NORTHERN EUROPEAN RUSSIA
pp 124-125
THE BALTIC STATES AND BELARUS
pp 118-119
SOUTHERN EUROPEAN RUSSIA
pp 126-127
ROMANIA, MOLDOVA & UKRAINE
pp 116-117
BULGARIA & GREECE
pp 114-115
ASIA pp 148 – 163
NORTHEASTERN CHINA, MONGOLIA & KOREA
pp162-163
WESTERN CHINA
pp158-159
AFGHANISTAN & PAKISTAN
pp148-149
EASTERN CHINA
pp160-161
NORTHERN INDIA & THE HIMALAYAN STATES
pp152-153
SOUTHERN INDIA & SRI LANKA
pp154-155
Svalbard
p 92
SCANDINAVIA, FINLAND & ICELAND
pp92-93
THE RUSSIAN FEDERATION
pp122-123
EUROPE
pp 84-127
(also see inset)
KAZAKHSTAN
pp144-145
ASIA
pp 128-173
(also see inset)
TURKEY & THE CAUCASUS
pp136-137
CENTRAL ASIA
pp146-147
THE MEDITERRANEAN
pp 120-121
Cyprus
pp 121
THE NEAR EAST
pp138-139
IRAN & THE GULF STATES
pp142-143
MAINLAND EAST ASIA
pp 156-157
JAPAN
pp 164-165
Izu-shoto, Ogasawara-shoto & Kazan-retto
p 165
THE PACIFIC OCEAN
pp 192-193
Ryukyu Islands
p 165
Sakishima-shoto
p 165
NORTH AFRICA
pp 74-75
THE ARABIAN PENINSULA
pp140-141
SOUTH ASIA
pp150-151
Mariana Islands
p 188
Wake Island
p 189
MAINLAND SOUTHEAST ASIA
pp 166-167
Saipan
p 188
MICRONESIA
pp 188-189
Guam
p 188
Yap
p 188
Chuuk Islands
p 189
Pohnpei
p 189
Marshall Islands
p 189
Babeldaob
p 188
Majuro Atoll
p 189
AFRICA
pp 66-83
EAST AFRICA
pp 80-81
Palau
p 188
Micronesia
pp 188-189
Kosrae
p 189
Maldives
p 151
Nauru
p 189
Tarawa
p 190
CENTRAL AFRICA
pp 78-79
WESTERN MARITIME SOUTHEAST ASIA
pp 168-169
EASTERN MARITIME SOUTHEAST ASIA
pp 170-171
Kiribati
p 191
Seychelles
p 172
Tuvalu
p 190
Funafuti Atoll
p 190
Comoro Islands
p 172
THE INDIAN OCEAN
pp 172-173
MELANESIA
pp 186-187
AUSTRALASIA & OCEANIA
pp 174-193
Madagascar
p 172
Mauritius
p 173
Réunion
p 173
SOUTHERN AFRICA
pp 82-83
AUSTRALIA
pp 180-181
SOUTHEAST AUSTRALIA
pp 182-183
NEW ZEALAND
pp 184-185
ANTARCTICA
pp 194-195

WORLD ATLAS

CONCISE

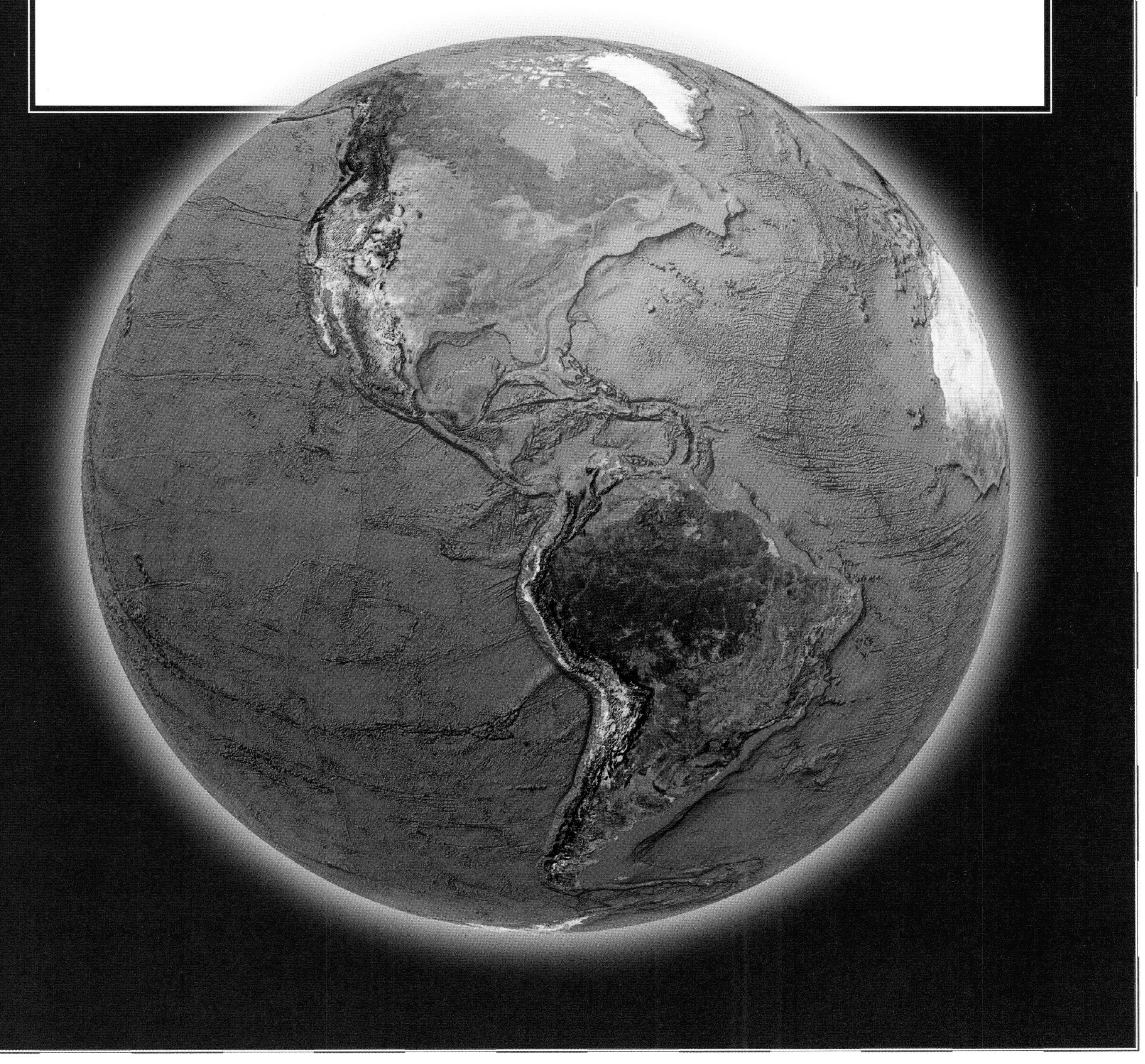

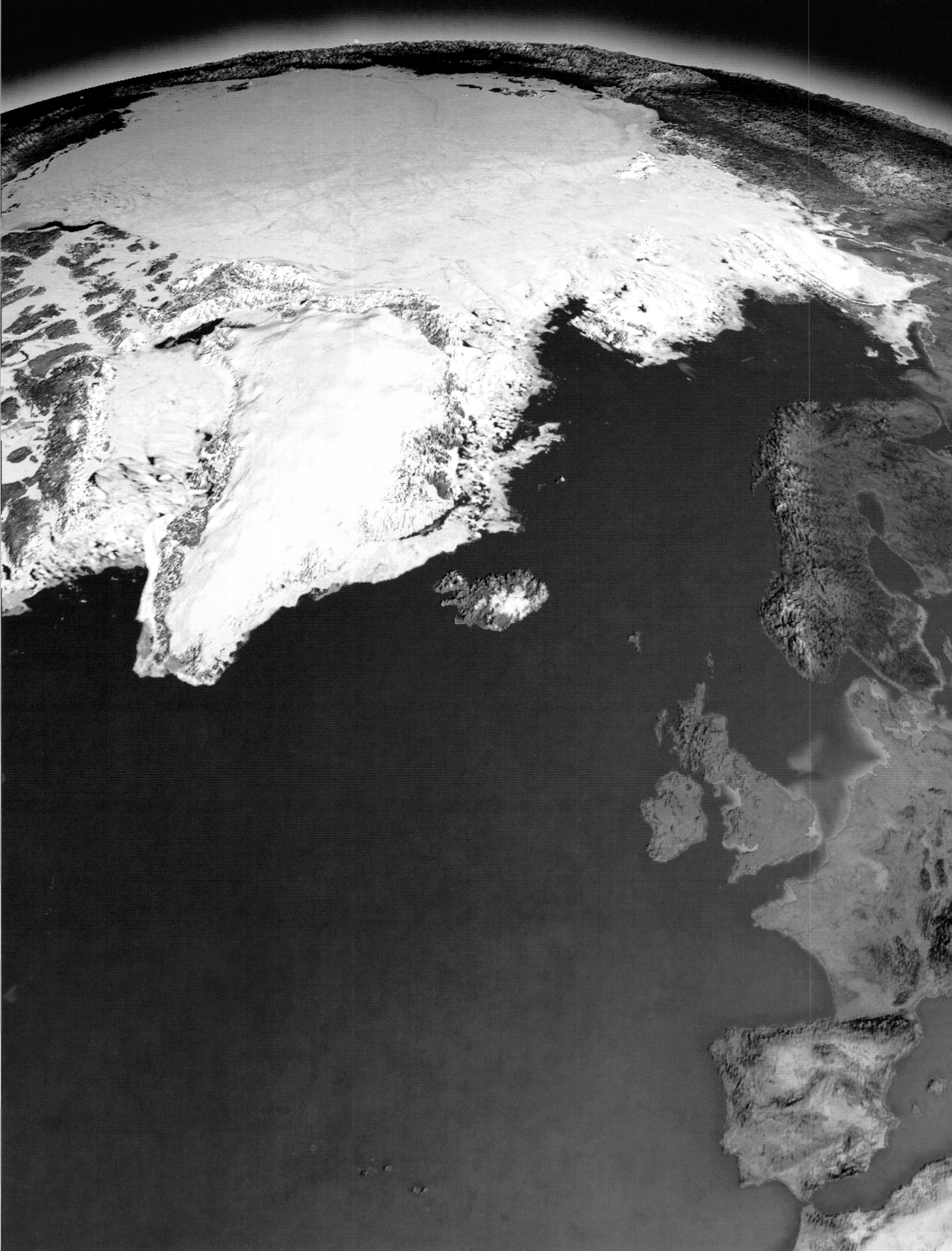

London • New York • Melbourne • Munich • Delhi

WORLD ATLAS

CONCISE

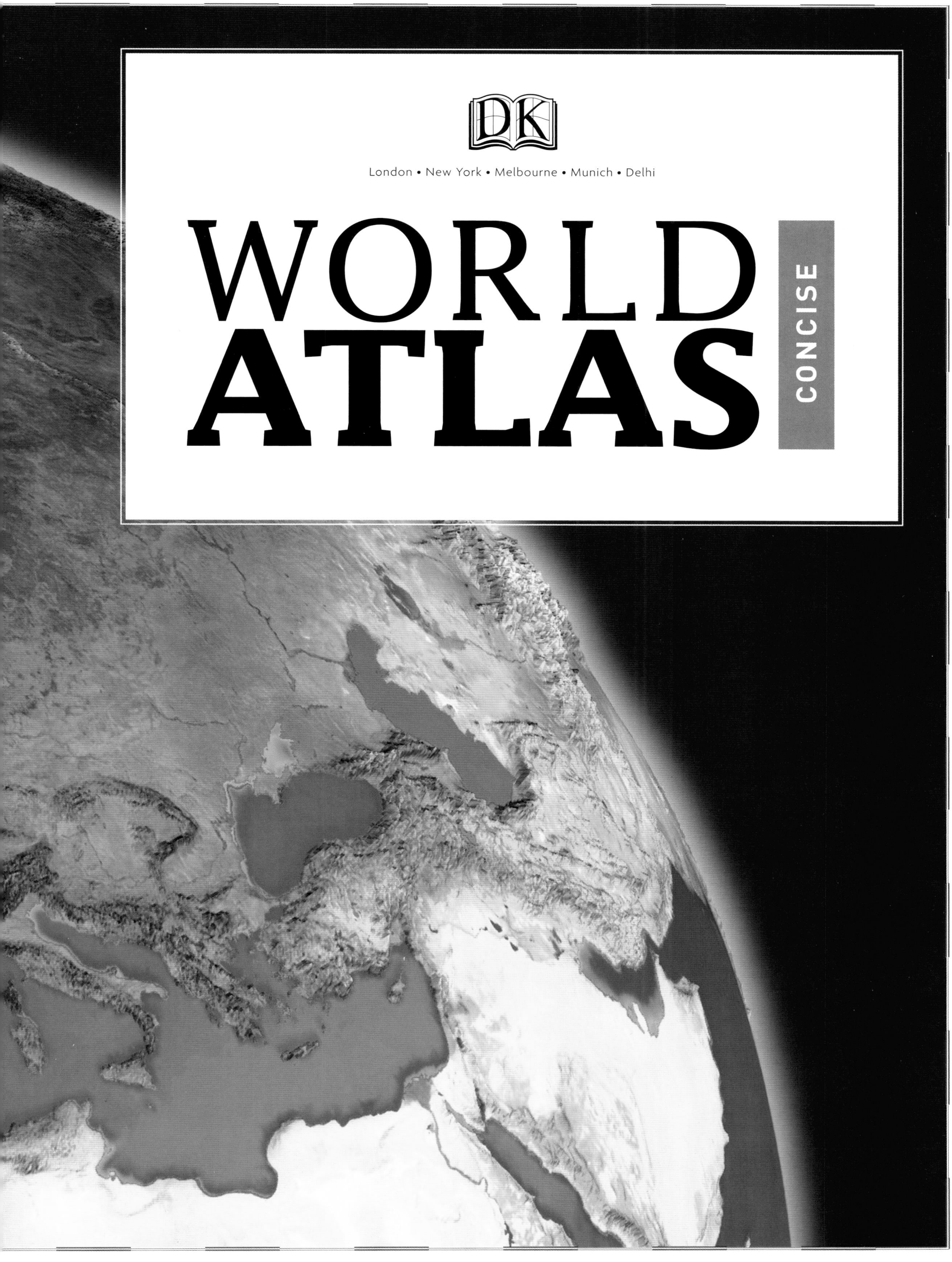

LONDON, NEW YORK, MELBOURNE, MUNICH, DELHI

FOR THE SIXTH EDITION

Publisher Jonathan Metcalf **Art Director** Philip Ormerod **Associate Publisher** Liz Wheeler
Senior Cartographic Editor Simon Mumford **Cartographers** Encompass Graphics Ltd, Brighton, UK
Index database David Roberts **Jacket Designer** Mark Cavanagh
Production Controller Gemma Sharpe **Producer** Rebekah Parsons-King

General Geographical Consultants

Physical Geography Denys Brunsden, Emeritus Professor, Department of Geography, King's College, London
Human Geography Professor J Malcolm Wagstaff, Department of Geography, University of Southampton
Place Names Caroline Burgess, Permanent Committee on Geographical Names, London
Boundaries International Boundaries Research Unit, Mountjoy Research Centre, University of Durham

Digital Mapping Consultants

DK Cartopia developed by George Galfalvi and XMap Ltd, London
Professor Jan-Peter Muller, Department of Photogrammetry and Surveying, University College, London
Cover globes, planets and information on the Solar System provided by Philip Eales and Kevin Tildsley, Planetary Visions Ltd, London

Regional Consultants

North America Dr David Green, Department of Geography, King's College, London • Jim Walsh, Head of Reference, Wessell Library, Tufts University, Medford, Massachussetts
South America Dr David Preston, School of Geography, University of Leeds **Europe** Dr Edward M Yates, formerly of the Department of Geography, King's College, London
Africa Dr Philip Amis, Development Administration Group, University of Birmingham • Dr Ieuan Ll Griffiths, Department of Geography, University of Sussex
Dr Tony Binns, Department of Geography, University of Sussex
Central Asia Dr David Turnock, Department of Geography, University of Leicester **South and East Asia** Dr Jonathan Rigg, Department of Geography, University of Durham
Australasia and Oceania Dr Robert Allison, Department of Geography, University of Durham

Acknowledgments

Digital terrain data created by Eros Data Center, Sioux Falls, South Dakota, USA. Processed by GVS Images Inc, California, USA and Planetary Visions Ltd, London, UK
Cambridge International Reference on Current Affairs (CIRCA), Cambridge, UK • Digitization by Robertson Research International, Swanley, UK • Peter Clark
British Isles maps generated from a dataset supplied by Map Marketing Ltd/European Map Graphics Ltd in combination with DK Cartopia copyright data

DORLING KINDERSLEY CARTOGRAPHY

Editor-in-Chief Andrew Heritage **Managing Cartographer** David Roberts **Senior Cartographic Editor** Roger Bullen
Editorial Direction Louise Cavanagh **Database Manager** Simon Lewis **Art Direction** Chez Picthall

Cartographers
Pamela Alford • James Anderson • Caroline Bowie • Dale Buckton • Tony Chambers • Jan Clark • Bob Croser • Martin Darlison • Damien Demaj • Claire Ellam • Sally Gable
Jeremy Hepworth • Geraldine Horner • Chris Jackson • Christine Johnston • Julia Lunn • Michael Martin • Ed Merritt • James Mills-Hicks • Simon Mumford • John Plumer
John Scott • Ann Stephenson • Gail Townsley • Julie Turner • Sarah Vaughan • Jane Voss • Scott Wallace • Iorwerth Watkins • Bryony Webb • Alan Whitaker • Peter Winfield

Digital Maps Created in DK Cartopia by
Tom Coulson • Thomas Robertshaw
Philip Rowles • Rob Stokes
Managing Editor
Lisa Thomas
Editors
Thomas Heath • Wim Jenkins • Jane Oliver
Siobhan Ryan • Elizabeth Wyse
Editorial Research
Helen Dangerfield • Andrew Rebeiro-Hargrave
Additional Editorial Assistance
Debra Clapson • Robert Damon • Ailsa Heritage
Constance Novis • Jayne Parsons • Chris Whitwell

Placenames Database Team
Natalie Clarkson • Ruth Duxbury • Caroline Falce • John Featherstone • Dan Gardiner
Ciárán Hynes • Margaret Hynes • Helen Rudkin • Margaret Stevenson • Annie Wilson
Senior Managing Art Editor
Philip Lord
Designers
Scott David • Carol Ann Davis • David Douglas • Rhonda Fisher
Karen Gregory • Nicola Liddiard • Paul Williams
Illustrations
Ciárán Hughes • Advanced Illustration, Congleton, UK
Picture Research
Melissa Albany • James Clarke • Anna Lord
Christine Rista • Sarah Moule • Louise Thomas

First published in Great Britain in 2001 by Dorling Kindersley Limited, 80 Strand, London WC2R 0RL.

A Penguin Company

9 8 7 6 5 4

003 - 188130 - April/2013

Second Edition 2003. Reprinted with revisions 2004. Third Edition 2005. Fourth Edition 2008. Fifth Edition 2011. Sixth Edition 2013.

A CIP catalogue record for this book is available from the British Library.

ISBN: 978-1-4093-6450-4

Printed and bound in Hong Kong.

Discover more at **www.dk.com**

Introduction

EVERYTHING YOU NEED TO KNOW ABOUT OUR PLANET TODAY

For many, the outstanding legacy of the twentieth century was the way in which the Earth shrank. In the third millennium, it is increasingly important for us to have a clear vision of the world in which we live. The human population has increased fourfold since 1900. The last scraps of *terra incognita* – the polar regions and ocean depths – have been penetrated and mapped. New regions have been colonized and previously hostile realms claimed for habitation. The growth of air transport and mass tourism allows many of us to travel further, faster, and more frequently than ever before. In doing so we are given a bird's-eye view of the Earth's surface denied to our forebears.

At the same time, the amount of information about our world has grown enormously. Our multimedia environment hurls uninterrupted streams of data at us, on the printed page, through the airwaves and across our television, computer, and phone screens; events from all corners of the globe reach us instantaneously, and are witnessed as they unfold. Our sense of stability and certainty has been eroded; instead, we are aware that the world is in a constant state of flux and change. Natural disasters, man-made cataclysms, and conflicts between nations remind us daily of the enormity and fragility of our domain. The ongoing threat of international terrorism throws into very stark relief the difficulties that arise when trying to 'know' or 'understand' our planet and its many cultures.

The current crisis in our 'global' culture has made the need greater than ever before for everyone to possess an atlas. The **CONCISE** WORLD **ATLAS** has been conceived to meet this need.
At its core, like all atlases, it seeks to define where places are, to describe their main characteristics, and to locate them in relation to other places. Every attempt has been made to make the information on the maps as clear, accurate, and accessible as possible using the latest digital cartographic techniques. In addition, each page of the atlas provides a wealth of further information, bringing the maps to life. Using photographs, diagrams, 'at-a-glance' maps, introductory texts, and captions, the atlas builds up a detailed portrait of those features – cultural, political, economic, and geomorphological – that make each region unique and which are also the main agents of change.

This sixth edition of the **CONCISE** WORLD **ATLAS** incorporates hundreds of revisions and updates affecting every map and every page, distilling the burgeoning mass of information available through modern technology into an extraordinarily detailed and reliable view of our world.

CONTENTS

Introduction v
Contents ..... vi–vii
How to use this Atlas ..... viii–ix

THE WORLD

The solar system ..... x–xi
The physical world ..... xii–xiii
Structure of the Earth ..... xiv–xv
Shaping the landscape ..... xvi–xvii
The world's oceans ..... xviii–xix
The global climate ..... xx–xxi
Life on Earth ..... xxii–xxiii
Population and settlement ..... xxiv–xxv
The economic system ..... xxvi–xxvii
The political world ..... xxviii–xxix
States and boundaries ..... xxx–xxxi
International disputes xxxii

ATLAS OF THE WORLD

North America

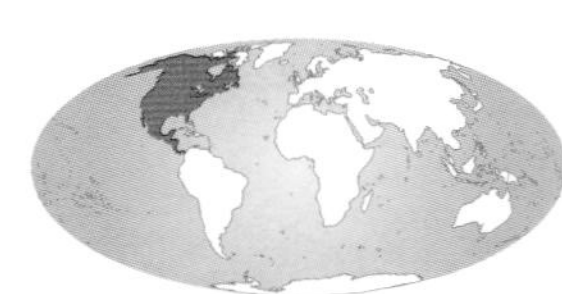

NORTH AMERICA 1
PHYSICAL NORTH AMERICA 2–3
POLITICAL NORTH AMERICA 4–5
NORTH AMERICAN RESOURCES 6–7
Canada 8–9
Canada: Western Provinces 10–11
Alberta, British Columbia, Manitoba, Saskatchewan, Yukon
Canada: Eastern Provinces 12–13
New Brunswick, Newfoundland & Labrador, Nova Scotia, Ontario, Prince Edward Island, Québec, St Pierre & Miquelon
Southeastern Canada 14–15
Southern Ontario, Southern Québec
United States of America 16–17
USA: Northeastern States 18–19
Connecticut, Maine, Massachussetts, New Hampshire, New Jersey, New York, Pennsylvania, Rhode Island, Vermont
USA: Mid-Eastern States 20–21
Delaware, District of Columbia, Kentucky, Maryland, North Carolina, South Carolina, Tennessee, Virginia, West Virginia
USA: Southern States 22–23
Alabama, Florida, Georgia, Louisiana, Mississippi
USA: Texas 24–25
USA: South Midwestern States 26–27
Arkansas, Kansas, Missouri, Oklahoma
USA: Upper Plains States 28–29
Iowa, Minnesota, Nebraska, North Dakota, South Dakota
USA: Great Lakes States 30–31
Illinois, Indiana, Michigan, Ohio, Wisconsin
USA: North Mountain States 32–33
Idaho, Montana, Oregon, Washington, Wyoming
USA: California & Nevada 34–35
USA: South Mountain States 36–37
Arizona, Colorado, New Mexico, Utah
USA: Hawaii & Alaska 38–39
Mexico 40–41
Central America 42–43
Belize, Costa Rica, El Salvador, Guatemala, Honduras, Nicaragua, Panama
The Caribbean 44–45
Anguilla, Antigua & Barbuda, Aruba, Bahamas, Barbados, Bonaire, British Virgin Islands, Cayman Islands, Cuba, Curaçao, Dominica, Dominican Republic, Grenada, Guadeloupe, Haiti, Jamaica, Martinique, Montserrat, Navassa Island, Puerto Rico, St Kitts & Nevis, St Lucia, St Vincent & the Grenadines, Sint Maarten, Trinidad & Tobago, Turks & Caicos Islands, Virgin Islands (US)

South America

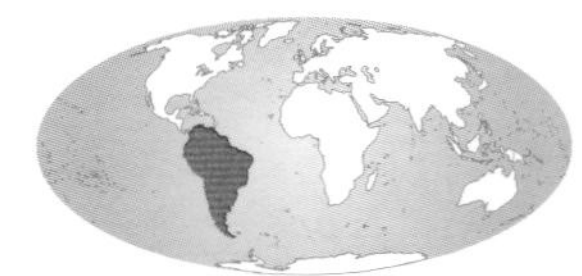

SOUTH AMERICA 46–47
PHYSICAL SOUTH AMERICA 48–49
POLITICAL SOUTH AMERICA 50–51
SOUTH AMERICAN RESOURCES 52–53
Northern South America 54–55
Colombia, French Guiana, Guyana, Surinam, Venezuela
Western South America 56–57
Bolivia, Ecuador, Peru
Brazil 58–59
Eastern South America 60–61
Southeast Brazil, Northeast Argentina, Uruguay
Southern South America 62–63
Argentina, Chile, Paraguay
The Atlantic Ocean 64–65

Africa

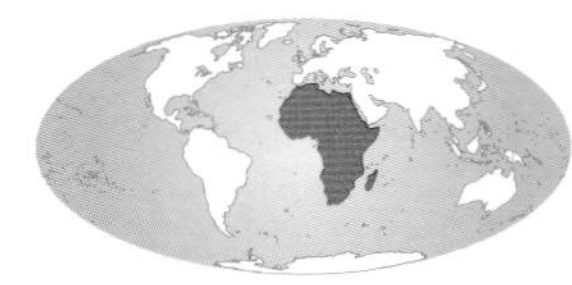

AFRICA 66–67
PHYSICAL AFRICA 68–69
POLITICAL AFRICA 70–71
AFRICAN RESOURCES 72–73
North Africa 74–75
Algeria, Egypt, Libya, Morocco, Tunisia, Western Sahara
West Africa 76–77
Benin, Burkina, Cape Verde, Gambia, Ghana, Guinea, Guinea-Bissau, Ivory Coast, Liberia, Mali, Mauritania, Niger, Nigeria, Senegal, Sierra Leone, Togo
Central Africa 78–79
Cameroon, Central African Republic, Chad, Congo, Dem. Rep. Congo, Equatorial Guinea, Gabon, Sao Tome & Principe
East Africa 80–81
Burundi, Djibouti, Eritrea, Ethiopia, Kenya, Rwanda, Somalia, South Sudan, Sudan, Tanzania, Uganda
Southern Africa 82–83
Angola, Botswana, Lesotho, Malawi, Mozambique, Namibia, South Africa, Swaziland, Zambia, Zimbabwe

Europe

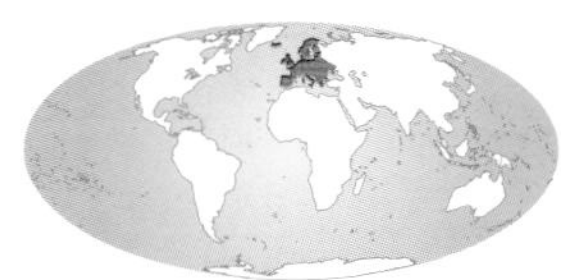

EUROPE 84–85

PHYSICAL EUROPE 86–87

POLITICAL EUROPE 88–89

EUROPEAN RESOURCES 90–91

Scandinavia, Finland & Iceland 92–93
Denmark, Finland, Iceland, Norway, Svalbard, Sweden

Southern Scandinavia 94–95
Denmark, Faeroe Islands, Southern Norway, Southern Sweden

The British Isles 96–97
Channel Islands, Ireland, Isle of Man, United Kingdom

The Low Countries 98–99
Belgium, Luxembourg, Netherlands

Germany 100–101

France 102–103
France, Monaco

The Iberian Peninsula 104–105
Andorra, Gibraltar, Portugal, Spain

The Italian Peninsula 106–107
Italy, San Marino, Vatican City

The Alpine States 108–109
Austria, Liechtenstein, Slovenia, Switzerland

Central Europe 110–111
Czech Republic, Hungary, Poland, Slovakia

Southeast Europe 112–113
Albania, Bosnia & Herzegovina, Croatia, Kosovo, Macedonia, Montenegro, Serbia

Bulgaria & Greece 114–115
(including European Turkey)

Romania, Moldova & Ukraine 116–117

The Baltic States & Belarus 118–119
Belarus, Estonia, Latvia, Lithuania, Kaliningrad

The Mediterranean 120–121

The Russian Federation 122–123

Northern European Russia 124–125

Southern European Russia 126–127

Asia

ASIA 128–129

PHYSICAL ASIA 130–131

POLITICAL ASIA 132–133

ASIAN RESOURCES 134–135

Turkey & the Caucasus 136–137
Armenia, Azerbaijan, Georgia, Turkey

The Near East 138–139
Iraq, Israel, Jordan, Lebanon, Syria

The Arabian Peninsula 140–141
Bahrain, Kuwait, Oman, Qatar, Saudi Arabia, United Arab Emirates, Yemen

Iran & the Gulf States 142–143
Bahrain, Iran, Kuwait, Qatar, United Arab Emirates

Kazakhstan 144–145

Central Asia 146–147
Kyrgyzstan, Tajikistan, Turkmenistan, Uzbekistan

Afghanistan & Pakistan 148–149

South Asia 150–151
Bangladesh, Bhutan, India, Maldives, Nepal, Pakistan, Sri Lanka

Northern India & the Himalayan States 152–153
Bangladesh, Bhutan, Nepal, Northern India

Southern India & Sri Lanka 154–155

Mainland East Asia 156–157
China, Mongolia, North Korea, South Korea, Taiwan

Western China 158–159

Eastern China 160–161
Eastern China, Taiwan

Northeastern China, Mongolia & Korea 162–163
Mongolia, Northeastern China, North Korea, South Korea

Japan 164–165

Mainland Southeast Asia 166–167
Burma, Cambodia, Laos, Paracel Islands, Thailand, Vietnam

West Maritime Southeast Asia 168–169
Brunei, Indonesia, Malaysia, Singapore

East Maritime Southeast Asia 170–171
East Timor, Indonesia, Philippines

The Indian Ocean 172–173

Australasia & Oceania

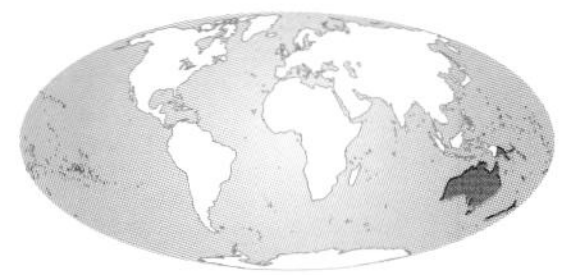

AUSTRALASIA & OCEANIA 174–175

POLITICAL AUSTRALASIA & OCEANIA 176–177

AUSTRALASIAN & OCEANIAN RESOURCES 178–179

Australia 180–181

Southeast Australia 182–183
New South Wales, South Australia, Tasmania, Victoria

New Zealand 184–185

Melanesia 186–187
Fiji, New Caledonia, Papua New Guinea, Solomon Islands, Vanuatu

Micronesia 188–189
Guam, Marshall Islands, Micronesia, Nauru, Northern Mariana Islands, Palau, Wake Island

Polynesia 190–191
Cook Islands, Easter Island, French Polynesia, Kiribati, Niue, Pitcairn Islands, Tokelau, Tuvalu, Wallis & Futuna

The Pacific Ocean 192–193

Antarctica 194–195

The Arctic 196–197

INDEX–GAZETTEER

Geographical comparisons 198–199

Countries of the world including The time zones 200–207

Geographical glossary 208–210

Geographical names 211

Index 212–349

Acknowledgements 350

Key to maps

Regional

Physical features

elevation

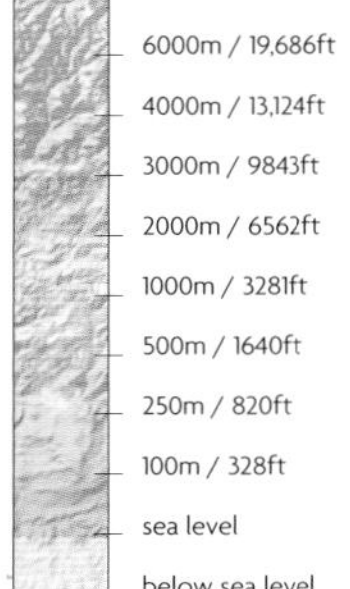

6000m / 19,686ft
4000m / 13,124ft
3000m / 9843ft
2000m / 6562ft
1000m / 3281ft
500m / 1640ft
250m / 820ft
100m / 328ft
sea level
below sea level

- elevation above sea level (mountain height)
- volcano
- pass
- elevation below sea level (depression depth)

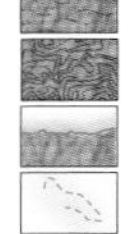

- sand desert
- lava flow
- coastline
- reef
- atoll

sea depth

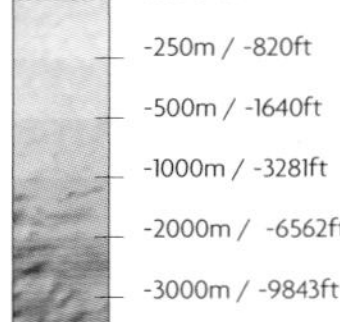

sea level
-250m / -820ft
-500m / -1640ft
-1000m / -3281ft
-2000m / -6562ft
-3000m / -9843ft

- seamount / guyot symbol
- undersea spot depth

Drainage features

- main river
- secondary river
- tertiary river
- minor river
- main seasonal river
- secondary seasonal river
- canal
- waterfall
- rapids
- dam
- perennial lake
- seasonal lake
- perennial salt lake
- seasonal salt lake
- reservoir

- salt flat / salt pan
- marsh / salt marsh
- mangrove
- wadi
- spring / well / waterhole / oasis

Ice features

- ice cap / sheet
- ice shelf
- glacier / snowfield
- summer pack ice limit
- winter pack ice limit

Communications

- motorway / highway
- motorway / highway (under construction)
- major road
- minor road
- tunnel (road)
- main line
- minor line
- tunnel (rail)
- international airport

Borders

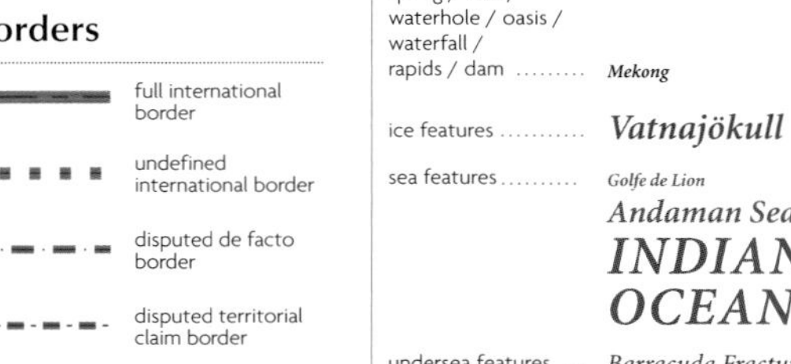

- full international border
- undefined international border
- disputed de facto border
- disputed territorial claim border
- indication of country extent (Pacific only)
- indication of dependent territory extent (Pacific only)
- demarcation/ cease fire line
- autonomous / federal region border
- other 1st order internal administrative border
- 2nd order internal administrative border

Settlements

- built up area

settlement population symbols

- more than 5 million
- 1 million to 5 million
- 500,000 to 1 million
- 100,000 to 500,000
- 50,000 to 100,000
- 10,000 to 50,000
- fewer than 10,000
- country/dependent territory capital city
- autonomous / federal region / other 1st order internal administrative centre
- 2nd order internal administrative centre

Miscellaneous features

- ancient wall
- site of interest
- scientific station

Graticule features

- lines of latitude and longitude / Equator
- Tropics / Polar circles
- 45° degrees of longitude / latitude

Typographic key

Physical features

landscape features	*Namib Desert* *Massif Central* *ANDES*
headland	*Nordkapp*
elevation / volcano / pass	Mount Meru 4556 m
drainage features	*Lake Geneva*
rivers / canals spring / well / waterhole / oasis / waterfall / rapids / dam	*Mekong*
ice features	*Vatnajökull*
sea features	*Golfe de Lion* *Andaman Sea* *INDIAN OCEAN*
undersea features	*Barracuda Fracture Zone*

Regions

country	ARMENIA
dependent territory with parent state	NIUE (to NZ)
region outside feature area	ANGOLA
autonomous / federal region	MINAS GERAIS
other 1st order internal administrative region	MINSKAYA VOBLASTS'
2nd order internal administrative region	Vaucluse
cultural region	New England

Settlements

capital city	BEIJING
dependent territory capital city	FORT-DE-FRANCE
other settlements	Chicago Adana Tizi Ozou Yonezawa Farnham

Miscellaneous

sites of interest / miscellaneous	Valley of the Kings
Tropics / Polar circles	*Antarctic Circle*

How to use this Atlas

The atlas is organized by continent, moving eastwards from the International Date Line. The opening section describes the world's structure, systems and its main features. The Atlas of the World which follows, is a continent-by-continent guide to today's world, starting with a comprehensive insight into the physical, political and economic structure of each continent, followed by integrated mapping and descriptions of each region or country.

The world

The introductory section of the Atlas deals with every aspect of the planet, from physical structure to human geography, providing an overall picture of the world we live in. Complex topics such as the landscape of the Earth, climate, oceans, population and economic patterns are clearly explained with the aid of maps, diagrams drawn from the latest information.

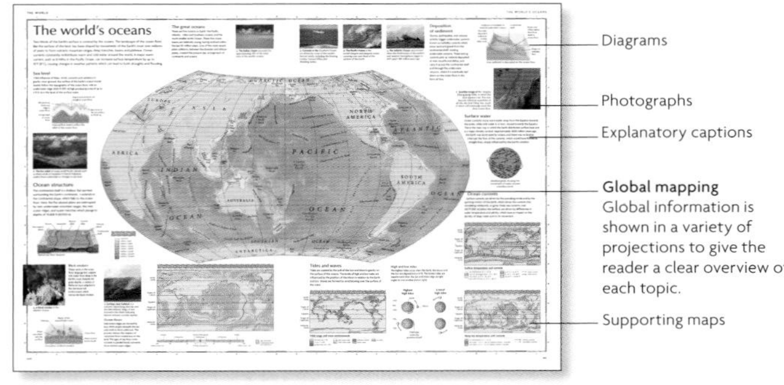

The world's oceans
Diagrams
Photographs
Explanatory captions
Global mapping
Global information is shown in a variety of projections to give the reader a clear overview of each topic.
Supporting maps

The political continent

The political portrait of the continent is a vital reference point for every continental section, showing the position of countries relative to one another, and the relationship between human settlement and geographic location. The complex mosaic of languages spoken in each continent is mapped, as is the effect of communications networks on the pattern of settlement.

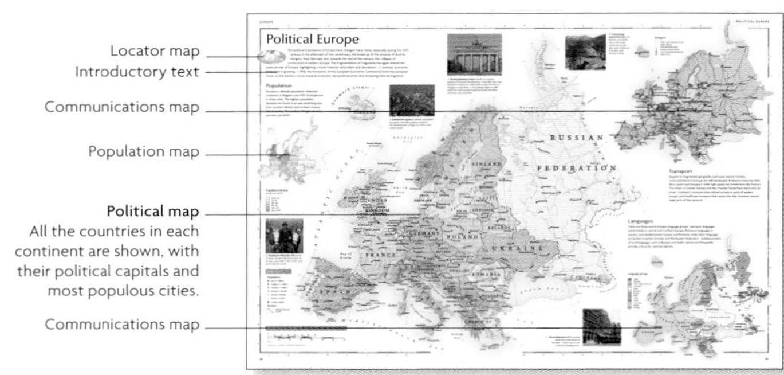

Political Europe
Locator map
Introductory text
Communications map
Population map
Political map
All the countries in each continent are shown, with their political capitals and most populous cities.
Communications map

Continental resources

The Earth's rich natural resources, including oil, gas, minerals and fertile land, have played a key role in the development of society. These pages show the location of minerals and agricultural resources on each continent, and how they have been instrumental in dictating industrial growth and the varieties of economic activity across the continent.

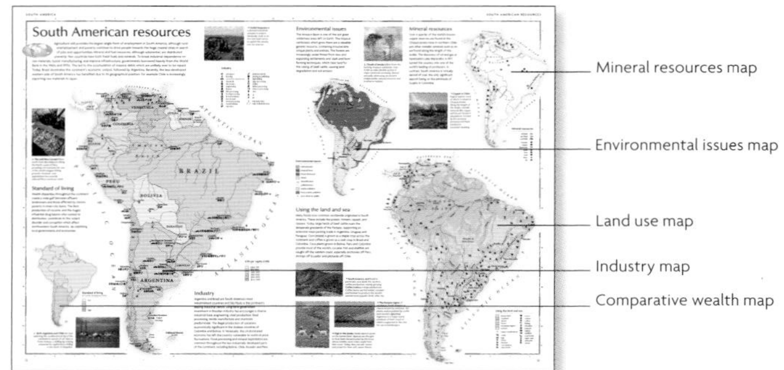

South American resources
Mineral resources map
Environmental issues map
Land use map
Industry map
Comparative wealth map

The physical continent

The astonishing variety of landforms, and the dramatic forces that created and continue to shape the landscape, are explained in the continental physical spread. Cross-sections, illustrations and terrain maps highlight the different parts of the continent, showing how nature's forces have produced the landscapes we see today.

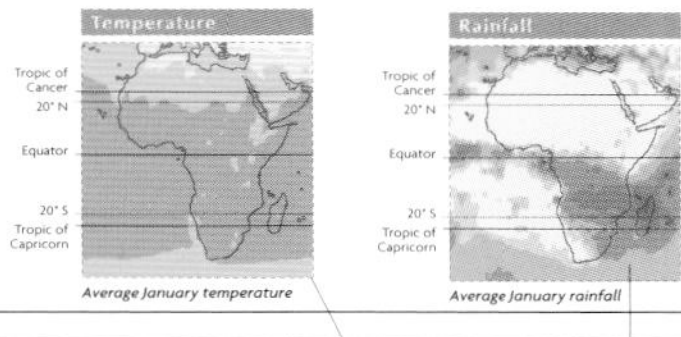
Temperature
Rainfall
Tropic of Cancer
Equator
Tropic of Capricorn
Average January temperature
Average January rainfall

Climate charts
Rainfall and temperature charts clearly show the continental patterns of rainfall and temperature.

Climate map
Climatic regions vary across each continent. The map displays the differing climatic regions, as well as daily hours of sunshine at selected weather stations.

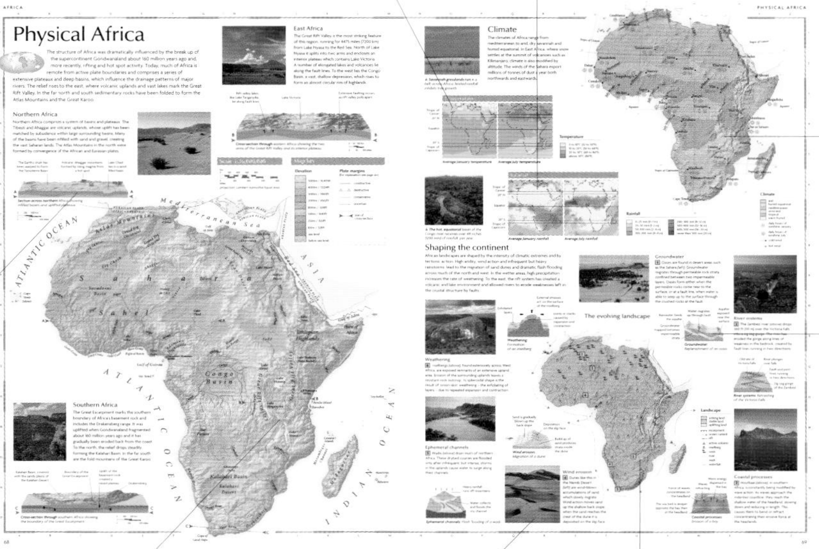
Physical Africa

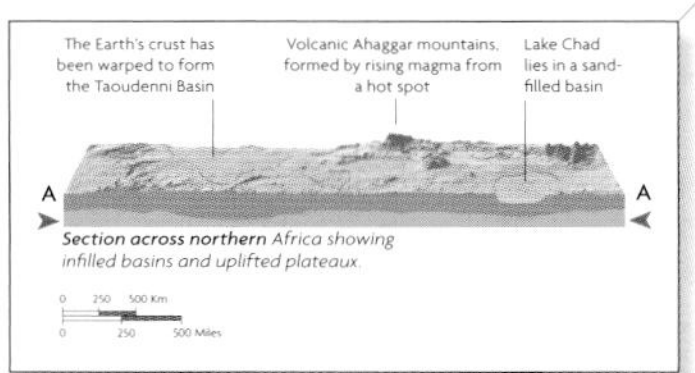
The Earth's crust has been warped to form the Taoudenni Basin
Volcanic Ahaggar mountains, formed by rising magma from a hot spot
Lake Chad lies in a sand-filled basin
A
A
Section across northern Africa showing infilled basins and uplifted plateaux.

Cross-sections
Detailed cross-sections through selected parts of the continent show the underlying geomorphic structure.

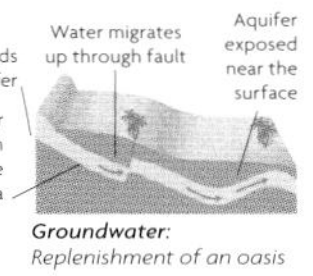
Rainwater feeds the aquifer
Water migrates up through fault
Aquifer exposed near the surface
Groundwater trapped between impermeable strata
Groundwater: Replenishment of an oasis

Landform diagrams
The complex formation of many typical landforms is summarized in these easy-to-understand illustrations.

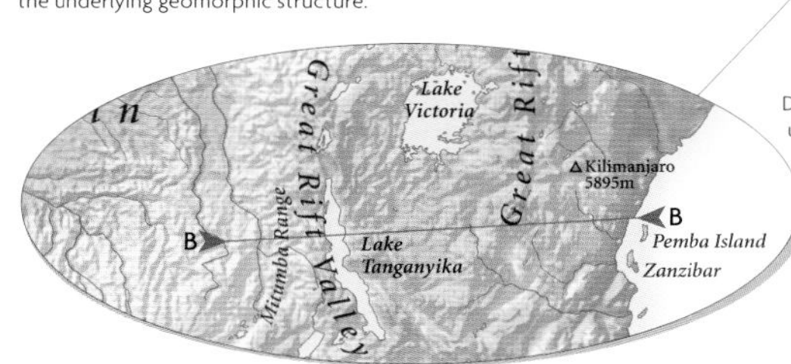
Lake Victoria
Great Rift Valley
Kilimanjaro 5895m
Lake Tanganyika
Pemba Island
Zanzibar
B
B

Main physical map
Detailed satellite data has been used to create an accurate and visually striking picture of the surface of the continent.

Photographs
A wide range of beautiful photographs bring the world's regions to life.

Landscape evolution map
The physical shape of each continent is affected by a variety of forces which continually sculpt and modify the landscape. This map shows the major processes which affect different parts of the continent.

Regional mapping

The main body of the Atlas is a unique regional map set, with detailed information on the terrain, the human geography of the region and its infrastructure. Around the edge of the map, additional 'at-a-glance' maps, give an instant picture of regional industry, land use and agriculture. The detailed terrain map (shown in perspective), focuses on the main physical features of the region, and is enhanced by annotated illustrations, and photographs of the physical structure.

Key to transport symbols
❶ Extent of national paved road network.
❷ Extent of motorways, freeways or major national highways.
❸ Extent of commercial rail network.
❹ Extent of inland waterways navigable by commercial craft.

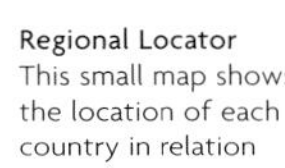

The transport network

❶	340,090 miles (544,144 km)	4813 miles (7703 km)	❷
❸	12,872 miles (20,592 km)	2108 miles (3389 km)	❹

New York's commercial success is tied historically to its transport connections. The Erie Canal, completed in 1825, opened up the Great Lakes and the interior to New York's markets and carried a stream of immigrants into the Midwest.

Transport network
The differing extent of the transport network for each region is shown here, along with key facts about the transport system.

Regional Locator
This small map shows the location of each country in relation to its continent.

Key to main map
A key to the population symbols and land heights accompanies the main map.

World locator
This locates the continent in which the region is found on a small world map.

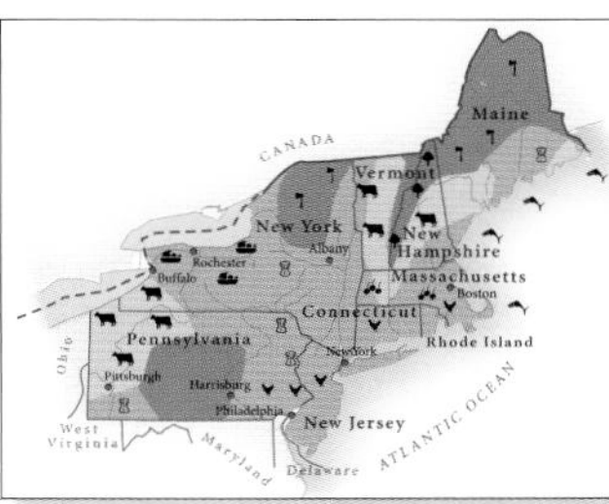
CANADA
Maine
Vermont
New Hampshire
Massachusetts
Boston
New York
Connecticut
Rhode Island
Pennsylvania
New Jersey
ATLANTIC OCEAN

Land use map
This shows the different types of land use which characterize the region, as well as indicating the principal agricultural activities.

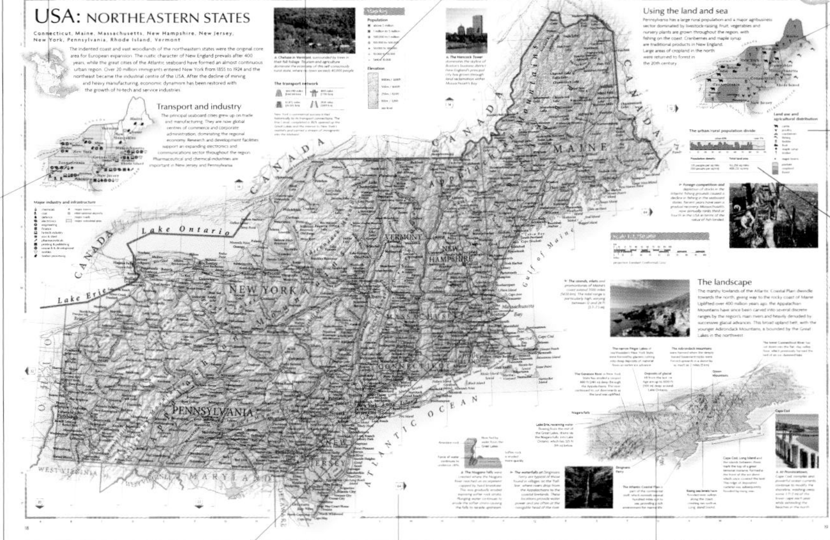
USA: NORTHEASTERN STATES

Map keys
Each supporting map has its own key.

Grid reference
The framing grid provides a location reference for each place listed in the Index.

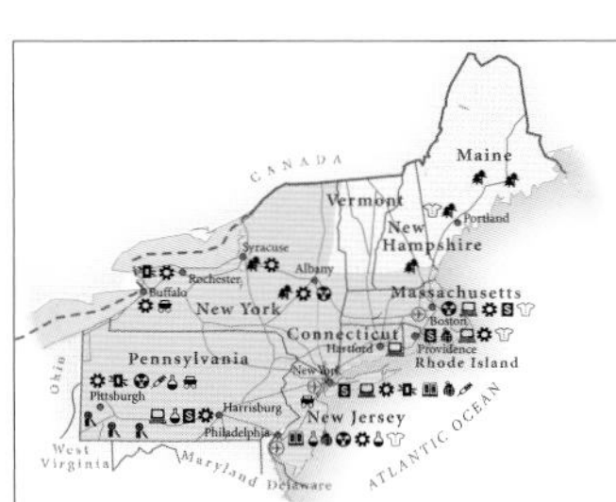
CANADA
Maine
Vermont
New Hampshire
Massachusetts
New York
Connecticut
Rhode Island
Pennsylvania
New Jersey

Transport and industry map
The main industrial areas are mapped, and the most important industrial and economic activities of the region are shown.

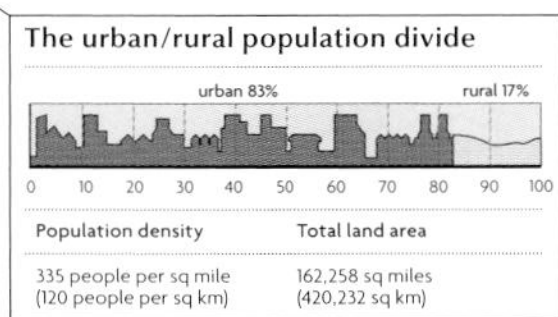
The urban/rural population divide
urban 83%
rural 17%
0 10 20 30 40 50 60 70 80 90 100
Population density
Total land area
335 people per sq mile (120 people per sq km)
162,258 sq miles (420,232 sq km)

Urban/rural population divide
The proportion of people in the region who live in urban and rural areas, as well as the overall population density and land area are clearly shown in these simple graphics.

Continuation symbols
These symbols indicate where adjacent maps can be found.

Landscape map
The computer-generated terrain model accurately portrays an oblique view of the landscape. Annotations highlight the most important geographic features of the region.

Nashua
Lowell
Lawrence
Gloucester
Beverly
Salem
Lynn
Massachusetts Bay
Cambridge
Boston
Quincy
Worcester
Framingham
Brockton
Providence
Plymouth
Cape Cod
Provincetown

Main regional map
A wealth of information is displayed on the main map, building up a rich portrait of the interaction between the physical landscape and the human and political geography of each region. The key to the regional maps can be found on page viii.

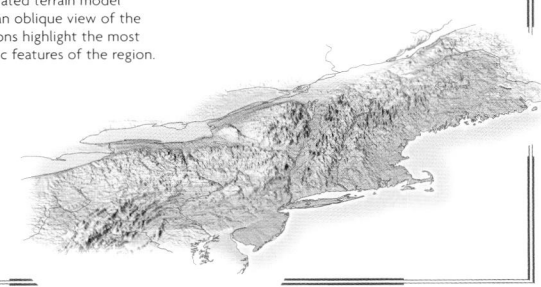

The Solar System

Nine major planets, their satellites and countless minor planets (asteroids) orbit the Sun to form the Solar System. The Sun, our nearest star, creates energy from nuclear reactions deep within its interior, providing all the light and heat which make life on Earth possible. The Earth is unique in the Solar System in that it supports life: its size, gravitational pull and distance from the Sun have all created the optimum conditions for the evolution of life. The planetary images seen here are composites derived from actual spacecraft images (not shown to scale).

Orbits

All the Solar System's planets and dwarf planets orbit the Sun in the same direction and (apart from Pluto) roughly in the same plane. All the orbits have the shapes of ellipses (stretched circles). However in most cases, these ellipses are close to being circular: only Pluto and Eris have very elliptical orbits. Orbital period (the time it takes an object to orbit the Sun) increases with distance from the Sun. The more remote objects not only have further to travel with each orbit, they also move more slowly.

Mercury

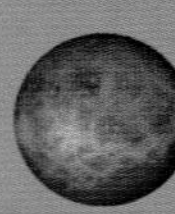

Venus

Earth

Mars

Ceres
(dwarf
planet)

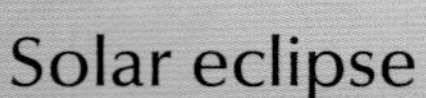
Jupiter

The Sun

⊖ *Diameter:* *864,948 miles (1,392,000 km)*
● *Mass:* *1990 million million million million tons*

The Sun was formed when a swirling cloud of dust and gas contracted, pulling matter into its centre. When the temperature at the centre rose to 1,000,000°C, nuclear fusion – the fusing of hydrogen into helium, creating energy – occurred, releasing a constant stream of heat and light.

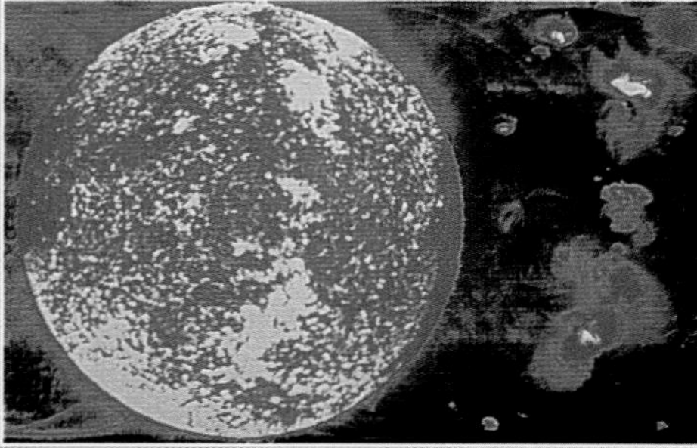

▲ ***Solar flares are*** *sudden bursts of energy from the Sun's surface. They can be 125,000 miles (200,000 km) long.*

The formation of the Solar System

The cloud of dust and gas thrown out by the Sun during its formation cooled to form the Solar System. The smaller planets nearest the Sun are formed of minerals and metals. The outer planets were formed at lower temperatures, and consist of swirling clouds of gases.

Solar eclipse

A solar eclipse occurs when the Moon passes between Earth and the Sun, casting its shadow on Earth's surface. During a total eclipse *(below)*, viewers along a strip of Earth's surface, called the area of totality, see the Sun totally blotted out for a short time, as the umbra (Moon's full shadow) sweeps over them. Outside this area is a larger one, where the Sun appears only partly obscured, as the penumbra (partial shadow) passes over.

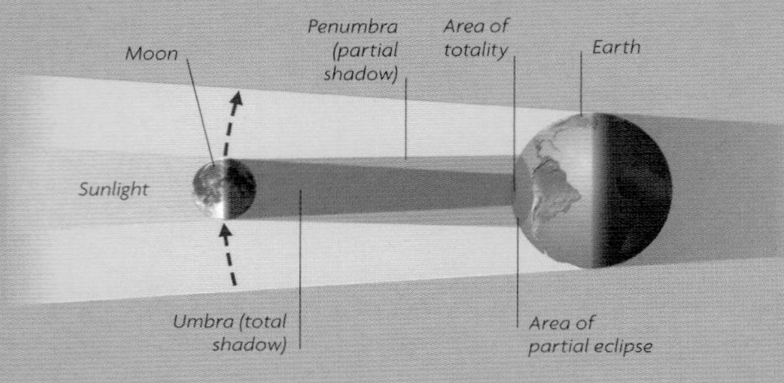
Moon
Penumbra (partial shadow)
Area of totality
Earth
Sunlight
Umbra (total shadow)
Area of partial eclipse

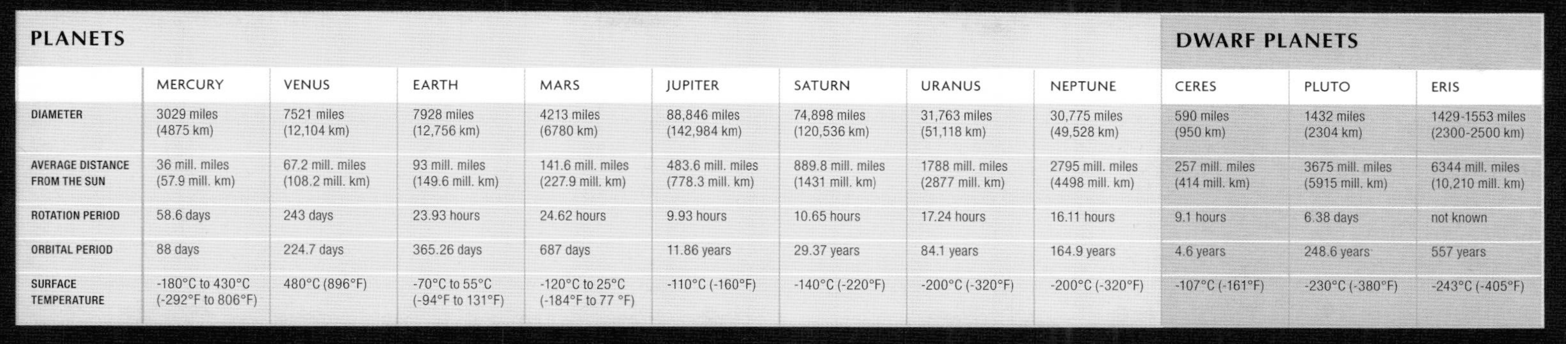

PLANETS									DWARF PLANETS		
	MERCURY	VENUS	EARTH	MARS	JUPITER	SATURN	URANUS	NEPTUNE	CERES	PLUTO	ERIS
DIAMETER	3029 miles (4875 km)	7521 miles (12,104 km)	7928 miles (12,756 km)	4213 miles (6780 km)	88,846 miles (142,984 km)	74,898 miles (120,536 km)	31,763 miles (51,118 km)	30,775 miles (49,528 km)	590 miles (950 km)	1432 miles (2304 km)	1429-1553 miles (2300-2500 km)
AVERAGE DISTANCE FROM THE SUN	36 mill. miles (57.9 mill. km)	67.2 mill. miles (108.2 mill. km)	93 mill. miles (149.6 mill. km)	141.6 mill. miles (227.9 mill. km)	483.6 mill. miles (778.3 mill. km)	889.8 mill. miles (1431 mill. km)	1788 mill. miles (2877 mill. km)	2795 mill. miles (4498 mill. km)	257 mill. miles (414 mill. km)	3675 mill. miles (5915 mill. km)	6344 mill. miles (10,210 mill. km)
ROTATION PERIOD	58.6 days	243 days	23.93 hours	24.62 hours	9.93 hours	10.65 hours	17.24 hours	16.11 hours	9.1 hours	6.38 days	not known
ORBITAL PERIOD	88 days	224.7 days	365.26 days	687 days	11.86 years	29.37 years	84.1 years	164.9 years	4.6 years	248.6 years	557 years
SURFACE TEMPERATURE	-180°C to 430°C (-292°F to 806°F)	480°C (896°F)	-70°C to 55°C (-94°F to 131°F)	-120°C to 25°C (-184°F to 77 °F)	-110°C (-160°F)	-140°C (-220°F)	-200°C (-320°F)	-200°C (-320°F)	-107°C (-161°F)	-230°C (-380°F)	-243°C (-405°F)

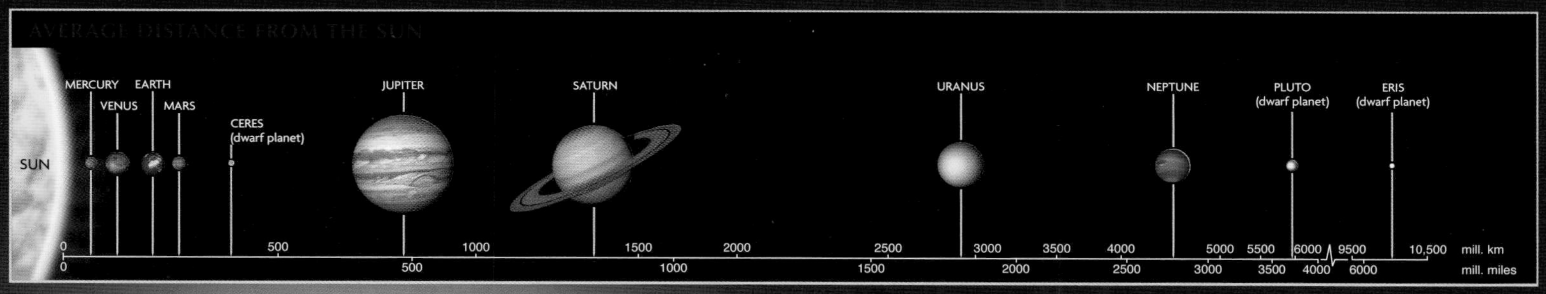
AVERAGE DISTANCE FROM THE SUN
SUN
MERCURY
VENUS
EARTH
MARS
CERES (dwarf planet)
JUPITER
SATURN
URANUS
NEPTUNE
PLUTO (dwarf planet)
ERIS (dwarf planet)
0 500 1000 1500 2000 2500 3000 3500 4000 5000 5500 6000 9500 10,500 mill. km
0 500 1000 1500 2000 2500 3000 3500 4000 6000 mill. miles

Saturn

Uranus

Neptune

Pluto (dwarf planet)

Eris (dwarf planet)

Space debris

Millions of objects, remnants of planetary formation, circle the Sun in a zone lying between Mars and Jupiter: the asteroid belt. Fragments of asteroids break off to form meteoroids, which can reach the Earth's surface. Comets, composed of ice and dust, originated outside our Solar System. Their elliptical orbit brings them close to the Sun and into the inner Solar System.

▲ ***Meteor Crater** in Arizona is 4200 ft (1300 m) wide and 660 ft (200 m) deep. It was formed over 10,000 years ago.*

Possible and actual meteorite craters

Map key
Possible impact craters
Meteorite impact craters

▲ ***The orbit of** Halley's Comet brings it close to the Earth every 76 years. It last visited in 1986.*

Halley's Comet

Earth's orbit

Halley's orbit

Orbit of Halley's Comet around the Sun

The Earth's atmosphere

During the early stages of the Earth's formation, ash, lava, carbon dioxide and water vapour were discharged onto the surface of the planet by constant volcanic eruptions. The water formed the oceans, while carbon dioxide entered the atmosphere or was dissolved in the oceans. Clouds, formed of water droplets, reflected some of the Sun's radiation back into space. The Earth's temperature stabilized and early life forms began to emerge, converting carbon dioxide into life-giving oxygen.

▲ ***It is thought** that the gases that make up the Earth's atmosphere originated deep within the interior, and were released many millions of years ago during intense volcanic actvity, similar to this eruption at Mount St. Helens.*

The physical world

The Earth's surface is constantly being transformed: it is uplifted, folded and faulted by tectonic forces; weathered and eroded by wind, water and ice. Sometimes change is dramatic, the spectacular results of earthquakes or floods. More often it is a slow process lasting millions of years. A physical map of the world represents a snapshot of the ever-evolving architecture of the Earth. This terrain map shows the whole surface of the Earth, both above and below the sea.

The world in section

These cross-sections around the Earth, one in the northern hemisphere; one straddling the Equator, reveal the limited areas of land above sea level in comparison with the extent of the sea floor. The greater erosive effects of weathering by wind and water limit the upward elevation of land above sea level, while the deep oceans retain their dramatic mountain and trench profiles.

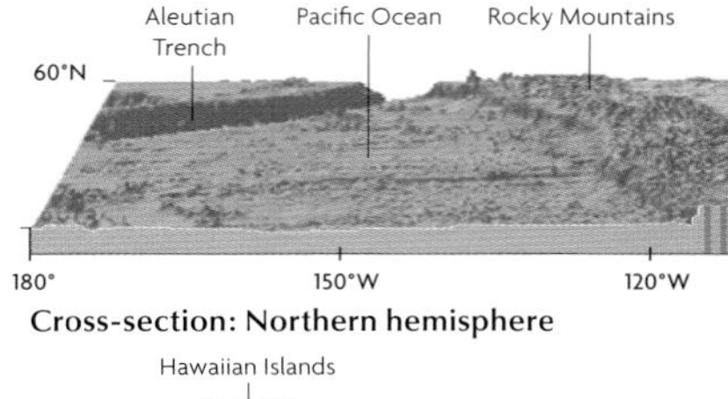
Aleutian Trench
Pacific Ocean
Rocky Mountains
60°N
180°
150°W
120°W

Cross-section: Northern hemisphere

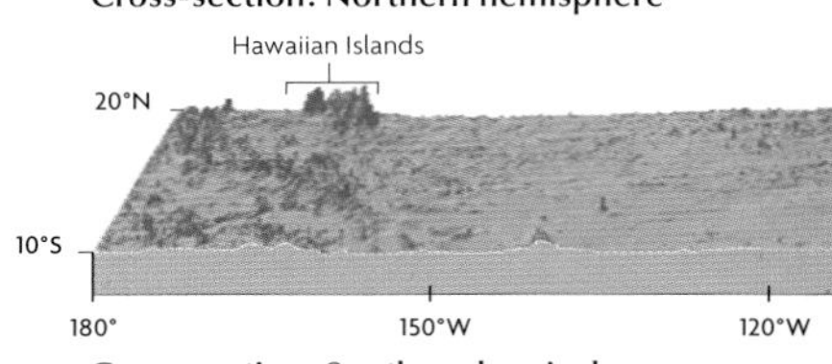
Hawaiian Islands
20°N
10°S
180°
150°W
120°W

Cross-section: Southern hemisphere

Map key

Elevation	Sea depth
6000m / 19,686ft	sea level
4000m / 13,124ft	-250m / -820ft
3000m / 9843ft	-2000m / -6562ft
2000m / 6562ft	-4000m / -13,124ft
1000m / 3281ft	
500m / 1640ft	
250m / 820ft	
100m / 328ft	
sea level	
below sea level	

ARCTIC OCEAN
Beaufort Sea
Chukchi Sea
Arctic Circle
Bering Strait
Brooks Range
Alaska Range
Mount McKinley (Denali) 6194m
Bering Sea
Aleutian Basin
Aleutian Islands
Aleutian Trench
Gulf of Alaska
Mackenzie Mts
Victoria Island
Queen Elizabeth Islands
Ellesmere Island
Baffin Island
Baffin Bay
Greenland
Great Bear Lake
Great Slave Lake
Hudson Strait
Peninsule d'Ungava
Davis Strait
Denmark Strait
Iceland
Jan Mayen
Hudson Bay
Belcher Islands
Labrador Sea
Reykjanes Basin
Reykjanes Ridge
Iceland Basin
Coast Mts
Athabasca
Saskatchewan
Canadian Shield
Laurentian Mountains
Labrador Basin
Charlie-Gibbs Fracture Zone
Vancouver Island

Fraser
Columbia
Lake Winnipeg
Lake Superior
Great Lakes
Lake Huron
Missouri
Rocky Mountains
NORTH AMERICA
Great Plains
Newfoundland
Grand Banks of Newfoundland
Newfoundland Basin
Nova Scotia
Lake Ontario
Lake Michigan
Lake Erie
Cape Cod
Snake
Coast Ranges
Mendocino Fracture Zone
Pioneer Fracture Zone
San Francisco Bay
Great Basin
Death Valley -86m
Colorado
Arkansas
Ohio
Tennessee
Appalachian Mts
Delaware Bay
Chesapeake Bay
Oceanographer Fracture Zone
Mid-Atlantic Ridge
Azores
Strait of Gibraltar
Rio Grande
Red River
Mississippi
Murray Fracture Zone
Bermuda
Blake Plateau
North American Basin
Atlantis Fracture Zone
Madeira
Hawaiian Islands
Tropic of Cancer
Molokai Fracture Zone
Gulf of California
Lower California
Sierra Madre Occidental
Sierra Madre Oriental
Gulf of Mexico
Straits of Florida
Bahamas
Sargasso Sea
Nares Plain
Canary Islands
Canary Basin

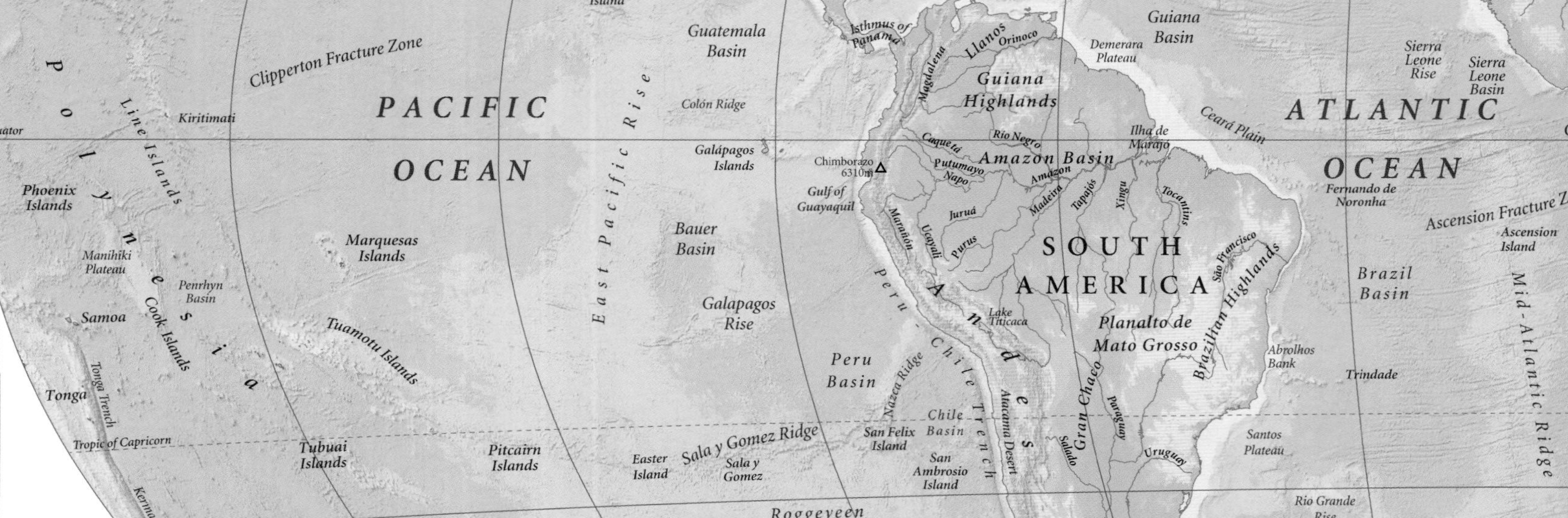
Hawai'i
Johnston Atoll
Mexico Basin
Yucatan Peninsula
Cuba
Puerto Rico Trench
Hispaniola
Greater Antilles
West Indies
Clarion Fracture Zone
Revillagigedo Islands
Sierra Madre del Sur
Middle America Trench
Caribbean Sea
Barracuda Fracture Zone
Cape Verde Islands
Cape Verde Terrace
Lesser Antilles
Clipperton Island
Guatemala Basin
Isthmus of Panama
Llanos
Orinoco
Demerara Plateau
Guiana Basin
Sierra Leone Rise
Sierra Leone Basin
Clipperton Fracture Zone
Guiana Highlands
Magdalena
Polynesia
Line Islands
Kiritimati
PACIFIC OCEAN
Colón Ridge
East Pacific Rise
Ceará Plain
ATLANTIC OCEAN
Equator
Rio Negro
Caquetá
Putumayo
Napo
Amazon Basin
Amazon
Ilha de Marajó
Galápagos Islands
Chimborazo 6310m
Gulf of Guayaquil
Phoenix Islands
Fernando de Noronha
Ascension Fracture Zone
Ascension Island
Marquesas Islands
Bauer Basin
Marañón
Ucayali
Juruá
Purus
Madeira
Tapajós
Xingu
Tocantins
São Francisco
SOUTH AMERICA
Brazil Basin
Manihiki Plateau
Penrhyn Basin
Cook Islands
Samoa
Tuamotu Islands
Galapagos Rise
Peru-Chile Trench
Andes
Lake Titicaca
Planalto de Mato Grosso
Brazilian Highlands
Abrolhos Bank
Trindade
Mid-Atlantic Ridge
Tonga
Tonga Trench
Peru Basin
Nazca Ridge
Chile Basin
Atacama Desert
Gran Chaco
Paraguay
Tropic of Capricorn

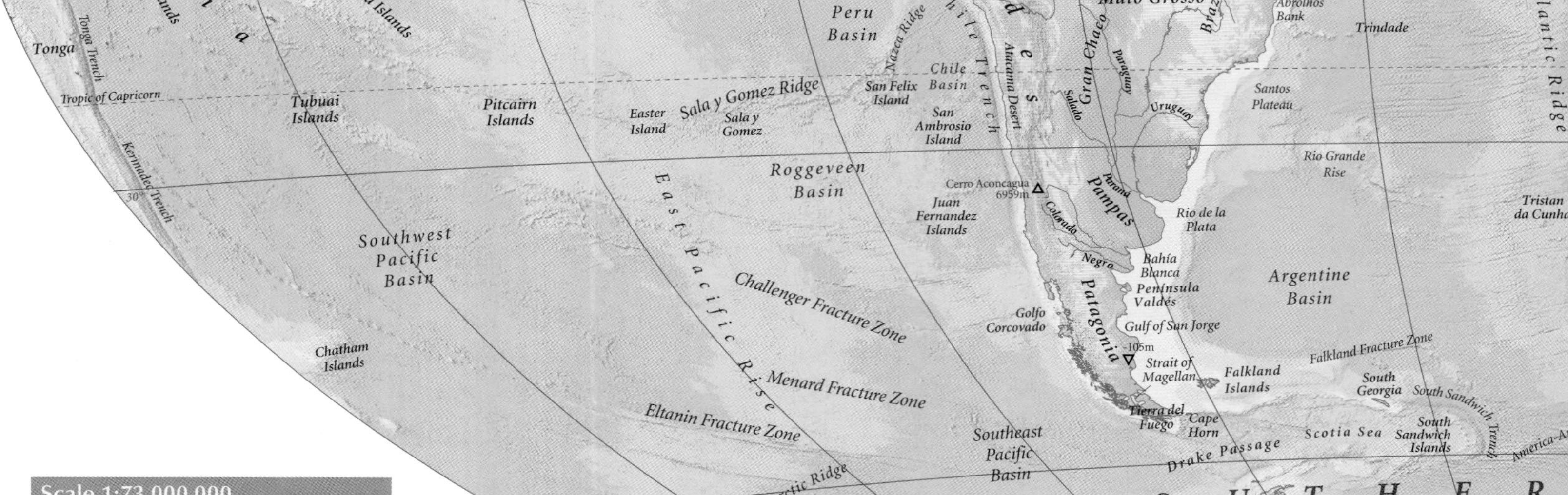
Tubuai Islands
Pitcairn Islands
Easter Island
Sala y Gomez Ridge
Sala y Gomez
San Felix Island
San Ambrosio Island
Salado
Uruguay
Santos Plateau
Rio Grande Rise
Kermadec Trench
Roggeveen Basin
Cerro Aconcagua 6959m
Juan Fernandez Islands
Colorado
Paraná
Pampas
Río de la Plata
Tristan da Cunha
Southwest Pacific Basin
East Pacific Rise
Negro
Bahía Blanca
Península Valdés
Argentine Basin
Gough Island
Challenger Fracture Zone
Patagonia
Golfo Corcovado
Gulf of San Jorge
-105m
Strait of Magellan
Falkland Islands
Falkland Fracture Zone
South Georgia
South Sandwich Trench
Chatham Islands
Menard Fracture Zone
Eltanin Fracture Zone
Southeast Pacific Basin
Tierra del Fuego
Cape Horn
Drake Passage
Scotia Sea
South Sandwich Islands
America-Antarctica Ridge
Pacific-Antarctic Ridge
SOUTHERN
Bellingshausen Sea
Antarctic Peninsula
Weddell Sea
Amundsen Plain
Amundsen Sea
Antarctic Circle
Ronne Ice Shelf
ANT
Ross Sea
Marie Byrd Land
Ross Ice Shelf

Scale 1:73,000,000

Km 0 250 500 1000 1500 2000

Miles 0 250 500 1000 1500 2000

projection: Wagner VII

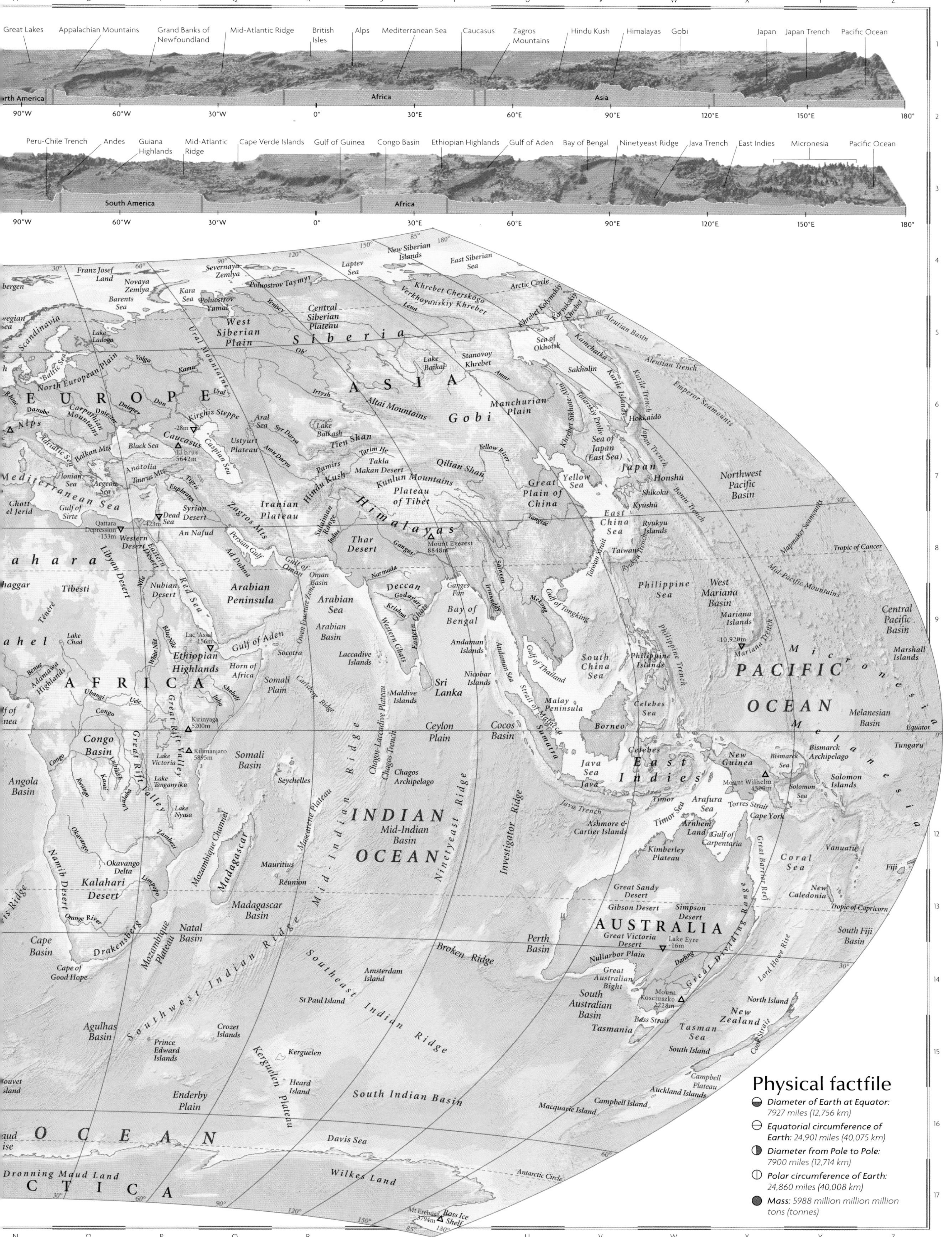
N O P Q R S T U V W X Y Z
Great Lakes
Appalachian Mountains
Grand Banks of Newfoundland
Mid-Atlantic Ridge
British Isles
Alps
Mediterranean Sea
Caucasus
Zagros Mountains
Hindu Kush
Himalayas
Gobi
Japan
Japan Trench
Pacific Ocean
orth America
Africa
Asia
90°W 60°W 30°W 0° 30°E 60°E 90°E 120°E 150°E 180°
Peru-Chile Trench
Andes
Guiana Highlands
Mid-Atlantic Ridge
Cape Verde Islands
Gulf of Guinea
Congo Basin
Ethiopian Highlands
Gulf of Aden
Bay of Bengal
Ninetyeast Ridge
Java Trench
East Indies
Micronesia
Pacific Ocean
South America
Africa
90°W 60°W 30°W 0° 30°E 60°E 90°E 120°E 150°E 180°
Franz Josef Land
Novaya Zemlya
Barents Sea
Kara Sea
Severnaya Zemlya
Poluostrov Taymyr
Laptev Sea
New Siberian Islands
East Siberian Sea
Poluostrov Yamal
West Siberian Plain
Central Siberian Plateau
Siberia
Arctic Circle
Sea of Okhotsk
Aleutian Basin
Aleutian Trench
Kamchatka
Sakhalin
Kurile Islands
Kurile Trench
Emperor Seamounts
Scandinavia
Lake Ladoga
Baltic Sea
North European Plain
Volga
Ural Mountains
Kama
Ural
EUROPE
ASIA
Lake Baikal
Stanovoy Khrebet
Amur
Manchurian Plain
Irtysh
Altai Mountains
Gobi
Rhine
Danube
Carpathian Mountains
Dniester
Dnieper
Don
Kirghiz Steppe
Aral Sea
Syr Darya
Lake Balkash
Tien Shan
Alps
Adriatic Sea
Balkan Mts
Black Sea
Caucasus
-28m
Elbrus 5642m
Caspian Sea
Ustyurt Plateau
Amu Darya
Tarim He
Takla Makan Desert
Yellow River
Qilian Shan
Sea of Japan (East Sea)
Japan
Honshū
Hokkaidō
Japan Trench
Mediterranean Sea
Ionian Sea
Aegean Sea
Anatolia
Taurus Mts
Tigris
Euphrates
Pamirs
Hindu Kush
Kunlun Mountains
Plateau of Tibet
Great Plain of China
Yellow Sea
Shikoku
Kyūshū
Northwest Pacific Basin
Bonin Trench
Chott el Jerid
Gulf of Sirte
Syrian Desert
Dead Sea
-423m
Zagros Mts
Iranian Plateau
Himalayas
Yangtze
East China Sea
Ryukyu Islands
Mapmaker Seamounts
Qattara Depression -133m
Western Desert
Eastern Desert
An Nafud
Persian Gulf
Sulaiman Range
Indus
Thar Desert
Ganges
Mount Everest 8848m
Taiwan
Taiwan Strait
Ryukyu Trench
Tropic of Cancer
Sahara
Libyan Desert
Nile
Nubian Desert
Red Sea
Ad Dahna
Arabian Peninsula
Gulf of Oman
Oman Basin
Narmada
Deccan
Godavari
Krishna
Ganges Fan
Salween
Irrawaddy
Mekong
Philippine Sea
West Mariana Basin
Mid-Pacific Mountains
Ahaggar
Tibesti
Ténéré
Arabian Sea
Owen Fracture Zone
Western Ghats
Eastern Ghats
Bay of Bengal
Gulf of Tongking
Mariana Islands
Central Pacific Basin
Sahel
Lake Chad
Blue Nile
White Nile
Lac 'Assal -156m
Gulf of Aden
Arabian Basin
Andaman Islands
Andaman Sea
Philippine Trench
-10,920m
Mariana Trench
Marshall Islands
Benue
Adamawa Highlands
Ethiopian Highlands
Socotra
Laccadive Islands
Gulf of Thailand
South China Sea
Philippine Islands
Micronesia
Horn of Africa
Somali Plain
Carlsberg Ridge
Maldive Islands
Sri Lanka
Nicobar Islands
PACIFIC OCEAN
AFRICA
Ubangi
Uele
Great Rift Valley
Shebeli
Juba
Malay Peninsula
Strait of Malacca
Celebes Sea
Melanesian Basin
Congo
Kirinyaga 5200m
Chagos-Laccadive Plateau
Ceylon Plain
Cocos Basin
Sumatra
Borneo
Equator
Congo Basin
Lualaba
Lake Victoria
Kilimanjaro 5895m
Somali Basin
Chagos Trench
Chagos Archipelago
Celebes
East Indies
New Guinea
Bismarck Sea
Bismarck Archipelago
Tungaru
Angola Basin
Kasai
Kwango
Lake Tanganyika
Seychelles
Mid-Indian Ridge
Java Sea
Java
Mount Wilhelm 4509m
Solomon Islands
Solomon Sea
Lake Nyasa
Zambezi
Mozambique Channel
Mascarene Plateau
INDIAN OCEAN
Mid-Indian Basin
Ninetyeast Ridge
Investigator Ridge
Java Trench
Timor
Timor Sea
Arafura Sea
Torres Strait
Cape York
Ashmore & Cartier Islands
Arnhem Land
Gulf of Carpentaria
Okavango
Okavango Delta
Madagascar
Mauritius
Réunion
Kimberley Plateau
Great Barrier Reef
Coral Sea
Vanuatu
Fiji
Namib Desert
Kalahari Desert
Limpopo
Great Sandy Desert
New Caledonia
Orange River
Madagascar Basin
Gibson Desert
Simpson Desert
Tropic of Capricorn
Cape Basin
Drakensberg
Mozambique Plateau
Natal Basin
AUSTRALIA
Great Victoria Desert
Lake Eyre -16m
Great Dividing Range
South Fiji Basin
Perth Basin
Broken Ridge
Darling
Nullarbor Plain
Lord Howe Rise
Cape of Good Hope
Southwest Indian Ridge
Amsterdam Island
Great Australian Bight
Southeast Indian Ridge
St Paul Island
South Australian Basin
Mount Kosciuszko 2228m
North Island
New Zealand
Agulhas Basin
Crozet Islands
Prince Edward Islands
Bass Strait
Tasmania
Tasman Sea
Cook Strait
South Island
Kerguelen
Kerguelen Plateau
Heard Island
Campbell Plateau
Auckland Islands
Bouvet Island
Enderby Plain
South Indian Basin
Macquarie Island
Campbell Island
OCEAN
Davis Sea
Dronning Maud Land
Wilkes Land
Antarctic Circle
ANTARCTICA
Mt Erebus 3794m
Ross Ice Shelf
N O P Q R S T U V W X Y Z

Physical factfile

- *Diameter of Earth at Equator: 7927 miles (12,756 km)*
- *Equatorial circumference of Earth: 24,901 miles (40,075 km)*
- *Diameter from Pole to Pole: 7900 miles (12,714 km)*
- *Polar circumference of Earth: 24,860 miles (40,008 km)*
- *Mass: 5988 million million million tons (tonnes)*

Structure of the Earth

The Earth as it is today is just the latest phase in a constant process of evolution which has occurred over the past 4.5 billion years. The Earth's continents are neither fixed nor stable; over the course of the Earth's history, propelled by currents rising from the intense heat at its centre, the great plates on which they lie have moved, collided, joined together, and separated. These processes continue to mould and transform the surface of the Earth, causing earthquakes and volcanic eruptions and creating oceans, mountain ranges, deep ocean trenches and island chains.

Inside the Earth

The Earth's hot inner core ismade up of solid iron, while the outer core is composed of liquid iron and nickel. The mantle nearest the core is viscous, whereas the rocky upper mantle is fairly rigid. The crust is the rocky outer shell of the Earth. Together, the upper mantle and the crust form the lithosphere.

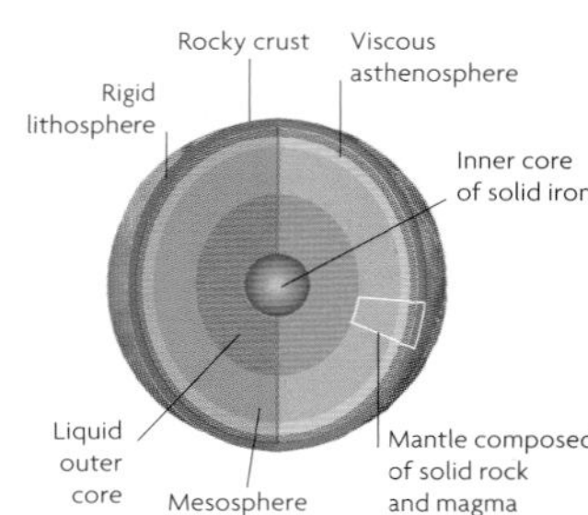

Rocky crust
Viscous asthenosphere
Rigid lithosphere
Inner core of solid iron
Liquid outer core
Mesosphere
Mantle composed of solid rock and magma

The dynamic Earth

The Earth's crust is made up of eight major (and several minor) rigid continental and oceanic tectonic plates, which fit closely together. The positions of the plates are not static. They are constantly moving relative to one another. The type of movement between plates affects the way in which they alter the structure of the Earth. The oldest parts of the plates, known as shields, are the most stable parts of the Earth and little tectonic activity occurs here.

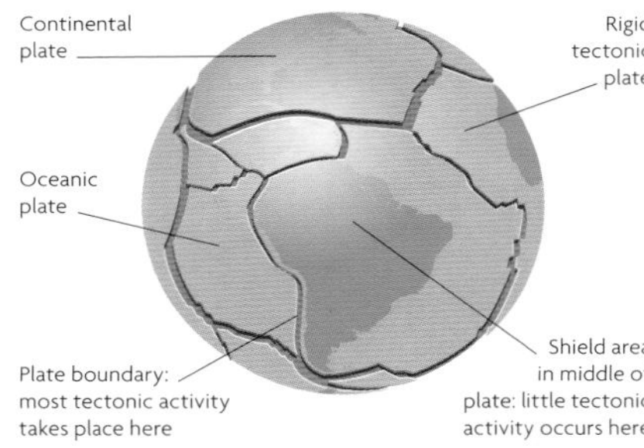

Continental plate
Rigid tectonic plate
Oceanic plate
Plate boundary: most tectonic activity takes place here
Shield area in middle of plate: little tectonic activity occurs here

Inner core
Outer core
Subduction zone
Ocean crust
Movement of plate
Mid-ocean ridge
Lithosphere
Asthenosphere
Mesosphere
Continental crust

Convection currents

Deep within the Earth, at its inner core, temperatures may exceed 8100°F (4500°C). This heat warms rocks in the mesosphere which rise through the partially molten mantle, displacing cooler rocks just below the solid crust, which sink, and are warmed again by the heat of the mantle. This process is continually repeated, creating convection currents which form the moving force beneath the Earth's crust.

Plate boundaries

The boundaries between the plates are the areas where most tectonic activity takes place. Three types of movement occur at plate boundaries: the plates can either move towards each other, move apart, or slide past each other. The effect this has on the Earth's structure depends on whether the margin is between two continental plates, two oceanic plates or an oceanic and continental plate.

▲ ***The Mid-Atlantic Ridge*** *rises above sea level in Iceland, producing geysers and volcanoes.*

Mid-ocean ridges

Mid-ocean ridges are formed when two adjacent oceanic plates pull apart, allowing magma to force its way up to the surface, which then cools to form solid rock. Vast amounts of volcanic material are discharged at these mid-ocean ridges which can reach heights of 10,000 ft (3000 m).

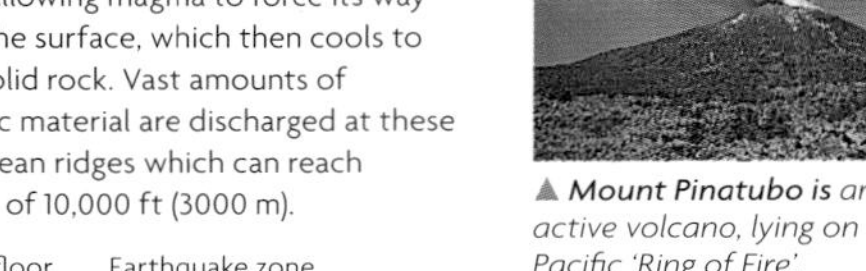

Ocean floor
Earthquake zone
Magma pushed upwards along centre of ridge
Solid mantle

Formation of a mid-ocean ridge

▲ ***Mount Pinatubo*** *is an active volcano, lying on the Pacific 'Ring of Fire'.*

Ocean plates meeting

△△ Oceanic crust is denser and thinner than continental crust; on average it is 3 miles (5 km) thick, while continental crust averages 18–24 miles (30–40 km). When oceanic plates of similar density meet, the crust is contorted as one plate overrides the other, forming deep sea trenches and volcanic island arcs above sea level.

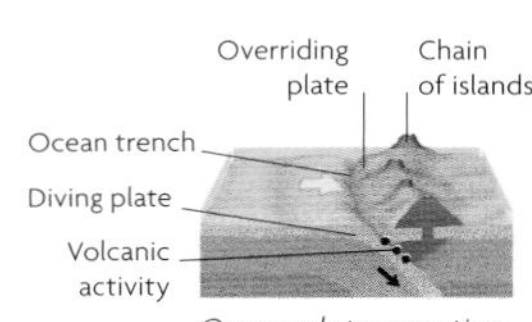

Overriding plate
Chain of islands
Ocean trench
Diving plate
Volcanic activity

Ocean plates meeting to form an island arc

Tectonic activity

- uncertain plate boundary
- volcanic zone
- earthquake zone
- hot spot
- rift valley

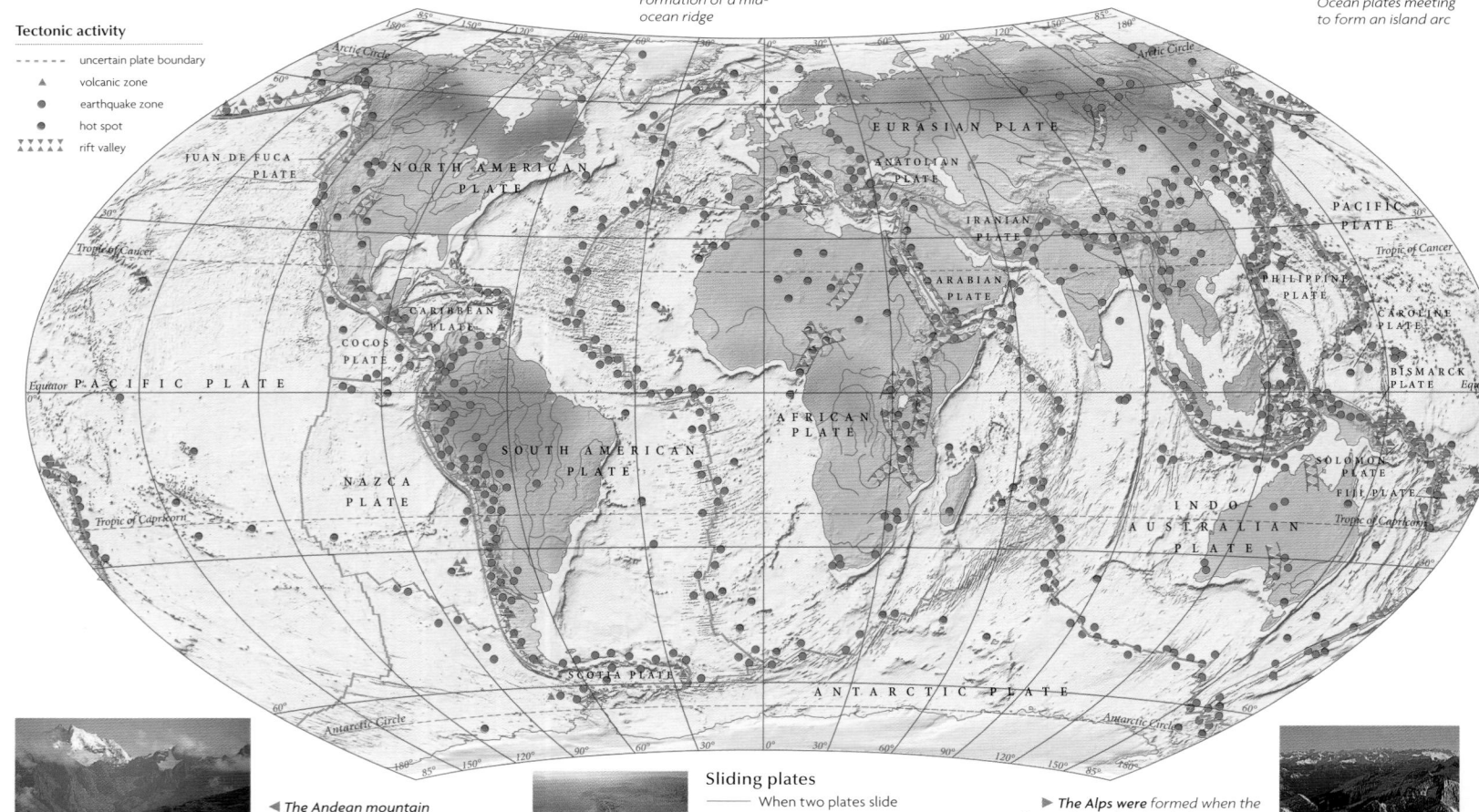

JUAN DE FUCA PLATE · NORTH AMERICAN PLATE · EURASIAN PLATE · ANATOLIAN PLATE · IRANIAN PLATE · ARABIAN PLATE · PACIFIC PLATE · PHILIPPINE PLATE · CAROLINE PLATE · BISMARCK PLATE · CARIBBEAN PLATE · COCOS PLATE · PACIFIC PLATE · AFRICAN PLATE · SOUTH AMERICAN PLATE · NAZCA PLATE · SOLOMON PLATE · FIJI PLATE · INDO-AUSTRALIAN PLATE · SCOTIA PLATE · ANTARCTIC PLATE

Arctic Circle · Tropic of Cancer · Equator · Tropic of Capricorn · Antarctic Circle

Diving plates

△△ When an oceanic and a continental plate meet, the denser oceanic plate is driven underneath the continental plate, which is crumpled by the collision to form mountain ranges. As the ocean plate plunges downward, it heats up, and molten rock (magma) is forced up to the surface.

◀ ***The Andean mountain*** *chain is the typical result of the impact of a diving plate.*

Oceanic plate dives under continental plate
Mountains thrust up by collision
Earthquake zone
Continental plate

Diving plate

▲ ***The deep fracture*** *caused by the sliding plates of the San Andreas Fault can be clearly seen in parts of California.*

Sliding plates

When two plates slide past each other, friction is caused along the fault line which divides them. The plates do not move smoothly, and the uneven movement causes earthquakes.

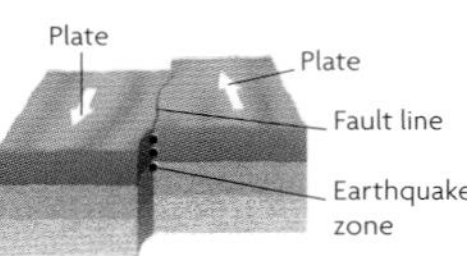

Plate
Plate
Fault line
Earthquake zone

Sliding plates

▶ ***The Alps were*** *formed when the African Plate collided with the Eurasian Plate, about 65 million years ago.*

Plate buckles as it collides
Mountains thrust upwards
Earthquake zone
Crust thickens in response to the impact

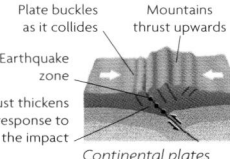

Continental plates colliding to form a mountain range

Colliding plates

▲▲▲ When two continental plates collide, great mountain chains are thrust upwards as the crust buckles and folds under the force of the impact.

Continental drift

Although the plates which make up the Earth's crust move only a few centimetres in a year, over the millions of years of the Earth's history, its continents have moved many thousands of kilometres, to create new continents, oceans and mountain chains.

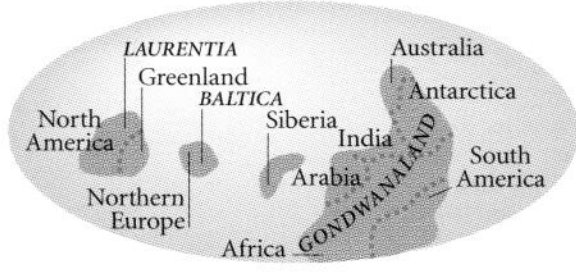
LAURENTIA
Greenland
BALTICA
Australia
Antarctica
North America
Siberia
India
South America
Arabia
Northern Europe
Africa
GONDWANALAND

1: Cambrian period

570–510 million years ago. Most continents are in tropical latitudes. The supercontinent of Gondwanaland reaches the South Pole.

Greenland
SIBERIA
LAURENTIA /BALTICA
Northern Europe
South Asia
Kazakhstania
North America
Africa
Australia
Arabia
South America
India
Antarctica
GONDWANALAND

2: Devonian period

408–362 million years ago. The continents of Gondwanaland and Laurentia are drifting northwards.

ANGARALAND
Siberia
LAURENTIA
Greenland
Northwest China
North America
Northern Europe
Antarctica
Australia
South America
Arabia
Africa
GONDWANALAND

3: Carboniferous period

362–290 million years ago. The Earth is dominated by three continents; Laurentia, Angaraland and Gondwanaland.

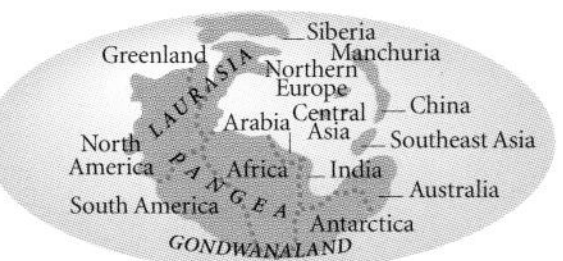
Greenland
Siberia
Manchuria
Northern Europe
LAURASIA
China
Arabia
Central Asia
Southeast Asia
North America
Africa
India
Australia
South America
PANGEA
Antarctica
GONDWANALAND

4: Triassic period

245–208 million years ago. All three major continents have joined to form the super-continent of Pangea.

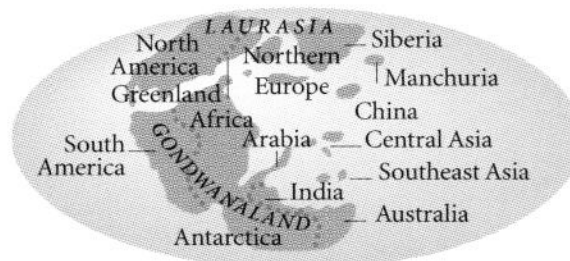
LAURASIA
North America
Northern Europe
Siberia
Greenland
Manchuria
China
Africa
South America
Arabia
Central Asia
Southeast Asia
India
Australia
GONDWANALAND
Antarctica

5: Jurassic period

208–145 million years ago. The super-continent of Pangea begins to break up, causing an overall rise in sea levels.

LAURASIA
Greenland
Siberia
Northern Europe
Manchuria
North America
China
Spain
Turkey
Africa
Arabia
Central Asia
South America
Southeast Asia
India
Australia
GONDWANALAND
Antarctica

6: Cretaceous period

145–65 million years ago. Warm shallow seas cover much of the land: sea levels are about 80 ft (25 m) above present levels.

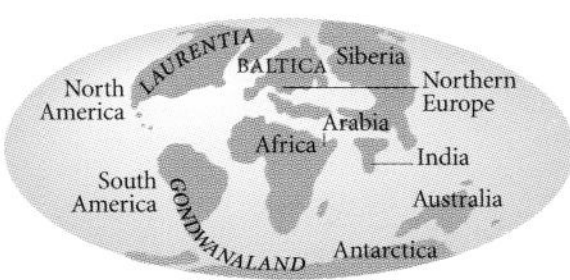
LAURENTIA
BALTICA
Siberia
North America
Northern Europe
Arabia
Africa
India
South America
Australia
GONDWANALAND
Antarctica

7: Tertiary period

65–2 million years ago. Although the world's geography is becoming more recognizable, major events such as the creation of the Himalayan mountain chain, are still to occur during this period.

Continental shields

The centres of the Earth's continents, known as shields, were established between 2500 and 500 million years ago; some contain rocks over three billion years old. They were formed by a series of turbulent events: plate movements, earthquakes and volcanic eruptions. Since the Pre-Cambrian period, over 570 million years ago, they have experienced little tectonic activity, and today, these flat, low-lying slabs of solidified molten rock form the stable centres of the continents. They are bounded or covered by successive belts of younger sedimentary rock.

Canadian (Laurentian)
Scandinavian (Fenno-Scandian)
Siberian
Korean
Indian
African
Guiana (Venezuelan)
Brazilian
Australian
Antarctic

The Hawai'ian island chain

A hot spot lying deep beneath the Pacific Ocean pushes a plume of magma from the Earth's mantle up through the Pacific Plate to form volcanic islands. While the hot spot remains stationary, the plate on which the islands sit is moving slowly. A long chain of islands has been created as the plate passes over the hot spot.

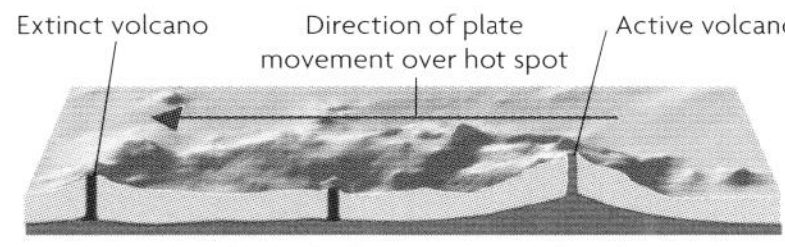
Extinct volcano
Direction of plate movement over hot spot
Active volcano

Cross-section through the Hawai'ian Islands

Evolution of the Hawai'ian Islands

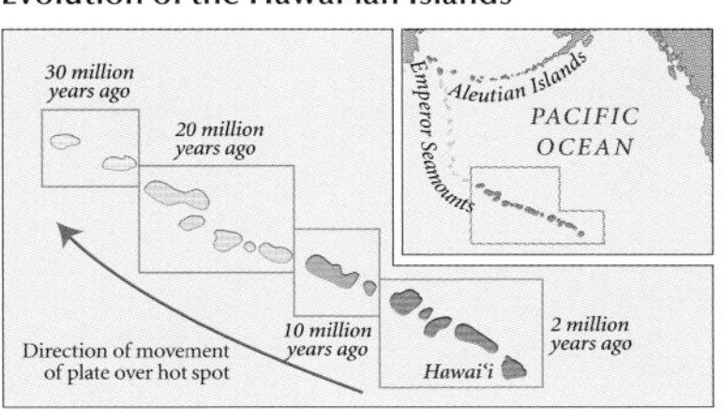
30 million years ago
20 million years ago
10 million years ago
2 million years ago
Hawai'i
Direction of movement of plate over hot spot
Emperor Seamounts
Aleutian Islands
PACIFIC OCEAN

Creation of the Himalayas

Between 10 and 20 million years ago, the Indian subcontinent, part of the ancient continent of Gondwanaland, collided with the continent of Asia. The Indo-Australian Plate continued to move northwards, displacing continental crust and uplifting the Himalayas, the world's highest mountain chain.

Movements of India

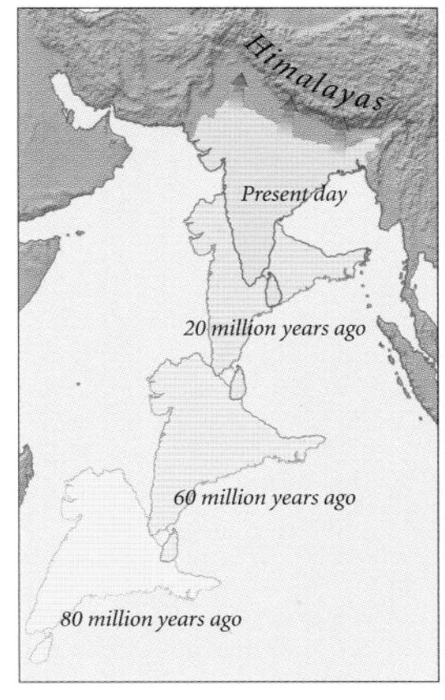
Himalayas
Present day
20 million years ago
60 million years ago
80 million years ago

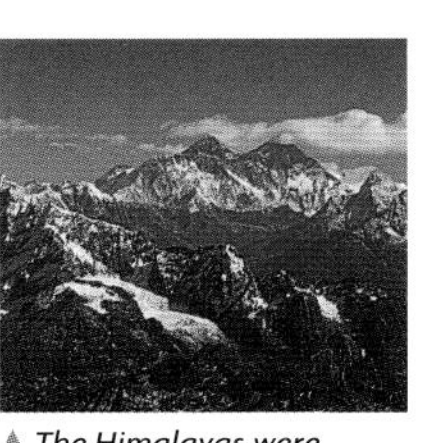
Force of collision pushes up mountains

Cross-section through the Himalayas

▲ ***The Himalayas were** uplifted when the Indian subcontinent collided with Asia.*

The Earth's geology

The Earth's rocks are created in a continual cycle. Exposed rocks are weathered and eroded by wind, water and chemicals and deposited as sediments. If they pass into the Earth's crust they will be transformed by high temperatures and pressures into metamorphic rocks or they will melt and solidify as igneous rocks.

Sandstone

[8] Sandstones are sedimentary rocks formed mainly in deserts, beaches and deltas. Desert sandstones are formed of grains of quartz which have been well rounded by wind erosion.

▲ ***Rock stacks** of desert sandstone, at Bryce Canyon National Park, Utah, USA.*

◀ ***Extrusive igneous rocks** are formed during volcanic eruptions, as here in Hawai'i.*

Andesite

[7] Andesite is an extrusive igneous rock formed from magma which has solidified on the Earth's crust after a volcanic eruption.

▲ ***Gneiss formations in** Norway's Jotunheimen Mountains.*

Gneiss

[1] Gneiss is a metamorphic rock made at great depth during the formation of mountain chains, when intense heat and pressure transform sedimentary or igneous rocks.

◀ ***Basalt columns at** Giant's Causeway, Northern Ireland, UK.*

Basalt

[2] Basalt is an igneous rock, formed when small quantities of magma lying close to the Earth's surface cool rapidly.

Limestone

[3] Limestone is a sedimentary rock, which is formed mainly from the calcite skeletons of marine animals which have been compressed into rock.

▲ ***Limestone hills, Guilin,** China.*

Coral

[4] Coral reefs are formed from the skeletons of millions of individual corals.

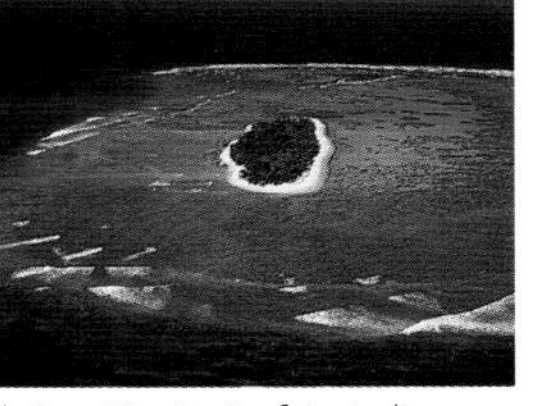

▲ ***Great Barrier Reef,** Australia.*

Geological regions

- continental shield
- sedimentary cover
- coral formation
- igneous rock types

Mountain ranges

- Alpine (new)
- Hercynian (old)
- Caledonian (ancient)

Schist

[6] Schist is a metamorphic rock formed during mountain building, when temperature and pressure are comparatively high. Both mudstones and shales reform into schist under these conditions.

▶ ***Schist formations in** the Atlas Mountains, northwestern Africa.*

Granite

[5] Granite is an intrusive igneous rock formed from magma which has solidified deep within the Earth's crust. The magma cools slowly, producing a coarse-grained rock.

▶ ***Namibia's Namaqualand Plateau** is formed of granite.*

Shaping the landscape

The basic material of the Earth's surface is solid rock: valleys, deserts, soil, and sand are all evidence of the powerful agents of weathering, erosion, and deposition which constantly shape and transform the Earth's landscapes. Water, either flowing continually in rivers or seas, or frozen and compacted into solid sheets of ice, has the most clearly visible impact on the Earth's surface. But wind can transport fragments of rock over huge distances and strip away protective layers of vegetation, exposing rock surfaces to the impact of extreme heat and cold.

Coastal water

The world's coastlines are constantly changing; every day, tides deposit, sift and sort sand, and gravel on the shoreline. Over longer periods, powerful wave action erodes cliffs and headlands and carves out bays.

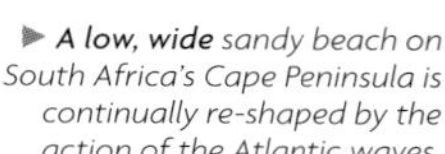

► ***A low, wide** sandy beach on South Africa's Cape Peninsula is continually re-shaped by the action of the Atlantic waves.*

▲ ***The sheer chalk** cliffs at Seven Sisters in southern England are constantly under attack from waves.*

Water

Less than 2% of the world's water is on the land, but it is the most powerful agent of landscape change. Water, as rainfall, groundwater and rivers, can transform landscapes through both erosion and deposition. Eroded material carried by rivers forms the world's most fertile soils.

▲ ***Waterfalls such as** the Iguaçu Falls on the border between Argentina and southern Brazil, erode the underlying rock, causing the falls to retreat.*

Groundwater

In regions where there are porous rocks such as chalk, water is stored underground in large quantities; these reservoirs of water are known as aquifers. Rain percolates through topsoil into the underlying bedrock, creating an underground store of water. The limit of the saturated zone is called the water table.

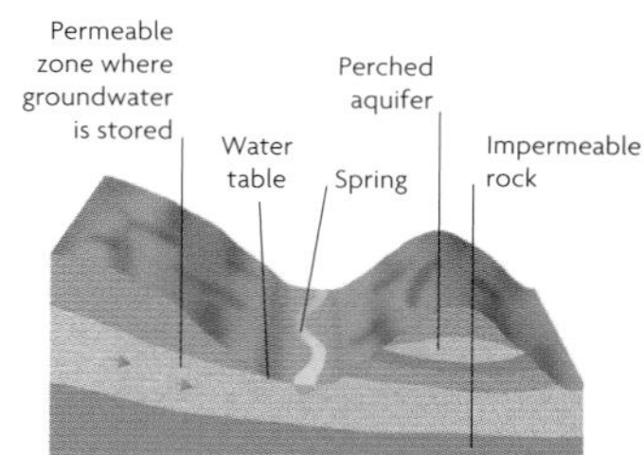
Permeable zone where groundwater is stored
Water table
Perched aquifer
Spring
Impermeable rock

Storage of groundwater in an aquifer

World river systems

drainage basin

World river systems: Sediment deposited annually per drainage basin

tons per sq mile per year: 9120, 6080, 1520, 760
tonnes per sq km per year: 2400, 1600, 400, 200 and less

Rivers

Rivers erode the land by grinding and dissolving rocks and stones. Most erosion occurs in the river's upper course as it flows through highland areas. Rock fragments are moved along the river bed by fast-flowing water and deposited in areas where the river slows down, such as flat plains, or where the river enters seas or lakes.

River valleys

Over long periods of time rivers erode uplands to form characteristic V-shaped valleys with smooth sides.

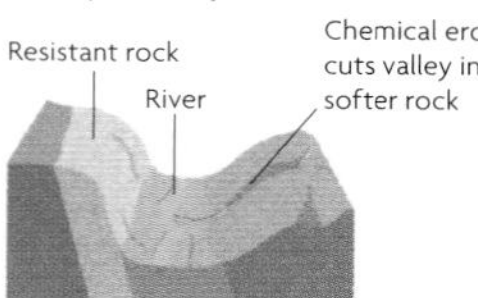
Resistant rock
River
Chemical erosion cuts valley in softer rock

River valley erosion

Deltas

When a river deposits its load of silt and sediment (alluvium) on entering the sea, it may form a delta. As this material accumulates, it chokes the mouth of the river, forcing it to create new channels to reach the sea.

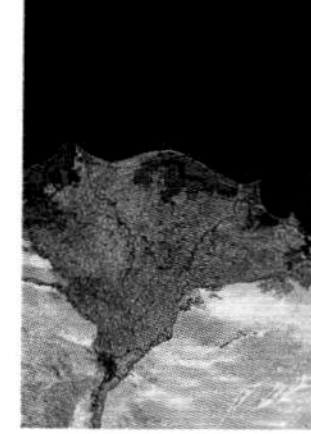

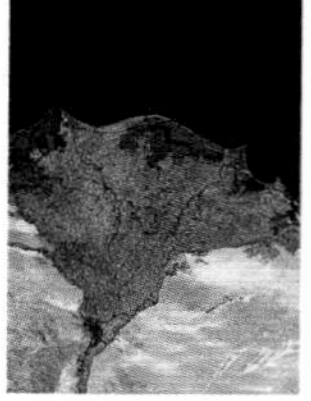

► ***The Nile forms** a broad delta as it flows into the Mediterranean.*

Drainage basins

The drainage basin is the area of land drained by a major trunk river and its smaller branch rivers or tributaries. Drainage basins are separated from one another by natural boundaries known as watersheds.

Watershed — Major trunk river — Alps — Dolomites — Apennines — Tributary river — Delta — River mouth — Po Valley

The drainage basin of the Po river, northern Italy.

Meanders

In their lower courses, rivers flow slowly. As they flow across the lowlands, they form looping bends called meanders.

▲ ***The Mississippi River** forms meanders as it flows across the southern US.*

▲ ***The meanders of** Utah's San Juan River have become deeply incised.*

◄ ***Mud is deposited** by China's Yellow River in its lower course.*

Deposition

When rivers have deposited large quantities of fertile alluvium, they are forced to find new channels through the alluvium deposits, creating braided river systems.

Landslides

Heavy rain and associated flooding on slopes can loosen underlying rocks, which crumble, causing the top layers of rock and soil to slip.

► ***A huge landslide** in the Swiss Alps has left massive piles of rocks and pebbles called scree.*

▲ ***A deep gully** in the French Alps caused by the scouring of upper layers of turf.*

Gullies

In areas where soil is thin, rainwater is not effectively absorbed, and may flow overland. The water courses downhill in channels, or gullies, and may lead to rapid erosion of soil.

Ice

During its long history, the Earth has experienced a number of glacial episodes when temperatures were considerably lower than today. During the last Ice Age, 18,000 years ago, ice covered an area three times larger than it does today. Over these periods, the ice has left a remarkable legacy of transformed landscapes.

Glaciers

Glaciers are formed by the compaction of snow into 'rivers' of ice. As they move over the landscape, glaciers pick up and carry a load of rocks and boulders which erode the landscape they pass over, and are eventually deposited at the end of the glacier.

▲ ***A massive glacier*** *advancing down a valley in southern Argentina.*

Glacial valleys

Glaciers can erode much more powerfully than rivers. They form steep-sided, flat-bottomed valleys with a typical U-shaped profile. Valleys created by tributary glaciers, whose floors have not been eroded to the same depth as the main glacial valley floor, are called hanging valleys

▲ ***The U-shaped profile*** *and piles of morainic debris are characteristic of a valley once filled by a glacier.*

▲ ***A series of*** *hanging valleys high up in the Chilean Andes.*

▲ ***The profile of*** *the Matterhorn has been formed by three cirques lying 'back-to-back'.*

Cirques

Cirques are basin-shaped hollows which mark the head of a glaciated valley. Where neighboring cirques meet, they are divided by sharp rock ridges called arêtes. It is these arêtes which give the Matterhorn its characteristic profile.

Fjords

Fjords are ancient glacial valleys flooded by the sea following the end of a period of glaciation. Beneath the water, the valley floor can be 4000 ft (1300 m) deep.

▲ ***A fjord fills*** *a former glacial valley in southern New Zealand.*

Past and present world ice-cover and glacial features

Past and present world ice cover and glacial features

- extent of last Ice Age
- loess deposits
- post-glacial feature
- glacial feature
- present day ice cover
- glacial field

Post-glacial features

When a glacial episode ends, the retreating ice leaves many features. These include depositional ridges called moraines, which may be eroded into low hills known as drumlins; sinuous ridges called eskers; kames, which are rounded hummocks; depressions known as kettle holes; and windblown loess deposits.

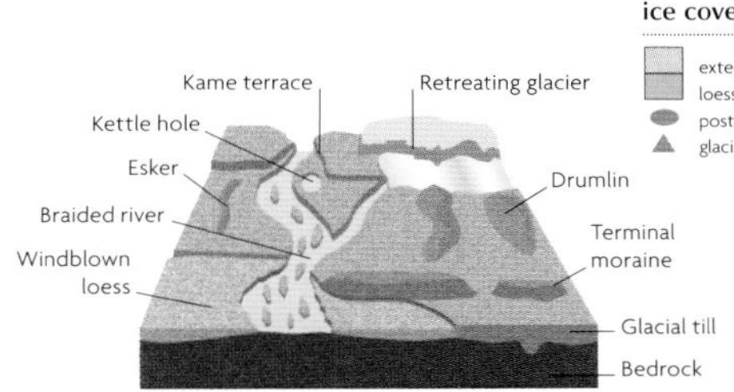
Kame terrace
Retreating glacier
Kettle hole
Esker
Drumlin
Braided river
Terminal moraine
Windblown loess
Glacial till
Bedrock

Post-glacial landscape features

Ice shattering

Water drips into fissures in rocks and freezes, expanding as it does so. The pressure weakens the rock, causing it to crack, and eventually to shatter into polygonal patterns.

▲ ***Irregular polygons show*** *through the sedge-grass tundra in the Yukon, Canada.*

Periglaciation

Periglacial areas occur near to the edge of ice sheets. A layer of frozen ground lying just beneath the surface of the land is known as permafrost. When the surface melts in the summer, the water is unable to drain into the frozen ground, and so 'creeps' downhill, a process known as solifluction.

Wind

Strong winds can transport rock fragments great distances, especially where there is little vegetation to protect the rock. In desert areas, wind picks up loose, unprotected sand particles, carrying them over great distances. This powerfully abrasive debris is blasted at the surface by the wind, eroding the landscape into dramatic shapes.

Prevailing winds and dust trajectories

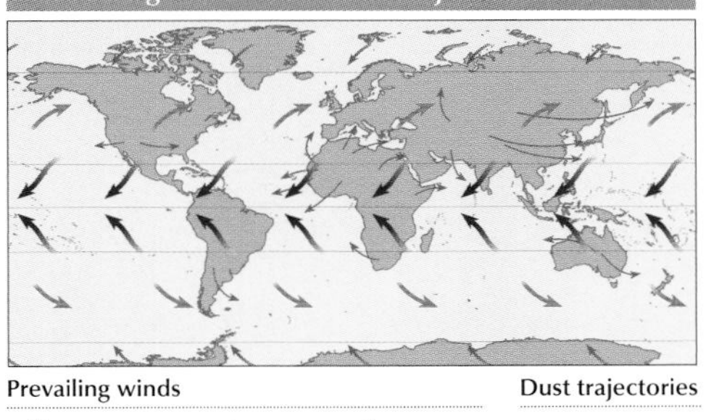

Prevailing winds

- northeast trade / southeast trade
- westerly / westerly
- polar easterly / polar easterly

Dust trajectories

- trajectory of aeolian dust

Hot and cold deserts

Main desert types

- hot arid
- semi-arid
- cold polar

Temperature

Most of the world's deserts are in the tropics. The cold deserts which occur elsewhere are arid because they are a long way from the rain-giving sea. Rock in deserts is exposed because of lack of vegetation and is susceptible to changes in temperature; extremes of heat and cold can cause both cracks and fissures to appear in the rock.

Deposition

The rocky, stony floors of the world's deserts are swept and scoured by strong winds. The smaller, finer particles of sand are shaped into surface ripples, dunes, or sand mountains, which rise to a height of 650 ft (200 m). Dunes usually form single lines, running perpendicular to the direction of the prevailing wind. These long, straight ridges can extend for over 100 miles (160 km).

▲ ***Barchan dunes*** *in the Arabian Desert.*

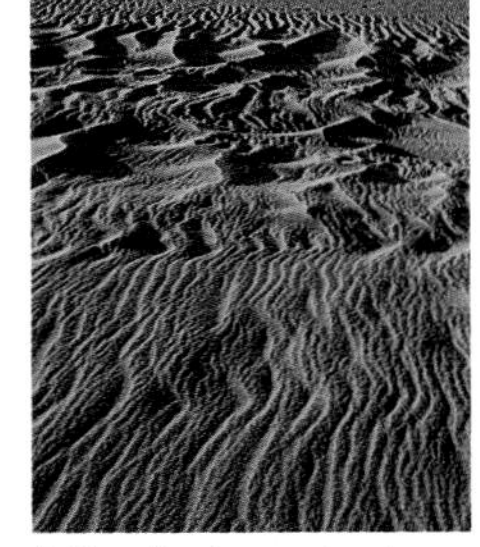

▲ ***Complex dune system*** *in the Sahara.*

Heat

Fierce sun can heat the surface of rock, causing it to expand more rapidly than the cooler, underlying layers. This creates tensions which force the rock to crack or break up. In arid regions, the evaporation of water from rock surfaces dissolves certain minerals within the water, causing salt crystals to form in small openings in the rock. The hard crystals force the openings to widen into cracks and fissures.

▲ ***The cracked and*** *parched floor of Death Valley, California. This is one of the hottest deserts on Earth.*

Desert abrasion

Abrasion creates a wide range of desert landforms from faceted pebbles and wind ripples in the sand, to large-scale features such as yardangs (low, streamlined ridges), and scoured desert pavements.

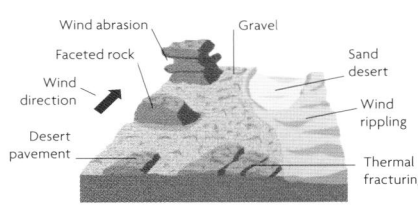

Wind abrasion
Gravel
Faceted rock
Sand desert
Wind direction
Wind rippling
Desert pavement
Thermal fracturing

Features of a desert surface

◀ ***This dry valley*** *at Ellesmere Island in the Canadian Arctic is an example of a cold desert. The cracked floor and scoured slopes are features also found in hot deserts.*

Dunes

Dunes are shaped by wind direction and sand supply. Where sand supply is limited, crescent-shaped barchan dunes are formed.

Types of dune

Wind direction

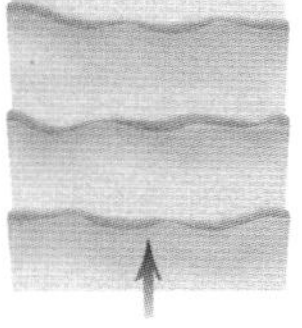
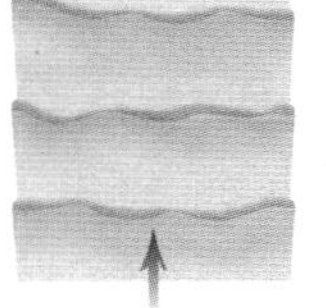

Transverse dune

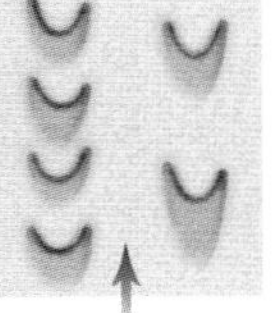

Barchan dune

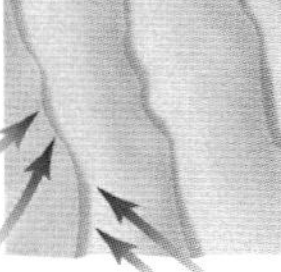

Linear dune

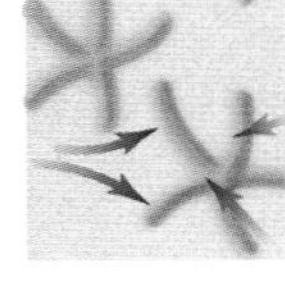

Star dune

The world's oceans

Two-thirds of the Earth's surface is covered by the oceans. The landscape of the ocean floor, like the surface of the land, has been shaped by movements of the Earth's crust over millions of years to form volcanic mountain ranges, deep trenches, basins and plateaux. Ocean currents constantly redistribute warm and cold water around the world. A major warm current, such as El Niño in the Pacific Ocean, can increase surface temperature by up to 10°F (8°C), causing changes in weather patterns which can lead to both droughts and flooding.

The great oceans

There are five oceans on Earth: the Pacific, Atlantic, Indian and Southern oceans, and the much smaller Arctic Ocean. These five ocean basins are relatively young, having evolved within the last 80 million years. One of the most recent plate collisions, between the Eurasian and African plates, created the present-day arrangement of continents and oceans.

▲ ***The Indian Ocean** accounts for approximately 20% of the total area of the world's oceans.*

Sea level

If the influence of tides, winds, currents and variations in gravity were ignored, the surface of the Earth's oceans would closely follow the topography of the ocean floor, with an underwater ridge 3000 ft (915 m) high producing a rise of up to 3 ft (1 m) in the level of the surface water.

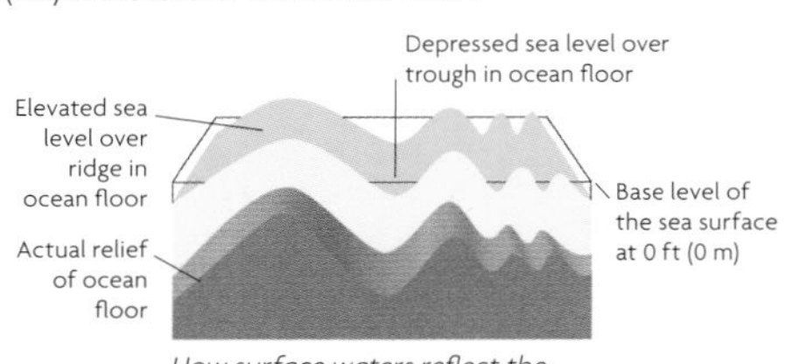

Depressed sea level over trough in ocean floor
Elevated sea level over ridge in ocean floor
Base level of the sea surface at 0 ft (0 m)
Actual relief of ocean floor

How surface waters reflect the relief of the ocean floor

▲ ***The low relief** of many small Pacific islands such as these atolls at Huahine in French Polynesia makes them vulnerable to changes in sea level.*

Ocean structure

The continental shelf is a shallow, flat sea-bed surrounding the Earth's continents. It extends to the continental slope, which falls to the ocean floor. Here, the flat abyssal plains are interrupted by vast, underwater mountain ranges, the mid-ocean ridges, and ocean trenches which plunge to depths of 35,828 ft (10,920 m).

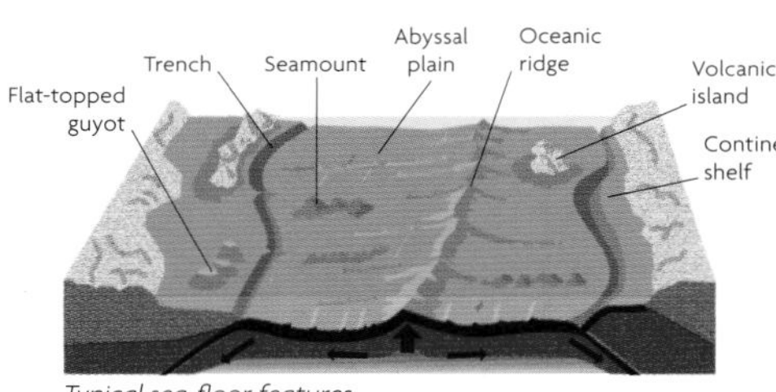

Flat-topped guyot
Trench
Seamount
Abyssal plain
Oceanic ridge
Volcanic island
Continental shelf

Typical sea-floor features

Ocean depth

Sea level
200m / 656ft
1000m / 3281ft
2000m / 6562ft
3000m / 9843ft
4000m / 13,124ft
5000m / 16,400ft
6000m / 19,686ft

EUROPE
ASIA
AFRICA
AUSTRALIA
ANTARCTICA
INDIAN OCEAN
SOUTHERN
ARCTIC
Arctic Circle
Tropic of Cancer
Equator
Tropic of Capricorn
Antarctic Circle
Barents Sea
Kara Sea
Laptev Sea
East Siberian Sea
North Sea
Baltic Sea
Sea of Okhotsk
Black Sea
Caspian Sea
Adriatic Sea
Mediterranean Sea
Sea of Japan (East Sea)
Kurile Trench
Emperor Seamounts
Japan Trench
Northwest Pacific Basin
Yellow Sea
East China Sea
Persian Gulf
Red Sea
Arabian Sea
Bay of Bengal
Taiwan Strait
Mid-Pacific Mountains
Philippine Sea
Mariana Trench
Gulf of Thailand
South China Sea
Sunda Shelf
Strait of Malacca
Celebes Sea
Gulf of Guinea
Carlsberg Ridge
Chagos-Laccadive Plateau
Somali Basin
Mid-Indian Basin
Ninetyeast Ridge
Mid-Indian Ridge
Bismarck Sea
Solomon Sea
Melanesian Basin
Angola Basin
Mozambique Channel
Mascarene Plateau
Arafura Sea
Timor Sea
Coral Sea
Great Barrier Reef
Walvis Ridge
Madagascar Basin
Perth Basin
Cape Basin
Mozambique Plateau
South Australian Basin
Bass Strait
Tasman Sea
Southwest Indian Ridge
Agulhas Basin
Southeast Indian Ridge
Kerguelen Plateau
South Indian Basin
Enderby Plain

▲ ***A black smoker** in the Atlantic Ocean.*

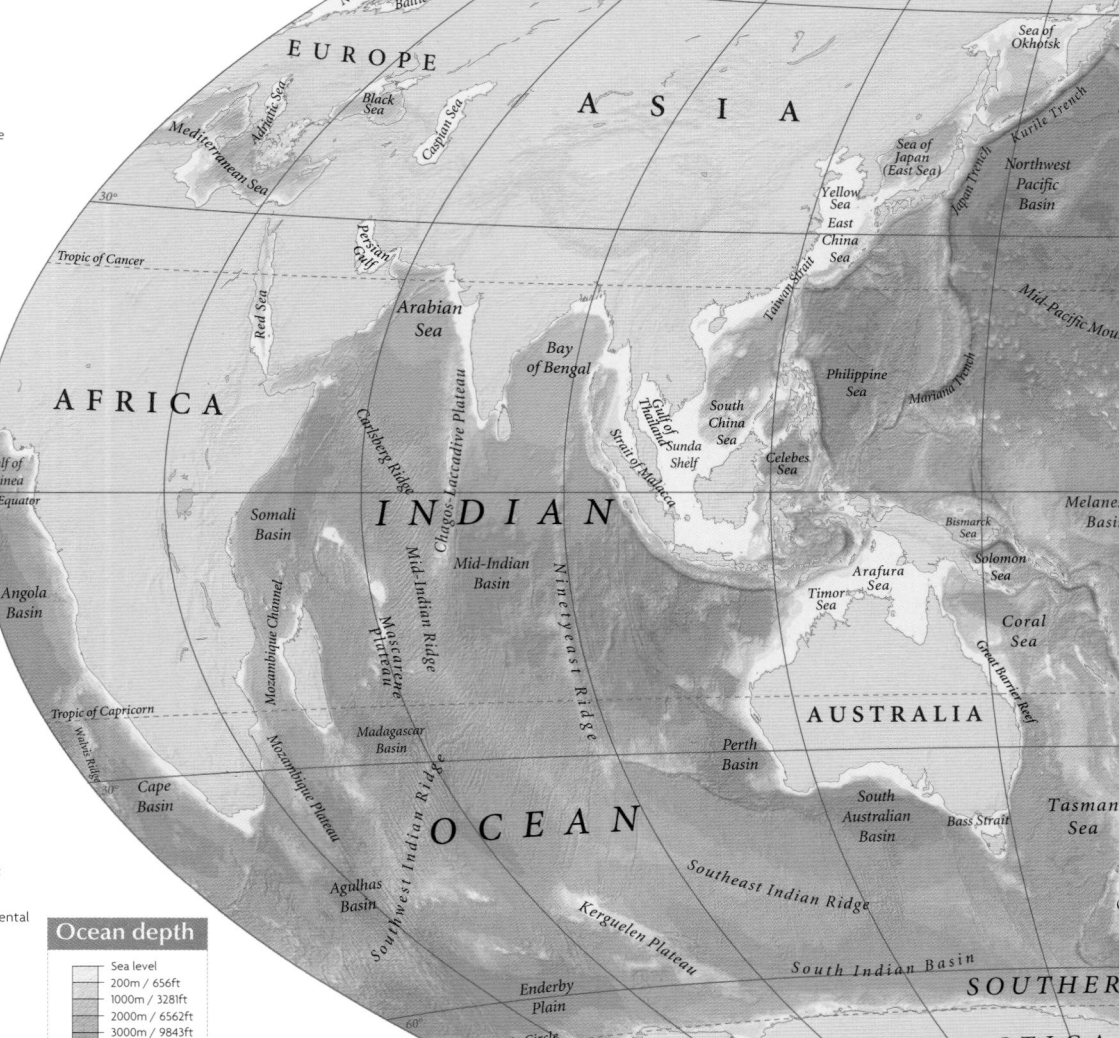

Black smokers

These vents in the ocean floor disgorge hot, sulphur-rich water from deep in the Earth's crust. Despite the great depths, a variety of lifeforms have adapted to the chemical-rich environment which surrounds black smokers.

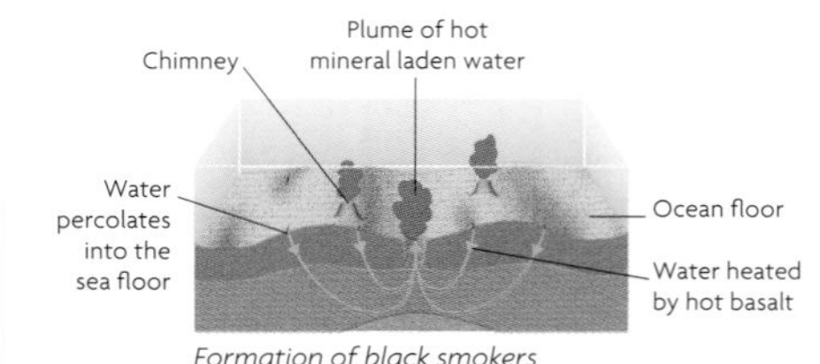

Chimney
Plume of hot mineral laden water
Water percolates into the sea floor
Ocean floor
Water heated by hot basalt

Formation of black smokers

▲ ***Surtsey, near Iceland,** is a volcanic island lying directly over the Mid-Atlantic Ridge. It was formed in the 1960s following intense volcanic activity nearby.*

Ocean floors

Mid-ocean ridges are formed by lava which erupts beneath the sea and cools to form solid rock. This process mirrors the creation of volcanoes from cooled lava on the land. The ages of sea floor rocks increase in parallel bands outwards from central ocean ridges.

Ages of the ocean floor

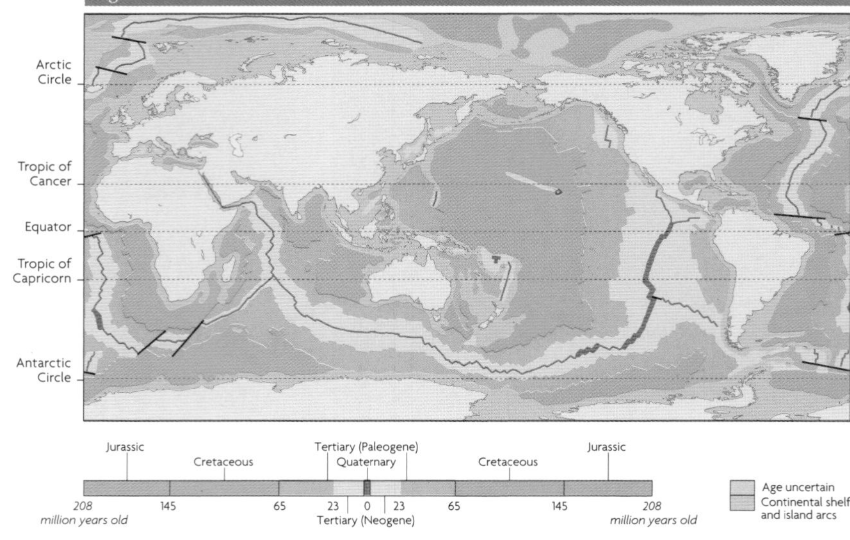

Arctic Circle
Tropic of Cancer
Equator
Tropic of Capricorn
Antarctic Circle

Jurassic | Cretaceous | Tertiary (Paleogene) | Quaternary | Cretaceous | Jurassic

208 million years old · 145 · 65 · 23 · 0 · 23 · 65 · 145 · 208 million years old

Tertiary (Neogene)

Age uncertain
Continental shelf and island arcs

▲ **Currents in the** *Southern Ocean are driven by some of the world's fiercest winds, including the Roaring Forties, Furious Fifties and Shrieking Sixties.*

▲ ***The Pacific Ocean*** *is the world's largest and deepest ocean, covering over one-third of the surface of the Earth.*

▲ ***The Atlantic Ocean*** *was formed when the landmasses of the eastern and western hemispheres began to drift apart 180 million years ago.*

Deposition of sediment

Storms, earthquakes, and volcanic activity trigger underwater currents known as turbidity currents which scour sand and gravel from the continental shelf, creating underwater canyons. These strong currents pick up material deposited at river mouths and deltas, and carry it across the continental shelf and through the underwater canyons, where it is eventually laid down on the ocean floor in the form of fans.

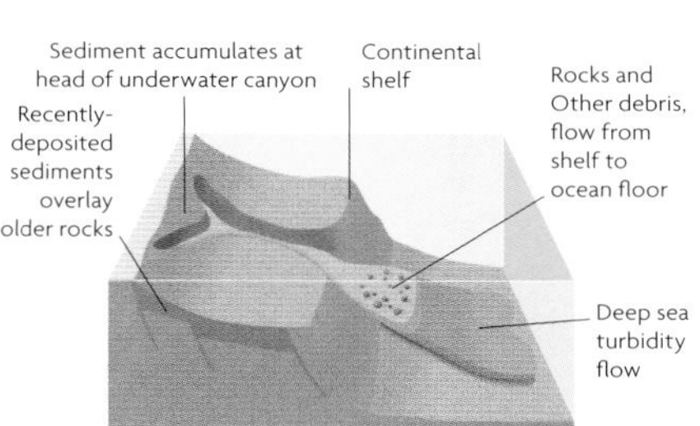
Sediment accumulates at head of underwater canyon
Continental shelf
Recently-deposited sediments overlay older rocks
Rocks and Other debris, flow from shelf to ocean floor
Deep sea turbidity flow

How sediment is deposited on the ocean floor

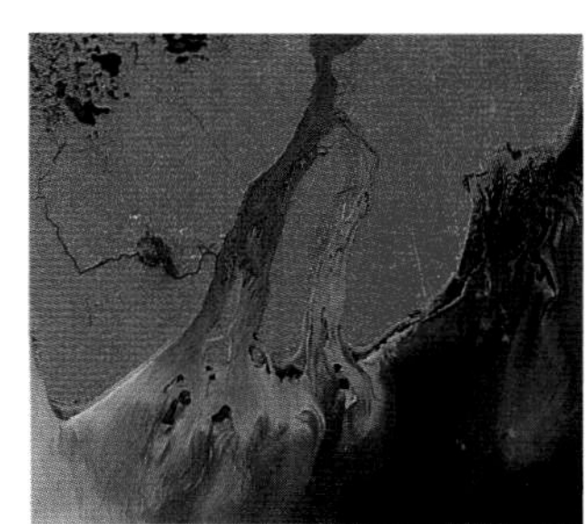

► ***Satellite image of*** *the Yangtze (Chang Jiang) Delta, in which the land appears red. The river deposits immense quantities of silt into the East China Sea, much of which will eventually reach the deep ocean floor.*

Surface water

Ocean currents move warm water away from the Equator towards the poles, while cold water is, in turn, moved towards the Equator. This is the main way in which the Earth distributes surface heat and is a major climatic control. Approximately 4000 million years ago, the Earth was dominated by oceans and there was no land to interrupt the flow of the currents, which would have flowed as straight lines, simply influenced by the Earth's rotation.

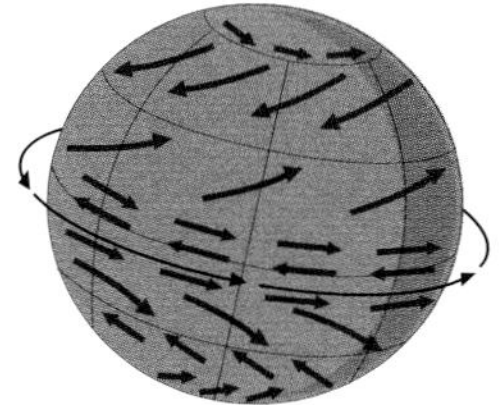

Idealized globe showing the movement of water around a landless Earth.

Ocean currents

Surface currents are driven by the prevailing winds and by the spinning motion of the Earth, which drives the currents into circulating whirlpools, or gyres. Deep sea currents, over 330 ft (100 m) below the surface, are driven by differences in water temperature and salinity, which have an impact on the density of deep water and on its movement.

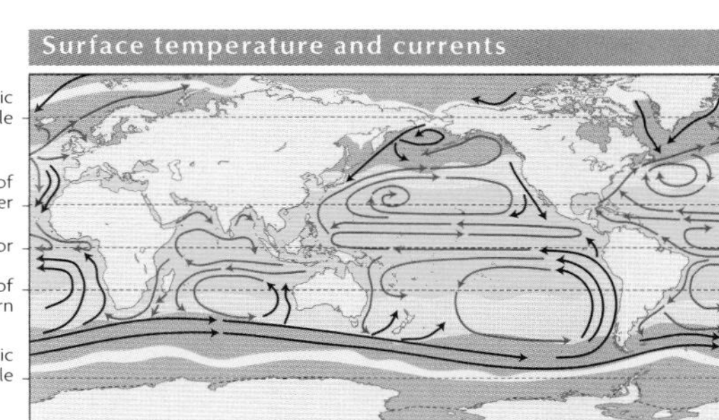
Surface temperature and currents
Arctic Circle
Tropic of Cancer
Equator
Tropic of Capricorn
Antarctic Circle

Surface temperature and currents

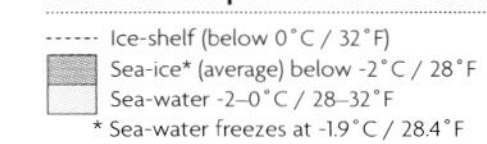
Ice-shelf (below 0°C / 32°F)
Sea-ice* (average) below -2°C / 28°F
Sea-water -2–0°C / 28–32°F
* Sea-water freezes at -1.9°C / 28.4°F

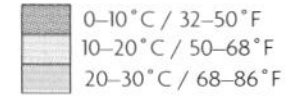
0–10°C / 32–50°F
10–20°C / 50–68°F
20–30°C / 68–86°F

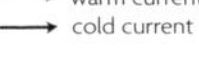
warm current
cold current

Tides and waves

Tides are created by the pull of the Sun and Moon's gravity on the surface of the oceans. The levels of high and low tides are influenced by the position of the Moon in relation to the Earth and Sun. Waves are formed by wind blowing over the surface of the water.

Tidal range and wave environments

Arctic Circle

Tropic of Cancer

Equator

Tropic of Capricorn

Antarctic Circle

Tidal range and wave environments

less than 2m / 7ft; 2–4m / 7–13ft; greater than 4m / 13ft; east coast swell; west coast swell; tropical cyclone storm wave; ice-shelf

High and low tides

The highest tides occur when the Earth, the Moon and the Sun are aligned *(below left)*. The lowest tides are experienced when the Sun and Moon align at right angles to one another *(below right)*.

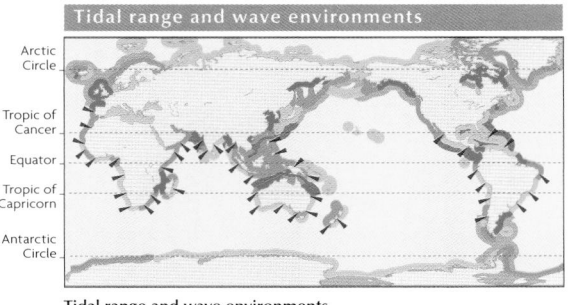

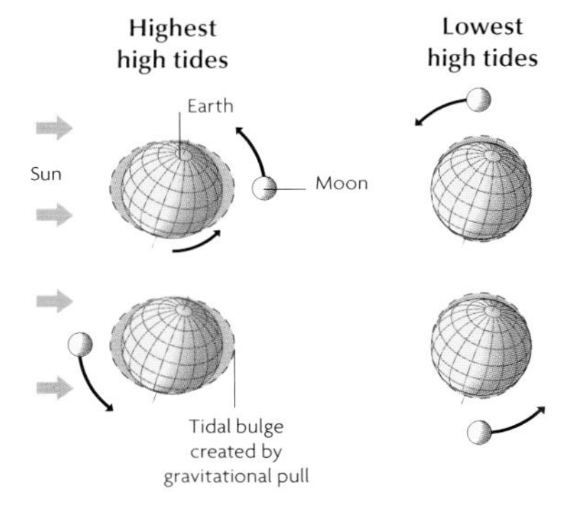
Highest high tides
Lowest high tides
Earth
Sun
Moon
Tidal bulge created by gravitational pull

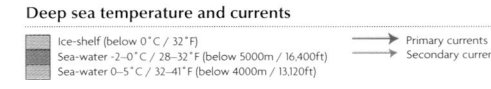

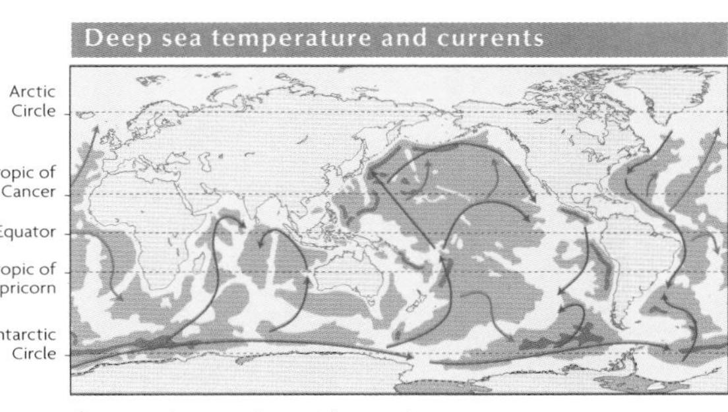
Deep sea temperature and currents
Arctic Circle
Tropic of Cancer
Equator
Tropic of Capricorn
Antarctic Circle

Deep sea temperature and currents

Ice-shelf (below 0°C / 32°F)

Sea-water -2–0°C / 28–32°F (below 5000m / 16,400ft)

Sea-water 0–5°C / 32–41°F (below 4000m / 13,120ft)

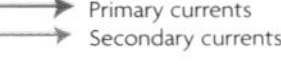
Primary currents
Secondary currents

The global climate

The Earth's climatic types consist of stable patterns of weather conditions averaged out over a long period of time. Different climates are categorized according to particular combinations of temperature and humidity. By contrast, weather consists of short-term fluctuations in wind, temperature and humidity conditions. Different climates are determined by latitude, altitude, the prevailing wind and circulation of ocean currents. Longer-term changes in climate, such as global warming or the onset of ice ages, are punctuated by shorter-term events which comprise the day-to-day weather of a region, such as frontal depressions, hurricanes and blizzards.

The atmosphere, wind and weather

The Earth's atmosphere has been compared to a giant ocean of air which surrounds the planet. Its circulation patterns are similar to the currents in the oceans and are influenced by three factors; the Earth's orbit around the Sun and rotation about its axis, and variations in the amount of heat radiation received from the Sun. If both heat and moisture were not redistributed between the Equator and the poles, large areas of the Earth would be uninhabitable.

◀ ***Heavy fogs**, as here in southern England, form as moisture-laden air passes over cold ground.*

Temperature

The world can be divided into three major climatic zones, stretching like large belts across the latitudes: the tropics which are warm; the cold polar regions and the temperate zones which lie between them. Temperatures across the Earth range from above 30°C (86°F) in the deserts to as low as -55°C (-70°F) at the poles. Temperature is also controlled by altitude; because air becomes cooler and less dense the higher it gets, mountainous regions are typically colder than those areas which are at, or close to, sea level.

Average January temperatures

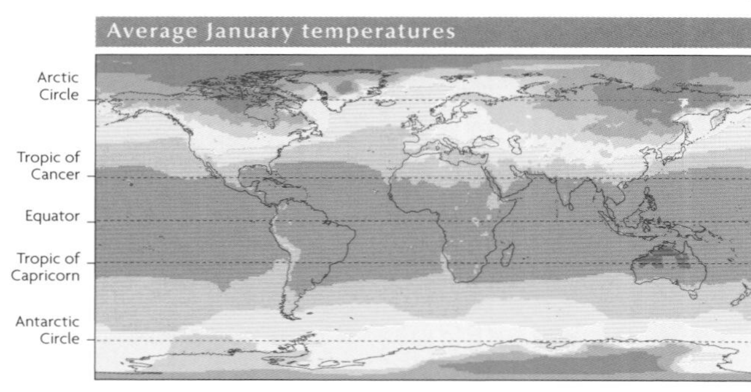
Arctic Circle
Tropic of Cancer
Equator
Tropic of Capricorn
Antarctic Circle

Average July temperatures

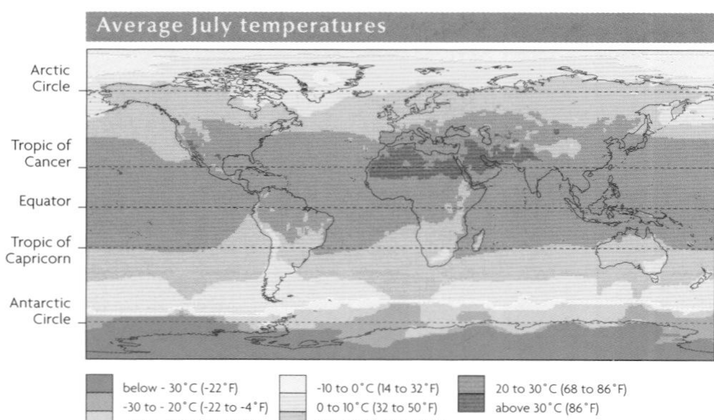
Arctic Circle
Tropic of Cancer
Equator
Tropic of Capricorn
Antarctic Circle

below - 30°C (-22°F)
-30 to - 20°C (-22 to -4°F)
-20 to - 10°C (-4 to 14°F)
-10 to 0°C (14 to 32°F)
0 to 10°C (32 to 50°F)
10 to 20°C (50 to 68°F)
20 to 30°C (68 to 86°F)
above 30°C (86°F)

Global air circulation

Air does not simply flow from the Equator to the poles, it circulates in giant cells known as Hadley and Ferrel cells. As air warms it expands, becoming less dense and rising; this creates areas of low pressure. As the air rises it cools and condenses, causing heavy rainfall over the tropics and slight snowfall over the poles. This cool air then sinks, forming high pressure belts. At surface level in the tropics these sinking currents are deflected polewards as the westerlies and towards the equator as the trade winds. At the poles they become the polar easterlies.

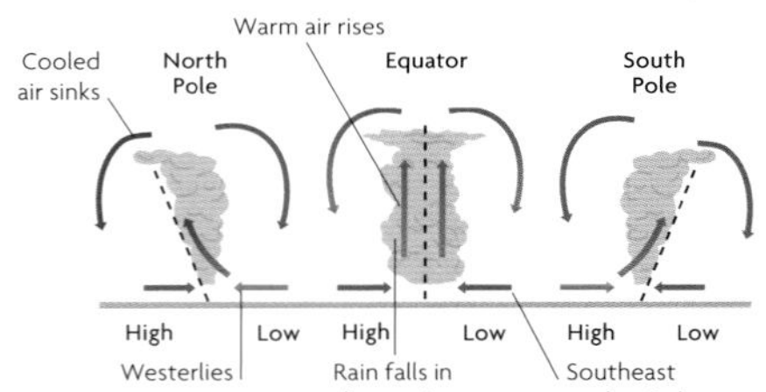
Warm air rises
Cooled air sinks
North Pole
Equator
South Pole
High
Low
High
Low
High
Low
Westerlies
Rain falls in the tropics
Southeast trade winds

▲ ***The Antarctic pack ice** expands its area by almost seven times during the winter as temperatures drop and surrounding seas freeze.*

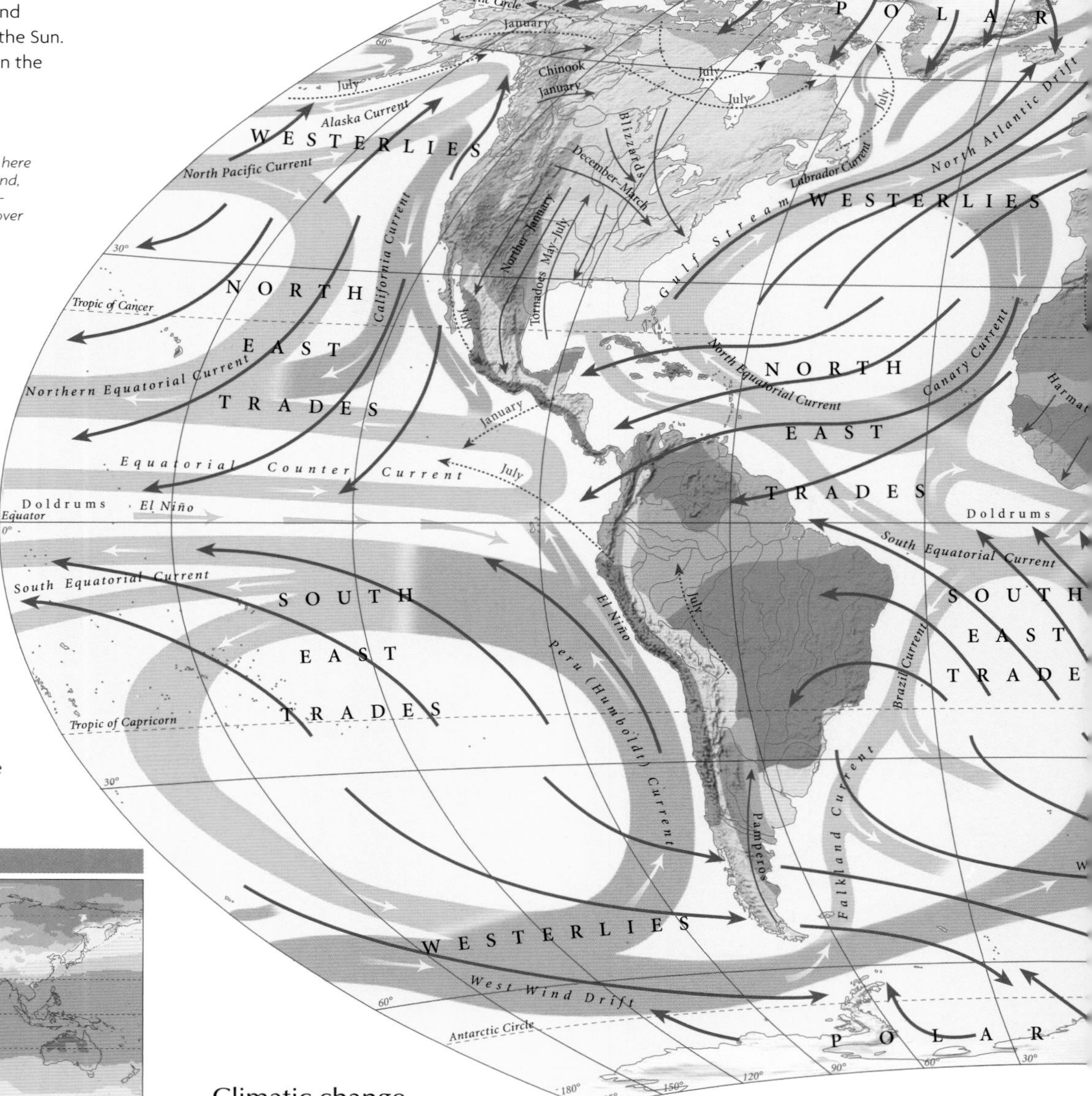
Arctic Circle
January
July
Chinook
January
Blizzards
December-March
POLAR
Alaska Current
WESTERLIES
North Pacific Current
California Current
Northern-January
Northern-May-July
Tornadoes
Labrador Current
North Atlantic Drift
Gulf Stream
WESTERLIES
Tropic of Cancer
NORTH EAST TRADES
Northern Equatorial Current
North Equatorial Current
NORTH EAST TRADES
Canary Current
Equatorial Counter Current
January
July
Doldrums
El Niño
Equator
Doldrums
South Equatorial Current
South Equatorial Current
SOUTH EAST TRADES
El Niño
July
Peru (Humboldt) Current
Brazil Current
SOUTH EAST TRADE
Tropic of Capricorn
Falkland Current
Pamperos
WESTERLIES
West Wind Drift
Antarctic Circle
POLAR

Climatic change

The Earth is currently in a warm phase between ice ages. Warmer temperatures result in higher sea levels as more of the polar ice caps melt. Most of the world's population lives near coasts, so any changes which might cause sea levels to rise, could have a potentially disastrous impact.

▲ ***This ice fair,** painted by Pieter Brueghel the Younger in the 17th century, shows the Little Ice Age which peaked around 300 years ago.*

The greenhouse effect

Gases such as carbon dioxide are known as 'greenhouse gases' because they allow shortwave solar radiation to enter the Earth's atmosphere, but help to stop longwave radiation from escaping. This traps heat, raising the Earth's temperature. An excess of these gases, such as that which results from the burning of fossil fuels, helps trap more heat and can lead to global warming.

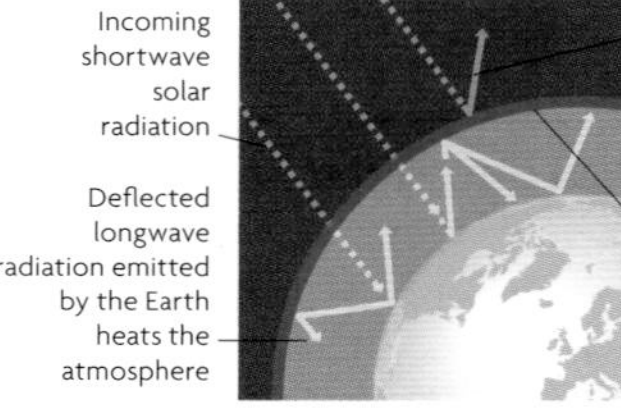
Incoming shortwave solar radiation
Deflected shortwave solar radiation
Deflected longwave radiation emitted by the Earth heats the atmosphere
Greenhouse gases prevent the escape of longwave radiation

▲ *The islands of the Caribbean, Mexico's Gulf coast and the southeastern USA are often hit by hurricanes formed far out in the Atlantic.*

Oceanic water circulation

In general, ocean currents parallel the movement of winds across the Earth's surface. Incoming solar energy is greatest at the Equator and least at the poles. So, water in the oceans heats up most at the Equator and flows polewards, cooling as it moves north or south towards the Arctic or Antarctic. The flow is eventually reversed and cold water currents move back towards the Equator. These ocean currents act as a vast system for moving heat from the Equator towards the poles and are a major influence on the distribution of the Earth's climates.

▲ ***In marginal climatic** zones years of drought can completely dry out the land and transform grassland to desert.*

Tilt and rotation

The tilt and rotation of the Earth during its annual orbit largely control the distribution of heat and moisture across its surface, which correspondingly controls its large-scale weather patterns. As the Earth annually rotates around the Sun, half its surface is receiving maximum radiation, creating summer and winter seasons. The angle of the Earth means that on average the tropics receive two and a half times as much heat from the Sun each day as the poles.

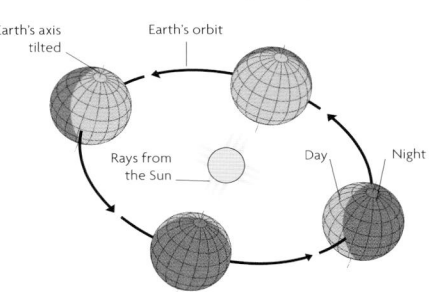

Earth's axis tilted
Earth's orbit
Rays from the Sun
Day
Night

Map key

Climate zones		Ocean currents	Prevailing winds	Local winds
ice cap	mediterranean	warm	warm	warm
subarctic	semi-arid	cold	cold	cold
tundra	arid			June seasonal*
continental	hot humid			* (seasonal winds which can either be warm or cold)
temperate	humid equatorial			
warm temperate	tropical			

▲ ***The wide range** of environments found in the Andes is strongly related to their altitude, which modifies climatic influences. While the peaks are snow-capped, many protected interior valleys are semi-tropical.*

The Coriolis effect

The rotation of the Earth influences atmospheric circulation by deflecting winds and ocean currents. Winds blowing in the northern hemisphere are deflected to the right and those in the southern hemisphere are deflected to the left, creating large-scale patterns of wind circulation, such as the northeast and southeast trade winds and the westerlies. This effect is greatest at the poles and least at the Equator.

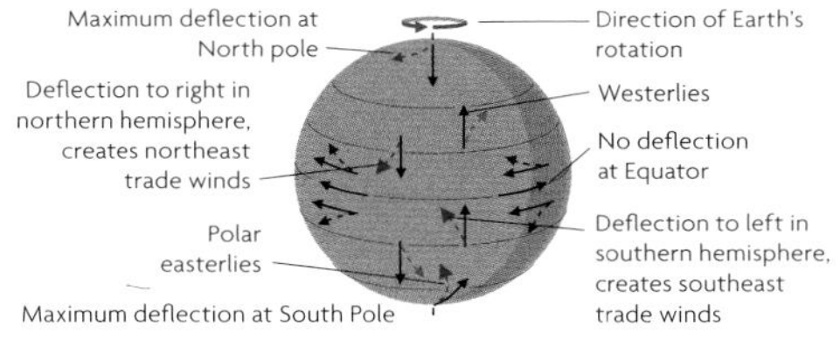
Maximum deflection at North pole
Deflection to right in northern hemisphere, creates northeast trade winds
Polar easterlies
Maximum deflection at South Pole
Direction of Earth's rotation
Westerlies
No deflection at Equator
Deflection to left in southern hemisphere, creates southeast trade winds

Precipitation

When warm air expands, it rises and cools, and the water vapour it carries condenses to form clouds. Heavy, regular rainfall is characteristic of the equatorial region, while the poles are cold and receive only slight snowfall. Tropical regions have marked dry and rainy seasons, while in the temperate regions rainfall is relatively unpredictable.

▲ ***Monsoon rains, which** affect southern Asia from May to September, are caused by sea winds blowing across the warm land.*

▲ ***Heavy tropical rainstorms** occur frequently in Papua New Guinea, often causing soil erosion and landslides in cultivated areas.*

Average January rainfall

Arctic Circle
Tropic of Cancer
Equator
Tropic of Capricorn
Antarctic Circle

Average July rainfall

Arctic Circle
Tropic of Cancer
Equator
Tropic of Capricorn
Antarctic Circle

0–25 mm (0–1 in)
25–50 mm (1–2 in)
50–100 mm (2–4 in)
100–200 mm (4–8 in)
200–300 mm (8–12 in)
300–400 mm (12–16 in)
400–500 mm (16–20 in)
above 500 mm (20 in)

▲ ***The intensity of** some blizzards in Canada and the northern USA can give rise to snowdrifts as high as 10 ft (3 m).*

▲ ***The Atacama Desert** in Chile is one of the driest places on Earth, with an average rainfall of less than 2 inches (50 mm) per year.*

▲ ***Violent thunderstorms occur** along advancing cold fronts, when cold, dry air masses meet warm, moist air, which rises rapidly, its moisture condensing into thunderclouds. Rain and hail become electrically charged, causing lightning.*

The rainshadow effect

When moist air is forced to rise by mountains, it cools and the water vapour falls as precipitation, either as rain or snow. Only the dry, cold air continues over the mountains, leaving inland areas with little or no rain. This is called the rainshadow effect and is one reason for the existence of the Mojave Desert in California, which lies east of the Coast Ranges.

Moist air travels inland from the sea
As air rises it cools and condenses leading to cloud
Dry air in 'shadow' of mountain

The rainshadow effect

Life on Earth

A unique combination of an oxygen-rich atmosphere and plentiful water is the key to life on Earth. Apart from the polar ice caps, there are few areas which have not been colonized by animals or plants over the course of the Earth's history. Plants process sunlight to provide them with their energy, and ultimately all the Earth's animals rely on plants for survival. Because of this reliance, plants are known as primary producers, and the availability of nutrients and temperature of an area is defined as its primary productivity, which affects the quantity and type of animals which are able to live there. This index is affected by climatic factors – cold and aridity restrict the quantity of life, whereas warmth and regular rainfall allow a greater diversity of species.

Biogeographical regions

The Earth can be divided into a series of biogeographical regions, or biomes, ecological communities where certain species of plant and animal co-exist within particular climatic conditions. Within these broad classifications, other factors including soil richness, altitude and human activities such as urbanization, intensive agriculture and deforestation, affect the local distribution of living species within each biome.

Polar regions

A layer of permanent ice at the Earth's poles covers both seas and land. Very little plant and animal life can exist in these harsh regions.

Tundra

A desolate region, with long, dark freezing winters and short, cold summers. With virtually no soil and large areas of permanently frozen ground known as permafrost, the tundra is largely treeless, though it is briefly clothed by small flowering plants in the summer months.

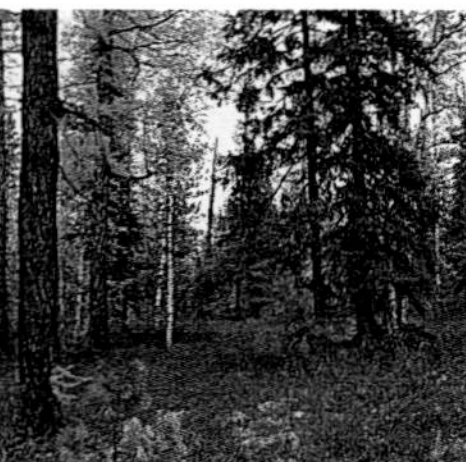

Needleleaf forests

With milder summers than the tundra and less wind, these areas are able to support large forests of coniferous trees.

Broadleaf forests

Much of the northern hemisphere was once covered by deciduous forests, which occurred in areas with marked seasonal variations. Most deciduous forests have been cleared for human settlement.

Temperate rainforests

In warmer wetter areas, such as southern China, temperate deciduous forests are replaced by evergreen forest.

Deserts

Deserts are areas with negligible rainfall. Most hot deserts lie within the tropics; cold deserts are dry because of their distance from the moisture-providing sea.

Mediterranean

Hot, dry summers and short winters typify these areas, which were once covered by evergreen shrubs and woodland, but have now been cleared by humans for agriculture.

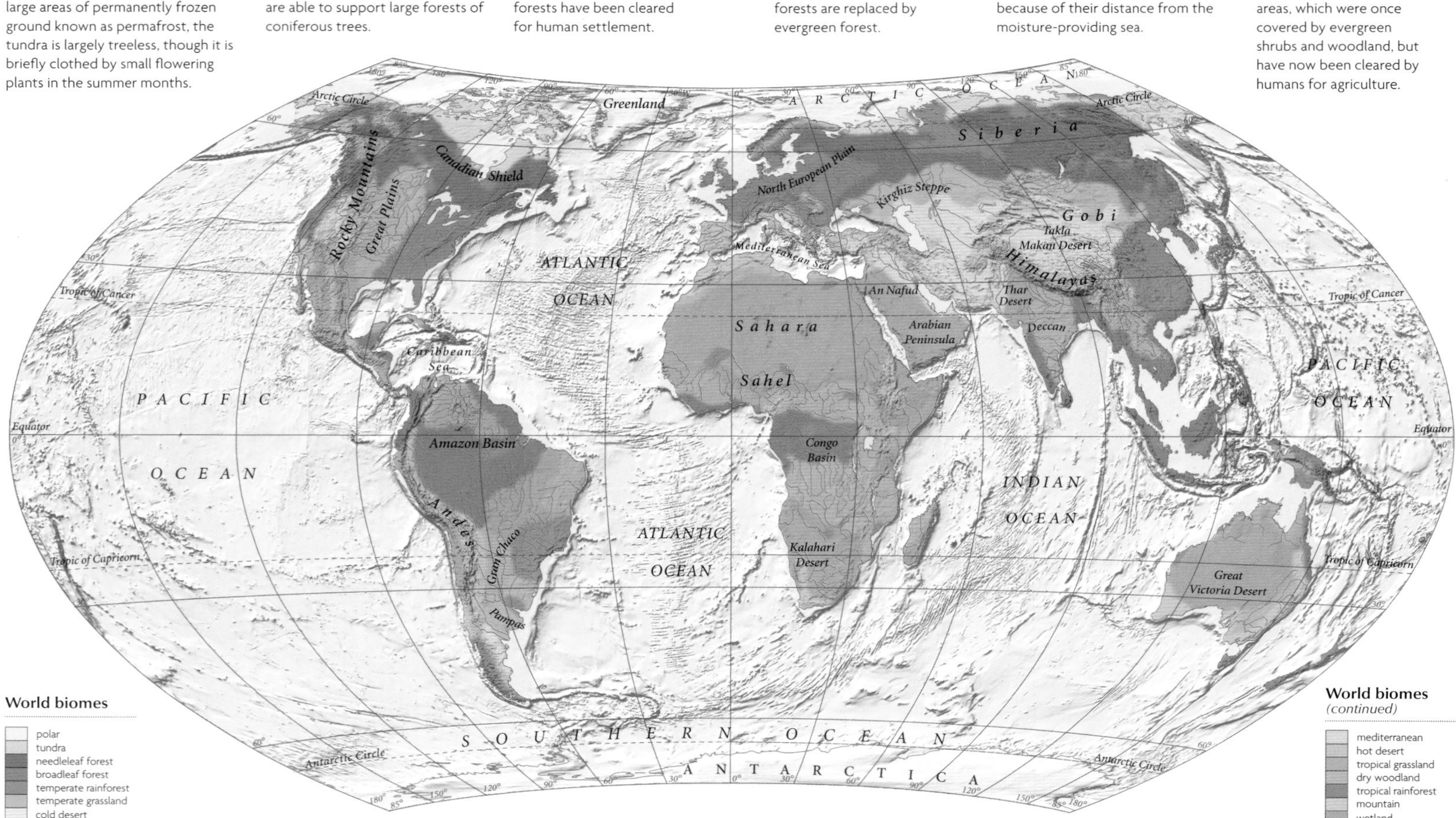
Arctic Circle
Greenland
ARCTIC OCEAN
Siberia
Rocky Mountains
Great Plains
Canadian Shield
North European Plain
Kirghiz Steppe
Gobi
Takla Makan Desert
Himalayas
Mediterranean Sea
ATLANTIC OCEAN
Tropic of Cancer
An Nafud
Thar Desert
Arabian Peninsula
Deccan
Sahara
Sahel
Caribbean Sea
PACIFIC OCEAN
Equator
Amazon Basin
Congo Basin
INDIAN OCEAN
Andes
Gran Chaco
Pampas
Kalahari Desert
Great Victoria Desert
Tropic of Capricorn
SOUTHERN OCEAN
Antarctic Circle
ANTARCTICA
World biomes
polar
tundra
needleleaf forest
broadleaf forest
temperate rainforest
temperate grassland
cold desert
World biomes (continued)
mediterranean
hot desert
tropical grassland
dry woodland
tropical rainforest
mountain
wetland

Tropical and temperate grasslands

The major grassland areas are found in the centres of the larger continental landmasses. In Africa's tropical savannah regions, seasonal rainfall alternates with drought. Temperate grasslands, also known as steppes and prairies are found in the northern hemisphere, and in South America, where they are known as the pampas.

Dry woodlands

Trees and shrubs, adapted to dry conditions, grow widely spaced from one another, interspersed by savannah grasslands.

Tropical rainforests

Characterized by year-round warmth and high rainfall, tropical rainforests contain the highest diversity of plant and animal species on Earth.

Mountains

Though the lower slopes of mountains may be thickly forested, only ground-hugging shrubs and other vegetation will grow above the tree line which varies according to both altitude and latitude.

Wetlands

Rarely lying above sea level, wetlands are marshes, swamps and tidal flats. Some, with their moist, fertile soils, are rich feeding grounds for fish and breeding grounds for birds. Others have little soil structure and are too acidic to support much plant and animal life.

Biodiversity

The number of plant and animal species, and the range of genetic diversity within the populations of each species, make up the Earth's biodiversity. The plants and animals which are endemic to a region – that is, those which are found nowhere else in the world – are also important in determining levels of biodiversity. Human settlement and intervention have encroached on many areas of the world once rich in endemic plant and animal species. Increasing international efforts are being made to monitor and conserve the biodiversity of the Earth's remaining wild places.

Animal adaptation

The degree of an animal's adaptability to different climates and conditions is extremely important in ensuring its success as a species. Many animals, particularly the largest mammals, are becoming restricted to ever-smaller regions as human development and modern agricultural practices reduce their natural habitats. In contrast, humans have been responsible – both deliberately and accidentally – for the spread of some of the world's most successful species. Many of these introduced species are now more numerous than the indigenous animal populations.

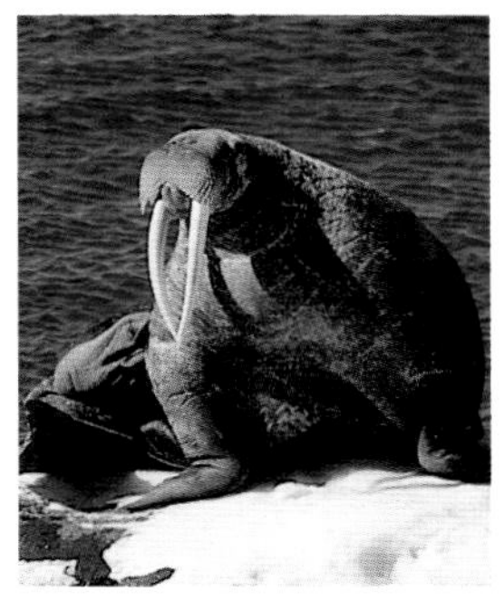

Polar animals

The frozen wastes of the polar regions are able to support only a small range of species which derive their nutritional requirements from the sea. Animals such as the walrus *(left)* have developed insulating fat, stocky limbs and double-layered coats to enable them to survive in the freezing conditions.

Desert animals

Many animals which live in the extreme heat and aridity of the deserts are able to survive for days and even months with very little food or water. Their bodies are adapted to lose heat quickly and to store fat and water. The Gila monster *(above)* stores fat in its tail.

Amazon rainforest

The vast Amazon Basin is home to the world's greatest variety of animal species. Animals are adapted to live at many different levels from the treetops to the tangled undergrowth which lies beneath the canopy. The sloth *(below)* hangs upside down in the branches. Its fur grows from its stomach to its back to enable water to run off quickly.

Diversity of animal species

Number of animal species per country

- more than 2000
- 1000–1999
- 700–999
- 400–699
- 200–399
- 100–199
- 0–99
- data not available

Marine biodiversity

The oceans support a huge variety of different species, from the world's largest mammals like whales and dolphins down to the tiniest plankton. The greatest diversities occur in the warmer seas of continental shelves, where plants are easily able to photosynthesize, and around coral reefs, where complex ecosystems are found. On the ocean floor, nematodes can exist at a depth of more than 10,000 ft (3000 m) below sea level.

High altitudes

Few animals exist in the rarefied atmosphere of the highest mountains. However, birds of prey such as eagles and vultures *(above)*, with their superb eyesight can soar as high as 23,000 ft (7000 m) to scan for prey below.

Urban animals

The growth of cities has reduced the amount of habitat available to many species. A number of animals are now moving closer into urban areas to scavenge from the detritus of the modern city *(left)*. Rodents, particularly rats and mice, have existed in cities for thousands of years, and many insects, especially moths, quickly develop new colouring to provide them with camouflage.

Endemic species

Isolated areas such as Australia and the island of Madagascar, have the greatest range of endemic species. In Australia, these include marsupials such as the kangaroo *(below)*, which carry their young in pouches on their bodies. Destruction of habitat, pollution, hunting, and predators introduced by humans, are threatening this unique biodiversity.

Plant adaptation

Environmental conditions, particularly climate, soil type and the extent of competition with other organisms, influence the development of plants into a number of distinctive forms. Similar conditions in quite different parts of the world create similar adaptations in the plants, which may then be modified by other, local, factors specific to the region.

Cold conditions

In areas where temperatures rarely rise above freezing, plants such as lichens *(left)* and mosses grow densely, close to the ground.

Rainforests

Most of the world's largest and oldest plants are found in rainforests; warmth and heavy rainfall provide ideal conditions for vast plants like the world's largest flower, the rafflesia *(left)*.

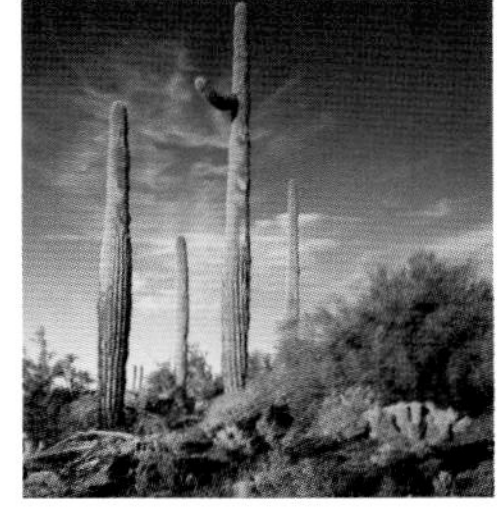

Hot, dry conditions

Arid conditions lead to the development of plants whose surface area has been reduced to a minimum to reduce water loss. In cacti *(above)*, which can survive without water for months, leaves are minimal or not present at all.

Ancient plants

Some of the world's most primitive plants still exist today, including algae, cycads and many ferns *(above)*, reflecting the success with which they have adapted to changing conditions.

Diversity of plant species

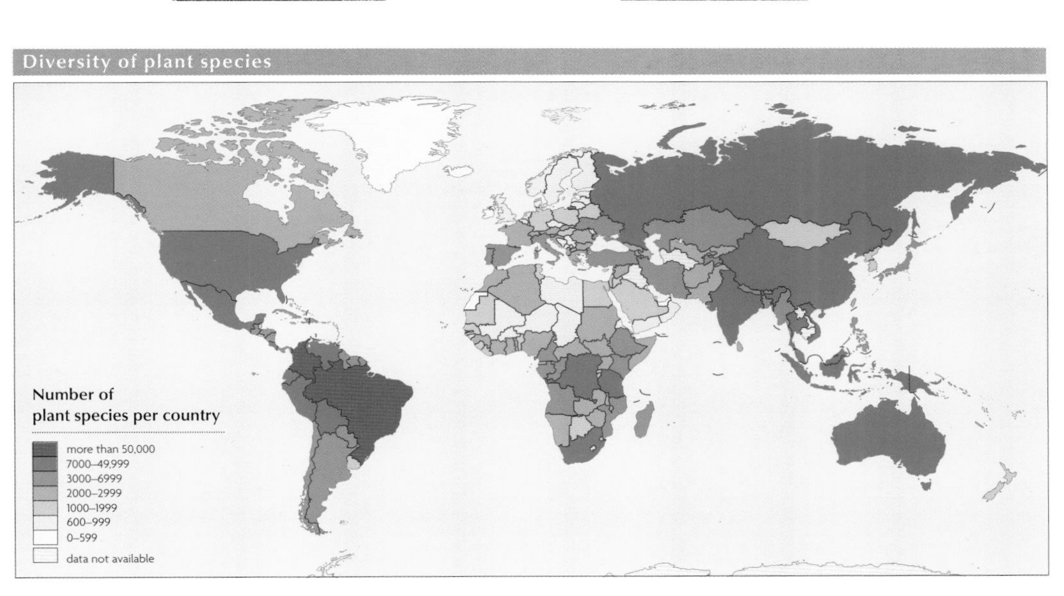
Number of plant species per country
more than 50,000
7000–49,999
3000–6999
2000–2999
1000–1999
600–999
0–599
data not available

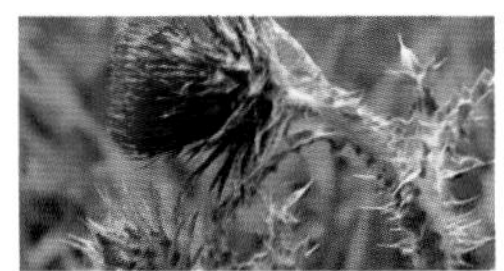

Resisting predators

A great variety of plants have developed devices including spines *(above)*, poisons, stinging hairs and an unpleasant taste or smell to deter animal predators.

Weeds

Weeds such as bindweed *(above)* are fast-growing, easily dispersed, and tolerant of a number of different environments, enabling them to quickly colonize suitable habitats. They are among the most adaptable of all plants.

Population and settlement

The Earth's population is projected to rise from its current level of about 7 billion to reach some 10.5 billion by 2050. The global distribution of this rapidly growing population is very uneven, and is dictated by climate, terrain and natural and economic resources. The great majority of the Earth's people live in coastal zones, and along river valleys. Deserts cover over 20% of the Earth's surface, but support less than 5% of the world's population. It is estimated that over half of the world's population live in cities – most of them in Asia – as a result of mass migration from rural areas in search of jobs. Many of these people live in the so-called 'megacities', some with populations as great as 40 million.

Patterns of settlement

The past 200 years have seen the most radical shift in world population patterns in recorded history.

Nomadic life

All the world's peoples were hunter-gatherers 10,000 years ago. Today nomads, who live by following available food resources, account for less than 0.0001% of the world's population. They are mainly pastoral herders, moving their livestock from place to place in search of grazing land.

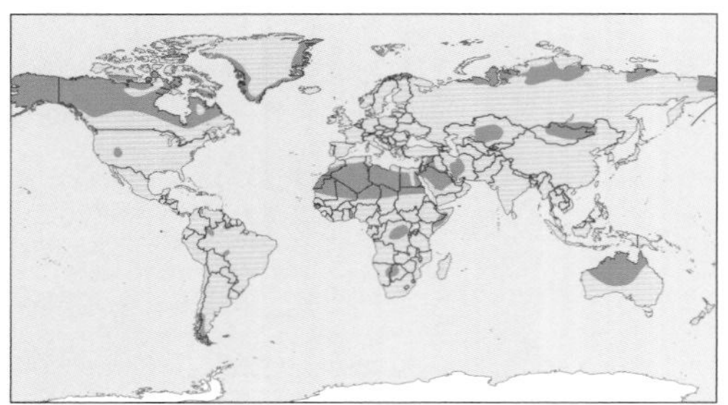

Nomadic population

Nomadic population area

The growth of cities

In 1900 there were only 14 cities in the world with populations of more than a million, mostly in the northern hemisphere. Today, as more and more people in the developing world migrate to towns and cities, there are over 70 cities whose population exceeds 5 million, and around 490 million-cities.

Million-cities in 1900

Million-cities in 1900

• Cities over 1 million population

Million-cities in 2005

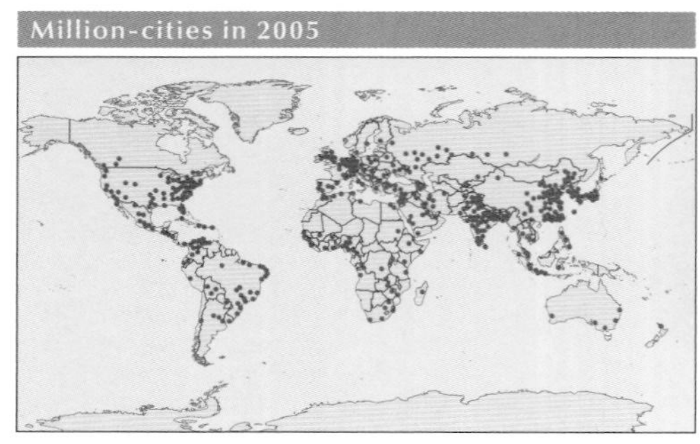

Million-cities in 2005

• Cities over 1 million population

North America

The eastern and western seaboards of the USA, with huge expanses of interconnected cities, towns and suburbs, are vast, densely-populated megalopolises. Central America and the Caribbean also have high population densities. Yet, away from the coasts and in the wilderness of northern Canada the land is very sparsely settled.

▲ ***Vancouver on Canada's*** *west coast, grew up as a port city. In recent years it has attracted many Asian immigrants, particularly from the Pacific Rim.*

▲ ***North America's central*** *plains, the continent's agricultural heartland, are thinly populated and highly productive.*

Europe

With its temperate climate, and rich mineral and natural resources, Europe is generally very densely settled. The continent acts as a magnet for economic migrants from the developing world, and immigration is now widely restricted. Birth rates in Europe are generally low, and in some countries, such as Germany, the populations have stabilized at zero growth, with a fast-growing elderly population.

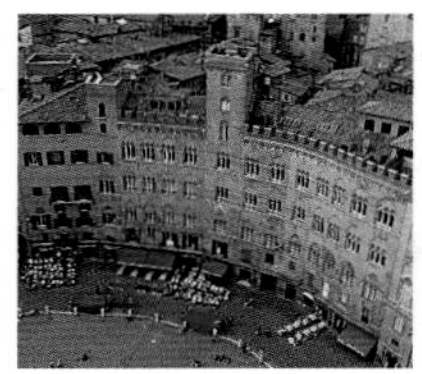

▲ ***Many European cities,*** *like Siena, once reflected the 'ideal' size for human settlements. Modern technological advances have enabled them to grow far beyond the original walls.*

▲ ***Within the densely-populated*** *Netherlands the reclamation of coastal wetlands is vital to provide much-needed land for agriculture and settlement.*

Population density (inhabitants per sq km)

200–1000
100–200
50–100
20–50
10–20
5–10
1–5
Less than 1

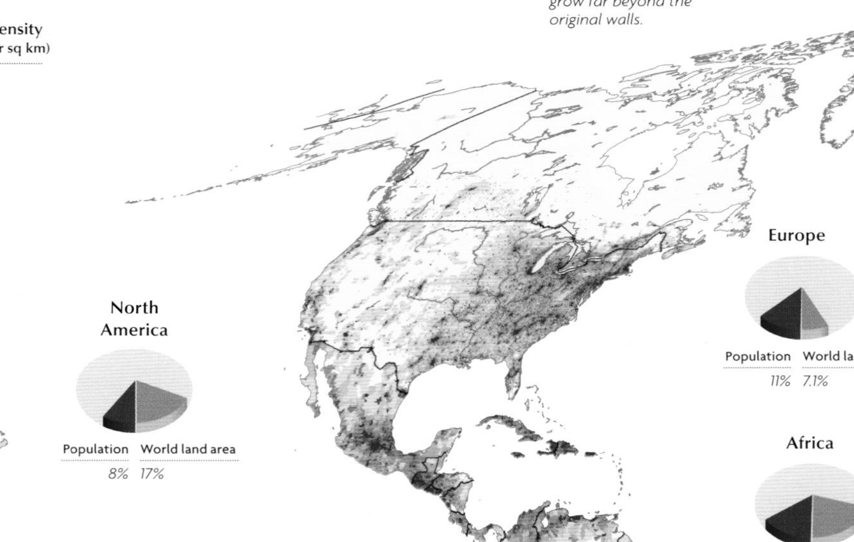

North America
Population 8% · World land area 17%

Europe
Population 11% · World land area 7.1%

Africa
Population 14% · World land area 20.2%

South America
Population 6% · World land area 11.8%

South America

Most settlement in South America is clustered in a narrow belt in coastal zones and in the northern Andes. During the 20th century, cities such as São Paulo and Buenos Aires grew enormously, acting as powerful economic magnets to the rural population. Shanty towns have grown up on the outskirts of many major cities to house these immigrants, often lacking basic amenities.

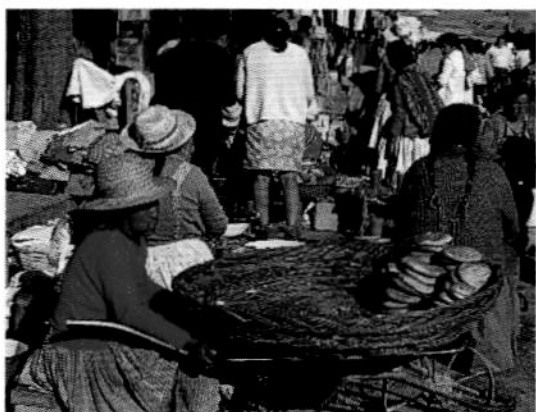

▲ ***Many people in*** *western South America live at high altitudes in the Andes, both in cities and in villages such as this one in Bolivia.*

▲ ***Venezuela is one*** *of the most highly urbanized countries in South America, with nearly 90% of the population living in cities such as Caracas.*

Africa

The arid climate of much of Africa means that settlement of the continent is sparse, focusing in coastal areas and fertile regions such as the Nile Valley. Africa still has a high proportion of nomadic agriculturalists, although many are now becoming settled, and the population is predominantly rural.

▲ ***Cities such as*** Nairobi (above), *Cairo and Johannesburg have grown rapidly in recent years, although only Cairo has a significant population on a global scale.*

▲ ***Traditional lifestyles and*** *homes persist across much of Africa, which has a higher proportion of rural or village-based population than any other continent.*

Asia

Most Asian settlement originally centred around the great river valleys such as the Indus, the Ganges and the Yangtze. Today, almost 60% of the world's population lives in Asia, many in burgeoning cities – particularly in the economically-buoyant Pacific Rim countries. Even rural population densities are high in many countries; practices such as terracing in Southeast Asia making the most of the available land.

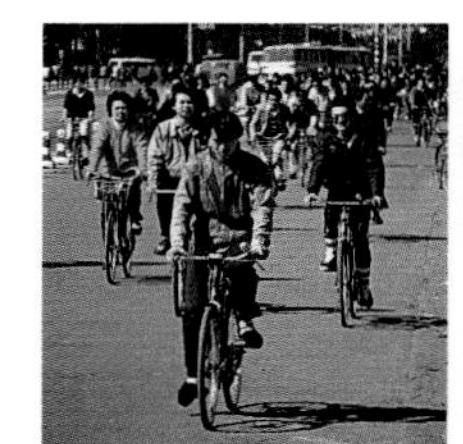

▲ ***Many of China's*** *cities are now vast urban areas with populations of more than 5 million people.*

▲ ***This stilt village*** *in Bangladesh is built to resist the regular flooding. Pressure on land, even in rural areas, forces many people to live in marginal areas.*

Population structures

Population pyramids are an effective means of showing the age structures of different countries, and highlighting changing trends in population growth and decline. The typical pyramid for a country with a growing, youthful population, is broad-based *(left)*, reflecting a high birth rate and a far larger number of young rather than elderly people. In contrast, countries with populations whose numbers are stabilizing have a more balanced distribution of people in each age band, and may even have lower numbers of people in the youngest age ranges, indicating both a high life expectancy, and that the population is now barely replacing itself *(right)*. The Russian Federation *(centre)* shows a marked decline in population due to a combination of a high death rate and low birth rate. The government has taken steps to reverse this trend by providing improved child support and health care. Immigration is also seen as vital to help sustain the population.

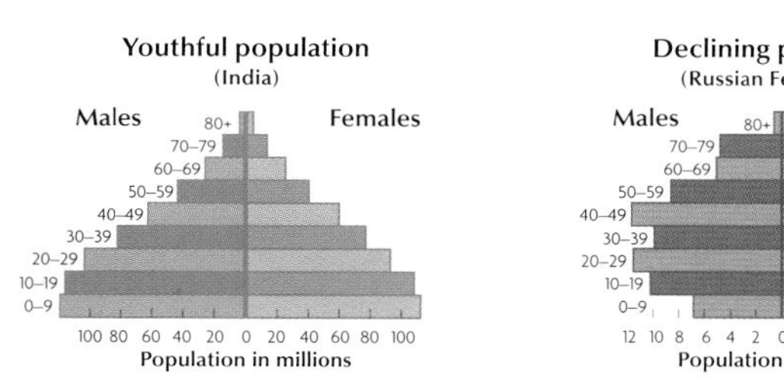
Youthful population
(India)
Males
Females
80+
70–79
60–69
50–59
40–49
30–39
20–29
10–19
0–9
100 80 60 40 20 0 20 40 60 80 100
Population in millions

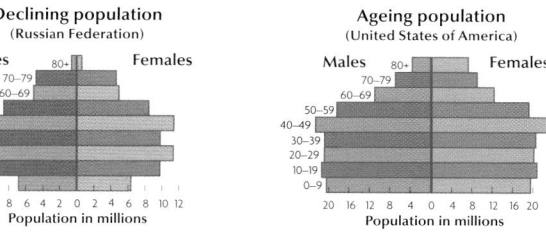

Declining population
(Russian Federation)
Males Females
80+ 70–79 60–69 50–59 40–49 30–39 20–29 10–19 0–9
12 10 8 6 4 2 0 2 4 6 8 10 12
Population in millions

Ageing population
(United States of America)
Males Females
80+ 70–79 60–69 50–59 40–49 30–39 20–29 10–19 0–9
20 16 12 8 4 0 4 8 12 16 20
Population in millions

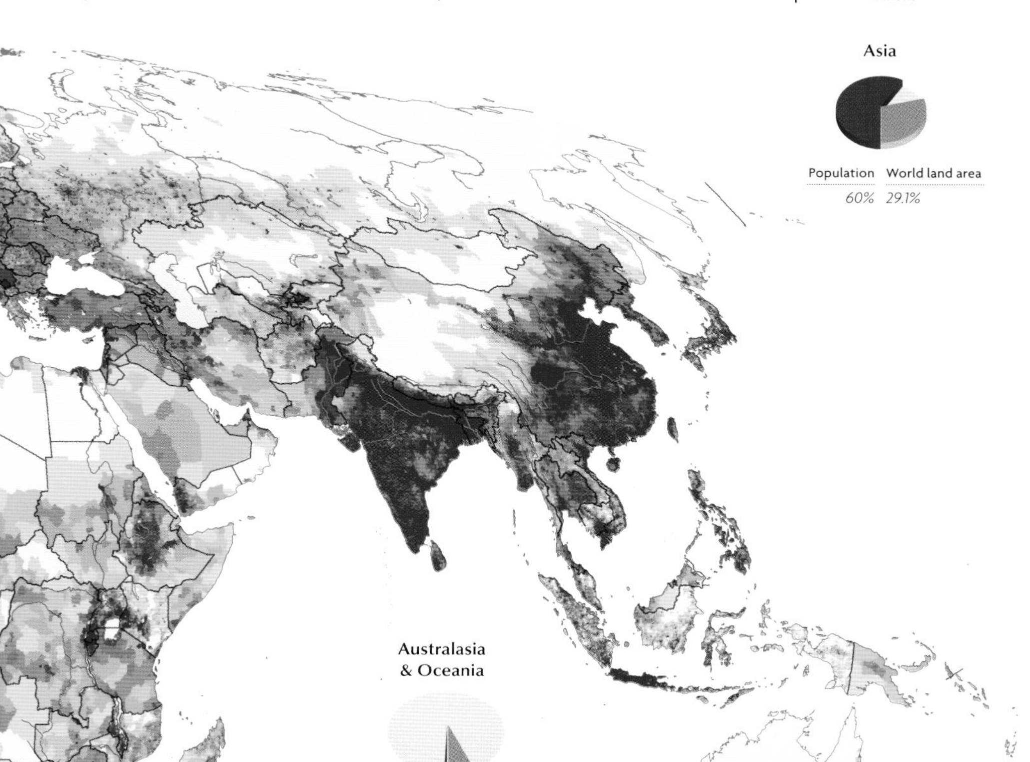

Asia
Population 60% World land area 29.1%

Australasia & Oceania
Population 1% World land area 5.9%

Antarctica
Population 0% World land area 8.9%

Population growth

Improvements in food supply and advances in medicine have both played a major role in the remarkable growth in global population, which has increased five-fold over the last 150 years. Food supplies have risen with the mechanization of agriculture and improvements in crop yields. Better nutrition, together with higher standards of public health and sanitation, have led to increased longevity and higher birth rates.

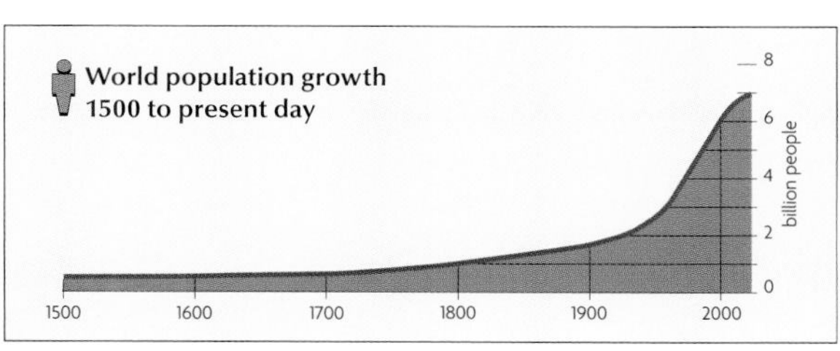
World population growth
1500 to present day
8
6
4
2
0
billion people
1500
1600
1700
1800
1900
2000

World nutrition

Two-thirds of the world's food supply is consumed by the industrialized nations, many of which have a daily calorific intake far higher than is necessary for their populations to maintain a healthy body weight. In contrast, in the developing world, about 800 million people do not have enough food to meet their basic nutritional needs.

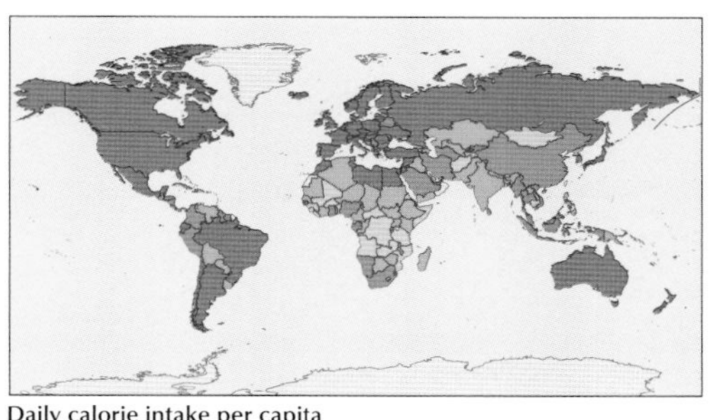

Daily calorie intake per capita

above 3000
2500–2999
2000–2499
below 2000
data not available

World life expectancy

Improved public health and living standards have greatly increased life expectancy in the developed world, where people can now expect to live twice as long as they did 100 years ago. In many of the world's poorest nations, inadequate nutrition and disease, means that the average life expectancy still does not exceed 45 years.

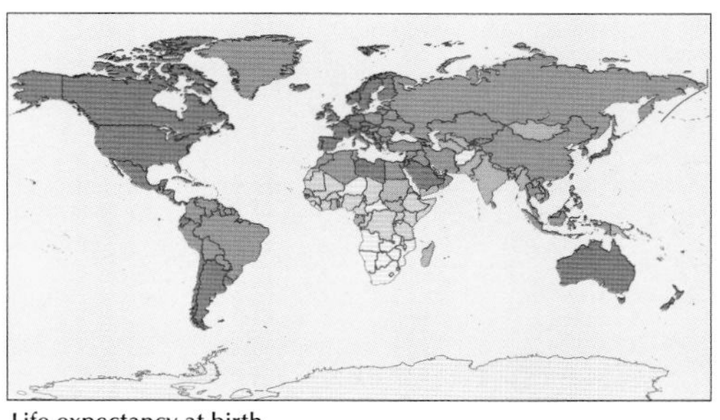

Life expectancy at birth

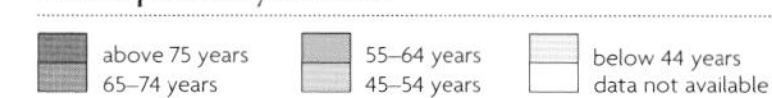
above 75 years
65–74 years
55–64 years
45–54 years
below 44 years
data not available

Australasia and Oceania

This is the world's most sparsely settled region. The peoples of Australia and New Zealand live mainly in the coastal cities, with only scattered settlements in the arid interior. The Pacific islands can only support limited populations because of their remoteness and lack of resources.

▶ ***Brisbane, on Australia's*** *Gold Coast is the most rapidly expanding city in the country. The great majority of Australia's population lives in cities near the coasts.*

◀ ***The remote highlands*** *of Papua New Guinea are home to a wide variety of peoples, many of whom still subsist by traditional hunting and gathering.*

Average world birth rates

Birth rates are much higher in Africa, Asia and South America than in Europe and North America. Increased affluence and easy access to contraception are both factors which can lead to a significant decline in a country's birth rate.

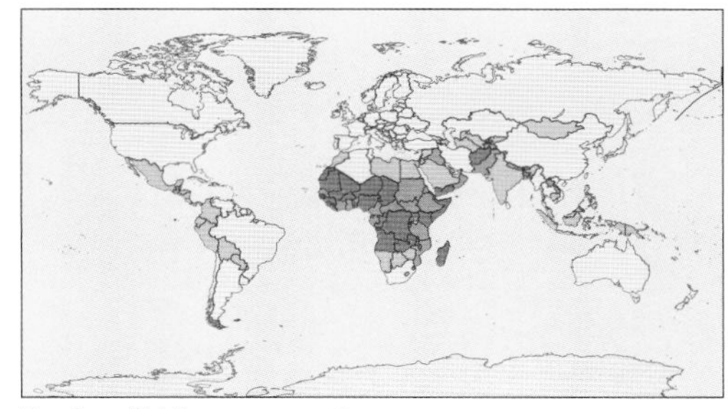

Number of births (per 1000 people)

above 40
30–39
20–29
below 20
data not available

World infant mortality

In parts of the developing world infant mortality rates are still high; access to medical services such as immunization, adequate nutrition and the promotion of breast-feeding have been important in combating infant mortality.

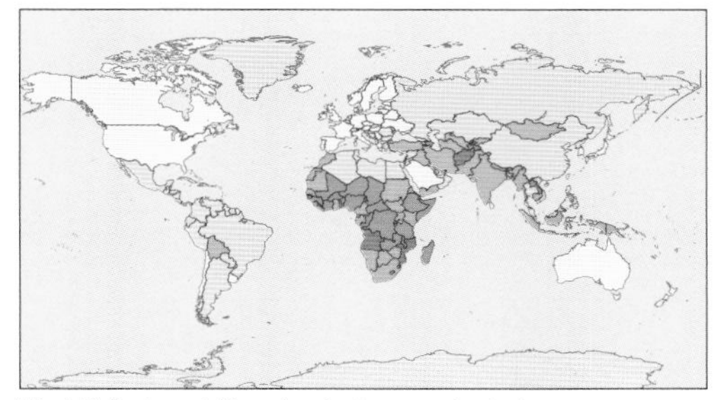

World infant mortality rates (deaths per 1000 live births)

above 125
75–124
35–74
15–34
below 15
data not available

The economic system

The wealthy countries of the developed world, with their aggressive, market-led economies and their access to productive new technologies and international markets, dominate the world economic system. At the other extreme, many of the countries of the developing world are locked in a cycle of national debt, rising populations and unemployment. In 2008 a major financial crisis swept the world's banking sector leading to a huge downturn in the global economy. Despite this, China overtook Japan in 2010 to become the world's second largest economy.

Trade blocs

EU
CACM
NAFTA
SADC
ASEAN
ECOWAS
LAIA
CEEAC

Trade blocs

International trade blocs are formed when groups of countries, often already enjoying close military and political ties, join together to offer mutually preferential terms of trade for both imports and exports. Increasingly, global trade is dominated by three main blocs: the EU, NAFTA, and ASEAN. They are supplanting older trade blocs such as the Commonwealth, a legacy of colonialism.

International trade flows

World trade acts as a stimulus to national economies, encouraging growth. Over the last three decades, as heavy industries have declined, services – banking, insurance, tourism, airlines and shipping – have taken an increasingly large share of world trade. Manufactured articles now account for nearly two-thirds of world trade; raw materials and food make up less than a quarter of the total.

Shipping
Ships carry 80% of international cargo, and extensive container ports, where cargo is stored, are vital links in the international transport network.

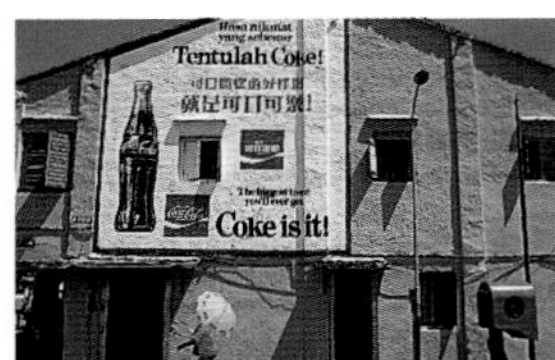
Tentulah Coke!
Coke is it!

Multinationals
Multinational companies are increasingly penetrating inaccessible markets. The reach of many American commodities is now global.

Primary products
Many countries, particularly in the Caribbean and Africa, are still reliant on primary products such as rubber and coffee, which makes them vulnerable to fluctuating prices.

Service industries
Service industries such as banking, tourism and insurance were the fastest-growing industrial sector in the last half of the 20th century. Lloyds of London is the centre of the world insurance market.

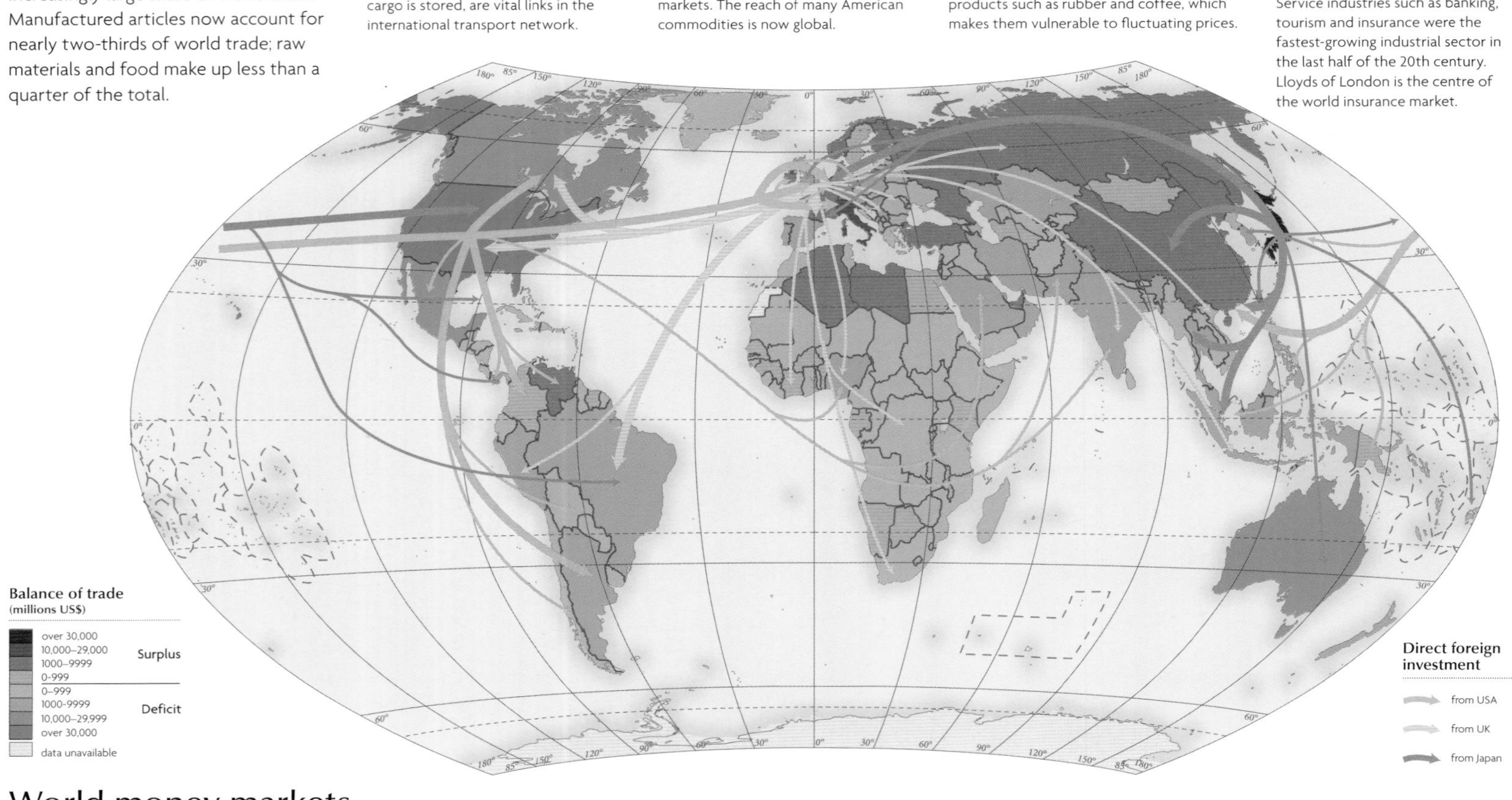
Balance of trade
(millions US$)
over 30,000
10,000–29,000
1000–9999
0–999
Surplus
0–999
1000–9999
10,000–29,999
over 30,000
Deficit
data unavailable
Direct foreign investment
from USA
from UK
from Japan

World money markets

The financial world has traditionally been dominated by three major centres – Tokyo, New York and London, which house the headquarters of stock exchanges, multinational corporations and international banks. Their geographic location means that, at any one time in a 24-hour day, one major market is open for trading in shares, currencies and commodities. Since the late 1980s, technological advances have enabled transactions between financial centres to occur at ever-greater speed, and new markets have sprung up throughout the world.

Major money markets

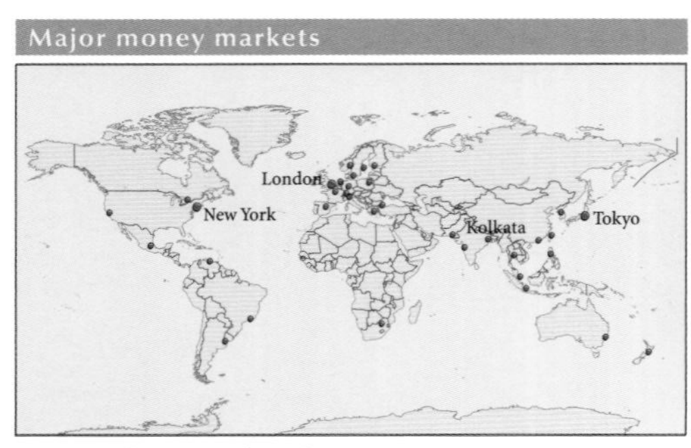
London
New York
Kolkata
Tokyo

Location of major stock markets

● Major stock markets

▲ *The Tokyo Stock Market crashed in 1990, leading to slow-down in the growth of the world's most powerful economy, and a refocusing on economic policy away from export-led growth and towards the domestic market.*

New stock markets

New stock markets are now opening in many parts of the world, where economies have recently emerged from state controls. In Moscow and Beijing, and several countries in eastern Europe, newly-opened stock exchanges reflect the transition to market-driven economies.

▲ *Dealers at the Kolkata Stock Market. The Indian economy has been opened up to foreign investment and many multinationals now have bases there.*

The developing world

International trade in capital and currency is dominated by the rich nations of the northern hemisphere. In parts of Africa and Asia, where exports of any sort are extremely limited, home-produced commodities are simply sold in local markets.

▲ *Markets have thrived in communist Vietnam since the introduction of a liberal economic policy.*

World wealth disparity

A global assessment of Gross Domestic Product (GDP) by nation reveals great disparities. The developed world, with only a quarter of the world's population, has 80% of the world's manufacturing income. Civil war, conflict and political instability further undermine the economic self-sufficiency of many of the world's poorest nations.

Urban sprawl

Cities are expanding all over the developing world, attracting economic migrants in search of work and opportunities. In cities such as Rio de Janeiro, housing has not kept pace with the population explosion, and squalid shanty towns *(favelas)* rub shoulders with middle-class housing.

▲ **The favelas of** *Rio de Janeiro sprawl over the hills surrounding the city.*

▲ ***Cities such as*** *Detroit have been badly hit by the decline in heavy industry.*

Urban decay

Although the USA still dominates the global economy, it faces deficits in both the federal budget and the balance of trade. Vast discrepancies in personal wealth, high levels of unemployment, and the dismantling of welfare provisions throughout the 1980s have led to severe deprivation in several of the inner cities of North America's industrial heartland.

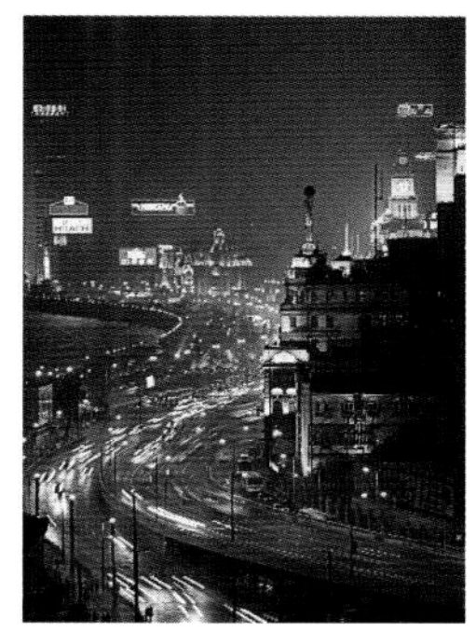

◄ ***Foreign investment has*** *encouraged new infrastructure development in cities like Shanghai.*

Booming cities

Since the 1980s the Chinese government has set up special industrial zones, such as Shanghai, where foreign investment is encouraged through tax incentives. Migrants from rural China pour into these regions in search of work, creating 'boomtown' economies.

Comparative world wealth

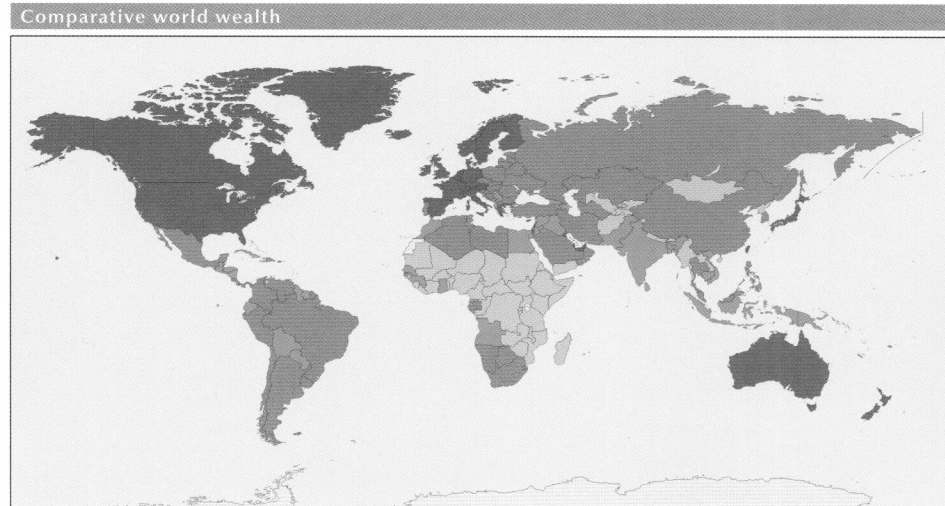

World economies - average GDP per capita (US$)

- above 20,000
- 5000–20,000
- 2000–5000
- below 2000
- data unavailable

Economic 'tigers'

The economic 'tigers' of the Pacific Rim – China, Singapore, and South Korea – have grown faster than Europe and the USA over the last decade. Their export- and service-led economies have benefited from stable government, low labour costs, and foreign investment.

▲ ***Hong Kong, with*** *its fine natural harbour, is one of the most important ports in Asia.*

Agricultural economies

In parts of the developing world, people survive by subsistence farming – only growing enough food for themselves and their families. With no surplus product, they are unable to exchange goods for currency, the only means of escaping the poverty trap. In other countries, farmers have been encouraged to concentrate on growing a single crop for the export market. This reliance on cash crops leaves farmers vulnerable to crop failure and to changes in the market price of the crop.

▲ ***The Ugandan uplands*** *are fertile, but poor infrastructure hampers the export of cash crops.*

▲ ***A shopping arcade*** *in Paris displays a great profusion of luxury goods.*

The affluent West

The capital cities of many countries in the developed world are showcases for consumer goods, reflecting the increasing importance of the service sector, and particularly the retail sector, in the world economy. The idea of shopping as a leisure activity is unique to the western world. Luxury goods and services attract visitors, who in turn generate tourist revenue.

Tourism

In 2004, there were over 940 million tourists worldwide. Tourism is now the world's biggest single industry, employing 130 million people, though frequently in low-paid unskilled jobs. While tourists are increasingly exploring inaccessible and less-developed regions of the world, the benefits of the industry are not always felt at a local level. There are also worries about the environmental impact of tourism, as the world's last wildernesses increasingly become tourist attractions.

▲ ***Botswana's Okavango Delta*** *is an area rich in wildlife. Tourists make safaris to the region, but the impact of tourism is controlled.*

Money flows

In 2008 a global financial crisis swept through the world's economic system. The crisis triggered the failure of several major financial institutions and lead to increased borrowing costs known as the "credit crunch". A consequent reduction in economic activity together with rising inflation forced many governments to introduce austerity measures to reduce borrowing and debt, particulary in Europe where massive "bailouts" were needed to keep some European single currency (Euro) countries solvent.

◄ ***In rural Southeast Asia,*** *babies are given medical checks by UNICEF as part of a global aid programme sponsored by the UN.*

Tourist arrivals

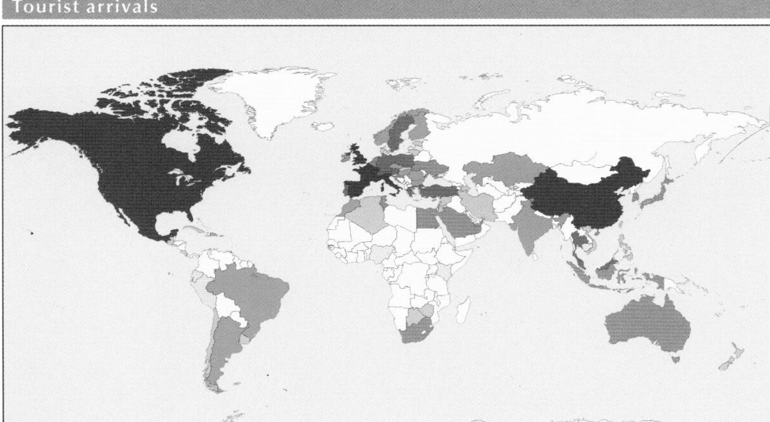

Tourist arrivals

- over 20 million
- 10–20 million
- 5–10 million
- 2.5–5 million
- 1–2.5 million
- 700,000–999,000
- under 700,000
- data unavailable

International debt

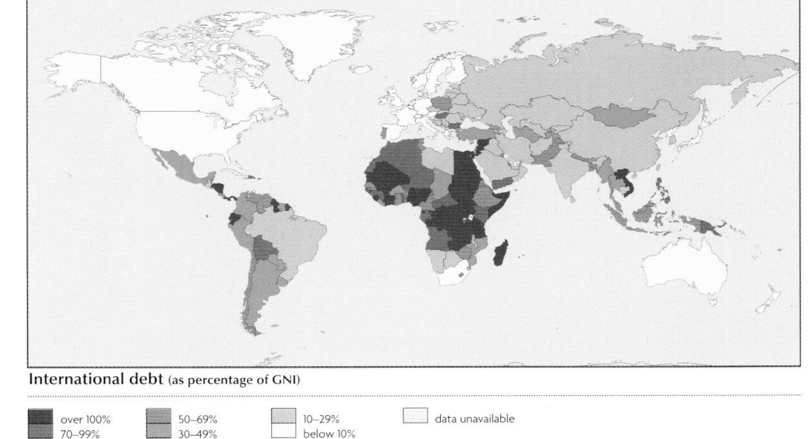

International debt (as percentage of GNI)

- over 100%
- 70–99%
- 50–69%
- 30–49%
- 10–29%
- below 10%
- data unavailable

The political world

There are 196 independent countries in the world today. With the exception of Antarctica, where territorial claims have been deferred by international treaty, every land area of the Earth's surface either belongs to, or is claimed by, one country or another. The largest country in the world is the Russian Federation, the smallest is Vatican City. Some 60 overseas dependent territories remain, administered variously by France, Australia, Denmark, New Zealand, Norway, Portugal, the UK, the US and the Netherlands.

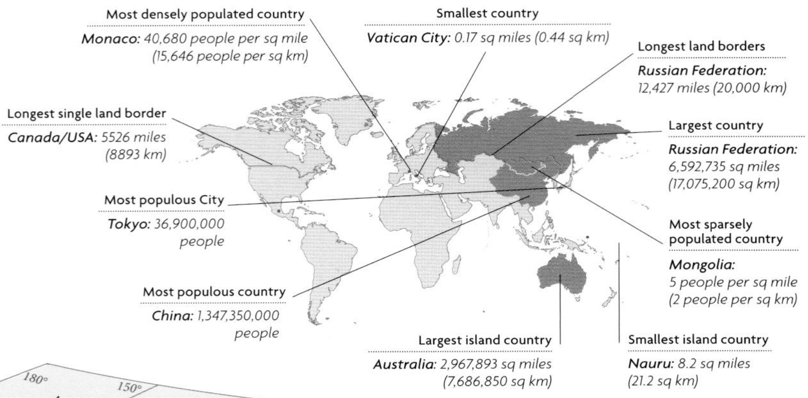

Most densely populated country
Monaco: 40,680 people per sq mile (15,646 people per sq km)

Smallest country
Vatican City: 0.17 sq miles (0.44 sq km)

Longest land borders
Russian Federation: 12,427 miles (20,000 km)

Longest single land border
Canada/USA: 5526 miles (8893 km)

Largest country
Russian Federation: 6,592,735 sq miles (17,075,200 sq km)

Most populous City
Tokyo: 36,900,000 people

Most sparsely populated country
Mongolia: 5 people per sq mile (2 people per sq km)

Most populous country
China: 1,347,350,000 people

Largest island country
Australia: 2,967,893 sq miles (7,686,850 sq km)

Smallest island country
Nauru: 8.2 sq miles (21.2 sq km)

International borders

The map shows three main types of boundary between states. Full borders represent internationally agreed and recognized territorial boundaries. Undefined borders exist where no fixed boundary between states has been demarcated; the boundaries indicated in this way show approximate areas of sovereignty. A disputed border is indicated where a *de facto* territorial boundary exists, which is not agreed or is subject to arbitration.

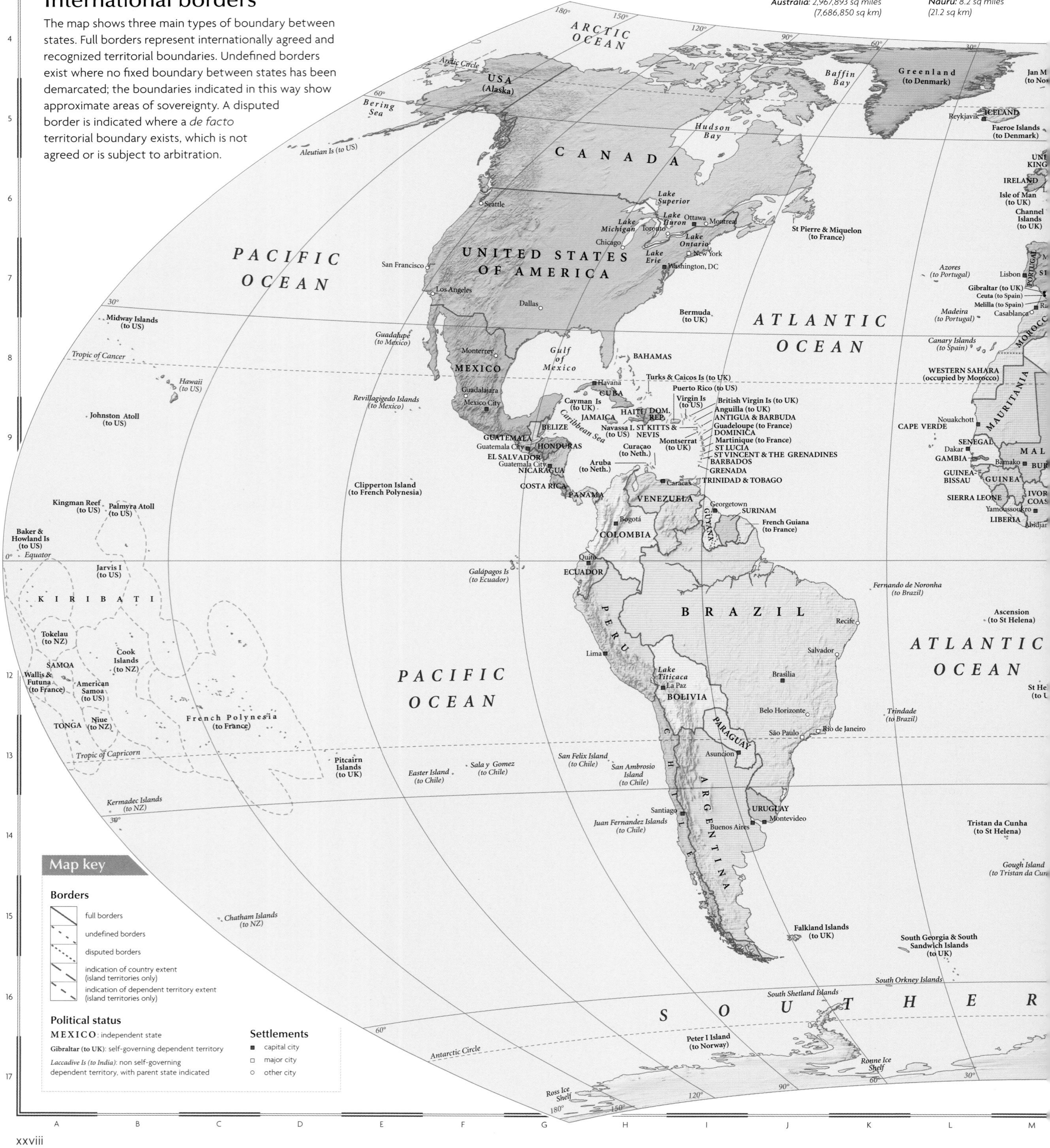

Map key

Borders

- full borders
- undefined borders
- disputed borders
- indication of country extent (island territories only)
- indication of dependent territory extent (island territories only)

Political status

MEXICO: independent state

Gibraltar (to UK): self-governing dependent territory

Laccadive Is (to India): non self-governing dependent territory, with parent state indicated

Settlements

- capital city
- major city
- other city

ARCTIC OCEAN
PACIFIC OCEAN
ATLANTIC OCEAN
USA (Alaska)
CANADA
UNITED STATES OF AMERICA
MEXICO
Greenland (to Denmark)
ICELAND
Faeroe Islands (to Denmark)
IRELAND
Isle of Man (to UK)
Channel Islands (to UK)
Bering Sea
Hudson Bay
Baffin Bay
Gulf of Mexico
Caribbean Sea
Aleutian Is (to US)
Seattle
San Francisco
Los Angeles
Dallas
Chicago
Toronto
Ottawa
Montreal
New York
Washington, DC
Lake Superior
Lake Michigan
Lake Huron
Lake Ontario
Lake Erie
St Pierre & Miquelon (to France)
Bermuda (to UK)
Azores (to Portugal)
Madeira (to Portugal)
Canary Islands (to Spain)
Lisbon
Gibraltar (to UK)
Ceuta (to Spain)
Melilla (to Spain)
Casablanca
Reykjavik
Midway Islands (to US)
Tropic of Cancer
Hawaii (to US)
Johnston Atoll (to US)
Guadalupe (to Mexico)
Revillagigedo Islands (to Mexico)
Monterrey
Guadalajara
Mexico City
BAHAMAS
Turks & Caicos Is (to UK)
Havana
CUBA
Cayman Is (to UK)
JAMAICA
HAITI
DOM. REP.
Puerto Rico (to US)
Virgin Is (to US)
British Virgin Is (to UK)
Anguilla (to UK)
ANTIGUA & BARBUDA
Guadeloupe (to France)
DOMINICA
Martinique (to France)
ST LUCIA
ST VINCENT & THE GRENADINES
BARBADOS
GRENADA
TRINIDAD & TOBAGO
ST KITTS & NEVIS
Navassa I. (to US)
Montserrat (to UK)
Curaçao (to Neth.)
Aruba (to Neth.)
BELIZE
GUATEMALA
Guatemala City
HONDURAS
EL SALVADOR
NICARAGUA
COSTA RICA
PANAMA
Caracas
VENEZUELA
Georgetown
GUYANA
SURINAM
French Guiana (to France)
Bogotá
COLOMBIA
Quito
ECUADOR
Galápagos Is (to Ecuador)
PERU
Lima
BRAZIL
Recife
Salvador
Brasília
Belo Horizonte
Rio de Janeiro
São Paulo
Lake Titicaca
La Paz
BOLIVIA
PARAGUAY
Asuncion
CHILE
ARGENTINA
Santiago
Buenos Aires
URUGUAY
Montevideo
Clipperton Island (to French Polynesia)
Western Sahara (occupied by Morocco)
MAURITANIA
MOROCCO
Nouakchott
CAPE VERDE
SENEGAL
Dakar
GAMBIA
GUINEA-BISSAU
GUINEA
SIERRA LEONE
LIBERIA
Yamoussoukro
Abidjan
Bamako
Fernando de Noronha (to Brazil)
Ascension (to St Helena)
Trindade (to Brazil)
Kingman Reef (to US)
Palmyra Atoll (to US)
Baker & Howland Is (to US)
Equator
Jarvis I (to US)
KIRIBATI
Tokelau (to NZ)
Cook Islands (to NZ)
SAMOA
Wallis & Futuna (to France)
American Samoa (to US)
Niue (to NZ)
TONGA
French Polynesia (to France)
Tropic of Capricorn
Pitcairn Islands (to UK)
Easter Island (to Chile)
Sala y Gomez (to Chile)
San Felix Island (to Chile)
San Ambrosio Island (to Chile)
Juan Fernandez Islands (to Chile)
Kermadec Islands (to NZ)
Chatham Islands (to NZ)
Tristan da Cunha (to St Helena)
Gough Island
Falkland Islands (to UK)
South Georgia & South Sandwich Islands (to UK)
South Orkney Islands
South Shetland Islands
SOUTHER
Peter I Island (to Norway)
Antarctic Circle
Arctic Circle
Ronne Ice Shelf
Ross Ice Shelf

The world in 1914

The early years of the 20th century saw the mainly European colonial empires reaching their greatest extents by 1914. Two world wars inaugurated their disintegration, but even in 1950 there were only 82 independent countries. Since then, over 100 have gained their independence, culminating in the breakup of the Soviet Union and former Yugoslavia in the early 1990s.

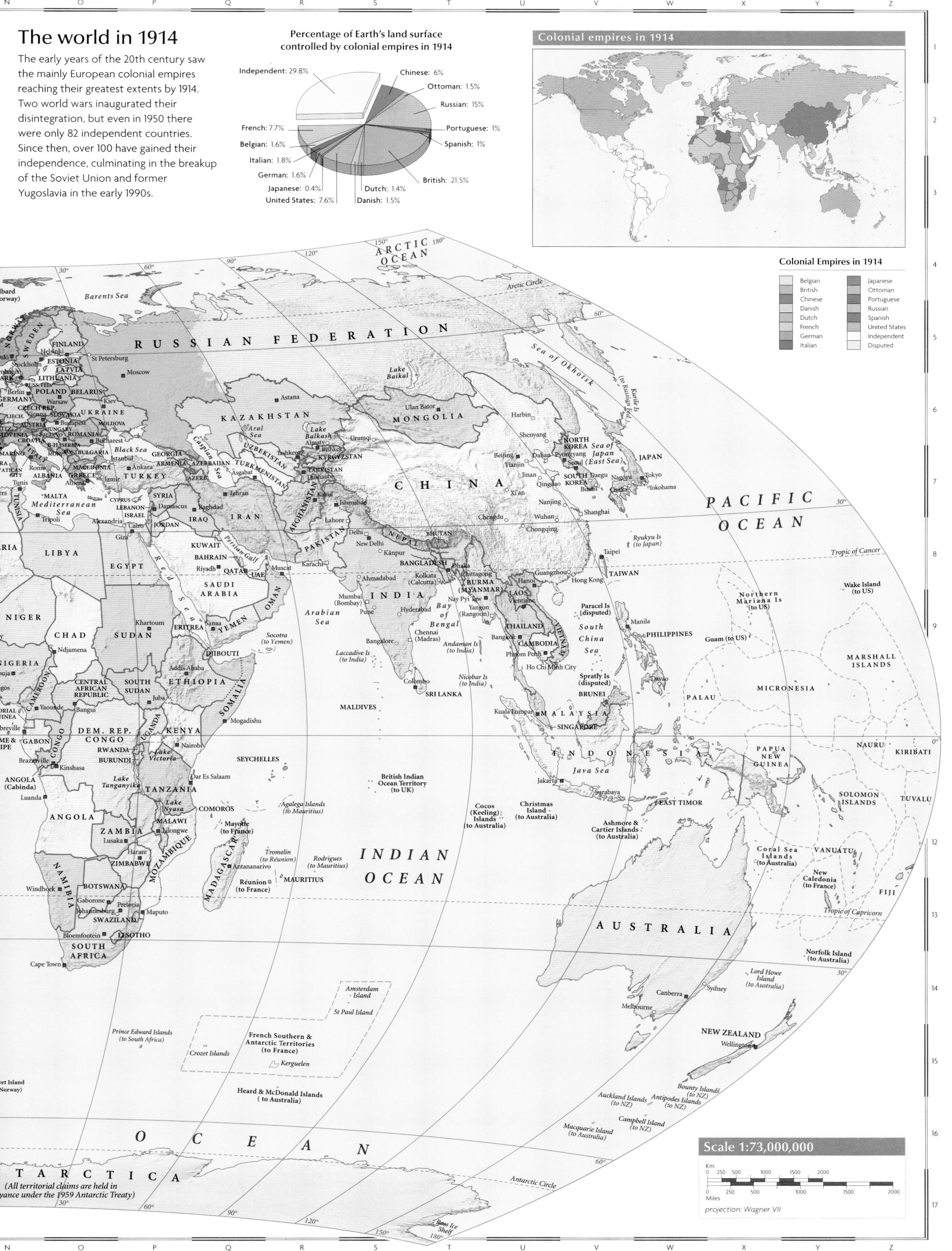
N O P Q R S T U V W X Y Z
1 2 3 4 5 6 7 8 9 12 13 14 15 16 17
Percentage of Earth's land surface controlled by colonial empires in 1914
Independent: 29.8%
Chinese: 6%
Ottoman: 1.5%
Russian: 15%
Portuguese: 1%
Spanish: 1%
British: 21.5%
Dutch: 1.4%
Danish: 1.5%
United States: 7.6%
Japanese: 0.4%
German: 1.6%
Italian: 1.8%
Belgian: 1.6%
French: 7.7%
Colonial empires in 1914
Colonial Empires in 1914
Belgian
British
Chinese
Danish
Dutch
French
German
Italian
Japanese
Ottoman
Portuguese
Russian
Spanish
United States
Independent
Disputed
ARCTIC OCEAN
Arctic Circle
Barents Sea
RUSSIAN FEDERATION
Sea of Okhotsk
Kurile Is (to Russian Fed.)
Lake Baikal
MONGOLIA
Ulan Bator
KAZAKHSTAN
Astana
Aral Sea
Caspian Sea
Lake Balkash
UZBEKISTAN
TURKMENISTAN
KYRGYZSTAN
TAJIKISTAN
AFGHANISTAN
PAKISTAN
CHINA
NEPAL
BHUTAN
BANGLADESH
INDIA
IRAN
IRAQ
TURKEY
SYRIA
SAUDI ARABIA
YEMEN
OMAN
EGYPT
LIBYA
SUDAN
CHAD
NIGER
NIGERIA
ETHIOPIA
SOMALIA
KENYA
TANZANIA
ANGOLA
ZAMBIA
NAMIBIA
BOTSWANA
SOUTH AFRICA
MOZAMBIQUE
MADAGASCAR
NORTH KOREA
SOUTH KOREA
JAPAN
Sea of Japan (East Sea)
TAIWAN
PHILIPPINES
THAILAND
CAMBODIA
VIETNAM
LAOS
BURMA (MYANMAR)
MALAYSIA
SINGAPORE
INDONESIA
Java Sea
EAST TIMOR
PAPUA NEW GUINEA
AUSTRALIA
NEW ZEALAND
PACIFIC OCEAN
INDIAN OCEAN
Arabian Sea
Bay of Bengal
South China Sea
Red Sea
Persian Gulf
Black Sea
Mediterranean Sea
Tropic of Cancer
Tropic of Capricorn
MICRONESIA
MARSHALL ISLANDS
PALAU
NAURU
KIRIBATI
TUVALU
SOLOMON ISLANDS
VANUATU
FIJI
New Caledonia (to France)
Norfolk Island (to Australia)
Lord Howe Island (to Australia)
Coral Sea Islands (to Australia)
Northern Mariana Is (to US)
Guam (to US)
Wake Island (to US)
Ryukyu Is (to Japan)
Paracel Is (disputed)
Spratly Is (disputed)
Andaman Is (to India)
Nicobar Is (to India)
Laccadive Is (to India)
Socotra (to Yemen)
MALDIVES
SRI LANKA
SEYCHELLES
British Indian Ocean Territory (to UK)
Cocos (Keeling) Islands (to Australia)
Christmas Island (to Australia)
Ashmore & Cartier Islands (to Australia)
COMOROS
Mayotte (to France)
Agalega Islands (to Mauritius)
Tromelin (to Réunion)
Rodrigues (to Mauritius)
Réunion (to France)
MAURITIUS
Amsterdam Island
St Paul Island
French Southern & Antarctic Territories (to France)
Crozet Islands
Kerguelen
Prince Edward Islands (to South Africa)
Heard & McDonald Islands (to Australia)
Auckland Islands (to NZ)
Antipodes Islands (to NZ)
Bounty Islands (to NZ)
Campbell Island (to NZ)
Macquarie Island (to Australia)
OCEAN
ANTARCTICA
(All territorial claims are held in abeyance under the 1959 Antarctic Treaty)
Antarctic Circle
Ross Ice Shelf
Scale 1:73,000,000
Km 0 250 500 1000 1500 2000
Miles 0 250 500 1000 1500 2000
projection: Wagner VII

A B C D E F G H I J K L M

States and boundaries

There are almost 200 sovereign states in the world today; in 1950 there were only 82. Over the last half-century national self-determination has been a driving force for many states with a history of colonialism and oppression. As more borders have been added to the world map, the number of international border disputes has increased.

In many cases, where the impetus towards independence has been religious or ethnic, disputes with minority groups have also caused violent internal conflict. While many newly-formed states have moved peacefully towards independence, successfully establishing government by multiparty democracy, dictatorship by military regime or individual despot is often the result of the internal power-struggles which characterize the early stages in the lives of new nations.

The nature of politics

Democracy is a broad term: it can range from the ideal of multiparty elections and fair representation to, in countries such as Singapore, a thin disguise for single-party rule. In despotic regimes, on the other hand, a single, often personal authority has total power; institutions such as parliament and the military are mere instruments of the dictator.

◀ *The stars and stripes of the US flag are a potent symbol of the country's status as a federal democracy.*

The changing world map

Decolonization

In 1950, large areas of the world remained under the control of a handful of European countries *(page xxix)*. The process of decolonization had begun in Asia, where, following the Second World War, much of south and southeast Asia sought and achieved self-determination. In the 1960s, a host of African states achieved independence, so that by 1965, most of the larger tracts of the European overseas empires had been substantially eroded. The final major stage in decolonization came with the break-up of the Soviet Union and the Eastern bloc after 1990. The process continues today as the last toeholds of European colonialism, often tiny island nations, press increasingly for independence.

▲ ***Icons of communism,*** *including statues of former leaders such as Lenin and Stalin, were destroyed when the Soviet bloc was dismantled in 1989, creating several new nations.*

New nations 1945–1965

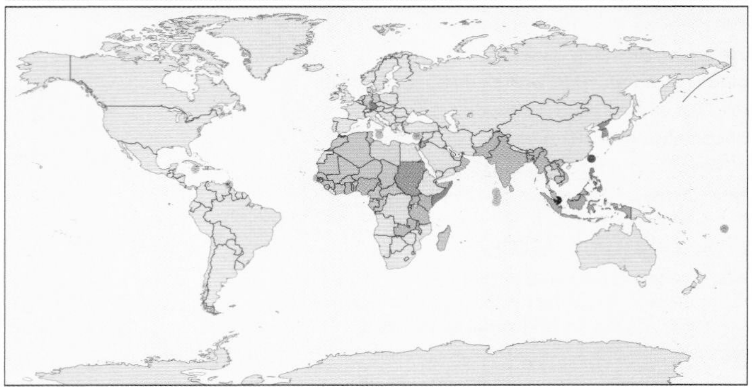

New nations 1965–present

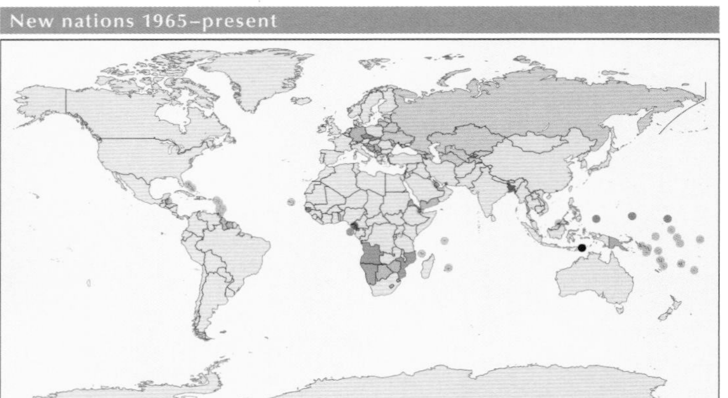

▲ ***Iran has been*** *one of the modern world's few true theocracies; Islam has an impact on every aspect of political life.*

▲ ***North Korea is*** *an independent communist republic. Power was transferred directly to Kim Jong-un in 2012 following the death of his father Kim Jong-il.*

Administration at the time of independence

Australia
Aust/NZ/UK
Belgium
China
Czechoslovakia
Egypt/UK
Ethiopia
France
France/UK
Indonesia
Italy
Japan
Malaysia
Netherlands
New Zealand
Pakistan
Portugal
South Africa
Spain
Sudan
UK
Unified country
USA
USSR
Yugoslavia

◀ ***Afghanistan*** *has suffered decades of war and occupation resulting in widespread destruction. The hardline Taliban government were ousted by a US-led coalition in 2001 but efforts to stabilise the country are still continuing over ten years later.*

◀ ***In early 2011,*** *Egypt underwent a revolution, part of the so called "Arab Spring", which resulted in the ousting of President Hosni Mubarak after nearly 30 years in power.*

▲ ***In Brunei the*** *Sultan has ruled by decree since 1962; power is closely tied to the royal family. The Sultan's brothers are responsible for finance and foreign affairs.*

Types of government

- Multiparty democracy for more than 10 yrs
- Multiparty democracy within last 10 yrs
- Single-party government
- Military regime
- Theocracy
- Monarchy
- Non-party system
- Transitional regime
- Current civil unrest

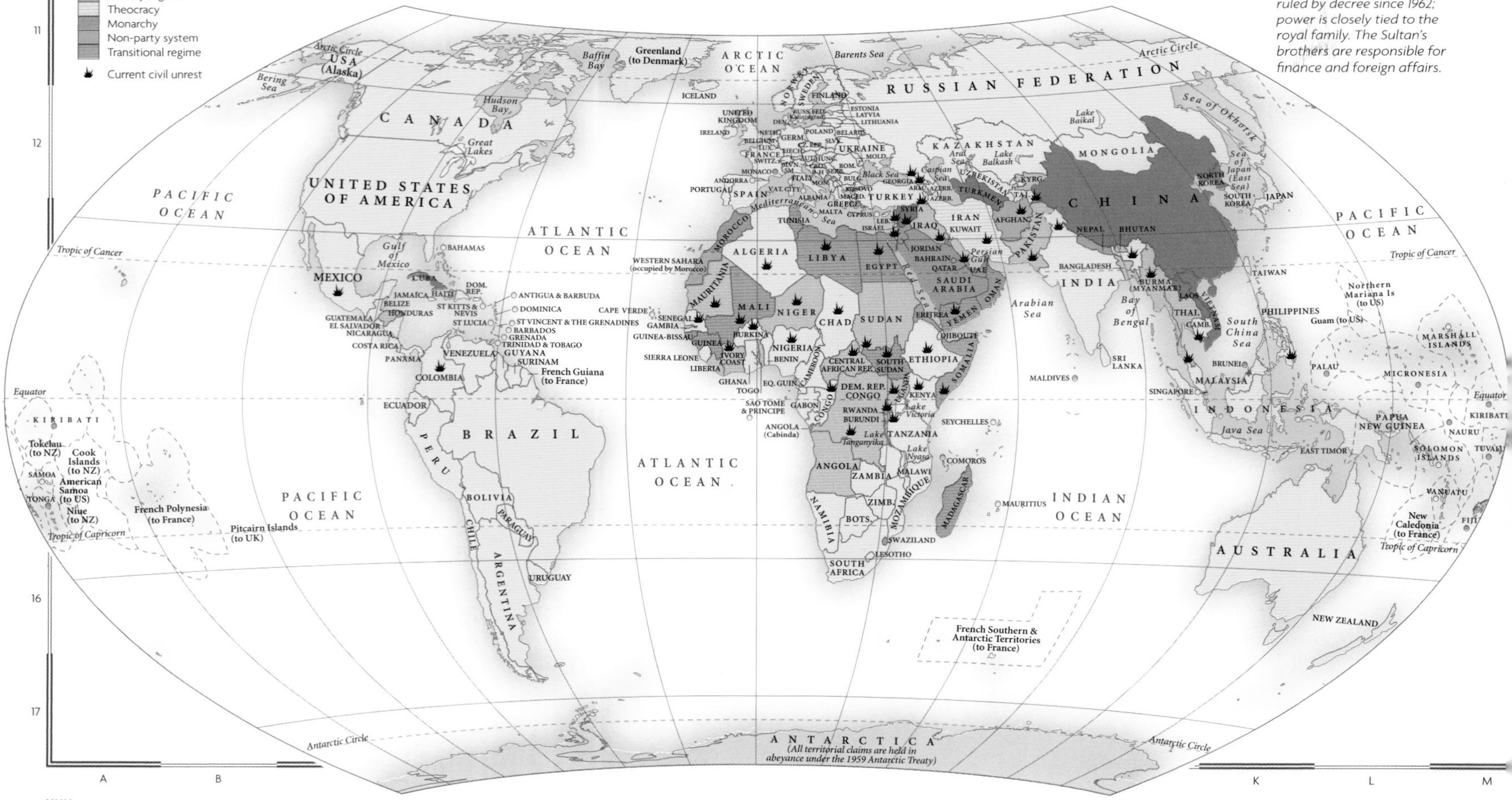

ANTARCTICA (All territorial claims are held in abeyance under the 1959 Antarctic Treaty)

A B K L M

Lines on the map

The determination of international boundaries can use a variety of criteria. Many of the borders between older states follow physical boundaries; some mirror religious and ethnic differences; others are the legacy of complex histories of conflict and colonialism, while others have been imposed by international agreements or arbitration.

Post-colonial borders

When the European colonial empires in Africa were dismantled during the second half of the 20th century, the outlines of the new African states mirrored colonial boundaries. These boundaries had been drawn up by colonial administrators, often based on inadequate geographical knowledge. Such arbitrary boundaries were imposed on people of different languages, racial groups, religions and customs. This confused legacy often led to civil and international war.

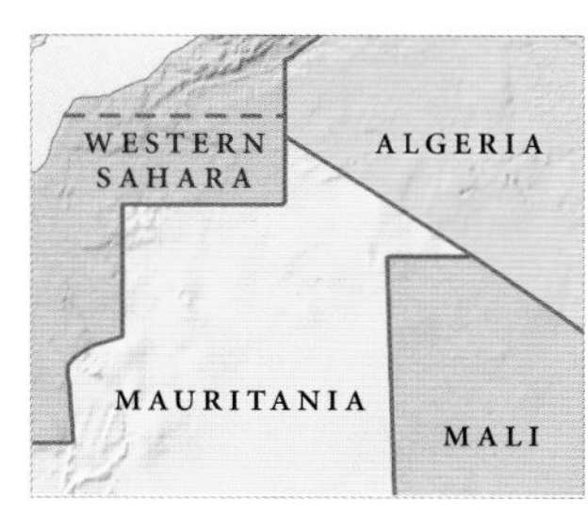
WESTERN SAHARA
ALGERIA
MAURITANIA
MALI

▲ *The conflict that has plagued many African countries since independence has caused millions of people to become refugees.*

Enclaves

The shifting political map over the course of history has frequently led to anomalous situations. Parts of national territories may become isolated by territorial agreement, forming an enclave. The West German part of the city of Berlin, which until 1989 lay a hundred miles (160 km) within East German territory, was a famous example.

Baltic Sea
ESTONIA
RUSSIAN FEDERATION
LATVIA
LITHUANIA
RUSS. FED. (Kaliningrad)
POLAND
BELARUS

▲ *Since the independence of Lithuania and Belarus, the peoples of the Russian enclave of Kaliningrad have become physically isolated.*

Antarctica

When Antarctic exploration began a century ago, seven nations, Australia, Argentina, Britain, Chile, France, New Zealand and Norway, laid claim to the new territory. In 1961 the Antarctic Treaty, now signed by 45 nations, agreed to hold all territorial claims in abeyance.

Brazilian zone of interest
British claim
Norwegian claim (undefined limits)
ATLANTIC OCEAN
Antarctic Circle
Australian claim
Argentinian claim
Chilean claim
PACIFIC OCEAN
INDIAN OCEAN
New Zealand claim
French claim
Australian claim

Geometric borders

Straight lines and lines of longitude and latitude have occasionally been used to determine international boundaries; and indeed the world's second longest continuous international boundary, between Canada and the USA, follows the 49th Parallel for over one-third of its course. Many Canadian, American and Australian internal administrative boundaries are similarly determined using a geometric solution.

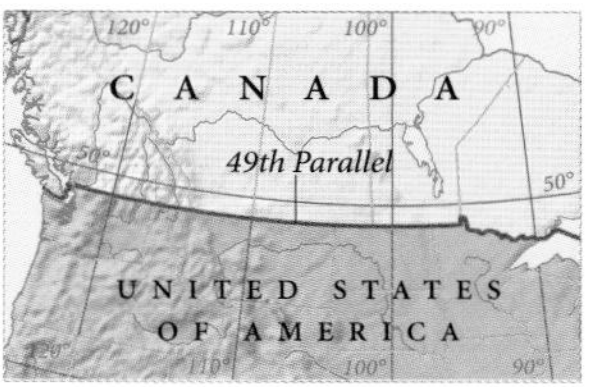
CANADA
49th Parallel
UNITED STATES OF AMERICA

▲ *Different farming techniques in Canada and the USA clearly mark the course of the international boundary in this satellite map.*

World boundaries

Dates from which current boundaries have existed
1990–present
1966–1989
1946–1965
1915–1945
1850–1914
1800–1849
Pre-1800

Physical borders

Many of the world's countries are divided by physical borders: lakes, rivers, mountains. The demarcation of such boundaries can, however, lead to disputes. Control of waterways, water supplies and fisheries are frequent causes of international friction.

Lake borders

Countries which lie next to lakes usually fix their borders in the middle of the lake. Unusually the Lake Nyasa border between Malawi and Tanzania runs along Tanzania's shore.

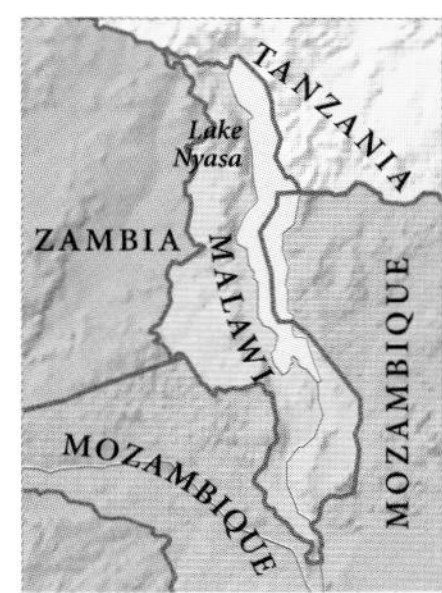
TANZANIA
Lake Nyasa
ZAMBIA
MALAWI
MOZAMBIQUE
MOZAMBIQUE

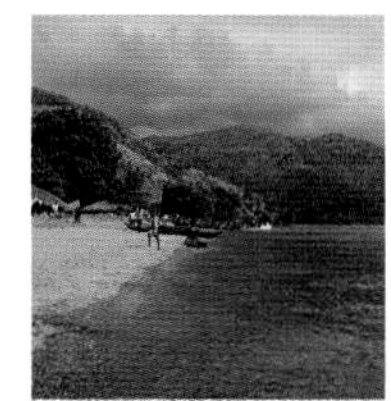

▲ *Complicated agreements between colonial powers led to the awkward division of Lake Nyasa.*

River borders

Rivers alone account for one-sixth of the world's borders. Many great rivers form boundaries between a number of countries. Changes in a river's course and interruptions of its natural flow can lead to disputes, particularly in areas where water is scarce. The centre of the river's course is the nominal boundary line.

GERMANY
Danube
SLOVAKIA
UKRAINE
AUSTRIA
HUNGARY
ROMANIA
CROATIA
SERBIA
Danube
BULGARIA

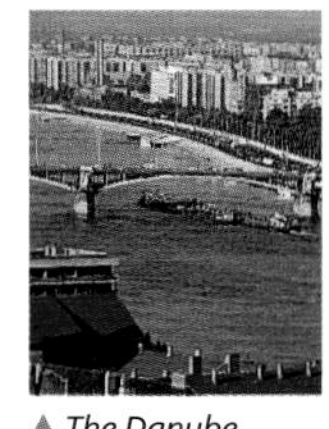

▲ *The Danube forms all or part of the border between nine European nations.*

Mountain borders

Mountain ranges form natural barriers and are the basis for many major borders, particularly in Europe and Asia. The watershed is the conventional boundary demarcation line, but its accurate determination is often problematic.

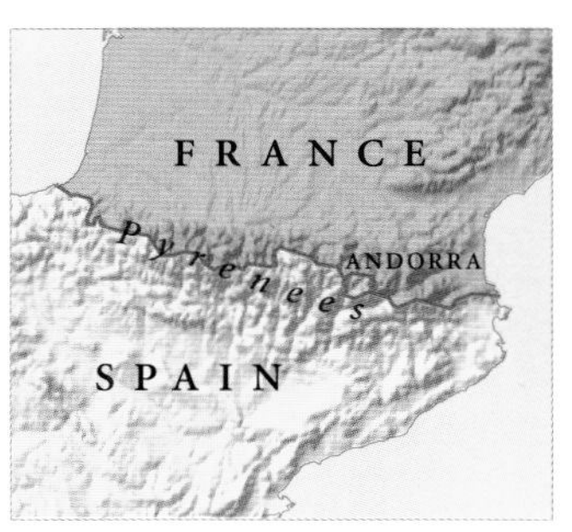
FRANCE
Pyrenees
ANDORRA
SPAIN

▲ *The Pyrenees form a natural mountain border between France and Spain.*

Shifting boundaries – Poland

Borders between countries can change dramatically over time. The nations of eastern Europe have been particularly affected by changing boundaries. Poland is an example of a country whose boundaries have changed so significantly that it has literally moved around Europe. At the start of the 16th century, Poland was the largest nation in Europe. Between 1772 and 1795, it was absorbed into Prussia, Austria and Russia, and it effectively ceased to exist. After the First World War, Poland became an independent country once more, but its borders changed again after the Second World War following invasions by both Soviet Russia and Nazi Germany.

Moscow
POLAND
Warsaw
Kiev

▲ *In 1634, Poland was the largest nation in Europe, its eastern boundary reaching towards Moscow.*

Moscow
PRUSSIA
Warsaw
RUSSIA
Kiev
AUSTRIA

▲ *From 1772–1795, Poland was gradually partitioned between Austria, Russia and Prussia. Its eastern boundary receded by over 100 miles (160 km).*

Moscow
POLAND
Warsaw
Kiev

▲ *Following the First World War, Poland was reinstated as an independent state, but it was less than half the size it had been in 1634.*

Moscow
POLAND
Warsaw
Kiev

▲ *After the Second World War the Baltic Sea border was extended westwards, but much of the eastern territory was annexed by Russia.*

International disputes

There are more than 60 disputed borders or territories in the world today. Although many of these disputes can be settled by peaceful negotiation, some areas have become a focus for international conflict. Ethnic tensions have been a major source of territorial disagreement throughout history, as has the ownership of, and access to, valuable natural resources. The turmoil of the post-colonial era in many parts of Africa is partly a result of the 19th century 'carve-up' of the continent, which created potential for conflict by drawing often arbitrary lines through linguistic and cultural areas.

Jammu and Kashmir

Disputes over Jammu and Kashmir have caused three serious wars between India and Pakistan since 1947. Pakistan wishes to annex the largely Muslim territory, while India refuses to cede any territory or to hold a referendum, and also lays claim to the entire territory. Most international maps show the 'line of control' agreed in 1972 as the *de facto* border. In addition India has territorial disputes with neighbouring China. The situation is further complicated by a Kashmiri independence movement, active since the late 1980s.

▲ ***Indian army troops*** *maintain their positions in the mountainous terrain of northern Kashmir.*

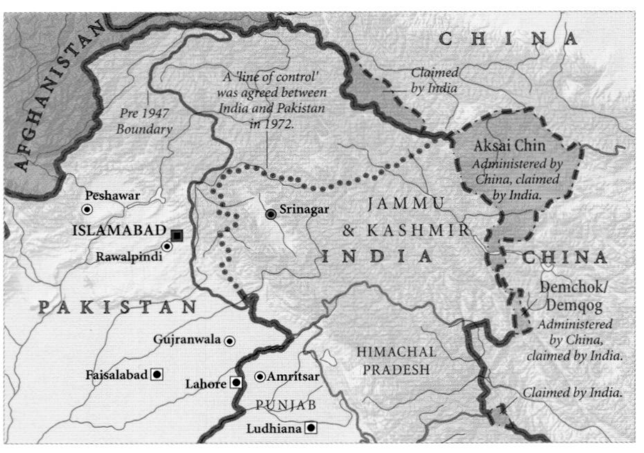
AFGHANISTAN
CHINA
Claimed by India
A 'line of control' was agreed between India and Pakistan in 1972.
Pre 1947 Boundary
Aksai Chin
Administered by China, claimed by India.
Peshawar
Srinagar
JAMMU & KASHMIR
ISLAMABAD
Rawalpindi
INDIA
CHINA
PAKISTAN
Demchok/ Demqog
Administered by China, claimed by India.
Gujranwala
HIMACHAL PRADESH
Faisalabad
Lahore
Amritsar
PUNJAB
Claimed by India.
Ludhiana

North and South Korea

Since 1953, the *de facto* border between North and South Korea has been a ceasefire line which straddles the 38th Parallel and is designated as a demilitarized zone. Both countries have heavy fortifications and troop concentrations behind this zone.

CHINA
NORTH KOREA
PYONGYANG
SEOUL
SOUTH KOREA
Yellow Sea

▲ ***Heavy fortifications on*** *the border between North and South Korea.*

ΛΕΥΤΕΡΙΑ ΣΤΗΝ ΚΥ
FREEDOM FOR CY

▲ ***The so-called*** *'green line' divides Cyprus into Greek and Turkish sectors.*

Cyprus

Cyprus was partitioned in 1974, following an invasion by Turkish troops. The south is now the Greek Cypriot Republic of Cyprus, while the self-proclaimed Turkish Republic of Northern Cyprus is recognized only by Turkey.

TURKISH REPUBLIC OF NORTHERN CYPRUS
(recognized only by Turkey)
Mediterranean Sea
Kyrenia Mountains
Karpasia
NICOSIA
CYPRUS
Troodos
UK Sovereign Base Area
Lárnaka
UK Sovereign Base Area
Lemesós (Limassol)
Mediterranean Sea

Conflicts and international disputes

- UN peacekeeping missions 2002-2012
- Major active territorial or border disputes
- Countries involved in internal conflict
- Active territorial or border disputes and internal conflict

RUSSIAN FEDERATION · Kurile Islands · NORTH KOREA · SOUTH KOREA · CHINA · Aksai Chin · Jammu and Kashmir · Arunachal Pradesh · Senkaku Islands · TAIWAN · Paracel Islands · PHILIPPINES · Spratly Islands · MALAYSIA · EAST TIMOR · BRITISH INDIAN OCEAN TERRITORY · TAJIKISTAN · AFGHANISTAN · PAKISTAN · IRAN · IRAQ · INDIA · BHUTAN · BANGLADESH · BURMA (MYANMAR) · THAILAND · CAMBODIA · VIETNAM · Chechnya · MOLDOVA · GEORGIA · ARMENIA · AZERBAIJAN · TURKEY · SYRIA · CYPRUS · LEBANON · ISRAEL · CROATIA · B&H · KOSOVO · BULGARIA · MACEDONIA · SPAIN · Gibraltar · Ceuta · Melilla · MOROCCO · ALGERIA · LIBYA · EGYPT · WESTERN SAHARA · MAURITANIA · MALI · NIGER · CHAD · SUDAN · ERITREA · YEMEN · SOMALIA · SENEGAL · BURKINA · NIGERIA · SIERRA LEONE · LIBERIA · IVORY COAST · BENIN · CAMEROON · C.A.R. · SOUTH SUDAN · ETHIOPIA · UGANDA · KENYA · DEM. REP. CONGO · CONGO · RWANDA · BURUNDI · Cabinda · ANGOLA · ZAMBIA · ZIMBABWE · BOTSWANA · MEXICO · CUBA · Guantanamo Bay · BELIZE · HAITI · VENEZUELA · GUYANA · SURINAM · French Guiana · COLOMBIA · ECUADOR · PERU · BRAZIL · BOLIVIA · CHILE · URUGUAY · ARGENTINA · Falkland Islands

The Falkland Islands

The British dependent territory of the Falkland Islands was invaded by Argentina in 1982, sparking a full-scale war with the UK. Tensions ran high during 2012 in the build up to the thirtieth anniversary of the conflict.

◀ ***British warships in*** *Falkland Sound during the 1982 war with Argentina.*

JERUSALEM · Jenin · Tulkarm · Qalqiliya · Nablus · WEST BANK · ISRAEL · Ramallah · 'Auja et Tahta · Nu'eima · Jericho · Bethlehem · Hebron (Israel retains 15% control) · Dead Sea · JORDAN

Palestinian control · Mixed control · Israeli settlement block · Israeli settlement · Palestinian settlement · West Bank fence

Israel

Israel was created in 1948 following the 1947 UN Resolution (147) on Palestine. Until 1979 Israel had no borders, only ceasefire lines from a series of wars in 1948, 1967 and 1973. Treaties with Egypt in 1979 and Jordan in 1994 led to these borders being defined and agreed. Negotiations over Israeli settlements and Palestinian self-government have seen little effective progress since 2000.

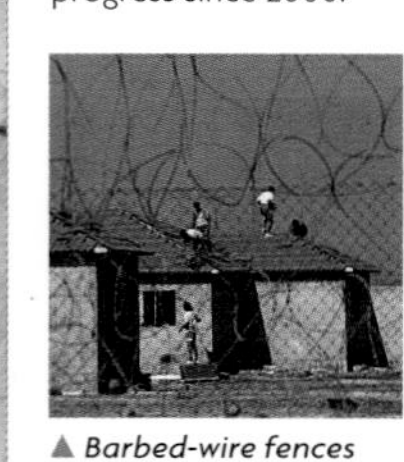
LEBANON
Mediterranean Sea
GOLAN HEIGHTS
SYRIA
WEST BANK
GAZA STRIP
ISRAEL
JORDAN
EGYPT

▲ ***Barbed-wire fences*** *surround a settlement in the Golan Heights.*

Former Yugoslavia

Following the disintegration in 1991 of the communist state of Yugoslavia, the breakaway states of Croatia and Bosnia and Herzegovina came into conflict with the 'parent' state (consisting of Serbia and Montenegro). Warfare focused on ethnic and territorial ambitions in Bosnia. The tenuous Dayton Accord of 1995 sought to recognize the post-1990 borders, whilst providing for ethnic partition and required international peace-keeping troops to maintain the terms of the peace.

CROATIA
Sava
Bihać
Brčko
Banja Luka
Bosna
Tuzla
Jajce
BOSNIA &
Srebrenica
Drina
HERZEGOVINA
SERBIA
Gornji Vakuf
Goražde
Split
SARAJEVO
Adriatic Sea
Mostar
Republika Srpska
Federacija Bosna i Hercegovina
MONTENEGRO
Dubrovnik

▲ ***Most claimant states*** *have small military garrisons on the Spratly Islands.*

The Spratly Islands

The site of potential oil and natural gas reserves, the Spratly Islands in the South China Sea have been claimed by China, Vietnam, Taiwan, Malaysia and the Philippines since the Japanese gave up a wartime claim in 1951.

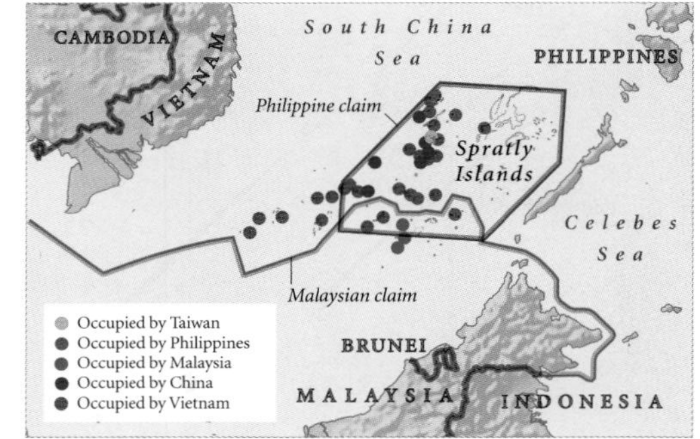
CAMBODIA
South China Sea
PHILIPPINES
VIETNAM
Philippine claim
Spratly Islands
Celebes Sea
Malaysian claim
Occupied by Taiwan
Occupied by Philippines
Occupied by Malaysia
Occupied by China
Occupied by Vietnam
BRUNEI
MALAYSIA
INDONESIA

ATLAS OF THE WORLD

THE MAPS IN THIS ATLAS ARE ARRANGED CONTINENT BY CONTINENT, STARTING FROM THE INTERNATIONAL DATE LINE, AND MOVING EASTWARDS. THE MAPS PROVIDE A UNIQUE VIEW OF TODAY'S WORLD, COMBINING TRADITIONAL CARTOGRAPHIC TECHNIQUES WITH THE LATEST REMOTE-SENSED AND DIGITAL TECHNOLOGY.

A
B
C
D
E
F
G
H
I
J
K
L
M
ARCTIC OCEAN
North Pole
Franz Josef Land
East Siberian Sea
Sea of Okhotsk
Chukchi Sea
Greenland Sea
Norwegian
Greenland
Nordøstrundingen
Kap Morris Jesup
King Frederik VIII Land
King Christian X Land
Ellesmere Island
Queen Elizabeth Islands
Beaufort Sea
Point Barrow
Bering Strait
Bering Sea
Aleutian Basin
Bowers Ridge
Anadyrskiy Zaliv
St Lawrence Island
Nunivak Island
Norton Sound
Kuskokwim Bay
Bristol Bay
Aleutian Islands
Aleutian Range
Alaska Peninsula
Alaska Range
Kenai Mountains
Brooks Range
Kuril Trench
Kamchatka
PACIFIC PLATE
NORTH AMERICAN PLATE
Gulf of Alaska
Patton Seamount
Queen Charlotte Islands
Union Seamount
Cobb Seamount
Vancouver Island
Cascadia Basin
Mendocino Fracture Zone
Pioneer Fracture Zone
Murray Fracture Zone
Molokai Fracture Zone
Clarion Fracture Zone
Clipperton Fracture Zone
Siqueiros Fracture Zone
Tropic of Cancer
Equator
PACIFIC OCEAN
Mackenzie Bay
McClure Strait
Banks Island
Parry Islands
Viscount Melville Sound
Prince of Wales Island
Victoria Island
Amundsen Gulf
Mackenzie Mountains
Great Bear Lake
Coronation Gulf
Queen Maud Gulf
Boothia Peninsula
Gulf of Boothia
McClintock Channel
Jones Sound
Lancaster Sound
Baffin Bay
Baffin Island
Davis Strait
Nettilling Lake
Foxe Basin
Amadjuak Lake
Cumberland Sound
Frobisher Bay
Hudson Strait
Foxe Channel
Southampton Island
Coats Island
Mansel Island
Péninsule d'Ungava
Hudson Bay
Belcher Islands
James Bay
Arctic Circle
Garry Lake
Baker Lake
Dubawnt Lake
Great Slave Lake
Lake Athabasca
Wollaston Lake
Reindeer Lake
Churchill
Canadian Shield
Lake Winnipeg
Lake Manitoba
Lake of the Woods
Lake Nipigon
Lac Mistassini
La Grande Rivière
Rocky Mountains
NORTH AMERICA
Great Plains
Great Lakes
Lake Superior
Lake Michigan
Lake Huron
Lake Erie
Lake Ontario
Lake St Clair
Ontario Peninsula
Niagara Falls
Black Hills
Lake Oahe
Great Salt Lake
Great Basin
Columbia Plateau
Harney Basin
Mount Rainier
Coast Mountains
Coast Ranges
Sierra Nevada
San Francisco Bay
Monterey Bay
Delgada Fan
Gorda Ridges
JUAN DE FUCA PLATE
Mount Whitney
Lake Mead
Lake Powell
Grand Canyon
Mojave Desert
Painted Desert
Colorado Plateau
Sonoran Desert
Mount Elbert
Baldy Peak 3476m
Appalachian Mountains
Allegheny Mountains
Blue Ridge
Mount Mitchell 2037m
Cumberland Plateau
Long Island
Delaware Bay
Chesapeake Bay
Cape Hatteras
Cape Lookout
Blake Plateau
Cape Canaveral
Lake Okeechobee
The Everglades
Straits of Florida
Mississippi Delta
Mississippi Fan
Galveston Bay
Sigsbee Escarpment
Apalachee Bay
Tampa Bay
Gulf of Mexico
Mexico Basin
Campeche Bank
Yucatan Channel
Yucatan Peninsula
Yucatan Basin
Bay of Campeche
Cuba
Cayman Trench
Jamaica
Gulf of Honduras
Nicaraguan Rise
Colombian Basin
Lake Nicaragua
Mosquito Gulf
Gulf of Darién
Isthmus of Panama
Gulf of Panama
Península de Azuero
Panama Basin
Cocos Ridge
Colón Ridge
Guatemala Basin
Tehuantepec Ridge
Golfo de Tehuantepec
Middle America Trench
COCOS PLATE
CARIBBEAN PLATE
NAZCA PLATE
East Pacific Rise
Albatross Plateau
Clipperton Seamounts
Clipperton Island
Mathematicians Seamounts
Revillagigedo Islands
Orozco Fracture Zone
Sierra Madre del Sur
Sierra Madre Occidental
Sierra Madre Oriental
Citlaltépetl 5700m
Cabo San Lucas
Lower California
Gulf of California
Islas Alijos
Río Grande
Caribbean Sea

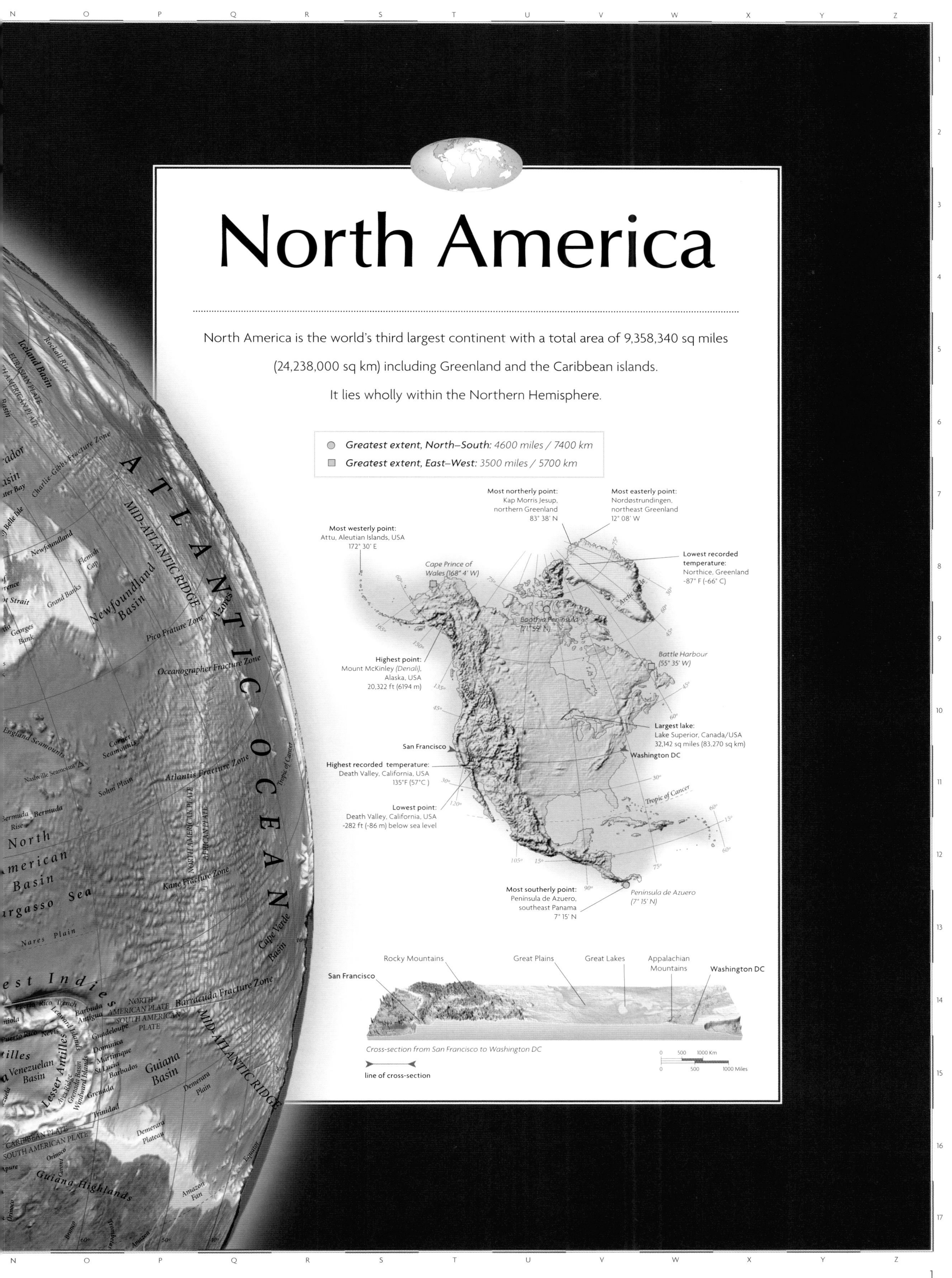
North America
North America is the world's third largest continent with a total area of 9,358,340 sq miles (24,238,000 sq km) including Greenland and the Caribbean islands.
It lies wholly within the Northern Hemisphere.
Greatest extent, North–South: 4600 miles / 7400 km
Greatest extent, East–West: 3500 miles / 5700 km
Most northerly point: Kap Morris Jesup, northern Greenland 83° 38' N
Most easterly point: Nordøstrundingen, northeast Greenland 12° 08' W
Most westerly point: Attu, Aleutian Islands, USA 172° 30' E
Cape Prince of Wales (168° 4' W)
Lowest recorded temperature: Northice, Greenland -87° F (-66° C)
Boothia Peninsula (71° 59' N)
Battle Harbour (55° 35' W)
Highest point: Mount McKinley (Denali), Alaska, USA 20,322 ft (6194 m)
Largest lake: Lake Superior, Canada/USA 32,142 sq miles (83,270 sq km)
San Francisco
Washington DC
Highest recorded temperature: Death Valley, California, USA 135°F (57°C)
Lowest point: Death Valley, California, USA -282 ft (-86 m) below sea level
Tropic of Cancer
Most southerly point: Peninsula de Azuero, southeast Panama 7° 15' N
Peninsula de Azuero (7° 15' N)
Rocky Mountains
Great Plains
Great Lakes
Appalachian Mountains
San Francisco
Washington DC
Cross-section from San Francisco to Washington DC
line of cross-section
0 500 1000 Km
0 500 1000 Miles
ATLANTIC OCEAN
MID-ATLANTIC RIDGE
Newfoundland Basin
Grand Banks
Flemish Cap
Pico Fracture Zone
Azores
Oceanographer Fracture Zone
Corner Seamounts
Atlantis Fracture Zone
Sohm Plain
Nashville Seamount
Tropic of Cancer
NORTH AMERICAN PLATE
AFRICAN PLATE
Kane Fracture Zone
Bermuda
North American Basin
Sargasso Sea
Nares Plain
Cape Verde Basin
West Indies
Barracuda Fracture Zone
NORTH AMERICAN PLATE
SOUTH AMERICAN PLATE
Lesser Antilles
Venezuelan Basin
Guiana Basin
Demerara Plain
Demerara Plateau
CARIBBEAN PLATE
SOUTH AMERICAN PLATE
Guiana Highlands
Amazon Fan
Equator
Iceland Basin
Rockall Rise
EURASIAN PLATE
NORTH AMERICAN PLATE
Charlie-Gibbs Fracture Zone
Newfoundland
Georges Bank
Barbados
Trinidad
Dominica
Martinique
St Lucia
Grenada
Guadeloupe
Antigua
Barbuda
Nevis

Physical North America

The North American continent can be divided into a number of major structural areas: the Western Cordillera, the Canadian Shield, the Great Plains and Central Lowlands, and the Appalachians. Other smaller regions include the Gulf Atlantic Coastal Plain which borders the southern coast of North America from the southern Appalachians to the Great Plains. This area includes the expanding Mississippi Delta. A chain of volcanic islands, running in an arc around the margin of the Caribbean Plate, lie to the east of the Gulf of Mexico.

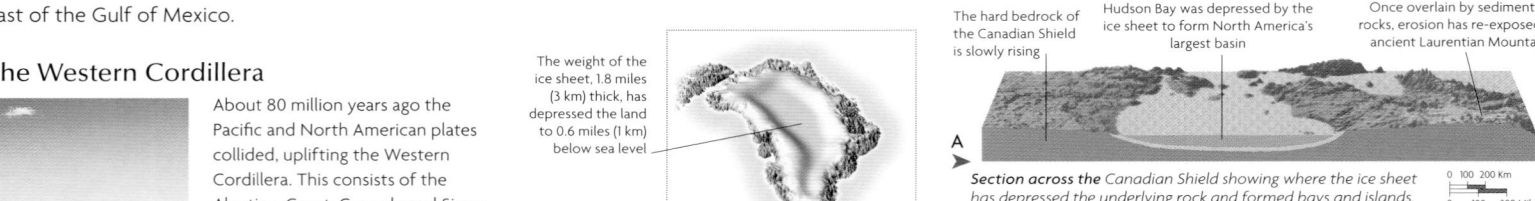

The Western Cordillera

About 80 million years ago the Pacific and North American plates collided, uplifting the Western Cordillera. This consists of the Aleutian, Coast, Cascade and Sierra Nevada mountains, and the inland Rocky Mountains. These run parallel from the Arctic to Mexico.

The weight of the ice sheet, 1.8 miles (3 km) thick, has depressed the land to 0.6 miles (1 km) below sea level

▲ *This computer-generated view shows the ice-covered island of Greenland without its ice cap.*

Volcanic rock

Strata have been thrust eastward along fault lines

The Rocky Mountain Trench is the longest linear fault on the continent

B B

***Cross-section through the** Western Cordillera showing direction of mountain building.* ⟶

0 50 100 Km
0 50 100 Miles

The Canadian Shield

Spanning northern Canada and Greenland, this geologically stable plain forms the heart of the continent, containing rocks over two billion years old. A long history of weathering and repeated glaciation has scoured the region, leaving flat plains, gentle hummocks, numerous small basins and lakes, and the bays and islands of the Arctic.

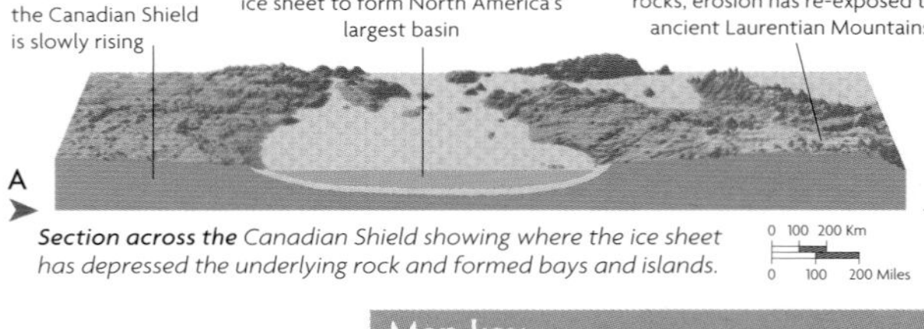

The hard bedrock of the Canadian Shield is slowly rising
Hudson Bay was depressed by the ice sheet to form North America's largest basin
Once overlain by sedimentary rocks, erosion has re-exposed the ancient Laurentian Mountains
A
A
0 100 200 Km
0 100 200 Miles

***Section across the** Canadian Shield showing where the ice sheet has depressed the underlying rock and formed bays and islands.*

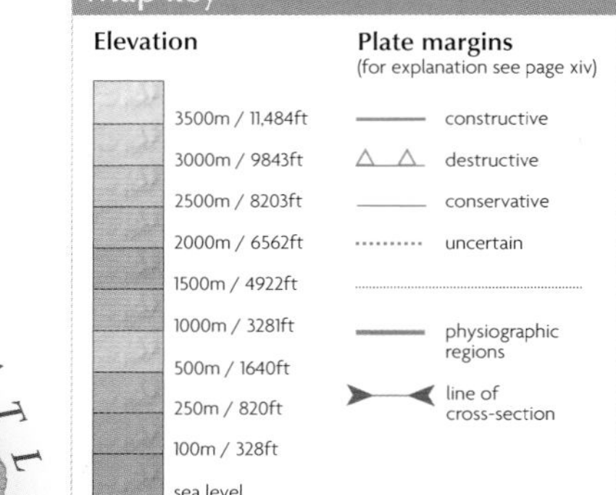

Map key
Elevation
3500m / 11,484ft
3000m / 9843ft
2500m / 8203ft
2000m / 6562ft
1500m / 4922ft
1000m / 3281ft
500m / 1640ft
250m / 820ft
100m / 328ft
sea level
Plate margins
(for explanation see page xiv)
constructive
destructive
conservative
uncertain
physiographic regions
line of cross-section

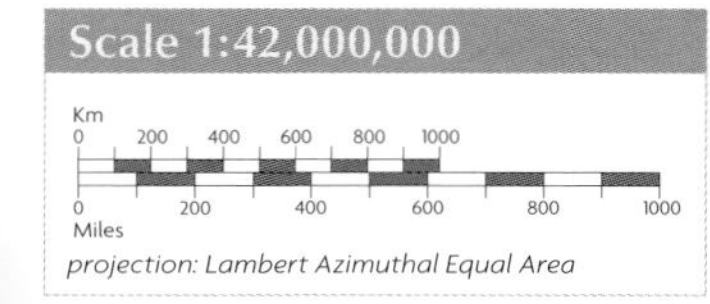

Scale 1:42,000,000
Km 0 200 400 600 800 1000
0 200 400 600 800 1000 Miles
projection: Lambert Azimuthal Equal Area

ASIA
Bering Strait
Bering Sea
Aleutian Islands
Aleutian Range
Alaska Range
Mount McKinley 6194m
Brooks Range
Beaufort Sea
Mackenzie Delta
Mackenzie
Mackenzie Mountains
Gulf of Alaska
NORTH AMERICAN PLATE
PACIFIC PLATE
JUAN DE FUCA PLATE
Coast Mountains
WESTERN CORDILLERA
ROCKY MOUNTAINS
Great Bear Lake
Great Slave Lake
Lake Athabasca
Reindeer Lake
CANADIAN SHIELD
CENTRAL LOWLANDS
GREAT PLAINS
Greenland
Baffin Bay
Baffin Island
Davis Strait
Foxe Basin
Hudson Strait
Labrador Sea
Labrador
ATLANTIC OCEAN
Hudson Bay
Laurentian Mountains
Newfoundland
Nova Scotia
St Lawrence
Lake Winnipeg
Lake Manitoba
Lake Superior
Lake Huron
Lake Ontario
Lake Michigan
Lake Erie
Great Lakes
Cape Cod
Missouri
Ohio
Mississippi
Arkansas
Appalachian Mountains
APPALACHIANS
GULF ATLANTIC COASTAL PLAIN
Cascade Range
Mount Rainier 4392m
Mount St Helens 2549m
Great Basin
Great Salt Lake
Colorado
Colorado Plateau
Sierra Nevada
San Joaquin Valley
San Andreas Fault
Death Valley -86m
Grand Canyon
Mojave Desert
Sonoran Desert
Lower California
Gulf of California
Sierra Madre Occidental
Sierra Madre Oriental
Rio Grande
Mississippi Delta
Gulf of Mexico
Yucatan Peninsula
Volcán Pico de Orizaba 5700m
Sierra Madre del Sur
PACIFIC OCEAN
CARIBBEAN PLATE
Lake Nicaragua
Isthmus of Panama
Caribbean Sea
West Indies
Greater Antilles
Lesser Antilles
SOUTH AMERICA
SOUTH AMERICAN PLATE
A A B B C C D D

The Great Plains and Central Lowlands

Deposits left by retreating glaciers and rivers have made this vast flat area very fertile. In the north this is the result of glaciation, with deposits up to one mile (1.7 km) thick, covering the basement rock. To the south and west, the massive Missouri/Mississippi river system has for centuries deposited silt across the plains, creating broad, flat flood plains and deltas.

Sedimentary layers overlay domed basement rock

Upland rivers drain south towards the Mississippi Basin

Confluence of the Missouri and Mississippi rivers

D D

***Section across the** Great Plains and Central Lowlands showing river systems and structure.*

0 200 400 Km
0 200 400 Miles

The Appalachians

The Appalachian Mountains, uplifted about 400 million years ago, are some of the oldest in the world. They have been lowered and rounded by erosion and now slope gently towards the Atlantic across a broad coastal plain.

Horizontal strata

Sedimentary strata folded and faulted into ridges and valleys

Softer strata has been crumpled against the harder basement rock

Hard basement rock

C C

***Cross-section through the** Appalachians showing the numerous folds, which have subsequently been weathered to create a rounded relief.*

0 25 50 Km
0 25 50 Miles

Climate

North America's climate includes extremes ranging from freezing Arctic conditions in Alaska and Greenland, to desert in the southwest, and tropical conditions in southeastern Florida, the Caribbean and Central America. Central and southern regions are prone to severe storms including tornadoes and hurricanes.

▲ *'Tornado alley' in the Mississippi Valley suffers frequent tornadoes.*

▲ *Much of the southwest is semi-desert; receiving less than 12 inches (300 mm) of rainfall a year.*

Climate
ice cap
tundra
subarctic
cool continental
warm humid
semi-arid
arid
humid equatorial
tropical
daily hours of sunshine, January
daily hours of sunshine, July
direction of hurricanes
tornado zones
Nome
Fairbanks
Aklavik
Kugluktuk
Resolute
Eismitte
Iqaluit
Haines Junction
Juneau
Fort Vermillon
Fort St John
Churchill
Happy Valley - Goose Bay
Torbay
Vancouver
Medicine Hat
Winnipeg
Montréal
Toronto
Boise
Sioux City
New York
Salt Lake City
San Francisco
Denver
Las Vegas
Phoenix
Los Angeles
Little Rock
Atlanta
Cape Hatteras
Houston
Guaymas
Chihuahua
New Orleans
Miami
Nassau
Tropic of Cancer
Arctic Circle
Santo Domingo
Fort-de-France
Mérida
Kingston
Acapulco
San Salvador
San José
Temperature
Arctic Circle
60° N
40° N
Tropic of Cancer
20° N

Average January temperature *Average July temperature*

Temperature
below -30°C (-22°F)
-30 to -20°C (-22 to -4°F)
-20 to -10°C (-4 to 14°F)
-10 to 0°C (14 to 32°F)
0 to 10°C (32 to 50°F)
10 to 20°C (50 to 68°F)
20 to 30°C (68 to 86°F)
above 30°C (86°F)
Rainfall
Arctic Circle
60° N
40° N
Tropic of Cancer
20° N

Average January rainfall *Average July rainfall*

Rainfall
0–25 mm (0–1 in)
25–50 mm (1–2 in)
50–100 mm (2–4 in)
100–200 mm (4–8 in)
200–300 mm (8–12 in)
300–400 mm (12–16 in)
400–500 mm (16–20 in)
more than 500 mm (20 in)

◀ *The lush, green mountains of the Lesser Antilles receive annual rainfalls of up to 360 inches (9000 mm).*

Shaping the continent

Glacial processes affect much of northern Canada, Greenland and the Western Cordillera. Along the western coast of North America, Central America and the Caribbean, underlying plates moving together lead to earthquakes and volcanic eruptions. The vast river systems, fed by mountain streams, constantly erode and deposit material along their paths.

Volcanic activity

1 Mount St Helens volcano *(right)* in the Cascade Range erupted violently in May 1980, killing 57 people and levelling large areas of forest. The lateral blast filled a valley for 15 miles (25 km) with debris.

Molten rock at volcano's core
Vertical eruption
Lateral explosion increases extent of damage
Landslide fills valley

Volcanic activity: *Eruption of Mount St Helens*

Periglaciation

2 The ground in the far north is nearly always frozen: the surface thaws only in summer. This freeze-thaw process produces features such as pingos *(left)*; formed by the freezing of groundwater. With each successive winter ice accumulates producing a mound with a core of ice.

Ice core pushes up ground to form pingo
Unfrozen lake
Groundwater attracted to ice core

Periglaciation: *Formation of a pingo in the Mackenzie Delta*

Post-glacial lakes

3 A chain of lakes from Great Bear Lake to the Great Lakes *(above)* was created as the ice retreated northwards. Glaciers scoured hollows in the softer lowland rock. Glacial deposits at the lip of the hollows, and ridges of harder rock, trapped water to form lakes.

Retreating glacier
Ice-scoured hollow filled with glacial meltwater to form a lake
Harder rock creates a barrier between lakes
Softer lowland rock

Post-glacial lakes: *Formation of the Great Lakes*

The evolving landscape

Landscape
limestone region
sinking land
stable land
uplifting land
active volcano
area of tectonic activity
limit of permafrost
maximum limit of glaciation
ocean current

Seismic activity

5 The San Andreas Fault *(above)* places much of the North America's west coast under constant threat from earthquakes. It is caused by the Pacific Plate grinding past the North American Plate at a faster rate, though in the same direction.

Pacific Plate
San Andreas Fault
Fault is caused by faster movement of Pacific Plate
North American Plate

Seismic activity: *Action of the San Andreas Fault*

River erosion

6 The Grand Canyon *(above)* in the Colorado Plateau was created by the downward erosion of the Colorado River, combined with the gradual uplift of the plateau, over the past 30 million years. The contours of the canyon formed as the softer rock layers eroded into gentle slopes, and the hard rock layers into cliffs. The depth varies from 3855–6560 ft (1175–2000 m).

Soft rock is easily eroded into gentle slopes
Hard rock resists erosion
Colorado River cuts down through rock

River Erosion: *Formation of the Grand Canyon*

Weathering

4 The Yucatan Peninsula is a vast, flat limestone plateau in southern Mexico. Weathering action from both rainwater and underground streams has enlarged fractures in the rock to form caves and hollows, called sinkholes *(above)*.

Porous limestone plateau
Rainwater erodes porous rock forming sinkholes
Sea level
Underground stream further erodes rock

Weathering: *Water erosion on the Yucatan Peninsula*

Political North America

Democracy is well established in some parts of the continent but is a recent phenomenon in others. The economically dominant nations of Canada and the USA have a long democratic tradition but elsewhere, notably in the countries of Central America, political turmoil has been more common. In Nicaragua and Haiti, harsh dictatorships have only recently been superseded by democratically-elected governments. North America's largest countries, Canada, Mexico and the USA have federal state systems, sharing political power between national and state governments. The USA has intervened militarily on several occasions in Central America and the Caribbean to protect its strategic interests.

Transport

In the 19th century, railways were used to open up the North American continent. Air transport is now more common for long distance passenger travel, although railways are still extensively used for bulk freight transport. Waterways, like the Mississippi River, are important for the transport of bulk materials, and the Panama Canal is a vital link between the Pacific Ocean and the Caribbean. In the 20th century, road transport increased massively in North America, with the introduction of cheap, mass-produced motor cars and extensive highway construction.

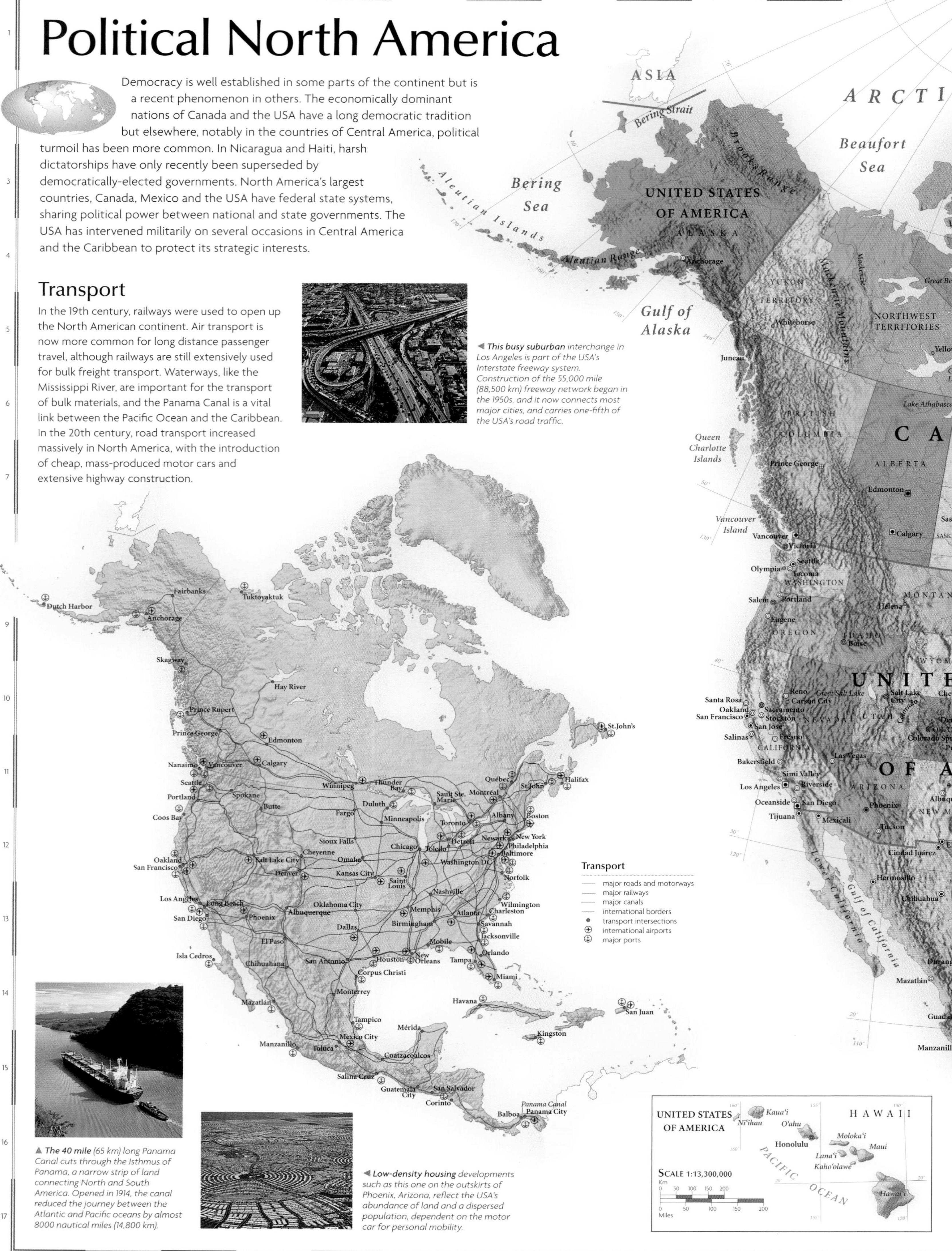

ASIA
Bering Strait
ARCTIC
Beaufort Sea
Bering Sea
Aleutian Islands
Aleutian Range
Brooks Range
UNITED STATES OF AMERICA
ALASKA
Anchorage
YUKON TERRITORY
Whitehorse
Mackenzie Mountains
NORTHWEST TERRITORIES
Great Bear Lake
Yellowknife
Great Slave Lake
Gulf of Alaska
Juneau
Lake Athabasca
BRITISH COLUMBIA
Queen Charlotte Islands
Prince George
ALBERTA
Edmonton
Vancouver Island
Vancouver
Victoria
Calgary
Olympia
Seattle
Tacoma
WASHINGTON
Salem
Portland
Eugene
OREGON
MONTANA
Helena
IDAHO
Boise
Santa Rosa
Oakland
San Francisco
Sacramento
Reno
Carson City
Great Salt Lake
Salt Lake City
Stockton
San Jose
NEVADA
UTAH
Salinas
Fresno
CALIFORNIA
Las Vegas
Bakersfield
Simi Valley
Los Angeles
Riverside
ARIZONA
Oceanside
San Diego
Tijuana
Mexicali
Phoenix
Tucson
Ciudad Juárez
Hermosillo
Chihuahua
Gulf of California
Durango
Mazatlán
Guadalajara
Manzanillo
Transport
major roads and motorways
major railways
major canals
international borders
transport intersections
international airports
major ports
Dutch Harbor
Fairbanks
Tuktoyaktuk
Skagway
Hay River
Prince Rupert
Edmonton
St.John's
Nanaimo
Calgary
Winnipeg
Thunder Bay
Québec
Halifax
Spokane
Butte
Duluth
Sault Ste. Marie
Montréal
Saint John
Coos Bay
Fargo
Minneapolis
Toronto
Albany
Boston
Sioux Falls
Detroit
Newark
New York
Cheyenne
Chicago
Toledo
Philadelphia
Baltimore
Omaha
Washington DC
Denver
Kansas City
Norfolk
Saint Louis
Nashville
Long Beach
Oklahoma City
Albuquerque
Memphis
Wilmington
Charleston
Atlanta
Birmingham
Savannah
Dallas
El Paso
Mobile
Jacksonville
Isla Cedros
San Antonio
Houston
New Orleans
Tampa
Orlando
Chihuahua
Corpus Christi
Miami
Monterrey
Havana
San Juan
Mazatlán
Tampico
Mérida
Kingston
Manzanillo
Mexico City
Toluca
Coatzacoalcos
Salina Cruz
Guatemala City
San Salvador
Corinto
Panama Canal
Balboa
Panama City
UNITED STATES OF AMERICA
HAWAII
Ni'ihau
Kaua'i
O'ahu
Honolulu
Moloka'i
Maui
Lana'i
Kaho'olawe
Hawai'i
PACIFIC OCEAN
SCALE 1:13,300,000

◀ **This busy suburban** *interchange in Los Angeles is part of the USA's Interstate freeway system. Construction of the 55,000 mile (88,500 km) freeway network began in the 1950s, and it now connects most major cities, and carries one-fifth of the USA's road traffic.*

▲ **The 40 mile** *(65 km) long Panama Canal cuts through the Isthmus of Panama, a narrow strip of land connecting North and South America. Opened in 1914, the canal reduced the journey between the Atlantic and Pacific oceans by almost 8000 nautical miles (14,800 km).*

◀ **Low-density housing** *developments such as this one on the outskirts of Phoenix, Arizona, reflect the USA's abundance of land and a dispersed population, dependent on the motor car for personal mobility.*

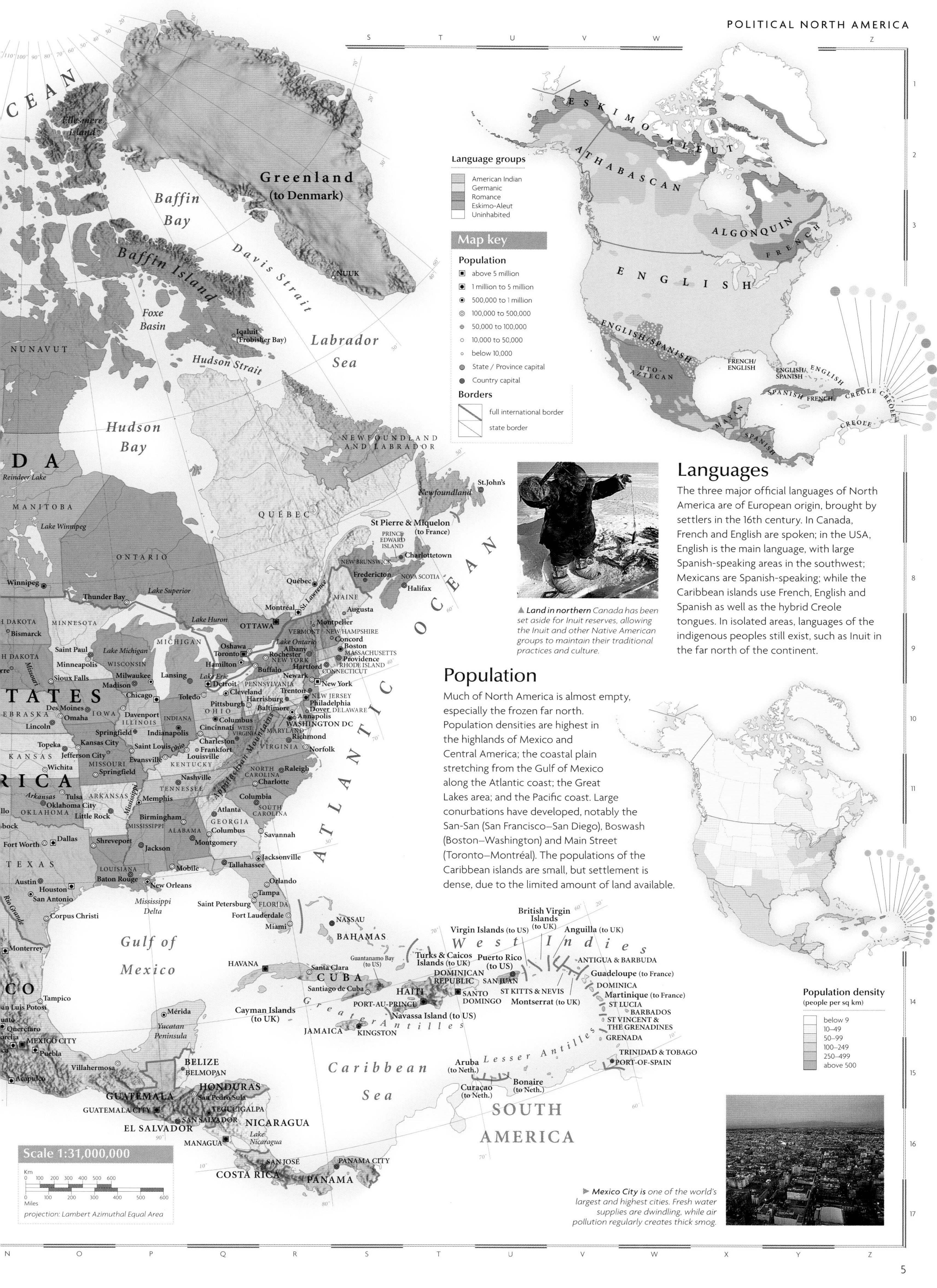
Language groups
American Indian
Germanic
Romance
Eskimo-Aleut
Uninhabited
ESKIMO-ALEUT
ATHABASCAN
ALGONQUIN
FRENCH
ENGLISH
ENGLISH/SPANISH
UTO-AZTECAN
FRENCH/ENGLISH
ENGLISH/SPANISH
ENGLISH
SPANISH
FRENCH
CREOLE
MAYAN
SPANISH
Map key
Population
above 5 million
1 million to 5 million
500,000 to 1 million
100,000 to 500,000
50,000 to 100,000
10,000 to 50,000
below 10,000
State / Province capital
Country capital
Borders
full international border
state border
Population density
(people per sq km)
below 9
10–49
50–99
100–249
250–499
above 500
Scale 1:31,000,000
projection: Lambert Azimuthal Equal Area
Greenland
(to Denmark)
Baffin Bay
Baffin Island
Davis Strait
NUUK
Foxe Basin
Iqaluit (Frobisher Bay)
Labrador Sea
Hudson Strait
NUNAVUT
Hudson Bay
NEWFOUNDLAND AND LABRADOR
QUÉBEC
ONTARIO
MANITOBA
Newfoundland
St.John's
St Pierre & Miquelon (to France)
ATLANTIC OCEAN
Gulf of Mexico
WEST INDIES
Caribbean Sea
SOUTH AMERICA
CUBA
HAVANA
BAHAMAS
NASSAU
HAITI
PORT-AU-PRINCE
DOMINICAN REPUBLIC
SANTO DOMINGO
JAMAICA
KINGSTON
Puerto Rico (to US)
SAN JUAN
BELIZE
BELMOPAN
HONDURAS
TEGUCIGALPA
GUATEMALA
GUATEMALA CITY
EL SALVADOR
SAN SALVADOR
NICARAGUA
MANAGUA
COSTA RICA
SAN JOSÉ
PANAMA
PANAMA CITY
MEXICO CITY
OTTAWA
WASHINGTON DC

▲ *Land in northern* Canada has been set aside for Inuit reserves, allowing the Inuit and other Native American groups to maintain their traditional practices and culture.

Languages

The three major official languages of North America are of European origin, brought by settlers in the 16th century. In Canada, French and English are spoken; in the USA, English is the main language, with large Spanish-speaking areas in the southwest; Mexicans are Spanish-speaking; while the Caribbean islands use French, English and Spanish as well as the hybrid Creole tongues. In isolated areas, languages of the indigenous peoples still exist, such as Inuit in the far north of the continent.

Population

Much of North America is almost empty, especially the frozen far north. Population densities are highest in the highlands of Mexico and Central America; the coastal plain stretching from the Gulf of Mexico along the Atlantic coast; the Great Lakes area; and the Pacific coast. Large conurbations have developed, notably the San-San (San Francisco–San Diego), Boswash (Boston–Washington) and Main Street (Toronto–Montréal). The populations of the Caribbean islands are small, but settlement is dense, due to the limited amount of land available.

▶ *Mexico City is* one of the world's largest and highest cities. Fresh water supplies are dwindling, while air pollution regularly creates thick smog.

North American resources

The two northern countries of Canada and the USA are richly endowed with natural resources which have helped to fuel economic development. The USA is the world's largest economy, although today it is facing stiff competition from the Far East. Mexico has relied on oil revenues but there are hopes that the North American Free Trade Agreement (NAFTA), will encourage trade growth with Canada and the USA. The poorer countries of Central America and the Caribbean depend largely on cash crops and tourism.

Industry

The modern, industrialized economies of the USA and Canada contrast sharply with those of Mexico, Central America and the Caribbean. Manufacturing is especially important in the USA; vehicle production is concentrated around the Great Lakes, while electronic and hi-tech industries are increasingly found in the western and southern states. Mexico depends on oil exports and assembly work, taking advantage of cheap labour. Many Central American and Caribbean countries rely heavily on agricultural exports.

◀ *After its purchase from Russia in 1867, Alaska's frozen lands were largely ignored by the USA. Oil reserves similar in magnitude to those in eastern Texas were discovered in Prudhoe Bay, Alaska in 1968. Freezing temperatures and a fragile environment hamper oil extraction.*

Standard of living

The USA and Canada have one of the highest overall standards of living in the world. However, many people still live in poverty, especially in inner city ghettos and some rural areas. Central America and the Caribbean are markedly poorer than their wealthier northern neighbours. Haiti is the poorest country in the western hemisphere.

Standard of living
(UN human development index)

- high
- low

▲ *Fish such as cod, flounder and plaice are caught in the Grand Banks, off the Newfoundland coast, and processed in many North Atlantic coastal settlements.*

▲ *South of San Francisco, 'Silicon Valley' is both a national and international centre for hi-tech industries, electronic industries and research institutions.*

▲ *The health of the Wall Street stock market in New York is the standard measure of the state of the world's economy.*

▲ *Multinational companies rely on cheap labour and tax benefits to facilitate the assembly of vehicle parts in Mexican factories.*

ARCTIC OCEAN · Beaufort Sea · Bering Sea · Baffin Bay · Greenland (to Denmark) · Labrador Sea · Hudson Strait · Hudson Bay · Gulf of Alaska · CANADA · USA · UNITED STATES OF AMERICA · PACIFIC OCEAN · ATLANTIC OCEAN · Gulf of Mexico · MEXICO · Caribbean Sea · West Indies · Greater Antilles · Lesser Antilles

Industry

- aerospace
- brewing
- car/vehicle manufacture
- chemicals
- defence
- electronics
- engineering
- film industry
- finance
- food processing
- hi-tech industry
- iron & steel
- pharmaceuticals
- printing & publishing
- research & development
- shipbuilding
- sugar processing
- textiles
- timber processing
- tobacco processing
- coal
- oil
- gas
- industrial cities
- major industrial areas

GNI per capita (US$)

- below 1999
- 2000–4999
- 5000–9999
- 10,000–19,999
- 20,000–24,999
- above 25,000
Virgin Islands (to US)
British Virgin Islands (to UK)
Anguilla (to UK)
ST KITTS & NEVIS
ANTIGUA & BARBUDA
Montserrat (to UK)
Guadeloupe (to France)
DOMINICA
ST LUCIA
BARBADOS
ST VINCENT & THE GRENADINES
GRENADA
TRINIDAD & TOBAGO
Port-of-Spain
Turks & Caicos Islands (to UK)
Puerto Rico (to US)
San Juan
BAHAMAS
CUBA
HAITI
DOMINICAN REPUBLIC
Santo Domingo
Port-au-Prince
Cayman Islands (to UK)
JAMAICA
Navassa Island (to US)
Aruba (to Neth.)
Curaçao (to Neth.)
Bonaire (to Neth.)
VENEZUELA
COLOMBIA
GUATEMALA
Guatemala City
BELIZE
HONDURAS
Tegucigalpa
EL SALVADOR
San Salvador
NICARAGUA
Managua
COSTA RICA
San José
PANAMA
Panama City

Environmental issues

Many fragile environments are under threat throughout the region. In Haiti, all the primary rainforest has been destroyed, while air pollution from factories and cars in Mexico City is amongst the worst in the world. Elsewhere, industry and mining pose threats, particularly in the delicate arctic environment of Alaska where oil spills have polluted coastlines and decimated fish stocks.

Mineral resources

Fossil fuels are exploited in considerable quantities throughout the continent. Coal mining in the Appalachians is declining but vast open pits exist further west in Wyoming. Oil and natural gas are found in Alaska, Texas, the Gulf of Mexico, and the Canadian West. Canada has large quantities of nickel, while Jamaica has considerable deposits of bauxite, and Mexico has large reserves of silver.

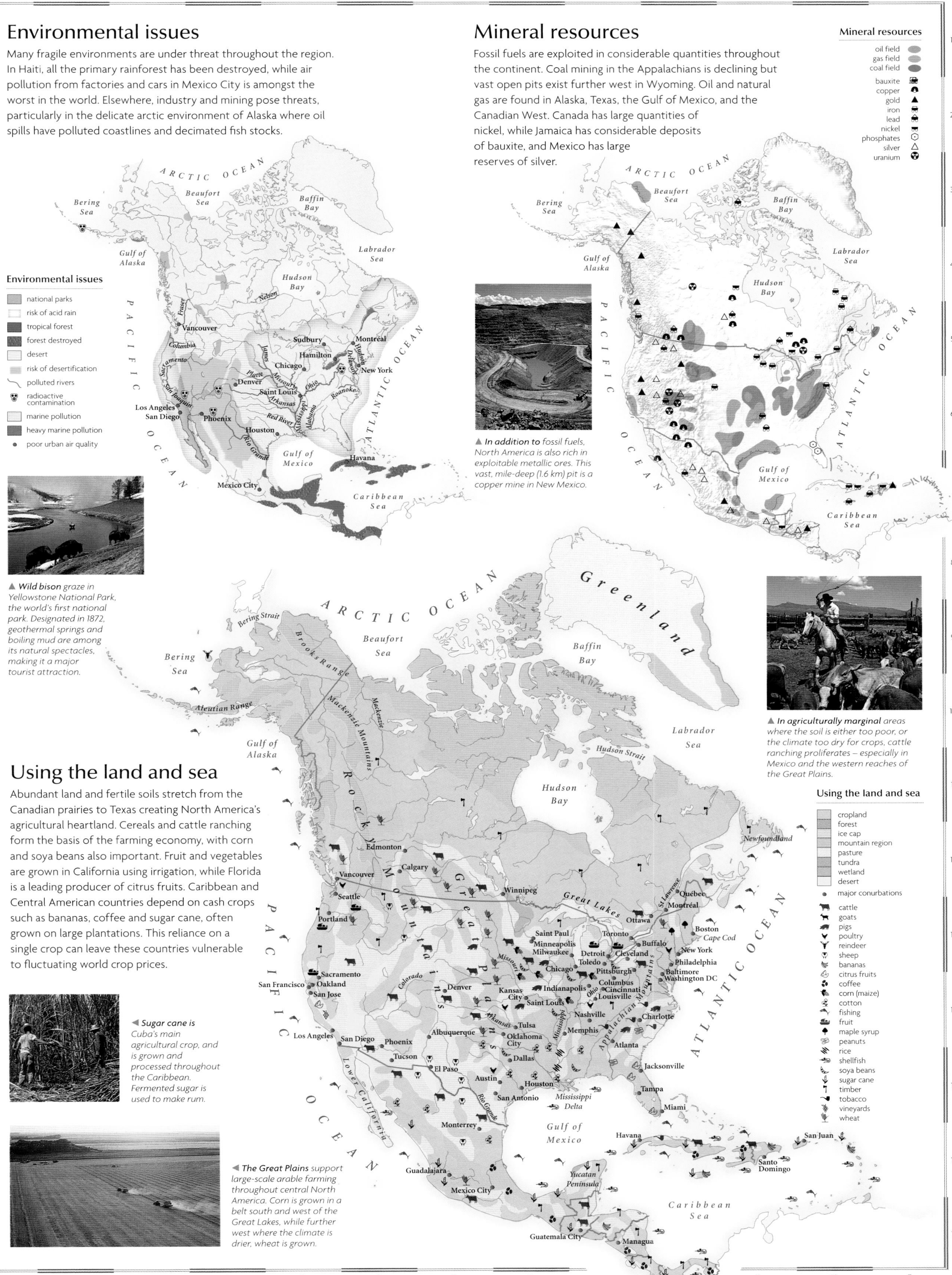
Environmental issues
national parks
risk of acid rain
tropical forest
forest destroyed
desert
risk of desertification
polluted rivers
radioactive contamination
marine pollution
heavy marine pollution
poor urban air quality
Mineral resources
oil field
gas field
coal field
bauxite
copper
gold
iron
lead
nickel
phosphates
silver
uranium
Using the land and sea
cropland
forest
ice cap
mountain region
pasture
tundra
wetland
desert
major conurbations
cattle
goats
pigs
poultry
reindeer
sheep
bananas
citrus fruits
coffee
corn (maize)
cotton
fishing
fruit
maple syrup
peanuts
rice
shellfish
soya beans
sugar cane
timber
tobacco
vineyards
wheat
ARCTIC OCEAN
PACIFIC OCEAN
ATLANTIC OCEAN
Greenland
Bering Sea
Beaufort Sea
Baffin Bay
Labrador Sea
Hudson Bay
Gulf of Alaska
Gulf of Mexico
Caribbean Sea

▲ **Wild bison** graze in Yellowstone National Park, the world's first national park. Designated in 1872, geothermal springs and boiling mud are among its natural spectacles, making it a major tourist attraction.

▲ **In addition to** fossil fuels, North America is also rich in exploitable metallic ores. This vast, mile-deep (1.6 km) pit is a copper mine in New Mexico.

▲ **In agriculturally marginal** areas where the soil is either too poor, or the climate too dry for crops, cattle ranching proliferates – especially in Mexico and the western reaches of the Great Plains.

Using the land and sea

Abundant land and fertile soils stretch from the Canadian prairies to Texas creating North America's agricultural heartland. Cereals and cattle ranching form the basis of the farming economy, with corn and soya beans also important. Fruit and vegetables are grown in California using irrigation, while Florida is a leading producer of citrus fruits. Caribbean and Central American countries depend on cash crops such as bananas, coffee and sugar cane, often grown on large plantations. This reliance on a single crop can leave these countries vulnerable to fluctuating world crop prices.

◀ **Sugar cane is** Cuba's main agricultural crop, and is grown and processed throughout the Caribbean. Fermented sugar is used to make rum.

◀ **The Great Plains** support large-scale arable farming throughout central North America. Corn is grown in a belt south and west of the Great Lakes, while further west where the climate is drier, wheat is grown.

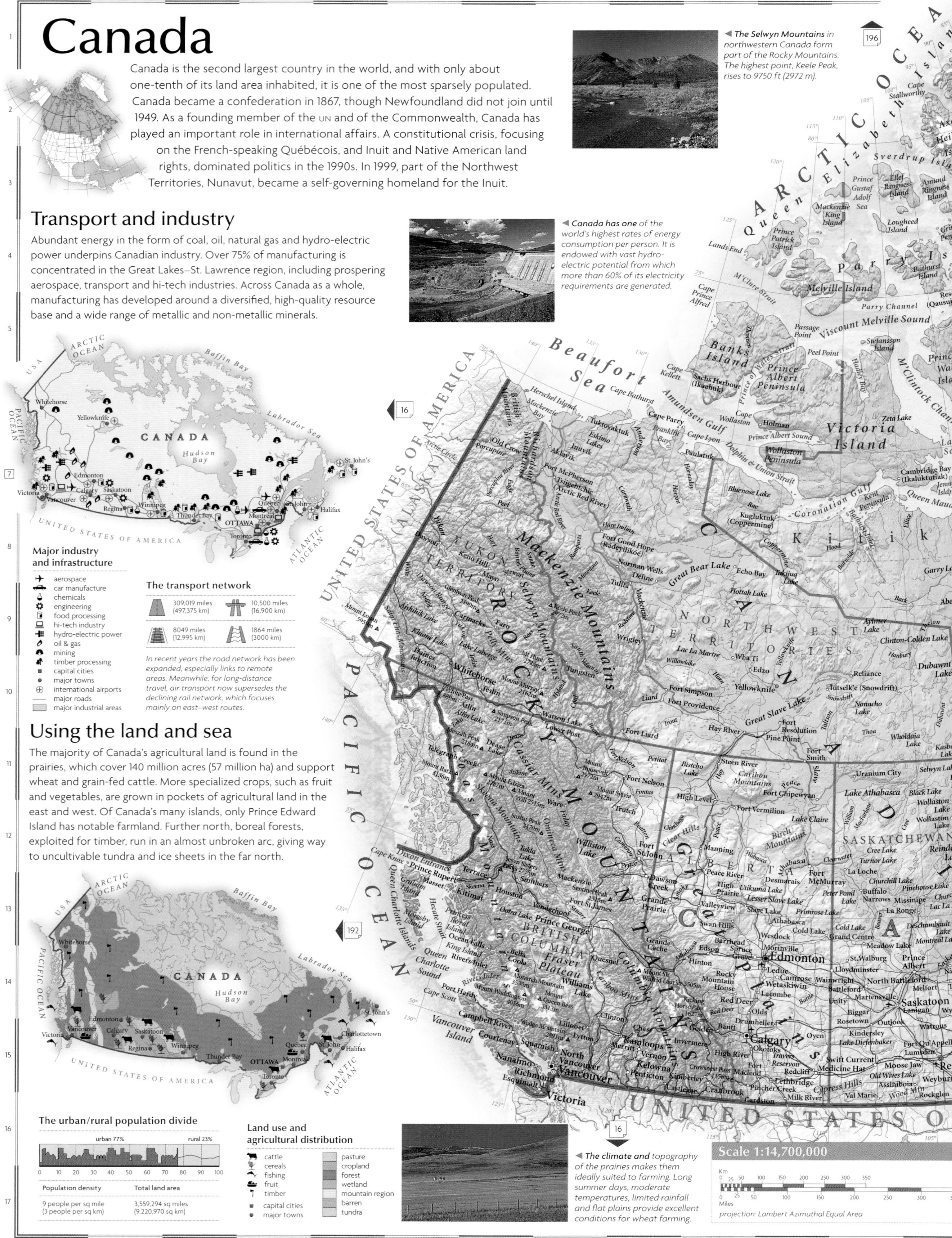

ARCTIC OCEAN
Beaufort Sea
PACIFIC OCEAN
UNITED STATES OF AMERICA (ALASKA)
ROCKY MOUNTAINS
Mackenzie Mountains
YUKON TERRITORY
NORTHWEST TERRITORIES
BRITISH COLUMBIA
ALBERTA
SASKATCHEWAN
Victoria Island
Banks Island
Queen Elizabeth Islands
Great Bear Lake
Great Slave Lake
Lake Athabasca
Edmonton
Calgary
Vancouver
Victoria
Saskatoon
Whitehorse
Yellowknife
UNITED STATES OF AMERICA

196
16
192
16

Canada

Canada is the second largest country in the world, and with only about one-tenth of its land area inhabited, it is one of the most sparsely populated. Canada became a confederation in 1867, though Newfoundland did not join until 1949. As a founding member of the UN and of the Commonwealth, Canada has played an important role in international affairs. A constitutional crisis, focusing on the French-speaking Québécois, and Inuit and Native American land rights, dominated politics in the 1990s. In 1999, part of the Northwest Territories, Nunavut, became a self-governing homeland for the Inuit.

◀ *The Selwyn Mountains in northwestern Canada form part of the Rocky Mountains. The highest point, Keele Peak, rises to 9750 ft (2972 m).*

Transport and industry

Abundant energy in the form of coal, oil, natural gas and hydro-electric power underpins Canadian industry. Over 75% of manufacturing is concentrated in the Great Lakes–St. Lawrence region, including prospering aerospace, transport and hi-tech industries. Across Canada as a whole, manufacturing has developed around a diversified, high-quality resource base and a wide range of metallic and non-metallic minerals.

◀ *Canada has one of the world's highest rates of energy consumption per person. It is endowed with vast hydro-electric potential from which more than 60% of its electricity requirements are generated.*

Major industry and infrastructure

- aerospace
- car manufacture
- chemicals
- engineering
- food processing
- hi-tech industry
- hydro-electric power
- oil & gas
- mining
- timber processing
- capital cities
- major towns
- international airports
- major roads
- major industrial areas

The transport network

309,019 miles (497,375 km)	10,500 miles (16,900 km)
8049 miles (12,995 km)	1864 miles (3000 km)

In recent years the road network has been expanded, especially links to remote areas. Meanwhile, for long-distance travel, air transport now supersedes the declining rail network, which focuses mainly on east–west routes.

Using the land and sea

The majority of Canada's agricultural land is found in the prairies, which cover 140 million acres (57 million ha) and support wheat and grain-fed cattle. More specialized crops, such as fruit and vegetables, are grown in pockets of agricultural land in the east and west. Of Canada's many islands, only Prince Edward Island has notable farmland. Further north, boreal forests, exploited for timber, run in an almost unbroken arc, giving way to uncultivable tundra and ice sheets in the far north.

The urban/rural population divide

urban 77% · rural 23%

Population density	Total land area
9 people per sq mile (3 people per sq km)	3,559,294 sq miles (9,220,970 sq km)

Land use and agricultural distribution

- cattle
- cereals
- fishing
- fruit
- timber
- capital cities
- major towns
- pasture
- cropland
- forest
- wetland
- mountain region
- barren
- tundra

◀ *The climate and topography of the prairies makes them ideally suited to farming. Long summer days, moderate temperatures, limited rainfall and flat plains provide excellent conditions for wheat farming.*

Scale 1:14,700,000

projection: Lambert Azimuthal Equal Area

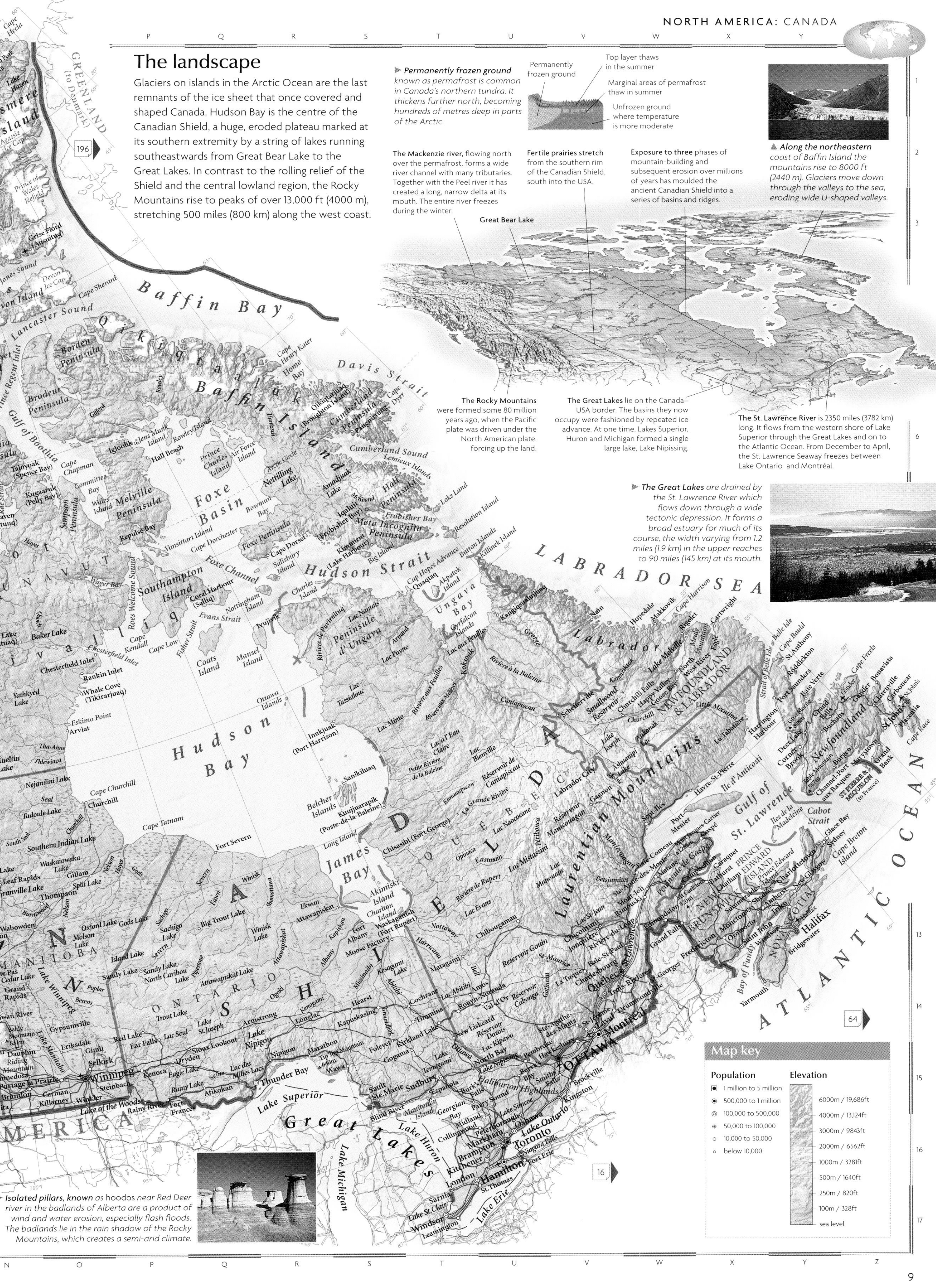

Top layer thaws in the summer
Permanently frozen ground
Marginal areas of permafrost thaw in summer
Unfrozen ground where temperature is more moderate
Great Bear Lake
Baffin Bay
Davis Strait
Baffin Island
Foxe Basin
Hudson Strait
LABRADOR SEA
Hudson Bay
James Bay
Labrador
NEWFOUNDLAND & LABRADOR
Laurentian Mountains
Gulf of St. Lawrence
ATLANTIC OCEAN
Great Lakes
Lake Superior
Lake Huron
Lake Michigan
Lake Ontario
Lake Erie
OTTAWA
Montréal
Québec
Toronto
Winnipeg
Halifax
Map key
Population
1 million to 5 million
500,000 to 1 million
100,000 to 500,000
50,000 to 100,000
10,000 to 50,000
below 10,000
Elevation
6000m / 19,686ft
4000m / 13,124ft
3000m / 9843ft
2000m / 6562ft
1000m / 3281ft
500m / 1640ft
250m / 820ft
100m / 328ft
sea level

The landscape

Glaciers on islands in the Arctic Ocean are the last remnants of the ice sheet that once covered and shaped Canada. Hudson Bay is the centre of the Canadian Shield, a huge, eroded plateau marked at its southern extremity by a string of lakes running southeastwards from Great Bear Lake to the Great Lakes. In contrast to the rolling relief of the Shield and the central lowland region, the Rocky Mountains rise to peaks of over 13,000 ft (4000 m), stretching 500 miles (800 km) along the west coast.

► ***Permanently frozen ground*** *known as permafrost is common in Canada's northern tundra. It thickens further north, becoming hundreds of metres deep in parts of the Arctic.*

▲ ***Along the northeastern*** *coast of Baffin Island the mountains rise to 8000 ft (2440 m). Glaciers move down through the valleys to the sea, eroding wide U-shaped valleys.*

The Mackenzie river, flowing north over the permafrost, forms a wide river channel with many tributaries. Together with the Peel river it has created a long, narrow delta at its mouth. The entire river freezes during the winter.

Fertile prairies stretch from the southern rim of the Canadian Shield, south into the USA.

Exposure to three phases of mountain-building and subsequent erosion over millions of years has moulded the ancient Canadian Shield into a series of basins and ridges.

The Rocky Mountains were formed some 80 million years ago, when the Pacific plate was driven under the North American plate, forcing up the land.

The Great Lakes lie on the Canada–USA border. The basins they now occupy were fashioned by repeated ice advance. At one time, Lakes Superior, Huron and Michigan formed a single large lake, Lake Nipissing.

The St. Lawrence River is 2350 miles (3782 km) long. It flows from the western shore of Lake Superior through the Great Lakes and on to the Atlantic Ocean. From December to April, the St. Lawrence Seaway freezes between Lake Ontario and Montréal.

► ***The Great Lakes*** *are drained by the St. Lawrence River which flows down through a wide tectonic depression. It forms a broad estuary for much of its course, the width varying from 1.2 miles (1.9 km) in the upper reaches to 90 miles (145 km) at its mouth.*

► ***Isolated pillars, known*** *as hoodos near Red Deer river in the badlands of Alberta are a product of wind and water erosion, especially flash floods. The badlands lie in the rain shadow of the Rocky Mountains, which creates a semi-arid climate.*

196
64
16

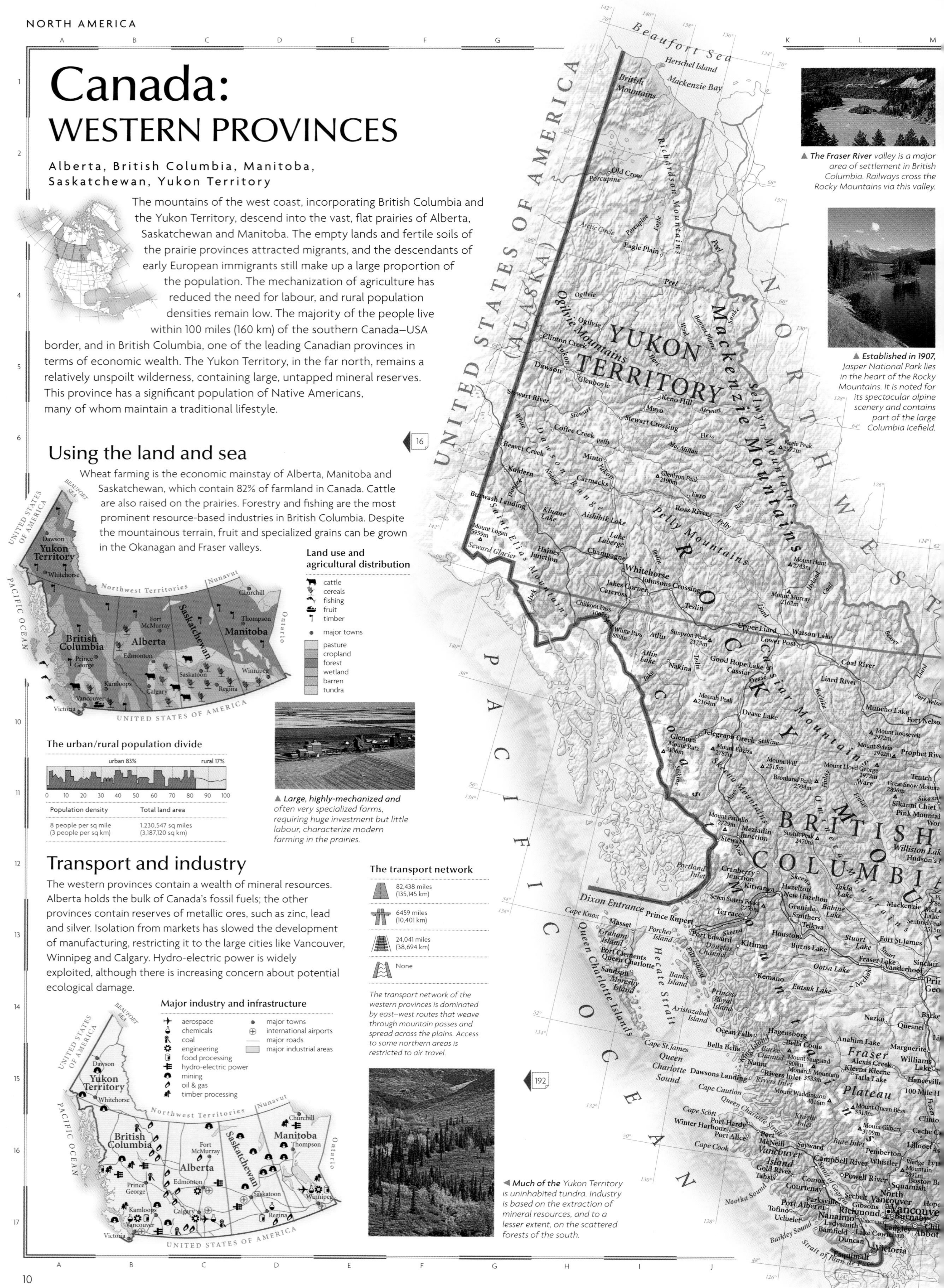

Canada: WESTERN PROVINCES

Alberta, British Columbia, Manitoba, Saskatchewan, Yukon Territory

The mountains of the west coast, incorporating British Columbia and the Yukon Territory, descend into the vast, flat prairies of Alberta, Saskatchewan and Manitoba. The empty lands and fertile soils of the prairie provinces attracted migrants, and the descendants of early European immigrants still make up a large proportion of the population. The mechanization of agriculture has reduced the need for labour, and rural population densities remain low. The majority of the people live within 100 miles (160 km) of the southern Canada–USA border, and in British Columbia, one of the leading Canadian provinces in terms of economic wealth. The Yukon Territory, in the far north, remains a relatively unspoilt wilderness, containing large, untapped mineral reserves. This province has a significant population of Native Americans, many of whom maintain a traditional lifestyle.

Using the land and sea

Wheat farming is the economic mainstay of Alberta, Manitoba and Saskatchewan, which contain 82% of farmland in Canada. Cattle are also raised on the prairies. Forestry and fishing are the most prominent resource-based industries in British Columbia. Despite the mountainous terrain, fruit and specialized grains can be grown in the Okanagan and Fraser valleys.

Land use and agricultural distribution

cattle
cereals
fishing
fruit
timber
major towns
pasture
cropland
forest
wetland
barren
tundra

The urban/rural population divide

urban 83%
rural 17%
0 10 20 30 40 50 60 70 80 90 100

Population density	Total land area
8 people per sq mile (3 people per sq km)	1,230,547 sq miles (3,187,120 sq km)

▲ *Large, highly-mechanized and often very specialized farms, requiring huge investment but little labour, characterize modern farming in the prairies.*

Transport and industry

The western provinces contain a wealth of mineral resources. Alberta holds the bulk of Canada's fossil fuels; the other provinces contain reserves of metallic ores, such as zinc, lead and silver. Isolation from markets has slowed the development of manufacturing, restricting it to the large cities like Vancouver, Winnipeg and Calgary. Hydro-electric power is widely exploited, although there is increasing concern about potential ecological damage.

The transport network

Roads	82,438 miles (135,145 km)
Motorways	6459 miles (10,401 km)
Railways	24,041 miles (38,694 km)
Waterways	None

The transport network of the western provinces is dominated by east–west routes that weave through mountain passes and spread across the plains. Access to some northern areas is restricted to air travel.

Major industry and infrastructure

aerospace
chemicals
coal
engineering
food processing
hydro-electric power
mining
oil & gas
timber processing
major towns
international airports
major roads
major industrial areas

▲ ***The Fraser River** valley is a major area of settlement in British Columbia. Railways cross the Rocky Mountains via this valley.*

▲ ***Established in 1907,** Jasper National Park lies in the heart of the Rocky Mountains. It is noted for its spectacular alpine scenery and contains part of the large Columbia Icefield.*

◀ ***Much of the** Yukon Territory is uninhabited tundra. Industry is based on the extraction of mineral resources, and to a lesser extent, on the scattered forests of the south.*

16
192

The landscape

The massive Rocky Mountains form a continental divide between rivers flowing eastward and westward. East of the mountains, stretching from the Arctic Circle south into the USA, lie the interior plains. Covered with glacial deposits from the last Ice Age, these are interspersed with hilly regions and long, steep escarpments.

Mount Logan rises 19,551 ft (5959 m). It is the highest peak in Canada.

The Columbia Icefield in the Rocky Mountains is the source of two major rivers, the Athabasca and the North Saskatchewan.

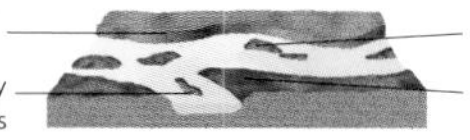

Vegetated island

Bar

Sand flat

River flow is diverted by deposited sediments

▲ ***Braided rivers are*** *shallow and fast-flowing. The interlaced branches are formed when excess sediments, which can no longer be transported, are deposited. The sediments collect in the river channel forming bars and sand flats. Islands form when the bars are colonized by vegetation.*

▲ ***Across the tundra*** *of northern Manitoba, widespread permafrost inhibits water from permeating the soil. This causes rivers like the Churchill to flow in many channels, which can be frozen for up to six months during the winter.*

The badlands of Alberta were created when east-flowing rivers, swollen by meltwater at the end of the last Ice Age, cut deep, wide canyons producing eroded, barren landscapes.

South Saskatchewan River

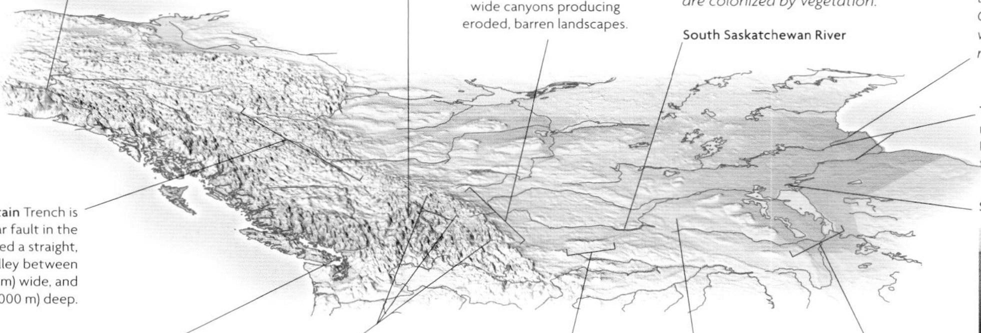

The Nelson and Churchill rivers drain northward across the Canadian Shield to Hudson Bay. The shield covers three-fifths of Saskatchewan.

Setting Lake

The Rocky Mountain Trench is the longest linear fault in the world. It has formed a straight, flat-bottomed valley between 2–9 miles (4–15 km) wide, and up to 3280 ft (1000 m) deep.

Hundreds of islands dot the fjord-indented coast of British Columbia; the largest is Vancouver Island.

Three major passes cut through the Rocky Mountains: Yellowhead, Kicking Horse and Crowsnest. They are all used as transport routes through the mountains.

The Alberta and Saskatchewan plains bear strong testament to past glaciations. The Assiniboine, Saskatchewan and Qu'Appelle rivers occupy flat-bottomed, steep-sided valleys eroded during the last Ice Age by glacial meltwater.

▲ ***Ancient granite outcrops,*** *part of the Canadian Shield, rise above the surface of Setting Lake, which was initially formed by meltwater from the last Ice Age.*

The Cypress Hills rise to 4806 ft (1465 m) above the surrounding plain. Having escaped the last glaciation they contain unique plant and animal life. The silvery lupine, bunchberry and lodgepole pine all grow in the cool, moist climate of the hills.

The lowlands of Manitoba are a basin that once held the vast post-glacial Lake Agassiz, remnants of which include Lake Winnipeg, Lake Winnipegosis and Lake Manitoba.

Map key

Population

- 500,000 to 1 million
- 100,000 to 500,000
- 50,000 to 100,000
- 10,000 to 50,000
- below 10,000

Elevation

- 6000m / 19,686ft
- 4000m / 13,124ft
- 3000m / 9843ft
- 2000m / 6562ft
- 1000m / 3281ft
- 500m / 1640ft
- 250m / 820ft
- 100m / 328ft
- sea level

Scale 1:8,250,000

Km 0 25 50 100 150 200 250

Miles 0 25 50 100 150 200 250

projection: Lambert Conformal Conic

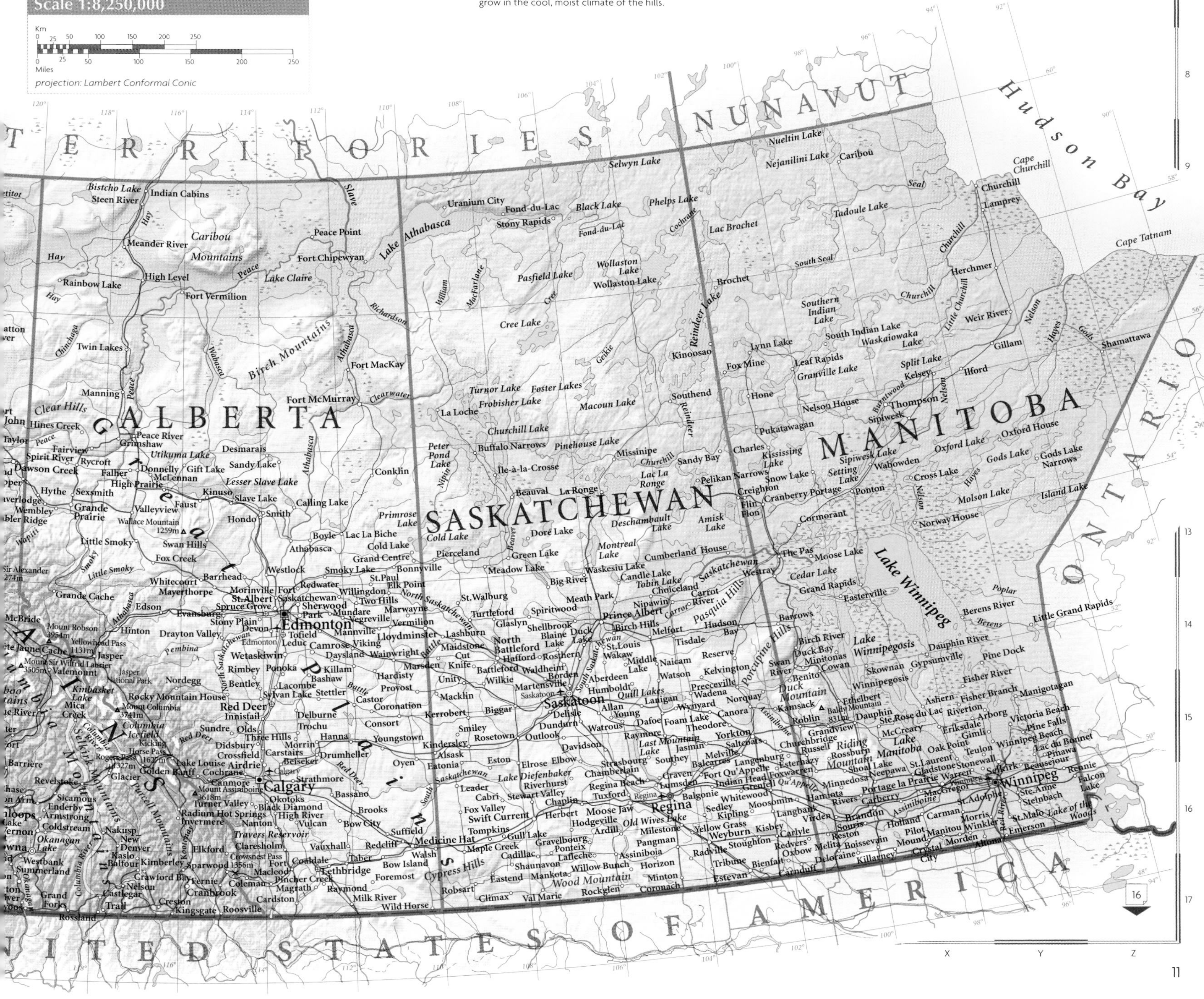

TERRITORIES NUNAVUT ALBERTA SASKATCHEWAN MANITOBA ONTARIO UNITED STATES OF AMERICA Hudson Bay

16

Canada: EASTERN PROVINCES

New Brunswick, Newfoundland & Labrador, Nova Scotia, Ontario, Prince Edward Island, Québec, *St Pierre & Miquelon (to France)*

Colonized by both the English and the French during the 16th century, Canada's eastern provinces are still marked by their dual influences. They contain the last fragment of once-sizeable French territories, the islands of St Pierre and Miquelon. French remains Canada's second official language and Québec's first language. The population of the eastern provinces is highly concentrated in the south, especially along the border with the USA. A recent decline in fishing in the Atlantic provinces has encouraged a steady flow of westerly migration to more prosperous regions. The north, around Hudson Bay, remains snow-covered for most of the year and the indigenous Inuit people make up the bulk of its sparse population.

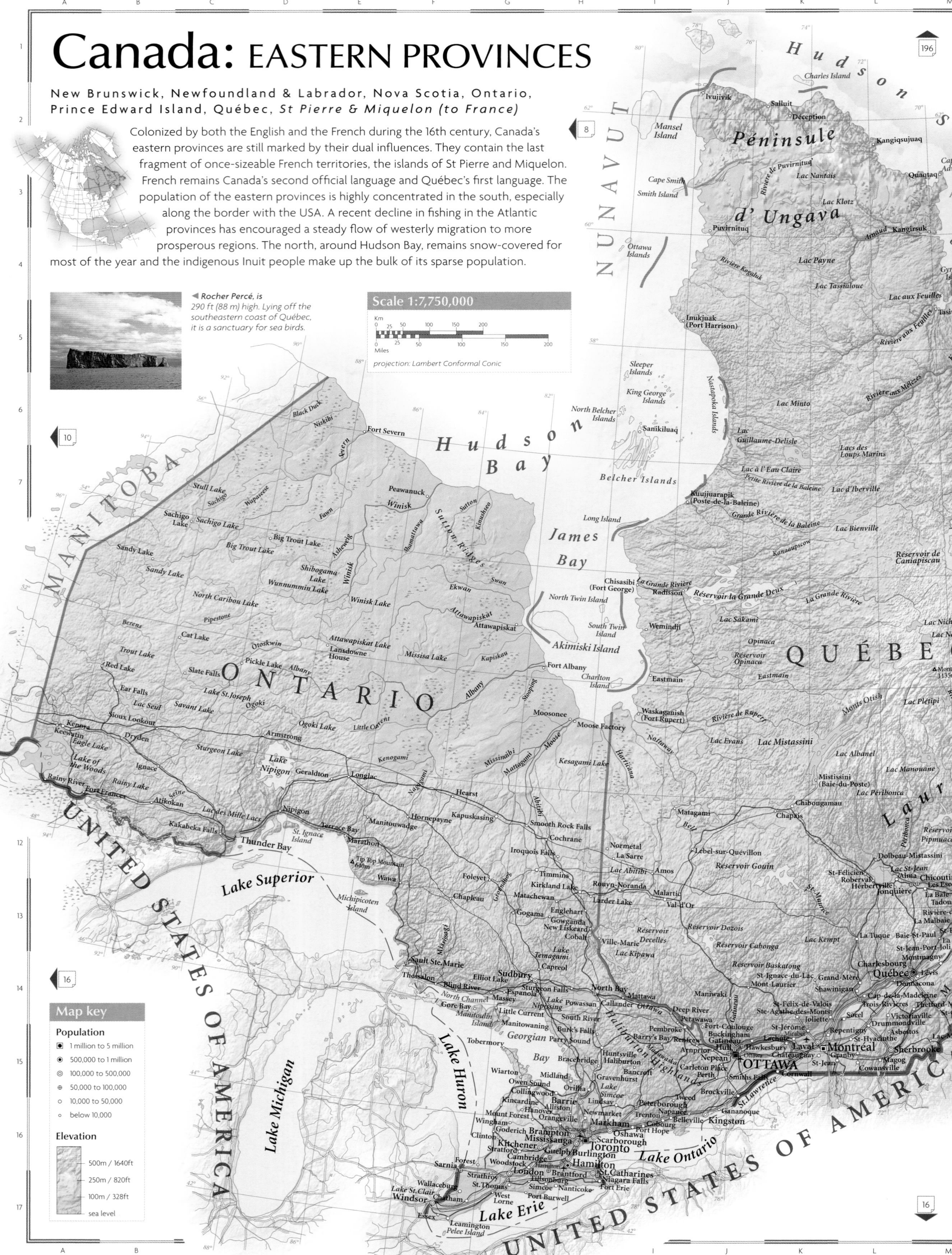

Scale 1:7,750,000
Km
Miles
projection: Lambert Conformal Conic
Hudson Bay
James Bay
ONTARIO
QUÉBEC
NUNAVUT
MANITOBA
UNITED STATES OF AMERICA
Péninsule d' Ungava
Lake Superior
Lake Michigan
Lake Huron
Georgian Bay
Lake Ontario
Lake Erie
Akimiski Island
Belcher Islands
Thunder Bay
Sault Ste. Marie
Sudbury
North Bay
OTTAWA
Montréal
Québec
Toronto
Hamilton
London
Windsor
Kingston
Sherbrooke
Trois-Rivières
Moosonee
Timmins
Kapuskasing
Kenora
Map key
Population
1 million to 5 million
500,000 to 1 million
100,000 to 500,000
50,000 to 100,000
10,000 to 50,000
below 10,000
Elevation
500m / 1640ft
250m / 820ft
100m / 328ft
sea level

◄ Rocher Percé, is 290 ft (88 m) high. Lying off the southeastern coast of Québec, it is a sanctuary for sea birds.

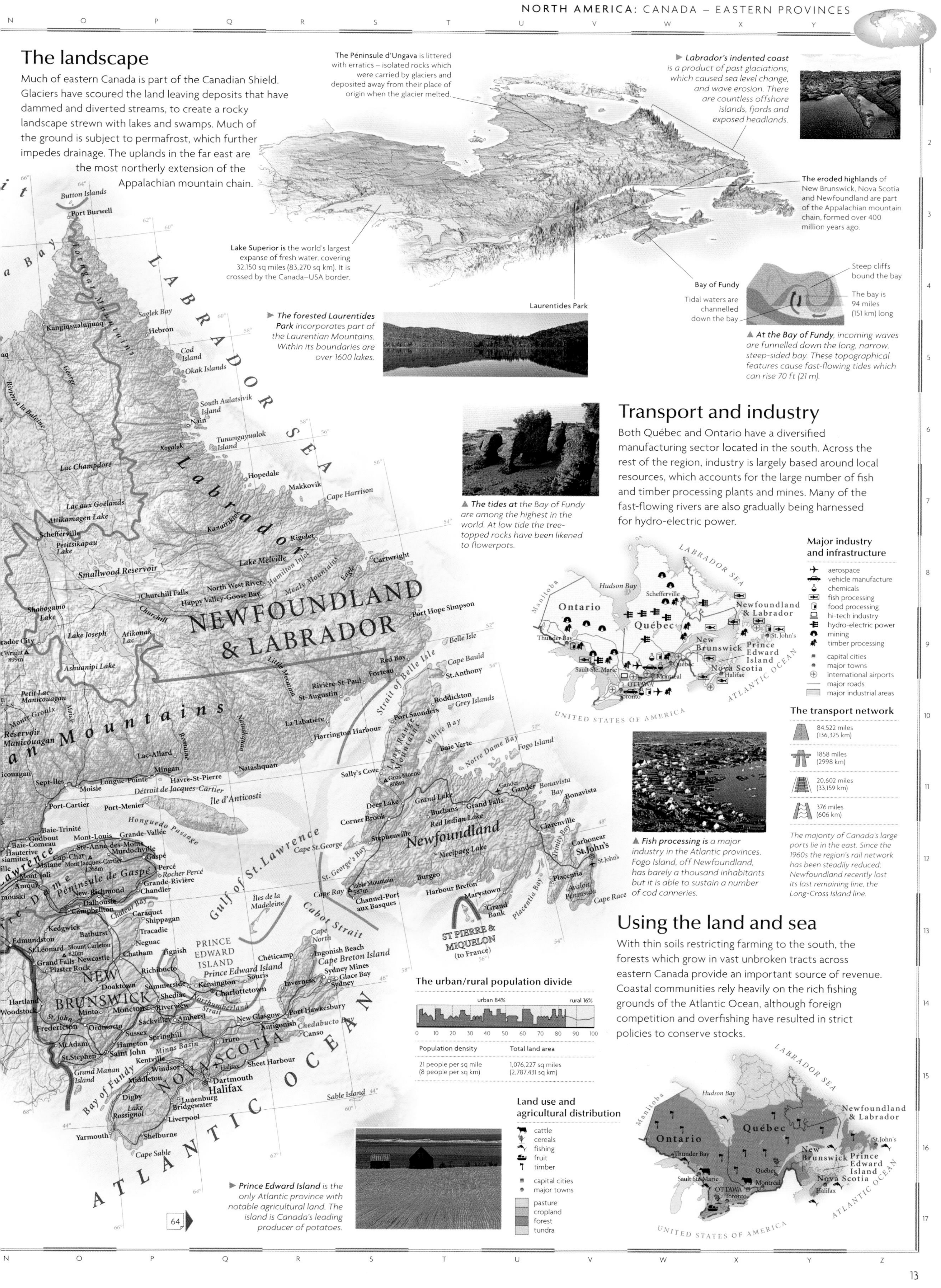

LABRADOR SEA
Labrador
NEWFOUNDLAND & LABRADOR
Newfoundland
ATLANTIC OCEAN
Gulf of St. Lawrence
Cabot Strait
Strait of Belle Isle
Torngat Mountains
Button Islands
Port Burwell
Saglek Bay
Hebron
Kangiqsualujjuaq
Cod Island
Okak Islands
South Aulatsivik Island
Nain
Tunungayualok Island
Kogaluk
Lac Champdoré
Hopedale
Makkovik
Cape Harrison
Lac aux Goélands
Attikamagen Lake
Schefferville
Petitsikapau Lake
Kanairiktok
Rigolet
Lake Melville
Hamilton Inlet
Mealy Mountains
Eagle
Cartwright
Smallwood Reservoir
Churchill Falls
North West River
Happy Valley-Goose Bay
Churchill
Port Hope Simpson
Shabogamo Lake
Lake Joseph
Atikonak Lac
Ashuanipi Lake
Belle Isle
Red Bay
Cape Bauld
St.Anthony
Forteau
Little Mecatina
Rivière-St-Paul
St-Augustin
Roddickton
Grey Islands
Petit Lac Manicouagan
Monts Groulx
Réservoir Manicouagan
Moisie
Natashquan
Romaine
La Tabatière
Harrington Harbour
Port Saunders
Long Range Mountains
White Bay
Baie Verte
Notre Dame Bay
Fogo Island
Lac-Allard
Mingan
Havre-St-Pierre
Sept-Iles
Longue-Pointe
Détroit de Jacques-Cartier
Île d'Anticosti
Port-Cartier
Port-Menier
Honguedo Passage
Baie-Trinité
Godbout
Baie-Comeau
Mont-Louis
Grande-Vallée
Ste-Anne-des-Monts
Murdochville
Cap-Chat
Matane
Mont Jacques-Cartier 1268m
Gaspé
Percé
Rocher Percé
Péninsule de Gaspé
Grande-Rivière
Chandler
Mont-Joli
Amqui
New-Richmond
Dalhousie
Campbellton
Chaleur Bay
Caraquet
Shippagan
Tracadie
Kedgwick
Bathurst
Edmundston
St.Léonard
Mount Carleton 820m
Grand Falls
Newcastle
Plaster Rock
Neguac
Chatham
Tignish
PRINCE EDWARD ISLAND
Prince Edward Island
Richibucto
NEW BRUNSWICK
Doaktown
Summerside
Kensington
Souris
Charlottetown
Shediac
Northumberland Strait
Hartland
Woodstock
Minto
Moncton
Riverview
Fredericton
Oromocto
Sackville
Amherst
Sussex
Springhill
McAdam
Hampton
Saint John
St.Stephen
Minas Basin
Truro
Kentville
Windsor
Grand Manan Island
Bay of Fundy
Middleton
NOVA SCOTIA
Halifax
Dartmouth
Sheet Harbour
Digby
Lunenburg
Bridgewater
Lake Rossignol
Liverpool
Yarmouth
Shelburne
Cape Sable
Sable Island
Iles de la Madeleine
Chéticamp
Cape North
Ingonish Beach
Cape Breton Island
Sydney Mines
Glace Bay
Sydney
Inverness
New Glasgow
Port Hawkesbury
Antigonish
Chedabucto Bay
Canso
Sally's Cove
Gros Morne 808m
Deer Lake
Grand Lake
Corner Brook
Buchans
Grand Falls
Red Indian Lake
Gander
Bonavista Bay
Bonavista
Clarenville
Trinity Bay
Carbonear
St.John's
Cape St.George
St. George's Bay
Stephenville
Meelpaeg Lake
Burgeo
Table Mountain 587m
Cape Ray
Channel-Port aux Basques
Harbour Breton
Marystown
Placentia Bay
Placentia
Avalon Peninsula
Cape Race
Grand Bank
ST PIERRE & MIQUELON (to France)
64
Major industry and infrastructure
aerospace
vehicle manufacture
chemicals
fish processing
food processing
hi-tech industry
hydro-electric power
mining
timber processing
capital cities
major towns
international airports
major roads
major industrial areas
Hudson Bay
Manitoba
Ontario
Québec
Newfoundland & Labrador
New Brunswick
Prince Edward Island
Nova Scotia
Thunder Bay
Sault Ste. Marie
OTTAWA
Toronto
Montreal
Québec
Halifax
St.John's
UNITED STATES OF AMERICA
The transport network
84,522 miles (136,325 km)
1858 miles (2998 km)
20,602 miles (33,159 km)
376 miles (606 km)
The urban/rural population divide
urban 84%
rural 16%
0 10 20 30 40 50 60 70 80 90 100
Population density
21 people per sq mile (8 people per sq km)
Total land area
1,076,227 sq miles (2,787,431 sq km)
Land use and agricultural distribution
cattle
cereals
fishing
fruit
timber
capital cities
major towns
pasture
cropland
forest
tundra
Steep cliffs bound the bay
The bay is 94 miles (151 km) long
Tidal waters are channelled down the bay
Bay of Fundy
Laurentides Park

The landscape

Much of eastern Canada is part of the Canadian Shield. Glaciers have scoured the land leaving deposits that have dammed and diverted streams, to create a rocky landscape strewn with lakes and swamps. Much of the ground is subject to permafrost, which further impedes drainage. The uplands in the far east are the most northerly extension of the Appalachian mountain chain.

The Péninsule d'Ungava is littered with erratics – isolated rocks which were carried by glaciers and deposited away from their place of origin when the glacier melted.

Lake Superior is the world's largest expanse of fresh water, covering 32,150 sq miles (83,270 sq km). It is crossed by the Canada–USA border.

► ***Labrador's indented coast*** *is a product of past glaciations, which caused sea level change, and wave erosion. There are countless offshore islands, fjords and exposed headlands.*

The eroded highlands of New Brunswick, Nova Scotia and Newfoundland are part of the Appalachian mountain chain, formed over 400 million years ago.

► ***The forested Laurentides Park*** *incorporates part of the Laurentian Mountains. Within its boundaries are over 1600 lakes.*

▲ ***At the Bay of Fundy****, incoming waves are funnelled down the long, narrow, steep-sided bay. These topographical features cause fast-flowing tides which can rise 70 ft (21 m).*

▲ ***The tides at*** *the Bay of Fundy are among the highest in the world. At low tide the tree-topped rocks have been likened to flowerpots.*

Transport and industry

Both Québec and Ontario have a diversified manufacturing sector located in the south. Across the rest of the region, industry is largely based around local resources, which accounts for the large number of fish and timber processing plants and mines. Many of the fast-flowing rivers are also gradually being harnessed for hydro-electric power.

The majority of Canada's large ports lie in the east. Since the 1960s the region's rail network has been steadily reduced; Newfoundland recently lost its last remaining line, the Long-Cross Island line.

▲ ***Fish processing*** *is a major industry in the Atlantic provinces. Fogo Island, off Newfoundland, has barely a thousand inhabitants but it is able to sustain a number of cod canneries.*

Using the land and sea

With thin soils restricting farming to the south, the forests which grow in vast unbroken tracts across eastern Canada provide an important source of revenue. Coastal communities rely heavily on the rich fishing grounds of the Atlantic Ocean, although foreign competition and overfishing have resulted in strict policies to conserve stocks.

► ***Prince Edward Island*** *is the only Atlantic province with notable agricultural land. The island is Canada's leading producer of potatoes.*

Southeastern Canada

Southern Ontario, Southern Québec

The southern parts of Québec and Ontario form the economic heart of Canada. The two provinces are divided by their language and culture; in Québec, French is the main language, whereas English is spoken in Ontario. Separatist sentiment in Québec has led to a provincial referendum on the question of a sovereignty association with Canada. The region contains Canada's capital, Ottawa, and its two largest cities: Toronto, the centre of commerce, and Montréal, the cultural and administrative heart of French Canada.

▲ *The port at Montréal is situated on the St. Lawrence Seaway. A network of 16 locks allows sea-going vessels access to routes once plied by fur-trappers and early settlers.*

Transport and industry

The cities of southern Québec and Ontario, and their hinterlands, form the heart of Canadian manufacturing industry. Toronto is Canada's leading financial centre, and Ontario's motor and aerospace industries have developed around the city. A major centre for nickel mining lies to the north of Toronto. Most of Québec's industry is located in Montréal, the oldest port in North America. Chemicals, paper manufacture and the construction of transport equipment are leading industrial activities.

▶ *Niagara Falls lies on the border between Canada and the USA. It comprises a system of two falls: American Falls, in New York, is separated from Horseshoe Falls, in Ontario, by Goat Island. Horseshoe Falls, seen here, plunges 184 ft (56 m) and is 2500 ft (762 m) wide.*

Major industry and infrastructure

- car manufacture
- chemicals
- engineering
- finance
- food processing
- hi-tech industry
- mining
- iron & steel
- textiles
- paper industry
- timber processing
- capital cities
- major towns
- international airports
- major roads
- major industrial areas

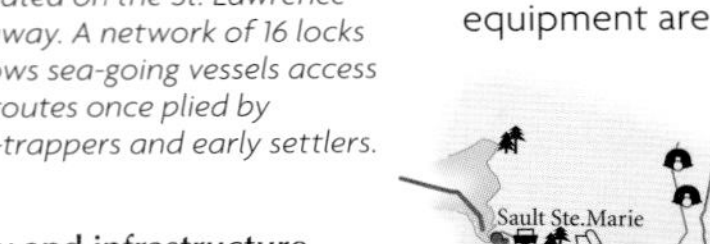

Sault Ste.Marie
North Bay
Québec
Ontario
Montreal
OTTAWA
Toronto
Lake Huron
Lake Ontario
Lake Erie
New Brunswick
UNITED STATES OF AMERICA

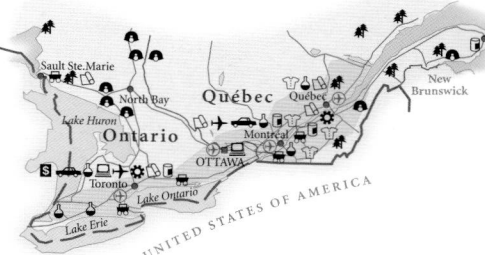

The transport network

The opening of the St. Lawrence Seaway in 1959 finally allowed ocean-going ships (up to 24,000 tons (tonnes)) access to the interior of Canada, creating a vital trading route.

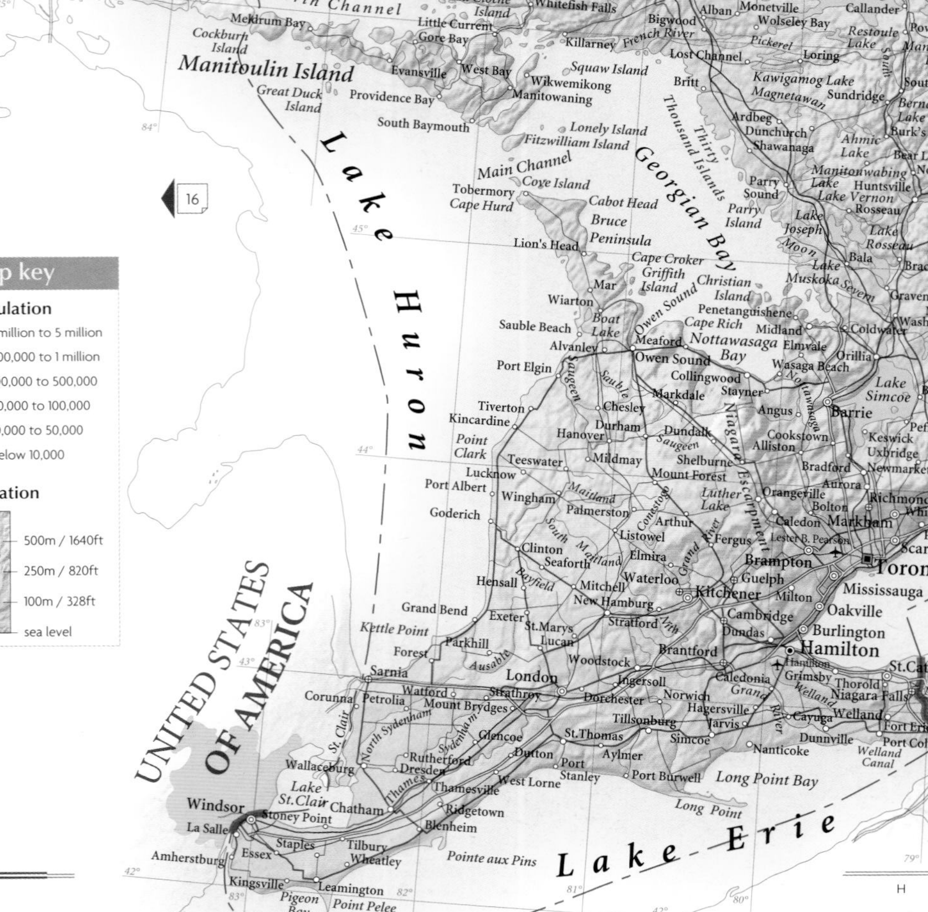

ONTARIO
QUÉBEC
Lake Superior
Lake Huron
Lake Ontario
Lake Erie
Georgian Bay
Manitoulin Island
North Channel
Haliburton Highlands
UNITED STATES OF AMERICA
Sault Ste.Marie
Sudbury
North Bay
Timmins
Toronto
Hamilton
Kitchener
London
Windsor
Mississauga
Brampton
Oshawa
Barrie
Kingston
St.Catharines
Niagara Falls
OTTAWA

Map key

Population

- 1 million to 5 million
- 500,000 to 1 million
- 100,000 to 500,000
- 50,000 to 100,000
- 10,000 to 50,000
- below 10,000

Elevation

- 500m / 1640ft
- 250m / 820ft
- 100m / 328ft
- sea level

16

16

▶ *Montréal, on the banks of the St. Lawrence River, is Québec's leading metropolitan centre and one of Canada's two largest cities – Toronto is the other. Montréal clearly reflects French culture and traditions.*

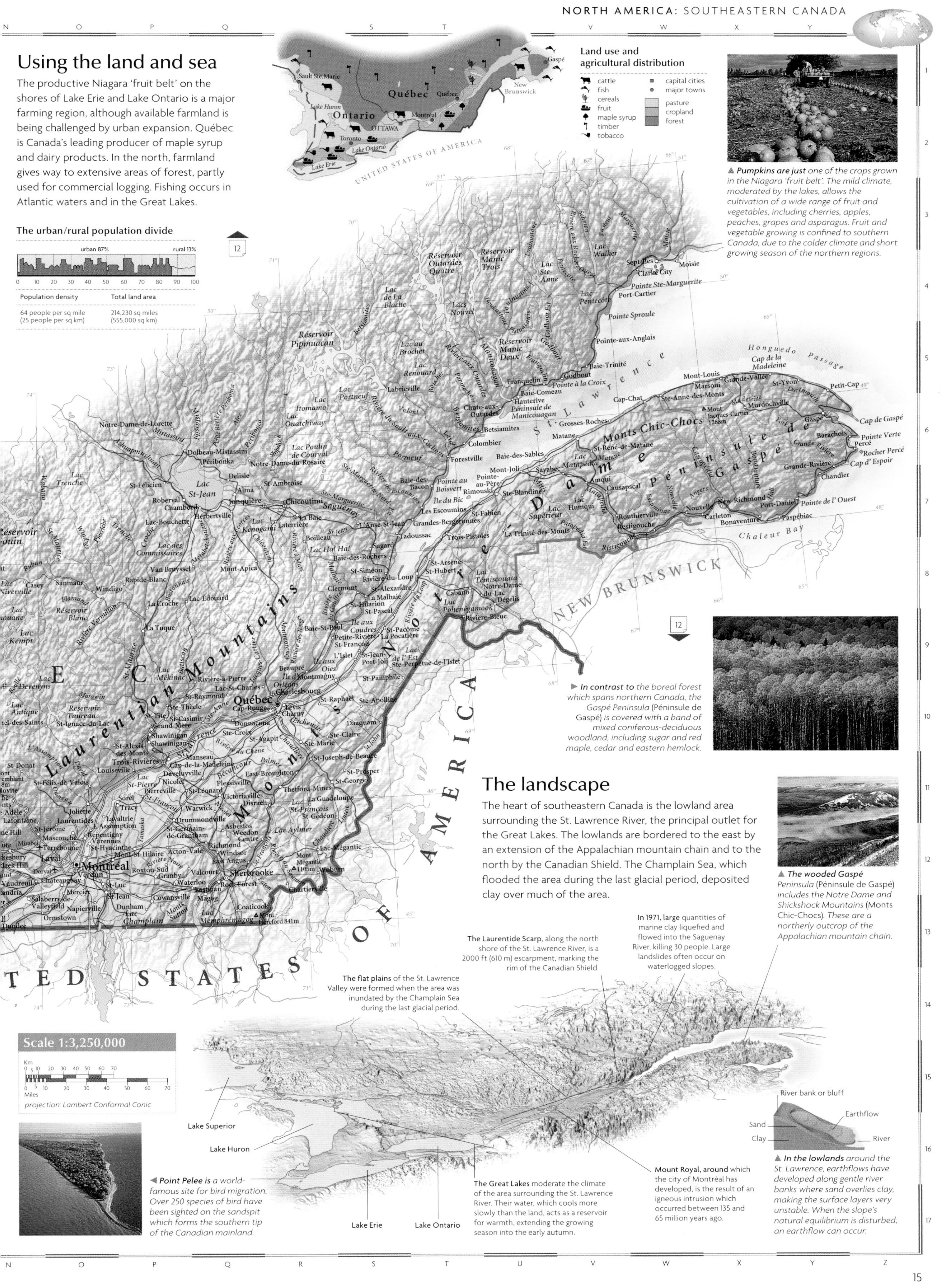
Land use and agricultural distribution
cattle
fish
cereals
fruit
maple syrup
timber
tobacco
capital cities
major towns
pasture
cropland
forest
Québec
Ontario
OTTAWA
Montréal
Toronto
Sault Ste.Marie
Lake Huron
Lake Ontario
Lake Erie
Gaspé
New Brunswick
UNITED STATES OF AMERICA
The urban/rural population divide
urban 87%
rural 13%
0 10 20 30 40 50 60 70 80 90 100
Population density
64 people per sq mile (25 people per sq km)
Total land area
214,230 sq miles (555,000 sq km)
Scale 1:3,250,000
Km
Miles
projection: Lambert Conformal Conic
Laurentian Mountains
Monts Notre-Dame
Péninsule de Gaspé
Monts Chic-Chocs
St Lawrence
Honguedo Passage
Chaleur Bay
NEW BRUNSWICK
UNITED STATES OF AMERICA
Québec
Montréal
Sherbrooke
Trois-Rivières
Chicoutimi
Lac St-Jean
Réservoir Manicouagan
Sept-Îles
Rimouski
Gaspé
Mont Jacques-Cartier 1268m
Mont Mégantic 1105m
Mont Hereford 841m
Lake Superior
Lake Huron
Lake Erie
Lake Ontario
River bank or bluff
Earthflow
Sand
Clay
River

Using the land and sea

The productive Niagara 'fruit belt' on the shores of Lake Erie and Lake Ontario is a major farming region, although available farmland is being challenged by urban expansion. Québec is Canada's leading producer of maple syrup and dairy products. In the north, farmland gives way to extensive areas of forest, partly used for commercial logging. Fishing occurs in Atlantic waters and in the Great Lakes.

▲ *Pumpkins are just one of the crops grown in the Niagara 'fruit belt'. The mild climate, moderated by the lakes, allows the cultivation of a wide range of fruit and vegetables, including cherries, apples, peaches, grapes and asparagus. Fruit and vegetable growing is confined to southern Canada, due to the colder climate and short growing season of the northern regions.*

► *In contrast to the boreal forest which spans northern Canada, the Gaspé Peninsula (Péninsule de Gaspé) is covered with a band of mixed coniferous-deciduous woodland, including sugar and red maple, cedar and eastern hemlock.*

The landscape

The heart of southeastern Canada is the lowland area surrounding the St. Lawrence River, the principal outlet for the Great Lakes. The lowlands are bordered to the east by an extension of the Appalachian mountain chain and to the north by the Canadian Shield. The Champlain Sea, which flooded the area during the last glacial period, deposited clay over much of the area.

▲ *The wooded Gaspé Peninsula (Péninsule de Gaspé) includes the Notre Dame and Shickshock Mountains (Monts Chic-Chocs). These are a northerly outcrop of the Appalachian mountain chain.*

In 1971, large quantities of marine clay liquefied and flowed into the Saguenay River, killing 30 people. Large landslides often occur on waterlogged slopes.

The Laurentide Scarp, along the north shore of the St. Lawrence River, is a 2000 ft (610 m) escarpment, marking the rim of the Canadian Shield.

The flat plains of the St. Lawrence Valley were formed when the area was inundated by the Champlain Sea during the last glacial period.

◄ *Point Pelee is a world-famous site for bird migration. Over 250 species of bird have been sighted on the sandspit which forms the southern tip of the Canadian mainland.*

The Great Lakes moderate the climate of the area surrounding the St. Lawrence River. Their water, which cools more slowly than the land, acts as a reservoir for warmth, extending the growing season into the early autumn.

Mount Royal, around which the city of Montréal has developed, is the result of an igneous intrusion which occurred between 135 and 65 million years ago.

▲ *In the lowlands around the St. Lawrence, earthflows have developed along gentle river banks where sand overlies clay, making the surface layers very unstable. When the slope's natural equilibrium is disturbed, an earthflow can occur.*

The United States of America

COTERMINOUS USA (FOR ALASKA AND HAWAII SEE PAGES 38-39)

The USA's progression from frontier territory to economic and political superpower has taken less than 200 years. The 48 coterminous states, along with the outlying states of Alaska and Hawaii, are part of a federal union, held together by the guiding principles of the US Constitution, which enshrines the ideals of democracy and liberty for all. Abundant fertile land and a rich resource-base fuelled and sustained the USA's economic development. With the spread of agriculture and the growth of trade and industry came the need for a larger workforce, which was supplied by millions of immigrants, many seeking an escape from poverty and political or religious persecution. Immigration continues today, particularly from Central America and Asia.

▲ ***Washington DC** was established as the site for the nation's capital in 1790. It is home to the seat of national government, on Capitol Hill, as well as the President's official residence, the White House.*

► ***The clear waters** of Niagara Falls cascade 190 ft (58 m) into the gorge below. It is one of America's most famous spectacles and a leading tourist attraction. The falls are slowly receding and the gorge may one day stretch from Lake Ontario to Lake Erie.*

▲ ***Mount Rainier** is a dormant volcano in the Cascade Range, Washington. This 14,090 ft (4392 m) peak is flanked by the most extensive glacier outside Alaska.*

Scale 1:12,700,000

Km 0 25 50 100 150 200 250 300 350 400

Miles 0 25 50 100 150 200 250 300 350 400

projection: Lambert Azimuthal Equal Area

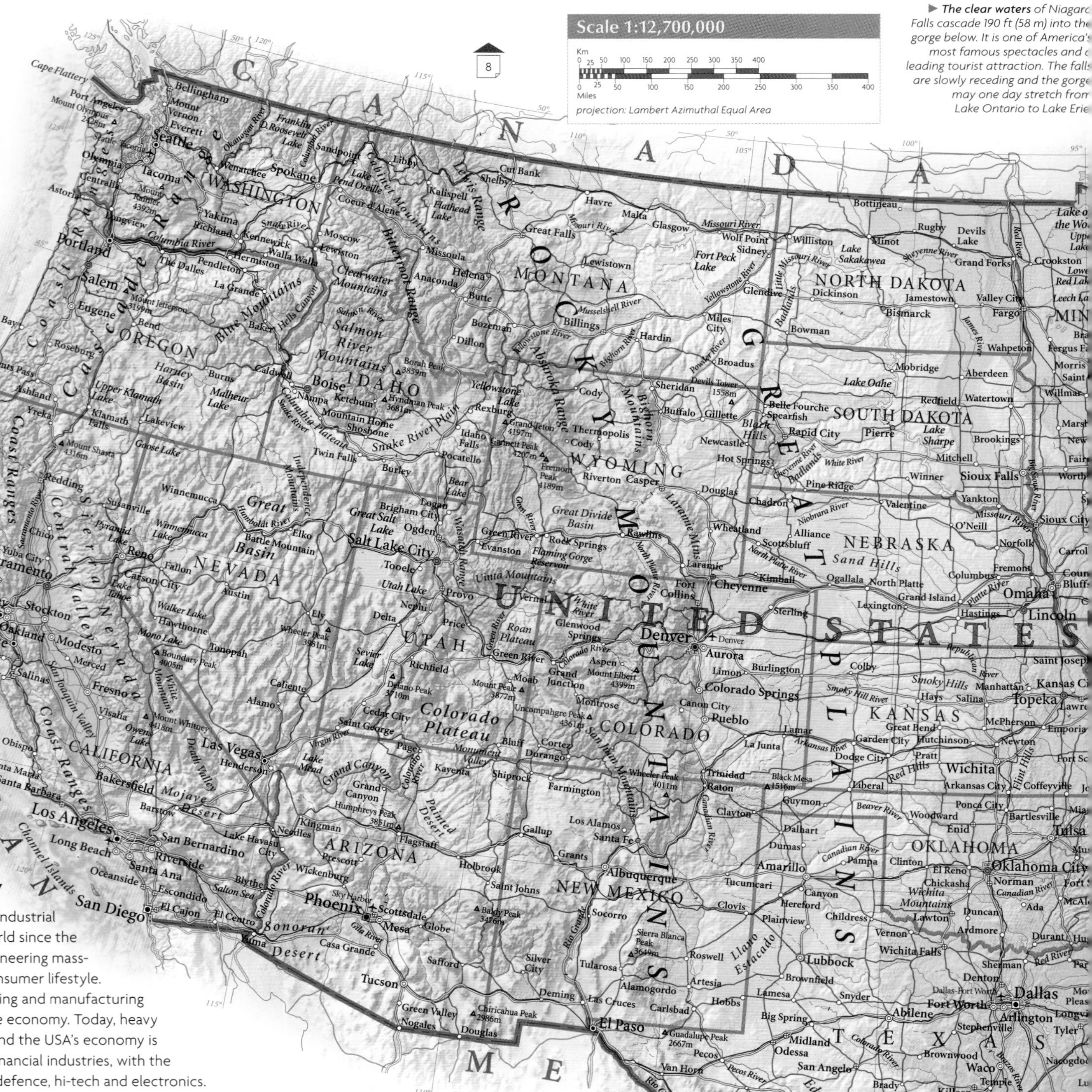

8

192

40

Transport and industry

The USA has been the industrial powerhouse of the world since the Second World War, pioneering mass-production and the consumer lifestyle. Initially, heavy engineering and manufacturing in the northeast led the economy. Today, heavy industry has declined and the USA's economy is driven by service and financial industries, with the most important being defence, hi-tech and electronics.

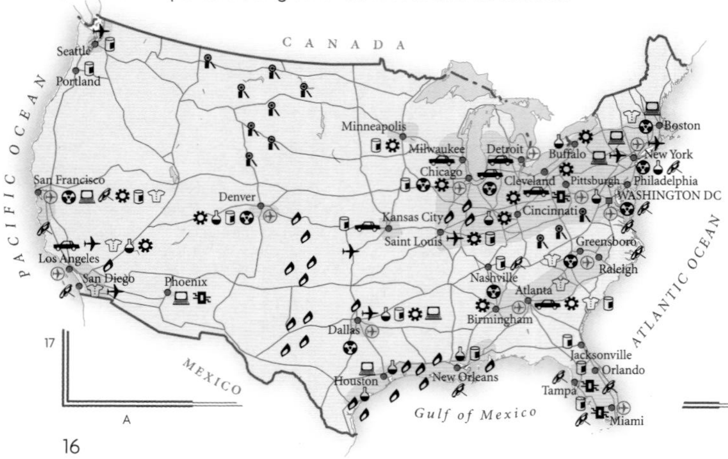

The transport network

3,875,040 miles (6,240,000 km)		52,388 miles (84,361 km)	
148,308 miles (235,238 km)		25,467 miles (41,009 km)	

Transport in the USA is dominated by the car which, with the extensive Interstate Highway system, allows great personal mobility. Today, internal air flights between major cities provide the most rapid cross-country travel.

Major industry and infrastructure

- aerospace
- car manufacture
- chemicals
- coal
- electronics
- engineering
- food processing
- hi-tech industry
- oil & gas
- research & development
- textiles
- tourism
- capital cities
- major towns
- international airports
- major roads
- major industrial areas

The landscape

The high, rugged mountain ranges of the west are about 80 million years old, geologically young compared to the old, eroded, Appalachian mountain chain, which dates from when North America and Europe were joined together as part of the supercontinent Pangaea, 400 million years ago. In contrast, the Great Plains and Mississippi Basin have a low relief and fertile soils.

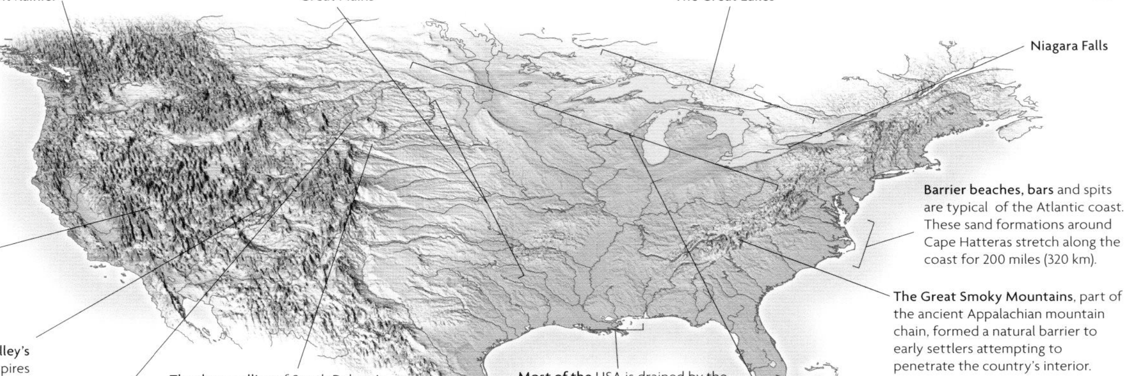

Mount Rainier

Great Plains

The Great Lakes

Niagara Falls

Barrier beaches, bars and spits are typical of the Atlantic coast. These sand formations around Cape Hatteras stretch along the coast for 200 miles (320 km).

The Great Smoky Mountains, part of the ancient Appalachian mountain chain, formed a natural barrier to early settlers attempting to penetrate the country's interior.

The Everglades are a vast area of saw-grass swamp covering 4000 sq miles (10,300 sq km) of southern Florida.

Death Valley, California, 282 ft (86 m) below sea level, is the lowest point in the western hemisphere, and one of the hottest places on Earth. Temperatures of 135° F (57° C) have been recorded here.

Monument Valley's striking sandstone spires and pillars *(buttes)* have been formed by the action of wind, water, heat and cold.

The deep gullies of South Dakota's badlands are created by periodic, torrential rainfall, which erodes the soft soils and rocks. Their form has been greatly affected by changes in land use.

Most of the USA is drained by the great Mississippi River system. At its mouth, where levées are breached, floodwaters are carried to the swamps through a series of channels. This region is known as the bayou.

◀ ***Devils Tower**, in Wyoming is a 1280 ft (390 m) intrusion of basalt rock, which cooled to form octagonal pillars.In 1906 it became the first US National Monument.*

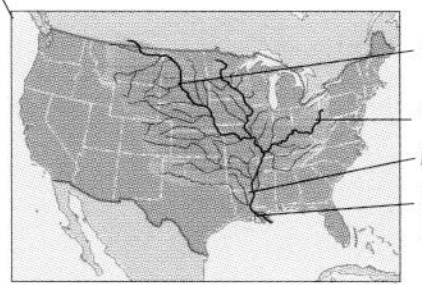

Missouri River

Ohio River

Mississippi River

Mississippi Delta

▲ ***The massive drainage** basin of the Mississippi covers 1,250,000 sq miles (3,200,000 sq km). It includes all areas drained by the Mississippi and its chief tributaries, the Missouri and Ohio rivers, and drains the entire region from the Appalachians to the Rockies.*

Map key

Population

- above 5 million
- 1 million to 5 million
- 500,000 to 1 million
- 100,000 to 500,000
- 50,000 to 100,000
- 10,000 to 50,000
- below 10,000

Elevation

- 4000m / 13,124ft
- 3000m / 9843ft
- 2000m / 6562ft
- 1000m / 3281ft
- 500m / 1640ft
- 250m / 820ft
- 100m / 328ft
- sea level

8

64

64

Using the land and sea

Over half of the USA's land area is utilized for agriculture, typified by the large cereal farms and cattle ranches of the Great Plains and Midwest prairie regions. Although wheat and corn are still primary crops, a diverse range of fruits and vegetables are grown in the fertile areas, particularly near the east and west coasts. Despite the abundance of cultivable land, inadequate soil management has resulted in a third of the topsoil being lost through wind and water erosion.

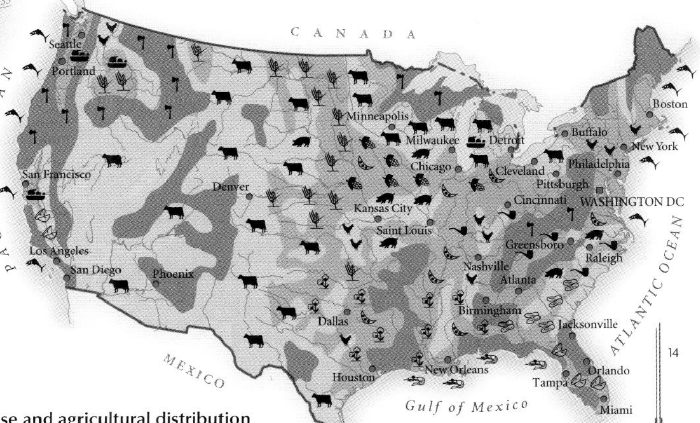

Land use and agricultural distribution

- cattle
- pigs
- poultry
- citrus fruits
- cotton
- fishing
- fruit
- corn (maize)
- peanuts
- shellfish
- soya beans
- timber
- tobacco
- wheat
- capital cities
- major towns
- pasture
- cropland
- forest
- wetland
- desert
- mountain region

The urban/rural population divide

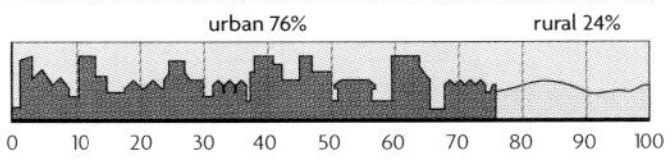

urban 76% | rural 24%

0 10 20 30 40 50 60 70 80 90 100

Population density	Total land area
98 people per sq mile (38 people per sq km)	2,959,045 sq miles (7,663,631 sq km)

▶ ***Fakahatchee Strand** is part of the extensive sub-tropical swamps in the Florida Everglades. The swamps support a wide variety of animal life, including many rare birds, fish, alligators and crocodiles.*

◀ ***Farming on the** Great Plains and in the Midwest is characterized by large-scale, mechanized wheat farms.*

USA: NORTHEASTERN STATES

Connecticut, Maine, Massachusetts, New Hampshire, New Jersey, New York, Pennsylvania, Rhode Island, Vermont

The indented coast and vast woodlands of the northeastern states were the original core area for European expansion. The rustic character of New England prevails after 400 years, while the great cities of the Atlantic seaboard have formed an almost continuous urban region. Over 20 million immigrants entered New York from 1855 to 1924 and the northeast became the industrial centre of the USA. After the decline of mining and heavy manufacturing, economic dynamism has been restored with the growth of hi-tech and service industries.

▲ ***Chelsea in Vermont,*** *surrounded by trees in their fall foliage. Tourism and agriculture dominate the economy of this self-consciously rural state, where no town exceeds 40,000 people.*

The transport network

340,090 miles (544,144 km)

4813 miles (7700 km)

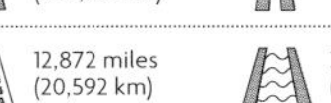

12,872 miles (20,592 km)

2108 miles (3389 km)

New York's commercial success is tied historically to its transport connections. The Erie Canal, completed in 1825, opened up the Great Lakes and the interior to New York's markets and carried a stream of immigrants into the Midwest.

Map key

Population

- above 5 million
- 1 million to 5 million
- 500,000 to 1 million
- 100,000 to 500,000
- 50,000 to 100,000
- 10,000 to 50,000
- below 10,000

Elevation

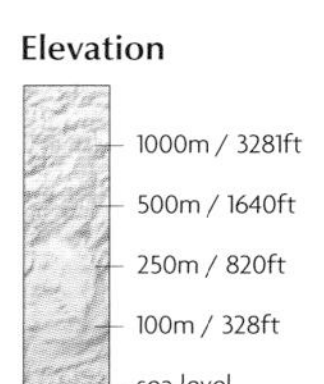

1000m / 3281ft
500m / 1640ft
250m / 820ft
100m / 328ft
sea level

Transport and industry

The principal seaboard cities grew up on trade and manufacturing. They are now global centres of commerce and corporate administration, dominating the regional economy. Research and development facilities support an expanding electronics and communications sector throughout the region. Pharmaceutical and chemical industries are important in New Jersey and Pennsylvania.

CANADA
Maine
Vermont
New Hampshire
Portland
Syracuse
Albany
Rochester
Buffalo
New York
Massachusetts
Boston
Connecticut
Hartford
Providence
Rhode Island
Pennsylvania
New York
Pittsburgh
Harrisburg
New Jersey
Philadelphia
Ohio
West Virginia
Maryland
Delaware
ATLANTIC OCEAN

Major industry and infrastructure

- chemicals
- coal
- defence
- electronics
- engineering
- finance
- hi-tech industry
- iron & steel
- pharmaceuticals
- printing & publishing
- research & development
- textiles
- timber processing
- major towns
- international airports
- major roads
- major industrial area

14 32 20 22 64

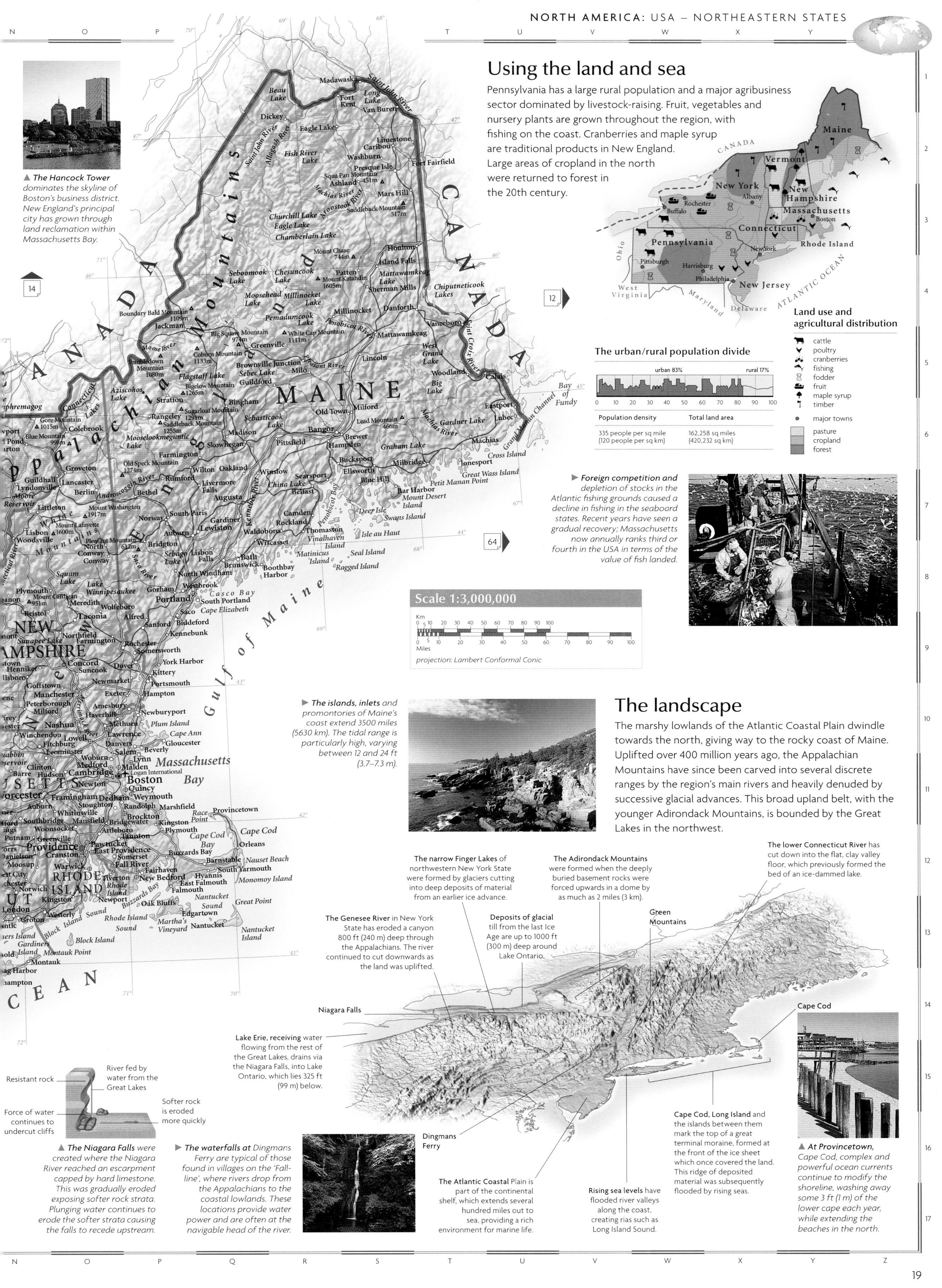
N O P T U V W X Y
1 2 3 4 5 6 7 8 9 10 11 12 13 14 15 16 17
14
12
64
MAINE
CANADA
Appalachian Mountains
Gulf of Maine
Massachusetts Bay
NEW HAMPSHIRE
RHODE ISLAND
Cape Cod
Bay of Fundy
Boston
Portland
Bangor
Augusta
Providence
Concord
Mount Katahdin 1605m
Mount Washington 1917m
Moosehead Lake
Canada
Maine
Vermont
New York
New Hampshire
Massachusetts
Connecticut
Rhode Island
Pennsylvania
New Jersey
Ohio
West Virginia
Maryland
Delaware
Atlantic Ocean
Buffalo
Rochester
Albany
Pittsburgh
Harrisburg
Philadelphia
New York
Land use and agricultural distribution
cattle
poultry
cranberries
fishing
fodder
fruit
maple syrup
timber
major towns
pasture
cropland
forest
The urban/rural population divide
urban 83%
rural 17%
0 10 20 30 40 50 60 70 80 90 100
Population density
335 people per sq mile (120 people per sq km)
Total land area
162,258 sq miles (420,232 sq km)
Scale 1:3,000,000
Km
Miles
projection: Lambert Conformal Conic
The narrow Finger Lakes of northwestern New York State were formed by glaciers cutting into deep deposits of material from an earlier ice advance.
The Adirondack Mountains were formed when the deeply buried basement rocks were forced upwards in a dome by as much as 2 miles (3 km).
The lower Connecticut River has cut down into the flat, clay valley floor, which previously formed the bed of an ice-dammed lake.
The Genesee River in New York State has eroded a canyon 800 ft (240 m) deep through the Appalachians. The river continued to cut downwards as the land was uplifted.
Deposits of glacial till from the last Ice Age are up to 1000 ft (300 m) deep around Lake Ontario.
Green Mountains
Niagara Falls
Cape Cod
Lake Erie, receiving water flowing from the rest of the Great Lakes, drains via the Niagara Falls, into Lake Ontario, which lies 325 ft (99 m) below.
Dingmans Ferry
The Atlantic Coastal Plain is part of the continental shelf, which extends several hundred miles out to sea, providing a rich environment for marine life.
Rising sea levels have flooded river valleys along the coast, creating rias such as Long Island Sound.
Cape Cod, Long Island and the islands between them mark the top of a great terminal moraine, formed at the front of the ice sheet which once covered the land. This ridge of deposited material was subsequently flooded by rising seas.
Resistant rock
River fed by water from the Great Lakes
Softer rock is eroded more quickly
Force of water continues to undercut cliffs

▲ *The Hancock Tower dominates the skyline of Boston's business district. New England's principal city has grown through land reclamation within Massachusetts Bay.*

Using the land and sea

Pennsylvania has a large rural population and a major agribusiness sector dominated by livestock-raising. Fruit, vegetables and nursery plants are grown throughout the region, with fishing on the coast. Cranberries and maple syrup are traditional products in New England. Large areas of cropland in the north were returned to forest in the 20th century.

▶ *Foreign competition and depletion of stocks in the Atlantic fishing grounds caused a decline in fishing in the seaboard states. Recent years have seen a gradual recovery; Massachusetts now annually ranks third or fourth in the USA in terms of the value of fish landed.*

▶ *The islands, inlets and promontories of Maine's coast extend 3500 miles (5630 km). The tidal range is particularly high, varying between 12 and 24 ft (3.7–7.3 m).*

The landscape

The marshy lowlands of the Atlantic Coastal Plain dwindle towards the north, giving way to the rocky coast of Maine. Uplifted over 400 million years ago, the Appalachian Mountains have since been carved into several discrete ranges by the region's main rivers and heavily denuded by successive glacial advances. This broad upland belt, with the younger Adirondack Mountains, is bounded by the Great Lakes in the northwest.

▲ *The Niagara Falls were created where the Niagara River reached an escarpment capped by hard limestone. This was gradually eroded exposing softer rock strata. Plunging water continues to erode the softer strata causing the falls to recede upstream.*

▶ *The waterfalls at Dingmans Ferry are typical of those found in villages on the 'Fall-line', where rivers drop from the Appalachians to the coastal lowlands. These locations provide water power and are often at the navigable head of the river.*

▲ *At Provincetown, Cape Cod, complex and powerful ocean currents continue to modify the shoreline, washing away some 3 ft (1 m) of the lower cape each year, while extending the beaches in the north.*

USA: MID-EASTERN STATES

Delaware, District of Columbia, Kentucky, Maryland, North Carolina, South Carolina, Tennessee, Virginia, West Virginia

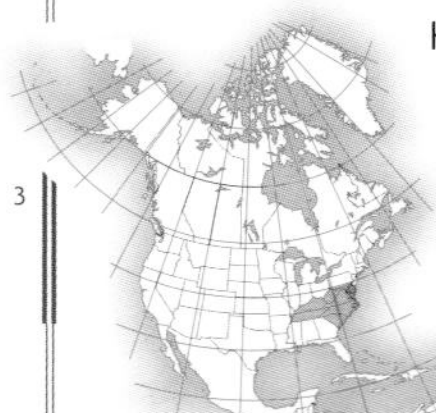

Key events in the history of the USA took place in this diverse region, which became the front line in the Civil War of 1861–65 between North and South. Strong regional contrasts exist between the fertile coastal plains, the isolated upcountry of the Appalachian Mountains and the cotton-growing areas of the Mississippi lowlands to the west. Whilst coal mining, a traditional industry in the Appalachians, has declined in recent years leaving much rural poverty, service industries elsewhere have increased, especially in the US federal capital, Washington DC.

Map key

Population

- 500,000 to 1 million
- 100,000 to 500,000
- 50,000 to 100,000
- 10,000 to 50,000
- below 10,000

Elevation

- 6000m / 19,686ft
- 4000m / 13,124ft
- 3000m / 9843ft
- 2000m / 6562ft
- 1000m / 3281ft
- 500m / 1640ft
- 250m / 820ft
- 100m / 328ft
- sea level

Scale 1:3,250,000

Km 0 5 10 20 30 40 50 60 70 80

Miles 0 5 10 20 30 40 50 60 70 80

projection: Lambert Conformal Conic

▲ *The Bluegrass region of Kentucky centres on the town of Lexington. This exceptionally fertile rolling plain is well known for its thoroughbred horse-breeding ranches.*

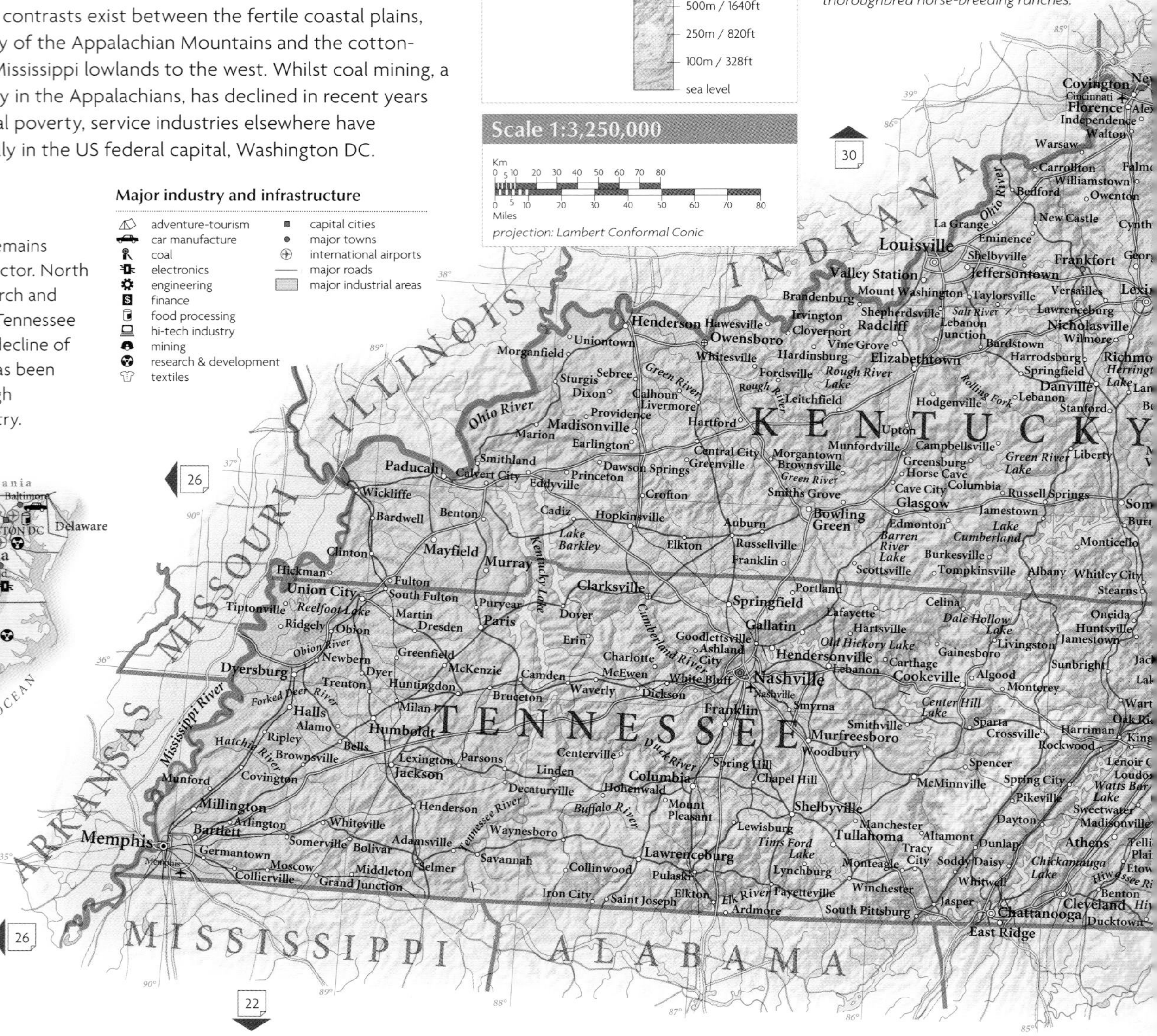

Transport and industry

In the urbanized northeast, manufacturing remains important, alongside a burgeoning service sector. North Carolina is a major centre for industrial research and development. Traditional industries include Tennessee whiskey, and textiles in South Carolina. The decline of open-cast coal mining in the Appalachians has been hastened by environmental controls, although adventure-tourism is a flourishing new industry.

Major industry and infrastructure

- adventure-tourism
- car manufacture
- coal
- electronics
- engineering
- finance
- food processing
- hi-tech industry
- mining
- research & development
- textiles
- capital cities
- major towns
- international airports
- major roads
- major industrial areas

The transport network

452,218 miles (723,548 km)	5737 miles (8267 km)
18,336 miles (29,503 km)	4404 miles (7081 km)

Tennessee's rivers are part of an important inland bulk-transport network. Memphis is connected with New Orleans in the south, and with cities as distant as Minneapolis, Sioux City, Chicago and Pittsburgh, via the Mississippi and its tributaries.

The landscape

The eastern tributaries of the Mississippi drain the interior lowlands. The Cumberland Plateau and the parallel ranges of the Appalachians have been successively uplifted and eroded over time, with the eastern side reduced to a series of foothills known as the Piedmont. The broad coastal plain gradually falls away into salt marshes, lagoons and offshore bars, broken by flooded estuaries along the shores of the Atlantic.

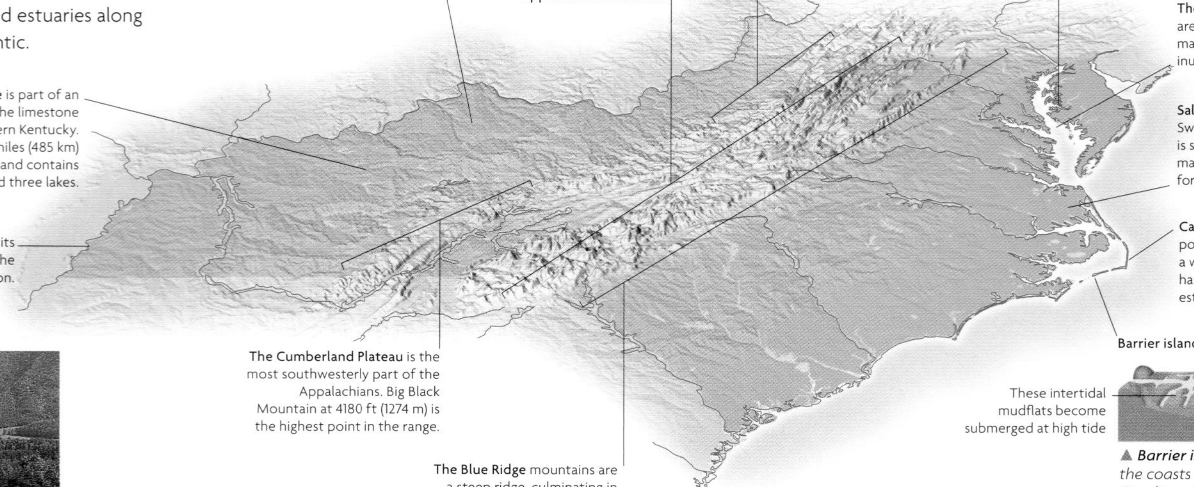

Natural Bridge in eastern Kentucky is an arch 78 ft (26 m) long and 65 ft (20 m) high. It has been shaped from resistant sandstone by gradual weathering processes, which removed the softer rock lying underneath.

The Allegheny Mountains form the northwestern edge of the Appalachian mountain chain. Continuous folding has formed rich seams of bituminous coal.

◄ *Farmland on the eastern shores of Chesapeake Bay is sustained by artificial drainage. The area also provides refuge for a variety of waterfowl.*

Appalachian Mountains

The many inlets of Chesapeake Bay are the flooded tributaries of the main river valley, which have been inundated by rising sea levels.

The Mammoth Cave is part of an extensive cave system in the limestone region of southwestern Kentucky. It stretches for over 300 miles (485 km) on five different levels and contains three rivers and three lakes.

Salt marshes such as Great Dismal Swamp, develop where the coast is sheltered. Vast areas of such marshland have been reclaimed for farmland and settlement.

The Mississippi River and its tributary the Ohio River form the western border of the region.

Cape Hatteras is the easternmost point of an offshore barrier island; a wave-deposited sand-bar which has become permanent, establishing its own vegetation.

Barrier islands

The Cumberland Plateau is the most southwesterly part of the Appalachians. Big Black Mountain at 4180 ft (1274 m) is the highest point in the range.

These intertidal mudflats become submerged at high tide

Tidal inlet

Barrier island

The Blue Ridge mountains are a steep ridge, culminating in Mount Mitchell, the highest point in the Appalachians, at 6684 ft (2037 m).

◄ *The Great Smoky Mountains form the western escarpment of the Appalachians. The region is heavily forested, with over 130 species of tree.*

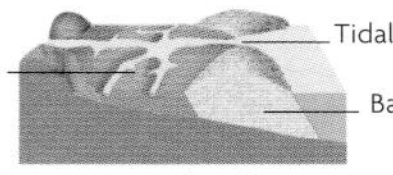

▲ *Barrier islands are common along the coasts of North and South Carolina. As sea levels rise, wave action builds up ridges of sand and pebbles parallel to the coast, separated by lagoons or intertidal mudflats, which are flooded at high tide.*

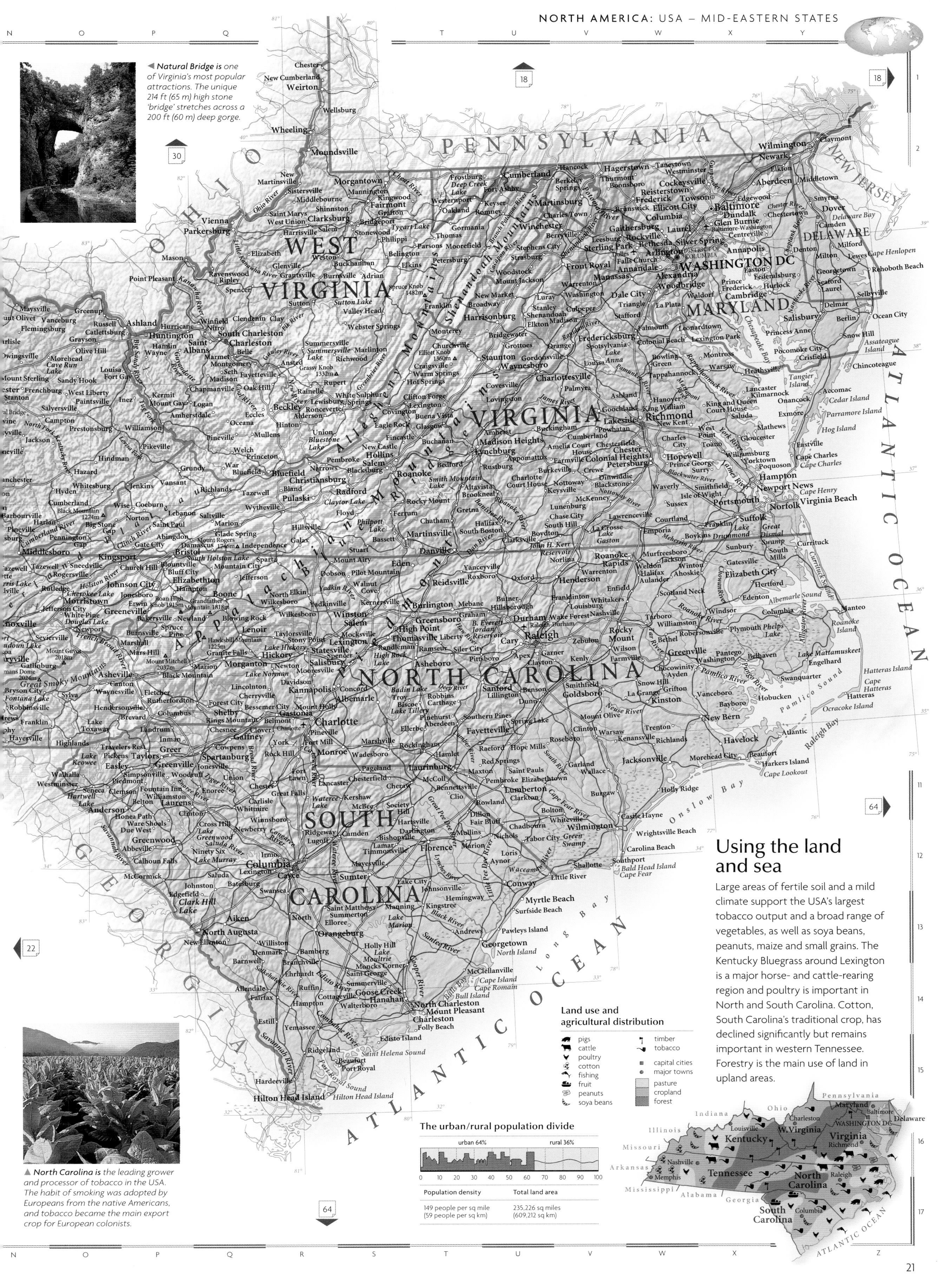

PENNSYLVANIA
OHIO
WEST VIRGINIA
VIRGINIA
MARYLAND
DELAWARE
NEW JERSEY
WASHINGTON DC
NORTH CAROLINA
SOUTH CAROLINA
GEORGIA
ATLANTIC OCEAN
Appalachian Mountains
Allegheny Mountains
Blue Ridge Mountains
Shenandoah Mountains
Great Smoky Mountains
Onslow Bay
Long Bay
Pamlico Sound
Albemarle Sound
Chesapeake Bay
Delaware Bay
Land use and agricultural distribution
pigs
cattle
poultry
cotton
fishing
fruit
peanuts
soya beans
timber
tobacco
capital cities
major towns
pasture
cropland
forest
The urban/rural population divide
urban 64%
rural 36%
0 10 20 30 40 50 60 70 80 90 100
Population density
149 people per sq mile (59 people per sq km)
Total land area
235,226 sq miles (609,212 sq km)

◀ **Natural Bridge** is *one of Virginia's most popular attractions. The unique 214 ft (65 m) high stone 'bridge' stretches across a 200 ft (60 m) deep gorge.*

▲ **North Carolina** is *the leading grower and processor of tobacco in the USA. The habit of smoking was adopted by Europeans from the native Americans, and tobacco became the main export crop for European colonists.*

Using the land and sea

Large areas of fertile soil and a mild climate support the USA's largest tobacco output and a broad range of vegetables, as well as soya beans, peanuts, maize and small grains. The Kentucky Bluegrass around Lexington is a major horse- and cattle-rearing region and poultry is important in North and South Carolina. Cotton, South Carolina's traditional crop, has declined significantly but remains important in western Tennessee. Forestry is the main use of land in upland areas.

USA: SOUTHERN STATES

Alabama, Florida, Georgia, Louisiana, Mississippi

The South has maintained a separate identity and outlook throughout the history of the USA. Defeat in the American Civil War (1861–65) brought chronic poverty to the Confederate states, while the subsequent liberation of four million black slaves began a struggle not resolved until the 1960s, when the Civil Rights movement achieved an end to legal racial segregation. Since then many parts of the region have experienced rapid change: tourism and retirement communities, together with agriculture, have fuelled growth in Florida whilst defence-related industries have boosted the growth of cities such as Miami and Atlanta. Despite these changes, many people retain a strong attachment to their history: in Louisiana, French is still spoken in Cajun communities near the coast.

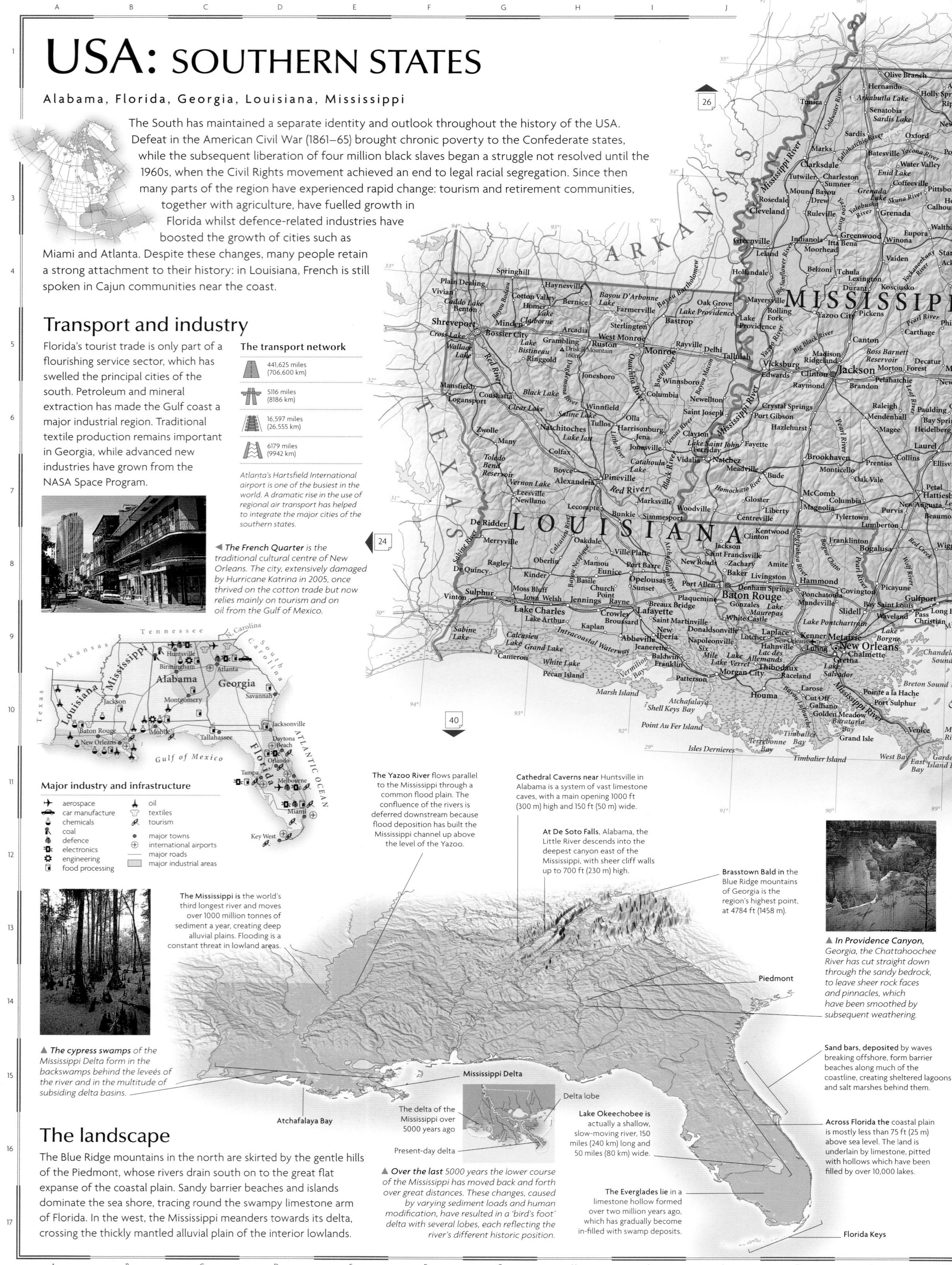

ARKANSAS
MISSISSIPPI
LOUISIANA
TEXAS
26
24
40

Transport and industry

Florida's tourist trade is only part of a flourishing service sector, which has swelled the principal cities of the south. Petroleum and mineral extraction has made the Gulf coast a major industrial region. Traditional textile production remains important in Georgia, while advanced new industries have grown from the NASA Space Program.

The transport network

441,625 miles (706,600 km)

5116 miles (8186 km)

16,597 miles (26,555 km)

6179 miles (9942 km)

Atlanta's Hartsfield International airport is one of the busiest in the world. A dramatic rise in the use of regional air transport has helped to integrate the major cities of the southern states.

◄ ***The French Quarter** is the traditional cultural centre of New Orleans. The city, extensively damaged by Hurricane Katrina in 2005, once thrived on the cotton trade but now relies mainly on tourism and on oil from the Gulf of Mexico.*

Tennessee
N. Carolina
South Carolina
Arkansas
Texas
Mississippi
Alabama
Georgia
Louisiana
Florida
Huntsville
Birmingham
Atlanta
Savannah
Jackson
Montgomery
Baton Rouge
New Orleans
Mobile
Tallahassee
Jacksonville
Daytona Beach
Orlando
Tampa
Melbourne
Miami
Key West
Gulf of Mexico
ATLANTIC OCEAN

Major industry and infrastructure

aerospace · car manufacture · chemicals · coal · defence · electronics · engineering · food processing · oil · textiles · tourism · major towns · international airports · major roads · major industrial areas

▲ ***The cypress swamps** of the Mississippi Delta form in the backswamps behind the levees of the river and in the multitude of subsiding delta basins.*

The Mississippi is the world's third longest river and moves over 1000 million tonnes of sediment a year, creating deep alluvial plains. Flooding is a constant threat in lowland areas.

The Yazoo River flows parallel to the Mississippi through a common flood plain. The confluence of the rivers is deferred downstream because flood deposition has built the Mississippi channel up above the level of the Yazoo.

Cathedral Caverns near Huntsville in Alabama is a system of vast limestone caves, with a main opening 1000 ft (300 m) high and 150 ft (50 m) wide.

At De Soto Falls, Alabama, the Little River descends into the deepest canyon east of the Mississippi, with sheer cliff walls up to 700 ft (230 m) high.

Brasstown Bald in the Blue Ridge mountains of Georgia is the region's highest point, at 4784 ft (1458 m).

▲ ***In Providence Canyon**, Georgia, the Chattahoochee River has cut straight down through the sandy bedrock, to leave sheer rock faces and pinnacles, which have been smoothed by subsequent weathering.*

Piedmont
Mississippi Delta
Atchafalaya Bay
Delta lobe
Florida Keys

The delta of the Mississippi over 5000 years ago

Present-day delta

▲ *Over the last 5000 years the lower course of the Mississippi has moved back and forth over great distances. These changes, caused by varying sediment loads and human modification, have resulted in a 'bird's foot' delta with several lobes, each reflecting the river's different historic position.*

Lake Okeechobee is actually a shallow, slow-moving river, 150 miles (240 km) long and 50 miles (80 km) wide.

The Everglades lie in a limestone hollow formed over two million years ago, which has gradually become in-filled with swamp deposits.

Sand bars, deposited by waves breaking offshore, form barrier beaches along much of the coastline, creating sheltered lagoons and salt marshes behind them.

Across Florida the coastal plain is mostly less than 75 ft (25 m) above sea level. The land is underlain by limestone, pitted with hollows which have been filled by over 10,000 lakes.

The landscape

The Blue Ridge mountains in the north are skirted by the gentle hills of the Piedmont, whose rivers drain south on to the great flat expanse of the coastal plain. Sandy barrier beaches and islands dominate the sea shore, tracing round the swampy limestone arm of Florida. In the west, the Mississippi meanders towards its delta, crossing the thickly mantled alluvial plain of the interior lowlands.

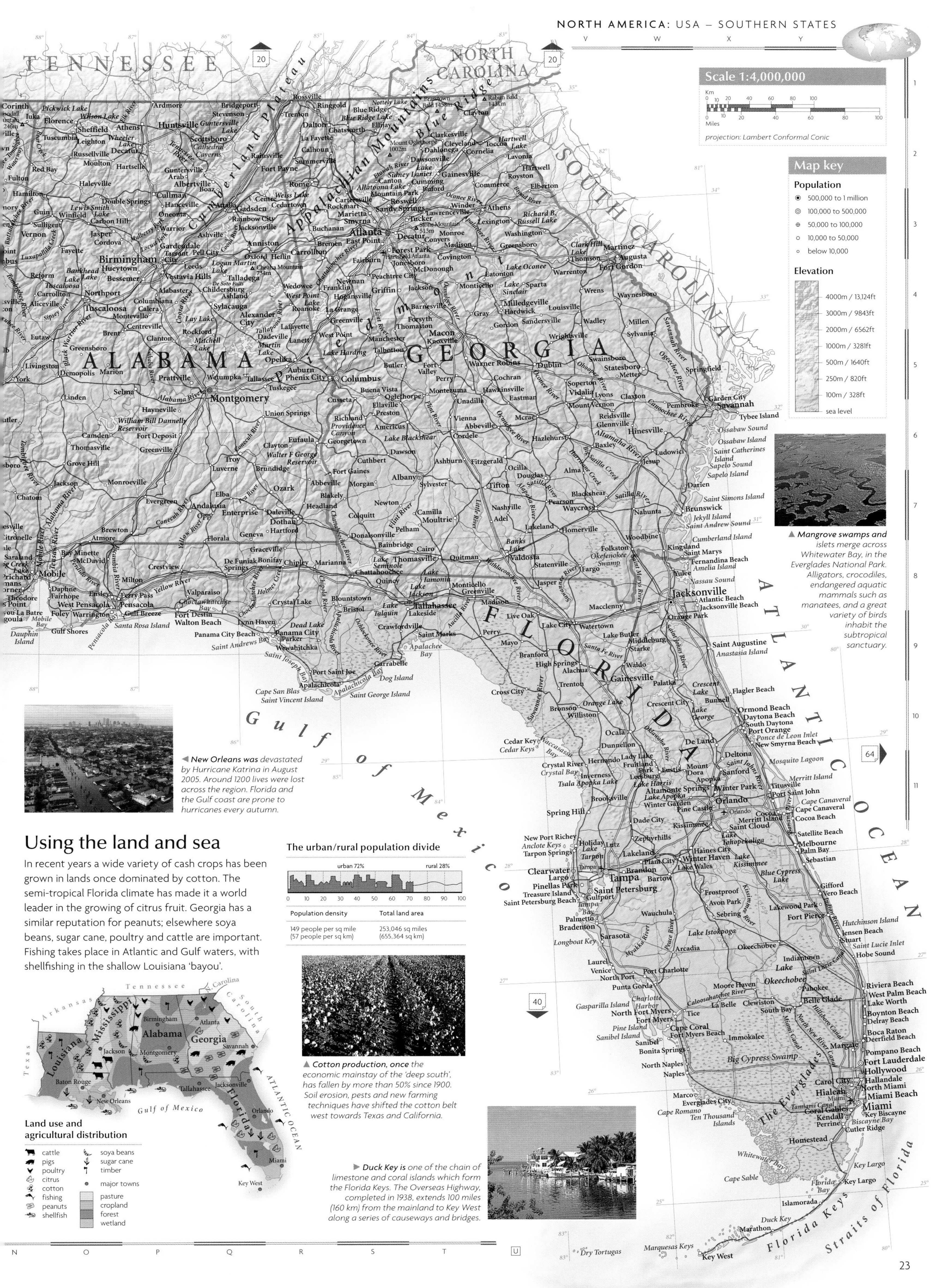

Scale 1:4,000,000
projection: Lambert Conformal Conic
Map key
Population
500,000 to 1 million
100,000 to 500,000
50,000 to 100,000
10,000 to 50,000
below 10,000
Elevation
4000m / 13,124ft
3000m / 9843ft
2000m / 6562ft
1000m / 3281ft
500m / 1640ft
250m / 820ft
100m / 328ft
sea level
TENNESSEE
NORTH CAROLINA
SOUTH CAROLINA
ALABAMA
GEORGIA
FLORIDA
Gulf of Mexico
ATLANTIC OCEAN
Straits of Florida
Florida Keys

▲ **Mangrove swamps and** islets merge across Whitewater Bay, in the Everglades National Park. Alligators, crocodiles, endangered aquatic mammals such as manatees, and a great variety of birds inhabit the subtropical sanctuary.

◀ **New Orleans was** devastated by Hurricane Katrina in August 2005. Around 1200 lives were lost across the region. Florida and the Gulf coast are prone to hurricanes every autumn.

Using the land and sea

In recent years a wide variety of cash crops has been grown in lands once dominated by cotton. The semi-tropical Florida climate has made it a world leader in the growing of citrus fruit. Georgia has a similar reputation for peanuts; elsewhere soya beans, sugar cane, poultry and cattle are important. Fishing takes place in Atlantic and Gulf waters, with shellfishing in the shallow Louisiana 'bayou'.

The urban/rural population divide

urban 72% | rural 28%

Population density	Total land area
149 people per sq mile (57 people per sq km)	253,046 sq miles (655,364 sq km)

▲ **Cotton production, once** the economic mainstay of the 'deep south', has fallen by more than 50% since 1900. Soil erosion, pests and new farming techniques have shifted the cotton belt west towards Texas and California.

▶ **Duck Key is** one of the chain of limestone and coral islands which form the Florida Keys. The Overseas Highway, completed in 1938, extends 100 miles (160 km) from the mainland to Key West along a series of causeways and bridges.

Tennessee
N. Carolina
South Carolina
Arkansas
Texas
Louisiana
Mississippi
Alabama
Georgia
Florida
Birmingham
Atlanta
Jackson
Montgomery
Savannah
Baton Rouge
New Orleans
Tallahassee
Jacksonville
Orlando
Miami
Key West
Gulf of Mexico
ATLANTIC OCEAN

Land use and agricultural distribution

cattle, pigs, poultry, citrus, cotton, fishing, peanuts, shellfish, soya beans, sugar cane, timber, major towns, pasture, cropland, forest, wetland

USA: Texas

First explored by Spaniards moving north from Mexico in search of gold, Texas was controlled by Spain and then Mexico, before becoming an independent republic in 1836, and joining the Union of States in 1845. During the 19th century, many of the migrants who came to Texas raised cattle on the abundant land; in the 20th century, they were joined by prospectors attracted by the promise of oil riches. Today, although natural resources, especially oil, still form the basis of its wealth, the diversified Texan economy includes thriving hi-tech and finance industries. The major urban centres, home to 80% of the population, lie in the south and east, and include Houston, the 'oil-city', and Dallas–Fort Worth. Hispanic influences remain strong, especially in the south and west.

▲ ***Dallas was founded*** *in 1841 as a prairie trading post and its development was stimulated by the arrival of railroads. Cotton and then oil funded the town's early growth. Today, the modern, high-rise skyline of Dallas reflects the city's position as a leading centre of banking, insurance and the petroleum industry in the southwest.*

36

Using the land

Cotton production and livestock-raising, particularly cattle, dominate farming, although crop failures and the demands of local markets have led to some diversification. Following the introduction of modern farming techniques, cotton production spread out from the east to the plains of western Texas. Cattle ranches are widespread, while sheep and goats are raised on the dry Edwards Plateau.

Land use and agricultural distribution

- cattle
- goats
- sheep
- cereals
- cotton
- major towns
- pasture
- cropland
- forest
- barren

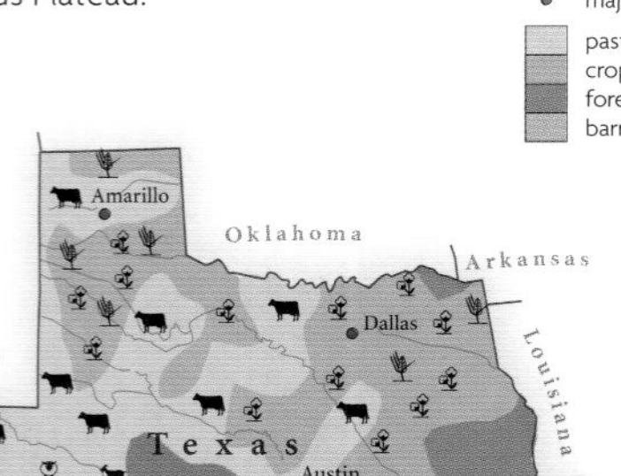
Amarillo
Oklahoma
Arkansas
New Mexico
Dallas
Louisiana
El Paso
Texas
Austin
Houston
San Antonio
MEXICO

The urban/rural population divide

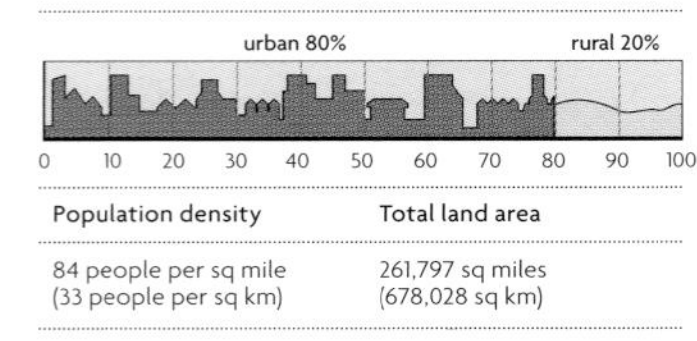
urban 80%
rural 20%
0 10 20 30 40 50 60 70 80 90 100

Population density	Total land area
84 people per sq mile (33 people per sq km)	261,797 sq miles (678,028 sq km)

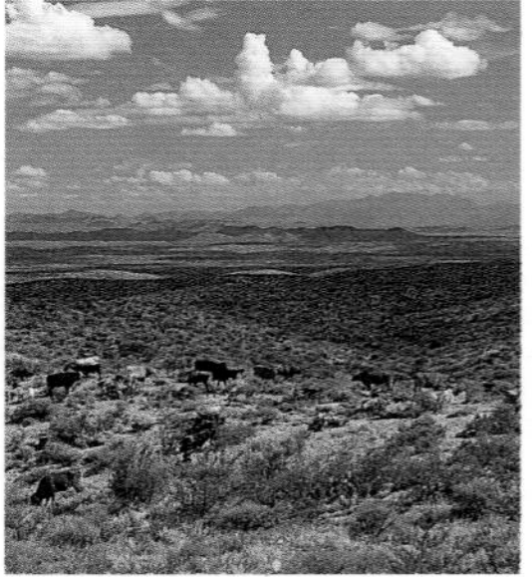

▲ ***The huge cattle*** *ranches of Texas developed during the 19th century when land was plentiful and could be acquired cheaply. Today, more cattle and sheep are raised in Texas than in any other state.*

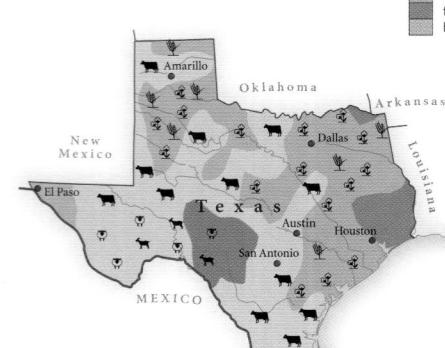

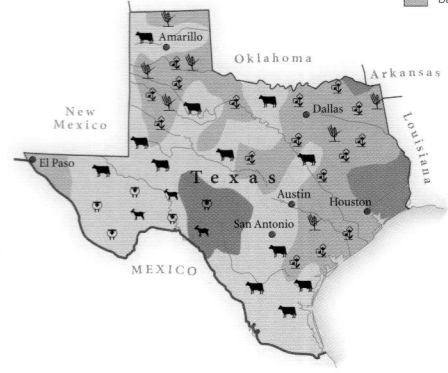

The landscape

Texas is made up of a series of massive steps descending from the mountains and high plains of the west and northwest to the coastal lowlands in the southeast. Many of the state's borders are delineated by water. The Rio Grande flows from the Rocky Mountains to the Gulf of Mexico, marking the border with Mexico.

▲ ***Cap Rock Escarpment*** *juts out from the plains, running 200 miles (320 km) from north to south. Its height varies from 300 ft (90 m) rising to sheer cliffs up to 1000 ft (300 m).*

40

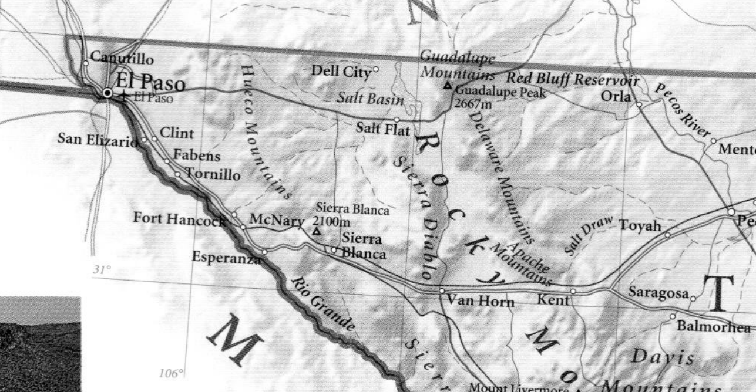

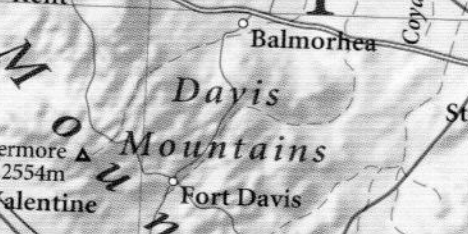

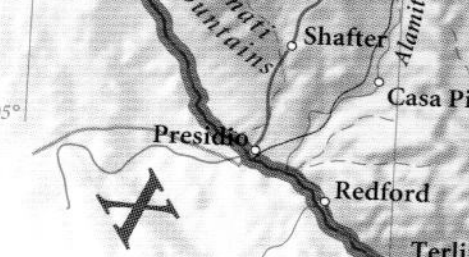

The Llano Estacado or Staked Plain in northern Texas is known for its harsh environment. In the north, freezing winds carrying ice and snow sweep down from the Rocky Mountains, and to the south, sandstorms frequently blow up, scouring anything in their paths. Flash floods, in the wide, flat river beds that remain dry for most of the year, are another hazard.

The Red River flows for 1300 miles (2090 km), marking most of the northern border of Texas. A dam and reservoir along its course provide vital irrigation and hydro-electric power to the surrounding area.

The Guadalupe Mountains lie in the southern Rocky Mountains. They incorporate Guadalupe Peak, the highest in Texas, rising 8749 ft (2667 m).

Sabine River

Extensive forests of pine and cypress grow in the eastern corner of the coastal lowlands where the average rainfall is 45 inches (1145 mm) a year. This is higher than the rest of the state and over twice the average in the west.

The Rio Grande flows from the Rocky Mountains through semi-arid land, supporting sparse vegetation. The river actually shrinks along its course, losing more water through evaporation and seepage than it gains from its tributaries and rainfall.

In the coastal lowlands of southeastern Texas the Earth's crust is warping, causing the land to subside and allowing the sea to invade. Around Galveston, the rate of downward tilting is 6 inches (15 cm) per year. Erosion of the coast is also exacerbated by hurricanes.

Big Bend National Park

◀ ***Flowing through*** *1500 ft (450 m) high gorges, the shallow, muddy Rio Grande makes a 90° bend, which marks the southern border of Big Bend National Park, giving it its name. The area is a mixture of forested mountains, deserts and canyons.*

Edwards Plateau is a limestone outcrop. It is part of the Great Plains, bounded to the southeast by the Balcones Escarpment, which marks the southerly limit of the plains.

Padre Island

Laguna Madre in southern Texas has been almost completely cut off from the sea by Padre Island. This sand bank was created by wave action, carrying and depositing material along the coast. The process is known as longshore drift.

Oil deposits

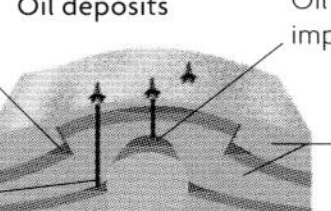
Oil trapped by fault
Oil deposits migrate through reservoir rocks such as shale
Oil accumulates beneath impermeable cap rock
Impermeable rock strata
Salt dome

▲ ***Oil deposits are*** *found beneath much of Texas. They collect as oil migrates upwards through porous layers of rock until it is trapped, either by a cap of rock above a salt dome, or by a fault line which exposes impermeable rock through which the oil cannot rise.*

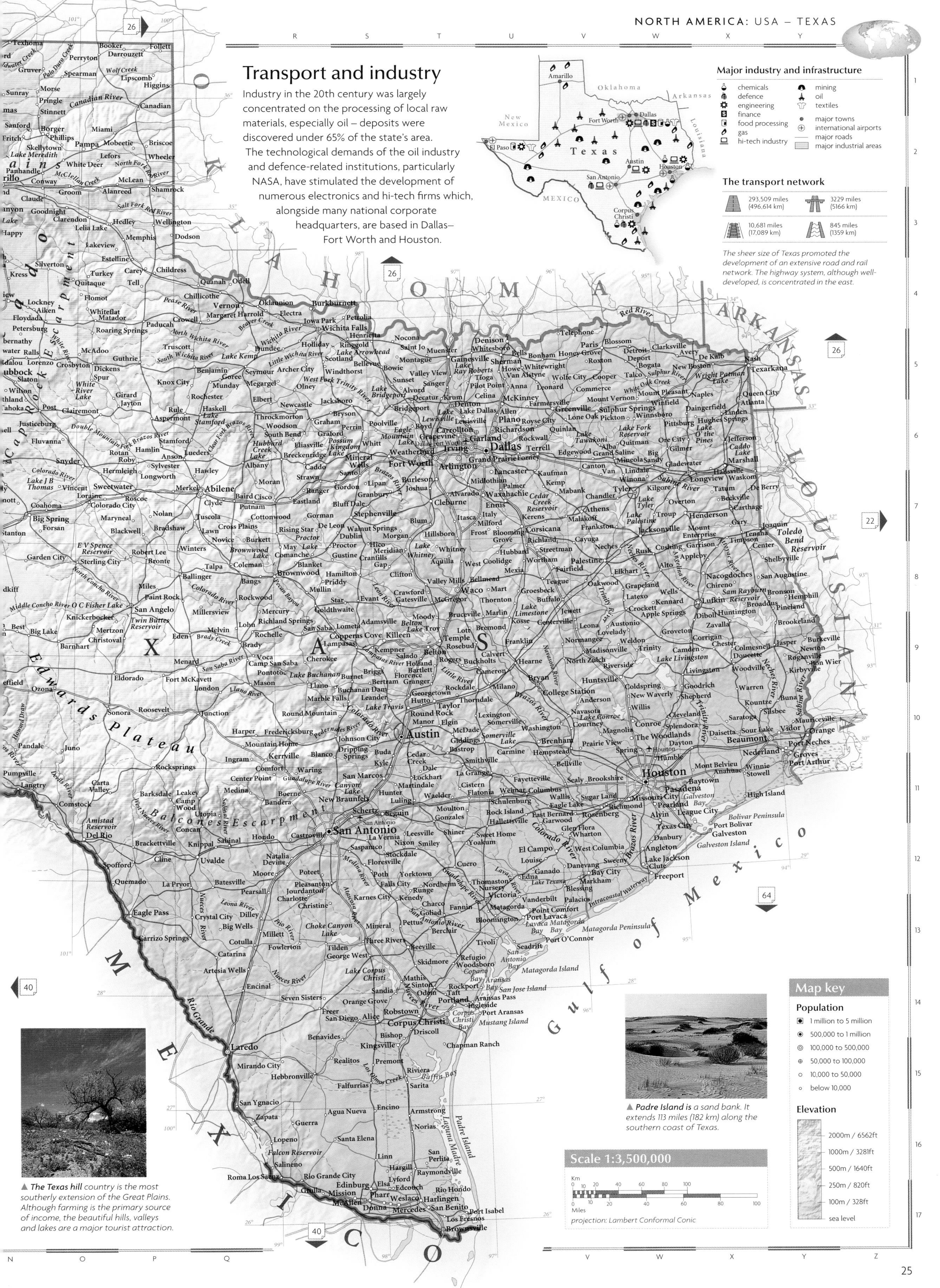
Transport and industry
Industry in the 20th century was largely concentrated on the processing of local raw materials, especially oil – deposits were discovered under 65% of the state's area. The technological demands of the oil industry and defence-related institutions, particularly NASA, have stimulated the development of numerous electronics and hi-tech firms which, alongside many national corporate headquarters, are based in Dallas–Fort Worth and Houston.
Major industry and infrastructure
chemicals
defence
engineering
finance
food processing
gas
hi-tech industry
mining
oil
textiles
major towns
international airports
major roads
major industrial areas
The transport network
293,509 miles (496,614 km)
3229 miles (5166 km)
10,681 miles (17,089 km)
845 miles (1359 km)
The sheer size of Texas promoted the development of an extensive road and rail network. The highway system, although well-developed, is concentrated in the east.
Map key
Population
1 million to 5 million
500,000 to 1 million
100,000 to 500,000
50,000 to 100,000
10,000 to 50,000
below 10,000
Elevation
2000m / 6562ft
1000m / 3281ft
500m / 1640ft
250m / 820ft
100m / 328ft
sea level
Scale 1:3,500,000
projection: Lambert Conformal Conic
Gulf of Mexico
OKLAHOMA
ARKANSAS
LOUISIANA
TEXAS
MEXICO
Dallas
Fort Worth
Houston
San Antonio
Austin
Corpus Christi
El Paso
Amarillo
Laredo
Edwards Plateau
Balcones Escarpment
Rio Grande
Padre Island

▲ The Texas hill country is the most southerly extension of the Great Plains. Although farming is the primary source of income, the beautiful hills, valleys and lakes are a major tourist attraction.

▲ Padre Island is a sand bank. It extends 113 miles (182 km) along the southern coast of Texas.

USA: SOUTH MIDWESTERN STATES

Arkansas, Kansas, Missouri, Oklahoma

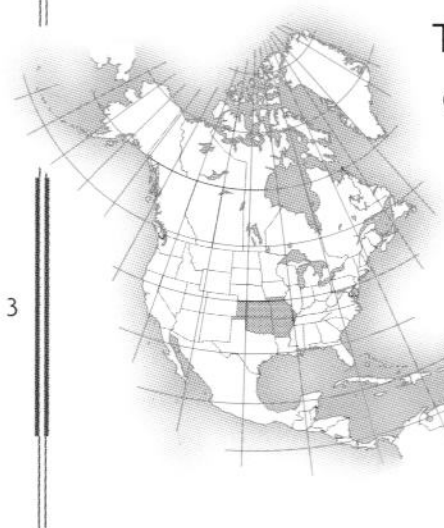

The expansion of the USA focused on this region in the mid-19th century. Settlers spread from the confluence of the Missouri and Mississippi rivers up onto the Great Plains. This treeless expanse, which early explorers had called the 'Great American Desert', was turned into one of the world's richest agricultural regions; but periodic droughts, coupled with over-intensive farming, led to the 'Dustbowl' soil erosion crisis of the 1930s, the abandonment of many farms, and a mass exodus to the west coast. The land has since recovered, although the mechanization of agriculture has led to a decline in the rural population. In recent years, suburban residential development has spread rapidly across the wooded Ozark Plateau in the east of the region.

Transport and industry

The processing of agricultural products, such as brewing and meat packing, has been traditionally important in these states. In Kansas and Oklahoma, diversified manufacturing now supplements income from fossil fuels; Wichita has become a world centre for aeronautical engineering, an industry which also employs many people in neighbouring Missouri.

Major industry and infrastructure

- aerospace
- engineering
- finance
- food processing
- gas
- mining
- oil
- vehicle manufacture
- major towns
- international airports
- major roads
- major industrial areas

The transport network

380,307 miles (608,491 km)		4068 miles (6508 km)	
16,185 miles (25,896 km)		1994 miles (3208 km)	

The Arkansas River and its tributaries allow access to over half of the USA's navigable inland waterways. A system of locks and dams along the river provides Tulsa in Oklahoma with a navigable water route to the Gulf of Mexico.

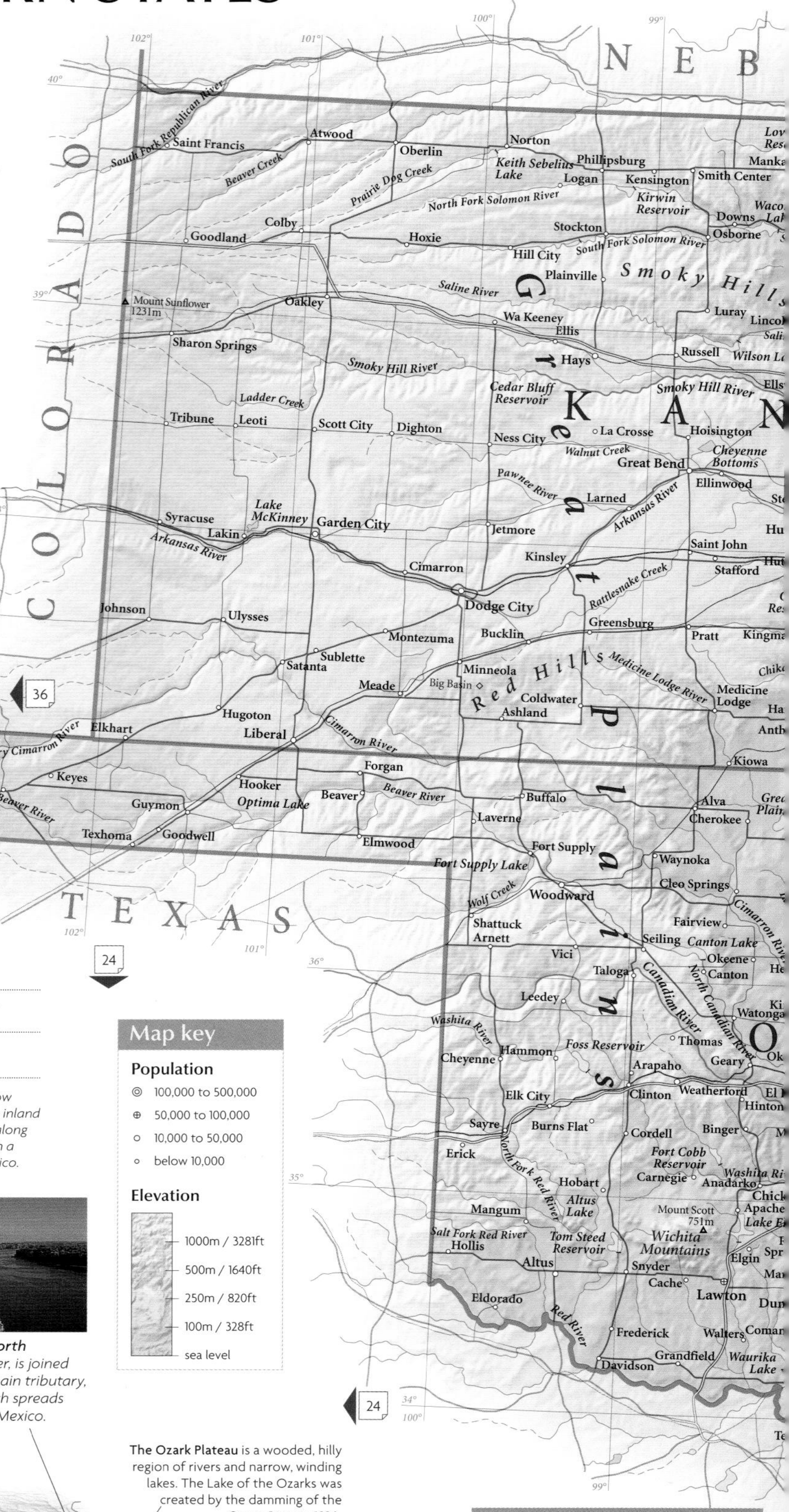

▶ ***Agricultural produce** from the plains is moved by barges along the Mississippi. The river now carries a far greater tonnage of freight than any other waterway system in the USA.*

The landscape

Most of the region consists of high, treeless plains, which gradually descend east from the Rocky Mountains. Drainage follows this slope, with rivers flowing towards the alluvial lowlands of the Mississippi in the southeast. Between the plains and the lowlands lie various ranges of wooded hills, including the deeply incised Ozark Plateau.

▲ ***The Mississippi, North** America's longest river, is joined by the Missouri, its main tributary, on a flood plain which spreads south to the Gulf of Mexico.*

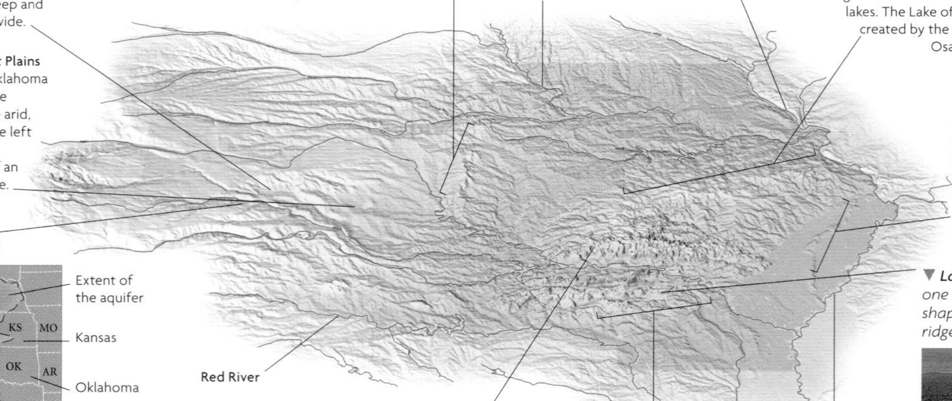

Collapsed limestone caverns led to the formation of Big Basin in Kansas; a depression 100 ft (33 m) deep and 1 mile (1.6 km) wide.

The Great Salt Plains of northern Oklahoma cover 45 sq mile (116 sq km). The arid, white flats were left by the gradual evaporation of an ancient salt lake.

Underground water reserves

Flint Hills is the region's easternmost major escarpment. Steep, grassy uplands are interspersed with rocky, wooded ravines and outcrops of limestone and chert.

Missouri River

The Ozark Plateau is a wooded, hilly region of rivers and narrow, winding lakes. The Lake of the Ozarks was created by the damming of the Osage River in 1930.

Crowleys Ridge is a long, sandy ridge, rising from the Mississippi flood plain. It was formed over thousands of years by the deposition of sand blown eastwards from the Great Plains.

Red River

Devil's Den is a dry badland area. The rugged landscape, strewn with large boulders, is the eroded remnant of a spur extending from the Arbuckle mountains to the west.

Ouachita Mountains

Mississippi River

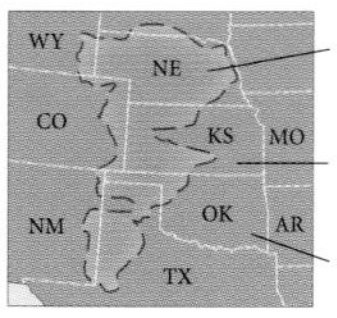

Extent of the aquifer

Kansas

Oklahoma

▲ ***The Ogallala Aquifer,** beneath the Great Plains, is the largest known source of underground water in the world. There is concern about the rapid depletion of this finite water supply by irrigation schemes.*

▼ ***Lake Ouachita,** in Arkansas is one of a number of irregularly-shaped lakes found among the ridges of the Ouachita Mountains.*

▲ ***The landscape of** northeast Kansas is interlaced by rivers which have cut broad wooded valleys through the gentle hills. All the rivers in Kansas form part of the massive Missouri/Mississippi drainage basin.*

Map key

Population

- 100,000 to 500,000
- 50,000 to 100,000
- 10,000 to 50,000
- below 10,000

Elevation

- 1000m / 3281ft
- 500m / 1640ft
- 250m / 820ft
- 100m / 328ft
- sea level

Scale 1:3,250,000

projection: Lambert Conformal Conic

28
36
24

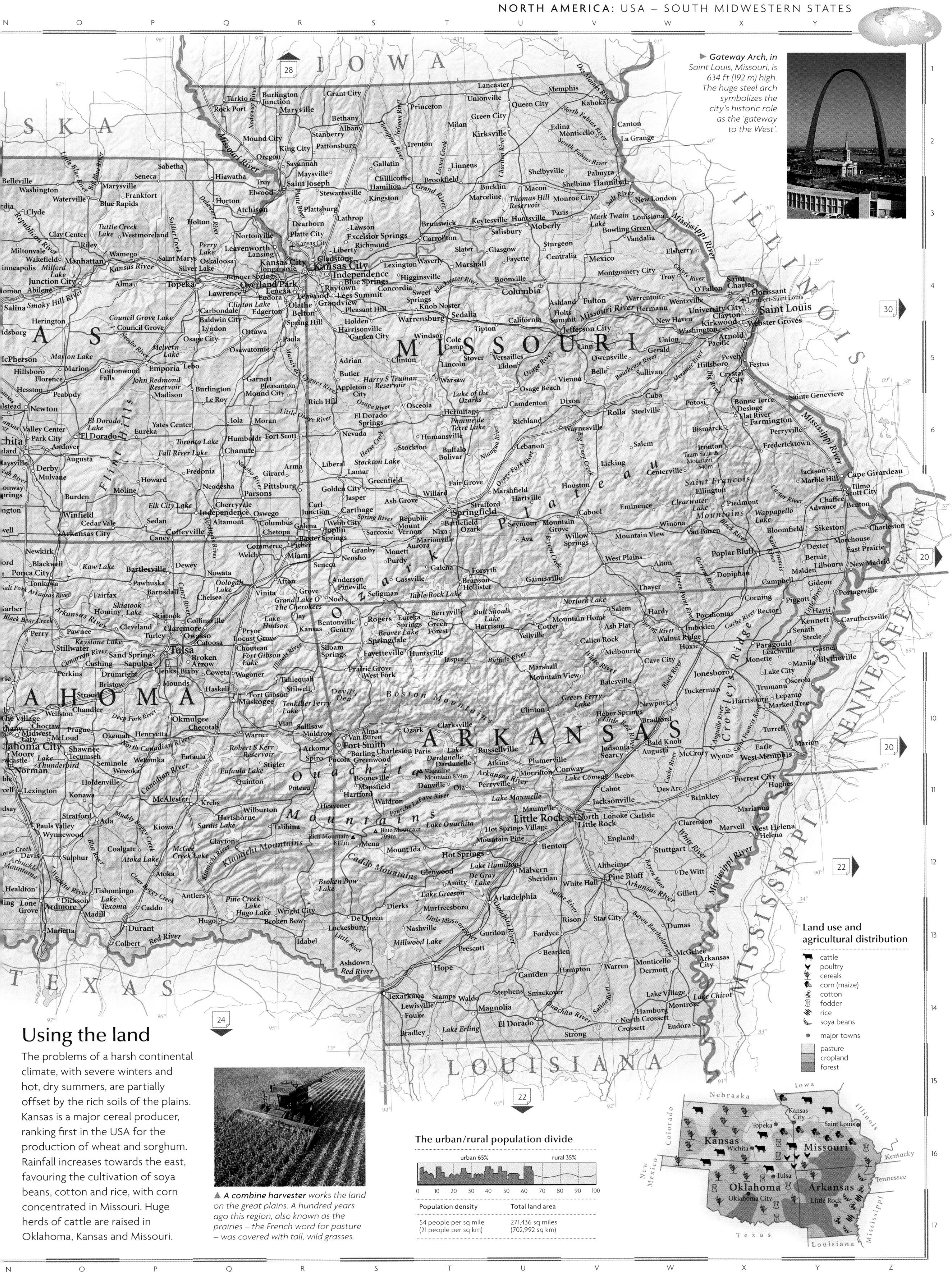
IOWA
MISSOURI
ARKANSAS
AHOMA
SKA
ILLINOIS
KENTUCKY
TENNESSEE
MISSISSIPPI
LOUISIANA
TEXAS
Ozark Plateau
Ouachita Mountains
Boston Mountains
Saint Louis
Kansas City
Springfield
Little Rock
Tulsa
Fort Smith
Jefferson City
Mississippi River
Missouri River
Arkansas River
Land use and agricultural distribution
cattle
poultry
cereals
corn (maize)
cotton
fodder
rice
soya beans
major towns
pasture
cropland
forest

▶ *Gateway Arch, in Saint Louis, Missouri, is 634 ft (192 m) high. The huge steel arch symbolizes the city's historic role as the 'gateway to the West'.*

Using the land

The problems of a harsh continental climate, with severe winters and hot, dry summers, are partially offset by the rich soils of the plains. Kansas is a major cereal producer, ranking first in the USA for the production of wheat and sorghum. Rainfall increases towards the east, favouring the cultivation of soya beans, cotton and rice, with corn concentrated in Missouri. Huge herds of cattle are raised in Oklahoma, Kansas and Missouri.

▲ ***A combine harvester** works the land on the great plains. A hundred years ago this region, also known as the prairies – the French word for pasture – was covered with tall, wild grasses.*

The urban/rural population divide

urban 65% — rural 35%

Population density	Total land area
54 people per sq mile (21 people per sq km)	271,436 sq miles (702,992 sq km)

USA: UPPER PLAINS STATES

Iowa, Minnesota, Nebraska, North Dakota, South Dakota

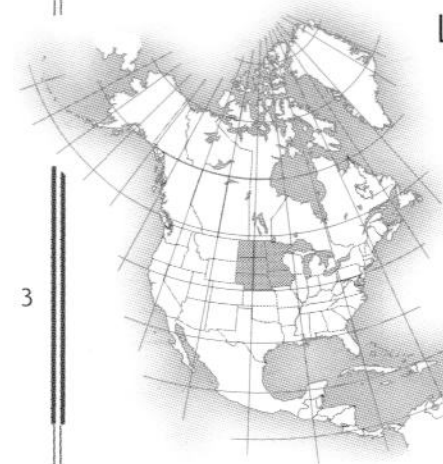

Lying at the very heart of the North American continent, much of this region was acquired from France as part of the Louisiana Purchase in 1803. The area was largely by-passed by the early waves of westward migrants. When Europeans did settle, during the 19th century, they displaced the Native Americans who lived on the plains. The settlers planted arable crops and raised cattle on the immensely fertile prairie land, founding an agrarian tradition which flourishes today. Most of this region remains rural; of the five states, only in Minnesota has there been significant diversification away from agriculture and resource-based industries into the hi-tech and service sectors.

Using the land

The popular image of these states as agricultural is entirely justified; prairies stretch uninterrupted across most of the area. Croplands fall into two regions: the wheat belt of the plains, and the corn belt of the central USA. Cash crops, such as soya beans, are grown to supplement incomes. Livestock, particularly pigs and cattle, are raised throughout this region.

The urban/rural population divide

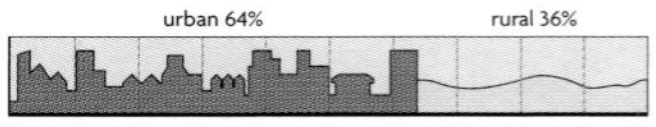

urban 64% — rural 36%

Population density	Total land area
31 people per sq mile (12 people per sq km)	357,212 sq miles (925,143 sq km)

Dark, fertile prairie soils in the southeast provide Minnesota's most productive farmland. Hot, humid summers create a long growing season for corn cultivation.

Land use and agricultural distribution

- cattle
- pigs
- corn (maize)
- soya beans
- wheat
- major towns
- pasture
- cropland
- forest
- wetland

Transport and industry

Food processing and the production of farm machinery are supported by the large agricultural sector. Mineral exploitation is also an important activity: gold is mined in the ore-rich Black Hills of South Dakota, and both North Dakota and Nebraska are emerging as major petroleum producers.

The transport network

504,522 miles (807,235 km)	3422 miles (5475 km)
16,940 miles (27,104 km)	683 miles (1098 km)

Nebraska's central location has made it an important transport artery for east–west traffic. Minnesota's road network radiates out from the hub of the twin cities, Minneapolis–Saint Paul.

Water erosion along the Little Missouri River has carried away sedimentary deposits, creating rugged landscapes known as badlands.

Major industry and infrastructure

- coal
- engineering
- electronics
- finance
- food processing
- oil & gas
- mining
- major towns
- international airports
- major roads
- major industrial areas

The landscape

These states straddle the Great Plains and the lowlands of the central USA, with Minnesota lying in a transition zone between the eastern forests and the prairies. The region was shaped by repeated ice advances and retreats, leaving a flat relief, broken only by the numerous lakes and broad river networks which drain the prairies.

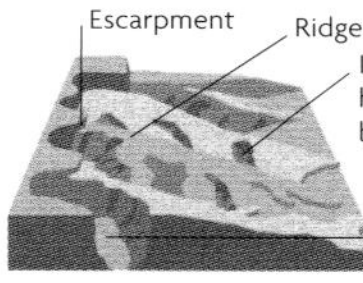

Escarpment

Ridge

In permeable strata hollows are formed by small mudslides

Water flowing into gullies erodes back the escarpment

Badlands are formed by stormwater run-off which flows down the impermeable strata of the escarpment and saturates the permeable strata leading to mudslides and the formation of gullies.

In the badlands of North and South Dakota, horizontal layers of sandstone have been eroded by rivers, leaving a landscape of narrow gullies, sharp crests and pinnacles.

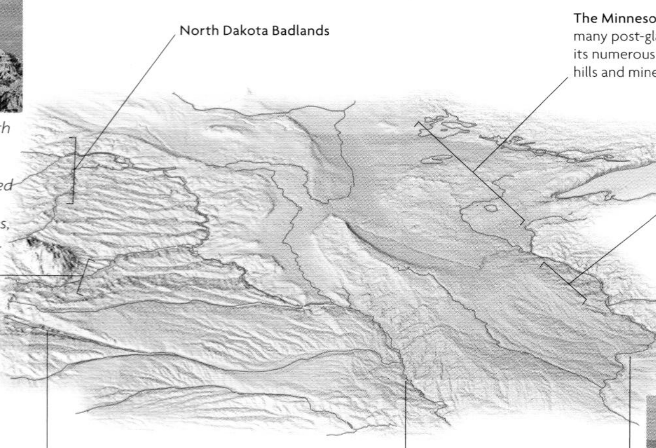

North Dakota Badlands

South Dakota Badlands

The Minnesota landscape contains many post-glacial features, including its numerous lakes, boulder-strewn hills and mineral-rich deposits.

Although it escaped the last glaciation, the limestone bedrock of southeastern Minnesota has been eroded by surface and subterranean streams, leaving a network of underground caverns and steepsided valleys.

Missouri River

Mississippi River

Chimney Rock is a remnant of an ancient land surface, eroded by the North Platte River. The tip of its spire stands 500 ft (150 m) above the plain.

In northeastern Iowa, the Mississippi and its tributaries have deeply incised the underlying bedrock creating a hilly terrain, with bluffs standing 300 ft (90 m) above the valley.

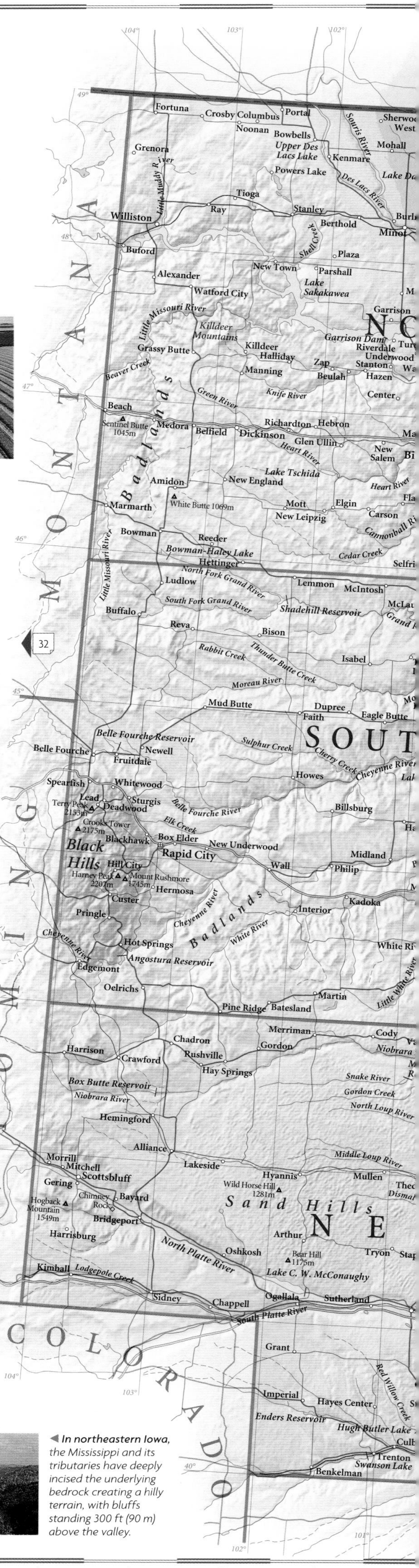

32

▶ *Along the shores of Lake Superior in Minnesota, the average number of frost-free days can be as few as 90, and frosts may occur in any month of the year.*

Map key

Population

- ◎ 100,000 to 500,000
- ⊕ 50,000 to 100,000
- ○ 10,000 to 50,000
- ◦ below 10,000

Elevation

- 2000m / 6562ft
- 1000m / 3281ft
- 500m / 1640ft
- 250m / 820ft
- 100m / 328ft
- sea level

Scale 1:3,500,000

Km 0 10 20 40 60 80 100 120

Miles 0 10 20 40 60 80 100 120

projection: Lambert Conformal Conic

USA: GREAT LAKES STATES

Illinois, Indiana, Michigan, Ohio, Wisconsin

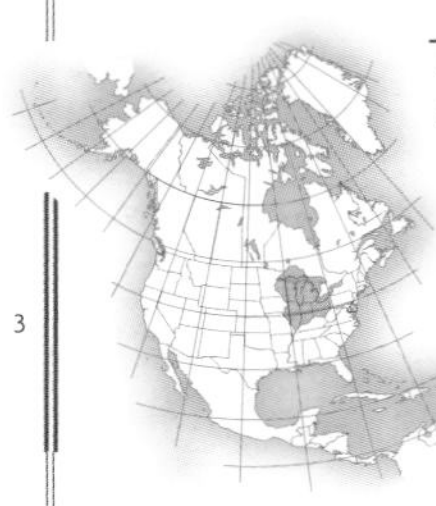

The states bordering the Great Lakes developed rapidly in the second half of the 19th century as a result of improvements in communications: rail to the west and waterways to the south and east. Fertile land and good links with growing eastern seaboard cities encouraged the development of agriculture and food processing. Migrants from Europe and other parts of the USA flooded into the region and for much of the 20th century the region's economy boomed. However, in recent years heavy industry has declined, earning the region the unwanted label the 'Rustbelt'.

Transport and industry

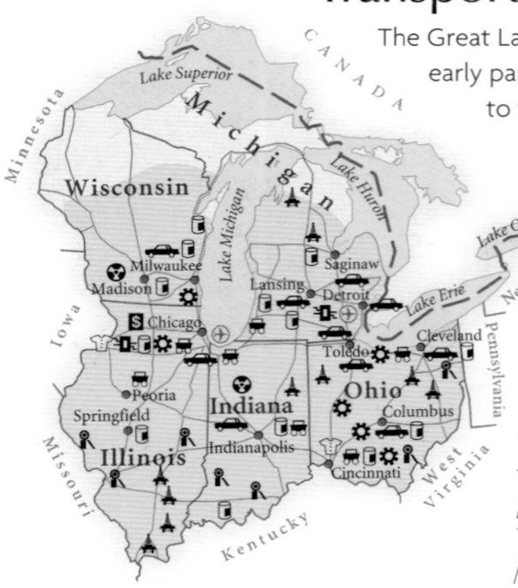

The Great Lakes region is the centre of the USA's car industry. Since the early part of the 20th century, its prosperity has been closely linked to the fortunes of automobile manufacturing. Iron and steel production has expanded to meet demand from this industry. In the 1970s, nationwide recession, cheaper foreign competition in the automobile sector, pollution in and around the Great Lakes and the collapse of the meat-packing industry, centred on Chicago, forced these states to diversify their industrial base. New industries have emerged, notably electronics, service and finance industries.

The transport network

540,682 miles (865,091 km)	6550 miles (10,480 km)
24,928 miles (39,884 km)	2330 miles (3748 km)

Few areas of the USA have a comparable transport system. Chicago is a principal transport terminus with a dense network of roads, railways and Interstate freeways radiating from the city.

Major industry and infrastructure

- car manufacture
- coal
- electronics
- engineering
- finance
- food processing
- iron & steel
- oil
- research & development
- textiles
- major towns
- international airports
- major roads
- major industrial areas

▶ ***Ever since Ransom Olds** and Henry Ford started mass-producing automobiles in Detroit early in the 20th century, the city's name has become synonymous with the American automotive industry.*

The landscape

Much of this region shows the impact of glaciation which lasted until about 10,000 years ago, and extended as far south as Illinois and Ohio. Although the relief of the region slopes towards the Great Lakes, because the ice sheets blocked northerly drainage, most of the rivers today flow southwards, forming part of the massive Mississippi/Missouri drainage basin.

◀ ***The dunes near** Sleeping Bear Point rise 400 ft (120 m) from the banks of Lake Michigan. They are constantly being resculpted by wind action.*

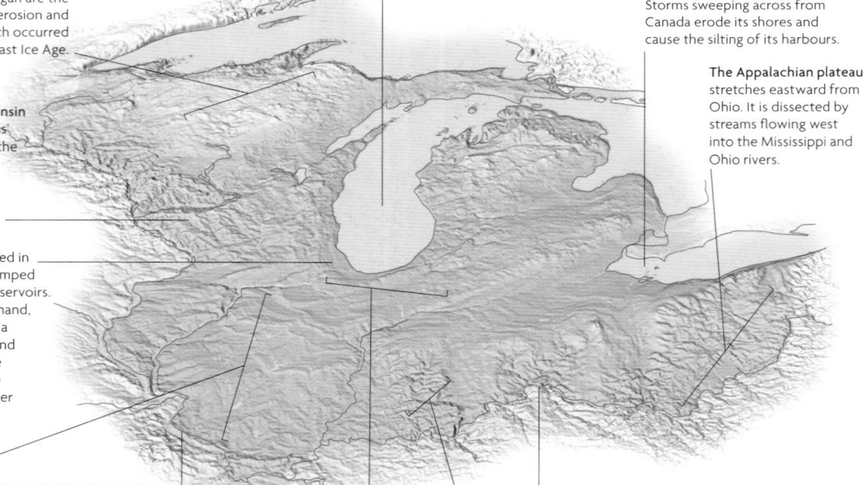

Lake Michigan

The many lakes and marshes of Wisconsin and Michigan are the result of glacial erosion and deposition which occurred during the last Ice Age.

Lake Erie is the shallowest of the five Great Lakes. Its average depth is about 62 ft (19 m). Storms sweeping across from Canada erode its shores and cause the silting of its harbours.

The Appalachian plateau stretches eastward from Ohio. It is dissected by streams flowing west into the Mississippi and Ohio rivers.

Southwestern Wisconsin is known as a 'driftless' area. Unlike most of the region, low hills protected it from erosion by the advancing ice sheet.

Most of the water used in northern Illinois is pumped from underground reservoirs. Due to increased demand, many areas now face a water shortage. Around Joliet, the water table was lowered by more than 700 ft (210 m) over the last century.

Illinois plains

Mississippi River

Ohio River

▲ ***The plains of** Illinois are characteristic of drift landscapes, scoured and flattened by glacial erosion and covered with fertile glacial deposits.*

Relic landforms from the last glaciation, such as shallow basins and ridges, cover all but the south of this region. Ridges, known as moraines, up to 300 ft (100 m) high, lie to the south of Lake Michigan.

Unlike the level prairie to the north, southern Indiana is relatively rugged. Limestone in the hills has been dissolved by water, producing features such as sinkholes and underground caves.

Glacial till

Present-day river or stream

Channels caused by outwash from melting glacier

Most recent till deposits

Older till sheet

Bedrock

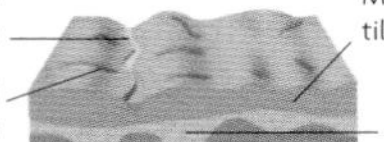

▲ ***As a result** of successive glacial depositions, the total depth of till along the former southern margin of the Laurentide ice sheet can exceed 1300 ft (400 m).*

28

28

26

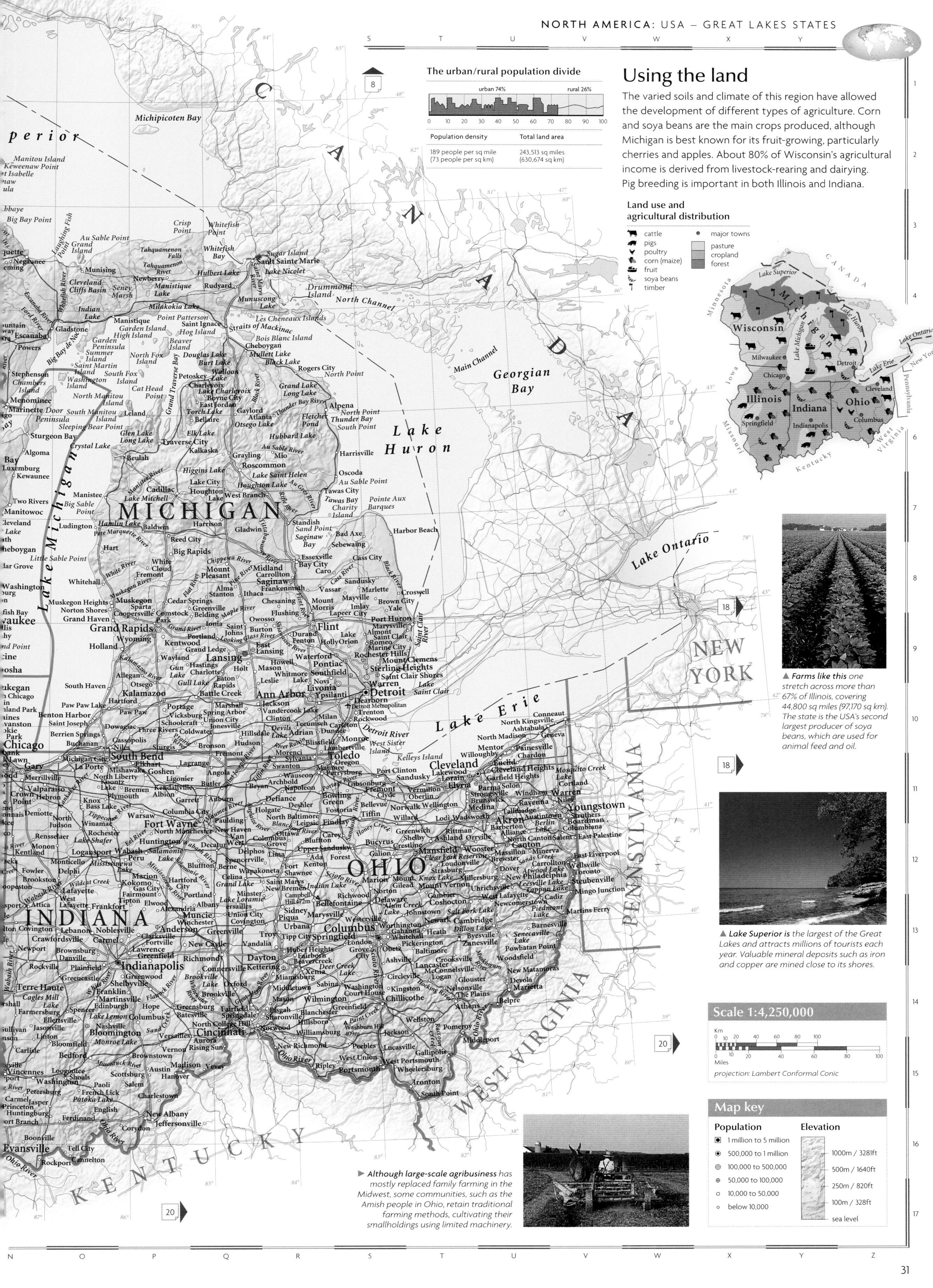
CANADA
MICHIGAN
INDIANA
OHIO
PENNSYLVANIA
NEW YORK
WEST VIRGINIA
KENTUCKY
Lake Michigan
Lake Huron
Lake Erie
Lake Ontario
Georgian Bay
Detroit
Chicago
Cleveland
Toledo
Columbus
Indianapolis
Cincinnati
Grand Rapids
Lansing
Flint
Fort Wayne
Dayton
Akron
Youngstown
Evansville

The urban/rural population divide

urban 74% | rural 26%

0 10 20 30 40 50 60 70 80 90 100

Population density	Total land area
189 people per sq mile (73 people per sq km)	243,513 sq miles (630,674 sq km)

Using the land

The varied soils and climate of this region have allowed the development of different types of agriculture. Corn and soya beans are the main crops produced, although Michigan is best known for its fruit-growing, particularly cherries and apples. About 80% of Wisconsin's agricultural income is derived from livestock-rearing and dairying. Pig breeding is important in both Illinois and Indiana.

Land use and agricultural distribution

cattle, pigs, poultry, corn (maize), fruit, soya beans, timber

major towns; pasture, cropland, forest

▲ **Farms like this** *one stretch across more than 67% of Illinois, covering 44,800 sq miles (97,170 sq km). The state is the USA's second largest producer of soya beans, which are used for animal feed and oil.*

▲ **Lake Superior** *is the largest of the Great Lakes and attracts millions of tourists each year. Valuable mineral deposits such as iron and copper are mined close to its shores.*

► ***Although large-scale agribusiness** has mostly replaced family farming in the Midwest, some communities, such as the Amish people in Ohio, retain traditional farming methods, cultivating their smallholdings using limited machinery.*

Scale 1:4,250,000

Km 0 10 20 40 60 80 100

Miles 0 10 20 40 60 80 100

projection: Lambert Conformal Conic

Map key

Population

- 1 million to 5 million
- 500,000 to 1 million
- 100,000 to 500,000
- 50,000 to 100,000
- 10,000 to 50,000
- below 10,000

Elevation

- 1000m / 3281ft
- 500m / 1640ft
- 250m / 820ft
- 100m / 328ft
- sea level

USA: NORTH MOUNTAIN STATES

Idaho, Montana, Oregon, Washington, Wyoming

The remoteness of the northwestern states, coupled with the rugged landscape, ensured that this was one of the last areas settled by Europeans in the 19th century. Fur-trappers and gold-prospectors followed the Snake River westwards as it wound its way through the Rocky Mountains. The states of the northwest have pioneered many conservationist policies, with the USA's first national park opened at Yellowstone in 1872. More recently, the Cascades and Rocky Mountains have become havens for adventure tourism. The mountains still serve to isolate the western seaboard from the rest of the continent. This isolation has encouraged west coast cities to expand their trade links with countries of the Pacific Rim.

▲ *The Snake River has cut down into the basalt of the Columbia Basin to form Hells Canyon, the deepest in the USA, with cliffs up to 7900 ft (2408 m) high.*

Map key

Population	Elevation
500,000 to 1 million	4000m / 13,124ft
100,000 to 500,000	3000m / 9843ft
50,000 to 100,000	2000m / 6562ft
10,000 to 50,000	1000m / 3281ft
below 10,000	500m / 1640ft
	250m / 820ft
	100m / 328ft
	sea level

Using the land

Wheat farming in the east gives way to cattle ranching as rainfall decreases. Irrigated farming in the Snake River valley produces large yields of potatoes and other vegetables. Dairying and fruit-growing take place in the wet western lowlands between the mountain ranges.

The urban/rural population divide

urban 74% — rural 26%

Population density	Total land area
26 people per sq mile (10 people per sq km)	487,970 sq miles (1,263,716 sq km)

Scale 1:4,250,000

projection: Lambert Conformal Conic

▶ *Fine-textured, volcanic soils in the hilly Palouse region of eastern Washington are susceptible to erosion.*

Land use and agricultural distribution

cattle, poultry, cereals, fruit, potatoes, timber, major towns, pasture, cropland, forest

Transport and industry

Minerals and timber are extremely important in this region. Uranium, precious metals, copper and coal are all mined, the latter in vast open-cast pits in Wyoming; oil and natural gas are extracted further north. Manufacturing, notably related to the aerospace and electronics industries, is important in western cities.

CANADA
PACIFIC OCEAN
Seattle
Tacoma
Spokane
Washington
Pasco
Portland
Salem
Eugene
Oregon
Lewiston
Great Falls
Helena
Montana
Billings
Boise
Idaho
Pocatello
Twin Falls
Casper
Wyoming
Cheyenne
California
Nevada
Utah
Colorado

The transport network

- 347,857 miles (556,571 km)
- 4200 miles (6720 km)
- 12,354 miles (19,766 km)
- 1108 miles (1782 km)

The Union Pacific Railroad has been in service across Wyoming since 1867. The route through the Rocky Mountains is now shared with the Interstate 80, a major east–west highway.

Major industry and infrastructure

adventure tourism, aerospace, coal, chemicals, electronics, food processing, mining, oil & gas, timber processing, major towns, international airports, major roads, major industrial areas

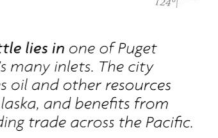

◀ *Seattle lies in one of Puget Sound's many inlets. The city receives oil and other resources from Alaska, and benefits from expanding trade across the Pacific.*

◀ *Crater Lake, Oregon, is 6 miles (10 km) wide and 1800 ft (600 m) deep. It marks the site of a volcanic cone, which collapsed after an eruption within the last 7000 years.*

8 192 34 34

The landscape

The Rocky Mountains are flanked by lower parallel ranges, which spread onto the Great Plains in the east and surmount the broad lava plateau which extends westwards. The Cascade Range divides the Columbia Basin from the coastlands, where the low areas skirting Puget Sound are broken by the steep, volcanic Olympic Mountains and the wooded hills of the Coast Ranges.

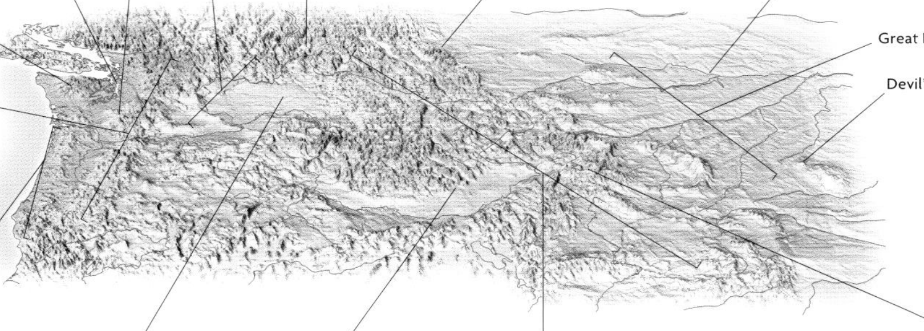

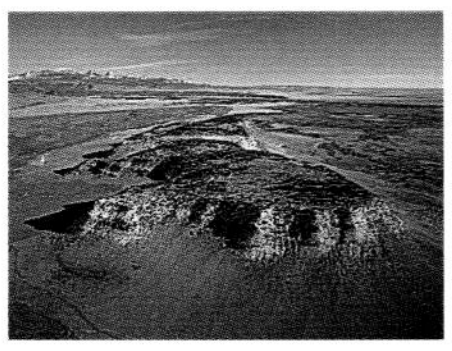

Glacial valleys on the seaward side of the Olympic Mountains receive about 142 inches (3600 mm) of rain per year, supporting the only true rainforest of the northern hemisphere.

Puget Sound

Mount St Helens erupted in 1980, killing 57 people and devastating a huge area.

Columbia Basin

Grand Coulee and the lesser *coulées* (ravines) were cut by cataclysmic floods, from the release of an ice-dammed lake, at the end of the last Ice Age.

The Continental Divide, or watershed, crosses the Lewis Range. From here, rivers flow east to Hudson Bay, south to the Gulf of Mexico and west to the Pacific Ocean.

▶ ***Piney Buttes are*** *the remnants of an older, higher land surface gradually weathered and eroded into isolated outcrops with flat tops and steep sides.*

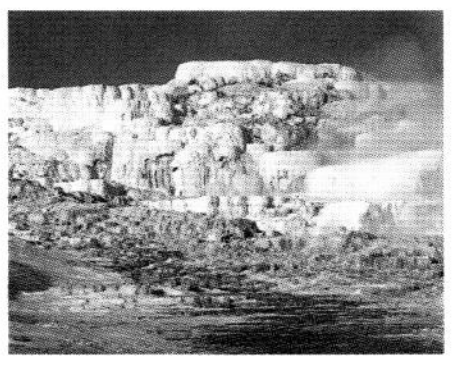

Great Plains

Devil's Tower

The Cascades are glacially scoured volcanic mountains, the highest of which is Mount Rainier, a dormant volcano at 14,409 ft (4392 m).

Molten rock cools, forming parallel columns

Surrounding strata eroded away

Molten rock wells up from the Earth's core

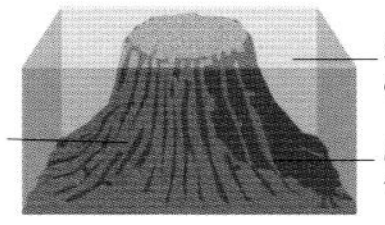

▲ ***Devil's Tower in*** *Wyoming is an igneous intrusion, formed below the Earth's surface. Molten rock intruded through cracks in the overlying strata and cooled. Over time, the softer rock layers have been eroded away, leaving only the tower standing.*

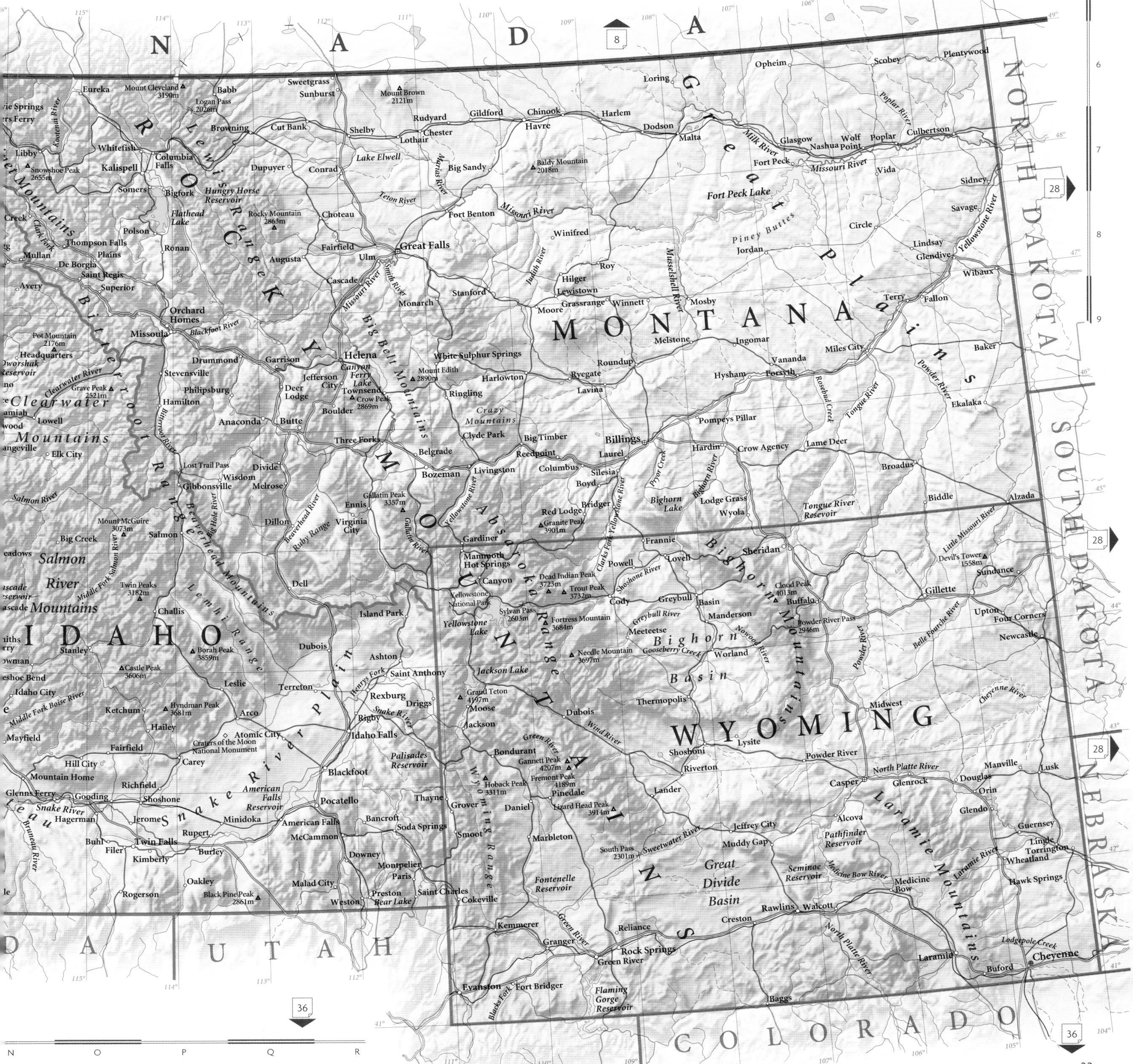

Coast Ranges

The plateaux of the Columbia and Snake rivers represent one of the world's largest accumulations of lava. Over 5 million years ago, successive flows of molten basalt buried the existing land surface by up to 450 ft (150 m).

The contorted rock shapes at 'Craters of the Moon' National Monument in Idaho were left 2000 years ago by the sporadic upwelling of viscous lava from fissures in the basalt plateau.

Rocky Mountains

▲ ***Water from the*** *hot springs in Yellowstone National Park deposits minerals as it cools in rock pools. Long periods of deposition have created these rock terraces.*

USA: CALIFORNIA & NEVADA

The 'Gold Rush' of 1849 attracted the first major wave of European settlers to the USA's west coast. The pleasant climate, beautiful scenery and dynamic economy continue to attract immigrants – despite the ever-present danger of earthquakes – and California has become the USA's most populous state. The population is concentrated in the vast conurbations of Los Angeles, San Francisco and San Diego; new immigrants include people from South Korea, the Philippines, Vietnam and Mexico. Nevada's arid lands were initially exploited for minerals; in recent years, revenue from mining has been superseded by income from the tourist and gambling centres of Las Vegas and Reno.

Map key

Population	Elevation
1 million to 5 million	4000m / 13,124ft
500,000 to 1 million	3000m / 9843ft
100,000 to 500,000	2000m / 6562ft
50,000 to 100,000	1000m / 3281ft
10,000 to 50,000	500m / 1640ft
below 10,000	250m / 820ft
	100m / 328ft
	sea level

Scale 1:3,250,000

Km 0 5 10 20 30 40 50 60 70 80

0 5 10 20 30 40 50 60 70 80 Miles

projection: Lambert Conformal Conic

Transport and industry

Nevada's rich mineral reserves ushered in a period of mining wealth which has now been replaced by revenue generated from gambling. California supports a broad set of activities including defence-related industries and research and development facilities. 'Silicon Valley', near San Francisco, is a world leading centre for micro-electronics, while tourism and the Los Angeles film industry also generate large incomes.

DUNES
OASIS
CASINO

◀ *Gambling was legalized in Nevada in 1931. Las Vegas has since become the centre of this multi-million dollar industry.*

Oregon
Idaho
Utah
Nevada
Reno
Ely
Sacramento
Carson City
San Francisco
Oakland
San Jose
California
Las Vegas
Bakersfield
Arizona
PACIFIC OCEAN
Los Angeles
San Diego
MEXICO

Major industry and infrastructure

- aerospace
- car manufacture
- defence
- film industry
- finance
- food processing
- gambling
- hi-tech industry
- mining
- pharmaceuticals
- research & development
- textiles
- tourism
- major towns
- international airports
- major roads
- major industrial areas

The transport network

211,459 miles (338,334 km)	2944 miles (4710 km)
7822 miles (12,595 km)	190 miles (360 km)

In California, the motor vehicle is a vital part of daily life, and an extensive freeway system runs throughout the state, cementing its position as the most important mode of transport.

The landscape

The broad Central Valley divides California's coastal mountains from the Sierra Nevada. The San Andreas Fault, running beneath much of the state, is the site of frequent earth tremors and sometimes more serious earthquakes. East of the Sierra Nevada, the landscape is characterized by the basin and range topography with stony deserts and many salt lakes.

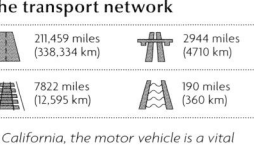

Rising molten rock causes stretching of the Earth's crust

Extensive cracking (faulting) uplifted a series of ridges

As ridges are eroded they fill intervening valleys with sediments

▲ **Molten rock (magma)** *welling up to form a dome in the Earth's interior, causes the brittle surface rocks to stretch and crack. Some areas were uplifted to form mountains (ranges), while others sunk to form flat valleys (basins).*

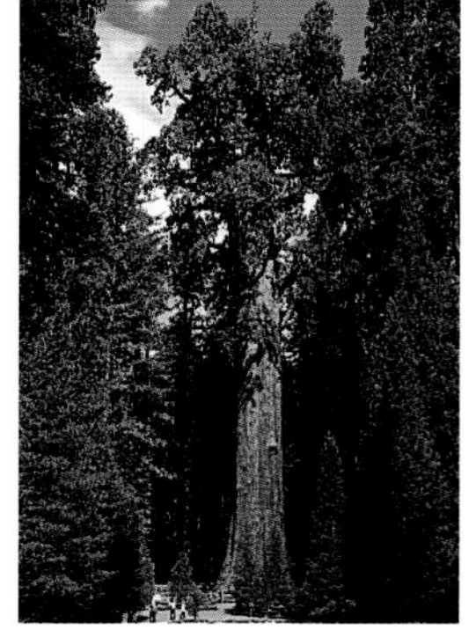

◀ ***The General Sherman*** *sequoia tree in Sequoia National Park is 2500 years old and at 275 ft (84 m) is one of the largest living things on earth.*

Most of California's agriculture is confined to the fertile and extensively irrigated Central Valley, running between the Coast Ranges and the Sierra Nevada. It incorporates the San Joaquin and Sacramento valleys.

The dramatic granitic rock formations of Half Dome and El Capitan, and the verdant coniferous forests, attract millions of visitors annually to Yosemite National Park in the Sierra Nevada.

Sierra Nevada

The Great Basin dominates most of Nevada's topography containing large open basins, punctuated by eroded features such as *buttes* and *mesas*. River flow tends to be seasonal, dependent upon spring showers and winter snow melt.

Wheeler Peak is home to some of the world's oldest trees, bristlecone pines, which live for up to 5000 years.

When the Hoover Dam across the Colorado River was completed in 1936, it created Lake Mead, one of the largest artificial lakes in the world, extending for 115 miles (285 km) upstream.

The San Andreas Fault is a transverse fault which extends for 650 miles (1050 km) through California. Major earthquakes occur when the land either side of the fault moves at different rates. San Francisco was devastated by an earthquake in 1906.

Death Valley

Amargosa Desert

▶ ***Named by migrating*** *settlers in 1849, Death Valley is the driest, hottest place in North America, as well as being the lowest point on land in the western hemisphere, at 282 ft (86 m) below sea level.*

The sparsely populated Mojave Desert receives less than 8 inches (200 mm) of rainfall a year. It is used extensively for weapons-testing and military purposes.

The Salton Sea was created accidentally between 1905 and 1907 when an irrigation channel from the Colorado River broke out of its banks and formed this salty 300 sq mile (777 sq km), land-locked lake.

▲ ***The Sierra Nevada*** *create a 'rainshadow', preventing rain from reaching much of Nevada. Pacific air masses, passing over the mountains, are stripped of their moisture.*

Using the land

California is the USA's leading agricultural producer, although low rainfall makes irrigation essential. The long growing season and abundant sunshine allow many crops to be grown in the fertile Central Valley including grapes, citrus fruits, vegetables and cotton. Almost 17 million acres (6.8 million hectares) of California's forests are used commercially. Nevada's arid climate and poor soil are largely unsuitable for agriculture; 85% of its land is state owned and large areas are used for underground testing of nuclear weapons.

Land use and agricultural distribution

- cattle
- citrus fruits
- fruit
- irrigation
- timber
- vineyards
- major towns
- pasture
- cropland
- forest
- desert

Oregon
Idaho
Nevada
Utah
Reno
Sacramento
San Francisco
California
Las Vegas
Arizona
PACIFIC OCEAN
Los Angeles
San Diego
MEXICO

▲ ***Without considerable irrigation,*** *this fertile valley at Palm Springs would still be part of the Sonoran Desert. California's farmers account for about 80% of the state's total water usage.*

The urban/rural population divide

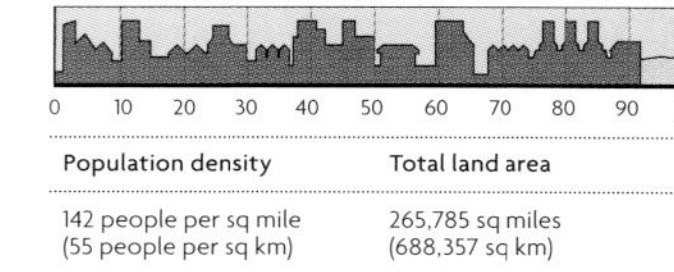
urban 92%
rural 8%
0 10 20 30 40 50 60 70 80 90 100

Population density	Total land area
142 people per sq mile (55 people per sq km)	265,785 sq miles (688,357 sq km)

192

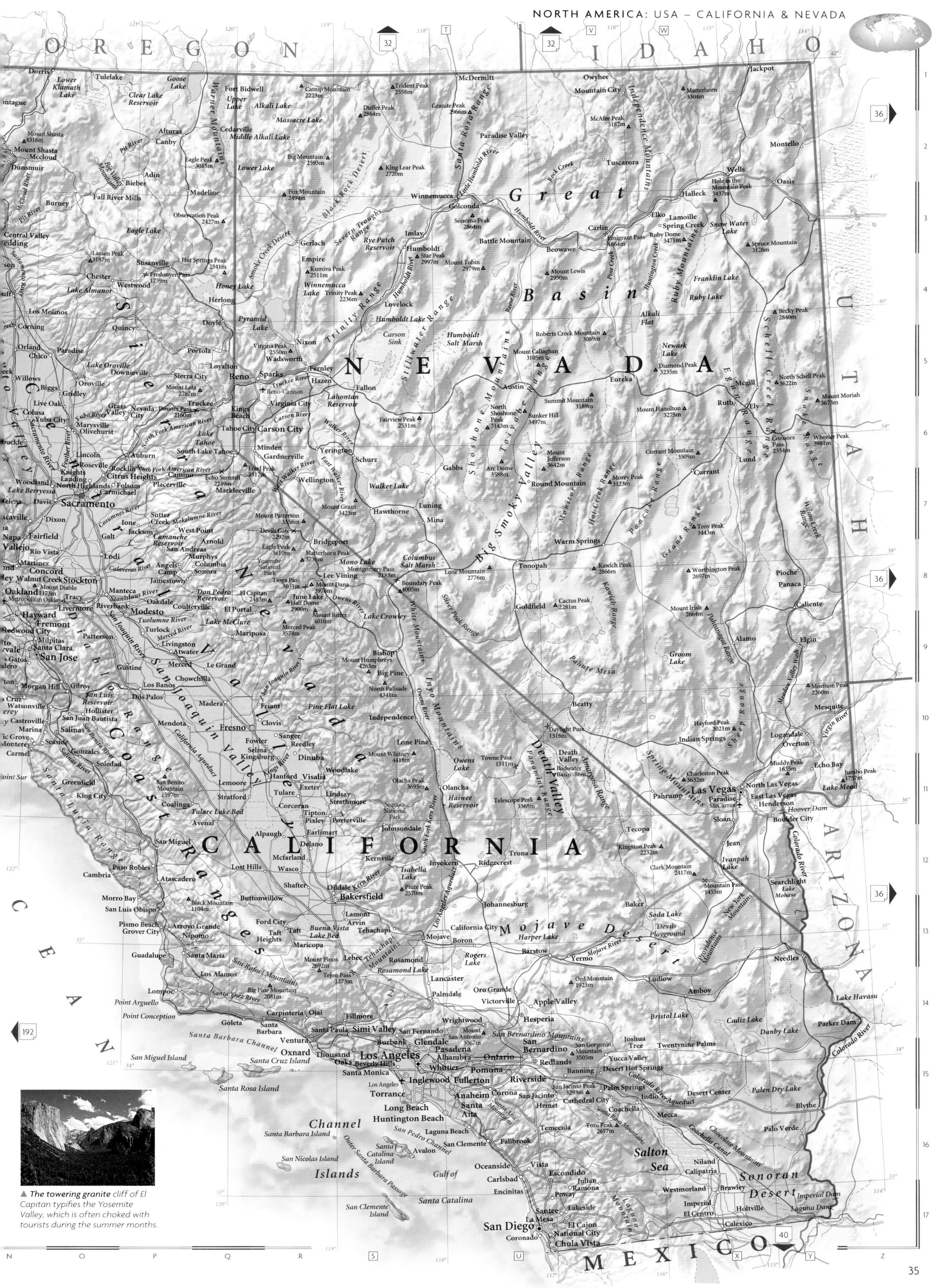
OREGON
IDAHO
UTAH
ARIZONA
MEXICO
NEVADA
CALIFORNIA
Great Basin
OCEAN
Sierra Nevada
Coast Ranges
Diablo Range
Central Valley
San Joaquin Valley
Mojave Desert
Sonoran Desert
Death Valley
Channel Islands
Santa Barbara Channel
Gulf of Santa Catalina
Santa Lucia Range
Salton Sea
Lake Tahoe
Mono Lake
Pyramid Lake
Walker Lake
Lake Mead
Lake Havasu
Owens Lake
Colorado River
Humboldt River
Black Rock Desert
Smoke Creek Desert
Ruby Mountains
Independence Mountains
Santa Rosa Range
Toiyabe Range
Shoshone Mountains
Monitor Range
White Mountains
Inyo Mountains
Spring Mountains
Sheep Range
Snake Range
Schell Creek Range
Egan Range
Carson City
Reno
Sparks
Las Vegas
North Las Vegas
Henderson
Boulder City
Hoover Dam
Elko
Ely
Winnemucca
Tonopah
Goldfield
Austin
Eureka
Fallon
Hawthorne
Beatty
Pahrump
Mesquite
Caliente
Wells
Jackpot
Sacramento
San Francisco
Oakland
San Jose
Stockton
Modesto
Fresno
Bakersfield
Visalia
Los Angeles
Long Beach
Santa Ana
Anaheim
Riverside
San Bernardino
Pasadena
Glendale
Ontario
Palm Springs
Barstow
Lancaster
Palmdale
Victorville
Needles
Blythe
El Centro
Calexico
San Diego
Chula Vista
Oceanside
Santa Barbara
Ventura
Oxnard
San Luis Obispo
Salinas
Monterey
Redding
Chico
Yosemite National Park
Sequoia National Park
Mount Whitney 4418m
Mount Shasta 4316m
Lassen Peak 3187m
Boundary Peak 4005m
Wheeler Peak 3981m
Badwater Basin -86m
Daylight Pass 1316m
Mountain Pass 1455m
Tioga Pass 3031m
Donner Pass 2160m
San Gorgonio Mountain 3505m
Charleston Peak 3632m
Santa Catalina Island
San Clemente Island
San Nicolas Island
Santa Cruz Island
Santa Rosa Island
San Miguel Island
Point Conception
Point Arguello

▲ The towering granite cliff of El Capitan typifies the Yosemite Valley, which is often choked with tourists during the summer months.

USA: SOUTH MOUNTAIN STATES

Arizona, Colorado, New Mexico, Utah

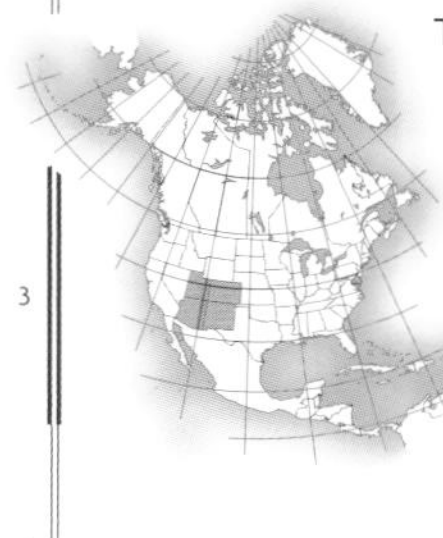

This arid region, characterized by expansive plateaux and spectacular canyons is home to several distinct peoples. The ruins of cliff dwellings built a thousand years ago by the Anasazi people still exist today, and native Americans own one-third of the land in Arizona. Spanish and Mexican conquest and settlement left a hispanic presence which is strongest in New Mexico. The Mormons, who came to the Great Salt Lake seeking religious freedom in 1847, were among the earliest Anglo-American settlers and now make up over 70% of Utah's population. The region's mineral wealth drove rapid development in the 20th century, yet the constraints of a fragile environment, including widespread water shortages, may limit prospects for growth.

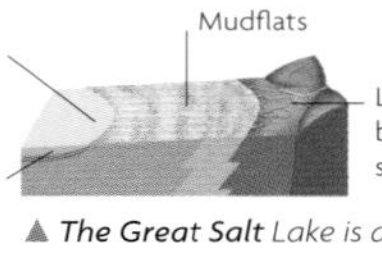

When water evaporates it leaves a salt pan
Mudflats
Lake is fed by seasonal snow melt
Water level of lake varies according to quantity of run-off received from snow melt

▲ *The Great Salt Lake is an ephemeral lake; it can remain dry for extended periods, leaving a pan of evaporated mineral salts in its centre.*

The landscape

The arid, rocky expanse of the Colorado Plateau is dissected by immense canyons of the Colorado River. Desert lies to the north and south and branches of the Rocky Mountains run to the east and west. The Great Salt Lake and Desert lie within the Great Basin, a barren region of parallel mountain ranges which extends into Arizona.

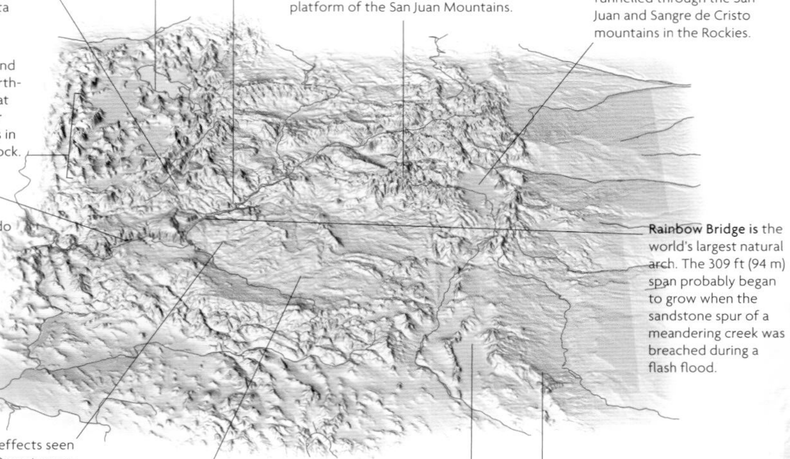

Over 13 million years of weathering has created thousands of spires and pinnacles from the alternating rock strata of Bryce Canyon.
Lake Powell
The Rio Grande has its source in several meltwater streams, which have cut deep valleys into the platform of the San Juan Mountains.
Sand dunes, 600 ft (180 m) high, have been deposited in San Luis Valley, by winds funnelled through the San Juan and Sangre de Cristo mountains in the Rockies.
The parallel basins and ridges, which run north-south along the Great Basin, reflect a major series of block-faults in the underlying bedrock.
Parts of the Grand Canyon, which cuts through the Colorado Plateau, are 16 miles (25 km) wide. The Colorado River has cut down 6262 ft (2000 m), exposing rock strata more than 2 billion years old.
Rainbow Bridge is the world's largest natural arch. The 309 ft (94 m) span probably began to grow when the sandstone spur of a meandering creek was breached during a flash flood.
The striking colour effects seen in the Painted Desert come from minerals such as gypsum and haematite, combined with ambient heat and dust.
Shifting gypsum sands produce a constantly changing land surface, overwhelming plants and any other obstacles in Tularosa Valley.
Petrified Forest
Carlsbad Caverns

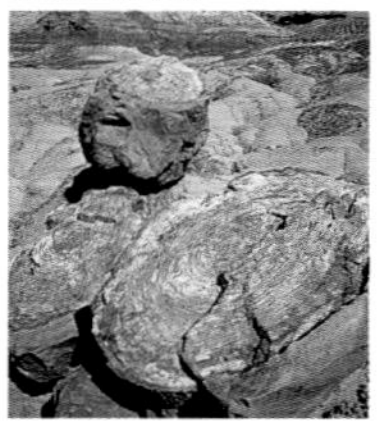

► *In the arid landscape of Petrified Forest National Park in Arizona, the grain of prehistoric trees has been preserved as a fossil imprint in the rocks. The bog-preserved trees were gradually turned to stone by seeping mineral-rich water.*

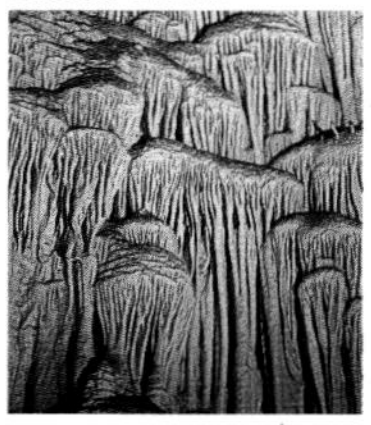

► *The intricate stalactites of Carlsbad Caverns have grown with the seepage of calcium-rich water, over the last 100,000 years. The huge caves are home to around 100,000 Mexican freetail bats.*

Transport and industry

New industries have helped reduce the region's dependence on the extraction of minerals and fossil fuels. Precision manufacture has grown rapidly, particularly in Arizona and Colorado. Salt Lake City and Denver are well-established financial centres and New Mexico, the USA's main producer of uranium, is a prominent region for nuclear research. Colorado is the USA's most important centre for winter sports.

The transport network

Roads	232,434 miles (373,986 km)	Motorways	4059 miles (6515 km)
Railways	8627 miles (13,881 km)	Waterways	none

The Colorado Rockies are crossed by 32 mountain passes, some as high as 12,183 ft (3713 m). The Eisenhower Tunnel west of Denver carries Interstate Highway 70 straight through the Continental Divide.

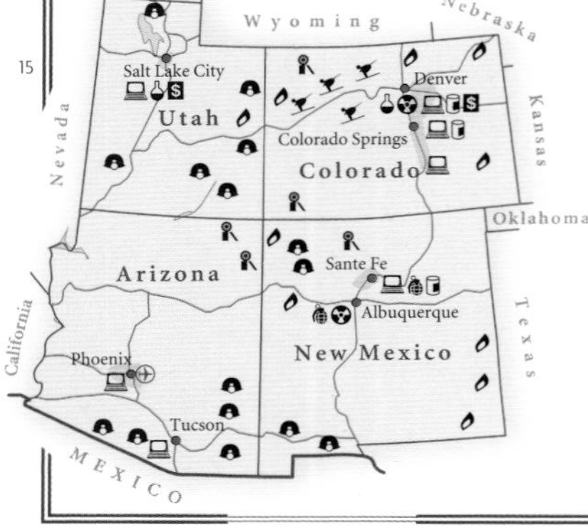

Major industry and infrastructure

- chemicals
- coal
- defence
- finance
- food processing
- hi-tech industry
- oil & gas
- mining
- research & development
- winter sports
- major towns
- international airports
- major roads
- major industrial areas

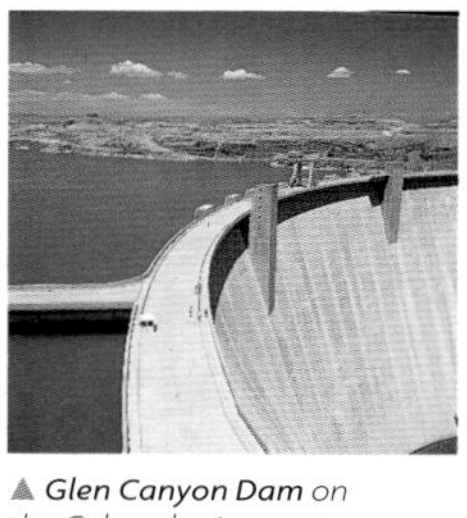

Idaho
Wyoming
Nebraska
Salt Lake City
Denver
Utah
Kansas
Nevada
Colorado Springs
Colorado
Oklahoma
Arizona
Santa Fe
Albuquerque
Texas
California
Phoenix
New Mexico
Tucson
MEXICO

▲ *Glen Canyon Dam on the Colorado river was completed in 1964. It provides hydro-electric power and irrigation water as part of a long-term federal project to harness the river.*

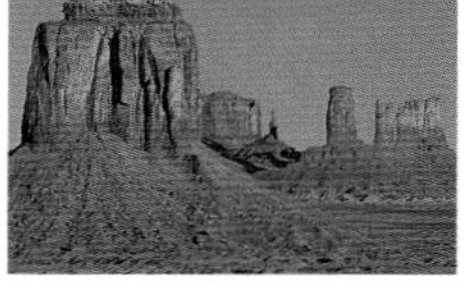

◄ *The flat tablelands (mesas), and the isolated pinnacles (buttes) which rise from the floor of Monument Valley are the resistant remnants of an earlier land surface, gradually cut back by erosion under arid conditions.*

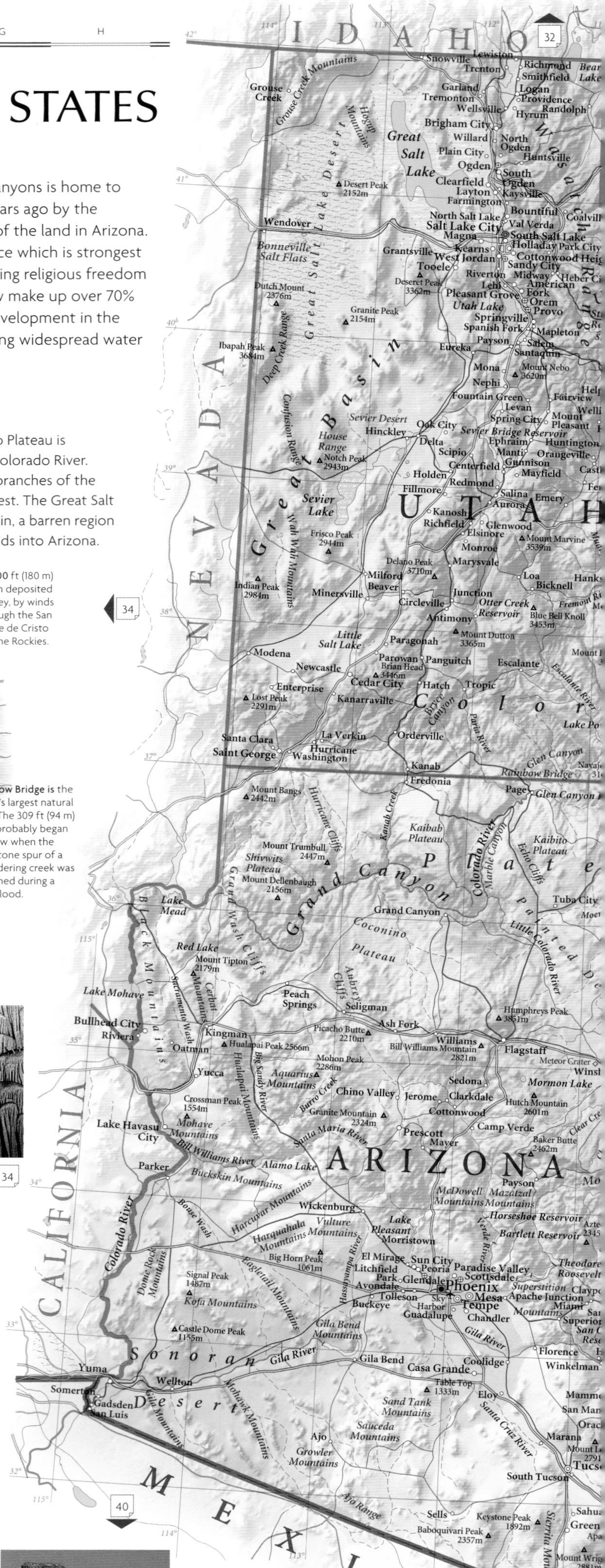

32
34
34
40

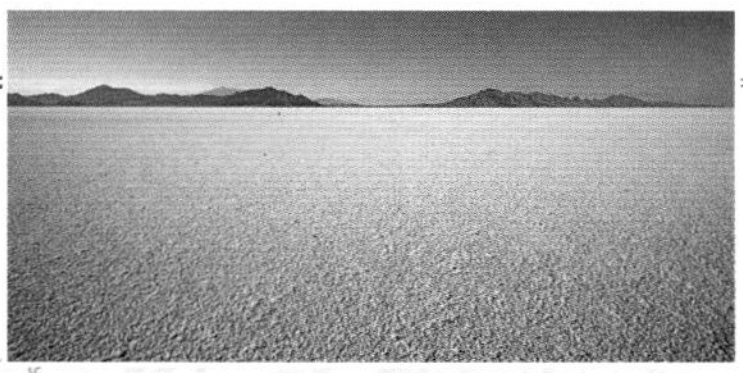

◀ *The Bonneville Salt Flats are in the Great Salt Lake. Sodium chloride (salt), magnesium, and other minerals are commercially extracted from these flats.*

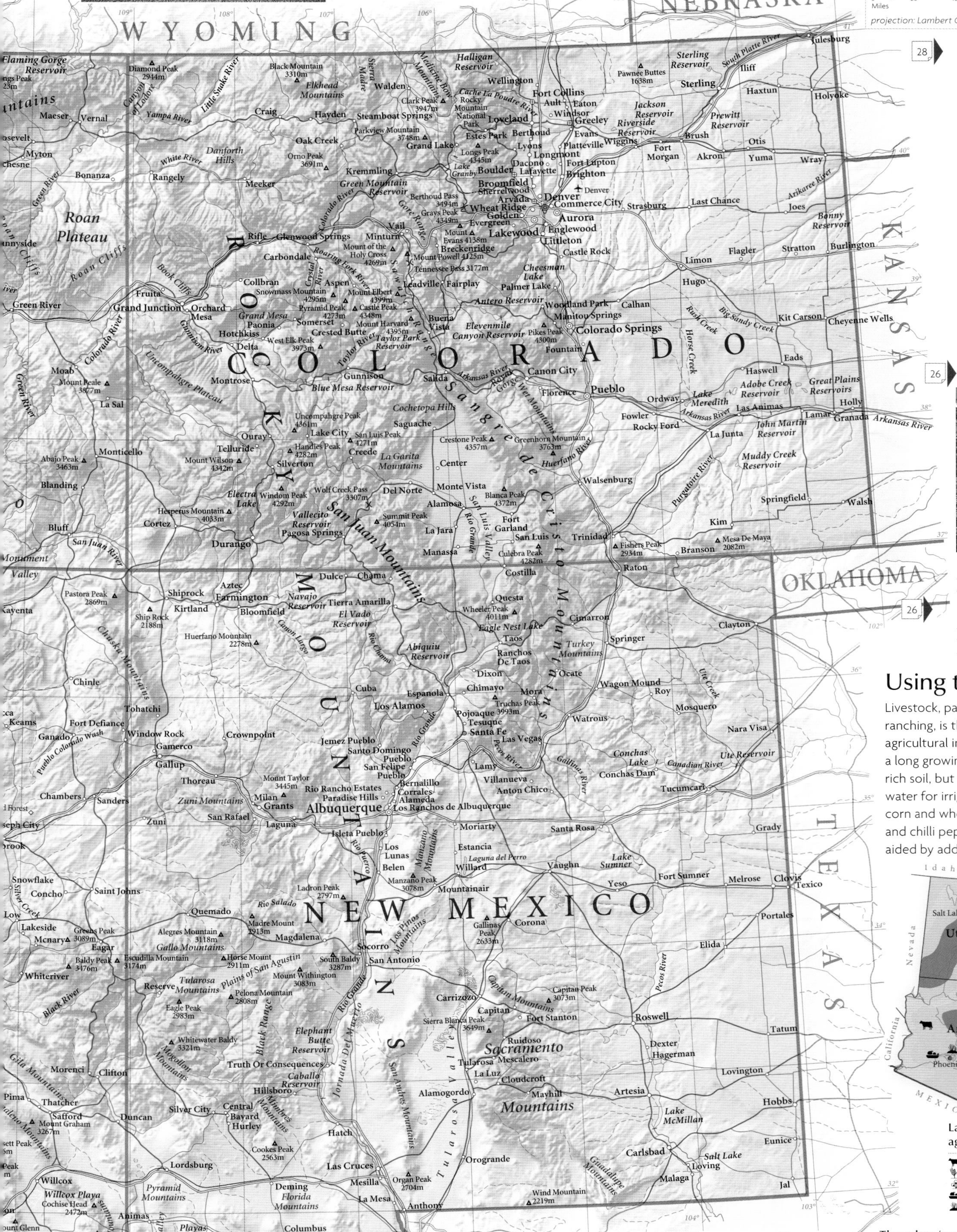

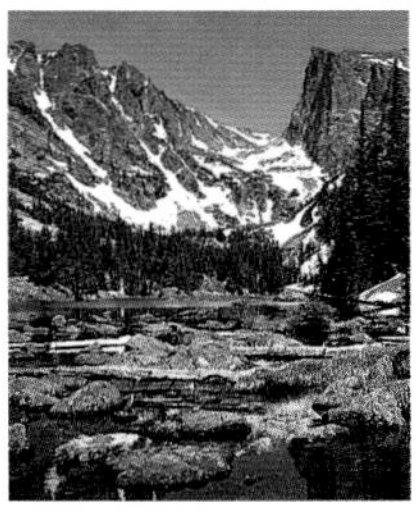

Scale 1:4,000,000

projection: Lambert Conformal Conic

Map key

Population

- 500,000 to 1 million
- 100,000 to 500,000
- 50,000 to 100,000
- 10,000 to 50,000
- below 10,000

Elevation

- 4000m / 13124ft
- 3000m / 9843ft
- 2000m / 6562ft
- 1000m / 3281ft
- 500m / 1640ft
- 250m / 820ft
- 100m / 328ft
- sea level

▲ *A glacially-eroded valley in Rocky Mountain National Park, Colorado. There are 1500 peaks exceeding 10,000 ft (3000 m) within the state, six times the number of major mountains found in the Swiss Alps.*

Using the land

Livestock, particularly cattle-ranching, is the main source of agricultural income. The region has a long growing season and areas of rich soil, but depends heavily on water for irrigation. Crops include corn and wheat in eastern areas, and chilli peppers, fruit and cotton aided by additional irrigation.

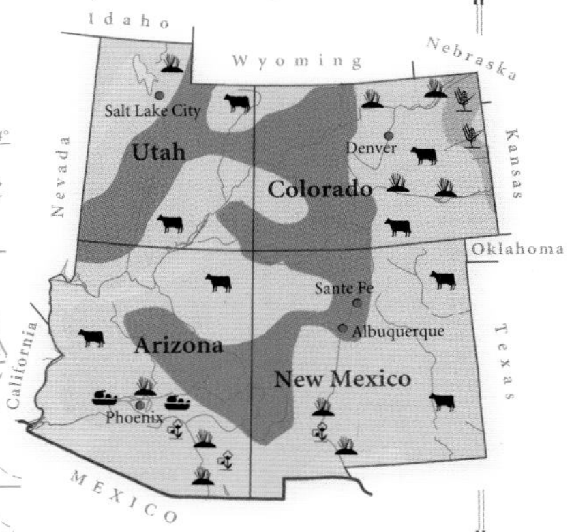

Land use and agricultural distribution

- cattle
- cereals
- cotton
- fruit
- irrigation
- major towns
- pasture
- cropland
- forest
- desert

The urban/rural population divide

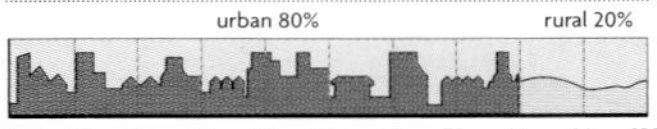

urban 80% / rural 20%

Population density	Total land area
34 people per sq mile (13 people per sq km)	424,852 sq miles (1,089,965 sq km)

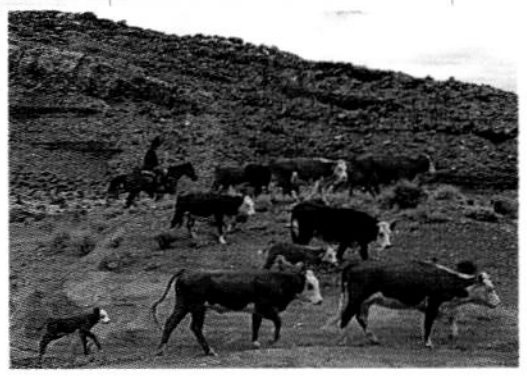

► *Cattle-ranching was introduced to New Mexico via Texas in the 19th century, and has become the principal agricultural land use across this region.*

USA: HAWAII

The 122 islands of the Hawai'ian archipelago – which are part of Polynesia – are the peaks of the world's largest volcanoes. They rise approximately 6 miles (9.7 km) from the floor of the Pacific Ocean. The largest, the island of Hawai'i, remains highly active. Hawaii became the USA's 50th state in 1959. A tradition of receiving immigrant workers is reflected in the islands' ethnic diversity, with peoples drawn from around the rim of the Pacific. Only 9% of the current population are native Polynesians.

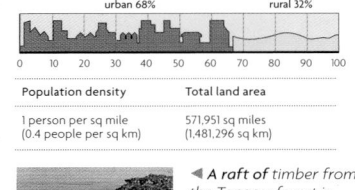

▲ *The island of* Moloka'i *is formed from volcanic rock. Mature sand dunes cover the rocks in coastal areas.*

Transport and industry

Tourism dominates the economy, with over 90% of the population employed in services. The naval base at Pearl Harbor is also a major source of employment. Industry is concentrated on the island of O'ahu and relies mostly on imported materials, while agricultural produce is processed locally.

The transport network

4102 miles (6600 km)	43 miles (69 km)
none	none

Hawaii relies on ocean-surface transportation. Honolulu is the main focus of this network, bringing foreign trade and the markets of mainland USA to Hawaii's outer islands.

◀ *Haleakala's extinct volcanic crater is the world's largest. The giant caldera, containing many secondary cones, is 2000 ft (600 m) deep and 20 miles (32 km) in circumference.*

Major industry and infrastructure

- food processing
- military base
- textiles
- tourism
- major towns
- international airports
- major roads
- major industrial areas

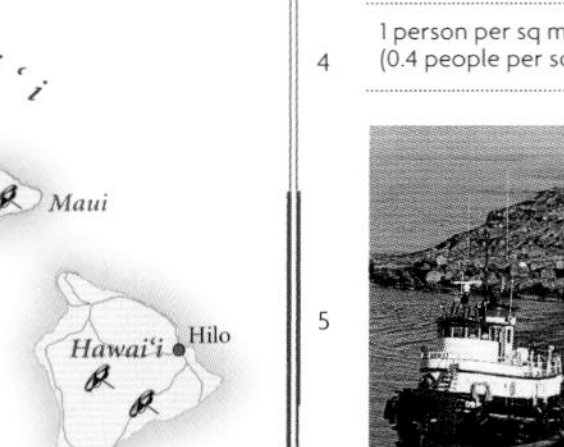

Ni'ihau
Kaua'i
O'ahu
Honolulu
Moloka'i
Lāna'i
Kaho'olawe
Maui
Hawai'i
Hilo
Hawai'i
PACIFIC OCEAN

Using the land and sea

The ice-free coastline of Alaska provides access to salmon fisheries and more than 129 million acres (52.2 million ha) of forest. Most of Alaska is uncultivable, and around 90% of food is imported. Barley, hay and hothouse products are grown around Anchorage, where dairy farming is also concentrated.

The urban/rural population divide

urban 68% | rural 32%

Population density	Total land area
1 person per sq mile (0.4 people per sq km)	571,951 sq miles (1,481,296 sq km)

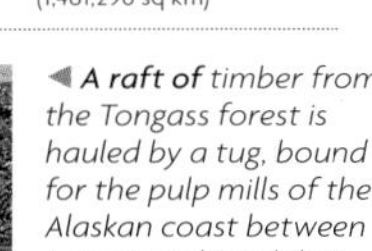

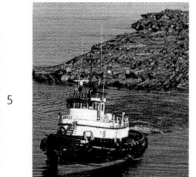

◀ *A raft of timber from the Tongass forest is hauled by a tug, bound for the pulp mills of the Alaskan coast between Juneau and Ketchikan.*

Scale 1:4,000,000

projection: Lambert Conformal Conic

Map key

Population

- 100,000 to 500,000
- 50,000 to 100,000
- 10,000 to 50,000
- below 10,000

Elevation

- 4000m / 13,124ft
- 3000m / 9843ft
- 2000m / 6562ft
- 1000m / 3281ft
- 500m / 1640ft
- 250m / 820ft
- 100m / 328ft
- sea level

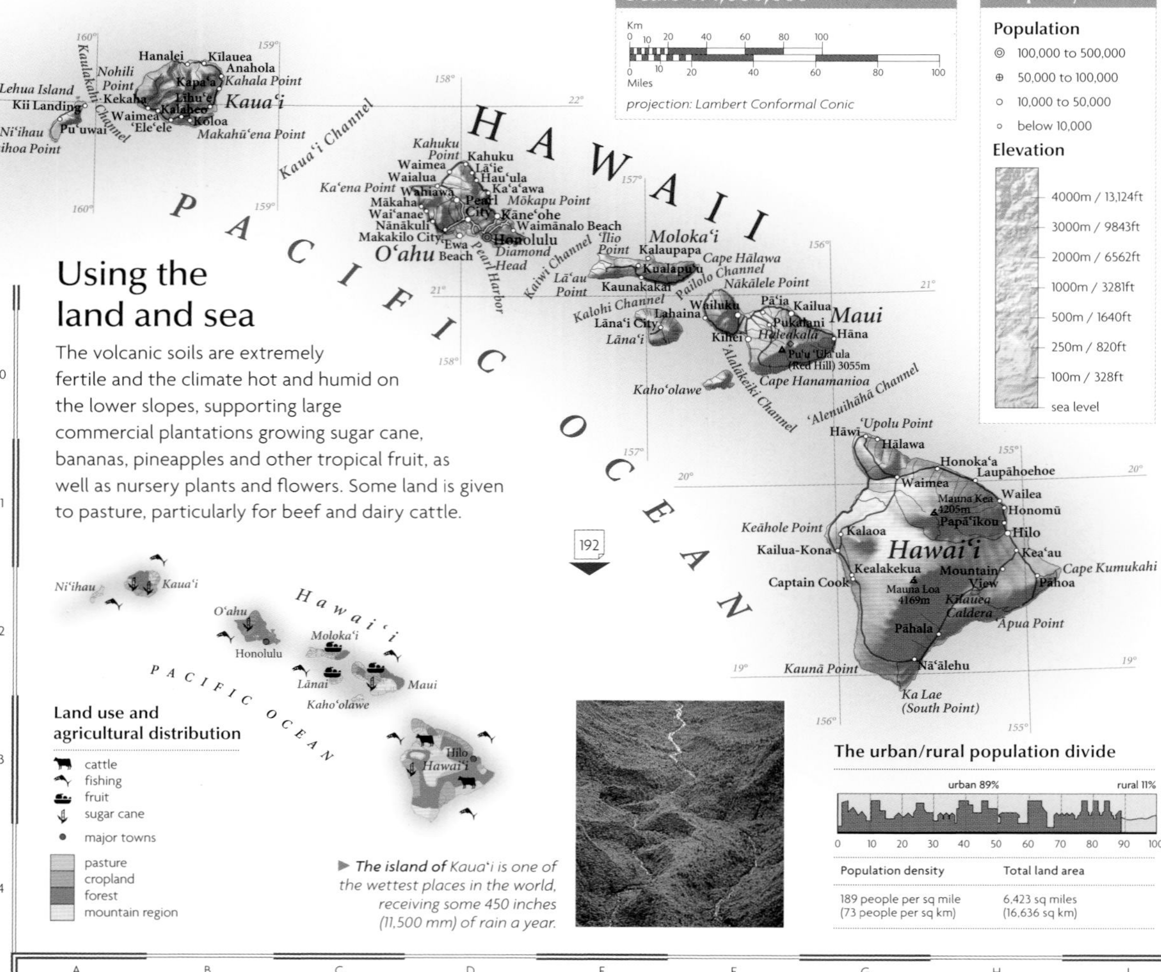

HAWAII
PACIFIC OCEAN
Ni'ihau
Lehua Island
Kii Landing
Kawaihoa Point
Pu'uwai
Kaulakahi Channel
Hanalei
Kīlauea
Anahola
Kahala Point
Nohili Point
Kekaha
Waimea
'Ele'ele
Kapa'a
Līhu'e
Kalaheo
Koloa
Kaua'i
Makahū'ena Point
Kaua'i Channel
Kahuku Point
Kahuku
Lā'ie
Hau'ula
Ka'a'awa
Ka'ena Point
Waimea
Waialua
Wahiawā
Mākaha
Wai'anae
Nānākuli
Makakilo City
Pearl City
Ewa Beach
Mōkapu Point
Kāne'ohe
Waimānalo Beach
Honolulu
Diamond Head
O'ahu
Pearl Harbor
Kaiwi Channel
Moloka'i
'Īlio Point
Kalaupapa
Cape Hālawa
Pailolo Channel
Nākālele Point
Lā'au Point
Kaunakakai
Kalohi Channel
Lahaina
Wailuku
Pā'ia
Kailua
Lāna'i City
Lāna'i
Kīhei
Pukalani
Haleakalā
Maui
Hāna
Pu'u 'Ula'ula (Red Hill) 3055m
Cape Hanamanioa
Kaho'olawe
'Alalākeiki Channel
'Alenuihāhā Channel
'Upolu Point
Hāwī
Hālawa
Honoka'a
Laupāhoehoe
Waimea
Wailea
Mauna Kea 4205m
Honomū
Pāpa'ikou
Hilo
Keāhole Point
Kalaoa
Kailua-Kona
Hawai'i
Kea'au
Cape Kumukahi
Captain Cook
Kealakekua
Mountain View
Pāhoa
Mauna Loa 4169m
Kīlauea Caldera
Pāhala
Apua Point
Kaunā Point
Nā'ālehu
Ka Lae (South Point)

192

Using the land and sea

The volcanic soils are extremely fertile and the climate hot and humid on the lower slopes, supporting large commercial plantations growing sugar cane, bananas, pineapples and other tropical fruit, as well as nursery plants and flowers. Some land is given to pasture, particularly for beef and dairy cattle.

Land use and agricultural distribution

- cattle
- fishing
- fruit
- sugar cane
- major towns
- pasture
- cropland
- forest
- mountain region

► *The island of* Kaua'i *is one of the wettest places in the world, receiving some 450 inches (11,500 mm) of rain a year.*

The urban/rural population divide

urban 89% | rural 11%

Population density	Total land area
189 people per sq mile (73 people per sq km)	6,423 sq miles (16,636 sq km)

CHUKCHI SEA
RUSSIAN FEDERATION
Bering Strait
BERING SEA
Cape Lisburne
Point Hope
Arctic Circle
Shishmaref
Little Diomede Island
Cape Prince of Wales
Port Clarence
Teller
Nome
Cape Douglas
Cape Rodney
Cape Nome
Northwest Cape
Gambell
Savoonga
Saint Lawrence Island
Southwest Cape
Camp Kulowiye
Northeast Cape
Southeast Cape
Emmonak
Alakanuk
Sheldons Point
Mountain Village
Scammon Bay
Hooper Bay
Chevak
Hall Island
Glory of Russia Cape
Saint Matthew Island
Upright Cape
Pinnacle Island
Newtok
Tanunak
Toksook
Nightmute
Mekoryuk
Nunivak Island
Cape Mohican
Roberts Mountain 510m
Chefornak
Kipnuk
Kwigillingok
Cape Mendenhall
Kuskokwim Bay
Saint Paul Island
Saint Paul
Pribilof Islands
Saint George Island
Saint George

122

192

Map key

Population

- 100,000 to 500,000
- 50,000 to 100,000
- 10,000 to 50,000
- below 10,000

Elevation

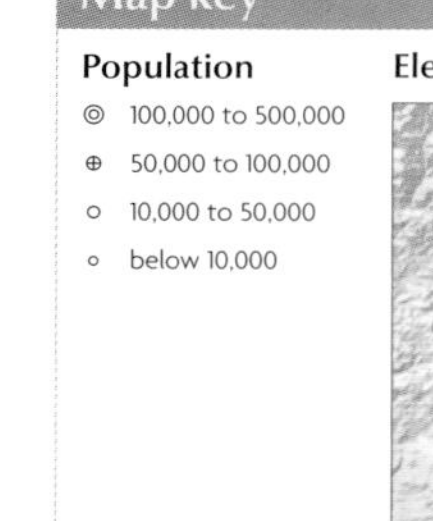

- 4000m / 13,124ft
- 3000m / 9843ft
- 2000m / 6562ft
- 1000m / 3281ft
- 500m / 1640ft
- 250m / 820ft
- 100m / 328ft
- sea level

Scale 1:9,000,000

projection: Lambert Conformal Conic

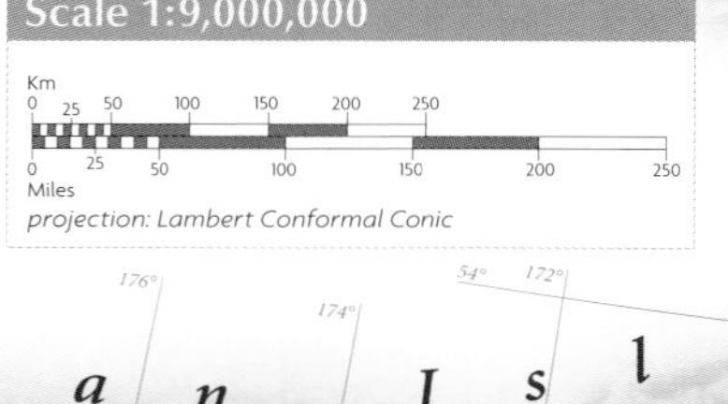

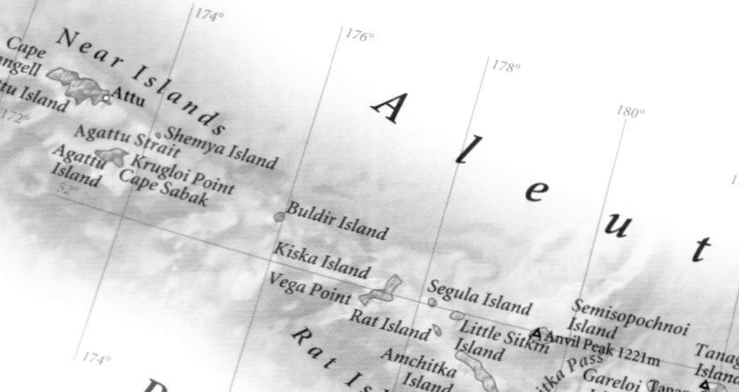

Aleutian Islands
PACIFIC OCEAN
Near Islands
Cape Wrangell
Attu Island
Attu
Shemya Island
Agattu Strait
Agattu Island
Krugloi Point
Cape Sabak
Buldir Island
Kiska Island
Vega Point
Rat Island
Rat Islands
Segula Island
Little Sitkin Island
Amchitka Island
Semisopochnoi Island
Anvil Peak 1221m
Amchitka Pass
Gareloi Island
Tanaga Island
Tanaga Volcano 1806m
Kanaga Island
Kanaga Volcano 1307m
Great Sitkin Island
Cape Sasmik
Adak Island
Kagalaska Island
Delarof Islands
Andreanof Islands
Atka Island
Atka
Seguam Island
Seguam Pass
Amlia Island
Amukta Pass

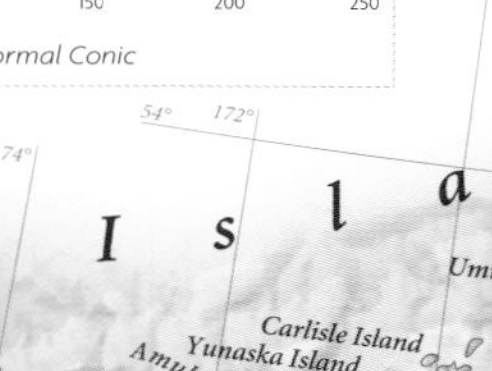

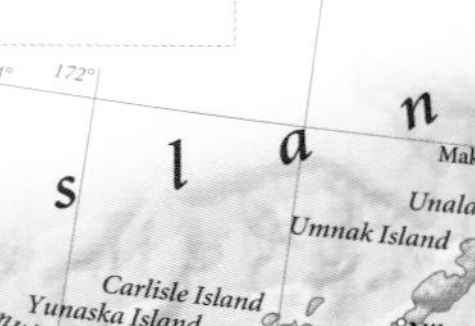

Yunaska Island
Carlisle Island
Herbert Island
Amukta Island
Islands of Four Mountains
Umnak Island
Nikolski
Fox Islands
Unalaska Island
Dutch Harbor
Makushin Volcano 2036m
Akutan Island
Akutan
Akun Island
Unimak Pass
Unimak Island
Shishaldin Volcano 2857m
Pogromni Volcano 2002m
Tigalda Island
Avatanak Island
Krenitzin Islands

USA: ALASKA

Almost 650,000 people live in Alaska, a wilderness of ice, forest, mountains and plains, purchased from Russia in 1867 and twice the size of Texas. The discovery of large oil reserves has brought prosperity to the USA's 'last frontier', while advancing the need to preserve natural habitats and the traditional livelihoods of indigenous peoples such as the Aleuts and Inupiaq.

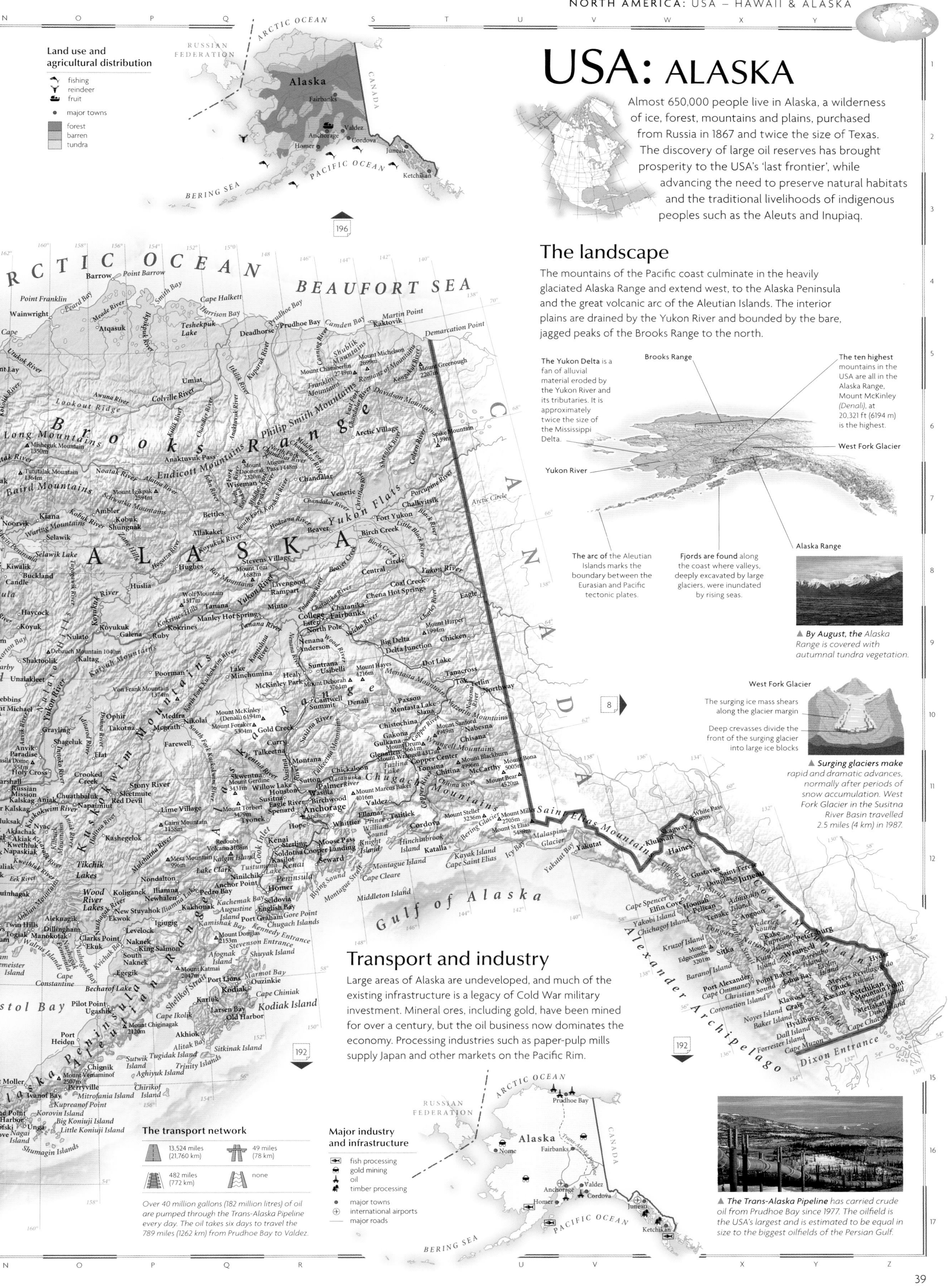

Land use and agricultural distribution
fishing
reindeer
fruit
major towns
forest
barren
tundra
ARCTIC OCEAN
RUSSIAN FEDERATION
CANADA
Alaska
Fairbanks
Anchorage
Valdez
Cordova
Homer
Juneau
Ketchikan
PACIFIC OCEAN
BERING SEA
196
ARCTIC OCEAN
BEAUFORT SEA
Brooks Range
ALASKA
CANADA
Gulf of Alaska
Alexander Archipelago
Dixon Entrance
192
8
The Yukon Delta is a fan of alluvial material eroded by the Yukon River and its tributaries. It is approximately twice the size of the Mississippi Delta.
Brooks Range
The ten highest mountains in the USA are all in the Alaska Range, Mount McKinley (Denali), at 20,321 ft (6194 m) is the highest.
West Fork Glacier
Yukon River
The arc of the Aleutian Islands marks the boundary between the Eurasian and Pacific tectonic plates.
Fjords are found along the coast where valleys, deeply excavated by large glaciers, were inundated by rising seas.
Alaska Range
West Fork Glacier
The surging ice mass shears along the glacier margin
Deep crevasses divide the front of the surging glacier into large ice blocks
The transport network
13,524 miles (21,760 km)
49 miles (78 km)
482 miles (772 km)
none
Major industry and infrastructure
fish processing
gold mining
oil
timber processing
major towns
international airports
major roads
Prudhoe Bay
Trans-Alaska Pipeline
Nome

The landscape

The mountains of the Pacific coast culminate in the heavily glaciated Alaska Range and extend west, to the Alaska Peninsula and the great volcanic arc of the Aleutian Islands. The interior plains are drained by the Yukon River and bounded by the bare, jagged peaks of the Brooks Range to the north.

▲ *By August, the Alaska Range is covered with autumnal tundra vegetation.*

▲ *Surging glaciers make rapid and dramatic advances, normally after periods of snow accumulation. West Fork Glacier in the Susitna River Basin travelled 2.5 miles (4 km) in 1987.*

Transport and industry

Large areas of Alaska are undeveloped, and much of the existing infrastructure is a legacy of Cold War military investment. Mineral ores, including gold, have been mined for over a century, but the oil business now dominates the economy. Processing industries such as paper-pulp mills supply Japan and other markets on the Pacific Rim.

Over 40 million gallons (182 million litres) of oil are pumped through the Trans-Alaska Pipeline every day. The oil takes six days to travel the 789 miles (1262 km) from Prudhoe Bay to Valdez.

▲ *The Trans-Alaska Pipeline has carried crude oil from Prudhoe Bay since 1977. The oilfield is the USA's largest and is estimated to be equal in size to the biggest oilfields of the Persian Gulf.*

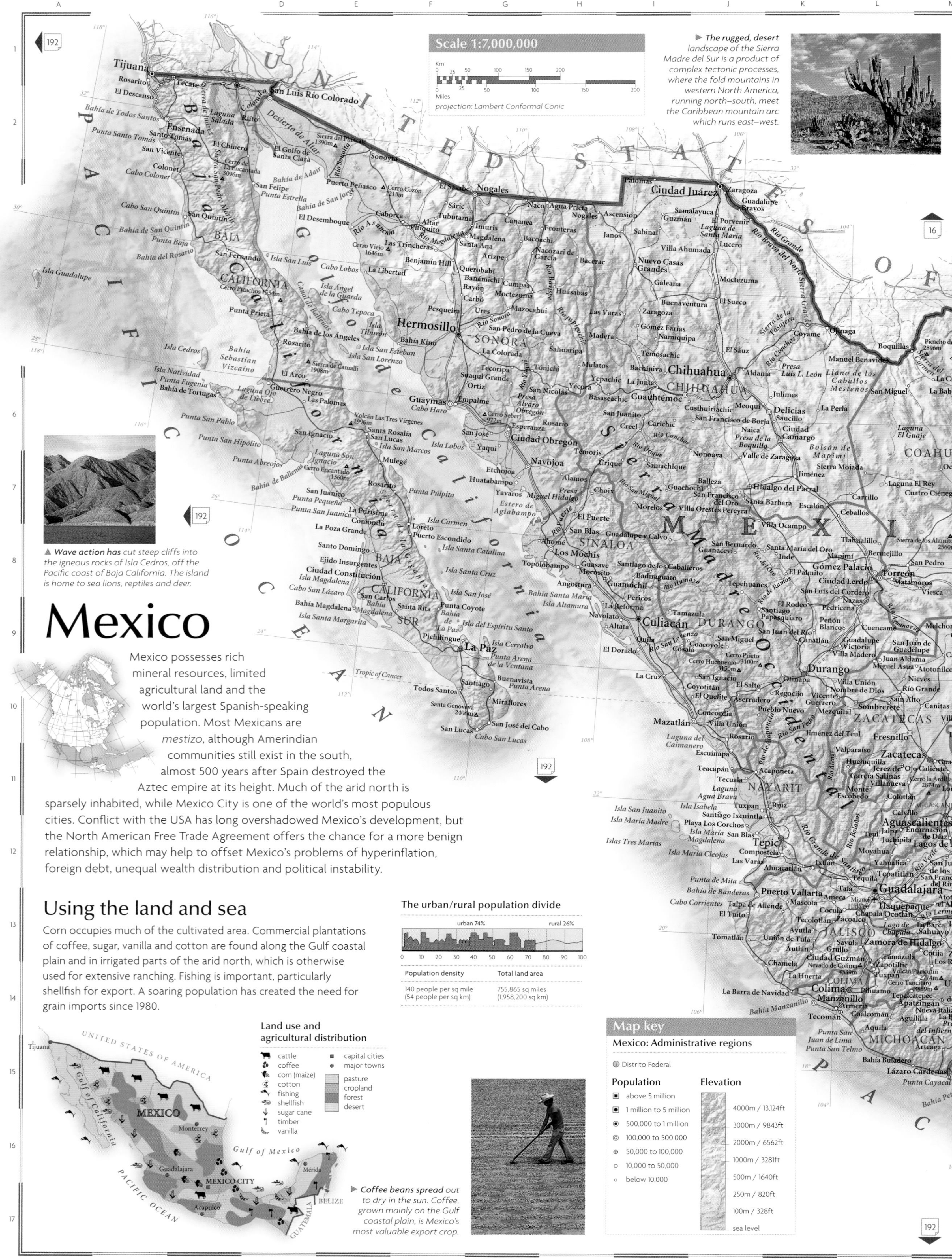

Scale 1:7,000,000
Km 0 25 50 100 150 200
Miles 0 25 50 100 150 200
projection: Lambert Conformal Conic
UNITED STATES OF AMERICA
PACIFIC OCEAN
Golfo de California
Sierra Madre Occidental
MEXICO
BAJA CALIFORNIA
BAJA CALIFORNIA SUR
SONORA
CHIHUAHUA
SINALOA
DURANGO
NAYARIT
ZACATECAS
JALISCO
COLIMA
MICHOACÁN
Tropic of Cancer

▶ **The rugged, desert** landscape of the Sierra Madre del Sur is a product of complex tectonic processes, where the fold mountains in western North America, running north–south, meet the Caribbean mountain arc which runs east–west.

▲ **Wave action has** cut steep cliffs into the igneous rocks of Isla Cedros, off the Pacific coast of Baja California. The island is home to sea lions, reptiles and deer.

Mexico

Mexico possesses rich mineral resources, limited agricultural land and the world's largest Spanish-speaking population. Most Mexicans are *mestizo*, although Amerindian communities still exist in the south, almost 500 years after Spain destroyed the Aztec empire at its height. Much of the arid north is sparsely inhabited, while Mexico City is one of the world's most populous cities. Conflict with the USA has long overshadowed Mexico's development, but the North American Free Trade Agreement offers the chance for a more benign relationship, which may help to offset Mexico's problems of hyperinflation, foreign debt, unequal wealth distribution and political instability.

Using the land and sea

Corn occupies much of the cultivated area. Commercial plantations of coffee, sugar, vanilla and cotton are found along the Gulf coastal plain and in irrigated parts of the arid north, which is otherwise used for extensive ranching. Fishing is important, particularly shellfish for export. A soaring population has created the need for grain imports since 1980.

The urban/rural population divide

urban 74% | rural 26%

0 10 20 30 40 50 60 70 80 90 100

Population density	Total land area
140 people per sq mile (54 people per sq km)	755,865 sq miles (1,958,200 sq km)

Land use and agricultural distribution

cattle
coffee
corn (maize)
cotton
fishing
shellfish
sugar cane
timber
vanilla
capital cities
major towns
pasture
cropland
forest
desert

UNITED STATES OF AMERICA
Tijuana
Gulf of California
MEXICO
Monterrey
Gulf of Mexico
Mérida
Guadalajara
MEXICO CITY
Acapulco
PACIFIC OCEAN
BELIZE
GUATEMALA

▶ **Coffee beans spread** out to dry in the sun. Coffee, grown mainly on the Gulf coastal plain, is Mexico's most valuable export crop.

Map key

Mexico: Administrative regions

① Distrito Federal

Population

- above 5 million
- 1 million to 5 million
- 500,000 to 1 million
- 100,000 to 500,000
- 50,000 to 100,000
- 10,000 to 50,000
- below 10,000

Elevation

- 4000m / 13,124ft
- 3000m / 9843ft
- 2000m / 6562ft
- 1000m / 3281ft
- 500m / 1640ft
- 250m / 820ft
- 100m / 328ft
- sea level

Sierra Madre Oriental
Rio Grande
Sierra Madre Occidental
Río Balsas
Popocatépetl
Formation of the Gulf of California
Direction of plate movement
Baja California
Transform fault
Edge of continental crust
Gulf of California
Spreading oceanic ridge
UNITED STATES OF AMERICA
MEXICO
Gulf of Mexico
PACIFIC OCEAN
BELIZE
GUATEMALA
Major industry and infrastructure
brewing
car manufacture
chemicals
electronics
fish processing
maquiladoras
mining
oil & gas
textiles
capital cities
major towns
international airports
major roads
major industrial areas
The transport network
67,564 miles (108,746 km)
3994 miles (6429 km)
16,561 miles (26,656 km)
1801 miles (2900 km)
Yucatan Channel
Bahía de Campeche
Yucatan Peninsula
Istmo de Tehuantepec
Golfo de Tehuantepec
Sierra Madre del Sur
Sierra Madre Oriental
PACIFIC OCEAN

The landscape

The great central plateau rises gently southwards from the Rio Grande, isolated from the coastal plains by the Sierra Madre Oriental and Occidental. The two ranges converge from east and west respectively, culminating in high volcanic peaks around Mexico City. Further ranges of the Sierra Madre rise to the south of the Balsas basin, skirted by the low-lying Isthmus of Tehuantepec *(Istmo de Tehuantepec)* and Yucatan Peninsula.

The long, narrow, extremely arid peninsula of Baja (lower) California is an elongated granite block, separated from the mainland by the flooded rift valley of the Gulf of California *(Golfo de California)*.

Wave action has constructed sand bars which shelter lagoons along the shore of the Gulf coastal plain.

The dormant cone of Volcán Pico de Orizaba is, at 18,700 ft (5700 m), the highest peak in Mexico. In North America, only Mount McKinley and Mount Logan are taller.

▲ ***Tropical rainforest abounds*** *in the Yucatan Peninsula, a broad, low limestone shelf. Rivers are rare due to the porous nature of limestone, so the forest is mostly fed by streams and underground water.*

The heavily-forested Isthmus of Tehuantepec *(Istmo de Tehuantepec)* is a graben; a low-lying trough created by downward movement of the bedrock between two fault lines.

▲ ***The Gulf of California*** (Golfo de California) *began to open out about 4 million years ago as a result of rifting and plate displacement along transform faults.*

▲ ***Popocatépetl is a*** *dormant volcano, part of the Pacific 'Ring of Fire'. The crater is over half a mile (1 km) wide.*

The unstable, earthquake-prone, upland basin around Mexico City was once a region of shallow lakes. Flood control measures and domestic consumption over the last four centuries have caused the virtual disappearance of this surface water.

The highlands of Chiapas are a series of *horsts*, blocks of land thrust upwards between two fault lines. Volcanic cones have developed where lava has flowed out from the faults.

16

Transport and industry

Oil and gas on the Gulf coast are Mexico's main sources of export income. Metal mining has declined but the country remains a leading global producer of silver. Manufacturing is heavily concentrated around the Mexico City metropolitan area, while the duty-free movement of goods in the USA border region, under the *Maquiladora* (twin plant) scheme, has created new hi-tech and service growth centres.

▲ ***A stone figure*** *reclines by the Temple of Warriors, within the Mayan city of Chichén-Itzá. The Maya civilization flourished across the Yucatan Peninsula between 200 and 900 AD.*

Fast, modern highways or autopistas now link Mexico City with Toluca, Puebla and other satellite cities, yet distant centres like Chihuahua are still served by narrow roads and an outdated rail network.

58
42
42

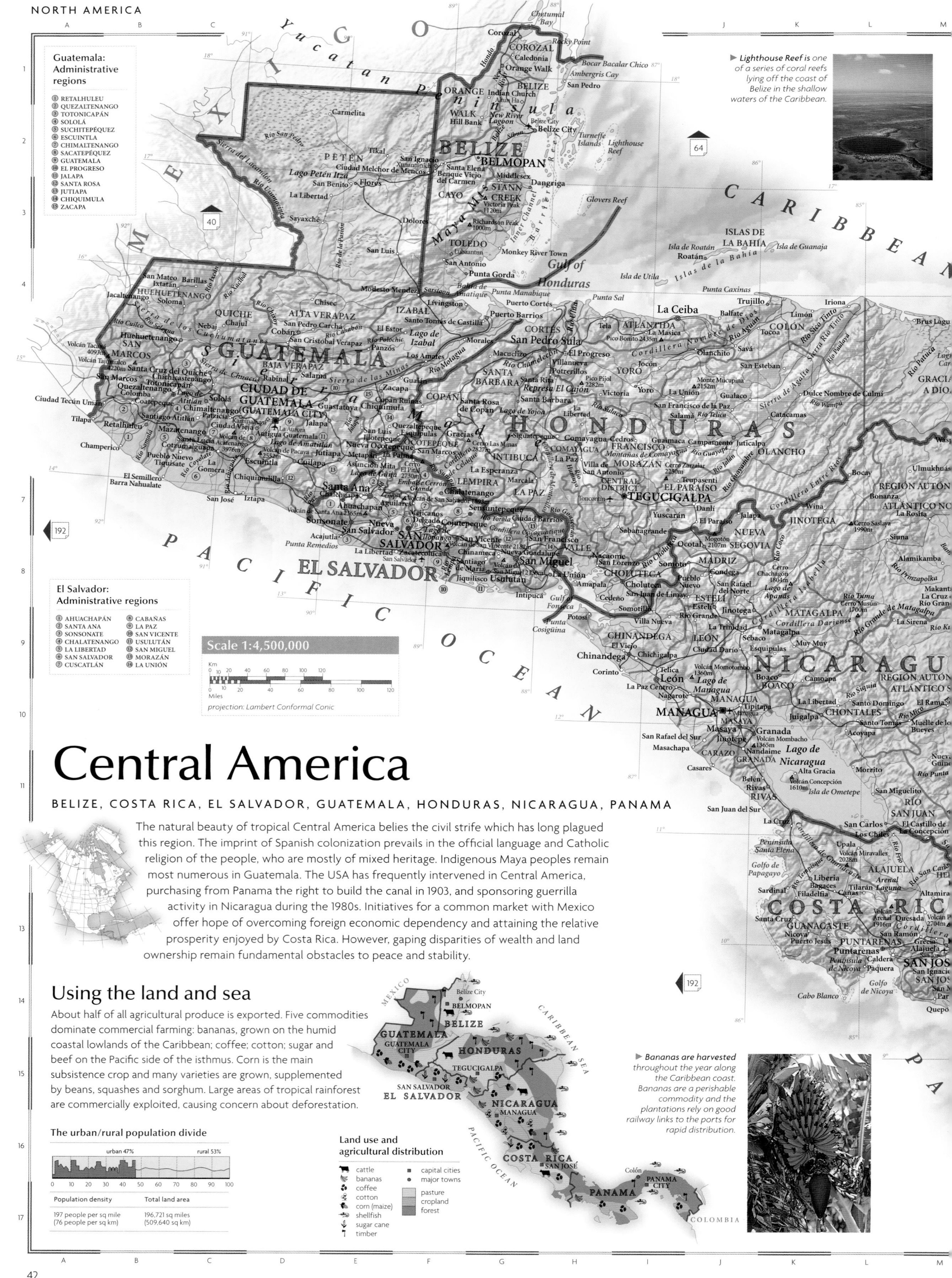

Guatemala: Administrative regions
1 RETALHULEU
2 QUEZALTENANGO
3 TOTONICAPÁN
4 SOLOLÁ
5 SUCHITEPÉQUEZ
6 ESCUINTLA
7 CHIMALTENANGO
8 SACATEPÉQUEZ
9 GUATEMALA
10 EL PROGRESO
11 JALAPA
12 SANTA ROSA
13 JUTIAPA
14 CHIQUIMULA
15 ZACAPA
El Salvador: Administrative regions
1 AHUACHAPÁN
2 SANTA ANA
3 SONSONATE
4 CHALATENANGO
5 LA LIBERTAD
6 SAN SALVADOR
7 CUSCATLÁN
8 CABAÑAS
9 LA PAZ
10 SAN VICENTE
11 USULUTÁN
12 SAN MIGUEL
13 MORAZÁN
14 LA UNIÓN
Scale 1:4,500,000
projection: Lambert Conformal Conic
MEXICO
Yucatan Peninsula
BELIZE
BELMOPAN
Belize City
GUATEMALA
CIUDAD DE GUATEMALA (GUATEMALA CITY)
HONDURAS
TEGUCIGALPA
EL SALVADOR
SAN SALVADOR
NICARAGUA
MANAGUA
COSTA RICA
SAN JOSÉ
Gulf of Honduras
CARIBBEAN
PACIFIC OCEAN
Lago de Nicaragua
Lighthouse Reef
Glovers Reef
La Ceiba
San Pedro Sula
León
Granada
Lago Petén Itzá
Gulf of Fonseca

► **Lighthouse Reef** *is one of a series of coral reefs lying off the coast of Belize in the shallow waters of the Caribbean.*

Central America

BELIZE, COSTA RICA, EL SALVADOR, GUATEMALA, HONDURAS, NICARAGUA, PANAMA

The natural beauty of tropical Central America belies the civil strife which has long plagued this region. The imprint of Spanish colonization prevails in the official language and Catholic religion of the people, who are mostly of mixed heritage. Indigenous Maya peoples remain most numerous in Guatemala. The USA has frequently intervened in Central America, purchasing from Panama the right to build the canal in 1903, and sponsoring guerrilla activity in Nicaragua during the 1980s. Initiatives for a common market with Mexico offer hope of overcoming foreign economic dependency and attaining the relative prosperity enjoyed by Costa Rica. However, gaping disparities of wealth and land ownership remain fundamental obstacles to peace and stability.

Using the land and sea

About half of all agricultural produce is exported. Five commodities dominate commercial farming: bananas, grown on the humid coastal lowlands of the Caribbean; coffee; cotton; sugar and beef on the Pacific side of the isthmus. Corn is the main subsistence crop and many varieties are grown, supplemented by beans, squashes and sorghum. Large areas of tropical rainforest are commercially exploited, causing concern about deforestation.

The urban/rural population divide

urban 47% | rural 53%

Population density	Total land area
197 people per sq mile (76 people per sq km)	196,721 sq miles (509,640 sq km)

Land use and agricultural distribution

cattle, bananas, coffee, cotton, corn (maize), shellfish, sugar cane, timber; capital cities, major towns; pasture, cropland, forest

► *Bananas are harvested throughout the year along the Caribbean coast. Bananas are a perishable commodity and the plantations rely on good railway links to the ports for rapid distribution.*

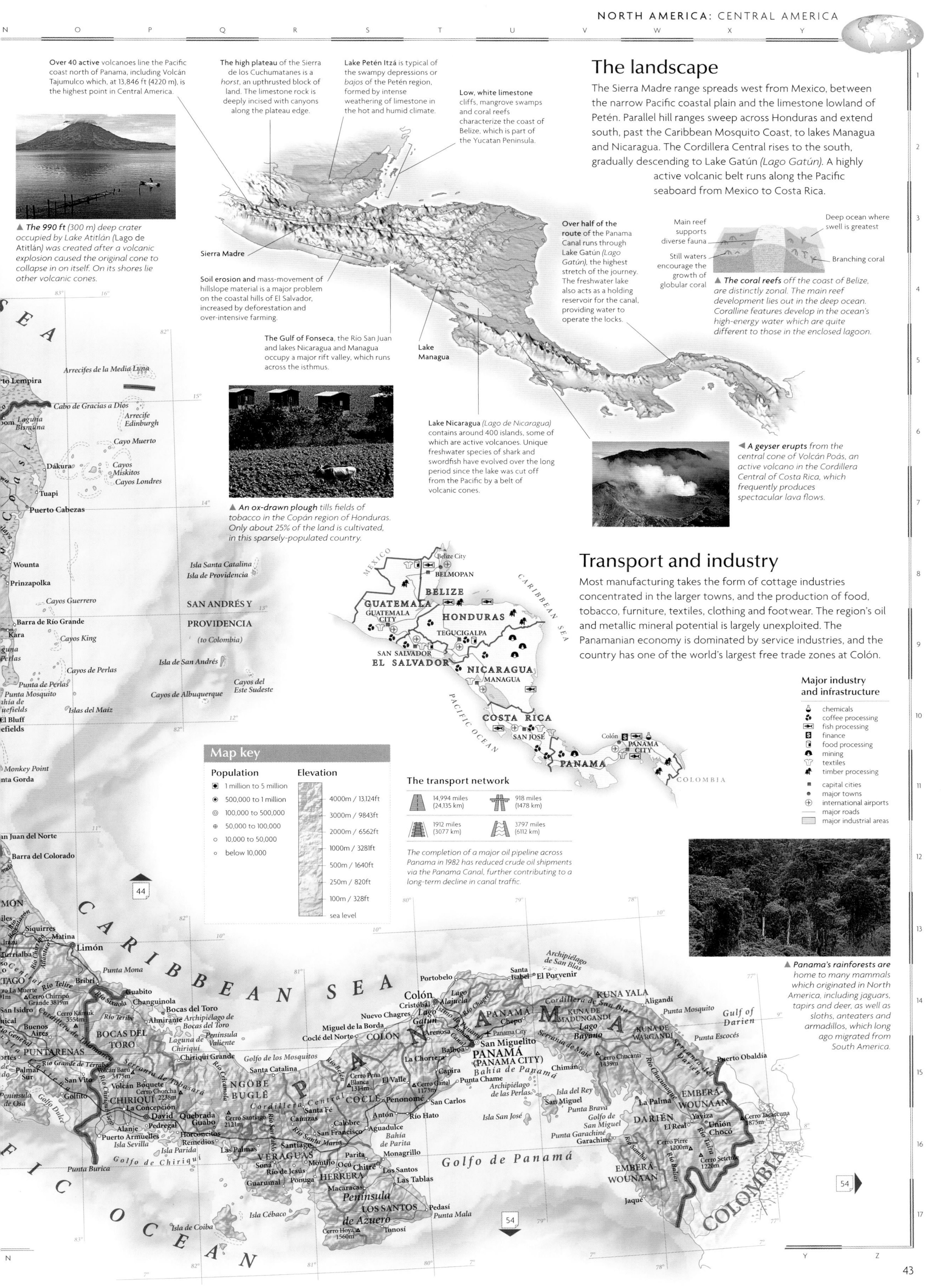

The landscape

The Sierra Madre range spreads west from Mexico, between the narrow Pacific coastal plain and the limestone lowland of Petén. Parallel hill ranges sweep across Honduras and extend south, past the Caribbean Mosquito Coast, to lakes Managua and Nicaragua. The Cordillera Central rises to the south, gradually descending to Lake Gatún *(Lago Gatún)*. A highly active volcanic belt runs along the Pacific seaboard from Mexico to Costa Rica.

Over 40 active volcanoes line the Pacific coast north of Panama, including Volcán Tajumulco which, at 13,846 ft (4220 m), is the highest point in Central America.

The high plateau of the Sierra de los Cuchumatanes is a *horst*, an upthrusted block of land. The limestone rock is deeply incised with canyons along the plateau edge.

Lake Petén Itzá is typical of the swampy depressions or *bajos* of the Petén region, formed by intense weathering of limestone in the hot and humid climate.

Low, white limestone cliffs, mangrove swamps and coral reefs characterize the coast of Belize, which is part of the Yucatan Peninsula.

▲ *The 990 ft (300 m) deep crater occupied by Lake Atitlán (Lago de Atitlán) was created after a volcanic explosion caused the original cone to collapse in on itself. On its shores lie other volcanic cones.*

Sierra Madre

Soil erosion and mass-movement of hillslope material is a major problem on the coastal hills of El Salvador, increased by deforestation and over-intensive farming.

The Gulf of Fonseca, the Río San Juan and lakes Nicaragua and Managua occupy a major rift valley, which runs across the isthmus.

Lake Managua

Over half of the route of the Panama Canal runs through Lake Gatún *(Lago Gatún)*, the highest stretch of the journey. The freshwater lake also acts as a holding reservoir for the canal, providing water to operate the locks.

Main reef supports diverse fauna

Still waters encourage the growth of globular coral

Deep ocean where swell is greatest

Branching coral

▲ *The coral reefs off the coast of Belize, are distinctly zonal. The main reef development lies out in the deep ocean. Coralline features develop in the ocean's high-energy water which are quite different to those in the enclosed lagoon.*

▲ *An ox-drawn plough tills fields of tobacco in the Copán region of Honduras. Only about 25% of the land is cultivated, in this sparsely-populated country.*

Lake Nicaragua *(Lago de Nicaragua)* contains around 400 islands, some of which are active volcanoes. Unique freshwater species of shark and swordfish have evolved over the long period since the lake was cut off from the Pacific by a belt of volcanic cones.

◀ *A geyser erupts from the central cone of Volcán Poás, an active volcano in the Cordillera Central of Costa Rica, which frequently produces spectacular lava flows.*

Transport and industry

Most manufacturing takes the form of cottage industries concentrated in the larger towns, and the production of food, tobacco, furniture, textiles, clothing and footwear. The region's oil and metallic mineral potential is largely unexploited. The Panamanian economy is dominated by service industries, and the country has one of the world's largest free trade zones at Colón.

Major industry and infrastructure

- chemicals
- coffee processing
- fish processing
- finance
- food processing
- mining
- textiles
- timber processing
- capital cities
- major towns
- international airports
- major roads
- major industrial areas

The transport network

14,994 miles (24,135 km)	918 miles (1478 km)	1912 miles (3077 km)	3797 miles (6112 km)

The completion of a major oil pipeline across Panama in 1982 has reduced crude oil shipments via the Panama Canal, further contributing to a long-term decline in canal traffic.

▲ *Panama's rainforests are home to many mammals which originated in North America, including jaguars, tapirs and deer, as well as sloths, anteaters and armadillos, which long ago migrated from South America.*

Map key

Population	Elevation
1 million to 5 million	4000m / 13,124ft
500,000 to 1 million	3000m / 9843ft
100,000 to 500,000	2000m / 6562ft
50,000 to 100,000	1000m / 3281ft
10,000 to 50,000	500m / 1640ft
below 10,000	250m / 820ft
	100m / 328ft
	sea level

44

54

54

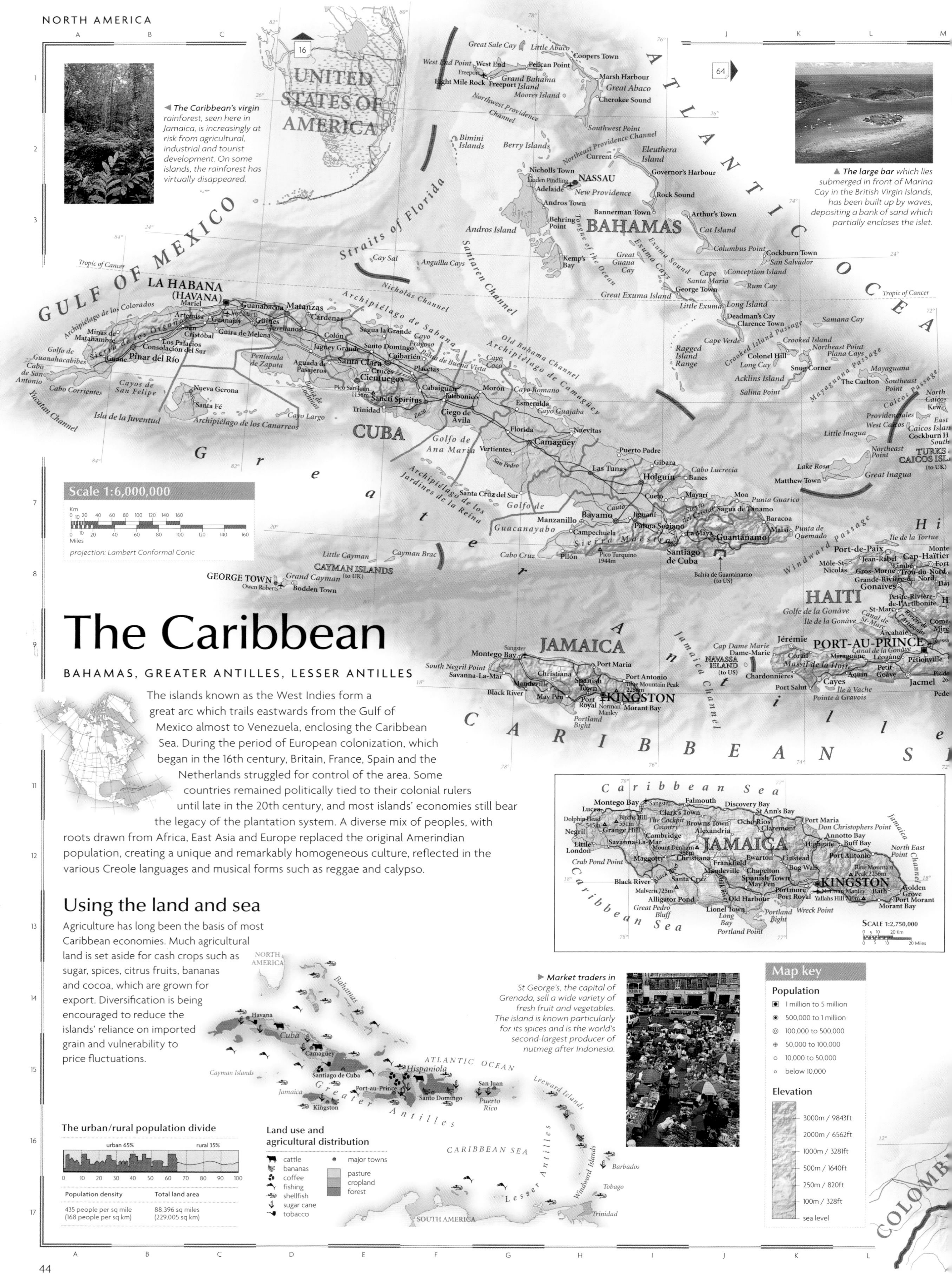
UNITED STATES OF AMERICA
GULF OF MEXICO
Straits of Florida
ATLANTIC OCEAN
BAHAMAS
NASSAU
New Providence
Andros Island
Eleuthera Island
Great Abaco
Grand Bahama Island
Freeport
Cat Island
Great Exuma Island
Long Island
Crooked Island
Acklins Island
Mayaguana
Great Inagua
Little Inagua
TURKS CAICOS ISLANDS (to UK)
Tropic of Cancer
LA HABANA (HAVANA)
Matanzas
Pinar del Río
Isla de la Juventud
Nueva Gerona
Cienfuegos
Santa Clara
Sancti Spíritus
Trinidad
Ciego de Avila
Camagüey
Las Tunas
Holguín
Bayamo
Manzanillo
Santiago de Cuba
Guantánamo
Bahía de Guantánamo (to US)
Pico Turquino 1944m
Sierra Maestra
CUBA
Yucatan Channel
Cayman Brac
Little Cayman
CAYMAN ISLANDS (to UK)
GEORGE TOWN
Grand Cayman
Bodden Town
Windward Passage
HAITI
PORT-AU-PRINCE
Cap-Haïtien
Gonaïves
Jérémie
Jacmel
Golfe de la Gonâve
Île de la Gonâve
NAVASSA ISLAND (to US)
Jamaica Channel
JAMAICA
Montego Bay
KINGSTON
Spanish Town
May Pen
Mandeville
Port Antonio
Port Maria
Black River
Savanna-La-Mar
Blue Mountain Peak 2256m
CARIBBEAN SEA
Greater Antilles
Scale 1:6,000,000
projection: Lambert Conformal Conic
SCALE 1:2,750,000
Map key
Population
1 million to 5 million
500,000 to 1 million
100,000 to 500,000
50,000 to 100,000
10,000 to 50,000
below 10,000
Elevation
3000m / 9843ft
2000m / 6562ft
1000m / 3281ft
500m / 1640ft
250m / 820ft
100m / 328ft
sea level
Land use and agricultural distribution
cattle
bananas
coffee
fishing
shellfish
sugar cane
tobacco
major towns
pasture
cropland
forest
ATLANTIC OCEAN
Hispaniola
Leeward Islands
Windward Islands
Lesser Antilles
Barbados
Tobago
Trinidad
SOUTH AMERICA
The urban/rural population divide
urban 65%
rural 35%
Population density
435 people per sq mile (168 people per sq km)
Total land area
88,396 sq miles (229,005 sq km)

◀ *The Caribbean's virgin rainforest, seen here in Jamaica, is increasingly at risk from agricultural, industrial and tourist development. On some islands, the rainforest has virtually disappeared.*

▲ *The large bar which lies submerged in front of Marina Cay in the British Virgin Islands, has been built up by waves, depositing a bank of sand which partially encloses the islet.*

The Caribbean

BAHAMAS, GREATER ANTILLES, LESSER ANTILLES

The islands known as the West Indies form a great arc which trails eastwards from the Gulf of Mexico almost to Venezuela, enclosing the Caribbean Sea. During the period of European colonization, which began in the 16th century, Britain, France, Spain and the Netherlands struggled for control of the area. Some countries remained politically tied to their colonial rulers until late in the 20th century, and most islands' economies still bear the legacy of the plantation system. A diverse mix of peoples, with roots drawn from Africa, East Asia and Europe replaced the original Amerindian population, creating a unique and remarkably homogeneous culture, reflected in the various Creole languages and musical forms such as reggae and calypso.

Using the land and sea

Agriculture has long been the basis of most Caribbean economies. Much agricultural land is set aside for cash crops such as sugar, spices, citrus fruits, bananas and cocoa, which are grown for export. Diversification is being encouraged to reduce the islands' reliance on imported grain and vulnerability to price fluctuations.

▶ *Market traders in St George's, the capital of Grenada, sell a wide variety of fresh fruit and vegetables. The island is known particularly for its spices and is the world's second-largest producer of nutmeg after Indonesia.*

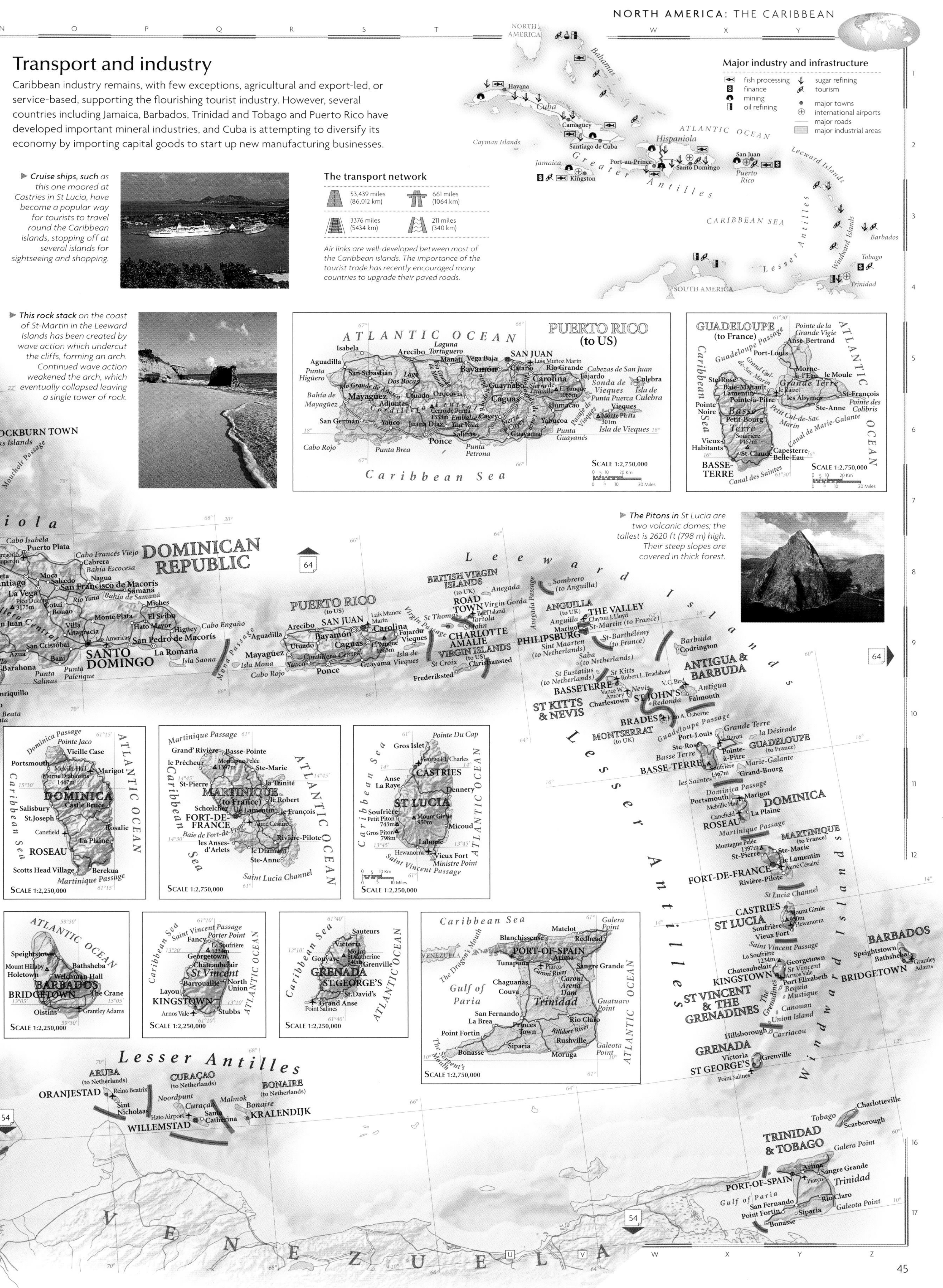
Major industry and infrastructure
fish processing
finance
mining
oil refining
sugar refining
tourism
major towns
international airports
major roads
major industrial areas
The transport network
53,439 miles (86,012 km)
661 miles (1064 km)
3376 miles (5434 km)
211 miles (340 km)
PUERTO RICO (to US)
GUADELOUPE (to France)
DOMINICAN REPUBLIC
DOMINICA
MARTINIQUE (to France)
ST LUCIA
BARBADOS
St Vincent
GRENADA
Trinidad
Leeward Islands
Lesser Antilles
Windward Islands
ATLANTIC OCEAN
Caribbean Sea
VENEZUELA

Transport and industry

Caribbean industry remains, with few exceptions, agricultural and export-led, or service-based, supporting the flourishing tourist industry. However, several countries including Jamaica, Barbados, Trinidad and Tobago and Puerto Rico have developed important mineral industries, and Cuba is attempting to diversify its economy by importing capital goods to start up new manufacturing businesses.

Air links are well-developed between most of the Caribbean islands. The importance of the tourist trade has recently encouraged many countries to upgrade their paved roads.

► ***Cruise ships, such** as this one moored at Castries in St Lucia, have become a popular way for tourists to travel round the Caribbean islands, stopping off at several islands for sightseeing and shopping.*

► ***This rock stack** on the coast of St-Martin in the Leeward Islands has been created by wave action which undercut the cliffs, forming an arch. Continued wave action weakened the arch, which eventually collapsed leaving a single tower of rock.*

► ***The Pitons** in St Lucia are two volcanic domes; the tallest is 2620 ft (798 m) high. Their steep slopes are covered in thick forest.*

South America

Reaching from the humid tropics down into the cold south Atlantic, South America has an area of 6,886,000 sq miles (17,835,000 sq km). There are 12 separate countries, with the largest, Brazil, covering almost half the continent.

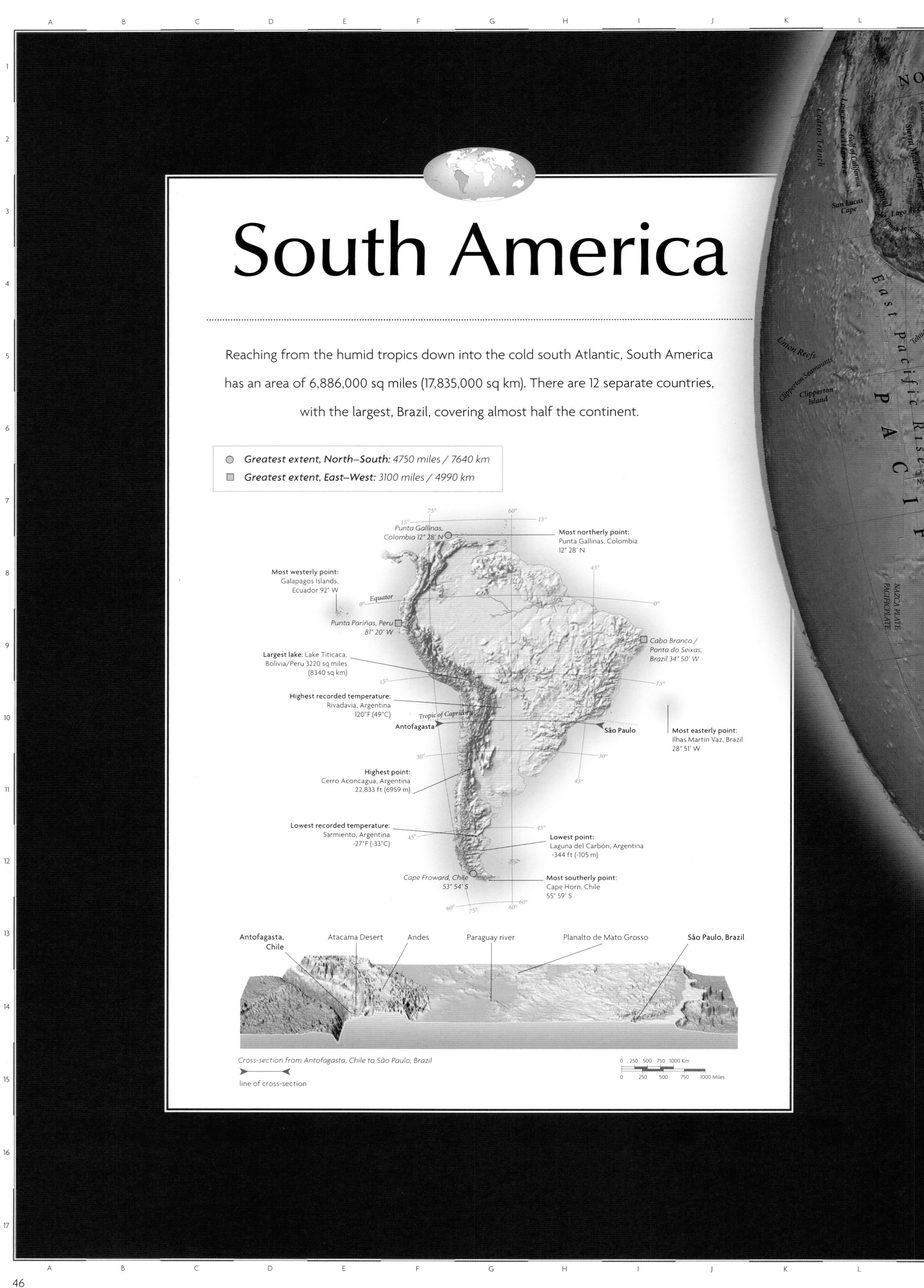

Greatest extent, North–South: 4750 miles / 7640 km
Greatest extent, East–West: 3100 miles / 4990 km
Punta Gallinas, Colombia 12° 28' N
Most northerly point: Punta Gallinas, Colombia 12° 28' N
Most westerly point: Galapagos Islands, Ecuador 92° W
Equator
Punta Pariñas, Peru 81° 20' W
Cabo Branco / Ponta do Seixas, Brazil 34° 50' W
Largest lake: Lake Titicaca, Bolivia/Peru 3220 sq miles (8340 sq km)
Highest recorded temperature: Rivadavia, Argentina 120°F (49°C)
Tropic of Capricorn
Antofagasta
São Paulo
Most easterly point: Ilhas Martin Vaz, Brazil 28° 51' W
Highest point: Cerro Aconcagua, Argentina 22,833 ft (6959 m)
Lowest recorded temperature: Sarmiento, Argentina -27°F (-33°C)
Lowest point: Laguna del Carbón, Argentina -344 ft (-105 m)
Cape Froward, Chile 53° 54' S
Most southerly point: Cape Horn, Chile 55° 59' S
Antofagasta, Chile
Atacama Desert
Andes
Paraguay river
Planalto de Mato Grosso
São Paulo, Brazil
line of cross-section
0 250 500 750 1000 Km
0 250 500 750 1000 Miles
Cedros Trench
Lower California
Gulf of California
Sierra Madre Occidental
Sierra Madre Oriental
Rio Grande
San Lucas Cape
Lago de Chapala
East Pacific Rise
Union Reefs
Clipperton Seamounts
Clipperton Island
PACIFIC
NAZCA PLATE
PACIFIC PLATE

Cross-section from Antofagasta, Chile to São Paulo, Brazil

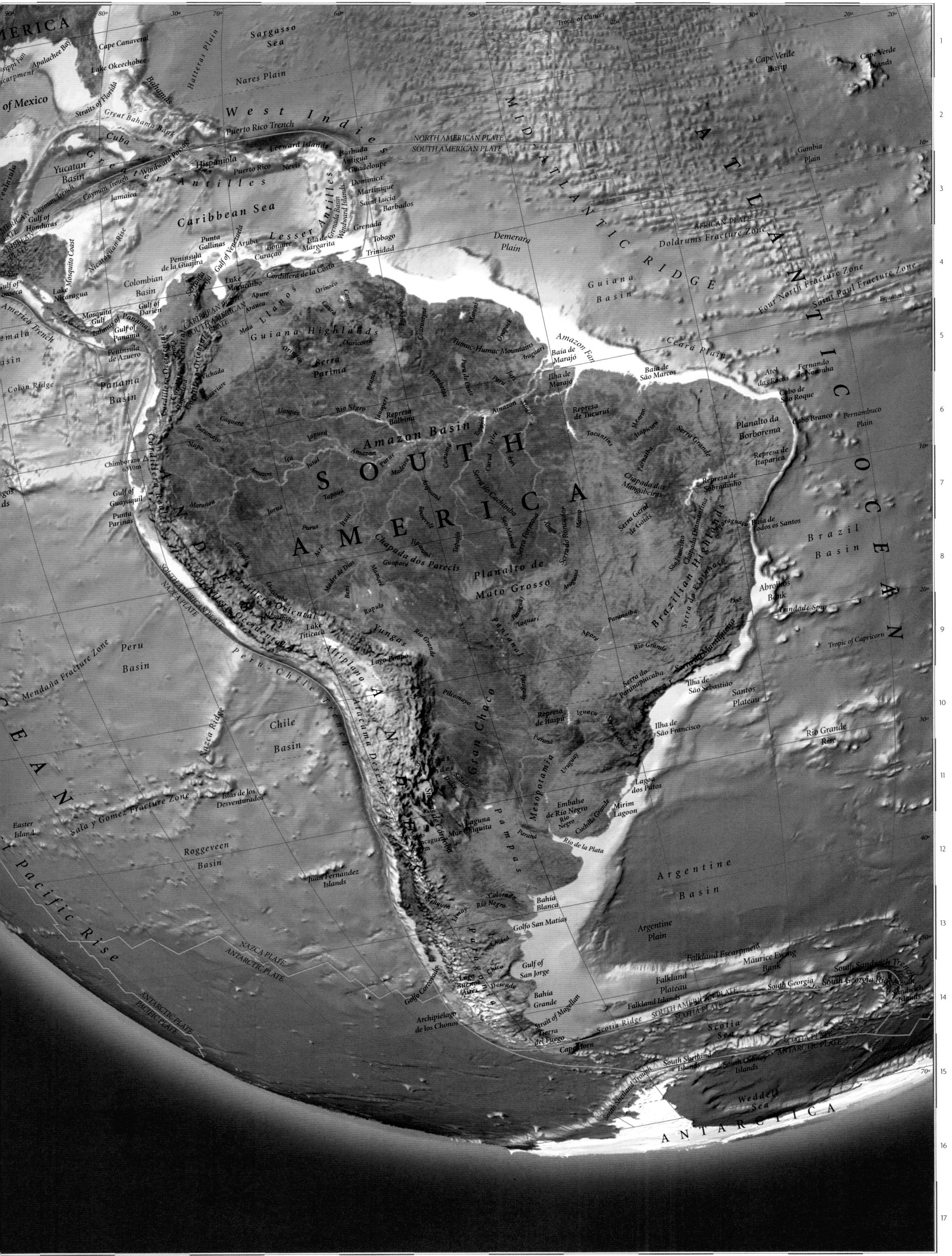
SOUTH AMERICA
ATLANTIC OCEAN
MID-ATLANTIC RIDGE
West Indies
Greater Antilles
Lesser Antilles
Caribbean Sea
Sargasso Sea
Nares Plain
Puerto Rico Trench
NORTH AMERICAN PLATE
SOUTH AMERICAN PLATE
Cape Verde Basin
Cape Verde Islands
Gambia Plain
Doldrums Fracture Zone
Four North Fracture Zone
Saint Paul Fracture Zone
Guiana Basin
Demerara Plain
Ceara Plain
Amazon Fan
Amazon Basin
Guiana Highlands
Llanos
ANDES
Brazilian Highlands
Planalto de Mato Grosso
Chapada dos Parecis
Planalto da Borborema
Gran Chaco
Pampas
Patagonia
Altiplano
Atacama Desert
Peru-Chile Trench
Peru Basin
Chile Basin
Mendaña Fracture Zone
Sala y Gomez Fracture Zone
Nazca Ridge
Roggeveen Basin
East Pacific Rise
NAZCA PLATE
ANTARCTIC PLATE
PACIFIC PLATE
Brazil Basin
Argentine Basin
Argentine Plain
Santos Plateau
Rio Grande Rise
Falkland Plateau
Falkland Escarpment
Maurice Ewing Bank
Scotia Sea
Scotia Ridge
SCOTIA PLATE
South Georgia
South Sandwich Trench
South Sandwich Islands
South Shetland Islands
South Orkney Islands
Weddell Sea
ANTARCTICA
Cape Horn
Tierra del Fuego
Strait of Magellan
Lake Titicaca
Amazon
Tropic of Cancer
Tropic of Capricorn
Equator

Physical South America

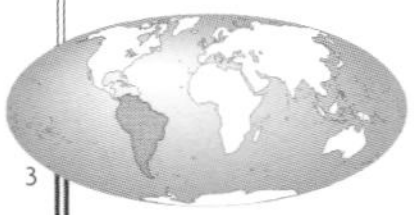

Three major physiographic regions characterize South America. The oldest, the ancient Brazilian Shield and the smaller Guiana and Patagonian shields, form the stable core of the continent. Stretching along the entire west coast are the younger Andean fold mountains with many summits rising to 20,000 ft (6100 m). These two diverse regions are separated by a number of sedimentary basins carrying South America's large river systems to the sea. These include the massive Amazon Basin and the basin of the Gran Chaco.

The Amazon Basin and Guiana Shield

The Amazon river occupies a large depression in the Earth's crust, formed by the uplift of the Andes. It is covered by thick volcanic deposits and layers of alluvium – these have been laid down by the Amazon's many tributaries. To the north is the smaller Guiana Shield.

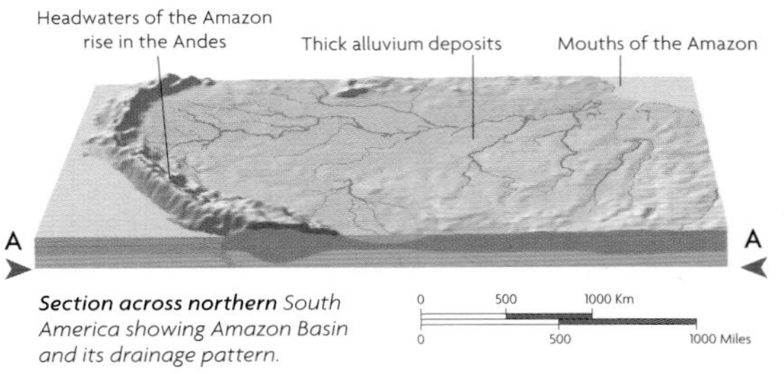

Headwaters of the Amazon rise in the Andes
Thick alluvium deposits
Mouths of the Amazon

Section across northern South America showing Amazon Basin and its drainage pattern.

Scale 1:30,500,000

projection: Lambert Azimuthal Equal Area

The Andean Uplands

The Andean Uplands run along the west coast of South America. They are being uplifted as the Nazca Plate is subducted beneath the South American Plate. They contain some of the world's largest volcanoes, such as Cotopaxi, and Lake Titicaca which occupies a dormant site. The far south has many large ice-sheets and a fragmented coastline.

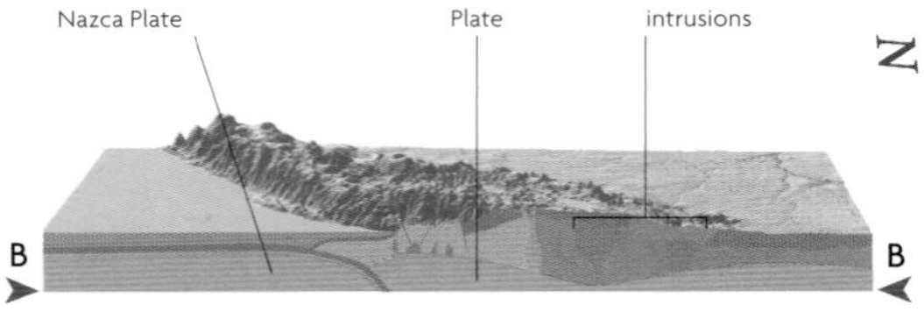

Nazca Plate
South American Plate
Volcanic intrusions

Cross-section through the Andes showing the subduction of the Nazca Plate beneath the South American Plate.

The Brazilian Shield and Gran Chaco

The immense Brazilian Shield underlies more than one-third of South America. It is pitted with numerous volcanic intrusions, and a large basaltic plateau exists between the Paraná river and the Atlantic Ocean. The flat Gran Chaco lies to the west of the shield, covered by sedimentary deposits eroded from the Andes, and transported by South America's mighty rivers.

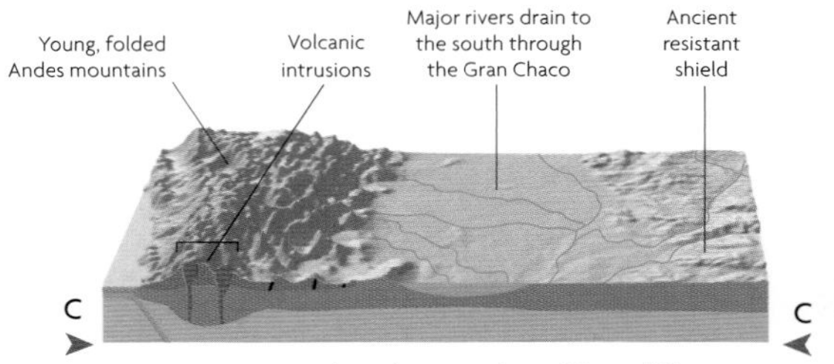

Young, folded Andes mountains
Volcanic intrusions
Major rivers drain to the south through the Gran Chaco
Ancient resistant shield

Section across central South America showing the flat basin of the Gran Chaco and the ancient Brazilian Shield.

Map key

Elevation

- 6000m / 19,686ft
- 4000m / 13,124ft
- 3000m / 9843ft
- 2000m / 6562ft
- 1000m / 3281ft
- 500m / 1640ft
- 250m / 820ft
- 100m / 328ft
- sea level

Plate margins (for explanation see page xiv)

- constructive
- destructive
- conservative
- uncertain
- physiographic regions
- line of cross-section

Maracaibo
Caracas
Georgetown
Cayenne
Bogotá
Quito
Equator
Manaus
Belém
Altos
Recife
Lima
La Paz
Santa Cruz
Brasília
Belo Horizonte
La Quiaca
Tropic of Capricorn
Rio de Janeiro
Antofagasta
Asunción
Córdoba
Porto Alegre
Santiago
Buenos Aires
Montevideo
Concepción
Pamperos
Stanley
Temperature
Equator
20° S
Tropic of Capricorn
40° S
Rainfall
Smooth summit dissected by deep gorges
Rainfall
Run-off surges down caverns as waterfalls
Scarp face left after soil has moved to the base of the slope
Failure plane
Toe of debris slide
Whitewater river
Blackwater river
Little erosion in shield areas
Confluence of whitewater with blackwater
Fold axis
Anticline
Syncline
Fold axis
Confined stream in the mountains
Subsequent fan
Mountain front
Fan forms as stream emerges onto the plain
Unstable front in deep water, where ice is fracturing
Original extent of glacier
Icebergs
Stable front
Glacier was grounded against a shoal

Climate

The climate of South America is influenced by three principal factors: the seasonal shift of high pressure air masses over the tropics, cold ocean currents along the western coast, affecting temperature and precipitation, and the mountain barrier produced by the Andes, which creates a rain shadow over much of the south.

▲ *Mild winters and cool summers typify the extensive Pampas grasslands of Argentina.*

▲ *Chile's hyper-arid Atacama Desert is renowned as one of the driest places on Earth.*

Climate

- tundra
- cool continental
- warm humid
- semi-arid
- arid
- humid equatorial
- tropical
- daily hours of sunshine, January
- daily hours of sunshine, July
- cold wind

Average January temperature · *Average July temperature*

Temperature

- below -30°C (-22°F)
- -30 to -20°C (-22 to -4°F)
- -20 to -10°C (-4 to 14°F)
- -10 to 0°C (14 to 32°F)
- 0 to 10°C (32 to 50°F)
- 10 to 20°C (50°F)
- 20 to 30°C (68 to 86°F)
- above 30°C (86°F)

Average January rainfall · *Average July rainfall*

Rainfall

- 0–25 mm (0–1 in)
- 25–50 mm (1–2 in)
- 50–100 mm (2–4 in)
- 100–200 mm (4–8 in)
- 200–300 mm (8–12 in)
- 300–400 mm (12–16 in)
- 400–500 mm (16–20 in)
- more than 500 mm (20 in)

▲ *Tropical conditions are found across over half of South America. When both rainfall and temperatures are high, hot humid rainforests prevail.*

Shaping the continent

South America's active tectonic belt has been extensively folded over millions of years; landslides are still frequent in the mountains. The large river systems that erode the mountains flow across resistant shield areas, depositing sediment. Present-day glaciation affects the distinctive landscape of the far south.

Mass movement

6 Debris slides are common in the highlands of South America *(left)*. They occur where soil on a slope is saturated by rainwater and therefore less stable. The actual slides are often triggered by earthquakes.

Mass movement: *A section of a debris slide*

Chemical weathering

1 Table mountains *(left)* are the eroded remnants of an ancient upland. As water percolates along cracks in these high, flat-topped mountains it forms intricate cave systems. Chemical weathering also isolates large blocks which then collapse, accumulating as rockfalls at the foot of scarp slopes.

Chemical weathering: *Erosion of the Guyana Shield*

River systems

2 Along the Amazon *(above)* there is a great variation in rates of erosion. As the headwaters of the Amazon flow down from the Andes, they erode and transport vast quantities of sediment, and are known as whitewaters. Across the shield areas erosion rates are very low. These rivers, carrying rotting vegetation, are called blackwaters.

River systems: *Suspended sediments in the Amazon*

The evolving landscape

Landscape

- uplifting land
- stable land
- sinking land
- glacier
- ocean current
- aluvial fan
- inselberg
- river

Folding

5 Folding occurs beneath the surface under high temperatures and pressures. Rocks become sufficiently malleable to flow and not fracture as tectonic plates collide. In the Valley of the Moon in Chile *(above)*, anticlines (or upfolds) and synclines (or troughs) have been exploited by erosion.

Folding: *Synclines and anticlines*

Deposition

4 Large alluvial fans are found extensively across South America *(above)*. Confined mountain rivers, carrying large quantities of eroded material, emerge from a mountain gorge onto the plains, where they deposit their load in huge fans.

Deposition: *Formation of an alluvial fan*

Glaciation: *Retreating glacier in Patagonia*

Glaciation

3 As fjord glaciers in Patagonia *(above)* retreat, they become grounded on shoals. In deeper water the base of the glacier becomes unstable, and icebergs break off (calve) until the glacier snout grounds once more.

Political South America

Modern South America's political boundaries have their origins in the territorial endeavours of explorers during the 16th century, who claimed almost the entire continent for Portugal and Spain. The Portuguese land in the east later evolved into the federal states of Brazil, while the Spanish vice-royalties eventually emerged as separate independent nation-states in the early 19th century. South America's growing population has become increasingly urbanized, with the expansion of coastal cities into large conurbations like Rio de Janeiro and Buenos Aires. In Brazil, Argentina, Chile and Uruguay, a succession of military dictatorships has given way to fragile, but strengthening, democracies.

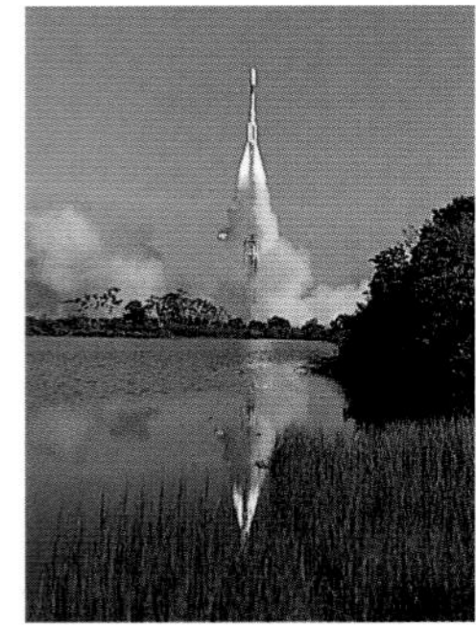

◀ ***Europe retains a*** *small foothold in South America. Kourou in French Guiana was the site chosen by the European Space Agency to launch the Ariane rocket. As a result of its status as a French overseas department, French Guiana is actually part of the European Union.*

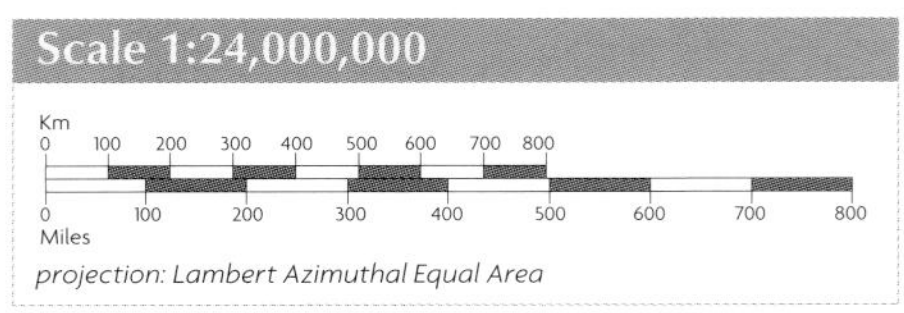
Scale 1:24,000,000
Km
0 100 200 300 400 500 600 700 800
0 100 200 300 400 500 600 700 800
Miles
projection: Lambert Azimuthal Equal Area

Transport

Most major road and rail routes are confined to the coastal regions by the forbidding natural barriers of the Andes mountains and the Amazon Basin. Few major cross-continental routes exist, although Buenos Aires serves as a transport centre for the main rail links to La Paz and Valparaíso, while the construction of the Trans-Amazon and Pan-American Highways have made direct road travel possible from Recife to Lima and from Puerto Montt up the coast into central America. A new waterway project is proposed to transform the Paraguay river into a major shipping route, although it involves considerable wetland destruction.

▶ ***South America's most*** *extensive rail network is centred on the Argentinian capital, Buenos Aires.The construction of new rail lines from this important port, allowed the colonization of the Pampas lands for agriculture.*

Transport

- major roads and motorways
- major railways
- international borders
- transport intersections
- international airports
- major ports

Languages

Prior to European exploration in the 16th century, a diverse range of indigenous languages were spoken across the continent. With the arrival of Iberian settlers, Spanish became the dominant language, with Portuguese spoken in Brazil, and Native American languages such as Quechua and Guaraní, becoming concentrated in the continental interior. Today this pattern persists, although successive European colonization has led to Dutch being spoken in Surinam, English in Guyana, and French in French Guiana, while in large urban areas, Japanese and Chinese are increasingly common.

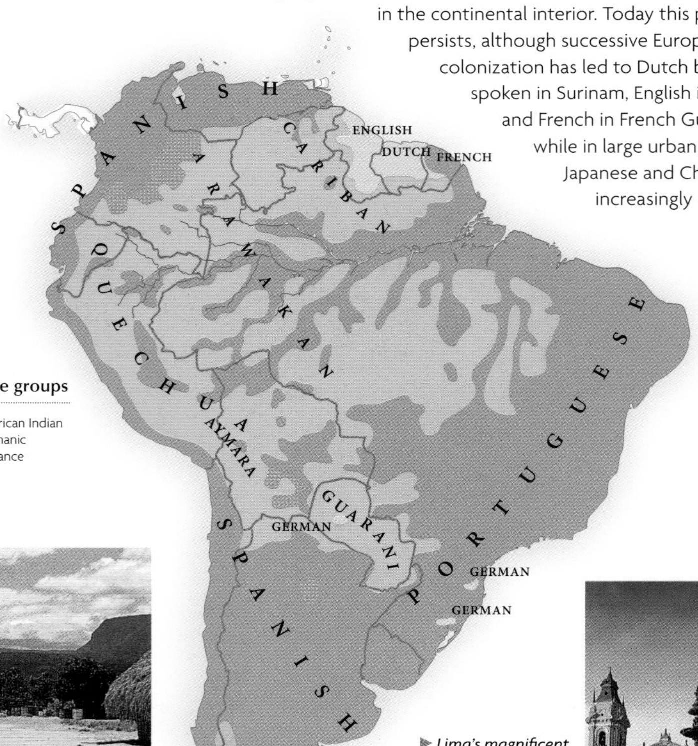

Language groups

- American Indian
- Germanic
- Romance

▶ ***Chile's main port,*** *Valparaíso, is a vital national shipping centre, in addition to playing a key role in the growing trade with Pacific nations. The country's awkward, elongated shape means that sea transport is frequently used for internal travel and communications in Chile.*

▲ ***Indigenous South American*** *lifestyles have not been totally submerged by European cultures and languages. The continental interior, and particularly the Amazon Basin, is still home to many different ethnic peoples.*

▶ ***Lima's magnificent cathedral*** *reflects South America's colonial past with its unmistakably Spanish style. In July 1821, Peru became the last Spanish colony on the mainland to declare independence.*

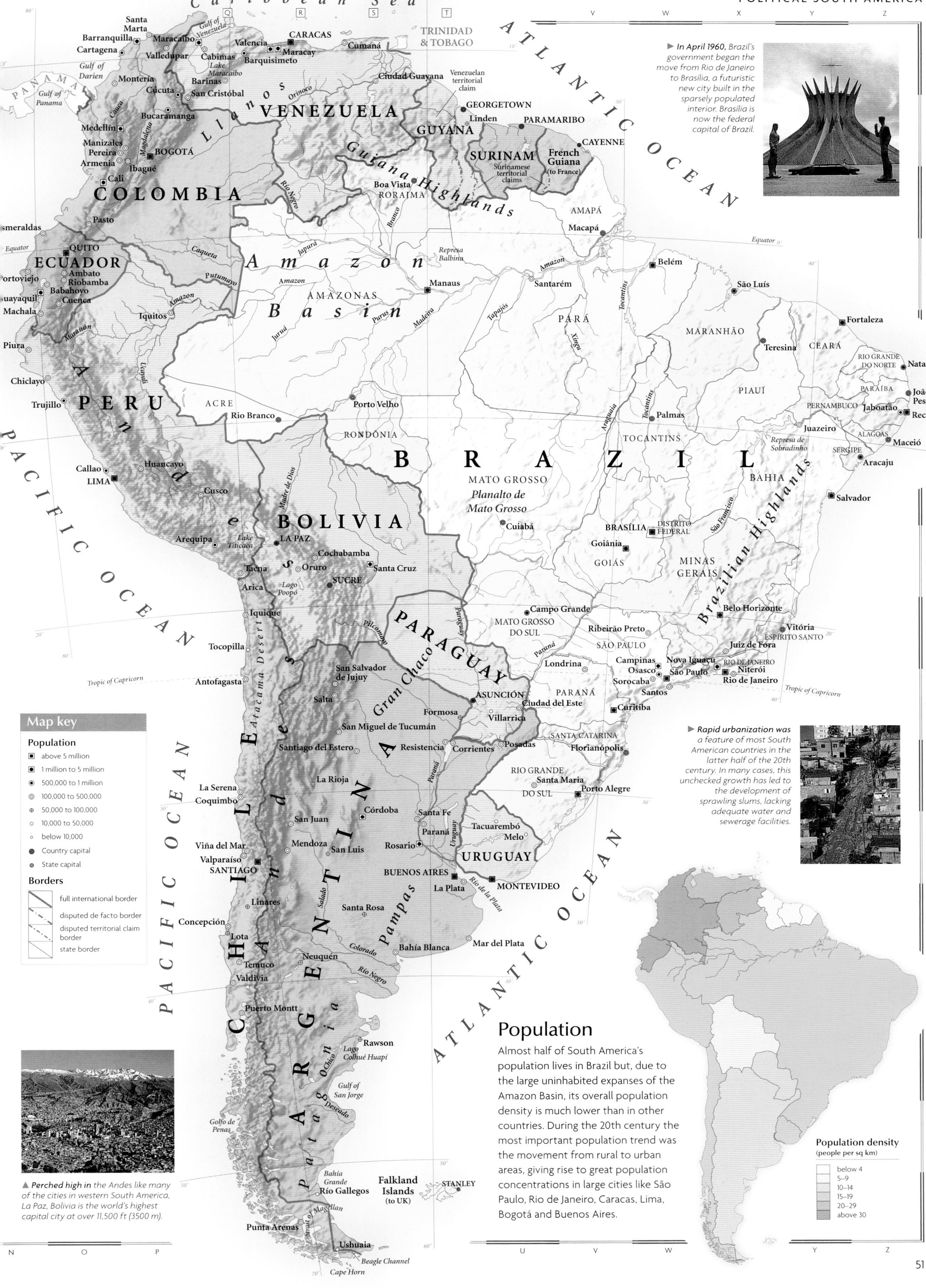

▶ *In April 1960, Brazil's government began the move from Rio de Janeiro to Brasília, a futuristic new city built in the sparsely populated interior. Brasília is now the federal capital of Brazil.*

▶ *Rapid urbanization was a feature of most South American countries in the latter half of the 20th century. In many cases, this unchecked growth has led to the development of sprawling slums, lacking adequate water and sewerage facilities.*

▲ *Perched high in the Andes like many of the cities in western South America, La Paz, Bolivia is the world's highest capital city at over 11,500 ft (3500 m).*

Map key

Population
- above 5 million
- 1 million to 5 million
- 500,000 to 1 million
- 100,000 to 500,000
- 50,000 to 100,000
- 10,000 to 50,000
- below 10,000
- Country capital
- State capital

Borders
- full international border
- disputed de facto border
- disputed territorial claim border
- state border

Population

Almost half of South America's population lives in Brazil but, due to the large uninhabited expanses of the Amazon Basin, its overall population density is much lower than in other countries. During the 20th century the most important population trend was the movement from rural to urban areas, giving rise to great population concentrations in large cities like São Paulo, Rio de Janeiro, Caracas, Lima, Bogotá and Buenos Aires.

Population density (people per sq km)
- below 4
- 5–9
- 10–14
- 15–19
- 20–29
- above 30

South American resources

Agriculture still provides the largest single form of employment in South America, although rural unemployment and poverty continue to drive people towards the huge coastal cities in search of jobs and opportunities. Mineral and fuel resources, although substantial, are distributed unevenly; few countries have both fossil fuels and minerals. To break industrial dependence on raw materials, boost manufacturing, and improve infrastructure, governments borrowed heavily from the World Bank in the 1960s and 1970s. This led to the accumulation of massive debts which are unlikely ever to be repaid. Today, Brazil dominates the continent's economic output, followed by Argentina. Recently, the less-developed western side of South America has benefited due to its geographical position; for example Chile is increasingly exporting raw materials to Japan.

Ciudad Guayana is a planned industrial complex in eastern Venezuela, built as an iron and steel centre to exploit the nearby iron ore reserves.

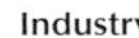

Industry

- aerospace
- brewing
- car/vehicle manufacture
- chemicals
- electronics
- engineering
- finance
- fish processing
- food processing
- hi-tech industry
- iron & steel
- meat processing
- metal refining
- narcotics
- pharmaceuticals
- printing & publishing
- shipbuilding
- sugar processing
- textiles
- timber processing
- tobacco processing
- wine
- oil
- gas
- industrial cities
- major industrial areas

The cold Peru Current flows north from the Antarctic along the Pacific coast of Peru, providing rich nutrients for one of the world's largest fishing grounds. However, over-exploitation has severely reduced Peru's anchovy catch.

Standard of living

Wealth disparities throughout the continent create a wide gulf between affluent landowners and those afflicted by chronic poverty in inner-city slums. The illicit production of cocaine, and the hugely influential drug barons who control its distribution, contribute to the violent disorder and corruption which affect northwestern South America, de-stabilizing local governments and economies.

Standard of living
(UN human development index)

- low
- high

GNI per capita (US$)

- below 999
- 1000–1999
- 2000–2999
- 3000–3999
- 4000–4999
- above 5000

Both Argentina and Chile are now exploring the southernmost tip of the continent in search of oil. Here in Punta Arenas, a drilling rig is being prepared for exploratory drilling in the Strait of Magellan.

Industry

Argentina and Brazil are South America's most industrialized countries and São Paulo is the continent's leading industrial centre. Long-term government investment in Brazilian industry has encouraged a diverse industrial base; engineering, steel production, food processing, textile manufacture and chemicals predominate. The illegal production of cocaine is economically significant in the Andean countries of Colombia and Bolivia. In Venezuela, the oil-dominated economy has left the country vulnerable to world oil price fluctuations. Food processing and mineral exploitation are common throughout the less industrially developed parts of the continent, including Bolivia, Chile, Ecuador and Peru.

Environmental issues

The Amazon Basin is one of the last great wilderness areas left on Earth. The tropical rainforests which grow there are a valuable genetic resource, containing innumerable unique plants and animals. The forests are increasingly under threat from new and expanding settlements and 'slash and burn' farming techniques, which clear land for the raising of beef cattle, causing land degradation and soil erosion.

▲ ***Clouds of smoke** billow from the burning Amazon rainforest. Over 11,500 sq miles (30,000 sq km) of virgin rainforest are being cleared annually, destroying an ancient, irreplaceable, natural resource and biodiverse habitat.*

Environmental issues

- national parks
- tropical forest
- forest destroyed
- desert
- risk of desertification
- polluted rivers
- marine pollution
- heavy marine pollution
- poor urban air quality

Mineral resources

Over a quarter of the world's known copper reserves are found at the Chuquicamata mine in northern Chile, and other metallic minerals such as tin are found along the length of the Andes. The discovery of oil and gas at Venezuela's Lake Maracaibo in 1917 turned the country into one of the world's leading oil producers. In contrast, South America is virtually devoid of coal, the only significant deposit being on the peninsula of Guajira in Colombia.

◀ ***Copper is Chile's** largest export, most of which is mined at Chuquicamata. Along the length of the Andes, metallic minerals like copper and tin are found in abundance, formed by the excessive pressures and heat involved in mountain-building.*

Mineral resources

- oil field
- gas field
- coal field
- bauxite
- copper
- diamonds
- gold
- iron
- lead
- silver
- tin

Using the land and sea

Many foods now common worldwide originated in South America. These include the potato, tomato, squash, and cassava. Today, large herds of beef cattle roam the temperate grasslands of the Pampas, supporting an extensive meat-packing trade in Argentina, Uruguay and Paraguay. Corn (maize) is grown as a staple crop across the continent and coffee is grown as a cash crop in Brazil and Colombia. Coca plants grown in Bolivia, Peru and Colombia provide most of the world's cocaine. Fish and shellfish are caught off the western coast, especially anchovies off Peru, shrimps off Ecuador and pilchards off Chile.

◀ ***South America, and** Brazil in particular, now leads the world in coffee production, mainly growing* Coffea arabica *in large plantations. Coffee beans are harvested, roasted and brewed to produce the world's second most popular drink, after tea.*

◀ ***The Pampas region** of southeast South America is characterized by extensive, flat plains, and populated by cattle and ranchers (gauchos). Argentina is a major world producer of beef, much of which is exported to the USA for use in hamburgers.*

◀ ***High in the Andes,** hardy alpacas graze on the barren land. Alpacas are thought to have been domesticated by the Incas, whose nobility wore robes made from their wool. Today, they are still reared and prized for their soft, warm fleeces.*

Using the land and sea

- barren land
- cropland
- desert
- forest
- mountain region
- pasture
- major conurbations
- cattle
- pigs
- sheep
- bananas
- corn (maize)
- citrus fruits
- cocoa
- cotton
- coffee
- fishing
- oil palms
- peanuts
- rubber
- shellfish
- soya beans
- sugar cane
- vineyards
- wheat

Northern South America

COLOMBIA, GUYANA, SURINAM, VENEZUELA, French Guiana (to France)

Fringed by the Pacific and Atlantic oceans and the Caribbean Sea, South America's northern region has a rich range of natural resources, some exploited for centuries by colonial powers including the Spanish, French, Dutch and British, others still to be fully explored. The prospects for further economic development in Colombia, Guyana and Surinam are blighted by drug-related violence and political instability. Venezuela, despite huge incomes from its oil reserves, remains less developed in other industrial sectors. French Guiana is an overseas *département* of France, now seeking greater autonomy. Most of the major population centres, such as Bogotá, have grown up in the temperate conditions of the high Andes or, like Caracas, at strategic points along the Caribbean coast.

▶ *Flowers grown in Colombia are exported all over the world, and include fine carnations and roses. Here, workers are cutting roses which have been grown in plastic greenhouses.*

Map key

Population

- 1 million to 5 million
- 500,000 to 1 million
- 100,000 to 500,000
- 50,000 to 100,000
- 10,000 to 50,000
- below 10,000

Elevation

- 4000m / 13,124ft
- 3000m / 9843ft
- 2000m / 6562ft
- 1000m / 3281ft
- 500m / 1640ft
- 250m / 820ft
- 100m / 328ft
- sea level

42

192

56

▲ *Large open squares like the Plaza de Bolívar in Bogotá are characteristic of many cities founded by the Spanish.*

◀ *Scattered farms and villages have grown up on the gentle slopes of this Colombian river valley, utilizing the fertile soils for farming.*

Scale 1:7,250,000

Km 0 25 50 100 150 200

Miles 0 25 50 100 150 200

projection: Lambert Azimuthal Equal Area

56

58

▲ *The Orinoco river flows from its source in the southern Guiana Highlands to form a broad delta on Venezuela's Atlantic coast. One of its distributary channels opens into a wide bay called the Serpent's Mouth.*

Transport and industry

Many mineral resources are mined in Colombia, including fuels, gold and precious and semi-precious stones. Revenues from coffee and exports of illegal narcotics are crucial to the economy. Venezuela's major economic activity is the oil industry around Lake Maracaibo *(Lago de Maracaibo)*. Sugar and bauxite are exported from Guyana and Surinam.

The transport network

31,720 miles (51,054 km)

3411 miles (5490 km)

2448 miles (3940 km)

22,429 miles (36,100 km)

Rivers are an important means of transport in Colombia; many are extensively navigable. The Pan-American Highway runs through Colombia. In Venezuela, much infrastructure investment is linked to the oil industry.

Major industry and infrastructure

chemicals
finance
food processing
iron & steel
narcotics
mining
oil
oil refining
pharmaceuticals
textiles
timber processing

capital cities
major towns
international airports
major roads
major industrial areas

▲ ***Vast oil reserves** around Lake Maracaibo* (Lago de Maracaibo) *form the focus of Venezuelan industry. Incomes from oil are used to invest in other industries and in the development of infrastructure.*

Using the land

The Andean basins support cereals and potatoes. Livestock graze at higher altitudes and on the drier tropical grasslands known as the *llanos*; hardy goats are reared in scrubland areas. Grown at higher elevations, coffee is an important cash crop, as is cotton, sugar cane, bananas, citrus fruits, cocoa and rice, farmed on the Caribbean lowlands. Coca is the most widely-grown narcotic plant, with heroin poppies grown in Colombia and marijuana in lowland areas throughout the region.

Land use and agricultural distribution

cattle
goats
bananas
cereals
coffee
cotton
sugar cane

capital cities
major towns

pasture
cropland
forest
wetlands
mountain region

The urban/rural population divide

urban 80% | rural 20%

0 10 20 30 40 50 60 70 80 90 100

Population density	Total land area
78 people per sq mile (30 people per sq km)	1,111,317 sq miles (2,879,060 sq km)

64

58

▲ *The Sierra Nevada de Santa Marta is a granite massif which rises sharply from the Caribbean lowlands to snow-covered peaks, the tallest of which is 18,947 ft (5775 m) high.*

Lake Maracaibo *(Lago de Maracaibo)* is not a true lake but a shallow inlet of the Caribbean Sea. It is the main source of Venezuela's oil.

In the Guiana Highlands, Venezuela's most remote region, the ancient crystalline rocks contain deposits of iron ore, gold and diamonds.

Angel Falls *(Salto Ángel)*, at 3212 ft (979 m), is the world's highest waterfall.

Igneous intrusions into the crystalline plateau which forms most of central Guyana have led to the many rapids which characterize Guyana's rivers.

Guiana Shield

Alluvial plains

Inselbergs

Table mountains

▲ ***The Guiana Shield** is one of the oldest land surfaces in the world – probably formed more than 4 billion years ago. Chemical weathering over millions of years has created flat-topped table mountains and large numbers of inselbergs.*

The drainage basin of the Magdalena River and the Cauca, its main tributary, covers over 20% of Colombia's total surface area.

Over 80% of Surinam is covered by tropical rainforest.

The landscape

At its northernmost reaches, in western Colombia and Venezuela, the great Andean mountain chain splits into three distinct ranges: the Cordillera Oriental, Cordillera Central and Cordillera Occidental, intercut by a complex series of lesser ranges and basins. The relief becomes lower toward the coast and the interior plains of the northern Amazon Basin, rising again into the tropical hills of the Guiana Highlands.

Cordillera Occidental

Cordillera Central

Cordillera Oriental

Colombia's eastern lowlands are known locally as *llanos*, meaning grasslands.

Potaru river

► ***The Potaru river** descends 741 ft (226 m) over a sandstone ledge at the Kaieteur Falls in Guyana.*

Most of the land in French Guiana is low-lying; here, the rocks of the Guiana Highlands have been eroded by rivers flowing towards the sea.

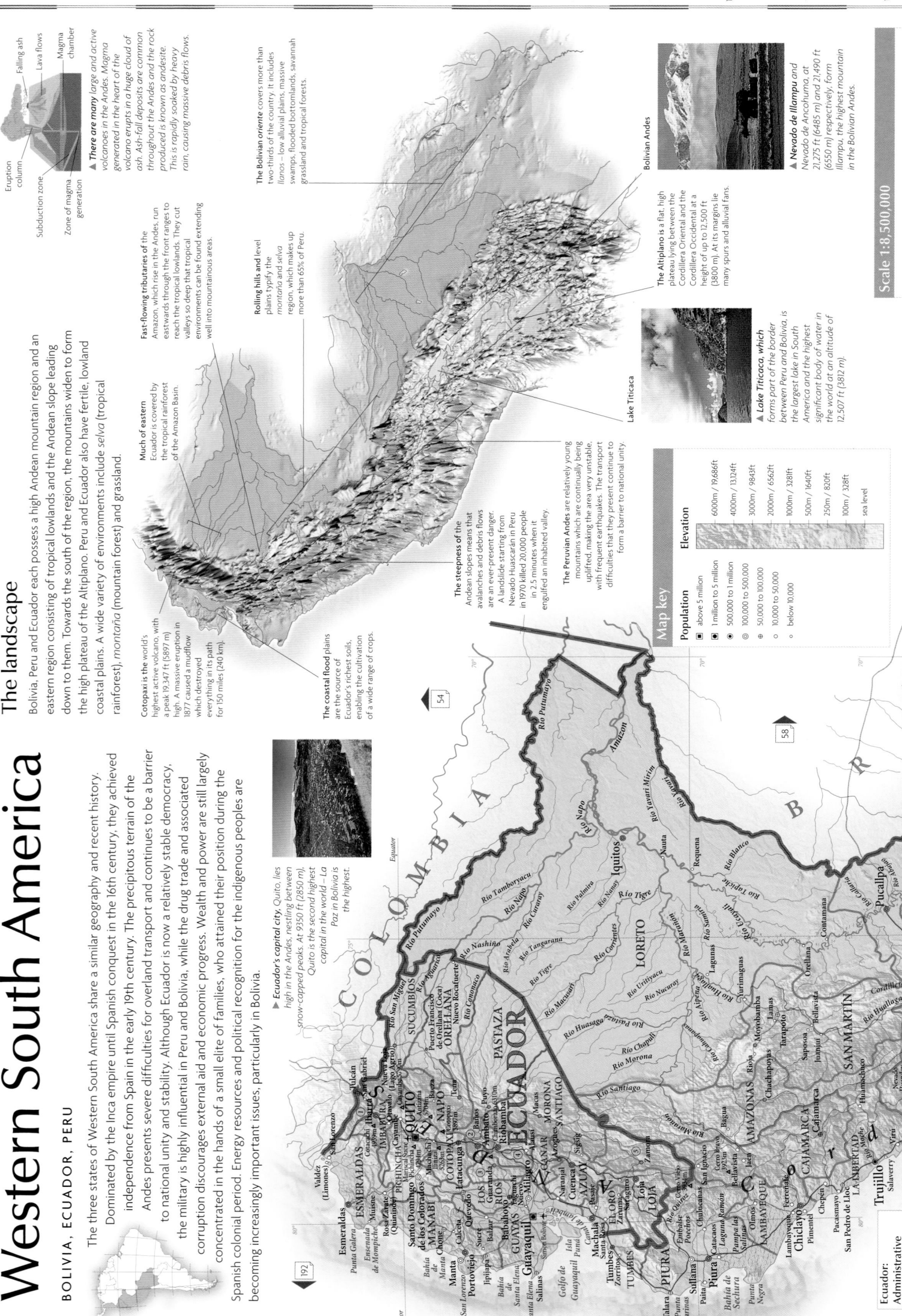

Western South America

BOLIVIA, ECUADOR, PERU

The three states of Western South America share a similar geography and recent history. Dominated by the Inca empire until Spanish conquest in the 16th century, they achieved independence from Spain in the early 19th century. The precipitous terrain of the Andes presents severe difficulties for overland transport and continues to be a barrier to national unity and stability. Although Ecuador is now a relatively stable democracy, the military is highly influential in Peru and Bolivia, while the drug trade and associated corruption discourages external aid and economic progress. Wealth and power are still largely concentrated in the hands of a small elite of families, who attained their position during the Spanish colonial period. Energy resources and political recognition for the indigenous peoples are becoming increasingly important issues, particularly in Bolivia.

The landscape

Bolivia, Peru and Ecuador each possess a high Andean mountain region and an eastern region consisting of tropical lowlands and the Andean slope leading down to them. Towards the south of the region, the mountains widen to form the high plateau of the Altiplano. Peru and Ecuador also have fertile, lowland coastal plains. A wide variety of environments include *selva* (tropical rainforest), *montaña* (mountain forest) and grassland.

Eruption column
Falling ash
Lava flows
Subduction zone
Magma chamber
Zone of magma generation

▲ ***There are many** large and active volcanoes in the Andes. Magma generated in the heart of the volcano erupts in a huge cloud of ash. Ash-fall deposits are common throughout the Andes and the rock produced is known as andesite. This is rapidly soaked by heavy rain, causing massive debris flows.*

Cotopaxi is the world's highest active volcano, with a peak 19,347 ft (5897 m) high. A massive eruption in 1877 caused a mudflow which destroyed everything in its path for 150 miles (240 km).

Much of eastern Ecuador is covered by the tropical rainforest of the Amazon Basin.

Fast-flowing tributaries of the Amazon, which rise in the Andes, run eastwards through the front ranges to reach the tropical lowlands. They cut valleys so deep that tropical environments can be found extending well into mountainous areas.

Rolling hills and level plains typify the *montaña* and *selva* region, which makes up more than 65% of Peru.

The Bolivian *oriente* covers more than two-thirds of the country. It includes *llanos* – low alluvial plains, massive swamps, flooded bottomlands, savannah grassland and tropical forests.

The coastal flood plains are the source of Ecuador's richest soils, enabling the cultivation of a wide range of crops.

The steepness of the Andean slopes means that avalanches and debris flows are an ever-present danger. A landslide starting from Nevado Huascarán in Peru in 1970 killed 20,000 people in 2.5 minutes when it engulfed an inhabited valley.

The Peruvian Andes are relatively young mountains which are continually being uplifted, making the area very unstable, with frequent earthquakes. The transport difficulties that they present continue to form a barrier to national unity.

Lake Titicaca

▲ ***Lake Titicaca, which** forms part of the border between Peru and Bolivia, is the largest lake in South America and the highest significant body of water in the world at an altitude of 12,507 ft (3812 m).*

The Altiplano is a flat, high plateau lying between the Cordillera Oriental and the Cordillera Occidental at a height of up to 12,500 ft (3800 m). At its margins lie many spurs and alluvial fans.

Bolivian Andes

▲ ***Nevado de Illampu** and Nevado de Ancohuma, at 21,275 ft (6485 m) and 21,490 ft (6550 m) respectively, form Illampu, the highest mountain in the Bolivian Andes.*

▶ ***Ecuador's capital city**, Quito, lies high in the Andes, nestling between snow-capped peaks. At 9350 ft (2850 m), Quito is the second highest capital in the world – La Paz in Bolivia is the highest.*

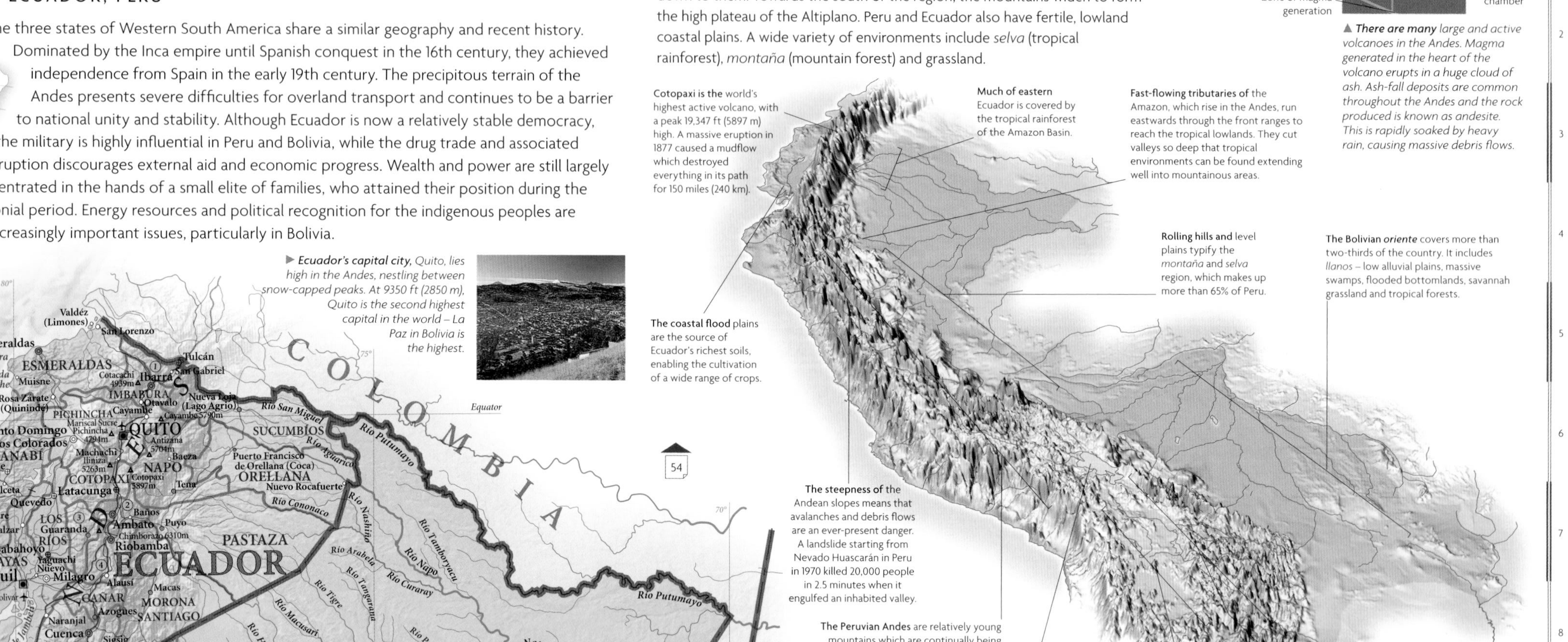
COLOMBIA
BRAZIL
ECUADOR
PERU
QUITO
Guayaquil
Iquitos
Pucallpa
Trujillo
Chiclayo
Piura
LORETO
PASTAZA
AMAZONAS
SAN MARTÍN
CAJAMARCA
Amazon
Equator

192
54
58

Map key

Population
- above 5 million
- 1 million to 5 million
- 500,000 to 1 million
- 100,000 to 500,000
- 50,000 to 100,000
- 10,000 to 50,000
- below 10,000

Elevation
- 6000m / 19,686ft
- 4000m / 13,124ft
- 3000m / 9843ft
- 2000m / 6562ft
- 1000m / 3281ft
- 500m / 1640ft
- 250m / 820ft
- 100m / 328ft
- sea level

Ecuador: Administrative regions
1. CARCHI
2. TUNGURAHUA
3. BOLÍVAR
4. CHIMBORAZO
5. ZAMORA CHINCHIPE

Scale 1:8,500,000

projection: Lambert Azimuthal Equal Area

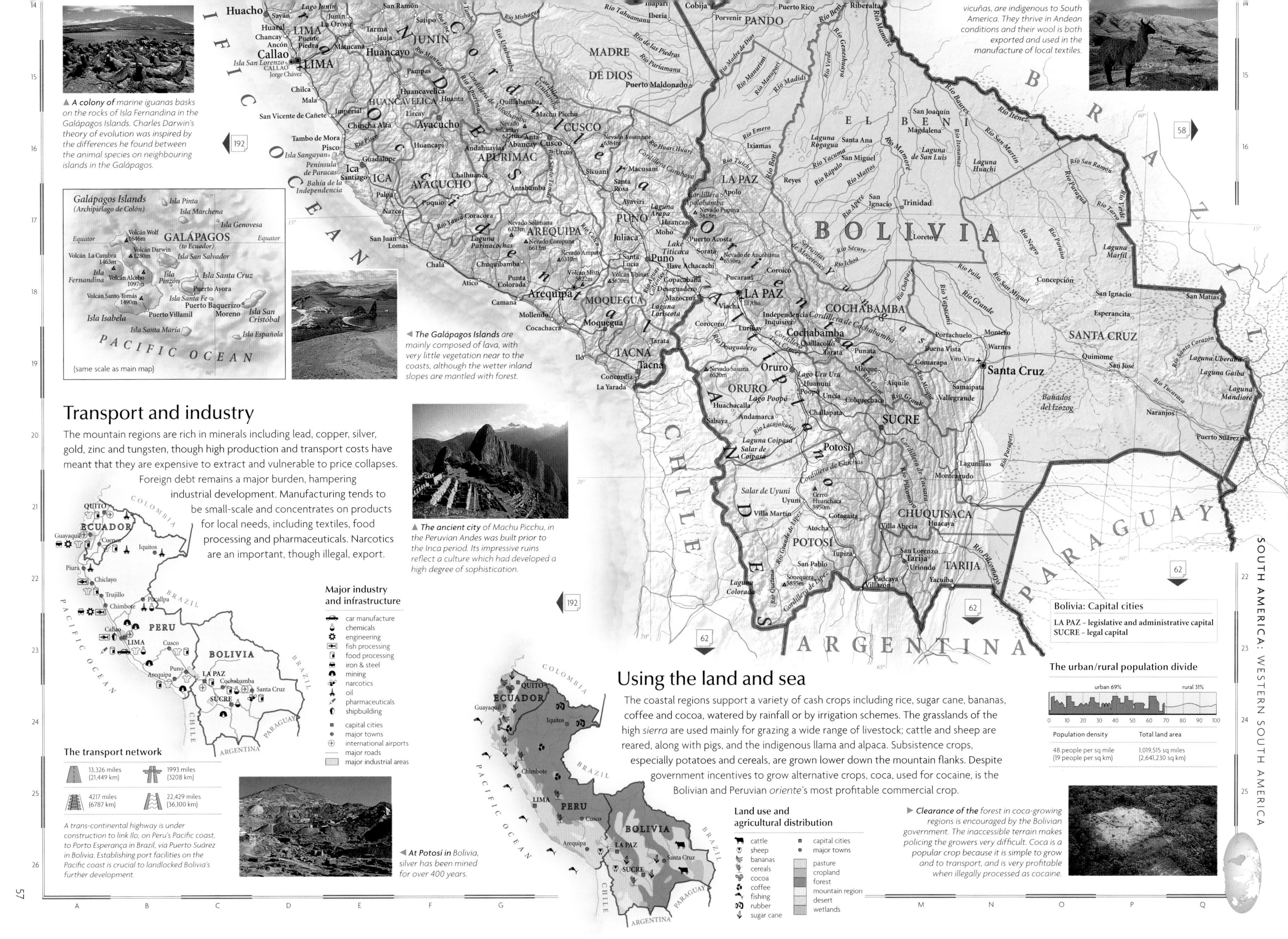
PACIFIC OCEAN
BRAZIL
BOLIVIA
PARAGUAY
ARGENTINA
CHILE
Cordillera Oriental
Cordillera Occidental
Altiplano
ANDES
LA PAZ
Santa Cruz
Cochabamba
SUCRE
Potosí
Oruro
LIMA
Callao
Arequipa
Cusco
Bolivia: Capital cities
LA PAZ – legislative and administrative capital
SUCRE – legal capital
The urban/rural population divide
urban 69%
rural 31%
Population density
48 people per sq mile (19 people per sq km)
Total land area
1,019,515 sq miles (2,641,230 sq km)
The transport network
13,326 miles (21,449 km)
1993 miles (3208 km)
4217 miles (6787 km)
22,429 miles (36,100 km)
Major industry and infrastructure
car manufacture
chemicals
engineering
fish processing
food processing
iron & steel
mining
narcotics
oil
pharmaceuticals
shipbuilding
capital cities
major towns
international airports
major roads
major industrial areas
Land use and agricultural distribution
cattle
sheep
bananas
cereals
cocoa
coffee
fishing
rubber
sugar cane
capital cities
major towns
pasture
cropland
forest
mountain region
desert
wetlands
Galápagos Islands (Archipiélago de Colón)
(same scale as main map)

▲ *A colony of* marine iguanas basks on the rocks of Isla Fernandina in the Galápagos Islands. Charles Darwin's theory of evolution was inspired by the differences he found between the animal species on neighbouring islands in the Galápagos.

vicuñas, are indigenous to South America. They thrive in Andean conditions and their wool is both exported and used in the manufacture of local textiles.

◀ *The Galápagos Islands* are mainly composed of lava, with very little vegetation near to the coasts, although the wetter inland slopes are mantled with forest.

Transport and industry

The mountain regions are rich in minerals including lead, copper, silver, gold, zinc and tungsten, though high production and transport costs have meant that they are expensive to extract and vulnerable to price collapses. Foreign debt remains a major burden, hampering industrial development. Manufacturing tends to be small-scale and concentrates on products for local needs, including textiles, food processing and pharmaceuticals. Narcotics are an important, though illegal, export.

▲ *The ancient city* of Machu Picchu, in the Peruvian Andes was built prior to the Inca period. Its impressive ruins reflect a culture which had developed a high degree of sophistication.

A trans-continental highway is under construction to link Ilo, on Peru's Pacific coast, to Porto Esperança in Brazil, via Puerto Suárez in Bolivia. Establishing port facilities on the Pacific coast is crucial to landlocked Bolivia's further development.

◀ *At Potosí in* Bolivia, silver has been mined for over 400 years.

Using the land and sea

The coastal regions support a variety of cash crops including rice, sugar cane, bananas, coffee and cocoa, watered by rainfall or by irrigation schemes. The grasslands of the high *sierra* are used mainly for grazing a wide range of livestock; cattle and sheep are reared, along with pigs, and the indigenous llama and alpaca. Subsistence crops, especially potatoes and cereals, are grown lower down the mountain flanks. Despite government incentives to grow alternative crops, coca, used for cocaine, is the Bolivian and Peruvian *oriente*'s most profitable commercial crop.

▶ *Clearance of the* forest in coca-growing regions is encouraged by the Bolivian government. The inaccessible terrain makes policing the growers very difficult. Coca is a popular crop because it is simple to grow and to transport, and is very profitable when illegally processed as cocaine.

Brazil

Brazil is the largest country in South America, with a population of 191 million – almost half the combined total of the continent. The 26 states which make up the federal republic of Brazil are administered from the purpose-built capital, Brasília. Tropical rainforest, covering more than one-third of the country, contains rich natural resources, but great tracts are sacrificed to agriculture, industry and urban expansion on a daily basis. Most of Brazil's multi-ethnic population now live in cities, some of which are vast areas of urban sprawl; São Paulo is one of the world's biggest conurbations, with more than 20 million inhabitants. Although prosperity is a reality for some, many people still live in great poverty, and mounting foreign debts continue to damage Brazil's prospects of economic advancement.

Using the land

Brazil has immense natural resources, including minerals and hardwoods, many of which are found in the fragile rainforest. Brazil is the world's leading coffee grower and a major producer of livestock, sugar and orange juice concentrate. Soya beans for animal feed, particularly for poultry feed, have become the country's most significant crop.

The urban/rural population divide

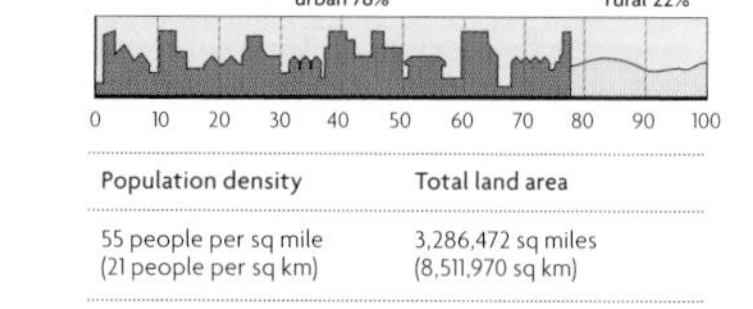
urban 78%
rural 22%
0 10 20 30 40 50 60 70 80 90 100

Population density	Total land area
55 people per sq mile (21 people per sq km)	3,286,472 sq miles (8,511,970 sq km)

Land use and agricultural distribution

- cattle
- pigs
- sheep
- citrus fruits
- coffee
- cotton
- soya beans
- sugar cane
- timber
- capital cities
- major towns
- pasture
- cropland
- forest

The fecundity of parts of Brazil's rainforest results from exceptionally high levels of rainfall and the quantities of silt deposited by the Amazon river system.

The landscape

The Amazon Basin, containing the largest area of tropical rainforest on Earth, covers nearly half of Brazil. It is bordered by two shield areas: in the south by the Brazilian Highlands, and in the north by the Guiana Highlands. The east coast is dominated by a great escarpment which runs for 1600 miles (2565 km).

Brazil's highest mountain is the Pico da Neblina which was only discovered in 1962. It is 9888 ft (3014 m) high.

The flood plains which border the Amazon river are made up of a variety of different features including shallow lakes and swamps, mangrove forests in the tidal delta area and fertile levées on river banks and point bars.

The Amazon Basin is the largest river basin in the world. The Amazon river and over a thousand tributaries drain an area of 2,375,000 sq miles (6,150,000 sq km) and carry one-fifth of the world's fresh water out to sea.

The ancient Brazilian Highlands have a varied topography. Their plateaux, hills and deep valleys are bordered by highly-eroded mountains containing important mineral deposits. They are drained by three great river systems, the Amazon, the Paraguay–Paraná and the São Francisco.

The São Francisco Basin has a climate unique in Brazil. Known as the 'drought polygon', it has almost no rain during the dry season, leading to regular disastrous droughts.

Guiana Highlands

Pantanal wetlands

The northeastern scrublands are known as the *caatinga*, a virtually impenetrable thorny woodland, sometimes intermixed with cacti where water is scarce.

The Pantanal region *in the south of Brazil is an extension of the Gran Chaco plain. The swamps and marshes of this area are renowned for their beauty, and abundant and unique wildlife, including wildfowl and these caimans, a type of crocodile.*

The famous Sugar Loaf Mountain (*Pão de Açúcar*) which overlooks Rio de Janeiro is a fine example of a volcanic plug a domed core of solidified lava left after the slopes of the original volcano have eroded away.

Deep natural harbours such as Baia de Guanabara were created where the steep slopes of the Serra da Mantiqueira plunge directly into the ocean.

The Iguaçu river *surges over the spectacular Iguaçu Falls (Saltos do Iguaçu) towards the Paraná river. Falls like these are increasingly under pressure from large-scale hydro-electric projects such as that at Itaipú.*

Hillslope gullying

Rainfall / Direction of growth / Overland water flow / Water seeps through hillslope / Gully

Large-scale gullies are *common in Brazil, particularly on hillslopes from which vegetation has been removed. Gullies grow headwards (up the slope), aided by a combination of erosion through water seepage and rainwater runoff.*

Map key

Population	Elevation
above 5 million	3000m / 9843ft
1 million to 5 million	2000m / 6562ft
500,000 to 1 million	1000m / 3281ft
100,000 to 500,000	500m / 1640ft
50,000 to 100,000	250m / 820ft
10,000 to 50,000	100m / 328ft
below 10,000	sea level

54
54
64
54
56

Scale 1:14,250,000

projection: Lambert Azimuthal Equal Area

Transport and industry

Brazilian industry is diverse and well developed, in part as a result of past government incentives, including the prohibition of imports. Industries which have benefited include car manufacture, petrochemicals and micro-electronics. Textiles, clothing and footwear are among Brazil's most successful exports. The country's services and tourism sectors are also expanding rapidly.

The transport network

- 101,893 miles (164,000 km)
- 3293 miles (5300 km)
- 18,889 miles (30,403 km)
- 31,065 miles (50,000 km)

An extensive new road network is being built to link Brazil's main centres. Investment is needed to update the antiquated railway system. In São Paulo, the subway system is being extended to accommodate the expanding population.

Major industry and infrastructure

car manufacture, chemicals, electronics, finance, food processing, iron & steel, mining, oil, printing & publishing, textiles, timber processing, tourism, capital cities, major towns, international airports, major roads, major industrial areas

▶ ***Brazil's urban population** has grown by over 6% per year since the mid-1970s – at current population levels a rate of nearly 6 million people annually. In Rio de Janeiro prosperous neighbourhoods exist alongside over 450 shanty towns or favelas, some of which house as many as 250,000 people.*

▶ ***A gaucho** in traditional costume herds beef cattle on the grasslands of the Rio Grande do Sul in southern Brazil.*

◀ ***Picinguaba Beach lies** in Serra do Mar State Park in São Paulo state. São Paulo's beaches stretch for 386 miles (622 km) along the Atlantic coast.*

Eastern South America

URUGUAY, NORTHEAST ARGENTINA, SOUTHEAST BRAZIL

The vast conurbations of Rio de Janeiro, São Paulo and Buenos Aires form the core of South America's highly-urbanized eastern region. São Paulo state, with over 40 million inhabitants, is among the world's 20 most powerful economies, and São Paulo is the fastest growing city on the continent. Rio de Janeiro and Buenos Aires, transformed in the last hundred years from port cities to great metropolitan areas each with more than 10 million inhabitants, typify the unstructured growth and wealth disparities of South America's great cities. In Uruguay, two fifths of the population lives in the capital, Montevideo, which faces Buenos Aires across the River Plate *(Río de la Plata)*. Immigration from the countryside has created severe pressure on the urban infrastructure, particularly on available housing, leading to a profusion of crowded shanty settlements *(favelas* or *barrios)*.

Using the land

Most of Uruguay and the Pampas of northern Argentina are devoted to the rearing of livestock, especially cattle and sheep, which are central to both countries' economies. Soya beans, first produced in Brazil's Rio Grande do Sul, are now more widely grown for large-scale export, as are cereals, sugar cane and grapes. Subsistence crops, including potatoes, corn and sugar beet, are grown on the remaining arable land.

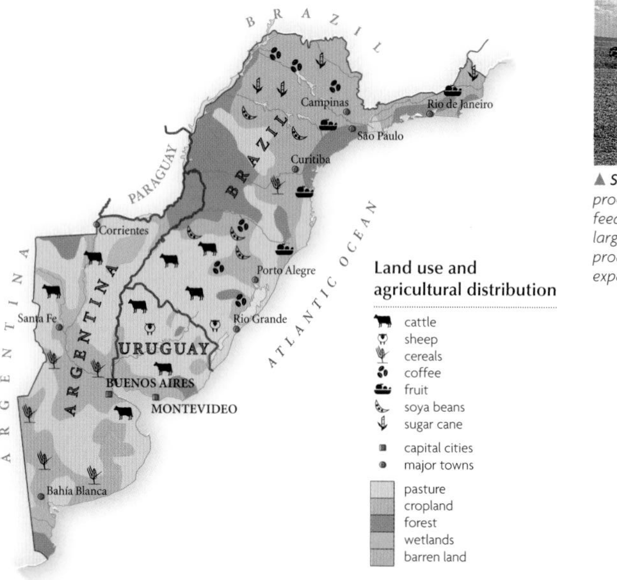
BRAZIL
PARAGUAY
ARGENTINA
URUGUAY
ATLANTIC OCEAN
Campinas
Rio de Janeiro
São Paulo
Curitiba
Corrientes
Porto Alegre
Rio Grande
Santa Fe
BUENOS AIRES
MONTEVIDEO
Bahía Blanca

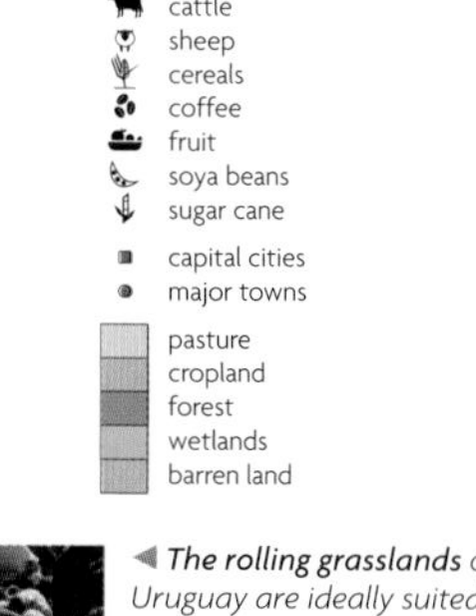
Land use and agricultural distribution
cattle
sheep
cereals
coffee
fruit
soya beans
sugar cane
capital cities
major towns
pasture
cropland
forest
wetlands
barren land

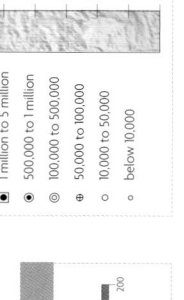

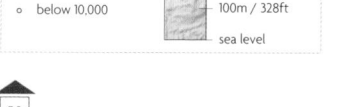

◀ ***The rolling grasslands*** *of Uruguay are ideally suited to the rearing of cattle. Beef is the country's main export commodity, valued at over one billion US dollars in 2006.*

Scale 1:7,000,000

Km 0 25 50 100 150 200

Miles 0 25 50 100 150 200

projection: Lambert Azimuthal Equal Area

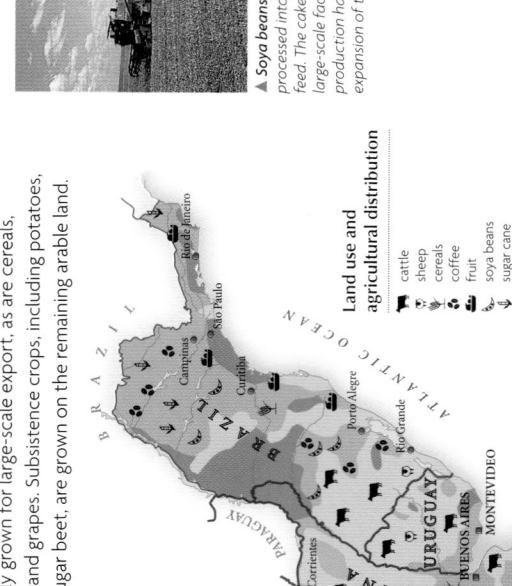

▲ ***Soya beans are*** *harvested, pressed, and processed into soya cake, which is used as animal feed. The cake is fed mainly to chickens on large-scale factory farms, and the growth in soya production has been an important factor in the expansion of the Brazilian poultry trade.*

Transport and industry

Southeast Brazil is home to much of the important motor and capital goods industry, largely based around São Paulo; iron and steel production is also concentrated in this region. Uruguay's economy continues to be based mainly on the export of livestock products including meat and leather goods. Buenos Aires is Argentina's chief port, and the region has a varied and sophisticated economic base including service-based industries such as finance and publishing, as well as primary processing.

Map key

Population

- above 5 million
- 1 million to 5 million
- 500,000 to 1 million
- 100,000 to 500,000
- 50,000 to 100,000
- 10,000 to 50,000
- below 10,000

Elevation

- 2000m / 6562ft
- 1000m / 3281ft
- 500m / 1640ft
- 250m / 820ft
- 100m / 328ft
- sea level

Major industry and infrastructure

- car manufacture
- chemicals
- engineering
- finance
- food processing
- iron & steel
- meat processing
- printing & publishing
- shipbuilding
- textiles
- timber processing
- capital cities
- major towns
- international airports
- major roads
- major industrial areas

The transport network

Throughout the region, road networks need to be expanded to cope with urban development. Plans are underway to build a bridge over the River Plate (Rio de la Plata) to link Colonia and Buenos Aires.

▲ ***The Itaipú dam*** *on the Paraná river is one of the largest hydro-electric projects in the world, jointly financed by Brazil and Paraguay.*

▶ ***Rio de Janeiro's*** *annual carnival, Mardi Gras, which ushers in the start of Lent, is an extravagant five-day parade through the city, characterized by fantastically decorated floats*

58

62

64

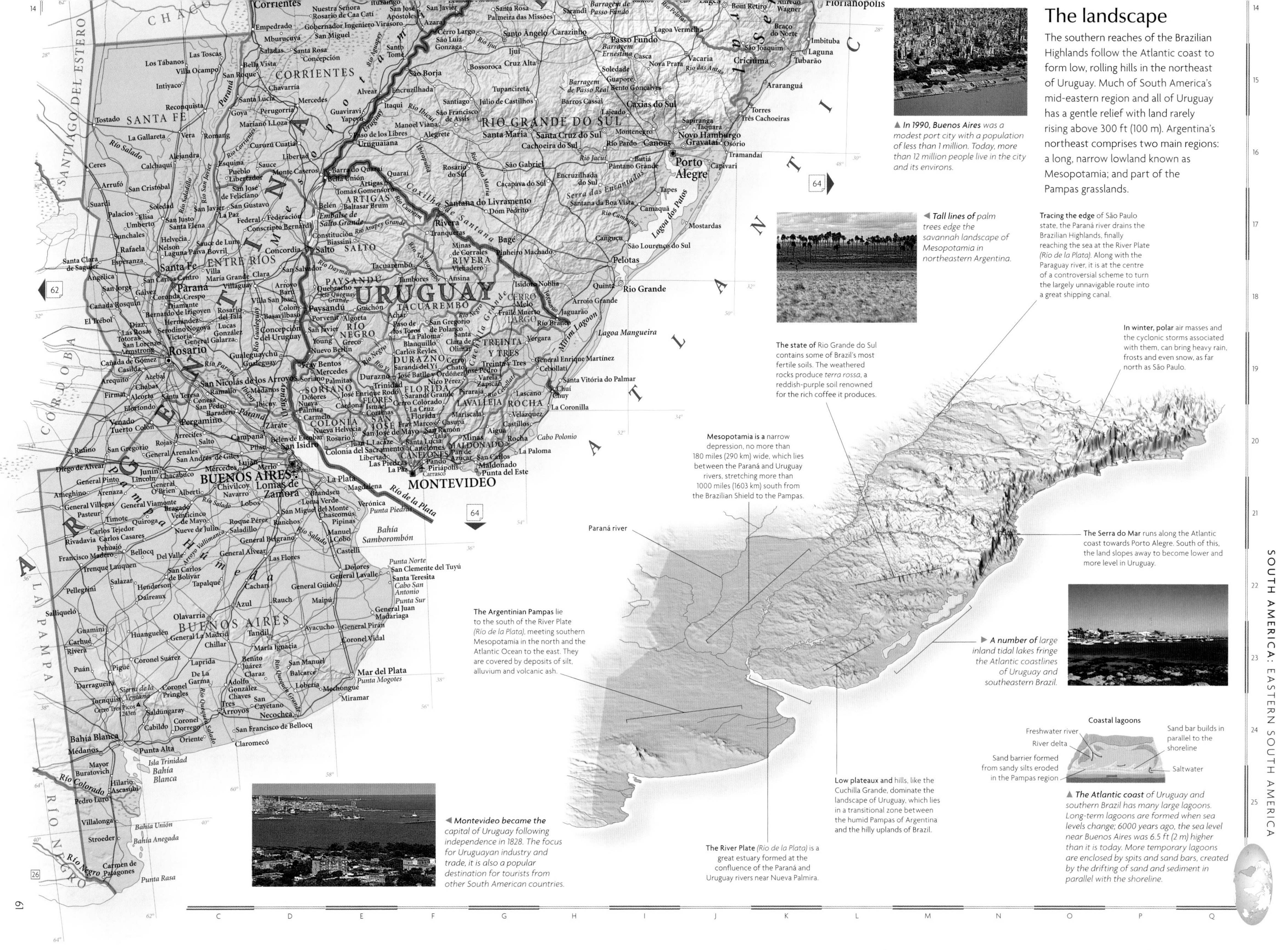
ARGENTINA
URUGUAY
RIO GRANDE DO SUL
BUENOS AIRES
MONTEVIDEO
Porto Alegre
Rosario
Mar del Plata
ATLANTIC
Río de la Plata
Paraná river
Coastal lagoons
Freshwater river
River delta
Sand barrier formed from sandy silts eroded in the Pampas region
Sand bar builds in parallel to the shoreline
Saltwater

The landscape

The southern reaches of the Brazilian Highlands follow the Atlantic coast to form low, rolling hills in the northeast of Uruguay. Much of South America's mid-eastern region and all of Uruguay has a gentle relief with land rarely rising above 300 ft (100 m). Argentina's northeast comprises two main regions: a long, narrow lowland known as Mesopotamia; and part of the Pampas grasslands.

▲ *In 1990, **Buenos Aires** was a modest port city with a population of less than 1 million. Today, more than 12 million people live in the city and its environs.*

◀ ***Tall lines of** palm trees edge the savannah landscape of Mesopotamia in northeastern Argentina.*

Tracing the edge of São Paulo state, the Paraná river drains the Brazilian Highlands, finally reaching the sea at the River Plate *(Río de la Plata)*. Along with the Paraguay river, it is at the centre of a controversial scheme to turn the largely unnavigable route into a great shipping canal.

In winter, polar air masses and the cyclonic storms associated with them, can bring heavy rain, frosts and even snow, as far north as São Paulo.

The state of Rio Grande do Sul contains some of Brazil's most fertile soils. The weathered rocks produce *terra rossa*, a reddish-purple soil renowned for the rich coffee it produces.

Mesopotamia is a narrow depression, no more than 180 miles (290 km) wide, which lies between the Paraná and Uruguay rivers, stretching more than 1000 miles (1603 km) south from the Brazilian Shield to the Pampas.

The Serra do Mar runs along the Atlantic coast towards Porto Alegre. South of this, the land slopes away to become lower and more level in Uruguay.

The Argentinian Pampas lie to the south of the River Plate *(Río de la Plata)*, meeting southern Mesopotamia in the north and the Atlantic Ocean to the east. They are covered by deposits of silt, alluvium and volcanic ash.

▶ ***A number of** large inland tidal lakes fringe the Atlantic coastlines of Uruguay and southeastern Brazil.*

◀ ***Montevideo became the** capital of Uruguay following independence in 1828. The focus for Uruguayan industry and trade, it is also a popular destination for tourists from other South American countries.*

The River Plate *(Río de la Plata)* is a great estuary formed at the confluence of the Paraná and Uruguay rivers near Nueva Palmira.

Low plateaux and hills, like the Cuchilla Grande, dominate the landscape of Uruguay, which lies in a transitional zone between the humid Pampas of Argentina and the hilly uplands of Brazil.

▲ ***The Atlantic coast** of Uruguay and southern Brazil has many large lagoons. Long-term lagoons are formed when sea levels change; 6000 years ago, the sea level near Buenos Aires was 6.5 ft (2 m) higher than it is today. More temporary lagoons are enclosed by spits and sand bars, created by the drifting of sand and sediment in parallel with the shoreline.*

62
64
64
26

Southern South America

ARGENTINA, CHILE, PARAGUAY

South America's cone-shaped southern region is shared by Argentina and Chile, two overwhelmingly urbanized nations whose populations live mainly in or around the capital cities, Buenos Aires and Santiago. The people are largely *mestizo* or of European origin; in the early 20th century Argentina absorbed waves of new European immigrants, many from Italy and Germany. Paraguay is far less urbanized than its neighbours, with a homogeneous population of mixed Spanish and Guaraní origin, who retain their Indian roots through the Guaraní language. Though most Paraguayans live in the southeast, near Asunción, the indigenous Indians live in the sparsely populated Gran Chaco. The Gran Chaco is also home to some of Argentina's minority indigenous peoples, who otherwise live mainly in Andean regions. Chile's estimated 800,000 Mapauche Indians live almost exclusively in the south.

Transport and industry

Food processing and agricultural exports remain a fundamental part of Argentina's economy. The growth of manufacturing is regularly hampered by hyper-inflation and massive foreign debts. The world's most important copper-producer and one of the top twenty gold producers, Chile also has a thriving wine and grape industry. Most Paraguayan exports involve primary processing, although domestic goods are produced for home markets.

▲ **Chuquicamata copper mine,** *lies on a desert plateau near Calama in the Andes of northern Chile. It is the world's largest open-cast copper mine.*

▲ **Boiling water and** *steam emerge from a volcanic vent, one of the Tatio geysers which lie at the foot of Cerro de Tocorpuri near Chile's border with Bolivia.*

▶ **Floodwaters cover the** *land in the Gran Chaco, partly submerging its vegetation of fan palms and hyacinths.*

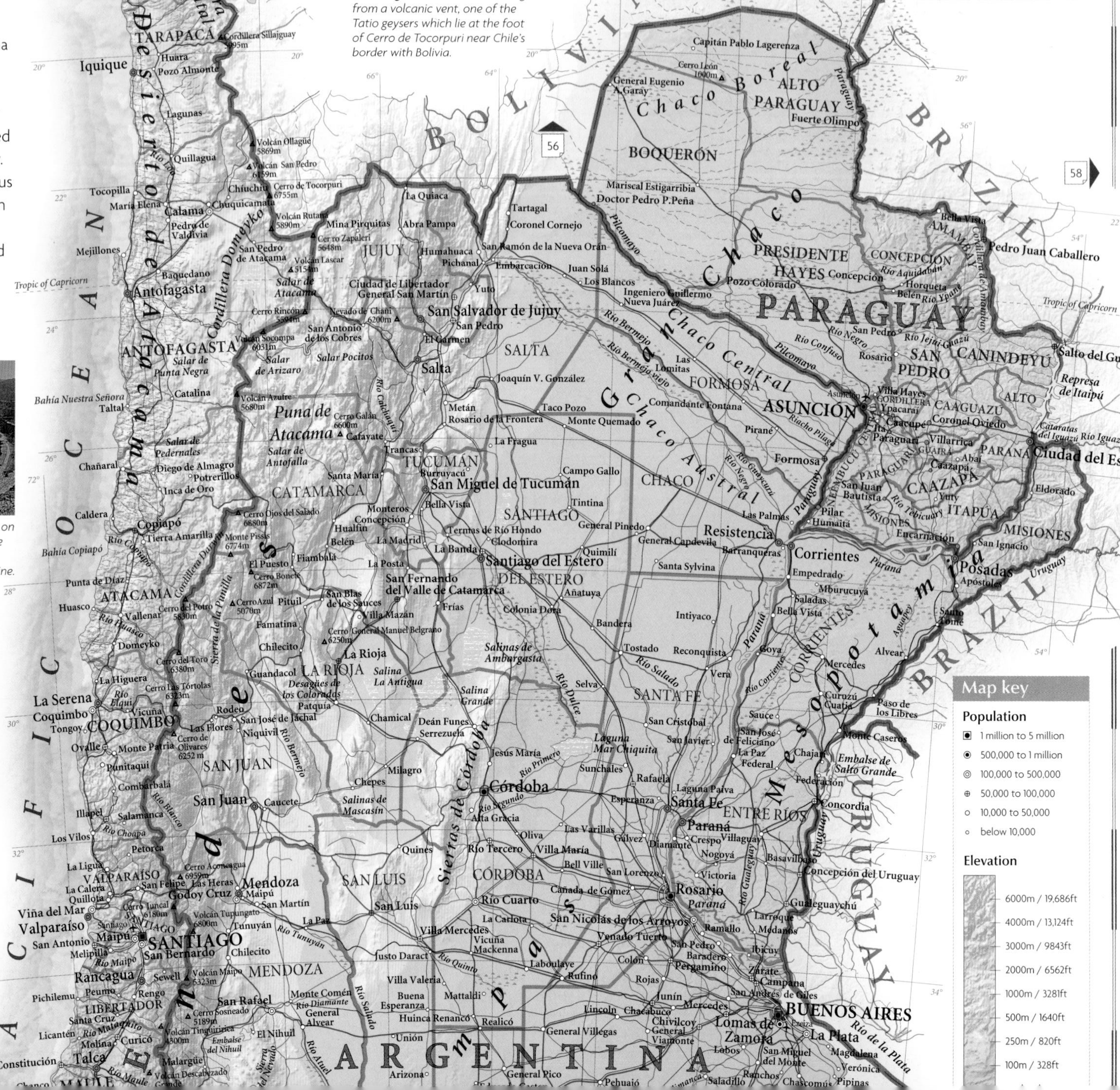

Major industry and infrastructure

- chemicals
- engineering
- food processing
- meat processing
- mining
- oil
- textiles
- timber processing
- capital cities
- major towns
- international airports
- major roads
- major industrial areas

The transport network

55,062 miles (93,453 km)	3038 miles (4889 km)
26,811 miles (43,153 km)	9180 miles (14,775 km)

Argentina's state transport system is undergoing privatization, though the outmoded rail network requires updating. Paraguay requires foreign investment to upgrade its roads and railways. Essential internal air routes, especially across the Andes, are well developed in all three countries.

Map key

Population

- 1 million to 5 million
- 500,000 to 1 million
- 100,000 to 500,000
- 50,000 to 100,000
- 10,000 to 50,000
- below 10,000

Elevation

- 6000m / 19,686ft
- 4000m / 13,124ft
- 3000m / 9843ft
- 2000m / 6562ft
- 1000m / 3281ft
- 500m / 1640ft
- 250m / 820ft
- 100m / 328ft

56
58

The landscape

The Andes run from north to south, forming a precipitous natural border between Chile and Argentina. East of the Andes are the scrublands of the Gran Chaco and the plains of the Pampas, which extend northward towards Paraguay. In the far southwest, Chile's indented Pacific coastline has many features typical of areas which have been affected by glaciation.

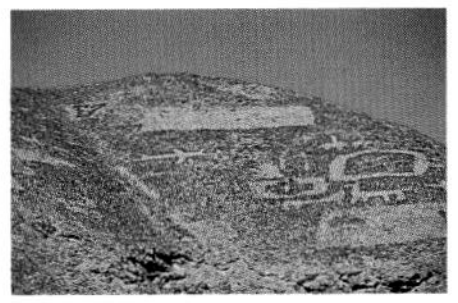

▲ *The Atacama Desert* (Desierto de Atacama) *in Chile is one of the driest places on Earth where some areas have never recorded any rain. It contains a number of salt lakes.*

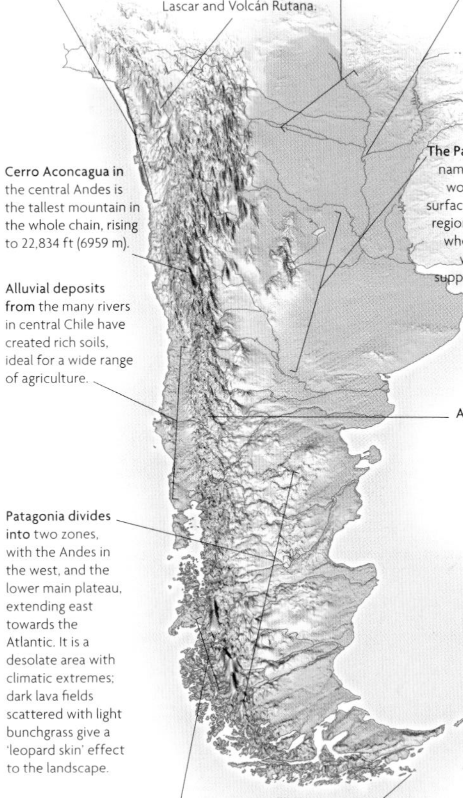

The Gran Chaco combines poor drainage, extremely hot temperatures and thorn-infested scrub to make it one of South America's most inhospitable regions.

Landlocked Paraguay relies on its river system for access to the sea and to produce hydro-electric power. The most important river system is the Paraguay–Paraná which provides links into neighbouring countries including Brazil, Uruguay and Argentina.

Most of the highest mountains in Chile's northern Andes are volcanoes like Volcán Lascar and Volcán Rutana.

The Pampas derive their name from an Indian word meaning flat surface. The dry western region is largely desert, whereas the east is well-watered, supporting temperate grasses.

Cerro Aconcagua in the central Andes is the tallest mountain in the whole chain, rising to 22,834 ft (6959 m).

Alluvial deposits from the many rivers in central Chile have created rich soils, ideal for a wide range of agriculture.

Andes

Patagonia divides into two zones, with the Andes in the west, and the lower main plateau, extending east towards the Atlantic. It is a desolate area with climatic extremes; dark lava fields scattered with light bunchgrass give a 'leopard skin' effect to the landscape.

The Patagonian ice sheet is the world's third largest ice field, covering 6560 sq miles (17,000 sq km). Patagonia also contains many typical features from past glaciations. These include glacial lakes, U-shaped valleys, fjords and deep-cut channels.

Cape Horn is the most southerly point of South America. The severity of the Roaring Forties winds makes the Horn one of the world's most treacherous shipping regions.

Argentinian Pampas

Jet stream

Rainfall

Windblown particles

Thick layer of loess sediments

Ice-capped Andes are source of loess

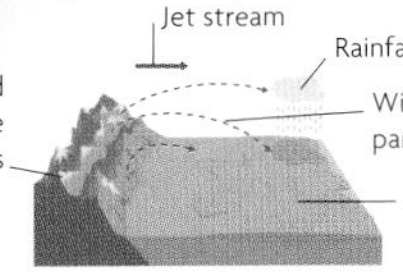

▲ *A thick, fertile layer of loess lies in the basin underlying the Argentinian Pampas. It has been laid down following successive periods of glaciation. The minute loess particles are transported as dust and deposited by a downward air motion, or following rainfall.*

192

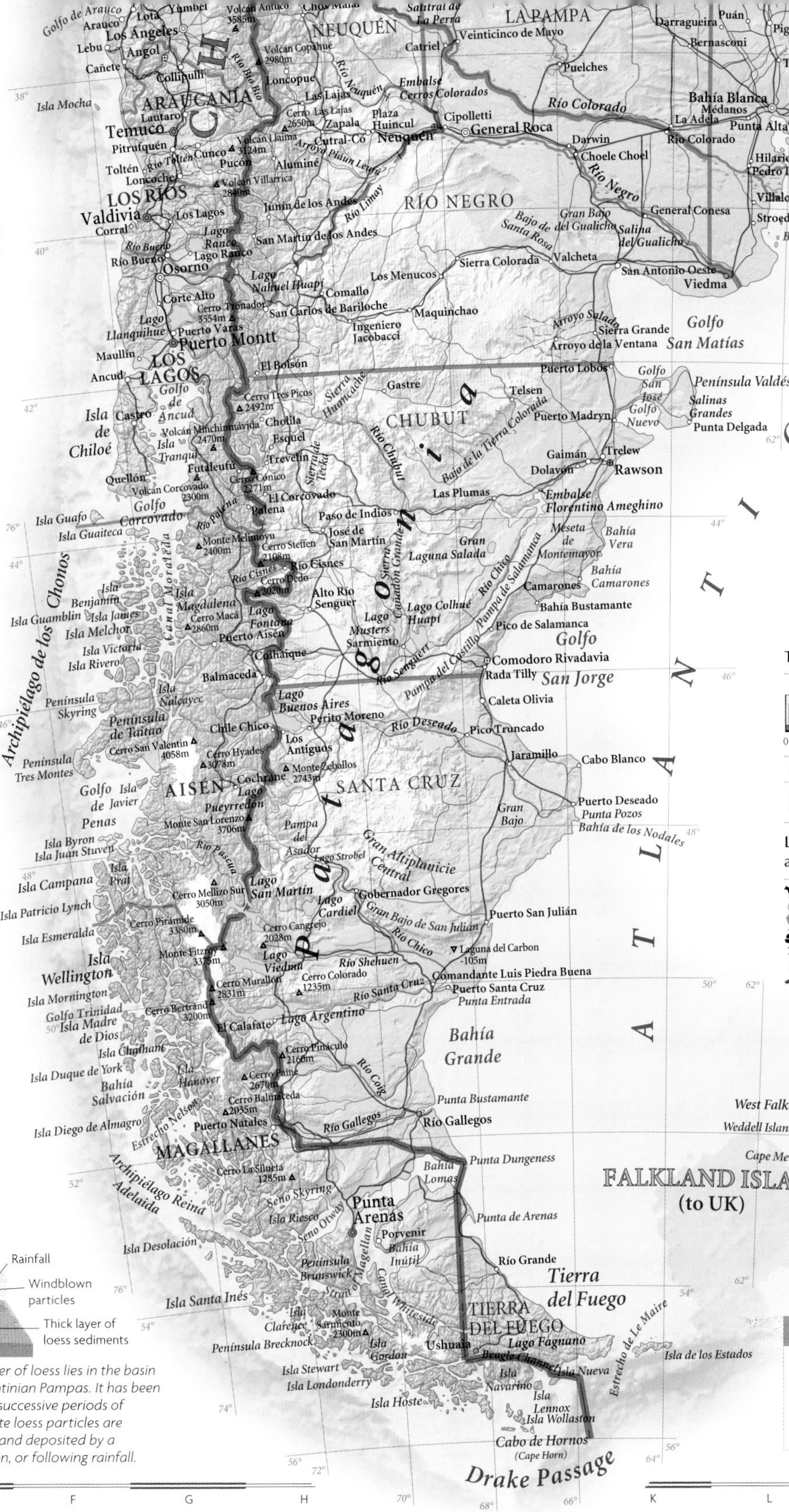

64

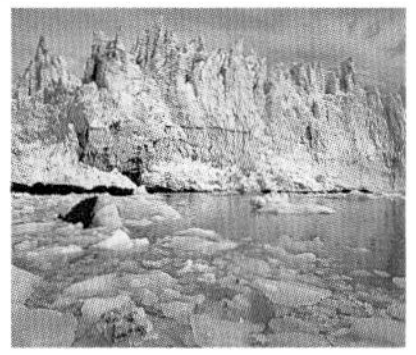

FALKLAND ISLANDS (to UK)

Scale 1:9,750,000

projection: Lambert Azimuthal Equal Area

▲ *Great blocks of ice break away from the jagged blue peaks of these ice mountains to form icebergs off the coast of Patagonia, Argentina's most southerly region.*

Using the land and sea

The rich plains of the Pampas support massive herds of cattle, producing meat, milk and hides essential to the domestic and export markets of both Argentina and Paraguay. Wheat and fruit are Argentina's other major agricultural products. A wide range of soft fruits, citrus fruits and more specialized crops such as walnuts, and grapes for wine and the table, are grown in Chile's fertile Central Valley, while the landscape to the south is dominated by forestry, mainly growing commercial radiata pine. Paraguay is self-sufficient in wheat and other staples. Cotton, coffee, tobacco and oilseeds such as soya, are the major export crops.

The urban/rural population divide

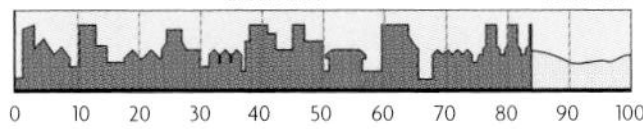

urban 84% · rural 16%

0 10 20 30 40 50 60 70 80 90 100

Population density	Total land area
40 people per sq mile (15 people per sq km)	1,498,757 sq miles (3,882,790 sq km)

Land use and agricultural distribution

cattle, sheep, cereals, fruit, grapes, timber, fishing

capital cities, major towns

pasture, cropland, forest, barren land, mountain region, desert

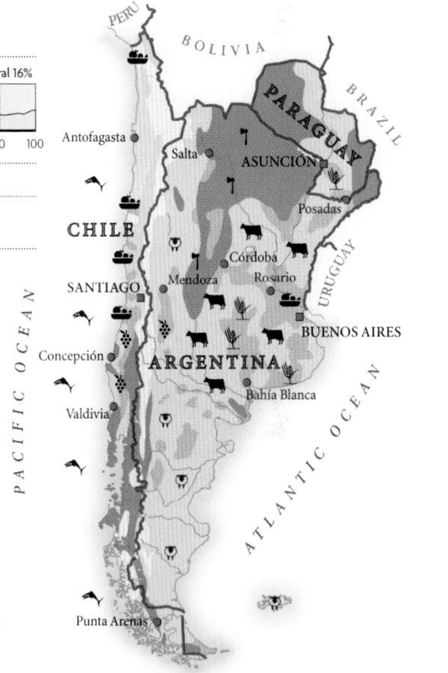

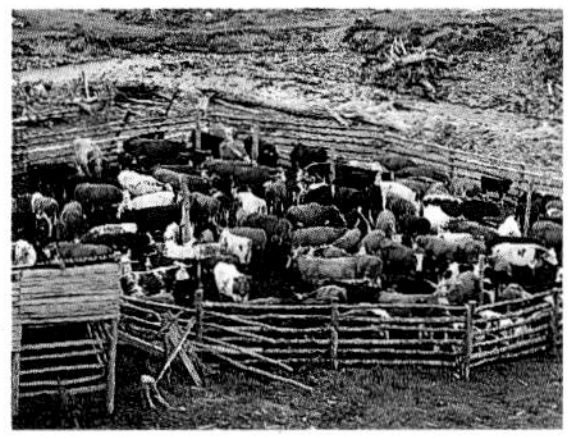

▲ *Charred tree stumps surround a cattle enclosure on the island of Tierra del Fuego in southern Argentina. Forest clearance to provide grazing land for cattle is of major environmental concern.*

The Atlantic Ocean

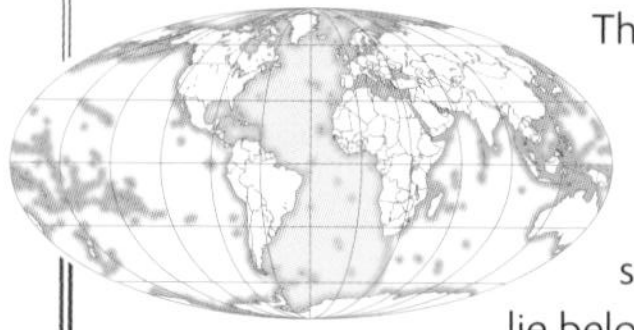

The Atlantic is the youngest of the world's oceans, formed about 180 million years ago when the landmasses of the eastern and western hemispheres separated. Its underwater topography is dominated by the Mid-Atlantic Ridge, a huge mountain system running north to south along the centre of the ocean. Although most of the ridge's peaks lie below the sea, some emerge as volcanic islands, like Iceland and the Azores. The Atlantic contains a wealth of resources, including substantial oil and gas reserves and rich fishing grounds. Until the 1950s, the north Atlantic was the world's busiest shipping route; cheaper air transport and alternative routes have shifted patterns of world trade.

▲ **Surtsey near Iceland**, *lies on the Mid-Atlantic Ridge. The island was formed in 1963 following a volcanic eruption caused by sea-floor spreading.*

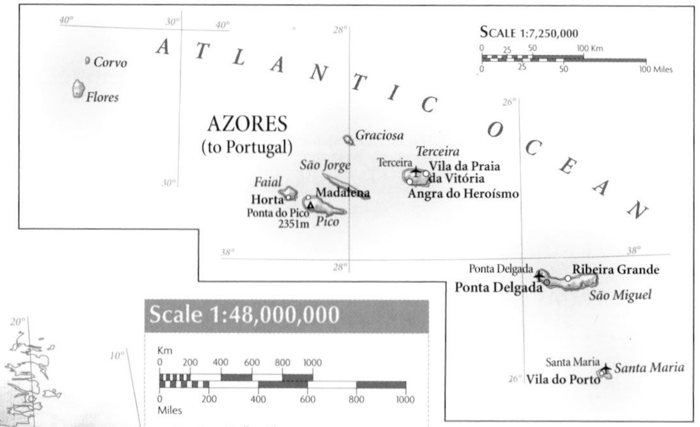

Resources

Development of the oil and gas reserves in the Atlantic began in the 1940s around the Gulf of Mexico. Since then other areas have been exploited, including the North Sea, the west coast of Africa and the area east of Newfoundland and Nova Scotia. There is also extensive mining of sand, gravel and shell deposits by the USA and UK. For centuries, the north Atlantic's fishing grounds have been utilized more heavily than other oceans, leading to a serious decline in many fish stocks.

Resources (including wildlife)

- fish
- whales
- aggregates
- oil & gas
- major towns
- major ports

▲ **Fishing in the** *seas around northwestern Europe dates back over 1500 years. The high nutrient content of the seas makes them ideal breeding grounds for many species of fish.*

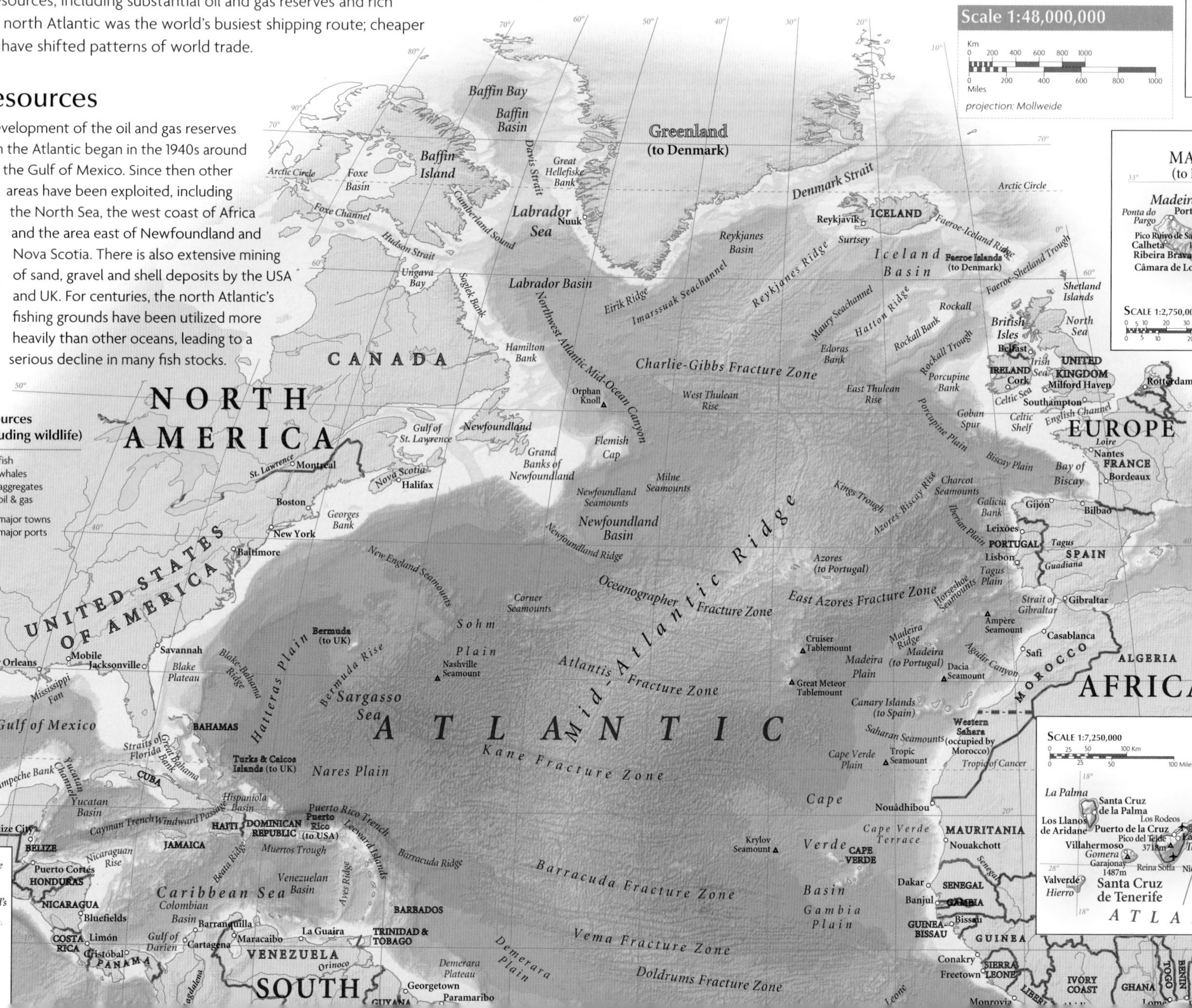

▲ **On 5 January 1993,** *the oil tanker Braer ran aground in the Shetland Islands, spilling 83,660 tons (85,000 tonnes) of light crude oil into the ocean, devastating the local marine ecosystem.*

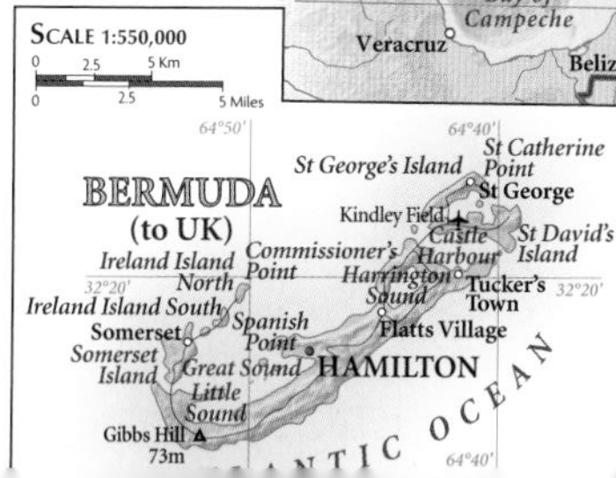

Scale 1:48,000,000

projection: Mollweide

AZORES (to Portugal) — Scale 1:7,250,000

MADEIRA (to Portugal) — Scale 1:2,750,000

ISLAS CANARIAS (CANARY ISLANDS) (to Spain) — Scale 1:7,250,000

BERMUDA (to UK) — Scale 1:550,000

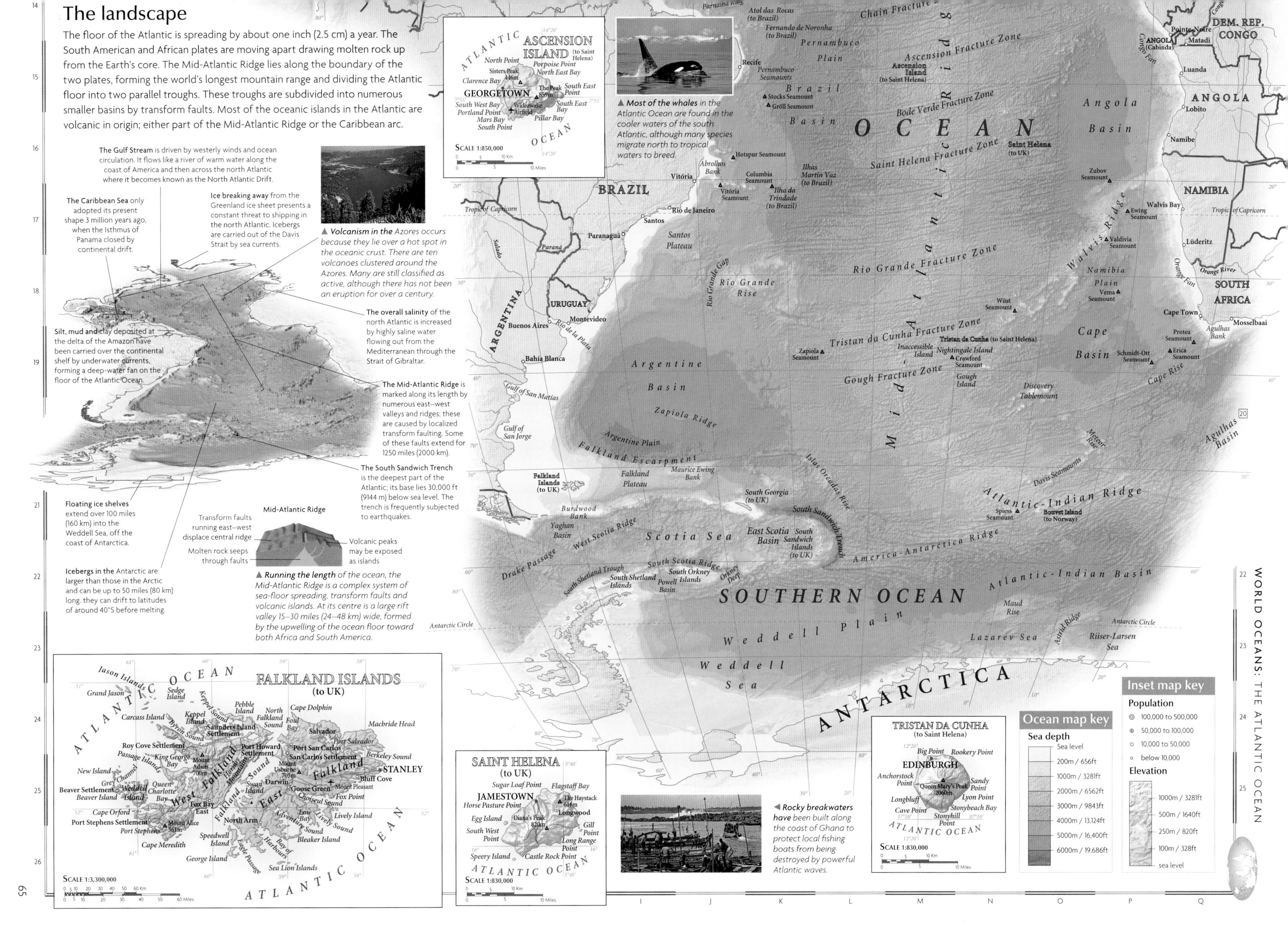

ASCENSION ISLAND (to Saint Helena)
ATLANTIC OCEAN
North Point
Porpoise Point
North East Bay
Sisters Peak 446m
Clarence Bay
GEORGETOWN
The Peak 859m
South East Point
South West Bay
Portland Point
Wideawake Airfield
South East Bay
Mars Bay
Pillar Bay
South Point
SCALE 1:850,000
Atol das Rocas (to Brazil)
Fernando de Noronha (to Brazil)
Pernambuco Plain
Recife
Pernambuco Seamounts
Stocks Seamount
Gröll Seamount
Brazil Basin
Ascension Fracture Zone
Ascension Island (to Saint Helena)
Bode Verde Fracture Zone
Saint Helena Fracture Zone
Saint Helena (to UK)
OCEAN
Mid-Atlantic Ridge
Chain Fracture
Hotspur Seamount
Abrolhos Bank
Vitória
Vitória Seamount
Columbia Seamount
Ilha da Trindade (to Brazil)
Ilhas Martin Vaz (to Brazil)
BRAZIL
Rio de Janeiro
Santos
Santos Plateau
Paranaguá
Tropic of Capricorn
Salado
Paraná
URUGUAY
Montevideo
Río de la Plata
Buenos Aires
ARGENTINA
Bahía Blanca
Gulf of San Matías
Gulf of San Jorge
Rio Grande Gap
Rio Grande Rise
Rio Grande Fracture Zone
Argentine Basin
Zapiola Ridge
Zapiola Seamount
Argentine Plain
Falkland Escarpment
Falkland Plateau
Maurice Ewing Bank
Falkland Islands (to UK)
Burdwood Bank
Yaghan Basin
West Scotia Ridge
Drake Passage
Scotia Sea
South Georgia (to UK)
Islas Orcadas Rise
South Sandwich Trench
East Scotia Basin
South Sandwich Islands (to UK)
South Scotia Ridge
South Orkney Islands
Powell Basin
Orkney Deep
South Shetland Trough
South Shetland Islands
Antarctic Circle
SOUTHERN OCEAN
Weddell Plain
Weddell Sea
America-Antarctica Ridge
Atlantic-Indian Basin
Maud Rise
Lazarev Sea
Astrid Ridge
Riiser-Larsen Sea
ANTARCTICA
Tristan da Cunha Fracture Zone
Tristan da Cunha (to Saint Helena)
Inaccessible Island
Nightingale Island
Crawford Seamount
Gough Fracture Zone
Gough Island
Discovery Tablemount
Wüst Seamount
Meteor Rise
Davis Seamounts
Atlantic-Indian Ridge
Spiess Seamount
Bouvet Island (to Norway)
Angola Basin
Zubov Seamount
Walvis Ridge
Ewing Seamount
Valdivia Seamount
Namibia Plain
Vema Seamount
Cape Basin
Schmidt-Ott Seamount
Erica Seamount
Protea Seamount
Cape Rise
Agulhas Basin
Agulhas Bank
DEM. REP. CONGO
Congo
Congo Fan
Pointe-Noire
ANGOLA (Cabinda)
Matadi
Luanda
ANGOLA
Lobito
Namibe
NAMIBIA
Walvis Bay
Tropic of Capricorn
Lüderitz
Orange River
Orange Fan
SOUTH AFRICA
Cape Town
Mosselbaai
Mid-Atlantic Ridge
Transform faults running east–west displace central ridge
Molten rock seeps through faults
Volcanic peaks may be exposed as islands
FALKLAND ISLANDS (to UK)
Jason Islands
Grand Jason
Sedge Island
Carcass Island
Keppel Island
Keppel Sound
Pebble Island
Saunders Island Settlement
North Falkland Sound
Cape Dolphin
Foul Bay
Salvador
Port Salvador
Macbride Head
Byron Sound
Roy Cove Settlement
Passage Islands
King George Bay
Mount Adam 700m
Port Howard Settlement
Port San Carlos
San Carlos Settlement
Berkeley Sound
STANLEY
Mount Usborne 705m
Bluff Cove
Mount Pleasant
New Island
Grey Channel
Weddell Island
Queen Charlotte Bay
West Falkland
Falkland Sound
Swan Island
Darwin
Goose Green
East Falkland
Choiseul Sound
Fox Point
Beaver Settlement
Beaver Island
Fox Bay East
Low Bay
Lively Island
Lively Sound
Cape Orford
Port Stephens Settlement
Port Stephens
Mount Alice 361m
North Arm
Adventure Sound
Bleaker Island
Speedwell Island
Eagle Passage
Bay of Harbours
Cape Meredith
George Island
Sea Lion Islands
ATLANTIC OCEAN
SCALE 1:3,300,000
SAINT HELENA (to UK)
Sugar Loaf Point
Flagstaff Bay
JAMESTOWN
The Haystack 616m
Horse Pasture Point
Longwood
Egg Island
Diana's Peak 823m
Gill Point
South West Point
Long Range Point
Speery Island
Castle Rock Point
ATLANTIC OCEAN
SCALE 1:830,000
TRISTAN DA CUNHA (to Saint Helena)
Big Point
Rookery Point
EDINBURGH
Anchorstock Point
Queen Mary's Peak 2060m
Sandy Point
Longbluff
Lyon Point
Cave Point
Stonybeach Bay
Stonyhill Point
ATLANTIC OCEAN
SCALE 1:830,000
Ocean map key
Sea depth
Sea level
200m / 656ft
1000m / 3281ft
2000m / 6562ft
3000m / 9843ft
4000m / 13,124ft
5000m / 16,400ft
6000m / 19,686ft
Inset map key
Population
100,000 to 500,000
50,000 to 100,000
10,000 to 50,000
below 10,000
Elevation
1000m / 3281ft
500m / 1640ft
250m / 820ft
100m / 328ft
sea level

The landscape

The floor of the Atlantic is spreading by about one inch (2.5 cm) a year. The South American and African plates are moving apart drawing molten rock up from the Earth's core. The Mid-Atlantic Ridge lies along the boundary of the two plates, forming the world's longest mountain range and dividing the Atlantic floor into two parallel troughs. These troughs are subdivided into numerous smaller basins by transform faults. Most of the oceanic islands in the Atlantic are volcanic in origin; either part of the Mid-Atlantic Ridge or the Caribbean arc.

The Gulf Stream is driven by westerly winds and ocean circulation. It flows like a river of warm water along the coast of America and then across the north Atlantic where it becomes known as the North Atlantic Drift.

The Caribbean Sea only adopted its present shape 3 million years ago, when the Isthmus of Panama closed by continental drift.

Ice breaking away from the Greenland ice sheet presents a constant threat to shipping in the north Atlantic. Icebergs are carried out of the Davis Strait by sea currents.

▲ ***Volcanism in the*** *Azores occurs because they lie over a hot spot in the oceanic crust. There are ten volcanoes clustered around the Azores. Many are still classified as active, although there has not been an eruption for over a century.*

Silt, mud and clay deposited at the delta of the Amazon have been carried over the continental shelf by underwater currents, forming a deep-water fan on the floor of the Atlantic Ocean.

The overall salinity of the north Atlantic is increased by highly saline water flowing out from the Mediterranean through the Strait of Gibraltar.

The Mid-Atlantic Ridge is marked along its length by numerous east–west valleys and ridges; these are caused by localized transform faulting. Some of these faults extend for 1250 miles (2000 km).

The South Sandwich Trench is the deepest part of the Atlantic; its base lies 30,000 ft (9144 m) below sea level. The trench is frequently subjected to earthquakes.

Floating ice shelves extend over 100 miles (160 km) into the Weddell Sea, off the coast of Antarctica.

Icebergs in the Antarctic are larger than those in the Arctic and can be up to 50 miles (80 km) long. they can drift to latitudes of around 40°S before melting.

▲ ***Running the length*** *of the ocean, the Mid-Atlantic Ridge is a complex system of sea-floor spreading, transform faults and volcanic islands. At its centre is a large rift valley 15–30 miles (24–48 km) wide, formed by the upwelling of the ocean floor toward both Africa and South America.*

▲ ***Most of the whales*** *in the Atlantic Ocean are found in the cooler waters of the south Atlantic, although many species migrate north to tropical waters to breed.*

◀ ***Rocky breakwaters have*** *been built along the coast of Ghana to protect local fishing boats from being destroyed by powerful Atlantic waves.*

Africa

The world's second largest continent, Africa covers an area of 11,712,434 sq miles (30,355,000 sq km). It has 57 separate countries, including Madagascar, Comoros, Mauritius and the Seychelles in the Indian Ocean – the highest number of any continent.

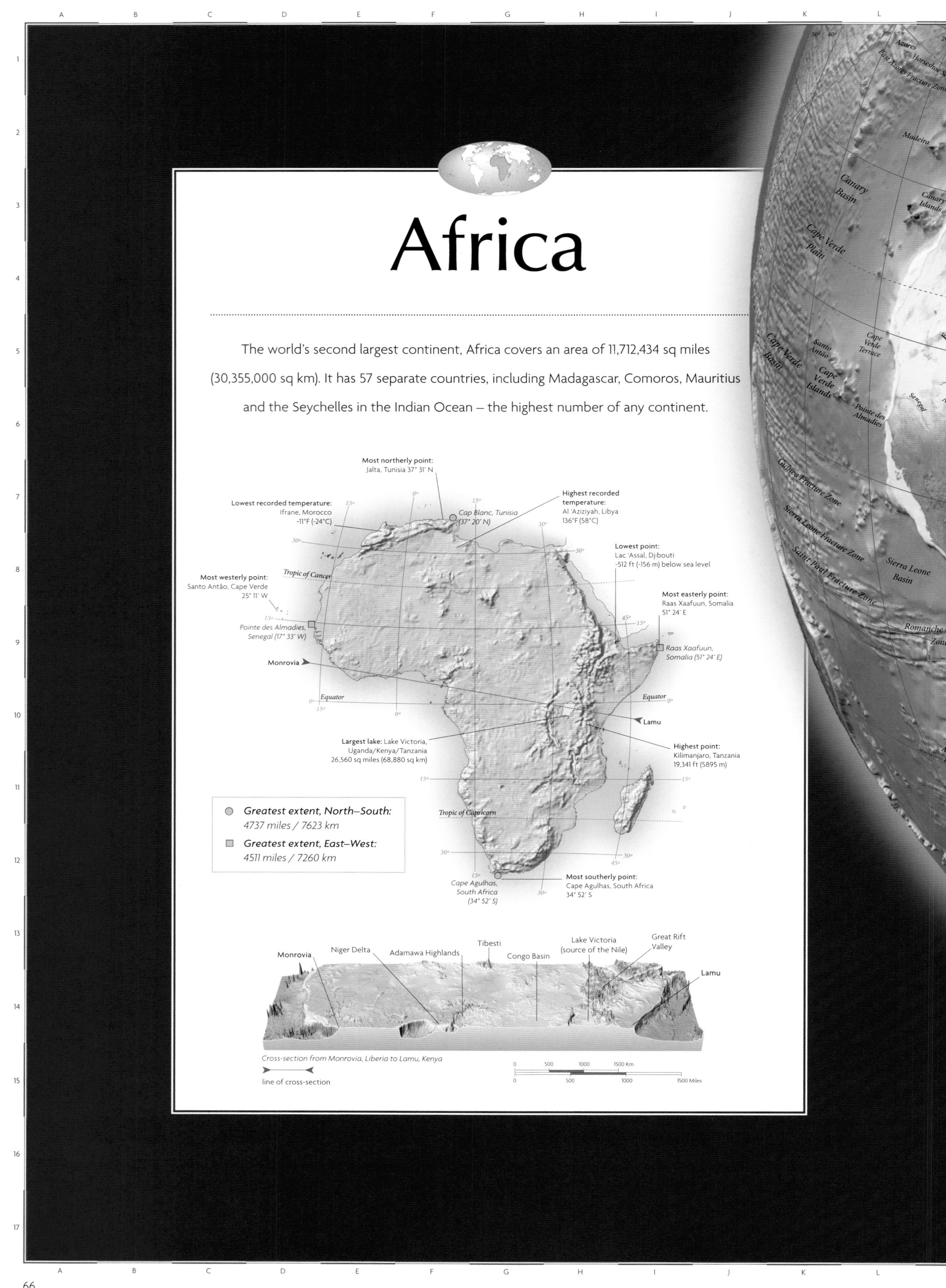

Most northerly point:
Jalta, Tunisia 37° 31' N
Cap Blanc, Tunisia (37° 20' N)
Lowest recorded temperature:
Ifrane, Morocco
-11°F (-24°C)
Highest recorded temperature:
Al 'Aziziyah, Libya
136°F (58°C)
Lowest point:
Lac 'Assal, Djibouti
-512 ft (-156 m) below sea level
Most westerly point:
Santo Antão, Cape Verde
25° 11' W
Most easterly point:
Raas Xaafuun, Somalia
51° 24' E
Pointe des Almadies, Senegal (17° 33' W)
Raas Xaafuun, Somalia (51° 24' E)
Tropic of Cancer
Monrovia
Equator
Lamu
Largest lake: Lake Victoria, Uganda/Kenya/Tanzania
26,560 sq miles (68,880 sq km)
Highest point:
Kilimanjaro, Tanzania
19,341 ft (5895 m)
Tropic of Capricorn
Greatest extent, North–South:
4737 miles / 7623 km
Greatest extent, East–West:
4511 miles / 7260 km
Cape Agulhas, South Africa (34° 52' S)
Most southerly point:
Cape Agulhas, South Africa
34° 52' S
Monrovia
Niger Delta
Adamawa Highlands
Tibesti
Congo Basin
Lake Victoria (source of the Nile)
Great Rift Valley
Lamu
Cross-section from Monrovia, Liberia to Lamu, Kenya
line of cross-section
0 500 1000 1500 Km
0 500 1000 1500 Miles
Azores
East Azores Fracture Zone
Madeira
Canary Basin
Canary Islands
Cape Verde Plain
Cape Verde Terrace
Santo Antão
Cape Verde Basin
Cape Verde Islands
Pointe des Almadies
Senegal
Guinea Fracture Zone
Sierra Leone Fracture Zone
Saint Paul Fracture Zone
Sierra Leone Basin

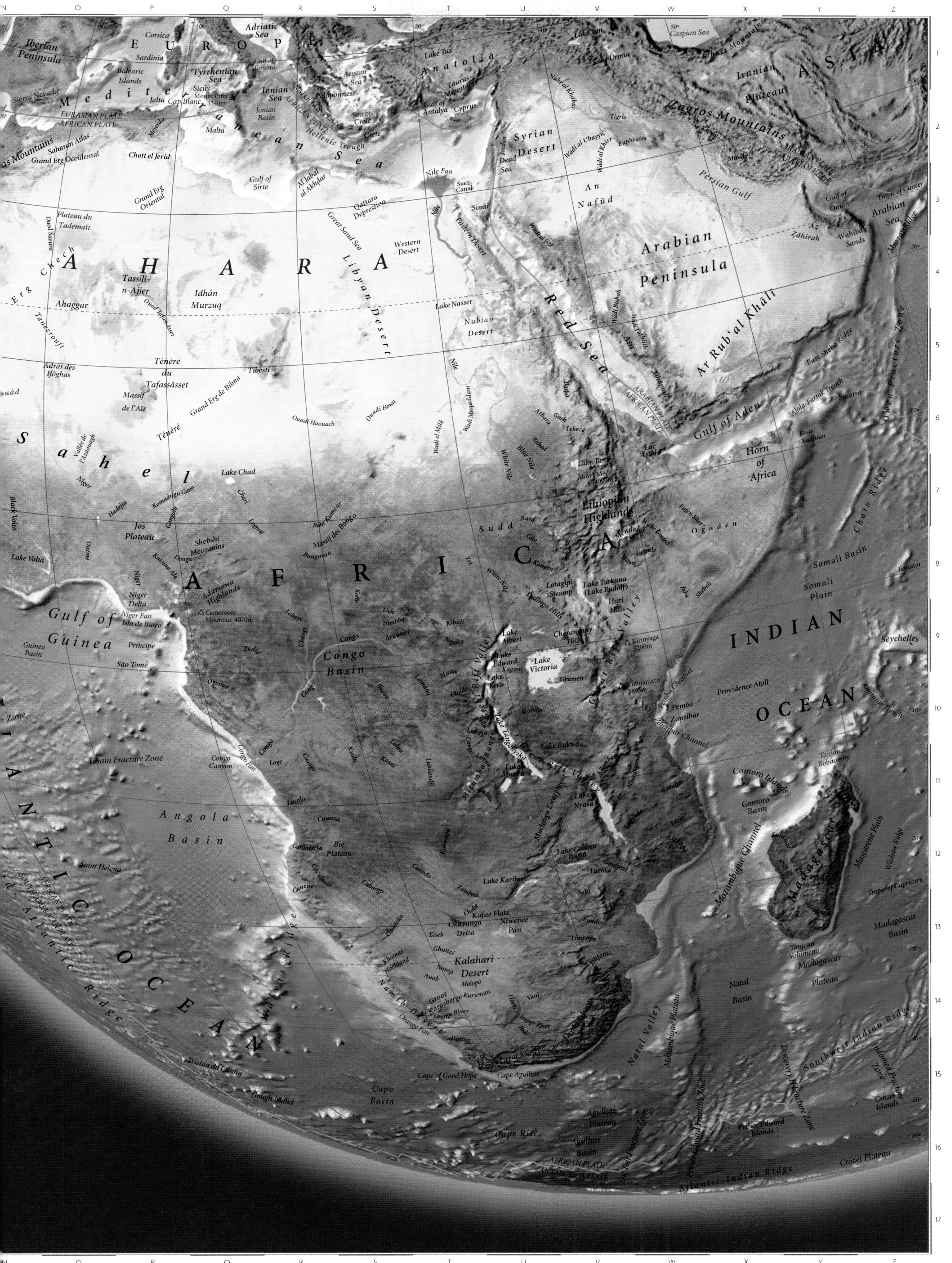

EUROPE
Iberian Peninsula
Corsica
Sardinia
Balearic Islands
Adriatic Sea
Tyrrhenian Sea
Sicily
Mount Etna 3340m
Ionian Sea
Ionian Basin
Malta
Mediterranean Sea
Aegean Sea
Peloponnese
Sea of Crete
Crete
Hellenic Trough
EURASIAN PLATE
AFRICAN PLATE
Anatolia
Lake Tuz
Taurus Mountains
Gulf of Antalya
Cyprus
Caspian Sea
Lake Urmia
Iranian Plateau
ASIA
Zagros Mountains
Syrian Desert
Jordan
Dead Sea
Euphrates
Tigris
Persian Gulf
Gulf of Oman
Tropic of Cancer
Arabian Sea
Saharan Atlas
Grand Erg Occidental
Chott el Jerid
Gulf of Sirte
Grand Erg Oriental
Al Jabal al Akhdar
Qattara Depression
Nile Fan
Suez Canal
Sinai
Nile
Eastern Desert
An Nafūd
Arabian Peninsula
Plateau du Tademaït
Great Sand Sea
Western Desert
SAHARA
Libyan Desert
Tassili-n-Ajjer
Idhān Murzuq
Ahaggar
Erg Chech
Tanezrouft
Lake Nasser
Nubian Desert
Red Sea
Ar Rubʻ al Khālī
Adrar des Ifôghas
Ténéré du Tafassâsset
Tibesti
Massif de l'Aïr
Grand Erg de Bilma
Ténéré
Sahel
Gulf of Aden
Socotra
Horn of Africa
Lake Chad
Lake Tana
Ethiopian Highlands
Ogaden
Sudd
AFRICA
Black Volta
Jos Plateau
Shebshi Mountains
Lake Volta
Massif des Bongo
Somali Basin
Equator
Lake Turkana (Lake Rudolf)
Huri Hills
Adamawa Highlands
Niger Delta
Gulf of Guinea
Niger Fan
Isla de Bioco
Cameroon Mountain 4070m
Príncipe
São Tomé
Guinea Basin
Congo
Congo Basin
Lake Albert
Lake Edward
Lake Kivu
Lake Victoria
Kirinyaga 5200m
Kilimanjaro 5895m
Somali Plain
INDIAN OCEAN
Seychelles
Providence Atoll
Pemba
Zanzibar
Lake Tanganyika
Lake Rukwa
Lake Mweru
Chain Fracture Zone
Congo Canyon
Comoro Islands
Comoro Basin
Tanjona Bobaomby
Lake Nyasa
Angola Basin
Bié Plateau
Mozambique Channel
Madagascar
Saint Helena
Lake Kariba
Lake Cabora Bassa
Kafue Flats
Okavango Delta
Ntwetwe Pan
Tropic of Capricorn
Madagascar Basin
Kalahari Desert
Tanjona Vohimena
Madagascar Plateau
Natal Basin
Walvis Ridge
ATLANTIC OCEAN
Orange River
Great Karoo
Natal Valley
Mozambique Plateau
Southwest Indian Ridge
Tristan da Cunha
Cape of Good Hope
Cape Agulhas
Cape Basin
Gough Island
Agulhas Plateau
Cape Rise
Agulhas Basin
Prince Edward Islands
Crozet Islands
Crozet Plateau
AFRICAN PLATE
ANTARCTIC PLATE
Atlantic-Indian Ridge

N O P Q R S T U V W X Y Z

Physical Africa

The structure of Africa was dramatically influenced by the break up of the supercontinent Gondwanaland about 160 million years ago and, more recently, rifting and hot spot activity. Today, much of Africa is remote from active plate boundaries and comprises a series of extensive plateaux and deep basins, which influence the drainage patterns of major rivers. The relief rises to the east, where volcanic uplands and vast lakes mark the Great Rift Valley. In the far north and south sedimentary rocks have been folded to form the Atlas Mountains and the Great Karoo.

East Africa

The Great Rift Valley is the most striking feature of this region, running for 4475 miles (7200 km) from Lake Nyasa to the Red Sea. North of Lake Nyasa it splits into two arms and encloses an interior plateau which contains Lake Victoria. A number of elongated lakes and volcanoes lie along the fault lines. To the west lies the Congo Basin, a vast, shallow depression, which rises to form an almost circular rim of highlands.

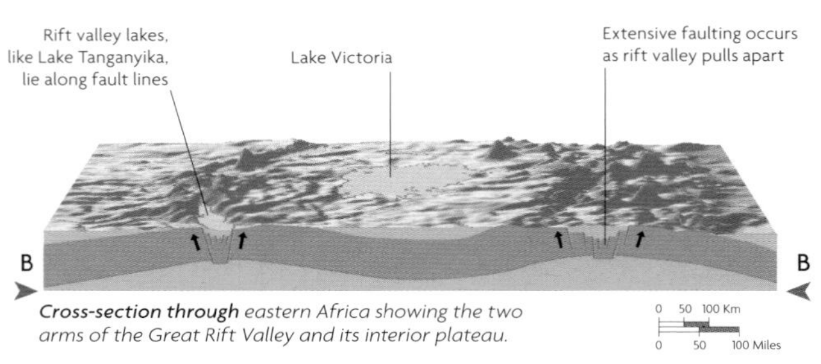
Rift valley lakes, like Lake Tanganyika, lie along fault lines
Lake Victoria
Extensive faulting occurs as rift valley pulls apart
B
B
0 50 100 Km
0 50 100 Miles

***Cross-section through** eastern Africa showing the two arms of the Great Rift Valley and its interior plateau.*

Northern Africa

Northern Africa comprises a system of basins and plateaux. The Tibesti and Ahaggar are volcanic uplands, whose uplift has been matched by subsidence within large surrounding basins. Many of the basins have been infilled with sand and gravel, creating the vast Saharan lands. The Atlas Mountains in the north were formed by convergence of the African and Eurasian plates.

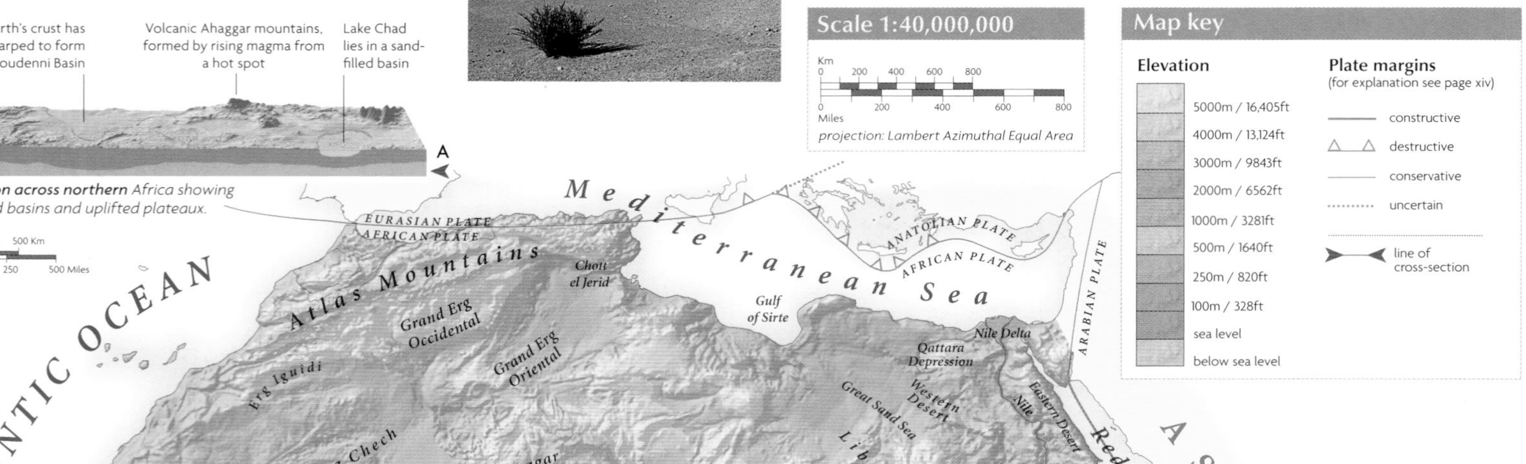
The Earth's crust has been warped to form the Taoudenni Basin
Volcanic Ahaggar mountains, formed by rising magma from a hot spot
Lake Chad lies in a sand-filled basin
A
A
0 250 500 Km
0 250 500 Miles

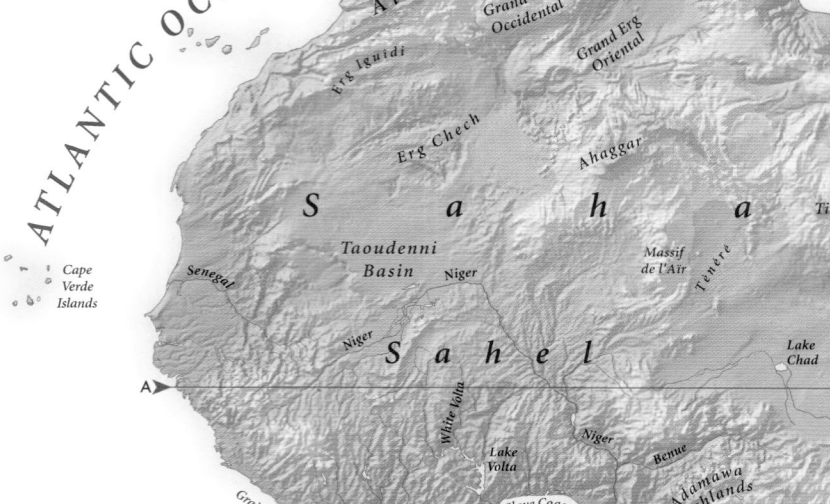

***Section across northern** Africa showing infilled basins and uplifted plateaux.*

Scale 1:40,000,000

Km 0 200 400 600 800
Miles 0 200 400 600 800

projection: Lambert Azimuthal Equal Area

Map key

Elevation

- 5000m / 16,405ft
- 4000m / 13,124ft
- 3000m / 9843ft
- 2000m / 6562ft
- 1000m / 3281ft
- 500m / 1640ft
- 250m / 820ft
- 100m / 328ft
- sea level
- below sea level

Plate margins
(for explanation see page xiv)

- constructive
- destructive
- conservative
- uncertain
- line of cross-section

Mediterranean Sea
EURASIAN PLATE
AFRICAN PLATE
ANATOLIAN PLATE
AFRICAN PLATE
ARABIAN PLATE
ARABIAN PLATE
AFRICAN PLATE
ATLANTIC OCEAN
ASIA
Atlas Mountains
Chott el Jerid
Gulf of Sirte
Grand Erg Occidental
Grand Erg Oriental
Erg Iguidi
Erg Chech
Ahaggar
Sahara
Tibesti
Nile Delta
Qattara Depression
Western Desert
Great Sand Sea
Libyan Desert
Eastern Desert
Nile
Red Sea
Lake Nasser
Nubian Desert
Cape Verde Islands
Taoudenni Basin
Niger
Senegal
Massif de l'Aïr
Ténéré
Sahel
Lake Chad
Blue Nile
White Nile
Lake Tana
Gulf of Aden
Horn of Africa
Ethiopian Highlands
White Volta
Lake Volta
Benue
Adamawa Highlands
Massif des Bongo
Sudd
Grain Coast
Ivory Coast
Gold Coast
Slave Coast
Bight of Benin
Niger Delta
Cameroon Mountain 4070m
Ubangi
Shebeli
Lake Turkana (Lake Rudolf)
Gulf of Guinea
Congo
Lake Albert
Juba
São Tomé
Congo Basin
Lake Victoria
Great Rift Valley
Kilimanjaro 5895m
Seychelles
Mitumba Range
Lake Tanganyika
Pemba Island
Zanzibar
Bié Plateau
Lake Nyasa
Comoro Islands
Zambezi
Mozambique Channel
Madagascar
Okavango Delta
Kalahari Basin
Kalahari Desert
Namib Desert
Limpopo
Mauritius
Réunion
INDIAN OCEAN
Orange River
Drakensberg
Great Karoo
Cape of Good Hope

Southern Africa

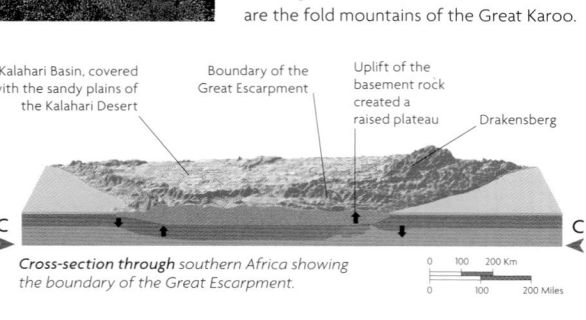

The Great Escarpment marks the southern boundary of Africa's basement rock and includes the Drakensberg range. It was uplifted when Gondwanaland fragmented about 160 million years ago and it has gradually been eroded back from the coast. To the north, the relief drops steadily, forming the Kalahari Basin. In the far south are the fold mountains of the Great Karoo.

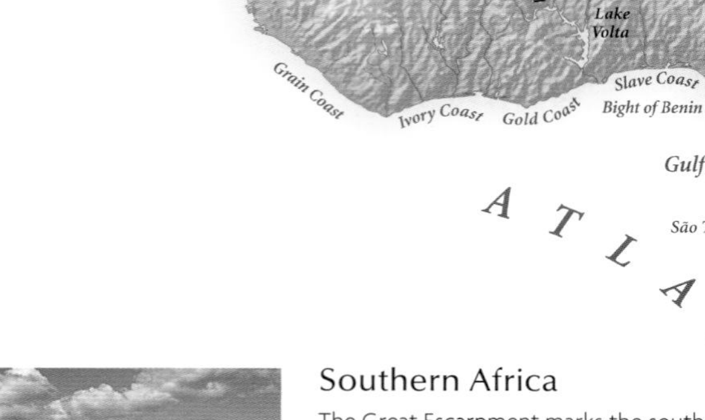
Kalahari Basin, covered with the sandy plains of the Kalahari Desert
Boundary of the Great Escarpment
Uplift of the basement rock created a raised plateau
Drakensberg
C
C
0 100 200 Km
0 100 200 Miles

***Cross-section through** southern Africa showing the boundary of the Great Escarpment.*

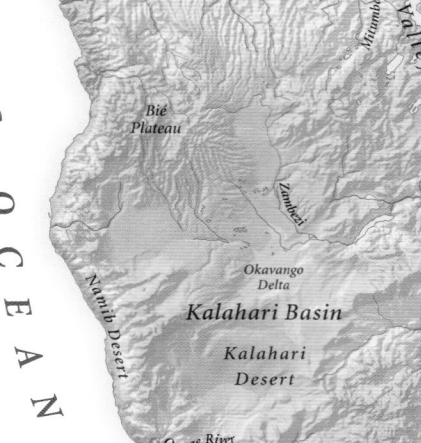

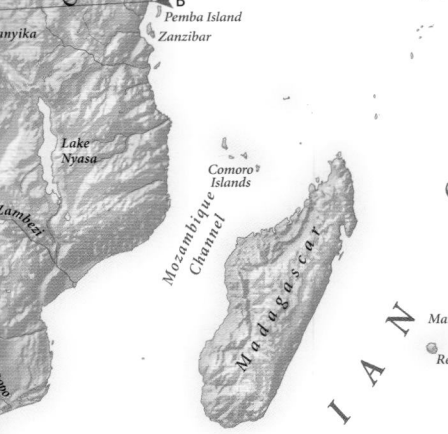

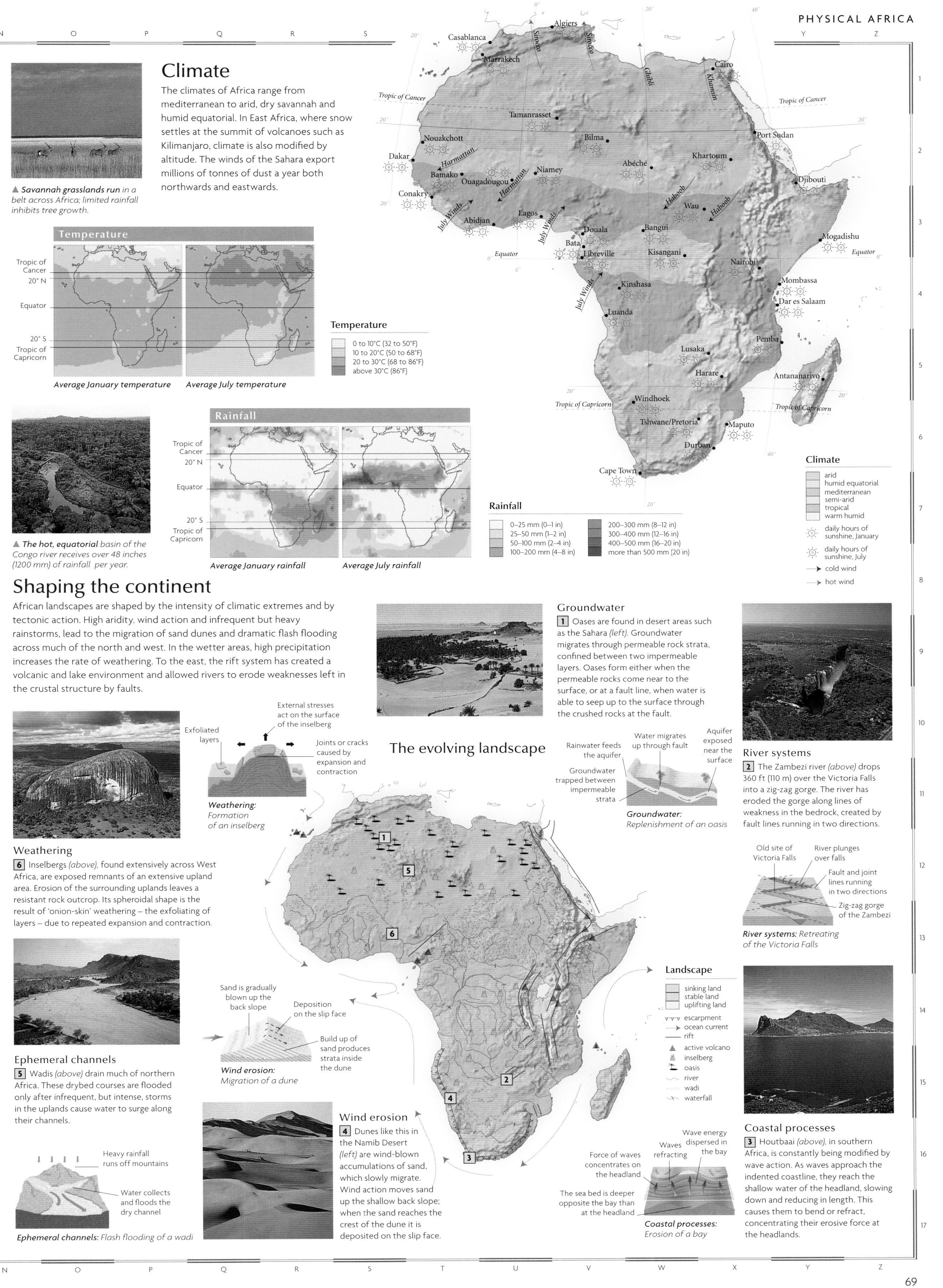

N O P Q R S T U V W X Y Z
1 2 3 4 5 6 7 8 9 10 11 12 13 14 15 16 17
Algiers
Casablanca
Marrakech
Sirocco
Sirocco
Ghibli
Khamsin
Cairo
Tropic of Cancer
Tropic of Cancer
Tamanrasset
Nouakchott
Bilma
Port Sudan
Dakar
Harmattan
Khartoum
Abéché
Bamako
Niamey
Ouagadougou
Harmattan
Djibouti
Conakry
Haboob
Haboob
Wau
July Winds
Lagos
Abidjan
July Winds
Douala
Bangui
Mogadishu
Bata
Libreville
Kisangani
Equator
Equator
Nairobi
Mombassa
July Winds
Kinshasa
Dar es Salaam
Luanda
Pemba
Lusaka
Harare
Antananarivo
Tropic of Capricorn
Windhoek
Tropic of Capricorn
Tshwane/Pretoria
Maputo
Durban
Cape Town
Temperature
Tropic of Cancer
20° N
Equator
20° S
Tropic of Capricorn
Temperature
0 to 10°C (32 to 50°F)
10 to 20°C (50 to 68°F)
20 to 30°C (68 to 86°F)
above 30°C (86°F)
Average January temperature
Average July temperature
Rainfall
Tropic of Cancer
20° N
Equator
20° S
Tropic of Capricorn
Average January rainfall
Average July rainfall
Rainfall
0–25 mm (0–1 in)
25–50 mm (1–2 in)
50–100 mm (2–4 in)
100–200 mm (4–8 in)
200–300 mm (8–12 in)
300–400 mm (12–16 in)
400–500 mm (16–20 in)
more than 500 mm (20 in)
Climate
arid
humid equatorial
mediterranean
semi-arid
tropical
warm humid
daily hours of sunshine, January
daily hours of sunshine, July
cold wind
hot wind
Exfoliated layers
External stresses act on the surface of the inselberg
Joints or cracks caused by expansion and contraction
Weathering: Formation of an inselberg
The evolving landscape
Rainwater feeds the aquifer
Water migrates up through fault
Aquifer exposed near the surface
Groundwater trapped between impermeable strata
Groundwater: Replenishment of an oasis
1
5
6
2
4
3
Sand is gradually blown up the back slope
Deposition on the slip face
Build up of sand produces strata inside the dune
Wind erosion: Migration of a dune
Landscape
sinking land
stable land
uplifting land
escarpment
ocean current
rift
active volcano
inselberg
oasis
river
wadi
waterfall
Old site of Victoria Falls
River plunges over falls
Fault and joint lines running in two directions
Zig-zag gorge of the Zambezi
River systems: Retreating of the Victoria Falls
Heavy rainfall runs off mountains
Water collects and floods the dry channel
Ephemeral channels: Flash flooding of a wadi
Wave energy dispersed in the bay
Waves refracting
Force of waves concentrates on the headland
The sea bed is deeper opposite the bay than at the headland
Coastal processes: Erosion of a bay

Climate

The climates of Africa range from mediterranean to arid, dry savannah and humid equatorial. In East Africa, where snow settles at the summit of volcanoes such as Kilimanjaro, climate is also modified by altitude. The winds of the Sahara export millions of tonnes of dust a year both northwards and eastwards.

▲ ***Savannah grasslands run** in a belt across Africa; limited rainfall inhibits tree growth.*

▲ ***The hot, equatorial** basin of the Congo river receives over 48 inches (1200 mm) of rainfall per year.*

Shaping the continent

African landscapes are shaped by the intensity of climatic extremes and by tectonic action. High aridity, wind action and infrequent but heavy rainstorms, lead to the migration of sand dunes and dramatic flash flooding across much of the north and west. In the wetter areas, high precipitation increases the rate of weathering. To the east, the rift system has created a volcanic and lake environment and allowed rivers to erode weaknesses left in the crustal structure by faults.

Weathering

6 Inselbergs *(above)*, found extensively across West Africa, are exposed remnants of an extensive upland area. Erosion of the surrounding uplands leaves a resistant rock outcrop. Its spheroidal shape is the result of 'onion-skin' weathering – the exfoliating of layers – due to repeated expansion and contraction.

Ephemeral channels

5 Wadis *(above)* drain much of northern Africa. These drybed courses are flooded only after infrequent, but intense, storms in the uplands cause water to surge along their channels.

Groundwater

1 Oases are found in desert areas such as the Sahara *(left)*. Groundwater migrates through permeable rock strata, confined between two impermeable layers. Oases form either when the permeable rocks come near to the surface, or at a fault line, when water is able to seep up to the surface through the crushed rocks at the fault.

River systems

2 The Zambezi river *(above)* drops 360 ft (110 m) over the Victoria Falls into a zig-zag gorge. The river has eroded the gorge along lines of weakness in the bedrock, created by fault lines running in two directions.

Wind erosion

4 Dunes like this in the Namib Desert *(left)* are wind-blown accumulations of sand, which slowly migrate. Wind action moves sand up the shallow back slope; when the sand reaches the crest of the dune it is deposited on the slip face.

Coastal processes

3 Houtbaai *(above)*, in southern Africa, is constantly being modified by wave action. As waves approach the indented coastline, they reach the shallow water of the headland, slowing down and reducing in length. This causes them to bend or refract, concentrating their erosive force at the headlands.

Political Africa

The political map of modern Africa only emerged following the end of the Second World War. Over the next half-century, all of the countries formerly controlled by European powers gained independence from their colonial rulers – only Liberia and Ethiopia were never colonized.

The post-colonial era has not been an easy period for many countries, but there have been moves towards multi-party democracy across much of the continent. In South Africa, democratic elections replaced the internationally-condemned apartheid system only in 1994. Other countries have still to find political stability; corruption in government and ethnic tensions are serious problems. National infrastructures, based on the colonial transport systems built to exploit Africa's resources, are often inappropriate for independent economic development.

BERBER
ARABIC
TUAREG
TEDA
FULANI
MANDINGO
MOSI
HAUSA
KANURI
AKAN
EVE
YORUBA
IBO
ARABIC
BEJA
TIGRAI
AMHARA
GALLA
DINKA
SOMALI
AZANDE
MASAI
SWAHILI
BANTU
MALAGASY
SAN
KHOI
AFRIKAANS

Language groups

- Afro-Asiatic (Hamito-Semitic)
- Niger-Congo
- Nilo-Saharan
- Khoisan
- Indo-European
- Austronesian

Languages

Three major world languages act as *lingua francas* across the African continent: Arabic in North Africa; English in southern and eastern Africa and Nigeria; and French in Central and West Africa, and in Madagascar. A huge number of African languages are spoken as well – over 2000 have been recorded, with more than 400 in Nigeria alone – reflecting the continuing importance of traditional cultures and values. In the north of the continent, the extensive use of Arabic reflects Middle Eastern influences while Bantu languages are widely spoken across much of southern Africa.

Official African languages

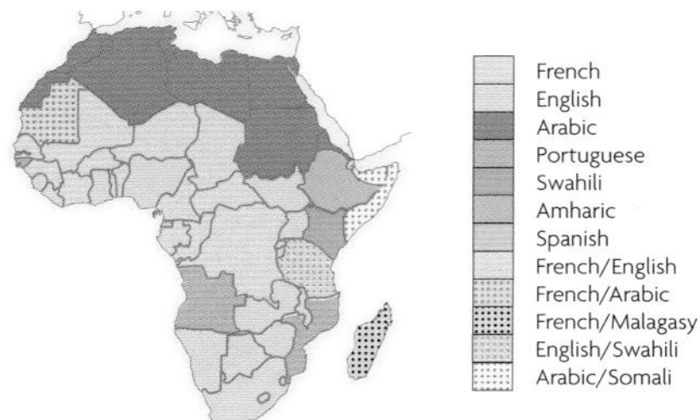
French
English
Arabic
Portuguese
Swahili
Amharic
Spanish
French/English
French/Arabic
French/Malagasy
English/Swahili
Arabic/Somali

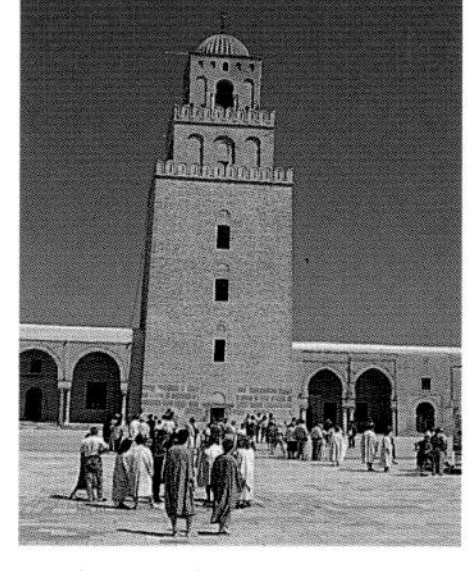

▲ *Islamic influences are evident throughout North Africa. The Great Mosque at Kairouan, Tunisia, is Africa's holiest Islamic place.*

▲ *In northeastern Nigeria, people speak Kanuri – a dialect of the Nilo-Saharan language group.*

Madeira (to Portugal)
MOROCCO
Agadir
Canary Islands (to Spain)
LAÂYOUNE
Western Sahara (Occupied by Morocco)
Tropic of Cancer
CAPE VERDE
PRAIA
MAURITANIA
NOUAKCHOTT
Senegal
SENEGAL
DAKAR
Kaolack
GAMBIA
BANJUL
BAMAKO
GUINEA-BISSAU
BISSAU
GUINEA
CONAKRY
FREETOWN
Koidu
SIERRA LEONE
YAMOUSSOUKRO
MONROVIA
LIBERIA

Transport

African railways were built to aid the exploitation of natural resources, and most offer passage only from the interior to the coastal cities, leaving large parts of the continent untouched – five land-locked countries have no railways at all. The Congo, Nile and Niger river networks offer limited access to land within the continental interior, but have a number of waterfalls and cataracts which prevent navigation from the sea. Many roads were developed in the 1960s and 1970s, but economic difficulties are making the maintenance and expansion of the networks difficult.

► *South Africa has the largest concentration of railways in Africa. Over 20,000 miles (32,000 km) of routes have been built since 1870.*

▲ *Traditional means of transport, such as the camel, are still widely used across the less accessible parts of Africa.*

◄ *The Congo river, though not suitable for river transport along its entire length, forms a vital link for people and goods in its navigable reaches.*

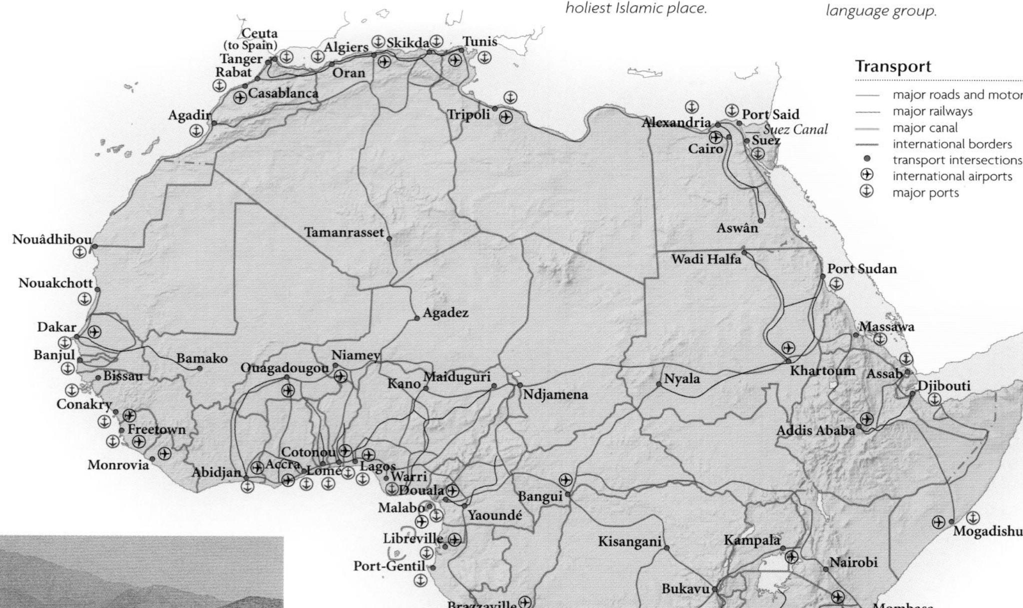
Ceuta (to Spain)
Tanger
Rabat
Casablanca
Agadir
Algiers
Oran
Skikda
Tunis
Tripoli
Alexandria
Port Said
Suez Canal
Cairo
Suez
Aswân
Wadi Halfa
Port Sudan
Tamanrasset
Nouâdhibou
Nouakchott
Dakar
Banjul
Bissau
Conakry
Freetown
Monrovia
Bamako
Ouagadougou
Niamey
Agadez
Kano
Maiduguri
Ndjamena
Nyala
Khartoum
Massawa
Assab
Djibouti
Addis Ababa
Abidjan
Accra
Lomé
Cotonou
Lagos
Warri
Douala
Malabo
Yaoundé
Bangui
Libreville
Port-Gentil
Mogadishu
Kisangani
Kampala
Nairobi
Bukavu
Mombasa
Brazzaville
Kinshasa
Pointe-Noire
Matadi
Kananga
Kalemie
Dodoma
Dar es Salaam
Mbeya
Luanda
Lobito
Lubumbashi
Namibe
Lusaka
Nampula
Livingstone
Harare
Tsumeb
Bulawayo
Beira
Antananarivo
Toamasina
Walvis Bay
Windhoek
Pretoria/Tshwane
Johannesburg
Maputo
Keetmanshoop
Durban
Cape Town
Port Elizabeth
Transport
major roads and motorways
major railways
major canal
international borders
transport intersections
international airports
major ports

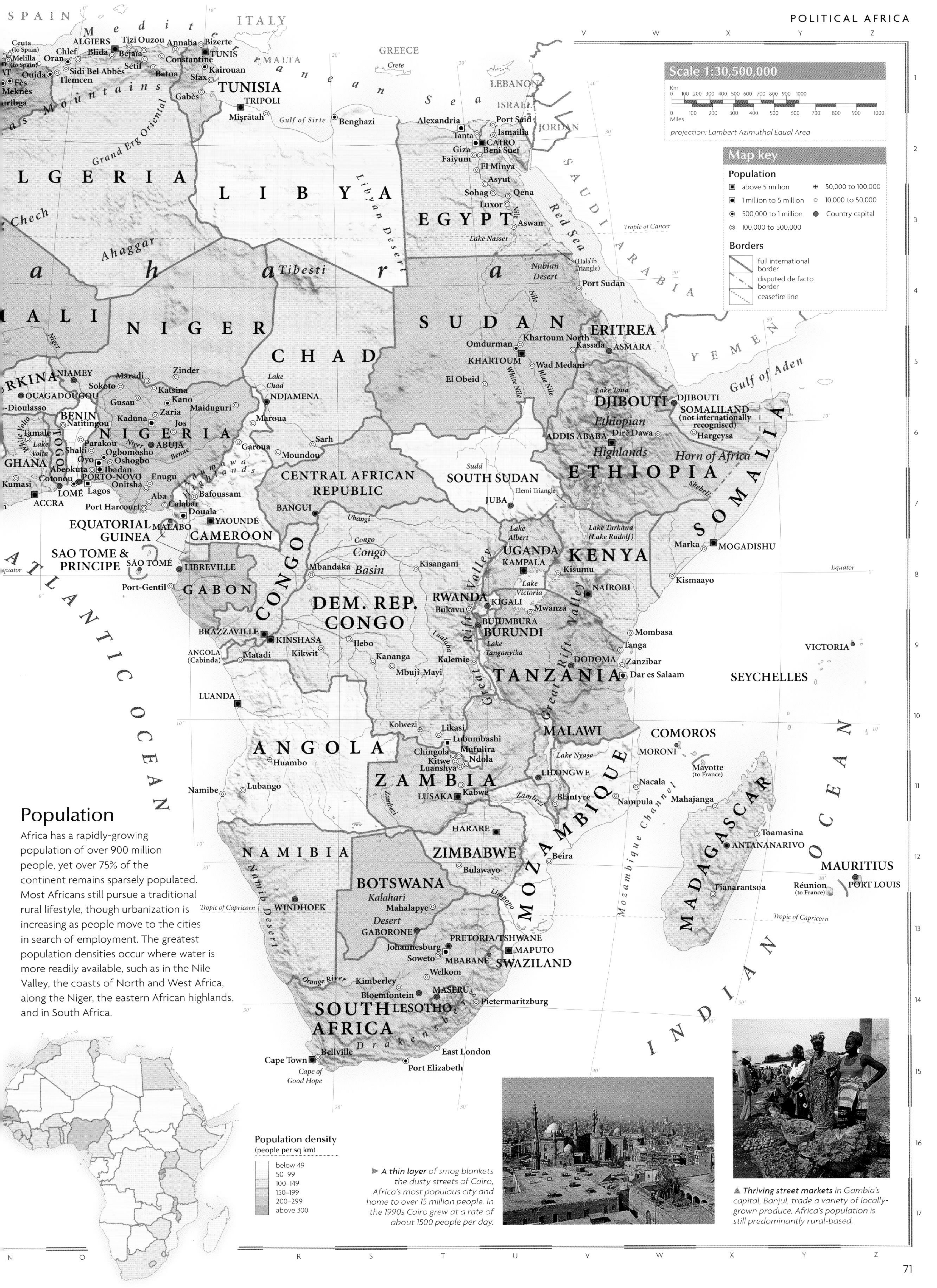
Scale 1:30,500,000
Km
Miles
projection: Lambert Azimuthal Equal Area
Map key
Population
above 5 million
1 million to 5 million
500,000 to 1 million
100,000 to 500,000
50,000 to 100,000
10,000 to 50,000
Country capital
Borders
full international border
disputed de facto border
ceasefire line
Population density
(people per sq km)
below 49
50–99
100–149
150–199
200–299
above 300
ALGERIA
LIBYA
EGYPT
TUNISIA
MALI
NIGER
CHAD
SUDAN
SOUTH SUDAN
ERITREA
DJIBOUTI
SOMALILAND (not internationally recognised)
ETHIOPIA
SOMALIA
NIGERIA
BENIN
TOGO
GHANA
CAMEROON
EQUATORIAL GUINEA
SAO TOME & PRINCIPE
GABON
CONGO
CENTRAL AFRICAN REPUBLIC
DEM. REP. CONGO
UGANDA
KENYA
RWANDA
BURUNDI
TANZANIA
ANGOLA
ZAMBIA
MALAWI
MOZAMBIQUE
ZIMBABWE
NAMIBIA
BOTSWANA
SOUTH AFRICA
LESOTHO
SWAZILAND
MADAGASCAR
COMOROS
SEYCHELLES
MAURITIUS
ATLANTIC OCEAN
INDIAN OCEAN
Mediterranean Sea
Red Sea
Gulf of Aden
Mozambique Channel
Sahara
Tropic of Cancer
Equator
Tropic of Capricorn

Population

Africa has a rapidly-growing population of over 900 million people, yet over 75% of the continent remains sparsely populated. Most Africans still pursue a traditional rural lifestyle, though urbanization is increasing as people move to the cities in search of employment. The greatest population densities occur where water is more readily available, such as in the Nile Valley, the coasts of North and West Africa, along the Niger, the eastern African highlands, and in South Africa.

▶ ***A thin layer*** *of smog blankets the dusty streets of Cairo, Africa's most populous city and home to over 15 million people. In the 1990s Cairo grew at a rate of about 1500 people per day.*

▲ ***Thriving street markets*** *in Gambia's capital, Banjul, trade a variety of locally-grown produce. Africa's population is still predominantly rural-based.*

African resources

The economies of most African countries are dominated by subsistence and cash crop agriculture, with limited industrialization. Manufacturing industry is largely confined to South Africa. Many countries depend on a single resource, such as copper or gold, or a cash crop, such as coffee, for export income, which can leave them vulnerable to fluctuations in world commodity prices. In order to diversify their economies and develop a wider industrial base, investment from overseas is being actively sought by many African governments.

Industry

Many African industries concentrate on the extraction and processing of raw materials. These include the oil industry, food processing, mining and textile production. South Africa accounts for over half of the continent's industrial output with much of the remainder coming from the countries along the northern coast. Over 60% of Africa's workforce is employed in agriculture.

◀ *The unspoilt natural splendour of wildlife reserves, like the Serengeti National Park in Tanzania, attract tourists to Africa from around the globe. The tourist industry in Kenya and Tanzania is particularly well developed, where it accounts for almost 10% of GNI.*

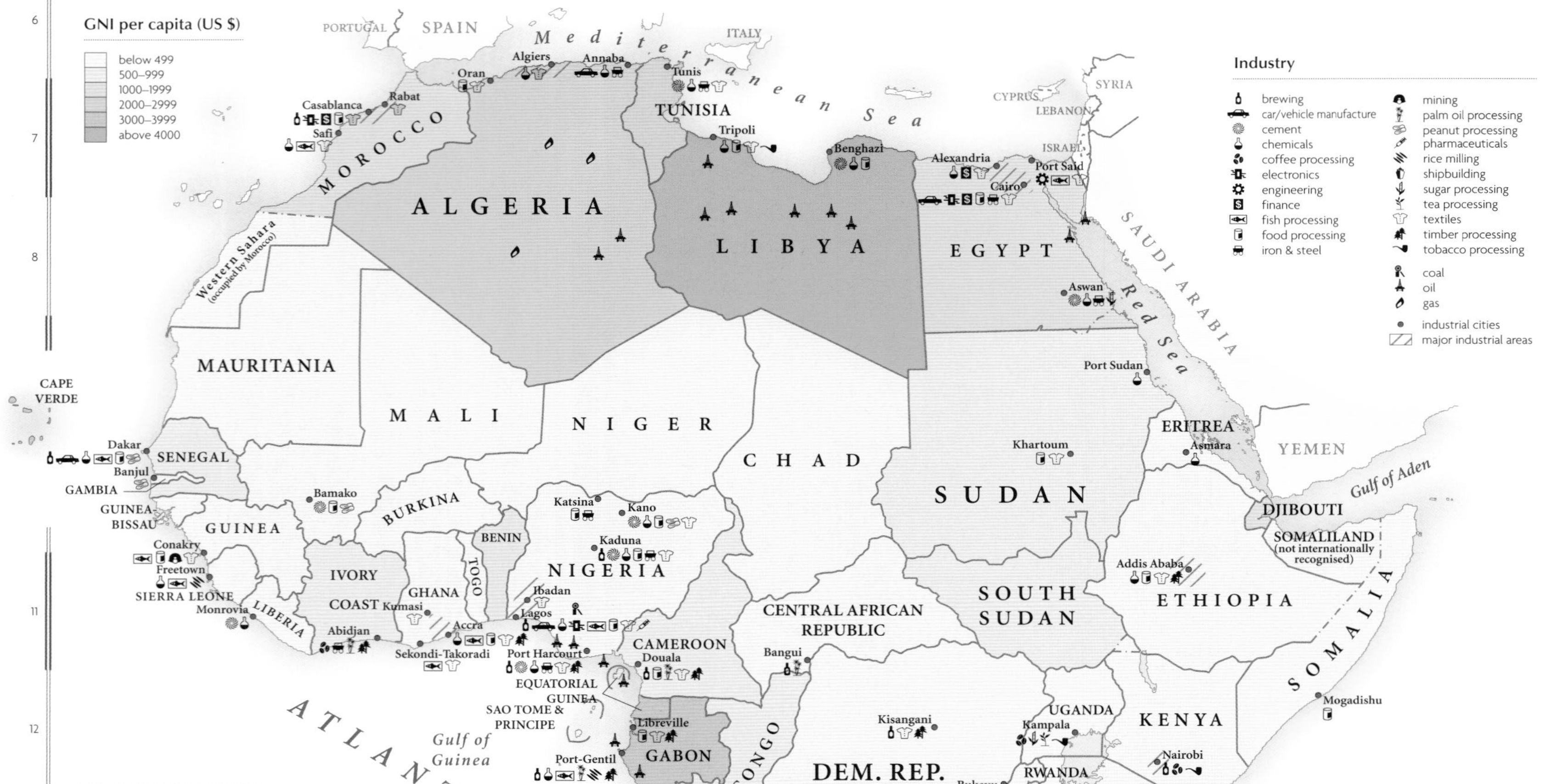

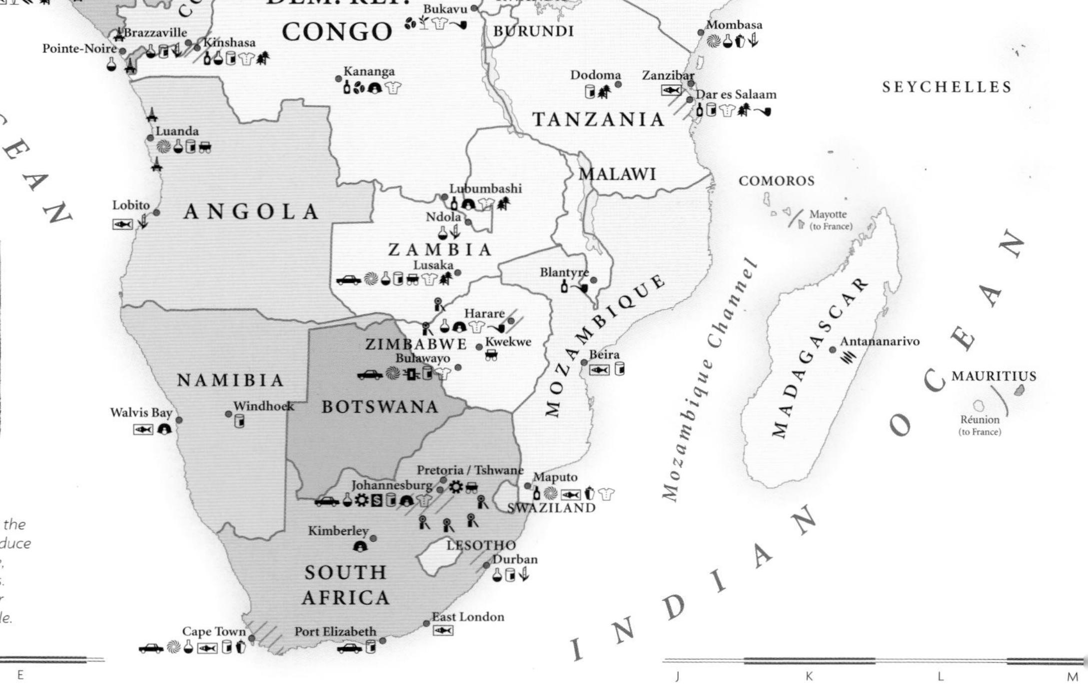

Standard of living

Since the 1960s most countries in Africa have seen significant improvements in life expectancy, healthcare and education. However, 28 of the 30 most deprived countries in the world are African, and the continent as a whole lies well behind the rest of the world in terms of meeting many basic human needs.

Standard of living
(UN human development index)

high

low

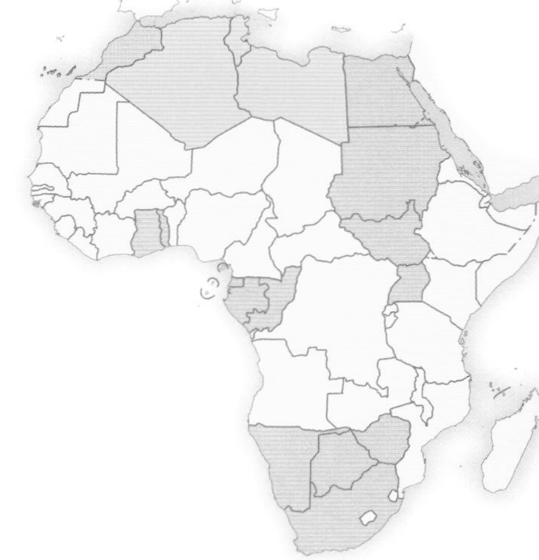

GNI per capita (US $)

- below 499
- 500–999
- 1000–1999
- 2000–2999
- 3000–3999
- above 4000

Industry

- brewing
- car/vehicle manufacture
- cement
- chemicals
- coffee processing
- electronics
- engineering
- finance
- fish processing
- food processing
- iron & steel
- mining
- palm oil processing
- peanut processing
- pharmaceuticals
- rice milling
- shipbuilding
- sugar processing
- tea processing
- textiles
- timber processing
- tobacco processing
- coal
- oil
- gas
- industrial cities
- major industrial areas

PORTUGAL SPAIN Mediterranean Sea ITALY CYPRUS SYRIA LEBANON ISRAEL SAUDI ARABIA Red Sea YEMEN Gulf of Aden

Algiers Oran Annaba Tunis Casablanca Rabat Safi Tripoli Benghazi Alexandria Port Said Cairo Aswan Port Sudan

MOROCCO ALGERIA TUNISIA LIBYA EGYPT Western Sahara (occupied by Morocco) MAURITANIA MALI NIGER CHAD SUDAN ERITREA DJIBOUTI SOMALILAND (not internationally recognised) ETHIOPIA SOUTH SUDAN SOMALIA

CAPE VERDE Dakar SENEGAL Banjul GAMBIA GUINEA-BISSAU GUINEA Conakry Freetown SIERRA LEONE Monrovia LIBERIA Bamako BURKINA IVORY COAST Abidjan Kumasi GHANA Accra Sekondi-Takoradi TOGO BENIN NIGERIA Katsina Kano Kaduna Ibadan Lagos Port Harcourt Khartoum Asmara Addis Ababa

CAMEROON Douala EQUATORIAL GUINEA SAO TOME & PRINCIPE Gulf of Guinea ATLANTIC OCEAN Libreville GABON Port-Gentil CONGO Brazzaville Pointe-Noire Kinshasa CENTRAL AFRICAN REPUBLIC Bangui DEM. REP. CONGO Kisangani Bukavu Kananga UGANDA Kampala RWANDA BURUNDI KENYA Nairobi Mombasa Mogadishu TANZANIA Dodoma Zanzibar Dar es Salaam SEYCHELLES

Luanda Lobito ANGOLA ZAMBIA Lubumbashi Ndola Lusaka MALAWI Blantyre COMOROS Mayotte (to France) Harare ZIMBABWE Kwekwe Bulawayo MOZAMBIQUE Beira Mozambique Channel MADAGASCAR Antananarivo MAURITIUS Réunion (to France) INDIAN OCEAN

NAMIBIA Walvis Bay Windhoek BOTSWANA Pretoria / Tshwane Johannesburg Maputo SWAZILAND Kimberley LESOTHO Durban SOUTH AFRICA East London Cape Town Port Elizabeth

◀ *The discovery of oil in the swampy Niger Delta during the 1960s made Nigeria one of Africa's richer nations. As world oil prices fell in the 1980s, the Nigerian economy faltered.*

▶ *Exotic rugs and brightly-coloured textiles are sold in a street market along the banks of the river Nile in Luxor, Egypt.*

◀ *The Rössing uranium mines in Namibia are one of the largest in the world. Canada and Australia produce over half the world's uranium ore, used to fuel nuclear power plants. Elsewhere, South Africa and Niger also mine uranium on a large scale.*

Environmental issues

One of Africa's most serious environmental problems occurs in marginal areas such as the Sahel where scrub and forest clearance, often for cooking fuel, combined with overgrazing, are causing desertification. Game reserves in southern and eastern Africa have helped to preserve many endangered animals, although the needs of growing populations have led to conflict over land use, and poaching is a serious problem.

Mineral resources

Africa's ancient plateaux contain some of the world's most substantial reserves of precious stones and metals. About 15% of the world's gold is mined in South Africa; Zambia has great copper deposits; and diamonds are mined in Botswana, Dem. Rep. Congo and South Africa. Oil has brought great economic benefits to Algeria, Libya and Nigeria.

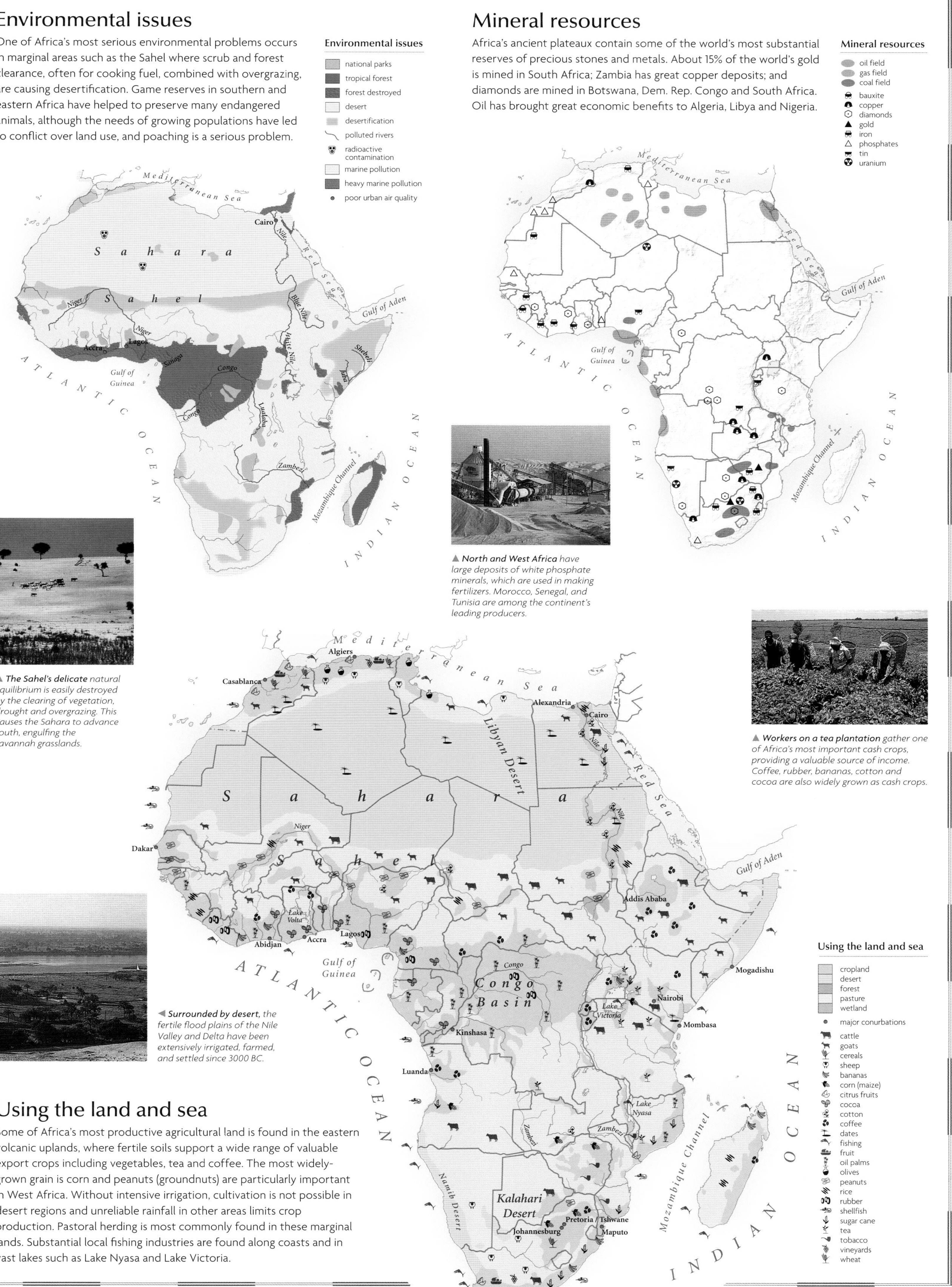

Environmental issues
national parks
tropical forest
forest destroyed
desert
desertification
polluted rivers
radioactive contamination
marine pollution
heavy marine pollution
poor urban air quality
Mineral resources
oil field
gas field
coal field
bauxite
copper
diamonds
gold
iron
phosphates
tin
uranium
Using the land and sea
cropland
desert
forest
pasture
wetland
major conurbations
cattle
goats
cereals
sheep
bananas
corn (maize)
citrus fruits
cocoa
cotton
coffee
dates
fishing
fruit
oil palms
olives
peanuts
rice
rubber
shellfish
sugar cane
tea
tobacco
vineyards
wheat

▲ *North and West Africa have large deposits of white phosphate minerals, which are used in making fertilizers. Morocco, Senegal, and Tunisia are among the continent's leading producers.*

▲ *The Sahel's delicate natural equilibrium is easily destroyed by the clearing of vegetation, drought and overgrazing. This causes the Sahara to advance south, engulfing the savannah grasslands.*

▲ *Workers on a tea plantation gather one of Africa's most important cash crops, providing a valuable source of income. Coffee, rubber, bananas, cotton and cocoa are also widely grown as cash crops.*

◀ *Surrounded by desert, the fertile flood plains of the Nile Valley and Delta have been extensively irrigated, farmed, and settled since 3000 BC.*

Using the land and sea

Some of Africa's most productive agricultural land is found in the eastern volcanic uplands, where fertile soils support a wide range of valuable export crops including vegetables, tea and coffee. The most widely-grown grain is corn and peanuts (groundnuts) are particularly important in West Africa. Without intensive irrigation, cultivation is not possible in desert regions and unreliable rainfall in other areas limits crop production. Pastoral herding is most commonly found in these marginal lands. Substantial local fishing industries are found along coasts and in vast lakes such as Lake Nyasa and Lake Victoria.

North Africa

ALGERIA, EGYPT, LIBYA, MOROCCO, TUNISIA, WESTERN SAHARA

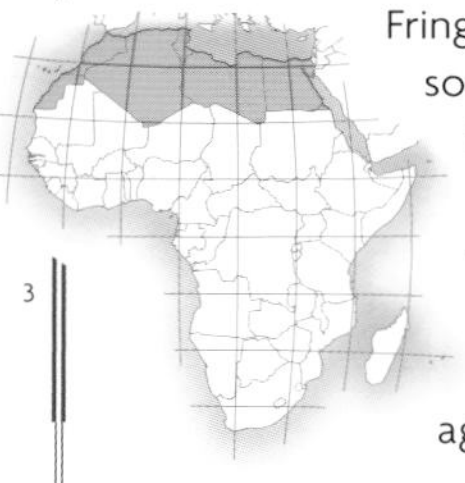

Fringed by the Mediterranean along the northern coast and by the arid Sahara in the south, North Africa reflects the influence of many invaders, both European and, most importantly, Arab, giving the region an almost universal Islamic flavour and a common Arabic language. The countries lying to the west of Egypt are often referred to as the Maghreb, an Arabic term for 'west'. Today, Morocco and Tunisia exploit their culture and landscape for tourism, while rich oil and gas deposits aid development in Libya and Algeria, despite political turmoil. Egypt, with its fertile, Nile-watered agricultural land and varied industrial base, is the most populous nation.

▲ **These rock piles** in Algeria's Ahaggar mountains are the result of weathering caused by extremes of temperature. Great cracks or joints appear in the rocks, which are then worn and smoothed by the wind.

The landscape

The Atlas Mountains, which extend across much of Morocco, northern Algeria and Tunisia, are part of the fold mountain system which also runs through much of southern Europe. They recede to the south and east, becoming a steppe landscape before meeting the Sahara desert which covers more than 90% of the region. The sediments of the Sahara overlie an ancient plateau of crystalline rock, some of which is more than four billion years old.

Map key

Population
- above 5 million
- 1 million to 5 million
- 500,000 to 1 million
- 100,000 to 500,000
- 50,000 to 100,000
- 10,000 to 50,000
- below 10,000

Elevation
- 4000m / 13,124ft
- 3000m / 9843ft
- 2000m / 6562ft
- 1000m / 3281ft
- 500m / 1640ft
- 250m / 820ft
- 100m / 328ft
- sea level

Scale 1:12,250,000

projection: Lambert Azimuthal Equal Area

104
120
64
76
76

◀ **The town of** Tiznit, Morocco, lies in an oasis in the desert. Crops and trees grow on the fertile land surrounding the town.

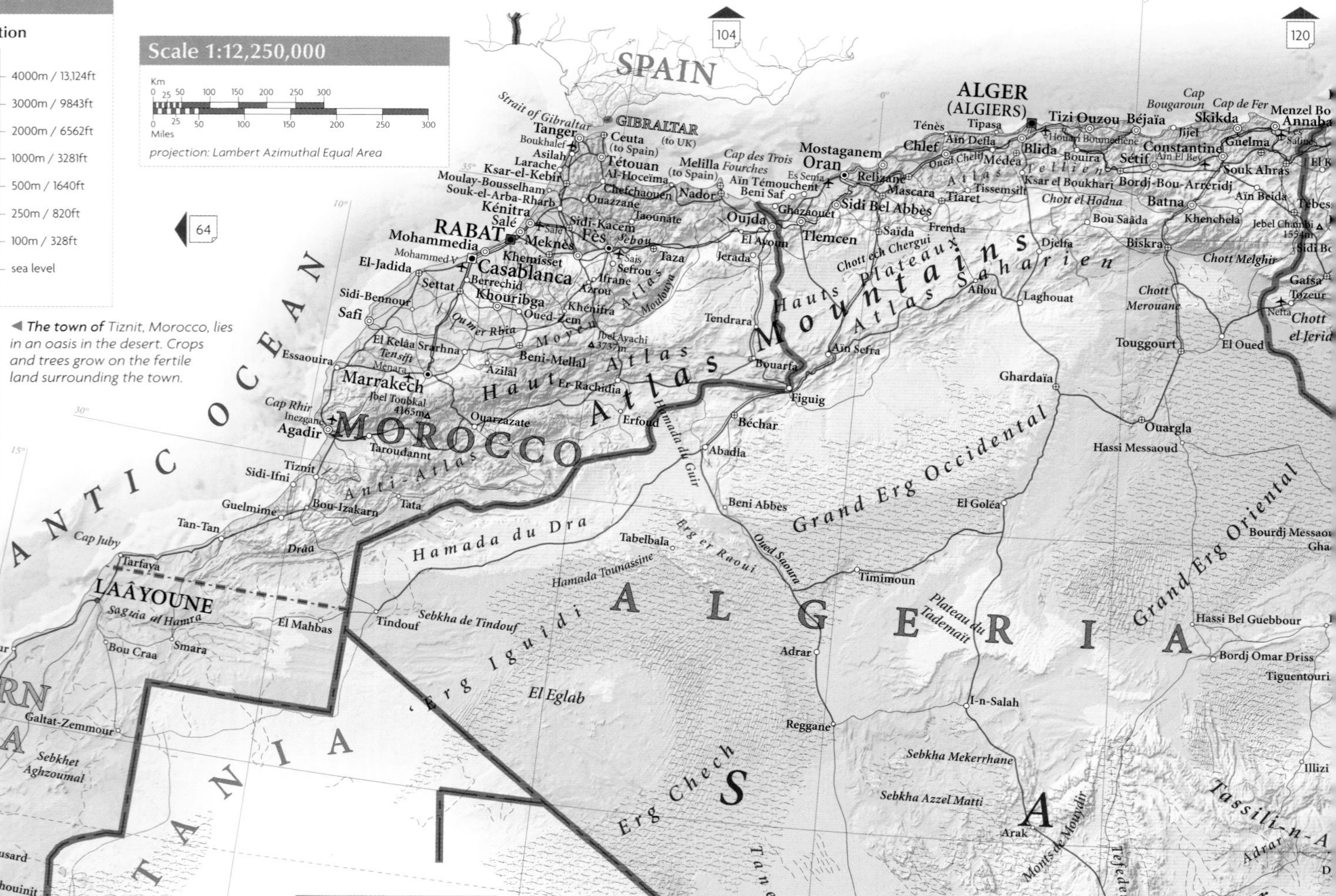

▶ **The Grand Erg Occidental** is one of Algeria's great Saharan sand seas. Wind force and direction determines the nature of landforms such as the linear or seif dunes in the foreground.

Using the land and sea

Sheltered valleys in the Atlas Mountains, the Nile Valley and Delta, and the Mediterranean coast are the main sources of good farming land. A wide variety of valuable crops including cereals, rice and cotton, and woods such as cedar and cork, are grown. Typical Mediterranean crops such as olives, figs, dates and citrus fruits also thrive in these areas. The Nile Valley is particularly fertile, and most of Egypt's population lives close to the river. Elsewhere, irrigation is essential to improve crop yields on the desert margins.

Land use and agricultural distribution

- goats
- sheep
- cereals
- citrus fruits
- cork
- cotton
- dates
- fishing
- olives
- vineyards
- capital cities
- major towns
- pasture
- cropland
- forest
- desert

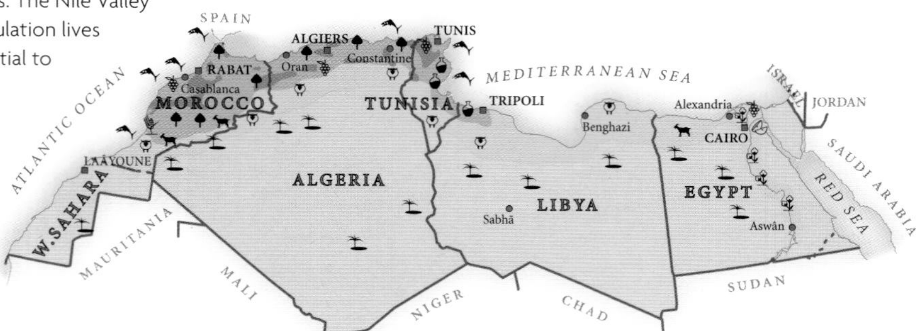

The urban/rural population divide

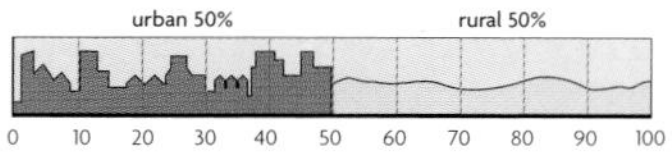

urban 50% | rural 50%

Population density	Total land area
65 people per sq mile (25 people per sq km)	2,215,020 sq miles (5,738,394 sq km)

▲ **Many North African** nomads, such as the Bedouin, maintain a traditional pastoral lifestyle on the desert fringes, moving their herds of sheep, goats and camels from place to place – crossing country borders in order to find sufficient grazing land.

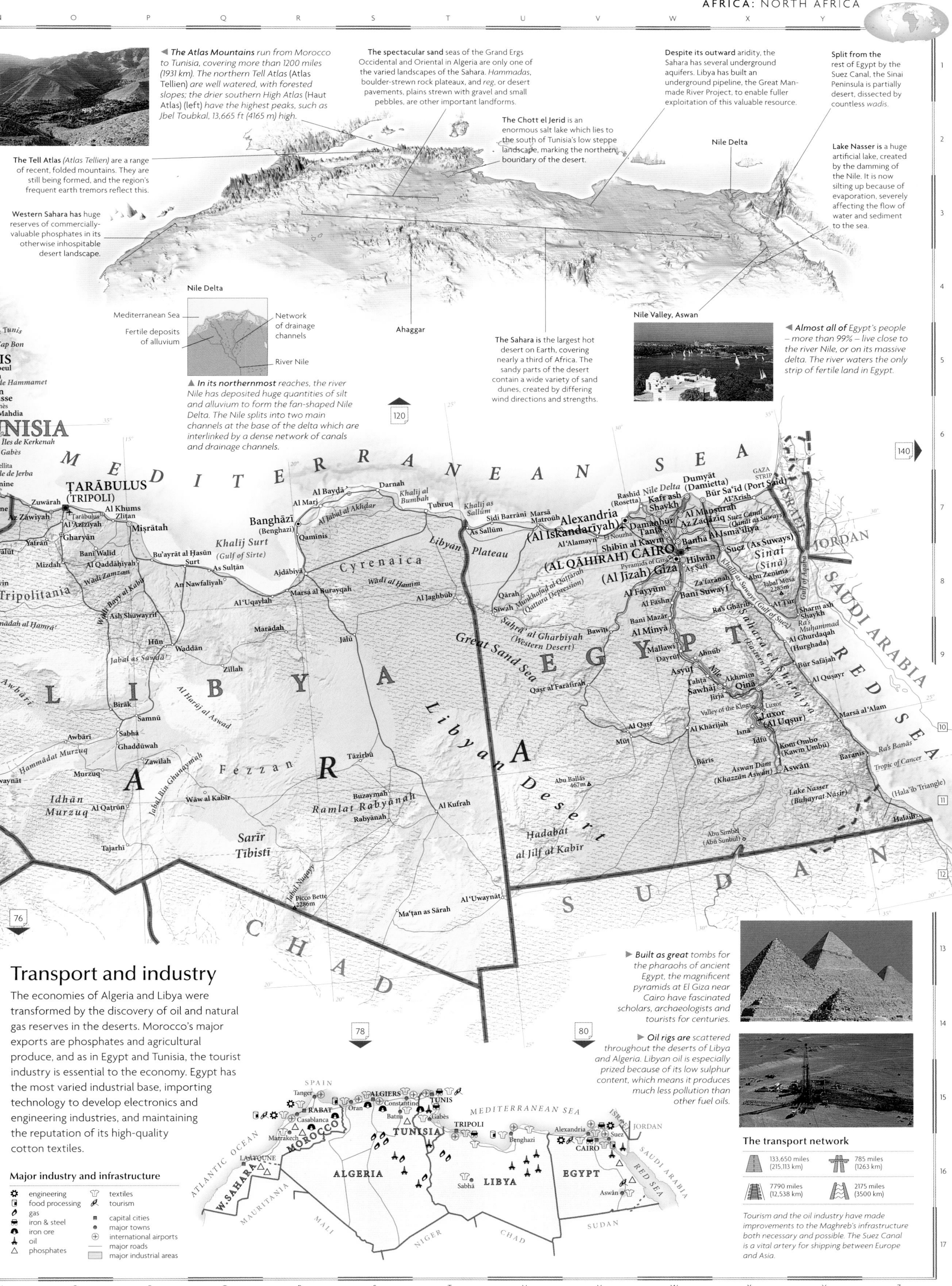
Nile Delta
Ahaggar
Mediterranean Sea
Fertile deposits of alluvium
Network of drainage channels
River Nile
Nile Valley, Aswan
120
140
76
78
80
MEDITERRANEAN SEA
ṬARĀBULUS (TRIPOLI)
Banghāzī (Benghazi)
Khalīj Surt (Gulf of Sirte)
Tripolitania
Cyrenaica
LIBYA
Fezzan
Ramlat Rabyānah
Sarīr Tībistī
Libyan Desert
Great Sand Sea
Libyan Plateau
Alexandria (Al Iskandarīyah)
(AL QĀHIRAH) CAIRO
(Al Jīzah) Giza
EGYPT
Sinai (Sīnā')
SAUDI ARABIA
RED SEA
Tropic of Cancer
(Hala'ib Triangle)
Lake Nasser (Buḥayrat Nāṣir)
Aswān
Luxor (Al Uqṣur)
Aswan Dam (Khazzān Aswān)
Abu Simbel (Abū Sunbul)
SUDAN
CHAD
JORDAN
ISRAEL
GAZA STRIP
TUNISIA
Ḥadabat al Jilf al Kabīr
Picco Bette 2286m
Jabal Mūsá 2285m
Abu Ballās 467m

◀ *The Atlas Mountains run from Morocco to Tunisia, covering more than 1200 miles (1931 km). The northern Tell Atlas* (Atlas Tellien) *are well watered, with forested slopes; the drier southern High Atlas* (Haut Atlas) (left) *have the highest peaks, such as Jbel Toubkal, 13,665 ft (4165 m) high.*

The Tell Atlas *(Atlas Tellien)* are a range of recent, folded mountains. They are still being formed, and the region's frequent earth tremors reflect this.

Western Sahara has huge reserves of commercially-valuable phosphates in its otherwise inhospitable desert landscape.

The spectacular sand seas of the Grand Ergs Occidental and Oriental in Algeria are only one of the varied landscapes of the Sahara. *Hammadas*, boulder-strewn rock plateaux, and *reg*, or desert pavements, plains strewn with gravel and small pebbles, are other important landforms.

The Chott el Jerid is an enormous salt lake which lies to the south of Tunisia's low steppe landscape, marking the northern boundary of the desert.

Despite its outward aridity, the Sahara has several underground aquifers. Libya has built an underground pipeline, the Great Man-made River Project, to enable fuller exploitation of this valuable resource.

Split from the rest of Egypt by the Suez Canal, the Sinai Peninsula is partially desert, dissected by countless *wadis*.

Lake Nasser is a huge artificial lake, created by the damming of the Nile. It is now silting up because of evaporation, severely affecting the flow of water and sediment to the sea.

▲ *In its northernmost reaches, the river Nile has deposited huge quantities of silt and alluvium to form the fan-shaped Nile Delta. The Nile splits into two main channels at the base of the delta which are interlinked by a dense network of canals and drainage channels.*

The Sahara is the largest hot desert on Earth, covering nearly a third of Africa. The sandy parts of the desert contain a wide variety of sand dunes, created by differing wind directions and strengths.

◀ *Almost all of Egypt's people – more than 99% – live close to the river Nile, or on its massive delta. The river waters the only strip of fertile land in Egypt.*

Transport and industry

The economies of Algeria and Libya were transformed by the discovery of oil and natural gas reserves in the deserts. Morocco's major exports are phosphates and agricultural produce, and as in Egypt and Tunisia, the tourist industry is essential to the economy. Egypt has the most varied industrial base, importing technology to develop electronics and engineering industries, and maintaining the reputation of its high-quality cotton textiles.

Major industry and infrastructure

- engineering
- food processing
- gas
- iron & steel
- iron ore
- oil
- phosphates
- textiles
- tourism
- capital cities
- major towns
- international airports
- major roads
- major industrial areas

▶ *Built as great tombs for the pharaohs of ancient Egypt, the magnificent pyramids at El Giza near Cairo have fascinated scholars, archaeologists and tourists for centuries.*

▶ *Oil rigs are scattered throughout the deserts of Libya and Algeria. Libyan oil is especially prized because of its low sulphur content, which means it produces much less pollution than other fuel oils.*

The transport network

133,650 miles (215,113 km)	785 miles (1263 km)
7790 miles (12,538 km)	2175 miles (3500 km)

Tourism and the oil industry have made improvements to the Maghreb's infrastructure both necessary and possible. The Suez Canal is a vital artery for shipping between Europe and Asia.

West Africa

BENIN, BURKINA, CAPE VERDE, GAMBIA, GHANA, GUINEA, GUINEA-BISSAU, IVORY COAST, LIBERIA, MALI, MAURITANIA, NIGER, NIGERIA, SENEGAL, SIERRA LEONE, TOGO

West Africa is an immensely diverse region, encompassing the desert landscapes and mainly Muslim populations of the southern Saharan countries, and the tropical rainforests of the more humid south, with a great variety of local languages and cultures. The rich natural resources and accessibility of the area were quickly exploited by Europeans; most of the Africans taken by slave traders came from this region, causing serious depopulation. The very different influences of West Africa's leading colonial powers, Britain and France, remain today, reflected in the languages and institutions of the countries they once governed.

The dry scrub of the Sahel is only suitable for grazing herd animals like these cattle in Mali.

Scale 1:10,000,000

Km 0 25 50 100 150 200 250

Miles 0 25 50 100 150 200 250

projection: Lambert Azimuthal Equal Area

Transport and industry

Abundant natural resources including oil and metallic minerals are found in much of West Africa, although investment is required for their further exploitation. Nigeria experienced an oil boom during the 1970s but subsequent growth has been sporadic. Most industry in other countries has a primary basis, including mining, logging and food processing.

The transport network

62,154 miles (100,038 km)	1037 miles (1669 km)
6752 miles (10,867 km)	10,192 miles (16,405 km)

The road and rail systems are most developed near the coasts. Some of the land-locked countries remain disadvantaged by the difficulty of access to ports, and their poor road networks.

Major industry and infrastructure

- chemicals
- cotton spinning
- food processing
- mining
- oil
- palm oil processing
- peanut processing
- textiles
- vehicle manufacture
- capital cities
- major towns
- international airports
- major roads
- major industrial areas

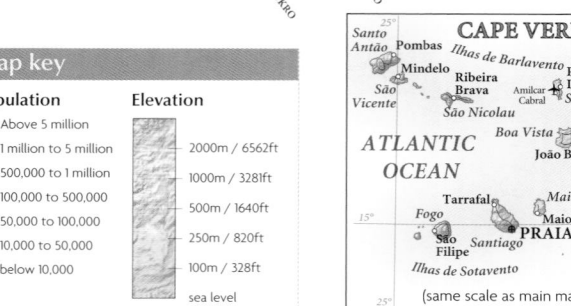

Map key

Population

- Above 5 million
- 1 million to 5 million
- 500,000 to 1 million
- 100,000 to 500,000
- 50,000 to 100,000
- 10,000 to 50,000
- below 10,000

Elevation

- 2000m / 6562ft
- 1000m / 3281ft
- 500m / 1640ft
- 250m / 820ft
- 100m / 328ft
- sea level

CAPE VERDE (same scale as main map)

The southern regions of West Africa still contain great swathes of tropical rainforest, including some of the world's most prized hardwood trees, such as mahogany and iroko.

Using the land and sea

The humid southern regions are most suitable for cultivation; in these areas, cash crops such as coffee, cotton, cocoa and rubber are grown in large quantities. Peanuts (groundnuts) are grown throughout West Africa. In the north, advancing desertification has made the Sahel increasingly unviable for cultivation, and pastoral farming is more common. Great herds of sheep, cattle and goats are grazed on the savannah grasses, and fishing is important in coastal and delta areas.

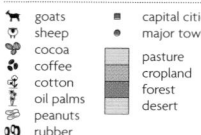

The Gambia, mainland Africa's smallest country, produces great quantities of peanuts (groundnuts). Winnowing is used to separate the nuts from their stalks.

MOROCCO
W. SAHARA
ALGERIA
LIBYA
SAHARA
MAURITANIA
NOUAKCHOTT
MALI
NIGER
CHAD
DAKAR
SENEGAL
BANJUL
GAMBIA
BISSAU
GUINEA-BISSAU
GUINEA
BAMAKO
BURKINA
NIAMEY
OUAGADOUGOU
NIGERIA
ABUJA
CONAKRY
FREETOWN
SIERRA LEONE
MONROVIA
LIBERIA
IVORY COAST
YAMOUSSOUKRO
GHANA
ACCRA
TOGO
LOME
BENIN
PORTO-NOVO
Lagos
CAMEROON
ATLANTIC OCEAN

Land use and agricultural distribution

- goats
- sheep
- cocoa
- coffee
- cotton
- oil palms
- peanuts
- rubber
- shellfish
- capital cities
- major towns
- pasture
- cropland
- forest
- desert

The urban/rural population divide

urban 36% | rural 64%

0 10 20 30 40 50 60 70 80 90 100

Population density	Total land area
104 people per sq mile (40 people per sq km)	2,337,137 sq miles (6,054,760 sq km)

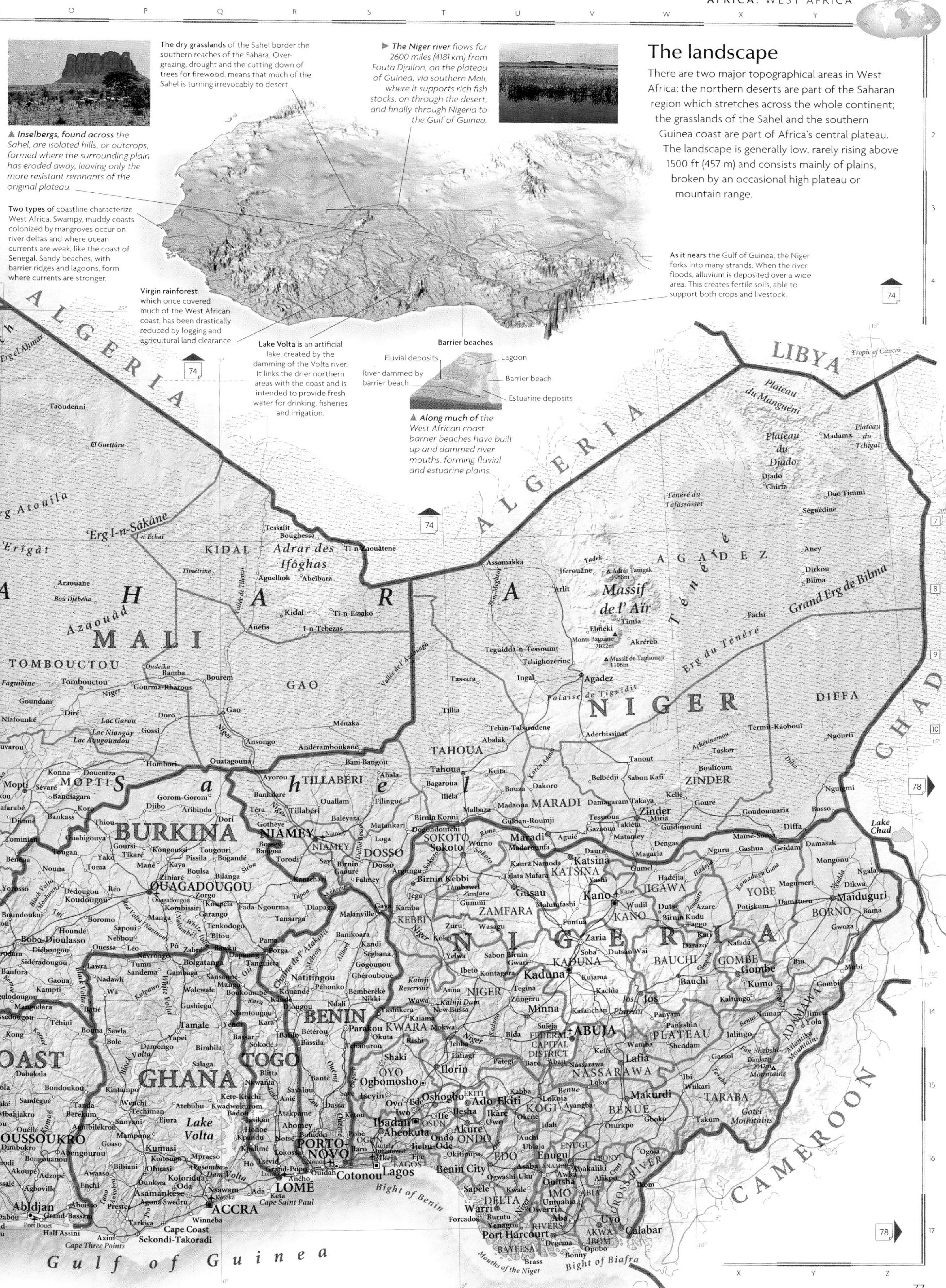
ALGERIA
LIBYA
MALI
NIGER
NIGERIA
BURKINA
GHANA
TOGO
BENIN
CHAD
CAMEROON
Gulf of Guinea
Bight of Benin
Bight of Biafra
Lake Volta
Lake Chad
Tropic of Cancer
NIAMEY
OUAGADOUGOU
ACCRA
LOMÉ
PORTO-NOVO
ABUJA
Lagos
Cotonou
Kano
Kaduna
Agadez
Tombouctou
Massif de l' Aïr
Adrar des Ifôghas
Grand Erg de Bilma
Erg du Ténéré
Fluvial deposits
Lagoon
River dammed by barrier beach
Barrier beach
Estuarine deposits
Barrier beaches

The landscape

There are two major topographical areas in West Africa: the northern deserts are part of the Saharan region which stretches across the whole continent; the grasslands of the Sahel and the southern Guinea coast are part of Africa's central plateau. The landscape is generally low, rarely rising above 1500 ft (457 m) and consists mainly of plains, broken by an occasional high plateau or mountain range.

▲ *Inselbergs, found across the Sahel, are isolated hills, or outcrops, formed where the surrounding plain has eroded away, leaving only the more resistant remnants of the original plateau.*

The dry grasslands of the Sahel border the southern reaches of the Sahara. Overgrazing, drought and the cutting down of trees for firewood, means that much of the Sahel is turning irrevocably to desert.

► ***The Niger river** flows for 2600 miles (4181 km) from Fouta Djallon, on the plateau of Guinea, via southern Mali, where it supports rich fish stocks, on through the desert, and finally through Nigeria to the Gulf of Guinea.*

Two types of coastline characterize West Africa. Swampy, muddy coasts colonized by mangroves occur on river deltas and where ocean currents are weak, like the coast of Senegal. Sandy beaches, with barrier ridges and lagoons, form where currents are stronger.

Virgin rainforest which once covered much of the West African coast, has been drastically reduced by logging and agricultural land clearance.

Lake Volta is an artificial lake, created by the damming of the Volta river. It links the drier northern areas with the coast and is intended to provide fresh water for drinking, fisheries and irrigation.

As it nears the Gulf of Guinea, the Niger forks into many strands. When the river floods, alluvium is deposited over a wide area. This creates fertile soils, able to support both crops and livestock.

▲ ***Along much of** the West African coast, barrier beaches have built up and dammed river mouths, forming fluvial and estuarine plains.*

Central Africa

CAMEROON, CENTRAL AFRICAN REPUBLIC, CHAD, CONGO, DEM. REP. CONGO, EQUATORIAL GUINEA, GABON, SAO TOME & PRINCIPE

The great rainforest basin of the Congo river embraces most of remote Central Africa. The interior was largely unknown to Europeans until late in the 19th century, when its tribal kingdoms were split – principally between France and Belgium – with Sao Tome and Principe the lone Portuguese territory, and Equatorial Guinea controlled by Spain. Open democracy and regional economic integration are important goals for these nations – several of which have only recently emerged from restrictive regimes – and investment is needed to improve transport infrastructures. Many of the small, but fast-growing and increasingly urban population, speak French, the regional *lingua franca*, along with several hundred Pygmy, Bantu and Sudanic dialects.

Transport and industry

Large reserves of valuable minerals are found in Central Africa: copper, cobalt and diamonds are mined in Dem. Rep. Congo and manganese in Gabon. Congo, Cameroon, Gabon and Equatorial Guinea have oil deposits and oil has also been recently discovered in Chad. Goods such as palm oil and rubber are processed for export.

▲ The ancient rocks *of Dem. Rep. Congo hold immense and varied mineral reserves. This open pit copper mine is at Kolwezi in the far south.*

LIBYA
NIGER
SUDAN
CHAD
NDJAMENA
SOUTH SUDAN
NIGERIA
CAMEROON
CENTRAL AFRICAN REPUBLIC
BANGUI
Douala
YAOUNDE
MALABO
EQ. GUINEA
SAO TOME & PRINCIPE
LIBREVILLE
CONGO
DEM. REP. CONGO
Kisangani
UGANDA
RWANDA
BURUNDI
Port-Gentil
GABON
BRAZZAVILLE
KINSHASA
Bukavu
Kananga
TANZANIA
ANGOLA (CABINDA)
ANGOLA
ATLANTIC OCEAN
Kolwezi
Lubumbashi
ZAMBIA

Major industry and infrastructure

- brewing
- chemicals
- cobalt
- copper
- diamonds
- food processing
- manganese
- oil
- palm oil processing
- textiles
- tin
- capital cities
- major towns
- international airports
- major roads
- major industrial areas

The transport network

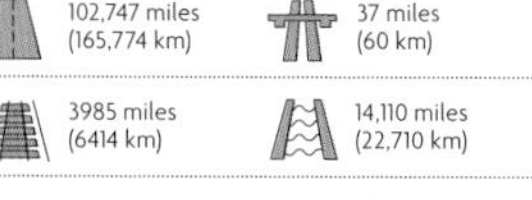

102,747 miles (165,774 km)	37 miles (60 km)
3985 miles (6414 km)	14,110 miles (22,710 km)

The Trans-Gabon railway, which began operating in 1987, has opened up new sources of timber and manganese. Elsewhere, much investment is needed to update and improve road, rail and water transport.

76

The landscape

Lake Chad lies in a desert basin bounded by the volcanic Tibesti mountains in the north, plateaux in the east and, in the south, the broad watershed of the Congo basin. The vast circular depression of the Congo is isolated from the coastal plain by the granite Massif du Chaillu. To the northwest, the volcanoes and fold mountains of the Cameroon Ridge *(Dorsale Camerounaise)* extend as islands into the Gulf of Guinea. The high fold mountains fringing the east of the Congo Basin fall steeply to the lakes of the Great Rift Valley.

◀ **A plug of** *resistant lava, at the southwestern end of the Cameroon Ridge* (Dorsale Camerounaise), *is all that remains of an eroded volcano.*

The volcanic massif of Cameroon Mountain occupies an area which remains volcanically active.

Gulf of Guinea

Massif du Chaillu

Lake Chad is the remnant of an inland sea, which once occupied much of the surrounding basin. A series of droughts since the 1970s has reduced the area of this shallow freshwater lake to about 1000 sq miles (2599 sq km).

The lake-like expansion of the Congo river at Stanley Pool is the lowest point of the interior basin, although the river still descends more than 1000 ft (300 m) to reach the sea.

The Tibesti mountains are the highest in the Sahara. They were pushed up by the movement of the African Plate over a hot spot, which first formed the northern Ahaggar mountains and is now thought to lie under the Great Rift Valley.

The Congo river is second only to the Amazon in the volume of water it carries, and in the size of its drainage basin.

Lake Tanganyika, the world's second deepest lake, is the largest of a series of linear 'ribbon' lakes occupying a trench within the Great Rift Valley.

Rich mineral deposits in the 'Copper Belt' of Dem. Rep. Congo were formed under intense heat and pressure when the ancient African Shield was uplifted to form the region's mountains.

74

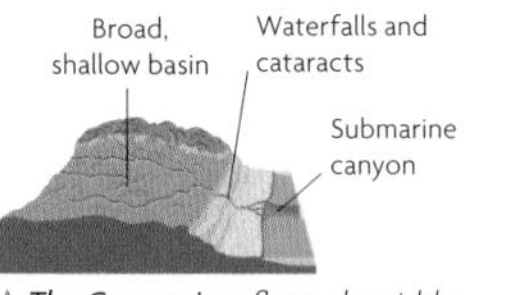
Broad, shallow basin
Waterfalls and cataracts
Submarine canyon

▲ The Congo river *flows sluggishly through the rainforest of the interior basin. Towards the coast, the river drops steeply in a series of waterfalls and cataracts. At this point, the erosional power of the river becomes so great that it has formed a deep submarine canyon offshore.*

▲ Virgin tropical rainforest *covers the Ruwenzori range on the borders of Dem. Rep. Congo and Uganda.*

▲ The vast sand *flats surrounding Lake Chad were once covered by water. Changing climatic patterns caused the lake to shrink, and desert now covers much of its previous area.*

Map key

Population

- 1 million to 5 million
- 500,000 to 1 million
- 100,000 to 500,000
- 50,000 to 100,000
- 10,000 to 50,000
- below 10,000

Elevation

- 4000m / 13,124ft
- 3000m / 9843ft
- 2000m / 6562ft
- 1000m / 3281ft
- 500m / 1640ft
- 250m / 820ft
- 100m / 328ft
- sea level

Scale 1:10,500,000

projection: Lambert Azimuthal Equal Area

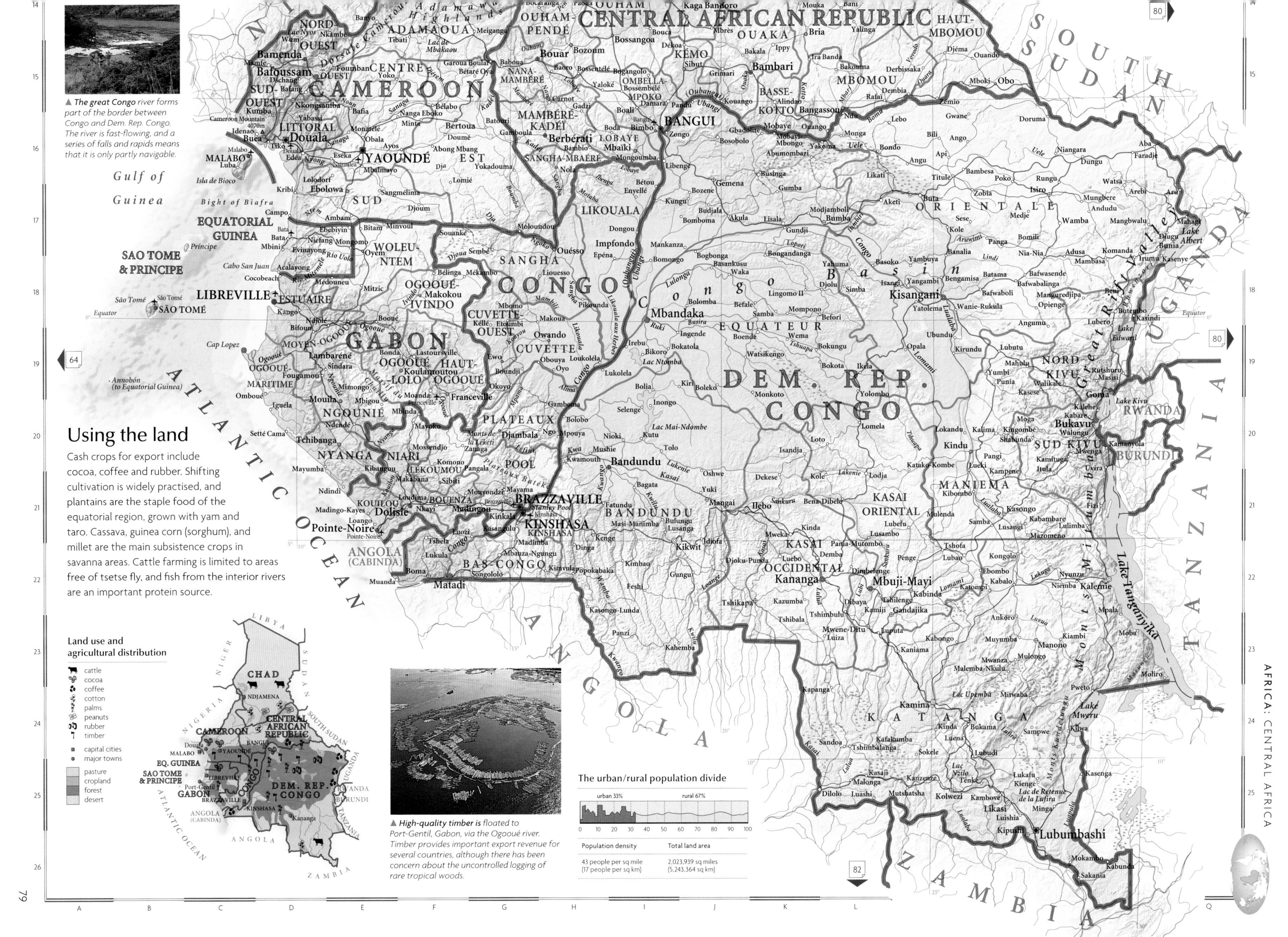
CENTRAL AFRICAN REPUBLIC
CAMEROON
EQUATORIAL GUINEA
SAO TOME & PRINCIPE
GABON
CONGO
DEM. REP. CONGO
SOUTH SUDAN
UGANDA
RWANDA
BURUNDI
TANZANIA
ZAMBIA
ANGOLA
ANGOLA (CABINDA)
ATLANTIC OCEAN
Gulf of Guinea
Bight of Biafra
Lake Tanganyika
Congo Basin
BANGUI
YAOUNDÉ
MALABO
LIBREVILLE
SÃO TOMÉ
BRAZZAVILLE
KINSHASA
Land use and agricultural distribution
cattle
cocoa
coffee
cotton
palms
peanuts
rubber
timber
capital cities
major towns
pasture
cropland
forest
desert
The urban/rural population divide
urban 33%
rural 67%
Population density
43 people per sq mile (17 people per sq km)
Total land area
2,023,939 sq miles (5,243,364 sq km)

▲ *The great Congo* river forms part of the border between Congo and Dem. Rep. Congo. The river is fast-flowing, and a series of falls and rapids means that it is only partly navigable.

Using the land

Cash crops for export include cocoa, coffee and rubber. Shifting cultivation is widely practised, and plantains are the staple food of the equatorial region, grown with yam and taro. Cassava, guinea corn (sorghum), and millet are the main subsistence crops in savanna areas. Cattle farming is limited to areas free of tsetse fly, and fish from the interior rivers are an important protein source.

▲ *High-quality timber is* floated to Port-Gentil, Gabon, via the Ogooué river. Timber provides important export revenue for several countries, although there has been concern about the uncontrolled logging of rare tropical woods.

East Africa

BURUNDI, DJIBOUTI, ERITREA, ETHIOPIA, KENYA, RWANDA, SOMALIA, SOUTH SUDAN, SUDAN, TANZANIA, UGANDA

The countries of East Africa divide into two distinct cultural regions. Sudan and the 'Horn' nations have been influenced by the Middle East; Ethiopia was the home of one of the earliest Christian civilizations, and Sudan reflects both Muslim and Christian influences, while the southern countries share a closer cultural affinity with other sub-Saharan nations. Some of Africa's most densely populated countries lie in this region, and the needs of a growing number of people have put pressure on marginal lands and fragile environments. Although most East African economies remain strongly agricultural, Kenya has developed a varied industrial base.

The landscape

East Africa's most significant landscape feature is the Great Rift Valley, which formed during the most recent phase of continental movement when the rigid basement rocks cracked and buckled. Great blocks of land were raised and lowered, creating huge flat-bottomed valleys and steep escarpments, sometimes covered by volcanic extrusions in highland areas.

◀ ***This dome at** Gonder, in Ethiopia, is a volcanic intrusion, formed when molten rock pushed up the surface of the Earth and then solidified, leaving an outcrop of igneous rock.*

Ephemeral lake forms at far edge of slope

Central block slopes towards main fault

Boundary fault

▲ ***The eastern arm** of the Great Rift Valley is gradually being pulled apart; however the forces on one side are greater than the other causing the land to slope. This affects regional drainage which migrates down the slope.*

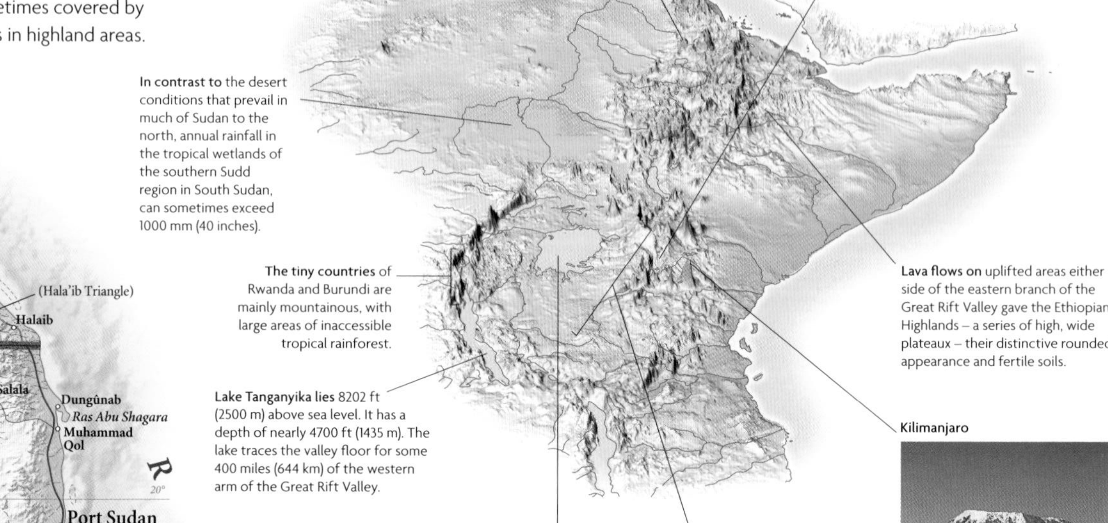

In contrast to the desert conditions that prevail in much of Sudan to the north, annual rainfall in the tropical wetlands of the southern Sudd region in South Sudan, can sometimes exceed 1000 mm (40 inches).

The tiny countries of Rwanda and Burundi are mainly mountainous, with large areas of inaccessible tropical rainforest.

Lake Tanganyika lies 8202 ft (2500 m) above sea level. It has a depth of nearly 4700 ft (1435 m). The lake traces the valley floor for some 400 miles (644 km) of the western arm of the Great Rift Valley.

Lake Victoria occupies a vast basin between the two arms of the Great Rift Valley. It is the world's second largest lake in terms of surface area, extending 26,560 sq miles (68,880 sq km). The lake contains numerous islands and coral reefs.

A vast plateau lies between the eastern and western rift valleys in Kenya, Uganda and western Tanzania. It has been levelled by long periods of erosion to form a peneplain, but is dotted with inselbergs – outcrops of more resistant rocks.

Lava flows on uplifted areas either side of the eastern branch of the Great Rift Valley gave the Ethiopian Highlands – a series of high, wide plateaux – their distinctive rounded appearance and fertile soils.

Kilimanjaro

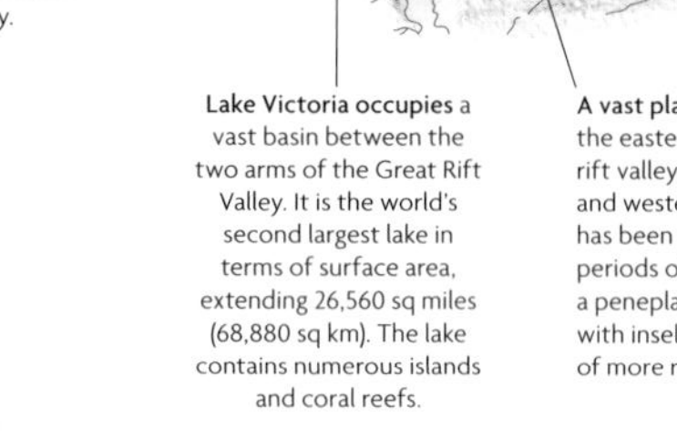

▲ ***An extinct volcano,** Kilimanjaro is Africa's highest mountain, rising 19,340 ft (5895 m). Once famed for its snow-capped peak, this has almost completely melted due to changing climatic conditions.*

▶ ***The Kassala region** in eastern Sudan is watered by the Atbara river, an important tributary of the Nile. Most of the population is engaged in agriculture, growing cotton and cereals.*

74
78
140

EGYPT · LIBYA · CHAD · SUDAN · ERITREA · ETHIOPIA · DJIBOUTI · YEMEN · SOMALILAND (not internationally recognized)
RED SEA · Gulf of Aden · Lake Nasser · Nubian Desert · Libyan Desert · Danakil Desert
KHARTOUM · Omdurman · Khartoum North · Port Sudan · Kassala · El Obeid · Wad Medani · ASMERA · DJIBOUTI · Gonder · Bahir Dar · Dire Dawa
NORTHERN · RIVER NILE · RED SEA · KASSALA · KHARTOUM · NORTHERN KORDOFAN · NORTHERN DARFUR · WESTERN DARFUR · SOUTHERN DARFUR · SOUTHERN KORDOFAN · WHITE NILE · SINNAR · GEZIRA · GEDAREF · BLUE NILE · UPPER NILE · TIGRAY · AMARA · AFAR · BINSHANGUL GUMUZ · AWDAL · SANAAG · BARI

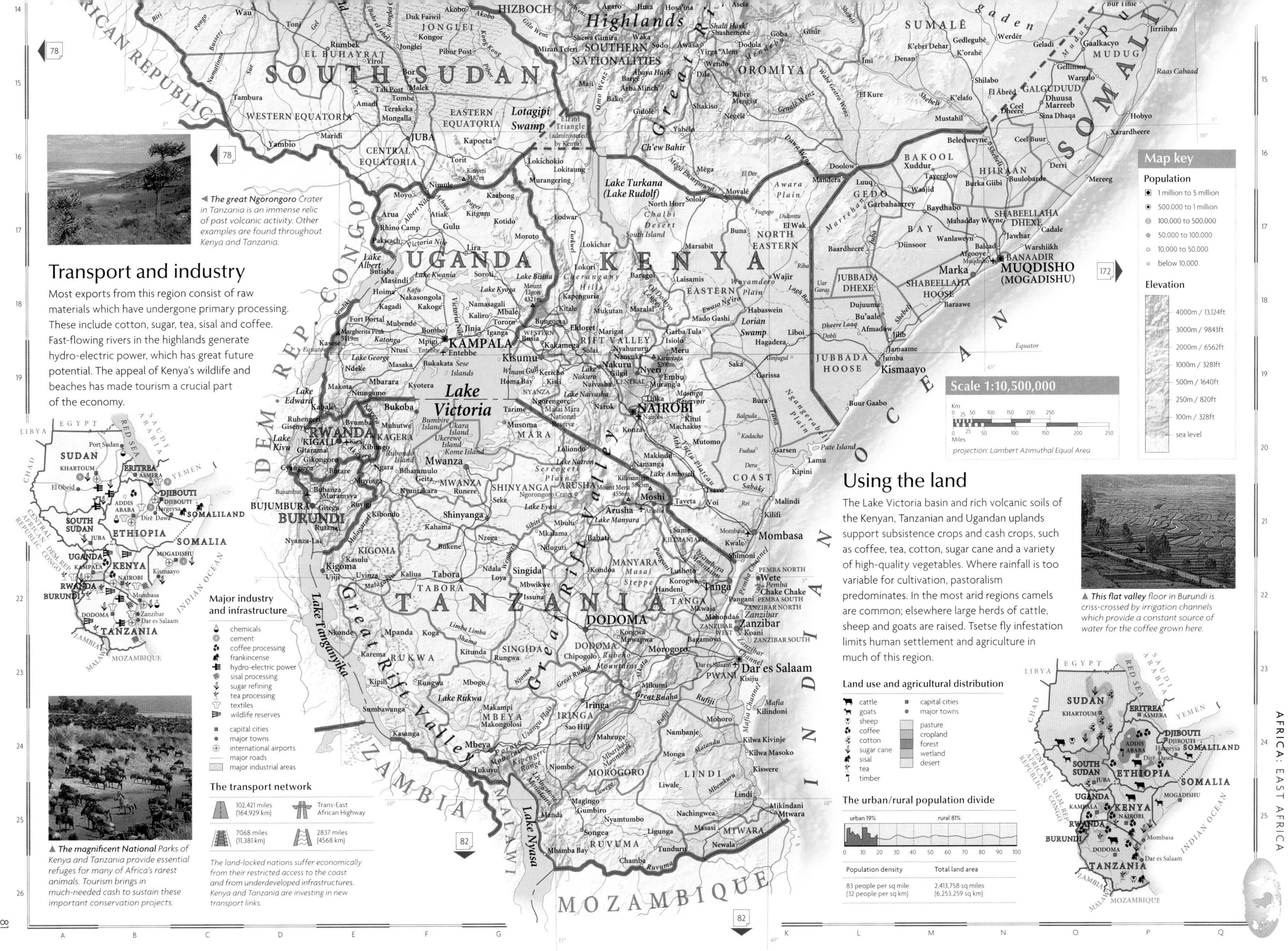
SOUTH SUDAN
UGANDA
KENYA
TANZANIA
SOMALIA
DEM. REP. CONGO
RWANDA
BURUNDI
ZAMBIA
MALAWI
MOZAMBIQUE
INDIAN OCEAN
Lake Victoria
Lake Turkana (Lake Rudolf)
Lake Tanganyika
Lake Nyasa
Great Rift Valley
KAMPALA
NAIROBI
DODOMA
Dar es Salaam
MUQDISHO (MOGADISHU)
Mombasa
Zanzibar
Kismaayo
Map key
Population
1 million to 5 million
500,000 to 1 million
100,000 to 500,000
50,000 to 100,000
10,000 to 50,000
below 10,000
Elevation
4000m / 13,124ft
3000m / 9843ft
2000m / 6562ft
1000m / 3281ft
500m / 1640ft
250m / 820ft
100m / 328ft
sea level
Scale 1:10,500,000
projection: Lambert Azimuthal Equal Area

78

172

82

◀ *The great Ngorongoro Crater in Tanzania is an immense relic of past volcanic activity. Other examples are found throughout Kenya and Tanzania.*

Transport and industry

Most exports from this region consist of raw materials which have undergone primary processing. These include cotton, sugar, tea, sisal and coffee. Fast-flowing rivers in the highlands generate hydro-electric power, which has great future potential. The appeal of Kenya's wildlife and beaches has made tourism a crucial part of the economy.

Major industry and infrastructure

- chemicals
- cement
- coffee processing
- frankincense
- hydro-electric power
- sisal processing
- sugar refining
- tea processing
- textiles
- wildlife reserves
- capital cities
- major towns
- international airports
- major roads
- major industrial areas

The transport network

- 102,421 miles (164,929 km)
- 7068 miles (11,381 km)
- Trans-East African Highway
- 2837 miles (4568 km)

The land-locked nations suffer economically from their restricted access to the coast and from underdeveloped infrastructures. Kenya and Tanzania are investing in new transport links.

▲ *The magnificent National Parks of Kenya and Tanzania provide essential refuges for many of Africa's rarest animals. Tourism brings in much-needed cash to sustain these important conservation projects.*

Using the land

The Lake Victoria basin and rich volcanic soils of the Kenyan, Tanzanian and Ugandan uplands support subsistence crops and cash crops, such as coffee, tea, cotton, sugar cane and a variety of high-quality vegetables. Where rainfall is too variable for cultivation, pastoralism predominates. In the most arid regions camels are common; elsewhere large herds of cattle, sheep and goats are raised. Tsetse fly infestation limits human settlement and agriculture in much of this region.

▲ *This flat valley floor in Burundi is criss-crossed by irrigation channels which provide a constant source of water for the coffee grown here.*

Land use and agricultural distribution

- cattle
- goats
- sheep
- coffee
- cotton
- sugar cane
- sisal
- tea
- timber
- capital cities
- major towns
- pasture
- cropland
- forest
- wetland
- desert

The urban/rural population divide

urban 19% | rural 81%

Population density	Total land area
83 people per sq mile (32 people per sq km)	2,413,758 sq miles (6,253,259 sq km)

Southern Africa

ANGOLA, BOTSWANA, LESOTHO, MALAWI, MOZAMBIQUE, NAMIBIA, SOUTH AFRICA, SWAZILAND, ZAMBIA, ZIMBABWE

Africa's vast southern plateau has been a contested homeland for disparate peoples for many centuries. The European incursion began with the slave trade and quickened in the 19th century, when the discovery of enormous mineral wealth secured South Africa's regional economic dominance. The struggle against white minority rule led to strife in Namibia, Zimbabwe, and the former Portuguese territories of Angola and Mozambique. South Africa's notorious apartheid laws, which denied basic human rights to more than 75% of the people, led to the state being internationally ostracized until 1994, when the first fully democratic elections inaugurated a new era of racial justice.

Transport and industry

South Africa, the world's largest exporter of gold, has a varied economy which generates about 75% of the region's income and draws migrant labour from neighbouring states. Angola exports petroleum; Botswana and Namibia rely on diamond mining; and Zambia is seeking to diversify its economy to compensate for declining copper reserves.

◀ **Almost all new** *mining ventures in Zimbabwe are now subject to government control. This mine at Bindura in northeastern Zimbabwe produces nickel, one of the country's top three minerals in terms of economic value.*

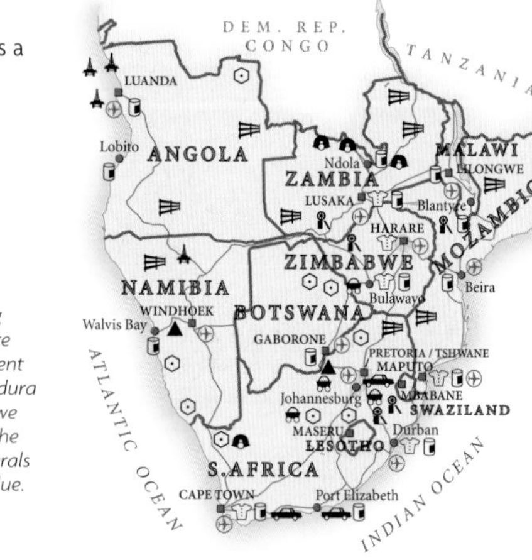

DEM. REP. CONGO
TANZANIA
LUANDA
Lobito
ANGOLA
ZAMBIA
Ndola
LUSAKA
MALAWI
LILONGWE
Blantyre
HARARE
MOZAMBIQUE
ZIMBABWE
Bulawayo
Beira
NAMIBIA
WINDHOEK
Walvis Bay
BOTSWANA
GABORONE
PRETORIA / TSHWANE
MAPUTO
Johannesburg
MBABANE
SWAZILAND
MASERU
LESOTHO
Durban
S. AFRICA
CAPE TOWN
Port Elizabeth
ATLANTIC OCEAN
INDIAN OCEAN

Major industry and infrastructure

car manufacture	gold	capital cities
coal	oil	major towns
copper	textiles	international airports
diamonds	uranium	major roads
food processing	wildlife reserves	major industrial areas

78

The landscape

Most of southern Africa rests on a concave plateau comprising the Kalahari basin and a mountainous fringe, skirted by a coastal plain which widens out in Mozambique. The plateau extends north, towards the Planalto de Bié in Angola, the Congo Basin and the lake-filled troughs of the Great Rift Valley. The eastern region is drained by the Zambezi and Limpopo rivers, and the Orange is the major western river.

Thousands of years of evaporating water have produced the Etosha Pan, one of the largest salt flats in the world. Lake and river sediments in the area indicate that the region was once less arid.

▲ **Finger Rock, near** *Khorixas, Namibia is a remnant of a former land surface, which has been denuded by erosion over the last 5 million years. These occasional stacks of partially weathered rocks interrupt the plains of the dry southern interior.*

Khorixas, Namibia

Planalto de Bié

Namib Desert

The Kalahari Desert is the largest continuous sand surface in the world. Iron oxide gives a distinctive red colour to the windblown sand, which, in eastern areas covers the bedrock by over 200 ft (60 m).

The Okavango/Cubango river flows from the Planalto de Bié to the swamplands of the Okavango Delta, one of the world's largest inland deltas, where it divides into countless distributary channels, feeding out into the desert.

At Victoria Falls, the Zambezi river has cut a spectacular gorge taking advantage of large joints in the basalt, which were first formed as the lava cooled and contracted.

▶ **The fast-flowing Zambezi** *river cuts a deep, wide channel as it flows along the Zimbabwe/Zambia border.*

Lake Nyasa occupies one of the deep troughs of the Great Rift Valley, where the land has been displaced downwards by as much as 3000 ft (920 m).

Great Rift Valley

Limpopo river

Bushveld intrusion

Volcanic lava, over 250 million years old, caps the peaks of the Drakensberg range, which lie on the mountainous rim of southern Africa's interior plateau.

The Orange River, one of the longest in Africa, rises in Lesotho and is the only major river in the south which flows westward, rather than to the east coast.

The mountains of the Little Karoo are composed of sedimentary rocks which have been substantially folded and faulted.

Broad, flat-topped mountains characterize the Great Karoo, which have been cut from level rock strata under extremely arid conditions.

The transport network

84,213 miles (135,609 km)	746 miles (1202 km)
23,208 miles (37,372 km)	3815 miles (6144 km)

Southern Africa's Cape-gauge rail network is by far the largest in the continent. About two-thirds of the 20,000 mile (32,000 km) system lies within South Africa. Lines such as the Harare–Bulawayo route have become corridors for industrial growth.

▲ **Following a series** *of droughts, this baobab tree in Zimbabwe now stands alone in a field once filled by sugar cane. The thick trunk and small leaves of the baobab help it to conserve water, enabling it to survive even in drought conditions.*

Bushveld intrusion

Gabbro and peridotite

Magnetite

Platinum minerals

Granite

Chromite

▲ **The Bushveld intrusion** *lies on South Africa's high 'veld'. Molten magma intruded into the Earth's crust creating a saucer-shaped feature, more than 180 miles (300 km) across, containing regular layers of precious minerals, overlain by a dome of granite.*

Scale 1:10,500,000

Km 0 25 50 100 150 200 250 300

Miles 0 25 50 100 150 200 250 300

projection: Lambert Azimuthal Equal Area

Map key

Population

- 1 million to 5 million
- 500,000 to 1 million
- 100,000 to 500,000
- 50,000 to 100,000
- 10,000 to 50,000
- below 10,000

Elevation

- 3000m / 9843ft
- 2000m / 6562ft
- 1000m / 3281ft
- 500m / 1640ft
- 250m / 820ft
- 100m / 328ft
- sea level

South Africa: Capital cities

PRETORIA / TSHWANE – administrative capital
CAPE TOWN – legislative capital
BLOEMFONTEIN – judicial capital

78

80

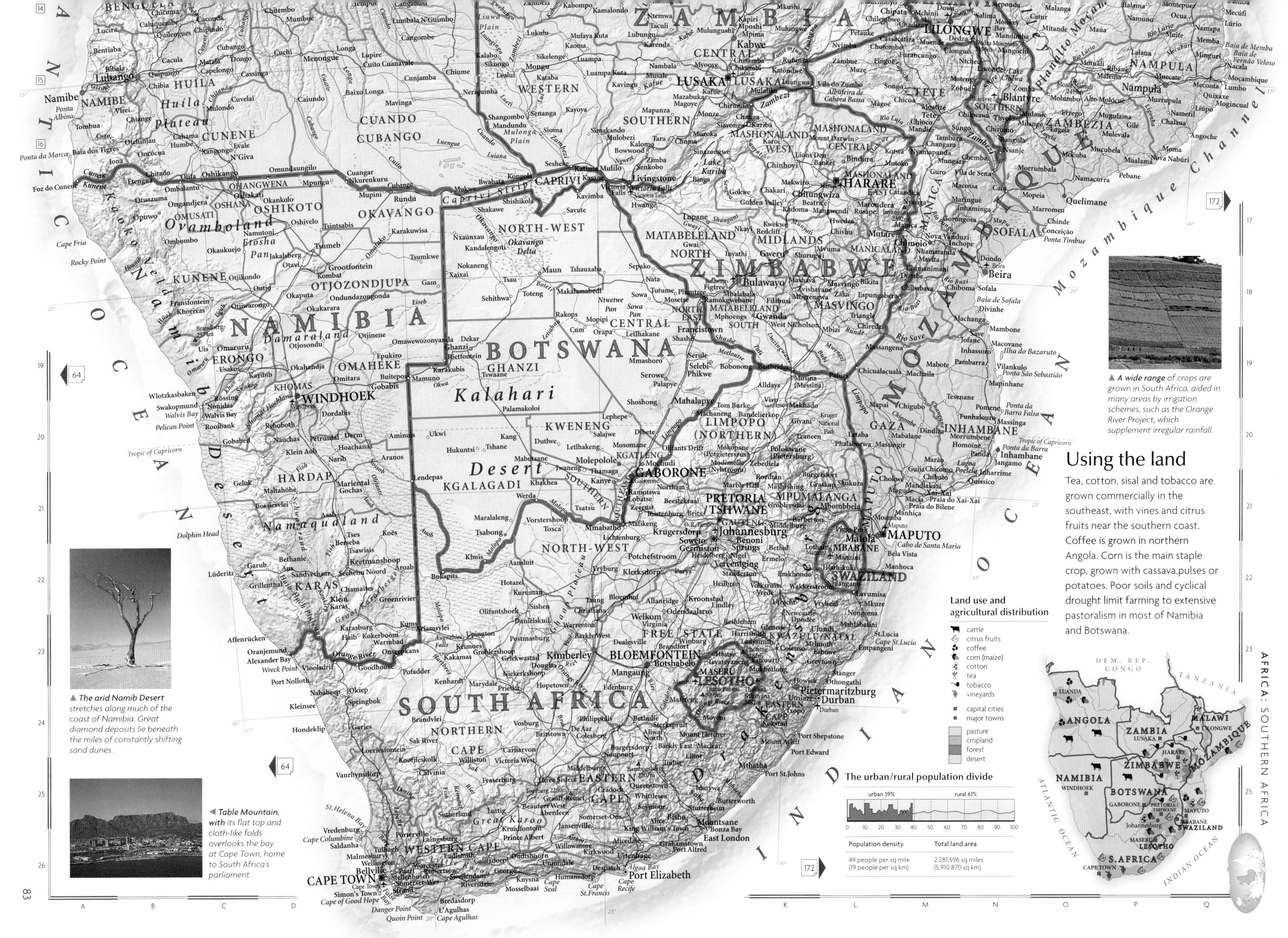
ZAMBIA
MOZAMBIQUE
ZIMBABWE
BOTSWANA
NAMIBIA
SOUTH AFRICA
SWAZILAND
LESOTHO
Kalahari
Desert
Namib Desert
INDIAN OCEAN
Mozambique Channel
Using the land
Tea, cotton, sisal and tobacco are grown commercially in the southeast, with vines and citrus fruits near the southern coast. Coffee is grown in northern Angola. Corn is the main staple crop, grown with cassava,pulses or potatoes. Poor soils and cyclical drought limit farming to extensive pastoralism in most of Namibia and Botswana.
Land use and agricultural distribution
cattle
citrus fruits
coffee
corn (maize)
cotton
tea
tobacco
vineyards
capital cities
major towns
pasture
cropland
forest
desert
The urban/rural population divide
urban 39%
rural 61%
Population density
49 people per sq mile (19 people per sq km)
Total land area
2,281,596 sq miles (5,910,870 sq km)

▲ A wide range of crops are grown in South Africa, aided in many areas by irrigation schemes, such as the Orange River Project, which supplement irregular rainfall.

▲ The arid Namib Desert stretches along much of the coast of Namibia. Great diamond deposits lie beneath the miles of constantly shifting sand dunes.

◄ Table Mountain, with its flat top and cloth-like folds overlooks the bay at Cape Town, home to South Africa's parliament.

ARCTIC OCEAN
North Pole
Ellesmere Island
King Frederik VIII Land
Greenland
King Christian X Land
Greenland Sea
Spitsbergen
Franz Josef Land
Ostrov Rudol'fa
Severnaya Zemlya
Laptev Sea
Poluostrov Taymyr
Kara Sea
Mys Flissingskiy
Novaya Zemlya
Barents Sea
Bjørnøya
Barents Trough
North Cape
Nordkinn
Murmansk Rise
Kara Strait
Poluostrov Yamal
Baydaratskaya Guba
Gulf of Ob
Yenisey
West Siberian Plain
Ural Mountains
Ostrov Kolguyev
Poluostrov Kanin
Pechora
Timanskiy Kryazh
Mezen'
Denmark Strait
Arctic Circle
Kolbeinsey Ridge
Iceland Plateau
Jan Mayen
Jan Mayen Fracture Zone
Jan Mayen Ridge
Norwegian Sea
Norwegian Basin
Vøring Plateau
Bjargtangar
Iceland
Vatnajökull
Reykjanes Ridge
Faeroe-Iceland Ridge
Faeroe Islands
Iceland Basin
Bill Baileys Bank
Faeroe-Shetland Trough
Shetland Islands
Hatton Ridge
Rockall Rise
Feni Ridge
Rockall Trough
ATLANTIC OCEAN
Tromsøflaket
Fugløya Bank
Vesterålen
Lofoten
Kebnekaise 2117m
Inarijärvi
Kola Peninsula
Ozero Imandra
White Sea
Onega Bay
Ozero Vygozero
Lake Onega
Lake Ladoga
Northern Dvina
Traena Bank
Scandinavia
Gulf of Bothnia
Umeälven
Oulujoki
Ljusnan
Galdhøpiggen 2469m
Viking Bank
Åland
Gulf of Finland
Lake Peipus
Lake Ilmen
Rybinsk Reservoir
Gor'kiy Reservoir
Kuybyshev Reservoir
Vänern
Vättern
Gotland
Gulf of Riga
Lake Pskov
Orkney Islands
Outer Hebrides
Ben Nevis 1343m
Grampian Mountains
North Channel
Norwegian Trench
Jutland Bank
Skagerrak
Kattegat
North Sea
Great Fisher Bank
Jutland
Sjælland
Baltic Sea
British Isles
Ireland
Irish Sea
Shannon
Snowdon 1085m
Pennines
Trent
Severn
Britain
Thames
Dogger Bank
Frisian Islands
Celtic Sea
Celtic Shelf
St. George's Channel
Bristol Channel
Strait of Dover
Land's End
English Channel
Channel Islands
Porcupine Plain
North European Plain
Western Dvina
Neman
Elbe
Oder
Warta
Vistula
Bug
Dnieper
Pripet Marshes
Desna
Central Russian Upland
Volga Upland
Moskva
Oka
Don
Khoper
EUROPE
Harz
Ardennes
Rhine
Meuse
Moselle
Seine
Marne
Loire
Cher
Vienne
Black Forest
Vosges
Danube
Lake Constance
Kiev Reservoir
Kremenchuk Reservoir
Dnieper Lowlands
Dniester
Podil's'ka Vysochina
Pivdennyy Buh
Carpathian Mountains
Tisza
Siret
Prut
Black Sea Lowland
Sea of Azov
Crimea
Kerch Strait
Tsimlyansk Reservoir
Volga
Donets
Manych
Yergeni
Kirghiz
Bakony
Lake Balaton
Great Hungarian Plain
Drava
Sava
Transylvanian Alps
Danube
Balkan Mountains
Maritsa
Black Sea
Bosporus
Sea of Marmara
Charcot Seamounts
Azores-Biscay Rise
Biscay Plain
Bay of Biscay
Garonne
Dordogne
Lot
Massif Central
Cévennes
Rhône
Saône
Lake Geneva
Lake Garda
Po
Adriatic Sea
Dinaric Alps
Corno Grande 2912m
Apennines
Theta Gap
Galicia Bank
Iberian Plain
Miño
Cordillera Cantábrica
Duero
Douro
Iberian Peninsula
Aragon
Ebro
Sistema Ibérico
Sistema Central
Gulf of Lion
Ligurian Sea
Corsica
Strait of Bonifacio
Sardinia
Tyrrhenian Sea
Tyrrhenian Basin
Adriatic Basin
Lake Ohrid
Lake Prespa
Gulf of Taranto
Strait of Otranto
Aegean Sea
Anatolia
Lake Tuz
Tagus
Tagus Plain
Cabo da Roca
Guadiana
Sierra Morena
Guadalquivir
Júcar
Segura
Gulf of Valencia
Balearic Islands
Algerian Basin
Horseshoe Seamounts
Gorringe Ridge
Cabo de São Vicente
Punta de Tarifa
Sistemas Béticos
Sierra Nevada
Ampère Seamount
Strait of Gibraltar
Alboran Sea
Mediterranean Sea
Strait of Sicily
Mount Etna 3340m
Messina
Sicily
Malta
Ionian Sea
Ionian Basin
Peloponnese
Mirtoan Sea
Sea of Crete
Rhodes Basin
Gulf of Antalya
Taurus Mountains
Cyprus
Cyprus Basin
Mediterranean Ridge
Levantine Basin
Nile Fan
Suez Canal
Nile
EURASIAN PLATE
AFRICAN PLATE
ANATOLIAN PLATE
NORTH AMERICAN PLATE
Seine Plain
Seine Seamount
Madeira
Oued Chelif
Tell Atlas
Atlas Mountains
Sebou
Moulouya
Oum er Rbia
Middle Atlas
High Atlas
Saharan Atlas
Agadir Canyon
Dacia Seamount
Canary Islands
Chott el Jerid
Gulf of Sirte
Grand Erg Occidental
Grand Erg Oriental
Qattara Depression -133m
Western Desert
Libyan Desert
AFRICA
SAHARA
'Erg Iguidi
Erg Chech

Europe

Europe is the world's second smallest continent, covering 4,053,309 sq miles (10,498,000 sq km). It comprises 46 separate countries, including Turkey and the Russian Federation, although the greater parts of these nations lie in Asia.

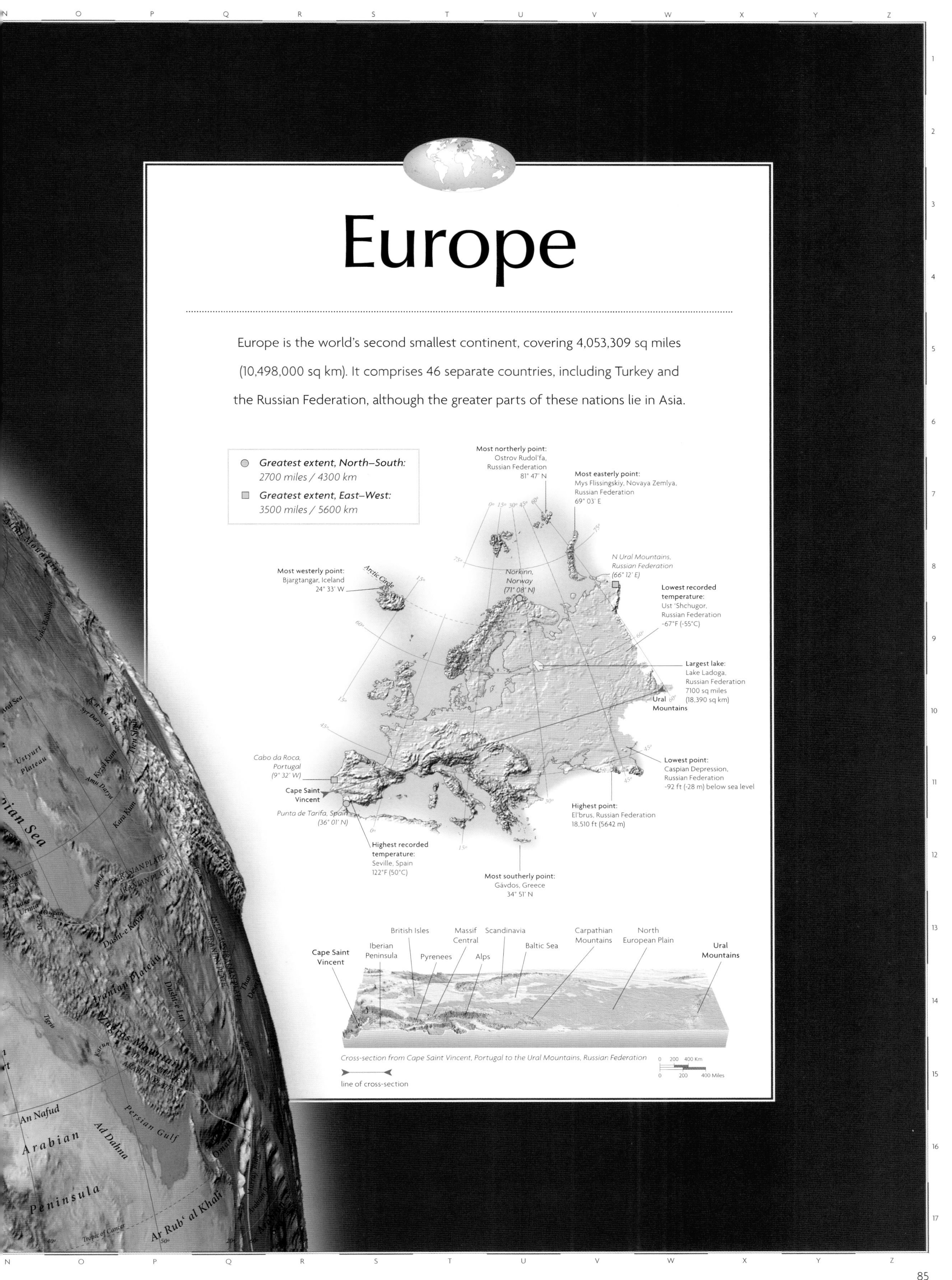

Greatest extent, North–South:
2700 miles / 4300 km
Greatest extent, East–West:
3500 miles / 5600 km
Most northerly point:
Ostrov Rudol'fa, Russian Federation
81° 47' N
Most easterly point:
Mys Flissingskiy, Novaya Zemlya, Russian Federation
69° 03' E
N Ural Mountains, Russian Federation
(66° 12' E)
Most westerly point:
Bjargtangar, Iceland
24° 33' W
Arctic Circle
Norkinn, Norway
(71° 08' N)
Lowest recorded temperature:
Ust 'Shchugor, Russian Federation
-67°F (-55°C)
Largest lake:
Lake Ladoga, Russian Federation
7100 sq miles
(18,390 sq km)
Ural Mountains
Cabo da Roca, Portugal
(9° 32' W)
Cape Saint Vincent
Punta de Tarifa, Spain
(36° 01' N)
Lowest point:
Caspian Depression, Russian Federation
-92 ft (-28 m) below sea level
Highest point:
El'brus, Russian Federation
18,510 ft (5642 m)
Highest recorded temperature:
Seville, Spain
122°F (50°C)
Most southerly point:
Gávdos, Greece
34° 51' N
Cape Saint Vincent
Iberian Peninsula
British Isles
Pyrenees
Massif Central
Alps
Scandinavia
Baltic Sea
Carpathian Mountains
North European Plain
Ural Mountains
Cross-section from Cape Saint Vincent, Portugal to the Ural Mountains, Russian Federation
0 200 400 Km
0 200 400 Miles
line of cross-section
Aral Sea
Ustyurt Plateau
Kara Kum
Iranian Plateau
Dasht-e Kavir
Dasht-e Lut
Zagros Mountains
Tigris
Persian Gulf
An Nafud
Arabian Peninsula
Ad Dahna
Ar Rub' al Khali
Tropic of Cancer

Physical Europe

The physical diversity of Europe belies its relatively small size. To the northwest and south it is enclosed by mountains. The older, rounded Atlantic Highlands of Scandinavia and the British Isles lie to the north and the younger, rugged peaks of the Alpine Uplands to the south. In between lies the North European Plain, stretching 2485 miles (4000 km) from The Fens in England to the Ural Mountains in Russia. South of the plain lies a series of gently folded sedimentary rocks separated by ancient plateaux, known as massifs.

The North European Plain

Rising less than 1000 ft (300 m) above sea level, the North European Plain strongly reflects past glaciation. Ridges of both coarse moraine and finer, windblown deposits have accumulated over much of the region. The ice sheet also diverted a number of river channels from their original courses.

Glacial lakes

Rivers were diverted from their original course by the ice sheet

A layer of glacial sediments covers the North European Plain

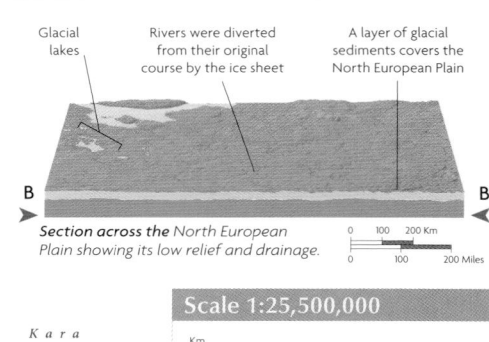

***Section across the** North European Plain showing its low relief and drainage.*

The Atlantic Highlands

The Atlantic Highlands were formed by compression against the Scandinavian Shield during the Caledonian mountain-building period over 500 million years ago. The highlands were once part of a continuous mountain chain, now divided by the North Sea and a submerged rift valley.

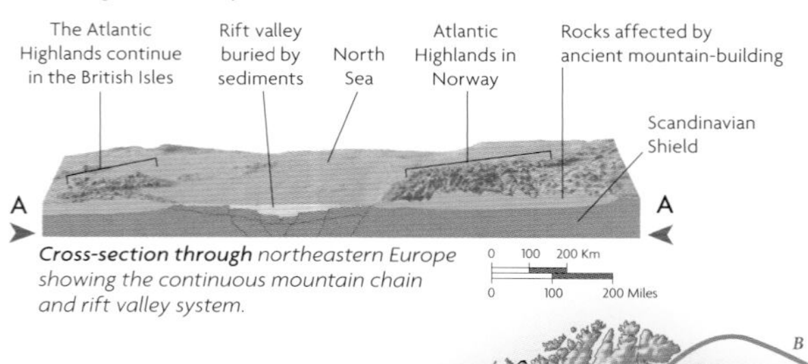
The Atlantic Highlands continue in the British Isles
Rift valley buried by sediments
North Sea
Atlantic Highlands in Norway
Rocks affected by ancient mountain-building
Scandinavian Shield
A
A
0 100 200 Km
0 100 200 Miles

***Cross-section through** northeastern Europe showing the continuous mountain chain and rift valley system.*

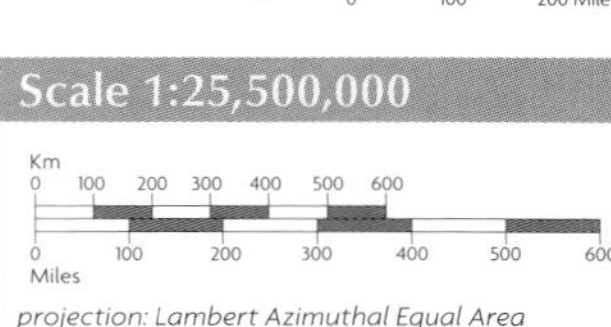
Scale 1:25,500,000
Km 0 100 200 300 400 500 600
Miles 0 100 200 300 400 500 600
projection: Lambert Azimuthal Equal Area

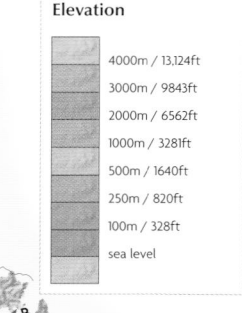

Map key

Elevation

- 4000m / 13,124ft
- 3000m / 9843ft
- 2000m / 6562ft
- 1000m / 3281ft
- 500m / 1640ft
- 250m / 820ft
- 100m / 328ft
- sea level

Plate margins (for explanation see page xiv)

- constructive
- destructive
- conservative
- uncertain
- physiographic regions
- line of cross-section

The plateaux and lowlands

The uplifted plateaux or massifs of southern central Europe are the result of long-term erosion, later followed by uplift. They are the source areas of many of the rivers which drain Europe's lowlands. In some of the higher reaches, fractures have enabled igneous rocks from deep in the Earth to reach the surface.

The Alpine uplands

The collision of the African and European continents, which began about 65 million years ago, folded and then uplifted a series of mountain ranges running across southern Europe and into Asia. Two major lines of folding can be traced: one includes the Pyrenees, the Alps and the Carpathian Mountains; the other incorporates the Apennines and the Dinaric Alps.

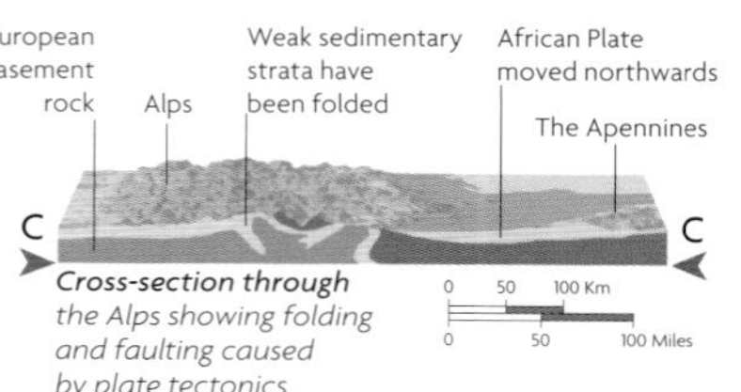
European basement rock
Alps
Weak sedimentary strata have been folded
African Plate moved northwards
The Apennines
C
C
0 50 100 Km
0 50 100 Miles

***Cross-section through** the Alps showing folding and faulting caused by plate tectonics.*

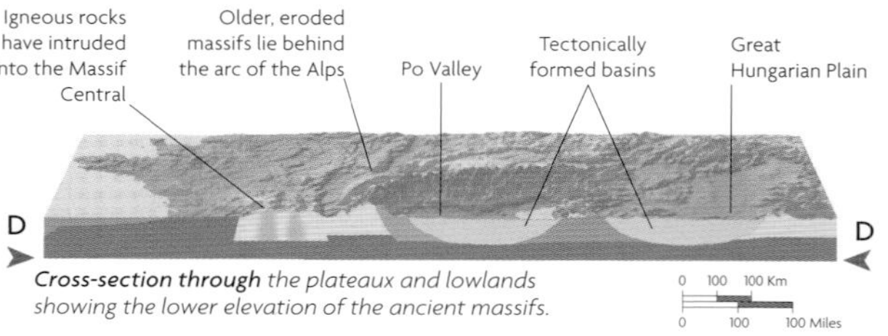
Igneous rocks have intruded into the Massif Central
Older, eroded massifs lie behind the arc of the Alps
Po Valley
Tectonically formed basins
Great Hungarian Plain
D
D
0 100 100 Km
0 100 100 Miles

***Cross-section through** the plateaux and lowlands showing the lower elevation of the ancient massifs.*

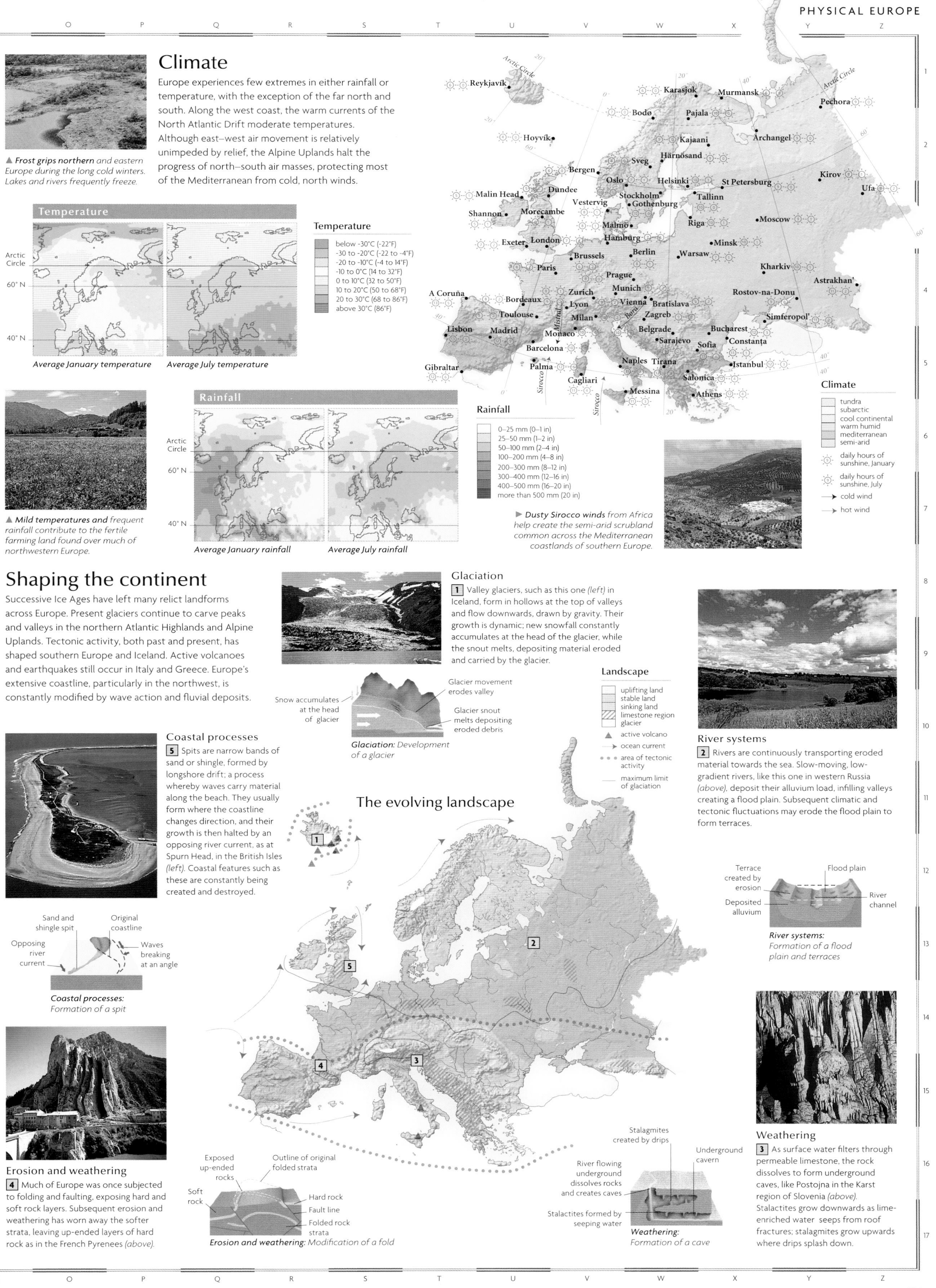
N O P Q R S T U V W X Y Z
1 2 3 4 5 6 7 8 9 10 11 12 13 14 15 16 17
Arctic Circle
Reykjavík
Karasjok
Murmansk
Pechora
Bodø
Pajala
Hoyvík
Kajaani
Archangel
Härnösand
Sveg
Bergen
Oslo
Helsinki
St Petersburg
Kirov
Ufa
Malin Head
Dundee
Stockholm
Tallinn
Shannon
Morecambe
Vestervig
Gothenburg
Riga
Moscow
Malmö
Exeter
London
Hamburg
Minsk
Brussels
Berlin
Warsaw
Paris
Prague
Kharkiv
Astrakhan'
A Coruña
Zurich
Munich
Rostov-na-Donu
Bordeaux
Lyon
Vienna
Bratislava
Toulouse
Mistral
Milan
Zagreb
Bora
Simferopol'
Lisbon
Madrid
Monaco
Belgrade
Bucharest
Sarajevo
Sofia
Constanța
Barcelona
Naples
Tirana
Istanbul
Gibraltar
Palma
Sirocco
Cagliari
Salonica
Messina
Athens
Temperature
Arctic Circle
60° N
40° N
below -30°C (-22°F)
-30 to -20°C (-22 to -4°F)
-20 to -10°C (-4 to 14°F)
-10 to 0°C (14 to 32°F)
0 to 10°C (32 to 50°F)
10 to 20°C (50 to 68°F)
20 to 30°C (68 to 86°F)
above 30°C (86°F)
Rainfall
0–25 mm (0–1 in)
25–50 mm (1–2 in)
50–100 mm (2–4 in)
100–200 mm (4–8 in)
200–300 mm (8–12 in)
300–400 mm (12–16 in)
400–500 mm (16–20 in)
more than 500 mm (20 in)
Climate
tundra
subarctic
cool continental
warm humid
mediterranean
semi-arid
daily hours of sunshine, January
daily hours of sunshine, July
cold wind
hot wind
Snow accumulates at the head of glacier
Glacier movement erodes valley
Glacier snout melts depositing eroded debris
Landscape
uplifting land
stable land
sinking land
limestone region
glacier
active volcano
ocean current
area of tectonic activity
maximum limit of glaciation
Terrace created by erosion
Flood plain
River channel
Deposited alluvium
Sand and shingle spit
Original coastline
Opposing river current
Waves breaking at an angle
Exposed up-ended rocks
Outline of original folded strata
Soft rock
Hard rock
Fault line
Folded rock strata
Stalagmites created by drips
Underground cavern
River flowing underground dissolves rocks and creates caves
Stalactites formed by seeping water

Climate

Europe experiences few extremes in either rainfall or temperature, with the exception of the far north and south. Along the west coast, the warm currents of the North Atlantic Drift moderate temperatures. Although east–west air movement is relatively unimpeded by relief, the Alpine Uplands halt the progress of north–south air masses, protecting most of the Mediterranean from cold, north winds.

▲ ***Frost grips northern*** *and eastern Europe during the long cold winters. Lakes and rivers frequently freeze.*

Average January temperature

Average July temperature

▲ ***Mild temperatures and*** *frequent rainfall contribute to the fertile farming land found over much of northwestern Europe.*

Average January rainfall

Average July rainfall

▶ ***Dusty Sirocco winds*** *from Africa help create the semi-arid scrubland common across the Mediterranean coastlands of southern Europe.*

Shaping the continent

Successive Ice Ages have left many relict landforms across Europe. Present glaciers continue to carve peaks and valleys in the northern Atlantic Highlands and Alpine Uplands. Tectonic activity, both past and present, has shaped southern Europe and Iceland. Active volcanoes and earthquakes still occur in Italy and Greece. Europe's extensive coastline, particularly in the northwest, is constantly modified by wave action and fluvial deposits.

Glaciation

1 Valley glaciers, such as this one *(left)* in Iceland, form in hollows at the top of valleys and flow downwards, drawn by gravity. Their growth is dynamic; new snowfall constantly accumulates at the head of the glacier, while the snout melts, depositing material eroded and carried by the glacier.

Glaciation: *Development of a glacier*

River systems

2 Rivers are continuously transporting eroded material towards the sea. Slow-moving, low-gradient rivers, like this one in western Russia *(above)*, deposit their alluvium load, infilling valleys creating a flood plain. Subsequent climatic and tectonic fluctuations may erode the flood plain to form terraces.

River systems: *Formation of a flood plain and terraces*

Coastal processes

5 Spits are narrow bands of sand or shingle, formed by longshore drift; a process whereby waves carry material along the beach. They usually form where the coastline changes direction, and their growth is then halted by an opposing river current, as at Spurn Head, in the British Isles *(left)*. Coastal features such as these are constantly being created and destroyed.

Coastal processes: *Formation of a spit*

The evolving landscape

Erosion and weathering

4 Much of Europe was once subjected to folding and faulting, exposing hard and soft rock layers. Subsequent erosion and weathering has worn away the softer strata, leaving up-ended layers of hard rock as in the French Pyrenees *(above)*.

Erosion and weathering: *Modification of a fold*

Weathering

3 As surface water filters through permeable limestone, the rock dissolves to form underground caves, like Postojna in the Karst region of Slovenia *(above)*. Stalactites grow downwards as lime-enriched water seeps from roof fractures; stalagmites grow upwards where drips splash down.

Weathering: *Formation of a cave*

Political Europe

The political boundaries of Europe have changed many times, especially during the 20th century in the aftermath of two world wars, the break-up of the empires of Austria-Hungary, Nazi Germany and, towards the end of the century, the collapse of communism in eastern Europe. The fragmentation of Yugoslavia has again altered the political map of Europe, highlighting a trend towards nationalism and devolution. In contrast, economic federalism is growing. In 1958, the formation of the European Economic Community (now the European Union or EU) started a move towards economic and political union and increasing internal migration.

Population

Europe is a densely populated, urbanized continent; in Belgium over 90% of people live in urban areas. The highest population densities are found in an area stretching east from southern Britain and northern France, into Germany. The northern fringes are only sparsely populated.

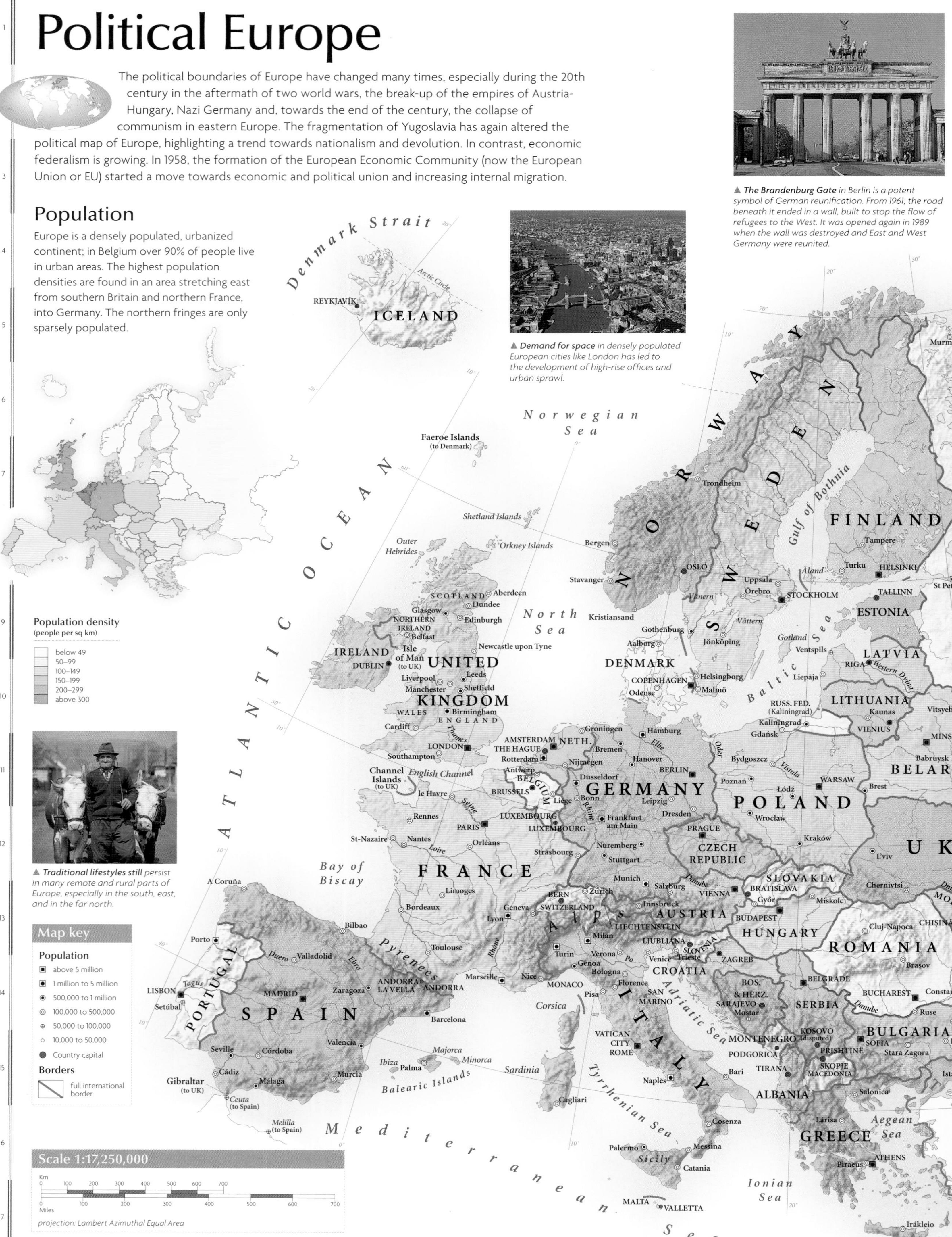
Population density
(people per sq km)
below 49
50–99
100–149
150–199
200–299
above 300
Map key
Population
above 5 million
1 million to 5 million
500,000 to 1 million
100,000 to 500,000
50,000 to 100,000
10,000 to 50,000
Country capital
Borders
full international border
Scale 1:17,250,000
Km
Miles
projection: Lambert Azimuthal Equal Area
Denmark Strait
ICELAND
REYKJAVÍK
Norwegian Sea
Faeroe Islands (to Denmark)
ATLANTIC OCEAN
Shetland Islands
Orkney Islands
Outer Hebrides
North Sea
NORWAY
SWEDEN
FINLAND
Gulf of Bothnia
OSLO
STOCKHOLM
HELSINKI
TALLINN
ESTONIA
LATVIA
RIGA
LITHUANIA
VILNIUS
Baltic Sea
DENMARK
COPENHAGEN
IRELAND
DUBLIN
UNITED KINGDOM
SCOTLAND
NORTHERN IRELAND
WALES
ENGLAND
LONDON
English Channel
Channel Islands (to UK)
NETH.
AMSTERDAM
THE HAGUE
BELGIUM
BRUSSELS
LUXEMBOURG
GERMANY
BERLIN
POLAND
WARSAW
FRANCE
PARIS
Bay of Biscay
SPAIN
MADRID
PORTUGAL
LISBON
ANDORRA
Pyrenees
SWITZERLAND
BERN
LIECHTENSTEIN
AUSTRIA
VIENNA
CZECH REPUBLIC
PRAGUE
SLOVAKIA
BRATISLAVA
HUNGARY
BUDAPEST
SLOVENIA
LJUBLJANA
CROATIA
ZAGREB
BOS. & HERZ.
SARAJEVO
SERBIA
BELGRADE
KOSOVO (disputed)
PRISHTINE
MONTENEGRO
PODGORICA
ALBANIA
TIRANA
MACEDONIA
SKOPJE
GREECE
ATHENS
BULGARIA
SOFIA
ROMANIA
BUCHAREST
ITALY
ROME
VATICAN CITY
SAN MARINO
MONACO
MALTA
VALLETTA
Alps
Adriatic Sea
Tyrrhenian Sea
Ionian Sea
Aegean Sea
Mediterranean Sea
Balearic Islands
Corsica
Sardinia
Sicily
Crete
Gibraltar (to UK)
Ceuta (to Spain)
Melilla (to Spain)
RUSS. FED. (Kaliningrad)
BELARUS
MINSK
UKRAINE

▲ **The Brandenburg Gate** in Berlin is a potent symbol of German reunification. From 1961, the road beneath it ended in a wall, built to stop the flow of refugees to the West. It was opened again in 1989 when the wall was destroyed and East and West Germany were reunited.

▲ **Demand for space** in densely populated European cities like London has led to the development of high-rise offices and urban sprawl.

▲ **Traditional lifestyles still** persist in many remote and rural parts of Europe, especially in the south, east, and in the far north.

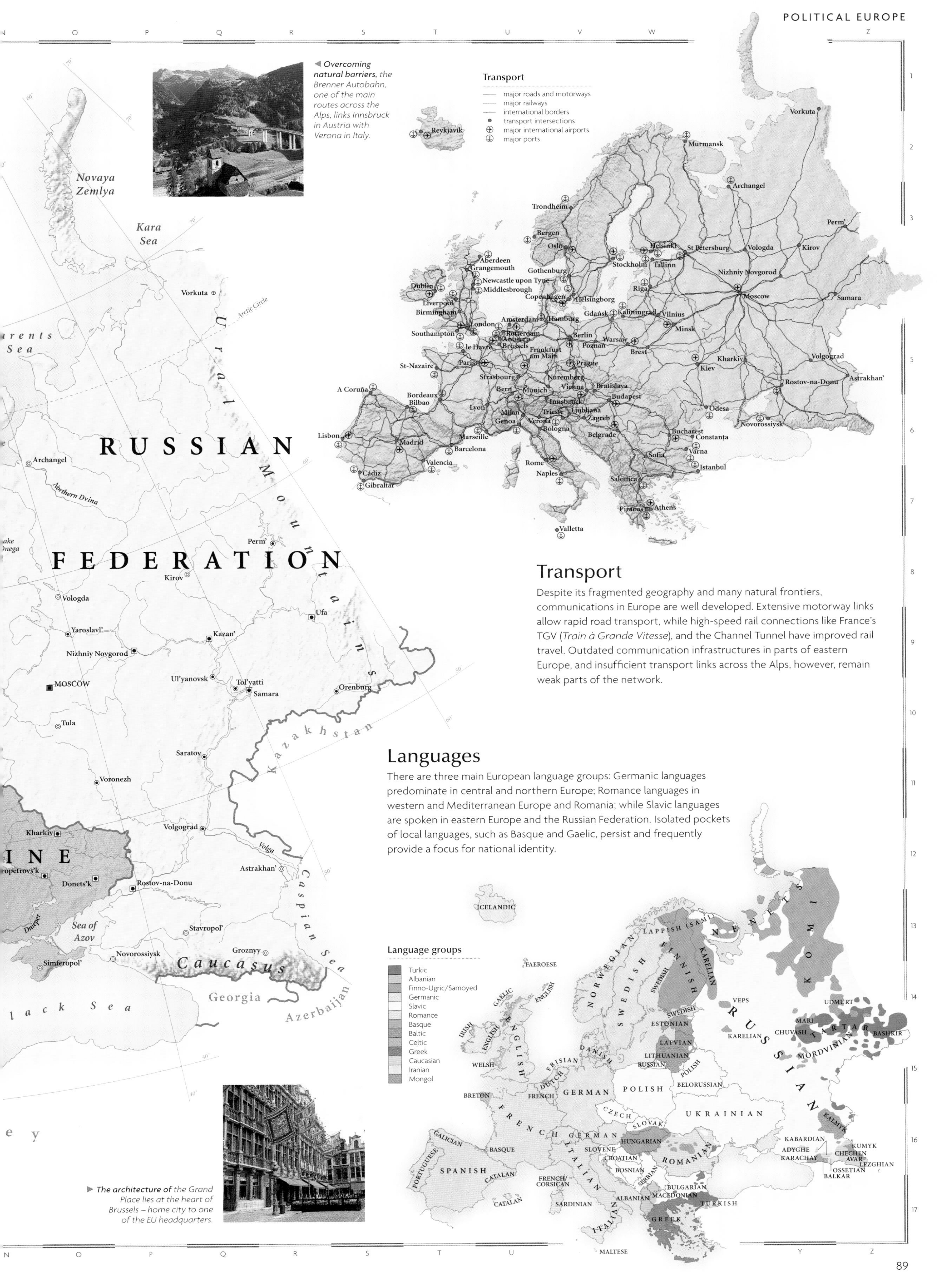

Novaya Zemlya
Kara Sea
Barents Sea
Vorkuta
Arctic Circle
Ural Mountains
RUSSIAN FEDERATION
Archangel
Northern Dvina
Perm'
Kirov
Vologda
Yaroslavl'
Kazan'
Ufa
Nizhniy Novgorod
MOSCOW
Ul'yanovsk
Tol'yatti
Samara
Orenburg
Tula
Kazakhstan
Saratov
Voronezh
Kharkiv
Volgograd
Volga
Astrakhan'
Donets'k
Rostov-na-Donu
Caspian Sea
Sea of Azov
Dnieper
Stavropol'
Groznyy
Simferopol'
Novorossiysk
Caucasus
Georgia
Azerbaijan
Black Sea
Transport
major roads and motorways
major railways
international borders
transport intersections
major international airports
major ports
Language groups
Turkic
Albanian
Finno-Ugric/Samoyed
Germanic
Slavic
Romance
Basque
Baltic
Celtic
Greek
Caucasian
Iranian
Mongol

◄ *Overcoming natural barriers,* the Brenner Autobahn, one of the main routes across the Alps, links Innsbruck in Austria with Verona in Italy.

► *The architecture of* the Grand Place lies at the heart of Brussels – home city to one of the EU headquarters.

Transport

Despite its fragmented geography and many natural frontiers, communications in Europe are well developed. Extensive motorway links allow rapid road transport, while high-speed rail connections like France's TGV (*Train à Grande Vitesse*), and the Channel Tunnel have improved rail travel. Outdated communication infrastructures in parts of eastern Europe, and insufficient transport links across the Alps, however, remain weak parts of the network.

Languages

There are three main European language groups: Germanic languages predominate in central and northern Europe; Romance languages in western and Mediterranean Europe and Romania; while Slavic languages are spoken in eastern Europe and the Russian Federation. Isolated pockets of local languages, such as Basque and Gaelic, persist and frequently provide a focus for national identity.

European resources

Europe's large tracts of fertile, accessible land, combined with its generally temperate climate, have allowed a greater percentage of land to be used for agricultural purposes than in any other continent. Extensive coal and iron ore deposits were used to create steel and manufacturing industries during the 19th and 20th centuries. Today, although natural resources have been widely exploited, and heavy industry is of declining importance, the growth of hi-tech and service industries has enabled Europe to maintain its wealth.

Industry

Europe's wealth was generated by the rise of industry and colonial exploitation during the 19th century. The mining of abundant natural resources made Europe the industrial centre of the world. Adaptation has been essential in the changing world economy, and a move to service-based industries has been widespread except in eastern Europe, where heavy industry still dominates.

▲ **Countries like Hungary** *are still struggling to modernize inefficient factories left over from extensive, centrally-planned industrialization during the communist era.*

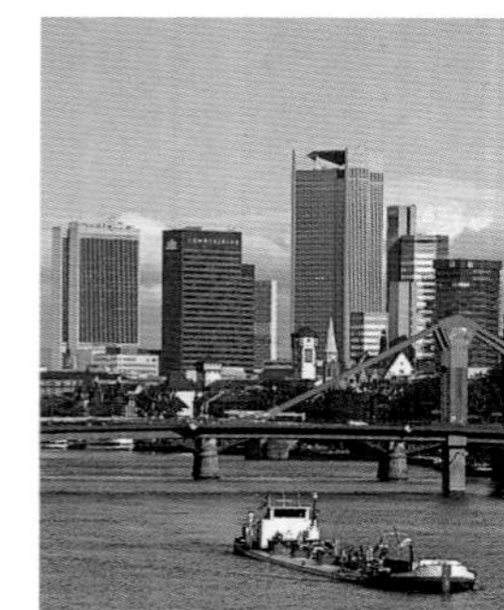

◀ **Frankfurt am Main** *is an example of a modern service-based city. The skyline is dominated by headquarters from the worlds of banking and commerce.*

▲ **Other power sources** *are becoming more attractive as fossil fuels run out; 16% of Europe's electricity is now provided by hydro-electric power.*

Standard of living

Living standards in western Europe are among the highest in the world, although there is a growing sector of homeless, jobless people. Eastern Europeans have lower overall standards of living – a legacy of stagnated economies.

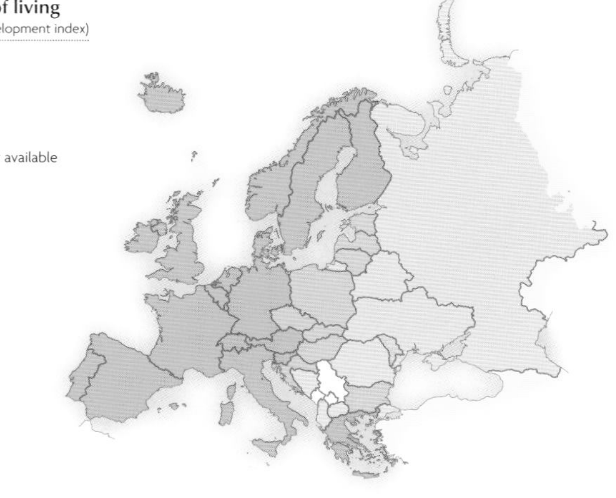
Standard of living
(UN human development index)
low
high
data not available

▶ **Skiing brings millions** *of tourists to the slopes each year, which means that even unproductive, marginal land is used to create wealth in the French, Swiss, Italian and Austrian Alps.*

GNI per capita (US $)

- below 1999
- 2000–4999
- 5000–9999
- 10,000–19,999
- 20,000–24,999
- above 25,000

Industry

- aerospace
- brewing
- car/vehicle manufacture
- chemicals
- defence
- electronics
- engineering
- finance
- food processing
- hi-tech industry
- iron & steel
- pharmaceuticals
- printing & publishing
- shipbuilding
- textiles
- timber processing
- wine
- coal
- oil
- gas
- industrial cities
- major industrial areas

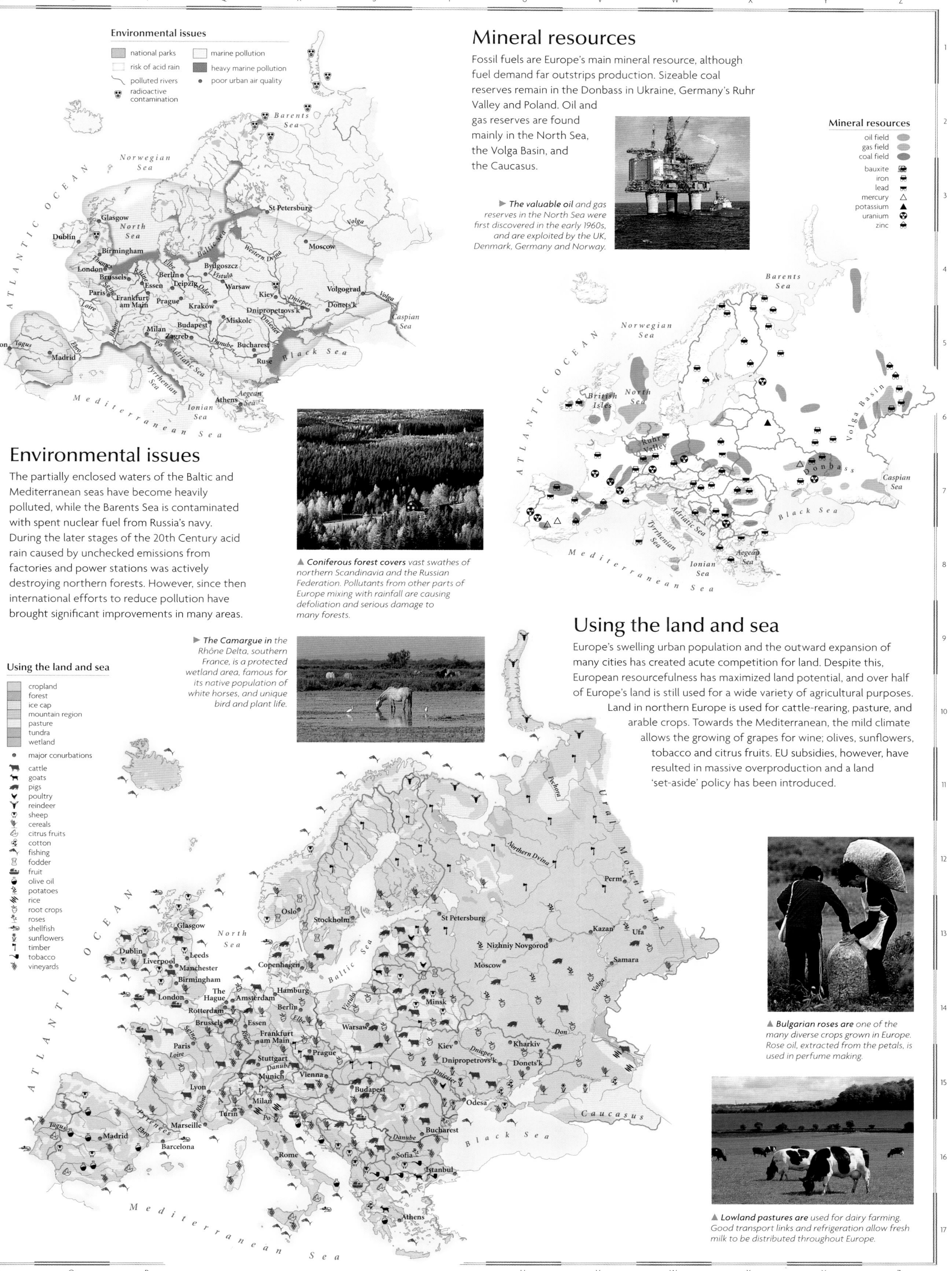
Environmental issues
national parks
marine pollution
risk of acid rain
heavy marine pollution
polluted rivers
poor urban air quality
radioactive contamination
Mineral resources
oil field
gas field
coal field
bauxite
iron
lead
mercury
potassium
uranium
zinc
Using the land and sea
cropland
forest
ice cap
mountain region
pasture
tundra
wetland
major conurbations
cattle
goats
pigs
poultry
reindeer
sheep
cereals
citrus fruits
cotton
fishing
fodder
fruit
olive oil
potatoes
rice
root crops
roses
shellfish
sunflowers
timber
tobacco
vineyards

Mineral resources

Fossil fuels are Europe's main mineral resource, although fuel demand far outstrips production. Sizeable coal reserves remain in the Donbass in Ukraine, Germany's Ruhr Valley and Poland. Oil and gas reserves are found mainly in the North Sea, the Volga Basin, and the Caucasus.

▶ *The valuable oil and gas reserves in the North Sea were first discovered in the early 1960s, and are exploited by the UK, Denmark, Germany and Norway.*

Environmental issues

The partially enclosed waters of the Baltic and Mediterranean seas have become heavily polluted, while the Barents Sea is contaminated with spent nuclear fuel from Russia's navy. During the later stages of the 20th Century acid rain caused by unchecked emissions from factories and power stations was actively destroying northern forests. However, since then international efforts to reduce pollution have brought significant improvements in many areas.

▲ *Coniferous forest covers vast swathes of northern Scandinavia and the Russian Federation. Pollutants from other parts of Europe mixing with rainfall are causing defoliation and serious damage to many forests.*

▶ *The Camargue in the Rhône Delta, southern France, is a protected wetland area, famous for its native population of white horses, and unique bird and plant life.*

Using the land and sea

Europe's swelling urban population and the outward expansion of many cities has created acute competition for land. Despite this, European resourcefulness has maximized land potential, and over half of Europe's land is still used for a wide variety of agricultural purposes. Land in northern Europe is used for cattle-rearing, pasture, and arable crops. Towards the Mediterranean, the mild climate allows the growing of grapes for wine; olives, sunflowers, tobacco and citrus fruits. EU subsidies, however, have resulted in massive overproduction and a land 'set-aside' policy has been introduced.

▲ *Bulgarian roses are one of the many diverse crops grown in Europe. Rose oil, extracted from the petals, is used in perfume making.*

▲ *Lowland pastures are used for dairy farming. Good transport links and refrigeration allow fresh milk to be distributed throughout Europe.*

Scandinavia, Finland & Iceland

DENMARK, NORWAY, SWEDEN, FINLAND, ICELAND

Jutting into the Arctic Circle, this northern swathe of Europe has some of the continent's harshest environments, but benefits from great reserves of oil, gas and natural evergreen forests. While most early settlers came from the south, migrants to Finland came from the east, giving it a distinct language and culture. Since the late 19th century, the Scandinavian states have developed strong egalitarian traditions. Today, their welfare benefits systems are among the most extensive in the world, and standards of living are high. The Lapps, or Sami, maintain their traditional lifestyle in the northern regions of Norway, Sweden and Finland.

The landscape

Glaciers up to 10,000 ft (3000 m) deep covered most of Scandinavia and Finland during the last Ice Age. The effects of glaciation mark the entire landscape, from the mountains to the lowlands, across the tundra landscape of Lapland, and the lake districts of Sweden and Finland.

Lapland, north of the Arctic Circle, is an area of undulating fells and plains known as tundra. The subsoil is permanently frozen and therefore impermeable. There are many peat bogs. Pools reappear in the summer when the surface thaws.

The Lofoten Islands were one of the first areas exposed as the ice sheet melted.

Halti mountain is Finland's highest point, at 4356 ft (1328 m).

Geysers are a by-product of Iceland's volcanic activity. Geysir, Iceland's largest spring, gives them their name.

Oulujärvi

◀ ***Finland's landscape was*** *fashioned by ice action. Glaciers gouged out its distinctive shallow lake basins, such as Oulujärvi, and left debris called moraines in their wake.*

Fjords

▲ ***The fjords on*** *the western coast of Norway were once gentle river valleys. Their deep floors and steep sides were carved out by glaciers during the last Ice Age, and they were later flooded by the sea.*

Sjælland coast

▲ ***On the coast*** *of Sjælland, these cliffs have been eroded by the sea, exposing layers of chalk and limestone.*

Slower rates of uplift 0.1 in/yr (3 mm/yr)

Area of maximum yearly uplift 0.3 in/yr (9 mm/yr)

▲ ***Scandinavia is still*** *recovering from the last Ice Age, when ice depressed the land by 2000 ft (600 m). This gradual uplift is known as isostatic rebound.*

Scale 1:5,500,000

projection: Lambert Conformal Conic

(same scale as main map)

SCALE 1:9,000,000

projection: Lambert Conformal Conic

Using the land and sea

The cold climate, short growing season, poorly developed soil, steep slopes, and exposure to high winds across northern regions means that most agriculture is concentrated, with the population, in the south. Most of Finland and much of Norway and Sweden are covered by dense forests of pine, spruce and birch, which supply the timber industries.

ARCTIC OCEAN
BARENTS SEA
RUSSIAN FE
FINNMARK
TROMS
NORDLAND
LAPPI
Lapland
Nordkapp (North Cape)
Hammerfest
Tromsø
Narvik
Kiruna
Bodø
Kebnekaise 2117m
Halti 1328m

Land use and agricultural distribution

fishing, pigs, reindeer, sheep, cereals, timber, capital cities, major towns, pasture, cropland, forest, mountain region, tundra

The urban/rural population divide

urban 77% rural 23%

Population density — Total land area

122

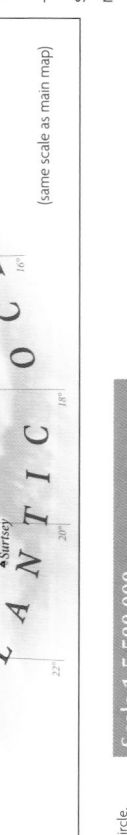

▲ ***Many Lappish people,*** *in addition to traditional reindeer herding, now also make their living from fishing and farming, or working in cities. Tourism provides some with an extra source of income.*

▲ ***Sweden is one*** *of the world's largest producers of wood and wood-based products. The traditional movement of logs by floating them down rivers has now been largely replaced by the use of trucks.*

Map key

Population

- 1 million to 5 million
- 500,000 to 1 million
- 100,000 to 500,000
- 50,000 to 100,000
- 10,000 to 50,000
- below 10,000

Elevation

- 2000m / 6562ft
- 1000m / 3281ft
- 500m / 1640ft
- 250m / 820ft
- 100m / 328ft
- sea level

Transport and industry

Norway derives its premier industry, the production of oil and gas, from the North Sea, while Denmark exploits its own oil and gas reserves. Hydro-electric power is a major industry, particularly in Sweden and Iceland. Timber processing remains significant in Finland and Sweden, but metal and engineering industries are increasingly important. In Iceland, fish products are the main source of export earnings.

The transport network

- 226,735 miles (364,936 km)
- 2042 miles (3286 km)
- 13,704 miles (22,057 km)
- 6,661 miles (10,721 km)

Although roads now reach most areas, the railways are markedly less developed. Much of the north is not served by rail and must rely on air and sea services for long distance travel and freight transportation.

Major industry and infrastructure

- car manufacture
- engineering
- fish processing
- hydro-electric power
- nuclear power
- oil & gas
- timber processing
- capital cities
- major towns
- international airports
- major roads
- major industrial areas

► ***The use of*** *geothermal power in Iceland began half a century ago. Today geothermal power stations supply 89% of the country's domestic heating requirements.*

100

Southern Scandinavia

SOUTHERN NORWAY, SOUTHERN SWEDEN, DENMARK

Scandinavia's economic and political hub is the more habitable and accessible southern region. Many of the area's major cities are on the southern coasts, including Oslo and Stockholm, the capitals of Norway and Sweden. In Denmark, most of the population and the capital, Copenhagen, are located on its many islands. A cultural unity links the three Scandinavian countries. Their main languages, Danish, Swedish and Norwegian, are mutually intelligible, and they all retain their monarchies, although the parliaments have legislative control.

Using the land

Agriculture in southern Scandinavia is highly mechanized although farms are small. Denmark is the most intensively farmed country and its western pastureland is used mainly for pig farming. Cereal crops including wheat, barley and oats, predominate in eastern Denmark and in the far south of Sweden. Southern Norway and Sweden have large tracts of forest which are exploited for logging.

The urban/rural population divide

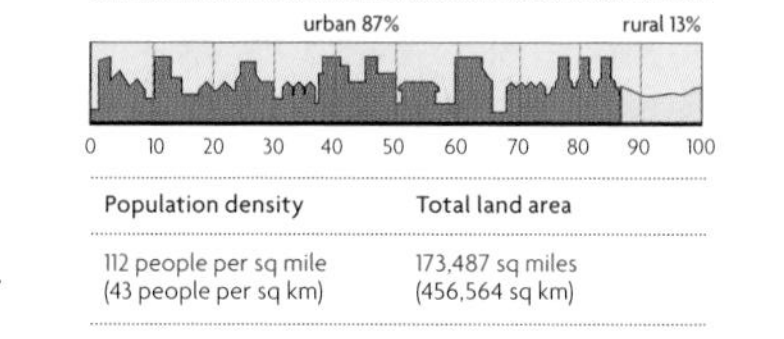

urban 87%
rural 13%
0 10 20 30 40 50 60 70 80 90 100

Population density	Total land area
112 people per sq mile (43 people per sq km)	173,487 sq miles (456,564 sq km)

Land use and agricultural distribution

cattle, pigs, sheep, cereals, fodder, root crops, timber

capital cities, major towns

pasture, cropland, forest, mountain region

The landscape

Southern Scandinavia, with the exception of Norway, has a flatter terrain than the rest of the region. Denmark and southern Sweden are both extensions of the North European Plain. In this area, because of glacial deposition rather than erosion, the soils are deeper and more fertile.

Acid rain, caused by industrial pollution carried north from elsewhere in Europe, harms plant and animal life in Scandinavian forests and lakes. The region's surface rocks lack lime to neutralize the acid, so making the problem more serious.

◀ *In the past, glaciers such as this one in Olden, Norway, were much larger. Today, many are retreating to yield the spectacular glacial scenery.*

The peak of Glittertind in the Jotunheimen mountains is 8110 ft (2472 m) high.

Distinctive low ridges, called eskers, are found across southern Sweden. They are formed from sand and gravel deposits left by retreating glaciers.

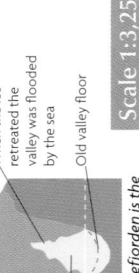

▲ ***Limestone pillars eroded*** *by the sea dot the coast of Gotland and surrounding islands.*

The lakes of southern Sweden remain from a period when the land was completely flooded. As the ice which covered the area melted, the land rose, leaving lakes in shallow, ice-scoured depressions. Sweden has over 90,000 lakes.

Denmark's flat and fertile soils are formed on glacial deposits between 100–160 ft (30–50 m) deep.

Vänern in Sweden is the largest lake in Scandinavia. It covers an area of 2080 sq miles (5390 sq km).

Sognefjorden

Erosion by glaciers deepened existing river valleys

Sea level

When the ice retreated the valley was flooded by the sea

Old valley floor

▲ ***Sognefjorden is the*** *deepest of Norway's many fjords. It drops to 4291 ft (1308 m) below sea level.*

▲ ***In Norway winters*** *are longer and colder inland than in coastal areas, where the warm current of the North Atlantic Drift moderates the climate.*

Scale 1:3,250,000

projection: Lambert Conformal Conic

Map key

Population

- 1 million to 5 million
- 500,000 to 1 million
- 100,000 to 500,000
- 50,000 to 100,000
- 10,000 to 50,000
- below 10,000

Elevation

- 2000m / 6562ft
- 1000m / 3281ft
- 500m / 1640ft
- 250m / 820ft
- 100m / 328ft

96

92

92

NORWAY
SWEDEN
DENMARK
GERMANY
FINLAND
OSLO
STOCKHOLM
KØBENHAVN (COPENHAGEN)
Göteborg (Gothenburg)
NORTH SEA
Skagerrak
Kattegat
BALTIC SEA
Gotland
Öland
Bornholm
Jylland
Sjælland
FAEROE ISLANDS (to Denmark)
TÓRSHAVN
ATLANTIC OCEAN
(same scale as main map)
96
100
110
The transport network
133,712 miles (215,666 km)
1160 miles (1872 km)
8180 miles (13,195 km)
3668 miles (5197 km)
Major industry and infrastructure
car manufacture
electronics
engineering
furniture industry
iron & steel
shipbuilding
food processing
capital cities
major towns
international airports
major roads
major industrial areas

▲ **Shipbuilding in Gothenburg** has declined in recent years as manufacturers in other sectors have come to the fore. One of these is the car firm, Volvo, a major employer in Gothenburg.

Transport and industry

In Denmark and Norway food processing is a major industry. Swedish iron and steel production supports car manufacturers such as Saab and Volvo. Nearly half of Norway's income comes from North Sea oil and gas reserves. Denmark's successful hi-tech, high-profit electronics and light engineering industries largely use imported raw materials.

A major addition to the transport network in this region is the Oresund bridge and tunnel project connecting Copenhagen in Denmark with Malmö in Sweden.

▶ **More than half** the land in Denmark is used for agriculture. Grains, particularly wheat and barley, are the main crops cultivated.

▶ **Sand deposited by** glaciers at the end of the last Ice Age, has been fashioned by wind and waves into dunes, creating heathlands along the northwestern coast of Jylland.

The British Isles

UNITED KINGDOM, IRELAND

The British Isles have for centuries played a central role in European and world history. England, Wales, Scotland and Northern Ireland together form the United Kingdom (UK), while the southern portion of Ireland is an independent country, self-governing since 1921. Although England has tended to be the politically and economically dominant partner in the UK, the Scots, Welsh and Irish maintain independent cultures, distinct national identities and languages. Southeastern England is the most densely populated part of this crowded region, with over eight million people living in and around the London area.

▲ ***The valley of** Glen Coe in the Scottish Highlands is a U-shaped valley, typical of the north and west of the British Isles, where glaciers shaped much of the landscape.*

Transport and industry

The British Isles' industrial base was founded primarily on coal, iron and textiles, based largely in the north. Today, the most productive sectors include hi-tech industries clustered mainly in southeastern England, chemicals, finance and the service sector, particularly tourism.

Major industry and infrastructure

- car manufacture
- chemicals
- engineering
- hi-tech industry
- iron & steel
- tourism
- capital cities
- major towns
- international airports
- major roads
- major industrial areas

The transport network

285,947 miles (460,240 km)		2023 miles (3578 km)	
11,825 miles (19,032km)		3976 miles (6400 km)	

The UK's congested roads have become a major focus of environmental concern in recent years. No longer an island, the UK was finally linked to continental Europe by the Channel Tunnel in 1994.

◀ ***Clew Bay in** western Ireland, is characteristic of the heavily indented west coast, where deep wide-mouthed bays separate the mountains of Mayo, Donegal and Kerry as they thrust out into the Atlantic Ocean.*

64

92

The landscape

Rugged uplands dominate the landscape of Scotland, Wales and northern England. All the peaks in the British Isles over 4000 ft (1219 m) lie in highland Scotland. Lowland England rises into several ranges of rolling hills, including the older Mendips, and the Cotswolds and the Chilterns, which were formed at the same time as the Alps in southern Europe.

Over 600 islands, mostly uninhabited, lie west and north of the Scottish mainland.

Ben Nevis at 4409 ft (1343 m) is the highest peak in the UK.

The Pennines, sometimes called 'the backbone of England', are formed of limestones and grits.

The lowlands of Scotland, drained by the Tay, Forth and Clyde rivers, are centred on a rift valley. The region contains valuable coal reserves.

Thousands of hexagonal basalt columns form Giant's Causeway on the north coast of Antrim. These were created by volcanic activity.

The British Isles have no large-scale river systems. The Shannon is the longest, at 230 miles (370 km).

Peat bogs dot the poorly-drained Irish lowlands.

Snowdon is the highest mountain in England and Wales reaching 3556 ft (1085 m).

Lake District

Mendip Hills

Chiltern Hills

▲ ***Ullswater in the** Lake District fills a deep valley formed by glacial erosion.*

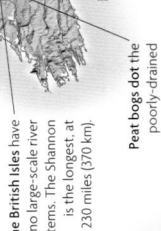

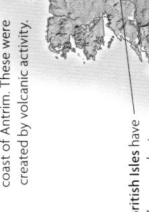

The Fens are a low-lying area reclaimed from the sea.

The Cotswold Hills are characterized by a series of limestone ridges overlooking clay vales.

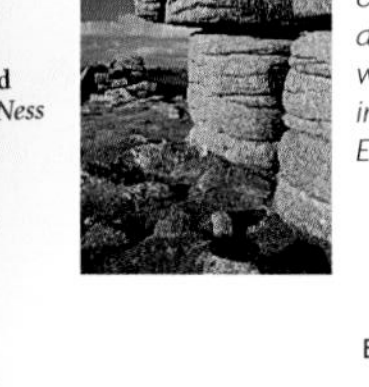

◀ ***Dartmoor, studded with** tors, is an exposed part of a vast granite dome, formed when molten rock intruded into the Earth's crust.*

Durdle Door

▲ ***Coastal erosion around** the British Isles forms striking features such as this limestone arch, Durdle Door in Dorset.*

Black Ven, Lyme Regis

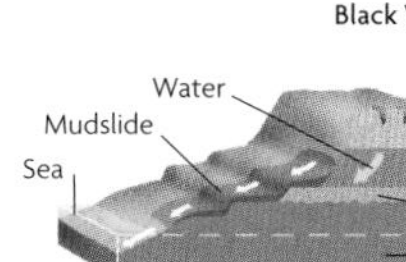

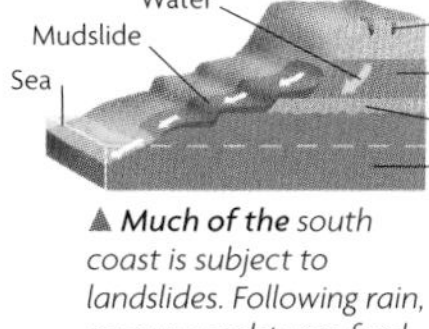

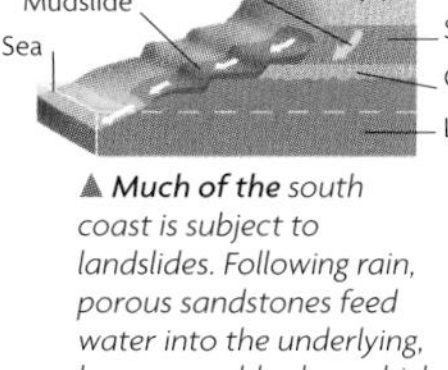

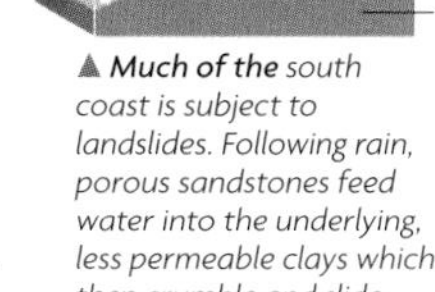

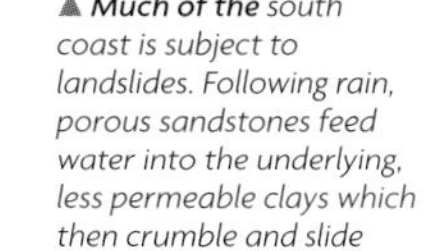

Water
Mudslide
Sea
Cracks
Sandstone
Clay
Limestone

▲ ***Much of the** south coast is subject to landslides. Following rain, porous sandstones feed water into the underlying, less permeable clays which then crumble and slide into the sea.*

Map key

Population

- above 5 million
- 1 million to 5 million
- 500,000 to 1 million
- 100,000 to 500,000
- 50,000 to 100,000
- 10,000 to 50,000
- below 10,000

Elevation

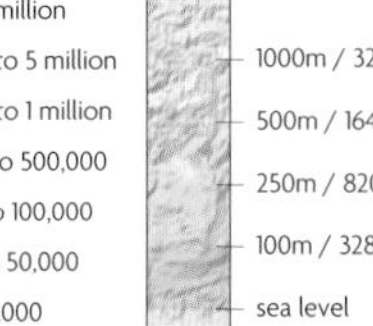

1000m / 3281ft
500m / 1640ft
250m / 820ft
100m / 328ft
sea level

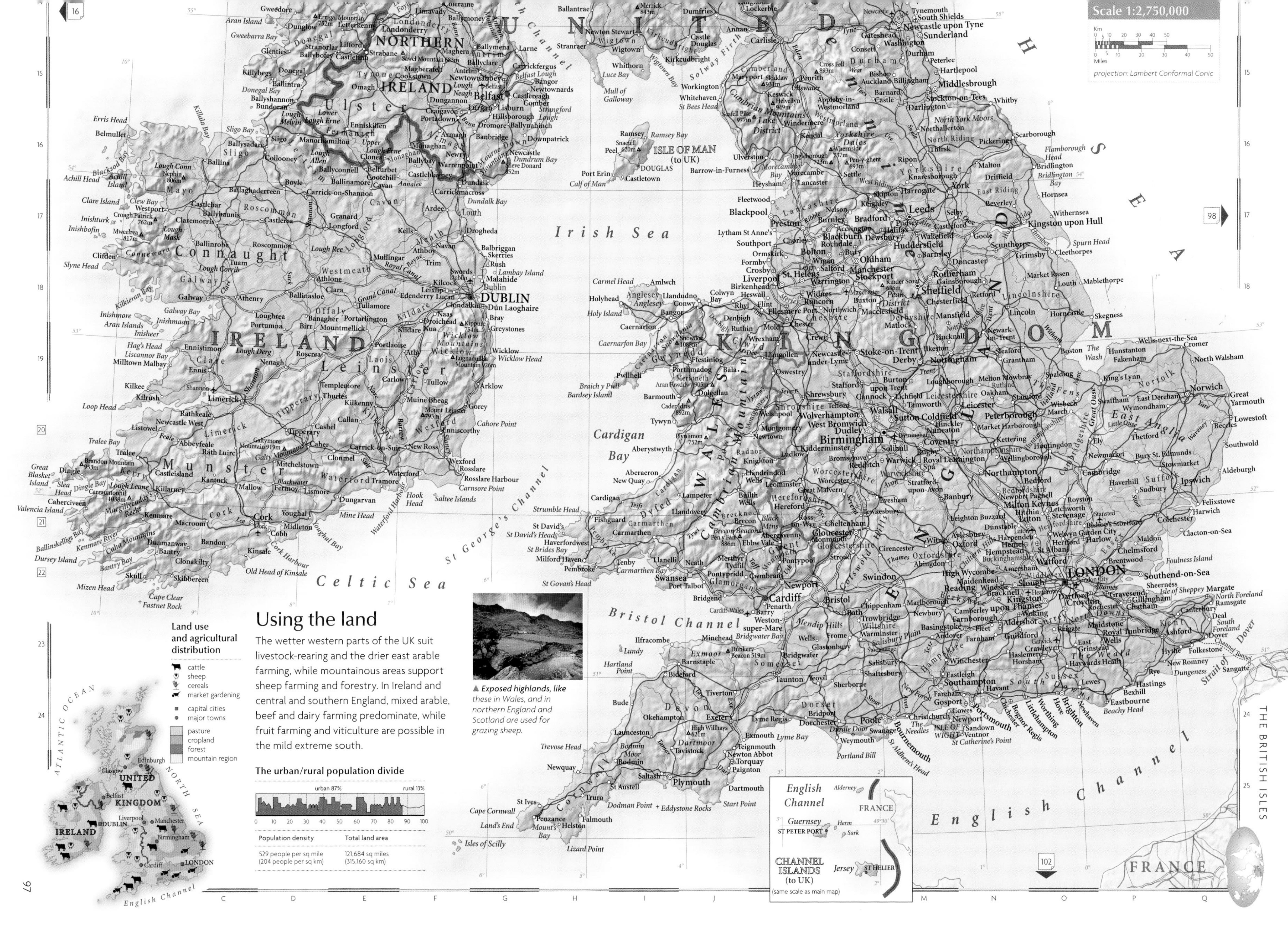
Scale 1:2,750,000
projection: Lambert Conformal Conic
UNITED KINGDOM
IRELAND
NORTHERN IRELAND
WALES
ENGLAND
FRANCE
NORTH SEA
Irish Sea
Celtic Sea
St George's Channel
Bristol Channel
English Channel
Cardigan Bay
DUBLIN
LONDON
Belfast
Cardiff
Birmingham
Manchester
Liverpool
Leeds
Bristol
Plymouth
Cork
Galway
Limerick
Ulster
Connaught
Leinster
Munster
ISLE OF MAN (to UK)
CHANNEL ISLANDS (to UK)
(same scale as main map)
Land use and agricultural distribution
cattle
sheep
cereals
market gardening
capital cities
major towns
pasture
cropland
forest
mountain region

Using the land

The wetter western parts of the UK suit livestock-rearing and the drier east arable farming, while mountainous areas support sheep farming and forestry. In Ireland and central and southern England, mixed arable, beef and dairy farming predominate, while fruit farming and viticulture are possible in the mild extreme south.

The urban/rural population divide

urban 87% — rural 13%

Population density	Total land area
529 people per sq mile (204 people per sq km)	121,684 sq miles (315,160 sq km)

▲ **Exposed highlands, like** these in Wales, and in northern England and Scotland are used for grazing sheep.

The Low Countries

BELGIUM, LUXEMBOURG, NETHERLANDS

One of northwestern Europe's strategic crossroads, the Low Countries are united by a common history in which they have often been a battleground in European wars. For over a thousand years they were ruled by foreign powers. Even after they achieved independence, the three countries maintained close links, later forming the world's first totally free labour and goods market, the Benelux Economic Union, which became the core of the European Community (now the European Union or EU). These states have remained at the forefront of wider European co-operation; Brussels, The Hague and Luxembourg are hosts to major institutions of the EU.

The landscape

The main geographical regions of the Netherlands are the northern glacial heathlands, the low-lying lands of the Rhine and Maas/Meuse, the reclaimed polders, and the dune coast and islands. Belgium includes part of the Ardennes, together with the coalfields on its northern flanks, and the fertile Flanders plain.

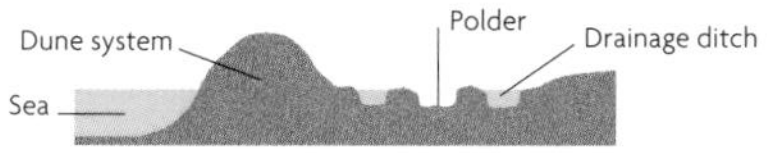

Dune system
Polder
Drainage ditch
Sea

▲ ***Extensive sand dune** systems along the coast have prevented flooding of the land. Behind the dunes, marshy land is drained to form polders, usable land suitable for agriculture.*

Schoorl

◀ ***Heathlands, like these** at Schoorl, are found along the coast of the Netherlands. Much of the coast was breached by the sea in the 5th century, creating its distinctive inlets and islands.*

▲ ***One-third of the** Netherlands lies below sea level and flooding is a constant threat. Barrages have been built across the mouths of many rivers to contain floodwaters.*

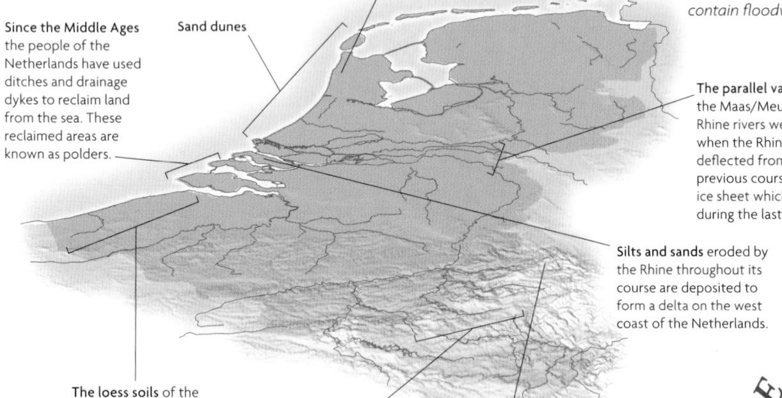

Since the Middle Ages the people of the Netherlands have used ditches and drainage dykes to reclaim land from the sea. These reclaimed areas are known as polders.

Sand dunes

The parallel valleys of the Maas/Meuse and Rhine rivers were created when the Rhine was deflected from its previous course by the ice sheet which formed during the last Ice Age.

Silts and sands eroded by the Rhine throughout its course are deposited to form a delta on the west coast of the Netherlands.

The loess soils of the Flanders Plain in western Belgium provide excellent conditions for arable farming.

Ardennes

Hautes Fagnes is the highest part of Belgium. The bogs and streams in this upland region result from high rainfall and low temperatures.

▶ ***Uplifted and folded** 220 million years ago, the Ardennes have since been reduced to relatively level plateaux, then sharply incised by rivers such as the Maas/Meuse.*

Transport and industry

In the western Netherlands, a massive, sprawling industrialized zone encompasses many new hi-tech and service industries. Belgium's central region has emerged as the country's light manufacturing and services centre. Luxembourg city is home to more than 160 banks and the European headquarters of many international companies.

Major industry and infrastructure

- aerospace
- finance
- engineering
- hi-tech industry
- pharmaceuticals
- textiles
- capital cities
- major towns
- international airports
- major roads
- major industrial areas

NETHERLANDS
AMSTERDAM
THE HAGUE
BELGIUM
BRUSSELS
LUXEMBOURG
NORTH SEA
GERMANY
FRANCE

The transport network

140,588 miles (226,281 km)
2565 miles (4129 km)
4099 miles (6598 km)
4134 miles (6653 km)

The Low Countries hold a key position on the North Sea, containing Europe's two largest ports, Rotterdam and Antwerp, which are connected to a comprehensive system of inland waterways.

NETHERLANDS
GERMANY
NORTH SEA
Waddenzee
Waddeneilanden
IJsselmeer
GRONINGEN
FRYSLÂN (FRIESLAND)
DRENTHE
OVERIJSSEL
FLEVOLAND
GELDERLAND
UTRECHT
NOORD-HOLLAND
ZUID-HOLLAND
AMSTERDAM
'S-GRAVENHAGE (THE HAGUE)
Rotterdam
Utrecht
Groningen
Leeuwarden
Zwolle
Arnhem
Apeldoorn
Enschede

100

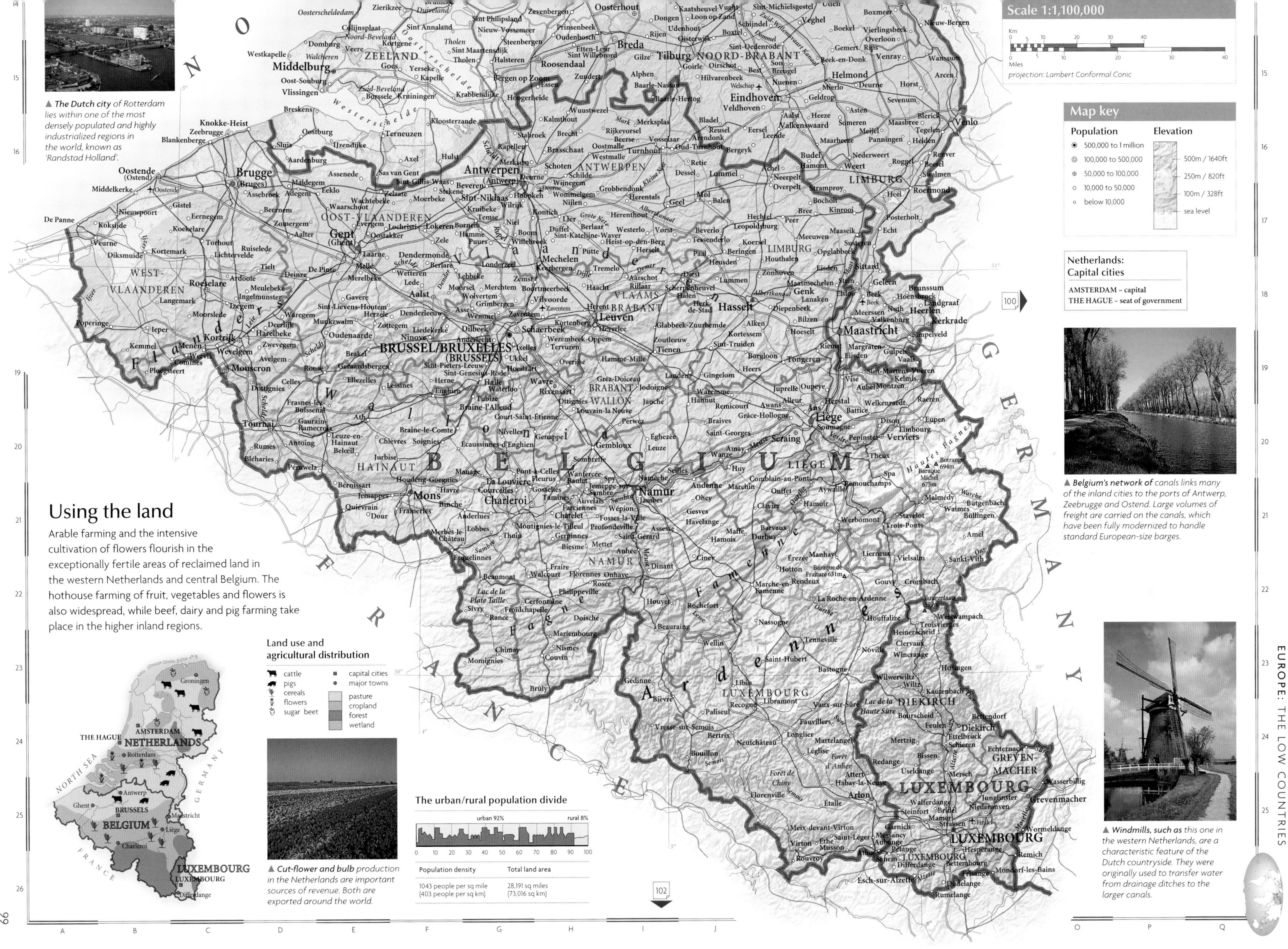
Scale 1:1,100,000
Km 0 5 10 20 30 40
Miles 0 5 10 20 30 40
projection: Lambert Conformal Conic
Map key
Population
500,000 to 1 million
100,000 to 500,000
50,000 to 100,000
10,000 to 50,000
below 10,000
Elevation
500m / 1640ft
250m / 820ft
100m / 328ft
sea level
Netherlands: Capital cities
AMSTERDAM – capital
THE HAGUE – seat of government
NORTH SEA
GERMANY
FRANCE
BELGIUM
LUXEMBOURG
Land use and agricultural distribution
cattle
pigs
cereals
flowers
sugar beet
capital cities
major towns
pasture
cropland
forest
wetland
THE HAGUE
AMSTERDAM
NETHERLANDS
Rotterdam
Groningen
Antwerp
Ghent
BRUSSELS
Maastricht
Liège
Charleroi
The urban/rural population divide
urban 92%
rural 8%
0 10 20 30 40 50 60 70 80 90 100
Population density
1043 people per sq mile
(403 people per sq km)
Total land area
28,191 sq miles
(73,016 sq km)
100
102

▲ **The Dutch city** of Rotterdam lies within one of the most densely populated and highly industrialized regions in the world, known as 'Randstad Holland'.

▲ **Belgium's network of** canals links many of the inland cities to the ports of Antwerp, Zeebrugge and Ostend. Large volumes of freight are carried on the canals, which have been fully modernized to handle standard European-size barges.

Using the land

Arable farming and the intensive cultivation of flowers flourish in the exceptionally fertile areas of reclaimed land in the western Netherlands and central Belgium. The hothouse farming of fruit, vegetables and flowers is also widespread, while beef, dairy and pig farming take place in the higher inland regions.

▲ **Cut-flower and bulb** production in the Netherlands are important sources of revenue. Both are exported around the world.

▲ **Windmills, such as** this one in the western Netherlands, are a characteristic feature of the Dutch countryside. They were originally used to transfer water from drainage ditches to the larger canals.

Germany

Despite the devastation of its industry and infrastructure during the Second World War and its separation from eastern Germany during the Cold War, West Germany made a rapid recovery in the following generation to become Europe's most formidable economic power. When the Berlin Wall was dismantled in 1989, the two halves of Germany were politically united for the first time in 40 years. Complete social and economic unity remain a longer term goal, as East German industry and society adapt to a free market. Germany has been a key player in the creation of the European Union (EU) and in moves toward a single European currency.

Using the land

Germany has a large, efficient agricultural sector, and produces more than three-quarters of its own food. The major crops grown are cereals and sugar beet on the more fertile soils, and root crops, rye, oats and fodder on the poorer soils of the northern plains and central uplands. Southern Germany is also a principal producer of high quality wines. Vineyards cover the slopes surrounding the Rhine and its tributaries.

Land use and agricultural distribution

cattle
pigs
cereals
sugar beet
vineyards
capital cities
major towns
pasture
cropland
forest

The urban/rural population divide

urban 87% | rural 13%

Population density	Total land area
612 people per sq mile (236 people per sq km)	13,804 sq miles (356,910 sq km)

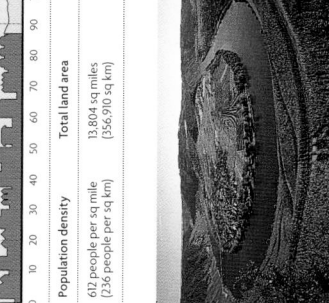

▲ *The Moselle river* flows through the Rhine State Uplands (Rheinisches Schiefergebirge). *During a period of uplift, pre-existing river meanders were deeply incised, to form its present dramatic contours.*

The landscape

The plains of northern Germany, the volcanic plateaux and mountains of the central uplands, and the Bavarian Alps are the three principal geographic regions in Germany. North to south the land rises steadily from barely 300 ft (90 m) in the plains to 6500 ft (2000 m) in the Bavarian Alps, which are a small but distinct region in the far south.

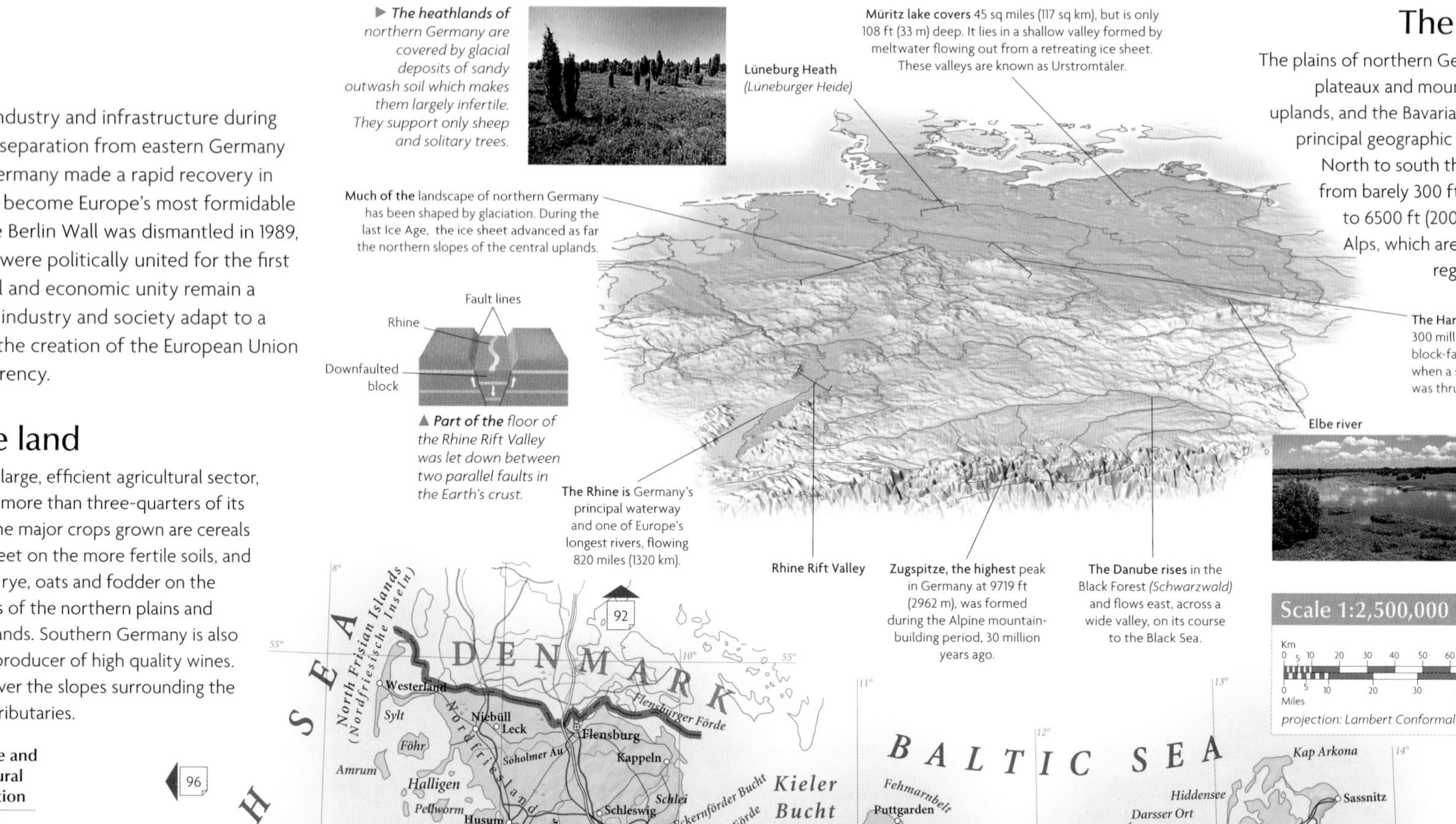
Lüneburg Heath
(Lüneburger Heide)
Fault lines
Rhine
Downfaulted block
Elbe river
Rhine Rift Valley

▶ *The heathlands of northern Germany are covered by glacial deposits of sandy outwash soil which makes them largely infertile. They support only sheep and solitary trees.*

Much of the landscape of northern Germany has been shaped by glaciation. During the last Ice Age, the ice sheet advanced as far the northern slopes of the central uplands.

▲ *Part of the floor of the Rhine Rift Valley was let down between two parallel faults in the Earth's crust.*

The Rhine is Germany's principal waterway and one of Europe's longest rivers, flowing 820 miles (1320 km).

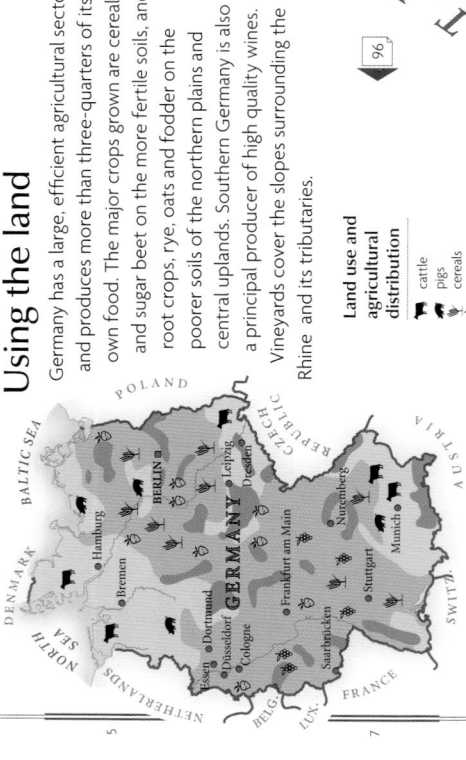

Müritz lake covers 45 sq miles (117 sq km), but is only 108 ft (33 m) deep. It lies in a shallow valley formed by meltwater flowing out from a retreating ice sheet. These valleys are known as Urstromtäler.

Zugspitze, the highest peak in Germany at 9719 ft (2962 m), was formed during the Alpine mountain-building period, 30 million years ago.

The Danube rises in the Black Forest *(Schwarzwald)* and flows east, across a wide valley, on its course to the Black Sea.

The Harz Mountains were formed 300 million years ago. They are block-faulted mountains, formed when a section of the Earth's crust was thrust up between two faults.

◀ *The Elbe flows in wide meanders across the north German plain to the North Sea. At its mouth it is 10 miles (16 km) wide.*

Scale 1:2,500,000

projection: Lambert Conformal Conic

92
96
98
110

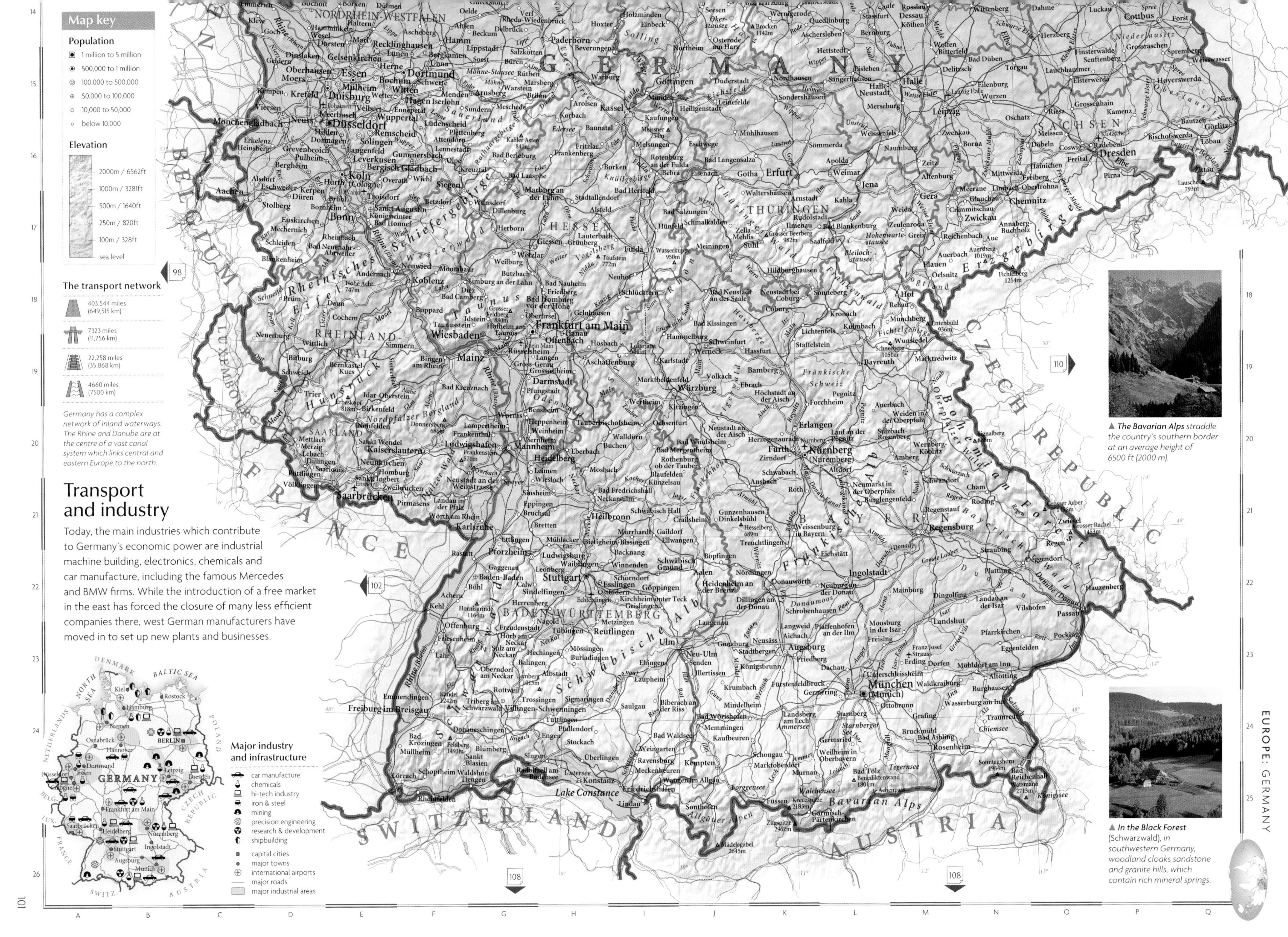
Map key
Population
1 million to 5 million
500,000 to 1 million
100,000 to 500,000
50,000 to 100,000
10,000 to 50,000
below 10,000
Elevation
2000m / 6562ft
1000m / 3281ft
500m / 1640ft
250m / 820ft
100m / 328ft
sea level
The transport network
403,544 miles (649,515 km)
7323 miles (11,756 km)
22,258 miles (35,868 km)
4660 miles (7500 km)
Germany has a complex network of inland waterways. The Rhine and Danube are at the centre of a vast canal system which links central and eastern Europe to the north.
GERMANY
CZECH REPUBLIC
AUSTRIA
SWITZERLAND
FRANCE
LUXEMBOURG
BELGIUM
Major industry and infrastructure
car manufacture
chemicals
hi-tech industry
iron & steel
mining
precision engineering
research & development
shipbuilding
capital cities
major towns
international airports
major roads
major industrial areas

Transport and industry

Today, the main industries which contribute to Germany's economic power are industrial machine building, electronics, chemicals and car manufacture, including the famous Mercedes and BMW firms. While the introduction of a free market in the east has forced the closure of many less efficient companies there, west German manufacturers have moved in to set up new plants and businesses.

▲ *The Bavarian Alps straddle the country's southern border at an average height of 6500 ft (2000 m).*

▲ *In the Black Forest* (Schwarzwald), *in southwestern Germany, woodland cloaks sandstone and granite hills, which contain rich mineral springs.*

France

FRANCE, MONACO

A major centre of culture and fashion, and a leading producer of both industrial and agricultural goods, France is a key player in the push towards European unity. The founder of modern Republican government in the 18th century, France has been closely involved in European events for many centuries. The Paris Basin is the most highly populated area; Île de France is home to over 11 million people. Large parts of rural France remain thinly populated, particularly the mountainous Massif Central, Pyrenees and southern Alps.

◀ *The chalk cliffs of Normandy (Normandie) and southeastern England form part of a single geological region, now divided in two by the English Channel.*

The landscape

France's landscape was fashioned by two phases of mountain-building. The northwestern peninsula, the Massif Central and the Vosges date from 220 million years ago. The complex folds of the Alps and Pyrenees, the gently-folded Jura, and the low-lying sedimentary areas of the Paris, Garonne and Rhône basins started to form 65 million years ago.

The coast of Brittany *(Bretagne)* is highly indented where deep valleys in the northwestern peninsula were drowned by the sea.

The Normandy *(Normandie)* coastline is characterized by high chalk cliffs.

▲ *The Paris Basin consists of a layered sequence of sedimentary rocks. Fertile soils over much of the area make good agricultural land.*

The coastline of France is 2141 miles (3427 km) long.

The gently rounded summits of the Vosges are over 200 million years old.

The folded Jura form low ridges and long narrow valleys.

The Biscay coast, like the Mediterranean, is characterized by flat sandy beaches, interspersed with lagoons.

The Alps were forced up during several phases of mountain-building beginning 65 million years ago.

Garonne Basin

Rhône Basin

Corsica's northeastern peninsula has dramatic cliffs of folded limestone.

The Dordogne region contains spectacular examples of limestone scenery including caves and gorges.

The Pyrenees form a natural border between France and Spain.

The ancient Massif Central, disturbed by the formation of the Alps, is subject to volcanism that only ceased during the last 10,000 years.

Rhône Delta

Rhône

Delta plain

The marshes of the Camargue

◀ *The volcanic landscape of the Auvergne where the cones of its extinct volcanoes have worn away to leave 'plugs' of lava.*

▲ *Deposition in the Rhône Delta is wave-dominated. Sea currents carry river sediments extending the delta plain westwards.*

Transport and industry

Today the main French growth industries are hi-tech, including micro-electronics, telecommunications and aerospace. Other important sectors are the nuclear industry, only rivalled in scale by that of the USA, car manufacture, dominated by the giants Renault and Peugeot and a highly diversified tourist industry.

Major industry and infrastructure

- aerospace industry
- car manufacture
- chemicals
- engineering
- hi-tech industry
- nuclear power
- tourism
- capital cities
- major towns
- international airports
- major roads
- major industrial areas

The transport network

555,473 miles (894,050 km)	7305 miles (11,758 km)
10,399 miles (16,737 km)	1159 miles (1863 km)

The French TGV (Train à Grande Vitesse) leads the world in high-speed train technology, and provides a service which can be faster, door-to-door, than air travel.

64

104

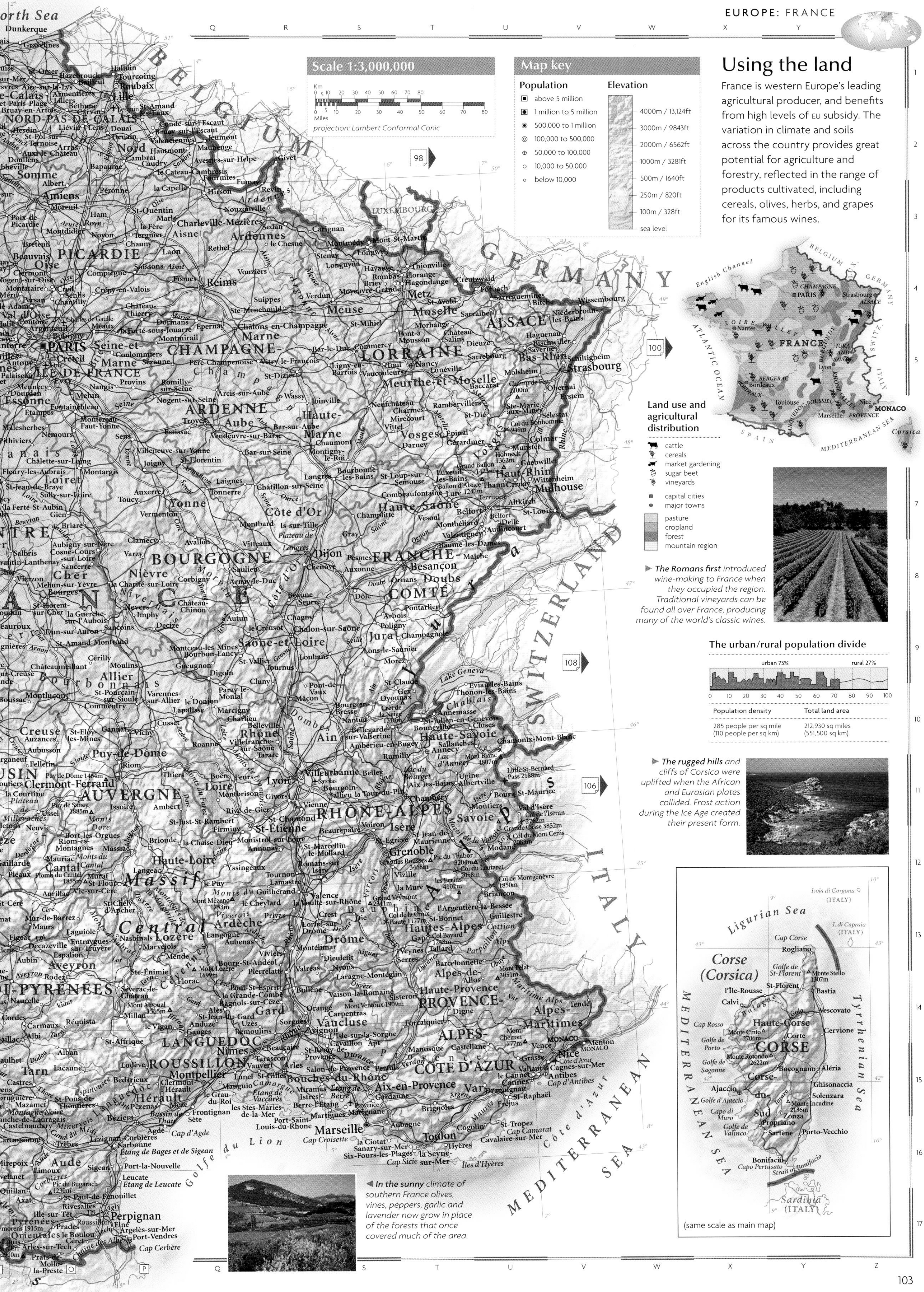
Scale 1:3,000,000
Km
Miles
projection: Lambert Conformal Conic
Map key
Population
above 5 million
1 million to 5 million
500,000 to 1 million
100,000 to 500,000
50,000 to 100,000
10,000 to 50,000
below 10,000
Elevation
4000m / 13,124ft
3000m / 9843ft
2000m / 6562ft
1000m / 3281ft
500m / 1640ft
250m / 820ft
100m / 328ft
sea level
Land use and agricultural distribution
cattle
cereals
market gardening
sugar beet
vineyards
capital cities
major towns
pasture
cropland
forest
mountain region
The urban/rural population divide
urban 73%
rural 27%
Population density
285 people per sq mile (110 people per sq km)
Total land area
212,930 sq miles (551,500 sq km)
North Sea
BELGIUM
LUXEMBOURG
GERMANY
SWITZERLAND
ITALY
MONACO
MEDITERRANEAN SEA
Golfe du Lion
Corse (Corsica)
Ligurian Sea
Tyrrhenian Sea
Sardinia (ITALY)
PARIS
Strasbourg
Lyon
Marseille
Nice
Toulouse
Bordeaux
Nantes
ATLANTIC OCEAN
English Channel
SPAIN
(same scale as main map)
98
100
106
108

Using the land

France is western Europe's leading agricultural producer, and benefits from high levels of EU subsidy. The variation in climate and soils across the country provides great potential for agriculture and forestry, reflected in the range of products cultivated, including cereals, olives, herbs, and grapes for its famous wines.

▶ *The Romans first introduced wine-making to France when they occupied the region. Traditional vineyards can be found all over France, producing many of the world's classic wines.*

▶ *The rugged hills and cliffs of Corsica were uplifted when the African and Eurasian plates collided. Frost action during the Ice Age created their present form.*

◀ *In the sunny climate of southern France olives, peppers, garlic and lavender now grow in place of the forests that once covered much of the area.*

The Iberian peninsula

ANDORRA, GIBRALTAR, PORTUGAL, SPAIN (Azores, Canary Islands, Madeira on p.64)

The Iberian peninsula is separated from the rest of Europe by the Pyrenees, and at its most southerly point is only 5 miles (8 km) from North Africa. The location of Iberia has been central to its diverse history. The Greeks, Carthaginians, Romans, Visigoths and most recently the Moors, invaded Iberia at various times. For much of the 20th century, both Spain and Portugal were governed by right-wing dictators. Since the establishment of democratic governments in the mid-1970s, modernization has been rapid and both countries are now among the most popular of European holiday destinations.

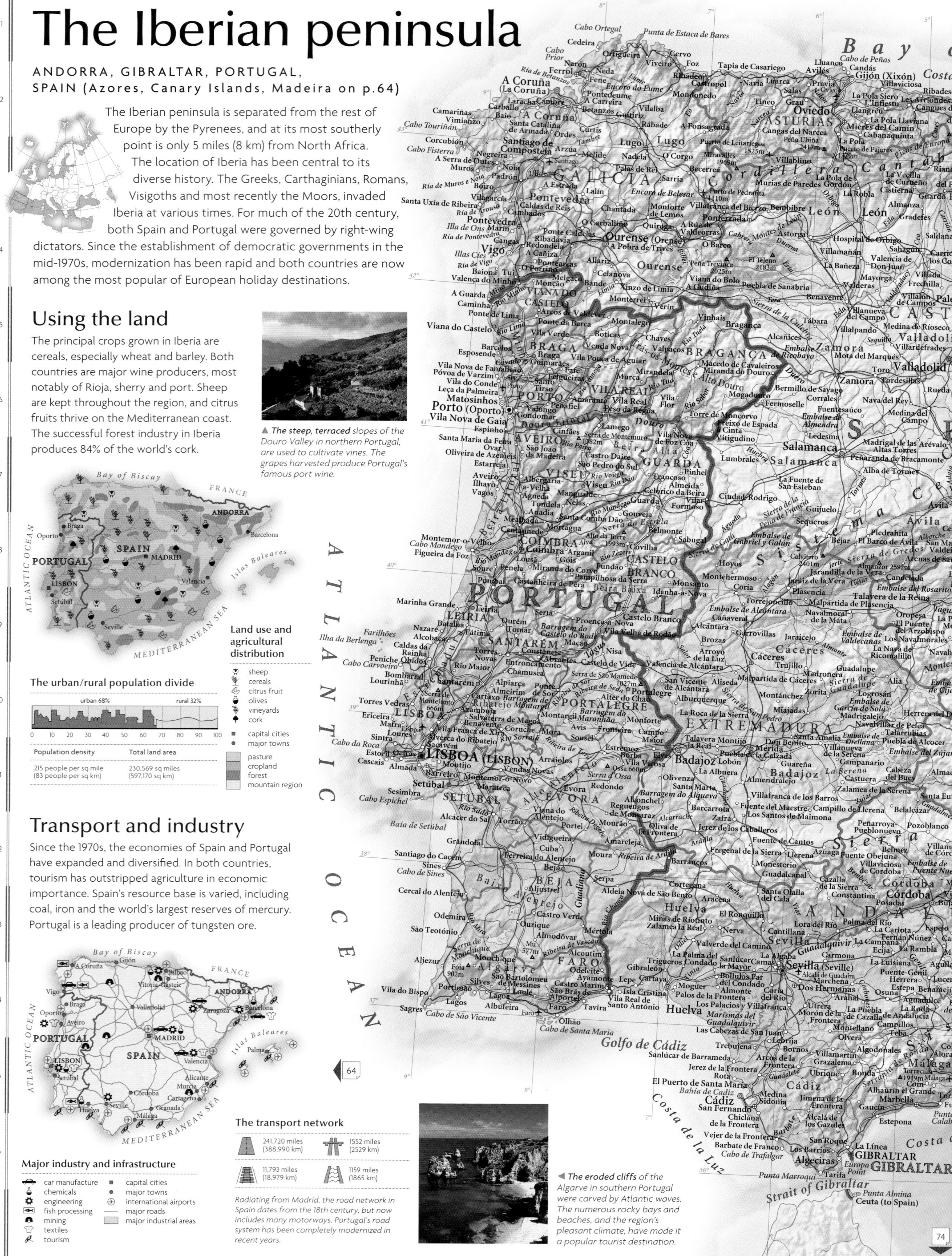

Using the land

The principal crops grown in Iberia are cereals, especially wheat and barley. Both countries are major wine producers, most notably of Rioja, sherry and port. Sheep are kept throughout the region, and citrus fruits thrive on the Mediterranean coast. The successful forest industry in Iberia produces 84% of the world's cork.

▲ ***The steep, terraced** slopes of the Douro Valley in northern Portugal, are used to cultivate vines. The grapes harvested produce Portugal's famous port wine.*

Land use and agricultural distribution

- sheep
- cereals
- citrus fruit
- olives
- vineyards
- cork
- capital cities
- major towns
- pasture
- cropland
- forest
- mountain region

The urban/rural population divide

urban 68% — rural 32%

Population density	Total land area
215 people per sq mile (83 people per sq km)	230,569 sq miles (597,170 sq km)

Transport and industry

Since the 1970s, the economies of Spain and Portugal have expanded and diversified. In both countries, tourism has outstripped agriculture in economic importance. Spain's resource base is varied, including coal, iron and the world's largest reserves of mercury. Portugal is a leading producer of tungsten ore.

Major industry and infrastructure

- car manufacture
- chemicals
- engineering
- fish processing
- mining
- textiles
- tourism
- capital cities
- major towns
- international airports
- major roads
- major industrial areas

The transport network

241,720 miles (388,990 km)	1552 miles (2529 km)
11,793 miles (18,979 km)	1159 miles (1865 km)

Radiating from Madrid, the road network in Spain dates from the 18th century, but now includes many motorways. Portugal's road system has been completely modernized in recent years.

◀ ***The eroded cliffs** of the Algarve in southern Portugal were carved by Atlantic waves. The numerous rocky bays and beaches, and the region's pleasant climate, have made it a popular tourist destination.*

64

74

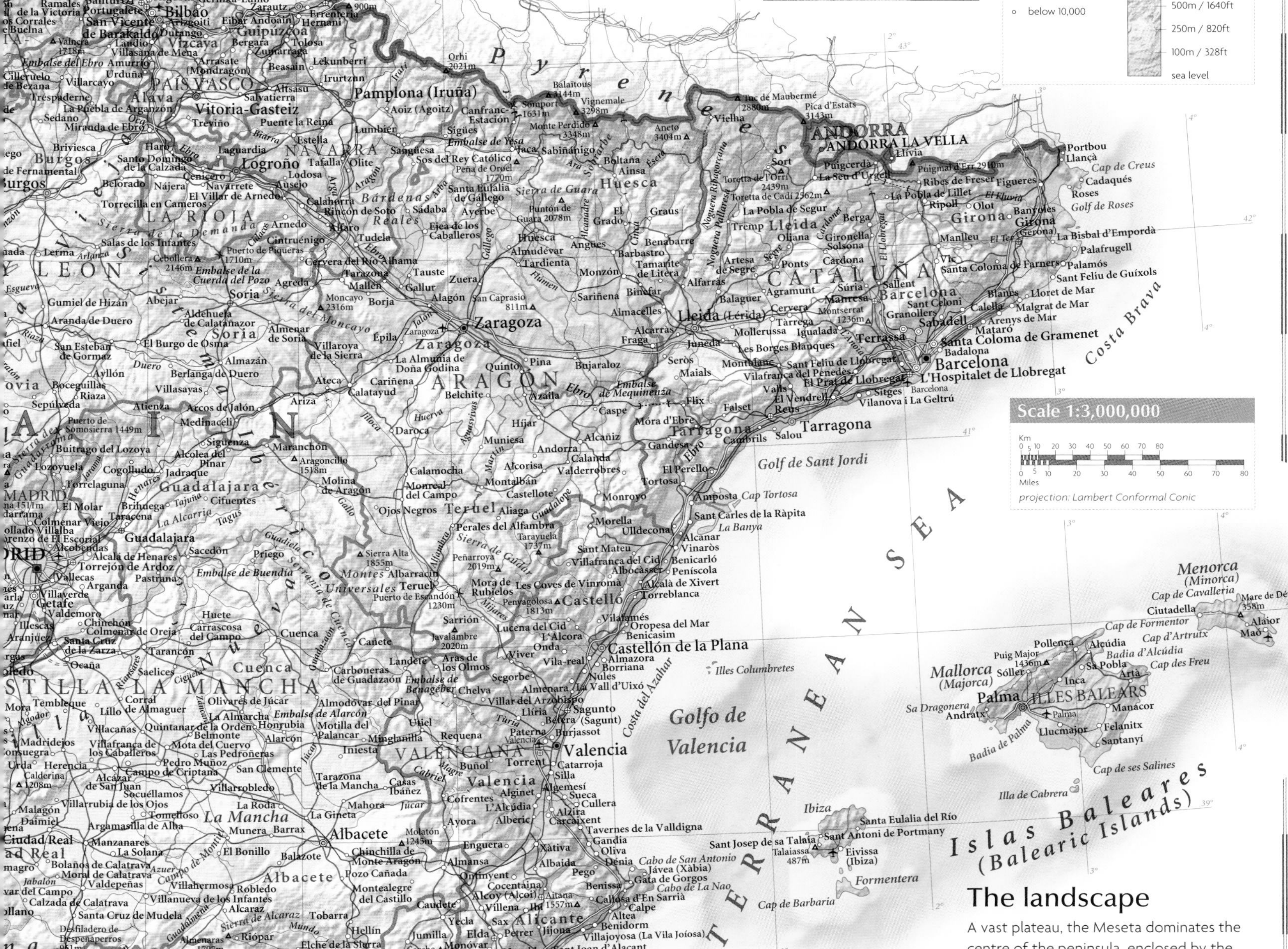

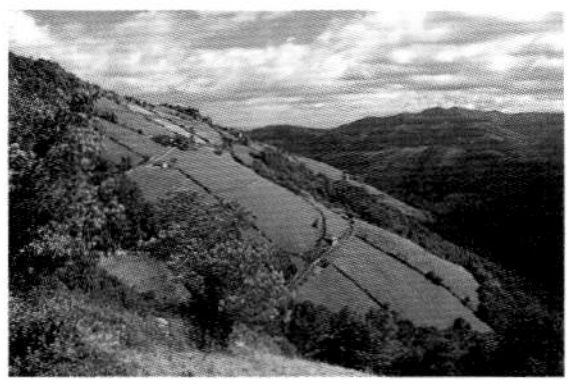

▶ *The climate in northwestern Spain is milder in both summer and winter than in the rest of the country, creating a verdant environment, more commonly associated with northwestern Europe.*

Map key

Population

- 1 million to 5 million
- 500,000 to 1 million
- 100,000 to 500,000
- 50,000 to 100,000
- 10,000 to 50,000
- below 10,000

Elevation

- 3000m / 9843ft
- 2000m / 6562ft
- 1000m / 3281ft
- 500m / 1640ft
- 250m / 820ft
- 100m / 328ft
- sea level

Scale 1:3,000,000

projection: Lambert Conformal Conic

The landscape

A vast plateau, the Meseta dominates the centre of the peninsula, enclosed by the Cordillera Cantábrica to the north and the Sierra Morena to the south. It is drained by three major rivers, the Douro/Duero, the Tagus, and the Guadalquivir. The peninsula experiences great variations in climate and rainfall, both regionally and locally.

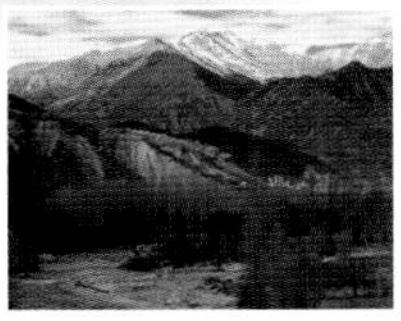

▲ *The Pyrenees form Iberia's northeastern boundary, running for 270 miles (440 km), dividing the peninsula from the rest of Europe.*

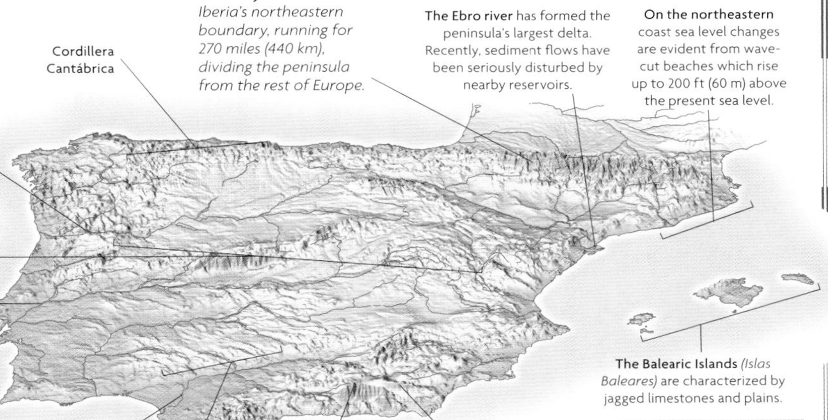

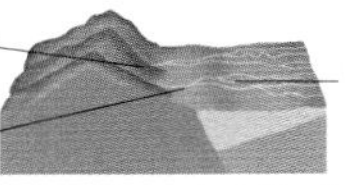

The Ebro river has formed the peninsula's largest delta. Recently, sediment flows have been seriously disturbed by nearby reservoirs.

On the northeastern coast sea level changes are evident from wave-cut beaches which rise up to 200 ft (60 m) above the present sea level.

Cordillera Cantábrica

Douro/Duero river

The Meseta plateau averages 1970 ft (600 m) in height and is now largely dry and treeless.

Tagus River

The Balearic Islands *(Islas Baleares)* are characterized by jagged limestones and plains.

Mountain front

Weathered material

Pediment

▲ *Pediments are characteristic of semi-arid lands across Iberia. A pediment is a flat, low-lying, eroded platform, cut into the bedrock. Weathered material is transported by streams and deposited in broad fan shapes on the pediment.*

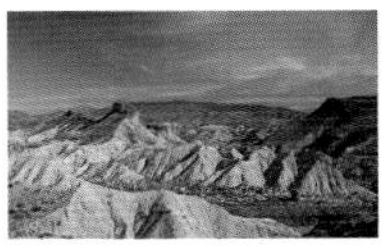

The Guadalquivir river brings vital irrigation water to the plains, and like many of Iberia's rivers, is prone to flooding.

Sierra Morena

The Sierra Nevada in southern Spain contain Iberia's highest peak, Mulhacén, which rises 11,418 ft (3481 m).

▶ *In the Sierra de los Filabres deforestation and overgrazing, which cause soil erosion, have created semi-desert badlands.*

The Italian peninsula

ITALY, SAN MARINO, VATICAN CITY

The Italian peninsula is a land of great contrasts. Until unification in 1861, Italy was a collection of independent states, whose competitiveness during the Renaissance resulted in the architectural and artistic magnificence of cities such as Rome, Florence and Venice. The majority of Italy's population and economic activity is concentrated in the north, centred on the sophisticated industrial city of Milan. Southern Italy, the *Mezzogiorno*, has a harsh and difficult terrain, and remains far less developed than the north. Attempts to attract industry and investment in the south are frequently deterred by the entrenched network of organized crime and corruption.

The landscape

The mainly mountainous and hilly Italian peninsula took its present form following a collision between the African and Eurasian tectonic plates. The Alps in the northwest rise to a high point of 15,772 ft (4807 m) at Mont Blanc *(Monte Bianco)* on the French border, while the Apennines *(Appennino)* form a rugged backbone, running along the entire length of the country.

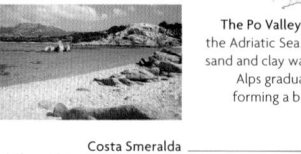

▶ ***The island of** Sardinia is an ancient land mass; an uplifted section of very old igneous rocks. Its rugged mountainous regions provide pasture for sheep and goats, while its valleys support some agriculture.*

Mont Blanc *(Monte Bianco)*

▲ ***The Dolomites** (Alpi Dolomitiche) are formed of thick limestones, overlying weaker marine strata. They have distinctive serrated peaks and many massive landslides occur.*

The Po Valley once formed part of the Adriatic Sea. Sediments of gravel, sand and clay washed down from the Alps gradually filling the bay and forming a broad, cultivable plain.

The distinctive square shape of the Gulf of Taranto *(Golfo di Taranto)* was defined by numerous block faults. Earthquakes are common in this region.

Costa Smeralda

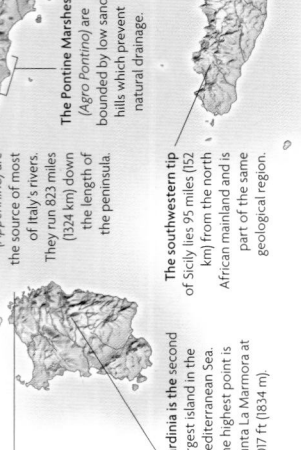

The Apennines *(Appennino)* are the source of most of Italy's rivers. They run 823 miles (1324 km) down the length of the peninsula.

The Pontine Marshes *(Agro Pontino)* are bounded by low sand hills which prevent natural drainage.

Vesuvius *(Vesuvio)*

Sardinia is the second largest island in the Mediterranean Sea. The highest point is Punta La Marmora at 6017 ft (1834 m).

The southwestern tip of Sicily lies 95 miles (152 km) from the north African mainland and is part of the same geological region.

The Strait of Messina *(Stretto di Messina)* is between 2 and 12 miles (3–19 km) wide, and is a rich fishing ground.

Sicily is the largest island in the Mediterranean at 9926 sq miles (25,708 sq km).

Vesuvius *(Vesuvio)*

Monte Somma

Old crater

Present-day crater has developed within the old crater of Monte Somma

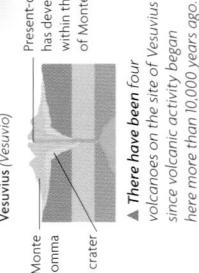

▲ ***There have been** four volcanoes on the site of Vesuvius since volcanic activity began here more than 10,000 years ago.*

Using the land

Italy produces 95% of its own food. The best farming land is in the Po Valley in northern Italy, where soft wheat and rice are grown. Irrigation is essential to agriculture in much of the south. Italy is a major producer and exporter of citrus fruits, olives, tomatoes and wine.

The urban/rural population divide

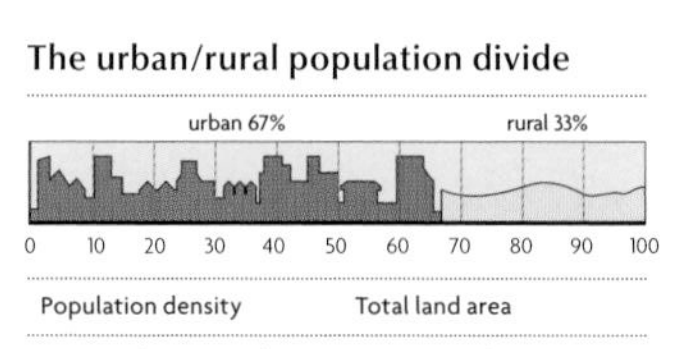
urban 67%
rural 33%
0 10 20 30 40 50 60 70 80 90 100

Population density	Total land area
506 people per sq mile (195 people per sq km)	116,320 sq miles (301,270 sq km)

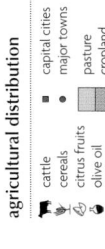

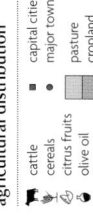

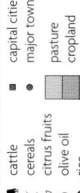

Land use and agricultural distribution

cattle
cereals
citrus fruits
olive oil
rice
capital cities
major towns
pasture
cropland
forest

Scale 1:2,750,000

projection: Lambert Conformal Conic

108
108
108
112
120
102

Corse (Corsica)
Sardegna (Sardinia)
SARDEGNA
Strait of Bonifacio
LAZIO
ABRUZZO
MOLISE
CAMPANIA
PUGLIA
BASILICATA
CALABRIA
SICILIA
Sicilia (Sicily)
VATICAN CITY
ROMA (ROME)
Napoli (Naples)
Bari
Taranto
Palermo
Catania
Cagliari
Isole Eolie
Tyrrhenian Sea
Ionian Sea
Strait of Otranto
Golfo di Taranto
Strait of Sicily
Malta Channel
MEDITERRANEAN SEA

◀ **Tuscany (Toscana) has** long produced grapes and olives. Sandstones form its higher reaches, while clays and alluvial soils fill its fertile valleys.

▲ **Vatican City in** Rome is the smallest independent state in the world. As the seat of the Catholic Church it is home to the Pope, spiritual head of 18% of the world's population.

▶ **Capri** (Isola di Capri), unlike other islands in the Gulf of Naples (Golfo di Napoli), is not of volcanic origin, but is part of the limestone chain of the Apennines (Appennino).

◀ **Winter flooding of** St Mark's Square, Venice, means tourists and residents have to cross it on planks. Action is needed to prevent Venice from sinking into the lagoon which surrounds it.

▲ **Italy is the** largest wine producer in the world. Vineyards, such as this one in the Chianti region of central Italy, are found all over the mainland, and on the islands of Sicily and Sardinia.

▲ **The Promontory of** Gargano (Promontorio del Gargano) is a limestone plateau that juts out into the Adriatic Sea. Wave erosion has resulted in a jagged coastline characterized by headlands and bays.

Map key

Population

- 1 million to 5 million
- 500,000 to 1 million
- 100,000 to 500,000
- 50,000 to 100,000
- 10,000 to 50,000
- below 10,000

Elevation

- 4000m / 13,124ft
- 3000m / 9843ft
- 2000m / 6562ft
- 1000m / 3281ft
- 500m / 1640ft
- 250m / 820ft
- 100m / 328ft
- sea level

Transport and industry

Although Italy has a large public sector, numerous relatively small enterprises dominate the private sector. Manufacturing is located mainly in the north and focuses on high-quality product design and engineering, using imported raw materials. Tourism is important throughout the country.

The transport network

- 298,167 miles (479,908 km)
- 4014 miles (6460 km)
- 10,133 miles (16,310 km)
- 1491 miles (2400 km)

Historically of great importance, sea ports now handle only 16% of Italy's exports. Congestion is a major problem on the roads, many town centres having developed around medieval street plans.

Major industry and infrastructure

- aerospace
- car manufacture
- finance
- hi-tech industry
- iron & steel
- textiles
- tourism
- capital cities
- major towns
- international airports
- major roads
- major industrial areas

The Alpine states

AUSTRIA, LIECHTENSTEIN, SLOVENIA, SWITZERLAND

The Alpine countries of Austria, Switzerland, Liechtenstein and Slovenia form a narrow strip across western Europe's geographical core, lying on the main north–south trading routes across the Alps. Switzerland, politically neutral since 1815, is an important international meeting place and houses one of the headquarters of the United Nations, although it only became a member in 2002. Austria, once at the heart of the great Habsburg Empire has been a fully independent nation since 1955, and maintains a deserved reputation as an international centre of culture. Slovenia declared independence from the former Yugoslavia in 1991 and despite initial economic hardship, is now starting to achieve the prosperity enjoyed by its Alpine neighbours.

Using the land

The Alpine region's mountainous terrain discourages cultivation over much of the land area. The primary agricultural activity is the raising of dairy and beef cattle on the pasture land of the lower mountain slopes. Austria is self-supporting in grains, and crops such as wheat, barley and grapes are grown on the east Austrian lowlands. Woodlands are more prevalent in the eastern Alps; both Austria and Slovenia have large tracts of forest.

Land use and agricultural distribution

cattle
pigs
cereals
vineyards
capital cities
major towns
pasture
cropland
forest
mountain region

The Matterhorn, on the Swiss-Italian border, is one of the highest mountains in the Alps, at 14,692 ft (4478 m). The term 'horn' refers to its distinctive peak, formed by three glaciers eroding hollows, known as cirques, in each of its sides.

100
102
106
102

The landscape

The Alps occupy three-fifths of Switzerland, most of southern Austria and the northwest of Slovenia. They were formed by the collision of the African and Eurasian tectonic plates, which began 65 million years ago. Their complex geology is reflected in the differing heights and rock types of the various ranges. The Rhine flows along Liechtenstein's border with Switzerland, creating a broad flood plain in the north and west of Liechtenstein. In the far northeast and east are a number of lowland regions, including the Vienna Basin, Burgenland and the plain of the Danube. Slovenia's major rivers flow across the lower eastern regions; in the west, the rivers flow largely underground through the limestone Karst region.

Original height after uplift and folding
Folded strata are overturned creating a *nappe*
Eurasian Plate
Present-day height of Alps
African Plate

The convergence of the African and Eurasian plates compressed and folded huge masses of rock strata. As the plates continued to move together, the folded strata were overturned, creating complex nappes. Much of the rock strata has since been eroded, resulting in the current topography of the Alps.

Constricted as it cuts through ridges in the Alps, the Danube meanders across the lowlands, where uplift combined with river erosion has deepened meanders.

The Vienna Basin lies mainly below 390 ft (120 m). It gradually subsided and filled with sediment as the Alps were uplifted.

Neusiedler See straddles the border of Austria and Hungary; the area around it provides some of the best wine-growing land in Austria.

The mountains of the Jura form a natural border between Switzerland and France. Their marine limestones date from over 200 million years ago. When the Alps were formed the Jura were folded into a series of parallel ridges and troughs.

The Austrian Alps comprise three distinct mountain ranges, separated by deep trenches. The northern and southern ranges are rugged limestones, while the Tauern range is formed of crystalline rocks.

The first road through the Brenner Pass was built in 1772, although it has been used as a mountain route since Roman times. It is the lowest of the main Alpine passes at 4298 ft (1374 m).

Tectonic activity has resulted in dramatic changes in land height over very short distances. Lake Geneva, lying at 1221 ft (372 m) is only 43 miles (70 km) away from the 15,772 ft (4807 m) peak of Mont Blanc, on the France–Italy border.

The Bernese Alps (*Berner Alpen*) contain the Aletsch, which at 15 miles (24 km) is the longest Alpine glacier.

The Rhine, like other major Alpine rivers, follows a broad, flat trough between the mountains. Along part of its course, the Rhine forms the boundary between Switzerland and Liechtenstein.

Karst region

The deep, blue lakes of the Karst region are part of a drainage network which runs largely underground through this limestone area.

The limestone cave system at Postojna extends for more than 10 miles (16 km) and includes caverns reaching 125 ft (40 m) in height and width.

The Tauern range in the central Austrian Alps contains the highest mountain in Austria, the towering Grossglockner, rising 12,461 ft (3798 m).

CZECH REPUBLIC
SLOVAKIA
HUNGARY
AUSTRIA
SLOVENIA
CROATIA
ITALY
GERMANY
WIEN (VIENNA)
LJUBLJANA
Scale 1:2,000,000
projection: Lambert Conformal Conic

The urban/rural population divide

urban 66% rural 34%

Population density	Total land area
314 people per sq mile (121 people per sq km)	56,135 sq miles (145,390 sq km)

◀ In this mountainous region, the flatter, more accessible areas are often used for both cattle grazing and recreation.

◀ These converging glaciers are marked by dark lines of moraine. This eroded material is carried by glaciers, and deposited as the ice melts.

▶ The Austrian Tirol contains some of the most spectacular Alpine scenery. Snow cover is a permanent feature in the highest reaches.

Map key

Population

- 1 million to 5 million
- 500,000 to 1 million
- 100,000 to 500,000
- 50,000 to 100,000
- 10,000 to 50,000
- below 10,000

Elevation

- 4000m / 13,124ft
- 3000m / 9843ft
- 2000m / 6562ft
- 1000m / 3281ft
- 500m / 1640ft
- 250m / 820ft
- 100m / 328ft
- sea level

Transport and industry

All four nations concentrate on high-quality manufacturing and services. Austrian iron and steel production is complemented by construction industries; and Slovenia, traditionally the industrial powerhouse of the western Balkans has increasingly diversified industries. Liechtenstein and Switzerland, lacking raw materials, produce pharmaceuticals and precision instruments, such as watches, and act as international banking centres. The spectacular scenery of the region encourages tourism all year round.

The transport network

181,107 miles (291,497 km)	2116 miles (3405 km)
6368 miles (10,249 km)	993 miles (1598 km)

Tunnels and passes through the Alps are an important feature of this region. The NEAT project, providing two new high-speed rail links between Basel and Milan, was given approval in 1992.

Major industry and infrastructure

- car manufacture
- chemicals
- engineering
- finance
- food processing
- iron & steel
- pharmaceuticals
- textiles
- tourism
- watch making
- winter sports
- capital cities
- major towns
- international airports
- major roads
- major industrial areas

▲ The Schönbrunn Palace in Vienna was the summer residence of the Habsburg monarchy. Today, it is a major tourist attraction.

Central Europe

CZECH REPUBLIC, HUNGARY, POLAND, SLOVAKIA

When Slovakia and the Czech Republic became separate countries in 1993, they joined Hungary and Poland in a new role as independent nation states, following centuries of shifting boundaries and imperial strife. This turbulent history bequeathed the region a rich cultural heritage, shared through the works of its many great writers and composers, and celebrated in the vibrant historic capitals of Prague, Budapest and Warsaw. Having shaken off years of Soviet domination in 1989, these states are confronting the challenge of winning commercial investment to modernize outmoded industries as they integrate their economies with those of the European Union.

The landscape

The forested Carpathian Mountains, uplifted with the Alps, lie southeast of the older Bohemian Massif, which contains the Sudeten and Krusné Hory *(Erzgebirge)* ranges. They divide the fertile plains of the Danube to the south and the Vistula *(Wisla)*, which flows north across vast expanses of glacial deposits into the Baltic Sea.

Hot mineral springs occur where geothermally heated water wells up through faults and fractures in the rocks of the Sudeten Mountains.

Pomerania is a sandy coastal region of glacially-formed lakes stretching west from the Vistula *(Wisla)*.

Longshore currents moving east along the Baltic coast have built a 40 mile (65 km) spit composed of material from the Vistula *(Wisla)* river.

▲ ***The Biebrza river*** *has left meanders and oxbow lakes as it flows across low-lying ground.*

Gerlachovsky stít, in the Tatra Mountains, is Slovakia's highest mountain, at 8711ft (2655 m).

Krusné Hory *(Erzgebirge)*

Bohemian Massif

Carpathian Mountains

Danube river

◀ ***The Berounka river*** *cuts through the precipitous wooded landscape of the Bohemian Massif, banked by a broad flood plain.*

The Slovak Ore Mountains *(Slovenské Rudohorie)* are noted for their mineral resources, including high-grade iron ore.

The Great Hungarian Plain formed by the flood plain of the Danube is a mixture of steppe and cultivated land, covering nearly half of Hungary's total area.

Bluff

Direction of flow

Slip-off slope

▲ ***Meanders form as*** *rivers flow across plains at a low gradient. A steep cliff or bluff, forms on the outside curve, and a gentler slip-off slope on the inside bend.*

Transport and industry

Heavy industry has dominated post-war life in Central Europe. Poland has large coal reserves, having inherited the Silesian coalfield from Germany after the Second World War, allowing the export of large quantities of coal, along with other minerals. Hungary specializes in consumer goods and services, while Slovakia's industrial base is still relatively small. The Czech Republic's traditional glassworks and breweries bring some stability to its precarious Soviet-built manufacturing sector.

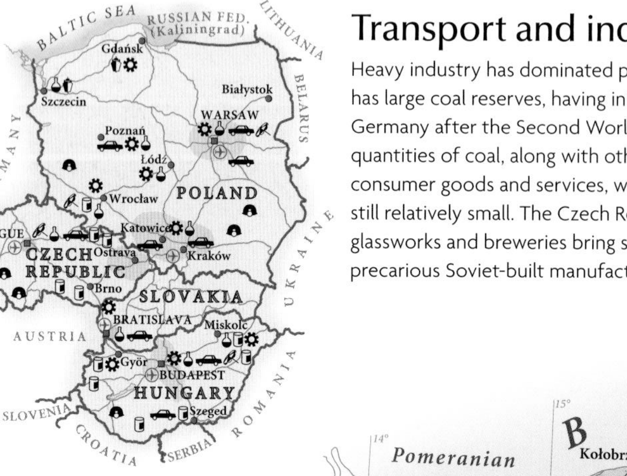
BALTIC SEA
RUSSIAN FED. (Kaliningrad)
LITHUANIA
BELARUS
UKRAINE
ROMANIA
SERBIA
CROATIA
SLOVENIA
AUSTRIA
GERMANY
Gdańsk
Szczecin
Białystok
WARSAW
Poznań
Łódź
POLAND
Wrocław
PRAGUE
CZECH REPUBLIC
Ostrava
Katowice
Kraków
Brno
SLOVAKIA
BRATISLAVA
Miskolc
Győr
BUDAPEST
HUNGARY
Szeged

Major industry and infrastructure

- car manufacture
- chemicals
- engineering
- food processing
- mining
- shipbuilding
- tourism
- capital cities
- major towns
- international airports
- major roads
- major industrial areas

The transport network

213,997 miles (344,600 km)

817 miles (1315 km)

27,479 miles (44,249 km)

3784 miles (6094 km)

The huge growth of tourism and business has prompted major investment in the transport infrastructure, with new road-building schemes within and between the main cities of the region.

▲ ***Budapest, the capital*** *of Hungary, straddles the Danube. It comprises the historic towns of Buda, on the west bank, and Pest, which contains the Parliament Building, seen here on the far bank.*

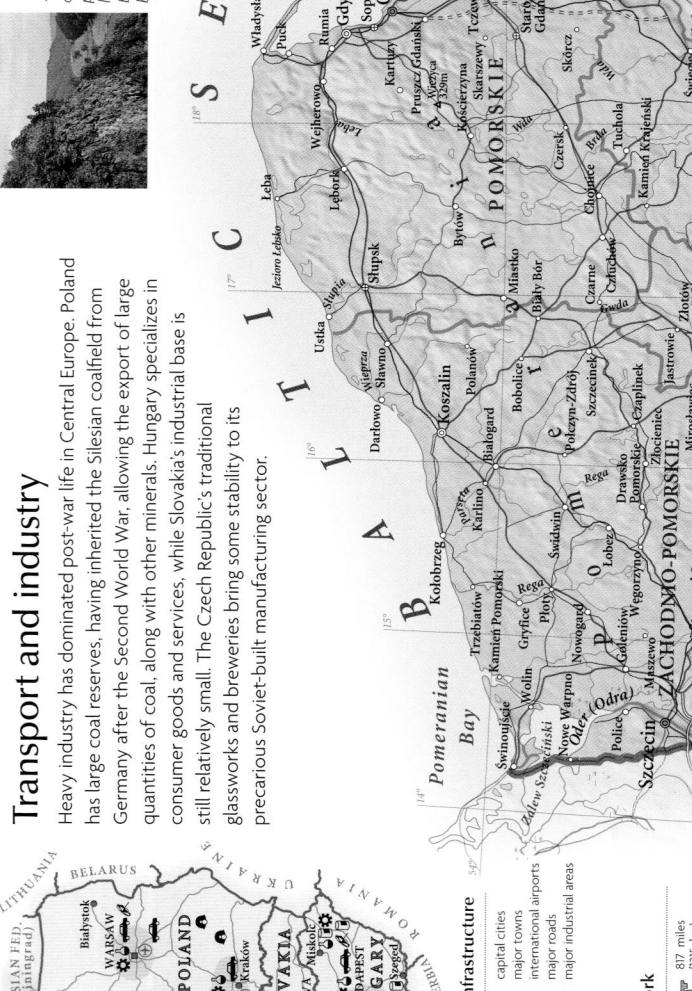

118

118

Map key
Population
1 million to 5 million
500,000 to 1 million
100,000 to 500,000
50,000 to 100,000
10,000 to 50,000
below 10,000
Elevation
2000m / 6562ft
1000m / 3281ft
500m / 1640ft
250m / 820ft
100m / 328ft
sea level
Scale 1:2,750,000
projection: Lambert Conformal Conic
Land use and agricultural distribution
cattle
pigs
cereals
potatoes
root crops
timber
vineyards
capital cities
major towns
pasture
cropland
forest
The urban/rural population divide
urban 65%
rural 35%
Population density
312 people per sq mile (120 people per sq km)
Total land area
201,561 sq miles (522,180 sq km)
CZECH REPUBLIC
SLOVAKIA
HUNGARY
POLAND
AUSTRIA
GERMANY
UKRAINE
ROMANIA
SERBIA
CROATIA
SLOVENIA
PRAHA (PRAGUE)
BRATISLAVA
BUDAPEST

Using the land

Cereals, sugar beet and potatoes are Central Europe's main crops, along with hops for the Czech breweries, sweet peppers for paprika, sunflowers and vines in milder areas. The plains of Poland and Hungary are well-suited to livestock-rearing, while forestry is important in the mountains of Slovakia.

▲ *Hay, used to feed livestock, is one of the major crops grown on the fertile foothills of Slovakia's Tatra Mountains.*

▶ *The upper Dunajec river of Poland and eastern Slovakia forms a gorge through the Pieniny range of the Carpathian Mountains.*

Southeast Europe

ALBANIA, BOSNIA & HERZEGOVINA, CROATIA, KOSVOVO, MACEDONIA, MONTENEGRO, SERBIA

For 46 years the federation of Yugoslavia held together the most diverse ethnic region in Europe, along the picturesque mountain hinterland of the Dalmatian coast. Economic collapse resulted in internal tensions. In the early 1990s, civil war broke out in both Croatia and Bosnia as the ethnic populations struggled to establish their own exclusive territories. Peace was only restored by the UN after NATO launched air strikes in 1995. Montenegro voted to split from Serbia in 2006. More recently, Kosovo controversially declared independence from Serbia in 2008, although this may take some time to be fully recognized. Neighbouring Albania is slowly improving its fragile economy but remains one of Europe's poorest nations.

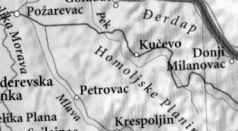

▲ **Hot, dry summers** and mild winters offer excellent conditions for viticulture in Montenegro. The precipitous Dinaric Alps have kept this region relatively isolated for centuries.

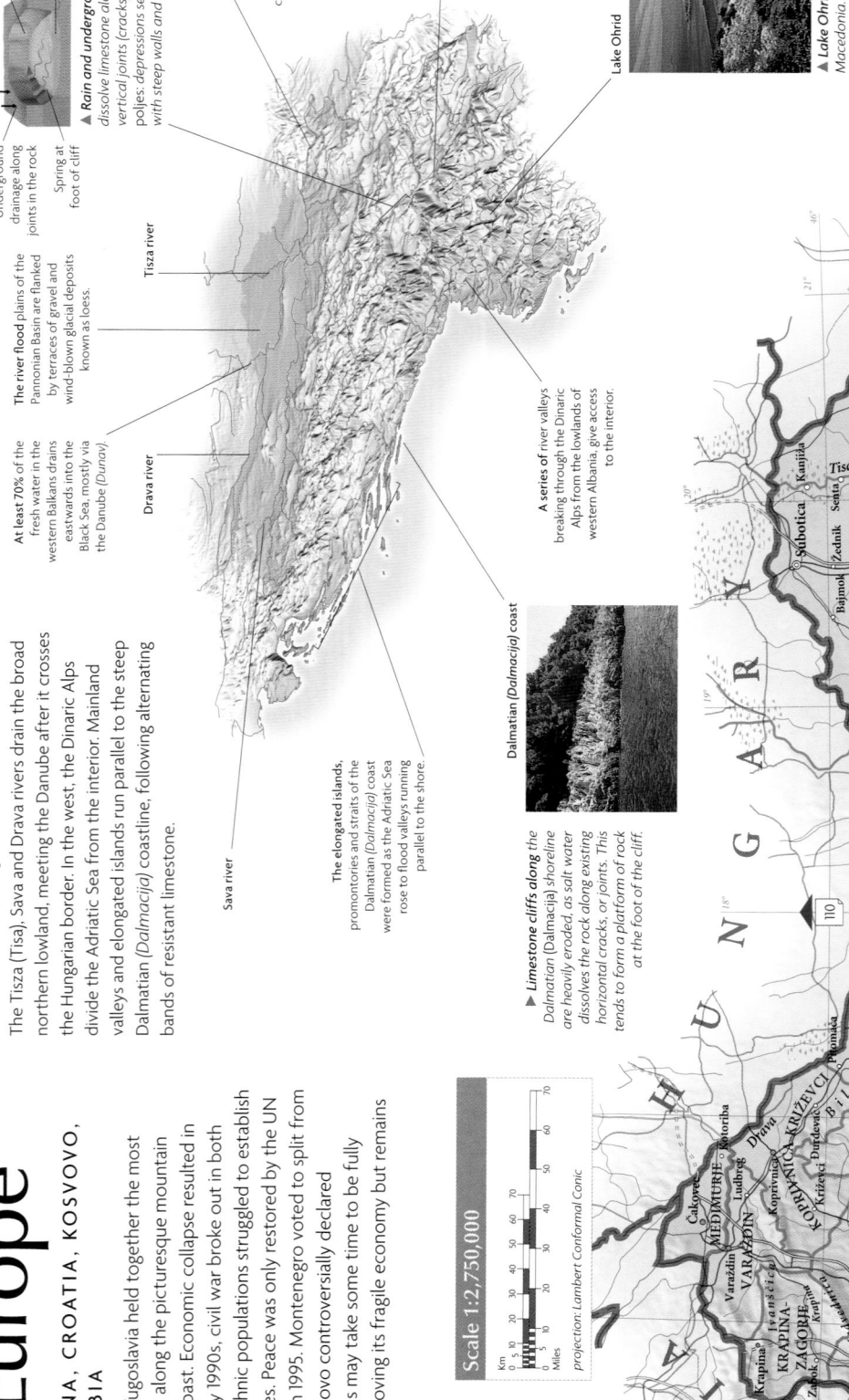

Scale 1:2,750,000

projection: Lambert Conformal Conic

The landscape

The Tisza (Tisa), Sava and Drava rivers drain the broad northern lowland, meeting the Danube after it crosses the Hungarian border. In the west, the Dinaric Alps divide the Adriatic Sea from the interior. Mainland valleys and elongated islands run parallel to the steep Dalmatian *(Dalmacija)* coastline, following alternating bands of resistant limestone.

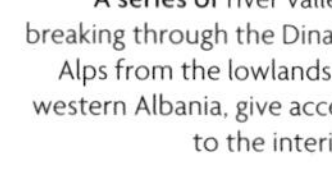
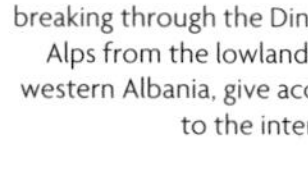
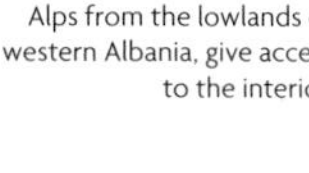
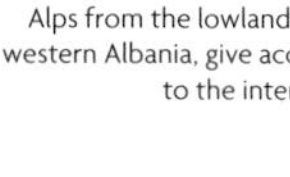
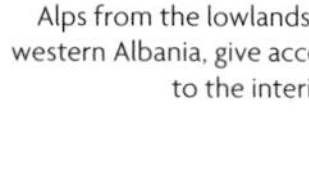
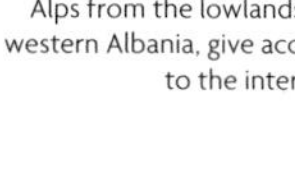
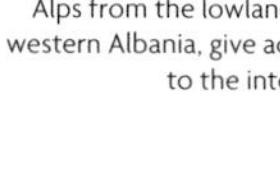
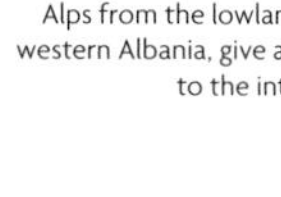
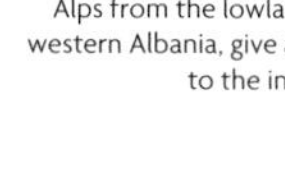
At least 70% of the fresh water in the western Balkans drains eastwards into the Black Sea, mostly via the Danube *(Dunav)*.
The river flood plains of the Pannonian Basin are flanked by terraces of gravel and wind-blown glacial deposits known as loess.
Drava river
Tisza river
Sava river
At Iron Gate *(Derdap)*, on the border with Romania, the Danube narrows and cuts through foothills of the Balkan and Carpathian mountains, forming the deepest gorge in Europe.
The elongated islands, promontories and straits of the Dalmatian *(Dalmacija)* coast were formed as the Adriatic Sea rose to flood valleys running parallel to the shore.
A major earthquake at Skopje, Macedonia, in 1963 killed 1000 people. The whole region lies on an active crustal plate margin.
Dalmatian *(Dalmacija)* coast
A series of river valleys breaking through the Dinaric Alps from the lowlands of western Albania, give access to the interior.
Lake Ohrid

▶ **Limestone cliffs along** *the Dalmatian* (Dalmacija) *shoreline are heavily eroded, as salt water dissolves the rock along existing horizontal cracks, or joints. This tends to form a platform of rock at the foot of the cliff.*

Poljes in the Kosovo region

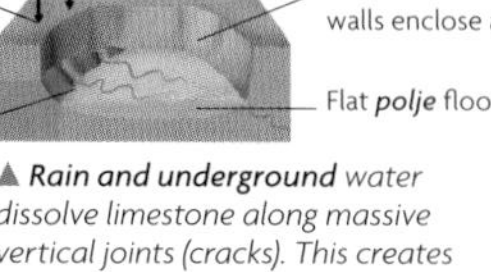
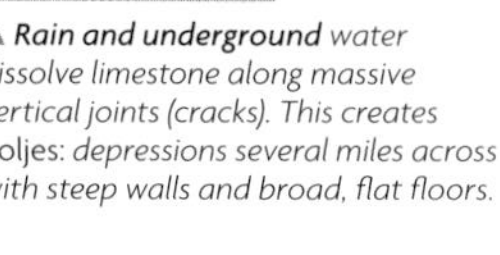
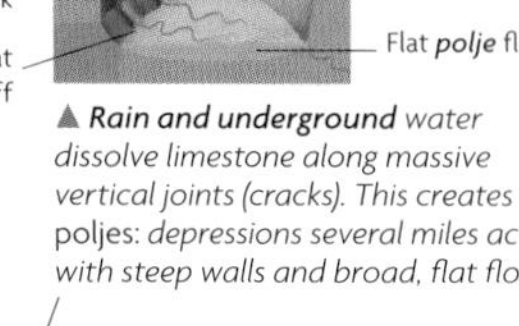
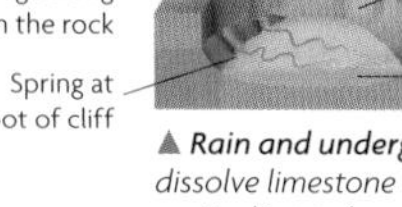
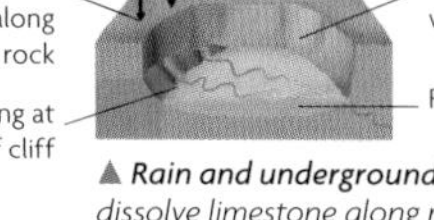
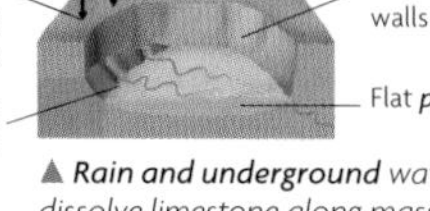
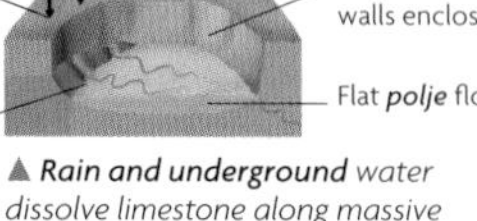
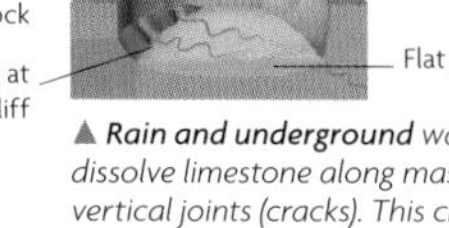
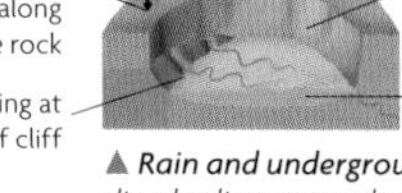

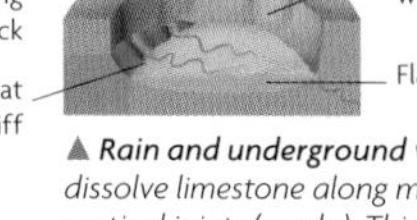

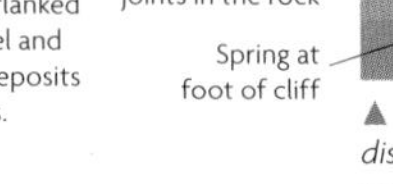

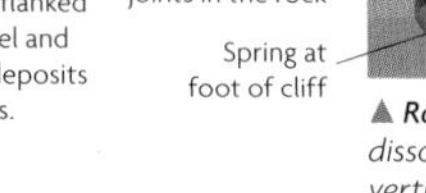
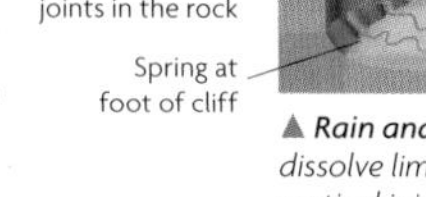

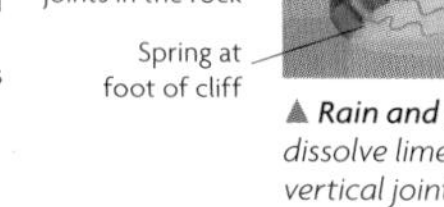
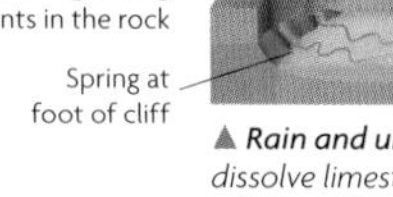

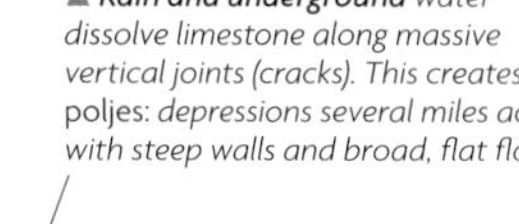
Underground drainage along joints in the rock
Sheer limestone walls enclose all sides
Spring at foot of cliff
Flat *polje* floor

▲ **Rain and underground** *water dissolve limestone along massive vertical joints (cracks). This creates* poljes: *depressions several miles across with steep walls and broad, flat floors.*

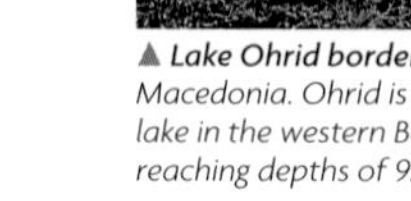
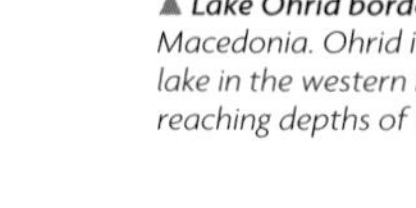
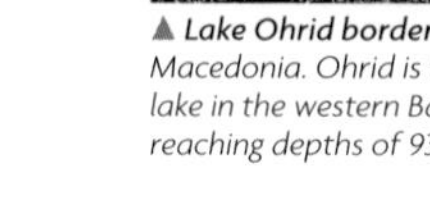
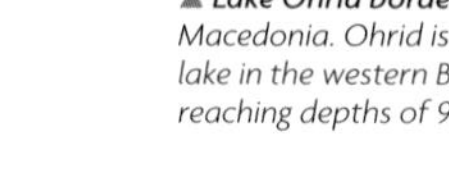
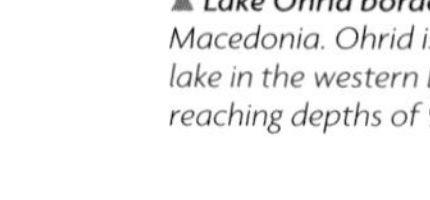
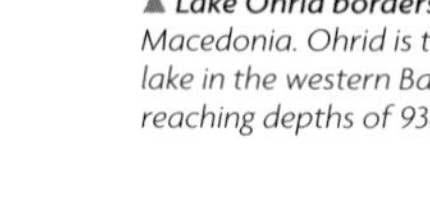
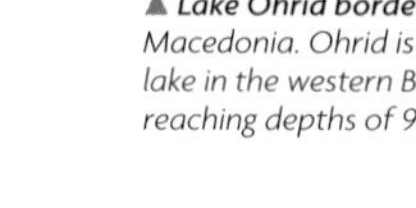
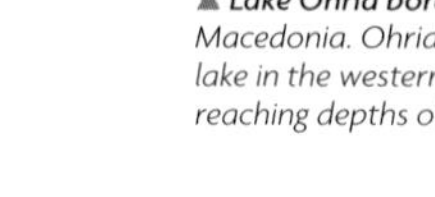
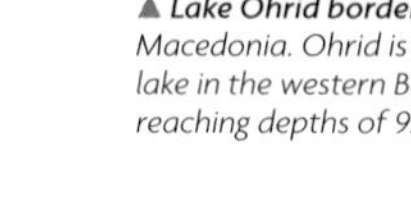
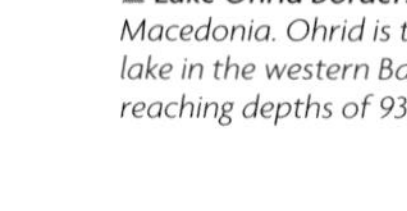
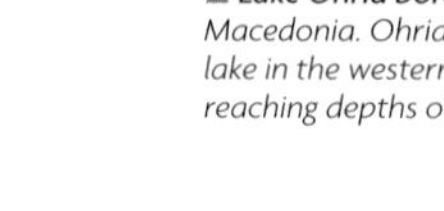
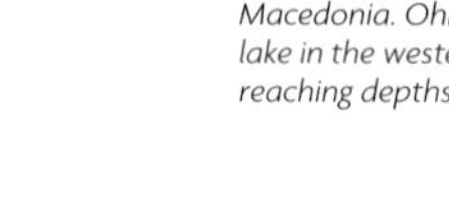
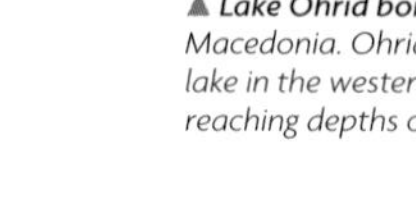
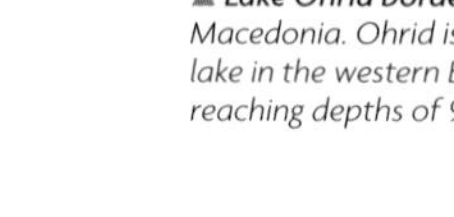
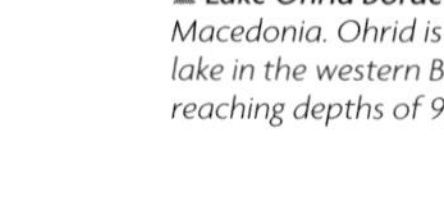
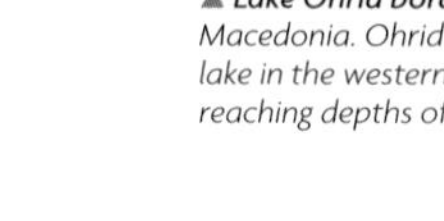
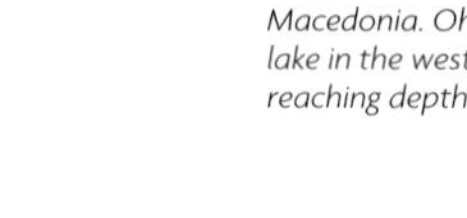
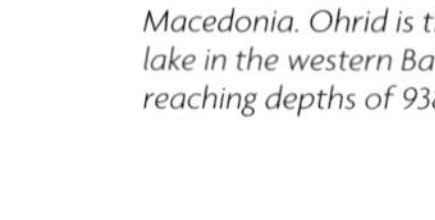
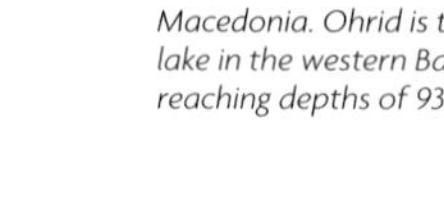
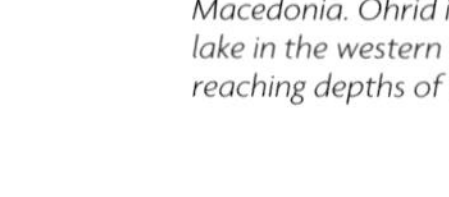
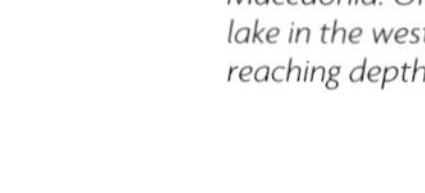

▲ **Lake Ohrid borders** *Albania and Macedonia. Ohrid is the deepest lake in the western Balkans, reaching depths of 938 ft (286 m).*

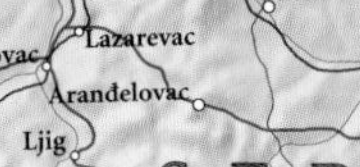

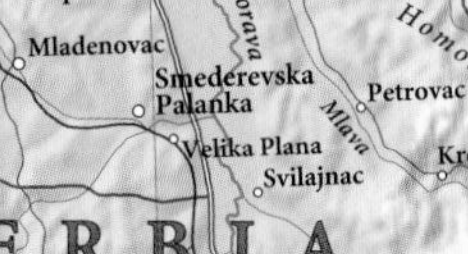

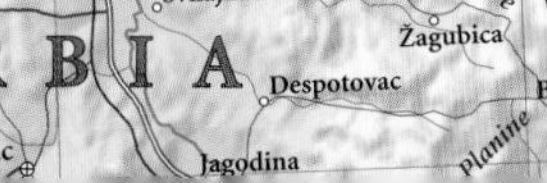

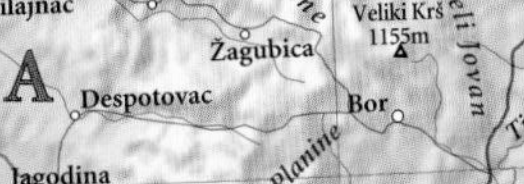

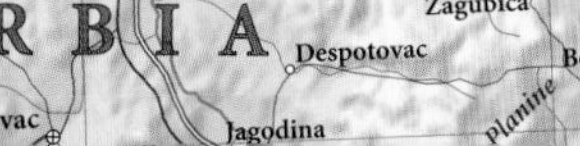

SLOVENIA
HUNGARY
ROMANIA
CROATIA
VOJVODINA
BOSNIA & HERZEGOVINA
SERBIA
ZAGREB
BEOGRAD (BELGRADE)
Gulf of Trieste

108
110
116
120
114

MONTENEGRO
KOSOVO
PRISHTINË (PRISTINA)
(Full independence not yet recognized)
MACEDONIA
SKOPJE
PODGORICA
ALBANIA
TIRANË (TIRANA)
DUBROVNIK-NERETVA
Adriatic Sea
Strait of Otranto
GREECE
BULGARIA
114

Major industry and infrastructure
aluminium refining
car manufacture
chemicals
engineering
food processing
hydro-electric power
mining
shipbuilding
textiles
timber processing
capital cities
major towns
international airports
major roads

The transport network
46,996 miles (75,642 km)
685 miles (1103 km)
5413 miles (8713 km)
879 miles (1415 km)

Land use and agricultural distribution
pigs
sheep
cereals
fruit
olives
sugar beet
timber
tobacco
vineyards
capital cities
major towns
pasture
cropland
forest
mountain region

Map key
Population
1 million to 5 million
500,000 to 1 million
100,000 to 500,000
50,000 to 100,000
10,000 to 50,000
below 10,000
Elevation
2000m / 6562ft
1000m / 3281ft
500m / 1640ft
250m / 820ft
100m / 328ft
sea level

◀ **The historic centre** of Mostar in southern Bosnia, with its famous 16th-century Turkish bridge, was destroyed by shelling during 1993. The bridge was rebuilt and opened again in 2004.

Transport and industry

Processing industries based on the region's wealth of mineral reserves predominate in Albania and Macedonia. In other regions, industrial plants have been commandeered, if not destroyed in the war and mineral extraction has severely declined. The fast-flowing rivers found throughout the Dinaric Alps are exploited to generate hydro-electric power.

In February 2008, Kosovo (a UN Protectorate within Serbia since 1999) declared independence. Although recognized by several countries, this decision has proved controversial with other states wary of setting a precedent for separatist groups within their own borders. It is therefore likely to be some time before Kosovo becomes universally recognized.

The war resulted in the destruction or disintegration of infrastructure for transport, communications and power supply, though this is now in the process of recovery.

▶ ***Industrial processing plants** were established throughout Albania by the Hoxha regime, which collapsed in 1992. They remain incongruous among the villages of one of Europe's most conservative rural societies.*

▲ ***The ancient Croatian** port of Dubrovnik was one of the former Yugoslavia's most popular tourist resorts and an important point of access to the sea along the Dalmatian (Dalmacija) coast. Shelling of the old city by Serb forces in 1991 provoked international condemnation.*

Using the land

Crops of wheat, maize, sugar beet, vegetables and fruit are widely grown. The hilly terrain is suited to forestry and livestock farming. The mild, mediterranean climate of the coastal regions provides ideal conditions for growing vines and olives. Albania's largely agricultural economy has been adversely affected by the recent dismantling of state farms.

◀ ***Sweet red peppers** are dried in the sun, ready to make paprika. Macedonia's economy is mainly agricultural and its fertile soils support a broad range of crops.*

The urban/rural population divide

urban 51% — rural 49%

Population density	Total land area
240 people per sq mile (93 people per sq km)	95,038 sq miles (246,278 sq km)

▶ ***The Tara river** is one of Montenegro's major rivers. It flows into the Danube via the Drina and Sava rivers. Along its course the Tara has eroded spectacular gorges up to 3280 ft (1000 m) deep.*

Bulgaria & Greece

Including EUROPEAN TURKEY

Greece is renowned as the original hearth of western civilization. The rugged terrain and numerous islands have profoundly affected its development, creating a strong agricultural and maritime tradition. In the past 50 years, this formerly rural society has rapidly urbanized, with one third of the population now living in the capital, Athens, and in the northern city of Salonica. Bulgaria, dominated for centuries by the Ottoman Turks, became part of the eastern bloc after the Second World War, only slowly emerging from Soviet influence in 1989. Moves towards democracy led to some instability in Bulgaria and Greece, now outweighed by the challenge of integration with the European Union.

Transport and industry

Soviet investment introduced heavy industry into Bulgaria, and the processing of agricultural produce, such as tobacco, is important throughout the country. Both countries have substantial shipyards and Greece has one of the world's largest merchant fleets. Many small craft workshops, producing textiles and processed foods, are clustered around Greek cities. The service and construction sectors have profited from the successful tourist industry.

ROMANIA
BULGARIA
SOFIA
Pleven
Ruse
Varna
Burgas
Stara Zagora
Plovdiv
BLACK SEA
SERBIA
MACEDONIA
TURKEY
Istanbul
ALBANIA
GREECE
Salonica
Larisa
Volos
Aegean Sea
Ionian Sea
Patra
Corinth
ATHENS
Irakleio
MEDITERRANEAN SEA

Major industry and infrastructure

- chemicals
- engineering
- food processing
- shipbuilding
- textiles
- tourism
- capital cities
- major towns
- international airports
- major roads
- major industrial areas

The transport network

- 103,930 miles (167,630 km)
- 345 miles (557 km)
- 4346 miles (6995 km)
- 294 miles (474 km)

Bulgaria's railways require investment to revive an outdated infrastructure. In Greece, despite a developing road network, ferry-boats remain the most effective form of transport in many areas.

▲ ***A towering pinnacle** at Metéora in central Greece is home to the monastery of Roussanou. The 24 rock towers which dominate the plain of Thessaly (Thessalia) are remnants of an old plateau. Long-term weathering along fissures in the rock has worn away the rest of the plateau.*

The landscape

Bulgaria's Balkan mountains divide the Danubian Plain *(Dunavska Ravnina)* and Maritsa Basin, meeting the Black Sea in the east along sandy beaches. The steep Rhodope Mountains form a natural barrier with Greece, while the younger Pindus form a rugged central spine which descends into the Aegean Sea to give a vast archipelago of over 2000 islands, the largest of which is Crete.

Balkan Mountains
Maritsa Basin
Rhodope Mountains
Pindus Mountains
Kythira
Karpathos
Rhodes
Crete
Limestone rocks exposed by erosion of metamorphic rocks
Mount Olympus
Ancient metamorphic rock, formed miles below the surface
Younger limestones created in shallow seas

The Danube, Europe's second longest river, forms most of Bulgaria's northern border. The Danubian plain *(Dunavska Ravnina)*, extending from the southern bank, is extremely fertile.

Mount Olympus is the mythical home of the Greek Gods and, at 9570 ft (2917 m), is the highest mountain in Greece.

The islands of Crete, Kythira, Karpathos and Rhodes are part of an arc which bends southeastwards from the Peloponnese, forming the southern boundary of the Aegean.

The Peloponnese consist of several mountainous peninsulas, linked to the mainland by the Isthmus of Corinth. The Corinth Canal *(Dioryga Korinthou)*, built in 1893, cuts through the isthmus, linking the Aegean and Ionian seas.

Corinth Canal *(Dioryga Korinthou)*

▲ ***Mount Olympus** is a composite of rocks formed by two major tectonic events. First the older metamorphic rocks were thrust over the limestones, then two million years ago regional warping and subsequent erosion, re-exposed the limestone.*

▲ ***The Arda river** cuts through the Rhodope Mountains in rugged, rocky gorges.*

▲ ***Layers of black** volcanic ash still cover the island of Santorini. This volcano last erupted 3500 years ago, but still shows signs of volcanic activity.*

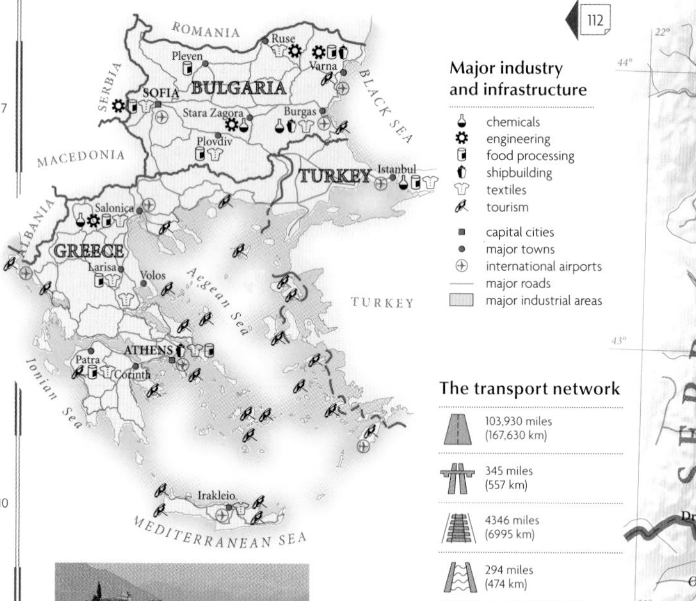

ROMANIA
SERBIA
BULGARIA
TURKEY
MACEDONIA
BLACK SEA
SOFIA
ISTANBUL
Scale 1:2,750,000
projection: Lambert Conformal Conic

112
116
112

Map key
Population
above 5 million
1 million to 5 million
500,000 to 1 million
100,000 to 500,000
50,000 to 100,000
10,000 to 50,000
below 10,000
Elevation
3000m / 9843ft
2000m / 6562ft
1000m / 3281ft
500m / 1640ft
250m / 820ft
100m / 328ft
sea level
Land use and agricultural distribution
cattle
fishing
goats
sheep
cereals
citrus fruits
cotton
olives
roses
tobacco
vineyards
capital cities
major towns
pasture
cropland
forest
mountain region
The urban/rural population divide
urban 65%
rural 35%
0 10 20 30 40 50 60 70 80 90 100
Population density
245 people per sq mile
(95 people per sq km)
Total land area
102,353 sq miles
(265,164 sq km)
ROMANIA
BULGARIA
SOFIA
BLACK SEA
TURKEY
MACEDONIA
ALBANIA
GREECE
ATHENS
Aegean Sea
Ionian Sea
MEDITERRANEAN SEA
ALBANIA
GREECE
TURKEY
Aegean Sea
VÓREION AIGAÍON
NÓTION AIGAÍON
Ionian Sea
Ióniа Nisiá (Ionian Islands)
Píndos (Pindus Mountains)
DYTIKÍ MAKEDONÍA
KENTRIKÍ MAKEDONÍA
THESSALÍA
ÍPEIROS
STEREÁ ELLÁDA
DYTIKÍ ELLÁDA
ATTIKÍ
PELOPÓNNISOS
Pelopónnisos
Athína (Athens)
Kykládes (Cyclades)
Dodekánisa (Dodecanese)
Kríti (Crete)
Kritikó Pélagos (Sea of Crete)
Karpáthio Pélagos
Mirtóo Pelagos
Évvoia (Euboea)
Vóreies Sporádes
Chalkidikí
ÁGION ÓROS
Lésvos (Lesbos)
Chíos
Sámos
Ródos (Rhodes)
Kárpathos
Iráklеio
MEDITERRANEAN SEA
ÇANAKKALE
112
136
120

▲ *The dry scrubland* seen here at Vasilikí in Crete, is characteristic of much of southern Greece, and is caused by centuries of forest clearance and soil degradation. Landslides are also common.

▶ *These terraces,* built on the hillside at Naxos, an island of the Cyclades group, help to guard against soil erosion.

Using the land and sea

The fertile plains of Bulgaria support cattle, fruit, vegetables, tobacco and cereal cultivation, while also providing traditional industries with grapes for wine, sunflowers for oil, and roses for perfume. Over half of Greece is barren upland. Citrus fruit, olives and tobacco are widely exported, yet much of rural life is still characterized by subsistence cropping and goat herding.

Romania, Moldova & Ukraine

The industrial, social and cultural make-up of Romania and the former Soviet states of Moldova and Ukraine still bear the imprint of their communist past. As part of the USSR, Ukraine was a leading agricultural, industrial and energy producer. These industries, like those in Moldova and Romania, are now being reoriented more firmly towards western markets. As a result of shifting borders, and Soviet policy actively encouraging Russian immigration into other Soviet states like Ukraine and Moldova, all three countries now contain large numbers of foreign nationals. Moldovans and Romanians are still close in terms of language and culture, although Moldova is striving to remain an independent nation.

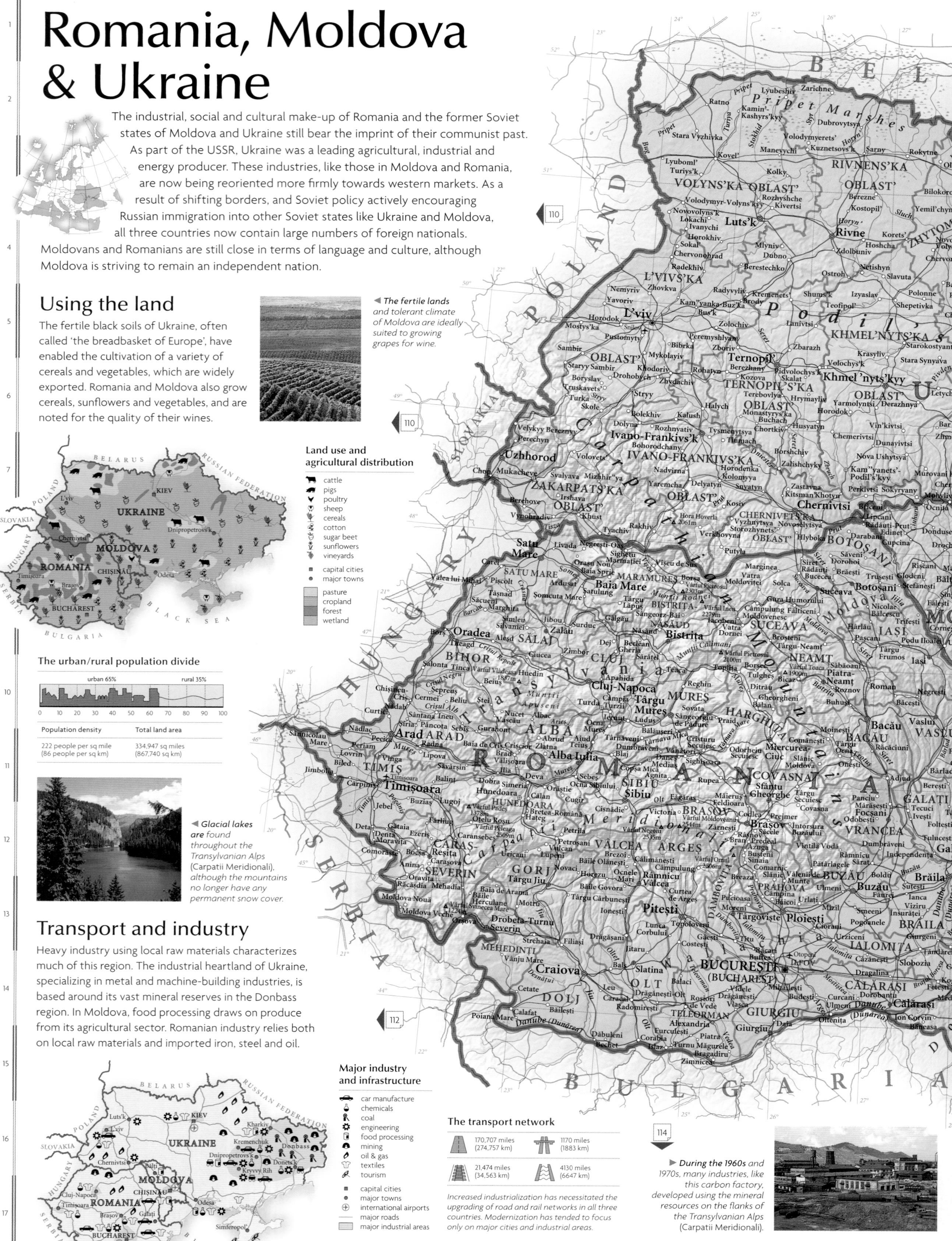

BELARUS
POLAND
UKRAINE
MOLDOVA
ROMANIA
HUNGARY
SLOVAKIA
SERBIA
BULGARIA
Carpathian Mountains
Transylvania
Pripet Marshes
Podil's'ka
BUCUREŞTI (BUCHAREST)
Cluj-Napoca
Timişoara
Arad
Oradea
Braşov
Sibiu
Craiova
Piteşti
Ploieşti
Iaşi
Bacău
Galaţi
Brăila
L'viv
Luts'k
Rivne
Ternopil'
Ivano-Frankivs'k
Uzhhorod
Chernivtsi
Khmel'nyts'kyy
Danube (Dunărea)

Using the land

The fertile black soils of Ukraine, often called 'the breadbasket of Europe', have enabled the cultivation of a variety of cereals and vegetables, which are widely exported. Romania and Moldova also grow cereals, sunflowers and vegetables, and are noted for the quality of their wines.

◀ *The fertile lands and tolerant climate of Moldova are ideally suited to growing grapes for wine.*

Land use and agricultural distribution

- cattle
- pigs
- poultry
- sheep
- cereals
- cotton
- sugar beet
- sunflowers
- vineyards
- capital cities
- major towns
- pasture
- cropland
- forest
- wetland

The urban/rural population divide

urban 65% | rural 35%

0 10 20 30 40 50 60 70 80 90 100

Population density	Total land area
222 people per sq mile (86 people per sq km)	334,947 sq miles (867,740 sq km)

◀ *Glacial lakes are found throughout the Transylvanian Alps (Carpatii Meridionali), although the mountains no longer have any permanent snow cover.*

Transport and industry

Heavy industry using local raw materials characterizes much of this region. The industrial heartland of Ukraine, specializing in metal and machine-building industries, is based around its vast mineral reserves in the Donbass region. In Moldova, food processing draws on produce from its agricultural sector. Romanian industry relies both on local raw materials and imported iron, steel and oil.

Major industry and infrastructure

- car manufacture
- chemicals
- coal
- engineering
- food processing
- mining
- oil & gas
- textiles
- tourism
- capital cities
- major towns
- international airports
- major roads
- major industrial areas

The transport network

170,707 miles (274,757 km)	1170 miles (1883 km)
21,474 miles (34,563 km)	4130 miles (6647 km)

Increased industrialization has necessitated the upgrading of road and rail networks in all three countries. Modernization has tended to focus only on major cities and industrial areas.

▶ *During the 1960s and 1970s, many industries, like this carbon factory, developed using the mineral resources on the flanks of the Transylvanian Alps (Carpatii Meridionali).*

110
110
112
114

Scale 1:3,500,000
Km
Miles
projection: Lambert Conformal Conic
Map key
Population
1 million to 5 million
500,000 to 1 million
100,000 to 500,000
50,000 to 100,000
10,000 to 50,000
below 10,000
Elevation
2000m / 6562ft
1000m / 3281ft
500m / 1640ft
250m / 820ft
100m / 328ft
sea level
118
122
120
126
RUSSIAN FEDERATION
UKRAINE
BLACK SEA
Sea of Azov
Gulf of Taganrog
Black Sea Lowland
Dnieper Lowland
CHERNIHIVS'KA OBLAST'
SUMS'KA OBLAST'
KYYIVS'KA OBLAST'
POLTAVS'KA OBLAST'
KHARKIVS'KA OBLAST'
LUHANS'KA OBLAST'
CHERKAS'KA OBLAST'
KIROVOHRADS'KA OBLAST'
DNIPROPETROVS'KA OBLAST'
DONETS'KA OBLAST'
ZAPORIZ'KA OBLAST'
MYKOLAYIVS'KA OBLAST'
ODES'KA OBLAST'
KHERSONS'KA OBLAST'
AVTONOMNA RESPUBLIKA KRYM
Kyyiv (Kiev)
Chernihiv
Sumy
Kharkiv
Poltava
Luhans'k
Donets'k
Dnipropetrovs'k
Zaporizhzhya
Kirovohrad
Cherkasy
Kremenchuk
Kryvyy Rih
Mykolayiv
Kherson
Odesa
Simferopol'
Sevastopol'
Yalta
Kerch
Mariupol'
Melitopol'
Berdyans'k
Zhytomyr
Chisinau
Tiraspol
Tulcea
Constanța
Kerch Strait
Old glaciated valley
Water has eroded a new post-glacial valley
Steppe landscape covers two-thirds of Ukraine. These flat, treeless grasslands extend from central Europe to central Asia.
Most of the major rivers in southeastern Europe, like the Danube, the Dniester and Dnieper flow south and east to the Black Sea.
The Codrii Hills dominate the landscape of central Moldova; they are intersected by deep, flat valleys and ravines.
Anti-clockwise currents have created the sandspits which fringe the Sea of Azov.
Uplifted and folded at the same time as the Alps, some 250 miles (400 km) of the eastern Carpathian Mountains contain ancient volcanic cones and craters.
The Apuseni Mountains (Muntii Apuseni) are rich in mineral deposits, including gold and iron ore.
Transylvanian Alps (Carpatii Meridionali)
The Danube forms a natural border between Romania and Bulgaria.
The three branches of the Danube Delta (Delta Dunării) form a triangle of wetlands covering some 1950 sq miles (5050 sq km).
At Kryms'ki Hory, three flat-topped, parallel limestone ridges run 80 miles (128 km) along the southern coast of the Crimean (Krym) Peninsula.

▲ **The Swallow's Nest** *castle at Yalta is one of many tourist resorts on the Crimean (Krym) coast, dubbed the 'Russian Riviera'.*

▲ **Balkas are common** *throughout Ukraine. They are large U-shaped valleys, formed during the last Ice Age, which contain narrower, deep valleys. These were incised by a sudden flow of water, following an ice melt.*

The landscape

Vast flat lowlands and gently rolling hills cover most of southeastern Europe. In the southwest, the Carpathian Mountains form a gentle arc. To the south of the Carpathian Mountains lies the Danube Plain, across which the Danube river flows to the Black Sea. To the north and east, the hills of Moldova level out into low plains, running east to the steppes of Ukraine.

► **Divided into crystalline** *massifs, the southern arm of the Carpathian Mountains, the Transylvanian Alps* (Carpatii Meridionali)*, extend 170 miles (274 km) across southwestern Romania.*

The Baltic states & Belarus

BELARUS, ESTONIA, LATVIA, LITHUANIA, Kaliningrad

Occupying Europe's main corridor to Russia, the four distinct cultures of Estonia, Latvia, Lithuania and Belarus share a history of struggle for nationhood against the interests of more powerful neighbours. As the first republics to declare their independence from the Soviet Union in 1990–91, the Baltic states of Estonia, Latvia and Lithuania sought an economic role in the EU, while reaffirming their European cultural roots through the church and a strong musical tradition. Meanwhile, Belarus has shown economic and political allegiance to Russia by joining the Commonwealth of Independent States.

▲ *The seaport of* Riga *is Latvia's capital and the centre of economic and cultural life. With a 32% Russian minority in Latvia, language and the right to national citizenship are key issues.*

Using the land

Across the four nations cattle and pig farming are widespread, together with diverse arable crops, including flax for making linen, potatoes used to produce vodka, cereals and other vegetables. Almost a third of the land is forested; demand for timber has increased the importance of forest management.

Land use and agricultural distribution

- cattle
- pigs
- cereals
- flax
- potatoes
- timber
- capital cities
- major towns
- pasture
- cropland
- forest
- wetland

The urban/rural population divide

urban 69% | rural 31%

0 10 20 30 40 50 60 70 80 90 100

Population density	Total land area
122 people per sq mile (47 people per sq km)	145,006 sq miles (375,656 sq km)

▶ *A pine forest in northern Belarus. Conifers in the north give way to hardwood forest further south. Timber mills are supplied with logs floated along the country's many navigable waterways.*

▲ *The Western Dvina river provides hydro-electric power and, during the summer months, access to the Baltic Sea. The lower course of the river freezes from December to April.*

Map key

Population

- 1 million to 5 million
- 500,000 to 1 million
- 100,000 to 500,000
- 50,000 to 100,000
- 10,000 to 50,000
- below 10,000

Elevation

- 250m / 820ft
- 100m / 328ft
- sea level

122
122

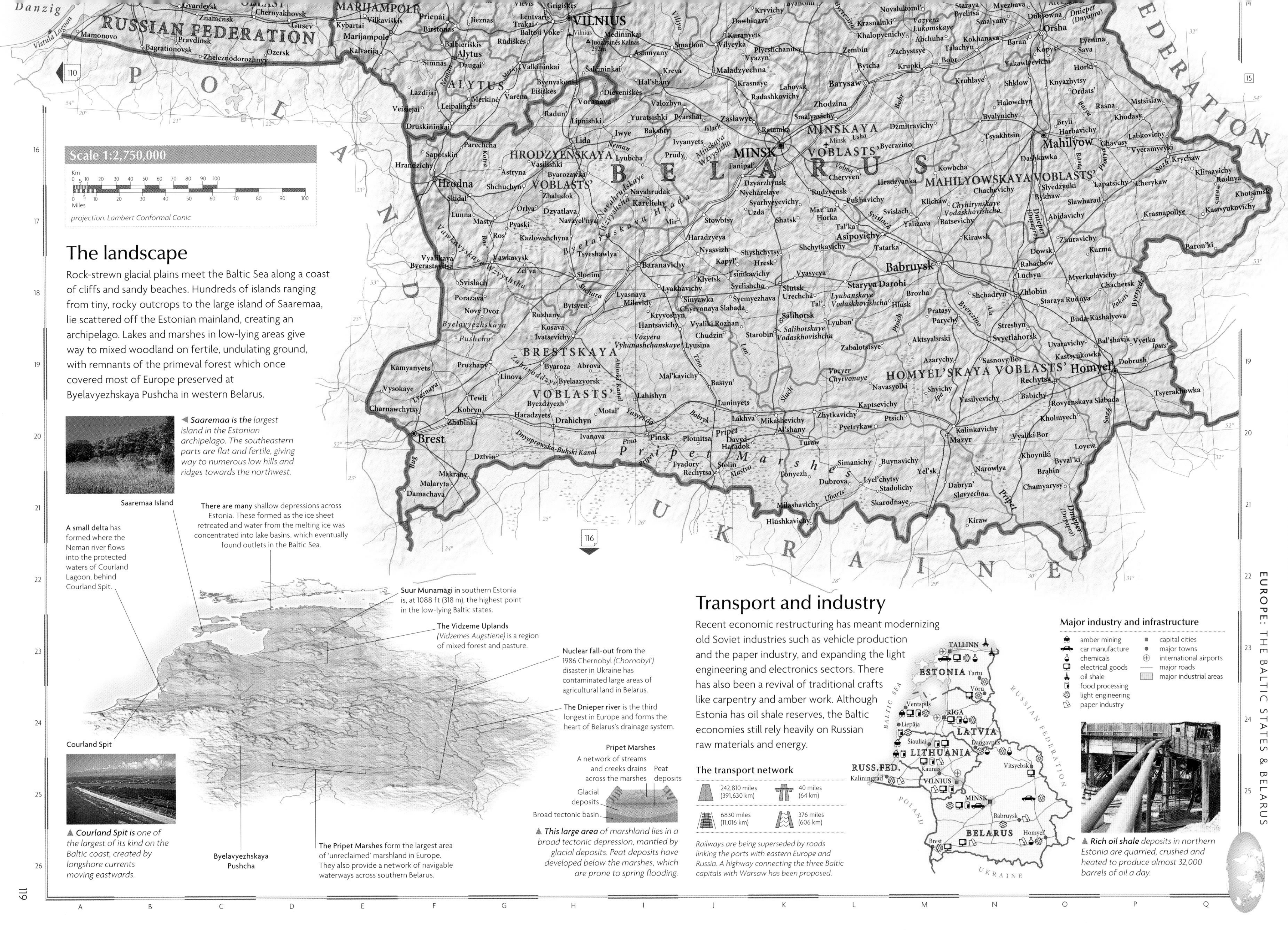

RUSSIAN FEDERATION
POLAND
UKRAINE
BELARUS
VILNIUS
MINSK
Brest
Hrodna
Babruysk
Homyel'
Mahilyow
Orsha
HRODZYENSKAYA VOBLASTS'
MINSKAYA VOBLASTS'
MAHILYOWSKAYA VOBLASTS'
BRESTSKAYA VOBLASTS'
HOMYEL'SKAYA VOBLASTS'
Pripet Marshes
Dnieper (Dnyapro)
Pripet
Scale 1:2,750,000
projection: Lambert Conformal Conic
110
116
15
Saaremaa Island
Courland Spit
Byelavyezhskaya Pushcha
Pripet Marshes
A network of streams and creeks drains across the marshes
Peat deposits
Glacial deposits
Broad tectonic basin
242,810 miles (391,630 km)
40 miles (64 km)
6830 miles (11,016 km)
376 miles (606 km)
TALLINN
ESTONIA
RIGA
LATVIA
LITHUANIA
RUSS.FED.
BALTIC SEA
amber mining
car manufacture
chemicals
electrical goods
oil shale
food processing
light engineering
paper industry
capital cities
major towns
international airports
major roads
major industrial areas

The landscape

Rock-strewn glacial plains meet the Baltic Sea along a coast of cliffs and sandy beaches. Hundreds of islands ranging from tiny, rocky outcrops to the large island of Saaremaa, lie scattered off the Estonian mainland, creating an archipelago. Lakes and marshes in low-lying areas give way to mixed woodland on fertile, undulating ground, with remnants of the primeval forest which once covered most of Europe preserved at Byelavyezhskaya Pushcha in western Belarus.

◀ *Saaremaa is the largest island in the Estonian archipelago. The southeastern parts are flat and fertile, giving way to numerous low hills and ridges towards the northwest.*

A small delta has formed where the Neman river flows into the protected waters of Courland Lagoon, behind Courland Spit.

There are many shallow depressions across Estonia. These formed as the ice sheet retreated and water from the melting ice was concentrated into lake basins, which eventually found outlets in the Baltic Sea.

Suur Munamägi in southern Estonia is, at 1088 ft (318 m), the highest point in the low-lying Baltic states.

The Vidzeme Uplands *(Vidzemes Augstiene)* is a region of mixed forest and pasture.

Nuclear fall-out from the 1986 Chernobyl *(Chornobyl')* disaster in Ukraine has contaminated large areas of agricultural land in Belarus.

The Dnieper river is the third longest in Europe and forms the heart of Belarus's drainage system.

▲ ***Courland Spit** is one of the largest of its kind on the Baltic coast, created by longshore currents moving eastwards.*

The Pripet Marshes form the largest area of 'unreclaimed' marshland in Europe. They also provide a network of navigable waterways across southern Belarus.

▲ ***This large area** of marshland lies in a broad tectonic depression, mantled by glacial deposits. Peat deposits have developed below the marshes, which are prone to spring flooding.*

Transport and industry

Recent economic restructuring has meant modernizing old Soviet industries such as vehicle production and the paper industry, and expanding the light engineering and electronics sectors. There has also been a revival of traditional crafts like carpentry and amber work. Although Estonia has oil shale reserves, the Baltic economies still rely heavily on Russian raw materials and energy.

The transport network

Railways are being superseded by roads linking the ports with eastern Europe and Russia. A highway connecting the three Baltic capitals with Warsaw has been proposed.

Major industry and infrastructure

▲ ***Rich oil shale** deposits in northern Estonia are quarried, crushed and heated to produce almost 32,000 barrels of oil a day.*

The Mediterranean

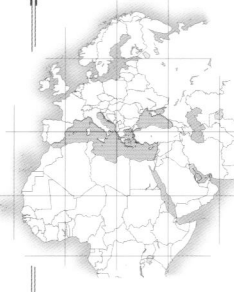

The Mediterranean Sea stretches over 2500 miles (4000 km) east to west, separating Europe from Africa. At its most westerly point it is connected to the Atlantic Ocean through the Strait of Gibraltar. In the east, the Suez canal, opened in 1869, gives passage to the Indian Ocean. In the northeast, linked by the Sea of Marmara, lies the Black Sea. The Mediterranean is bordered by almost 30 states and territories, and more than 100 million people live on its shores and islands. Throughout history, the Mediterranean has been a focal area for many great empires and civilizations, reflected in the variety of cultures found on its shores. Since the 1960s, development along the southern coast of Europe has expanded rapidly to accommodate increasing numbers of tourists and to enable the exploitation of oil and gas reserves. This has resulted in rising levels of pollution, threatening the future of the sea.

▲ *Monaco is just one of the luxurious resorts scattered along the Riviera, which stretches along the coast from Cannes in France to La Spezia in Italy. The region's mild winters and hot summers have attracted wealthy tourists since the early 19th century.*

ATLANTIC OCEAN
Bay of Biscay
FRANCE
SPAIN
PORTUGAL
ANDORRA
MONACO
SWITZERLAND
ITALY
MOROCCO
ALGERIA
TUNISIA
MEDITERRANEAN
Algerian Basin
Tyrrhenian Sea
Tyrrhenian Basin
Ligurian Sea
Alboran Sea
Islas Baleares (Balearic Islands)
Mallorca (Majorca)
Menorca (Minorca)
Ibiza
Formentera
Sardegna (Sardinia) (to Italy)
Corse (Corsica) (to France)
Sicilia (Sicily)
LISBOA (LISBON)
MADRID
ROMA (ROME)
VATICAN CITY
RABAT
ALGER (ALGIERS)
TUNIS
VALLETTA
ṬARĀBULUS (TRIPOLI)
Barcelona
Valencia
Marseille
Lyon
Toulouse
Bordeaux
Milano (Milan)
Torino (Turin)
Genova (Genoa)
Napoli (Naples)
Palermo
Cagliari
Porto
Sevilla (Seville)
Málaga
Granada
Córdoba
Zaragoza
Casablanca
Fès
Marrakech
Oran
Constantine
Sfax
Gabès
GIBRALTAR (to UK)
Strait of Gibraltar
Ceuta (Part of Spain)
Melilla (Part of Spain)
Strait of Bonifacio
Strait of Sicily
Pyrenees
Sistema Central
Sierra Morena
Sistemas Béticos
Massif Central
Atlas Tellien
Hauts Plateaux
Haut Atlas
Atlas Saharien
Massif de l'Aurès
Atlas Mountains

The landscape

The Mediterranean Sea is almost totally landlocked, joined to the Atlantic Ocean through the Strait of Gibraltar, which is only 8 miles (13 km) wide. Lying on an active plate margin, sea floor movements have formed a variety of basins, troughs and ridges. A submarine ridge running from Tunisia to the island of Sicily divides the Mediterranean into two distinct basins. The western basin is characterized by broad, smooth abyssal (or ocean) plains. In contrast, the eastern basin is dominated by a large ridge system, running east to west.

The narrow Strait of Gibraltar inhibits water exchange between the Mediterranean Sea and the Atlantic Ocean, producing a high degree of salinity and a low tidal range within the Mediterranean. The lack of tides has encouraged the build-up of pollutants in many semi-enclosed bays.

Main surface current

Dense currents sink below surface

Denser, more saline currents flow back to Atlantic

▲ *Because the Mediterranean is almost enclosed by land, its circulation is quite different to the oceans. There is one major current which flows in from the Atlantic and moves east. Currents flowing back to the Atlantic are denser and flow below the main current.*

Industrial pollution flowing from the Dnieper and Danube rivers has destroyed a large proportion of the fish population that used to inhabit the upper layers of the Black Sea.

The Ionian Basin is the deepest in the Mediterranean, reaching depths of 16,800 ft (5121 m).

The edge of the Eurasian Plate is edged by a continental shelf. In the Mediterranean Sea this is widest at the Ebro Fan where it extends 60 miles (96 km).

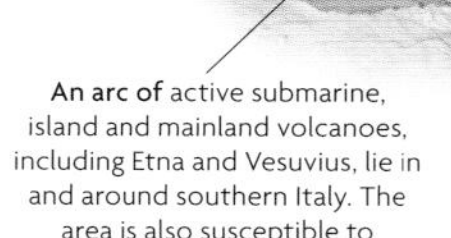

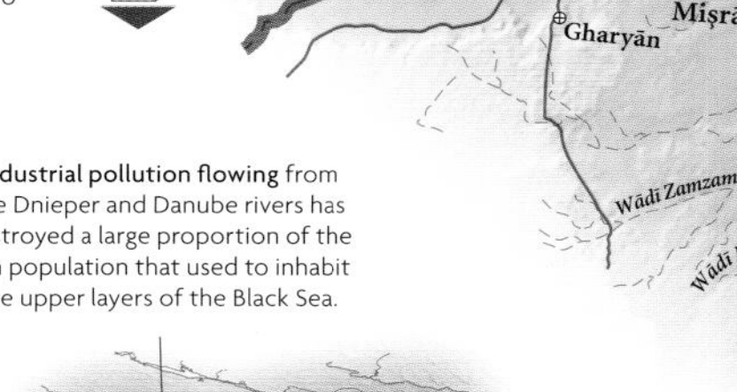

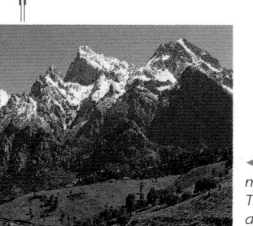

◀ *The Atlas Mountains are a range of fold mountains which lie in Morocco and Algeria. They run parallel to the Mediterranean, forming a topographical and climatic divide between the Mediterranean coast and the western Sahara.*

An arc of active submarine, island and mainland volcanoes, including Etna and Vesuvius, lie in and around southern Italy. The area is also susceptible to earthquakes and landslides.

Nutrient flows into the eastern Mediterranean, and sediment flows to the Nile Delta have been severely lowered by the building of the Aswan Dam across the Nile in Egypt. This is causing the delta to shrink.

Oxygen in the Black Sea dissolved only in its upp layers; at depths below 300 ft (70–100 m) the se 'dead' and can support lifeforms other than specially-adapted bacte

The Suez Canal, opened in extends 100 miles (160 km) Port Said to the Gulf of Sue

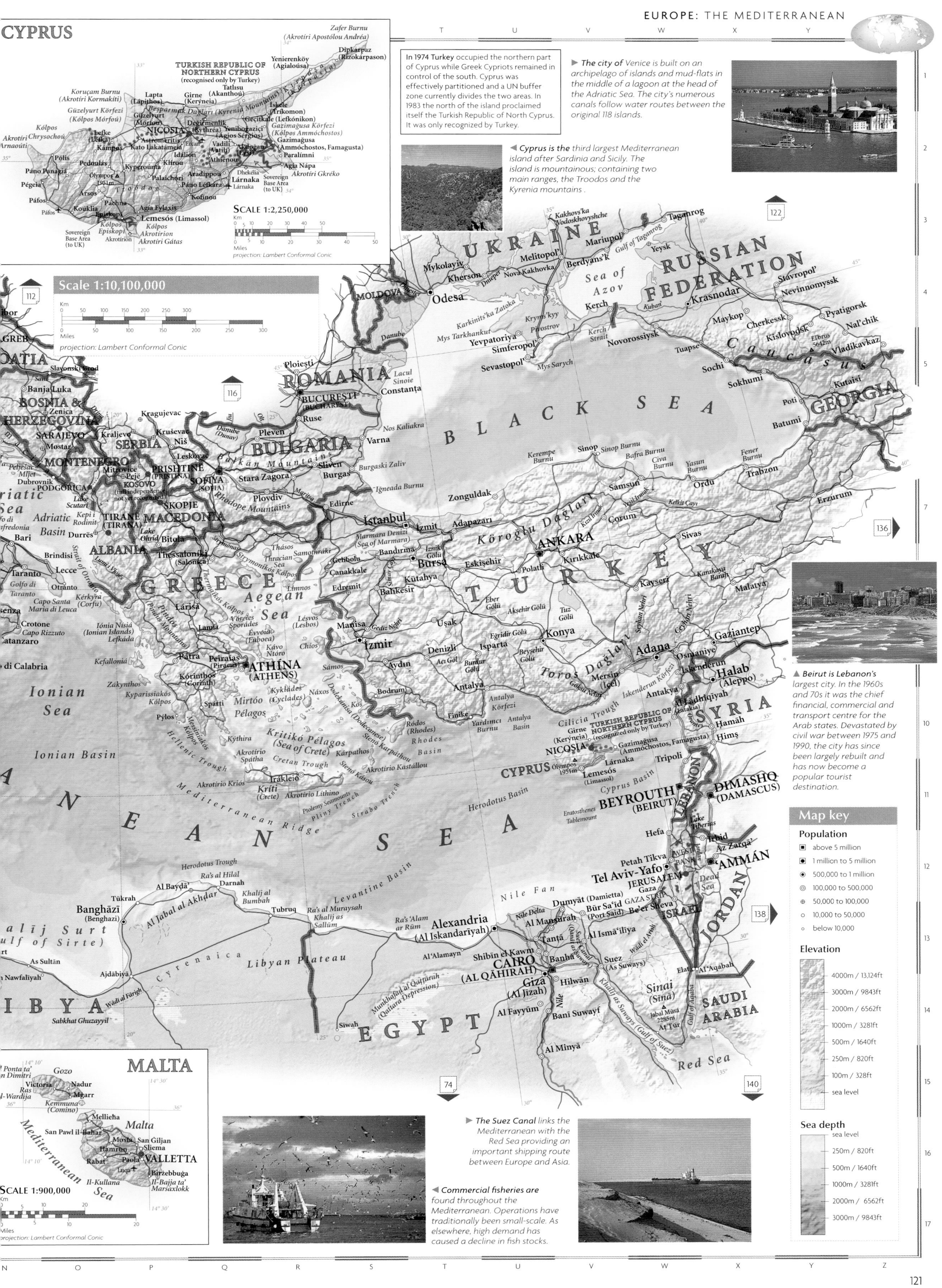
CYPRUS
TURKISH REPUBLIC OF NORTHERN CYPRUS (recognised only by Turkey)
NICOSIA
Lemesós (Limassol)
Lárnaka
Gazimagusa (Ammóchostos, Famagusta)
SCALE 1:2,250,000
projection: Lambert Conformal Conic
Scale 1:10,100,000
projection: Lambert Conformal Conic
UKRAINE
RUSSIAN FEDERATION
MOLDOVA
ROMANIA
BUCUREŞTI (BUCHAREST)
BULGARIA
SOFIYA (SOFIA)
SERBIA
BOSNIA & HERZEGOVINA
SARAJEVO
MONTENEGRO
PODGORICA
KOSOVO
PRISHTINË (PRIŠTINA)
MACEDONIA
SKOPJE
ALBANIA
TIRANË (TIRANA)
GREECE
ATHÍNA (ATHENS)
TURKEY
ANKARA
İstanbul
GEORGIA
SYRIA
DIMASHQ (DAMASCUS)
LEBANON
BEYROUTH (BEIRUT)
JERUSALEM
ISRAEL
JORDAN
'AMMĀN
EGYPT
CAIRO (AL QĀHIRAH)
SAUDI ARABIA
LIBYA
BLACK SEA
Sea of Azov
Aegean Sea
Ionian Sea
Adriatic Sea
MEDITERRANEAN SEA
Red Sea
MALTA
VALLETTA
Gozo
Mediterranean Sea
SCALE 1:900,000
projection: Lambert Conformal Conic

In 1974 Turkey occupied the northern part of Cyprus while Greek Cypriots remained in control of the south. Cyprus was effectively partitioned and a UN buffer zone currently divides the two areas. In 1983 the north of the island proclaimed itself the Turkish Republic of North Cyprus. It was only recognized by Turkey.

► *The city of Venice is built on an archipelago of islands and mud-flats in the middle of a lagoon at the head of the Adriatic Sea. The city's numerous canals follow water routes between the original 118 islands.*

◄ *Cyprus is the third largest Mediterranean island after Sardinia and Sicily. The island is mountainous; containing two main ranges, the Troodos and the Kyrenia mountains .*

▲ *Beirut is Lebanon's largest city. In the 1960s and 70s it was the chief financial, commercial and transport centre for the Arab states. Devastated by civil war between 1975 and 1990, the city has since been largely rebuilt and has now become a popular tourist destination.*

Map key

Population
- above 5 million
- 1 million to 5 million
- 500,000 to 1 million
- 100,000 to 500,000
- 50,000 to 100,000
- 10,000 to 50,000
- below 10,000

Elevation
- 4000m / 13,124ft
- 3000m / 9843ft
- 2000m / 6562ft
- 1000m / 3281ft
- 500m / 1640ft
- 250m / 820ft
- 100m / 328ft
- sea level

Sea depth
- sea level
- 250m / 820ft
- 500m / 1640ft
- 1000m / 3281ft
- 2000m / 6562ft
- 3000m / 9843ft

► *The Suez Canal links the Mediterranean with the Red Sea providing an important shipping route between Europe and Asia.*

◄ *Commercial fisheries are found throughout the Mediterranean. Operations have traditionally been small-scale. As elsewhere, high demand has caused a decline in fish stocks.*

The Russian Federation

The Cold War era of global relations was concluded in 1991 with the formal dissolution of the Soviet Union. The Russian Federation declared its separate sovereignty from the foundering communist empire following independence declarations from a number of former Soviet republics. As the leading member of the Commonwealth of Independent States, the Russian Federation has a central role in the development of post-Soviet Eurasia. Crossing 11 time zones, the Russian Federation is almost twice the size of the USA, and with more than 150 ethnic minorities and 21 autonomous republics, regionalist dissent within its own territory remains a danger.

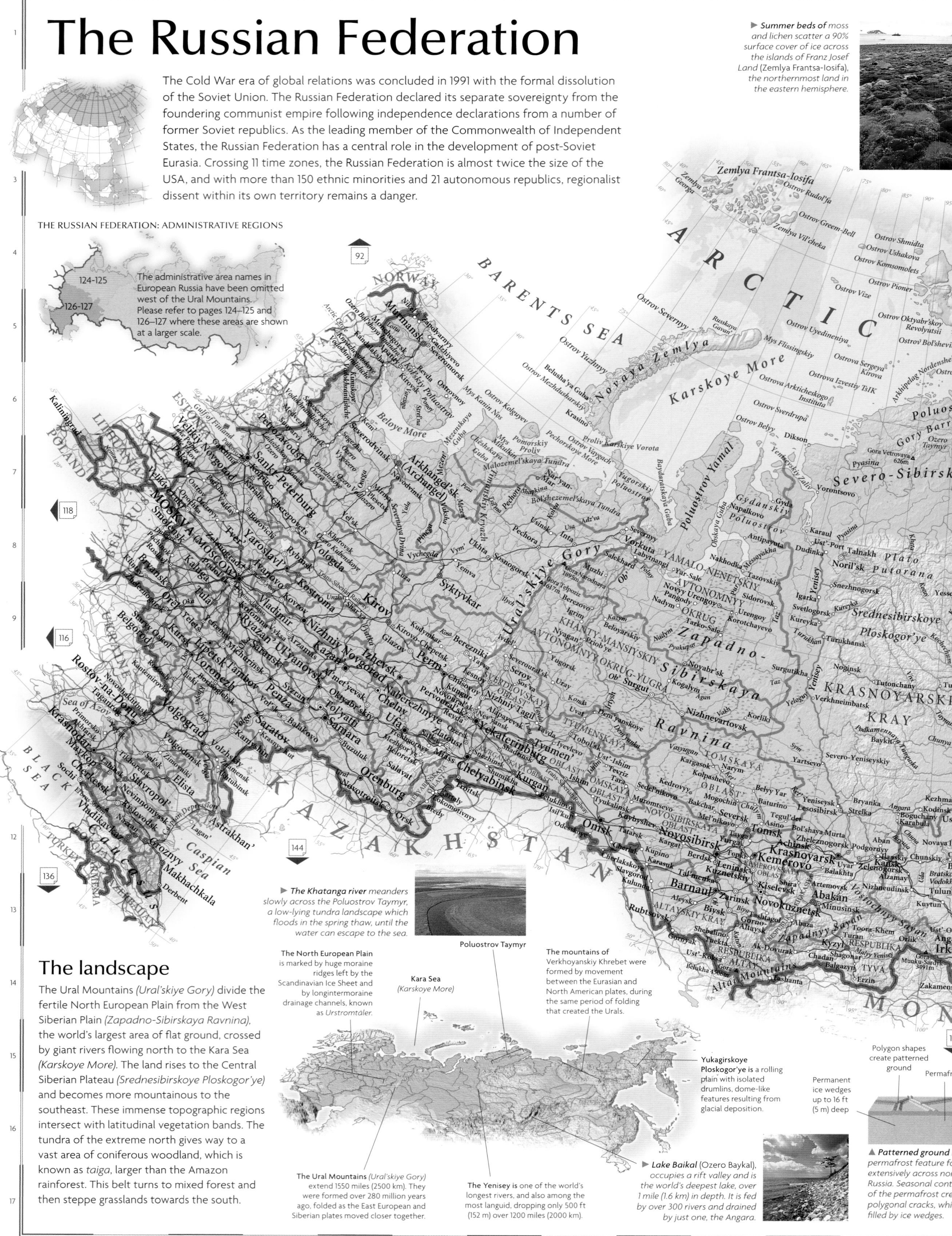
THE RUSSIAN FEDERATION: ADMINISTRATIVE REGIONS
124-125
126-127
The administrative area names in European Russia have been omitted west of the Ural Mountains. Please refer to pages 124–125 and 126–127 where these areas are shown at a larger scale.
92
118
116
136
144
BARENTS SEA
ARCTIC
Zemlya Frantsa-Iosifa
Novaya Zemlya
Karskoye More
Beloye More
Sea of Azov
BLACK SEA
Caspian Sea
KAZAKHSTAN
NORWAY
FINLAND
ESTONIA
LATVIA
LITHUANIA
POLAND
BELARUS
UKRAINE
GEORGIA
Ural'skiye Gory
Zapadno-Sibirskaya Ravnina
Srednesibirskoye Ploskogor'ye
Plato Putorana
Severo-Sibirsk
Poluostrov Yamal
Gydanskiy Poluostrov
YAMALO-NENETSKIY AVTONOMNYY OKRUG
KHANTY-MANSIYSKIY AVTONOMNYY OKRUG-YUGRA
KRASNOYARSKIY KRAY
TOMSKAYA OBLAST'
NOVOSIBIRSKAYA OBLAST'
ALTAYSKIY KRAY
RESPUBLIKA ALTAY
RESPUBLIKA TYVA
Altai Mountains
Kaliningrad
Sankt-Peterburg
Petrozavodsk
Murmansk
Arkhangel'sk (Archangel)
Severodvinsk
Vologda
Yaroslavl'
MOSKVA (MOSCOW)
Smolensk
Bryansk
Kursk
Belgorod
Voronezh
Lipetsk
Tambov
Ryazan'
Vladimir
Ivanovo
Kostroma
Nizhniy Novgorod
Kazan'
Izhevsk
Kirov
Syktyvkar
Perm'
Yekaterinburg
Chelyabinsk
Tyumen'
Kurgan
Omsk
Novosibirsk
Tomsk
Kemerovo
Barnaul
Novokuznetsk
Krasnoyarsk
Abakan
Noril'sk
Vorkuta
Salekhard
Surgut
Nizhnevartovsk
Orenburg
Samara
Saratov
Ul'yanovsk
Penza
Volgograd
Astrakhan'
Rostov-na-Donu
Krasnodar
Stavropol'
Elista
Makhachkala
Groznyy
Vladikavkaz
Caucasus
Derbent
Orsk
Ufa
Dikson
Igarka
Turukhansk
Yeniseysk
Rubtsovsk

► Summer beds of moss and lichen scatter a 90% surface cover of ice across the islands of Franz Josef Land (Zemlya Frantsa-Iosifa), the northernmost land in the eastern hemisphere.

► **The Khatanga river** meanders slowly across the Poluostrov Taymyr, a low-lying tundra landscape which floods in the spring thaw, until the water can escape to the sea.

The landscape

The Ural Mountains *(Ural'skiye Gory)* divide the fertile North European Plain from the West Siberian Plain *(Zapadno-Sibirskaya Ravnina)*, the world's largest area of flat ground, crossed by giant rivers flowing north to the Kara Sea *(Karskoye More)*. The land rises to the Central Siberian Plateau *(Srednesibirskoye Ploskogor'ye)* and becomes more mountainous to the southeast. These immense topographic regions intersect with latitudinal vegetation bands. The tundra of the extreme north gives way to a vast area of coniferous woodland, which is known as *taiga*, larger than the Amazon rainforest. This belt turns to mixed forest and then steppe grasslands towards the south.

The North European Plain is marked by huge moraine ridges left by the Scandinavian Ice Sheet and by longintermoraine drainage channels, known as *Urstromtäler*.

Kara Sea *(Karskoye More)*

Poluostrov Taymyr

The mountains of Verkhoyanskiy Khrebet were formed by movement between the Eurasian and North American plates, during the same period of folding that created the Urals.

Yukagirskoye Ploskogor'ye is a rolling plain with isolated drumlins, dome-like features resulting from glacial deposition.

The Ural Mountains *(Ural'skiye Gory)* extend 1550 miles (2500 km). They were formed over 280 million years ago, folded as the East European and Siberian plates moved closer together.

The Yenisey is one of the world's longest rivers, and also among the most languid, dropping only 500 ft (152 m) over 1200 miles (2000 km).

► **Lake Baikal** (Ozero Baykal), occupies a rift valley and is the world's deepest lake, over 1 mile (1.6 km) in depth. It is fed by over 300 rivers and drained by just one, the Angara.

Polygon shapes create patterned ground

Permafro

Permanent ice wedges up to 16 ft (5 m) deep

▲ **Patterned ground i**
permafrost feature fo
extensively across nor
Russia. Seasonal contr
of the permafrost cre
polygonal cracks, whic
filled by ice wedges.

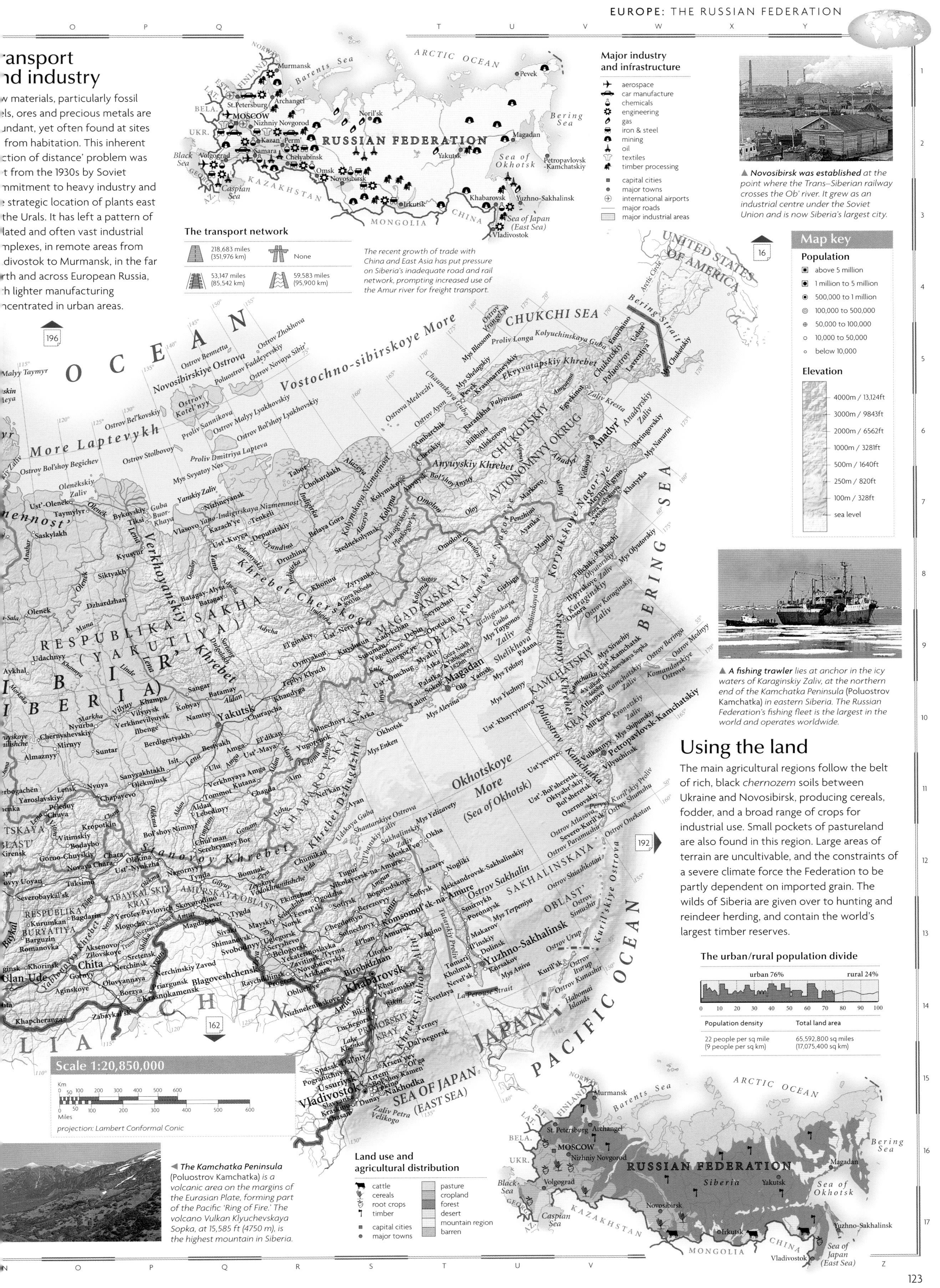

O P Q T U V W X Y
Major industry and infrastructure
aerospace
car manufacture
chemicals
engineering
gas
iron & steel
mining
oil
textiles
timber processing
capital cities
major towns
international airports
major roads
major industrial areas
RUSSIAN FEDERATION
ARCTIC OCEAN
Map key
Population
above 5 million
1 million to 5 million
500,000 to 1 million
100,000 to 500,000
50,000 to 100,000
10,000 to 50,000
below 10,000
Elevation
4000m / 13,124ft
3000m / 9843ft
2000m / 6562ft
1000m / 3281ft
500m / 1640ft
250m / 820ft
100m / 328ft
sea level
Scale 1:20,850,000
projection: Lambert Conformal Conic
Land use and agricultural distribution
cattle
cereals
root crops
timber
capital cities
major towns
pasture
cropland
forest
desert
mountain region
barren

ransport
nd industry

w materials, particularly fossil els, ores and precious metals are undant, yet often found at sites from habitation. This inherent ction of distance' problem was t from the 1930s by Soviet mmitment to heavy industry and strategic location of plants east the Urals. It has left a pattern of lated and often vast industrial mplexes, in remote areas from divostok to Murmansk, in the far rth and across European Russia, h lighter manufacturing ncentrated in urban areas.

The transport network

218,683 miles (351,976 km)	None
53,147 miles (85,542 km)	59,583 miles (95,900 km)

The recent growth of trade with China and East Asia has put pressure on Siberia's inadequate road and rail network, prompting increased use of the Amur river for freight transport.

▲ ***Novosibirsk was established** at the point where the Trans-Siberian railway crosses the Ob' river. It grew as an industrial centre under the Soviet Union and is now Siberia's largest city.*

▲ ***A fishing trawler** lies at anchor in the icy waters of Karaginskiy Zaliv, at the northern end of the Kamchatka Peninsula (Poluostrov Kamchatka) in eastern Siberia. The Russian Federation's fishing fleet is the largest in the world and operates worldwide.*

Using the land

The main agricultural regions follow the belt of rich, black *chernozem* soils between Ukraine and Novosibirsk, producing cereals, fodder, and a broad range of crops for industrial use. Small pockets of pastureland are also found in this region. Large areas of terrain are uncultivable, and the constraints of a severe climate force the Federation to be partly dependent on imported grain. The wilds of Siberia are given over to hunting and reindeer herding, and contain the world's largest timber reserves.

The urban/rural population divide

urban 76% — rural 24%

Population density	Total land area
22 people per sq mile (9 people per sq km)	65,592,800 sq miles (17,075,400 sq km)

◀ ***The Kamchatka Peninsula** (Poluostrov Kamchatka) is a volcanic area on the margins of the Eurasian Plate, forming part of the Pacific 'Ring of Fire.' The volcano Vulkan Klyuchevskaya Sopka, at 15,585 ft (4750 m), is the highest mountain in Siberia.*

Northern European Russia

Reaching into the Arctic Circle, this region of lakeland, forest and tundra is historically bound to Europe by St Petersburg, the old imperial capital of Tsarist Russia and home to a third of the region's population. Communist rule from Moscow left the north politically marginalized, contributing to the present problems of outmoded industry, poor infrastructure and serious environmental neglect. However, with borders embracing Finland, Norway, the Baltic and the northern sea route to the Atlantic, the region's success in foreign trade is now of prime importance to the Russian economy.

The landscape

The ancient bedrock of the Scandinavian Shield lies exposed across the glacially scoured Khibiny Mountains of the Kola Peninsula *(Kol'skiy Poluostrov)*, becoming mantled with till towards the North European Plain. The Valdai Hills *(Valdayskaya Vozvyshennost')* form an important watershed for the plain's rivers, while thick forest veils a complicated topography of moraines, lakes and ground disturbed by frost action. The Ural Mountains *(Ural'skiye Gory)* form a border with Asia in the east.

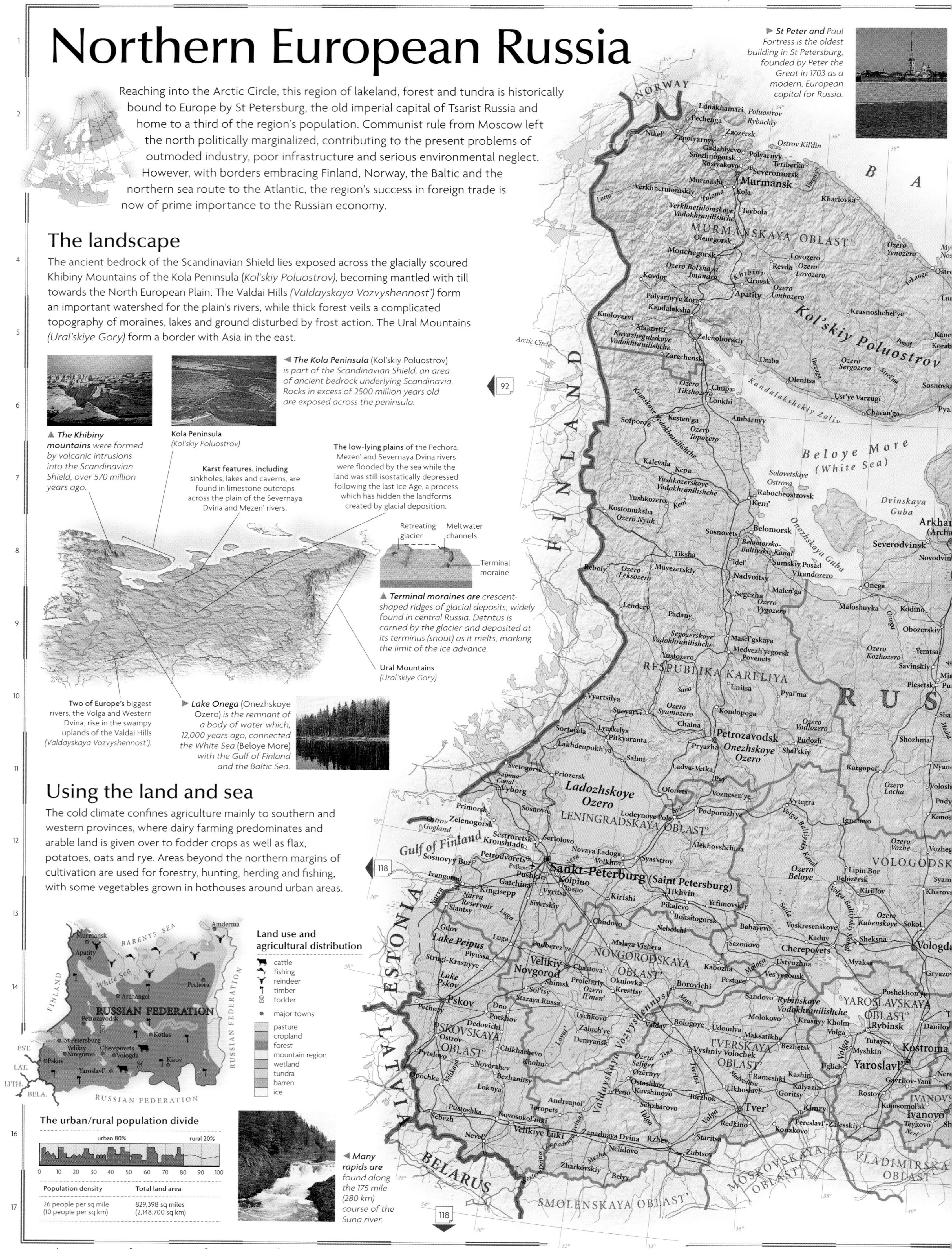

NORWAY
FINLAND
ESTONIA
LATVIA
BELARUS
Murmansk
Severomorsk
Kola
Apatity
Kirovsk
Kandalaksha
Kol'skiy Poluostrov
MURMANSKAYA OBLAST'
Beloye More (White Sea)
Onezhskaya Guba
Dvinskaya Guba
Severodvinsk
Belomorsk
Kem'
Kostomuksha
Segezha
Medvezh'yegorsk
RESPUBLIKA KARELIYA
Petrozavodsk
Onezhskoye Ozero
Ladozhskoye Ozero
Vyborg
Gulf of Finland
Sankt-Peterburg (Saint Petersburg)
Kolpino
Kronshtadt
Petrodvorets
LENINGRADSKAYA OBLAST'
Tikhvin
Kirishi
Lake Peipus
Pskov
PSKOVSKAYA OBLAST'
Velikiy Novgorod
NOVGORODSKAYA OBLAST'
Valdayskaya Vozvyshennost'
Velikiye Luki
Tver'
TVERSKAYA OBLAST'
Cherepovets
Vologda
VOLOGODSKAYA
Rybinsk
Yaroslavl'
YAROSLAVSKAYA OBLAST'
Kostroma
Ivanovo
SMOLENSKAYA OBLAST'
MOSKOVSKAYA OBLAST'
VLADIMIRSKAYA OBLAST'
Arctic Circle
92
118

▶ **St Peter and Paul** *Fortress is the oldest building in St Petersburg, founded by Peter the Great in 1703 as a modern, European capital for Russia.*

◀ ***The Kola Peninsula*** (Kol'skiy Poluostrov) *is part of the Scandinavian Shield, an area of ancient bedrock underlying Scandinavia. Rocks in excess of 2500 million years old are exposed across the peninsula.*

▲ ***The Khibiny mountains*** *were formed by volcanic intrusions into the Scandinavian Shield, over 570 million years ago.*

Kola Peninsula *(Kol'skiy Poluostrov)*

Karst features, including sinkholes, lakes and caverns, are found in limestone outcrops across the plain of the Severnaya Dvina and Mezen' rivers.

The low-lying plains of the Pechora, Mezen' and Severnaya Dvina rivers were flooded by the sea while the land was still isostatically depressed following the last Ice Age, a process which has hidden the landforms created by glacial deposition.

Retreating glacier
Meltwater channels
Terminal moraine

▲ ***Terminal moraines are*** *crescent-shaped ridges of glacial deposits, widely found in central Russia. Detritus is carried by the glacier and deposited at its terminus (snout) as it melts, marking the limit of the ice advance.*

Ural Mountains *(Ural'skiye Gory)*

Two of Europe's biggest rivers, the Volga and Western Dvina, rise in the swampy uplands of the Valdai Hills *(Valdayskaya Vozvyshennost').*

▶ ***Lake Onega*** *(Onezhskoye Ozero) is the remnant of a body of water which, 12,000 years ago, connected the White Sea* (Beloye More) *with the Gulf of Finland and the Baltic Sea.*

Using the land and sea

The cold climate confines agriculture mainly to southern and western provinces, where dairy farming predominates and arable land is given over to fodder crops as well as flax, potatoes, oats and rye. Areas beyond the northern margins of cultivation are used for forestry, hunting, herding and fishing, with some vegetables grown in hothouses around urban areas.

BARENTS SEA
Amderma
Murmansk
Apatity
White Sea
Archangel
Pechora
RUSSIAN FEDERATION
Petrozavodsk
St Petersburg
Velikiy Novgorod
Cherepovets
Vologda
Kotlas
Kirov
Pskov
Yaroslavl'
FINLAND
EST.
LAT.
LITH.
BELA.

Land use and agricultural distribution

- cattle
- fishing
- reindeer
- timber
- fodder
- major towns
- pasture
- cropland
- forest
- mountain region
- wetland
- tundra
- barren
- ice

The urban/rural population divide

urban 80%
rural 20%
0 10 20 30 40 50 60 70 80 90 100

Population density	Total land area
26 people per sq mile (10 people per sq km)	829,398 sq miles (2,148,700 sq km)

◀ ***Many rapids are*** *found along the 175 mile (280 km) course of the Suna river.*

Scale 1:6,000,000
Km
Miles
projection: Lambert Conformal Conic
Map key
Population
1 million to 5 million
500,000 to 1 million
100,000 to 500,000
50,000 to 100,000
10,000 to 50,000
below 10,000
Elevation
1000m / 3281ft
500m / 1640ft
250m / 820ft
100m / 328ft
sea level
Major industry and infrastructure
chemicals
coal
defence
engineering
food processing
hydro-electric power
mining
oil & gas
textiles
timber processing
major towns
international airports
major roads
major industrial areas
The transport network
53,700 miles (85,920 km)
None
10,300 miles (16,572 km)
12,500 miles (20,000 km)
BARENTS SEA
White Sea
FINLAND
RUSSIAN FEDERATION
Murmansk
Apatity
Archangel
Petrozavodsk
St Petersburg
Cherepovets
Vologda
Velikiy Novgorod
Pskov
Yaroslavl'
Kotlas
Kirov
Pechora
Amderma
Ostrov Vaygach
Ostrov Kolguyev
Ostrov Dolgiy
Yugorskiy Poluostrov
NENETSKIY AVTONOMNYY OKRUG
RESPUBLIKA KOMI
ARKHANGEL'SKAYA OBLAST'
KIROVSKAYA OBLAST'
PERMSKIY KRAY
UDMURTSKAYA RESPUBLIKA
NIZHEGORODSKAYA OBLAST'
KOSTROMSKAYA OBLAST'
RESPUBLIKA MARIY EL
RESPUBLIKA TATARSTAN
RESPUBLIKA BASHKORTOSTAN
SVERDLOVSKAYA OBLAST'
KHANTY-MANSIYSKIY AVTONOMNYY OKRUG
YAMALO-NENETSKIY AVTONOMNYY OKRUG
Bol'shezemel'skaya Tundra
Malozemel'skaya Tundra
Timanskiy Kryazh
Ural'skiye Gory
Polyarnyy Ural
Severnyy Ural
Sredniy Ural
Severnyye Uvaly
Gryada Chernysheva
Syktyvkar
Vorkuta
Ukhta
Inta
Usinsk
Nar'yan-Mar
Perm'
Solikamsk
Berezniki
Arctic Circle

◄ ***The Ural Mountains*** *(Ural'skiye Gory) form the traditional boundary between Europe and Asia. Elevations rarely exceed 6000 ft (1830 m). The region is extremely barren in the far northern latitudes.*

Transport and industry

The ports of St Petersburg, Murmansk and Archangel serve a regional economy led by large-scale resource extraction. Nickel, iron ore and apatite are mined in the Kola Peninsula *(Kol'skiy Poluostrov)*, and fossil fuels in the Pechora Basin. Paper production is central to Archangel's vast timber industry, while St Petersburg, drawing on ample labour, has become a major manufacturing centre.

Railways linking remote industrial centres with the region's ports are the principal means of supply, although the impressive system of canals, linking natural waterways, is used for freight haulage during the summer.

► ***Ice forces the*** *port at St Petersburg to close in winter, yet Murmansk, on the Barents Sea, remains open, its waters prevented from freezing by warmer ocean currents extending from the North Atlantic Drift.*

BALTIC SEA
LITHUANIA
POLAND
BELARUS
UKRAINE
RUSSIA
Sea of Azov
BLACK SEA
KALININGRADSKAYA OBLAST'
Kaliningrad
MOSKVA (MOSCOW)
Smolensk
Bryansk
Kursk
Voronezh
Rostov-na-Donu
Krasnodar
Sochi
Salt dome
Sedimentary strata
Salt dome is forced up and through the rock strata
Salts are forced upwards by denser overlying strata

▶ *Kaliningrad has been a Russian enclave since 1945. The port is an important centre for the Russian Federation's Baltic fishing fleet.*

◀ *St Basil's Cathedral, completed in 1561, stands in Moscow's Red Square next to the Kremlin; the original fortified stronghold of the city.*

Southern European Russia

This region, divided from Asia by desert, seas and mountains, has exerted a powerful influence both east and west since the 13th century. Over 70 years of Communist rule produced a highly urbanized, industrial society dominated by Moscow, which was the capital of the Soviet Union until 1991. Almost two-thirds of the Russian Federation's population live in this core area, with a relatively high *per capita* share of its wealth. However, the rapid growth of a market economy has caused great social upheaval, with rising crime and political instability.

The landscape

Ancient folds in the deep sedimentary strata of the North European Plain have created a sequence of high and low regions. The Central Russian Upland *(Srednerusskaya Vozvyshennost')* in the west is deeply incised by rivers draining into the lowland of the Oka and Don rivers. In the east the Volga, Europe's longest river, flows south to the Caspian Sea, dividing the Volga Uplands *(Privolzhskaya Vozvyshennost')* from the foothills of the Ural Mountains *(Ural'skiye Gory)*. The Caucasus mountains and the Black Sea form a natural border to the southwest.

▲ *A plantation of Scots pine helps consolidate the loose sandy soils of the Meshchera Lowland* (Meshcherskaya Nizina)*, which lies on the bed of an old glacial lake.*

The Smolensk-Moscow Upland *(Smolensko-Moskovskaya Vozvyshennost')* is a series of terminal moraine ridges marking the southern extent of the last glaciation.

Glacial till covers the bedrock to the north of the North European Plain, giving a gentle surface relief.

The lowland of the Oka and Don rivers lies over a broad trough, between the upfolds of the Volga Uplands *(Privolzhskaya Vozvyshennost')* to the east, and the Central Russian Upland *(Srednerusskaya Vozvyshennost')* to the west.

The southern Ural Mountains *(Ural'skiye Gory)* consist of several parallel ranges of ancient fold mountains running from north to south.

Central Russian Upland *(Srednerusskaya Vozvyshennost')*.

The flood plain of the Volga forms a long oasis of verdant vegetation, contrasting with the aridity of the surrounding Caspian hinterland.

The marshlands of the Volga Delta are visited by over 260 species of bird each year, migrating between South Africa and Arctic Siberia.

The Caspian Depression is a large downfold (or syncline) which became flooded, forming the Caspian Sea. The shoreline is 98 ft (30 m) below sea level.

Drifting sand occupies large areas of the south, forming dunes up to 50 ft (15 m) high.

◀ *The Caucasus mountains run from the Black Sea to the Caspian Sea. They include El'brus which, at 18,511 ft (5642 m), is the highest point in Europe. It is still uplifting at a rate of 0.4 inches (10 mm) per year.*

▲ *Salt domes, rounded hills up to 500 ft (150 m) high, are produced as less dense rock salts are displaced under the extreme pressure of denser, overlying strata and forced up towards the surface creating domes. They are widespread in the Caspian Depression.*

Scale 1:6,000,000
Km
Miles
projection: Lambert Conformal Conic
Map key
Population
above 5 million
1 million to 5 million
500,000 to 1 million
100,000 to 500,000
50,000 to 100,000
10,000 to 50,000
below 10,000
Elevation
4000m / 13,124ft
3000m / 9843ft
2000m / 6562ft
1000m / 3281ft
500m / 1640ft
250m / 820ft
100m / 328ft
sea level
RUSSIAN FEDERATION
KAZAKHSTAN
RESPUBLIKA KALMYKIYA
RESPUBLIKA BASHKORTOSTAN
RESPUBLIKA TATARSTAN
ORENBURGSKAYA OBLAST'
SARATOVSKAYA OBLAST'
SAMARSKAYA OBLAST'
VOLGOGRADSKAYA OBLAST'
ASTRAKHANSKAYA OBLAST'
KIROVSKAYA OBLAST'
UDMURTSKAYA RESPUBLIKA
Caspian Depression
Caspian Sea
Ural'skiye Gory
AZERBAIJAN
GEORGIA
Kazan'
Samara
Saratov
Volgograd
Astrakhan'
Orenburg
Ufa
Izhevsk
Penza
Makhachkala
Elista
144
136
136

Using the land

In the cold, humid north and in the southern Urals *(Ural'skiye Gory)*, small grains, potatoes and flax are commonly rotated with legumes which support livestock farming. The rich chernozem (or black earth) areas support diverse crops such as sugar beet, hemp, sunflowers, millet and vegetables. Further south, aridity restricts husbandry to extensive grazing, with intensive fruit and rice cultivation along the oasis of the Volga.

The urban/rural population divide

urban 71% — rural 29%

Population density	Total land area
119 people per sq mile (46 people per sq km)	705,916 sq miles (1,828,800 sq km)

Land use and agricultural distribution

sheep, flax, potatoes, rice, sunflowers, sugar beet, timber; capital cities, major towns; pasture, cropland, forest, wetland, mountain region, tundra

Transport and industry

Manufacturing is largely based around Moscow and the Volga region, which became a major industrial area during the Second World War. Both Moscow and Nizhniy Novgorod are centres of skilled labour for light manufacturing and engineering. Most of Russia's main chemical plants are located along the Volga, and one of the world's largest car factories was recently opened in Tol'yatti. Processing and machine construction plants use oil, gas and hydro-electric power from the Volga Basin and metallic minerals from the Urals *(Ural'skiye Gory)* and Kursk.

◀ Industrial plants are massed along the Volga. Environmental stress from decades of unbridled industrial development has prompted widespread concern about pollution levels.

The transport network

250,000 miles (402,000 km)	None
28,000 miles (44,800 km)	16,300 miles (26,080 km)

Seventy private and national flag airlines have been created from the reorganization of the state airline Aeroflot, which maintained the world's largest fleet of aircraft during the Soviet era.

Major industry and infrastructure

aerospace, car manufacture, chemicals, defence, electronics, engineering, gas, mining, oil, textiles; capital cities, major towns, international airports, major roads, major industrial areas

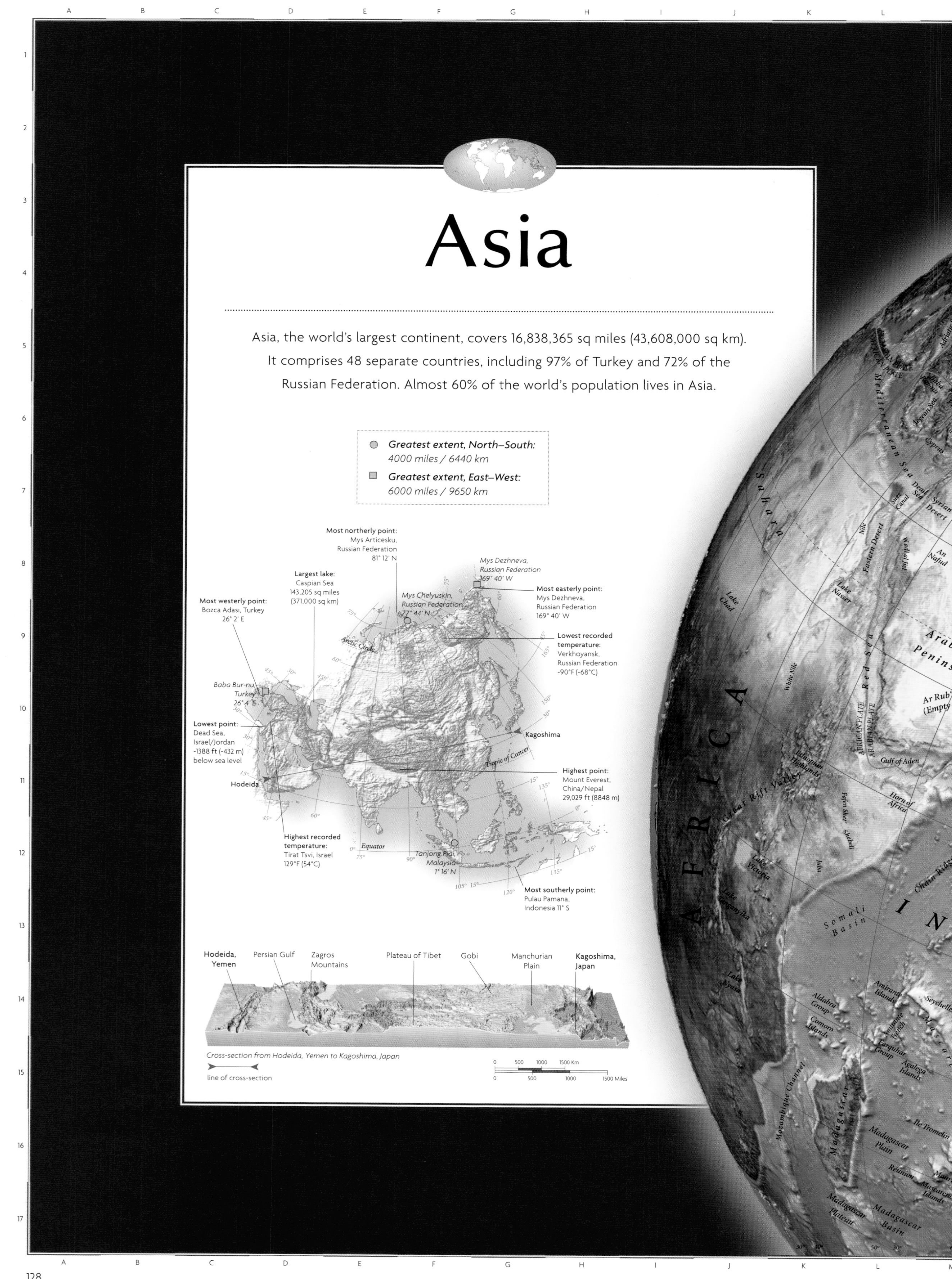

Asia

Asia, the world's largest continent, covers 16,838,365 sq miles (43,608,000 sq km). It comprises 48 separate countries, including 97% of Turkey and 72% of the Russian Federation. Almost 60% of the world's population lives in Asia.

Greatest extent, North–South:
4000 miles / 6440 km
Greatest extent, East–West:
6000 miles / 9650 km
Most northerly point:
Mys Articesku,
Russian Federation
81° 12' N
Largest lake:
Caspian Sea
143,205 sq miles
(371,000 sq km)
Most westerly point:
Bozca Adasi, Turkey
26° 2' E
Mys Dezhneva,
Russian Federation
169° 40' W
Mys Chelyuskin,
Russian Federation
77° 44' N
Most easterly point:
Mys Dezhneva,
Russian Federation
169° 40' W
Lowest recorded
temperature:
Verkhoyansk,
Russian Federation
-90°F (-68°C)
Arctic Circle
Baba Bur-nu,
Turkey
26° 4' E
Lowest point:
Dead Sea,
Israel/Jordan
-1388 ft (-432 m)
below sea level
Kagoshima
Tropic of Cancer
Highest point:
Mount Everest,
China/Nepal
29,029 ft (8848 m)
Hodeida
Highest recorded
temperature:
Tirat Tsvi, Israel
129°F (54°C)
Equator
Tanjong Piai,
Malaysia
1° 16' N
Most southerly point:
Pulau Pamana,
Indonesia 11° S
Hodeida,
Yemen
Persian Gulf
Zagros
Mountains
Plateau of Tibet
Gobi
Manchurian
Plain
Kagoshima,
Japan
Cross-section from Hodeida, Yemen to Kagoshima, Japan
line of cross-section
0 500 1000 1500 Km
0 500 1000 1500 Miles
Mediterranean Sea
Aegean Sea
Cyprus
Sahara
Suez Canal
Dead Sea
Syrian Desert
Nile
Eastern Desert
Wadi al Jarir
An Nafud
Lake Nasser
Lake Chad
Red Sea
Arabian Peninsula
White Nile
Ar Rub' al Khali (Empty Quarter)
AFRICA
AFRICAN PLATE
ARABIAN PLATE
Ethiopian Highlands
Gulf of Aden
Great Rift Valley
Horn of Africa
Jubba
Shabeelle
Lake Victoria
Lake Tanganyika
Somali Basin
Lake Nyasa
Amirante Islands
Seychelles
Aldabra Group
Comoro Islands
Farquhar Group
Agalega Islands
Mozambique Channel
Madagascar
Île Tromelin
Madagascar Plain
Réunion
Mascarene Islands
Madagascar Plateau
Madagascar Basin

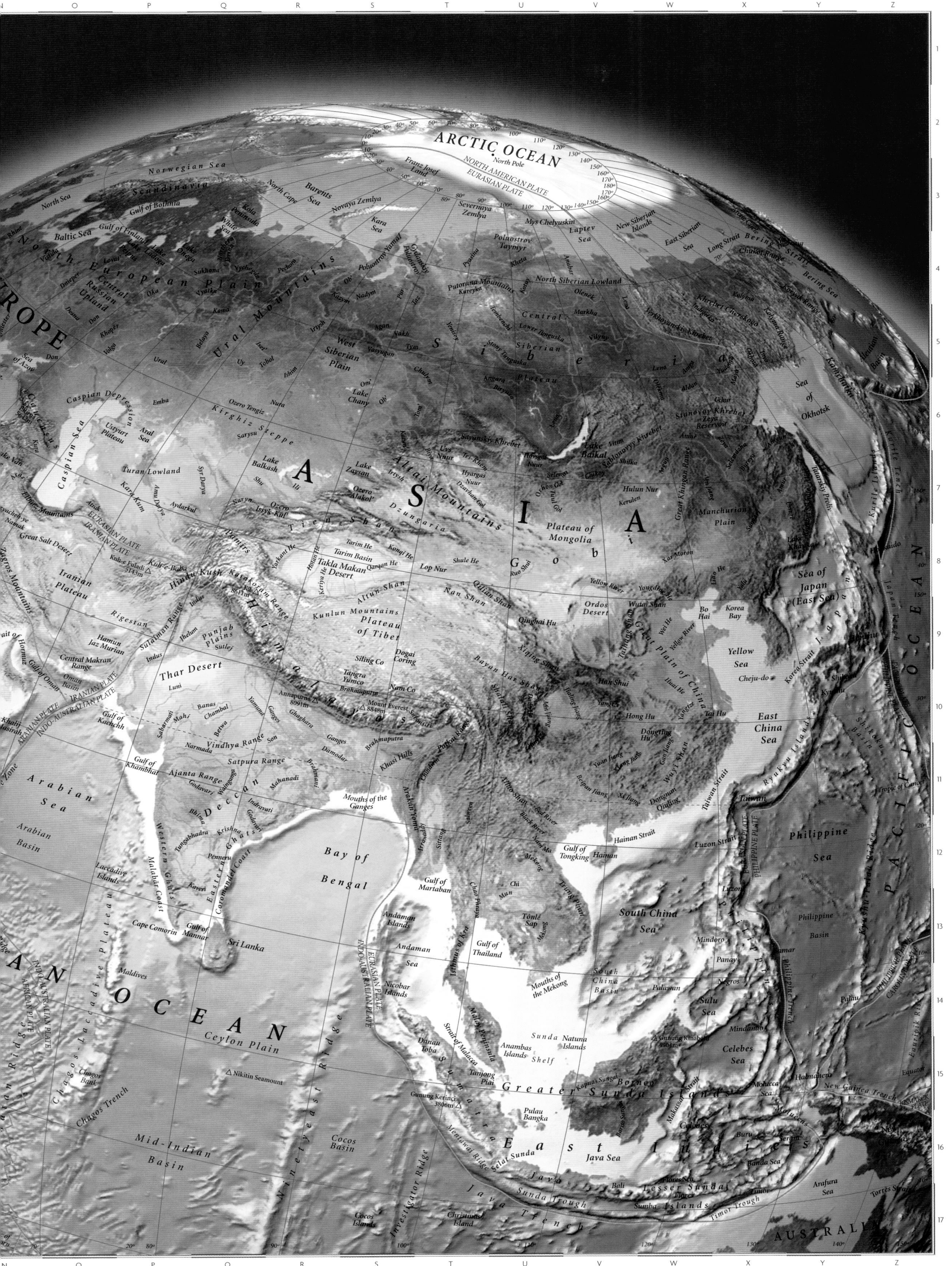
ARCTIC OCEAN
North Pole
NORTH AMERICAN PLATE
EURASIAN PLATE
Norwegian Sea
Barents Sea
Kara Sea
Laptev Sea
East Siberian Sea
Bering Sea
Sea of Okhotsk
North Sea
Baltic Sea
Scandinavia
North European Plain
Central Russian Upland
Ural Mountains
West Siberian Plain
Central Siberian Plateau
Siberia
North Siberian Lowland
Putorana Mountains
Novaya Zemlya
Severnaya Zemlya
Franz Josef Land
New Siberian Islands
EUROPE
ASIA
Caspian Sea
Caspian Depression
Aral Sea
Kirghiz Steppe
Turan Lowland
Lake Balkash
Lake Baikal
Altai Mountains
Tien Shan
Dzungaria
Plateau of Mongolia
Gobi
Tarim Basin
Takla Makan Desert
Pamirs
Hindu Kush
Karakoram Range
Iranian Plateau
Zagros Mountains
Kunlun Mountains
Plateau of Tibet
Himalayas
Mount Everest 8848m
Annapurna 8091m
Thar Desert
Deccan
Western Ghats
Eastern Ghats
Arabian Sea
Bay of Bengal
Sri Lanka
Manchurian Plain
Great Plain of China
Yellow Sea
East China Sea
Sea of Japan (East Sea)
Korea Bay
Bo Hai
Taiwan
South China Sea
Gulf of Tongking
Gulf of Thailand
Andaman Sea
Philippine Sea
Celebes Sea
Sulu Sea
Java Sea
Banda Sea
Arafura Sea
East Indies
Greater Sunda Islands
Lesser Sunda Islands
Sunda Shelf
Borneo
Sumatra
Malay Peninsula
Java Trench
Sunda Trough
Timor Trough
INDIAN OCEAN
Ceylon Plain
Mid-Indian Basin
Cocos Basin
Ninetyeast Ridge
Chagos-Laccadive Plateau
Chagos Trench
PACIFIC OCEAN
Kurile Islands
Japan
Ryukyu Islands
Philippines
Philippine Basin
Shikoku Basin
New Guinea Trench
AUSTRALIA
EURASIAN PLATE
INDO-AUSTRALIAN PLATE
ARABIAN PLATE
IRANIAN PLATE
PHILIPPINE PLATE

Physical Asia

The structure of Asia can be divided into two distinct regions. The landscape of northern Asia consists of old mountain chains, shields, plateaux and basins, like the Ural Mountains in the west and the Central Siberian Plateau to the east. To the south of this region, are a series of plateaux and basins, including the vast Plateau of Tibet and the Tarim Basin. In contrast, the landscapes of southern Asia are much younger, formed by tectonic activity beginning about 65 million years ago, leading to an almost continuous mountain chain running from Europe, across much of Asia, and culminating in the mighty Himalayan mountain belt, formed when the Indo-Australian Plate collided with the Eurasian Plate. They are still being uplifted today. North of the mountains lies a belt of deserts, including the Gobi and the Takla Makan. In the far south, tectonic activity has formed narrow island arcs, extending over 4000 miles (7000 km). To the west lies the Arabian Shield, once part of the African Plate. As it was rifted apart from Africa, the Arabian Plate collided with the Eurasian Plate, uplifting the Zagros Mountains.

Coastal Lowlands and Island Arcs

The coastal plains that fringe Southeast Asia contain many large delta systems, caused by high levels of rainfall and erosion of the Himalayas, the Plateau of Tibet and relict loess deposits. To the south is an extensive island archipelago, lying on the drowned Sunda Shelf. Most of these islands are volcanic in origin, caused by the subduction of the Indo-Australian Plate beneath the Eurasian Plate.

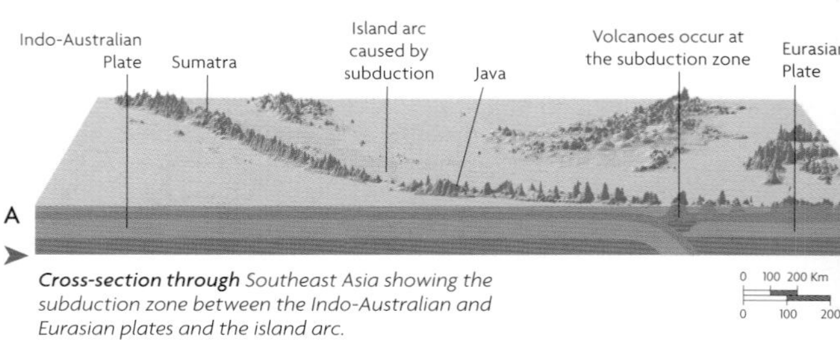
Indo-Australian Plate
Sumatra
Island arc caused by subduction
Java
Volcanoes occur at the subduction zone
Eurasian Plate
A

Cross-section through Southeast Asia showing the subduction zone between the Indo-Australian and Eurasian plates and the island arc.

0 100 200 Km
0 100 200

The Indian Shield and Himalayan System

The large shield area beneath the Indian subcontinent is between 2.5 and 3.5 billion years old. As the floor of the southern Indian Ocean spread, it pushed the Indian Shield north. This was eventually driven beneath the Plateau of Tibet. This process closed up the ancient Tethys Sea and uplifted the world's highest mountain chain, the Himalayas. Much of the uplifted rock strata was from the seabed of the Tethys Sea, partly accounting for the weakness of the rocks and the high levels of erosion found in the Himalayas.

Indo-Gangetic Depression
Crushed sediment from seabed of the Tethys Sea
Himalayas
Thrust zone
Plateau of Tibet
B B

Cross-section through the Himalayas showing thrust faulting of the rock strata.

0 50 100 Km
0 50 100 Miles

East Asian Plains and Uplands

Several, small, isolated shield areas, such as the Shandong Peninsula, are found in east Asia. Between these stable shield areas, large river systems like the Yangtze and the Yellow River have deposited thick layers of sediment, forming extensive alluvial plains. The largest of these is the Great Plain of China, the relief of which does not rise above 300 ft (100 m).

ARCTIC OCEAN
PACIFIC OCEAN
INDIAN OCEAN
EUROPE
AFRICA
AUSTRALIA
SIBERIAN PLATEAU & PLAIN
Central Siberian Plateau
West Siberian Plain
Siberia
EAST SIBERIAN MOUNTAINS
Ural Mountains
Kirghiz Steppe
TURAN BASIN & KAZAKH UPLANDS
Altai Mountains
Plateau of Mongolia
Gobi
CENTRAL ASIAN PLATEAUX & BASINS
Tien Shan
Takla Makan Desert
Kunlun Mountains
Qilian Shan
Plateau of Tibet
Himalayas
Mount Everest 8848m
K2 8611m
Khyber Pass 1080m
Hindu Kush
ARABIAN SHIELD
Syrian Desert
IRANIAN PLATEAU
Iranian Plateau
Zagros Mountains
Arabian Peninsula
Ar Rub' al Khali (Empty Quarter)
INDIAN SHIELD & HIMALAYAN SYSTEM
Thar Desert
Deccan
Western Ghats
Eastern Ghats
Sri Lanka
EAST ASIAN PLAINS & UPLANDS
COASTAL LOWLANDS & ISLAND ARCS
Great Plain of China
Sichuan Pendi
Shandong Peninsula
Kara Sea
Laptev Sea
East Siberian Sea
Chukchi Sea
Bering Sea
Sea of Okhotsk
Sea of Japan (East Sea)
Yellow Sea
East China Sea
South China Sea
Philippine Sea
Bay of Bengal
Arabian Sea
Black Sea
Caspian Sea
Aral Sea
Lake Balkash
Lake Baikal
Red Sea
Persian Gulf
Gulf of Oman
Gulf of Aden
Mediterranean Sea
Sea of Azov
Andaman Sea
Gulf of Thailand
Sulu Sea
Celebes Sea
Java Sea
Flores Sea
Banda Sea
Timor Sea
Arafura Sea
Coral Sea
Kamchatka
Sakhalin
Hokkaido
Honshu
Shikoku
Kyushu
Taiwan
Luzon
Philippines
Mindanao
Borneo
Sumatra
Java
New Guinea
Moluccas
Sunda Islands
NORTH AMERICAN PLATE
EURASIAN PLATE
PACIFIC PLATE
PHILIPPINE PLATE
INDO-AUSTRALIAN PLATE
ARABIAN PLATE
AFRICAN PLATE
ANATOLIAN PLATE
IRANIAN PLATE
CAROLINE PLATE

Map key

Elevation

6000m / 19,686ft
4000m / 13,124ft
3000m / 9843ft
2000m / 6562ft
1000m / 3281ft
500m / 1640ft
250m / 820ft
100m / 328ft
sea level

Plate margins (for explanation see page x)

constructive
destructive
conservative
uncertain

physiographic regions

line of cross-section

Scale 1:63,000,000

Km 0 250 500 1000 1500
Miles 0 250 500 1000 1500

projection: Lambert Azimuthal Equal Area

The Arabian Shield and Iranian Plateau

Approximately five million years ago, rifting of the continental crust split the Arabian Plate from the African Plate and flooded the Red Sea. As this rift spread, the Arabian Plate collided with the Eurasian Plate, transforming part of the Tethys seabed into the Zagros Mountains which run northwest-southeast across western Iran.

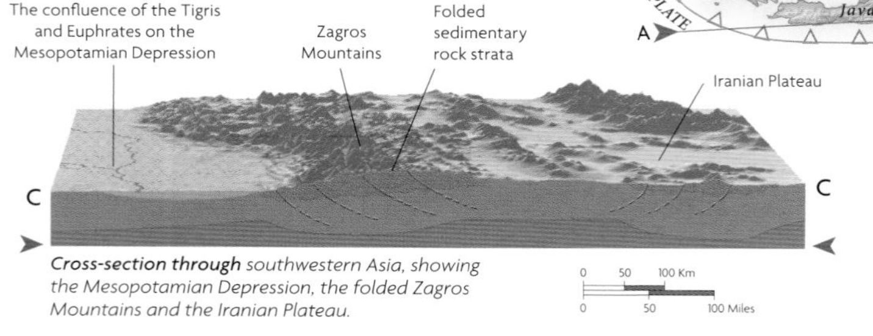
The confluence of the Tigris and Euphrates on the Mesopotamian Depression
Zagros Mountains
Folded sedimentary rock strata
Iranian Plateau
C
C

Cross-section through southwestern Asia, showing the Mesopotamian Depression, the folded Zagros Mountains and the Iranian Plateau.

0 50 100 Km
0 50 100 Miles

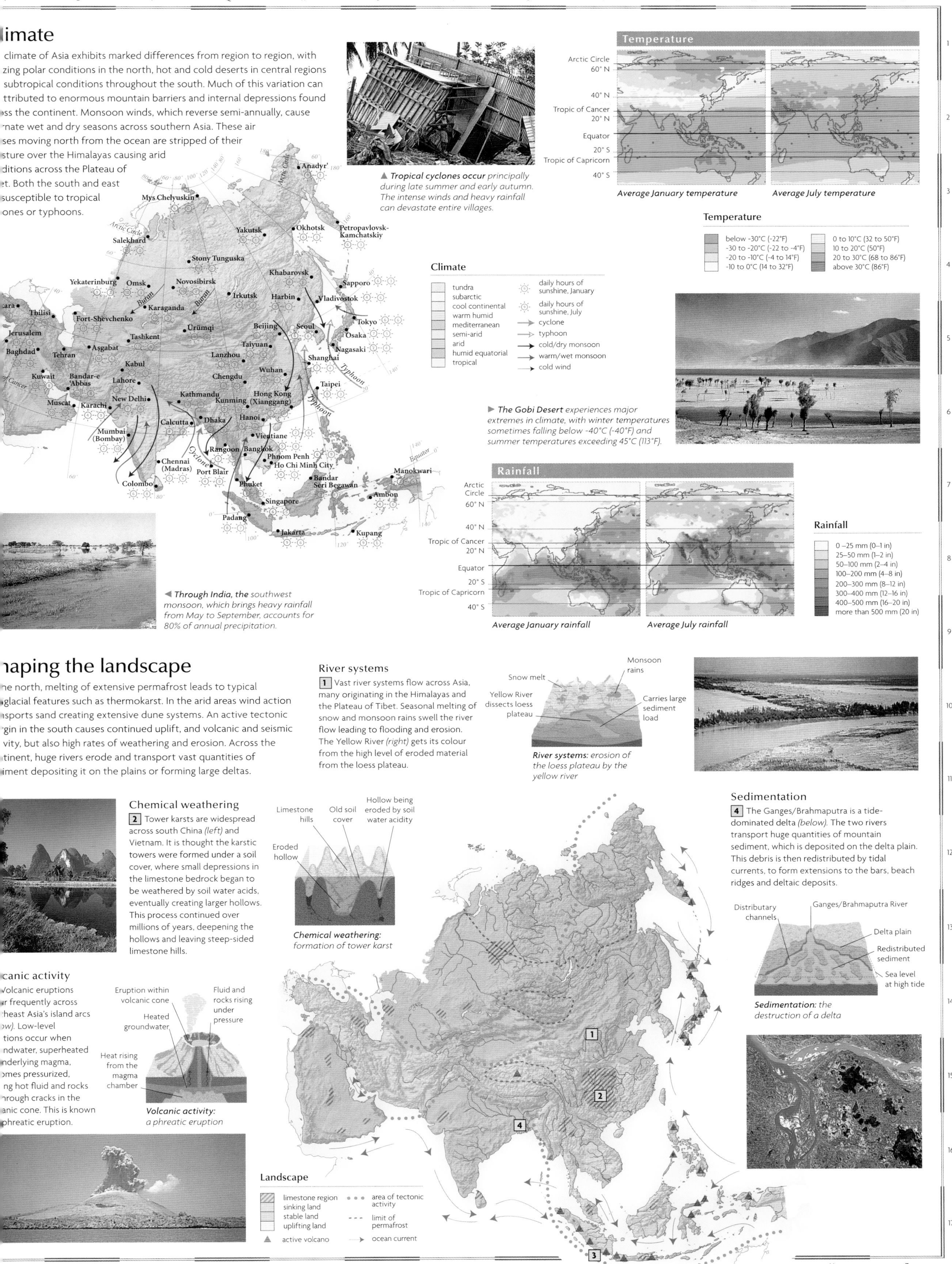

limate

climate of Asia exhibits marked differences from region to region, with zing polar conditions in the north, hot and cold deserts in central regions subtropical conditions throughout the south. Much of this variation can ttributed to enormous mountain barriers and internal depressions found ss the continent. Monsoon winds, which reverse semi-annually, cause rnate wet and dry seasons across southern Asia. These air ses moving north from the ocean are stripped of their sture over the Himalayas causing arid ditions across the Plateau of et. Both the south and east susceptible to tropical ones or typhoons.

▲ ***Tropical cyclones occur** principally during late summer and early autumn. The intense winds and heavy rainfall can devastate entire villages.*

Temperature
Arctic Circle
60° N
40° N
Tropic of Cancer
20° N
Equator
20° S
Tropic of Capricorn
40° S
Average January temperature
Average July temperature
Temperature
below -30°C (-22°F)
-30 to -20°C (-22 to -4°F)
-20 to -10°C (-4 to 14°F)
-10 to 0°C (14 to 32°F)
0 to 10°C (32 to 50°F)
10 to 20°C (50°F)
20 to 30°C (68 to 86°F)
above 30°C (86°F)
Climate
tundra
subarctic
cool continental
warm humid
mediterranean
semi-arid
arid
humid equatorial
tropical
daily hours of sunshine, January
daily hours of sunshine, July
cyclone
typhoon
cold/dry monsoon
warm/wet monsoon
cold wind
Anadyr'
Mys Chelyuskin
Salekhard
Yakutsk
Okhotsk
Petropavlovsk-Kamchatskiy
Stony Tunguska
Khabarovsk
Yekaterinburg
Omsk
Novosibirsk
Irkutsk
Harbin
Sapporo
Vladivostok
Tbilisi
Fort-Shevchenko
Karaganda
Tokyo
Jerusalem
Tashkent
Ürümqi
Beijing
Seoul
Osaka
Baghdad
Tehran
Asgabat
Taiyuan
Nagasaki
Lanzhou
Shanghai
Kuwait
Bandar-e 'Abbas
Kabul
Wuhan
Typhoon
Lahore
Chengdu
Taipei
Muscat
Karachi
New Delhi
Kathmandu
Kunming
Hong Kong (Xianggang)
Calcutta
Dhaka
Hanoi
Mumbai (Bombay)
Vientiane
Rangoon
Bangkok
Phnom Penh
Ho Chi Minh City
Chennai (Madras)
Port Blair
Cyclone
Manokwari
Colombo
Phuket
Bandar Seri Begawan
Ambon
Singapore
Padang
Jakarta
Kupang
Buran

▶ ***The Gobi Desert** experiences major extremes in climate, with winter temperatures sometimes falling below -40°C (-40°F) and summer temperatures exceeding 45°C (113°F).*

Rainfall
Arctic Circle
60° N
40° N
Tropic of Cancer
20° N
Equator
20° S
Tropic of Capricorn
40° S
Average January rainfall
Average July rainfall
Rainfall
0–25 mm (0–1 in)
25–50 mm (1–2 in)
50–100 mm (2–4 in)
100–200 mm (4–8 in)
200–300 mm (8–12 in)
300–400 mm (12–16 in)
400–500 mm (16–20 in)
more than 500 mm (20 in)

◀ ***Through India, the** southwest monsoon, which brings heavy rainfall from May to September, accounts for 80% of annual precipitation.*

haping the landscape

ne north, melting of extensive permafrost leads to typical glacial features such as thermokarst. In the arid areas wind action nsports sand creating extensive dune systems. An active tectonic gin in the south causes continued uplift, and volcanic and seismic vity, but also high rates of weathering and erosion. Across the tinent, huge rivers erode and transport vast quantities of iment depositing it on the plains or forming large deltas.

River systems

1 Vast river systems flow across Asia, many originating in the Himalayas and the Plateau of Tibet. Seasonal melting of snow and monsoon rains swell the river flow leading to flooding and erosion. The Yellow River *(right)* gets its colour from the high level of eroded material from the loess plateau.

Monsoon rains
Snow melt
Yellow River dissects loess plateau
Carries large sediment load

***River systems:** erosion of the loess plateau by the yellow river*

Chemical weathering

2 Tower karsts are widespread across south China *(left)* and Vietnam. It is thought the karstic towers were formed under a soil cover, where small depressions in the limestone bedrock began to be weathered by soil water acids, eventually creating larger hollows. This process continued over millions of years, deepening the hollows and leaving steep-sided limestone hills.

Limestone hills
Old soil cover
Hollow being eroded by soil water acidity
Eroded hollow

***Chemical weathering:** formation of tower karst*

Sedimentation

4 The Ganges/Brahmaputra is a tide-dominated delta *(below)*. The two rivers transport huge quantities of mountain sediment, which is deposited on the delta plain. This debris is then redistributed by tidal currents, to form extensions to the bars, beach ridges and deltaic deposits.

Distributary channels
Ganges/Brahmaputra River
Delta plain
Redistributed sediment
Sea level at high tide

***Sedimentation:** the destruction of a delta*

canic activity

Volcanic eruptions r frequently across heast Asia's island arcs ow). Low-level tions occur when ndwater, superheated nderlying magma, omes pressurized, ng hot fluid and rocks hrough cracks in the anic cone. This is known phreatic eruption.

Eruption within volcanic cone
Fluid and rocks rising under pressure
Heated groundwater
Heat rising from the magma chamber

***Volcanic activity:** a phreatic eruption*

1
2
3
4
Landscape
limestone region
sinking land
stable land
uplifting land
active volcano
area of tectonic activity
limit of permafrost
ocean current

Political Asia

Asia is the world's largest continent, encompassing many different and discrete realms, from the desert Arab lands of the southwest to the subtropical archipelago of Indonesia; from the vast barren wastes of Siberia to the fertile river valleys of China and South Asia, seats of some of the world's most ancient civilizations. The collapse of the Soviet Union has fragmented the north of the continent into the Siberian portion of the Russian Federation, and the new republics of Central Asia. Strong religious traditions heavily influence the politics of South and Southwest Asia. Hindu and Muslim rivalries threaten to upset the political equilibrium in South Asia where India – in terms of population – remains the world's largest democracy. Communist China, another population giant, is reasserting its position as a world political and economic power, while on its doorstep, the dynamic Pacific Rim countries, led by Japan, continue to assert their worldwide economic force.

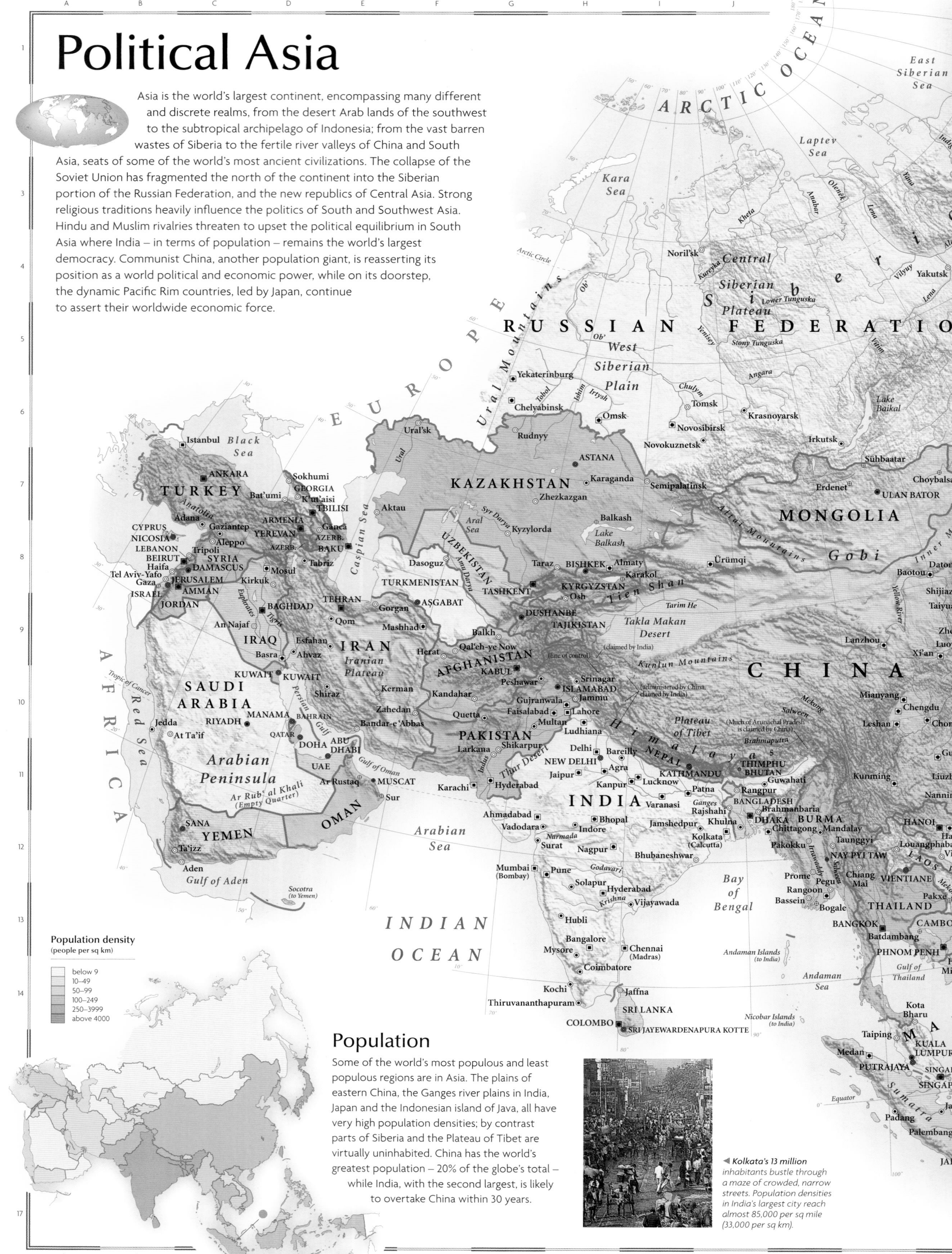
ARCTIC OCEAN
East Siberian Sea
Laptev Sea
Kara Sea
Arctic Circle
Noril'sk
Central Siberian Plateau
Lower Tunguska
Stony Tunguska
Angara
Yakutsk
RUSSIAN FEDERATION
West Siberian Plain
Ural Mountains
EUROPE
Yekaterinburg
Chelyabinsk
Tomsk
Omsk
Krasnoyarsk
Novosibirsk
Novokuznetsk
Irkutsk
Lake Baikal
Süchbaatar
Ural'sk
Rudnyy
ASTANA
Karaganda
Semipalatinsk
KAZAKHSTAN
Zhezkazgan
Aral Sea
Syr Darya
Kyzylorda
Balkash
Lake Balkash
MONGOLIA
ULAN BATOR
Erdenet
Choybalsan
Altai Mountains
Gobi
Istanbul
Black Sea
ANKARA
TURKEY
Anatolia
Sokhumi
GEORGIA
Bat'umi
K'ut'aisi
TBILISI
ARMENIA
YEREVAN
Gäncä
AZERB.
BAKU
Aktau
Caspian Sea
CYPRUS
NICOSIA
Adana
Gaziantep
Aleppo
LEBANON
BEIRUT
Tripoli
SYRIA
DAMASCUS
Haifa
Tel Aviv-Yafo
Gaza
JERUSALEM
AMMAN
ISRAEL
JORDAN
Mosul
Tabriz
Kirkuk
BAGHDAD
Euphrates
Tigris
TEHRAN
Qom
IRAQ
An Najaf
Basra
Esfahan
Ahvaz
IRAN
Iranian Plateau
KUWAIT
Shiraz
Kerman
Zahedan
Bandar-e 'Abbas
Dasoguz
UZBEKISTAN
Amu Darya
TURKMENISTAN
ASGABAT
Gorgan
Mashhad
TASHKENT
BISHKEK
Almaty
Karakol
KYRGYZSTAN
Osh
DUSHANBE
TAJIKISTAN
Taraz
Tien Shan
Ürümqi
Tarim He
Takla Makan Desert
Balkh
Herat
Qal'eh-ye Now
AFGHANISTAN
KABUL
Kandahar
Peshawar
ISLAMABAD
Srinagar
Jammu
Quetta
Gujranwala
Faisalabad
Lahore
Multan
PAKISTAN
Larkana
Shikarpur
Indus
Thar Desert
Karachi
Hyderabad
Kunlun Mountains
Himalaya
Plateau of Tibet
CHINA
Ludhiana
Delhi
NEW DELHI
Bareilly
Agra
Jaipur
Kanpur
Lucknow
NEPAL
KATHMANDU
THIMPHU
BHUTAN
Guwahati
Patna
Varanasi
INDIA
Ganges
Rajshahi
BANGLADESH
DHAKA
Khulna
Rangpur
Brahmanbaria
Chittagong
Ahmadabad
Vadodara
Bhopal
Indore
Narmada
Surat
Nagpur
Jamshedpur
Kolkata (Calcutta)
Bhubaneshwar
Mumbai (Bombay)
Pune
Godavari
Solapur
Hyderabad
Krishna
Vijayawada
Hubli
Bangalore
Mysore
Chennai (Madras)
Coimbatore
Kochi
Thiruvananthapuram
Jaffna
SRI LANKA
COLOMBO
SRI JAYEWARDENAPURA KOTTE
Bay of Bengal
Andaman Islands (to India)
Nicobar Islands (to India)
Andaman Sea
BURMA
Mandalay
Taunggyi
Pakokku
NAY PYI TAW
Prome
Pegu
Rangoon
Bassein
Bogale
Chiang Mai
THAILAND
BANGKOK
Batdambang
PHNOM PENH
Gulf of Thailand
VIENTIANE
LAOS
HANOI
Luang Prabang
Kunming
Lanzhou
Xi'an
Mianyang
Chengdu
Leshan
Baotou
Inner Mongolia
Yellow River
Mekong
Salween
Brahmaputra
SAUDI ARABIA
RIYADH
Jedda
At Ta'if
MANAMA
BAHRAIN
QATAR
DOHA
ABU DHABI
UAE
Persian Gulf
Gulf of Oman
Ar Rustaq
MUSCAT
Sur
OMAN
Arabian Peninsula
Ar Rub' al Khali (Empty Quarter)
SANA
YEMEN
Ta'izz
Aden
Gulf of Aden
Socotra (to Yemen)
Red Sea
AFRICA
Tropic of Cancer
Arabian Sea
INDIAN OCEAN
Kota Bharu
Taiping
KUALA LUMPUR
Medan
PUTRAJAYA
Sumatra
Padang
Palembang
Equator
Population density (people per sq km)
below 9
10–49
50–99
100–249
250–3999
above 4000

Population

Some of the world's most populous and least populous regions are in Asia. The plains of eastern China, the Ganges river plains in India, Japan and the Indonesian island of Java, all have very high population densities; by contrast parts of Siberia and the Plateau of Tibet are virtually uninhabited. China has the world's greatest population – 20% of the globe's total – while India, with the second largest, is likely to overtake China within 30 years.

◀ *Kolkata's 13 million inhabitants bustle through a maze of crowded, narrow streets. Population densities in India's largest city reach almost 85,000 per sq mile (33,000 per sq km).*

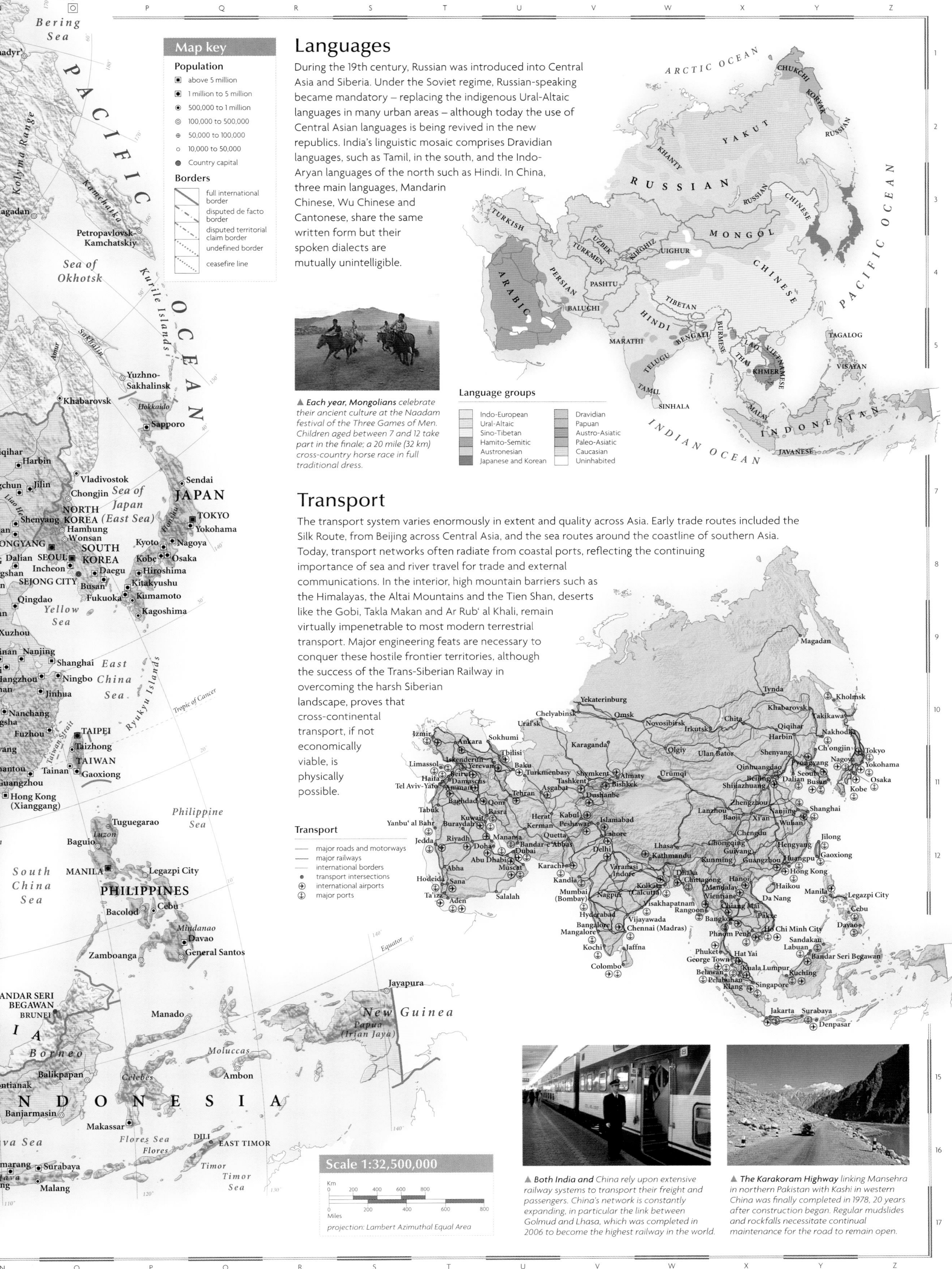
Map key
Population
above 5 million
1 million to 5 million
500,000 to 1 million
100,000 to 500,000
50,000 to 100,000
10,000 to 50,000
Country capital
Borders
full international border
disputed de facto border
disputed territorial claim border
undefined border
ceasefire line
Language groups
Indo-European
Ural-Altaic
Sino-Tibetan
Hamito-Semitic
Austronesian
Japanese and Korean
Dravidian
Papuan
Austro-Asiatic
Paleo-Asiatic
Caucasian
Uninhabited
Transport
major roads and motorways
major railways
international borders
transport intersections
international airports
major ports
Scale 1:32,500,000
projection: Lambert Azimuthal Equal Area

Languages

During the 19th century, Russian was introduced into Central Asia and Siberia. Under the Soviet regime, Russian-speaking became mandatory – replacing the indigenous Ural-Altaic languages in many urban areas – although today the use of Central Asian languages is being revived in the new republics. India's linguistic mosaic comprises Dravidian languages, such as Tamil, in the south, and the Indo-Aryan languages of the north such as Hindi. In China, three main languages, Mandarin Chinese, Wu Chinese and Cantonese, share the same written form but their spoken dialects are mutually unintelligible.

▲ *Each year, Mongolians celebrate their ancient culture at the Naadam festival of the Three Games of Men. Children aged between 7 and 12 take part in the finale; a 20 mile (32 km) cross-country horse race in full traditional dress.*

Transport

The transport system varies enormously in extent and quality across Asia. Early trade routes included the Silk Route, from Beijing across Central Asia, and the sea routes around the coastline of southern Asia. Today, transport networks often radiate from coastal ports, reflecting the continuing importance of sea and river travel for trade and external communications. In the interior, high mountain barriers such as the Himalayas, the Altai Mountains and the Tien Shan, deserts like the Gobi, Takla Makan and Ar Rubʻ al Khali, remain virtually impenetrable to most modern terrestrial transport. Major engineering feats are necessary to conquer these hostile frontier territories, although the success of the Trans-Siberian Railway in overcoming the harsh Siberian landscape, proves that cross-continental transport, if not economically viable, is physically possible.

▲ *Both India and China rely upon extensive railway systems to transport their freight and passengers. China's network is constantly expanding, in particular the link between Golmud and Lhasa, which was completed in 2006 to become the highest railway in the world.*

▲ *The Karakoram Highway linking Mansehra in northern Pakistan with Kashi in western China was finally completed in 1978, 20 years after construction began. Regular mudslides and rockfalls necessitate continual maintenance for the road to remain open.*

Asian resources

Although agriculture remains the economic mainstay of most Asian countries, the number of people employed in agriculture has steadily declined, as new industries have been developed during the past 30 years. China, Indonesia, Malaysia, Thailand and Turkey have all experienced far-reaching structural change in their economies, while the breakup of the Soviet Union has created a new economic challenge in the Central Asian republics. The countries of the Persian Gulf illustrate the rapid transformation from rural nomadism to modern, urban society which oil wealth has brought to parts of the continent. Asia's most economically dynamic countries, Japan, Singapore, South Korea, and Taiwan, fringe the Pacific Ocean and are known as the Pacific Rim. In contrast, other Southeast Asian countries like Laos and Cambodia remain both economically and industrially underdeveloped.

Industry

East Asian industry leads the continent in both productivity and efficiency; electronics, hi-tech industries, car manufacture and shipbuilding are important. The so-called economic 'tigers' of the Pacific Rim are Japan, South Korea and Taiwan and in recent years China has rediscovered its potential as an economic superpower. Heavy industries such as engineering, chemicals, and steel typify the industrial complexes along the corridor created by the Trans-Siberian Railway, the Fergana Valley in Central Asia, and also much of the huge industrial plain of east China. The discovery of oil in the Persian Gulf has brought immense wealth to countries that previously relied on subsistence agriculture on marginal desert land.

Standard of living

Despite Japan's high standards of living, and Southwest Asia's oil-derived wealth, immense disparities exist across the continent. Afghanistan remains one of the world's most underdeveloped nations, as do the mountain states of Nepal and Bhutan. Further rapid population growth is exacerbating poverty and overcrowding in many parts of India and Bangladesh.

Standard of living
(UN human development index)

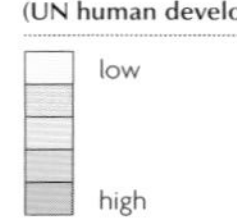

low
high

▲ **On a small** island at the southern tip of the Malay Peninsula lies Singapore, one of the Pacific Rim's most vibrant economic centres. Multinational banking and finance form the core of the city's wealth.

GNI per capita (US$)

- below 1999
- 2000–4999
- 5000–9999
- 10,000–19,999
- 20,000–24,999
- above 25,000

Industry

- aerospace
- brewing
- car/vehicle manufacture
- cement
- chemicals
- electronics
- engineering
- finance
- fish processing
- food processing
- hi-tech industry
- iron & steel
- pharmaceuticals
- printing & publishing
- shipbuilding
- sugar processing
- tea processing
- textiles
- timber processing
- tobacco processing
- coal
- oil
- gas
- industrial cities
- major industrial areas

ARCTIC OCEAN
PACIFIC OCEAN
Sea of Okhotsk
RUSSIAN FEDERATION
KAZAKHSTAN
MONGOLIA
CHINA
JAPAN
NORTH KOREA
SOUTH KOREA
TURKEY
IRAQ
IRAN
SAUDI ARABIA
AFGHANISTAN
PAKISTAN
INDIA
Arabian Sea
INDIAN OCEAN
South China Sea
MALAYSIA
INDONESIA

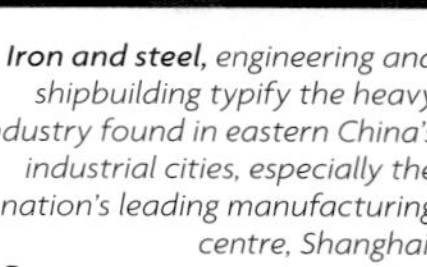

▲ **Iron and steel,** engineering and shipbuilding typify the heavy industry found in eastern China's industrial cities, especially the nation's leading manufacturing centre, Shanghai.

◀ **Traditional industries are** still crucial to many rural economies across Asia. Here, on the Vietnamese coast, salt has been extracted from seawater by evaporation and is being loaded into a van to take to market.

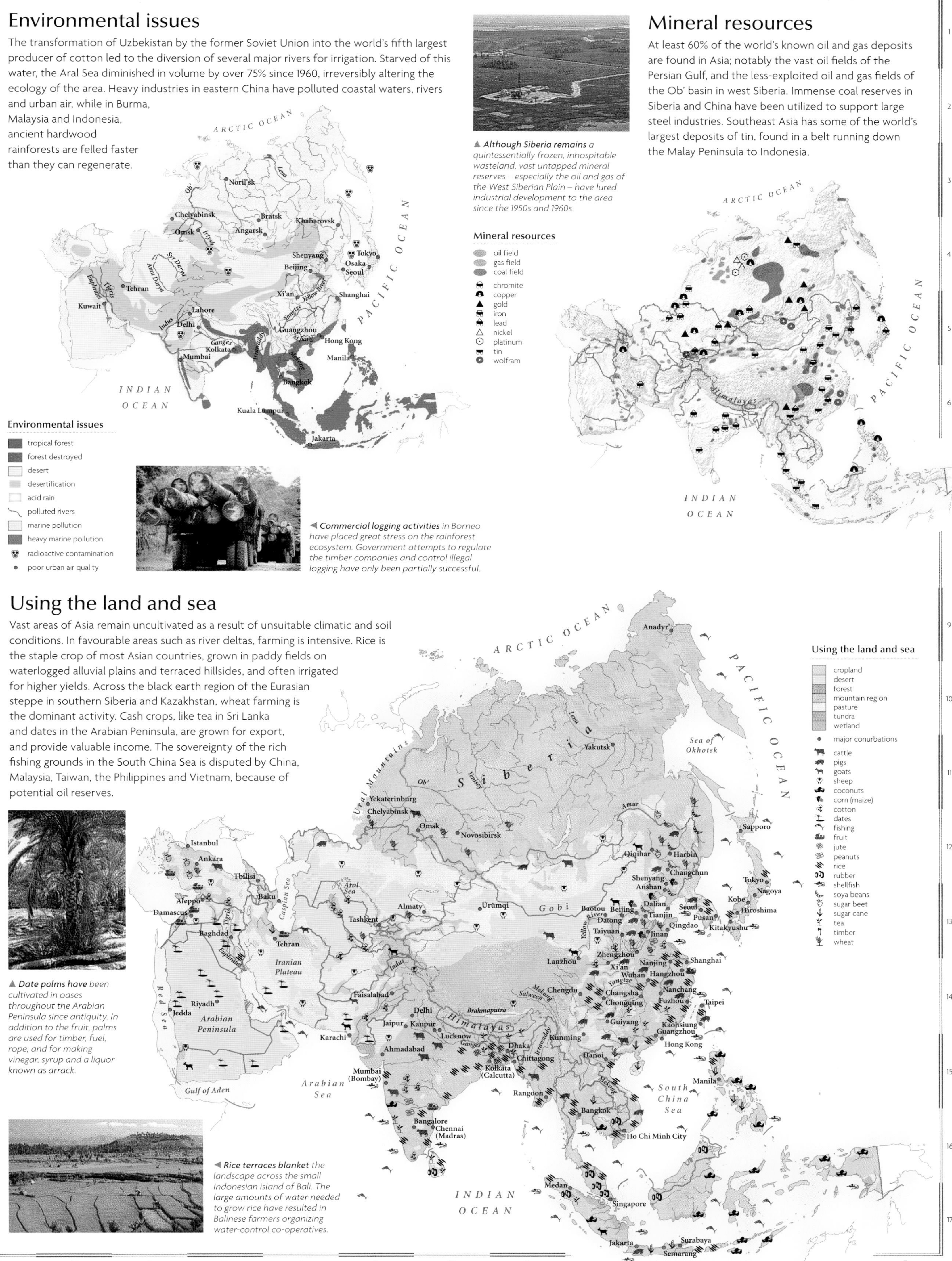

Environmental issues

The transformation of Uzbekistan by the former Soviet Union into the world's fifth largest producer of cotton led to the diversion of several major rivers for irrigation. Starved of this water, the Aral Sea diminished in volume by over 75% since 1960, irreversibly altering the ecology of the area. Heavy industries in eastern China have polluted coastal waters, rivers and urban air, while in Burma, Malaysia and Indonesia, ancient hardwood rainforests are felled faster than they can regenerate.

ARCTIC OCEAN
PACIFIC OCEAN
INDIAN OCEAN
Noril'sk
Chelyabinsk
Omsk
Bratsk
Angarsk
Khabarovsk
Shenyang
Beijing
Tokyo
Osaka
Seoul
Tehran
Kuwait
Xi'an
Shanghai
Lahore
Delhi
Guangzhou
Hong Kong
Kolkata
Mumbai
Manila
Bangkok
Kuala Lumpur
Jakarta
Environmental issues
tropical forest
forest destroyed
desert
desertification
acid rain
polluted rivers
marine pollution
heavy marine pollution
radioactive contamination
poor urban air quality

▲ *Although Siberia remains a quintessentially frozen, inhospitable wasteland, vast untapped mineral reserves – especially the oil and gas of the West Siberian Plain – have lured industrial development to the area since the 1950s and 1960s.*

◀ ***Commercial logging activities** in Borneo have placed great stress on the rainforest ecosystem. Government attempts to regulate the timber companies and control illegal logging have only been partially successful.*

Mineral resources

At least 60% of the world's known oil and gas deposits are found in Asia; notably the vast oil fields of the Persian Gulf, and the less-exploited oil and gas fields of the Ob' basin in west Siberia. Immense coal reserves in Siberia and China have been utilized to support large steel industries. Southeast Asia has some of the world's largest deposits of tin, found in a belt running down the Malay Peninsula to Indonesia.

Mineral resources
oil field
gas field
coal field
chromite
copper
gold
iron
lead
nickel
platinum
tin
wolfram
ARCTIC OCEAN
PACIFIC OCEAN
INDIAN OCEAN
Himalayas

Using the land and sea

Vast areas of Asia remain uncultivated as a result of unsuitable climatic and soil conditions. In favourable areas such as river deltas, farming is intensive. Rice is the staple crop of most Asian countries, grown in paddy fields on waterlogged alluvial plains and terraced hillsides, and often irrigated for higher yields. Across the black earth region of the Eurasian steppe in southern Siberia and Kazakhstan, wheat farming is the dominant activity. Cash crops, like tea in Sri Lanka and dates in the Arabian Peninsula, are grown for export, and provide valuable income. The sovereignty of the rich fishing grounds in the South China Sea is disputed by China, Malaysia, Taiwan, the Philippines and Vietnam, because of potential oil reserves.

Using the land and sea
cropland
desert
forest
mountain region
pasture
tundra
wetland
major conurbations
cattle
pigs
goats
sheep
coconuts
corn (maize)
cotton
dates
fishing
fruit
jute
peanuts
rice
rubber
shellfish
soya beans
sugar beet
sugar cane
tea
timber
wheat
ARCTIC OCEAN
PACIFIC OCEAN
INDIAN OCEAN
Siberia
Sea of Okhotsk
Anadyr'
Yakutsk
Ural Mountains
Ob'
Yenisey
Lena
Amur
Yekaterinburg
Chelyabinsk
Omsk
Novosibirsk
Sapporo
Istanbul
Ankara
Tbilisi
Baku
Caspian Sea
Aral Sea
Aleppo
Damascus
Baghdad
Tigris
Euphrates
Tehran
Iranian Plateau
Tashkent
Almaty
Ürümqi
Gobi
Qiqihar
Harbin
Changchun
Shenyang
Anshan
Dalian
Baotou
Beijing
Tianjin
Datong
Taiyuan
Jinan
Qingdao
Seoul
Pusan
Tokyo
Nagoya
Kobe
Hiroshima
Kitakyushu
Lanzhou
Zhengzhou
Xi'an
Nanjing
Shanghai
Wuhan
Hangzhou
Chengdu
Changsha
Chongqing
Nanchang
Fuzhou
Taipei
Guiyang
Kaohsiung
Guangzhou
Hong Kong
Kunming
Hanoi
Red Sea
Riyadh
Jedda
Arabian Peninsula
Gulf of Aden
Arabian Sea
Karachi
Faisalabad
Indus
Delhi
Jaipur
Kanpur
Lucknow
Himalayas
Brahmaputra
Ganges
Ahmadabad
Dhaka
Chittagong
Kolkata (Calcutta)
Mumbai (Bombay)
Rangoon
Bangalore
Chennai (Madras)
Bangkok
Ho Chi Minh City
Mekong
Salween
Irrawaddy
South China Sea
Manila
Medan
Singapore
Jakarta
Semarang
Surabaya

▲ ***Date palms have** been cultivated in oases throughout the Arabian Peninsula since antiquity. In addition to the fruit, palms are used for timber, fuel, rope, and for making vinegar, syrup and a liquor known as arrack.*

◀ ***Rice terraces blanket** the landscape across the small Indonesian island of Bali. The large amounts of water needed to grow rice have resulted in Balinese farmers organizing water-control co-operatives.*

Turkey & the Caucasus

ARMENIA, AZERBAIJAN, GEORGIA, TURKEY

This region occupies the fragmented junction between Europe, Asia and the Russian Federation. Sunni Islam provides a common identity for the secular state of Turkey, which the revered leader Kemal Atatürk established from the remnants of the Ottoman Empire after the First World War. Turkey has a broad resource base and expanding trade links with Europe, but the east is relatively undeveloped and strife between the state and a large Kurdish minority has yet to be resolved. Georgia is similarly challenged by ethnic separatism, while the Christian state of Armenia and the mainly Muslim and oil-rich Azerbaijan are locked in conflict over the territory of Nagorno-Karabakh.

Transport and industry

Turkey leads the region's well-diversified economy. Petrochemicals, textiles, engineering and food processing are the main industries. Azerbaijan is able to export oil, while the other states rely heavily on hydro-electric power and imported fuel. Georgia produces precision machinery. War and earthquake damage have devastated Armenia's infrastructure.

▲ *Azerbaijan has substantial oil reserves, located in and around the Caspian Sea. They were some of the earliest oilfields in the world to be exploited.*

Major industry and infrastructure

- carpet weaving
- cement
- chemicals
- coal
- engineering
- food processing
- oil
- textiles
- tourism
- vehicle manufacture
- capital cities
- major towns
- international airports
- major roads
- major industrial areas

The transport network

- 114,867 miles (184,882 km)
- 5778 miles (9300 km)
- 8120 miles (13,069 km)
- 745 miles (1200 km)

Physical and political barriers have severely limited communications between Armenia, Georgia and Azerbaijan. Turkey has a relatively well-developed transport network.

Using the land and sea

Turkey is largely self-sufficient in food. The irrigated Black Sea coastlands have the world's highest yields of hazelnuts. Tobacco, cotton, sultanas, tea and figs are the region's main cash crops and a great range of fruit and vegetables are grown. Wine grapes are among the labour-intensive crops which allow full use of limited agricultural land in the Caucasus. Sturgeon fishing is particularly important in Azerbaijan.

Land use and agricultural distribution

- cattle
- goats
- cotton
- fishing
- fruit
- hazelnuts
- olives
- sugar beet
- tobacco
- vineyards
- capital cities
- major towns
- pasture
- cropland
- forest

The urban/rural population divide

urban 72% — rural 28%

Population density	Total land area
238 people per sq mile (92 people per sq km)	368,912 sq miles (955,730 sq km)

▲ *For many centuries, Istanbul has held tremendous strategic importance as a crucial gateway between Europe and Asia. Founded by the Greeks as Byzantium, the city became the centre of the East Roman Empire and was known as Constantinople to the Romans. From the 15th century onwards the city became the centre of the great Ottoman Empire.*

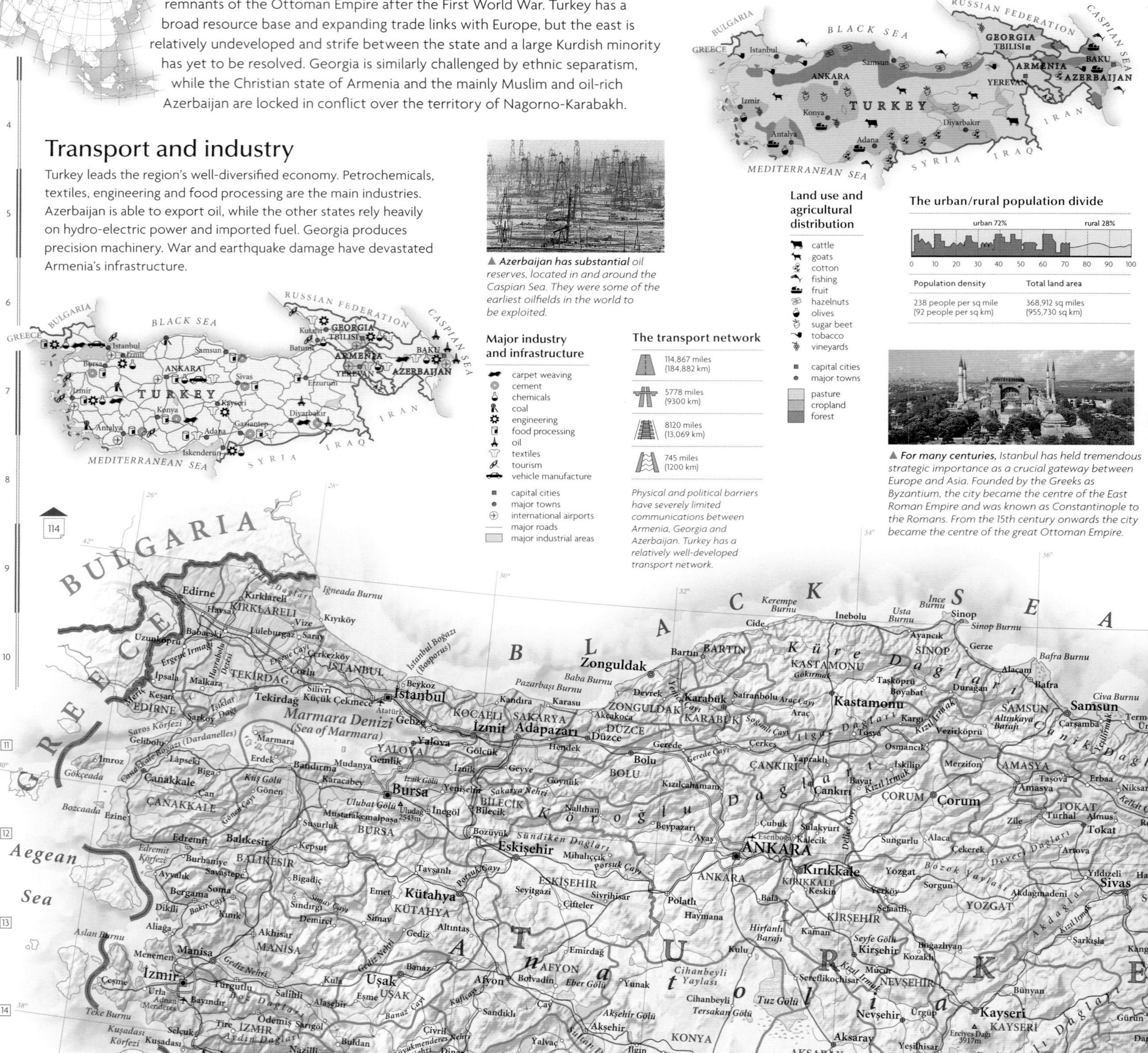

BULGARIA
GREECE
BLACK SEA
Aegean Sea
MEDITERRANEAN SEA
İstanbul
Ankara
İzmir
Bursa
Konya
Antalya
Adana
Kayseri
Samsun
Mersin (İçel)
Marmara Denizi (Sea of Marmara)

114
120

The landscape

The deeply-eroded hills and salty basins of the Anatolian Plateau are bordered by several mountain ranges along the Black Sea coast, and the limestone Taurus Mountains *(Toros Daglari)* in the south. A lowland trough divides the Caucasus and the Lesser Caucasus, which form a formidable barrier of peaks in the north.

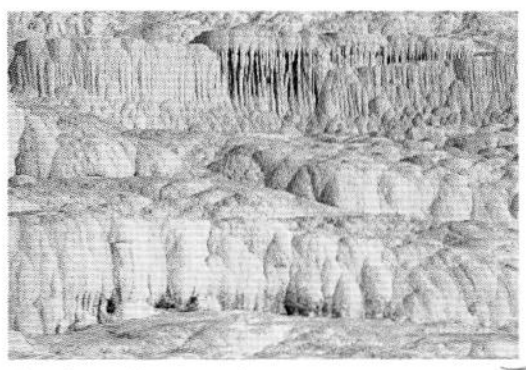

Limestone weathering in the Anatolian Plateau

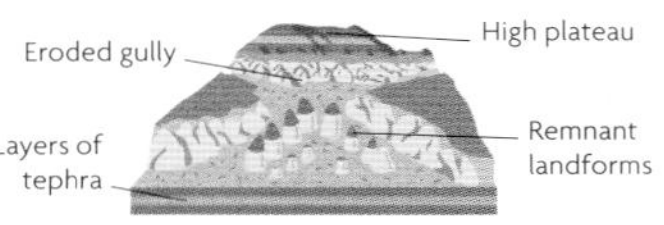

Eroded gully
High plateau
Layers of tephra
Remnant landforms

▲ *In central Turkey, rainwater has chemically weathered away numerous layers of limestone, leaving isolated outcrops and pinnacles and deep eroded gullies.*

► *The Caucasus are fold mountains, which formed around the same time as the Taurus Mountains (Toros Daglari) around 65 million years ago and have since been modified by volcanic erruptions.*

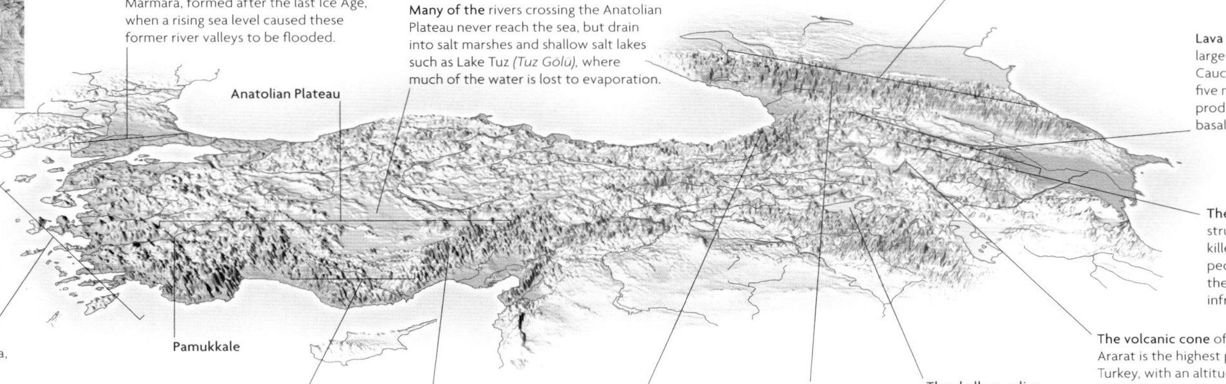

▲ *The white rock terraces at Pamukkale in western Turkey were formed when underground water, heated by volcanic activity, dissolved minerals in the rocks. When the water reached the surface and evaporated the minerals were left behind in these extraordinary formations.*

The straits of the Bosporus and the Dardanelles, respectively linking the Black and Mediterranean seas with the Sea of Marmara, formed after the last Ice Age, when a rising sea level caused these former river valleys to be flooded.

Many of the rivers crossing the Anatolian Plateau never reach the sea, but drain into salt marshes and shallow salt lakes such as Lake Tuz *(Tuz Gölü)*, where much of the water is lost to evaporation.

Anatolian Plateau

Lava has flowed over large areas of the Lesser Caucasus within the last five million years, producing extensive basalt plateaux.

The earthquake that struck Armenia in 1988 killed over 55,000 people and devastated the country's infrastructure.

Pamukkale

Long, parallel mountain ranges run from east to west into the Aegean Sea, which has risen since the last Ice Age to form a drowned coastline of numerous islands and extended inlets.

The volcanic cone of Mount Ararat is the highest peak in Turkey, with an altitude of 16,853 ft (5137 m).

The folded peaks of the Taurus Mountains *(Toros Daglari)* were formed 60–65 million years ago, at the same time as the Alps. The rock is mainly limestone, with deep caves, gorges and underground rivers.

The Cilician Gates *(Gulek Bogazi)*, a major pass through the Taurus Mountains *(Toros Daglari)*, is the point where streams flow from the interior plateau onto the lowland of Adana.

Thick, temperate forest veils the seaward slopes of the Kaçkar Daglari. The southern slopes, which lie in a rainshadow, are dry and barren.

The granite massif near Surami divides the lowlands of Georgia from the oil-rich basin of Azerbaijan's Kura river, which has built a large delta into the Caspian Sea.

The shallow, saline Lake Van *(Van Gölü)* is the largest lake in Turkey. Dry terraces mark a previous shoreline 181 ft (55 m) above the present water level.

Map key

Population

- above 5 million
- 1 million to 5 million
- 500,000 to 1 million
- 100,000 to 500,000
- 50,000 to 100,000
- 10,000 to 50,000
- below 10,000

Elevation

- 4000m / 13,124ft
- 3000m / 9843ft
- 2000m / 6562ft
- 1000m / 3281ft
- 500m / 1640ft
- 250m / 820ft
- 100m / 328ft
- sea level

► *Since the 6th century BC, the pinnacles and caves of east-central Anatolia have been utilized as dwellings. Many are still inhabited today.*

RUSSIAN FEDERATION
GEORGIA
ARMENIA
AZERBAIJAN
Caspian Sea
IRAN
IRAQ
SYRIA
TBILISI
YEREVAN
BAKI (Baku)

122
142
138
138

Scale 1:4,500,000

projection: Lambert Conformal Conic

▲ *The fisheries of Azerbaijan are noted for their hauls of sturgeon, and the Caspian Sea accounts for 80% of the world's total catch. However, stocks are now under serious threat due to overfishing.*

▲ *Traditional steam baths are found throughout the region, and are used for socializing as well as for bathing.*

The Near East

IRAQ, ISRAEL, JORDAN, LEBANON, SYRIA

Some of the world's oldest civilizations developed in this region – the Fertile Crescent – which is venerated by Jews, Muslims and Christians, but torn by competing religious, ethnic and national claims to the land. Turkish Ottoman rule ended with the First World War and the region was divided into areas administered by Britain and France. The UN endorsed calls for a Jewish homeland in what was then Palestine and in 1948 the state of Israel was declared. Hostility towards the Jewish state led to a series of wars with its Arab neighbours. After 2000, attempts to broker peaceful resolutions with both the Palestinian population and with adjacent Arab states were hampered by a revival of Islamic militarism and conflicting international interests in the oil-rich region. This led to an Israeli retrenchment and culminated in a US-led invasion of Iraq in 2003, which toppled the Ba'athist regime of Saddam Hussein in the name of a 'war on terror'.

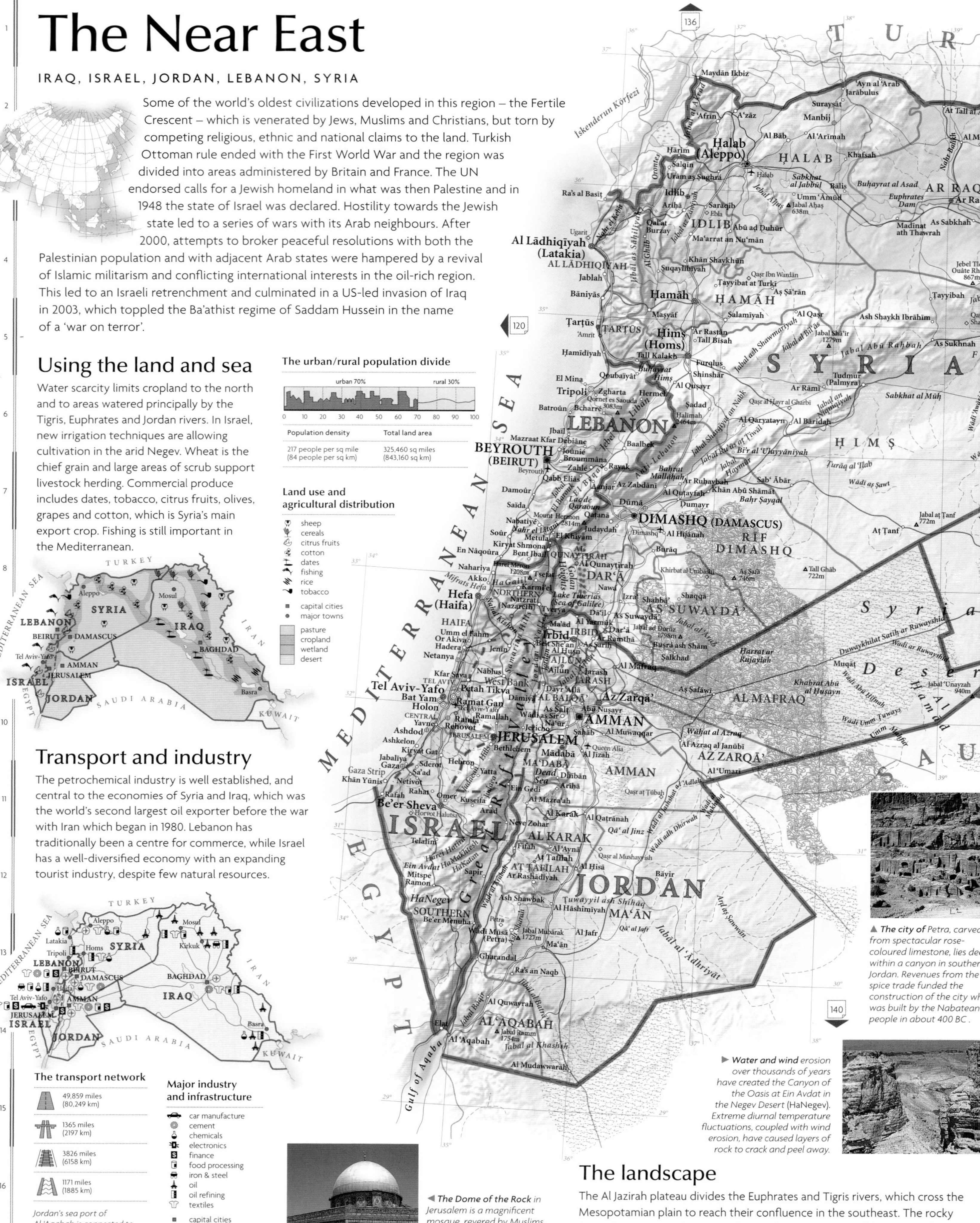

The urban/rural population divide
urban 70%
rural 30%
0 10 20 30 40 50 60 70 80 90 100
Population density
217 people per sq mile (84 people per sq km)
Total land area
325,460 sq miles (843,160 sq km)
Land use and agricultural distribution
sheep
cereals
citrus fruits
cotton
dates
fishing
rice
tobacco
capital cities
major towns
pasture
cropland
wetland
desert
The transport network
49,859 miles (80,249 km)
1365 miles (2197 km)
3826 miles (6158 km)
1171 miles (1885 km)
Major industry and infrastructure
car manufacture
cement
chemicals
electronics
finance
food processing
iron & steel
oil
oil refining
textiles
capital cities
major towns
international airports
major roads
major industrial areas
MEDITERRANEAN SEA
SYRIA
LEBANON
ISRAEL
JORDAN
IRAQ
EGYPT
TURKEY
IRAN
SAUDI ARABIA
KUWAIT
DIMASHQ (DAMASCUS)
BEYROUTH (BEIRUT)
JERUSALEM
AMMAN
Halab (Aleppo)
Tel Aviv-Yafo

Using the land and sea

Water scarcity limits cropland to the north and to areas watered principally by the Tigris, Euphrates and Jordan rivers. In Israel, new irrigation techniques are allowing cultivation in the arid Negev. Wheat is the chief grain and large areas of scrub support livestock herding. Commercial produce includes dates, tobacco, citrus fruits, olives, grapes and cotton, which is Syria's main export crop. Fishing is still important in the Mediterranean.

Transport and industry

The petrochemical industry is well established, and central to the economies of Syria and Iraq, which was the world's second largest oil exporter before the war with Iran which began in 1980. Lebanon has traditionally been a centre for commerce, while Israel has a well-diversified economy with an expanding tourist industry, despite few natural resources.

Jordan's sea port of Al 'Aqabah is connected to Damascus in Syria by road and rail. This route to the Red Sea provides for large exports of phosphate and trade with states in the Persian Gulf.

◀ ***The Dome of the Rock** in Jerusalem is a magnificent mosque, revered by Muslims. Close by is the Wailing Wall, the city's most sacred Jewish landmark and the Church of the Holy Sepulchre, a famous Christian place of worship.*

▲ ***The city of** Petra, carved from spectacular rose-coloured limestone, lies deep within a canyon in southern Jordan. Revenues from the spice trade funded the construction of the city which was built by the Nabatean people in about 400 BC.*

▶ ***Water and wind** erosion over thousands of years have created the Canyon of the Oasis at Ein Avdat in the Negev Desert (HaNegev). Extreme diurnal temperature fluctuations, coupled with wind erosion, have caused layers of rock to crack and peel away.*

The landscape

The Al Jazirah plateau divides the Euphrates and Tigris rivers, which cross the Mesopotamian plain to reach their confluence in the southeast. The rocky Syrian Desert extends west to the northern extremity of the Great Rift Valley, which runs from the mountains of Lebanon to the Gulf of Aqaba. The Jordan river flows south along this trough into the Dead Sea, divided from the Mediterranean coastal plain by a steep-sided plateau.

Map key
Population
1 million to 5 million
500,000 to 1 million
100,000 to 500,000
50,000 to 100,000
10,000 to 50,000
below 10,000
Elevation
4000m / 13,124ft
3000m / 9843ft
2000m / 6562ft
1000m / 3281ft
500m / 1640ft
250m / 820ft
100m / 328ft
sea level
Scale 1: 3,500,000
Km
Miles
projection: Lambert Conformal Conic
IRAQ
BAGHDAD
Al Mawşil (Mosul)
Al Başrah (Basra)
Kirkūk
Arbil
As Sulaymānīyah
An Najaf
Karbalā'
Al Ḩillah
An Nāşirīyah
Al 'Amārah
Al Kūt
Ad Dīwānīyah
As Samāwah
Ar Ramādī
Ba'qūbah
Tikrīt
Sāmarrā'
DAHŪK
ARBĪL
NĪNAWÁ
AS SULAYMĀNĪYAH
AT TA'MĪM
ŞALĀḨ AD DĪN
DIYĀLÁ
AL ANBĀR
BĀBIL
KARBALĀ'
WĀSIT
MAYSĀN
AL QĀDISĪYAH
DHĪ QĀR
AL BAŞRAH
AL MUTHANNÁ
AN NAJAF
Al Jazīrah
Kurdistan
IRAN
ARABIA
KUWAIT
Persian Gulf
Tigris
Euphrates
142
140
142
Dead Sea
Iraq Marshlands
Lake
Tigris
Dried salt marsh
Salt-covered alluvial plain
Euphrates

▶ **The island of** El Hlayaye near Saida in southern Lebanon is linked to the mainland by a bridge built as part of the fort in the 12th century.

▲ **The marshlands of** the Tigris/Euphrates Delta were for centuries home to the Marsh Arabs, who for centuries maintained a traditional and unique lifestyle. Attempts to destroy this by Saddam Hussein's regime through drainage and genocide have now been halted.

◀ **The shores of** the Dead Sea are the lowest land on the Earth's surface – 1388 ft (432 m) below sea level. This highly saline lake is fed by the Jordan river but has no outlet to the sea. The water level has continued to fall in recent years, due to increased use of the Jordan river for irrigation.

Ancient eruptions of lava formed the plateau of Jabal ad Duruz which is deeply weathered and eroded along the edge of the Great Rift Valley. The lava impounded the waters of the Jordan river to form the Sea of Galilee (Lake Tiberias).

The Nahr el Litani, Lebanon's only permanent river, flows along the fertile El Beqaa Valley, which runs for 110 miles (175 km), between the Jebel Liban and Anti-Lebanon mountains.

The gravel-strewn terrain of the Syrian Desert is interrupted by *wadis* – river valleys which remain dry for most of the year.

Great quantities of sediment, deposited by the Tigris and Euphrates rivers, have infilled the head of The Persian Gulf, shifting the coastline south by more than 150 miles (250 km) in the last 5000 years.

Extensive marshlands surround the lake of Hawr al Hammar, which is 70 miles (110 km) long.

▲ **The flood plains** of southern Iraq are crossed by the Tigris and Euphrates rivers. Salt marshes and alluvial plains crusted with salt cover much of the area. The many small lakes are filled with brackish water and the marshes are colonized by reeds.

The Arabian Peninsula

BAHRAIN, KUWAIT, OMAN, QATAR, SAUDI ARABIA, UNITED ARAB EMIRATES (UAE), YEMEN

Huge expanses of desert cover much of the Arabian Peninsula, limiting settlement to oases, the mountains along the Red Sea and coastal belts. The most populous area is the fertile highlands of Yemen. The Islamic faith and Arabic language give the region a cultural and religious unity, and the Saudi city of Mecca *(Makkah)* is Islam's most holy place, visited by over two million pilgrims each year. More than half the world's oil reserves are contained in this region, and the exploitation of oil and gas has brought great wealth, particularly to Saudi Arabia. Yemen and Oman are the least developed of the Arabian states, with large rural populations. Within Saudi Arabia over 86% of the people live in urban areas.

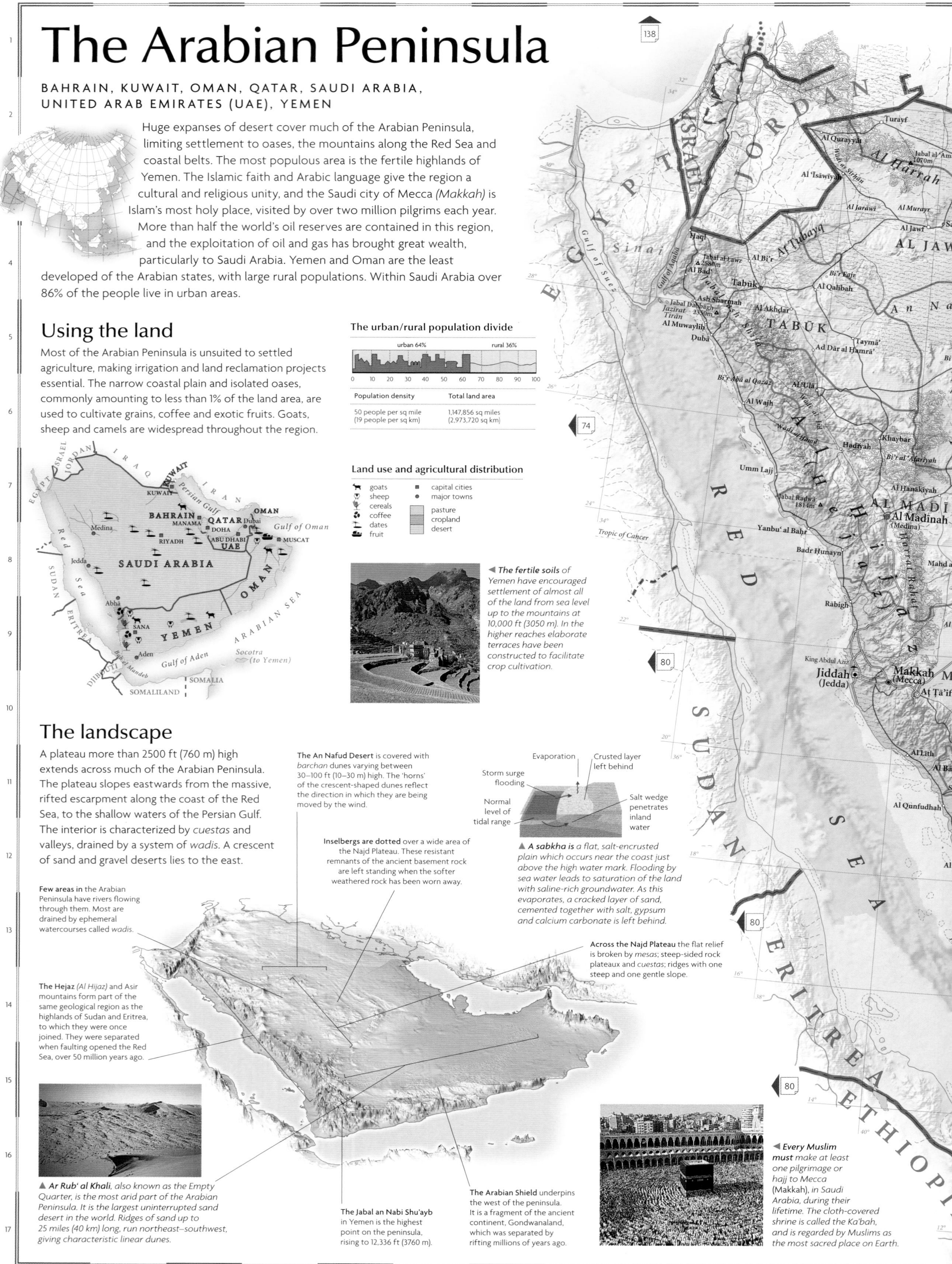

Using the land

Most of the Arabian Peninsula is unsuited to settled agriculture, making irrigation and land reclamation projects essential. The narrow coastal plain and isolated oases, commonly amounting to less than 1% of the land area, are used to cultivate grains, coffee and exotic fruits. Goats, sheep and camels are widespread throughout the region.

The urban/rural population divide

urban 64% — rural 36%

Population density	Total land area
50 people per sq mile (19 people per sq km)	1,147,856 sq miles (2,973,720 sq km)

Land use and agricultural distribution

goats, sheep, cereals, coffee, dates, fruit, capital cities, major towns, pasture, cropland, desert

◀ *The fertile soils of Yemen have encouraged settlement of almost all of the land from sea level up to the mountains at 10,000 ft (3050 m). In the higher reaches elaborate terraces have been constructed to facilitate crop cultivation.*

The landscape

A plateau more than 2500 ft (760 m) high extends across much of the Arabian Peninsula. The plateau slopes eastwards from the massive, rifted escarpment along the coast of the Red Sea, to the shallow waters of the Persian Gulf. The interior is characterized by *cuestas* and valleys, drained by a system of *wadis*. A crescent of sand and gravel deserts lies to the east.

The An Nafud Desert is covered with *barchan* dunes varying between 30–100 ft (10–30 m) high. The 'horns' of the crescent-shaped dunes reflect the direction in which they are being moved by the wind.

Inselbergs are dotted over a wide area of the Najd Plateau. These resistant remnants of the ancient basement rock are left standing when the softer weathered rock has been worn away.

Evaporation / Crusted layer left behind / Storm surge flooding / Normal level of tidal range / Salt wedge penetrates inland water

▲ ***A sabkha is** a flat, salt-encrusted plain which occurs near the coast just above the high water mark. Flooding by sea water leads to saturation of the land with saline-rich groundwater. As this evaporates, a cracked layer of sand, cemented together with salt, gypsum and calcium carbonate is left behind.*

Few areas in the Arabian Peninsula have rivers flowing through them. Most are drained by ephemeral watercourses called *wadis*.

Across the Najd Plateau the flat relief is broken by *mesas*; steep-sided rock plateaux and *cuestas*; ridges with one steep and one gentle slope.

The Hejaz *(Al Hijaz)* and Asir mountains form part of the same geological region as the highlands of Sudan and Eritrea, to which they were once joined. They were separated when faulting opened the Red Sea, over 50 million years ago.

▲ ***Ar Rub' al Khali**, also known as the Empty Quarter, is the most arid part of the Arabian Peninsula. It is the largest uninterrupted sand desert in the world. Ridges of sand up to 25 miles (40 km) long, run northeast–southwest, giving characteristic linear dunes.*

The Jabal an Nabi Shu'ayb in Yemen is the highest point on the peninsula, rising to 12,336 ft (3760 m).

The Arabian Shield underpins the west of the peninsula. It is a fragment of the ancient continent, Gondwanaland, which was separated by rifting millions of years ago.

◀ ***Every Muslim must** make at least one pilgrimage or hajj to Mecca (Makkah), in Saudi Arabia, during their lifetime. The cloth-covered shrine is called the Ka'bah, and is regarded by Muslims as the most sacred place on Earth.*

138

◀ *Saudi Arabia contains the world's largest oil reserves, lying mainly along the Persian Gulf coast. Each day the region produces around 10 million barrels of oil. Here, in the desert, excess oil is being burnt off.*

Transport and industry

The extraction and refining of oil and gas are the major industrial activities in the Arabian Peninsula. The region also has an active construction sector, with many Arab cities reflecting the wealth generated by the oil industry. The service sector is dominated by financial and technical institutions, which, like the construction sector, mainly serve the oil industry. Traditional handicrafts such as carpet-weaving are found in rural areas.

The transport network

44,832 miles (72,159 km)	673 miles (1083 km)
670 miles (1078 km)	none

Internal surface transport is poorly developed across the peninsula. Along the coast, commercial routes have developed, but connections between bordering states rely on major airports.

Major industry and infrastructure

- cement
- chemicals
- iron & steel
- oil
- oil refining
- food processing
- capital cities
- major towns
- international airports
- major roads
- major industrial areas

142

▶ *Seasonal watercourses or wadis drain much of the interior of the Arabian Peninsula. Although they remain dry for much of the year, they are prone to flash floods after heavy rains.*

Map key

Population

- 1 million to 5 million
- 500,000 to 1 million
- 100,000 to 500,000
- 50,000 to 100,000
- 10,000 to 50,000
- below 10,000

Elevation

- 3000m / 9843ft
- 2000m / 6562ft
- 1000m / 3281ft
- 500m / 1640ft
- 250m / 820ft
- 100m / 328ft
- sea level

Scale 1:8,250,000

Km 0 25 50 100 150 200 250

Miles 0 25 50 100 150 200 250

projection: Lambert Conformal Conic

80

Iran & the Gulf states

136

BAHRAIN, IRAN, KUWAIT, QATAR, UNITED ARAB EMIRATES (UAE)

The discovery of oil in the Persian Gulf in the 1930s brought great wealth to the surrounding states. The revenue was largely used to modernize industry and infrastructure, initiating great social change in these formerly agrarian countries. Today, over 90% of the people in the Gulf states live in urban areas, and foreign nationals make up a sizeable proportion of the population in Kuwait, Qatar and the United Arab Emirates. The importance of control of the oil reserves has led to a number of territorial disputes, including most recently the Iran–Iraq War (1980-88) and the First Gulf War (1991). Islam is practised almost exclusively throughout the region and two distinct strands are found; Sunni Muslims in Qatar, Kuwait and UAE, and Shi'a Muslims in Iran and Bahrain. In 1979 Iran became the world's largest theocracy.

138

Pyroclastic layers
Lava flow
Lava flow layers
Caspian Sea
Qolleh-ye Damavand
The Dasht-e Lut
ARMENIA
AZERBAIJAN
TURKEY
IRAQ
KUWAIT
SAUDI ARABIA
Tabrīz
Ardabīl
Orūmīyeh
Rasht
Zanjān
KORDESTĀN
Sanandaj
HAMADĀN
Hamadān
Kermānshāh (Bākhtarān)
KERMĀNSHĀH
LORESTĀN
Khorramābād
ĪLĀM
Dezfūl
KHŪZESTĀN
Ahvāz
Khorramshahr
Ābādān
AL KUWAYT (KUWAIT)
TURKMENISTAN
AFGHANISTAN
PAKISTAN
TEHRAN
IRAN
Esfahan
Kerman
Shiraz
Bandar-e-Abbas
BAHRAIN
MANAMA
QATAR
DOHA
ABU DHABI
U.A.E.
OMAN
Persian Gulf
Gulf of Oman

The landscape

The land rises steeply from the fragmented coastal lowlands bordering the Persian Gulf, to reach Iran's interior plateau, bounded by heavily-eroded mountain chains. An unstable plate boundary runs northwest to southeast across Iran causing frequent earthquakes. On the sandy west coast of the Persian Gulf, the relief is generally flat, with patches of salt marsh. Bahrain consists of two groups of islands, which are mostly small and rocky.

▲ *Qolleh-ye Damavand in the Elburz Mountains is a composite volcano. It comprises layers of lava and pyroclasts – fragmentary rocks which accumulate on the slopes of the volcano after being ejected into the air.*

▲ *Marine sediments from deep beneath the ancient Tethys Sea have been uplifted to form the Elburz Mountains, which stretch along the shores of the Caspian Sea, northern Iran.*

Lava and ash from previous volcanic activity covers a 200 mile (320 km) stretch from the border with Azerbaijan to the Caspian Sea.

Iran's two mountain chains, the Zagros and Elburz, were uplifted at the same time as the Alps in Europe, when the African Plate collided with the Eurasian Plate.

Dominated by a vast, semi-arid interior plateau, most of Iran lies above 1640 ft (500 m). The region is poorly drained with many of its basins remaining dry for months at a time.

The fierce Shamal wind affects much of this region. Every summer it blows dust south from the flood plains of the Tigris and Euphrates, reducing visibility to such an extent that Kuwait International Airport is frequently forced to close.

Autumn winds blowing across the Persian Gulf can reach speeds of up to 95 mph (150 kmph) causing severe storms, squalls and waterspouts.

Prolific springs tapping artesian water make cultivation possible across the north of Bahrain's main island. This provides a sharp contrast to the sandy plains in the south and west.

The oilfields of the Persian Gulf are formed from marine shale deposits lying in sedimentary basins at the margins of the Zagros Mountains.

Numerous islands lie along the southern coast of the Persian Gulf. Some of these are salt domes, created when less dense salts were displaced and forced up to the surface by denser, overlying strata.

◀ *The Dasht-e Lut covers a large portion of eastern Iran with its dry, wind-eroded plain of scattered sandstone pillars and salty depressions. During the summer, temperatures soar, making it one of the world's hottest, driest places.*

140

Using the land and sea

Along the coast of the Caspian Sea, desalinated water allows fruits and vegetables to be produced, although water shortages and desert soils still limit farming. Sheep are the most important livestock raised in Iran and commercial forests cover the northwest of the country. Shrimp stocks were decimated by pollution during the Gulf War, but fishing remains important for domestic and export markets.

◀ *All of the Gulf states have commercial fishing fleets. Before the discovery of oil, fishing was the region's leading industry.*

Land use and agricultural distribution

goats, sheep, cereals, citrus fruits, cotton, dates, fishing, timber; capital cities, major towns; pasture, cropland, forest, desert, wetland

The urban/rural population divide

urban 65% · rural 35%

0 10 20 30 40 50 60 70 80 90 100

Population density	Total land area
112 people per sq mile (43 people per sq km)	642,883 sq miles (1,665,500 sq km)

◀ *The Kuwait Towers in the centre of Kuwait are symbols of the vast wealth oil has brought to the country. Before 1960, the city had only one main street and was surrounded by a mud wall.*

◀ *Many volcanoes lie in Iran's 1200 mile (1930 km) volcanic belt, including the country's highest peak, the now-extinct Qolleh-ye Damavand at 18,600 ft (5671 m).*

▶ *Extensive oil and gas exploitation in the Gulf region has allowed the economic transformation of the Gulf states. Consequently, many of these states have a hugely improved per capita income compared to the 1960's.*

Transport and industry

Both onshore and offshore oil reserves are exploited throughout the region. Kuwait not only extracts but also refines 80% of its oil. Bahrain has diversified its economy to become the main commercial and financial centre in the Persian Gulf. Iran produces a wide range of products: textile mills are widespread and carpet-weaving is an important export industry.

Major industry and infrastructure

- carpet manufacture
- chemicals
- finance
- food processing
- oil
- oil refining
- textiles
- capital city
- major towns
- international airports
- major roads
- major industrial areas

The transport network

63,543 miles (102,274 km)	884 miles (1423 km)
3822 miles (6151 km)	562 miles (904 km)

Major towns and neighbouring countries are linked by adequate road networks, although rural areas are less well served. Bahrain is linked to the mainland by a 15 mile (25 km) long causeway.

Map key

Population

- above 5 million
- 1 million to 5 million
- 500,000 to 1 million
- 100,000 to 500,000
- 50,000 to 100,000
- 10,000 to 50,000
- below 10,000

Elevation

- 4000m / 13,124ft
- 3000m / 9843ft
- 2000m / 6562ft
- 1000m / 3281ft
- 500m / 1640ft
- 250m / 820ft
- 100m / 328ft
- sea level

Scale 1:6,000,000

Km 0 10 20 40 60 80 100 120 140 160 180 200

Miles 0 10 20 40 60 80 100 120 140 160 180 200

projection: Lambert Conformal Conic

Kazakhstan

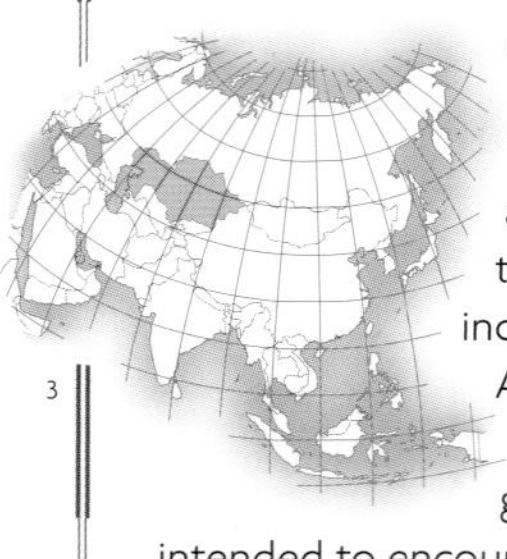

Abundant natural resources lie in the immense steppe grasslands, deserts and central plateau of the former Soviet republic of Kazakhstan. An intensive programme of industrial and agricultural development to exploit these resources during the Soviet era resulted in catastrophic industrial pollution, including fallout from nuclear testing and the shrinkage of the Aral Sea. Since independence, the government has encouraged foreign investment and liberalized the economy to promote growth. The adoption of Kazakh as the national language is intended to encourage a new sense of national identity in a state where living conditions for the majority remain harsh, both in cramped urban centres and impoverished rural areas.

Transport and industry

The single most important industry in Kazakhstan is mining, based around extensive oil deposits near the Caspian Sea, the world's largest chromium mine, and vast reserves of iron ore. Recent foreign investment has helped to develop industries including food processing and steel manufacture, and to expand the exploitation of mineral resources. The Russian space programme is still based at Baykonyr, near Kyzylorda in central Kazakhstan.

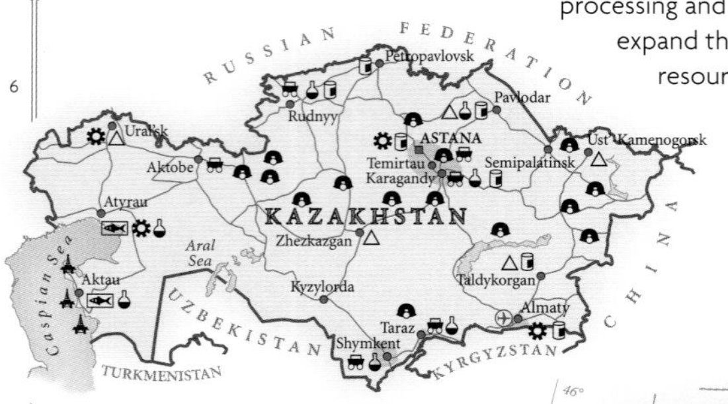

Major industry and infrastructure

- chemicals
- engineering
- fish processing
- food processing
- iron & steel
- metallurgy
- mining
- oil
- capital cities
- major towns
- international airports
- major roads
- major industrial areas

The transport network

- 48,263 miles (77,680 km)
- none
- 8483 miles (13,660 km)
- 3900 miles (2423 km)

Industrial areas in the north and east are well-connected to Russia. Air and rail links with Germany and China have been established through foreign investment. Better access to Baltic ports is being sought.

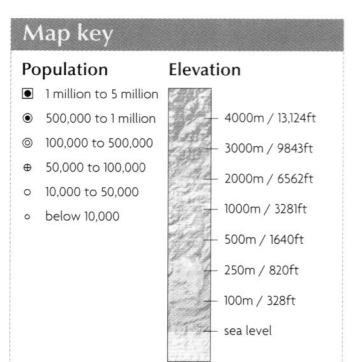

◄ An open-cast coal mine in Kazakhstan. Foreign investment is being actively sought by the Kazakh government in order to fully exploit the potential of the country's rich mineral reserves.

Using the land and sea

The rearing of large herds of sheep and goats on the steppe grasslands forms the core of Kazakh agriculture. Arable cultivation and cotton-growing in pasture and desert areas was encouraged during the Soviet era, but relative yields are low. The heavy use of fertilizers and the diversion of natural water sources for irrigation has degraded much of the land.

The urban/rural population divide

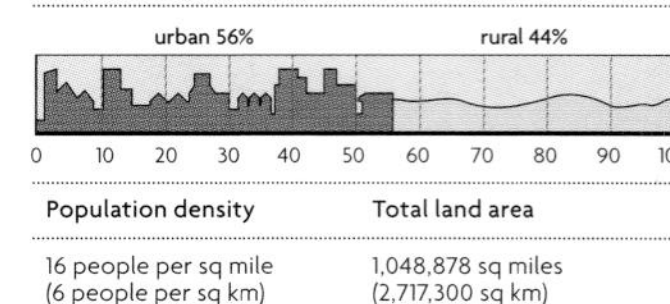

urban 56%
rural 44%
0 10 20 30 40 50 60 70 80 90 100

Population density	Total land area
16 people per sq mile (6 people per sq km)	1,048,878 sq miles (2,717,300 sq km)

Land use and agricultural distribution

- cattle
- goats
- sheep
- cotton
- fishing
- wheat
- capital cities
- major towns
- pasture
- cropland
- forest
- mountain region
- desert

RUSSIAN FEDERATION
KAZAKHSTAN
ASTANA
Rudnyy
Ural'sk
Karagandy
Semipalatinsk
Ust'-Kamenogorsk
Atyrau
Aral Sea
Caspian Sea
Aktau
Kyzylorda
Taldykorgan
Almaty
Shymkent
UZBEKISTAN
TURKMENISTAN
KYRGYZSTAN
CHINA

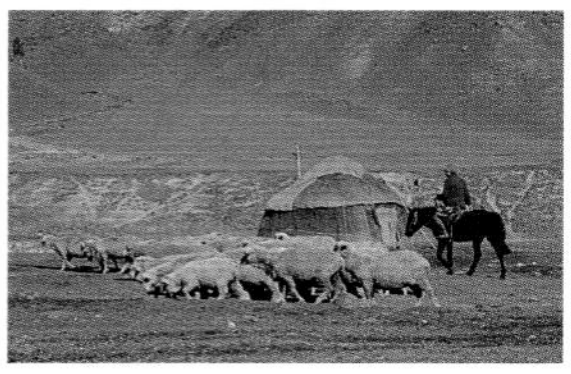

*◄ **The nomadic peoples** who moved their herds around the steppe grasslands are now largely settled, although echoes of their traditional lifestyle, in particular their superb riding skills, remain.*

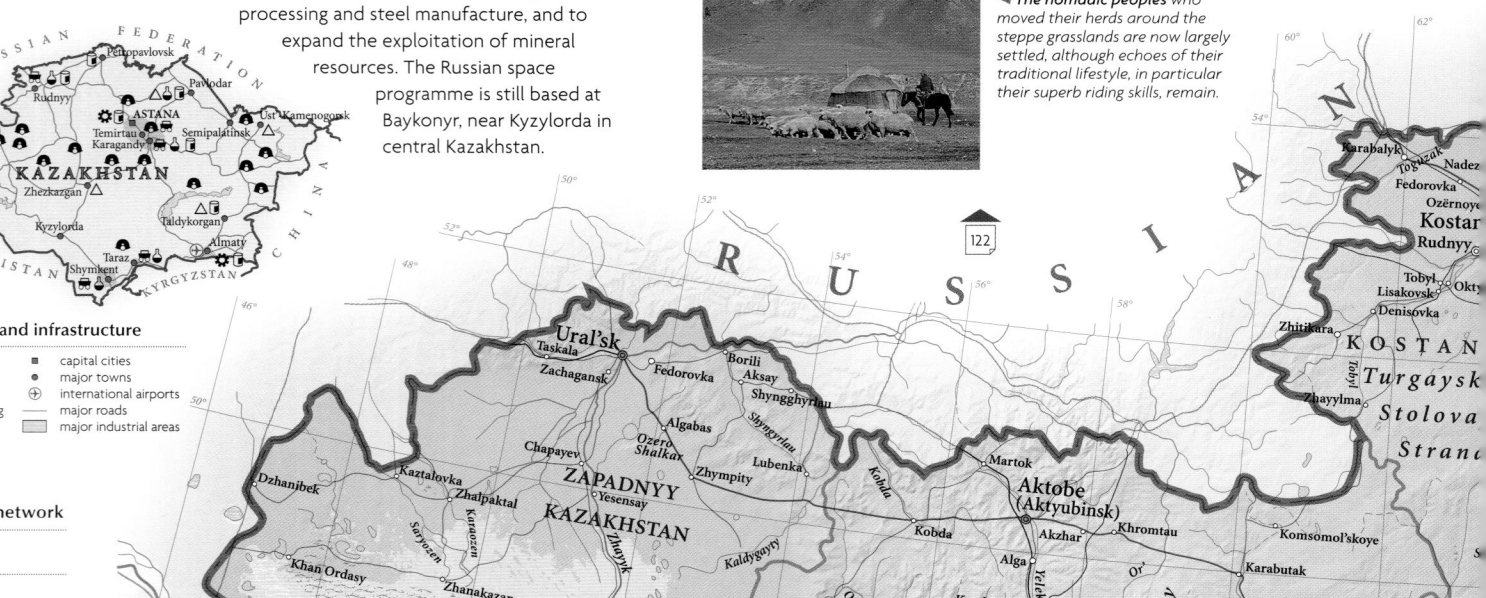

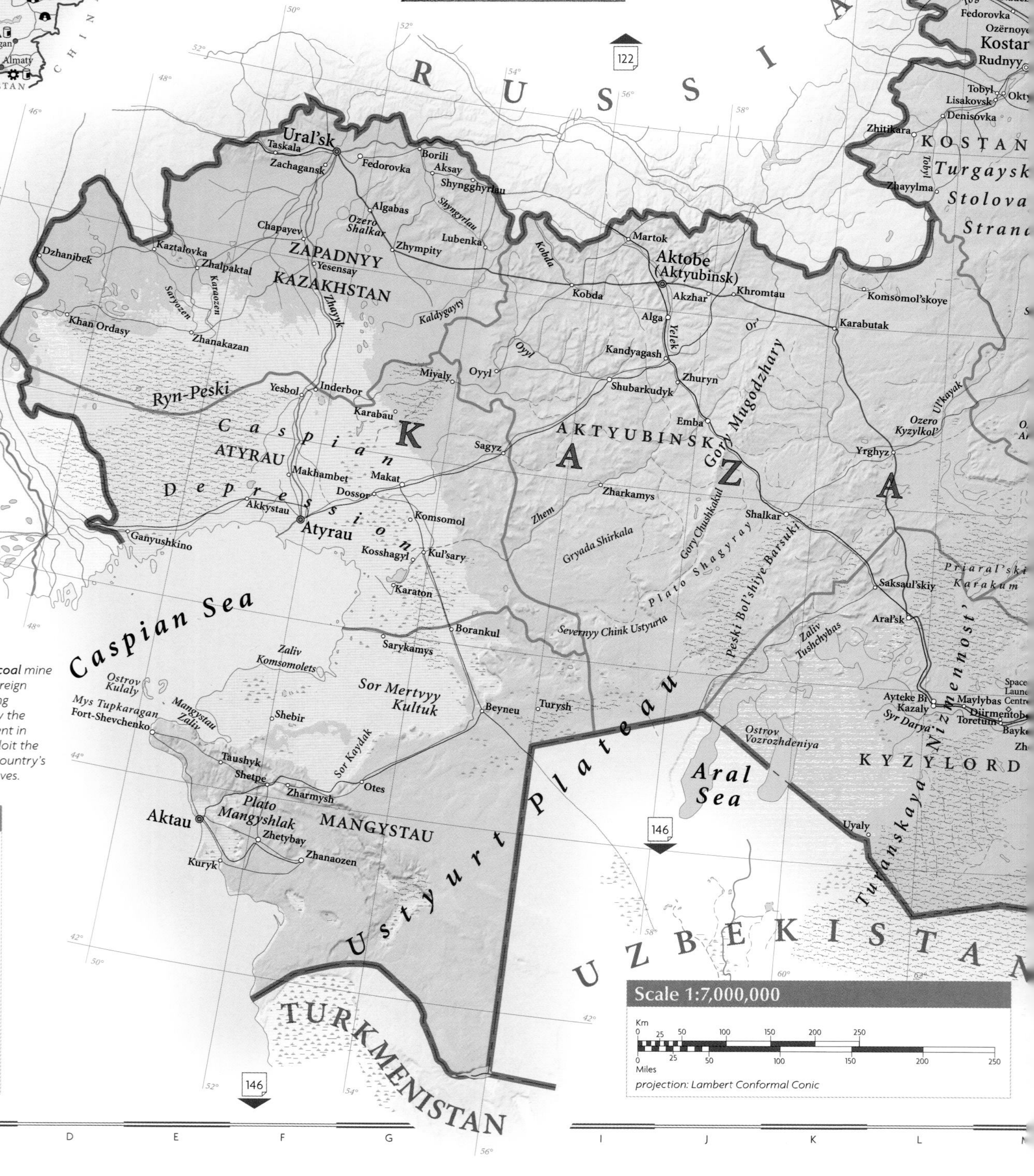

RUSSIA
KAZAKHSTAN
Ural'sk
Aktobe (Aktyubinsk)
Atyrau
Aktau
ZAPADNYY KAZAKHSTAN
AKTYUBINSK
ATYRAU
MANGYSTAU
KOSTANAY
KYZYLORDA
Caspian Depression
Caspian Sea
Aral Sea
Ustyurt Plateau
Ryn-Peski
Turgayskaya Stolovaya Strana
Gory Mugodzhary
Plato Mangyshlak
Sor Mertvyy Kultuk
Peski Bol'shiye Barsuki
Turanskaya Nizmennost'
UZBEKISTAN
TURKMENISTAN
Fort-Shevchenko
Beyneu
Aral'sk
Shalkar
Kandyagash
Emba
Rudnyy
Kostanay
Zhanaozen
Kuryk
Ganyushkino
Makat
Dossor
Kul'sary
Karabutak
Yrghyz
Kazaly
Baykonyr

122
146

Map key

Population

- 1 million to 5 million
- 500,000 to 1 million
- 100,000 to 500,000
- 50,000 to 100,000
- 10,000 to 50,000
- below 10,000

Elevation

- 4000m / 13,124ft
- 3000m / 9843ft
- 2000m / 6562ft
- 1000m / 3281ft
- 500m / 1640ft
- 250m / 820ft
- 100m / 328ft
- sea level

Scale 1:7,000,000

Km 0 25 50 100 150 200 250
Miles 0 25 50 100 150 200 250

projection: Lambert Conformal Conic

The landscape

Stretching more than 1250 miles (2000 km) from the Caspian Sea in the west to China in the east, more than 40% of Kazakhstan is covered by steppe grasslands which give way to barren desert in the south. The land rises eastwards towards the mineral-rich central plateau, to form the Altai Mountains.

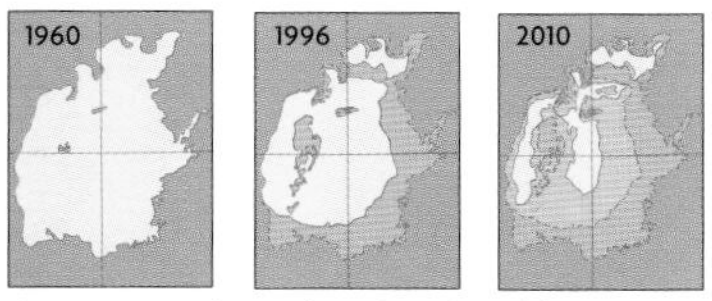

1960 1996 2010

▲ *Since 1960, the Aral Sea has shrunk by 90%, become extremely saline, and lost all but five of its once-abundant fish species. Factors in this ecological disaster include the excessive use of fertilizers, defoliants and the diversion of its main source rivers for the irrigation of desert lands.*

The Caspian Sea is the largest body of inland water in the world.

The desert of Peski Bol'shiye Barsuki is mainly sandy, displaying a number of classic dune formations. Groundwater supports a small amount of vegetation.

A large number of salt lakes fill depressions in the rolling uplands of central Kazakhstan.

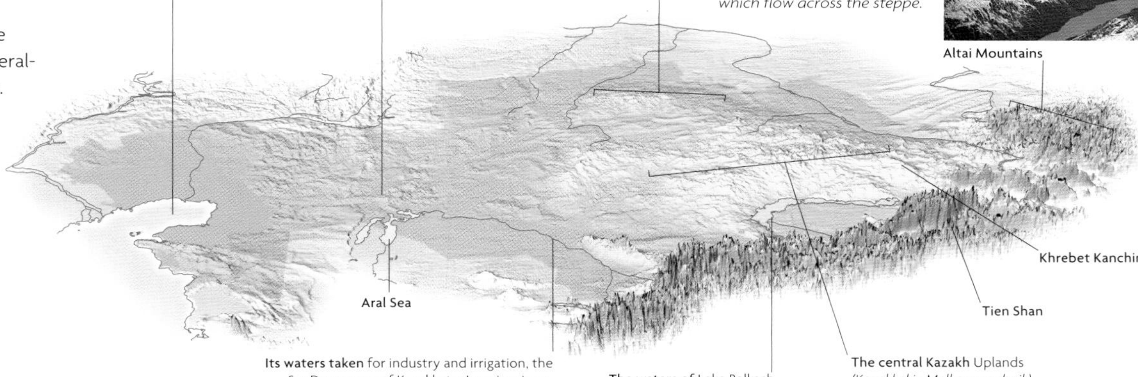

► ***The Altai Mountains*** *lie on Kazakhstan's eastern borders with China and the Russian Federation. Cold and largely barren, they are the source of many of the rivers which flow across the steppe.*

Altai Mountains

Khrebet Kanchingiz

Tien Shan

Aral Sea

Its waters taken for industry and irrigation, the Syr Darya, one of Kazakhstan's major rivers, now barely reaches the Aral Sea which it used to fill. Like many Kazakh rivers it has been heavily polluted with chemicals and its flow has been restricted by up to 60%.

The waters of Lake Balkash (*Ozero Balkash*), unlike those of the Aral Sea, are still able to support a fishing industry.

The central Kazakh Uplands (*Kazakhskiy Melkosopochnik*) contain much of the country's mineral riches. The landscape is largely flat with occasional rocky outcrops and hillocks.

► ***Immense stretches of*** *steppe grasslands characterize much of the Kazakh landscape. These lowland areas have been used for arable cultivation in recent years, although problems with irrigation have meant that much of the land is being allowed to revert to its natural vegetation and pastoral usage.*

▲ ***Rows of pine*** *trees edge this valley near Almaty. The snow-covered slopes in the background are used for skiing.*

122

156

146

Central Asia

KYRGYZSTAN, TAJIKISTAN, TURKMENISTAN, UZBEKISTAN

The four republics that declared independence in 1991 were created in the early years of the Soviet Union, promoting ethnic divisions in a region whose common focus, since the 8th century, has been Islam. Traditional rural and nomadic ways of life have survived the Soviet era, while the benefits of modern industry and grand irrigation schemes have resulted in severe pollution in the delicate, arid environment of the steppe, particularly in Uzbekistan. Many ethnic minority groups are scattered among the four republics, with isolated communities in the mountains of Kyrgyzstan.

The current Islamic revival has brought hope of greater regional unity, in spite of religious factionalism which, in 1992, plunged Tajikistan into civil war.

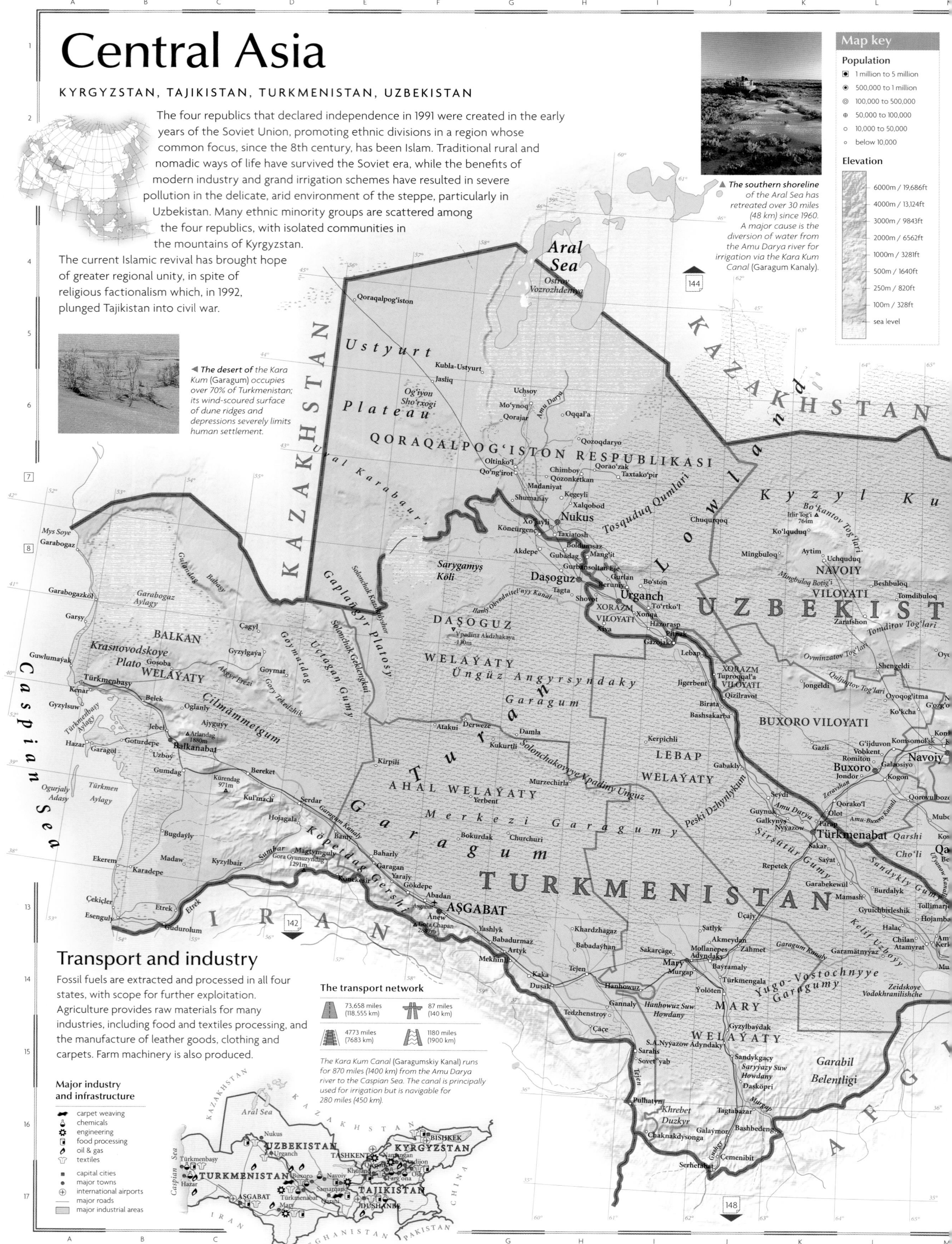

Map key
Population
1 million to 5 million
500,000 to 1 million
100,000 to 500,000
50,000 to 100,000
10,000 to 50,000
below 10,000
Elevation
6000m / 19,686ft
4000m / 13,124ft
3000m / 9843ft
2000m / 6562ft
1000m / 3281ft
500m / 1640ft
250m / 820ft
100m / 328ft
sea level
Aral Sea
Ostrov Vozrozhdeniya
KAZAKHSTAN
Qoraqalpog'iston
Ustyurt Plateau
Kubla-Ustyurt
Jasliq
Og'iyon Sho'rxogi
Uchsoy
Mo'ynoq
Qorajar
Amu Darya
Oqqal'a
Qozoqdaryo
QORAQALPOG'ISTON RESPUBLIKASI
Ural Karabaur
Oltinko'l
Qo'ng'irot
Chimboy
Qorao'zak
Qozonketkan
Taxtako'pir
Madaniyat
Shumanay
Kegeyli
Xalqobod
Nukus
Tosquduq Qumlari
Xo'jayli
Köneürgenç
Taxiatosh
Boldumsaz
Akdepe
Gubadag
Mang'it
Gurbansoltan Eje
Sarygamyş Köli
Daşoguz
Gurlan
Bo'ston
Beruniy
Urganch
Tagta
Shovot
XORAZM VILOYATI
To'rtko'l
Xonqa
Xiva
Hazorasp
Pitnak
Gazojak
Chuqurqoq
Lowland
Kyzyl Kum
Bo'kantov Tog'lari
Itdir Tog'i 764m
Ko'lquduq
Mingbuloq
Aytim
Uchquduq
NAVOIY VILOYATI
Mingbuloq Botig'i
Beshbuloq
Tomdibuloq
UZBEKISTAN
Zarafshon
Tomditov Tog'lari
Ovminzatov Tog'lari
Quljuqtov Tog'lari
Shengeldi
Jongeldi
Oyoqog'itma
Ko'kcha
Mys Soye
Garabogaz
Garabogazköl
Garabogaz Aylagy
Gulanadag
Babasy
Garşy
Gaplaňgyr Platosy
Solonchak Kazakhlyshor
Solonchak Geklengskui
DAŞOGUZ WELAÝATY
Vpadina Akdzhakaya -130m
Üngüz Angyrsyndaky Garagum
Ilanly Obvodnitel'nyy Kanal
BALKAN WELAÝATY
Krasnovodskoye Plato
Gosoba
Çagyl
Gyzylgaýa
Goymat
Goymatdag
Uçtagan Gumy
Akgyr Erezi
Gory Tekedzhik
Gumbuzdag
Gwulumaýak
Türkmenbaşy
Kenar
Belek
Oglanly
Gyzylsuw
Türkmenbaşy Aylagy
Jebel
Ajyguyy
Arlandag 1880m
Balkanabat
Çilmämmetgum
Hazar
Goturdepe
Garagöl
Uzboý
Gumdag
Bereket
Kürendag 971m
Kul'mach
Serdar
Caspian Sea
Ogurjaly Adasy
Türkmen Aylagy
Hojagala
Bugdaýly
Madaw
Kyzylbair
Sumbar
Magtymguly
Gora Gyunuzyndag 1291m
Ekerem
Karadepe
Çekiçler
Esenguly
Etrek
Gudurolum
IRAN
Kopetdag Gershi
Garagum Kanaly
Baharly
Garagan
Yarajy
Gökdepe
Abadan
Aşgabat
Anew
Gora Chapan 2839m
Kunekesir
Atakui
Derweze
Damla
Kukurtli
Kirpili
Turan
AHAL WELAÝATY
Yerbent
Murzechirla
Solonchakovyye Vpadiny Unguz
Merkezi Garagumy
Bokurdak
Churchuri
Garagum
TURKMENISTAN
Kerpichli
LEBAP WELAÝATY
Lebap
Jigerbent
XORAZM Tuproqqal'a VILOYATI
Qizilravot
Birata
Bashsakarba
BUXORO VILOYATI
Gabakly
Peski Dzhynlykum
Seydi
Amu Darya
Guynuk
Galkynyş
Nyyazow
Farap
Türkmenabat
Sakar
Saýat
Repetek
Sirşütür Gumy
Garabekewül
Mamash
Burdalyk
Sandykly Gumy
Gyuichbirleshik
Halaç
Chilan
Atamyrat
Garamätnyýaz
Tollimarjon
Hojambaz
Kelif Uzboýy
Gazli
G'ijduvon
Komsomol'sk
Vobkent
Romiton
Buxoro
Navoiy
Galaosiyo
Jondor
Kogon
Zeravshan
Qorako'l
Olot
Amu-Buxoro Kanali
Qorovulbozor
Qarshi
Cho'li
Ulyanovo Kanal
Kazakhdzhagaz
Babadaýhan
Yashlyk
Babadurmaz
Artyk
Mekhinli
Kaka
Duşak
Tejen
Hanhowuz
Sakarçäge
Mollanepes
Adyndaky
Akmeydan
Zähmet
Şatlyk
Üçajy
Mary
Murgap
Baýramaly
Türkmengala
Ýolöten
Yugo-Vostochnyye Garagumy
Zeidskoye Vodokhranilishche
Gannaly
Hanhowuz Suw Howdany
Tedzhenstroy
Çäçe
MARY WELAÝATY
Gyzylbaýdak
S.A.Nyýazow Adyndaky
Sarahs
Sovet'yab
Sandykgaçy
Saryýazy Suw Howdany
Daşköpri
Garabil Belentligi
Pulhatyn
Khrebet Duzkyr
Tagtabazar
Bashbedeng
Galaýmor
Chaknakdysonga
Serhetabat
Gushgy
Çemenibit
AFGHANISTAN
Murgap
Tejen
144
142
148

▲ The southern shoreline of the Aral Sea has retreated over 30 miles (48 km) since 1960. A major cause is the diversion of water from the Amu Darya river for irrigation via the Kara Kum Canal (Garagum Kanaly).

◀ The desert of the Kara Kum (Garagum) occupies over 70% of Turkmenistan; its wind-scoured surface of dune ridges and depressions severely limits human settlement.

Transport and industry

Fossil fuels are extracted and processed in all four states, with scope for further exploitation. Agriculture provides raw materials for many industries, including food and textiles processing, and the manufacture of leather goods, clothing and carpets. Farm machinery is also produced.

The transport network

73,658 miles (118,555 km)

87 miles (140 km)

4773 miles (7683 km)

1180 miles (1900 km)

The Kara Kum Canal (Garagumskiy Kanal) runs for 870 miles (1400 km) from the Amu Darya river to the Caspian Sea. The canal is principally used for irrigation but is navigable for 280 miles (450 km).

Major industry and infrastructure

carpet weaving
chemicals
engineering
food processing
oil & gas
textiles
capital cities
major towns
international airports
major roads
major industrial areas

KAZAKHSTAN
Aral Sea
Nukus
UZBEKISTAN
Urganch
BISHKEK
KYRGYZSTAN
TASHKENT
Namangan
Andijon
Farg'ona
Osh
Khujand
Caspian Sea
Türkmenbaşy
TURKMENISTAN
Buxoro
Navoiy
Samarqand
Hazar
AŞGABAT
Türkmenabat
Qarshi
TAJIKISTAN
DUSHANBE
CHINA
IRAN
AFGHANISTAN
PAKISTAN

The landscape

The great Tien Shan and Pamir ranges meet in a succession of high mountain chains. These mountains encircle the fertile Fergana Valley and reach west into the desert of the Kyzyl Kum, dividing the Syr Darya and Amu Darya rivers. Sandy steppeland extends to the shores of the Caspian Sea, with the desert of the Kara Kum *(Garagum)* in the south. The Amu Darya drains into the Aral Sea in the north.

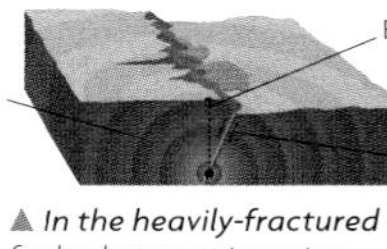

The Amu Darya is the only river in Central Asia with a sufficient volume of water to cross the desert of the Kara Kum *(Garagum)* from the Pamirs to the Aral Sea, where it forms a delta largely vegetated by scrub grasses.

Shock waves travel through ground

Epicentre

Fault

▲ ***In the heavily-fractured** and faulted mountain region, earthquakes are common, caused by the sudden release of tension along active fault lines.*

◀ ***Bare mountains provide** a stark background to the croplands along the Naryn river in Kyrgyzstan. Irrigation is essential for cultivation in this dry region.*

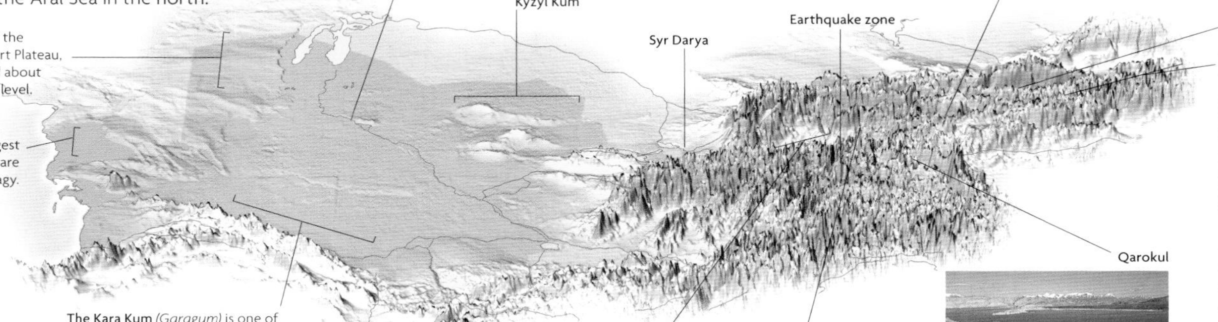

Naryn river

Ozero Issyk-Kul' lies at an altitude of 5193 ft (1584 m). The lake remains ice-free throughout the year, due to the slight salinity of the water.

Salt marshes fill many of the depressions in the Ustyurt Plateau, a barren, rocky tableland about 650 ft (200 m) above sea level.

Kyzyl Kum

Earthquake zone

Syr Darya

Tien Shan

Some of the world's largest deposits of marine salts are found in Garabogaz Aylagy. This shallow, saline gulf has an average depth of only 33 ft (10 m), and a very high evaporation rate, producing the salty deposits.

▲ ***The Tien Shan** extend from China in the east, reaching heights over 24,420 ft (7443 m) and branching into many parallel ranges in the west.*

Qarokul

The Kara Kum *(Garagum)* is one of the world's largest expanses of sand. Wind action has created a terrain of shifting, crescent-shaped sand dunes known as *barchans*.

A series of major rock faults has created the Fergana Valley, a deep depression surrounded by high mountains. Water from the Syr Darya river and from underground sources supports intensive agriculture, despite minimal rainfall.

Mount Communism *(Qullai Kommunizm)*, in the northern Pamirs, was so named for being the highest point in the former Soviet Union, rising to 24,590 ft (7495 m).

◀ ***Nestling high in** the Pamir range, and fed by glacial meltwater, Qarokul is the largest of the lakes in this region.*

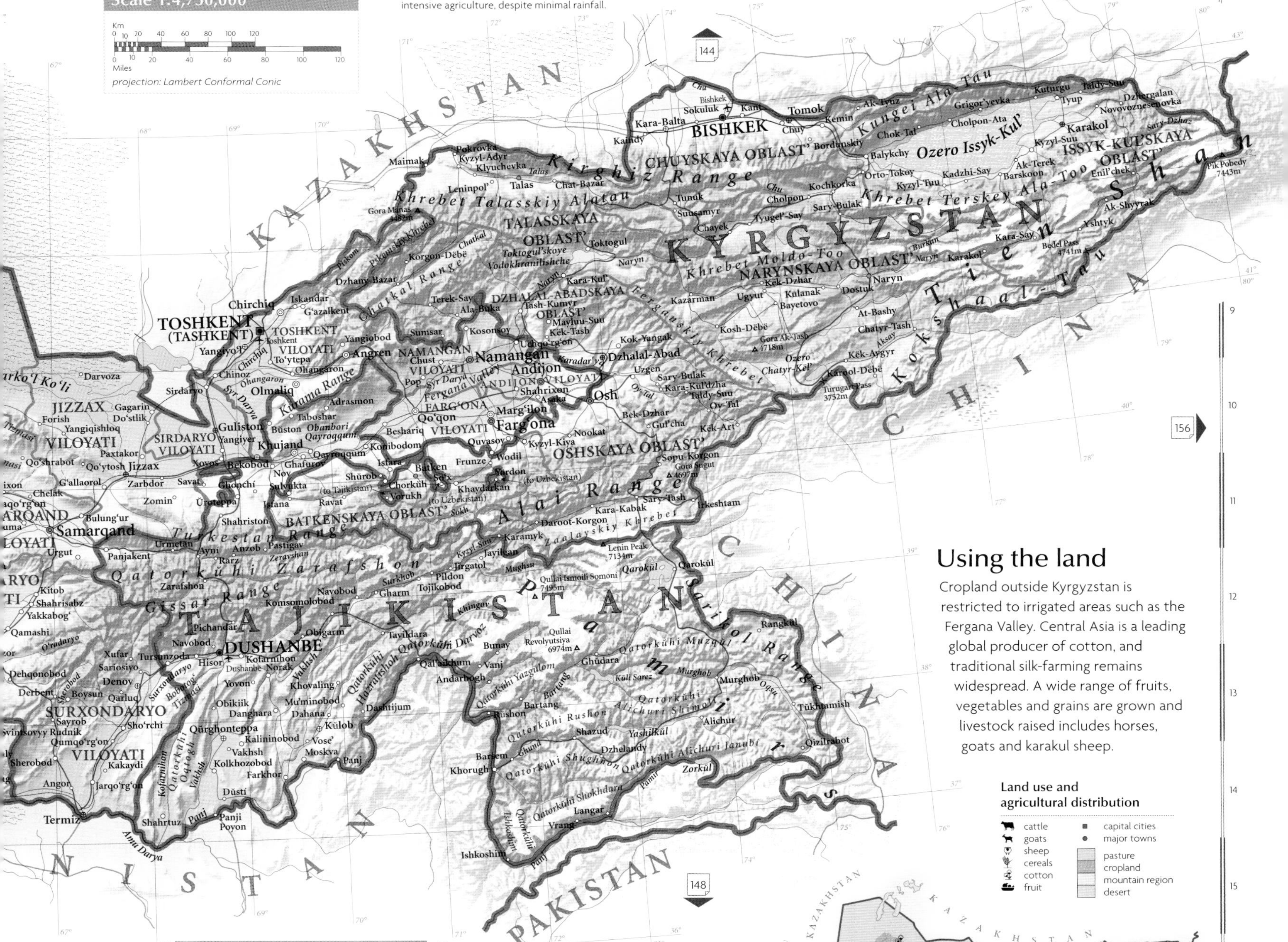

Scale 1:4,750,000

Km 0 10 20 40 60 80 100 120

Miles 0 10 20 40 60 80 100 120

projection: Lambert Conformal Conic

144

156

148

Using the land

Cropland outside Kyrgyzstan is restricted to irrigated areas such as the Fergana Valley. Central Asia is a leading global producer of cotton, and traditional silk-farming remains widespread. A wide range of fruits, vegetables and grains are grown and livestock raised includes horses, goats and karakul sheep.

Land use and agricultural distribution

cattle
goats
sheep
cereals
cotton
fruit
capital cities
major towns
pasture
cropland
mountain region
desert

▶ ***Plentiful sunshine, rich** soils and massive irrigation schemes have made Uzbekistan the world's fifth largest cotton producer, although water shortages now prevent any further expansion of irrigated land.*

The urban/rural population divide

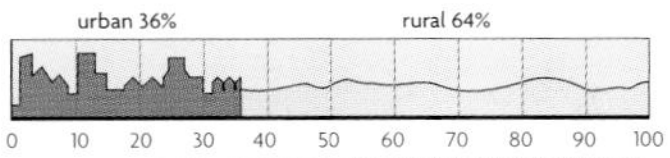

urban 36% rural 64%

0 10 20 30 40 50 60 70 80 90 100

Population density	Total land area
88 people per sq mile (34 people per sq km)	492,961 sq miles (1,277,100 sq km)

Afghanistan & Pakistan

Pakistan was created by the partition of British India in 1947, becoming the western arm of a new Islamic state for Indian Muslims; the eastern sector, in Bengal, seceded to become the separate country of Bangladesh in 1971. Over half of Pakistan's 158 million people live in the Punjab, at the fertile head of the great Indus Basin. The river sustains a national economy based on irrigated agriculture, including cotton for the vital textiles industry. Afghanistan, a mountainous, landlocked country, with an ancient and independent culture, has been wracked by war since 1979. Factional strife escalated into an international conflict in late 2001, as US-led troops ousted the militant and fundamentally Islamist *taliban* regime as part of their 'war on terror'.

◄ **The town of** Bamian lies high in the Hindu Kush west of Kabul. Between the 2nd and 5th centuries two huge statues of Buddha were carved into the nearby rock,the largest of which stood 125 ft (38 m) high. The statues were destroyed by the taliban regime in March 2001.

Transport and industry

Pakistan is highly dependent on the cotton textiles industry, although diversified manufacture is expanding around cities such as Karachi and Lahore. Afghanistan's limited industry is based mainly on the processing of agricultural raw materials and includes traditional crafts such as carpet-making.

Major industry and infrastructure

- carpet weaving
- chemicals
- engineering
- finance
- food processing
- iron & steel
- oil & gas
- textiles
- capital cities
- major towns
- international airports
- major roads
- major industrial areas

The transport network

- 96,154 miles (154,763 km)
- 211 miles (340 km)
- 4852 miles (7814 km)
- 745 miles (1200 km)

The Karakoram Highway was completed after 20 years of construction in 1978. It breaches the Himalayan mountain barrier providing a commercial motor route linking lowland Pakistan and China.

► ***The Karakoram Highway*** *is one of the highest major roads in the world. It took over 24,000 workers almost 20 years to complete.*

The landscape

Afghanistan's topography is dominated by the mountains of the Hindu Kush, which spread south and west into numerous mountain spurs. The dry plateau of southwestern Afghanistan extends into Pakistan and the hills which overlook the great Indus Basin. In northern Pakistan the Hindu Kush, Himalayan and Karakoram ranges meet to form one of the world's highest mountain regions.

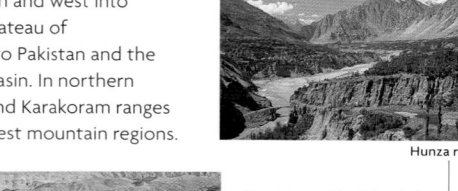

◄ ***The Hunza river*** *rises in the northern Karakoram Range, running for 120 miles (193 km) before joining the Gilgit river.*

► ***The arid Hindu Kush*** *makes much of Afghanistan uninhabitable, with over 50% of the land lying above 6500 ft (2000 m).*

Hunza river

The plains and foothills which extend from the northern slopes of the Hindu Kush are part of the great grassy steppe lands of Central Asia.

Hindu Kush

K2 (Mount Godwin Austen), in the Karakoram Range, is the second highest mountain in the world, at an altitude of 28,251 ft (8611 m).

Frequent earthquakes mean that mountain-building processes are continuing in this region, as the Indo-Australian Plate drifts northwards, colliding with the Eurasian Plate.

Some of the largest glaciers outside the polar regions are found in the Karakoram Range, including Siachen Glacier *(Siachen Muztagh)*, which is 40 miles (72 km) long.

Himalayas

Mountain chains running southwest from the Hindu Kush into Pakistan form a barrier to the humid winds which blow from the Indian Ocean, creating arid conditions across southern Afghanistan.

The soils of the Punjab plain are nourished by enormous quantities of sediment, carried from the Himalayas by the five tributaries of the Indus river.

Glacis covered by coarse-grained sediment

Sediments washed down from mountains accumulate on glacis slopes

Fine sediments deposited on salt flats are removed by wind erosion.

Bedrock

The Indus Basin is part of the Indus-Ganges lowland, a vast depression which has been filled with layers of sediment over the last 50 million years. These deposits are estimated to be over 16,400 ft (5000 m) deep.

The Indus Delta is prone to heavy flooding and high levels of salinity. It remains a largely uncultivated wilderness area.

▲ ***Glacis are gentle,*** *debris-covered slopes which lead into salt flats or deserts. They typically occur at the base of mountains in arid regions such as Afghanistan.*

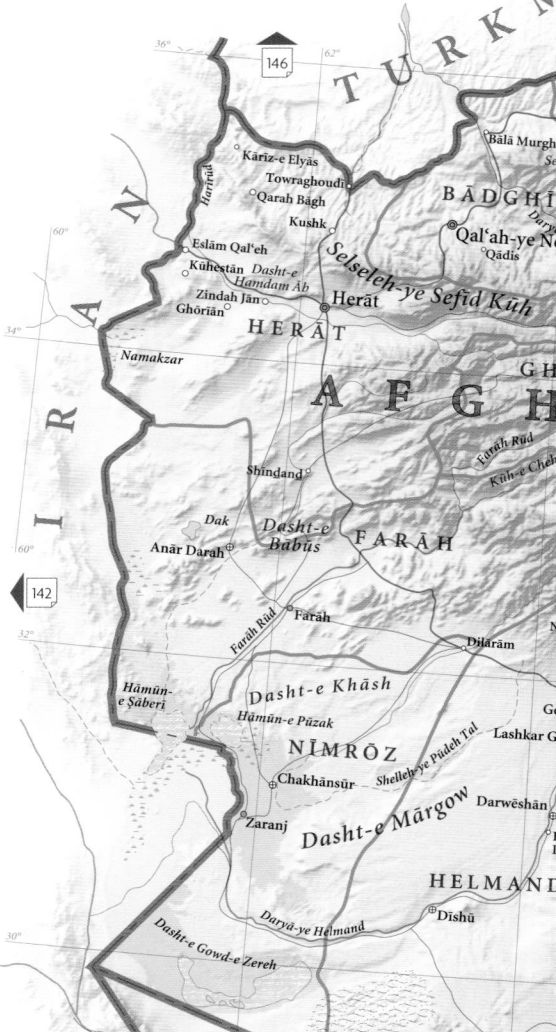

Scale 1:5,000,000

projection: Lambert Conformal Conic

146

142

142

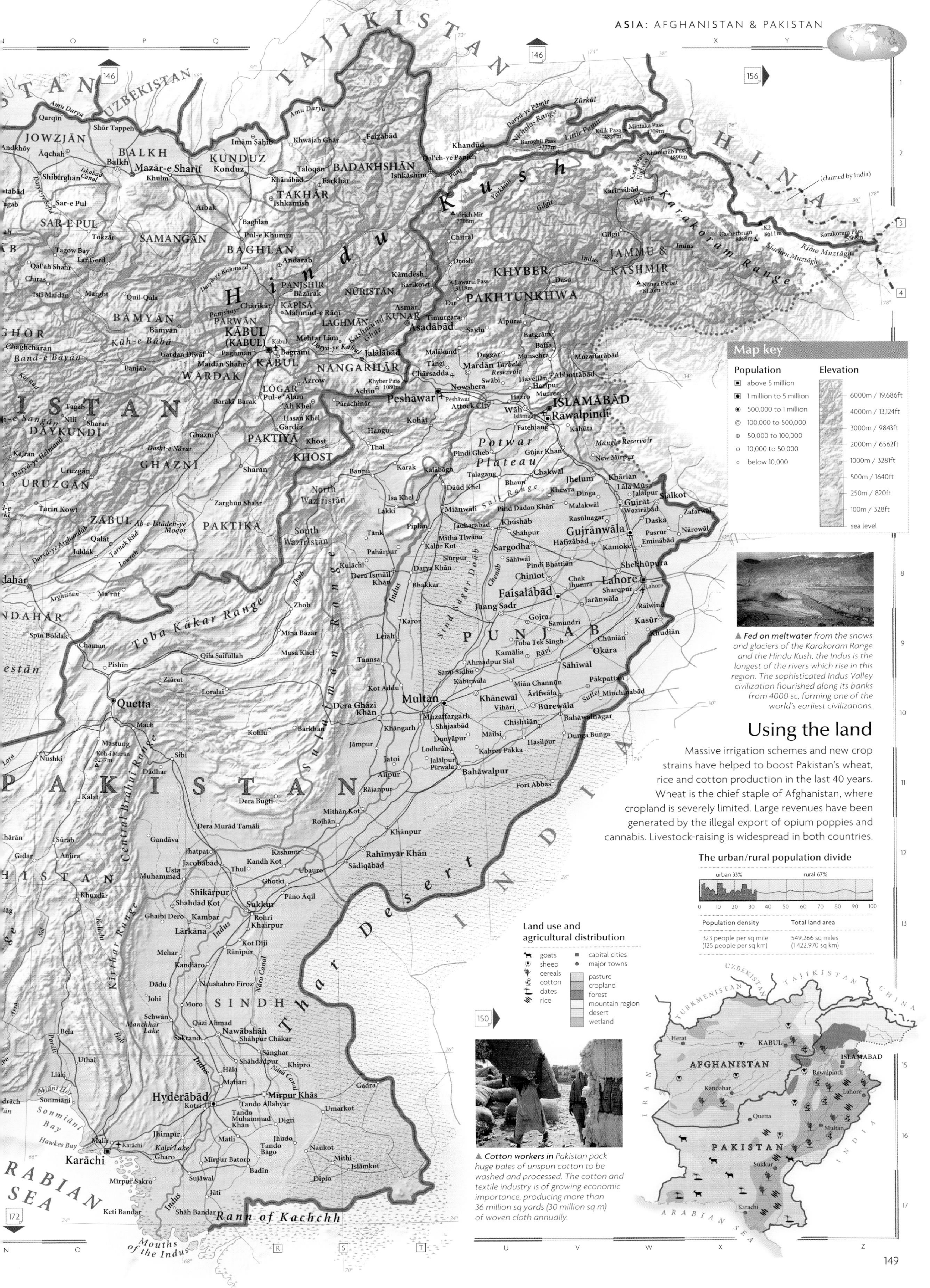

TAJIKISTAN
UZBEKISTAN
CHINA
PAKISTAN
INDIA
ARABIAN SEA
Hindu Kush
Karakoram Range
Thar Desert
Toba Kākar Range
Sulaimān Range
Kirthar Range
Central Brāhui Range
Potwar Plateau
Salt Range
Sind Sāgar Doāb
Rann of Kachchh
Mouths of the Indus
Sonmiāni Bay
Hawkes Bay
JOWZJĀN
BALKH
KUNDUZ
BADAKHSHĀN
TAKHĀR
SAR-E PUL
SAMANGĀN
BAGHLĀN
BĀMYĀN
PARWĀN
KĀPĪSĀ
PANJSHĪR
NŪRISTĀN
LAGHMĀN
KUNAR
NANGARHĀR
KĀBUL
WARDAK
LŌGAR
PAKTIYĀ
KHŌST
GHAZNĪ
URUZGĀN
DĀYKUNDĪ
ZĀBUL
PAKTĪKĀ
GHŌR
KHYBER PAKHTUNKHWA
JAMMU & KASHMIR
PUNJAB
SINDH
North Wazīristān
South Wazīristān
KĀBUL (KABUL)
ISLĀMĀBĀD
Rāwalpindi
Peshāwar
Lahore
Faisalābād
Gujrānwāla
Multān
Quetta
Hyderābād
Karāchi
Sukkur
Bahāwalpur
Mazār-e Sharīf
Jalālābād
Tirich Mir 7708m
K2 8611m
Nanga Parbat 8126m
Gasherbrum 8068m
Khyber Pass 1080m
Lowarai Pass 3118m
Kilik Pass 4827m
Mintaka Pass 4709m
Khunjerab Pass 4890m
Karakoram Pass 5569m
(claimed by India)
Map key
Population
above 5 million
1 million to 5 million
500,000 to 1 million
100,000 to 500,000
50,000 to 100,000
10,000 to 50,000
below 10,000
Elevation
6000m / 19,686ft
4000m / 13,124ft
3000m / 9843ft
2000m / 6562ft
1000m / 3281ft
500m / 1640ft
250m / 820ft
100m / 328ft
sea level
The urban/rural population divide
urban 33%
rural 67%
0 10 20 30 40 50 60 70 80 90 100
Population density
323 people per sq mile (125 people per sq km)
Total land area
549,266 sq miles (1,422,970 sq km)
Land use and agricultural distribution
goats
sheep
cereals
cotton
dates
rice
capital cities
major towns
pasture
cropland
forest
mountain region
desert
wetland
AFGHANISTAN
PAKISTAN
KABUL
ISLAMABAD
Herat
Kandahar
Quetta
Rawalpindi
Lahore
Multan
Sukkur
Karachi
TURKMENISTAN
IRAN

▲ *Fed on meltwater* from the snows and glaciers of the Karakoram Range and the Hindu Kush, the Indus is the longest of the rivers which rise in this region. The sophisticated Indus Valley civilization flourished along its banks from 4000 BC, forming one of the world's earliest civilizations.

Using the land

Massive irrigation schemes and new crop strains have helped to boost Pakistan's wheat, rice and cotton production in the last 40 years. Wheat is the chief staple of Afghanistan, where cropland is severely limited. Large revenues have been generated by the illegal export of opium poppies and cannabis. Livestock-raising is widespread in both countries.

▲ *Cotton workers in* Pakistan pack huge bales of unspun cotton to be washed and processed. The cotton and textile industry is of growing economic importance, producing more than 36 million sq yards (30 million sq m) of woven cloth annually.

South Asia

BANGLADESH, BHUTAN, INDIA, MALDIVES, NEPAL, PAKISTAN, SRI LANKA

More than one-fifth of the world's population lives in the south Asian subcontinent. Great cultural diversity has come from a long succession of foreign invaders, including Hindu Aryans, Islamic Moguls and the British, whose empire incorporated the princely states of the Maharajas and extended to the borders of Nepal and Bhutan in the Himalayas. Independent since 1947, India is the world's largest democracy, and at the current rate of growth, may overtake China as the world's most populous country during the 21st century. There are points of tension in the region over claims for independence by the Sikhs in the Indian Punjab and the Tamil separatists in Sri Lanka, and the long-standing dispute with Pakistan over Jammu and Kashmir in the north.

◀ *The towering Karakoram and Hindu Kush ranges, formed at the same time as the Himalayas, dominate Pakistan's northern borders. K2 on the border of northern Pakistan is the second highest mountain on Earth, at 28,251 ft (8611 m).*

The landscape

South Asia is effectively isolated from the rest of Asia by desert along the western flank of Pakistan, and a continuous wall of mountains, dominated by the Himalayas, to the north and east. The great basins of the Indus and Ganges separate this mountain fringe from the rolling plateau of the Indian peninsula, which is bordered by a line of coastal hills, the Eastern and Western Ghats.

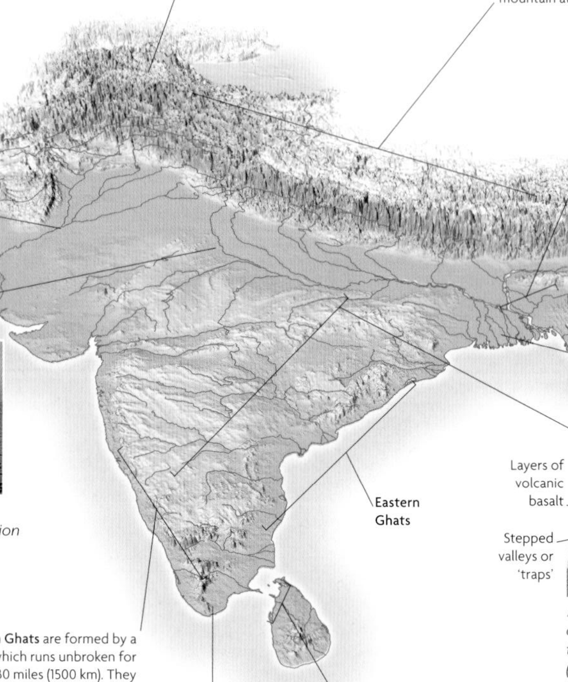

The Indus river flows more than 1970 miles (3180 km) from southwestern Tibet to its mouth on the Arabian Sea. It has an estimated catchment area of 450,000 sq miles (1,165,500 sq km).

The coast of western Pakistan is a staircase of folded rock strata caused by successive periods of rapid uplift.

◀ *The Indus valley near Skardu in northern Pakistan has been partially infilled by great quantities of eroded sediment. Most of this is carried from the region's bare slopes by swollen rivers during the spring thaw and mass movement activity.*

The Himalayas are the highest and most extensive mountain system in the world. They were formed when the Indo-Australian Plate collided with the Eurasian Plate about 40 million years ago, thrusting up huge masses of land and creating a 'ripple' effect, which formed lesser mountain ranges in Tibet and Southeast Asia. Mount Everest is the world's tallest mountain at 29,029 ft (8848 m).

Almost all of Bangladesh lies in the immense delta formed by the Ganges and the Brahmaputra which merge and flow out into the Bay of Bengal.

Bharatpur
Ganges delta
Deccan plateau
Eastern Ghats
Layers of volcanic basalt
Stepped valleys or 'traps'

▲ *Rivers flowing from the Himalayas into a broad depression in northern India have formed marshes around Bharatpur. They are now a sanctuary for numerous bird species.*

The Western Ghats are formed by a fault scarp which runs unbroken for more than 930 miles (1500 km). They reach their highest point at the southern Cardamom Hills.

Trivandrum in southern India normally receives the first of the monsoon rains, which are essential to south Asian agriculture and moderate the extreme summer heat. The monsoon then moves northwards over a period of about two months.

Coastal deposition has formed many typical features along the western coast of Sri Lanka. These include spits and bars, sometimes enclosing lagoons.

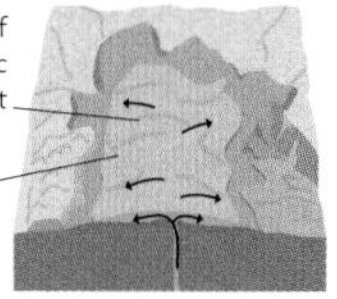

▲ *The Deccan plateau covers an area of more than 123,553 sq miles (320,000 sq km). It is formed of deep layers of volcanic basalt, reaching thicknesses of more than 9800 ft (3000 m) towards the coast. Distinctive stepped valleys cut in the basalt plateau by rivers are known as 'traps'.*

146 156 156 156 148 142

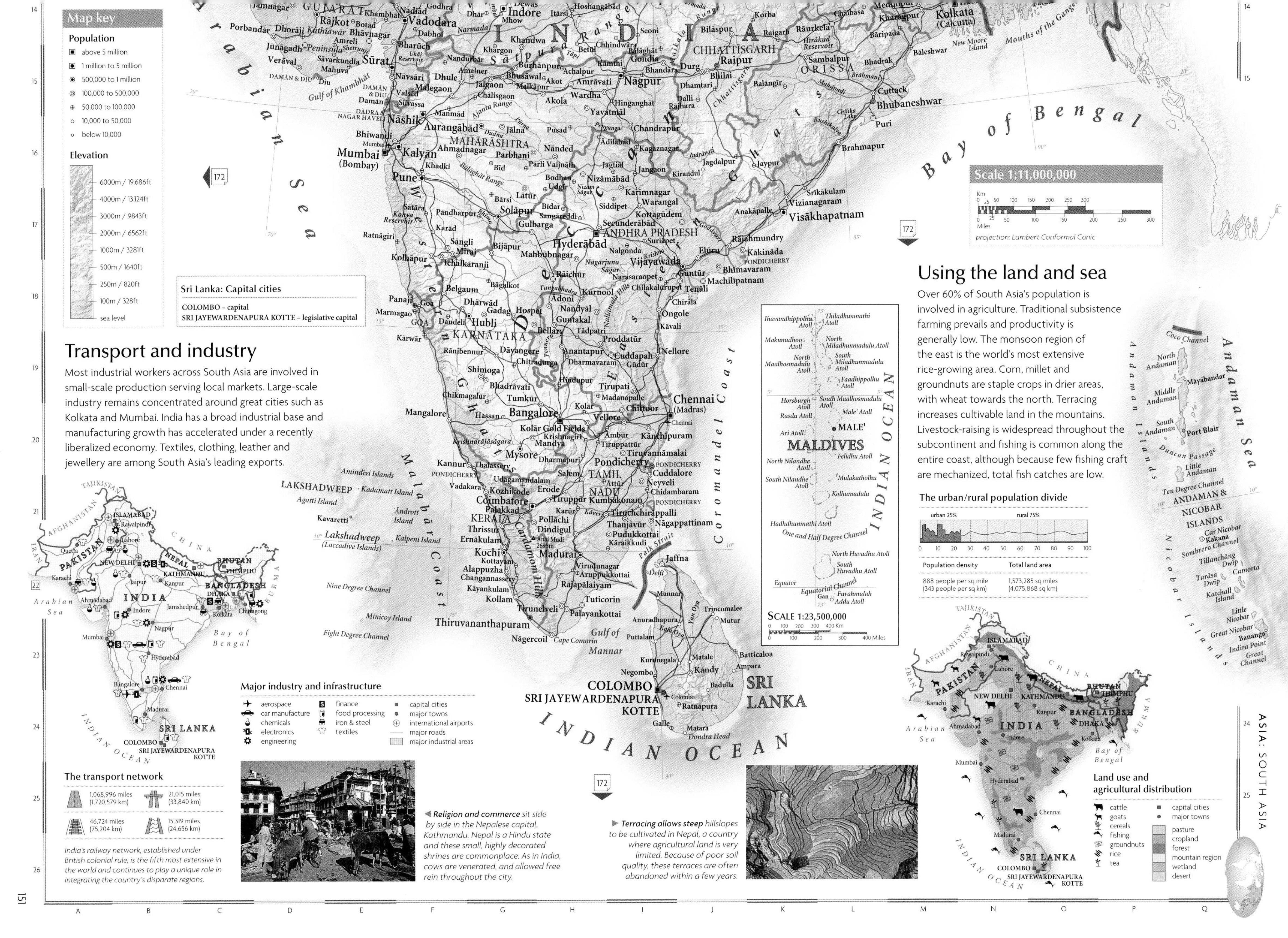
Map key
Population
above 5 million
1 million to 5 million
500,000 to 1 million
100,000 to 500,000
50,000 to 100,000
10,000 to 50,000
below 10,000
Elevation
6000m / 19,686ft
4000m / 13,124ft
3000m / 9843ft
2000m / 6562ft
1000m / 3281ft
500m / 1640ft
250m / 820ft
100m / 328ft
sea level
Scale 1:11,000,000
projection: Lambert Conformal Conic
SCALE 1:23,500,000
MALDIVES
INDIA
SRI LANKA
Arabian Sea
Bay of Bengal
Andaman Sea
INDIAN OCEAN
Coromandel Coast
Malabār Coast
Western Ghats
Eastern Ghats
Deccan
Mumbai (Bombay)
Kolkata (Calcutta)
Chennai (Madras)
Hyderābād
Bangalore
COLOMBO
SRI JAYEWARDENAPURA KOTTE
MALE'
LAKSHADWEEP
ANDAMAN & NICOBAR ISLANDS
Port Blair
Lakshadweep (Laccadive Islands)
Nine Degree Channel
Eight Degree Channel
Ten Degree Channel
Gulf of Mannar
Palk Strait
Cape Comorin

Sri Lanka: Capital cities

COLOMBO – capital
SRI JAYEWARDENAPURA KOTTE – legislative capital

Transport and industry

Most industrial workers across South Asia are involved in small-scale production serving local markets. Large-scale industry remains concentrated around great cities such as Kolkata and Mumbai. India has a broad industrial base and manufacturing growth has accelerated under a recently liberalized economy. Textiles, clothing, leather and jewellery are among South Asia's leading exports.

Major industry and infrastructure

aerospace, car manufacture, chemicals, electronics, engineering, finance, food processing, iron & steel, textiles, capital cities, major towns, international airports, major roads, major industrial areas

The transport network

1,068,996 miles (1,720,579 km)	21,015 miles (33,840 km)
46,724 miles (75,204 km)	15,319 miles (24,656 km)

India's railway network, established under British colonial rule, is the fifth most extensive in the world and continues to play a unique role in integrating the country's disparate regions.

◀ ***Religion and commerce*** *sit side by side in the Nepalese capital, Kathmandu. Nepal is a Hindu state and these small, highly decorated shrines are commonplace. As in India, cows are venerated, and allowed free rein throughout the city.*

▶ ***Terracing allows steep*** *hillslopes to be cultivated in Nepal, a country where agricultural land is very limited. Because of poor soil quality, these terraces are often abandoned within a few years.*

Using the land and sea

Over 60% of South Asia's population is involved in agriculture. Traditional subsistence farming prevails and productivity is generally low. The monsoon region of the east is the world's most extensive rice-growing area. Corn, millet and groundnuts are staple crops in drier areas, with wheat towards the north. Terracing increases cultivable land in the mountains. Livestock-raising is widespread throughout the subcontinent and fishing is common along the entire coast, although because few fishing craft are mechanized, total fish catches are low.

The urban/rural population divide

urban 25% / rural 75%

Population density	Total land area
888 people per sq mile (343 people per sq km)	1,573,285 sq miles (4,075,868 sq km)

Land use and agricultural distribution

cattle, goats, cereals, fishing, groundnuts, rice, tea, capital cities, major towns, pasture, cropland, forest, mountain region, wetland, desert

Northern India & the Himalayan states

BANGLADESH, BHUTAN, NEPAL, Arunachal Pradesh, Assam, Bihar, Chandigarh, Delhi, Haryana, Himachal Pradesh, Jammu & Kashmir, Jharkhand, Manipur, Meghalaya, Mizoram, Nagaland, Punjab, Rajasthan, Sikkim, Tripura, Uttarakhand, Uttar Pradesh, West Bengal

The Ganges and Brahmaputra river basins and the massive mountain barrier of the Himalayas define this region's landscape and have served to reinforce potent cultural and religious differences among its people. Hinduism pervades most aspects of national life and is a growing political force within India, a secular country which also encompasses the centre of Sikhism at Amritsar and the world's largest Muslim minority. Nepal is a crowded mountain state, which faces severe ecological problems from deforestation, while the tiny Himalayan Buddhist kingdom of Bhutan is emerging from long-term isolation, to welcome selected visitors. The Muslim state of Bangladesh, formerly East Pakistan, is one of the world's most densely populated countries and one of the poorest, with more than 145 million people living largely on the massive Ganges/Brahmaputra delta. Many Bangladeshis live under threat of repeated, catastrophic floods.

Scale 1:6,500,000
projection: Lambert Conformal Conic
AFGHANISTAN
CHINA
PAKISTAN
INDIA
JAMMU AND KASHMIR
HIMACHAL PRADESH
PUNJAB
HARYANA
UTTARAKHAND
UTTAR PRADESH
RĀJASTHĀN
GUJARAT
MADHYA PRADESH
FAR WESTERN
Thar Desert
Karakoram Range
Zāskār Range
Ladakh Range
Pīr Panjāl Range
Arāvali Range
Aksai Chin (Administered by China, claimed by India)
(Claimed by India)
(Line of control)
Demchok/Dêmqog (Administered by China, claimed by India)
K2 8611m
Srīnagar
Jammu
Amritsar
Ludhiāna
Chandigarh
Shimla
Dehra Dūn
DELHI
NEW DELHI
Meerut
Ghāziābād
Farīdābād
Bareilly
Āgra
Jaipur
Jodhpur
Bīkāner
Ajmer
Udaipur
Kota
Kānpur
Lucknow
Allahābād
Jhānsi
Tropic of Cancer
148
154
156
NEPAL
BHUTAN
BANGLADESH
BAY OF BENGAL
KATHMANDU
THIMPHU
DHAKA
Kolkata

The Golden Temple *in Amritsar, the most sacred shrine of the Sikh religion, was the scene of violent clashes between Sikh separatists and government forces in 1984.*

Map key

Population

- 1 million to 5 million
- 500,000 to 1 million
- 100,000 to 500,000
- 50,000 to 100,000
- 10,000 to 50,000
- below 10,000

Elevation

- 6000m / 19,686ft
- 4000m / 13,124ft
- 3000m / 9843ft
- 2000m / 6562ft
- 1000m / 3281ft
- 500m / 1640ft
- 250m / 820ft
- 100m / 328ft
- sea level

Transport and industry

Textiles, engineering, chemicals and electronics are leading industries in north India. The plateau of Chota Nagpur provides ore for iron and steel production in the major industrial region northeast of Kolkata. Bangladesh processes jute and Nepal has a small manufacturing sector based on agricultural produce, while Bhutan's limited industry is concentrated in the southern lowland area.

Major industry and infrastructure

- adventure tourism
- car manufacture
- chemicals
- coal
- electronics
- engineering
- finance
- food processing
- iron & steel
- jute processing
- oil
- tea processing
- textiles
- capital cities
- major towns
- international airports
- major roads
- major industrial areas

The transport network

Over 60% of Bangladesh's internal trade is carried by boat. The country has a very disjointed land transport network, with no bridges over the Brahmaputra and few road crossings on the Ganges river.

The landscape

Most of the region is drained by the Ganges river, which meets the Brahmaputra in Bangladesh to form an immense delta before flowing into the Bay of Bengal. The Himalayas extend eastwards over 1500 miles (2400 km), from the parallel ranges running through Jammu and Kashmir. The Thar Desert occupies the southwest.

The Pir Panjal range in southwestern Kashmir rises to elevations of 12,500 ft (3810 m). Despite the freezing conditions, settlements and extensive pastures are found above the tree line.

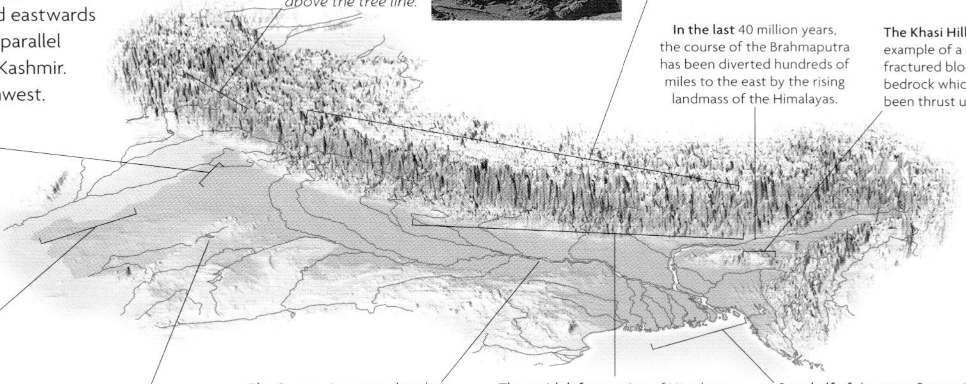

The northern ranges of the Himalayas contain the highest mountains in the world, with average heights of more than 23,000 ft (7000 m) and many peaks higher than 26,000 ft (8000 m).

In the last 40 million years, the course of the Brahmaputra has been diverted hundreds of miles to the east by the rising landmass of the Himalayas.

The Khasi Hills are an example of a *horst*, a fractured block of bedrock which has been thrust upwards.

▲ ***The summit of*** *Machhapuchhre rises to 22,942 ft (6993 m). It is also known as the 'Fish's Tail' because of its distinctive peak.*

The Indian Punjab lies mainly to the west of the Ganges watershed and its rivers flow into the Indus. Control of this water resource has been a source of great friction with neighbouring Pakistan.

The border between India and Pakistan runs through the Thar Desert, an area of sandy *seif* dunes 50–100 ft (15–30 m) in height. Fossils found in the desert indicate that the dunes, stabilized by vegetation, have been in their current position for about 3000 years.

Debris slides in the middle Himalayas

Soil blocks
Slide plain
Debris fans at base of slope

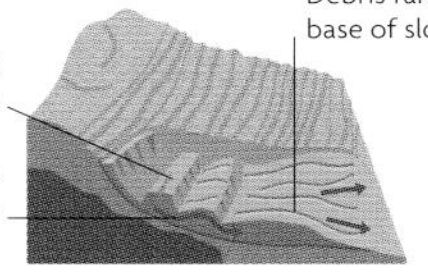

▲ ***Soil loss*** *in the middle Himalayas has largely been attributed to debris slides, where large blocks of soil are mobilized by saturation along a slide plane. Once mobile, the soil slides down the slope, gaining speed and thinning to form a fan at the base of the slope.*

Sambhar Salt Lake in Rajasthan is India's largest lake. Unlike most of the Himalayan lakes which are glacial in origin – formed in ice-scoured basins or as the result of depositional damming – it is an ephemeral salt lake filled periodically by flash flooding.

The Ganges river, sacred to the Hindu people, drains a vast lowland area at the base of the Himalayas. The northern plains are covered by sandy deposits, broken by mud-banks formed when the river floods.

The rapid deforestation of Himalayan valleys has led to acute soil erosion and increased rates of rainwater run-off, both cited as possible causes of the worsening floods downstream in the Ganges/Brahmaputra delta, although natural rates are high and may be the real cause.

Over half of the great Ganges/Brahmaputra delta floods each year during the monsoon as rivers, swollen by meltwater from the Himalayas and by excess rainwater, break their banks and fertilize the land with nutrient-rich sediment.

Using the land

Grain production dominates land use. Rice is most widely grown in the east. Irrigation and new crop strains have dramatically increased yields in the Punjab, a major wheat-producing area. River flood plains are intensively farmed and livestock-herding is widespread, particularly in Bhutan. Regional crops include jute in Bangladesh, tea in Assam, cardamom in Sikkim and saffron in Kashmir.

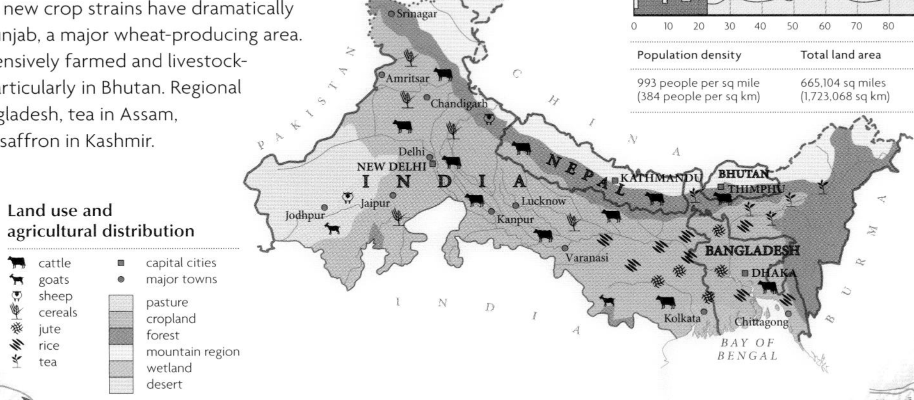

The urban/rural population divide

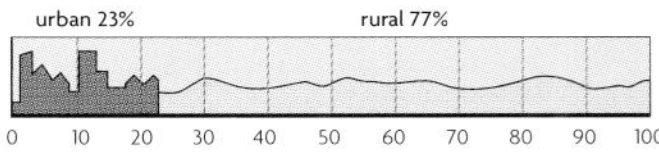

urban 23% | rural 77%

0 10 20 30 40 50 60 70 80 90 100

Population density	Total land area
993 people per sq mile (384 people per sq km)	665,104 sq miles (1,723,068 sq km)

Land use and agricultural distribution

cattle, goats, sheep, cereals, jute, rice, tea, capital cities, major towns, pasture, cropland, forest, mountain region, wetland, desert

▲ ***An adverse climate,*** *steep slopes and poor soils limit crop cultivation in Bhutan, which is a largely agrarian economy. Rice, corn and wheat are the main staples, although orchards are being established as the soil and climate suit this type of farming.*

156

166

172

▲ ***Flooded streets*** *in Dhaka, Bangladesh are a testament to the region's vulnerability to flooding. In 1988 alone, 75% of the country was flooded, leaving thousands of people dead and over 25 million homeless.*

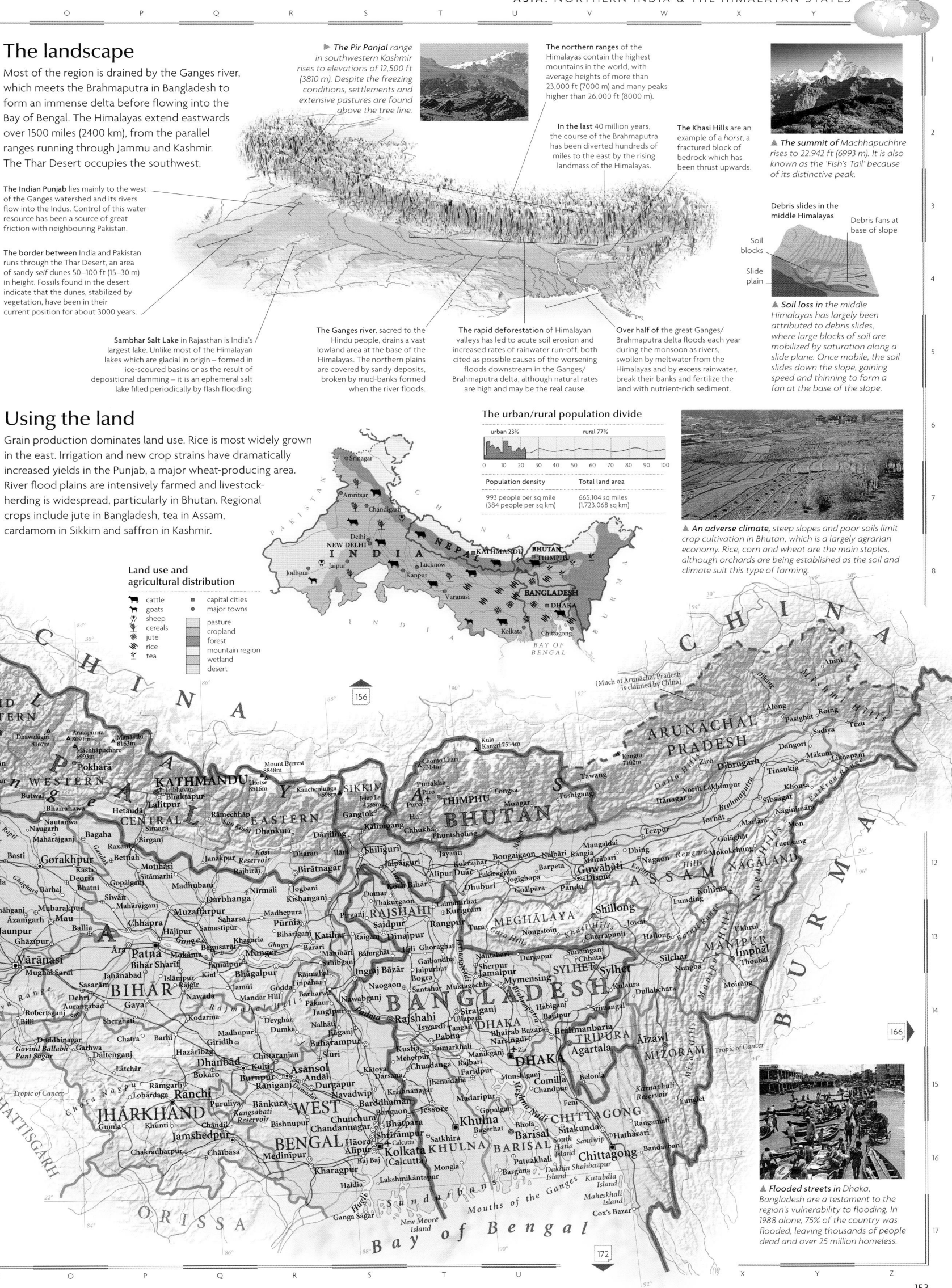

Southern India & Sri Lanka

SRI LANKA, Andhra Pradesh, Chhattisgarh, Dadra & Nagar Haveli, Daman & Diu, Goa, Gujarat, Karnataka, Kerala, Lakshadweep, Madhya Pradesh, Maharashtra, Orissa, Pondicherry, Tamil Nadu

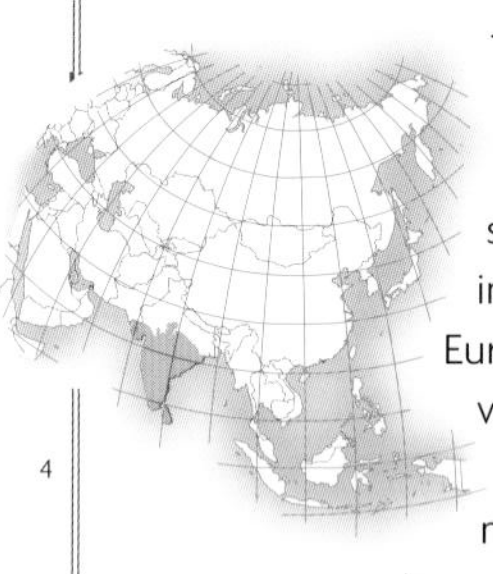

The unique and highly independent southern states reflect the diverse and decentralized nature of India, which has fourteen official languages. The southern half of the peninsula lay beyond the reach of early invaders from the north and retained the distinct and ancient culture of Dravidian peoples such as the Tamils, whose language is spoken in preference to Hindi throughout southern India. The interior plateau of southern India is less densely populated than the coastal lowlands, where the European colonial imprint is strongest. Urban and industrial growth is accelerating, but southern India's vast population remains predominantly rural. The island of Sri Lanka has two distinct cultural groups; the mainly Buddhist Sinhalese majority, and the Tamil minority whose struggle for a homeland in the northeast has led to prolonged civil war.

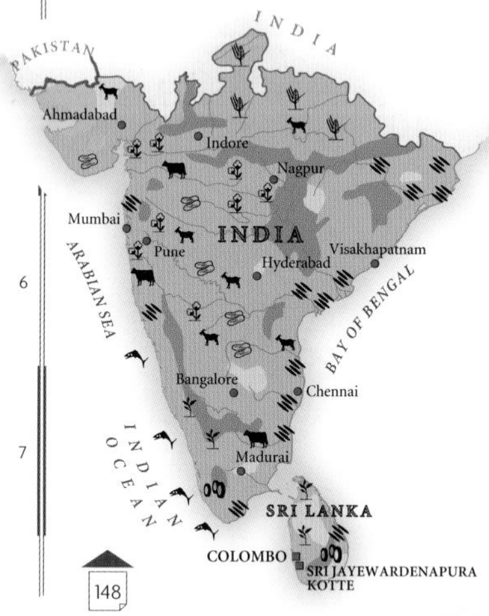

Using the land and sea

Rice is the main staple in the east, in Sri Lanka and along the humid Malabar Coast. Groundnuts are grown on the Deccan plateau, with wheat, corn and chickpeas, towards the north. Sri Lanka is a leading exporter of tea, coconuts and rubber. Cotton plantations supply local mills around Nagpur and Mumbai. Fishing supports many communities in Kerala and the Laccadive Islands.

The urban/rural population divide

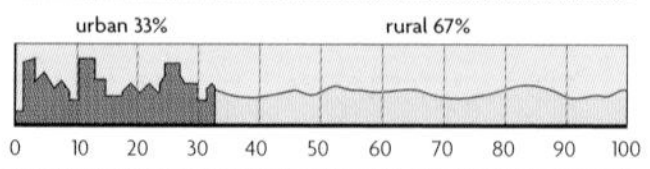

urban 33% rural 67%

Population density	Total land area
730 people per sq mile (282 people per sq km)	698,295 sq miles (1,809,054 sq km)

Land use and agricultural distribution

cattle, goats, cereals, cotton, fishing, groundnuts, rice, rubber, tea, capital cities, major towns, pasture, cropland, forest, wetland

The landscape

The undulating Deccan plateau underlies most of southern India; it slopes gently down towards the east and is largely enclosed by the Ghats coastal hill ranges. The Western Ghats run continuously along the Arabian Sea coast, while the Eastern Ghats are interrupted by rivers which follow the slope of the plateau and flow across broad lowlands into the Bay of Bengal. The plateaux and basins of Sri Lanka's central highlands are surrounded by a broad plain.

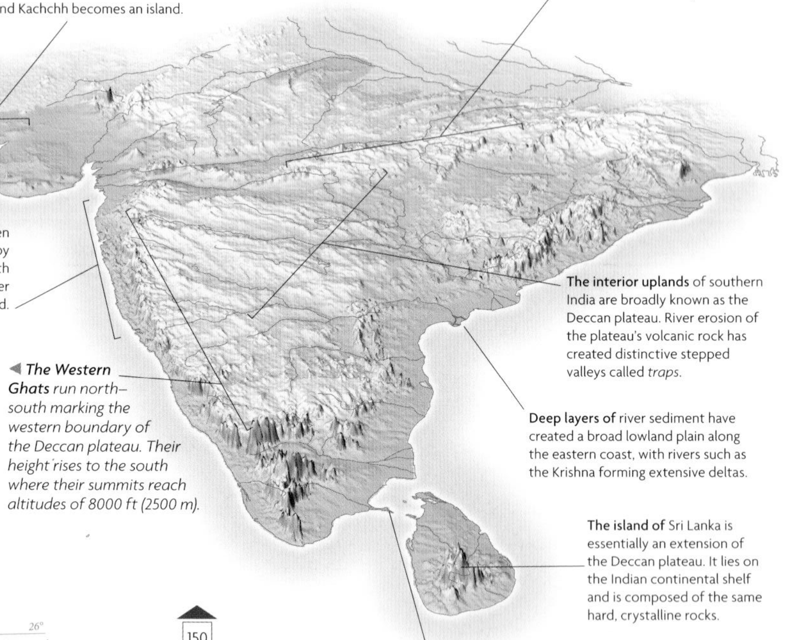

The Rann of Kachchh tidal marshes encircle the low-lying Kachchh peninsula. For several months during the rainy season the water level of the marshes rises and Kachchh becomes an island.

Along the northern boundary of the Deccan plateau, old basement rocks are interspersed with younger sedimentary strata. This creates spectacular scarplands, cut by numerous waterfalls along the softer sedimentary strata.

The Konkan coast, which runs between Daman and Goa, is characterized by rocky headlands, and bays with crescent-shaped beaches. Flooded river valleys known as *rias* extend inland.

The interior uplands of southern India are broadly known as the Deccan plateau. River erosion of the plateau's volcanic rock has created distinctive stepped valleys called *traps*.

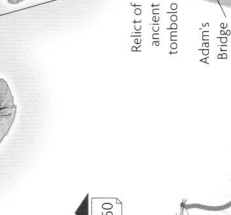

◀ ***The Western Ghats*** *run north–south marking the western boundary of the Deccan plateau. Their height rises to the south where their summits reach altitudes of 8000 ft (2500 m).*

Deep layers of river sediment have created a broad lowland plain along the eastern coast, with rivers such as the Krishna forming extensive deltas.

The island of Sri Lanka is essentially an extension of the Deccan plateau. It lies on the Indian continental shelf and is composed of the same hard, crystalline rocks.

Adam's Bridge

Relict of ancient tombolo — Ocean currents cause sediment build up — Adam's Bridge — Sri Lanka

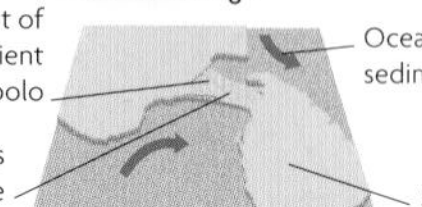

▲ ***Adam's Bridge (Rama's Bridge)*** *is a chain of sandy shoals lying about 4 ft (1.2 m) under the sea between India and Sri Lanka. They once formed the world's longest tombolo, or land bridge, before the sea level began to rise several thousand years ago.*

148 150 150 150 172

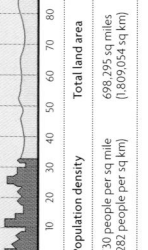

Map key

Population

- above 5 million
- 1 million to 5 million
- 500,000 to 1 million
- 100,000 to 500,000
- 50,000 to 100,000
- 10,000 to 50,000
- below 10,000

Elevation

- 2000m / 6562ft
- 1000m / 3281ft
- 500m / 1640ft
- 250m / 820ft
- 100m / 328ft
- sea level

◀ *Sea pencils thrive* on the coral reefs around the coast of the Laccadive Islands and Sri Lanka. The reefs support an amazing diversity of marine life, but are increasingly under threat from growing coastal populations.

Sri Lanka: Capital cities

COLOMBO – capital
SRI JAYEWARDENAPURA KOTTE – legislative capital

▲ *Local fisheries around* Sri Lanka afford great potential for exploitation. However, many fishermen living on the coastal fringes saw their livelihoods destroyed by the devastating effects of the Asian tsunami in 2004.

Scale 1:7,000,000

projection: Lambert Conformal Conic

▲ *The great triumphal* arch of Charminar, built in 1591, epitomizes the fine Islamic architecture which the Moghuls brought from the north to Hyderabad, the capital of Andhra Pradesh.

Transport and industry

South India has a broad industrial base, with three leading regions. Around Mumbai, Bangalore and Ahmadabad, cotton mills and chemical plants make use of cheap hydro-electric power generated in the Western Ghats. Light engineering and textiles are well established to the south and west of Chennai. Sri Lanka's industry is based mainly on the processing of agricultural products.

Major industry and infrastructure

- aerospace
- car manufacture
- chemicals
- electronics
- engineering
- food processing
- iron & steel
- pharmaceuticals
- printing & publishing
- shipbuilding
- tea processing
- textiles
- tobacco processing
- capital cities
- major towns
- international airports
- major roads
- major industrial areas

The transport network

India's hard-surfaced road network has grown almost tenfold since independence, yet many villages are still only accessible on foot, even in densely-populated rural areas.

▶ *Mumbai is one* of the largest and most densely-populated cities in the world. It is the centre of India's textile trade and has important finance and commerce sectors.

172

Mainland East Asia

CHINA, MONGOLIA, NORTH KOREA, SOUTH KOREA, TAIWAN

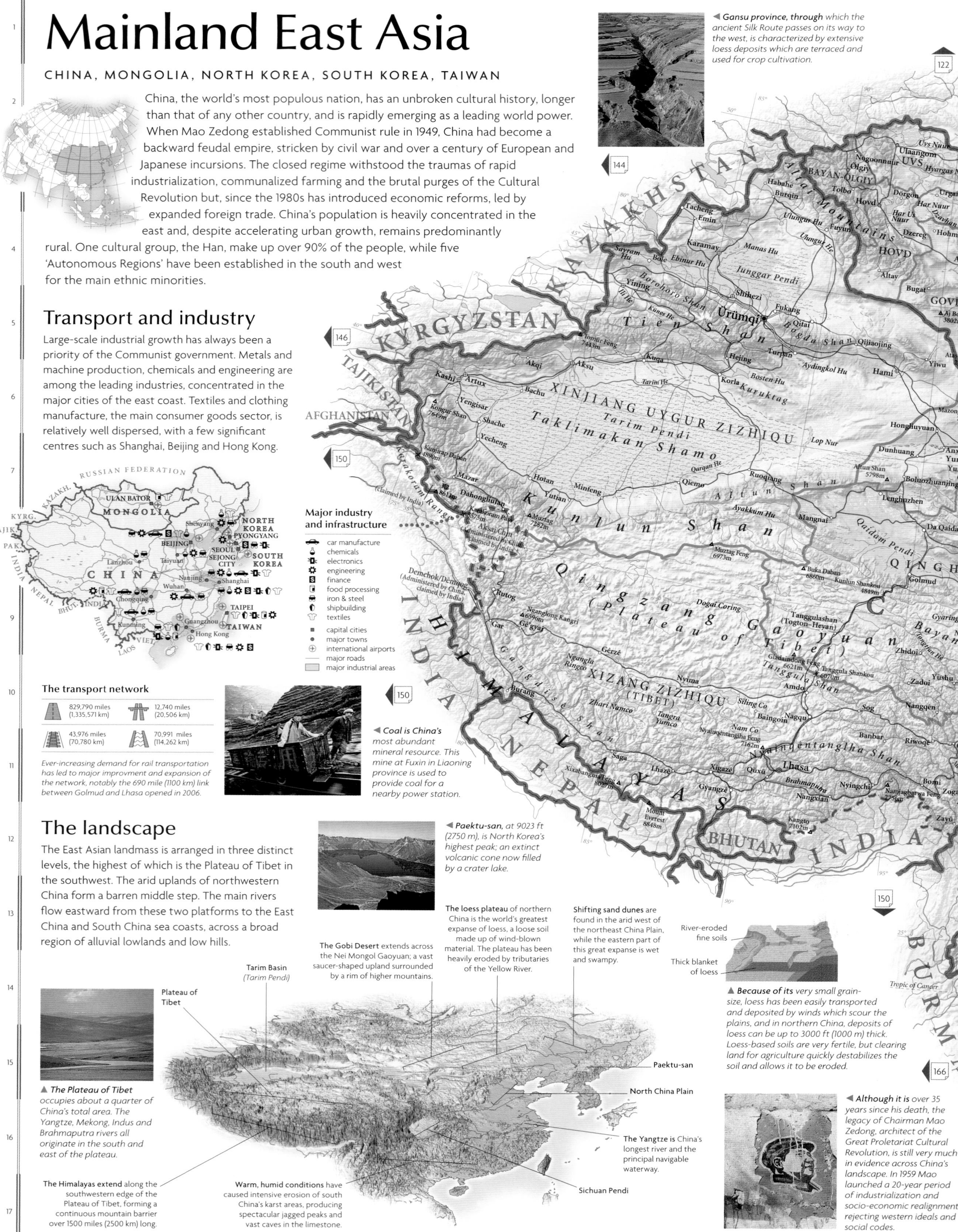

China, the world's most populous nation, has an unbroken cultural history, longer than that of any other country, and is rapidly emerging as a leading world power. When Mao Zedong established Communist rule in 1949, China had become a backward feudal empire, stricken by civil war and over a century of European and Japanese incursions. The closed regime withstood the traumas of rapid industrialization, communalized farming and the brutal purges of the Cultural Revolution but, since the 1980s has introduced economic reforms, led by expanded foreign trade. China's population is heavily concentrated in the east and, despite accelerating urban growth, remains predominantly rural. One cultural group, the Han, make up over 90% of the people, while five 'Autonomous Regions' have been established in the south and west for the main ethnic minorities.

◀ **Gansu province, through** *which the ancient Silk Route passes on its way to the west, is characterized by extensive loess deposits which are terraced and used for crop cultivation.*

Transport and industry

Large-scale industrial growth has always been a priority of the Communist government. Metals and machine production, chemicals and engineering are among the leading industries, concentrated in the major cities of the east coast. Textiles and clothing manufacture, the main consumer goods sector, is relatively well dispersed, with a few significant centres such as Shanghai, Beijing and Hong Kong.

Major industry and infrastructure
car manufacture
chemicals
electronics
engineering
finance
food processing
iron & steel
shipbuilding
textiles
capital cities
major towns
international airports
major roads
major industrial areas

The transport network

829,790 miles (1,335,571 km)		12,740 miles (20,506 km)	
43,976 miles (70,780 km)		70,991 miles (114,262 km)	

Ever-increasing demand for rail transportation has led to major improvment and expansion of the network, notably the 690 mile (1100 km) link between Golmud and Lhasa opened in 2006.

◀ **Coal is China's** *most abundant mineral resource. This mine at Fuxin in Liaoning province is used to provide coal for a nearby power station.*

The landscape

The East Asian landmass is arranged in three distinct levels, the highest of which is the Plateau of Tibet in the southwest. The arid uplands of northwestern China form a barren middle step. The main rivers flow eastward from these two platforms to the East China and South China sea coasts, across a broad region of alluvial lowlands and low hills.

◀ **Paektu-san,** *at 9023 ft (2750 m), is North Korea's highest peak; an extinct volcanic cone now filled by a crater lake.*

▲ **The Plateau of Tibet** *occupies about a quarter of China's total area. The Yangtze, Mekong, Indus and Brahmaputra rivers all originate in the south and east of the plateau.*

Plateau of Tibet
Tarim Basin (Tarim Pendi)
Paektu-san
North China Plain
Sichuan Pendi
River-eroded fine soils
Thick blanket of loess

The Gobi Desert extends across the Nei Mongol Gaoyuan; a vast saucer-shaped upland surrounded by a rim of higher mountains.

The loess plateau of northern China is the world's greatest expanse of loess, a loose soil made up of wind-blown material. The plateau has been heavily eroded by tributaries of the Yellow River.

Shifting sand dunes are found in the arid west of the northeast China Plain, while the eastern part of this great expanse is wet and swampy.

The Yangtze is China's longest river and the principal navigable waterway.

The Himalayas extend along the southwestern edge of the Plateau of Tibet, forming a continuous mountain barrier over 1500 miles (2500 km) long.

Warm, humid conditions have caused intensive erosion of south China's karst areas, producing spectacular jagged peaks and vast caves in the limestone.

▲ **Because of its** *very small grain-size, loess has been easily transported and deposited by winds which scour the plains, and in northern China, deposits of loess can be up to 3000 ft (1000 m) thick. Loess-based soils are very fertile, but clearing land for agriculture quickly destabilizes the soil and allows it to be eroded.*

◀ **Although it is** *over 35 years since his death, the legacy of Chairman Mao Zedong, architect of the Great Proletariat Cultural Revolution, is still very much in evidence across China's landscape. In 1959 Mao launched a 20-year period of industrialization and socio-economic realignment, rejecting western ideals and social codes.*

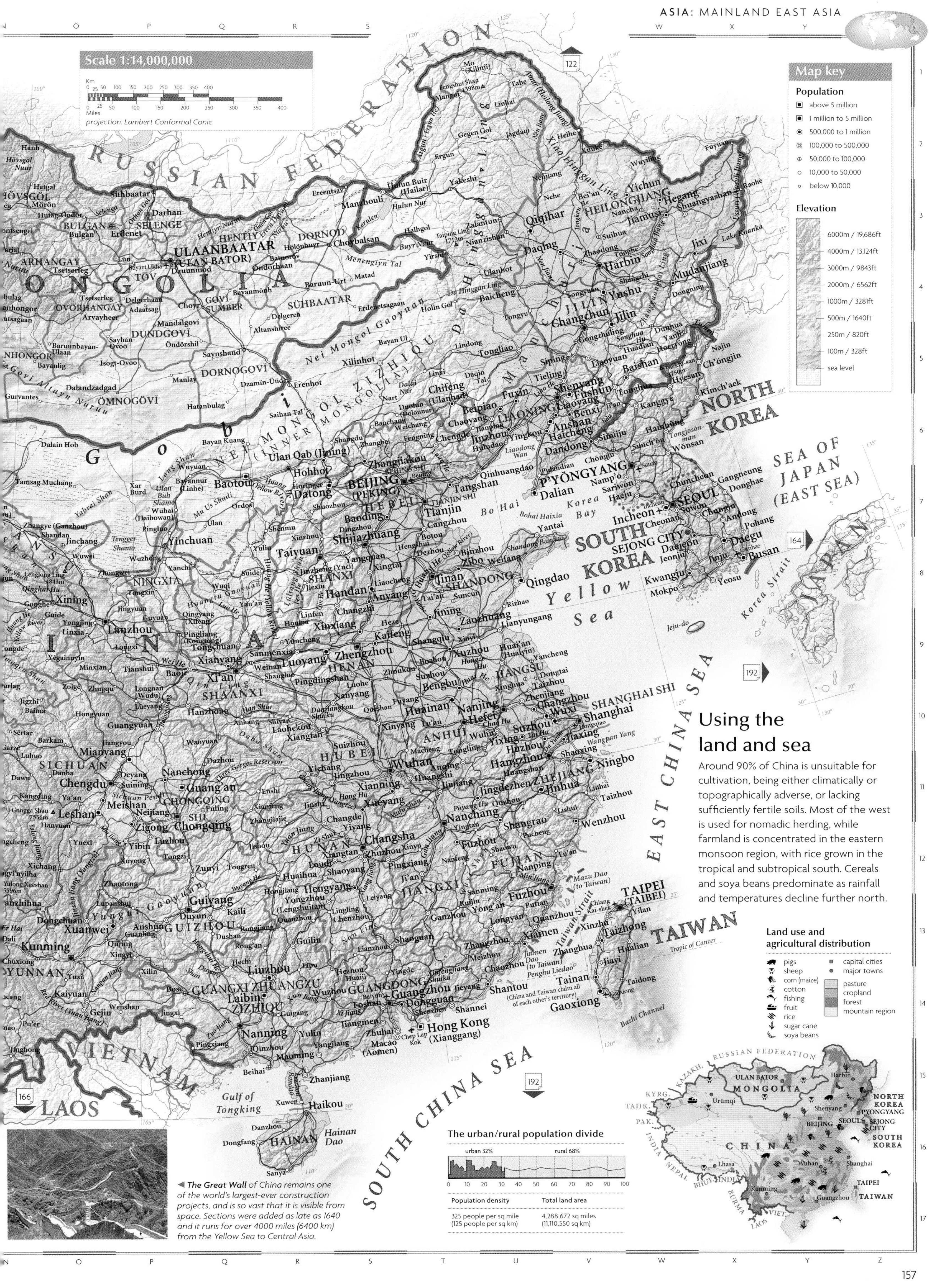
Scale 1:14,000,000
Km
Miles
projection: Lambert Conformal Conic
Map key
Population
above 5 million
1 million to 5 million
500,000 to 1 million
100,000 to 500,000
50,000 to 100,000
10,000 to 50,000
below 10,000
Elevation
6000m / 19,686ft
4000m / 13,124ft
3000m / 9843ft
2000m / 6562ft
1000m / 3281ft
500m / 1640ft
250m / 820ft
100m / 328ft
sea level
RUSSIAN FEDERATION
MONGOLIA
CHINA
NORTH KOREA
SOUTH KOREA
JAPAN
TAIWAN
VIETNAM
LAOS
SEA OF JAPAN (EAST SEA)
Yellow Sea
EAST CHINA SEA
SOUTH CHINA SEA
Land use and agricultural distribution
pigs
sheep
corn (maize)
cotton
fishing
fruit
rice
sugar cane
soya beans
capital cities
major towns
pasture
cropland
forest
mountain region
The urban/rural population divide
urban 32%
rural 68%
Population density
325 people per sq mile (125 people per sq km)
Total land area
4,288,672 sq miles (11,110,550 sq km)

Using the land and sea

Around 90% of China is unsuitable for cultivation, being either climatically or topographically adverse, or lacking sufficiently fertile soils. Most of the west is used for nomadic herding, while farmland is concentrated in the eastern monsoon region, with rice grown in the tropical and subtropical south. Cereals and soya beans predominate as rainfall and temperatures decline further north.

◀ *The Great Wall* of China remains one of the world's largest-ever construction projects, and is so vast that it is visible from space. Sections were added as late as 1640 and it runs for over 4000 miles (6400 km) from the Yellow Sea to Central Asia.

Western China

Gansu, Ningxia, Qinghai, Tibet, Xinjiang

The plateaux and basins of China's dry, desolate western domain are sparsely populated and largely undeveloped, although they have rich mineral reserves; they also form a critical buffer zone for China, in a geographically important and culturally sensitive part of the Asian continent. Across most of the west, the Han Chinese are outnumbered by a range of cultural groups, including the Uygur, the largest group of the various semi-nomadic Muslim peoples from Central Asia. The remote, inhospitable Plateau of Tibet is the world's coldest and highest plateau. It has been occupied by the Chinese since 1950. Tibet is one of western China's five 'Autonomous Regions', but its reclusive Buddhist culture has been systematically undermined by the Chinese government.

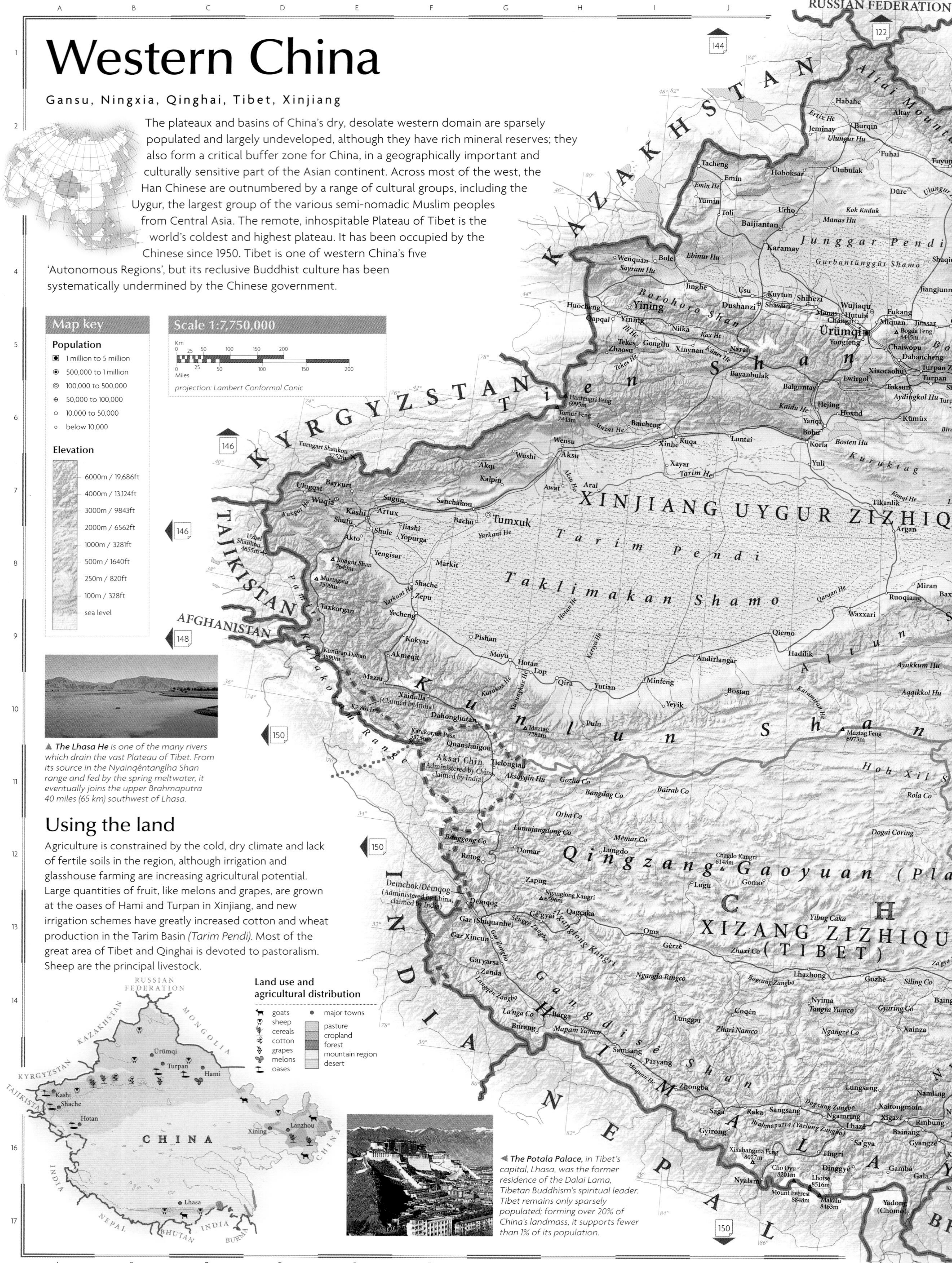

Map key
Population
1 million to 5 million
500,000 to 1 million
100,000 to 500,000
50,000 to 100,000
10,000 to 50,000
below 10,000
Elevation
6000m / 19,686ft
4000m / 13,124ft
3000m / 9843ft
2000m / 6562ft
1000m / 3281ft
500m / 1640ft
250m / 820ft
100m / 328ft
sea level
Scale 1:7,750,000
Km
Miles
projection: Lambert Conformal Conic
RUSSIAN FEDERATION
KAZAKHSTAN
KYRGYZSTAN
TAJIKISTAN
AFGHANISTAN
INDIA
NEPAL
XINJIANG UYGUR ZIZHIQU
XIZANG ZIZHIQU (TIBET)
Tarim Pendi
Taklimakan Shamo
Junggar Pendi
Tien Shan
Kunlun Shan
Altun Shan
Qingzang Gaoyuan (Plateau of Tibet)
Gangdisê Shan
Karakoram Range
Pamirs
Ürümqi
Yining
Kashi
Hotan
Aksu
Kuqa
Korla
Turpan
Shache
Yecheng
Qiemo
Ruoqiang
Aksai Chin (Administered by China, claimed by India)
Demchok/Dêmqog (Administered by China, claimed by India)
K2 8611m
Mount Everest 8848m
Cho Oyu 8201m
Lhotse 8516m
Makalu 8463m
Muztagata 7509m
Kongur Shan 7649m
Hantengri Feng 6995m
Tomür Feng 7443m
Bogda Feng 5445m
Muztag 7282m
Muztag Feng 6973m
Chagdo Kangri 6148m
Nganglong Kangri 6596m
Xixabangma Feng 8027m
Tarim He
Yarkant He
Hotan He
Keriya He
Ili He
Kax He
Ertix He
Ulungur Hu
Bosten Hu
Brahmaputra (Yarlung Zangbo)
Bangong Co
Mapam Yumco
Zhari Namco
Ngangla Ringco
Dogai Coring
Hoh Xil Shan
Kuruktag
144
146
146
148
150
150
150
150
122

▲ *The Lhasa He* is one of the many rivers which drain the vast Plateau of Tibet. From its source in the Nyainqêntanglha Shan range and fed by the spring meltwater, it eventually joins the upper Brahmaputra 40 miles (65 km) southwest of Lhasa.

Using the land

Agriculture is constrained by the cold, dry climate and lack of fertile soils in the region, although irrigation and glasshouse farming are increasing agricultural potential. Large quantities of fruit, like melons and grapes, are grown at the oases of Hami and Turpan in Xinjiang, and new irrigation schemes have greatly increased cotton and wheat production in the Tarim Basin *(Tarim Pendi)*. Most of the great area of Tibet and Qinghai is devoted to pastoralism. Sheep are the principal livestock.

Land use and agricultural distribution

goats, sheep, cereals, cotton, grapes, melons, oases; major towns; pasture, cropland, forest, mountain region, desert

◀ *The Potala Palace*, in Tibet's capital, Lhasa, was the former residence of the Dalai Lama, Tibetan Buddhism's spiritual leader. Tibet remains only sparsely populated; forming over 20% of China's landmass, it supports fewer than 1% of its population.

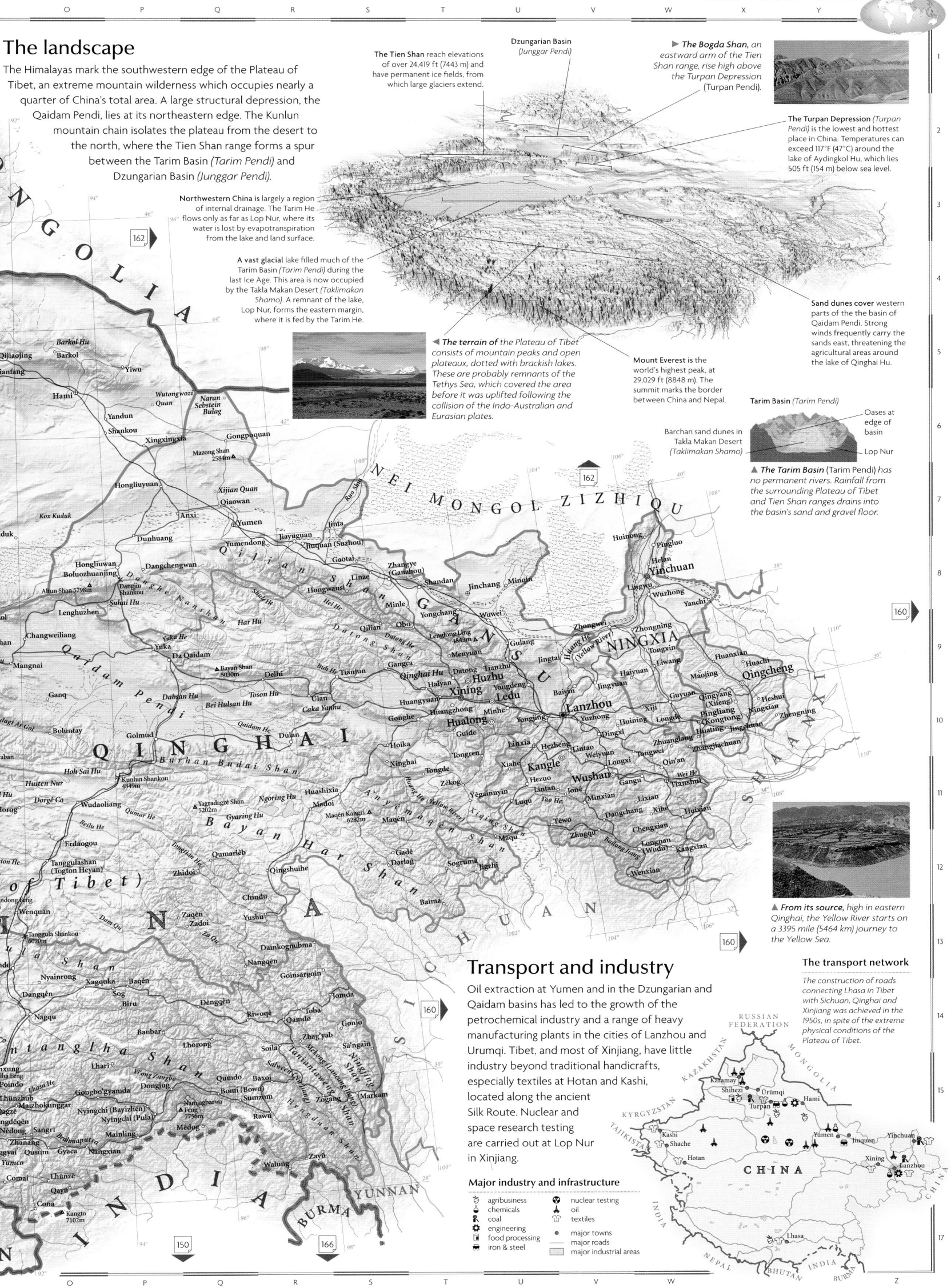

The landscape

The Himalayas mark the southwestern edge of the Plateau of Tibet, an extreme mountain wilderness which occupies nearly a quarter of China's total area. A large structural depression, the Qaidam Pendi, lies at its northeastern edge. The Kunlun mountain chain isolates the plateau from the desert to the north, where the Tien Shan range forms a spur between the Tarim Basin *(Tarim Pendi)* and Dzungarian Basin *(Junggar Pendi)*.

The Tien Shan reach elevations of over 24,419 ft (7443 m) and have permanent ice fields, from which large glaciers extend.

Dzungarian Basin *(Junggar Pendi)*

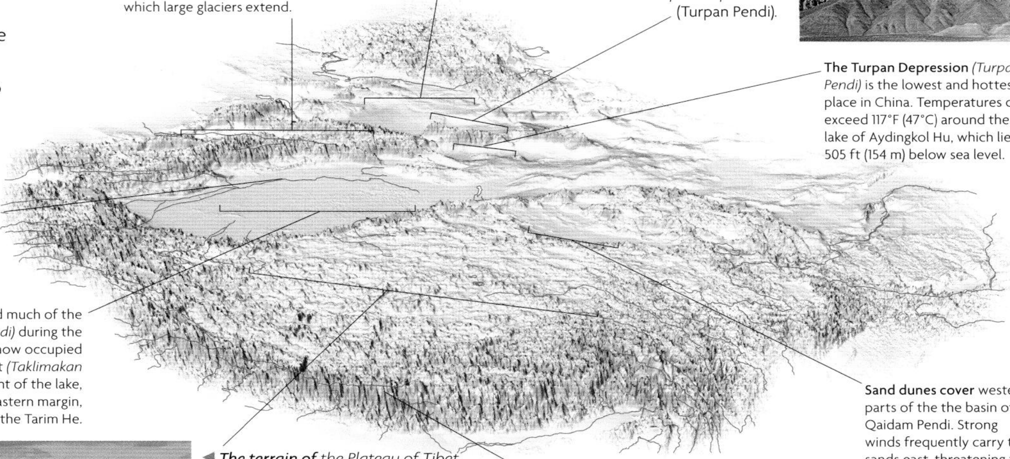

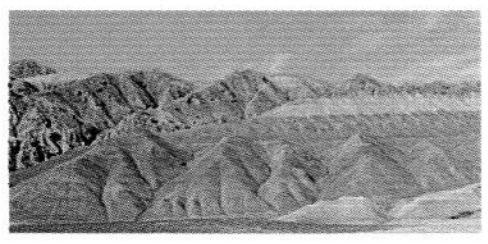

▶ ***The Bogda Shan**, an eastward arm of the Tien Shan range, rise high above the Turpan Depression* (Turpan Pendi).

The Turpan Depression *(Turpan Pendi)* is the lowest and hottest place in China. Temperatures can exceed 117°F (47°C) around the lake of Aydingkol Hu, which lies 505 ft (154 m) below sea level.

Northwestern China is largely a region of internal drainage. The Tarim He flows only as far as Lop Nur, where its water is lost by evapotranspiration from the lake and land surface.

A vast glacial lake filled much of the Tarim Basin *(Tarim Pendi)* during the last Ice Age. This area is now occupied by the Takla Makan Desert *(Taklimakan Shamo)*. A remnant of the lake, Lop Nur, forms the eastern margin, where it is fed by the Tarim He.

Sand dunes cover western parts of the the basin of Qaidam Pendi. Strong winds frequently carry the sands east, threatening the agricultural areas around the lake of Qinghai Hu.

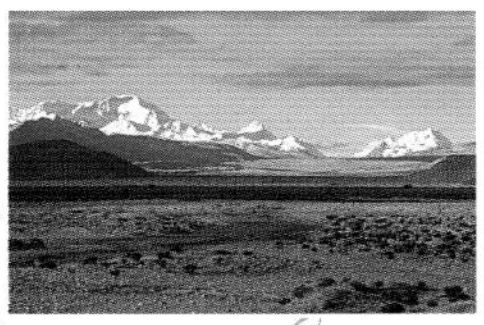

◀ ***The terrain of** the Plateau of Tibet consists of mountain peaks and open plateaux, dotted with brackish lakes. These are probably remnants of the Tethys Sea, which covered the area before it was uplifted following the collision of the Indo-Australian and Eurasian plates.*

Mount Everest is the world's highest peak, at 29,029 ft (8848 m). The summit marks the border between China and Nepal.

Tarim Basin *(Tarim Pendi)*

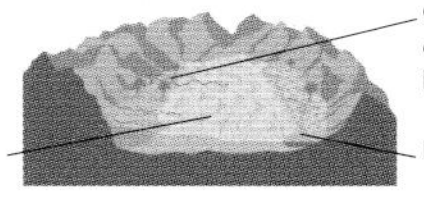

Oases at edge of basin

Barchan sand dunes in Takla Makan Desert *(Taklimakan Shamo)*

Lop Nur

▲ ***The Tarim Basin** (Tarim Pendi) has no permanent rivers. Rainfall from the surrounding Plateau of Tibet and Tien Shan ranges drains into the basin's sand and gravel floor.*

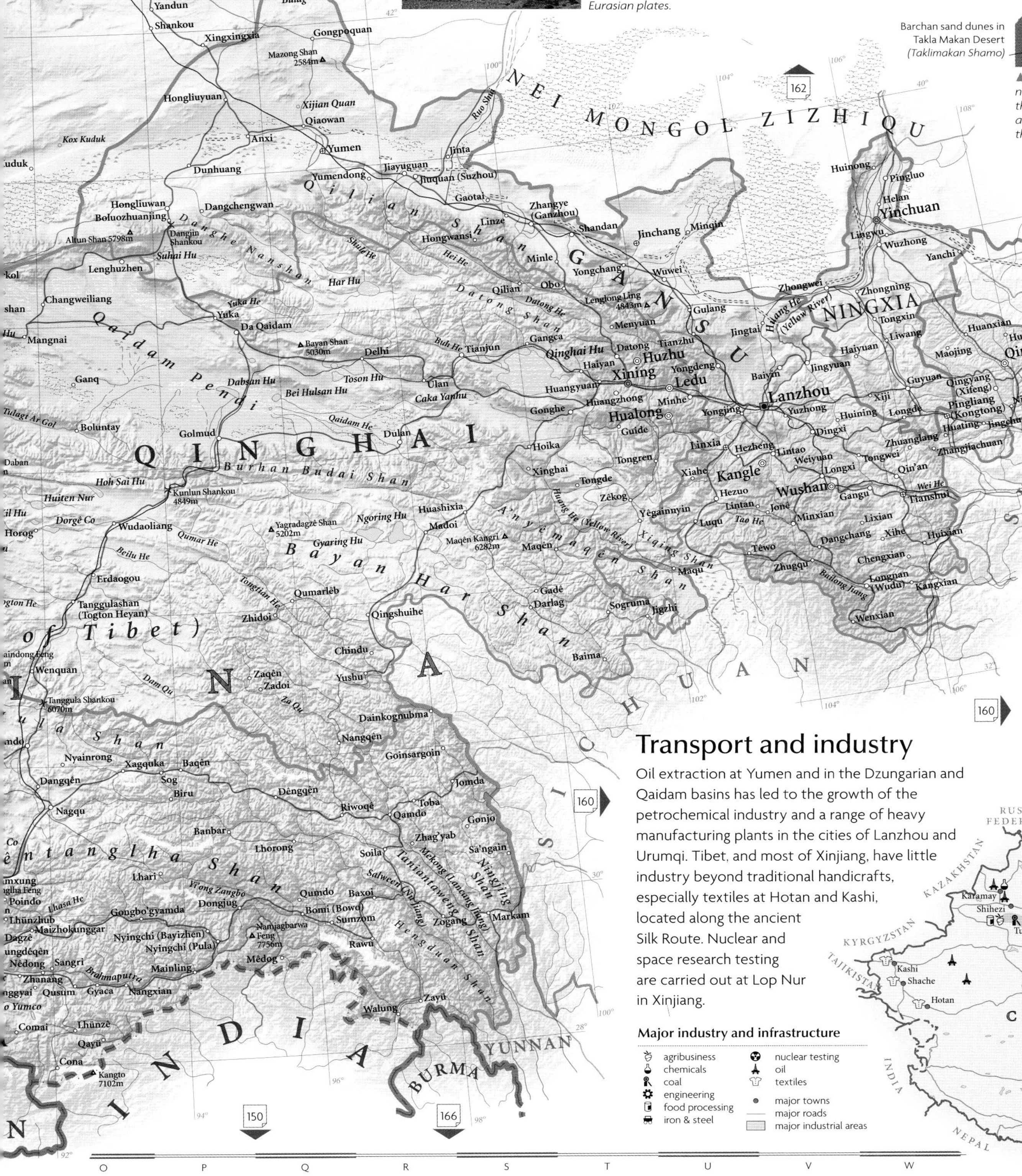

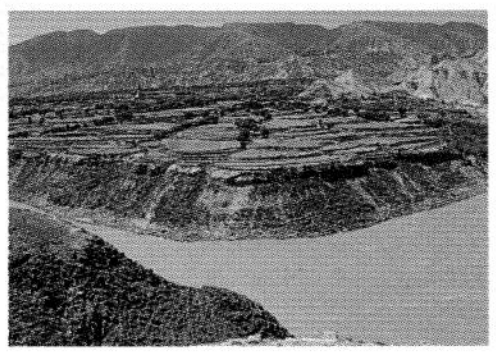

▲ ***From its source,** high in eastern Qinghai, the Yellow River starts on a 3395 mile (5464 km) journey to the Yellow Sea.*

MONGOLIA

NEI MONGOL ZIZHIQU

GANSU

NINGXIA

QINGHAI

Plateau of Tibet

INDIA

BURMA

YUNNAN

SICHUAN

SHAANXI

162

160

150

166

Transport and industry

Oil extraction at Yumen and in the Dzungarian and Qaidam basins has led to the growth of the petrochemical industry and a range of heavy manufacturing plants in the cities of Lanzhou and Urumqi. Tibet, and most of Xinjiang, have little industry beyond traditional handicrafts, especially textiles at Hotan and Kashi, located along the ancient Silk Route. Nuclear and space research testing are carried out at Lop Nur in Xinjiang.

The transport network

The construction of roads connecting Lhasa in Tibet with Sichuan, Qinghai and Xinjiang was achieved in the 1950s, in spite of the extreme physical conditions of the Plateau of Tibet.

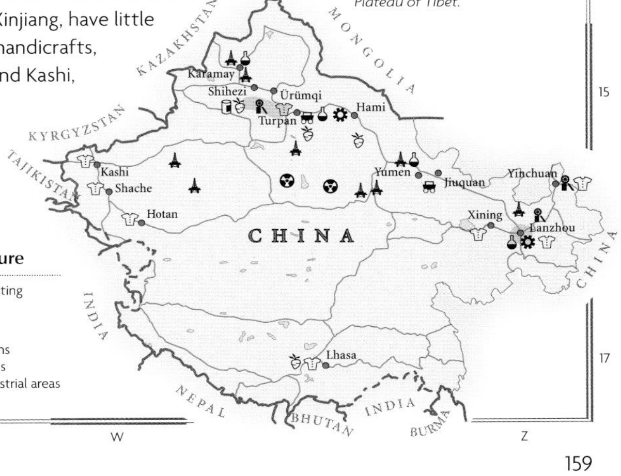

Major industry and infrastructure

- agribusiness
- chemicals
- coal
- engineering
- food processing
- iron & steel
- nuclear testing
- oil
- textiles
- major towns
- major roads
- major industrial areas

Eastern China

TAIWAN, Anhui, Beijing, Chongqing, Fujian, Guangdong, Guangxi, Guizhou, Hainan, Hebei, Henan, Hubei, Hunan, Jiangsu, Jiangxi, Shaanxi, Shandong, Shanghai, Shanxi, Sichuan, Tianjin, Yunnan, Zhejiang

The east is China's heartland. Massive industrial development since 1949 has transformed much of the densely populated rural landscape, in a region still prone to flooding and drought. Over 30 cities have populations of over a million, including the giant metropolis of Shanghai and the capital Beijing, which has been China's cultural and political centre since the 13th century. The ethnically diverse southwest and the oil-rich interior provinces of Sichuan and Shaanxi have largely missed out on the remarkable economic growth occurring in designated free-trade areas along the coasts of the South and East China seas. The republic of Taiwan was established in 1949 by Chinese nationalists ousted from the mainland by the victorious Communist forces. Taiwan now has one of the strongest economies in the world but its sovereignty is not recognized by China. Hong Kong provides a major international trade link for China; a 99-year 'lease' period of British control was concluded in 1997.

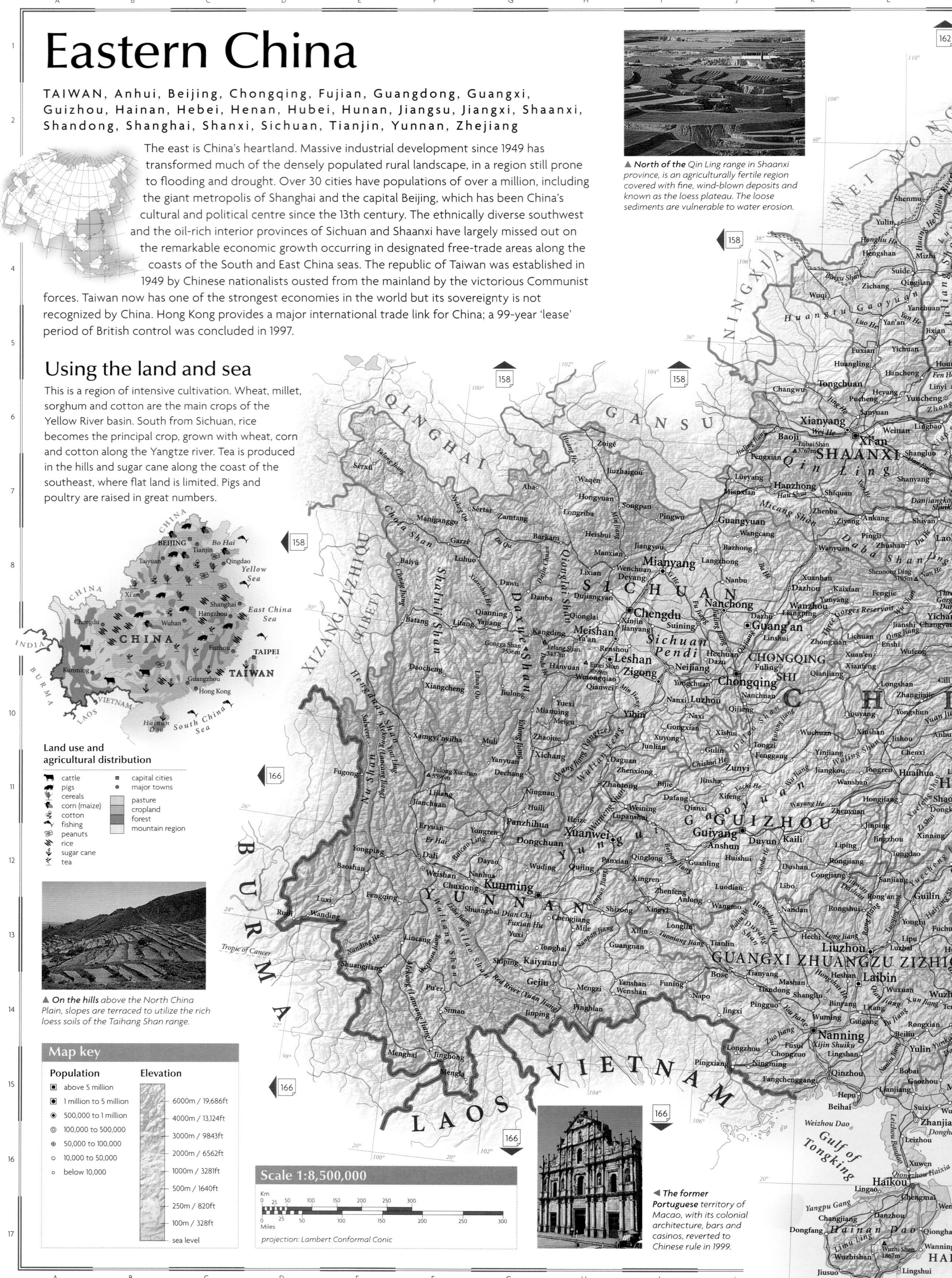

▲ **North of the** *Qin Ling range in Shaanxi province, is an agriculturally fertile region covered with fine, wind-blown deposits and known as the loess plateau. The loose sediments are vulnerable to water erosion.*

Using the land and sea

This is a region of intensive cultivation. Wheat, millet, sorghum and cotton are the main crops of the Yellow River basin. South from Sichuan, rice becomes the principal crop, grown with wheat, corn and cotton along the Yangtze river. Tea is produced in the hills and sugar cane along the coast of the southeast, where flat land is limited. Pigs and poultry are raised in great numbers.

Land use and agricultural distribution

cattle
pigs
cereals
corn (maize)
cotton
fishing
peanuts
rice
sugar cane
tea
capital cities
major towns
pasture
cropland
forest
mountain region

▲ **On the hills** *above the North China Plain, slopes are terraced to utilize the rich loess soils of the Taihang Shan range.*

Map key

Population
above 5 million
1 million to 5 million
500,000 to 1 million
100,000 to 500,000
50,000 to 100,000
10,000 to 50,000
below 10,000
Elevation
6000m / 19,686ft
4000m / 13,124ft
3000m / 9843ft
2000m / 6562ft
1000m / 3281ft
500m / 1640ft
250m / 820ft
100m / 328ft
sea level
Scale 1:8,500,000
projection: Lambert Conformal Conic

◀ **The former** *Portuguese territory of Macao, with its colonial architecture, bars and casinos, reverted to Chinese rule in 1999.*

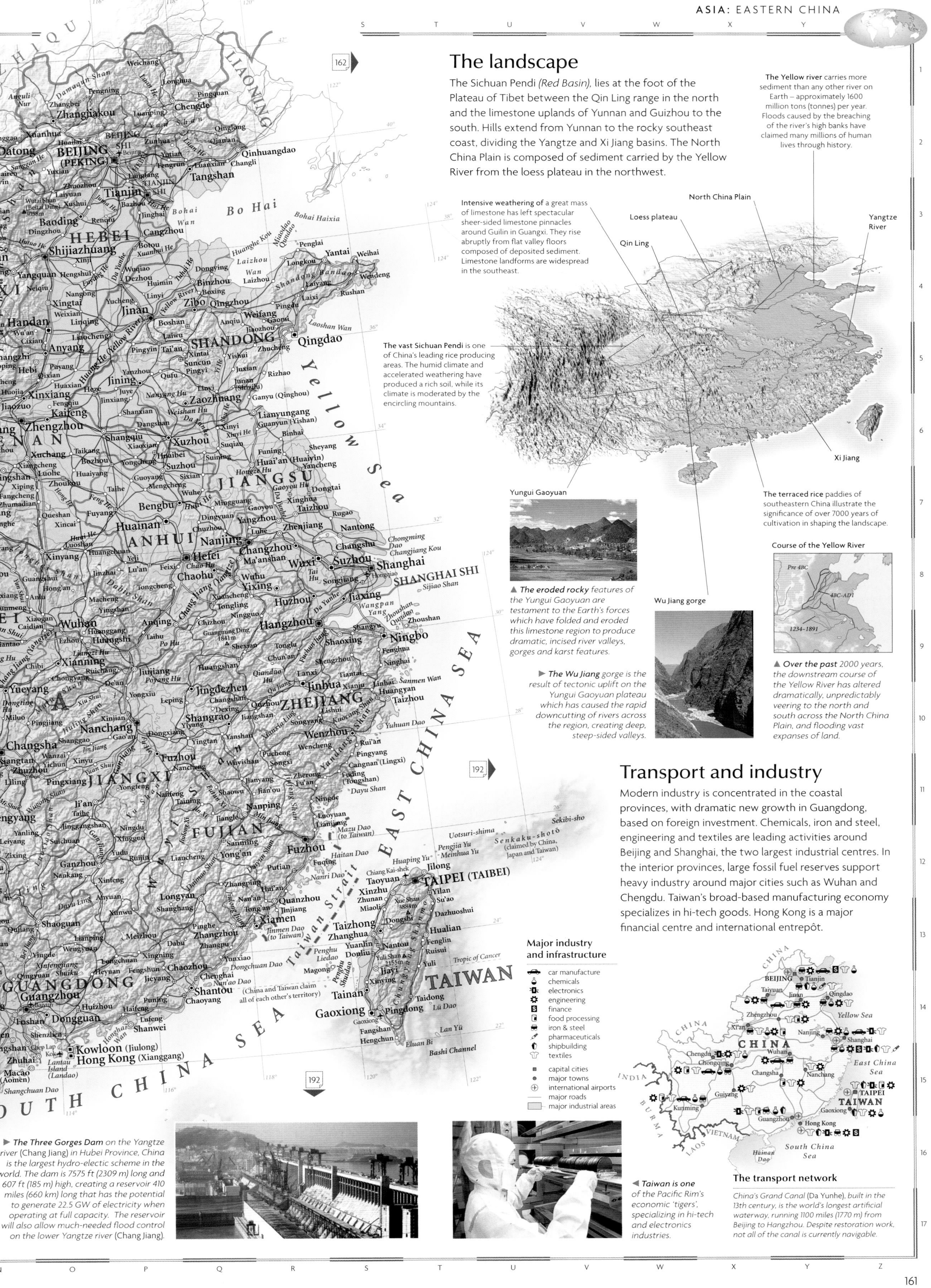
North China Plain
Loess plateau
Qin Ling
Yangtze River
Xi Jiang
Yungui Gaoyuan
Wu Jiang gorge
Course of the Yellow River
Pre 4BC
4BC–AD11
1234–1891
Major industry and infrastructure
car manufacture
chemicals
electronics
engineering
finance
food processing
iron & steel
pharmaceuticals
shipbuilding
textiles
capital cities
major towns
international airports
major roads
major industrial areas

The landscape

The Sichuan Pendi *(Red Basin)*, lies at the foot of the Plateau of Tibet between the Qin Ling range in the north and the limestone uplands of Yunnan and Guizhou to the south. Hills extend from Yunnan to the rocky southeast coast, dividing the Yangtze and Xi Jiang basins. The North China Plain is composed of sediment carried by the Yellow River from the loess plateau in the northwest.

The Yellow river carries more sediment than any other river on Earth – approximately 1600 million tons (tonnes) per year. Floods caused by the breaching of the river's high banks have claimed many millions of human lives through history.

Intensive weathering of a great mass of limestone has left spectacular sheer-sided limestone pinnacles around Guilin in Guangxi. They rise abruptly from flat valley floors composed of deposited sediment. Limestone landforms are widespread in the southeast.

The vast Sichuan Pendi is one of China's leading rice producing areas. The humid climate and accelerated weathering have produced a rich soil, while its climate is moderated by the encircling mountains.

The terraced rice paddies of southeastern China illustrate the significance of over 7000 years of cultivation in shaping the landscape.

▲ ***The eroded rocky** features of the Yungui Gaoyuan are testament to the Earth's forces which have folded and eroded this limestone region to produce dramatic, incised river valleys, gorges and karst features.*

► ***The Wu Jiang** gorge is the result of tectonic uplift on the Yungui Gaoyuan plateau which has caused the rapid downcutting of rivers across the region, creating deep, steep-sided valleys.*

▲ ***Over the past** 2000 years, the downstream course of the Yellow River has altered dramatically, unpredictably veering to the north and south across the North China Plain, and flooding vast expanses of land.*

Transport and industry

Modern industry is concentrated in the coastal provinces, with dramatic new growth in Guangdong, based on foreign investment. Chemicals, iron and steel, engineering and textiles are leading activities around Beijing and Shanghai, the two largest industrial centres. In the interior provinces, large fossil fuel reserves support heavy industry around major cities such as Wuhan and Chengdu. Taiwan's broad-based manufacturing economy specializes in hi-tech goods. Hong Kong is a major financial centre and international entrepôt.

► ***The Three Gorges Dam** on the Yangtze river* (Chang Jiang) *in Hubei Province, China is the largest hydro-electic scheme in the world. The dam is 7575 ft (2309 m) long and 607 ft (185 m) high, creating a reservoir 410 miles (660 km) long that has the potential to generate 22.5 GW of electricity when operating at full capacity. The reservoir will also allow much-needed flood control on the lower Yangtze river* (Chang Jiang).

◄ ***Taiwan** is one of the Pacific Rim's economic 'tigers', specializing in hi-tech and electronics industries.*

The transport network

China's Grand Canal (Da Yunhe), built in the 13th century, is the world's longest artificial waterway, running 1100 miles (1770 m) from Beijing to Hangzhou. Despite restoration work, not all of the canal is currently navigable.

Northeastern China, Mongolia & Korea

MONGOLIA, NORTH KOREA, SOUTH KOREA, Heilongjiang, Inner Mongolia, Jilin, Liaoning

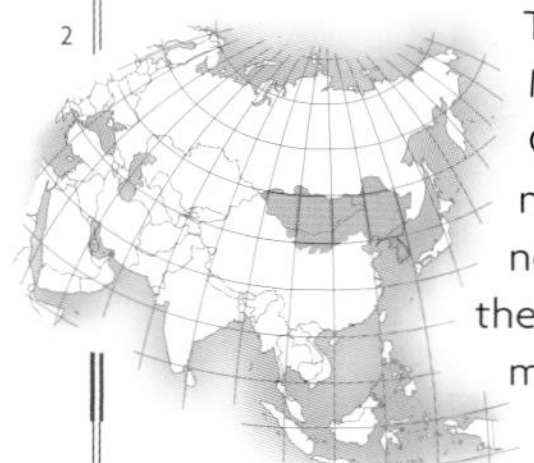

This northerly region has for centuries been a domain of shifting borders and competing colonial powers. Mongolia was the heartland of Chinghiz Khan's vast Mongol empire in the 13th century, while northeastern China was home to the Manchus, China's last ruling dynasty (1644–1911). The mineral and forest wealth of the northeast helped make this China's principal region of heavy industry, although the outdated state factories now face decline. South Korea's state-led market economy has grown dramatically and Seoul is now one of the world's largest cities. The austere communist regime of North Korea has isolated itself from the expanding markets of the Pacific Rim and faces continuing economic stagnation.

▲ ***The Eurasian steppe*** *stretches from the mouth of the Danube in Europe, to Mongolia. In Mongolia, nomadic people have lived in felt huts called yurts or gers, for thousands of years.*

Map key

Population

- above 5 million
- 1 million to 5 million
- 500,000 to 1 million
- 100,000 to 500,000
- 50,000 to 100,000
- 10,000 to 50,000
- below 10,000

Elevation

- 4000m / 13,124ft
- 3000m / 9843ft
- 2000m / 6562ft
- 1000m / 3281ft
- 500m / 1640ft
- 250m / 820ft
- 100m / 328ft
- sea level

Scale 1:7,750,000

Km 0 25 50 100 150 200

Miles 0 25 50 100 150 200

projection: Lambert Conformal Conic

RUSSIAN FEDERATION
MONGOLIA
BAYAN-ÖLGIY
UVS
HÖVSGÖL
SELENGE
DARHAN UUL
BULGAN
ARHANGAY
ULAANBAATAR (ULAN BATOR)
TÖV
ZAVHAN
HOVD
GOVĬ-ALTAY
BAYANHONGOR
ÖVÖRHANGAY
DUNDGOVĬ
ÖMNÖGOVĬ
XINJIANG UYGUR ZIZHIQU
GANSU
NINGXIA
NEI
Altai Mountains
Hangayn Nuruu
Govĭ Altayn Nuruu
Badain Jaran Shamo
Tengger Shamo
Yabrai Shan
Lang Shan
Helan Shan

The landscape

The great North China Plain is largely enclosed by mountain ranges including the Great and Lesser Khingan Ranges (*Da Hinggan Ling* and *Xiao Hinggan Ling*) in the north, and the Changbai Shan, which extend south into the rugged peninsula of Korea. The broad steppeland plateau of Nei Mongol Gaoyuan borders the southeastern edge of the great cold desert of the Gobi which extends west across the southern reaches of Mongolia. In northwest Mongolia the Altai Mountains and various lesser ranges are interspersed with lakeland basins.

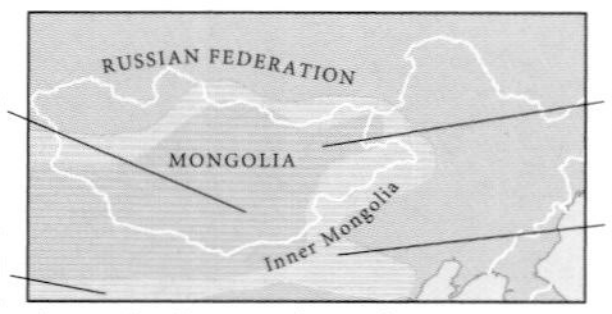

RUSSIAN FEDERATION
MONGOLIA
Inner Mongolia
Gobi
Semi-arid zone
Desert zone
Ordos Desert (Mu Us Shadi)

▲ ***Much of Mongolia*** *and Inner Mongolia is a vast desert area. To the south and east, a semi-arid region extends into China proper.*

▲ ***The Gobi desert*** *stretches from Central Asia, through Mongolia and into China. Bare rock surfaces, rather than sand dunes, typify the cold desert landscape of the Gobi.*

Tributaries of the Amur river follow U-shaped valleys through the Great Khingan Range (*Da Hinggan Ling*). These were cut by ice-age glaciers between 3 and 10 million years ago.

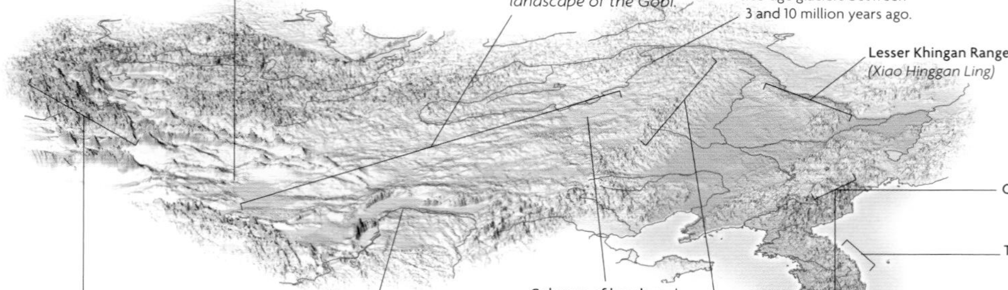

Lesser Khingan Range (Xiao Hinggan Ling)
Changbai Shan
Taebaek-sanmaek

The Altai Mountains are the highest and longest of the mountain ranges which extend into Mongolia from the northwest. These mountains provide one of the last refuges for the endangered snow leopard.

The Yellow River sweeps north around the Ordos Desert (*Mu Us Shadi*), bringing water to an otherwise barren region.

Columns of basalt rock protrude in occasional clusters from the flat surface of the eastern Gobi. Their regular, six-sided form was produced when the rock cooled and contracted from its molten state.

Great Khingan Range (*Da Hinggan Ling*)

A crater lake occupies the 9023 ft (2750 m) snowy summit of the extinct volcano Paektu-san, the highest peak in the mountains of the Changbai Shan.

◀ ***The wooded mountain*** *range of T'aebaek-sanmaek forms the backbone of the Korean peninsula, running north–south along the eastern coastline.*

Transport and industry

North Korea's centrally-planned economy is strongly oriented towards heavy industry, while South Korea has a broad manufacturing base which includes textiles, steel, electronics, and one of the world's largest shipbuilding industries. Mongolia and Inner Mongolia's great mineral resource potential is largely undeveloped. The heavy industrial region around Shenyang produces iron, steel, chemicals and cement on a massive scale.

▲ **Ulan Bator, the** Mongolian capital bears many of the hallmarks of Soviet-style central planning, the result of economic and industrial assistance from the Soviet Union following Mongolian independence in 1921.

The transport network

Liaoning has China's most comprehensive railway network, the legacy of the Japanese occupation of Manchuria in the 20th century. The railways are used primarily for freight transport.

Major industry and infrastructure

- car manufacture
- chemicals
- coal
- electronics
- engineering
- finance
- food processing
- iron & steel
- pharmaceuticals
- shipbuilding
- textiles
- capital cities
- major towns
- international airports
- major roads
- major industrial areas

▶ ***While North Korea** has remained politically and economically isolated from the rest of the world, South Korea has enjoyed immense economic growth. It has benefited considerably from US economic aid in the aftermath of the Korean war of 1950–1953.*

South Korea: Capital cities

SEOUL – capital
SEJONG CITY – administrative capital

Using the land and sea

Mongolia and Inner Mongolia rely heavily on livestock farming, with only about 1% of the land area cultivated. Northeastern China produces wheat, corn, soya beans and sugar beet. The cool climate limits the range of crops and large upland areas of the northeast remain forested. Rice is the staple food of North and South Korea. The latter has become a leading ocean-fishing nation.

Land use and agricultural distribution

- goats
- pigs
- sheep
- corn (maize)
- fishing
- rice
- soya beans
- sugar beet
- wheat
- capital cities
- major towns
- pasture
- cropland
- forest
- mountain region
- desert

122
160

Japan

In the years since the end of the Second World War, Japan has become the world's most dynamic industrial nation. The country comprises a string of over 4000 islands which lie in a great northeast to southwest arc in the northwest Pacific. Four major islands: Hokkaido, Honshu, Shikoku and Kyushu are home to the great majority of Japan's population of 128 million people, although the mountainous terrain of the central region means that most cities are situated on the coast. A densely populated industrial belt stretches along much of Honshu's southern coast, including Japan's crowded capital, Tokyo. Alongside its spectacular economic growth and the increasing westernization of its cities, Japan still maintains a most singular culture, reflected in its traditional food, formal behavioural codes, unique Shinto religion and a deep reverence for the emperor.

Using the land and sea

Although only about 11% of Japan is suitable for cultivation, substantial government support, a favour climate and intensive farming methods enable the country to be virtually self-sufficient in rice production. Northern Hokkaido, the largest and most productive farming region, has an open terrain climate similar to that of the US Midwest, and produces over half of Japan's cereal requirements. Farm are being encouraged to diversify by growing fruit, vegetables and wheat, as well as raising livestock.

Land use and agricultural distribution
cattle
pigs
fishing
cereals
citrus fruits
fruit
herbs
rice
root crops
tobacco
capital cities
major towns
pasture
cropland
forest
The urban/rural population divide
urban 78%
rural 22%
0 10 20 30 40 50 60 70 80 90 100
Population density
885 people per sq mile (342 people per sq km)
Total land area
145,869 sq miles (377,800 sq km)
Sea of Japan (East Sea)
PACIFIC OCEAN
JAPAN
Sapporo
Hachinohe
Fukushima
Hitachi
TOKYO
Yokohama
Toyama
Tsuruga
Nagoya
Osaka
Kobe
Hiroshima
Fukuoka
Nagasaki
Kagoshima
Sea of Japan
Philippine Sea
East China Sea
Korea Strait
Kyūshū
Shikoku
Honshu

▶ **Cutting terraces maximizes** *the limited agricultural land, enabling Japan to produce large quantities of rice.*

The landscape

The islands of Japan lie on the Pacific 'Ring of Fire', and form a series of clearly defined arcs. The largely mountainous landscape was formed very recently in geological terms. Volcanic eruptions and earthquakes continue to reshape the terrain and to shake the country's complex infrastructure. There is no one continuous mountain range; the mountains divide into many small land blocks separated by lowlands and dissected by numerous river valleys.

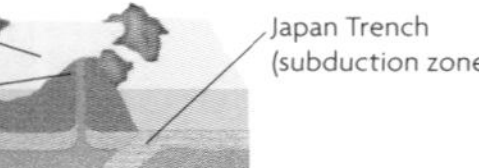
Sea of Japan (East Sea)
Active volcanic island
Japan Trench (subduction zone)

▲ ***Japan is part*** *of an arc of volcanic islands, formed by the Pacific Plate diving under the Eurasian Plate. This process generates intense stress which is periodically released as earthquakes.*

◀ ***Mount Fuji is*** *Japan's highest mountain, rising 12,388 ft (3776 m) above the Kanto Plain in the central region of Honshu. The flat land below is suitable for growing crops such as tea. Like many Japanese mountains, it is revered as a sacred site.*

A number of rivers which emerge from the volcanic parts of northwestern Honshu are so highly acidic that their water is unsuitable for irrigation and consumption.

▶ ***Trees cling to*** *the sheer slopes of the waterfalls on the northern island of Hokkaido. The island's climate is similar to that in northern Europe, with long, cold winters and short, warm summers.*

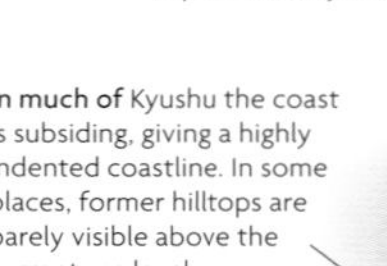

In much of Kyushu the coast is subsiding, giving a highly indented coastline. In some places, former hilltops are barely visible above the current sea level.

Mount Fuji

There are over 60 active volcanoes – like Asahi-dake, Hokkaido's highest peak – throughout Japan. This accounts for more than 10% of the world's total.

Rising land on the Pacific coast of Honshu leads to typical features such as raised beaches, some lying over 1000 ft (300 m) above sea level.

The Inland Sea *(Seto-naikai)* has resulted from the depression of faulted blocks which has allowed sea water to invade the region between northern Shikoku and western Honshu.

Strong southeasterly winds blowing onshore during the winter create sand dunes which extend for miles along the eastern coasts.

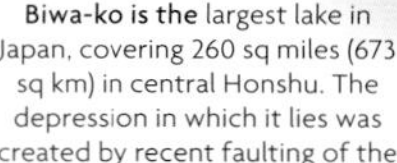

Biwa-ko is the largest lake in Japan, covering 260 sq miles (673 sq km) in central Honshu. The depression in which it lies was created by recent faulting of the underlying rocks.

157

▼ ***Autumnal trees near*** *Gifu, on central Honshu, create a spectacular display. Native trees on this island include camphor, pasania, Japanese evergreen oak, camellia and holly.*

▶ ***The Kobe earthquake*** *in January 1995 highlighted Japan's vulnerability to earthquakes, despite technological advances. It shattered much of the infrastructure of this important port. More than 5000 people died as buildings and overhead highways collapsed and fires broke out.*

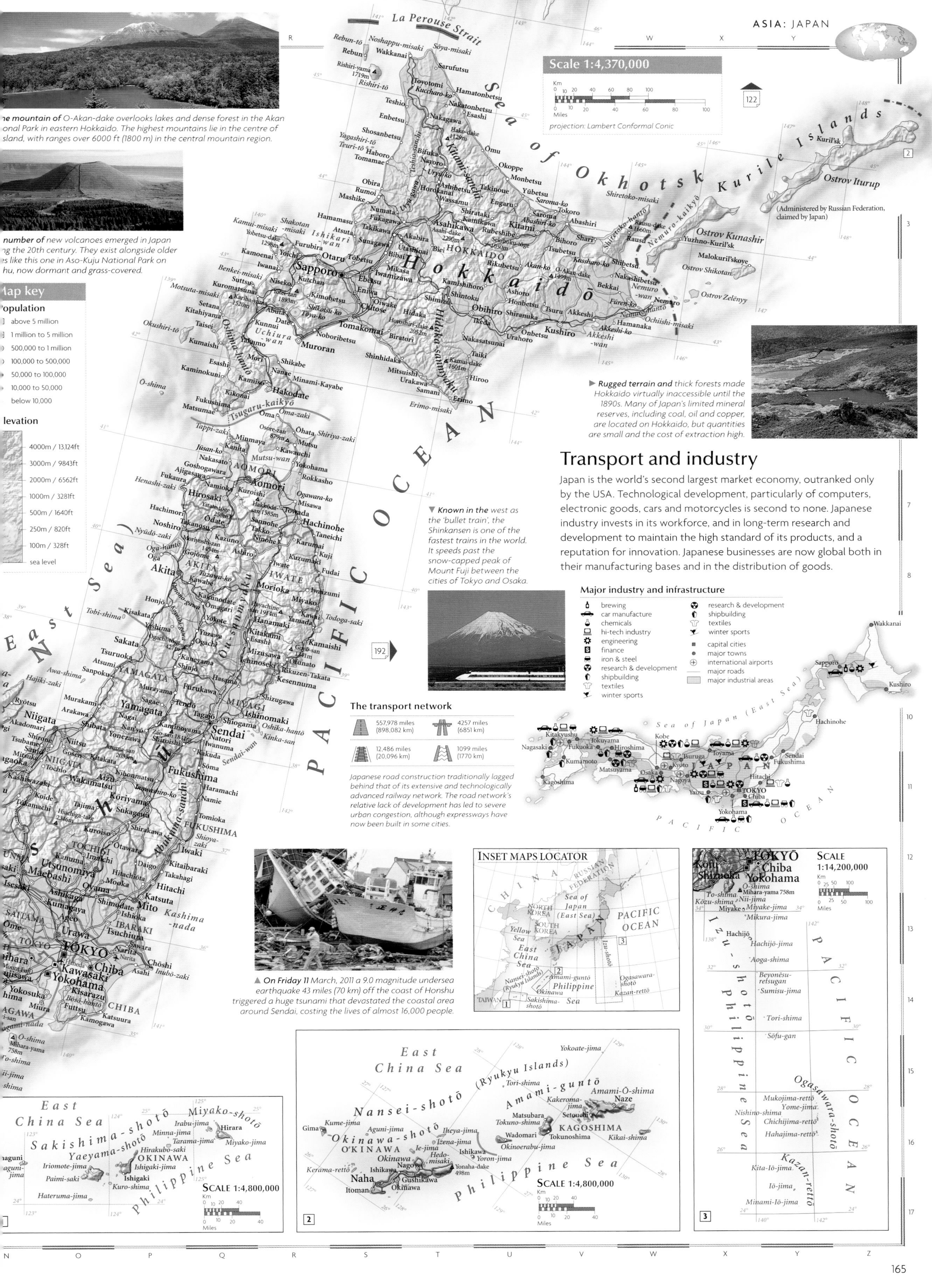
La Perouse Strait
Sea of Okhotsk
Kuril Islands
Hokkaidō
PACIFIC OCEAN
East Sea)
Scale 1:4,370,000
projection: Lambert Conformal Conic
(Administered by Russian Federation, claimed by Japan)
Map key
Population
above 5 million
1 million to 5 million
500,000 to 1 million
100,000 to 500,000
50,000 to 100,000
10,000 to 50,000
below 10,000
Elevation
4000m / 13,124ft
3000m / 9843ft
2000m / 6562ft
1000m / 3281ft
500m / 1640ft
250m / 820ft
100m / 328ft
sea level
Major industry and infrastructure
brewing
car manufacture
chemicals
hi-tech industry
engineering
finance
iron & steel
research & development
shipbuilding
textiles
winter sports
capital cities
major towns
international airports
major roads
major industrial areas
INSET MAPS LOCATOR
SCALE 1:14,200,000
SCALE 1:4,800,000
East China Sea
Philippine Sea

…he mountain of O-Akan-dake overlooks lakes and dense forest in the Akan …onal Park in eastern Hokkaido. The highest mountains lie in the centre of …sland, with ranges over 6000 ft (1800 m) in the central mountain region.

…number of new volcanoes emerged in Japan …ng the 20th century. They exist alongside older …es like this one in Aso-Kuju National Park on …hu, now dormant and grass-covered.

▶ Rugged terrain and thick forests made Hokkaido virtually inaccessible until the 1890s. Many of Japan's limited mineral reserves, including coal, oil and copper, are located on Hokkaido, but quantities are small and the cost of extraction high.

Transport and industry

Japan is the world's second largest market economy, outranked only by the USA. Technological development, particularly of computers, electronic goods, cars and motorcycles is second to none. Japanese industry invests in its workforce, and in long-term research and development to maintain the high standard of its products, and a reputation for innovation. Japanese businesses are now global both in their manufacturing bases and in the distribution of goods.

▼ Known in the west as the 'bullet train', the Shinkansen is one of the fastest trains in the world. It speeds past the snow-capped peak of Mount Fuji between the cities of Tokyo and Osaka.

The transport network

557,978 miles (898,082 km)	4257 miles (6851 km)
12,486 miles (20,096 km)	1099 miles (1770 km)

Japanese road construction traditionally lagged behind that of its extensive and technologically advanced railway network. The road network's relative lack of development has led to severe urban congestion, although expressways have now been built in some cities.

▲ On Friday 11 March, 2011 a 9.0 magnitude undersea earthquake 43 miles (70 km) off the coast of Honshu triggered a huge tsunami that devastated the coastal area around Sendai, costing the lives of almost 16,000 people.

Mainland Southeast Asia

BURMA, CAMBODIA, LAOS, THAILAND, VIETNAM

Thickly forested mountains, intercut by the broad valleys of five great rivers characterize the landscape of Southeast Asia's mainland countries. Agriculture remains the main activity for much of the population, which is concentrated in the river flood plains and deltas. Linked ethnic and cultural roots give the region a distinct identity. Most people on the mainland are Theravada Buddhists, and the Philippines is the only predominantly Christian country in Southeast Asia. Foreign intervention began in the 16th century with the opening of the spice trade; Cambodia, Laos and Vietnam were French colonies until the end of the Second World War, Burma was under British control. Only Thailand was never colonized. Today, Thailand is poised to play a leading role in the economic development of the Pacific Rim, and Laos and Vietnam have begun to mend the devastation of the Vietnam War, and to develop their economies. With continuing political instability and a shattered infrastructure, Cambodia faces an uncertain future, while Burma is seeking investment and the ending of its long isolation from the world community.

▲ *The Irrawaddy river is Burma's vital central artery, watering the ricefields and providing a rich source of fish, as well as an important transport link, particularly for local traffic.*

The landscape

A series of mountain ranges runs north–south through the mainland, formed as the result of the collision between the Eurasian Plate and the Indian subcontinent, which created the Himalayas. They are interspersed by the valleys of a number of great rivers. On their passage to the sea these rivers have deposited sediment, forming huge, fertile flood plains and deltas.

The coastline of the Isthmus of Kra

Longshore drift
Eroded coastline
Spit
Lagoon
Wave attack

◄ *The east and west coasts of the Isthmus of Kra differ greatly. The tectonically uplifting west coast is exposed to the harsh south-westerly monsoon and is heavily eroded. On the east coast, longshore currents produce depositional features such as spits and lagoons.*

Hkakabo Razi is the highest point in mainland Southeast Asia. It rises 19,300 ft (5885 m) at the border between China and Burma.

Mountains dominate the Laotian landscape with more than 90% of the land lying more than 600 ft (180 m) above sea level. The mountains of the Chaîne Annamitique form the country's eastern border.

The Red River delta in northern Vietnam is fringed to the north by steep-sided, round-topped limestone hills, typical of karst scenery.

The Irrawaddy river runs virtually north–south, draining the plains of northern Burma. The Irrawaddy delta is the country's main rice-growing area.

Salween River

Isthmus of Kra

Malay Peninsula

Tonle Sap, a freshwater lake, drains into the Mekong delta via the Mekong river. It is the largest lake in Southeast Asia.

The Mekong river flows through southern China and Burma, then for much of its length forms the border between Laos and Thailand, flowing through Cambodia before terminating in a vast delta on the southern Vietnamese coast.

▲ *The coast of the Isthmus of Kra, in southeast Thailand has many small, precipitous islands like these, formed by chemical erosion on limestone, which is weathered along vertical cracks. The humidity of the climate in Southeast Asia increases the rate of weathering.*

◄ *The fast-flowing waters of the Mekong river cascade over this waterfall in Champasak province in Laos. The force of the water erodes rocks at the base of the fall.*

Using the land and sea

The fertile flood plains of rivers such as the Mekong and Salween, and the humid climate, enable the production of rice throughout the region. Cambodia, Burma and Laos still have substantial forests, producing hardwoods such as teak and rosewood. Cash crops include tropical fruits such as coconuts, bananas and pineapples, rubber, oil palm, sugar cane and the jute substitute, kenaf. Pigs and cattle are the main livestock raised. Large quantities of marine and freshwater fish are caught throughout the region.

▲ *Commercial logging – still widespread in Burma – has now been stopped in Thailand because of over-exploitation of the tropical rainforest.*

The urban/rural population divide

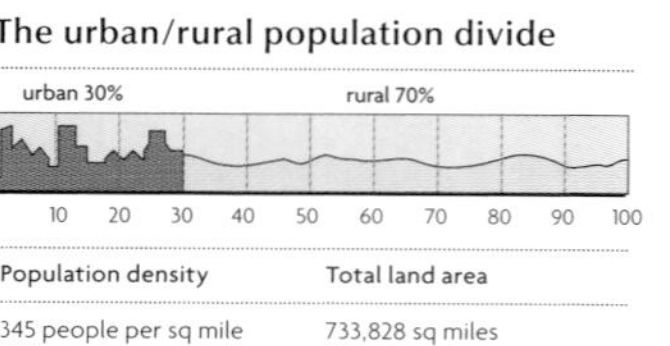
urban 30%
rural 70%
0 10 20 30 40 50 60 70 80 90 100

Population density	Total land area
345 people per sq mile (133 people per sq km)	733,828 sq miles (1,901,110 sq km)

INDIA
BANGLADESH
CHINA
BURMA
Mandalay
NAY PYI TAW
HANOI
Gulf of Tongking
Bay of Bengal
VIENTIANE
LAOS
Hue
Rangoon
THAILAND
BANGKOK
VIETNAM
CAMBODIA
Andaman Sea
PHNOM PENH
South China Sea
Ho Chi Minh City
Gulf of Thailand
MALAYSIA

Land use and agricultural distribution

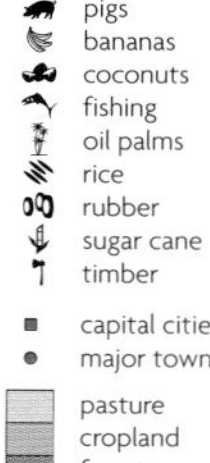
cattle
pigs
bananas
coconuts
fishing
oil palms
rice
rubber
sugar cane
timber
capital cities
major towns
pasture
cropland
forest
wetland

152
172
168

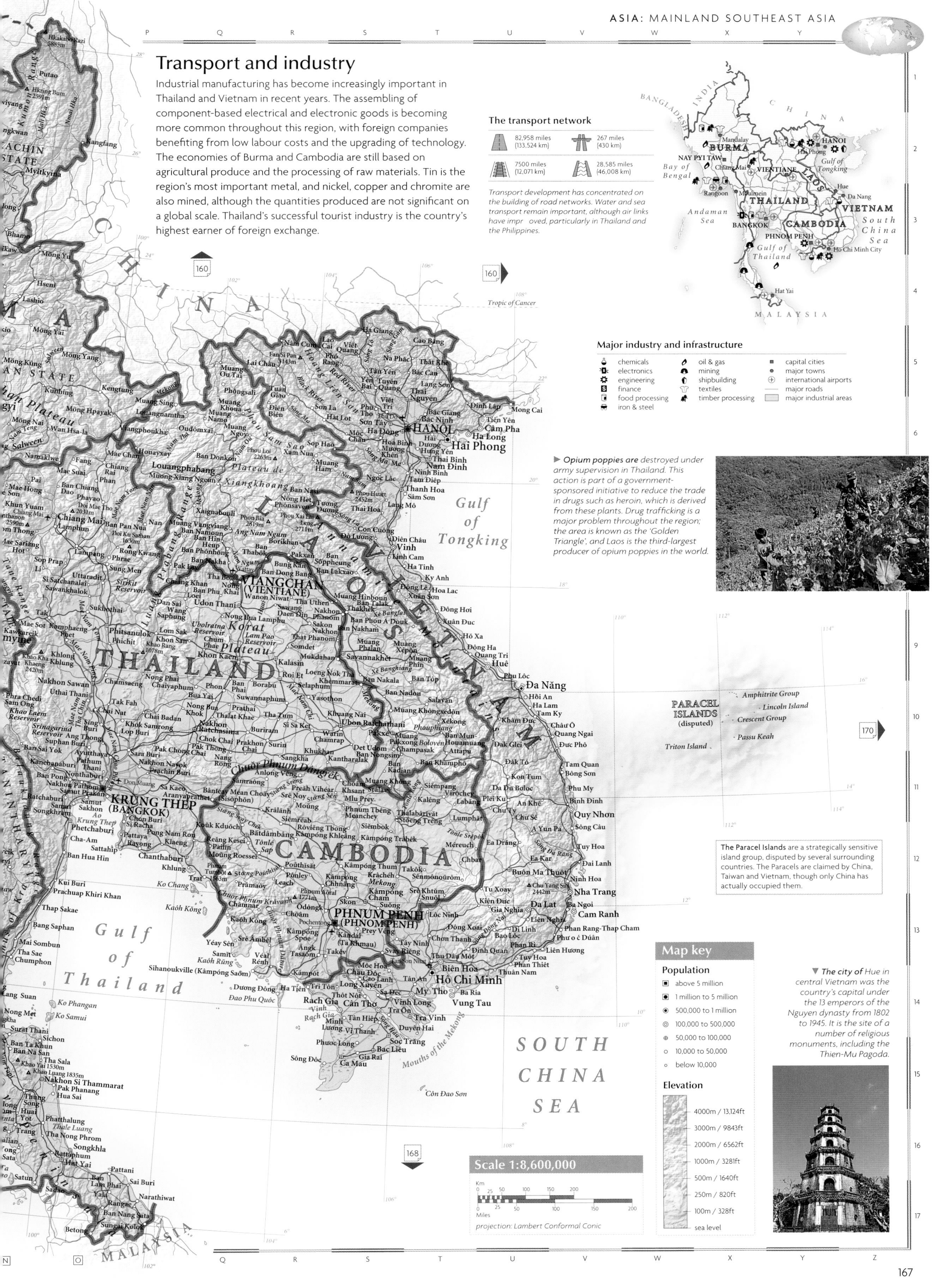
CHINA
LAOS
VIETNAM
THAILAND
CAMBODIA
HANOI
Hai Phong
VIANGCHAN (VIENTIANE)
KRUNG THEP (BANGKOK)
PHNUM PENH (PHNOM PENH)
Hô Chi Minh
Đa Năng
Huê
Gulf of Tongking
Gulf of Thailand
SOUTH CHINA SEA
PARACEL ISLANDS (disputed)
Amphitrite Group
Lincoln Island
Crescent Group
Passu Keah
Triton Island
MALAYSIA
Tropic of Cancer
Korat Plateau
Mouths of the Mekong
Côn Đao Sơn
BANGLADESH
INDIA
BURMA
NAY PYI TAW
Mandalay
Rangoon
Moulmein
Chiang Mai
VIENTIANE
BANGKOK
PHNOM PENH
HANOI
Hai Phong
Da Nang
Ho Chi Minh City
Hat Yai
Bay of Bengal
Andaman Sea
Gulf of Thailand
South China Sea
Gulf of Tongking
160
160
168
170
Scale 1:8,600,000
Km 0 25 50 100 150 200
Miles 0 25 50 100 150 200
projection: Lambert Conformal Conic

Transport and industry

Industrial manufacturing has become increasingly important in Thailand and Vietnam in recent years. The assembling of component-based electrical and electronic goods is becoming more common throughout this region, with foreign companies benefiting from low labour costs and the upgrading of technology. The economies of Burma and Cambodia are still based on agricultural produce and the processing of raw materials. Tin is the region's most important metal, and nickel, copper and chromite are also mined, although the quantities produced are not significant on a global scale. Thailand's successful tourist industry is the country's highest earner of foreign exchange.

The transport network

82,958 miles (133,524 km)	267 miles (430 km)
7500 miles (12,071 km)	28,585 miles (46,008 km)

Transport development has concentrated on the building of road networks. Water and sea transport remain important, although air links have impr oved, particularly in Thailand and the Philippines.

Major industry and infrastructure

chemicals, electronics, engineering, finance, food processing, iron & steel, oil & gas, mining, shipbuilding, textiles, timber processing, capital cities, major towns, international airports, major roads, major industrial areas

► *Opium poppies are destroyed under army supervision in Thailand. This action is part of a government-sponsored initiative to reduce the trade in drugs such as heroin, which is derived from these plants. Drug trafficking is a major problem throughout the region; the area is known as the 'Golden Triangle', and Laos is the third-largest producer of opium poppies in the world.*

The Paracel Islands are a strategically sensitive island group, disputed by several surrounding countries. The Paracels are claimed by China, Taiwan and Vietnam, though only China has actually occupied them.

Map key

Population

- above 5 million
- 1 million to 5 million
- 500,000 to 1 million
- 100,000 to 500,000
- 50,000 to 100,000
- 10,000 to 50,000
- below 10,000

Elevation

- 4000m / 13,124ft
- 3000m / 9843ft
- 2000m / 6562ft
- 1000m / 3281ft
- 500m / 1640ft
- 250m / 820ft
- 100m / 328ft
- sea level

▼ *The city of Hue in central Vietnam was the country's capital under the 13 emperors of the Nguyen dynasty from 1802 to 1945. It is the site of a number of religious monuments, including the Thien-Mu Pagoda.*

Western Maritime Southeast Asia

BRUNEI, INDONESIA, MALAYSIA, SINGAPORE

The world's largest archipelago, Indonesia's myriad islands stretch 3100 miles (5000 km) eastwards across the Pacific, from the Malay Peninsula to western New Guinea. Only about 1500 of the 13,677 islands are inhabited and the huge, predominently Muslim population is unevenly distributed, with some two-thirds crowded onto the western islands of Java, Madura and Bali. The national government is trying to resettle large numbers of people from these islands to other parts of the country to reduce population pressure there. Malaysia, split between the mainland and the east Malaysian states of Sabah and Sarawak on Borneo, has a diverse population, as well as a fast-growing economy, although the pace of its development is still far outstripped by that of Singapore. This small island nation is the financial and commercial capital of Southeast Asia. The Sultanate of Brunei in northern Borneo, one of the world's last princely states, has an extremely high standard of living, based on its oil revenues.

The landscape

Indonesia's western islands are characterized by rugged volcanic mountains cloaked with dense tropical forest, which slope down to coastal plains covered by thick alluvial swamps. The Sunda Shelf, an extension of the Eurasian Plate, lies between Java, Bali, Sumatra and Borneo. These islands' mountains rise from a base below the sea, and they were once joined together by dry land, which has since been submerged by rising sea levels.

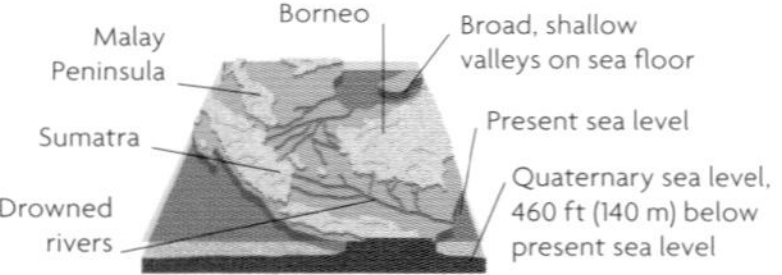
Borneo
Malay Peninsula
Broad, shallow valleys on sea floor
Sumatra
Present sea level
Drowned rivers
Quaternary sea level, 460 ft (140 m) below present sea level

▲ *The Sunda Shelf underlies this whole region. It is one of the largest submarine shelves in the world, covering an area of 714,285 sq miles (1,850,000 sq km). During the early Quaternary period, when sea levels were lower, the shelf was exposed.*

◄ *On January 24, 2005 a 9.2 magnitude earthquake off the coast of Sumatra triggered a devastating tsunami that was up to 90 ft (30 m) high in places. The death toll was estimated to be around 230,000 people from fourteen different countries around the Indian Ocean.*

Malay Peninsula has a rugged east coast, but the west coast, fronting the Strait of Malacca, has many sheltered beaches and bays. The two coasts are divided by the Banjaran Titiwangsa, which run the length of the peninsula.

Gunung Kinabalu is the highest peak in Malaysia, rising 13,455 ft (4101 m).

◄ *The river of Sungai Mahakam cuts through the central highlands of Borneo, the third largest island in the world, with a total area of 290,000 sq miles (757,050 sq km). Although mountainous, Borneo is one of the most stable of the Indonesian islands, with little volcanic activity.*

The island of Krakatau *(Pulau Rakata)*, lying between Sumatra and Java, was all but destroyed in 1883, when the volcano erupted. The release of gas and dust into the atmosphere disrupted cloud cover and global weather patterns for several years.

Gunung Semeru

Indonesia has more than 220 volcanoes, most of which are still active. They are strung out along the island arc from Sumatra through the Lesser Sunda Islands, into the Moluccas and Celebes.

Transport and industry

Singapore has a thriving economy based on international trade and finance. Annual trade through the port is among the highest of any in the world. Indonesia's western islands still depend on natural resources, particularly petroleum, gas and wood, although the economy is rapidly diversifying with manufactured exports including garments, consumer electronics and footwear. A high-profile aircraft industry has developed in Bandung on Java. Malaysia has a fast-growing and varied manufacturing sector, although oil, gas and timber remain important resource-based industries.

► *Ranks of gleaming skyscrapers, new motorways and infrastructure construction reflect the investment which is pouring into Southeast Asian cities like the Malaysian capital, Kuala Lumpur. Traditional housing and markets still exist amidst the new developments. Many of the city's inhabitants subsist at a level far removed from the prosperity implied by its outward modernity.*

Malaysia: Capital cities
KUALA LUMPUR – capital
PUTRAJAYA – administrative capital

THAILAND
Malay Peninsula
Strait of Malacca
Sumatra
INDIAN OCEAN
Kepulauan Mentawai
Selat Mentawai
166
172
Kota Bharu
George Town
Kangar
Alor Setar
PERLIS
KEDAH
PINANG
Butterworth
Ipoh
PERAK
Taiping
KELANTAN
TERENGGANU
Kuala Terengganu
Kuala Lipis
PAHANG
Kuantan
SELANGOR
KUALA LUMPUR
PUTRAJAYA
Shah Alam
Klang
Pelabuhan Klang
Seremban
NEGERI SEMBILAN
MELAKA
Melaka
Muar
Batu Pahat
JOHOR
Johor Bahru
SINGAPORE
Tanjungpinang
RIAU
Pekanbaru
Dumai
Banda Aceh
Pulau Weh
Pulau Breueh
Sigli
Lhoksukon
Idi
Langsa
ACEH
Calang
Meulaboh
Pangkalanbrandan
Belawan
Binjai
Medan
Tebingtinggi
Pematangsiantar
Labuhanhaji
Pulau Simeulue
Sinabang
Danau Toba
Pulau Samosir
Sibolga
SUMATERA UTARA
Padangsidempuan
Gunungsitoli
Pulau Nias
Telukdalam
Kepulauan Batu
Kepulauan Banyak
Equator
Bukittinggi
Padangpanjang
Padang
SUMATERA BARAT
Solok
Pulau Siberut
Pulau Sipura
Pulau Pagai Utara
Pulau Pagai Selatan
JAMBI
Jambi
Sungaipenuh
Gunung Kerinci 3804m
BENGKULU
Bengkulu
Palembang
Pulau Enggano
Krui
Danau Ranau
Bukitkemuning

Using the land and sea

Rice is the most important arable crop in Indonesia and Malaysia, and both countries manage to meet almost all of their domestic demand. Malaysian rubber accounts for 25% of world production and is the main cash crop, grown on plantations and small farms, along with oil palms and copra. Timber is exported from both Malaysia and Indonesia. Modern agricultural techniques enable Singapore to produce fruits and vegetables despite a shortage of suitable land.

▶ *Spiral cuts in the bark of this rubber palm show where it has been tapped. Sophisticated 'cloning' techniques mean that trees which produce consistently high quantities of rubber can be easily reproduced.*

e transport network

165,272 miles (266,010 km)

958 miles (1,542 km)

5,061 miles (8,146 km)

18,070 miles (29,084 km)

apore's metro system, npleted in 1991, is among most efficient in the ·ld. Malaysia has several , modern highways and st roads are paved. onesia's many islands ke improvement of the ping infrastructure riority.

Major industry and infrastructure

- aerospace
- copra processing
- chemicals
- electronics
- engineering
- finance
- food processing
- iron & steel
- oil
- ship building
- timber processing
- textiles
- capital cities
- major towns
- international airports
- major roads
- major industrial areas

Land use and agricultural distribution

- coconuts
- fishing
- oil palms
- rice
- rubber
- shellfish
- sugar cane
- timber
- capital cities
- major towns
- pasture
- cropland
- forest
- wetland

The urban/rural population divide

urban 44% | rural 56%

0 10 20 30 40 50 60 70 80 90 100

Population density	Total land area
297 people per sq mile (115 people per sq km)	828,356 sq miles (2,146,000 sq km)

▼ *This tiny island near Kota Kinabalu, in Sabah, eastern Malaysia, is a part of a designated national park. Thickly forested, it is surrounded by broad, sandy beaches and shallow inland seas.*

▲ *The volcano of Gunung Semeru in eastern Java lies on the Pacific 'Ring of Fire'. It is part of the ancient Tennegger volcano and remains highly active.*

Scale 1:8,750,000

Km 0 25 50 100 150 200

Miles 0 25 50 100 150 200

projection: Mercator

Map key

Population

- above 5 million
- 1 million to 5 million
- 500,000 to 1 million
- 100,000 to 500,000
- 50,000 to 100,000
- 10,000 to 50,000
- below 10,000

Elevation

- 4000m / 13,124ft
- 3000m / 9843ft
- 2000m / 6562ft
- 1000m / 3281ft
- 500m / 1640ft
- 250m / 820ft
- 100m / 328ft
- sea level

166
170

Eastern Maritime Southeast Asia

EAST TIMOR, INDONESIA, PHILIPPINES

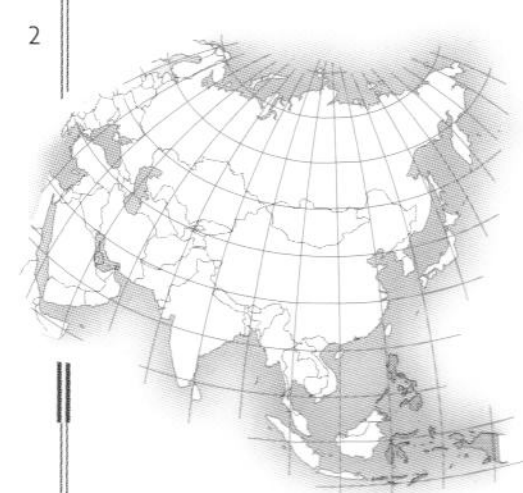

The Philippines takes its name from Philip II of Spain who was king when the islands were colonized during the 16th century. Almost 400 years of Spanish, and later US, rule have left their mark on the country's culture; English is widely spoken and over 90% of the population is Christian. The Philippines' economy is agriculturally based – inadequate infrastructure and electrical power shortages have so far hampered faster industrial growth. Indonesia's eastern islands are less economically developed than the rest of the country. Papua (Irian Jaya), which constitutes the western portion of New Guinea, is one of the world's last great wildernesses. East Timor is the newest independent state in the world, gaining full autonomy in 2002.

▲ ***The traditional boat-shaped** houses of the Toraja people in Sulawesi. Although now Christian, the Toraja still practice the animist traditions and rituals of their ancestors. They are famous for their elaborate funeral ceremonies and burial sites in cliffside caves.*

The landscape

Located on the Pacific 'Ring of Fire' the Philippines' 7100 islands are subject to frequent earthquakes and volcanic activity. Their terrain is largely mountainous, with narrow coastal plains and interior valleys and plains. Luzon and Mindanao are by far the largest islands and comprise roughly 66% of the country's area. Indonesia's eastern islands are mountainous and dotted with volcanoes, both active and dormant.

► ***Lake Taal on** the Philippines island of Luzon lies within the crater of an immense volcano that erupted twice in the 20th century, first in 1911 and again in 1965, causing the deaths of more than 3200 people.*

The Spratly Islands are a strategically sensitive island group, disputed by several surrounding countries. The Spratlys are claimed by China, Taiwan, Vietnam, Malaysia and the Philippines and are particularly important as they lie on oil and gas deposits.

***Mindanao has five** mountain ranges many of which have large numbers of active volcanoes. Lying just west of the Philippines Trench, which forms the boundary between the colliding Philippine and Eurasian plates, the entire island chain is subject to earthquakes and volcanic activity.*

***The 1000 islands** of the Moluccas are the fabled Spice Islands of history, whose produce attracted traders from around the globe. Most of the northern and central Moluccas have dense vegetation and rugged mountainous interiors where elevations often exceed 3000 feet (9144 m).*

▲ ***Bohol in the** southern Philippines is famous for its so-called 'chocolate hills'. There are more than 1000 of these regular mounds on the island. The hills are limestone in origin, the smoothed remains of an earlier cycle of erosion. Their brown appearance in the dry season gives them their name.*

The four-pronged island of Celebes is the product of complex tectonic activity which ruptured and then reattached small fragments of the Earth's crust to form the island's many peninsulas.

Coral islands such as Timor in eastern Indonesia show evidence of very recent and dramatic movements of the Earth's plates. Reefs in Timor have risen by as much as 4000 ft (1300 m) in the last million years.

The Pegunungan Jayawijaya range in central Papua (Irian Jaya) contains the world's highest range of limestone mountains, some with peaks more than 16,400 ft (5000 m) high. Heavy rainfall and high temperatures, which promote rapid weathering, have led to the creation of large underground caves and river systems such as the river of Sungai Baliem.

Using the land and sea

Indonesia's eastern islands are less intensively cultivated than those in the west. Coconuts, coffee and spices such as cloves and nutmeg are the major commercial crops while rice, corn and soya beans are grown for local consumption. The Philippines' rich, fertile soils support year-round production of a wide range of crops. The country is one of the world's largest producers of coconuts and a major exporter of coconut products, including one-third of the world's copra. Although much of the arable land is given over to rice and corn, the main staple food crops, tropical fruits such as bananas, pineapples and mangos,and sugar cane are also grown for export.

◄ ***The terracing of** land to restrict soil erosion and create flat surfaces for agriculture is a common practice throughout Southeast Asia, particularly where land is scarce. These terraces are on Luzon in the Philippines.*

Land use and agricultural distribution

coconuts, fishing, rice, rubber, shellfish, sugar cane

capital cities, major towns

pasture, cropland, forest, wetland

The urban/rural population divide

urban 45% — rural 55%

Population density	Total land area
258 people per sq mile (160 people per sq km)	654,771 sq miles (1,053,755 sq km)

▲ ***More than two-thirds** of Papua's (Irian Jaya) land area is heavily forested and the population of around 1.5 million live mainly in isolated tribal groups using more than 80 distinct languages.*

168

Transport and industry

The Philippines' economy is primarily a mixture of agriculture and light industry. The manufacturing sector is still developing; many factories are licensees of foreign companies producing finished goods for export. Mining is also important – the country's chromite, nickel and copper deposits are among the largest in the world. Agriculture is the main activity in eastern Indonesia. Most industry has a primary basis, including logging, food-processing and mining. Nickel, the most important metal, is produced on Sulawesi, in Papua (Irian Jaya), and in the Moluccas.

The transport network

- 16,652 miles (26,800 km)
- None
- 500 miles (805 km)
- 8704 miles (14,008 km)

Sulawesi has some good roads, but on Papua (Irian Jaya) and the Moluccas there are few road interconnections between major settled areas. Water and sea transport remain important although air links have improved in the Philippines.

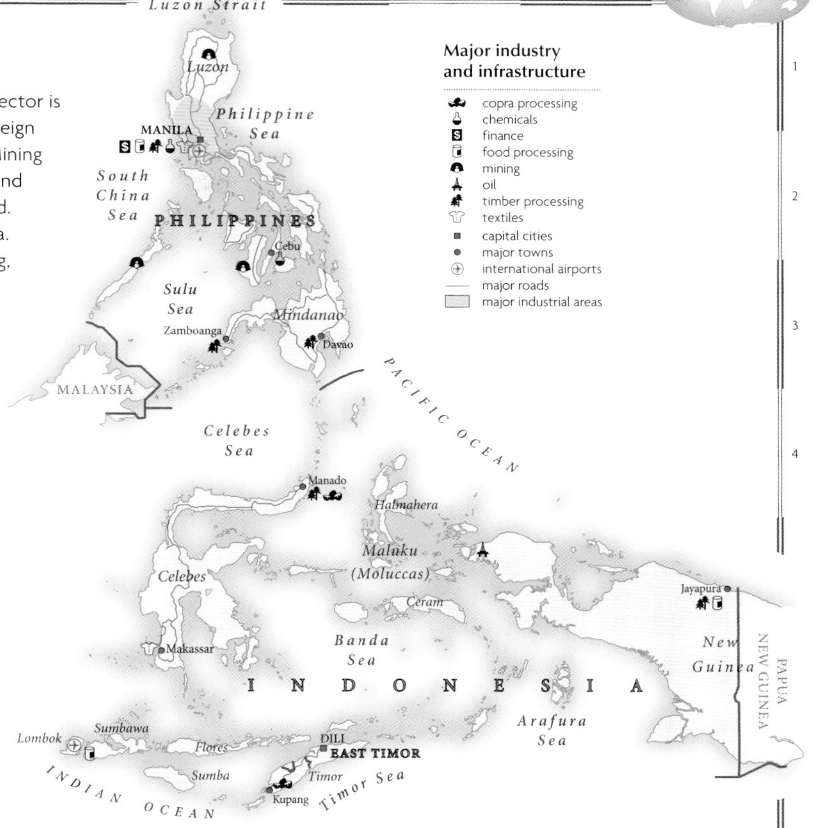

Major industry and infrastructure

- copra processing
- chemicals
- finance
- food processing
- mining
- oil
- timber processing
- textiles
- capital cities
- major towns
- international airports
- major roads
- major industrial areas

▲ *Manila is the* Philippines' chief port and transport centre, and the focus of the country's commercial, industrial and cultural activities. Much of the city lies below sea level, and it suffers from floods during the rainy summer season.

Map key

Population

- above 5 million
- 1 million to 5 million
- 500,000 to 1 million
- 100,000 to 500,000
- 50,000 to 100,000
- 10,000 to 50,000
- below 10,000

Elevation

- 4000m / 13,124ft
- 3000m / 9843ft
- 2000m / 6562ft
- 1000m / 3281ft
- 500m / 1640ft
- 250m / 820ft
- 100m / 328ft
- sea level

Scale 1:,11,800,000

Km 0 50 100 200 300 400

Miles 0 50 100 200 300 400

projection: Mercator

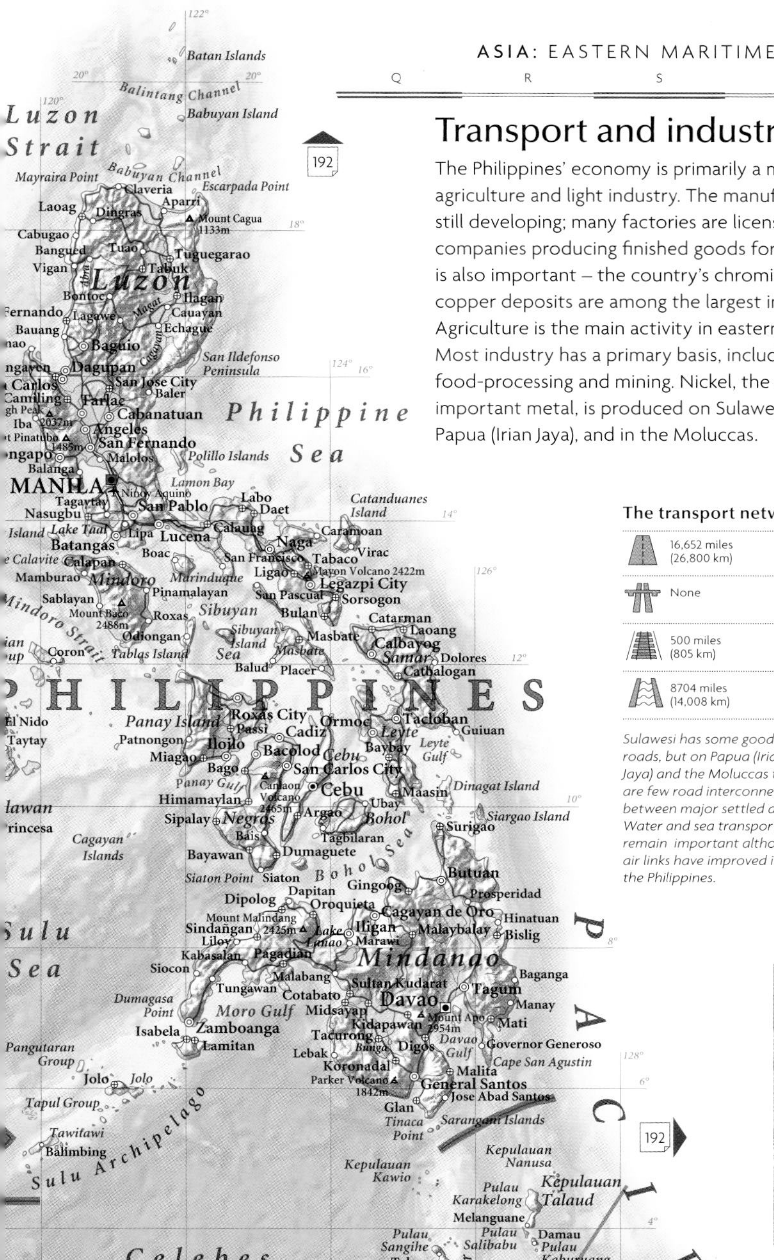

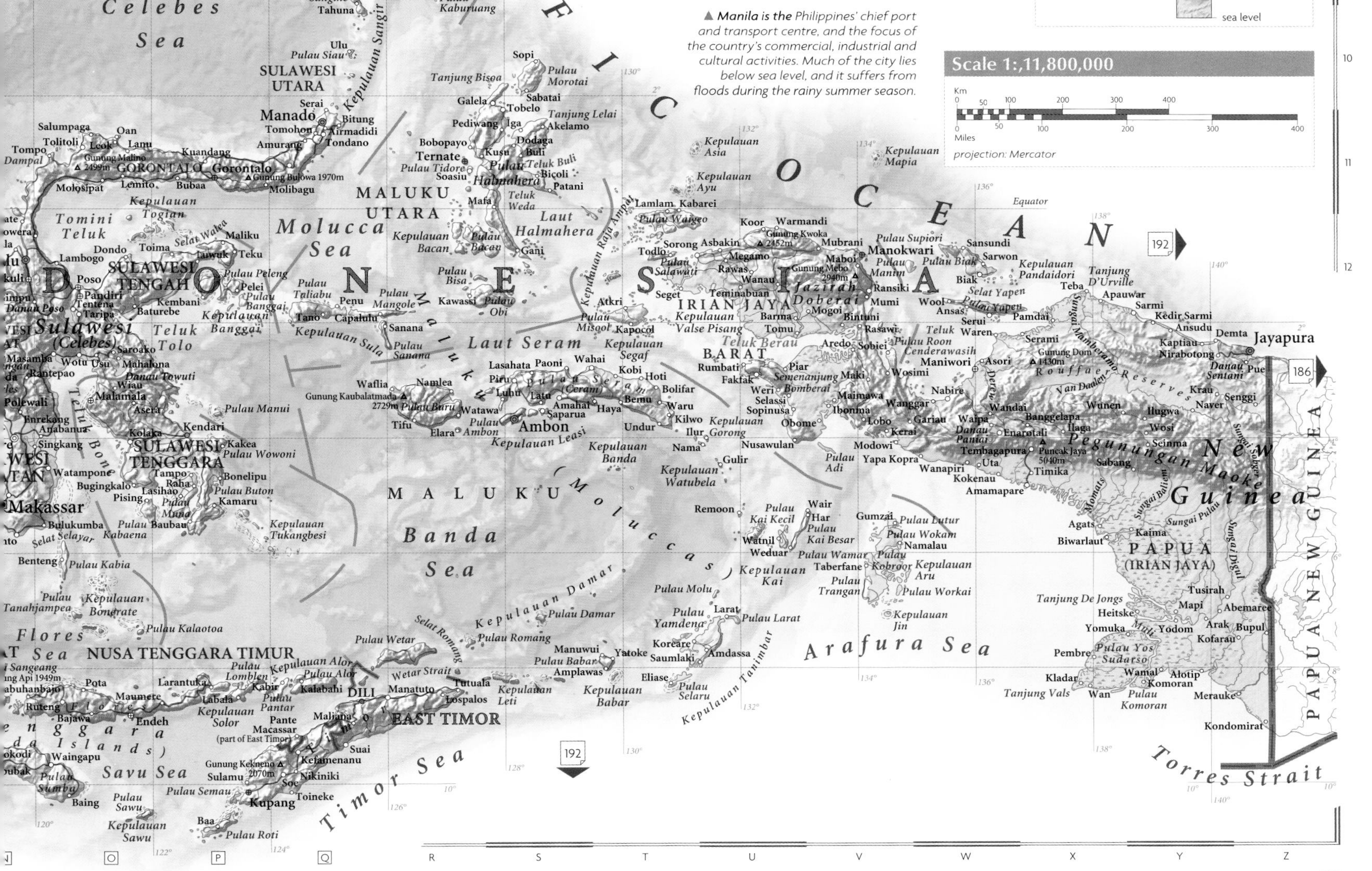

The Indian Ocean

Despite being the smallest of the three major oceans, the evolution of the Indian Ocean was the most complex. The ocean basin was formed during the break up of the supercontinent Gondwanaland, when the Indian subcontinent moved northeast, Africa moved west and Australia separated from Antarctica. Like the Pacific Ocean, the warm waters of the Indian Ocean are punctuated by coral atolls and islands. About one-fifth of the world's population – over 1000 million people – live on its shores. Those people living along the northern coasts are constantly threatened by flooding and typhoons caused by the monsoon winds.

The landscape

The Indian Ocean began forming about 150 million years ago, but in its present form it is relatively young, only about 36 million years old. Along the three subterranean mountain chains of its mid-ocean ridge the seafloor is still spreading. The Indian Ocean has fewer trenches than other oceans and only a narrow continental shelf around most of its surrounding land.

Sediments come from Ganges/ Brahmaputra river system

Submarine canyons transport sediment to fan – some of these are more than 1500 miles (2500 km) long

Sri Lanka

▲ *The Ganges Fan is one of the world's largest submarine accumulations of sediment, extending far beyond Sri Lanka. It is fed by the Ganges/Brahmaputra river system, whose sediment is carried through a network of underwater canyons at the edge of the continental shelf.*

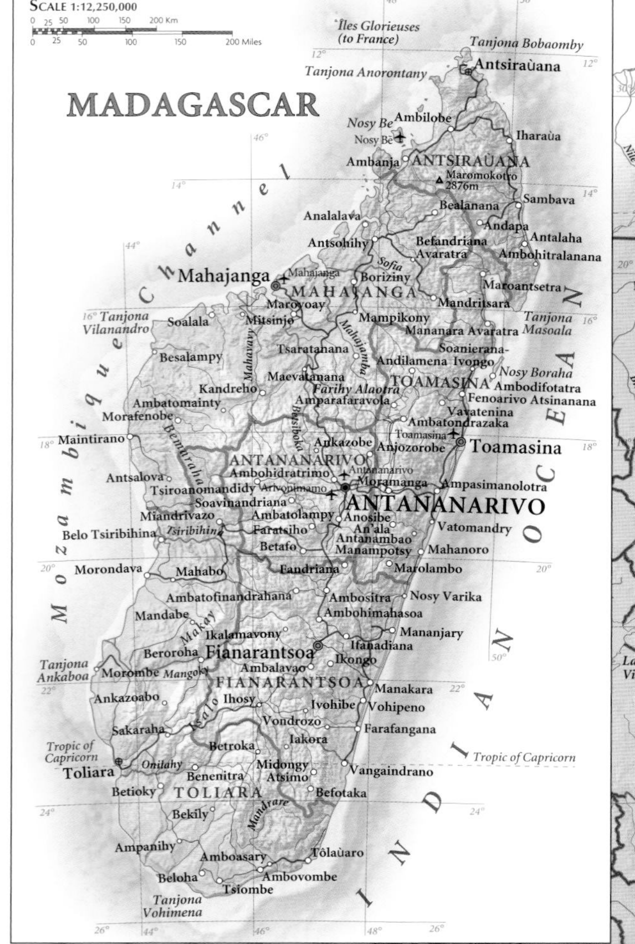
SCALE 1:12,250,000
MADAGASCAR
Îles Glorieuses (to France)
Tanjona Bobaomby
Antsiraùana
Tanjona Anorontany
Nosy Be
Ambilobe
Iharaùa
ANTSIRAÙANA
Maromokotro 2876m
Sambava
Analalava
Andapa
Antalaha
Antsohihy
Befandriana Avaratra
Ambohitralanana
Mahajanga
MAHAJANGA
Maroantsetra
Mandritsara
Marovoay
Tanjona Vilanandro
Soalala
Mitsinjo
Mampikony
Mananara Avaratra
Tanjona Masoala
Besalampy
Tsaratanana
Soanierana-Ivongo
Andilamena
Nosy Boraha
Maevatanana
Fenoarivo Atsinanana
Kandreho
TOAMASINA
Ambatomainty
Amparafaravola
Morafenobe
Ambatondrazaka
Maintirano
Ankazobe
Anjozorobe
Toamasina
ANTANANARIVO
Ambohidratrimo
Antsalova
Tsiroanomandidy
Moramanga
Ampasimanolotra
Soavinandriana
ANTANANARIVO
Miandrivazo
Ambatolampy
Anosibe An'ala
Vatomandry
Belo Tsiribihina
Faratsiho
Betafo
Antanambao Manampotsy
Mahanoro
Morondava
Mahabo
Fandriana
Marolambo
Ambatofinandrahana
Ambositra
Nosy Varika
Mandabe
Ambohimahasoa
Ikalamavony
Mananjary
Beroroha
Fianarantsoa
Ifanadiana
Tanjona Ankaboa
Morombe
Ambalavao
Ikongo
FIANARANTSOA
Manakara
Ankazoabo
Ihosy
Ivohibe
Vohipeno
Vondrozo
Farafangana
Sakaraha
Iakora
Betroka
Tropic of Capricorn
Toliara
Midongy Atsimo
Vangaindrano
Benenitra
TOLIARA
Betioky
Befotaka
Bekily
Ampanihy
Tôlaùaro
Amboasary
Beloha
Ambovombe
Tsiombe
Tanjona Vohimena
Mozambique Channel
INDIAN OCEAN

The mid-oceanic ridge runs from the Arabian Sea. It diverges east of Madagascar, one arm runs southwest to join the Mid-Atlantic Ridge, the other branches southeast, joining the Pacific-Antarctic Ridge, southeast of Tasmania.

The Ninetyeast Ridge takes its name from the line of longitude it follows. It is the world's longest and straightest under-sea ridge.

Two of the world's largest rivers flow into the Indian Ocean; the Indus and the Ganges/ Brahmaputra. Both have deposited enormous fans of sediment.

Indus River

▶ *A large proportion of the coast of Thailand, on the Isthmus of Kra, is stabilized by mangrove thickets. They act as an important breeding ground for wildlife.*

The Java Trench is the world's longest, it runs 1600 miles (2570 km) from the southwest of Java, but is only 50 miles (80 km) wide.

The circulation in the northern Indian Ocean is controlled by the monsoon winds. Biannually these winds reverse their pattern, causing a reversal in the surface currents and alternative high and low pressure conditions over Asia and Australia.

The Kerguelen Islands in the Southern Ocean were created by a hot spot in the Earth's crust. The islands were formed in succession as the Antarctic Plate moved slowly over the hot spot.

The relief of Madagascar rises from a low-lying coastal strip in the east, to the central plateau. The plateau is also a major watershed separating Madagascar's three main river basins.

▶ *The central group of the Seychelles are mountainous, granite islands. They have a narrow coastal belt and lush, tropical vegetation cloaks the highlands.*

Resources

Many of the small islands in the Indian Ocean rely exclusively on tuna-fishing and tourism to maintain their economies. Most fisheries are artisanal, although large-scale tuna-fishing does take place in the Seychelles, Mauritius and the western Indian Ocean. Other resources include oil in The Gulf, pearls in the Red Sea and tin from deposits off the shores of Burma, Thailand and Indonesia.

Suez
Kuwait
ASIA
Mumbai
Rangoon
Arabian Sea
Bay of Bengal
South China Sea
Singapore
AFRICA
Mombasa
Java Sea
INDIAN OCEAN
Timor Sea
Toamasina
AUSTRALIA
Fremantle
SOUTHERN OCEAN
ANTARCTICA

Resources (including wildlife)

- fish
- penguins
- shellfish
- whales
- oil & gas
- tin deposits
- tourism
- major towns
- major ports

▶ *The recent use of large drag nets for tuna-fishing has not only threatened the livelihoods of many small-scale fisheries, but also caused widespread environmental concern about the potential impact on other marine species.*

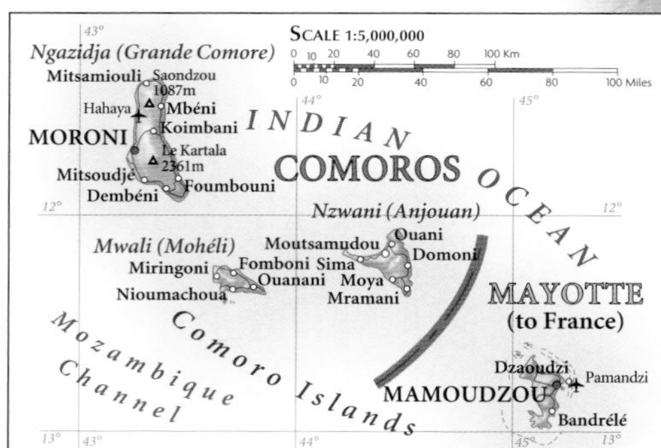
SCALE 1:5,000,000
Ngazidja (Grande Comore)
Mitsamiouli
Saondzou 1087m
Hahaya
Mbéni
MORONI
Koimbani
Le Kartala 2361m
INDIAN OCEAN
COMOROS
Mitsoudjé
Dembéni
Foumbouni
Nzwani (Anjouan)
Ouani
Mwali (Mohéli)
Moutsamudou
Domoni
Miringoni
Fomboni
Sima
Ouanani
Moya
Nioumachoua
Mramani
MAYOTTE (to France)
Comoro Islands
Mozambique Channel
Dzaoudzi
Pamandzi
MAMOUDZOU
Bandrélé

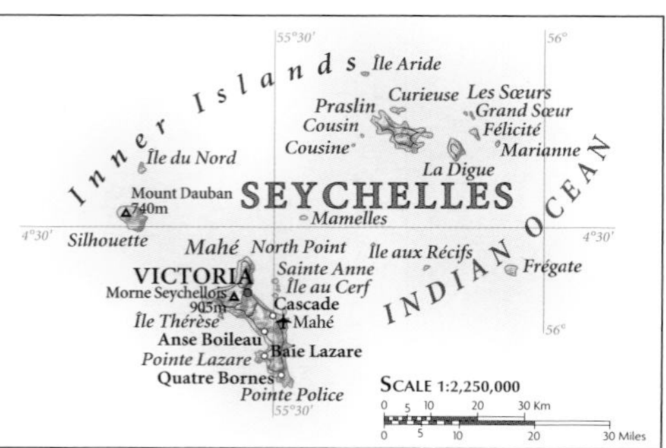
Inner Islands
Ile Aride
Praslin
Curieuse
Les Sœurs
Grand Sœur
Cousin
Félicité
Cousine
Marianne
Ile du Nord
La Digue
Mount Dauban 740m
SEYCHELLES
Mamelles
Silhouette
Mahé
North Point
Ile aux Récifs
Frégate
VICTORIA
Sainte Anne
Morne Seychellois 905m
Ile au Cerf
Cascade
Ile Thérèse
Mahé
Anse Boileau
Baie Lazare
Pointe Lazare
Quatre Bornes
Pointe Police
INDIAN OCEAN
SCALE 1:2,250,000

▲ *Coral reefs support an enormous diversity of animal and plant life. Many species of tropical fish, like these squirrel fish, live and feed around the profusion of reefs and atolls in the Indian Ocean.*

Suez
EGYPT
Red Sea
Yanbu' al Bahr
Port Sudan
SUDAN
ERITREA
Massawa
DJIBOUTI
Djibouti
ETHIOPIA
KENYA
Lake Victoria
TANZANIA
Mombasa
Tanga
Pemba
Zanzibar
Dar es Salaam
Mafia
Lake Nyasa
MOZAMBIQUE
Nacala
Quelimane
Beira
Mozambique Channel
Bassas da India
Ile Europa
Tropic of Capricorn
Maputo
SWAZILAND
LESOTHO
Durban
SOUTH AFRICA
East London
Cape Town
Port Elizabeth
Mosselbaai
Agulhas Bank
Natal Basin
Transkei Basin
Agulhas Plateau
Agulhas Basin
Atlantic-Indian Ridge
Atlantic-Indian Basin

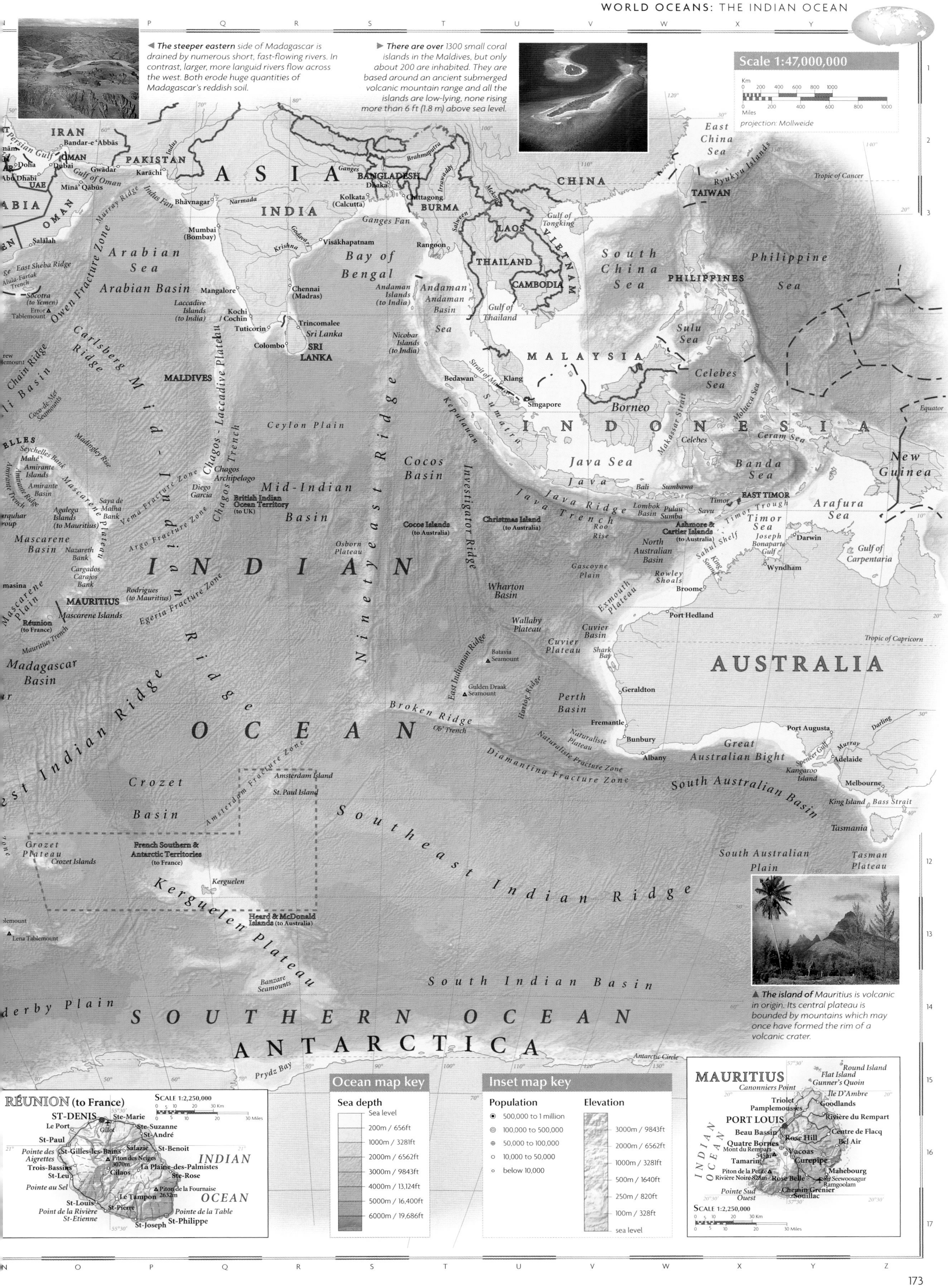

Scale 1:47,000,000
Km 0 200 400 600 800 1000
Miles 0 200 400 600 800 1000
projection: Mollweide
IRAN
Bandar-e 'Abbās
Persian Gulf
OMAN
Doha
Dubai
Abu Dhabi
UAE
Gwādar
Gulf of Oman
Mina' Qābūs
PAKISTAN
Karāchi
Indus
ASIA
Ganges
BANGLADESH
Dhaka
Brahmaputra
Irrawaddy
Mekong
CHINA
Murray Ridge
Indus Fan
Bhāvnagar
Narmada
INDIA
Kolkata (Calcutta)
Chittagong
BURMA
Ganges Fan
Salween
LAOS
Gulf of Tongking
VIETNAM
Mumbai (Bombay)
Godavari
Krishna
Visākhapatnam
Rangoon
THAILAND
CAMBODIA
Sālālah
Arabian Sea
Bay of Bengal
East Sheba Ridge
Alula-Fartak Trench
Owen Fracture Zone
Arabian Basin
Mangalore
Chennai (Madras)
Andaman Islands (to India)
Andaman Sea
Andaman Basin
Gulf of Thailand
Socotra (to Yemen)
Error Tablemount
Laccadive Islands (to India)
Kochi / Cochin
Tuticorin
Trincomalee
Sri Lanka
Colombo
SRI LANKA
Nicobar Islands (to India)
Carlsberg Ridge
Chain Ridge
Coco-de-Mer Seamounts
Laccadive Plateau
MALDIVES
Mid-Indian Ridge
Ninetyeast Ridge
Ceylon Plain
Chagos - Laccadive Plateau
Chagos Trench
Chagos Archipelago
Diego Garcia
British Indian Ocean Territory (to UK)
Mid-Indian Basin
Cocos Basin
Investigator Ridge
Cocos Islands (to Australia)
Christmas Island (to Australia)
Osborn Plateau
Kepulauan
Sumatra
Strait of Malacca
Bedawan
Klang
Singapore
MALAYSIA
Borneo
INDONESIA
Java Sea
Java
Java Ridge
Java Trench
Bali
Sumbawa
Lombok Basin
Pulau Sumba
Savu
Timor
EAST TIMOR
Timor Trough
Timor Sea
Roo Rise
Ashmore & Cartier Islands (to Australia)
Sahul Shelf
Joseph Bonaparte Gulf
Darwin
Arafura Sea
Gulf of Carpentaria
Wyndham
King Sound
North Australian Basin
Rowley Shoals
Broome
Gascoyne Plain
Exmouth Plateau
Port Hedland
South China Sea
PHILIPPINES
Philippine Sea
Sulu Sea
Celebes Sea
Makassar Strait
Molucca Sea
Celebes
Ceram Sea
Banda Sea
New Guinea
Equator
East China Sea
Ryukyu Islands
TAIWAN
Tropic of Cancer
Seychelles Bank
Mahé
Amirante Islands
Amirante Trench
Amirante Ridge
Amirante Basin
Mascarene Plateau
Madingley Rise
Agalega Islands (to Mauritius)
Saya de Malha Bank
Vema Fracture Zone
Argo Fracture Zone
Mascarene Basin
Nazareth Bank
Cargados Carajos Bank
Rodrigues (to Mauritius)
MAURITIUS
Mascarene Islands
Réunion (to France)
Mauritius Trench
Mascarene Plain
Egeria Fracture Zone
INDIAN OCEAN
Madagascar Basin
Wharton Basin
Wallaby Plateau
Cuvier Basin
Cuvier Plateau
Shark Bay
Batavia Seamount
Gulden Draak Seamount
East Indiaman Ridge
Hartog Ridge
Perth Basin
Geraldton
Fremantle
Bunbury
Albany
Naturaliste Plateau
Naturaliste Fracture Zone
Broken Ridge
Ob' Trench
Diamantina Fracture Zone
Tropic of Capricorn
AUSTRALIA
Port Augusta
Darling
Murray
Spencer Gulf
Adelaide
Kangaroo Island
Great Australian Bight
South Australian Basin
Melbourne
King Island
Bass Strait
Tasmania
South Australian Plain
Tasman Plateau
Southwest Indian Ridge
Crozet Basin
Amsterdam Fracture Zone
Amsterdam Island
St. Paul Island
Southeast Indian Ridge
Crozet Plateau
Crozet Islands
French Southern & Antarctic Territories (to France)
Kerguelen
Kerguelen Plateau
Heard & McDonald Islands (to Australia)
Lena Tablemount
Banzare Seamounts
South Indian Basin
Enderby Plain
SOUTHERN OCEAN
ANTARCTICA
Prydz Bay
Antarctic Circle
RÉUNION (to France)
SCALE 1:2,250,000
ST-DENIS
Ste-Marie
Le Port
Ste-Suzanne
St-André
St-Paul
Salazie
St-Benoit
Pointe des Aigrettes
St-Gilles-les-Bains
Piton des Neiges 3070m
Trois-Bassins
Cilaos
La Plaine-des-Palmistes
St-Leu
Ste-Rose
INDIAN
Pointe au Sel
Piton de la Fournaise 2632m
Le Tampon
OCEAN
St-Louis
St-Pierre
Pointe de la Rivière St-Etienne
Pointe de la Table
St-Joseph
St-Philippe
Ocean map key
Sea depth
Sea level
200m / 656ft
1000m / 3281ft
2000m / 6562ft
3000m / 9843ft
4000m / 13,124ft
5000m / 16,400ft
6000m / 19,686ft
Inset map key
Population
500,000 to 1 million
100,000 to 500,000
50,000 to 100,000
10,000 to 50,000
below 10,000
Elevation
3000m / 9843ft
2000m / 6562ft
1000m / 3281ft
500m / 1640ft
250m / 820ft
100m / 328ft
sea level
MAURITIUS
Round Island
Flat Island
Gunner's Quoin
Canonniers Point
Île D'Ambre
Triolet
Goodlands
Pamplemousses
Rivière du Rempart
PORT LOUIS
Beau Bassin
Rose Hill
Centre de Flacq
Bel Air
Quatre Bornes
Mont du Rempart 545m
Vacoas
Tamarin
Curepipe
INDIAN OCEAN
Piton de la Petite Rivière Noire 828m
Mahebourg
Rose Belle
Sir Seewoosagur Ramgoolam
Chemin Grenier
Pointe Sud Ouest
Souillac
SCALE 1:2,250,000

◀ *The steeper eastern* side of Madagascar is drained by numerous short, fast-flowing rivers. In contrast, larger, more languid rivers flow across the west. Both erode huge quantities of Madagascar's reddish soil.

▶ *There are over* 1300 small coral islands in the Maldives, but only about 200 are inhabited. They are based around an ancient submerged volcanic mountain range and all the islands are low-lying, none rising more than 6 ft (1.8 m) above sea level.

▲ *The island of* Mauritius is volcanic in origin. Its central plateau is bounded by mountains which may once have formed the rim of a volcanic crater.

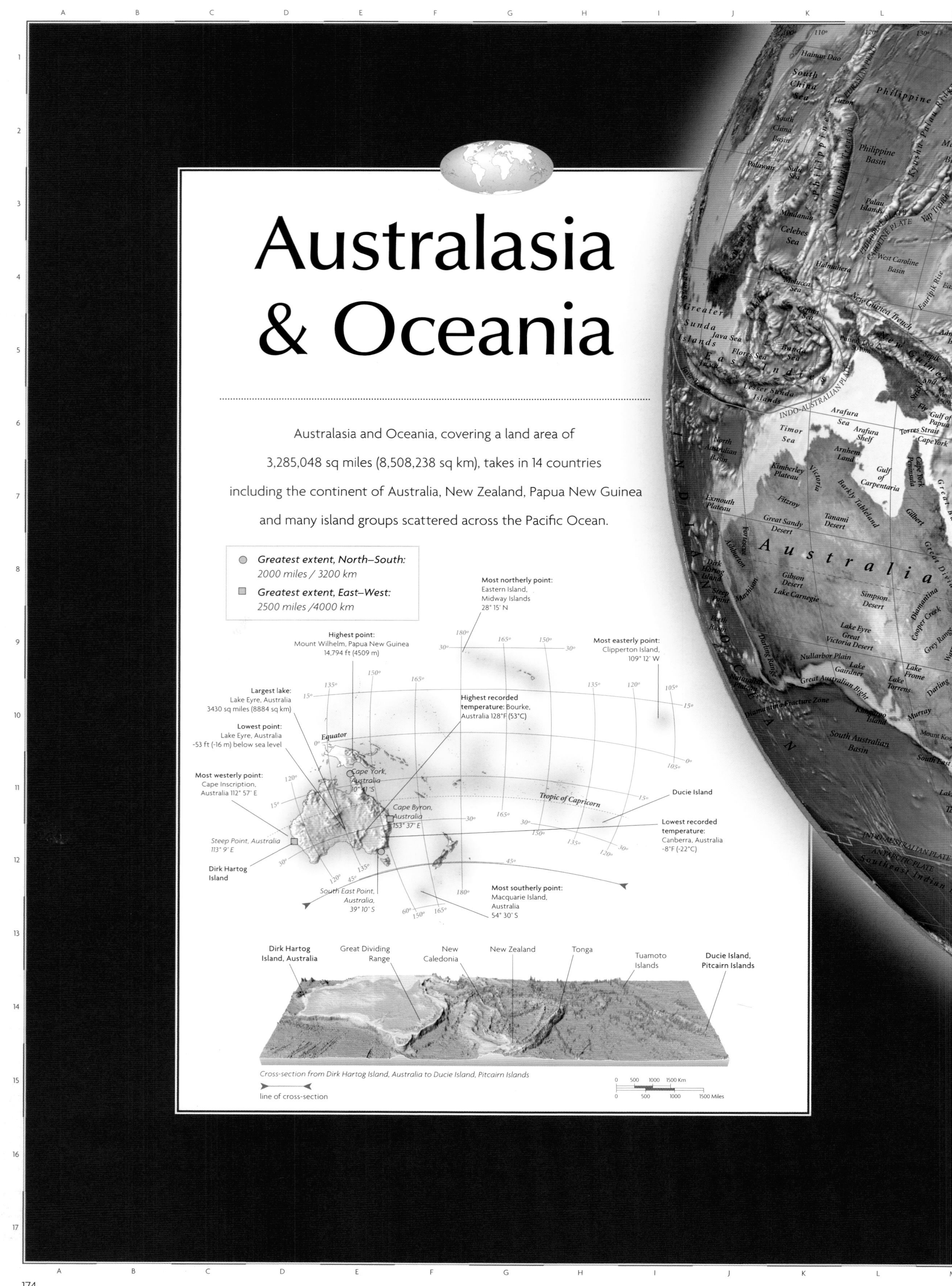

Australasia & Oceania
Australasia and Oceania, covering a land area of 3,285,048 sq miles (8,508,238 sq km), takes in 14 countries including the continent of Australia, New Zealand, Papua New Guinea and many island groups scattered across the Pacific Ocean.
Greatest extent, North–South: 2000 miles / 3200 km
Greatest extent, East–West: 2500 miles /4000 km
Most northerly point: Eastern Island, Midway Islands 28° 15' N
Highest point: Mount Wilhelm, Papua New Guinea 14,794 ft (4509 m)
Most easterly point: Clipperton Island, 109° 12' W
Largest lake: Lake Eyre, Australia 3430 sq miles (8884 sq km)
Highest recorded temperature: Bourke, Australia 128°F (53°C)
Lowest point: Lake Eyre, Australia -53 ft (-16 m) below sea level
Equator
Most westerly point: Cape Inscription, Australia 112° 57' E
Cape York, Australia 10° 41' S
Cape Byron, Australia 153° 37' E
Tropic of Capricorn
Ducie Island
Lowest recorded temperature: Canberra, Australia -8°F (-22°C)
Steep Point, Australia 113° 9' E
Dirk Hartog Island
South East Point, Australia, 39° 10' S
Most southerly point: Macquarie Island, Australia 54° 30' S
Dirk Hartog Island, Australia
Great Dividing Range
New Caledonia
New Zealand
Tonga
Tuamoto Islands
Ducie Island, Pitcairn Islands
Cross-section from Dirk Hartog Island, Australia to Ducie Island, Pitcairn Islands
line of cross-section
0 500 1000 1500 Km
0 500 1000 1500 Miles
South China Sea
Philippine Basin
Celebes Sea
Java Sea
Flores Sea
Banda Sea
Arafura Sea
Timor Sea
Gulf of Carpentaria
Great Sandy Desert
Tanami Desert
Gibson Desert
Simpson Desert
Great Victoria Desert
Nullarbor Plain
Great Australian Bight
Australia
South Australian Basin

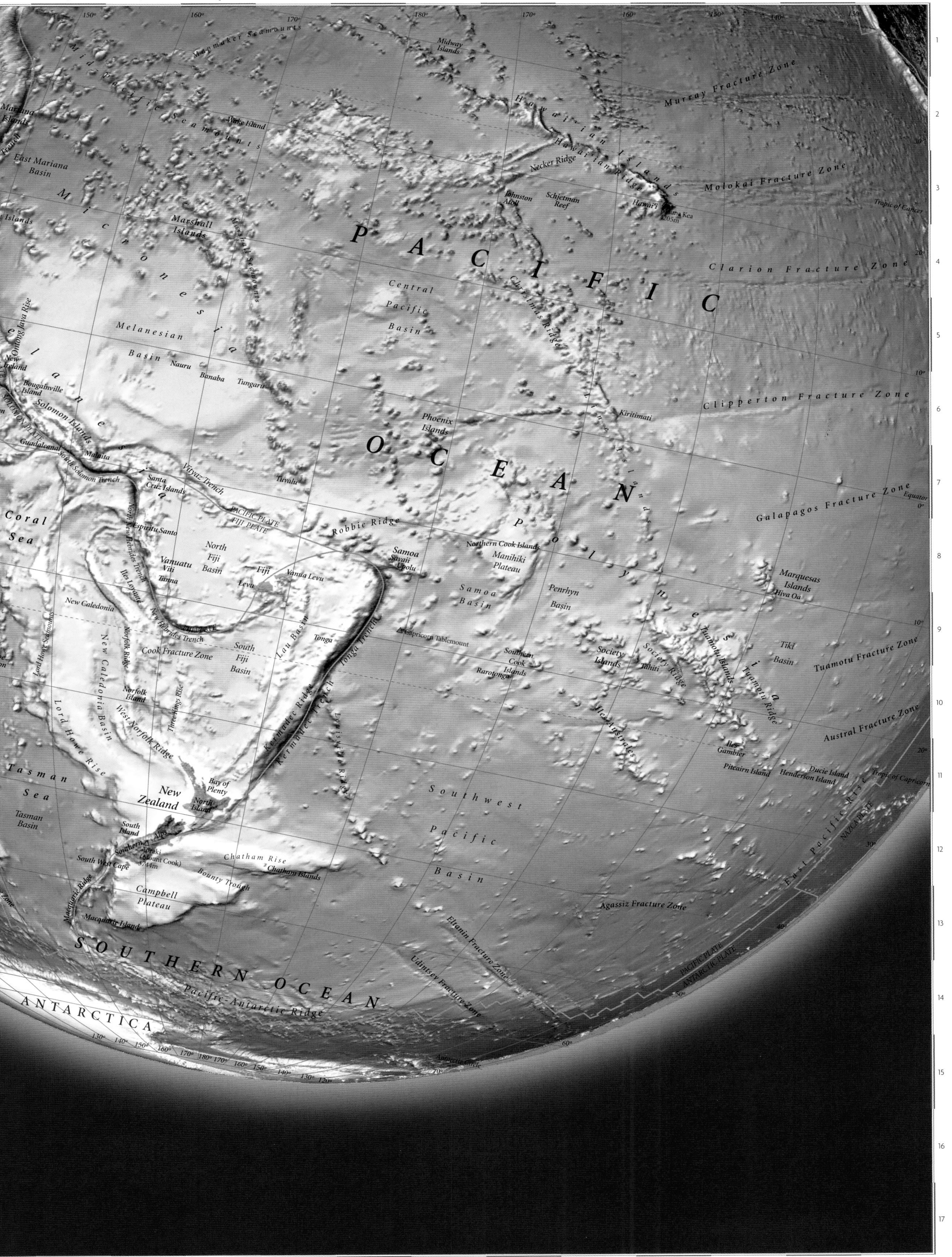
O P Q R S T U V W X Y Z
1 2 3 4 5 6 7 8 9 10 11 12 13 14 15 16 17
PACIFIC
OCEAN
SOUTHERN OCEAN
ANTARCTICA
Micronesia
Melanesia
Polynesia
Midway Islands
Murray Fracture Zone
Hawaiian Islands
Hawaiian Ridge
Necker Ridge
Molokai Fracture Zone
Tropic of Cancer
Johnston Atoll
Schjetman Reef
Mid-Pacific Seamounts
Wake Island
Mariana Islands
East Mariana Basin
Marshall Islands
Clarion Fracture Zone
Central Pacific Basin
Christmas Ridge
Melanesian Basin
Ontong Java Rise
Nauru
Banaba
Tungaru
New Ireland
Bougainville Island
Solomon Islands
Guadalcanal
Malaita
South Solomon Trench
Clipperton Fracture Zone
Kiritimati
Line Islands
Phoenix Islands
Tuvalu
Santa Cruz Islands
Vityaz Trench
Coral Sea
Espiritu Santo
PACIFIC PLATE
FIJI PLATE
Robbie Ridge
Galapagos Fracture Zone
Equator
North Fiji Basin
Vanuatu
Viti
Fiji
Vanua Levu
Samoa
Savaii
Upolu
Northern Cook Islands
Manihiki Plateau
Marquesas Islands
Hiva Oa
New Hebrides Trench
Îles Loyauté
New Caledonia
Samoa Basin
Penrhyn Basin
Lau Basin
Tonga
Tonga Trench
Capricorn Tablemount
Lord Howe Seamounts
Norfolk Ridge
New Caledonia Basin
Cook Fracture Zone
South Fiji Basin
Southern Cook Islands
Rarotonga
Society Islands
Tahiti
Society Ridge
Tuamotu Islands
Tuamotu Ridge
Tiki Basin
Tuamotu Fracture Zone
Norfolk Island
West Norfolk Ridge
Three Kings Rise
Kermadec Ridge
Kermadec Trench
Louisville Ridge
Îles Australes
Austral Fracture Zone
Îles Gambier
Pitcairn Island
Henderson Island
Ducie Island
Tropic of Capricorn
Lord Howe Rise
Tasman Sea
Tasman Basin
New Zealand
Bay of Plenty
North Island
South Island
Southern Alps
South West Cape
Chatham Rise
Chatham Islands
Bounty Trough
Southwest Pacific Basin
East Pacific Rise
NAZCA PLATE
Campbell Plateau
Macquarie Ridge
Macquarie Island
Agassiz Fracture Zone
Eltanin Fracture Zone
Udintsev Fracture Zone
Pacific-Antarctic Ridge
PACIFIC PLATE
ANTARCTIC PLATE
Antarctic Circle

Political Australasia & Oceania

Vast expanses of ocean separate this geographically fragmented realm, characterized more by each country's isolation than by any political unity. Australia's and New Zealand's traditional ties with the United Kingdom, as members of the Commonwealth, are now being called into question as Australasian and Oceanian nations are increasingly looking to forge new relationships with neighbouring Asian countries like Japan. External influences have featured strongly in the politics of the Pacific Islands; the various territories of Micronesia were largely under US control until the late 1980s, and France, New Zealand, the USA and the UK still have territories under colonial rule in Polynesia. Nuclear weapons-testing by Western superpowers was widespread during the Cold War period, but has now been discontinued.

◀ ***Western Australia's mineral*** *wealth has transformed its state capital, Perth, into one of Australia's major cities. Perth is one of the world's most isolated cities – over 2500 miles (4000 km) from the population centres of the eastern seaboard.*

Scale 1:35,500,000

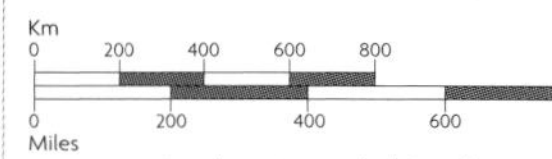
Km
0
200
400
600
800
0
200
400
600
800
Miles

projection: Lambert Azimuthal Equal Area

Population

Density of settlement in the region is generally low. Australia is one of the least densely populated countries on Earth with over 80% of its population living within 25 miles (40 km) of the coast – mostly in the southeast of the country. New Zealand, and the island groups of Melanesia, Micronesia and Polynesia, are much more densely populated, although many of the smaller islands remain uninhabited.

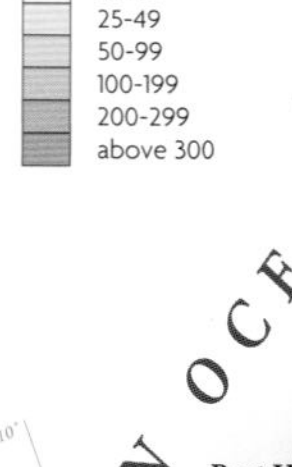
Population density
(people per sq km)
below 4
5-24
25-49
50-99
100-199
200-299
above 300

▲ ***The myriad of*** *small coral islands which are scattered across the Pacific Ocean are often uninhabited, as they offer little shelter from the weather, often no fresh water, and only limited food supplies.*

◀ ***The planes of*** *the Australian Royal Flying Doctor Service are able to cover large expanses of barren land quickly, bringing medical treatment to the most inaccessible and far-flung places.*

Philippine Sea
Northern Mariana Islands (to US)
Mariana Islands
Saipan
Guam (to US)
HAGÅTÑA
Micronesia
Bikini Atoll
Yap
Chuuk
Pohnpei
PALIKIR
Kosrae
Caroline Islands
MELEKEOK
Babeldaob
PALAU
MICRONESIA
Melanesia
PAPUA NEW GUINEA
Bismarck Sea
New Ireland
Wewak
Rabaul
New Britain
New Guinea
Madang
Ubai
Arawa
Bougainville Island
Solomon Islands
Mount Hagen
Lae
Solomon Sea
Tapini
New Georgia Islands
HONIARA
Guadalcanal
PORT MORESBY
Santa Cruz Islands
Arafura Sea
Torres Strait
Equator
Timor Sea
Coral Sea
Coral Sea Islands (to Australia)
New Caledonia (to France)
NOUMÉA
INDIAN OCEAN
Darwin
Arnhem Land
Katherine
Joseph Bonaparte Gulf
Gulf of Carpentaria
Cape York Peninsula
Great Barrier Reef
Cairns
Normanton
Townsville
Wyndham
Kimberley Plateau
NORTHERN TERRITORY
Hughenden
Mackay
Derby
Tennant Creek
Mount Isa
Tanami Desert
QUEENSLAND
Rockhampton
Broome
Barcaldine
Great Dividing Range
Great Sandy Desert
Alice Springs
Simpson Desert
Charleville
Miles
Port Hedland
Toowoomba
Brisbane
AUSTRALIA
Cunnamulla
Grafton
Hamersley Range
Gibson Desert
Lake Eyre North
Grey Range
Bourke
SOUTH AUSTRALIA
WESTERN AUSTRALIA
Wilcannia
Darling
NEW SOUTH WALES
Dubbo
Newcastle
Lake Torrens
Flinders Ranges
Sydney
Carnavon
Great Victoria Desert
Lake Everard
Lake Gairdner
Port Augusta
Campbelltown
Wollongong
Tropic of Capricorn
Mount Magnet
Ceduna
Whyalla
Murray
Wagga Wagga
CANBERRA
AUSTRALIAN CAPITAL TERRITORY
Nullarbor Plain
Kalgoorlie
Great Australian Bight
Adelaide
Bendigo
Geraldton
Kangaroo Island
Horsham
VICTORIA
Ballarat
Melbourne
Geelong
Mount Gambier
Tasman Sea
Perth
Esperance
Bass Strait
Launceston
Albany
TASMANIA
Tasmania
Hobart
Lord Howe Island (to Australia)

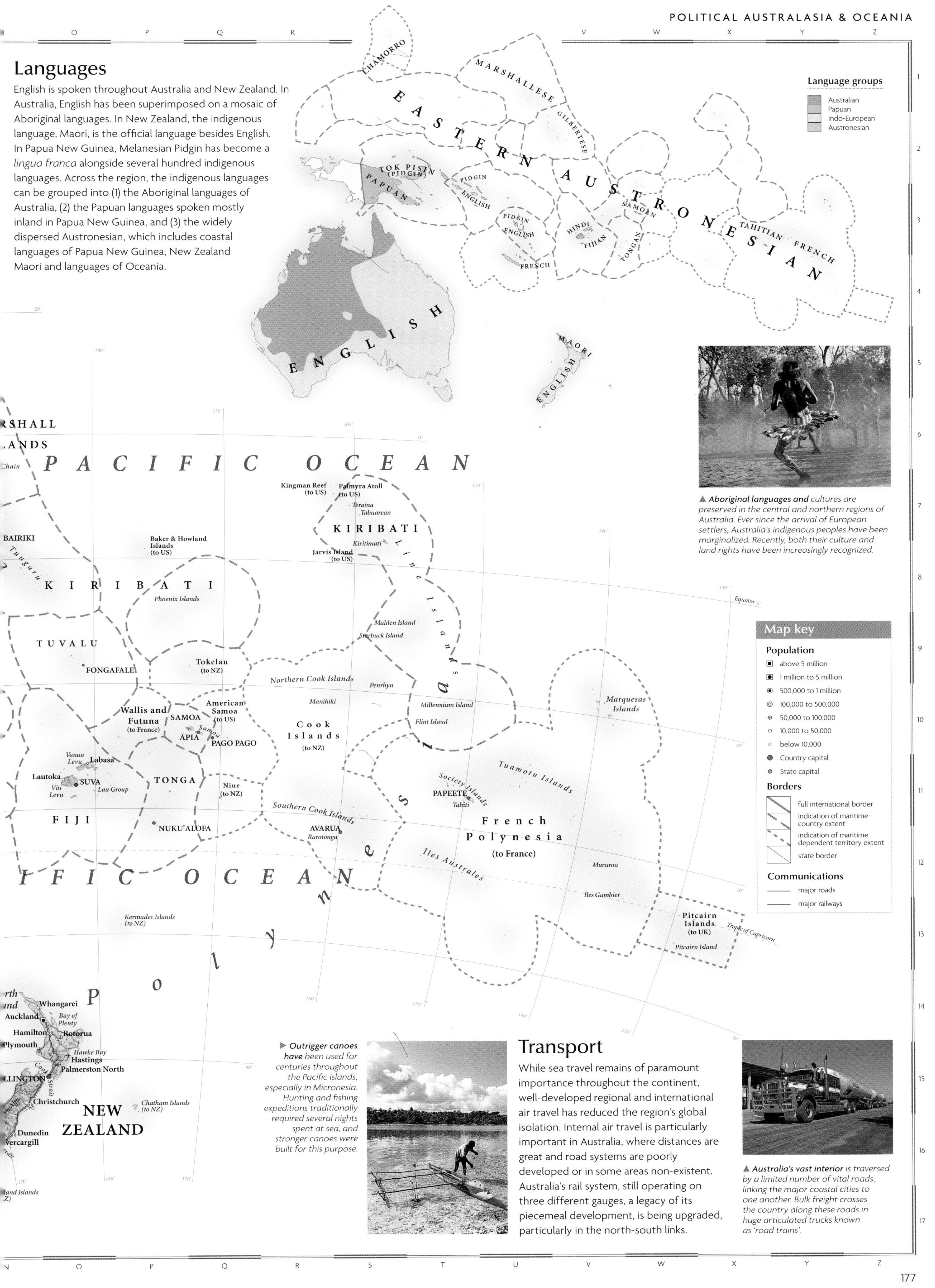
Language groups
Australian
Papuan
Indo-European
Austronesian
EASTERN AUSTRONESIAN
CHAMORRO
MARSHALLESE
GILBERTESE
TOK PISIN (PIDGIN)
PAPUAN
PIDGIN ENGLISH
PIDGIN ENGLISH
FRENCH
HINDI
FIJIAN
SAMOAN
TONGAN
TAHITIAN FRENCH
ENGLISH
MAORI
ENGLISH
PACIFIC OCEAN
Kingman Reef (to US)
Palmyra Atoll (to US)
Teraina
Tabuarean
KIRIBATI
Kiritimati
Jarvis Island (to US)
Line Islands
Baker & Howland Islands (to US)
BAIRIKI
Tungaru
KIRIBATI
Phoenix Islands
Malden Island
Starbuck Island
TUVALU
FONGAFALE
Tokelau (to NZ)
Northern Cook Islands
Penrhyn
Manihiki
Millennium Island
Flint Island
Marquesas Islands
Wallis and Futuna (to France)
SAMOA
American Samoa (to US)
ĀPIA
PAGO PAGO
Cook Islands (to NZ)
Vanua Levu
Labasa
Lautoka
SUVA
Viti Levu
Lau Group
TONGA
Niue (to NZ)
FIJI
NUKU'ALOFA
Southern Cook Islands
AVARUA
Rarotonga
Tuamotu Islands
Society Islands
PAPEETE
Tahiti
French Polynesia (to France)
Îles Australes
Mururoa
Îles Gambier
Pitcairn Islands (to UK)
Pitcairn Island
Tropic of Capricorn
Equator
Kermadec Islands (to NZ)
Polynesia
Whangarei
Auckland
Bay of Plenty
Hamilton
Rotorua
Plymouth
Hawke Bay
Hastings
Palmerston North
Cook Strait
Christchurch
NEW ZEALAND
Chatham Islands (to NZ)
Dunedin
Map key
Population
above 5 million
1 million to 5 million
500,000 to 1 million
100,000 to 500,000
50,000 to 100,000
10,000 to 50,000
below 10,000
Country capital
State capital
Borders
full international border
indication of maritime country extent
indication of maritime dependent territory extent
state border
Communications
major roads
major railways

Languages

English is spoken throughout Australia and New Zealand. In Australia, English has been superimposed on a mosaic of Aboriginal languages. In New Zealand, the indigenous language, Maori, is the official language besides English. In Papua New Guinea, Melanesian Pidgin has become a *lingua franca* alongside several hundred indigenous languages. Across the region, the indigenous languages can be grouped into (1) the Aboriginal languages of Australia, (2) the Papuan languages spoken mostly inland in Papua New Guinea, and (3) the widely dispersed Austronesian, which includes coastal languages of Papua New Guinea, New Zealand Maori and languages of Oceania.

▲ ***Aboriginal languages and** cultures are preserved in the central and northern regions of Australia. Ever since the arrival of European settlers, Australia's indigenous peoples have been marginalized. Recently, both their culture and land rights have been increasingly recognized.*

▶ ***Outrigger canoes have** been used for centuries throughout the Pacific islands, especially in Micronesia. Hunting and fishing expeditions traditionally required several nights spent at sea, and stronger canoes were built for this purpose.*

Transport

While sea travel remains of paramount importance throughout the continent, well-developed regional and international air travel has reduced the region's global isolation. Internal air travel is particularly important in Australia, where distances are great and road systems are poorly developed or in some areas non-existent. Australia's rail system, still operating on three different gauges, a legacy of its piecemeal development, is being upgraded, particularly in the north-south links.

▲ ***Australia's vast interior** is traversed by a limited number of vital roads, linking the major coastal cities to one another. Bulk freight crosses the country along these roads in huge articulated trucks known as 'road trains'.*

Australasian & Oceanian resources

Natural resources are of major economic importance throughout Australasia and Oceania. Australia in particular is a major world exporter of raw materials such as coal, iron ore and bauxite, while New Zealand's agricultural economy is dominated by sheep-raising. Trade with western Europe has declined significantly in the last 20 years, and the Pacific Rim countries of Southeast Asia are now the main trading partners, as well as a source of new settlers to the region. Australasia and Oceania's greatest resources are its climate and environment; tourism increasingly provides a vital source of income for the whole continent.

▲ *The largely unpolluted waters of the Pacific Ocean support rich and varied marine life, much of which is farmed commercially. Here, oysters are gathered for market off the coast of New Zealand's South Island.*

Northern Mariana Islands (to US)

Saipan

Guam (to US)

PALAU

► *Huge flocks of sheep are a common sight in New Zealand, where they outnumber people by 12 to 1. New Zealand is one of the world's largest exporters of wool and frozen lamb.*

Standard of living

In marked contrast to its neighbour, Australia, with one of the world's highest life expectancies and standards of living, Papua New Guinea is one of the world's least developed countries. In addition, high population growth and urbanization rates throughout the Pacific islands contribute to overcrowding. The Aboriginal and Maori people of Australia and New Zealand have been isolated for many years. Recently, their traditional land ownership rights have begun to be legally recognized in an effort to ease their social and economic isolation, and to improve living standards.

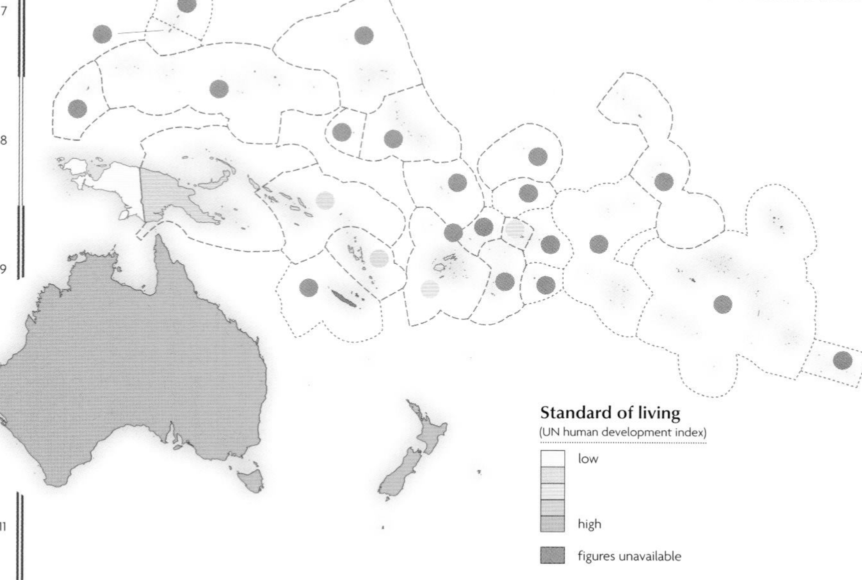
Standard of living
(UN human development index)
low
high
figures unavailable

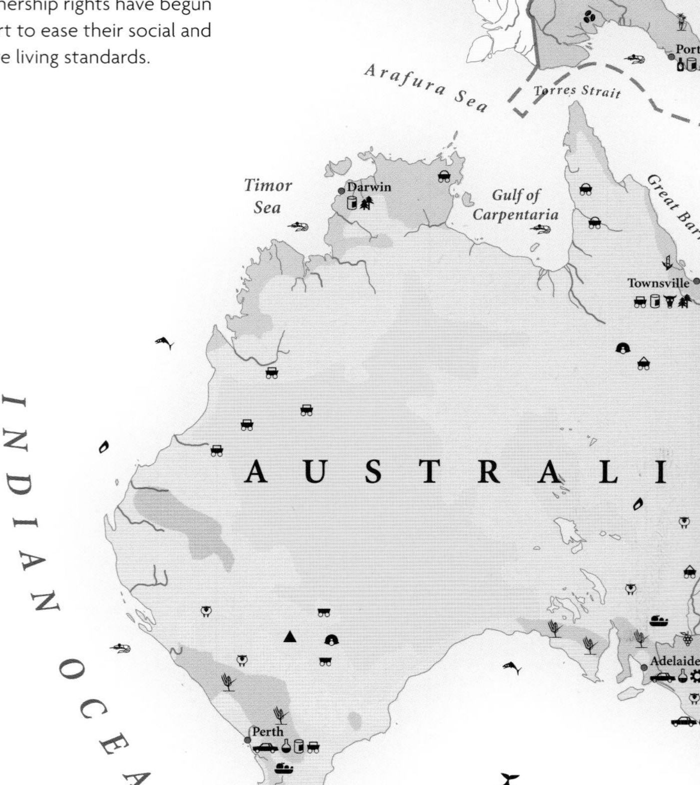
New Guinea
Arafura Sea
Torres Strait
Timor Sea
Darwin
Gulf of Carpentaria
Townsville
INDIAN OCEAN
Perth
Adelaide

Environmental issues

The prospect of rising sea levels poses a threat to many low-lying islands in the Pacific. Nuclear weapons-testing, once common throughout the region, was finally discontinued in 1996. Australia's ecological balance has been irreversibly altered by the introduction of alien species. Although it has the world's largest underground water reserve, the Great Artesian Basin, the availability of fresh water in Australia remains critical. Periodic droughts combined with over-grazing lead to desertification and increase the risk of devastating bush fires, and occasional flash floods.

Bikini Atoll

Eniwetak Atoll

Malden Island

Fangataufa

Coral Sea

PACIFIC OCEAN

INDIAN OCEAN

Murchison

Mackenzie

Darling

Murray

Sydney

Tasman Sea

Environmental issues

- national parks
- tropical forest
- forest destroyed
- desert
- desertification
- polluted rivers
- radioactive contamination
- marine pollution
- heavy marine pollution
- poor urban air quality

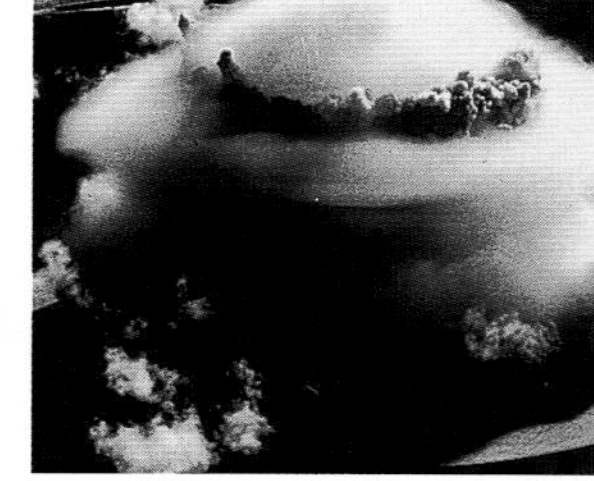

▲ ***In 1946 Bikini Atoll,** in the Marshall Islands, was chosen as the site for Operation Crossroads – investigating the effects of atomic bombs upon naval vessels. Further nuclear tests continued until the early 1990s. The long-term environmental effects are unknown.*

Agriculture, industry and minerals

Much of the region's industry is resource-based: sheep farming for wool and meat in Australia and New Zealand; mining in Australia and Papua New Guinea and fishing throughout the Pacific islands. Manufacturing is mainly limited to the large coastal cities in Australia and New Zealand, like Sydney, Adelaide, Melbourne, Brisbane, Perth and Auckland, although small-scale enterprises operate in the Pacific islands, concentrating on processing of fish and foods. Tourism continues to provide revenue to the area – in Fiji it accounts for 15% of GNP.

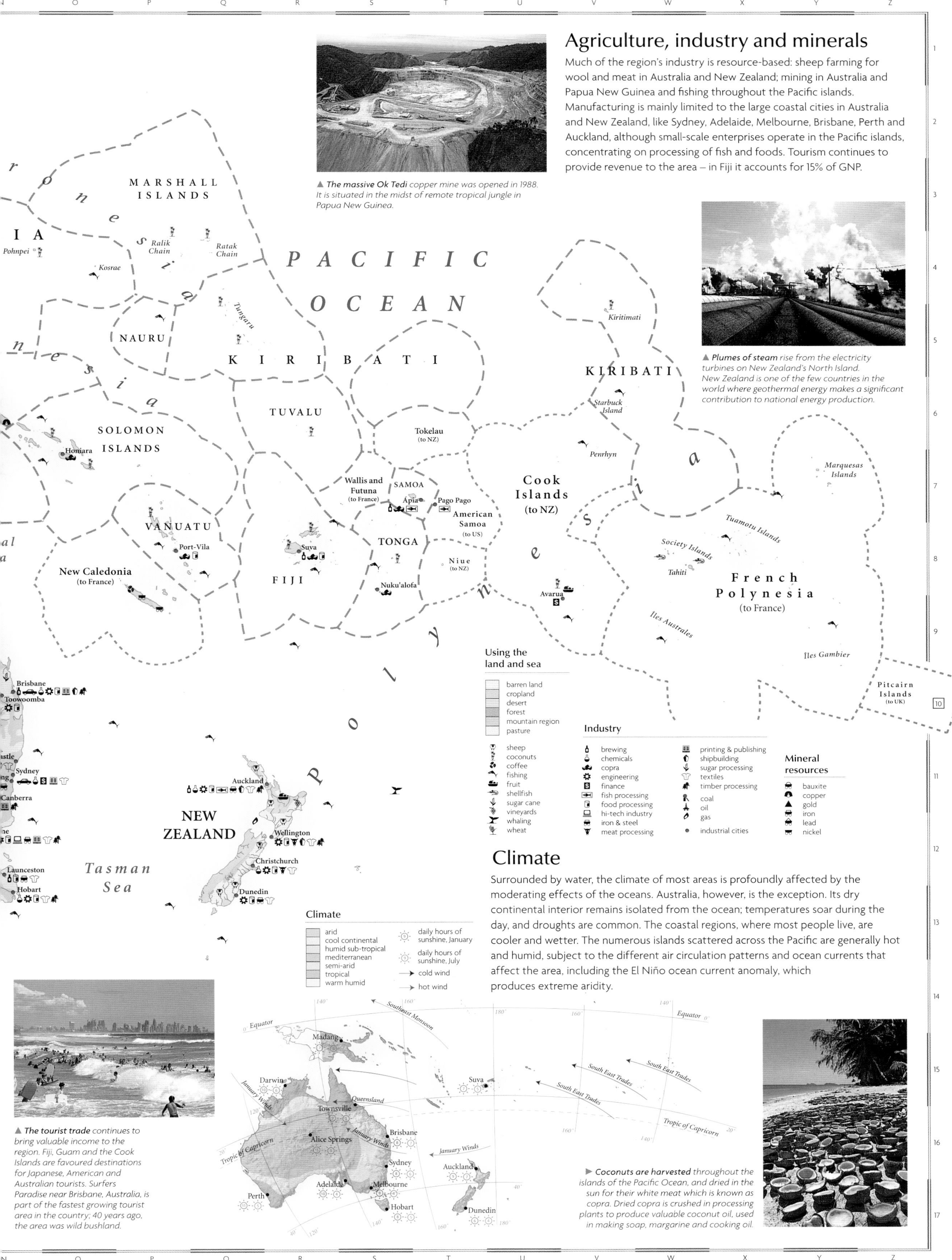
PACIFIC OCEAN
MARSHALL ISLANDS
Ralik Chain
Ratak Chain
Pohnpei
Kosrae
NAURU
KIRIBATI
Tungaru
Kiritimati
Starbuck Island
Penrhyn
TUVALU
SOLOMON ISLANDS
Honiara
Tokelau (to NZ)
Wallis and Futuna (to France)
SAMOA
Apia
Pago Pago
American Samoa (to US)
Cook Islands (to NZ)
Marquesas Islands
Tuamotu Islands
Society Islands
Tahiti
French Polynesia (to France)
VANUATU
Port-Vila
New Caledonia (to France)
Suva
FIJI
TONGA
Nuku'alofa
Niue (to NZ)
Avarua
Iles Australes
Iles Gambier
Pitcairn Islands (to UK)
Polynesia
Brisbane
Toowoomba
Sydney
Canberra
Launceston
Hobart
Tasman Sea
Auckland
NEW ZEALAND
Wellington
Christchurch
Dunedin
Using the land and sea
barren land
cropland
desert
forest
mountain region
pasture
sheep
coconuts
coffee
fishing
fruit
shellfish
sugar cane
vineyards
whaling
wheat
Industry
brewing
chemicals
copra
engineering
finance
fish processing
food processing
hi-tech industry
iron & steel
meat processing
printing & publishing
shipbuilding
sugar processing
textiles
timber processing
coal
oil
gas
industrial cities
Mineral resources
bauxite
copper
gold
iron
lead
nickel
Climate
arid
cool continental
humid sub-tropical
mediterranean
semi-arid
tropical
warm humid
daily hours of sunshine, January
daily hours of sunshine, July
cold wind
hot wind
Equator
Southeast Monsoon
Madang
Darwin
January Winds
Townsville
Queensland
Alice Springs
Brisbane
Tropic of Capricorn
Sydney
Adelaide
Melbourne
Perth
Hobart
Auckland
Dunedin
Suva
South East Trades

▲ **The massive Ok Tedi** copper mine was opened in 1988. It is situated in the midst of remote tropical jungle in Papua New Guinea.

▲ **Plumes of steam** rise from the electricity turbines on New Zealand's North Island. New Zealand is one of the few countries in the world where geothermal energy makes a significant contribution to national energy production.

Climate

Surrounded by water, the climate of most areas is profoundly affected by the moderating effects of the oceans. Australia, however, is the exception. Its dry continental interior remains isolated from the ocean; temperatures soar during the day, and droughts are common. The coastal regions, where most people live, are cooler and wetter. The numerous islands scattered across the Pacific are generally hot and humid, subject to the different air circulation patterns and ocean currents that affect the area, including the El Niño ocean current anomaly, which produces extreme aridity.

▲ **The tourist trade** continues to bring valuable income to the region. Fiji, Guam and the Cook Islands are favoured destinations for Japanese, American and Australian tourists. Surfers Paradise near Brisbane, Australia, is part of the fastest growing tourist area in the country; 40 years ago, the area was wild bushland.

▶ **Coconuts are harvested** throughout the islands of the Pacific Ocean, and dried in the sun for their white meat which is known as copra. Dried copra is crushed in processing plants to produce valuable coconut oil, used in making soap, margarine and cooking oil.

Australia

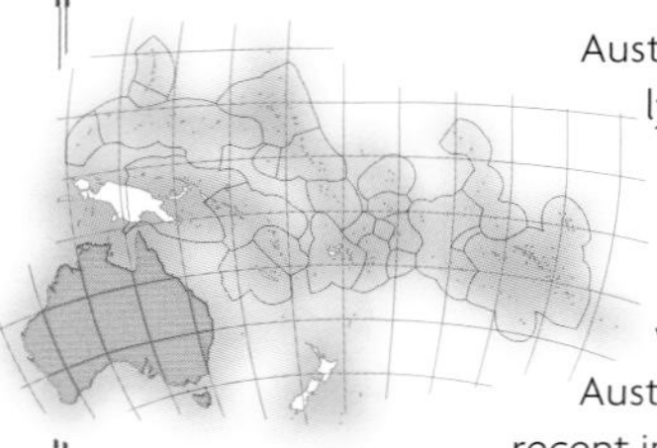

Australia is the world's smallest continent, a stable landmass lying between the Indian and Pacific oceans. Previously home to its aboriginal peoples only, since the end of the 18th century immigration has transformed the face of the country. Initially settlers came mainly from western Europe, particularly the UK, and for years Australia remained wedded to its British colonial past. More recent immigrants have come from eastern Europe, and from Asian countries such as Japan, South Korea and Indonesia. Australia is now forging strong trading links with these 'Pacific Rim' countries and its economic future seems to lie with Asia and the Americas, rather than Europe, its traditional partner.

◀ **Uluru (Ayers Rock),** *the world's largest free-standing rock, is a massive outcrop of red sandstone in Australia's desert centre. Wind and sandstorms have ground the rock into the smooth curves seen here. Uluru is revered as a sacred site by many aboriginal peoples.*

Scale 1:11,500,000

projection: Lambert Conformal Conic

Map key

Population

- 1 million to 5 million
- 500,000 to 1 million
- 100,000 to 500,000
- 50,000 to 100,000
- 10,000 to 50,000
- below 10,000

Elevation

- 2000m / 6562ft
- 1000m / 3281ft
- 500m / 1640ft
- 250m / 820ft
- 100m / 328ft
- sea level

154

Using the land

Over 104 million sheep are dispersed in vast herds around the country, contributing to a major export industry. Cattle-ranching is important, particularly in the west. Wheat, and grapes for Australia's wine industry, are grown mainly in the south. Much of the country is desert, unsuitable for agriculture unless irrigation is used.

The urban/rural population divide

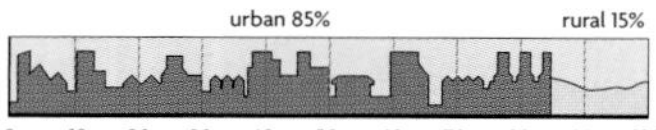

urban 85% — rural 15%

Population density	Total land area
6 people per sq mile (2 people per sq km)	2,967,893 sq miles (7,686,850 sq km)

Land use and agricultural distribution

- cattle
- sheep
- cereals
- sugar cane
- timber
- vineyards
- capital cities
- major towns
- pasture
- cropland
- forest
- desert
- mountain region

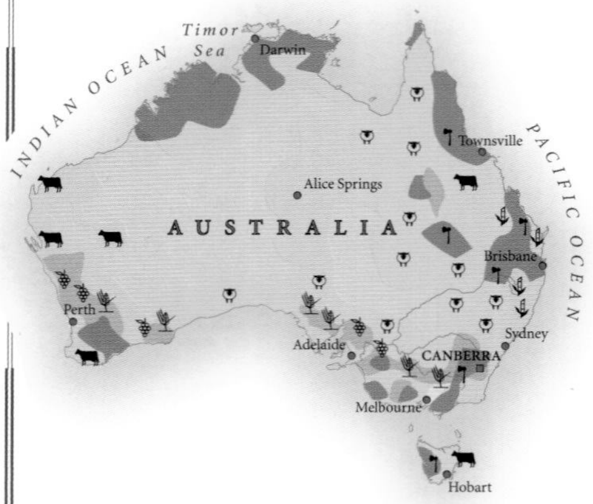

▲ ***Lines of ripening** vines stretch for miles in Barossa Valley, a major wine-growing region near Adelaide.*

The landscape

Australia consists of many eroded plateaux, lying firmly in the middle of the Indo-Australian Plate. It is the world's flattest continent, and the driest, after Antarctica. The coasts tend to be more hilly and fertile, especially in the east. The mountains of the Great Dividing Range form a natural barrier between the eastern coastal areas and the flat, dry plains and desert regions of the Australian 'outback.'

▲ ***The Great Barrier Reef** is the world's largest area of coral islands and reefs. It runs for about 1240 miles (2000 km) along the Queensland coast.*

▲ ***The Pinnacles are** a series of rugged sandstone pillars. Their strange shapes have been formed by water and wind erosion.*

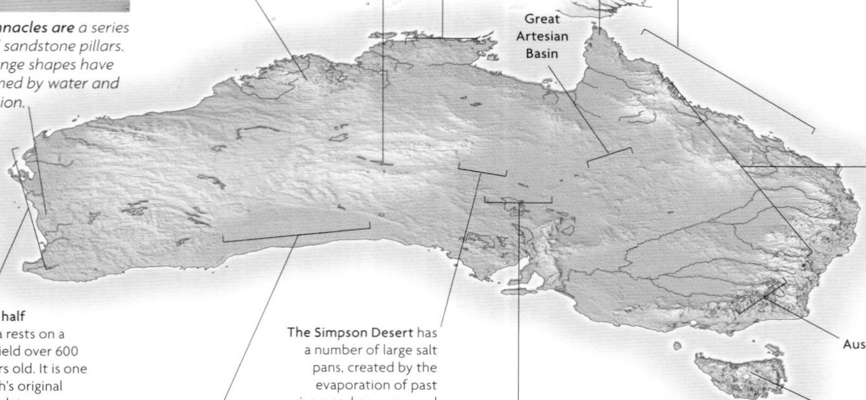

The ancient Kimberley Plateau is the source of some of Australia's richest mineral deposits, including diamonds.

Uluru (Ayers Rock)

Arnhem Land

The tropical rain forest of the Cape York Peninsula contains more than 600 different varieties of tree.

Great Artesian Basin

The Great Dividing Range forms a watershed between east- and west-flowing rivers. Erosion has created deep valleys, gorges and waterfalls where rivers tumble over escarpments on their way to the sea.

Australian Alps

More than half of Australia rests on a uniform shield over 600 million years old. It is one of the Earth's original geological plates.

The Nullarbor Plain is a low-lying limestone plateau which is so flat that the Trans-Australian Railway runs through it in a straight line for more than 300 miles (483 km).

The Simpson Desert has a number of large salt pans, created by the evaporation of past rivers and now sourced by seasonal rains. Some are crusted with gypsum, but most are covered by common salt crystals.

The Lake Eyre basin, lying 51 ft (16 m) below sea level, is one of the largest inland drainage systems in the world, covering an area of more than 500,000 sq miles (1,300,000 sq km).

Tasmania has the same geological structure as the Australian Alps. During the last period of glaciation, 18,000 years ago, sea levels were some 300 ft (100 m) lower and it was joined to the mainland.

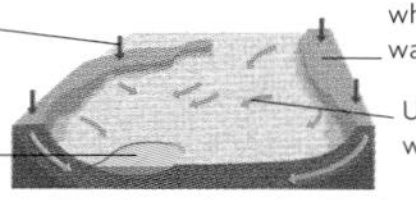

Great Artesian Basin

Rainwater replenishes aquifer

Aquifers from which artesian water is obtained

Underground water movements

Lake Eyre

▲ ***The Great Artesian Basin** underlies nearly 20% of the total area of Australia, providing a valuable store of underground water, essential to Australian agriculture. The ephemeral rivers which drain the northern part of the basin have highly braided courses and, in consequence, the area is known as 'channel country.'*

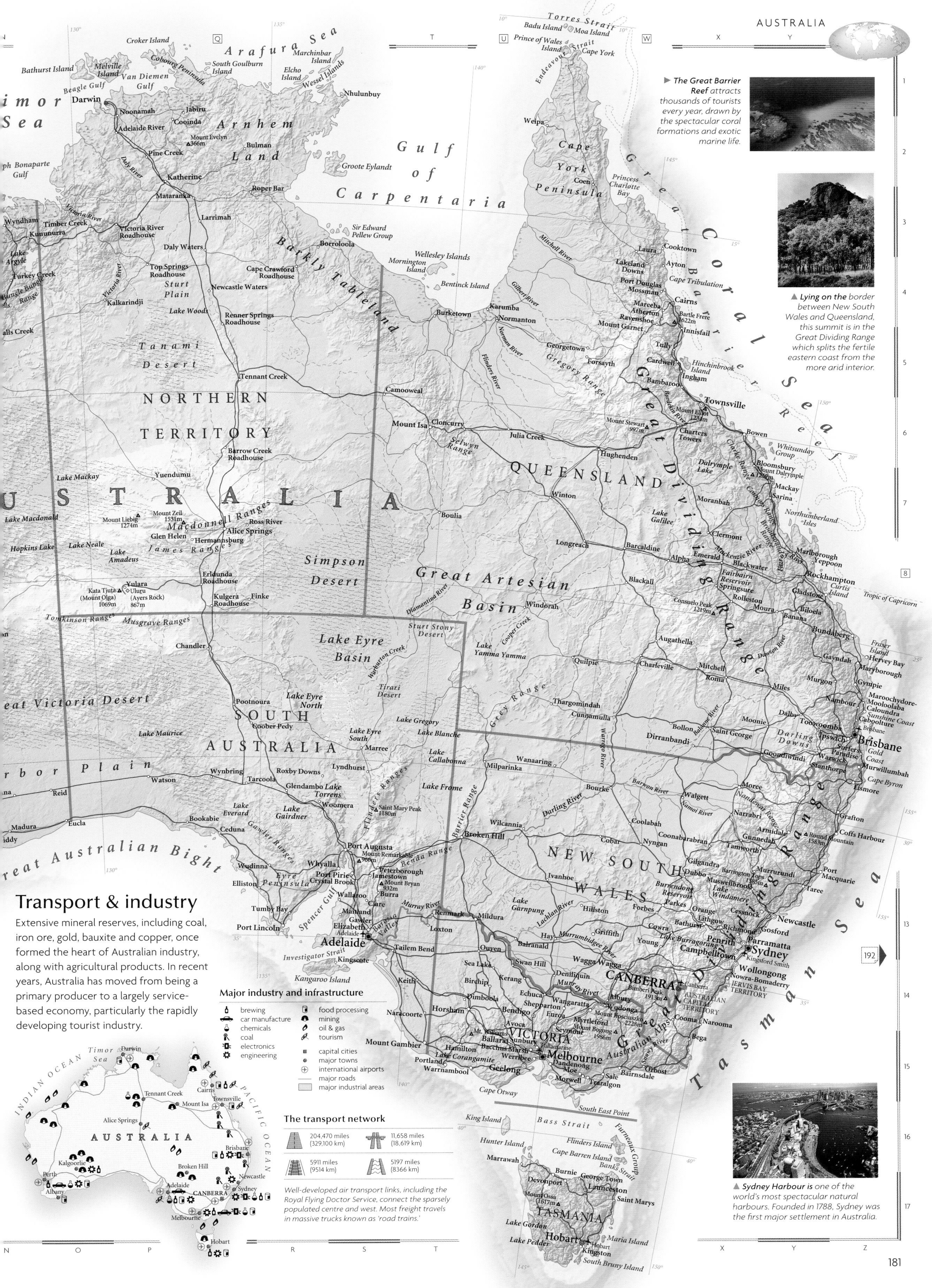
Torres Strait
Badu Island
Moa Island
Prince of Wales Island
Cape York
Croker Island
Arafura Sea
Bathurst Island
Melville Island
Van Diemen Gulf
Coburg Peninsula
South Goulburn Island
Marchinbar Island
Elcho Island
Wessel Islands
Nhulunbuy
Beagle Gulf
Darwin
Timor Sea
Noonamah
Jabiru
Cooinda
Adelaide River
Arnhem Land
Mount Evelyn 366m
Bulman
Pine Creek
Gulf of Carpentaria
Groote Eylandt
Joseph Bonaparte Gulf
Daly River
Katherine
Mataranka
Roper Bar
Weipa
Cape York Peninsula
Coen
Princess Charlotte Bay
Great Barrier Reef
Coral Sea
Wyndham
Timber Creek
Kununurra
Victoria River
Victoria River Roadhouse
Larrimah
Sir Edward Pellew Group
Borroloola
Daly Waters
Barkly Tableland
Wellesley Islands
Mornington Island
Mitchell River
Cooktown
Laura
Lake Argyle
Turkey Creek
Top Springs Roadhouse
Sturt Plain
Cape Crawford Roadhouse
Bentinck Island
Lakeland Downs
Port Douglas
Mossman
Cape Tribulation
Bungle Bungle Range
Kalkarindji
Newcastle Waters
Gilbert River
Cairns
Mareeba
Atherton
Ravenshoe
Mount Garnet
Bartle Frere 1622m
Innisfail
Lake Woods
Renner Springs Roadhouse
Burketown
Karumba
Normanton
Halls Creek
Tanami Desert
Norman River
Flinders River
Georgetown
Forsayth
Gregory Range
Tully
Cardwell
Hinchinbrook Island
Ingham
Bambaroo
Tennant Creek
Camooweal
NORTHERN TERRITORY
Mount Isa
Cloncurry
Selwyn Range
Julia Creek
Mount Stewart 997m
Burdekin River
Mount Elliot 1234m
Townsville
Charters Towers
Bowen
Whitsunday Group
Hughenden
Barrow Creek Roadhouse
Lake Mackay
Yuendumu
QUEENSLAND
Dalrymple Lake
Clarke Range
Bloomsbury
Mount Dalrymple 1280m
Mackay
Sarina
Great Dividing Range
AUSTRALIA
Winton
Moranbah
Northumberland Isles
Lake Macdonald
Mount Liebig 1274m
Mount Zeil 1531m
Macdonnell Ranges
Ross River
Alice Springs
Boulia
Lake Galilee
Glen Helen
Hermannsburg
Clermont
Hopkins Lake
Lake Neale
Lake Amadeus
James Range
Longreach
Barcaldine
Alpha
Emerald
Mackenzie River
Blackwater
Marlborough
Yeppoon
Simpson Desert
Erldunda Roadhouse
Great Artesian Basin
Fairbairn Reservoir
Springsure
Blackall
Rockhampton
Curtis Island
Gladstone
Tropic of Capricorn
Kata Tjuta (Mount Olga) 1069m
Yulara
Uluru (Ayers Rock) 867m
Kulgera Roadhouse
Finke
Diamantina River
Windorah
Consuelo Peak 1219m
Rolleston
Moura
Biloela
Banana
Tomkinson Ranges
Musgrave Ranges
Sturt Stony Desert
Bundaberg
Cooper Creek
Augathella
Fraser Island
Hervey Bay
Maryborough
Chandler
Lake Eyre Basin
Lake Yamma Yamma
Warburton Creek
Dawson River
Gayndah
Quilpie
Charleville
Mitchell
Roma
Murgon
Gympie
Great Victoria Desert
Tirari Desert
Lake Eyre North
Pootnoura
Grey Range
Thargomindah
Cunnamulla
Miles
Nambour
Maroochydore-Mooloolaba
Caloundra
Sunshine Coast
Caboolture
SOUTH AUSTRALIA
Coober Pedy
Lake Gregory
Lake Blanche
Lake Eyre South
Marree
Warrego River
Balonne River
Bollon
Dirranbandi
Saint George
Moonie
Dalby
Toowoomba
Darling Downs
Ipswich
Brisbane
Surfers Paradise
Gold Coast
Warwick
Stanthorpe
Goondiwindi
Lake Maurice
Lake Callabonna
Milparinka
Wanaaring
Murwillumbah
Nullarbor Plain
Watson
Wynbring
Tarcoola
Roxby Downs
Lyndhurst
Lake Frome
Bourke
Barwon River
Walgett
Moree
Cape Byron
Lismore
Reid
Glendambo
Lake Torrens
Woomera
Flinders Ranges
Barrier Range
Darling River
Namoi River
Narrabri
Nandewar Range
Saint Mary Peak 1180m
Lake Everard
Lake Gairdner
Bookabie
Madura
Eucla
Ceduna
Gawler Ranges
Wilcannia
Coolabah
Armidale
Grafton
Gunnedah
Round Mountain 1583m
Coffs Harbour
Broken Hill
Cobar
Nyngan
Coonabarabran
Tamworth
Great Australian Bight
Port Augusta
Mount Remarkable 960m
Whyalla
Port Pirie
Crystal Brook
Peterborough
Jamestown
Mount Bryan 932m
Burra
Benda Range
Wudinna
Eyre Peninsula
Elliston
NEW SOUTH WALES
Ivanhoe
Gilgandra
Dubbo
Barrington Tops 1585m
Murrurundi
Port Macquarie
Taree
Burrendong Reservoir
Muswellbrook
Lake Windamere
Parkes
Forbes
Orange
Cessnock
Lithgow
Newcastle
Gosford
Bathurst
Richmond
Penrith
Parramatta
Sydney
Kingsford Smith
Tumby Bay
Spencer Gulf
Wallaroo
Clare
Mallala
Gawler
Elizabeth
Adelaide
Barossa Valley
Murray River
Renmark
Mildura
Loxton
Lake Garnpung
Lachlan River
Hillston
Cowra
Young
Lake Burragorang
Campbelltown
Wollongong
Nowra-Bomaderry
JERVIS BAY TERRITORY
Port Lincoln
Investigator Strait
Kingscote
Kangaroo Island
Tailem Bend
Ouyen
Balranald
Hay
Murrumbidgee River
Griffith
Wagga Wagga
CANBERRA
Canberra
Bimberi Peak 1913m
AUSTRALIAN CAPITAL TERRITORY
Sea Lake
Swan Hill
Deniliquin
Keith
Birchip
Kerang
Murray River
Albury
Wodonga
Tasman Sea
Dimboola
Echuca
Shepparton
Wangaratta
Bendigo
Euroa
Naracoorte
Horsham
Mount Kosciuszko 2228m
Cooma
Narooma
Avoca
Myrtleford
Mount Bogong 1986m
Australian Alps
Bega
Mt. Williams
Ballarat
VICTORIA
Seymour
Bacchus Marsh
Sunbury
Snowy River
Mount Gambier
Hamilton
Tullamarine
Melbourne
Lake Corangamite
Werribee
Dandenong
Orbost
Portland
Geelong
Moe
Warrnambool
Sale
Bairnsdale
Morwell
Traralgon
Cape Otway
South East Point
King Island
Bass Strait
Furneaux Group
Hunter Island
Flinders Island
Cape Barren Island
Banks Strait
Marrawah
Burnie
George Town
Devonport
Launceston
Mount Ossa 1617m
Saint Marys
TASMANIA
Lake Gordon
Lake Pedder
Hobart
Maria Island
Kingston
South Bruny Island
Major industry and infrastructure
brewing
car manufacture
chemicals
coal
electronics
engineering
food processing
mining
oil & gas
tourism
capital cities
major towns
international airports
major roads
major industrial areas
Timor Sea
Darwin
INDIAN OCEAN
PACIFIC OCEAN
Tennant Creek
Cairns
Townsville
Mount Isa
Alice Springs
AUSTRALIA
Brisbane
Kalgoorlie
Broken Hill
Newcastle
Perth
Adelaide
Sydney
CANBERRA
Albany
Melbourne
Hobart
The transport network
204,470 miles (329,100 km)
11,658 miles (18,619 km)
5911 miles (9514 km)
5197 miles (8366 km)

Transport & industry

Extensive mineral reserves, including coal, iron ore, gold, bauxite and copper, once formed the heart of Australian industry, along with agricultural products. In recent years, Australia has moved from being a primary producer to a largely service-based economy, particularly the rapidly developing tourist industry.

Well-developed air transport links, including the Royal Flying Doctor Service, connect the sparsely populated centre and west. Most freight travels in massive trucks known as 'road trains.'

▶ **The Great Barrier Reef** *attracts thousands of tourists every year, drawn by the spectacular coral formations and exotic marine life.*

▲ **Lying on the** *border between New South Wales and Queensland, this summit is in the Great Dividing Range which splits the fertile eastern coast from the more arid interior.*

▲ **Sydney Harbour is** *one of the world's most spectacular natural harbours. Founded in 1788, Sydney was the first major settlement in Australia.*

192

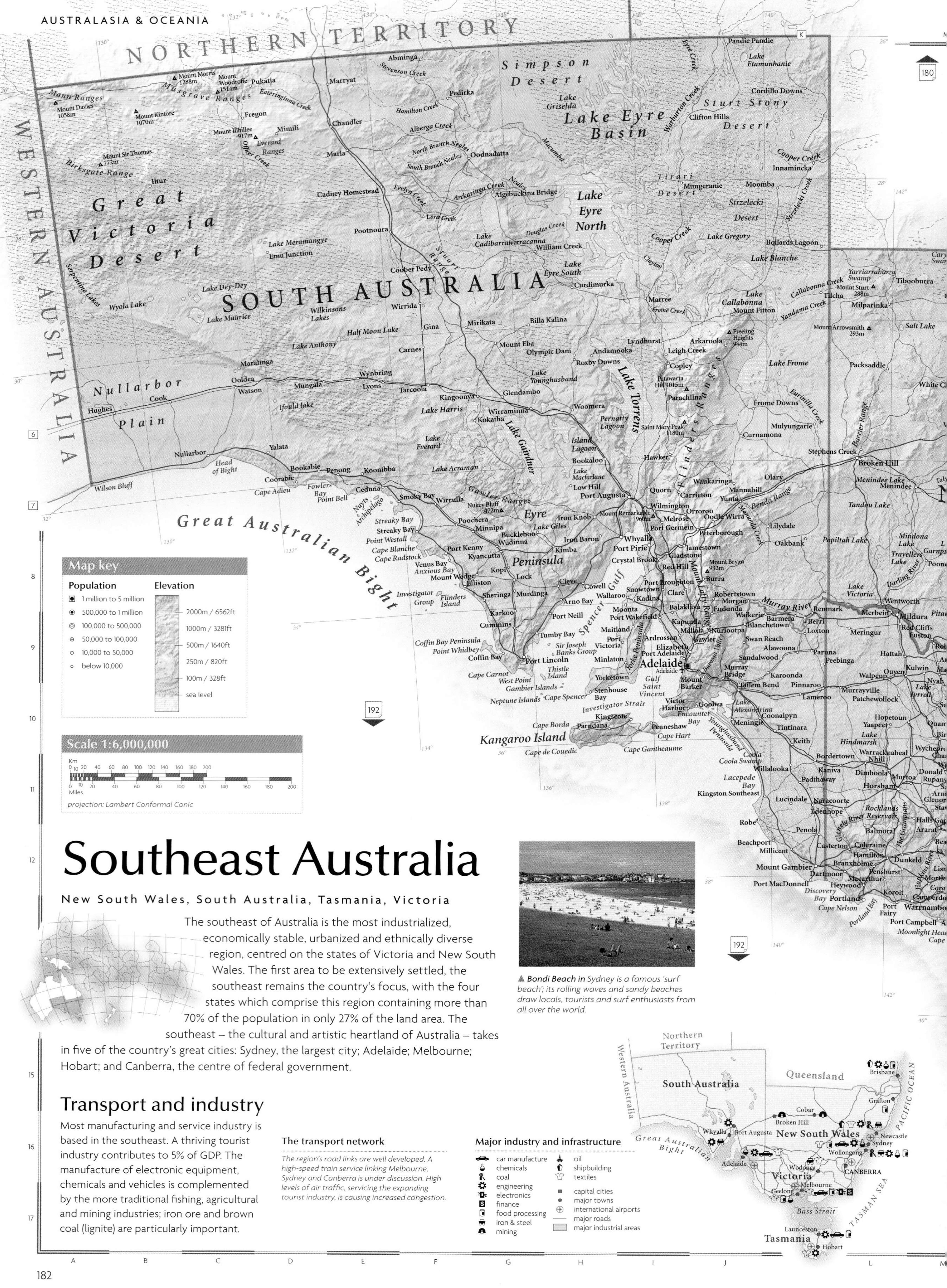
NORTHERN TERRITORY
WESTERN AUSTRALIA
SOUTH AUSTRALIA
Simpson Desert
Lake Eyre Basin
Sturt Stony Desert
Great Victoria Desert
Nullarbor Plain
Lake Eyre North
Lake Torrens
Flinders Ranges
Eyre Peninsula
Great Australian Bight
Spencer Gulf
Gulf Saint Vincent
Kangaroo Island
Investigator Strait
Adelaide
Port Augusta
Whyalla
Port Lincoln
Coober Pedy
Murray River
Mount Gambier
180
192
Map key
Population
1 million to 5 million
500,000 to 1 million
100,000 to 500,000
50,000 to 100,000
10,000 to 50,000
below 10,000
Elevation
2000m / 6562ft
1000m / 3281ft
500m / 1640ft
250m / 820ft
100m / 328ft
sea level
Scale 1:6,000,000
Km
Miles
projection: Lambert Conformal Conic

Southeast Australia

New South Wales, South Australia, Tasmania, Victoria

The southeast of Australia is the most industrialized, economically stable, urbanized and ethnically diverse region, centred on the states of Victoria and New South Wales. The first area to be extensively settled, the southeast remains the country's focus, with the four states which comprise this region containing more than 70% of the population in only 27% of the land area. The southeast – the cultural and artistic heartland of Australia – takes in five of the country's great cities: Sydney, the largest city; Adelaide; Melbourne; Hobart; and Canberra, the centre of federal government.

▲ *Bondi Beach in Sydney is a famous 'surf beach'; its rolling waves and sandy beaches draw locals, tourists and surf enthusiasts from all over the world.*

Transport and industry

Most manufacturing and service industry is based in the southeast. A thriving tourist industry contributes to 5% of GDP. The manufacture of electronic equipment, chemicals and vehicles is complemented by the more traditional fishing, agricultural and mining industries; iron ore and brown coal (lignite) are particularly important.

The transport network

The region's road links are well developed. A high-speed train service linking Melbourne, Sydney and Canberra is under discussion. High levels of air traffic, servicing the expanding tourist industry, is causing increased congestion.

Major industry and infrastructure

car manufacture
chemicals
coal
engineering
electronics
finance
food processing
iron & steel
mining
oil
shipbuilding
textiles
capital cities
major towns
international airports
major roads
major industrial areas
Northern Territory
Western Australia
South Australia
Queensland
New South Wales
Victoria
Tasmania
PACIFIC OCEAN
TASMAN SEA
Bass Strait
Great Australian Bight
Brisbane
Grafton
Cobar
Broken Hill
Whyalla
Port Augusta
Newcastle
Sydney
Wollongong
CANBERRA
Adelaide
Wodonga
Melbourne
Geelong
Launceston
Hobart

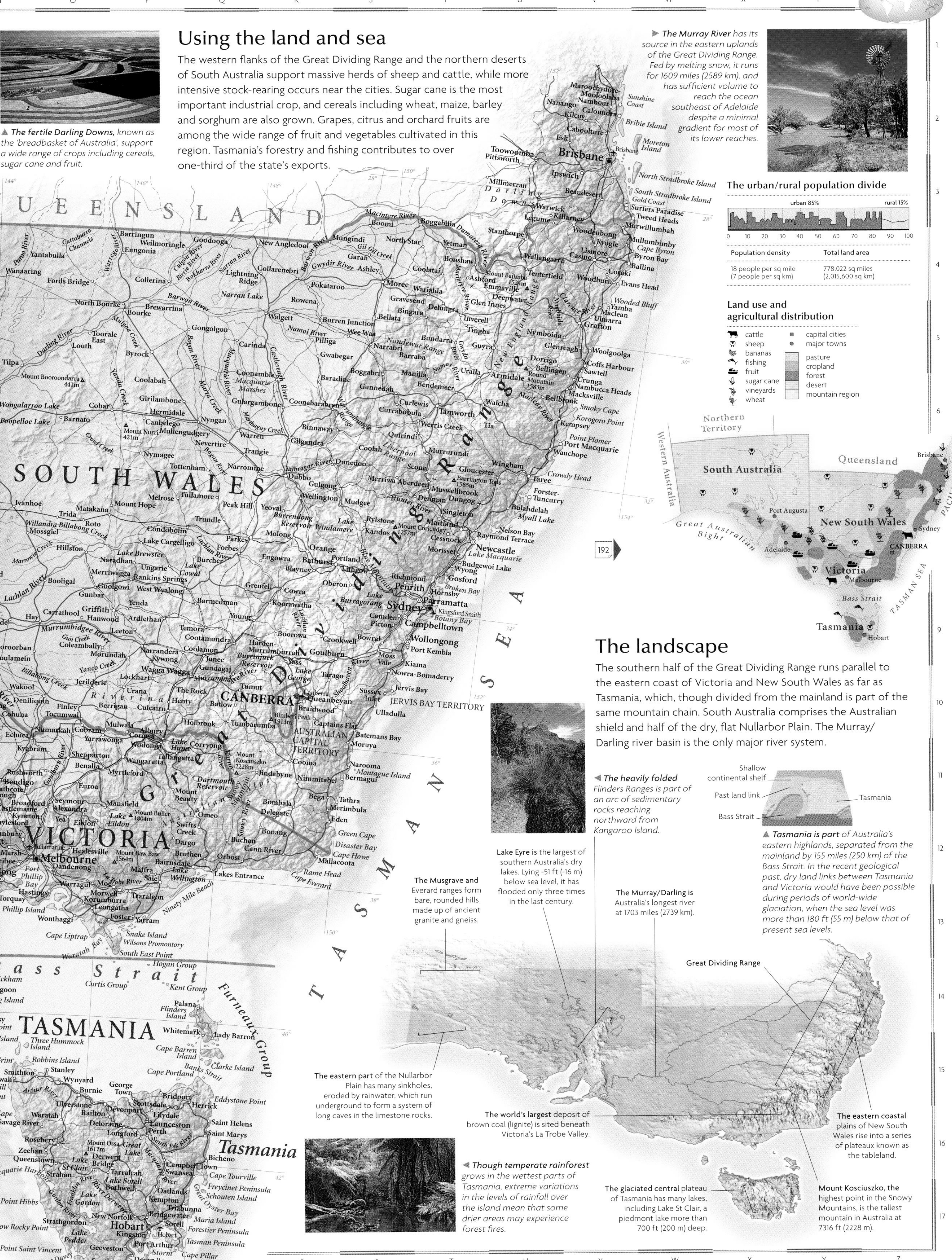
QUEENSLAND
NEW SOUTH WALES
VICTORIA
TASMANIA
Tasmania
Great Dividing Range
TASMAN SEA
Bass Strait
CANBERRA
AUSTRALIAN CAPITAL TERRITORY
JERVIS BAY TERRITORY
Brisbane
Sydney
Melbourne
Hobart
192
The urban/rural population divide
urban 85%
rural 15%
0 10 20 30 40 50 60 70 80 90 100
Population density
18 people per sq mile (7 people per sq km)
Total land area
778,022 sq miles (2,015,600 sq km)
Land use and agricultural distribution
cattle
sheep
bananas
fishing
fruit
sugar cane
vineyards
wheat
capital cities
major towns
pasture
cropland
forest
desert
mountain region
Northern Territory
Western Australia
South Australia
Queensland
New South Wales
Victoria
Tasmania
PACIFIC OCEAN
TASMAN SEA
Great Australian Bight
Port Augusta
Adelaide
Shallow continental shelf
Past land link
Bass Strait
Tasmania
Great Dividing Range

Using the land and sea

The western flanks of the Great Dividing Range and the northern deserts of South Australia support massive herds of sheep and cattle, while more intensive stock-rearing occurs near the cities. Sugar cane is the most important industrial crop, and cereals including wheat, maize, barley and sorghum are also grown. Grapes, citrus and orchard fruits are among the wide range of fruit and vegetables cultivated in this region. Tasmania's forestry and fishing contributes to over one-third of the state's exports.

▲ *The fertile Darling Downs, known as the 'breadbasket of Australia', support a wide range of crops including cereals, sugar cane and fruit.*

▶ *The Murray River has its source in the eastern uplands of the Great Dividing Range. Fed by melting snow, it runs for 1609 miles (2589 km), and has sufficient volume to reach the ocean southeast of Adelaide despite a minimal gradient for most of its lower reaches.*

The landscape

The southern half of the Great Dividing Range runs parallel to the eastern coast of Victoria and New South Wales as far as Tasmania, which, though divided from the mainland is part of the same mountain chain. South Australia comprises the Australian shield and half of the dry, flat Nullarbor Plain. The Murray/Darling river basin is the only major river system.

◀ *The heavily folded Flinders Ranges is part of an arc of sedimentary rocks reaching northward from Kangaroo Island.*

▲ *Tasmania is part of Australia's eastern highlands, separated from the mainland by 155 miles (250 km) of the Bass Strait. In the recent geological past, dry land links between Tasmania and Victoria would have been possible during periods of world-wide glaciation, when the sea level was more than 180 ft (55 m) below that of present sea levels.*

Lake Eyre is the largest of southern Australia's dry lakes. Lying -51 ft (-16 m) below sea level, it has flooded only three times in the last century.

The Musgrave and Everard ranges form bare, rounded hills made up of ancient granite and gneiss.

The Murray/Darling is Australia's longest river at 1703 miles (2739 km).

The eastern part of the Nullarbor Plain has many sinkholes, eroded by rainwater, which run underground to form a system of long caves in the limestone rocks.

The world's largest deposit of brown coal (lignite) is sited beneath Victoria's La Trobe Valley.

The eastern coastal plains of New South Wales rise into a series of plateaux known as the tableland.

◀ *Though temperate rainforest grows in the wettest parts of Tasmania, extreme variations in the levels of rainfall over the island mean that some drier areas may experience forest fires.*

The glaciated central plateau of Tasmania has many lakes, including Lake St Clair, a piedmont lake more than 700 ft (200 m) deep.

Mount Kosciuszko, the highest point in the Snowy Mountains, is the tallest mountain in Australia at 7316 ft (2228 m).

New Zealand

Lying 1500 miles east-southeast of Australia, New Zealand was originally settled by the Maori, a people with Polynesian roots. It was one of the last major landmasses to be visited by Europeans. The islands' rugged topography means that most settlement has concentrated in coastal areas. People of European origin make up about 70% of the population of 4 million, following immigration from the 1920s onwards. Many recent settlers have come from Asia, including India and China, and a number of the Pacific islands. Although the Maori now make up a minority of less than half a million, their ancient claims to at least half of national territory are gaining increasing legal credence.

The landscape

New Zealand comprises two large islands and many scattered smaller islands. On South Island the Alpine Fault marks the boundary between the Pacific and Indo-Australian plates. Tectonic activity has strongly influenced the formation of the Southern Alps, snow-capped mountains with several peaks over 9800 ft (3000 m). North Island has a lower and less extensive mountain region, containing forested hills, a central volcanic plateau and downlands.

Mountain-building in the Southern Alps

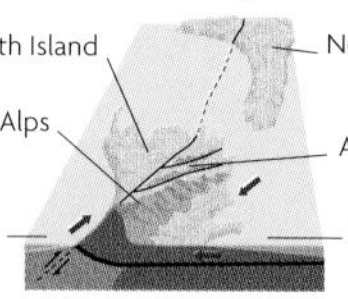

South Island
North Island
Southern Alps
Alpine Fault
Indo-Australian Plate
Pacific Plate

▲ *The Southern Alps have been formed by 'slip' faulting. The Indo-Australian and Pacific plates run in opposite directions along the Alpine Fault. Although they slide past each other, they are also being thrust over one another, causing the continental crust of the Pacific Plate to be uplifted to form the Alps.*

◀ ***The Northland region** is characterized by many coastal inlets. These are lined by mangrove swamps, signalling the change to a subtropical climate in the far north of the island.*

◀ ***The Rotorua and** Taupo valleys have some of the largest and most spectacular thermal springs in New Zealand. These occur when superheated groundwater rises to the surface through joints in the rocks.*

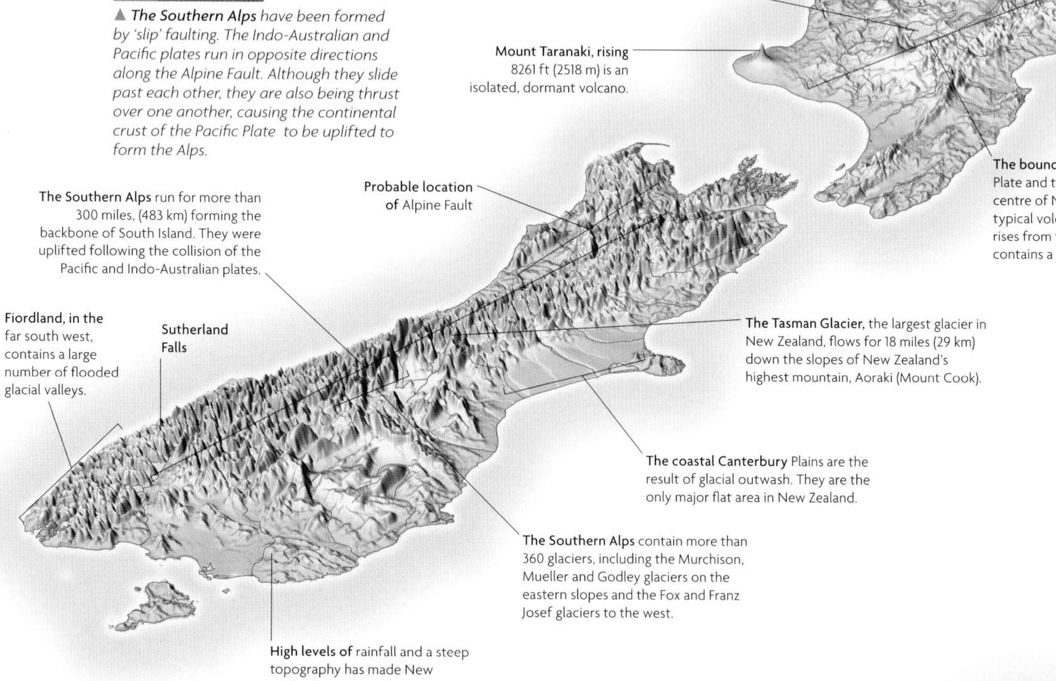

▶ ***Clouds of steam** rise from White Island, an active, offshore volcano lying in the Bay of Plenty, off the northern coast of North Island.*

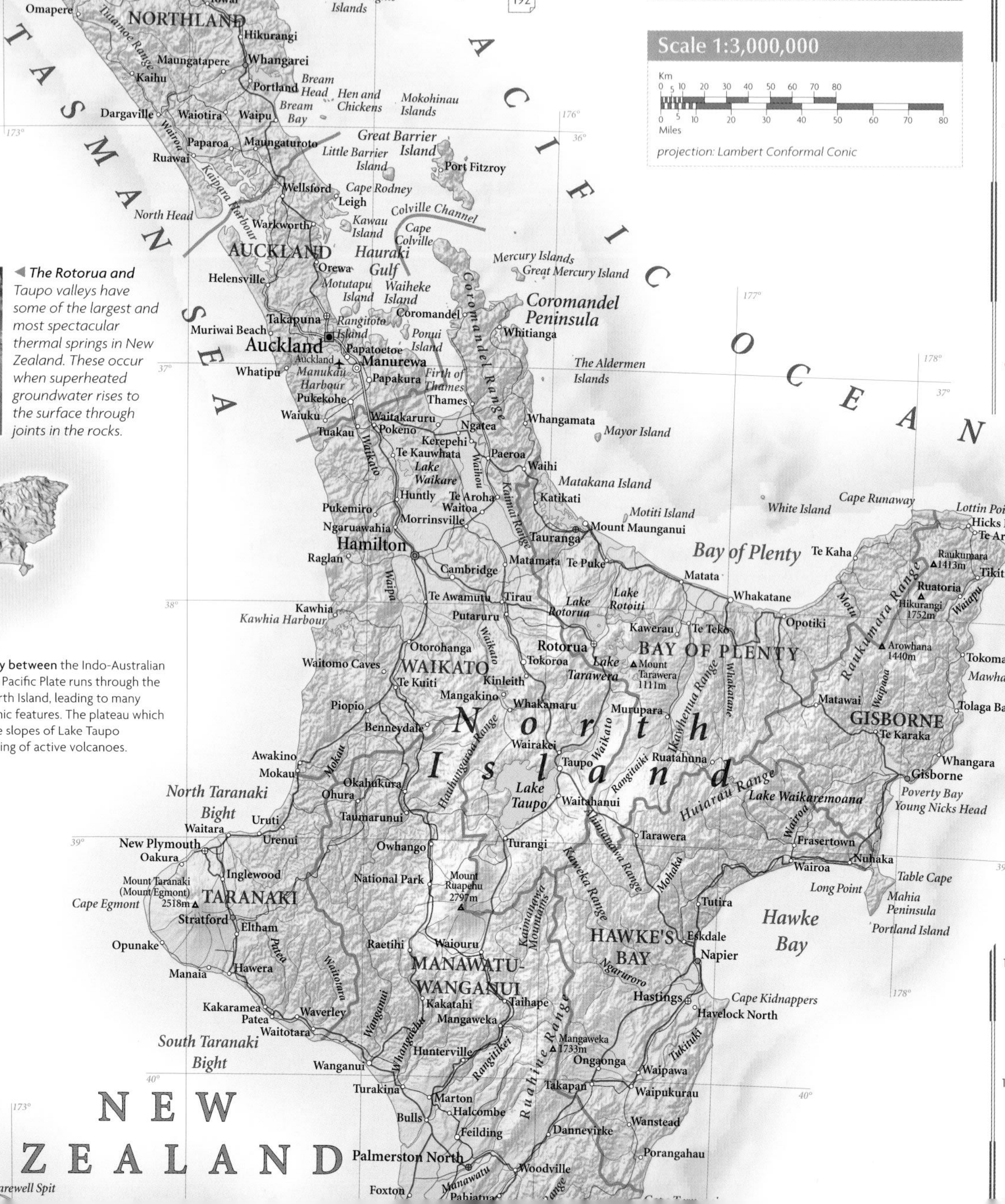

Northland
Rotorua

Lake Taupo is New Zealand's largest inland lake. It occupies the crater of an extinct volcano.

Mount Taranaki, rising 8261 ft (2518 m) is an isolated, dormant volcano.

The boundary between the Indo-Australian Plate and the Pacific Plate runs through the centre of North Island, leading to many typical volcanic features. The plateau which rises from the slopes of Lake Taupo contains a string of active volcanoes.

Probable location of Alpine Fault

The Southern Alps run for more than 300 miles, (483 km) forming the backbone of South Island. They were uplifted following the collision of the Pacific and Indo-Australian plates.

Fiordland, in the far south west, contains a large number of flooded glacial valleys.

Sutherland Falls

The Tasman Glacier, the largest glacier in New Zealand, flows for 18 miles (29 km) down the slopes of New Zealand's highest mountain, Aoraki (Mount Cook).

The coastal Canterbury Plains are the result of glacial outwash. They are the only major flat area in New Zealand.

The Southern Alps contain more than 360 glaciers, including the Murchison, Mueller and Godley glaciers on the eastern slopes and the Fox and Franz Josef glaciers to the west.

High levels of rainfall and a steep topography has made New Zealand's rivers swift-running. In the southern reaches of both islands, rivers such as the Mokoreta form broad, braided streams.

Scale 1:3,000,000

Km 0 5 10 20 30 40 50 60 70 80
Miles 0 5 10 20 30 40 50 60 70 80

projection: Lambert Conformal Conic

192

TASMAN SEA
PACIFIC OCEAN
NEW ZEALAND
North Island

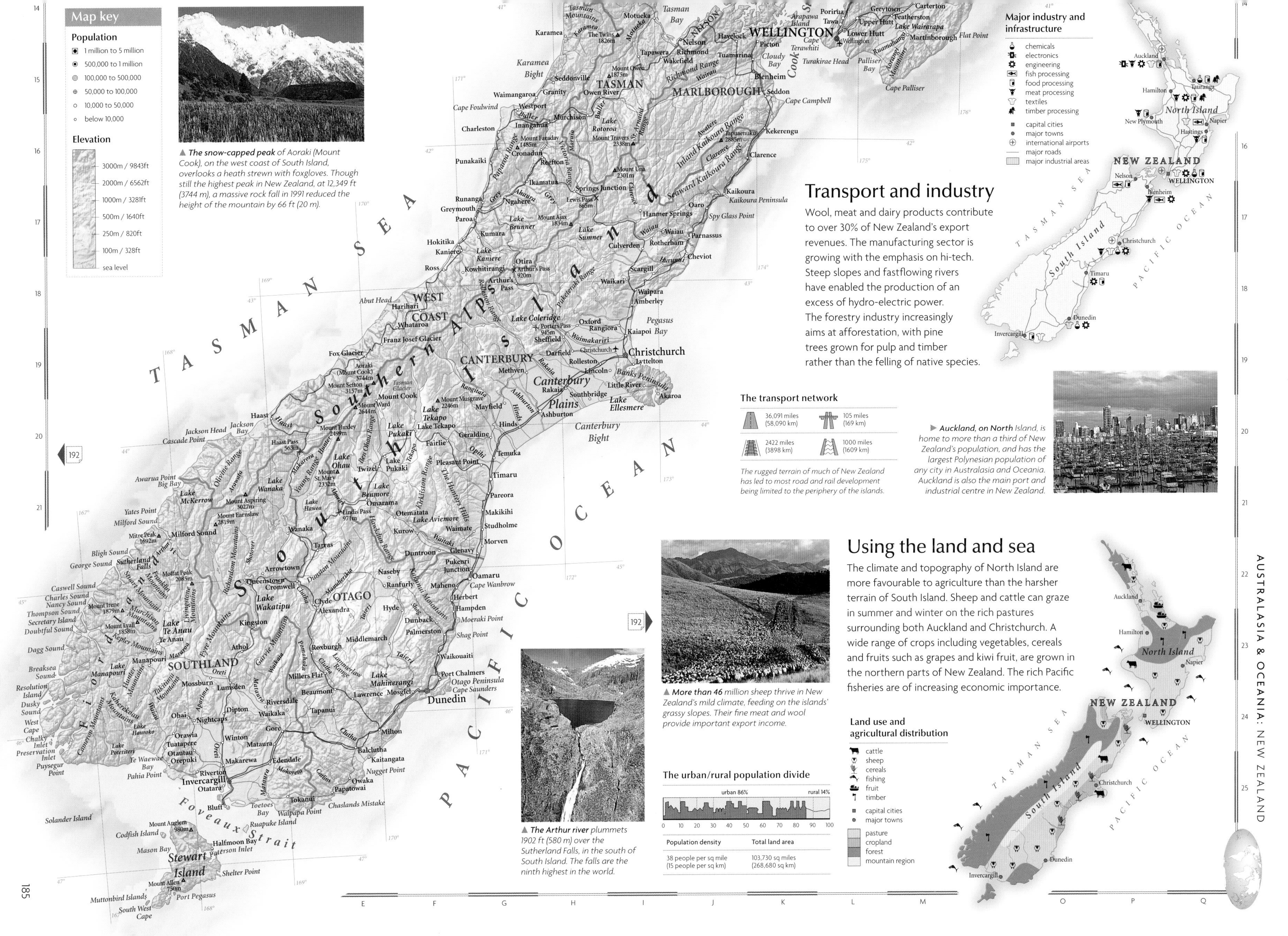

Map key
Population
1 million to 5 million
500,000 to 1 million
100,000 to 500,000
50,000 to 100,000
10,000 to 50,000
below 10,000
Elevation
3000m / 9843ft
2000m / 6562ft
1000m / 3281ft
500m / 1640ft
250m / 820ft
100m / 328ft
sea level
TASMAN SEA
PACIFIC OCEAN
South Island
Southern Alps
Fiordland
Foveaux Strait
Stewart Island
WEST COAST
CANTERBURY
OTAGO
SOUTHLAND
TASMAN
MARLBOROUGH
NELSON
WELLINGTON
Christchurch
Dunedin
Invercargill
Canterbury Plains
Canterbury Bight
Aoraki (Mount Cook) 3744m
Major industry and infrastructure
chemicals
electronics
engineering
fish processing
food processing
meat processing
textiles
timber processing
capital cities
major towns
international airports
major roads
major industrial areas
NEW ZEALAND
North Island
Land use and agricultural distribution
cattle
sheep
cereals
fishing
fruit
timber
capital cities
major towns
pasture
cropland
forest
mountain region

▲ *The snow-capped peak* of Aoraki (Mount Cook), on the west coast of South Island, overlooks a heath strewn with foxgloves. Though still the highest peak in New Zealand, at 12,349 ft (3744 m), a massive rock fall in 1991 reduced the height of the mountain by 66 ft (20 m).

Transport and industry

Wool, meat and dairy products contribute to over 30% of New Zealand's export revenues. The manufacturing sector is growing with the emphasis on hi-tech. Steep slopes and fastflowing rivers have enabled the production of an excess of hydro-electric power. The forestry industry increasingly aims at afforestation, with pine trees grown for pulp and timber rather than the felling of native species.

The transport network

36,091 miles (58,090 km)	105 miles (169 km)
2422 miles (3898 km)	1000 miles (1609 km)

The rugged terrain of much of New Zealand has led to most road and rail development being limited to the periphery of the islands.

▶ *Auckland, on North Island,* is home to more than a third of New Zealand's population, and has the largest Polynesian population of any city in Australasia and Oceania. Auckland is also the main port and industrial centre in New Zealand.

Using the land and sea

The climate and topography of North Island are more favourable to agriculture than the harsher terrain of South Island. Sheep and cattle can graze in summer and winter on the rich pastures surrounding both Auckland and Christchurch. A wide range of crops including vegetables, cereals and fruits such as grapes and kiwi fruit, are grown in the northern parts of New Zealand. The rich Pacific fisheries are of increasing economic importance.

▲ *More than 46* million sheep thrive in New Zealand's mild climate, feeding on the islands' grassy slopes. Their fine meat and wool provide important export income.

▲ *The Arthur river* plummets 1902 ft (580 m) over the Sutherland Falls, in the south of South Island. The falls are the ninth highest in the world.

The urban/rural population divide

urban 86% | rural 14%

Population density	Total land area
38 people per sq mile (15 people per sq km)	103,730 sq miles (268,680 sq km)

192

192

Melanesia

FIJI, New Caledonia *(to France)*, PAPUA NEW GUINEA, SOLOMON ISLANDS, VANUATU

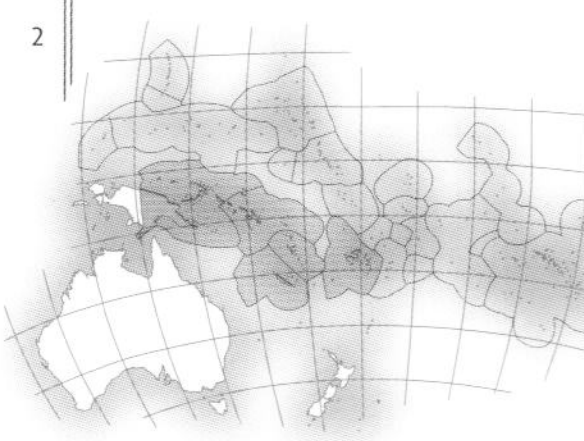

Lying in the southwest Pacific Ocean, northeast of Australia and south of the Equator, the islands of Melanesia form one of the three geographic divisions (along with Polynesia and Micronesia) of Oceania. Melanesia's name derives from the Greek melas, 'black', and nesoi, 'islands'. Most of the larger islands are volcanic in origin. The smaller islands tend to be coral atolls and are mainly uninhabited. Rugged mountains, covered by dense rainforest, take up most of the land area. Melanesian's cultivate yams, taro, and sweet potatoes for local consumption and live in small, usually dispersed, homesteads.

▲ **Huli tribesmen from** *Southern Highlands Province in Papua New Guinea parade in ceremonial dress, their powdered wigs decorated with exotic plumage and their faces and bodies painted with coloured pigments.*

Map key

Population

- 100,000 to 500,000
- 50,000 to 100,000
- 10,000 to 50,000
- below 10,000

Elevation

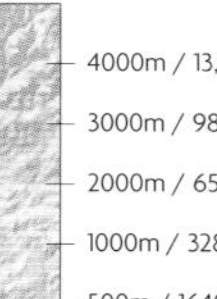

4000m / 13,124ft
3000m / 9843ft
2000m / 6562ft
1000m / 3281ft
500m / 1640ft
250m / 820ft
100m / 328ft
sea level

168

192

180

◀ **Lying close to** *the banks of the Sepik river in northern Papua New Guinea, this building is known as the Spirit House. It is constructed from leaves and twigs, ornately woven and trimmed into geometric patterns. The house is decorated with a mask and topped by a carved statue.*

▲ **On one of** *Vanuatu's many islands, beach houses stand at the water's edge, surrounded by coconut palms and other tropical vegetation. The unspoilt beaches and tranquillity of its islands are drawing ever-larger numbers of tourists to Vanuatu.*

Transport and Industry

The processing of natural resources generates significant export revenue for the countries of Melanesia. The region relies mainly on copra, tuna and timber exports, with some production of cocoa and palm oil. The islands have substantial mineral resources including the world's largest copper reserves on Bougainville Island; gold, and potential oil and natural gas. Tourism has become the fastest growing sector in most of the countries' economies.

◀ **On New Caledonia's** *main island, relatively high interior plateaux descend to coastal plains. Nickel is the most important mineral resource, but the hills also harbour metallic deposits including chrome, cobalt, iron, gold, silver and copper.*

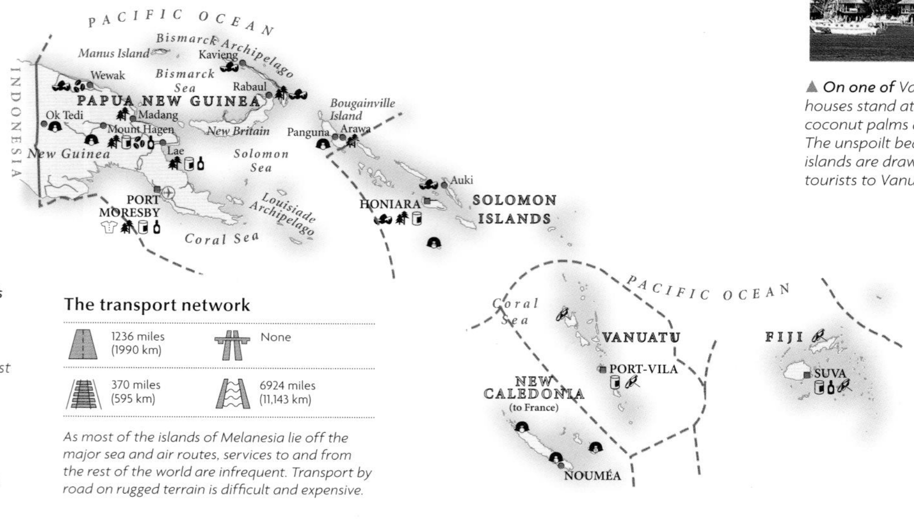

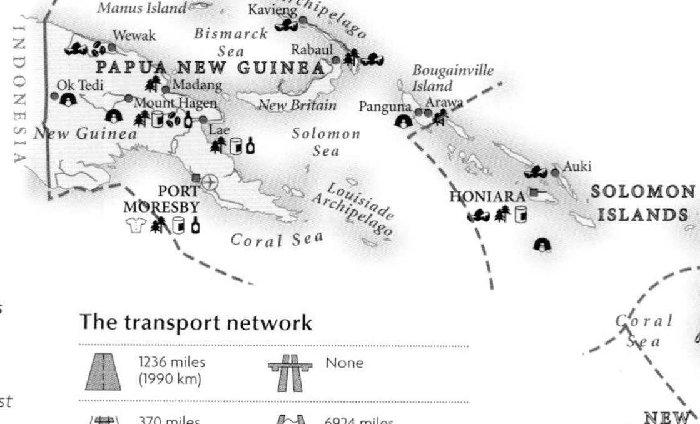

PACIFIC OCEAN
Bismarck Archipelago
Manus Island
Kavieng
INDONESIA
Wewak
Bismarck Sea
Rabaul
PAPUA NEW GUINEA
Madang
Ok Tedi
Mount Hagen
New Britain
Bougainville Island
Panguna
Arawa
New Guinea
Lae
Solomon Sea
PORT MORESBY
Louisiade Archipelago
Coral Sea
HONIARA
Auki
SOLOMON ISLANDS

The transport network

1236 miles (1990 km)		None	
370 miles (595 km)		6924 miles (11,143 km)	

As most of the islands of Melanesia lie off the major sea and air routes, services to and from the rest of the world are infrequent. Transport by road on rugged terrain is difficult and expensive.

PACIFIC OCEAN

Coral Sea

VANUATU

PORT-VILA

NEW CALEDONIA (to France)

NOUMÉA

FIJI

SUVA

Major industry and infrastructure

- beverages
- coffee processing
- copra processing
- food processing
- mining
- textiles
- timber processing
- tourism
- capital cities
- major towns
- international airports
- major roads

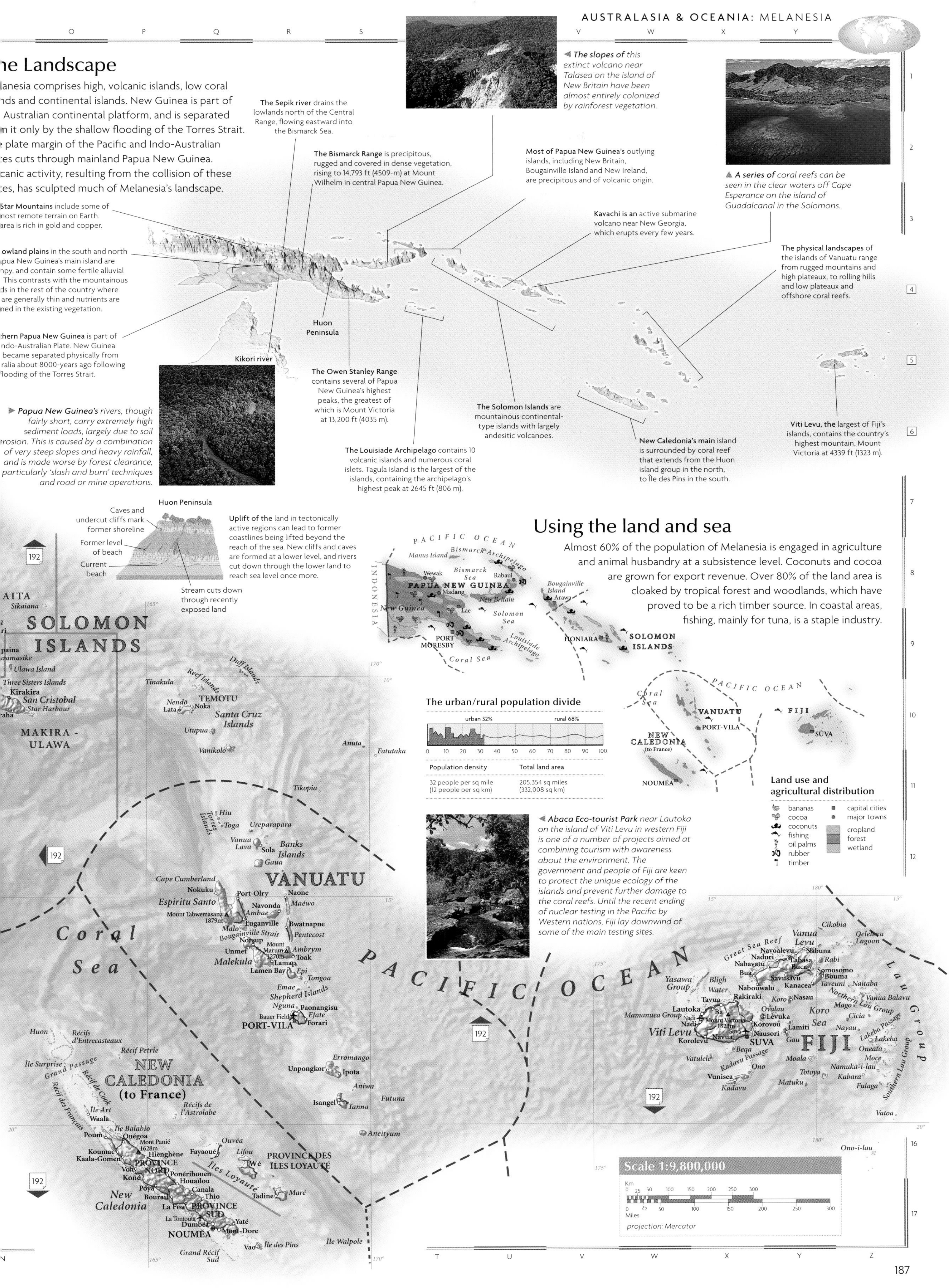
O P Q R S V W X Y
1 2 3 4 5 6 7 8 9 10 11 12 16 17
ne Landscape
lanesia comprises high, volcanic islands, low coral
nds and continental islands. New Guinea is part of
Australian continental platform, and is separated
n it only by the shallow flooding of the Torres Strait.
plate margin of the Pacific and Indo-Australian
es cuts through mainland Papua New Guinea.
canic activity, resulting from the collision of these
es, has sculpted much of Melanesia's landscape.
◀ The slopes of this extinct volcano near Talasea on the island of New Britain have been almost entirely colonized by rainforest vegetation.
▲ A series of coral reefs can be seen in the clear waters off Cape Esperance on the island of Guadalcanal in the Solomons.
The Sepik river drains the lowlands north of the Central Range, flowing eastward into the Bismarck Sea.
The Bismarck Range is precipitous, rugged and covered in dense vegetation, rising to 14,793 ft (4509-m) at Mount Wilhelm in central Papua New Guinea.
Most of Papua New Guinea's outlying islands, including New Britain, Bougainville Island and New Ireland, are precipitous and of volcanic origin.
Star Mountains include some of nost remote terrain on Earth. area is rich in gold and copper.
Kavachi is an active submarine volcano near New Georgia, which erupts every few years.
owland plains in the south and north pua New Guinea's main island are npy, and contain some fertile alluvial This contrasts with the mountainous ds in the rest of the country where are generally thin and nutrients are ned in the existing vegetation.
The physical landscapes of the islands of Vanuatu range from rugged mountains and high plateaux, to rolling hills and low plateaux and offshore coral reefs.
Huon Peninsula
hern Papua New Guinea is part of ndo-Australian Plate. New Guinea became separated physically from ralia about 8000-years ago following looding of the Torres Strait.
Kikori river
The Owen Stanley Range contains several of Papua New Guinea's highest peaks, the greatest of which is Mount Victoria at 13,200 ft (4035 m).
The Solomon Islands are mountainous continental-type islands with largely andesitic volcanoes.
▶ Papua New Guinea's rivers, though fairly short, carry extremely high sediment loads, largely due to soil erosion. This is caused by a combination of very steep slopes and heavy rainfall, and is made worse by forest clearance, particularly 'slash and burn' techniques and road or mine operations.
The Louisiade Archipelago contains 10 volcanic islands and numerous coral islets. Tagula Island is the largest of the archipelago's highest peak at 2645 ft (806 m).
New Caledonia's main island is surrounded by coral reef that extends from the Huon island group in the north, to Île des Pins in the south.
Viti Levu, the largest of Fiji's islands, contains the country's highest mountain, Mount Victoria at 4339 ft (1323 m).
Huon Peninsula
Caves and undercut cliffs mark former shoreline
Former level of beach
Current beach
Stream cuts down through recently exposed land
Uplift of the land in tectonically active regions can lead to former coastlines being lifted beyond the reach of the sea. New cliffs and caves are formed at a lower level, and rivers cut down through the lower land to reach sea level once more.
Using the land and sea
Almost 60% of the population of Melanesia is engaged in agriculture and animal husbandry at a subsistence level. Coconuts and cocoa are grown for export revenue. Over 80% of the land area is cloaked by tropical forest and woodlands, which have proved to be a rich timber source. In coastal areas, fishing, mainly for tuna, is a staple industry.
PACIFIC OCEAN
Manus Island
Bismarck Archipelago
Wewak
Bismarck Sea
Rabaul
INDONESIA
PAPUA NEW GUINEA
Madang
New Guinea
New Britain
Lae
Bougainville Island
Arawa
Solomon Sea
PORT MORESBY
Louisiade Archipelago
Coral Sea
HONIARA
SOLOMON ISLANDS
The urban/rural population divide
urban 32%
rural 68%
0 10 20 30 40 50 60 70 80 90 100
Population density
32 people per sq mile (12 people per sq km)
Total land area
205,354 sq miles (332,008 sq km)
Coral Sea
PACIFIC OCEAN
VANUATU
PORT-VILA
FIJI
SUVA
NEW CALEDONIA (to France)
NOUMÉA
Land use and agricultural distribution
bananas
cocoa
coconuts
fishing
oil palms
rubber
timber
capital cities
major towns
cropland
forest
wetland
◀ Abaca Eco-tourist Park near Lautoka on the island of Viti Levu in western Fiji is one of a number of projects aimed at combining tourism with awareness about the environment. The government and people of Fiji are keen to protect the unique ecology of the islands and prevent further damage to the coral reefs. Until the recent ending of nuclear testing in the Pacific by Western nations, Fiji lay downwind of some of the main testing sites.
192
SOLOMON ISLANDS
MAKIRA - ULAWA
Ulawa Island
Three Sisters Islands
Kirakira
San Cristobal
Star Harbour
Duff Islands
Reef Islands
Tinakula
Nendö
Lata
Noka
TEMOTU
Santa Cruz Islands
Utupua
Vanikolo
Anuta
Fatutaka
Tikopia
Hiu
Torres Islands
Toga
Ureparapara
Vanua Lava
Sola
Banks Islands
Gaua
VANUATU
Cape Cumberland
Nokuku
Port-Olry
Naone
Espiritu Santo
Maéwo
Mount Tabwemasana 1879m
Navonda
Ambae
Luganville
Malo
Bwatnapne
Bougainville Strait
Pentecost
Norsup
Mount Marum 1270m
Ambrym
Unmet
Malekula
Toak
Lamap
Lamen Bay
Epi
Tongoa
Emae
Shepherd Islands
Nguna
Paonangisu
Bauer Field
Efate
Forari
PORT-VILA
Coral Sea
PACIFIC OCEAN
Erromango
Unpongkor
Ipota
Aniwa
Futuna
Isangel
Tanna
Aneityum
Huon
Récifs d'Entrecasteaux
Récif Petrie
Île Surprise
Grand Passage
NEW CALEDONIA (to France)
Récif de Cook
Récif des Français
Île Art
Waala
Récifs de l'Astrolabe
Île Balabio
Ouégoa
Poum
Mont Panié 1628m
Hienghène
Koumac
Kaala-Gomen
PROVINCE NORD
Voh
Koné
Ponérihouen
Houailou
Ouvéa
Fayaoué
Lifou
Wé
PROVINCE DES ÎLES LOYAUTÉ
Îles Loyauté
Poya
Bourail
Canala
Thio
New Caledonia
La Foa
PROVINCE SUD
La Tontouta
Dumbéa
Yaté
NOUMÉA
Mont-Dore
Tadine
Maré
Vao
Île des Pins
Grand Récif Sud
Île Walpole
Great Sea Reef
Vanua Levu
Cikobia
Qelelevu Lagoon
Navoalevu
Nabuna
Naduri
Labasa
Rabi
Nabavatu
Buca
Somosomo
Bua
Savusavu
Bouma
Yasawa Group
Bligh Water
Nabouwalu
Kanacea
Taveuni
Naitaba
Tavua
Rakiraki
Koro
Nasau
Northern Lau Group
Vanua Balavu
Lautoka
Ovalau
Koro Sea
Mago
Mamanuca Group
Nadi
Ba
Mount Victoria 1324m
Levuka
Cicia
Lau Group
Viti Levu
Korovou
Lamiti
Nayau
Korolevu
Navua
Nausori
SUVA
Gau
Lakeba Passage
Lakeba
FIJI
Vatulele
Beqa
Kadavu Passage
Moala
Oneata
Moce
Ono
Totoya
Namuka-i-lau
Vunisea
Kadavu
Matuku
Kabara
Fulaga
Southern Lau Group
Vatoa
Ono-i-lau
Scale 1:9,800,000
Km 0 25 50 100 150 200 250 300
Miles 0 25 50 100 150 200 300
projection: Mercator
T U V W X Y Z

Micronesia

MARSHALL ISLANDS, MICRONESIA, NAURU, PALAU, Guam, Northern Mariana Islands, Wake Island

The Micronesian islands lie in the western reaches of the Pacific Ocean and are all part of the same volcanic zone. The Federated States of Micronesia is the largest group, with more than 600 atolls and forested volcanic islands in an area of more than 1120 sq miles (2900 sq km). Micronesia is a mixture of former colonies, overseas territories and dependencies. Most of the region still relies on aid and subsidies to sustain economies limited by resources, isolation, and an emigrating population, drawn to New Zealand and Australia by the attractions of a western lifestyle.

Palau

Palau is an archipelago of over 200 islands, only eight of which are inhabited. It was the last remaining UN trust territory in the Pacific, controlled by the USA until 1994, when it became independent. The economy operates on a subsistence level, with coconuts and cassava the principal crops. Fishing licences and tourism provide foreign currency.

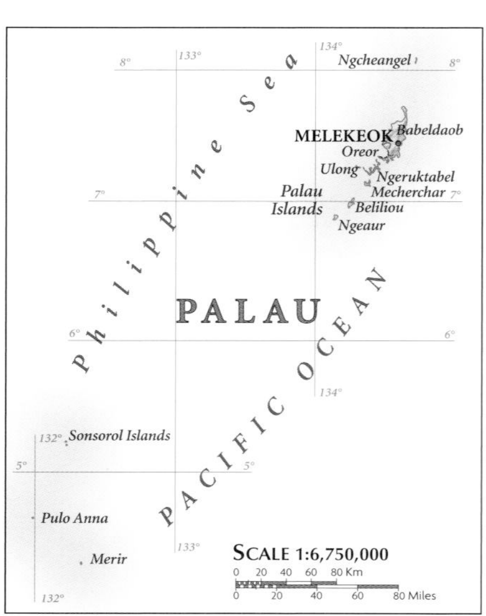
Philippine Sea
Ngcheangel
MELEKEOK
Babeldaob
Oreor
Ulong
Ngeruktabel
Mecherchar
Palau Islands
Beliliou
Ngeaur
PALAU
PACIFIC OCEAN
Sonsorol Islands
Pulo Anna
Merir
SCALE 1:6,750,000

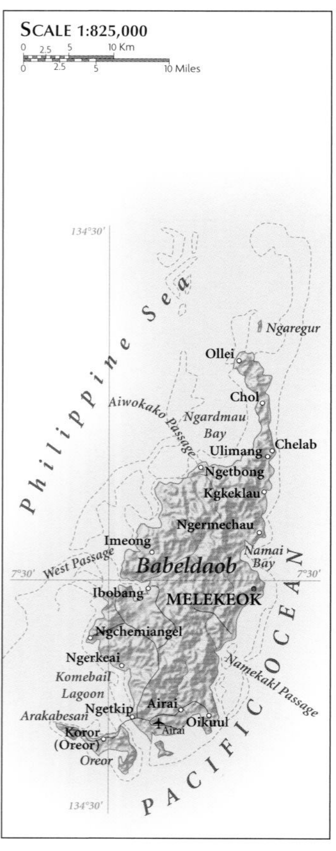
SCALE 1:825,000
Philippine Sea
Ngaregur
Ollei
Chol
Aiwokako Passage
Ngardmau Bay
Chelab
Ulimang
Ngetbong
Kgkeklau
Ngermechau
Imeong
Namai Bay
West Passage
Babeldaob
Ibobang
MELEKEOK
Ngchemiangel
Ngerkeai
Komebail Lagoon
Namekakl Passage
Ngetkip
Airai
Arakabesan
Koror (Oreor)
Oikul
Oreor
PACIFIC OCEAN

Guam *(to US)*

Lying at the southern end of the Mariana Islands, Guam is an important US military base and tourist destination. Social and political life is dominated by the indigenous Chamorro, who make up just under half the population, although the increasing prevalence of western culture threatens Guam's traditional social stability.

◀ *The tranquillity of these coastal lagoons, at Inarajan in southern Guam, belies the fact that the island lies in a region where typhoons are common.*

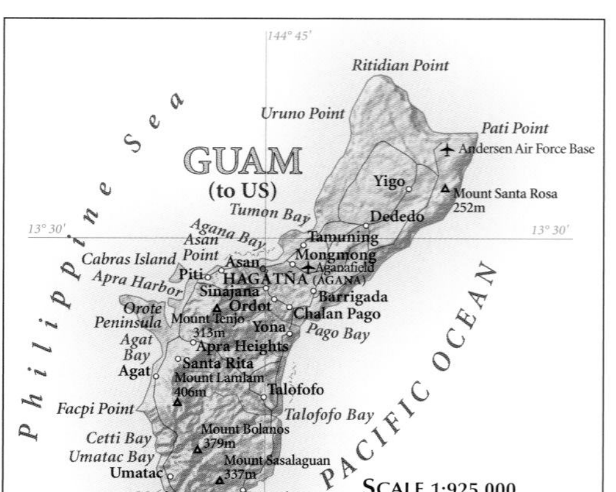
Ritidian Point
Philippine Sea
Uruno Point
Pati Point
Andersen Air Force Base
GUAM (to US)
Yigo
Mount Santa Rosa 252m
Tumon Bay
Dededo
Agana Bay
Tamuning
Cabras Island
Asan Point
Mongmong
Apra Harbor
Piti
HAGÅTÑA (AGANA)
Sinajana
Barrigada
Ordot
Orote Peninsula
Chalan Pago
Yona
Pago Bay
Agat Bay
Apra Heights
Agat
Santa Rita
Mount Lamlam 406m
Talofofo
Facpi Point
Talofofo Bay
Mount Bolanos 379m
Cetti Bay
Umatac Bay
Umatac
Mount Sasalaguan 337m
Merizo
Inarajan
Cocos Island
Aga Point
PACIFIC OCEAN
SCALE 1:925,000

Northern Mariana Islands *(to US)*

A US Commonwealth territory, the Northern Marianas comprise the whole of the Mariana archipelago except for Guam. The islands retain their close links with the United States and continue to receive US aid. Tourism, though bringing in much-needed revenue, has speeded the decline of the traditional subsistence economy. Most of the population lives on Saipan.

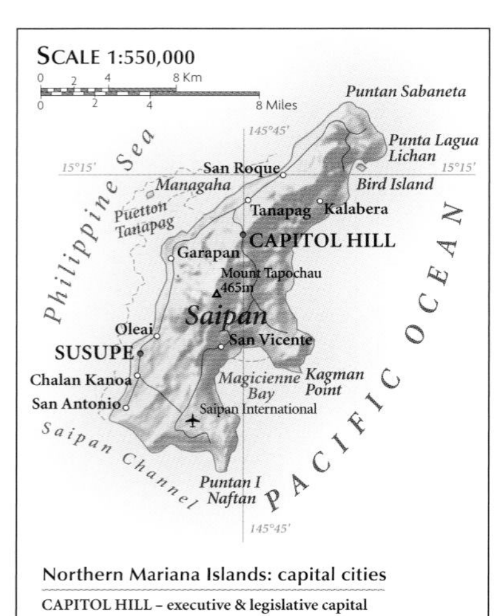
SCALE 1:550,000
Puntan Sabaneta
Punta Lagua Lichan
Philippine Sea
San Roque
Managaha
Bird Island
Puetton Tanapag
Tanapag
Kalabera
CAPITOL HILL
Garapan
Mount Tapochau 465m
Saipan
Oleai
SUSUPE
San Vicente
Chalan Kanoa
Magicienne Bay
Kagman Point
San Antonio
Saipan International
Saipan Channel
Puntan I Naftan
PACIFIC OCEAN
Northern Mariana Islands: capital cities
CAPITOL HILL – executive & legislative capital
SUSUPE – judicial capital

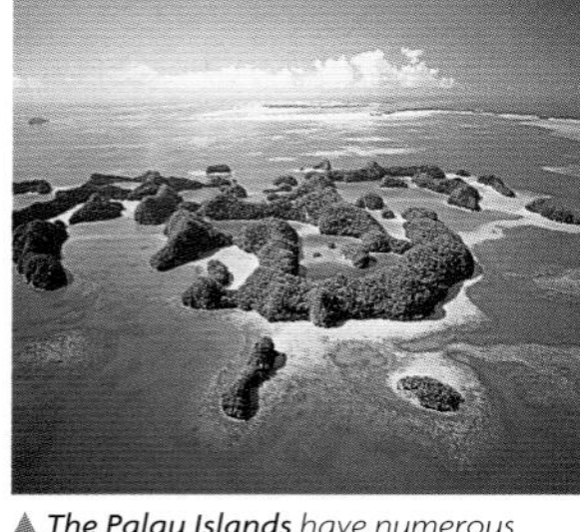

▲ *The Palau Islands have numerous hidden lakes and lagoons. These sustain their own ecosystems which have developed in isolation. This has produced adaptations in the animals and plants which are often unique to each lake.*

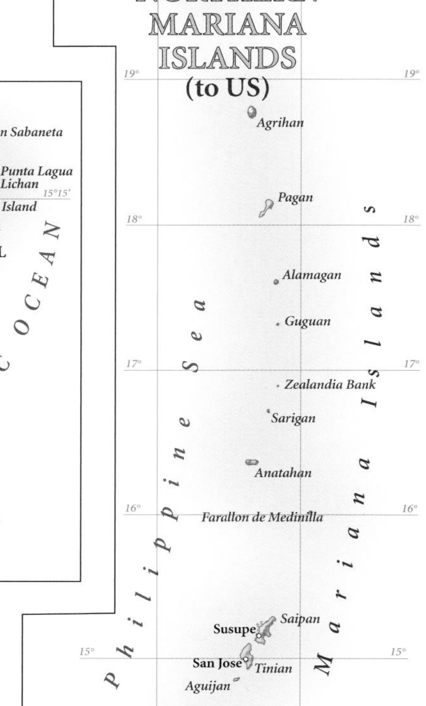
Farallon de Pajaros
Supply Reef
PACIFIC OCEAN
Maug Islands
Asuncion Island
NORTHERN MARIANA ISLANDS (to US)
Agrihan
Pagan
Alamagan
Guguan
Zealandia Bank
Sarigan
Anatahan
Farallon de Medinilla
Mariana Islands
Philippine Sea
Susupe
Saipan
San Jose
Tinian
Aguijan
Rota
GUAM (to US)
HAGÅTÑA
Dededo
PACIFIC OCEAN
SCALE 1:5,500,000

Micronesia

A mixture of high volcanic islands and low-lying coral atolls, the Federated States of Micronesia include all the Caroline Islands except Palau. Pohnpei, Kosrae, Chuuk and Yap are the four main island cluster states, each of which has its own language, with English remaining the official language. Nearly half the population is concentrated on Pohnpei, the largest island. Independent since 1986, the islands continue to receive considerable aid from the USA which supplements an economy based primarily on fishing and copra processing.

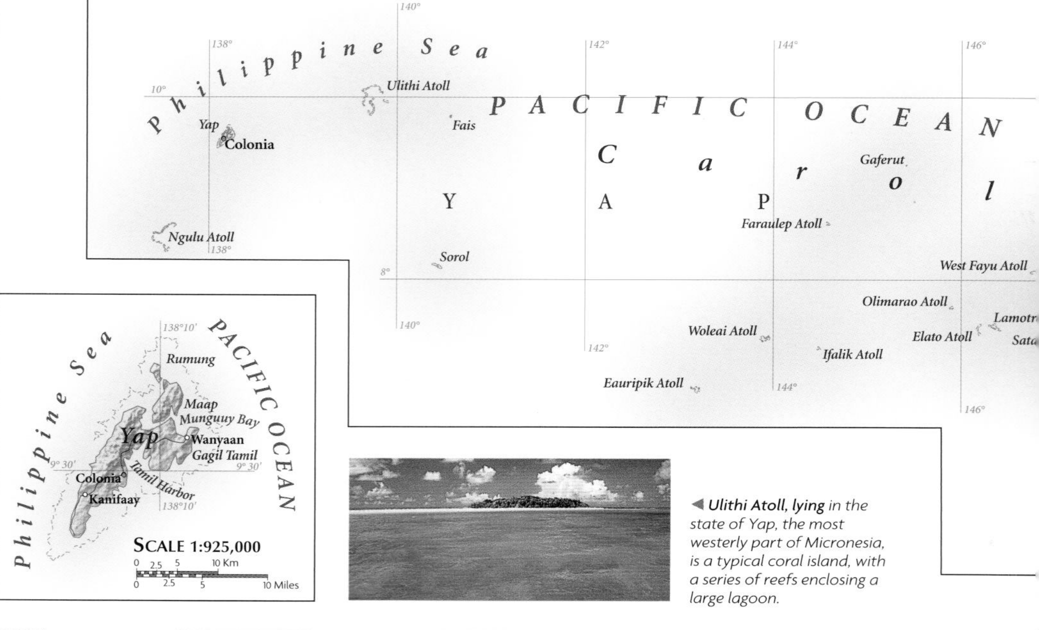
Philippine Sea
Ulithi Atoll
PACIFIC OCEAN
Yap
Colonia
Fais
Caroline
YAP
Gaferut
Ngulu Atoll
Faraulep Atoll
Sorol
West Fayu Atoll
Olimarao Atoll
Woleai Atoll
Elato Atoll
Ifalik Atoll
Eauripik Atoll
Philippine Sea
Rumung
PACIFIC OCEAN
Maap
Munguuy Bay
Wanyaan
Gagil Tamil
Yap
Tamil Harbor
Colonia
Kanifaay
SCALE 1:925,000

◀ *Ulithi Atoll, lying in the state of Yap, the most westerly part of Micronesia, is a typical coral island, with a series of reefs enclosing a large lagoon.*

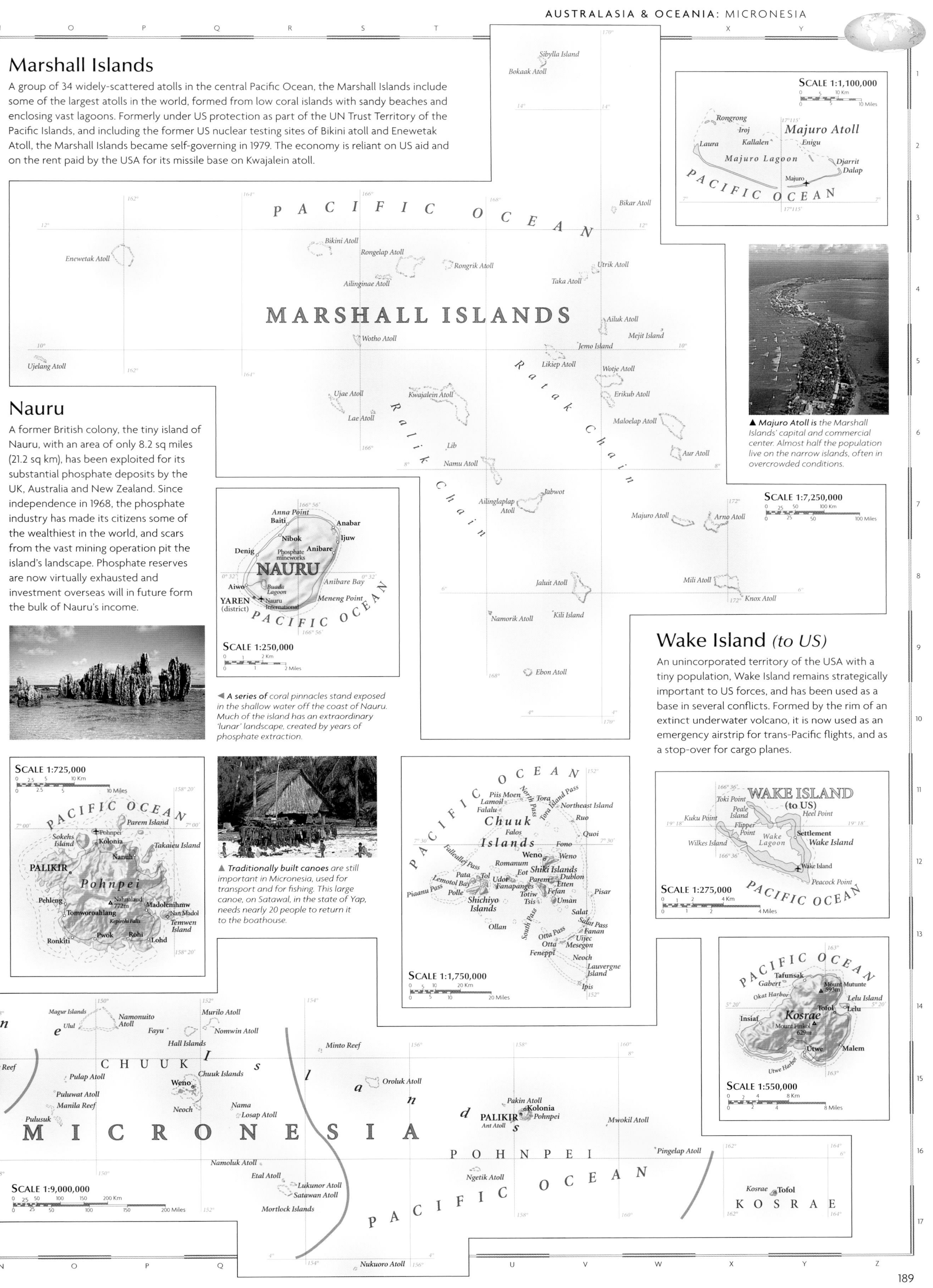

PACIFIC OCEAN
MARSHALL ISLANDS
Sibylla Island
Bokaak Atoll
Bikar Atoll
Enewetak Atoll
Bikini Atoll
Rongelap Atoll
Rongrik Atoll
Ailinginae Atoll
Utrik Atoll
Taka Atoll
Ailuk Atoll
Mejit Island
Jemo Island
Wotho Atoll
Ujelang Atoll
Likiep Atoll
Wotje Atoll
Erikub Atoll
Ratak Chain
Ralik Chain
Ujae Atoll
Kwajalein Atoll
Lae Atoll
Maloelap Atoll
Aur Atoll
Lib
Namu Atoll
Jabwot
Ailinglaplap Atoll
Majuro Atoll
Arno Atoll
Mili Atoll
Knox Atoll
Jaluit Atoll
Kili Island
Namorik Atoll
Ebon Atoll
SCALE 1:7,250,000
SCALE 1:1,100,000
Majuro Atoll
Rongrong
Iroj
Laura
Kallalen
Enigu
Majuro Lagoon
Djarrit
Dalap
Majuro
NAURU
Anna Point
Baiti
Anabar
Nibok
Ijuw
Denig
Phosphate mineworks
Anibare
Anibare Bay
Aiwo
Buada Lagoon
Meneng Point
YAREN (district)
Nauru International
SCALE 1:250,000
WAKE ISLAND (to US)
Toki Point
Peale Island
Heel Point
Kuku Point
Flipper Point
Wake Lagoon
Settlement
Wake Island
Wilkes Island
Peacock Point
SCALE 1:275,000
Chuuk Islands
Weno
Tol
Shichiyo Islands
Fefan
Uman
SCALE 1:1,750,000
Pohnpei
PALIKIR
Kolonia
Nahnalaud 772m
SCALE 1:725,000
Kosrae
Tofol
Lelu
Malem
Utwe
SCALE 1:550,000
MICRONESIA
CHUUK
POHNPEI
KOSRAE
Islands
SCALE 1:9,000,000

Marshall Islands

A group of 34 widely-scattered atolls in the central Pacific Ocean, the Marshall Islands include some of the largest atolls in the world, formed from low coral islands with sandy beaches and enclosing vast lagoons. Formerly under US protection as part of the UN Trust Territory of the Pacific Islands, and including the former US nuclear testing sites of Bikini atoll and Enewetak Atoll, the Marshall Islands became self-governing in 1979. The economy is reliant on US aid and on the rent paid by the USA for its missile base on Kwajalein atoll.

▲ **Majuro Atoll** is the Marshall Islands' capital and commercial center. Almost half the population live on the narrow islands, often in overcrowded conditions.

Nauru

A former British colony, the tiny island of Nauru, with an area of only 8.2 sq miles (21.2 sq km), has been exploited for its substantial phosphate deposits by the UK, Australia and New Zealand. Since independence in 1968, the phosphate industry has made its citizens some of the wealthiest in the world, and scars from the vast mining operation pit the island's landscape. Phosphate reserves are now virtually exhausted and investment overseas will in future form the bulk of Nauru's income.

◀ **A series of** coral pinnacles stand exposed in the shallow water off the coast of Nauru. Much of the island has an extraordinary 'lunar' landscape, created by years of phosphate extraction.

Wake Island *(to US)*

An unincorporated territory of the USA with a tiny population, Wake Island remains strategically important to US forces, and has been used as a base in several conflicts. Formed by the rim of an extinct underwater volcano, it is now used as an emergency airstrip for trans-Pacific flights, and as a stop-over for cargo planes.

▲ **Traditionally built canoes** are still important in Micronesia, used for transport and for fishing. This large canoe, on Satawal, in the state of Yap, needs nearly 20 people to return it to the boathouse.

Polynesia

KIRIBATI, TUVALU, Cook Islands, Easter Island, French Polynesia, Niue, Pitcairn Islands, Tokelau, Wallis & Futuna

The numerous island groups of Polynesia lie to the east of Australia, scattered over a vast area in the south Pacific. The islands are a mixture of low-lying coral atolls, some of which enclose lagoons, and the tips of great underwater volcanoes. The populations on the islands are small, and most people are of Polynesian origin, as are the Maori of New Zealand. Local economies remain simple, relying mainly on subsistence crops, mineral deposits – many now exhausted – fishing and tourism.

Tuvalu

A chain of nine coral atolls, 360 miles (579 km) long with a land area of just over 9 sq miles (23 sq km), Tuvalu is one of the world's smallest and most isolated states. As the Ellice Islands, Tuvalu was linked to the Gilbert Islands (now part of Kiribati) as a British colony until independence in 1978. Politically and socially conservative, Tuvaluans live by fishing and subsistence farming.

▲ **Funafuti Atoll contains** *more than 40% of Tuvalu's people, giving it an extremely high population density.*

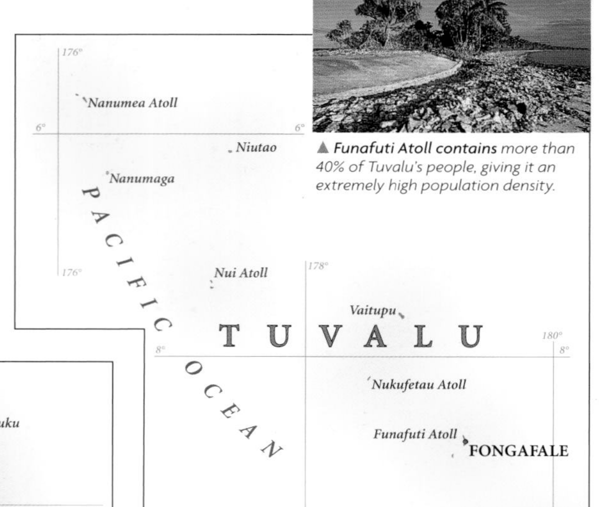
Nanumea Atoll
Niutao
Nanumaga
PACIFIC OCEAN
Nui Atoll
Vaitupu
TUVALU

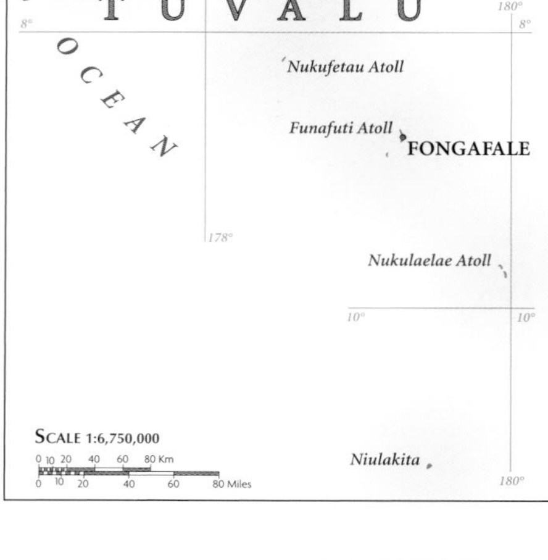
Nukufetau Atoll
Funafuti Atoll
FONGAFALE
Nukulaelae Atoll
Niulakita
SCALE 1:6,750,000

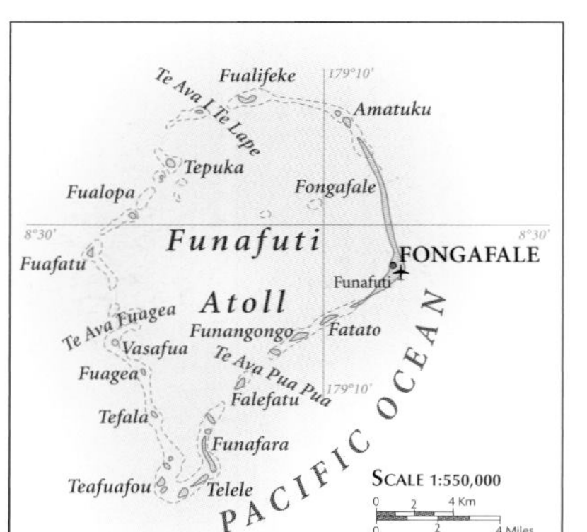
Fualifeke
Te Ava I Te Lape
Amatuku
Tepuka
Fualopa
Fongafale
Funafuti Atoll
Fuafatu
FONGAFALE
Funafuti
Te Ava Fuagea
Vasafua
Funangongo
Fatato
Fuagea
Te Ava Pua Pua
Falefatu
Tefala
Funafara
Teafuafou
Telele
PACIFIC OCEAN
SCALE 1:550,000

Kiribati

A former British colony, Kiribati became independent in 1979. Banaba's phosphate deposits ran out in 1980, following decades of exploitation by the British. Economic development remains slow and most agriculture is at a subsistence level, though coconuts provide export income, and underwater agriculture is being developed.

PACIFIC OCEAN
Iku
Buariki
Taratai
Abaokoro
Marenanuka
Nabeina
Tarawa
Tabiteuea
Bikeman
Bonriki
Betio
Bikenebu
Tarawa
Eita
BAIRIKI
Banraeaba
SCALE 1:1,100,000

▶ **With the exception** *of Banaba all the islands in Kiribati's three groups are low-lying, coral atolls. This aerial view shows the sparsely vegetated islands, intercut by many small lagoons.*

Tokelau *(to New Zealand)*

A low-lying coral atoll, Tokelau is a dependent territory of New Zealand with few natural resources. Although a 1990 cyclone destroyed crops and infrastructure, a tuna cannery and the sale of fishing licences have raised revenue and a catamaran link between the islands has increased their tourism potential. Tokelau's small size and economic weakness makes independence from New Zealand unlikely.

▲ **Fishermen cast their** *nets to catch small fish in the shallow waters off Atafu Atoll, the most westerly island in Tokelau.*

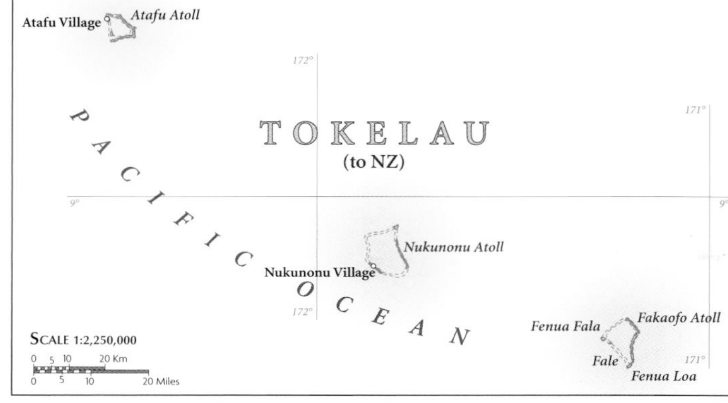
Atafu Village
Atafu Atoll
TOKELAU
(to NZ)
PACIFIC OCEAN
Nukunonu Atoll
Nukunonu Village
Fenua Fala
Fakaofo Atoll
Fale
Fenua Loa
SCALE 1:2,250,000

Wallis & Futuna
(to France)

In contrast to other French overseas territories in the south Pacific, the inhabitants of Wallis and Futuna have shown little desire for greater autonomy. A subsistence economy produces a variety of tropical crops, while foreign currency remittances come from expatriates and from the sale of licences to Japanese and Korean fishing fleets.

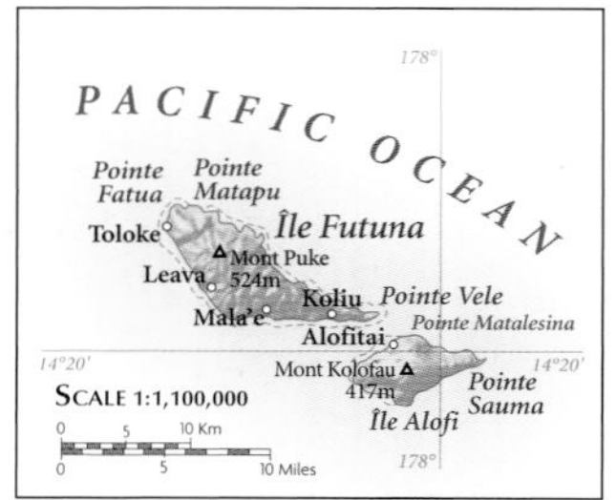
PACIFIC OCEAN
Pointe Fatua
Pointe Matapu
Toloke
Île Futuna
Mont Puke 524m
Leava
Kolia
Pointe Vele
Mala'e
Pointe Matalesina
Alofitai
Mont Kolofau 417m
Pointe Sauma
Île Alofi
SCALE 1:1,100,000

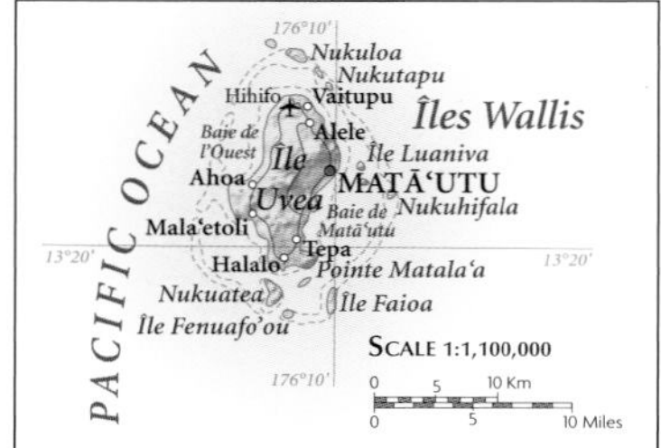
PACIFIC OCEAN
Nukuloa
Nukutapu
Hihifo
Vaitupu
Îles Wallis
Baie de l'Ouest
Alele
Ahoa
Île Luaniva
Île Uvea
MATĀ'UTU
Mala'etoli
Baie de Matā'utu
Nukuhifala
Tepa
Halalo
Pointe Matala'a
Nukuatea
Île Faioa
Île Fenuafo'ou
SCALE 1:1,100,000

Cook Islands *(to New Zealand)*

A mixture of coral atolls and volcanic peaks, the Cook Islands achieved self-government in 1965 but exist in free association with New Zealand. A diverse economy includes pearl and giant clam farming, and an ostrich farm, plus tourism and banking. A 1991 friendship treaty with France provides for French surveillance of territorial waters.

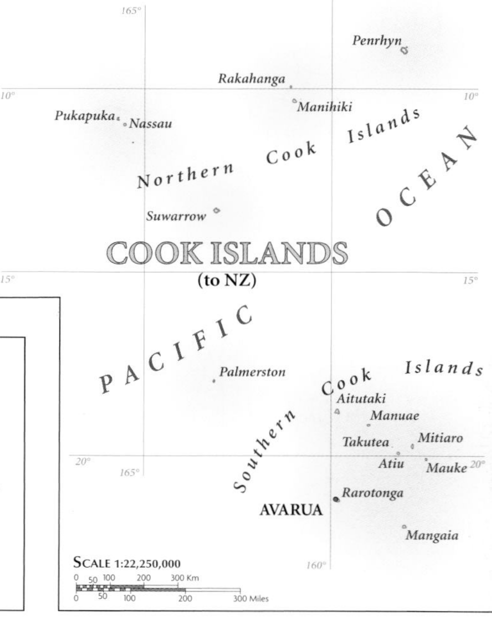
Penrhyn
Rakahanga
Manihiki
Pukapuka
Nassau
Northern Cook Islands
OCEAN
Suwarrow
COOK ISLANDS
(to NZ)
PACIFIC
Palmerston
Southern Cook Islands
Aitutaki
Manuae
Takutea
Mitiaro
Atiu
Mauke
Rarotonga
AVARUA
Mangaia
SCALE 1:22,250,000

▲ **Palm trees fringe** *the white sands of a beach on Aitutaki in the Southern Cook Islands, where tourism is of increasing economic importance.*

Niue *(to New Zealand)*

Niue, the world's largest coral island, is self-governing but exists in free association with New Zealand. Tropical fruits are grown for local consumption; tourism and the sale of postage stamps provide foreign currency. The lack of local job prospects has led more than 10,000 Niueans to emigrate to New Zealand, which has now invested heavily in Niue's economy in the hope of reversing this trend.

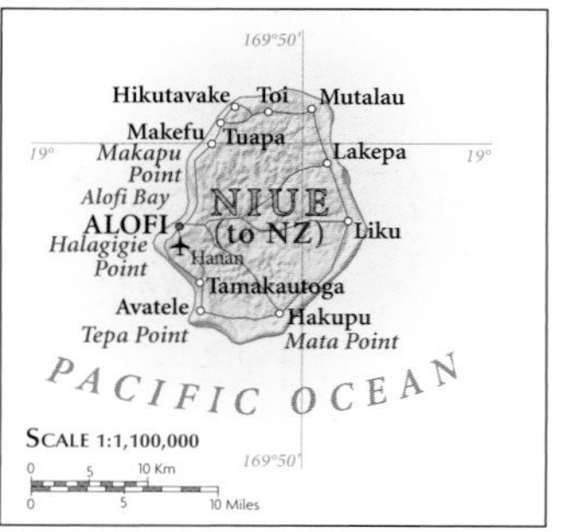
Hikutavake
Toi
Mutalau
Makefu
Tuapa
Makapu Point
Lakepa
Alofi Bay
NIUE (to NZ)
ALOFI
Halagigie Point
Liku
Tamakautoga
Avatele
Hakupu
Tepa Point
Mata Point
PACIFIC OCEAN
SCALE 1:1,100,000

▲ **Waves have cut** *back the original coastline, exposing a sandy beach, near Mutalau in the northeast corner of Niue.*

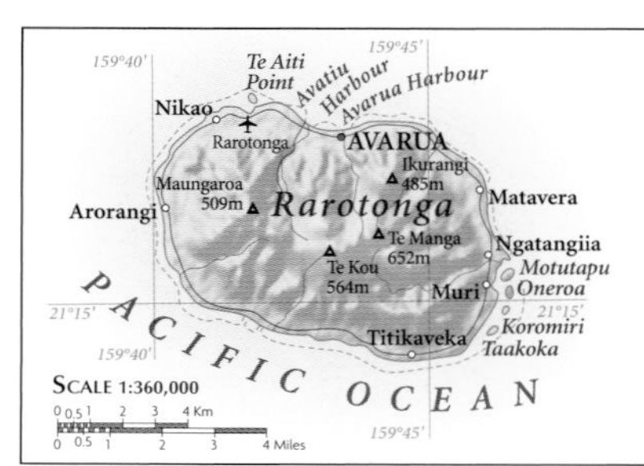
Te Aiti Point
Avatiu Harbour
Avarua Harbour
Nikao
Rarotonga
AVARUA
Ikurangi
Maungaroa 509m
Rarotonga
Matavera
Arorangi
Te Manga 652m
Ngatangiia
Te Kou 564m
Muri
Motutapu
Oneroa
Titikaveka
Koromiri
Taakoka
PACIFIC OCEAN
SCALE 1:360,000

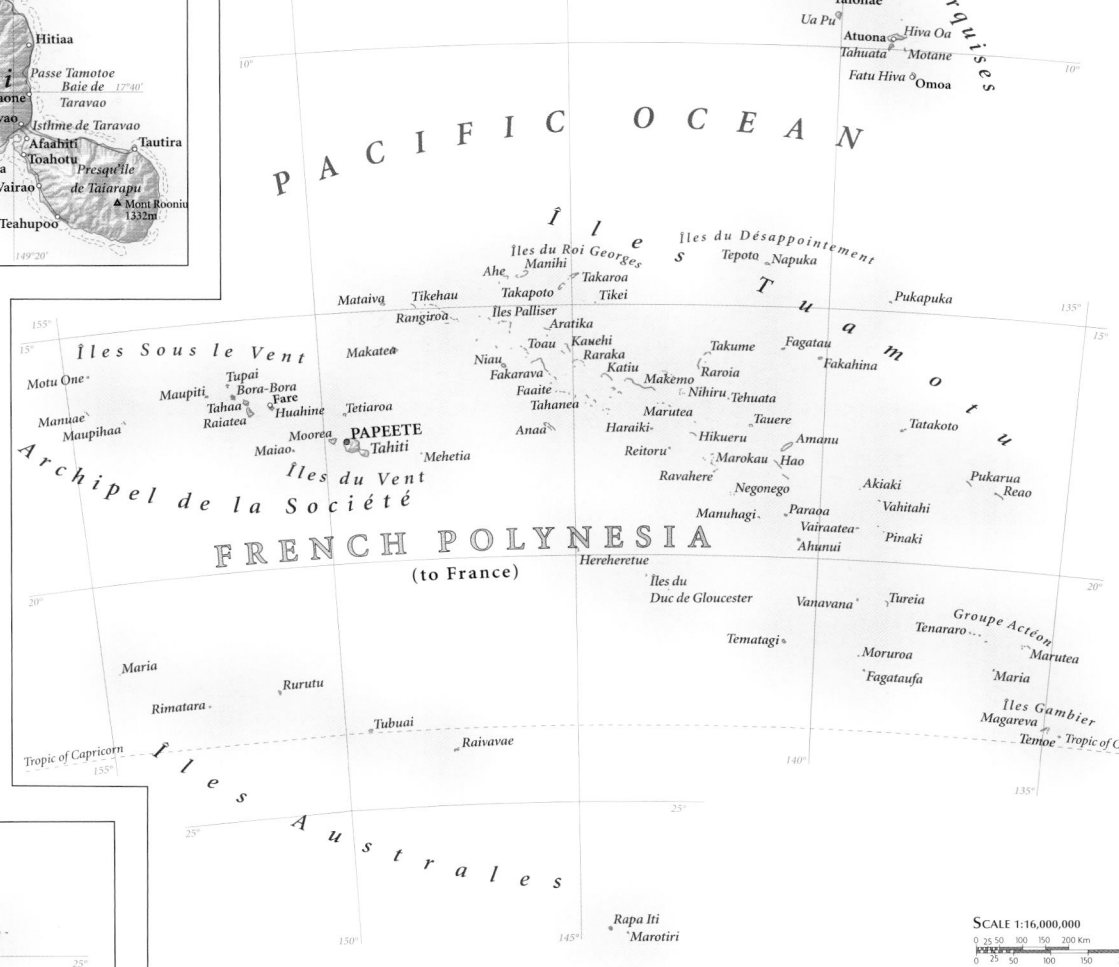

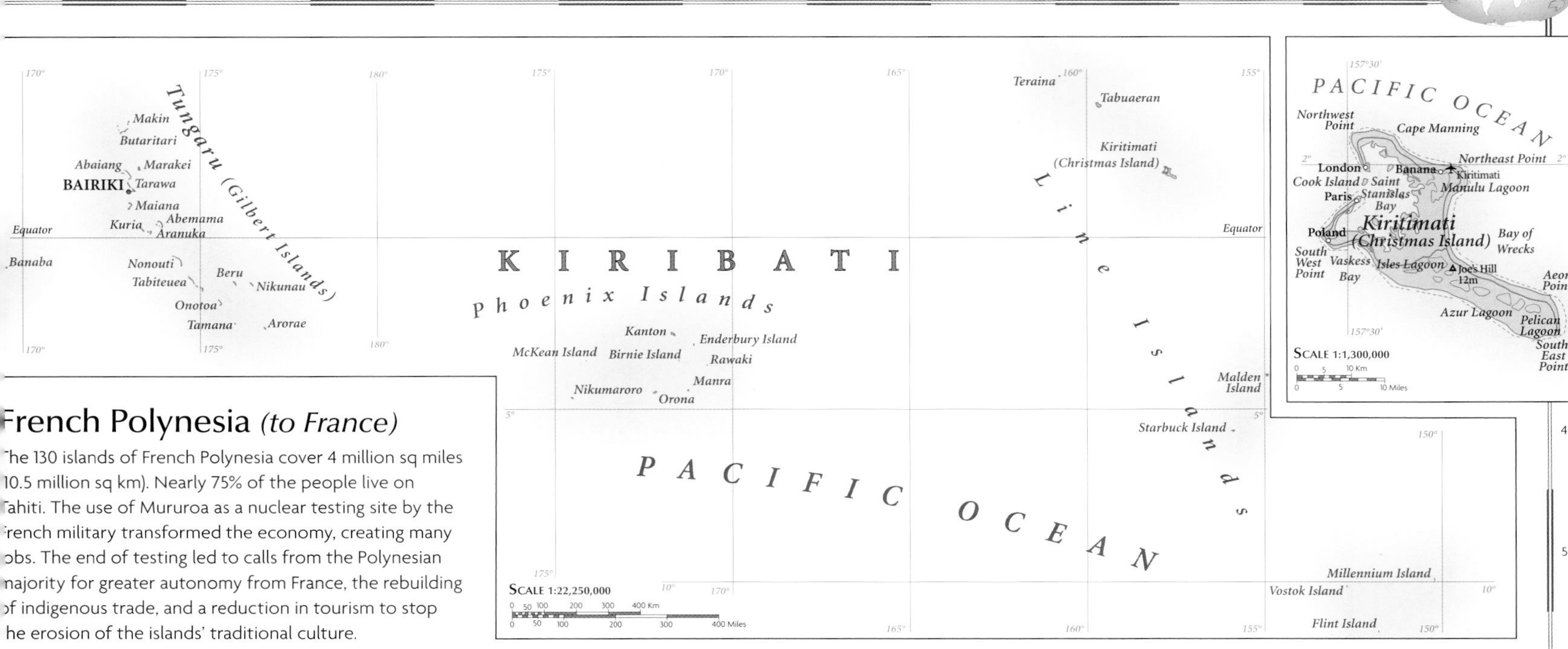
Makin
Butaritari
Tungaru (Gilbert Islands)
Abaiang
Marakei
BAIRIKI
Tarawa
Maiana
Abemama
Kuria
Aranuka
Equator
Banaba
Nonouti
Tabiteuea
Beru
Nikunau
Onotoa
Tamana
Arorae
KIRIBATI
Phoenix Islands
Kanton
Enderbury Island
McKean Island
Birnie Island
Rawaki
Manra
Nikumaroro
Orona
Teraina
Tabuaeran
Kiritimati (Christmas Island)
Line Islands
Malden Island
Starbuck Island
PACIFIC OCEAN
Millennium Island
Vostok Island
Flint Island
SCALE 1:22,250,000
PACIFIC OCEAN
Northwest Point
Cape Manning
Northeast Point
London
Banana
Kiritimati
Cook Island
Saint Stanislas Bay
Manulu Lagoon
Paris
Poland
Kiritimati (Christmas Island)
Bay of Wrecks
South West Point
Vaskess Bay
Isles Lagoon
Joe's Hill 12m
Aeon Point
Azur Lagoon
Pelican Lagoon
South East Point
SCALE 1:1,300,000

French Polynesia *(to France)*

The 130 islands of French Polynesia cover 4 million sq miles (10.5 million sq km). Nearly 75% of the people live on Tahiti. The use of Mururoa as a nuclear testing site by the French military transformed the economy, creating many jobs. The end of testing led to calls from the Polynesian majority for greater autonomy from France, the rebuilding of indigenous trade, and a reduction in tourism to stop the erosion of the islands' traditional culture.

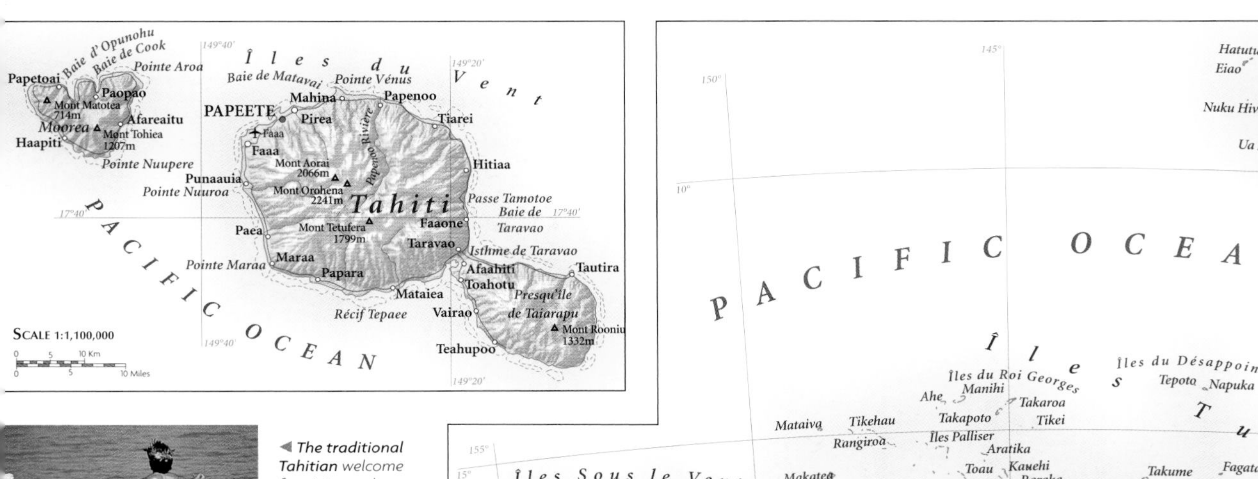
Papetoai
Baie d'Opunohu
Baie de Cook
Pointe Aroa
Paopao
Mont Matotea 714m
Afareaitu
Moorea
Mont Tohiea 1207m
Haapiti
Pointe Nuupere
Îles du Vent
Baie de Matavai
Pointe Vénus
Mahina
Papenoo
PAPEETE
Pirea
Tiarei
Faaa
Punaauia
Pointe Nuuroa
Mont Aorai 2066m
Mont Orohena 2241m
Tahiti
Hitiaa
Passe Tamotoe
Baie de Taravao
Paea
Mont Tetufera 1799m
Faaone
Taravao
Isthme de Taravao
Pointe Maraa
Maraa
Papara
Afaahiti
Toahotu
Tautira
Presqu'île de Taiarapu
Mataiea
Récif Tepaee
Vairao
Mont Rooniu 1332m
Teahupoo
PACIFIC OCEAN
SCALE 1:1,100,000

◀ The traditional Tahitian welcome for visitors, who are greeted by parties of canoes, has become a major tourist attraction.

Pitcairn Islands *(to UK)*

Britain's most isolated dependency, Pitcairn Island was first populated by mutineers from the HMS *Bounty* in 1790. Emigration is further depleting the already limited gene pool of the island's inhabitants, with associated social and health problems. Barter, fishing and subsistence farming form the basis of the economy although postage stamp sales provide foreign currency earnings, and offshore mineral exploitation may boost the economy in future.

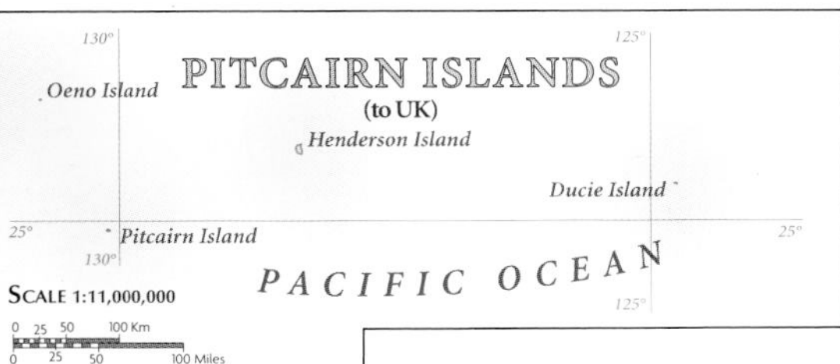
Oeno Island
PITCAIRN ISLANDS
(to UK)
Henderson Island
Ducie Island
Pitcairn Island
PACIFIC OCEAN
SCALE 1:11,000,000

◀ The Pitcairn Islanders rely on regular airdrops from New Zealand and periodic visits by supply vessels to provide them with basic commodities.

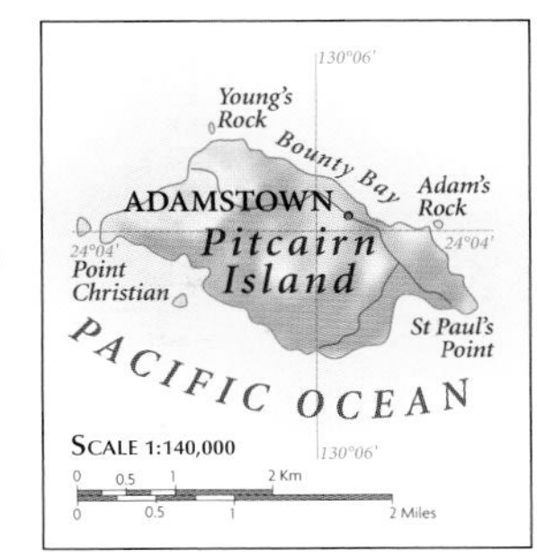
Young's Rock
Bounty Bay
ADAMSTOWN
Adam's Rock
Pitcairn Island
Point Christian
St Paul's Point
PACIFIC OCEAN
SCALE 1:140,000

PACIFIC OCEAN
Hatutu
Eiao
Îles Marquises
Nuku Hiva
Ua Huka
Taiohae
Ua Pu
Atuona
Hiva Oa
Tahuata
Motane
Fatu Hiva
Omoa
Îles Tuamotu
Îles du Roi Georges
Îles du Désappointement
Manihi
Ahe
Tepoto
Napuka
Takaroa
Takapoto
Tikei
Mataiva
Tikehau
Rangiroa
Îles Palliser
Aratika
Pukapuka
Îles Sous le Vent
Makatea
Toau
Kauehi
Raraka
Katiu
Takume
Fagatau
Fakahina
Motu One
Maupiti
Tupai
Bora-Bora
Niau
Fakarava
Faaite
Makemo
Raroia
Nihiru
Tehuata
Tahaa
Fare
Huahine
Tetiaroa
Tahanea
Manuae
Maupihaa
Raiatea
Moorea
PAPEETE
Tahiti
Anaa
Marutea
Haraiki
Tauere
Amanu
Tatakoto
Maiao
Mehetia
Îles du Vent
Reitoru
Hikueru
Marokau
Hao
Archipel de la Société
Ravahere
Negonego
Akiaki
Pukarua
Reao
Manuhagi
Paraoa
Vahitahi
Vairaatea
Pinaki
Ahunui
FRENCH POLYNESIA
(to France)
Hereheretue
Îles du Duc de Gloucester
Vanavana
Tureia
Groupe Actéon
Tenararo
Marutea
Tematagi
Maria
Moruroa
Fagataufa
Maria
Rurutu
Rimatara
Îles Gambier
Magareva
Temoe
Tubuai
Raivavae
Tropic of Capricorn
Îles Australes
Rapa Iti
Marotiri
SCALE 1:16,000,000

Easter Island *(to Chile)*

One of the most easterly islands in Polynesia, Easter Island *(Isla de Pascua)* – also known as Rapa Nui, is part of Chile. The mainly Polynesian inhabitants support themselves by farming, which is mainly of a subsistence nature, and includes cattle rearing and crops such as sugar cane, bananas, corn, gourds and potatoes. In recent years, tourism has become the most important source of income and the island sustains a small commercial airport.

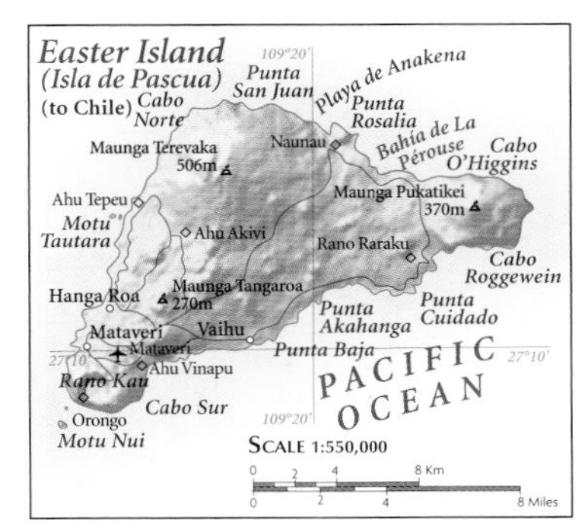
Easter Island
(Isla de Pascua)
(to Chile)
Cabo Norte
Punta San Juan
Playa de Anakena
Punta Rosalia
Bahía de La Pérouse
Cabo O'Higgins
Maunga Terevaka 506m
Naunau
Maunga Pukatikei 370m
Ahu Tepeu
Motu Tautara
Ahu Akivi
Rano Raraku
Cabo Roggewein
Hanga Roa
Maunga Tangaroa 270m
Punta Akahanga
Punta Cuidado
Mataveri
Vaihu
Ahu Vinapu
Punta Baja
Rano Kau
Orongo
Cabo Sur
Motu Nui
PACIFIC OCEAN
SCALE 1:550,000

▲ The Naunau, a series of huge stone statues overlook Playa de Anakena, on Easter Island. Carved from a soft volcanic rock, they were erected between 400 and 900 years ago.

The Pacific Ocean

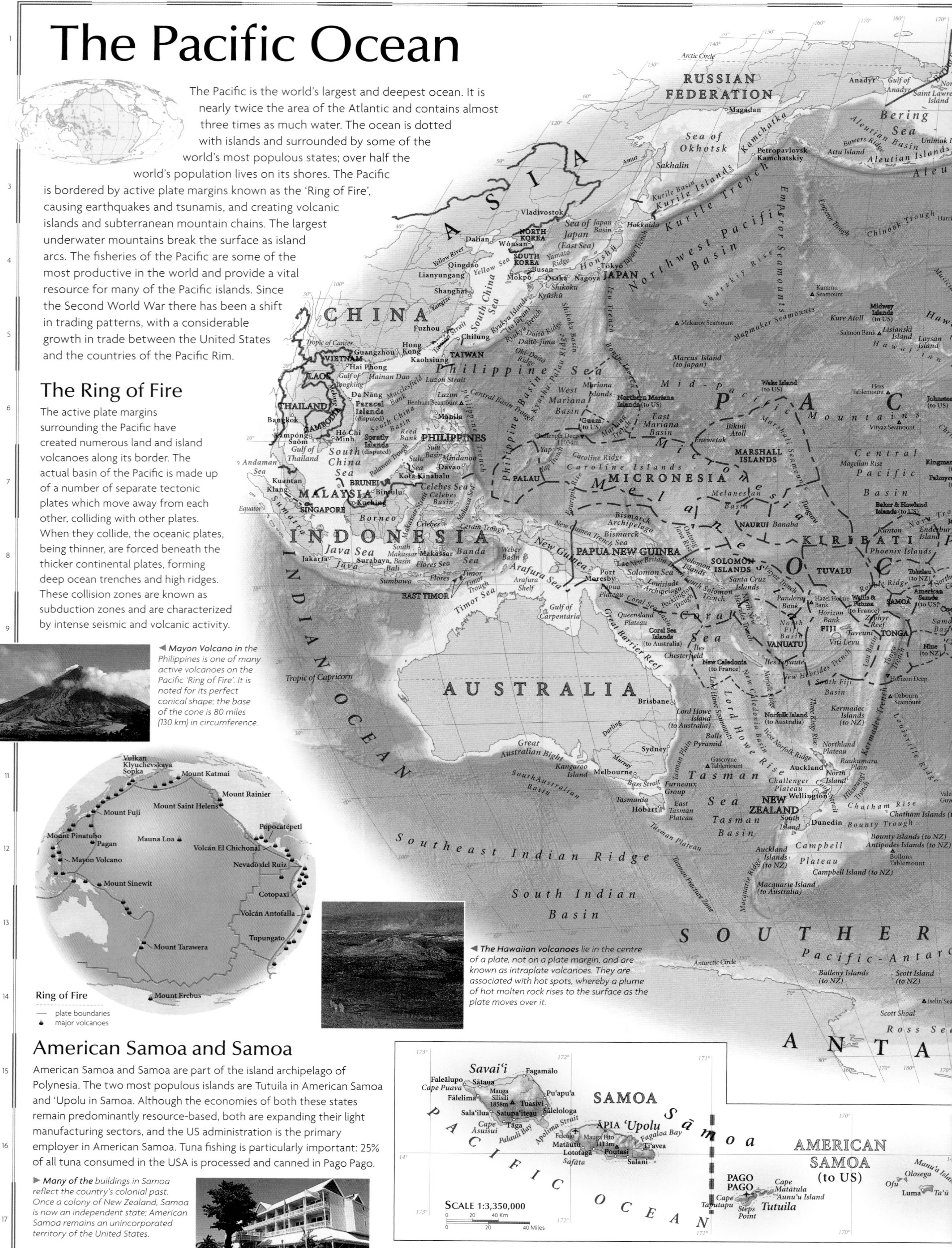
RUSSIAN FEDERATION
ASIA
CHINA
JAPAN
NORTH KOREA
SOUTH KOREA
TAIWAN
VIETNAM
LAOS
THAILAND
CAMBODIA
PHILIPPINES
MALAYSIA
SINGAPORE
BRUNEI
INDONESIA
EAST TIMOR
PAPUA NEW GUINEA
SOLOMON ISLANDS
AUSTRALIA
NEW ZEALAND
MICRONESIA
PALAU
MARSHALL ISLANDS
NAURU
KIRIBATI
TUVALU
VANUATU
FIJI
TONGA
SAMOA
INDIAN OCEAN
Sea of Okhotsk
Sea of Japan (East Sea)
Bering Sea
South China Sea
Philippine Sea
Java Sea
Banda Sea
Arafura Sea
Timor Sea
Coral Sea
Tasman Sea
Solomon Sea
Celebes Sea
Northwest Pacific Basin
Central Pacific Basin
Kurile Trench
Emperor Seamounts
Mariana Trench
Southeast Indian Ridge
South Indian Basin
Tropic of Cancer
Tropic of Capricorn
Equator
Arctic Circle
Antarctic Circle
Ring of Fire
plate boundaries
major volcanoes
Vulkan Klyuchevskaya Sopka
Mount Katmai
Mount Rainier
Mount Saint Helens
Mount Fuji
Popocatépetl
Mount Pinatubo
Pagan
Mauna Loa
Volcán El Chichonal
Mayon Volcano
Nevado del Ruiz
Mount Sinewit
Cotopaxi
Volcán Antofalla
Tupungato
Mount Tarawera
Mount Erebus
Savai'i
'Upolu
SAMOA
ĀPIA
AMERICAN SAMOA (to US)
PAGO PAGO
Tutuila
PACIFIC OCEAN
SCALE 1:3,350,000

The Pacific is the world's largest and deepest ocean. It is nearly twice the area of the Atlantic and contains almost three times as much water. The ocean is dotted with islands and surrounded by some of the world's most populous states; over half the world's population lives on its shores. The Pacific is bordered by active plate margins known as the 'Ring of Fire', causing earthquakes and tsunamis, and creating volcanic islands and subterranean mountain chains. The largest underwater mountains break the surface as island arcs. The fisheries of the Pacific are some of the most productive in the world and provide a vital resource for many of the Pacific islands. Since the Second World War there has been a shift in trading patterns, with a considerable growth in trade between the United States and the countries of the Pacific Rim.

The Ring of Fire

The active plate margins surrounding the Pacific have created numerous land and island volcanoes along its border. The actual basin of the Pacific is made up of a number of separate tectonic plates which move away from each other, colliding with other plates. When they collide, the oceanic plates, being thinner, are forced beneath the thicker continental plates, forming deep ocean trenches and high ridges. These collision zones are known as subduction zones and are characterized by intense seismic and volcanic activity.

◀ *Mayon Volcano in the Philippines is one of many active volcanoes on the Pacific 'Ring of Fire'. It is noted for its perfect conical shape; the base of the cone is 80 miles (130 km) in circumference.*

◀ *The Hawaiian volcanoes lie in the centre of a plate, not on a plate margin, and are known as intraplate volcanoes. They are associated with hot spots, whereby a plume of hot molten rock rises to the surface as the plate moves over it.*

American Samoa and Samoa

American Samoa and Samoa are part of the island archipelago of Polynesia. The two most populous islands are Tutuila in American Samoa and 'Upolu in Samoa. Although the economies of both these states remain predominantly resource-based, both are expanding their light manufacturing sectors, and the US administration is the primary employer in American Samoa. Tuna fishing is particularly important: 25% of all tuna consumed in the USA is processed and canned in Pago Pago.

▶ *Many of the buildings in Samoa reflect the country's colonial past. Once a colony of New Zealand, Samoa is now an independent state; American Samoa remains an unincorporated territory of the United States.*

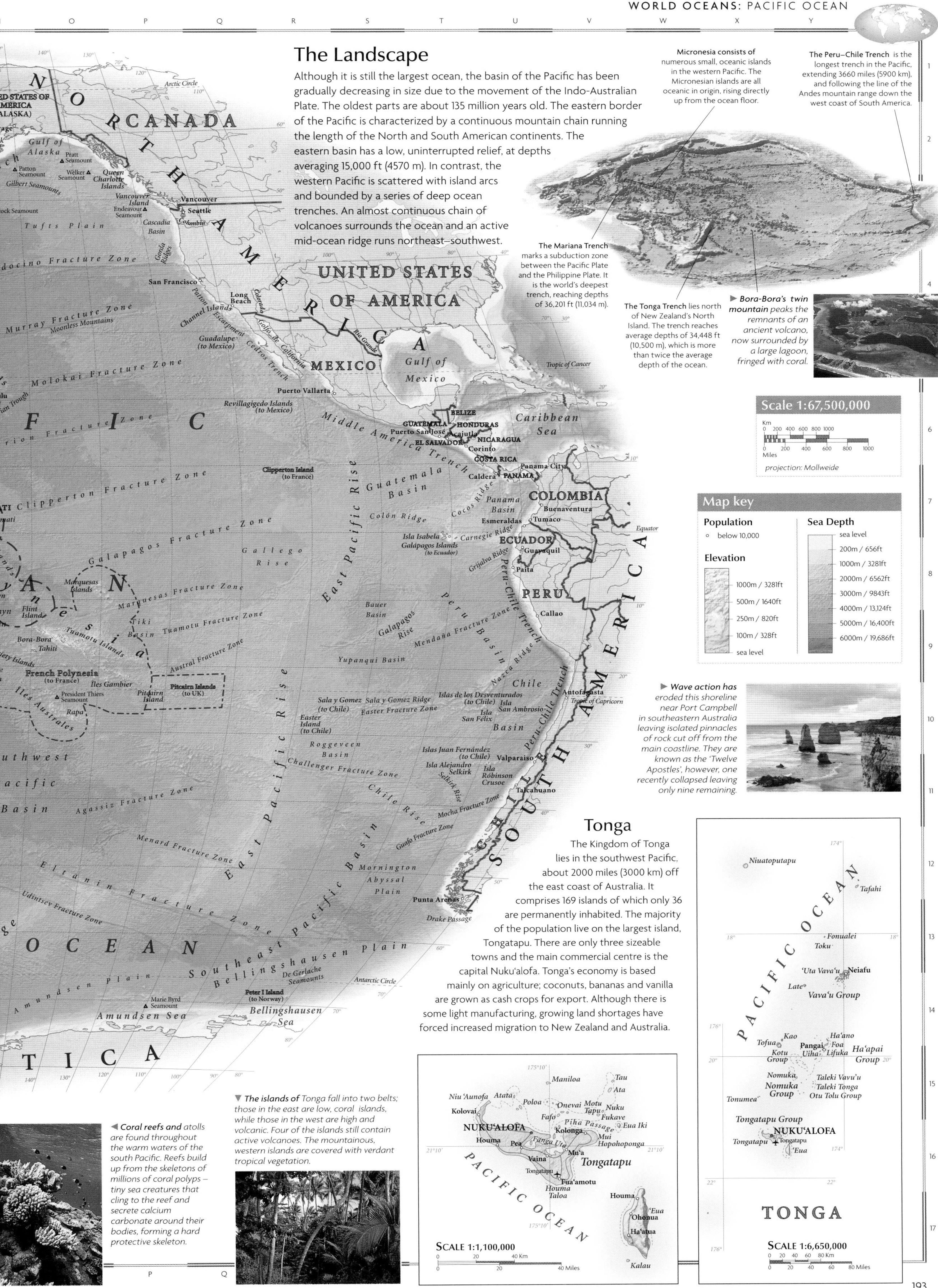

The Landscape

Although it is still the largest ocean, the basin of the Pacific has been gradually decreasing in size due to the movement of the Indo-Australian Plate. The oldest parts are about 135 million years old. The eastern border of the Pacific is characterized by a continuous mountain chain running the length of the North and South American continents. The eastern basin has a low, uninterrupted relief, at depths averaging 15,000 ft (4570 m). In contrast, the western Pacific is scattered with island arcs and bounded by a series of deep ocean trenches. An almost continuous chain of volcanoes surrounds the ocean and an active mid-ocean ridge runs northeast–southwest.

Micronesia consists of numerous small, oceanic islands in the western Pacific. The Micronesian islands are all oceanic in origin, rising directly up from the ocean floor.

The Peru–Chile Trench is the longest trench in the Pacific, extending 3660 miles (5900 km), and following the line of the Andes mountain range down the west coast of South America.

The Mariana Trench marks a subduction zone between the Pacific Plate and the Philippine Plate. It is the world's deepest trench, reaching depths of 36,201 ft (11,034 m).

The Tonga Trench lies north of New Zealand's North Island. The trench reaches average depths of 34,448 ft (10,500 m), which is more than twice the average depth of the ocean.

► *Bora-Bora's twin* ***mountain*** *peaks the remnants of an ancient volcano, now surrounded by a large lagoon, fringed with coral.*

Scale 1:67,500,000

projection: Mollweide

Map key

Population: below 10,000

Elevation: 1000m / 3281ft; 500m / 1640ft; 250m / 820ft; 100m / 328ft; sea level

Sea Depth: sea level; 200m / 656ft; 1000m / 3281ft; 2000m / 6562ft; 3000m / 9843ft; 4000m / 13,124ft; 5000m / 16,400ft; 6000m / 19,686ft

► *Wave action has eroded this shoreline near Port Campbell in southeastern Australia leaving isolated pinnacles of rock cut off from the main coastline. They are known as the 'Twelve Apostles', however, one recently collapsed leaving only nine remaining.*

Tonga

The Kingdom of Tonga lies in the southwest Pacific, about 2000 miles (3000 km) off the east coast of Australia. It comprises 169 islands of which only 36 are permanently inhabited. The majority of the population live on the largest island, Tongatapu. There are only three sizeable towns and the main commercial centre is the capital Nuku'alofa. Tonga's economy is based mainly on agriculture; coconuts, bananas and vanilla are grown as cash crops for export. Although there is some light manufacturing, growing land shortages have forced increased migration to New Zealand and Australia.

◄ ***Coral reefs and*** *atolls are found throughout the warm waters of the south Pacific. Reefs build up from the skeletons of millions of coral polyps – tiny sea creatures that cling to the reef and secrete calcium carbonate around their bodies, forming a hard protective skeleton.*

▼ ***The islands of*** *Tonga fall into two belts; those in the east are low, coral islands, while those in the west are high and volcanic. Four of the islands still contain active volcanoes. The mountainous, western islands are covered with verdant tropical vegetation.*

SCALE 1:1,100,000

TONGA

SCALE 1:6,650,000

Antarctica

The ice-covered continent of Antarctica, which is the Earth's most southerly region, has for over 200 years drawn explorers and entrepreneurs seeking challenge and riches in its wintry lands. The extreme climate has deterred any large-scale settlement of the continent, and though commercial hunters built outposts in the past, habitation is now limited to scientific bases. The Antarctic Treaty, which came into force in 1961, provides for international governance and scientific co-operation in place of potential territorial conflict.

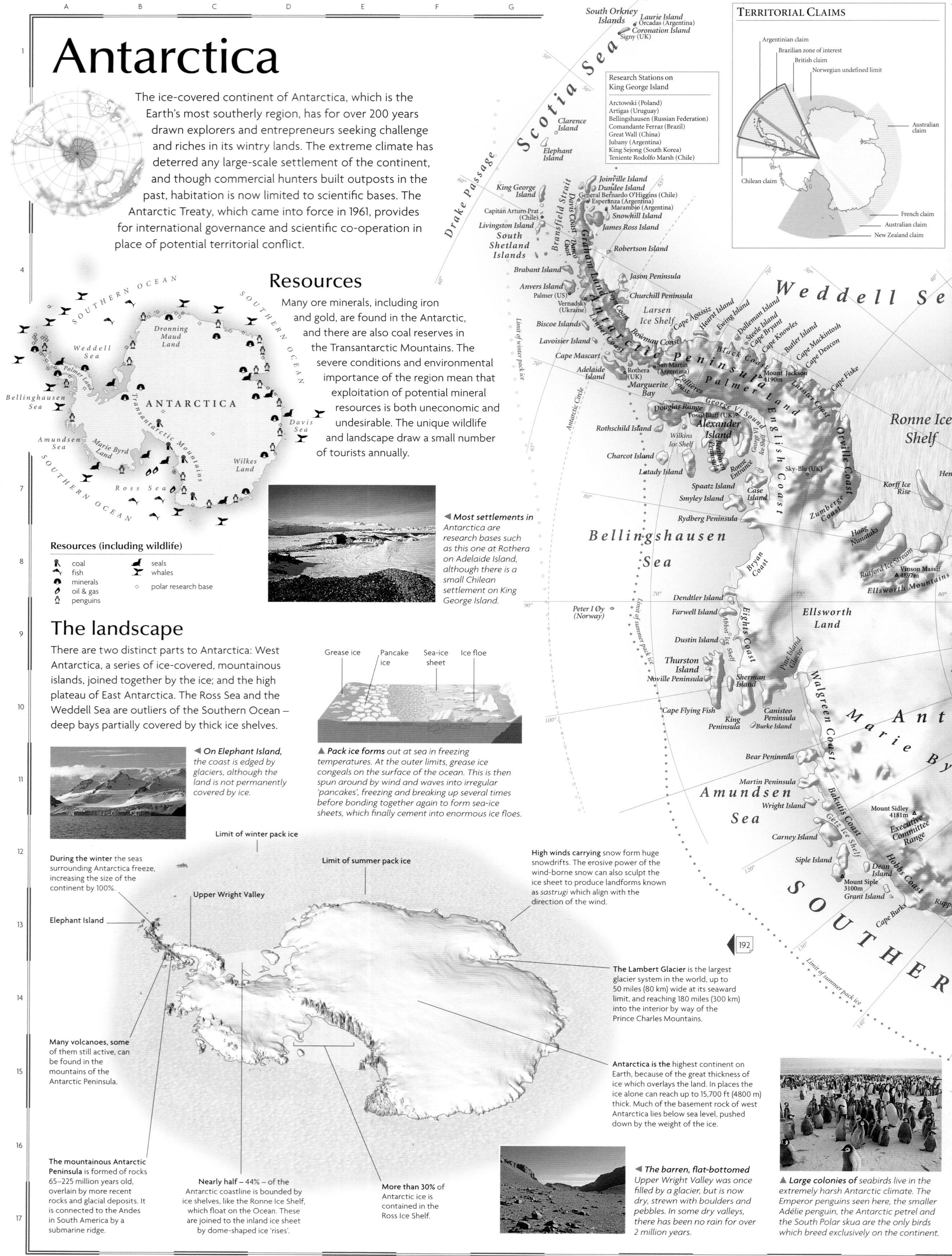

TERRITORIAL CLAIMS
Argentinian claim
Brazilian zone of interest
British claim
Norwegian undefined limit
Australian claim
Chilean claim
French claim
Australian claim
New Zealand claim
Research Stations on King George Island
Arctowski (Poland)
Artigas (Uruguay)
Bellingshausen (Russian Federation)
Comandante Ferraz (Brazil)
Great Wall (China)
Jubany (Argentina)
King Sejong (South Korea)
Teniente Rodolfo Marsh (Chile)
Resources (including wildlife)
coal
fish
minerals
oil & gas
penguins
seals
whales
polar research base
Grease ice
Pancake ice
Sea-ice sheet
Ice floe
Limit of winter pack ice
Limit of summer pack ice
Upper Wright Valley
Elephant Island

Resources

Many ore minerals, including iron and gold, are found in the Antarctic, and there are also coal reserves in the Transantarctic Mountains. The severe conditions and environmental importance of the region mean that exploitation of potential mineral resources is both uneconomic and undesirable. The unique wildlife and landscape draw a small number of tourists annually.

◀ *Most settlements in Antarctica are research bases such as this one at Rothera on Adelaide Island, although there is a small Chilean settlement on King George Island.*

The landscape

There are two distinct parts to Antarctica: West Antarctica, a series of ice-covered, mountainous islands, joined together by the ice; and the high plateau of East Antarctica. The Ross Sea and the Weddell Sea are outliers of the Southern Ocean – deep bays partially covered by thick ice shelves.

◀ ***On Elephant Island,** the coast is edged by glaciers, although the land is not permanently covered by ice.*

▲ ***Pack ice forms** out at sea in freezing temperatures. At the outer limits, grease ice congeals on the surface of the ocean. This is then spun around by wind and waves into irregular 'pancakes', freezing and breaking up several times before bonding together again to form sea-ice sheets, which finally cement into enormous ice floes.*

During the winter the seas surrounding Antarctica freeze, increasing the size of the continent by 100%.

High winds carrying snow form huge snowdrifts. The erosive power of the wind-borne snow can also sculpt the ice sheet to produce landforms known as *sastrugi* which align with the direction of the wind.

The Lambert Glacier is the largest glacier system in the world, up to 50 miles (80 km) wide at its seaward limit, and reaching 180 miles (300 km) into the interior by way of the Prince Charles Mountains.

Many volcanoes, some of them still active, can be found in the mountains of the Antarctic Peninsula.

Antarctica is the highest continent on Earth, because of the great thickness of ice which overlays the land. In places the ice alone can reach up to 15,700 ft (4800 m) thick. Much of the basement rock of west Antarctica lies below sea level, pushed down by the weight of the ice.

The mountainous Antarctic Peninsula is formed of rocks 65–225 million years old, overlain by more recent rocks and glacial deposits. It is connected to the Andes in South America by a submarine ridge.

Nearly half – 44% – of the Antarctic coastline is bounded by ice shelves, like the Ronne Ice Shelf, which float on the Ocean. These are joined to the inland ice sheet by dome-shaped ice 'rises'.

More than 30% of Antarctic ice is contained in the Ross Ice Shelf.

◀ ***The barren, flat-bottomed** Upper Wright Valley was once filled by a glacier, but is now dry, strewn with boulders and pebbles. In some dry valleys, there has been no rain for over 2 million years.*

▲ ***Large colonies of** seabirds live in the extremely harsh Antarctic climate. The Emperor penguins seen here, the smaller Adélie penguin, the Antarctic petrel and the South Polar skua are the only birds which breed exclusively on the continent.*

192

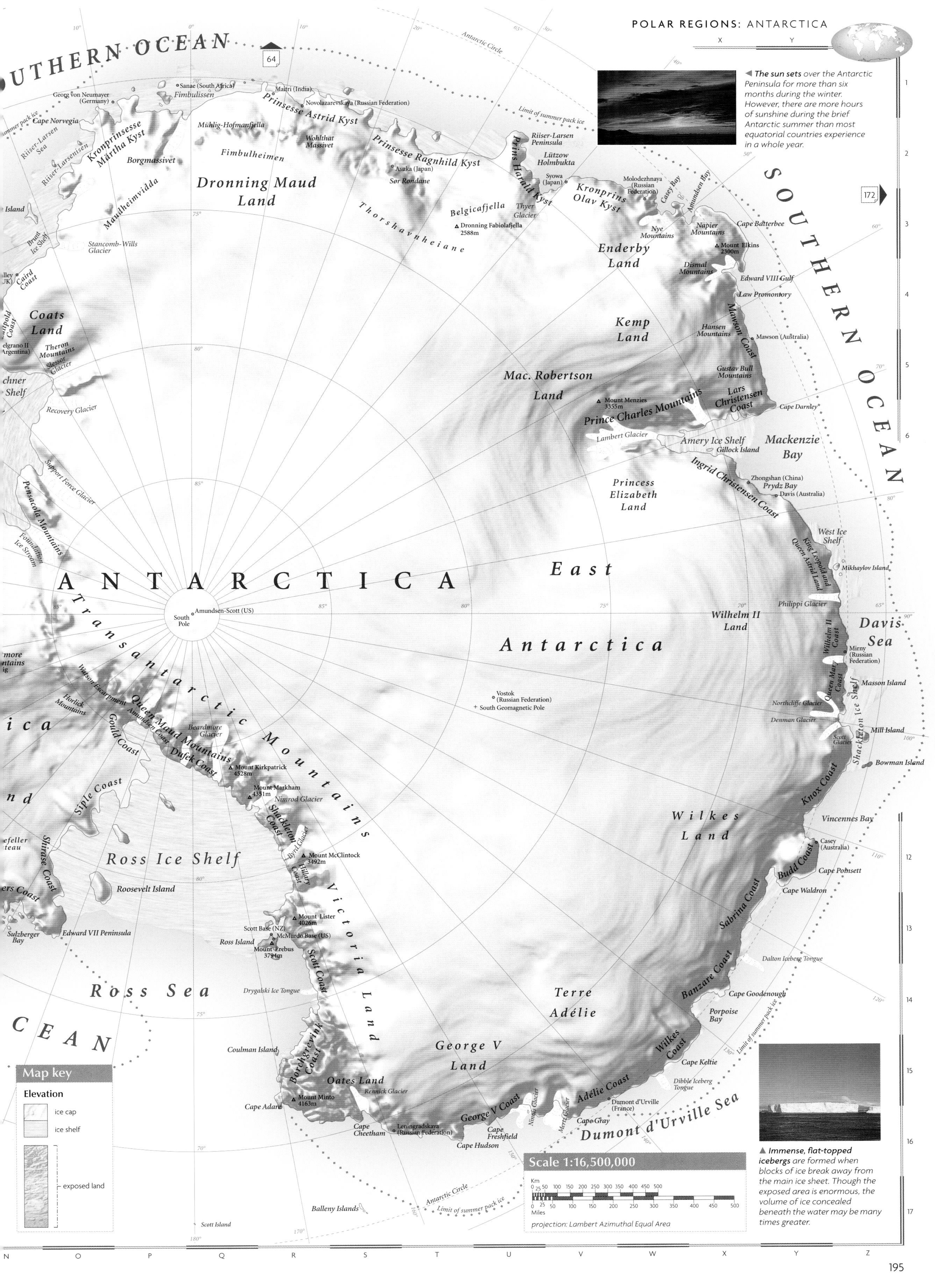
SOUTHERN OCEAN
64
Sanae (South Africa)
Fimbulisen
Maitri (India)
Novolazarevskaya (Russian Federation)
Georg von Neumayer (Germany)
Prinsesse Astrid Kyst
Cape Norvegia
Riiser-Larsen Sea
Riiser-Larsenisen
Kronprinsesse Märtha Kyst
Mühlig-Hofmanfjella
Wohlthat Massivet
Prinsesse Ragnhild Kyst
Asuka (Japan)
Sør Rondane
Limit of summer pack ice
Riiser-Larsen Peninsula
Lützow Holmbukta
Prins Harald Kyst
Syowa (Japan)
Borgmassivet
Fimbulheimen
Dronning Maud Land
Maudheimvidda
Thorshavnheiane
Belgicafjella
Dronning Fabiolafjella 2588m
Thyer Glacier
Kronprins Olav Kyst
Molodezhnaya (Russian Federation)
Casey Bay
Amundsen Bay
Antarctic Circle
Island
Brunt Ice Shelf
Stancomb-Wills Glacier
Caird Coast
Coats Land
Theron Mountains
Slessor Glacier
Recovery Glacier
Nye Mountains
Napier Mountains
Cape Batterbee
Mount Elkins 2300m
Enderby Land
Dismal Mountains
Edward VIII Gulf
Law Promontory
Kemp Land
Hansen Mountains
Mawson Coast
Mawson (Australia)
Gustav Bull Mountains
Mac. Robertson Land
Mount Menzies 3355m
Prince Charles Mountains
Lars Christensen Coast
Cape Darnley
Lambert Glacier
Amery Ice Shelf
Gillock Island
Mackenzie Bay
SOUTHERN OCEAN
172
Ingrid Christensen Coast
Zhongshan (China)
Prydz Bay
Davis (Australia)
Princess Elizabeth Land
Support Force Glacier
Pensacola Mountains
Foundation Ice Stream
West Ice Shelf
King Leopold and Queen Astrid Land
Mikhaylov Island
ANTARCTICA
East
South Pole
Amundsen-Scott (US)
Philippi Glacier
Wilhelm II Land
Davis Sea
Antarctica
Wilhelm II Coast
Mirny (Russian Federation)
Transantarctic Mountains
Watson Escarpment
Horlick Mountains
Queen Maud Mountains
Amundsen Coast
Gould Coast
Vostok (Russian Federation)
South Geomagnetic Pole
Queen Mary Coast
Masson Island
Northcliffe Glacier
Denman Glacier
Shackleton Ice Shelf
Mill Island
Scott Glacier
Bowman Island
Beardmore Glacier
Dufek Coast
Mount Kirkpatrick 4528m
Mount Markham 4351m
Nimrod Glacier
Siple Coast
Shackleton Coast
Knox Coast
Wilkes Land
Vincennes Bay
Ross Ice Shelf
Byrd Glacier
Mount McClintock 3492m
Hillary Coast
Casey (Australia)
Budd Coast
Cape Poinsett
Shirase Coast
Roosevelt Island
Victoria Land
Cape Waldron
Sabrina Coast
Mount Lister 4026m
Scott Base (NZ)
McMurdo Base (US)
Ross Island
Mount Erebus 3794m
Sulzberger Bay
Edward VII Peninsula
Dalton Iceberg Tongue
Scott Coast
Banzare Coast
Ross Sea
Drygalski Ice Tongue
Terre Adélie
Cape Goodenough
Porpoise Bay
Borchgrevink Coast
George V Land
Wilkes Coast
Coulman Island
Limit of summer pack ice
Cape Keltie
Oates Land
Rennick Glacier
Dibble Iceberg Tongue
Mount Minto 4163m
Adélie Coast
Dumont d'Urville (France)
Cape Adare
George V Coast
Ninnis Glacier
Mertz Glacier
Cape Gray
Dumont d'Urville Sea
Cape Cheetham
Leningradskaya (Russian Federation)
Cape Freshfield
Cape Hudson
Antarctic Circle
Balleny Islands
Scott Island
Map key
Elevation
ice cap
ice shelf
exposed land
Scale 1:16,500,000
Km
Miles
projection: Lambert Azimuthal Equal Area

◀ ***The sun sets*** *over the Antarctic Peninsula for more than six months during the winter. However, there are more hours of sunshine during the brief Antarctic summer than most equatorial countries experience in a whole year.*

▲ ***Immense, flat-topped icebergs*** *are formed when blocks of ice break away from the main ice sheet. Though the exposed area is enormous, the volume of ice concealed beneath the water may be many times greater.*

The Arctic

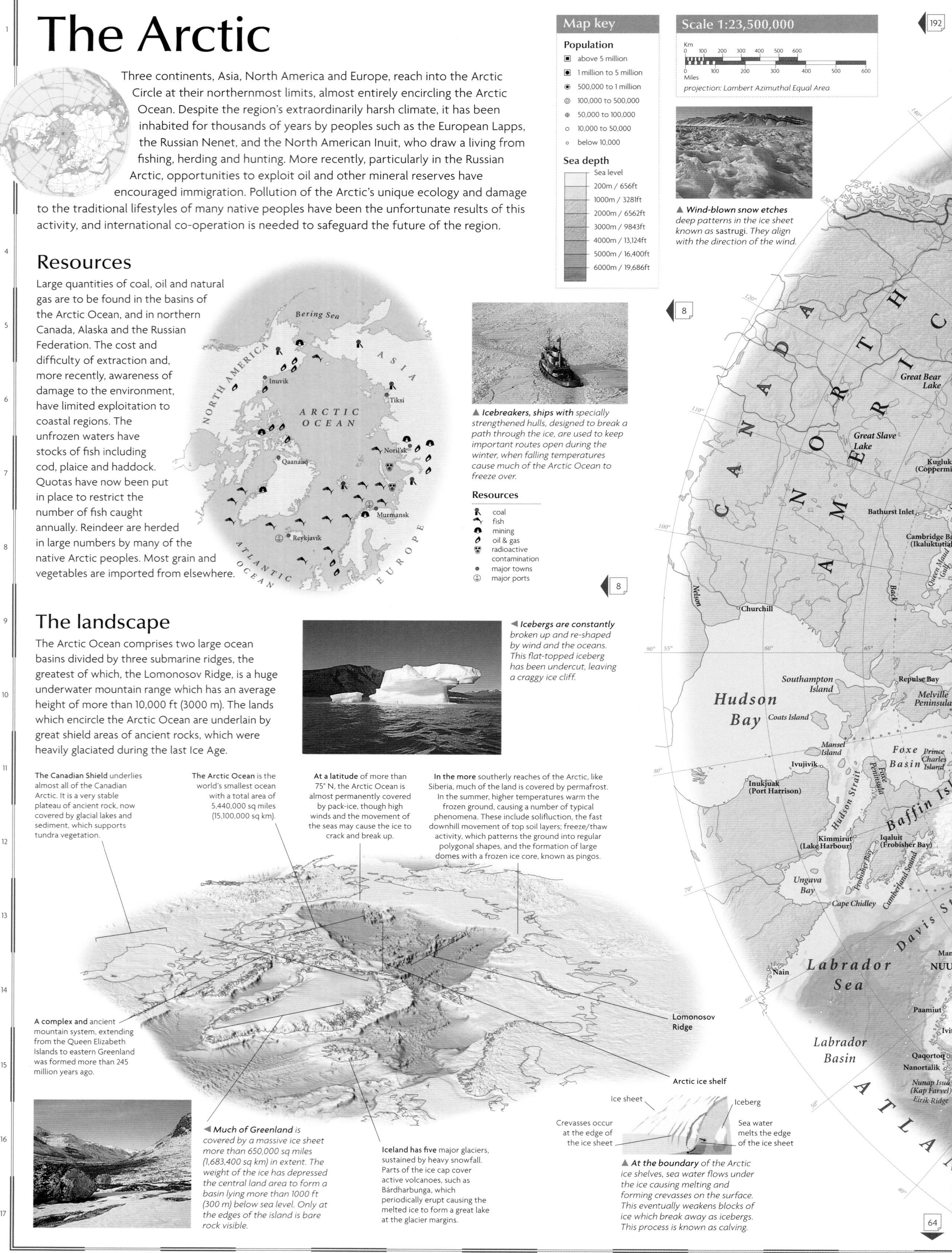

Map key
Population
above 5 million
1 million to 5 million
500,000 to 1 million
100,000 to 500,000
50,000 to 100,000
10,000 to 50,000
below 10,000
Sea depth
Sea level
200m / 656ft
1000m / 3281ft
2000m / 6562ft
3000m / 9843ft
4000m / 13,124ft
5000m / 16,400ft
6000m / 19,686ft
Scale 1:23,500,000
projection: Lambert Azimuthal Equal Area
Bering Sea
NORTH AMERICA
ASIA
ARCTIC OCEAN
Inuvik
Tiksi
Noril'sk
Qaanaaq
Murmansk
Reykjavík
ATLANTIC OCEAN
EUROPE
Resources
coal
fish
mining
oil & gas
radioactive contamination
major towns
major ports
Lomonosov Ridge
Arctic ice shelf
Ice sheet
Iceberg
Crevasses occur at the edge of the ice sheet
Sea water melts the edge of the ice sheet
CANADA
NORTH AMERICA
Great Bear Lake
Great Slave Lake
Kugluktuk (Coppermine)
Bathurst Inlet
Cambridge Bay (Ikaluktutiak)
Queen Maud Gulf
Back
Nelson
Churchill
Southampton Island
Hudson Bay
Coats Island
Repulse Bay
Melville Peninsula
Mansel Island
Ivujivik
Foxe Basin
Prince Charles Island
Foxe Peninsula
Inukjuak (Port Harrison)
Hudson Strait
Baffin Island
Kimmirut (Lake Harbour)
Iqaluit (Frobisher Bay)
Frobisher Bay
Cumberland Sound
Ungava Bay
Cape Chidley
Davis Strait
Nain
Labrador Sea
Paamiut
Labrador Basin
Qaqortoq
Nanortalik
Nunap Isua (Kap Farvel)
Eirik Ridge
ATLANTIC

Three continents, Asia, North America and Europe, reach into the Arctic Circle at their northernmost limits, almost entirely encircling the Arctic Ocean. Despite the region's extraordinarily harsh climate, it has been inhabited for thousands of years by peoples such as the European Lapps, the Russian Nenet, and the North American Inuit, who draw a living from fishing, herding and hunting. More recently, particularly in the Russian Arctic, opportunities to exploit oil and other mineral reserves have encouraged immigration. Pollution of the Arctic's unique ecology and damage to the traditional lifestyles of many native peoples have been the unfortunate results of this activity, and international co-operation is needed to safeguard the future of the region.

▲ **Wind-blown snow etches** *deep patterns in the ice sheet known as sastrugi. They align with the direction of the wind.*

Resources

Large quantities of coal, oil and natural gas are to be found in the basins of the Arctic Ocean, and in northern Canada, Alaska and the Russian Federation. The cost and difficulty of extraction and, more recently, awareness of damage to the environment, have limited exploitation to coastal regions. The unfrozen waters have stocks of fish including cod, plaice and haddock. Quotas have now been put in place to restrict the number of fish caught annually. Reindeer are herded in large numbers by many of the native Arctic peoples. Most grain and vegetables are imported from elsewhere.

▲ **Icebreakers, ships with** *specially strengthened hulls, designed to break a path through the ice, are used to keep important routes open during the winter, when falling temperatures cause much of the Arctic Ocean to freeze over.*

The landscape

The Arctic Ocean comprises two large ocean basins divided by three submarine ridges, the greatest of which, the Lomonosov Ridge, is a huge underwater mountain range which has an average height of more than 10,000 ft (3000 m). The lands which encircle the Arctic Ocean are underlain by great shield areas of ancient rocks, which were heavily glaciated during the last Ice Age.

◀ **Icebergs are constantly** *broken up and re-shaped by wind and the oceans. This flat-topped iceberg has been undercut, leaving a craggy ice cliff.*

The Canadian Shield underlies almost all of the Canadian Arctic. It is a very stable plateau of ancient rock, now covered by glacial lakes and sediment, which supports tundra vegetation.

The Arctic Ocean is the world's smallest ocean with a total area of 5,440,000 sq miles (15,100,000 sq km).

At a latitude of more than 75° N, the Arctic Ocean is almost permanently covered by pack-ice, though high winds and the movement of the seas may cause the ice to crack and break up.

In the more southerly reaches of the Arctic, like Siberia, much of the land is covered by permafrost. In the summer, higher temperatures warm the frozen ground, causing a number of typical phenomena. These include solifluction, the fast downhill movement of top soil layers; freeze/thaw activity, which patterns the ground into regular polygonal shapes, and the formation of large domes with a frozen ice core, known as pingos.

A complex and ancient mountain system, extending from the Queen Elizabeth Islands to eastern Greenland was formed more than 245 million years ago.

◀ **Much of Greenland** *is covered by a massive ice sheet more than 650,000 sq miles (1,683,400 sq km) in extent. The weight of the ice has depressed the central land area to form a basin lying more than 1000 ft (300 m) below sea level. Only at the edges of the island is bare rock visible.*

Iceland has five major glaciers, sustained by heavy snowfall. Parts of the ice cap cover active volcanoes, such as Bárdharbunga, which periodically erupt causing the melted ice to form a great lake at the glacier margins.

▲ **At the boundary** *of the Arctic ice shelves, sea water flows under the ice causing melting and forming crevasses on the surface. This eventually weakens blocks of ice which break away as icebergs. This process is known as calving.*

192
8
8
64

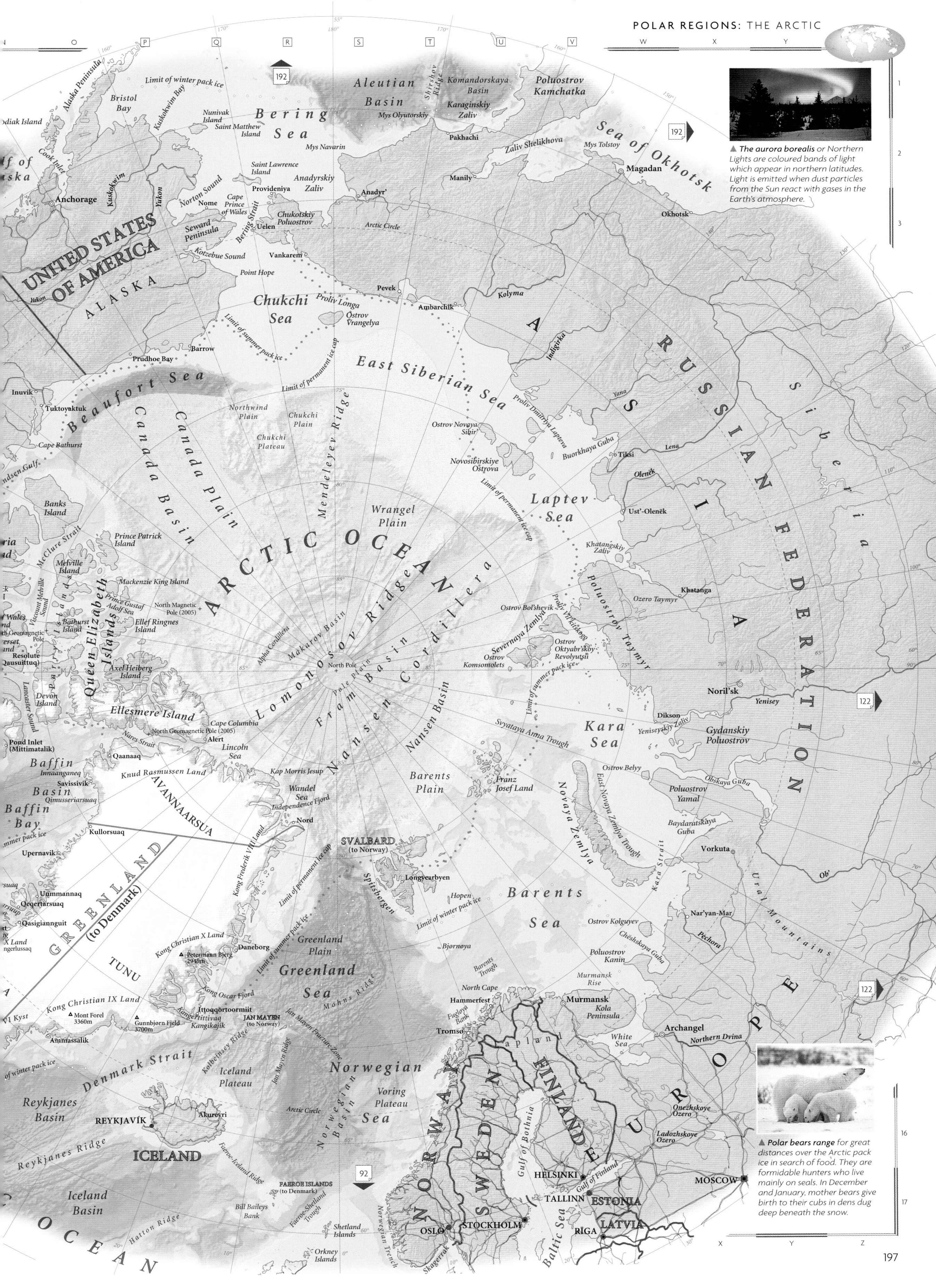

Aleutian Basin
Bering Sea
Bristol Bay
Alaska Peninsula
Kuskokwim Bay
Limit of winter pack ice
Nunivak Island
Saint Matthew Island
Saint Lawrence Island
Shirshov Ridge
Komandorskaya Basin
Karaginskiy Zaliv
Mys Olyutorskiy
Poluostrov Kamchatka
Pakhachi
Mys Navarin
Anadyrskiy Zaliv
Anadyr'
Manily
Zaliv Shelikhova
Mys Tolstoy
Magadan
Sea of Okhotsk
Okhotsk
Anchorage
Cook Inlet
Kuskokwim
Yukon
Norton Sound
Nome
Cape Prince of Wales
Provideniya
Bering Strait
Chukotskiy Poluostrov
Uelen
Arctic Circle
Seward Peninsula
Kotzebue Sound
Vankarem
Point Hope
UNITED STATES OF AMERICA
ALASKA
Chukchi Sea
Proliv Longa
Ostrov Vrangelya
Pevek
Ambarchik
Kolyma
Limit of summer pack ice
Limit of permanent ice cap
Barrow
Prudhoe Bay
Beaufort Sea
Inuvik
Tuktoyaktuk
Cape Bathurst
East Siberian Sea
Indigirka
Northwind Plain
Chukchi Plain
Chukchi Plateau
Canada Basin
Canada Plain
Mendeleyev Ridge
Ostrov Novaya Sibir'
Novosibirskiye Ostrova
Proliv Dmitriya Lapteva
Buorkhaya Guba
Tiksi
Yana
Lena
Olenëk
RUSSIAN FEDERATION
Siberia
Laptev Sea
Ust'-Olenëk
Banks Island
Wrangel Plain
ARCTIC OCEAN
Prince Patrick Island
McClure Strait
Melville Island
Viscount Melville Sound
Mackenzie King Island
Prince Gustaf Adolf Sea
North Magnetic Pole (2005)
Ellef Ringnes Island
Bathurst Island
Queen Elizabeth Islands
Parry Islands
Resolute (Qausuittuq)
Axel Heiberg Island
Lomonosov Ridge
Makarov Basin
Alpha Cordillera
North Pole
Pole Plain
Fram Basin
Nansen Cordillera
Nansen Basin
Khatangskiy Zaliv
Poluostrov Taymyr
Khatanga
Ozero Taymyr
Ostrov Bol'shevik
Severnaya Zemlya
Ostrov Oktyabr'skoy Revolyutsii
Ostrov Komsomolets
Proliv Vil'kitskogo
Noril'sk
Yenisey
Dikson
Yeniseyskiy Zaliv
Gydanskiy Poluostrov
Kara Sea
Svyataya Anna Trough
Devon Island
Lancaster Sound
Ellesmere Island
Cape Columbia
North Geomagnetic Pole (2005)
Alert
Nares Strait
Lincoln Sea
Pond Inlet (Mittimatalik)
Baffin Basin
Qaanaaq
Knud Rasmussen Land
Savissivik
Baffin Bay
Kap Morris Jesup
Wandel Sea
Independence Fjord
Nord
Barents Plain
Franz Josef Land
Novaya Zemlya
East Novaya Zemlya Trough
Ostrov Belyy
Obskaya Guba
Poluostrov Yamal
Baydaratskaya Guba
Vorkuta
Kara Strait
Ob'
Ural Mountains
AVANNAARSUA
Kullorsuaq
Upernavik
SVALBARD (to Norway)
Spitsbergen
Longyearbyen
Hopen
Limit of winter pack ice
Barents Sea
Ostrov Kolguyev
Nar'yan-Mar
Pechora
Chëshskaya Guba
Poluostrov Kanin
GREENLAND (to Denmark)
Uummannaq
Qeqertarsuaq
Qasigiannguit
Kong Frederik VIII Land
Kong Christian X Land
Daneborg
Petermann Bjerg 2940m
Greenland Plain
Greenland Sea
Bjørnøya
Barents Trough
Murmansk Rise
TUNU
Kong Oscar Fjord
Ittoqqortoormiit
Kangertittivaq
JAN MAYEN (to Norway)
Mohns Ridge
North Cape
Hammerfest
Murmansk
Kola Peninsula
Kong Christian IX Land
Mont Forel 3360m
Gunnbjørn Fjeld 3700m
Ammassalik
Jan Mayen Fracture Zone
Fugløya Bank
Tromsø
White Sea
Archangel
Northern Dvina
Denmark Strait
Kolbeinsey Ridge
Iceland Plateau
Jan Mayen Ridge
Norwegian Sea
Lapland
FINLAND
SWEDEN
NORWAY
EUROPE
Voring Plateau
Reykjanes Basin
REYKJAVÍK
Akureyri
Arctic Circle
Norwegian Basin
Gulf of Bothnia
Onezhskoye Ozero
Ladozhskoye Ozero
Reykjanes Ridge
ICELAND
Faeroe-Iceland Ridge
FAEROE ISLANDS (to Denmark)
HELSINKI
Gulf of Finland
TALLINN
ESTONIA
MOSCOW
Iceland Basin
Bill Baileys Bank
Faeroe-Shetland Trough
Norwegian Trench
Shetland Islands
OSLO
STOCKHOLM
Baltic Sea
RIGA
LATVIA
Hatton Ridge
Orkney Islands
Skagerrak
OCEAN

▲ **The aurora borealis** *or Northern Lights are coloured bands of light which appear in northern latitudes. Light is emitted when dust particles from the Sun react with gases in the Earth's atmosphere.*

▲ **Polar bears range** *for great distances over the Arctic pack ice in search of food. They are formidable hunters who live mainly on seals. In December and January, mother bears give birth to their cubs in dens dug deep beneath the snow.*

Geographical comparisons

Largest countries

Russian Federation	6,592,735 sq miles	(17,075,200 sq km)
Canada	3,855,171 sq miles	(9,984,670 sq km)
USA	3,717,792 sq miles	(9,629,091 sq km)
China	3,705,386 sq miles	(9,596,960 sq km)
Brazil	3,286,470 sq miles	(8,511,965 sq km)
Australia	2,967,893 sq miles	(7,686,850 sq km)
India	1,269,339 sq miles	(3,287,590 sq km)
Argentina	1,068,296 sq miles	(2,766,890 sq km)
Kazakhstan	1,049,150 sq miles	(2,717,300 sq km)
Algeria	919,590 sq miles	(2,381,740 sq km)

Smallest countries

Vatican City	0.17 sq miles	(0.44 sq km)
Monaco	0.75 sq miles	(1.95 sq km)
Nauru	8.2 sq miles	(21.2 sq km)
Tuvalu	10 sq miles	(26 sq km)
San Marino	24 sq miles	(61 sq km)
Liechtenstein	62 sq miles	(160 sq km)
Marshall Islands	70 sq miles	(181 sq km)
St. Kitts & Nevis	101 sq miles	(261 sq km)
Maldives	116 sq miles	(300 sq km)
Malta	124 sq miles	(320 sq km)

Largest islands

To the nearest 1000 – or 100,000 for the largest

Greenland	849,400 sq miles	(2,200,000 sq km)
New Guinea	312,000 sq miles	(808,000 sq km)
Borneo	292,222 sq miles	(757,050 sq km)
Madagascar	229,300 sq miles	(594,000 sq km)
Sumatra	202,300 sq miles	(524,000 sq km)
Baffin Island	183,800 sq miles	(476,000 sq km)
Honshu	88,800 sq miles	(230,000 sq km)
Britain	88,700 sq miles	(229,800 sq km)
Victoria Island	81,900 sq miles	(212,000 sq km)
Ellesmere Island	75,700 sq miles	(196,000 sq km)

Richest countries

GNI per capita, in US$

Monaco	188,150
Liechtenstein	137,070
Norway	88,890
Qatar	80,440
Luxembourg	78,130
Switzerland	76,380
Denmark	60,390
Sweden	53,230
Netherlands	49,730
Kuwait	48,900

Poorest countries

GNI per capita, in US$

Dem. Rep. Congo	190
Liberia	240
Burundi	250
Sierra Leone	340
Malawi	340
Niger	360
Ethiopia	400
Afghanistan	400
Madagascar	430
Eritrea	430
Guinea	440
Mozambique	470

Most populous countries

China	1,347,300,000
India	1,240,000,000
USA	314,500,000
Indonesia	237,600,000
Brazil	193,300,000
Pakistan	180,800,000
Nigeria	166,500,000
Bangladesh	152,500,000
Russian Federation	143,200,000
Japan	127,500,000

Least populous countries

Vatican City	821
Nauru	9,378
Tuvalu	10,619
Palau	21,032
Monaco	30,510
San Marino	32,140
Liechtenstein	36,713
St Kitts & Nevis	50,726
Marshall Islands	64,480
Dominica	73,126
Andorra	85,082
Antigua & Barbuda	89,018

Most densely populated countries

Monaco	40,680 people per sq mile	(15,641 per sq km)
Singapore	22,034 people per sq mile	(8525 per sq km)
Vatican City	4918 people per sq mile	(1900 per sq km)
Bahrain	4762 people per sq mile	(1841 per sq km)
Maldives	3400 people per sq mile	(1315 per sq km)
Malta	3226 people per sq mile	(1250 per sq km)
Bangladesh	2911 people per sq mile	(1124 per sq km)
Taiwan	1860 people per sq mile	(718 per sq km)
Mauritius	1811 people per sq mile	(699 per sq km)
Barbados	1807 people per sq mile	(698 per sq km)

Most sparsely populated countries

Mongolia	5 people per sq mile	(2 per sq km)
Namibia	7 people per sq mile	(3 per sq km)
Australia	8 people per sq mile	(3 per sq km)
Surinam	8 people per sq mile	(3 per sq km)
Iceland	8 people per sq mile	(3 per sq km)
Mauriania	9 people per sq mile	(4 per sq km)
Botswana	9 people per sq mile	(4 per sq km)
Libya	9 people per sq mile	(4 per sq km)
Canada	10 people per sq mile	(4 per sq km)
Guyana	11 people per sq mile	(4 per sq km)

Most widely spoken languages

1. Chinese (Mandarin)	6. Arabic
2. English	7. Bengali
3. Hindi	8. Portuguese
4. Spanish	9. Malay-Indonesian
5. Russian	10. French

Largest conurbations

Population

Tokyo	36,900,000
Delhi	21,900,000
Mexico City	20,100,000
New York - Newark	20,100,000
São Paulo	19,600,000
Shanghai	19,500,000
Mumbai	19,400,000
Beijing	15,000,000
Dhaka	14,900,000
Kolkata	14,300,000
Karachi	13,500,000
Buenos Aires	13,400,000
Los Angeles	13,200,000
Rio de Janeiro	11,800,000
Manilla	11,600,000
Moscow	11,500,000
Osaka	11,400,000
Cairo	11,400,000
Istanbul	10,900,000
Lagos	10,800,000
Paris	10,500,000
Guangzhou	10,500,000
Shenzhen	10,200,000
Seoul	9,700,000
Chongqing	9,700,000

Countries with the most land borders

14: China	(Afghanistan, Bhutan, Burma, India, Kazakhstan, Kyrgyzstan, Laos, Mongolia, Nepal, North Korea, Pakistan, Russian Federation, Tajikistan, Vietnam)
14: Russian Federation	(Azerbaijan, Belarus, China, Estonia, Finland, Georgia, Kazakhstan, Latvia, Lithuania, Mongolia, North Korea, Norway, Poland, Ukraine)
10: Brazil	(Argentina, Bolivia, Colombia, French Guiana, Guyana, Paraguay, Peru, Surinam, Uruguay, Venezuela)
9: Congo, Dem. Rep.	(Angola, Burundi, Central African Republic, Congo, Rwanda, South Sudan, Tanzania, Uganda, Zambia)
9: Germany	(Austria, Belgium, Czech Republic, Denmark, France, Luxembourg, Netherlands, Poland, Switzerland)
8: Austria	(Czech Republic, Germany, Hungary, Italy, Liechtenstein, Slovakia, Slovenia, Switzerland)
8: France	(Andorra, Belgium, Germany, Italy, Luxembourg, Monaco, Spain, Switzerland)
8: Tanzania	(Burundi, Dem. Rep. Congo, Kenya, Malawi, Mozambique, Rwanda, Uganda, Zambia)
8: Turkey	(Armenia, Azerbaijan, Bulgaria, Georgia, Greece, Iran, Iraq, Syria)
8: Zambia	(Angola, Botswana, Dem. Rep.Congo, Malawi, Mozambique, Namibia, Tanzania, Zimbabwe)

Longest rivers

Nile (NE Africa)	4160 miles	(6695 km)
Amazon (South America)	4049 miles	(6516 km)
Yangtze (China)	3915 miles	(6299 km)
Mississippi/Missouri (USA)	3710 miles	(5969 km)
Ob'-Irtysh (Russian Federation)	3461 miles	(5570 km)
Yellow River (China)	3395 miles	(5464 km)
Congo (Central Africa)	2900 miles	(4667 km)
Mekong (Southeast Asia)	2749 miles	(4425 km)
Lena (Russian Federation)	2734 miles	(4400 km)
Mackenzie (Canada)	2640 miles	(4250 km)
Yenisey (Russian Federation)	2541 miles	(4090km)

Highest mountains

Height above sea level

Everest	29,029 ft	(8848 m)
K2	28,253 ft	(8611 m)
Kangchenjunga I	28,210 ft	(8598 m)
Makalu I	27,767 ft	(8463 m)
Cho Oyu	26,907 ft	(8201 m)
Dhaulagiri I	26,796 ft	(8167 m)
Manaslu I	26,783 ft	(8163 m)
Nanga Parbat I	26,661 ft	(8126 m)
Annapurna I	26,547 ft	(8091 m)
Gasherbrum I	26,471 ft	(8068 m)

Largest bodies of inland water

With area and depth

Caspian Sea	143,243 sq miles (371,000 sq km)	3215 ft (980 m)
Lake Superior	31,151 sq miles (83,270 sq km)	1289 ft (393 m)
Lake Victoria	26,828 sq miles (69,484 sq km)	328 ft (100 m)
Lake Huron	23,436 sq miles (60,700 sq km)	751 ft (229 m)
Lake Michigan	22,402 sq miles (58,020 sq km)	922 ft (281 m)
Lake Tanganyika	12,703 sq miles (32,900 sq km)	4700 ft (1435 m)
Great Bear Lake	12,274 sq miles (31,790 sq km)	1047 ft (319 m)
Lake Baikal	11,776 sq miles (30,500 sq km)	5712 ft (1741 m)
Great Slave Lake	10,981 sq miles (28,440 sq km)	459 ft (140 m)
Lake Erie	9,915 sq miles (25,680 sq km)	197 ft (60 m)

Deepest ocean features

Challenger Deep, Mariana Trench (Pacific)	36,201 ft	(11,034 m)
Vityaz III Depth, Tonga Trench (Pacific)	35,704 ft	(10,882 m)
Vityaz Depth, Kurile-Kamchatka Trench (Pacific)	34,588 ft	(10,542 m)
Cape Johnson Deep, Philippine Trench (Pacific)	34,441 ft	(10,497 m)
Kermadec Trench (Pacific)	32,964 ft	(10,047 m)
Ramapo Deep, Japan Trench (Pacific)	32,758 ft	(9984 m)
Milwaukee Deep, Puerto Rico Trench (Atlantic)	30,185 ft	(9200 m)
Argo Deep, Torres Trench (Pacific)	**30,070 ft**	**(9165 m)**
Meteor Depth, South Sandwich Trench (Atlantic)	30,000 ft	(9144 m)
Planet Deep, New Britain Trench (Pacific)	29,988 ft	(9140 m)

Greatest waterfalls

Mean flow of water

Boyoma (Dem. Rep. Congo)	600,400 cu. ft/sec	(17,000 cu.m/sec)
Khône (Laos/Cambodia)	410,000 cu. ft/sec	(11,600 cu.m/sec)
Niagara (USA/Canada)	195,000 cu. ft/sec	(5500 cu.m/sec)
Grande, Salto (Uruguay)	160,000 cu. ft/sec	(4500 cu.m/sec)
Paulo Afonso (Brazil)	100,000 cu. ft/sec	(2800 cu.m/sec)
Urubupungá, Salto do (Brazil)	97,000 cu. ft/sec	(2750 cu.m/sec)
Iguaçu (Argentina/Brazil)	62,000 cu. ft/sec	(1700 cu.m/sec)
Maribondo, Cachoeira do (Brazil)	53,000 cu. ft/sec	(1500 cu.m/sec)
Victoria (Zimbabwe)	39,000 cu. ft/sec	(1100 cu.m/sec)
Murchison Falls (Uganda)	42,000 cu. ft/sec	(1200 cu.m/sec)
Churchill (Canada)	35,000 cu. ft/sec	(1000 cu.m/sec)
Kaveri Falls (India)	33,000 cu. ft/sec	(900 cu.m/sec)

Highest waterfalls

* Indicates that the total height is a single leap

Angel (Venezuela)	3212 ft	(979 m)
Tugela (South Africa)	3110 ft	(948 m)
Utigard (Norway)	2625 ft	(800 m)
Mongefossen (Norway)	2539 ft	(774 m)
Mtarazi (Zimbabwe)	2500 ft	(762 m)
Yosemite (USA)	2425 ft	(739 m)
Ostre Mardola Foss (Norway)	2156 ft	(657 m)
Tyssestrengane (Norway)	2119 ft	(646 m)
***Cuquenan** (Venezuela)	2001 ft	(610 m)
Sutherland (New Zealand)	1903 ft	(580 m)
***Kjellfossen** (Norway)	1841 ft	(561 m)

Largest deserts

NB – Most of Antarctica is a polar desert, with only 50mm of precipitation annually

Sahara	3,450,000 sq miles	(9,065,000 sq km)
Gobi	500,000 sq miles	(1,295,000 sq km)
Ar Rub al Khali	289,600 sq miles	(750,000 sq km)
Great Victorian	249,800 sq miles	(647,000 sq km)
Sonoran	120,000 sq miles	(311,000 sq km)
Kalahari	120,000 sq miles	(310,800 sq km)
Kara Kum	115,800 sq miles	(300,000 sq km)
Takla Makan	100,400 sq miles	(260,000 sq km)
Namib	52,100 sq miles	(135,000 sq km)
Thar	33,670 sq miles	(130,000 sq km)

Hottest inhabited places

Djibouti (Djibouti)	86° F	(30 °C)
Tombouctou (Mali) **Tirunelveli** (India) **Tuticorin** (India)	84.7° F	(29.3 °C)
Nellore (India) **Santa Marta** (Colombia)	84.5° F	(29.2 °C)
Aden (Yemen) **Madurai** (India) **Niamey** (Niger)	84° F	(28.9 °C)
Hodeida (Yemen) **Ouagadougou** (Burkina) **Thanjavur** (India) **Tiruchchirappalli** (India)	83.8° F	(28.8 °C)

Driest inhabited places

Aswân (Egypt)	0.02 in	(0.5 mm)
Luxor (Egypt)	0.03 in	(0.7 mm)
Arica (Chile)	0.04 in	(1.1 mm)
Ica (Peru)	0.1 in	(2.3 mm)
Antofagasta (Chile)	0.2 in	(4.9 mm)
Al Minya (Egypt)	0.2 in	(5.1 mm)
Asyut (Egypt)	0.2 in	(5.2 mm)
Callao (Peru)	0.5 in	(12.0 mm)
Trujillo (Peru)	0.55 in	(14.0 mm)
Al Fayyum (Egypt)	0.8 in	(19.0 mm)

Wettest inhabited places

Mawsynram (India)	467 in	(11,862 mm)
Mount Waialeale (Hawaii, USA)	460 in	(11,684 mm)
Cherrapunji (India)	450 in	(11,430 mm)
Cape Debundsha (Cameroon)	405 in	(10,290 mm)
Quibdo (Colombia)	354 in	(8892 mm)
Buenaventura (Colombia)	265 in	(6743 mm)
Monrovia (Liberia)	202 in	(5131 mm)
Pago Pago (American Samoa)	196 in	(4990 mm)
Mawlamyine (Burma)	191 in	(4852 mm)
Lae (Papua New Guinea)	183 in	(4645 mm)

The time zones

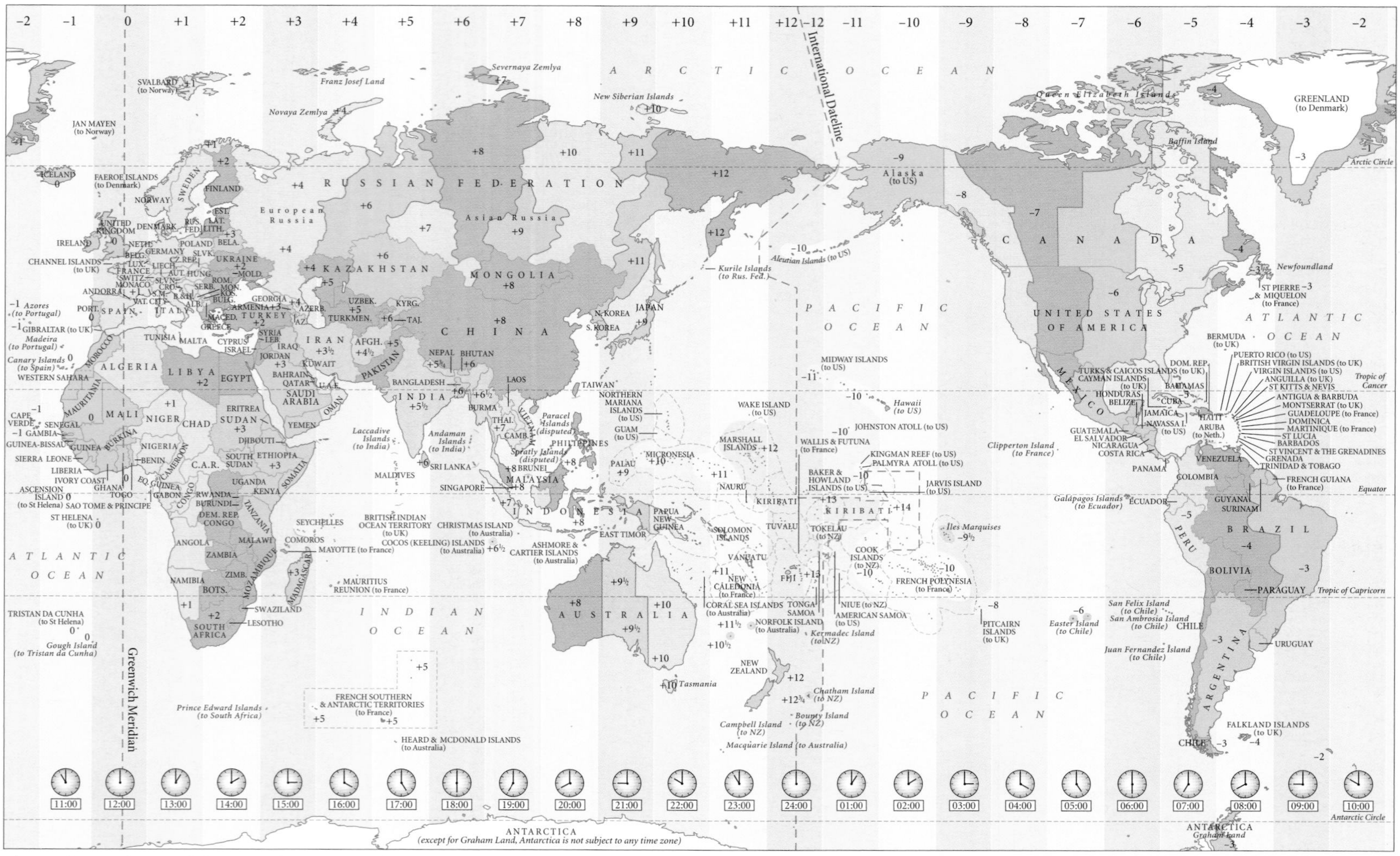

The numbers at the top of the map indicate the number of hours each time zone is ahead or behind Coordinated Universal Time (UTC). The clocks and 24-hour times given at the bottom of the map show the time in each time zone when it is 12:00 hours noon (UTC)

Time Zones

Because Earth is a rotating sphere, the Sun shines on only half of its surface at any one time. Thus, it is simultaneously morning, evening and night time in different parts of the world *(see diagram below)*. Because of these disparities, each country or part of a country adheres to a local time.

A region of Earth's surface within which a single local time is used is called a time zone. There are 24 one hour time zones around the world, arranged roughly in longitudinal bands.

Standard Time

Standard time is the official local time in a particular country or part of a country. It is defined by the time zone or zones associated with that country or region. Although time zones are arranged roughly in longitudinal bands, in many places the borders of a zone do not fall exactly on longitudinal meridians, as can be seen on the map *(above)*, but are determined by geographical factors or by borders between countries or parts of countries. Most countries have just one time zone and one standard time, but some large countries (such as the USA, Canada and Russia) are split between several time zones, so standard time varies across those countries. For example, the coterminous United States straddles four time zones and so has four standard times, called the Eastern, Central, Mountain and Pacific standard times. China is unusual in that just one standard time is used for the whole country, even though it extends across 60° of longitude from west to east.

Day and night around the world

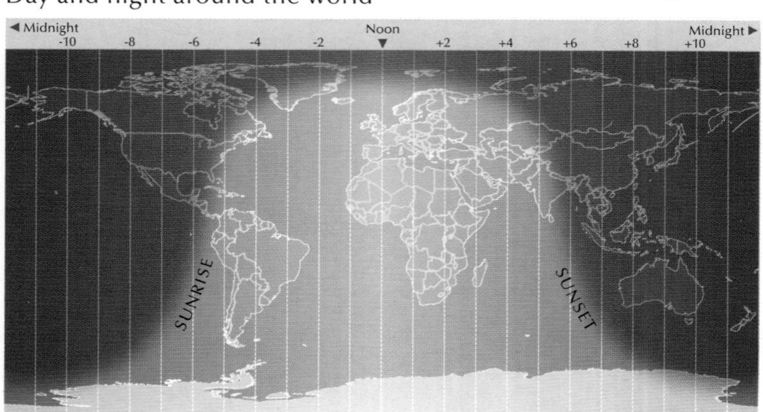
◀ Midnight
-10
-8
-6
-4
-2
Noon
+2
+4
+6
+8
Midnight ▶
+10
SUNRISE
SUNSET

Coordinated Universal Time (UTC)

Coordinated Universal Time (UTC) is a reference by which the local time in each time zone is set. For example, Australian Western Standard Time (the local time in Western Australia) is set 8 hours ahead of UTC (it is UTC+8) whereas Eastern Standard Time in the United States is set 5 hours behind UTC (it is UTC-5). UTC is a successor to, and closely approximates, Greenwich Mean Time (GMT). However, UTC is based on an atomic clock, whereas GMT is determined by the Sun's position in the sky relative to the 0° longitudinal meridian, which runs through Greenwich, UK.

The International Dateline

The International Dateline is an imaginary line from pole to pole that roughly corresponds to the 180° longitudinal meridian. It is an arbitrary marker between calendar days. The dateline is needed because of the use of local times around the world rather than a single universal time. When moving from west to east across the dateline, travellers have to set their watches back one day. Those travelling in the opposite direction, from east to west, must add a day.

Daylight Saving Time

Daylight saving is a summertime adjustment to the local time in a country or region, designed to cause a higher proportion of its citizens' waking hours to pass during daylight. To follow the system, timepieces are advanced by an hour on a pre-decided date in spring and reverted back in autumn. About half of the world's nations use daylight saving.

Countries of the World

There are currently 196 independent countries in the world and almost 60 dependencies. Antarctica is the only land area on Earth that is not officially part of, and does not belong to, any single country.

In 1950, the world comprised 82 countries. In the decades following, many more states came into being as they achieved independence from their former colonial rulers. Most recent additions were caused by the breakup of the former Soviet Union in 1991, and the former Yugoslavia in 1992, which swelled the ranks of independent states. In July 2011, South Sudan became the latest country to be formed after declaring independence from Sudan.

Country factfile key

Formation Date of independence / date current borders were established

Population Total population / population density – based on total *land* area

Languages An asterisk (*) denotes the official language(s)

Calorie consumption Average number of calories consumed daily per person

AFGHANISTAN
Central Asia

Official name Islamic Republic of Afghanistan
Formation 1919 / 1919
Capital Kabul
Population 32.4 million / 50 people per sq km (129 people per sq mile)
Total area 647,500 sq. km (250,000 sq. miles)
Languages Pashtu*, Tajik, Dari*, Farsi, Uzbek, Turkmen
Religions Sunni Muslim 80%, Shi'a Muslim 19%, Other 1%
Ethnic mix Pashtun 38%, Tajik 25%, Hazara 19%, Uzbek and Turkmen 15%, Other 3%
Government Nonparty system
Currency Afghani = 100 puls
Literacy rate rate 28%
Calorie consumption 1539 kilocalories

ALBANIA
Southeast Europe

Official name Republic of Albania
Formation 1912 / 1921
Capital Tirana
Population 3.2 million / 117 people per sq km (302 people per sq mile)
Total area 28,748 sq. km (11,100 sq. miles)
Languages Albanian*, Greek
Religions Sunni Muslim 70%, Albanian Orthodox 20%, Roman Catholic 10%
Ethnic mix Albanian 98%, Greek 1%, Other 1%
Government Parliamentary system
Currency Lek = 100 qindarka (qintars)
Literacy rate 96%
Calorie consumption 2903 kilocalories

ALGERIA
North Africa

Official name People's Democratic Republic of Algeria
Formation 1962 / 1962
Capital Algiers
Population 36 million / 15 people per sq km (39 people per sq mile)
Total area 2,381,740 sq. km (919,590 sq. miles)
Languages Arabic*, Tamazight (Kabyle, Shawia, Tamashek), French
Religions Sunni Muslim 99%, Christian and Jewish 1%
Ethnic mix Arab 75%, Berber 24%, European and Jewish 1%
Government Presidential system
Currency Algerian dinar = 100 centimes
Literacy rate 75%
Calorie consumption 3239 kilocalories

ANDORRA
Southwest Europe

Official name Principality of Andorra
Formation 1278 / 1278
Capital Andorra la Vella
Population 85,082 / 183 people per sq km (473 people per sq mile)
Total area 468 sq. km (181 sq. miles)
Languages Spanish, Catalan*, French, Portuguese
Religions Roman Catholic 94%, Other 6%
Ethnic mix Spanish 46%, Andorran 28%, Other 18%, French 8%
Government Parliamentary system
Currency Euro = 100 cents
Literacy rate 99%
Calorie consumption Not available

ANGOLA
Southern Africa

Official name Republic of Angola
Formation 1975 / 1975
Capital Luanda
Population 19.6 million / 16 people per sq km (41 people per sq mile)
Total area 1,246,700 sq. km (481,351 sq. miles)
Languages Portuguese*, Umbundu, Kimbundu, Kikongo
Religions Roman Catholic 68%, Protestant 20%, Indigenous beliefs 12%
Ethnic mix Ovimbundu 37%, Kimbundu 25%, Other 25%, Bakongo 13%
Government Presidential system
Currency Readjusted kwanza = 100 lwei
Literacy rate 70%
Calorie consumption 2079 kilocalories

ANTIGUA & BARBUDA
West Indies

Official name Antigua and Barbuda
Formation 1981 / 1981
Capital St. John's
Population 89,018 / 202 people per sq km (524 people per sq mile)
Total area 442 sq. km (170 sq. miles)
Languages English*, English patois
Religions Anglican 45%, Other Protestant 42%, Roman Catholic 10%, Other 2%, Rastafarian 1%
Ethnic mix Black African 95%, Other 5%
Government Parliamentary system
Currency East Caribbean dollar = 100 cents
Literacy rate 99%
Calorie consumption 2373 kilocalories

ARGENTINA
South America

Official name Republic of Argentina
Formation 1816 / 1816
Capital Buenos Aires
Population 40.8 million / 15 people per sq km (39 people per sq mile)
Total area 2,766,890 sq. km (1,068,296 sq. miles)
Languages Spanish*, Italian, Amerindian languages
Religions Roman Catholic 70%, Other 18%, Protestant 9%, Muslim 2%, Jewish 1%
Ethnic mix Indo-European 97%, Mestizo 2%, Amerindian 1%
Government Presidential system
Currency Argentine peso = 100 centavos
Literacy rate 98%
Calorie consumption 2918 kilocalories

ARMENIA
Southwest Asia

Official name Republic of Armenia
Formation 1991 / 1991
Capital Yerevan
Population 3.1 million / 104 people per sq km (269 people per sq mile)
Total area 29,800 sq. km (11,506 sq. miles)
Languages Armenian*, Azeri, Russian
Religions Armenian Apostolic Church (Orthodox) 88%, Armenian Catholic Church 6%, Other 6%
Ethnic mix Armenian 98%, Other 1%, Yezidi 1%
Government Parliamentary system
Currency Dram = 100 luma
Literacy rate 99%
Calorie consumption 2806 kilocalories

AUSTRALIA
Australasia & Oceania

Official name Commonwealth of Australia
Formation 1901 / 1901
Capital Canberra
Population 22.6 million / 3 people per sq km (8 people per sq mile)
Total area 7,686,850 sq. km (2,967,893 sq. miles)
Languages English*, Italian, Cantonese, Greek, Arabic, Vietnamese, Aboriginal languages
Religions Roman Catholic 26%, Nonreligious 19%, Anglican 19%, Other 17%, Other Christian 13%, United Church 6%
Ethnic mix European 92%, Asian 7%, Aboriginal and Other 1%
Government Parliamentary system
Currency Australian dollar = 100 cents
Literacy rate 99%
Calorie consumption 3261 kilocalories

AUSTRIA
Central Europe

Official name Republic of Austria
Formation 1918 / 1919
Capital Vienna
Population 8.4 million / 102 people per sq km (263 people per sq mile)
Total area 83,858 sq. km (32,378 sq. miles)
Languages German*, Croatian, Slovenian, Hungarian (Magyar)
Religions Roman Catholic 78%, Nonreligious 9%, Other (including Jewish and Muslim) 8%, Protestant 5%
Ethnic mix Austrian 93%, Croat, Slovene, and Hungarian 6%, Other 1%
Government Parliamentary system
Currency Euro = 100 cents
Literacy rate 99%
Calorie consumption 3800 kilocalories

AZERBAIJAN
Southwest Asia

Official name Republic of Azerbaijan
Formation 1991 / 1991
Capital Baku
Population 9.3 million / 107 people per sq km (278 people per sq mile)
Total area 86,600 sq. km (33,436 sq. miles)
Languages Azeri*, Russian
Religions Shi'a Muslim 68%, Sunni Muslim 26%, Russian Orthodox 3%, Armenian Apostolic Church (Orthodox) 2%, Other 1%
Ethnic mix Azeri 91%, Other 3%, Lazs 2%, Armenian 2%, Russian 2%
Government Presidential system
Currency New manat = 100 gopik
Literacy rate 99%
Calorie consumption 3072 kilocalories

BAHAMAS
West Indies

Official name Commonwealth of the Bahamas
Formation 1973 / 1973
Capital Nassau
Population 300,000 / 30 people per sq km (78 people per sq mile)
Total area 13,940 sq. km (5382 sq. miles)
Languages English*, English Creole, French Creole
Religions Baptist 32%, Anglican 20%, Roman Catholic 19%, Other 17%, Methodist 6%, Church of God 6%
Ethnic mix Black African 85%, European 12%, Asian and Hispanic 3%
Government Parliamentary system
Currency Bahamian dollar = 100 cents
Literacy rate 96%
Calorie consumption 2750 kilocalories

BAHRAIN
Southwest Asia

Official name Kingdom of Bahrain
Formation 1971 / 1971
Capital Manama
Population 1.3 million / 1841 people per sq km (4762 people per sq mile)
Total area 620 sq. km (239 sq. miles)
Languages Arabic
Religions Muslim (mainly Shi'a) 99%, Other 1%
Ethnic mix Bahraini 63%, Asian 19%, Other Arab 10%, Iranian 8%
Government Mixed monarchical–parliamentary system
Currency Bahraini dinar = 1000 fils
Literacy rate 91%
Calorie consumption Not available

BANGLADESH
South Asia

Official name People's Republic of Bangladesh
Formation 1971 / 1971
Capital Dhaka
Population 150 million / 1124 people per sq km (2911 people per sq mile)
Total area 144,000 sq. km (55,598 sq. miles)
Languages Bengali*, Urdu, Chakma, Marma (Magh), Garo, Khasi, Santhali, Tripuri, Mro
Religions Muslim (mainly Sunni) 88%, Hindu 11%, Other 1%
Ethnic mix Bengali 98%, Other 2%
Government Parliamentary system
Currency Taka = 100 poisha
Literacy rate 56%
Calorie consumption 2481 kilocalories

BARBADOS
West Indies

Official name Barbados
Formation 1966 / 1966
Capital Bridgetown
Population 300,000 / 698 people per sq km (1807 people per sq mile)
Total area 430 sq. km (166 sq. miles)
Languages Bajan (Barbadian English), English*
Religions Anglican 40%, Other 24%, Nonreligious 17%, Pentecostal 8%, Methodist 7%, Roman Catholic 4%
Ethnic mix Black African 92%, White 3%, Other 3%, Mixed race 2%
Government Parliamentary system
Currency Barbados dollar = 100 cents
Literacy rate 99%
Calorie consumption 3021 kilocalories

BELARUS
Eastern Europe

Official name Republic of Belarus
Formation 1991 / 1991
Capital Minsk
Population 9.6 million / 46 people per sq km (120 people per sq mile)
Total area 207,600 sq. km (80,154 sq. miles)
Languages Belarussian*, Russian*
Religions Orthodox Christian 80%, Roman Catholic 14%, Other 4%, Protestant 2%
Ethnic mix Belarussian 81%, Russian 11%, Polish 4%, Ukrainian 2%, Other 2%
Government Presidential system
Currency Belarussian rouble = 100 kopeks
Literacy rate 99%
Calorie consumption 3186 kilocalories

BELGIUM
Northwest Europe

Official name Kingdom of Belgium
Formation 1830 / 1919
Capital Brussels
Population 10.8 million / 329 people per sq km (852 people per sq mile)
Total area 30,510 sq. km (11,780 sq. miles)
Languages Dutch*, French*, German*
Religions Roman Catholic 88%, Other 10%, Muslim 2%
Ethnic mix Fleming 58%, Walloon 33%, Other 6%, Italian 2%, Moroccan 1%
Government Parliamentary system
Currency Euro = 100 cents
Literacy rate 99%
Calorie consumption 3721 kilocalories

BELIZE
Central America

Official name Belize
Formation 1981 / 1981
Capital Belmopan
Population 300,000 / 13 people per sq km (34 people per sq mile)
Total area 22,966 sq. km (8867 sq. miles)
Languages English Creole, Spanish, English*, Mayan, Garifuna (Carib)
Religions Roman Catholic 62%, Other 13%, Anglican 12%, Methodist 6%, Mennonite 4%, Seventh-day Adventist 3%
Ethnic mix Mestizo 49%, Creole 25%, Maya 11%, Garifuna 6%, Other 6%, Asian Indian 3%
Government Parliamentary system
Currency Belizean dollar = 100 cents
Literacy rate 75%
Calorie consumption 2680 kilocalories

BENIN
West Africa

Official name Republic of Benin
Formation 1960 / 1960
Capital Porto-Novo
Population 9.1 million / 82 people per sq km (213 people per sq mile)
Total area 112,620 sq. km (43,483 sq. miles)
Languages Fon, Bariba, Yoruba, Adja, Houeda, Somba, French*
Religions Indigenous beliefs and Voodoo 50%, Christian 30%, Muslim 20%
Ethnic mix Fon 41%, Other 21%, Adja 16%, Yoruba 12%, Bariba 10%
Government Presidential system
Currency CFA franc = 100 centimes
Literacy rate 42%
Calorie consumption 2592 kilocalories

BHUTAN
South Asia

Official name Kingdom of Bhutan
Formation 1656 / 1865
Capital Thimphu
Population 700,000 / 15 people per sq km (39 people per sq mile)
Total area 47,000 sq. km (18,147 sq. miles)
Languages Dzongkha*, Nepali, Assamese
Religions Mahayana Buddhist 75%, Hindu 25%
Ethnic mix Bhutanese 50%, Nepalese 35%, Other 15%
Government Mixed monarchical–parliamentary system
Currency Ngultrum = 100 chetrum
Literacy rate 56%
Calorie consumption Not available

BOLIVIA
South America

Official name Plurinational State of Bolivia
Formation 1825 / 1938
Capital La Paz (administrative); Sucre (judicial)
Population 10.1 million / 9 people per sq km (24 people per sq mile)
Total area 1,098,580 sq. km (424,162 sq. miles)
Languages Aymara*, Quechua*, Spanish*
Religions Roman Catholic 93%, Other 7%
Ethnic mix Quechua 37%, Aymara 32%, Mixed race 13%, European 10%, Other 8%
Government Presidential system
Currency Boliviano = 100 centavos
Literacy rate 91%
Calorie consumption 2172 kilocalories

BOSNIA & HERZEGOVINA
Southeast Europe

Official name Bosnia and Herzegovina
Formation 1992 / 1992
Capital Sarajevo
Population 3.8 million / 74 people per sq km (192 people per sq mile)
Total area 51,129 sq. km (19,741 sq. miles)
Languages Bosnian*, Serbian*, Croatian*
Religions Muslim (mainly Sunni) 40%, Orthodox Christian 31%, Roman Catholic 15%, Other 10%, Protestant 4%
Ethnic mix Bosniak 48%, Serb 34%, Croat 16%, Other 2%
Government Parliamentary system
Currency Marka = 100 pfeninga
Literacy rate 98%
Calorie consumption 3070 kilocalories

BOTSWANA
Southern Africa

Official name Republic of Botswana
Formation 1966 / 1966
Capital Gaborone
Population 2 million / 4 people per sq km (9 people per sq mile)
Total area 600,370 sq. km (231,803 sq. miles)
Languages Setswana, English*, Shona, San, Khoikhoi, isiNdebele
Religions Christian (mainly Protestant) 70%, Nonreligious 20%, Traditional beliefs 6%, Other (including Muslim) 4%
Ethnic mix Tswana 79%, Kalanga 11%, Other 10%
Government Presidential system
Currency Pula = 100 thebe
Literacy rate 84%
Calorie consumption 2164 kilocalories

BRAZIL
South America

Official name Federative Republic of Brazil
Formation 1822 / 1828
Capital Brasilia
Population 197 million / 23 people per sq km (60 people per sq mile)
Total area 8,511,965 sq. km (3,286,470 sq. miles)
Languages Portuguese*, German, Italian, Spanish, Polish, Japanese, Amerindian languages
Religions Roman Catholic 74%, Protestant 15%, Atheist 7%, Other 3%, Afro-American Spiritist 1%
Ethnic mix White 54%, Mixed race 38%, Black 6%, Other 2%
Government Presidential system
Currency Real = 100 centavos
Literacy rate 90%
Calorie consumption 3173 kilocalories

BRUNEI
Southeast Asia

Official name Sultanate of Brunei
Formation 1984 / 1984
Capital Bandar Seri Begawan
Population 400,000 / 76 people per sq km (197 people per sq mile)
Total area 5770 sq. km (2228 sq. miles)
Languages Malay*, English, Chinese
Religions Muslim (mainly Sunni) 66%, Buddhist 14%, Other 10%, Christian 10%
Ethnic mix Malay 67%, Chinese 16%, Other 11%, Indigenous 6%
Government Monarchy
Currency Brunei dollar = 100 cents
Literacy rate 95%
Calorie consumption 3088 kilocalories

BULGARIA
Southeast Europe

Official name Republic of Bulgaria
Formation 1908 / 1947
Capital Sofia
Population 7.4 million / 67 people per sq km (173 people per sq mile)
Total area 110,910 sq. km (42,822 sq. miles)
Languages Bulgarian*, Turkish, Romani
Religions Bulgarian Orthodox 83%, Muslim 12%, Other 4%, Roman Catholic 1%
Ethnic mix Bulgarian 84%, Turkish 9%, Roma 5%, Other 2%
Government Parliamentary system
Currency Lev = 100 stotinki
Literacy rate 98%
Calorie consumption 2791 kilocalories

BURKINA
West Africa

Official name Burkina Faso
Formation 1960 / 1960
Capital Ouagadougou
Population 17 million / 62 people per sq km (161 people per sq mile)
Total area 274,200 sq. km (105,869 sq. miles)
Languages Mossi, Fulani, French*, Tuareg, Dyula, Songhai
Religions Muslim 55%, Christian 25%, Traditional beliefs 20%
Ethnic mix Mossi 48%, Other 21%, Peul 10%, Lobi 7%, Bobo 7%, Mandé 7%
Government Presidential system
Currency CFA franc = 100 centimes
Literacy rate 29%
Calorie consumption 2647 kilocalories

BURMA (MYANMAR)
Southeast Asia

Official name Union of Myanmar
Formation 1948 / 1948
Capital Nay Pyi Taw
Population 48.3 million / 73 people per sq km (190 people per sq mile)
Total area 678,500 sq. km (261,969 sq. miles)
Languages Burmese*, Shan, Karen, Rakhine, Chin, Yangbye, Kachin, Mon
Religions Buddhist 89%, Christian 4%, Muslim 4%, Other 2%, Animist 1%
Ethnic mix Burman (Bamah) 68%, Other 12%, Shan 9%, Karen 7%, Rakhine 4%
Government Presidential system
Currency Kyat = 100 pyas
Literacy rate 92%
Calorie consumption 2493 kilocalories

BURUNDI
Central Africa

Official name Republic of Burundi
Formation 1962 / 1962
Capital Bujumbura
Population 8.6 million / 335 people per sq km (868 people per sq mile)
Total area 27,830 sq. km (10,745 sq. miles)
Languages Kirundi*, French*, Kiswahili
Religions Roman Catholic 62%, Traditional beliefs 23%, Muslim 10%, Protestant 5%
Ethnic mix Hutu 85%, Tutsi 14%, Twa 1%
Government Presidential system
Currency Burundian franc = 100 centimes
Literacy rate 67%
Calorie consumption 1604 kilocalories

CAMBODIA
Southeast Asia

Official name Kingdom of Cambodia
Formation 1953 / 1953
Capital Phnom Penh
Population 14.3 million / 81 people per sq km (210 people per sq mile)
Total area 181,040 sq. km (69,900 sq. miles)
Languages Khmer*, French, Chinese, Vietnamese, Cham
Religions Buddhist 93%, Muslim 6%, Christian 1%
Ethnic mix Khmer 90%, Vietnamese 5%, Other 4%, Chinese 1%
Government Parliamentary system
Currency Riel = 100 sen
Literacy rate 78%
Calorie consumption 2382 kilocalories

CAMEROON
Central Africa

Official name Republic of Cameroon
Formation 1960 / 1961
Capital Yaoundé
Population 20 million / 43 people per sq km (111 people per sq mile)
Total area 475,400 sq. km (183,567 sq. miles)
Languages Bamileke, Fang, Fulani, French*, English*
Religions Roman Catholic 35%, Traditional beliefs 25%, Muslim 22%, Protestant 18%
Ethnic mix Cameroon highlanders 31%, Other 21%, Equatorial Bantu 19%, Kirdi 11%, Fulani 10%, Northwestern Bantu 8%
Government Presidential system
Currency CFA franc = 100 centimes
Literacy rate 71%
Calorie consumption 2457 kilocalories

CANADA
North America

Official name Canada
Formation 1867 / 1949
Capital Ottawa
Population 34.3 million / 4 people per sq km (10 people per sq mile)
Total area 9,984,670 sq. km (3,855,171 sq. miles)
Languages English*, French*, Chinese, Italian, German, Ukrainian, Portuguese, Inuktitut, Cree
Religions Roman Catholic 44%, Protestant 29%, Other and nonreligious 27%
Ethnic mix European 66%, Other 32%, Amerindian 2%
Government Parliamentary system
Currency Canadian dollar = 100 cents
Literacy rate 99%
Calorie consumption 3399 kilocalories

CAPE VERDE
Atlantic Ocean

Official name Republic of Cape Verde
Formation 1975 / 1975
Capital Praia
Population 500,000 / 124 people per sq km (321 people per sq mile)
Total area 4033 sq. km (1557 sq. miles)
Languages Portuguese Creole, Portuguese*
Religions Roman Catholic 97%, Other 2%, Protestant (Church of the Nazarene) 1%
Ethnic mix Mestiço 71%, African 28%, European 1%
Government Mixed presidential–parliamentary system
Currency Escudo = 100 centavos
Literacy rate 85%
Calorie consumption 2644 kilocalories

CENTRAL AFRICAN REPUBLIC
Central Africa

Official name Central African Republic
Formation 1960 / 1960
Capital Bangui
Population 4.5 million / 7 people per sq km (19 people per sq mile)
Total area 622,984 sq. km (240,534 sq. miles)
Languages Sango, Banda, Gbaya, French*
Religions Traditional beliefs 35%, Roman Catholic 25%, Protestant 25%, Muslim 15%
Ethnic mix Baya 33%, Banda 27%, Other 17%, Mandjia 13%, Sara 10%
Government Presidential system
Currency CFA franc = 100 centimes
Literacy rate 55%
Calorie consumption 2181 kilocalories

CHAD
Central Africa

Official name Republic of Chad
Formation 1960 / 1960
Capital N'Djamena
Population 11.5 million / 9 people per sq km (24 people per sq mile)
Total area 1,284,000 sq. km (495,752 sq. miles)
Languages French*, Sara, Arabic*, Maba
Religions Muslim 51%, Christian 35%, Animist 7%, Traditional beliefs 7%
Ethnic mix Other 30%, Sara 28%, Mayo-Kebbi 12%, Arab 12%, Ouaddai 9%, Kanem-Bornou 9%
Government Presidential system
Currency CFA franc = 100 centimes
Literacy rate 34%
Calorie consumption 2074 kilocalories

CHILE
South America

Official name Republic of Chile
Formation 1818 / 1883
Capital Santiago
Population 17.3 million / 23 people per sq km (60 people per sq mile)
Total area 756,950 sq. km (292,258 sq. miles)
Languages Spanish*, Amerindian languages
Religions Roman Catholic 89%, Other and nonreligious 11%
Ethnic mix Mestizo and European 90%, Other Amerindian 9%, Mapuche 1%
Government Presidential system
Currency Chilean peso = 100 centavos
Literacy rate 99%
Calorie consumption 2908 kilocalories

CHINA
East Asia

Official name People's Republic of China
Formation 960 / 1999
Capital Beijing
Population 1.35 billion / 144 people per sq km (374 people per sq mile)
Total area 9,596,960 sq. km (3,705,386 sq. miles)
Languages Mandarin*, Wu, Cantonese, Hsiang, Min, Hakka, Kan
Religions Nonreligious 59%, Traditional beliefs 20%, Other 13%, Buddhist 6%, Muslim 2%
Ethnic mix Han 92%, Other 4%, Hui 1%, Miao 1%, Manchu 1%, Zhuang 1%
Government One-party state
Currency Renminbi (known as yuan) = 10 jiao = 100 fen
Literacy rate 94%
Calorie consumption 3036 kilocalories

COLOMBIA
South America

Official name Republic of Colombia
Formation 1819 / 1903
Capital Bogotá
Population 46.9 million / 45 people per sq km (117 people per sq mile)
Total area 1,138,910 sq. km (439,733 sq. miles)
Languages Spanish*, Wayuu, Páez, and other Amerindian languages
Religions Roman Catholic 95%, Other 5%
Ethnic mix Mestizo 58%, White 20%, European–African 14%, African 4%, African–Amerindian 3%, Amerindian 1%
Government Presidential system
Currency Colombian peso = 100 centavos
Literacy rate 93%
Calorie consumption 2717 kilocalories

COMOROS
Indian Ocean

Official name Union of the Comoros
Formation 1975 / 1975
Capital Moroni
Population 800,000 / 359 people per sq km (929 people per sq mile)
Total area 2170 sq. km (838 sq. miles)
Languages Arabic*, Comoran*, French*
Religions Muslim (mainly Sunni) 98%, Other 1%, Roman Catholic 1%
Ethnic mix Comoran 97%, Other 3%
Government Presidential system
Currency Comoros franc = 100 centimes
Literacy rate 74%
Calorie consumption 2139 kilocalories

CONGO
Central Africa

Official name Republic of the Congo
Formation 1960 / 1960
Capital Brazzaville
Population 4.1 million / 12 people per sq km (31 people per sq mile)
Total area 342,000 sq. km (132,046 sq. miles)
Languages Kongo, Teke, Lingala, French*
Religions Traditional beliefs 50%, Roman Catholic 35%, Protestant 13%, Muslim 2%
Ethnic mix Bakongo 51%, Teke 17%, Other 16%, Mbochi 11%, Mbédé 5%
Government Presidential system
Currency CFA franc = 100 centimes
Literacy rate 87%
Calorie consumption 2056 kilocalories

CONGO, DEM. REP.
Central Africa

Official name Democratic Republic of the Congo
Formation 1960 / 1960
Capital Kinshasa
Population 67.8 million / 30 people per sq km (77 people per sq mile)
Total area 2,345,410 sq. km (905,563 sq. miles)
Languages Kiswahili, Tshiluba, Kikongo, Lingala, French*
Religions Roman Catholic 50%, Protestant 20%, Traditional beliefs and other 10%, Muslim 10%, Kimbanguist 10%
Ethnic mix Other 55%, Mongo, Luba, Kongo, and Mangbetu-Azande 45%
Government Presidential system
Currency Congolese franc = 100 centimes
Literacy rate 67%
Calorie consumption 1585 kilocalories

COSTA RICA
Central America

Official name Republic of Costa Rica
Formation 1838 / 1838
Capital San José
Population 4.7 million / 92 people per sq km (238 people per sq mile)
Total area 51,100 sq. km (19,730 sq. miles)
Languages Spanish*, English Creole, Bribri, Cabecar
Religions Roman Catholic 71%, Evangelical 14%, Nonreligious 11%, Other 4%
Ethnic mix Mestizo and European 94%, Black 3%, Other 1%, Chinese 1%, Amerindian 1%
Government Presidential system
Currency Costa Rican colón = 100 céntimos
Literacy rate 96%
Calorie consumption 2886 kilocalories

CROATIA
Southeast Europe

Official name Republic of Croatia
Formation 1991 / 1991
Capital Zagreb
Population 4.4 million / 78 people per sq km (202 people per sq mile)
Total area 56,542 sq. km (21,831 sq. miles)
Languages Croatian*
Religions Roman Catholic 88%, Other 7%, Orthodox Christian 4%, Muslim 1%
Ethnic mix Croat 90%, Other 5%, Serb 5%
Government Parliamentary system
Currency Kuna = 100 lipa
Literacy rate 99%
Calorie consumption 3130 kilocalories

CUBA
West Indies

Official name Republic of Cuba
Formation 1902 / 1902
Capital Havana
Population 11.3 million / 102 people per sq km (264 people per sq mile)
Total area 110,860 sq. km (42,803 sq. miles)
Languages Spanish
Religions Nonreligious 49%, Roman Catholic 40%, Atheist 6%, Other 4%, Protestant 1%
Ethnic mix Mulatto (mixed race) 51%, White 37%, Black 11%, Chinese 1%
Government One-party state
Currency Cuban peso = 100 centavos
Literacy rate 99%
Calorie consumption 3258 kilocalories

CYPRUS
Southeast Europe

Official name Republic of Cyprus
Formation 1960 / 1960
Capital Nicosia
Population 1.1 million / 119 people per sq km (308 people per sq mile)
Total area 9250 sq. km (3571 sq. miles)
Languages Greek*, Turkish*
Religions Orthodox Christian 78%, Muslim 18%, Other 4%
Ethnic mix Greek 81%, Turkish 11%, Other 8%
Government Presidential system
Currency Euro (new Turkish lira in TRNC) = 100 cents (euro); 100 kurus (Turkish lira)
Literacy rate 98%
Calorie consumption 2678 kilocalories

CZECH REPUBLIC
Central Europe

Official name Czech Republic
Formation 1993 / 1993
Capital Prague
Population 10.5 million / 133 people per sq km (345 people per sq mile)
Total area 78,866 sq. km (30,450 sq. miles)
Languages Czech*, Slovak, Hungarian (Magyar)
Religions Roman Catholic 39%, Atheist 38%, Other 18%, Protestant 3%, Hussite 2%
Ethnic mix Czech 90%, Moravian 4%, Other 4%, Slovak 2%
Government Parliamentary system
Currency Czech koruna = 100 haleru
Literacy rate 99%
Calorie consumption 3305 kilocalories

DENMARK
Northern Europe

Official name Kingdom of Denmark
Formation 950 / 1944
Capital Copenhagen
Population 5.6 million / 132 people per sq km (342 people per sq mile)
Total area 43,094 sq. km (16,639 sq. miles)
Languages Danish
Religions Evangelical Lutheran 95%, Roman Catholic 3%, Muslim 2%
Ethnic mix Danish 96%, Other (including Scandinavian and Turkish) 3%, Faeroese and Inuit 1%
Government Parliamentary system
Currency Danish krone = 100 øre
Literacy rate 99%
Calorie consumption 3378 kilocalories

DJIBOUTI
East Africa

Official name Republic of Djibouti
Formation 1977 / 1977
Capital Djibouti
Population 900,000 / 39 people per sq km (101 people per sq mile)
Total area 22,000 sq. km (8494 sq. miles)
Languages Somali, Afar, French*, Arabic*
Religions Muslim (mainly Sunni) 94%, Christian 6%
Ethnic mix Issa 60%, Afar 35%, Other 5%
Government Presidential system
Currency Djibouti franc = 100 centimes
Literacy rate 70%
Calorie consumption 2419 kilocalories

DOMINICA
West Indies

Official name Commonwealth of Dominica
Formation 1978 / 1978
Capital Roseau
Population 73,126 / 98 people per sq km (253 people per sq mile)
Total area 754 sq. km (291 sq. miles)
Languages French Creole, English*
Religions Roman Catholic 77%, Protestant 15%, Other 8%
Ethnic mix Black 87%, Mixed race 9%, Carib 3%, Other 1%
Government Parliamentary system
Currency East Caribbean dollar = 100 cents
Literacy rate 88%
Calorie consumption 3147 kilocalories

DOMINICAN REPUBLIC
West Indies

Official name Dominican Republic
Formation 1865 / 1865
Capital Santo Domingo
Population 10.1 million / 209 people per sq km (541 people per sq mile)
Total area 48,380 sq. km (18,679 sq. miles)
Languages Spanish*, French Creole
Religions Roman Catholic 95%, Other and nonreligious 5%
Ethnic mix Mixed race 73%, European 16%, African 11%
Government Presidential system
Currency Dominican Republic peso = 100 centavos
Literacy rate 88%
Calorie consumption 2491 kilocalories

EAST TIMOR
Southeast Asia

Official name Democratic Republic of Timor-Leste
Formation 2002 / 2002
Capital Dili
Population 1.2 million / 82 people per sq km (213 people per sq mile)
Total area 14,874 sq. km (5756 sq. miles)
Languages Tetum (Portuguese/Austronesian)*, Bahasa Indonesia, Portuguese*
Religions Roman Catholic 95%, Other (including Muslim and Protestant) 5%
Ethnic mix Papuan groups approx 85%, Indonesian approx 13%, Chinese 2%
Government Parliamentary system
Currency US dollar = 100 cents
Literacy rate 51%
Calorie consumption 2076 kilocalories

ECUADOR
South America

Official name Republic of Ecuador
Formation 1830 / 1942
Capital Quito
Population 14.7 million / 53 people per sq km (138 people per sq mile)
Total area 283,560 sq. km (109,483 sq. miles)
Languages Spanish*, Quechua, other Amerindian languages
Religions Roman Catholic 95%, Protestant, Jewish, and other 5%
Ethnic mix Mestizo 77%, White 11%, Amerindian 7%, Black 5%
Government Presidential system
Currency US dollar = 100 cents
Literacy rate 84%
Calorie consumption 2267 kilocalories

EGYPT
North Africa

Official name Arab Republic of Egypt
Formation 1936 / 1982
Capital Cairo
Population 82.5 million / 83 people per sq km (215 people per sq mile)
Total area 1,001,450 sq. km (386,660 sq. miles)
Languages Arabic*, French, English, Berber
Religions Muslim (mainly Sunni) 90%, Coptic Christian and other 9%, Other Christian 1%
Ethnic mix Egyptian 99%, Nubian, Armenian, Greek, and Berber 1%
Government Transitional regime
Currency Egyptian pound = 100 piastres
Literacy rate 72%
Calorie consumption 3349 kilocalories

EL SALVADOR
Central America

Official name Republic of El Salvador
Formation 1841 / 1841
Capital San Salvador
Population 6.2 million / 299 people per sq km (775 people per sq mile)
Total area 21,040 sq. km (8124 sq. miles)
Languages Spanish
Religions Roman Catholic 80%, Evangelical 18%, Other 2%
Ethnic mix Mestizo 90%, White 9%, Amerindian 1%
Government Presidential system
Currency Salvadorean colón & US dollar = 100 centavos (colón); 100 cents (US dollar)
Literacy rate 84%
Calorie consumption 2574 kilocalories

EQUATORIAL GUINEA
Central Africa

Official name Republic of Equatorial Guinea
Formation 1968 / 1968
Capital Malabo
Population 700,000 / 25 people per sq km (65 people per sq mile)
Total area 28,051 sq. km (10,830 sq. miles)
Languages Spanish*, Fang, Bubi, French*
Religions Roman Catholic 90%, Other 10%
Ethnic mix Fang 85%, Other 11%, Bubi 4%
Government Presidential system
Currency CFA franc = 100 centimes
Literacy rate 93%
Calorie consumption Not available

ERITREA
East Africa

Official name State of Eritrea
Formation 1993 / 2002
Capital Asmara
Population 5.4 million / 46 people per sq km (119 people per sq mile)
Total area 121,320 sq. km (46,842 sq. miles)
Languages Tigrinya*, English*, Tigre, Afar, Arabic*, Saho, Bilen, Kunama, Nara, Hadareb
Religions Christian 50%, Muslim 48%, Other 2%
Ethnic mix Tigray 50%, Tigre 31%, Other 9%, Afar 5%, Saho 5%
Government Transitional regime
Currency Nakfa = 100 cents
Literacy rate 67%
Calorie consumption 1640 kilocalories

ESTONIA
Northeast Europe

Official name Republic of Estonia
Formation 1991 / 1991
Capital Tallinn
Population 1.3 million / 29 people per sq km (75 people per sq mile)
Total area 45,226 sq. km (17,462 sq. miles)
Languages Estonian*, Russian
Religions Evangelical Lutheran 56%, Orthodox Christian 25%, Other 19%
Ethnic mix Estonian 69%, Russian 25%, Other 4%, Ukrainian 2%
Government Parliamentary system
Currency Euro = 100 cents
Literacy rate 99%
Calorie consumption 3163 kilocalories

ETHIOPIA
East Africa

Official name Federal Democratic Republic of Ethiopia
Formation 1896 / 2002
Capital Addis Ababa
Population 84.7 million / 76 people per sq km (198 people per sq mile)
Total area 1,127,127 sq. km (435,184 sq. miles)
Languages Amharic*, Tigrinya, Galla, Sidamo, Somali, English, Arabic
Religions Orthodox Christian 40%, Muslim 40%, Traditional beliefs 15%, Other 5%
Ethnic mix Oromo 40%, Amhara 25%, Other 13%, Sidama 9%, Tigray 7%, Somali 6%
Government Parliamentary system
Currency Birr = 100 cents
Literacy rate 36%
Calorie consumption 2097 kilocalories

FIJI
Australasia & Oceania

Official name Republic of the Fiji Islands
Formation 1970 / 1970
Capital Suva
Population 900,000 / 49 people per sq km (128 people per sq mile)
Total area 18,270 sq. km (7054 sq. miles)
Languages Fijian, English*, Hindi, Urdu, Tamil, Telugu
Religions Hindu 38%, Methodist 37%, Roman Catholic 9%, Muslim 8%, Other 8%
Ethnic mix Melanesian 51%, Indian 44%, Other 5%
Government Transitional regime
Currency Fiji dollar = 100 cents
Literacy rate 94%
Calorie consumption 2996 kilocalories

FINLAND
Northern Europe

Official name Republic of Finland
Formation 1917 / 1947
Capital Helsinki
Population 5.4 million / 18 people per sq km (46 people per sq mile)
Total area 337,030 sq. km (130,127 sq. miles)
Languages Finnish*, Swedish*, Sámi
Religions Evangelical Lutheran 83%, Other 15%, Orthodox Christian 1%, Roman Catholic 1%
Ethnic mix Finnish 93%, Other (including Sámi) 7%
Government Parliamentary system
Currency Euro = 100 cents
Literacy rate 99%
Calorie consumption 3240 kilocalories

FRANCE
Western Europe

Official name French Republic
Formation 987 / 1919
Capital Paris
Population 63.1 million / 115 people per sq km (297 people per sq mile)
Total area 547,030 sq. km (211,208 sq. miles)
Languages French*, Provençal, German, Breton, Catalan, Basque
Religions Roman Catholic 88%, Muslim 8%, Protestant 2%, Buddhist 1%, Jewish 1%
Ethnic mix French 90%, North African (mainly Algerian) 6%, German (Alsace) 2%, Breton 1%, Other (including Corsicans) 1%
Government Mixed presidential–parliamentary system
Currency Euro = 100 cents
Literacy rate 99%
Calorie consumption 3531 kilocalories

GABON
Central Africa

Official name Gabonese Republic
Formation 1960 / 1960
Capital Libreville
Population 1.5 million / 6 people per sq km (15 people per sq mile)
Total area 267,667 sq. km (103,346 sq. miles)
Languages Fang, French*, Punu, Sira, Nzebi, Mpongwe
Religions Christian (mainly Roman Catholic) 55%, Traditional beliefs 40%, Other 4%, Muslim 1%
Ethnic mix Fang 26%, Shira-punu 24%, Other 16%, Foreign residents 15%, Nzabi-duma 11%, Mbédé-Teke 8%
Government Presidential system
Currency CFA franc = 100 centimes
Literacy rate 88%
Calorie consumption 2745 kilocalories

GAMBIA
West Africa

Official name Republic of the Gambia
Formation 1965 / 1965
Capital Banjul
Population 1.8 million / 180 people per sq km (466 people per sq mile)
Total area 11,300 sq. km (4363 sq. miles)
Languages Mandinka, Fulani, Wolof, Jola, Soninke, English*
Religions Sunni Muslim 90%, Christian 8%, Traditional beliefs 2%
Ethnic mix Mandinka 42%, Fulani 18%, Wolof 16%, Jola 10%, Serahuli 9%, Other 5%
Government Presidential system
Currency Dalasi = 100 butut
Literacy rate 46%
Calorie consumption 2643 kilocalories

GEORGIA
Southwest Asia

Official name Georgia
Formation 1991 / 1991
Capital Tbilisi
Population 4.3 million / 62 people per sq km (160 people per sq mile)
Total area 69,700 sq. km (26,911 sq. miles)
Languages Georgian*, Russian, Azeri, Armenian, Mingrelian, Ossetian, Abkhazian* (in Abkhazia)
Religions Georgian Orthodox 74%, Muslim 10%, Russian Orthodox 10%, Armenian Apostolic Church (Orthodox) 4%, Other 2%
Ethnic mix Georgian 84%, Azeri 6%, Armenian 6%, Russian 2%, Ossetian 1%, Other 1%
Government Presidential system
Currency Lari = 100 tetri
Literacy rate 99%
Calorie consumption 2743 kilocalories

GERMANY
Northern Europe

Official name Federal Republic of Germany
Formation 1871 / 1990
Capital Berlin
Population 82.2 million / 235 people per sq km (609 people per sq mile)
Total area 357,021 sq. km (137,846 sq. miles)
Languages German*, Turkish
Religions Protestant 34%, Roman Catholic 33%, Other 30%, Muslim 3%
Ethnic mix German 92%, Other European 3%, Other 3%, Turkish 2%
Government Parliamentary system
Currency Euro = 100 cents
Literacy rate 99%
Calorie consumption 3549 kilocalories

GHANA
West Africa

Official name Republic of Ghana
Formation 1957 / 1957
Capital Accra
Population 25 million / 109 people per sq km (281 people per sq mile)
Total area 238,540 sq. km (92,100 sq. miles)
Languages Twi, Fanti, Ewe, Ga, Adangbe, Gurma, Dagomba (Dagbani), English*
Religions Christian 69%, Muslim 16%, Traditional beliefs 9%, Other 6%
Ethnic mix Akan 49%, Mole-Dagbani 17%, Ewe 13%, Other 9%, Ga and Ga-Adangbe 8%, Guan 4%
Government Presidential system
Currency Cedi = 100 pesewas
Literacy rate 67%
Calorie consumption 2934 kilocalories

GREECE
Southeast Europe

Official name Hellenic Republic
Formation 1829 / 1947
Capital Athens
Population 11.4 million / 87 people per sq km (226 people per sq mile)
Total area 131,940 sq. km (50,942 sq. miles)
Languages Greek*, Turkish, Macedonian, Albanian
Religions Orthodox Christian 98%, Muslim 1%, Other 1%
Ethnic mix Greek 98%, Other 2%
Government Parliamentary system
Currency Euro = 100 cents
Literacy rate 97%
Calorie consumption 3661 kilocalories

GRENADA
West Indies

Official name Grenada
Formation 1974 / 1974
Capital St. George's
Population 109,011 / 321 people per sq km (832 people per sq mile)
Total area 340 sq. km (131 sq. miles)
Languages English*, English Creole
Religions Roman Catholic 68%, Anglican 17%, Other 15%
Ethnic mix Black African 82%, Mulatto (mixed race) 13%, East Indian 3%, Other 2%
Government Parliamentary system
Currency East Caribbean dollar = 100 cents
Literacy rate 96%
Calorie consumption 2456 kilocalories

GUATEMALA
Central America

Official name Republic of Guatemala
Formation 1838 / 1838
Capital Guatemala City
Population 14.8 million / 136 people per sq km (354 people per sq mile)
Total area 108,890 sq. km (42,042 sq. miles)
Languages Quiché, Mam, Cakchiquel, Kekchí, Spanish*
Religions Roman Catholic 65%, Protestant 33%, Other and nonreligious 2%
Ethnic mix Amerindian 60%, Mestizo 30%, Other 10%
Government Presidential system
Currency Quetzal = 100 centavos
Literacy rate 74%
Calorie consumption 2244 kilocalories

GUINEA
West Africa

Official name Republic of Guinea
Formation 1958 / 1958
Capital Conakry
Population 10.2 million / 41 people per sq km (107 people per sq mile)
Total area 245,857 sq. km (94,925 sq. miles)
Languages Pulaar, Malinké, Soussou, French*
Religions Muslim 85%, Christian 8%, Traditional beliefs 7%
Ethnic mix Peul 40%, Malinké 30%, Soussou 20%, Other 10%
Government Transitional regime
Currency Guinea franc = 100 centimes
Literacy rate 40%
Calorie consumption 2652 kilocalories

GUINEA-BISSAU
West Africa

Official name Republic of Guinea-Bissau
Formation 1974 / 1974
Capital Bissau
Population 1.5 million / 53 people per sq km (138 people per sq mile)
Total area 36,120 sq. km (13,946 sq. miles)
Languages Portuguese Creole, Balante, Fulani, Malinké, Portuguese*
Religions Traditional beliefs 50%, Muslim 40%, Christian 10%
Ethnic mix Balante 30%, Fulani 20%, Other 16%, Mandyako 14%, Mandinka 13%, Papel 7%
Government Transitional regime
Currency CFA franc = 100 centimes
Literacy rate 52%
Calorie consumption 2476 kilocalories

GUYANA
South America

Official name Cooperative Republic of Guyana
Formation 1966 / 1966
Capital Georgetown
Population 800,000 / 4 people per sq km (11 people per sq mile)
Total area 214,970 sq. km (83,000 sq. miles)
Languages English Creole, Hindi, Tamil, Amerindian languages, English*
Religions Christian 57%, Hindu 28%, Muslim 10%, Other 5%
Ethnic mix East Indian 43%, Black African 30%, Mixed race 17%, Amerindian 9%, Other 1%
Government Presidential system
Currency Guyanese dollar = 100 cents
Literacy rate 99%
Calorie consumption 2718 kilocalories

HAITI
West Indies

Official name Republic of Haiti
Formation 1804 / 1844
Capital Port-au-Prince
Population 10.1 million / 366 people per sq km (949 people per sq mile)
Total area 27,750 sq. km (10,714 sq. miles)
Languages French Creole*, French*
Religions Roman Catholic 55%, Protestant 28%, Other (including Voodoo) 16%, Nonreligious 1%
Ethnic mix Black African 95%, Mulatto (mixed race) and European 5%
Government Presidential system
Currency Gourde = 100 centimes
Literacy rate 62%
Calorie consumption 1979 kilocalories

HONDURAS
Central America

Official name Republic of Honduras
Formation 1838 / 1838
Capital Tegucigalpa
Population 7.8 million / 70 people per sq km (181 people per sq mile)
Total area 112,090 sq. km (43,278 sq. miles)
Languages Spanish*, Garífuna (Carib), English Creole
Religions Roman Catholic 97%, Protestant 3%
Ethnic mix Mestizo 90%, Black 5%, Amerindian 4%, White 1%
Government Presidential system
Currency Lempira = 100 centavos
Literacy rate 84%
Calorie consumption 2694 kilocalories

HUNGARY
Central Europe

Official name Hungary
Formation 1918 / 1947
Capital Budapest
Population 10 million / 108 people per sq km (280 people per sq mile)
Total area 93,030 sq. km (35,919 sq. miles)
Languages Hungarian (Magyar)*
Religions Roman Catholic 52%, Calvinist 16%, Other 15%, Nonreligious 14%, Lutheran 3%
Ethnic mix Magyar 90%, Roma 4%, German 3%, Serb 2%, Other 1%
Government Parliamentary system
Currency Forint = 100 fillér
Literacy rate 99%
Calorie consumption 3477 kilocalories

ICELAND
Northwest Europe

Official name Republic of Iceland
Formation 1944 / 1944
Capital Reykjavík
Population 300,000 / 3 people per sq km (8 people per sq mile)
Total area 103,000 sq. km (39,768 sq. miles)
Languages Icelandic*
Religions Evangelical Lutheran 84%, Other (mostly Christian) 10%, Roman Catholic 3%, Nonreligious 3%
Ethnic mix Icelandic 94%, Other 5%, Danish 1%
Government Parliamentary system
Currency Icelandic króna = 100 aurar
Literacy rate 99%
Calorie consumption 3376 kilocalories

INDIA
South Asia

Official name Republic of India
Formation 1947 / 1947
Capital New Delhi
Population 1.24 billion / 418 people per sq km (1081 people per sq mile)
Total area 3,287,590 sq. km (1,269,339 sq. miles)
Languages Hindi*, English*, Urdu, Bengali, Marathi, Telugu, Tamil, Bihari, Gujarati, Kanarese
Religions Hindu 81%, Muslim 13%, Christian 2%, Sikh 2%, Buddhist 1%, Other 1%
Ethnic mix Indo-Aryan 72%, Dravidian 25%, Mongoloid and other 3%
Government Parliamentary system
Currency Indian rupee = 100 paise
Literacy rate 66%
Calorie consumption 2321 kilocalories

INDONESIA
Southeast Asia

Official name Republic of Indonesia
Formation 1949 / 1999
Capital Jakarta
Population 242 million / 135 people per sq km (349 people per sq mile)
Total area 1,919,440 sq. km (741,096 sq. miles)
Languages Javanese, Sundanese, Madurese, Bahasa Indonesian*, Dutch
Religions Sunni Muslim 86%, Protestant 6%, Roman Catholic 3%, Hindu 2%, Other 2%, Buddhist 1%
Ethnic mix Javanese 41%, Other 29%, Sundanese 15%, Coastal Malays 12%, Madurese 3%
Government Presidential system
Currency Rupiah = 100 sen
Literacy rate 92%
Calorie consumption 2646 kilocalories

IRAN
Southwest Asia

Official name Islamic Republic of Iran
Formation 1502 / 1990
Capital Tehran
Population 74.8 million / 46 people per sq km (118 people per sq mile)
Total area 1,648,000 sq. km (636,293 sq. miles)
Languages Farsi*, Azeri, Luri, Gilaki, Mazanderani, Kurdish, Turkmen, Arabic, Baluchi
Religions Shi'a Muslim 89%, Sunni Muslim 9%, Other 2%
Ethnic mix Persian 51%, Azari 24%, Other 10%, Lur and Bakhtiari 8%, Kurdish 7%
Government Islamic theocracy
Currency Iranian rial = 100 dinars
Literacy rate 85%
Calorie consumption 3143 kilocalories

IRAQ
Southwest Asia

Official name Republic of Iraq
Formation 1932 / 1990
Capital Baghdad
Population 32.7 million / 75 people per sq km (194 people per sq mile)
Total area 437,072 sq. km (168,753 sq. miles)
Languages Arabic*, Kurdish*, Turkic languages, Armenian, Assyrian
Religions Shi'a Muslim 60%, Sunni Muslim 35%, Other (including Christian) 5%
Ethnic mix Arab 80%, Kurdish 15%, Turkmen 3%, Other 2%
Government Parliamentary system
Currency New Iraqi dinar = 1000 fils
Literacy rate 78%
Calorie consumption 2197 kilocalories

IRELAND
Northwest Europe

Official name Ireland
Formation 1922 / 1922
Capital Dublin
Population 4.5 million / 65 people per sq km (169 people per sq mile)
Total area 70,280 sq. km (27,135 sq. miles)
Languages English*, Irish Gaelic*
Religions Roman Catholic 87%, Other and nonreligious 10%, Anglican 3%
Ethnic mix Irish 99%, Other 1%
Government Parliamentary system
Currency Euro = 100 cents
Literacy rate 99%
Calorie consumption 3617 kilocalories

ISRAEL
Southwest Asia

Official name State of Israel
Formation 1948 / 1994
Capital Jerusalem (not internationally recognized)
Population 7.6 million / 374 people per sq km (968 people per sq mile)
Total area 20,770 sq. km (8019 sq. miles)
Languages Hebrew*, Arabic*, Yiddish, German, Russian, Polish, Romanian, Persian
Religions Jewish 76%, Muslim (mainly Sunni) 16%, Other 4%, Druze 2%, Christian 2%
Ethnic mix Jewish 76%, Arab 20%, Other 4%
Government Parliamentary system
Currency Shekel = 100 agorot
Literacy rate 99%
Calorie consumption 3569 kilocalories

ITALY
Southern Europe

Official name Italian Republic
Formation 1861 / 1947
Capital Rome
Population 60.8 million / 207 people per sq km (536 people per sq mile)
Total area 301,230 sq. km (116,305 sq. miles)
Languages Italian*, German, French, Rhaeto-Romanic, Sardinian
Religions Roman Catholic 85%, Other and nonreligious 13%, Muslim 2%
Ethnic mix Italian 94%, Other 4%, Sardinian 2%
Government Parliamentary system
Currency Euro = 100 cents
Literacy rate 99%
Calorie consumption 3627 kilocalories

IVORY COAST
West Africa

Official name Republic of Côte d'Ivoire
Formation 1960 / 1960
Capital Yamoussoukro
Population 20.2 million / 64 people per sq km (165 people per sq mile)
Total area 322,460 sq. km (124,502 sq. miles)
Languages Akan, French*, Krou, Voltaique
Religions Muslim 38%, Traditional beliefs 25%, Roman Catholic 25%, Other 6%, Protestant 6%
Ethnic mix Akan 42%, Voltaique 18%, Mandé du Nord 17%, Krou 11%, Mandé du Sud 10%, Other 2%
Government Presidential system
Currency CFA franc = 100 centimes
Literacy rate 55%
Calorie consumption 2670 kilocalories

JAMAICA
West Indies

Official name Jamaica
Formation 1962 / 1962
Capital Kingston
Population 2.8 million / 259 people per sq km (670 people per sq mile)
Total area 10,990 sq. km (4243 sq. miles)
Languages English Creole, English*
Religions Other and nonreligious 45%, Other Protestant 20%, Church of God 18%, Baptist 10%, Anglican 7%
Ethnic mix Black 91%, Mulatto (mixed race) 7%, European and Chinese 1%, East Indian 1%
Government Parliamentary system
Currency Jamaican dollar = 100 cents
Literacy rate 86%
Calorie consumption 2807 kilocalories

JAPAN
East Asia

Official name Japan
Formation 1590 / 1972
Capital Tokyo
Population 126 million / 336 people per sq km (870 people per sq mile)
Total area 377,835 sq. km (145,882 sq. miles)
Languages Japanese*, Korean, Chinese
Religions Shinto and Buddhist 76%, Buddhist 16%, Other (including Christian) 8%
Ethnic mix Japanese 99%, Other (mainly Korean) 1%
Government Parliamentary system
Currency Yen = 100 sen
Literacy rate 99%
Calorie consumption 2723 kilocalories

JORDAN
Southwest Asia

Official name Hashemite Kingdom of Jordan
Formation 1946 / 1967
Capital Amman
Population 6.3 million / 71 people per sq km (183 people per sq mile)
Total area 92,300 sq. km (35,637 sq. miles)
Languages Arabic*
Religions Sunni Muslim 92%, Christian 6%, Other 2%
Ethnic mix Arab 98%, Circassian 1%, Armenian 1%
Government Monarchy
Currency Jordanian dinar = 1000 fils
Literacy rate 92%
Calorie consumption 2977 kilocalories

KAZAKHSTAN
Central Asia

Official name Republic of Kazakhstan
Formation 1991 / 1991
Capital Astana
Population 16.2 million / 6 people per sq km (15 people per sq mile)
Total area 2,717,300 sq. km (1,049,150 sq. miles)
Languages Kazakh*, Russian, Ukrainian, German, Uzbek, Tatar, Uighur
Religions Muslim (mainly Sunni) 47%, Orthodox Christian 44%, Other 7%, Protestant 2%
Ethnic mix Kazakh 57%, Russian 27%, Other 8%, Uzbek 3%, Ukrainian 3%, German 2%
Government Presidential system
Currency Tenge = 100 tiyn
Literacy rate 99%
Calorie consumption 3284 kilocalories

KENYA
East Africa

Official name Republic of Kenya
Formation 1963 / 1963
Capital Nairobi
Population 41.6 million / 73 people per sq km (190 people per sq mile)
Total area 582,650 sq. km (224,961 sq. miles)
Languages Kiswahili*, English*, Kikuyu, Luo, Kalenjin, Kamba
Religions Christian 80%, Muslim 10%, Traditional beliefs 9%, Other 1%
Ethnic mix Other 28%, Kikuyu 22%, Luo 14%, Luhya 14%, Kalenjin 11%, Kamba 11%
Government Mixed Presidential–Parliamentary system
Currency Kenya shilling = 100 cents
Literacy rate 87%
Calorie consumption 2092 kilocalories

KIRIBATI
Australasia & Oceania

Official name Republic of Kiribati
Formation 1979 / 1979
Capital Bairiki (Tarawa Atoll)
Population 101,998 / 144 people per sq km (372 people per sq mile)
Total area 717 sq. km (277 sq. miles)
Languages English*, Kiribati
Religions Roman Catholic 55%, Kiribati Protestant Church 36%, Other 9%
Ethnic mix Micronesian 99%, Other 1%
Government Elections involving informal groupings
Currency Australian dollar = 100 cents
Literacy rate 99%
Calorie consumption 2866 kilocalories

KOSOVO (not yet recognised)
Southeast Europe

Official name Republic of Kosovo
Formation 2008 / 2008
Capital Pristina
Population 1.73 million / 159 people per sq km (412 people per sq mile)
Total area 10,908 sq. km (4212 sq. miles)
Languages Albanian*, Serbian*, Bosniak, Gorani, Roma, Turkish
Religions Muslim 92%, Roman Catholic 4%, Orthodox Christian 4%
Ethnic mix Albanian 92%, Serb 4%, Bosniak and Gorani 2%, Turkish 1%, Roma 1%
Government Parliamentary system
Currency Euro = 100 cents
Literacy rate 92%
Calorie consumption Not available

KUWAIT
Southwest Asia

Official name State of Kuwait
Formation 1961 / 1961
Capital Kuwait City
Population 2.8 million / 157 people per sq km (407 people per sq mile)
Total area 17,820 sq. km (6880 sq. miles)
Languages Arabic*, English
Religions Sunni Muslim 45%, Shi'a Muslim 40%, Christian, Hindu, and other 15%
Ethnic mix Kuwaiti 45%, Other Arab 35%, South Asian 9%, Other 7%, Iranian 4%
Government Monarchy
Currency Kuwaiti dinar = 1000 fils
Literacy rate 94%
Calorie consumption 3681 kilocalories

KYRGYZSTAN
Central Asia

Official name Kyrgyz Republic
Formation 1991 / 1991
Capital Bishkek
Population 5.4 million / 27 people per sq km (70 people per sq mile)
Total area 198,500 sq. km (76,641 sq. miles)
Languages Kyrgyz*, Russian*, Uzbek, Tatar, Ukrainian
Religions Muslim (mainly Sunni) 70%, Orthodox Christian 30%
Ethnic mix Kyrgyz 69%, Uzbek 14%, Russian 9%, Other 6%, Dungan 1%, Uighur 1%
Government Presidential system
Currency Som = 100 tyiyn
Literacy rate 99%
Calorie consumption 2791 kilocalories

LAOS
Southeast Asia

Official name Lao People's Democratic Republic
Formation 1953 / 1953
Capital Vientiane
Population 6.3 million / 27 people per sq km (71 people per sq mile)
Total area 236,800 sq. km (91,428 sq. miles)
Languages Lao*, Mon-Khmer, Yao, Vietnamese, Chinese, French
Religions Buddhist 65%, Other (including animist) 34%, Christian 1%
Ethnic mix Lao Loum 66%, Lao Theung 30%, Lao Soung 2%, Other 2%
Government One-party state
Currency New kip = 100 at
Literacy rate 73%
Calorie consumption 2377 kilocalories

LATVIA
Northeast Europe

Official name Republic of Latvia
Formation 1991 / 1991
Capital Riga
Population 2.2 million / 34 people per sq km (88 people per sq mile)
Total area 64,589 sq. km (24,938 sq. miles)
Languages Latvian*, Russian
Religions Other 43%, Lutheran 24%, Roman Catholic 18%, Orthodox Christian 15%
Ethnic mix Latvian 59%, Russian 28%, Belarussian 4%, Other 4%, Ukrainian 3%, Polish 2%
Government Parliamentary system
Currency Lats = 100 santimi
Literacy rate 99%
Calorie consumption 2923 kilocalories

LEBANON
Southwest Asia

Official name Republic of Lebanon
Formation 1941 / 1941
Capital Beirut
Population 4.3 million / 420 people per sq km (1089 people per sq mile)
Total area 10,400 sq. km (4015 sq. miles)
Languages Arabic*, French, Armenian, Assyrian
Religions Muslim 60%, Christian 39%, Other 1%
Ethnic mix Arab 95%, Armenian 4%, Other 1%
Government Parliamentary system
Currency Lebanese pound = 100 piastres
Literacy rate 90%
Calorie consumption 3153 kilocalories

LESOTHO
Southern Africa

Official name Kingdom of Lesotho
Formation 1966 / 1966
Capital Maseru
Population 2.2 million / 72 people per sq km (188 people per sq mile)
Total area 30,355 sq. km (11,720 sq. miles)
Languages English*, Sesotho*, isiZulu
Religions Christian 90%, Traditional beliefs 10%
Ethnic mix Sotho 99%, European and Asian 1%
Government Parliamentary system
Currency Loti & South African rand = 100 lisente
Literacy rate 90%
Calorie consumption 2371 kilocalories

LIBERIA
West Africa

Official name Republic of Liberia
Formation 1847 / 1847
Capital Monrovia
Population 4.1 million / 43 people per sq km (110 people per sq mile)
Total area 111,370 sq. km (43,000 sq. miles)
Languages Kpelle, Vai, Bassa, Kru, Grebo, Kissi, Gola, Loma, English*
Religions Christian 40%, Traditional beliefs 40%, Muslim 20%
Ethnic mix Indigenous tribes (12 groups) 49%, Kpellé 20%, Bassa 16%, Gio 8%, Krou 7%
Government Presidential system
Currency Liberian dollar = 100 cents
Literacy rate 59%
Calorie consumption 2261 kilocalories

LIBYA
North Africa

Official name Libya
Formation 1951 / 1951
Capital Tripoli
Population 6.4 million / 4 people per sq km (9 people per sq mile)
Total area 1,759,540 sq. km (679,358 sq. miles)
Languages Arabic*, Tuareg
Religions Muslim (mainly Sunni) 97%, Other 3%
Ethnic mix Arab and Berber 97%, Other 3%
Government Transitional regime
Currency Libyan dinar = 1000 dirhams
Literacy rate 89%
Calorie consumption 3157 kilocalories

LIECHTENSTEIN
Central Europe

Official name Principality of Liechtenstein
Formation 1719 / 1719
Capital Vaduz
Population 36,713 / 229 people per sq km (592 people per sq mile)
Total area 160 sq. km (62 sq. miles)
Languages German*, Alemannish dialect, Italian
Religions Roman Catholic 79%, Other 13%, Protestant 8%
Ethnic mix Liechtensteiner 66%, Other 12%, Swiss 10%, Austrian 6%, German 3%, Italian 3%
Government Parliamentary system
Currency Swiss franc = 100 rappen/centimes
Literacy rate 99%
Calorie consumption Not available

LITHUANIA
Northeast Europe

Official name Republic of Lithuania
Formation 1991 / 1991
Capital Vilnius
Population 3.3 million / 51 people per sq km (131 people per sq mile)
Total area 65,200 sq. km (25,174 sq. miles)
Languages Lithuanian*, Russian
Religions Roman Catholic 79%, Other 15%, Russian Orthodox 4%, Protestant 2%
Ethnic mix Lithuanian 85%, Polish 6%, Russian 5%, Other 3%, Belarussian 1%
Government Parliamentary system
Currency Litas = 100 centu
Literacy rate 99%
Calorie consumption 3486 kilocalories

LUXEMBOURG
Northwest Europe

Official name Grand Duchy of Luxembourg
Formation 1867 / 1867
Capital Luxembourg-Ville
Population 500,000 / 193 people per sq km (501 people per sq mile)
Total area 2586 sq. km (998 sq. miles)
Languages Luxembourgish*, German*, French*
Religions Roman Catholic 97%, Protestant, Orthodox Christian, and Jewish 3%
Ethnic mix Luxembourger 62%, Foreign residents 38%
Government Parliamentary system
Currency Euro = 100 cents
Literacy rate 99%
Calorie consumption 3637 kilocalories

MACEDONIA
Southeast Europe

Official name Republic of Macedonia
Formation 1991 / 1991
Capital Skopje
Population 2.1 million / 82 people per sq km (212 people per sq mile)
Total area 25,333 sq. km (9781 sq. miles)
Languages Macedonian*, Albanian*, Turkish, Romani, Serbian
Religions Orthodox Christian 65%, Muslim 29%, Roman Catholic 4%, Other 2%
Ethnic mix Macedonian 64%, Albanian 25%, Turkish 4%, Roma 3%, Serb 2%, Other 2%
Government Mixed presidential–parliamentary system
Currency Macedonian denar = 100 deni
Literacy rate 97%
Calorie consumption 2983 kilocalories

MADAGASCAR
Indian Ocean

Official name Republic of Madagascar
Formation 1960 / 1960
Capital Antananarivo
Population 21.3 million / 37 people per sq km (95 people per sq mile)
Total area 587,040 sq. km (226,656 sq. miles)
Languages Malagasy*, French*, English*
Religions Traditional beliefs 52%, Christian (mainly Roman Catholic) 41%, Muslim 7%
Ethnic mix Other Malay 46%, Merina 26%, Betsimisaraka 15%, Betsileo 12%, Other 1%
Government Transitional regime
Currency Ariary = 5 iraimbilanja
Literacy rate 64%
Calorie consumption 2117 kilocalories

MALAWI
Southern Africa

Official name Republic of Malawi
Formation 1964 / 1964
Capital Lilongwe
Population 15.4 million / 164 people per sq km (424 people per sq mile)
Total area 118,480 sq. km (45,745 sq. miles)
Languages Chewa, Lomwe, Yao, Ngoni, English*
Religions Protestant 55%, Roman Catholic 20%, Muslim 20%, Traditional beliefs 5%
Ethnic mix Bantu 99%, Other 1%
Government Presidential system
Currency Malawi kwacha = 100 tambala
Literacy rate 74%
Calorie consumption 2318 kilocalories

MALAYSIA
Southeast Asia

Official name Federation of Malaysia
Formation 1963 / 1965
Capital Kuala Lumpur; Putrajaya (administrative)
Population 28.9 million / 88 people per sq km (228 people per sq mile)
Total area 329,750 sq. km (127,316 sq. miles)
Languages Bahasa Malaysia*, Malay, Chinese, Tamil, English
Religions Muslim (mainly Sunni) 61%, Buddhist 19%, Christian 9%, Hindu 6%, Other 5%
Ethnic mix Malay 53%, Chinese 26%, Indigenous tribes 12%, Indian 8%, Other 1%
Government Parliamentary system
Currency Ringgit = 100 sen
Literacy rate 92%
Calorie consumption 2902 kilocalories

MALDIVES
Indian Ocean

Official name Republic of Maldives
Formation 1965 / 1965
Capital Male'
Population 394,491 / 1315 people per sq km (3400 people per sq mile)
Total area 300 sq. km (116 sq. miles)
Languages Dhivehi (Maldivian), Sinhala, Tamil, Arabic
Religions Sunni Muslim 100%
Ethnic mix Arab–Sinhalese–Malay 100%
Government Presidential system
Currency Rufiyaa = 100 laari
Literacy rate 97%
Calorie consumption 2720 kilocalories

MALI
West Africa

Official name Republic of Mali
Formation 1960 / 1960
Capital Bamako
Population 15.8 million / 13 people per sq km (34 people per sq mile)
Total area 1,240,000 sq. km (478,764 sq. miles)
Languages Bambara, Fulani, Senufo, Soninke, French*
Religions Muslim (mainly Sunni) 90%, Traditional beliefs 6%, Christian 4%
Ethnic mix Bambara 52%, Other 14%, Fulani 11%, Saracolé 7%, Soninka 7%, Tuareg 5%, Mianka 4%
Government Transitional regime
Currency CFA franc = 100 centimes
Literacy rate 23%
Calorie consumption 2624 kilocalories

MALTA
Southern Europe

Official name Republic of Malta
Formation 1964 / 1964
Capital Valletta
Population 400,000 / 1250 people per sq km (3226 people per sq mile)
Total area 316 sq. km (122 sq. miles)
Languages Maltese*, English*
Religions Roman Catholic 98%, Other and nonreligious 2%
Ethnic mix Maltese 96%, Other 4%
Government Parliamentary system
Currency Euro = 100 cents
Literacy rate 92%
Calorie consumption 3438 kilocalories

MARSHALL ISLANDS
Australasia & Oceania

Official name Republic of the Marshall Islands
Formation 1986 / 1986
Capital Majuro
Population 68,480 / 378 people per sq km (978 people per sq mile)
Total area 181 sq. km (70 sq. miles)
Languages Marshallese*, English*, Japanese, German
Religions Protestant 90%, Roman Catholic 8%, Other 2%
Ethnic mix Micronesian 90%, Other 10%
Government Presidential system
Currency US dollar = 100 cents
Literacy rate 91%
Calorie consumption Not available

MAURITANIA
West Africa

Official name Islamic Republic of Mauritania
Formation 1960 / 1960
Capital Nouakchott
Population 3.5 million / 3 people per sq km (9 people per sq mile)
Total area 1,030,700 sq. km (397,953 sq. miles)
Languages Hassaniyah Arabic*, Wolof, French
Religions Sunni Muslim 100%
Ethnic mix Maure 81%, Wolof 7%, Tukolor 5%, Other 4%, Soninka 3%
Government Presidential system
Currency Ouguiya = 5 khoums
Literacy rate 58%
Calorie consumption 2856 kilocalories

MAURITIUS
Indian Ocean

Official name Republic of Mauritius
Formation 1968 / 1968
Capital Port Louis
Population 1.3 million / 699 people per sq km (1811 people per sq mile)
Total area 1860 sq. km (718 sq. miles)
Languages French Creole, Hindi, Urdu, Tamil, Chinese, English*, French
Religions Hindu 48%, Roman Catholic 24%, Muslim 17%, Protestant 9%, Other 2%
Ethnic mix Indo-Mauritian 68%, Creole 27%, Sino-Mauritian 3%, Franco-Mauritian 2%
Government Parliamentary system
Currency Mauritian rupee = 100 cents
Literacy rate 88%
Calorie consumption 2993 kilocalories

MEXICO
North America

Official name United Mexican States
Formation 1836 / 1848
Capital Mexico City
Population 115 million / 60 people per sq km (156 people per sq mile)
Total area 1,972,550 sq. km (761,602 sq. miles)
Languages Spanish*, Nahuatl, Mayan, Zapotec, Mixtec, Otomi, Totonac, Tzotzil, Tzeltal
Religions Roman Catholic 77%, Other 14%, Protestant 6%, Nonreligious 3%
Ethnic mix Mestizo 60%, Amerindian 30%, European 9%, Other 1%
Government Presidential system
Currency Mexican peso = 100 centavos
Literacy rate 93%
Calorie consumption 3146 kilocalories

MICRONESIA
Australasia & Oceania

Official name Federated States of Micronesia
Formation 1986 / 1986
Capital Palikir (Pohnpei Island)
Population 106,487 / 152 people per sq km (393 people per sq mile)
Total area 702 sq. km (271 sq. miles)
Languages Trukese, Pohnpeian, Kosraean, Yapese, English*
Religions Roman Catholic 50%, Protestant 47%, Other 3%
Ethnic mix Chuukese 49%, Pohnpeian 24%, Other 14%, Kosraean 6%, Yapese 5%, Asian 2%
Government Nonparty system
Currency US dollar = 100 cents
Literacy rate 81%
Calorie consumption Not available

MOLDOVA
Southeast Europe

Official name Republic of Moldova
Formation 1991 / 1991
Capital Chisinau
Population 3.5 million / 104 people per sq km (269 people per sq mile)
Total area 33,843 sq. km (13,067 sq. miles)
Languages Moldovan*, Ukrainian, Russian
Religions Orthodox Christian 93%, Other 6%, Baptist 1%
Ethnic mix Moldovan 84%, Ukrainian 7%, Gagauz 5%, Russian 2%, Bulgarian 1%, Other 1%
Government Parliamentary system
Currency Moldovan leu = 100 bani
Literacy rate 99%
Calorie consumption 2707 kilocalories

MONACO
Southern Europe

Official name Principality of Monaco
Formation 1861 / 1861
Capital Monaco-Ville
Population 30,510 / 15646 people per sq km (40680 people per sq mile)
Total area 1.95 sq. km (0.75 sq. miles)
Languages French*, Italian, Monégasque, English
Religions Roman Catholic 89%, Protestant 6%, Other 5%
Ethnic mix French 47%, Other 21%, Italian 16%, Monégasque 16%
Government Mixed monarchical–parliamentary system
Currency Euro = 100 cents
Literacy rate 99%
Calorie consumption Not available

MONGOLIA
East Asia

Official name Mongolia
Formation 1924 / 1924
Capital Ulan Bator
Population 2.8 million / 2 people per sq km (5 people per sq mile)
Total area 1,565,000 sq. km (604,247 sq. miles)
Languages Khalkha Mongolian, Kazakh, Chinese, Russian
Religions Tibetan Buddhist 50%, Nonreligious 40%, Shamanist and Christian 6%, Muslim 4%
Ethnic mix Khalkh 95%, Kazakh 4%, Other 1%
Government Mixed presidential–parliamentary system
Currency Tugrik (tögrög) = 100 möngö
Literacy rate 98%
Calorie consumption 2434 kilocalories

MONTENEGRO
Southeast Europe

Official name Montenegro
Formation 2006 / 2006
Capital Podgorica
Population 600,000 / 43 people per sq km (113 people per sq mile)
Total area 13,812 sq. km (5332 sq. miles)
Languages Montenegrin*, Serbian, Albanian, Bosniak, Croatian
Religions Orthodox Christian 74%, Muslim 18%, Roman Catholic 4%, Other 4%
Ethnic mix Montenegrin 43%, Serb 32%, Other 12%, Bosniak 8%, Albanian 5%
Government Parliamentary system
Currency Euro = 100 cents
Literacy rate 98%
Calorie consumption 2887 kilocalories

MOROCCO
North Africa

Official name Kingdom of Morocco
Formation 1956 / 1969
Capital Rabat
Population 32.3 million / 72 people per sq km (187 people per sq mile)
Total area 446,300 sq. km (172,316 sq. miles)
Languages Arabic*, Tamazight (Berber), French, Spanish
Religions Muslim (mainly Sunni) 99%, Other (mostly Christian) 1%
Ethnic mix Arab 70%, Berber 29%, European 1%
Government Mixed monarchical–parliamentary system
Currency Moroccan dirham = 100 centimes
Literacy rate 56%
Calorie consumption 3264 kilocalories

MOZAMBIQUE
Southern Africa

Official name Republic of Mozambique
Formation 1975 / 1975
Capital Maputo
Population 23.9 million / 30 people per sq km (79 people per sq mile)
Total area 801,590 sq. km (309,494 sq. miles)
Languages Makua, Xitsonga, Sena, Lomwe, Portuguese*
Religions Traditional beliefs 56%, Christian 30%, Muslim 14%
Ethnic mix Makua Lomwe 47%, Tsonga 23%, Malawi 12%, Shona 11%, Yao 4%, Other 3%
Government Presidential system
Currency New metical = 100 centavos
Literacy rate 55%
Calorie consumption 2112 kilocalories

NAMIBIA
Southern Africa

Official name Republic of Namibia
Formation 1990 / 1994
Capital Windhoek
Population 2.3 million / 3 people per sq km (7 people per sq mile)
Total area 825,418 sq. km (318,694 sq. miles)
Languages Ovambo, Kavango, English*, Bergdama, German, Afrikaans
Religions Christian 90%, Traditional beliefs 10%
Ethnic mix Ovambo 50%, Other tribes 22%, Kavango 9%, Damara 7%, Herero 7%, Other 5%
Government Presidential system
Currency Namibian dollar & South African rand = 100 cents
Literacy rate 88%
Calorie consumption 2151 kilocalories

NAURU
Australasia & Oceania

Official name Republic of Nauru
Formation 1968 / 1968
Capital Yaren District
Population 9378 / 447 people per sq km (1158 people per sq mile)
Total area 21 sq. km (8.1 sq. miles)
Languages Nauruan*, Kiribati, Chinese, Tuvaluan, English
Religions Nauruan Congregational Church 60%, Roman Catholic 35%, Other 5%
Ethnic mix Nauruan 93%, Chinese 5%, European 1%, Other Pacific islanders 1%
Government Nonparty system
Currency Australian dollar = 100 cents
Literacy rate 95%
Calorie consumption Not available

NEPAL
South Asia

Official name Federal Democratic Republic of Nepal
Formation 1769 / 1769
Capital Kathmandu
Population 30.5 million / 223 people per sq km (577 people per sq mile)
Total area 140,800 sq. km (54,363 sq. miles)
Languages Nepali*, Maithili, Bhojpuri
Religions Hindu 81%, Buddhist 11%, Muslim 4%, Other (including Christian) 4%
Ethnic mix Other 52%, Chhetri 16%, Hill Brahman 13%, Tharu 7%, Magar 7%, Tamang 5%
Government Transitional regime
Currency Nepalese rupee = 100 paisa
Literacy rate 59%
Calorie consumption 2443 kilocalories

NETHERLANDS
Northwest Europe

Official name Kingdom of the Netherlands
Formation 1648 / 1839
Capital Amsterdam; The Hague (administrative)
Population 16.7 million / 492 people per sq km (1275 people per sq mile)
Total area 41,526 sq. km (16,033 sq. miles)
Languages Dutch*, Frisian
Religions Roman Catholic 36%, Other 34%, Protestant 27%, Muslim 3%
Ethnic mix Dutch 82%, Other 12%, Surinamese 2%, Turkish 2%, Moroccan 2%
Government Parliamentary system
Currency Euro = 100 cents
Literacy rate 99%
Calorie consumption 3261 kilocalories

NEW ZEALAND
Australasia & Oceania

Official name New Zealand
Formation 1947 / 1947
Capital Wellington
Population 4.4 million / 16 people per sq km (42 people per sq mile)
Total area 268,680 sq. km (103,737 sq. miles)
Languages English*, Maori*
Religions Anglican 24%, Other 22%, Presbyterian 18%, Nonreligious 16%, Roman Catholic 15%, Methodist 5%
Ethnic mix European 75%, Maori 15%, Other 7%, Samoan 3%
Government Parliamentary system
Currency New Zealand dollar = 100 cents
Literacy rate 99%
Calorie consumption 3172 kilocalories

NICARAGUA
Central America

Official name Republic of Nicaragua
Formation 1838 / 1838
Capital Managua
Population 5.9 million / 50 people per sq km (129 people per sq mile)
Total area 129,494 sq. km (49,998 sq. miles)
Languages Spanish*, English Creole, Miskito
Religions Roman Catholic 80%, Protestant Evangelical 17%, Other 3%
Ethnic mix Mestizo 69%, White 17%, Black 9%, Amerindian 5%
Government Presidential system
Currency Córdoba oro = 100 centavos
Literacy rate 80%
Calorie consumption 2517 kilocalories

NIGER
West Africa

Official name Republic of Niger
Formation 1960 / 1960
Capital Niamey
Population 16.1 million / 13 people per sq km (33 people per sq mile)
Total area 1,267,000 sq. km (489,188 sq. miles)
Languages Hausa, Djerma, Fulani, Tuareg, Teda, French*
Religions Muslim 99%, Other (including Christian) 1%
Ethnic mix Hausa 53%, Djerma and Songhai 21%, Tuareg 11%, Fulani 7%, Kanuri 6%, Other 2%
Government Presidential system
Currency CFA franc = 100 centimes
Literacy rate 30%
Calorie consumption 2489 kilocalories

NIGERIA
West Africa

Official name Federal Republic of Nigeria
Formation 1960 / 1961
Capital Abuja
Population 162 million / 178 people per sq km (462 people per sq mile)
Total area 923,768 sq. km (356,667 sq. miles)
Languages Hausa, English*, Yoruba, Ibo
Religions Muslim 50%, Christian 40%, Traditional beliefs 10%
Ethnic mix Other 29%, Hausa 21%, Yoruba 21%, Ibo 18%, Fulani 11%
Government Presidential system
Currency Naira = 100 kobo
Literacy rate 61%
Calorie consumption 2711 kilocalories

NORTH KOREA
East Asia

Official name Democratic People's Republic of Korea
Formation 1948 / 1953
Capital Pyongyang
Population 24.5 million / 203 people per sq km (527 people per sq mile)
Total area 120,540 sq. km (46,540 sq. miles)
Languages Korean*
Religions Atheist 100%
Ethnic mix Korean 100%
Government One-party state
Currency North Korean won = 100 chon
Literacy rate 99%
Calorie consumption 2078 kilocalories

NORWAY
Northern Europe

Official name Kingdom of Norway
Formation 1905 / 1905
Capital Oslo
Population 4.9 million / 16 people per sq km (41 people per sq mile)
Total area 324,220 sq. km (125,181 sq. miles)
Languages Norwegian* (Bokmål "book language" and Nynorsk "new Norsk"), Sámi
Religions Evangelical Lutheran 88%, Other and nonreligious 8%, Muslim 2%, Pentecostal 1%, Roman Catholic 1%
Ethnic mix Norwegian 93%, Other 6%, Sámi 1%
Government Parliamentary system
Currency Norwegian krone = 100 øre
Literacy rate 99%
Calorie consumption 3453 kilocalories

OMAN
Southwest Asia

Official name Sultanate of Oman
Formation 1951 / 1951
Capital Muscat
Population 2.8 million / 13 people per sq km (34 people per sq mile)
Total area 212,460 sq. km (82,031 sq. miles)
Languages Arabic*, Baluchi, Farsi, Hindi, Punjabi
Religions Ibadi Muslim 75%, Other Muslim and Hindu 25%
Ethnic mix Arab 88%, Baluchi 4%, Persian 3%, Indian and Pakistani 3%, African 2%
Government Monarchy
Currency Omani rial = 1000 baisa
Literacy rate 87%
Calorie consumption Not available

PAKISTAN
South Asia

Official name Islamic Republic of Pakistan
Formation 1947 / 1971
Capital Islamabad
Population 177 million / 229 people per sq km (594 people per sq mile)
Total area 803,940 sq. km (310,401 sq. miles)
Languages Punjabi, Sindhi, Pashtu, Urdu*, Baluchi, Brahui
Religions Sunni Muslim 77%, Shi'a Muslim 20%, Hindu 2%, Christian 1%
Ethnic mix Punjabi 56%, Pathan (Pashtun) 15%, Sindhi 14%, Mohajir 7%, Baluchi 4%, Other 4%
Government Presidential system
Currency Pakistani rupee = 100 paisa
Literacy rate 56%
Calorie consumption 2423 kilocalories

PALAU
Australasia & Oceania

Official name Republic of Palau
Formation 1994 / 1994
Capital Melekeok
Population 21,032 / 41 people per sq km (107 people per sq mile)
Total area 458 sq. km (177 sq. miles)
Languages Palauan, English, Japanese, Angaur, Tobi, Sonsorolese
Religions Christian 66%, Modekngei 34%
Ethnic mix Palauan 74%, Filipino 16%, Other 6%, Chinese and other Asian 4%
Government Nonparty system
Currency US dollar = 100 cents
Literacy rate 98%
Calorie consumption Not available

PANAMA
Central America

Official name Republic of Panama
Formation 1903 / 1903
Capital Panama City
Population 3.6 million / 47 people per sq km (123 people per sq mile)
Total area 78,200 sq. km (30,193 sq. miles)
Languages English Creole, Spanish*, Amerindian languages, Chibchan languages
Religions Roman Catholic 84%, Protestant 15%, Other 1%
Ethnic mix Mestizo 70%, Black 14%, White 10%, Amerindian 6%
Government Presidential system
Currency Balboa & US dollar = 100 centésimos
Literacy rate 94%
Calorie consumption 2606 kilocalories

PAPUA NEW GUINEA
Australasia & Oceania

Official name Independent State of Papua New Guinea
Formation 1975 / 1975
Capital Port Moresby
Population 7 million / 15 people per sq km (40 people per sq mile)
Total area 462,840 sq. km (178,703 sq. miles)
Languages Pidgin English, Papuan, English*, Motu, 800 (est.) native languages
Religions Protestant 60%, Roman Catholic 37%, Other 3%
Ethnic mix Melanesian and mixed race 100%
Government Parliamentary system
Currency Kina = 100 toea
Literacy rate 60%
Calorie consumption 2193 kilocalories

PARAGUAY
South America

Official name Republic of Paraguay
Formation 1811 / 1938
Capital Asunción
Population 6.6 million / 17 people per sq km (43 people per sq mile)
Total area 406,750 sq. km (157,046 sq. miles)
Languages Guaraní, Spanish*, German
Religions Roman Catholic 90%, Protestant (including Mennonite) 10%
Ethnic mix Mestizo 91%, Other 7%, Amerindian 2%
Government Presidential system
Currency Guaraní = 100 céntimos
Literacy rate 95%
Calorie consumption 2518 kilocalories

PERU
South America

Official name Republic of Peru
Formation 1824 / 1941
Capital Lima
Population 29.4 million / 23 people per sq km (59 people per sq mile)
Total area 1,285,200 sq. km (496,223 sq. miles)
Languages Spanish*, Quechua*, Aymara
Religions Roman Catholic 81%, Other 19%
Ethnic mix Amerindian 45%, Mestizo 37%, White 15%, Other 3%
Government Presidential system
Currency New sol = 100 céntimos
Literacy rate 90%
Calorie consumption 2563 kilocalories

PHILIPPINES
Southeast Asia

Official name Republic of the Philippines
Formation 1946 / 1946
Capital Manila
Population 94.9 million / 318 people per sq km (824 people per sq mile)
Total area 300,000 sq. km (115,830 sq. miles)
Languages Filipino, English, Tagalog, Cebuano, Ilocano, Hiligaynon, many other local languages
Religions Roman Catholic 81%, Protestant 9%, Muslim 5%, Other (including Buddhist) 5%
Ethnic mix Other 34%, Tagalog 28%, Cebuano 13%, Ilocano 9%, Hiligaynon 8%, Bisaya 8%
Government Presidential system
Currency Philippine peso = 100 centavos
Literacy rate 95%
Calorie consumption 2580 kilocalories

POLAND
Northern Europe

Official name Republic of Poland
Formation 1918 / 1945
Capital Warsaw
Population 38.3 million / 126 people per sq km (326 people per sq mile)
Total area 312,685 sq. km (120,728 sq. miles)
Languages Polish*
Religions Roman Catholic 93%, Other and nonreligious 5%, Orthodox Christian 2%
Ethnic mix Polish 98%, Other 2%
Government Parliamentary system
Currency Zloty = 100 groszy
Literacy rate 99%
Calorie consumption 3392 kilocalories

PORTUGAL
Southwest Europe

Official name Republic of Portugal
Formation 1139 / 1640
Capital Lisbon
Population 10.7 million / 116 people per sq km (301 people per sq mile)
Total area 92,391 sq. km (35,672 sq. miles)
Languages Portuguese*
Religions Roman Catholic 92%, Protestant 4%, Nonreligious 3%, Other 1%
Ethnic mix Portuguese 98%, African and other 2%
Government Parliamentary system
Currency Euro = 100 cents
Literacy rate 95%
Calorie consumption 3617 kilocalories

QATAR
Southwest Asia

Official name State of Qatar
Formation 1971 / 1971
Capital Doha
Population 1.9 million / 173 people per sq km (447 people per sq mile)
Total area 11,437 sq. km (4416 sq. miles)
Languages Arabic*
Religions Muslim (mainly Sunni) 95%, Other 5%
Ethnic mix Qatari 20%, Indian 20%, Other Arab 20%, Nepalese 13%, Filipino 10%, Other 10%, Pakistani 7%
Government Monarchy
Currency Qatar riyal = 100 dirhams
Literacy rate 95%
Calorie consumption Not available

ROMANIA
Southeast Europe

Official name Romania
Formation 1878 / 1947
Capital Bucharest
Population 21.4 million / 93 people per sq km (241 people per sq mile)
Total area 237,500 sq. km (91,699 sq. miles)
Languages Romanian*, Hungarian (Magyar), Romani, German
Religions Romanian Orthodox 87%, Protestant 5%, Roman Catholic 5%, Greek Orthodox 1%, Greek Catholic (Uniate) 1%, Other 1%
Ethnic mix Romanian 89%, Magyar 7%, Roma 3%, Other 1%
Government Presidential system
Currency New Romanian leu = 100 bani
Literacy rate 98%
Calorie consumption 3487 kilocalories

RUSSIAN FEDERATION
Europe / Asia

Official name Russian Federation
Formation 1480 / 1991
Capital Moscow
Population 143 million / 8 people per sq km (22 people per sq mile)
Total area 17,075,200 sq. km (6,592,735 sq. miles)
Languages Russian*, Tatar, Ukrainian, Chavash, various other national languages
Religions Orthodox Christian 75%, Muslim 14%, Other 11%
Ethnic mix Russian 80%, Other 12%, Tatar 4%, Ukrainian 2%, Bashkir 1%, Chavash 1%
Government Mixed Presidential–Parliamentary system
Currency Russian rouble = 100 kopeks
Literacy rate 99%
Calorie consumption 3172 kilocalories

RWANDA
Central Africa

Official name Republic of Rwanda
Formation 1962 / 1962
Capital Kigali
Population 10.9 million / 437 people per sq km (1132 people per sq mile)
Total area 26,338 sq. km (10,169 sq. miles)
Languages Kinyarwanda*, French*, Kiswahili, English*
Religions Christian 94%, Muslim 5%, Traditional beliefs 1%
Ethnic mix Hutu 85%, Tutsi 14%, Other (including Twa) 1%
Government Presidential system
Currency Rwanda franc = 100 centimes
Literacy rate 71%
Calorie consumption 2188 kilocalories

ST KITTS & NEVIS
West Indies

Official name Federation of Saint Christopher and Nevis
Formation 1983 / 1983
Capital Basseterre
Population 50,726 / 141 people per sq km (365 people per sq mile)
Total area 261 sq. km (101 sq. miles)
Languages English*, English Creole
Religions Anglican 33%, Methodist 29%, Other 22%, Moravian 9%, Roman Catholic 7%
Ethnic mix Black 95%, Mixed race 3%, White 1%, Other and Amerindian 1%
Government Parliamentary system
Currency East Caribbean dollar = 100 cents
Literacy rate 98%
Calorie consumption 2546 kilocalories

ST LUCIA
West Indies

Official name Saint Lucia
Formation 1979 / 1979
Capital Castries
Population 162,178 / 266 people per sq km (687 people per sq mile)
Total area 620 sq. km (239 sq. miles)
Languages English*, French Creole
Religions Roman Catholic 90%, Other 10%
Ethnic mix Black 83%, Mulatto (mixed race) 13%, Asian 3%, Other 1%
Government Parliamentary system
Currency East Caribbean dollar = 100 cents
Literacy rate 95%
Calorie consumption 2710 kilocalories

ST VINCENT & THE GRENADINES
West Indies

Official name Saint Vincent and the Grenadines
Formation 1979 / 1979
Capital Kingstown
Population 103,537 / 305 people per sq km (790 people per sq mile)
Total area 389 sq. km (150 sq. miles)
Languages English*, English Creole
Religions Anglican 47%, Methodist 28%, Roman Catholic 13%, Other 12%
Ethnic mix Black 66%, Mulatto (mixed race) 19%, Other 12%, Carib 2%, Asian 1%
Government Parliamentary system
Currency East Caribbean dollar = 100 cents
Literacy rate 88%
Calorie consumption 2914 kilocalories

SAMOA
Australasia & Oceania

Official name Independent State of Samoa
Formation 1962 / 1962
Capital Apia
Population 200,000 / 71 people per sq km (183 people per sq mile)
Total area 2860 sq. km (1104 sq. miles)
Languages Samoan*, English*
Religions Christian 99%, Other 1%
Ethnic mix Polynesian 91%, Euronesian 7%, Other 2%
Government Parliamentary system
Currency Tala = 100 sene
Literacy rate 99%
Calorie consumption 2997 kilocalories

SAN MARINO
Southern Europe

Official name Republic of San Marino
Formation 1631 / 1631
Capital San Marino
Population 32,140 / 527 people per sq km (1339 people per sq mile)
Total area 61 sq. km (23.6 sq. miles)
Languages Italian*
Religions Roman Catholic 93%, Other and nonreligious 7%
Ethnic mix Sammarinese 88%, Italian 10%, Other 2%
Government Parliamentary system
Currency Euro = 100 cents
Literacy rate 99%
Calorie consumption Not available

SÃO TOMÉ & PRÍNCIPE
West Africa

Official name Democratic Republic of São Tomé and Príncipe
Formation 1975 / 1975
Capital São Tomé
Population 200,000 / 208 people per sq km (539 people per sq mile)
Total area 1001 sq. km (386 sq. miles)
Languages Portuguese Creole, Portuguese*
Religions Roman Catholic 84%, Other 16%
Ethnic mix Black 90%, Portuguese and Creole 10%
Government Presidential system
Currency Dobra = 100 céntimos
Literacy rate 89%
Calorie consumption 2734 kilocalories

SAUDI ARABIA
Southwest Asia

Official name Kingdom of Saudi Arabia
Formation 1932 / 1932
Capital Riyadh
Population 28.1 million / 13 people per sq km (34 people per sq mile)
Total area 1,960,582 sq. km (756,981 sq. miles)
Languages Arabic*
Religions Sunni Muslim 85%, Shi'a Muslim 15%
Ethnic mix Arab 72%, Foreign residents (mostly south and southeast Asian) 20%, Afro-Asian 8%
Government Monarchy
Currency Saudi riyal = 100 halalat
Literacy rate 86%
Calorie consumption 3076 kilocalories

SENEGAL
West Africa

Official name Republic of Senegal
Formation 1960 / 1960
Capital Dakar
Population 12.8 million / 66 people per sq km (172 people per sq mile)
Total area 196,190 sq. km (75,749 sq. miles)
Languages Wolof, Pulaar, Serer, Diola, Mandinka, Malinké, Soninké, French*
Religions Sunni Muslim 95%, Christian (mainly Roman Catholic) 4%, Traditional beliefs 1%
Ethnic mix Wolof 43%, Serer 15%, Peul 14%, Other 14%, Toucouleur 9%, Diola 5%
Government Presidential system
Currency CFA franc = 100 centimes
Literacy rate 50%
Calorie consumption 2479 kilocalories

SERBIA
Southeast Europe

Official name Republic of Serbia
Formation 2006 / 2008
Capital Belgrade
Population 9.9 million / 128 people per sq km (331 people per sq mile)
Total area 77,453 sq. km (29,905 sq. miles)
Languages Serbian*, Hungarian (Magyar)
Religions Orthodox Christian 85%, Roman Catholic 6%, Other 6%, Muslim 3%
Ethnic mix Serb 83%, Other 10%, Magyar 4%, Bosniak 2%, Roma 1%
Government Parliamentary system
Currency Serbian dinar = 100 para
Literacy rate 98%
Calorie consumption 2823 kilocalories

SEYCHELLES
Indian Ocean

Official name Republic of Seychelles
Formation 1976 / 1976
Capital Victoria
Population 90,024 / 333 people per sq km (866 people per sq mile)
Total area 455 sq. km (176 sq. miles)
Languages French Creole*, English*, French*
Religions Roman Catholic 82%, Anglican 6%, Other (including Muslim) 6%, Other Christian 3%, Hindu 2%, Seventh-day Adventist 1%
Ethnic mix Creole 89%, Indian 5%, Other 4%, Chinese 2%
Government Presidential system
Currency Seychelles rupee = 100 cents
Literacy rate 92%
Calorie consumption 2426 kilocalories

SIERRA LEONE
West Africa

Official name Republic of Sierra Leone
Formation 1961 / 1961
Capital Freetown
Population 6 million / 84 people per sq km (217 people per sq mile)
Total area 71,740 sq. km (27,698 sq. miles)
Languages Mende, Temne, Krio, English*
Religions Muslim 60%, Christian 30%, Traditional beliefs 10%
Ethnic mix Mende 35%, Temne 32%, Other 21%, Limba 8%, Kuranko 4%
Government Presidential system
Currency Leone = 100 cents
Literacy rate 41%
Calorie consumption 2162 kilocalories

SINGAPORE
Southeast Asia

Official name Republic of Singapore
Formation 1965 / 1965
Capital Singapore
Population 5.2 million / 8525 people per sq km (22034 people per sq mile)
Total area 648 sq. km (250 sq. miles)
Languages Mandarin*, Malay*, Tamil*, English*
Religions Buddhist 55%, Taoist 22%, Muslim 16%, Hindu, Christian, and Sikh 7%
Ethnic mix Chinese 74%, Malay 14%, Indian 9%, Other 3%
Government Parliamentary system
Currency Singapore dollar = 100 cents
Literacy rate 95%
Calorie consumption Not available

SLOVAKIA
Central Europe

Official name Slovak Republic
Formation 1993 / 1993
Capital Bratislava
Population 5.5 million / 112 people per sq km (290 people per sq mile)
Total area 48,845 sq. km (18,859 sq. miles)
Languages Slovak*, Hungarian (Magyar), Czech
Religions Roman Catholic 69%, Nonreligious 13%, Other 13%, Greek Catholic (Uniate) 4%, Orthodox Christian 1%
Ethnic mix Slovak 86%, Magyar 10%, Roma 2%, Czech 1%, Other 1%
Government Parliamentary system
Currency Euro = 100 cents
Literacy rate 99%
Calorie consumption 2881 kilocalories

SLOVENIA
Central Europe

Official name Republic of Slovenia
Formation 1991 / 1991
Capital Ljubljana
Population 2 million / 99 people per sq km (256 people per sq mile)
Total area 20,253 sq. km (7820 sq. miles)
Languages Slovenian*
Religions Roman Catholic 58%, Other 28%, Atheist 10%, Orthodox Christian 2%, Muslim 2%
Ethnic mix Slovene 83%, Other 12%, Serb 2%, Croat 2%, Bosniak 1%
Government Parliamentary system
Currency Euro = 100 cents
Literacy rate 99%
Calorie consumption 3275 kilocalories

SOLOMON ISLANDS
Australasia & Oceania

Official name Solomon Islands
Formation 1978 / 1978
Capital Honiara
Population 600,000 / 21 people per sq km (56 people per sq mile)
Total area 28,450 sq. km (10,985 sq. miles)
Languages English*, Pidgin English, Melanesian Pidgin, c.120 others
Religions Church of Melanesia (Anglican) 34%, Roman Catholic 19%, South Seas Evangelical Church 17%, Methodist 11%, Seventh-day Adventist 10%, Other 9%
Ethnic mix Melanesian 93%, Polynesian 4%, Micronesian 2%, Other 1%
Government Parliamentary system
Currency Solomon Islands dollar = 100 cents
Literacy rate 77%
Calorie consumption 2439 kilocalories

SOMALIA
East Africa

Official name Federal Republic of Somalia
Formation 1960 / 1960
Capital Mogadishu
Population 9.6 million / 15 people per sq km (40 people per sq mile)
Total area 637,657 sq. km (246,199 sq. miles)
Languages Somali*, Arabic*, English, Italian
Religions Sunni Muslim 99%, Christian 1%
Ethnic mix Somali 85%, Other 15%
Government Transitional regime
Currency Somali shilin = 100 senti
Literacy rate 24%
Calorie consumption 1762 kilocalories

SOUTH AFRICA
Southern Africa

Official name Republic of South Africa
Formation 1934 / 1994
Capital Pretoria (Tshwane); Cape Town; Bloemfontein
Population 50.5 million / 41 people per sq km (107 people per sq mile)
Total area 1,219,912 sq. km (471,008 sq. miles)
Languages English, isiZulu, isiXhosa, Afrikaans, Sepedi, Setswana, Sesotho, Xitsonga, siSwati, Tshivenda, isiNdebele
Religions Christian 68%, Traditional beliefs and animist 29%, Muslim 2%, Hindu 1%
Ethnic mix Black 89%, White 9%, Asian 2%
Government Presidential system
Currency Rand = 100 cents
Literacy rate 89%
Calorie consumption 3017 kilocalories

SOUTH KOREA
East Asia

Official name Republic of Korea
Formation 1948 / 1953
Capital Seoul
Population 48.4 million / 490 people per sq km (1270 people per sq mile)
Total area 98,480 sq. km (38,023 sq. miles)
Languages Korean*
Religions Mahayana Buddhist 47%, Protestant 38%, Roman Catholic 11%, Confucianist 3%, Other 1%
Ethnic mix Korean 100%
Government Presidential system
Currency South Korean won = 100 chon
Literacy rate 99%
Calorie consumption 3200 kilocalories

SOUTH SUDAN
East Africa

Official name Republic of South Sudan
Formation 2011 / 2011
Capital Juba
Population 8.3 million / 13 people per sq km (33 people per sq mile)
Total area 644,329 sq. km (248,777 sq. miles)
Languages Arabic, Dinka, Nuer, Zande, Bari, Shilluk, Lotuko
Religions Over half of the population follow Christian or traditional beliefs.
Ethnic mix Dinka 40%, Nuer 15%, Bari 10%, Shilluk/Anwak 10%, Azande 10%, Arab 10%, Other 5%
Government Transitional regime
Currency South Sudan pound = 100 piastres
Literacy rate 37%
Calorie consumption Not available

SPAIN
Southwest Europe

Official name Kingdom of Spain
Formation 1492 / 1713
Capital Madrid
Population 46.5 million / 93 people per sq km (241 people per sq mile)
Total area 504,782 sq. km (194,896 sq. miles)
Languages Spanish*, Catalan*, Galician*, Basque*
Religions Roman Catholic 96%, Other 4%
Ethnic mix Castilian Spanish 72%, Catalan 17%, Galician 6%, Basque 2%, Other 2%, Roma 1%
Government Parliamentary system
Currency Euro = 100 cents
Literacy rate 98%
Calorie consumption 3239 kilocalories

SRI LANKA
South Asia

Official name Democratic Socialist Republic of Sri Lanka
Formation 1948 / 1948
Capital Colombo; Sri Jayewardenapura Kotte
Population 21 million / 324 people per sq km (840 people per sq mile)
Total area 65,610 sq. km (25,332 sq. miles)
Languages Sinhala*, Tamil*, Sinhala-Tamil, English
Religions Buddhist 69%, Hindu 15%, Muslim 8%, Christian 8%
Ethnic mix Sinhalese 74%, Tamil 18%, Moor 7%, Other 1%
Government Mixed presidential–parliamentary system
Currency Sri Lanka rupee = 100 cents
Literacy rate 91%
Calorie consumption 2426 kilocalories

SUDAN
East Africa

Official name Republic of the Sudan
Formation 1956 / 2011
Capital Khartoum
Population 34 million / 18 people per sq km (47 people per sq mile)
Total area 1,861,481 sq. km (718,722 sq. miles)
Languages Arabic, Nubian, Beja, Fur
Religions Nearly the whole population is Muslim (mainly Sunni)
Ethnic mix Arab 60%, Other 18%, Nubian 10%, Beja 8%, Fur 3%, Zaghawa 1%
Government Presidential system
Currency New Sudanese pound = 100 piastres
Literacy rate 70%
Calorie consumption 2326 kilocalories

SURINAM
South America

Official name Republic of Surinam
Formation 1975 / 1975
Capital Paramaribo
Population 500,000 / 3 people per sq km (8 people per sq mile)
Total area 163,270 sq. km (63,039 sq. miles)
Languages Sranan (creole), Dutch*, Javanese, Sarnami Hindi, Saramaccan, Chinese, Carib
Religions Hindu 27%, Protestant 25%, Roman Catholic 23%, Muslim 20%, Traditional beliefs 5%
Ethnic mix East Indian 27%, Creole 18%, Black 15%, Javanese 15%, Mixed race 13%, Other 6%, Amerindian 4%, Chinese 2%
Government Parliamentary system
Currency Surinamese dollar = 100 cents
Literacy rate 95%
Calorie consumption 2548 kilocalories

SWAZILAND
Southern Africa

Official name Kingdom of Swaziland
Formation 1968 / 1968
Capital Mbabane
Population 1.2 million / 70 people per sq km (181 people per sq mile)
Total area 17,363 sq. km (6704 sq. miles)
Languages English*, siSwati*, isiZulu, Xitsonga
Religions Traditional beliefs 40%, Other 30%, Roman Catholic 20%, Muslim 10%
Ethnic mix Swazi 97%, Other 3%
Government Monarchy
Currency Lilangeni = 100 cents
Literacy rate 87%
Calorie consumption 2249 kilocalories

SWEDEN
Northern Europe

Official name Kingdom of Sweden
Formation 1523 / 1921
Capital Stockholm
Population 9.4 million / 23 people per sq km (59 people per sq mile)
Total area 449,964 sq. km (173,731 sq. miles)
Languages Swedish*, Finnish, Sámi
Religions Evangelical Lutheran 75%, Other 13%, Muslim 5%, Other Protestant 5%, Roman Catholic 2%
Ethnic mix Swedish 86%, Foreign-born or first-generation immigrant 12%, Finnish and Sámi 2%
Government Parliamentary system
Currency Swedish krona = 100 öre
Literacy rate 99%
Calorie consumption 3125 kilocalories

SWITZERLAND
Central Europe

Official name Swiss Confederation
Formation 1291 / 1857
Capital Bern
Population 7.7 million / 194 people per sq km (501 people per sq mile)
Total area 41,290 sq. km (15,942 sq. miles)
Languages German*, Swiss-German, French*, Italian*, Romansch
Religions Roman Catholic 42%, Protestant 35%, Other and nonreligious 19%, Muslim 4%
Ethnic mix German 64%, French 20%, Other 9.5%, Italian 6%, Romansch 0.5%
Government Parliamentary system
Currency Swiss franc = 100 rappen/centimes
Literacy rate 99%
Calorie consumption 3454 kilocalories

SYRIA
Southwest Asia

Official name Syrian Arab Republic
Formation 1941 / 1967
Capital Damascus
Population 20.8 million / 113 people per sq km (293 people per sq mile)
Total area 184,180 sq. km (71,498 sq. miles)
Languages Arabic*, French, Kurdish, Armenian, Circassian, Turkic languages, Assyrian, Aramaic
Religions Sunni Muslim 74%, Alawi 12%, Christian 10%, Druze 3%, Other 1%
Ethnic mix Arab 90%, Kurdish 9%, Armenian, Turkmen, and Circassian 1%
Government One-party state
Currency Syrian pound = 100 piastres
Literacy rate 84%
Calorie consumption 3212 kilocalories

TAIWAN
East Asia

Official name Republic of China (ROC)
Formation 1949 / 1949
Capital Taipei
Population 23.2 million / 718 people per sq km (1860 people per sq mile)
Total area 35,980 sq. km (13,892 sq. miles)
Languages Amoy Chinese, Mandarin Chinese*, Hakka Chinese
Religions Buddhist, Confucianist, and Taoist 93%, Christian 5%, Other 2%
Ethnic mix Han Chinese (pre-20th-century migration) 84%, Han Chinese (20th-century migration) 14%, Aboriginal 2%
Government Presidential system
Currency Taiwan dollar = 100 cents
Literacy rate 98%
Calorie consumption 2673 kilocalories

TAJIKISTAN
Central Asia

Official name Republic of Tajikistan
Formation 1991 / 1991
Capital Dushanbe
Population 7 million / 49 people per sq km (127 people per sq mile)
Total area 143,100 sq. km (55,251 sq. miles)
Languages Tajik*, Uzbek, Russian
Religions Sunni Muslim 95%, Shi'a Muslim 3%, Other 2%
Ethnic mix Tajik 80%, Uzbek 15%, Other 3%, Russian 1%, Kyrgyz 1%
Government Presidential system
Currency Somoni = 100 diram
Literacy rate 99%
Calorie consumption 2106 kilocalories

TANZANIA
East Africa

Official name United Republic of Tanzania
Formation 1964 / 1964
Capital Dodoma
Population 46.2 million / 52 people per sq km (135 people per sq mile)
Total area 945,087 sq. km (364,898 sq. miles)
Languages Kiswahili*, Sukuma, Chagga, Nyamwezi, Hehe, Makonde, Yao, Sandawe, English*
Religions Christian 63%, Muslim 35%, Other 2%
Ethnic mix Native African (over 120 tribes) 99%, European, Asian, and Arab 1%
Government Presidential system
Currency Tanzanian shilling = 100 cents
Literacy rate 73%
Calorie consumption 2137 kilocalories

THAILAND
Southeast Asia

Official name Kingdom of Thailand
Formation 1238 / 1907
Capital Bangkok
Population 69.5 million / 136 people per sq km (352 people per sq mile)
Total area 514,000 sq. km (198,455 sq. miles)
Languages Thai*, Chinese, Malay, Khmer, Mon, Karen, Miao
Religions Buddhist 95%, Muslim 4%, Other (including Christian) 1%
Ethnic mix Thai 83%, Chinese 12%, Malay 3%, Khmer and Other 2%
Government Parliamentary system
Currency Baht = 100 satang
Literacy rate 94%
Calorie consumption 2862 kilocalories

TOGO
West Africa

Official name Republic of Togo
Formation 1960 / 1960
Capital Lomé
Population 6.2 million / 114 people per sq km (295 people per sq mile)
Total area 56,785 sq. km (21,924 sq. miles)
Languages Ewe, Kabye, Gurma, French*
Religions Christian 47%, Traditional beliefs 33%, Muslim 14%, Other 6%
Ethnic mix Ewe 46%, Other African 41%, Kabye 12%, European 1%
Government Presidential system
Currency CFA franc = 100 centimes
Literacy rate 57%
Calorie consumption 2363 kilocalories

TONGA
Australasia & Oceania

Official name Kingdom of Tonga
Formation 1970 / 1970
Capital Nuku'alofa
Population 106,146 / 147 people per sq km (382 people per sq mile)
Total area 748 sq. km (289 sq. miles)
Languages English*, Tongan*
Religions Free Wesleyan 41%, Other 17%, Roman Catholic 16%, Church of Jesus Christ of Latter-day Saints 14%, Free Church of Tonga 12%
Ethnic mix Tongan 98%, Other 2%
Government Monarchy
Currency Pa'anga (Tongan dollar) = 100 seniti
Literacy rate 99%
Calorie consumption Not available

TRINIDAD & TOBAGO
West Indies

Official name Republic of Trinidad and Tobago
Formation 1962 / 1962
Capital Port-of-Spain
Population 1.3 million / 253 people per sq km (656 people per sq mile)
Total area 5128 sq. km (1980 sq. miles)
Languages English Creole, English*, Hindi, French, Spanish
Religions Roman Catholic 26%, Hindu 23%, Other and nonreligious 23%, Anglican 8%, Baptist 7%, Pentecostal 7%, Muslim 6%
Ethnic mix East Indian 40%, Black 38%, Mixed race 20%, Other 2%
Government Parliamentary system
Currency Trinidad and Tobago dollar = 100 cents
Literacy rate 99%
Calorie consumption 2751 kilocalories

TUNISIA
North Africa

Official name Republic of Tunisia
Formation 1956 / 1956
Capital Tunis
Population 10.6 million / 68 people per sq km (177 people per sq mile)
Total area 163,610 sq. km (63,169 sq. miles)
Languages Arabic*, French
Religions Muslim (mainly Sunni) 98%, Christian 1%, Jewish 1%
Ethnic mix Arab and Berber 98%, Jewish 1%, European 1%
Government Transitional regime
Currency Tunisian dinar = 1000 millimes
Literacy rate 78%
Calorie consumption 3314 kilocalories

TURKEY
Asia / Europe

Official name Republic of Turkey
Formation 1923 / 1939
Capital Ankara
Population 73.6 million / 96 people per sq km (248 people per sq mile)
Total area 780,580 sq. km (301,382 sq. miles)
Languages Turkish*, Kurdish, Arabic, Circassian, Armenian, Greek, Georgian, Ladino
Religions Muslim (mainly Sunni) 99%, Other 1%
Ethnic mix Turkish 70%, Kurdish 20%, Other 8%, Arab 2%
Government Parliamentary system
Currency Turkish lira = 100 kurus
Literacy rate 91%
Calorie consumption 3666 kilocalories

TURKMENISTAN
Central Asia

Official name Turkmenistan
Formation 1991 / 1991
Capital Ashgabat
Population 5.1 million / 10 people per sq km (27 people per sq mile)
Total area 488,100 sq. km (188,455 sq. miles)
Languages Turkmen*, Uzbek, Russian, Kazakh, Tatar
Religions Sunni Muslim 89%, Orthodox Christian 9%, Other 2%
Ethnic mix Turkmen 85%, Other 6%, Uzbek 5%, Russian 4%
Government One-party state
Currency New manat = 100 tenge
Literacy rate 99%
Calorie consumption 2878 kilocalories

TUVALU
Australasia & Oceania

Official name Tuvalu
Formation 1978 / 1978
Capital Fongafale (Funafuti Atoll)
Population 10,619 / 408 people per sq km (1062 people per sq mile)
Total area 26 sq. km (10 sq. miles)
Languages Tuvaluan, Kiribati, English*
Religions Church of Tuvalu 97%, Baha'i 1%, Seventh-day Adventist 1%, Other 1%
Ethnic mix Polynesian 96%, Micronesian 4%
Government Nonparty system
Currency Australian dollar and Tuvaluan dollar = 100 cents
Literacy rate 98%
Calorie consumption Not available

UGANDA
East Africa

Official name Republic of Uganda
Formation 1962 / 1962
Capital Kampala
Population 34.5 million / 173 people per sq km (448 people per sq mile)
Total area 236,040 sq. km (91,135 sq. miles)
Languages Luganda, Nkole, Chiga, Lango, Acholi, Teso, Lugbara, English*
Religions Christian 85%, Muslim (mainly Sunni) 12%, Other 3%
Ethnic mix Other 50%, Baganda 17%, Banyakole 10%, Basoga 9%, Iteso 7%, Bakiga 7%
Government Presidential system
Currency New Uganda shilling = 100 cents
Literacy rate 74%
Calorie consumption 2260 kilocalories

UKRAINE
Eastern Europe

Official name Ukraine
Formation 1991 / 1991
Capital Kiev
Population 45.2 million / 75 people per sq km (194 people per sq mile)
Total area 603,700 sq. km (223,089 sq. miles)
Languages Ukrainian*, Russian, Tatar
Religions Christian (mainly Orthodox) 95%, Other 5%
Ethnic mix Ukrainian 78%, Russian 17%, Other 5%
Government Presidential system
Currency Hryvna = 100 kopiykas
Literacy rate 99%
Calorie consumption 3198 kilocalories

UNITED ARAB EMIRATES
Southwest Asia

Official name United Arab Emirates
Formation 1971 / 1972
Capital Abu Dhabi
Population 7.9 million / 94 people per sq km (245 people per sq mile)
Total area 82,880 sq. km (32,000 sq. miles)
Languages Arabic*, Farsi, Indian and Pakistani languages, English
Religions Muslim (mainly Sunni) 96%, Christian, Hindu, and other 4%
Ethnic mix Asian 60%, Emirian 25%, Other Arab 12%, European 3%
Government Monarchy
Currency UAE dirham = 100 fils
Literacy rate 90%
Calorie consumption 3245 kilocalories

UNITED KINGDOM
Northwest Europe

Official name United Kingdom of Great Britain and Northern Ireland
Formation 1707 / 1922
Capital London
Population 62.4 million / 258 people per sq km (669 people per sq mile)
Total area 244,820 sq. km (94,525 sq. miles)
Languages English*, Welsh*, Scottish Gaelic, Irish Gaelic
Religions Anglican 45%, Other and nonreligious 36%, Roman Catholic 9%, Presbyterian 4%, Muslim 3%, Methodist 2%, Hindu 1%
Ethnic mix English 80%, Scottish 9%, West Indian, Asian, and other 5%, Northern Irish 3%, Welsh 3%
Government Parliamentary system
Currency Pound sterling = 100 pence
Literacy rate 99%
Calorie consumption 3432 kilocalories

UNITED STATES
North America

Official name United States of America
Formation 1776 / 1959
Capital Washington D.C.
Population 313 million / 34 people per sq km (88 people per sq mile)
Total area 9,626,091 sq. km (3,717,792 sq. miles)
Languages English, Spanish, Chinese, French, German, Tagalog, Vietnamese, Italian, Korean, Russian, Polish
Religions Protestant 52%, Roman Catholic 25%, Other and nonreligious 20%, Jewish 2%, Muslim 1%
Ethnic mix White 62%, Hispanic 13%, Black American/African 13%, Other 7%, Asian 4%, Native American 1%
Government Presidential system
Currency US dollar = 100 cents
Literacy rate 99%
Calorie consumption 3688 kilocalories

URUGUAY
South America

Official name Eastern Republic of Uruguay
Formation 1828 / 1828
Capital Montevideo
Population 3.4 million / 19 people per sq km (50 people per sq mile)
Total area 176,220 sq. km (68,039 sq. miles)
Languages Spanish*
Religions Roman Catholic 66%, Other and nonreligious 30%, Jewish 2%, Protestant 2%
Ethnic mix White 90%, Mestizo 6%, Black 4%
Government Presidential system
Currency Uruguayan peso = 100 centésimos
Literacy rate 98%
Calorie consumption 2808 kilocalories

UZBEKISTAN
Central Asia

Official name Republic of Uzbekistan
Formation 1991 / 1991
Capital Tashkent
Population 27.8 million / 62 people per sq km (161 people per sq mile)
Total area 447,400 sq. km (172,741 sq. miles)
Languages Uzbek*, Russian, Tajik, Kazakh
Religions Sunni Muslim 88%, Orthodox Christian 9%, Other 3%
Ethnic mix Uzbek 80%, Russian 6%, Other 6%, Tajik 5%, Kazakh 3%
Government Presidential system
Currency Som = 100 tiyin
Literacy rate 99%
Calorie consumption 2618 kilocalories

VANUATU
Australasia & Oceania

Official name Republic of Vanuatu
Formation 1980 / 1980
Capital Port Vila
Population 200,000 / 16 people per sq km (42 people per sq mile)
Total area 12,200 sq. km (4710 sq. miles)
Languages Bislama* (Melanesian pidgin), English*, French*, other indigenous languages
Religions Presbyterian 37%, Other 19%, Anglican 15%, Roman Catholic 15%, Traditional beliefs 8%, Seventh-day Adventist 6%
Ethnic mix ni-Vanuatu 94%, European 4%, Other 2%
Government Parliamentary system
Currency Vatu = 100 centimes
Literacy rate 82%
Calorie consumption 2841 kilocalories

VATICAN CITY
Southern Europe

Official name State of the Vatican City
Formation 1929 / 1929
Capital Vatican City
Population 836 / 1900 people per sq km (4918 people per sq mile)
Total area 0.44 sq. km (0.17 sq. miles)
Languages Italian*, Latin*
Religions Roman Catholic 100%
Ethnic mix The current pope is German, though most popes for the last 500 years have been Italian. Cardinals are from many nationalities, but Italians form the largest group. Most of the resident lay persons are Italian.
Government Papal state
Currency Euro = 100 cents
Literacy rate 99%
Calorie consumption Not available

VENEZUELA
South America

Official name Bolivarian Republic of Venezuela
Formation 1830 / 1830
Capital Caracas
Population 29.4 million / 33 people per sq km (86 people per sq mile)
Total area 912,050 sq. km (352,143 sq. miles)
Languages Spanish*, Amerindian languages
Religions Roman Catholic 96%, Protestant 2%, Other 2%
Ethnic mix Mestizo 69%, White 20%, Black 9%, Amerindian 2%
Government Presidential system
Currency Bolívar fuerte = 100 céntimos
Literacy rate 95%
Calorie consumption 3014 kilocalories

VIETNAM
Southeast Asia

Official name Socialist Republic of Vietnam
Formation 1976 / 1976
Capital Hanoi
Population 88.8 million / 273 people per sq km (707 people per sq mile)
Total area 329,560 sq. km (127,243 sq. miles)
Languages Vietnamese*, Chinese, Thai, Khmer, Muong, Nung, Miao, Yao, Jarai
Religions Other 74%, Buddhist 14%, Roman Catholic 7%, Cao Dai 3%, Protestant 2%
Ethnic mix Vietnamese 86%, Other 8%, Muong 2%, Tay 2%, Thai 2%
Government One-party state
Currency Dông = 10 hao = 100 xu
Literacy rate 93%
Calorie consumption 2690 kilocalories

YEMEN
Southwest Asia

Official name Republic of Yemen
Formation 1990 / 1990
Capital Sana
Population 24.8 million / 44 people per sq km (114 people per sq mile)
Total area 527,970 sq. km (203,849 sq. miles)
Languages Arabic*
Religions Sunni Muslim 55%, Shi'a Muslim 42%, Christian, Hindu, and Jewish 3%
Ethnic mix Arab 99%, Afro-Arab, Indian, Somali, and European 1%
Government Transitional regime
Currency Yemeni rial = 100 fils
Literacy rate 62%
Calorie consumption 2109 kilocalories

ZAMBIA
Southern Africa

Official name Republic of Zambia
Formation 1964 / 1964
Capital Lusaka
Population 13.5 million / 18 people per sq km (47 people per sq mile)
Total area 752,614 sq. km (290,584 sq. miles)
Languages Bemba, Tonga, Nyanja, Lozi, Lala-Bisa, Nsenga, English*
Religions Christian 63%, Traditional beliefs 36%, Muslim and Hindu 1%
Ethnic mix Bemba 34%, Other African 26%, Tonga 16%, Nyanja 14%, Lozi 9%, European 1%
Government Presidential system
Currency Zambian kwacha = 100 ngwee
Literacy rate 71%
Calorie consumption 1879 kilocalories

ZIMBABWE
Southern Africa

Official name Republic of Zimbabwe
Formation 1980 / 1980
Capital Harare
Population 12.8 million / 33 people per sq km (86 people per sq mile)
Total area 390,580 sq. km (150,803 sq. miles)
Languages Shona, isiNdebele, English*
Religions Syncretic (Christian/traditional beliefs) 50%, Christian 25%, Traditional beliefs 24%, Other (including Muslim) 1%
Ethnic mix Shona 71%, Ndebele 16%, Other African 11%, White 1%, Asian 1%
Government Presidential system
Currency Zimbabwe dollar suspended in 2009; US dollar, South African rand, euro, UK pound, and Botswanan pula are legal tender
Literacy rate 92%
Calorie consumption 2219 kilocalories

GLOSSARY

This glossary lists all geographical, technical and foreign language terms which appear in the text, followed by a brief definition of the term. Any acronyms used in the text are also listed in full. Terms in italics are for cross-reference and indicate that the word is separately defined in the glossary.

A

Aboriginal The original (indigenous) inhabitants of a country or continent. Especially used with reference to Australia.

Abyssal plain A broad plain found in the depths of the ocean, more than 10,000 ft (3000 m) below sea level.

Acid rain Rain, sleet, snow or mist which has absorbed waste gases from fossil-fuelled power stations and vehicle exhausts, becoming more acid. It causes severe environmental damage.

Adaptation The gradual evolution of plants and animals so that they become better suited to survive and reproduce in their *environment*.

Afforestation The planting of new forest in areas which were once forested but have been cleared.

Agribusiness A term applied to activities such as the growing of crops, rearing of animals or the manufacture of farm machinery, which eventually leads to the supply of agricultural produce at market.

Air mass A huge, homogeneous mass of air, within which horizontal patterns of temperature and *humidity* are consistent. Air masses are separated by *fronts*.

Alliance An agreement between two or more states, to work together to achieve common purposes.

Alluvial fan A large fan-shaped deposit of fine sediments deposited by a river as it emerges from a narrow, mountain valley onto a broad, open *plain*.

Alluvium Material deposited by rivers. Nowadays usually only applied to finer particles of silt and clay.

Alpine Mountain *environment*, between the *treeline* and the level of permanent snow cover.

Alpine mountains Ranges of mountains formed between 30 and 65 million years ago, by *folding*, in west and central Europe.

Amerindian A term applied to people *indigenous* to North, Central and South America.

Animal husbandry The business of rearing animals.

Antarctic circle The parallel which lies at *latitude* of 66° 32' S.

Anticline A geological *fold* that forms an arch shape, curving upwards in the rock *strata*.

Anticyclone An area of relatively high atmospheric pressure.

Aquaculture Collective term for the farming of produce derived from the sea, including fish-farming, the cultivation of shellfish, and plants such as seaweed.

Aquifer A body of rock which can absorb water. Also applied to any rock strata that have sufficient porosity to yield *groundwater* through wells or springs.

Arable Land which has been ploughed and is being used, or is suitable, for growing crops.

Archipelago A group or chain of islands.

Arctic Circle The parallel which lies at a *latitude* of 66° 32' N.

Arête A thin, jagged mountain ridge which divides two adjacent *cirques*, found in regions where *glaciation* has occurred.

Arid Dry. An area of low rainfall, where the rate of *evaporation* may be greater than that of *precipitation*. Often defined as those areas that receive less than one inch (25 mm) of rain a year. In these areas only drought-resistant plants can survive.

Artesian well A naturally occurring source of underground water, stored in an *aquifer*.

Artisanal Small-scale, manual operation, such as fishing, using little or no machinery.

ASEAN Association of Southeast Asian Nations. Established in 1967 to promote economic, social and cultural co-operation. Its members include Brunei, Indonesia, Malaysia, Philippines, Singapore and Thailand.

Aseismic A region where *earthquake* activity has ceased.

Asteroid A minor planet circling the Sun, mainly between the orbits of Mars and Jupiter.

Asthenosphere A zone of hot, partially melted rock, which underlies the *lithosphere*, within the Earth's *crust*.

Atmosphere The envelope of odourless, colourless and tasteless gases surrounding the Earth, consisting of *oxygen* (23%), *nitrogen* (75%), argon (1%), *carbon dioxide* (0.03%), as well as tiny proportions of other gases.

Atmospheric pressure The pressure created by the action of gravity on the gases surrounding the Earth.

Atoll A ring-shaped island or *coral reef* often enclosing a *lagoon* of sea water.

Avalanche The rapid movement of a mass of snow and ice down a steep slope. Similar movements of other materials are described as *rock avalanches* or *landslides* and *sand avalanches*.

B

Badlands A landscape that has been heavily eroded and dissected by rainwater, and which has little or no vegetation.

Back slope The gentler windward slope of a sand *dune* or gentler slope of a *cuesta*.

Bajos An *alluvial fan* deposited by a river at the base of mountains and hills which encircle *desert* areas.

Bar, coastal An offshore strip of sand or shingle, either above or below the water. Usually parallel to the shore but sometimes crescent-shaped or at an oblique angle.

Barchan A crescent-shaped sand *dune*, formed where wind direction is very consistent. The horns of the crescent point downwind and where there is enough sand the barchan is mobile.

Barrio A Spanish term for the shanty towns – self-built settlements – which are clustered around many South and Central American cities (*see also Favela*).

Basalt Dark, fine-grained *igneous rock*. Formed near the Earth's surface from fast-cooling *lava*.

Base level The level below which flowing water cannot erode the land.

Basement rock A mass of ancient rock often of *Pre-Cambrian age*, covered by a layer of more recent *sedimentary rocks*. Commonly associated with *shield* areas.

Beach Lake or sea shore where waves break and there is an accumulation of loose material – mud, sand, shingle or pebbles.

Bedrock Solid, consolidated and relatively unweathered rock, found on the surface of the land or just below a layer of soil or *weathered* rock.

Biodiversity The quantity of animal or plant species in a given area.

Biomass The total mass of organic matter – plants and animals – in a given area. It is usually measured in kilogrammes per square metre. Plant biomass is proportionally greater than that of animals, except in cities.

Biosphere The zone just above and below the Earth's surface, where all plants and animals live.

Blizzard A severe windstorm with snow and sleet. Visibility is often severely restricted.

Bluff The steep bank of a *meander*, formed by the erosive action of a river.

Boreal forest Tracts of mainly coniferous forest found in northern *latitudes*.

Breccia A type of rock composed of sharp fragments, cemented by a fine-grained material such as clay.

Butte An isolated, flat-topped hill with steep or vertical sides, buttes are the eroded remnants of a former land surface.

C

Caatinga Portuguese (Brazilian) term for thorny woodland growing in areas of pale granitic soils.

CACM Central American Common Market. Established in 1960 to further economic ties between its members, which are Costa Rica, El Salvador, Guatemala, Honduras and Nicaragua.

Calcite Hexagonal crystals of calcium carbonate.

Caldera A huge volcanic vent, often containing a number of smaller vents, and sometimes a crater lake.

Carbon cycle The transfer of carbon to and from the *atmosphere*. This occurs on land through *photosynthesis*. In the sea, *carbon dioxide* is absorbed, some returning to the air and some taken up into the bodies of sea creatures.

Carbon dioxide A colourless, odourless gas (CO_2) which makes up 0.03% of the *atmosphere*.

Carbonation The process whereby rocks are broken down by carbonic acid. Carbon dioxide in the air dissolves in rainwater, forming carbonic acid. *Limestone* terrain can be rapidly eaten away.

Cash crop A single crop grown specifically for export sale, rather than for local use. Typical examples include coffee, tea and citrus fruits.

Cassava A type of grain meal, used to produce tapioca. A staple crop in many parts of Africa.

Castle kopje Hill or rock outcrop, especially in southern Africa, where steep sides, and a summit composed of blocks, give a castle-like appearance.

Cataracts A series of stepped waterfalls created as a river flows over a band of hard, resistant rock.

Causeway A raised route through marshland or a body of water.

CEEAC Economic Community of Central African States. Established in 1983 to promote regional co-operation and if possible, establish a common market between 16 Central African nations.

Chemical weathering The chemical reactions leading to the decomposition of rocks. Types of chemical weathering include *carbonation*, *hydrolysis* and *oxidation*.

Chernozem A fertile soil, also known as 'black earth' consisting of a layer of dark topsoil, rich in decaying vegetation, overlying a lighter chalky layer.

Cirque Armchair-shaped basin, found in mountain regions, with a steep back, or rear, wall and a raised rock lip, often containing a lake (or *tarn*). The cirque floor has been eroded by a *glacier*, while the back wall is eroded both by the *glacier* and by *weathering*.

Climate The average weather conditions in a given area over a period of years, sometimes defined as 30 years or more.

Cold War A period of hostile relations between the USA and the Soviet Union and their allies after the Second World War.

Composite volcano Also known as a strato-volcano, the volcanic cone is composed of alternating deposits of *lava* and *pyroclastic* material.

Compound A substance made up of *elements* chemically combined in a consistent way.

Condensation The process whereby a gas changes into a liquid. For example, water vapour in the *atmosphere* condenses around tiny airborne particles to form droplets of water.

Confluence The point at which two rivers meet.

Conglomerate Rock composed of large, water-worn or rounded pebbles, held together by a natural cement.

Coniferous forest A forest type containing trees which are generally, but not necessarily, *evergreen* and have slender, needle-like leaves and which reproduce by means of seeds contained in a cone.

Continental drift The theory that the continents of today are fragments of one or more prehistoric *supercontinents* which have moved across the Earth's surface, creating ocean basins. The theory has been superseded by a more sophisticated one – *plate tectonics*.

Continental shelf An area of the continental crust, below sea level, which slopes gently. It is separated from the deep ocean by a much more steeply inclined *continental slope*.

Continental slope A steep slope running from the edge of the *continental shelf* to the ocean floor.

Conurbation A vast metropolitan area created by the expansion of towns and cities into a virtually continuous urban area.

Cool continental A rainy *climate* with warm summers [warmest month below 76°F (22°C)] and often severe winters [coldest month below 32°F (0°C)].

Copra The dried, white kernel of a coconut, from which coconut oil is extracted.

Coral reef An underwater barrier created by colonies of the coral polyp. Polyps secrete a protective skeleton of calcium carbonate, and reefs develop as live polyps build on the skeletons of dead generations.

Core The centre of the Earth, consisting of a dense mass of iron and nickel. It is thought that the outer core is molten or liquid, and that the hot inner core is solid due to extremely high pressures.

Coriolis effect A deflecting force caused by the rotation of the Earth. In the northern hemisphere a body, such as an *air mass* or ocean current, is deflected to the right, and in the southern hemisphere to the left. This prevents winds from blowing straight from areas of high to low pressure.

Coulées A US / Canadian term for a ravine formed by river *erosion*.

Craton A large block of the Earth's *crust* which has remained stable for a long period of *geological time*. It is made up of ancient *shield* rocks.

Cretaceous A period of *geological time* beginning about 145 million years ago and lasting until about 65 million years ago.

Crevasse A deep crack in a *glacier*.

Crust The hard, thin outer shell of the Earth. The crust floats on the *mantle*, which is softer and more dense. Under the oceans (oceanic crust) the crust is 3.7–6.8 miles (6–11 km) thick. Continental crust averages 18–24 miles (30–40 km).

Crystalline rock Rocks formed when molten *magma* crystallizes (*igneous rocks*) or when heat or pressure cause re-crystallization (*metamorphic rocks*). Crystalline rocks are distinct from *sedimentary rocks*.

Cuesta A hill which rises into a steep slope on one side but has a gentler gradient on its other slope.

Cyclone An area of low *atmospheric pressure*, occurring where the air is warm and relatively low in density, causing low level winds to spiral. *Hurricanes* and *typhoons* are tropical cyclones.

D

De facto
1 Government or other activity that takes place, or exists in actuality if not by right.
2 A border, which exists in practice, but which is not officially recognized by all the countries it adjoins.

Deciduous forest A forest of trees which shed their leaves annually at a particular time or season. In *temperate* climates the fall of leaves occurs in the Autumn. Some *coniferous* trees, such as the larch, are deciduous. Deciduous vegetation contrasts with *evergreen*, which keeps its leaves for more than a year.

Defoliant Chemical spray used to remove foliage (leaves) from trees.

Deforestation The act of cutting down and clearing large areas of forest for human activities, such as agricultural land or urban development.

Delta Low-lying, fan-shaped area at a river mouth, formed by the *deposition* of successive layers of *sediment*. Slowing as it enters the sea, a river deposits sediment and may, as a result, split into numerous smaller channels, known as *distributaries*.

Denudation The combined effect of *weathering*, *erosion* and *mass movement*, which, over long periods, exposes underlying rocks.

Deposition The laying down of material that has accumulated:
(1) after being *eroded* and then transported by physical forces such as wind, ice or water;
(2) as organic remains, such as coal and coral;
(3) as the result of *evaporation* and chemical *precipitation*.

Depression
1 In climatic terms it is a large low pressure system.
2 A complex *fold*, producing a large valley, which incorporates both a *syncline* and an *anticline*.

Desert An *arid* region of low rainfall, with little vegetation or animal life, which is adapted to the dry conditions. The term is now applied not only to hot tropical and subtropical regions, but to arid areas of the continental interiors and to the ice deserts of the *Arctic* and *Antarctic*.

Desertification The gradual extension of *desert* conditions in *arid* or *semi-arid* regions, as a result of climatic change or human activity, such as over-grazing and *deforestation*.

Despot A ruler with absolute power. Despots are often associated with oppressive regimes.

Detritus Piles of rock deposited by an erosive agent such as a river or *glacier*.

Distributary A minor branch of a river, which does not rejoin the main stream, common at *deltas*.

Diurnal Daily, something that occurs each day. Diurnal temperature refers to the variation in temperature over the course of a full day and night.

Divide A US term describing the area of high ground separating two *drainage basins*.

Donga A steep-sided *gully*, resulting from *erosion* by a river or by floods.

Dormant A term used to describe a *volcano* which is not currently erupting. They differ from extinct volcanoes as dormant volcanoes are still considered likely to erupt in the future.

Drainage basin The area drained by a single river system, its boundary is marked by a *watershed* or *divide*.

Drought A long period of continuously low rainfall.

Drumlin A long, streamlined hillock composed of material deposited by a *glacier*. They often occur in groups known as swarms.

Dune A mound or ridge of sand, shaped, and often moved, by the wind. They are found in hot *deserts* and on low-lying coasts where onshore winds blow across sandy beaches.

Dyke A wall constructed in low-lying areas to contain floodwaters or protect from high tides.

E

Earthflow The rapid movement of soil and other loose surface material down a slope, when saturated by water. Similar to a mudflow but not as fast-flowing, due to a lower percentage of water.

Earthquake Sudden movements of the Earth's *crust*, causing the ground to shake. Frequently occurring at *tectonic plate* margins. The shock, or series of shocks, spreads out from an *epicentre*.

EC The European Community (*see* EU).

Ecosystem A system of living organisms – plants and animals – interacting with their *environment*.

ECOWAS Economic Community of West African States. Established in 1975, it incorporates 16 West African states and aims to promote closer regional and economic co-operation.

Element
1 A constituent of the *climate* – *precipitation*, *humidity*, temperature, *atmospheric pressure* or wind.
2 A substance that cannot be separated into simpler substances by chemical means.

El Niño A climatic phenomenon, the El Niño effect occurs about 14 times each century and leads to major shifts in global air circulation. It is associated with unusually warm currents off the coasts of Peru, Ecuador and Chile. The anomaly can last for up to two years.

Environment The conditions created by the surroundings (both natural and artificial) within which an organism lives. In human geography the word includes the surrounding economic, cultural and social conditions.

Eon (aeon) Traditionally a long, but indefinite, period of *geological time*.

Ephemeral A non-permanent feature, often used in connection with seasonal rivers or lakes in dry areas.

Epicentre The point on the Earth's surface directly above the underground origin – or focus – of an *earthquake*.

Equator The line of *latitude* which lies equidistant between the North and South Poles.

Erg An extensive area of sand *dunes*, particularly in the Sahara Desert.

Erosion The processes which wear away the surface of the land. *Glaciers*, wind, rivers, waves and currents all carry debris which causes *erosion*. Some definitions also include *mass movement* due to gravity as an agent of erosion.

Escarpment A steep slope at the margin of a level, upland surface. In a landscape created by *folding*, escarpments (or scarps) frequently lie behind a more gentle backward slope.

Esker A narrow, winding ridge of sand and gravel deposited by streams of water flowing beneath or at the edge of a *glacier*.

Erratic A rock transported by a *glacier* and deposited some distance from its place of origin.

Eustacy A world-wide fall or rise in ocean levels.

EU The European Union. Established in 1965, it was formerly known as the EEC (European Economic Community) and then the EC (European Community). Its members are Austria, Belgium, Denmark, Finland, France, Germany, Greece, Ireland, Italy, Luxembourg, Netherlands, Portugal, Spain, Sweden and UK. It seeks to establish an integrated European common market and eventual federation.

Evaporation The process whereby a liquid or solid is turned into a gas or vapour. Also refers to the diffusion of water vapour into the *atmosphere* from exposed water surfaces such as lakes and seas.

Evapotranspiration The loss of moisture from the Earth's surface through a combination of *evaporation*, and *transpiration* from the leaves of plants.

Evergreen Plants with long-lasting leaves, which are not shed annually or seasonally.

Exfoliation A kind of *weathering* whereby scale-like flakes of rock are peeled or broken off by the development of salt crystals in water within the rocks. *Groundwater*, which contains dissolved salts, seeps to the surface and evaporates, precipitating a film of salt crystals, which expands causing fine cracks. As these grow, flakes of rock break off.

Extrusive rock *Igneous* rock formed when molten material (*magma*) pours forth at the Earth's surface and cools rapidly. It usually has a glassy texture.

F

Factionalism The actions of one or more minority political group acting against the interests of the majority government.

Fault A fracture or crack in rock, where strains (*tectonic* movement) have caused blocks to move, vertically or laterally, relative to each other.

Fauna Collective name for the animals of a particular period of time, or region.

Favela Brazilian term for the shanty towns or self-built, temporary dwellings which have grown up around the edge of many South and Central American cities.

Ferrel cell A component in the global pattern of air circulation, which rises in the colder *latitudes* (60° N and S) and descends in warmer *latitudes* (30° N and S). The Ferrel cell forms part of the world's three-cell air circulation pattern, with the *Hadley* and Polar cells.

Fissure A deep crack in a rock or a *glacier*.

Fjord A deep, narrow inlet, created when the sea inundates the *U-shaped valley* created by a *glacier*.

Flash flood A sudden, short-lived rise in the water level of a river or stream, or surge of water down a dry river channel, or *wadi*, caused by heavy rainfall.

Flax A plant used to make linen.

Flood plain The broad, flat part of a river valley, adjacent to the river itself, formed by *sediment* deposited during flooding.

Flora The collective name for the plants of a particular period of time or region.

Flow The movement of a river within its banks, particularly in terms of the speed and volume of water.

Fold A bend in the rock *strata* of the Earth's *crust*, resulting from compression.

Fossil The remains, or traces, of a dead organism preserved in the Earth's *crust*.

Fossil dune A *dune* formed in a once-*arid* region which is now wetter. *Dunes* normally move with the wind, but in these cases vegetation makes them stable.

Fossil fuel Fuel – coal, natural gas or oil – composed of the fossilized remains of plants and animals.

Front The boundary between two *air masses*, which contrast sharply in temperature and *humidity*.

Frontal depression An area of low pressure caused by rising warm air. They are generally 600–1200 miles (1000–2000 km) in diameter. Within *depressions* there are both warm and cold fronts.

Frost shattering A form of *weathering* where water freezes in cracks, causing expansion. As temperatures fluctuate and the ice melts and refreezes, it eventually causes the rocks to shatter and fragments of rock to break off.

G

Gaucho South American term for a stock herder or cowboy who works on the grassy *plains* of Paraguay, Uruguay and Argentina.

Geological time-scale The chronology of the Earth's history as revealed in its rocks. Geological time is divided into a number of periods: *eon*, era, period, epoch, age and chron (the shortest). These units are not of uniform length.

Geosyncline A concave fold (*syncline*) or large depression in the Earth's *crust*, extending hundreds of kilometres. This basin contains a deep layer of sediment, especially at its centre, from the land masses around it.

Geothermal energy Heat derived from hot rocks within the Earth's *crust* and resulting in hot springs, steam or hot rocks at the surface. The energy is generated by rock movements, and from the breakdown of radioactive elements occurring under intense pressure.

GDP Gross Domestic Product. The total value of goods and services produced by a country excluding income from foreign countries.

Geyser A jet of steam and hot water that intermittently erupts from vents in the ground in areas that are, or were, *volcanic*. Some geysers occasionally reach heights of 196 ft (60 m).

Ghetto An area of a city or region occupied by an overwhelming majority of people from one racial or religious group, who may be subject to persecution or containment.

Glaciation The growth of *glaciers* and *ice sheets*, and their impact on the landscape.

Glacier A body of ice moving downslope under the influence of gravity and consisting of compacted and frozen snow. A glacier is distinct from an *ice sheet*, which is wider and less confined by features of the landscape.

Glacio-eustacy A world-wide change in the level of the oceans, caused when the formation of *ice sheets* takes up water or when their melting returns water to the ocean. The formation of ice sheets in the *Pleistocene* epoch, for example, caused sea level to drop by about 320 ft (100 m).

Glaciofluvial To do with glacial *meltwater*, the landforms it creates and its processes; *erosion*, transportation and *deposition*. Glaciofluvial effects are more powerful and rapid where they occur within or beneath the *glacier*, rather than beyond its edge.

Glacis A gentle slope or *pediment*.

Global warming An increase in the average temperature of the Earth. At present the *greenhouse effect* is thought to contribute to this.

GNP Gross National Product. The total value of goods and services produced by a country.

Gondwanaland The *supercontinent* thought to have existed over 200 million years ago in the southern hemisphere. Gondwanaland is believed to have comprised today's Africa, Madagascar, Australia, parts of South America, *Antarctica* and the Indian subcontinent.

Graben A block of rock let down between two parallel *faults*. Where the graben occurs within a valley, the structure is known as a *rift valley*.

Grease ice Slicks of ice which form in *Antarctic* seas, when ice crystals are bonded together by wind and wave action.

Greenhouse effect A change in the temperature of the *atmosphere*. Short-wave solar radiation travels through the *atmosphere* unimpeded to the Earth's surface, whereas outgoing, long-wave terrestrial radiation is absorbed by materials that re-radiate it back to the Earth. Radiation trapped in this way, by water vapour, carbon dioxide and other 'greenhouse gases', keeps the Earth warm. As more *carbon dioxide* is released into the atmosphere by the burning of *fossil fuels*, the greenhouse effect may cause a global increase in temperature.

Groundwater Water that has seeped into the pores, cavities and cracks of rocks or into soil and water held in an *aquifer*.

Gully A deep, narrow channel eroded in the landscape by *ephemeral* streams.

Guyot A small, flat-topped submarine mountain, formed as a result of subsidence which occurs during *sea-floor spreading*.

Gypsum A soft mineral *compound* (hydrated calcium sulphate), used as the basis of many forms of plaster, including plaster of Paris.

H

Hadley cell A large-scale component in the global pattern of air circulation. Warm air rises over the *Equator* and blows at high altitude towards the poles, sinking in subtropical regions (30° N and 30° S) and creating high pressure. The air then flows at the surface towards the *Equator* in the form of trade winds. There is one cell in each hemisphere. Named after G Hadley, who published his theory in 1735.

Hamada An Arabic word for a plateau of bare rock in a *desert*.

Hanging valley A tributary valley which ends suddenly, high above the bed of the main valley. The effect is found where the main valley has been more deeply eroded by a *glacier*, than has the tributary valley. A stream in a hanging valley will descend to the floor of the main valley as a waterfall or *cataract*.

Headwards The action of a river eroding back upstream, as opposed to the normal process of downstream *erosion*. Headwards erosion is often associated with *gullying*.

Hoodos Pinnacles of rock which have been worn away by *weathering* in *semi-arid* regions.

Horst A block of the Earth's *crust* which has been left upstanding by the sinking of adjoining blocks along fault lines.

Hot spot A region of the Earth's *crust* where high thermal activity occurs, often leading to volcanic eruptions. Hot spots often occur far from plate boundaries, but their movement is associated with *plate tectonics*.

Humid equatorial Rainy *climate* with no winter, where the coolest month is generally above 64°F (18°C).

Humidity The relative amount of moisture held in the Earth's *atmosphere*.

Hurricane
1 A tropical *cyclone* occurring in the Caribbean and western North Atlantic. *2* A wind of more than 65 knots (75 kmph).

Hydro-electric power Energy produced by harnessing the rapid movement of water down steep mountain slopes to drive turbines to generate electricity.

Hydrolysis The chemical breakdown of rocks in reaction with water, forming new compounds.

I

Ice Age A period in the Earth's history when surface temperatures in the temperate *latitudes* were much lower and *ice sheets* expanded considerably. There have been *ice ages* from *Pre-Cambrian* times onwards. The most recent began two million years ago and ended 10,000 years ago.

Ice cap A permanent dome of ice in highland areas. The term ice cap is often seen as distinct from *ice sheet*, which denotes a much wider covering of ice; and is also used refer to the very extensive polar and Greenland ice caps.

Ice floe A large, flat mass of ice floating free on the ocean surface. It is usually formed after the break-up of winter ice by heavy storms.

Ice sheet A continuous, very thick layer of ice and snow. The term is usually used of ice masses which are continental in extent.

Ice shelf A floating mass of ice attached to the edge of a coast. The seaward edge is usually a sheer cliff up to 100 ft (30 m) high.

Ice wedge Massive blocks of ice up to 6.5 ft (2 m) wide at the top and extending 32 ft (10 m) deep. They are found in cracks in *polygonally-patterned* ground in *periglacial* regions.

Iceberg A large mass of ice in a lake or a sea, which has broken off from a floating *ice sheet* (an *ice shelf*) or from a *glacier*.

Igneous rock Rock formed when molten material, *magma*, from the hot, lower layers of the Earth's *crust*, cools, solidifies and crystallizes, either within the Earth's *crust* (*intrusive*) or on the surface (*extrusive*).

IMF International Monetary Fund. Established in 1944 as a UN agency, it contains 182 members around the world and is concerned with world monetary stability and economic development.

Incised meander A *meander* where the river, following its original course, cuts deeply into *bedrock*. This may occur when a mature, meandering river begins to erode its bed much more vigorously after the surrounding land has been uplifted.

Indigenous People, plants or animals native to a particular region.

Infrastructure The communications and services – roads, railways and telecommunications – necessary for the functioning of a country or region.

Inselberg An isolated, steep-sided hill, rising from a low *plain* in *semi-arid* and *savannah* landscapes. Inselbergs are usually composed of a rock, such as granite, which resists *erosion*.

Interglacial A period of global *climate*, between two *ice ages*, when temperatures rise and *ice sheets* and *glaciers* retreat.

Intraplate volcano A *volcano* which lies in the centre of one of the Earth's *tectonic plates*, rather than, as is more common, at its edge. They are thought to have been formed by a *hot spot*.

Intrusion (intrusive igneous rock) Rock formed when molten material, *magma*, penetrates existing rocks below the Earth's surface before cooling and solidifying. These rocks cool more slowly than extrusive rock and therefore tend to have coarser grains.

Irrigation The artificial supply of agricultural water to dry areas, often involving the creation of canals and the diversion of natural watercourses.

Island arc A curved chain of islands. Typically, such an arc fringes an ocean trench, formed at the margin between two *tectonic plates*. As one plate overrides another, *earthquakes* and volcanic activity are common and the islands themselves are often volcanic cones.

Isostasy The state of equilibrium which the Earth's *crust* maintains as its lighter and heavier parts float on the denser underlying mantle.

Isthmus A narrow strip of land connecting two larger landmasses or islands.

J

Jet stream A narrow belt of westerly winds in the *troposphere*, at altitudes above 39,000 ft (12,000 m). Jet streams tend to blow more strongly in winter and include: the subtropical jet stream; the *polar* front jet stream in mid-*latitudes*; the *Arctic* jet stream; and the polar-night jet stream.

Joint A crack in a rock, formed where blocks of rock have not shifted relative to each other, as is the case with a *fault*. Joints are created by *folding*; by shrinkage in *igneous rock* as it cools or *sedimentary rock* as it dries out; and by the release of pressure in a rock mass when overlying materials are removed by *erosion*.

Jute A plant fibre used to make coarse ropes, sacks and matting.

K

Kame A mound of stratified sand and gravel with steep sides, deposited in a *crevasse* by *meltwater* running over a *glacier*. When the ice retreats, this forms an undulating terrain of hummocks.

Karst A barren *limestone* landscape created by carbonic acid in streams and rainwater, in areas where *limestone* is close to the surface. Typical features include caverns, tower-like hills, *sinkholes* and flat limestone pavements.

Kettle hole A round hollow formed in a glacial deposit by a detached block of glacial ice, which later melted. They can fill with water to form kettle-lakes.

L

Lagoon A shallow stretch of coastal salt-water behind a partial barrier such as a sandbank or *coral reef*. Lagoon is also used to describe the water encircled by an *atoll*.

LAIA Latin American Integration Association. Established in 1980, its members are Argentina, Bolivia, Brazil, Chile, Colombia, Ecuador, Mexico, Paraguay, Peru, Uruguay and Venezuela. It aims to promote economic co-operation between member states.

Landslide The sudden downslope movement of a mass of rock or earth on a slope, caused either by heavy rain; the impact of waves; an *earthquake* or human activity.

Laterite A hard red deposit left by *chemical weathering* in tropical conditions, and consisting mainly of oxides of iron and aluminium.

Latitude The angular distance from the *Equator*, to a given point on the Earth's surface. Imaginary lines of *latitude* running parallel to the Equator encircle the Earth, and are measured in degrees north or south of the Equator. The Equator is 0°, the poles 90° South and North respectively. Also called parallels.

Laurasia In the theory of *continental drift*, the northern part of the great *supercontinent* of *Pangaea*. Laurasia is said to consist of N America, Greenland and all of Eurasia north of the Indian subcontinent.

Lava The molten rock, *magma*, which erupts onto the Earth's surface through a *volcano*, or through a *fault* or crack in the Earth's *crust*. Lava refers to the rock both in its molten and in its later, solidified form.

Leaching The process whereby water dissolves minerals and moves them down through layers of soil or rock.

Levée A raised bank alongside the channel of a river. Levées are either human-made or formed in times of flood when the river overflows its channel, slows and deposits much of its *sediment* load.

Lichen An organism which is the symbiotic product of an algae and a fungus. Lichens form in tight crusts on stones and trees, and are resistant to extreme cold. They are often found in tundra regions.

Lignite Low-grade coal, also known as brown coal. Found in large deposits in eastern Europe.

Limestone A porous *sedimentary* rock formed from carbonate materials.

Lingua franca The language adopted as the common language between speakers whose native languages are different. This is common in former colonial states.

Lithosphere The rigid upper layer of the Earth, comprising the *crust* and the upper part of the *mantle*.

Llanos Vast grassland *plains* of northern South America.

Loess Fine-grained, yellow deposits of unstratified silts and sands. Loess is believed to be wind-carried *sediment* created in the last *Ice Age*. Some deposits may later have been redistributed by rivers. Loess-derived soils are of high quality, fertile and easy to work.

Longitude A division of the Earth which pinpoints how far east or west a given place is from the Prime Meridian (0°) which runs through the Royal Observatory at Greenwich, England (UK). Imaginary lines of longitude are drawn around the world from pole to pole. The world is divided into 360 degrees.

Longshore drift The transport of sand and silt along the coast, carried by waves hitting the beach at an angle.

M

Magma Underground, molten rock, which is very hot and highly charged with gas. It is generated at great pressure, at depths 10 miles (16 km) or more below the Earth's surface. It can issue as *lava* at the Earth's surface or, more often, solidify below the surface as *intrusive igneous rock*.

Mantle The layer of the Earth between the *crust* and the *core*. It is about 1800 miles (2900 km) thick. The uppermost layer of the mantle is the soft, 125 mile (200 km) thick *asthenosphere* on which the more rigid *lithosphere* floats.

Maquiladoras Factories on the Mexico side of the Mexico/US border, which are allowed to import raw materials and components duty-free and use low-cost labour to assemble the goods, finally exporting them for sale in the US.

Market gardening The intensive growing of fruit and vegetables close to large local markets.

Mass movement Downslope movement of weathered materials such as rock, often helped by rainfall or glacial *meltwater*. Mass movement may be a gradual process or rapid, as in a *landslide* or rockfall.

Massif A single very large mountain or an area of mountains with uniform characteristics and clearly-defined boundaries.

Meander A loop-like bend in a river, which is found typically in the lower, mature reaches of a river but can form wherever the valley is wide and the slope gentle.

Mediterranean climate A temperate *climate* of hot, dry summers and warm, damp winters. This is typical of the western fringes of the world's continents in the warm temperate regions between *latitudes* of 30° and 40° (north and south).

Meltwater Water resulting from the melting of a *glacier* or *ice sheet*.

Mesa A broad, flat-topped hill, characteristic of *arid* regions.

Mesosphere A layer of the Earth's *atmosphere*, between the *stratosphere* and the *thermosphere*. Extending from about 25–50 miles (40–80 km) above the surface of the Earth.

Mestizo A person of mixed *Amerindian* and European origin.

Metallurgy The refining and working of metals.

Metamorphic rocks Rocks which have been altered from their original form, in terms of texture, composition and structure by intense heat, pressure, or by the introduction of new chemical substances – or a combination of more than one of these.

Meteor A body of rock, metal or other material, which travels through space at great speeds. Meteors are visible as they enter the Earth's *atmosphere* as shooting stars and fireballs.

Meteorite The remains of a *meteor* that has fallen to Earth.

Meteoroid A *meteor* which is still travelling in space, outside the Earth's *atmosphere*.

Mezzogiorno A term applied to the southern portion of Italy.

Milankovitch hypothesis A theory suggesting that there are a series of cycles which slightly alter the Earth's position when rotating about the Sun. The cycles identified all affect the amount of *radiation* the Earth receives at different *latitudes*. The theory is seen as a key factor in the cause of *ice ages*.

Millet A grain-crop, forming part of the staple diet in much of Africa.

Mistral A strong, dry, cold northerly or north-westerly wind, which blows from the Massif Central of France to the Mediterranean Sea. It is common in winter and its cold blasts can cause crop damage in the Rhône Delta, in France.

Mohorovicic discontinuity (Moho) The structural divide at the margin between the Earth's *crust* and the *mantle*. On average it is 20 miles (35 km) below the continents and 6 miles (10 km) below the oceans. The different densities of the *crust* and the mantle cause *earthquake* waves to accelerate at this point.

Monarchy A form of government in which the head of state is a single hereditary monarch. The monarch may be a mere figurehead, or may retain significant authority.

Monsoon A wind which changes direction bi-annually. The change is caused by the reversal of pressure over landmasses and the adjacent oceans. Because the inflowing moist winds bring rain, the term monsoon is also used to refer to the rains themselves. The term is derived from and most commonly refers to the seasonal winds of south and east Asia.

Montaña Mountain areas along the west coast of South America.

Moraine Debris, transported and deposited by a *glacier* or *ice sheet* in unstratified, mixed, piles of rock, boulders, pebbles and clay.

Mountain-building The formation of *fold* mountains by tectonic activity. Also known as orogeny, mountain-building often occurs on the margin where two *tectonic plates* collide. The periods when most mountain-building occurred are known as orogenic phases and lasted many millions of years.

Mudflow An *avalanche* of mud which occurs when a mass of soil is drenched by rain or melting snow. It is a type of *mass movement*, faster than an *earthflow* because it is lubricated by water.

N

Nappe A mass of rocks which has been overfolded by repeated thrust *faulting*.

NAFTA The North American Free Trade Association. Established in 1994 between Canada, Mexico and the US to set up a free-trade zone.

NASA The National Aeronautics and Space Administration. It is a US government agency established in 1958 to develop manned and unmanned space programmes.

NATO The North Atlantic Treaty Organization. Established in 1949 to promote mutual defence and co-operation between its members, which are Belgium, Canada, Czech Republic, Denmark, France, Germany, Greece, Iceland, Italy, Luxembourg, the Netherlands, Norway, Portugal, Poland, Spain, Turkey, UK, and US.

Nitrogen The odourless, colourless gas which makes up 78% of the atmosphere. Within the soil, it is a vital nutrient for plants.

Nomads (nomadic) Wandering communities who move around in search of suitable pasture for their herds of animals.

Nuclear fusion A technique used to create a new nucleus by the merging of two lighter ones, resulting in the release of large quantities of energy.

O

Oasis A fertile area in the midst of a *desert*, usually watered by an underground *aquifer*.

Oceanic ridge A mid-ocean ridge formed, according to the theory of *plate tectonics*, when plates drift apart and hot *magma* pours through to form new oceanic *crust*.

Oligarchy The government of a state by a small, exclusive group of people – such as an elite class or a family group.

Onion-skin weathering The *weathering* away or *exfoliation* of a rock or outcrop by the peeling off of surface layers.

Oriente A flatter region lying to the east of the Andes in South America.

Outwash plain *Glaciofluvial* material (typically clay, sand and gravel) carried beyond an ice sheet by *meltwater* streams, forming a broad, flat deposit.

Oxbow lake A crescent-shaped lake formed on a river *flood plain* when a river erodes the outside bend of a *meander*, making the neck of the *meander* narrower until the river cuts across the neck. The meander is cut off and is dammed off with sediment, creating an oxbow lake. Also known as a cut-off or mortlake.

Oxidation A form of *chemical weathering* where *oxygen* dissolved in water reacts with minerals in rocks – particularly iron – to form oxides. Oxidation causes brown or yellow staining on rocks, and eventually leads to the break down of the rock.

Oxygen A colourless, odourless gas which is one of the main constituents of the Earth's *atmosphere* and is essential to life on Earth.

Ozone layer A layer of enriched *oxygen* (O_3) within the stratosphere, mostly between 18–50 miles (30–80 km) above the Earth's surface. It is vital to the existence of life on Earth because it absorbs harmful shortwave ultraviolet radiation, while allowing beneficial longer wave ultraviolet radiation to penetrate to the Earth's surface.

P

Pacific Rim The name given to the economically-dynamic countries bordering the Pacific Ocean.

Pack ice Ice masses more than 10 ft (3 m) thick which form on the sea surface and are not attached to a landmass.

Pancake ice Thin discs of ice, up to 8 ft (2.4 m) wide which form when slicks of *grease ice* are tossed together by winds and stormy seas.

Pangaea In the theory of continental drift, Pangaea is the original great land mass which, about 190 million years ago, began to split into Gondwanaland in the south and Laurasia in the north, separated by the Tethys Sea.

Pastoralism Grazing of livestock– usually sheep, goats or cattle. Pastoralists in many drier areas have traditionally been *nomadic*.

Parallel *see Latitude.*

Peat Ancient, partially-decomposed vegetation found in wet, boggy conditions where there is little *oxygen*. It is the first stage in the development of coal and is often dried for use as fuel. It is also used to improve soil quality.

Pediment A gently-sloping ramp of *bedrock* below a steeper slope, often found at mountain edges in *desert* areas, but also in other climatic zones. Pediments may include depositional elements such as *alluvial fans*.

Peninsula A thin strip of land surrounded on three of its sides by water. Large examples include Florida and Korea.

Per capita Latin term meaning 'for each person'.

Periglacial Regions on the edges of *ice sheets* or *glaciers* or, more commonly, cold regions experiencing intense frost action, *permafrost* or both. Periglacial climates bring long, freezing winters and short, mild summers.

Permafrost Permanently frozen ground, typical of *Arctic* regions. Although a layer of soil above the permafrost melts in summer, the melted water does not drain through the permafrost.

Permeable rocks Rocks through which water can seep, because they are either porous or cracked.

Pharmaceuticals The manufacture of medicinal drugs.

Phreatic eruption A volcanic eruption which occurs when *lava* combines with *groundwater*, superheating the water and causing a sudden emission of steam at the surface.

Physical weathering (mechanical weathering) The breakdown of rocks by physical, as opposed to chemical, processes. Examples include: changes in pressure or temperature; the effect of windblown sand; the pressure of growing salt crystals in cracks within rock; and the expansion and contraction of water within rock as it freezes and thaws.

Pingo A dome of earth with a core of ice, found in *tundra* regions. Pingos are formed either when *groundwater* freezes and expands, pushing up the land surface, or when trapped, freezing water in a lake expands and pushes up lake *sediments* to form the pingo dome.

Placer A belt of mineral-bearing rock *strata* lying at or close to the Earth's surface, from which minerals can be easily extracted.

Plain A flat, level region of land, often relatively low-lying.

Plateau A highland tract of flat land.

Plate *see Tectonic plates.*

Plate tectonics The study of *tectonic plates*, which helps to explain *continental drift*, mountain formation and volcanic activity. The movement of tectonic plates may be explained by the currents of rock rising and falling from within the Earth's *mantle*, as it heats up and then cools. The boundaries of the plates are known as plate margins and most mountains, *earthquakes* and *volcanoes* occur at these margins. Constructive margins are moving apart; destructive margins are crunching together and conservative margins are sliding past one another.

Pleistocene A period of *geological time* spanning from about 5.2 million years ago to 1.6 million years ago.

Plutonic rock *Igneous* rocks found deep below the surface. They are coarse-grained because they cooled and solidified slowly.

Polar The zones within the *Arctic* and *Antarctic* circles.

Polje A long, broad *depression* found in *karst* (*limestone*) regions.

Polygonal patterning Typical ground patterning, found in areas where the soil is subject to severe frost action, often in *periglacial* regions.

Porosity A measure of how much water can be held within a rock or a soil. Porosity is measured as the percentage of holes or pores in a material, compared to its total volume. For example, the porosity of slate is less than 1%, whereas that of gravel is 25–35%.

Prairies Originally a French word for grassy *plains* with few or no trees.

Pre-Cambrian The earliest period of *geological time* dating from over 570 million years ago.

Precipitation The fall of moisture from the *atmosphere* onto the surface of the Earth, whether as dew, hail, rain, sleet or snow.

Pyramidal peak A steep, isolated mountain summit, formed when the back walls of three or more *cirques* are cut back and move towards each other. The cliffs around such a horned peak, or horn, are divided by sharp *arêtes*. The Matterhorn in the Swiss Alps is an example.

Pyroclasts Fragments of rock ejected during volcanic eruptions.

Q

Quaternary The current period of *geological time*, which started about 1.6 million years ago.

R

Radiation The emission of energy in the form of particles or waves. Radiation from the sun includes heat, light, ultraviolet rays, gamma rays and X-rays. Only some of the solar energy radiated into space reaches the Earth.

Rainforest Dense forests in tropical zones with high rainfall, temperature and *humidity*. Strictly, the term applies to the equatorial rainforest in tropical lowlands with constant rainfall and no seasonal change. The Congo and Amazon basins are examples. The term is applied more loosely to lush forest in other climates. Within rainforests organic life is dense and varied: at least 40% of all plant and animal species are found here and there may be as many as 100 tree species per hectare.

Rainshadow An area which experiences low rainfall, because of its position on the leeward side of a mountain range.

Reg A large area of stony *desert*, where tightly-packed gravel lies on top of clayey sand. A reg is formed where the wind blows away the finer sand.

Remote-sensing Method of obtaining information about the *environment* using unmanned equipment, such as a satellite, which relays the information to a point where it is collected and used.

Resistance The capacity of a rock to resist *denudation*, by processes such as *weathering* and *erosion*.

Ria A flooded *V-shaped river valley* or estuary, flooded by a rise in sea level (*eustacy*) or sinking land. It is shorter than a *fjord* and gets deeper as it meets the sea.

Rift valley A long, narrow depression in the Earth's *crust*, formed by the sinking of rocks between two *faults*.

River channel The trough which contains a river and is moulded by the flow of water within it.

Roche moutonée A rock found in a glaciated valley. The side facing the flow of the *glacier* has been smoothed and rounded, while the other side has been left more rugged because the *glacier*, as it flows over it, has plucked out frozen fragments and carried them away.

Runoff Water draining from a land surface by flowing across it.

S

Sabkha The floor of an isolated *depression* which occurs in an *arid environment* – usually covered by salt deposits and devoid of vegetation.

SADC Southern African Development Community. Established in 1992 to promote economic integration between its member states, which are Angola, Botswana, Lesotho, Malawi, Mauritius, Mozambique, Namibia, South Africa, Swaziland, Tanzania, Zambia and Zimbabwe.

Salt plug A rounded hill produced by the upward doming of rock *strata* caused by the movement of salt or other evaporite deposits under intense pressure.

Sastrugi Ice ridges formed by wind action. They lie parallel to the direction of the wind.

Savannah Open grassland found between the zone of *deserts*, and that of tropical *rainforests* in the tropics and subtropics. Scattered trees and shrubs are found in some kinds of savannah. A savannah *climate* usually has wet and dry seasons.

Scarp *see Escarpment.*

Scree Piles of rock fragments beneath a cliff or rock face, caused by mechanical *weathering*, especially *frost shattering*, where the expansion and contraction of freezing and thawing water within the rock, gradually breaks it up.

Sea-floor spreading The process whereby *tectonic plates* move apart, allowing hot *magma* to erupt and solidify. This forms a new sea floor and, ultimately, widens the ocean.

Seamount An isolated, submarine mountain or hill, probably of volcanic origin.

Season A period of time linked to regular changes in the weather, especially the intensity of solar *radiation*.

Sediment Grains of rock transported and deposited by rivers, sea, ice or wind.

Sedimentary rocks Rocks formed from the debris of pre-existing rocks or of organic material. They are found in many *environments* – on the ocean floor, on beaches, rivers and *deserts*. Organically-formed sedimentary rocks include coal and chalk. Other sedimentary rocks, such as flint, are formed by chemical processes. Most of these rocks contain *fossils*, which can be used to date them.

Seif A sand *dune* which lies parallel to the direction of the prevailing wind. Seifs form steep-sided ridges, sometimes extending for miles.

Seismic activity Movement within the Earth, such as an *earthquake* or *tremor*.

Selva A region of wet forest found in the Amazon Basin.

Semi-arid, semi-desert The *climate* and landscape which lies between *savannah* and *desert* or between savannah and a *mediterranean* climate. In semi-arid conditions there is a little more moisture than in a true *desert*; and more patches of drought-resistant vegetation can survive.

Shale (marine shale) A compacted *sedimentary rock*, with fine-grained particles. Marine shale is formed on the seabed. Fuel such as oil may be extracted from it.

Sheetwash Water which runs downhill in thin sheets without forming channels. It can cause *sheet erosion*.

Sheet erosion The washing away of soil by a thin film or sheet of water, known as *sheetwash*.

Shield A vast stable block of the Earth's *crust*, which has experienced little or no *mountain-building*.

Sierra The Spanish word for mountains.

Sinkhole A circular *depression* in a *limestone* region. They are formed by the collapse of an underground cave system or the *chemical weathering* of the *limestone*.

Sisal A plant-fibre used to make matting.

Slash and burn A farming technique involving the cutting down and burning of scrub forest, to create agricultural land. After a number of seasons this land is abandoned and the process is repeated. This practice is common in Africa and South America.

Slip face The steep leeward side of a sand *dune* or slope. Opposite side to a *back slope*.

Soil A thin layer of rock particles mixed with the remains of dead plants and animals. This occurs naturally on the surface of the Earth and provides a medium for plants to grow.

Soil creep The very gradual downslope movement of rock debris and soil, under the influence of gravity. This is a type of *mass movement*.

Soil erosion The wearing away of soil more quickly than it is replaced by natural processes. Soil can be carried away by wind as well as by water. Human activities, such as over-grazing and the clearing of land for farming, accelerate the process in many areas.

Solar energy Energy derived from the Sun. Solar energy is converted into other forms of energy. For example, the wind and waves, as well as the creation of plant material in photosynthesis, depend on solar energy.

Solifluction A kind of *soil creep*, where water in the surface layer has saturated the soil and rock debris which slips slowly downhill. It often happens where frozen top-layer deposits thaw, leaving frozen layers below them.

Sorghum A type of grass found in South America, similar to sugar cane. When refined it is used to make molasses.

Spit A thin linear deposit of sand or shingle extending from the sea shore. Spits are formed as angled waves shift sand along the beach, eventually extending a ridge of sand beyond a change in the angle of the coast. Spits are common where the coastline bends, especially at estuaries.

Squash A type of edible gourd.

Stack A tall, isolated pillar of rock near a coastline, created as wave action erodes away the adjacent rock.

Stalactite A tapering cylinder of mineral deposit, hanging from the roof of a cave in a *karst* area. It is formed by calcium carbonate, dissolved in water, which drips through the roof of a *limestone* cavern.

Stalagmite A cone of calcium carbonate, similar to a *stalactite*, rising from the floor of a *limestone* cavern and formed when drops of water fall from the roof of a *limestone* cave. If the water has dripped from a *stalactite* above the stalagmite, the two may join to form a continuous pillar.

Staple crop The main crop on which a country is economically and or physically reliant. For example, the major crop grown for large-scale local consumption in South Asia is rice.

Steppe Large areas of dry grassland in the northern hemisphere – particularly found in southeast Europe and central Asia.

Strata The plural of stratum, a distinct, virtually horizontal layer of deposited material, lying parallel to other layers.

Stratosphere A layer of the *atmosphere*, above the *troposphere*, extending from about 7–30 miles (11–50 km) above the Earth's surface. In the lower part of the stratosphere, the temperature is relatively stable and there is little moisture.

Strike-slip fault Occurs where plates move sideways past each other and blocks of rocks move horizontally in relation to each other, not up or down as in normal *faults*.

Subduction zone A region where two *tectonic plates* collide, forcing one beneath the other. Typically, a dense oceanic plate dips below a lighter continental plate, melting in the heat of the *asthenosphere*. This is why the zone is also called a destructive margin (*see Plate tectonics*). These zones are characterized by *earthquakes*, volcanoes, *mountain-building* and the development of oceanic trenches and *island arcs*.

Submarine canyon A steep-sided valley, which extends along the *continental shelf* to the ocean floor. Often formed by *turbidity currents*.

Submarine fan Deposits of silt and *alluvium*, carried by large rivers forming great fan-shaped deposits on the ocean floor.

Subsistence agriculture An agricultural practice, whereby enough food is produced to support the farmer and his dependents, but not providing any surplus to generate an income.

Subtropical A term applied loosely to *climates* which are nearly tropical or tropical for a part of the year – areas north or south of the *tropics* but outside the *temperate zone*.

Supercontinent A large continent that breaks up to form smaller continents or which forms when smaller continents merge. In the theory of *continental drift*, the supercontinents are *Pangaea*, *Gondwanaland* and *Laurasia*.

Sustainable development An approach to development, applied to economies across the world which exploit natural resources without destroying them or the *environment*.

Syncline A basin-shaped downfold in rock *strata*, created when the *strata* are compressed, for example where *tectonic plates* collide.

T

Tableland A highland area with a flat or gently undulating surface.

Taiga The belt of *coniferous* forest found in the north of Asia and North America. The conifers are adapted to survive low temperatures and long periods of snowfall.

Tarn A Scottish term for a small mountain lake, usually found at the head of a *glacier*.

Tectonic plates Plates, or tectonic plates, are the rigid slabs which form the Earth's outer shell, the *lithosphere*. Eight big plates and several smaller ones have been identified.

Temperate A moderate *climate* without extremes of temperature, typical of the mid-*latitudes* between the *tropics* and the *polar* circles.

Theocracy A state governed by religious laws – today Iran is the world's largest theocracy.

Thermokarst Subsidence created by the thawing of ground ice in *periglacial* areas, creating depressions.

Thermosphere A layer of the Earth's *atmosphere* which lies above the *mesophere*, about 60–300 miles (100–500 km) above the Earth

Terraces Steps cut into steep slopes to create flat surfaces for cultivating crops. They also help reduce soil *erosion* on unconsolidated slopes. They are most common in heavily-populated parts of Southeast Asia.

Till Unstratified glacial deposits or drift left by a *glacier* or *ice sheet*. Till includes mixtures of clay, sand, gravel and boulders.

Topography The typical shape and features of a given area such as land height and terrain.

Tombolo A large sand *spit* which attaches part of the mainland to an island.

Tornado A violent, spiralling windstorm, with a centre of very low pressure. Wind speeds reach 200 mph (320 kmph) and there is often thunder and heavy rain.

Transform fault In *plate tectonics*, a *fault* of continental scale, occurring where two plates slide past each other, staying close together for example, the San Andreas Fault, USA. The jerky, uneven movement creates *earthquakes* but does not destroy or add to the Earth's *crust*

Transpiration The loss of water vapour through the pores (or stomata) of plants. The process helps to return moisture to the *atmosphere*.

Trap An area of fine-grained *igneous rock* which has been extruded and cooled on the Earth's surface in stages, forming a series of steps or terraces.

Treeline The line beyond which trees cannot grow, dependent on *latitude* and altitude, as well as local factors such as soil.

Tremor A slight *earthquake*.

Trench (oceanic trench) A long, deep trough in the ocean floor, formed, according to the theory of *plate tectonics*, when two plates collide and one dives under the other, creating a *subduction zone*.

Tropics The zone between the *Tropic of Cancer* and the *Tropic of Capricorn* where the *climate* is hot. Tropical climate is also applied to areas rather further north and south of the *Equator* where the climate is similar to that of the true tropics.

Tropic of Cancer A line of *latitude* or imaginary circle round the Earth, lying at 23° 28' N.

Tropic of Capricorn A line of *latitude* or imaginary circle round the Earth, lying at 23° 28' S.

Troposphere The lowest layer of the Earth's *atmosphere*. From the surface, it reaches a height of between 4–10 miles (7–16 km). It is the most turbulent zone of the atmosphere and accounts for the generation of most of the world's weather. The layer above it is called the *stratosphere*.

Tsunami A huge wave created by shock waves from an *earthquake* under the sea. Reaching speeds of up to 600 mph (960 kmph), the wave may increase to heights of 50 ft (15 m) on entering coastal waters; and it can cause great damage.

Tundra The treeless *plains* of the *Arctic Circle*, found south of the *polar* region of permanent ice and snow, and north of the belt of *coniferous* forests known as *taiga*. In this region of long, very cold winters, vegetation is usually limited to mosses, *lichens*, sedges and rushes, although flowers and dwarf shrubs blossom in the brief summer.

Turbidity current An oceanic feature. A turbidity current is a mass of *sediment*-laden water which has substantial erosive power. Turbidity currents are thought to contribute to the formation of *submarine canyons*.

Typhoon A kind of *hurricane* (or tropical cyclone) bringing violent winds and heavy rain, a typhoon can do great damage. They occur in the South China Sea, especially around the Philippines.

U

U-shaped valley A river valley that has been deepened and widened by a *glacier*. They are characteristically flat-bottomed and steep-sided and generally much deeper than river valleys.

UN United Nations. Established in 1945, it contains 188 nations and aims to maintain international peace and security, and promote co-operation over economic, social, cultural and humanitarian problems.

UNICEF United Nations Children's Fund. A UN organization set up to promote family and child related programmes.

Urstromtäler A German word used to describe *meltwater* channels which flowed along the front edge of the advancing *ice sheet* during the last Ice Age, 18,000–20,000 years ago.

V

V-shaped valley A typical valley eroded by a river in its upper course.

Virgin rainforest Tropical *rainforest* in its original state, untouched by human activity such as logging, clearance for agriculture, settlement or road building.

Viticulture The cultivation of grapes for wine.

Volcano An opening or vent in the Earth's *crust* where molten rock, *magma*, erupts. Volcanoes tend to be conical but may also be a crack in the Earth's surface or a hole blasted through a mountain. The magma is accompanied by other materials such as gas, steam and fragments of rock, or *pyroclasts*. They tend to occur on destructive or constructive *tectonic plate* margins.

W-Z

Wadi The dry bed left by a torrent of water. Also classified as a *ephemeral* stream, found in *arid* and *semi-arid* regions, which are subject to sudden and often severe flash flooding.

Warm humid climate A rainy climate with warm summers and mild winters.

Water cycle The continuous circulation of water between the Earth's surface and the *atmosphere*. The processes include *evaporation* and *transpiration* of moisture into the atmosphere, and its return as *precipitation*, some of which flows into lakes and oceans.

Water table The upper level of *groundwater* saturation in permeable rock *strata*.

Watershed The dividing line between one *drainage basin* – an area where all streams flow into a single river system – and another. In the US, watershed also means the whole drainage basin of a single river system – its catchment area.

Waterspout A rotating column of water in the form of cloud, mist and spray which form on open water. Often has the appearance of a small *tornado*.

Weathering The decay and break-up of rocks at or near the Earth's surface, caused by water, wind, heat or ice, organic material or the *atmosphere*. *Physical weathering* includes the effects of frost and temperature changes. Biological weathering includes the effects of plant roots, burrowing animals and the acids produced by animals, especially as they decay after death. *Carbonation* and *hydrolysis* are among many kinds of *chemical weathering*.

Geographical names

The following glossary lists all geographical terms occurring on the maps and in main-entry names in the Index-Gazetteer. These terms may precede, follow or be run together with the proper element of the name; where they precede it the term is reversed for indexing purposes - thus Poluostrov Yamal is indexed as Yamal, Poluostrov.

Key

Geographical term
Language, Term

A

Å *Danish, Norwegian*, River
Āb *Persian*, River
Adrar *Berber*, Mountains
Agía, Ágios *Greek*, Saint
Air *Indonesian*, River
Akrotírio *Greek*, Cape, point
Alpen *German*, Alps
Alt- *German*, Old
Altiplanicie *Spanish*, Plateau
Älv, -älven *Swedish*, River
-ån *Swedish*, River
Anse *French*, Bay
'Aqabat *Arabic*, Pass
Archipiélago *Spanish*, Archipelago
Arcipelago *Italian*, Archipelago
Arquipélago *Portuguese*, Archipelago
Arrecife(s) *Spanish*, Reef(s)
Aru *Tamil*, River
Augstiene *Latvian*, Upland
Aukštuma *Lithuanian*, Upland
Aust- *Norwegian*, Eastern
Avtonomnyy Okrug *Russian*, Autonomous district
Āw *Kurdish*, River
'Ayn *Arabic*, Spring, well
'Ayoûn *Arabic*, Wells

B

Baelt *Danish*, Strait
Bahía *Spanish*, Bay
Baḥr *Arabic*, River
Baía *Portuguese*, Bay
Baie *French*, Bay
Bañado *Spanish*, Marshy land
Bandao *Chinese*, Peninsula
Banjaran *Malay*, Mountain range
Barajı *Turkish*, Dam
Barragem *Portuguese*, Reservoir
Bassin *French*, Basin
Batang *Malay*, Stream
Beinn, Ben *Gaelic*, Mountain
-berg *Afrikaans, Norwegian*, Mountain
Besar *Indonesian, Malay*, Big
Birkat, Birket *Arabic*, Lake, well,
Boğazı *Turkish*, Strait, defile
Boka *Serbo-Croatian*, Bay
Bol'sh-aya, -iye, -oy, -oye *Russian*, Big
Botigh(i) *Uzbek*, Depression basin
-bre(en) *Norwegian*, Glacier
Bredning *Danish*, Bay
Bucht *German*, Bay
Bugt(en) *Danish*, Bay
Buḥayrat *Arabic*, Lake, reservoir
Buḥeiret *Arabic*, Lake
Bukit *Malay*, Mountain
-bukta *Norwegian*, Bay
bukten *Swedish*, Bay
Bulag *Mongolian*, Spring
Bulak *Uighur*, Spring
Burnu *Turkish*, Cape, point
Buuraha *Somali*, Mountains

C

Cabo *Portuguese*, Cape
Caka *Tibetan*, Salt lake
Canal *Spanish*, Channel
Cap *French*, Cape
Capo *Italian*, Cape, headland
Cascada *Portuguese*, Waterfall
Cayo(s) *Spanish*, Islet(s), rock(s)
Cerro *Spanish*, Hill
Chaîne *French*, Mountain range
Chapada *Portuguese*, Hills, upland
Chau *Cantonese*, Island
Chāy *Turkish*, River
Chhâk *Cambodian*, Bay
Chhu *Tibetan*, River
-chōsuji *Korean*, Reservoir
Chott *Arabic*, Depression, salt lake
Chŭli *Uzbek*, Grassland, steppe
Ch'ün-tao *Chinese*, Island group
Chuŏr Phnum *Cambodian*, Mountains
Ciudad *Spanish*, City, town
Co *Tibetan*, Lake
Colline(s) *French*, Hill(s)
Cordillera *Spanish*, Mountain range
Costa *Spanish*, Coast
Côte *French*, Coast
Coxilha *Portuguese*, Mountains
Cuchilla *Spanish*, Mountains

D

Daban *Mongolian, Uighur*, Pass
Dağı *Azerbaijani, Turkish*, Mountain
Dağları *Azerbaijani, Turkish*, Mountains
-dake *Japanese*, Peak
-dal(en) *Norwegian*, Valley
Danau *Indonesian*, Lake
Dao *Chinese*, Island
Đao *Vietnamese*, Island
Daryā *Persian*, River
Daryācheh *Persian*, Lake
Dasht *Persian*, Desert, plain
Dawḥat *Arabic*, Bay
Denizi *Turkish*, Sea
Dere *Turkish*, Stream
Desierto *Spanish*, Desert
Dili *Azerbaijani*, Spit
-do *Korean*, Island
Dooxo *Somali*, Valley
Düzü *Azerbaijani*, Steppe
-dwīp *Bengali*, Island

E

-eilanden *Dutch*, Islands
Embalse *Spanish*, Reservoir
Ensenada *Spanish*, Bay
Erg *Arabic*, Dunes
Estany *Catalan*, Lake
Estero *Spanish*, Inlet
Estrecho *Spanish*, Strait
Étang *French*, Lagoon, lake
-ey *Icelandic*, Island
Ezero *Bulgarian, Macedonian*, Lake
Ezers *Latvian*, Lake

F

Feng *Chinese*, Peak
-fjella *Norwegian*, Mountain
Fjord *Danish*, Fjord
-fjord(en) *Danish, Norwegian, Swedish*, fjord
-fjördhur *Icelandic*, Fjord
Fleuve *French*, River
Fliegu *Maltese*, Channel
-fljór *Icelandic*, River
-flói *Icelandic*, Bay
Forêt *French*, Forest

G

-gan *Japanese*, Rock
-gang *Korean*, River
Ganga *Hindi, Nepali, Sinhala*, River
Gaoyuan *Chinese*, Plateau
Garagumy *Turkmen*, Sands
-gawa *Japanese*, River
Gebel *Arabic*, Mountain
-gebirge *German*, Mountain range
Ghadīr *Arabic*, Well
Ghubbat *Arabic*, Bay
Gjiri *Albanian*, Bay
Gol *Mongolian*, River
Golfe *French*, Gulf
Golfo *Italian, Spanish*, Gulf
Göl(ü) *Turkish*, Lake
Golyam, -a *Bulgarian*, Big
Gora *Russian, Serbo-Croatian*, Mountain
Góra *Polish*, mountain
Gory *Russian*, Mountain
Gryada *Russian*, ridge
Guba *Russian*, Bay
-gundo *Korean*, island group
Gunung *Malay*, Mountain

H

Ḥadd *Arabic*, Spit
-haehyŏp *Korean*, Strait
Haff *German*, Lagoon
Hai *Chinese*, Bay, lake, sea
Haixia *Chinese*, Strait
Ḥammādah *Arabic*, Desert
Ḥammādat *Arabic*, Rocky plateau
Hāmūn *Persian*, Lake
-hantō *Japanese*, Peninsula
Har, Haré *Hebrew*, Mountain
Ḥarrat *Arabic*, Lava-field
Hav(et) *Danish*, Swedish, Sea
Hawr *Arabic*, Lake
Hāyk' *Amharic*, Lake
He *Chinese*, River
-hegység *Hungarian*, Mountain range
Heide *German*, Heath, moorland
Helodrano *Malagasy*, Bay
Higashi- *Japanese*, East(ern)
Ḥiṣā' *Arabic*, Well
Hka *Burmese*, River
-ho *Korean*, Lake
Ḥolot *Hebrew*, Dunes
Hora *Belarussian, Czech*, Mountain
Hrada *Belarussian*, Mountain, ridge
Hsi *Chinese*, River
Hu *Chinese*, Lake
Huk *Danish*, Point

I

Île(s) *French*, Island(s)
Ilha(s) *Portuguese*, Island(s)
Ilhéu(s) *Portuguese*, Islet(s)
-isen *Norwegian*, Ice shelf
Imeni *Russian*, In the name of
Inish- *Gaelic*, Island
Insel(n) *German*, Island(s)
Irmağı, Irmak *Turkish*, River
Isla(s) *Spanish*, Island(s)
Isola (Isole) *Italian*, Island(s)

J

Jabal *Arabic*, Mountain
Jāl *Arabic*, Ridge
-järv *Estonian*, Lake
-järvi *Finnish*, Lake
Jazā'ir *Arabic*, Islands
Jazīrat *Arabic*, Island
Jazīreh *Persian*, Island
Jebel *Arabic*, Mountain
Jezero *Serbo-Croatian*, Lake
Jezioro *Polish*, Lake
Jiang *Chinese*, River
-jima *Japanese*, Island
Jižní *Czech*, Southern
-jõgi *Estonian*, River
-joki *Finnish*, River
-jökull *Icelandic*, Glacier
Jūn *Arabic*, Bay
Juzur *Arabic*, Islands

K

Kaikyō *Japanese*, Strait
-kaise *Lappish*, Mountain
Kali *Nepali*, River
Kalnas *Lithuanian*, Mountain
Kalns *Latvian*, Mountain
Kang *Chinese*, Harbour
Kangri *Tibetan*, Mountain(s)
Kaôh *Cambodian*, Island
Kapp *Norwegian*, Cape
Káto *Greek*, Lower
Kavīr *Persian*, Desert
K'edi *Georgian*, Mountain range
Kediet *Arabic*, Mountain
Kepi *Albanian*, Cape, point
Kepulauan *Indonesian, Malay*, Island group
Khalīg, Khalīj *Arabic*, Gulf
Khawr *Arabic*, Inlet
Khola *Nepali*, River
Khrebet *Russian*, Mountain range
Ko *Thai*, Island
-ko *Japanese*, Inlet, lake
Kólpos *Greek*, Bay
-kopf *German*, Peak
Körfäzi *Azerbaijani*, Bay
Körfezi *Turkish*, Bay
Kõrgustik *Estonian*, Upland
Kosa *Russian, Ukrainian*, Spit
Koshi *Nepali*, River
Kou *Chinese*, River-mouth
Kowtal *Persian*, Pass
Kray *Russian*, Region, territory
Kryazh *Russian*, Ridge
Kuduk *Uighur*, Well
Kūh(hā) *Persian*, Mountain(s)
-kul' *Russian*, Lake
Kŭl(i) *Tajik, Uzbek*, Lake
-kundo *Korean*, Island group
-kysten *Norwegian*, Coast
Kyun *Burmese*, Island

L

Laaq *Somali*, Watercourse
Lac *French*, Lake
Lacul *Romanian*, Lake
Lagh *Somali*, Stream
Lago *Italian, Portuguese, Spanish*, Lake
Lagoa *Portuguese*, Lagoon
Laguna *Italian, Spanish*, Lagoon, lake
Laht *Estonian*, Bay
Laut *Indonesian*, Bay
Lembalemba *Malagasy*, Plateau
Lerr *Armenian*, Mountain
Lernnashghtʻa *Armenian*, Mountain range
Les *Czech*, Forest
Lich *Armenian*, Lake
Liehtao *Chinese*, Island group
Liqeni *Albanian*, Lake
Límni *Greek*, Lake
Ling *Chinese*, Mountain range
Llano *Spanish*, Plain, prairie
Lumi *Albanian*, River
Lyman *Ukrainian*, Estuary

M

Madīnat *Arabic*, City, town
Mae Nam *Thai*, River
-mägi *Estonian*, Hill
Maja *Albanian*, Mountain
Mal *Albanian*, Mountains
Mal-aya, -oye, -yy, *Russian*, Small
-man *Korean*, Bay
Mar *Spanish*, Sea
Marios *Lithuanian*, Lake
Massif *French*, Mountains
Meer *German*, Lake
-meer *Dutch*, Lake
Melkosopochnik *Russian*, Plain
-meri *Estonian*, Sea
Mifraẓ *Hebrew*, Bay
Minami- *Japanese*, South(ern)
-misaki *Japanese*, Cape, point
Monkhafad *Arabic*, Depression
Montagne(s) *French*, Mountain(s)
Montañas *Spanish*, Mountains
Mont(s) *French*, Mountain(s)
Monte *Italian, Portuguese*, Mountain
More *Russian*, Sea
Mörön *Mongolian*, River
Mys *Russian*, Cape, point

N

-nada *Japanese*, Open stretch of water
Nadi *Bengali*, River
Nagor'ye *Russian*, Upland
Naḥal *Hebrew*, River
Nahr *Arabic*, River
Nam *Laotian*, River
Namakzār *Persian*, Salt desert
Né-a, -on, -os *Greek*, New
Nedre- *Norwegian*, Lower
-neem *Estonian*, Cape, point
Nehri *Turkish*, River
-nes *Norwegian*, Cape, point
Nevado *Spanish*, Mountain (snow-capped)
Nieder- *German*, Lower
Nishi- *Japanese*, West(ern)
-nísi *Greek*, Island
Nisoi *Greek*, Islands
Nizhn-eye, -iy, -iye, -yaya *Russian*, Lower
Nizmennost' *Russian*, Lowland, plain
Nord *Danish, French, German*, North
Norte *Portuguese, Spanish*, North
Nos *Bulgarian*, Point, spit
Nosy *Malagasy*, Island
Nov-a, -i, *Bulgarian, Serbo-Croatian*, New
Nov-aya, -o, -oye, -yy, -yye *Russian*, New
Now-a, -e, -y *Polish*, New
Nur *Mongolian*, Lake
Nuruu *Mongolian*, Mountains
Nuur *Mongolian*, Lake
Nyzovyna *Ukrainian*, Lowland, plain

O

-ø *Danish*, Island
Ober- *German*, Upper
Oblast' *Russian*, Province
Órmos *Greek*, Bay
Orol(i) *Uzbek*, Island
Øster- *Norwegian*, Eastern
Ostrov(a) *Russian*, Island(s)
Otok *Serbo-Croatian*, Island
Oued *Arabic*, Watercourse
-oy *Faeroese*, Island
-øy(a) *Norwegian*, Island
Oya *Sinhala*, River
Ozero *Russian, Ukrainian*, Lake

P

Passo *Italian*, Pass
Pegunungan *Indonesian, Malay*, Mountain range
Pélagos *Greek*, Sea
Pendi *Chinese*, Basin
Penisola *Italian*, Peninsula
Pertuis *French*, Strait
Peski *Russian*, Sands
Phanom *Thai*, Mountain
Phou *Laotian*, Mountain
Pi *Chinese*, Point
Pic *Catalan, French*, Peak
Pico *Portuguese, Spanish*, Peak
-piggen *Danish*, Peak
Pik *Russian*, Peak
Pivostriv *Ukrainian*, Peninsula
Planalto *Portuguese*, Plateau
Planina, Planini *Bulgarian, Macedonian, Serbo-Croatian*, Mountain range
Plato *Russian*, Plateau
Ploskogor'ye *Russian*, Upland
Poluostrov *Russian*, Peninsula
Ponta *Portuguese*, Point
Porthmós *Greek*, Strait
Pótamos *Greek*, River
Presa *Spanish*, Dam
Prokhod *Bulgarian*, Pass
Proliv *Russian*, Strait
Pulau *Indonesian Malay*, Island
Pulu *Malay*, Island
Punta *Spanish*, Point
Pushcha *Belorussian*, Forest
Puszcza *Polish*, Forest

Q

Qā' *Arabic*, Depression
Qalamat *Arabic*, Well
Qatorkŭh(i) *Tajik*, Mountain
Qiuling *Chinese*, Hills
Qolleh *Persian*, Mountain
Qu *Tibetan*, Stream
Quan *Chinese*, Well
Qulla(i) *Tajik*, Peak
Qundao *Chinese*, Island group

R

Raas *Somali*, Cape
-rags *Latvian*, Cape
Ramlat *Arabic*, Sands
Ra's *Arabic*, Cape, headland, point
Ravnina *Bulgarian, Russian*, Plain
Récif *French*, Reef
Recife *Portuguese*, Reef
Reka *Bulgarian*, River
Represa (Rep.) *Portuguese, Spanish*, Reservoir
Reshteh *Persian*, Mountain range
Respublika *Russian*, Republic, first-order administrative division
Respublika(si) *Uzbek*, Republic, first-order administrative division
-retsugan *Japanese*, Chain of rocks
-rettō *Japanese*, Island chain
Riacho *Spanish*, Stream
Riban' *Malagasy*, Mountains
Rio *Portuguese*, River
Río *Spanish*, River
Riu *Catalan*, River
Rivier *Dutch*, River
Rivière *French*, River
Rowd *Pashtu*, River
Rt *Serbo-Croatian*, Point
Rūd *Persian*, River
Rūdkhāneh *Persian*, River
Rudohorie *Slovak*, Mountains
Ruisseau *French*, Stream

S

-saar *Estonian*, Island
-saari *Finnish*, Island
Sabkhat *Arabic*, Salt marsh
Sāgar(a) *Hindi*, Lake, reservoir
Ṣaḥrā' *Arabic*, Desert
Saint, Sainte *French*, Saint
Salar *Spanish*, Salt-pan
Salto *Portuguese, Spanish*, Waterfall
Samudra *Sinhala*, Reservoir
-san *Japanese, Korean*, Mountain
-sanchi *Japanese*, Mountains
-sandur *Icelandic*, Beach
Sankt *German, Swedish*, Saint
-sanmaek *Korean*, Mountain range
-sanmyaku *Japanese*, Mountain range
San, Santa, Santo *Italian, Portuguese, Spanish*, Saint
São *Portuguese*, Saint
Sarīr *Arabic*, Desert
Sebkha, Sebkhet *Arabic*, Depression, salt marsh
Sedlo *Czech*, Pass
See *German*, Lake
Selat *Indonesian*, Strait
Selatan *Indonesian*, Southern
-selkä *Finnish*, Lake, ridge
Selseleh *Persian*, Mountain range
Serra *Portuguese*, Mountain
Serranía *Spanish*, Mountain
-seto *Japanese*, Channel, strait
Sever-naya, -noye, -nyy, -o *Russian*, Northern
Sha'īb *Arabic*, Watercourse
Shākh *Kurdish*, Mountain
Shamo *Chinese*, Desert
Shan *Chinese*, Mountain(s)
Shankou *Chinese*, Pass
Shanmo *Chinese*, Mountain range
Shaṭṭ *Arabic*, Distributary
Shet' *Amharic*, River
Shi *Chinese*, Municipality
-shima *Japanese*, Island
Shiqqat *Arabic*, Depression
-shotō *Japanese*, Group of islands
Shuiku *Chinese*, Reservoir
Shŭrkhog(i) *Uzbek*, Salt marsh
Sierra *Spanish*, Mountains
Sint *Dutch*, Saint
-sjø(en) *Norwegian*, Lake
-sjön *Swedish*, Lake
Solonchak *Russian*, Salt lake
Solonchakovyye Vpadiny *Russian*, Salt basin, wetlands
Son *Vietnamese*, Mountain
Sông *Vietnamese*, River
Sør- *Norwegian*, Southern
-spitze *German*, Peak
Star-á, -é *Czech*, Old
Star-aya, -oye, -yy, -yye *Russian*, Old
Stenó *Greek*, Strait
Step' *Russian*, Steppe
Štít *Slovak*, Peak
Stœng *Cambodian*, River
Stolovaya Strana *Russian*, Plateau
Stredné *Slovak*, Middle
Střední *Czech*, Middle
Stretto *Italian*, Strait
Su Anbarı *Azerbaijani*, Reservoir
-suidō *Japanese*, Channel, strait
Sund *Swedish*, Sound, strait
Sungai *Indonesian, Malay*, River
Suu *Turkish*, River

T

Tal *Mongolian*, Plain
Tandavan' *Malagasy*, Mountain range
Tangorombohitr' *Malagasy*, Mountain massif
Tanjung *Indonesian, Malay*, Cape, point
Tao *Chinese*, Island
Ṭaraq *Arabic*, Hills
Tassili *Berber*, Mountain, plateau
Tau *Russian*, Mountain(s)
Taungdan *Burmese*, Mountain range
Techníti Límni *Greek*, Reservoir
Tekojärvi *Finnish*, Reservoir
Teluk *Indonesian, Malay*, Bay
Tengah *Indonesian*, Middle
Terara *Amharic*, Mountain
Timur *Indonesian*, Eastern
-tind(an) *Norwegian*, Peak
Tizma(si) *Uzbek*, Mountain range, ridge
-tō *Japanese*, island
Tog *Somali*, Valley
-tōge *Japanese*, pass
Togh(i) *Uzbek*, mountain
Tônlé *Cambodian*, Lake
Top *Dutch*, Peak
-tunturi *Finnish*, Mountain
Ṭurāq *Arabic*, hills
Tur'at *Arabic*, Channel

U

Udde(n) *Swedish*, Cape, point
'Uqlat *Arabic*, Well
Utara *Indonesian*, Northern
Uul *Mongolian*, Mountains

V

Väin *Estonian*, Strait
Vallée *French*, Valley
Varful *Romanian*, Peak
-vatn *Icelandic*, Lake
-vatnet *Norwegian*, Lake
Velayat *Turkmen*, Province
-vesi *Finnish*, Lake
Vestre- *Norwegian*, Western
-vidda *Norwegian*, Plateau
-vík *Icelandic*, Bay
-viken *Swedish*, Bay, inlet
Vinh *Vietnamese*, Bay
Víztárloló *Hungarian*, Reservoir
Vodaskhovishcha *Belarussian*, Reservoir
Vodokhranilishche (Vdkhr.) *Russian*, Reservoir
Vodoskhovyshche (Vdskh.) *Ukrainian*, Reservoir
Volcán *Spanish*, Volcano
Vostochn-o, yy *Russian*, Eastern
Vozvyshennost' *Russian*, Upland, plateau
Vozyera *Belarussian*, Lake
Vpadina *Russian*, Depression
Vrchovina *Czech*, Mountains
Vrh *Croat, Slovene*, Peak
Vychodné *Slovak*, Eastern
Vysochyna *Ukrainian*, Upland
Vysočina *Czech*, Upland

W

Waadi *Somali*, Watercourse
Wādī *Arabic* Watercourse
Wāḥat, Wâhat *Arabic*, Oasis
Wald *German*, Forest
Wan *Chinese*, Bay
Way *Indonesian*, River
Webi *Somali*, River
Wenz *Amharic*, River
Wiloyat(i) *Uzbek*, Province
Wyżyna *Polish*, Upland
Wzgórza *Polish*, Upland
Wzvyshsha *Belarussian*, Upland

X

Xé *Laotian*, River
Xi *Chinese*, Stream

Y

-yama *Japanese*, Mountain
Yanchi *Chinese*, Salt lake
Yanhu *Chinese*, Salt lake
Yarımadası *Azerbaijani, Turkish*, Peninsula
Yaylası *Turkish*, Plateau
Yazovir *Bulgarian*, Reservoir
Yoma *Burmese*, Mountains
Ytre- *Norwegian*, Outer
Yu *Chinese*, Islet
Yunhe *Chinese*, Canal
Yuzhn-o, -yy *Russian*, Southern

Z

-zaki *Japanese*, Cape, point
Zaliv *Bulgarian, Russian*, Bay
-zan *Japanese*, Mountain
Zangbo *Tibetan*, River
Zapadn-aya, -o, -yy *Russian*, Western
Západné *Slovak*, Western
Západní *Czech*, Western
Zatoka *Polish, Ukrainian*, Bay
-zee *Dutch*, Sea
Zemlya *Russian*, Earth, land
Zizhiqu *Chinese*, Autonomous region

Index

Glossary of Abbreviations

This glossary provides a comprehensive guide to the abbreviations used in this Atlas, and in the Index.

A
abbrev. abbreviated
AD Anno Domini
Afr. Afrikaans
Alb. Albanian
Amh. Amharic
anc. ancient
approx. approximately
Ar. Arabic
Arm. Armenian
ASEAN Association of South East Asian Nations
ASSR Autonomous Soviet Socialist Republic
Aust. Australian
Az. Azerbaijani
Azerb. Azerbaijan

B
Basq. Basque
BC before Christ
Bel. Belorussian
Ben. Bengali
Ber. Berber
B-H Bosnia-Herzegovina
bn billion (one thousand million)
BP British Petroleum
Bret. Breton
Brit. British
Bul. Bulgarian
Bur. Burmese

C
C central
C. Cape
°C degrees Centigrade
CACM Central America Common Market
Cam. Cambodian
Cant. Cantonese
CAR Central African Republic
Cast. Castilian
Cat. Catalan
CEEAC Central America Common Market
Chin. Chinese
CIS Commonwealth of Independent States
cm centimetre(s)
Cro. Croat
Cz. Czech
Czech Rep. Czech Republic

D
Dan. Danish
Div. Divehi
Dom. Rep. Dominican Republic
Dut. Dutch

E
E east
EC *see* EU
EEC *see* EU
ECOWAS Economic Community of West African States
ECU European Currency Unit
EMS European Monetary System
Eng. English
est estimated
Est. Estonian
EU European Union (previously European Community [EC], European Economic Community [EEC])

F
°F degrees Fahrenheit
Faer. Faeroese
Fij. Fijian
Fin. Finnish
Fr. French
Fris. Frisian
ft foot/feet
FYROM Former Yugoslav Republic of Macedonia

G
g gram(s)
Gael. Gaelic
Gal. Galician
GDP Gross Domestic Product (the total value of goods and services produced by a country excluding income from foreign countries)
Geor. Georgian
Ger. German
Gk Greek
GNP Gross National Product (the total value of goods and services produced by a country)

H
Heb. Hebrew
HEP hydro-electric power
Hind. Hindi
hist. historical
Hung. Hungarian

I
I. Island
Icel. Icelandic
in inch(es)
In. Inuit (Eskimo)
Ind. Indonesian
Intl International
Ir. Irish
Is Islands
It. Italian

J
Jap. Japanese

K
Kaz. Kazakh
kg kilogram(s)
Kir. Kirghiz
km kilometre(s)
km² square kilometre (singular)
Kor. Korean
Kurd. Kurdish

L
L. Lake
LAIA Latin American Integration Association
Lao. Laotian
Lapp. Lappish
Lat. Latin
Latv. Latvian
Liech. Liechtenstein
Lith. Lithuanian
Lus. Lusatian
Lux. Luxembourg

M
m million/metre(s)
Mac. Macedonian
Maced. Macedonia
Mal. Malay
Malg. Malagasy
Malt. Maltese
mi. mile(s)
Mong. Mongolian
Mt. Mountain
Mts Mountains

N
N north
NAFTA North American Free Trade Agreement
Nep. Nepali
Neth. Netherlands
Nic. Nicaraguan
Nor. Norwegian
NZ New Zealand

P
Pash. Pashtu
PNG Papua New Guinea
Pol. Polish
Poly. Polynesian
Port. Portuguese
prev. previously

R
Rep. Republic
Res. Reservoir
Rmsch Romansch
Rom. Romanian
Rus. Russian
Russ. Fed. Russian Federation

S
S south
SADC Southern Africa Development Community
SCr. Serbian, Croatian
Sinh. Sinhala
Slvk Slovak
Slvn. Slovene
Som. Somali
Sp. Spanish
St., St Saint
Strs Straits
Swa. Swahili
Swe. Swedish
Switz. Switzerland

T
Taj. Tajik
Th. Thai
Thai. Thailand
Tib. Tibetan
Turk. Turkish
Turkm. Turkmenistan

U
UAE United Arab Emirates
Uigh. Uighur
UK United Kingdom
Ukr. Ukrainian
UN United Nations
Urd. Urdu
US/USA United States of America
USSR Union of Soviet Socialist Republics
Uzb. Uzbek

V
var. variant
Vdkhr. Vodokhranilishche (Russian for reservoir)
Vdskh. Vodoskhovyshche (Ukrainian for reservoir)
Vtn. Vietnamese

W
W west
Wel. Welsh

This index lists all the placenames and features shown on the regional and continental maps in this Atlas. Placenames are referenced to the largest scale map on which they appear. The policy followed throughout the Atlas is to use the local spelling or local name at regional level; commonly-used English language names may occasionally be added (in parentheses) where this is an aid to identification e.g. Firenze (Florence). English names, where they exist, have been used for all international features e.g. oceans and country names; they are also used on the continental maps and in the introductory World Today section; these are then fully cross-referenced to the local names found on the regional maps. The index also contains commonly-found alternative names and variant spellings, which are also fully cross-referenced.

All main entry names are those of settlements unless otherwise indicated by the use of italicized definitions or representative symbols, which are keyed at the foot of each page.

1

10 M16 **100 Mile House** *var.* Hundred Mile House. British Columbia, SW Canada *51°39′N 121°19′W*
25 de Mayo *see* Veinticinco de Mayo
26 Bakı Komissarı *see* Häsänabad
26 Baku Komissarlary Adyndaky *see* Uzboý

A

Aa *see* Gauja
95 G24 **Aabenraa** *var.* Åbenrå, *Ger.* Apenrade. Syddanmark, SW Denmark *55°03′N 09°26′E*
95 G20 **Aabybro** *var.* Åbybro. Nordjylland, N Denmark *57°09′N 09°32′E*
101 C16 **Aachen** *Dut.* Aken, *Fr.* Aix-la-Chapelle; *anc.* Aquae Grani, Aquisgranum. Nordrhein-Westfalen, W Germany *50°47′N 06°06′E*
Aaiún *see* Laâyoune
95 M24 **Aakirkeby** *var.* Åkirkeby. Bornholm, E Denmark *55°04′N 14°56′E*
95 G20 **Aalborg** *var.* Ålborg, Ålborg-Nørresundby; *anc.* Alburgum. Nordjylland, N Denmark *57°03′N 09°56′E*
Aalborg Bugt *see* Ålborg Bugt
101 J21 **Aalen** Baden-Württemberg, S Germany *48°50′N 10°06′E*
95 G21 **Aalestrup** *var.* Ålestrup. Midtjylland, NW Denmark *56°42′N 09°31′E*
98 I11 **Aalsmeer** Noord-Holland, C Netherlands *52°17′N 04°43′E*
99 F18 **Aalst** Oost-Vlaanderen, C Belgium *50°57′N 04°03′E*
99 K18 **Aalst** *Fr.* Alost. Noord-Brabant, S Netherlands *51°23′N 05°29′E*
98 O12 **Aalten** Gelderland, E Netherlands *51°56′N 06°35′E*
99 D17 **Aalter** Oost-Vlaanderen, NW Belgium *51°05′N 03°28′E*
Aanaar *see* Inari
Aanaarjävri *see* Inarijärvi
93 M17 **Äänekoski** Länsi-Suomi, W Finland *62°34′N 25°45′E*
138 H7 **Aanjar** *var.* ʻAnjar. C Lebanon *33°45′N 35°56′E*
83 G21 **Aansluit** Northern Cape, N South Africa *26°41′S 22°24′E*
Aar *see* Aare
108 F7 **Aarau** Aargau, N Switzerland *47°22′N 08°00′E*
108 D8 **Aarberg** Bern, W Switzerland *47°19′N 07°54′E*
99 D16 **Aardenburg** Zeeland, SW Netherlands *51°16′N 03°27′E*
108 D8 **Aare** *var.* Aar. ≈ W Switzerland
108 F7 **Aargau** *Fr.* Argovie. ◆ *canton* N Switzerland
Aarhus *see* Århus
Aarlen *see* Arlon
95 G21 **Aars** *var.* Års. Nordjylland, N Denmark *56°49′N 09°32′E*
99 I17 **Aarschot** Vlaams Brabant, C Belgium *50°59′N 04°50′E*
Aassi, Nahr el *see* Orontes
Aat *see* Ath
160 G7 **Aba** *prev.* Ngawa. Sichuan, C China *32°51′N 101°46′E*
79 P16 **Aba** Orientale, NE Dem. Rep. Congo *03°52′N 30°14′E*
77 V17 **Aba** Abia, S Nigeria *05°06′N 07°22′E*
140 J6 **Abā al Qazāz, Biʼr** *well* NW Saudi Arabia
Abā as Suʻūd *see* Najrān
59 G14 **Abacaxis, Rio** ≈ NW Brazil
Abaco Island *see* Great Abaco/Little Abaco
Abaco Island *see* Great Abaco, N Bahamas
142 K10 **Ābādān** Khūzestān, SW Iran *30°24′N 48°18′E*
146 F13 **Abadan** *prev.* Bezmein, Büzmeýin, *Rus.* Byuzmeyin. Ahal Welaýaty, C Turkmenistan *38°08′N 57°53′E*
143 O10 **Ābādeh** Fārs, C Iran *31°06′N 52°40′E*
74 H8 **Abadla** W Algeria *31°04′N 02°39′W*
59 M20 **Abaeté** Minas Gerais, SE Brazil *19°10′S 45°24′W*
62 P7 **Abaí** Caazapá, S Paraguay *25°58′S 55°54′W*
Abai *see* Blue Nile
191 O2 **Abaiang** *var.* Apia; *prev.* Charlotte Island. *atoll* Tungaru, W Kiribati
Abaj *see* Abay
77 U15 **Abaji** Federal Capital District, C Nigeria *08°35′N 06°54′E*
37 O7 **Abajo Peak** ▲ Utah, W USA *37°51′N 109°28′W*
77 V16 **Abakaliki** Ebonyi, SE Nigeria *06°18′N 08°07′E*
122 K13 **Abakan** Respublika Khakasiya, S Russian Federation *53°43′N 91°25′E*
77 S11 **Abala** Tillabéri, SW Niger *14°55′N 03°27′E*
77 U11 **Abalak** Tahoua, C Niger *15°28′N 06°18′E*
119 N14 **Abalyanka** *Rus.* Obolyanka. ≈ N Belarus
122 L12 **Aban** Krasnoyarskiy Kray, S Russian Federation *56°41′N 96°04′E*
143 P9 **Āb Anbār-e Kān Sorkh** Yazd, C Iran *31°22′N 53°38′E*
57 G16 **Abancay** Apurímac, SE Peru *13°37′S 72°52′W*
190 H2 **Abaokoro** *atoll* Tungaru, W Kiribati
Abariringa *see* Kanton
143 P10 **Abarkūh** Yazd, C Iran *31°07′N 53°17′E*
165 V3 **Abashiri** *var.* Abasiri. Hokkaidō, NE Japan *44°N 144°15′E*
165 U3 **Abashiri-ko** ◎ Hokkaidō, NE Japan
Abasiri *see* Abashiri
41 P10 **Abasolo** Tamaulipas, C Mexico *24°02′N 98°18′W*
186 F9 **Abau** Central, S Papua New Guinea *10°04′S 148°34′E*
145 R10 **Abay** *var.* Abaj. Karaganda, C Kazakhstan *49°38′N 72°50′E*
81 I15 **Ābaya Hāykʼ** *Eng.* Lake Margherita, *It.* Abbaia. ◎ SW Ethiopia
Ābay Wenz *see* Blue Nile
122 K13 **Abaza** Respublika Khakasiya, S Russian Federation *52°40′N 89°58′E*
Abbaia *see* Ābaya Hāykʼ
143 Q13 **Āb Bārīk** Fārs, S Iran
107 C18 **Abbasanta** Sardegna, Italy, C Mediterranean Sea *40°08′N 08°49′E*
Abbatis Villa *see* Abbeville
30 M3 **Abbaye, Point** *headland* Michigan, N USA *46°58′N 88°08′W*
Abbazia *see* Opatija
Abbé, Lake *see* Abhe, Lake
103 N2 **Abbeville** *anc.* Abbatis Villa. Somme, N France *50°06′N 01°50′E*
23 R7 **Abbeville** Alabama, S USA *31°35′N 85°16′W*
23 U6 **Abbeville** Georgia, SE USA *31°58′N 83°18′W*
22 I9 **Abbeville** Louisiana, S USA *29°58′N 92°08′W*
21 P12 **Abbeville** South Carolina, SE USA *34°10′N 82°23′W*
97 B20 **Abbeyfeale** *Ir.* Mainistir na Féile. SW Ireland *52°24′N 09°21′W*
106 D8 **Abbiategrasso** Lombardia, NW Italy *45°24′N 08°55′E*
93 I14 **Abborrträsk** Norrbotten, N Sweden *65°24′N 19°33′E*
194 J9 **Abbot Ice Shelf** *ice shelf* Antarctica
10 M17 **Abbotsford** British Columbia, SW Canada *49°02′N 122°18′W*
30 K6 **Abbotsford** Wisconsin, N USA *44°57′N 90°19′W*
149 U5 **Abbottābād** Khyber Pakhtunkhwa, NW Pakistan *34°12′N 73°15′E*
119 M14 **Abchuha** *Rus.* Obchuga. Minskaya Voblastsʼ, NW Belarus *54°30′N 29°22′E*
98 I10 **Abcoude** Utrecht, C Netherlands *52°17′N 04°59′E*
139 N2 **ʻAbd al ʻAzīz, Jabal** ⛰ NE Syria
141 U17 **ʻAbd al Kūrī** *island* SE Yemen
127 U6 **Abdulino** Orenburgskaya Oblastʼ, W Russian Federation *53°37′N 53°39′E*
78 J10 **Abéché** *var.* Abécher, Abeshr. Ouaddaï, SE Chad *13°49′N 20°49′E*
Abécher *see* Abéché
143 S8 **Āb-e Garm va Sard** Yazd, E Iran
77 R8 **Abeïbara** Kidal, NE Mali *19°07′N 01°52′E*
105 P5 **Abejar** Castilla y León, N Spain *41°48′N 02°47′W*
54 E9 **Abejorral** Antioquia, W Colombia *05°48′N 75°28′W*
Abela *see* Ávila
Abellinum *see* Avellino
92 Q2 **Abeløya** *island* Kong Karls Land, E Svalbard
80 I13 **Ābeltī** Oromīya, C Ethiopia *08°09′N 37°31′E*
191 O2 **Abemama** *var.* Apamama; *prev.* Roger Simpson Island. *atoll* Tungaru, W Kiribati
171 Y15 **Abemaree** *var.* Abermarre. Papua, E Indonesia *07°03′S 140°10′E*
77 O16 **Abengourou** E Ivory Coast *06°42′N 03°27′W*
Åbenrå *see* Aabenraa
101 L22 **Abens** ≈ SE Germany
77 S16 **Abeokuta** Ogun, SW Nigeria *07°07′N 03°21′E*
97 I20 **Aberaeron** SW Wales, United Kingdom *52°15′N 04°15′W*
Aberbrothock *see* Arbroath
Abercorn *see* Mbala
29 R6 **Abercrombie** North Dakota, N USA *46°25′N 96°42′W*
183 T7 **Aberdeen** New South Wales, SE Australia *32°09′S 150°55′E*
11 T15 **Aberdeen** Saskatchewan, S Canada *52°15′N 106°19′W*
83 H25 **Aberdeen** Eastern Cape, S South Africa *32°30′S 24°00′E*
96 L9 **Aberdeen** *anc.* Devana. NE Scotland, United Kingdom *57°10′N 02°04′W*
21 X2 **Aberdeen** Maryland, NE USA *39°28′N 76°09′W*
23 N3 **Aberdeen** Mississippi, S USA *33°49′N 88°32′W*
21 T10 **Aberdeen** North Carolina, SE USA *35°07′N 79°25′W*
29 P8 **Aberdeen** South Dakota, N USA *45°27′N 98°29′W*
32 F8 **Aberdeen** Washington, NW USA *46°57′N 123°48′W*
96 K9 **Aberdeen** *cultural region* NE Scotland, United Kingdom
8 L8 **Aberdeen Lake** ◎ Nunavut, NE Canada
96 J10 **Aberfeldy** C Scotland, United Kingdom *56°38′N 03°49′W*
97 K21 **Abergavenny** *anc.* Gobannium. SE Wales, United Kingdom *51°50′N 03°W*
Abergwaun *see* Fishguard
Abermarre *see* Abemaree
25 N5 **Abernathy** Texas, SW USA *33°49′N 101°50′W*
Abersee *see* Wolfgangsee
Abertawe *see* Swansea
Aberteifi *see* Cardigan
32 I15 **Abert, Lake** ◎ Oregon, NW USA
97 I20 **Aberystwyth** W Wales, United Kingdom *52°25′N 04°05′W*
Abeshr *see* Abéché
Ábeskovvu *see* Abisko
106 F10 **Abetone** Toscana, C Italy *44°09′N 10°42′E*
125 V5 **Abezʼ** Respublika Komi, NW Russian Federation *66°32′N 61°41′E*
142 M5 **Āb Garm** Qazvin, N Iran
141 N12 **Abhā** ʻAsīr, SW Saudi Arabia *18°16′N 42°32′E*
142 M5 **Abhar** Zanjān, NW Iran *36°05′N 49°18′E*
Abhé Bad/Ābhē Bid Hāykʼ *see* Abhe, Lake
80 K12 **Abhe, Lake** *var.* Lake Abbé, *Amh.* Ābhē Bid Hāykʼ, *Som.* Abhé Bad. ◎ Djibouti/Ethiopia
77 V17 **Abia** ◆ *state* SE Nigeria
139 V9 **ʻAbīd ʻAlī** Wāsiţ, E Iraq *32°20′N 45°58′E*
119 O17 **Abidavichy** *Rus.* Obidovichi. Mahilyowskaya Voblastsʼ, E Belarus *53°20′N 30°25′E*
115 L15 **Abide** Çanakkale, NW Turkey *40°04′N 26°13′E*
77 N17 **Abidjan** S Ivory Coast *05°19′N 04°01′W*
Āb-i-Istāda *see* Īstādeh-ye Moqor, Āb-e-
27 N4 **Abilene** Kansas, C USA *38°55′N 97°14′W*
25 Q7 **Abilene** Texas, SW USA *32°27′N 99°44′W*
Abindonia *see* Abingdon
97 M21 **Abingdon** *anc.* Abindonia. S England, United Kingdom *51°41′N 01°17′W*
30 K12 **Abingdon** Illinois, N USA *40°48′N 90°24′W*
21 P8 **Abingdon** Virginia, NE USA *36°42′N 81°59′W*
Abingdon *see* Pinta, Isla
18 J15 **Abington** Pennsylvania, NE USA *40°06′N 75°05′W*
126 K14 **Abinsk** Krasnodarskiy Kray, SW Russian Federation *44°51′N 38°12′E*
37 R9 **Abiquiu Reservoir** ⊞ New Mexico, SW USA
Āb-i-safed *see* Sefīd, Darya-ye
92 I10 **Abisko** *Lapp.* Ábeskovvu. Norrbotten, N Sweden *68°21′N 18°50′E*
12 G12 **Abitibi** ≈ Ontario, S Canada
12 H12 **Abitibi, Lac** ◎ Ontario/Québec, S Canada
80 J10 **Ābīy Ādī** Tigray, N Ethiopia *13°40′N 38°57′E*
118 H6 **Abja-Paluoja** Viljandimaa, S Estonia *58°08′N 25°20′E*
Abkhazia *see* Apkhazeti
182 F1 **Abminga** South Australia *26°07′S 134°49′E*
75 W9 **Abnūb** *var.* Abnûb. C Egypt *27°18′N 31°09′E*
Abnûb *see* Abnūb
Åbo *see* Turku
152 G9 **Abohar** Punjab, N India *30°11′N 74°14′E*
77 O17 **Aboisso** SE Ivory Coast *05°26′N 03°13′W*
78 H5 **Abo, Massif dʼ** ⛰ NW Chad
77 R16 **Abomey** S Benin *07°14′N 02°00′E*
79 F16 **Abong Mbang** Est, SE Cameroon *03°58′N 13°10′E*
111 L23 **Abony** Pest, C Hungary *47°10′N 20°00′E*
78 J11 **Abou-Déïa** Salamat, SE Chad *11°30′N 19°18′E*
Aboudouhour *see* Abū aḑ Ḑuhūr
Abou Kémal *see* Abū Kamāl
Abou Simbel *see* Abū Sunbul
137 T12 **Abovyan** C Armenia *40°16′N 44°33′E*
141 P15 **Abrād, Wādī** *seasonal river* W Yemen
Abraham Bay *see* The Carlton
104 G10 **Abrantes** *var.* Abrántes. Santarém, C Portugal *39°28′N 08°12′W*
62 J4 **Abra Pampa** Jujuy, N Argentina *22°47′S 65°41′W*
Abrashlare *see* Brezovo
54 G7 **Abrego** Norte de Santander, N Colombia *08°08′N 73°14′W*
Abrene *see* Pytalovo
40 C7 **Abreojos, Punta** *headland* NW Mexico *26°43′N 113°36′W*
65 J16 **Abrolhos Bank** *undersea feature* W Atlantic Ocean *18°30′S 38°45′W*
119 H19 **Abrova** *Rus.* Obrovo. Brestskaya Voblastsʼ, SW Belarus *52°30′N 25°34′E*
116 G11 **Abrud** *Ger.* Gross-Schlatten, *Hung.* Abrudbánya. Alba, SW Romania *46°16′N 23°05′E*
Abrudbánya *see* Abrud
118 E6 **Abruka** *island* SW Estonia
107 J15 **Abruzzese, Appennino** ⛰ C Italy
107 J14 **Abruzzo** ◆ *region* C Italy
141 N14 **ʻAbs** *var.* Sūq ʻAbs. W Yemen *16°42′N 42°55′E*
33 T12 **Absaroka Range** ⛰ Montana/Wyoming, NW USA
137 Z11 **Abşeron Yarımadası** *Rus.* Apsheronskiy Poluostrov. *peninsula* E Azerbaijan
143 N6 **Āb Shīrīn** Eşfahān, C Iran *34°17′N 51°17′E*
139 X10 **Abtān** Maysān, SE Iraq *31°37′N 47°06′E*
109 R6 **Abtenau** Salzburg, NW Austria *47°33′N 13°21′E*
152 E14 **Ābu** Rājasthān, N India *24°41′N 72°50′E*
164 E12 **Abu** Yamaguchi, Honshū, SW Japan *34°30′N 131°26′E*
138 I4 **Abū aḑ Ḑuhūr** *Fr.* Aboudouhour. Idlib, NW Syria *35°30′N 37°00′E*
143 P17 **Abū al Abyaḑ** *island* C United Arab Emirates
138 K10 **Abū al Ḩuşayn, Khabrat** ◎ N Jordan
139 R8 **Abū al Jīr** Al Anbār, C Iraq *33°16′N 42°55′E*
139 Y12 **Abū al Khaşīb** *var.* Abul Khasib. Al Başrah, SE Iraq *30°26′N 48°00′E*
139 U12 **Abū at Tubrah, Thaqb** *well* S Iraq
Abu Balâs *see* Abu Ballâs
75 V11 **Abu Ballās** *var.* Abu Balâs. ▲ SW Egypt *24°28′N 27°36′E*
Abu Dhabi *see* Abū Z̧abī
139 R8 **Abū Farūkh** Al Anbār, C Iraq *33°06′N 43°18′E*
80 C12 **Abu Gabra** Southern Darfur, W Sudan *11°02′N 26°50′E*
139 P10 **Abū Ghār, Shaʻīb** *dry watercourse* S Iraq
80 G7 **Abu Hamed** River Nile, N Sudan *19°32′N 33°20′E*
139 O5 **Abū Ḩardān** *var.* Hajîne. Dayr az Zawr, E Syria *34°45′N 40°49′E*
139 T7 **Abū Ḩasāwīyah** Diyālá, E Iraq *33°52′N 44°47′E*
138 K10 **Abū Ḩifnah, Wādī** *dry watercourse* N Jordan
77 V15 **Abuja** ● (Nigeria) Federal Capital District, C Nigeria *09°04′N 07°28′E*
139 R9 **Abū Jahaf, Wādī** *dry watercourse* C Iraq
56 F12 **Abujao, Río** ≈ E Peru
139 U12 **Abū Jasrah** Al Muthanná, S Iraq *30°43′N 44°50′E*
139 O6 **Abū Kamāl** *Fr.* Abou Kémal. Dayr az Zawr, E Syria *34°29′N 40°56′E*
165 P12 **Abukuma-sanchi** ⛰ Honshū, C Japan
Abula *see* Ávila
Abul Khasib *see* Abū al Khaşīb
79 K16 **Abumombazi** *var.* Abumonbazi. Equateur, N Dem. Rep. Congo *03°43′N 22°06′E*
Abumonbazi *see* Abumombazi
59 D15 **Abunā** Rondônia, W Brazil *09°41′S 65°20′W*
56 K13 **Abunã, Rio** *var.* Río Abuná. ≈ Bolivia/Brazil
138 G10 **Abū Nuşayr** *var.* Abu Nuseir. ʻAmmān, W Jordan *32°03′N 35°58′E*
Abu Nuseir *see* Abū Nuşayr
139 T12 **Abū Qabr** Al Muthanná, S Iraq *31°03′N 44°34′E*
138 K5 **Abū Raḩbah, Jabal** ⛰ C Syria
139 S5 **Abū Rajāsh** Şalāḩ ad Dīn, N Iraq *34°47′N 43°36′E*
139 W13 **Abū Raqrāq, Ghadīr** *well* S Iraq
152 E14 **Ābu Road** Rājasthān, N India *24°29′N 72°47′E*
80 I6 **Abu Shagara, Ras** *headland* NE Sudan *18°04′N 38°31′E*
Abu Simbel *see* Abū Sunbul
139 U12 **Abū Sudayrah** Al Muthanná, S Iraq *30°55′N 44°58′E*
139 T10 **Abū Şukhayr** Al Qādisīyah, S Iraq *31°54′N 44°27′E*
Abū Sunbul *see* Abū Sunbul
185 E18 **Abut Head** *headland* South Island, New Zealand *43°06′S 170°16′E*
80 E9 **Abu ʻUrug** Northern Kordofan, C Sudan *15°52′N 30°25′E*
80 K12 **Ābuyē Mēda** ▲ C Ethiopia *10°28′N 39°44′E*

◆ Country
● Country Capital
◇ Dependent Territory
○ Dependent Territory Capital
◆ Administrative Regions
✈ International Airport
▲ Mountain
⛰ Mountain Range
Volcano
≈ River
◎ Lake
⊞ Reservoir

80 D11 **Abu Zabad** Southern Kordofan, C Sudan 12°21′N 29°16′E
143 P16 **Abū Ẓabī** *var.* Abū Ẓabi, *Eng.* Abu Dhabi. ● (United Arab Emirates) Abū Ẓaby, C United Arab Emirates 24°30′N 54°20′E
Abū Ẓabī *see* Abū Ẓabī
75 X8 **Abu Zenīma** E Egypt 29°01′N 33°08′E
95 N17 **Åby** Östergötland, S Sweden 58°40′N 16°10′E
Abyad, Al Baḥr al *see* White Nile
Åbybro *see* Aabybro
80 D13 **Abyei** Southern Kordofan, S Sudan 09°35′N 28°28′E
80 D13 **Abyei Area** *disputed region* Southern Kordofan, S Sudan
Abyla *see* Ávila
Abymes *see* les Abymes
Abyssinia *see* Ethiopia
Açâba *see* Assaba
54 F11 **Acacías** Meta, C Colombia 03°59′N 73°46′W
58 L13 **Açailândia** Maranhão, E Brazil 04°51′S 47°26′W
Acaill *see* Achill Island
42 E8 **Acajutla** Sonsonate, W El Salvador 13°34′N 89°50′W
79 D17 **Acalayong** SW Equatorial Guinea 01°05′N 09°34′E
41 N13 **Acámbaro** Guanajuato, C Mexico 20°01′N 100°42′W
54 C6 **Acandí** Chocó, NW Colombia 08°32′N 77°20′W
104 H4 **A Cañiza** *var.* La Cañiza. Galicia, NW Spain 42°13′N 08°16′W
40 J11 **Acaponeta** Nayarit, C Mexico 22°30′N 105°21′W
40 J11 **Acaponeta, Río de** ≈ C Mexico
41 O16 **Acapulco** *var.* Acapulco de Juárez. Guerrero, S Mexico 16°51′N 99°53′W
Acapulco de Juárez *see* Acapulco
55 T13 **Acarai Mountains** *Sp.* Serra Acaraí. ▲▲ Brazil/Guyana
Acaraí, Serra *see* Acarai Mountains
58 O13 **Acaraú** Ceará, NE Brazil 04°35′S 37°37′W
54 J6 **Acarigua** Portuguesa, N Venezuela 09°35′N 69°12′W
104 H2 **A Carreira** Galicia, NW Spain 43°21′N 08°12′W
42 C6 **Acatenango, Volcán de** △ S Guatemala 14°30′N 90°52′W
41 Q15 **Acatlán** *var.* Acatlán de Osorio. Puebla, S Mexico 18°12′N 98°02′W
Acatlán de Osorio *see* Acatlán
41 S15 **Acayucan** *var.* Acayucán. Veracruz-Llave, E Mexico 17°59′N 94°58′W
Accho *see* Akko
21 Y5 **Accomac** Virginia, NE USA 37°43′N 75°41′N
77 Q17 **Accra** ● (Ghana)SE Ghana 05°33′N 00°15′W
97 L17 **Accrington** NW England, United Kingdom 53°46′N 02°21′W
61 B19 **Acebal** Santa Fe, C Argentina 33°14′S 60°50′W
168 H8 **Aceh** *off.* Daerah Istimewa Aceh, *var.* Acheen, Achin, Atchin, Atjeh. ◈ *autonomous district* NW Indonesia
107 M18 **Acerenza** Basilicata, S Italy 40°46′N 15°51′E
107 K17 **Acerra** *anc.* Acerrae. Campania, S Italy 40°56′N 14°22′E
Acerrae *see* Acerra
57 J17 **Achacachi** La Paz, W Bolivia 16°01′S 68°44′W
54 K7 **Achaguas** Apure, C Venezuela 07°46′N 68°14′W
154 H12 **Achalpur** *prev.* Elichpur, Ellichpur. Mahārāshtra, C India 21°19′N 77°30′E
61 F18 **Achar** Tacuarembó, C Uruguay 32°20′S 56°15′W
137 R10 **Ach'ara** *prev.* Achara, *var.* Ajaria. ◈ *autonomous republic* SW Georgia
Achara *see* Ach'ara
115 H19 **Acharnés** *var.* Aharnes; *prev.* Akharnaí. Attikí, C Greece 38°09′N 23°58′E
Ach'asar Lerr *see* Achk'asari, Mta
Acheen *see* Aceh
99 K16 **Achel** Limburg, NE Belgium 51°15′N 05°31′E
115 D16 **Achelóos** *var.* Akhelóos, Aspropótamos; *anc.* Achelous. ≈ W Greece
Achelous *see* Achelóos
163 W8 **Acheng** Heilongjiang, NE China 45°32′N 126°56′E
109 N6 **Achenkirch** Tirol, W Austria 47°31′N 11°42′E
101 L24 **Achenpass** *pass* Austria/Germany
109 N7 **Achensee** ◎ W Austria
101 F22 **Achern** Baden-Württemberg, SW Germany 48°37′N 08°04′E
115 C16 **Acherón** ≈ W Greece
77 W11 **Achétinamou** ≈ S Niger
152 J12 **Achhnera** Uttar Pradesh, N India 27°10′N 77°45′E
42 C7 **Achiguate, Río** ≈ S Guatemala
97 A16 **Achill Head** *Ir.* Ceann Acla. *headland* W Ireland 53°58′N 10°14′W
97 A16 **Achill Island** *Ir.* Acaill. *island* W Ireland
100 H11 **Achim** Niedersachsen, NW Germany 53°01′N 09°01′E
149 S5 **Achīn** Nangarhār, E Afghanistan 34°04′N 70°41′E
Achin *see* Aceh
122 K12 **Achinsk** Krasnoyarskiy Kray, S Russian Federation 56°21′N 90°25′E
162 E5 **Achit Nuur** ◎ NW Mongolia
137 T11 **Achk'asari, Mta** *Arm.* Ach'asar Lerr. ▲ Armenia/Georgia 41°09′N 43°55′E
126 K13 **Achuyevo** Krasnodarskiy Kray, SW Russian Federation 46°00′N 38°01′E
81 F16 **Achwa** *var.* Aswa. ≈ N Uganda
136 E15 **Acıgöl** *salt lake* SW Turkey
107 L24 **Acireale** Sicilia, Italy, C Mediterranean Sea 37°36′N 15°10′E
Aciris *see* Agri
25 N7 **Ackerly** Texas, SW USA 32°31′N 101°43′W
22 M4 **Ackerman** Mississippi, S USA 33°18′N 89°10′W
29 W13 **Ackley** Iowa, C USA 42°33′N 93°03′W
44 J5 **Acklins Island** *island* SE Bahamas
Acla, Ceann *see* Achill Head
62 H11 **Aconcagua, Cerro** ▲ W Argentina 32°36′S 69°53′W
Açores/Açores, Arquipélago dos/Açores, Ilhas dos *see* Azores
104 H2 **A Coruña** *Cast.* La Coruña, *Eng.* Corunna; *anc.* Caronium. Galicia, NW Spain 43°22′N 08°24′W
104 G2 **A Coruña** *Cast.* La Coruña. ◈ *province* Galicia, NW Spain
42 L10 **Acoyapa** Chontales, S Nicaragua 11°58′N 85°10′W
106 H13 **Acquapendente** Lazio, C Italy 42°44′N 11°52′E
106 J13 **Acquasanta Terme** Marche, C Italy 42°46′N 13°24′E
106 I13 **Acquasparta** Lazio, C Italy 42°41′N 12°31′E
106 C9 **Acqui Terme** Piemonte, NW Italy 44°41′N 08°28′E
Acrae *see* Palazzola Acreide
182 F7 **Acraman, Lake** *salt lake* South Australia
59 A15 **Acre** *off.* Estado do Acre. ◈ *state* W Brazil
Acre *see* Akko
59 C16 **Acre, Rio** ≈ W Brazil
107 N20 **Acri** Calabria, SW Italy 39°30′N 16°22′E
Acte *see* Ágion Óros
191 Y12 **Actéon, Groupe** *island group* Îles Tuamotu, SE French Polynesia
15 P12 **Acton-Vale** Québec, SE Canada 45°39′N 72°31′W
41 P13 **Actopan** *var.* Actopán. Hidalgo, C Mexico 20°19′N 98°59′W
Açu *see* Assu
Acunum Acusio *see* Montélimar
77 Q17 **Ada** SE Ghana 05°47′N 00°42′E
112 L8 **Ada** Vojvodina, N Serbia 45°48′N 20°08′E
29 R5 **Ada** Minnesota, N USA 47°18′N 96°31′W
31 R12 **Ada** Ohio, N USA 40°46′N 83°49′W
27 O12 **Ada** Oklahoma, C USA 34°47′N 96°41′W
162 L8 **Adaatsag** *var.* Tavin. Dundgovĭ, C Mongolia 46°27′N 105°43′E
Ada Bazar *see* Adapazarı
40 D3 **Adair, Bahía de** *bay* NW Mexico
104 M7 **Adaja** ≈ N Spain
38 H17 **Adak Island** *island* Aleutian Islands, Alaska, USA
Adalia *see* Antalya
Adalia, Gulf of *see* Antalya Körfezi
141 X9 **Adam** N Oman 22°22′N 57°30′E
Adama *see* Nazrēt
60 I8 **Adamantina** São Paulo, S Brazil 21°41′S 51°04′W
79 E14 **Adamaoua** *Eng.* Adamawa. ◈ *province* N Cameroon
68 F11 **Adamaoua, Massif d'** *Eng.* Adamawa Highlands. *plateau* NW Cameroon
77 Y14 **Adamawa** ◈ *state* E Nigeria
Adamawa *see* Adamaoua
Adamawa Highlands *see* Adamaoua, Massif d'
106 F6 **Adamello** ▲ N Italy 46°09′N 10°33′E
81 J14 **Ādamī Tulu** Oromīya, C Ethiopia 07°52′N 38°39′E
63 M23 **Adam, Mount** *var.* Monte Independencia. ▲ West Falkland, Falkland Islands 51°36′S 60°00′W
29 R16 **Adams** Nebraska, C USA 40°25′N 96°30′W
18 H8 **Adams** New York, NE USA 43°48′N 75°57′W
29 Q3 **Adams** North Dakota, N USA 48°23′N 98°01′W
155 I23 **Adam's Bridge** *chain of shoals* NW Sri Lanka
32 H10 **Adams, Mount** ▲ Washington, NW USA 46°12′N 121°29′W
Adam's Peak *see* Sri Pada
191 R16 **Adam's Rock** *island* Pitcairn Island, Pitcairn Islands
191 P16 **Adamstown** ○ (Pitcairn Islands)Pitcairn Island, Pitcairn Islands 25°04′S 130°05′W
20 G10 **Adamsville** Tennessee, S USA 35°14′N 88°23′W
25 S9 **Adamsville** Texas, SW USA 31°15′N 98°09′W
141 O17 **'Adan** *Eng.* Aden. SW Yemen 12°51′N 45°05′E
136 K16 **Adana** *var.* Seyhan. Adana, S Turkey 37°N 35°19′E
136 K16 **Adana** *var.* Seyhan. ◈ *province* S Turkey
Adâncata *see* Horlivka
169 V12 **Adang, Teluk** *bay* Borneo, C Indonesia
136 F11 **Adapazarı** *prev.* Ada Bazar. Sakarya, NW Turkey 40°49′N 30°24′E
80 H8 **Adarama** River Nile, NE Sudan 17°04′N 34°57′E
195 Q16 **Adare, Cape** *cape* Antarctica
Adâvâni *see* Ādoni
106 E6 **Adda** *anc.* Addua. ≈ N Italy
80 A13 **Adda** ≈ W South Sudan
143 Q17 **Ad Ḍab'īyah** Abū Ẓaby, C United Arab Emirates 24°17′N 54°08′E
143 O18 **Ad Ḍafrah** *desert* S United Arab Emirates
141 Q6 **Ad Dahnā'** *desert* E Saudi Arabia
74 A11 **Ad Dakhla** *var.* Dakhla. SW Western Sahara 23°46′N 15°56′W
Ad Dalanj *see* Dilling
Ad Damar *see* Ed Damer
Ad Damazīn *see* Ed Damazin
173 N2 **Ad Dāmir** *see* Ed Damer
Ad Dammām *desert* NE Saudi Arabia
141 R6 **Ad Dammān** *var.* Dammām. Ash Sharqīyah, NE Saudi Arabia 26°23′N 50°05′E
Ad Dāmūr *see* Damoûr
140 K5 **Ad Dār al Ḥamrā'** Tabūk, NW Saudi Arabia 27°22′N 37°46′E
140 M13 **Ad Darb** Jīzān, SW Saudi Arabia 17°45′N 42°15′E
141 O8 **Ad Dawādimī** Ar Riyāḍ, C Saudi Arabia 24°32′N 44°21′E
143 N16 **Ad Dawḥah** *Eng.* Doha. ● (Qatar) C Qatar 25°15′N 51°36′E
143 N16 **Ad Dawḥah** *Eng.* Doha. ✈ C Qatar 25°11′N 51°37′E
139 S6 **Ad Dawr** Ṣalāḥ ad Dīn, N Iraq 34°30′N 43°49′E
139 Y12 **Ad Dayr** *var.* Dayr, Shahbān. Al Baṣrah, E Iraq 30°45′N 47°36′E
Addi Arkay *see* Ādī Ārk'ay
139 X15 **Ad Dibdibah** *physical region* Iraq/Kuwait
Ad Diffah *see* Libyan Plateau
Addis Ababa *see* Ādīs Ābeba
Addison *see* Webster Springs
139 U10 **Ad Dīwānīyah** *var.* Diwaniyah. C Iraq 32°00′N 44°57′E
Addoo Atoll *see* Addu Atoll
Addua *see* Adda
151 K22 **Addu Atoll** *var.* Addoo Atoll, Seenu Atoll. *atoll* S Maldives
Ad Dujail *see* Ad Dujayl
139 T7 **Ad Dujayl** *var.* Ad Dujail. Ṣalāḥ ad Dīn, N Iraq 33°49′N 44°16′E
Ad Duwēm *see* Ed Dueim
99 D16 **Adegem** Oost-Vlaanderen, NW Belgium 51°12′N 03°31′E
23 U7 **Adel** Georgia, SE USA 31°08′N 83°25′W
29 U14 **Adel** Iowa, C USA 41°36′N 94°01′W
182 I9 **Adelaide** *state capital* South Australia 34°56′S 138°36′E
44 H2 **Adelaide** New Providence, N Bahamas 24°59′N 77°30′W
182 I9 **Adelaide** ✈ South Australia 34°55′S 138°31′E
194 H6 **Adelaide Island** *island* Antarctica
181 P2 **Adelaide River** Northern Territory, N Australia 13°12′S 131°06′E
76 M10 **'Adel Bagrou** Hodh ech Chargui, SE Mauritania 15°33′N 07°04′W
186 D6 **Adelbert Range** ▲▲ N Papua New Guinea
180 K3 **Adele Island** *island* Western Australia
107 O17 **Adelfia** Puglia, SE Italy 41°01′N 16°52′E
195 V16 **Adélie Coast** *physical region* Antarctica
195 V14 **Adélie, Terre** *physical region* Antarctica
Adelnau *see* Odolanów
Adelsberg *see* Postojna
Aden *see* Khormaksar
Aden *see* 'Adan
141 Q17 **Aden, Gulf of** *gulf* SW Arabian Sea
77 V10 **Aderbissinat** Agadez, C Niger 15°30′N 07°57′E
Adhaim *see* Al 'Uẓaym
143 R16 **Adh Dhayd** *var.* Al Dhaid. Ash Shāriqah, NE United Arab Emirates 25°19′N 55°51′E
140 M4 **'Adhfā'** *spring/well* NW Saudi Arabia 29°15′N 41°24′E
138 I13 **'Ādhriyāt, Jabāl al** ▲▲ S Jordan
80 I10 **Ādī Ārk'ay** *var.* Addi Arkay. Āmara, N Ethiopia 13°18′N 37°56′E
182 C7 **Adieu, Cape** *headland* South Australia 32°01′S 132°12′E
106 H8 **Adige** *Ger.* Etsch. ≈ N Italy
80 J10 **Ādīgrat** Tigray, N Ethiopia 14°17′N 39°27′E
154 I13 **Ādilābād** *var.* Ādilābād. Andhra Pradesh, C India 19°40′N 78°31′E
35 P2 **Adin** California, W USA 41°10′N 120°57′W
171 V14 **Adi, Pulau** *island* E Indonesia
18 K8 **Adirondack Mountains** ▲▲ New York, NE USA
80 J13 **Ādīs Ābeba** *Eng.* Addis Ababa. ● (Ethiopia) Ādīs Ābeba, C Ethiopia 8°59′N 38°43′E
80 J13 **Ādīs Ābeba** ✈ Ādīs Ābeba, C Ethiopia 08°58′N 38°53′E
80 I11 **Ādīs Zemen** Āmara, N Ethiopia 12°00′N 37°43′E
Adi Ugri *see* Mendefera
137 N15 **Adıyaman** Adıyaman, SE Turkey 37°46′N 38°15′E
137 N15 **Adıyaman** ◈ *province* S Turkey
116 L11 **Adjud** Vrancea, E Romania 46°07′N 27°10′E
45 T6 **Adjuntas** C Puerto Rico 18°10′N 66°42′W
Adjuntas, Presa de las *see* Vicente Guerrero, Presa
Ādkup *see* Erikub Atoll
126 L15 **Adler** Krasnodarskiy Kray, SW Russian Federation 43°25′N 39°58′E
Adler *see* Orlice
108 G7 **Adliswil** Zürich, NW Switzerland 47°19′N 08°32′E
32 G7 **Admiralty Inlet** *inlet* Washington, NW USA
39 X13 **Admiralty Island** *island* Alexander Archipelago, Alaska, USA
186 E5 **Admiralty Islands** *island group* N Papua New Guinea
136 B14 **Adnan Menderes** ✈ (İzmir) İzmir, W Turkey 38°16′N 27°09′E
37 V6 **Adobe Creek Reservoir** ▣ Colorado, C USA
77 T16 **Ado-Ekiti** Ekiti, SW Nigeria 07°42′N 05°13′E
Adola *see* Kibre Mengist
61 C23 **Adolfo González Chaues** Buenos Aires, E Argentina 38°02′S 60°05′W
155 H17 **Ādoni** *var.* Adavāni. Andhra Pradesh, C India 15°38′N 77°16′E
102 K15 **Adour** *anc.* Aturus. ≈ SW France
Adowa *see* Ādwa
105 O15 **Adra** Andalucía, S Spain 36°45′N 03°01′W
107 L24 **Adrano** Sicilia, Italy, C Mediterranean Sea 37°39′N 14°49′E
74 I9 **Adrar** C Algeria 27°56′N 00°12′W
76 K7 **Adrar** ◈ *region* C Mauritania
74 L11 **Adrar** ▲ SE Algeria
74 A12 **Adrar Souttouf** ▲▲ SW Western Sahara
Adrasman *see* Adrasmon
147 Q10 **Adrasmon** *Rus.* Adrasman. NW Tajikistan 40°38′N 69°56′E
78 K10 **Adré** Ouaddaï, E Chad 13°26′N 22°14′E
106 H9 **Adria** *anc.* Atria, Hadria, Hatria. Veneto, NE Italy 45°03′N 12°04′E
31 R10 **Adrian** Michigan, N USA 41°54′N 84°02′W
29 S11 **Adrian** Minnesota, N USA 43°38′N 95°55′W
27 R5 **Adrian** Missouri, C USA 38°24′N 94°21′W
24 M2 **Adrian** Texas, SW USA 35°16′N 102°39′W
21 S4 **Adrian** West Virginia, NE USA 38°53′N 80°14′W
Adrianople/Adrianopolis *see* Edirne
121 P7 **Adriatic Basin** *undersea feature* Adriatic Sea, N Mediterranean Sea 42°00′N 17°30′E
Adriatico, Mare *see* Adriatic Sea
106 L13 **Adriatic Sea** *Alb.* Deti Adriatik, *It.* Mare Adriatico, *SCr.* Jadransko More, *Slvn.* Jadransko Morje. *sea* N Mediterranean Sea
Adriatik, Deti *see* Adriatic Sea
Adua *see* Ādwa
Aduana del Sásabe *see* El Sásabe
79 O17 **Adusa** Orientale, NE Dem. Rep. Congo 01°25′N 28°05′E
118 J13 **Adutiškis** Vilnius, E Lithuania 55°09′N 26°34′E
27 Y7 **Advance** Missouri, C USA 37°06′N 89°54′W
65 D25 **Adventure Sound** *bay* East Falkland, Falkland Islands
80 J10 **Ādwa** *var.* Adowa, *It.* Adua. Tigray, N Ethiopia 14°08′N 38°51′E
123 Q8 **Adycha** ≈ NE Russian Federation
126 L14 **Adygeya, Respublika** ◈ *autonomous republic* SW Russian Federation
Adzhikui *see* Ajyguýy
77 N17 **Adzopé** SE Ivory Coast 06°07′N 03°49′W
125 U4 **Adz'va** ≈ NW Russian Federation
125 U5 **Adz'vavom** Respublika Komi, NW Russian Federation 66°35′N 59°13′E
Ædua *see* Autun
115 K19 **Aegean Islands** *island group* Greece/Turkey
Aegean North *see* Vóreion Aigaíon
115 I17 **Aegean Sea** *Gk.* Aigaíon Pelagos, Aigaío Pélagos, *Turk.* Ege Denizi. *sea* NE Mediterranean Sea
Aegean South *see* Nótion Aigaíon
118 H3 **Aegviidu** *Ger.* Charlottenhof. Harjumaa, NW Estonia 59°17′N 25°37′E
Aegyptus *see* Egypt
Aelana *see* Al 'Aqabah
Aelok *see* Ailuk Atoll
Aelōninae *see* Ailinginae Atoll
Aelōnlaplap *see* Ailinglaplap Atoll
Æmilia *see* Emilia-Romagna
Æmilianum *see* Millau
Aemona *see* Ljubljana
Aenaria *see* Ischia
Aeolian Islands *see* Eolie, Isole
191 Z3 **Aeon Point** *headland* Kiritimati, NE Kiribati 01°46′N 157°11′W
Æsernia *see* Isernia
104 G3 **A Estrada** Galicia, NW Spain 42°41′N 08°29′W
115 C18 **Aetós** Itháki, Iónia Nísoi, Greece, C Mediterranean Sea 38°21′N 20°40′E
191 Q8 **Afaahiti** Tahiti, W French Polynesia 17°43′S 149°18′W
139 U10 **'Afak** Al Qādisīyah, C Iraq 32°04′N 45°17′E
Afanasjevo *see* Afanas'yevo
125 T14 **Afanas'yevo** *var.* Afanasjevo. Kirovskaya Oblast', NW Russian Federation 58°55′N 53°13′E
Afándou *see* Afántou
115 O23 **Afántou** *var.* Afándou. Ródos, Dodekánisa, Greece, Aegean Sea 36°17′N 28°10′E
80 K11 **Āfar** ◈ *region* NE Ethiopia
Afar Depression *see* Danakil Desert
191 O7 **Afareaitu** Moorea, W French Polynesia 17°33′S 149°47′W
140 L7 **'Afarīyah, Bi'r al** *well* NW Saudi Arabia
Afars et des Issas, Territoire Français des *see* Djibouti
83 D22 **Affenrücken** Karas, SW Namibia 28°05′S 15°49′E
Afghānestān, Dowlat-e Eslāmī-ye *see* Afghanistan
148 M6 **Afghanistan** *off.* Islamic Republic of Afghanistan, *Per.* Dowlat-e Eslāmī-ye Afghānestān; *prev.* Republic of Afghanistan. ◆ *islamic state* C Asia
Afgoi *see* Afgooye
81 N17 **Afgooye** *It.* Afgoi. Shabeellaha Hoose, S Somalia 02°09′N 45°07′E
141 N8 **'Afif** Ar Riyāḍ, C Saudi Arabia 23°57′N 42°57′E
77 V17 **Afikpo** Ebonyi, S Nigeria 05°52′N 07°58′E
Afiun Karahissar *see* Afyon
109 V6 **Aflenz Kurort** Steiermark, E Austria 47°33′N 15°14′E
74 J6 **Aflou** N Algeria 34°09′N 02°06′E
81 L18 **Afmadow** Jubbada Hoose, S Somalia 0°24′N 42°04′E
39 Q14 **Afognak Island** *island* Alaska, USA
104 J2 **A Fonsagrada** Galicia, NW Spain 43°09′N 07°03′W
186 E9 **Afore** Northern, S Papua New Guinea 09°10′S 148°30′E
59 O15 **Afrânio** Pernambuco, E Brazil 08°32′S 40°54′W
66-67 **Africa** *continent*
68 L11 **Africa, Horn of** *physical region* Ethiopia/Somalia
172 K11 **Africana Seamount** *undersea feature* SW Indian Ocean 37°10′S 29°10′E
86 A14 **African Plate** *tectonic plate*
138 I2 **'Afrīn** Ḥalab, N Syria 36°31′N 36°51′E
136 M15 **Afşin** Kahramanmaraş, C Turkey 38°14′N 36°54′E
98 J7 **Afsluitdijk** *dam* N Netherlands
29 U15 **Afton** Iowa, C USA 41°01′N 94°12′W
29 W9 **Afton** Minnesota, N USA 44°54′N 92°46′W
27 R8 **Afton** Oklahoma, C USA 36°41′N 94°57′W
136 F14 **Afyon** *prev.* Afyonkarahisar. Afyon, W Turkey 38°46′N 30°32′E
136 F14 **Afyon** *var.* Afiun Karahissar, Afyonkarahisar. ◈ *province* W Turkey
Afyonkarahisar *see* Afyon
Agadès *see* Agadez
77 V10 **Agadez** *prev.* Agadès. Agadez, C Niger 16°57′N 07°56′E
77 W8 **Agadez** ◈ *department* N Niger
74 E8 **Agadir** SW Morocco 30°30′N 09°37′W
64 M9 **Agadir Canyon** *undersea feature* SE Atlantic Ocean 32°30′N 12°50′W
145 R12 **Agadyr'** Karaganda, C Kazakhstan 48°15′N 72°55′E
173 O7 **Agalega Islands** *island group* N Mauritius
42 K6 **Agalta, Sierra de** ▲▲ E Honduras
122 I10 **Agan** ≈ C Russian Federation
Agana/Agaña *see* Hagåtña
188 B15 **Agana Bay** *bay* NW Guam
171 Kk13 **Agano-gawa** ≈ Honshū, C Japan
188 B17 **Aga Point** *headland* S Guam
154 G9 **Agar** Madhya Pradesh, C India 23°44′N 76°01′E
81 I14 **Āgaro** Oromīya, C Ethiopia 07°52′N 36°36′E
153 V15 **Agartala** *state capital* Tripura, NE India 23°49′N 91°15′E
194 I5 **Agassiz, Cape** *headland* Antarctica 68°29′S 62°59′W
175 V13 **Agassiz Fracture Zone** *tectonic feature* S Pacific Ocean
9 N2 **Agassiz Ice Cap** *Ice feature* Nunavut, N Canada
188 B16 **Agat** W Guam 13°20′N 144°38′E
188 B16 **Agat Bay** *bay* W Guam
Agatha *see* Agde
115 M20 **Agathónisi** *island* Dodekánisa, Greece, Aegean Sea
171 X14 **Agats** Papua, E Indonesia 05°33′S 138°07′E
155 C21 **Agatti Island** *island* Lakshadweep, India, N Indian Ocean
38 D16 **Agattu Island** *island* Aleutian Islands, Alaska, USA
38 D16 **Agattu Strait** *strait* Aleutian Islands, Alaska, USA
14 B8 **Agawa** ≈ Ontario, S Canada
14 B8 **Agawa Bay** *lake bay* Ontario, S Canada
77 N17 **Agboville** SE Ivory Coast 05°55′N 04°15′W
137 V12 **Ağdam** *Rus.* Agdam. SW Azerbaijan 40°04′N 46°00′E
Agdam *see* Ağdam
103 P16 **Agde** *anc.* Agatha. Hérault, S France 43°19′N 03°29′E
103 P16 **Agde, Cap d'** *headland* S France 43°17′N 03°30′E
Agedabia *see* Ajdābiyā
102 L14 **Agen** *anc.* Aginnum. Lot-et-Garonne, SW France 44°12′N 00°37′E
Agendicum *see* Sens
165 O13 **Ageo** Saitama, Honshū, S Japan 35°58′N 139°36′E
109 R5 **Ager** ≈ N Austria
Agere Hiywet *see* Hägere Hiywet
108 G8 **Ägerisee** ◎ W Switzerland
142 M10 **Āghā Jārī** Khūzestān, SW Iran 30°48′N 49°45′E
39 P15 **Aghiyuk Island** *island* Alaska, USA
74 B12 **Aghouinit** SE Western Sahara 22°14′N 13°10′W
Aghri Dagh *see* Büyükağrı Dağı
74 B10 **Aghzoumal, Sebkhet** *var.* Sebjet Agsumal. *salt lake* E Western Sahara
115 F15 **Agiá** *var.* Ayiá. Thessalía, C Greece 39°43′N 22°45′E
40 G7 **Agiabampo, Estero de** *estuary* NW Mexico
121 P3 **Agía Fýlaxis** *var.* Ayia Phyla. S Cyprus 34°43′N 33°02′E
Agialoúsa *see* Yenierenköy
115 M21 **Agía Marína** Léros, Dodekánisa, Greece, Aegean Sea 37°09′N 26°51′E
121 Q2 **Agía Nápa** *var.* Ayia Napa. E Cyprus 34°59′N 34°00′E
115 L16 **Agía Paraskeví** Lésvos, E Greece 39°13′N 26°19′E
115 J15 **Agías Eirínis, Akrotírio** *headland* Límnos, E Greece 39°47′N 25°21′E
Agiasós *see* Agiassós
115 L17 **Agiassós** *var.* Agiasós, Ayiásos, Ayiássos. Lésvos, E Greece 39°05′N 26°23′E
Aginnum *see* Agen
123 O14 **Aginskoye** Zabaykal'skiy Kray, S Russian Federation 51°10′N 114°32′E
115 I14 **Ágion Óros** *Eng.* Mount Athos. ◈ *monastic republic* NE Greece
115 H14 **Ágion Óros** *var.* Akte, Aktí; *anc.* Acte. *peninsula* NE Greece
114 D13 **Ágios Achílleios** *religious building* Dytikí Makedonía, N Greece
115 J16 **Ágios Efstrátios** *var.* Áyios Evstrátios, Hagios Evstrátios. *island* E Greece 39°34′N 24°58′E
115 H20 **Ágios Geórgios** *island* Kykládes, Greece, Aegean Sea
Ágios Geórgios *see* Ro
115 E21 **Ágios Ilías** ▲ S Greece 36°57′N 22°19′E
115 K25 **Ágios Ioánnis, Akrotírio** *headland* Kriti, Greece, E Mediterranean Sea 35°19′N 25°46′E
115 L20 **Ágios Kírykos** *var.* Áyios Kírikos. Ikaría, Dodekánisa, Greece, Aegean Sea 37°34′N 26°15′E
115 K25 **Ágios Nikólaos** *var.* Áyios Nikólaos. Kriti, Greece, E Mediterranean Sea 35°12′N 25°43′E
115 D16 **Ágios Nikolaos** Thessalía, C Greece 39°33′N 21°21′E
115 H14 **Agíou Órous, Kólpos** *gulf* N Greece
107 K24 **Agira** *anc.* Agyrium. Sicilia, Italy, C Mediterranean Sea 37°39′N 14°32′E
115 G20 **Agkístri** *island* S Greece
114 G12 **Agkistro** *var.* Angistro. ▲ NE Greece 41°21′N 23°29′E
103 O17 **Agly** ≈ S France
Agnetheln *see* Agnita
14 E10 **Agnew Lake** ◎ Ontario, S Canada
77 O16 **Agnibilékrou** E Ivory Coast 07°10′N 03°11′W
116 I11 **Agnita** *Ger.* Agnetheln, *Hung.* Szentágota. Sibiu, SW Romania 45°59′N 24°40′E
107 K15 **Agnone** Molise, C Italy 41°49′N 14°21′E
164 K14 **Ago** Mie, Honshū, SW Japan 34°18′N 136°50′E
106 C8 **Agogna** ≈ N Italy
Agoitz *see* Aoiz
Agoiz *see* Aoiz
77 P17 **Agona Swedru** *var.* Swedru. SE Ghana 05°31′N 00°42′W
Agordat *see* Ak'ordat
Agosta *see* Augusta
103 N15 **Agout** ≈ S France
152 J12 **Āgra** Uttar Pradesh, N India 27°09′N 78°E
Agra and Oudh, United Provinces of *see* Uttar Pradesh
Agram *see* Zagreb
105 U5 **Agramunt** Cataluña, NE Spain 41°48′N 01°07′E
105 Q5 **Agreda** Castilla y León, N Spain 41°51′N 01°55′W
137 S13 **Ağrı** *var.* Karaköse; *prev.* Karakılısse. Ağrı, NE Turkey 39°44′N 43°04′E
137 S13 **Ağrı** ◈ *province* NE Turkey
107 N19 **Agri** *anc.* Aciris. ≈ S Italy
Agri Dagi *see* Büyükağrı Dağı
107 J24 **Agrigento** *Gk.* Akragas; *prev.* Girgenti. Sicilia, Italy, C Mediterranean Sea 37°19′N 13°33′E
188 K4 **Agrihan** *island* N Northern Mariana Islands
115 L17 **Agriliá, Akrotírio** *prev.* Ákra Maléas. *cape* Lésvos, E Greece
115 D18 **Agrínio** *prev.* Agrinion. Dytikí Elláda, W Greece 38°38′N 21°25′E
Agrinion *see* Agrínio
115 G17 **Agriovótano** Évvoia, C Greece 39°00′N 23°18′E
107 L18 **Agropoli** Campania, S Italy 40°22′N 14°59′E
127 T3 **Agryz** Udmurtskaya Respublika, NW Russian Federation 56°27′N 52°58′E
137 U11 **Ağstafa** *Rus.* Akstafa. NW Azerbaijan 41°06′N 45°28′E
137 X11 **Ağsu** *Rus.* Akhsu. C Azerbaijan
Agsumal, Sebjet *see* Aghzoumal, Sebkhet
40 J11 **Agua Brava, Laguna** *lagoon* W Mexico
54 F7 **Aguachica** Cesar, N Colombia 08°16′N 73°35′W
59 J20 **Agua Clara** Mato Grosso do Sul, SW Brazil 20°21′S 52°58′W
44 D5 **Aguada de Pasajeros** Cienfuegos, C Cuba 22°23′N 80°51′W
54 J5 **Aguada Grande** Lara, N Venezuela 10°38′N 69°29′W
45 S5 **Aguadilla** W Puerto Rico 18°27′N 67°08′W
43 S16 **Aguadulce** Coclé, S Panama 08°16′N 80°31′W
104 L14 **Aguadulce** Andalucía, S Spain 37°15′N 04°59′W
41 O8 **Agualeguas** Nuevo León, NE Mexico 26°17′N 99°30′W
40 L9 **Aguanaval, Río** ≈ C Mexico
42 J5 **Aguán, Río** ≈ N Honduras
25 R16 **Agua Nueva** Texas, SW USA 26°57′N 98°34′W
60 J8 **Aguapeí, Rio** ≈ S Brazil
61 E14 **Aguapey, Río** ≈ NE Argentina
40 G3 **Agua Prieta** Sonora, NW Mexico 31°16′N 109°33′W
104 G5 **A Guarda** *var.* A Guardia, Laguardia, La Guardia. Galicia, NW Spain 41°54′N 08°53′W
A Guardia *see* A Guarda
56 E6 **Aguarico, Río** ≈ Ecuador/Peru
55 O6 **Aguasay** Monagas, NE Venezuela 09°25′N 63°44′W
40 M12 **Aguascalientes** Aguascalientes, C Mexico 21°54′N 102°17′W
40 L12 **Aguascalientes** ◈ *state* C Mexico
57 I18 **Aguas Calientes, Río** ≈ S Peru
105 R7 **Aguasvivas** ≈ NE Spain
60 J7 **Água Vermelha, Represa de** ▣ S Brazil
56 E12 **Aguaytía** Ucayali, C Peru 09°02′S 75°30′W
104 I5 **A Gudiña** *var.* La Gudiña. Galicia, NW Spain 42°04′N 07°08′W
104 G7 **Águeda** Aveiro, N Portugal 40°34′N 08°28′W
104 J8 **Agueda** ≈ Portugal/Spain
77 Q8 **Aguelhok** Kidal, NE Mali 19°18′N 00°50′E
77 V12 **Aguié** Maradi, S Niger 13°28′N 07°43′E
188 K8 **Aguijan** *island* S Northern Mariana Islands
104 M14 **Aguilar** *var.* Aguilar de la Frontera. Andalucía, S Spain 37°31′N 04°40′W
104 M3 **Aguilar de Campóo** Castilla y León, N Spain 42°47′N 04°15′W
Aguilar de la Frontera *see* Aguilar
42 F7 **Aguilares** San Salvador, C El Salvador 13°56′N 89°09′W
105 Q14 **Aguilas** Murcia, SE Spain 37°24′N 01°36′W
40 L15 **Aguililla** Michoacán, SW Mexico 18°43′N 102°45′W
Agulhas *see* L'Agulhas
172 J11 **Agulhas Bank** *undersea feature* SW Indian Ocean 35°30′S 21°00′E
172 K11 **Agulhas Basin** *undersea feature* SW Indian Ocean 47°00′S 27°00′E
83 F26 **Agulhas, Cape** *Afr.* Kaap Agulhas. *headland* SW South Africa 34°51′S 19°59′E
Agulhas, Kaap *see* Agulhas, Cape
60 O9 **Agulhas Negras, Pico das** ▲ SE Brazil 22°21′S 44°39′W
172 K11 **Agulhas Plateau** *undersea feature* SW Indian Ocean 40°00′S 26°00′E
165 S16 **Aguni-jima** *island* Nansei-shotō, SW Japan
Agurain *see* Salvatierra
54 G5 **Agustín Codazzi** *var.* Codazzi. Cesar, N Colombia 10°02′N 73°15′W
Agyrium *see* Agira
74 L12 **Ahaggar** *high plateau region* SE Algeria
146 E12 **Ahal Welaýaty** *Rus.* Akhalskiy Velayat. ◈ *province* C Turkmenistan
142 K2 **Ahar** Āzarbāyjān-e Sharqī, NW Iran 38°25′N 47°07′E
Aharnes *see* Acharnés
138 J3 **Aḥaṣ, Jabal** ▲ NW Syria
138 J3 **Aḥaṣ, Jebal** ▲ W Syria
185 G16 **Ahaura** ≈ South Island, New Zealand
100 E13 **Ahaus** Nordrhein-Westfalen, NW Germany 52°04′N 07°01′E
191 U9 **Ahe** *atoll* Îles Tuamotu, C French Polynesia
184 N10 **Ahimanawa Range** ▲▲ North Island, New Zealand
119 I19 **Ahinski Kanal** *Rus.* Oginskiy Kanal. *canal* SW Belarus
186 G10 **Ahioma** SE Papua New Guinea 10°20′S 150°35′E
184 I2 **Ahipara** Northland, North Island, New Zealand 35°11′S 173°07′E
184 I2 **Ahipara Bay** *bay* SE Tasman Sea
Áhkájávrre *see* Akkajaure
Áhkká *see* Akka
39 N13 **Ahklun Mountains** ▲▲ Alaska, USA
137 R14 **Ahlat** Bitlis, E Turkey 38°45′N 42°28′E
101 F14 **Ahlen** Nordrhein-Westfalen, W Germany 51°46′N 07°53′E
154 D10 **Ahmadābād** *var.* Ahmedabad. Gujarāt, W India 23°03′N 72°40′E
143 R10 **Ahmadābād** Kermān, C Iran 35°51′N 59°36′E
Ahmadi *see* Al Aḥmadī
Ahmad Khel *see* Ḥasan Khēl
155 F14 **Ahmadnagar** *var.* Ahmednagar. Mahārāshtra, W India 19°08′N 74°48′E
149 T9 **Ahmadpur Siāl** Punjab, E Pakistan 30°40′N 71°52′E
77 N5 **Aḥmar, 'Erg el** *desert* N Mali
80 K13 **Ahmar Mountains** ▲▲ C Ethiopia
Ahmedabad *see* Ahmadābād
Ahmednagar *see* Ahmadnagar
114 N12 **Ahmetbey** Kırklareli, NW Turkey 41°26′N 27°35′E
14 H12 **Ahmic Lake** ◎ Ontario, S Canada
190 G12 **Ahoa** Île Uvea, E Wallis and Futuna 13°17′S 176°12′W
40 G8 **Ahomé** Sinaloa, C Mexico 25°55′N 109°10′W
21 X8 **Ahoskie** North Carolina, SE USA 36°17′N 76°59′W
101 D17 **Ahr** ≈ W Germany
143 N12 **Ahram** *var.* Ahrom. Būshehr, S Iran 28°52′N 51°18′E
100 J9 **Ahrensburg** Schleswig-Holstein, N Germany 53°41′N 10°14′E
Ahrom *see* Ahram
93 L17 **Ähtäri** Länsi-Suomi, W Finland 62°34′N 24°08′E
40 K12 **Ahuacatlán** Nayarit, C Mexico 21°02′N 104°30′W
42 E7 **Ahuachapán** Ahuachapán, W El Salvador 13°55′N 89°51′W
42 A9 **Ahuachapán** ◈ *department* W El Salvador
191 V16 **Ahu Akivi** *var.* Siete Moai. *ancient monument* Easter Island, Chile, E Pacific Ocean
191 W11 **Ahunui** *atoll* Îles Tuamotu, C French Polynesia
185 E20 **Ahuriri** ≈ South Island, New Zealand
95 L22 **Åhus** Skåne, S Sweden 55°55′N 14°18′E
Ahu Tahira *see* Ahu Vinapu
191 V16 **Ahu Tepeu** *ancient monument* Easter Island, Chile, E Pacific Ocean
191 V17 **Ahu Vinapu** *var.* Ahu Tahira. *ancient monument* Easter Island, Chile, E Pacific Ocean
142 L9 **Ahvāz** *var.* Ahwāz; *prev.* Nāsiri. Khūzestān, SW Iran 31°20′N 48°38′E
Ahvenanmaa *see* Åland
141 Q16 **Aḥwar** SW Yemen 13°34′N 46°41′E
Ahwāz *see* Ahvāz
94 H7 **Åi Åfjord** *var.* Åi Åfjord, Årnes. Sør-Trøndelag, C Norway 63°57′N 10°12′E
see also Åi Åfjord
Åi Åfjord *see* Åi Åfjord
149 P3 **Aibak** *var.* Haibak; *prev.* Äybak, Samangān. Samangān, NE Afghanistan 36°16′N 68°04′E
101 K22 **Aichach** Bayern, SE Germany 48°26′N 11°06′E
164 L14 **Aichi** *off.* Aichi-ken, *var.* Aiti. ◈ *prefecture* Honshū, SW Japan
Aïdin *see* Aydın
Aidussina *see* Ajdovščina
Aifir, Clochán an *see* Giant's Causeway
Aigaíon Pelagos/Aigaío Pélagos *see* Aegean Sea
109 S3 **Aigen im Mühlkreis** Oberösterreich, N Austria 48°39′N 13°57′E
115 G20 **Aígina** *var.* Aíyina, Egina. Aígina, C Greece 37°45′N 23°26′E
115 G20 **Aígina** *island* S Greece
115 E18 **Aígio** *var.* Egio; *prev.* Aíyion. Dytikí Elláda, S Greece 38°15′N 22°05′E
108 C10 **Aigle** Vaud, SW Switzerland 46°20′N 06°58′E
103 P14 **Aigoual, Mont** ▲ S France 44°09′N 03°34′E
173 O16 **Aigrettes, Pointe des** *headland* W Réunion 21°02′S 55°14′E
61 G19 **Aiguá** *var.* Aigua. Maldonado, S Uruguay 34°13′S 54°46′W
103 S13 **Aigues** ≈ SE France
103 N10 **Aigurande** Indre, C France 46°26′N 01°49′E
Ai-hun *see* Heihe
163 N10 **Aikawa** Niigata, Sado, C Japan 38°04′N 138°15′E
21 Q13 **Aiken** South Carolina, SE USA 33°34′N 81°44′W
25 N4 **Aiken** Texas, SW USA 34°06′N 101°51′W

◆ Country ● Country Capital ◇ Dependent Territory ○ Dependent Territory Capital ◈ Administrative Regions ✈ International Airport ▲ Mountain ▲▲ Mountain Range △ Volcano ≈ River ◎ Lake ▣ Reservoir

160 F13 **Ailao Shan** ▲▲ SW China
189 R4 **Ailinginae Atoll** *var.* Aelōninae. *atoll* Ralik Chain, SW Marshall Islands
189 T7 **Ailinglaplap Atoll** *var.* Aelōnlaplap. *atoll* Ralik Chain, S Marshall Islands
Aillionn, Loch *see* Allen, Lough
96 H13 **Ailsa Craig** *island* SW Scotland, United Kingdom
189 V5 **Ailuk Atoll** *var.* Aelok. *atoll* Ratak Chain, NE Marshall Islands
123 R11 **Aim** Khabarovskiy Kray, E Russian Federation 58°45′N 134°08′E
45 Q12 **Aimé Césaire** ✈ (Fort-de-France) C Martinique 14°34′N 61°00′W
103 R11 **Ain** ◐ *department* E France
103 S10 **Ain** ≈ E France
118 G7 **Ainaži** *Est.* Heinaste, *Ger.* Hainasch. N Latvia 57°51′N 24°24′E
74 L6 **Aïn Beida** NE Algeria 35°52′N 07°25′E
76 K4 **'Aïn Ben Tili** Tiris Zemmour, N Mauritania 25°58′N 09°30′W
74 J5 **Aïn Defla** *var.* Aïn Eddefla. N Algeria 36°16′N 01°58′E
Aïn Eddefla *see* Aïn Defla
74 L5 **Ain El Bey** ✈ (Constantine) NE Algeria 36°15′N 06°36′E
115 C19 **Aínos** ▲ Kefallonía, Iónia Nísoi, Greece, C Mediterranean Sea 38°08′N 20°39′E
105 T4 **Ainsa** Aragón, NE Spain 42°25′N 00°08′E
74 I7 **Aïn Sefra** NW Algeria 32°45′N 00°32′W
29 N13 **Ainsworth** Nebraska, C USA 42°33′N 99°51′W
Aintab *see* Gaziantep
74 H5 **Aïn Témouchent** N Algeria 35°18′N 01°09′W
186 C6 **Aiome** Madang, N Papua New Guinea 05°08′S 144°45′E
Aïoun el Atrous/Aïoun el Atroûss *see* 'Ayoûn el 'Atroûs
54 E11 **Aipe** Huila, C Colombia 03°15′N 75°17′W
56 D9 **Aipena, Río** ≈ N Peru
57 L19 **Aiquile** Cochabamba, C Bolivia 18°10′S 65°10′W
Aïr *see* Aïr, Massif de l'
188 E10 **Airai** Babeldaob, C Palau
188 E10 **Airai** ✈ (Oreor) Babeldaob, N Palau 07°22′N 134°34′E
168 I11 **Airbangis** Sumatera, NW Indonesia 0°12′N 99°22′E
11 Q16 **Airdrie** Alberta, SW Canada 51°20′N 114°00′W
96 I12 **Airdrie** S Scotland, United Kingdom 55°52′N 03°59′W
Air du Azbine *see* Aïr, Massif de l'
97 M17 **Aire** ≈ N England, United Kingdom
102 K15 **Aire-sur-l'Adour** Landes, SW France 43°43′N 00°16′W
103 O1 **Aire-sur-la-Lys** Pas-de-Calais, N France 50°39′N 02°24′E
9 Q6 **Air Force Island** *island* Baffin Island, Nunavut, NE Canada
169 Q13 **Airhitam, Teluk** *bay* Borneo, C Indonesia
171 Q11 **Airmadidi** Sulawesi, N Indonesia 01°25′N 124°59′E
77 V8 **Aïr, Massif de l'** *var.* Aïr, Air du Azbine, Asben. ▲▲ NC Niger
108 G10 **Airolo** Ticino, S Switzerland 46°32′N 08°38′E
102 K9 **Airvault** Deux-Sèvres, W France 46°51′N 00°07′W
101 K19 **Aisch** ≈ S Germany
63 G20 **Aisén** *off.* Región Aisén del General Carlos Ibañez del Campo, *var.* Aysen. ◐ *region* S Chile
10 H7 **Aishihik Lake** ◎ Yukon Territory, W Canada
103 P3 **Aisne** ◐ *department* N France
103 R4 **Aisne** ≈ NE France
109 T4 **Aist** ≈ N Austria
114 K13 **Aisými** Anatolikí Makedonía kai Thráki, NE Greece 41°00′N 25°55′E
105 S11 **Aitana** ▲ E Spain 38°39′N 00°15′W
186 B5 **Aitape** *var.* Eitape. Sandaun, NW Papua New Guinea 03°10′S 142°17′E
Aiti *see* Aichi
29 V6 **Aitkin** Minnesota, N USA 46°31′N 93°42′W
115 D18 **Aitolikó** *var.* Etoliko; *prev.* Aitolikón. Dytikí Elláda, C Greece 38°26′N 21°21′E
Aitolikón *see* Aitolikó
190 L15 **Aitutaki** *island* S Cook Islands
116 H11 **Aiud** *Ger.* Strassburg, *Hung.* Nagyenyed; *prev.* Engeten. Alba, SW Romania 46°19′N 23°43′E
118 I9 **Aiviekste** ≈ C Latvia
189 Q8 **Aiwo** SW Nauru 0°32′S 166°54′E
188 E8 **Aiwokako Passage** *passage* Babeldaob, N Palau
Aix *see* Aix-en-Provence
103 S15 **Aix-en-Provence** *var.* Aix; *anc.* Aquae Sextiae. Bouches-du-Rhône, SE France 43°31′N 05°27′E
Aix-la-Chapelle *see* Aachen
103 T11 **Aix-les-Bains** Savoie, E France 45°40′N 05°55′E
186 A6 **Aiyang, Mount** ▲ NW Papua New Guinea 05°03′S 141°15′E
Aíyina *see* Aígina
Aíyion *see* Aígio
153 W15 **Āīzawl** *state capital* Mizoram, NE India 23°41′N 92°45′E
118 H9 **Aizkraukle** S Latvia 56°39′N 25°07′E
118 C9 **Aizpute** W Latvia 56°43′N 21°32′E
165 O11 **Aizuwakamatsu** Fukushima, Honshū, C Japan 37°30′N 139°58′E
103 X15 **Ajaccio** Corse, France, C Mediterranean Sea 41°54′N 08°43′E
103 X15 **Ajaccio, Golfe d'** *gulf* Corse, France, C Mediterranean Sea
41 Q15 **Ajalpán** Puebla, S Mexico 18°26′N 97°20′W
154 F13 **Ajanta Range** ▲▲ C India
Ajaria *see* Ach'ara
Ajastan *see* Armenia
93 G14 **Ajaureforsen** Västerbotten, N Sweden 65°31′N 15°44′E
185 H17 **Ajax, Mount** ▲ South Island, New Zealand 42°34′S 172°06′E
162 F9 **Aj Bogd Uul** ▲ SW Mongolia 44°49′N 95°01′E
75 R8 **Ajdābiyā** *var.* Agedabia, Ajdābiyah. NE Libya 30°46′N 20°14′E
Ajdābiyah *see* Ajdābiyā
109 S12 **Ajdovščina** *Ger.* Haidenschaft, *It.* Aidussina. W Slovenia 45°52′N 13°55′E
165 Q7 **Ajigasawa** Aomori, Honshū, C Japan 40°45′N 140°11′E
Ajjinena *see* El Geneina
111 H23 **Ajka** Veszprém, W Hungary 47°18′N 17°32′E
138 G9 **'Ajlūn** Irbid, N Jordan 32°20′N 35°45′E
138 H9 **'Ajlūn, Jabal** ▲▲ W Jordan
Ájluokta *see* Drag
143 R15 **'Ajmān** *var.* Ajman, 'Ujmān. 'Ajmān, NE United Arab Emirates 25°36′N 55°42′E
152 G12 **Ajmer** *var.* Ajmere. Rājasthān, N India 26°29′N 74°40′E
36 J15 **Ajo** Arizona, SW USA 32°22′N 112°51′W
105 N2 **Ajo, Cabo de** *headland* N Spain 43°31′N 03°36′W
36 J16 **Ajo Range** ▲▲ Arizona, SW USA
146 C14 **Ajyguýy** *Rus.* Adzhikui. Balkan Welaýaty, W Turkmenistan 39°46′N 53°57′E
Akaba *see* Al 'Aqabah
165 T3 **Akabira** Hokkaidō, NE Japan 43°30′N 142°04′E
165 N10 **Akadomari** Niigata, Sado, C Japan 37°54′N 138°24′E
81 E20 **Akagera** ≈ Rwanda/Tanzania
191 W16 **Akahanga, Punta** *headland* Easter Island, Chile, E Pacific Ocean
80 J13 **Āk'ak'i** Oromīya, C Ethiopia 08°50′N 38°51′E
155 G15 **Akalkot** Mahārāshtra, W India 17°36′N 76°10′E
Akamagaseki *see* Shimonoseki
165 V3 **Akan** Hokkaidō, NE Japan 44°06′N 144°03′E
165 U4 **Akan** Hokkaidō, NE Japan 43°09′N 144°08′E
165 U4 **Akan-ko** ◎ Hokkaidō, NE Japan
Akanthoú *see* Tatlısu
185 I19 **Akaroa** Canterbury, South Island, New Zealand 43°48′S 172°58′E
80 E6 **Akasha** Northern, N Sudan 21°03′N 30°46′E
164 I13 **Akashi** *var.* Akasi. Hyōgo, Honshū, SW Japan 34°39′N 135°00′E
139 N7 **'Akāsh, Wādī** *var.* Wādī 'Ukash. *dry watercourse* W Iraq
Akasi *see* Akashi
92 K11 **Äkäsjokisuu** Lappi, N Finland 67°28′N 23°44′E
137 S11 **Akbaba Dağı** ▲ Armenia/Turkey 41°04′N 43°28′E
Akbük Limanı *see* Güllük Körfezi
127 V8 **Akbulak** Orenburgskaya Oblast', W Russian Federation 51°01′N 55°35′E
137 O11 **Akçaabat** Trabzon, NE Turkey 41°00′N 39°36′E
137 N15 **Akçadağ** Malatya, C Turkey 38°21′N 37°59′E
136 G11 **Akçakoca** Düzce, NW Turkey 41°05′N 31°08′E
Akchakaya, Vpadina *see* Akdzhakaya, Vpadina
76 H7 **Akchâr** *desert* W Mauritania
Akchatau *see* Akshatau
136 L13 **Akdağlar** ▲▲ C Turkey
136 E17 **Ak Dağları** ▲▲ SW Turkey
136 K13 **Akdağmadeni** Yozgat, C Turkey 39°40′N 35°52′E
146 G8 **Akdepe** *prev.* Ak-Tepe, Leninsk, *Turkm.* Lenin. Daşoguz Welaýat, N Turkmenistan 42°10′N 59°17′E
Ak-Dere *see* Byala
121 P2 **Akdoğan** *Gk.* Lýsi. C Cyprus 35°06′N 33°42′E
122 J14 **Ak-Dovurak** Respublika Tyva, S Russian Federation 51°09′N 90°36′E
146 F9 **Akdzhakaya, Vpadina** *var.* Vpadina Akchakaya. *depression* N Turkmenistan
171 S11 **Akelamo** Pulau Halmahera, E Indonesia 01°27′N 128°39′E
Aken *see* Aachen
Akermanceaster *see* Bath
95 P15 **Åkersberga** Stockholm, C Sweden 59°28′N 18°19′E
95 H15 **Akershus** ◐ *county* S Norway
79 L16 **Aketi** Orientale, N Dem. Rep. Congo 02°44′N 23°46′E
146 C10 **Akgyr Erezi** *Rus.* Gryada Akkyr. *hill range* NW Turkmenistan
Akhalskiy Velayat *see* Ahal Welaýaty
137 S10 **Akhaltsikhe** *prev.* Akhalts'ikhe. SW Georgia 41°39′N 43°04′E
Akhalts'ikhe *see* Akhaltsikhe
Akhangaran *see* Ohangaron
Akharnaí *see* Acharnés
75 R7 **Akhḑar, Al Jabal al** *hill range* NE Libya
Akhelóös *see* Achelóos
39 Q15 **Akhiok** Kodiak Island, Alaska, USA 56°57′N 154°12′W
136 C13 **Akhisar** Manisa, W Turkey 38°54′N 27°50′E
75 X10 **Akhmīm** *var.* Akhmîm; *anc.* Panopolis. C Egypt 26°35′N 31°48′E
152 H6 **Akhnūr** Jammu and Kashmir, NW India 32°53′N 74°46′E
Akhsu *see* Ağsu
114 N10 **Akhtopol** Burgas, E Bulgaria 42°06′N 27°57′E
127 P11 **Akhtuba** ≈ SW Russian Federation
127 P11 **Akhtubinsk** Astrakhanskaya Oblast', SW Russian Federation 48°17′N 46°14′E
Akhtyrka *see* Okhtyrka
164 H14 **Aki** Kōchi, Shikoku, SW Japan 33°30′N 133°53′E
39 N12 **Akiachak** Alaska, USA 60°54′N 161°25′W
39 N12 **Akiak** Alaska, USA 60°54′N 161°12′W
191 X11 **Akiaki** *atoll* Îles Tuamotu, E French Polynesia
12 H9 **Akimiski Island** *island* Nunavut, C Canada
136 K17 **Akıncı Burnu** *headland* S Turkey 36°21′N 35°47′E
Akıncılar *see* Selçuk
117 U10 **Akinovka** Zaporiz'ka Oblast', S Ukraine
Åkirkeby *see* Aakirkeby
165 P8 **Akita** Akita, Honshū, C Japan 39°44′N 140°06′E
165 Q8 **Akita** *off.* Akita-ken. ◐ *prefecture* Honshū, C Japan
76 H8 **Akjoujt** *prev.* Fort-Repoux. Inchiri, W Mauritania 19°42′N 14°28′W
92 H11 **Akka** *Lapp.* Áhkká. ▲ N Sweden 67°33′N 17°27′E
92 H11 **Akkajaure** *Lapp.* Áhkájávrre. ◎ N Sweden
Akkala *see* Oqqal'a
155 L25 **Akkaraipattu** Eastern Province, E Sri Lanka 07°13′N 81°51′E
145 P13 **Akkense** *Kaz.* Aqkengse. Karaganda, C Kazakhstan 46°39′N 68°06′E
Akkerman *see* Bilhorod-Dnistrovs'kyy
127 W8 **Akkermanovka** Orenburgskaya Oblast', W Russian Federation 51°11′N 58°03′E
165 V4 **Akkeshi** Hokkaidō, NE Japan 43°03′N 144°49′E
165 V4 **Akkeshi-ko** ◎ Hokkaidō, NE Japan
165 V5 **Akkeshi-wan** *bay* NW Pacific Ocean
138 F8 **Akko** *Eng.* Acre, *Fr.* Saint-Jean-d'Acre, *Bibl.* Accho, Ptolemaïs. Northern, N Israel 32°55′N 35°04′E
145 Q8 **Akkol'** *Kaz.* Aqköl; *prev.* Alekseyevka, *Kaz.* Alekseevka. Akmola, C Kazakhstan 51°58′N 70°58′E
145 T14 **Akkol'** *Kaz.* Aqköl. Almaty, SE Kazakhstan 45°01′N 75°38′E
145 Q16 **Akkol'** *Kaz.* Aqköl. Zhambyl, C Kazakhstan 43°25′N 70°47′E
144 M11 **Akkol', Ozero** *prev.* Ozero Zhaman-Akkol. ◎ C Kazakhstan
98 L6 **Akkrum** Fryslân, N Netherlands 53°01′N 05°52′E
145 U8 **Akku** *Kaz.* Aqqū; *prev.* Lebyazh'ye. Pavlodar, NE Kazakhstan 51°29′N 77°48′E
144 F12 **Akkystau** *Kaz.* Aqqystaū. Atyrau, SW Kazakhstan 47°17′N 51°03′E
8 G6 **Aklavik** Northwest Territories, NW Canada 68°15′N 135°02′W
118 B9 **Akmenrags** *prev.* Akmeņrags. *headland* W Latvia 56°49′N 21°03′E
Akmeņrags *see* Akmenrags
158 E9 **Akmeqit** Xinjiang Uygur Zizhiqu, NW China 37°10′N 76°59′E
146 J14 **Akmeydan** Mary Welaýaty, C Turkmenistan 37°50′N 62°08′E
145 P9 **Akmola** *off.* Akmolinskaya Oblast', *Kaz.* Aqmola Oblysy; *prev.* Tselinogradskaya Oblast. ◐ *province* C Kazakhstan
Akmola *see* Astana
Akmolinsk *see* Astana
Akmolinskaya Oblast' *see* Akmola
Aknavásár *see* Târgu Ocna
118 I11 **Aknīste** S Latvia 56°09′N 25°43′E
81 G14 **Akobo** Jonglei, E South Sudan 07°50′N 33°05′E
81 G14 **Akobo** *var.* Ākobowenz. ≈ Ethiopia/Sudan
Ākobowenz *see* Akobo
154 H12 **Akola** Mahārāshtra, C India 20°44′N 77°00′E
80 J9 **Ak'ordat** *var.* Agordat, Akurdet. C Eritrea 15°33′N 38°01′E
77 Q16 **Akosombo Dam** *dam* SE Ghana
154 H12 **Akot** Mahārāshtra, C India 20°45′N 77°00′E
77 N16 **Akoupé** SE Ivory Coast 06°19′N 03°54′W
12 M3 **Akpatok Island** *island* Nunavut, E Canada
158 G7 **Akqi** Xinjiang Uygur Zizhiqu, NW China 40°51′N 78°20′E
138 I2 **Akrād, Jabal al** ▲▲ N Syria
Akragas *see* Agrigento
92 H3 **Akranes** Vesturland, W Iceland 64°19′N 22°01′W
139 S2 **Ākrē** *Ar.* 'Aqrah. Dahūk, N Iraq 36°46′N 43°52′E
95 C16 **Åkrehamn** Rogaland, S Norway 59°15′N 15°13′E
77 V9 **Akrérèb** Agadez, C Niger 17°45′N 09°01′E
115 D22 **Akrítas, Akrotírio** *headland* S Greece 36°43′N 21°52′E
37 V3 **Akron** Colorado, C USA 40°09′N 103°12′W
29 R12 **Akron** Iowa, C USA 42°49′N 96°33′W
31 U12 **Akron** Ohio, N USA 41°05′N 81°31′W
Akrotiri *see* Akrotírion
Akrotiri Bay *see* Akrotírion, Kólpos
Akrotírio Kastállou *see* Kástelo, Akrotírio
121 P3 **Akrotírion** *var.* Akrotiri. *UK air base* S Cyprus34°36′N 32°57′E
121 P3 **Akrotírion, Kólpos** *var.* Akrotiri Bay. *bay* S Cyprus
121 O3 **Akrotiri Sovereign Base Area** *UK military installation* S Cyprus
158 F11 **Aksai Chin** *Chin.* Aksayqin. *disputed region* China/India
Aksaj *see* Aksay
136 I15 **Aksaray** Aksaray, C Turkey 38°23′N 33°50′E
136 I15 **Aksaray** ◐ *province* C Turkey
144 G8 **Aksay** *var.* Aksaj, *Kaz.* Aqsay. Zapadnyy Kazakhstan, NW Kazakhstan 51°11′N 53°00′E
127 O11 **Aksay** Volgogradskaya Oblast', SW Russian Federation 47°59′N 43°54′E
147 W10 **Ak-say** *var.* Toxkan He. ≈ China/Kyrgyzstan
Aksay/Aksay Kazakzu Zizhixian *see* Boluozhuanjing/Hongliuwan
Aksayqin *see* Aksai Chin
158 G11 **Aksayqin Hu** ◎ NW China
136 G14 **Akşehir** Konya, W Turkey 38°22′N 31°24′E
136 G14 **Akşehir Gölü** ◎ C Turkey
136 G16 **Akseki** Antalya, SW Turkey 37°03′N 31°46′E
123 P13 **Aksenovo-Zilovskoye** Zabaykal'skiy Kray, S Russian Federation 53°01′N 117°26′E
145 S12 **Akshatau** *Kaz.* Aqshataū; *prev.* Akchatau. Karaganda, C Kazakhstan 47°59′N 74°02′E
145 V11 **Akshatau, Khrebet** ▲▲ E Kazakhstan
147 Y8 **Ak-Shyyrak** Issyk-Kul'skaya Oblast', E Kyrgyzstan 41°46′N 78°34′E
Akstafa *see* Ağstafa
158 H7 **Aksu** Xinjiang Uygur Zizhiqu, NW China 41°17′N 80°15′E
145 R8 **Aksu** *Kaz.* Aqsū. Akmola, N Kazakhstan 52°31′N 72°00′E
145 W13 **Aksu** *Kaz.* Aqsū. Almaty, SE Kazakhstan 45°31′N 79°28′E
145 T8 **Aksu** *var.* Jermak, *Kaz.* Ermak; *prev.* Yermak. Pavlodar, NE Kazakhstan 52°03′N 76°55′E
145 V13 **Aksu** *Kaz.* Aqsū. ≈ SE Kazakhstan
145 Y11 **Aksuat** *Kaz.* Aqsūat. Vostochnyy Kazakhstan, SE Kazakhstan 48°16′N 83°39′E
145 X11 **Aksuat** *Kaz.* Aqsūat. Vostochnyy Kazakhstan, E Kazakhstan 47°48′N 82°51′E
127 S4 **Aksubayevo** Respublika Tatarstan, W Russian Federation 54°52′N 50°50′E
158 H7 **Aksu He** *Rus.* Sary-Dzhaz. ≈ China/Kyrgyzstan *see also* Sary-Dzhaz
80 J10 **Āksum** Tigray, N Ethiopia 14°06′N 38°42′E
145 O12 **Aktas** *Kaz.* Aqtas. Karaganda, C Kazakhstan 48°03′N 66°21′E
Aktash *see* Oqtosh
147 V9 **Ak-Tash, Gora** ▲ C Kyrgyzstan 40°53′N 74°39′E
145 R10 **Aktau** *Kaz.* Aqtaū. Karaganda, C Kazakhstan 50°13′N 73°06′E
144 E11 **Aktau** *Kaz.* Aqtaū; *prev.* Shevchenko. Mangistau, W Kazakhstan 43°37′N 51°14′E
Aktau, Khrebet *see* Oqtogh, Qatorkŭhi. SW Tajikistan
Aktau, Khrebet *see* Oqtov Tizmasi, C Uzbekistan
Akte *see* Ágion Óros
Ak-Tepe *see* Akdepe
147 X7 **Ak-Terek** Issyk-Kul'skaya Oblast', E Kyrgyzstan 42°14′N 77°46′E
Aktí *see* Ágion Óros
Aktjubinsk/Aktyubinsk *see* Aktobe
158 E8 **Akto** Xinjiang Uygur Zizhiqu, NW China 39°07′N 75°43′E
144 I10 **Aktobe** *Kaz.* Aqtöbe; *prev.* Aktjubinsk, Aktyubinsk. Aktyubinsk, NW Kazakhstan 50°18′N 57°10′E
145 V12 **Aktogay** *Kaz.* Aqtoghay. Vostochnyy Kazakhstan, E Kazakhstan 46°56′N 79°40′E
119 M18 **Aktsyabrski** *Rus.* Oktyabr'skiy; *prev.* Karpilovka. Homyel'skaya Voblasts', SE Belarus 52°38′N 28°53′E
144 H11 **Aktyubinsk** *off.* Aktyubinskaya Oblast', *Kaz.* Aqtöbe Oblysy. ◐ *province* W Kazakhstan
Aktyubinsk *see* Aktobe
147 W7 **Ak-Tyuz** *var.* Aktyuz. Chuyskaya Oblast', N Kyrgyzstan 42°50′N 76°05′E
79 J17 **Akula** Equateur, NW Dem. Rep. Congo 02°21′N 20°13′E
164 C15 **Akune** Kagoshima, Kyūshū, SW Japan 32°00′N 130°12′E
38 L16 **Akun Island** *island* Aleutian Islands, Alaska, USA
Akurdet *see* Ak'ordat
77 T16 **Akure** Ondo, SW Nigeria 07°18′N 05°13′E
92 J2 **Akureyri** Nordhurland Eystra, N Iceland 65°40′N 18°07′W
38 L17 **Akutan** Akutan Island, Alaska, USA 54°08′N 165°47′W
38 K17 **Akutan Island** *island* Aleutian Islands, Alaska, USA
77 V17 **Akwa Ibom** ◐ *state* SE Nigeria
Akyab *see* Sittwe
127 W7 **Ak"yar** Respublika Bashkortostan, W Russian Federation 51°51′N 58°13′E
144 J10 **Akzhar** *prev.* Novorossiyskiy, Novorossiyskoye. Aktyubinsk, NW Kazakhstan 50°14′N 57°57′E
145 Y11 **Akzhar** *Kaz.* Aqzhar. Vostochnyy Kazakhstan, E Kazakhstan 47°36′N 83°38′E
94 F13 **Ål** Buskerud, S Norway 60°37′N 08°33′E
119 N18 **Ala** *Rus.* Ola. ≈ SE Belarus
23 P5 **Alabama** *off.* State of Alabama, *also known as* Camellia State, Heart of Dixie, The Cotton State, Yellowhammer State. ◐ *state* S USA
23 P6 **Alabama River** ≈ Alabama, S USA
23 P4 **Alabaster** Alabama, S USA 33°14′N 86°49′W
139 U10 **Al 'Abd Allāh** *var.* Al Abdullah. Al Qādisīyah, S Iraq 32°06′N 45°08′E
139 W14 **Al Abṭīyah** *well* S Iraq
147 S9 **Ala-Buka** Dzhalal-Abadskaya Oblast', W Kyrgyzstan 41°22′N 71°27′E
136 J12 **Alaca** Çorum, N Turkey 40°10′N 34°52′E
136 K10 **Alaçam** Samsun, N Turkey 41°36′N 35°35′E
Alacant *see* Alicante
23 V9 **Alachua** Florida, SE USA 29°48′N 82°29′W
137 S13 **Aladağlar** ▲▲ W Turkey
136 K15 **Ala Dağları** ▲▲ C Turkey
162 I5 **Alag-Erdene** *var.* Manhan. Hövsgöl, N Mongolia 50°05′N 100°01′E
127 O16 **Alagir** Respublika Severnaya Osetiya, SW Russian Federation 43°02′N 44°10′E
106 B6 **Alagna Valsesia** Valle d'Aosta, NW Italy 45°51′N 07°50′E
103 P12 **Alagnon** ≈ C France
59 P16 **Alagoas** *off.* Estado de Alagoas. ◐ *state* E Brazil
59 P17 **Alagoinhas** Bahia, E Brazil 12°09′S 38°21′W
105 R5 **Alagón** Aragón, NE Spain 41°46′N 01°07′W
104 J9 **Alagón** ≈ W Spain
93 K16 **Alahärmä** Länsi-Suomi, W Finland 63°15′N 22°50′E
al Ahdar *see* Al Akhḑar
Álaheaieatnu *see* Altaelva
142 K12 **Al Aḩmadī** *var.* Ahmadi. E Kuwait 29°02′N 48°01′E
Al Ain *see* Al 'Ayn
105 Z8 **Alaior** *prev.* Alayor. Menorca, Spain, W Mediterranean Sea 39°56′N 04°08′E
147 T11 **Alai Range** *Rus.* Alayskiy Khrebet. ▲▲ Kyrgyzstan/Tajikistan
Alais *see* Alès
141 X11 **Al 'Ajā'iz** E Oman 19°33′N 57°12′E
141 X11 **Al 'Ajā'iz** *oasis* SE Oman
93 L16 **Alajärvi** Länsi-Suomi, W Finland 63°00′N 23°50′E
118 K4 **Alajõe** Ida-Virumaa, NE Estonia 59°00′N 27°26′E
42 M13 **Alajuela** Alajuela, C Costa Rica 10°00′N 84°12′W
42 L12 **Alajuela** *off.* Provincia de Alajuela. ◐ *province* N Costa Rica
43 T14 **Alajuela, Lago** ◎ C Panama
38 M11 **Alakanuk** Alaska, USA 62°41′N 164°37′W
140 K5 **Al Akhḑar** *var.* al Ahdar. Tabūk, NW Saudi Arabia 28°04′N 37°13′E
Alaköl *see* Alakol', Ozero
145 X13 **Alakol', Ozero** *Kaz.* Alaköl. ◎ SE Kazakhstan
124 I5 **Alakurtti** Murmanskaya Oblast', NW Russian Federation 66°57′N 30°27′E
38 F10 **Alalākeiki Channel** *var.* Alalakeiki Channel. *channel* Hawaii, USA, C Pacific Ocean
75 U8 **Al 'Alamayn** *var.* El 'Alamein. N Egypt 30°50′N 28°57′E
139 R1 **Al 'Amādīyah** Dahūk, N Iraq 37°09′N 43°27′E
188 K5 **Alamagan** *island* C Northern Mariana Islands
139 X10 **Al 'Amārah** *var.* Amara. Maysān, E Iraq 31°51′N 47°10′E
80 J11 **Ālamat'ā** Tigray, N Ethiopia 12°22′N 39°32′E
37 R11 **Alameda** New Mexico, SW USA 35°09′N 106°37′W
121 T13 **'Alam el Rûm, Râs** *headland* N Egypt 31°21′N 27°23′E
Alamícamba *see* Alamikamba
42 M8 **Alamikamba** *var.* Alamícamba. Región Autónoma Atlántico Norte, NE Nicaragua 13°26′N 84°09′W
24 K11 **Alamito Creek** ≈ Texas, SW USA
40 M8 **Alamitos, Sierra de los** ▲ NE Mexico 26°15′N 102°14′W
41 Q12 **Álamo** Veracruz-Llave, C Mexico 20°55′N 97°41′W
35 X9 **Alamo** Nevada, W USA 37°21′N 115°08′W
20 F9 **Alamo** Tennessee, S USA 35°47′N 89°09′W
37 S14 **Alamogordo** New Mexico, SW USA 32°52′N 105°57′W
36 J12 **Alamo Lake** ⊞ Arizona, SW USA
40 H7 **Alamos** Sonora, NW Mexico 26°59′N 108°53′W
37 S7 **Alamosa** Colorado, C USA 37°25′N 105°51′W
93 J20 **Åland** *var.* Aland Islands, *Fin.* Ahvenanmaa. ◐ *province* SW Finland
88 K9 **Åland** *var.* Aland Islands, *Fin.* Ahvenanmaa. *island group* SW Finland
Aland Islands *see* Åland
Aland Sea *see* Ålands Hav
95 Q14 **Ålands Hav** *var.* Aland Sea. *strait* Baltic Sea/Gulf of Bothnia
43 P16 **Alanje** Chiriquí, SW Panama 08°26′N 82°33′W
25 O2 **Alanreed** Texas, SW USA 35°12′N 100°45′W
136 G17 **Alanya** Antalya, S Turkey 36°32′N 32°02′E
23 U7 **Alapaha River** ≈ Florida/Georgia, SE USA
122 G10 **Alapayevsk** Sverdlovskaya Oblast', C Russian Federation 57°48′N 61°50′E
138 F14 **Al 'Aqabah** *var.* Akaba, Aqaba, 'Aqaba; *anc.* Aelana, Elath. Al 'Aqabah, SW Jordan 29°32′N 35°00′E
138 G14 **Al 'Aqabah** *off.* Muḩāfaẓat Al 'Aqabah. ◐ *governorate* SW Jordan
Al 'Arabīyah as Su'ūdīyah *see* Saudi Arabia
al Araïch *see* Larache
105 Q10 **Alarcón** Castilla-La Mancha, C Spain 39°32′N 02°05′W
105 Q9 **Alarcón, Embalse de** ⊞ C Spain
138 J2 **Al 'Arīmah** *Fr.* Arime. Ḩalab, N Syria 36°27′N 37°41′E
75 X7 **Al 'Arīsh** *var.* El 'Arîsh. NE Egypt 33°00′N 31°00′E
141 P6 **Al Arṭāwīyah** Ar Riyāḑ, N Saudi Arabia 26°34′N 45°20′E
Alasca, Golfo de *see* Alaska, Gulf of
136 D14 **Alaşehir** Manisa, W Turkey 38°19′N 28°30′E
139 N5 **Al 'Ashārah** *var.* Ashara. Dayr az Zawr, E Syria 34°51′N 40°36′E
Al Ashkhara *see* Al Ashkharah
141 Z9 **Al Ashkharah** *var.* Al Ashkhara. NE Oman 21°47′N 59°30′E
Al 'Aṣimah *see* 'Ammān
39 P8 **Alaska** *off.* State of Alaska, *also known as* Land of the Midnight Sun, The Last Frontier, Seward's Folly; *prev.* Russian America. ◐ *state* NW USA
39 T13 **Alaska, Gulf of** *var.* Golfo de Alasca. *gulf* Canada/USA
39 O15 **Alaska Peninsula** *peninsula* Alaska, USA
39 Q11 **Alaska Range** ▲▲ Alaska, USA
Al-Asnam *see* Chlef
106 B10 **Alassio** Liguria, NW Italy 44°01′N 08°12′E
137 Y12 **Älät** *Rus.* Alyat; *prev.* Alyaty-Pristan'. SE Azerbaijan 39°57′N 49°24′E
Alat *see* Olot
139 S13 **Al 'Athāmīn** An Najaf, S Iraq 30°27′N 43°41′E
39 P7 **Alatna River** ≈ Alaska, USA
107 J15 **Alatri** Lazio, C Italy 41°43′N 13°21′E
Alattio *see* Alta
127 P5 **Alatyr'** Chuvashskaya Respublika, W Russian Federation 54°50′N 46°28′E
56 C7 **Alausí** Chimborazo, C Ecuador 02°11′S 78°52′W
105 O3 **Álava** *Basq.* Araba. ◐ *province* País Vasco, N Spain
137 T11 **Alaverdi** N Armenia 41°06′N 44°37′E
Alavo *see* Alavus
93 N14 **Ala-Vuokki** Oulu, E Finland 64°46′N 29°29′E
93 K17 **Alavus** *Swe.* Alavo. Länsi-Suomi, W Finland 62°33′N 23°38′E
Al 'Awābī *see* Awābī
139 P6 **Al 'Awānī** Al Anbār, W Iraq 34°28′N 41°43′E
75 U12 **Al Awaynāt** SE Libya 21°46′N 24°51′E
Al Awaynāt *see* Al 'Uwaynāt
182 K9 **Alawoona** South Australia 34°45′S 140°28′E
Alaykel'/Alay-Kuu *see* Këk-Art
143 R17 **Al 'Ayn** *var.* Al Ain. Abū Ẓaby, E United Arab Emirates 24°13′N 55°44′E
143 R17 **Al 'Ayn** *var.* Al Ain. ✈ Abū Ẓaby, E United Arab Emirates 24°16′N 55°31′E
138 G12 **Al 'Aynā** Al Karak, W Jordan 30°59′N 35°43′E
Alayor *see* Alaior
Alayskiy Khrebet *see* Alai Range
123 S6 **Alazeya** ≈ NE Russian Federation
139 U8 **Al 'Azīzīyah** *var.* Aziziya. Wāsiṭ, E Iraq 32°54′N 45°05′E
120 M12 **Al 'Azīzīyah** NW Libya 32°32′N 13°01′E
138 I10 **Al Azraq al Janūbī** Az Zarqā', N Jordan 31°49′N 36°48′E
106 B9 **Alba** *anc.* Alba Pompeia. Piemonte, NW Italy 44°42′N 08°02′E
25 V6 **Alba** Texas, SW USA 32°47′N 95°37′W
116 G11 **Alba** ◐ *county* W Romania
139 P3 **Al Ba'āj** Nīnawá, N Iraq 36°02′N 41°43′E
138 J2 **Al Bāb** Ḩalab, N Syria 36°24′N 37°32′E
116 G10 **Albac** *Hung.* Fehérvölgy; *prev.* Álbák. Alba, SW Romania 46°27′N 22°58′E
105 Q11 **Albacete** Castilla-La Mancha, C Spain 39°N 01°52′W
105 P11 **Albacete** ◐ *province* Castilla-La Mancha, C Spain
140 I4 **Al Bad'** Tabūk, NW Saudi Arabia 28°28′N 35°00′E
104 L7 **Alba de Tormes** Castilla y León, N Spain 40°50′N 05°30′W
139 P3 **Al Bādī** Nīnawá, N Iraq 35°57′N 41°37′E
141 V8 **Al Badī'ah** ✈ (Abū Ẓaby) Abū Ẓaby, C United Arab Emirates 24°27′N 54°39′E
143 P17 **Al Badī'ah** *var.* Al Bedei'ah. *spring/well* C United Arab Emirates 23°44′N 53°50′E
95 H19 **Ålbæk** Nordjylland, N Denmark 57°33′N 10°24′E
139 Q7 **Al Baghdādī** *var.* Khān al Baghdādī. Al Anbār, SW Iraq 33°60′N 42°50′E
Al Bāha *see* Al Bāḩah
140 M11 **Al Bāḩah** *var.* Al Bāha. Al BāḨah, SW Saudi Arabia 20°01′N 41°29′E
140 M11 **Al Bāḩah** *var.* Minṭaqat al Bāḩah. ◐ *province* W Saudi Arabia
Al Baḩrayn *see* Bahrain
105 S11 **Albaida** Valenciana, E Spain 38°51′N 00°31′W
116 H11 **Alba Iulia** *Ger.* Weissenburg, *Hung.* Gyulafehérvár; *prev.* Bălgrad, Karlsburg, Károly-Fehérvár. Alba, W Romania 46°06′N 23°33′E
Álbák *see* Albac
138 G10 **Al Balqā'** *off.* Muḩāfaẓat al Balqā', *var.* Balqā'. ◐ *governorate* NW Jordan
14 F11 **Alban** Ontario, S Canada 46°07′N 80°37′W
103 O15 **Alban** Tarn, S France 43°52′N 02°30′E
12 K11 **Albanel, Lac** ◎ Québec, SE Canada
113 L20 **Albania** *off.* Republic of Albania, *Alb.* Republika e Shqipqërisë, Shqipëria; *prev.* People's Socialist Republic of Albania. ◆ *republic* SE Europe
Albania *see* Aubagne
107 H15 **Albano Laziaie** Lazio, C Italy 41°44′N 12°40′E
180 J14 **Albany** Western Australia 35°03′S 117°54′E
23 S7 **Albany** Georgia, SE USA 31°35′N 84°09′W
31 P13 **Albany** Indiana, N USA 40°18′N 85°14′W
20 L8 **Albany** Kentucky, S USA 36°42′N 85°08′W
29 U7 **Albany** Minnesota, N USA 45°39′N 94°33′W
27 R2 **Albany** Missouri, C USA 40°15′N 94°15′W
18 L10 **Albany** *state capital* New York, NE USA 42°39′N 73°45′W
32 G12 **Albany** Oregon, NW USA 44°38′N 123°06′W
25 Q6 **Albany** Texas, SW USA 32°44′N 99°18′W
12 F10 **Albany** ≈ Ontario, S Canada
Alba Pompeia *see* Alba
Alba Regia *see* Székesfehérvár
138 J6 **Al Bāridah** *var.* Bāridah. Ḩimş, C Syria 34°15′N 37°39′E
139 Q11 **Al Barīt** Al Anbār, S Iraq 31°16′N 42°28′E
105 R8 **Albarracín** Aragón, NE Spain 40°24′N 01°25′W
139 Y12 **Al Başrah** *Eng.* Basra, *hist.* Busra, Bussora. Al Başrah, SE Iraq 30°30′N 47°50′E
139 V11 **Al Baṭḩā'** Dhī Qār, SE Iraq 31°06′N 45°54′E
141 X8 **Al Bāṭinah** *var.* Batinah. *coastal region* N Oman
0 H16 **Albatross Plateau** *undersea feature* E Pacific Ocean 10°00′N 103°00′W
Al Batrūn *see* Batroûn
121 Q12 **Al Bayḑā'** *var.* Beida. NE Libya 32°46′N 21°43′E
141 P16 **Al Bayḑā'** *var.* Al Beida. SW Yemen 13°58′N 45°38′E
Al Bedei'ah *see* Al Badī'ah
Al Beida *see* Al Bayḑā'
21 S10 **Albemarle** *var.* Albermarle. North Carolina, SE USA 35°21′N 80°12′W
Albemarle Island *see* Isabela, Isla
21 N8 **Albemarle Sound** *inlet* W Atlantic Ocean
106 B10 **Albenga** Liguria, NW Italy 44°04′N 08°13′E
104 L8 **Alberche** ≈ C Spain
103 O17 **Albères, Chaîne des** *var.* les Albères, Montes Albères. ▲▲ France/Spain
Albères, Montes *see* Albères, Chaîne des
182 F2 **Alberga Creek** *seasonal river* South Australia
104 G7 **Albergaria-a-Velha** Aveiro, N Portugal 40°42′N 08°28′W
105 S10 **Alberic** Valenciana, E Spain 39°07′N 00°31′W
Albermarle *see* Albemarle
107 P18 **Alberobello** Puglia, SE Italy 40°47′N 17°14′E
108 J7 **Alberschwende** Vorarlberg, W Austria 47°28′N 09°50′E
103 O3 **Albert** Somme, N France 50°N 02°38′E
11 O12 **Alberta** ◐ *province* SW Canada
Albert Edward Nyanza *see* Edward, Lake
61 C20 **Alberti** Buenos Aires, E Argentina 35°03′S 60°15′W
111 K23 **Albertirsa** Pest, C Hungary 47°15′N 19°36′E
99 I16 **Albertkanaal** *canal* N Belgium
79 P17 **Albert, Lake** *var.* Albert Nyanza, Lac Mobutu Sese Seko. ◎ Uganda/Dem. Rep. Congo
29 V11 **Albert Lea** Minnesota, N USA 43°39′N 93°22′W
81 F16 **Albert Nile** ≈ NW Uganda
Albert Nyanza *see* Albert, Lake
103 T11 **Albertville** Savoie, E France 45°41′N 06°24′E
23 Q2 **Albertville** Alabama, S USA 34°16′N 86°12′W
Albertville *see* Kalemie
103 N15 **Albi** *anc.* Albiga. Tarn, S France 43°55′N 02°09′E
29 W15 **Albia** Iowa, C USA 41°01′N 92°48′W
Albiga *see* Albi
55 X9 **Albina** Marowijne, NE Surinam 05°29′N 54°08′W
83 A15 **Albina, Ponta** *headland* SW Angola 15°52′S 11°45′E
30 M16 **Albion** Illinois, N USA 38°22′N 88°03′W
31 P11 **Albion** Indiana, N USA 41°23′N 85°26′W
29 P14 **Albion** Nebraska, C USA 41°41′N 98°00′W
18 E9 **Albion** New York, NE USA 43°13′N 78°09′W
18 B12 **Albion** Pennsylvania, NE USA 41°52′N 80°18′W
Al Biqā' *see* El Beqaa
140 J4 **Al Bi'r** *var.* Bi'r Ibn Hirmās. Tabūk, NW Saudi Arabia 28°52′N 36°16′E
140 M12 **Al Birk** Makkah, SW Saudi Arabia 18°13′N 41°36′E
141 Q9 **Al Biyāḑ** *desert* C Saudi Arabia
98 H13 **Alblasserdam** Zuid-Holland, SW Netherlands 51°52′N 04°40′E
Albocácer *see* Albocàsser
105 T8 **Albocàsser** *Cast.* Albocácer. Valenciana, E Spain 40°21′N 00°01′E
Albona *see* Labin
105 O17 **Alborán, Isla de** *island* S Spain
Alborán, Mar de *see* Alboran Sea
105 N17 **Alboran Sea** *Sp.* Mar de Alborán. *sea* SW Mediterranean Sea
Ålborg *see* Aalborg
95 H21 **Ålborg Bugt** *var.* Aalborg Bugt. *bay* N Denmark
Ålborg-Nørresundby *see* Aalborg
143 O5 **Alborz, Reshteh-ye Kūhhā-ye** *Eng.* Elburz Mountains. ▲▲ N Iran
105 Q14 **Albox** Andalucía, S Spain 37°22′N 02°08′W
101 H23 **Albstadt** Baden-Württemberg, SW Germany 48°13′N 09°01′E
104 G14 **Albufeira** Beja, S Portugal 37°05′N 08°15′W
139 P5 **Ālbū Gharz, Sabkhat** ◎ W Iraq
105 O15 **Albuñol** Andalucía, S Spain 36°48′N 03°11′W
37 Q11 **Albuquerque** New Mexico, SW USA 35°05′N 106°38′W
141 W8 **Al Buraymī** *var.* Buraimi. N Oman 24°16′N 55°48′E
143 R17 **Al Buraymī** *var.* Buraimi. *spring/well* Oman/United Arab Emirates 24°27′N 55°33′E
Al Burayqah *see* Marsá al Burayqah
Alburgum *see* Aalborg
104 I10 **Alburquerque** Extremadura, W Spain 39°12′N 07°00′W
181 V14 **Albury** New South Wales, SE Australia 36°03′S 146°53′E
141 T14 **Al Buzūn** SE Yemen 15°40′N 50°53′E
93 G17 **Alby** Västernorrland, C Sweden 62°30′N 15°25′E
Albyn, Glen *see* Mor, Glen
104 G12 **Alcácer do Sal** Setúbal, W Portugal 38°22′N 08°29′W
Alcalá de Chisvert/Alcalá de Chivert *see* Alcalà de Xivert
104 K14 **Alcalá de Guadaira** Andalucía, S Spain 37°20′N 05°50′W
105 O8 **Alcalá de Henares** *Ar.* Alkal'a; *anc.* Complutum. Madrid, C Spain 40°28′N 03°22′W
104 K16 **Alcalá de los Gazules** Andalucía, S Spain 36°29′N 05°43′W
105 T8 **Alcalà de Xivert** *var.* Alcalá de Chisvert, *Cast.* Alcalá de Chivert. Valenciana, E Spain 40°19′N 00°13′E
105 N14 **Alcalá La Real** Andalucía, S Spain 37°28′N 03°55′W
107 I23 **Alcamo** Sicilia, Italy, C Mediterranean Sea 37°58′N 12°58′E
105 T4 **Alcanadre** ≈ NE Spain
105 T8 **Alcanar** Cataluña, NE Spain 40°33′N 00°28′E
104 J5 **Alcañices** Castilla y León, N Spain 41°41′N 06°21′W

◆ Country
● Country Capital
◇ Dependent Territory
○ Dependent Territory Capital
◐ Administrative Regions
✈ International Airport
▲ Mountain
▲▲ Mountain Range
☼ Volcano
≈ River
◎ Lake
⊞ Reservoir

105 *T7* **Alcañiz** Aragón, NE Spain *41°03′N 00°09′W*
104 *I9* **Alcántara** Extremadura, W Spain *39°42′N 06°54′W*
104 *J9* **Alcántara, Embalse de** ⊠ W Spain
105 *R13* **Alcantarilla** Murcia, SE Spain *37°59′N 01°12′W*
105 *P11* **Alcaraz** Castilla-La Mancha, C Spain *38°40′N 02°29′W*
105 *P12* **Alcaraz, Sierra de** ▲▲ C Spain
104 *I12* **Alcarrache** ≈ SW Spain
105 *T6* **Alcarràs** Cataluña, NE Spain *41°34′N 00°31′E*
105 *N14* **Alcaudete** Andalucía, S Spain *37°35′N 04°05′W*
Alcázar *see* Ksar-el-Kebir
105 *O10* **Alcázar de San Juan** ***anc.*** Alce. Castilla-La Mancha, C Spain *39°24′N 03°12′W*
Alcazarquivir *see* Ksar-el-Kebir
Alce *see* Alcázar de San Juan
57 *B17* **Alcebo, Volcán** ⛰ Galapagos Islands, Ecuador, E Pacific Ocean *0°25′S 91°06′W*
139 *X12* **Al Chabā'ish** ***var.*** Al Kaba'ish. Dhī Qār, SE Iraq *30°58′N 47°02′E*
117 *Y7* **Alchevs'k** ***prev.*** Kommunarsk, Voroshilovsk. Luhans'ka Oblast', E Ukraine *48°29′N 38°52′E*
Alcira *see* Alzira
21 *N9* **Alcoa** Tennessee, S USA *35°47′N 83°58′W*
104 *F9* **Alcobaça** Leiria, C Portugal *39°32′N 08°59′W*
105 *N8* **Alcobendas** Madrid, C Spain *40°32′N 03°38′W*
Alcoi *see* Alcoy
105 *P7* **Alcolea del Pinar** Castilla-La Mancha, C Spain *41°02′N 02°28′W*
104 *I11* **Alconchel** Extremadura, W Spain *38°31′N 07°04′W*
Alcora *see* L'Alcora
105 *N8* **Alcorcón** Madrid, C Spain *40°20′N 03°52′W*
105 *S7* **Alcorisa** Aragón, NE Spain *40°53′N 00°23′W*
61 *B19* **Alcorta** Santa Fe, C Argentina *33°32′S 61°07′W*
104 *H14* **Alcoutim** Faro, S Portugal *37°28′N 07°29′W*
33 *W15* **Alcova** Wyoming, C USA *42°33′N 106°40′W*
105 *S11* **Alcoy** ***Cat.*** Alcoi. Valenciana, E Spain *38°42′N 00°29′W*
105 *Y9* **Alcúdia** Mallorca, Spain, W Mediterranean Sea *39°51′N 03°06′E*
105 *Y9* **Alcúdia, Badia d'** *bay* Mallorca, Spain, W Mediterranean Sea
172 *M7* **Aldabra Group** *island group* SW Seychelles
139 *U10* **Al Daghghārah** Bābil, C Iraq *32°10′N 44°57′E*
40 *J5* **Aldama** Chihuahua, N Mexico *28°50′N 105°52′W*
41 *P11* **Aldama** Tamaulipas, C Mexico *22°54′N 98°05′W*
123 *Q11* **Aldan** Respublika Sakha (Yakutiya), NE Russian Federation *58°31′N 125°15′E*
123 *Q10* **Aldan** ≈ NE Russian Federation
Aldar *see* Aldarhaan
al Dar al Baida *see* Rabat
162 *G7* **Aldarhaan** ***var.*** Aldar. Dzavhan, W Mongolia *47°43′N 96°36′E*
97 *Q20* **Aldeburgh** E England, United Kingdom *52°12′N 01°36′E*
105 *P5* **Aldehuela de Calatañazor** Castilla y León, N Spain *41°42′N 02°46′W*
Aldeia Nova *see* Aldeia Nova de São Bento
104 *H13* **Aldeia Nova de São Bento** ***var.*** Aldeia Nova. Beja, S Portugal *37°55′N 07°24′W*
29 *V11* **Alden** Minnesota, N USA *43°40′N 93°34′W*
184 *N6* **Aldermen Islands, The** *island group* N New Zealand
97 *L25* **Alderney** *island* Channel Islands
97 *N22* **Aldershot** S England, United Kingdom *51°15′N 00°47′W*
21 *R6* **Alderson** West Virginia, NE USA *37°43′N 80°38′W*
Al Dhaid *see* Adh Dhayd
98 *L5* **Aldtsjerk** ***Dutch.*** Oudkerk. Fryslân, N Netherlands *53°16′N 05°52′E*
30 *J11* **Aledo** Illinois, N USA *41°12′N 90°45′W*
76 *H9* **Aleg** Brakna, SW Mauritania *17°03′N 13°53′W*
64 *Q10* **Alegranza** *island* Islas Canarias, Spain, NE Atlantic Ocean
37 *P12* **Alegres Mountain** ▲ New Mexico, SW USA *34°09′N 108°11′W*
61 *F15* **Alegrete** Rio Grande do Sul, S Brazil *29°46′S 55°46′W*
61 *C16* **Alejandra** Santa Fe, C Argentina *29°54′S 59°50′W*
193 *T11* **Alejandro Selkirk, Isla** *island* Islas Juan Fernández, Chile, E Pacific Ocean
124 *I12* **Alëkhovshchina** Leningradskaya Oblast', NW Russian Federation *60°22′N 33°57′E*
39 *O13* **Aleknagik** Alaska, USA *59°16′N 158°37′W*
Aleksandriya *see* Oleksandriya
Aleksandropol' *see* Gyumri
126 *L3* **Aleksandrov** Vladimirskaya Oblast', W Russian Federation *56°24′N 38°42′E*
113 *N14* **Aleksandrovac** Serbia, C Serbia *43°28′N 21°05′E*
127 *R9* **Aleksandrov Gay** Saratovskaya Oblast', W Russian Federation *50°08′N 48°34′E*
127 *U6* **Aleksandrovka** Orenburgskaya Oblast', W Russian Federation *52°47′N 54°14′E*
Aleksandrovka *see* Oleksandrivka
125 *V13* **Aleksandrovsk** Permskiy Kray, NW Russian Federation *59°12′N 57°27′E*
Aleksandrovsk *see* Zaporizhzhya
127 *N14* **Aleksandrovskoye** Stavropol'skiy Kray, SW Russian Federation *44°43′N 42°56′E*
123 *T12* **Aleksandrovsk-Sakhalinskiy** Ostrov Sakhalin, Sakhalinskaya Oblast', SE Russian Federation *50°55′N 142°12′E*
110 *J10* **Aleksandrów Kujawski** Kujawskio-pormorskie, C Poland *52°52′N 18°40′E*
110 *K12* **Aleksandrów Łódzki** Łódzkie, C Poland *51°49′N 19°19′E*
114 *J8* **Aleksandŭr Stamboliyski, Yazovir** ⊠ N Bulgaria
Alekseevka *see* Akkol', Akmola, Kazakhstan
Alekseevka *see* Terekty
145 *P7* **Alekseyevka** ***Kaz.*** Alekseevka. Akmola, N Kazakhstan *53°32′N 69°30′E*
126 *L9* **Alekseyevka** Belgorodskaya, W Russian Federation *50°35′N 38°41′E*
127 *S7* **Alekseyevka** Samarskaya Oblast', W Russian Federation *52°37′N 51°20′E*
Alekseyevka *see* Akkol', Akmola, Kazakhstan
Alekseyevka *see* Terekty, Vostochnyy Kazakhstan, Kazakhstan
127 *R4* **Alekseyevskoye** Respublika Tatarstan, W Russian Federation *55°18′N 50°11′E*
126 *K5* **Aleksin** Tul'skaya Oblast', W Russian Federation *54°30′N 37°08′E*
113 *O14* **Aleksinac** Serbia, SE Serbia *43°33′N 21°43′E*
190 *G11* **Alele** Île Uvea, E Wallis and Futuna *13°14′S 176°09′W*
95 *N20* **Ålem** Kalmar, S Sweden *56°57′N 16°25′E*
102 *L6* **Alençon** Orne, N France *48°26′N 00°04′E*
58 *I12* **Alenquer** Pará, NE Brazil *01°58′S 54°45′W*
38 *G10* **'Alenuihaha Channel** ***var.*** Alenuihaha Channel. *channel* Hawai'i, USA, C Pacific Ocean
Alep/Aleppo *see* Ḥalab
103 *Y15* **Aléria** Corse, France, C Mediterranean Sea *42°06′N 09°29′E*
197 *Q11* **Alert** Ellesmere Island, Nunavut, N Canada *82°28′N 62°13′W*
103 *Q14* **Alès** ***prev.*** Alais. Gard, S France *44°08′N 04°05′E*
116 *G9* **Aleşd** ***Hung.*** Élesd. Bihor, SW Romania *47°03′N 22°22′E*
106 *C9* **Alessandria** ***Fr.*** Alexandrie. Piemonte, N Italy *44°54′N 08°37′E*
Ålestrup *see* Aalestrup
94 *D9* **Ålesund** Møre og Romsdal, S Norway *62°28′N 06°11′E*
108 *E10* **Aletschhorn** ▲ SW Switzerland *46°33′N 08°01′E*
197 *S1* **Aleutian Basin** *undersea feature* Bering Sea *57°00′N 177°00′E*
38 *H17* **Aleutian Islands** *island group* Alaska, USA
39 *P14* **Aleutian Range** ▲▲ Alaska, USA
0 *B5* **Aleutian Trench** *undersea feature* S Bering Sea *57°00′N 177°00′W*
123 *T10* **Alevina, Mys** *cape* E Russian Federation
15 *Q6* **Alex** ≈ Québec, SE Canada
28 *J3* **Alexander** North Dakota, N USA *47°48′N 103°38′W*
39 *W14* **Alexander Archipelago** *island group* Alaska, USA
Alexanderbaai *see* Alexander Bay
83 *D23* **Alexander Bay** ***Afr.*** Alexanderbaai. Northern Cape, W South Africa *28°40′S 16°30′E*
23 *Q5* **Alexander City** Alabama, S USA *32°56′N 85°57′W*
194 *J6* **Alexander Island** *island* Antarctica
Alexander Range *see* Kirghiz Range
183 *O12* **Alexandra** Victoria, SE Australia *37°12′S 145°43′E*
185 *D22* **Alexandra** Otago, South Island, New Zealand *45°15′S 169°25′E*
115 *F14* **Alexándreia** ***var.*** Alexándria. Kentrikí Makedonía, N Greece *40°38′N 22°27′E*
Alexandretta *see* İskenderun
Alexandretta, Gulf of *see* İskenderun Körfezi
15 *N13* **Alexandria** Ontario, SE Canada *45°19′N 74°37′W*
121 *U13* **Alexandria** ***Ar.*** Al Iskandarīyah. N Egypt *31°07′N 29°51′E*
44 *J12* **Alexandria** C Jamaica *18°18′N 77°21′W*
116 *J15* **Alexandria** Teleorman, S Romania *43°58′N 25°18′E*
31 *P13* **Alexandria** Indiana, N USA *40°15′N 85°40′W*
20 *M4* **Alexandria** Kentucky, S USA *38°59′N 84°22′W*
22 *H7* **Alexandria** Louisiana, S USA *31°19′N 92°27′W*
29 *T7* **Alexandria** Minnesota, N USA *45°54′N 95°22′W*
29 *Q11* **Alexandria** South Dakota, N USA *43°39′N 97°46′W*
21 *W4* **Alexandria** Virginia, NE USA *38°49′N 77°06′W*
Alexándria *see* Alexándreia
18 *I7* **Alexandria Bay** New York, NE USA *44°20′N 75°54′W*
Alexandrie *see* Alessandria
182 *J10* **Alexandrina, Lake** ◎ South Australia
114 *K13* **Alexandroúpoli** ***var.*** Alexandroúpolis, ***Turk.*** Dedeagaç, Dedeagach. Anatolikí Makedonía kai Thráki, NE Greece *40°52′N 25°53′E*
Alexandroúpolis *see* Alexandroúpoli
10 *L15* **Alexis Creek** British Columbia, SW Canada *52°06′N 123°25′W*
122 *I13* **Aleysk** Altayskiy Kray, S Russian Federation *52°32′N 82°46′E*
139 *S8* **Al Fallūjah** ***var.*** Falluja. Al Anbār, C Iraq *33°21′N 43°46′E*
105 *R8* **Alfambra** ≈ E Spain
Al Faqa *see* Faq'
141 *R15* **Al Farḍah** C Yemen *14°51′N 48°33′E*
105 *Q4* **Alfaro** La Rioja, N Spain *42°13′N 01°45′W*
105 *U5* **Alfarràs** Cataluña, NE Spain *41°50′N 00°34′E*
Al Fāshir *see* El Fasher
75 *W8* **Al Fashn** ***var.*** El Fashn. C Egypt *28°49′N 30°54′E*
114 *M7* **Alfatar** Silistra, NE Bulgaria *43°56′N 27°17′E*
139 *S5* **Al Fatḥah** Şalāḩ ad Dīn, C Iraq *35°06′N 43°34′E*
139 *Q3* **Al Fatsī** Nīnawá, N Iraq *36°04′N 42°39′E*
139 *Z13* **Al Fāw** ***var.*** Fao. Al Başrah, SE Iraq *29°55′N 48°26′E*
75 *W8* **Al Fayyūm** ***var.*** El Faiyûm. N Egypt *29°19′N 30°50′E*
115 *D20* **Alfeiós** ***prev.*** Alfiós; ***anc.*** Alpheius, Alpheus. ≈ S Greece
100 *I13* **Alfeld** Niedersachsen, C Germany *51°58′N 09°49′E*
Alfiós *see* Alfeiós
Alföld *see* Great Hungarian Plain
94 *C11* **Ålfotbreen** *glacier* S Norway
19 *P9* **Alfred** Maine, NE USA *43°29′N 70°44′W*
18 *F11* **Alfred** New York, NE USA *42°15′N 77°47′W*
61 *K14* **Alfredo Wagner** Santa Catarina, S Brazil *27°40′S 49°22′W*
94 *M12* **Alfta** Gävleborg, C Sweden *61°20′N 16°05′E*
140 *K12* **Al Fuḥayḥīl** ***var.*** Fahaheel. SE Kuwait *29°01′N 48°05′E*
139 *Q6* **Al Fuḥaymī** Al Anbār, C Iraq *34°18′N 42°09′E*
143 *S16* **Al Fujayrah** ***Eng.*** Fujairah. Al Fujayrah, NE United Arab Emirates *25°09′N 56°18′E*
143 *S16* **Al Fujayrah** ***Eng.*** Fujairah. ✈ Al Fujayrah, NE United Arab Emirates *25°04′N 56°12′E*
Al-Furāt *see* Euphrates
144 *I10* **Alga** ***Kaz.*** Algha. Aktyubinsk, NW Kazakhstan *49°56′N 57°19′E*
144 *G9* **Algabas** ***Kaz.*** Alghabas. Zapadnyy Kazakhstan, NW Kazakhstan *50°43′N 52°09′E*
95 *C17* **Ålgård** Rogaland, S Norway *58°45′N 05°52′E*
104 *G14* **Algarve** *cultural region* S Portugal
182 *G3* **Algebuckina Bridge** South Australia *28°03′S 135°48′E*
104 *K16* **Algeciras** Andalucía, SW Spain *36°08′N 05°27′W*
105 *S10* **Algemesí** Valenciana, E Spain *39°11′N 00°27′W*
Al-Genain *see* El Geneina
120 *F9* **Alger** ***var.*** Algiers, El Djazaïr, Al Jazair. ● (Algeria) N Algeria *36°47′N 02°58′E*
74 *H9* **Algeria** ***off.*** Democratic and Popular Republic of Algeria. ◆ *republic* N Africa
Algeria, Democratic and Popular Republic of *see* Algeria
120 *J8* **Algerian Basin** ***var.*** Balearic Plain. *undersea feature* W Mediterranean Sea
Algha *see* Alga
138 *I4* **Al Ghāb** *Valley* NW Syria
141 *X10* **Al Ghābah** ***var.*** Ghaba. C Oman *21°22′N 57°14′E*
Alghabas *see* Algabas
141 *U14* **Al Ghayḍah** E Yemen *16°15′N 52°13′E*
140 *M6* **Al Ghazālah** Ḥā'il, NW Saudi Arabia *26°55′N 41°23′E*
107 *B17* **Alghero** Sardegna, Italy, C Mediterranean Sea *40°34′N 08°19′E*
95 *M20* **Älghult** Kronoberg, S Sweden *57°00′N 15°34′E*
75 *X9* **Al Ghurdaqah** ***var.*** Ghurdaqah, Hurghada. E Egypt *27°17′N 33°47′E*
Algiers *see* Alger
105 *S10* **Alginet** Valenciana, E Spain *39°16′N 00°28′W*
83 *I26* **Algoa Bay** *bay* S South Africa
104 *L15* **Algodonales** Andalucía, S Spain *36°54′N 05°24′W*
105 *N9* **Algodor** ≈ C Spain
Al Golea *see* El Goléa
31 *N6* **Algoma** Wisconsin, N USA *44°41′N 87°24′W*
29 *U12* **Algona** Iowa, C USA *43°04′N 94°13′W*
20 *L8* **Algood** Tennessee, S USA *36°12′N 85°27′W*
105 *O2* **Algorta** País Vasco, N Spain *43°20′N 03°00′W*
61 *E18* **Algorta** Río Negro, W Uruguay *32°26′S 57°18′W*
Al Haba *see* Haba
139 *Q10* **Al Habbārīyah** Al Anbār, S Iraq *32°16′N 42°12′E*
Al Hadhar *see* Al Ḥaḍr
139 *Q4* **Al Ḥaḍr** ***var.*** Al Hadhar; ***anc.*** Hatra. Nīnawýa, NW Iraq *35°34′N 42°44′E*
139 *T13* **Al Ḥajarah** *desert* S Iraq
141 *W8* **Al Ḥajar al Gharbī** ▲▲ N Oman
141 *Y8* **Al Ḥajar ash Sharqī** ▲▲ NE Oman
141 *R15* **Al Hajarayn** C Yemen *15°29′N 48°24′E*
138 *L10* **Al Ḥamād** *desert* Jordan/Saudi Arabia
Al Hamad *see* Syrian Desert
75 *N9* **Al Ḥamādah al Ḥamrā'** ***var.*** Al Ḥamrā'. *desert* NW Libya
105 *N15* **Alhama de Granada** Andalucía, S Spain *37°00′N 03°59′W*
105 *R13* **Alhama de Murcia** Murcia, SE Spain *37°51′N 01°25′W*
35 *T15* **Alhambra** California, W USA *34°08′N 118°06′W*
139 *T12* **Al Ḥammām** An Najaf, S Iraq *31°09′N 44°04′E*
141 *X8* **Al Ḥamrā'** NE Oman *23°07′N 57°23′E*
Al Ḥamrā' *see* Al Ḥamādah al Ḥamrā'
141 *O6* **Al Ḥamūdīyah** *spring/well* N Saudi Arabia *27°05′N 44°24′E*
140 *M7* **Al Ḥanākīyah** Al Madīnah, W Saudi Arabia *24°55′N 40°31′E*
139 *W14* **Al Ḥanīyah** *escarpment* Iraq/Saudi Arabia
139 *Y12* **Al Ḥārithah** Al Başrah, SE Iraq *30°43′N 47°44′E*
140 *L3* **Al Ḥarrah** *desert* NW Saudi Arabia
75 *Q10* **Al Harūj al Aswad** *desert* C Libya
Al Hasaifin *see* Al Ḥusayfin
139 *N2* **Al Ḥasakah** ***var.*** Al Hasijah, El Haseke, ***Fr.*** Hassetché. Al Ḥasakah, NE Syria *36°22′N 40°44′E*
139 *O2* **Al Ḥasakah** ***off.*** Muḥāfaẓat al Ḥasakah, ***var.*** Al Hasakah, Āl Hasakah, Hasakah, Hassakeh. ◈ *governorate* NE Syria
Al Hasakah *see* Al Ḥasakah
Al Hasakah *see* 'Āmūdah
139 *T9* **Al Hāshimīyah** Bābil, C Iraq *32°24′N 44°39′E*
138 *G13* **Al Hāshimīyah** Ma'ān, S Jordan *30°31′N 35°46′E*
Al Hasijah *see* Al Ḥasakah
104 *M15* **Alhaurín el Grande** Andalucía, S Spain *36°39′N 04°41′W*
141 *Q16* **Al Ḥawrā** S Yemen *13°54′N 47°36′E*
139 *V10* **Al Ḥayy** ***var.*** Kut al Hai, Kūt al Ḥayy. Wāsiţ, E Iraq *32°11′N 46°03′E*
141 *U11* **Al Ḥibāk** *desert* E Saudi Arabia
138 *H8* **Al Hījānah** ***var.*** Hejanah, Hijanah. Rīf Dimashq, W Syria *33°23′N 36°34′E*
140 *K7* **Al Ḥijāz** ***Eng.*** Hejaz. *physical region* NW Saudi Arabia
Al Hilbeh *see* 'Ulayyānīyah, Bi'r al
139 *T9* **Al Ḥillah** ***var.*** Hilla. Bābil, C Iraq *32°28′N 44°29′E*
139 *T9* **Al Hindīyah** ***var.*** Hindiya. Bābil, C Iraq *32°32′N 44°14′E*
138 *G12* **Al Ḥisā** Aţ Ţafīlah, W Jordan *30°49′N 35°58′E*
74 *G5* **Al-Hoceïma** ***var.*** al Hoceima, Al-Hoceima, Alhucemas; ***prev.*** Villa Sanjurjo. N Morocco *35°14′N 03°56′W*
Alhucemas *see* Al-Hoceïma
105 *N17* **Alhucemas, Peñon de** *island group* S Spain
141 *N15* **Al Ḥudaydah** ***Eng.*** Hodeida. W Yemen *15°N 42°50′E*
141 *N15* **Al Ḥudaydah** ***var.*** Hodeida. ✈ W Yemen *14°45′N 43°01′E*
140 *M4* **Al Ḥudūd ash Shamālīyah** ***var.*** Minṭaqat al Ḥudūd ash Shamālīyah, ***Eng.*** Northern Border Region. ◈ *province* N Saudi Arabia
141 *S7* **Al Hufūf** ***var.*** Hofuf. Ash Sharqīyah, NE Saudi Arabia *25°21′N 49°34′E*
al-Hurma *see* Al Khurmah
141 *X7* **Al Ḥusayfin** ***var.*** Al Hasaifin. N Oman *24°33′N 56°33′E*
138 *G9* **Al Ḥuṣn** ***var.*** Husn. Irbid, N Jordan *32°29′N 35°53′E*
139 *U9* **'Alī** Wāsiţ, E Iraq *32°43′N 45°21′E*
104 *L10* **Alia** Extremadura, W Spain *39°25′N 05°12′W*
143 *P9* **'Alīābād** Yazd, C Iran *36°55′N 54°33′E*
'Alīābad *see* Qā'emshahr
105 *S7* **Aliaga** Aragón, NE Spain *40°40′N 00°42′W*
136 *B13* **Aliağa** İzmir, W Turkey *38°49′N 26°59′E*
Aliákmon *see* Aliákmonas
115 *F14* **Aliákmonas** ***prev.*** Aliákmon; ***anc.*** Haliacmon. ≈ N Greece
139 *W9* **'Alī al Gharbī** Maysān, E Iraq *32°28′N 46°42′E*
139 *U11* **'Alī al Ḥassūnī** Al Qādisīyah, S Iraq *31°25′N 44°50′E*
115 *G18* **Alíartos** Stereá Elláda, C Greece *38°23′N 23°06′E*
Äli-Bayramlı *see* Şirvan
114 *P12* **Alibey Barajī** ⊠ NW Turkey
77 *S13* **Alibori** ≈ N Benin
112 *M10* **Alibunar** Vojvodina, NE Serbia *45°06′N 20°59′E*
105 *S12* **Alicante** ***Cat.*** Alacant, ***Lat.*** Lucentum. Valenciana, SE Spain *38°21′N 00°29′W*
105 *S12* **Alicante** ◈ *province* Valenciana, SE Spain
105 *S12* **Alicante** ✈ Murcia, E Spain *38°21′N 00°29′W*
83 *I25* **Alice** Eastern Cape, S South Africa *32°47′S 26°50′E*
25 *S14* **Alice** Texas, SW USA *27°45′N 98°06′W*
83 *I25* **Alicedale** Eastern Cape, S South Africa *33°19′S 26°05′E*
65 *B25* **Alice, Mount** *hill* West Falkland, Falkland Islands
107 *P20* **Alice, Punta** *headland* S Italy *39°24′N 17°09′E*
181 *Q7* **Alice Springs** Northern Territory, C Australia *23°42′S 133°52′E*
23 *N4* **Aliceville** Alabama, S USA *33°07′N 88°09′W*
147 *U13* **Alichur** SE Tajikistan *37°49′N 73°45′E*
147 *U14* **Alichuri Janubí, Qatorkŭhi** ***Rus.*** Yuzhno-Alichurskiy Khrebet. ▲▲ SE Tajikistan
147 *U13* **Alichuri Shimolí, Qatorkŭhi** ***Rus.*** Severo-Alichurskiy Khrebet. ▲▲ SE Tajikistan
107 *K22* **Alicudi, Isola** *island* Isole Eolie, S Italy
Alifu Atoll *see* Ari Atoll
43 *W14* **Aligandí** Kuna Yala, NE Panama *09°15′N 78°05′W*
152 *J11* **Alīgarh** Uttar Pradesh, N India *27°54′N 78°04′E*
142 *M7* **Alīgūdarz** Lorestān, W Iran *33°24′N 49°19′E*
163 *U5* **Alihe** ***var.*** Oroqen Zizhiqi. Nei Mongol Zizhiqu, N China *50°34′N 123°40′E*
0 *F12* **Alijos, Islas** *islets* California, SW USA
149 *R6* **'Alī Kbel** ***Pash.*** 'Alī Khēl. Paktīkā, E Afghanistan *33°55′N 69°49′E*
149 *R6* **'Alī Khēl** ***var.*** Ali Khel, Jajı; ***prev.*** 'Alī Kheyl. Paktiyā, SE Afghanistan *33°55′N 69°46′E*
'Alī Khēl *see* 'Alī Kbel, Paktīkā, Afghanistan
Ali Khel *see* 'Alī Kheyl, Paktīā, Afghanistan
'Alī Kheyl *see* 'Alī Khēl
141 *V17* **Al Ikhwān** *island group* SE Yemen
Aliki *see* Alykí
79 *H19* **Alima** ≈ C Congo
Al Imārāt al 'Arabīyahal Muttaḥidah *see* United Arab Emirates
115 *N23* **Alimía** *island* Dodekánisa, Greece, Aegean Sea
55 *V12* **Alimimuni Piek** ▲ S Surinam *02°26′N 55°46′W*
79 *K15* **Alindao** Basse-Kotto, S Central African Republic *04°58′N 21°16′E*
95 *J18* **Alingsås** Västra Götaland, S Sweden *57°55′N 12°30′E*
81 *K18* **Alinjugul** *spring/well* E Kenya *0°03′S 40°31′E*
149 *S11* **Alīpur** Punjab, E Pakistan *29°22′N 70°59′E*
153 *T12* **Alīpur Duār** West Bengal, NE India *26°28′N 89°25′E*
18 *B14* **Aliquippa** Pennsylvania, NE USA *40°36′N 80°15′W*
80 *L12* **'Ali Sabieh** ***var.*** 'Alī Sabīḥ. S Djibouti *11°07′N 42°44′E*
'Alī Sabīḥ *see* 'Ali Sabieh
140 *K3* **Al 'Īsāwīyah** Al Jawf, NW Saudi Arabia *30°41′N 37°58′E*
104 *J10* **Aliseda** Extremadura, W Spain *39°25′N 06°42′W*
139 *T8* **Al Iskandarīyah** Bābil, C Iraq *32°53′N 44°22′E*
Al Iskandarīyah *see* Alexandria
123 *T6* **Aliskerovo** Chukotskiy Avtonomnyy Okrug, NE Russian Federation *67°40′N 167°37′E*
75 *W7* **Al Ismā'īlīya** ***var.*** Ismailia, Ismâ'ilîya. N Egypt *30°32′N 32°13′E*
114 *H13* **Alistráti** Kentrikí Makedonía, NE Greece *41°03′N 23°58′E*
39 *P15* **Alitak Bay** *bay* Kodiak Island, Alaska, USA
Al Ittiḥād *see* Madīnat ash Sha'b
115 *H18* **Alivéri** ***var.*** Alivérion. Évvoia, C Greece *38°24′N 24°02′E*
Alivérion *see* Alivéri
Aliwal-Noord *see* Aliwal North
83 *I24* **Aliwal North** ***Afr.*** Aliwal-Noord. Eastern Cape, SE South Africa *30°42′S 26°43′E*
121 *Q13* **Al Jabal al Akhḍar** ▲▲ NE Libya
138 *H13* **Al Jafr** Ma'ān, S Jordan *30°18′N 36°13′E*
75 *T8* **Al Jaghbūb** NE Libya *29°45′N 24°31′E*
142 *K11* **Al Jahrā'** ***var.*** Al Jahrah, Jahra. C Kuwait *29°18′N 47°36′E*
Al Jahrah *see* Al Jahrā'
Al Jamāhīrīyah al 'Arabīyah al Lībīyah ash Sha'bīyah al Ishtirākīy *see* Libya
140 *K3* **Al Jarāwī** *spring/well* NW Saudi Arabia *30°12′N 38°48′E*
141 *X11* **Al Jawārah** *oasis* SE Oman
140 *L3* **Al Jawf** ***off.*** Jauf. Al Jawf, NW Saudi Arabia *29°51′N 39°49′E*
140 *L4* **Al Jawf** ***var.*** Minṭaqat al Jawf. ◈ *province* N Saudi Arabia
Al Jawlān *see* Golan Heights
Al Jazair *see* Alger
139 *N4* **Al Jazīrah** *physical region* Iraq/Syria
104 *F14* **Aljezur** Faro, S Portugal *37°18′N 08°49′W*
139 *S13* **Al Jīl** An Najaf, S Iraq *30°28′N 43°57′E*
138 *G11* **Al Jīzah** ***var.*** Jiza. 'Ammān, N Jordan *31°42′N 35°57′E*
Al Jīzah *see* Giza
Al Jubail *see* Al Jubayl
141 *S6* **Al Jubayl** ***var.*** Al Jubail. Ash Sharqīyah, NE Saudi Arabia *27°N 49°36′E*
141 *T10* **Āl Juḥaysh, Qalamat** *well* SE Saudi Arabia
143 *N15* **Al Jumaylīyah** N Qatar *25°37′N 51°05′E*
Al Junaynah *see* El Geneina
104 *G13* **Aljustrel** Beja, S Portugal *37°52′N 08°10′W*
Al Kaba'ish *see* Al Chabā'ish
Al-Kadhimain *see* Al Kāẓimīyah
Al Kāf *see* El Kef
Alkal'a *see* Alcalá de Henares
35 *W4* **Alkali Flat** *salt flat* Nevada, W USA
35 *Q1* **Alkali Lake** ◎ Nevada, W USA
141 *Z9* **Al Kāmil** NE Oman *22°14′N 58°15′E*
138 *G11* **Al Karak** ***var.*** El Kerak, Karak, Kerak; ***anc.*** Kir Moab, Kir of Moab. Al Karak, W Jordan *31°11′N 35°42′E*
138 *G12* **Al Karak** ***off.*** Muḥāfaẓat al Karak. ◈ *governorate* W Jordan
139 *W8* **Al Karmashīyah** Wāsiţ, E Iraq *32°57′N 46°10′E*
Al-Kashaniya *see* Al Qash'ānīyah
Al-Kasr al-Kebir *see* Ksar-el-Kebir
139 *T8* **Al Kāẓimīyah** ***var.*** Al-Kadhimain, Kadhimain. Baghdād, C Iraq *33°22′N 44°20′E*
99 *J18* **Alken** Limburg, NE Belgium *50°52′N 05°19′E*
141 *X8* **Al Khābūrah** ***var.*** Khabura. N Oman *23°57′N 57°06′E*
Al Khalīl *see* Hebron
139 *T7* **Al Khāliş** Diyālá, C Iraq *33°51′N 44°33′E*
Al Khaluf *see* Khalūf
75 *W10* **Al Khārijah** ***var.*** El Khârga. C Egypt *25°31′N 30°36′E*
141 *Q8* **Al Kharj** Ar Riyāḍ, C Saudi Arabia *24°12′N 47°12′E*
141 *W6* **Al Khaşab** ***var.*** Khasab. N Oman *26°11′N 56°18′E*
Al Khaur *see* Al Khawr
143 *N15* **Al Khawr** ***var.*** Al Khaur, Al Khor. N Qatar *25°40′N 51°33′E*
142 *K12* **Al Khīrān** ***var.*** Al Khiran. SE Kuwait *28°34′N 48°21′E*
141 *W9* **Al Khīrān** *spring/well* NW Oman *22°31′N 55°42′E*
Al Khiyām *see* El Khiyam
Al-Khobar *see* Al Khubar
Al Khor *see* Al Khawr
141 *S6* **Al Khubar** ***var.*** Al-Khobar. Ash Sharqīyah, NE Saudi Arabia *26°00′N 50°00′E*
120 *M12* **Al Khums** ***var.*** Homs, Khoms, Khums. NW Libya *32°39′N 14°16′E*
141 *R15* **Al Khuraybah** C Yemen *15°05′N 48°17′E*
140 *M9* **Al Khurmah** ***var.*** al-Hurma. Makkah, W Saudi Arabia *21°59′N 42°00′E*
141 *V9* **Al Kidan** *desert* NE Saudi Arabia
127 *V4* **Alkino-2** Respublika Bashkortostan, W Russian Federation *54°30′N 55°40′E*
98 *H9* **Alkmaar** Noord-Holland, NW Netherlands *52°37′N 04°45′E*
139 *T10* **Al Kūfah** ***var.*** Kufa. An Najaf, S Iraq *32°02′N 44°25′E*
75 *T11* **Al Kufrah** SE Libya *24°11′N 23°19′E*
141 *T10* **Al Kursū'** *desert* E Saudi Arabia
139 *V9* **Al Kūt** ***var.*** Kūt al 'Amārah, Kut al Imara. Wāsiţ, E Iraq *32°30′N 45°51′E*
Al-Kuwait *see* Al Kuwayt
Al Kuwayr *see* Guwēr
142 *K11* **Al Kuwayt** ***var.*** Al-Kuwait, ***Eng.*** Kuwait, Kuwait City; ***prev.*** Qurein. ● (Kuwait) E Kuwait *29°23′N 48°00′E*
142 *K11* **Al Kuwayt** ✈ C Kuwait *29°13′N 47°57′E*
115 *G19* **Alkyonidón, Kólpos** *gulf* C Greece
141 *N4* **Al Labbah** *physical region* N Saudi Arabia
138 *G4* **Al Lādhiqīyah** ***Eng.*** Latakia, ***Fr.*** Lattaquié; ***anc.*** Laodicea, Laodicea ad Mare. Al Lādhiqīyah, W Syria *35°31′N 35°47′E*
138 *H4* **Al Lādhiqīyah** ***off.*** Muḥāfaẓat al Ļādhiqīyah, ***var.*** Al Lathqiyah, Latakia, Lattakia. ◈ *governorate* W Syria
19 *R2* **Allagash River** ≈ Maine, NE USA
152 *M13* **Allahābād** Uttar Pradesh, N India *25°27′N 81°50′E*
143 *S3* **Allāh Dāgh, Reshteh-ye** ▲▲ NE Iran
39 *Q8* **Allakaket** Alaska, USA *66°34′N 152°39′W*
141 *X12* **Al Lakbī** S Oman *18°27′N 56°37′E*
11 *T15* **Allan** Saskatchewan, S Canada *51°50′N 105°59′W*
Allanmyo *see* Aunglan
83 *I22* **Allanridge** Free State, C South Africa *27°45′S 26°40′E*
104 *H4* **Allariz** Galicia, NW Spain *42°11′N 07°48′W*
139 *R11* **Al Laşaf** ***var.*** Al Lussuf. An Najaf, S Iraq *31°38′N 43°16′E*
Al Lathqiyah *see* Al Lādhiqīyah
23 *S2* **Allatoona Lake** ⊠ Georgia, SE USA
83 *J19* **Alldays** Limpopo, NE South Africa *22°39′S 29°04′E*
Alle *see* Łyna
31 *P10* **Allegan** Michigan, N USA *42°31′N 85°51′W*
18 *E14* **Allegheny Mountains** ▲▲ NE USA
18 *E12* **Allegheny Plateau** ▲▲ New York/Pennsylvania, NE USA
18 *D11* **Allegheny Reservoir** ⊠ New York/Pennsylvania, NE USA
18 *E12* **Allegheny River** ≈ New York/Pennsylvania, NE USA
22 *K9* **Allemands, Lac des** ◎ Louisiana, S USA
25 *U6* **Allen** Texas, SW USA *33°06′N 96°40′W*
21 *R14* **Allendale** South Carolina, SE USA *33°01′N 81°19′W*
41 *N6* **Allende** Coahuila, NE Mexico *28°22′N 100°50′W*
41 *O9* **Allende** Nuevo León, NE Mexico *25°20′N 100°01′W*
97 *D16* **Allen, Lough** ***Ir.*** Loch Aillionn. ◎ NW Ireland
185 *B26* **Allen, Mount** ▲ Stewart Island, Southland, SW New Zealand *47°05′S 167°49′E*
109 *V2* **Allensteig** Niederösterreich, N Austria *48°40′N 15°24′E*
Allenstein *see* Olsztyn
18 *I14* **Allentown** Pennsylvania, NE USA *40°37′N 75°30′W*
155 *G23* **Alleppey** ***var.*** Alappuzha. Kerala, SW India *09°30′N 76°22′E* ***see also*** Alappuzha
100 *J12* **Aller** ≈ NW Germany
29 *V16* **Allerton** Iowa, C USA *40°42′N 93°22′W*
99 *K19* **Alleur** Liège, E Belgium *50°40′N 05°33′E*
101 *J25* **Allgäuer Alpen** ▲▲ Austria/Germany
28 *J13* **Alliance** Nebraska, C USA *42°08′N 102°54′W*
31 *U12* **Alliance** Ohio, N USA *40°55′N 81°06′W*
103 *O10* **Allier** ◈ *department* N France
139 *R13* **Al Līfīyah** *well* An Najaf, S Iraq
44 *J13* **Alligator Pond** C Jamaica *17°52′N 77°34′W*
21 *Y9* **Alligator River** ≈ North Carolina, SE USA
29 *W12* **Allison** Iowa, C USA *42°45′N 92°48′W*
14 *G14* **Alliston** Ontario, S Canada *44°09′N 79°51′W*
140 *L11* **Al Līth** Makkah, SW Saudi Arabia *21°N 41°E*
Al Liwā' *see* Līwā
96 *J12* **Alloa** C Scotland, United Kingdom *56°07′N 03°49′W*
103 *U14* **Allos** Alpes-de-Haute-Provence, SE France *44°16′N 06°37′E*
108 *D6* **Allschwil** Basel Landschaft, NW Switzerland *47°34′N 07°32′E*
Al Lubnān *see* Lebanon
141 *N14* **Al Luḥayyah** W Yemen *15°44′N 42°45′E*
14 *K12* **Allumettes, Île des** *island* Québec, SE Canada
Al Lussuf *see* Al Laşaf
109 *S5* **Alm** ≈ N Austria
15 *Q7* **Alma** Québec, SE Canada *48°32′N 71°41′W*
27 *S10* **Alma** Arkansas, C USA *35°28′N 94°13′W*
23 *V7* **Alma** Georgia, SE USA *31°32′N 82°27′W*
27 *P4* **Alma** Kansas, C USA *39°01′N 96°17′W*
31 *Q8* **Alma** Michigan, N USA *43°22′N 84°39′W*
29 *O17* **Alma** Nebraska, C USA *40°06′N 99°21′W*
30 *I7* **Alma** Wisconsin, N USA *44°21′N 91°54′W*
139 *R12* **Al Ma'ānīyah** *well* An Najaf, S Iraq
Alma-Ata *see* Almaty
Alma-Atinskaya Oblast' *see* Almaty
105 *T5* **Almacelles** Cataluña, NE Spain *41°44′N 00°26′E*
104 *F11* **Almada** Setúbal, W Portugal *38°40′N 09°09′W*
104 *L11* **Almadén** Castilla-La Mancha, C Spain *38°47′N 04°50′W*
66 *L6* **Almadies, Pointe des** *headland* W Senegal *14°44′N 17°31′W*
140 *L7* **Al Madīnah** ***Eng.*** Medina. Al Madīnah, W Saudi Arabia *24°25′N 39°29′E*
140 *L7* **Al Madīnah** ***off.*** Minṭaqat al Madīnah. ◈ *province* W Saudi Arabia
138 *H9* **Al Mafraq** ***var.*** Mafraq. Al Mafraq, N Jordan *32°20′N 36°12′E*
138 *J10* **Al Mafraq** ***off.*** Muḥāfaẓat al Mafraq. ◈ *governorate* NW Jordan
141 *R15* **Al Maghārīm** C Yemen *15°00′N 47°49′E*
105 *N11* **Almagro** Castilla-La Mancha, C Spain *38°54′N 03°43′W*
Al Maḥallah al Kubrá *see* El Maḥalla el Kubra
139 *T9* **Al Maḥāwīl** ***var.*** Khān al Maḥāwīl. Bābil, C Iraq *32°39′N 44°28′E*
Al Mahdīyah *see* Mahdia
139 *T8* **Al Maḥmūdīyah** ***var.*** Mahmudiya. Baghdād, C Iraq *33°04′N 44°22′E*
141 *T14* **Al Mahrah** ▲▲ E Yemen
141 *P7* **Al Majma'ah** Ar Riyāḍ, C Saudi Arabia *25°55′N 45°19′E*
139 *Q11* **Al Makmīn** *well* S Iraq
139 *Q1* **Al Mālikīyah** ***var.*** Malkiye. Al Ḥasakah, N Syria *37°12′N 42°13′E*
Almalyk *see* Olmaliq
Al Mamlakah *see* Morocco
Al Mamlaka al Urdunīya al Hashemīyah *see* Jordan
143 *Q18* **Al Manādir** ***var.*** Al Manadir. *desert* Oman/United Arab Emirates
142 *L15* **Al Manāmah** ***Eng.*** Manama. ● (Bahrain) N Bahrain *26°13′N 50°33′E*
139 *O5* **Al Manāşif** ▲▲ E Syria
35 *O4* **Almanor, Lake** ⊠ California, W USA
105 *R11* **Almansa** Castilla-La Mancha, C Spain *38°52′N 01°06′W*
75 *W7* **Al Manşūrah** ***var.*** Manşûra, El Manşûra. N Egypt *31°03′N 31°23′E*
104 *L3* **Almanza** Castilla y León, N Spain *42°40′N 05°01′W*
104 *L8* **Almanzor** ▲ W Spain *40°13′N 05°18′W*
105 *P14* **Almanzora** ≈ SE Spain
139 *S9* **Al Mardah** Karbalā', C Iraq *32°35′N 43°30′E*
Al-Mariyya *see* Almería
75 *R7* **Al Marj** ***var.*** Barka, ***It.*** Barce. NE Libya *32°30′N 20°54′E*
138 *L2* **Al Mashrafah** Ar Raqqah, N Syria *36°25′N 39°07′E*
141 *X8* **Al Maşna'ah** ***var.*** Al Muşana'a. NE Oman *23°45′N 57°38′E*
Almassora *see* Almazora
Almatinskaya Oblast' *see* Almaty
145 *U15* **Almaty** ***var.*** Alma-Ata. Almaty, SE Kazakhstan *43°19′N 76°55′E*
145 *S14* **Almaty** ***off.*** Almatinskaya Oblast', ***Kaz.*** Almaty Oblysy; ***prev.*** Alma-Atinskaya Oblast'. ◈ *province* SE Kazakhstan
145 *U15* **Almaty** ✈ Almaty, SE Kazakhstan *43°15′N 76°57′E*
Almaty Oblysy *see* Almaty
al-Mawailih *see* Al Muwayliḥ
139 *R3* **Al Mawşil** ***Eng.*** Mosul. Nīnawá, N Iraq *36°21′N 43°08′E*
139 *N5* **Al Mayādīn** ***var.*** Mayadin, ***Fr.*** Meyadine. Dayr az Zawr, E Syria *35°00′N 40°31′E*
139 *X10* **Al Maymūnah** ***var.*** Maimuna. Maysān, SE Iraq *31°43′N 46°55′E*
141 *N5* **Al Mayyāh** Ḥā'il, N Saudi Arabia *27°57′N 42°53′E*
Al Ma'zam *see* Al Ma'zim
105 *P6* **Almazán** Castilla y León, N Spain *41°29′N 02°31′W*
141 *W8* **Al Ma'zim** ***var.*** Al Ma'zam. NW Oman *23°22′N 56°16′E*
123 *N11* **Almaznyy** Respublika Sakha (Yakutiya), NE Russian Federation *62°19′N 114°14′E*
105 *T9* **Almazora** ***Cat.*** Almassora. Valenciana, E Spain *39°55′N 00°02′W*
Al Mazra' *see* Al Mazra'ah
138 *G11* **Al Mazra'ah** ***var.*** Al Mazra', Mazra'a. Al Karak, W Jordan *31°18′N 35°32′E*
101 *G15* **Alme** ≈ W Germany
104 *I7* **Almeida** Guarda, N Portugal *40°43′N 06°53′W*
104 *G10* **Almeirim** Santarém, C Portugal *39°12′N 08°37′W*
98 *O10* **Almelo** Overijssel, E Netherlands *52°22′N 06°42′E*
105 *S9* **Almenara** Valenciana, E Spain *39°46′N 00°14′W*
105 *P12* **Almenaras** ▲ S Spain *38°31′N 02°27′W*
105 *P5* **Almenar de Soria** Castilla y León, N Spain *41°41′N 02°12′W*
104 *J6* **Almendra, Embalse de** ⊠ Castilla y León, NW Spain
104 *J11* **Almendralejo** Extremadura, W Spain *38°41′N 06°25′W*
98 *J10* **Almere** ***var.*** Almere-stad. Flevoland, C Netherlands *52°22′N 05°12′E*
98 *J10* **Almere-Buiten** Flevoland, C Netherlands *52°24′N 05°15′E*
98 *J10* **Almere-Haven** Flevoland, C Netherlands *52°20′N 05°13′E*
Almere-stad *see* Almere
105 *P15* **Almería** ***Ar.*** Al-Mariyya; ***anc.*** Unci, ***Lat.*** Portus Magnus. Andalucía, S Spain *36°50′N 02°26′W*
105 *P14* **Almería** ◈ *province* Andalucía, S Spain
105 *P15* **Almería, Golfo de** *gulf* S Spain
127 *S5* **Al'met'yevsk** Respublika Tatarstan, W Russian Federation *54°53′N 52°20′E*
95 *L21* **Älmhult** Kronoberg, S Sweden *56°32′N 14°10′E*
141 *U9* **Al Miḥrāḍ** *desert* NE Saudi Arabia
Al Mīnā' *see* El Mina
104 *L17* **Almina, Punta** *headland* Ceuta, Spain, N Africa *35°54′N 05°16′W*
75 *W9* **Al Minyā** ***var.*** El Minya, Minya. C Egypt *28°06′N 30°40′E*
Al Miqdādīyah *see* Al Muqdādīyah
43 *P14* **Almirante** Bocas del Toro, NW Panama *09°20′N 82°22′W*
Almirós *see* Almyrós
140 *M9* **Al Mislaḥ** *spring/well* W Saudi Arabia *22°46′N 40°47′E*
Almissa *see* Omiš
104 *G13* **Almodôvar** ***var.*** Almodóvar. Beja, S Portugal *37°31′N 08°03′W*

◆ Country
● Country Capital
◇ Dependent Territory
○ Dependent Territory Capital
◈ Administrative Regions
✈ International Airport
▲ Mountain
▲▲ Mountain Range
⛰ Volcano
≈ River
◎ Lake
⊠ Reservoir

104 M11 **Almodóvar del Campo** Castilla-La Mancha, C Spain 38°43′N 04°10′W
105 Q9 **Almodóvar del Pinar** Castilla-La Mancha, C Spain 39°44′N 01°55′W
31 S9 **Almont** Michigan, N USA 42°53′N 83°02′W
14 L13 **Almonte** Ontario, SE Canada 45°13′N 76°12′W
104 J14 **Almonte** Andalucía, S Spain 37°16′N 06°31′W
104 K9 **Almonte** ≈ W Spain
152 K9 **Almora** Uttarakhand, N India 29°36′N 79°40′E
104 M8 **Almorox** Castilla-La Mancha, C Spain 40°13′N 04°22′W
141 S7 **Al Mubarraz** Ash Sharqīyah, E Saudi Arabia 25°28′N 49°34′E
Al Muḍaibī see Al Muḍaybī
138 G15 **Al Mudawwarah** Ma'ān, SW Jordan 29°20′N 36°E
141 Y9 **Al Muḍaybī** var. Al Muḍaibī. NE Oman 22°35′N 58°08′E
Almudébar see Almudévar
105 S5 **Almudévar** var. Almudébar. Aragón, NE Spain 42°03′N 00°34′W
141 S15 **Al Mukallā** var. Mukalla. SE Yemen 14°36′N 49°07′E
141 N16 **Al Mukhā** Eng. Mocha. SW Yemen 13°18′N 43°17′E
105 N15 **Almuñécar** Andalucía, S Spain 36°44′N 03°41′W
139 U7 **Al Muqdādīyah** var. Al Miqdādīyah. Diyālá, C Iraq 33°58′N 44°58′E
140 L3 **Al Murayr** spring/well NW Saudi Arabia 30°06′N 39°54′E
136 M12 **Almus** Tokat, N Turkey 40°22′N 36°54′E
Al Muṣana'a see Al Maṣna'ah
139 T9 **Al Musayyib** var. Musaiyib. Bābil, C Iraq 32°47′N 44°20′E
139 V9 **Al Muwaffaqīyah** Wāsiṭ, S Iraq 32°19′N 45°22′E
138 H10 **Al Muwaqqar** var. El Muwaqqar. 'Ammān, W Jordan 31°49′N 36°06′E
140 J5 **Al Muwayliḥ** var. al-Mawailih. Tabūk, NW Saudi Arabia 27°39′N 35°33′E
115 F17 **Almyrós** var. Almirós. Thessalía, C Greece 39°11′N 22°45′E
115 I24 **Almyroú, Órmos** bay Kríti, Greece, E Mediterranean Sea
Al Nūwfalīyah see An Nawfalīyah
96 L13 **Alnwick** N England, United Kingdom 55°27′N 01°44′W
Al Obayyid see El Obeid
Al Odaid see Al 'Udayd
190 B16 **Alofi** ○ (Niue) W Niue 19°01′S 169°55′E
190 A16 **Alofi Bay** bay W Niue, C Pacific Ocean
190 E13 **Alofi, Île** island S Wallis and Futuna
190 E13 **Alofitai** Île Alofi, W Wallis and Futuna 14°21′S 178°03′W
Aloha State see Hawai'i
118 G7 **Aloja** N Latvia 57°47′N 24°53′E
153 X10 **Along** Arunāchal Pradesh, NE India 28°15′N 94°56′E
115 H16 **Alónnisos** island Vóreies Sporádes, Greece, Aegean Sea
104 M15 **Álora** Andalucía, S Spain 36°50′N 04°43′W
171 Q16 **Alor, Kepulauan** island group E Indonesia
171 Q16 **Alor, Pulau** prev. Ombai. island Kepulauan Alor, E Indonesia
171 O16 **Alor, Selat** strait Flores Sea/Savu Sea
168 I7 **Alor Setar** var. Alor Star, Alur Setar. Kedah, Peninsular Malaysia 06°06′N 100°23′E
Alor Star see Alor Setar
Alost see Aalst
154 F9 **Ālot** Madhya Pradesh, C India 23°56′N 75°40′E
186 G10 **Alotau** Milne Bay, SE Papua New Guinea 10°20′S 150°23′E
171 Y16 **Alotip** Papua, E Indonesia 08°07′S 140°06′E
Al Oued see El Oued
35 R12 **Alpaugh** California, W USA 35°52′N 119°29′W
Alpen see Alps
31 R6 **Alpena** Michigan, N USA 45°04′N 83°27′W
Alpes see Alps
103 S14 **Alpes-de-Haute-Provence** ◈ department SE France
103 U14 **Alpes-Maritimes** ◈ department SE France
181 W8 **Alpha** Queensland, E Australia 23°40′S 146°38′E
197 R9 **Alpha Cordillera** var. Alpha Ridge. undersea feature Arctic Ocean 85°30′N 125°00′W
Alpha Ridge see Alpha Cordillera
Alpheius see Alfeiós
99 I15 **Alphen** Noord-Brabant, S Netherlands 51°29′N 04°57′E
Alphen see Alphen aan den Rijn
98 H11 **Alphen aan den Rijn** var. Alphen. Zuid-Holland, C Netherlands 52°08′N 04°40′E
Alpheus see Alfeiós
Alpi see Alps
104 G10 **Alpiarça** Santarém, C Portugal 39°15′N 08°35′W
24 K10 **Alpine** Texas, SW USA 30°22′N 103°40′W
108 F8 **Alpnach** Unterwalden, W Switzerland 46°56′N 08°17′E
108 D11 **Alps** Fr. Alpes, Ger. Alpen, It. Alpi. ▲▲ C Europe
141 W8 **Al Qābil** var. Qabil. N Oman 23°55′N 55°50′E
Al Qaḍārif see Gedaref
75 P8 **Al Qaddāḥiyah** N Libya 31°21′N 15°16′E
Al Qāhirah see Cairo
140 K4 **Al Qalībah** Tabūk, NW Saudi Arabia 28°29′N 37°40′E
139 O1 **Al Qāmishlī** var. Kamishli, Qamishly. Al Ḥasakah, NE Syria 37°N 41°E
138 I6 **Al Qaryatayn** var. Qaryatayn, Fr. Qariateïne. Ḥimṣ, C Syria 34°13′N 37°13′E
142 K11 **Al Qash'āniyah** var. Al-Kashaniya. NE Kuwait 29°59′N 47°42′E
141 N7 **Al Qaşīm** var. Minṭaqat Qaşīm, Qassim. ◈ province C Saudi Arabia
75 V10 **Al Qaşr** var. Al Qaşr var. El Qaşr. C Egypt 25°43′N 28°54′E
138 J5 **Al Qaşr** Ḥimṣ, C Syria 35°06′N 37°39′E
Al Qaşr see Al Qaşr
Al Qaşrayn see Kasserine
141 S6 **Al Qaṭīf** Ash Sharqīyah, NE Saudi Arabia 26°27′N 50°01′E
138 G11 **Al Qaṭrānah** var. El Qatrani, Qatrana. Al Karak, W Jordan 31°14′N 36°03′E
75 P11 **Al Qaṭrūn** SW Libya 24°57′N 14°40′E
Al Qayrawān see Kairouan
Al-Qsar al-Kbir see Ksar-el-Kebir
Al Qubayyāt see Qoubaïyât
Al Quds/Al Quds ash Sharīf see Jerusalem
104 H12 **Alqueva, Barragem do** ⊞ Portugal/Spain
138 G8 **Al Qunayṭirah** var. El Kuneitra, El Quneitra, Kuneitra, Qunaytra. Al Qunayṭirah, SW Syria 33°08′N 35°49′E
138 G8 **Al Qunayṭirah** off. Muḥāfaẓat al Qunayṭirah, var. El Q'unayṭirah, Qunaytirah, Fr. Kuneitra. ◈ governorate SW Syria
140 M11 **Al Qunfudhah** Makkah, SW Saudi Arabia 19°19′N 41°03′E
140 K2 **Al Qurayyāt** Al Jawf, NW Saudi Arabia 31°25′N 37°26′E
139 Y11 **Al Qurnah** var. Kurna. Al Baṣrah, SE Iraq 31°01′N 47°27′E
75 Y10 **Al Quşayr** var. Al Quşayr var. Qusair, Quseir. E Egypt 26°05′N 34°16′E
139 V12 **Al Quşayr** Al Muthannā, S Iraq 30°36′N 45°52′E
138 I6 **Al Quşayr** var. El Quseir, Quşayr, Fr. Kousseir. Ḥimṣ, W Syria 34°36′N 36°36′E
Al Quşayr see Al Quşayr
138 H7 **Al Quṭayfah** var. Quṭayfe, Quteife, Fr. Kouteifé. Rīf Dimashq, W Syria 33°44′N 36°33′E
141 P8 **Al Quwayʻiyah** Ar Riyāḍ, C Saudi Arabia 24°06′N 45°18′E
Al Quwayr see Guwêr
138 F14 **Al Quwayrah** var. El Quweira. Al 'Aqabah, SW Jordan 29°47′N 35°18′E
Al Rayyan see Ar Rayyān
Al Ruweis see Ar Ruways
95 G24 **Als** Ger. Alsen. island SW Denmark
103 U5 **Alsace** Ger. Elsass; anc. Alsatia. ◈ region NE France
11 R16 **Alsask** Saskatchewan, S Canada 51°24′N 109°55′W
Alsasua see Altsasu
Alsatia see Alsace
101 C16 **Alsdorf** Nordrhein-Westfalen, W Germany 50°52′N 06°09′E
10 G8 **Alsek** ≈ Canada/USA
Alsen see Als
101 F19 **Alsenz** ≈ W Germany
101 H17 **Alsfeld** Hessen, C Germany 50°45′N 09°14′E
119 K20 **Al'shany** Rus. Ol'shany. Brestskaya Voblasts', SW Belarus 52°05′N 27°21′E
Alsókubin see Dolný Kubín
118 C9 **Alsunga** W Latvia 56°59′N 21°31′E
Alt see Olt
92 K9 **Alta** Fin. Alattio. Finnmark, N Norway 69°58′N 23°17′E
29 T12 **Alta** Iowa, C USA 42°40′N 95°17′W
108 I7 **Altach** Vorarlberg, W Austria 47°22′N 09°39′E
92 K9 **Altaelva** Lapp. Álaheaieatnu. ≈ N Norway
92 J8 **Altafjorden** fjord NE Norwegian Sea
62 K10 **Alta Gracia** Córdoba, C Argentina 31°42′S 64°25′W
42 K11 **Alta Gracia** Rivas, SW Nicaragua 11°35′N 85°38′W
54 H4 **Altagracia** Zulia, NW Venezuela 10°44′N 71°30′W
54 M5 **Altagracia de Orituco** Guárico, N Venezuela 09°54′N 66°24′W
Altai see Altai Mountains
129 T7 **Altai Mountains** var. Altai, Chin. Altay Shan, Rus. Altay. ▲▲ Asia/Europe
23 V6 **Altamaha River** ≈ Georgia, SE USA
58 J13 **Altamira** Pará, NE Brazil 03°13′S 52°15′W
54 D12 **Altamira** Huila, S Colombia 02°04′N 75°47′W
42 M13 **Altamira** Alajuela, N Costa Rica 10°25′N 84°21′W
41 Q11 **Altamira** Tamaulipas, C Mexico 22°25′N 97°55′W
30 L15 **Altamont** Illinois, N USA 39°03′N 88°45′W
27 Q7 **Altamont** Kansas, C USA 37°11′N 95°18′W
32 H16 **Altamont** Oregon, NW USA 42°12′N 121°44′W
20 K10 **Altamont** Tennessee, S USA 35°28′N 85°42′W
23 X11 **Altamonte Springs** Florida, SE USA 28°39′N 81°22′W
107 O17 **Altamura** anc. Lupatia. Puglia, SE Italy 40°50′N 16°33′E
40 H9 **Altamura, Isla** island C Mexico
Altan see Erdenehayrhan
Altanbulag see Bayanhayrhan
163 Q7 **Altan Emel** var. Xin Barag Youqi. Nei Mongol Zizhiqu, N China 48°37′N 116°40′E
Altan-Ovoo see Tsenher
163 N9 **Altanshiree** var. Chamdmani. Dornigovĭ, SE Mongolia 45°36′N 110°30′E
Altanteel see Dzereg
162 D5 **Altantsögts** var. Tsagaantüngi. Bayan-Ölgiy, NW Mongolia 49°06′N 90°26′E
40 F3 **Altar** Sonora, NW Mexico 30°41′N 111°53′W
40 D2 **Altar, Desierto de** var. Sonoran Desert. desert Mexico/USA see also Sonoran Desert
Altar, Desierto de see Sonoran Desert
105 Q8 **Alta, Sierra** ▲ N Spain 40°29′N 01°36′W
40 H9 **Altata** Sinaloa, C Mexico 24°40′N 107°54′W
42 D4 **Alta Verapaz** off. Departamento de Alta Verapaz. ◈ department C Guatemala
Alta Verapaz, Departamento de see Alta Verapaz
107 L18 **Altavilla Silentia** Campania, S Italy 40°32′N 15°06′E
21 T7 **Altavista** Virginia, NE USA 37°06′N 79°17′W
158 L2 **Altay** Xinjiang Uygur Zizhiqu, NW China 47°51′N 88°06′E
162 D6 **Altay** var. Chihertey. Bayan-Ölgiy, W Mongolia 48°10′N 89°35′E
162 G8 **Altay** prev. Yösönbulag. Govĭ-Altay, W Mongolia 46°23′N 96°17′E
162 E8 **Altay** var. Bor-Üdzüür. Hovd, W Mongolia 45°46′N 92°13′E
Altay see Altai Mountains, Asia/Europe
Altay see Bayantes, Mongolia
122 J14 **Altay, Respublika** var. Gornyy Altay; prev. Gorno-Altayskaya Respublika. ◈ autonomous republic S Russian Federation
Altay Shan see Altai Mountains
123 I13 **Altayskiy Kray** ◈ territory S Russian Federation
Altbetsche see Bečej
101 L20 **Altdorf** Bayern, SE Germany 49°23′N 11°22′E
108 G8 **Altdorf** var. Altorf. Uri, C Switzerland 46°53′N 08°38′E
105 T11 **Altea** Valenciana, E Spain 38°37′N 00°03′W
100 L10 **Alte Elde** ≈ N Germany
101 M16 **Altenburg** Thüringen, E Germany 50°59′N 12°27′E
Altenburg see Bucureşti, Romania
Altenburg see Baia de Criş, Romania
100 P12 **Alte Oder** ≈ NE Germany
104 H10 **Alter do Chão** Portalegre, C Portugal 39°12′N 07°40′W
92 I10 **Altevatnet** Lapp. Álttesjávri. ◎ N Norway
27 V12 **Altheimer** Arkansas, C USA 34°19′N 91°51′W
109 T9 **Althofen** Kärnten, S Austria 46°52′N 14°27′E
114 H7 **Altimir** Vratsa, NW Bulgaria 43°33′N 23°48′E
136 K11 **Altınkaya Barajı** ⊞ N Turkey
139 S3 **Altin Köprü** var. Altun Kupri. At Ta'mīm, N Iraq 35°50′N 44°10′E
136 E13 **Altıntaş** Kütahya, W Turkey 39°05′N 30°07′E
57 K18 **Altiplano** physical region W South America
Altkanischa see Kanjiža
103 U7 **Altkirch** Haut-Rhin, NE France 47°37′N 07°14′E
Altlublau see Stará L'ubovňa
100 L12 **Altmark** cultural region N Germany
Altmoldowa see Moldova Veche
25 W8 **Alto** Texas, SW USA 31°39′N 95°04′W
104 H11 **Alto Alentejo** physical region S Portugal
59 I19 **Alto Araguaia** Mato Grosso, C Brazil 17°19′S 53°10′W
58 L12 **Alto Bonito** Pará, NE Brazil 01°48′S 46°18′W
83 O15 **Alto Molócuè** Zambézia, NE Mozambique 15°38′S 37°42′E
30 K15 **Alton** Illinois, N USA 38°53′N 90°10′W
27 W8 **Alton** Missouri, C USA 36°41′N 91°25′W
11 X17 **Altona** Manitoba, S Canada 49°06′N 97°35′W
18 E14 **Altoona** Pennsylvania, NE USA 40°32′N 78°23′W
30 J6 **Altoona** Wisconsin, N USA 44°49′N 91°22′W
62 N3 **Alto Paraguay** off. Departamento del Alto Paraguay. ◈ department N Paraguay
Alto Paraguay, Departamento del see Alto Paraguay
59 L17 **Alto Paraíso de Goiás** Goiás, S Brazil 14°04′S 47°15′W
62 P6 **Alto Paraná** off. Departamento del Alto Paraná. ◈ department E Paraguay
Alto Paraná see Paraná
Alto Paraná, Departamento del see Alto Paraná
59 L15 **Alto Parnaíba** Maranhão, E Brazil 09°08′S 45°56′W
56 H13 **Alto Purús, Río** ≈ E Peru
Altorf see Altdorf
63 H19 **Alto Río Senguer** var. Alto Río Senguerr. Chubut, S Argentina 45°01′S 70°55′W
Alto Río Senguerr see Alto Río Senguer
41 Q13 **Altotonga** Veracruz-Llave, E Mexico 19°46′N 97°14′W
101 N23 **Altötting** Bayern, SE Germany 48°12′N 12°37′E
Altpasua see Stara Pazova
Altraga see Bayandzürh
105 P3 **Altsasu** Cast. Alsasua. Navarra, N Spain 42°54′N 02°10′W
Alt-Schwanenburg see Gulbene
Altsohl see Zvolen
108 I7 **Altstätten** Sankt Gallen, NE Switzerland 47°22′N 09°33′E
Álttesjávri see Altevatnet
42 G1 **Altun Ha** ruins Belize, N Belize
Altun Kupri see Altin Köprü
158 D8 **Altun Shan** ▲ C China 39°19′N 93°37′E
158 L9 **Altun Shan** var. Altyn Tagh. ▲▲ NW China
35 P2 **Alturas** California, W USA 41°28′N 120°32′W
26 K12 **Altus** Oklahoma, C USA 34°39′N 99°21′W
26 K11 **Altus Lake** ⊞ Oklahoma, C USA
Altvater see Praděd
Altyn Tagh see Altun Shan
Alu see Shortland Island
al-'Ubaila see Al 'Ubaylah
139 O6 **Al 'Ubaydī** Al Anbār, W Iraq 34°22′N 41°15′E
141 T9 **Al 'Ubaylah** var. al-'Ubaila. Ash Sharqīyah, E Saudi Arabia 22°02′N 50°57′E
141 T9 **Al 'Ubaylah** spring/well E Saudi Arabia 22°02′N 50°56′E
Al Ubayyiḍ see El Obeid
141 T7 **Al 'Udayd** var. Al Odaid. Abū Ẓaby, W United Arab Emirates 24°34′N 51°27′E
118 J8 **Alūksne** Ger. Marienburg. NE Latvia 57°26′N 27°02′E
140 K6 **Al 'Ulā** Al Madīnah, NW Saudi Arabia 26°39′N 37°55′E
173 N4 **Alula-Fartak Trench** var. Illaue Fartak Trench. undersea feature W Indian Ocean 14°04′N 51°47′E
138 I11 **Al 'Umarī** 'Ammān, E Jordan 37°30′N 31°30′E
31 S13 **Alum Creek Lake** ⊞ Ohio, N USA
63 H15 **Aluminé** Neuquén, C Argentina 39°15′S 71°00′W
95 O14 **Alunda** Uppsala, C Sweden 60°04′N 18°04′E
117 T14 **Alupka** Avtonomna Respublika Krym, S Ukraine 44°24′N 34°01′E
75 P8 **Al 'Uqaylah** N Libya 30°13′N 19°12′E
Al Uqşur see Luxor
Al Urdunn see Jordan
168 J9 **Alur Panal** bay Sumatera, W Indonesia
Alur Setar see Alor Setar
141 V10 **Al 'Urūq al Mu'tariḍah** salt lake SE Saudi Arabia
139 Q7 **Ālūs** Al Anbār, C Iraq 34°05′N 42°27′E
117 T13 **Alushta** Avtonomna Respublika Krym, S Ukraine 44°41′N 34°24′E
151 G22 **Aluva** var. Alwaye. Kerala, SW India 10°06′N 76°23′E see also Alwaye
75 N11 **Al 'Uwaynāt** var. Al Awaynāt. SW Libya 25°47′N 10°34′E
139 T6 **Al 'Uẓaym** var. Adhaim. Diyālá, E Iraq 34°12′N 44°31′E
26 L8 **Alva** Oklahoma, C USA 36°48′N 98°40′W
104 H8 **Alva** ≈ N Portugal
95 J18 **Älvängen** Västra Götaland, S Sweden 57°56′N 12°09′E
14 F14 **Alvanley** Ontario, S Canada 44°33′N 81°05′W
41 S14 **Alvarado** Veracruz-Llave, E Mexico 18°47′N 95°45′W
25 T7 **Alvarado** Texas, SW USA 32°24′N 97°12′W
58 D13 **Alvarães** Amazonas, NW Brazil 03°13′S 64°53′W
40 G6 **Álvaro Obregón, Presa** ⊞ W Mexico
94 H10 **Alvdal** Hedmark, S Norway 62°07′N 10°39′E
94 K12 **Älvdalen** Dalarna, C Sweden 61°13′N 14°04′E
61 E15 **Alvear** Corrientes, NE Argentina 29°05′S 56°35′W
104 F10 **Alverca do Ribatejo** Lisboa, C Portugal 38°56′N 09°01′W
95 L20 **Alvesta** Kronoberg, S Sweden 56°52′N 14°34′E
25 W12 **Alvin** Texas, SW USA 29°25′N 95°14′W
94 O13 **Älvkarleby** Uppsala, C Sweden 60°34′N 17°30′E
25 S5 **Alvord** Texas, SW USA 33°22′N 97°39′W
93 G18 **Älvros** Jämtland, C Sweden 62°04′N 14°30′E
92 J13 **Älvsbyn** Norrbotten, N Sweden 65°41′N 21°00′E
142 K12 **Al Wafrā'** SE Kuwait 28°38′N 47°57′E
140 J6 **Al Wajh** Tabūk, NW Saudi Arabia 26°16′N 36°30′E
143 N16 **Al Wakrah** var. Wakra. C Qatar 25°09′N 51°36′E
138 M8 **al Walaj, Sha'īb** dry watercourse W Iraq
152 I11 **Alwar** Rājasthān, N India 27°32′N 76°35′E
141 Q5 **Al Wari'ah** Ash Sharqīyah, N Saudi Arabia 27°54′N 47°23′E
155 G22 **Alwaye** var. Aluva. Kerala, SW India 10°06′N 76°23′E see also Aluva
Alxa Zuoqi see Bayan Hot
Alx Youqi see Ehen Hudag
Al Yaman see Yemen
138 G9 **Al Yarmūk** Irbid, N Jordan 32°41′N 35°55′E
Alyat/Alyaty-Pristan' see Älät
115 I14 **Alykí** var. Aliki. Thásos, N Greece 40°36′N 24°45′E
119 F14 **Alytus** Pol. Olita. Alytus, S Lithuania 54°24′N 24°02′E
119 F15 **Alytus** ◈ province S Lithuania
101 N23 **Alz** ≈ SE Germany
33 Y11 **Alzada** Montana, NW USA 45°00′N 104°24′W
122 L12 **Alzamay** Irkutskaya Oblast', S Russian Federation 55°33′N 98°36′E
99 M25 **Alzette** ≈ S Luxembourg
105 S10 **Alzira** var. Alcira; anc. Saetabicula, Suero. Valenciana, E Spain 39°10′N 00°27′W
Al Zubair see Az Zubayr
181 O8 **Amadeus, Lake** seasonal lake Northern Territory, C Australia
81 E15 **Amadi** Western Equatoria, SW South Sudan 05°32′N 30°20′E
9 R7 **Amadjuak Lake** ◎ Baffin Island, Nunavut, N Canada
95 J23 **Amager** island E Denmark
165 N14 **Amagi-san** ▲ Honshū, S Japan 34°51′N 138°57′E
171 S13 **Amahai** var. Masohi. Pulau Seram, E Indonesia 03°19′S 128°56′E
38 M16 **Amak Island** island Alaska, USA
164 C15 **Amakusa** prev. Hondo. Kumamoto, Shimo-jima, SW Japan 32°28′N 130°12′E
164 B14 **Amakusa-nada** gulf SW Japan
95 J16 **Åmål** Västra Götaland, S Sweden 59°04′N 12°41′E
54 E8 **Amalfi** Antioquia, N Colombia 06°54′N 75°04′W
107 L18 **Amalfi** Campania, S Italy 40°37′N 14°35′E
115 D19 **Amaliáda** var. Amaliás. Dytikí Elláda, S Greece 37°48′N 21°21′E
Amaliás see Amaliáda
154 F12 **Amalner** Mahārāshtra, C India 21°03′N 75°04′E
171 W14 **Amamapare** Papua, E Indonesia 04°51′S 136°44′E
59 H21 **Amambaí, Serra de** var. Cordillera de Amambay, Serra de Amambay. ▲ Brazil/Paraguay see also Amambay, Cordillera de
62 P4 **Amambay** off. Departamento del Amambay. ◈ department E Paraguay
62 P5 **Amambay, Cordillera de** var. Serra de Amambaí, Serra de Amambay. ▲ Brazil/Paraguay see also Amambaí, Serra de
Amambay, Departamento del see Amambay
Amambay, Serra de see Amambaí, Serra de/Amambay, Cordillera de
165 U16 **Amami-guntō** island group SW Japan
165 V15 **Amami-Ō-shima** island S Japan
186 A5 **Amanab** Sandaun, NW Papua New Guinea 03°38′S 141°16′E
106 J13 **Amandola** Marche, C Italy 42°58′N 13°22′E
107 N21 **Amantea** Calabria, SW Italy 39°06′N 16°05′E
191 W10 **Amanu** island Îles Tuamotu, C French Polynesia
58 J10 **Amapá** Amapá, NE Brazil 02°00′N 50°50′W
58 J11 **Amapá** off. Estado de Amapá; prev. Território de Amapá. ◈ state NE Brazil
Amapá, Estado de see Amapá
42 H8 **Amapala** Valle, S Honduras 13°16′N 87°39′W
Amapá, Território de see Amapá
80 J12 **Āmara** var. Amhara. ◈ N Ethiopia
Amara see Al 'Amārah
104 H6 **Amarante** Porto, N Portugal 41°16′N 08°05′W
166 M5 **Amarapura** Mandalay, C Burma (Myanmar) 21°54′N 96°01′E
Amardalay see Delgertsogt
104 I12 **Amareleja** Beja, S Portugal 38°12′N 07°13′W
35 V11 **Amargosa Range** ▲▲ California, W USA
25 N2 **Amarillo** Texas, SW USA 35°13′N 101°50′W
Amarinthos see Amárynthos
107 K15 **Amaro, Monte** ▲ C Italy 42°03′N 14°06′E
115 H18 **Amárynthos** var. Amarinthos. Évvoia, C Greece 38°24′N 23°53′E
Amasia see Amasya
136 K12 **Amasya** anc. Amasia. Amasya, N Turkey 40°37′N 35°50′E
136 K11 **Amasya** ◈ province N Turkey
42 F4 **Amatique, Bahía de** bay Gulf of Honduras, W Caribbean Sea
42 D6 **Amatitlán, Lago de** ◎ S Guatemala
107 J14 **Amatrice** Lazio, C Italy 42°38′N 13°19′E
190 C8 **Amatuku** atoll C Tuvalu
99 J20 **Amay** Liège, E Belgium 50°33′N 05°19′E
48 F7 **Amazon** Sp. Amazonas. ≈ Brazil/Peru
59 C14 **Amazonas** off. Estado do Amazonas. ◈ state N Brazil
54 G15 **Amazonas** off. Comisaria del Amazonas. ◈ province SE Colombia
56 C10 **Amazonas** off. Departamento de Amazonas. ◈ department N Peru
54 M12 **Amazonas** off. Territorio Amazonas. ◈ federal territory S Venezuela
Amazonas see Amazon
Amazonas, Comisaria del see Amazonas
Amazonas, Departamento de see Amazonas
Amazonas, Estado do see Amazonas
Amazonas, Territorio see Amazonas
48 F7 **Amazon Basin** basin N South America
47 V5 **Amazon Fan** undersea feature W Atlantic Ocean 05°00′N 47°30′W
58 K11 **Amazon, Mouths of the** delta NE Brazil
187 R13 **Ambae** var. Aoba, Omba. island C Vanuatu
152 I9 **Ambāla** Haryāna, NW India 30°19′N 76°49′E
155 J26 **Ambalangoda** Southern Province, SW Sri Lanka 06°14′N 80°03′E
155 K26 **Ambalantota** Southern Province, S Sri Lanka 06°07′N 81°01′E
172 I6 **Ambalavao** Fianarantsoa, C Madagascar 21°50′S 46°56′E
54 E10 **Ambalema** Tolima, C Colombia 04°49′N 74°48′W
79 E17 **Ambam** Sud, S Cameroon 02°23′N 11°17′E
172 J2 **Ambanja** Antsiranana, N Madagascar 13°40′S 48°27′E
123 T6 **Ambarchik** Respublika Sakha (Yakutiya), NE Russian Federation 69°33′N 162°08′E
62 K9 **Ambargasta, Salinas de** salt lake C Argentina
124 J6 **Ambarnyy** Respublika Kareliya, NW Russian Federation 65°53′N 33°44′E
56 C7 **Ambato** Tungurahua, C Ecuador 01°18′S 78°39′W
172 I6 **Ambato Finandrahana** Fianarantsoa, SE Madagascar 20°33′S 46°48′E
172 I5 **Ambatolampy** Antananarivo, C Madagascar 19°21′S 47°27′E
172 H4 **Ambatomainty** Mahajanga, W Madagascar 17°40′S 45°39′E
172 J4 **Ambatondrazaka** Toamasina, C Madagascar 17°49′S 48°28′E
101 L20 **Amberg** var. Amberg in der Oberpfalz. Bayern, SE Germany 49°26′N 11°52′E
Amberg in der Oberpfalz see Amberg
42 H1 **Ambergris Cay** island NE Belize
103 S11 **Ambérieu-en-Bugey** Ain, E France 45°57′N 05°21′E
185 I18 **Amberley** Canterbury, South Island, New Zealand 43°09′S 172°43′E
103 P11 **Ambert** Puy-de-Dôme, C France 45°33′N 03°45′E
Ambianum see Amiens
76 J11 **Ambidédi** Kayes, SW Mali 14°37′N 11°49′W
154 M10 **Ambikāpur** Chhattīsgarh, C India 23°09′N 83°12′E
172 J2 **Ambilobe** Antsiranana, N Madagascar 13°10′S 49°03′E
39 O7 **Ambler** Alaska, USA 67°05′N 157°51′W
Amblève see Amel
Ambo see Hägere Hiywet
172 I8 **Amboasary** Toliara, S Madagascar 25°01′S 46°23′E
172 J4 **Ambodifotatra** var. Ambodifototra. Toamasina, E Madagascar 16°59′S 49°51′E
Amboenten see Ambunten
172 I5 **Ambohidratrimo** Antananarivo, C Madagascar 18°48′S 47°26′E
172 I6 **Ambohimahasoa** Fianarantsoa, SE Madagascar 21°07′S 47°13′E
172 K3 **Ambohitralanana** Antsirañana, NE Madagascar 15°13′S 50°28′E
Amboina see Ambon
102 M8 **Amboise** Indre-et-Loire, C France 47°25′N 01°00′E
171 S13 **Ambon** prev. Amboina, Amboyna. Pulau Ambon, E Indonesia 03°41′S 128°10′E
171 S13 **Ambon, Pulau** island E Indonesia
81 I20 **Amboseli, Lake** ◎ Kenya/Tanzania
172 I6 **Ambositra** Fianarantsoa, SE Madagascar 20°31′S 47°15′E
172 I8 **Ambovombe** Toliara, S Madagascar 25°10′S 46°06′E
35 W14 **Amboy** California, W USA 34°33′N 115°44′W
30 L11 **Amboy** Illinois, N USA 41°42′N 89°19′W
Amboyna see Ambon
Ambracia see Árta
Ambre, Cap d' see Bobaomby, Tanjona
18 B14 **Ambridge** Pennsylvania, NE USA 40°33′N 80°11′W
Ambrim see Ambrym
82 A11 **Ambriz** Bengo, NW Angola 07°55′S 13°11′E
Ambrizete see N'Zeto
187 R13 **Ambrym** var. Ambrim. island C Vanuatu
169 T16 **Ambunten** prev. Amboenten. Pulau Madura, E Indonesia 06°55′S 113°45′E
186 B6 **Ambunti** East Sepik, NW Papua New Guinea 04°12′S 142°49′E
155 I20 **Āmbūr** Tamil Nādu, SE India 12°48′N 78°44′E
38 E17 **Amchitka Island** island Aleutian Islands, Alaska, USA
38 F17 **Amchitka Pass** strait Aleutian Islands, Alaska, USA
141 R15 **'Amd** C Yemen 15°10′N 47°58′E
78 J10 **Am Dam** Ouaddaï, E Chad 12°46′N 20°29′E
171 U16 **Amdassa** Pulau Yamdena, E Indonesia 07°40′S 131°24′E
125 U1 **Amderma** Nenetskiy Avtonomnyy Okrug, NW Russian Federation 69°45′N 61°36′E
159 N14 **Amdo** Xizang Zizhiqu, W China 32°15′N 91°43′E
40 K13 **Ameca** Jalisco, SW Mexico 20°34′N 104°03′W
41 P14 **Amecameca** var. Amecameca de Juárez. México, C Mexico 19°08′N 98°48′W
Amecameca de Juárez see Amecameca
61 A20 **Ameghino** Buenos Aires, E Argentina 34°51′S 62°28′W
99 M21 **Amel** Fr. Amblève. Liège, E Belgium 50°20′N 06°13′E
98 K4 **Ameland** Fris. It Amelân. island Waddeneilanden, N Netherlands
Amelân, It see Ameland
107 H14 **Amelia** Umbria, C Italy 42°33′N 12°26′E
21 V6 **Amelia Court House** Virginia, NE USA 37°20′N 77°59′W
23 W8 **Amelia Island** island Florida, SE USA
18 L12 **Amenia** New York, NE USA 41°51′N 73°31′W
America see United States of America
65 M21 **America-Antarctica Ridge** undersea feature S Atlantic Ocean
America in Miniature see Maryland
60 L9 **Americana** São Paulo, S Brazil 22°44′S 47°19′W
33 Q15 **American Falls** Idaho, NW USA 42°47′N 112°51′W
33 Q15 **American Falls Reservoir** ⊞ Idaho, NW USA
36 L3 **American Fork** Utah, W USA 40°24′N 111°47′W
192 K16 **American Samoa** ◇ US unincorporated territory W Polynesia
23 S6 **Americus** Georgia, SE USA 32°04′N 84°13′W
98 K12 **Amerongen** Utrecht, C Netherlands 52°00′N 05°30′E
98 K11 **Amersfoort** Utrecht, C Netherlands 52°09′N 05°23′E
97 N21 **Amersham** SE England, United Kingdom 51°40′N 00°37′W
30 I5 **Amery** Wisconsin, N USA 45°18′N 92°20′W
195 W6 **Amery Ice Shelf** ice shelf Antarctica
29 V13 **Ames** Iowa, C USA 42°01′N 93°37′W
19 P10 **Amesbury** Massachusetts, NE USA 42°51′N 70°55′W
Amestratus see Mistretta
115 F18 **Amfíkleia** var. Amfiklia. Stereá Elláda, C Greece 38°38′N 22°35′E
Amfiklia see Amfíkleia
115 D17 **Amfilochía** var. Amfilokhía. Dytikí Elláda, C Greece 38°52′N 21°09′E
Amfilokhía see Amfilochía
114 H13 **Amfípoli** anc. Amphipolis. site of ancient city Kentrikí Makedonía, NE Greece
115 F18 **Ámfissa** Stereá Elláda, C Greece 38°32′N 22°22′E
123 Q10 **Amga** Respublika Sakha (Yakutiya), NE Russian Federation 60°55′N 131°45′E
123 Q11 **Amga** ≈ NE Russian Federation
163 R7 **Amgalang** var. Xin Barag Zuoqi. Nei Mongol Zizhiqu, N China 48°12′N 118°15′E
123 V5 **Amguema** ≈ NE Russian Federation
123 S12 **Amgun'** ≈ SE Russian Federation
Amhara see Āmara
13 P15 **Amherst** Nova Scotia, SE Canada 45°50′N 64°14′W
18 M11 **Amherst** Massachusetts, NE USA 42°22′N 72°31′W
18 D10 **Amherst** New York, NE USA 42°57′N 78°47′W
24 M4 **Amherst** Texas, SW USA 33°59′N 102°24′W
21 U6 **Amherst** Virginia, NE USA 37°35′N 79°04′W
Amherst see Kyaikkami
14 C18 **Amherstburg** Ontario, S Canada 42°05′N 83°06′W
21 Q6 **Amherstdale** West Virginia, NE USA 37°46′N 81°46′W
14 K15 **Amherst Island** island Ontario, SE Canada
Amida see Diyarbakır
28 J6 **Amidon** North Dakota, N USA 46°29′N 103°19′W
103 O3 **Amiens** anc. Ambianum, Samarobriva. Somme, N France 49°54′N 02°18′E
139 P8 **'Āmij, Wādī** var. Wadi 'Amiq. dry watercourse W Iraq
136 L17 **Amik Ovası** ◎ S Turkey
76 E9 **Amilcar Cabral** ✈ Sal, NE Cape Verde
Amilhayt, Wādī see Umm al Ḥayt, Wādī
Amindaion/Amindeo see Amýntaio
155 C21 **Amīndīvi Islands** island group Lakshadweep, India, N Indian Ocean
139 U6 **Amīn Ḥabīb** Diyālá, E Iraq 34°17′N 45°10′E
83 E20 **Aminuis** Omaheke, E Namibia 23°43′S 19°21′E
'Amiq, Wadi see 'Āmij, Wādī
142 J7 **Amīrābād** Īlām, NW Iran 33°20′N 46°16′E
Amirante Bank see Amirante Ridge
173 N6 **Amirante Basin** undersea feature W Indian Ocean 07°00′S 54°00′E
173 N6 **Amirante Islands** var. Amirantes Group. island group C Seychelles
173 N7 **Amirante Ridge** var. Amirante Bank. undersea feature W Indian Ocean 06°00′S 53°10′E
Amirantes Group see Amirante Islands
173 N7 **Amirante Trench** undersea feature W Indian Ocean 08°00′S 52°30′E
11 U13 **Amisk Lake** ◎ Saskatchewan, C Canada
Amistad, Presa de la see Amistad Reservoir
25 O12 **Amistad Reservoir** var. Presa de la Amistad. ⊞ Mexico/USA
Amisus see Samsun
22 K8 **Amite** var. Amite City. Louisiana, S USA 30°40′N 90°30′W
Amite City see Amite
27 T12 **Amity** Arkansas, C USA 34°15′N 93°27′W
154 H11 **Amla** prev. Amulla. Madhya Pradesh, C India 21°53′N 78°10′E
38 I17 **Amlia Island** island Aleutian Islands, Alaska, USA
97 I18 **Amlwch** NW Wales, United Kingdom 53°25′N 04°23′W
Ammaia see Portalegre
138 H10 **'Ammān** var. Amman; anc. Philadelphia, Bibl. Rabbah Ammon, Rabbath Ammon. ● (Jordan) 'Ammān, NW Jordan 31°57′N 35°56′E
138 H10 **'Ammān** off. Muḥāfazat 'Ammān; prev. Al 'Aşimah. ◈ governorate NW Jordan
'Ammān, Muḥāfazat see 'Ammān
93 N14 **Ämmänsaari** Oulu, E Finland 64°51′N 28°58′E
92 H13 **Ammarnäs** Västerbotten, N Sweden 65°58′N 16°10′E
197 O15 **Ammassalik** var. Angmagssalik. Tunu, S Greenland 65°51′N 37°30′W
101 K24 **Ammer** ≈ SE Germany
101 K24 **Ammersee** ◎ SE Germany
98 J13 **Ammerzoden** Gelderland, C Netherlands 51°46′N 05°07′E
Ammóchostos see Gazimağusa
Ammóchostos, Kólpos see Gazimağusa Körfezi
Amnok-kang see Yalu
Amoea see Portalegre
Amoentai see Amuntai
Amoerang see Amurang
143 O4 **Āmol** var. Amul. Māzandarān, N Iran 36°31′N 52°24′E
115 K21 **Amorgós** Amorgós, Kykládes, Greece, Aegean Sea 36°49′N 25°54′E
115 K22 **Amorgós** island Kykládes, Greece, Aegean Sea
23 N3 **Amory** Mississippi, S USA 33°58′N 88°29′W
12 I13 **Amos** Québec, SE Canada 48°34′N 78°08′W
95 G15 **Åmot** Buskerud, S Norway 59°52′N 09°55′E
95 E15 **Åmot** Telemark, S Norway 59°34′N 07°59′E
95 J15 **Åmotfors** Värmland, C Sweden 59°46′N 12°24′E
76 L10 **Amourj** Hodh ech Chargui, SE Mauritania 16°04′N 07°12′W
Amoy see Xiamen
172 H7 **Ampanihy** Toliara, SW Madagascar 24°40′S 44°45′E
155 L25 **Ampara** var. Amparai. Eastern Province, E Sri Lanka 07°17′N 81°41′E
172 J4 **Amparafaravola** Toamasina, E Madagascar 17°33′S 48°13′E
Amparai see Ampara
60 M9 **Amparo** São Paulo, S Brazil 22°40′S 46°49′W
172 J5 **Ampasimanolotra** Toamasina, E Madagascar 18°49′S 49°04′E
57 H17 **Ampato, Nevado** ▲ S Peru 15°52′S 71°51′W
101 L23 **Amper** ≈ SE Germany
64 M9 **Ampère Seamount** undersea feature E Atlantic Ocean 35°05′N 13°00′W
Amphipolis see Amfípoli
167 X10 **Amphitrite Group** island group N Paracel Islands
171 T16 **Amplawas** var. Emplawas. Pulau Babar, E Indonesia 08°01′S 129°42′E
105 U7 **Amposta** Cataluña, NE Spain 40°43′N 00°34′E
15 V7 **Amqui** Québec, SE Canada 48°28′N 67°27′W
141 O14 **'Amrān** W Yemen 15°39′N 43°59′E
Amraoti see Amrāvati
154 H12 **Amrāvati** prev. Amraoti. Mahārāshtra, C India 20°56′N 77°45′E
154 C11 **Amreli** Gujarāt, W India 21°36′N 71°20′E

◆ Country ● Country Capital ◇ Dependent Territory ○ Dependent Territory Capital ◈ Administrative Regions ✈ International Airport ▲ Mountain ▲▲ Mountain Range Volcano ≈ River ◎ Lake ⊞ Reservoir

108 *H6* **Amriswil** Thurgau, NE Switzerland *47°33′N 09°18′E*
138 *H5* **'Amrīt** *ruins* Tarṭūs, W Syria
152 *H7* **Amritsar** Punjab, N India *31°38′N 74°55′E*
152 *J10* **Amroha** Uttar Pradesh, N India *28°54′N 78°29′E*
100 *G7* **Amrum** *island* NW Germany
93 *I15* **Åmsele** Västerbotten, N Sweden *64°31′N 19°24′E*
98 *I10* **Amstelveen** Noord-Holland, C Netherlands *52°18′N 04°50′E*
98 *I10* **Amsterdam** ● (Netherlands) Noord-Holland, C Netherlands *52°22′N 04°54′E*
18 *K10* **Amsterdam** New York, NE USA *42°56′N 74°11′W*
173 *Q11* **Amsterdam Fracture Zone** *tectonic feature* S Indian Ocean
173 *R11* **Amsterdam Island** *island* NE French Southern and Antarctic Territories
109 *U4* **Amstetten** Niederösterreich, N Austria *48°08′N 14°52′E*
78 *J11* **Am Timan** Salamat, SE Chad *11°02′N 20°17′E*
146 *L12* **Amu-Buxoro Kanali** *var.* Aral-Bukhorskiy Kanal. *canal* C Uzbekistan
139 *O1* **'Āmūdah** *var.* Amude. Al Ḥasakah, N Syria *37°06′N 40°56′E*
147 *O15* **Amu Darya** *Rus.* Amudar'ya, *Taj.* Dar"yoi Amu, *Turkm.* Amyderya, *Uzb.* Amudaryo; *anc.* Oxus. ≈ C Asia
Amu-Dar'ya *see* Amyderýa
Amudar'ya/Amudaryo/ Amu, Dar"yoi *see* Amu Darya
Amude *see* 'Āmūdah
140 *L3* **'Amūd, Jabal al** ▲ NW Saudi Arabia *30°59′N 39°17′E*
38 *J17* **Amukta Island** *island* Aleutian Islands, Alaska, USA
38 *I17* **Amukta Pass** *strait* Aleutian Islands, Alaska, USA
Amul *see* Āmol
Amulla *see* Amla
Amundsen Basin *see* Fram Basin
195 *X3* **Amundsen Bay** *bay* Antarctica
195 *P10* **Amundsen Coast** *physical region* Antarctica
193 *O14* **Amundsen Plain** *undersea feature* S Pacific Ocean
195 *Q9* **Amundsen-Scott** *US research station* Antarctica *89°59′S 10°00′E*
194 *J11* **Amundsen Sea** *sea* S Pacific Ocean
94 *M12* **Amungen** ◎ C Sweden
169 *U13* **Amuntai** *prev.* Amoentai. Borneo, C Indonesia *02°24′S 115°14′E*
129 *W6* **Amur** *Chin.* Heilong Jiang. ≈ China/Russian Federation
171 *Q11* **Amurang** *prev.* Amoerang. Sulawesi, C Indonesia *01°12′N 124°37′E*
105 *O3* **Amurrio** País Vasco, N Spain *43°03′N 03°00′W*
123 *S13* **Amursk** Khabarovskiy Kray, SE Russian Federation *50°13′N 136°34′E*
123 *Q12* **Amurskaya Oblast'** ◈ *province* SE Russian Federation
80 *G7* **'Amur, Wadi** ≈ NE Sudan
115 *C17* **Amvrakikós Kólpos** *gulf* W Greece
Amvrosiyevka *see* Amvrosiyivka
117 *X8* **Amvrosiyivka** *Rus.* Amvrosiyevka. Donets'ka Oblast', SE Ukraine *47°46′N 38°30′E*
146 *M14* **Amyderýa** *Rus.* Amu-Dar'ya. Lebap Welaýaty, NE Turkmenistan *37°58′N 65°14′E*
Amyderya *see* Amu Darya
114 *E13* **Amýntaio** *var.* Amindeo; *prev.* Amíndaion. Dytikí Makedonía, N Greece *40°42′N 21°42′E*
14 *B6* **Amyot** Ontario, S Canada *48°28′N 84°58′W*
191 *U10* **Anaa** *atoll* Îles Tuamotu, C French Polynesia
Anabanoea *see* Anabanua
171 *N14* **Anabanua** *prev.* Anabanoea. Sulawesi, C Indonesia *03°58′S 120°07′E*
189 *R8* **Anabar** NE Nauru *0°30′S 166°56′E*
123 *N8* **Anabar** ≈ NE Russian Federation
An Abhainn Mhór *see* Blackwater
55 *O6* **Anaco** Anzoátegui, NE Venezuela *09°30′N 64°28′W*
33 *Q10* **Anaconda** Montana, NW USA *46°09′N 112°56′W*
32 *H7* **Anacortes** Washington, NW USA *48°30′N 122°36′W*
26 *M11* **Anadarko** Oklahoma, C USA *35°04′N 98°16′W*
114 *N12* **Ana Dere** ≈ NW Turkey
104 *G8* **Anadia** Aveiro, N Portugal *40°26′N 08°27′W*
Anadolu Dağları *see* Doğu Karadeniz Dağları
123 *V6* **Anadyr'** Chukotskiy Avtonomnyy Okrug, NE Russian Federation *64°41′N 177°22′E*
123 *V6* **Anadyr'** ≈ NE Russian Federation
Anadyr, Gulf of *see* Anadyrskiy Zaliv
129 *X4* **Anadyrskiy Khrebet** *var.* Chukot Range. ▲▲ NE Russian Federation
123 *W6* **Anadyrskiy Zaliv** *Eng.* Gulf of Anadyr. *gulf* NE Russian Federation
115 *K22* **Anáfi** *anc.* Anaphe. *island* Kykládes, Greece, Aegean Sea
107 *J15* **Anagni** Lazio, C Italy *41°43′N 13°12′E*
'Ānah *see* 'Annah
35 *T15* **Anaheim** California, W USA *33°50′N 117°54′W*
10 *L15* **Anahim Lake** British Columbia, SW Canada *52°26′N 125°13′W*
38 *B8* **Anahola** Kaua'i, Hawai'i, USA, C Pacific Ocean *22°09′N 159°19′W*
41 *O7* **Anáhuac** Nuevo León, NE Mexico *27°13′N 100°09′W*
25 *X11* **Anahuac** Texas, SW USA *29°44′N 94°41′W*
155 *G22* **Anai Mudi** ▲ S India *10°16′N 77°08′E*
Anaiza *see* 'Unayzah
155 *M15* **Anakāpalle** Andhra Pradesh, E India *17°42′N 83°06′E*
191 *W15* **Anakena, Playa de** *beach* Easter Island, Chile, E Pacific Ocean
39 *Q7* **Anaktuvuk Pass** Alaska, USA *68°08′N 151°44′W*
39 *Q6* **Anaktuvuk River** ≈ Alaska, USA
172 *J3* **Analalava** Mahajanga, NW Madagascar *14°38′S 47°46′E*
44 *F6* **Ana Maria, Golfo de** *gulf* N Caribbean Sea
Anambas Islands *see* Anambas, Kepulauan
169 *N8* **Anambas, Kepulauan** *var.* Anambas Islands. *island group* W Indonesia
77 *U17* **Anambra** ◈ *state* SE Nigeria
29 *N4* **Anamoose** North Dakota, N USA *47°50′N 100°14′W*
29 *Y13* **Anamosa** Iowa, C USA *42°06′N 91°17′W*
136 *H17* **Anamur** İçel, S Turkey *36°06′N 32°49′E*
136 *H17* **Anamur Burnu** *headland* S Turkey *36°03′N 32°49′E*
154 *O12* **Ānandapur** *var.* Anandpur. Orissa, E India *21°14′N 86°10′E*
Anandpur *see* Ānandapur
155 *H18* **Anantapur** Andhra Pradesh, S India *14°41′N 77°36′E*
152 *H5* **Anantnāg** *var.* Islamabad. Jammu and Kashmir, NW India *33°44′N 75°11′E*
Ananyev *see* Anan'yiv
117 *O9* **Anan'yiv** *Rus.* Ananyev. Odes'ka Oblast', SW Ukraine *47°43′N 29°51′E*
126 *J14* **Anapa** Krasnodarskiy Kray, SW Russian Federation *44°55′N 37°20′E*
Anaphe *see* Anáfi
59 *K18* **Anápolis** Goiás, C Brazil *16°19′S 48°58′W*
143 *R10* **Anār** Kermān, C Iran *30°49′N 55°18′E*
Anár *see* Inari
143 *P7* **Anārak** Eşfahān, C Iran *33°21′N 53°43′E*
Anar Dara *see* Anār Darreh
148 *J7* **Anār Darreh** *var.* Anar Dara. Farāh, W Afghanistan *32°45′N 61°38′E*
Anárjohka *see* Inarijoki
23 *X9* **Anastasia Island** *island* Florida, SE USA
188 *K7* **Anatahan** *island* C Northern Mariana Islands
128 *M6* **Anatolia** *plateau* C Turkey
86 *F14* **Anatolian Plate** *tectonic feature* Asia/Europe
114 *H13* **Anatolikí Makedonía kai Thráki** *Eng.* Macedonia East and Thrace. ◈ *region* NE Greece
Anatom *see* Aneityum
62 *L8* **Añatuya** Santiago del Estero, N Argentina *28°28′S 62°52′W*
An Baile Meánach *see* Ballymena
An Bhearú *see* Barrow
An Bhóinn *see* Boyne
An Blascaod Mór *see* Great Blasket Island
An Cabhán *see* Cavan
An Caisleán Nua *see* Newcastle
An Caisleán Riabhach *see* Castlerea, Ireland
An Caisleán Riabhach *see* Castlereagh
56 *C13* **Ancash** *off.* Departamento de Ancash. ◈ *department* W Peru
Ancash, Departamento de *see* Ancash
An Cathair *see* Caher
102 *J8* **Ancenis** Loire-Atlantique, NW France *47°23′N 01°10′W*
An Chanáil Ríoga *see* Royal Canal
An Cheacha *see* Caha Mountains
39 *R11* **Anchorage** Alaska, USA *61°13′N 149°52′W*
39 *R12* **Anchorage** ✈ Alaska, USA *61°08′N 150°00′W*
39 *Q13* **Anchor Point** Alaska, USA *59°46′N 151°49′W*
An Chorr Chríochach *see* Cookstown
65 *M24* **Anchorstock Point** *headland* W Tristan da Cunha *37°07′S 12°21′W*
An Clár *see* Clare
An Clochán *see* Clifden
An Clochán Liath *see* Dunglow
23 *U12* **Anclote Keys** *island group* Florida, SE USA
An Cóbh *see* Cobh
57 *J17* **Ancohuma, Nevado de** ▲ W Bolivia *15°51′S 68°33′W*
An Comar *see* Comber
57 *D14* **Ancón** Lima, W Peru *11°45′S 77°08′W*
106 *J12* **Ancona** Marche, C Italy *43°38′N 13°30′E*
Ancuabe *see* Ancuabi
82 *Q13* **Ancuabi** *var.* Ancuabe. Cabo Delgado, NE Mozambique *13°00′S 39°50′E*
63 *F17* **Ancud** *prev.* San Carlos de Ancud. Los Lagos, S Chile *41°53′S 73°50′W*
63 *G17* **Ancud, Golfo de** *gulf* S Chile
Ancyra *see* Ankara
163 *V8* **Anda** Heilongjiang, NE China *46°25′N 125°20′E*
57 *G16* **Andahuaylas** Apurímac, S Peru *13°39′S 73°24′W*
An Daingean *see* Dingle
153 *R15* **Andāl** West Bengal, NE India *23°35′N 87°14′E*
94 *E9* **Åndalsnes** Møre og Romsdal, S Norway *62°33′N 07°42′E*
104 *K13* **Andalucía** *Eng.* Andalusia. ◈ *autonomous community* S Spain
23 *P7* **Andalusia** Alabama, S USA *31°18′N 86°29′W*
Andalusia *see* Andalucía
151 *Q21* **Andaman and Nicobar Islands** *var.* Andamans and Nicobars. ◈ *union territory* India, NE Indian Ocean
173 *T4* **Andaman Basin** *undersea feature* NE Indian Ocean *10°00′N 94°00′E*
151 *P19* **Andaman Islands** *island group* India, NE Indian Ocean
Andamans and Nicobars *see* Andaman and Nicobar Islands
173 *T4* **Andaman Sea** *sea* NE Indian Ocean
57 *K19* **Andamarca** Oruro, C Bolivia *18°46′S 67°31′W*
182 *H5* **Andamooka** South Australia *30°26′S 137°12′E*
141 *Y9* **'Andām, Wādī** *seasonal river* NE Oman
172 *J3* **Andapa** Antsirañana, NE Madagascar *14°39′S 49°40′E*
149 *R4* **Andarāb** *var.* Banow. Baghlān, NE Afghanistan *35°36′N 69°18′E*
Andarbag *see* Andarbogh
147 *S13* **Andarbogh** *Rus.* Andarbag, Anderbak. S Tajikistan *37°51′N 71°45′E*
109 *Z5* **Andau** Burgenland, E Austria *47°47′N 17°02′E*
108 *I10* **Andeer** Graubünden, S Switzerland *46°36′N 09°24′E*
92 *H9* **Andenes** Nordland, C Norway *69°18′N 16°10′E*
99 *J20* **Andenne** Namur, SE Belgium *50°29′N 05°06′E*
77 *S11* **Andéramboukane** Gao, E Mali *15°24′N 03°03′E*
Anderbak *see* Andarbogh
99 *G18* **Anderlecht** Brussels, C Belgium *50°50′N 04°18′E*
99 *G21* **Anderlues** Hainaut, S Belgium *50°24′N 04°16′E*
108 *G9* **Andermatt** Uri, C Switzerland *46°39′N 08°36′E*
101 *E17* **Andernach** *anc.* Antunnacum. Rheinland-Pfalz, SW Germany *50°26′N 07°24′E*
188 *D15* **Andersen Air Force Base** *air base* NE Guam *13°34′N 144°55′E*
39 *R9* **Anderson** Alaska, USA *64°20′N 149°11′W*
35 *N4* **Anderson** California, W USA *40°26′N 122°21′W*
31 *P13* **Anderson** Indiana, N USA *40°06′N 85°40′W*
27 *R8* **Anderson** Missouri, C USA *36°39′N 94°26′W*
21 *P11* **Anderson** South Carolina, SE USA *34°30′N 82°39′W*
25 *V10* **Anderson** Texas, SW USA *30°29′N 96°00′W*
95 *K20* **Anderstorp** Jönköping, S Sweden *57°17′N 13°38′E*
54 *D9* **Andes** Antioquia, W Colombia *05°40′N 75°56′W*
47 *P7* **Andes** ▲▲ W South America
29 *P12* **Andes, Lake** ◎ South Dakota, N USA
92 *H9* **Andfjorden** *fjord* E Norwegian Sea
155 *H16* **Andhra Pradesh** ◈ *state* E India
98 *J8* **Andijk** Noord-Holland, NW Netherlands *52°38′N 05°00′E*
147 *S10* **Andijon** *Rus.* Andizhan. Andijon Viloyati, E Uzbekistan *40°46′N 72°19′E*
147 *S10* **Andijon Viloyati** *Rus.* Andizhanskaya Oblast'. ◈ *province* E Uzbekistan
Andikíthira *see* Antikýthira
172 *J4* **Andilamena** Toamasina, C Madagascar *17°00′S 48°35′E*
142 *L8* **Andīmeshk** *var.* Andimishk; *prev.* Salehābād. Khūzestān, SW Iran *32°30′N 48°26′E*
Andimishk *see* Andīmeshk
Andipáros *see* Antíparos
Andipaxi *see* Antípaxoi
Andípsara *see* Antípsara
136 *L16* **Andırın** Kahramanmaraş, S Turkey *37°33′N 36°18′E*
158 *J8* **Andirlangar** Xinjiang Uygur Zizhiqu, NW China *37°38′N 83°40′E*
Andírrion *see* Antírrio
Ándissa *see* Ántissa
Andizhan *see* Andijon
Andizhanskaya Oblast' *see* Andijon Viloyati
149 *N2* **Andkhvōy** *prev.* Andkhvoy. Fāryāb, N Afghanistan *36°56′N 65°08′E*
105 *Q2* **Andoain** País Vasco, N Spain *43°13′N 02°02′W*
163 *Y15* **Andong** *Jap.* Antō. E South Korea *36°34′N 128°44′E*
109 *R4* **Andorf** Oberösterreich, N Austria *48°22′N 13°33′E*
105 *S7* **Andorra** Aragón, NE Spain *40°59′N 00°27′W*
105 *V4* **Andorra** *off.* Principality of Andorra, *Cat.* Valls d'Andorra, *Fr.* Vallée d'Andorre. ◆ *monarchy* SW Europe
Andorra *see* Andorra la Vella
105 *V4* **Andorra la Vella** *var.* Andorra, *Fr.* Andorre la Vielle, *Sp.* Andorra la Vieja. ● (Andorra) C Andorra *42°30′N 01°30′E*
Andorra la Vieja *see* Andorra la Vella
Andorra, Principality of *see* Andorra
Andorra, Valls d'/Andorra, Vallée d' *see* Andorra
Andorre la Vielle *see* Andorra la Vella
97 *M22* **Andover** S England, United Kingdom *51°13′N 01°28′W*
27 *N6* **Andover** Kansas, C USA *37°42′N 97°08′W*
92 *G10* **Andøya** *island* C Norway
60 *I8* **Andradina** São Paulo, S Brazil *20°54′S 51°19′W*
105 *X9* **Andratx** Mallorca, Spain, W Mediterranean Sea *39°35′N 02°25′E*
39 *N10* **Andreafsky River** ≈ Alaska, USA
38 *H17* **Andreanof Islands** *island group* Aleutian Islands, Alaska, USA
124 *H16* **Andreapol'** Tverskaya Oblast', W Russian Federation *56°38′N 32°17′E*
Andreas, Cape *see* Zafer Burnu
Andreevka *see* Kabanbay
21 *N10* **Andrews** North Carolina, SE USA *35°19′N 84°01′W*
21 *T13* **Andrews** South Carolina, SE USA *33°27′N 79°33′W*
24 *M7* **Andrews** Texas, SW USA *32°19′N 102°34′W*
173 *N5* **Andrew Tablemount** *var.* Gora Andryu. *undersea feature* W Indian Ocean *06°45′N 50°30′E*
Andreyevka *see* Kabanbay
107 *N17* **Andria** Puglia, SE Italy *41°13′N 16°17′E*
113 *K16* **Andrijevica** E Montenegro *42°45′N 19°45′E*
115 *E20* **Andrítsaina** Pelopónnisos, S Greece *37°29′N 21°52′E*
An Droichead Nua *see* Newbridge
Andropov *see* Rybinsk
115 *J19* **Ándros** Ándros, Kykládes, Greece, Aegean Sea *37°49′N 24°54′E*
115 *J20* **Ándros** *island* Kykládes, Greece, Aegean Sea
19 *O7* **Androscoggin River** ≈ Maine/New Hampshire, NE USA
44 *F3* **Andros Island** *island* NW Bahamas
127 *R7* **Androsovka** Samarskaya Oblast', W Russian Federation *52°41′N 49°34′E*
44 *G3* **Andros Town** Andros Island, NW Bahamas *24°40′N 77°47′W*
155 *D21* **Āndrott Island** *island* Lakshadweep, India, N Indian Ocean
117 *N5* **Andrushivka** Zhytomyrs'ka Oblast', N Ukraine *50°01′N 29°02′E*
111 *K17* **Andrychów** Małopolskie, S Poland *49°51′N 19°18′E*
Andryu, Gora *see* Andrew Tablemount
92 *I10* **Andselv** Troms, N Norway *69°05′N 18°30′E*
79 *O17* **Andudu** Orientale, NE Dem. Rep. Congo *02°26′N 28°39′E*
105 *N13* **Andújar** *anc.* Illiturgis. Andalucía, SW Spain *38°02′N 04°03′W*
82 *C12* **Andulo** Bié, W Angola *11°29′S 16°43′E*
103 *Q14* **Anduze** Gard, S France *44°03′N 03°59′E*
An Earagail *see* Errigal Mountain
95 *L19* **Aneby** Jönköping, S Sweden *57°50′N 14°45′E*
Anécho *see* Aného
77 *Q9* **Anéfis** Kidal, NE Mali *18°05′N 00°38′E*
45 *U8* **Anegada** *island* NE British Virgin Islands
61 *B25* **Anegada, Bahía** *bay* E Argentina
45 *U9* **Anegada Passage** *passage* Anguilla/British Virgin Islands
77 *R17* **Aného** *var.* Anécho; *prev.* Petit-Popo. S Togo *06°14′N 01°36′E*
197 *D17* **Aneityum** *var.* Anatom; *prev.* Kéamu. *island* S Vanuatu
117 *N10* **Anenii Noi** *Rus.* Novyye Aneny. C Moldova *46°52′N 29°10′E*
186 *F7* **Anepmete** New Britain, E Papua New Guinea *05°47′S 148°37′E*
105 *U4* **Aneto** ▲ NE Spain *42°36′N 00°37′E*
146 *F13* **Änew** *Rus.* Annau. Ahal Welaýaty, C Turkmenistan *37°51′N 58°22′E*
Änewetak *see* Enewetak Atoll
77 *Y8* **Aney** Agadez, NE Niger *19°22′N 13°00′E*
An Fheoir *see* Nore
122 *L12* **Angara** ≈ C Russian Federation
122 *M13* **Angarsk** Irkutskaya Oblast', S Russian Federation *52°31′N 103°55′E*
Angaur *see* Ngeaur
93 *G17* **Ånge** Västernorrland, C Sweden *62°31′N 15°40′E*
Angel *see* Úhlava
40 *D4* **Ángel de la Guarda, Isla** *island* NW Mexico
171 *O3* **Angeles** *off.* Angeles City. Luzon, N Philippines *15°16′N 120°37′E*
Angeles City *see* Angeles
Angel Falls *see* Ángel, Salto
95 *J22* **Ängelholm** Skåne, S Sweden *56°14′N 12°52′E*
61 *A17* **Angélica** Santa Fe, C Argentina *31°33′S 61°33′W*
25 *W8* **Angelina River** ≈ Texas, SW USA
55 *Q9* **Ángel, Salto** *Eng.* Angel Falls. *waterfall* E Venezuela
95 *M15* **Ängelsberg** Västmanland, C Sweden *59°57′N 16°01′E*
35 *P8* **Angels Camp** California, W USA *38°03′N 120°31′W*
109 *W7* **Anger** Steiermark, SE Austria *47°16′N 15°41′E*
Angerapp *see* Ozersk
Angerburg *see* Węgorzewo
93 *H15* **Ångermanälven** ≈ N Sweden
100 *P11* **Angermünde** Brandenburg, NE Germany *53°02′N 13°59′E*
102 *K7* **Angers** *anc.* Juliomagus. Maine-et-Loire, NW France *47°30′N 00°33′W*
15 *W7* **Angers** ≈ Québec, SE Canada
93 *J16* **Ängesön** *island* N Sweden
Angistro *see* Ágkistro
114 *H13* **Angítis** ≈ NE Greece
167 *R13* **Ângk Tasaôm** *prev.* Angtassom. Takêv, S Cambodia
185 *C25* **Anglem, Mount** ▲ Stewart Island, Southland, SW New Zealand *46°44′S 167°56′E*
97 *I18* **Anglesey** *cultural region* NW Wales, United Kingdom
97 *I18* **Anglesey** *island* NW Wales, United Kingdom
102 *I15* **Anglet** Pyrénées-Atlantiques, SW France *43°29′N 01°30′W*
25 *W12* **Angleton** Texas, SW USA *29°10′N 95°27′W*
Anglia *see* England
14 *H9* **Angliers** Québec, SE Canada *47°33′N 79°17′W*
Anglo-Egyptian Sudan *see* Sudan
Angmagssalik *see* Ammassalik
167 *Q7* **Ang Nam Ngum** ◎ C Laos
79 *N16* **Ango** Orientale, N Dem. Rep. Congo *04°01′N 25°52′E*
83 *Q15* **Angoche** Nampula, E Mozambique *16°10′S 39°58′E*
63 *G14* **Angol** Araucanía, C Chile *37°47′S 72°45′W*
31 *Q11* **Angola** Indiana, N USA *41°37′N 85°00′W*
82 *A9* **Angola** *off.* Republic of Angola; *prev.* People's Republic of Angola, Portuguese West Africa. ◆ *republic* SW Africa
65 *P15* **Angola Basin** *undersea feature* E Atlantic Ocean *15°00′S 03°00′E*
Angola, People's Republic of *see* Angola
Angola, Republic of *see* Angola
39 *X13* **Angoon** Admiralty Island, Alaska, USA *57°33′N 134°30′W*
147 *O14* **Angor** Surkhondaryo Viloyati, S Uzbekistan *37°30′N 67°06′E*
Angora *see* Ankara
186 *C6* **Angoram** East Sepik, NW Papua New Guinea *04°04′S 144°04′E*
40 *H8* **Angostura** Sinaloa, C Mexico *25°18′N 108°10′W*
Angostura *see* Ciudad Bolívar
41 *U17* **Angostura, Presa de la** ▣ SE Mexico
28 *J11* **Angostura Reservoir** ▣ South Dakota, N USA
102 *L11* **Angoulême** *anc.* Iculisma. Charente, W France *45°39′N 00°10′E*
102 *K11* **Angoumois** *cultural region* W France
64 *O2* **Angra do Heroísmo** Terceira, Azores, Portugal, NE Atlantic Ocean *38°40′N 27°14′W*
60 *O10* **Angra dos Reis** Rio de Janeiro, SE Brazil *22°59′S 44°17′W*
Angra Pequena *see* Lüderitz
147 *Q10* **Angren** Toshkent Viloyati, E Uzbekistan *41°05′N 70°18′E*
Angtassom *see* Ângk Tasaôm
167 *O10* **Ang Thong** *var.* Angthong. Ang Thong, C Thailand *14°35′N 100°25′E*
Angthong *see* Ang Thong
79 *M16* **Angu** Orientale, N Dem. Rep. Congo *03°38′N 24°14′E*
105 *S5* **Angües** Aragón, NE Spain *42°07′N 00°10′W*
45 *U9* **Anguilla** ◇ *UK dependent territory* E West Indies
45 *V9* **Anguilla** *island* E West Indies
44 *F4* **Anguilla Cays** *islets* SW Bahamas
Angul *see* Anugul
161 *N1* **Anguli Nur** ◎ E China
79 *O18* **Angumu** Orientale, E Dem. Rep. Congo *0°10′S 27°42′E*
14 *G14* **Angus** Ontario, S Canada *44°19′N 79°52′W*
96 *J10* **Angus** *cultural region* E Scotland, United Kingdom
59 *K19* **Anhangüera** Goiás, S Brazil *18°12′S 48°19′W*
99 *I21* **Anhée** Namur, S Belgium *50°18′N 04°52′E*
95 *I21* **Anholt** *island* C Denmark
160 *M11* **Anhua** *var.* Dongping. Hunan, S China *28°25′N 111°10′E*
161 *P8* **Anhui** *var.* Anhui Sheng, Anhwei, Wan. ◈ *province* E China
AnhuiSheng/Anhwei Wan *see* Anhui
39 *O11* **Aniak** Alaska, USA *61°34′N 159°31′W*
39 *O12* **Aniak River** ≈ Alaska, USA
An Iarmhí *see* Westmeath
189 *R8* **Anibare** E Nauru *0°31′S 166°56′E*
189 *R8* **Anibare Bay** *bay* E Nauru, W Pacific Ocean
Anicium *see* le Puy
115 *K22* **Ánidro** *island* Kykládes, Greece, Aegean Sea
77 *R15* **Anié** C Togo *07°48′N 01°12′E*
77 *Q15* **Anié** ≈ C Togo
102 *J16* **Anie, Pic d'** ▲ SW France *42°56′N 00°44′W*
127 *Y7* **Anikhovka** Orenburgskaya Oblast', W Russian Federation *51°27′N 60°17′E*
14 *G9* **Anima Nipissing Lake** ◎ Ontario, S Canada
37 *O16* **Animas** New Mexico, SW USA *31°55′N 108°49′W*
37 *P16* **Animas Peak** ▲ New Mexico, SW USA *31°34′N 108°46′W*
37 *P16* **Animas Valley** *valley* New Mexico, SW USA
116 *F13* **Anina** *Ger.* Steierdorf, *Hung.* Stájerlakanina; *prev.* Ştaierdorf-Anina, Steierdorf-Anina, Steyerlak-Anina. Caraş-Severin, SW Romania *45°05′N 21°51′E*
29 *U14* **Anita** Iowa, C USA *41°27′N 94°45′W*
123 *U14* **Aniva, Mys** *headland* Ostrov Sakhalin, SE Russian Federation *46°02′N 143°25′E*
187 *S15* **Aniwa** *island* S Vanuatu
93 *M19* **Anjalankoski** Etelä-Suomi, S Finland *60°39′N 26°54′E*
'Anjar *see* Aanjar
Anjiangying *see* Luanping
14 *B8* **Anjigami Lake** ◎ Ontario, S Canada
149 *N13* **Anjīra** Baluchistān, SW Pakistan *28°19′N 66°19′E*
164 *K14* **Anjō** *var.* Anzyô. Aichi, Honshū, SW Japan *34°56′N 137°05′E*
102 *J8* **Anjou** *cultural region* NW France
Anjouan *see* Nzwani
172 *J4* **Anjozorobe** Antananarivo, C Madagascar *18°22′S 47°52′E*
163 *W13* **Anju** W North Korea *39°36′N 125°44′E*
98 *M5* **Anjum** *Fris.* Eanjum. Fryslân, N Netherlands *53°22′N 06°09′E*
172 *G6* **Ankaboa, Tanjona** *prev./Fr.* Cap Saint-Vincent. *headland* W Madagascar *21°57′S 43°16′E*
160 *L7* **Ankang** *prev.* Xing'an. Shaanxi, C China *32°45′N 109°00′E*
136 *I12* **Ankara** *prev.* Angora; *anc.* Ancyra. ● (Turkey) Ankara, C Turkey *39°55′N 32°50′E*
136 *H12* **Ankara** ◈ *province* C Turkey
95 *N19* **Ankarsrum** Kalmar, S Sweden *57°40′N 16°19′E*
172 *H6* **Ankazoabo** Toliara, SW Madagascar *22°18′S 44°30′E*
172 *I4* **Ankazobe** Antananarivo, C Madagascar *18°20′S 47°07′E*
29 *V14* **Ankeny** Iowa, C USA *41°43′N 93°37′W*
167 *V11* **An Khê** Gia Lai, C Vietnam *13°57′N 108°39′E*
100 *O9* **Anklam** Mecklenburg-Vorpommern, NE Germany *53°51′N 13°42′E*
80 *K13* **Ānkober** Āmara, N Ethiopia *09°36′N 39°44′E*
77 *O17* **Ankobra** ≈ S Ghana
79 *N22* **Ankoro** Katanga, SE Dem. Rep. Congo *06°45′S 26°58′E*
99 *L24* **Anlier, Forêt d'** *forest* SE Belgium
160 *I13* **Anlong** *var.* Xin'an. Guizhou, S China *25°05′N 105°29′E*
An Longfort *see* Longford
167 *R11* **Ânlong Vêng** Siĕmréab, NW Cambodia *14°16′N 104°08′E*
An Lorgain *see* Lurgan
161 *N8* **Anlu** Hubei, C China *31°15′N 113°41′E*
An Mhí *see* Meath
An Mhuir Cheilteach *see* Celtic Sea
An Muileann gCearr *see* Mullingar
93 *F16* **Ånn** Jämtland, C Sweden *63°19′N 12°34′E*
126 *M8* **Anna** Voronezhskaya Oblast', W Russian Federation *51°31′N 40°23′E*
30 *L17* **Anna** Illinois, N USA *37°27′N 89°15′W*
25 *U5* **Anna** Texas, SW USA *33°21′N 96°33′W*
74 *L5* **Annaba** *prev.* Bône. NE Algeria *36°55′N 07°47′E*
An Nabatīyah at Taḥtā *see* Nabatîyé
101 *N17* **Annaberg-Buchholz** Sachsen, E Germany *50°35′N 13°01′E*
109 *T9* **Annabichl** ✈ (Klagenfurt) Kärnten, S Austria *46°39′N 14°21′E*
140 *M5* **An Nafūd** *desert* NW Saudi Arabia
139 *P6* **'Annah** *var.* 'Ānah. Al Anbār, NW Iraq *34°50′N 42°00′E*
139 *P6* **An Nāḥiyah** Al Anbār, W Iraq *34°24′N 41°33′E*
139 *T10* **An Najaf** *var.* Najaf. An Najaf, S Iraq *31°59′N 44°19′E*
21 *V5* **Anna, Lake** ▣ Virginia, NE USA
97 *F16* **Annalee** ≈ N Ireland
167 *S9* **Annamite Mountains** *var.* annamsescordillera, *Fr.* Chaîne Annamitique, *Lao.* Phou Louang. ▲▲ C Laos
Annamitique, Chaîne *see* Annamite Mountains
Annamses Cordillera *see* Annamite Mountains
97 *J14* **Annan** S Scotland, United Kingdom *55°N 03°20′W*
29 *U8* **Annandale** Minnesota, N USA *45°15′N 94°07′W*
21 *W4* **Annandale** Virginia, NE USA *38°48′N 77°10′W*
189 *Q7* **Anna Point** *headland* N Nauru *0°30′S 166°56′E*
21 *X3* **Annapolis** *state capital* Maryland, NE USA *38°59′N 76°30′W*
188 *A10* **Anna, Pulo** *island* S Palau
153 *O10* **Annapurṇa** ▲ C Nepal *28°30′N 83°50′E*
An Nāqūrah *see* En Nâqoûra
31 *R10* **Ann Arbor** Michigan, N USA *42°17′N 83°45′W*
An Nás *see* Naas
139 *W12* **An Nāṣirīyah** *var.* Nasiriya. Dhī Qār, SE Iraq *31°04′N 46°17′E*
139 *W11* **An Naṣr** Dhī Qār, E Iraq *31°34′N 46°08′E*
Annau *see* Änew
121 *O13* **An Nawfalīyah** *var.* Al Nūwfalīyah. N Libya *30°46′N 17°48′E*
19 *P10* **Ann, Cape** *headland* Massachusetts, NE USA *42°39′N 70°35′W*
180 *I10* **Annean, Lake** ◎ Western Australia
Anneciacum *see* Annecy
103 *T11* **Annecy** *anc.* Anneciacum. Haute-Savoie, E France *45°53′N 06°09′E*
103 *T11* **Annecy, Lac d'** ◎ E France
103 *T10* **Annemasse** Haute-Savoie, E France *46°10′N 06°13′E*
39 *Z14* **Annette Island** *island* Alexander Archipelago, Alaska, USA
An Nhon *see* Binh Đinh
An Nīl al Abyaḍ *see* White Nile
An Nīl al Azraq *see* Blue Nile
23 *Q3* **Anniston** Alabama, S USA *33°39′N 85°49′W*
79 *A19* **Annobón** *island* W Equatorial Guinea
103 *R12* **Annonay** Ardèche, E France *45°15′N 04°40′E*
44 *K12* **Annotto Bay** C Jamaica *18°16′N 76°47′W*
141 *R5* **An Nu'ayrīyah** *var.* Narıya. Ash Sharqīyah, NE Saudi Arabia *27°30′N 48°30′E*
182 *M9* **Annuello** Victoria, SE Australia *34°54′S 142°50′E*
139 *Q10* **An Nukhayb** Al Anbār, S Iraq *32°02′N 42°15′E*
139 *U9* **An Nu'mānīyah** Wāsiṭ, E Iraq *32°34′N 45°23′E*
Áno Arkhánai *see* Archánes
115 *J25* **Anógeia** *var.* Anogia, Anóyia. Kríti, Greece, E Mediterranean Sea *35°17′N 24°53′E*
Anogia *see* Anógeia
29 *V8* **Anoka** Minnesota, N USA *45°15′N 93°26′W*
An Ómaigh *see* Omagh
172 *I1* **Anorontany, Tanjona** *Fr.* Cap Saint-Sébastien. *headland* N Madagascar
172 *J5* **Anosibe An'Ala** Toamasina, E Madagascar *19°24′S 48°11′E*
Anóyia *see* Anógeia
An Pointe *see* Warrenpoint
161 *P9* **Anqing** Anhui, E China *30°32′N 116°59′E*
161 *Q5* **Anqiu** Shandong, E China *36°25′N 119°10′E*
An Ráth *see* Ráth Luirc
An Ribhéar *see* Kenmare River
An Ros *see* Rush
99 *K19* **Ans** Liège, E Belgium *50°39′N 05°32′E*
Anşāb *see* Nişāb
171 *W12* **Ansas** Papua, E Indonesia *01°44′S 135°52′E*
101 *J20* **Ansbach** Bayern, SE Germany *49°18′N 10°36′E*
An Sciobairín *see* Skibbereen
An Scoil *see* Skull
An Seancheann *see* Old Head of Kinsale
45 *Y5* **Anse-Bertrand** Grande Terre, N Guadeloupe *16°28′N 61°31′W*
172 *H17* **Anse Boileau** Mahé, NE Seychelles *04°43′S 55°29′E*
45 *S11* **Anse La Raye** NW Saint Lucia *13°57′N 61°01′W*
54 *D9* **Anserma** Caldas, W Colombia *05°15′N 75°47′W*
109 *T4* **Ansfelden** Oberösterreich, N Austria *48°12′N 14°17′E*
163 *U12* **Anshan** Liaoning, NE China *41°06′N 122°55′E*
160 *J12* **Anshun** Guizhou, S China *26°15′N 105°58′E*
61 *F17* **Ansina** Tacuarembó, C Uruguay *31°58′S 55°28′W*
29 *O15* **Ansley** Nebraska, C USA *41°16′N 99°22′W*
25 *P6* **Anson** Texas, SW USA *32°45′N 99°55′W*
77 *Q10* **Ansongo** Gao, E Mali *15°39′N 00°33′E*
An Srath Bán *see* Strabane
21 *R5* **Ansted** West Virginia, NE USA *38°08′N 81°06′W*
171 *Y13* **Ansudu** Papua, E Indonesia *02°09′S 139°19′E*
57 *G15* **Anta** Cusco, S Peru *13°30′S 72°08′W*
57 *G16* **Antabamba** Apurímac, C Peru *14°23′S 72°54′W*
Antafalva *see* Kovačica
136 *L17* **Antakya** *anc.* Antioch, Antiochia. Hatay, S Turkey *36°12′N 36°10′E*
172 *K3* **Antalaha** Antsirañana, NE Madagascar *14°53′S 50°16′E*
136 *F17* **Antalya** *prev.* Adalia; *anc.* Attaleia, *Bibl.* Attalia. Antalya, SW Turkey *36°53′N 30°42′E*
136 *F17* **Antalya** ◈ *province* SW Turkey
136 *F16* **Antalya** ✈ Antalya, SW Turkey *36°53′N 30°45′E*
121 *U10* **Antalya Basin** *undersea feature* E Mediterranean Sea
Antalya, Gulf of *see* Antalya Körfezi
136 *F16* **Antalya Körfezi** *var.* Gulf of Adalia, *Eng.* Gulf of Antalya. *gulf* SW Turkey
172 *J5* **Antanambao Manampotsy** Toamasina, E Madagascar *19°30′S 48°36′E*
172 *I5* **Antananarivo** *prev.* Tananarive. ● (Madagascar) Antananarivo, C Madagascar *18°52′S 47°30′E*
172 *I4* **Antananarivo** ◈ *province* C Madagascar
172 *J5* **Antananarivo** ✈ Antananarivo, C Madagascar *18°52′S 47°30′E*
An tAonach *see* Nenagh
194-195 **Antarctica** *continent*
194 *I5* **Antarctic Peninsula** *peninsula* Antarctica
61 *J15* **Antas, Rio das** ≈ S Brazil
189 *U16* **Ant Atoll** *atoll* Caroline Islands, E Micronesia
An Teampall Mór *see* Templemore
Antep *see* Gaziantep
104 *M15* **Antequera** *anc.* Anticaria, Antiquaria. Andalucía, S Spain *37°01′N 04°34′W*
Antequera *see* Oaxaca
37 *S5* **Antero Reservoir** ▣ Colorado, C USA
26 *M7* **Anthony** Kansas, C USA *37°10′N 98°02′W*
37 *R16* **Anthony** New Mexico, SW USA *32°00′N 106°36′W*
182 *D5* **Anthony, Lake** *salt lake* South Australia
74 *E8* **Anti-Atlas** ▲▲ SW Morocco
103 *U15* **Antibes** *anc.* Antipolis. Alpes-Maritimes, SE France *43°35′N 07°07′E*
103 *U15* **Antibes, Cap d'** *headland* SE France *43°33′N 07°08′E*
Anticaria *see* Antequera
13 *Q11* **Anticosti, Île d'** *Eng.* Anticosti Island. *island* Québec, E Canada
Anticosti Island *see* Anticosti, Île d'
102 *K3* **Antifer, Cap d'** *headland* N France *49°43′N 00°10′E*
30 *L6* **Antigo** Wisconsin, N USA *45°10′N 89°10′W*
13 *Q15* **Antigonish** Nova Scotia, SE Canada *45°39′N 62°00′W*
64 *P11* **Antigua** Fuerteventura, Islas Canarias, NE Atlantic Ocean
45 *X10* **Antigua** *island* S Antigua and Barbuda, Leeward Islands
Antigua *see* Antigua Guatemala
45 *W9* **Antigua and Barbuda** ◆ *commonwealth republic* E West Indies
42 *C6* **Antigua Guatemala** *var.* Antigua. Sacatepéquez, SW Guatemala *14°33′N 90°42′W*
41 *P11* **Antiguo Morelos** *var.* Antiguo-Morelos. Tamaulipas, C Mexico *22°35′N 99°08′W*
115 *F19* **Antíkyras, Kólpos** *gulf* C Greece
115 *G24* **Antikýthira** *var.* Andikíthira. *island* S Greece
138 *I7* **Anti-Lebanon** *var.* Jebel esh Sharqi, *Ar.* Al Jabal ash Sharqī, *Fr.* Anti-Liban. ▲▲ Lebanon/Syria
Anti-Liban *see* Anti-Lebanon
115 *M22* **Antimácheia** Kos, Dodekánisa, Greece *47°19′N 07°54′E*
115 *I22* **Antímilos** *island* Kykládes, Greece, Aegean Sea
36 *L6* **Antimony** Utah, W USA *38°07′N 112°00′W*
An tInbhear Mór *see* Arklow
30 *M10* **Antioch** Illinois, N USA *42°28′N 88°06′W*
Antioch *see* Antakya
102 *I10* **Antioche, Pertuis d'** *inlet* W France
Antiochia *see* Antakya
54 *D8* **Antioquia** Antioquia, C Colombia *06°36′N 75°53′W*
54 *E8* **Antioquia** *off.* Departamento de Antioquia. ◈ *province* C Colombia
Antioquia, Departamento de *see* Antioquia
115 *J21* **Antíparos** *var.* Andipáros. *island* Kykládes, Greece, Aegean Sea
115 *B17* **Antípaxoi** *var.* Andipaxi. *island* Iónia Nísiá, Greece, C Mediterranean Sea
122 *J8* **Antipayuta** Yamalo-Nenetskiy Avtonomnyy Okrug, N Russian Federation *69°08′N 76°43′E*
192 *L12* **Antipodes Islands** *island group* S New Zealand
Antipolis *see* Antibes
115 *J18* **Antípsara** *var.* Andípsara. *island* E Greece
Antiquaria *see* Antequera
15 *N10* **Antique, Lac** ◎ Québec, SE Canada
115 *E18* **Antírrio** *var.* Andírrion. Dytikí Elláda, C Greece *38°20′N 21°46′E*

◆ Country
● Country Capital
◇ Dependent Territory
○ Dependent Territory Capital
◈ Administrative Regions
✈ International Airport
▲ Mountain
▲▲ Mountain Range
Volcano
≈ River
◎ Lake
▣ Reservoir

115 K16 **Ántissa** *var.* Ándissa. Lésvos, E Greece *39°15′N 26°00′E*
An tIúr *see* Newry
Antivari *see* Bar
56 C6 **Antizana** ▲ N Ecuador *0°29′S 78°08′W*
27 Q13 **Antlers** Oklahoma, C USA *34°15′N 95°38′W*
93 J14 **Antnäs** Norrbotten, N Sweden *65°32′N 21°53′E*
Antō *see* Andong
62 G5 **Antofagasta** Antofagasta, N Chile *23°40′S 70°23′W*
62 G6 **Antofagasta** *off.* Región de Antofagasta. ◈ *region* N Chile
Antofagasta, Región de *see* Antofagasta
62 I7 **Antofalla, Salar de** *salt lake* NW Argentina
99 D20 **Antoing** Hainaut, SW Belgium *50°34′N 03°26′E*
43 S16 **Antón** Coclé, C Panama *08°23′N 80°15′W*
24 M5 **Anton** Texas, SW USA *33°48′N 102°09′W*
37 T11 **Anton Chico** New Mexico, SW USA *35°12′N 105°09′W*
60 K12 **Antonina** Paraná, S Brazil *25°28′S 48°43′W*
188 C16 **Antonio B. Won Pat International** ✈ (Agana) C Guam *13°28′N 144°48′E*
103 O5 **Antony** Hauts-de-Seine, N France *48°45′N 02°17′E*
Antratsit *see* Antratsyt
117 Y8 **Antratsyt** *Rus.* Antratsit. Luhans'ka Oblast', E Ukraine *48°07′N 39°05′E*
97 G15 **Antrim** *Ir.* Aontroim. NE Northern Ireland, United Kingdom *54°43′N 06°13′W*
97 G14 **Antrim** *Ir.* Aontroim. *cultural region* NE Northern Ireland, United Kingdom
97 G14 **Antrim Mountains** ▲▲ NE Northern Ireland, United Kingdom
172 H5 **Antsalova** Mahajanga, W Madagascar *18°40′S 44°37′E*
Antserana *see* Antsirañana
An tSionainn *see* Shannon
172 J2 **Antsirañana** *var.* Antserana; *prev.* Antsirane, Diégo-Suarez. Antsirañana, N Madagascar *12°19′S 49°17′E*
172 J2 **Antsirañana** ◈ *province* N Madagascar
Antsirane *see* Antsirañana
An tSiúir *see* Suir
118 I7 **Antsla** *Ger.* Anzen. Võrumaa, SE Estonia *57°52′N 26°33′E*
An tSláine *see* Slaney
172 J3 **Antsohihy** Mahajanga, NW Madagascar *14°50′S 47°58′E*
63 G14 **Antuco, Volcán** ☒ C Chile *37°29′S 71°25′W*
169 W10 **Antu, Gunung** ▲ Borneo, N Indonesia *0°57′N 118°51′E*
An Tullach *see* Tullow
An-tung *see* Dandong
Antunnacum *see* Andernach
Antwerp *see* Antwerpen
99 G16 **Antwerpen** *Eng.* Antwerp, *Fr.* Anvers. Antwerpen, N Belgium *51°13′N 04°25′E*
99 H16 **Antwerpen** *Eng.* Antwerp. ◈ *province* N Belgium
An Uaimh *see* Navan
154 N12 **Anugul** *var.* Angul. Orissa, E India *20°51′N 84°59′E*
152 F9 **Anūpgarh** Rājasthān, NW India *29°10′N 73°14′E*
154 K10 **Anūppur** Madhya Pradesh, C India *23°05′N 81°45′E*
155 K24 **Anuradhapura** North Central Province, C Sri Lanka *08°20′N 80°25′E*
Anvers *see* Antwerpen
194 G4 **Anvers Island** *island* Antarctica
39 N11 **Anvik** Alaska, USA *62°39′N 160°12′W*
39 N10 **Anvik River** ≈ Alaska, USA
38 F17 **Anvil Peak** ▲ Semisopochnoi Island, Alaska, USA *51°59′N 179°36′E*
159 P7 **Anxi** *var.* Yuanquan. Gansu, N China *40°32′N 95°50′E*
182 F8 **Anxious Bay** *bay* South Australia
161 O5 **Anyang** Henan, C China *36°11′N 114°18′E*
159 S11 **A'nyêmaqên Shan** ▲▲ C China
118 H12 **Anykščiai** Utena, E Lithuania *55°30′N 25°34′E*
161 P13 **Anyuan** *var.* Xinshan. Jiangxi, S China *25°10′N 115°25′E*
123 T7 **Anyuysk** Chukotskiy Avtonomnyy Okrug, NE Russian Federation *68°22′N 161°33′E*
123 T7 **Anyuyskiy Khrebet** ▲▲ NE Russian Federation
54 D8 **Anzá** Antioquia, C Colombia *06°18′N 75°54′W*
Anzen *see* Antsla
107 I16 **Anzio** Lazio, C Italy *41°28′N 12°38′E*
55 O6 **Anzoátegui** *off.* Estado Anzoátegui. ◈ *state* NE Venezuela
Anzoátegui, Estado *see* Anzoátegui
147 P12 **Anzob** W Tajikistan *39°24′N 68°55′E*
Anzyō *see* Anjō
Aoba *see* Ambae
165 X13 **Aoga-shima** *island* Izu-shotō, SE Japan
Aohan Qi *see* Xinhui
105 R3 **Aoiz** *Bas.* Agoitz, *var.* Agoiz. Navarra, N Spain *42°47′N 01°23′W*
167 O11 **Ao Krung Thep** *var.* Krung Thep Mahanakhon, *Eng.* Bangkok. ● (Thailand) Bangkok, C Thailand *13°44′N 100°30′E*
186 M9 **Aola** *var.* Tenaghau. Guadalcanal, C Solomon Islands *09°32′S 160°28′E*
166 M15 **Ao Luk Nua** Krabi, SW Thailand *08°21′N 98°43′E*
Aomen *see* Macao
172 N8 **Aomori** Aomori, Honshū, C Japan *40°50′N 140°43′E*
172 N8 **Aomori** *off.* Aomori-ken. ◈ *prefecture* Honshū, C Japan
Aomori-ken *see* Aomori
Aontroim *see* Antrim
115 C15 **Aóos** *var.* Vijosa, Vijosë, *Alb.* Lumi i Vjosës. ≈ Albania/Greece *see also* Vjosës, Lumi i
Aóos *see* Vjosës, Lumi i
191 Q7 **Aorai, Mont** ☒ Tahiti, W French Polynesia *17°36′S 149°29′W*
185 E19 **Aoraki** *prev.* Aorangi, Mount Cook. ▲ South Island, New Zealand *43°38′S 170°05′E*
167 R13 **Aôral, Phnum** *prev.* Phnom Aural. ▲ W Cambodia *12°01′N 104°10′E*
Aorangi *see* Aoraki
185 L15 **Aorangi Mountains** ▲▲ North Island, New Zealand
184 H13 **Aorere** ≈ South Island, New Zealand
106 A7 **Aosta** *anc.* Augusta Praetoria. Valle d'Aosta, NW Italy *45°43′N 07°20′E*
77 O11 **Aougoundou, Lac** ◎ S Mali
76 K9 **Aoukâr** *var.* Aouker. *plateau* C Mauritania
78 J13 **Aouk, Bahr** ≈ Central African Republic/Chad
Aouker *see* Aoukâr
74 B11 **Aousard** SE Western Sahara *22°42′N 14°22′W*
164 H12 **Aoya** Tottori, Honshū, SW Japan *35°31′N 134°01′E*
Aoyang *see* Shanggao
78 H5 **Aozou** Borkou-Ennedi-Tibesti, N Chad *22°01′N 17°11′E*
26 M11 **Apache** Oklahoma, C USA *34°57′N 98°21′W*
36 L14 **Apache Junction** Arizona, SW USA *33°25′N 111°33′W*
24 J9 **Apache Mountains** ▲▲ Texas, SW USA
36 M16 **Apache Peak** ▲ Arizona, SW USA *31°50′N 110°25′W*
116 H10 **Apahida** Cluj, NW Romania *46°49′N 23°45′E*
23 T9 **Apalachee Bay** *bay* Florida, SE USA
23 T3 **Apalachee River** ≈ Georgia, SE USA
23 S10 **Apalachicola** Florida, SE USA *29°43′N 84°58′W*
23 S10 **Apalachicola Bay** *bay* Florida, SE USA
23 R9 **Apalachicola River** ≈ Florida, SE USA
Apam *see* Apan
Apamama *see* Abemama
41 P14 **Apan** *var.* Apam. Hidalgo, C Mexico *19°48′N 98°25′W*
42 J8 **Apanás, Lago de** ◎ NW Nicaragua
54 H14 **Apaporis, Río** ≈ Brazil/Colombia
185 C23 **Aparima** ≈ South Island, New Zealand
171 O1 **Aparri** Luzon, N Philippines *18°16′N 121°42′E*
112 J9 **Apatin** Vojvodina, NW Serbia *45°40′N 19°01′E*
124 J4 **Apatity** Murmanskaya Oblast', NW Russian Federation *67°34′N 33°26′E*
55 X9 **Apatou** NW French Guiana *05°10′N 54°22′W*
40 M14 **Apatzingán** *var.* Apatzingán de la Constitución. Michoacán, SW Mexico *19°05′N 102°20′W*
Apatzingán de la Constitución *see* Apatzingán
171 X12 **Apauwar** Papua, E Indonesia *01°36′S 138°10′E*
Apaxtla *see* Apaxtla de Castrejón
41 O15 **Apaxtla de Castrejón** *var.* Apaxtla. Guerrero, S Mexico *18°06′N 99°55′W*
118 J7 **Ape** NE Latvia *57°32′N 26°42′E*
98 L11 **Apeldoorn** Gelderland, E Netherlands *52°13′N 05°57′E*
Apennines *see* Appennino
Apenrade *see* Aabenraa
57 L17 **Apere, Río** ≈ C Bolivia
55 W11 **Apetina** Sipaliwini, SE Surinam *03°30′N 55°03′W*
21 U9 **Apex** North Carolina, SE USA *35°43′N 78°51′W*
79 M16 **Api** Orientale, N Dem. Rep. Congo *03°40′N 25°26′E*
152 M9 **Api** ▲ NW Nepal *30°07′N 80°57′E*
192 H16 **Āpia** ● (Samoa) Upolu, SE Samoa *13°50′S 171°47′W*
Apia *see* Abaiang
60 K11 **Apiaí** São Paulo, S Brazil *24°29′S 48°51′W*
170 M16 **Api, Gunung** ▲ Pulau Sangeang, S Indonesia *08°09′S 119°03′E*
187 N9 **Apio** Maramasike Island, N Solomon Islands *09°36′S 161°25′E*
41 O15 **Apipilulco** Guerrero, S Mexico *18°11′N 99°40′W*
41 P14 **Apizaco** Tlaxcala, S Mexico *19°26′N 98°09′W*
137 Q8 **Apkhazeti** *var.* Abkhazia; *prev.* Ap'khazet'i. ◈ *autonomous republic* NW Georgia
Ap'khazet'i *see* Apkhazeti
104 I4 **A Pobla de Trives** *Cast.* Puebla de Trives. Galicia, NW Spain *42°21′N 07°16′W*
55 U9 **Apoera** Sipaliwini, NW Surinam *05°12′N 57°13′W*
115 O23 **Apolakkiá** Ródos, Dodekánisa, Greece, Aegean Sea *36°02′N 27°48′E*
101 L16 **Apolda** Thüringen, C Germany *51°02′N 11°31′E*
192 H16 **Apolima Strait** *strait* C Pacific Ocean
182 M13 **Apollo Bay** Victoria, SE Australia *38°40′S 143°44′E*
Apollonia *see* Sozopol
57 J16 **Apolo** La Paz, W Bolivia *14°48′S 68°31′W*
57 J16 **Apolobamba, Cordillera** ▲▲ Bolivia/Peru
171 Q8 **Apo, Mount** ☒ Mindanao, S Philippines *06°54′N 125°16′E*
23 W11 **Apopka** Florida, SE USA *28°40′N 81°30′W*
23 W11 **Apopka, Lake** ◎ Florida, SE USA
59 I19 **Aporé, Rio** ≈ SW Brazil
30 K2 **Apostle Islands** *island group* Wisconsin, N USA
Apostolas Andreas, Cape *see* Zafer Burnu
61 F14 **Apóstoles** Misiones, NE Argentina *27°54′S 55°45′W*
Apostólou Andréa, Akrotíri *see* Zafer Burnu
117 S9 **Apostolove** *Rus.* Apostolovo. Dnipropetrovs'ka Oblast', E Ukraine *47°40′N 33°45′E*
Apostolovo *see* Apostolove
17 S10 **Appalachian Mountains** ▲▲ E USA
95 K14 **Äppelbo** Dalarna, C Sweden *60°30′N 14°00′E*
98 N7 **Appelscha** *Fris.* Appelskea. Fryslân, N Netherlands *52°57′N 06°19′E*
Appelskea *see* Appelscha
106 G11 **Appennino** *Eng.* Apennines. ▲▲ Italy/San Marino
107 L17 **Appennino Campano** ▲▲ C Italy
108 I7 **Appenzell** Inner-Rhoden, NW Switzerland *47°20′N 09°25′E*
Appenzell *former canton see* Ausser-Rhoden, Inner-Rhoden
55 V12 **Appikalo** Sipaliwini, S Surinam *02°07′N 56°16′W*
98 O5 **Appingedam** Groningen, NE Netherlands *53°18′N 06°52′E*
25 X8 **Appleby** Texas, SW USA *31°43′N 94°36′W*
97 L15 **Appleby-in-Westmorland** Cumbria, NW England, United Kingdom *54°35′N 02°26′W*
30 K10 **Apple River** ≈ Illinois, N USA
30 I5 **Apple River** ≈ Wisconsin, N USA
25 W9 **Apple Springs** Texas, SW USA *31°13′N 94°57′W*
29 S8 **Appleton** Minnesota, N USA *45°12′N 96°01′W*
30 M7 **Appleton** Wisconsin, N USA *44°17′N 88°24′W*
27 S5 **Appleton City** Missouri, C USA *38°11′N 94°01′W*
35 U14 **Apple Valley** California, W USA *34°30′N 117°11′W*
29 V9 **Apple Valley** Minnesota, N USA *44°43′N 93°13′W*
21 U6 **Appomattox** Virginia, NE USA *37°21′N 78°51′W*
188 B16 **Apra Harbor** *harbour* W Guam
188 B16 **Apra Heights** W Guam
106 F6 **Aprica, Passo dell'** *pass* N Italy
107 M15 **Apricena** *anc.* Hadria Picena. Puglia, SE Italy *41°47′N 15°27′E*
114 I9 **Apriltsi** Lovech, N Bulgaria *42°50′N 24°54′E*
126 L14 **Apsheronsk** Krasnodarskiy Kray, SW Russian Federation *44°27′N 39°45′E*
Apsheronskiy Poluostrov *see* Abşeron Yarımadası
103 S15 **Apt** *anc.* Apta Julia. Vaucluse, SE France *43°54′N 05°24′E*
Apta Julia *see* Apt
38 H12 **'Apua Point** *var.* Apua Point. *headland* Hawai'i, USA, C Pacific Ocean *19°15′N 155°13′W*
60 I10 **Apucarana** Paraná, S Brazil *23°34′S 51°28′W*
Apulia *see* Puglia
54 K8 **Apure** *off.* Estado Apure. ◈ *state* C Venezuela
Apure, Estado *see* Apure
54 J7 **Apure, Río** ≈ W Venezuela
57 F16 **Apurímac** *off.* Departamento de Apurímac. ◈ *department* C Peru
Apurímac, Departamento de *see* Apurímac
57 F15 **Apurímac, Río** ≈ S Peru
116 G10 **Apuseni, Munţii** ▲▲ W Romania
Aqaba/'Aqaba *see* Al 'Aqabah
138 F15 **Aqaba, Gulf of** *var.* Gulf of Elat, *Ar.* Khalīj al 'Aqabah; *anc.* Sinus Aelaniticus. *gulf* NE Red Sea
139 R7 **'Aqabah** Al Anbār, C Iraq *33°33′N 42°55′E*
'Aqabah, Khalīj al *see* Aqaba, Gulf of
149 O2 **Āqchah** *var.* Āqcheh. Jowzjān, N Afghanistan *37°N 66°07′E*
Āqcheh *see* Āqchah
Aqkengse *see* Akkense
Aqköl *see* Akkol'
Aqmola *see* Astana
Aqmola Oblysy *see* Akmola
158 L10 **Aqqikkol Hu** ◎ NW China
Aqqū *see* Akku
Aqqystaū *see* Akkystau
'Aqrah *see* Ākrē
Aqsay *see* Aksay
Aqshataū *see* Akshatau
Aqsū *see* Aksu
Aqsūat *see* Aksuat
Aqtas *see* Aktas
Aqtaū *see* Aktau
Aqtöbe *see* Aktobe
Aqtöbe Oblysy *see* Aktyubinsk
Aqtoghay *see* Aktogay
Aquae Augustae *see* Dax
Aquae Calidae *see* Bath
Aquae Flaviae *see* Chaves
Aquae Grani *see* Aachen
Aquae Panoniae *see* Baden
Aquae Sextiae *see* Aix-en-Provence
Aquae Solis *see* Bath
Aquae Tarbelicae *see* Dax
36 J11 **Aquarius Mountains** ▲▲ Arizona, SW USA
62 O5 **Aquidabán, Río** ≈ E Paraguay
59 H20 **Aquidauana** Mato Grosso do Sul, S Brazil *20°27′S 55°45′W*
40 L15 **Aquila** Michoacán, S Mexico *18°36′N 103°32′W*
Aquila/Aquila degli Abruzzi *see* L'Aquila
25 T8 **Aquilla** Texas, SW USA *31°51′N 97°13′W*
44 L9 **Aquin** S Haiti *18°16′N 73°24′W*
Aquisgranum *see* Aachen
102 J13 **Aquitaine** ◈ *region* SW France
Aqzhar *see* Akzhar
153 P13 **Āra** *prev.* Arrah. Bihār, N India *25°34′N 84°40′E*
105 S4 **Ara** ≈ NE Spain
23 P2 **Arab** Alabama, S USA *34°19′N 86°30′W*
Araba *see* Álava
138 G12 **'Arabah, Wādī al** *Heb.* Ha'Arava. *dry watercourse* Israel/Jordan
117 U12 **Arabats'ka Strilka, Kosa** *spit* S Ukraine
117 U12 **Arabats'ka Zatoka** *gulf* S Ukraine
'Arab, Baḩr al *see* Arab, Bahr el
80 C12 **Arab, Bahr el** *var.* Baḩr al 'Arab. ≈ S Sudan
56 E7 **Arabela, Río** ≈ N Peru
173 O4 **Arabian Basin** *undersea feature* N Arabian Sea *11°30′N 65°00′E*
Arabian Desert *see* Sahara el Sharqîya
141 N9 **Arabian Peninsula** *peninsula* SW Asia
85 P15 **Arabian Plate** *tectonic feature* Africa/Asia/Europe
141 W14 **Arabian Sea** *sea* NW Indian Ocean
Arabicus, Sinus *see* Red Sea
'Arabī, Khalīj al *see* Persian Gulf
Arabistan *see* Khūzestān
'Arabīyah as Su'ūdīyah, Al Mamlakah al *see* Saudi Arabia
'Arabīyah Jumhūrīyah, Miṣr al *see* Egypt
138 I9 **'Arab, Jabal al** ▲▲ S Syria
Arab Republic of Egypt *see* Egypt
139 Y12 **'Arab, Shaṭṭ al** *Eng.* Shatt al Arab, *Per.* Arvand Rūd. ≈ Iran/Iraq
136 I11 **Araç** Kastamonu, N Turkey *41°14′N 33°20′E*
59 P16 **Aracaju** *state capital* Sergipe, E Brazil *10°45′S 37°07′W*
54 F5 **Aracataca** Magdalena, N Colombia *10°38′N 74°09′W*
58 P13 **Aracati** Ceará, E Brazil *04°32′S 37°45′W*
60 J8 **Araçatuba** São Paulo, S Brazil *21°12′S 50°24′W*
136 I11 **Araç Çayı** ≈ N Turkey
104 J13 **Aracena** Andalucía, S Spain *37°54′N 06°33′W*
115 F20 **Arachnaío** ▲▲ S Greece
115 D16 **Árachthos** *var.* Arta, *prev.* Árakhthos; *anc.* Arachthus. ≈ W Greece
Arachthus *see* Árachthos
59 N19 **Araçuai** Minas Gerais, SE Brazil *16°52′S 42°03′W*
138 F11 **'Arad** Southern, S Israel *31°16′N 35°09′E*
116 F11 **Arad** Arad, W Romania *46°12′N 21°20′E*
116 F11 **Arad** ◈ *county* W Romania
78 J9 **Arada** Biltine, NE Chad *15°00′N 20°38′E*
143 P18 **'Arādah** Abū Ẓaby, S United Arab Emirates *22°57′N 53°24′E*
Aradhippou *see* Aradippou
121 Q3 **Aradippou** *var.* Aradhippou. SE Cyprus *34°57′N 33°37′E*
174 K6 **Arafura Sea** *Ind.* Laut Arafuru. *sea* W Pacific Ocean
174 L6 **Arafura Shelf** *undersea feature* C Arafura Sea
Arafuru, Laut *see* Arafura Sea
59 J18 **Aragarças** Goiás, C Brazil *15°55′S 52°12′W*
Aragats, Gora *see* Aragats Lerr
137 T12 **Aragats Lerr** *Rus.* Gora Aragats. ▲ W Armenia *40°31′N 44°06′E*
32 E14 **Arago, Cape** *headland* Oregon, NW USA *43°17′N 124°25′W*
105 R6 **Aragón** *autonomous community* E Spain
105 Q4 **Aragón** ≈ NE Spain
107 I24 **Aragona** Sicilia, Italy, C Mediterranean Sea *37°25′N 13°37′E*
105 Q7 **Aragoncillo** ▲ C Spain *40°59′N 02°01′W*
54 L5 **Aragua** *off.* Estado Aragua. ◈ *state* N Venezuela
55 N6 **Aragua de Barcelona** Anzoátegui, NE Venezuela *09°30′N 64°51′W*
55 O5 **Aragua de Maturín** Monagas, NE Venezuela *09°58′N 63°30′W*
Aragua, Estado *see* Aragua
59 K15 **Araguaia, Río** *var.* Araguaya. ≈ C Brazil
59 K19 **Araguari** Minas Gerais, SE Brazil *18°38′S 48°13′W*
58 J11 **Araguari, Rio** ≈ SW Brazil
Araguaya *see* Araguaia, Río
104 K14 **Arahal** Andalucía, S Spain *37°15′N 05°33′W*
165 N11 **Arai** Niigata, Honshū, C Japan *37°02′N 138°17′E*
Árainn *see* Inishmore
Árainn Mhór *see* Aran Island
Ara Jovis *see* Aranjuez
74 J11 **Arak** C Algeria *25°17′N 03°45′E*
171 Y15 **Arak** Papua, E Indonesia *07°14′S 139°40′E*
142 M7 **Arāk** *prev.* Sultānābād. Markazī, W Iran *34°07′N 49°39′E*
188 D10 **Arakabesan** *island* Palau Islands, N Palau
55 S7 **Arakaka** NW Guyana *07°37′N 59°58′W*
Arakan State *see* Rakhine State
166 K5 **Arakan Yoma** ▲▲ W Burma (Myanmar)
165 O10 **Arakawa** Niigata, Honshū, C Japan *38°06′N 139°25′E*
Árakhthos *see* Árachthos
Araks/Arak's *see* Aras
158 H7 **Aral** Xinjiang Uygur Zizhiqu, NW China *40°40′N 81°19′E*
Aral *see* Aralsk, Kazakhstan
Aral *see* Vose', Tajikistan
Aral-Bukhorskiy Kanal *see* Amu-Buxoro Kanali
137 T12 **Aralık** Iğdır, E Turkey *39°54′N 44°28′E*
146 H5 **Aral Sea** *Kaz.* Aral Tengizi, *Rus.* Aral'skoye More, *Uzb.* Orol Dengizi. *inland sea* Kazakhstan/Uzbekistan
144 L13 **Aral'sk** *Kaz.* Aral. Kzylorda, SW Kazakhstan *46°48′N 61°40′E*
Aral'skoye More/Aral Tengizi *see* Aral Sea
41 O10 **Aramberri** Nuevo León, NE Mexico *24°05′N 99°52′W*
186 B8 **Aramia** ≈ SW Papua New Guinea
105 N5 **Aranda de Duero** Castilla y León, N Spain *41°40′N 03°41′W*
112 M12 **Aranđelovac** *prev.* Arandjelovac. Serbia, C Serbia *44°18′N 20°32′E*
Arandjelovac *see* Aranđelovac
97 J19 **Aran Fawddwy** ▲ NW Wales, United Kingdom *52°48′N 03°42′W*
97 C14 **Aran Island** *Ir.* Árainn Mhór. *island* NW Ireland
97 A18 **Aran Islands** *island group* W Ireland
105 N9 **Aranjuez** *anc.* Ara Jovis. Madrid, C Spain *40°02′N 03°37′W*
83 E20 **Aranos** Hardap, SE Namibia *24°10′S 19°08′E*
25 U14 **Aransas Bay** *inlet* Texas, SW USA
25 T14 **Aransas Pass** Texas, SW USA *27°54′N 97°09′W*
191 O3 **Aranuka** *prev.* Nanouki. *atoll* Tungaru, W Kiribati
143 N6 **Ārān-va-Bidgol** *var.* Golārā. Eşfahān, C Iran *34°03′N 51°30′E*
167 Q11 **Aranyaprathet** Prachin Buri, S Thailand *13°42′N 102°32′E*
Aranyosaszatal *see* Zlatý Stôl
Aranyosgyéres *see* Câmpia Turzii
Aranyosmarót *see* Zlaté Moravce
164 C14 **Arao** Kumamoto, Kyūshū, SW Japan *32°58′N 130°26′E*
77 O8 **Araouane** Tombouctou, N Mali *18°53′N 03°31′W*
26 L10 **Arapaho** Oklahoma, C USA *35°34′N 98°57′W*
29 N16 **Arapahoe** Nebraska, C USA *40°18′N 99°54′W*
57 I16 **Arapa, Laguna** ◎ S Peru
185 K14 **Arapawa Island** *island* C New Zealand
61 E17 **Arapey Grande, Río** ≈ N Uruguay
59 P16 **Arapiraca** Alagoas, E Brazil *09°45′S 36°40′W*
140 M3 **'Ar'ar** Al Ḥudūd ash Shamālīyah, NW Saudi Arabia *31°N 41°E*
54 G15 **Araracuara** Caquetá, S Colombia *0°36′S 72°24′W*
61 K15 **Araranguá** Santa Catarina, S Brazil *29°00′S 49°30′W*
60 L8 **Araraquara** São Paulo, S Brazil *21°46′S 48°08′W*
59 O13 **Araras** Ceará, E Brazil *04°08′S 40°30′W*
58 I14 **Araras** Pará, N Brazil *06°04′S 54°34′W*
60 L9 **Araras** São Paulo, S Brazil *22°21′S 47°21′W*
60 H11 **Araras, Serra das** ▲▲ S Brazil
137 U12 **Ararat** S Armenia *39°49′N 44°45′E*
182 M12 **Ararat** Victoria, SE Australia *37°20′S 143°00′E*
Ararat, Mount *see* Büyükağrı Dağı
140 M3 **'Ar'ar, Wādī** *dry watercourse* Iraq/Saudi Arabia
129 N7 **Aras** *Arm.* Arak's, *Az.* Araz Nehri, *Per.* Rūd-e Aras, *Rus.* Araks; *prev.* Araxes. ≈ SW Asia
Aras de Alpuente *see* Aras de los Olmos
105 R9 **Aras de los Olmos** *prev.* Aras de Alpuente. Valenciana, E Spain *39°55′N 01°09′W*
137 S13 **Aras Güneyi Dağları** ▲▲ NE Turkey
Aras, Rūd-e *see* Aras
191 U9 **Aratika** *atoll* Îles Tuamotu, C French Polynesia
Aratürük *see* Yiwu
54 I8 **Arauca** Arauca, NE Colombia *07°03′N 70°47′W*
54 I8 **Arauca** *off.* Intendencia de Arauca. ◈ *province* NE Colombia
Arauca, Intendencia de *see* Arauca
63 G15 **Araucanía** *off.* Región de la Araucanía. ◈ *region* C Chile
Araucanía, Región de la *see* Araucanía
54 L7 **Arauca, Río** ≈ Colombia/Venezuela
63 F14 **Arauco** Bío Bío, C Chile *37°15′S 73°22′W*
63 F14 **Arauco, Golfo de** *gulf* S Chile
54 H8 **Arauquita** Arauca, C Colombia *06°57′N 71°19′W*
Arausio *see* Orange
152 F13 **Arāvali Range** ▲▲ N India
186 J7 **Arawa** Bougainville Island, NE Papua New Guinea *06°15′S 155°35′E*
185 C20 **Arawata** ≈ South Island, New Zealand
186 F7 **Arawe Islands** *island group* E Papua New Guinea
59 L20 **Araxá** Minas Gerais, SE Brazil *19°37′S 46°50′W*
Araxes *see* Aras
55 O5 **Araya** Sucre, N Venezuela *10°34′N 64°15′W*
Araz Nehri *see* Aras
105 P4 **Arba** ≈ N Spain
81 I15 **Ārba Minch'** Southern Nationalities, S Ethiopia *06°02′N 37°34′E*
139 U4 **Arbat** As Sulaymānīyah, NE Iraq *35°26′N 45°34′E*
107 D19 **Arbatax** Sardegna, Italy, C Mediterranean Sea *39°57′N 09°42′E*
Arbe *see* Rab
Arbela *see* Arbīl
139 S3 **Arbīl** *var.* Erbil, Irbīl, *Kurd.* Hawlêr; *anc.* Arbela. Arbīl, N Iraq *36°12′N 44°01′E*
95 M16 **Arboga** Västmanland, C Sweden *59°24′N 15°50′E*
95 M16 **Arbogaån** ≈ C Sweden
103 S9 **Arbois** Jura, E France *46°54′N 05°45′E*
54 D6 **Arboletes** Antioquia, NW Colombia *08°52′N 76°25′W*
11 X15 **Arborg** Manitoba, S Canada *50°52′N 97°20′W*
94 N12 **Arbrå** Gävleborg, C Sweden *61°27′N 16°21′E*
96 K10 **Arbroath** *anc.* Aberbrothock. E Scotland, United Kingdom *56°34′N 02°35′W*
35 N6 **Arbuckle** California, W USA *39°00′N 122°05′W*
27 N12 **Arbuckle Mountains** ▲▲ Oklahoma, C USA
162 I5 **Arbulag** *var.* Mandal. Hövsgöl, N Mongolia *49°55′N 99°21′E*
Arbuzinka *see* Arbuzynka
117 Q8 **Arbuzynka** *Rus.* Arbuzinka. Mykolayivs'ka Oblast', S Ukraine *47°54′N 31°19′E*
103 U12 **Arc** ≈ E France
102 J13 **Arcachon** Gironde, SW France *44°40′N 01°11′W*
102 J13 **Arcachon, Bassin d'** *inlet* SW France
18 E10 **Arcade** New York, NE USA *42°32′N 78°19′W*
23 W14 **Arcadia** Florida, SE USA *27°13′N 81°51′W*
22 H5 **Arcadia** Louisiana, S USA *32°33′N 92°55′W*
30 J7 **Arcadia** Wisconsin, N USA *44°15′N 91°30′W*
Arcae Remorum *see* Châlons-en-Champagne
44 L9 **Arcahaie** C Haiti *18°46′N 72°32′W*
34 K3 **Arcata** California, W USA *40°51′N 124°06′W*
35 U6 **Arc Dome** ▲ Nevada, W USA *38°52′N 117°20′W*
107 J16 **Arce** Lazio, C Italy *41°35′N 13°34′E*
41 O15 **Arcelia** Guerrero, S Mexico *18°20′N 100°16′W*
99 M15 **Arcen** Limburg, SE Netherlands *51°28′N 06°10′E*
115 J25 **Archánes** *var.* Áno Arkhánai, Epáno Archánes; *prev.* Epáno Arkhánai. Kríti, Greece, E Mediterranean Sea *35°12′N 25°10′E*
Archangel *see* Arkhangel'sk
Archangel Bay *see* Chëshskaya Guba
115 O23 **Archángelos** *var.* Arhangelos, Arkhángelos. Ródos, Dodekánisa, Greece, Aegean Sea *36°13′N 28°07′E*
114 F7 **Archar** ≈ NW Bulgaria
31 R11 **Archbold** Ohio, N USA *41°31′N 84°18′W*
105 R12 **Archena** Murcia, SE Spain *38°07′N 01°17′W*
25 R5 **Archer City** Texas, SW USA *33°36′N 98°37′W*
104 M14 **Archidona** Andalucía, S Spain *37°06′N 04°23′W*
65 B25 **Arch Islands** *island group* SW Falkland Islands
106 G13 **Arcidosso** Toscana, C Italy *42°52′N 11°30′E*
103 Q5 **Arcis-sur-Aube** Aube, N France *48°32′N 04°09′E*
182 F3 **Arckaringa Creek** *seasonal river* South Australia
106 G7 **Arco** Trentino-Alto Adige, N Italy *45°53′N 10°52′E*
33 Q14 **Arco** Idaho, NW USA *43°38′N 113°18′W*
30 M14 **Arcola** Illinois, N USA *39°39′N 88°19′W*
105 P6 **Arcos de Jalón** Castilla y León, N Spain *41°12′N 02°13′W*
104 K15 **Arcos de la Frontera** Andalucía, S Spain *36°45′N 05°49′W*
104 G5 **Arcos de Valdevez** Viana do Castelo, N Portugal *41°51′N 08°25′W*
59 P15 **Arcoverde** Pernambuco, E Brazil *08°23′S 37°W*
102 H5 **Arcovest, Pointe de l'** *headland* NW France *48°49′N 02°58′W*
Arctic Mid Oceanic Ridge *see* Nansen Cordillera
197 R8 **Arctic Ocean** *ocean*
8 G7 **Arctic Red River** ≈ Northwest Territories/Yukon Territory, NW Canada
Arctic Red River *see* Tsiigehtchic
39 S6 **Arctic Village** Alaska, USA *68°07′N 145°32′W*
194 H1 **Arctowski** *Polish research station* South Shetland Islands, Antarctica *61°57′S 58°23′W*
114 I12 **Arda** *var.* Ardhas, *Gk.* Árdas. ≈ Bulgaria/Greece *see also* Ardas
142 L2 **Ardabīl** *var.* Ardebil. Ardabīl, NW Iran *38°15′N 48°18′E*
142 L2 **Ardabīl** *off.* Ostān-e Ardabīl. ◈ *province* NW Iran
Ardabīl, Ostān-e *see* Ardabīl
137 R11 **Ardahan** Ardahan, NE Turkey *41°08′N 42°41′E*
137 S11 **Ardahan** ◈ *province* Ardahan, Turkey
143 P8 **Ardakān** Yazd, C Iran *32°20′N 53°59′E*
94 E12 **Årdalstangen** Sogn Og Fjordane, S Norway *61°14′N 07°45′E*
137 R11 **Ardanuç** Artvin, NE Turkey *41°07′N 42°04′E*
114 L12 **Ardas** *var.* Ardhas, *Bul.* Arda. ≈ Bulgaria/Greece *see also* Arda
138 I13 **Ard aş Şawwān** *var.* Ardh es Suwwān. *plain* S Jordan
127 P5 **Ardatov** Respublika Mordoviya, W Russian Federation *54°49′N 46°13′E*
14 G12 **Ardbeg** Ontario, S Canada *45°38′N 80°05′W*
Ardeal *see* Transylvania
Ardebil *see* Ardabīl
103 Q13 **Ardèche** ◈ *department* E France
103 Q13 **Ardèche** ≈ C France
97 F17 **Ardee** *Ir.* Baile Átha Fhirdhia. Louth, NE Ireland *53°52′N 06°33′W*
103 Q3 **Ardennes** ◈ *department* NE France
99 J23 **Ardennes** *physical region* Belgium/France
137 Q11 **Ardeşen** Rize, NE Turkey *41°14′N 41°00′E*
143 O7 **Ardestān** *var.* Ardistan. Eşfahān, C Iran *33°29′N 52°17′E*
108 J9 **Ardez** Graubünden, SE Switzerland *46°47′N 10°09′E*
Ardhas *see* Arda/Ardas
Ardh es Suwwān *see* Ard aş Şawwān
Ardila *see* Ardila, Ribeira de
104 I12 **Ardila, Ribeira de** *Sp.* Ardilla. ≈ Portugal/Spain *see also* Ardilla
Ardila, Ribeira de *see* Ardilla
11 T17 **Ardill** Saskatchewan, S Canada *49°56′N 105°49′W*
104 I12 **Ardilla** *Port.* Ribeira de Ardila. ≈ Portugal/Spain *see also* Ardila, Ribeira de
40 M11 **Ardilla, Cerro la** ▲ C Mexico *22°15′N 102°33′W*
114 J12 **Ardino** Kŭrdzhali, S Bulgaria *41°38′N 25°22′E*
Ardistan *see* Ardestān
183 P9 **Ardlethan** New South Wales, SE Australia *34°24′S 146°52′E*
Ard Mhacha *see* Armagh
23 P1 **Ardmore** Alabama, S USA *34°59′N 86°51′W*
27 N13 **Ardmore** Oklahoma, C USA *34°11′N 97°08′W*
20 J10 **Ardmore** Tennessee, S USA *35°00′N 86°48′W*
96 G10 **Ardnamurchan, Point of** *headland* N Scotland, United Kingdom *56°42′N 06°15′W*
Ardni *see* Arnøya
99 C17 **Ardooie** West-Vlaanderen, W Belgium *50°59′N 03°10′E*
182 I9 **Ardrossan** South Australia *34°27′S 137°54′E*
116 H9 **Ardusat** *Hung.* Erdőszáda. Maramureş, N Romania *47°36′N 23°25′E*
93 F16 **Åre** Jämtland, C Sweden *63°25′N 13°04′E*
79 P16 **Arebi** Orientale, NE Dem. Rep. Congo *02°47′N 29°35′E*
45 T5 **Arecibo** C Puerto Rico *18°29′N 66°44′W*
171 V13 **Aredo** Papua, E Indonesia *02°27′S 133°59′E*
59 P14 **Areia Branca** Rio Grande do Norte, E Brazil *04°53′S 37°03′W*
119 O14 **Arekhawsk** *Rus.* Orekhovsk. Vitsyebskaya Voblasts', N Belarus *54°42′N 30°30′E*
Arel *see* Arlon
Arelas/Arelate *see* Arles
Arenal, Embalse de *see* Arenal Laguna
42 L12 **Arenal Laguna** *var.* Embalse de Arenal. ◎ NW Costa Rica
42 L13 **Arenal, Volcán** ☒ NW Costa Rica *10°21′N 84°42′W*
34 K6 **Arena, Point** *headland* California, W USA *38°57′N 123°44′W*
59 H17 **Arenápolis** Mato Grosso, W Brazil *14°25′S 56°52′W*
40 G10 **Arena, Punta** *headland* NW Mexico *23°28′N 109°24′W*
104 L8 **Arenas de San Pedro** Castilla y León, N Spain *40°12′N 05°05′W*
63 I24 **Arenas, Punta de** *headland* S Argentina *53°10′S 68°15′W*
61 B20 **Arenaza** Buenos Aires, E Argentina *34°55′S 61°45′W*
95 F17 **Arendal** Aust-Agder, S Norway *58°27′N 08°45′E*
99 J16 **Arendonk** Antwerpen, N Belgium *51°18′N 05°06′E*
43 T15 **Arenosa** Panamá, N Panama *09°02′N 79°57′W*
Arensburg *see* Kuressaare
105 W5 **Arenys de Mar** Cataluña, NE Spain *41°35′N 02°33′E*
106 C9 **Arenzano** Liguria, NW Italy *44°25′N 08°43′E*
115 F22 **Areópoli** *prev.* Areópolis. Pelopónnisos, S Greece *36°40′N 22°24′E*
Areópolis *see* Areópoli
57 H18 **Arequipa** Arequipa, SE Peru *16°24′S 71°33′W*
57 G17 **Arequipa** *off.* Departamento de Arequipa. ◈ *department* Arequia SW Peru
Arequipa, Departamento de *see* Arequipa
61 B19 **Arequito** Santa Fe, C Argentina *33°09′S 61°28′W*
104 M7 **Arévalo** Castilla y León, N Spain *41°04′N 04°44′W*
106 H12 **Arezzo** *anc.* Arretium. Toscana, C Italy *43°28′N 11°50′E*
105 Q4 **Arga** ≈ N Spain
Argaeus *see* Erciyes Dağı
115 G17 **Argalastí** Thessalía, C Greece *39°13′N 23°13′E*
105 O10 **Argamasilla de Alba** Castilla-La Mancha, C Spain *39°08′N 03°05′W*
158 L8 **Argan** Xinjiang Uygur Zizhiqu, NW China *40°09′N 88°16′E*
105 O8 **Arganda** Madrid, C Spain *40°19′N 03°26′W*
104 H8 **Arganil** Coimbra, N Portugal *40°13′N 08°03′W*
171 P6 **Argao** Cebu, C Philippines *09°52′N 123°33′E*
153 V15 **Argartala** Tripura, NE India *23°49′N 91°15′E*
123 N9 **Arga-Sala** ≈ Respublika Sakha (Yakutiya), NE Russian Federation
103 P17 **Argelès-sur-Mer** Pyrénées-Orientales, S France *42°33′N 03°01′E*
103 T15 **Argens** ≈ SE France
106 H9 **Argenta** Emilia-Romagna, N Italy *44°37′N 11°49′E*
102 K5 **Argentan** Orne, N France *48°45′N 00°01′W*
103 N12 **Argentat** Corrèze, C France *45°06′N 01°57′E*
106 A9 **Argentera** Piemonte, NE Italy *44°25′N 06°57′E*
103 N5 **Argenteuil** Val-d'Oise, N France *48°57′N 02°13′E*
62 K13 **Argentina** *off.* Argentine Republic. ◆ *republic* S South America
Argentina Basin *see* Argentine Basin
Argentine Abyssal Plain *see* Argentine Plain
65 I19 **Argentine Basin** *var.* Argentina Basin. *undersea feature* SW Atlantic Ocean *45°00′S 45°00′W*
65 I20 **Argentine Plain** *var.* Argentine Abyssal Plain. *undersea feature* SW Atlantic Ocean *47°31′S 50°00′W*
Argentine Republic *see* Argentina
Argentine Rise *see* Falkland Plateau
63 H22 **Argentino, Lago** ◎ S Argentina
102 K8 **Argenton-Château** Deux-Sèvres, W France *46°59′N 00°22′W*
102 M9 **Argenton-sur-Creuse** Indre, C France *46°34′N 01°32′E*
Argentoratum *see* Strasbourg
116 I12 **Argeş** ◈ *county* S Romania
116 K14 **Argeş** ≈ S Romania
149 O8 **Arghandāb, Daryā-ye** ≈ SE Afghanistan
Arghastān *see* Arghistān
Arghestān *see* Arghistān
149 O8 **Arghistān** *Pash.* Arghastān; *prev.* Arghestān. ≈ SE Afghanistan
Argirocastro *see* Gjirokastër
80 E7 **Argo** Northern, N Sudan *19°31′N 30°25′E*
173 P7 **Argo Fracture Zone** *tectonic feature* C Indian Ocean
115 F20 **Argolikós Kólpos** *gulf* S Greece
103 R4 **Argonne** *physical region* NE France
115 F20 **Árgos** Pelopónnisos, S Greece *37°38′N 22°43′E*
139 S1 **Argōsh** Dahūk, N Iraq *37°07′N 44°13′E*
115 D14 **Árgos Orestikó** Dytikí Makedonía, N Greece *40°27′N 21°15′E*
115 B19 **Argostóli** *var.* Argostólion. Kefallonía, Iónia Nisiá, Greece, C Mediterranean Sea *38°13′N 20°29′E*
Argostólion *see* Argostóli
Argovie *see* Aargau
35 O14 **Arguello, Point** *headland* California, W USA *34°34′N 120°39′W*
127 P16 **Argun** Chechenskaya Respublika, SW Russian Federation *43°16′N 45°53′E*

◆ Country
● Country Capital
◇ Dependent Territory
○ Dependent Territory Capital
◈ Administrative Regions
✈ International Airport
▲ Mountain
▲▲ Mountain Range
☒ Volcano
≈ River
◎ Lake
▣ Reservoir

157 *T2* **Argun** *Chin.* Ergun He, *Rus.* Argun'. ≈ China/Russian Federation
77 *T12* **Argungu** Kebbi, NW Nigeria 12°45′N 04°24′E
Arguut *see* Guchin-Us
181 *N3* **Argyle, Lake** *salt lake* Western Australia
96 *G12* **Argyll** *cultural region* W Scotland, United Kingdom
Argyrokastron *see* Gjirokastër
162 *I7* **Arhangay** ⬖ *province* C Mongolia
Arhangelos *see* Archángelos
95 *G22* **Århus** *var.* Aarhus. Midtjylland, C Denmark 56°09′N 10°11′E
139 *T1* **Ārī** Arbīl, E Iraq 37°07′N 44°34′E
Aria *see* Herāt
83 *F22* **Ariamsvlei** Karas, SE Namibia 28°08′S 19°50′E
107 *L17* **Ariano Irpino** Campania, S Italy 41°08′N 15°00′E
54 *F11* **Ariari, Río** ≈ C Colombia
151 *K19* **Ari Atoll** *var.* Alifu Atoll. *atoll* C Maldives
77 *P11* **Aribinda** N Burkina 14°12′N 00°50′W
62 *G2* **Arica** *hist.* San Marcos de Arica. Arica y Parinacota, N Chile 18°31′S 70°18′W
54 *H16* **Arica** Amazonas, S Colombia 02°09′S 71°48′W
62 *G2* **Arica** ✈ Arica y Parinacota, N Chile 18°30′S 70°20′W
62 *H2* **Arica y Parinacota** ⬖ *region* N Chile
114 *E13* **Aridaía** *var.* Aridea, Aridhaía. Dytikí Makedonía, N Greece 40°59′N 22°04′E
Aridea *see* Aridaía
172 *I15* **Aride, Île** *island* Inner Islands, NE Seychelles
Aridhaía *see* Aridaía
103 *N17* **Ariège** ⬖ *department* S France
102 *M16* **Ariège** *var.* la Riege. ≈ Andorra/France
116 *H11* **Arieş** ≈ W Romania
149 *U10* **Ārifwāla** Punjab, E Pakistan 30°15′N 73°08′E
Ariguaní *see* El Difícil
138 *G11* **Arīhā** Al Karak, W Jordan 31°25′N 35°47′E
138 *I3* **Arīḥā** *var.* Arīhā. Idlib, W Syria 35°50′N 36°36′E
Arīhā *see* Arīḥā
Arīḥā *see* Jericho
37 *W4* **Arikaree River** ≈ Colorado/Nebraska, C USA
112 *L13* **Arilje** Serbia, W Serbia 43°45′N 20°06′E
45 *U14* **Arima** Trinidad, Trinidad and Tobago 10°38′N 61°17′W
Arime *see* Al 'Arīmah
Ariminum *see* Rimini
59 *H16* **Arinos, Rio** ≈ W Brazil
40 *M14* **Ario de Rosales** *var.* Ario de Rosáles. Michoacán, SW Mexico 19°12′N 101°42′W
Ario de Rosáles *see* Ario de Rosales
118 *F12* **Ariogala** Kaunas, C Lithuania 55°16′N 23°30′E
47 *T7* **Aripuanã** ≈ W Brazil
59 *E15* **Ariquemes** Rondônia, W Brazil 09°55′S 63°06′W
121 *W13* **'Arīsh, Wādi el** ≈ NE Egypt
54 *K6* **Arismendi** Barinas, C Venezuela 08°29′N 68°22′W
10 *J14* **Aristazabal Island** *island* SW Canada
60 *F13* **Aristóbulo del Valle** Misiones, NE Argentina 27°09′S 54°54′W
172 *I5* **Arivonimamo** ✈ (Antananarivo) Antananarivo, C Madagascar 19°00′S 47°11′E
Arixang *see* Wenquan
105 *Q6* **Ariza** Aragón, NE Spain 41°19′N 02°03′W
62 *I6* **Arizaro, Salar de** *salt lake* NW Argentina
105 *O2* **Arizgoiti** *var.* Basauri. País Vasco, N Spain 43°13′N 02°54′W
62 *K13* **Arizona** San Luis, C Argentina 35°44′S 65°16′W
36 *J12* **Arizona** *off.* State of Arizona, ***also known as*** Copper State, Grand Canyon State. ⬖ *state* SW USA
40 *G4* **Arizpe** Sonora, NW Mexico 30°20′N 110°11′W
95 *J16* **Årjäng** Värmland, C Sweden 59°24′N 12°09′E
143 *P8* **Arjenān** Yazd, C Iran 32°19′N 53°48′E
92 *I13* **Arjeplog** *Lapp.* Árjepluovve. Norrbotten, N Sweden 66°04′N 18°E
Árjepluovve *see* Arjeplog
54 *E5* **Arjona** Bolívar, N Colombia 10°14′N 75°22′W
105 *N13* **Arjona** Andalucía, S Spain 37°56′N 04°04′W
123 *S10* **Arka** Khabarovskiy Kray, E Russian Federation 60°04′N 142°17′E
22 *L2* **Arkabutla Lake** ⊠ Mississippi, S USA
127 *O7* **Arkadak** Saratovskaya Oblast', W Russian Federation 51°55′N 43°29′E
27 *T13* **Arkadelphia** Arkansas, C USA 34°07′N 93°06′W
115 *J25* **Arkalochóri** ; *prev.* Arkalokhórion. Kríti, Greece, E Mediterranean Sea 35°09′N 25°15′E
Arkalohori/Arkalokhórion *see* Arkalochóri
145 *O10* **Arkalyk** *Kaz.* Arqalyq. Kostanay, N Kazakhstan 50°17′N 66°51′E
27 *U10* **Arkansas** *off.* State of Arkansas, ***also known as*** The Land of Opportunity. ⬖ *state* S USA
27 *W14* **Arkansas City** Arkansas, C USA 33°36′N 91°12′W
27 *O7* **Arkansas City** Kansas, C USA 37°03′N 97°02′W
16 *K11* **Arkansas River** ≈ C USA
182 *J5* **Arkaroola** South Australia 30°21′S 139°20′E
Arkhángelos *see* Archángelos
124 *L8* **Arkhangel'sk** *Eng.* Archangel. Arkhangel'skaya Oblast', NW Russian Federation 64°32′N 40°40′E
124 *L9* **Arkhangel'skaya Oblast'** ⬖ *province* NW Russian Federation
127 *O14* **Arkhangel'skoye** Stavropol'skiy Kray, SW Russian Federation 44°37′N 44°03′E
123 *R14* **Arkhara** Amurskaya Oblast', S Russian Federation 49°20′N 130°04′E
97 *G19* **Arklow** *Ir.* An tInbhear Mór. SE Ireland 52°48′N 06°09′W
115 *M20* **Arkoí** *island* Dodekánisa, Greece, Aegean Sea
27 *R11* **Arkoma** Oklahoma, C USA 35°19′N 94°27′W
100 *O7* **Arkona, Kap** *headland* NE Germany 54°40′N 13°24′E
95 *N17* **Arkösund** Östergötland, S Sweden 58°28′N 16°55′E
122 *J6* **Arkticheskogo Instituta, Ostrova** *island* N Russian Federation
95 *O15* **Arlanda** ✈ (Stockholm) Stockholm, C Sweden 59°40′N 17°58′E
146 *C11* **Arlandag** *Rus.* Gora Arlan. ▲ W Turkmenistan 39°39′N 54°28′E
Arlan, Gora *see* Arlandag
105 *O5* **Arlanza** ≈ N Spain
105 *N5* **Arlanzón** ≈ N Spain
103 *R15* **Arles** *var.* Arles-sur-Rhône; *anc.* Arelas, Arelate. Bouches-du-Rhône, SE France 43°41′N 04°38′E
Arles-sur-Rhône *see* Arles
103 *O17* **Arles-sur-Tech** Pyrénées-Orientales, S France 42°27′N 02°37′E
29 *U9* **Arlington** Minnesota, N USA 44°36′N 94°04′W
29 *R15* **Arlington** Nebraska, C USA 41°27′N 96°21′W
32 *J11* **Arlington** Oregon, NW USA 45°43′N 120°10′W
29 *R10* **Arlington** South Dakota, N USA 44°21′N 97°07′W
20 *E10* **Arlington** Tennessee, S USA 35°17′N 89°40′W
25 *T6* **Arlington** Texas, SW USA 32°44′N 97°05′W
21 *W4* **Arlington** Virginia, NE USA 38°54′N 77°09′W
32 *H7* **Arlington** Washington, NW USA 48°12′N 122°07′W
30 *M10* **Arlington Heights** Illinois, N USA 42°08′N 88°03′W
77 *U8* **Arlit** Agadez, C Niger 18°54′N 07°25′E
99 *L24* **Arlon** *Dut.* Aarlen, *Ger.* Arel, *Lat.* Orolaunum. Luxembourg, SE Belgium 49°41′N 05°49′E
27 *R7* **Arma** Kansas, C USA 37°32′N 94°42′W
97 *F16* **Armagh** *Ir.* Ard Mhacha. S Northern Ireland, United Kingdom 54°15′N 06°33′W
97 *F16* **Armagh** *cultural region* S Northern Ireland, United Kingdom
102 *K15* **Armagnac** *cultural region* S France
103 *Q7* **Armançon** ≈ C France
60 *K10* **Armando Laydner, Represa** ⊠ S Brazil
115 *M24* **Armathía** *island* SE Greece
137 *T12* **Armavir** *prev.* Hoktemberyan, *Rus.* Oktemberyan. SW Armenia 40°09′N 43°58′E
126 *M14* **Armavir** Krasnodarskiy Kray, SW Russian Federation 44°59′N 41°07′E
54 *E10* **Armenia** Quindío, W Colombia 04°32′N 75°40′W
137 *T12* **Armenia** *off.* Republic of Armenia, *var.* Ajastan, *Arm.* Hayastani Hanrapetut'yun; *prev.* Armenian Soviet Socialist Republic. ◆ *republic* SW Asia
Armenian Soviet Socialist Republic *see* Armenia
Armenia, Republic of *see* Armenia
Armenierstadt *see* Gherla
103 *O1* **Armentières** Nord, N France 50°41′N 02°53′E
40 *K14* **Armería** Colima, SW Mexico 18°55′N 103°59′W
183 *T5* **Armidale** New South Wales, SE Australia 30°32′S 151°40′E
29 *P11* **Armour** South Dakota, N USA 43°19′N 98°21′W
61 *B18* **Armstrong** Santa Fe, C Argentina 32°46′S 61°39′W
11 *N16* **Armstrong** British Columbia, SW Canada 50°27′N 119°14′W
12 *D11* **Armstrong** Ontario, S Canada 50°20′N 89°02′W
29 *U11* **Armstrong** Iowa, C USA 43°24′N 94°28′W
25 *S16* **Armstrong** Texas, SW USA 26°55′N 97°47′W
117 *S11* **Armyans'k** *Rus.* Armyansk. Avtonomna Respublika Krym, S Ukraine 46°05′N 33°43′E
115 *H14* **Arnaía** *Cont.* Arnea. Kentrikí Makedonía, N Greece 40°30′N 23°36′E
121 *N2* **Arnaoúti, Akrotíri** *var.* Arnaoútis, Cape Arnaouti. *headland* W Cyprus 35°06′N 32°16′E
Arnaouti, Cape/Arnaoútis *see* Arnaoúti, Akrotíri
12 *L4* **Arnaud** ≈ Québec, E Canada
103 *Q8* **Arnay-le-Duc** Côte d'Or, C France 47°08′N 04°27′E
Arnea *see* Arnaía
105 *Q4* **Arnedo** La Rioja, N Spain 42°14′N 02°05′W
95 *I14* **Årnes** Akershus, S Norway 60°07′N 11°28′E
Årnes *see* Åi Åfjord
26 *K9* **Arnett** Oklahoma, C USA 36°08′N 99°46′W
98 *L12* **Arnhem** Gelderland, SE Netherlands 51°59′N 05°54′E
181 *Q2* **Arnhem Land** *physical region* Northern Territory, N Australia
106 *F11* **Arno** ≈ C Italy
Arņo *see* Arno Atoll
189 *W7* **Arno Atoll** *var.* Arņo. *atoll* Ratak Chain, NE Marshall Islands
182 *H8* **Arno Bay** South Australia 33°55′S 136°31′E
35 *Q8* **Arnold** California, W USA 38°15′N 120°19′W
27 *X5* **Arnold** Missouri, C USA 38°25′N 90°22′W
29 *N15* **Arnold** Nebraska, C USA 41°25′N 100°11′W
109 *R10* **Arnoldstein** *Slvn.* Pod Klošter. Kärnten, S Austria 46°34′N 13°43′E
103 *N9* **Arnon** ≈ C France
45 *P14* **Arnos Vale** ✈ (Kingstown) Saint Vincent, SE Saint Vincent and the Grenadines 13°08′N 61°13′W
92 *I8* **Arnøya** *Lapp.* Árdni. *island* N Norway
14 *L12* **Arnprior** Ontario, SE Canada 45°31′N 76°11′W
101 *G15* **Arnsberg** Nordrhein-Westfalen, W Germany 51°24′N 08°04′E
101 *K16* **Arnstadt** Thüringen, C Germany 50°50′N 10°57′E
Arnswalde *see* Choszczno
54 *K5* **Aroa** Yaracuy, N Venezuela 10°26′N 68°54′W
83 *E21* **Aroab** Karas, SE Namibia 26°47′S 19°40′E
Ároania *see* Chelmós
191 *O6* **Aroa, Pointe** *headland* Moorea, W French Polynesia 17°27′S 149°45′W
Aroe Islands *see* Aru, Kepulauan
101 *H15* **Arolsen** Niedersachsen, C Germany 51°23′N 09°00′E
106 *C7* **Arona** Piemonte, NE Italy 45°45′N 08°33′E
19 *R3* **Aroostook River** ≈ Canada/USA
Arop Island *see* Long Island
38 *M12* **Aropuk Lake** ◎ Alaska, USA
191 *P4* **Arorae** *atoll* Tungaru, W Kiribati
190 *G16* **Arorangi** Rarotonga, S Cook Islands 21°13′S 159°49′W
108 *I9* **Arosa** Graubünden, S Switzerland 46°48′N 09°42′E
104 *F4* **Arousa, Ría de** *estuary* E Atlantic Ocean
184 *P8* **Arowhana** ▲ North Island, New Zealand 38°07′S 177°52′E
137 *V12* **Arp'a** *Az.* Arpaçay. ≈ Armenia/Azerbaijan
137 *S11* **Arpaçay** Kars, NE Turkey 40°51′N 43°20′E
Arpaçay *see* Arp'a
Arqalyq *see* Arkalyk
149 *N14* **Arra** ≈ SW Pakistan
Arrabona *see* Győr
Arrah *see* Āra
Ar Rahad *see* Er Rahad
139 *R9* **Ar Raḥḥālīyah** Al Anbār, C Iraq 32°53′N 43°21′E
60 *Q10* **Arraial do Cabo** Rio de Janeiro, SE Brazil 22°57′S 42°00′W
104 *H11* **Arraiolos** Évora, S Portugal 38°44′N 07°59′W
139 *R8* **Ar Ramādī** *var.* Ramadi, Rumadiya. Al Anbār, SW Iraq 33°27′N 43°19′E
138 *J6* **Ar Rāmī** Ḥimş, C Syria 34°32′N 37°54′E
Ar Rams *see* Rams
138 *H9* **Ar Ramthā** *var.* Ramtha. Irbid, N Jordan 32°34′N 36°00′E
96 *H13* **Arran, Isle of** *island* SW Scotland, United Kingdom
138 *L3* **Ar Raqqah** *var.* Rakka; *anc.* Nicephorium. Ar Raqqah, N Syria 35°57′N 39°03′E
138 *L3* **Ar Raqqah** *off.* Muḥāfaẓat al Raqqah, *var.* Raqqah, *Fr.* Rakka. ⬖ *governorate* N Syria
103 *O2* **Arras** *anc.* Nemetocenna. Pas-de-Calais, N France 50°17′N 02°46′E
105 *P3* **Arrasate** *Cast.* Mondragón. País Vasco, N Spain 43°04′N 02°30′W
138 *G12* **Ar Rashādīyah** Aṭ ṭafīlah, W Jordan 30°42′N 35°38′E
138 *I5* **Ar Rastān** *var.* Rastâne. Ḥimş, W Syria 34°57′N 36°43′E
139 *X12* **Ar Raṭāwī** Al Başrah, E Iraq 30°37′N 47°12′E
102 *L15* **Arrats** ≈ S France
141 *N10* **Ar Rawḍah** Makkah, S Saudi Arabia 21°19′N 42°48′E
141 *Q15* **Ar Rawḍah** S Yemen 14°26′N 47°14′E
142 *K11* **Ar Rawḍatayn** *var.* Raudhatain. N Kuwait 29°80′N 47°50′E
143 *N16* **Ar Rayyān** *var.* Al Rayyan. C Qatar 25°18′N 51°29′E
102 *L17* **Arreau** Hautes-Pyrénées, S France 42°55′N 00°21′E
64 *Q11* **Arrecife** *var.* Arrecife de Lanzarote, Puerto Arrecife. Lanzarote, Islas Canarias, NE Atlantic Ocean 28°57′N 13°33′W
Arrecife de Lanzarote *see* Arrecife
43 *P6* **Arrecife Edinburgh** *reef* NE Nicaragua
61 *C19* **Arrecifes** Buenos Aires, E Argentina 34°06′S 60°09′W
102 *F6* **Arrée, Monts d'** ▲▲ NW France
Ar Refā'ī *see* Ar Rifā'ī
Arretium *see* Arezzo
Arriaca *see* Guadalajara
109 *S9* **Arriach** Kärnten, S Austria 46°43′N 13°52′E
41 *T16* **Arriaga** Chiapas, SE Mexico 16°14′N 93°54′W
41 *N12* **Arriaga** San Luis Potosí, C Mexico 21°55′N 101°23′W
139 *W10* **Ar Rifā'ī** *var.* Ar Refā'ī. Dhī Qār, SE Iraq 31°47′N 46°07′E
139 *V12* **Ar Riḥāb** *salt flat* S Iraq
Arriondas *see* Les Arriondes
141 *Q7* **Ar Riyāḍ** *Eng.* Riyadh. ● (Saudi Arabia) Ar Riyāḍ, C Saudi Arabia 24°50′N 46°50′E
141 *O8* **Ar Riyāḍ** *off.* Minṭaqat ar Riyāḍ. ⬖ *province* C Saudi Arabia
141 *S15* **Ar Riyān** S Yemen 14°43′N 49°18′E
Arrö *see* Ærø
61 *H18* **Arroio Grande** Rio Grande do Sul, S Brazil 32°15′S 53°02′W
102 *K15* **Arros** ≈ S France
103 *Q9* **Arroux** ≈ C France
25 *R5* **Arrowhead, Lake** ⊠ Texas, SW USA
182 *L5* **Arrowsmith, Mount** *hill* New South Wales, SE Australia
185 *D21* **Arrowtown** Otago, South Island, New Zealand 44°57′S 168°51′E
61 *D17* **Arroyo Barú** Entre Ríos, E Argentina 31°52′S 58°26′W
104 *J10* **Arroyo de la Luz** Extremadura, W Spain 39°28′N 06°36′W
63 *J16* **Arroyo de la Ventana** Río Negro, SE Argentina 41°41′S 66°03′W
35 *P13* **Arroyo Grande** California, W USA 35°07′N 120°35′W
Ar Ru'ays *see* Ar Ruways
141 *R11* **Ar Rub' al Khālī** *Eng.* Empty Quarter, Great Sandy Desert. *desert* SW Asia
139 *V13* **Ar Ruḍaymah** Al Muthanná, S Iraq 30°20′N 45°26′E
61 *A16* **Arrufó** Santa Fe, C Argentina 30°15′S 61°45′W
138 *I7* **Ar Ruḥaybah** *var.* Ruhaybeh, *Fr.* Rouhaïbé. Rīf Dimashq, W Syria 33°45′N 36°40′E
139 *V15* **Ar Rukhaymīyah** *well* S Iraq
139 *U11* **Ar Rumaythah** *var.* Rumaitha. Al Muthanná, S Iraq 31°31′N 45°15′E
141 *X8* **Ar Rustāq** *var.* Rostak, Rustaq. N Oman 23°34′N 57°25′E
139 *N8* **Ar Ruṭbah** *var.* Rutba. Al Anbār, SW Iraq 33°03′N 40°16′E
140 *M3* **Ar Rūthīyah** *spring/well* NW Saudi Arabia 31°18′N 41°23′E
ar-Ruwaida *see* Ar Ruwayḍah
141 *O8* **Ar Ruwayḍah** *var.* ar-Ruwaida. Jīzān, C Saudi Arabia 23°48′N 44°44′E
143 *N15* **Ar Ruways** *var.* Al Ruweis, Ar Ru'ays, Ruwais. N Qatar 26°08′N 51°13′E
143 *O17* **Ar Ruways** *var.* Ar Ru'ays. Abū Ẓaby, W United Arab Emirates 24°09′N 52°57′E
Års *see* Aars
Arsanias *see* Murat Nehri
123 *S15* **Arsen'yev** Primorskiy Kray, SE Russian Federation 44°09′N 133°28′E
155 *G19* **Arsikere** Karnātaka, W India 13°20′N 76°13′E′N
127 *R3* **Arsk** Respublika Tatarstan, W Russian Federation 56°07′N 49°54′E
94 *N10* **Årskogen** Gävleborg, C Sweden 62°07′N 17°19′E
121 *O3* **Ársos** C Cyprus 34°51′N 32°46′E
94 *N13* **Årsunda** Gävleborg, C Sweden 60°31′N 16°45′E
115 *C17* **Árta** *anc.* Ambracia. Ípeiros, W Greece 39°08′N 20°59′E
105 *Y9* **Artà** Mallorca, Spain, W Mediterranean Sea 39°42′N 03°20′E
Arta *see* Árachthos
137 *T12* **Artashat** S Armenia 39°57′N 44°34′E
40 *M15* **Arteaga** Michoacán, SW Mexico 18°22′N 102°18′W
123 *S15* **Artem** Primorskiy Kray, SE Russian Federation 43°24′N 132°20′E
44 *C4* **Artemisa** La Habana, W Cuba 22°49′N 82°47′W
117 *W7* **Artemivs'k** Donets'ka Oblast', E Ukraine 48°35′N 37°58′E
122 *K13* **Artemovsk** Krasnoyarskiy Kray, S Russian Federation 54°22′N 93°24′E
105 *U5* **Artesa de Segre** Cataluña, NE Spain 41°54′N 01°03′E
37 *U14* **Artesia** New Mexico, SW USA 32°50′N 104°24′W
25 *Q14* **Artesia Wells** Texas, SW USA 28°13′N 99°18′W
108 *G8* **Arth** Schwyz, C Switzerland 47°05′N 08°39′E
14 *F15* **Arthur** Ontario, S Canada 43°49′N 80°31′W
30 *M14* **Arthur** Illinois, N USA 39°42′N 88°28′W
28 *L14* **Arthur** Nebraska, C USA 41°35′N 101°42′W
29 *Q5* **Arthur** North Dakota, N USA 47°03′N 97°12′W
185 *B21* **Arthur** ≈ South Island, New Zealand
18 *B13* **Arthur, Lake** ⊠ Pennsylvania, NE USA
183 *N15* **Arthur River** ≈ Tasmania, SE Australia
185 *G18* **Arthur's Pass** Canterbury, South Island, New Zealand 42°59′S 171°33′E
185 *G17* **Arthur's Pass** *pass* South Island, New Zealand
44 *I3* **Arthur's Town** Cat Island, C Bahamas 24°34′N 75°39′W
44 *M9* **Artibonite, Rivière de l'** ≈ C Haiti
61 *E16* **Artigas** *prev.* San Eugenio, San Eugenio del Cuareim. Artigas, N Uruguay 30°25′S 56°28′W
61 *E16* **Artigas** ⬖ *department* N Uruguay
194 *H1* **Artigas** *Uruguayan research station* Antarctica 61°57′S 58°23′W
137 *T11* **Art'ik** W Armenia 40°38′N 43°58′E
187 *O16* **Art, Île** *island* Îles Belep, W New Caledonia
103 *O2* **Artois** *cultural region* N France
136 *L12* **Artova** Tokat, N Turkey 40°04′N 36°17′E
105 *Y9* **Artrutx, Cap d'** *var.* Cabo Dartuch. *cape* Menorca, Spain, W Mediterranean Sea
Artsiz *see* Artsyz
117 *N11* **Artsyz** *Rus.* Artsiz. Odes'ka Oblast', SW Ukraine 45°59′N 29°26′E
158 *E7* **Artux** Xinjiang Uygur Zizhiqu, NW China 39°40′N 76°10′E
137 *R11* **Artvin** Artvin, NE Turkey 41°12′N 41°48′E
137 *R11* **Artvın** ⬖ *province* NE Turkey
146 *G14* **Artyk** Ahal Welaýaty, C Turkmenistan 37°32′N 59°16′E
79 *Q16* **Aru** Orientale, NE Dem. Rep. Congo 02°53′N 30°50′E
81 *E17* **Arua** NW Uganda 03°02′N 30°56′E
104 *I4* **A Rúa de Valdeorras** *var.* La Rúa. Galicia, NW Spain 42°22′N 07°12′W
Aruângua *see* Luangwa
45 *O15* **Aruba** *var.* Oruba. ◇ *Dutch autonomous region* S West Indies
47 *Q4* **Aruba** *island* Aruba, Lesser Antilles
Aru Islands *see* Aru, Kepulauan
171 *W15* **Aru, Kepulauan** *Eng.* Aru Islands; *prev.* Aroe Islands. *island group* E Indonesia
153 *W10* **Arunāchal Pradesh** *prev.* North East Frontier Agency, North East Frontier Agency of Assam. ⬖ *state* NE India
Arun Qi *see* Naji
155 *H23* **Aruppukkottai** Tamil Nādu, SE India 09°31′N 78°03′E
81 *I20* **Arusha** Arusha, N Tanzania 03°23′S 36°40′E
81 *I21* **Arusha** ⬖ *region* E Tanzania
81 *I20* **Arusha** ✈ Arusha, N Tanzania 03°26′S 37°07′E
54 *C9* **Arusí, Punta** *headland* NW Colombia 05°36′N 77°30′W
155 *J23* **Aruvi Aru** ≈ NW Sri Lanka
79 *M17* **Aruwimi** *var.* Ituri (upper course). ≈ NE Dem. Rep. Congo
Árva *see* Orava
37 *T4* **Arvada** Colorado, C USA 39°48′N 105°06′W
Arvand Rūd *see* 'Arab, Shaṭṭ al
162 *J8* **Arvayheer** Övörhangay, C Mongolia 46°13′N 102°47′E
9 *O10* **Arviat** *prev.* Eskimo Point. Nunavut, C Canada 61°10′N 94°15′W
93 *I14* **Arvidsjaur** Norrbotten, N Sweden 65°34′N 19°12′E
95 *J15* **Arvika** Värmland, C Sweden 59°41′N 12°38′E
92 *J8* **Årviksand** Troms, N Norway 70°10′N 20°30′E
35 *S13* **Arvin** California, W USA 35°12′N 118°52′W
163 *S8* **Arxan** Nei Mongol Zizhiqu, N China 47.11N 119.58′E
145 *P7* **Arykbalyk** *Kaz.* Aryqbalyq. Severnyy Kazakhstan, N Kazakhstan 53°00′N 68°11′E
Aryqbalyq *see* Arykbalyk
145 *P17* **'Arys'** *prev.* Arys'. Yuzhnyy Kazakhstan, S Kazakhstan 42°26′N 68°49′E
Arys' *see* 'Arys'
Arys *see* Orzysz
Arys Köli *see* Arys, Ozero
145 *O14* **Arys, Ozero** *Kaz.* Arys Köli. ◎ C Kazakhstan
107 *D16* **Arzachena** Sardegna, Italy, C Mediterranean Sea 41°05′N 09°21′E
127 *O4* **Arzamas** Nizhegorodskaya Oblast', W Russian Federation 55°25′N 43°51′E
141 *V13* **Arzāt** S Oman 17°00′N 54°18′E
104 *H3* **Arzúa** Galicia, NW Spain 42°55′N 08°10′W
111 *A16* **Aš** *Ger.* Asch. Karlovarský Kraj, W Czech Republic 50°18′N 12°12′E
95 *H15* **Ås** Akershus, S Norway 59°40′N 10°50′E
Åsa *see* Asaa
95 *H20* **Asaa** *var.* Åsa. Nordjylland, N Denmark 57°07′N 10°24′E
83 *E21* **Asab** Karas, S Namibia 25°29′S 17°59′E
77 *U16* **Asaba** Delta, S Nigeria 06°10′N 06°44′E
76 *J10* **Assaba** *var.* Açâba. ⬖ *region* S Mauritania
149 *S4* **Asadābād** *var.* Asaḏābād; *prev.* Chaghasarāy. Kunar, E Afghanistan 34°52′N 71°09′E
Asaḏābād *see* Asadābād
138 *K3* **Asad, Buḥayrat al** *Eng.* Lake Assad. ◎ N Syria
63 *H20* **Asador, Pampa del** *plain* S Argentina
165 *P14* **Asahi** Chiba, Honshū, S Japan 35°43′N 140°38′E
164 *M11* **Asahi** Toyama, Honshū, SW Japan 36°56′N 137°34′E
165 *T13* **Asahi-dake** ▲ Hokkaidō, N Japan 43°42′N 142°50′E
165 *T3* **Asahikawa** Hokkaidō, N Japan 43°46′N 142°23′E
147 *S10* **Asaka** *Rus.* Assake; *prev.* Leninsk. Andijon Viloyati, E Uzbekistan 40°39′N 72°16′E
77 *P17* **Asamankese** SE Ghana 05°47′N 00°41′W
188 *B15* **Asan** W Guam 13°28′N 144°43′E
188 *B15* **Asan Point** *headland* W Guam
153 *R15* **Āsānsol** West Bengal, NE India 23°40′N 86°59′E
80 *K12* **Āsayita** Āfar, NE Ethiopia 11°35′S 41°23′E
171 *T12* **Asbakin** Papua, E Indonesia 0°45′S 131°40′E
Asben *see* Aïr, Massif de l'
15 *Q12* **Asbestos** Québec, SE Canada 45°46′N 71°56′W
29 *Y13* **Asbury** Iowa, C USA 42°30′N 90°45′W
18 *K15* **Asbury Park** New Jersey, NE USA 40°13′N 74°00′W
41 *Z12* **Ascención, Bahiá de la** *bay* NW Caribbean Sea
40 *I3* **Ascensión** Chihuahua, N Mexico 31°07′N 107°59′W
65 *M14* **Ascension Fracture Zone** *tectonic feature* C Atlantic Ocean
65 *G14* **Ascension Island** ◇ *dependency of St.Helena* C Atlantic Ocean
65 *N16* **Ascension Island** *island* C Atlantic Ocean
Asch *see* Aš
109 *S3* **Aschach an der Donau** Oberösterreich, N Austria 48°22′N 14°00′E
101 *H18* **Aschaffenburg** Bayern, SW Germany 49°58′N 09°10′E
101 *F14* **Ascheberg** Nordrhein-Westfalen, W Germany 51°46′N 07°36′E
101 *L14* **Aschersleben** Sachsen-Anhalt, C Germany 51°46′N 11°28′E
106 *G12* **Asciano** Toscana, C Italy 43°15′N 11°32′E
106 *J13* **Ascoli Piceno** *anc.* Asculum Picenum. Marche, C Italy 42°51′N 13°34′E
107 *M17* **Ascoli Satriano** *anc.* Asculub, Ausculum Apulum. Puglia, SE Italy 41°13′N 15°32′E
108 *G11* **Ascona** Ticino, S Switzerland 46°10′N 08°45′E
Asculub *see* Ascoli Satriano
Asculum Picenum *see* Ascoli Piceno
80 *L11* **'Aseb** *var.* Assab, *Amh.* Āseb. SE Eritrea 13°04′N 42°36′E
95 *M20* **Åseda** Kronoberg, S Sweden 57°10′N 15°20′E
127 *T6* **Asekeyevo** Orenburgskaya Oblast', W Russian Federation 53°36′N 52°53′E
81 *J14* **Āsela** *var.* Asella, Aselle, Asselle. Oromīya, C Ethiopia 07°55′N 39°08′E
93 *H15* **Åsele** Västerbotten, N Sweden 64°10′N 17°20′E
Asella/Aselle *see* Āsela
98 *N7* **Assen** Drenthe, NE Netherlands 53°N 06°34′E
94 *K12* **Åsen** Dalarna, C Sweden 61°18′N 13°49′E
114 *J11* **Asenovgrad** *prev.* Stanimaka. Plovdiv, C Bulgaria 42°00′N 24°53′E
171 *O13* **Asera** Sulawesi, C Indonesia 03°24′S 121°42′E
95 *E17* **Åseral** Vest-Agder, S Norway 58°37′N 07°27′E
118 *J3* **Aseri** *var.* Asserien, *Ger.* Asserin. Ida-Virumaa, NE Estonia 59°29′N 26°51′E
104 *G3* **A Serra de Outes** Galicia, NW Spain 42°50′N 08°54′W
40 *J10* **Aserradero** Durango, W Mexico
146 *F13* **Aşgabat** *prev.* Ashgabat, Ashkhabad, Poltoratsk. ● (Turkmenistan) Ahal Welaýaty, C Turkmenistan 37°58′N 58°22′E
146 *F13* **Aşgabat** ✈ Ahal Welaýaty, C Turkmenistan 38°06′N 58°10′E
95 *H16* **Åsgårdstrand** Vestfold, S Norway 59°22′N 10°27′E
Ashara *see* Al 'Ashārah
23 *T6* **Ashburn** Georgia, SE USA 31°42′N 83°39′W
185 *G19* **Ashburton** Canterbury, South Island, New Zealand 43°55′S 171°47′E
185 *G19* **Ashburton** ≈ South Island, New Zealand
180 *H8* **Ashburton River** ≈ Western Australia
145 *V10* **Ashchysu** ≈ E Kazakhstan
10 *M16* **Ashcroft** British Columbia, SW Canada 50°41′N 121°17′W
138 *E10* **Ashdod** *anc.* Azotos, *Lat.* Azotus. Central, W Israel 31°48′N 34°38′E
27 *S14* **Ashdown** Arkansas, C USA 33°40′N 94°09′W
21 *T9* **Asheboro** North Carolina, SE USA 35°42′N 79°50′W
11 *X15* **Ashern** Manitoba, S Canada 51°10′N 98°22′W
21 *P10* **Asheville** North Carolina, SE USA 35°36′N 82°33′W
12 *E8* **Asheweig** ≈ Ontario, C Canada
27 *V9* **Ash Flat** Arkansas, C USA 36°13′N 91°36′W
183 *T4* **Ashford** New South Wales, SE Australia 29°18′S 151°09′E
97 *P22* **Ashford** SE England, United Kingdom 51°09′N 00°52′E
36 *K11* **Ash Fork** Arizona, SW USA 35°12′N 112°31′W
Ashgabat *see* Aşgabat
27 *T7* **Ash Grove** Missouri, C USA 37°19′N 93°35′W
165 *O12* **Ashikaga** *var.* Asikaga. Tochigi, Honshū, S Japan 36°21′N 139°26′E
165 *Q8* **Ashiro** Iwate, Honshū, C Japan 40°04′N 141°00′E
164 *F15* **Ashizuri-misaki** Shikoku, SW Japan
138 *E10* **Ashkelon** *prev.* Ashqelon. Southern, C Israel 31°40′N 34°35′E
Ashkhabad *see* Aşgabat
23 *Q4* **Ashland** Alabama, S USA 33°16′N 85°50′W
26 *K7* **Ashland** Kansas, C USA 37°12′N 99°47′W
21 *P5* **Ashland** Kentucky, S USA 38°28′N 82°40′W
19 *S2* **Ashland** Maine, NE USA 46°36′N 68°24′W
22 *M1* **Ashland** Mississippi, S USA 34°51′N 89°10′W
27 *U4* **Ashland** Missouri, C USA 38°46′N 92°15′W
29 *S15* **Ashland** Nebraska, C USA 41°01′N 96°21′W
31 *T12* **Ashland** Ohio, N USA 40°52′N 82°19′W
32 *G15* **Ashland** Oregon, NW USA 42°11′N 122°42′W
21 *W6* **Ashland** Virginia, NE USA 37°45′N 77°28′W
30 *K3* **Ashland** Wisconsin, N USA 46°34′N 90°54′W
20 *I8* **Ashland City** Tennessee, S USA 36°16′N 87°05′W
183 *S4* **Ashley** New South Wales, SE Australia 29°21′S 149°49′E
29 *O7* **Ashley** North Dakota, N USA 46°00′N 99°22′W
173 *W7* **Ashmore and Cartier Islands** ◇ *Australian external territory* E Indian Ocean
119 *I14* **Ashmyany** *Rus.* Oshmyany. Hrodzyenskaya Voblasts', W Belarus 54°24′N 25°57′E
18 *K12* **Ashokan Reservoir** ⊠ New York, NE USA
165 *U4* **Ashoro** Hokkaidō, NE Japan 43°16′N 143°33′E
Ashqelon *see* Ashkelon
Ashraf *see* Behshahr
139 *O3* **Ash Shadādah** *var.* Ash Shaddādah, Jisr ash Shadadi, Shaddādī, Shedadi, Tell Shedadi. Al Ḥasakah, NE Syria 36°00′N 40°42′E
Ash Shaddādah *see* Ash Shadādah
139 *Y12* **Ash Shāfī** Al Başrah, E Iraq 30°49′N 47°30′E
139 *R4* **Ash Shakk** *var.* Shaykh. Şalāḥ ad Dīn, C Iraq 35°15′N 43°27′E
Ash Sham/Ash Shām *see* Rīf Dimashq
139 *T10* **Ash Shāmīyah** *var.* Shamiya. Al Qādisīyah, C Iraq 31°56′N 44°37′E
139 *Y13* **Ash Shāmīyah** *var.* Al Bādiyah al Janūbīyah. *desert* S Iraq
139 *T11* **Ash Shanāfīyah** *var.* Ash Shināfīyah. Al Qādisīyah, S Iraq 31°35′N 44°38′E
138 *G13* **Ash Sharāh** *var.* Esh Sharā. ▲▲ W Jordan
143 *R16* **Ash Shāriqah** *Eng.* Sharjah. Ash Shāriqah, NE United Arab Emirates 25°22′N 55°28′E
143 *R16* **Ash Shāriqah** *var.* Sharjah. ✈ Ash Shāriqah, NE United Arab Emirates 25°19′N 55°37′E
140 *I4* **Ash Sharmah** *var.* Šarma. Tabūk, NW Saudi Arabia 28°02′N 35°16′E
139 *R4* **Ash Sharqāṭ** Nīnawýa, NW Iraq 35°31′N 43°15′E
141 *S10* **Ash Sharqīyah** *off.* Al Minṭaqah ash Sharqīyah, *Eng.* Eastern Region. ⬖ *province* E Saudi Arabia
Ash Sharqīyah *see* Al 'Ubaylah
139 *W11* **Ash Shaṭrah** *var.* Shatra. Dhī Qār, SE Iraq 31°26′N 46°10′E
138 *G13* **Ash Shawbak** Ma'ān, W Jordan 30°32′N 35°34′E
138 *L5* **Ash Shaykh Ibrāhīm** Ḥimş, C Syria 35°03′N 38°50′E
141 *O17* **Ash Shaykh 'Uthmān** SW Yemen 12°53′N 45°00′E
141 *S15* **Ash Shiḥr** SE Yemen 14°45′N 49°24′E
Ash Shināfīyah *see* Ash Shanāfīyah
141 *V12* **Ash Shişar** *var.* Shisur. SW Oman 18°13′N 53°35′E
139 *S13* **Ash Shubrūm** *well* S Iraq
141 *R10* **Ash Shuqqān** *desert* E Saudi Arabia
75 *O9* **Ash Shuwayrif** *var.* Ash Shwayrif. N Libya 29°54′N 14°16′E
Ash Shwayrif *see* Ash Shuwayrif
31 *U10* **Ashtabula** Ohio, N USA 41°54′N 80°46′W
29 *Q5* **Ashtabula, Lake** ⊠ North Dakota, N USA
137 *T12* **Ashtarak** W Armenia 40°18′N 44°22′E
142 *M6* **Āshtīān** *var.* Āshtiyān. Markazī, W Iran 34°23′N 49°55′E
Āshtiyān *see* Āshtīān
33 *R13* **Ashton** Idaho, NW USA 44°04′N 111°27′W
13 *O10* **Ashuanipi Lake** ◎ Newfoundland and Labrador, E Canada
15 *P6* **Ashuapmushuan** ≈ Québec, SE Canada
23 *Q3* **Ashville** Alabama, S USA 33°50′N 86°15′W
31 *S14* **Ashville** Ohio, N USA 39°43′N 82°57′W
30 *K3* **Ashwabay, Mount** *hill* Wisconsin, N USA
128-129 **Asia** *continent*
171 *T11* **Asia, Kepulauan** *island group* E Indonesia
154 *N13* **Āsika** Orissa, E India 19°38′N 84°41′E
Asikaga *see* Ashikaga
93 *M18* **Asikkala** *var.* Vääksy. Etelä-Suomi, S Finland 61°09′N 25°36′E
74 *G5* **Asilah** N Morocco 35°32′N 06°04′W
'Aşī, Nahr al *see* Orontes
107 *B16* **Asinara, Isola** *island* W Italy
122 *J12* **Asino** Tomskaya Oblast', C Russian Federation 56°56′N 86°02′E
119 *O14* **Asintorf** *Rus.* Osintorf. Vitsyebskaya Voblasts', N Belarus 54°43′N 30°35′E
119 *L17* **Asipovichy** *Rus.* Osipovichi. Mahilyowskaya Voblasts', C Belarus 53°18′N 28°40′E
141 *N12* **'Asīr** *off.* Minṭaqat 'Asīr. ⬖ *province* SW Saudi Arabia
140 *M11* **'Asīr** *Eng.* Asir. ▲▲ SW Saudi Arabia
'Asīr, Minṭaqat *see* 'Asīr
139 *X10* **Askal** Maysān, E Iraq 31°45′N 47°07′E
137 *P13* **Aşkale** Erzurum, NE Turkey 39°56′N 40°39′E
117 *T11* **Askaniya-Nova** Khersons'ka Oblast', S Ukraine 46°27′N 33°54′E
95 *H15* **Asker** Akershus, S Norway 59°52′N 10°26′E
95 *L17* **Askersund** Örebro, C Sweden 58°55′N 14°55′E
Askī Kalak *see* Eski Kaļak
95 *I15* **Askim** Østfold, S Norway 59°15′N 11°10′E
127 *V3* **Askino** Respublika Bashkortostan, W Russian Federation 56°07′N 56°39′E
115 *D14* **Áskio** ▲▲ N Greece
152 *L9* **Askot** Uttarakhand, N India 29°44′N 80°20′E
94 *C12* **Askvoll** Sogn Og Fjordane, S Norway 61°21′N 05°04′E
136 *A13* **Aslan Burnu** *headland* W Turkey 38°44′N 26°43′E
136 *L16* **Aslantaş Barajı** ⊠ S Turkey
149 *S4* **Asmār** *var.* Bar Kunar. Kunar, E Afghanistan 34°59′N 71°29′E
Asmara *see* Asmera
80 *I9* **Asmera** *var.* Asmara. ● (Eritrea) C Eritrea 15°15′N 38°58′E
95 *L21* **Åsnen** ◎ S Sweden
115 *F19* **Asopós** ≈ S Greece
171 *W13* **Asori** Papua, E Indonesia 02°37′S 136°06′E
80 *G12* **Āsosa** Bīnishangul Gumuz, W Ethiopia 10°06′N 34°27′E
32 *M10* **Asotin** Washington, NW USA 46°18′N 117°03′W
Aspadana *see* Eşfahān
Aspang *see* Aspang Markt
109 *X6* **Aspang Markt** *var.* Aspang. Niederösterreich, E Austria 47°34′N 16°06′E
105 *S12* **Aspe** Valenciana, E Spain 38°21′N 00°43′W
37 *R5* **Aspen** Colorado, C USA 39°12′N 106°49′W
25 *P6* **Aspermont** Texas, SW USA 33°08′N 100°14′W
Asphaltites, Lacus *see* Dead Sea
Aspinwall *see* Colón
185 *C20* **Aspiring, Mount** ▲ South Island, New Zealand 44°21′S 168°47′E
115 *B16* **Asprókavos, Akrotírio** *headland* Kérkyra, Iónia Nísiá, Greece, C Mediterranean Sea 39°22′N 20°07′E
Aspropótamos *see* Achelóos
Assab *see* 'Aseb
138 *L4* **As Sabkhah** *var.* Sabkha. Ar Raqqah, NE Syria 35°30′N 35°54′E
139 *U6* **As Sa'dīyah** Diyālá, E Iraq 34°11′N 45°09′E
Assad, Lake *see* Asad, Buḥayrat al
138 *I8* **Aş Şafā** ▲ S Syria 33°03′N 37°07′E
138 *I10* **Aş Şafāwī** Al Mafraq, N Jordan 37°12′N 32°30′E
75 *W8* **Aş Şaff** *var.* El Şaff. N Egypt 29°34′N 31°16′E
139 *N2* **Aş Şafīḥ** Al Ḥasakah, N Syria 36°42′N 40°12′E
Aş Şaḥrā' ash Sharqīyah *see* Sahara el Sharqîya
Assake *see* Asaka
As Salamīyah *see* Salamīyah
141 *Q4* **As Sālimī** *var.* Salemy. SW Kuwait 29°07′N 46°41′E
67 *W7* **'Assal, Lac** ◎ C Djibouti
75 *T7* **As Sallūm** *var.* Salûm. NW Egypt 31°31′N 25°09′E
139 *T13* **As Salmān** Al Muthanná, S Iraq 30°29′N 44°34′E
138 *G10* **As Salṭ** *var.* Salt. Al Balqā', NW Jordan 32°03′N 35°44′E

◆ Country
● Country Capital
◇ Dependent Territory
○ Dependent Territory Capital
⬖ Administrative Regions
✈ International Airport
▲ Mountain
▲▲ Mountain Range
Volcano
≈ River
◎ Lake
⊠ Reservoir

142 M16 **As Salwā** var. Salwa, Salwah. S Qatar 24°44′N 50°52′E
153 V12 **Assam** ◆ state NE India
Assamaka see Assamakka
77 T8 **Assamakka** var. Assamaka. Agadez, NW Niger 19°24′N 05°53′E
139 U11 **As Samāwah** var. Samawa. Al Muthanná, S Iraq 31°17′N 45°06′E
As Saqia al Hamra see Saguia al Hamra
138 J4 **Aş Şā'rān** Ḩamāh, C Syria 35°15′N 37°28′E
138 G9 **Aş Şarīḩ** Irbid, N Jordan 32°31′N 35°54′E
21 Z5 **Assateague Island** island Maryland, NE USA
139 O6 **As Sayyāl** var. Sayyāl. Dayr az Zawr, E Syria 34°37′N 40°52′E
99 G18 **Asse** Vlaams Brabant, C Belgium 50°55′N 04°12′E
99 D16 **Assebroek** West-Vlaanderen, NW Belgium 51°12′N 03°16′E
Asselle see Āsela
107 C20 **Assemini** Sardegna, Italy, C Mediterranean Sea 39°16′N 08°58′E
99 E16 **Assenede** Oost-Vlaanderen, NW Belgium 51°15′N 03°43′E
95 G24 **Assens** Syddtjylland, C Denmark 55°16′N 09°54′N
Asserien/Asserin see Aseri
99 I21 **Assesse** Namur, SE Belgium 50°22′N 05°01′E
141 Y8 **As Sīb** var. Seeb. NE Oman 23°40′N 58°03′E
139 Z13 **As Sībah** var. Sibah. Al Başrah, SE Iraq 30°13′N 47°24′E
11 T17 **Assiniboia** Saskatchewan, S Canada 49°39′N 105°59′W
11 V15 **Assiniboine** ≈ Manitoba, S Canada
11 P16 **Assiniboine, Mount** ▲ Alberta/British Columbia, SW Canada 50°54′N 115°43′W
Assiout see Asyūţ
60 J9 **Assis** São Paulo, S Brazil 22°37′S 50°25′W
106 I13 **Assisi** Umbria, C Italy 43°04′N 12°36′E
Assiut see Asyūţ
Assling see Jesenice
Assouan see Aswān
59 P14 **Assu** var. Açu. Rio Grande do Norte, E Brazil 05°33′S 36°55′W
Assuan see Aswān
142 K12 **Aş Şubayḩīyah** var. Subiyah. S Kuwait 28°55′N 47°57′E
141 R16 **As Sufāl** S Yemen 14°06′N 48°42′E
138 L5 **As Sukhnah** var. Sukhne, Fr. Soukhné. Ḩimş, C Syria 34°56′N 38°52′E
139 U4 **As Sulaymānīyah** var. Sulaimaniya, Kurd. Slêmānî. As Sulaymānīyah, NE Iraq 35°32′N 45°27′E
141 P11 **As Sulayyil** Ar Riyāḑ, S Saudi Arabia 20°29′N 45°33′E
121 O13 **As Sulţān** N Libya 31°01′N 17°21′E
141 Q5 **Aş Şummān** desert N Saudi Arabia
141 Q16 **Aş Şurrah** SW Yemen 13°56′N 46°23′E
139 N4 **Aş Şuwār** var. Şuwār. Dayr az Zawr, E Syria 35°31′N 40°37′E
138 H9 **As Suwaydā'** var. El Suweida, Es Suweida, Suweida, Fr. Soueida. As Suwaydā', SW Syria 32°43′N 36°33′E
138 H9 **As Suwaydā'** off. Muḩāfaẓat as Suwaydā', var. As Suwaydā, Suwaydá, Suweida. ◆ governorate S Syria
141 Z9 **As Suwayḩ** NE Oman 22°07′N 59°42′E
141 X8 **As Suwayq** var. Suwaik. N Oman 23°49′N 57°30′E
139 T8 **Aş Şuwayrah** var. Suwaira. Wāsiţ, E Iraq 32°57′N 44°47′E
As Suways see Suez
Asta Colonia see Asti
Astacus see İzmit
115 M23 **Astakída** island SE Greece
145 Q9 **Astana** prev. Akmola, Akmolinsk, Tselinograd, Aqmola. ● (Kazakhstan) Akmola, N Kazakhstan 51°13′N 71°25′E
142 M3 **Āstāneh** var. Āstāneh-ye Ashrafīyeh. Gīlān, NW Iran 37°17′N 49°58′E
Āstāneh-ye Ashrafīyeh see Āstāneh
Asta Pompeia see Asti
137 Y14 **Astara** S Azerbaijan 38°28′N 48°51′E
Astarabad see Gorgān
99 L15 **Asten** Noord-Brabant, SE Netherlands 51°24′N 05°45′E
Asterābād see Gorgān
106 C8 **Asti** anc. Asta Colonia, Asta Pompeia, Hasta Colonia, Hasta Pompeia. Piemonte, NW Italy 44°54′N 08°11′E
Astigi see Ecija
Astipálaia see Astypálaia
148 L16 **Astola Island** island SW Pakistan
152 H4 **Astor** Jammu and Kashmir, NW India 35°21′N 74°52′E
104 K4 **Astorga** anc. Asturica Augusta. Castilla y León, N Spain 42°27′N 06°04′W
32 F10 **Astoria** Oregon, NW USA 46°12′N 123°50′W
0 F8 **Astoria Fan** undersea feature E Pacific Ocean 45°15′N 126°15′W
95 J22 **Åstorp** Skåne, S Sweden 56°09′N 12°57′E
Astrabad see Gorgān
127 Q13 **Astrakhan'** Astrakhanskaya Oblast', SW Russian Federation 46°20′N 48°01′E
Astrakhan-Bazar see Cälilabad
127 Q11 **Astrakhanskaya Oblast'** ◆ province SW Russian Federation
93 J15 **Åsträsk** Västerbotten, N Sweden 64°38′N 20°00′E
Astrida see Butare
65 O22 **Astrid Ridge** undersea feature S Atlantic Ocean
187 P15 **Astrolabe, Récifs de l'** reef C New Caledonia
121 P2 **Astromerítis** N Cyprus 35°09′N 33°02′E
115 F20 **Ástros** Pelopónnisos, S Greece 37°24′N 22°43′E
119 G16 **Astryna** Rus. Ostryna. Hrodzyenskaya Voblasts', W Belarus 53°44′N 24°33′E
104 J2 **Asturias** ◆ autonomous community NW Spain
Asturias see Oviedo
Asturica Augusta see Astorga
115 L22 **Astypálaia** var. Astipálaia, It. Stampalia. island Kykládes, Greece, Aegean Sea
192 G16 **Āsuisui, Cape** headland Savai'i, W Samoa 13°44′S 172°29′W
195 S2 **Asuka** Japanese research station Antarctica 71°49′S 23°52′E
62 O6 **Asunción** ● (Paraguay) Central, S Paraguay 25°17′S 57°36′W
62 O6 **Asunción** ✈ Central, S Paraguay 25°15′S 57°40′W
188 K3 **Asuncion Island** island N Northern Mariana Islands
42 E6 **Asunción Mita** Jutiapa, SE Guatemala 14°20′N 89°42′W
Asunción Nochixtlán see Nochixtlán
40 E3 **Asunción, Río** ≈ NW Mexico
95 M18 **Åsunden** ◎ S Sweden
118 K11 **Asvyeya** Rus. Osveya. Vitsyebskaya Voblasts', N Belarus 56°00′N 28°05′E
Aswa see Achwa
75 X11 **Aswān** var. Assouan, Assuan, Aswân; anc. Syene. SE Egypt 24°03′N 32°59′E
Aswân see Aswān
Aswan Dam see Khazzān Aswān
75 W9 **Asyūţ** var. Assiout, Assiut, Asyût, Siut; anc. Lycopolis. C Egypt 27°06′N 31°11′E
Asyût see Asyūţ
193 W15 **Ata** island Tongatapu Group, SW Tonga
62 G8 **Atacama** off. Región de Atacama. ◆ region C Chile
Atacama Desert see Atacama, Desierto de
62 H4 **Atacama, Desierto de** Eng. Atacama Desert. desert N Chile
62 I6 **Atacama, Puna de** ▲ NW Argentina
Atacama, Región de see Atacama
62 I5 **Atacama, Salar de** salt lake N Chile
54 E11 **Ataco** Tolima, C Colombia 03°36′N 75°23′W
190 H8 **Atafu Atoll** island NW Tokelau
190 H8 **Atafu Village** Atafu Atoll, NW Tokelau 08°40′S 172°40′W
74 K12 **Atakor** ▲ SE Algeria
77 R14 **Atakora, Chaîne de l'** var. Atakora Mountains. ▲ N Benin
Atakora Mountains see Atakora, Chaîne de l'
77 R16 **Atakpamé** C Togo 07°32′N 01°08′E
146 F11 **Atakui** Ahal Welaýaty, C Turkmenistan 40°04′N 58°03′E
58 B13 **Atalaia do Norte** Amazonas, N Brazil 04°22′S 70°10′W
146 M14 **Atamyrat** prev. Kerki. Lebap Welaýaty, E Turkmenistan 37°52′N 65°06′E
76 I7 **Aţâr** Adrar, W Mauritania 20°30′N 13°03′W
162 G10 **Atas Bogd** ▲ SW Mongolia 43°17′N 96°47′E
35 P12 **Atascadero** California, W USA 35°28′N 120°40′W
25 S13 **Atascosa River** ≈ Texas, SW USA
145 R11 **Atasu** Karaganda, C Kazakhstan 48°42′N 71°38′E
145 R12 **Atasu** ≈ Karaganda, C Kazakhstan
193 V15 **Atata** island Tongatapu Group, S Tonga
136 H10 **Atatürk** ✈ (İstanbul) İstanbul, NW Turkey 40°58′N 28°50′E
137 N16 **Atatürk Barajı** ⊞ S Turkey
115 O23 **Atavýros** prev. Attávyros. Ródos, Dodekánisa, Aegean Sea 36°10′N 27°50′E
115 O23 **Atávyros** prev. Attávyros. ▲ Ródos, Dodekánisa, Greece, Aegean Sea 36°10′N 27°50′E
Atax see Aude
80 G8 **Atbara** var. 'Aţbārah. River Nile, NE Sudan 17°42′N 34°E
80 H8 **Atbara** var. Nahr 'Aţbarah. ≈ Eritrea/Sudan
'Aţbārah/'Aţbarah, Nahr see Atbara
145 P9 **Atbasar** Akmola, N Kazakhstan 51°49′N 68°18′E
At-Bashi see At-Bashy
147 W9 **At-Bashy** var. At-Bashi. Narynskaya Oblast', C Kyrgyzstan 41°07′N 75°48′E
22 I10 **Atchafalaya Bay** bay Louisiana, S USA
22 I8 **Atchafalaya River** ≈ Louisiana, S USA
Atchin see Aceh
27 Q3 **Atchison** Kansas, C USA 39°31′N 95°07′W
77 P16 **Atebubu** C Ghana 07°47′N 01°00′W
105 Q6 **Ateca** Aragón, NE Spain 41°20′N 01°49′W
40 K11 **Atengo, Río** ≈ C Mexico
Aternum see Pescara
107 K15 **Atessa** Abruzzo, C Italy 42°03′N 14°25′E
Ateste see Este
99 E19 **Ath** var. Aat. Hainaut, SW Belgium 50°38′N 03°47′E
11 Q13 **Athabasca** Alberta, SW Canada 54°44′N 113°15′W
11 Q12 **Athabasca** var. Athabaska. ≈ Alberta, SW Canada
11 R10 **Athabasca, Lake** ◎ Alberta/ Saskatchewan, SW Canada
Athabaska see Athabasca
115 C16 **Athamánon** ▲ C Greece
97 F17 **Athboy** Ir. Baile Átha Buí. E Ireland 53°38′N 06°55′W
Athenae see Athína
97 C18 **Athenry** Ir. Baile Átha an Rí. W Ireland 53°19′N 08°49′W
23 P2 **Athens** Alabama, S USA 34°48′N 86°58′W
23 T3 **Athens** Georgia, SE USA 33°57′N 83°24′W
31 T14 **Athens** Ohio, N USA 39°20′N 82°06′W
20 M10 **Athens** Tennessee, S USA 35°27′N 84°38′W
25 V7 **Athens** Texas, SW USA 32°12′N 95°51′W
Athens see Athína
115 B18 **Athéras, Akrotírio** headland Kefalloniá, Iónia Nísiá, Greece, C Mediterranean Sea 38°20′N 20°24′E
181 W4 **Atherton** Queensland, NE Australia 17°18′S 145°29′E
81 I19 **Athi** ≈ S Kenya
121 Q2 **Athíenou** SE Cyprus 35°01′N 33°31′E
115 H19 **Athína** Eng. Athens, prev. Athínai; anc. Athenae. ● (Greece) Attikí, C Greece 37°59′N 23°44′E
Athínai see Athína
139 S10 **Athīyah** An Najaf, C Iraq 32°01′N 44°04′E
97 D18 **Athlone** Ir. Baile Átha Luain. C Ireland 53°25′N 07°56′W
155 F16 **Athni** Karnātaka, W India 16°43′N 75°04′E
185 C23 **Athol** Southland, South Island, New Zealand 45°30′S 168°35′E
19 N11 **Athol** Massachusetts, NE USA 42°35′N 72°11′W
115 I15 **Áthos** ▲ NE Greece 40°10′N 24°21′E
Athos, Mount see Ágion Óros
Ath Thawrah see Madīnat ath Thawrah
141 P5 **Ath Thumāmī** spring/well N Saudi Arabia 27°56′N 45°06′E
99 L25 **Athus** Luxembourg, SE Belgium 49°34′N 05°50′E
97 E19 **Athy** Ir. Baile Átha Í. C Ireland 52°59′N 06°59′W
78 I10 **Ati** Batha, C Chad 13°11′N 18°20′E
81 F16 **Atiak** NW Uganda 03°14′N 32°05′E
57 G17 **Atico** Arequipa, SW Peru 16°13′S 73°13′W
105 O6 **Atienza** Castilla-La Mancha, C Spain 41°12′N 02°52′W
39 Q6 **Atigun Pass** pass Alaska, USA
12 B12 **Atikokan** Ontario, S Canada 48°45′N 91°38′W
13 O9 **Atikonak Lac** ◎ Newfoundland and Labrador, E Canada
42 C6 **Atitlán, Lago de** ◎ W Guatemala
190 L16 **Atiu** island S Cook Islands
Atjeh see Aceh
123 T9 **Atka** Magadanskaya Oblast', E Russian Federation 60°45′N 151°35′E
38 H17 **Atka** Atka Island, Alaska, USA 52°12′N 174°14′W
38 H17 **Atka Island** island Aleutian Islands, Alaska, USA
127 O7 **Atkarsk** Saratovskaya Oblast', W Russian Federation 52°15′N 43°48′E
27 U11 **Atkins** Arkansas, C USA 35°15′N 92°56′W
29 O13 **Atkinson** Nebraska, C USA 42°31′N 98°57′W
171 T12 **Atkri** Papua, E Indonesia 01°45′S 130°04′E
41 O13 **Atlacomulco** var. Atlacomulco de Fabela. México, C Mexico 19°49′N 99°54′W
Atlacomulco de Fabela see Atlacomulco
23 S3 **Atlanta** state capital Georgia, SE USA 33°45′N 84°23′W
31 R6 **Atlanta** Michigan, N USA 45°01′N 84°07′W
25 X6 **Atlanta** Texas, SW USA 33°06′N 94°09′W
29 T15 **Atlantic** Iowa, C USA 41°24′N 95°00′W
21 Y10 **Atlantic** North Carolina, SE USA 34°52′N 76°20′W
23 W8 **Atlantic Beach** Florida, SE USA 30°19′N 81°24′W
18 J17 **Atlantic City** New Jersey, NE USA 39°23′N 74°27′W
172 L14 **Atlantic-Indian Basin** undersea feature SW Indian Ocean 60°00′S 15°00′E
172 K13 **Atlantic-Indian Ridge** undersea feature SW Indian Ocean 53°00′S 15°00′E
54 E4 **Atlántico** off. Departamento del Atlántico. ◆ province NW Colombia
64-65 **Atlantic Ocean** ocean
Atlántico, Departamento del see Atlántico
42 K7 **Atlántico Norte, Región Autónoma** prev. Zelaya Norte. ◆ autonomous region NE Nicaragua
42 L10 **Atlántico Sur, Región Autónoma** prev. Zelaya Sur. ◆ autonomous region SE Nicaragua
42 I5 **Atlántida** ◆ department N Honduras
77 Y15 **Atlantika Mountains** ▲ E Nigeria
64 J10 **Atlantis Fracture Zone** tectonic feature NW Atlantic Ocean
74 H7 **Atlas Mountains** ▲ NW Africa
123 V11 **Atlasova, Ostrov** island SE Russian Federation
123 V10 **Atlasovo** Kamchatskiy Kray, E Russian Federation 55°42′N 159°35′E
120 G11 **Atlas Saharien** var. Saharan Atlas. ▲ Algeria/Morocco
Atlas, Tell see Atlas Tellien
120 H10 **Atlas Tellien** Eng. Tell Atlas. ▲ N Algeria
10 I9 **Atlin** British Columbia, W Canada 59°31′N 133°41′W
10 I9 **Atlin Lake** ◎ British Columbia, W Canada
41 P14 **Atlixco** Puebla, S Mexico 18°55′N 98°26′W
94 B11 **Atløyna** island S Norway
155 I17 **Ātmakūr** Andhra Pradesh, C India 15°52′N 78°42′E
23 O8 **Atmore** Alabama, S USA 31°01′N 87°29′W
101 J20 **Atmühl** ≈ S Germany
94 I11 **Atna** ≈ S Norway
164 E13 **Atō** Yamaguchi, Honshū, SW Japan 34°24′N 131°42′E
57 L21 **Atocha** Potosí, S Bolivia 20°55′S 66°14′W
27 P12 **Atoka** Oklahoma, C USA 34°22′N 96°08′W
27 O12 **Atoka Lake** var. Atoka Reservoir. ⊞ Oklahoma, C USA
Atoka Reservoir see Atoka Lake
33 Q14 **Atomic City** Idaho, NW USA 43°26′N 112°48′W
40 L10 **Atotonilco** Zacatecas, C Mexico 24°12′N 102°46′W
Atotonilco see Atotonilco el Alto
40 M13 **Atotonilco el Alto** var. Atotonilco. Jalisco, SW Mexico 20°35′N 102°30′W
77 N7 **Atouila, 'Erg** desert N Mali
41 N16 **Atoyac** var. Atoyac de Alvarez. Guerrero, S Mexico 17°12′N 100°28′W
Atoyac de Alvarez see Atoyac
41 P15 **Atoyac, Río** ≈ S Mexico
39 O5 **Atqasuk** Alaska, USA 70°28′N 157°24′W
Atrak/Atrak, Rūd-e see Etrek
95 J20 **Ätran** ≈ S Sweden
54 C7 **Atrato, Río** ≈ NW Colombia
Atrek see Etrek
107 K14 **Atri** Abruzzo, C Italy 42°35′N 13°59′E
Atria see Adria
165 P9 **Atsumi** Yamagata, Honshū, C Japan 38°38′N 139°36′E
165 S3 **Atsuta** Hokkaidō, NE Japan 43°28′N 141°24′E
143 Q17 **Aţ Ţaff** desert C United Arab Emirates
138 G12 **Aţ Ţafīlah** var. Et Tafila, Tafila. Aţ Ţafīlah, W Jordan 30°52′N 35°36′E
138 G12 **Aţ Ţafīlah** off. Muḩāfaẓat aţ Ţafīlah. ◆ governorate W Jordan
140 L10 **Aţ Ţā'if** Makkah, W Saudi Arabia 21°50′N 40°50′E
Attaleia/Attalia see Antalya
23 Q3 **Attalla** Alabama, S USA 34°01′N 86°05′W
138 L2 **At Tall al Abyaḑ** var. Tall al Abyaḑ, Tell Abyad, Fr. Tell Abiad. Ar Raqqah, N Syria 36°36′N 38°56′E
138 L7 **At Tanf** Ḩimş, S Syria 33°29′N 38°39′E
163 N9 **Attanshiree** Dornogovĭ, SE Mongolia 45°36′N 110°30′E
167 T10 **Attapu** var. Attopeu, Samakhixai. Attapu, S Laos 14°48′N 106°51′E
139 S10 **At Taqtaqānah** An Najaf, C Iraq 32°03′N 43°54′E
Attávyros see Atávyros
12 G9 **Attawapiskat** Ontario, C Canada 52°55′N 82°26′W
12 F9 **Attawapiskat** ≈ Ontario, S Canada
12 D9 **Attawapiskat Lake** ◎ Ontario, C Canada
At Taybé see Ţayyibah
101 F16 **Attendorn** Nordrhein-Westfalen, W Germany 51°07′N 07°54′E
109 R5 **Attersee** Salzburg, NW Austria 47°55′N 13°31′E
109 R5 **Attersee** ◎ N Austria
99 L24 **Attert** Luxembourg, SE Belgium 49°45′N 05°47′E
138 M4 **At Tibnī** var. Tibnī. Dayr az Zawr, NE Syria 35°30′N 39°48′E
31 N13 **Attica** Indiana, N USA 40°17′N 87°15′W
18 E10 **Attica** New York, NE USA 42°51′N 78°13′W
Attica see Attikí
13 N7 **Attikamagen Lake** ◎ Newfoundland and Labrador, E Canada
115 H20 **Attikí** Eng. Attica. ◆ region C Greece
19 O12 **Attleboro** Massachusetts, NE USA 41°55′N 71°15′W
109 R5 **Attnang** Oberösterreich, N Austria 48°02′N 13°44′E
149 U6 **Attock City** Punjab, E Pakistan 33°52′N 72°20′E
Attopeu see Attapu
25 X8 **Attoyac River** ≈ Texas, SW USA
38 D16 **Attu** Attu Island, Alaska, USA 52°53′N 173°18′E
139 Y12 **Aţ Ţūbah** Al Başrah, E Iraq 30°29′N 47°28′E
140 K4 **Aţ Ţubayq** plain Jordan/ Saudi Arabia
38 C16 **Attu Island** island Aleutian Islands, Alaska, USA
75 X8 **Aţ Ţūr** var. El Ţûr. NE Egypt 28°14′N 33°36′E
155 I21 **Āttūr** Tamil Nādu, SE India 11°34′N 78°39′E
141 N17 **At Turbah** SW Yemen 12°42′N 43°31′E
62 I12 **Atuel, Río** ≈ C Argentina
191 X7 **Atuona** Hiva Oa, NE French Polynesia 09°47′S 139°03′W
Aturus see Adour
95 M18 **Åtvidaberg** Östergötland, S Sweden 58°12′N 16°00′E
35 P9 **Atwater** California, W USA 37°19′N 120°33′W
29 T8 **Atwater** Minnesota, N USA 45°08′N 94°48′W
26 I2 **Atwood** Kansas, C USA 39°48′N 101°03′W
31 U12 **Atwood Lake** ⊞ Ohio, N USA
127 P5 **Atyashevo** Respublika Mordoviya, W Russian Federation 54°36′N 46°04′E
144 F12 **Atyrau** prev. Gur'yev. Atyrau, W Kazakhstan 47°07′N 51°56′E
144 E11 **Atyrau** off. Atyrauskaya Oblast', var.Kaz. Atyraū Oblysy; prev. Gur'yevskaya Oblast'. ◆ province W Kazakhstan
Atyraū Oblysy/ Atyrauskaya Oblast' see Atyrau
Atyrauskaya Oblast' see Atyrau
108 J7 **Au** Vorarlberg, NW Austria 47°19′N 10°01′E
186 B4 **Aua Island** island NW Papua New Guinea
103 S16 **Aubagne** anc. Albania. Bouches-du-Rhône, SE France 43°17′N 05°35′E
99 L25 **Aubange** Luxembourg, SE Belgium 49°35′N 05°49′E
103 Q6 **Aube** ◆ department N France
103 R6 **Aube** ≈ N France
99 L19 **Aubel** Liège, E Belgium 50°45′N 05°49′E
103 Q13 **Aubenas** Ardèche, E France 44°37′N 04°24′E
103 O8 **Aubigny-sur-Nère** Cher, C France 47°30′N 02°27′E
103 O13 **Aubin** Aveyron, S France 44°30′N 02°18′E
103 O13 **Aubrac, Monts d'** ▲ S France
36 J10 **Aubrey Cliffs** cliff Arizona, SW USA
23 R5 **Auburn** Alabama, S USA 32°37′N 85°30′W
35 P6 **Auburn** California, W USA 38°53′N 121°03′W
30 K14 **Auburn** Illinois, N USA 39°35′N 89°45′W
31 Q11 **Auburn** Indiana, N USA 41°22′N 85°03′W
20 J7 **Auburn** Kentucky, S USA 36°52′N 86°42′W
19 P8 **Auburn** Maine, NE USA 44°05′N 70°15′W
19 N11 **Auburn** Massachusetts, NE USA 42°11′N 71°47′W
29 S16 **Auburn** Nebraska, C USA 40°23′N 95°50′W
18 H10 **Auburn** New York, NE USA 42°55′N 76°31′W
32 H8 **Auburn** Washington, NW USA 47°18′N 122°13′W
103 N11 **Aubusson** Creuse, C France 45°58′N 02°10′E
118 E10 **Auce** Ger. Autz. SW Latvia 56°28′N 22°54′E
102 L15 **Auch** Lat. Augusta Auscorum, Elimberrum. Gers, S France 43°40′N 00°37′E
77 U16 **Auchi** Edo, S Nigeria 07°01′N 06°17′E
23 T9 **Aucilla River** ≈ Florida/ Georgia, SE USA
184 L6 **Auckland** Auckland, North Island, New Zealand 36°53′S 174°46′E
184 K5 **Auckland** off. Auckland Region. ◆ region North Island, New Zealand
184 L6 **Auckland** ✈ Auckland, North Island, New Zealand 37°01′S 174°49′E
192 J12 **Auckland Islands** island group S New Zealand
Auckland Region see Auckland
103 O16 **Aude** ◆ department S France
103 N16 **Aude** anc. Atax. ≈ S France
Audenarde see Oudenaarde
Audern see Audru
102 E6 **Audierne** Finistère, NW France 48°01′N 04°30′W
102 E6 **Audierne, Baie d'** bay NW France
103 U7 **Audincourt** Doubs, E France 47°29′N 06°50′E
118 G5 **Audru** Ger. Audern. Pärnumaa, SW Estonia 58°24′N 24°22′E
29 T14 **Audubon** Iowa, C USA 41°44′N 94°56′W
101 N17 **Aue** Sachsen, E Germany 50°35′N 12°42′E
100 H12 **Aue** ≈ NW Germany
100 L9 **Auerbach** Bayern, SE Germany 49°41′N 11°41′E
101 M17 **Auerbach** Sachsen, E Germany 50°30′N 12°24′E
108 I10 **Auererrhein** ≈ SW Switzerland
101 N17 **Auersberg** ▲ E Germany 50°30′N 12°42′E
181 W9 **Augathella** Queensland, E Australia 25°54′S 146°38′E
31 Q12 **Auglaize River** ≈ Ohio, N USA
83 F22 **Augrabies Falls** waterfall W South Africa
31 R7 **Au Gres River** ≈ Michigan, N USA
Augsbourg see Augsburg
101 K22 **Augsburg** Fr. Augsbourg; anc. Augusta Vindelicorum. Bayern, S Germany 48°22′N 10°54′E
180 I14 **Augusta** Western Australia 34°18′S 115°10′E
107 L25 **Augusta** It. Agosta. Sicilia, Italy, C Mediterranean Sea 37°14′N 15°14′E
27 W11 **Augusta** Arkansas, C USA 35°16′N 91°21′W
23 V3 **Augusta** Georgia, SE USA 33°29′N 81°58′W
27 O6 **Augusta** Kansas, C USA 37°40′N 96°59′W
19 Q7 **Augusta** state capital Maine, NE USA 44°20′N 69°44′W
33 Q8 **Augusta** Montana, NW USA 47°28′N 112°23′W
Augusta see London
Augusta Auscorum see Auch
Augusta Emerita see Mérida
Augusta Praetoria see Aosta
Augusta Suessionum see Soissons
Augusta Trajana see Stara Zagora
Augusta Treverorum see Trier
Augusta Vangionum see Worms
Augusta Vindelicorum see Augsburg
95 G24 **Augustenborg** Ger. Augustenburg. Syddanmark, SW Denmark 54°57′N 09°53′E
Augustenburg see Augustenborg
39 Q13 **Augustine Island** island Alaska, USA
14 L9 **Augustines, Lac des** ◎ Québec, SE Canada
Augustobona Tricassium see Troyes
Augustodunum see Autun
Augustodurum see Bayeux
Augustoritum Lemovicensium see Limoges
110 O8 **Augustów** Rus. Avgustov. Podlaskie, NE Poland 53°52′N 22°58′E
Augustow Canal see Augustowski, Kanał
110 O8 **Augustowski, Kanał** Eng. Augustow Canal, Rus. Avgustovskiy Kanal. canal NE Poland
180 I9 **Augustus, Mount** ▲ Western Australia 24°42′S 117°42′E
Aujuittuq see Grise Fiord
186 M9 **Auki** Malaita, N Solomon Islands 08°48′S 160°45′E
21 W8 **Aulander** North Carolina, SE USA 36°15′N 77°16′W
180 L7 **Auld, Lake** salt lake C Western Australia
Aulie Ata/Auliye-Ata see Taraz
Äülieköl see Auliyekol'
144 M8 **Auliyekol'** Kaz. Äülieköl; prev. Semiozernoye. Kostanay, N Kazakhstan 52°22′N 64°06′E
106 E10 **Aulla** Toscana, C Italy 44°15′N 10°00′E
102 F6 **Aulne** ≈ NW France
37 T3 **Ault** Colorado, C USA 40°34′N 104°43′W
95 F22 **Aulum** var. Avlum. Midtjylland, C Denmark 56°16′N 08°48′E
103 N3 **Aumale** Seine-Maritime, N France 49°45′N 01°43′E
Auminzatau, Gory see Ovminzatovo Tog'lari
77 T14 **Auna** Niger, W Nigeria 10°13′N 04°43′E
166 L6 **Aunglan** var. Allanmyo, Myaydo. Magway, C Burma (Myanmar) 19°25′N 95°13′E
95 H21 **Auning** Midtjylland, C Denmark 56°26′N 10°23′E
192 K17 **'Aunu'u Island** island W American Samoa
83 E20 **Auob** var. Oup. ≈ Namibia/South Africa
93 K19 **Aura** Länsi-Suomi, SW Finland 60°37′N 22°35′E
109 R5 **Aurach** ≈ N Austria
Aural, Phnom see Aôral, Phnum
153 O14 **Aurangābād** Bihār, N India 24°46′N 84°23′E
154 F13 **Aurangābād** Mahārāshtra, C India 19°52′N 75°22′E
189 V7 **Aur Atoll** atoll E Marshall Islands
102 G7 **Auray** Morbihan, NW France 47°40′N 02°59′W
94 G13 **Aurdal** Oppland, S Norway 60°51′N 09°25′E
94 F8 **Aure** Møre og Romsdal, S Norway 63°16′N 08°31′E
29 T12 **Aurelia** Iowa, C USA 42°42′N 95°26′W
Aurelia Aquensis see Baden-Baden
Aurelianum see Orléans
120 J10 **Aurès, Massif de l'** ▲ NE Algeria
100 F10 **Aurich** Niedersachsen, NW Germany 53°28′N 07°28′E
103 O13 **Aurillac** Cantal, C France 44°56′N 02°26′E
Aurine, Alpi see Zillertaler Alpen
Aurium see Ourense
14 H15 **Aurora** Ontario, S Canada 44°00′N 79°26′W
55 S8 **Aurora** NW Guyana 06°46′N 59°45′W
37 T4 **Aurora** Colorado, C USA 39°42′N 104°51′W
30 M11 **Aurora** Illinois, N USA 41°46′N 88°19′W
31 Q15 **Aurora** Indiana, N USA 39°01′N 84°55′W
29 W4 **Aurora** Minnesota, N USA 47°31′N 92°14′W
27 S8 **Aurora** Missouri, C USA 36°58′N 93°43′W
29 P16 **Aurora** Nebraska, C USA 40°52′N 98°00′W
36 J5 **Aurora** Utah, W USA 38°55′N 111°55′W
Aurora see San Francisco, Philippines
Aurora see Maéwo, Vanuatu
94 F10 **Aursjøen** ◎ S Norway
94 I9 **Aursunden** ◎ S Norway
83 D21 **Aus** Karas, SW Namibia 26°38′S 16°19′E
Ausa see Vic
14 E16 **Ausable** ≈ Ontario, S Canada
31 O3 **Au Sable Point** headland Michigan, N USA 46°40′N 86°08′W
31 S7 **Au Sable Point** headland Michigan, N USA 44°19′N 83°20′W
31 R6 **Au Sable River** ≈ Michigan, N USA
57 H16 **Ausangate, Nevado** ▲ C Peru 13°47′S 71°13′W
Auschwitz see Oświęcim
Ausculum Apulum see Ascoli Satriano
105 Q4 **Ausejo** La Rioja, N Spain 42°21′N 02°10′W
108 H7 **Ausser Rhoden** ◆ canton NE Switzerland
Ausser Rhoden/Inner Rhoden see Ausser Rhoden
Aussig see Ústí nad Labem
95 F17 **Aust-Agder** ◆ county S Norway
92 P2 **Austfonna** glacier NE Svalbard
31 P15 **Austin** Indiana, N USA 38°45′N 85°48′W
29 W11 **Austin** Minnesota, N USA 43°40′N 92°58′W
35 U5 **Austin** Nevada, W USA 39°30′N 117°05′W
25 S10 **Austin** state capital Texas, S USA 30°16′N 97°45′W
180 J10 **Austin, Lake** salt lake Western Australia
31 V11 **Austintown** Ohio, N USA 41°06′N 80°45′W
25 V9 **Austonio** Texas, SW USA 31°09′N 95°39′W
Australes, Archipel des see Australes, Îles
Australes et Antarctiques Françaises, Terres see French Southern and Antarctic Territories
191 T14 **Australes, Îles** var. Archipel des Australes, Îles Tubuai, Tubuai Islands, Eng. Austral Islands. island group SW French Polynesia
175 Y11 **Austral Fracture Zone** tectonic feature S Pacific Ocean
174 M8 **Australia** continent
181 O7 **Australia** off. Commonwealth of Australia. ◆ commonwealth republic
Australia, Commonwealth of see Australia
183 Q12 **Australian Alps** ▲ SE Australia
183 R11 **Australian Capital Territory** prev. Federal Capital Territory. ◆ territory SE Australia
Australie, Bassin Nord de l' see North Australian Basin
Austral Islands see Australes, Îles
Austrava see Ostrov
109 T6 **Austria** off. Republic of Austria, Ger. Österreich. ◆ republic C Europe
Austria, Republic of see Austria
92 K3 **Austurland** ◆ region SE Iceland
92 G10 **Austvågøya** island C Norway
Ausuituq see Grise Fiord
58 G13 **Autazes** Amazonas, N Brazil 03°37′S 59°08′W
102 M16 **Auterive** Haute-Garonne, S France 43°22′N 01°28′E
Autesiodorum see Auxerre
103 N2 **Authie** ≈ N France
Autissiodorum see Auxerre
40 K14 **Autlán** var. Autlán de Navarro. Jalisco, SW Mexico 19°48′N 104°20′W
Autlán de Navarro see Autlán
Autricum see Chartres
103 Q9 **Autun** anc. Ædua, Augustodunum. Saône-et-Loire, C France 46°58′N 04°18′E
Autz see Auce
99 H20 **Auvelais** Namur, S Belgium 50°27′N 04°38′E
103 P11 **Auvergne** ◆ region C France
102 M12 **Auvézère** ≈ W France
103 P7 **Auxerre** anc. Autesiodorum, Autissiodorum. Yonne, C France 47°48′N 03°35′E
103 N2 **Auxi-le-Château** Pas-de-Calais, N France 50°14′N 02°06′E
103 S8 **Auxonne** Côte d'Or, C France 47°12′N 05°22′E
55 P9 **Auyan Tebuy** ▲ SE Venezuela 05°48′N 62°27′W
103 O10 **Auzances** Creuse, C France 46°01′N 02°29′E
27 U8 **Ava** Missouri, C USA 36°57′N 92°39′W
142 M5 **Āvaj** Qazvīn, N Iran
95 C15 **Avaldsnes** Rogaland, S Norway 59°21′N 05°16′E
103 Q8 **Avallon** Yonne, C France 47°30′N 03°54′E
102 K6 **Avaloirs, Mont des** ▲ NW France 48°27′N 00°11′W
35 S16 **Avalon** Santa Catalina Island, California, W USA 33°20′N 118°19′W
18 J17 **Avalon** New Jersey, NE USA 39°04′N 74°42′W
13 V13 **Avalon Peninsula** peninsula Newfoundland and Labrador, E Canada
Avanersuaq see Avannaarsua
197 Q11 **Avannaarsua** var Avanersuaq, Dan. Nordgrønland. ◆ province N Greenland
60 K10 **Avaré** São Paulo, S Brazil 23°06′S 48°57′W
Avaricum see Bourges
190 H16 **Avarua** ○ (Cook Islands) Rarotonga, S Cook Islands 21°12′S 159°46′E
190 H16 **Avarua Harbour** harbour Rarotonga, S Cook Islands
Avasfelsőfalu see Negreşti-Oaş
38 L17 **Avatanak Island** island Aleutian Islands, Alaska, USA
190 B16 **Avatele** S Niue 19°06′S 169°55′E
190 H15 **Avatiu Harbour** harbour Rarotonga, S Cook Islands
Avdeyevka see Avdiyivka
114 J13 **Ávdira** Anatolikí Makedonía kai Thrákí, NE Greece 40°58′N 24°58′E
117 X8 **Avdiyivka** Rus. Avdeyevka. Donets'ka Oblast', SE Ukraine 48°06′N 37°46′E
Avdzaga see Gurvanbulag
104 G6 **Ave** ≈ N Portugal
104 G7 **Aveiro** anc. Talabriga. Aveiro, W Portugal 40°38′N 08°40′W
104 G7 **Aveiro** ◆ district N Portugal
Avela see Ávila
99 D18 **Avelgem** West-Vlaanderen, W Belgium 50°46′N 03°25′E
61 D20 **Avellaneda** Buenos Aires, E Argentina 34°43′S 58°23′W
107 L17 **Avellino** anc. Abellinum. Campania, S Italy 40°54′N 14°46′E
35 Q12 **Avenal** California, W USA 36°00′N 120°07′W
Avenio see Avignon
94 E8 **Averøya** island S Norway
107 K17 **Aversa** Campania, S Italy 40°58′N 14°13′E
33 N9 **Avery** Idaho, NW USA 47°14′N 115°48′W
25 W5 **Avery** Texas, SW USA 33°33′N 94°46′W
Aves, Islas de see Las Aves, Islas
Avesnes see Avesnes-sur-Helpe
103 Q2 **Avesnes-sur-Helpe** var. Avesnes. Nord, N France 50°08′N 03°57′E
64 G12 **Aves Ridge** undersea feature SE Caribbean Sea 14°00′N 63°30′W
95 M14 **Avesta** Dalarna, C Sweden 60°09′N 16°10′E
103 O14 **Aveyron** ◆ department S France
103 N14 **Aveyron** ≈ S France
107 J15 **Avezzano** Abruzzo, C Italy 42°02′N 13°26′E
115 D16 **Avgó** ▲ C Greece 39°31′N 21°24′E
Avgustov see Augustów
Avgustovskiy Kanal see Augustowski, Kanał
96 J9 **Aviemore** N Scotland, United Kingdom 57°06′N 04°01′W
185 F21 **Aviemore, Lake** ◎ South Island, New Zealand
103 R15 **Avignon** anc. Avenio. Vaucluse, SE France 43°57′N 04°49′E
104 M7 **Ávila** var. Avila; anc. Abela, Abula, Abyla, Avela. Castilla y León, C Spain 40°39′N 04°42′W
104 L8 **Ávila** ◆ province Castilla y León, C Spain
104 K2 **Avilés** Asturias, NW Spain 43°33′N 05°55′W
118 J4 **Avinurme** Ger. Awwinorm. Ida-Virumaa, NE Estonia 58°58′N 26°53′E
104 H10 **Avis** Portalegre, C Portugal 39°03′N 07°53′W
Avlum see Aulum
182 M11 **Avoca** Victoria, SE Australia 37°09′S 143°34′E
29 T14 **Avoca** Iowa, C USA 41°27′N 95°20′W
182 M11 **Avoca River** ≈ Victoria, SE Australia
107 L25 **Avola** Sicilia, Italy, C Mediterranean Sea 36°54′N 15°08′E
18 F10 **Avon** New York, NE USA 42°53′N 77°41′W
29 P12 **Avon** South Dakota, N USA 43°00′N 98°03′W
97 M23 **Avon** ≈ S England, United Kingdom
97 L20 **Avon** ≈ C England, United Kingdom
36 K13 **Avondale** Arizona, SW USA 33°25′N 112°20′W
23 X13 **Avon Park** Florida, SE USA 27°36′N 81°30′W
102 J5 **Avranches** Manche, N France 48°42′N 01°21′W
Avveel see Ivalo, Finland
186 M6 **Avuavu** var. Kolotambu. Guadalcanal, C Solomon Islands 09°52′S 160°25′E
103 O3 **Avure** ≈ N France

◆ Country
● Country Capital
◇ Dependent Territory
○ Dependent Territory Capital
◆ Administrative Regions
✈ International Airport
▲ Mountain
▲ Mountain Range
Volcano
≈ River
◎ Lake
⊞ Reservoir

Avveel *see* Ivalo, Finland
Avvil *see* Ivalo
77 O17 **Awaaso** *var.* Awaso. SW Ghana 06°10′N 02°18′W
141 X8 **Awābī** *var.* Al 'Awābī. NE Oman 23°20′N 57°35′E
184 L9 **Awakino** Waikato, North Island, New Zealand 38°40′S 174°37′E
142 M15 **'Awālī** C Bahrain 26°07′N 50°33′E
99 K19 **Awans** Liège, E Belgium 50°39′N 05°30′E
184 I2 **Awanui** Northland, North Island, New Zealand 35°01′S 173°16′E
148 M14 **Awārān** Baluchistān, SW Pakistan 26°31′N 65°10′E
81 K16 **Awara Plain** *plain* NE Kenya
80 M13 **Āwarē** Sumalē, E Ethiopia 08°12′N 44°09′E
138 M6 **'Awāriḍ, Wādī** *dry watercourse* E Syria
185 B20 **Awarua Point** *headland* South Island, New Zealand 44°15′S 168°03′E
81 J14 **Āwasa** Southern Nationalities, S Ethiopia 06°54′N 38°26′E
80 K13 **Āwash** Āfar, NE Ethiopia 08°59′N 40°16′E
80 K12 **Āwash** *var.* Hawash. ≈ C Ethiopia
Awaso *see* Awaaso
158 H7 **Awat** Xinjiang Uygur Zizhiqu, NW China 40°36′N 80°22′E
185 J15 **Awatere** ≈ South Island, New Zealand
75 O10 **Awbārī** SW Libya 26°35′N 12°46′E
75 N9 **Awbāri, Idhān** *var.* Edeyen d'Oubari. *desert* Algeria/Libya
80 M12 **Awdal** *off.* Gobolka Awdal. ◈ N Somalia
80 C13 **Aweil** Northern Bahr el Ghazal, NW South Sudan 08°42′N 27°20′E
96 H11 **Awe, Loch** ◎ W Scotland, United Kingdom
77 U16 **Awka** Anambra, SW Nigeria 06°12′N 07°04′E
39 O6 **Awuna River** ≈ Alaska, USA
Awwinorm *see* Avinurme
Ax *see* Dax
Axarfjördhur *see* Öxarfjördhur
103 N17 **Axat** Aude, S France 42°47′N 02°14′E
99 F16 **Axel** Zeeland, SW Netherlands 51°16′N 03°55′E
197 P9 **Axel Heiberg Island** *var.* Axel Heiburg. *island* Nunavut, N Canada
Axel Heiburg *see* Axel Heiberg Island
77 O17 **Axim** S Ghana 04°53′N 02°14′W
114 F13 **Axiós** *var.* Vardar. ≈ Greece/FYR Macedonia *see also* Vardar
Axiós *see* Vardar
103 N17 **Ax-les-Thermes** Ariège, S France 42°43′N 01°49′E
120 D11 **Ayachi, Jbel** ▲ C Morocco 32°30′N 05°00′W
61 D22 **Ayacucho** Buenos Aires, E Argentina 37°09′S 58°30′W
57 F15 **Ayacucho** Ayacucho, S Peru 13°10′S 74°15′W
57 E16 **Ayacucho** *off.* Departamento de Ayacucho. ◈ *department* SW Peru
Ayacucho, Departamento de *see* Ayacucho
145 W11 **Ayagoz** *var.* Ayaguz, *Kaz.* Ayaköz; *prev.* Sergiopol. Vostochnyy Kazakhstan, E Kazakhstan 47°54′N 80°25′E
145 V12 **Ayagoz** *var.* Ayaguz, *Kaz.* Ayakoz. ≈ E Kazakhstan
Ayaguz *see* Ayagoz
Ayakagytma *see* Oyoqog'itma
Ayakkuduk *see* Oyoqquduq
158 L10 **Ayakkum Hu** ◎ NW China
Ayaköz *see* Ayagoz
104 H14 **Ayamonte** Andalucía, S Spain 37°13′N 07°24′W
123 S11 **Ayan** Khabarovskiy Kray, E Russian Federation 56°27′N 138°09′E
136 J10 **Ayancık** Sinop, N Turkey 41°56′N 34°35′E
55 S9 **Ayanganna Mountain** ▲ C Guyana 05°21′N 59°54′W
77 U16 **Ayangba** Kogi, C Nigeria 07°36′N 07°10′E
123 U7 **Ayanka** Krasnoyarskiy Kray, E Russian Federation 63°42′N 167°31′E
54 E7 **Ayapel** Córdoba, NW Colombia 08°16′N 75°10′W
136 H12 **Ayaş** Ankara, N Turkey 40°02′N 32°21′E
57 I16 **Ayaviri** Puno, S Peru 14°53′S 70°35′W
Āybak *see* Aibak
147 N10 **Aydarko'l Ko'li** *Rus.* Ozero Aydarkul'. ◎ C Uzbekistan
Aydarkul', Ozero *see* Aydarko'l Ko'li
21 W10 **Ayden** North Carolina, SE USA 35°28′N 77°25′W
136 C15 **Aydın** *var.* Aïdin; *anc.* Tralles Aydin. Aydın, SW Turkey 37°51′N 27°51′E
136 C15 **Aydın** *var.* Aïdin. ◈ *province* SW Turkey
136 I17 **Aydıncık** İçel, S Turkey 36°08′N 33°17′E
136 C15 **Aydın Dağları** ▲▲ W Turkey
158 L6 **Aydingkol Hu** ◎ NW China
127 X7 **Aydyrlinskiy** Orenburgskaya Oblast', W Russian Federation 52°03′N 59°54′E
105 S4 **Ayerbe** Aragón, NE Spain 42°16′N 00°41′W
Ayers Rock *see* Uluṟu
166 K8 **Ayeyarwady** *var.* Irrawaddy. ◈ *division* SW Burma (Myanmar)
Ayeyarwady *see* Irrawaddy
Ayiá *see* Agiá
Ayia Napa *see* Agía Nápa
Ayia Phyla *see* Agía Fýlaxis
Ayiásos/Ayiássos *see* Agiassós
Áyios Evstrátios *see* Ágios Efstrátios
Áyios Kírikos *see* Ágios Kírykos
Áyios Nikólaos *see* Ágios Nikólaos
80 I11 **Āykel** Āmara, N Ethiopia 12°33′N 37°01′E
123 N9 **Aykhal** Respublika Sakha (Yakutiya), NE Russian Federation 66°07′N 110°25′E
14 J12 **Aylen Lake** ◎ Ontario, SE Canada
97 N21 **Aylesbury** SE England, United Kingdom 51°50′N 00°50′W
105 O6 **Ayllón** Castilla y León, N Spain 41°25′N 03°23′W
14 F17 **Aylmer** Ontario, S Canada 42°46′N 80°57′W
14 L12 **Aylmer** Québec, SE Canada 45°23′N 75°51′W
15 R12 **Aylmer, Lac** ◎ Québec, SE Canada
8 L9 **Aylmer Lake** ◎ Northwest Territories, NW Canada
145 V14 **Aynabulak** *Kaz.* Aynabulaq. Almaty, SE Kazakhstan 44°37′N 77°59′E
Aynabulaq *see* Aynabulak
138 K2 **'Ayn al 'Arab** Ḥalab, N Syria 36°55′N 38°21′E
Aynayn *see* 'Aynīn
139 V12 **'Ayn Ḥamūd** Dhī Qār, S Iraq 30°51′N 45°37′E
147 P12 **Ayní** *prev.* Varzimanor Ayni. W Tajikistan 39°24′N 68°30′E
140 M10 **'Aynīn** *var.* Aynayn. *spring/well* SW Saudi Arabia 20°52′N 41°41′E
21 U12 **Aynor** South Carolina, SE USA 33°59′N 79°11′W
139 Q7 **'Ayn Zāzūh** Al Anbār, C Iraq 33°29′N 42°34′E
153 N12 **Ayodhya** Uttar Pradesh, N India 26°47′N 82°12′E
123 S6 **Ayon, Ostrov** *island* NE Russian Federation
105 R11 **Ayora** Valenciana, E Spain 39°04′N 01°04′W
77 Q11 **Ayorou** Tillabéri, W Niger 14°45′N 00°54′E
79 E16 **Ayos** Centre, S Cameroon 03°53′N 12°31′E
76 L5 **'Ayoûn 'Abd el Mâlek** *well* N Mauritania
76 K10 **'Ayoûn el 'Atroûs** *var.* Aïoun el Atrous, Aïoun el Atroûss. Hodh el Gharbi, SE Mauritania 16°38′N 09°36′W
96 I13 **Ayr** W Scotland, United Kingdom 55°28′N 04°38′W
96 I13 **Ayr** ≈ W Scotland, United Kingdom
96 I13 **Ayrshire** *cultural region* SW Scotland, United Kingdom
Aysen *see* Aisén
80 L12 **Āysha** Sumalē, E Ethiopia 10°36′N 42°31′E
144 L14 **Ayteke Bi** *Kaz.* Zhangaqazaly; *prev.* Novokazalinsk. Kzylorda, SW Kazakhstan 45°53′N 62°10′E
146 K8 **Aytim** Navoiy Viloyati, N Uzbekistan 42°15′N 63°25′E
181 W4 **Ayton** Queensland, NE Australia 15°54′S 145°19′E
114 M9 **Aytos** Burgas, E Bulgaria 42°43′N 27°14′E
171 T11 **Ayu, Kepulauan** *island group* E Indonesia
167 U12 **A Yun Pa** *prev.* Cheo Reo. Gia Lai, S Vietnam 13°19′N 108°27′E
169 V11 **Ayu, Tanjung** *headland* Borneo, N Indonesia 0°25′N 117°34′E
41 P16 **Ayutlá** *var.* Ayutla de los Libres. Guerrero, S Mexico 16°51′N 99°16′W
40 K13 **Ayutla** Jalisco, C Mexico 20°07′N 104°18′W
Ayutla de los Libres *see* Ayutlá
167 O11 **Ayutthaya** *var.* Phra Nakhon Si Ayutthaya. Phra Nakhon Si Ayutthaya, C Thailand 14°20′N 100°35′E
136 B13 **Ayvalık** Balıkesir, W Turkey 39°18′N 26°42′E
99 L20 **Aywaille** Liège, E Belgium 50°28′N 05°40′E
141 R13 **'Aywat aş Şay'ar, Wādī** *seasonal river* N Yemen
Azaffal *see* Azeffâl
105 T9 **Azahar, Costa del** *coastal region* E Spain
105 S6 **Azaila** Aragón, NE Spain 41°17′N 00°20′W
104 F10 **Azambuja** Lisboa, C Portugal 39°04′N 08°52′W
153 N13 **Āzamgarh** Uttar Pradesh, N India 26°03′N 83°10′E
77 O9 **Azaouâd** *desert* C Mali
77 S10 **Azaouagh, Vallée de l'** *var.* Azaouak. ≈ W Niger
Azaouak *see* Azaouagh, Vallée de l'
61 F14 **Azara** Misiones, NE Argentina 28°03′S 55°42′W
Azaran *see* Hashtrūd
Azärbaycan/Azärbaycan Respublikasī *see* Azerbaijan
Āzarbāyjān-e Bākhtarī *see* Āzarbāyjān-e Gharbī
142 I4 **Āzarbāyjān-e Gharbī** *off.* Ostān-e Āzarbāyjān-e Gharbī, *Eng.* West Azerbaijan; *prev.* Āzarbāyjān-e Bākhtarī. NW Iran
Āzarbāyjān-e Gharbī, Ostān-e *see* Āzarbāyjān-e Gharbī
Āzarbāyjān-e Khāvarī *see* Āzarbāyjān-e Sharqī
142 J3 **Āzarbāyjān-e Sharqī** *off.* Ostān-e Azarbāyjān-e Sharqī, *Eng.* East Azerbaijan; *prev.* Āzarbāyjān-e Khāvarī. ◈ *province* NW Iran
Āzarbāyjān-e Sharqī, Ostān-e *see* Āzarbāyjān-e Sharqī
77 W13 **Azare** Bauchi, N Nigeria 11°41′N 10°09′E
119 M19 **Azarychy** *Rus.* Ozarichi. Homyel'skaya Voblasts', SE Belarus 52°31′N 29°19′E
145 P13 **Azat, Gory** *hill* C Kazakhstan
102 L8 **Azay-le-Rideau** Indre-et-Loire, C France 47°16′N 00°25′E
138 I2 **A'zāz** Ḥalab, NW Syria 36°35′N 37°03′E
76 H7 **Azeffâl** *var.* Azaffal. *desert* Mauritania/Western Sahara
137 V12 **Azerbaijan** *off.* Azerbaijani Republic, *Az.* Azärbaycan, Azärbaycan Respublikasī; *prev.* Azerbaijan SSR. ◆ *republic* SE Asia
Azerbaijani Republic *see* Azerbaijan
Azerbaijan SSR *see* Azerbaijan
74 F7 **Azilal** C Morocco 31°58′N 06°53′W
Azimabad *see* Patna
19 O6 **Aziscohos Lake** ⊞ Maine, NE USA
Azizbekov *see* Vayk'
Azizie *see* Telish
Aziziya *see* Al 'Azīzīyah
127 T4 **Aznakayevo** Respublika Tatarstan, W Russian Federation 54°55′N 53°15′E
56 C8 **Azogues** Cañar, S Ecuador 02°44′S 78°48′W
64 N2 **Azores** *var.* Açores, Ilhas dos Açores, *Port.* Arquipélago dos Açores. *island group* Portugal, NE Atlantic Ocean
64 L8 **Azores-Biscay Rise** *undersea feature* E Atlantic Ocean 19°00′W 42°40′N
Azotos/Azotus *see* Ashdod
78 K11 **Azoum, Bahr** *seasonal river* SE Chad
126 L12 **Azov** Rostovskaya Oblast', SW Russian Federation 47°07′N 39°26′E
126 J13 **Azov, Sea of** *Rus.* Azovskoye More, *Ukr.* Azovs'ke More. *sea* NE Black Sea
Azovs'ke More/Azovskoye More *see* Azov, Sea of
138 I10 **Azraq, Wāḥat al** *oasis* N Jordan
Āzro *see* Āzrow
74 G6 **Azrou** C Morocco 33°30′N 05°12′W
149 R5 **Āzrow** *var.* Āzro. Lōgar, E Afghanistan 34°11′N 69°39′E
37 P8 **Aztec** New Mexico, SW USA 36°49′N 107°59′W
36 M13 **Aztec Peak** ▲ Arizona, SW USA 33°48′N 110°54′W
45 N9 **Azua** *var.* Azua de Compostela. S Dominican Republic 18°29′N 70°44′W
Azua de Compostela *see* Azua
104 K12 **Azuaga** Extremadura, W Spain 38°16′N 05°40′W
56 B8 **Azuay** ◈ *province* W Ecuador
164 C13 **Azuchi-Ō-shima** *island* SW Japan
105 O11 **Azuer** ≈ C Spain
43 S17 **Azuero, Península de** *peninsula* S Panama
62 I6 **Azufre, Volcán** *var.* Volcán Lastarria. ^ N Chile 25°16′S 68°35′W
116 J12 **Azuga** Prahova, SE Romania 45°27′N 25°34′E
61 C22 **Azul** Buenos Aires, E Argentina 36°46′S 59°50′W
62 I8 **Azul, Cerro** ▲ NW Argentina 28°28′S 68°43′W
56 E12 **Azul, Cordillera** ▲▲ C Peru
165 P11 **Azuma-san** ▲ Honshū, C Japan 37°44′N 140°05′E
103 V15 **Azur, Côte d'** *coastal region* SE France
191 Z3 **Azur Lagoon** ◎ Kiritimati, E Kiribati
'Azza *see* Gaza
Az Zāb al Kabīr *see* Great Zab
138 H7 **Az Zabdānī** *var.* Zabadani. Rīf Dimashq, W Syria 33°45′N 36°07′E
141 W8 **Aẓ Ẓāhirah** *desert* NW Oman
141 S6 **Aẓ Ẓahrān** *Eng.* Dhahran. Ash Sharqīyah, NE Saudi Arabia 26°18′N 50°02′E
141 R6 **Aẓ Ẓahrān al Khubar** *var.* Dhahran Al Khobar. ✈ Ash Sharqīyah, NE Saudi Arabia 26°28′N 49°42′E
75 W7 **Az Zaqāzīq** *var.* Zagazig. N Egypt 30°36′N 31°32′E
138 H10 **Az Zarqā'** *var.* Zarqa. Az Zarqā', NW Jordan 32°04′N 36°06′E
138 I11 **Az Zarqā'** *off.* Muḥāfazat az Zarqā', *var.* Zarqa. ◈ *governorate* N Jordan
75 O7 **Az Zāwiyah** *var.* Zawia. NW Libya 32°45′N 12°44′E
141 N15 **Az Zaydīyah** W Yemen 15°20′N 43°03′E
74 I11 **Azzel Matti, Sebkha** *var.* Sebkra Azz el Matti. *salt flat* C Algeria
141 P6 **Az Zilfī** Ar Riyāḍ, N Saudi Arabia 26°17′N 44°48′E
139 Y13 **Az Zubayr** *var.* Al Zubair. Al Başrah, SE Iraq 30°24′N 47°45′E
Az Zuqur *see* Jabal Zuqar, Jazīrat

B

187 X15 **Ba** *prev.* Mba. Viti Levu, W Fiji 17°35′S 177°40′E
Ba *see* Da Răng, Sông
171 P17 **Baa** Pulau Rote, C Indonesia 10°44′S 123°06′E
138 H7 **Baalbek** *var.* Ba'labakk; *anc.* Heliopolis. E Lebanon 34°00′N 36°15′E
108 G8 **Baar** Zug, N Switzerland 47°12′N 08°32′E
81 L17 **Baardheere** *var.* Bardere, *It.* Bardera. Gedo, SW Somalia 02°13′N 42°19′E
Baargaal *see* Bargaal
99 I15 **Baarle-Hertog** Antwerpen, N Belgium 51°26′N 04°56′E
99 I15 **Baarle-Nassau** Noord-Brabant, S Netherlands 51°27′N 04°56′E
98 J11 **Baarn** Utrecht, C Netherlands 52°13′N 05°16′E
162 H9 **Baatsagaan** *var.* Bayansayr. Bayanhongor, C Mongolia 45°36′N 99°27′E
114 D13 **Baba** *var.* Buševa, *Gk.* Varnoús. ▲▲ FYR Macedonia/Greece
76 H10 **Bababé** Brakna, W Mauritania 16°22′N 13°57′W
136 G10 **Baba Burnu** *headland* NW Turkey 41°18′N 31°24′E
117 N13 **Babadag** Tulcea, SE Romania 44°53′N 28°47′E
137 X10 **Babadağ Dağı** ▲ NE Azerbaijan 41°02′N 48°04′E
146 H14 **Babadaýhan** *Rus.* Babadaykhan; *prev.* Kirovsk. Ahal Welaýaty, C Turkmenistan 37°39′N 60°17′E
Babadaykhan *see* Babadaýhan
146 G14 **Babadurmaz** Ahal Welaýaty, C Turkmenistan 37°39′N 59°03′E
114 M12 **Babaeski** Kırklareli, NW Turkey 41°26′N 27°06′E
139 T4 **Bāba Gurgur** At Ta'mím, N Iraq 35°34′N 44°18′E
56 B7 **Babahoyo** *prev.* Bodegas. Los Ríos, C Ecuador 01°53′S 79°31′W
149 P5 **Bābā, Kūh-e** ▲▲ C Afghanistan
171 N12 **Babana** Sulawesi, C Indonesia 02°03′S 119°13′E
Babao *see* Qilian
171 Q12 **Babar, Kepulauan** *island group* E Indonesia
171 T12 **Babar, Pulau** *island* Kepulauan Babar, E Indonesia
Bābāsar Pass *see* Babusar Pass
Babashy, Gory *see* Babaşy
146 C9 **Babaşy** *Rus.* Gory Babashy. ▲▲ W Turkmenistan
168 M13 **Babat** Sumatera, W Indonesia 02°45′S 104°01′E
Babatag, Khrebet *see* Bototog', Tizmasi
81 H21 **Babati** Manyara, NE Tanzania 04°12′S 35°45′E
124 J13 **Babayevo** Vologodskaya Oblast', NW Russian Federation 59°23′N 35°52′E
127 Q15 **Babayurt** Respublika Dagestan, SW Russian Federation 43°38′N 46°49′E
33 P6 **Babb** Montana, NW USA 48°51′N 113°26′W
29 X4 **Babbitt** Minnesota, N USA 47°42′N 91°56′W
188 E9 **Babeldaob** *var.* Babeldaop, Babelthuap. *island* N Palau
Babeldaop *see* Babeldaob
141 N17 **Bab el Mandeb** *strait* Gulf of Aden/Red Sea
Babelthuap *see* Babeldaob
111 K17 **Babia Góra** *var.* Babia Hora. ▲ Poland/Slovakia 49°33′N 19°32′E
Babia Hora *see* Babia Góra
Babian Jiang *see* Black River
Babichi *see* Babichy
119 N19 **Babichy** *Rus.* Babichi. Homyel'skaya Voblasts', SE Belarus 52°17′N 30°00′E
112 I10 **Babina Greda** Vukovar-Srijem, E Croatia 45°09′N 18°33′E
10 K13 **Babine Lake** ◎ British Columbia, SW Canada
143 O4 **Bābol** *var.* Babul, Balfrush, Barfrush; *prev.* Barfurush. Māzandarān, N Iran 36°34′N 52°39′E
143 O4 **Bābolsar** *var.* Babulsar; *prev.* Meshed-i-Sar. Māzandarān, N Iran 36°41′N 52°39′E
36 L16 **Baboquivari Peak** ▲ Arizona, SW USA 31°46′N 111°36′W
79 G15 **Baboua** Nana-Mambéré, W Central African Republic 05°46′N 14°47′E
119 M17 **Babruysk** *Rus.* Bobruysk. Mahilyowskaya Voblasts', E Belarus 53°07′N 29°13′E
Babu *see* Hezhou
Babul *see* Bābol
Babulsar *see* Bābolsar
113 O19 **Babuna** ▲▲ C FYR Macedonia
113 O19 **Babuna** ≈ C FYR Macedonia
152 G4 **Babusar Pass** *prev.* Bābāsar Pass. *pass* India/Pakistan
148 K7 **Bābūs, Dasht-e** *Pash.* Bebas, Dasht-i. ▲▲ W Afghanistan
171 O1 **Babuyan Channel** *channel* N Philippines
171 O1 **Babuyan Islands** *island* N Philippines
139 T9 **Babylon** *site of ancient city* C Iraq
112 J9 **Bač** *Ger.* Batsch. Vojvodina, NW Serbia 45°24′N 19°17′E
58 M13 **Bacabal** Maranhão, E Brazil 04°15′S 44°45′W
41 Y14 **Bacalar** Quintana Roo, SE Mexico 18°38′N 88°17′W
41 Y14 **Bacalar Chico, Boca** *strait* SE Mexico
171 Q12 **Bacan, Kepulauan** *island group* E Indonesia
171 S12 **Bacan, Pulau** *prev.* Batjan. *island* Maluku, E Indonesia
116 L10 **Bacău** *Hung.* Bákó. Bacău, NE Romania 46°36′N 26°56′E
116 K11 **Bacău** ◈ *county* E Romania
Băc Bô, Vinh *see* Tongking, Gulf of
167 T5 **Băc Can** *var.* Bach Thong. Băc Thai, N Vietnam 22°07′N 105°50′E
103 T5 **Baccarat** Meurthe-et-Moselle, NE France 48°27′N 06°46′E
183 N12 **Bacchus Marsh** Victoria, SE Australia 37°41′S 144°30′E
40 H4 **Bacerac** Sonora, NW Mexico 30°27′N 108°55′W
116 L10 **Băceşti** Vaslui, E Romania 46°50′N 27°14′E
167 T6 **Băc Giang** Ha Băc, N Vietnam 21°17′N 106°12′E
54 I5 **Bachaquero** Zulia, NW Venezuela 09°57′N 71°09′W
Bacher *see* Pohorje
118 M13 **Bacheykava** *Rus.* Bocheykovo. Vitsyebskaya Voblasts', N Belarus 55°01′N 29°09′E
40 I5 **Bachíniva** Chihuahua, N Mexico 28°41′N 107°13′W
Bach Thong *see* Băc Can
158 G8 **Bachu** Xinjiang Uygur Zizhiqu, NW China 39°46′N 78°30′E
9 N8 **Back** ≈ Nunavut, N Canada
112 K10 **Bačka Palanka** *prev.* Palanka. Serbia, NW Serbia 44°22′N 20°57′E
112 K8 **Bačka Topola** *Hung.* Topolya; *prev. Hung.* Bácstopolya. Vojvodina, N Serbia 45°48′N 19°39′E
95 J17 **Bäckefors** Västra Götaland, S Sweden 58°49′N 12°07′E
Bäckermühle Schulzenmühle *see* Żywiec
95 L16 **Bäckhammar** Värmland, C Sweden 59°09′N 14°13′E
112 K9 **Bački Petrovac** *Hung.* Petrőcz; *prev.* Petrovac, Petrovácz. Vojvodina, NW Serbia 45°22′N 19°34′E
101 I21 **Backnang** Baden-Württemberg, SW Germany 48°57′N 09°26′E
167 S15 **Bac Liêu** *var.* Vinh Loi. Minh Hai, S Vietnam 09°17′N 105°44′E
167 T6 **Băc Ninh** Ha Băc, N Vietnam 21°10′N 106°04′E
40 G4 **Bacoachi** Sonora, NW Mexico 30°36′N 110°00′W
171 P6 **Bacolod** *off.* Bacolod City. Negros, C Philippines 10°43′N 122°58′E
Bacolod City *see* Bacolod
171 O4 **Baco, Mount** ▲ Mindoro, N Philippines 12°50′N 121°08′E
111 K25 **Bácsalmás** Bács-Kiskun, S Hungary 46°07′N 19°20′E
Bácsjózseffalva *see* Žednik
111 J24 **Bács-Kiskun** *off.* Bács-Kiskun Megye. ◈ *county* S Hungary
Bács-Kiskun Megye *see* Bács-Kiskun
Bácsszenttamás *see* Srbobran
Bácstopolya *see* Bačka Topola
Bactra *see* Balkh
Bada *see* Xilin
155 F21 **Badagara** *var.* Vadakara. Kerala, SW India 11°36′N 75°34′E *see also* Vadakara
101 M24 **Bad Aibling** Bayern, SE Germany 47°52′N 12°00′E
162 I13 **Badain Jaran Shamo** *desert* N China
104 I11 **Badajoz** *anc.* Pax Augusta. Extremadura, W Spain 38°53′N 06°58′W
104 J11 **Badajoz** ◈ *province* Extremadura, W Spain
149 S2 **Badakhshān** ◈ *province* NE Afghanistan
105 W6 **Badalona** *anc.* Baetulo. Cataluña, E Spain 41°27′N 02°15′E
154 O11 **Bādāmpāhārh** *var.* Bādāmapāhārh. Orissa, E India 22°04′N 86°06′E
169 O10 **Badas, Kepulauan** *island group* W Indonesia
109 S6 **Bad Aussee** Salzburg, E Austria 47°35′N 13°44′E
31 S8 **Bad Axe** Michigan, N USA 43°48′N 83°00′W
101 G16 **Bad Berleburg** Nordrhein-Westfalen, W Germany 51°03′N 08°24′E
101 L17 **Bad Blankenburg** Thüringen, C Germany 50°43′N 11°19′E
Bad Borseck *see* Borsec
101 G18 **Bad Camberg** Hessen, W Germany 50°18′N 08°15′E
100 L8 **Bad Doberan** Mecklenburg-Vorpommern, N Germany 54°06′N 11°55′E
101 N14 **Bad Düben** Sachsen, E Germany 51°35′N 12°34′E
109 X4 **Baden** *var.* Baden bei Wien; *anc.* Aquae Panoniae, Thermae Pannonicae. Niederösterreich, NE Austria 48°01′N 16°14′E
108 F9 **Baden** Aargau, N Switzerland 47°28′N 08°19′E
101 G21 **Baden-Baden** *anc.* Aurelia Aquensis. Baden-Württemberg, SW Germany 48°46′N 08°14′E
Baden bei Wien *see* Baden
101 G22 **Baden-Württemberg** *Fr.* Bade-Wurtemberg. ◈ *state* SW Germany
112 A10 **Baderna** Istra, NW Croatia 45°12′N 13°45′E
Bade-Wurtemberg *see* Baden-Württemberg
101 H20 **Bad Fredrichshall** Baden-Württemberg, S Germany 49°13′N 09°15′E
100 P11 **Bad Freienwalde** Brandenburg, NE Germany 52°47′N 14°04′E
109 Q8 **Badgastein** *var.* Gastein. Salzburg, NW Austria 47°07′N 13°09′E
Badger State *see* Wisconsin
148 L4 **Bādghīs** ◈ *province* NW Afghanistan
109 T5 **Bad Hall** Oberösterreich, N Austria 48°03′N 14°13′E
101 J14 **Bad Harzburg** Niedersachsen, C Germany 51°52′N 10°34′E
101 I16 **Bad Hersfeld** Hessen, C Germany 50°52′N 09°42′E
98 I10 **Badhoevedorp** Noord-Holland, C Netherlands 52°21′N 04°46′E
109 Q8 **Bad Hofgastein** Salzburg, NW Austria 47°11′N 13°07′E
Bad Homburg *see* Bad Homburg vor der Höhe
101 G18 **Bad Homburg vor der Höhe** *var.* Bad Homburg. Hessen, W Germany 50°14′N 08°37′E
101 E17 **Bad Honnef** Nordrhein-Westfalen, W Germany 50°39′N 07°13′E
149 Q17 **Badīn** Sind, SE Pakistan 24°38′N 68°53′E
21 S10 **Badin Lake** ⊞ North Carolina, SE USA
40 I8 **Badiraguato** Sinaloa, C Mexico 25°21′N 107°31′W
109 R6 **Bad Ischl** Oberösterreich, N Austria 47°43′N 13°36′E
Badjawa *see* Bajawa
Badje-Sohppar *see* Övre Soppero
101 J18 **Bad Kissingen** Bayern, SE Germany 50°12′N 10°04′E
Bad Königswart *see* Lázně Kynžvart
101 F19 **Bad Kreuznach** Rheinland-Pfalz, SW Germany 49°51′N 07°52′E
101 F24 **Bad Krozingen** Baden-Württemberg, SW Germany 47°55′N 07°43′E
101 G16 **Bad Laasphe** Nordrhein-Westfalen, W Germany 50°57′N 08°24′E
28 J6 **Badlands** *physical region* North Dakota/South Dakota, N USA
101 K16 **Bad Langensalza** Thüringen, C Germany 51°05′N 10°40′E
109 T3 **Bad Leonfelden** Oberösterreich, N Austria 48°31′N 14°17′E
101 I20 **Bad Mergentheim** Baden-Württemberg, SW Germany 49°30′N 09°46′E
101 H17 **Bad Nauheim** Hessen, W Germany 50°22′N 08°45′E
101 E17 **Bad Neuenahr-Ahrweiler** Rheinland-Pfalz, W Germany 50°33′N 07°07′E
Bad Neustadt *see* Bad Neustadt an der Saale
101 J18 **Bad Neustadt an der Saale** *var.* Bad Neustadt. Berlin, C Germany 50°21′N 10°13′E
Badnur *see* Betūl
100 H13 **Bad Oeynhausen** Nordrhein-Westfalen, NW Germany 52°12′N 08°48′E
100 J9 **Bad Oldesloe** Schleswig-Holstein, N Germany 53°49′N 10°22′E
77 Q16 **Badou** C Togo 07°37′N 00°37′E
Bad Polzin *see* Połczyn-Zdrój
100 H13 **Bad Pyrmont** Niedersachsen, C Germany 51°58′N 09°16′E
109 X9 **Bad Radkersburg** Steiermark, SE Austria 46°40′N 16°02′E
139 V8 **Badrah** Wāsiţ, E Iraq 33°06′N 45°58′E
Badrah *see* Tarialan
101 N24 **Bad Reichenhall** Bayern, SE Germany 47°43′N 12°52′E
140 K8 **Badr Ḥunayn** Al Madīnah, W Saudi Arabia 23°46′N 38°45′E
152 K8 **Badrīnāth** ▲ N India 30°44′N 79°29′E
28 M10 **Bad River** ≈ South Dakota, N USA
30 K4 **Bad River** ≈ Wisconsin, N USA
100 H13 **Bad Salzuflen** Nordrhein-Westfalen, NW Germany 52°06′N 08°45′E
101 J16 **Bad Salzungen** Thüringen, C Germany 50°48′N 10°15′E
109 V8 **Bad Sankt Leonhard im Lavanttal** Kärnten, S Austria 46°55′N 14°51′E
100 K9 **Bad Schwartau** Schleswig-Holstein, N Germany 53°55′N 10°42′E
101 L24 **Bad Tölz** Bayern, SE Germany 47°44′N 11°34′E
181 U1 **Badu Island** *island* Queensland, NE Australia
155 K25 **Badulla** Uva Province, C Sri Lanka 06°59′N 81°03′E
109 X5 **Bad Vöslau** Niederösterreich, NE Austria 47°58′N 16°13′E
101 I24 **Bad Waldsee** Baden-Württemberg, S Germany 47°54′N 09°44′E
35 U11 **Badwater Basin** *depression* California, W USA
101 J20 **Bad Windsheim** Bayern, C Germany 49°30′N 10°25′E
101 J23 **Bad Wörishofen** Bayern, S Germany 48°00′N 10°36′E
100 G10 **Bad Zwischenahn** Niedersachsen, NW Germany 53°10′N 08°01′E
104 M13 **Baena** Andalucía, S Spain 36°37′N 04°20′W
163 V15 **Baengnyong-do** *prev.* Paengnyŏng. *island* NW South Korea
Baeterrae/Baeterrae Septimanorum *see* Béziers
Baetic Cordillera/Baetic Mountains *see* Béticos, Sistemas
Baetulo *see* Badalona
57 K18 **Baeza** Napo, NE Ecuador 0°30′S 77°52′W
105 N13 **Baeza** Andalucía, S Spain 38°00′N 03°28′W
79 D15 **Bafang** Ouest, W Cameroon 05°10′N 10°11′E
76 H12 **Bafatá** C Guinea-Bissau 12°09′N 14°38′W
149 U5 **Baffa** Khyber Pakhtunkhwa, NW Pakistan 34°30′N 73°18′E
197 O11 **Baffin Basin** *undersea feature* N Labrador Sea
197 N12 **Baffin Bay** *bay* Canada/Greenland
25 T15 **Baffin Bay** *inlet* Texas, SW USA
196 M12 **Baffin Island** *island* Nunavut, NE Canada
79 E15 **Bafia** Centre, C Cameroon 04°49′N 11°14′E
77 R14 **Bafilo** NE Togo 09°23′N 01°20′E
76 J12 **Bafing** ≈ W Africa
76 J12 **Bafoulabé** Kayes, W Mali 13°43′N 10°49′W
79 D15 **Bafoussam** Ouest, W Cameroon 05°31′N 10°25′E
143 R9 **Bāfq** Yazd, C Iran 31°35′N 55°21′E
136 L10 **Bafra** Samsun, N Turkey 41°34′N 35°56′E
136 L10 **Bafra Burnu** *headland* N Turkey 41°42′N 36°02′E
143 S12 **Bāft** Kermān, S Iran 29°12′N 56°36′E
79 N18 **Bafwabalinga** Orientale, NE Dem. Rep. Congo 0°52′N 26°55′E
79 N18 **Bafwaboli** Orientale, NE Dem. Rep. Congo 0°36′N 26°08′E
79 N17 **Bafwasende** Orientale, NE Dem. Rep. Congo 01°00′N 27°09′E
42 K13 **Bagaces** Guanacaste, NW Costa Rica 10°31′N 85°18′W
153 O12 **Bagaha** Bihār, N India 27°08′N 84°04′E
155 F16 **Bāgalkot** Karnātaka, W India 16°11′N 75°42′E
81 J22 **Bagamoyo** Pwani, E Tanzania 06°26′S 38°55′E
Bagan Datok *see* Bagan Datuk
168 J8 **Bagan Datuk** *var.* Bagan Datok. Perak, Peninsular Malaysia 03°58′N 100°47′E
171 R7 **Baganga** Mindanao, S Philippines 07°31′N 126°34′E
168 J9 **Bagansiapiapi** *var.* Pasirpangarayan. Sumatera, W Indonesia 02°06′N 100°52′E
162 M8 **Baganuur** *var.* Nüürst. Töv, C Mongolia 47°44′N 108°22′E
Bagaria *see* Bagheria
77 T11 **Bagaroua** Tahoua, W Niger 14°34′N 04°24′E
79 I20 **Bagata** Bandundu, W Dem. Rep. Congo 03°47′S 17°57′E
Bagdad *see* Baghdad
123 O13 **Bagdarin** Respublika Buryatiya, S Russian Federation 54°27′N 113°34′E
61 G17 **Bagé** Rio Grande do Sul, S Brazil 31°22′S 54°06′W
Bagenalstown *see* Muine Bheag
153 T16 **Bagerhat** *var.* Bagherhat. Khulna, S Bangladesh 22°40′N 89°48′E
103 P16 **Bages et de Sigean, Étang de** ◎ S France
33 W17 **Baggs** Wyoming, C USA 41°02′N 107°39′W
154 F11 **Bāgh** Madhya Pradesh, C India 22°22′N 74°49′E
139 T8 **Baghdad** *var.* Bagdad, *Eng.* Baghdad. ● Baghdād, C Iraq 33°20′N 44°26′E
139 T8 **Baghdād** ✈ (Baghdād) Baghdād, C Iraq 33°20′N 44°26′E
Baghdad *see* Baghdad
Bagherhat *see* Bagerhat
107 J23 **Bagheria** *var.* Bagaria. Sicilia, Italy, C Mediterranean Sea 38°05′N 13°31′E
143 S10 **Bāghīn** Kermān, C Iran 30°50′N 57°00′E
149 Q3 **Baghlān** Baghlān, NE Afghanistan 36°11′N 68°44′E
149 Q3 **Baghlān** *var.* Bāghlān. ◈ *province* NE Afghanistan
Bāghlān *see* Baghlān
148 M7 **Bāghrān** Helmand, S Afghanistan 32°55′N 64°57′E
29 T4 **Bagley** Minnesota, N USA 47°31′N 95°24′W
106 H10 **Bagnacavallo** Emilia-Romagna, C Italy 44°00′N 12°59′E
102 K16 **Bagnères-de-Bigorre** Hautes-Pyrénées, S France 43°04′N 00°09′E
102 L17 **Bagnères-de-Luchon** Hautes-Pyrénées, S France 42°46′N 00°34′E
106 F11 **Bagni di Lucca** Toscana, C Italy 44°01′N 10°38′E
106 H11 **Bagno di Romagna** Emilia-Romagna, C Italy 43°51′N 11°57′E
103 R14 **Bagnols-sur-Cèze** Gard, S France 44°10′N 04°37′E
162 M14 **Bag Nur** ◎ N China
166 L8 **Bago** *var.* Pegu. Bago, SW Burma (Myanmar) 17°18′N 96°31′E
171 P6 **Bago** *off.* Bago City. Negros, C Philippines 10°30′N 122°49′E
166 L7 **Bago** *var.* Pegu. ◈ *division* S Burma (Myanmar)
Bago City *see* Bago
76 M13 **Bagoé** ≈ Ivory Coast/Mali
Bagrāmē *see* Bagrāmī
149 R5 **Bagrāmī** *var.* Bagrāmē. Kâbōl, E Afghanistan 34°29′N 69°16′E
119 B14 **Bagrationovsk** *Ger.* Preussisch Eylau. Kaliningradskaya Oblast', W Russian Federation 54°24′N 20°39′E
Bagrax *see* Bohu
Bagrax Hu *see* Bosten Hu
56 C10 **Bagua** Amazonas, NE Peru 05°37′S 78°36′W
171 O2 **Baguio** *off.* Baguio City. Luzon, N Philippines 16°25′N 120°36′E
Baguio City *see* Baguio
77 V9 **Bagzane, Monts** ▲ N Niger 17°48′N 08°43′E
Bāḥah, Minṭaqat al *see* Al Bāḥah
Bahama Islands *see* Bahamas
44 H3 **Bahamas** *off.* Commonwealth of the Bahamas. ◆ *commonwealth republic* N West Indies
0 L13 **Bahamas** *var.* Bahama Islands. *island group* N West Indies
Bahamas, Commonwealth of the *see* Bahamas
153 S15 **Baharampur** *prev.* Berhampore. West Bengal, NE India 24°06′N 88°19′E
146 E12 **Baharly** *var.* Bäherden, *Rus.* Bakharden; *prev.* Bakherden. Ahal Welaýaty, C Turkmenistan 38°30′N 57°18′E
149 U10 **Bahāwalnagar** Punjab, E Pakistan 30°00′N 73°03′E
149 T11 **Bahāwalpur** Punjab, E Pakistan 29°25′N 71°40′E
136 L16 **Bahçe** Osmaniye, S Turkey 37°14′N 36°34′E
160 J8 **Ba He** ≈ C China
Bäherden *see* Baharly
59 N16 **Bahia** *off.* Estado da Bahia. ◈ *state* E Brazil
61 B24 **Bahía Blanca** Buenos Aires, E Argentina 38°43′S 62°19′W
40 L15 **Bahía Bufadero** Michoacán, SW Mexico
63 J19 **Bahía Bustamante** Chubut, SE Argentina 45°06′S 66°30′W
40 D5 **Bahía de los Ángeles** Baja California Norte, NW Mexico
40 C6 **Bahía de Tortugas** Baja California Sur, NW Mexico 27°42′N 114°54′W
Bahia, Estado da *see* Bahia
42 J4 **Bahía, Islas de la** *Eng.* Bay Islands. *island group* N Honduras
40 E5 **Bahía Kino** Sonora, NW Mexico 28°48′N 111°55′W
40 E9 **Bahía Magdalena** *var.* Puerto Magdalena. Baja California Sur, NW Mexico 24°34′N 112°07′W
54 C8 **Bahía Solano** *var.* Ciudad Mutis, Solano. Chocó, W Colombia 06°13′N 77°27′W
80 I11 **Bahir Dar** *var.* Bahr Dar, Bahrdar Giyorgis. Āmara, N Ethiopia 11°34′N 37°23′E
141 X8 **Bahlā'** *var.* Bahlah, Bahlat. NW Oman 22°58′N 57°16′E
Bāhla *see* Bālān
Bahlah/Bahlat *see* Bahlā'
152 M11 **Bahraich** Uttar Pradesh, N India 27°35′N 81°36′E
143 M14 **Bahrain** *off.* State of Bahrain, Dawlat al Bahrayn, *Ar.* Al Baḥrayn, *prev.* Bahrein; *anc.* Tylos, Tyros. ◆ *monarchy* SW Asia
142 M14 **Bahrain** ✈ C Bahrain 26°15′N 50°39′E
142 M15 **Bahrain, Gulf of** *gulf* Persian Gulf, NW Arabian Sea
Bahrain, State of *see* Bahrain
138 I7 **Baḥrat Mallāḥah** ◎ W Syria
Bahrayn, Dawlat al *see* Bahrain
Bahr Dar/Bahrdar Giyorgis *see* Bahir Dar
Bahrein *see* Bahrain
Bahr el, Azraq *see* Blue Nile
Bahr el Gebel *see* Central Equatoria
Bahr el Jebel *see* Central Equatoria
80 E13 **Bahr ez Zaref** ≈ Jonglei, E South Sudan
67 R8 **Bahr Kameur** ≈ N Central African Republic
Bahr Tabariya, Sea of *see* Tiberias, Lake
143 W15 **Bāhū Kalāt** Sīstān va Balūchestān, SE Iran 25°42′N 61°28′E

◆ Country
● Country Capital
◇ Dependent Territory
○ Dependent Territory Capital
◈ Administrative Regions
✈ International Airport
▲ Mountain
▲▲ Mountain Range
^ Volcano
≈ River
◎ Lake
⊞ Reservoir

118 N13 **Bahushewsk** *Rus.* Bogushëvsk. Vitsyebskaya Voblasts', NE Belarus 54°51′N 30°13′E
Bai *see* Tagow Bāy
116 G13 **Baia de Aramă** Mehedinți, SW Romania 45°00′N 22°43′E
116 G11 **Baia de Criş** *Ger.* Altenburg, *Hung.* Körösbánya. Hunedoara, SW Romania 46°10′N 22°41′E
83 A16 **Baia dos Tigres** Namibe, SW Angola 16°36′S 11°44′E
82 A13 **Baia Farta** Benguela, W Angola 12°38′S 13°12′E
116 H9 **Baia Mare** *Ger.* Frauenbach, *Hung.* Nagybánya; *prev.* Neustadt. Maramureş, NW Romania 47°40′N 23°35′E
116 H8 **Baia Sprie** *Ger.* Mittelstadt, *Hung.* Felsőbánya. Maramureş, NW Romania 47°40′N 23°42′E
78 G13 **Baïbokoum** Logone-Oriental, SW Chad 07°46′N 15°43′E
160 F12 **Baicao Ling** ▲▲ SW China
163 U9 **Baicheng** *var.* Pai-ch'eng; *prev.* T'aon-an. Jilin, NE China 45°32′N 122°51′E
158 I6 **Baicheng** *var.* Bay. Xinjiang Uygur Zizhiqu, NW China 41°49′N 81°45′E
116 J13 **Băicoi** Prahova, SE Romania 45°02′N 25°51′E
Baidoa *see* Baydhabo
15 U6 **Baie-Comeau** Québec, SE Canada 49°12′N 68°10′W
15 U6 **Baie-des-Sables** Québec, SE Canada 48°41′N 67°55′W
15 T7 **Baie-des-Bacon** Québec, SE Canada 48°31′N 69°17′W
15 S8 **Baie-des-Rochers** Québec, SE Canada 47°57′N 69°50′W
Baie-du-Poste *see* Mistissini
172 H17 **Baie Lazare** Mahé, NE Seychelles 04°45′S 55°29′E
45 Y5 **Baie-Mahault** Basse Terre, C Guadeloupe 16°16′N 61°35′W
15 R9 **Baie-St-Paul** Québec, SE Canada 47°27′N 70°30′W
15 V5 **Baie-Trinité** Québec, SE Canada 49°25′N 67°20′W
13 T11 **Baie Verte** Newfoundland and Labrador, SE Canada 49°55′N 56°12′W
Baiguan *see* Shangyu
Baihe *see* Erdaobaihe
139 U11 **Bā'ij al Mahdī** Al Muthanná, S Iraq 31°21′N 44°57′E
Baiji *see* Bayjī
Baikal, Lake *see* Baykal, Ozero
Bailādila *see* Kirandul
Baile an Chaistil *see* Ballycastle
Baile an Róba *see* Ballinrobe
Baile an tSratha *see* Ballintra
Baile Átha an Rí *see* Athenry
Baile Átha Buí *see* Athboy
Baile Átha Cliath *see* Dublin
Baile Átha Fhirdhia *see* Ardee
Baile Átha Í *see* Athy
Baile Átha Luain *see* Athlone
Baile Átha Troim *see* Trim
Baile Brigín *see* Balbriggan
Baile Easa Dara *see* Ballysadare
116 I13 **Băile Govora** Vâlcea, SW Romania 45°00′N 24°08′E
116 F13 **Băile Herculane** *Ger.* Herkulesbad, *Hung.* Herkulesfürdő. Caraş-Severin, SW Romania 44°51′N 22°24′E
Baile Locha Riach *see* Loughrea
Baile Mhistéala *see* Mitchelstown
Baile Monaidh *see* Ballymoney
105 N12 **Bailén** Andalucía, S Spain 38°06′N 03°46′W
Baile na hInse *see* Ballynahinch
Baile na Lorgan *see* Castleblayney
Baile na Mainistreach *see* Newtownabbey
Baile Nua na hArda *see* Newtownards
116 I12 **Băile Olăneşti** Vâlcea, SW Romania 45°14′N 24°18′E
116 H14 **Băileşti** Dolj, SW Romania 44°01′N 23°20′E
163 N12 **Bailingmiao** *var.* Darhan Muminggan Lianheqi. Nei Mongol Zizhiqu, N China 41°41′N 110°25′E
58 K11 **Bailique, Ilha** *island* NE Brazil
103 O1 **Bailleul** Nord, N France 50°43′N 02°43′E
78 H12 **Ba Illi** Chari-Baguirmi, SW Chad 10°31′N 16°29′E
159 V12 **Bailong Jiang** ≈ C China
82 C13 **Bailundo** *Port.* Vila Teixeira da Silva. Huambo, C Angola 12°12′S 15°52′E
159 T13 **Baima** *var.* Sêraitang. Qinghai, C China 32°55′N 100°44′E
Baima *see* Baxoi
186 C8 **Baimuru** Gulf, S Papua New Guinea 07°34′S 144°49′E
158 M16 **Bainang** Xizang Zizhiqu, W China 28°57′N 89°31′E
23 S8 **Bainbridge** Georgia, SE USA 30°54′N 84°33′W
171 O17 **Baing** Pulau Sumba, SE Indonesia 10°09′S 120°34′E
158 M14 **Baingoin** *var.* Pubao. Xizang Zizhiqu, W China 31°22′N 90°00′E
104 G2 **Baio** Galicia, NW Spain 43°08′N 08°58′W
104 G4 **Baiona** Galicia, NW Spain 42°06′N 08°49′W
163 V7 **Baiquan** Heilongjiang, NE China 47°37′N 126°04′E
Bā'ir *see* Bāyir
158 I11 **Bairab Co** ◎ W China
25 Q7 **Baird** Texas, SW USA 32°23′N 99°24′W
39 N7 **Baird Mountains** ▲▲ Alaska, USA
Baireuth *see* Bayreuth
190 H3 **Bairiki** ● (Kiribati) Tarawa, NW Kiribati 01°20′N 173°01′E
Bairin Youqi *see* Daban
Bairin Zuoqi *see* Lindong
Bairkum *see* Bayyrkum
183 P12 **Bairnsdale** Victoria, SE Australia 37°51′S 147°38′E
171 P6 **Bais** Negros, S Philippines 09°36′N 123°07′E
102 L15 **Baïse** *var.* Baise. ≈ S France
Baise *see* Baïse
163 W11 **Baishan** *prev.* Hunjiang. Jilin, NE China 41°57′N 126°31′E
Baishan *see* Mashan
118 F12 **Baisogala** Šiauliai, C Lithuania 55°38′N 23°44′E
189 Q7 **Baiti** N Nauru 0°30′S 166°55′E
Baitou Shan *see* Paektu-san
104 G13 **Baixo Alentejo** *physical region* S Portugal
64 P5 **Baixo, Ilhéu de** *island* Madeira, Portugal, NE Atlantic Ocean
83 E15 **Baixo Longa** Cuando Cubango, SE Angola 15°39′S 18°39′E
159 V10 **Baiyin** Gansu, C China 36°33′N 104°11′E
160 E8 **Baiyü** *var.* Jianshe. Sichuan, C China 30°37′N 97°15′E
161 N14 **Baiyun** ✈ (Guangzhou) Guangdong, S China 23°12′N 113°19′E
160 K4 **Baiyu Shan** ▲▲ C China
111 J25 **Baja** Bács-Kiskun, S Hungary 46°13′N 18°56′E
40 C4 **Baja California** *Eng.* Lower California. *peninsula* NW Mexico
40 C4 **Baja California Norte** ◈ *state* NW Mexico
40 E9 **Baja California Sur** ◈ *state* NW Mexico
Bājah *see* Béja
Bajan *see* Bayan
191 V16 **Baja, Punta** *headland* Easter Island, Chile, E Pacific Ocean 27°10′S 109°21′W
40 B4 **Baja, Punta** *headland* NW Mexico 29°57′N 115°48′W
55 R5 **Baja, Punta** *headland* NE Venezuela
42 D5 **Baja Verapaz** *off.* Departamento de Baja Verapaz. ◈ *department* C Guatemala
Baja Verapaz, Departamento de *see* Baja Verapaz
171 N16 **Bajawa** *prev.* Badjawa. Flores, S Indonesia 08°46′S 120°59′E
153 S16 **Baj Baj** *prev.* Budge-Budge. West Bengal, E India 22°29′N 88°11′E
141 N15 **Bājil** W Yemen 15°05′N 43°16′E
183 U4 **Bajimba, Mount** ▲ New South Wales, SE Australia 29°19′S 152°04′E
112 K13 **Bajina Bašta** Serbia, W Serbia 43°58′N 19°33′E
153 U14 **Bajitpur** Dhaka, E Bangladesh 24°12′N 90°57′E
112 K8 **Bajmok** Vojvodina, NW Serbia 45°59′N 19°25′E
Bajo Boquete *see* Boquete
113 L17 **Bajram Curri** Kukës, N Albania 42°23′N 20°06′E
79 J14 **Bakala** Ouaka, C Central African Republic 06°03′N 20°31′E
127 T4 **Bakaly** Respublika Bashkortostan, W Russian Federation 55°10′N 53°46′E
Bakan *see* Shimonoseki
145 U14 **Bakanas** *Kaz.* Baqanas. Almaty, SE Kazakhstan 44°50′N 76°13′E
145 V12 **Bakanas** *Kaz.* Baqanas. ≈ E Kazakhstan
149 R4 **Bākārak** Panjshīr, NE Afghanistan 35°16′N 69°28′E
145 U14 **Bakbakty** *Kaz.* Baqbaqty. Almaty, SE Kazakhstan 44°36′N 76°41′E
122 J12 **Bakchar** Tomskaya Oblast', C Russian Federation 56°58′N 81°59′E
76 I11 **Bakel** E Senegal 14°54′N 12°26′W
35 W13 **Baker** California, W USA 35°15′N 116°04′W
22 J8 **Baker** Louisiana, S USA 30°35′N 91°10′W
33 Y9 **Baker** Montana, NW USA 46°22′N 104°16′W
32 L12 **Baker** Oregon, NW USA 44°46′N 117°50′W
192 L7 **Baker and Howland Islands** ◇ *US unincorporated territory* W Polynesia
36 L12 **Baker Butte** ▲ Arizona, SW USA 34°24′N 111°22′W
39 X15 **Baker Island** *island* Alexander Archipelago, Alaska, USA
9 N9 **Baker Lake** *var.* Qamanittuaq. Nunavut, N Canada 64°20′N 96°10′W
9 N9 **Baker Lake** ◎ Nunavut, N Canada
32 H6 **Baker, Mount** ▲ Washington, NW USA 48°46′N 121°48′W
35 R13 **Bakersfield** California, W USA 35°22′N 119°01′W
24 M9 **Bakersfield** Texas, SW USA 30°54′N 102°21′W
21 P9 **Bakersville** North Carolina, SE USA 36°01′N 82°09′W
Bakhābī *see* Bū Khābī
Bakharden *see* Baharly
Bakhardok *see* Bokurdak
143 U5 **Bākharz, Kuhhā-ye** ▲▲ NE Iran
152 D13 **Bākhāsar** Rājasthān, NW India 24°42′N 71°11′E
Bakhchisaray *see* Bakhchysaray
117 T13 **Bakhchysaray** *Rus.* Bakhchisaray. Avtonomna Respublika Krym, S Ukraine 44°44′N 33°53′E
Bakherden *see* Baharly
117 R3 **Bakhmach** Chernihivs'ka Oblast', N Ukraine 51°10′N 32°48′E
Bākhtarān *see* Kermānshāh
143 Q11 **Bakhtegān, Daryācheh-ye** ◎ C Iran
Bakhty *see* Bakty
137 Z11 **Bakı** *Eng.* Baku. ● (Azerbaijan) E Azerbaijan 40°24′N 49°51′E
80 M12 **Baki** Awdal, N Somalia 10°10′N 43°45′E
137 Z11 **Bakı** ✈ E Azerbaijan 40°26′N 49°55′E
136 C13 **Bakır Çayı** ≈ W Turkey
92 L1 **Bakkafjördhur** Austurland, NE Iceland 66°01′N 14°49′W
92 L1 **Bakkaflói** *sea area* W Norwegian Sea
81 I15 **Bako** Southern Nationalities, S Ethiopia 05°45′N 36°39′E
76 L15 **Bako** NW Ivory Coast 09°08′N 07°40′W
Bákó *see* Bacău
111 H23 **Bakony** *Eng.* Bakony Mountains, *Ger.* Bakonywald. ▲▲ W Hungary
Bakony Mountains/Bakonywald *see* Bakony
81 M16 **Bakool** *off.* Gobolka Bakool. ◈ *region* W Somalia
Bakool, Gobolka *see* Bakool
79 L15 **Bakouma** Mbomou, SE Central African Republic 05°42′N 22°43′E
127 N15 **Baksan** Kabardino-Balkarskaya Respublika, SW Russian Federation 43°43′N 43°31′E
119 I16 **Bakshty** Hrodzyenskaya Voblasts', W Belarus 53°56′N 26°11′E
145 X12 **Bakty** *prev.* Bakhty. Vostochnyy Kazakhstan, E Kazakhstan 46°41′N 82°45′E
Baku *see* Bakı
194 K12 **Bakutis Coast** *physical region* Antarctica
Bakwanga *see* Mbuji-Mayi
145 O15 **Bakyrly** Yuzhnyy Kazakhstan, S Kazakhstan 44°30′N 67°41′E
14 H13 **Bala** Ontario, S Canada 45°01′N 79°37′W
136 I13 **Balâ** Ankara, C Turkey 39°34′N 33°07′E
97 J19 **Bala** NW Wales, United Kingdom 52°54′N 03°31′W
170 L7 **Balabac Island** *island* W Philippines
Balabac, Selat *see* Balabac Strait
169 V5 **Balabac Strait** *var.* Selat Balabac. *strait* Malaysia/Philippines
Ba'labakk *see* Baalbek
187 P16 **Balabio, Île** *island* Province Nord, W New Caledonia
116 I14 **Balaci** Teleorman, S Romania 44°21′N 24°55′E
139 S7 **Balad** Şalāḩ ad Dīn, N Iraq 34°00′N 44°07′E
139 U7 **Balad Rūz** Diyālá, E Iraq 33°42′N 45°04′E
154 J11 **Bālāghāt** Madhya Pradesh, C India 21°48′N 80°11′E
155 F14 **Bālāghāt Range** ▲▲ W India
103 X14 **Balagne** *physical region* Corse, France, C Mediterranean Sea
105 U5 **Balaguer** Cataluña, NE Spain 41°48′N 00°48′E
105 S3 **Balaïtous** *var.* Pic de Balaitous. ▲ France/Spain 42°51′N 00°17′W
Balaitous, Pic de *see* Balaïtous
Bálák *see* Ballangen
127 O3 **Balakhna** Nizhegorodskaya Oblast', W Russian Federation 56°26′N 43°43′E
122 L12 **Balakhta** Krasnoyarskiy Kray, S Russian Federation 55°22′N 91°24′E
182 I9 **Balaklava** South Australia 34°10′S 138°22′E
Balakleya *see* Balakliya
117 V6 **Balakliya** *Rus.* Balakleya. Kharkivs'ka Oblast', E Ukraine 49°27′N 36°53′E
127 Q7 **Balakovo** Saratovskaya Oblast', W Russian Federation 52°03′N 47°47′E
83 P14 **Balama** Cabo Delgado, N Mozambique 13°18′S 38°39′E
169 U6 **Balambangan, Pulau** *island* East Malaysia
Bālā Morghāb *see* Bālā Murghāb
148 L3 **Bālā Murghāb** *prev.* Bālā Morghāb. Laghmān, NW Afghanistan 35°38′N 63°21′E
152 E11 **Bālān** *prev.* Bāhla. Rājasthān, NW India 27°45′N 71°32′E
116 J10 **Bălan** *Hung.* Balánbánya. Harghita, C Romania 46°39′N 25°47′E
Balánbánya *see* Bălan
171 O3 **Balanga** Luzon, N Philippines 14°40′N 120°32′E
154 M12 **Balāngīr** *prev.* Bolangir. Orissa, E India 20°41′N 83°30′E
127 N8 **Balashov** Saratovskaya Oblast', W Russian Federation 51°32′N 43°14′E
Balasore *see* Bāleshwar
111 K21 **Balassagyarmat** Nógrád, N Hungary 48°06′N 19°17′E
29 S10 **Balaton** Minnesota, N USA 44°13′N 95°52′W
111 H24 **Balaton** *var.* Lake Balaton, *Ger.* Plattensee. ◎ W Hungary
111 I23 **Balatonfüred** *var.* Füred. Veszprém, W Hungary 46°59′N 17°53′E
Balaton, Lake *see* Balaton
116 I11 **Bălăuşeri** *Ger.* Bladenmarkt, *Hung.* Balavásár. Mureş, C Romania 46°24′N 24°41′E
Balavásár *see* Bălăuşeri
105 Q11 **Balazote** Castilla-La Mancha, C Spain 38°54′N 02°09′W
Balázsfalva *see* Blaj
119 F14 **Balbieriškis** Kaunas, S Lithuania 54°29′N 23°52′E
186 J7 **Balbi, Mount** ▲ Bougainville Island, NE Papua New Guinea 05°51′S 154°58′E
58 F11 **Balbina, Represa** ▣ NW Brazil
43 T15 **Balboa** Panamá, C Panama 08°55′N 79°36′W
97 G17 **Balbriggan** *Ir.* Baile Brigín. E Ireland 53°37′N 06°11′W
Balbunar *see* Kubrat
81 N17 **Balcad** Shabeellaha Dhexe, C Somalia 02°19′N 45°19′E
61 D23 **Balcarce** Buenos Aires, E Argentina 37°51′S 58°16′W
11 U16 **Balcarres** Saskatchewan, S Canada 50°49′N 103°31′W
114 O8 **Balchik** Dobrich, NE Bulgaria 43°25′N 28°11′E
185 E24 **Balclutha** Otago, South Island, New Zealand 46°15′S 169°45′E
25 Q12 **Balcones Escarpment** *escarpment* Texas, SW USA
18 F14 **Bald Eagle Creek** ≈ Pennsylvania, NE USA
Baldenburg *see* Biały Bór
21 V12 **Bald Head Island** *island* North Carolina, SE USA
27 W10 **Bald Knob** Arkansas, C USA 35°18′N 91°34′W
30 K17 **Bald Knob** *hill* Illinois, N USA
Baldohn *see* Baldone
118 G9 **Baldone** *Ger.* Baldohn. W Latvia 56°46′N 24°18′E
22 I9 **Baldwin** Louisiana, S USA 29°50′N 91°32′W
31 P7 **Baldwin** Michigan, N USA 43°54′N 85°50′W
27 Q4 **Baldwin City** Kansas, C USA 38°43′N 95°12′W
39 N8 **Baldwin Peninsula** *headland* Alaska, USA 66°45′N 162°19′W
18 H9 **Baldwinsville** New York, NE USA 43°09′N 76°19′W
23 N2 **Baldwyn** Mississippi, S USA 34°30′N 88°38′W
11 W15 **Baldy Mountain** ▲ Manitoba, S Canada 51°29′N 100°46′W
33 T7 **Baldy Mountain** ▲ Montana, NW USA 48°09′N 109°39′W
37 O13 **Baldy Peak** ▲ Arizona, SW USA 33°56′N 109°37′W
Bâle *see* Basel
Balearic Plain *see* Algerian Basin
Baleares *see* Illes Baleares
105 X11 **Baleares, Islas** *Eng.* Balearic Islands. *island group* Spain, W Mediterranean Sea
Baleares Major *see* Mallorca
Balearic Islands *see* Baleares, Islas
Balearis Minor *see* Menorca
169 S9 **Baleh, Batang** ≈ East Malaysia
12 J8 **Baleine, Grande Rivière de la** ≈ Québec, E Canada
12 K7 **Baleine, Petite Rivière de la** ≈ Québec, SE Canada
12 K7 **Baleine, Petite Rivière de la** ≈ Québec, NE Canada
13 N6 **Baleine, Rivière à la** ≈ Québec, E Canada
99 J16 **Balen** Antwerpen, N Belgium 51°12′N 05°12′E
171 O3 **Baler** Luzon, N Philippines 15°47′N 121°30′E
154 P11 **Bāleshwar** *prev.* Balasore. Orissa, E India 21°31′N 86°59′E
77 S12 **Baléyara** Tillabéri, W Niger 13°48′N 02°57′E
127 T1 **Balezino** Udmurtskaya Respublika, NW Russian Federation 57°57′N 53°03′E
42 J4 **Balfate** Colón, N Honduras 15°47′N 86°24′W
11 O17 **Balfour** British Columbia, SW Canada 49°39′N 116°57′W
29 N3 **Balfour** North Dakota, N USA 47°55′N 100°34′W
Balfrush *see* Bābol
122 L14 **Balgazyn** Respublika Tyva, S Russian Federation 50°53′N 95°12′E
11 U16 **Balgonie** Saskatchewan, S Canada 50°30′N 104°12′W
Bălgrad *see* Alba Iulia
81 J19 **Balguda** *spring/well* S Kenya 01°28′S 39°50′E
158 K6 **Balguntay** Xinjiang Uygur Zizhiqu, NW China 42°45′N 86°18′E
141 R16 **Balḩāf** S Yemen 14°02′N 48°16′E
152 F13 **Bāli** Rājasthān, N India 25°10′N 73°20′E
169 U17 **Bali** ◈ *province* S Indonesia
169 T17 **Bali** *island* C Indonesia
111 K16 **Balice** ✈ (Kraków) Małopolskie, S Poland 49°57′N 19°49′E
171 Y14 **Baliem, Sungai** ≈ Papua, E Indonesia
136 C12 **Balıkesir** Balıkesir, W Turkey 39°38′N 27°52′E
136 C12 **Balıkesir** ◈ *province* NW Turkey
138 L3 **Balīkh, Nahr** ≈ N Syria
169 V12 **Balikpapan** Borneo, C Indonesia 01°15′S 116°50′E
169 T16 **Bali, Laut** *Eng.* Bali Sea. *sea* C Indonesia
171 N9 **Balimbing** Tawitawi, SW Philippines 05°10′N 120°00′E
186 B8 **Balimo** Western, SW Papua New Guinea 08°00′S 143°00′E
Bálinc *see* Balinţ
101 H23 **Balingen** Baden-Württemberg, SW Germany 48°16′N 08°51′E
116 F11 **Balinţ** *Hung.* Bálinc. Timiş, W Romania 45°48′N 21°54′E
171 O1 **Balintang Channel** *channel* N Philippines
138 K3 **Bālis** Ḩalab, N Syria 36°01′N 38°03′E
Bali Sea *see* Bali, Laut
98 K7 **Balk** Fryslân, N Netherlands 52°54′N 05°34′E
146 B11 **Balkanabat** *Rus.* Nebitdag. Balkan Welaýaty, W Turkmenistan 39°33′N 54°19′E
121 R6 **Balkan Mountains** *Bul./SCr.* Stara Planina. ▲▲ Bulgaria/Serbia
Balkanskiy Welayat *see* Balkan Welaýaty
146 B9 **Balkan Welaýaty** *Rus.* Balkanskiy Velayat. ◈ *province* W Turkmenistan
145 T13 **Balkash** *Kaz.* Balqash; *prev.* Balkhash. Karaganda, SE Kazakhstan 46°52′N 74°55′E
145 P8 **Balkashino** Akmola, N Kazakhstan 52°36′N 68°46′E
145 T13 **Balkash, Ozero** *Eng.* Lake Balkhash, *Kaz.* Balqash; *prev.* Ozero Balkhash. ◎ SE Kazakhstan
149 O2 **Balkh** *anc.* Bactra. Balkh, N Afghanistan 36°46′N 66°54′E
149 P2 **Balkh** ◈ *province* N Afghanistan
Balkhash *see* Balkash
Balkhash, Lake *see* Balkash, Ozero
Balkhash, Ozero *see* Balkash, Ozero
Balla Balla *see* Mbalabala
96 H10 **Ballachulish** N Scotland, United Kingdom 56°40′N 05°10′W
180 M12 **Balladonia** Western Australia 32°21′S 123°32′E
97 C16 **Ballaghaderreen** *Ir.* Bealach an Doirín. C Ireland 53°51′N 08°29′W
92 H10 **Ballangen** *Lapp.* Bálák. Nordland, NW Norway 68°18′N 16°48′E
97 H14 **Ballantrae** W Scotland, United Kingdom 55°05′N 05°W
183 N12 **Ballarat** Victoria, SE Australia 37°36′S 143°51′E
180 K11 **Ballard, Lake** *salt lake* Western Australia
Ballari *see* Bellary
76 L11 **Ballé** Koulikoro, W Mali 15°18′N 08°31′W
40 D7 **Ballenas, Bahía de** *bay* NW Mexico
40 D5 **Ballenas, Canal de** *channel* NW Mexico
195 R17 **Balleny Islands** *island group* Antarctica
40 J7 **Balleza** *var.* San Pablo Balleza. Chihuahua, N Mexico 26°55′N 106°21′W
114 M13 **Ballı** Tekirdağ, NW Turkey 40°48′N 27°03′E
153 O13 **Ballia** Uttar Pradesh, N India 25°45′N 84°09′E
183 V4 **Ballina** New South Wales, SE Australia 28°50′S 153°37′E
97 C16 **Ballina** *Ir.* Béal an Átha. W Ireland 54°07′N 09°09′W
97 D16 **Ballinamore** *Ir.* Béal an Átha Móir. NW Ireland 54°03′N 07°47′W
97 D18 **Ballinasloe** *Ir.* Béal Átha na Sluaighe. W Ireland 53°20′N 08°13′W
25 P8 **Ballinger** Texas, SW USA 31°44′N 99°57′W
97 C17 **Ballinrobe** *Ir.* Baile an Róba. W Ireland 53°37′N 09°14′W
97 A21 **Ballinskelligs Bay** *Ir.* Bá na Scealg. *inlet* SW Ireland
97 D15 **Ballintra** *Ir.* Baile an tSratha. NW Ireland 54°35′N 08°07′W
103 T7 **Ballon d'Alsace** ▲ NE France 47°50′N 06°54′E
Ballon de Guebwiller *see* Grand Ballon
113 K21 **Ballsh** *var.* Ballshi. Fier, SW Albania 40°35′N 19°45′E
Ballshi *see* Ballsh
98 K4 **Ballum** Fryslân, N Netherlands 53°27′N 05°40′E
97 F16 **Ballybay** *Ir.* Béal Átha Beithe. N Ireland 54°08′N 06°54′W
97 E14 **Ballybofey** *Ir.* Bealach Féich. NW Ireland 54°49′N 07°47′W
97 G14 **Ballycastle** *Ir.* Baile an Chaistil. N Northern Ireland, United Kingdom 55°12′N 06°14′W
97 G15 **Ballyclare** *Ir.* Bealach Cláir. E Northern Ireland, United Kingdom 54°45′N 06°W
97 E16 **Ballyconnell** *Ir.* Béal Átha Conaill. N Ireland 54°07′N 07°35′W
97 C17 **Ballyhaunis** *Ir.* Beál Átha hAmhnais. W Ireland 53°45′N 08°45′W
97 G14 **Ballymena** *Ir.* An Baile Meánach. NE Northern Ireland, United Kingdom 54°52′N 06°17′W
97 F14 **Ballymoney** *Ir.* Baile Monaidh. NE Northern Ireland, United Kingdom 55°10′N 06°30′W
97 G15 **Ballynahinch** *Ir.* Baile na hInse. SE Northern Ireland, United Kingdom 54°24′N 05°54′W
97 D16 **Ballysadare** *Ir.* Baile Easa Dara. NW Ireland 54°13′N 08°30′W
97 D15 **Ballyshannon** *Ir.* Béal Átha Seanaidh. NW Ireland 54°30′N 08°11′W
63 H19 **Balmaceda** Aisén, S Chile 45°52′S 72°43′W
63 G23 **Balmaceda, Cerro** ▲ S Chile 51°27′S 73°26′W
111 N22 **Balmazújváros** Hajdú-Bihar, E Hungary 47°36′N 21°18′E
108 E10 **Balmhorn** ▲ SW Switzerland 46°27′N 07°41′E
182 L12 **Balmoral** Victoria, SE Australia 37°16′S 141°38′E
24 K9 **Balmorhea** Texas, SW USA 30°58′N 103°44′W
Balneario Claromecó *see* Claromecó
148 M12 **Balochistan** *prev.* Baluchistan, Beluchistan. ◈ *province* SW Pakistan
82 B13 **Balombo** *Port.* Norton de Matos, Vila Norton de Matos. Benguela, W Angola 12°21′S 14°46′E
82 B13 **Balombo** ≈ W Angola
181 X10 **Balonne River** ≈ Queensland, E Australia
152 E13 **Bālotra** Rājasthān, N India 25°50′N 72°21′E
145 V14 **Balpyk Bi** *prev.* Kirovskiy, *Kaz.* Kīrov. Almaty, SE Kazakhstan 44°54′N 78°13′E
Balqā'/Balqā', Muḩāfaẓat al *see* Al Balqā'
Balqash *see* Balkhash/Balkhash, Ozero
152 M12 **Balrāmpur** Uttar Pradesh, N India 27°25′N 82°10′E
182 M9 **Balranald** New South Wales, SE Australia 34°39′S 143°33′E
116 H14 **Balş** Olt, S Romania 44°20′N 24°06′E
14 H11 **Balsam Creek** Ontario, S Canada 46°26′N 79°10′W
30 I5 **Balsam Lake** Wisconsin, N USA 45°27′N 92°28′W
14 I14 **Balsam Lake** ◎ Ontario, SE Canada
59 M14 **Balsas** Maranhão, E Brazil 07°30′S 46°W
40 M15 **Balsas, Río** *var.* Río Mexcala. ≈ S Mexico
43 W16 **Balsas, Río** ≈ SE Panama
119 O18 **Bal'shavik** *Rus.* Bol'shevik. Homyel'skaya Voblasts', SE Belarus 52°34′N 30°53′E
95 O15 **Bålsta** Uppsala, C Sweden 59°31′N 17°32′E
108 E7 **Balsthal** Solothurn, NW Switzerland 47°18′N 07°42′E
117 O8 **Balta** Odes'ka Oblast', SW Ukraine 47°58′N 29°39′E
105 N5 **Baltanás** Castilla y León, N Spain 41°56′N 04°12′W
61 E16 **Baltasar Brum** Artigas, N Uruguay 30°44′S 57°19′W
116 M9 **Bălţi** *Rus.* Bel'tsy. N Moldova 47°45′N 27°57′E
Baltic Port *see* Paldiski
118 B10 **Baltic Sea** *Ger.* Ostee, *Rus.* Baltiskoye More. *sea* N Europe
21 X3 **Baltimore** Maryland, NE USA 39°17′N 76°37′W
31 T13 **Baltimore** Ohio, N USA 39°48′N 82°33′W
21 X3 **Baltimore-Washington** ✈ Maryland, E USA 39°10′N 76°40′W
Baltischport/Baltiski *see* Paldiski
Baltiskoye More *see* Baltic Sea
119 A14 **Baltiysk** *Ger.* Pillau. Kaliningradskaya Oblast', W Russian Federation 54°39′N 19°54′E
Baltkrievija *see* Belarus
119 H14 **Baltoji Voke** Vilnius, SE Lithuania 54°35′N 25°13′E
Balūchestān va Sīstān *see* Sīstān va Balūchestān
Baluchistan *see* Balochistan
171. P5 **Balud** Masbate, N Philippines 12°03′N 123°12′E
169 T9 **Balui, Batang** ≈ East Malaysia
153 S13 **Bālurghat** West Bengal, NE India 25°12′N 88°50′E
118 J8 **Balvi** NE Latvia 57°07′N 27°14′E
147 W7 **Balykchy** *Kir.* Ysyk-Köl; *prev.* Issyk-Kul', Rybach'ye. Issyk-Kul'skaya Oblast', NE Kyrgyzstan 42°29′N 76°08′E
56 B7 **Balzar** Guayas, W Ecuador 01°25′S 79°54′W
108 I8 **Balzers** S Liechtenstein 47°04′N 09°32′E
143 T12 **Bam** Kermān, SE Iran 29°08′N 58°27′E
77 Y13 **Bama** Borno, NE Nigeria 11°28′N 13°46′E
76 L12 **Bamako** ● (Mali) Capital District, SW Mali 12°39′N 08°02′W
77 P10 **Bamba** Gao, C Mali 17°03′N 01°19′W
42 M8 **Bambana, Río** ≈ NE Nicaragua
79 J15 **Bambari** Ouaka, C Central African Republic 05°45′N 20°37′E
181 W5 **Bambaroo** Queensland, NE Australia 19°00′S 146°16′E
101 K19 **Bamberg** Bayern, SE Germany 49°54′N 10°53′E
21 R14 **Bamberg** South Carolina, SE USA 33°16′N 81°02′W
79 M16 **Bambesa** Orientale, N Dem. Rep. Congo 03°25′N 25°43′E
76 G11 **Bambey** W Senegal 14°43′N 16°26′W
79 H16 **Bambio** Sangha-Mbaéré, SW Central African Republic 03°57′N 16°54′E
83 I24 **Bamboesberge** ▲ S South Africa 31°24′S 26°10′E
79 D14 **Bamenda** Nord-Ouest, W Cameroon 05°55′N 10°09′E
10 K17 **Bamfield** Vancouver Island, British Columbia, SW Canada 48°48′N 125°05′W
Bami *see* Bamy
79 J14 **Bamingui** Bamingui-Bangoran, C Central African Republic 07°38′N 20°06′E
78 J13 **Bamingui** ≈ N Central African Republic
78 J13 **Bamingui-Bangoran** ◈ *prefecture* N Central African Republic
143 V13 **Bampūr** Sīstān va Balūchestān, SE Iran 27°13′N 60°28′E
186 C8 **Bamu** ≈ SW Papua New Guinea
146 E12 **Bamy** *Rus.* Bami. Ahal Welaýaty, C Turkmenistan 38°42′N 56°47′E
149 P4 **Bāmyān** *prev.* Bāmīān. Bāmyān, NE Afghanistan 34°50′N 67°50′E
149 O4 **Bāmyān** *prev.* Bāmīān. ◈ *province* C Afghanistan
Bán *see* Bánovce nad Bebravou
81 N17 **Banaadir** *off.* Gobolka Banaadir. ◈ *region* S Somalia
Banaadir, Gobolka *see* Banaadir
191 N3 **Banaba** *var.* Ocean Island. *island* Tungaru, W Kiribati
59 O14 **Banabuiú, Açude** ▣ NE Brazil
57 O19 **Bañados del Izozog** *salt lake* SE Bolivia
97 D18 **Banagher** *Ir.* Beannchar. C Ireland 53°12′N 07°56′W
79 M17 **Banalia** Orientale, N Dem. Rep. Congo 01°33′N 25°23′E
76 L12 **Banamba** Koulikoro, W Mali 13°29′N 07°22′W
40 G4 **Banámichi** Sonora, NW Mexico 30°00′N 110°14′W
181 Y9 **Banana** Queensland, E Australia 24°33′S 150°07′E
191 Z2 **Banana** *prev.* Main Camp. Kiritimati, E Kiribati 02°00′N 157°25′W
59 K16 **Bananal, Ilha do** *island* C Brazil
23 Y12 **Banana River** *lagoon* Florida, SE USA
151 Q22 **Bananga** Andaman and Nicobar Islands, India, NE Indian Ocean 06°57′N 93°54′E
Banaras *see* Vārānasi
114 N13 **Banarlı** Tekirdağ, NW Turkey 41°04′N 27°21′E
152 H12 **Banās** ≈ N India
75 Z11 **Banās, Rās** *headland* E Egypt 23°55′N 35°47′E
112 N10 **Banatski Karlovac** Vojvodina, NE Serbia 45°03′N 21°02′E
141 P16 **Banā, Wādī** *dry watercourse* SW Yemen
136 E14 **Banaz** Uşak, W Turkey 38°47′N 29°46′E
136 E14 **Banaz Çayı** ≈ W Turkey
159 P14 **Banbar** *var.* Coka. Xizang Zizhiqu, W China 31°01′N 94°43′E
97 G15 **Banbridge** *Ir.* Droichead na Banna. SE Northern Ireland, United Kingdom 54°21′N 06°16′W
Ban Bua Yai *see* Bua Yai
97 M21 **Banbury** S England, United Kingdom 52°04′N 01°20′W
167 O7 **Ban Chiang Dao** Chiang Mai, NW Thailand 19°22′N 98°59′E
96 K9 **Banchory** NE Scotland, United Kingdom 58°05′N 00°35′W
14 J13 **Bancroft** Ontario, SE Canada 45°03′N 77°52′W
33 R15 **Bancroft** Idaho, NW USA 42°43′N 111°54′W
29 U11 **Bancroft** Iowa, C USA 43°17′N 94°13′W
154 I9 **Bānda** Madhya Pradesh, C India 24°01′N 78°59′E
152 L13 **Bānda** Uttar Pradesh, N India 25°28′N 80°20′E
168 F7 **Banda Aceh** *var.* Banda Atjeh; *prev.* Koetaradja, Kutaradja, Kutaraja. Sumatera, W Indonesia 05°30′N 95°20′E
Banda Atjeh *see* Banda Aceh
171 S14 **Banda, Kepulauan** *island group* E Indonesia
Banda, Laut *see* Banda Sea
77 N17 **Bandama** *var.* Bandama Fleuve. ≈ S Ivory Coast
77 N15 **Bandama Blanc** ≈ C Ivory Coast
Bandama Fleuve *see* Bandama
Bandar 'Abbās *see* Bandar-e 'Abbās
153 W16 **Bandarban** Chittagong, SE Bangladesh 22°13′N 92°13′E
80 Q13 **Bandarbeyla** *var.* Bender Beila, Bender Beyla. Bari, NE Somalia 09°28′N 50°48′E
143 R14 **Bandar-e 'Abbās** *var.* Bandar 'Abbās; *prev.* Gombroon. Hormozgān, S Iran 27°11′N 56°11′E
142 M3 **Bandar-e Anzalī** Gīlān, NW Iran 37°26′N 49°29′E
143 N12 **Bandar-e Būshehr** *var.* Būshehr, *Eng.* Bushire. Būshehr, S Iran 28°59′N 50°50′E
143 O13 **Bandar-e Dayyer** *var.* Deyyer. Būshehr, SE Iran 27°50′N 51°55′E
142 M11 **Bandar-e Gonāveh** *var.* Deyyer; *prev.* Gonāveh. Būshehr, SW Iran 29°33′N 50°39′E
143 T15 **Bandar-e Jāsk** *var.* Jāsk. Hormozgān, SE Iran 25°35′N 58°06′E
143 O13 **Bandar-e Kangān** *var.* Kangān. Būshehr, S Iran 25°50′N 57°30′E
143 R14 **Bandar-e Khamīr** Hormozgān, S Iran 27°00′N 55°50′E
Bandar-e Langeh *see* Bandar-e Lengeh
143 Q14 **Bandar-e Lengeh** *var.* Bandar-e Langeh, Lingeh. Hormozgān, S Iran 26°34′N 54°52′E
142 L10 **Bandar-e Māhshahr** *var.* Māh-Shahr; *prev.* Bandar-e Ma'shūr. Khūzestān, SW Iran 30°34′N 49°10′E
Bandar-e Ma'shūr *see* Bandar-e Māhshahr
143 O14 **Bandar-e Nakhīlū** Hormozgān, S Iran
Bandar-e Shāh *see* Bandar-e Torkaman
143 P4 **Bandar-e Torkaman** *var.* Bandar-e Torkeman, Bandar-e Torkman; *prev.* Bandar-e Shāh. Golestán, N Iran 36°55′N 54°05′E
Bandar-e Torkeman/Bandar-e Torkman *see* Bandar-e Torkaman
Bandar Kassim *see* Boosaaso
168 M15 **Bandar Lampung** *var.* Bandarlampung, Tanjungkarang-Telukbetung; *prev.* Tandjoengkarang, Tanjungkarang, Teloekbetoeng, Telukbetung. Sumatera, W Indonesia 05°28′S 105°16′E
Bandarlampung *see* Bandar Lampung
Bandar Maharani *see* Muar
Bandar Masulipatnam *see* Machilīpatnam
Bandar Penggaram *see* Batu Pahat
169 T7 **Bandar Seri Begawan** *prev.* Brunei Town. ● (Brunei) N Brunei 04°56′N 114°58′E
169 T7 **Bandar Seri Begawan** ✈ N Brunei 04°56′N 114°58′E
171 R15 **Banda Sea** *var.* Laut Banda. *sea* E Indonesia
104 H5 **Bande** Galicia, NW Spain 42°01′N 07°58′W
59 G15 **Bandeirantes** Mato Grosso, W Brazil 09°04′S 57°53′W
59 N20 **Bandeira, Pico da** ▲ SE Brazil 20°25′S 41°45′W
83 K19 **Bandelierkop** Limpopo, NE South Africa 23°21′S 29°46′E
62 L8 **Bandera** Santiago del Estero, N Argentina 28°53′S 62°15′W
25 Q11 **Bandera** Texas, SW USA 29°44′N 99°06′W
40 J13 **Banderas, Bahía de** *bay* W Mexico
77 O11 **Bandiagara** Mopti, C Mali 14°20′N 03°37′W
152 I12 **Bāndīkūi** Rājasthān, N India 27°01′N 76°33′E
136 C11 **Bandırma** *var.* Penderma. Balıkesir, NW Turkey 40°21′N 27°58′E
Bandjarmasin *see* Banjarmasin
Bandoeng *see* Bandung
97 C21 **Bandon** *Ir.* Droicheadna Bandan. SW Ireland 51°44′N 08°44′W
32 E14 **Bandon** Oregon, NW USA 43°07′N 124°24′W
167 R8 **Ban Dong Bang** Nong Khai, E Thailand 18°00′N 104°08′E
167 Q6 **Ban Donkon** Oudômxai, N Laos 20°20′N 101°37′E
172 J14 **Bandrélé** SE Mayotte
79 H20 **Bandundu** *prev.* Banningville. Bandundu, W Dem. Rep. Congo 03°19′S 17°24′E
79 I21 **Bandundu** *off.* Région de Bandundu. ◈ *region* W Dem. Rep. Congo
Bandundu, Région de *see* Bandundu
169 O16 **Bandung** *prev.* Bandoeng. Jawa, C Indonesia 06°47′S 107°28′E
116 L15 **Băneasa** Constanţa, SW Romania 45°56′N 27°55′E
142 J4 **Bāneh** Kordestān, N Iran 35°58′N 45°54′E
44 I7 **Banes** Holguín, E Cuba 20°58′N 75°43′W
11 P16 **Banff** Alberta, SW Canada 51°10′N 115°34′W
96 K8 **Banff** NE Scotland, United Kingdom 57°39′N 02°33′W
96 K8 **Banff** *cultural region* NE Scotland, United Kingdom
Bánffyhunyad *see* Huedin
77 N14 **Banfora** SW Burkina 10°36′N 04°45′W
155 H19 **Bangalore** *var.* Bengalooru. *state capital* Karnātaka, S India 12°58′N 77°35′E
153 S16 **Bangaon** West Bengal, NE India 23°01′N 88°50′E
79 L15 **Bangassou** Mbomou, SE Central African Republic 04°51′N 22°55′E
186 D7 **Bangeta, Mount** ▲ C Papua New Guinea 06°11′S 147°02′E
171 P12 **Banggai, Kepulauan** *island group* C Indonesia
171 Q12 **Banggai, Pulau** *island* Kepulauan Banggai, N Indonesia
171 X13 **Banggelapa** Papua, E Indonesia 03°47′S 136°53′E

◆ Country
● Country Capital
◇ Dependent Territory
○ Dependent Territory Capital
◈ Administrative Regions
✈ International Airport
▲ Mountain
▲▲ Mountain Range
⛰ Volcano
≈ River
◎ Lake
▣ Reservoir

Banggi *see* Banggi, Pulau
169 *V6* **Banggi, Pulau** *var.* Banggi. *island* East Malaysia
152 *K5* **Banggong Co** *var.* Pangong Tso. ◎ China/India ***see also*** Pangong Tso
121 *P13* **Banghāzī** ***Eng.*** Bengazi, Benghazi, ***It.*** Bengasi. NE Libya *32°07′N 20°04′E*
Bang Hieng *see* Xé Banghiang
169 *O13* **Bangka-Belitung** ***off.*** Propinsi Bangka-Belitung. ◐ *province* W Indonesia
169 *P11* **Bangkai, Tanjung** ***var.*** Bankai. *headland* Borneo, N Indonesia *0°21′N 108°53′E*
169 *S16* **Bangkalan** Pulau Madura, C Indonesia *07°05′S 112°44′E*
169 *N12* **Bangka, Pulau** *island* W Indonesia
169 *N13* **Bangka, Selat** *strait* Sumatera, W Indonesia
169 *N13* **Bangka, Selat** ***var.*** Selat Likupang. *strait* Sulawesi, N Indonesia
168 *J11* **Bangkinang** Sumatera, W Indonesia *0°21′N 100°52′E*
168 *K12* **Bangko** Sumatera, W Indonesia *02°05′S 102°20′E*
Bangkok *see* Ao Krung Thep
Bangkok, Bight of *see* Krung Thep, Ao
153 *T14* **Bangladesh** ***off.*** People's Republic of Bangladesh; ***prev.*** East Pakistan. ◆ *republic* S Asia
Bangladesh, People's Republic of *see* Bangladesh
167 *V13* **Ba Ngoi** Khanh Hoa, S Vietnam *11°56′N 109°07′E*
Ba Ngoi *see* Cam Ranh
Bangong Co *see* Pangong Tso
97 *I18* **Bangor** NW Wales, United Kingdom *53°13′N 04°08′W*
97 *G15* **Bangor** ***Ir.*** Beannchar. E Northern Ireland, United Kingdom *54°40′N 05°40′W*
19 *R6* **Bangor** Maine, NE USA *44°48′N 68°47′W*
18 *I14* **Bangor** Pennsylvania, NE USA *40°52′N 75°12′W*
67 *R8* **Bangoran** ≈ S Central African Republic
Bang Phra *see* Trat
Bang Pla Soi *see* Chon Buri
25 *Q8* **Bangs** Texas, SW USA *31°43′N 99°07′W*
167 *N13* **Bang Saphan** *var.* Bang Saphan Yai. Prachuap Khiri Khan, SW Thailand *11°10′N 99°33′E*
Bang Saphan Yai *see* Bang Saphan
36 *I8* **Bangs, Mount** ▲ Arizona, SW USA *36°47′N 113°51′W*
93 *E15* **Bangsund** Nord-Trøndelag, C Norway *64°22′N 11°22′E*
171 *O2* **Bangued** Luzon, N Philippines *17°36′N 120°40′E*
79 *I15* **Bangui** ● (Central African Republic) Ombella-Mpoko, SW Central African Republic *04°21′N 18°32′E*
79 *I15* **Bangui** ✈ Ombella-Mpoko, SW Central African Republic *04°19′N 18°34′E*
83 *N16* **Bangula** Southern, S Malawi *16°38′S 35°04′E*
Bangwaketse *see* Southern
82 *K12* **Bangweulu, Lake** ***var.*** Lake Bengweulu. ◎ N Zambia
121 *V13* **Banhā** ***var.*** Benha. N Egypt *30°28′N 31°11′E*
Ban Hat Yai *see* Hat Yai
167 *Q7* **Ban Hin Heup** Viangchan, C Laos *18°37′N 102°19′E*
Ban Houayxay/Ban Houei Sai *see* Houayxay
167 *O12* **Ban Hua Hin** ***var.*** Hua Hin. Prachuap Khiri Khan, SW Thailand *12°34′N 99°58′E*
79 *L14* **Bani** Haute-Kotto, E Central African Republic *07°06′N 22°51′E*
45 *O9* **Baní** S Dominican Republic *18°19′N 70°21′W*
77 *N12* **Bani** ≈ S Mali
Bāmīān *see* Bāmyān
Banias *see* Bāniyās
77 *S11* **Bani Bangou** Tillabéri, SW Niger *15°04′N 02°40′E*
76 *M12* **Banifing** ***var.*** Ngorolaka. ≈ Burkina/Mali
Banijska Palanka *see* Glina
77 *R13* **Banikoara** N Benin *11°18′N 02°26′E*
75 *W9* **Banī Mazār** ***var.*** Beni Mazâr. C Egypt *28°29′N 30°48′E*
114 *K8* **Baniski Lom** ≈ N Bulgaria
21 *U7* **Banister River** ≈ Virginia, NE USA
121 *V14* **Banī Suwayf** ***var.*** Beni Suef. N Egypt *29°09′N 31°04′E*
75 *O8* **Banī Walīd** NW Libya *31°46′N 13°59′E*
138 *H5* **Bāniyās** ***var.*** Banias, Baniyas, Paneas. Tarṭūs, W Syria *35°12′N 35°57′E*
113 *K14* **Banja** Serbia, W Serbia *43°33′N 19°35′E*
Banjak, Kepulauan *see* Banyak, Kepulauan
112 *J12* **Banja Koviljača** Serbia, W Serbia *44°31′N 19°11′E*
112 *G11* **Banja Luka** ◐ Republika Srpska, NW Bosnia and Herzegovina
169 *T13* **Banjarmasin** ***prev.*** Bandjarmasin. Borneo, C Indonesia *03°22′S 114°33′E*
76 *F11* **Banjul** ***prev.*** Bathurst. ● (Gambia) W Gambia *13°26′N 16°43′W*
76 *F11* **Banjul** ✈ W Gambia *13°18′N 16°39′W*
Bank *see* Bankä
137 *Y13* **Bankä** ***Rus.*** Bank. SE Azerbaijan *39°25′N 49°13′E*
167 *S11* **Ban Kadian** ***var.*** Ban Kadiene. Champasak, S Laos *14°25′N 105°42′E*
Ban Kadiene *see* Ban Kadian
Bankai *see* Bangkai, Tanjung
166 *M14* **Ban Kam Phuam** Phangnga, SW Thailand *09°16′N 98°24′E*
Ban Kantang *see* Kantang
77 *O11* **Bankass** Mopti, S Mali *14°05′N 03°30′W*
95 *L19* **Bankeryd** Jönköping, S Sweden *57°51′N 14°07′E*
83 *K16* **Banket** Mashonaland West, N Zimbabwe *17°23′S 30°24′E*
167 *T11* **Ban Khamphô** Attapu, S Laos *14°35′N 106°18′E*
23 *O4* **Bankhead Lake** ⊠ Alabama, S USA
77 *Q11* **Bankilaré** Tillabéri, SW Niger *14°34′N 00°41′E*
Banks, Îles *see* Banks Islands
10 *I14* **Banks Island** *island* British Columbia, SW Canada
187 *R12* **Banks Islands** ***Fr.*** Îles Banks. *island group* N Vanuatu
23 *U8* **Banks Lake** ◎ Georgia, SE USA
32 *K8* **Banks Lake** ⊠ Washington, NW USA
185 *I19* **Banks Peninsula** *peninsula* South Island, New Zealand
183 *Q15* **Banks Strait** *strait* SW Tasman Sea
Ban Kui Nua *see* Kui Buri
153 *R16* **Bānkura** West Bengal, NE India *23°14′N 87°05′E*
167 *S8* **Ban Lakxao** ***var.*** Lak Sao. Bolikhamxai, C Laos *18°10′N 104°58′E*
167 *O16* **Ban Lam Phai** Songkhla, SW Thailand *06°43′N 100°57′E*
Ban Mae Sot *see* Mae Sot
Ban Mae Suai *see* Mae Suai
Ban Mak Khaeng *see* Udon Thani
166 *M3* **Banmauk** Sagaing, N Burma (Myanmar) *24°26′N 95°54′E*
Banmo *see* Bhamo
167 *T10* **Ban Mun-Houamuang** S Laos *15°11′N 106°44′E*
97 *F14* **Bann** ***var.*** Lower Bann, Upper Bann. ≈ N Northern Ireland, United Kingdom
167 *S10* **Ban Nadou** Salavan, S Laos *15°51′N 105°38′E*
167 *S9* **Ban Nakala** Savannakhét, S Laos *16°14′N 105°09′E*
167 *Q8* **Ban Nakha** Viangchan, C Laos *18°13′N 102°29′E*
167 *S9* **Ban Nakham** Khammouan, S Laos *17°10′N 105°25′E*
167 *P7* **Ban Namoun** Xaignabouli, N Laos *18°40′N 101°34′E*
167 *O17* **Ban Nang Sata** Yala, SW Thailand *06°15′N 101°13′E*
167 *N15* **Ban Na San** Surat Thani, SW Thailand *08°53′N 99°17′E*
167 *R7* **Ban Nasi** Xiangkhoang, N Laos *19°37′N 103°33′E*
44 *I3* **Bannerman Town** Eleuthera Island, C Bahamas *24°38′N 76°09′W*
35 *V15* **Banning** California, W USA *33°55′N 116°52′W*
Banningville *see* Bandundu
167 *S11* **Ban Nongsim** Champasak, S Laos *14°45′N 106°00′E*
149 *S7* **Bannu** ***prev.*** Edwardesabad. Khyber Pakhtunkhwa, NW Pakistan *33°00′N 70°36′E*
Bañolas *see* Banyoles
56 *C7* **Baños** Tungurahua, C Ecuador *01°26′S 78°24′W*
Bánovce *see* Bánovce nad Bebravou
111 *I19* **Bánovce nad Bebravou** ***var.*** Bánovce, ***Hung.*** Bán. Trenčiansky Kraj, W Slovakia *48°43′N 18°15′E*
112 *I12* **Banovići** ◐ Federacija Bosna I Hercegovina, E Bosnia and Herzegovina
Banow *see* Andarāb
Ban Pak Phanang *see* Pak Phanang
167 *O7* **Ban Pan Nua** Lampang, NW Thailand *18°51′N 99°57′E*
167 *Q9* **Ban Phai** Khon Kaen, E Thailand *16°00′N 102°42′E*
167 *Q8* **Ban Phônhông** ***var.*** Phônhông. C Laos *18°29′N 102°26′E*
167 *T9* **Ban Phou A Douk** Khammouan, C Laos *17°12′N 106°07′E*
167 *Q8* **Ban Phu** Uthai Thani, W Thailand
167 *O11* **Ban Pong** Ratchaburi, W Thailand *13°49′N 99°53′E*
190 *I3* **Banraeaba** Tarawa, W Kiribati *01°20′N 173°02′E*
167 *N10* **Ban Sai Yok** Kanchanaburi, W Thailand *14°24′N 98°54′E*
Ban Sattahip/Ban Sattahipp *see* Sattahip
Ban Sichon *see* Sichon
Ban Si Racha *see* Si Racha
111 *J19* **Banská Bystrica** ***Ger.*** Neusohl, ***Hung.*** Besztercebánya. Banskobystricky Kraj, C Slovakia *48°46′N 19°08′E*
111 *K20* **Banskobystrický Kraj** ◐ *region* C Slovakia
167 *R8* **Ban Sôppheung** Bolikhamxai, C Laos *18°33′N 104°18′E*
Ban Sop Prap *see* Sop Prap
152 *G15* **Bānswāra** Rājasthān, N India *23°32′N 74°28′E*
167 *N15* **Ban Ta Khun** Surat Thani, SW Thailand *08°53′N 98°52′E*
Ban Takua Pa *see* Takua Pa
167 *S8* **Ban Talak** Khammouan, C Laos *17°33′N 105°40′E*
77 *R15* **Bantè** W Benin *08°25′N 01°58′E*
167 *Q11* **Bânteay Méan Choăy** ***var.*** Sisŏphŏn. Bătdâmbâng, NW Cambodia *13°37′N 102°58′E*
167 *N16* **Banten** ***off.*** Propinsi Banten. ◐ *province* W Indonesia
Propinsi Banten *see* Banten
167 *Q8* **Ban Thabôk** Bolikhamxai, C Laos *18°21′N 103°12′E*
167 *T9* **Ban Tôp** Savannakhét, S Laos *16°07′N 106°07′E*
97 *B21* **Bantry** ***Ir.*** Beanntraí. Cork, SW Ireland *51°41′N 09°27′W*
97 *A21* **Bantry Bay** ***Ir.*** Bá Bheanntraí. *bay* SW Ireland
155 *F19* **Bantvāl** ***var.*** Bantwāl. Karnātaka, E India *12°57′N 75°04′E*
Bantwāl *see* Bantvāl
114 *N9* **Banya** Burgas, E Bulgaria *42°46′N 27°49′E*
168 *G10* **Banyak, Kepulauan** ***prev.*** Kepulauan Banjak. *island group* NW Indonesia
105 *U8* **Banya, La** *headland* E Spain *40°34′N 00°37′E*
79 *E14* **Banyo** Adamaoua, NW Cameroon *06°47′N 11°50′E*
105 *X4* **Banyoles** ***var.*** Bañolas. Cataluña, NE Spain *42°07′N 02°46′E*
167 *N16* **Ban Yong Sata** Trang, SW Thailand *07°09′N 99°42′E*
195 *X14* **Banzare Coast** *physical region* Antarctica
173 *Q14* **Banzare Seamounts** *undersea feature* S Indian Ocean
Banzart *see* Bizerte
163 *Q12* **Baochang** ***var.*** Taibus Qi. Nei Mongol Zizhiqu, N China *41°55′N 115°22′E*
161 *O3* **Baoding** ***var.*** Pao-ting; ***prev.*** Tsingyuan. Hebei, E China *38°47′N 115°30′E*
Baoebaoe *see* Baubau
Baoi, Oileán *see* Dursey Island
160 *J6* **Baoji** ***var.*** Pao-chi, Paoki. Shaanxi, C China *34°23′N 107°16′E*
163 *U9* **Baokang** ***var.*** Hoqin Zuoyi Zhongji. Nei Mongol Zizhiqu, N China *44°08′N 123°18′E*
186 *L8* **Baolo** Santa Isabel, N Solomon Islands *07°41′S 158°47′E*
167 *U13* **Bao Lôc** Lâm Đông, S Vietnam *11°33′N 107°48′E*
163 *Z7* **Baoqing** Heilongjiang, NE China *46°15′N 132°12′E*
Baoqing *see* Shaoyang
79 *H15* **Baoro** Nana-Mambéré, W Central African Republic *05°40′N 16°00′E*
160 *E12* **Baoshan** ***var.*** Pao-shan. Yunnan, SW China *25°05′N 99°07′E*
163 *N13* **Baotou** ***var.*** Pao-t'ou, Paotow. Nei Mongol Zizhiqu, N China *40°38′N 109°59′E*
76 *L14* **Baoulé** ≈ S Mali
76 *K12* **Baoulé** ≈ W Mali
Bao Yèn *see* Phô Rang
103 *O2* **Bapaume** Pas-de-Calais, N France *50°06′N 02°50′E*
14 *J13* **Baptiste Lake** ◎ Ontario, SE Canada
Bapu *see* Meigu
Baqanas *see* Bakanas
Baqbaqty *see* Bakbakty
159 *P14* **Baqên** ***var.*** Dartang. Xizang Zizhiqu, W China *31°50′N 94°08′E*
138 *F14* **Bāqir, Jabal** ▲▲ S Jordan
139 *T7* **Ba'qūbah** ***var.*** Qubba. Diyālá, C Iraq *33°45′N 44°40′E*
62 *H5* **Baquedano** Antofagasta, N Chile *23°20′S 69°50′W*
Baquerizo Moreno *see* Puerto Baquerizo Moreno
113 *J18* **Bar** ***It.*** Antivari. S Montenegro *42°02′N 19°09′E*
116 *M6* **Bar** Vinnyts'ka Oblast', C Ukraine *49°05′N 27°40′E*
80 *E10* **Bara** Northern Kordofan, C Sudan *13°42′N 30°21′E*
81 *M18* **Baraawe** ***It.*** Brava. Shabeellaha Hoose, S Somalia *01°10′N 43°59′E*
152 *M12* **Bāra Banki** Uttar Pradesh, N India *26°56′N 81°11′E*
30 *L8* **Baraboo** Wisconsin, N USA *43°27′N 89°45′W*
30 *K8* **Baraboo Range** *hill range* Wisconsin, N USA
Baracaldo *see* San Vicente de Barakaldo
15 *Y6* **Barachois** Québec, SE Canada *48°37′N 64°14′W*
44 *J7* **Baracoa** Guantánamo, E Cuba *20°23′N 74°31′W*
61 *C19* **Baradero** Buenos Aires, E Argentina *33°50′S 59°30′W*
183 *R6* **Baradine** New South Wales, SE Australia *30°55′S 149°03′E*
Baraf Daja Islands *see* Damar, Kepulauan
Baragarh *see* Bargarh
81 *I17* **Baragoi** Rift Valley, W Kenya *01°39′N 36°46′E*
45 *N9* **Barahona** SW Dominican Republic *18°13′N 71°07′W*
153 *W13* **Barail Range** ▲▲ NE India
Baraka *see* Barka
80 *G10* **Barakat** Gezira, C Sudan *14°18′N 33°32′E*
Barakī *see* Barakī Barak
149 *Q6* **Barakī Barak** ***var.*** Barakī, Baraki Rajan. Lōgar, E Afghanistan *33°58′N 68°58′E*
Baraki Rajan *see* Barakī Barak
154 *N11* **Bārākot** Orissa, E India *21°35′N 85°00′E*
55 *S7* **Barama River** ≈ N Guyana
155 *E14* **Bārāmati** Mahārāshtra, W India *18°12′N 74°39′E*
152 *H5* **Bāramūla** Jammu and Kashmir, NW India *34°15′N 74°24′E*
119 *N14* **Baran'** Vitsyebskaya Voblasts', NE Belarus *54°29′N 30°18′E*
152 *I14* **Bārān** Rājasthān, N India *25°08′N 76°32′E*
139 *U4* **Barānān, Shākh-i** ▲▲ E Iraq
119 *I17* **Baranavichy** ***Pol.*** Baranowicze, ***Rus.*** Baranovichi. Brestskaya Voblasts', SW Belarus *53°08′N 26°02′E*
123 *T6* **Baranikha** Chukotskiy Avtonomnyy Okrug, NE Russian Federation *68°29′N 168°13′E*
75 *Y11* **Baranīs** ***var.*** Berenice, Mînâ Baranîs. SE Egypt *23°58′N 35°29′E*
116 *M4* **Baranivka** Zhytomyrs'ka Oblast', N Ukraine *50°16′N 27°40′E*
39 *W14* **Baranof Island** *island* Alexander Archipelago, Alaska, USA
Baranovichi/Baranowicze *see* Baranavichy
111 *N15* **Baranów Sandomierski** Podkarpackie, SE Poland *50°28′N 21°31′E*
111 *I26* **Baranya** ***off.*** Baranya Megye. ◐ *county* S Hungary
Baranya Megye *see* Baranya
153 *R13* **Barāri** Bihār, NE India *25°31′N 87°23′E*
22 *L10* **Barataria Bay** *bay* Louisiana, S USA
Barat Daya, Kepulauan *see* Damar, Kepulauan
118 *L12* **Baravukha** ***Rus.*** Borovukha. Vitsyebskaya Voblasts', N Belarus *55°34′N 28°36′E*
54 *E11* **Baraya** Huila, C Colombia *03°11′N 75°04′W*
59 *M21* **Barbacena** Minas Gerais, SE Brazil *21°13′S 43°47′W*
54 *B13* **Barbacoas** Nariño, SW Colombia *01°38′N 78°08′W*
54 *L6* **Barbacoas** Aragua, N Venezuela *09°29′N 66°58′W*
45 *Z13* **Barbados** ◆ *commonwealth republic* SE West Indies
47 *S3* **Barbados** *island* Barbados
105 *U11* **Barbaria, Cap de** ***var.*** Cabo de Berberia. *headland* Formentera, E Spain *38°39′N 01°24′E*
114 *N13* **Barbaros** Tekirdağ, NW Turkey *40°55′N 27°28′E*
74 *A11* **Barbas, Cap** *headland* S Western Sahara *22°14′N 16°45′W*
105 *T5* **Barbastro** Aragón, NE Spain *42°02′N 00°07′E*
104 *K16* **Barbate** ≈ SW Spain
104 *K16* **Barbate de Franco** Andalucía, S Spain *36°11′N 05°55′W*
83 *K21* **Barberton** Mpumalanga, NE South Africa *25°48′S 31°03′E*
31 *U12* **Barberton** Ohio, N USA *41°02′N 81°37′W*
102 *K12* **Barbezieux-St-Hilaire** Charente, W France *45°28′N 00°09′W*
54 *G9* **Barbosa** Boyaca, C Colombia *05°57′N 73°37′W*
21 *N7* **Barbourville** Kentucky, S USA *36°52′N 83°54′W*
45 *W9* **Barbuda** *island* N Antigua and Barbuda
181 *W8* **Barcaldine** Queensland, E Australia *23°33′S 145°21′E*
Barcarozsnyó *see* Râşnov
104 *I11* **Barcarrota** Extremadura, W Spain *38°31′N 06°51′W*
Barcău *see* Berettyó
Barce *see* Al Marj
107 *L23* **Barcellona** ***var.*** Barcellona Pozzo di Gotto. Sicilia, Italy, C Mediterranean Sea *38°10′N 15°15′E*
Barcellona Pozzo di Gotto *see* Barcellona
105 *W6* **Barcelona** ***anc.*** Barcino, Barcinona. Cataluña, E Spain *41°25′N 02°10′E*
55 *N5* **Barcelona** Anzoátegui, NE Venezuela *10°08′N 64°43′W*
105 *S5* **Barcelona** ◐ *province* Cataluña, NE Spain
105 *W6* **Barcelona** ✈ Cataluña, E Spain *41°25′N 02°10′E*
103 *U14* **Barcelonnette** Alpes-de-Haute-Provence, SE France *44°24′N 06°37′E*
58 *E12* **Barcelos** Amazonas, N Brazil *0°59′S 62°58′W*
104 *G5* **Barcelos** Braga, N Portugal *41°32′N 08°37′W*
110 *I10* **Barcin** ***Ger.*** Bartschin. Kujawski-pomorskie, C Poland *52°51′N 17°55′E*
Barcino/Barcinona *see* Barcelona
Barcoo *see* Cooper Creek
111 *H26* **Barcs** Somogy, SW Hungary *45°58′N 17°26′E*
137 *W11* **Bärdä** ***Rus.*** Barda. C Azerbaijan *40°25′N 47°07′E*
Barda *see* Bärdä
78 *H5* **Bardaï** Borkou-Ennedi-Tibesti, N Chad *21°21′N 16°56′E*
139 *R2* **Bardaṛash** Dahūk, N Iraq *36°32′N 43°36′E*
139 *Q7* **Bardasah** Al Anbār, SW Iraq *34°02′N 42°28′E*
153 *S16* **Barddhamān** West Bengal, NE India *23°10′N 88°03′E*
111 *N18* **Bardejov** ***Ger.*** Bartfeld, ***Hung.*** Bártfa. Presovský Kraj, E Slovakia *49°17′N 21°18′E*
105 *R4* **Bárdenas Reales** *physical region* N Spain
Bardera/Bardere *see* Baardheere
Bardesīr *see* Bardsīr
92 *K3* **Bárdharbunga** ▲ C Iceland *64°39′N 17°30′W*
92 *K2* **Bárdhárdalur** ≈ C Iceland
106 *E9* **Bardi** Emilia-Romagna, C Italy *44°39′N 09°44′E*
106 *A8* **Bardonecchia** Piemonte, W Italy *45°04′N 06°40′E*
97 *H19* **Bardsey Island** *island* NW Wales, United Kingdom
143 *S11* **Bardsīr** ***var.*** Bardesīr, Mashīz. Kermān, C Iran *29°58′N 56°29′E*
20 *L6* **Bardstown** Kentucky, S USA *37°49′N 85°29′W*
Barduli *see* Barletta
20 *G7* **Bardwell** Kentucky, S USA *36°52′N 89°01′W*
152 *K11* **Bareilly** ***var.*** Bareli. Uttar Pradesh, N India *28°20′N 79°24′E*
Bareli *see* Bareilly
Baren *see* Jiashi
98 *H13* **Barendrecht** Zuid-Holland, SW Netherlands *51°52′N 04°31′E*
102 *M3* **Barentin** Seine-Maritime, N France *49°33′N 00°57′E*
92 *N3* **Barentsburg** Spitsbergen, W Svalbard *78°01′N 14°19′E*
Barentsevo More/Barents Havet *see* Barents Sea
92 *O3* **Barentsøya** *island* E Svalbard
197 *T11* **Barents Plain** *undersea feature* N Barents Sea
125 *P3* **Barents Sea** ***Nor.*** Barents Havet, ***Rus.*** Barentsevo More. *sea* Arctic Ocean
197 *U14* **Barents Trough** *undersea feature* SW Barents Sea *75°00′N 29°00′E*
80 *I9* **Barentu** W Eritrea *15°08′N 37°35′E*
102 *J3* **Barfleur** Manche, N France *49°41′N 01°18′W*
102 *J3* **Barfleur, Pointe de** *headland* N France *49°46′N 01°09′W*
Barfrush/Barfurush *see* Bābol
158 *H14* **Barga** Xizang Zizhiqu, W China *30°51′N 81°20′E*
80 *Q12* **Bargaal** ***prev.*** Baargaal. Bari, NE Somalia *11°12′N 51°04′E*
154 *M12* **Bargarh** ***var.*** Baragarh. Orissa, E India *21°25′N 83°35′E*
105 *N9* **Bargas** Castilla-La Mancha, C Spain *39°56′N 04°00′W*
81 *I15* **Bargē** Southern Nationalities, S Ethiopia *06°11′N 37°04′E*
106 *A9* **Barge** Piemonte, NE Italy *44°49′N 07°21′E*
153 *U16* **Barguna** Barisal, S Bangladesh *22°09′N 90°07′E*
Bärguşad *see* Vorotan
123 *N13* **Barguzin** Respublika Buryatiya, S Russian Federation *53°37′N 109°47′E*
153 *O13* **Barhaj** Uttar Pradesh, N India *26°16′N 83°44′E*
183 *N10* **Barham** New South Wales, SE Australia *35°39′S 144°09′E*
152 *J12* **Barhan** Uttar Pradesh, N India *27°21′N 78°11′E*
19 *S7* **Bar Harbor** Mount Desert Island, Maine, NE USA *44°23′N 68°14′W*
153 *R14* **Barharwa** Jhārkhand, NE India *24°52′N 87°47′E*
153 *P15* **Barhi** Jhārkhand, N India *24°19′N 85°25′E*
107 *O17* **Bari** ***var.*** Bari delle Puglie; ***anc.*** Barium. Puglia, SE Italy *41°06′N 16°52′E*
80 *P12* **Bari** ***Off.*** Gobolka Bari. ◐ *region* NE Somalia
167 *T14* **Ba Ria** ***var.*** Châu Thanh. Ba Ria-Vung Tau, S Vietnam *10°30′N 107°10′E*
Bāridah *see* Al Bāridah
Bari delle Puglie *see* Bari
Bari, Gobolka *see* Bari
Barikot *see* Barīkowṯ
149 *T4* **Barīkowṯ** ***var.*** Barikot. Kunar, NE Afghanistan *35°18′N 71°36′E*
42 *C4* **Barillas** ***var.*** Santa Cruz Barillas. Huehuetenango, NW Guatemala *15°50′N 91°20′W*
54 *J6* **Barinas** Barinas, W Venezuela *08°36′N 70°15′W*
54 *I7* **Barinas** ***off.*** Estado Barinas; ***prev.*** Zamora. ◐ *state* C Venezuela
Barinas, Estado *see* Barinas
54 *I6* **Barinitas** Barinas, NW Venezuela *08°45′N 70°26′W*
154 *P11* **Bāripada** Orissa, E India *21°56′N 86°43′E*
60 *K9* **Bariri** São Paulo, S Brazil *22°04′S 48°46′W*
75 *W11* **Bārīs** ***var.*** Bârîs. S Egypt *24°28′N 30°39′E*
152 *G14* **Bari Sādri** Rājasthān, N India *24°25′N 74°28′E*
153 *U16* **Barisal** Barisal, S Bangladesh *22°41′N 90°20′E*
153 *U16* **Barisal** ◐ *division* S Bangladesh
168 *I10* **Barisan, Pegunungan** ▲▲ Sumatera, W Indonesia
169 *T12* **Barito, Sungai** ≈ Borneo, C Indonesia
Barium *see* Bari
Bårjås *see* Porjus
80 *I9* **Barka** ***var.*** Baraka, ***Ar.*** Khawr Barakah. *seasonal river* Eritrea/Sudan
Barka *see* Al Marj
160 *H8* **Barkam** Sichuan, C China *31°56′N 102°22′E*
118 *J9* **Barkava** C Latvia *56°43′N 26°34′E*
10 *M15* **Barkerville** British Columbia, SW Canada *53°06′N 121°35′W*
14 *J12* **Bark Lake** ◎ Ontario, SE Canada
20 *H7* **Barkley, Lake** ⊠ Kentucky/Tennessee, S USA
10 *K17* **Barkley Sound** *inlet* British Columbia, W Canada
83 *J24* **Barkly East** ***Afr.*** Barkly-Oos. Eastern Cape, SE South Africa *30°58′S 27°35′E*
Barkly-Oos *see* Barkly East
181 *S4* **Barkly Tableland** *plateau* Northern Territory/Queensland, N Australia
Barkly-Wes *see* Barkly West
83 *H22* **Barkly West** ***Afr.*** Barkly-Wes. Northern Cape, N South Africa *28°32′S 24°32′E*
159 *O5* **Barkol** ***var.*** Barkol Kazak Zizhixian. Xinjiang Uygur Zizhiqu, NW China *43°37′N 93°01′E*
159 *O5* **Barkol Hu** ◎ NW China
Barkol Kazak Zizhixian *see* Barkol
30 *J3* **Bark Point** *headland* Wisconsin, N USA *46°53′N 91°11′W*
25 *P11* **Barksdale** Texas, SW USA *29°43′N 100°03′W*
Bar Kunar *see* Asmār
116 *L11* **Bârlad** ***prev.*** Bîrlad. Vaslui, E Romania *46°12′N 27°39′E*
116 *M11* **Bârlad** ***prev.*** Bîrlad. ≈ E Romania
76 *D9* **Barlavento, Ilhas de** ***var.*** Windward Islands. *island group* N Cape Verde
103 *R5* **Bar-le-Duc** ***var.*** Bar-sur-Ornain. Meuse, NE France *48°46′N 05°10′E*
180 *K11* **Barlee, Lake** ◎ Western Australia
180 *H8* **Barlee Range** ▲▲ Western Australia
107 *N16* **Barletta** ***anc.*** Barduli. Puglia, SE Italy *41°20′N 16°17′E*
110 *E10* **Barlinek** ***Ger.*** Berlinchen. Zachodnio-pomorskie, NW Poland *53°N 15°11′E*
27 *S11* **Barling** Arkansas, C USA *35°19′N 94°18′W*
171 *U12* **Barma** Papua, E Indonesia *01°55′S 132°57′E*
183 *Q9* **Barmedman** New South Wales, SE Australia *34°09′S 147°21′E*
Barmen-Elberfeld *see* Wuppertal
152 *D12* **Bārmer** Rājasthān, NW India *25°43′N 71°25′E*
182 *K9* **Barmera** South Australia *34°14′S 140°26′E*
97 *I19* **Barmouth** NW Wales, United Kingdom *52°44′N 04°04′W*
154 *F10* **Barnagar** Madhya Pradesh, C India *23°01′N 75°28′E*
152 *H9* **Barnāla** Punjab, NW India *30°26′N 75°33′E*
97 *L15* **Barnard Castle** N England, United Kingdom *54°35′N 01°55′W*
183 *O6* **Barnato** New South Wales, SE Australia *31°39′S 145°01′E*
112 *I13* **Barnaul** Altayskiy Kray, C Russian Federation *53°21′N 83°45′E*
109 *V8* **Bärnbach** Steiermark, SE Austria *47°05′N 15°07′E*
18 *K16* **Barnegat** New Jersey, NE USA *39°43′N 74°12′W*
23 *S4* **Barnesville** Georgia, SE USA *33°03′N 84°09′W*
29 *R6* **Barnesville** Minnesota, N USA *46°39′N 96°25′W*
31 *U13* **Barnesville** Ohio, N USA *39°59′N 81°10′W*
98 *K11* **Barneveld** ***var.*** Barnveld. Gelderland, C Netherlands *52°08′N 05°34′E*
25 *O9* **Barnhart** Texas, SW USA *31°07′N 101°09′W*
27 *P8* **Barnsdall** Oklahoma, C USA *36°33′N 96°09′W*
97 *M17* **Barnsley** N England, United Kingdom *53°34′N 01°28′W*
19 *Q12* **Barnstable** Massachusetts, NE USA *41°42′N 70°17′W*
97 *I23* **Barnstaple** SW England, United Kingdom *51°05′N 04°04′W*
Barnveld *see* Barneveld
21 *Q14* **Barnwell** South Carolina, SE USA *33°14′N 81°21′W*
77 *U15* **Baro** Niger, C Nigeria *08°35′N 06°28′E*
67 *U8* **Baro** ***var.*** Baro Wenz. ≈ Ethiopia/Sudan
Baro *see* Baro Wenz
Baroda *see* Vadodara
149 *U2* **Baroghil Pass** ***var.*** Kowtal-e Barowghīl. *pass* Afghanistan/Pakistan
119 *Q17* **Baron'ki** ***Rus.*** Boron'ki. Mahilyowskaya Voblasts', E Belarus *53°09′N 32°08′E*
182 *J9* **Barossa Valley** *valley* South Australia
Baroui *see* Salisbury
81 *H14* **Baro Wenz** ***var.*** Baro, Nahr Barū. ≈ Ethiopia/Sudan
Baro Wenz *see* Baro
Barowghīl, Kowtal-e *see* Baroghil Pass
153 *U12* **Barpeta** Assam, NE India *26°19′N 91°05′E*
31 *S7* **Barques, Pointe Aux** *headland* Michigan, N USA *44°04′N 82°57′W*
54 *I5* **Barquisimeto** Lara, NW Venezuela *10°03′N 69°18′W*
59 *N16* **Barra** Bahia, E Brazil *11°06′S 43°15′W*
96 *E9* **Barra** *island* NW Scotland, United Kingdom
183 *T5* **Barraba** New South Wales, SE Australia *30°24′S 150°37′E*
60 *L9* **Barra Bonita** São Paulo, S Brazil *22°30′S 48°35′W*
64 *J12* **Barracuda Fracture Zone** ***var.*** Fifteen Twenty Fracture Zone. *tectonic feature* SW Atlantic Ocean
64 *G11* **Barracuda Ridge** *undersea feature* N Atlantic Ocean
43 *N12* **Barra del Colorado** Limón, NE Costa Rica *10°44′N 83°35′W*
43 *N9* **Barra de Río Grande** Región Autónoma Atlántico Sur, E Nicaragua *12°56′N 83°30′W*
82 *A11* **Barra do Cuanza** Luanda, NW Angola *09°12′S 13°08′E*
60 *O9* **Barra do Piraí** Rio de Janeiro, SE Brazil *22°30′S 43°47′W*
61 *D16* **Barra do Quaraí** Rio Grande do Sul, SE Brazil *31°03′S 58°10′W*
59 *G14* **Barra do São Manuel** Pará, N Brazil *07°12′S 58°03′W*
83 *N19* **Barra Falsa, Ponta da** *headland* S Mozambique *22°57′S 35°36′E*
96 *E10* **Barra Head** *headland* NW Scotland, United Kingdom *56°46′N 07°37′W*
60 *O9* **Barra Mansa** Rio de Janeiro, SE Brazil *22°25′S 44°03′W*
57 *D14* **Barranca** Lima, W Peru *10°46′S 77°46′W*
54 *F8* **Barrancabermeja** Santander, N Colombia *07°01′N 73°51′W*
54 *H4* **Barrancas** La Guajira, N Colombia *10°59′N 72°46′W*
54 *J6* **Barrancas** Barinas, NW Venezuela *08°47′N 70°07′W*
55 *Q6* **Barrancas** Monagas, NE Venezuela *08°45′N 62°12′W*
54 *F6* **Barranco de Loba** Bolívar, N Colombia *08°56′N 74°07′W*
104 *I12* **Barrancos** Beja, S Portugal *38°08′N 06°59′W*
62 *N7* **Barranqueras** Chaco, N Argentina *27°29′S 58°54′W*
54 *E4* **Barranquilla** Atlántico, N Colombia *10°59′N 74°48′W*
83 *N20* **Barra, Ponta da** *headland* S Mozambique *23°46′S 35°33′E*
105 *P11* **Barrax** Castilla-La Mancha, C Spain *39°04′N 02°12′W*
19 *N11* **Barre** Massachusetts, NE USA *42°24′N 72°06′W*
18 *M7* **Barre** Vermont, NE USA *44°09′N 72°25′W*
59 *M17* **Barreiras** Bahia, E Brazil *12°09′S 44°58′W*
104 *F11* **Barreiro** Setúbal, W Portugal *38°40′N 09°05′W*
65 *C26* **Barren Island** *island* S Falkland Islands
20 *K7* **Barren River Lake** ⊠ Kentucky, S USA
60 *L7* **Barretos** São Paulo, S Brazil *20°33′S 48°33′W*
11 *P14* **Barrhead** Alberta, SW Canada *54°10′N 114°22′W*
14 *G14* **Barrie** Ontario, S Canada *44°22′N 79°42′W*
11 *N16* **Barrière** British Columbia, SW Canada *51°10′N 120°06′W*
14 *H8* **Barrière, Lac** ◎ Québec, SE Canada
182 *L6* **Barrier Range** *hill range* New South Wales, SE Australia
42 *G3* **Barrier Reef** *reef* E Belize
188 *C16* **Barrigada** C Guam *13°27′N 144°48′E*
Barrington Island *see* Santa Fe, Isla
183 *T7* **Barrington Tops** ▲ New South Wales, SE Australia *32°06′S 151°18′E*
183 *O4* **Barringun** New South Wales, SE Australia *29°02′S 145°45′E*
59 *K18* **Barro Alto** Goiás, S Brazil *15°07′S 48°56′W*
59 *N14* **Barro Duro** Piauí, NE Brazil *05°49′S 42°30′W*
30 *I5* **Barron** Wisconsin, N USA *45°24′N 91°50′W*
14 *J12* **Barron** ≈ Ontario, SE Canada
61 *H15* **Barros Cassal** Rio Grande do Sul, S Brazil *29°12′S 52°33′W*
45 *P14* **Barrouallie** Saint Vincent , W Saint Vincent and the Grenadines *13°14′N 61°17′W*
39 *O4* **Barrow** Alaska, USA *71°17′N 156°47′W*
97 *E20* **Barrow** ***Ir.*** An Bhearú. ≈ SE Ireland
181 *Q6* **Barrow Creek Roadhouse** Northern Territory, N Australia *21°30′S 133°52′E*
97 *J16* **Barrow-in-Furness** NW England, United Kingdom *54°07′N 03°14′W*
180 *G7* **Barrow Island** *island* Western Australia
39 *O4* **Barrow, Point** *headland* Alaska, USA *71°23′N 156°28′W*
11 *V14* **Barrows** Manitoba, S Canada *52°49′N 101°36′W*
97 *J22* **Barry** S Wales, United Kingdom *51°24′N 03°18′W*
14 *J12* **Barry's Bay** Ontario, SE Canada *45°30′N 77°41′W*
144 *K14* **Barsakel'mes, Ostrov** *island* SW Kazakhstan
Baršć Łužyca *see* Forst
147 *S14* **Barsem** S Tajikistan *37°36′N 71°43′E*
145 *V11* **Barshatas** Vostochnyy Kazakhstan, E Kazakhstan *48°13′N 78°33′E*
155 *F14* **Bārsi** Mahārāshtra, W India *18°14′N 75°42′E*
100 *I13* **Barsinghausen** Niedersachsen, C Germany *53°19′N 09°30′E*
147 *X8* **Barskoon** Issyk-Kul'skaya Oblast', E Kyrgyzstan *42°07′N 77°34′E*
100 *F10* **Barssel** Niedersachsen, NW Germany *53°10′N 07°46′E*
35 *U14* **Barstow** California, W USA *34°52′N 117°00′W*
24 *L8* **Barstow** Texas, SW USA *31°27′N 103°23′W*
103 *R6* **Bar-sur-Aube** Aube, NE France *48°13′N 04°43′E*
Bar-sur-Ornain *see* Bar-le-Duc
103 *Q6* **Bar-sur-Seine** Aube, N France *48°06′N 04°22′E*
147 *S13* **Bartang** S Tajikistan *38°06′N 71°48′E*
147 *T13* **Bartang** ≈ SE Tajikistan
Bartenstein *see* Bartoszyce
Bártfa/Bartfeld *see* Bardejov
100 *N7* **Barth** Mecklenburg-Vorpommern, NE Germany *54°21′N 12°43′E*
27 *W13* **Bartholomew, Bayou** ≈ Arkansas/Louisiana, S USA
55 *T8* **Bartica** N Guyana *06°24′N 58°36′W*
136 *H10* **Bartın** Bartın, NW Turkey *41°37′N 32°20′E*
136 *H10* **Bartın** ◐ *province* NW Turkey
181 *W4* **Bartle Frere** ▲ Queensland, E Australia *17°15′S 145°43′E*
27 *P8* **Bartlesville** Oklahoma, C USA *36°44′N 95°59′W*
29 *P14* **Bartlett** Nebraska, C USA *41°51′N 98°32′W*
20 *E10* **Bartlett** Tennessee, S USA *35°12′N 89°52′W*
25 *T9* **Bartlett** Texas, SW USA *30°47′N 97°25′W*
36 *L13* **Bartlett Reservoir** ⊠ Arizona, SW USA
19 *N6* **Barton** Vermont, NE USA *44°44′N 72°09′W*
110 *L7* **Bartoszyce** ***Ger.*** Bartenstein. Warmińsko-mazurskie, NE Poland *54°16′N 20°49′E*
23 *W12* **Bartow** Florida, SE USA *27°54′N 81°50′W*
Bartschin *see* Barcin
168 *J10* **Barumun, Sungai** ≈ Sumatera, W Indonesia
Barū, Nahr *see* Baro Wenz
169 *S17* **Barung, Nusa** *island* S Indonesia
168 *H9* **Barus** Sumatera, NW Indonesia *02°02′N 98°20′E*
162 *I9* **Baruunbayan-Ulaan** ***var.*** Höövör. Övörhangay, C Mongolia *45°10′N 101°19′E*
Baruunsuu *see* Tsogttsetsiy
163 *P8* **Baruun-Urt** Sühbaatar, E Mongolia *46°40′N 113°17′E*
43 *P15* **Barú, Volcán** ***var.*** Volcán de Chiriquí. ⛰ W Panama *08°49′N 82°32′W*
99 *K21* **Barvaux** Luxembourg, SE Belgium *50°21′N 05°30′E*
42 *M13* **Barva, Volcán** ⛰ NW Costa Rica *10°07′N 84°08′W*
117 *W6* **Barvinkove** Kharkivs'ka Oblast', E Ukraine *48°54′N 37°03′E*
154 *G11* **Barwāh** Madhya Pradesh, C India *22°17′N 76°01′E*
Bärwalde Neumark *see* Mieszkowice
154 *F11* **Barwāni** Madhya Pradesh, C India *22°02′N 74°56′E*
183 *P5* **Barwon River** ≈ New South Wales, SE Australia
119 *L15* **Barysaw** ***Rus.*** Borisov. Minskaya Voblasts', NE Belarus *54°14′N 28°30′E*
127 *Q6* **Barysh** Ul'yanovskaya Oblast', W Russian Federation *53°32′N 47°06′E*
117 *Q4* **Baryshivka** Kyyivs'ka Oblast', N Ukraine *50°21′N 31°21′E*
79 *J17* **Basankusu** Equateur, NW Dem. Rep. Congo *01°12′N 19°50′E*
117 *N11* **Basarabeasca** ***Rus.*** Bessarabka. SE Moldova *46°22′N 28°56′E*
116 *M14* **Basarabi** Constanţa, SW Romania *44°10′N 28°26′E*
40 *H6* **Basaseachic** Chihuahua, NW Mexico *28°18′N 108°13′W*
Basauri *see* Arizgoiti
61 *D18* **Basavilbaso** Entre Ríos, E Argentina *32°23′S 58°55′W*
79 *F21* **Bas-Congo** ***off.*** Région du Bas-Congo; ***prev.*** Bas-Zaïre. ◐ *region* SW Dem. Rep. Congo
108 *E6* **Basel** ***Eng.*** Basle, ***Fr.*** Bâle. Basel Stadt, NW Switzerland *47°33′N 07°36′E*
Baselland *see* Basel Landschaft
108 *E7* **Basel Landschaft** ***prev.*** Baselland ◐ *canton* NW Switzerland
108 *E6* **Basel Stadt** ◐ *canton* NW Switzerland
143 *T14* **Bashākerd, Kūhhā-ye** ▲▲ SE Iran
11 *Q15* **Bashaw** Alberta, SW Canada *52°40′N 112°53′W*
146 *K16* **Bashbedeng** Mary Welaýaty, S Turkmenistan *35°44′N 63°07′E*
161 *T15* **Bashi Channel** ***Chin.*** Pa-shih Hai-hsia. *channel* Philippines/Taiwan
Bashkiria *see* Bashkortostan, Respublika
122 *F11* **Bashkortostan, Respublika** ***prev.*** Bashkiria. ◐ *autonomous republic* W Russian Federation
127 *N6* **Bashmakovo** Penzenskaya Oblast', W Russian Federation *53°13′N 43°00′E*
146 *J10* **Bashsakarba** Lebap Welaýaty, NE Turkmenistan *40°25′N 62°16′E*
117 *R9* **Bashtanka** Mykolayivs'ka Oblast', S Ukraine *47°24′N 32°27′E*
22 *H8* **Basile** Louisiana, S USA *30°29′N 92°36′W*
107 *M18* **Basilicata** ◐ *region* S Italy
33 *V13* **Basin** Wyoming, C USA *44°22′N 108°02′W*
97 *N22* **Basingstoke** S England, United Kingdom *51°16′N 01°08′W*
143 *U8* **Başīrān** Khorāsān-e Janūbī, E Iran *31°57′N 59°07′E*

◆ Country ◇ Dependent Territory ◐ Administrative Regions ▲ Mountain ⛰ Volcano ◎ Lake
● Country Capital ○ Dependent Territory Capital ✈ International Airport ▲▲ Mountain Range ≈ River ⊠ Reservoir

112 B10 **Baška** It. Bescanuova. Primorje-Gorski Kotar, NW Croatia 44°58´N 14°46´E
137 T15 **Başkale** Van, SE Turkey 38°03´N 43°59´E
14 L10 **Baskatong, Réservoir** ▦ Québec, SE Canada
137 O14 **Baskil** Elazığ, E Turkey 38°38´N 38°47´E
Basle see Basel
154 H9 **Bāsoda** Madhya Pradesh, C India 23°54´N 77°58´E
79 L17 **Basoko** Orientale, N Dem. Rep. Congo 01°14´N 23°26´E
Basque Country, The see País Vasco
Basra see Al Başrah
103 U5 **Bas-Rhin** ◈ department NE France
Bassam see Grand-Bassam
11 Q16 **Bassano** Alberta, SW Canada 50°48´N 112°28´W
106 H7 **Bassano del Grappa** Veneto, NE Italy 45°45´N 11°45´E
77 Q15 **Bassar** var. Bassari. NW Togo 09°15´N 00°47´E
Bassari see Bassar
172 L9 **Bassas da India** island group W Madagascar
108 D7 **Bassecourt** Jura, W Switzerland 47°20´N 07°16´E
Bassein see Pathein
79 J15 **Basse-Kotto** ◈ prefecture S Central African Republic
102 J5 **Basse-Normandie** Eng. Lower Normandy. ◈ region N France
45 Q11 **Basse-Pointe** N Martinique 14°52´N 61°07´W
76 H12 **Basse Santa Su** E Gambia 13°18´N 14°10´W
Basse-Saxe see Niedersachsen
45 X6 **Basse-Terre** ○ (Guadeloupe) Basse Terre, SW Guadeloupe 16°08´N 61°40´W
45 V10 **Basseterre** ● (Saint Kitts and Nevis) Saint Kitts, Saint Kitts and Nevis 17°16´N 62°45´W
45 X6 **Basse Terre** island W Guadeloupe
29 O13 **Bassett** Nebraska, C USA 42°34´N 99°32´W
21 S7 **Bassett** Virginia, NE USA 36°45´N 79°59´W
37 N15 **Bassett Peak** ▲ Arizona, SW USA 32°30´N 110°16´W
76 M10 **Bassikounou** Hodh ech Chargui, SE Mauritania 15°55´N 05°59´W
77 R15 **Bassila** W Benin 08°25´N 01°58´E
Bass, Îlots de see Marotiri
31 O11 **Bass Lake** Indiana, N USA 41°12´N 86°35´W
183 O14 **Bass Strait** strait SE Australia
100 H11 **Bassum** Niedersachsen, NW Germany 52°52´N 08°44´E
29 X3 **Basswood Lake** ◎ Canada/USA
95 J21 **Båstad** Skåne, S Sweden 56°25´N 12°50´E
139 U2 **Basṭah** As Sulaymānīyah, E Iraq 36°20´N 45°14´E
153 N12 **Basti** Uttar Pradesh, N India 26°48´N 82°44´E
103 X14 **Bastia** Corse, France, C Mediterranean Sea 42°42´N 09°27´E
99 L23 **Bastogne** Luxembourg, SE Belgium 50°N 05°43´E
22 I5 **Bastrop** Louisiana, S USA 32°46´N 91°54´W
25 T11 **Bastrop** Texas, SW USA 30°07´N 97°21´W
93 J15 **Bastuträsk** Västerbotten, N Sweden 64°47´N 20°05´E
119 J19 **Bastyn'** Rus. Bostyn'. Brestskaya Voblasts', SW Belarus 52°23´N 26°45´E
Basuo see Dongfang
Basutoland see Lesotho
119 O15 **Basya** ≈ E Belarus
Bas-Zaïre see Bas-Congo
79 D17 **Bata** NW Equatorial Guinea 01°51´N 09°48´E
79 D17 **Bata** ✈ S Equatorial Guinea 01°55´N 09°48´E
Batae Coritanorum see Leicester
123 Q8 **Batagay** Respublika Sakha (Yakutiya), NE Russian Federation 67°36´N 134°44´E
123 P8 **Batagay-Alyta** Respublika Sakha (Yakutiya), NE Russian Federation 67°48´N 130°15´E
112 L10 **Batajnica** Vojvodina, N Serbia 44°55´N 20°17´E
136 H15 **Bataklık Gölü** ◎ S Turkey
114 H11 **Batak, Yazovir** ▦ SW Bulgaria
152 H7 **Batāla** Punjab, N India 31°48´N 75°12´E
104 F9 **Batalha** Leiria, C Portugal 39°40´N 08°50´W
79 N17 **Batama** Orientale, NE Dem. Rep. Congo 0°54´N 26°25´E
123 Q10 **Batamay** Respublika Sakha (Yakutiya), NE Russian Federation 63°28´N 129°33´E
160 F9 **Batang** var. Bazhong. Sichuan, C China 30°04´N 99°10´E
79 I14 **Batangafo** Ouham, NW Central African Republic 07°19´N 18°22´E
171 P8 **Batangas** off. Batangas City. Luzon, N Philippines 13°47´N 121°03´E
Batangas City see Batangas
Bătania see Battonya
171 Q10 **Batan Islands** island group N Philippines
60 L8 **Batatais** São Paulo, S Brazil 20°54´S 47°37´W
18 E10 **Batavia** New York, NE USA 43°00´N 78°11´W
Batavia see Jakarta
173 T9 **Batavia Seamount** undersea feature E Indian Ocean 27°42´S 100°36´E
126 L12 **Bataysk** Rostovskaya Oblast', SW Russian Federation 47°10´N 39°46´E
14 B9 **Batchawana** ≈ Ontario, S Canada
14 B9 **Batchawana Bay** Ontario, S Canada 46°55´N 84°36´W
167 Q12 **Bătdâmbâng** prev. Battambang. Bătdâmbâng, NW Cambodia 13°06´N 103°13´E
79 G20 **Batéké, Plateaux** plateau S Congo
183 S11 **Batemans Bay** New South Wales, SE Australia 35°45´S 150°09´E
21 Q13 **Batesburg** South Carolina, SE USA 33°54´N 81°33´W
28 K12 **Batesland** South Dakota, N USA 43°05´N 102°07´W
27 V10 **Batesville** Arkansas, C USA 35°45´N 91°39´W
31 Q14 **Batesville** Indiana, N USA 39°18´N 85°13´W
22 L2 **Batesville** Mississippi, S USA 34°18´N 89°56´W
25 Q13 **Batesville** Texas, SW USA 28°56´N 99°38´W
44 L13 **Bath** E Jamaica 17°57´N 76°22´W
97 L22 **Bath** hist. Akermanceaster; anc. Aquae Calidae, Aquae Solis. SW England, United Kingdom 51°23´N 02°22´W
19 Q8 **Bath** Maine, NE USA 43°54´N 69°49´W
18 F11 **Bath** New York, NE USA 42°20´N 77°16´W
Bath see Berkeley Springs
78 I10 **Batha** off. Préfecture du Batha. ◈ prefecture C Chad
78 I10 **Batha** seasonal river C Chad
Batha, Préfecture du see Batha
141 Y8 **Baṭhā', Wādī al** dry watercourse NE Oman
152 H9 **Bathinda** Punjab, NW India 30°14´N 74°54´E
98 M11 **Bathmen** Overijssel, E Netherlands 52°15´N 06°16´E
45 Z14 **Bathsheba** E Barbados 13°13´N 59°31´W
183 R8 **Bathurst** New South Wales, SE Australia 33°32´S 149°35´E
13 O13 **Bathurst** New Brunswick, SE Canada 47°37´N 65°40´W
Bathurst see Banjul
8 H6 **Bathurst, Cape** headland Northwest Territories, NW Canada 70°33´N 128°00´W
196 L8 **Bathurst Inlet** Nunavut, N Canada 66°23´N 107°00´W
196 L8 **Bathurst Inlet** inlet Nunavut, N Canada
181 N1 **Bathurst Island** island Northern Territory, N Australia
197 O9 **Bathurst Island** island Parry Islands, Nunavut, N Canada
77 O14 **Batié** SW Burkina 09°53´N 02°53´W
Batinah see Al Bāṭinah
141 Y9 **Bāṭin, Wādī al** dry watercourse SW Asia
15 P9 **Batiscan** ≈ Québec, SE Canada
136 F16 **BatıToroslar** ▲▲ SW Turkey
Batjan see Bacan, Pulau
147 R11 **Batken** Batenskaya Oblast', SW Kyrgyzstan 40°03´N 70°50´E
Batken Oblasty see Batkenskaya Oblast'
147 Q11 **Batkenskaya Oblast'** Kir. Batken Oblasty. ◈ province SW Kyrgyzstan
Batlle y Ordóñez see José Batlle y Ordóñez
183 Q10 **Batlow** New South Wales, SE Australia 35°32´S 148°09´E
137 Q15 **Batman** var. İluh. Batman, SE Turkey 37°52´N 41°06´E
137 Q15 **Batman** ◈ province SE Turkey
74 L6 **Batna** NE Algeria 35°34´N 06°10´E
163 O7 **Batnorov** var. Dundbürd. Hentiy, E Mongolia 47°55´N 111°37´E
Batoe see Batu, Kepulauan
162 K7 **Bat-Öldziy** var. Övt. Övörhangay, C Mongolia 46°50´N 102°15´E
Bat-Öldziyt see Dzaamar
22 J8 **Baton Rouge** state capital Louisiana, S USA 30°28´N 91°09´W
79 G15 **Batouri** Est, E Cameroon 04°26´N 14°27´E
138 G14 **Batrā', Jibāl al** ▲▲ S Jordan
138 G6 **Batroûn** var. Al Batrūn. N Lebanon 34°15´N 35°42´E
Batsch see Bač
Batsevichi see Batsevichy
119 M17 **Batsevichy** Rus. Batsevichi. Mahilyowskaya Voblasts', E Belarus 53°24´N 29°14´E
92 M7 **Båtsfjord** Finnmark, N Norway 70°37´N 29°42´E
Batshireet see Hentiy
162 L7 **Batsümber** var. Mandal. Töv, C Mongolia 48°24´N 106°47´E
Battambang see Bătdâmbâng
195 X3 **Batterbee, Cape** headland Antarctica
155 L24 **Batticaloa** Eastern Province, E Sri Lanka 07°44´N 81°43´E
99 L19 **Battice** Liège, E Belgium 50°39´N 05°50´E
107 L18 **Battipaglia** Campania, S Italy 40°36´N 14°59´E
11 R15 **Battle** ≈ Alberta/Saskatchewan, SW Canada
Battle Born State see Nevada
31 Q10 **Battle Creek** Michigan, N USA 42°20´N 85°10´W
27 T7 **Battlefield** Missouri, C USA 37°07´N 93°22´W
11 S15 **Battleford** Saskatchewan, S Canada 52°45´N 108°20´W
29 S6 **Battle Lake** Minnesota, N USA 46°16´N 95°42´W
35 U3 **Battle Mountain** Nevada, W USA 40°37´N 116°55´W
111 M25 **Battonya** Rom. Bătania. Békés, SE Hungary 46°16´N 21°00´E
162 J7 **Battsengel** var. Jargalant. Arhangay, C Mongolia 47°46´N 101°56´E
168 D11 **Batu, Kepulauan** prev. Batoe. island group W Indonesia
137 Q10 **Batumi** W Georgia 41°39´N 41°38´E
168 K10 **Batu Pahat** prev. Bandar Penggaram. Johor, Peninsular Malaysia 01°51´N 102°56´E
171 O12 **Baturebe** Sulawesi, N Indonesia 01°43´S 121°43´E
122 J12 **Baturino** Tomskaya Oblast', C Russian Federation 57°46´N 85°08´E
117 R3 **Baturyn** Chernihivs'ka Oblast', N Ukraine 51°20´N 32°54´E
138 F10 **Bat Yam** Tel Aviv, C Israel 32°01´N 34°45´E
127 Q4 **Batyrevo** Chuvashskaya Respublika, W Russian Federation 55°04´N 47°34´E
Batys Qazaqstan Oblysy see Zapadnyy Kazakhstan
102 F5 **Batz, Île de** island NW France
169 Q10 **Bau** Sarawak, East Malaysia 01°25´N 110°10´E
171 N2 **Bauang** Luzon, N Philippines 16°33´N 120°19´E
171 P14 **Baubau** var. Baoebaoe. Pulau Buton, C Indonesia 05°30´S 122°37´E
77 W14 **Bauchi** Bauchi, NE Nigeria 10°18´N 09°46´E
77 W14 **Bauchi** ◈ state C Nigeria
102 H7 **Baud** Morbihan, NW France 47°52´N 02°59´W
29 T2 **Baudette** Minnesota, N USA 48°42´N 94°36´W
193 S9 **Bauer Basin** undersea feature E Pacific Ocean 10°00´S 101°45´W
187 R14 **Bauer Field** var. Port Vila. ✈ (Port-Vila) Éfaté, C Vanuatu 17°42´S 168°21´E
13 T9 **Bauld, Cape** headland Newfoundland and Labrador, E Canada 51°35´N 55°22´W
103 T8 **Baume-les-Dames** Doubs, E France 47°22´N 06°20´E
101 I15 **Baunatal** Hessen, C Germany 51°15´N 09°25´E
107 D18 **Baunei** Sardegna, Italy, C Mediterranean Sea 40°04´N 09°36´E
57 M15 **Baures, Río** ≈ N Bolivia
60 K9 **Bauru** São Paulo, S Brazil 22°19´S 49°07´W
Baushar see Bawshar
118 G10 **Bauska** Ger. Bauske. S Latvia 56°25´N 24°11´E
Bauske see Bauska
101 Q15 **Bautzen** Lus. Budyšin. Sachsen, E Germany 51°11´N 14°29´E
145 Q16 **Bauyrzhan Momyshuly** Kaz. Baūyrzhan Momyshuly; prev. Burnoye. Zhambyl, S Kazakhstan 42°36´N 70°46´E
Bauzanum see Bolzano
Bavaria see Bayern
109 N7 **Bavarian Alps** Ger. Bayrische Alpen. ▲▲ Austria/Germany
Bavière see Bayern
40 H4 **Bavispe, Río** ≈ NW Mexico
127 T5 **Bavly** Respublika Tatarstan, W Russian Federation 54°20´N 53°21´E
169 P13 **Bawal, Pulau** island N Indonesia
169 T12 **Bawan** Borneo, C Indonesia 01°36´S 113°55´E
183 O12 **Baw Baw, Mount** ▲ Victoria, SE Australia 37°49´S 146°16´E
169 S15 **Bawean, Pulau** island S Indonesia
75 V9 **Bawīṭī** var. Bawîṭi. N Egypt 28°19´N 28°53´E
Bawîṭi see Bawīṭī
77 Q13 **Bawku** N Ghana 11°00´N 00°12´W
Bawlake see Bawlakhe
167 N7 **Bawlakhe** var. Bawlake. Kayah State, C Burma (Myanmar) 19°10´N 97°19´E
169 H11 **Bawo Ofuloa** Pulau Tanahmasa, W Indonesia 0°10´S 98°24´E
141 Y8 **Bawshar** var. Baushar. NE Oman 23°32´N 58°24´E
Ba Xian see Bazhou
Baxian see Bazhou
158 M8 **Baxkorgan** Xinjiang Uygur Zizhiqu, W China 39°05´N 90°00´E
23 V6 **Baxley** Georgia, SE USA 31°46´N 82°21´W
159 R15 **Baxoi** var. Baima. Xizang Zizhiqu, W China 30°01´N 96°53´E
29 W14 **Baxter** Iowa, C USA 41°49´N 93°09´W
29 U6 **Baxter** Minnesota, N USA 46°21´N 94°18´W
27 R8 **Baxter Springs** Kansas, C USA 37°01´N 94°45´W
81 M17 **Bay** off. Gobolka Bay. ◈ region SW Somalia
Bay see Baicheng
44 H7 **Bayamo** Granma, E Cuba 20°21´N 76°38´W
45 U5 **Bayamón** E Puerto Rico 18°24´N 66°09´W
163 W8 **Bayan** Heilongjiang, NE China 46°05´N 127°24´E
170 L16 **Bayan** prev. Bajan. Pulau Lombok, C Indonesia 08°16´S 116°28´E
162 M8 **Bayan** var. Maanĭt. Töv, C Mongolia 47°14´N 107°34´E
Bayan see Hölönbuyr, Dornod, Mongolia
Bayan see Ihhet, Dornogovĭ, Mongolia
Bayan see Bayan-Uul, Govĭ-Altay, Mongolia
Bayan see Bayanhutag, Hentiy, Mongolia
Bayan see Bürentogtoh, Hövsgol, Mongolia
152 I12 **Bayāna** Rājasthān, N India 26°55´N 77°18´E
149 N5 **Bāyān, Band-e** ▲▲ C Afghanistan
162 H8 **Bayanbulag** Bayanhongor, C Mongolia 46°46´N 98°07´E
Bayanbulag see Ömnödelger
158 J5 **Bayanbulak** Xinjiang Uygur Zizhiqu, W China 43°05´N 84°05´E
162 L7 **Bayanchandmanĭ** var. Ihsüüj. Töv, C Mongolia 48°12´N 106°23´E
162 J11 **Bayandalay** var. Dalay. Ömnögovĭ, S Mongolia 43°27´N 103°30´E
163 O9 **Bayandelger** var. Shireet. Sühbaatar, SE Mongolia 45°33´N 112°19´E
162 I5 **Bayandzürh** var. Altraga. Hövsgöl, N Mongolia 50°08´N 98°54´E
Bayan Gol see Dengkou, China
Bayangol see Bugat, Mongolia
162 I9 **Bayangovĭ** var. Örgön. Bayanhongor, C Mongolia 44°43´N 100°23´E
159 R12 **Bayan Har Shan** var. Bayan Khar. ▲▲ C China
162 G6 **Bayanhayrhan** var. Altanbulag. Dzavhan, N Mongolia 49°16´N 96°22´E
162 I8 **Bayanhongor** Bayanhongor, C Mongolia 46°08´N 100°42´E
162 H9 **Bayanhongor** ◈ province C Mongolia
162 K14 **Bayan Hot** var. Alxa Zuoqi. Nei Mongol Zizhiqu, N China 38°49´N 105°40´E
163 O8 **Bayanhutag** var. Bayan. Hentiy, C Mongolia 47°13´N 110°57´E
163 T9 **Bayan Huxu** var. Horqin Zuoyi Zhongqi. Nei Mongol Zizhiqu, N China 45°02´N 121°28´E
Bayan Khar see Bayan Har Shan
163 N12 **Bayan Kuang** prev. Bayan Obo. Nei Mongol Zizhiqu, N China 41°45´N 109°58´E
168 J7 **Bayan Lepas** ✈ (George Town) Pinang, Peninsular Malaysia 05°18´N 100°15´E
162 I10 **Bayanlig** var. Hatansuudal. Bayanhongor, C Mongolia 44°34´N 100°41´E
162 K13 **Bayan Mod** Nei Mongol Zizhiqu, N China 40°45´N 104°29´E
163 N8 **Bayanmönh** var. Ulaan-Ereg. Hentiy, E Mongolia 46°50´N 109°39´E
162 L12 **Bayannur** var. Linhe. Nei Mongol Zizhiqu, N China 40°46´N 107°27´E
Bayan Nuru see Xar Burd
162 E5 **Bayannuur** var. Tsul-Ulaan. Bayan-Ölgiy, W Mongolia 48°51´N 91°13´E
Bayan Obo see Bayan Kuang
43 V15 **Bayano, Lago** ◎ E Panama
162 C5 **Bayan-Ölgiy** ◈ province NW Mongolia
162 H9 **Bayan-Öndör** var. Bulgan. Bayanhongor, C Mongolia 44°48´N 98°39´E
162 K8 **Bayan-Öndör** var. Bumbat. Övörhangay, C Mongolia 46°30´N 104°08´E
162 L8 **Bayan-Önjüül** var. Ihhayrhan. Töv, C Mongolia 46°57´N 105°51´E
163 O7 **Bayan-Ovoo** var. Javhlant. Hentiy, E Mongolia 47°46´N 112°06´E
162 L11 **Bayan-Ovoo** var. Erdenetsogt. Ömnögovĭ, S Mongolia 42°54´N 106°16´E
Bayansayr see Baatsagaan
159 Q9 **Bayan Shan** ▲ C China 37°36´N 96°23´E
162 J9 **Bayanteeg** Övörhangay, C Mongolia 45°39´N 101°30´E
162 G5 **Bayantes** var. Altay. Dzavhan, N Mongolia 49°40´N 96°21´E
Bayantöhöm see Büren
162 M8 **Bayantsagaan** var. Dzogsool. Töv, C Mongolia 46°46´N 107°18´E
163 P7 **Bayantümen** var. Tsagaanders. Dornod, NE Mongolia 48°03´N 114°16´E
Bayan-Uhaa see Ih-Uul
163 R10 **Bayan Ul** var. Xi Ujimqin Qi. Nei Mongol Zizhiqu, N China 44°31´N 117°36´E
Bayan-Ulaan see Dzüünbayan-Ulaan
163 O7 **Bayan-Uul** var. Javarthushuu. Dornod, NE Mongolia 49°05´N 112°40´E
162 F7 **Bayan-Uul** var. Bayan. Govĭ-Altay, W Mongolia 47°05´N 95°13´E
162 M8 **Bayanuur** var. Tsul-Ulaan. Töv, C Mongolia 47°44´N 108°22´E
28 J14 **Bayard** Nebraska, C USA 41°45´N 103°19´W
37 P15 **Bayard** New Mexico, SW USA 32°45´N 108°07´W
103 T13 **Bayard, Col** pass SE France
Bayasgalant see Mönhhaan
136 J12 **Bayat** Çorum, N Turkey 40°34´N 34°07´E
171 P6 **Bayawan** Negros, C Philippines 09°22´N 122°50´E
143 R10 **Bayāẕ** Kermān, C Iran 30°41´N 55°29´E
171 Q6 **Baybay** Leyte, C Philippines 10°41´N 124°49´E
21 X10 **Bayboro** North Carolina, SE USA 35°08´N 76°49´W
137 P12 **Bayburt** Bayburt, NE Turkey 40°15´N 40°16´E
137 P12 **Bayburt** ◈ province NE Turkey
31 R8 **Bay City** Michigan, N USA 43°35´N 83°52´W
25 V12 **Bay City** Texas, SW USA 28°59´N 96°00´W
Baydarata Bay see Baydaratskaya Guba
122 J7 **Baydaratskaya Guba** var. Baydarata Bay. bay N Russian Federation
81 M16 **Baydhabo** var. Baydhowa, Isha Baydhabo, It. Baidoa. Bay, SW Somalia 03°08´N 43°39´E
Baydhowa see Baydhabo
101 N21 **Bayerischer Wald** ▲▲ SE Germany
101 K21 **Bayern** Eng. Bavaria, Fr. Bavière. ◈ state SE Germany
147 V9 **Bayetovo** Narynskaya Oblast', C Kyrgyzstan 41°14´N 74°55´E
102 K4 **Bayeux** anc. Augustodurum. Calvados, N France 49°16´N 00°42´W
14 E15 **Bayfield** ≈ Ontario, S Canada
145 O15 **Baygekum** Kaz. Bäygequm. Kzylorda, S Kazakhstan 44°15´N 66°34´E
Bäygequm see Baygekum
136 C14 **Bayındır** Izmir, SW Turkey 38°12´N 27°40´E
138 H12 **Bāyir** var. Bā'ir. Ma'ān, S Jordan 30°46´N 36°40´E
Bay Islands see Bahía, Islas de la
Bayizhen see Nyingchi
139 R5 **Bayjī** var. Baiji. Şalāḩ ad Dīn, N Iraq 34°56´N 43°29´E
Baykadam see Saudakent
123 N13 **Baykal, Ozero** Eng. Lake Baikal. ◎ S Russian Federation
123 M14 **Baykal'sk** Irkutskaya Oblast', S Russian Federation 51°30´N 104°03´E
137 R15 **Baykan** Siirt, SE Turkey 38°08´N 41°43´E
123 L11 **Baykit** Krasnoyarskiy Kray, C Russian Federation 61°37´N 96°23´E
145 N12 **Baykonur** var. Baykonyr. Karaganda, C Kazakhstan 47°50´N 75°33´E
Baykonur see Baykonyr
144 M14 **Baykonyr** var. Baykonur, Kaz. Bayqongyr; prev. Leninsk. Kyzylorda, S Kazakhstan 45°38´N 63°20´E
Baykonyr see Baykonur
158 E7 **Baykurt** Xinjiang Uygur Zizhiqu, W China 39°56´N 75°33´E
14 I9 **Bay, Lac** ◎ Québec, SE Canada
127 W6 **Baymak** Respublika Bashkortostan, W Russian Federation 52°34´N 58°20´E
23 O8 **Bay Minette** Alabama, S USA 30°52´N 87°46´W
143 O17 **Baynūnah** desert W United Arab Emirates
184 O8 **Bay of Plenty** off. Bay of Plenty Region. ◈ region North Island, New Zealand
Bay of Plenty Region see Bay of Plenty
191 Z3 **Bay of Wrecks** bay Kiritimati, E Kiribati
Bayonnaise Rocks see Beyonēsu-retsugan
102 I15 **Bayonne** anc. Lapurdum. Pyrénées-Atlantiques, SW France 43°30´N 01°28´W
22 H4 **Bayou D'Arbonne Lake** ▦ Louisiana, S USA
23 N9 **Bayou La Batre** Alabama, S USA 30°24´N 88°15´W
Bayou State see Mississippi
Bayqadam see Saudakent
Bayqongyr see Baykonyr
Bayram-Ali see Baýramaly
146 J14 **Baýramaly** var. Bayramaly; prev. Bayram-Ali. Mary Welaýaty, S Turkmenistan 37°33´N 62°08´E
101 L19 **Bayreuth** var. Baireuth. Bayern, SE Germany 49°57´N 11°34´E
Bayrische Alpen see Bavarian Alps
Bayrūt see Beyrouth
22 L9 **Bay Saint Louis** Mississippi, S USA 30°18´N 89°19´W
Baysān see Beit She'an
Bayshint see Öndörshireet
14 H13 **Bays, Lake of** ◎ Ontario, S Canada
22 M6 **Bay Springs** Mississippi, S USA 31°58´N 89°17´W
Bay State see Massachusetts
Baysun see Boysun
14 H13 **Baysville** Ontario, S Canada 45°10´N 79°03´W
141 N15 **Bayt al Faqīh** W Yemen 14°30´N 43°20´E
158 M4 **Baytik Shan** ▲▲ China/Mongolia
Bayt Laḩm see Bethlehem
25 W11 **Baytown** Texas, SW USA 29°43´N 94°59´W
169 V11 **Bayur, Tanjung** headland Borneo, N Indonesia 0°43´S 117°32´E
121 N14 **Bayy al Kabīr, Wādī** dry watercourse NW Libya
145 P17 **Bayyrkum** Kaz. Bayyrqum; prev. Bairkum. Yuzhnyy Kazakhstan, S Kazakhstan 41°57´N 68°05´E
Bayyrqum see Bayyrkum
105 P14 **Baza** Andalucía, S Spain 37°30´N 02°45´W
137 X10 **Bazardüzü Dağı** Rus. Gora Bazardyuzyu. ▲ N Azerbaijan 41°13´N 47°50´E
Bazardyuzyu, Gora see Bazardüzü Dağı
Bazargic see Dobrich
83 N18 **Bazaruto, Ilha do** island SE Mozambique
102 K14 **Bazas** Gironde, SW France 44°27´N 00°11´W
105 O14 **Baza, Sierra de** ▲▲ S Spain
160 J8 **Bazhong** var. Bazhou. Sichuan, C China 31°55´N 106°44´E
Bazhong see Batang
161 P3 **Bazhou** prev. Baxian, Ba Xian. Hebei, E China 39°05´N 116°24´E
Bazhou see Bazhong
14 M9 **Bazin** ≈ Québec, SE Canada
Bazin see Pezinok
139 Q7 **Bāzīyah** Al Anbār, C Iraq 33°50´N 42°41´E
138 H6 **Bcharré** var. Bcharreh, Bsharrī, Bsherri. NE Lebanon 34°16´N 36°01´E
Bcharreh see Bcharré
28 J5 **Beach** North Dakota, N USA 46°55´N 104°00´W
182 K12 **Beachport** South Australia 37°29´S 140°03´E
97 O23 **Beachy Head** headland SE England, United Kingdom 50°44´N 00°16´E
18 K13 **Beacon** New York, NE USA 41°30´N 73°54´W
63 J25 **Beagle Channel** channel Argentina/Chile
181 O1 **Beagle Gulf** gulf Northern Territory, N Australia
Bealach an Doirín see Ballaghaderreen
Bealach Cláir see Ballyclare
Bealach Féich see Ballybofey
172 J3 **Bealanana** Mahajanga, NE Madagascar 14°33´S 48°44´E
Béal an Átha see Ballina
Béal an Átha Móir see Ballinamore
Béal an Mhuirhead see Belmullet
Béal Átha Beithe see Ballybay
Béal Átha Conaill see Ballyconnell
Beál Átha hAmhnais see Ballyhaunis
Béal Átha na Sluaighe see Ballinasloe
Béal Átha Seanaidh see Ballyshannon
Bealdovuopmi see Peltovuoma
Béal Feirste see Belfast
Béal Tairbirt see Belturbet
Beanna Boirche see Mourne Mountains
Beannchar see Banagher, Ireland
Beannchar see Bangor, Northern Ireland, UK
Beanntraí see Bantry
Bearalváhki see Berlevåg
23 N2 **Bear Creek** ≈ Alabama/Mississippi, S USA
30 J13 **Bear Creek** ≈ Illinois, N USA
27 U13 **Bearden** Arkansas, C USA 33°43´N 92°37´W
195 Q10 **Beardmore Glacier** glacier Antarctica
30 K13 **Beardstown** Illinois, N USA 40°01´N 90°25´W
28 L14 **Bear Hill** ▲ Nebraska, C USA 41°24´N 101°49´W
Bear Island see Bjørnøya
14 H12 **Bear Lake** Ontario, S Canada 45°28´N 79°31´W
36 M1 **Bear Lake** ◎ Idaho/Utah, NW USA
39 U11 **Bear, Mount** ▲ Alaska, USA 61°16´N 141°09´W
102 J16 **Béarn** cultural region SW France
194 J11 **Bear Peninsula** peninsula Antarctica
152 I7 **Beās** ≈ India/Pakistan
105 P3 **Beasain** País Vasco, N Spain 43°03´N 02°11´W
105 O12 **Beas de Segura** Andalucía, S Spain 38°16´N 02°54´W
45 N10 **Beata, Cabo** headland SW Dominican Republic 17°34´N 71°25´W
45 N10 **Beata, Isla** island SW Dominican Republic
64 F11 **Beata Ridge** undersea feature N Caribbean Sea 16°00´N 72°30´W
29 R17 **Beatrice** Nebraska, C USA 40°14´N 96°43´W
83 L16 **Beatrice** Mashonaland East, NE Zimbabwe 18°15´S 30°55´E
11 N11 **Beatton** ≈ British Columbia, W Canada
11 N11 **Beatton River** British Columbia, W Canada 57°35´N 121°45´W
35 V10 **Beatty** Nevada, W USA 36°53´N 116°44´W
21 N6 **Beattyville** Kentucky, S USA 37°33´N 83°44´W
173 X16 **Beau Bassin** W Mauritius 20°13´S 57°27´E
103 R15 **Beaucaire** Gard, S France 43°49´N 04°37´E
14 I8 **Beauchastel, Lac** ◎ Québec, SE Canada
14 I10 **Beauchêne, Lac** ◎ Québec, SE Canada
183 V3 **Beaudesert** Queensland, E Australia 28°00´S 152°27´E
182 M12 **Beaufort** Victoria, SE Australia 37°27´S 143°24´E
21 X11 **Beaufort** North Carolina, SE USA 34°44´N 76°41´W
21 R15 **Beaufort** South Carolina, SE USA 32°23´N 80°40´W
38 M11 **Beaufort Sea** sea Arctic Ocean
Beaufort-Wes see Beaufort West
83 G25 **Beaufort West** Afr. Beaufort-Wes. Western Cape, SW South Africa 32°21´S 22°35´E
103 N7 **Beaugency** Loiret, C France 47°46´N 01°38´E
19 R1 **Beau Lake** ▦ Maine, NE USA
96 I8 **Beauly** N Scotland, United Kingdom 57°29´N 04°29´W
99 G21 **Beaumont** Hainaut, S Belgium 50°12´N 04°13´E
185 E23 **Beaumont** Otago, South Island, New Zealand 45°48´S 169°32´E
22 M7 **Beaumont** Mississippi, S USA 31°10´N 88°55´W
25 X10 **Beaumont** Texas, SW USA 30°05´N 94°06´W
102 M15 **Beaumont-de-Lomagne** Tarn-et-Garonne, S France 43°54´N 01°00´E
102 L6 **Beaumont-sur-Sarthe** Sarthe, NW France 48°15´N 00°07´E
103 R8 **Beaune** Côte d'Or, C France 47°02´N 04°50´E
15 R9 **Beaupré** Québec, SE Canada 47°03´N 70°52´W
102 J8 **Beaupréau** Maine-et-Loire, NW France 47°13´N 00°57´W
99 I22 **Beauraing** Namur, SE Belgium 50°07´N 04°57´E
103 R12 **Beaurepaire** Isère, E France 45°20´N 05°03´E
11 Y16 **Beausejour** Manitoba, S Canada 50°04´N 96°30´W
103 N4 **Beauvais** anc. Bellovacum, Caesaromagus. Oise, N France 49°27´N 02°04´E
11 S13 **Beauval** Saskatchewan, C Canada 55°10´N 107°37´W
102 I9 **Beauvoir-sur-Mer** Vendée, NW France 46°54´N 02°03´W
39 R8 **Beaver** Alaska, USA 66°22´N 147°31´W
26 J8 **Beaver** Oklahoma, C USA 36°48´N 100°32´W
18 B14 **Beaver** Pennsylvania, NE USA 40°39´N 80°19´W
36 K6 **Beaver** Utah, W USA 38°16´N 112°38´W
10 L9 **Beaver** ≈ British Columbia/Yukon Territory, W Canada
11 S13 **Beaver** ≈ Saskatchewan, C Canada
29 N17 **Beaver City** Nebraska, C USA 40°08´N 99°49´W
10 G6 **Beaver Creek** Yukon Territory, W Canada 62°20´N 140°45´W
31 R14 **Beavercreek** Ohio, N USA 39°42´N 83°58´W
39 S8 **Beaver Creek** ≈ Alaska, USA
26 H3 **Beaver Creek** ≈ Kansas/Nebraska, C USA
28 J5 **Beaver Creek** ≈ Montana/North Dakota, N USA
29 Q14 **Beaver Creek** ≈ Nebraska, C USA
25 Q4 **Beaver Creek** ≈ Texas, SW USA
30 M8 **Beaver Dam** Wisconsin, N USA 43°28´N 88°49´W
30 M8 **Beaver Dam Lake** ◎ Wisconsin, N USA
18 B14 **Beaver Falls** Pennsylvania, NE USA 40°45´N 80°20´W
33 P12 **Beaverhead Mountains** ▲▲ Idaho/Montana, NW USA
33 Q12 **Beaverhead River** ≈ Montana, NW USA
65 A25 **Beaver Island** island W Falkland Islands
31 P5 **Beaver Island** island Michigan, N USA
27 S9 **Beaver Lake** ▦ Arkansas, C USA
11 N13 **Beaverlodge** Alberta, W Canada 55°11´N 119°29´W
18 I8 **Beaver River** ≈ New York, NE USA
26 J8 **Beaver River** ≈ Oklahoma, C USA
18 B13 **Beaver River** ≈ Pennsylvania, NE USA
65 A25 **Beaver Settlement** Beaver Island, W Falkland Islands 51°30´S 61°15´W
Beaver State see Oregon
14 H14 **Beaverton** Ontario, S Canada 44°24´N 79°07´W
32 G11 **Beaverton** Oregon, NW USA 45°29´N 122°49´W
152 G12 **Beāwar** Rājasthān, N India 26°08´N 74°22´E
Bebas, Dasht-i see Bābūs, Dasht-e
60 L8 **Bebedouro** São Paulo, S Brazil 20°58´S 48°28´W
101 I16 **Bebra** Hessen, C Germany 50°59´N 09°46´E
41 W12 **Becal** Campeche, SE Mexico 19°49´N 90°28´W
15 Q11 **Bécancour** ≈ Québec, SE Canada
97 Q19 **Beccles** E England, United Kingdom 52°27´N 01°32´E
112 L9 **Bečej** Ger. Altbetsche, Hung. Óbecse, Rácz-Becse; prev. Magyar-Becse, Stari Bečej. Vojvodina, N Serbia 45°36´N 20°02´E
104 I3 **Becerréa** Galicia, NW Spain 42°51´N 07°10´W
74 H7 **Béchar** prev. Colomb-Béchar. W Algeria 31°38´N 02°11´W
39 O14 **Becharof Lake** ◎ Alaska, USA
116 H15 **Bechet** var. Bechetu. Dolj, SW Romania 43°45´N 23°57´E
Bechetu see Bechet
21 R6 **Beckley** West Virginia, NE USA 37°46´N 81°12´W
101 G14 **Beckum** Nordrhein-Westfalen, W Germany 51°45´N 08°03´E
25 X7 **Beckville** Texas, SW USA 32°14´N 94°27´W
35 X4 **Becky Peak** ▲ Nevada, W USA 39°59´N 114°33´W
116 I9 **Beclean** Hung. Bethlen; prev. Betlen. Bistriţa-Năsăud, N Romania 47°10´N 24°11´E
Bécs see Wien
111 H18 **Bečva** Ger. Betschau, Pol. Beczwa. ≈ E Czech Republic
Beczwa see Bečva
103 P15 **Bédarieux** Hérault, S France 43°37´N 03°10´E
120 B10 **Beddouza, Cap** headland W Morocco 32°35´N 09°16´W
80 I13 **Bedelē** Oromīya, C Ethiopia 08°25´N 36°21´E
147 Y8 **Bedel Pass** Rus. Pereval Bedel. pass China/Kyrgyzstan
Bedel, Pereval see Bedel Pass
95 H22 **Beder** Midtjylland, C Denmark 56°03´N 10°13´E
97 N20 **Bedford** E England, United Kingdom 52°08´N 00°29´W
31 O15 **Bedford** Indiana, N USA 38°51´N 86°29´W
29 U16 **Bedford** Iowa, C USA 40°40´N 94°43´W
20 L4 **Bedford** Kentucky, S USA 38°36´N 85°18´W
18 D15 **Bedford** Pennsylvania, NE USA 40°00´N 78°29´W
21 T6 **Bedford** Virginia, NE USA 37°20´N 79°31´W
97 N20 **Bedfordshire** cultural region E England, United Kingdom
127 N5 **Bednodem'yanovsk** Penzenskaya Oblast', W Russian Federation 53°55´N 43°14´E
98 N5 **Bedum** Groningen, NE Netherlands 53°18´N 06°36´E
27 V11 **Beebe** Arkansas, C USA 35°04´N 91°52´W
Beechy Group see Chichijima-rettō
45 T9 **Beef Island** ✈ (Road Town) Tortola, E British Virgin Islands 18°25´N 64°31´W
Beehive State see Utah
99 L18 **Beek** Limburg, SE Netherlands 50°56´N 05°47´E
99 L18 **Beek** ✈ (Maastricht) Limburg, SE Netherlands 50°55´N 05°47´E
99 K14 **Beek-en-Donk** Noord-Brabant, S Netherlands 51°31´N 05°37´E
138 F13 **Be'er Menuha** prev. Be'ér Menuẖa. Southern, S Israel 30°22´N 35°09´E
Be'ér Menuẖa see Be'er Menuha
99 D16 **Beernem** West-Vlaanderen, NW Belgium 51°09´N 03°18´E
99 I16 **Beerse** Antwerpen, N Belgium 51°20´N 04°52´E
Beersheba see Be'er Sheva
138 E11 **Be'er Sheva** var. Beersheba, Ar. Bir es Saba; prev. Be'ér Sheva'. Southern, S Israel 31°15´N 34°47´E
Be'ér Sheva' see Be'er Sheva
98 J13 **Beesd** Gelderland, C Netherlands 51°52´N 05°12´E
99 M16 **Beesel** Limburg, SE Netherlands 51°16´N 06°02´E
83 J21 **Beestekraal** North-West, N South Africa 25°21´S 27°40´E
194 J7 **Beethoven Peninsula** peninsula Alexander Island, Antarctica
Beetstersweach see Beetsterzwaag
98 M6 **Beetsterzwaag** Fris. Beetstersweach. Fryslân, N Netherlands 53°03´N 06°04´E
25 S13 **Beeville** Texas, SW USA 28°25´N 97°47´W
79 J18 **Befale** Equateur, NW Dem. Rep. Congo 0°25´N 20°48´E
Befandriana see Befandriana Avaratra
172 J3 **Befandriana Avaratra** var. Befandriana, Befandriana Nord. Mahajanga, NW Madagascar 15°14´S 48°33´E
Befandriana Nord see Befandriana Avaratra
79 K18 **Befori** Equateur, N Dem. Rep. Congo 0°09´N 22°18´E
172 I7 **Befotaka** Fianarantsoa, S Madagascar 23°49´S 47°00´E
183 R11 **Bega** New South Wales, SE Australia 36°43´S 149°50´E
102 G5 **Bégard** Côtes d'Armor, NW France 48°37´N 03°18´W
112 M9 **Begejski Kanal** canal Vojvodina, NE Serbia
94 G13 **Begna** ≈ S Norway
Begoml' see Byahoml'
Begovat see Bekobod
153 Q13 **Begusarai** Bihār, NE India 25°25´N 86°08´E
143 R9 **Behābād** Yazd, C Iran 32°23´N 59°50´E
Behagle see Laï
55 Z10 **Béhague, Pointe** headland E French Guiana 04°38´N 51°52´W
Behar see Bihār
142 M10 **Behbahān** var. Behbehān. Khūzestān, SW Iran 30°38´N 50°07´E
Behbehān see Behbahān
44 G3 **Behring Point** Andros Island, W Bahamas 24°28´N 77°44´W

◆ Country
● Country Capital
◇ Dependent Territory
○ Dependent Territory Capital
◈ Administrative Regions
✈ International Airport
▲ Mountain
▲▲ Mountain Range
Volcano
≈ River
◎ Lake
▦ Reservoir

143 P4 **Behshahr** *prev.* Ashraf. Māzandarān, N Iran *36°42′N 53°36′E*
163 V6 **Bei'an** Heilongjiang, NE China *48°16′N 126°29′E*
Beibunar *see* Sredishte
Beibu Wan *see* Tongking, Gulf of
Beida *see* Al Bayḍā'
80 H13 **Beigi** Oromīya, C Ethiopia *09°13′N 34°48′E*
160 L16 **Beihai** Guangxi Zhuangzu Zizhiqu, S China *21°29′N 109°10′E*
159 Q10 **Bei Hulsan Hu** ◎ C China
161 N13 **Bei Jiang** ~ S China
161 O2 **Beijing** *var.* Pei-ching, *Eng.* Peking; *prev.* Pei-p'ing. ● (China) Beijing Shi, E China *39°58′N 116°23′E*
161 P2 **Beijing** ✈ Beijing Shi, N China *39°54′N 116°22′E*
Beijing *see* Beijing Shi, China
161 O2 **Beijing Shi** *var.* Beijing, Jing, Pei-ching, *Eng.* Peking; *prev.* Pei-p'ing. ◈ *municipality* E China
76 G8 **Beïla** Trarza, W Mauritania *18°07′N 15°56′W*
98 N7 **Beilen** Drenthe, NE Netherlands *52°52′N 06°27′E*
160 L15 **Beiliu** *var.* Lingcheng. Guangxi Zhuangzu Zizhiqu, S China *22°50′N 110°22′E*
159 O12 **Beilu He** ~ W China
Beilul *see* Beylul
163 U12 **Beining** *prev.* Beizhen. Liaoning, NE China *41°34′N 121°51′E*
96 H8 **Beinn Dearg** ▲ N Scotland, United Kingdom *57°47′N 04°52′W*
Beinn MacDuibh *see* Ben Macdui
160 I12 **Beipan Jiang** ~ S China
163 T12 **Beipiao** Liaoning, NE China *41°49′N 120°45′E*
83 N17 **Beira** Sofala, C Mozambique *19°45′S 34°56′E*
83 N17 **Beira** ✈ Sofala, C Mozambique *19°39′S 35°05′E*
104 I7 **Beira Alta** *former province* N Portugal
104 H9 **Beira Baixa** *former province* C Portugal
104 G8 **Beira Litoral** *former province* N Portugal
Beirut *see* Beyrouth
Beisān *see* Beit She'an
11 Q16 **Beiseker** Alberta, SW Canada *51°20′N 113°34′W*
Beitai Ding *see* Wutai Shan
83 K19 **Beitbridge** Matabeleland South, S Zimbabwe *22°10′S 30°02′E*
Beit Lekhem *see* Bethlehem
138 G9 **Beit She'an** *Ar.* Baysān, Beisān; *anc.* Scythopolis, *prev.* Bet She'an. Northern, N Israel *32°30′N 35°30′E*
116 G10 **Beiuş** *Hung.* Belényes. Bihor, NW Romania *46°40′N 22°21′E*
Beizhen *see* Beining
104 H12 **Beja** *anc.* Pax Julia. Beja, SE Portugal *38°01′N 07°52′W*
74 M5 **Béja** *var.* Bājah. N Tunisia *36°45′N 09°04′E*
104 G13 **Beja** ◈ *district* S Portugal
120 I9 **Béjaïa** *var.* Bejaïa, *Fr.* Bougie; *anc.* Saldae. NE Algeria *36°49′N 05°03′E*
Bejaïa *see* Béjaïa
104 K8 **Béjar** Castilla y León, N Spain *40°24′N 05°45′W*
Bejraburi *see* Phetchaburi
Bekaa Valley *see* El Beqaa
Bekabad *see* Bekobod
Békás *see* Bicaz
169 O15 **Bekasi** Jawa, C Indonesia *06°14′S 106°595′E*
Bek-Budi *see* Qarshi
Bekdaş/Bekdash *see* Garabogaz
147 T10 **Bek-Dzhar** Oshskaya Oblast', SW Kyrgyzstan *40°22′N 73°08′E*
111 N24 **Békés** *Rom.* Bichiş. Békés, SE Hungary *46°45′N 21°09′E*
111 M24 **Békés** *off.* Békés Megye. ◈ *county* SE Hungary
111 M24 **Békéscsaba** *Rom.* Bichiş-Ciaba. Békés, SE Hungary *46°40′N 21°05′E*
Békés Megye *see* Békés
172 H7 **Bekily** Toliara, S Madagascar *24°12′S 45°20′E*
165 W4 **Bekkai** *var.* Betsukai. Hokkaidō, NE Japan *43°23′N 145°07′E*
139 S2 **Bēkma** Arbīl, E Iraq *36°40′N 44°15′E*
147 Q11 **Bekobod** *Rus.* Bekabad; *prev.* Begovat. Toshkent Viloyati, E Uzbekistan *40°17′N 69°11′E*
127 O7 **Bekovo** Penzenskaya Oblast', W Russian Federation *52°27′N 43°41′E*
Bel *see* Beliu
152 M13 **Bela** Uttar Pradesh, N India *25°55′N 82°00′E*
149 N15 **Bela** Baluchistān, SW Pakistan *26°12′N 66°20′E*
79 F15 **Bélabo** Est, C Cameroon *04°54′N 13°10′E*
112 N10 **Bela Crkva** *Ger.* Weisskirchen, *Hung.* Fehértemplom. Vojvodina, W Serbia *44°55′N 21°28′E*
173 Y16 **Bel Air** *var.* Rivière Sèche. E Mauritius
104 L12 **Belalcázar** Andalucía, S Spain *38°33′N 05°07′W*
113 P15 **Bela Palanka** Serbia, SE Serbia *43°13′N 22°19′E*
119 H16 **Belarus** *off.* Republic of Belarus, *var.* Belorussia, *Latv.* Baltkrievija; *prev.* Belorussian SSR, *Rus.* Belorusskaya SSR. ◆ *republic* E Europe
Belarus, Republic of *see* Belarus
Belau *see* Palau
59 H21 **Bela Vista** Mato Grosso do Sul, SW Brazil *22°04′S 56°25′W*
83 L21 **Bela Vista** Maputo, S Mozambique *26°20′S 32°40′E*
168 I8 **Belawan** Sumatera, W Indonesia *03°46′N 98°44′E*
Běla Woda *see* Weisswasser
127 U4 **Belaya** ~ W Russian Federation
123 R7 **Belaya Gora** Respublika Sakha (Yakutiya), NE Russian Federation *68°25′N 146°12′E*
126 M11 **Belaya Kalitiva** Rostovskaya Oblast', SW Russian Federation *48°09′N 40°43′E*
125 R14 **Belaya Kholunitsa** Kirovskaya Oblast', NW Russian Federation *58°54′N 50°52′E*
Belaya Tserkov' *see* Bila Tserkva
77 V11 **Belbédji** Zinder, S Niger *14°35′N 08°00′E*
111 K14 **Bełchatów** *var.* Belchatow. Łódzski, C Poland *51°23′N 19°20′E*
Belchatow *see* Bełchatów
Belcher, Îles *see* Belcher Islands
12 H7 **Belcher Islands** *Fr.* Îles Belcher. *island group* Nunavut, SE Canada
105 S6 **Belchite** Aragón, NE Spain *41°18′N 00°45′W*
29 O2 **Belcourt** North Dakota, N USA *48°50′N 99°44′W*
31 P9 **Belding** Michigan, N USA *43°06′N 85°13′W*
127 U5 **Belebey** Respublika Bashkortostan, W Russian Federation *54°04′N 54°13′E*
81 N16 **Beledweyne** *var.* Belet Huen, *It.* Belet Uen. Hiiraan, C Somalia *04°39′N 45°12′E*
146 B10 **Belek** Balkan Welaýaty, W Turkmenistan *39°57′N 53°51′E*
58 L12 **Belém** *var.* Pará. *state capital* Pará, N Brazil *01°27′S 48°29′W*
65 I14 **Belém Ridge** *undersea feature* C Atlantic Ocean
62 I7 **Belén** Catamarca, NW Argentina *27°36′N 67°00′W*
54 G9 **Belén** Boyacá, C Colombia *06°01′N 72°55′W*
42 J11 **Belén** Rivas, SW Nicaragua *11°30′N 85°55′W*
62 O5 **Belén** Concepción, C Paraguay *23°25′S 57°14′W*
61 D16 **Belén** Salto, N Uruguay *30°47′S 57°47′W*
37 R12 **Belen** New Mexico, SW USA *34°37′N 106°46′W*
61 D20 **Belén de Escobar** Buenos Aires, E Argentina *34°21′S 58°47′W*
114 J7 **Belene** Pleven, N Bulgaria *43°39′N 25°09′E*
114 J7 **Belene, Ostrov** *island* N Bulgaria
43 R15 **Belén, Río** ~ C Panama
Belényes *see* Beiuş
Embalse de Belesar *see* Belesar, Encoro de
104 H3 **Belesar, Encoro de** *Sp.* Embalse de Belesar. ⊠ NW Spain
Belet Huen/Belet Uen *see* Beledweyne
126 J5 **Belëv** Tul'skaya Oblast', W Russian Federation *53°48′N 36°07′E*
19 R7 **Belfast** Maine, NE USA *44°25′N 69°02′W*
97 G15 **Belfast** *Ir.* Béal Feirste. ◐ E Northern Ireland, United Kingdom *54°35′N 05°55′W*
97 G15 **Belfast Aldergrove** ✈ E Northern Ireland, United Kingdom *54°37′N 06°11′W*
97 G15 **Belfast Lough** *Ir.* Loch Lao. *inlet* E Northern Ireland, United Kingdom
28 K5 **Belfield** North Dakota, N USA *46°53′N 103°12′W*
103 U7 **Belfort** Territoire-de-Belfort, E France *47°38′N 06°52′E*
Belgard *see* Białogard
155 E17 **Belgaum** Karnātaka, W India *15°52′N 74°30′E*
Belgian Congo *see* Congo (Democratic Republic of)
België/Belgique *see* Belgium
99 F20 **Belgium** *off.* Kingdom of Belgium, *Dut.* België, *Fr.* Belgique. ◆ *monarchy* NW Europe
Belgium, Kingdom of *see* Belgium
126 J8 **Belgorod** Belgorodskaya Oblast', W Russian Federation *50°38′N 36°37′E*
Belgorod-Dnestrovskiy *see* Bilhorod-Dnistrovs'kyy
126 J8 **Belgorodskaya Oblast'** ◈ *province* W Russian Federation
Belgrad *see* Beograd
29 T8 **Belgrade** Minnesota, N USA *45°27′N 94°59′W*
33 S11 **Belgrade** Montana, NW USA *45°46′N 111°10′W*
Belgrade *see* Beograd
Belgrano, Cabo *see* Meredith, Cape
195 N5 **Belgrano II** *Argentinian research station* Antarctica *77°50′S 35°25′W*
21 X9 **Belhaven** North Carolina, SE USA *35°36′N 76°50′W*
107 I23 **Belice** *anc.* Hypsas. ~ Sicilia, Italy, C Mediterranean Sea
Belice *see* Belize/Belize City
Beli Drim *see* Drini i Bardhë
Beligrad *see* Berat
188 C8 **Beliliou** *prev.* Peleliu. *island* S Palau
114 L8 **Beli Lom, Yazovir** ⊠ NE Bulgaria
112 I8 **Beli Manastir** *Hung.* Pélmonostor; *prev.* Monostor. Osijek-Baranja, NE Croatia *45°46′N 16°38′E*
102 J13 **Bélin-Béliet** Gironde, SW France *44°30′N 00°48′W*
79 F17 **Bélinga** Ogooué-Ivindo, NE Gabon *01°05′N 13°12′E*
21 S4 **Belington** West Virginia, NE USA *39°01′N 79°57′W*
127 O6 **Belinskiy** Penzenskaya Oblast', W Russian Federation *52°58′N 43°25′E*
169 N12 **Belinyu** Pulau Bangka, W Indonesia *01°37′S 105°45′E*
169 O13 **Belitung, Pulau** *island* W Indonesia
116 F10 **Beliu** *Hung.* Bel. Arad, W Romania *46°31′N 21°57′E*
114 I9 **Beli Vit** ~ NW Bulgaria
42 G2 **Belize** *Sp.* Belice; *prev.* British Honduras, Colony of Belize. ◆ *commonwealth republic* Central America
42 F2 **Belize** *Sp.* Belice. ◈ *district* NE Belize
42 G2 **Belize** ~ Belize/Guatemala
Belize *see* Belize City
42 G2 **Belize City** *var.* Belize, *Sp.* Belice. Belize, NE Belize *17°29′N 88°10′W*
42 G2 **Belize City** ✈ Belize, NE Belize *17°31′N 88°15′W*
Belize, Colony of *see* Belize
Beljak *see* Villach
39 N16 **Belkofski** Alaska, USA *55°07′N 162°04′W*
123 O6 **Bel'kovskiy, Ostrov** *island* Novosibirskiye Ostrova, NE Russian Federation
14 J8 **Bell** ~ Québec, SE Canada
10 J15 **Bella Bella** British Columbia, SW Canada *52°04′N 128°07′W*
102 M10 **Bellac** Haute-Vienne, C France *46°07′N 01°04′E*
10 K15 **Bella Coola** British Columbia, SW Canada *52°23′N 126°46′W*
106 D6 **Bellagio** Lombardia, N Italy *45°58′N 09°15′E*
31 P6 **Bellaire** Michigan, N USA *44°59′N 85°12′W*
106 D6 **Bellano** Lombardia, N Italy *46°06′N 09°21′E*
155 G17 **Bellary** *var.* Ballari. Karnātaka, S India *15°11′N 76°54′E*
183 S5 **Bellata** New South Wales, SE Australia *29°58′S 149°49′E*
61 D16 **Bella Unión** Artigas, N Uruguay *30°18′S 57°35′W*
61 C14 **Bella Vista** Corrientes, NE Argentina *28°30′S 59°03′W*
62 J7 **Bella Vista** Tucumán, N Argentina *27°05′S 65°19′W*
62 P4 **Bella Vista** Amambay, C Paraguay *22°08′S 56°20′W*
56 B10 **Bellavista** Cajamarca, N Peru *05°43′S 78°48′W*
56 D11 **Bellavista** San Martín, N Peru *07°04′S 76°35′W*
183 U6 **Bellbrook** New South Wales, SE Australia *30°48′S 152°32′E*
27 V5 **Belle** Missouri, C USA *38°17′N 91°43′W*
21 Q5 **Belle** West Virginia, NE USA *38°13′N 81°32′W*
31 R13 **Bellefontaine** Ohio, N USA *40°22′N 83°45′W*
18 F14 **Bellefonte** Pennsylvania, NE USA *40°54′N 77°43′W*
28 J9 **Belle Fourche** South Dakota, N USA *44°40′N 103°50′W*
28 J9 **Belle Fourche Reservoir** ⊠ South Dakota, N USA
28 K9 **Belle Fourche River** ~ South Dakota/Wyoming, N USA
103 S10 **Bellegarde-sur-Valserine** Ain, E France *46°06′N 05°49′E*
23 Y14 **Belle Glade** Florida, SE USA *26°40′N 80°40′W*
102 G8 **Belle Île** *island* NW France
13 T9 **Belle Isle** *island* Belle Isle, Newfoundland and Labrador, E Canada
13 S10 **Belle Isle, Strait of** *strait* Newfoundland and Labrador, E Canada
Bellenz *see* Bellinzona
29 W14 **Belle Plaine** Iowa, C USA *41°54′N 92°16′W*
29 V9 **Belle Plaine** Minnesota, N USA *44°39′N 93°47′W*
14 I9 **Belleterre** Québec, SE Canada *47°24′N 78°40′W*
14 J15 **Belleville** Ontario, SE Canada *44°10′N 77°22′W*
103 R10 **Belleville** Rhône, E France *46°09′N 04°42′E*
30 K15 **Belleville** Illinois, N USA *38°31′N 89°58′W*
27 N3 **Belleville** Kansas, C USA *39°51′N 97°38′W*
29 Z13 **Bellevue** Iowa, C USA *42°15′N 90°25′W*
29 S15 **Bellevue** Nebraska, C USA *41°08′N 95°53′W*
31 S11 **Bellevue** Ohio, N USA *41°16′N 82°50′W*
25 S5 **Bellevue** Texas, SW USA *33°38′N 98°00′W*
32 H8 **Bellevue** Washington, NW USA *47°36′N 122°12′W*
55 Y11 **Bellevue de l'Inini, Montagnes** ▲▲ S French Guiana
103 S11 **Belley** Ain, E France *45°46′N 05°41′E*
Bellin *see* Kangirsuk
183 V6 **Bellingen** New South Wales, SE Australia *30°27′S 152°53′E*
97 L14 **Bellingham** N England, United Kingdom *55°09′N 02°16′W*
32 H6 **Bellingham** Washington, NW USA *48°46′N 122°29′W*
Belling Hausen Mulde *see* Southeast Pacific Basin
194 H2 **Bellingshausen** *Russian research station* South Shetland Islands, Antarctica *61°57′S 58°23′W*
Bellingshausen *see* Motu One
Bellingshausen Abyssal Plain *see* Bellingshausen Plain
196 R14 **Bellingshausen Plain** *var.* Bellingshausen Abyssal Plain. *undersea feature* SE Pacific Ocean *64°00′S 90°00′W*
194 I8 **Bellingshausen Sea** *sea* Antarctica
98 P6 **Bellingwolde** Groningen, NE Netherlands *53°07′N 07°10′E*
108 H11 **Bellinzona** *Ger.* Bellenz. Ticino, S Switzerland *46°12′N 09°02′E*
25 T8 **Bellmead** Texas, SW USA *31°36′N 97°02′W*
54 E8 **Bello** Antioquia, W Colombia *06°19′N 75°34′W*
61 B21 **Bellocq** Buenos Aires, E Argentina *35°55′S 61°32′W*
Bello Horizonte *see* Belo Horizonte
186 L10 **Bellona** *var.* Mungiki. *island* S Solomon Islands
Bellovacum *see* Beauvais
182 D7 **Bell, Point** *headland* South Australia *32°13′S 133°08′E*
20 F9 **Bells** Tennessee, S USA *35°42′N 89°05′W*
25 U5 **Bells** Texas, SW USA *33°36′N 96°24′W*
92 N3 **Bellsund** *inlet* SW Svalbard
106 H6 **Belluno** Veneto, NE Italy *46°08′N 12°13′E*
62 L11 **Bell Ville** Córdoba, C Argentina *32°35′S 62°41′W*
83 E26 **Bellville** Western Cape, SW South Africa *33°50′S 18°43′E*
25 U11 **Bellville** Texas, SW USA *29°57′N 96°15′W*
104 L12 **Belméz** Andalucía, S Spain *38°16′N 05°12′W*
29 V12 **Belmond** Iowa, C USA *42°51′N 93°36′W*
18 E11 **Belmont** New York, NE USA *42°14′N 78°02′W*
21 R10 **Belmont** North Carolina, SE USA *35°13′N 81°01′W*
59 O18 **Belmonte** Bahia, E Brazil *15°53′S 38°54′W*
104 I8 **Belmonte** Castelo Branco, C Portugal *40°21′N 07°20′W*
105 P10 **Belmonte** Castilla-La Mancha, C Spain *39°34′N 02°43′W*
42 G2 **Belmopan** ● (Belize) Cayo, C Belize *17°13′N 88°48′W*
97 B16 **Belmullet** *Ir.* Béal an Mhuirhead. Mayo, W Ireland *54°14′N 09°59′W*
99 E20 **Belœil** Hainaut, SW Belgium *50°33′N 03°45′E*
123 R13 **Belogorsk** Amurskaya Oblast', SE Russian Federation *50°53′N 128°24′E*
Belogorsk *see* Bilohirs'k
114 F7 **Belogradchik** Vidin, NW Bulgaria *43°37′N 22°42′E*
172 H8 **Beloha** Toliara, S Madagascar *25°09′S 45°04′E*
59 M20 **Belo Horizonte** *prev.* Bello Horizonte. *state capital* Minas Gerais, SE Brazil *19°54′S 43°54′W*
26 M3 **Beloit** Kansas, C USA *39°27′N 98°06′W*
30 L9 **Beloit** Wisconsin, N USA *42°31′N 89°01′W*
Belokorovichi *see* Novi Bilokorovychi
124 J8 **Belomorsk** Respublika Kareliya, NW Russian Federation *64°30′N 34°43′E*
124 J8 **Belomorsko-Baltiyskiy Kanal** *Eng.* White Sea-Baltic Canal, White Sea Canal. *canal* NW Russian Federation
153 V15 **Belonia** Tripura, NE India *23°15′N 91°25′E*
Beloozersk *see* Byelaazyorsk
Belopol'ye *see* Bilopillya
105 O4 **Belorado** Castilla y León, N Spain *42°25′N 03°11′W*
126 L14 **Belorechensk** Krasnodarskiy Kray, SW Russian Federation *44°46′N 39°53′E*
127 W5 **Beloretsk** Respublika Bashkortostan, W Russian Federation *53°56′N 58°26′E*
Belorussia/Belorussian SSR *see* Belarus
Belorusskaya Gryada *see* Byelaruskaya Hrada
Belorusskaya SSR *see* Belarus
Beloshchel'ye *see* Nar'yan-Mar
114 N8 **Beloslav** Varna, E Bulgaria *43°13′N 27°42′E*
Belostok *see* Białystok
Belo-sur-Tsiribihina *see* Belo Tsiribihina
172 H5 **Belo Tsiribihina** *var.* Belo-sur-Tsiribihina. Toliara, W Madagascar *19°40′S 44°30′E*
Belovár *see* Bjelovar
Belovezhskaya, Pushcha *see* Białowieska, Puszcza/ Byelavyezhskaya, Pushcha
114 H10 **Belovo** Pazardzhik, C Bulgaria *42°10′N 24°01′E*
Belovodsk *see* Bilovods'k
122 H9 **Beloyarskiy** Khanty-Mansiyskiy Avtonomnyy Okrug-Yugra, N Russian Federation *63°40′N 66°31′E*
124 K7 **Beloye More** *Eng.* White Sea. *sea* NW Russian Federation
124 K13 **Beloye, Ozero** ◎ NW Russian Federation
114 J10 **Belozem** Plovdiv, C Bulgaria *42°11′N 25°00′E*
124 K13 **Belozërsk** Vologodskaya Oblast', NW Russian Federation *59°59′N 37°49′E*
108 D8 **Belp** Bern, W Switzerland *46°54′N 07°31′E*
108 D8 **Belp** ✈ (Bern) Bern, C Switzerland *46°55′N 07°29′E*
107 L24 **Belpasso** Sicilia, Italy, C Mediterranean Sea *37°35′N 14°59′E*
31 U14 **Belpre** Ohio, N USA *39°14′N 81°34′W*
98 M8 **Belterwijde** ◎ N Netherlands
27 R4 **Belton** Missouri, C USA *38°48′N 94°31′W*
21 P11 **Belton** South Carolina, SE USA *34°31′N 82°29′W*
25 T9 **Belton** Texas, SW USA *31°04′N 97°30′W*
25 S9 **Belton Lake** ⊠ Texas, SW USA
Bel'tsy *see* Bălţi
97 E16 **Belturbet** *Ir.* Béal Tairbirt. Cavan, N Ireland *54°06′N 07°26′W*
Beluchistan *see* Balochistan
145 Z9 **Belukha, Gora** ▲ Kazakhstan/Russian Federation *49°50′N 86°44′E*
107 M20 **Belvedere Marittimo** Calabria, SW Italy *39°37′N 15°52′E*
30 L10 **Belvidere** Illinois, N USA *42°15′N 88°50′W*
18 J14 **Belvidere** New Jersey, NE USA *40°50′N 75°05′W*
Bely *see* Belyy
127 V8 **Belyayevka** Orenburgskaya Oblast', W Russian Federation *51°25′N 56°26′E*
Belynichi *see* Byalynichy
124 H17 **Belyy** *var.* Bely, Beyj. Tverskaya Oblast', W Russian Federation *55°51′N 32°57′E*
126 I6 **Belyye Berega** Bryanskaya Oblast', W Russian Federation *53°11′N 34°42′E*
122 J6 **Belyy, Ostrov** *island* N Russian Federation
122 J11 **Belyy Yar** Tomskaya Oblast', C Russian Federation *58°26′N 84°57′E*
100 N13 **Belzig** Brandenburg, NE Germany *52°09′N 12°37′E*
22 K4 **Belzoni** Mississippi, S USA *33°10′N 90°29′W*
172 H4 **Bemaraha** *var.* Plateau du Bemaraha. ▲▲ W Madagascar
Bemaraha, Plateau du *see* Bemaraha
82 B10 **Bembe** Uíge, NW Angola *07°03′S 14°25′E*
77 S14 **Bembèrèkè** *var.* Bimbéréké. N Benin *10°10′N 02°41′E*
104 K12 **Bembézar** ~ SW Spain
104 J3 **Bembibre** Castilla y León, N Spain *42°37′N 06°25′W*
29 T4 **Bemidji** Minnesota, N USA *47°27′N 94°53′W*
98 L12 **Bemmel** Gelderland, SE Netherlands *51°53′N 05°54′E*
171 T13 **Bemu** Pulau Seram, E Indonesia *03°21′S 129°58′E*
Benāb *see* Bonāb
105 T5 **Benabarre** *var.* Benavarn. Aragón, NE Spain *42°06′N 00°28′E*
Benaco *see* Garda, Lago di
79 L20 **Bena-Dibele** Kasai-Oriental, C Dem. Rep. Congo *04°01′S 22°50′E*
105 R9 **Benagéber, Embalse de** E Spain
183 O11 **Benalla** Victoria, SE Australia *36°33′S 146°00′E*
104 M14 **Benamejí** Andalucía, S Spain *37°16′N 04°33′W*
Benares *see* Vārānasi
Benavarn *see* Benabarre
104 F10 **Benavente** Santarém, C Portugal *38°59′N 08°49′W*
104 K5 **Benavente** Castilla y León, N Spain *42°N 05°40′W*
25 S15 **Benavides** Texas, SW USA *27°36′N 98°24′W*
96 F8 **Benbecula** *island* NW Scotland, United Kingdom
Bencovazzo *see* Benkovac
32 H13 **Bend** Oregon, NW USA *44°04′N 121°19′W*
182 K7 **Benda Range** ▲▲ South Australia
183 T6 **Bendemeer** New South Wales, SE Australia *30°54′S 151°12′E*
Bender *see* Tighina
Bender Beila/Bender Beyla *see* Bandarbeyla
Bender Cassim/Bender Qaasim *see* Boosaaso
Bendery *see* Tighina
183 N11 **Bendigo** Victoria, SE Australia *36°46′S 144°19′E*
118 E10 **Bēne** SW Latvia *56°30′N 23°04′E*
98 K13 **Beneden-Leeuwen** Gelderland, C Netherlands *51°52′N 05°32′E*
101 L24 **Benediktenwand** ▲ S Germany *47°39′N 11°28′E*
Benemérita de San Cristóbal *see* San Cristóbal
77 N12 **Bénéna** Ségou, S Mali *13°04′N 04°20′W*
172 I7 **Benenitra** Toliara, S Madagascar *23°25′S 45°06′E*
Beneschau *see* Benešov
Beneški Zaliv *see* Venice, Gulf of
111 D17 **Benešov** *Ger.* Beneschau. Středočeský Kraj, W Czech Republic *49°48′N 14°41′E*
107 L17 **Benevento** *anc.* Beneventum, Malventum. Campania, S Italy *41°07′N 14°45′E*
Beneventum *see* Benevento
173 S3 **Bengal, Bay of** *bay* N Indian Ocean
Bengalooru *see* Bangalore
79 M17 **Bengamisa** Orientale, N Dem. Rep. Congo *0°58′N 25°11′E*
Bengasi *see* Banghāzī
Bengazi *see* Banghāzī
161 P7 **Bengbu** *var.* Peng-pu. Anhui, E China *32°57′N 117°17′E*
32 L9 **Benge** Washington, NW USA *46°55′N 118°01′W*
Benghazi *see* Banghāzī
168 K10 **Bengkalis** Pulau Bengkalis, W Indonesia *01°27′N 102°10′E*
168 K10 **Bengkalis, Pulau** *island* W Indonesia
169 Q10 **Bengkayang** Borneo, C Indonesia *0°45′N 109°28′E*
168 K14 **Bengkulu** *prev.* Bengkoeloe, Benkoelen, Benkulen. Sumatera, W Indonesia *03°46′S 102°16′E*
168 K13 **Bengkulu** *off.* Propinsi Bengkulu; *prev.* Bengkoeloe, Benkoelen, Benkulen. ◈ *province* W Indonesia
Bengkulu, Propinsi *see* Bengkulu
82 A11 **Bengo** ◈ *province* W Angola
95 J16 **Bengtsfors** Västra Götaland, S Sweden *59°03′N 12°14′E*
82 B13 **Benguela** *var.* Benguella. Benguela, W Angola *12°35′S 13°30′E*
83 A14 **Benguela** ◈ *province* W Angola
Benguella *see* Benguela
138 F10 **Ben Gurion** ✈ Tel Aviv, C Israel *32°04′N 34°45′E*
Bengweulu, Lake *see* Bangweulu, Lake
Benha *see* Banhā
192 F6 **Benham Seamount** *undersea feature* W Philippine Sea *15°48′N 124°15′E*
96 H6 **Ben Hope** ▲ N Scotland, United Kingdom *58°25′N 04°36′W*
79 P18 **Beni** Nord-Kivu, NE Dem. Rep. Congo *0°31′N 29°30′E*
74 H8 **Beni Abbès** W Algeria *30°07′N 02°09′W*
105 T8 **Benicarló** Valenciana, E Spain *40°25′N 00°25′E*
105 T9 **Benicasim** *Cat.* Benicàssim. Valenciana, E Spain *40°03′N 00°03′E*
Benicàssim *see* Benicasim
105 T12 **Benidorm** Valenciana, SE Spain *38°33′N 00°09′W*
Beni Mazâr *see* Banī Mazār
121 C11 **Beni-Mellal** C Morocco *32°20′N 06°21′W*
77 R14 **Benin** *off.* Republic of Benin; *prev.* Dahomey. ◆ *republic* W Africa
77 S17 **Benin, Bight of** *gulf* W Africa
77 U16 **Benin City** Edo, SW Nigeria *06°23′N 05°40′E*
Benin, Republic of *see* Benin
57 K16 **Beni, Río** ~ N Bolivia
120 F10 **Beni Saf** *var.* Beni-Saf. NW Algeria *35°19′N 01°23′W*
Beni-Saf *see* Beni Saf
Benishangul *see* Bīnshangul Gumuz
105 T11 **Benissa** Valenciana, E Spain *38°43′N 00°03′E*
Beni Suef *see* Banī Suwayf
11 V15 **Benito** Manitoba, S Canada *51°57′N 101°24′W*
Benito *see* Uolo, Río
61 C23 **Benito Juárez** Buenos Aires, E Argentina *37°43′S 59°48′W*
41 P14 **Benito Juárez Internacional** ✈ (México) México, S Mexico *19°24′N 99°02′W*
25 P5 **Benjamin** Texas, SW USA *33°35′N 99°49′W*
58 B13 **Benjamin Constant** Amazonas, N Brazil *04°22′S 70°02′W*
40 F4 **Benjamín Hill** Sonora, NW Mexico *30°13′N 111°08′W*
63 F19 **Benjamín, Isla** *island* Archipiélago de los Chonos, S Chile
164 Q4 **Benkei-misaki** *headland* Hokkaidō, NE Japan *42°49′N 140°10′E*
28 L17 **Benkelman** Nebraska, C USA *40°04′N 101°30′W*
96 I7 **Ben Klibreck** ▲ N Scotland, United Kingdom *58°15′N 04°23′W*
Benkoelen/Bengkoeloe *see* Bengkulu
112 D13 **Benkovac** *It.* Bencovazzo. Zadar, SW Croatia *44°02′N 15°36′E*
Benkulen *see* Bengkulu
96 I11 **Ben Lawers** ▲ C Scotland, United Kingdom *56°33′N 04°13′W*
96 J9 **Ben Macdui** *var.* Beinn MacDuibh. ▲ C Scotland, United Kingdom *57°02′N 03°42′W*
96 G11 **Ben More** ▲ W Scotland, United Kingdom *56°26′N 06°00′W*
96 I11 **Ben More** ▲ C Scotland, United Kingdom *56°22′N 04°31′W*
96 H7 **Ben More Assynt** ▲ N Scotland, United Kingdom *58°09′N 04°51′W*
185 E20 **Benmore, Lake** ◎ South Island, New Zealand
98 L12 **Bennekom** Gelderland, SE Netherlands *52°00′N 05°40′E*
123 Q5 **Bennetta, Ostrov** *island* Novosibirskiye Ostrova, NE Russian Federation
21 T11 **Bennettsville** South Carolina, SE USA *34°36′N 79°40′W*
96 H10 **Ben Nevis** ▲ N Scotland, United Kingdom *56°80′N 05°00′W*
184 M9 **Benneydale** Waikato, North Island, New Zealand *38°31′S 175°22′E*
Bennichab *see* Bennichchâb
76 H8 **Bennichchâb** *var.* Bennichab. Inchiri, W Mauritania *19°26′N 15°21′W*
18 L10 **Bennington** Vermont, NE USA *42°51′N 73°09′W*
185 E20 **Ben Ohau Range** ▲▲ South Island, New Zealand
83 J21 **Benoni** Gauteng, NE South Africa *26°04′S 28°18′E*
172 J2 **Be, Nosy** *var.* Nossi-Bé. *island* NW Madagascar
Bénoué *see* Benue
42 F2 **Benque Viejo del Carmen** Cayo, W Belize *17°04′N 89°08′W*
101 G19 **Bensheim** Hessen, W Germany *49°41′N 08°38′E*
37 N16 **Benson** Arizona, SW USA *31°55′N 110°16′W*
29 S8 **Benson** Minnesota, N USA *45°19′N 95°36′W*
21 U10 **Benson** North Carolina, SE USA *35°22′N 78°33′W*
171 N15 **Benteng** Pulau Selayar, C Indonesia *06°07′S 120°28′E*
83 A14 **Bentiaba** Namibe, SW Angola *14°18′S 12°27′E*
181 T4 **Bentinck Island** *island* Wellesley Islands, Queensland, N Australia
80 E13 **Bentiu** Wahda, N South Sudan *09°14′N 29°49′E*
138 G8 **Bent Jbaïl** *var.* Bint Jubayl. S Lebanon *33°07′N 35°26′E*
11 Q15 **Bentley** Alberta, SW Canada *52°27′N 114°02′W*
61 I15 **Bento Gonçalves** Rio Grande do Sul, S Brazil *29°12′S 51°34′W*
27 U12 **Benton** Arkansas, C USA *34°34′N 92°35′W*
30 L16 **Benton** Illinois, N USA *38°00′N 88°55′W*
20 H7 **Benton** Kentucky, S USA *36°51′N 88°21′W*
22 G5 **Benton** Louisiana, S USA *32°41′N 93°44′W*
27 Y7 **Benton** Missouri, C USA *37°05′N 89°34′W*
20 M10 **Benton** Tennessee, S USA *35°10′N 84°39′W*
31 O10 **Benton Harbor** Michigan, N USA *42°07′N 86°27′W*
27 S9 **Bentonville** Arkansas, C USA *36°23′N 94°13′W*
77 V16 **Benue** ◈ *state* SE Nigeria
78 F13 **Benue** *Fr.* Bénoué. ~ Cameroon/Nigeria
163 V12 **Benxi** *prev.* Pen-ch'i, Penhsihu, Penki. Liaoning, NE China *41°20′N 123°45′E*
Benyakoni *see* Byenyakoni
112 K10 **Beočin** Vojvodina, N Serbia *45°13′N 19°43′E*
Beodericsworth *see* Bury St Edmunds
112 M11 **Beograd** *Eng.* Belgrade, *Ger.* Belgrad; *anc.* Singidunum. ● (Serbia) Serbia, N Serbia *44°48′N 20°27′E*
112 L11 **Beograd** *Eng.* Belgrade. ✈ Serbia, N Serbia *44°45′N 20°21′E*
76 M16 **Béoumi** C Ivory Coast *07°40′N 05°34′W*
35 V3 **Beowawe** Nevada, W USA *40°33′N 116°31′W*
164 E14 **Beppu** Ōita, Kyūshū, SW Japan *33°18′N 131°30′E*
187 X15 **Beqa** *prev.* Mbengga. *island* W Fiji
45 Y14 **Bequia** *island* C Saint Vincent and the Grenadines
113 L16 **Berane** *prev.* Ivangrad. E Montenegro *42°51′N 19°51′E*
113 L21 **Berat** *var.* Berati, *SCr.* Beligrad. Berat, C Albania *40°43′N 19°58′E*
113 L21 **Berat** ◈ *district* C Albania
Berătău *see* Berettyó
Berati *see* Berat
Beraun *see* Berounka, Czech Republic
Beraun *see* Beroun, Czech Republic
171 U13 **Berau, Teluk** *var.* MacCluer Gulf. *bay* Papua, E Indonesia
80 G8 **Berber** River Nile, NE Sudan *18°01′N 34°00′E*
80 N12 **Berbera** Woqooyi Galbeed, NW Somalia *10°24′N 45°02′E*
79 H16 **Berbérati** Mambéré-Kadéï, SW Central African Republic *04°14′N 15°50′E*
Berberia, Cabo de *see* Barbaria, Cap de
55 T9 **Berbice River** ~ NE Guyana
Berchid *see* Berrechid
103 N2 **Berck-Plage** Pas-de-Calais, N France *50°24′N 01°35′E*
25 T13 **Berclair** Texas, SW USA *28°33′N 97°32′W*
117 W10 **Berda** ~ SE Ukraine
Berdichev *see* Berdychiv
123 P10 **Berdigestyakh** Respublika Sakha (Yakutiya), NE Russian Federation *62°02′N 127°03′E*
122 J12 **Berdsk** Novosibirskaya Oblast', C Russian Federation *54°42′N 82°56′E*
117 W10 **Berdyans'k** *Rus.* Berdyansk; *prev.* Osipenko. Zaporiz'ka Oblast', SE Ukraine *46°46′N 36°49′E*
117 W10 **Berdyans'ka Kosa** *spit* SE Ukraine
117 V10 **Berdyans'ka Zatoka** *gulf* S Ukraine
117 N5 **Berdychiv** *Rus.* Berdichev. Zhytomyrs'ka Oblast', N Ukraine *49°54′N 28°39′E*
20 M6 **Berea** Kentucky, S USA *37°34′N 84°18′W*
Beregovo/Beregszász *see* Berehove
116 G8 **Berehove** *Cz.* Berehovo, *Hung.* Beregszász, *Rus.* Beregovo. Zakarpats'ka Oblast', W Ukraine *48°13′N 22°39′E*
Berehovo *see* Berehove
186 D9 **Bereina** Central, S Papua New Guinea *08°29′S 146°30′E*
146 C11 **Bereket** *prev. Rus.* Gazandzhyk, Kazandzhik, *Turkm.* Gazanjyk. Balkan Welaýaty, W Turkmenistan *39°17′N 55°27′E*
45 O12 **Berekua** S Dominica *15°14′N 61°19′W*
77 O16 **Berekum** W Ghana *07°27′N 02°35′W*
Berenice *see* Baranīs
11 O14 **Berens** ~ Manitoba/ Ontario, C Canada
11 X14 **Berens River** Manitoba, C Canada *52°22′N 97°00′W*
29 R12 **Beresford** South Dakota, N USA *43°02′N 96°45′W*
116 J4 **Berestechko** Volyns'ka Oblast', NW Ukraine *50°21′N 25°06′E*
116 M11 **Bereşti** Galaţi, E Romania *46°04′N 27°54′E*
117 U6 **Berestova** ~ E Ukraine
Beretău *see* Berettyó
111 N23 **Berettyó** *Rom.* Barcău; *prev.* Berătău, Beretău. ~ Hungary/Romania
111 N23 **Berettyóújfalu** Hajdú-Bihar, E Hungary *47°15′N 21°33′E*
Berëza/Bereza Kartuska *see* Byaroza
117 Q4 **Berezan'** Kyyivs'ka Oblast', N Ukraine *50°18′N 31°30′E*
117 Q10 **Berezanka** Mykolayivs'ka Oblast', S Ukraine *46°51′N 31°24′E*
116 J6 **Berezhany** *Pol.* Brzeżany. Ternopil's'ka Oblast', W Ukraine *49°29′N 25°00′E*
Berezina *see* Byarezina
Berezino *see* Byerazino
117 P10 **Berezivka** *Rus.* Berezovka. Odes'ka Oblast', SW Ukraine *47°12′N 30°56′E*
117 Q2 **Berezna** Chernihivs'ka Oblast', NE Ukraine *51°35′N 31°50′E*
116 L3 **Berezne** Rivnens'ka Oblast', NW Ukraine *51°00′N 26°46′E*
117 R9 **Bereznehuvate** Mykolayivs'ka Oblast', S Ukraine *47°18′N 32°52′E*
125 N10 **Bereznik** Arkhangel'skaya Oblast', NW Russian Federation *62°50′N 42°40′E*
125 U13 **Berezniki** Permskiy Kray, NW Russian Federation *59°26′N 56°49′E*
Berëzovka *see* Byarozawka, Belarus
Berezovka *see* Berezivka, Ukraine
122 H9 **Berezovo** Khanty-Mansiyskiy Avtonomnyy Okrug-Yugra, N Russian Federation *63°48′N 64°38′E*
127 O9 **Berezovskaya** Volgogradskaya Oblast', SW Russian Federation *50°17′N 43°58′E*
123 S13 **Berezovyy** Khabarovskiy Kray, E Russian Federation *51°42′N 135°39′E*
83 E25 **Berg** ~ W South Africa
Berg *see* Berg bei Rohrbach
105 V4 **Berga** Cataluña, NE Spain *42°06′N 01°41′E*
95 N20 **Berga** Kalmar, S Sweden *57°13′N 16°03′E*
136 B13 **Bergama** İzmir, W Turkey *39°08′N 27°10′E*
106 E7 **Bergamo** *anc.* Bergomum. Lombardia, N Italy *45°42′N 09°40′E*
105 P3 **Bergara** País Vasco, N Spain *43°05′N 02°25′W*
109 S3 **Berg bei Rohrbach** *var.* Berg. Oberösterreich, N Austria *48°34′N 14°02′E*
100 O6 **Bergen** Mecklenburg-Vorpommern, NE Germany *54°25′N 13°25′E*
101 I11 **Bergen** Niedersachsen, NW Germany *52°49′N 09°57′E*
98 H8 **Bergen** Noord-Holland, NW Netherlands *52°40′N 04°42′E*
94 C13 **Bergen** Hordaland, S Norway *60°24′N 05°19′E*
Bergen *see* Mons
55 W9 **Berg en Dal** Brokopondo, C Surinam *05°15′N 55°20′W*
99 G15 **Bergen op Zoom** Noord-Brabant, S Netherlands *51°30′N 04°17′E*
102 L13 **Bergerac** Dordogne, SW France *44°51′N 00°30′E*
99 J16 **Bergeyk** Noord-Brabant, S Netherlands *51°19′N 05°21′E*
101 D16 **Bergheim** Nordrhein-Westfalen, W Germany *50°57′N 06°39′E*
55 X10 **Bergi** Sipaliwini, E Surinam *04°36′N 54°24′W*
101 E16 **Bergisch Gladbach** Nordrhein-Westfalen, W Germany *50°59′N 07°09′E*
101 F14 **Bergkamen** Nordrhein-Westfalen, W Germany *51°32′N 07°41′E*
95 N21 **Bergkvara** Kalmar, S Sweden *56°22′N 16°04′E*
Bergomum *see* Bergamo
98 K13 **Bergse Maas** ~ S Netherlands

◆ Country
● Country Capital
◇ Dependent Territory
○ Dependent Territory Capital
◈ Administrative Regions
✈ International Airport
▲ Mountain
▲▲ Mountain Range
Volcano
~ River
◎ Lake
⊠ Reservoir

95 P15 **Bergshamra** Stockholm, C Sweden 59°37′N 18°40′E
94 N10 **Bergsjö** Gävleborg, C Sweden 62°00′N 17°10′E
93 J14 **Bergsviken** Norrbotten, N Sweden 65°16′N 21°24′E
Bergum *see* Burgum
98 M6 **Bergumer Meer** ◎ N Netherlands
94 N12 **Bergviken** ◎ C Sweden
168 M11 **Berhala, Selat** *strait* Sumatera, W Indonesia
Berhampore *see* Baharampur
99 J17 **Beringen** Limburg, NE Belgium 51°04′N 05°14′E
39 T12 **Bering Glacier** *glacier* Alaska, USA
Beringov Proliv *see* Bering Strait
192 L2 **Bering Sea** *sea* N Pacific Ocean
38 L9 **Bering Strait** *Rus.* Beringov Proliv. *strait* Bering Sea/ Chukchi Sea
Berislav *see* Beryslav
105 O15 **Berja** Andalucía, S Spain 36°51′N 02°56′W
94 H9 **Berkåk** Sør-Trøndelag, S Norway 62°50′N 10°01′E
98 N11 **Berkel** ≈ Germany/ Netherlands
35 N8 **Berkeley** California, W USA 37°52′N 122°16′W
65 E24 **Berkeley Sound** *sound* NE Falkland Islands
21 V2 **Berkeley Springs** *var.* Bath. West Virginia, NE USA 39°38′N 78°14′W
195 N6 **Berkner Island** *island* Antarctica
114 G8 **Berkovitsa** Montana, NW Bulgaria 43°15′N 23°05′E
97 M22 **Berkshire** *former county* S England, United Kingdom
99 H17 **Berlaar** Antwerpen, N Belgium 51°08′N 04°39′E
Berlanga *see* Berlanga de Duero
105 P6 **Berlanga de Duero** *var.* Berlanga. Castilla y León, N Spain 41°28′N 02°51′W
0 I16 **Berlanga Rise** *undersea feature* E Pacific Ocean 08°30′N 93°30′W
99 F17 **Berlare** Oost-Vlaanderen, NW Belgium 51°02′N 04°01′E
104 E9 **Berlenga, Ilha da** *island* C Portugal
92 M7 **Berlevåg** *Lapp.* Bearalváhki. Finnmark, N Norway 70°51′N 29°04′E
100 O12 **Berlin** ● (Germany) Berlin, NE Germany 52°31′N 13°26′E
21 Z4 **Berlin** Maryland, NE USA 38°19′N 75°13′W
19 O7 **Berlin** New Hampshire, NE USA 44°27′N 71°13′W
18 D16 **Berlin** Pennsylvania, NE USA 39°54′N 78°57′W
30 L7 **Berlin** Wisconsin, N USA 43°57′N 88°59′W
100 O12 **Berlin** ◈ *state* NE Germany
Berlinchen *see* Barlinek
31 U12 **Berlin Lake** ⊠ Ohio, N USA
183 R11 **Bermagui** New South Wales, SE Australia 36°26′S 150°01′E
40 L8 **Bermejillo** Durango, C Mexico 25°55′N 103°39′W
62 L5 **Bermejo, Río** ≈ N Argentina
62 I10 **Bermejo, Río** ≈ W Argentina
62 M6 **Bermejo viejo, Río** ≈ N Argentina
105 P2 **Bermeo** País Vasco, N Spain 43°25′N 02°44′W
104 K6 **Bermillo de Sayago** Castilla y León, N Spain 41°22′N 06°08′W
106 E6 **Bermina, Pizzo** *Rmsch.* Piz Bernina. ▲ Italy/Switzerland 46°22′N 09°52′E *see also* Bermina, Piz
64 A12 **Bermuda** *var.* Bermuda Islands, Bermudas; *prev.* Somers Islands. ◇ *UK crown colony* NW Atlantic Ocean
1 N11 **Bermuda** *var.* Great Bermuda, Long Island, Main Island. *island* Bermuda
Bermuda Islands *see* Bermuda
Bermuda-New England Seamount Arc *see* New England Seamounts
1 N11 **Bermuda Rise** *undersea feature* C Sargasso Sea 32°30′N 65°00′W
Bermudas *see* Bermuda
108 D8 **Bern** *Fr.* Berne. ● (Switzerland) Bern, W Switzerland 46°57′N 07°26′E
108 D9 **Bern** *Fr.* Berne. ◈ *canton* W Switzerland
37 R11 **Bernalillo** New Mexico, SW USA 35°18′N 106°33′W
14 H12 **Bernard Lake** ◎ Ontario, S Canada
61 B18 **Bernardo de Irigoyen** Santa Fe, NE Argentina 32°09′S 61°06′W
18 J14 **Bernardsville** New Jersey, NE USA 40°43′N 74°34′W
63 K14 **Bernasconi** La Pampa, C Argentina 37°55′S 63°44′W
100 O12 **Bernau** Brandenburg, NE Germany 52°41′N 13°36′E
102 L4 **Bernay** Eure, N France 49°05′N 00°36′E
101 L14 **Bernburg** Sachsen-Anhalt, C Germany 51°47′N 11°45′E
109 X5 **Berndorf** Niederösterreich, NE Austria 47°58′N 16°08′E
31 Q12 **Berne** Indiana, N USA 40°39′N 84°57′W
Berne *see* Bern
108 D10 **Berner Alpen** *var.* Berner Oberland, *Eng.* Bernese Oberland. ▲▲ SW Switzerland
Berner Oberland/Bernese Oberland *see* Berner Alpen
109 Y2 **Bernhardsthal** Niederösterreich, N Austria 48°40′N 16°51′E
22 H4 **Bernice** Louisiana, S USA 32°49′N 92°39′W
27 Y8 **Bernie** Missouri, C USA 36°40′N 89°58′W
180 G9 **Bernier Island** *island* Western Australia
Bernina Pass *see* Bernina, Passo del
108 J10 **Bernina, Passo del** *Eng.* Bernina Pass. *pass* SE Switzerland
108 J10 **Bernina, Piz** *It.* Pizzo Bernina. ▲ Italy/Switzerland 46°22′N 09°55′E *see also* Bermina, Pizzo
Bernina, Piz *see* Bermina, Pizzo
99 E20 **Bernissart** Hainaut, SW Belgium 50°29′N 03°37′E
101 E18 **Bernkastel-Kues** Rheinland-Pfalz, W Germany 49°55′N 07°04′E
Beroea *see* Ḩalab
172 H6 **Beroroha** Toliara, SW Madagascar 21°40′S 45°10′E
Béroubouay *see* Gbéroubouè
111 C17 **Beroun** *Ger.* Beraun. Středočeský Kraj, W Czech Republic 49°58′N 14°05′E
111 C16 **Berounka** *Ger.* Beraun. ≈ W Czech Republic
113 Q18 **Berovo** E FYR Macedonia 41°45′N 22°50′E
74 F6 **Berrechid** *var.* Berchid. W Morocco 33°16′N 07°32′W
103 R15 **Berre, Étang de** ◎ SE France
103 S15 **Berre-l'Étang** Bouches-du-Rhône, SE France 43°28′N 05°10′E
182 K9 **Berri** South Australia 34°16′S 140°35′E
31 O10 **Berrien Springs** Michigan, N USA 41°57′N 86°20′W
183 O10 **Berrigan** New South Wales, SE Australia 35°41′S 145°50′E
103 N9 **Berry** *cultural region* C France
35 N7 **Berryessa, Lake** ◎ California, W USA
44 G2 **Berry Islands** *island group* N Bahamas
27 T9 **Berryville** Arkansas, C USA 36°22′N 93°35′W
21 V3 **Berryville** Virginia, NE USA 39°08′N 77°59′W
83 D21 **Berseba** Karas, S Namibia 26°00′S 17°46′E
117 O8 **Bershad'** Vinnyts'ka Oblast', C Ukraine 48°20′N 29°30′E
28 L3 **Berthold** North Dakota, N USA 48°16′N 101°48′W
37 T3 **Berthoud** Colorado, C USA 40°18′N 105°04′W
37 S4 **Berthoud Pass** *pass* Colorado, C USA
79 F15 **Bertoua** Est, E Cameroon 04°34′N 13°42′E
25 S10 **Bertram** Texas, SW USA 30°44′N 98°03′W
63 G22 **Bertrand, Cerro** ▲ S Argentina 50°00′S 73°27′W
99 J23 **Bertrix** Luxembourg, SE Belgium 49°52′N 05°15′E
191 P3 **Beru** *var.* Peru. *atoll* Tungaru, W Kiribati
Beruni *see* Beruniy
146 I9 **Beruniy** *var.* Biruni, *Rus.* Beruni. Qoraqalpog'iston Respublikasi, W Uzbekistan 41°48′N 60°39′E
58 F13 **Beruri** Amazonas, NW Brazil 03°44′S 61°13′W
18 H14 **Berwick** Pennsylvania, NE USA 41°03′N 76°13′W
96 K12 **Berwick** *cultural region* SE Scotland, United Kingdom
96 L12 **Berwick-upon-Tweed** N England, United Kingdom 55°46′N 02°W
117 S10 **Beryslav** *Rus.* Berislav. Khersons'ka Oblast', S Ukraine 46°51′N 33°26′E
Berytus *see* Beyrouth
172 H4 **Besalampy** Mahajanga, W Madagascar 16°43′S 44°29′E
103 T8 **Besançon** *anc.* Besontium, Vesontio. Doubs, E France 47°14′N 06°01′E
103 P10 **Besbre** ≈ C France
Bescanuova *see* Baška
Besdan *see* Bezdan
Besed' *see* Byesyedz'
147 R10 **Besharyq** *Rus.* Besharyk; *prev.* Kirovo. Farg'ona Viloyati, E Uzbekistan 40°26′N 70°33′E
Besharyk *see* Besharyq
146 L9 **Beshbuloq** *Rus.* Beshulak. Navoiy Viloyati, N Uzbekistan 41°55′N 64°13′E
Beshenkovichi *see* Byeshankovichy
146 M13 **Beshkent** Qashqadaryo Viloyati, S Uzbekistan 38°47′N 65°42′E
Beshulak *see* Beshbuloq
112 L10 **Beška** Vojvodina, N Serbia 45°09′N 20°04′E
Beskra *see* Biskra
127 O16 **Beslan** Respublika Severnaya Osetiya, SW Russian Federation 43°12′N 44°33′E
113 P16 **Besna Kobila** ▲ SE Serbia 42°30′N 22°16′E
137 N16 **Besni** Adıyaman, S Turkey 37°42′N 37°53′E
Besontium *see* Besançon
121 Q2 **Beşparmak Dağları** *Eng.* Kyrenia Mountains. ▲▲ Cyprus
Bessarabka *see* Basarabeasca
92 O2 **Bessels, Kapp** *headland* C Svalbard 78°36′N 21°43′E
23 P4 **Bessemer** Alabama, S USA 33°24′N 86°57′W
30 K3 **Bessemer** Michigan, N USA 46°28′N 90°03′W
21 Q10 **Bessemer City** North Carolina, SE USA 35°16′N 81°16′W
102 M10 **Bessines-sur-Gartempe** Haute-Vienne, C France 46°06′N 01°22′E
99 K15 **Best** Noord-Brabant, S Netherlands 51°31′N 05°24′E
25 N9 **Best** Texas, SW USA 31°13′N 101°34′W
125 O11 **Bestuzhevo** Arkhangel'skaya Oblast', NW Russian Federation 61°36′N 43°54′E
123 M11 **Bestyakh** Respublika Sakha (Yakutiya), NE Russian Federation 61°25′N 129°05′E
Beszterce *see* Bistriţa
Besztercebánya *see* Banská Bystrica
172 I5 **Betafo** Antananarivo, C Madagascar 19°50′S 46°50′E
104 H2 **Betanzos** Galicia, NW Spain 43°17′N 08°17′W
104 G2 **Betanzos, Ría de** *estuary* NW Spain
79 G15 **Bétaré Oya** Est, E Cameroon 05°34′N 14°09′E
105 S9 **Bétera** Valenciana, E Spain 39°35′N 00°28′W
77 R15 **Bétérou** C Benin 09°13′N 02°18′E
83 K21 **Bethal** Mpumalanga, NE South Africa 26°27′S 29°28′E
30 K15 **Bethalto** Illinois, N USA 38°54′N 90°02′W
83 D21 **Bethanie** *var.* Bethanien, Bethany. Karas, S Namibia 26°32′S 17°11′E
Bethanien *see* Bethanie
27 S2 **Bethany** Missouri, C USA 40°15′N 94°03′W
27 N10 **Bethany** Oklahoma, C USA 35°31′N 97°37′W
Bethany *see* Bethanie
39 N12 **Bethel** Alaska, USA 60°47′N 161°45′W
19 P7 **Bethel** Maine, NE USA 44°24′N 70°47′W
21 W9 **Bethel** North Carolina, SE USA 35°46′N 77°21′W
18 B15 **Bethel Park** Pennsylvania, NE USA 40°21′N 80°03′W
21 W3 **Bethesda** Maryland, NE USA 39°00′N 77°05′W
83 J22 **Bethlehem** Free State, C South Africa 28°12′S 28°16′E
18 I14 **Bethlehem** Pennsylvania, NE USA 40°36′N 75°22′W
138 F10 **Bethlehem** *var.* Beit Lekhem, *Ar.* Bayt Laḩm, *Heb.* Bet Leḩem. C West Bank 31°43′N 35°12′E
Bethlen *see* Beclean
83 I24 **Bethulie** Free State, C South Africa 30°30′S 25°59′E
103 O1 **Béthune** Pas-de-Calais, N France 50°32′N 02°38′E
102 M3 **Béthune** ≈ N France
104 M14 **Béticos, Sistemas** *var.* Sistema Penibético, *Eng.* Baetic Cordillera, Baetic Mountains. ▲▲ S Spain
54 I6 **Betijoque** Trujillo, NW Venezuela 09°25′N 70°45′W
59 M20 **Betim** Minas Gerais, SE Brazil 19°56′S 44°10′W
190 H3 **Betio** Tarawa, W Kiribati 01°21′N 172°56′E
172 H7 **Betioky** Toliara, S Madagascar 23°42′S 44°22′E
Bet Leḩem *see* Bethlehem
Betlen *see* Beclean
167 O17 **Betong** Yala, SW Thailand 05°45′N 101°05′E
79 I16 **Bétou** Likouala, N Congo 03°08′N 18°31′E
145 P14 **Betpakdala** *prev.* Betpak-Dala *Kaz.* Betpaqdala. *plateau* S Kazakhstan
Betpak-Dala *see* Betpakdala
Betpaqdala *see* Betpakdala
172 H7 **Betroka** Toliara, S Madagascar 23°15′S 46°07′E
Betschau *see* Bečva
Bet She'an *see* Beit She'an
15 T6 **Betsiamites** Québec, SE Canada 48°56′N 68°40′W
15 T6 **Betsiamites** ≈ Québec, SE Canada
172 I4 **Betsiboka** ≈ N Madagascar
Betsukai *see* Bekkai
99 M25 **Bettembourg** Luxembourg, S Luxembourg 49°31′N 06°06′E
99 M23 **Bettendorf** Diekirch, NE Luxembourg 49°53′N 06°13′E
29 Z14 **Bettendorf** Iowa, C USA 41°31′N 90°31′W
Bette, Pic *see* Bette, Picco
75 R13 **Bette, Picco** *var.* Bikkū Bīttī, Pic Bette. ▲ S Libya 22°02′N 19°07′E
153 P12 **Bettiah** Bihār, N India 26°49′N 84°30′E
39 Q7 **Bettles** Alaska, USA 66°54′N 151°40′W
95 N17 **Bettna** Södermanland, C Sweden 58°52′N 16°40′E
154 H11 **Betūl** *prev.* Badnur. Madhya Pradesh, C India 21°55′N 77°54′E
154 H9 **Betwa** ≈ C India
101 F16 **Betzdorf** Rheinland-Pfalz, W Germany 50°47′N 07°50′E
82 C9 **Béu** Uíge, NW Angola 06°15′S 15°32′E
31 P6 **Beulah** Michigan, N USA 43°35′N 83°52′W
28 L5 **Beulah** North Dakota, N USA 47°16′N 101°48′W
98 M8 **Beulakerwijde** ◎ N Netherlands
98 L13 **Beuningen** Gelderland, SE Netherlands 51°52′N 05°47′E
Beuthen *see* Bytom
103 N7 **Beuvron** ≈ C France
99 F16 **Beveren** Oost-Vlaanderen, N Belgium 51°13′N 04°15′E
21 T9 **B. Everett Jordan Reservoir** *var.* Jordan Lake. ⊠ North Carolina, SE USA
97 N17 **Beverley** E England, United Kingdom 53°51′N 00°26′W
Beverley *see* Beverly
99 J17 **Beverlo** Limburg, NE Belgium 51°06′N 05°14′E
19 P11 **Beverly** Massachusetts, NE USA 42°33′N 70°49′W
32 J9 **Beverly** Washington, NW USA 46°50′N 119°57′W
Beverly *see* Beverley
35 S15 **Beverly Hills** California, W USA 34°02′N 118°25′W
101 I14 **Beverungen** Nordrhein-Westfalen, C Germany 51°39′N 09°22′E
98 H9 **Beverwijk** Noord-Holland, W Netherlands 52°29′N 04°40′E
108 C10 **Bex** Vaud, W Switzerland 46°15′N 07°00′E
97 P23 **Bexhill** *var.* Bexhill-on-Sea. SE England, United Kingdom 50°50′N 00°28′E
Bexhill-on-Sea *see* Bexhill
136 E17 **Bey Dağları** ▲▲ SW Turkey
Beyj *see* Belyy
136 E10 **Beykoz** İstanbul, NW Turkey 41°09′N 29°06′E
76 K15 **Beyla** SE Guinea 08°43′N 08°41′W
137 X12 **Beyläqan** *prev.* Zhdanov. SW Azerbaijan 39°43′N 47°38′E
80 L10 **Beylul** *var.* Beilul. SE Eritrea 13°10′N 42°27′E
144 H14 **Beyneu** *Kaz.* Beyneū. Mangistau, SW Kazakhstan 45°20′N 55°11′E
Beyneū *see* Beyneu
165 X14 **Beyonēsu-retsugan** *Eng.* Bayonnaise Rocks. *island group* SE Japan
136 G12 **Beypazarı** Ankara, NW Turkey 40°10′N 31°56′E
155 F21 **Beypore** Kerala, SW India 11°10′N 75°49′E
138 G7 **Beyrouth** *var.* Bayrūt, *Eng.* Beirut; *anc.* Berytus. ● (Lebanon) W Lebanon 33°55′N 35°31′E
138 G7 **Beyrouth** ✈ W Lebanon 33°52′N 35°30′E
136 G15 **Beyşehir** Konya, SW Turkey 37°40′N 31°43′E
136 G15 **Beyşehir Gölü** ◎ C Turkey
108 J7 **Bezau** Vorarlberg, NW Austria 47°24′N 09°55′E
112 J8 **Bezdan** *Ger.* Besdan, *Hung.* Bezdán. Vojvodina, NW Serbia 45°51′N 19°00′E
Bezdezh *see* Byezdzyezh
124 G15 **Bezhanitsy** Pskovskaya Oblast', W Russian Federation 56°57′N 29°53′E
124 K15 **Bezhetsk** Tverskaya Oblast', W Russian Federation 57°47′N 36°42′E
103 P16 **Béziers** *anc.* Baeterrae, Baeterrae Septimanorum, Julia Beterrae. Hérault, S France 43°21′N 03°13′E
Bezmein *see* Abadan
Bezwada *see* Vijayawāda
154 P12 **Bhadrak** *var.* Bhadrakh. Orissa, E India 21°04′N 86°30′N
Bhadrakh *see* Bhadrak
155 F19 **Bhadra Reservoir** ⊠ SW India
155 F18 **Bhadrāvati** Karnātaka, SW India 13°52′N 75°43′E
153 R14 **Bhāgalpur** Bihār, NE India 25°14′N 86°59′E
Bhairab *see* Bhairab Bazar
153 U14 **Bhairab Bazar** *var.* Bhairab. Dhaka, C Bangladesh 24°04′N 91°00′E
153 O11 **Bhairahawā** Western, S Nepal 27°31′N 83°27′E
149 S8 **Bhakkar** Punjab, E Pakistan 31°40′N 71°08′E
153 P11 **Bhaktapur** Central, C Nepal 27°47′N 85°21′E
167 N3 **Bhamo** *var.* Banmo. Kachin State, N Burma (Myanmar) 24°15′N 97°15′E
Bhāmragad *see* Bhāmragarh
154 K13 **Bhāmragarh** *var.* Bhāmragad. Mahārāshtra, C India 19°28′N 80°39′E
154 J12 **Bhandāra** Mahārāshtra, C India 21°10′N 79°41′E
Bhārat *see* India
152 J12 **Bharatpur** *prev.* Bhurtpore. Rājasthān, N India 27°14′N 77°29′E
154 D11 **Bharūch** Gujarāt, W India 21°48′N 72°55′E
155 E18 **Bhatkal** Karnātaka, W India 13°59′N 74°34′E
153 O13 **Bhatni** *var.* Bhatni Junction. Uttar Pradesh, N India 26°23′N 83°56′E
Bhatni Junction *see* Bhatni
153 S16 **Bhātpāra** West Bengal, NE India 22°55′N 88°30′E
149 U7 **Bhaun** Punjab, E Pakistan 32°53′N 72°48′E
Bhaunagar *see* Bhāvnagar
Bhavānīpātna *see* Bhawānipatna
155 H21 **Bhavānīsāgar** ⊠ S India
154 D11 **Bhāvnagar** *prev.* Bhaunagar. Gujarāt, W India 21°46′N 72°14′E
154 M13 **Bhawānipatna** *var.* Bhavānīpātna. Orissa, E India 19°56′N 83°09′E
Bheanntraí, Bá *see* Bantry Bay
Bheara, Béal an *see* Gweebarra Bay
154 K12 **Bhilai** Chhattīsgarh, C India 21°12′N 81°26′E
152 G13 **Bhīlwāra** Rājasthān, N India 25°23′N 74°39′E
155 E14 **Bhīma** ≈ S India
155 K16 **Bhimavaram** Andhra Pradesh, E India 16°34′N 81°35′E
154 I7 **Bhind** Madhya Pradesh, C India 26°33′N 78°47′E
152 E13 **Bhīnmāl** Rājasthān, N India 25°01′N 72°22′E
Bhir *see* Bīd
154 D13 **Bhiwandi** Mahārāshtra, W India 19°21′N 73°08′E
152 H10 **Bhiwāni** Haryāna, N India 28°50′N 76°10′E
152 L13 **Bhognīpur** Uttar Pradesh, N India 26°12′N 79°48′E
153 U16 **Bhola** Barisal, S Bangladesh 22°40′N 91°36′E
154 H10 **Bhopāl** *state capital* Madhya Pradesh, C India 23°17′N 77°25′E
155 J14 **Bhopālpatnam** Chhattīsgarh, C India 18°51′N 80°22′E
155 E14 **Bhor** Mahārāshtra, W India 18°10′N 73°55′E
154 O12 **Bhubaneshwar** *prev.* Bhubaneswar, Bhuvaneshwar. *state capital* Orissa, E India 20°16′N 85°51′E
Bhubaneswar *see* Bhubaneshwar
154 B9 **Bhuj** Gujarāt, W India 23°16′N 69°40′E
Bhuket *see* Phuket
Bhurtpore *see* Bharatpur
Bhusawal *see* Bhusāwal
154 G12 **Bhusāwal** *prev.* Bhusawal. Mahārāshtra, C India 21°01′N 75°50′E
153 T12 **Bhutan** *off.* Kingdom of Bhutan, *var.* Druk-yul. ◆ *monarchy* S Asia
Bhutan, Kingdom of *see* Bhutan
Bhuvaneshwar *see* Bhubaneshwar
143 T15 **Bīābān, Kūh-e** ▲▲ S Iran
77 V18 **Biafra, Bight of** *var.* Bight of Bonny. *bay* W Africa
171 W12 **Biak** Papua, E Indonesia 01°10′S 136°05′E
171 W12 **Biak, Pulau** *island* E Indonesia
110 P12 **Biała Podlaska** Lubelskie, E Poland 52°03′N 23°08′E
110 F7 **Białogard** *Ger.* Belgard. Zachodnio-pomorskie, NW Poland 54°01′N 15°59′E
110 P10 **Białowieska, Puszcza** *Bel.* Byelavyezhskaya Pushcha, *Rus.* Belovezhskaya Pushcha. *physical region* Belarus/Poland *see also* Byelavyezhskaya, Pushcha
Białowieska, Puszcza *see* Byelavyezhskaya Pushcha
110 G8 **Biały Bór** *Ger.* Baldenburg. Zachodnio-pomorskie, NW Poland 53°53′N 16°49′E
110 P9 **Białystok** *Rus.* Belostok, Bielostok. Podlaskie, NE Poland 53°08′N 23°09′E
107 L24 **Biancavilla** *prev.* Inessa. Sicilia, Italy, C Mediterranean Sea 37°38′N 14°52′E
Bianco, Monte *see* Blanc, Mont
Bianjiang *see* Xunke
76 L15 **Biankouma** W Ivory Coast 07°44′N 07°37′W
167 R7 **Bia, Phou** *var.* Pou Bia. ▲ C Laos 18°59′N 103°09′E
Bia, Pou *see* Bia, Phou
143 R5 **Bīārjmand** Semnān, N Iran 36°05′N 55°50′E
105 P4 **Biarra** ≈ NE Spain
102 I15 **Biarritz** Pyrénées-Atlantiques, SW France 43°25′N 01°40′W
108 H10 **Biasca** Ticino, S Switzerland 46°22′N 08°59′E
61 E17 **Biassini** Salto, N Uruguay 31°18′S 57°05′W
Biasteri *see* Laguardia
165 S3 **Bibai** Hokkaidō, NE Japan 43°21′N 141°53′E
83 B15 **Bibala** *Port.* Vila Arriaga. Namibe, SW Angola 14°46′S 13°21′E
104 I4 **Bibéi** ≈ NW Spain
Biberach *see* Biberach an der Riss
101 I23 **Biberach an der Riss** *var.* Biberach, *Ger.* Biberach an der Riß. Baden-Württemberg, S Germany 48°06′N 09°48′E
108 E7 **Biberist** Solothurn, NW Switzerland 47°11′N 07°34′E
77 O16 **Bibiani** SW Ghana 06°28′N 02°20′W
112 C13 **Bibinje** Zadar, SW Croatia 44°04′N 15°17′E
Biblical Gebal *see* Jbail
116 I5 **Bibrka** *Pol.* Bóbrka, *Rus.* Bobrka. L'vivs'ka Oblast', NW Ukraine 49°39′N 24°16′E
117 N10 **Bîc** ≈ S Moldova
113 M18 **Bicaj** Kukës, NE Albania 42°00′N 20°24′E
116 K10 **Bicaz** *Hung.* Békás. Neamţ, NE Romania 46°53′N 26°05′E
183 Q16 **Bicheno** Tasmania, SE Australia 41°56′S 148°15′E
Bichiş *see* Békés
Bichiş-Ciaba *see* Békéscsaba
Bichitra *see* Phichit
137 P8 **Bich'vinta** *Prev.* Bichvint'a, *Rus.* Pitsunda. NW Georgia 43°12′N 40°21′E
Bichvint'a *see* Bich'vinta
15 T7 **Bic, Île du** *island* Québec, SE Canada
32 J10 **Bickleton** Washington, NW USA 46°00′N 120°16′W
36 L6 **Bicknell** Utah, W USA 38°20′N 111°32′W
171 S11 **Bicoli** Pulau Halmahera, E Indonesia 0°34′N 128°33′E
111 J22 **Bicske** Fejér, C Hungary 47°30′N 18°36′E
155 F14 **Bīd** *prev.* Bhir. Mahārāshtra, W India 19°17′N 75°22′E
77 U15 **Bida** Niger, C Nigeria 09°06′N 06°02′E
155 H15 **Bīdar** Karnātaka, C India 17°56′N 77°35′E
141 Y8 **Bidbid** NE Oman 23°25′N 58°08′E
19 P9 **Biddeford** Maine, NE USA 43°29′N 70°27′W
98 L9 **Biddinghuizen** Flevoland, C Netherlands 52°28′N 05°41′E
33 X11 **Biddle** Montana, NW USA 45°04′N 105°21′W
97 J23 **Bideford** SW England, United Kingdom 51°01′N 04°12′W
82 D13 **Bié** ◈ *province* C Angola
35 O2 **Bieber** California, W USA 41°07′N 121°09′W
110 O9 **Biebrza** ≈ NE Poland
165 T3 **Biei** Hokkaidō, NE Japan 43°33′N 142°28′E
108 D8 **Biel** *Fr.* Bienne. Bern, W Switzerland 47°09′N 07°16′E
100 G13 **Bielefeld** Nordrhein-Westfalen, NW Germany 52°01′N 08°32′E
108 D8 **Bieler See** *Fr.* Lac de Bienne. ◎ W Switzerland
Bielitz/Bielitz-Biala *see* Bielsko-Biała
106 C7 **Biella** Piemonte, N Italy 45°34′N 08°04′E
Bielostok *see* Białystok
111 J17 **Bielsko-Biała** *Ger.* Bielitz, Bielitz-Biala. Śląskie, S Poland 49°49′N 19°01′E
110 P10 **Bielsk Podlaski** Białystok, E Poland 52°45′N 23°11′E
Bien Bien *see* Điện Biên Phu
Biên Đông *see* South China Sea
11 V17 **Bienfait** Saskatchewan, S Canada 49°06′N 102°47′W
167 T14 **Biên Hoa** Đông Nai, S Vietnam 10°58′N 106°50′E
Bienne *see* Biel
Bienne, Lac de *see* Bieler See
12 K8 **Bienville, Lac** ◎ Québec, C Canada
82 D13 **Bié, Planalto do** *var.* Bié Plateau. *plateau* C Angola
Bié Plateau *see* Bié, Planalto do
108 B9 **Bière** Vaud, W Switzerland 46°32′N 06°19′E
98 O4 **Bierum** Groningen, NE Netherlands 53°25′N 06°51′E
98 I13 **Biesbos** *var.* Biesbosch. *wetland* S Netherlands
Biesbosch *see* Biesbos
99 H21 **Biesme** Namur, S Belgium 50°19′N 04°43′E
101 H21 **Bietigheim-Bissingen** Baden-Württemberg, SW Germany 48°57′N 09°07′E
99 J23 **Bièvre** Namur, SE Belgium 49°56′N 05°01′E
79 D18 **Bifoun** Moyen-Ogooué, NW Gabon 0°15′S 10°24′E
165 T2 **Bifuka** Hokkaidō, NE Japan 44°28′N 142°20′E
136 C11 **Biga** Çanakkale, NW Turkey 40°13′N 27°14′E
136 C13 **Bigadiç** Balıkesir, W Turkey 39°24′N 28°08′E
26 J7 **Big Basin** *basin* Kansas, C USA
185 B20 **Big Bay** *bay* South Island, New Zealand
31 O5 **Big Bay de Noc** ◎ Michigan, N USA
31 N3 **Big Bay Point** *headland* Michigan, N USA 46°51′N 87°40′W
33 R10 **Big Belt Mountains** ▲▲ Montana, NW USA
29 N10 **Big Bend Dam** *dam* South Dakota, N USA
24 K12 **Big Bend National Park** *national park* Texas, S USA
22 K5 **Big Black River** ≈ Mississippi, S USA
27 O3 **Big Blue River** ≈ Kansas/ Nebraska, C USA
24 M10 **Big Canyon** ≈ Texas, SW USA
33 N12 **Big Creek** Idaho, NW USA 45°05′N 115°20′W
23 N8 **Big Creek Lake** ⊠ Alabama, S USA
23 X15 **Big Cypress Swamp** *wetland* Florida, SE USA
39 S9 **Big Delta** Alaska, USA 64°09′N 145°50′W
30 K6 **Big Eau Pleine Reservoir** ⊠ Wisconsin, N USA
19 P5 **Bigelow Mountain** ▲ Maine, NE USA 45°09′N 70°17′W
162 G9 **Biger** *var.* Jargalant. Govĭ-Altay, W Mongolia 45°39′N 97°10′E
29 U3 **Big Falls** Minnesota, N USA 48°13′N 93°48′W
33 P8 **Bigfork** Montana, NW USA 48°03′N 114°04′W
29 U3 **Big Fork River** ≈ Minnesota, N USA
11 S15 **Biggar** Saskatchewan, S Canada 52°03′N 107°59′W
180 L3 **Bigge Island** *island* Western Australia
35 O5 **Biggs** California, W USA 39°24′N 121°44′W
32 I11 **Biggs** Oregon, NW USA 45°39′N 120°49′W
14 K13 **Big Gull Lake** ◎ Ontario, SE Canada
37 P16 **Big Hachet Peak** ▲ New Mexico, SW USA 31°38′N 108°24′W
33 P11 **Big Hole River** ≈ Montana, NW USA
33 V13 **Bighorn Basin** *basin* Wyoming, C USA
33 U11 **Bighorn Lake** ◎ Montana/ Wyoming, N USA
33 W13 **Bighorn Mountains** ▲▲ Wyoming, C USA
36 J13 **Big Horn Peak** ▲ Arizona, SW USA 33°40′N 113°01′W
33 V11 **Bighorn River** ≈ Montana/ Wyoming, NW USA
9 S7 **Big Island** *island* Nunavut, NE Canada
39 O16 **Big Koniuji Island** *island* Shumagin Islands, Alaska, USA
25 N9 **Big Lake** Texas, SW USA 31°12′N 101°29′W
19 T5 **Big Lake** ◎ Maine, NE USA
30 I3 **Big Manitou Falls** *waterfall* Wisconsin, N USA
35 R2 **Big Mountain** ▲ Nevada, W USA 41°18′N 119°03′W
108 G10 **Bignasco** Ticino, S Switzerland 46°21′N 08°37′E
29 R16 **Big Nemaha River** ≈ Nebraska, C USA
76 G12 **Bignona** SW Senegal 12°49′N 16°16′W
Bigorra *see* Tarbes
Bigosovo *see* Bihosava
35 S10 **Big Pine** California, W USA 37°09′N 118°18′W
35 Q14 **Big Pine Mountain** ▲ California, W USA 34°41′N 119°37′W
27 V6 **Big Piney Creek** ≈ Missouri, C USA
65 M24 **Big Point** *headland* N Tristan da Cunha 37°10′S 12°18′W
31 P8 **Big Rapids** Michigan, N USA 43°42′N 85°28′W
30 K6 **Big Rib River** ≈ Wisconsin, N USA
14 L14 **Big Rideau Lake** ◎ Ontario, SE Canada
11 T14 **Big River** Saskatchewan, C Canada 53°48′N 106°55′W
27 X5 **Big River** ≈ Missouri, C USA
31 N7 **Big Sable Point** *headland* Michigan, N USA 44°03′N 86°30′W
33 S7 **Big Sandy** Montana, NW USA 48°08′N 110°09′W
25 W6 **Big Sandy** Texas, SW USA 32°34′N 95°06′W
37 V5 **Big Sandy Creek** ≈ Colorado, C USA
29 Q16 **Big Sandy Creek** ≈ Nebraska, C USA
29 V5 **Big Sandy Lake** ◎ Minnesota, N USA
36 J11 **Big Sandy River** ≈ Arizona, SW USA
21 P5 **Big Sandy River** ≈ S USA
23 V6 **Big Satilla Creek** ≈ Georgia, SE USA
29 R12 **Big Sioux River** ≈ Iowa/ South Dakota, N USA
35 U7 **Big Smoky Valley** *valley* Nevada, W USA
25 N7 **Big Spring** Texas, SW USA 32°15′N 101°30′W
19 Q5 **Big Squaw Mountain** ▲ Maine, NE USA 45°28′N 69°42′W
21 O7 **Big Stone Gap** Virginia, NE USA 36°52′N 82°45′W
29 Q8 **Big Stone Lake** ◎ Minnesota/South Dakota, N USA
22 K4 **Big Sunflower River** ≈ Mississippi, S USA
33 T11 **Big Timber** Montana, NW USA 45°50′N 109°57′W
12 D8 **Big Trout Lake** Ontario, C Canada 53°40′N 90°00′W
14 I12 **Big Trout Lake** ◎ Ontario, SE Canada
35 O2 **Big Valley Mountains** ▲▲ California, W USA
25 Q13 **Big Wells** Texas, SW USA 28°34′N 99°34′W
14 F11 **Bigwood** Ontario, S Canada 46°03′N 80°37′W
112 D11 **Bihać** ◈ Federacija Bosna I Hercegovina, NW Bosnia and Herzegovina
153 P14 **Bihār** *prev.* Behar. ◈ *state* N India
Bihār *see* Bihār Sharīf
81 F20 **Biharamulo** Kagera, NW Tanzania 02°37′S 31°20′E
153 R13 **Bihārīganj** Bihār, NE India 25°44′N 86°59′E
153 P14 **Bihār Sharīf** *var.* Bihār. Bihār, N India 25°13′N 85°31′E
116 F10 **Bihor** ◈ *county* NW Romania
165 V3 **Bihoro** Hokkaidō, NE Japan 43°50′N 144°05′E
118 K11 **Bihosava** *Rus.* Bigosovo. Vitsyebskaya Voblasts', NW Belarus 55°50′N 27°46′E
Bijagos Archipelago *see* Bijagós, Arquipélago dos
76 G13 **Bijagós, Arquipélago dos** *var.* Bijagos Archipelago. *island group* W Guinea-Bissau
155 F16 **Bijāpur** Karnātaka, C India 16°50′N 75°42′E
142 K5 **Bījār** Kordestān, W Iran 35°52′N 47°39′E
112 J11 **Bijeljina** Republika Srpska, NE Bosnia and Herzegovina 44°46′N 19°13′E
113 K15 **Bijelo Polje** E Montenegro 43°03′N 19°44′E
160 I11 **Bijie** Guizhou, S China 27°15′N 105°16′E
152 J10 **Bijnor** Uttar Pradesh, N India 29°22′N 78°09′E
152 F11 **Bīkāner** Rājasthān, NW India 28°01′N 73°22′E
189 V3 **Bikar Atoll** *var.* Pikaar. *atoll* Ratak Chain, N Marshall Islands
190 H3 **Bikeman** *atoll* Tungaru, W Kiribati
190 I3 **Bikenebu** Tarawa, W Kiribati
123 S14 **Bikin** Khabarovskiy Kray, SE Russian Federation 46°45′N 134°06′E
123 S14 **Bikin** ≈ SE Russian Federation
189 R3 **Bikini Atoll** *var.* Pikinni. *atoll* Ralik Chain, NW Marshall Islands
83 L17 **Bikita** Masvingo, E Zimbabwe 20°06′S 31°41′E
Bikkū Bīttī *see* Bette, Picco
79 I19 **Bikoro** Equateur, W Dem. Rep. Congo 0°45′S 18°09′E
141 Z9 **Bilād Banī Bū 'Alī** NE Oman 22°02′N 59°18′E
141 Z9 **Bilād Banī Bū Ḩasan** NE Oman 22°09′N 59°14′E
141 X9 **Bilād Manaḩ** *var.* Manaḩ. NE Oman 22°44′N 57°36′E
77 Q12 **Bilanga** C Burkina 12°35′N 00°08′W
152 F12 **Bilāra** Rājasthān, N India 26°10′N 73°48′E
152 K10 **Bilāri** Uttar Pradesh, N India 28°37′N 78°48′E
138 J5 **Bil'ās, Jabal al** ▲▲ C Syria
154 L11 **Bilāspur** Chhattīsgarh, C India 22°06′N 82°08′E
152 I8 **Bilāspur** Himāchal Pradesh, N India 31°18′N 76°48′E
168 J9 **Bila, Sungai** ≈ Sumatera, W Indonesia
137 Y13 **Biläsuvar** *Rus.* Bilyasuvar; *prev.* Pushkino. SE Azerbaijan 39°26′N 48°34′E
117 O5 **Bila Tserkva** *Rus.* Belaya Tserkov'. Kyyivs'ka Oblast', N Ukraine 49°49′N 30°08′E
167 N11 **Bilauktaung Range** *var.* Thanintari Taungdan. ▲▲ Burma (Myanmar)/ Thailand
105 O2 **Bilbao** *Basq.* Bilbo. País Vasco, N Spain 43°15′N 02°56′W
Bilbo *see* Bilbao
92 H2 **Bíldudalur** Vestfirdhir, NW Iceland 65°40′N 23°35′W
113 I16 **Bileća** ◈ Republika Srpska, S Bosnia and Herzegovina
136 E12 **Bilecik** Bilecik, NW Turkey 39°59′N 29°54′E
136 F12 **Bilecik** ◈ *province* NW Turkey
116 E11 **Biled** *Ger.* Billed, *Hung.* Billéd. Timiş, W Romania 45°55′N 20°55′E
111 O15 **Biłgoraj** Lubelskie, E Poland 50°31′N 22°41′E
117 P11 **Bilhorod-Dnistrovs'kyy** *Rus.* Belgorod-Dnestrovskiy, *Rom.* Cetatea Albă, *prev.* Akkerman; *anc.* Tyras. Odes'ka Oblast', SW Ukraine 46°10′N 30°19′E
79 M16 **Bili** Orientale, N Dem. Rep. Congo 04°07′N 25°09′E
123 T6 **Bilibino** Chukotskiy Avtonomnyy Okrug, NE Russian Federation 67°56′N 166°45′E
166 M8 **Bilin** Mon State, S Burma (Myanmar) 17°14′N 97°12′E
113 N21 **Bilisht** *var.* Bilishti. Korçë, SE Albania 40°36′N 21°00′E
Bilishti *see* Bilisht
183 N10 **Billabong Creek** *var.* Moulamein Creek. *seasonal river* New South Wales, SE Australia
182 G4 **Billa Kalina** South Australia 29°57′S 136°13′E
197 Q17 **Bill Baileys Bank** *undersea feature* N Atlantic Ocean 60°35′N 10°15′W
Billed/Billéd *see* Biled
153 N14 **Billi** Uttar Pradesh, N India 24°30′N 82°59′E
97 M15 **Billingham** N England, United Kingdom 54°36′N 01°17′W
33 U11 **Billings** Montana, NW USA 45°47′N 108°32′W
95 J16 **Billingsfors** Västra Götaland, S Sweden 58°57′N 12°14′E
Bill of Cape Clear, The *see* Clear, Cape
28 L9 **Billsburg** South Dakota, N USA 44°22′N 101°40′W
95 F23 **Billund** Syddtjylland, W Denmark 55°44′N 09°07′E
36 L11 **Bill Williams Mountain** ▲ Arizona, SW USA 35°12′N 112°12′W
36 I12 **Bill Williams River** ≈ Arizona, SW USA
77 Y8 **Bilma** Agadez, NE Niger 18°22′N 13°01′E
77 Y8 **Bilma, Grand Erg de** *desert* NE Niger
181 Y9 **Biloela** Queensland, E Australia 24°27′S 150°31′E
112 G8 **Bilo Gora** ▲▲ N Croatia
117 U13 **Bilohirs'k** *Rus.* Belogorsk; *prev.* Karasubazar. Avtonomna Respublika Krym, S Ukraine 45°04′N 34°35′E
Bilokorovychi *see* Novi Bilokorovychi
Bilokurakine *see* Bilokurakyne
117 X5 **Bilokurakyne** *var.* Bilokurakine. Luhans'ka Oblast', E Ukraine 49°32′N 38°44′E
117 T3 **Bilopillya** *Rus.* Belopol'ye. Sums'ka Oblast', NE Ukraine 51°09′N 34°17′E
117 Y6 **Bilovods'k** *Rus.* Belovodsk. Luhans'ka Oblast', E Ukraine 49°11′N 39°34′E
22 M9 **Biloxi** Mississippi, S USA 30°24′N 88°53′W
117 R10 **Bilozerka** Khersons'ka Oblast', S Ukraine 46°36′N 32°23′E
117 W7 **Bilozers'ke** Donets'ka Oblast', E Ukraine 48°29′N 37°03′E
98 J11 **Bilthoven** Utrecht, C Netherlands 52°07′N 05°12′E
78 K9 **Biltine** Biltine, E Chad 14°30′N 20°53′E
78 J9 **Biltine** *off.* Préfecture de Biltine. ◈ *prefecture* E Chad
Biltine, Préfecture de *see* Biltine

◆ Country
● Country Capital
◇ Dependent Territory
○ Dependent Territory Capital
◈ Administrative Regions
✈ International Airport
▲ Mountain
▲▲ Mountain Range
Volcano
≈ River
◎ Lake
⊠ Reservoir

Bilüü *see* Ulaanhus
Bilwi *see* Puerto Cabezas
Bilyasuvar *see* Biläsuvar
117 *O11* **Bilyayivka** Odes'ka Oblast', SW Ukraine *46°28´N 30°11´E*
99 *K18* **Bilzen** Limburg, NE Belgium *50°52´N 05°31´E*
Bimbéréké *see* Bembèrèkè
183 *R10* **Bimberi Peak** ▲ New South Wales, SE Australia *35°42´S 148°46´E*
77 *Q15* **Bimbila** E Ghana *08°54´N 00°05´E*
79 *I15* **Bimbo** Ombella-Mpoko, SW Central African Republic *04°19´N 18°27´E*
44 *F2* **Bimini Islands** *island group* W Bahamas
154 *I9* **Bīna** Madhya Pradesh, C India *24°09´N 78°10´E*
143 *T4* **Bīnālūd, Kūh-e** ▲▲ NE Iran
99 *F20* **Binche** Hainaut, S Belgium *50°25´N 04°10´E*
Bindloe Island *see* Marchena, Isla
83 *L16* **Bindura** Mashonaland Central, NE Zimbabwe *17°20´S 31°21´E*
105 *T5* **Binefar** Aragón, NE Spain *41°51´N 00°17´E*
83 *J16* **Binga** Matabeleland North, W Zimbabwe *17°40´S 27°22´E*
183 *T5* **Bingara** New South Wales, SE Australia *29°54´S 150°36´E*
101 *F18* **Bingen am Rhein** Rheinland-Pfalz, SW Germany *49°58´N 07°54´E*
26 *M11* **Binger** Oklahoma, C USA *35°19´N 98°19´W*
Bingerau *see* Węgrów
Bin Ghalfān, Jazā'ir *see* Ḥalāniyāt, Juzur al
19 *Q6* **Bingham** Maine, NE USA *45°01´N 69°51´W*
18 *H11* **Binghamton** New York, NE USA *42°06´N 75°55´W*
Bin Ghanīmah, Jabal *see* Bin Ghunaymah, Jabal
75 *P11* **Bin Ghunaymah, Jabal** *var.* Jabal Bin Ghanīmah. ▲▲ C Libya
139 *U3* **Bingird** As Sulaymānīyah, NE Iraq *36°03´N 45°03´E*
Bingmei *see* Congjiang
137 *P14* **Bingöl** Bingöl, E Turkey *38°54´N 40°29´E*
137 *P14* **Bingöl** ◈ *province* E Turkey
161 *R6* **Binhai** *var.* Dongkan. Jiangsu, E China *34°00´N 119°51´E*
167 *V11* **Binh Đinh** *var.* An Nhon. Binh Đinh, C Vietnam *13°53´N 109°07´E*
Binh Sơn *see* Châu Ô
Binimani *see* Bintimani
168 *I8* **Binjai** Sumatera, W Indonesia *03°37´N 98°30´E*
183 *R6* **Binnaway** New South Wales, SE Australia *31°34´S 149°24´E*
108 *E6* **Binningen** Basel Landschaft, NW Switzerland *47°32´N 07°35´E*
80 *H12* **Bīnshangul Gumuz** *var.* Benishangul. ◈ W Ethiopia
168 *J8* **Bintang, Banjaran** ▲▲ Peninsular Malaysia
168 *M10* **Bintan, Pulau** *island* Kepulauan Riau, W Indonesia
76 *J14* **Bintimani** *var.* Binimani. ▲ NE Sierra Leone *09°21´N 11°09´W*
Bint Jubayl *see* Bent Jbaïl
169 *S9* **Bintulu** Sarawak, East Malaysia *03°12´N 113°01´E*
169 *S9* **Bintuni** *prev.* Steenkool. Papua, E Indonesia *02°03´S 133°45´E*
163 *W8* **Binxian** *prev.* Binzhou. Heilongjiang, NE China *45°44´N 127°27´E*
160 *K14* **Binyang** *var.* Binzhou. Guangxi Zhuangzu Zizhiqu, S China *23°15´N 108°40´E*
161 *Q4* **Binzhou** Shandong, E China *37°23´N 118°03´E*
Binzhou *see* Binyang
Binzhou *see* Binxian
63 *G14* **Bío Bío** *var.* Región del Bío Bío. ◈ *region* C Chile
Bío Bío, Región del *see* Bío Bío
63 *G14* **Bío Bío, Río** ≈ C Chile
79 *C16* **Bioco, Isla de** *var.* Bioko, *Eng.* Fernando Po, *Sp.* Fernando Póo; *prev.* Macías Nguema Biyogo. *island* NW Equatorial Guinea
112 *D13* **Biograd na Moru** *It.* Zaravecchia. Zadar, SW Croatia *43°57´N 15°27´E*
Bioko *see* Bioco, Isla de
113 *F14* **Biokovo** ▲▲ S Croatia
Biorra *see* Birr
Bipontium *see* Zweibrücken
143 *W13* **Bīrag, Kūh-e** ▲▲ SE Iran
75 *O10* **Birāk** *var.* Brak. C Libya *27°32´N 14°17´E*
139 *S10* **Bi'r al Islām** Karbalā', C Iraq *32°15´N 43°40´E*
154 *N11* **Biramitrapur** *var.* Birmitrapur. Orissa, E India *22°24´N 84°42´E*
139 *T11* **Bi'r an Niṣf** An Najaf, S Iraq *31°22´N 44°07´E*
78 *L12* **Birao** Vakaga, NE Central African Republic *10°14´N 22°49´E*
146 *J10* **Birata** *Rus.* Darganata, Dargan-Ata. Lebap Welaýaty, NE Turkmenistan *40°30´N 62°09´E*
158 *M6* **Biratar Bulak** *well* NW China
153 *R12* **Birātnagar** Eastern, SE Nepal *26°28´N 87°16´E*
165 *R5* **Biratori** Hokkaidō, NE Japan *42°35´N 142°07´E*
39 *S8* **Birch Creek** Alaska, USA *66°17´N 145°54´W*
38 *M11* **Birch Creek** ≈ Alaska, USA
11 *T14* **Birch Hills** Saskatchewan, S Canada *52°58´N 105°22´W*
182 *M10* **Birchip** Victoria, SE Australia *36°01´S 142°55´E*
29 *X4* **Birch Lake** ◎ Minnesota, N USA
11 *Q11* **Birch Mountains** ▲▲ Alberta, W Canada
11 *V15* **Birch River** Manitoba, S Canada *52°22´N 101°03´W*
44 *H12* **Birchs Hill** *hill* W Jamaica
39 *R11* **Birchwood** Alaska, USA *61°24´N 149°28´W*
188 *I5* **Bird Island** *island* S Northern Mariana Islands
137 *N16* **Birecik** Şanlıurfa, S Turkey *37°03´N 37°59´E*
152 *M10* **Birendranagar** *var.* Surkhet. Mid Western, W Nepal *28°35´N 81°36´E*
Bir es Saba *see* Be'er Sheva
74 *A12* **Bir-Gandouz** SW Western Sahara *21°35´N 16°27´W*
153 *P12* **Birganj** Central, C Nepal *27°03´N 84°53´E*
81 *B14* **Biri** ≈ W South Sudan
Bi'r Ibn Hirmās *see* Al Bi'r
143 *U8* **Bīrjand** Khorāsān-e Janūbī, E Iran *32°54´N 59°14´E*
139 *T11* **Birkat Ḥāmid** *well* S Iraq
95 *F18* **Birkeland** Aust-Agder, S Norway *58°18´N 08°13´E*
101 *E19* **Birkenfeld** Rheinland-Pfalz, SW Germany *49°39´N 07°10´E*
97 *K18* **Birkenhead** NW England, United Kingdom *53°24´N 03°02´W*
109 *W7* **Birkfeld** Steiermark, SE Austria *47°21´N 15°40´E*
182 *A2* **Birksgate Range** ▲▲ South Australia
Bîrlad *see* Bârlad
145 *S15* **Birlik** *var.* Novotroickoje, Novotroitskoye; *prev.* Brlik. Zhambyl, SE Kazakhstan *43°39´N 73°45´E*
97 *K20* **Birmingham** C England, United Kingdom *52°30´N 01°50´W*
23 *P4* **Birmingham** Alabama, S USA *33°30´N 86°47´W*
97 *M20* **Birmingham** ✈ C England, United Kingdom *52°27´N 01°46´W*
Birmitrapur *see* Biramitrapur
Bir Moghrein *see* Bîr Mogreïn
76 *J4* **Bîr Mogreïn** *var.* Bir Moghrein; *prev.* Fort-Trinquet. Tiris Zemmour, N Mauritania *25°10´N 11°35´W*
191 *S4* **Birnie Island** *atoll* Phoenix Islands, C Kiribati
77 *S12* **Birnin Gaouré** *var.* Birni-Ngaouré. Dosso, SW Niger *12°59´N 03°02´E*
Birni-Ngaouré *see* Birnin Gaouré
77 *S12* **Birnin Kebbi** Kebbi, NW Nigeria *12°28´N 04°08´E*
77 *T12* **Birnin Konni** *var.* Birni-Nkonni. Tahoua, SW Niger *13°51´N 05°15´E*
Birni-Nkonni *see* Birnin Konni
77 *W13* **Birnin Kudu** Jigawa, N Nigeria *11°28´N 09°29´E*
123 *S16* **Birobidzhan** Yevreyskaya Avtonomnaya Oblast', SE Russian Federation *48°42´N 132°55´E*
97 *D18* **Birr** *var.* Parsonstown, *Ir.* Biorra. C Ireland *53°06´N 07°55´W*
183 *P4* **Birrie River** ≈ New South Wales/Queensland, SE Australia
108 *D7* **Birse** ≈ NW Switzerland
Birsen *see* Biržai
108 *E6* **Birsfelden** Basel Landschaft, NW Switzerland *47°33´N 07°37´E*
127 *U4* **Birsk** Respublika Bashkortostan, W Russian Federation *55°24´N 55°33´E*
119 *F14* **Birštonas** Kaunas, C Lithuania *54°37´N 24°00´E*
159 *P14* **Biru** Xinjiang Uygur Zizhiqu, W China *31°30´N 93°56´E*
Biruni *see* Beruniy
122 *L12* **Biryusa** ≈ C Russian Federation
122 *L12* **Biryusinsk** Irkutskaya Oblast', C Russian Federation *55°52´N 97°48´E*
118 *G10* **Biržai** *Ger.* Birsen. Panevėžys, NE Lithuania *56°12´N 24°47´E*
121 *P16* **Birżebbuġa** SE Malta *35°50´N 14°32´E*
Bisanthe *see* Tekirdağ
171 *R12* **Bisa, Pulau** *island* Maluku, E Indonesia
37 *N17* **Bisbee** Arizona, SW USA *31°27´N 109°55´W*
29 *O2* **Bisbee** North Dakota, N USA *48°36´N 99°21´W*
Biscaia, Baía de *see* Biscay, Bay of
102 *I13* **Biscarrosse et de Parentis, Étang de** ◎ SW France
104 *M1* **Biscay, Bay of** *Sp.* Golfo de Vizcaya, *Port.* Baía de Biscaia. *bay* France/Spain
23 *Z16* **Biscayne Bay** *bay* Florida, SE USA
64 *M7* **Biscay Plain** *undersea feature* SE Bay of Biscay *07°15´W 45°00´N*
107 *N17* **Bisceglie** Puglia, SE Italy *41°14´N 16°31´E*
Bischoflack *see* Škofja Loka
Bischofsburg *see* Biskupiec
109 *Q7* **Bischofshofen** Salzburg, NW Austria *47°25´N 13°13´E*
101 *P15* **Bischofswerda** Sachsen, E Germany *51°07´N 14°13´E*
103 *V5* **Bischwiller** Bas-Rhin, NE France *48°46´N 07°52´E*
21 *T10* **Biscoe** North Carolina, SE USA *35°20´N 79°46´W*
194 *G5* **Biscoe Islands** *island group* Antarctica
14 *E9* **Biscotasi Lake** ◎ Ontario, S Canada
14 *E9* **Biscotasing** Ontario, S Canada *47°16´N 82°04´W*
54 *J6* **Biscucuy** Portuguesa, NW Venezuela *09°22´N 69°59´W*
99 *M24* **Bissen** Luxembourg, C Luxembourg *49°47´N 06°04´E*
114 *K11* **Biser** Khaskovo, S Bulgaria *41°52´N 25°59´E*
113 *D15* **Biševo** *It.* Busi. *island* SW Croatia
141 *N12* **Bīshah, Wādī** *dry watercourse* C Saudi Arabia
147 *U7* **Bishkek** *var.* Pishpek; *prev.* Frunze. ● (Kyrgyzstan) Chuyskaya Oblast', N Kyrgyzstan *42°54´N 74°27´E*
147 *U7* **Bishkek** ✈ Chuyskaya Oblast', N Kyrgyzstan *42°55´N 74°37´E*
153 *R16* **Bishnupur** West Bengal, NE India *23°05´N 87°20´E*
83 *J25* **Bisho** Eastern Cape, S South Africa *32°46´S 27°21´E*
35 *S9* **Bishop** California, W USA *37°22´N 118°24´W*
25 *S15* **Bishop** Texas, SW USA *27°36´N 97°49´W*
97 *L15* **Bishop Auckland** N England, United Kingdom *54°41´N 01°41´W*
Bishop's Lynn *see* King's Lynn
97 *O21* **Bishop's Stortford** E England, United Kingdom *51°45´N 00°11´E*
21 *S12* **Bishopville** South Carolina, SE USA *34°18´N 80°15´W*
138 *M5* **Bishrī, Jabal** ▲▲ E Syria
163 *U4* **Bishui** Heilongjiang, NE China *52°06´N 123°42´E*
81 *G17* **Bisina, Lake** *prev.* Lake Salisbury. ◎ E Uganda
Biskara *see* Biskra
74 *L6* **Biskra** *var.* Beskra, Biskara. NE Algeria *34°51´N 05°44´E*
110 *M8* **Biskupiec** *Ger.* Bischofsburg. Warmińsko-Mazurskie, NE Poland *53°52´N 20°57´E*
171 *R7* **Bislig** Mindanao, S Philippines *08°10´N 126°19´E*
27 *X6* **Bismarck** Missouri, C USA *37°46´N 90°37´W*
28 *M5* **Bismarck** *state capital* North Dakota, N USA *46°49´N 100°47´W*
186 *D5* **Bismarck Archipelago** *island group* NE Papua New Guinea
129 *Z16* **Bismarck Plate** *tectonic feature* W Pacific Ocean
186 *D7* **Bismarck Range** ▲▲ N Papua New Guinea
186 *E6* **Bismarck Sea** *sea* W Pacific Ocean
137 *P15* **Bismil** Dıyarbakır, SE Turkey *37°53´N 40°38´E*
43 *N6* **Bismuna, Laguna** *lagoon* NE Nicaragua
Bisnulok *see* Phitsanulok
171 *R10* **Bisoa, Tanjung** *headland* Pulau Halmahera, N Indonesia *02°15´N 127°57´E*
28 *K7* **Bison** South Dakota, N USA *45°31´N 102°27´W*
93 *H17* **Bispgården** Jämtland, C Sweden *63°00´N 16°40´E*
76 *G13* **Bissau** ● (Guinea-Bissau) W Guinea-Bissau *11°52´N 15°39´W*
76 *G13* **Bissau** ✈ W Guinea-Bissau *11°53´N 15°41´W*
Bissojohka *see* Børselv
76 *G12* **Bissorã** W Guinea-Bissau *12°16´N 15°35´W*
11 *O10* **Bistcho Lake** ◎ Alberta, W Canada
22 *G5* **Bistineau, Lake** ⊠ Louisiana, S USA
Bistrica *see* Ilirska Bistrica
116 *I9* **Bistriţa** *Ger.* Bistritz, *Hung.* Beszterce; *prev.* Nösen. Bistriţa-Năsăud, N Romania *47°10´N 24°31´E*
116 *K10* **Bistriţa** *Ger.* Bistritz. ≈ NE Romania
116 *I9* **Bistriţa-Năsăud** ◈ *county* N Romania
Bistritz *see* Bistriţa
Bistritz ober Pernstein *see* Bystřice nad Pernštejnem
152 *L11* **Biswān** Uttar Pradesh, N India *27°30´N 81°00´E*
110 *M7* **Bisztynek** Warmińsko-Mazurskie, NE Poland *54°05´N 20°53´E*
79 *E17* **Bitam** Woleu-Ntem, N Gabon *02°05´N 11°30´E*
101 *D18* **Bitburg** Rheinland-Pfalz, SW Germany *49°58´N 06°31´E*
103 *U4* **Bitche** Moselle, NE France *49°01´N 07°27´E*
78 *I11* **Bitkine** Guéra, C Chad *11°59´N 18°13´E*
137 *R15* **Bitlis** Bitlis, SE Turkey *38°23´N 42°04´E*
137 *R14* **Bitlis** ◈ *province* E Turkey
Bitoeng *see* Bitung
113 *N20* **Bitola** *Turk.* Monastir; *prev.* Bitolj. S FYR Macedonia *41°01´N 21°22´E*
Bitolj *see* Bitola
107 *O17* **Bitonto** *anc.* Butuntum. Puglia, SE Italy *41°07´N 16°41´E*
77 *Q13* **Bitou** *var.* Bittou. SE Burkina *11°19´N 00°17´W*
155 *C20* **Bitra Island** *island* Lakshadweep, India, N Indian Ocean
101 *M14* **Bitterfeld** Sachsen-Anhalt, E Germany *51°37´N 12°18´E*
32 *O9* **Bitterroot Range** ▲▲ Idaho/Montana, NW USA
33 *P10* **Bitterroot River** ≈ Montana, NW USA
107 *D18* **Bitti** Sardegna, Italy, C Mediterranean Sea *40°30´N 09°31´E*
Bittou *see* Bitou
171 *Q11* **Bitung** *prev.* Bitoeng. Sulawesi, C Indonesia *01°28´N 125°13´E*
60 *I12* **Bituruna** Paraná, S Brazil *26°11´S 51°34´W*
77 *Y13* **Biu** Borno, E Nigeria *10°35´N 12°13´E*
Biumba *see* Byumba
164 *J13* **Biwa-ko** ◎ Honshū, SW Japan
171 *X14* **Biwarlaut** Papua, E Indonesia *05°44´S 138°14´E*
27 *P10* **Bixby** Oklahoma, C USA *35°56´N 95°52´W*
122 *J13* **Biya** ≈ S Russian Federation
122 *J13* **Biysk** Altayskiy Kray, S Russian Federation *52°34´N 85°09´E*
164 *H13* **Bizen** Okayama, Honshū, SW Japan *34°45´N 134°10´E*
Bizerta *see* Bizerte
120 *K10* **Bizerte** *Ar.* Banzart, *Eng.* Bizerta. N Tunisia *37°18´N 09°48´E*
Bizkaia *see* Vizcaya
92 *G2* **Bjargtangar** *headland* W Iceland *63°30´N 24°29´W*
Bjärnå *see* Perniö
95 *K22* **Bjärnum** Skåne, S Sweden *56°15´N 13°45´E*
93 *I16* **Bjästa** Västernorrland, C Sweden *63°12´N 18°30´E*
113 *I14* **Bjelašnica** ▲ SE Bosnia and Herzegovina *43°13´N 18°18´E*
112 *C10* **Bjelolasica** ▲ NW Croatia *45°13´N 14°56´E*
112 *F8* **Bjelovar** *Hung.* Belovár. Bjelovar-Bilogora, N Croatia *45°54´N 16°49´E*
112 *F8* **Bjelovar-Bilogora** *off.* Bjelovarsko-Bilogorska Županija. ◈ *province* NE Croatia
Bjelovarsko-Bilogorska Županija *see* Bjelovar-Bilogora
92 *H10* **Bjerkvik** Nordland, C Norway *68°31´N 16°08´E*
95 *G21* **Bjerringbro** Midtjylland, NW Denmark *56°23´N 09°40´E*
Bjeshkët e Namuna *see* North Albanian Alps
95 *L14* **Björbo** Dalarna, C Sweden *60°28´N 14°44´E*
95 *I15* **Bjørkelangen** Akershus, S Norway *59°54´N 11°33´E*
95 *O14* **Björklinge** Uppsala, C Sweden *60°03´N 17°33´E*
95 *P14* **Bjørkø-Arholma** Stockholm, C Sweden *59°51´N 19°01´E*
93 *I14* **Björksele** Västerbotten, N Sweden *64°58´N 18°30´E*
93 *I16* **Björna** Västernorrland, C Sweden *63°34´N 18°38´E*
95 *C14* **Bjørnafjorden** *fjord* S Norway
95 *L16* **Björneborg** Värmland, C Sweden *59°13´N 14°15´E*
Björneborg *see* Pori
95 *E14* **Bjornesfjorden** ◎ S Norway
92 *M9* **Bjørnevatn** Finnmark, N Norway *69°40´N 29°57´E*
197 *T13* **Bjørnøya** *Eng.* Bear Island. *island* N Norway
93 *I15* **Bjurholm** Västerbotten, N Sweden *63°57´N 19°16´E*
95 *J22* **Bjuv** Skåne, S Sweden *56°05´N 12°57´E*
76 *M12* **Bla** Ségou, W Mali *12°58´N 05°45´W*
181 *W8* **Blackall** Queensland, E Australia *24°26´S 145°32´E*
29 *V2* **Black Bay** *lake bay* Minnesota, N USA
27 *N9* **Black Bear Creek** ≈ Oklahoma, C USA
97 *K17* **Blackburn** NW England, United Kingdom *53°45´N 02°29´W*
39 *T11* **Blackburn, Mount** ▲ Alaska, USA *61°43´N 143°25´W*
35 *N5* **Black Butte Lake** ⊠ California, W USA
194 *J5* **Black Coast** *physical region* Antarctica
11 *Q16* **Black Diamond** Alberta, SW Canada *50°42´N 114°09´W*
18 *K11* **Black Dome** ▲ New York, NE USA *42°16´N 74°07´W*
113 *L18* **Black Drin** *Alb.* Lumi i Drinit të Zi, *SCr.* Crni Drim. ≈ Albania/FYR Macedonia
29 *U4* **Blackduck** Minnesota, N USA *47°45´N 94°33´W*
12 *D6* **Black Duck** ≈ Ontario, C Canada
33 *R14* **Blackfoot** Idaho, NW USA *43°11´N 112°20´W*
33 *P9* **Blackfoot River** ≈ Montana, NW USA
Black Forest *see* Schwarzwald
28 *J10* **Blackhawk** South Dakota, N USA *44°09´N 103°18´W*
28 *I10* **Black Hills** ▲▲ South Dakota/Wyoming, N USA
11 *T10* **Black Lake** ◎ Saskatchewan, C Canada
22 *G6* **Black Lake** ⊠ Louisiana, S USA
31 *Q5* **Black Lake** ◎ Michigan, N USA
18 *I7* **Black Lake** ◎ New York, NE USA
26 *F7* **Black Mesa** ▲ Oklahoma, C USA *37°00´N 103°07´W*
21 *P10* **Black Mountain** North Carolina, SE USA *35°37´N 82°19´W*
35 *P13* **Black Mountain** ▲ California, W USA *35°22´N 120°21´W*
37 *Q2* **Black Mountain** ▲ Colorado, C USA *40°47´N 107°23´W*
96 *K1* **Black Mountains** ▲▲ SE Wales, United Kingdom
36 *H10* **Black Mountains** ▲▲ Arizona, SW USA
21 *O7* **Black Mountains** ▲ Kentucky, E USA *36°54´N 82°53´W*
33 *Q16* **Black Pine Peak** ▲ Idaho, NW USA *42°07´N 113°07´W*
97 *K17* **Blackpool** NW England, United Kingdom *53°50´N 03°03´W*
37 *Q14* **Black Range** ▲▲ New Mexico, SW USA
44 *I12* **Black River** W Jamaica *18°02´N 77°52´W*
14 *J14* **Black River** ≈ Ontario, SE Canada
129 *U12* **Black River** *Chin.* Babian Jiang, Lixian Jiang, *Fr.* Rivière Noire, *Vtn.* Sông Đa. ≈ China/Vietnam
44 *I12* **Black River** ≈ W Jamaica
39 *T7* **Black River** ≈ Alaska, USA
37 *N13* **Black River** ≈ Arizona, SW USA
27 *X7* **Black River** ≈ Arkansas/Missouri, C USA
22 *I7* **Black River** ≈ Louisiana, S USA
31 *S8* **Black River** ≈ Michigan, N USA
31 *Q5* **Black River** ≈ Michigan, N USA
18 *I8* **Black River** ≈ New York, NE USA
21 *T13* **Black River** ≈ South Carolina, SE USA
30 *J7* **Black River** ≈ Wisconsin, N USA
30 *J7* **Black River Falls** Wisconsin, N USA *44°18´N 90°51´W*
35 *R3* **Black Rock Desert** *desert* Nevada, W USA
Black Sand Desert *see* Garagum
21 *S7* **Blacksburg** Virginia, NE USA *37°15´N 80°25´W*
136 *H10* **Black Sea** *var.* Euxine Sea, *Bul.* Cherno More, *Rom.* Marea Neagră, *Rus.* Chernoye More, *Turk.* Karadeniz, *Ukr.* Chorne More. *sea* Asia/Europe
117 *Q10* **Black Sea Lowland** *Ukr.* Prychornomor'ska Nyzovyna. *depression* SE Europe
33 *S17* **Blacks Fork** ≈ Wyoming, C USA
23 *V7* **Blackshear** Georgia, SE USA *31°18´N 82°14´W*
23 *S6* **Blackshear, Lake** ⊠ Georgia, SE USA
97 *A16* **Blacksod Bay** *Ir.* Cuan an Fhóid Duibh. *inlet* W Ireland
21 *V7* **Blackstone** Virginia, NE USA *37°04´N 78°00´W*
77 *O14* **Black Volta** *var.* Borongo, Mouhoun, Moun Hou, *Fr.* Volta Noire. ≈ W Africa
23 *O5* **Black Warrior River** ≈ Alabama, S USA
181 *X8* **Blackwater** Queensland, E Australia *23°34´S 148°51´E*
97 *D20* **Blackwater** *Ir.* An Abhainn Mhór. ≈ S Ireland
27 *T4* **Blackwater River** ≈ Missouri, C USA
21 *W7* **Blackwater River** ≈ Virginia, NE USA
Blackwater State *see* Nebraska
27 *N8* **Blackwell** Oklahoma, C USA *36°48´N 97°16´W*
25 *P7* **Blackwell** Texas, SW USA *32°05´N 100°19´W*
99 *J15* **Bladel** Noord-Brabant, S Netherlands *51°22´N 05°13´E*
Bladenmarkt *see* Bălăuşeri
114 *G11* **Blagoevgrad** *prev.* Gorna Dzhumaya. Blagoevgrad, W Bulgaria *42°01´N 23°05´E*
114 *G11* **Blagoevgrad** ◈ *province* SW Bulgaria
123 *Q14* **Blagoveshchensk** Amurskaya Oblast', SE Russian Federation *50°19´N 127°30´E*
127 *V4* **Blagoveshchensk** Respublika Bashkortostan, W Russian Federation *55°03´N 56°01´E*
102 *I7* **Blain** Loire-Atlantique, NW France *47°26´N 01°47´W*
29 *V8* **Blaine** Minnesota, N USA *45°09´N 93°13´W*
32 *H6* **Blaine** Washington, NW USA *48°59´N 122°45´W*
11 *T15* **Blaine Lake** Saskatchewan, S Canada *52°49´N 106°48´W*
29 *S14* **Blair** Nebraska, C USA *41°32´N 96°07´W*
96 *J10* **Blairgowrie** C Scotland, United Kingdom *56°19´N 03°25´W*
18 *C15* **Blairsville** Pennsylvania, NE USA *40°25´N 79°12´W*
116 *H11* **Blaj** *Ger.* Blasendorf, *Hung.* Balázsfalva. Alba, SW Romania *46°10´N 23°57´E*
64 *F9* **Blake-Bahama Ridge** *undersea feature* W Atlantic Ocean *29°00´N 73°30´W*
23 *S7* **Blakely** Georgia, SE USA *31°22´N 84°55´W*
64 *E10* **Blake Plateau** *var.* Blake Terrace. *undersea feature* W Atlantic Ocean *31°00´N 79°00´W*
30 *M1* **Blake Point** *headland* Michigan, N USA *48°11´N 88°25´W*
Blake Terrace *see* Blake Plateau
61 *B24* **Blanca, Bahía** *bay* E Argentina
56 *C12* **Blanca, Cordillera** ▲▲ W Peru
105 *T12* **Blanca, Costa** *physical region* SE Spain
37 *S7* **Blanca Peak** ▲ Colorado, C USA *37°34´N 105°29´W*
24 *I9* **Blanca, Sierra** ▲ Texas, SW USA *31°15´N 105°26´W*
120 *K9* **Blanc, Cap** *headland* N Tunisia *37°20´N 09°41´E*
Blanc, Cap *see* Nouâdhibou, Râs
31 *R12* **Blanchard River** ≈ Ohio, N USA
182 *E8* **Blanche, Cape** *headland* South Australia *33°03´S 134°10´E*
182 *J4* **Blanche, Lake** ◎ South Australia
31 *R14* **Blanchester** Ohio, N USA *39°17´N 83°59´W*
182 *J9* **Blanchetown** South Australia *34°21´S 139°36´E*
45 *U13* **Blanchisseuse** Trinidad, Trinidad and Tobago *10°47´N 61°18´W*
103 *T11* **Blanc, Mont** *It.* Monte Bianco. ▲ France/Italy *45°45´N 06°51´E*
25 *R11* **Blanco** Texas, SW USA *30°06´N 98°25´W*
42 *K14* **Blanco, Cabo** *headland* NW Costa Rica *09°34´N 85°06´W*
32 *D14* **Blanco, Cape** *headland* Oregon, NW USA *42°49´N 124°33´W*
62 *H10* **Blanco, Río** ≈ W Argentina
56 *F10* **Blanco, Río** ≈ NE Peru
15 *O9* **Blanc, Réservoir** ⊠ Québec, SE Canada
21 *R7* **Bland** Virginia, NE USA *37°06´N 81°08´W*
92 *I2* **Blanda** ≈ N Iceland
37 *O7* **Blanding** Utah, W USA *37°37´N 109°28´W*
105 *X5* **Blanes** Cataluña, NE Spain *41°41´N 02°48´E*
103 *N3* **Blangy-sur-Bresle** Seine-Maritime, N France *49°55´N 01°37´E*
111 *C18* **Blanice** *Ger.* Blanitz. ≈ SE Czech Republic
Blanitz *see* Blanice
99 *C16* **Blankenberge** West-Vlaanderen, NW Belgium *51°19´N 03°08´E*
101 *D17* **Blankenheim** Nordrhein-Westfalen, W Germany *50°26´N 06°41´E*
25 *R8* **Blanket** Texas, SW USA *31°49´N 98°47´W*
55 *O3* **Blanquilla, Isla** *var.* La Blanquilla. *island* N Venezuela
Blanquilla, La *see* Blanquilla, Isla
61 *F18* **Blanquillo** Durazno, C Uruguay *32°53´S 55°37´W*
111 *G18* **Blansko** *Ger.* Blanz. Jihomoravský Kraj, SE Czech Republic *49°22´N 16°39´E*
83 *N15* **Blantyre** *var.* Blantyre-Limbe. Southern, S Malawi *15°45´S 35°04´E*
83 *N15* **Blantyre** ✈ Southern, S Malawi *15°34´S 35°03´E*
Blantyre-Limbe *see* Blantyre
Blanz *see* Blansko
98 *J10* **Blaricum** Noord-Holland, C Netherlands *52°16´N 05°15´E*
Blasendorf *see* Blaj
Blatnitsa *see* Durankulak
113 *F15* **Blato** *It.* Blatta. Dubrovnik-Neretva, S Croatia *42°57´N 16°47´E*
Blatta *see* Blato
108 *E10* **Blatten** Valais, SW Switzerland *46°22´N 08°00´E*
101 *J20* **Blaufelden** Baden-Württemberg, SW Germany *49°21´N 10°01´E*
95 *E23* **Blåvands Huk** *headland* W Denmark *55°33´N 08°04´E*
102 *G6* **Blavet** ≈ NW France
102 *J12* **Blaye** Gironde, SW France
183 *R8* **Blayney** New South Wales, SE Australia *33°33´S 149°13´E*
65 *D25* **Bleaker Island** *island* SE Falkland Islands
109 *T10* **Bled** *Ger.* Veldes. NW Slovenia *46°23´N 14°06´E*
99 *D20* **Bléharies** Hainaut, SW Belgium *50°31´N 03°25´E*
109 *U9* **Bleiburg** *Slvn.* Pliberk. Kärnten, S Austria *46°36´N 14°49´E*
101 *L17* **Bleiloch-stausee** ⊠ C Germany
98 *H12* **Bleiswijk** Zuid-Holland, W Netherlands *52°01´N 04°32´E*
95 *L22* **Blekinge** ◈ *county* S Sweden
14 *D17* **Blenheim** Ontario, S Canada *42°20´N 81°59´W*
185 *K15* **Blenheim** Marlborough, South Island, New Zealand *41°32´S 174°E*
99 *M15* **Blerick** Limburg, SE Netherlands *51°22´N 06°10´E*
Blesae *see* Blois
25 *V13* **Blessing** Texas, SW USA *28°52´N 96°12´W*
14 *I10* **Bleu, Lac** ◎ Québec, SE Canada
Blibba *see* Blitta
120 *H10* **Blida** *var.* El Boulaida, El Boulaïda. N Algeria *36°30´N 02°50´E*
95 *P15* **Blidö** Stockholm, C Sweden *59°37´N 18°55´E*
95 *K18* **Blidsberg** Västra Götaland, S Sweden *57°55´N 13°30´E*
185 *A21* **Bligh Sound** *sound* South Island, New Zealand
187 *X14* **Bligh Water** *strait* NW Fiji
14 *D11* **Blind River** Ontario, S Canada *46°12´N 82°59´W*
31 *R11* **Blissfield** Michigan, N USA *41°49´N 83°51´W*
77 *R15* **Blitta** *prev.* Blibba. C Togo *08°19´N 00°59´E*
19 *O13* **Block Island** *island* Rhode Island, NE USA
19 *O13* **Block Island Sound** *sound* Rhode Island, NE USA
98 *H10* **Bloemendaal** Noord-Holland, W Netherlands *52°23´N 04°39´E*
83 *H23* **Bloemfontein** *var.* Mangaung. ● (South Africa-judicial capital) Free State, C South Africa *29°07´S 26°14´E*
83 *I22* **Bloemhof** North-West, NW South Africa *27°39´S 25°37´E*
102 *M7* **Blois** *anc.* Blesae. Loir-et-Cher, C France *47°36´N 01°20´E*
98 *L8* **Blokzijl** Overijssel, N Netherlands *52°46´N 05°58´E*
95 *N20* **Blomstermåla** Kalmar, S Sweden *56°58´N 16°19´E*
92 *I2* **Blönduós** Nordhurland Vestra, N Iceland *65°39´N 20°15´W*
110 *L11* **Błonie** Mazowieckie, C Poland *52°13´N 20°36´E*
97 *C14* **Bloody Foreland** *Ir.* Cnoc Fola. *headland* NW Ireland *55°09´N 08°18´W*
31 *N15* **Bloomfield** Indiana, N USA *39°01´N 86°58´W*
29 *X16* **Bloomfield** Iowa, C USA *40°45´N 92°24´W*
27 *Y8* **Bloomfield** Missouri, C USA *36°54´N 89°58´W*
37 *P9* **Bloomfield** New Mexico, SW USA *36°42´N 108°00´W*
25 *U7* **Blooming Grove** Texas, SW USA *32°05´N 96°43´W*
29 *W10* **Blooming Prairie** Minnesota, N USA *43°52´N 93°03´W*
30 *L13* **Bloomington** Illinois, N USA *40°28´N 88°59´W*
31 *O15* **Bloomington** Indiana, N USA *39°10´N 86°31´W*
29 *V9* **Bloomington** Minnesota, N USA *44°50´N 93°18´W*
25 *U13* **Bloomington** Texas, SW USA *28°39´N 96°53´W*
18 *H14* **Bloomsburg** Pennsylvania, NE USA *40°59´N 76°27´W*
181 *X7* **Bloomsbury** Queensland, NE Australia *20°47´S 148°35´E*
169 *R16* **Blora** Jawa, C Indonesia *06°55´S 111°29´E*
18 *G12* **Blossburg** Pennsylvania, NE USA *41°38´N 77°00´W*
25 *V5* **Blossom** Texas, SW USA *33°39´N 95°23´W*
123 *T5* **Blossom, Mys** *headland* Ostrov Vrangelya, NE Russian Federation *70°49´N 178°49´E*
23 *R8* **Blountstown** Florida, SE USA *30°26´N 85°03´W*
21 *P8* **Blountville** Tennessee, S USA *36°31´N 82°19´W*
21 *Q9* **Blowing Rock** North Carolina, SE USA *36°15´N 81°53´W*
108 *J8* **Bludenz** Vorarlberg, W Austria *47°10´N 09°50´E*
36 *L6* **Blue Bell Knoll** ▲ Utah, W USA *38°11´N 111°31´W*
23 *Y12* **Blue Cypress Lake** ◎ Florida, SE USA
29 *U11* **Blue Earth** Minnesota, N USA *43°38´N 94°06´W*
21 *Q7* **Bluefield** Virginia, NE USA *37°15´N 81°16´W*
21 *R7* **Bluefield** West Virginia, NE USA *37°16´N 81°13´W*
43 *N10* **Bluefields** Región Autónoma Atlántico Sur, SE Nicaragua *12°01´N 83°47´W*
43 *N10* **Bluefields, Bahía de** *bay* W Caribbean Sea
29 *Z14* **Blue Grass** Iowa, C USA *41°30´N 90°46´W*
Bluegrass State *see* Kentucky
Blue Hen State *see* Delaware
19 *S7* **Blue Hill** Maine, NE USA *44°25´N 68°36´W*
29 *P16* **Blue Hill** Nebraska, C USA *40°19´N 98°27´W*
30 *J5* **Blue Hills** *hill range* Wisconsin, N USA
34 *L3* **Blue Lake** California, W USA *40°52´N 124°00´W*
Blue Law State *see* Connecticut
37 *Q6* **Blue Mesa Reservoir** ⊠ Colorado, C USA
27 *S12* **Blue Mountain** ▲ Arkansas, C USA *34°42´N 94°04´W*
19 *O6* **Blue Mountain** ▲ New Hampshire, NE USA *44°48´N 71°26´W*
18 *K8* **Blue Mountain** ▲ New York, NE USA *43°52´N 74°24´W*
18 *H15* **Blue Mountain** *ridge* Pennsylvania, NE USA
44 *H10* **Blue Mountain Peak** ▲ E Jamaica *18°02´N 76°34´W*
183 *S8* **Blue Mountains** ▲▲ New South Wales, SE Australia
32 *L11* **Blue Mountains** ▲▲ Oregon/Washington, NW USA
80 *G12* **Blue Nile** ◈ *state* E Sudan
80 *H12* **Blue Nile** *var.* Abai, Bahr el, Azraq, *Amh.* Ābay Wenz, *Ar.* An Nīl al Azraq. ≈ Ethiopia/Sudan
8 *J7* **Bluenose Lake** ◎ Nunavut, NW Canada
27 *O3* **Blue Rapids** Kansas, C USA *39°39´N 96°38´W*
23 *S1* **Blue Ridge** Georgia, SE USA *34°51´N 84°19´W*
17 *S11* **Blue Ridge** *var.* Blue Ridge Mountains. ▲▲ North Carolina/Virginia, USA
23 *S1* **Blue Ridge Lake** ⊠ Georgia, SE USA
Blue Ridge Mountains *see* Blue Ridge
11 *N15* **Blue River** British Columbia, SW Canada *52°03´N 119°21´W*
27 *O12* **Blue River** ≈ Oklahoma, C USA
27 *R4* **Blue Springs** Missouri, C USA *39°01´N 94°16´W*
21 *R6* **Bluestone Lake** ⊠ West Virginia, NE USA
185 *C25* **Bluff** Southland, South Island, New Zealand *46°36´S 168°22´E*
37 *O8* **Bluff** Utah, W USA *37°15´N 109°36´W*
21 *P8* **Bluff City** Tennessee, S USA *36°28´N 82°15´W*
65 *E24* **Bluff Cove** East Falkland, Falkland Islands *51°45´S 58°11´W*
25 *S7* **Bluff Dale** Texas, SW USA *32°18´N 98°01´W*
183 *N15* **Bluff Hill Point** *headland* Tasmania, SE Australia *41°03´S 144°35´E*
31 *Q12* **Bluffton** Indiana, N USA *40°44´N 85°10´W*
31 *R12* **Bluffton** Ohio, N USA *40°54´N 83°53´W*
25 *T7* **Blum** Texas, SW USA *32°08´N 97°24´W*
101 *G24* **Blumberg** Baden-Württemberg, SW Germany *47°48´N 08°31´E*
60 *K13* **Blumenau** Santa Catarina, S Brazil *26°55´S 49°07´W*
29 *N9* **Blunt** South Dakota, N USA *44°30´N 99°58´E*
32 *H15* **Bly** Oregon, NW USA *42°22´N 121°04´W*
39 *R13* **Blying Sound** *sound* Alaska, USA
97 *M14* **Blyth** N England, United Kingdom *55°07´N 01°30´W*
35 *Y16* **Blythe** California, W USA *33°35´N 114°36´W*
27 *Y9* **Blytheville** Arkansas, C USA *35°56´N 89°55´W*
117 *V7* **Blyznyuky** Kharkivs'ka Oblast', E Ukraine *48°51´N 36°32´E*
95 *G16* **Bø** Telemark, S Norway *59°24´N 09°04´E*
76 *I15* **Bo** S Sierra Leone *07°58´N 11°45´W*
171 *O4* **Boac** Marinduque, N Philippines *13°26´N 121°50´E*
42 *K10* **Boaco** Boaco, S Nicaragua *12°28´N 85°45´W*
42 *J10* **Boaco** ◈ *department* C Nicaragua
79 *I15* **Boali** Ombella-Mpoko, SW Central African Republic *04°52´N 18°00´E*
Boalsert *see* Bolsward
31 *V12* **Boardman** Ohio, N USA *41°01´N 80°39´W*
32 *J11* **Boardman** Oregon, NW USA *45°50´N 119°42´W*
14 *F13* **Boat Lake** ◎ Ontario, S Canada
58 *F10* **Boa Vista** *state capital* Roraima, NW Brazil *02°51´N 60°43´W*
76 *D9* **Boa Vista** *island* Ilhas de Barlavento, E Cape Verde
23 *Q2* **Boaz** Alabama, S USA *34°12´N 86°10´W*
160 *L15* **Bobai** Guangxi Zhuangzu Zizhiqu, S China *22°09´N 109°57´E*
172 *J1* **Bobaomby, Tanjona** *Fr.* Cap d'Ambre. *headland* N Madagascar *11°58´S 49°13´E*
155 *M14* **Bobbili** Andhra Pradesh, E India *18°32´N 83°29´E*
106 *D9* **Bobbio** Emilia-Romagna, C Italy *44°48´N 09°27´E*
14 *I14* **Bobcaygeon** Ontario, SE Canada *44°32´N 78°33´W*
Bober *see* Bóbr
103 *O5* **Bobigny** Seine-St-Denis, N France *48°55´N 02°27´E*
77 *N13* **Bobo-Dioulasso** SW Burkina *11°12´N 04°21´W*
110 *G8* **Bobolice** *Ger.* Bublitz. Zachodnio-pomorskie, NW Poland *53°56´N 16°37´E*
83 *J19* **Bobonong** Central, E Botswana *21°58´S 28°26´E*
171 *R11* **Bobopayo** Pulau Halmahera, E Indonesia *01°07´N 127°26´E*
113 *J15* **Bobotov Kuk** ▲ N Montenegro *43°06´N 19°00´E*
114 *G10* **Bobovdol** Kyustendil, W Bulgaria *42°21´N 22°59´E*
119 *M15* **Bobr** Minskaya Voblasts', NW Belarus *54°20´N 29°16´E*
119 *M15* **Bobr** ≈ C Belarus
111 *E14* **Bóbr** *Eng.* Bobrawa, *Ger.* Bober. ≈ SW Poland
Bobrawa *see* Bóbr
Bobrik *see* Bobryk
Bobrinets *see* Bobrynets'
Bobrka/Bóbrka *see* Bibrka
126 *L8* **Bobrov** Voronezhskaya Oblast', W Russian Federation *51°10´N 40°03´E*
117 *Q4* **Bobrovytsya** Chernihivs'ka Oblast', N Ukraine *50°43´N 31°24´E*
Bobruysk *see* Babruysk
119 *J19* **Bobryk** *Rus.* Bobrik. ≈ SW Belarus
117 *Q8* **Bobrynets'** *Rus.* Bobrinets. Kirovohrads'ka Oblast', C Ukraine *48°02´N 32°10´E*
14 *K14* **Bobs Lake** ◎ Ontario, SE Canada
54 *I6* **Bobures** Zulia, NW Venezuela *09°15´N 71°10´W*
42 *H1* **Boca Bacalar Chico** *headland* N Belize *15°05´N 82°12´W*
112 *G11* **Bočac** ◈ Republika Srpska, NW Bosnia and Herzegovina
41 *R14* **Boca del Río** Veracruz-Llave, S Mexico *19°08´N 96°08´W*
55 *O4* **Boca de Pozo** Nueva Esparta, NE Venezuela *11°00´N 64°23´W*
59 *C15* **Boca do Acre** Amazonas, N Brazil *08°45´S 67°23´W*
55 *N12* **Boca Mavaca** Amazonas, S Venezuela *02°30´N 65°11´W*
79 *G14* **Bocaranga** Ouham-Pendé, W Central African Republic *07°07´N 15°40´E*

◆ Country ● Country Capital ◇ Dependent Territory ○ Dependent Territory Capital ◈ Administrative Regions ✈ International Airport ▲ Mountain ▲▲ Mountain Range ⛰ Volcano ≈ River ◎ Lake ⊠ Reservoir

23 Z15 **Boca Raton** Florida, SE USA 26°22′N 80°05′W
43 P14 **Bocas del Toro** Bocas del Toro, NW Panama 09°20′N 82°15′W
43 P15 **Bocas del Toro** *off.* Provincia de Bocas del Toro. ◆ *province* NW Panama
43 P15 **Bocas del Toro, Archipiélago de** *island group* NW Panama
Bocas del Toro, Provincia de *see* Bocas del Toro
42 L7 **Bocay** Jinotega, N Nicaragua 14°19′N 85°08′W
105 N6 **Boceguillas** Castilla y León, N Spain 41°20′N 03°39′W
Bocheykovo *see* Bacheykava
111 L17 **Bochnia** Małopolskie, SE Poland 49°58′N 20°27′E
99 K16 **Bocholt** Limburg, NE Belgium 51°10′N 05°37′E
101 D14 **Bocholt** Nordrhein-Westfalen, W Germany 51°50′N 06°37′E
101 E15 **Bochum** Nordrhein-Westfalen, W Germany 51°29′N 07°13′E
103 Y15 **Bocognano** Corse, France, C Mediterranean Sea 42°04′N 09°03′E
54 I6 **Boconó** Trujillo, NW Venezuela 09°17′N 70°17′W
116 F12 **Bocșa** *Ger.* Bokschen, *Hung.* Boksánbánya. Caraș-Severin, SW Romania 45°23′N 21°47′E
79 H15 **Boda** Lobaye, SW Central African Republic 04°17′N 17°25′E
94 L12 **Boda** Dalarna, C Sweden 61°00′N 15°15′E
95 O20 **Böda** Kalmar, S Sweden 57°16′N 17°04′E
95 L19 **Bodafors** Jönköping, S Sweden 57°30′N 14°40′E
123 O12 **Bodaybo** Irkutskaya Oblast', E Russian Federation 57°52′N 114°05′E
22 G5 **Bodcau, Bayou** *var.* Bodcau Creek. ≈ Louisiana, S USA
Bodcau Creek *see* Bodcau, Bayou
44 D8 **Bodden Town** *var.* Boddentown. Grand Cayman, SW Cayman Islands 19°20′N 81°14′W
Boddentown *see* Bodden Town
101 K14 **Bode** ≈ C Germany
34 L7 **Bodega Head** *headland* California, W USA 38°16′N 123°04′W
Bodegas *see* Babahoyo
98 H11 **Bodegraven** Zuid-Holland, C Netherlands 52°05′N 04°45′E
78 H8 **Bodélé** *depression* W Chad
92 J13 **Boden** Norrbotten, N Sweden 65°50′N 21°44′E
Bodensee *see* Constance, Lake, C Europe
65 M15 **Bode Verde Fracture Zone** *tectonic feature* E Atlantic Ocean
155 H14 **Bodhan** Andhra Pradesh, C India 18°40′N 77°51′E
Bodi *see* Jinst
155 H22 **Bodināyakkanūr** Tamil Nādu, SE India 10°02′N 77°18′E
108 H10 **Bodio** Ticino, S Switzerland 46°23′N 08°55′E
Bodjonegoro *see* Bojonegoro
97 I24 **Bodmin** SW England, United Kingdom 50°29′N 04°43′W
97 I24 **Bodmin Moor** *moorland* SW England, United Kingdom
92 G12 **Bodø** Nordland, C Norway 67°17′N 14°22′E
59 H20 **Bodoquena, Serra da** ▲▲ SW Brazil
136 B16 **Bodrum** Muğla, SW Turkey 37°01′N 27°28′E
Bodzafordulő *see* Întorsura Buzăului
99 L14 **Boekel** Noord-Brabant, SE Netherlands 51°35′N 05°42′E
Boeloekoemba *see* Bulukumba
103 Q11 **Boën** Loire, E France 45°45′N 04°01′E
79 K18 **Boende** Equateur, C Dem. Rep. Congo 0°12′S 20°54′E
25 R11 **Boerne** Texas, SW USA 29°47′N 98°44′W
Boeroe *see* Buru, Pulau
Boetoeng *see* Buton, Pulau
22 I5 **Boeuf River** ≈ Arkansas/Louisiana, S USA
76 H14 **Boffa** W Guinea 10°12′N 14°02′W
Bó Finne, Inis *see* Inishbofin
Boga *see* Bogë
166 L9 **Bogale** Ayeyarwady, SW Burma (Myanmar) 16°16′N 95°21′E
22 L8 **Bogalusa** Louisiana, S USA 30°47′N 89°51′W
77 Q12 **Bogandé** C Burkina 13°02′N 00°08′W
79 I15 **Bogangolo** Ombella-Mpoko, C Central African Republic 05°36′N 18°17′E
183 Q7 **Bogan River** ≈ New South Wales, SE Australia
25 W5 **Bogata** Texas, SW USA 33°28′N 95°12′W
111 D14 **Bogatynia** *Ger.* Reichenau. Dolnośląskie, SW Poland 50°53′N 14°55′E
136 K13 **Boğazlıyan** Yozgat, C Turkey 39°13′N 35°17′E
79 J17 **Bogbonga** Equateur, NW Dem. Rep. Congo 01°36′N 19°24′E
158 J14 **Bogcang Zangbo** ≈ W China
162 I9 **Bogd** *var.* Horiult. Bayanhongor, C Mongolia 45°09′N 100°50′E
162 J10 **Bogd** *var.* Hovd. Övörhangay, C Mongolia 44°43′N 102°08′E
158 L5 **Bogda Feng** ▲ NW China 43°51′N 88°14′E
114 I9 **Bogdan** ▲ C Bulgaria 42°37′N 24°28′E
113 Q20 **Bogdanci** SE FYR Macedonia 41°12′N 22°34′E
158 M5 **Bogda Shan** *var.* Po-ko-to Shan. ▲▲ NW China
113 K17 **Bogë** *var.* Boga. Shkodër, N Albania 42°25′N 19°38′E
Bogeda'er *see* Wenquan
Bogendorf *see* Łuków
95 G23 **Bogense** Syddtjylland, C Denmark 55°34′N 10°06′E
183 T3 **Boggabilla** New South Wales, SE Australia 28°37′S 150°21′E
183 S6 **Boggabri** New South Wales, SE Australia 30°44′S 150°00′E
186 D6 **Bogia** Madang, N Papua New Guinea 04°16′S 144°56′E
97 N23 **Bognor Regis** SE England, United Kingdom 50°47′N 00°41′W
Bogodukhov *see* Bohodukhiv
181 V15 **Bogong, Mount** ▲ Victoria, SE Australia 36°43′S 147°19′E
169 O16 **Bogor** *Dut.* Buitenzorg. Jawa, C Indonesia 06°34′S 106°45′E
126 L5 **Bogoroditsk** Tul'skaya Oblast', W Russian Federation 53°46′N 38°09′E
127 O3 **Bogorodsk** Nizhegorodskaya Oblast', W Russian Federation 56°06′N 43°29′E
Bogorodskoje *see* Bogorodskoye
123 S12 **Bogorodskoye** Khabarovskiy Kray, SE Russian Federation 52°22′N 140°33′E
125 R15 **Bogorodskoye** *var.* Bogorodskoje. Kirovskaya Oblast', NW Russian Federation 57°50′N 50°41′E
54 F10 **Bogotá** *prev.* Santa Fe, Santa Fe de Bogotá. ● (Colombia) Cundinamarca, C Colombia 04°38′N 74°05′W
153 T14 **Bogra** Rajshahi, N Bangladesh 24°52′N 89°28′E
Bogschan *see* Boldu
122 L12 **Boguchany** Krasnoyarskiy Kray, C Russian Federation 58°20′N 97°20′E
126 M9 **Boguchar** Voronezhskaya Oblast', W Russian Federation 49°57′N 40°34′E
76 H10 **Bogué** Brakna, SW Mauritania 16°36′N 14°15′W
22 K8 **Bogue Chitto** ≈ Louisiana/Mississippi, S USA
Bogushëvsk *see* Bahushewsk
Boguslav *see* Bohuslav
44 K12 **Bog Walk** C Jamaica 18°06′N 77°01′W
161 Q3 **Bo Hai** *var.* Gulf of Chihli. *gulf* NE China
161 R3 **Bohai Haixia** *strait* NE China
161 Q3 **Bohai Wan** *bay* NE China
111 C17 **Bohemia** *Cz.* Čechy, *Ger.* Böhmen. W Czech Republic
111 B18 **Bohemian Forest** *Cz.* Ceský Les, Šumava, *Ger.* Böhmerwald. ▲▲ C Europe
Bohemian-Moravian Highlands *see* Českomoravská Vrchovina
77 R16 **Bohicon** S Benin 07°14′N 02°04′E
109 S11 **Bohinjska Bistrica** *Ger.* Wocheiner Feistritz. NW Slovenia 46°16′N 13°55′E
Bohkká *see* Pokka
Böhmen *see* Bohemia
Böhmerwald *see* Bohemian Forest
Böhmisch-Krumau *see* Český Krumlov
Böhmisch-Leipa *see* Česká Lípa
Böhmisch-Mährische Höhe *see* Českomoravská Vrchovina
Böhmisch-Trübau *see* Česká Třebová
117 U5 **Bohodukhiv** *Rus.* Bogodukhov. Kharkivs'ka Oblast', E Ukraine 50°10′N 35°32′E
171 Q6 **Bohol** *island* C Philippines
171 Q7 **Bohol Sea** *var.* Mindanao Sea. *sea* S Philippines
116 I7 **Bohorodchany** Ivano-Frankivs'ka Oblast', W Ukraine 48°46′N 24°31′E
Böhöt *see* Öndörshil
158 K6 **Bohu** *var.* Bagrax. Xinjiang Uygur Zizhiqu, NW China 42°00′N 86°28′E
111 I17 **Bohumín** *Ger.* Oderberg; *prev.* Neuoderberg, Nový Bohumín. Moravskoslezský Kraj, E Czech Republic 49°55′N 18°20′E
117 P6 **Bohuslav** *Rus.* Boguslav. Kyyivs'ka Oblast', N Ukraine 49°33′N 30°53′E
58 F11 **Boiaçu** Roraima, N Brazil 0°27′S 61°46′W
107 K16 **Boiano** Molise, C Italy 41°28′N 14°28′E
15 R8 **Boilleau** Québec, SE Canada 48°06′N 70°49′W
59 O17 **Boipeba, Ilha de** *island* SE Brazil
104 G3 **Boiro** Galicia, NW Spain 42°39′N 08°53′W
31 Q5 **Bois Blanc Island** *island* Michigan, N USA
29 R7 **Bois de Sioux River** ≈ Minnesota, N USA
33 N14 **Boise** *var.* Boise City. *state capital* Idaho, NW USA 43°39′N 116°14′W
26 G8 **Boise City** Oklahoma, C USA 36°44′N 102°31′W
Boise City *see* Boise
33 N14 **Boise River, Middle Fork** ≈ Idaho, NW USA
Bois, Lac des *see* Woods, Lake of the
Bois-le-Duc *see* 's-Hertogenbosch
11 W17 **Boissevain** Manitoba, S Canada 49°14′N 100°02′W
15 T7 **Boisvert, Pointe au** *headland* Québec, SE Canada 48°34′N 69°07′W
100 K10 **Boizenburg** Mecklenburg-Vorpommern, N Germany 53°23′N 10°43′E
Bojador *see* Boujdour
113 K18 **Bojana** *Alb.* Bunë. ≈ Albania/Montenegro *see also* Bunë
Bojana *see* Bunë, Lumi i
143 S3 **Bojnūrd** *var.* Bujnurd. Khorāsān-e Shemālī, N Iran 37°31′N 57°24′E
169 R16 **Bojonegoro** *prev.* Bodjonegoro. Jawa, C Indonesia 07°06′S 111°50′E
189 T1 **Bokaak Atoll** *var.* Bokak, Taongi. *atoll* Ratak Chain, NE Marshall Islands
Bokak *see* Bokaak Atoll
146 K8 **Bo'kantov Tog'lari** *Rus.* Gory Bukantau. ▲ N Uzbekistan
153 Q15 **Bokāro** Jhārkhand, N India 23°46′N 85°55′E
79 I18 **Bokatola** Equateur, NW Dem. Rep. Congo 0°37′S 18°45′E
76 H13 **Boké** W Guinea 10°56′N 14°18′W
Bokhara *see* Buxoro
183 Q4 **Bokharra River** ≈ New South Wales/Queensland, SE Australia
147 X8 **Bokonbayevo** *Kir.* Kajisay; *prev.* Kadzhi-Say. Issyk-Kul'skaya Oblast', NE Kyrgyzstan 42°07′N 76°59′E
78 H11 **Bokoro** Chari-Baguirmi, W Chad 12°23′N 17°03′E
79 K19 **Bokota** Equateur, NW Dem. Rep. Congo 0°56′S 22°24′E
167 N13 **Bokpyin** Tanintharyi, S Burma (Myanmar) 11°16′N 98°47′E
Boksánbánya/Bokschen *see* Bocșa
83 F21 **Bokspits** Kgalagadi, SW Botswana 26°50′S 20°41′E
79 K18 **Bokungu** Equateur, C Dem. Rep. Congo 0°41′S 22°19′E
146 F12 **Bokurdak** *Rus.* Bakhardok. Ahal Welaýaty, C Turkmenistan 38°51′N 58°34′E
78 G10 **Bol** Lac, W Chad 13°27′N 14°40′E
76 G13 **Bolama** SW Guinea-Bissau 11°35′N 15°30′W
Bolangir *see* Balāngīr
Bolanos *see* Bolanos, Mount, Guam
Bolaños *see* Bolaños de Calatrava, Spain
105 N11 **Bolaños de Calatrava** *var.* Bolaños. Castilla-La Mancha, C Spain 38°55′N 03°39′W
188 B17 **Bolanos, Mount** *var.* Bolanos. ▲ S Guam 13°18′N 144°41′E
40 L12 **Bolaños, Río** ≈ C Mexico
115 M14 **Bolayır** Çanakkale, NW Turkey 40°31′N 26°46′E
102 L3 **Bolbec** Seine-Maritime, N France 49°34′N 00°31′E
116 L13 **Boldu** *var.* Bogschan. Buzău, SE Romania 45°18′N 27°15′E
146 H8 **Boldumsaz** *prev.* Kalinin, Kalininsk, Porsy. Daşoguz Welaýaty, N Turkmenistan 42°12′N 59°33′E
158 I4 **Bole** *var.* Bortala. Xinjiang Uygur Zizhiqu, NW China 44°52′N 82°06′E
77 O15 **Bole** NW Ghana 09°02′N 02°29′W
79 J19 **Boleko** Equateur, W Dem. Rep. Congo 01°27′S 19°52′E
111 E14 **Bolesławiec** *Ger.* Bunzlau. Dolnośląskie, SW Poland 51°16′N 15°34′E
127 R4 **Bolgar** *prev.* Kuybyshev. Respublika Tatarstan, W Russian Federation 54°58′N 49°03′E
77 P14 **Bolgatanga** N Ghana 10°45′N 00°52′W
Bolgrad *see* Bolhrad
117 N12 **Bolhrad** *Rus.* Bolgrad. Odes'ka Oblast', SW Ukraine 45°42′N 28°35′E
163 Y8 **Boli** Heilongjiang, NE China 45°45′N 130°32′E
79 I19 **Bolia** Bandundu, W Dem. Rep. Congo 01°34′S 18°24′E
93 J14 **Boliden** Västerbotten, N Sweden 64°52′N 20°20′E
171 T13 **Bolifar** Pulau Seram, E Indonesia 03°08′S 130°34′E
171 N2 **Bolinao** Luzon, N Philippines 16°22′N 119°52′E
54 C12 **Bolívar** Cauca, SW Colombia 01°52′N 76°56′W
27 T6 **Bolivar** Missouri, C USA 37°37′N 93°25′W
20 F10 **Bolivar** Tennessee, S USA 35°17′N 88°59′W
54 F7 **Bolívar** *off.* Departmento de Bolívar. ◆ *province* N Colombia
56 A13 **Bolívar** ◆ *province* C Ecuador
55 N9 **Bolívar** *off.* Estado Bolívar. ◆ *state* SE Venezuela
Bolívar, Departmento de *see* Bolívar
Bolívar, Estado *see* Bolívar
25 X12 **Bolivar Peninsula** *headland* Texas, SW USA 29°26′N 94°41′W
54 I6 **Bolívar, Pico** ▲ W Venezuela 08°33′N 71°05′W
57 K17 **Bolivia** *off.* Republic of Bolivia. ◆ *republic* W South America
Bolivia, Republic of *see* Bolivia
112 O13 **Boljevac** Serbia, E Serbia 43°50′N 21°57′E
Bolkenhain *see* Bolków
126 J5 **Bolkhov** Orlovskaya Oblast', W Russian Federation 53°28′N 36°00′E
111 F14 **Bolków** *Ger.* Bolkenhain. Dolnośląskie, SW Poland 50°55′N 15°49′E
182 K3 **Bollards Lagoon** South Australia 28°58′S 140°52′E
103 R14 **Bollène** Vaucluse, SE France 44°16′N 04°45′E
94 N12 **Bollnäs** Gävleborg, C Sweden 61°18′N 16°27′E
181 W10 **Bollon** Queensland, C Australia 28°07′S 147°28′E
192 L12 **Bollons Tablemount** *undersea feature* S Pacific Ocean 49°40′S 176°10′W
93 H17 **Bollstabruk** Västernorrland, C Sweden 63°00′N 17°41′E
Bollulos de Par del Condado *see* Bollulos Par del Condado
104 J14 **Bollulos Par del Condado** *var.* Bollulos de Par del Condado. Andalucía, S Spain 37°20′N 06°32′W
95 K21 **Bolmen** ◎ S Sweden
137 T10 **Bolnisi** S Georgia 41°28′N 44°34′E
79 H19 **Bolobo** Bandundu, W Dem. Rep. Congo 02°10′S 16°17′E
106 G10 **Bologna** Emilia-Romagna, N Italy 44°30′N 11°20′E
124 I15 **Bologoye** Tverskaya Oblast', W Russian Federation 57°54′N 34°04′E
79 J18 **Bolomba** Equateur, NW Dem. Rep. Congo 0°27′N 19°13′E
41 X13 **Bolonchén de Rejón** *var.* Bolonchén de Rejón. Campeche, SE Mexico 20°00′N 89°34′W
114 J13 **Boloústra, Akrotírio** *headland* NE Greece 40°56′N 24°58′E
167 L8 **Bolovén, Phouphiang** *Fr.* Plateau des Bolovens. *plateau* S Laos
Bolovens, Plateau des *see* Bolovén, Phouphiang
106 H13 **Bolsena** Lazio, C Italy 42°39′N 11°59′E
107 G14 **Bolsena, Lago di** ◎ C Italy
126 B3 **Bol'shakovo** *Ger.* Kreuzingen; *prev.* Gross-Skaisgirren. Kaliningradskaya Oblast', W Russian Federation 54°53′N 21°38′E
Bol'shaya Berëstovitsa *see* Vyalikaya Byerastavitsa
127 S7 **Bol'shaya Chernigovka** Samarskaya Oblast', W Russian Federation 52°07′N 50°49′E
127 S7 **Bol'shaya Glushitsa** Samarskaya Oblast', W Russian Federation 52°22′N 50°29′E
124 J4 **Bol'shaya Imandra, Ozero** ◎ NW Russian Federation
Bol'shaya Khobda *see* Kobda
126 M12 **Bol'shaya Martynovka** Rostovskaya Oblast', SW Russian Federation 47°19′N 41°40′E
122 K12 **Bol'shaya Murta** Krasnoyarskiy Kray, C Russian Federation 56°51′N 93°10′E
125 V4 **Bol'shaya Rogovaya** ≈ NW Russian Federation
125 U7 **Bol'shaya Synya** ≈ NW Russian Federation
145 V9 **Bol'shaya Vladimirovka** Vostochnyy Kazakhstan, E Kazakhstan 50°53′N 79°29′E
123 V11 **Bol'sheretsk** Kamchatskiy Kray, E Russian Federation 52°20′N 156°24′E
127 W3 **Bol'sheust'ikinskoye** Respublika Bashkortostan, W Russian Federation 56°00′N 58°13′E
Bol'shevik *see* Bal'shavik
122 L5 **Bol'shevik, Ostrov** *island* Severnaya Zemlya, N Russian Federation
125 U4 **Bol'shezemel'skaya Tundra** *physical region* NW Russian Federation
144 J13 **Bol'shiye Barsuki, Peski** *desert* SW Kazakhstan
123 T7 **Bol'shoy Anyuy** ≈ NE Russian Federation
123 N7 **Bol'shoy Begichev, Ostrov** *island* NE Russian Federation
123 S15 **Bol'shoye Kamen'** Primorskiy Kray, SE Russian Federation 43°06′N 132°21′E
127 O4 **Bol'shoye Murashkino** Nizhegorodskaya Oblast', W Russian Federation 55°46′N 44°48′E
127 W4 **Bol'shoy Iremel'** ▲ W Russian Federation 54°31′N 58°47′E
127 R7 **Bol'shoy Irgiz** ≈ W Russian Federation
123 Q6 **Bol'shoy Lyakhovskiy, Ostrov** *island* NE Russian Federation
123 Q11 **Bol'shoy Nimnyr** Respublika Sakha (Yakutiya), NE Russian Federation 57°55′N 125°34′E
Bol'shoy Rozhan *see* Vyaliki Rozhan
Bol'shoy Uzen' *see* Karaozen
40 K6 **Bolsón de Mapimí** ▲ NW Mexico
98 K6 **Bolsward** *Fris.* Boalsert. Fryslân, N Netherlands 53°04′N 05°31′E
105 T4 **Boltaña** Aragón, NE Spain 42°28′N 00°02′E
14 G15 **Bolton** Ontario, S Canada 43°52′N 79°45′W
97 K17 **Bolton** *prev.* Bolton-le-Moors. NW England, United Kingdom 53°35′N 02°26′W
21 V12 **Bolton** North Carolina, SE USA 34°22′N 78°26′W
Bolton-le-Moors *see* Bolton
136 G11 **Bolu** Bolu, NW Turkey 40°45′N 31°38′E
136 G11 **Bolu** ◆ *province* NW Turkey
186 G9 **Bolubolu** Goodenough Island, S Papua New Guinea 09°22′S 150°22′E
92 H1 **Bolungarvík** Vestfirdhir, NW Iceland 66°09′N 23°17′W
159 O10 **Boluntay** Qinghai, W China 36°30′N 92°11′E
159 P8 **Boluozhuanjing**, Aksay Kazakzu Zizhixian. Gansu, N China 39°25′N 94°09′E
136 F14 **Bolvadin** Afyon, W Turkey 38°43′N 31°02′E
114 M10 **Bolyarovo** *prev.* Pashkeni. Yambol, E Bulgaria 42°09′N 26°49′E
106 G6 **Bolzano** *Ger.* Bozen; *anc.* Bauzanum. Trentino-Alto Adige, N Italy 46°30′N 11°22′E
79 F22 **Boma** Bas-Congo, W Dem. Rep. Congo 05°42′S 13°05′E
183 R12 **Bombala** New South Wales, SE Australia 36°54′S 149°15′E
104 F10 **Bombarral** Leiria, C Portugal 39°15′N 09°09′W
Bombay *see* Mumbai
171 U13 **Bomberai, Semenanjung** *cape* Papua, E Indonesia
81 F18 **Bombo** S Uganda 0°36′N 32°33′E
162 I8 **Bömbögör** *var.* Dzadgay. Bayanhongor, C Mongolia 46°12′N 99°29′E
79 I17 **Bomboma** Equateur, NW Dem. Rep. Congo 02°23′N 19°03′E
59 I14 **Bom Futuro** Pará, N Brazil 06°27′S 54°44′W
159 Q15 **Bomi** *var.* Bowo, Zhamo. Xizang Zizhiqu, W China 29°43′N 96°12′E
79 N17 **Bomili** Orientale, NE Dem. Rep. Congo 01°45′N 27°01′E
59 N17 **Bom Jesus da Lapa** Bahia, E Brazil 13°16′S 43°23′W
60 Q8 **Bom Jesus do Itabapoana** Rio de Janeiro, SE Brazil 21°07′S 41°43′W
95 C15 **Bømlafjorden** *fjord* S Norway
95 B15 **Bømlo** *island* S Norway
12 Q12 **Bomnak** Amurskaya Oblast', SE Russian Federation 54°43′N 128°50′E
79 I17 **Bomongo** Equateur, NW Dem. Rep. Congo 01°22′N 18°21′E
61 K14 **Bom Retiro** Santa Catarina, S Brazil 27°45′S 49°31′W
79 L15 **Bomu** *var.* Mbomou, Mbomu, M'Bomu. ≈ Central African Republic/Dem. Rep. Congo
142 J3 **Bonāb** *var.* Benāb, Bunab. Āžarbāyjān-e Sharqī, N Iran 37°30′N 46°03′E
45 S9 **Bonaire** ◆ *Dutch autonomous region* S Caribbean Sea
45 Q16 **Bonaire** *island* Lesser Antilles
39 U11 **Bona, Mount** ▲ Alaska, USA 61°22′N 141°45′W
183 Q12 **Bonang** Victoria, SE Australia 37°13′S 148°43′E
42 L7 **Bonanza** Región Autónoma Atlántico Norte, NE Nicaragua 13°59′N 84°30′W
37 O4 **Bonanza** Utah, W USA 40°01′N 109°12′W
45 O9 **Bonao** C Dominican Republic 18°55′N 70°25′W
180 L3 **Bonaparte Archipelago** *island group* Western Australia
32 K6 **Bonaparte, Mount** ▲ Washington, NW USA 48°47′N 119°07′W
39 N11 **Bonasila Dome** ▲ Alaska, USA 62°24′N 160°28′W
45 T15 **Bonasse** Trinidad, Trinidad and Tobago 10°02′N 61°48′W
15 X7 **Bonaventure** Québec, SE Canada 48°03′N 65°30′W
15 X7 **Bonaventure** ≈ Québec, SE Canada
13 V11 **Bonavista** Newfoundland, Newfoundland and Labrador, SE Canada 48°38′N 53°08′W
13 U11 **Bonavista Bay** *inlet* NW Atlantic Ocean
79 E19 **Bonda** Ogooué-Lolo, C Gabon 0°50′S 12°28′E
127 N6 **Bondari** Tambovskaya Oblast', W Russian Federation 52°58′N 42°02′E
106 G9 **Bondeno** Emilia-Romagna, C Italy 44°53′N 11°24′E
30 L4 **Bond Falls Flowage** ◎ Michigan, N USA
79 L16 **Bondo** Orientale, N Dem. Rep. Congo 03°52′N 23°41′E
171 N17 **Bondokodi** Pulau Sumba, S Indonesia 09°36′S 119°01′E
77 O15 **Bondoukou** E Ivory Coast 08°03′N 02°45′W
Bondoukui/Bondoukuy *see* Boundoukui
169 T17 **Bondowoso** Jawa, C Indonesia 07°54′S 113°50′E
33 S14 **Bondurant** Wyoming, C USA 43°14′N 110°26′W
Bône *see* Annaba, Algeria
Bone *see* Watampone, Indonesia
30 I5 **Bone Lake** ◎ Wisconsin, N USA
171 P14 **Bonelipu** Pulau Buton, C Indonesia 04°42′S 123°09′E
171 O15 **Bonerate, Kepulauan** *var.* Macan. *island group* C Indonesia
29 O12 **Bonesteel** South Dakota, N USA 43°01′N 98°55′W
62 I8 **Bonete, Cerro** ▲ N Argentina 27°58′S 68°22′W
171 O14 **Bone, Teluk** *bay* Sulawesi, C Indonesia
108 D6 **Bonfol** Jura, NW Switzerland 47°28′N 07°08′E
153 U12 **Bongaigaon** Assam, NE India 26°30′N 90°31′E
79 K17 **Bongandanga** Equateur, NW Dem. Rep. Congo 01°28′N 21°03′E
78 L13 **Bongo, Massif des** *var.* Chaîne des Mongos. ▲ NE Central African Republic
78 G12 **Bongor** Mayo-Kébbi, SW Chad 10°18′N 15°20′E
77 N16 **Bongouanou** E Ivory Coast 06°39′N 04°12′W
167 V11 **Bông Sơn** *var.* Hoài Nhơn. Binh Đinh, C Vietnam 14°28′N 109°00′E
25 U5 **Bonham** Texas, SW USA 33°36′N 96°12′W
Bonhard *see* Bonyhád
103 U6 **Bonhomme, Col du** *pass* NE France
103 Y16 **Bonifacio** Corse, France, C Mediterranean Sea 41°24′N 09°09′E
Bonifacio, Bouches de/Bonifacio, Bouches de *see* Bonifacio, Strait of
103 Y16 **Bonifacio, Strait of** *Fr.* Bouches de Bonifacio, *It.* Bocche di Bonifacio. *strait* C Mediterranean Sea
23 Q8 **Bonifay** Florida, SE USA 30°49′N 85°42′W
Bonin Islands *see* Ogasawara-shotō
192 H5 **Bonin Trench** *undersea feature* NW Pacific Ocean
23 W15 **Bonita Springs** Florida, SE USA 26°19′N 81°48′W
42 I5 **Bonito, Pico** ▲ N Honduras 15°33′N 86°55′W
101 E17 **Bonn** Nordrhein-Westfalen, W Germany 50°44′N 07°06′E
92 H11 **Bonnåsjøen** Nordland, C Norway 67°35′N 15°39′E
14 J12 **Bonnechere** Ontario, SE Canada 45°39′N 77°36′W
14 J12 **Bonnechere** ≈ Ontario, SE Canada
33 N7 **Bonners Ferry** Idaho, NW USA 48°41′N 116°19′W
27 R4 **Bonner Springs** Kansas, C USA 39°03′N 94°52′W
102 L6 **Bonnétable** Sarthe, NW France 48°09′N 00°24′E
27 X6 **Bonne Terre** Missouri, C USA 37°55′N 90°33′W
10 J5 **Bonnet Plume** ≈ Yukon Territory, NW Canada
102 M6 **Bonneval** Eure-et-Loir, C France 48°12′N 01°23′E
103 T10 **Bonneville** Haute-Savoie, E France 46°05′N 06°25′E
36 J3 **Bonneville Salt Flats** *salt flat* Utah, W USA
77 U18 **Bonny** Rivers, S Nigeria 04°25′N 07°13′E
Bonny, Bight of *see* Biafra, Bight of
37 W4 **Bonny Reservoir** ⊠ Colorado, C USA
11 R14 **Bonnyville** Alberta, SW Canada 54°16′N 110°46′W
107 C18 **Bono** Sardegna, Italy, C Mediterranean Sea 40°24′N 09°01′E
Bononia *see* Vidin, Bulgaria
Bononia *see* Boulogne-sur-Mer, France
107 B18 **Bonorva** Sardegna, Italy, C Mediterranean Sea 40°27′N 08°46′E
30 M15 **Bonpas Creek** ≈ Illinois, N USA
190 I3 **Bonriki** Tarawa, W Kiribati 01°23′N 173°09′E
183 T4 **Bonshaw** New South Wales, SE Australia 29°06′S 151°15′E
76 I16 **Bonthe** SW Sierra Leone 07°32′N 12°30′W
171 N2 **Bontoc** Luzon, N Philippines 17°04′N 120°58′E
25 Y9 **Bon Wier** Texas, SW USA 30°43′N 93°40′W
111 J25 **Bonyhád** *Ger.* Bonhard. Tolna, S Hungary 46°20′N 18°31′E
Bonzabaai *see* Bonza Bay
83 J25 **Bonza Bay** *Afr.* Bonzabaai. Eastern Cape, S South Africa 32°58′S 27°58′E
182 D7 **Bookabie** South Australia 31°49′S 132°41′E
182 H6 **Bookaloo** South Australia 31°56′S 137°21′E
37 P5 **Book Cliffs** *cliff* Colorado/Utah, W USA
25 P1 **Booker** Texas, SW USA 36°27′N 100°32′W
76 K15 **Boola** SE Guinea 08°22′N 08°41′W
183 O8 **Booligal** New South Wales, SE Australia 33°56′S 144°54′E
99 G17 **Boom** Antwerpen, N Belgium 51°05′N 04°24′E
43 N6 **Boom** *var.* Boon. Región Autónoma Atlántico Norte, NE Nicaragua 14°52′N 83°36′W
183 S3 **Boomi** New South Wales, SE Australia 28°43′S 149°35′E
Boon *see* Boom
162 H9 **Bööncagaan Nuur** ◎ S Mongolia
29 V13 **Boone** Iowa, C USA 42°04′N 93°52′W
21 Q8 **Boone** North Carolina, SE USA 36°13′N 81°41′W
27 S11 **Booneville** Arkansas, C USA 35°09′N 93°57′W
21 N6 **Booneville** Kentucky, S USA 37°26′N 83°45′W
23 N2 **Booneville** Mississippi, S USA 34°39′N 88°34′W
21 V3 **Boonsboro** Maryland, NE USA 39°30′N 77°39′W
34 L6 **Boonville** California, W USA 38°58′N 123°21′W
31 N16 **Boonville** Indiana, N USA 38°03′N 87°16′W
27 U4 **Boonville** Missouri, C USA 38°58′N 92°43′W
18 I9 **Boonville** New York, NE USA 43°28′N 75°17′W
80 M12 **Booraama** Awdal, NW Somalia 09°58′N 43°15′E
183 O6 **Booroondarra, Mount** *hill* New South Wales, SE Australia
183 N9 **Booroorban** New South Wales, SE Australia 34°55′S 144°45′E
183 R9 **Boorowa** New South Wales, SE Australia 34°26′S 148°42′E
99 H17 **Boortmeerbeek** Vlaams Brabant, C Belgium 50°58′N 04°27′E
80 P11 **Boosaaso** *var.* Bandar Kassim, Bender Qaasim, Bosaso, *It.* Bender Cassim. Bari, N Somalia 11°26′N 49°37′E
19 Q8 **Boothbay Harbor** Maine, NE USA 43°52′N 69°35′W
Boothia Felix *see* Boothia Peninsula
9 N6 **Boothia, Gulf of** *gulf* Nunavut, NE Canada
9 N6 **Boothia Peninsula** *prev.* Boothia Felix. *peninsula* Nunavut, NE Canada
79 E18 **Booué** Ogooué-Ivindo, NE Gabon 00°03′S 11°58′E
101 J21 **Bopfingen** Baden-Württemberg, S Germany 48°51′N 10°21′E
101 F18 **Boppard** Rheinland-Pfalz, W Germany 50°13′N 07°36′E
62 M4 **Boquerón** *off.* Departmento de Boquerón. ◆ *department* W Paraguay
Boquerón, Departamento de *see* Boquerón
43 P15 **Boquete** *var.* Bajo Boquete. Chiriquí, W Panama 08°45′N 82°26′W
40 J6 **Boquilla, Presa de la** ⊠ N Mexico
40 L5 **Boquillas** *var.* Boquillas del Carmen. Coahuila, NE Mexico 29°10′N 102°55′W
Boquillas del Carmen *see* Boquillas
112 P12 **Bor** Serbia, E Serbia 44°05′N 22°07′E
81 F15 **Bor** Jonglei, E South Sudan 06°12′N 31°33′E
95 L20 **Bor** Jönköping, S Sweden 57°04′N 14°10′E
136 J15 **Bor** Niğde, S Turkey 37°49′N 35°00′E
191 S10 **Bora-Bora** *island* Îles Sous le Vent, W French Polynesia
167 Q9 **Borabu** Maha Sarakham, E Thailand 16°01′N 103°06′E
172 K4 **Boraha, Nosy** *island* E Madagascar
33 P13 **Borah Peak** ▲ Idaho, NW USA 44°21′N 113°53′W
145 U16 **Boralday** *prev.* Burunday. Almaty, SE Kazakhstan 43°21′N 76°48′E
145 Y11 **Boran** *prev.* Buran. Vostochnyy Kazakhstan, E Kazakhstan 48°00′N 85°09′E
144 G13 **Borankul** *prev.* Opornyy. Mangistau, SW Kazakhstan 46°09′N 54°32′E
95 J19 **Borås** Västra Götaland, S Sweden 57°44′N 12°55′E
143 N11 **Borāzjān** *var.* Borazjān. Būshehr, S Iran 29°19′N 51°12′E
Borazjān *see* Borāzjān
58 G13 **Borba** Amazonas, N Brazil 04°39′S 59°35′W
104 H11 **Borba** Évora, S Portugal 38°48′N 07°28′W
Borbetomagus *see* Worms
55 O7 **Borbón** Bolívar, E Venezuela 07°55′N 64°03′W
59 Q15 **Borborema, Planalto da** *plateau* NE Brazil
116 M14 **Borcea, Brațul** ≈ S Romania
Borchalo *see* Marneuli
195 R15 **Borchgrevink Coast** *physical region* Antarctica
137 Q11 **Borçka** Artvin, NE Turkey 41°24′N 41°38′E
98 N11 **Borculo** Gelderland, E Netherlands 52°07′N 06°31′E
182 G10 **Borda, Cape** *headland* South Australia 35°45′S 136°34′E
102 K13 **Bordeaux** *anc.* Burdigala. Gironde, SW France 44°49′N 00°33′W
11 T15 **Borden** Saskatchewan, S Canada 52°23′N 107°10′W
14 D8 **Borden Lake** ◎ Ontario, S Canada
9 N4 **Borden Peninsula** *peninsula* Baffin Island, Nunavut, NE Canada
182 K11 **Bordertown** South Australia 36°21′S 140°48′E
92 H2 **Bordheyri** Vestfirdhir, NW Iceland 65°12′N 21°09′W
95 B18 **Bordhoy** *Dan.* Bordø. *island* NE Faeroe Islands
106 B11 **Bordighera** Liguria, NW Italy 43°48′N 07°40′E
74 K5 **Bordj-Bou-Arreridj** *var.* Bordj Bou Arreridj, Bordj Bou Arréridj. N Algeria 36°02′N 04°49′E
74 L10 **Bordj Omar Driss** E Algeria 28°09′N 06°52′E
143 N13 **Bord Khūn** Hormozgān, S Iran
Bordø *see* Bordhoy
147 V7 **Bordunskiy** Chuyskaya Oblast', N Kyrgyzstan 42°37′N 75°31′E
95 M17 **Borensberg** Östergötland, S Sweden 58°33′N 15°15′E
Borgå *see* Porvoo
92 L2 **Borgarfjördhur** Austurland, NE Iceland 65°32′N 13°46′W
92 H3 **Borgarnes** Vesturland, W Iceland 64°33′N 21°55′W
93 G14 **Børgefjell** ▲ C Norway
98 O7 **Borger** Drenthe, NE Netherlands 52°54′N 06°48′E
25 N2 **Borger** Texas, SW USA 35°40′N 101°24′W
95 N20 **Borgholm** Kalmar, S Sweden 56°50′N 16°41′E
107 N22 **Borgia** Calabria, SW Italy 38°48′N 16°28′E
99 J18 **Borgloon** Limburg, NE Belgium 50°48′N 05°21′E
Borg Massif *see* Borgmassivet
195 P2 **Borgmassivet** *Eng.* Borg Massif. ▲ Antarctica
22 L9 **Borgne, Lake** ◎ Louisiana, S USA
106 C7 **Borgomanero** Piemonte, NE Italy 45°42′N 08°33′E
106 G10 **Borgo Panigale** ✕ (Bologna) Emilia-Romagna, N Italy 44°33′N 11°16′E
107 J15 **Borgorose** Lazio, C Italy 42°10′N 13°15′E
106 A9 **Borgo San Dalmazzo** Piemonte, N Italy 44°19′N 07°29′E
106 G11 **Borgo San Lorenzo** Toscana, C Italy 43°58′N 11°22′E
106 C6 **Borgosesia** Piemonte, NE Italy 45°41′N 08°21′E
106 E9 **Borgo Val di Taro** Emilia-Romagna, C Italy 44°29′N 09°48′E
106 G6 **Borgo Valsugana** Trentino-Alto Adige, N Italy 46°04′N 11°31′E
Borhoyn Tal *see* Dzamïn-Üüd
167 R8 **Borikhan** *var.* Borikhane. Bolikhamxai, C Laos 18°36′N 103°43′E
Borikhane *see* Borikhan
144 G8 **Borili** *prev.* Burlin. Zapadnyy Kazakhstan, NW Kazakhstan 51°25′N 52°42′E
Borislav *see* Boryslav
127 N8 **Borisoglebsk** Voronezhskaya Oblast', W Russian Federation 51°23′N 42°00′E
Borisov *see* Barysaw
Borisovgrad *see* Pŭrvomay
Borispol' *see* Boryspil'
172 I3 **Boriziny** *prev./Fr.* Port-Bergé. Mahajanga, NW Madagascar 15°31′S 47°40′E
105 Q5 **Borja** Aragón, NE Spain 41°50′N 01°32′W
Borjas Blancas *see* Les Borges Blanques
137 S10 **Borjomi** *Rus.* Borzhomi. C Georgia 41°50′N 43°24′E
118 L12 **Borkavichy** *Rus.* Borkovichi. Vitsyebskaya Voblasts', N Belarus 55°40′N 28°20′E
101 H16 **Borken** Hessen, C Germany 51°01′N 09°16′E
101 E14 **Borken** Nordrhein-Westfalen, W Germany 51°51′N 06°51′E
92 H10 **Borkenes** Troms, N Norway 68°46′N 16°10′E
78 H7 **Borkou-Ennedi-Tibesti** *off.* Préfecture du Borkou-Ennedi-Tibesti. ◆ *prefecture* N Chad
Borkou-Ennedi-Tibesti, Préfecture du *see* Borkou-Ennedi-Tibesti
Borkovichi *see* Borkavichy
100 E9 **Borkum** *island* NW Germany
81 K17 **Bor, Lagh** *var.* Lak Bor. *dry watercourse* NE Kenya
Bor, Lak *see* Bor, Lagh
95 M14 **Borlänge** Dalarna, C Sweden 60°29′N 15°25′E
106 C9 **Bormida** ≈ NW Italy
106 F6 **Bormio** Lombardia, N Italy 46°27′N 10°24′E
101 M16 **Borna** Sachsen, E Germany 51°07′N 12°30′E
98 O10 **Borne** Overijssel, E Netherlands 52°18′N 06°45′E
99 F17 **Bornem** Antwerpen, N Belgium 51°06′N 04°14′E
169 S10 **Borneo** *island* Brunei/Indonesia/Malaysia
101 E16 **Bornheim** Nordrhein-Westfalen, W Germany 50°46′N 06°58′E
95 L24 **Bornholm** ◆ *county* E Denmark
95 L24 **Bornholm** *island* E Denmark
77 Y13 **Borno** ◆ *state* NE Nigeria
104 K15 **Bornos** Andalucía, S Spain 36°50′N 05°42′W
162 L7 **Bornuur** Töv, C Mongolia 48°28′N 106°15′E
117 O4 **Borodyanka** Kyyivs'ka Oblast', N Ukraine 50°40′N 29°54′E
158 I5 **Borohoro Shan** ▲▲ NW China
77 O13 **Boromo** SW Burkina 11°47′N 02°54′W
35 T13 **Boron** California, W USA 35°00′N 117°42′W
Borongo *see* Black Volta
Boron'ki *see* Baron'ki
Borosjenő *see* Ineu
Borossebes *see* Sebiş

◆ Country ● Country Capital ◇ Dependent Territory ○ Dependent Territory Capital ◆ Administrative Regions ✕ International Airport ▲ Mountain ▲▲ Mountain Range ✱ Volcano ≈ River ◎ Lake ⊠ Reservoir

76 *L15* **Borotou** NW Ivory Coast *08°46′N 07°30′W*
117 *W6* **Borova** Kharkivs'ka Oblast', E Ukraine *49°22′N 37°39′E*
114 *H8* **Borovan** Vratsa, NW Bulgaria *43°25′N 23°45′E*
124 *I14* **Borovichi** Novgorodskaya Oblast', W Russian Federation *58°24′N 33°56′E*
Borovlje *see* Ferlach
114 *K8* **Borovo** Ruse, N Bulgaria *43°28′N 25°46′E*
112 *J9* **Borovo** Vukovar-Srijem, NE Croatia *45°22′N 18°57′E*
Borovoye *see* Burabay
126 *K4* **Borovsk** Kaluzhskaya Oblast', W Russian Federation *55°12′N 36°22′E*
145 *N7* **Borovskoye** Kostanay, N Kazakhstan *53°48′N 64°17′E*
Borovukha *see* Baravukha
95 *L23* **Borrby** Skåne, S Sweden *55°27′N 14°10′E*
105 *T9* **Borriana** *var.* Burriana. Valenciana, E Spain *39°54′N 00°05′W*
181 *R3* **Borroloola** Northern Territory, N Australia *16°09′S 136°18′E*
116 *F9* **Borş** Bihor, NW Romania *47°07′N 21°49′E*
116 *I9* **Borşa** *Hung.* Borsa. Maramureş, N Romania *47°40′N 24°37′E*
116 *J10* **Borsec** *Ger.* Bad Borseck, *Hung.* Borszék. Harghita, C Romania *46°58′N 25°32′E*
92 *K8* **Børselv** *Lapp.* Bissojohka. Finnmark, N Norway *70°18′N 25°35′E*
113 *L23* **Borsh** *var.* Borshi. Vlorë, S Albania *40°04′N 19°51′E*
Borshchev *see* Borshchiv
116 *K7* **Borshchiv** *Pol.* Borszczów, *Rus.* Borshchev. Ternopil's'ka Oblast', W Ukraine *48°48′N 26°00′E*
Borshi *see* Borsh
111 *L20* **Borsod-Abaúj-Zemplén** *off.* Borsod-Abaúj-Zemplén Megye. ◆ *county* NE Hungary
Borsod-Abaúj-Zemplén Megye *see* Borsod-Abaúj-Zemplén
99 *E15* **Borssele** Zeeland, SW Netherlands *51°26′N 03°45′E*
Borszczów *see* Borshchiv
Borszék *see* Borsec
Bortala *see* Bole
103 *O12* **Bort-les-Orgues** Corrèze, C France *45°28′N 02°31′E*
Bor u Českè Lípy *see* Nový Bor
Bor-Üdzüür *see* Altay
143 *N9* **Borūjen** Chahār Maḩall va Bakhtiārī, C Iran *32°N 51°09′E*
142 *L7* **Borūjerd** *var.* Burujird. Lorestān, W Iran *33°55′N 48°46′E*
116 *H6* **Boryslav** *Pol.* Borysław, *Rus.* Borislav. L'vivs'ka Oblast', NW Ukraine *49°18′N 23°28′E*
Borysław *see* Boryslav
117 *P4* **Boryspil'** *Rus.* Borispol'. Kyyivs'ka Oblast', N Ukraine *50°21′N 30°59′E*
117 *P4* **Boryspil'** *Rus.* Borispol'. ✈ (Kyyiv) Kyyivs'ka Oblast', N Ukraine *50°21′N 30°46′E*
Borzhomi *see* Borjomi
117 *R3* **Borzna** Chernihivs'ka Oblast', NE Ukraine *51°15′N 32°25′E*
123 *O14* **Borzya** Zabaykal'skiy Kray, S Russian Federation *50°18′N 116°24′E*
107 *B18* **Bosa** Sardegna, Italy, C Mediterranean Sea *40°18′N 08°28′E*
112 *F10* **Bosanska Dubica** *var.* Kozarska Dubica. ◆ Republika Srpska, NW Bosnia and Herzegovina
112 *G10* **Bosanska Gradiška** *var.* Gradiška. ◆ Republika Srpska, N Bosnia and Herzegovina
112 *F10* **Bosanska Kostajnica** *var.* Srpska Kostajnica. ◆ Republika Srpska, NW Bosnia and Herzegovina
112 *E11* **Bosanska Krupa** *var.* Krupa, Krupa na Uni. ◆ Federacija Bosna I Hercegovina, NW Bosnia and Herzegovina
112 *H10* **Bosanski Brod** *var.* Srpski Brod. ◆ Republika Srpska, N Bosnia and Herzegovina
112 *E10* **Bosanski Novi** *var.* Novi Grad. Republika Srpska, NW Bosnia and Herzegovina *45°03′N 16°23′E*
112 *E11* **Bosanski Petrovac** *var.* Petrovac. Federacija Bosna I Hercegovina, NW Bosnia and Herzegovina *44°34′N 16°21′E*
112 *I10* **Bosanski Šamac** *var.* Šamac. Republika Srpska, N Bosnia and Herzegovina *45°03′N 18°27′E*
112 *E12* **Bosansko Grahovo** *var.* Grahovo, Hrvatsko Grahovi. Federacija Bosna I Hercegovina, W Bosnia and Herzegovina *44°10′N 16°22′E*
Bosaso *see* Boosaaso
186 *B7* **Bosavi, Mount** ⛰ W Papua New Guinea *06°33′S 142°50′E*
160 *J14* **Bose** Guangxi Zhuangzu Zizhiqu, S China *23°55′N 106°32′E*
161 *Q5* **Boshan** Shandong, E China *36°32′N 117°47′E*
113 *P16* **Bosilegrad** *prev.* Bosiljgrad. Serbia, SE Serbia *42°30′N 22°30′E*
Bosiljgrad *see* Bosilegrad
Bösing *see* Pezinok
98 *H12* **Boskoop** Zuid-Holland, C Netherlands *52°04′N 04°40′E*
111 *G18* **Boskovice** *Ger.* Boskowitz. Jihomoravský Kraj, SE Czech Republic *49°30′N 16°39′E*
Boskowitz *see* Boskovice
112 *I10* **Bosna** ⚡ N Bosnia and Herzegovina
113 *G14* **Bosna I Hercegovina, Federacija** ◆ *republic* Bosnia and Herzegovina
112 *H12* **Bosnia and Herzegovina** *off.* Republic of Bosnia and Herzegovina. ◆ *republic* SE Europe
Bosnia and Herzegovina, Republic of *see* Bosnia and Herzegovina
79 *J16* **Bosobolo** Equateur, NW Dem. Rep. Congo *04°11′N 19°55′E*
165 *O14* **Bōsō-hantō** *peninsula* Honshū, S Japan
Bosora *see* Buşrá ash Shām
Bosphorus/Bosporus *see* İstanbul Boğazı
Bosporus Cimmerius *see* Kerch Strait
Bosporus Thracius *see* İstanbul Boğazı
Bosra *see* Buşrá ash Shām
79 *H14* **Bossangoa** Ouham, C Central African Republic *06°32′N 17°25′E*
Bossé Bangou *see* Bossey Bangou
79 *I15* **Bossembélé** Ombella-Mpoko, C Central African Republic *05°13′N 17°39′E*
79 *H15* **Bossentélé** Ouham-Pendé, W Central African Republic *05°36′N 16°37′E*
77 *R12* **Bossey Bangou** *var.* Bossé Bangou. Tillabéri, SW Niger *13°22′N 01°18′E*
22 *G5* **Bossier City** Louisiana, S USA *32°31′N 93°43′W*
83 *D20* **Bossiesvlei** Hardap, S Namibia *25°02′S 16°48′E*
77 *Y11* **Bosso** Diffa, SE Niger *13°42′N 13°18′E*
61 *F15* **Bossoroca** Rio Grande do Sul, S Brazil *28°45′S 54°54′W*
158 *J10* **Bostan** Xinjiang Uygur Zizhiqu, W China *41°20′N 83°15′E*
142 *K3* **Bostānābād** Āžarbāyjān-e Sharqī, N Iran *37°52′N 46°51′E*
158 *K6* **Bosten Hu** *var.* Bagrax Hu. ⊚ NW China
97 *O18* **Boston** *prev.* St.Botolph's Town. E England, United Kingdom *52°59′N 00°01′W*
19 *O11* **Boston** *state capital* Massachusetts, NE USA *42°22′N 71°04′W*
146 *I9* **Bo'ston** *Rus.* Bustan. Qoraqalpog'iston Respublikasi, W Uzbekistan *41°49′N 60°51′E*
10 *M17* **Boston Bar** British Columbia, SW Canada *49°54′N 121°22′W*
27 *T10* **Boston Mountains** ▲ Arkansas, C USA
15 *P8* **Bostonnais** ⚡ Québec, SE Canada
Bostyn' *see* Bastyn'
112 *J10* **Bosut** ⚡ E Croatia
154 *C11* **Botād** Gujarāt, W India *22°12′N 71°44′E*
145 *S10* **Botakara** *Kas.* Botaqara; *prev.* Ul'yanovskiy. Karaganda, C Kazakhstan *50°05′N 73°45′E*
183 *T9* **Botany Bay** *inlet* New South Wales, SE Australia
Botaqara *see* Botakara
83 *G18* **Boteti** *var.* Botletle. ⚡ N Botswana
114 *J9* **Botev** ▲ C Bulgaria *42°45′N 24°57′E*
114 *H9* **Botevgrad** *prev.* Orkhaniye. Sofiya, W Bulgaria *42°55′N 23°47′E*
93 *J16* **Bothnia, Gulf of** *Fin.* Pohjanlahti, *Swe.* Bottniska Viken. *gulf* N Baltic Sea
183 *P17* **Bothwell** Tasmania, SE Australia *42°24′S 147°01′E*
104 *H5* **Boticas** Vila Real, N Portugal *41°41′N 07°40′W*
55 *W10* **Boti-Pasi** Sipaliwini, C Surinam *04°15′N 55°27′W*
Botletle *see* Boteti
127 *P16* **Botlikh** Chechenskaya Respublika, SW Russian Federation *42°39′N 46°12′E*
117 *N10* **Botna** ⚡ E Moldova
116 *I9* **Botoşani** *Hung.* Botosány. Botoşani, NE Romania *47°44′N 26°41′E*
116 *K8* **Botoşani** ◆ *county* NE Romania
Botosány *see* Botoşani
147 *P12* **Bototog', Tizmasi** *Rus.* Khrebet Babatag. ▲ Tajikistan/Uzbekistan
161 *P4* **Botou** *prev.* Bozhen. Hebei, E China *38°09′N 116°37′E*
99 *M20* **Botrange** ▲ E Belgium *50°30′N 06°03′E*
107 *O21* **Botricello** Calabria, SW Italy *38°56′N 16°51′E*
83 *I23* **Botshabelo** Free State, C South Africa *29°15′S 26°51′E*
93 *J15* **Botsmark** Västerbotten, N Sweden *64°15′N 20°15′E*
83 *G19* **Botswana** *off.* Republic of Botswana. ◆ *republic* S Africa
Botswana, Republic of *see* Botswana
29 *N2* **Bottineau** North Dakota, N USA *48°50′N 100°28′W*
Bottniska Viken *see* Bothnia, Gulf of
60 *L9* **Botucatu** São Paulo, S Brazil *22°52′S 48°30′W*
76 *M16* **Bouaflé** C Ivory Coast *06°59′N 05°45′W*
77 *N16* **Bouaké** *var.* Bwake. C Ivory Coast *07°42′N 05°00′W*
79 *G14* **Bouar** Nana-Mambéré, W Central African Republic *05°58′N 15°38′E*
74 *H7* **Bouarfa** NE Morocco *32°33′N 01°54′W*
111 *B19* **Boubín** ▲ SW Czech Republic *49°00′N 13°51′E*
79 *I14* **Bouca** Ouham, W Central African Republic *06°57′N 18°18′E*
15 *T5* **Boucher** ⚡ Québec, SE Canada
103 *R15* **Bouches-du-Rhône** ◆ *department* SE France
74 *C9* **Bou Craa** *var.* Bu Craa. NW Western Sahara *26°32′N 12°52′W*
77 *O9* **Boû Djébéha** *oasis* C Mali
108 *C8* **Boudry** Neuchâtel, W Switzerland *46°57′N 06°46′E*
79 *F21* **Bouenza** ◆ *province* S Congo
186 *L2* **Bougainville, Cape** *cape* Western Australia
65 *E24* **Bougainville, Cape** *headland* East Falkland, Falkland Islands *51°18′S 58°28′W*
Bougainville, Détroit de *see* Bougainville Strait
186 *J7* **Bougainville Island** *island* NE Papua New Guinea
186 *I8* **Bougainville Strait** *strait* N Solomon Islands
187 *Q13* **Bougainville Strait** *Fr.* Détroit de Bougainville. *strait* C Vanuatu
120 *I9* **Bougaroun, Cap** *headland* NE Algeria *37°07′N 06°18′E*
77 *R8* **Boughessa** Kidal, NE Mali *20°05′N 02°13′E*
Bougie *see* Béjaïa
76 *L13* **Bougouni** Sikasso, SW Mali *11°25′N 07°28′W*
99 *J24* **Bouillon** Luxembourg, SE Belgium *49°47′N 05°04′E*
74 *K5* **Bouira** *var.* Bouïra. N Algeria *36°22′N 03°55′E*
74 *D8* **Bou-Izakarn** SW Morocco *29°12′N 09°43′W*
74 *B9* **Boujdour** *var.* Bojador. W Western Sahara *26°06′N 14°29′W*
74 *G5* **Boukhalef** ✈ (Tanger) N Morocco *35°45′N 05°53′W*
Boukombé *see* Boukoumbé
77 *R14* **Boukoumbé** *var.* Boukombé. C Benin *10°13′N 01°09′E*
76 *G6* **Boû Lanouâr** Dakhlet Nouâdhibou, W Mauritania *21°17′N 16°29′W*
37 *T4* **Boulder** Colorado, C USA *40°02′N 105°18′W*
33 *R10* **Boulder** Montana, NW USA *46°14′N 112°07′W*
35 *X12* **Boulder City** Nevada, W USA *35°58′N 114°49′W*
181 *T7* **Boulia** Queensland, C Australia *23°02′S 139°58′E*
15 *N10* **Boullé** ⚡ Québec, SE Canada
102 *J9* **Boulogne** ⚡ NW France
Boulogne *see* Boulogne-sur-Mer
102 *L16* **Boulogne-sur-Gesse** Haute-Garonne, S France *43°18′N 00°38′E*
103 *N1* **Boulogne-sur-Mer** *var.* Boulogne; *anc.* Bononia, Gesoriacum, Gessoriacum. Pas-de-Calais, N France *50°43′N 01°36′E*
77 *Q12* **Boulsa** C Burkina *12°41′N 00°29′W*
77 *W11* **Boultoum** Zinder, C Niger *14°43′N 10°22′E*
187 *Y14* **Bouma** Taveuni, N Fiji *16°49′S 179°50′W*
79 *G16* **Boumba** ⚡ SE Cameroon
76 *J9* **Boûmdeïd** *var.* Boumdeït. Assaba, S Mauritania *17°26′N 11°21′W*
Boumdeït *see* Boûmdeïd
115 *C17* **Boumistós** ▲ W Greece *38°48′N 20°59′E*
77 *O15* **Bouna** NE Ivory Coast *09°16′N 03°00′W*
19 *P4* **Boundary Bald Mountain** ▲ Maine, NE USA *45°45′N 70°10′W*
35 *S8* **Boundary Peak** ▲ Nevada, W USA *37°50′N 118°21′W*
76 *M14* **Boundiali** N Ivory Coast *09°30′N 06°31′W*
79 *G19* **Boundji** Cuvette, C Congo *01°05′S 15°18′E*
77 *O13* **Boundoukui** *var.* Bondoukui, Bondoukuy. W Burkina *11°51′N 03°47′W*
36 *L2* **Bountiful** Utah, W USA *40°53′N 111°52′W*
Bounty Basin *see* Bounty Trough
191 *Q16* **Bounty Bay** *bay* Pitcairn Island, C Pacific Ocean
192 *L12* **Bounty Islands** *island group* S New Zealand
175 *Q13* **Bounty Trough** *var.* Bounty Basin. *undersea feature* S Pacific Ocean
187 *P17* **Bourail** Province Sud, C New Caledonia *21°35′S 165°29′E*
27 *V5* **Bourbeuse River** ⚡ Missouri, C USA
103 *Q9* **Bourbon-Lancy** Saône-et-Loire, C France *46°39′N 03°48′E*
31 *N11* **Bourbonnais** Illinois, N USA *41°08′N 87°52′W*
103 *O10* **Bourbonnais** *cultural region* C France
103 *S7* **Bourbonne-les-Bains** Haute-Marne, N France *48°00′N 05°43′E*
Bourbon Vendée *see* la Roche-sur-Yon
74 *M8* **Bourdj Messaouda** E Algeria *30°18′N 09°19′E*
77 *Q10* **Bourem** Gao, C Mali *16°56′N 00°21′W*
Bourg *see* Bourg-en-Bresse
103 *N11* **Bourganeuf** Creuse, C France *45°57′N 01°47′E*
Burgas *see* Burgas
Bourge-en-Bresse *see* Bourg-en-Bresse
103 *S10* **Bourg-en-Bresse** *var.* Bourg, Bourge-en-Bresse. Ain, E France *46°12′N 05°13′E*
103 *O8* **Bourges** *anc.* Avaricum. Cher, C France *47°06′N 02°24′E*
103 *T11* **Bourget, Lac du** ⊚ E France
103 *P8* **Bourgogne** *Eng.* Burgundy. ◆ *region* E France
103 *S11* **Bourgoin-Jallieu** Isère, E France *45°34′N 05°16′E*
103 *R14* **Bourg-St-Andéol** Ardèche, E France *44°24′N 04°36′E*
103 *U11* **Bourg-St-Maurice** Savoie, E France *45°37′N 06°49′E*
108 *C11* **Bourg St. Pierre** Valais, SW Switzerland *45°54′N 07°10′E*
76 *H8* **Boû Rjeïmât** *well* W Mauritania
183 *P5* **Bourke** New South Wales, SE Australia *30°08′S 145°57′E*
97 *M24* **Bournemouth** S England, United Kingdom *50°43′N 01°54′W*
99 *M23* **Bourscheid** Diekirch, NE Luxembourg *49°55′N 06°04′E*
74 *K6* **Bou Saâda** *var.* Bou Saada. N Algeria *35°10′N 04°09′E*
36 *I13* **Bouse Wash** ⚡ Arizona, SW USA
103 *N10* **Boussac** Creuse, C France *46°20′N 02°12′E*
102 *M16* **Boussens** Haute-Garonne, S France *43°11′N 00°58′E*
78 *H12* **Bousso** *prev.* Fort-Bretonnet. Chari-Baguirmi, S Chad *10°32′N 16°45′E*
76 *H9* **Boutilimit** Trarza, SW Mauritania *17°33′N 14°42′W*
65 *D21* **Bouvet Island** ◇ *Norwegian dependency* S Atlantic Ocean
77 *U11* **Bouza** Tahoua, SW Niger *14°25′N 06°09′E*
109 *R10* **Bovec** *Ger.* Flitsch, *It.* Plezzo. NW Slovenia *46°21′N 13°33′E*
98 *J8* **Bovenkarspel** Noord-Holland, NW Netherlands *52°33′N 05°03′E*
29 *V5* **Bovey** Minnesota, N USA *47°18′N 93°25′W*
32 *M9* **Bovill** Idaho, NW USA *46°50′N 116°24′W*
24 *L4* **Bovina** Texas, SW USA *34°30′N 102°52′W*
107 *M17* **Bovino** Puglia, SE Italy *41°14′N 15°19′E*
61 *C17* **Bovril** Entre Ríos, E Argentina *31°24′S 59°25′W*
28 *L2* **Bowbells** North Dakota, N USA *48°48′N 102°15′W*
11 *Q16* **Bow City** Alberta, SW Canada *50°27′N 112°16′W*
29 *O8* **Bowdle** South Dakota, N USA *45°27′N 99°39′W*
181 *X6* **Bowen** Queensland, NE Australia *20°S 148°10′E*
192 *L2* **Bowers Ridge** *undersea feature* S Bering Sea *50°00′N 180°00′W*
25 *S5* **Bowie** Texas, SW USA *33°33′N 97°51′W*
11 *R17* **Bow Island** Alberta, SW Canada *49°53′N 111°24′W*
Bowkān *see* Būkān
20 *J7* **Bowling Green** Kentucky, S USA *37°00′N 86°29′W*
27 *V3* **Bowling Green** Missouri, C USA *39°21′N 91°11′W*
31 *R11* **Bowling Green** Ohio, N USA *41°22′N 83°40′W*
21 *W5* **Bowling Green** Virginia, NE USA *38°02′N 77°22′W*
28 *J6* **Bowman** North Dakota, N USA *46°11′N 103°26′W*
9 *Q7* **Bowman Bay** *bay* NW Atlantic Ocean
194 *I5* **Bowman Coast** *physical region* Antarctica
28 *J7* **Bowman-Haley Lake** ⊠ North Dakota, N USA
195 *Z11* **Bowman Island** *island* Antarctica
Bowo *see* Bomi
183 *S9* **Bowral** New South Wales, SE Australia *34°28′S 150°52′E*
186 *E8* **Bowutu Mountains** ▲ C Papua New Guinea
83 *I16* **Bowwood** Southern, S Zambia *17°09′S 26°16′E*
28 *I12* **Box Butte Reservoir** ⊠ Nebraska, C USA
28 *J10* **Box Elder** South Dakota, N USA *44°06′N 103°04′W*
95 *M18* **Boxholm** Östergötland, S Sweden *58°12′N 15°05′E*
Bo Xian/Boxian *see* Bozhou
161 *Q4* **Boxing** Shandong, E China *37°06′N 118°05′E*
99 *L14* **Boxmeer** Noord-Brabant, SE Netherlands *51°39′N 05°57′E*
99 *J14* **Boxtel** Noord-Brabant, S Netherlands *51°36′N 05°20′E*
136 *J10* **Boyabat** Sinop, N Turkey *41°27′N 34°45′E*
54 *F9* **Boyacá** *off.* Departamento de Boyacá. ◆ *province* C Colombia
Boyacá, Departamento de *see* Boyacá
117 *O4* **Boyarka** Kyyivs'ka Oblast', N Ukraine *50°19′N 30°20′E*
22 *H7* **Boyce** Louisiana, S USA *31°23′N 92°40′W*
114 *H8* **Boychinovtsi** Montana, NW Bulgaria *43°28′N 23°20′E*
33 *U11* **Boyd** Montana, NW USA *45°27′N 109°03′W*
25 *S6* **Boyd** Texas, SW USA *33°01′N 97°33′W*
21 *V8* **Boydton** Virginia, NE USA *36°40′N 78°26′W*
Boyer Ahmadī va Kohkīlūyeh *see* Kohgīlūyeh va Bowyer Aḩmad
29 *T13* **Boyer River** ⚡ Iowa, C USA
21 *W8* **Boykins** Virginia, NE USA *36°35′N 77°11′W*
11 *Q13* **Boyle** Alberta, SW Canada *54°38′N 112°45′W*
97 *D16* **Boyle** *Ir.* Mainistirna Búille. C Ireland *53°58′N 08°18′W*
97 *F17* **Boyne** *Ir.* An Bhóinn. ⚡ E Ireland
31 *Q5* **Boyne City** Michigan, N USA *45°13′N 85°00′W*
23 *Z14* **Boynton Beach** Florida, SE USA *26°31′N 80°04′W*
147 *O13* **Boysun** *Rus.* Baysun. Surkhondaryo Viloyati, S Uzbekistan *38°14′N 67°08′E*
Bozau *see* Întorsura Buzăului
136 *B12* **Bozcaada** *Island* Çanakkale, NW Turkey
136 *C14* **Boz Dağları** ▲ W Turkey
33 *S11* **Bozeman** Montana, NW USA *45°40′N 111°02′W*
Bozen *see* Bolzano
79 *J16* **Bozene** Equateur, NW Dem. Rep. Congo *02°56′N 19°15′E*
Bozhen *see* Botou
161 *P7* **Bozhou** *var.* Boxian, Bo Xian. Anhui, E China *33°46′N 115°44′E*
136 *H16* **Bozkır** Konya, S Turkey *37°10′N 32°15′E*
136 *K13* **Bozok Yaylası** *plateau* C Turkey
79 *H14* **Bozoum** Ouham-Pendé, W Central African Republic *06°17′N 16°26′E*
137 *N16* **Bozova** Sanlıurfa, S Turkey *37°23′N 38°33′E*
Bozrah *see* Buşrá ash Shām
136 *E12* **Bozüyük** Bilecik, NW Turkey *39°55′N 30°02′E*
106 *B9* **Bra** Piemonte, NW Italy *44°42′N 07°51′E*
194 *G4* **Brabant Island** *island* Antarctica
99 *I20* **Brabant Walloon** ◆ *province* C Belgium
113 *F15* **Brač** *var.* Brach, *It.* Brazza; *anc.* Brattia. *island* S Croatia
Bracara Augusta *see* Braga
107 *H15* **Bracciano** Lazio, C Italy *42°04′N 12°12′E*
107 *H14* **Bracciano, Lago di** ⊚ C Italy
14 *H13* **Bracebridge** Ontario, S Canada *45°02′N 79°19′W*
Brach *see* Brač
93 *G17* **Bräcke** Jämtland, C Sweden *62°43′N 15°30′E*
25 *P12* **Brackettville** Texas, SW USA *29°19′N 100°27′W*
97 *N22* **Bracknell** S England, United Kingdom *51°26′N 00°46′W*
61 *K14* **Braço do Norte** Santa Catarina, S Brazil *28°16′S 49°11′W*
116 *G11* **Brad** *Hung.* Brád. Hunedoara, SW Romania *45°52′N 23°00′E*
107 *N18* **Bradano** ⚡ S Italy
23 *V13* **Bradenton** Florida, SE USA *27°30′N 82°34′W*
45 *V10* **Brades** ○ (Montserrat: *de facto* capital, *de jure* capital, Plymouth, destroyed by volcano in 1995) N Montserrat *16°45′N 62°12′W*
14 *H14* **Bradford** Ontario, S Canada *44°09′N 79°34′W*
97 *L17* **Bradford** N England, United Kingdom *53°48′N 01°45′W*
27 *W10* **Bradford** Arkansas, C USA *35°25′N 91°27′W*
18 *D12* **Bradford** Pennsylvania, NE USA *41°57′N 78°38′W*
27 *T15* **Bradley** Arkansas, C USA *33°06′N 93°39′W*
25 *P7* **Bradshaw** Texas, SW USA *32°06′N 99°52′W*
25 *Q9* **Brady** Texas, SW USA *31°08′N 99°22′W*
25 *Q9* **Brady Creek** ⚡ Texas, SW USA
95 *G22* **Brædstrup** Syddanmark, C Denmark *55°58′N 09°38′E*
96 *J10* **Braemar** NE Scotland, United Kingdom *57°12′N 02°52′W*
116 *K8* **Brăeşti** Botoşani, NW Romania *47°50′N 26°26′E*
104 *G5* **Braga** *anc.* Bracara Augusta. Braga, NW Portugal *41°32′N 08°26′W*
104 *G5* **Braga** ◆ *district* N Portugal
116 *J15* **Bragadiru** Teleorman, S Romania *43°43′N 25°32′E*
61 *C20* **Bragado** Buenos Aires, E Argentina *35°10′S 60°29′W*
104 *J5* **Bragança** *Eng.* Braganza; *anc.* Julio Briga. Bragança, NE Portugal *41°47′N 06°46′W*
104 *I5* **Bragança** ◆ *district* N Portugal
60 *N9* **Bragança Paulista** São Paulo, S Brazil *22°55′S 46°30′W*
Braganza *see* Bragança
Bragin *see* Brahin
29 *V7* **Braham** Minnesota, N USA *45°43′N 93°10′W*
Brahe *see* Brda
Brahestad *see* Raahe
119 *O20* **Brahin** *Rus.* Bragin. Homyel'skaya Voblasts', SE Belarus *51°47′N 30°16′E*
153 *U15* **Brahmanbaria** Chittagong, E Bangladesh *23°58′N 91°04′E*
154 *O12* **Brāhmani** ⚡ E India
154 *N13* **Brahmapur** Orissa, E India *19°21′N 84°51′E*
129 *S10* **Brahmaputra** *var.* Padma, Tsangpo, *Ben.* Jamuna, *Chin.* Yarlung Zangbo Jiang, *Ind.* Bramaputra, Dihang, Siang. ⚡ S Asia
97 *H19* **Braich y Pwll** *headland* NW Wales, United Kingdom *52°47′N 04°46′W*
183 *R10* **Braidwood** New South Wales, SE Australia *35°26′S 149°48′E*
30 *M11* **Braidwood** Illinois, N USA *41°16′N 88°12′W*
116 *M13* **Brăila** Brăila, E Romania *45°17′N 27°57′E*
116 *L13* **Brăila** ◆ *county* SE Romania
99 *G19* **Braine-l'Alleud** Brabant Walloon, C Belgium *50°41′N 04°22′E*
99 *F19* **Braine-le-Comte** Hainaut, SW Belgium *50°37′N 04°08′E*
29 *U6* **Brainerd** Minnesota, N USA *46°22′N 94°10′W*
99 *J19* **Braives** Liège, E Belgium *50°37′N 05°09′E*
83 *H23* **Brak** ⚡ C South Africa
Brak *see* Birāk
99 *E18* **Brakel** Oost-Vlaanderen, SW Belgium *50°50′N 03°48′E*
98 *J13* **Brakel** Gelderland, C Netherlands *51°49′N 05°05′E*
76 *H9* **Brakna** ◆ *region* S Mauritania
95 *J17* **Brålanda** Västra Götaland, S Sweden *58°32′N 12°18′E*
Bramaputra *see* Brahmaputra
95 *F23* **Bramming** Syddtjylland, W Denmark *55°28′N 08°42′E*
14 *G15* **Brampton** Ontario, S Canada *43°42′N 79°46′W*
100 *F12* **Bramsche** Niedersachsen, NW Germany *52°25′N 07°58′E*
116 *J12* **Bran** *Ger.* Törzburg, *Hung.* Törcsvár. Braşov, S Romania *45°31′N 25°23′E*
29 *W8* **Branch** Minnesota, N USA *45°29′N 92°57′W*
21 *R14* **Branchville** South Carolina, SE USA *33°15′N 80°49′W*
47 *Y6* **Branco, Cabo** *headland* E Brazil *07°08′S 34°45′W*
58 *F11* **Branco, Rio** ⚡ N Brazil
108 *J8* **Brand** Vorarlberg, W Austria *47°07′N 09°45′E*
83 *B18* **Brandberg** ▲ NW Namibia *21°20′S 14°22′E*
95 *H14* **Brandbu** Oppland, S Norway *60°24′N 10°30′E*
95 *F22* **Brande** Midtjylland, W Denmark *55°57′N 09°08′E*
Brandebourg *see* Brandenburg
100 *M12* **Brandenburg** *var.* Brandenburg an der Havel. Brandenburg, NE Germany *52°25′N 12°34′E*
20 *K5* **Brandenburg** Kentucky, S USA *38°00′N 86°11′W*
100 *N12* **Brandenburg** *off.* Freie und Hansestadt Hamburg, *Fr.* Brandebourg. ◆ *state* NE Germany
Brandenburg an der Havel *see* Brandenburg
83 *I23* **Brandfort** Free State, C South Africa *28°42′S 26°28′E*
11 *W16* **Brandon** Manitoba, S Canada *49°50′N 99°57′W*
23 *V12* **Brandon** Florida, SE USA *27°56′N 82°17′W*
22 *L6* **Brandon** Mississippi, S USA *32°16′N 90°01′W*
97 *A20* **Brandon Mountain** *Ir.* Cnoc Bréanainn. ▲ SW Ireland *52°13′N 10°16′W*
Brandsen *see* Coronel Brandsen
95 *I14* **Brandval** Hedmark, S Norway *60°18′N 12°01′E*
83 *F24* **Brandvlei** Northern Cape, W South Africa *30°27′S 20°29′E*
23 *U9* **Branford** Florida, SE USA *29°57′N 82°54′W*
110 *K7* **Braniewo** *Ger.* Braunsberg. Warmińsko-mazurskie, N Poland *54°24′N 19°50′E*
194 *H3* **Bransfield Strait** *strait* Antarctica
37 *U8* **Branson** Colorado, C USA *37°01′N 103°52′W*
27 *T8* **Branson** Missouri, C USA *36°38′N 93°13′W*
14 *G16* **Brantford** Ontario, S Canada *43°09′N 80°17′W*
102 *L12* **Brantôme** Dordogne, SW France *45°21′N 00°37′E*
182 *L12* **Branxholme** Victoria, SE Australia *37°51′S 141°48′E*
Brasil *see* Brazil
59 *C16* **Brasiléia** Acre, W Brazil *10°59′S 48°45′W*
59 *K18* **Brasília** ● (Brazil) Distrito Federal, C Brazil *15°45′S 47°57′W*
Brasil, República Federativa do *see* Brazil
Braslav *see* Braslaw
118 *J12* **Braslaw** *Pol.* Brasław, *Rus.* Braslav. Vitsyebskaya Voblasts', N Belarus *55°38′N 27°02′E*
116 *J12* **Braşov** *Ger.* Kronstadt, *Hung.* Brassó; *prev.* Oraşul Stalin. Braşov, C Romania *45°40′N 25°35′E*
116 *I12* **Braşov** ◆ *county* C Romania
77 *U18* **Brass** Bayelsa, S Nigeria *04°19′N 06°21′E*
99 *H16* **Brasschaat** *var.* Brasschaet. Antwerpen, N Belgium *51°17′N 04°30′E*
Brasschaet *see* Brasschaat
169 *V8* **Brassey, Banjaran** *var.* Brassey Range. ▲ East Malaysia
Brassey Range *see* Brassey, Banjaran
Brassó *see* Braşov
23 *T1* **Brasstown Bald** ▲ Georgia, SE USA *34°52′N 83°48′W*
113 *K22* **Brataj** Vlorë, SW Albania *40°18′N 19°37′E*
114 *J10* **Bratan** *var.* Morozov. ▲ C Bulgaria *42°31′N 25°08′E*
111 *F21* **Bratislava** *Ger.* Pressburg, *Hung.* Pozsony. ● (Slovakia) Bratislavský Kraj, W Slovakia *48°10′N 17°10′E*
111 *H21* **Bratislavský Kraj** ◆ *region* W Slovakia
114 *H10* **Bratiya** ▲ C Bulgaria *42°36′N 24°08′E*
122 *M12* **Bratsk** Irkutskaya Oblast', C Russian Federation *56°20′N 101°50′E*
117 *Q8* **Brats'ke** Mykolayivs'ka Oblast', S Ukraine *47°52′N 31°34′E*
122 *M13* **Bratskoye Vodokhranilishche** *Eng.* Bratsk Reservoir. ⊠ S Russian Federation
Bratsk Reservoir *see* Bratskoye Vodokhranilishche
Brattia *see* Brač
94 *D9* **Brattvåg** Møre og Romsdal, S Norway *62°36′N 06°21′E*
112 *K12* **Bratunac** ◆ Republika Srpska, E Bosnia and Herzegovina
114 *J10* **Bratya Daskalovi** *prev.* Grozdovo. Stara Zagora, C Bulgaria *42°13′N 25°21′E*
109 *U2* **Braunau** ⚡ N Austria
Braunau *see* Braunau am Inn
109 *Q4* **Braunau am Inn** *var.* Braunau. Oberösterreich, N Austria *48°16′N 13°03′E*
Braunsberg *see* Braniewo
100 *J13* **Braunschweig** *Eng./Fr.* Brunswick. Niedersachsen, N Germany *52°16′N 10°32′E*
Brava *see* Baraawe
105 *Y6* **Brava, Costa** *coastal region* NE Spain
43 *V16* **Brava, Punta** *headland* E Panama *08°21′N 78°22′W*
95 *N17* **Bråviken** *inlet* S Sweden
56 *B10* **Bravo, Cerro** ▲ N Peru *05°33′S 79°10′W*
Bravo del Norte, Río/Bravo, Río *see* Grande, Rio
35 *X17* **Brawley** California, W USA *32°58′N 115°31′W*
97 *G18* **Bray** *Ir.* Bré. E Ireland *53°12′N 06°06′W*
59 *G16* **Brazil** *off.* Federative Republic of Brazil, *Port.* República Federativa do Brasil, *Sp.* Brasil; *prev.* United States of Brazil. ◆ *federal republic* South America
65 *K15* **Brazil Basin** *var.* Brazilian Basin, Brazil'skaya Kotlovina. *undersea feature* W Atlantic Ocean *15°00′S 25°00′W*
Brazil, Federative Republic of *see* Brazil
Brazilian Basin *see* Brazil Basin
Brazilian Highlands *see* Central, Planalto
Brazil'skaya Kotlovina *see* Brazil Basin
Brazil, United States of *see* Brazil
25 *U10* **Brazos River** ⚡ Texas, SW USA
Brazza *see* Brač
79 *G21* **Brazzaville** ● (Congo) Capital District, S Congo *04°14′S 15°14′E*
79 *G21* **Brazzaville** ✈ Pool, S Congo *04°15′S 15°15′E*
112 *J11* **Brčko** ◆ Republika Srpska, NE Bosnia and Herzegovina
110 *H8* **Brda** *Ger.* Brahe. ⚡ N Poland
Bré *see* Bray
185 *A23* **Breaksea Sound** *sound* South Island, New Zealand
184 *L4* **Bream Bay** *bay* North Island, New Zealand
184 *L4* **Bream Head** *headland* North Island, New Zealand *35°51′S 174°35′E*
Bréanainn, Cnoc *see* Brandon Mountain
45 *S6* **Brea, Punta** *headland* W Puerto Rico *17°56′N 66°55′W*
22 *I9* **Breaux Bridge** Louisiana, S USA *30°16′N 91°54′W*
116 *J13* **Breaza** Prahova, SE Romania *45°13′N 25°38′E*
169 *P16* **Brebes** Jawa, C Indonesia *06°54′S 109°00′E*
96 *K10* **Brechin** E Scotland, United Kingdom *56°45′N 02°38′W*
99 *H15* **Brecht** Antwerpen, N Belgium *51°21′N 04°33′E*
37 *S4* **Breckenridge** Colorado, C USA *39°28′N 106°02′W*
29 *R6* **Breckenridge** Minnesota, N USA *46°15′N 96°35′W*
25 *R6* **Breckenridge** Texas, SW USA *32°45′N 98°56′W*
97 *J21* **Brecknock** *cultural region* SE Wales, United Kingdom
63 *G25* **Brecknock, Península** *headland* S Chile *54°39′S 71°48′W*
111 *G19* **Břeclav** *Ger.* Lundenburg. Jihomoravský Kraj, SE Czech Republic *49°05′N 16°51′E*
97 *J21* **Brecon** E Wales, United Kingdom *51°58′N 03°26′W*
97 *J21* **Brecon Beacons** ▲ S Wales, United Kingdom
99 *I14* **Breda** Noord-Brabant, S Netherlands *51°35′N 04°46′E*
95 *K20* **Bredaryd** Jönköping, S Sweden *57°10′N 13°45′E*
83 *F26* **Bredasdorp** Western Cape, SW South Africa *34°32′S 20°02′E*
93 *H16* **Bredbyn** Västernorrland, N Sweden *63°28′N 18°04′E*
122 *F11* **Bredy** Chelyabinskaya Oblast', C Russian Federation *52°23′N 60°24′E*
99 *K17* **Bree** Limburg, NE Belgium *51°08′N 05°36′E*
67 *T15* **Breede** ⚡ S South Africa
98 *I7* **Breezand** Noord-Holland, NW Netherlands *52°52′N 04°47′E*
113 *P18* **Bregalnica** ⚡ E FYR Macedonia
108 *I6* **Bregenz** *anc.* Brigantium. Vorarlberg, W Austria *47°31′N 09°46′E*
108 *J7* **Bregenzer Wald** ▲ W Austria
114 *F6* **Bregovo** Vidin, NW Bulgaria *44°07′N 22°40′E*
102 *H5* **Bréhat, Île de** *island* NW France
92 *H2* **Breidhafjördhur** *bay* W Iceland
92 *L3* **Breidhdalsvík** Austurland, E Iceland *64°48′N 14°02′W*
108 *H9* **Breil** *Ger.* Brigels. Graubünden, S Switzerland *46°46′N 09°04′E*
92 *J8* **Breivikbotn** Finnmark, N Norway *70°36′N 22°19′E*
94 *I9* **Brekken** Sør-Trøndelag, S Norway *62°39′N 11°49′E*
94 *G7* **Brekstad** Sør-Trøndelag, S Norway *63°42′N 09°40′E*
94 *B10* **Bremangerlandet** *island* S Norway
Brême *see* Bremen
100 *H11* **Bremen** *Fr.* Brême. Bremen, NW Germany *53°06′N 08°48′E*
23 *R3* **Bremen** Georgia, SE USA *33°43′N 85°09′W*
31 *O11* **Bremen** Indiana, N USA *41°24′N 86°07′W*
100 *H10* **Bremen** *off.* Freie Hansestadt Bremen, *Fr.* Brême. ◆ *state* N Germany
100 *G9* **Bremerhaven** Bremen, NW Germany *53°33′N 08°35′E*
Bremersdorp *see* Manzini
32 *G8* **Bremerton** Washington, NW USA *47°34′N 122°37′W*
100 *H10* **Bremervörde** Niedersachsen, NW Germany *53°29′N 09°06′E*
25 *U9* **Bremond** Texas, SW USA *31°10′N 96°40′W*
25 *U10* **Brenham** Texas, SW USA *30°09′N 96°24′W*
108 *M8* **Brenner** Tirol, W Austria *47°10′N 11°51′E*
Brenner, Col du/Brennero, Passo del *see* Brenner Pass
108 *M8* **Brenner Pass** *var.* Brenner Sattel, *Fr.* Col du Brenner, *Ger.* Brennerpass, *It.* Passo del Brennero. *pass* Austria/Italy
Brennerpass *see* Brenner Pass
Brenner Sattel *see* Brenner Pass
108 *G10* **Brenno** ⚡ SW Switzerland
106 *F7* **Breno** Lombardia, N Italy *45°58′N 10°18′E*
23 *O5* **Brent** Alabama, S USA *32°54′N 87°10′W*
106 *H7* **Brenta** ⚡ NE Italy
97 *P21* **Brentwood** E England, United Kingdom *51°38′N 00°21′E*
18 *L14* **Brentwood** Long Island, New York, NE USA *40°46′N 73°12′W*
106 *F7* **Brescia** *anc.* Brixia. Lombardia, N Italy *45°33′N 10°13′E*
99 *D15* **Breskens** Zeeland, SW Netherlands *51°24′N 03°33′E*
Breslau *see* Wrocław
106 *H5* **Bressanone** *Ger.* Brixen. Trentino-Alto Adige, N Italy *46°44′N 11°41′E*
96 *M2* **Bressay** *island* NE Scotland, United Kingdom
102 *K9* **Bressuire** Deux-Sèvres, W France *46°50′N 00°29′W*
119 *F20* **Brest** *Pol.* Brześć nad Bugiem, *Rus.* Brest-Litovsk; *prev.* Brześć Litewski. Brestskaya Voblasts', SW Belarus *52°06′N 23°42′E*
102 *F5* **Brest** Finistère, NW France *48°24′N 04°31′W*
Brest-Litovsk *see* Brest
112 *A10* **Brestova** Istra, NW Croatia *45°09′N 14°13′E*
Brestskaya Oblast' *see* Brestskaya Voblasts'
119 *G19* **Brestskaya Voblasts'** *prev. Rus.* Brestskaya Oblast'. ◆ *province* SW Belarus
102 *G6* **Bretagne** *Eng.* Brittany, *Lat.* Britannia Minor. ◆ *region* NW France
116 *G12* **Bretea-Română** *Hung.* Oláhbrettye; *prev.* Bretea-Romînă. Hunedoara, W Romania *45°39′N 23°00′E*
Bretea-Romînă *see* Bretea-Română
103 *O3* **Breteuil** Oise, N France *49°37′N 02°18′E*
102 *I10* **Breton, Pertuis** *inlet* W France
22 *L10* **Breton Sound** *sound* Louisiana, S USA
184 *K2* **Brett, Cape** *headland* North Island, New Zealand *35°11′S 174°21′E*
101 *G21* **Bretten** Baden-Württemberg, SW Germany *49°01′N 08°42′E*
99 *K15* **Breugel** Noord-Brabant, S Netherlands *51°30′N 05°30′E*
106 *B6* **Breuil-Cervinia** *It.* Cervinia. Valle d'Aosta, NW Italy *45°57′N 07°37′E*
98 *I11* **Breukelen** Utrecht, C Netherlands *52°11′N 05°01′E*
21 *P10* **Brevard** North Carolina, SE USA *35°13′N 82°46′W*
38 *L9* **Brevig Mission** Alaska, USA *65°19′N 166°29′W*
95 *G16* **Brevik** Telemark, S Norway *59°05′N 09°42′E*

◆ Country
● Country Capital
◇ Dependent Territory
○ Dependent Territory Capital
◆ Administrative Regions
✈ International Airport
▲ Mountain
▲ Mountain Range
⛰ Volcano
⚡ River
⊚ Lake
⊠ Reservoir

- 183 *P5* **Brewarrina** New South Wales, SE Australia *30°01´S 146°50´E*
- 19 *R6* **Brewer** Maine, NE USA *44°46´N 68°44´W*
- 29 *T11* **Brewster** Minnesota, N USA *43°43´N 95°28´W*
- 29 *N14* **Brewster** Nebraska, C USA *41°57´N 99°52´W*
- 31 *U12* **Brewster** Ohio, N USA *40°42´N 81°36´W*
- **Brewster, Kap** *see* Kangikajik
- 183 *O8* **Brewster, Lake** ◎ New South Wales, SE Australia
- 23 *P7* **Brewton** Alabama, S USA *31°06´N 87°04´W*
- **Brezhnev** *see* Naberezhnyye Chelny
- 109 *W12* **Brežice** *Ger.* Rann. E Slovenia *45°54´N 15°35´E*
- 114 *G9* **Breznik** Pernik, W Bulgaria *42°45´N 22°54´E*
- 111 *K19* **Brezno** *Ger.* Bries, Briesen, *Hung.* Breznóbánya; *prev.* Brezno nad Hronom. Banskobystrický Kraj, C Slovakia *48°49´N 19°40´E*
- **Breznóbánya/Brezno nad Hronom** *see* Brezno
- 116 *I12* **Brezoi** Vâlcea, SW Romania *45°18´N 24°15´E*
- 114 *J10* **Brezovo** *prev.* Abrashlare. Plovdiv, C Bulgaria *42°19´N 25°05´E*
- 79 *K14* **Bria** Haute-Kotto, C Central African Republic *06°30´N 22°00´E*
- 103 *U13* **Briançon** *anc.* Brigantio. Hautes-Alpes, SE France *44°55´N 06°37´E*
- 36 *K7* **Brian Head** ▲ Utah, W USA *37°40´N 112°49´W*
- 103 *O7* **Briare** Loiret, C France *47°35´N 02°46´E*
- 183 *V2* **Bribie Island** *island* Queensland, E Australia
- 43 *O14* **Bribrí** Limón, E Costa Rica *09°37´N 82°51´W*
- 116 *L8* **Briceni** *var.* Brinceni, *Rus.* Brichany. N Moldova *48°21´N 27°02´E*
- **Bricgstow** *see* Bristol
- **Brichany** *see* Briceni
- 99 *M24* **Bridel** Luxembourg, C Luxembourg *49°40´N 06°03´E*
- 97 *J22* **Bridgend** S Wales, United Kingdom *51°30´N 03°37´W*
- 14 *I14* **Bridgenorth** Ontario, SE Canada *44°21´N 78°22´W*
- 23 *Q1* **Bridgeport** Alabama, S USA *34°57´N 85°42´W*
- 35 *R8* **Bridgeport** California, W USA *38°14´N 119°15´W*
- 18 *L13* **Bridgeport** Connecticut, NE USA *41°10´N 73°12´W*
- 31 *N15* **Bridgeport** Illinois, N USA *38°42´N 87°45´W*
- 28 *J14* **Bridgeport** Nebraska, C USA *41°37´N 103°07´W*
- 25 *S6* **Bridgeport** Texas, SW USA *33°12´N 97°45´W*
- 21 *S3* **Bridgeport** West Virginia, NE USA *39°17´N 80°15´W*
- 25 *S5* **Bridgeport, Lake** ⊠ Texas, SW USA
- 33 *U11* **Bridger** Montana, NW USA *45°16´N 108°55´W*
- 18 *I17* **Bridgeton** New Jersey, NE USA *39°24´N 75°10´W*
- 180 *J14* **Bridgetown** Western Australia *34°01´S 116°07´E*
- 45 *Y14* **Bridgetown** ● (Barbados) SW Barbados *13°05´N 59°36´W*
- 183 *P17* **Bridgewater** Tasmania, SE Australia *42°47´S 147°15´E*
- 13 *P16* **Bridgewater** Nova Scotia, SE Canada *44°19´N 64°30´W*
- 19 *P12* **Bridgewater** Massachusetts, NE USA *41°59´N 70°58´W*
- 29 *Q11* **Bridgewater** South Dakota, N USA *43°33´N 97°30´W*
- 21 *U5* **Bridgewater** Virginia, NE USA *38°22´N 78°58´W*
- 19 *P8* **Bridgton** Maine, NE USA *44°04´N 70°43´W*
- 97 *K23* **Bridgwater** SW England, United Kingdom *51°08´N 03°W*
- 97 *K22* **Bridgwater Bay** *bay* SW England, United Kingdom
- 97 *O16* **Bridlington** E England, United Kingdom *54°05´N 00°12´W*
- 97 *O16* **Bridlington Bay** *bay* E England, United Kingdom
- 183 *P15* **Bridport** Tasmania, SE Australia *41°03´S 147°26´E*
- 97 *K24* **Bridport** S England, United Kingdom *50°44´N 02°43´W*
- 103 *O5* **Brie** *cultural region* N France
- **Brieg** *see* Brzeg
- **Briel** *see* Brielle
- 98 *G12* **Brielle** *var.* Briel, Bril, *Eng.* The Brill. Zuid-Holland, SW Netherlands *51°54´N 04°10´E*
- 108 *E9* **Brienz** Bern, C Switzerland *46°45´N 08°00´E*
- 108 *E9* **Brienzer See** ◎ SW Switzerland
- **Bries/Briesen** *see* Brezno
- **Brietzig** *see* Brzesko
- 103 *S4* **Briey** Meurthe-et-Moselle, NE France *49°15´N 05°57´E*
- 108 *E10* **Brig** *Fr.* Brigue, *It.* Briga. Valais, SW Switzerland *46°19´N 08°E*
- **Briga** *see* Brig
- 101 *G24* **Brigach** ≈ S Germany
- 18 *K17* **Brigantine** New Jersey, NE USA *39°23´N 74°21´W*
- **Brigantio** *see* Briançon
- **Brigantium** *see* Bregenz
- **Brigels** *see* Breil
- 25 *S9* **Briggs** Texas, SW USA *30°52´N 97°55´W*
- 36 *L1* **Brigham City** Utah, W USA *41°30´N 112°00´W*
- 14 *J15* **Brighton** Ontario, SE Canada *44°01´N 77°44´W*
- 97 *O23* **Brighton** SE England, United Kingdom *50°50´N 00°10´W*
- 37 *T4* **Brighton** Colorado, C USA *39°58´N 104°46´W*
- 30 *K15* **Brighton** Illinois, N USA *39°01´N 90°09´W*
- 103 *T16* **Brignoles** Var, W France *43°25´N 06°03´E*
- **Brigue** *see* Brig
- 105 *O7* **Brihuega** Castilla-La Mancha, C Spain *40°45´N 02°52´W*
- 112 *A10* **Brijuni** *It.* Brioni. *island group* NW Croatia
- 76 *G12* **Brikama** W Gambia *13°13´N 16°37´W*
- **Bril** *see* Brielle
- **Brill, The** *see* Brielle
- 101 *G15* **Brilon** Nordrhein-Westfalen, W Germany *51°24´N 08°34´E*
- **Brinceni** *see* Briceni
- 107 *Q18* **Brindisi** *anc.* Brundisium, Brundusium. Puglia, SE Italy *40°39´N 17°55´E*
- 27 *W11* **Brinkley** Arkansas, C USA *34°53´N 91°11´W*
- **Brioni** *see* Brijuni
- 103 *P12* **Brioude** *anc.* Brivas. Haute-Loire, C France *45°18´N 03°23´E*
- **Briovera** *see* St-Lô
- 183 *U2* **Brisbane** *state capital* Queensland, E Australia *27°30´S 153°E*
- 183 *V2* **Brisbane** ✕ Queensland, E Australia *27°30´S 153°00´E*
- 25 *P2* **Briscoe** Texas, SW USA *35°34´N 100°17´W*
- 106 *H10* **Brisighella** Emilia-Romagna, C Italy *44°12´N 11°45´E*
- 108 *G11* **Brissago** Ticino, S Switzerland *46°07´N 08°40´E*
- 97 *K22* **Bristol** *anc.* Bricgstow. SW England, United Kingdom *51°27´N 02°35´W*
- 18 *M12* **Bristol** Connecticut, NE USA *41°40´N 72°56´W*
- 23 *R9* **Bristol** Florida, SE USA *30°25´N 84°58´W*
- 19 *N9* **Bristol** New Hampshire, NE USA *43°34´N 71°42´W*
- 29 *Q8* **Bristol** South Dakota, N USA *45°18´N 97°45´W*
- 21 *P8* **Bristol** Tennessee, S USA *36°36´N 82°11´W*
- 18 *M8* **Bristol** Vermont, NE USA *44°07´N 73°00´W*
- 39 *N14* **Bristol Bay** *bay* Alaska, USA
- 97 *I22* **Bristol Channel** *inlet* England/Wales, United Kingdom
- 35 *W14* **Bristol Lake** ◎ California, W USA
- 27 *P10* **Bristow** Oklahoma, C USA *35°49´N 96°23´W*
- 86 *C10* **Britain** *var.* Great Britain. *island* United Kingdom
- **Britannia Minor** *see* Bretagne
- 10 *L12* **British Columbia** *Fr.* Colombie-Britannique. ⬖ *province* SW Canada
- **British Guiana** *see* Guyana
- **British Honduras** *see* Belize
- 173 *Q7* **British Indian Ocean Territory** ◇ *UK dependent territory* C Indian Ocean
- 86 *B9* **British Isles** *island group* NW Europe
- 10 *I1* **British Mountains** ▲▲ Yukon Territory, NW Canada
- **British North Borneo** *see* Sabah
- **British Solomon Islands Protectorate** *see* Solomon Islands
- 45 *S8* **British Virgin Islands** *var.* Virgin Islands. ◇ *UK dependent territory* E West Indies
- 83 *J21* **Brits** North-West, N South Africa *25°39´S 27°47´E*
- 83 *H24* **Britstown** Northern Cape, W South Africa *30°36´S 23°30´E*
- 14 *F12* **Britt** Ontario, S Canada *45°46´N 80°34´W*
- 29 *V12* **Britt** Iowa, C USA *43°06´N 93°48´W*
- **Brittany** *see* Bretagne
- 29 *Q7* **Britton** South Dakota, N USA *45°47´N 97°45´W*
- **Briva Curretia** *see* Brive-la-Gaillarde
- **Briva Isarae** *see* Pontoise
- **Brivas** *see* Brioude
- **Brive** *see* Brive-la-Gaillarde
- 102 *M12* **Brive-la-Gaillarde** *prev.* Brive; *anc.* Briva Curretia. Corrèze, C France *45°09´N 01°31´E*
- 105 *O4* **Briviesca** Castilla y León, N Spain *42°33´N 03°19´W*
- **Brixen** *see* Bressanone
- **Brixia** *see* Brescia
- **Brlik** *see* Birlik
- **Brněnský Kraj** *see* Jihomoravský Kraj
- 111 *G18* **Brno** *Ger.* Brünn. Jihomoravský Kraj, SE Czech Republic *49°11´N 16°35´E*
- 96 *G7* **Broad Bay** *bay* NW Scotland, United Kingdom
- 25 *X8* **Broaddus** Texas, SW USA *31°18´N 94°16´W*
- 183 *O12* **Broadford** Victoria, SE Australia *37°07´S 145°04´E*
- 96 *G9* **Broadford** N Scotland, United Kingdom *57°14´N 05°54´W*
- 96 *J13* **Broad Law** ▲ S Scotland, United Kingdom *55°30´N 03°22´W*
- 23 *U3* **Broad River** ≈ Georgia, SE USA
- 21 *N8* **Broad River** ≈ North Carolina/South Carolina, SE USA
- 181 *Y8* **Broadsound Range** ▲▲ Queensland, E Australia
- 33 *X11* **Broadus** Montana, NW USA *45°28´N 105°22´W*
- 21 *U4* **Broadway** Virginia, NE USA *38°36´N 78°48´W*
- 118 *E9* **Brocēni** SW Latvia *56°41´N 22°31´E*
- 11 *U11* **Brochet** Manitoba, C Canada *57°55´N 101°40´W*
- 11 *U10* **Brochet, Lac** ◎ Manitoba, C Canada
- 15 *S5* **Brochet, Lac au** ◎ Québec, SE Canada
- 101 *K14* **Brocken** ▲ C Germany *51°48´N 10°38´E*
- 19 *O12* **Brockton** Massachusetts, NE USA *42°04´N 71°01´W*
- 14 *L14* **Brockville** Ontario, SE Canada *44°35´N 75°44´W*
- 18 *D13* **Brockway** Pennsylvania, NE USA *41°14´N 78°45´W*
- **Brod/Bród** *see* Slavonski Brod
- 9 *N5* **Brodeur Peninsula** *peninsula* Baffin Island, Nunavut, NE Canada
- 96 *H13* **Brodick** W Scotland, United Kingdom *55°34´N 05°10´W*
- **Brod na Savi** *see* Slavonski Brod
- 110 *K9* **Brodnica** *Ger.* Buddenbrock. Kujawski-pomorskie, C Poland *53°15´N 19°23´E*
- **Brod-Posavina** *see* Slavonski Brod-Posavina
- **Brodsko-Posavska Županija** *see* Slavonski Brod-Posavina
- 116 *J5* **Brody** L'vivs'ka Oblast', NW Ukraine *50°05´N 25°08´E*
- 98 *I10* **Broek-in-Waterland** Noord-Holland, C Netherlands *52°27´N 04°59´E*
- 32 *L13* **Brogan** Oregon, NW USA *44°15´N 117°34´W*
- 110 *N10* **Brok** Mazowieckie, C Poland *52°42´N 21°53´E*
- 27 *P9* **Broken Arrow** Oklahoma, C USA *36°03´N 95°47´W*
- 183 *T9* **Broken Bay** *bay* New South Wales, SE Australia
- 29 *N15* **Broken Bow** Nebraska, C USA *41°24´N 99°38´W*
- 27 *R13* **Broken Bow** Oklahoma, C USA *34°01´N 94°44´W*
- 27 *R12* **Broken Bow Lake** ⊠ Oklahoma, C USA
- 182 *L6* **Broken Hill** New South Wales, SE Australia *31°58´S 141°27´E*
- 173 *S10* **Broken Ridge** *undersea feature* S Indian Ocean *31°30´S 95°00´E*
- 186 *C6* **Broken Water Bay** *bay* W Bismarck Sea
- 55 *W10* **Brokopondo** Brokopondo, NE Surinam *05°04´N 55°00´W*
- 55 *W10* **Brokopondo** ⬖ *district* C Surinam
- **Bromberg** *see* Bydgoszcz
- 95 *L22* **Bromölla** Skåne, S Sweden *56°04´N 14°28´E*
- 97 *L20* **Bromsgrove** W England, United Kingdom *52°20´N 02°03´W*
- 95 *G20* **Brønderslev** Nordjylland, N Denmark *57°16´N 09°58´E*
- 106 *D8* **Broni** Lombardia, N Italy *45°04´N 09°18´E*
- 10 *K11* **Bronlund Peak** ▲ British Columbia, W Canada *57°27´N 126°43´W*
- 93 *F14* **Brønnøysund** Nordland, C Norway *65°38´N 12°15´E*
- 23 *V10* **Bronson** Florida, SE USA *29°25´N 82°38´W*
- 31 *Q11* **Bronson** Michigan, N USA *41°52´N 85°11´W*
- 25 *X8* **Bronson** Texas, SW USA *31°20´N 94°00´W*
- 107 *L24* **Bronte** Sicilia, Italy, C Mediterranean Sea *37°47´N 14°50´E*
- 25 *P8* **Bronte** Texas, SW USA *31°53´N 100°17´W*
- 25 *Y9* **Brookeland** Texas, SW USA *31°05´N 93°57´W*
- 170 *M7* **Brooke's Point** Palawan, W Philippines *08°54´N 117°54´E*
- 27 *T3* **Brookfield** Missouri, C USA *39°46´N 93°04´W*
- 22 *K7* **Brookhaven** Mississippi, S USA *31°34´N 90°26´W*
- 32 *E16* **Brookings** Oregon, NW USA *42°03´N 124°16´W*
- 29 *R10* **Brookings** South Dakota, N USA *44°15´N 96°46´W*
- 29 *W14* **Brooklyn** Iowa, C USA *41°43´N 92°27´W*
- 29 *U8* **Brooklyn Park** Minnesota, N USA *45°06´N 93°18´W*
- 21 *U7* **Brookneal** Virginia, NE USA *37°03´N 78°56´W*
- 11 *R16* **Brooks** Alberta, SW Canada *50°35´N 111°54´W*
- 25 *V11* **Brookshire** Texas, SW USA *29°47´N 95°57´W*
- 38 *L8* **Brooks Mountain** ▲ Alaska, USA *65°31´N 167°24´W*
- 38 *M11* **Brooks Range** ▲▲ Alaska, USA
- 31 *O12* **Brookston** Indiana, N USA *40°34´N 86°53´W*
- 23 *V11* **Brooksville** Florida, SE USA *28°33´N 82°23´W*
- 23 *N4* **Brooksville** Mississippi, S USA *33°13´N 88°34´W*
- 180 *J13* **Brookton** Western Australia *32°24´S 117°04´E*
- 31 *Q14* **Brookville** Indiana, N USA *39°25´N 85°00´W*
- 18 *D13* **Brookville** Pennsylvania, NE USA *41°07´N 79°05´W*
- 31 *Q14* **Brookville Lake** ⊠ Indiana, N USA
- 180 *K5* **Broome** Western Australia *17°58´S 122°15´E*
- 37 *S4* **Broomfield** Colorado, C USA *39°55´N 105°05´W*
- **Broos** *see* Orăştie
- 96 *J7* **Brora** N Scotland, United Kingdom *57°59´N 04°00´W*
- 96 *I7* **Brora** ≈ N Scotland, United Kingdom
- 95 *F23* **Brørup** Syddtjylland, W Denmark *55°29´N 09°01´E*
- 95 *L23* **Brösarp** Skåne, S Sweden *55°43´N 14°10´E*
- 116 *J9* **Broşteni** Suceava, NE Romania *47°14´N 25°43´E*
- 102 *M6* **Brou** Eure-et-Loir, C France *48°12´N 01°10´E*
- **Broucsella** *see* Brussel/Bruxelles
- **Broughton Bay** *see* Tongjosŏn-man
- **Broughton Island** *see* Qikiqtarjuaq
- 138 *G7* **Broummâna** C Lebanon *33°53´N 35°39´E*
- 22 *I9* **Broussard** Louisiana, S USA *30°09´N 91°57´W*
- 98 *E13* **Brouwersdam** *dam* SW Netherlands
- 98 *E13* **Brouwershaven** Zeeland, SW Netherlands *51°44´N 03°50´E*
- 117 *P4* **Brovary** Kyyivs'ka Oblast', N Ukraine *50°30´N 30°45´E*
- 95 *G20* **Brovst** Nordjylland, N Denmark *57°06´N 09°32´E*
- 31 *S8* **Brown City** Michigan, N USA *43°12´N 82°50´W*
- 24 *M6* **Brownfield** Texas, SW USA *33°11´N 102°16´W*
- 33 *Q7* **Browning** Montana, NW USA *48°33´N 113°00´W*
- 33 *R6* **Brown, Mount** ▲ Montana, NW USA *48°52´N 111°08´W*
- 0 *M9* **Browns Bank** *undersea feature* NW Atlantic Ocean *42°40´N 66°05´W*
- 31 *O14* **Brownsburg** Indiana, N USA *39°50´N 86°24´W*
- 18 *J16* **Browns Mills** New Jersey, NE USA *39°58´N 74°33´W*
- 44 *J12* **Browns Town** C Jamaica *18°28´N 77°22´W*
- 31 *P15* **Brownstown** Indiana, N USA *38°52´N 86°02´W*
- 29 *R8* **Browns Valley** Minnesota, N USA *45°36´N 96°49´W*
- 20 *K7* **Brownsville** Kentucky, S USA *37°10´N 86°18´W*
- 20 *F9* **Brownsville** Tennessee, S USA *35°35´N 89°15´W*
- 25 *T17* **Brownsville** Texas, SW USA *25°56´N 97°28´W*
- 55 *W10* **Brownsweg** Brokopondo, C Surinam
- 29 *U9* **Brownton** Minnesota, N USA *44°43´N 94°21´W*
- 19 *R5* **Brownville Junction** Maine, NE USA *45°20´N 69°04´W*
- 25 *R8* **Brownwood** Texas, SW USA *31°42´N 98°59´W*
- 25 *R8* **Brownwood Lake** ⊠ Texas, SW USA
- 104 *I9* **Brozas** Extremadura, W Spain *39°37´N 06°48´W*
- 119 *M18* **Brozha** Mahilyowskaya Voblasts', E Belarus *52°57´N 29°07´E*
- 103 *O2* **Bruay-en-Artois** Pas-de-Calais, N France *50°31´N 02°30´E*
- 103 *P2* **Bruay-sur-l'Escaut** Nord, N France *50°24´N 03°33´E*
- 14 *F13* **Bruce Peninsula** *peninsula* Ontario, S Canada
- 20 *H9* **Bruceton** Tennessee, S USA *36°02´N 88°14´W*
- 25 *T9* **Bruceville** Texas, SW USA *31°17´N 97°15´W*
- 101 *G21* **Bruchsal** Baden-Württemberg, SW Germany *49°07´N 08°35´E*
- 109 *Q7* **Bruck** Salzburg, NW Austria *47°18´N 12°51´E*
- **Bruck** *see* Bruck an der Mur
- 109 *Y4* **Bruck an der Leitha** Niederösterreich, NE Austria *48°02´N 16°47´E*
- 109 *V7* **Bruck an der Mur** *var.* Bruck. Steiermark, C Austria *47°25´N 15°17´E*
- 101 *M24* **Bruckmühl** Bayern, SE Germany *47°52´N 11°54´E*
- 168 *E7* **Brueuh, Pulau** *island* NW Indonesia
- **Bruges** *see* Brugge
- 108 *F6* **Brugg** Aargau, NW Switzerland *47°29´N 08°13´E*
- 99 *C16* **Brugge** *Fr.* Bruges. West-Vlaanderen, NW Belgium *51°13´N 03°14´E*
- 109 *R9* **Bruggen** Kärnten, S Austria *46°46´N 13°13´E*
- 101 *E16* **Brühl** Nordrhein-Westfalen, W Germany *50°50´N 06°55´E*
- 99 *F14* **Bruinisse** Zeeland, SW Netherlands *51°40´N 04°04´E*
- 169 *R9* **Bruit, Pulau** *island* East Malaysia
- 14 *K10* **Brûlé, Lac** ◎ Québec, SE Canada
- 30 *M4* **Brule River** ≈ Michigan/Wisconsin, N USA
- 99 *H23* **Brûly** Namur, S Belgium *49°55´N 04°31´E*
- 59 *N17* **Brumado** Bahia, E Brazil *14°14´S 41°38´W*
- 98 *M11* **Brummen** Gelderland, E Netherlands *52°05´N 06°10´E*
- 94 *H13* **Brumunddal** Hedmark, S Norway *60°54´N 11°00´E*
- 23 *Q6* **Brundidge** Alabama, S USA *31°43´N 85°49´W*
- **Brundisium/Brundusium** *see* Brindisi
- 33 *N15* **Bruneau River** ≈ Idaho, NW USA
- **Bruneck** *see* Brunico
- 169 *T8* **Brunei** *off.* Brunei Darussalam, *Mal.* Negara Brunei Darussalam. ◆ *monarchy* SE Asia
- 169 *T7* **Brunei Bay** *var.* Teluk Brunei. *bay* N Brunei
- **Brunei Darussalam** *see* Brunei
- **Brunei, Teluk** *see* Brunei Bay
- **Brunei Town** *see* Bandar Seri Begawan
- 106 *H5* **Brunico** *Ger.* Bruneck. Trentino-Alto Adige, N Italy *46°49´N 11°57´E*
- **Brünn** *see* Brno
- 185 *G17* **Brunner, Lake** ◎ South Island, New Zealand
- 99 *M18* **Brunssum** Limburg, SE Netherlands *50°57´N 05°59´E*
- 23 *W7* **Brunswick** Georgia, SE USA *31°09´N 81°30´W*
- 19 *Q8* **Brunswick** Maine, NE USA *43°54´N 69°58´W*
- 21 *V3* **Brunswick** Maryland, NE USA *39°18´N 77°37´W*
- 27 *T3* **Brunswick** Missouri, C USA *39°25´N 93°07´W*
- 31 *T11* **Brunswick** Ohio, N USA *41°14´N 81°50´W*
- **Brunswick** *see* Braunschweig
- 63 *H24* **Brunswick, Península** *headland* S Chile *53°30´S 71°27´W*
- 111 *H17* **Bruntál** *Ger.* Freudenthal. Moravskoslezský Kraj, E Czech Republic *50°00´N 17°27´E*
- 195 *N3* **Brunt Ice Shelf** *ice shelf* Antarctica
- **Brusa** *see* Bursa
- 114 *G7* **Brusartsi** Montana, NW Bulgaria *43°39´N 23°04´E*
- 37 *U3* **Brush** Colorado, C USA *40°15´N 103°37´W*
- 42 *M5* **Brus Laguna** Gracias a Dios, E Honduras *15°46´N 84°32´W*
- 60 *K13* **Brusque** Santa Catarina, S Brazil *27°07´S 48°54´W*
- **Brussa** *see* Bursa
- 99 *E18* **Brussel** *var.* Brussels, *Fr.* Bruxelles, *Ger.* Brüssel; *anc.* Broucsella. ● (Belgium) Brussels, C Belgium *50°52´N 04°21´E* *see also* Bruxelles
- **Brussel** *see* Bruxelles
- **Brüssel/Brussels** *see* Brussel/Bruxelles
- 117 *O5* **Brusyliv** Zhytomyrs'ka Oblast', N Ukraine *50°16´N 29°31´E*
- 183 *Q12* **Bruthen** Victoria, SE Australia *37°43´S 147°49´E*
- **Bruttium** *see* Calabria
- **Brüx** *see* Most
- 99 *E18* **Bruxelles** *var.* Brussels, *Dut.* Brussel, *Ger.* Brüssel; *anc.* Broucsella. ● Brussels, C Belgium *50°52´N 04°21´E* *see also* Brussel
- **Bruxelles** *see* Brussel
- 54 *J7* **Bruzual** Apure, W Venezuela *07°59´N 69°18´W*
- 31 *Q11* **Bryan** Ohio, N USA *41°30´N 84°34´W*
- 25 *U10* **Bryan** Texas, SW USA *30°40´N 96°23´W*
- 194 *J4* **Bryan Coast** *physical region* Antarctica
- 122 *L11* **Bryanka** Krasnoyarskiy Kray, C Russian Federation *59°01´N 93°13´E*
- 117 *Y7* **Bryanka** Luhans'ka Oblast', E Ukraine *48°30´N 38°45´E*
- 182 *J8* **Bryan, Mount** ▲ South Australia *33°25´S 138°59´E*
- 126 *I6* **Bryansk** Bryanskaya Oblast', W Russian Federation *53°16´N 34°07´E*
- 126 *H6* **Bryanskaya Oblast'** ⬖ *province* W Russian Federation
- 194 *J5* **Bryant, Cape** *headland* Antarctica
- 27 *U8* **Bryant Creek** ≈ Missouri, C USA
- 36 *K8* **Bryce Canyon** *canyon* Utah, W USA
- 119 *O15* **Bryli** Mahilyowskaya Voblasts', E Belarus *53°54´N 30°33´E*
- 95 *C17* **Bryne** Rogaland, S Norway *58°43´N 05°40´E*
- 25 *R6* **Bryson** Texas, SW USA *33°09´N 98°23´W*
- 21 *N10* **Bryson City** North Carolina, SE USA *35°26´N 83°27´W*
- 14 *K11* **Bryson, Lac** ◎ Québec, SE Canada
- 126 *K13* **Bryukhovetskaya** Krasnodarskiy Kray, SW Russian Federation *45°49´N 38°01´E*
- 111 *H15* **Brzeg** *Ger.* Brieg; *anc.* Civitas Altae Ripae. Opolskie, S Poland *50°52´N 17°27´E*
- 111 *G14* **Brzeg Dolny** *Ger.* Dyhernfurth. Dolnośląskie, SW Poland *51°15´N 16°40´E*
- **Brześć Litewski/Brześć nad Bugiem** *see* Brest
- 111 *L17* **Brzesko** *Ger.* Brietzig. Małopolskie, SE Poland *49°59´N 20°34´E*
- **Brzeżany** *see* Berezhany
- 110 *K12* **Brzeziny** Łódzkie, C Poland *51°49´N 19°41´E*
- **Brzostowica Wielka** *see* Vyalikaya Byerastavitsa
- 111 *O17* **Brzozów** Podkarpackie, SE Poland *49°38´N 22°00´E*
- **Bsharrī/Bsherri** *see* Bcharré
- 187 *X14* **Bua** Vanua Levu, N Fiji *16°48´S 178°36´E*
- 95 *J20* **Bua** Halland, S Sweden *57°14´N 12°07´E*
- 82 *M13* **Bua** ≈ C Malawi
- **Bua** *see* Čiovo
- 81 *L18* **Bu'aale** *It.* Buale. Jubbada Dhexe, SW Somalia *0°52´N 42°37´E*
- **Buache, Mount** *see* Mutunte, Mount
- 189 *Q8* **Buada Lagoon** *lagoon* Nauru, C Pacific Ocean
- 186 *M8* **Buala** Santa Isabel, E Solomon Islands *08°06´S 159°31´E*
- **Buale** *see* Bu'aale
- 190 *H1* **Buariki** *atoll* Tungaru, W Kiribati
- 167 *Q10* **Bua Yai** *var.* Ban Bua Yai. Nakhon Ratchasima, E Thailand *15°35´N 102°25´E*
- 75 *P8* **Bu'ayrāt al Ḩasūn** *var.* Buwayrāt al Hasūn. C Libya *31°22´N 15°41´E*
- 76 *H13* **Buba** S Guinea-Bissau *11°36´N 14°55´W*
- 171 *P11* **Bubaa** Sulawesi, N Indonesia *0°32´N 122°27´E*
- 81 *D20* **Bubanza** NW Burundi *03°04´S 29°22´E*
- 83 *K18* **Bubi** *prev.* Bubye. ≈ S Zimbabwe
- 142 *L11* **Būbīyan, Jazīrat** *island* E Kuwait
- **Bublitz** *see* Bobolice
- **Bubye** *see* Bubi
- 187 *Y13* **Buca** *prev.* Mbutha. Vanua Levu, N Fiji *16°39´S 179°51´E*
- 136 *F16* **Bucak** Burdur, SW Turkey *37°28´N 30°37´E*
- 54 *G8* **Bucaramanga** Santander, N Colombia *07°08´N 73°10´W*
- 107 *M18* **Buccino** Campania, S Italy *40°37´N 15°25´E*
- 116 *K9* **Bucecea** Botoşani, NE Romania *47°45´N 26°30´E*
- 116 *J6* **Buchach** *Pol.* Buczacz. Ternopil's'ka Oblast', W Ukraine *49°04´N 25°23´E*
- 183 *Q12* **Buchan** Victoria, SE Australia *37°26´S 148°11´E*
- 76 *J17* **Buchanan** *prev.* Grand Bassa. SW Liberia *05°53´N 10°03´W*
- 23 *R3* **Buchanan** Georgia, SE USA *33°48´N 85°11´W*
- 31 *O11* **Buchanan** Michigan, N USA *41°49´N 86°21´W*
- 21 *T6* **Buchanan** Virginia, NE USA *37°31´N 79°40´W*
- 25 *R10* **Buchanan Dam** Texas, SW USA *30°42´N 98°24´W*
- 25 *R10* **Buchanan, Lake** ⊠ Texas, SW USA
- 96 *L8* **Buchan Ness** *headland* NE Scotland, United Kingdom *57°28´N 01°46´W*
- 13 *T12* **Buchans** Newfoundland and Labrador, SE Canada *48°49´N 56°53´W*
- **Bucharest** *see* Bucureşti
- 101 *H20* **Buchen** Baden-Württemberg, SW Germany *49°31´N 09°18´E*
- 100 *I10* **Buchholz in der Nordheide** Niedersachsen, NW Germany *53°19´N 09°52´E*
- 108 *F7* **Buchs** Aargau, N Switzerland *47°24´N 08°04´E*
- 108 *I8* **Buchs** Sankt Gallen, NE Switzerland *47°10´N 09°28´E*
- 100 *H13* **Bückeburg** Niedersachsen, NW Germany *52°16´N 09°03´E*
- 36 *K14* **Buckeye** Arizona, SW USA *33°22´N 112°34´W*
- **Buckeye State** *see* Ohio
- 21 *S4* **Buckhannon** West Virginia, NE USA *38°59´N 80°14´W*
- 25 *T9* **Buckholts** Texas, SW USA *30°52´N 97°07´W*
- 96 *K8* **Buckie** NE Scotland, United Kingdom *57°39´N 02°56´W*
- 14 *M12* **Buckingham** Québec, SE Canada *45°35´N 75°25´W*
- 21 *U6* **Buckingham** Virginia, NE USA *37°33´N 78°34´W*
- 97 *N21* **Buckinghamshire** *cultural region* SE England, United Kingdom
- 39 *N8* **Buckland** Alaska, USA *65°58´N 161°07´W*
- 182 *G7* **Buckleboo** South Australia *32°55´S 136°11´E*
- 26 *K7* **Bucklin** Kansas, C USA *37°33´N 99°37´W*
- 27 *T3* **Bucklin** Missouri, C USA *39°46´N 92°53´W*
- 36 *I12* **Buckskin Mountains** ▲▲ Arizona, SW USA
- 19 *R7* **Bucksport** Maine, NE USA *44°34´N 68°46´W*
- 82 *A9* **Buco Zau** Cabinda, NW Angola *04°45´S 12°34´E*
- **Bu Craa** *see* Bou Craa
- 116 *K14* **Bucureşti** *Eng.* Bucharest, *Ger.* Bukarest, *prev.* Altenburg; *anc.* Cetatea Damboviţei. ● (Romania) Bucureşti, S Romania *44°27´N 26°06´E*
- 31 *S12* **Bucyrus** Ohio, N USA *40°47´N 82°57´W*
- **Buczacz** *see* Buchach
- 94 *E9* **Bud** Møre og Romsdal, S Norway *62°55´N 06°55´E*
- 25 *S11* **Buda** Texas, SW USA *30°05´N 97°50´W*
- 119 *O18* **Buda-Kashalyova** *Rus.* Buda-Koshelëvo. Homyel'skaya Voblasts', SE Belarus *52°43´N 30°34´E*
- **Buda-Koshelëvo** *see* Buda-Kashalyova
- 166 *L4* **Budalin** Sagaing, C Burma (Myanmar) *22°24´N 95°08´E*
- 111 *J22* **Budapest** *off.* Budapest Főváros, *SCr.* Budimpešta. ● (Hungary) Pest, N Hungary *47°30´N 19°03´E*
- **Budapest Főváros** *see* Budapest
- 152 *K11* **Budaun** Uttar Pradesh, N India *28°02´N 79°07´E*
- 141 *O9* **Budayyi'ah** *oasis* C Saudi Arabia
- 195 *Y12* **Budd Coast** *physical region* Antarctica
- **Buddenbrock** *see* Brodnica
- 107 *C17* **Budduso** Sardegna, Italy, C Mediterranean Sea *40°37´N 09°19´E*
- 97 *I23* **Bude** SW England, United Kingdom *50°50´N 04°33´W*
- 22 *J7* **Bude** Mississippi, S USA *31°27´N 90°51´W*
- **Budějovický Kraj** *see* Jihočeský Kraj
- 99 *K16* **Budel** Noord-Brabant, SE Netherlands *51°17´N 05°35´E*
- 100 *I8* **Büdelsdorf** Schleswig-Holstein, N Germany *54°20´N 09°40´E*
- 127 *O14* **Budënnovsk** Stavropol'skiy Kray, SW Russian Federation *44°46´N 44°07´E*
- 116 *K14* **Budeşti** Călăraşi, SE Romania *44°13´N 26°30´E*
- **Budge-Budge** *see* Baj Baj
- **Budgewoi** *see* Budgewoi Lake
- 183 *T8* **Budgewoi Lake** *var.* Budgewoi. New South Wales, SE Australia *33°14´S 151°34´E*
- 92 *I2* **Búdhardalur** Vesturland, W Iceland *65°07´N 21°45´W*
- **Budimpešta** *see* Budapest
- 79 *J16* **Budjala** Equateur, NW Dem. Rep. Congo *02°39´N 19°42´E*
- 106 *G10* **Budrio** Emilia-Romagna, C Italy *44°33´N 11°34´E*
- **Budslav** *see* Budslaw
- 119 *K14* **Budslaw** *Rus.* Budslav. Minskaya Voblasts', N Belarus *54°47´N 27°27´E*
- **Budua** *see* Budva
- 169 *R9* **Budu, Tanjung** *headland* East Malaysia *02°51´N 111°42´E*
- 113 *J17* **Budva** *It.* Budua. W Montenegro *42°17´N 18°49´E*
- **Budweis** *see* České Budějovice
- **Budyšin** *see* Bautzen
- 79 *D16* **Buea** Sud-Ouest, SW Cameroon *04°09´N 09°13´E*
- 103 *S13* **Buëch** ≈ SE France
- 18 *J17* **Buena** New Jersey, NE USA *39°30´N 74°55´W*
- 62 *K12* **Buena Esperanza** San Luis, C Argentina *34°45´S 65°15´W*
- 54 *C11* **Buenaventura** Valle del Cauca, W Colombia *03°54´N 77°02´W*
- 40 *I4* **Buenaventura** Chihuahua, N Mexico *29°50´N 107°30´W*
- 57 *M18* **Buena Vista** Santa Cruz, C Bolivia *17°28´S 63°37´W*
- 40 *G10* **Buenavista** Baja California Sur, NW Mexico *23°39´N 109°41´W*
- 37 *S5* **Buena Vista** Colorado, C USA *38°50´N 106°07´W*
- 23 *S5* **Buena Vista** Georgia, SE USA *32°19´N 84°31´W*
- 21 *T6* **Buena Vista** Virginia, NE USA *37°44´N 79°22´W*
- 44 *F5* **Buena Vista, Bahia de** *bay* N Cuba
- 35 *R13* **Buena Vista Lake Bed** ◎ California, W USA
- 105 *P8* **Buendía, Embalse de** ⊠ C Spain
- 63 *F16* **Bueno, Río** ≈ S Chile
- 62 *N12* **Buenos Aires** *hist.* Santa Maria del Buen Aire. ● (Argentina) Buenos Aires, E Argentina *34°40´S 58°30´W*
- 43 *O15* **Buenos Aires** Puntarenas, SE Costa Rica *09°10´N 83°23´W*
- 61 *C20* **Buenos Aires** *off.* Provincia de Buenos Aires. ⬖ *province* E Argentina
- 63 *H19* **Buenos Aires, Lago** *var.* Lago General Carrera. ◎ Argentina/Chile
- **Buenos Aires, Provincia de** *see* Buenos Aires
- 54 *C13* **Buesaco** Nariño, SW Colombia *01°22´N 77°07´W*
- 29 *U8* **Buffalo** Minnesota, N USA *45°11´N 93°50´W*
- 26 *T6* **Buffalo** Missouri, C USA *37°38´N 93°05´W*
- 18 *D10* **Buffalo** New York, NE USA *42°53´N 78°53´W*
- 27 *K8* **Buffalo** Oklahoma, C USA *36°51´N 99°38´W*
- 28 *J7* **Buffalo** South Dakota, N USA *45°25´N 103°35´W*
- 25 *V8* **Buffalo** Texas, SW USA *31°25´N 96°04´W*
- 33 *W12* **Buffalo** Wyoming, C USA *44°21´N 106°40´W*
- 29 *U11* **Buffalo Center** Iowa, C USA *43°23´N 93°57´W*
- 24 *M3* **Buffalo Lake** ⊠ Texas, SW USA
- 30 *K7* **Buffalo Lake** ⊠ Wisconsin, N USA
- 11 *S12* **Buffalo Narrows** Saskatchewan, C Canada *55°52´N 108°28´W*
- 27 *U9* **Buffalo River** ≈ Arkansas, C USA
- 29 *R5* **Buffalo River** ≈ Minnesota, N USA
- 20 *I10* **Buffalo River** ≈ Tennessee, S USA
- 30 *J6* **Buffalo River** ≈ Wisconsin, N USA
- 44 *L12* **Buff Bay** E Jamaica *18°18´N 76°40´W*
- 23 *T3* **Buford** Georgia, SE USA *34°07´N 84°00´W*
- 28 *J3* **Buford** North Dakota, N USA *48°00´N 103°58´W*
- 33 *Y17* **Buford** Wyoming, C USA *41°05´N 105°17´W*
- 116 *J14* **Buftea** Ilfov, S Romania *44°34´N 25°58´E*
- 84 *I9* **Bug** *Bel.* Zakhodni Buh, *Eng.* Western Bug, *Rus.* Zapadnyy Bug, *Ukr.* Zakhidnyy Buh. ≈ E Europe
- 54 *D11* **Buga** Valle del Cauca, W Colombia *03°53´N 76°17´W*
- **Buga** *see* Dörvöljin
- 103 *O17* **Bugarach, Pic du** ▲ S France *42°52´N 02°23´E*
- 162 *F8* **Bugat** *var.* Bayangol. Govĭ-Altay, SW Mongolia *45°33´N 94°22´E*
- 146 *B12* **Bugdaýly** *Rus.* Bugdayly. Balkan Welaýaty, W Turkmenistan *38°42´N 54°14´E*
- **Bugdayly** *see* Bugdaýly
- **Buggs Island Lake** *see* John H. Kerr Reservoir
- **Bughotu** *see* Santa Isabel
- 171 *O14* **Bugingkalo** Sulawesi, C Indonesia *04°49´S 121°42´E*
- 64 *P6* **Bugio** *island* Madeira, Portugal, NE Atlantic Ocean
- 92 *M8* **Bugøynes** Finnmark, N Norway *69°57´N 29°34´E*
- 125 *Q3* **Bugrino** Nenetskiy Avtonomnyy Okrug, NW Russian Federation *68°48´N 49°12´E*
- 127 *T5* **Bugul'ma** Respublika Tatarstan, W Russian Federation *54°31´N 52°45´E*
- **Bügür** *see* Luntai
- 127 *T6* **Buguruslan** Orenburgskaya Oblast', W Russian Federation *53°38´N 52°30´E*
- 159 *R9* **Buh He** ≈ C China
- 101 *F22* **Bühl** Baden-Württemberg, SW Germany *48°42´N 08°07´E*
- 33 *O15* **Buhl** Idaho, NW USA *42°36´N 114°45´W*
- 116 *K10* **Buhuşi** Bacău, E Romania *46°41´N 26°45´E*
- **Buie d'Istria** *see* Buje
- 97 *J20* **Builth Wells** E Wales, United Kingdom *52°07´N 03°28´W*
- 186 *J8* **Buin** Bougainville Island, NE Papua New Guinea *06°52´S 155°42´E*
- 108 *J9* **Buin, Piz** ▲ Austria/Switzerland *46°51´N 10°07´E*
- 127 *Q4* **Buinsk** Chuvashskaya Respublika, W Russian Federation *55°09´N 47°00´E*
- 127 *Q4* **Buinsk** Respublika Tatarstan, W Russian Federation *54°58´N 48°16´E*
- 163 *R8* **Buir Nur** *Mong.* Buyr Nuur. ◎ China/Mongolia *see also* Buyr Nuur
- **Buir Nur** *see* Buyr Nuur
- 98 *M5* **Buitenpost** *Fris.* Bûtenpost. Fryslân, N Netherlands *53°15´N 06°09´E*
- **Buitenzorg** *see* Bogor
- 83 *F19* **Buitepos** Omaheke, E Namibia *22°17´S 19°59´E*
- 105 *N7* **Buitrago del Lozoya** Madrid, C Spain *41°00´N 03°38´W*
- **Buj** *see* Buy
- 104 *M13* **Bujalance** Andalucía, S Spain *37°54´N 04°23´W*
- 113 *O17* **Bujanovac** SE Serbia *42°29´N 21°44´E*
- 105 *S6* **Bujaraloz** Aragón, NE Spain *41°29´N 00°10´W*
- 112 *A9* **Buje** *It.* Buie d'Istria. Istra, NW Croatia *45°23´N 13°40´E*
- **Bujnurd** *see* Bojnūrd
- 81 *D21* **Bujumbura** *prev.* Usumbura. ● (Burundi) W Burundi *03°25´S 29°24´E*
- 81 *D20* **Bujumbura** ✕ W Burundi *03°21´S 29°19´E*
- 159 *N11* **Buka Daban** *var.* Bukadaban Feng. ▲ C China *36°09´N 90°52´E*
- **Bukadaban Feng** *see* Buka Daban
- 186 *J6* **Buka Island** *island* NE Papua New Guinea
- 81 *F18* **Bukakata** S Uganda *0°18´S 31°57´E*
- 79 *N24* **Bukama** Katanga, SE Dem. Rep. Congo *09°13´S 25°52´E*
- 142 *J4* **Būkān** *var.* Bowkān. Āzarbāyjān-e Gharbī, NW Iran *36°31´N 46°10´E*
- **Bukantau, Gory** *see* Bo'kantov Tog'lari
- **Bukarest** *see* Bucureşti
- 79 *O19* **Bukavu** *prev.* Costermansville. Sud-Kivu, E Dem. Rep. Congo *02°19´S 28°49´E*
- 81 *F21* **Bukene** Tabora, NW Tanzania *04°15´S 32°51´E*
- 141 *W8* **Bū Khābī** *var.* Bakhābī. NW Oman *23°29´N 56°06´E*
- **Bukhara** *see* Buxoro
- **Bukharskaya Oblast'** *see* Buxoro Viloyati
- 168 *M14* **Bukitkemuning** Sumatera, W Indonesia *04°43´S 104°27´E*
- 168 *I11* **Bukittinggi** *prev.* Fort de Kock. Sumatera, W Indonesia *0°18´S 100°20´E*
- 111 *L21* **Bükk** ▲▲ NE Hungary
- 81 *F19* **Bukoba** Kagera, NW Tanzania *01°19´S 31°49´E*
- 113 *N20* **Bukovo** S FYR Macedonia *40°59´N 21°20´E*
- 108 *G6* **Bülach** Zürich, NW Switzerland *47°31´N 08°30´E*
- **Būlaevo** *see* Bulayevo
- **Bulag** *see* Tünel, Hövsgöl, Mongolia
- **Bulag** *see* Möngönmorīt, Töv, Mongolia
- **Bulagiyn Denj** *see* Bulgan
- 183 *U7* **Bulahdelah** New South Wales, SE Australia *32°24´S 152°13´E*
- 171 *P4* **Bulan** Luzon, N Philippines *12°40´N 123°55´E*
- 137 *N11* **Bulancak** Giresun, N Turkey *40°57´N 38°14´E*
- 152 *J10* **Bulandshahr** Uttar Pradesh, N India *28°30´N 77°49´E*
- 137 *R14* **Bulanık** Muş, E Turkey *39°04´N 42°16´E*
- 127 *V7* **Bulanovo** Orenburgskaya Oblast', W Russian Federation *52°27´N 55°08´E*
- 83 *J17* **Bulawayo** *var.* Buluwayo. Bulawayo, SW Zimbabwe *20°08´S 28°37´E*
- 83 *J17* **Bulawayo** ✕ Matabeleland North, SW Zimbabwe *20°00´S 28°36´E*

◆ Country
● Country Capital
◇ Dependent Territory
○ Dependent Territory Capital
⬖ Administrative Regions
✕ International Airport
▲ Mountain
▲▲ Mountain Range
Volcano
≈ River
◎ Lake
⊠ Reservoir

145 Q6 **Bulayevo** *Kaz.* Bülaevo. Severnyy Kazakhstan, N Kazakhstan *54°55′N 70°29′E*
136 D15 **Buldan** Denizli, SW Turkey *38°03′N 28°50′E*
154 G12 **Buldāna** Mahārāshtra, C India *20°31′N 76°18′E*
38 E16 **Buldir Island** *island* Aleutian Islands, Alaska, USA
Buldur *see* Burdur
162 I8 **Bulgan** *var.* Bulagiyn Denj. Arhangay, C Mongolia *47°14′N 100°56′E*
162 D7 **Bulgan** *var.* Jargalant. Bayan-Ölgiy, W Mongolia *46°56′N 91°07′E*
162 K6 **Bulgan** Bulgan, N Mongolia *50°31′N 101°30′E*
162 F7 **Bulgan** *var.* Bürenhayrhan. Hovd, W Mongolia *46°04′N 91°34′E*
162 J10 **Bulgan** Ömnögovĭ, S Mongolia *44°07′N 103°28′E*
162 J7 **Bulgan** ◈ *province* N Mongolia
Bulgan *see* Bayan-Öndör, Bayanhongor, C Mongolia
Bulgan *see* Darvi, Hovd, Mongolia
Bulgan *see* Tsagaan-Üür, Hövsgöl, Mongolia
114 H10 **Bulgaria** *off.* Republic of Bulgaria, *Bul.* Bŭlgariya; *prev.* People's Republic of Bulgaria. ◆ *republic* SE Europe
Bulgaria, People's Republic of *see* Bulgaria
Bulgaria, Republic of *see* Bulgaria
Bŭlgariya *see* Bulgaria
114 L9 **Bŭlgarka** ▲ E Bulgaria *42°43′N 26°19′E*
171 S11 **Buli** Pulau Halmahera, E Indonesia *0°56′N 128°17′E*
171 S11 **Buli, Teluk** *bay* Pulau Halmahera, E Indonesia
160 J13 **Buliu He** ≈ S China
Bullange *see* Büllingen
Bulla, Ostrov *see* Xärä Zirä Adasi
104 M11 **Bullaque** ≈ C Spain
105 Q13 **Bullas** Murcia, SE Spain *38°02′N 01°40′W*
80 M12 **Bullaxaar** Woqooyi Galbeed, NW Somalia *10°28′N 44°15′E*
108 C9 **Bulle** Fribourg, SW Switzerland *46°37′N 07°04′E*
185 G15 **Buller** ≈ South Island, New Zealand
183 P12 **Buller, Mount** ▲ Victoria, SE Australia *37°10′S 146°31′E*
36 H11 **Bullhead City** Arizona, SW USA *35°07′N 114°32′W*
99 N21 **Büllingen** *Fr.* Bullange. Liège, E Belgium *50°23′N 06°15′E*
Bullion State *see* Missouri
21 T14 **Bull Island** *island* South Carolina, SE USA
182 M4 **Bulloo River Overflow** *wetland* New South Wales, SE Australia
184 M12 **Bulls** Manawatu-Wanganui, North Island, New Zealand *40°10′S 175°22′E*
21 T14 **Bulls Bay** *bay* South Carolina, SE USA
27 U9 **Bull Shoals Lake** ⊡ Arkansas/Missouri, C USA
181 Q2 **Bulman** Northern Territory, N Australia *13°39′S 134°21′E*
162 I6 **Bulnayn Nuruu** ▲▲ N Mongolia
171 O11 **Bulowa, Gunung** ▲ Sulawesi, N Indonesia *0°33′N 123°39′E*
Bulqiza *see* Bulqizë
113 L19 **Bulqizë** *var.* Bulqiza. Dibër, C Albania *41°30′N 20°16′E*
Bulsar *see* Valsād
171 N14 **Bulukumba** *prev.* Boeloekoemba. Sulawesi, C Indonesia *05°35′S 120°13′E*
147 O11 **Bulung'ur** *Rus.* Bulungur; *prev.* Krasnogvardeysk. Samarqand Viloyati, C Uzbekistan *39°46′N 67°18′E*
79 I21 **Bulungu** Bandundu, SW Dem. Rep. Congo *04°36′S 18°34′E*
Bulungur *see* Bulung'ur
Buluwayo *see* Bulawayo
79 K17 **Bumba** Equateur, N Dem. Rep. Congo *02°14′N 22°25′E*
121 R12 **Bumbah, Khalīj al** *gulf* N Libya
Bumbat *see* Bayan-Öndör
81 F19 **Bumbire Island** *island* N Tanzania
169 V8 **Bum Bun, Pulau** *island* East Malaysia
81 J17 **Buna** North Eastern, NE Kenya *02°40′N 39°34′E*
25 Y10 **Buna** Texas, SW USA *30°25′N 94°00′W*
Bunab *see* Bonāb
Bunai *see* M'bunai
147 S13 **Bunay** S Tajikistan *38°29′N 71°41′E*
180 I13 **Bunbury** Western Australia *33°24′S 115°44′E*
97 E14 **Buncrana** *Ir.* Bun Cranncha. NW Ireland *55°08′N 07°27′W*
Bun Cranncha *see* Buncrana
181 Z9 **Bundaberg** Queensland, E Australia *24°50′S 152°16′E*
183 T5 **Bundarra** New South Wales, SE Australia *30°12′S 151°06′E*
100 G13 **Bünde** Nordrhein-Westfalen, NW Germany *52°12′N 08°34′E*
152 H13 **Būndi** Rājasthān, N India *25°28′N 75°42′E*
Bun Dobhráin *see* Bundoran
97 D15 **Bundoran** *Ir.* Bun Dobhráin. NW Ireland *54°30′N 08°11′W*
Bunë *see* Bojana
113 K18 **Bunë, Lumi i** *SCr.* Bojana. ≈ Albania/Montenegro *see also* Bojana
171 Q8 **Bunga** ≈ Mindanao, S Philippines
168 I12 **Bungalaut, Selat** *strait* W Indonesia
167 R8 **Bung Kan** Nong Khai, E Thailand *18°19′N 103°39′E*
181 N4 **Bungle Bungle Range** ▲▲ Western Australia
82 C10 **Bungo** Uíge, NW Angola *07°30′S 15°24′E*
81 G18 **Bungoma** Western, W Kenya *0°34′N 34°34′E*
164 F15 **Bungo-suidō** *strait* SW Japan
164 E14 **Bungo-Takada** Ōita, Kyūshū, SW Japan *33°34′N 131°28′E*
100 K8 **Bungsberg** *hill* N Germany
Bungur *see* Bunyu
79 P17 **Bunia** Orientale, NE Dem. Rep. Congo *01°33′N 30°16′E*
35 U6 **Bunker Hill** ▲ Nevada, W USA *39°16′N 117°06′W*
22 I7 **Bunkie** Louisiana, S USA *30°58′N 92°12′W*
23 X10 **Bunnell** Florida, SE USA *29°28′N 81°15′W*
105 S10 **Buñol** Valenciana, E Spain *39°25′N 00°47′W*
98 K11 **Bunschoten** Utrecht, C Netherlands *52°15′N 05°23′E*
136 K14 **Bünyan** Kayseri, C Turkey *38°51′N 35°50′E*
169 W8 **Bunyu** *var.* Bungur. Borneo, N Indonesia *03°33′N 117°50′E*
169 W8 **Bunyu, Pulau** *island* N Indonesia
Bunzlau *see* Bolesławiec
Buoddobohki *see* Patoniva
123 P7 **Buor-Khaya, Guba** *bay* N Russian Federation
123 P7 **Buor-Khaya, Guba** *bay* N Russian Federation
171 Z15 **Bupul** Papua, E Indonesia *07°24′S 140°57′E*
81 K19 **Bura** Coast, SE Kenya *01°06′S 40°01′E*
80 P12 **Buraan** Bari, N Somalia *10°03′N 49°08′E*
145 Q7 **Burabay** *prev.* Borovoye. Akmola, N Kazakhstan *53°07′N 70°20′E*
Buraida *see* Buraydah
Buraimi *see* Al Buraymī
Buran *see* Boran
158 G15 **Burang** Xizang Zizhiqu, W China *30°28′N 81°13′E*
Burao *see* Burco
138 H8 **Burāq** Dar'ā, S Syria *33°11′N 36°28′E*
141 O6 **Buraydah** *var.* Buraida. Al Qaşīm, N Saudi Arabia *26°50′N 44°E*
35 S15 **Burbank** California, W USA *34°10′N 118°25′W*
31 N11 **Burbank** Illinois, N USA *41°45′N 87°48′W*
183 Q8 **Burcher** New South Wales, SE Australia *33°29′S 147°16′E*
80 N13 **Burco** *var.* Burao, Bur'o. Togdheer, NW Somalia *09°29′N 45°31′E*
162 K8 **Bürd** *var.* Ongon. Övörhangay, C Mongolia *46°58′N 103°45′E*
146 L13 **Burdalyk** Lebap Welaýaty, E Turkmenistan *38°31′N 64°21′E*
181 W6 **Burdekin River** ≈ Queensland, NE Australia
27 O7 **Burden** Kansas, C USA *37°18′N 96°45′W*
Burdigala *see* Bordeaux
136 E15 **Burdur** *var.* Buldur. Burdur, SW Turkey *37°44′N 30°17′E*
136 E15 **Burdur** *var.* Buldur. ◈ *province* SW Turkey
136 E15 **Burdur Gölü** *salt lake* SW Turkey
65 H21 **Burdwood Bank** *undersea feature* SW Atlantic Ocean
80 I12 **Burē** Āmara, N Ethiopia *10°43′N 37°09′E*
80 H13 **Burē** Oromīya, C Ethiopia *08°13′N 35°09′E*
93 J15 **Bureå** Västerbotten, N Sweden *64°36′N 21°15′E*
162 K7 **Büreghangay** *var.* Darhan. Bulgan, C Mongolia *48°07′N 103°54′E*
101 G14 **Büren** Nordrhein-Westfalen, W Germany *51°34′N 08°34′E*
162 L8 **Büren** *var.* Bayantöhöm. Töv, C Mongolia *46°57′N 105°09′E*
162 K6 **Bürengiyn Nuruu** ▲▲ N Mongolia
Bürenhayrhan *see* Bulgan
162 I6 **Bürentogtoh** *var.* Bayan. Hövsgöl, C Mongolia *49°36′N 99°36′E*
149 U10 **Būrewāla** *var.* Mandi Būrewāla. Punjab, E Pakistan *30°05′N 72°47′E*
92 J9 **Burfjord** Troms, N Norway *69°55′N 21°54′E*
100 L13 **Burg** *var.* Burg an der Ihle, Burg bei Magdeburg. Sachsen-Anhalt, C Germany *52°17′N 11°51′E*
Burg an der Ihle *see* Burg
114 N10 **Burgas** *var.* Bourgas. Burgas, E Bulgaria *42°31′N 27°30′E*
114 M10 **Burgas** ◈ *province* E Bulgaria
114 N9 **Burgas** ✈ Burgas, E Bulgaria *42°35′N 27°33′E*
114 N10 **Burgaski Zaliv** *gulf* E Bulgaria
114 M10 **Burgasko Ezero** *lagoon* E Bulgaria
21 V11 **Burgaw** North Carolina, SE USA *34°33′N 77°56′W*
Burg bei Magdeburg *see* Burg
108 E8 **Burgdorf** Bern, NW Switzerland *47°03′N 07°38′E*
109 Y7 **Burgenland** *off.* Land Burgenland. ◈ *state* SE Austria
13 S13 **Burgeo** Newfoundland, Newfoundland and Labrador, SE Canada *47°37′N 57°38′W*
83 I24 **Burgersdorp** Eastern Cape, SE South Africa *31°00′S 26°20′E*
83 K20 **Burgersfort** Mpumalanga, NE South Africa *24°39′S 30°18′E*
101 N23 **Burghausen** Bayern, SE Germany *48°10′N 12°48′E*
139 O5 **Burghūth, Sabkhat al** ◎ E Syria
101 M20 **Burglengenfeld** Bayern, SE Germany *49°11′N 12°01′E*
41 P9 **Burgos** Tamaulipas, C Mexico *24°55′N 98°46′W*
105 N4 **Burgos** Castilla y León, N Spain *42°21′N 03°41′W*
105 N4 **Burgos** ◈ *province* Castilla y León, N Spain
Burgstadlberg *see* Hradiště
95 P20 **Burgsvik** Gotland, SE Sweden *57°01′N 18°18′E*
98 L6 **Burgum** *Dutch.* Bergum. Fryslân, N Netherlands *53°12′N 05°59′E*
Burgundy *see* Bourgogne
159 Q11 **Burhan Budai Shan** ▲▲ C China
136 B12 **Burhaniye** Balıkesir, W Turkey *39°29′N 26°59′E*
154 G12 **Burhānpur** Madhya Pradesh, C India *21°18′N 76°14′E*
127 W7 **Buribay** Respublika Bashkortostan, W Russian Federation *51°57′N 58°11′E*
43 O17 **Burica, Punta** *headland* Costa Rica/Panama *08°02′N 82°53′W*
167 Q10 **Buriram** *var.* Buri Ram, Puriramya. Buri Ram, E Thailand *15°01′N 103°06′E*
Buri Ram *see* Buriram
105 S10 **Burjassot** Valenciana, E Spain *39°33′N 00°26′W*
81 N16 **Burka Giibi** Hiiraan, C Somalia *03°52′N 45°07′E*
147 X8 **Burkan** ≈ E Kyrgyzstan
25 R4 **Burkburnett** Texas, SW USA *34°06′N 98°34′W*
29 O12 **Burke** South Dakota, N USA *43°09′N 99°18′W*
10 K15 **Burke Channel** *channel* British Columbia, W Canada
194 J10 **Burke Island** *island* Antarctica
20 L7 **Burkesville** Kentucky, S USA *36°48′N 85°21′W*
181 T4 **Burketown** Queensland, NE Australia *17°49′S 139°28′E*
25 Q8 **Burkett** Texas, SW USA *32°01′N 99°17′W*
25 Y9 **Burkeville** Texas, SW USA *30°58′N 93°41′W*
21 V7 **Burkeville** Virginia, NE USA *37°11′N 78°12′W*
77 O12 **Burkina** *off.* Burkina Faso; *prev.* Upper Volta. ◆ *republic* W Africa
Burkina *see* Burkina Faso
Burkina Faso *see* Burkina
194 L13 **Burks, Cape** *headland* Antarctica
14 H12 **Burk's Falls** Ontario, S Canada *45°38′N 79°25′W*
101 H23 **Burladingen** Baden-Württemberg, S Germany *48°18′N 09°05′E*
25 T7 **Burleson** Texas, SW USA *32°32′N 97°19′W*
33 P15 **Burley** Idaho, NW USA *42°32′N 113°47′W*
Burlin *see* Borili
14 G16 **Burlington** Ontario, S Canada *43°19′N 79°48′W*
37 W4 **Burlington** Colorado, C USA *39°17′N 102°17′W*
29 Y15 **Burlington** Iowa, C USA *40°48′N 91°05′W*
27 P5 **Burlington** Kansas, C USA *38°11′N 95°46′W*
21 T9 **Burlington** North Carolina, SE USA *36°05′N 79°27′W*
28 M3 **Burlington** North Dakota, N USA *48°16′N 101°25′W*
18 L7 **Burlington** Vermont, NE USA *44°28′N 73°14′W*
30 M9 **Burlington** Wisconsin, N USA *42°38′N 88°12′W*
27 Q1 **Burlington Junction** Missouri, C USA *40°27′N 95°04′W*
166 M4 **Burma** *off.* Union of Myanmar, Myanmar. ◆ *military dictatorship* SE Asia
10 L17 **Burnaby** British Columbia, SW Canada *49°16′N 122°58′W*
117 O12 **Burnas, Ozero** ◎ SW Ukraine
25 S10 **Burnet** Texas, SW USA *30°46′N 98°14′W*
35 O3 **Burney** California, W USA *40°52′N 121°42′W*
183 O16 **Burnie** Tasmania, SE Australia *41°07′S 145°52′E*
97 L17 **Burnley** NW England, United Kingdom *53°48′N 02°14′W*
Burnoye *see* Bauyrzhan Momyshuly
153 R15 **Burnpur** West Bengal, NE India *23°39′N 86°55′E*
32 K14 **Burns** Oregon, NW USA *43°35′N 119°03′W*
26 K11 **Burns Flat** Oklahoma, C USA *35°21′N 99°10′W*
20 M7 **Burnside** Kentucky, S USA *36°55′N 84°34′W*
8 K8 **Burnside** ≈ Nunavut, NW Canada
32 L15 **Burns Junction** Oregon, NW USA *42°46′N 117°51′W*
10 L13 **Burns Lake** British Columbia, SW Canada *54°14′N 125°45′W*
29 V9 **Burnsville** Minnesota, N USA *44°49′N 93°14′W*
21 P9 **Burnsville** North Carolina, SE USA *35°56′N 82°18′W*
21 R4 **Burnsville** West Virginia, NE USA *38°50′N 80°39′W*
14 I13 **Burnt River** ≈ Ontario, SE Canada
14 I11 **Burntroot Lake** ◎ Ontario, SE Canada
11 W12 **Burntwood** ≈ Manitoba, C Canada
Bur'o *see* Burco
158 L2 **Burqin** Xinjiang Uygur Zizhiqu, NW China *47°42′N 86°50′E*
182 J8 **Burra** South Australia *33°41′S 138°54′E*
183 S9 **Burragorang, Lake** ⊡ New South Wales, SE Australia
96 K5 **Burray** *island* NE Scotland, United Kingdom
113 L19 **Burrel** *var.* Burreli. Dibër, C Albania *41°36′N 20°00′E*
Burreli *see* Burrel
183 R8 **Burrendong Reservoir** ⊡ New South Wales, SE Australia
183 R5 **Burren Junction** New South Wales, SE Australia *30°06′S 149°01′E*
Burriana *see* Borriana
183 R10 **Burrinjuck Reservoir** ⊡ New South Wales, SE Australia
36 J12 **Burro Creek** ≈ Arizona, SW USA
40 M5 **Burro, Serranías del** ▲▲ NW Mexico
62 K7 **Burruyacú** Tucumán, N Argentina *26°30′S 64°45′W*
136 E12 **Bursa** *var.* Brussa, *prev.* Brusa; *anc.* Prusa. Bursa, NW Turkey *40°12′N 29°04′E*
136 D12 **Bursa** *var.* Brusa, Brussa. ◈ *province* NW Turkey
75 Y9 **Būr Safājah** *var.* Būr Safājah. E Egypt *26°43′N 33°55′E*
Būr Safājah *see* Būr Safājah
75 W7 **Būr Saʻīd** *var.* Port Said. N Egypt *31°17′N 32°18′E*
81 O14 **Bur Tinle** Nugaal, C Somalia *07°50′N 48°01′E*
31 Q5 **Burt Lake** ◎ Michigan, N USA
118 H7 **Burtnieks** *var.* Burtnieks Ezers. ◎ N Latvia
Burtnieks Ezers *see* Burtnieks
31 Q9 **Burton** Michigan, N USA *43°00′N 84°16′W*
Burton on Trent *see* Burton upon Trent
97 M19 **Burton upon Trent** *var.* Burton on Trent, Burton-upon-Trent. C England, United Kingdom *52°48′N 01°36′W*
93 J15 **Burträsk** Västerbotten, N Sweden *64°31′N 20°40′E*
Burubaytal *see* Burybaytal
Burujird *see* Borūjerd
Burultokay *see* Fuhai
141 R15 **Burūm** SE Yemen *14°22′N 48°53′E*
Burunday *see* Boralday
81 D21 **Burundi** *off.* Republic of Burundi; *prev.* Kingdom of Burundi, Urundi. ◆ *republic* C Africa
Burundi, Kingdom of *see* Burundi
Burundi, Republic of *see* Burundi
171 R13 **Buru, Pulau** *prev.* Boeroe. *island* E Indonesia
77 T17 **Burutu** Delta, S Nigeria *05°18′N 05°32′E*
10 G7 **Burwash Landing** Yukon Territory, W Canada *61°26′N 139°12′W*
29 O14 **Burwell** Nebraska, C USA *41°46′N 99°04′W*
97 L17 **Bury** NW England, United Kingdom *53°36′N 02°17′W*
123 N13 **Buryatiya, Respublika** *prev.* Buryatskaya ASSR. ◈ *autonomous republic* S Russian Federation
Buryatskaya ASSR *see* Buryatiya, Respublika
145 S14 **Burybaytal** *prev.* Burubaytal. Zhambyl, SE Kazakhstan *44°56′N 73°59′E*
117 S3 **Buryn'** Sums'ka Oblast', NE Ukraine *51°13′N 33°50′E*
97 P20 **Bury St Edmunds** *hist.* Beodericsworth. E England, United Kingdom *52°15′N 00°43′E*
114 G8 **Bŭrziya** ≈ NW Bulgaria
106 D9 **Busalla** Liguria, NW Italy *44°35′N 08°55′E*
163 Z16 **Busan** *off.* Pusan-gwangyŏksi, *var.* Vusan; *prev.* Pusan, *Jap.* Fusan. SE South Korea *35°11′N 129°04′E*
139 N5 **Buşayrah** Dayr az Zawr, E Syria *35°10′N 40°25′E*
Buševa *see* Baba
143 N12 **Būshehr** *off.* Ostān-e Būshehr. ◈ *province* SW Iran
Bushehr/Bushire *see* Bandar-e Būshehr
Būshehr, Ostān-e *see* Būshehr
25 N2 **Bushland** Texas, SW USA *35°11′N 102°04′W*
30 J12 **Bushnell** Illinois, N USA *40°33′N 90°30′W*
Busi *see* Biševo
81 G18 **Busia** SE Uganda *01°20′N 34°48′E*
Busiasch *see* Buziaş
79 K16 **Businga** Equateur, NW Dem. Rep. Congo *03°20′N 20°53′E*
79 J18 **Busira** ≈ NW Dem. Rep. Congo
116 I5 **Bus'k** *Rus.* Busk. L'vivs'ka Oblast', W Ukraine *49°59′N 24°34′E*
95 E14 **Buskerud** ◈ *county* S Norway
113 F14 **Buško Jezero** ⊡ SW Bosnia and Herzegovina
111 M15 **Busko-Zdrój** Świętokrzyskie, C Poland *50°28′N 20°44′E*
Busra *see* Al Başrah, Iraq
Buşrá *see* Buşrá ash Shām, Syria
138 H9 **Buşrá ash Shām** *var.* Bosora, Bosra, Bozrah, Buşrá. Dar'ā, S Syria *32°31′N 36°29′E*
180 I13 **Busselton** Western Australia *33°43′S 115°15′E*
81 C14 **Busseri** ≈ W South Sudan
106 E9 **Busseto** Emilia-Romagna, C Italy *45°00′N 10°06′E*
106 A8 **Bussoleno** Piemonte, NE Italy *45°11′N 07°07′E*
Bussora *see* Al Başrah
41 N7 **Bustamante** Nuevo León, NE Mexico *26°29′N 100°30′W*
63 I23 **Bustamante, Punta** *headland* S Argentina *51°35′S 68°58′W*
Bustan *see* Bo'ston
116 J12 **Buşteni** Prahova, SE Romania *45°23′N 25°32′E*
106 D7 **Busto Arsizio** Lombardia, N Italy *45°37′N 08°51′E*
147 Q10 **Būston** *Rus.* Buston. NW Tajikistan *40°31′N 69°21′E*
100 H8 **Büsum** Schleswig-Holstein, N Germany *54°08′N 08°52′E*
79 M16 **Buta** Orientale, N Dem. Rep. Congo *02°50′N 24°41′E*
81 E20 **Butare** *prev.* Astrida. S Rwanda *02°39′S 29°44′E*
191 O2 **Butaritari** *atoll* Tungaru, W Kiribati
Butawal *see* Butwal
96 H13 **Bute** *cultural region* SW Scotland, United Kingdom
162 K6 **Büteeliyn Nuruu** ▲▲ N Mongolia
10 L16 **Bute Inlet** *fjord* British Columbia, W Canada
96 H12 **Bute, Island of** *island* SW Scotland, United Kingdom
79 P18 **Butembo** Nord-Kivu, NE Dem. Rep. Congo *0°09′N 29°17′E*
Bûtenpost *see* Buitenpost
107 K25 **Butera** Sicilia, Italy, C Mediterranean Sea *37°12′N 14°12′E*
99 M20 **Bütgenbach** Liège, E Belgium *50°25′N 06°12′E*
Butha Qi *see* Zalantun
166 J5 **Buthidaung** Rakhine State, W Burma (Myanmar) *20°50′N 92°25′E*
61 I16 **Butiá** Rio Grande do Sul, S Brazil *30°09′S 51°55′W*
81 F17 **Butiaba** NW Uganda *01°48′N 31°21′E*
23 N6 **Butler** Alabama, S USA *32°05′N 88°13′W*
23 S5 **Butler** Georgia, SE USA *32°33′N 84°14′W*
31 Q11 **Butler** Indiana, N USA *41°25′N 84°52′W*
27 R5 **Butler** Missouri, C USA *38°17′N 94°21′W*
18 B14 **Butler** Pennsylvania, NE USA *40°51′N 79°52′W*
194 K5 **Butler Island** *island* Antarctica
21 U8 **Butner** North Carolina, SE USA *36°07′N 78°45′W*
171 P14 **Buton, Pulau** *var.* Pulau Butung; *prev.* Boetoeng. *island* C Indonesia
Bütow *see* Bytów
113 L23 **Butrintit, Liqeni i** ◎ S Albania
23 N3 **Buttahatchee River** ≈ Alabama/Mississippi, S USA
33 Q10 **Butte** Montana, NW USA *46°01′N 112°33′W*
29 O12 **Butte** Nebraska, C USA *42°54′N 98°51′W*
168 J7 **Butterworth** Pinang, Peninsular Malaysia *05°24′N 100°22′E*
83 J25 **Butterworth** *var.* Gcuwa. Eastern Cape, SE South Africa *32°20′S 28°09′E*
13 O3 **Button Islands** *island group* Nunavut, NE Canada
35 R13 **Buttonwillow** California, W USA *35°24′N 119°26′W*
171 Q7 **Butuan** *off.* Butuan City. Mindanao, S Philippines *08°57′N 125°33′E*
Butuan City *see* Butuan
Butung, Pulau *see* Buton, Pulau
Butuntum *see* Bitonto
126 M8 **Buturlinovka** Voronezhskaya Oblast', W Russian Federation *50°48′N 40°33′E*
153 O11 **Butwal** *var.* Butawal. Western, C Nepal *27°41′N 83°28′E*
101 G17 **Butzbach** Hessen, W Germany *50°26′N 08°40′E*
100 L9 **Bützow** Mecklenburg-Vorpommern, N Germany *53°49′N 11°58′E*
80 N13 **Buuhoodle** Togdheer, N Somalia *08°18′N 46°15′E*
81 N16 **Buulobarde** *var.* Buulo Berde. Hiiraan, C Somalia *03°52′N 45°37′E*
Buulo Berde *see* Buulobarde
80 P12 **Buuraha Cal Miskaat** ▲▲ NE Somalia
81 L19 **Buur Gaabo** Jubbada Hoose, S Somalia *01°14′S 41°48′E*
99 M22 **Buurgplaatz** ▲ N Luxembourg *50°09′N 06°02′E*
162 H8 **Buutsagaan** *var.* Buyant. Bayanhongor, C Mongolia *46°07′N 98°45′E*
Buwayrāt al Hasūn *see* Bu'ayrāt al Hasūn
146 L11 **Buxoro** *var.* Bokhara, *Rus.* Bukhara. Buxoro Viloyati, C Uzbekistan *39°51′N 64°23′E*
146 J11 **Buxoro Viloyati** *Rus.* Bukharskaya Oblast'. ◈ *province* C Uzbekistan
100 I10 **Buxtehude** Niedersachsen, NW Germany *53°29′N 09°42′E*
97 L18 **Buxton** C England, United Kingdom *53°18′N 01°52′W*
124 M14 **Buy** *var.* Buj. Kostromskaya Oblast', NW Russian Federation *58°27′N 41°31′E*
Buyanbat *see* Jargalant
162 D6 **Buyant** Bayan-Ölgiy, W Mongolia *48°31′N 89°36′E*
Buyant *see* Buutsagaan, Bayanhongor, Mongolia
Buyant *see* Otgon, Dzavhan, Mongolia
Buyant *see* Galshar, Hentiy, Mongolia
163 N10 **Buyant-Uhaa** Dornogovĭ, SE Mongolia *44°52′N 110°12′E*
162 M7 **Buyant Ukha** ✈ (Ulaanbaatar) Töv, N Mongolia
127 Q16 **Buynaksk** Respublika Dagestan, SW Russian Federation *42°53′N 47°03′E*
119 L20 **Buynavichy** *Rus.* Buynovichi. Homyel'skaya Voblasts', SE Belarus *51°52′N 28°33′E*
Buynovichi *see* Buynavichy
76 L16 **Buyo** SW Ivory Coast *06°16′N 07°03′W*
76 L16 **Buyo, Lac de** ⊡ W Ivory Coast
163 R7 **Buyr Nuur** *var.* Buir Nur. ◎ China/Mongolia *see also* Buir Nur
Buyr Nuur *see* Buir Nur
137 T13 **Büyükağrı Dağı** *var.* Aghri Dagh, Agri Dagi, Koh I Noh, Masis, *Eng.* Great Ararat, Mount Ararat. ▲ E Turkey *39°43′N 44°19′E*
137 R15 **Büyük Çayı** ≈ NE Turkey
114 O13 **Büyük Çekmece** Istanbul, NW Turkey *41°02′N 28°35′E*
114 N12 **Büyükkarıştıran** Kırklareli, NW Turkey *41°17′N 27°33′E*
115 L14 **Büyükkemikli Burnu** *cape* NW Turkey
136 E15 **Büyükmenderes Nehri** ≈ SW Turkey
Büyükzap Suyu *see* Great Zab
102 M9 **Buzançais** Indre, C France *46°53′N 01°25′E*
116 K13 **Buzău** Buzău, SE Romania *45°08′N 26°51′E*
116 K13 **Buzău** ◈ *county* SE Romania
116 L12 **Buzău** ≈ E Romania
75 S11 **Buzaymah** *var.* Bzīmah. SE Libya *24°53′N 22°01′E*
164 E13 **Buzen** Fukuoka, Kyūshū, SW Japan *33°37′N 131°06′E*
116 F12 **Buziaş** *Ger.* Busiasch, *Hung.* Buziásfürdő; *prev.* Buziás. Timiş, W Romania *45°38′N 21°36′E*
Buziás *see* Buziaş
Buziásfürdő *see* Buziaş
83 M18 **Búzi, Rio** ≈ C Mozambique
117 Q10 **Buz'kyy Lyman** *bay* S Ukraine
Büzmeýin *see* Abadan
127 T6 **Buzuluk** Orenburgskaya Oblast', W Russian Federation *52°47′N 52°16′E*
127 N8 **Buzuluk** ≈ SW Russian Federation
Buzuluk *see* Buzylyk
145 O8 **Buzylyk** *prev.* Buzuluk. Akmola, C Kazakhstan *51°53′N 66°09′E*
19 P12 **Buzzards Bay** Massachusetts, NE USA *41°45′N 70°37′W*
19 P13 **Buzzards Bay** *bay* Massachusetts, NE USA
83 G16 **Bwabata** Caprivi, NE Namibia *17°52′S 22°39′E*
186 H10 **Bwagaoia** Misima Island, SE Papua New Guinea *10°39′S 152°48′E*
Bwake *see* Bouaké
187 R13 **Bwatnapne** Pentecost, C Vanuatu *15°42′S 168°07′E*
119 K14 **Byahoml'** *Rus.* Begoml'. Vitsyebskaya Voblasts', N Belarus *54°44′N 28°04′E*
114 K8 **Byala** Ruse, N Bulgaria *43°27′N 25°44′E*
114 N9 **Byala** *prev.* Ak-Dere. Varna, E Bulgaria *42°52′N 27°53′E*
Byala Reka *see* Erythropótamos
114 H8 **Byala Slatina** Vratsa, NW Bulgaria *43°28′N 23°56′E*
119 N15 **Byalynichy** *Rus.* Belynichi. Mahilyowskaya Voblasts', E Belarus *54°00′N 29°42′E*
Byan Tumen *see* Choybalsan
119 L14 **Byarezina** *prev.* Byerezino, *Rus.* Berezina. ≈ C Belarus
119 G19 **Byaroza** *Pol.* Bereza Kartuska, *Rus.* Berëza. Brestskaya Voblasts', SW Belarus *52°32′N 24°59′E*
119 H16 **Byarozawka** *Rus.* Berëzovka. Hrodzyenskaya Voblasts', W Belarus *53°45′N 25°30′E*
Bybles *see* Jbail
111 O14 **Bychawa** Lubelskie, SE Poland *51°06′N 22°34′E*
Bychikha *see* Bychykha
118 N11 **Bychykha** *Rus.* Bychikha. Vitsyebskaya Voblasts', NE Belarus *55°41′N 29°59′E*
111 I14 **Byczyna** *Ger.* Pitschen. Opolskie, S Poland *51°06′N 18°13′E*
110 I10 **Bydgoszcz** *Ger.* Bromberg. Kujawski-pomorskie, C Poland *53°06′N 18°00′E*
119 H19 **Byelaazyorsk** *Rus.* Beloozersk. Brestskaya Voblasts', SW Belarus *52°28′N 25°10′E*
119 I17 **Byelaruskaya Hrada** *Rus.* Belorusskaya Gryada. *ridge* N Belarus
119 G18 **Byelavyezhskaya Pushcha** *Pol.* Puszcza Białowieska, *Rus.* Belovezhskaya Pushcha. *forest* Belarus/Poland *see also* Białowieska, Puszcza
Byelavyezhskaya, Pushcha *see* Białowieska, Puszcza
119 H15 **Byenyakoni** *Rus.* Benyakoni. Hrodzyenskaya Voblasts', W Belarus *54°15′N 25°22′E*
119 M16 **Byerazino** *Rus.* Berezino. Minskaya Voblasts', C Belarus *53°50′N 29°00′E*
118 L13 **Byerazino** *Rus.* Berezino. Vitsyebskaya Voblasts', N Belarus *54°54′N 28°12′E*
Byerezino *see* Byarezina
118 M13 **Byeshankovichy** *Rus.* Beshenkovichi. Vitsyebskaya Voblasts', N Belarus *55°03′N 29°27′E*
31 U13 **Byesville** Ohio, N USA *39°58′N 81°32′W*
119 P18 **Byesyedz'** *Rus.* Besed'. ≈ SE Belarus
119 H19 **Byezdzyezh** *Rus.* Bezdezh. Brestskaya Voblasts', SW Belarus *52°19′N 25°18′E*
93 J15 **Bygdeå** Västerbotten, N Sweden *64°03′N 20°49′E*
94 F12 **Bygdin** ◎ S Norway
93 J15 **Bygdsiljum** Västerbotten, N Sweden *64°20′N 20°31′E*
95 E17 **Bygland** Aust-Agder, S Norway *58°46′N 07°50′E*
95 E17 **Byglandsfjord** Aust-Agder, S Norway *58°42′N 07°51′E*
119 N16 **Bykhaw** *Rus.* Bykhov. Mahilyowskaya Voblasts', E Belarus *53°31′N 30°15′E*
Bykhov *see* Bykhaw
127 P9 **Bykovo** Volgogradskaya Oblast', SW Russian Federation *49°52′N 45°24′E*
123 P7 **Bykovsky** Respublika Sakha (Yakutiya), NE Russian Federation *71°57′N 129°07′E*
195 R12 **Byrd Glacier** *glacier* Antarctica
14 K10 **Byrd, Lac** ◎ Québec, SE Canada
183 P5 **Byrock** New South Wales, SE Australia *30°40′S 146°24′E*
30 L10 **Byron** Illinois, N USA *42°06′N 89°15′W*
183 V4 **Byron Bay** New South Wales, SE Australia *28°39′S 153°34′E*
183 V4 **Byron, Cape** *headland* New South Wales, E Australia *28°37′S 153°40′E*
63 F21 **Byron, Isla** *island* S Chile
Byron Island *see* Nikunau
65 B24 **Byron Sound** *sound* NW Falkland Islands
122 M6 **Byrranga, Gory** ▲▲ N Russian Federation
93 J14 **Byske** Västerbotten, N Sweden *64°58′N 21°10′E*
111 K18 **Bystrá** ▲ N Slovakia *49°10′N 19°49′E*
111 F18 **Bystřice nad Pernštejnem** *Ger.* Bistritz ober Pernstein. Vysočina, C Czech Republic *49°32′N 16°16′E*
Bystrovka *see* Kemin
111 G16 **Bystrzyca Kłodzka** *Ger.* Habelschwerdt. Wałbrzych, SW Poland *50°19′N 16°39′E*
111 I18 **Bytča** Žilinský Kraj, N Slovakia *49°15′N 18°32′E*
119 L15 **Bytcha** Minskaya Voblasts', NE Belarus *54°19′N 28°24′E*
Byteń/Byten' *see* Bytsyen'
111 J16 **Bytom** *Ger.* Beuthen. Śląskie, S Poland *50°21′N 18°51′E*
110 H7 **Bytów** *Ger.* Bütow. Pomorskie, N Poland *54°10′N 17°30′E*
119 H18 **Bytsyen'** *Pol.* Byteń, *Rus.* Byten'. Brestskaya Voblasts', SW Belarus *52°53′N 25°30′E*
81 E19 **Byumba** *var.* Biumba. N Rwanda *01°37′S 30°05′E*
Byuzmeyin *see* Abadan
119 O20 **Byval'ki** Homyel'skaya Voblasts', SE Belarus *51°51′N 30°38′E*
95 O20 **Byxelkrok** Kalmar, S Sweden *57°18′N 17°01′E*
Byzantium *see* İstanbul
Bzīmah *see* Buzaymah

C

62 O6 **Caacupé** Cordillera, S Paraguay *25°23′S 57°05′W*
62 P6 **Caaguazú** *off.* Departamento de Caaguazú. ◈ *department* C Paraguay
Caaguazú, Departamento de *see* Caaguazú
82 C13 **Caála** *var.* Kaala, *Port.* Vila Robert Williams. Huambo, C Angola *12°51′S 15°33′E*
62 P7 **Caazapá** Caazapá, S Paraguay *26°09′S 56°21′W*
62 P7 **Caazapá** *off.* Departamento de Caazapá. ◈ *department* SE Paraguay
Caazapá, Departamento de *see* Caazapá
81 P15 **Cabaad, Raas** *headland* C Somalia *06°13′N 49°01′E*
55 N10 **Cabadisocaña** Amazonas, S Venezuela *04°28′N 64°45′W*
44 F5 **Cabaiguán** Sancti Spíritus, C Cuba *22°04′N 79°32′W*
Caballeria, Cabo *see* Cavalleria, Cap de
37 Q14 **Caballo Reservoir** ⊡ New Mexico, SW USA
40 L6 **Caballos Mesteños, Llano de los** *plain* N Mexico
104 L2 **Cabanaquinta** Asturias, N Spain *43°10′N 05°37′W*
42 B9 **Cabañas** ◈ *department* E El Salvador
171 O3 **Cabanatuan** *off.* Cabanatuan City. Luzon, N Philippines *15°27′N 120°57′E*
Cabanatuan City *see* Cabanatuan
15 T8 **Cabano** Québec, SE Canada *47°40′N 68°56′W*
104 L11 **Cabeza del Buey** Extremadura, W Spain *38°44′N 05°13′W*
45 V5 **Cabezas de San Juan** *headland* E Puerto Rico *18°23′N 65°37′W*
105 N2 **Cabezón de la Sal** Cantabria, N Spain *43°19′N 04°14′W*
Cabhán *see* Cavan
61 B23 **Cabildo** Buenos Aires, E Argentina *38°28′S 61°50′W*
Cabillonum *see* Chalon-sur-Saône
54 H5 **Cabimas** Zulia, NW Venezuela *10°26′N 71°27′W*
82 A9 **Cabinda** *var.* Kabinda. Cabinda, NW Angola *05°34′S 12°12′E*
82 A9 **Cabinda** *var.* Kabinda. ◈ *province* NW Angola
33 N7 **Cabinet Mountains** ▲▲ Idaho/Montana, NW USA
82 B11 **Cabiri** Bengo, NW Angola *08°50′S 13°42′E*
63 J20 **Cabo Blanco** Santa Cruz, SE Argentina *47°13′S 65°43′W*
82 P13 **Cabo Delgado** *off.* Província de Cabo Delgado. ◈ *province* NE Mozambique
14 L9 **Cabonga, Réservoir** ⊡ Québec, SE Canada
27 V7 **Cabool** Missouri, C USA *37°07′N 92°06′W*
183 V2 **Caboolture** Queensland, E Australia *27°05′S 152°50′E*
Cabora Bassa, Lake *see* Cahora Bassa, Albufeira de
40 F3 **Caborca** Sonora, NW Mexico *30°44′N 112°06′W*
Cabo San Lucas *see* San Lucas
27 V11 **Cabot** Arkansas, C USA *34°58′N 92°01′W*
14 F12 **Cabot Head** *headland* Ontario, S Canada *45°13′N 81°17′W*
13 R13 **Cabot Strait** *strait* E Canada
Cabo Verde, Ilhas do *see* Cape Verde
104 M14 **Cabra** Andalucía, S Spain *37°28′N 04°28′W*
107 B19 **Cabras** Sardegna, Italy, C Mediterranean Sea *39°55′N 08°30′E*
188 A15 **Cabras Island** *island* W Guam
45 O8 **Cabrera** N Dominican Republic *19°40′N 69°54′W*
104 J4 **Cabrera** ≈ NW Spain
105 X10 **Cabrera, Illa de** *anc.* Capraria. *island* Islas Baleares, Spain, W Mediterranean Sea
105 Q15 **Cabrera, Sierra** ▲▲ S Spain
11 S16 **Cabri** Saskatchewan, S Canada *50°38′N 108°28′W*
105 R10 **Cabriel** ≈ E Spain
54 M7 **Cabruta** Guárico, C Venezuela *07°39′N 66°19′W*
171 N2 **Cabugao** Luzon, N Philippines *17°55′N 120°29′E*
54 G10 **Cabuyaro** Meta, C Colombia *04°21′N 72°47′W*
60 I13 **Caçador** Santa Catarina, S Brazil *26°47′S 51°00′W*
42 G8 **Cacaguatique, Cordillera** *var.* Cordillera. ▲▲ NE El Salvador
112 L13 **Čačak** Serbia, C Serbia *43°52′N 20°23′E*
55 Y10 **Cacao** NE French Guiana *04°37′N 52°29′W*
61 H16 **Caçapava do Sul** Rio Grande do Sul, S Brazil *30°28′S 53°29′W*
21 U3 **Cacapon River** ≈ West Virginia, NE USA
107 J23 **Caccamo** Sicilia, Italy, C Mediterranean Sea *37°56′N 13°40′E*
107 A17 **Caccia, Capo** *headland* Sardegna, Italy, C Mediterranean Sea *40°34′N 08°09′E*
146 H15 **Çäçe** *var.* Chäche, *Rus.* Chaacha. Ahal Welaýaty, S Turkmenistan *36°49′N 60°33′E*
59 G18 **Cáceres** Mato Grosso, W Brazil *16°05′S 57°40′W*
104 J10 **Cáceres** *Ar.* Qazris. Extremadura, W Spain *39°29′N 06°23′W*
104 J9 **Cáceres** ◈ *province* Extremadura, W Spain
Cachacrou *see* Scotts Head Village
61 C21 **Cacharí** Buenos Aires, E Argentina *36°24′S 59°32′W*
26 L12 **Cache** Oklahoma, C USA *34°37′N 98°37′W*
10 M16 **Cache Creek** British Columbia, SW Canada *50°49′N 121°20′W*
35 N6 **Cache Creek** ≈ California, W USA
37 S3 **Cache La Poudre River** ≈ Colorado, C USA
Cacheo *see* Cacheu
27 W11 **Cache River** ≈ Arkansas, C USA
30 L17 **Cache River** ≈ Illinois, N USA
76 G12 **Cacheu** *var.* Cacheo. W Guinea-Bissau *12°12′N 16°10′W*

◆ Country
● Country Capital
◇ Dependent Territory
○ Dependent Territory Capital
◈ Administrative Regions
✈ International Airport
▲ Mountain
▲▲ Mountain Range
Ӿ Volcano
≈ River
◎ Lake
⊡ Reservoir

59 I15 **Cachimbo** Pará, NE Brazil 09°21′S 54°58′W
59 H15 **Cachimbo, Serra do** ▲▲ C Brazil
82 D13 **Cachingues** Bié, C Angola 13°05′S 16°48′E
54 G7 **Cáchira** Norte de Santander, N Colombia 07°44′N 73°07′W
61 H16 **Cachoeira do Sul** Rio Grande do Sul, S Brazil 29°58′S 52°54′W
59 O20 **Cachoeiro de Itapemirim** Espírito Santo, SE Brazil 20°51′S 41°07′W
82 E12 **Cacolo** Lunda Sul, NE Angola 10°09′S 19°21′E
83 C14 **Caconda** Huíla, C Angola 13°43′S 15°03′E
82 A9 **Cacongo** Cabinda, NW Angola 05°13′S 12°08′E
35 U9 **Cactus Peak** ▲ Nevada, W USA 37°42′N 116°51′W
82 A11 **Cacuaco** Luanda, NW Angola 08°47′S 13°21′E
83 B14 **Cacula** Huíla, SW Angola 14°33′S 14°04′E
67 R12 **Caculuvar** ≈ SW Angola
59 P19 **Caçumba, Ilha** *island* SE Brazil
55 N10 **Cacuri** Amazonas, S Venezuela
81 N17 **Cadale** Shabeellaha Dhexe, E Somalia 02°48′N 46°19′E
105 X4 **Cadaqués** Cataluña, NE Spain 42°17′N 03°16′E
111 J18 **Čadca** *Hung.* Csaca. Žilinský Kraj, N Slovakia 49°27′N 18°46′E
27 P13 **Caddo** Oklahoma, C USA 34°07′N 96°15′W
25 R6 **Caddo** Texas, SW USA 32°42′N 98°40′W
25 X6 **Caddo Lake** ⊠ Louisiana/Texas, SW USA
27 S12 **Caddo Mountains** ▲▲ Arkansas, C USA
41 O8 **Cadereyta** Nuevo León, NE Mexico 25°35′N 99°54′W
97 J19 **Cader Idris** ▲ NW Wales, United Kingdom 52°43′N 03°57′W
182 F3 **Cadibarrawirracanna, Lake** *salt lake* South Australia
14 I7 **Cadillac** Québec, SE Canada 48°12′N 78°23′W
11 T17 **Cadillac** Saskatchewan, S Canada 49°43′N 107°41′W
102 K13 **Cadillac** Gironde, SW France 44°37′N 00°16′W
31 P7 **Cadillac** Michigan, N USA 44°15′N 85°23′W
105 V4 **Cadí, Toretta de** *prev.* Torre de Cadí. ▲ NE Spain 42°16′N 01°38′E
Torre de Cadí *see* Cadí, Toretta de
171 P5 **Cadiz** *off.* Cadiz City. Negros, C Philippines 10°58′N 123°18′E
104 J15 **Cádiz** *anc.* Gades, Gadier, Gadir, Gadire. Andalucía, SW Spain 36°32′N 06°18′W
20 H7 **Cadiz** Kentucky, S USA 36°52′N 87°50′W
31 U13 **Cadiz** Ohio, N USA 40°16′N 81°00′W
104 K15 **Cádiz** ◈ *province* Andalucía, SW Spain
104 I15 **Cadiz, Bahía de** *bay* SW Spain
Cadiz City *see* Cadiz
104 H15 **Cádiz, Golfo de** *Eng.* Gulf of Cadiz. *gulf* Portugal/Spain
Cadiz, Gulf of *see* Cádiz, Golfo de
35 X14 **Cadiz Lake** ◎ California, W USA
182 E2 **Cadney Homestead** South Australia 27°52′S 134°03′E
Cadurcum *see* Cahors
Caecae *see* Xaixai
102 K4 **Caen** Calvados, N France 49°10′N 00°20′W
Caene/Caenepolis *see* Qinā
Caerdydd *see* Cardiff
Caer Glou *see* Gloucester
Caer Gybi *see* Holyhead
Caerleon *see* Chester
Caer Luel *see* Carlisle
97 I18 **Caernarfon** *var.* Caernarvon, Carnarvon. NW Wales, United Kingdom 53°08′N 04°16′W
97 H18 **Caernarfon Bay** *bay* NW Wales, United Kingdom
97 I19 **Caernarvon** *cultural region* NW Wales, United Kingdom
Caernarvon *see* Caernarfon
Caesaraugusta *see* Zaragoza
Caesarea Mazaca *see* Kayseri
Caesarobriga *see* Talavera de la Reina
Caesarodunum *see* Tours
Caesaromagus *see* Beauvais
Caesena *see* Cesena
59 N17 **Caetité** Bahia, E Brazil 14°04′S 42°29′W
62 J6 **Cafayate** Salta, N Argentina 26°02′S 66°00′W
171 O2 **Cagayan** ≈ Luzon, N Philippines
171 Q7 **Cagayan de Oro** *off.* Cagayan de Oro City. Mindanao, S Philippines 08°29′N 124°38′E
Cagayan de Oro City *see* Cagayan de Oro
170 M8 **Cagayan de Tawi Tawi** *island* S Philippines
171 N6 **Cagayan Islands** *island group* C Philippines
31 O14 **Cagles Mill Lake** ⊠ Indiana, N USA
106 I12 **Cagli** Marche, C Italy 43°33′N 12°39′E
107 C20 **Cagliari** *anc.* Caralis. Sardegna, Italy, C Mediterranean Sea 39°15′N 09°06′E
107 C20 **Cagliari, Golfo di** *gulf* Sardegna, Italy, C Mediterranean Sea
103 U15 **Cagnes-sur-Mer** Alpes-Maritimes, SE France 43°40′N 07°09′E
54 L5 **Cagua** Aragua, N Venezuela 10°09′N 67°27′W
171 O1 **Cagua, Mount** ▲ Luzon, N Philippines 18°10′N 122°03′E
54 F13 **Caguán, Río** ≈ SW Colombia
45 U6 **Caguas** E Puerto Rico 18°14′N 66°02′W
146 C9 **Çagyl** *Rus.* Chagyl. Balkan Welaýaty, NW Turkmenistan 40°48′N 55°21′E
23 P5 **Cahaba River** ≈ Alabama, S USA
42 E5 **Cahabón, Río** ≈ C Guatemala
83 B15 **Cahama** Cunene, SW Angola 16°16′S 14°23′E
97 B21 **Caha Mountains** *Ir.* An Cheacha. ▲▲ SW Ireland
97 D20 **Caher** *Ir.* An Cathair. S Ireland 52°21′N 07°58′W
97 A21 **Caherciveen** *Ir.* Cathair Saidhbhín. SW Ireland 51°56′N 10°12′W
30 K15 **Cahokia** Illinois, N USA 38°34′N 90°11′W
83 L15 **Cahora Bassa, Albufeira de** *var.* Lake Cabora Bassa. ⊠ NW Mozambique
97 G20 **Cahore Point** *Ir.* Rinn Chathóir. *headland* SE Ireland 52°33′N 06°11′W
102 M14 **Cahors** *anc.* Cadurcum. Lot, S France 44°26′N 01°27′E
56 D9 **Cahuapanas, Río** ≈ N Peru
116 M12 **Cahul** *Rus.* Kagul. S Moldova 45°53′N 28°13′E
Cahul, Lacul *see* Kahul, Ozero
83 N16 **Caia** Sofala, C Mozambique 17°50′S 35°21′E
59 J19 **Caiapó, Serra do** ▲▲ C Brazil
44 F5 **Caibarién** Villa Clara, C Cuba 22°31′N 79°29′W
55 O5 **Caicara** Monagas, NE Venezuela 09°52′N 63°38′W
54 L5 **Caicara del Orinoco** Bolívar, C Venezuela 07°38′N 66°10′W
59 P14 **Caicó** Rio Grande do Norte, E Brazil 06°25′S 37°04′W
44 M6 **Caicos Islands** *island group* W Turks and Caicos Islands
44 L5 **Caicos Passage** *strait* Bahamas/Turks and Caicos Islands
161 O9 **Caidian** *prev.* Hanyang. Hubei, C China 30°37′N 114°02′E
Caiffa *see* Hefa
180 M12 **Caiguna** Western Australia 32°14′S 125°33′E
Cailli, Ceann *see* Hag's Head
40 J11 **Caimanero, Laguna del** *var.* Laguna del Camaronero. *lagoon* E Pacific Ocean
117 N10 **Căinari** *Rus.* Kaynary. C Moldova 46°43′N 29°00′E
57 L19 **Caine, Río** ≈ C Bolivia
Caiphas *see* Hefa
195 N4 **Caird Coast** *physical region* Antarctica
96 J9 **Cairn Gorm** ▲ C Scotland, United Kingdom 57°07′N 03°38′W
96 J9 **Cairngorm Mountains** ▲▲ C Scotland, United Kingdom
39 P12 **Cairn Mountain** ▲ Alaska, USA 61°07′N 155°23′W
181 W4 **Cairns** Queensland, NE Australia 16°51′S 145°43′E
121 V13 **Cairo** *var.* El Qâhira, *Ar.* Al Qāhirah. ● (Egypt) N Egypt 30°01′N 31°18′E
23 T8 **Cairo** Georgia, SE USA 30°52′N 84°12′W
30 L17 **Cairo** Illinois, N USA 37°00′N 89°10′W
75 V8 **Cairo** ✈ C Egypt 30°06′N 31°36′E
Caiseal *see* Cashel
Caisleán an Bharraigh *see* Castlebar
Caisleán na Finne *see* Castlefinn
96 J6 **Caithness** *cultural region* N Scotland, United Kingdom
83 D15 **Caiundo** Cuando Cubango, S Angola 15°41′S 17°28′E
56 C11 **Cajamarca** *prev.* Caxamarca. Cajamarca, NW Peru 07°09′S 78°32′W
56 B11 **Cajamarca** *off.* Departamento de Cajamarca. ◈ *department* N Peru
Cajamarca, Departamento de *see* Cajamarca
103 N14 **Cajarc** Lot, S France 44°28′N 01°51′E
42 G6 **Cajón, Represa El** ⊠ NW Honduras
59 N12 **Caju, Ilha do** *island* NE Brazil
159 R10 **Caka Yanhu** ◎ C China
112 E7 **Čakovec** *Ger.* Csakathurn, *Hung.* Csáktornya; *prev. Ger.* Tschakathurn. Medimurje, N Croatia 46°24′N 16°29′E
77 V17 **Calabar** Cross River, S Nigeria 04°56′N 08°25′E
14 K13 **Calabogie** Ontario, SE Canada 45°18′N 76°46′W
54 L6 **Calabozo** Guárico, C Venezuela 08°58′N 67°28′W
107 N20 **Calabria** *anc.* Bruttium. ◈ *region* SW Italy
104 M16 **Calaburra, Punta de** *headland* S Spain 36°30′N 04°38′W
116 G14 **Calafat** Dolj, SW Romania 43°59′N 22°57′E
Calafate *see* El Calafate
105 Q4 **Calahorra** La Rioja, N Spain 42°19′N 01°58′W
103 N1 **Calais** Pas-de-Calais, N France 51°N 01°54′E
19 T5 **Calais** Maine, NE USA 45°09′N 67°15′W
Calais, Pas de *see* Dover, Strait of
Calalen *see* Kallalen
62 H4 **Calama** Antofagasta, N Chile 22°26′S 68°54′W
Calamianes *see* Calamian Group
170 M5 **Calamian Group** *var.* Calamianes. *island group* W Philippines
105 R7 **Calamocha** Aragón, NE Spain 40°54′N 01°18′W
29 N14 **Calamus River** ≈ Nebraska, C USA
116 G12 **Călan** *Ger.* Kalan, *Hung.* Pusztakalán. Hunedoara, SW Romania 45°45′N 22°59′E
105 S7 **Calanda** Aragón, NE Spain 40°56′N 00°15′W
168 F9 **Calang** Sumatera, W Indonesia 04°37′N 95°37′E
171 N4 **Calapan** Mindoro, N Philippines 13°24′N 121°08′E
Călăras *see* Călărași
116 M9 **Călărași** *var.* Călăras, *Rus.* Kalarash. C Moldova 47°19′N 28°13′E
116 L14 **Călărași** Călărași, SE Romania 44°18′N 26°52′E
116 K14 **Călărași** ◈ *county* SE Romania
54 E10 **Calarca** Quindío, W Colombia 04°31′N 75°38′W
105 Q12 **Calasparra** Murcia, SE Spain 38°14′N 01°41′W
107 I23 **Calatafimi** Sicilia, Italy, C Mediterranean Sea 37°54′N 12°52′E
105 Q6 **Calatayud** Aragón, NE Spain 41°21′N 01°39′W
171 O4 **Calauag** Luzon, N Philippines 13°57′N 122°18′E
35 P8 **Calaveras River** ≈ California, W USA
171 N4 **Calavite, Cape** *headland* Mindoro, N Philippines 13°25′N 120°16′E
171 Q8 **Calbayog** *off.* Calbayog City. Samar, C Philippines 12°08′N 124°36′E
Calbayog City *see* Calbayog
22 G9 **Calcasieu Lake** ◎ Louisiana, S USA
22 H8 **Calcasieu River** ≈ Louisiana, S USA
56 B6 **Calceta** Manabí, W Ecuador 0°51′S 80°07′W
61 B16 **Calchaquí** Santa Fe, C Argentina 29°56′S 60°14′W
62 J6 **Calchaquí, Río** ≈ NW Argentina
58 J10 **Calçoene** Amapá, NE Brazil 02°29′N 51°01′W
153 S16 **Calcutta** ✈ West Bengal, N India 22°30′N 88°20′E
Calcutta *see* Kolkata
54 E9 **Caldas** *off.* Departamento de Caldas. ◈ *province* W Colombia
104 F10 **Caldas da Rainha** Leiria, W Portugal 39°24′N 09°08′W
Caldas, Departamento de *see* Caldas
104 G3 **Caldas de Reis** *var.* Caldas de Reyes. Galicia, NW Spain 42°36′N 08°39′W
Caldas de Reyes *see* Caldas de Reis
58 F13 **Caldeirão** Amazonas, NW Brazil 03°18′S 60°22′W
62 G7 **Caldera** Atacama, N Chile 27°05′S 70°48′W
42 L14 **Caldera** Puntarenas, W Costa Rica 09°55′N 84°51′W
105 N10 **Calderina** ▲ C Spain 39°18′N 03°49′W
137 T13 **Çaldıran** Van, E Turkey 39°10′N 43°52′E
32 M14 **Caldwell** Idaho, NW USA 43°39′N 116°41′W
27 N8 **Caldwell** Kansas, C USA 37°01′N 97°36′W
14 G15 **Caledon** Ontario, S Canada 43°51′N 79°58′W
83 I23 **Caledon** *var.* Mohokare. ≈ Lesotho/South Africa
42 G1 **Caledonia** Corozal, N Belize 18°14′N 88°29′W
14 G16 **Caledonia** Ontario, S Canada 43°04′N 79°57′W
29 X11 **Caledonia** Minnesota, N USA 43°37′N 91°30′W
105 X5 **Calella** *var.* Calella de la Costa. Cataluña, NE Spain 41°37′N 02°40′E
Calella de la Costa *see* Calella
23 P4 **Calera** Alabama, S USA 33°06′N 86°45′W
63 I19 **Caleta Olivia** Santa Cruz, SE Argentina 46°21′S 67°37′W
35 X17 **Calexico** California, W USA 32°39′N 115°28′W
97 H16 **Calf of Man** *island* SW Isle of Man
11 Q16 **Calgary** Alberta, SW Canada 51°05′N 114°05′W
11 Q16 **Calgary** ✈ Alberta, SW Canada 51°15′N 114°03′W
37 U5 **Calhan** Colorado, C USA 39°00′N 104°18′W
64 O5 **Calheta** Madeira, Portugal, NE Atlantic Ocean 32°42′N 17°12′W
23 R2 **Calhoun** Georgia, SE USA 34°30′N 84°57′W
20 I6 **Calhoun** Kentucky, S USA 37°32′N 87°15′W
22 M3 **Calhoun City** Mississippi, S USA 33°51′N 89°18′W
21 P12 **Calhoun Falls** South Carolina, SE USA 34°05′N 82°36′W
54 D11 **Cali** Valle del Cauca, W Colombia 03°24′N 76°30′W
27 V9 **Calico Rock** Arkansas, C USA 36°07′N 92°08′W
155 F21 **Calicut** *var.* Kozhikode. Kerala, SW India 11°17′N 75°49′E *see also* Kozhikode
35 Y9 **Caliente** Nevada, W USA 37°37′N 114°30′W
27 U5 **California** Missouri, C USA 38°39′N 92°35′W
18 B15 **California** Pennsylvania, NE USA 40°02′N 79°52′W
35 Q12 **California** *off.* State of California, *also known as* El Dorado, The Golden State. ◈ *state* W USA
35 P11 **California Aqueduct** *aqueduct* California, W USA
35 T13 **California City** California, W USA 35°06′N 117°55′W
40 F6 **California, Golfo de** *Eng.* Gulf of California; *prev.* Sea of Cortez. *gulf* W Mexico
California, Gulf of *see* California, Golfo de
137 Y13 **Cälilabad** *Rus.* Dzhalilabad; *prev.* Astrakhan-Bazar. S Azerbaijan 39°15′N 48°30′E
116 I12 **Călimănești** Vâlcea, SW Romania 45°14′N 24°20′E
116 J9 **Călimani, Munții** ▲▲ N Romania
Calinisc *see* Cupcina
35 X17 **Calipatria** California, W USA 33°07′N 115°30′W
Calisia *see* Kalisz
34 M7 **Calistoga** California, W USA 38°34′N 122°37′W
83 G25 **Calitzdorp** Western Cape, SW South Africa 33°32′S 21°41′E
41 W12 **Calkiní** Campeche, E Mexico 20°21′N 90°03′W
182 K4 **Callabonna Creek** *var.* Tilcha Creek. *seasonal river* New South Wales/South Australia
182 J4 **Callabonna, Lake** ◎ South Australia
102 G5 **Callac** Côtes d'Armor, NW France 48°28′N 03°22′W
35 U5 **Callaghan, Mount** ▲ Nevada, W USA 39°38′N 116°57′W
Callain *see* Callan
97 E19 **Callan** *Ir.* Callain. S Ireland 52°33′N 07°23′W
14 H11 **Callander** Ontario, S Canada 46°14′N 79°21′W
96 I11 **Callander** C Scotland, United Kingdom 56°15′N 04°16′W
98 H7 **Callantsoog** Noord-Holland, NW Netherlands 52°51′N 04°41′E
57 D14 **Callao** Callao, W Peru 12°03′S 77°10′W
57 D15 **Callao** *off.* Departamento del Callao. ◈ *constitutional province* W Peru
Callao, Departamento del *see* Callao
56 F11 **Callaria, Río** ≈ E Peru
Callatis *see* Mangalia
11 Q13 **Calling Lake** Alberta, W Canada 55°12′N 113°07′W
Callosa de Ensarriá *see* Callosa d'En Sarrià
105 T11 **Callosa d'En Sarrià** *var.* Callosa de Ensarriá. Valenciana, E Spain 38°40′N 00°08′W
105 S12 **Callosa de Segura** Valenciana, E Spain 38°07′N 00°53′W
29 X11 **Calmar** Iowa, C USA 43°10′N 91°51′W
Calmar *see* Kalmar
43 R16 **Calobre** Veraguas, C Panama 08°18′N 80°49′W
23 X14 **Caloosahatchee River** ≈ Florida, SE USA
183 V2 **Caloundra** Queensland, E Australia 26°48′S 153°08′E
Calp *see* Calpe
105 T11 **Calpe** *Cat.* Calp. Valenciana, E Spain 38°39′N 00°03′E
41 P14 **Calpulalpan** Tlaxcala, S Mexico 19°36′N 98°26′W
107 K25 **Caltagirone** Sicilia, Italy, C Mediterranean Sea 37°14′N 14°31′E
107 J24 **Caltanissetta** Sicilia, Italy, C Mediterranean Sea 37°30′N 14°01′E
82 E11 **Caluango** Lunda Norte, NE Angola 08°16′S 19°36′E
82 C12 **Calucinga** Bié, W Angola 11°18′S 16°12′E
82 B12 **Calulo** Cuanza Sul, NW Angola 09°58′S 14°56′E
83 B14 **Caluquembe** Huíla, W Angola 13°47′S 14°40′E
80 Q11 **Caluula** Bari, NE Somalia 11°55′N 50°51′E
102 K4 **Calvados** ◈ *department* N France
186 I10 **Calvados Chain, The** *island group* SE Papua New Guinea
25 U9 **Calvert** Texas, SW USA 30°58′N 96°40′W
20 H7 **Calvert City** Kentucky, S USA 37°01′N 88°21′W
103 X14 **Calvi** Corse, France, C Mediterranean Sea 42°34′N 08°44′E
40 L12 **Calvillo** Aguascalientes, C Mexico 21°51′N 102°18′W
83 F24 **Calvinia** Northern Cape, W South Africa 31°25′S 19°47′E
104 K8 **Calvitero** ▲ W Spain 40°16′N 05°48′W
101 G22 **Calw** Baden-Württemberg, SW Germany 48°43′N 08°43′E
Calydon *see* Kalydón
105 N11 **Calzada de Calatrava** Castilla-La Mancha, C Spain 38°42′N 03°46′W
Cama *see* Kama
82 C11 **Camabatela** Cuanza Norte, NW Angola 08°13′S 15°23′E
64 Q5 **Camacha** Porto Santo, Madeira, Portugal, NE Atlantic Ocean 32°41′N 16°52′W
14 L8 **Camachigama, Lac** ◎ Québec, SE Canada
40 M9 **Camacho** Zacatecas, C Mexico 24°23′N 102°20′W
82 D13 **Camacupa** *var.* General Machado, *Port.* Vila General Machado. Bié, C Angola 12°S 17°31′E
54 L7 **Camaguán** Guárico, C Venezuela 08°09′N 67°37′W
44 G6 **Camagüey** *prev.* Puerto Príncipe. Camagüey, C Cuba 21°24′N 77°55′W
44 G5 **Camagüey, Archipiélago de** *island group* C Cuba
40 D5 **Camalli, Sierra de** ▲ NW Mexico 28°21′N 113°26′W
57 G18 **Camana** *var.* Camaná. Arequipa, SW Peru 16°37′S 72°42′W
29 Z14 **Camanche** Iowa, C USA 41°47′N 90°15′W
35 P8 **Camanche Reservoir** ⊠ California, W USA
61 I16 **Camaquã** Rio Grande do Sul, S Brazil 30°50′S 51°47′W
61 H16 **Camaquã, Rio** ≈ S Brazil
64 P6 **Câmara de Lobos** Madeira, Portugal, NE Atlantic Ocean 32°38′N 16°59′W
103 U16 **Camarat, Cap** *headland* SE France 43°12′N 06°42′E
41 O8 **Camargo** Tamaulipas, C Mexico 26°16′N 98°49′W
103 R15 **Camargue** *physical region* SE France
104 F2 **Camariñas** Galicia, NW Spain 43°07′N 09°10′W
Camaronero, Laguna del *see* Caimanero, Laguna del
63 J18 **Camarones** Chubut, S Argentina 44°48′S 65°42′W
63 J18 **Camarones, Bahía** *bay* S Argentina
104 J14 **Camas** Andalucía, S Spain 37°24′N 06°01′W
167 S15 **Ca Mau** *var.* Quan Long. Minh Hai, S Vietnam 09°11′N 105°09′E
82 E11 **Camaxilo** Lunda Norte, NE Angola 08°19′S 18°53′E
104 G3 **Cambados** Galicia, NW Spain 42°31′N 08°49′W
Cambay, Gulf of *see* Khambhāt, Gulf of
Camberia *see* Chambéry
97 N22 **Camberley** SE England, United Kingdom 51°21′N 00°45′W
167 R12 **Cambodia** *off.* Kingdom of Cambodia, *var.* Democratic Kampuchea, Roat Kampuchea, *Cam.* Kampuchea; *prev.* People's Democratic Republic of Kampuchea. ◆ *republic* SE Asia
Cambodia, Kingdom of *see* Cambodia
102 I16 **Cambo-les-Bains** Pyrénées-Atlantiques, SW France 43°22′N 01°24′W
103 P2 **Cambrai** *Flem.* Kambryk, *prev.* Cambray; *anc.* Cameracum. Nord, N France 50°10′N 03°14′E
Cambray *see* Cambrai
104 H2 **Cambre** Galicia, NW Spain 43°18′N 08°21′W
35 O12 **Cambria** California, W USA 35°33′N 121°04′W
97 J20 **Cambrian Mountains** ▲▲ C Wales, United Kingdom
14 G16 **Cambridge** Ontario, S Canada 43°22′N 80°20′W
44 I12 **Cambridge** W Jamaica 18°18′N 77°54′W
184 M8 **Cambridge** Waikato, North Island, New Zealand 37°53′S 175°28′E
97 O20 **Cambridge** *Lat.* Cantabrigia. E England, United Kingdom 52°12′N 00°07′E
32 M12 **Cambridge** Idaho, NW USA 44°34′N 116°42′W
30 K11 **Cambridge** Illinois, N USA 41°18′N 90°11′W
21 Y4 **Cambridge** Maryland, NE USA 38°34′N 76°04′W
19 O11 **Cambridge** Massachusetts, NE USA 42°21′N 71°05′W
29 V7 **Cambridge** Minnesota, N USA 45°34′N 93°13′W
29 N16 **Cambridge** Nebraska, C USA 40°18′N 100°10′W
31 U13 **Cambridge** Ohio, NE USA 40°00′N 81°34′W
8 L7 **Cambridge Bay** *var.* Ikaluktutiak. Victoria Island, Nunavut, NW Canada 68°56′N 105°09′W
97 O20 **Cambridgeshire** *cultural region* E England, United Kingdom
105 U6 **Cambrils** *prev.* Cambrils de Mar. Cataluña, NE Spain 41°06′N 01°02′E
Cambrils de Mar *see* Cambrils
Cambundi-Catembo *see* Nova Gaia
137 N11 **Çam Burnu** *headland* N Turkey 41°07′N 37°48′E
183 S9 **Camden** New South Wales, SE Australia 34°04′S 150°40′E
23 O6 **Camden** Alabama, S USA 31°59′N 87°17′W
27 U14 **Camden** Arkansas, C USA 33°32′N 92°49′W
21 Y3 **Camden** Delaware, NE USA 39°06′N 75°30′W
19 R7 **Camden** Maine, NE USA 44°12′N 69°04′W
18 I16 **Camden** New Jersey, NE USA 39°55′N 75°07′W
18 I9 **Camden** New York, NE USA 43°21′N 75°45′W
21 R12 **Camden** South Carolina, SE USA 34°16′N 80°36′W
20 H8 **Camden** Tennessee, S USA 36°03′N 88°07′W
25 X9 **Camden** Texas, SW USA 30°55′N 94°43′W
39 S5 **Camden Bay** *bay* S Beaufort Sea
27 U6 **Camdenton** Missouri, C USA 38°01′N 92°44′W
Camellia State *see* Alabama
18 M7 **Camels Hump** ▲ Vermont, NE USA 44°18′N 72°50′W
117 N8 **Camenca** *Rus.* Kamenka. N Moldova 48°01′N 28°43′E
Cameracum *see* Cambrai
22 G9 **Cameron** Louisiana, S USA 29°48′N 93°19′W
25 T9 **Cameron** Texas, SW USA 30°51′N 96°58′W
30 J5 **Cameron** Wisconsin, N USA 45°25′N 91°42′W
10 M12 **Cameron** ≈ British Columbia, W Canada
185 A24 **Cameron Mountains** ▲▲ South Island, New Zealand
79 D15 **Cameroon** *off.* Republic of Cameroon, *Fr.* Cameroun. ◆ *republic* W Africa
79 D15 **Cameroon Mountain** ▲ SW Cameroon 04°12′N 09°00′E
Cameroon, Republic of *see* Cameroon
Cameroon Ridge *see* Camerounaise, Dorsale
Cameroun *see* Cameroon
79 E14 **Camerounaise, Dorsale** *Eng.* Cameroon Ridge. *ridge* NW Cameroon
136 B15 **Çamiçi Gölü** ◎ SW Turkey
171 N3 **Camiling** Luzon, N Philippines 15°41′N 120°22′E
23 T7 **Camilla** Georgia, SE USA 31°13′N 84°12′W
104 G5 **Caminha** Viana do Castelo, N Portugal 41°52′N 08°50′W
35 P7 **Camino** California, W USA 38°43′N 120°39′W
107 J24 **Cammarata** Sicilia, Italy, C Mediterranean Sea 37°36′N 13°39′E
42 K10 **Camoapa** Boaco, S Nicaragua 12°25′N 85°30′W
58 O13 **Camocim** Ceará, E Brazil 02°55′S 40°50′W
106 D10 **Camogli** Liguria, NW Italy 44°21′N 09°10′E
181 S5 **Camooweal** Queensland, C Australia 19°57′S 138°14′E
55 Y11 **Camopi** E French Guiana 03°12′N 52°19′W
151 Q22 **Camorta** *island* Nicobar Islands, India, NE Indian Ocean
42 I6 **Campamento** Olancho, C Honduras 14°36′N 86°38′W
61 D19 **Campana** Buenos Aires, E Argentina 34°10′S 58°57′W
63 F21 **Campana, Isla** *island* S Chile
104 K11 **Campanario** Extremadura, W Spain 38°52′N 05°36′W
107 L17 **Campania** *Eng.* Champagne. ◈ *region* S Italy
27 Y8 **Campbell** Missouri, C USA 36°29′N 90°04′W
185 K15 **Campbell, Cape** *headland* South Island, New Zealand 41°44′S 174°16′E
14 J14 **Campbellford** Ontario, SE Canada 44°18′N 77°48′W
31 R13 **Campbell Hill** *hill* Ohio, N USA
192 K13 **Campbell Island** *island* S New Zealand
175 P13 **Campbell Plateau** *undersea feature* SW Pacific Ocean 51°00′S 170°00′E
10 K17 **Campbell River** Vancouver Island, British Columbia, SW Canada 49°59′N 125°18′W
20 L6 **Campbellsville** Kentucky, S USA 37°20′N 85°21′W
13 O13 **Campbellton** New Brunswick, SE Canada 48°00′N 66°41′W
183 S9 **Campbelltown** New South Wales, SE Australia 34°04′S 150°46′E
183 P16 **Campbell Town** Tasmania, SE Australia 41°57′S 147°30′E
96 G13 **Campbeltown** W Scotland, United Kingdom 55°26′N 05°38′W
41 W13 **Campeche** Campeche, SE Mexico 19°47′N 90°29′W
41 W14 **Campeche** ◈ *state* SE Mexico
41 T14 **Campeche, Bahía de** *Eng.* Bay of Campeche. *bay* E Mexico
Campeche, Banco de *see* Campeche Bank
64 C11 **Campeche Bank** *Sp.* Banco de Campeche, Sonda de Campeche. *undersea feature* S Gulf of Mexico 22°00′N 90°00′W
Campeche, Bay of *see* Campeche, Bahía de
Campeche, Sonda de *see* Campeche Bank
44 H7 **Campechuela** Granma, E Cuba 20°15′N 77°17′W
182 M13 **Camperdown** Victoria, SE Australia 38°16′S 143°10′E
167 U6 **Câm Pha** Quang Ninh, N Vietnam 21°04′N 107°20′E
116 H10 **Câmpia Turzii** *Ger.* Jerischmarkt, *Hung.* Aranyosgyéres; *prev.* Cîmpia Turzii, Ghiriș, Gyéres. Cluj, NW Romania 46°33′N 23°53′E
104 K12 **Campillo de Llerena** Extremadura, W Spain 38°30′N 05°48′W
104 L15 **Campillos** Andalucía, S Spain 37°04′N 04°51′W
116 J13 **Câmpina** *prev.* Cîmpina. Prahova, SE Romania 45°08′N 25°44′E
59 Q15 **Campina Grande** Paraíba, E Brazil 07°15′S 35°50′W
60 L9 **Campinas** São Paulo, S Brazil 22°54′S 47°06′W
38 L10 **Camp Kulowiye** Saint Lawrence Island, Alaska, USA 63°15′N 168°45′W
79 D17 **Campo** *var.* Kampo. Sud, SW Cameroon 02°22′N 09°50′E
Campo *see* Ntem
59 N15 **Campo Alegre de Lourdes** Bahia, E Brazil 09°28′S 43°01′W
107 L16 **Campobasso** Molise, C Italy 41°34′N 14°40′E
107 H24 **Campobello di Mazara** Sicilia, Italy, C Mediterranean Sea 37°38′N 12°45′E
Campo Criptana *see* Campo de Criptana
105 O10 **Campo de Criptana** *var.* Campo Criptana. Castilla-La Mancha, C Spain 39°25′N 03°07′W
59 I16 **Campo de Diauarum** *var.* Pôsto Diuarum. Mato Grosso, W Brazil 11°08′S 53°16′W
54 E5 **Campo de la Cruz** Atlántico, N Colombia 10°23′N 74°52′W
105 P11 **Campo de Montiel** *physical region* C Spain
60 H12 **Campo Erê** Santa Catarina, S Brazil 26°24′S 53°04′W
62 L7 **Campo Gallo** Santiago del Estero, N Argentina 26°32′S 62°51′W
59 I20 **Campo Grande** *state capital* Mato Grosso do Sul, SW Brazil 20°24′S 54°35′W
60 K12 **Campo Largo** Paraná, S Brazil 25°27′S 49°29′W
58 N13 **Campo Maior** Piauí, E Brazil 04°50′S 42°12′W
104 I10 **Campo Maior** Portalegre, C Portugal 39°01′N 07°04′W
60 H10 **Campo Mourão** Paraná, S Brazil 24°01′S 52°24′W
59 L17 **Campos Belos** Goiás, S Brazil 13°11′S 46°47′W
60 N9 **Campos do Jordão** São Paulo, S Brazil 22°45′S 45°36′W
60 Q9 **Campos dos Goytacazes** Rio de Janeiro, SE Brazil 21°46′S 41°21′W
60 I13 **Campos Novos** Santa Catarina, S Brazil 27°22′S 51°11′W
59 O14 **Campos Sales** Ceará, E Brazil 07°01′S 40°21′W
25 Q9 **Camp San Saba** Texas, SW USA 30°57′N 99°16′W
21 N6 **Campton** Kentucky, S USA 37°44′N 83°35′W
116 I13 **Câmpulung** *prev.* Câmpulung-Mușcel, Cîmpulung. Argeș, S Romania 45°16′N 25°03′E
116 J9 **Câmpulung Moldovenesc** *var.* Cîmpulung Moldovenesc, *Ger.* Kimpolung, *Hung.* Hosszúmezjő. Suceava, NE Romania 47°32′N 25°34′E
Câmpulung-Mușcel *see* Câmpulung
Campus Stellae *see* Santiago de Compostela
36 L12 **Camp Verde** Arizona, SW USA 34°33′N 111°52′W
25 P11 **Camp Wood** Texas, SW USA 29°40′N 100°00′W
167 V13 **Cam Ranh** *prev.* Ba Ngoi. Khanh Hoa, S Vietnam 11°54′N 109°14′E
11 Q15 **Camrose** Alberta, SW Canada 53°01′N 112°48′W
Camulodunum *see* Colchester
136 B12 **Çan** Çanakkale, NW Turkey 40°03′N 27°03′E
18 L12 **Canaan** Connecticut, NE USA 42°00′N 73°17′W
11 O13 **Canada** ◆ *commonwealth republic* N North America
197 P6 **Canada Basin** *undersea feature* Arctic Ocean 80°00′N 145°00′W
61 B18 **Cañada de Gómez** Santa Fe, C Argentina 32°50′S 61°23′W
197 P6 **Canada Plain** *undersea feature* Arctic Ocean
61 A18 **Cañada Rosquín** Santa Fe, C Argentina 32°04′S 61°35′W
25 P1 **Canadian** Texas, SW USA 35°54′N 100°23′W
16 K12 **Canadian River** ≈ SW USA
8 L12 **Canadian Shield** *physical region* Canada
63 I18 **Cañadón Grande, Sierra** ▲▲ S Argentina
55 P9 **Canaima** Bolívar, SE Venezuela 09°41′N 72°33′W
136 B11 **Çanakkale** *var.* Dardanelli; *prev.* Chanak, Kale Sultanie. Çanakkale, W Turkey 40°09′N 26°25′E
136 B12 **Çanakkale** ◈ *province* NW Turkey
136 B11 **Çanakkale Boğazı** *Eng.* Dardanelles. *strait* NW Turkey
187 Q17 **Canala** Province Nord, C New Caledonia 21°31′S 165°57′E
59 A15 **Canamari** Amazonas, W Brazil 07°37′S 72°33′W
18 G10 **Canandaigua** New York, NE USA 42°52′N 77°14′W
18 F10 **Canandaigua Lake** ◎ New York, NE USA
40 G3 **Cananea** Sonora, NW Mexico 30°59′N 110°20′W
56 B8 **Cañar** ◈ *province* C Ecuador
64 N10 **Canarias, Islas** *Eng.* Canary Islands. ◈ *autonomous community* Spain, NE Atlantic Ocean
Canaries Basin *see* Canary Basin
44 C6 **Canarreos, Archipiélago de los** *island group* W Cuba
Canary Islands *see* Canarias, Islas
66 K3 **Canary Basin** *var.* Canaries Basin, Monaco Basin. *undersea feature* E Atlantic Ocean 30°00′N 25°00′W
42 L13 **Cañas** Guanacaste, NW Costa Rica 10°25′N 85°07′W
18 I10 **Canastota** New York, NE USA 43°04′N 75°45′W
40 K9 **Canatlán** Durango, C Mexico 24°33′N 104°45′W
104 J9 **Cañaveral** Extremadura, W Spain 39°47′N 06°24′W
23 Y11 **Canaveral, Cape** *headland* Florida, SE USA 28°27′N 80°31′W
59 O18 **Canavieiras** Bahia, E Brazil 15°44′S 38°58′W
43 R16 **Cañazas** Veraguas, W Panama 08°25′N 81°10′W
106 H6 **Canazei** Trentino-Alto Adige, N Italy 46°29′N 11°50′E
183 P6 **Canbelego** New South Wales, SE Australia 31°36′S 146°20′E
183 R10 **Canberra** ● (Australia) Australian Capital Territory, SE Australia 35°21′S 149°08′E
183 R10 **Canberra** ✈ Australian Capital Territory, SE Australia 35°19′S 149°12′E
35 P2 **Canby** California, W USA 41°27′N 120°51′W
29 S9 **Canby** Minnesota, N USA 44°42′N 96°17′W
103 N2 **Canche** ≈ N France
102 L13 **Cancon** Lot-et-Garonne, SW France 44°33′N 00°37′E
41 Z11 **Cancún** Quintana Roo, SE Mexico 21°05′N 86°48′W
104 K2 **Candás** Asturias, N Spain 43°35′N 05°45′W
102 J7 **Cande** Maine-et-Loire, NW France 47°33′N 01°03′W
41 W14 **Candelaria** Campeche, SE Mexico 18°10′N 91°00′W
24 J11 **Candelaria** Texas, SW USA 30°05′N 104°40′W
41 W15 **Candelaria, Río** ≈ Guatemala/Mexico
104 L8 **Candeleda** Castilla y León, N Spain 40°10′N 05°14′W
Candia *see* Irákleio
41 P8 **Cándido Aguilar** Tamaulipas, C Mexico 25°30′N 97°57′W
39 N8 **Candle** Alaska, USA 65°54′N 161°55′W
11 T14 **Candle Lake** Saskatchewan, C Canada 53°43′N 105°09′W
18 L13 **Candlewood, Lake** ⊠ Connecticut, NE USA
29 O3 **Cando** North Dakota, N USA 48°29′N 99°12′W
Canea *see* Chaniá
45 O12 **Canefield** ✈ (Roseau) SW Dominica 15°20′N 61°24′W
61 F20 **Canelones** *prev.* Guadalupe. Canelones, S Uruguay 34°32′S 56°17′W
61 E20 **Canelones** ◈ *department* S Uruguay
Canendiyú *see* Canindeyú
63 F14 **Cañete** Bío Bío, C Chile 37°48′S 73°25′W
105 Q9 **Cañete** Castilla-La Mancha, C Spain 40°03′N 01°39′W
Cañete *see* San Vicente de Cañete
27 P8 **Caney** Kansas, C USA 37°00′N 95°56′W
27 P8 **Caney River** ≈ Kansas/Oklahoma, C USA
105 S3 **Canfranc-Estación** Aragón, NE Spain 42°42′N 00°31′W
83 E14 **Cangamba** *Port.* Vila de Aljustrel. Moxico, E Angola 13°40′S 19°47′E
82 C12 **Cangandala** Malanje, NW Angola 09°47′S 16°27′E
104 G4 **Cangas** Galicia, NW Spain 42°16′N 08°46′W
104 J2 **Cangas del Narcea** Asturias, N Spain 43°10′N 06°32′W
Cangas de Onís *see* Cangues d'Onís
161 S11 **Cangnan** *var.* Lingxi. Zhejiang, SE China 27°29′N 120°23′E
82 C10 **Cangola** Uíge, NW Angola 07°54′S 15°57′E
83 E14 **Cangombe** Moxico, E Angola 14°27′S 20°05′E
63 H21 **Cangrejo, Cerro** ▲ S Argentina 49°19′S 72°18′W
61 H17 **Canguçu** Rio Grande do Sul, S Brazil 31°25′S 52°37′W
104 L2 **Cangues d'Onís** *var.* Cangas de Onís. Asturias, N Spain 43°21′N 05°08′W
161 P3 **Cangzhou** Hebei, E China 38°19′N 116°54′E
12 M7 **Caniapiscau** ≈ Québec, E Canada
12 M8 **Caniapiscau, Réservoir de** ⊠ Québec, C Canada
107 J24 **Canicattì** Sicilia, Italy, C Mediterranean Sea 37°22′N 13°51′E
136 L11 **Canik Dağları** ▲▲ N Turkey
105 P14 **Caniles** Andalucía, S Spain 37°24′N 02°41′W
59 B16 **Canindé** Acre, W Brazil 10°55′S 69°45′W
62 P6 **Canindeyú** *var.* Canendiyú, Canindiyú. ◈ *department* E Paraguay
Canindiyú *see* Canindeyú
194 J10 **Canisteo Peninsula** *peninsula* Antarctica
18 F11 **Canisteo River** ≈ New York, NE USA
40 M10 **Cañitas** *var.* Cañitas de Felipe Pescador. Zacatecas, C Mexico 23°35′N 102°39′W
Cañitas de Felipe Pescador *see* Cañitas
105 P15 **Canjáyar** Andalucía, S Spain 37°00′N 02°45′W

◆ Country ● Country Capital ◇ Dependent Territory ○ Dependent Territory Capital ◈ Administrative Regions ✈ International Airport ▲ Mountain ▲▲ Mountain Range Volcano ≈ River ◎ Lake ⊠ Reservoir

136 I12 **Çankırı** *var.* Chankiri; *anc.* Gangra, Germanicopolis. Çankın, N Turkey 40°36´N 33°35´E
136 I11 **Çankırı** *var.* Chankiri. ◐ *province* N Turkey
171 P6 **Canlaon Volcano** Negros, C Philippines 10°24´N 123°05´E
11 P16 **Canmore** Alberta, SW Canada 51°07´N 115°18´W
96 F9 **Canna** *island* NW Scotland, United Kingdom
155 F20 **Cannanore** *var.* Kannur, Jagatsinghapur. Kerala, SW India 11°53´N 75°23´E *see also* Kannur
31 O17 **Cannelton** Indiana, N USA 37°54´N 86°44´W
103 U15 **Cannes** Alpes-Maritimes, SE France 43°33´N 06°59´E
39 R5 **Canning River** Alaska, USA
106 C6 **Cannobio** Piemonte, NE Italy 46°04´N 08°39´E
97 L19 **Cannock** C England, United Kingdom 52°41´N 02°03´W
28 M6 **Cannonball River** North Dakota, N USA
29 W9 **Cannon Falls** Minnesota, N USA 44°30´N 92°54´W
18 I11 **Cannonsville Reservoir** New York, NE USA
183 R12 **Cann River** Victoria, SE Australia 37°34´S 149°11´E
61 I16 **Canoas** Rio Grande do Sul, S Brazil 29°42´S 51°07´W
61 I14 **Canoas, Rio** S Brazil
14 I12 **Canoe Lake** Ontario, SE Canada
60 J12 **Canoinhas** Santa Catarina, S Brazil 26°12´S 50°24´W
37 T6 **Canon City** Colorado, C USA 38°25´N 105°14´W
55 P8 **Caño Negro** Bolívar, SE Venezuela
173 X15 **Canonniers Point** *headland* N Mauritius
23 W6 **Canoochee River** Georgia, SE USA
11 V15 **Canora** Saskatchewan, S Canada 51°38´N 102°28´W
45 Y14 **Canouan** *island* S Saint Vincent and the Grenadines
13 R15 **Canso** Nova Scotia, SE Canada 45°20´N 61°00´W
104 M3 **Cantabria** ◐ *autonomous community* N Spain
104 K3 **Cantábrica, Cordillera** ▲▲ N Spain
Cantabrigia *see* Cambridge
103 O12 **Cantal** ◐ *department* C France
105 N6 **Cantalejo** Castilla y León, N Spain 41°15´N 03°57´W
103 O12 **Cantal, Monts du** ▲▲ C France
104 G8 **Cantanhede** Coimbra, C Portugal 40°21´N 08°37´W
Cantaño *see* Cataño
55 O6 **Cantaura** Anzoátegui, NE Venezuela 09°22´N 64°24´W
116 M11 **Cantemir** *Rus.* Kantemir. S Moldova 46°17´N 28°12´E
97 Q22 **Canterbury** *hist.* Cantwaraburh; *anc.* Durovernum, *Lat.* Cantuaria. SE England, United Kingdom 51°17´N 01°05´E
185 F19 **Canterbury** *off.* Canterbury Region. ◐ *region* South Island, New Zealand
185 H20 **Canterbury Bight** *bight* South Island, New Zealand
185 H19 **Canterbury Plains** *plain* South Island, New Zealand
Canterbury Region *see* Canterbury
167 S14 **Cân Thơ** Cân Thơ, S Vietnam 10°03´N 105°46´E
104 K13 **Cantillana** Andalucía, S Spain 37°34´N 05°48´W
59 N15 **Canto do Buriti** Piauí, NE Brazil 08°07´S 43°00´W
23 S2 **Canton** Georgia, SE USA 34°14´N 84°29´W
30 K12 **Canton** Illinois, N USA 40°33´N 90°02´W
22 L5 **Canton** Mississippi, S USA 32°36´N 90°02´W
27 V2 **Canton** Missouri, C USA 40°07´N 91°31´W
18 J7 **Canton** New York, NE USA 44°36´N 75°10´W
21 O10 **Canton** North Carolina, SE USA 35°31´N 82°50´W
31 U12 **Canton** Ohio, N USA 40°48´N 81°23´W
26 L9 **Canton** Oklahoma, C USA 36°03´N 98°35´W
18 G12 **Canton** Pennsylvania, NE USA 41°38´N 76°49´W
29 R11 **Canton** South Dakota, N USA 43°19´N 96°33´W
25 V7 **Canton** Texas, SW USA 32°33´N 95°51´W
Canton *see* Guangzhou
Canton Island *see* Kanton
26 L9 **Canton Lake** Oklahoma, C USA
106 D7 **Cantù** Lombardia, N Italy 45°44´N 09°98´E
Cantuaria/Cantwaraburh *see* Canterbury
39 R10 **Cantwell** Alaska, USA 63°23´N 148°57´W
59 O16 **Canudos** Bahia, E Brazil 09°51´S 39°08´W
47 T7 **Canumã, Rio** N Brazil
Canusium *see* Puglia, Canosa di
24 G7 **Canutillo** Texas, SW USA 31°53´N 106°34´W
25 N3 **Canyon** Texas, SW USA 34°58´N 101°56´W
33 S12 **Canyon** Wyoming, C USA 44°44´N 110°30´W
32 K13 **Canyon City** Oregon, NW USA 44°24´N 118°58´W
33 R10 **Canyon Ferry Lake** Montana, NW USA
25 S11 **Canyon Lake** Texas, SW USA
167 T5 **Cao Băng** *var.* Caobang. Cao Băng, N Vietnam 22°40´N 106°16´E
Caobang *see* Cao Băng
160 J12 **Caodu He** S China
Caohai *see* Weining
167 S14 **Cao Lanh** Đông Thap, S Vietnam 10°35´N 105°25´E
82 C11 **Caombo** Malanje, NW Angola 08°42´S 16°33´E
Caorach, Cuan na g *see* Sheep Haven
Caozhou *see* Heze
171 Q12 **Capalulu** Pulau Mangole, E Indonesia 01°51´S 125°53´E
54 K8 **Capanaparo, Río** Colomiba/Venezuela
58 L12 **Capanema** Pará, NE Brazil 01°08´S 47°07´W
60 L10 **Capão Bonito do Sul** São Paulo, S Brazil 24°01´S 48°23´W
60 I13 **Capão Doce, Morro do** ▲ S Brazil 26°37´S 51°28´W
54 I4 **Capatárida** Falcón, N Venezuela 11°11´N 70°37´W
102 I15 **Capbreton** Landes, SW France 43°40´N 01°25´W
Cap-Breton, Île du *see* Cape Breton Island
15 W6 **Cap-Chat** Québec, SE Canada 49°04´N 66°43´W
15 P11 **Cap-de-la-Madeleine** Québec, SE Canada 46°22´N 72°31´W
103 N13 **Capdenac** Aveyron, S France 44°35´N 02°06´E
Cap des Palmès *see* Palmas, Cape
183 Q15 **Cape Barren Island** *island* Furneaux Group, Tasmania, SE Australia
65 O18 **Cape Basin** *undersea feature* S Atlantic Ocean 37°00´S 07°00´E
13 R14 **Cape Breton Island** *Fr.* Île du Cap-Breton. *island* Nova Scotia, SE Canada
23 Y11 **Cape Canaveral** Florida, SE USA 28°24´N 80°36´W
21 Y6 **Cape Charles** Virginia, NE USA 37°16´N 76°01´W
77 P17 **Cape Coast** *prev.* Cape Coast Castle. S Ghana 05°10´N 01°13´W
Cape Coast Castle *see* Cape Coast
19 Q12 **Cape Cod Bay** *bay* Massachusetts, NE USA
23 W15 **Cape Coral** Florida, SE USA 26°33´N 81°57´W
181 R4 **Cape Crawford Roadhouse** Northern Territory, N Australia 16°39´S 135°44´E
9 Q7 **Cape Dorset** *var.* Kingait. Baffin Island, Nunavut, NE Canada 76°14´N 76°32´W
21 N8 **Cape Fear River** North Carolina, SE USA
27 Y7 **Cape Girardeau** Missouri, C USA 37°19´N 89°31´W
21 T14 **Cape Island** *island* South Carolina, SE USA
186 A6 **Capella** ▲ NW Papua New Guinea 05°00´S 141°09´E
98 H12 **Capelle aan den IJssel** Zuid-Holland, SW Netherlands 51°56´N 04°36´E
83 C15 **Capelongo** Huíla, C Angola 14°45´S 15°02´E
18 J17 **Cape May** New Jersey, NE USA 38°54´N 74°54´W
18 J17 **Cape May Court House** New Jersey, NE USA 39°03´N 74°46´W
Cape Palmas *see* Harper
8 I16 **Cape Parry** Northwest Territories, N Canada 70°10´N 124°33´W
65 P19 **Cape Rise** *undersea feature* SW Indian Ocean 42°00´S 15°00´E
Cape Saint Jacques *see* Vung Tau
Capesterre *see* Capesterre-Belle-Eau
45 Y6 **Capesterre-Belle-Eau** *var.* Capesterre. Basse Terre, S Guadeloupe 16°03´N 61°34´W
83 D26 **Cape Town** *var.* Ekapa, *Afr.* Kaapstad, Kapstad. ● (South Africa-legislative capital) Western Cape, SW South Africa 33°56´S 18°28´E
83 E26 **Cape Town** ✈ Western Cape, SW South Africa 31°51´S 21°06´E
76 D9 **Cape Verde** *off.* Republic of Cape Verde, *Port.* Cabo Verde, Ilhas do Cabo Verde. ◆ *republic* E Atlantic Ocean
64 L11 **Cape Verde Basin** *undersea feature* E Atlantic Ocean 15°00´N 30°00´W
66 K5 **Cape Verde Islands** *island group* E Atlantic Ocean
64 L10 **Cape Verde Plain** *undersea feature* E Atlantic Ocean 23°00´N 26°00´W
Cape Verde Plateau/Cape Verde Rise *see* Cape Verde Terrace
Cape Verde, Republic of *see* Cape Verde
64 L11 **Cape Verde Terrace** *var.* Cape Verde Plateau, Cape Verde Rise. *undersea feature* E Atlantic Ocean 18°00´N 20°00´W
181 V2 **Cape York Peninsula** *peninsula* Queensland, N Australia
44 M8 **Cap-Haïtien** *var.* Le Cap. N Haiti 19°44´N 72°12´W
43 T15 **Capira** Panamá, C Panama 08°48´N 79°51´W
14 K8 **Capitachouane** Québec, SE Canada
14 L8 **Capitachouane, Lac** Québec, SE Canada
37 T13 **Capitan** New Mexico, SW USA 33°33´N 105°34´W
194 G3 **Capitán Arturo Prat** *Chilean research station* South Shetland Islands, Antarctica 62°24´S 59°42´W
37 S13 **Capitan Mountains** ▲▲ New Mexico, SW USA
62 M3 **Capitán Pablo Lagerenza** *var.* Mayor Pablo Lagerenza. Chaco, N Paraguay 19°55´S 60°46´W
37 T13 **Capitan Peak** ▲ New Mexico, SW USA 33°35´N 105°15´W
188 H5 **Capitol Hill** ● (Northern Mariana Islands-legislative capital) Saipan, S Northern Mariana Islands
60 I9 **Capivara, Represa** S Brazil
61 J16 **Capivari** Rio Grande do Sul, S Brazil 30°08´S 50°32´W
113 H15 **Čapljina** Federicija Bosna I Hercegovina, S Bosnia and Herzegovina 43°07´N 17°42´E
83 M15 **Capoche** *var.* Kapoche. Mozambique/Zambia
Capo Delgado, Província de *see* Cabo Delgado
107 K17 **Capodichino** ✈ (Napoli) Campania, S Italy 40°53´N 14°15´E
Capodistria *see* Koper
106 E12 **Capraia, Isola di** *island* Arcipelago Toscano, C Italy
107 B16 **Caprara, Punta** *var.* Punta dello Scorno. *headland* Isola Asinara, W Italy 41°07´N 08°19´E
Capraria *see* Cabrera, Illa de
14 F10 **Capreol** Ontario, S Canada 46°43´N 80°56´W
107 K18 **Capri** Campania, S Italy 40°33´N 14°14´E
175 S9 **Capricorn Tablemount** *undersea feature* W Pacific Ocean 18°34´S 172°12´W
107 J18 **Capri, Isola di** *island* S Italy
83 G16 **Caprivi** ◐ *district* NE Namibia
Caprivi Concession *see* Caprivi Strip
83 F16 **Caprivi Strip** *Ger.* Caprivizipfel; *prev.* Caprivi Concession. *cultural region* NE Namibia
Caprivizipfel *see* Caprivi Strip
25 O5 **Cap Rock Escarpment** *cliffs* Texas, SW USA
15 R10 **Cap-Rouge** Québec, SE Canada 46°45´N 71°18´W
Cap Saint-Jacques *see* Vung Tau
38 F12 **Captain Cook** Hawaii, USA, C Pacific Ocean 19°30´N 155°55´W
183 R10 **Captains Flat** New South Wales, SE Australia 35°37´S 149°28´E
102 K14 **Captieux** Gironde, SW France 44°16´N 00°15´W
107 K17 **Capua** Campania, S Italy 41°06´N 14°13´E
54 F14 **Caquetá** *off.* Departamanto del Caquetá. ◐ *province* S Colombia
Caquetá, Departamanto del *see* Caquetá
54 E13 **Caquetá, Río** *var.* Rio Japurá, Yapurá. Brazil/Colombia *see also* Japurá, Rio
Caquetá, Río *see* Japurá, Rio
CAR *see* Central African Republic
Cara *see* Kara
57 I16 **Carabaya, Cordillera** ▲▲ E Peru
54 K5 **Carabobo** *off.* Estado Carabobo. ◐ *state* N Venezuela
Carabobo, Estado *see* Carabobo
116 I14 **Caracal** Olt, S Romania 44°07´N 24°18´E
58 F10 **Caracaraí** Rondônia, W Brazil 01°47´N 61°11´W
54 L5 **Caracas** ● (Venezuela) Distrito Federal, N Venezuela 10°29´N 66°54´W
54 I5 **Carache** Trujillo, N Venezuela 09°40´N 70°15´W
60 N10 **Caraguatatuba** São Paulo, S Brazil 23°37´S 45°24´W
48 I7 **Carajás, Serra dos** ▲▲ N Brazil
Caralis *see* Cagliari
54 E9 **Caramanta** Antioquia, W Colombia 05°36´N 75°38´W
171 P4 **Caramoan** Catanduanes Island, N Philippines 13°47´N 123°49´E
Caramurat *see* Mihail Kogălniceanu
116 F12 **Caransebeş** *Ger.* Karansebesch, *Hung.* Karánsebes. Caraş-Severin, SW Romania 45°23´N 22°13´E
Carapella *see* Carapelle
107 M16 **Carapelle** *var.* Carapella. SE Italy
55 O9 **Carapo** Bolívar, SE Venezuela
13 P13 **Caraquet** New Brunswick, SE Canada 47°48´N 64°59´W
Caras *see* Caraz
116 F12 **Caraşova** *Hung.* Krassóvár. Caraş-Severin, SW Romania 45°11´N 21°51´E
116 F12 **Caraş-Severin** ◐ *county* SW Romania
42 M5 **Caratasca, Laguna de** *lagoon* NE Honduras
58 C13 **Carauari** Amazonas, NW Brazil 04°55´S 66°57´W
Caravaca *see* Caravaca de la Cruz
105 Q12 **Caravaca de la Cruz** *var.* Caravaca. Murcia, SE Spain 38°06´N 01°51´W
106 E7 **Caravaggio** Lombardia, N Italy 45°31´N 09°39´E
107 C18 **Caravai, Passo di** *pass* Sardegna, Italy, C Mediterranean Sea
59 O19 **Caravelas** Bahia, E Brazil 17°45´S 39°15´W
56 C12 **Caraz** *var.* Caras. Ancash, W Peru 09°03´S 77°47´W
61 H14 **Carazinho** Rio Grande do Sul, S Brazil 28°16´S 52°46´W
42 J11 **Carazo** ◐ *department* SW Nicaragua
Carballiño *see* O Carballiño
104 G2 **Carballo** Galicia, NW Spain 43°13´N 08°41´W
11 W16 **Carberry** Manitoba, S Canada 49°52´N 99°20´W
40 F4 **Carbó** Sonora, NW Mexico 29°41´N 111°00´W
107 C20 **Carbonara, Capo** *headland* Sardegna, Italy, C Mediterranean Sea 39°06´N 09°31´E
37 Q5 **Carbondale** Colorado, C USA 39°24´N 107°12´W
30 L17 **Carbondale** Illinois, N USA 37°43´N 89°13´W
27 Q4 **Carbondale** Kansas, C USA 38°49´N 95°41´W
18 I13 **Carbondale** Pennsylvania, NE USA 41°34´N 75°30´W
13 V12 **Carbonear** Newfoundland, Newfoundland and Labrador, SE Canada 47°45´N 53°16´W
105 Q9 **Carboneras de Guadazaón** *var.* Carboneras de Guadazón. Castilla-La Mancha, C Spain 39°54´N 01°50´W
Carboneras de Guadazón *see* Carboneras de Guadazaón
23 O3 **Carbon Hill** Alabama, S USA 33°53´N 87°31´W
107 B20 **Carbonia** *var.* Carbonia Centro. Sardegna, Italy, C Mediterranean Sea 39°11´N 08°31´E
Carbonia Centro *see* Carbonia
63 I22 **Carbon, Laguna del** *depression* S Argentina 49°34´S 68°21´W
105 S10 **Carcaixent** Valenciana, E Spain 39°08´N 00°28´W
Carcaso *see* Carcassonne
65 B24 **Carcass Island** *island* NW Falkland Islands
103 O16 **Carcassonne** *anc.* Carcaso. Aude, S France 43°13´N 02°21´E
105 R12 **Carche** ▲ S Spain 38°24´N 01°11´W
56 A13 **Carchi** ◐ *province* N Ecuador
10 I8 **Carcross** Yukon Territory, W Canada 60°11´N 134°41´W
Cardamomes, Chaîne des *see* Krâvanh, Chuŏr Phnum
155 G22 **Cardamom Hills** ▲▲ SW India
Cardamom Mountains *see* Krâvanh, Chuŏr Phnum
104 M12 **Cardeña** Andalucía, S Spain 38°16´N 04°20´W
44 D4 **Cárdenas** Matanzas, W Cuba 23°02´N 81°12´W
41 O11 **Cárdenas** San Luis Potosí, C Mexico 22°03´N 99°30´W
41 U15 **Cárdenas** Tabasco, SE Mexico 18°00´N 93°21´W
63 H21 **Cardiel, Lago** S Argentina
97 K22 **Cardiff** *Wel.* Caerdydd. S Wales, United Kingdom 51°30´N 03°13´W
97 J22 **Cardiff-Wales** ✈ S Wales, United Kingdom 51°24´N 03°22´W
97 I21 **Cardigan** *Wel.* Aberteifi. SW Wales, United Kingdom 52°06´N 04°40´W
97 I20 **Cardigan** *cultural region* W Wales, United Kingdom
97 I20 **Cardigan Bay** *bay* W Wales, United Kingdom
19 N8 **Cardigan, Mount** ▲ New Hampshire, NE USA 43°39´N 71°52´W
14 M13 **Cardinal** Ontario, SE Canada 44°48´N 75°22´W
105 V5 **Cardona** Cataluña, NE Spain 41°55´N 01°41´E
61 E19 **Cardona** Soriano, SW Uruguay 33°53´S 57°18´W
105 V4 **Cardoner** NE Spain
11 Q17 **Cardston** Alberta, SW Canada 49°14´N 113°19´W
181 W5 **Cardwell** Queensland, NE Australia 18°24´S 146°06´E
116 G8 **Carei** *Ger.* Gross-Karol, Karol, *Hung.* Nagykároly; *prev.* Careii-Mari. Satu Mare, NW Romania 47°40´N 22°28´E
Careii-Mari *see* Carei
58 F13 **Careiro** Amazonas, NW Brazil 03°40´S 60°23´W
102 J4 **Carentan** Manche, N France 49°18´N 01°15´W
104 M2 **Cares** N Spain
33 P14 **Carey** Idaho, NW USA 43°17´N 113°58´W
31 S12 **Carey** Ohio, N USA 40°57´N 83°22´W
25 P4 **Carey** Texas, SW USA 34°28´N 100°18´W
180 L11 **Carey, Lake** Western Australia
173 O8 **Cargados Carajos Bank** *undersea feature* C Indian Ocean
102 G6 **Carhaix-Plouguer** Finistère, NW France 48°16´N 03°35´W
61 A22 **Carhué** Buenos Aires, E Argentina 37°10´S 62°45´W
55 O5 **Cariaco** Sucre, NE Venezuela 10°33´N 63°37´W
107 O20 **Cariati** Calabria, SW Italy 39°30´N 16°57´E
2 H17 **Caribbean Plate** *tectonic feature*
44 I11 **Caribbean Sea** *sea* W Atlantic Ocean
11 N15 **Cariboo Mountains** ▲▲ British Columbia, SW Canada
11 W9 **Caribou** Manitoba, C Canada 59°27´N 97°43´W
19 S2 **Caribou** Maine, NE USA 46°51´N 68°00´W
11 P10 **Caribou Mountains** ▲▲ Alberta, SW Canada
Caribrod *see* Dimitrovgrad
40 I6 **Carichic** Chihuahua, N Mexico 27°57´N 107°01´W
103 R3 **Carignan** Ardennes, N France 49°38´N 05°08´E
183 Q5 **Carinda** New South Wales, SE Australia 30°26´S 147°45´E
105 R6 **Cariñena** Aragón, NE Spain 41°20´N 01°13´W
107 I23 **Carini** Sicilia, Italy, C Mediterranean Sea 38°06´N 13°09´E
107 K17 **Carinola** Campania, S Italy 41°14´N 14°03´E
Carinthi *see* Kärnten
55 O5 **Caripe** Monagas, NE Venezuela 10°13´N 63°30´W
55 P5 **Caripito** Monagas, NE Venezuela 10°03´N 63°05´W
15 W7 **Carleton** Québec, SE Canada 48°07´N 66°07´W
31 S10 **Carleton** Michigan, N USA 42°03´N 83°23´W
13 O14 **Carleton, Mount** ▲ New Brunswick, SE Canada 47°10´N 66°54´W
14 L13 **Carleton Place** Ontario, SE Canada 45°08´N 76°09´W
35 V3 **Carlin** Nevada, W USA 40°40´N 116°09´W
30 K14 **Carlinville** Illinois, N USA 39°16´N 89°52´W
97 K14 **Carlisle** *anc.* Caer Luel, Luguvallium, Luguvallum. NW England, United Kingdom 54°54´N 02°55´W
27 V11 **Carlisle** Arkansas, C USA 34°46´N 91°45´W
31 N15 **Carlisle** Indiana, N USA 38°57´N 87°23´W
29 V14 **Carlisle** Iowa, C USA 41°30´N 93°29´W
21 N5 **Carlisle** Kentucky, S USA 38°19´N 84°02´W
18 F15 **Carlisle** Pennsylvania, NE USA 40°10´N 77°10´W
21 Q11 **Carlisle** South Carolina, SE USA 34°35´N 81°27´W
38 J17 **Carlisle Island** *island* Aleutian Islands, Alaska, USA
27 R7 **Carl Junction** Missouri, C USA 37°10´N 94°34´W
107 A20 **Carloforte** Sardegna, Italy, C Mediterranean Sea 39°10´N 08°17´E
Carlopago *see* Karlobag
61 B21 **Carlos Casares** Buenos Aires, E Argentina 35°39´S 61°28´W
61 E18 **Carlos Reyles** Durazno, C Uruguay 33°00´S 56°30´W
61 A21 **Carlos Tejedor** Buenos Aires, E Argentina 35°25´S 62°25´W
97 F19 **Carlow** *Ir.* Ceatharlach. SE Ireland 52°50´N 06°55´W
97 F19 **Carlow** *Ir.* Cheatharlach. *cultural region* SE Ireland
96 F7 **Carloway** NW Scotland, United Kingdom 58°17´N 06°48´W
35 U17 **Carlsbad** California, W USA 33°09´N 117°21´W
37 U15 **Carlsbad** New Mexico, SW USA 32°24´N 104°15´W
Carlsbad *see* Karlovy Vary
129 N13 **Carlsberg Ridge** *undersea feature* S Arabian Sea 06°00´N 61°00´E
Carlsruhe *see* Karlsruhe
29 W6 **Carlton** Minnesota, N USA 46°39´N 92°25´W
11 V17 **Carlyle** Saskatchewan, S Canada 49°39´N 102°18´W
30 L15 **Carlyle** Illinois, N USA 38°36´N 89°22´W
30 L15 **Carlyle Lake** Illinois, N USA
10 H7 **Carmacks** Yukon Territory, W Canada 62°04´N 136°21´W
106 B9 **Carmagnola** Piemonte, NW Italy 44°50´N 07°43´E
11 X16 **Carman** Manitoba, S Canada 49°32´N 97°59´W
Carmana/Carmania *see* Kermān
97 I21 **Carmarthen** SW Wales, United Kingdom 51°52´N 04°19´W
97 I21 **Carmarthen** *cultural region* SW Wales, United Kingdom
97 I22 **Carmarthen Bay** *inlet* SW Wales, United Kingdom
103 N14 **Carmaux** Tarn, S France 44°03´N 02°09´E
35 N11 **Carmel** California, W USA 36°32´N 121°54´W
31 O13 **Carmel** Indiana, N USA 39°58´N 86°07´W
18 L13 **Carmel** New York, NE USA 41°25´N 73°40´W
97 H18 **Carmel Head** *headland* NW Wales, United Kingdom 53°24´N 04°35´W
42 E2 **Carmelita** Petén, N Guatemala 17°33´N 90°11´W
61 D19 **Carmelo** Colonia, SW Uruguay 34°00´S 58°20´W
41 V14 **Carmen** *var.* Ciudad del Carmen. Campeche, SE Mexico 18°38´N 91°50´W
61 A25 **Carmen de Patagones** Buenos Aires, E Argentina 40°45´S 63°00´W
40 F8 **Carmen, Isla** *island* NW Mexico
40 M5 **Carmen, Sierra del** ▲▲ NW Mexico
30 M16 **Carmi** Illinois, N USA 38°05´N 88°09´W
35 O7 **Carmichael** California, W USA 38°36´N 121°21´W
Carmiel *see* Karmi'el
25 U11 **Carmine** Texas, SW USA 30°07´N 96°40´W
104 K14 **Carmona** Andalucía, S Spain 37°28´N 05°38´W
Carmona *see* Uíge
Carnaro *see* Kvarner
180 G9 **Carnarvon** Western Australia 24°57´S 113°38´E
14 I13 **Carnarvon** Ontario, SE Canada 45°03´N 78°41´W
83 G24 **Carnarvon** Northern Cape, W South Africa 30°59´S 22°08´E
Carnarvon *see* Caernarfon
180 K9 **Carnarvon Range** ▲▲ Western Australia
Carn Domhnach *see* Carndonagh
96 E13 **Carndonagh** *Ir.* Carn Domhnach. NW Ireland 55°15´N 07°15´W
11 V17 **Carnduff** Saskatchewan, S Canada 49°11´N 101°50´W
26 L11 **Carnegie** Oklahoma, C USA 35°06´N 98°36´W
180 L9 **Carnegie, Lake** *salt lake* Western Australia
193 U8 **Carnegie Ridge** *undersea feature* E Pacific Ocean 01°00´S 85°00´W
96 H9 **Carn Eige** ▲ N Scotland, United Kingdom 57°18´N 05°04´W
182 F5 **Carnes** South Australia 30°12´S 134°31´E
194 J12 **Carney Island** *island* Antarctica
18 H16 **Carneys Point** New Jersey, NE USA 39°38´N 75°29´W
Carniche, Alpi *see* Karnische Alpen
151 Q21 **Car Nicobar** *island* Nicobar Islands, India, NE Indian Ocean
79 H15 **Carnot** Mambéré-Kadéï, W Central African Republic 04°58´N 15°55´E
182 F10 **Carnot, Cape** *headland* South Australia 34°57´S 135°39´E
96 K11 **Carnoustie** E Scotland, United Kingdom 56°30´N 02°42´W
97 F20 **Carnsore Point** *Ir.* Ceann an Chairn. *headland* SE Ireland 52°10´N 06°22´W
8 H7 **Carnwath** Northwest Territories, NW Canada
31 R8 **Caro** Michigan, N USA 43°29´N 83°24´W
23 Z15 **Carol City** Florida, SE USA 25°56´N 80°15´W
59 L14 **Carolina** Maranhão, E Brazil 07°20´S 47°25´W
45 U5 **Carolina** E Puerto Rico 18°22´N 65°57´W
21 V12 **Carolina Beach** North Carolina, SE USA 34°02´N 77°53´W
Caroline Island *see* Millennium Island
189 N15 **Caroline Islands** *island group* C Micronesia
129 Z14 **Caroline Plate** *tectonic feature*
192 H7 **Caroline Ridge** *undersea feature* E Philippine Sea 08°00´N 150°00´E
Carolopois *see* Châlons-en-Champagne
45 V14 **Caroni Arena Dam** Trinidad, Trinidad and Tobago
Caronie, Monti *see* Nebrodi, Monti
55 P7 **Caroní, Río** E Venezuela
45 U14 **Caroni River** Trinidad, Trinidad and Tobago
Caronium *see* A Coruña
54 J5 **Carora** Lara, N Venezuela 10°12´N 70°07´W
86 F12 **Carpathian Mountains** *var.* Carpathians, *Cz./Pol.* Karpaty, *Ger.* Karpaten. ▲▲ E Europe
Carpathians *see* Carpathian Mountains
Carpathos/Carpathus *see* Kárpathos
116 H12 **Carpaţii Meridionalii** *var.* Alpi Transilvaniei, Carpaţii Sudici, *Eng.* South Carpathians, Transylvanian Alps, *Ger.* Südkarpaten, Transsylvanische Alpen, *Hung.* Déli-Kárpátok, Erdélyi-Havasok. ▲▲ C Romania
Carpaţii Sudici *see* Carpaţii Meridionalii
174 L7 **Carpentaria, Gulf of** *gulf* N Australia
Carpentoracte *see* Carpentras
103 R14 **Carpentras** *anc.* Carpentoracte. Vaucluse, SE France 44°03´N 05°03´E
106 F9 **Carpi** Emilia-Romagna, N Italy 44°47´N 10°53´E
116 E11 **Cărpiniş** *Hung.* Gyertyámos. Timiş, W Romania 45°46´N 20°53´E
35 R14 **Carpinteria** California, W USA 34°24´N 119°30´W
23 S9 **Carrabelle** Florida, SE USA 29°51´N 84°39´W
Carraig Aonair *see* Fastnet Rock
Carraig Fhearghais *see* Carrickfergus
Carraig Mhachaire Rois *see* Carrickmacross
Carraig na Siúire *see* Carrick-on-Suir
Carrantual *see* Carrauntoohil
106 E10 **Carrara** Toscana, C Italy 44°05´N 10°07´E
61 F20 **Carrasco** ✈ (Montevideo) Canelones, S Uruguay 34°51´S 56°00´W
105 P9 **Carrascosa del Campo** Castilla-La Mancha, C Spain 40°02´N 02°35´W
54 H4 **Carrasquero** Zulia, NW Venezuela 11°00´N 72°01´W
183 O9 **Carrathool** New South Wales, SE Australia 34°25´S 145°30´E
Carrauntohil *see* Carrauntoohil
97 B21 **Carrauntoohil** *Ir.* Carrantual, Carrauntohil, Corrán Tuathail. ▲ SW Ireland 51°98´N 09°53´W
45 Y15 **Carriacou** *island* N Grenada
97 G15 **Carrickfergus** *Ir.* Carraig Fhearghais. NE Northern Ireland, United Kingdom 54°43´N 05°49´W
97 F16 **Carrickmacross** *Ir.* Carraig Mhachaire Rois. N Ireland 53°58´N 06°43´W
97 D16 **Carrick-on-Shannon** *Ir.* Cora Droma Rúisc. NW Ireland 53°37´N 08°05´W
97 E20 **Carrick-on-Suir** *Ir.* Carraig na Siúire. S Ireland 52°21´N 07°25´W
182 I7 **Carrieton** South Australia 32°27´S 138°33´E
40 L7 **Carrillo** Chihuahua, N Mexico 25°53´N 103°54´W
29 O4 **Carrington** North Dakota, N USA 47°27´N 99°07´W
104 M4 **Carrión** N Spain
104 M4 **Carrión de los Condes** Castilla y León, N Spain 42°20´N 04°37´W
25 P13 **Carrizo Springs** Texas, SW USA 28°33´N 99°54´W
37 S13 **Carrizozo** New Mexico, SW USA 33°38´N 105°52´W
29 T13 **Carroll** Iowa, C USA 42°04´N 94°52´W
23 N4 **Carrollton** Alabama, S USA 33°13´N 88°05´W
23 R3 **Carrollton** Georgia, SE USA 33°33´N 85°04´W
30 K14 **Carrollton** Illinois, N USA 39°18´N 90°24´W
20 L4 **Carrollton** Kentucky, S USA 38°41´N 85°09´W
31 R8 **Carrollton** Michigan, N USA 43°27´N 83°55´W
27 T3 **Carrollton** Missouri, C USA 39°20´N 93°30´W
31 U12 **Carrollton** Ohio, N USA 40°34´N 81°05´W
25 T6 **Carrollton** Texas, SW USA 32°57´N 96°53´W
11 U14 **Carrot** Saskatchewan, S Canada
11 U14 **Carrot River** Saskatchewan, C Canada 53°18´N 103°32´W
18 J7 **Carry Falls Reservoir** New York, NE USA
136 L11 **Çarşamba** Samsun, N Turkey 41°13´N 36°43´E
28 L6 **Carson** North Dakota, N USA 46°26´N 101°34´W
35 Q6 **Carson City** *state capital* Nevada, W USA 39°10´N 119°46´W
35 R6 **Carson River** Nevada, W USA
35 S5 **Carson Sink** *salt flat* Nevada, W USA
11 Q16 **Carstairs** Alberta, SW Canada 51°35´N 114°02´W
Carstensz, Puntjak *see* Jaya, Puncak
54 E5 **Cartagena** *var.* Cartagena de los Indes. Bolívar, NW Colombia 10°24´N 75°33´W
105 R13 **Cartagena** *anc.* Carthago Nova. Murcia, SE Spain 37°36´N 00°59´W
54 E13 **Cartagena de Chaira** Caquetá, S Colombia 01°19´N 74°52´W
Cartagena de los Indes *see* Cartagena
54 D10 **Cartago** Valle del Cauca, W Colombia 04°45´N 75°55´W
43 N14 **Cartago** Cartago, C Costa Rica 09°50´N 83°54´W
42 M14 **Cartago** *off.* Provincia de Cartago. ◐ *province* C Costa Rica
Cartago, Provincia de *see* Cartago
25 O11 **Carta Valley** Texas, SW USA 29°46´N 100°37´W
104 F10 **Cartaxo** Santarém, C Portugal 39°10´N 08°47´W
104 I14 **Cartaya** Andalucía, S Spain 37°16´N 07°09´W
Carteret Islands *see* Tulun Islands
29 S15 **Carter Lake** Iowa, C USA 41°17´N 95°55´W
23 S3 **Cartersville** Georgia, SE USA 34°10´N 84°48´W
185 M14 **Carterton** Wellington, North Island, New Zealand 41°01´S 175°30´E
30 J13 **Carthage** Illinois, N USA 40°25´N 91°09´W
22 L5 **Carthage** Mississippi, S USA 32°43´N 89°31´W
27 R7 **Carthage** Missouri, C USA 37°10´N 94°20´W
18 I8 **Carthage** New York, NE USA 43°58´N 75°36´W
21 T10 **Carthage** North Carolina, SE USA 35°21´N 79°27´W
20 K8 **Carthage** Tennessee, S USA 36°14´N 85°59´W
25 X7 **Carthage** Texas, SW USA 32°10´N 94°21´W
74 M5 **Carthage** ✈ (Tunis) N Tunisia 36°51´N 10°12´E
Carthago Nova *see* Cartagena
14 E10 **Cartier** Ontario, S Canada 46°40´N 81°31´W
13 S8 **Cartwright** Newfoundland and Labrador, E Canada 53°40´N 57°W
55 P9 **Caruana de Montaña** Bolívar, SE Venezuela 05°16´N 63°12´W
59 Q15 **Caruaru** Pernambuco, E Brazil 08°15´S 35°55´W
55 P5 **Carúpano** Sucre, NE Venezuela 10°39´N 63°14´W
Carusbur *see* Cherbourg
58 M12 **Carutapera** Maranhão, E Brazil 01°12´S 45°57´W
27 Y9 **Caruthersville** Missouri, C USA 36°11´N 89°40´W
103 O1 **Carvin** Pas-de-Calais, N France 50°31´N 03°00´E
58 E12 **Carvoeiro** Amazonas, NW Brazil 01°24´S 61°59´W
104 E10 **Carvoeiro, Cabo** *headland* C Portugal 39°19´N 09°27´W
21 U9 **Cary** North Carolina, SE USA 35°47´N 78°46´W
182 M3 **Caryapundy Swamp** *wetland* New South Wales/Queensland, SE Australia
65 E24 **Carysfort, Cape** *headland* East Falkland, Falkland Islands 51°26´S 57°50´W
74 F6 **Casablanca** *Ar.* Dar-el-Beida. NW Morocco 33°39´N 07°31´W
60 M8 **Casa Branca** São Paulo, S Brazil 21°47´S 47°05´W
36 L14 **Casa Grande** Arizona, SW USA 32°52´N 111°45´W
106 C8 **Casale Monferrato** Piemonte, NW Italy 45°08´N 08°27´E
106 E8 **Casalpusterlengo** Lombardia, N Italy 45°10´N 09°37´E
54 H10 **Casanare** *off.* Intendencia de Casanare. ◐ *province* C Colombia
Casanare, Intendencia de *see* Casanare
55 P5 **Casanay** Sucre, NE Venezuela 10°30´N 63°25´W
24 K11 **Casa Piedra** Texas, SW USA 29°43´N 104°03´W
107 Q19 **Casarano** Puglia, SE Italy 40°01´N 18°10´E
42 J11 **Casares** Carazo, W Nicaragua 11°37´N 86°19´W
105 R10 **Casas Ibáñez** Castilla-La Mancha, C Spain 39°17´N 01°28´W
61 I14 **Casca** Rio Grande do Sul, S Brazil 28°39´S 51°55´W
172 I17 **Cascade** Mahé, NE Seychelles 04°39´S 55°29´E
33 N13 **Cascade** Idaho, NW USA 44°31´N 116°02´W
29 Y13 **Cascade** Iowa, C USA 42°18´N 91°00´W
33 R9 **Cascade** Montana, NW USA 47°15´N 111°46´W
185 B20 **Cascade Point** *headland* South Island, New Zealand 44°00´S 168°23´E
32 G13 **Cascade Range** ▲▲ Oregon/Washington, NW USA
33 N12 **Cascade Reservoir** Idaho, NW USA
0 E8 **Cascadia Basin** *undersea feature* NE Pacific Ocean 47°00´N 127°30´W
104 E11 **Cascais** Lisboa, C Portugal 38°41´N 09°25´W
15 W7 **Cascapédia** Québec, SE Canada
59 I22 **Cascavel** Ceará, E Brazil 04°10´S 38°15´W
60 G11 **Cascavel** Paraná, S Brazil 24°56´S 53°28´W
106 I13 **Cascia** Umbria, C Italy 42°45´N 13°01´E
106 F11 **Cascina** Toscana, C Italy 43°40´N 10°33´E
19 Q8 **Casco Bay** *bay* Maine, NE USA
194 J7 **Case Island** *island* Antarctica
106 B8 **Caselle** ✈ (Torino) Piemonte, NW Italy 45°06´N 07°41´E
107 K17 **Caserta** Campania, S Italy 41°05´N 14°20´E
15 N8 **Casey** Québec, SE Canada 47°50´N 74°09´W
30 M14 **Casey** Illinois, N USA 39°18´N 87°59´W
195 Y12 **Casey** *Australian research station* Antarctica 65°58´S 111°04´E
195 W3 **Casey Bay** *bay* Antarctica
80 Q11 **Caseyr, Raas** *headland* NE Somalia 11°51´S 51°16´E
97 D20 **Cashel** *Ir.* Caiseal. S Ireland 52°31´N 07°53´W
54 G6 **Casigua** Zulia, W Venezuela 08°46´N 72°30´W
61 B19 **Casilda** Santa Fe, C Argentina 33°05´S 61°10´W
Casim *see* General Toshevo
183 V4 **Casino** New South Wales, SE Australia 28°50´S 153°02´E
107 J16 **Cassino** *prev.* San Germano; *anc.* Casinum. Lazio, C Italy 41°29´N 13°50´E
Casinum *see* Cassino
111 E17 **Čáslav** *Ger.* Tschaslau. Střední Čechy, C Czech Republic 49°54´N 15°23´E
56 C13 **Casma** Ancash, C Peru 09°30´S 78°18´W
167 S7 **Ca, Sông** N Vietnam
107 K17 **Casoria** Campania, S Italy 40°54´N 14°28´E
105 T6 **Caspe** Aragón, NE Spain 41°14´N 00°03´W
33 X15 **Casper** Wyoming, C USA 42°48´N 106°22´W
84 M10 **Caspian Depression** *Kaz.* Kaspīy Mangy Oypaty, *Rus.* Prikaspiyskaya Nizmennost'. *depression* Kazakhstan/Russian Federation
130 D10 **Caspian Sea** *Az.* Xäzär Dänizi, *Kaz.* Kaspiy Tengizi, *Per.* Baḩr-e Khazar, Daryā-ye Khazar, *Rus.* Kaspiyskoye More. *inland sea* Asia/Europe

◆ Country
● Country Capital
◇ Dependent Territory
○ Dependent Territory Capital
◐ Administrative Regions
✈ International Airport
▲ Mountain
▲▲ Mountain Range
Volcano
River
Lake
Reservoir

83 L14 Cassacatiza Tete, NW Mozambique 14°20′S 32°24′E
Cassai see Kasai
82 F13 Cassamba Moxico, E Angola 13°07′S 20°22′E
107 N20 Cassano allo Ionio Calabria, SE Italy 39°46′N 16°16′E
31 S8 Cass City Michigan, N USA 43°36′N 83°10′W
Cassel see Kassel
14 M13 Casselman Ontario, SE Canada 45°18′N 75°05′W
29 R5 Casselton North Dakota, N USA 46°53′N 97°10′W
Cássia see Santa Rita de Cassia
10 J9 Cassiar British Columbia, W Canada 59°16′N 129°40′W
10 K10 Cassiar Mountains ▲ British Columbia, W Canada
83 C15 Cassinga Huíla, SW Angola 15°08′S 16°05′E
29 T4 Cass Lake Minnesota, N USA 47°22′N 94°36′W
29 T4 Cass Lake ◎ Minnesota, N USA
31 P10 Cassopolis Michigan, N USA 41°56′N 86°00′W
31 S8 Cass River ↝ Michigan, N USA
27 S8 Cassville Missouri, C USA 36°42′N 93°52′W
Castamoni see Kastamonu
58 L12 Castanhal Pará, NE Brazil 01°16′S 47°55′W
104 G8 Castanheira de Pêra Leiria, C Portugal 40°01′N 08°12′W
41 N7 Castaños Coahuila, NE Mexico 26°48′N 101°26′W
108 I10 Castasegna Graubünden, SE Switzerland 46°21′N 09°30′E
106 D8 Casteggio Lombardia, N Italy 45°02′N 09°10′E
107 K23 Castelbuono Sicilia, Italy, C Mediterranean Sea 37°56′N 14°05′E
107 K15 Castel di Sangro Abruzzo, C Italy 41°46′N 14°03′E
106 H7 Castelfranco Veneto Veneto, NE Italy 45°40′N 11°55′E
102 K14 Casteljaloux Lot-et-Garonne, SW France 44°19′N 00°03′E
107 L18 Castellabate var. Santa Maria di Castellabate. Campania, S Italy 40°16′N 14°57′E
107 I23 Castellammare del Golfo Sicilia, Italy, C Mediterranean Sea 38°02′N 12°53′E
107 H22 Castellammare, Golfo di gulf Sicilia, Italy, C Mediterranean Sea
103 U15 Castellane Alpes-de-Haute-Provence, SE France 43°49′N 06°34′E
107 O18 Castellaneta Puglia, SE Italy 40°38′N 16°57′E
106 E9 Castel l'Arquato Emilia-Romagna, C Italy 44°52′N 09°51′E
61 E21 Castelli Buenos Aires, E Argentina 36°07′S 57°47′W
105 S8 Castelló de la Plana var. Castellón de la Plana. ◆ province Valenciana, E Spain
Castelló de la Plana see Castellón de la Plana
Castellón see Castellón de la Plana
105 T9 Castellón de la Plana var. Castellón, Cat. Castelló de la Plana. Valenciana, E Spain 39°59′N 00°03′W
Castellón de la Plana see Castelló de la Plana
105 S7 Castellote Aragón, NE Spain 40°46′N 00°18′W
103 N16 Castelnaudary Aude, S France 43°18′N 01°57′E
102 L16 Castelnau-Magnoac Hautes-Pyrénées, S France 43°18′N 00°30′E
106 F10 Castelnovo ne' Monti Emilia-Romagna, C Italy 44°26′N 10°24′E
Castelnuovo see Herceg-Novi
104 H9 Castelo Branco Castelo Branco, C Portugal 39°50′N 07°30′W
104 H8 Castelo Branco ◆ district C Portugal
104 I10 Castelo de Vide Portalegre, C Portugal 39°25′N 07°27′W
104 G9 Castelo do Bode, Barragem do ⊠ C Portugal
106 G10 Castel San Pietro Terme Emilia-Romagna, C Italy 44°22′N 11°34′E
107 B17 Castelsardo Sardegna, Italy, C Mediterranean Sea 40°54′N 08°42′E
102 M14 Castelsarrasin Tarn-et-Garonne, S France 44°02′N 01°06′E
107 I24 Casteltermini Sicilia, Italy, C Mediterranean Sea 37°33′N 13°38′E
107 H24 Castelvetrano Sicilia, Italy, C Mediterranean Sea 37°40′N 12°46′E
182 L12 Casterton Victoria, SE Australia 37°37′S 141°22′E
102 J15 Castets Landes, SW France 43°55′N 01°08′W
106 H12 Castiglione del Lago Umbria, C Italy 43°07′N 12°02′E
106 F13 Castiglione della Pescaia Toscana, C Italy 42°46′N 10°53′E
106 F8 Castiglione delle Stiviere Lombardia, N Italy 45°24′N 10°31′E
104 M9 Castilla-La Mancha ◆ autonomous community NE Spain
Castilla-León see Castilla y León
105 N10 Castilla Nueva cultural region C Spain
105 N6 Castilla Vieja ◆ cultural region N Spain
104 L5 Castilla y León var. Castillia-León. ◆ autonomous community NW Spain
Castillo de Locubim see Castillo de Locubín
105 N14 Castillo de Locubín var. Castillo de Locubim. Andalucía, S Spain 37°32′N 03°56′W
102 K13 Castillon-la-Bataille Gironde, SW France 44°51′N 00°01′W
63 I19 Castillo, Pampa del plain S Argentina
61 G19 Castillos Rocha, SE Uruguay 34°12′S 53°52′W
97 B16 Castlebar Ir. Caisleán an Bharraigh. W Ireland 53°52′N 09°17′W
97 F16 Castleblayney Ir. Baile na Lorgan. N Ireland 54°07′N 06°44′W
45 O11 Castle Bruce E Dominica 15°24′N 61°26′W
36 M5 Castle Dale Utah, W USA 39°10′N 111°02′W
36 I14 Castle Dome Peak ▲ Arizona, SW USA 33°04′N 114°08′W
97 J14 Castle Douglas S Scotland, United Kingdom 54°56′N 03°56′W
97 E14 Castlefinn Ir. Caisleán na Finne. NW Ireland 54°47′N 07°35′W
97 M17 Castleford N England, United Kingdom 53°44′N 01°21′W
11 O17 Castlegar British Columbia, SW Canada 49°18′N 117°48′W
64 B12 Castle Harbour inlet Bermuda, NW Atlantic Ocean
21 V12 Castle Hayne North Carolina, SE USA 34°23′N 78°07′W
97 B20 Castleisland Ir. Oileán Ciarraí. SW Ireland 52°12′N 09°30′W
183 N12 Castlemaine Victoria, SE Australia 37°06′S 144°13′E
37 R5 Castle Peak ▲ Colorado, C USA 39°00′N 106°51′W
33 O13 Castle Peak ▲ Idaho, NW USA 44°02′N 114°42′W
184 N13 Castlepoint Wellington, North Island, New Zealand 40°54′S 176°13′E
97 D17 Castlerea Ir. An Caisleán Riabhach. W Ireland 53°45′N 08°32′W
97 G15 Castlereagh Ir. An Caisleán Riabhach. N Northern Ireland, United Kingdom 54°33′N 05°53′W
183 R6 Castlereagh River ↝ New South Wales, SE Australia
37 T5 Castle Rock Colorado, C USA 39°22′N 104°51′W
30 K7 Castle Rock Lake ⊠ Wisconsin, N USA
65 G25 Castle Rock Point headland S Saint Helena 16°02′S 05°45′W
97 I16 Castletown SE Isle of Man 54°05′N 04°39′W
29 R9 Castlewood South Dakota, N USA 44°43′N 97°01′W
11 R15 Castor Alberta, SW Canada 52°14′N 111°54′W
14 M13 Castor ↝ Ontario, SE Canada
27 X7 Castor River ↝ Missouri, C USA
Castra Albiensium see Castres
Castra Regina see Regensburg
103 N15 Castres anc. Castra Albiensium. Tarn, S France 43°36′N 02°15′E
98 H9 Castricum Noord-Holland, W Netherlands 52°33′N 04°40′E
45 S11 Castries ● (Saint Lucia) N Saint Lucia 14°01′N 60°59′W
60 J11 Castro Paraná, S Brazil 24°46′S 50°03′W
63 F17 Castro Los Lagos, W Chile 42°27′S 73°48′W
104 H7 Castro Daire Viseu, N Portugal 40°54′N 07°55′W
104 M13 Castro del Río Andalucía, S Spain 37°41′N 04°29′W
Castrogiovanni see Enna
104 H14 Castro Marim Faro, S Portugal 37°13′N 07°26′W
104 J2 Castropol Asturias, N Spain 43°30′N 07°01′W
105 O2 Castro-Urdiales var. Castro Urdiales. Cantabria, N Spain 43°23′N 03°11′W
104 G13 Castro Verde Beja, S Portugal 37°42′N 08°05′W
107 N19 Castrovillari Calabria, SW Italy 39°48′N 16°12′E
35 N10 Castroville California, W USA 36°46′N 121°46′W
25 R12 Castroville Texas, SW USA 29°21′N 98°52′W
104 K11 Castuera Extremadura, W Spain 38°44′N 05°33′W
61 F19 Casupá Florida, S Uruguay 34°09′S 55°38′W
185 A22 Caswell Sound sound South Island, New Zealand
137 Q13 Çat Erzurum, NE Turkey 39°40′N 41°03′E
42 K6 Catacamas Olancho, C Honduras 14°55′N 85°54′W
56 A10 Catacaos Piura, NW Peru 05°22′S 80°40′W
22 I7 Catahoula Lake ◎ Louisiana, S USA
137 S15 Çatak Van, SE Turkey 38°02′N 43°05′E
137 S15 Çatak Çayi ↝ SE Turkey
114 O12 Çatalca İstanbul, NW Turkey 41°09′N 28°28′E
114 O12 Çatalca Yarimadasi physical region NW Turkey
62 H6 Catalina Antofagasta, N Chile 25°19′S 69°37′W
Catalonia see Cataluña
105 U5 Cataluña Cat. Catalunya, Eng. Catalonia. ◆ autonomous community N Spain
Catalunya see Cataluña
62 I7 Catamarca off. Provincia de Catamarca. ◆ province NW Argentina
Catamarca see San Fernando del Valle de Catamarca
Catamarca, Provincia de see Catamarca
83 M16 Catandica Manica, C Mozambique 18°05′S 33°10′E
171 P4 Catanduanes Island island N Philippines
60 K8 Catanduva São Paulo, S Brazil 21°05′S 49°00′W
107 L24 Catania Sicilia, Italy, C Mediterranean Sea 37°31′N 15°04′E
107 M24 Catania, Golfo di gulf Sicilia, Italy, C Mediterranean Sea
45 U5 Cataño var. Cantaño. E Puerto Rico 18°26′N 66°06′W
107 O21 Catanzaro Calabria, SW Italy 38°53′N 16°36′E
107 O22 Catanzaro Marina var. Marina di Catanzaro. Calabria, S Italy 38°48′N 16°33′E
Marina di Catanzaro see Catanzaro Marina
25 Q14 Catarina Texas, SW USA 28°19′N 99°36′W
171 Q5 Catarman Samar, C Philippines 12°29′N 124°34′E
105 S10 Catarroja Valenciana, E Spain 39°24′N 00°24′W
21 R11 Catawba River ↝ North Carolina/South Carolina, SE USA
171 Q5 Catbalogan Samar, C Philippines 11°49′N 124°55′E
14 I14 Catchacoma Ontario, SE Canada 44°43′N 78°19′W
41 S15 Catemaco Veracruz-Llave, SE Mexico 18°28′N 95°10′W
Cathair na Mart see Westport
Cathair Saidhbhín see Caherciveen
31 P5 Cat Head Point headland Michigan, N USA 45°11′N 85°37′W
23 Q2 Cathedral Caverns cave Alabama, S USA
35 V16 Cathedral City California, W USA 33°45′N 116°27′W
24 K10 Cathedral Mountain ▲ Texas, SW USA 30°10′N 103°39′W
32 G10 Cathlamet Washington, NW USA 46°12′N 123°24′W
76 G13 Catió S Guinea-Bissau 11°13′N 15°10′W
55 O10 Catisimiña Bolívar, SE Venezuela 04°07′N 63°40′W
44 J3 Cat Island island C Bahamas
12 B9 Cat Lake Ontario, S Canada 51°47′N 91°52′W
21 P5 Catlettsburg Kentucky, S USA 38°24′N 82°37′W
185 D24 Catlins ↝ South Island, New Zealand
35 R1 Catnip Mountain ▲ Nevada, W USA 41°53′N 119°19′W
41 Z11 Catoche, Cabo headland SE Mexico 21°36′N 87°04′W
27 P9 Catoosa Oklahoma, C USA 36°11′N 95°45′W
41 N10 Catorce San Luis Potosí, C Mexico 23°42′N 100°49′W
63 I14 Catriel Río Negro, C Argentina 37°54′S 67°52′W
62 K13 Catriló La Pampa, C Argentina 36°28′S 63°20′W
58 F11 Catrimani Roraima, N Brazil 0°24′N 61°30′W
58 E10 Catrimani, Rio ↝ N Brazil
18 K11 Catskill New York, NE USA 42°13′N 73°52′W
18 K11 Catskill Creek ↝ New York, NE USA
18 J11 Catskill Mountains ▲ New York, NE USA
18 D11 Cattaraugus Creek ↝ New York, NE USA
Cattaro see Kotor
Cattaro, Bocche di see Kotorska, Boka
107 I24 Cattolica Eraclea Sicilia, Italy, C Mediterranean Sea 37°27′N 13°24′E
83 B14 Catumbela ↝ W Angola
83 N14 Catur Niassa, N Mozambique 13°50′S 35°43′E
82 C10 Cauale ↝ NE Angola
171 O2 Cauayan Luzon, N Philippines 16°55′N 121°46′E
54 C12 Cauca off. Departamento del Cauca. ◆ province SW Colombia
47 P5 Cauca ↝ SE Venezuela
Cauca, Departamento del see Cauca
58 P13 Caucaia Ceará, E Brazil 03°44′S 38°45′W
54 E7 Cauca, Río ↝ N Colombia
54 E7 Caucasia Antioquia, NW Colombia 07°59′N 75°13′W
137 Q8 Caucasus Rus. Kavkaz. ▲ Georgia/Russian Federation
62 I10 Caucete San Juan, W Argentina 31°38′S 68°16′W
105 R11 Caudete Castilla-La Mancha, C Spain 38°42′N 01°00′W
103 P2 Caudry Nord, N France 50°07′N 03°24′E
82 D11 Caungula Lunda Norte, NE Angola 08°22′S 18°37′E
62 G13 Cauquenes Maule, C Chile 35°58′S 72°22′W
55 N8 Caura, Río ↝ C Venezuela
15 V7 Causapscal Québec, SE Canada 48°22′N 67°14′W
117 N10 Căuşeni Rus. Kaushany. E Moldova 46°37′N 29°21′E
102 M14 Caussade Tarn-et-Garonne, S France 44°10′N 01°31′E
102 K17 Cauterets Hautes-Pyrénées, S France 42°53′N 00°08′W
10 J15 Caution, Cape headland British Columbia, SW Canada 51°10′N 127°43′W
44 H7 Cauto ↝ E Cuba
Cauvery see Kāveri
102 L3 Caux, Pays de physical region N France
107 L18 Cava de' Tirreni Campania, S Italy 40°42′N 14°42′E
104 G6 Cávado ↝ N Portugal
Cavaia see Kavajë
103 R15 Cavaillon Vaucluse, SE France 43°51′N 05°01′E
103 U16 Cavalaire-sur-Mer Var, SE France 43°10′N 06°31′E
106 G6 Cavalese Ger. Gablös. Trentino-Alto Adige, N Italy 46°18′N 11°29′E
29 Q2 Cavalier North Dakota, N USA 48°47′N 97°37′W
76 L17 Cavalla var. Cavally, Cavally Fleuve. ↝ Ivory Coast/ Liberia
105 Y8 Cavalleria, Cap de var. Cabo Caballeria. headland Menorca, Spain, W Mediterranean Sea 40°04′N 04°06′E
184 K2 Cavalli Islands island group N New Zealand
Cavally/Cavally Fleuve see Cavalla
97 E16 Cavan Ir. Cabhán. N Ireland 54°N 07°21′W
97 E16 Cavan Ir. An Cabhán. cultural region N Ireland
106 H8 Cavarzere Veneto, NE Italy 45°08′N 12°05′E
27 W9 Cave City Arkansas, C USA 35°56′N 91°33′W
20 K7 Cave City Kentucky, S USA 37°08′N 85°57′W
65 M25 Cave Point headland S Tristan da Cunha
21 N5 Cave Run Lake ⊠ Kentucky, S USA
58 K11 Caviana de Fora, Ilha var. Ilha Caviana. island N Brazil
Caviana, Ilha see Caviana de Fora, Ilha
113 I16 Cavtat It. Ragusavecchia. Dubrovnik-Neretva, SE Croatia 42°36′N 18°13′E
Cawnpore see Kānpur
Caxamarca see Cajamarca
58 A13 Caxias Amazonas, W Brazil 04°27′S 71°27′W
58 N13 Caxias Maranhão, E Brazil 04°53′S 43°20′W
61 I15 Caxias do Sul Rio Grande do Sul, S Brazil 29°14′S 51°10′W
42 J4 Caxinas, Punta headland N Honduras 16°01′N 86°02′W
82 B11 Caxito Bengo, NW Angola 08°34′S 13°38′E
136 F14 Çay Afyon, W Turkey 38°35′N 31°01′E
40 L15 Cayacal, Punta var. Punta Mongrove. headland S Mexico 17°55′N 102°09′W
56 C6 Cayambe Pichincha, N Ecuador 0°02′N 78°08′W
56 C6 Cayambe ▲ N Ecuador 0°00′S 77°58′W
21 R12 Cayce South Carolina, SE USA 33°58′N 81°04′W
55 Y10 Cayenne ○ (French Guiana) NE French Guiana 04°55′N 52°18′W
55 Y10 Cayenne ✕ NE French Guiana 04°55′N 52°18′W
44 K10 Cayes var. Les Cayes. SW Haiti 18°10′N 73°48′W
45 U6 Cayey C Puerto Rico 18°06′N 66°11′W
45 U6 Cayey, Sierra de ▲ E Puerto Rico
103 N14 Caylus Tarn-et-Garonne, S France 44°13′N 01°42′E
44 E8 Cayman Brac island E Cayman Islands
44 D8 Cayman Islands ◇ UK dependent territory W West Indies
64 D11 Cayman Trench undersea feature NW Caribbean Sea 19°00′N 80°00′W
47 O3 Cayman Trough undersea feature NW Caribbean Sea 18°00′N 81°00′W
80 O13 Caynabo Togdheer, N Somalia 08°55′N 46°28′E
42 F3 Cayo ◆ district SW Belize
Cayo see San Ignacio
43 N9 Cayos Guerrero reef E Nicaragua
43 O9 Cayos King reef E Nicaragua
44 E4 Cay Sal islet SW Bahamas
14 G16 Cayuga Ontario, S Canada 42°57′N 79°49′W
25 V8 Cayuga Texas, SW USA 31°55′N 95°57′W
18 G10 Cayuga Lake ◎ New York, NE USA
104 K13 Cazalla de la Sierra Andalucía, S Spain 37°56′N 05°46′W
116 L14 Căzăneşti Ialomiţa, SE Romania 44°36′N 27°03′E
102 M16 Cazères Haute-Garonne, S France 43°15′N 01°11′E
112 E10 Cazin ◆ Federacija Bosna I Hercegovina, NW Bosnia and Herzegovina
82 G13 Cazombo Moxico, E Angola 11°54′S 22°56′E
105 O13 Cazorla Andalucía, S Spain 37°55′N 03°W
Cazza see Sušac
104 L4 Cea ↝ NW Spain
Ceadâr-Lunga see Ciadîr-Lunga
Ceanannas see Kells
Ceann Toirc see Kanturk
58 O13 Ceará off. Estado do Ceará. ◆ state C Brazil
Ceará see Fortaleza
Ceara Abyssal Plain see Ceará Plain
Ceará, Estado do see Ceará
59 Q14 Ceará Mirim Rio Grande do Norte, E Brazil 05°30′S 35°51′W
64 J13 Ceará Plain var. Ceara Abyssal Plain. undersea feature W Atlantic Ocean 0°00′S 36°30′W
64 I13 Ceará Ridge undersea feature C Atlantic Ocean
Ceatharlach see Carlow
43 Q17 Cébaco, Isla island SW Panama
40 K7 Ceballos Durango, C Mexico 26°33′N 104°07′W
61 G19 Cebollatí Rocha, E Uruguay 33°15′S 53°46′W
61 G19 Cebollatí, Río ↝ E Uruguay
105 P5 Cebollera ▲ N Spain 42°01′N 02°40′W
104 M8 Cebreros Castilla y León, N Spain 40°27′N 04°28′W
171 P6 Cebu off. Cebu City. Cebu, C Philippines 10°17′N 123°46′E
171 P6 Cebu island C Philippines
Cebu City see Cebu
107 J16 Ceccano Lazio, C Italy 41°34′N 13°20′E
Čechy see Bohemia
106 F12 Cecina Toscana, C Italy 43°19′N 10°31′E
26 K4 Cedar Bluff Reservoir ⊠ Kansas, C USA
30 M8 Cedarburg Wisconsin, N USA 43°18′N 87°58′W
36 J7 Cedar City Utah, W USA 37°40′N 113°03′W
25 T11 Cedar Creek Texas, SW USA 30°04′N 97°30′W
28 L7 Cedar Creek ↝ North Dakota, N USA
25 U7 Cedar Creek Reservoir ⊠ Texas, SW USA
29 W13 Cedar Falls Iowa, C USA 42°31′N 92°27′W
31 N8 Cedar Grove Wisconsin, N USA 43°31′N 87°48′W
21 Y6 Cedar Island island Virginia, NE USA
23 U11 Cedar Key Cedar Keys, Florida, SE USA 29°08′N 83°03′W
23 U11 Cedar Keys island group Florida, SE USA
11 V14 Cedar Lake ◎ Manitoba, C Canada
14 I11 Cedar Lake ◎ Ontario, SE Canada
24 M6 Cedar Lake ◎ Texas, SW USA
29 X13 Cedar Rapids Iowa, C USA 41°58′N 91°40′W
29 X14 Cedar River ↝ Iowa/ Minnesota, C USA
29 O14 Cedar River ↝ Nebraska, C USA
31 P8 Cedar Springs Michigan, N USA 43°13′N 85°33′W
23 R3 Cedartown Georgia, SE USA 34°00′N 85°16′W
27 O7 Cedar Vale Kansas, C USA 37°06′N 96°30′W
35 Q2 Cedarville California, W USA 41°30′N 120°10′W
104 H1 Cedeira Galicia, NW Spain 43°40′N 08°03′W
42 H8 Cedeño Choluteca, S Honduras 13°10′N 87°25′W
41 N10 Cedral San Luis Potosí, C Mexico 23°47′N 100°40′W
42 I6 Cedros Francisco Morazán, C Honduras 14°38′N 86°42′W
40 M9 Cedros Zacatecas, C Mexico 24°39′N 101°47′W
40 B5 Cedros, Isla island W Mexico
193 R5 Cedros Trench undersea feature E Pacific Ocean 27°45′N 115°45′W
182 E7 Ceduna South Australia 32°09′S 133°43′E
110 D10 Cedynia Ger. Zehden. Zachodnio-pomorskie, W Poland 52°54′N 14°15′E
80 P12 Ceelaayo Sanaag, N Somalia 11°18′N 49°20′E
81 O16 Ceel Buur It. El Bur. Galguduud, C Somalia 04°36′N 46°33′E
81 N15 Ceel Dheere var. Ceel Dher, It. El Dere. Galguduud, C Somalia 05°18′N 46°07′E
Ceel Dher see Ceel Dheere
80 O12 Ceerigaabo var. Erigabo, Erigavo. Sanaag, N Somalia 10°34′N 47°22′E
107 J23 Cefalù anc. Cephaloedium. Sicilia, Italy, C Mediterranean Sea 38°02′N 14°02′E
105 N6 Cega ↝ Castilla y León, N Spain
111 K23 Cegléd prev. Czegléd. Pest, C Hungary 47°10′N 19°47′E
113 N18 Čegrane W FYR Macedonia 41°50′N 20°59′E
105 Q13 Cehegín Murcia, SE Spain 38°04′N 01°48′W
136 K12 Çekerek Yozgat, N Turkey 40°04′N 35°30′E
146 B13 Çekiçler Rus. Chekishlyar, Turkm. Chekichler. Balkan Welaýaty, W Turkmenistan 37°35′N 53°52′E
107 J15 Celano Abruzzo, C Italy 42°06′N 13°33′E
104 H4 Celanova Galicia, NW Spain 42°09′N 07°58′W
42 F6 Celaque, Cordillera de ▲ W Honduras
41 N13 Celaya Guanajuato, C Mexico 20°32′N 100°48′W
Celebes see Sulawesi
192 F7 Celebes Basin undersea feature SE South China Sea 04°00′N 122°00′E
192 F7 Celebes Sea Ind. Laut Sulawesi. sea Indonesia/ Philippines
41 W12 Celestún Yucatán, E Mexico 20°50′N 90°22′W
31 Q12 Celina Ohio, N USA 40°34′N 84°35′W
20 L8 Celina Tennessee, S USA 36°32′N 85°30′W
25 U5 Celina Texas, SW USA 33°19′N 96°46′W
112 G11 Čelinac Donji Republika Srpska, N Bosnia and Herzegovina 44°43′N 17°19′E
109 V10 Celje Ger. Cilli. C Slovenia 46°16′N 15°14′E
111 G23 Celldömölk Vas, W Hungary 47°16′N 17°10′E
100 J12 Celle var. Zelle. Niedersachsen, N Germany 52°38′N 10°05′E
99 D19 Celles Hainaut, SW Belgium 50°42′N 03°25′E
104 I7 Celorico da Beira Guarda, N Portugal 40°38′N 07°24′W
Celovec see Klagenfurt
64 M7 Celtic Sea Ir. An Mhuir Cheilteach. sea SW British Isles
64 N7 Celtic Shelf undersea feature E Atlantic Ocean 07°00′W 49°15′N
114 L13 Çeltik Gölu ◎ NW Turkey
146 J17 Çemenibit prev. Rus. Chemenibit. Mary Welaýaty, S Turkmenistan 35°27′N 62°19′E
113 M14 Čemerno ▲ C Serbia
105 Q12 Cenajo, Embalse del ⊠ S Spain
171 V13 Cenderawasih, Teluk var. Teluk Irian, Teluk Sarera. bay W Pacific Ocean
105 P4 Cenicero La Rioja, N Spain 42°29′N 02°38′W
106 E9 Ceno ↝ NW Italy
102 K13 Cenon Gironde, SW France 44°51′N 00°33′W
14 K13 Centennial Lake ◎ Ontario, SE Canada
Centennial State see Colorado
37 S7 Center Colorado, C USA 37°45′N 106°06′W
29 Q13 Center Nebraska, C USA 42°33′N 97°51′W
28 M5 Center North Dakota, N USA 47°07′N 101°18′W
25 X8 Center Texas, SW USA 31°49′N 94°10′W
29 W8 Center City Minnesota, N USA 45°25′N 92°48′W
36 L5 Centerfield Utah, W USA 39°07′N 111°49′W
20 K9 Center Hill Lake ⊠ Tennessee, S USA
29 X13 Center Point Iowa, C USA 42°11′N 91°47′W
25 R11 Center Point Texas, SW USA 29°56′N 99°01′W
29 W16 Centerville Iowa, C USA 40°47′N 92°51′W
27 W7 Centerville Missouri, C USA 37°27′N 91°01′W
29 R12 Centerville South Dakota, N USA 43°07′N 96°57′W
20 I9 Centerville Tennessee, S USA 35°45′N 87°29′W
25 V9 Centerville Texas, SW USA 31°17′N 95°59′W
40 M5 Centinela, Picacho del ▲ NE Mexico 29°07′N 102°40′W
106 G9 Cento Emilia-Romagna, N Italy 44°43′N 11°16′E
Centrafricaine, République see Central African Republic
39 S8 Central Alaska, USA 65°34′N 144°48′W
37 P15 Central New Mexico, SW USA 32°46′N 108°09′W
83 H18 Central ◆ district E Botswana
138 E10 Central ◆ district C Israel
81 I19 Central ◆ province C Kenya
82 M13 Central ◆ region C Malawi
153 P12 Central ◆ zone C Nepal
186 E9 Central prev. Central. ◆ province S Papua New Guinea
63 I21 Central ◆ department C Paraguay
155 K25 Central ◆ province C Sri Lanka
83 J14 Central ◆ province C Zambia
117 P11 Central ✕ (Odesa) Odes'ka Oblast', SW Ukraine 46°26′N 30°41′E
Central see Centre
Central see Central
Central see Rennell and Bellona
79 H14 Central African Republic var. République Centrafricaine, abbrev. CAR; prev. Ubangi-Shari, Oubangui-Chari, Territoire de l'Oubangui-Chari. ◆ republic C Africa
192 C6 Central Basin Trough undersea feature W Pacific Ocean 16°45′N 130°00′E
Central Borneo see Kalimantan Tengah
149 P12 Central Brāhui Range ▲ W Pakistan
Central Celebes see Sulawesi Tengah
29 Y13 Central City Iowa, C USA 42°12′N 91°31′W
20 I6 Central City Kentucky, S USA 37°17′N 87°07′W
29 P15 Central City Nebraska, C USA 41°04′N 97°59′W
48 D6 Central, Cordillera ▲ W Bolivia
54 D11 Central, Cordillera ▲ W Colombia
42 M13 Central, Cordillera ▲ C Costa Rica
45 N9 Central, Cordillera ▲ C Dominican Republic
43 R16 Central, Cordillera ▲ C Panama
45 S6 Central, Cordillera ▲ Puerto Rico
42 H7 Central District var. Tegucigalpa. ◆ district C Honduras
81 E16 Central Equatoria var. Bahr el Gebel, Bahr el Jebel. ◆ state S South Sudan
Central Group see Inner Islands
30 L15 Centralia Illinois, N USA 38°31′N 89°07′W
27 U4 Centralia Missouri, C USA 39°12′N 92°08′W
32 G9 Centralia Washington, NW USA 46°43′N 122°57′W
Central Indian Ridge see Mid-Indian Ridge
Central Java see Jawa Tengah
Central Kalimantan see Kalimantan Tengah
148 L14 Central Makrān Range ▲ W Pakistan
192 K7 Central Pacific Basin undersea feature C Pacific Ocean 05°00′N 175°00′W
59 M19 Central, Planalto var. Brazilian Highlands. ▲ E Brazil
32 F15 Central Point Oregon, NW USA 42°22′N 122°55′W
Central Provinces and Berar see Madhya Pradesh
186 B6 Central Range ▲ NW Papua New Guinea
Central Russian Upland see Srednerusskaya Vozvyshennost'
Central Siberian Plateau/ Central Siberian Uplands see Srednesibirskoye Ploskogor'ye
104 K8 Central, Sistema ▲ C Spain
Central Sulawesi see Sulawesi Tengah
35 N3 Central Valley California, W USA 40°39′N 122°21′W
35 P8 Central Valley valley California, W USA
23 Q3 Centre Alabama, S USA 34°09′N 85°40′W
79 E15 Centre Eng. Central. ◆ province C Cameroon
102 M8 Centre ◆ region N France
173 Y16 Centre de Flacq E Mauritius 20°12′S 57°43′E
55 Y9 Centre Spatial Guyanais space station N French Guiana
23 O5 Centreville Alabama, S USA 32°58′N 87°08′W
21 X3 Centreville Maryland, NE USA 39°03′N 76°04′W
22 J7 Centreville Mississippi, S USA 31°05′N 91°04′W
Centum Cellae see Civitavecchia
160 M14 Cenxi Guangxi Zhuangzu Zizhiqu, S China 22°58′N 111°00′E
Ceos see Tziá
Cephaloedium see Cefalù
112 I9 Čepin Hung. Csepén. Osijek-Baranja, E Croatia 45°32′N 18°33′E
Ceram see Seram, Pulau
Ceram Sea see Seram, Laut
192 G8 Ceram Trough undersea feature W Pacific Ocean
Cerasus see Giresun
36 I10 Cerbat Mountains ▲ Arizona, SW USA
103 P17 Cerbère, Cap headland S France 42°28′N 03°15′E
104 F13 Cercal do Alentejo Setúbal, S Portugal 37°48′N 08°40′W
111 A18 Čerchov Ger. Czerkow. ▲ W Czech Republic 49°24′N 12°47′E
103 O13 Cère ↝ C France
Cerede see Sète
61 A16 Ceres Santa Fe, C Argentina 29°55′S 61°55′W
59 K18 Ceres Goiás, C Brazil 15°21′S 49°34′W
Ceresio see Lugano, Lago di
103 O17 Céret Pyrénées-Orientales, S France 42°30′N 02°44′E
54 E6 Cereté Córdoba, NW Colombia 08°54′N 75°51′W
172 I17 Cerf, Île au island Inner Islands, NE Seychelles
99 G22 Cerfontaine Namur, S Belgium 50°08′N 04°25′E
Cergy-Pontoise see Pontoise
107 N16 Cerignola Puglia, SE Italy 41°17′N 15°53′E
Cerigo see Kýthira
103 O9 Cérilly Allier, C France 46°38′N 02°51′E
136 I11 Çerkeş Çankin, N Turkey 40°51′N 32°52′E
136 D10 Çerkezköy Tekirdağ, NW Turkey 41°17′N 28°00′E
109 T12 Cerknica Ger. Zirknitz. SW Slovenia 45°48′N 14°21′E
109 S11 Cerkno W Slovenia 46°07′N 13°58′E
116 F10 Cermei Hung. Csermő. Arad, W Romania 46°33′N 21°51′E
137 O15 Çermik Diyarbakır, SE Turkey 38°09′N 39°27′E
112 I10 Cerna Vukovar-Srijem, E Croatia 45°10′N 18°36′E
Cernăuţi see Chernivtsi
116 M14 Cernavodă Constanţa, SW Romania 44°20′N 28°03′E
103 U7 Cernay Haut-Rhin, NE France 47°49′N 07°11′E
Černice see Schwarzach
41 O8 Cerralvo Nuevo León, NE Mexico 26°10′N 99°40′W
40 G9 Cerralvo, Isla island NW Mexico
107 L16 Cerreto Sannita Campania, S Italy 41°17′N 14°39′E
113 L20 Cërrik var. Cerriku. Elbasan, C Albania 41°01′N 19°55′E
Cerriku see Cërrik
41 O11 Cerritos San Luis Potosí, C Mexico 22°25′N 100°16′W
60 K11 Cerro Azul Paraná, S Brazil 24°48′S 49°14′W
61 F18 Cerro Chato Treinta y Tres, E Uruguay 33°04′S 55°08′W
61 F19 Cerro Colorado Florida, S Uruguay 33°52′S 55°33′W
56 E13 Cerro de Pasco Pasco, C Peru 10°43′S 76°15′W
61 G14 Cerro Largo Rio Grande do Sul, S Brazil 28°10′S 54°43′W
61 G18 Cerro Largo ◆ department NE Uruguay
42 E7 Cerrón Grande, Embalse ⊠ N El Salvador
63 I14 Cerros Colorados, Embalse ◎ W Argentina
105 V5 Cervera Cataluña, NE Spain 41°40′N 01°16′E
104 M3 Cervera del Pisuerga Castilla y León, N Spain 42°51′N 04°30′W
105 Q5 Cervera del Río Alhama La Rioja, N Spain 42°01′N 01°58′W
107 H15 Cerveteri Lazio, C Italy 42°00′N 12°06′E
106 H10 Cervia Emilia-Romagna, N Italy 44°14′N 12°22′E
106 J7 Cervignano del Friuli Friuli-Venezia Giulia, NE Italy 45°49′N 13°18′E
107 L17 Cervinara Campania, S Italy 41°02′N 14°36′E
Cervinia see Breuil-Cervinia
106 B6 Cervino, Monte var. Matterhorn. ▲ Italy/ Switzerland 46°00′N 07°39′E
see also Matterhorn
Cervino, Monte see Matterhorn
103 Y14 Cervione Corse, France, C Mediterranean Sea 42°22′N 09°28′E
104 I1 Cervo Galicia, NW Spain 43°39′N 07°25′W
54 F5 Cesar off. Departamento del Cesar. ◆ province N Colombia
Cesar, Departamento del see Cesar
106 H10 Cesena anc. Caesena. Emilia-Romagna, N Italy 44°09′N 12°14′E
106 I10 Cesenatico Emilia-Romagna, N Italy 44°12′N 12°24′E
118 H8 Cēsis Ger. Wenden. C Latvia 57°19′N 25°17′E
111 D15 Česká Lípa Ger. Böhmisch-Leipa. Liberecký Kraj, N Czech Republic 50°43′N 14°35′E
Česká Republika see Czech Republic
111 F17 Česká Třebová Ger. Böhmisch-Trübau. Pardubický Kraj, C Czech Republic 49°54′N 16°27′E
111 D19 České Budějovice Ger. Budweis. Jihočeský Kraj, S Czech Republic 48°58′N 14°29′E
111 D19 České Velenice Jihočeský Kraj, S Czech Republic 48°49′N 14°57′E
111 E18 Českomoravská Vrchovina var. Českomoravská Vysočina, Eng. Bohemian-Moravian Highlands, Ger. Böhmisch-Mährische Höhe. ▲ S Czech Republic
Českomoravská Vysočina see Českomoravská Vrchovina
111 C19 Český Krumlov var. Böhmisch-Krumau, Ger. Krummau. Jihočeský Kraj, S Czech Republic 48°48′N 14°18′E
Ceský Les see Bohemian Forest
112 F8 Česma ↝ N Croatia
136 A14 Çeşme İzmir, W Turkey 38°19′N 26°20′E
Cess see Cestos
183 T8 Cessnock New South Wales, SE Australia 32°51′S 151°21′E
76 K17 Cestos var. Cess. ↝ S Liberia
118 I9 Cesvaine E Latvia 56°58′N 26°15′E
116 G14 Cetate Dolj, SW Romania 44°06′N 23°01′E
Cetatea Albă see Bilhorod-Dnistrovs'kyy
Cetatea Damboviţei see Bucureşti
113 J17 Cetinje It. Cettigne. S Montenegro 42°23′N 18°55′E
107 N20 Cetraro Calabria, S Italy 39°30′N 15°59′E
Cette see Sète
188 A17 Cetti Bay bay SW Guam
Cettigne see Cetinje
104 L17 Ceuta var. Sebta. Ceuta, Spain, N Africa 35°53′N 05°19′W
88 C16 Ceuta enclave Spain, N Africa
106 B9 Ceva Piemonte, NE Italy 44°24′N 08°01′E
103 P14 Cévennes ▲ S France
108 G10 Cevio Ticino, S Switzerland 46°18′N 08°36′E
136 K16 Ceyhan Adana, S Turkey 37°02′N 35°48′E
136 K17 Ceyhan Nehri ↝ S Turkey
137 P17 Ceylanpınar Şanlıurfa, SE Turkey 36°53′N 40°02′E
Ceylon see Sri Lanka
173 R6 Ceylon Plain undersea feature N Indian Ocean 04°00′S 82°00′E
Ceyre to the Caribs see Marie-Galante
103 Q14 Cèze ↝ S France
Chaacha see Çäçe

◆ Country
● Country Capital
◇ Dependent Territory
○ Dependent Territory Capital
◆ Administrative Regions
✕ International Airport
▲ Mountain
▲ Mountain Range
Volcano
↝ River
◎ Lake
⊠ Reservoir

127 P6 **Chaadayevka** Penzenskaya Oblast', W Russian Federation 53°07´N 45°55´E
167 O12 **Cha-Am** Phetchaburi, SW Thailand 12°48´N 99°58´E
143 W15 **Chābahār** *var.* Chāh Bahār, Chahbar. Sīstān va Balūchestān, SE Iran 25°21´N 60°38´E
Chabaricha *see* Khabarikha
61 B19 **Chabas** Santa Fe, C Argentina 33°16´S 61°23´W
103 T10 **Chablais** *physical region* E France
61 B20 **Chacabuco** Buenos Aires, E Argentina 34°40´S 60°27´W
42 K8 **Chachagón, Cerro** ▲ N Nicaragua 13°18´N 85°39´W
56 C10 **Chachapoyas** Amazonas, NW Peru 06°13´S 77°54´W
Chäche *see* Çäçe
119 O18 **Chachersk** *Rus.* Chechersk. Homyel'skaya Voblasts', SE Belarus 52°54´N 30°54´E
119 N16 **Chachevichy** *Rus.* Chechevichi. Mahilyowskaya Voblasts', E Belarus 53°31´N 29°51´E
61 B14 **Chaco** *off.* Provincia de Chaco. ◈ *province* NE Argentina
Chaco *see* Gran Chaco
62 M6 **Chaco Austral** *physical region* N Argentina
62 M3 **Chaco Boreal** *physical region* N Paraguay
62 M6 **Chaco Central** *physical region* N Argentina
39 Y15 **Chacon, Cape** *headland* Prince of Wales Island, Alaska, USA 54°41´N 132°00´W
Chaco, Provincia de *see* Chaco
78 H9 **Chad** *off.* Republic of Chad, *Fr.* Tchad. ◆ *republic* C Africa
122 K14 **Chadan** Respublika Tyva, S Russian Federation 51°16´N 91°25´E
21 U12 **Chadbourn** North Carolina, SE USA 34°19´N 78°49´W
83 L14 **Chadiza** Eastern, E Zambia 14°04´S 32°27´E
67 Q7 **Chad, Lake** *Fr.* Lac Tchad. ◎ C Africa
Chad, Republic of *see* Chad
28 J12 **Chadron** Nebraska, C USA 42°48´N 102°57´W
Chadyr-Lunga *see* Ciadîr-Lunga
163 W14 **Chaeryŏng** SW North Korea 38°22´N 125°35´E
105 P17 **Chafarinas, Islas** *island group* S Spain
27 Y7 **Chaffee** Missouri, C USA 37°10´N 89°39´W
148 L12 **Chāgai Hills** *var.* Chāh Gay. ▲▲ Afghanistan/Pakistan
123 Q11 **Chagda** Respublika Sakha (Yakutiya), NE Russian Federation 58°43´N 130°38´E
Chaghasarāy *see* Asadābād
149 N5 **Chaghcharān** *var.* Chakhcharan, Cheghcheran, Qala Āhangarān. Gōwr, C Afghanistan 34°28´N 65°18´E
103 R9 **Chagny** Saône-et-Loire, C France 46°54´N 04°45´E
173 Q7 **Chagos Archipelago** *var.* Oil Islands. *island group* British Indian Ocean Territory
129 O15 **Chagos Bank** *undersea feature* C Indian Ocean 06°15´S 72°00´E
129 O14 **Chagos-Laccadive Plateau** *undersea feature* N Indian Ocean 03°00´S 73°00´E
173 Q7 **Chagos Trench** *undersea feature* N Indian Ocean 07°00´S 73°30´E
43 T14 **Chagres, Río** ≈ C Panama
45 U14 **Chaguanas** Trinidad, Trinidad and Tobago 10°31´N 61°25´W
54 M6 **Chaguaramas** Guárico, N Venezuela 09°23´N 66°18´W
Chagyl *see* Çagyl
Chahār Maḩāll and Bakhtiyāri *see* Chahār Maḩāl va Bakhtīārī
Chahār Maḩall va Bakhtīārī, Ostān-e *see* Chahār Maḩāl va Bakhtīārī
142 M9 **Chahār Maḩāl va Bakhtīārī** *off.* Ostān-e Chahār Maḩall va Bakhtīārī, *var.* Chahār Maḩāll and Bakhtiyāri. ◈ *province* SW Iran
Chāh Bahār/Chahbar *see* Chābahār
143 V13 **Chāh Derāz** Sīstān va Balūchestān, SE Iran 27°07´N 60°01´E
Chāh Gay *see* Chāgai Hills
167 P10 **Chai Badan** Lop Buri, C Thailand 15°08´N 101°03´E
153 Q16 **Chāībāsa** Jhārkhand, N India 22°31´N 85°50´E
79 E19 **Chaillu, Massif du** ▲▲ C Gabon
167 O10 **Chai Nat** *var.* Chainat, Jainat, Jayanath. Chai Nat, C Thailand 15°10´N 100°10´E
Chainat *see* Chai Nat
65 M14 **Chain Fracture Zone** *tectonic feature* E Atlantic Ocean
173 N5 **Chain Ridge** *undersea feature* W Indian Ocean 06°00´N 54°00´E
Chairn, Ceann an *see* Carnsore Point
158 L5 **Chaiwopu** Xinjiang Uygur Zizhiqu, W China 43°32´N 87°55´E
167 Q10 **Chaiyaphum** *var.* Jayabum. Chaiyaphum, C Thailand 15°46´N 101°55´E
62 N10 **Chajarí** Entre Ríos, E Argentina 30°45´S 57°57´W
42 C5 **Chajul** Quiché, W Guatemala 15°28´N 91°02´W
83 K16 **Chakari** Mashonaland West, N Zimbabwe 18°05´S 29°51´E
148 J9 **Chakhānsūr** Nīmrōz, SW Afghanistan 31°11´N 62°06´E
Chakhānsūr *see* Nīmrōz
Chakhcharan *see* Chaghcharān
149 V8 **Chak Jhumra** *var.* Jhumra. Punjab, E Pakistan 31°33´N 73°14´E
146 I16 **Chaknakdysonga** Ahal Welaýaty, S Turkmenistan 35°39´N 61°24´E
153 P16 **Chakradharpur** Jhāarkhand, N India 22°42´N 85°38´E
152 J8 **Chakrāta** Uttarakhand, N India 30°42´N 77°52´E
149 U7 **Chakwāl** Punjab, NE Pakistan 32°56´N 72°53´E
57 F17 **Chala** Arequipa, SW Peru 15°52´S 74°13´W
102 K12 **Chalais** Charente, W France 45°16´N 00°02´E
108 D10 **Chalais** Valais, SW Switzerland 46°18´N 07°37´E
115 J20 **Chalándri** *var.* Halandri; *prev.* Khalándrion. *prehistoric site* Sýros, Kykládes, Greece, Aegean Sea
188 H6 **Chalan Kanoa** Saipan, S Northern Mariana Islands 15°08´S 145°43´E
188 C16 **Chalan Pago** C Guam
Chalap Dalam/Chalap Dalan *see* Chehel Abdālān, Kūh-e
42 F7 **Chalatenango** Chalatenango, N El Salvador 14°04´N 88°53´W
42 A9 **Chalatenango** ◈ *department* NW El Salvador
83 P15 **Chalaua** Nampula, NE Mozambique 16°04´S 39°08´E
81 I16 **Chalbi Desert** *desert* N Kenya
42 D7 **Chalchuapa** Santa Ana, W El Salvador 13°59´N 89°41´W
Chalcidice *see* Chalkidikí
Chalcis *see* Chalkída
Chālderān *see* Sīāh Chashmeh
103 N6 **Châlette-sur-Loing** Loiret, C France 48°01´N 02°45´E
15 X8 **Chaleur Bay** *Fr.* Baie des Chaleurs. *bay* New Brunswick/Québec, E Canada
Chaleurs, Baie des *see* Chaleur Bay
57 G16 **Chalhuanca** Apurímac, S Peru 14°17´S 73°15´W
154 F12 **Chālisgaon** Mahārāshtra, C India 20°29´N 75°10´E
115 N23 **Chálki** *island* Dodekánisa, Greece, Aegean Sea
115 F16 **Chalkiádes** Thessalía, C Greece 39°24´N 22°25´E
115 H18 **Chalkída** *var.* Halkida, *prev.* Khalkís; *anc.* Chalcis. Evvoia, E Greece 38°27´N 23°38´E
115 G14 **Chalkidikí** *var.* Khalkidhikí; *anc.* Chalcidice. *peninsula* NE Greece
185 A24 **Chalky Inlet** *inlet* South Island, New Zealand
39 S7 **Chalkyitsik** Alaska, USA 66°39´N 143°43´W
102 I9 **Challans** Vendée, NW France 46°51´N 01°52´W
57 K19 **Challapata** Oruro, SW Bolivia 18°50´S 66°45´W
192 H6 **Challenger Deep** *undersea feature* W Pacific Ocean 11°20´N 142°12´E
Challenger Deep *see* Mariana Trench
193 S11 **Challenger Fracture Zone** *tectonic feature* SE Pacific Ocean
192 K11 **Challenger Plateau** *undersea feature* E Tasman Sea
33 P13 **Challis** Idaho, NW USA 44°31´N 114°14´W
22 L9 **Chalmette** Louisiana, S USA 29°56´N 89°57´W
124 J11 **Chalna** Respublika Kareliya, NW Russian Federation 61°53´N 33°59´E
103 Q5 **Châlons-en-Champagne** *prev.* Châlons-sur-Marne, *hist.* Arcae Remorum; *anc.* Carolopois. Marne, NE France 48°58´N 04°22´E
Châlons-sur-Marne *see* Châlons-en-Champagne
103 R9 **Chalon-sur-Saône** *anc.* Cabillonum. Saône-et-Loire, C France 46°47´N 04°51´E
Chaltel, Cerro *see* Fitzroy, Monte
102 M11 **Châlus** Haute-Vienne, C France 45°38´N 01°00´E
143 N4 **Chālūs** Māzandarān, N Iran 36°40´N 51°25´E
101 N20 **Cham** Bayern, SE Germany 49°13´N 12°40´E
108 F7 **Cham** Zug, N Switzerland 47°11´N 08°28´E
37 R8 **Chama** New Mexico, SW USA 36°54´N 106°34´W
Cha Mai *see* Thung Song
83 E22 **Chamaites** Karas, S Namibia 27°15´S 17°52´E
149 O9 **Chaman** Baluchistān, SW Pakistan 30°55´N 66°27´E
37 R9 **Chama, Rio** ≈ New Mexico, SW USA
152 I6 **Chamba** Himāchal Pradesh, N India 32°33´N 76°10´E
81 I25 **Chamba** Ruvuma, S Tanzania 11°33´S 37°01´E
150 H12 **Chambal** ≈ C India
11 U16 **Chamberlain** Saskatchewan, S Canada 50°49´N 105°29´W
29 O11 **Chamberlain** South Dakota, N USA 43°48´N 99°19´W
19 R3 **Chamberlain Lake** ◎ Maine, NE USA
39 S5 **Chamberlin, Mount** ▲ Alaska, USA 69°16´N 144°54´W
37 O11 **Chambers** Arizona, SW USA 35°11´N 109°25´W
18 F16 **Chambersburg** Pennsylvania, NE USA 39°54´N 77°39´W
31 N5 **Chambers Island** *island* Wisconsin, N USA
103 T11 **Chambéry** *anc.* Camberia. Savoie, E France 45°34´N 05°56´E
82 L12 **Chambeshi** Northern, NE Zambia 10°55´S 31°07´E
82 L12 **Chambeshi** ≈ NE Zambia
74 M6 **Chambi, Jebel** *var.* Jabal ash Sha'nabī. ▲ W Tunisia 35°16´N 08°39´E
15 Q7 **Chambord** Québec, SE Canada 48°25´N 72°02´W
139 U11 **Chamcham** Al Muthanná, S Iraq 31°17´N 45°05´E
139 T4 **Chamchamāḽ** At Ta'mím, N Iraq 35°32´N 44°50´E
Chamdmanī *see* Altanshiree
40 J14 **Chamela** Jalisco, SW Mexico 19°31´N 105°02´W
42 G5 **Chamelecón, Río** ≈ NW Honduras
62 J9 **Chamical** La Rioja, C Argentina 30°21´S 66°19´W
115 L23 **Chamilí** *island* Kykládes, Greece, Aegean Sea
167 Q13 **Châmnar** Kaôh Kông, SW Cambodia 11°45´N 103°32´E
152 K9 **Chamoli** Uttarakhand, N India 30°22´N 79°19´E
103 U11 **Chamonix-Mont-Blanc** Haute-Savoie, E France 45°55´N 06°52´E
154 L11 **Chāmpa** Chhattīsgarh, C India 22°02´N 82°42´E
10 H8 **Champagne** Yukon Territory, W Canada 60°48´N 136°22´W
103 Q5 **Champagne** *cultural region* N France
Champagne *see* Campania
103 Q5 **Champagne-Ardenne** ◈ *region* N France
103 S9 **Champagnole** Jura, E France 46°44´N 05°55´E
30 M13 **Champaign** Illinois, N USA 40°07´N 88°15´W
167 S10 **Champasak** Champasak, S Laos 14°50´N 105°51´E
103 U6 **Champ de Feu** ▲ NE France 48°24´N 07°15´E
13 O7 **Champdoré, Lac** ◎ Québec, NE Canada
42 B6 **Champerico** Retalhuleu, SW Guatemala 14°18´N 91°54´W
108 C11 **Champéry** Valais, SW Switzerland 46°12´N 06°52´E
18 L6 **Champlain** New York, NE USA 44°58´N 73°25´W
18 L9 **Champlain Canal** *canal* New York, NE USA
15 P13 **Champlain, Lac** ◎ Québec, Canada/USA *see also* Champlain, Lake
18 L7 **Champlain, Lake** ◎ Canada/USA *see also* Champlain, Lac
103 S7 **Champlitte** Haute-Saône, E France 47°36´N 05°31´E
41 W13 **Champotón** Campeche, SE Mexico 19°18´N 90°43´W
104 G10 **Chamusca** Santarém, C Portugal 39°21´N 08°29´W
119 O20 **Chamyarysy** *Rus.* Chemerisy. Homyel'skaya Voblasts', SE Belarus 51°42´N 30°27´E
127 P5 **Chamzinka** Respublika Mordoviya, W Russian Federation 54°22´N 45°22´E
Chanáil Mhór, An *see* Grand Canal
Chanak *see* Çanakkale
62 G7 **Chañaral** Atacama, N Chile 26°19´S 70°34´W
104 H13 **Chança, Rio** *var.* Chanza. ≈ Portugal/Spain
57 D14 **Chancay** Lima, W Peru 11°36´S 77°14´W
Chan-chiang/Chanchiang *see* Zhanjiang
62 G13 **Chanco** Maule, C Chile 35°43´S 72°35´W
39 R7 **Chandalar** Alaska, USA 67°30´N 148°29´W
39 R6 **Chandalar River** ≈ Alaska, USA
152 L10 **Chandan Chauki** Uttar Pradesh, N India 28°32´N 80°43´E
153 S16 **Chandannagar** *prev.* Chandernagore. West Bengal, E India 22°52´N 88°21´E
152 K10 **Chandausi** Uttar Pradesh, N India 28°27´N 78°43´E
22 M10 **Chandeleur Islands** *island group* Louisiana, S USA
22 M9 **Chandeleur Sound** *sound* N Gulf of Mexico
Chandernagore *see* Chandannagar
152 I8 **Chandīgarh** *state capital* Punjab, N India 30°41´N 76°51´E
153 Q16 **Chāndil** Jhārkhand, NE India 22°58´N 86°04´E
182 D2 **Chandler** South Australia 26°59´S 133°22´E
15 Y7 **Chandler** Québec, SE Canada 48°21´N 64°41´W
36 L14 **Chandler** Arizona, SW USA 33°18´N 111°50´W
27 O10 **Chandler** Oklahoma, C USA 35°43´N 96°54´W
25 V7 **Chandler** Texas, SW USA 32°18´N 95°28´W
39 Q6 **Chandler River** ≈ Alaska, USA
56 H13 **Chandles, Río** ≈ E Peru
162 H9 **Chandmanĭ** *var.* Talshand. Govĭ-Altayĭ, C Mongolia 45°21´N 98°00´E
162 E7 **Chandmanĭ** *var.* Urdgol. Hovd, W Mongolia 47°39´N 92°46´E
14 J13 **Chandos Lake** ◎ Ontario, SE Canada
153 U15 **Chandpur** Chittagong, C Bangladesh 23°13´N 90°43´E
154 I13 **Chandrapur** Mahārāshtra, C India 19°58´N 79°21´E
83 J15 **Changa** Southern, S Zambia 16°24´S 28°27´E
Chang'an *see* Rong'an, Guangxi Zhuangzu Zizhiqu, S China
Changan *see* Xi'an, Shaanxi, C China
155 G23 **Changanācheri** *var.* Changannassery. Kerala, SW India 09°26´N 76°31´E *see also* Changannassery
83 M19 **Changane** ≈ S Mozambique
83 M16 **Changara** Tete, NW Mozambique 16°54´S 33°15´E
163 X11 **Changbai** *var.* Changbai Chaoxianzu Zizhixian. Jilin, NE China 41°25´N 128°08´E
Changbai Chaoxianzu Zizhixian *see* Changbai
163 X11 **Changbai Shan** ▲▲ NE China
163 V10 **Changchun** *var.* Ch'angch'un, Ch'ang-ch'un; *prev.* Hsinking. *province capital* Jilin, NE China 43°53´N 125°18´E
Ch'angch'un/Ch'ang-ch'un *see* Changchun
160 M10 **Changde** Hunan, S China 29°04´N 111°42´E
Changhua *see* Zhanghua
168 L10 **Changi** ✈ (Singapore) E Singapore 01°22´N 103°58´E
158 L5 **Changji** Xinjiang Uygur Zizhiqu, NW China 44°02´N 87°12´E
160 L17 **Changjiang** *var.* Changjiang Lizu Zizhixian, Shiliu. Hainan, S China 19°16´N 109°09´E
157 R11 **Chang Jiang** *var.* Yangtze Kiang, *Eng.* Yangtze. ≈ C China
157 N12 **Chang Jiang** *Eng.* Yangtze. ≈ SW China
161 S8 **Changjiang Kou** *delta* E China
Changjiang Lizu Zizhixian *see* Changjiang
Changkiakow *see* Zhangjiakou
167 F12 **Chang, Ko** *island* S Thailand
161 Q2 **Changli** Hebei, E China 39°44´N 119°13´E
163 V10 **Changling** Jilin, NE China 44°15´N 124°03´E
Changning *see* Xunwu
161 N11 **Changsha** *var.* Ch'angsha, Ch'ang-sha. *province capital* Hunan, S China 28°10´N 113°E
Ch'angsha/Ch'ang-sha *see* Changsha
161 Q10 **Changshan** Zhejiang, SE China 28°54´N 118°30´E
163 V14 **Changshan Qundao** *island group* NE China
161 S8 **Changshu** *var.* Ch'ang-shu. Jiangsu, E China 31°39´N 120°45´E
Ch'ang-shu *see* Changshu
163 V11 **Changtu** Liaoning, NE China 42°50´N 123°59´E
43 P14 **Changuinola** Bocas del Toro, NW Panama 09°28´N 82°31´W
159 N9 **Changweiliang** Qinghai, W China 38°24´N 92°08´E
160 K6 **Changwu** *var.* Zhaoren. Shaanxi, C China 35°12´N 107°46´E
163 U13 **Changxing Dao** *island* N China
160 M9 **Changyang** *var.* Longzhouping. Hubei, C China 30°45´N 111°13´E
163 W14 **Changyŏn** SW North Korea 38°19´N 125°15´E
161 N5 **Changzhi** Shanxi, C China 36°10´N 113°02´E
161 R8 **Changzhou** Jiangsu, E China 31°45´N 119°58´E
115 H24 **Chaniá** *var.* Hania, Khaniá, *Eng.* Canea; *anc.* Cydonia. Kríti, Greece, E Mediterranean Sea 35°31´N 24°00´E
62 J5 **Chañi, Nevado de** ▲ NW Argentina 24°09´S 65°44´W
115 H24 **Chanión, Kólpos** *gulf* Kríti, Greece, E Mediterranean Sea
Chankiri *see* Çankırı
30 M11 **Channahon** Illinois, N USA 41°25´N 88°13´W
155 H20 **Channapatna** Karnātaka, E India 12°43´N 77°14´E
97 K26 **Channel Islands** *Fr.* Iles Normandes. *island group* S English Channel
35 R16 **Channel Islands** *island group* California, W USA
13 S13 **Channel-Port aux Basques** Newfoundland and Labrador, SE Canada 47°35´N 59°02´W
Channel, The *see* English Channel
97 Q23 **Channel Tunnel** *tunnel* France/United Kingdom
24 M2 **Channing** Texas, SW USA 35°41´N 102°21´W
Chantabun/Chantaburi *see* Chanthaburi
104 H3 **Chantada** Galicia, NW Spain 42°36´N 07°46´W
167 P12 **Chanthaburi** *var.* Chantabun, Chantaburi. Chantaburi, S Thailand 12°35´N 102°08´E
103 O4 **Chantilly** Oise, N France 49°12´N 02°28´E
139 V12 **Chanūn as Sa'ūdī** Dhī Qār, S Iraq 31°04´N 46°00´E
27 Q6 **Chanute** Kansas, C USA 37°40´N 95°27´W
Chanza *see* Chança, Rio
Ch'ao-an/Chaochow *see* Chaozhou
161 P8 **Chao Hu** ◎ E China
167 P11 **Chao Phraya, Mae Nam** ≈ C Thailand
163 T8 **Chaor He** *prev.* Qulin Gol. ≈ NE China
Chaouèn *see* Chefchaouen
161 P14 **Chaoyang** Guangdong, S China 23°17´N 116°33´E
163 T12 **Chaoyang** Liaoning, NE China 41°34´N 120°29´E
Chaoyang *see* Jiayin, Heilongjiang, China
Chaoyang *see* Huinan, Jilin China
161 Q14 **Chaozhou** *var.* Chaoan, Chao'an, Ch'ao-an; *prev.* Chaochow. Guangdong, SE China 23°42´N 116°36´E
58 N13 **Chapadinha** Maranhão, E Brazil 03°45´S 43°23´W
12 K12 **Chapais** Québec, SE Canada 49°47´N 74°54´W
40 L13 **Chapala** Jalisco, SW Mexico 20°20´N 103°10´W
40 L13 **Chapala, Lago de** ◎ C Mexico
146 F13 **Chapan, Gora** ▲ C Turkmenistan 37°48´N 58°03´E
57 M18 **Chapare, Río** ≈ C Bolivia
54 E11 **Chaparral** Tolima, C Colombia 03°45´N 75°30´W
144 F9 **Chapayev** Zapadnyy Kazakhstan, NW Kazakhstan 50°12´N 51°09´E
123 O11 **Chapayevo** Respublika Sakha (Yakutiya), NE Russian Federation 60°03´N 117°19´E
127 R6 **Chapayevsk** Samarskaya Oblast', W Russian Federation 52°57´N 49°42´E
60 H13 **Chapecó** Santa Catarina, S Brazil 27°14´S 52°41´W
60 I13 **Chapecó, Rio** ≈ S Brazil
20 J9 **Chapel Hill** Tennessee, S USA 35°38´N 86°40´W
44 J12 **Chapelton** C Jamaica 18°05´N 77°16´W
14 C8 **Chapleau** Ontario, SE Canada 47°50´N 83°24´W
14 D7 **Chapleau** ≈ Ontario, S Canada
11 T16 **Chaplin** Saskatchewan, S Canada 50°27´N 106°37´W
126 M6 **Chaplygin** Lipetskaya Oblast', W Russian Federation 53°13´N 39°58´E
117 S11 **Chaplynka** Khersons'ka Oblast', S Ukraine 46°20´N 33°34´E
9 O6 **Chapman, Cape** *headland* Nunavut, NE Canada 69°15´N 89°09´W
25 T15 **Chapman Ranch** Texas, SW USA 27°32´N 97°25´W
Chapman's *see* Okwa
21 P5 **Chapmanville** West Virginia, NE USA 37°58´N 82°01´W
28 K15 **Chappell** Nebraska, C USA 41°05´N 102°28´W
Chapra *see* Chhapra
56 D9 **Chapuli, Río** ≈ N Peru
76 I6 **Châr** *well* N Mauritania
123 P12 **Chara** Zabaykal'skiy Kray, S Russian Federation 56°57´N 118°05´E
123 O11 **Chara** ≈ C Russian Federation
54 G8 **Charala** Santander, C Colombia 06°17´N 73°09´W
41 N10 **Charcas** San Luis Potosí, C Mexico 23°09´N 101°10´W
25 T13 **Charco** Texas, SW USA 28°42´N 97°35´E
194 H7 **Charcot Island** *island* Antarctica
64 M8 **Charcot Seamounts** *undersea feature* E Atlantic Ocean 11°30´W 45°00´N
Chardara *see* Shardara
Chardarinskoye Vodokhranilishche *see* Shardarinskoye Vodokhranilishche
31 U11 **Chardon** Ohio, N USA 41°34´N 81°12´W
44 K9 **Chardonnières** SW Haiti 18°16´N 74°10´W
Chardzhev *see* Türkmenabat
Chardzhevskaya Oblast *see* Lebap Welaýaty
Chardzhou/Chardzhui *see* Türkmenabat
102 L11 **Charente** ◈ *department* W France
102 J11 **Charente** ≈ W France
102 J10 **Charente-Maritime** ◈ *department* W France
137 U12 **Ch'arents'avan** C Armenia 40°23´N 44°41´E
78 I12 **Chari** *var.* Shari. ≈ Central African Republic/Chad
78 G11 **Chari-Baguirmi** *off.* Préfecture du Chari-Baguirmi. ◈ *prefecture* SW Chad
Chari-Baguirmi, Préfecture du *see* Chari-Baguirmi
149 Q4 **Chārīkār** Parwān, NE Afghanistan 35°01´N 69°11´E
29 V15 **Chariton** Iowa, C USA 41°00´N 93°18´W
27 U3 **Chariton River** ≈ Missouri, C USA
55 T7 **Charity** NW Guyana 07°22´N 58°34´W
31 R7 **Charity Island** *island* Michigan, N USA
Chärjew *see* Türkmenabat
Chärjew Oblasty *see* Lebap Welaýaty
Charkhlik/Charkhliq *see* Ruoqiang
99 G20 **Charleroi** Hainaut, S Belgium 50°25´N 04°27´E
11 V12 **Charles** Manitoba, C Canada 55°27´N 100°58´W
15 R10 **Charlesbourg** Québec, SE Canada 46°50´N 71°15´W
21 Y7 **Charles, Cape** *headland* Virginia, NE USA 37°09´N 75°57´W
29 W12 **Charles City** Iowa, C USA 43°04´N 92°40´W
21 W6 **Charles City** Virginia, NE USA 37°21´N 77°05´W
103 O5 **Charles de Gaulle** ✈ (Paris) Seine-et-Marne, N France 49°04´N 02°36´E
12 K1 **Charles Island** *island* Nunavut, NE Canada
Charles Island *see* Santa María, Isla
30 K9 **Charles Mound** *hill* Illinois, N USA
185 A22 **Charles Sound** *sound* South Island, New Zealand
185 G15 **Charleston** West Coast, South Island, New Zealand 41°54´S 171°25´E
27 S11 **Charleston** Arkansas, C USA 35°19´N 94°02´W
30 M14 **Charleston** Illinois, N USA 39°30´N 88°10´W
22 L3 **Charleston** Mississippi, S USA 34°00´N 90°03´W
27 Z7 **Charleston** Missouri, C USA 36°54´N 89°22´W
21 T15 **Charleston** South Carolina, SE USA 32°48´N 79°57´W
21 Q5 **Charleston** *state capital* West Virginia, NE USA 38°21´N 81°38´W
14 L14 **Charleston Lake** ◎ Ontario, SE Canada
35 W11 **Charleston Peak** ▲ Nevada, W USA 36°16´N 115°40´W
45 W10 **Charlestown** Nevis, Saint Kitts and Nevis 17°08´N 62°37´W
31 P16 **Charlestown** Indiana, N USA 38°27´N 85°40´W
18 M9 **Charlestown** New Hampshire, NE USA 43°14´N 72°23´W
21 V3 **Charles Town** West Virginia, NE USA 39°18´N 77°54´W
181 W9 **Charleville** Queensland, E Australia 26°25´S 146°18´E
103 R3 **Charleville-Mézières** Ardennes, N France 49°45´N 04°43´E
31 P5 **Charlevoix** Michigan, N USA 45°19´N 85°15´W
31 Q6 **Charlevoix, Lake** ◎ Michigan, N USA
39 T9 **Charley River** ≈ Alaska, USA
64 J6 **Charlie-Gibbs Fracture Zone** *tectonic feature* N Atlantic Ocean
103 Q10 **Charlieu** Loire, E France 46°11´N 04°10´E
31 Q9 **Charlotte** Michigan, N USA 42°33´N 84°50´W
21 R10 **Charlotte** North Carolina, SE USA 35°14´N 80°51´W
20 I8 **Charlotte** Tennessee, S USA 36°11´N 87°18´W
25 R13 **Charlotte** Texas, SW USA 28°51´N 98°42´W
21 R10 **Charlotte** ✈ North Carolina, SE USA 35°12´N 80°54´W
45 T9 **Charlotte Amalie** *prev.* Saint Thomas. ○ (Virgin Islands (US)) Saint Thomas, N Virgin Islands (US) 18°22´N 64°56´W
21 U7 **Charlotte Court House** Virginia, NE USA 37°04´N 78°37´W
23 W14 **Charlotte Harbor** *inlet* Florida, SE USA
Charlotte Island *see* Abaiang
95 J15 **Charlottenberg** Värmland, C Sweden 59°53´N 12°17´E
Charlottenhof *see* Aegviidu
21 U5 **Charlottesville** Virginia, NE USA 38°02´N 78°29´W
13 Q14 **Charlottetown** *province capital* Prince Edward Island, Prince Edward Island, SE Canada 46°14´N 63°09´W
Charlotte Town *see* Roseau, Dominica
Charlotte Town *see* Gouyave, Grenada
45 Z16 **Charlotteville** Tobago, Trinidad and Tobago 11°16´N 60°33´W
182 M11 **Charlton** Victoria, SE Australia 36°18´S 143°19´E
12 H10 **Charlton Island** *island* Northwest Territories, C Canada
103 T6 **Charmes** Vosges, NE France 48°19´N 06°19´E
119 F19 **Charnawchytsy** *Rus.* Chernavchitsy. Brestskaya Voblasts', SW Belarus 52°13´N 23°44´E
15 R10 **Charny** Québec, SE Canada 46°43´N 71°15´W
149 T5 **Chārsadda** Khyber Pakhtunkhwa, NW Pakistan 34°12´N 71°46´E
Charshanga/ Charshangngy/ Charshangy *see* Köýtendag
Charsk *see* Shar
181 W6 **Charters Towers** Queensland, NE Australia 20°02´S 146°20´E
15 R12 **Chartierville** Québec, SE Canada 45°19´N 71°13´W
102 M6 **Chartres** *anc.* Autricum, Civitas Carnutum. Eure-et-Loir, C France 48°27´N 01°27´E
Charyn *see* Sharyn
Charyn *see* Sharyn
61 D21 **Chascomús** Buenos Aires, E Argentina 35°34´S 58°01´W
11 N16 **Chase** British Columbia, SW Canada 50°49´N 119°41´W
21 U7 **Chase City** Virginia, NE USA 36°48´N 78°27´W
19 S4 **Chase, Mount** ▲ Maine, NE USA 46°06´N 68°30´W
118 M13 **Chashniki** Vitsyebskaya Voblasts', N Belarus 54°52´N 29°10´E
115 D15 **Chásia** ▲▲ C Greece
29 V9 **Chaska** Minnesota, N USA 44°47´N 93°36´W
185 D25 **Chaslands Mistake** *headland* South Island, New Zealand 46°37´S 169°21´E
125 R11 **Chasovo** Respublika Komi, NW Russian Federation 61°58´N 50°34´E
Chasovo *see* Vazhgort
124 H14 **Chastova** Novgorodskaya Oblast', NW Russian Federation 58°37´N 32°05´E
143 R3 **Chāt** Golestān, N Iran 37°52´N 55°27´E
Chatak *see* Chhatak
Chatang *see* Zhanang
39 R9 **Chatanika** Alaska, USA 65°06´N 147°28´W
39 R9 **Chatanika River** ≈ Alaska, USA
147 T8 **Chat-Bazar** Talasskaya Oblast', NW Kyrgyzstan 42°29´N 72°37´E
45 Y14 **Chateaubelair** Saint Vincent, W Saint Vincent and the Grenadines 13°15´N 61°05´W
102 J7 **Châteaubriant** Loire-Atlantique, NW France 47°43´N 01°22´W
103 Q8 **Château-Chinon** Nièvre, C France 47°04´N 03°50´E
108 C10 **Château d'Oex** Vaud, W Switzerland 46°28´N 07°09´E
102 L7 **Château-du-Loir** Sarthe, NW France 47°40´N 00°25´E
102 M6 **Châteaudun** Eure-et-Loir, C France 48°04´N 01°20´E
102 K7 **Château-Gontier** Mayenne, NW France 47°49´N 00°42´W
15 O13 **Châteauguay** Québec, SE Canada 45°22´N 73°44´W
102 F6 **Châteaulin** Finistère, NW France 48°12´N 04°07´W
103 N9 **Châteaumeillant** Cher, C France 46°33´N 02°10´E
102 K11 **Châteauneuf-sur-Charente** Charente, W France 45°34´N 00°33´W
102 M7 **Château-Renault** Indre-et-Loire, C France 47°34´N 00°52´E
103 N9 **Châteauroux** *prev.* Indreville. Indre, C France 46°50´N 01°43´E
103 T5 **Château-Salins** Moselle, NE France 48°50´N 06°29´E
103 P4 **Château-Thierry** Aisne, N France 49°03´N 03°24´E
99 H21 **Châtelet** Hainaut, S Belgium 50°24´N 04°32´E
Châtelherault *see* Châtellerault
102 L9 **Châtellerault** *var.* Châtelherault. Vienne, W France 46°49´N 00°33´E
29 X10 **Chatfield** Minnesota, N USA 43°51´N 92°11´W
13 O14 **Chatham** New Brunswick, SE Canada 47°02´N 65°30´W
14 D17 **Chatham** Ontario, S Canada 42°24´N 82°11´W
97 P22 **Chatham** SE England, United Kingdom 51°23´N 00°31´E
30 K14 **Chatham** Illinois, N USA 39°40´N 89°42´W
21 T7 **Chatham** Virginia, NE USA 36°49´N 79°26´W
63 F22 **Chatham, Isla** *island* S Chile
175 R12 **Chatham Island** *island* Chatham Islands, New Zealand
Chatham Island *see* San Cristóbal, Isla
Chatham Island Rise *see* Chatham Rise
175 R12 **Chatham Islands** *island group* New Zealand, SW Pacific Ocean
175 Q12 **Chatham Rise** *var.* Chatham Island Rise. *undersea feature* S Pacific Ocean
39 X13 **Chatham Strait** *strait* Alaska, USA
Chathóir, Rinn *see* Cahore Point
102 M9 **Châtillon-sur-Indre** Indre, C France 46°58´N 01°10´E
103 Q7 **Châtillon-sur-Seine** Côte d'Or, C France 47°51´N 04°30´E
147 S8 **Chatkal** *Uzb.* Chotqol. ≈ Kyrgyzstan/Uzbekistan
147 R9 **Chatkal Range** *Rus.* Chatkal'skiy Khrebet. ▲▲ Kyrgyzstan/Uzbekistan
Chatkal'skiy Khrebet *see* Chatkal Range
23 N7 **Chatom** Alabama, S USA 31°28´N 88°15´W
Chatrapur *see* Chhatrapur
143 S10 **Chatrūd** Kermān, C Iran 30°39´N 56°57´E
23 S2 **Chatsworth** Georgia, SE USA 34°46´N 84°46´W
Chāttagām *see* Chittagong
23 S8 **Chattahoochee** Florida, SE USA 30°40´N 84°51´W
23 R8 **Chattahoochee River** ≈ SE USA
20 L10 **Chattanooga** Tennessee, S USA 35°05´N 85°16´W
147 V10 **Chatyr-Kël', Ozero** ◎ C Kyrgyzstan
147 W9 **Chatyr-Tash** Narynskaya Oblast', C Kyrgyzstan 40°54´N 76°22´E
15 R12 **Chaudière** ≈ Québec, SE Canada
167 S14 **Châu Đốc** *var.* Chauphu, Chau Phu. An Giang, S Vietnam 10°53´N 105°07´E
152 D13 **Chauhtan** *prev.* Chohtan. Rājasthān, NW India 25°27´N 71°08´E
166 L5 **Chauk** Magway, W Burma (Myanmar) 20°52´N 94°50´E
103 R6 **Chaumont** *prev.* Chaumont-en-Bassigny. Haute-Marne, N France 48°07´N 05°08´E
Chaumont-en-Bassigny *see* Chaumont
123 T5 **Chaunskaya Guba** *bay* NE Russian Federation
103 P3 **Chauny** Aisne, N France 49°37´N 03°13´E
167 U10 **Châu Ô** *var.* Binh Sơn. Quang Ngai, C Vietnam 15°18´N 108°45´E
Chau Phu *see* Châu Đốc
102 I5 **Chausey, Îles** *island group* N France
Chausy *see* Chavusy
18 C11 **Chautauqua Lake** ◎ New York, NE USA
ChâuThanh *see* Ba Ria
102 L9 **Chauvigny** Vienne, W France 46°35´N 00°37´E
124 L6 **Chavan'ga** Murmanskaya Oblast', NW Russian Federation 66°07´N 37°44´E
14 K10 **Chavannes, Lac** ◎ Québec, SE Canada
Chavantes, Represa de *see* Xavantes, Represa de
61 D15 **Chavarría** Corrientes, NE Argentina 28°57´S 58°35´W
Chavash Respubliki *see* Chuvashskaya Respublika
104 I5 **Chaves** *anc.* Aquae Flaviae. Vila Real, N Portugal 41°44´N 07°28´W
Chávez, Isla *see* Santa Cruz, Isla
82 G13 **Chavuma** North Western, NW Zambia 13°04´S 22°43´E
119 O16 **Chavusy** *Rus.* Chausy. Mahilyowskaya Voblasts', E Belarus 53°48´N 30°58´E
Chayan *see* Shayan
147 U8 **Chayek** Narynskaya Oblast', C Kyrgyzstan 41°54´N 74°28´E
139 T6 **Chāy Khānah** Diyālá, E Iraq 34°19´N 44°33´E
125 T16 **Chaykovskiy** Permskiy Kray, NW Russian Federation 56°45´N 54°09´E
167 T12 **Chbar** Môndól Kiri, E Cambodia 12°46´N 107°10´E
23 Q4 **Cheaha Mountain** ▲ Alabama, S USA 33°29´N 85°48´W
Cheatharlach *see* Carlow
21 S2 **Cheat River** ≈ NE USA
111 A16 **Cheb** *Ger.* Eger. Karlovarský Kraj, W Czech Republic 50°05´N 12°23´E
127 Q3 **Cheboksary** Chuvashskaya Respublika, W Russian Federation 56°06´N 47°15´E
31 Q5 **Cheboygan** Michigan, N USA 45°40´N 84°28´W
Chechaouèn *see* Chefchaouen
Chechenia *see* Chechenskaya Respublika
127 O15 **Chechenskaya Respublika** *Eng.* Chechenia, Chechnia, *Rus.* Chechnya. ◈ *autonomous republic* SW Russian Federation
67 N4 **Chech, Erg** *desert* Algeria/ Mali
Chechevichi *see* Chachevichy
Che-chiang *see* Zhejiang
Chechnia/Chechnya *see* Chechenskaya Respublika
Chech'ŏn *see* Jecheon
111 L15 **Chęciny** Świętokrzyskie, S Poland 50°51´N 20°31´E
27 Q10 **Checotah** Oklahoma, C USA 35°28´N 95°31´W
13 R15 **Chedabucto Bay** *inlet* Nova Scotia, E Canada
166 J7 **Cheduba Island** *island* W Burma (Myanmar)
37 T5 **Cheesman Lake** ⊠ Colorado, C USA
195 S16 **Cheetham, Cape** *headland* Antarctica 70°26´S 162°40´E
74 G5 **Chefchaouen** *var.* Chaouèn, Chechaouèn, *Sp.* Xauen. N Morocco 35°10´N 05°16´W
Chefoo *see* Yantai
38 M12 **Chefornak** Alaska, USA 60°09´N 164°09´W
123 R13 **Chegdomyn** Khabarovskiy Kray, SE Russian Federation 51°09´N 132°58´E
76 M4 **Chegga** Tiris Zemmour, NE Mauritania 25°27´N 05°49´W
Cheghcheran *see* Chaghcharān
32 G9 **Chehalis** Washington, NW USA 46°39´N 122°57´W
32 G9 **Chehalis River** ≈ Washington, NW USA
148 M6 **Chehel Abdālān, Kūh-e** *var.* Chalap Dalam, *Pash.* Chalap Dalan. ▲▲ C Afghanistan
115 D14 **Cheimadítis, Límni** *var.* Límni Cheimadítis. ◎ N Greece
Cheimadítis, Límni *see* Cheimadítis, Límni
103 U15 **Cheiron, Mont** ▲ SE France 43°49´N 07°00´E
163 Y17 **Cheju** ✈ S South Korea 33°31´N 126°29´E
Cheju *see* Jeju
Cheju-do *see* Jeju-do
Cheju-haehyeop *see* Jeju-haehyeop
Cheju Strait *see* Jeju-haehyeop
Chekiang *see* Zhejiang
Chekichler/Chekishlyar *see* Çekiçler
188 F8 **Chelab** Babeldaob, N Palau

◆ Country
● Country Capital
◇ Dependent Territory
○ Dependent Territory Capital
◈ Administrative Regions
✈ International Airport
▲ Mountain
▲▲ Mountain Range
Volcano
≈ River
◎ Lake
⊠ Reservoir

147 N11 **Chelak** Rus. Chelek. Samarqand Viloyati, C Uzbekistan 39°55′N 66°45′E
32 J7 **Chelan, Lake** ▣ Washington, NW USA
Chelek see Chelak
Cheleken see Hazar
Chélif/Chéliff see Chelif, Oued
74 J5 **Chelif, Oued** var. Chélif, Chéliff, Chellif, Shellif. ≈ N Algeria
Chelkar see Shalkar
Chelkar Ozero see Shalkar, Ozero
Chellif see Chelif, Oued
111 P14 **Chełm** Rus. Kholm. Lubelskie, SE Poland 51°08′N 23°29′E
110 I9 **Chełmno** Ger. Culm, Kulm. Kujawski-pomorskie, C Poland 53°21′N 18°27′E
115 E19 **Chelmós** var. Ároania. ▲▲ S Greece
14 F10 **Chelmsford** Ontario, S Canada 46°33′N 81°16′W
97 P21 **Chelmsford** E England, United Kingdom 51°44′N 00°28′E
110 J9 **Chełmża** Ger. Culmsee, Kulmsee. Kujawski-pomorskie, C Poland 53°11′N 18°34′E
27 Q8 **Chelsea** Oklahoma, C USA 36°32′N 95°25′W
18 M8 **Chelsea** Vermont, NE USA 43°58′N 72°29′W
97 L21 **Cheltenham** C England, United Kingdom 51°54′N 02°04′W
105 R9 **Chelva** Valenciana, E Spain 39°45′N 01°00′W
122 G11 **Chelyabinsk** Chelyabinskaya Oblast′, C Russian Federation 55°12′N 61°25′E
122 F11 **Chelyabinskaya Oblast′** ◈ province C Russian Federation
123 N5 **Chelyuskin, Mys** headland N Russian Federation 77°42′N 104°13′E
41 Y12 **Chemax** Yucatán, SE Mexico 20°41′N 87°54′W
83 N16 **Chemba** Sofala, C Mozambique 17°11′S 34°53′E
82 J13 **Chembe** Luapula, NE Zambia 11°58′S 28°45′E
Chemenibit see Çemenibit
Chemerisy see Chamyarysy
116 K7 **Chemerivtsi** Khmel′nyts′ka Oblast′, W Ukraine 49°00′N 26°21′E
102 J8 **Chemillé** Maine-et-Loire, NW France 47°15′N 00°42′W
173 X17 **Chemin Grenier** S Mauritius 20°29′S 57°28′E
101 N16 **Chemnitz** prev. Karl-Marx-Stadt. Sachsen, E Germany 50°50′N 12°55′E
Chemulpo see Incheon
32 H14 **Chemult** Oregon, NW USA 43°14′N 121°48′W
18 G12 **Chemung River** ≈ New York/Pennsylvania, NE USA
149 U8 **Chenāb** ≈ India/Pakistan
39 S9 **Chena Hot Springs** Alaska, USA 65°06′N 146°02′W
18 I11 **Chenango River** ≈ New York, NE USA
168 J7 **Chenderoh, Tasik** ◎ Peninsular Malaysia
15 Q11 **Chêne, Rivière du** ≈ Québec, SE Canada
32 L8 **Cheney** Washington, NW USA 47°29′N 117°34′W
26 M6 **Cheney Reservoir** ▣ Kansas, C USA
Chengchiatun see Liaoyuan
Ch′eng-chou/Chengchow see Zhengzhou
161 P1 **Chengde** var. Jehol. Hebei, E China 41°N 117°57′E
160 I9 **Chengdu** var. Chengtu, Ch′eng-tu. province capital Sichuan, C China 30°41′N 104°03′E
161 Q14 **Chenghai** Guangdong, S China 23°30′N 116°42′E
Chenghsien see Zhengzhou
160 H13 **Chengjiang** Yunnan, SW China 24°40′N 102°55′E
Chengjiang see Taihe
160 L17 **Chengmai** var. Jinjiang. Hainan, S China 19°45′N 109°56′E
Chengtu/Ch′eng-tu see Chengdu
Chengwen see Chindu
159 W12 **Chengxian** var. Cheng Xiang. Gansu, C China 33°42′N 105°45′E
Cheng Xiang see Chengxian
Chengyang see Juxian
Chengzhong see Ningming
Chenkiang see Zhenjiang
155 J19 **Chennai** prev. Madras. state capital Tamil Nādu, S India 13°05′N 80°18′E
155 J19 **Chennai** ✈ Tamil Nādu, S India 13°07′N 80°13′E
103 R8 **Chenôve** Côte d′Or, C France 47°16′N 05°00′E
Chenstokhov see Częstochowa
160 L11 **Chenxi** var. Chenyang. Hunan, S China 28°02′N 110°15′E
Chen Xian/Chenxian/Chen Xiang see Chenzhou
Chenyang see Chenxi
161 N12 **Chenzhou** var. Chenxian, Chen Xian, Chen Xiang. Hunan, S China 25°51′N 113°01′E
163 X15 **Cheonan** Jap. Tenan; prev. Ch′ŏnan. W South Korea 36°51′N 127°11′E
163 W13 **Cheongju** prev. Chŏngju. W North Korea 39°44′N 125°13′E
Cheo Reo see A Yun Pa
114 I11 **Chepelare** Smolyan, S Bulgaria 41°44′N 24°41′E
114 I11 **Chepelarska Reka** ≈ S Bulgaria
56 B11 **Chepén** La Libertad, C Peru 07°15′S 79°23′W
62 J10 **Chepes** La Rioja, C Argentina 31°19′S 66°40′W
161 O15 **Chep Lap Kok** ✈ S China 22°23′N 114°11′E
43 U14 **Chepo** Panamá, C Panama 09°09′N 79°03′W
Chepping Wycombe see High Wycombe
125 R14 **Cheptsa** ≈ NW Russian Federation
30 K3 **Chequamegon Point** headland Wisconsin, N USA 46°42′N 90°45′W
103 O8 **Cher** ◈ department C France
102 M8 **Cher** ≈ C France
Cherangani Hills see Cherangany Hills
81 H17 **Cherangany Hills** var. Cherangani Hills. ▲▲ W Kenya
21 S11 **Cheraw** South Carolina, SE USA 34°42′N 79°52′W
102 I3 **Cherbourg** anc. Carusbur. Manche, N France 49°40′N 01°36′W
127 R5 **Cherdakly** Ul′yanovskaya Oblast′, W Russian Federation 54°21′N 48°54′E
125 U12 **Cherdyn′** Permskiy Kray, NW Russian Federation 60°21′N 56°39′E
124 J14 **Cherekha** ≈ W Russian Federation
122 M13 **Cheremkhovo** Irkutskaya Oblast′, S Russian Federation 53°16′N 102°44′E
Cheren see Keren
124 K14 **Cherepovets** Vologodskaya Oblast′, NW Russian Federation 59°09′N 37°50′E
125 O11 **Cherevkovo** Arkhangel′skaya Oblast′, NW Russian Federation 61°45′N 45°16′E
74 I6 **Chergui, Chott ech** salt lake NW Algeria
Cherikov see Cherykaw
117 P6 **Cherkas′ka Oblast′** var. Cherkasy, Rus. Cherkasskaya Oblast′. ◈ province C Ukraine
Cherkasskaya Oblast′ see Cherkas′ka Oblast′
Cherkassy see Cherkasy
117 Q6 **Cherkasy** Rus. Cherkassy. Cherkas′ka Oblast′, C Ukraine 49°26′N 32°05′E
Cherkasy see Cherkas′ka Oblast′
126 M15 **Cherkessk** Karachayevo-Cherkesskaya Respublika, SW Russian Federation 44°12′N 42°06′E
122 H12 **Cherlak** Omskaya Oblast′, C Russian Federation 54°06′N 74°59′E
122 H12 **Cherlakskoye** Omskaya Oblast′, C Russian Federation 53°42′N 74°23′E
125 U13 **Chermoz** Permskiy Kray, NW Russian Federation 58°49′N 56°07′E
Chernavchitsy see Charnawchytsy
125 T3 **Chernaya** Nenetskiy Avtonomnyy Okrug, NW Russian Federation 68°36′N 56°34′E
125 T4 **Chernaya** ≈ NW Russian Federation
Chernigov see Chernihiv
Chernigovskaya Oblast′ see Chernihivs′ka Oblast′
117 Q2 **Chernihiv** Rus. Chernigov. Chernihivs′ka Oblast′, NE Ukraine 51°28′N 31°19′E
Chernihiv see Chernihivs′ka Oblast′
117 V9 **Chernihivka** Zaporiz′ka Oblast′, SE Ukraine 47°11′N 36°10′E
117 P2 **Chernihivs′ka Oblast′** var. Chernihiv, Rus. Chernigovskaya Oblast′. ◈ province NE Ukraine
114 I9 **Cherni Osŭm** ≈ N Bulgaria
116 J8 **Chernivets′ka Oblast′** var. Chernivtsi, Rus. Chernovitskaya Oblast′. ◈ province W Ukraine
114 I9 **Cherni Vit** ≈ NW Bulgaria
114 G10 **Cherni Vrŭkh** ▲ W Bulgaria 42°33′N 23°18′E
116 K8 **Chernivtsi** Ger. Czernowitz, Rom. Cernăuţi, Rus. Chernovtsy. Chernivets′ka Oblast′, W Ukraine 48°18′N 25°55′E
116 M7 **Chernivtsi** Vinnyts′ka Oblast′, C Ukraine 48°33′N 28°06′E
Chernivtsi see Chernivets′ka Oblast′
Chernobyl′ see Chornobyl′
Cherno More see Black Sea
Chernomorskoye see Chornomors′ke
145 T7 **Chernoretsk** prev. Chernoretskoye. Pavlodar, NE Kazakhstan 52°51′N 76°37′E
Chernoretskoye see Chernoretsk
Chernovitskaya Oblast′ see Chernivets′ka Oblast′
Chernovtsy see Chernivtsi
145 U8 **Chernoye** Pavlodar, NE Kazakhstan 51°40′N 77°33′E
Chernoye More see Black Sea
125 U16 **Chernushka** Permskiy Kray, NW Russian Federation 56°30′N 56°07′E
117 N4 **Chernyakhiv** Rus. Chernyakhov. Zhytomyrs′ka Oblast′, N Ukraine 50°30′N 28°38′E
Chernyakhov see Chernyakhiv
119 C14 **Chernyakhovsk** Ger. Insterburg. Kaliningradskaya Oblast′, W Russian Federation 54°36′N 21°49′E
126 K8 **Chernyanka** Belgorodskaya Oblast′, W Russian Federation 50°59′N 37°54′E
125 V5 **Chernyshëva, Gryada** ▲▲ NW Russian Federation
144 J14 **Chernyshëva, Zaliv** gulf SW Kazakhstan
123 O10 **Chernyshevskiy** Respublika Sakha (Yakutiya), NE Russian Federation 62°57′N 112°29′E
127 P13 **Chernyye Zemli** plain SW Russian Federation
Chërnyy Irtysh see Ertix He, China/Kazakhstan
Chërnyy Irtysh see Kara Irtysh, Kazakhstan
127 V7 **Chernyy Otrog** Orenburgskaya Oblast′, W Russian Federation 52°03′N 56°09′E
29 T12 **Cherokee** Iowa, C USA 42°45′N 95°33′W
26 M8 **Cherokee** Oklahoma, C USA 36°45′N 98°22′W
25 R9 **Cherokee** Texas, SW USA 30°56′N 98°42′W
21 O8 **Cherokee Lake** ▣ Tennessee, S USA
Cherokees, Lake O′ The see Grand Lake O′ The Cherokees
44 H1 **Cherokee Sound** Great Abaco, N Bahamas 26°16′N 77°03′W
153 V13 **Cherrapunji** Meghālaya, NE India 25°16′N 91°42′E
28 L9 **Cherry Creek** ≈ South Dakota, N USA
18 J16 **Cherry Hill** New Jersey, NE USA 39°55′N 75°01′W
27 Q7 **Cherryvale** Kansas, C USA 37°16′N 95°33′W
21 Q10 **Cherryville** North Carolina, SE USA 35°22′N 81°22′W
Cherski Range see Cherskogo, Khrebet
123 T6 **Cherskiy** Respublika Sakha (Yakutiya), NE Russian Federation 68°45′N 161°15′E
123 R8 **Cherskogo, Khrebet** var. Cherski Range. ▲▲ NE Russian Federation
Cherso see Cres
126 L10 **Chertkovo** Rostovskaya Oblast′, SW Russian Federation 49°22′N 40°10′E
Cherven′ see Chervyen′
114 H8 **Cherven Bryag** Pleven, N Bulgaria 43°16′N 24°06′E
116 M4 **Chervonoarmiys′k** Zhytomyrs′ka Oblast′, N Ukraine 50°27′N 28°15′E
Chervonograd see Chervonohrad
116 I4 **Chervonohrad** Rus. Chervonograd. L′vivs′ka Oblast′, NW Ukraine 50°25′N 24°10′E
117 W6 **Chervonooskil′s′ke Vodoskhovyshche** Rus. Krasnoosol′skoye Vodokhranilishche. ▣ NE Ukraine
Chervonoye, Ozero see Chyrvonaye, Vozyera
117 S4 **Chervonozavods′ke** Poltavs′ka Oblast′, C Ukraine 50°24′N 33°22′E
119 L16 **Chervyen′** Rus. Cherven′. Minskaya Voblasts′, C Belarus 53°42′N 28°26′E
119 P16 **Cherykaw** Rus. Cherikov. Mahilyowskaya Voblasts′, E Belarus 53°34′N 31°23′E
31 R9 **Chesaning** Michigan, N USA 43°10′N 84°07′W
21 X5 **Chesapeake Bay** inlet NE USA
Chesha Bay see Chëshskaya Guba
Cheshevlya see Tsyeshawlya
97 K18 **Cheshire** cultural region C England, United Kingdom
125 P5 **Chëshskaya Guba** var. Archangel Bay, Chesha Bay, Dvina Bay. bay NW Russian Federation
14 F14 **Chesley** Ontario, S Canada 44°17′N 81°06′W
21 Q10 **Chesnee** South Carolina, SE USA 35°09′N 81°51′W
97 K18 **Chester** Wel. Caerleon, hist. Legaceaster, Lat. Deva, Devana Castra. C England, United Kingdom 53°12′N 02°54′W
35 O4 **Chester** California, W USA 40°18′N 121°14′W
30 K16 **Chester** Illinois, N USA 37°54′N 89°49′W
33 S7 **Chester** Montana, NW USA 48°30′N 110°59′W
18 I16 **Chester** Pennsylvania, NE USA 39°51′N 75°21′W
21 R1 **Chester** South Carolina, SE USA 34°43′N 81°14′W
25 X9 **Chester** Texas, SW USA 30°55′N 94°36′W
21 W6 **Chester** Virginia, NE USA 37°22′N 77°27′W
21 R11 **Chester** West Virginia, NE USA 40°34′N 80°33′W
97 M18 **Chesterfield** C England, United Kingdom 53°15′N 01°25′W
21 S11 **Chesterfield** South Carolina, SE USA 34°44′N 80°04′W
21 W6 **Chesterfield** Virginia, NE USA 37°22′N 77°31′W
192 J9 **Chesterfield, Îles** island group NW New Caledonia
9 O9 **Chesterfield Inlet** Nunavut, NW Canada 63°19′N 90°57′W
9 O9 **Chesterfield Inlet** inlet Nunavut, N Canada
21 Y3 **Chester River** ≈ Delaware/Maryland, NE USA
21 X3 **Chestertown** Maryland, NE USA 39°13′N 76°04′W
19 R4 **Chesuncook Lake** ◎ Maine, NE USA
30 J5 **Chetek** Wisconsin, N USA 45°19′N 91°37′W
13 R14 **Chéticamp** Nova Scotia, SE Canada 46°14′N 61°19′W
27 Q8 **Chetopa** Kansas, C USA 37°02′N 95°05′W
41 Y14 **Chetumal** var. Payo Obispo. Quintana Roo, SE Mexico 18°32′N 88°16′W
Chetumal, Bahia/Chetumal, Bahía de see Chetumal Bay
42 G1 **Chetumal Bay** var. Bahia Chetumal, Bahía de Chetumal. bay Belize/Mexico
10 M13 **Chetwynd** British Columbia, W Canada 55°42′N 121°36′W
38 M11 **Chevak** Alaska, USA 61°31′N 165°35′W
36 M12 **Chevelon Creek** ≈ Arizona, SW USA
185 J17 **Cheviot** Canterbury, South Island, New Zealand 42°48′S 173°17′E
96 L13 **Cheviot Hills** hill range England/Scotland, United Kingdom
96 L13 **Cheviot, The** ▲ NE England, United Kingdom 55°28′N 02°10′W
14 M11 **Chevreuil, Lac du** ◎ Québec, SE Canada
81 I16 **Ch′ew Bahir** var. Lake Stefanie. ◎ Ethiopia/Kenya
32 L7 **Chewelah** Washington, NW USA 48°16′N 117°42′W
26 K10 **Cheyenne** Oklahoma, C USA 35°37′N 99°43′W
33 Z17 **Cheyenne** state capital Wyoming, C USA 41°08′N 104°46′W
26 L5 **Cheyenne Bottoms** ◎ Kansas, C USA
16 J8 **Cheyenne River** ≈ South Dakota/Wyoming, N USA
37 W5 **Cheyenne Wells** Colorado, C USA 38°49′N 102°21′W
108 C9 **Cheyres** Vaud, W Switzerland 46°48′N 06°48′E
Chezdi-Oşorheiu see Târgu Secuiesc
153 P13 **Chhapra** prev. Chapra. Bihār, N India 25°50′N 84°42′E
153 V13 **Chhatak** var. Chatak. Sylhet, NE Bangladesh 25°02′N 91°33′E
154 J9 **Chhatarpur** Madhya Pradesh, C India 24°54′N 79°35′E
154 N13 **Chhatrapur** prev. Chatrapur. Orissa, E India 19°26′N 85°02′E
154 K2 **Chhattīsgarh** ◈ state E India
154 L12 **Chhattīsgarh** plain C India
154 I11 **Chhindwāra** Madhya Pradesh, C India 22°04′N 78°58′E
153 T12 **Chhukha** SW Bhutan 27°02′N 89°36′E
Chiai see Jiayi
Chia-i see Jiayi
Chia-mu-ssu see Jiamusi
83 B15 **Chiange** Port. Vila de Almoster. Huíla, SW Angola 15°44′S 13°54′E
Chiang-hsi see Jiangxi
161 S12 **Chiang Kai-shek** ✈ (T′aipei) N Taiwan 25°09′N 121°20′E
167 P8 **Chiang Khan** Loei, E Thailand 17°51′N 101°43′E
167 O7 **Chiang Mai** var. Chiangmai, Chiengmai, Kiangmai. Chiang Mai, NW Thailand 18°48′N 98°59′E
167 O7 **Chiang Mai** ✈ Chiang Mai, NW Thailand 18°44′N 98°53′E
Chiangmai see Chiang Mai
167 O6 **Chiang Rai** var. Chianpai, Chienrai, Muang Chiang Rai. Chiang Rai, NW Thailand 19°56′N 99°51′E
Chiang-su see Jiangsu
Chianning/Chian-ning see Nanjing
Chianpai see Chiang Rai
106 G12 **Chianti** cultural region C Italy
Chiapa see Chiapa de Corzo
41 U16 **Chiapa de Corzo** var. Chiapa. Chiapas, SE Mexico 16°42′N 92°59′W
41 V16 **Chiapas** ◈ state SE Mexico
106 J12 **Chiaravalle** Marche, C Italy 43°36′N 13°19′E
107 N22 **Chiaravalle Centrale** Calabria, SW Italy 38°40′N 16°25′E
106 E7 **Chiari** Lombardia, N Italy 45°33′N 10°00′E
108 H12 **Chiasso** Ticino, S Switzerland 45°51′N 09°02′E
137 S9 **Chiatura** prev. Chiat′ura. C Georgia 42°13′N 43°11′E
Chiat′ura see Chiatura
41 P15 **Chiautla** var. Chiautla de Tapia. Puebla, S Mexico 18°16′N 98°31′W
Chiautla de Tapia see Chiautla
106 D10 **Chiavari** Liguria, NW Italy 44°19′N 09°19′E
106 E6 **Chiavenna** Lombardia, N Italy 46°19′N 09°22′E
Chiayi see Jiayi
Chiazza see Piazza Armerina
165 O14 **Chiba** var. Tiba. Chiba, Honshū, S Japan 35°37′N 140°06′E
165 O13 **Chiba** off. Chiba-ken, var. Tiba. ◈ prefecture Honshū, S Japan
83 M18 **Chibabava** Sofala, C Mozambique 20°17′S 33°39′E
Chiba-ken see Chiba
161 O10 **Chibi** prev. Puqi. Hubei, C China 29°45′N 113°55′E
83 B15 **Chibia** Port. João de Almeida, Vila João de Almeida. Huíla, SW Angola 15°11′S 13°41′E
83 M18 **Chiboma** Sofala, C Mozambique 20°06′S 33°54′E
82 J12 **Chibondo** Luapula, N Zambia 10°42′S 28°42′E
82 K11 **Chibote** Luapula, NE Zambia 09°52′S 29°33′E
12 K12 **Chibougamau** Québec, SE Canada 49°56′N 74°24′W
164 H11 **Chiburi-jima** island Oki-shotō, SW Japan
83 M20 **Chibuto** Gaza, S Mozambique 24°40′S 33°33′E
31 N11 **Chicago** Illinois, N USA 41°51′N 87°39′W
31 N11 **Chicago Heights** Illinois, N USA 41°30′N 87°38′W
15 W6 **Chic-Chocs, Monts** Eng. Shickshock Mountains. ▲▲ Québec, SE Canada
39 W13 **Chichagof Island** island Alexander Archipelago, Alaska, USA
57 K20 **Chichas, Cordillera de** ▲▲ SW Bolivia
41 X12 **Chichén-Itzá, Ruinas** ruins Yucatán, SE Mexico
97 N23 **Chichester** SE England, United Kingdom 50°50′N 00°48′W
42 C5 **Chichicastenango** Quiché, W Guatemala 14°55′N 91°06′W
42 I9 **Chichigalpa** Chinandega, NW Nicaragua 12°35′N 87°04′W
Ch′i-ch′i-ha-erh see Qiqihar
165 X16 **Chichijima-rettō** Eng. Beechy Group. island group SE Japan
54 K4 **Chichiriviche** Falcón, N Venezuela 10°58′N 68°17′W
39 R11 **Chickaloon** Alaska, USA 61°48′N 148°27′W
20 L10 **Chickamauga Lake** ▣ Tennessee, S USA
23 N7 **Chickasawhay River** ≈ Mississippi, S USA
26 M11 **Chickasha** Oklahoma, C USA 35°03′N 97°57′W
39 T9 **Chicken** Alaska, USA 64°04′N 141°56′W
104 J16 **Chiclana de la Frontera** Andalucía, S Spain 36°26′N 06°09′W
56 B11 **Chiclayo** Lambayeque, NW Peru 06°47′S 79°47′W
35 N5 **Chico** California, W USA 39°42′N 121°51′W
83 L15 **Chicoa** Tete, NW Mozambique 15°45′S 32°25′E
83 M20 **Chicomo** Gaza, S Mozambique 24°29′S 34°15′E
18 M11 **Chicopee** Massachusetts, NE USA 42°08′N 72°34′W
63 I19 **Chico, Río** ≈ SE Argentina
63 I21 **Chico, Río** ≈ S Argentina
27 W14 **Chicot, Lake** ◎ Arkansas, C USA
15 R7 **Chicoutimi** Québec, SE Canada 48°24′N 71°04′W
15 Q8 **Chicoutimi** ≈ Québec, SE Canada
83 L19 **Chicualacuala** Gaza, SW Mozambique 22°06′S 31°42′E
83 B14 **Chicuma** Benguela, C Angola 13°33′S 14°41′E
155 J21 **Chidambaram** Tamil Nādu, SE India 11°25′N 79°42′E
196 K13 **Chidley, Cape** headland Newfoundland and Labrador, E Canada 60°25′N 64°39′W
101 N24 **Chiemsee** ◎ SE Germany
Chiengmai see Chiang Mai
Chienrai see Chiang Rai
106 B8 **Chieri** Piemonte, NW Italy 45°01′N 07°49′E
106 F8 **Chiese** ≈ N Italy
107 K14 **Chieti** var. Teate. Abruzzo, C Italy 42°22′N 14°10′E
99 E19 **Chièvres** Hainaut, SW Belgium 50°34′N 03°49′E
163 S12 **Chifeng** var. Ulanhad. Nei Mongol Zizhiqu, N China 42°17′N 118°56′E
82 F13 **Chifumage** ≈ E Angola
82 M13 **Chifunda** Eastern, NE Zambia 11°57′S 32°36′E
Chiganak see Shyganak
39 P15 **Chiginagak, Mount** ▲ Alaska, USA 57°10′N 157°00′W
Chigirin see Chyhyryn
41 P13 **Chignahuapan** Puebla, S Mexico 19°52′N 98°03′W
39 O15 **Chignik** Alaska, USA 56°18′N 158°24′W
83 M19 **Chigombe** ≈ S Mozambique
54 D7 **Chigorodó** Antioquia, NW Colombia 07°42′N 76°45′W
83 M19 **Chigubo** Gaza, S Mozambique 22°50′S 33°30′E
Chihertey see Altay
Chih-fu see Yantai
Chihli see Hebei
Chihli, Gulf of see Bo Hai
40 J6 **Chihuahua** Chihuahua, NW Mexico 28°40′N 106°06′W
40 I6 **Chihuahua** ◈ state N Mexico
Chiili see Shiyeli
26 M7 **Chikaskia River** ≈ Kansas/Oklahoma, C USA
155 H19 **Chik Ballāpur** Karnātaka, W India 13°28′N 77°42′E
124 G15 **Chikhachevo** Pskovskaya Oblast′, W Russian Federation 57°17′N 29°51′E
155 F19 **Chikmagalūr** Karnātaka, W India 13°20′N 75°46′E
129 V7 **Chikoy** ≈ C Russian Federation
83 J15 **Chikumbi** Lusaka, C Zambia 15°11′S 28°20′E
82 M13 **Chikwa** Eastern, NE Zambia 11°39′S 32°45′E
Chikwana see Chikwawa
83 N15 **Chikwawa** var. Chikwana. Southern, S Malawi 16°03′S 34°48′E
155 J16 **Chilakalūrupet** Andhra Pradesh, E India 16°09′N 80°13′E
146 L14 **Chilan** Lebap Welaýaty, E Turkmenistan 37°57′N 64°58′E
Chilapa see Chilapa de Alvarez
41 P16 **Chilapa de Alvarez** var. Chilapa. Guerrero, S Mexico 17°38′N 99°11′W
155 J25 **Chilaw** North Western Province, W Sri Lanka 07°34′N 79°48′E
57 D15 **Chilca** Lima, W Peru 12°35′S 76°41′W
23 Q4 **Childersburg** Alabama, S USA 33°16′N 86°21′W
25 P4 **Childress** Texas, SW USA 34°25′N 100°14′W
63 G14 **Chile** off. Republic of Chile. ◆ republic SW South America
47 R10 **Chile Basin** undersea feature E Pacific Ocean 33°00′S 80°00′W
63 H20 **Chile Chico** Aisén, W Chile 46°34′S 71°44′W
62 I9 **Chilecito** La Rioja, NW Argentina 29°10′S 67°30′W
62 H12 **Chilecito** Mendoza, W Argentina 33°53′S 69°03′W
83 L14 **Chilembwe** Eastern, E Zambia 13°54′S 31°38′E
Chile, Republic of see Chile
193 S11 **Chile Rise** undersea feature SE Pacific Ocean 40°00′S 90°00′W
117 N13 **Chilia, Braţul** ≈ SE Romania
Chilia-Nouă see Kiliya
Chilik see Shelek
Chilik see Shelek
154 O13 **Chilika Lake** var. Chilka Lake. ◎ E India
82 J13 **Chililabombwe** Copperbelt, C Zambia 12°20′S 27°52′E
Chi-lin see Jilin
Chilka Lake see Chilika Lake
10 H9 **Chilkoot Pass** pass British Columbia, W Canada
Chill Ala, Cuan see Killala Bay
62 G13 **Chillán** Bío Bío, C Chile 36°37′S 72°10′W
61 C22 **Chillar** Buenos Aires, E Argentina 37°16′S 59°58′W
Chill Chiaráin, Cuan see Kilkieran Bay
30 K12 **Chillicothe** Illinois, N USA 40°55′N 89°29′W
27 S3 **Chillicothe** Missouri, C USA 39°47′N 93°33′W
31 S14 **Chillicothe** Ohio, N USA 39°20′N 83°00′W
25 Q4 **Chillicothe** Texas, SW USA 34°15′N 99°31′W
10 M17 **Chilliwack** British Columbia, SW Canada 49°09′N 121°54′W
Chill Mhantáin, Ceann see Wicklow Head
Chill Mhantáin, Sléibhte see Wicklow Mountains
108 C10 **Chillon** Vaud, W Switzerland 46°24′N 06°56′E
Chil′mamedkum, Peski/Chilmämetgum see Çilmämmetgum
63 F17 **Chiloé, Isla de** var. Isla Grande de Chiloé. island W Chile
32 H15 **Chiloquin** Oregon, NW USA 42°33′N 121°33′W
41 O16 **Chilpancingo** var. Chilpancingo de los Bravos. Guerrero, S Mexico 17°33′N 99°30′W
Chilpancingo de los Bravos see Chilpancingo
97 N21 **Chiltern Hills** hill range S England, United Kingdom
30 M7 **Chilton** Wisconsin, N USA 44°04′N 88°10′W
82 F11 **Chiluage** Lunda Sul, NE Angola 09°32′S 21°48′E
82 N12 **Chilumba** prev. Deep Bay. Northern, N Malawi 10°27′S 34°12′E
Chilung see Jilong
83 N15 **Chilwa, Lake** var. Lago Chirua, Lake Shirwa. ◎ SE Malawi
167 R10 **Chi, Mae Nam** ≈ E Thailand
42 C6 **Chimaltenango** Chimaltenango, C Guatemala 14°40′N 90°48′W
42 A2 **Chimaltenango** off. Departamento de Chimaltenango. ◈ department S Guatemala
Chimaltenango, Departamento de see Chimaltenango
43 V15 **Chimán** Panamá, E Panama 08°42′N 78°35′W
83 M17 **Chimanimani** prev. Mandidzudzure, Melsetter. Manicaland, E Zimbabwe 19°48′S 32°52′E
99 G22 **Chimay** Hainaut, S Belgium 50°03′N 04°20′E
37 S10 **Chimayo** New Mexico, SW USA 36°00′N 105°55′W
Chimbay see Chimboy
56 A13 **Chimborazo** ◈ province C Ecuador
56 C7 **Chimborazo** 🌋 C Ecuador 01°29′S 78°50′W
56 C12 **Chimbote** Ancash, W Peru 09°04′S 78°34′W
146 H7 **Chimboy** Rus. Chimbay. Qoraqalpog′iston Respublikasi, NW Uzbekistan 43°03′N 59°52′E
186 D7 **Chimbu** ◈ province C Papua New Guinea
54 F6 **Chimichagua** Cesar, N Colombia 09°19′N 73°51′W
Chimishliya see Cimişlia
Chimkent see Shymkent
Chimkentskaya Oblast′ see Yuzhnyy Kazakhstan
28 I14 **Chimney Rock** rock Nebraska, C USA
83 M17 **Chimoio** Manica, C Mozambique 19°08′S 33°29′E
82 K11 **Chimpembe** Northern, NE Zambia 09°31′S 29°33′E
41 O8 **China** Nuevo León, NE Mexico 25°42′N 99°15′W
156 M9 **China** off. People′s Republic of China, Chin. Chung-hua Jen-min Kung-ho-kuo, Zhonghua Renmin Gongheguo; prev. Chinese Empire. ◆ republic E Asia
19 Q7 **China Lake** ◎ Maine, NE USA
42 F8 **Chinameca** San Miguel, E El Salvador 13°30′N 88°20′W*
Chi-nan/Chinan see Jinan
42 H9 **Chinandega** Chinandega, NW Nicaragua 12°37′N 87°08′W
42 H9 **Chinandega** ◈ department NW Nicaragua
China, People′s Republic of see China
China, Republic of see Taiwan
24 J11 **Chinati Mountains** ▲▲ Texas, SW USA
Chinaz see Chinoz
57 E15 **Chincha Alta** Ica, SW Peru 13°25′S 76°07′W
11 N11 **Chinchaga** ≈ Alberta, SW Canada
Chin-chiang see Quanzhou
Chinchilla see Chinchilla de Monte Aragón
105 Q11 **Chinchilla de Monte Aragón** var. Chinchilla. Castilla-La Mancha, C Spain 38°56′N 01°44′W
54 D10 **Chinchiná** Caldas, W Colombia 04°59′N 75°37′W
105 O8 **Chinchón** Madrid, C Spain 40°08′N 03°26′W
41 Z14 **Chinchorro, Banco** island SE Mexico
Chin-chou/Chinchow see Jinzhou
21 Z5 **Chincoteague** Assateague Island, Virginia, NE USA 37°55′N 75°22′W
83 O17 **Chinde** Zambézia, NE Mozambique 18°35′S 36°28′E
Chin-do see Jin-do
159 R13 **Chindu** var. Chengwen; prev. Chuqung. Qinghai, C China 33°19′N 97°08′E
Chindwin see Chindwinn
166 M2 **Chindwinn** var. Chindwin. ≈ N Burma (Myanmar)
Chinese Empire see China
Ch′ing Hai see Qinghai Hu, China
Chinghai see Qinghai
Chingildi see Shengeldi
Chingirlau see Shyngghyrlau
82 J13 **Chingola** Copperbelt, C Zambia 12°31′S 27°53′E
Ching-Tao/Ch′ing-tao see Qingdao
82 C13 **Chinguar** Huambo, C Angola 12°33′S 16°25′E
76 I7 **Chinguețti** var. Chinguetti. Adrar, C Mauritania 20°25′N 12°24′W
Chinhae see Jinhae
166 K4 **Chin Hills** ▲▲ W Burma (Myanmar)
83 K16 **Chinhoyi** prev. Sinoia. Mashonaland West, N Zimbabwe 17°22′S 30°12′E
Chinhsien see Jinzhou
39 Q14 **Chiniak, Cape** headland Kodiak Island, Alaska, USA 57°37′N 152°10′W
14 G10 **Chiniguchi Lake** ◎ Ontario, S Canada
149 U8 **Chinīot** Punjab, NE Pakistan 31°40′N 73°00′E
Chinju see Jinju
Chinkai see Jinhae
78 M13 **Chinko** ≈ E Central African Republic
37 O9 **Chinle** Arizona, SW USA 36°09′N 109°33′W
Chinmen Tao see Jinmen Dao
Chinnchâr see Shinshār
Chinnereth see Tiberias, Lake
164 C12 **Chino** var. Tino. Nagano, Honshū, S Japan 36°00′N 138°10′E
102 L8 **Chinon** Indre-et-Loire, C France 47°10′N 00°15′E
33 T7 **Chinook** Montana, NW USA 48°35′N 109°13′W
Chinook State see Washington
192 L4 **Chinook Trough** undersea feature N Pacific Ocean
36 K11 **Chino Valley** Arizona, SW USA 34°45′N 112°27′W
147 P10 **Chinoz** Rus. Chinaz. Toshkent Viloyati, E Uzbekistan 40°58′N 68°46′E
82 L12 **Chinsali** Northern, NE Zambia 10°33′S 32°05′E
166 K5 **Chin State** ◈ state W Burma (Myanmar)
Chinsura see Chunchura
Chin-tō see Jin-do
54 E6 **Chinú** Córdoba, NW Colombia 09°07′N 75°25′W
99 K24 **Chiny, Forêt de** forest SE Belgium
83 M15 **Chioco** Tete, NW Mozambique 16°22′S 32°50′E
106 H8 **Chioggia** anc. Fossa Claudia. Veneto, NE Italy 45°14′N 12°17′E
114 H12 **Chionótrypa** ▲ NE Greece 41°16′N 24°06′E
115 L18 **Chíos** var. Hios, Khíos, It. Scio, Turk. Sakiz-Adasi. Chíos, E Greece 38°23′N 26°07′E
115 K18 **Chíos** var. Khíos. island E Greece
83 M14 **Chipata** prev. Fort Jameson. Eastern, E Zambia 13°40′S 32°42′E
83 C14 **Chipindo** Huíla, C Angola 13°53′S 15°47′E
23 R8 **Chipley** Florida, SE USA 30°46′N 85°32′W
155 D15 **Chiplūn** Mahārāshtra, W India 17°32′N 73°32′E
81 H22 **Chipogolo** Dodoma, C Tanzania 06°52′S 36°03′E
23 R8 **Chipola River** ≈ Florida, SE USA
97 L22 **Chippenham** S England, United Kingdom 51°28′N 02°07′W
30 J6 **Chippewa Falls** Wisconsin, N USA 44°56′N 91°25′W
30 J4 **Chippewa, Lake** ▣ Wisconsin, N USA
31 Q8 **Chippewa River** ≈ Michigan, N USA
30 I6 **Chippewa River** ≈ Wisconsin, N USA
Chipping Wycombe see High Wycombe
114 G8 **Chiprovtsi** Montana, NW Bulgaria 43°23′N 22°53′E
19 T4 **Chiputneticook Lakes** lakes Canada/USA
56 D13 **Chiquián** Ancash, W Peru 10°09′S 78°08′W
41 Y11 **Chiquilá** Quintana Roo, SE Mexico 21°25′N 87°20′W
42 E6 **Chiquimula** Chiquimula, SE Guatemala 14°46′N 89°32′W
42 A3 **Chiquimula** off. Departamento de Chiquimula. ◈ department SE Guatemala
Chiquimula, Departamento de see Chiquimula
42 D7 **Chiquimulilla** Santa Rosa, S Guatemala 14°06′N 90°23′W
54 F9 **Chiquinquirá** Boyacá, C Colombia 05°37′N 73°51′W
155 J17 **Chīrāla** Andhra Pradesh, E India 15°49′N 80°21′E
149 N4 **Chīras** Gōwr, N Afghanistan 35°15′N 65°39′E
152 H11 **Chirāwa** Rājasthān, N India 28°12′N 75°42′E
Chirchik see Chirchiq
147 Q9 **Chirchiq** Rus. Chirchik. Toshkent Viloyati, E Uzbekistan 41°30′N 69°32′E
147 P10 **Chirchiq** ≈ E Uzbekistan
Chire see Shire
83 L18 **Chiredzi** Masvingo, SE Zimbabwe 21°00′S 31°38′E
25 X8 **Chireno** Texas, SW USA 31°30′N 94°21′W
77 X7 **Chirfa** Agadez, NE Niger 21°01′N 12°41′E
37 O16 **Chiricahua Mountains** ▲▲ Arizona, SW USA
37 O16 **Chiricahua Peak** ▲ Arizona, SW USA 31°51′N 109°17′W
54 F6 **Chiriguaná** Cesar, N Colombia 09°24′N 73°38′W
39 P15 **Chirikof Island** island Alaska, USA
43 P16 **Chiriquí** off. Provincia de Chiriquí. ◈ province SW Panama
43 P17 **Chiriquí, Golfo de** Eng. Chiriqui Gulf. gulf SW Panama
43 P15 **Chiriquí Grande** Bocas del Toro, W Panama 08°58′N 82°08′W
Chiriqui Gulf see Chiriquí, Golfo de
43 P15 **Chiriquí, Laguna de** lagoon NW Panama
Chiriquí, Provincia de see Chiriquí
43 O16 **Chiriquí Viejo, Río** ≈ W Panama
Chiriquí, Volcán de see Barú, Volcán
83 N15 **Chiromo** Southern, S Malawi 16°32′S 35°07′E
114 J10 **Chirpan** Stara Zagora, C Bulgaria 42°12′N 25°20′E
43 N14 **Chirripó Atlántico, Río** ≈ E Costa Rica
Chirripó, Cerro see Chirripó Grande, Cerro
Chirripó del Pacífico, Río see Chirripó, Río
43 N14 **Chirripó Grande, Cerro** var. Cerro Chirripó. ▲ SE Costa Rica 09°31′N 83°28′W
43 N13 **Chirripó, Río** var. Río Chirripó del Pacífico. ≈ NE Costa Rica
Chirua, Lago see Chilwa, Lake
83 J15 **Chirundu** Southern, S Zambia 16°03′S 28°50′E
29 W8 **Chisago City** Minnesota, N USA 45°22′N 92°53′W
83 J14 **Chisamba** Central, C Zambia 15°00′S 28°22′E
39 T10 **Chisana** Alaska, USA 62°09′N 142°07′W
82 I13 **Chisasa** North Western, NW Zambia 12°09′S 25°30′E
12 I9 **Chisasibi** prev. Fort George. Québec, C Canada 53°50′N 79°01′W
42 D4 **Chisec** Alta Verapaz, C Guatemala 15°50′N 90°18′W
127 U5 **Chishmy** Respublika Bashkortostan, W Russian Federation 54°33′N 55°21′E

◆ Country
● Country Capital
◇ Dependent Territory
○ Dependent Territory Capital
◈ Administrative Regions
✈ International Airport
▲ Mountain
▲▲ Mountain Range
🌋 Volcano
≈ River
◎ Lake
▣ Reservoir

29 V4 **Chisholm** Minnesota, N USA 47°29′N 92°52′W
149 U10 **Chishtiān** *var.* Chishtiān Mandi. Punjab, E Pakistan 29°44′N 72°54′E
Chishtiān Mandi *see* Chishtiān
160 I11 **Chishui He** C China
Chisimaio/Chisimayu *see* Kismaayo
117 N10 **Chişinău** *Rus.* Kishinev. ● (Moldova) C Moldova 47°N 28°51′E
117 N10 **Chişinău** ✕ S Moldova 46°54′N 28°56′E
Chişinău-Criş *see* Chişineu-Criş
116 F10 **Chişineu-Criş** *Hung.* Kisjenő; *prev.* Chişinău-Criş. Arad, W Romania 46°33′N 21°30′E
83 K14 **Chisomo** Central, C Zambia 13°30′S 30°37′E
106 A8 **Chisone** NW Italy
24 K12 **Chisos Mountains** ▲ Texas, SW USA
39 T10 **Chistochina** Alaska, USA 62°34′N 144°39′W
127 R4 **Chistopol'** Respublika Tatarstan, W Russian Federation 55°20′N 50°39′E
145 O8 **Chistopol'ye** Severnyy Kazakhstan, N Kazakhstan 52°37′N 67°14′E
123 O13 **Chita** Zabaykal'skiy Kray, S Russian Federation 52°03′N 113°35′E
83 B16 **Chitado** Cunene, SW Angola 17°16′S 13°54′E
Chitaldroog/Chitaldrug *see* Chitradurga
83 C15 **Chitanda** S Angola
Chitangwiza *see* Chitungwiza
82 F10 **Chitato** Lunda Norte, NE Angola 07°23′S 20°46′E
83 C14 **Chitembo** Bié, C Angola 13°33′S 16°47′E
39 T11 **Chitina** Alaska, USA 61°31′N 144°26′W
39 T11 **Chitina River** Alaska, USA
82 M11 **Chitipa** Northern, NW Malawi 09°41′S 33°19′E
165 S4 **Chitose** *var.* Titose. Hokkaidō, NE Japan 42°51′N 141°40′E
155 G18 **Chitradurga** *prev.* Chitaldroog, Chitaldrug. Karnātaka, W India 14°16′N 76°23′E
149 T3 **Chitrāl** Khyber Pakhtunkhwa, NW Pakistan 35°51′N 71°47′E
43 S16 **Chitré** Herrera, S Panama 07°57′N 80°26′W
153 V16 **Chittagong** *Ben.* Chāttagām. Chittagong, SE Bangladesh 22°20′N 91°48′E
153 U16 **Chittagong** ◐ *division* E Bangladesh
153 Q15 **Chittaranjan** West Bengal, NE India 23°52′N 86°40′E
152 G14 **Chittaurgarh** *var.* Chittorgarh. Rājasthān, N India 24°54′N 74°42′E
155 I19 **Chittoor** Andhra Pradesh, E India 13°13′N 79°06′E
Chittorgarh *see* Chittaurgarh
155 G21 **Chittūr** Kerala, SW India 10°42′N 76°46′E
83 K16 **Chitungwiza** *prev.* Chitangwiza. Mashonaland East, NE Zimbabwe 18°S 31°06′E
62 H4 **Chiuchiu** Antofagasta, N Chile 22°13′S 68°34′W
82 F12 **Chiumbe** *var.* Tshiumbe. Angola/Dem. Rep. Congo
83 F15 **Chiume** Moxico, E Angola 15°08′S 21°09′E
83 K13 **Chiundaponde** Northern, NE Zambia 12°14′S 30°40′E
106 H13 **Chiusi** Toscana, C Italy 43°00′N 11°56′E
54 J5 **Chivacoa** Yaracuy, N Venezuela 10°10′N 68°54′W
106 B8 **Chivasso** Piemonte, NW Italy 45°13′N 07°54′E
83 L17 **Chivhu** *prev.* Enkeldoorn. Midlands, C Zimbabwe 19°01′S 30°54′E
61 C20 **Chivilcoy** Buenos Aires, E Argentina 34°55′S 60°00′W
82 N12 **Chiweta** Northern, N Malawi 10°36′S 34°09′E
42 D4 **Chixoy, Río** *var.* Río Negro, Río Salinas. Guatemala/Mexico
82 H13 **Chizela** North Western, NW Zambia 13°11′S 24°59′E
125 O5 **Chizha** Nenetskiy Avtonomnyy Okrug, NW Russian Federation 67°04′N 44°19′E
161 Q9 **Chizhou** *var.* Guichi. Anhui, E China 30°39′N 117°29′E
164 I12 **Chizu** Tottori, Honshū, SW Japan 35°15′N 134°14′E
Chkalov *see* Orenburg
74 J5 **Chlef** *var.* Ech Cheliff, Ech Chleff; *prev.* Al-Asnam, El Asnam, Orléansville. NW Algeria 36°11′N 01°21′E
115 G18 **Chlómo** ▲ C Greece 38°36′N 22°57′E
111 M15 **Chmielnik** Świętokrzyskie, C Poland 50°37′N 20°43′E
167 S11 **Chŏâm Khsant** Preăh Vihéar, N Cambodia 14°13′N 104°56′E
62 G10 **Choapa, Río** *var.* Choapo. C Chile
Choapas *see* Las Choapas
Choapo *see* Choapa, Río
Choarta *see* Chwārtā
67 T13 **Chobe** N Botswana
14 K8 **Chochocouane** Québec, SE Canada
110 E13 **Chocianów** *Ger.* Kotzenan. Dolnośląskie, SW Poland 51°23′N 15°55′E
54 C9 **Chocó** *off.* Departamento del Chocó. ◐ *province* W Colombia
Chocó, Departamento del *see* Chocó
35 X16 **Chocolate Mountains** California, W USA
21 W9 **Chocowinity** North Carolina, SE USA 35°33′N 77°03′W
27 N10 **Choctaw** Oklahoma, C USA 35°30′N 97°16′W
23 Q8 **Choctawhatchee Bay** *bay* Florida, SE USA
23 Q8 **Choctawhatchee River** Florida, SE USA
Chodau *see* Chodov
163 V14 **Ch'o-do** *island* SW North Korea
Chodorów *see* Khodoriv
111 A16 **Chodov** *Ger.* Chodau. Karlovarský Kraj, W Czech Republic 50°15′N 12°45′E
110 G10 **Chodzież** Wielkopolskie, C Poland 53°N 16°55′E
63 J15 **Choele Choel** Río Negro, C Argentina 39°19′S 65°42′W
83 L14 **Chofombo** Tete, NW Mozambique 14°43′S 31°48′E
Chohtan *see* Chauhtan
11 U14 **Choiceland** Saskatchewan, C Canada 53°28′N 104°26′W
186 K8 **Choiseul** ◐ *province* NW Solomon Islands
186 K8 **Choiseul** *var.* Lauru. *island* NW Solomon Islands
63 M23 **Choiseul Sound** *sound* East Falkland, Falkland Islands
40 H7 **Choix** Sinaloa, C Mexico 26°43′N 108°20′W
110 D10 **Chojna** Zachodnio-pomorskie, W Poland 52°56′N 14°25′E
110 H8 **Chojnice** *Ger.* Konitz. Pomorskie, N Poland 53°41′N 17°34′E
111 F14 **Chojnów** *Ger.* Hainau, Haynau. Dolnośląskie, SW Poland 51°16′N 15°55′E
167 Q10 **Chok Chai** Nakhon Ratchasima, C Thailand 14°45′N 102°10′E
80 I12 **Ch'ok'ē** *var.* Choke Mountains. ▲ NW Ethiopia
25 R13 **Choke Canyon Lake** Texas, SW USA
Choke Mountains *see* Ch'ok'ē
Chokpar *see* Shokpar
147 W7 **Chok-Tal** *var.* Choktal. Issyk-Kul'skaya Oblast', E Kyrgyzstan 42°37′N 76°45′E
Choktal *see* Chok-Tal
Chókué *see* Chokwè
123 R7 **Chokurdakh** Respublika Sakha (Yakutiya), NE Russian Federation 70°38′N 148°18′E
83 L20 **Chokwè** *var.* Chókué. Gaza, S Mozambique 24°27′S 32°55′E
188 F8 **Chol** Babeldaob, N Palau
160 E8 **Chola Shan** C China
102 J8 **Cholet** Maine-et-Loire, NW France 47°03′N 00°52′W
63 H17 **Cholila** Chubut, W Argentina 42°33′S 71°28′W
Cholo *see* Thyolo
147 V8 **Cholpon** Narynskaya Oblast', C Kyrgyzstan 42°07′N 75°25′E
147 X7 **Cholpon-Ata** Issyk-Kul'skaya Oblast', E Kyrgyzstan 42°39′N 77°05′E
41 P14 **Cholula** Puebla, S Mexico 19°03′N 98°19′W
42 I8 **Choluteca** Choluteca, S Honduras 13°15′N 87°10′W
42 H8 **Choluteca** ◐ *department* S Honduras
42 H8 **Choluteca, Río** SW Honduras
83 I15 **Choma** Southern, S Zambia 16°48′S 26°58′E
153 T11 **Chomo Lhari** ▲ NW Bhutan 27°59′N 89°24′E
167 N7 **Chom Thong** Chiang Mai, NW Thailand 18°25′N 98°44′E
111 B15 **Chomutov** *Ger.* Komotau. Ústecký Kraj, NW Czech Republic 50°28′N 13°24′E
123 N11 **Chona** C Russian Federation
Ch'ŏnan *see* Cheonan
167 P11 **Chon Buri** *prev.* Bang Pla Soi. Chon Buri, S Thailand 13°24′N 100°59′E
56 B6 **Chone** Manabí, W Ecuador 0°44′S 80°04′W
Chong'an *see* Wuyishan
163 W13 **Ch'ŏngch'ŏn-gang** W North Korea
163 Y11 **Ch'ŏngjin** NE North Korea 41°48′N 129°44′E
Chŏngju *see* Cheongju
161 S8 **Chongming Dao** *island* E China
160 J10 **Chongqing** *var.* Ch'ung-ching, Ch'ung-ch'ing, Chungking, Pahsien, Tchongking, Yuzhou. Chongqing Shi, C China 29°34′N 106°27′E
Chŏngup *see* Chŏnju
161 O10 **Chongyang** *var.* Tiancheng. Hubei, C China 29°35′N 114°03′E
160 J15 **Chongzuo** *prev.* Taiping. Guangxi Zhuangzu Zizhiqu, S China 22°18′N 107°23′E
163 Y16 **Chŏnju** *prev.* Chŏngup, Chŏngup, *Jap.* Seiyu. SW South Korea 35°51′N 127°08′E
Chŏnju *see* Chŏnju
Chŏnju *see* Jeonju
Chonnacht *see* Connaught
Chonogol *see* Erdenetsagaan
63 F19 **Chonos, Archipiélago de los** *island group* S Chile
42 K10 **Chontales** ◐ *department* S Nicaragua
167 T13 **Chon Thanh** Sông Be, S Vietnam 11°25′N 106°38′E
158 K17 **Cho Oyu** *var.* Qowowuyag. ▲ China/Nepal 28°07′N 86°37′E
116 G7 **Chop** *Cz.* Čop, *Hung.* Csap. Zakarpats'ka Oblast', W Ukraine 48°26′N 22°13′E
21 Y3 **Choptank River** Maryland, NE USA
115 J22 **Chóra** *prev.* Íos. Íos, Kykládes, Greece, Aegean Sea 36°42′N 25°16′E
115 H25 **Chóra Sfakíon** *var.* Sfákia. Kríti, Greece, E Mediterranean Sea 35°12′N 24°05′E
Chorcaí, Cuan *see* Cork Harbour
43 P15 **Chorcha, Cerro** ▲ W Panama 08°39′N 82°07′W
Chorku *see* Chorkŭh
147 R11 **Chorkŭh** *Rus.* Chorku. N Tajikistan 40°04′N 70°30′E
97 K17 **Chorley** NW England, United Kingdom 53°40′N 02°38′W
Chorne More *see* Black Sea
117 R5 **Chornobay** Cherkas'ka Oblast', C Ukraine 49°40′N 32°20′E
117 O3 **Chornobyl'** *Rus.* Chernobyl'. Kyyivs'ka Oblast', N Ukraine 51°17′N 30°15′E
117 R12 **Chornomors'ke** *Rus.* Chernomorskoye. Avtonomna Respublika Krym, S Ukraine 45°29′N 32°45′E
117 R4 **Chornukhy** Poltavs'ka Oblast', C Ukraine 50°15′N 32°57′E
Chorokh/Chorokhi *see* Çoruh Nehri
110 O9 **Choroszcz** Podlaskie, NE Poland 53°10′N 23°E
116 K6 **Chortkiv** *Rus.* Chortkov. Ternopil's'ka Oblast', W Ukraine 49°01′N 25°46′E
Chortkov *see* Chortkiv
Chorum *see* Çorum
110 M9 **Chorzele** Mazowieckie, C Poland 53°16′N 20°53′E
111 J16 **Chorzów** *Ger.* Königshütte; *prev.* Królewska Huta. Śląskie, S Poland 50°17′N 18°58′E
163 W12 **Ch'osan** N North Korea 40°45′N 125°52′E
Chośebuz *see* Cottbus
Chōsen-kaikyō *see* Korea Strait
164 P14 **Chōshi** *var.* Tyôsi. Chiba, Honshū, S Japan 35°44′N 140°48′E
63 H14 **Chos Malal** Neuquén, W Argentina 37°23′S 70°16′W
Chosŏn-minjujuŭi-inmin-kanghwaguk *see* North Korea
110 E9 **Choszczno** *Ger.* Arnswalde. Zachodnio-pomorskie, NW Poland 53°10′N 15°24′E
153 O15 **Chota Nāgpur** *plateau* N India
33 R8 **Choteau** Montana, NW USA 47°48′N 112°40′W
Chotqol *see* Chatkal
14 M8 **Chouart** Québec, SE Canada
76 I7 **Choûm** Adrar, C Mauritania 21°19′N 12°59′W
27 Q9 **Chouteau** Oklahoma, C USA 36°11′N 95°20′W
21 X8 **Chowan River** North Carolina, SE USA
35 Q10 **Chowchilla** California, W USA 37°06′N 120°15′W
163 P7 **Choybalsan** *prev.* Byan Tumen. Dornod, E Mongolia 48°03′N 114°32′E
163 Q7 **Choybalsan** *var.* Hulstay. Dornod, NE Mongolia 48°25′N 114°56′E
162 M9 **Choyr** Govĭ Sumber, C Mongolia 46°20′N 108°21′E
185 I19 **Christchurch** Canterbury, South Island, New Zealand 43°31′S 172°39′E
97 M24 **Christchurch** S England, United Kingdom 50°44′N 01°45′W
185 I18 **Christchurch** ✕ Canterbury, South Island, New Zealand 43°28′S 172°33′E
44 J12 **Christiana** C Jamaica 18°13′N 77°29′W
83 H22 **Christiana** Free State, C South Africa 27°55′S 25°10′E
115 J23 **Christiána** *var.* Christiani. *island* Kykládes, Greece, Aegean Sea
Christiani *see* Christiána
Christiania *see* Oslo
14 G13 **Christian Island** *island* Ontario, S Canada
191 P16 **Christian, Point** *headland* Pitcairn Island, Pitcairn Islands 25°04′S 130°08′E
38 M11 **Christian River** Alaska, USA
Christiansand *see* Kristiansand
21 S7 **Christiansburg** Virginia, NE USA 37°07′N 80°26′W
95 G23 **Christiansfeld** Syddanmark, SW Denmark 55°21′N 09°30′E
Christianshåb *see* Qasigiannguit
39 X14 **Christian Sound** *inlet* Alaska, USA
45 T9 **Christiansted** Saint Croix, S Virgin Islands (US) 17°43′N 64°42′W
Christiansund *see* Kristiansund
25 R13 **Christine** Texas, SW USA 28°47′N 98°30′W
173 U7 **Christmas Island** ◇ *Australian external territory* E Indian Ocean
129 T17 **Christmas Island** *island* E Indian Ocean
Christmas Island *see* Kiritimati
192 M7 **Christmas Ridge** *undersea feature* C Pacific Ocean
30 L16 **Christopher** Illinois, N USA 37°58′N 89°03′W
25 P9 **Christoval** Texas, SW USA 31°09′N 100°30′W
111 F17 **Chrudim** Pardubický Kraj, C Czech Republic 49°58′N 15°49′E
115 K25 **Chrýsi** *island* SE Greece
121 N2 **Chrysochoú, Kólpos** *var.* Khrysokhou Bay. *bay* E Mediterranean Sea
114 I13 **Chrysoúpoli** *var.* Hrisoupoli; *prev.* Khrisoúpolis. Anatolikí Makedonía kai Thráki, NE Greece 40°59′N 24°42′E
111 K16 **Chrzanów** *var.* Chrzanow, *Ger.* Zaumgarten. Śląskie, S Poland 50°10′N 19°21′E
Chu *see* Shu
42 C5 **Chuacús, Sierra de** W Guatemala
153 S15 **Chuadanga** Khulna, W Bangladesh 23°38′N 88°52′E
Chuan *see* Sichuan
Ch'uan-chou *see* Quanzhou
Chuankou *see* Minhe
39 O11 **Chuathbaluk** Alaska, USA 61°36′N 159°14′W
Chubek *see* Moskva
63 I17 **Chubut** *off.* Provincia de Chubut. ◐ *province* S Argentina
Chubut, Provincia de *see* Chubut
63 I17 **Chubut, Río** SE Argentina
43 V15 **Chucanti, Cerro** ▲ E Panama 08°48′N 78°27′W
Ch'u-chiang *see* Shaoguan
43 W15 **Chucunaque, Río** E Panama
Chudin *see* Chudzin
116 M5 **Chudniv** Zhytomyrs'ka Oblast', N Ukraine 50°02′N 28°06′E
124 H13 **Chudovo** Novgorodskaya Oblast', W Russian Federation 59°07′N 31°42′E
Chudskoye Ozero *see* Peipus, Lake
119 J18 **Chudzin** *Rus.* Chudin. Brestskaya Voblasts', SW Belarus 52°44′N 26°59′E
39 Q13 **Chugach Islands** *island group* Alaska, USA
39 S11 **Chugach Mountains** ▲ Alaska, USA
164 G12 **Chūgoku-sanchi** ▲ Honshū, SW Japan
Chuguyev *see* Chuhuyiv
Chugqênsumdo *see* Jigzhi
117 V5 **Chuhuyiv** *var.* Chuguyev. Kharkivs'ka Oblast', E Ukraine 49°51′N 36°44′E
61 H19 **Chuí** Rio Grande do Sul, S Brazil 33°45′S 53°23′W
Chuí *see* Chuy
Chu-Iliyskiye Gory *see* Gory Shu-Ile
Chukai *see* Cukai
Chukchi Avtonomnyy Okrug *see* Chukotskiy Avtonomnyy Okrug
Chukchi Peninsula *see* Chukotskiy Poluostrov
197 R6 **Chukchi Plain** *undersea feature* Arctic Ocean
197 R6 **Chukchi Plateau** *undersea feature* Arctic Ocean
197 R4 **Chukchi Sea** *Rus.* Chukotskoye More. *sea* Arctic Ocean
125 N14 **Chukhloma** Kostromskaya Oblast', NW Russian Federation 58°42′N 42°39′E
Chukotka *see* Chukotskiy Avtonomnyy Okrug
Chukot Range *see* Anadyrskiy Khrebet
123 V6 **Chukotskiy Avtonomnyy Okrug** *var.* Chukchi Avtonomnyy Okrug, Chukotka. ◐ *autonomous district* NE Russian Federation
123 W5 **Chukotskiy, Mys** *headland* NE Russian Federation 64°15′N 173°03′W
123 V5 **Chukotskiy Poluostrov** *Eng.* Chukchi Peninsula. *peninsula* NE Russian Federation
Chukotskoye More *see* Chukchi Sea
Chukurkak *see* Chuqurqoq
Chulakkurgan *see* Sholakkorgan
35 U17 **Chula Vista** California, W USA 32°38′N 117°04′W
123 Q12 **Chul'man** Respublika Sakha (Yakutiya), NE Russian Federation 56°50′N 124°47′E
56 B9 **Chulucanas** Piura, NW Peru 05°08′S 80°10′W
122 J12 **Chulym** C Russian Federation
152 K6 **Chumar** Jammu and Kashmir, N India 32°38′N 78°36′E
114 K9 **Chumerna** ▲ C Bulgaria 42°45′N 25°58′E
123 R12 **Chumikan** Khabarovskiy Kray, E Russian Federation 54°41′N 135°12′E
167 Q9 **Chum Phae** Khon Kaen, C Thailand 16°31′N 102°09′E
167 N13 **Chumphon** *var.* Jumporn. Chumphon, SW Thailand 10°30′N 99°11′E
167 O9 **Chumsaeng** *var.* Chum Saeng. Nakhon Sawan, C Thailand 15°52′N 100°18′E
Chum Saeng *see* Chumsaeng
122 L12 **Chuna** C Russian Federation
161 R9 **Chun'an** *var.* Qiandaohu; *prev.* Pailing. Zhejiang, SE China 29°37′N 118°59′E
Chunan *see* Zhunan
Chuncheng *see* Yangchun
163 Y14 **Chuncheon** *Jap.* Shunsen; *prev.* Ch'unch'ŏn. N South Korea 37°52′N 127°48′E
Ch'unch'ŏn *see* Chuncheon
153 S16 **Chunchura** *prev.* Chinsura. West Bengal, NE India 22°54′N 88°20′E
Chundzha *see* Shonzhy
Ch'ung-ch'ing/Ch'ung-ching *see* Chongqing
Chung-hua Jen-min Kung-ho-kuo *see* China
163 Y15 **Chungju** *Jap.* Chūshū; *prev.* Ch'ungju. C South Korea 36°57′N 127°50′E
Ch'ungju *see* Chungju
Chungking *see* Chongqing
161 T14 **Chungyang Shanmo** *Chin.* Taiwan Shan. ▲ C Taiwan
149 V9 **Chūniān** Punjab, E Pakistan 30°57′N 74°01′E
122 L12 **Chunskiy** Irkutskaya Oblast', S Russian Federation 56°10′N 99°15′E
122 M11 **Chunya** C Russian Federation
124 J6 **Chupa** Respublika Kareliya, NW Russian Federation 66°15′N 33°02′E
125 P8 **Chuprovo** Respublika Komi, NW Russian Federation 64°16′N 46°27′E
57 G17 **Chuquibamba** Arequipa, SW Peru 15°47′S 72°44′W
62 H4 **Chuquicamata** Antofagasta, N Chile 22°20′S 68°56′W
57 L21 **Chuquisaca** ◐ *department* S Bolivia
Chuquisaca *see* Sucre
Chuqung *see* Chindu
146 I8 **Chuqurqoq** *Rus.* Chukurkak. Qoraqalpog'iston Respublikasi, NW Uzbekistan 42°44′N 61°33′E
127 T2 **Chur** Udmurtskaya Respublika, NW Russian Federation 57°06′N 52°57′E
108 I9 **Chur** *Fr.* Coire, *It.* Coira, *Rmsch.* Cuera, Quera; *anc.* Curia Rhaetorum. Graubünden, E Switzerland 46°52′N 09°32′E
123 Q10 **Churapcha** Respublika Sakha (Yakutiya), NE Russian Federation 61°59′N 132°06′E
11 V16 **Churchbridge** Saskatchewan, S Canada 50°55′N 101°53′W
21 O8 **Church Hill** Tennessee, S USA 36°31′N 82°42′W
11 X9 **Churchill** Manitoba, C Canada 58°46′N 94°10′W
11 X10 **Churchill** Manitoba/Saskatchewan, C Canada
13 P9 **Churchill** Newfoundland and Labrador, E Canada
11 Y9 **Churchill, Cape** *headland* Manitoba, C Canada
13 P9 **Churchill Falls** Newfoundland and Labrador, E Canada 53°38′N 64°00′W
11 S12 **Churchill Lake** Saskatchewan, C Canada
19 Q3 **Churchill Lake** Maine, NE USA
194 I5 **Churchill Peninsula** *peninsula* Antarctica
22 H8 **Church Point** Louisiana, S USA 30°24′N 92°13′W
29 O3 **Churchs Ferry** North Dakota, N USA 48°15′N 99°12′W
146 G12 **Churchuri** Ahal Welaýaty, C Turkmenistan 38°55′N 59°13′E
21 T5 **Churchville** Virginia, NE USA 38°13′N 79°10′W
152 G10 **Chūru** Rājasthān, NW India 28°18′N 75°00′E
54 J4 **Churuguara** Falcón, N Venezuela 10°52′N 69°35′W
167 U11 **Chư Sê** Gia Lai, C Vietnam 13°38′N 108°06′E
144 J12 **Chushkakul, Gory** ▲ SW Kazakhstan
Chūshū *see* Chungju
37 O9 **Chuska Mountains** ▲ Arizona/New Mexico, SW USA
Chu, Sông *see* Sam, Nam
125 V14 **Chusovoy** Permskiy Kray, NW Russian Federation 58°17′N 57°54′E
147 R10 **Chust** Namangan Viloyati, E Uzbekistan 40°58′N 71°12′E
Chust *see* Khust
15 U6 **Chute-aux-Outardes** Québec, SE Canada 49°07′N 68°25′W
117 U5 **Chutove** Poltavs'ka Oblast', C Ukraine 49°45′N 35°11′E
167 U11 **Chư Ty** *var.* Đưc Co. Gia Lai, C Vietnam 13°48′N 107°41′E
189 O15 **Chuuk** *var.* Truk. ◐ *state* C Micronesia
189 P15 **Chuuk Islands** *var.* Hogoley Islands; *prev.* Truk Islands. *island group* Caroline Islands, C Micronesia
Chuvashia *see* Chuvashskaya Respublika
Chuvashiya *see* Chuvashskaya Respublika
127 P4 **Chuvashskaya Respublika** *var.* Chuvashiya, *Eng.* Chuvashia. ◐ *autonomous republic* W Russian Federation
Chuwārtah *see* Chwārtā
Chu Xian/Chuxian *see* Chuzhou
160 G13 **Chuxiong** Yunnan, SW China 25°02′N 101°32′E
147 V7 **Chuy** Chuyskaya Oblast', N Kyrgyzstan 42°45′N 75°11′E
61 H19 **Chuy** *var.* Chuí. Rocha, E Uruguay 33°42′S 53°27′W
123 O11 **Chuya** Respublika Sakha (Yakutiya), NE Russian Federation 59°30′N 112°26′E
Chüy Oblasty *see* Chuyskaya Oblast'
147 U8 **Chuyskaya Oblast'** *Kir.* Chüy Oblasty. ◐ *province* N Kyrgyzstan
161 Q7 **Chuzhou** *var.* Chuxian, Chu Xian. Anhui, E China 32°20′N 118°18′E
139 U3 **Chwārtā** *var.* Choarta, Chuwārtah. As Sulaymānīyah, NE Iraq 35°11′N 45°59′E
119 N16 **Chyhirynskaye Vodaskhovishcha** E Belarus
117 R6 **Chyhyryn** *Rus.* Chigirin. Cherkas'ka Oblast', N Ukraine 49°03′N 32°40′E
119 J18 **Chyrvonaya Slabada** *Rus.* Krasnaya Slabada, Krasnaya Sloboda. Minskaya Voblasts', S Belarus 52°51′N 27°10′E
119 L19 **Chyrvonaye, Vozyera** *Rus.* Ozero Chervonoye. SE Belarus
117 N11 **Ciadîr-Lunga** *var.* Ceadâr-Lunga, *Rus.* Chadyr-Lunga. S Moldova 46°03′N 28°50′E
169 P16 **Ciamis** *prev.* Tjiamis. Jawa, C Indonesia 07°20′S 108°21′E
107 I16 **Ciampino** ✕ Lazio, C Italy 41°48′N 12°36′E
169 N16 **Cianjur** *prev.* Tjiandjoer. Jawa, C Indonesia 06°50′S 107°09′E
60 H10 **Cianorte** Paraná, S Brazil 23°42′S 52°31′W
Ciarraí *see* Kerry
112 N13 **Ćićevac** Serbia, E Serbia 43°44′N 21°25′E
187 Z14 **Cicia** *prev.* Thithia. *island* Lau Group, E Fiji
105 P4 **Cidacos** N Spain
136 I10 **Cide** Kastamonu, N Turkey 41°53′N 33°01′E
110 L10 **Ciechanów** *prev.* Zichenau. Mazowieckie, C Poland 52°53′N 20°37′E
110 O10 **Ciechanowiec** *Ger.* Rudelstadt. Podlaskie, E Poland 52°43′N 22°30′E
110 J10 **Ciechocinek** Kujawsko-pomorskie, C Poland 52°53′N 18°49′E
44 F6 **Ciego de Ávila** Ciego de Ávila, C Cuba 21°50′N 78°44′W
54 F4 **Ciénaga** Magdalena, N Colombia 11°01′N 74°15′W
54 E6 **Ciénaga de Oro** Córdoba, NW Colombia 08°54′N 75°39′W
44 E5 **Cienfuegos** Cienfuegos, C Cuba 22°10′N 80°27′W
104 F4 **Cíes, Illas** *island group* NW Spain
111 P16 **Cieszanów** Podkarpackie, SE Poland 50°15′N 23°09′E
111 J17 **Cieszyn** *Cz.* Těšín, *Ger.* Teschen. Śląskie, S Poland 49°45′N 18°35′E
105 R12 **Cieza** Murcia, SE Spain 38°14′N 01°25′W
136 F13 **Çifteler** Eskişehir, W Turkey 39°25′N 31°00′E
105 P7 **Cifuentes** Castilla-La Mancha, C Spain 40°47′N 02°37′W
Ciganak *see* Shyganak
105 P9 **Cigüela** C Spain
136 H14 **Cihanbeyli** Konya, C Turkey 38°40′N 32°55′E
136 H14 **Cihanbeyli Yaylası** *plateau* C Turkey
104 L10 **Cijara, Embalse de** C Spain
169 P16 **Cikalong** Jawa, S Indonesia 07°46′S 108°13′E
169 N16 **Cikawung** Jawa, S Indonesia 06°49′S 105°29′E
187 Y13 **Cikobia** *prev.* Thikombia. *island* N Fiji
169 P17 **Cilacap** *prev.* Tjilatjap. Jawa, C Indonesia 07°44′S 109°E
173 O16 **Cilaos** C Réunion 21°08′S 55°28′E
137 S11 **Çıldır** Ardahan, NE Turkey 41°08′N 43°08′E
137 S11 **Çıldır Gölü** NE Turkey
160 M10 **Cili** Hunan, S China 29°24′N 110°59′E
Cilician Gates *see* Gülek Boğazı
121 V10 **Cilicia Trough** *undersea feature* E Mediterranean Sea
Cill Airne *see* Killarney
Cill Chainnigh *see* Kilkenny
Cill Chaoi *see* Kilkee
Cill Choca *see* Kilcock
Cill Dara *see* Kildare
105 N3 **Cilleruelo de Bezana** Castilla y León, N Spain 42°58′N 03°50′W
Cilli *see* Celje
Cill Mhantáin *see* Wicklow
Cill Rois *see* Kilrush
146 C11 **Çilmämmetgum** *Rus.* Peski Chil'mamedkum, *Turkm.* Chilmämetgum. *desert* Balkan Welaýaty, W Turkmenistan
137 Z11 **Çilov Adası** *Rus.* Ostrov Zhiloy. *island* E Azerbaijan
26 J6 **Cimarron** Kansas, C USA 37°49′N 100°20′W
37 T9 **Cimarron** New Mexico, SW USA 36°30′N 104°55′W
26 M9 **Cimarron River** Kansas/Oklahoma, C USA
117 N11 **Cimişlia** *Rus.* Chimishliya. S Moldova 46°31′N 28°45′E
Cimpia Turzii *see* Câmpia Turzii
Cîmpina *see* Câmpina
Cîmpulung *see* Câmpulung
Cîmpulung Moldovenesc *see* Câmpulung Moldovenesc
137 P15 **Çınar** Diyarbakır, SE Turkey 37°45′N 40°22′E
54 J8 **Cinaruco, Río** Colombia/Venezuela
Cina Selatan, Laut *see* South China Sea
105 T5 **Cinca** NE Spain
112 G13 **Cincar** ▲ SW Bosnia and Herzegovina 43°55′N 17°05′E
31 Q15 **Cincinnati** Ohio, N USA 39°04′N 84°34′W
21 M4 **Cincinnati** ✕ Kentucky, S USA 39°03′N 84°39′W
Cinco de Outubro *see* Xá-Muteba
136 C15 **Çine** Aydın, SW Turkey 37°37′N 28°03′E
99 J21 **Ciney** Namur, SE Belgium 50°17′N 05°06′E
104 H6 **Cinfães** Viseu, N Portugal 41°04′N 08°06′W
106 J12 **Cingoli** Marche, C Italy 43°25′N 13°09′E
41 U16 **Cintalapa** *var.* Cintalapa de Figueroa. Chiapas, SE Mexico 16°42′N 93°40′W
Cintalapa de Figueroa *see* Cintalapa
103 X14 **Cinto, Monte** ▲ Corse, France, C Mediterranean Sea 42°22′N 08°57′E
Cintra *see* Sintra
105 Q5 **Cintruénigo** Navarra, N Spain 42°05′N 01°50′W
Cionn tSáile *see* Kinsale
116 K13 **Ciorani** Prahova, SE Romania 44°49′N 26°25′E
113 E14 **Čiovo** *It.* Bua. *island* S Croatia
Cipiúr *see* Kippure
63 I15 **Cipolletti** Río Negro, C Argentina 38°55′S 68°W
120 L7 **Circeo, Capo** *headland* C Italy 41°15′N 13°03′E
39 S8 **Circle** *var.* Circle City. Alaska, USA 65°51′N 144°04′W
33 X8 **Circle** Montana, NW USA 47°25′N 105°32′W
Circle City *see* Circle
31 S14 **Circleville** Ohio, N USA 39°36′N 82°57′W
36 K6 **Circleville** Utah, W USA 38°10′N 112°16′W
169 P16 **Cirebon** *prev.* Tjirebon. Jawa, S Indonesia 06°46′S 108°33′E
97 L21 **Cirencester** *anc.* Corinium, Corinium Dobunorum. C England, United Kingdom 51°44′N 01°59′W
Cirkvenica *see* Crikvenica
107 O20 **Cirò** Calabria, SW Italy 39°22′N 17°02′E
107 O20 **Cirò Marina** Calabria, S Italy 39°21′N 17°07′E
102 K14 **Ciron** SW France
Cirquenizza *see* Crikvenica
25 R7 **Cisco** Texas, SW USA 32°23′N 98°58′W
116 I12 **Cisnădie** *Ger.* Heltau, *Hung.* Nagydisznód. Sibiu, SW Romania 45°42′N 24°09′E
63 G18 **Cisnes, Río** S Chile
25 T11 **Cistern** Texas, SW USA 29°46′N 97°12′W
104 L3 **Cistierna** Castilla y León, N Spain 42°47′N 05°08′W
Citharista *see* la Ciotat
Citlaltépetl *see* Orizaba, Volcán Pico de
55 X10 **Citron** NW French Guiana 04°49′N 53°55′W
23 N7 **Citronelle** Alabama, S USA 31°05′N 88°13′W
35 O7 **Citrus Heights** California, W USA 38°42′N 121°18′W
106 H7 **Cittadella** Veneto, NE Italy 45°37′N 11°46′E
106 H13 **Città della Pieve** Umbria, C Italy 42°57′N 12°01′E
106 H12 **Città di Castello** Umbria, C Italy 43°27′N 12°13′E
107 I14 **Cittaducale** Lazio, C Italy 42°24′N 12°55′E
107 N22 **Cittanova** Calabria, SW Italy 38°21′N 16°05′E
Cittavecchia *see* Stari Grad
116 G10 **Ciucea** *Hung.* Csucsa. Cluj, NW Romania 46°58′N 22°50′E
116 M13 **Ciucurova** Tulcea, SE Romania 44°57′N 28°24′E
Ciudad Acuña *see* Villa Acuña
41 N15 **Ciudad Altamirano** Guerrero, S Mexico 18°20′N 100°40′W
42 G7 **Ciudad Barrios** San Miguel, NE El Salvador 13°46′N 88°13′W
54 I7 **Ciudad Bolívar** Barinas, NW Venezuela 08°22′N 70°37′W
55 N7 **Ciudad Bolívar** *prev.* Angostura. Bolívar, E Venezuela 08°08′N 63°31′W
40 K6 **Ciudad Camargo** Chihuahua, N Mexico 27°42′N 105°10′W
40 E8 **Ciudad Constitución** Baja California Sur, NW Mexico 25°09′N 111°43′W
Ciudad Cortés *see* Cortés
41 V17 **Ciudad Cuauhtémoc** Chiapas, SE Mexico 15°38′N 91°59′W
42 J9 **Ciudad Darío** *var.* Dario. Matagalpa, W Nicaragua 12°42′N 86°10′W
Ciudad de Dolores Hidalgo *see* Dolores Hidalgo
42 C6 **Ciudad de Guatemala** *Eng.* Guatemala City; *prev.* Santiago de los Caballeros. ● (Guatemala) Guatemala, C Guatemala 14°38′N 90°29′W
Ciudad del Carmen *see* Carmen
62 Q6 **Ciudad del Este** *prev.* Cuidad Presidente Stroessner, Presidente Stroessner, Puerto Presidente Stroessner. Alto Paraná, SE Paraguay 25°34′S 54°40′W
62 K5 **Ciudad de Libertador General San Martín** *var.* Libertador General San Martín. Jujuy, C Argentina 23°50′S 64°45′W
Ciudad Delicias *see* Delicias
41 O11 **Ciudad del Maíz** San Luis Potosí, C Mexico 22°26′N 99°36′W
Ciudad de México *see* México
54 J7 **Ciudad de Nutrias** Barinas, NW Venezuela 08°03′N 69°17′W
Ciudad de Panama *see* Panamá
55 P7 **Ciudad Guayana** *prev.* San Tomé de Guayana, Santo Tomé de Guayana. Bolívar, NE Venezuela 08°22′N 62°37′W
40 K14 **Ciudad Guzmán** Jalisco, SW Mexico 19°40′N 103°30′W
41 V17 **Ciudad Hidalgo** Chiapas, SE Mexico 14°40′N 92°11′W
41 N14 **Ciudad Hidalgo** Michoacán, SW Mexico 19°40′N 100°34′W
40 J3 **Ciudad Juárez** Chihuahua, N Mexico 31°39′N 106°26′W
40 L8 **Ciudad Lerdo** Durango, C Mexico 25°34′N 103°30′W
41 Q11 **Ciudad Madero** *var.* Villa Cecilia. Tamaulipas, C Mexico 22°18′N 97°56′W
41 P11 **Ciudad Mante** Tamaulipas, C Mexico 22°43′N 99°02′W
42 F2 **Ciudad Melchor de Mencos** *var.* Melchor de Mencos. Petén, NE Guatemala 17°03′N 89°12′W
41 P8 **Ciudad Miguel Alemán** Tamaulipas, C Mexico 26°20′N 99°56′W
Ciudad Mutis *see* Bahía Solano
40 G6 **Ciudad Obregón** Sonora, NW Mexico 27°32′N 109°53′W
54 I5 **Ciudad Ojeda** Zulia, NW Venezuela 10°12′N 71°17′W
55 P7 **Ciudad Piar** Bolívar, E Venezuela 07°25′N 63°19′W
Ciudad Porfirio Díaz *see* Piedras Negras
Ciudad Presidente Stroessner *see* Ciudad del Este
Ciudad Quesada *see* Quesada
105 N11 **Ciudad Real** Castilla-La Mancha, C Spain 38°59′N 03°55′W
105 N11 **Ciudad Real** ◐ *province* Castilla-La Mancha, C Spain
104 J7 **Ciudad-Rodrigo** Castilla y León, N Spain 40°36′N 06°33′W
42 A6 **Ciudad Tecún Umán** San Marcos, SW Guatemala 14°40′N 92°06′W
Ciudad Trujillo *see* Santo Domingo
41 P12 **Ciudad Valles** San Luis Potosí, C Mexico 21°59′N 99°01′W
41 O10 **Ciudad Victoria** Tamaulipas, C Mexico 23°44′N 99°07′W
42 C6 **Ciudad Vieja** Suchitepéquez, S Guatemala 14°30′N 90°46′W
116 L8 **Ciuhuru** *var.* Reuţel. N Moldova
105 Z8 **Ciutadella** *var.* Ciutadella de Menorca. Menorca, Spain, W Mediterranean Sea 40°N 03°50′E
Ciutadella Ciutadella de Menorca *see* Ciutadella
136 L11 **Civa Burnu** *headland* N Turkey 41°22′N 36°39′E
106 J7 **Cividale del Friuli** Friuli-Venezia Giulia, NE Italy 46°06′N 13°25′E
107 H14 **Civita Castellana** Lazio, C Italy 42°16′N 12°24′E
106 J12 **Civitanova Marche** Marche, C Italy 43°18′N 13°41′E
Civitas Altae Ripae *see* Brzeg
Civitas Carnutum *see* Chartres
Civitas Eburovicum *see* Évreux
Civitas Nemetum *see* Speyer
107 G15 **Civitavecchia** *anc.* Centum Cellae, Trajani Portus. Lazio, C Italy 42°05′N 11°47′E
102 L10 **Civray** Vienne, W France 46°10′N 00°18′E
136 E14 **Çivril** Denizli, W Turkey 38°18′N 29°43′E
161 O5 **Cixian** Hebei, E China 36°19′N 114°22′E
137 R16 **Cizre** Şırnak, SE Turkey 37°21′N 42°11′E
Clacton *see* Clacton-on-Sea
97 Q21 **Clacton-on-Sea** *var.* Clacton. E England, United Kingdom 51°48′N 01°09′E
22 H5 **Claiborne, Lake** Louisiana, S USA
102 L10 **Clain** W France
11 Q11 **Claire, Lake** Alberta, C Canada
25 O6 **Clairemont** Texas, SW USA 33°09′N 100°45′W
34 M3 **Clair Engle Lake** California, W USA
18 B15 **Clairton** Pennsylvania, NE USA 40°17′N 79°52′W
32 F7 **Clallam Bay** Washington, NW USA 48°13′N 124°16′W
103 P8 **Clamecy** Nièvre, C France 47°28′N 03°30′E
23 P5 **Clanton** Alabama, S USA 32°50′N 86°37′W
61 D17 **Clara** Entre Ríos, E Argentina 31°50′S 58°48′W
97 E18 **Clara** *Ir.* Clóirtheach. C Ireland 53°20′N 07°36′W
29 T9 **Clara City** Minnesota, N USA 44°57′N 95°22′W

◆ Country
● Country Capital
◇ Dependent Territory
○ Dependent Territory Capital
◐ Administrative Regions
✕ International Airport
▲ Mountain
▲ Mountain Range
Volcano
River
Lake
Reservoir

61 D23 **Claraz** Buenos Aires, E Argentina 37°56′S 59°18′W
Clár Chlainne Mhuiris *see* Claremorris
182 I8 **Clare** South Australia 33°49′S 138°35′E
97 C19 **Clare** *Ir.* An Clár. *cultural region* W Ireland
97 C18 **Clare** W Ireland
97 A16 **Clare Island** *Ir.* Cliara. *island* W Ireland
44 J12 **Claremont** C Jamaica 18°23′N 77°11′W
29 W10 **Claremont** Minnesota, N USA 44°01′N 93°00′W
19 N9 **Claremont** New Hampshire, NE USA 43°21′N 72°18′W
27 Q9 **Claremore** Oklahoma, C USA 36°20′N 95°37′W
97 C17 **Claremorris** *Ir.* Clár Chlainne Mhuiris. W Ireland 53°47′N 09°W
185 J16 **Clarence** Canterbury, South Island, New Zealand 42°08′S 173°54′E
185 J16 **Clarence** South Island, New Zealand
65 F15 **Clarence Bay** *bay* Ascension Island, C Atlantic Ocean
63 H25 **Clarence, Isla** *island* S Chile
194 H2 **Clarence Island** *island* South Shetland Islands, Antarctica
183 V5 **Clarence River** New South Wales, SE Australia
44 J5 **Clarence Town** Long Island, C Bahamas 23°03′N 74°57′W
27 W12 **Clarendon** Arkansas, C USA 34°41′N 91°19′W
25 O3 **Clarendon** Texas, SW USA 34°57′N 100°54′W
13 U12 **Clarenville** Newfoundland, Newfoundland and Labrador, SE Canada 48°10′N 54°00′W
11 Q17 **Claresholm** Alberta, SW Canada 50°02′N 113°33′W
29 T16 **Clarinda** Iowa, C USA 40°44′N 95°02′W
55 N5 **Clarines** Anzoátegui, NE Venezuela 09°56′N 65°11′W
29 V12 **Clarion** Iowa, C USA 42°43′N 93°43′W
18 C13 **Clarion** Pennsylvania, NE USA 41°11′N 79°21′W
193 O6 **Clarion Fracture Zone** *tectonic feature* NE Pacific Ocean
18 D13 **Clarion River** Pennsylvania, NE USA
29 Q9 **Clark** South Dakota, N USA 44°50′N 97°44′W
36 K11 **Clarkdale** Arizona, SW USA 34°46′N 112°03′W
15 W4 **Clarke City** Québec, SE Canada 50°09′N 66°36′W
183 Q15 **Clarke Island** *island* Furneaux Group, Tasmania, SE Australia
181 X6 **Clarke Range** ▲▲ Queensland, E Australia
23 T2 **Clarkesville** Georgia, SE USA 34°36′N 83°31′W
29 S9 **Clarkfield** Minnesota, N USA 44°48′N 95°49′W
33 N7 **Clark Fork** Idaho, NW USA 48°06′N 116°10′W
33 N8 **Clark Fork** Idaho/Montana, NW USA
21 P13 **Clark Hill Lake** *var.* J.Storm Thurmond Reservoir. Georgia/South Carolina, SE USA
39 Q12 **Clark, Lake** Alaska, USA
35 W12 **Clark Mountain** ▲ California, W USA 35°30′N 115°34′W
37 S3 **Clark Peak** ▲ Colorado, C USA 40°36′N 105°57′W
14 D14 **Clark, Point** *headland* Ontario, S Canada 44°04′N 81°45′W
21 S3 **Clarksburg** West Virginia, NE USA 39°16′N 80°22′W
22 K2 **Clarksdale** Mississippi, S USA 34°12′N 90°34′W
33 U12 **Clarks Fork Yellowstone River** Montana/Wyoming, NW USA
29 R14 **Clarkson** Nebraska, C USA 41°42′N 97°07′W
39 O13 **Clarks Point** Alaska, USA 58°50′N 158°33′W
18 I13 **Clarks Summit** Pennsylvania, NE USA 41°29′N 75°42′W
32 M10 **Clarkston** Washington, NW USA 46°25′N 117°02′W
44 J12 **Clark's Town** C Jamaica 18°25′N 77°32′W
27 T10 **Clarksville** Arkansas, C USA 35°29′N 93°29′W
31 P13 **Clarksville** Indiana, N USA 40°01′N 85°54′W
20 I8 **Clarksville** Tennessee, S USA 36°32′N 87°22′W
25 W5 **Clarksville** Texas, SW USA 33°37′N 95°04′W
21 U8 **Clarksville** Virginia, NE USA 36°36′N 78°36′W
21 U11 **Clarkton** North Carolina, SE USA 34°28′N 78°39′W
61 C24 **Claromecó** *var.* Balneario Claromecó. Buenos Aires, E Argentina 38°51′S 60°01′W
25 N3 **Claude** Texas, SW USA 35°06′N 101°22′W
Clausentum *see* Southampton
171 O1 **Claveria** Luzon, N Philippines 18°36′N 121°04′E
99 J20 **Clavier** Liège, E Belgium 50°27′N 05°21′E
23 W6 **Claxton** Georgia, SE USA 32°09′N 81°54′W
21 R4 **Clay** West Virginia, NE USA 38°28′N 81°17′W
27 N3 **Clay Center** Kansas, C USA 39°22′N 97°08′W
29 P16 **Clay Center** Nebraska, C USA 40°31′N 98°03′W
21 Y2 **Claymont** Delaware, NE USA 39°48′N 75°27′W
36 M14 **Claypool** Arizona, SW USA 33°24′N 110°50′W
23 R6 **Clayton** Alabama, S USA 31°52′N 85°27′W
23 T1 **Clayton** Georgia, SE USA 34°52′N 83°24′W
22 J5 **Clayton** Louisiana, S USA 31°43′N 91°32′W
27 X5 **Clayton** Missouri, C USA 38°39′N 90°21′W
37 V9 **Clayton** New Mexico, SW USA 36°27′N 103°12′W
21 V9 **Clayton** North Carolina, SE USA 35°39′N 78°27′W
27 Q12 **Clayton** Oklahoma, C USA 34°35′N 95°21′W
45 V9 **Clayton J. Lloyd** ✈ (The Valley) C Anguilla 18°12′N 63°02′W
182 I4 **Clayton River** *seasonal river* South Australia
21 R7 **Claytor Lake** Virginia, NE USA
27 P13 **Clear Boggy Creek** Oklahoma, C USA
97 B22 **Clear, Cape** *var.* The Bill of Cape Clear, *Ir.* Ceann Cléire. *headland* SW Ireland 51°25′N 09°31′W
36 M12 **Clear Creek** Arizona, SW USA
39 S12 **Cleare, Cape** *headland* Montague Island, Alaska, USA 59°46′N 147°54′W
18 E13 **Clearfield** Pennsylvania, NE USA 41°02′N 78°27′W
36 L2 **Clearfield** Utah, W USA 41°06′N 112°03′W
25 Q6 **Clear Fork Brazos River** Texas, SW USA
31 T12 **Clear Fork Reservoir** Ohio, N USA
11 N12 **Clear Hills** ▲▲ Alberta, SW Canada
34 M6 **Clearlake** California, W USA 38°57′N 122°38′W
29 V12 **Clear Lake** Iowa, C USA 43°07′N 93°27′W
29 R9 **Clear Lake** South Dakota, N USA 44°45′N 96°40′W
34 M6 **Clear Lake** California, W USA
22 G6 **Clear Lake** Louisiana, S USA
35 P1 **Clear Lake Reservoir** California, W USA
11 N16 **Clearwater** British Columbia, SW Canada 51°38′N 120°02′W
23 U12 **Clearwater** Florida, SE USA 27°58′N 82°46′W
11 R12 **Clearwater** Alberta/Saskatchewan, C Canada
27 W7 **Clearwater Lake** Missouri, C USA
33 N10 **Clearwater Mountains** ▲▲ Idaho, NW USA
33 N10 **Clearwater River** Idaho, NW USA
29 S4 **Clearwater River** Minnesota, N USA
25 T7 **Cleburne** Texas, SW USA 32°21′N 97°24′W
32 I9 **Cle Elum** Washington, NW USA 47°12′N 120°56′W
97 O17 **Cleethorpes** E England, United Kingdom 53°34′N 00°02′W
Cléire, Ceann *see* Clear, Cape
21 O11 **Clemson** South Carolina, SE USA 34°40′N 82°50′W
21 Q4 **Clendenin** West Virginia, NE USA 38°29′N 81°21′W
26 M9 **Cleo Springs** Oklahoma, C USA 36°25′N 98°25′W
Clerk Island *see* Onotoa
181 X8 **Clermont** Queensland, E Australia 22°47′S 147°41′E
15 S8 **Clermont** Québec, SE Canada 47°41′N 70°15′W
103 O4 **Clermont** Oise, N France 49°23′N 02°26′E
29 X12 **Clermont** Iowa, C USA 43°00′N 91°39′W
103 P11 **Clermont-Ferrand** Puy-de-Dôme, C France 45°47′N 03°05′E
103 Q15 **Clermont-l'Hérault** Hérault, S France 43°37′N 03°25′E
99 M22 **Clervaux** Diekirch, N Luxembourg 50°03′N 06°02′E
106 G6 **Cles** Trentino-Alto Adige, N Italy 46°22′N 11°04′E
182 H8 **Cleve** South Australia 33°43′S 136°30′E
Cleve *see* Kleve
23 T2 **Cleveland** Georgia, SE USA 34°36′N 83°45′W
22 K3 **Cleveland** Mississippi, S USA 33°45′N 90°43′W
31 T11 **Cleveland** Ohio, N USA 41°30′N 81°42′W
27 O9 **Cleveland** Oklahoma, C USA 36°18′N 96°27′W
20 L10 **Cleveland** Tennessee, S USA 35°10′N 84°51′W
25 W10 **Cleveland** Texas, SW USA 30°19′N 95°06′W
31 N7 **Cleveland** Wisconsin, N USA 43°58′N 87°45′W
31 O4 **Cleveland Cliffs Basin** Michigan, N USA
31 U11 **Cleveland Heights** Ohio, N USA 41°30′N 81°34′W
33 P6 **Cleveland, Mount** ▲ Montana, NW USA 48°55′N 113°51′W
Cleves *see* Kleve
97 B16 **Clew Bay** *Ir.* Cuan Mó. *inlet* W Ireland
23 Y14 **Clewiston** Florida, SE USA 26°45′N 80°55′W
Cliara *see* Clare Island
97 A17 **Clifden** *Ir.* An Clochán. Galway, W Ireland 53°29′N 10°14′W
37 O14 **Clifton** Arizona, SW USA 33°03′N 109°18′W
18 K14 **Clifton** New Jersey, NE USA 40°50′N 74°28′W
25 S8 **Clifton** Texas, SW USA 31°43′N 97°36′W
21 S6 **Clifton Forge** Virginia, NE USA 37°49′N 79°50′W
182 I1 **Clifton Hills** South Australia 27°03′S 138°49′E
11 S17 **Climax** Saskatchewan, S Canada 49°12′N 108°22′W
21 O8 **Clinch River** Tennessee/Virginia, S USA
25 P12 **Cline** Texas, SW USA 29°14′N 100°07′W
21 N10 **Clingmans Dome** ▲ North Carolina/Tennessee, SE USA 35°33′N 83°30′W
24 H8 **Clint** Texas, SW USA 31°35′N 106°13′W
10 M16 **Clinton** British Columbia, SW Canada 51°06′N 121°31′W
14 E15 **Clinton** Ontario, S Canada 43°36′N 81°33′W
27 U10 **Clinton** Arkansas, C USA 35°34′N 92°28′W
30 L10 **Clinton** Illinois, N USA 40°09′N 88°57′W
29 Z14 **Clinton** Iowa, C USA 41°50′N 90°11′W
20 G7 **Clinton** Kentucky, S USA 36°39′N 89°00′W
22 J8 **Clinton** Louisiana, S USA 30°52′N 91°01′W
19 N11 **Clinton** Massachusetts, NE USA 42°25′N 71°40′W
31 R10 **Clinton** Michigan, N USA 42°04′N 83°58′W
22 K5 **Clinton** Mississippi, S USA 32°22′N 90°22′W
27 S5 **Clinton** Missouri, C USA 38°22′N 93°51′W
21 V10 **Clinton** North Carolina, SE USA 35°00′N 78°19′W
26 L10 **Clinton** Oklahoma, C USA 35°31′N 98°58′W
21 Q12 **Clinton** South Carolina, SE USA 34°28′N 81°52′W
21 M9 **Clinton** Tennessee, S USA 36°07′N 84°08′W
8 L9 **Clinton-Colden Lake** Northwest Territories, NW Canada
10 H5 **Clinton Creek** Yukon Territory, NW Canada 64°24′N 140°35′W
30 L13 **Clinton Lake** Illinois, N USA
27 Q4 **Clinton Lake** Kansas, N USA
21 T11 **Clio** South Carolina, SE USA 34°34′N 79°33′W
193 O7 **Clipperton Fracture Zone** *tectonic feature* E Pacific Ocean
193 Q7 **Clipperton Island** ◇ *French dependency of French Polynesia* E Pacific Ocean
46 K6 **Clipperton Island** *island* E Pacific Ocean
0 F16 **Clipperton Seamounts** *undersea feature* E Pacific Ocean 08°00′N 111°00′W
102 J8 **Clisson** Loire-Atlantique, NW France 47°06′N 01°19′W
62 K7 **Clodomira** Santiago del Estero, N Argentina 27°35′S 64°14′W
Cloich na Coillte *see* Clonakilty
Clóirtheach *see* Clara
97 C21 **Clonakilty** *Ir.* Cloich na Coillte. SW Ireland 51°37′N 08°54′W
181 T6 **Cloncurry** Queensland, C Australia 20°45′S 140°30′E
97 F18 **Clondalkin** *Ir.* Cluain Dolcáin. E Ireland 53°19′N 06°24′W
97 E16 **Clones** *Ir.* Cluain Eois. N Ireland 54°11′N 07°14′W
97 D20 **Clonmel** *Ir.* Cluain Meala. S Ireland 52°21′N 07°42′W
100 G11 **Cloppenburg** Niedersachsen, NW Germany 52°51′N 08°03′E
29 W6 **Cloquet** Minnesota, N USA 46°43′N 92°27′W
37 S14 **Cloudcroft** New Mexico, SW USA 32°57′N 105°44′W
33 W12 **Cloud Peak** ▲ Wyoming, C USA 44°22′N 107°10′W
185 K14 **Cloudy Bay** *inlet* South Island, New Zealand
21 R10 **Clover** South Carolina, SE USA 35°06′N 81°13′W
34 M6 **Cloverdale** California, W USA 38°49′N 123°03′W
20 J5 **Cloverport** Kentucky, S USA 37°50′N 86°37′W
35 Q10 **Clovis** California, W USA 36°48′N 119°43′W
37 W12 **Clovis** New Mexico, SW USA 34°22′N 103°12′W
14 K13 **Cloyne** Ontario, SE Canada 44°48′N 77°09′W
Cluain Dolcáin *see* Clondalkin
Cluain Eois *see* Clones
Cluainín *see* Manorhamilton
Cluain Meala *see* Clonmel
116 H10 **Cluj** ◈ *county* NW Romania
Cluj *see* Cluj-Napoca
116 H10 **Cluj-Napoca** *Ger.* Klausenburg, *Hung.* Kolozsvár; *prev.* Cluj. Cluj, NW Romania 46°47′N 23°36′E
Clunia *see* Feldkirch
103 R10 **Cluny** Saône-et-Loire, C France 46°25′N 04°38′E
103 T10 **Cluses** Haute-Savoie, E France 46°04′N 06°34′E
106 E7 **Clusone** Lombardia, N Italy 45°56′N 10°00′E
25 W12 **Clute** Texas, SW USA 29°01′N 95°24′W
185 D23 **Clutha** South Island, New Zealand
97 J18 **Clwyd** *cultural region* NE Wales, United Kingdom
185 D22 **Clyde** Otago, South Island, New Zealand 45°12′S 169°21′E
27 N3 **Clyde** Kansas, C USA 39°35′N 97°24′W
29 P2 **Clyde** North Dakota, N USA 48°44′N 98°51′W
31 S11 **Clyde** Ohio, N USA 41°18′N 82°58′W
25 Q7 **Clyde** Texas, SW USA 32°24′N 99°29′W
14 K13 **Clyde** Ontario, SE Canada
96 J13 **Clyde** W Scotland, United Kingdom
96 H12 **Clydebank** S Scotland, United Kingdom 55°54′N 04°24′W
96 H13 **Clyde, Firth of** *inlet* S Scotland, United Kingdom
33 S11 **Clyde Park** Montana, NW USA 45°56′N 110°39′W
35 W16 **Coachella** California, W USA 33°38′N 116°10′W
35 W16 **Coachella Canal** *canal* California, W USA
40 I9 **Coacoyole** Durango, C Mexico 24°30′N 106°33′W
25 N7 **Coahoma** Texas, SW USA 32°18′N 101°18′W
10 K8 **Coal** Yukon Territory, NW Canada
40 L14 **Coalcomán** *var.* Coalcomán de Matamoros. Michoacán, S Mexico 18°49′N 103°13′W
Coalcomán de Matamoros *see* Coalcomán
39 T8 **Coal Creek** Alaska, USA 65°21′N 143°08′W
11 Q17 **Coaldale** Alberta, SW Canada 49°42′N 112°36′W
27 P12 **Coalgate** Oklahoma, C USA 34°33′N 96°15′W
35 P11 **Coalinga** California, W USA 36°08′N 120°21′W
10 L9 **Coal River** British Columbia, W Canada 59°38′N 126°45′W
21 Q6 **Coal River** West Virginia, NE USA
36 M2 **Coalville** Utah, W USA 40°56′N 111°22′W
58 E13 **Coari** Amazonas, N Brazil 04°08′S 63°07′W
104 I7 **Côa, Rio** N Portugal
59 D14 **Coari, Rio** NW Brazil
81 J20 **Coast** ◈ *province* SE Kenya
Coast *see* Pwani
10 G12 **Coast Mountains** *Fr.* Chaîne Côtière. ▲▲ Canada/USA
16 C7 **Coast Ranges** ▲▲ W USA
96 I12 **Coatbridge** S Scotland, United Kingdom 55°52′N 04°01′W
42 B6 **Coatepeque** Quezaltenango, SW Guatemala 14°42′N 91°50′W
18 H16 **Coatesville** Pennsylvania, NE USA 39°58′N 75°47′W
15 Q13 **Coaticook** Québec, SE Canada 45°07′N 71°46′W
9 P9 **Coats Island** *island* Nunavut, NE Canada
195 O4 **Coats Land** *physical region* Antarctica
41 T14 **Coatzacoalcos** *var.* Quetzalcoalco; *prev.* Puerto México. Veracruz-Llave, E Mexico 18°06′N 94°26′W
41 S14 **Coatzacoalcos, Río** SE Mexico
116 M15 **Cobadin** Constanța, SW Romania 44°05′N 28°13′E
14 H9 **Cobalt** Ontario, S Canada 47°24′N 79°41′W
42 D5 **Cobán** Alta Verapaz, C Guatemala 15°28′N 90°20′W
183 O6 **Cobar** New South Wales, SE Australia 31°31′S 145°51′E
18 F12 **Cobb Hill** ▲ Pennsylvania, NE USA 41°52′N 77°52′W
0 D8 **Cobb Seamount** *undersea feature* E Pacific Ocean 47°00′N 131°00′W
14 K12 **Cobden** Ontario, SE Canada 45°36′N 76°54′W
97 D21 **Cobh** *Ir.* An Cóbh; *prev.* Cove of Cork, Queenstown. SW Ireland 51°51′N 08°17′W
57 J14 **Cobija** Pando, NW Bolivia 11°04′S 68°49′W
Coblence/Coblenz *see* Koblenz
18 J10 **Cobleskill** New York, NE USA 42°40′N 74°29′W
14 I15 **Cobourg** Ontario, SE Canada 43°57′N 78°06′W
181 P1 **Cobourg Peninsula** *headland* Northern Territory, N Australia 11°27′S 132°33′E
183 O10 **Cobram** Victoria, SE Australia 35°56′S 145°36′E
82 N13 **Cóbuè** Niassa, N Mozambique 12°08′S 34°46′E
101 K18 **Coburg** Bayern, SE Germany 50°16′N 10°58′E
19 Q5 **Coburn Mountain** ▲ Maine, NE USA 45°28′N 70°07′W
57 H18 **Cocachacra** Arequipa, SW Peru 17°05′S 71°45′W
59 J17 **Cocalinho** Mato Grosso, W Brazil 14°22′S 51°00′W
Cocanada *see* Kākināda
105 S11 **Cocentaina** Valenciana, E Spain 38°44′N 00°27′W
57 L18 **Cochabamba** *hist.* Oropeza. Cochabamba, C Bolivia 17°23′S 66°10′W
57 K18 **Cochabamba** ◈ *department* C Bolivia
57 L18 **Cochabamba, Cordillera de** ▲▲ C Bolivia
101 E18 **Cochem** Rheinland-Pfalz, W Germany 50°09′N 07°09′E
37 R6 **Cochetopa Hills** ▲▲ Colorado, C USA
155 G22 **Cochin** *var.* Kochchi, Kochi. Kerala, SW India 09°56′N 76°15′E *see also* Kochi
44 D5 **Cochinos, Bahía de** *Eng.* Bay of Pigs. *bay* SE Cuba
37 O16 **Cochise Head** ▲ Arizona, SW USA 32°03′N 109°19′W
23 U5 **Cochran** Georgia, SE USA 32°23′N 83°21′W
11 P16 **Cochrane** Alberta, SW Canada 51°15′N 114°25′W
12 G12 **Cochrane** Ontario, S Canada 49°04′N 81°02′W
63 G20 **Cochrane** Aisén, S Chile 47°16′S 72°33′W
11 U10 **Cochrane** Manitoba/Saskatchewan, C Canada
Cochrane, Lago *see* Pueyrredón, Lago
Cocibolca *see* Nicaragua, Lago de
Cockade State *see* Maryland
44 M6 **Cockburn Harbour** South Caicos, S Turks and Caicos Islands 21°28′N 71°30′W
14 C11 **Cockburn Island** *island* Ontario, S Canada
44 J3 **Cockburn Town** San Salvador, E Bahamas 24°01′N 74°31′W
21 X2 **Cockeysville** Maryland, NE USA 39°29′N 76°34′W
181 N12 **Cocklebiddy** Western Australia 32°02′S 125°54′E
44 I12 **Cockpit Country, The** *physical region* W Jamaica
43 S16 **Coclé** *off.* Provincia de Coclé. ◈ *province* C Panama
43 S15 **Coclé del Norte** Colón, C Panama 09°04′N 80°32′W
Coclé, Provincia de *see* Coclé
23 Y12 **Cocoa** Florida, SE USA 28°23′N 80°44′W
23 Y12 **Cocoa Beach** Florida, SE USA 28°19′N 80°36′W
79 D17 **Cocobeach** Estuaire, NW Gabon 0°59′N 09°34′E
44 G5 **Coco, Cayo** *island* C Cuba
151 Q19 **Coco Channel** *strait* Andaman Sea/Bay of Bengal
173 N6 **Coco-de-Mer Seamounts** *undersea feature* W Indian Ocean 0°30′N 56°00′E
36 K10 **Coconino Plateau** *plain* Arizona, SW USA
43 N6 **Coco, Río** *var.* Río Wanki, Segoviao Wangkí. Honduras/Nicaragua
173 T7 **Cocos Basin** *undersea feature* E Indian Ocean 05°00′S 94°00′E
188 B17 **Cocos Island** *island* S Guam
Cocos Island Ridge *see* Cocos Ridge
129 S17 **Cocos Islands** *island group* E Indian Ocean
173 T8 **Cocos (Keeling) Islands** ◇ *Australian external territory* E Indian Ocean
0 G15 **Cocos Plate** *tectonic feature*
193 T7 **Cocos Ridge** *var.* Cocos Island Ridge. *undersea feature* E Pacific Ocean 05°30′N 86°00′W
40 K13 **Cocula** Jalisco, SW Mexico 20°22′N 103°50′W
107 D17 **Coda Cavallo, Capo** *headland* Sardegna, Italy, C Mediterranean Sea 40°49′N 09°43′E
58 E13 **Codajás** Amazonas, N Brazil 03°50′S 62°12′W
Codazzi *see* Agustín Codazzi
19 Q12 **Cod, Cape** *headland* Massachusetts, NE USA 41°50′N 69°56′W
185 B25 **Codfish Island** *island* SW New Zealand
106 H9 **Codigoro** Emilia-Romagna, N Italy 44°50′N 12°07′E
13 P5 **Cod Island** *island* Newfoundland and Labrador, E Canada
116 J12 **Codlea** *Ger.* Zeiden, *Hung.* Feketehalom. Brașov, C Romania 45°43′N 25°27′E
58 M13 **Codó** Maranhão, E Brazil 04°28′S 43°51′W
106 E8 **Codogno** Lombardia, N Italy 45°10′N 09°42′E
116 M10 **Codrii** *hill range* C Moldova
45 W9 **Codrington** Barbuda, Antigua and Barbuda 17°43′N 61°49′W
106 J7 **Codroipo** Friuli-Venezia Giulia, NE Italy 45°58′N 13°00′E
28 M12 **Cody** Nebraska, C USA 42°54′N 101°13′W
33 U12 **Cody** Wyoming, C USA 43°31′N 109°04′W
21 P7 **Coeburn** Virginia, NE USA 36°56′N 82°27′W
54 E10 **Coello** Tolima, W Colombia 04°15′N 74°52′W
Coemba *see* Cuemba
181 V2 **Coen** Queensland, NE Australia 14°03′S 143°16′E
101 E14 **Coesfeld** Nordrhein-Westfalen, W Germany 51°55′N 07°10′E
32 M8 **Coeur d'Alene** Idaho, NW USA 47°40′N 116°46′W
32 M8 **Coeur d'Alene Lake** Idaho, NW USA
98 O8 **Coevorden** Drenthe, NE Netherlands 52°39′N 06°45′E
10 H6 **Coffee Creek** Yukon Territory, W Canada 62°52′N 139°05′W
30 L15 **Coffeen Lake** Illinois, N USA
22 L3 **Coffeeville** Mississippi, S USA 33°58′N 89°40′W
27 Q8 **Coffeyville** Kansas, C USA 37°02′N 95°37′W
182 G9 **Coffin Bay** South Australia 34°39′S 135°30′E
182 F9 **Coffin Bay Peninsula** *peninsula* South Australia
183 V5 **Coffs Harbour** New South Wales, SE Australia 30°18′S 153°08′E
105 R10 **Cofrentes** Valenciana, E Spain 39°14′N 01°04′W
117 N10 **Cogîlnic** *Ukr.* Kohyl'nyk. Moldova/Ukraine
102 K11 **Cognac** *anc.* Compniacum. Charente, W France 45°42′N 00°19′W
106 B7 **Cogne** Valle d'Aosta, NW Italy 45°37′N 07°27′E
103 U16 **Cogolin** Var, SE France 43°15′N 06°30′E
105 O7 **Cogolludo** Castilla-La Mancha, C Spain 40°58′N 03°05′W
Cohalm *see* Rupea
92 K8 **Čohkarášša** *var.* Cuokkarašša. ▲ N Norway 69°57′N 24°38′E
Čohkkiras *see* Jukkasjärvi
18 F11 **Cohocton River** New York, NE USA
18 L10 **Cohoes** New York, NE USA 42°46′N 73°42′W
183 N10 **Cohuna** Victoria, SE Australia 35°51′S 144°15′E
43 P17 **Coiba, Isla de** *island* SW Panama
63 H23 **Coig, Río** S Argentina
63 G19 **Coihaique** *var.* Coyhaique. Aisén, S Chile 45°32′S 72°00′W
155 G21 **Coimbatore** Tamil Nādu, S India 11°N 76°57′E
104 G8 **Coimbra** *anc.* Conimbria, Conimbriga. Coimbra, W Portugal 40°12′N 08°25′W
104 G8 **Coimbra** ◈ *district* N Portugal
104 L15 **Coín** Andalucía, S Spain 36°40′N 04°45′W
Coin de Mire *see* Gunner's Quoin
57 J20 **Coipasa, Laguna** W Bolivia
57 J20 **Coipasa, Salar de** *salt lake* W Bolivia
Coira/Coire *see* Chur
Coirib, Loch *see* Corrib, Lough
54 K6 **Cojedes** *off.* Estado Cojedes. ◈ *state* N Venezuela
Cojedes, Estado *see* Cojedes
42 F7 **Cojutepeque** Cuscatlán, C El Salvador 13°43′N 88°56′W
Coka *see* Banbar
33 S16 **Cokeville** Wyoming, C USA 42°03′N 110°55′W
182 M13 **Colac** Victoria, SE Australia 38°22′S 143°38′E
59 O20 **Colatina** Espírito Santo, SE Brazil 19°35′S 40°37′W
27 O13 **Colbert** Oklahoma, C USA 33°51′N 96°30′W
100 L12 **Colbitz-Letzinger Heide** *heathland* N Germany
26 I3 **Colby** Kansas, C USA 39°24′N 101°04′W
57 H17 **Colca, Río** SW Peru
97 P21 **Colchester** *hist.* Colneceaste; *anc.* Camulodunum. E England, United Kingdom 51°54′N 00°54′E
19 N13 **Colchester** Connecticut, NE USA 41°34′N 72°17′W
38 M16 **Cold Bay** Alaska, USA 55°11′N 162°43′W
11 R14 **Cold Lake** Alberta, SW Canada 54°26′N 110°16′W
11 R13 **Cold Lake** Alberta/Saskatchewan, S Canada
29 U8 **Cold Spring** Minnesota, N USA 45°27′N 94°25′W
25 W10 **Coldspring** Texas, SW USA 30°34′N 95°10′W
11 N17 **Coldstream** British Columbia, SW Canada 50°13′N 119°09′W
96 L13 **Coldstream** SE Scotland, United Kingdom 55°39′N 02°19′W
14 H13 **Coldwater** Ontario, S Canada 44°43′N 79°36′W
26 K7 **Coldwater** Kansas, C USA 37°16′N 99°20′W
31 Q10 **Coldwater** Michigan, N USA 41°56′N 85°00′W
25 N1 **Coldwater Creek** Oklahoma/Texas, SW USA
22 K2 **Coldwater River** Mississippi, S USA
183 O9 **Coleambally** New South Wales, SE Australia 34°48′S 145°54′E
19 O6 **Colebrook** New Hampshire, NE USA 44°52′N 71°27′W
27 T5 **Cole Camp** Missouri, C USA 38°27′N 93°12′W
39 T6 **Coleen River** Alaska, USA
11 P17 **Coleman** Alberta, SW Canada 49°36′N 114°26′W
25 Q8 **Coleman** Texas, SW USA 31°50′N 99°27′W
Çölemerik *see* Hakkâri
83 K22 **Colenso** KwaZulu/Natal, E South Africa 28°44′S 29°50′E
182 L12 **Coleraine** Victoria, SE Australia 37°39′S 141°42′E
97 F14 **Coleraine** *Ir.* Cúil Raithin. N Northern Ireland, United Kingdom 55°08′N 06°40′W
185 G18 **Coleridge, Lake** South Island, New Zealand
83 H24 **Colesberg** Northern Cape, C South Africa 30°41′S 25°08′E
22 H7 **Colfax** Louisiana, S USA 31°31′N 92°42′W
32 L9 **Colfax** Washington, NW USA 46°52′N 117°21′W
30 J6 **Colfax** Wisconsin, N USA 45°00′N 91°44′W
63 I19 **Colhué Huapí, Lago** S Argentina
45 Z6 **Colibris, Pointe des** *headland* Grande Terre, E Guadeloupe 16°15′N 61°10′W
106 D6 **Colico** Lombardia, N Italy 46°08′N 09°24′E
99 E14 **Colijnsplaat** Zeeland, SW Netherlands 51°36′N 03°47′E
40 L14 **Colima** Colima, S Mexico 19°13′N 103°46′W
40 K14 **Colima** ◈ *state* SW Mexico
40 L14 **Colima, Nevado de** C Mexico 19°36′N 103°36′W
59 M14 **Colinas** Maranhão, E Brazil 06°02′S 44°15′W
96 F10 **Coll** *island* W Scotland, United Kingdom
105 N7 **Collado Villalba** *var.* Villalba. Madrid, C Spain 40°38′N 04°00′W
183 R4 **Collarenebri** New South Wales, SE Australia 29°31′S 148°33′E
37 P5 **Collbran** Colorado, C USA 39°14′N 107°57′W
106 G12 **Colle di Val d'Elsa** Toscana, C Italy 43°26′N 11°06′E
39 R9 **College** Alaska, USA 64°49′N 148°06′W
32 K10 **College Place** Washington, NW USA 46°03′N 118°23′W
25 U10 **College Station** Texas, SW USA 30°38′N 96°21′W
183 P4 **Collerina** New South Wales, SE Australia 29°41′S 146°36′E
180 I13 **Collie** Western Australia 33°20′S 116°06′E
180 L4 **Collier Bay** *bay* Western Australia
21 F10 **Collierville** Tennessee, S USA 35°02′N 89°39′W
106 F11 **Collina, Passo della** *pass* C Italy
14 G14 **Collingwood** Ontario, S Canada 44°30′N 80°14′W
184 I13 **Collingwood** Tasman, South Island, New Zealand 40°40′S 172°40′E
22 L7 **Collins** Mississippi, S USA 31°39′N 89°33′W
30 K15 **Collinsville** Illinois, N USA 38°40′N 89°58′W
27 P9 **Collinsville** Oklahoma, C USA 36°21′N 95°50′W
20 H10 **Collinwood** Tennessee, S USA 35°10′N 87°44′W
Collipo *see* Leiria
63 G14 **Collipulli** Araucanía, C Chile 37°55′S 72°30′W
97 D16 **Collooney** *Ir.* Cúil Mhuine. NW Ireland 54°11′N 08°29′W
29 R10 **Colman** South Dakota, N USA 43°58′N 96°48′W
103 U6 **Colmar** *Ger.* Kolmar. Haut-Rhin, NE France 48°05′N 07°21′E
104 M15 **Colmenar** Andalucía, S Spain 36°54′N 04°20′W
Colmenar *see* Colmenar de Oreja
105 O9 **Colmenar de Oreja** *var.* Colmenar. Madrid, C Spain 40°06′N 03°25′W
105 N7 **Colmenar Viejo** Madrid, C Spain 40°39′N 03°46′W
25 X9 **Colmesneil** Texas, SW USA 30°54′N 94°25′W
Cöln *see* Köln
Colneceaste *see* Colchester
59 G15 **Colniza** Mato Grosso, W Brazil 09°16′S 59°25′W
Cologne *see* Köln
42 B6 **Colomba** Quezaltenango, SW Guatemala 14°45′N 91°39′W
Colomb-Béchar *see* Béchar
54 E11 **Colombia** Huila, C Colombia 03°24′N 74°49′W
54 G10 **Colombia** *off.* Republic of Colombia. ◆ *republic* N South America
64 E12 **Colombian Basin** *undersea feature* SW Caribbean Sea 13°00′N 76°00′W
Colombia, Republic of *see* Colombia
Colombie-Britannique *see* British Columbia
15 T6 **Colombier** Québec, SE Canada 48°51′N 68°52′W
155 J25 **Colombo** ● (Sri Lanka) Western Province, W Sri Lanka 06°55′N 79°52′E
155 J25 **Colombo** ✈ Western Province, SW Sri Lanka 06°50′N 79°59′E
29 N11 **Colome** South Dakota, N USA 43°13′N 99°42′W
61 B19 **Colón** Buenos Aires, E Argentina 33°53′S 61°06′W
61 D18 **Colon** Entre Ríos, E Argentina 32°10′S 58°16′W
44 D5 **Colón** Matanzas, C Cuba 22°43′N 80°54′W
43 T14 **Colón** *prev.* Aspinwall. Colón, C Panama 09°04′N 80°33′W
42 K5 **Colón** ◈ *department* NE Honduras
43 S15 **Colón** *off.* Provincia de Colón. ◈ *province* N Panama
57 A16 **Colón, Archipiélago de** *var.* Islas de los Galápagos, *Eng.* Galapagos Islands, Tortoise Islands. *island group* Ecuador, E Pacific Ocean
44 K5 **Colonel Hill** Crooked Island, SE Bahamas 22°43′N 74°12′W
40 C3 **Colonet** Baja California Norte, NW Mexico 31°00′N 116°1′W
40 B3 **Colonet, Cabo** *headland* NW Mexico 30°57′N 116°19′W
188 G14 **Colonia** Yap, W Micronesia 09°29′N 138°06′E
61 D19 **Colonia** ◈ *department* SW Uruguay
Colonia *see* Kolonia, Micronesia
Colonia *see* Colonia del Sacramento, Uruguay
Colonia Agrippina *see* Köln
61 D20 **Colonia del Sacramento** *var.* Colonia. Colonia, SW Uruguay 34°29′S 57°48′W
62 L8 **Colonia Dora** Santiago del Estero, N Argentina 28°34′S 62°59′W
Colonia Julia Fanestris *see* Fano
21 W5 **Colonial Beach** Virginia, NE USA 38°15′N 76°57′W
21 V6 **Colonial Heights** Virginia, NE USA 37°15′N 77°24′W
Colón, Provincia de *see* Colón
193 S7 **Colón Ridge** *undersea feature* E Pacific Ocean 02°00′N 96°00′W
96 F12 **Colonsay** *island* W Scotland, United Kingdom
57 K22 **Colorada, Laguna** SW Bolivia
37 R6 **Colorado** *off.* State of Colorado, *also known as* Centennial State, Silver State. ◈ *state* C USA
63 H22 **Colorado, Cerro** ▲ S Argentina 49°58′S 71°38′W
25 O7 **Colorado City** Texas, SW USA 32°24′N 100°51′W
36 M7 **Colorado Plateau** *plateau* W USA
61 A24 **Colorado, Río** E Argentina
43 N12 **Colorado, Río** NE Costa Rica
Colorado, Río *see* Colorado River
16 F12 **Colorado River** *var.* Río Colorado. Mexico/USA
16 K14 **Colorado River** Texas, SW USA
35 W15 **Colorado River Aqueduct** *aqueduct* California, W USA
44 A4 **Colorados, Archipiélago de los** *island group* NW Cuba
62 J9 **Colorados, Desagües de los** W Argentina
37 T5 **Colorado Springs** Colorado, C USA 38°50′N 104°47′W
40 L11 **Colotlán** Jalisco, SW Mexico 22°08′N 103°15′W
57 L19 **Colquechaca** Potosí, C Bolivia 18°40′S 66°00′W
23 S7 **Colquitt** Georgia, SE USA 31°10′N 84°43′W
29 R11 **Colton** South Dakota, N USA 43°47′N 96°55′W
32 M10 **Colton** Washington, NW USA 46°34′N 117°10′W
35 P8 **Columbia** California, W USA 38°01′N 120°22′W
30 K16 **Columbia** Illinois, N USA 38°26′N 90°12′W
20 L7 **Columbia** Kentucky, S USA 37°05′N 85°19′W
22 I6 **Columbia** Louisiana, S USA 32°05′N 92°03′W
21 W3 **Columbia** Maryland, NE USA 39°13′N 76°51′W
22 L7 **Columbia** Mississippi, S USA 31°15′N 89°50′W
27 U4 **Columbia** Missouri, C USA 38°56′N 92°19′W
21 Y9 **Columbia** North Carolina, SE USA 35°55′N 76°15′W
18 G16 **Columbia** Pennsylvania, NE USA 40°01′N 76°30′W
21 Q12 **Columbia** *state capital* South Carolina, SE USA 34°00′N 81°02′W
20 I9 **Columbia** Tennessee, S USA 35°37′N 87°02′W
0 F9 **Columbia** Canada/USA
32 K9 **Columbia Basin** *basin* Washington, NW USA
197 Q10 **Columbia, Cape** *headland* Ellesmere Island, Nunavut, NE Canada
31 Q12 **Columbia City** Indiana, N USA 41°09′N 85°29′W
21 W3 **Columbia, District of** ◈ *federal district* NE USA
33 P7 **Columbia Falls** Montana, NW USA 48°22′N 114°10′W
11 O15 **Columbia Icefield** *ice field* Alberta/British Columbia, S Canada
11 O15 **Columbia, Mount** ▲ Alberta/British Columbia, SW Canada 52°07′N 117°30′W
11 N15 **Columbia Mountains** ▲▲ British Columbia, SW Canada
23 P4 **Columbiana** Alabama, S USA 33°10′N 86°36′W
31 V12 **Columbiana** Ohio, N USA 40°53′N 80°41′W
32 M14 **Columbia Plateau** *plateau* Idaho/Oregon, NW USA
29 P7 **Columbia Road Reservoir** South Dakota, N USA
65 K16 **Columbia Seamount** *undersea feature* C Atlantic Ocean 20°30′S 32°00′W
83 D25 **Columbine, Cape** *headland* SW South Africa 32°50′S 17°39′E
105 U9 **Columbretes, Illes** *prev.* Islas Columbretes. *island group* E Spain
Columbretes, Islas *see* Columbretes, Illes
23 R5 **Columbus** Georgia, SE USA 32°29′N 84°58′W
31 P14 **Columbus** Indiana, N USA 39°12′N 85°55′W
27 R7 **Columbus** Kansas, C USA 37°09′N 94°52′W
23 N4 **Columbus** Mississippi, S USA 33°30′N 88°25′W
33 U11 **Columbus** Montana, NW USA 45°38′N 109°15′W
29 Q15 **Columbus** Nebraska, C USA 41°25′N 97°22′W
37 Q16 **Columbus** New Mexico, SW USA 31°49′N 107°38′W
21 P10 **Columbus** North Carolina, SE USA 35°15′N 82°09′W
28 K2 **Columbus** North Dakota, N USA 48°52′N 102°47′W
31 S13 **Columbus** *state capital* Ohio, N USA 39°58′N 83°W
25 U11 **Columbus** Texas, SW USA 29°42′N 96°35′W
30 L8 **Columbus** Wisconsin, N USA 43°21′N 89°00′W
31 R12 **Columbus Grove** Ohio, N USA 40°55′N 84°03′W
29 Y15 **Columbus Junction** Iowa, C USA 41°16′N 91°21′W
44 J3 **Columbus Point** *headland* Cat Island, C Bahamas 24°07′N 75°19′W
35 T8 **Columbus Salt Marsh** *salt marsh* Nevada, W USA
35 N6 **Colusa** California, W USA 39°10′N 122°03′W

◆ Country
● Country Capital
◇ Dependent Territory
○ Dependent Territory Capital
◈ Administrative Regions
✈ International Airport
▲ Mountain
▲▲ Mountain Range
Volcano
River
Lake
Reservoir

32 L7 **Colville** Washington, NW USA 48°33′N 117°54′W
184 M5 **Colville, Cape** *headland* North Island, New Zealand 36°28′S 175°20′E
184 M5 **Colville Channel** *channel* North Island, New Zealand
39 P6 **Colville River** ≈ Alaska, USA
97 J18 **Colwyn Bay** N Wales, United Kingdom 53°18′N 03°43′W
106 H9 **Comacchio** *var.* Commachio; *anc.* Comactium. Emilia-Romagna, N Italy 44°41′N 12°10′E
106 H9 **Comacchio, Valli di** *lagoon* Adriatic Sea, N Mediterranean Sea
Comactium *see* Comacchio
41 V17 **Comalapa** Chiapas, SE Mexico 15°42′N 92°06′W
41 U15 **Comalcalco** Tabasco, SE Mexico 18°16′N 93°05′W
63 H16 **Comallo** Río Negro, SW Argentina 40°58′S 70°13′W
26 M12 **Comanche** Oklahoma, C USA 34°22′N 97°57′W
25 R8 **Comanche** Texas, SW USA 31°55′N 98°36′W
194 H2 **Comandante Ferraz** *Brazilian research station* Antarctica 61°57′S 58°23′W
62 N6 **Comandante Fontana** Formosa, N Argentina 25°19′S 59°42′W
63 I22 **Comandante Luis Peidra Buena** Santa Cruz, S Argentina 50°04′S 68°55′W
59 O18 **Comandatuba** Bahia, SE Brazil 15°13′S 39°00′W
116 K11 **Comănești** *Hung.* Kománfalva. Bacău, SW Romania 46°25′N 26°29′E
57 M19 **Comarapa** Santa Cruz, C Bolivia 17°53′S 64°30′W
116 J13 **Comarnic** Prahova, SE Romania 45°18′N 25°37′E
42 H6 **Comayagua** Comayagua, W Honduras 14°30′N 87°39′W
42 H6 **Comayagua** ◈ *department* W Honduras
42 I6 **Comayagua, Montañas de** ⛰ C Honduras
21 R15 **Combahee River** ≈ South Carolina, SE USA
62 G10 **Combarbalá** Coquimbo, C Chile 31°15′S 71°03′W
103 S7 **Combeaufontaine** Haute-Saône, E France 47°43′N 05°52′E
97 G15 **Comber** *Ir.* An Comar. E Northern Ireland, United Kingdom 54°33′N 05°45′W
99 K20 **Comblain-au-Pont** Liège, E Belgium 50°29′N 05°36′E
102 I6 **Combourg** Ille-et-Vilaine, NW France 48°21′N 01°44′W
44 M9 **Comendador** *prev.* Elías Piña. W Dominican Republic 18°53′N 71°42′W
Comer See *see* Como, Lago di
25 R11 **Comfort** Texas, SW USA 29°58′N 98°54′W
153 V15 **Comilla** *Ben.* Kumillā. Chittagong, E Bangladesh 23°28′N 91°10′E
99 B18 **Comines** Hainaut, W Belgium 50°46′N 02°58′E
Comino *see* Kemmuna
107 D18 **Comino, Capo** *headland* Sardegna, Italy, C Mediterranean Sea 40°32′N 09°49′E
107 K25 **Comiso** Sicilia, Italy, C Mediterranean Sea 36°57′N 14°37′E
41 V16 **Comitán** *var.* Comitán de Domínguez. Chiapas, SE Mexico 16°15′N 92°06′W
Comitán de Domínguez *see* Comitán
Commachio *see* Comacchio
Commander Islands *see* Komandorskiye Ostrova
103 O10 **Commentry** Allier, C France 46°18′N 02°46′E
23 T2 **Commerce** Georgia, SE USA 34°12′N 83°27′W
27 R8 **Commerce** Oklahoma, C USA 36°55′N 94°52′W
25 V5 **Commerce** Texas, SW USA 33°16′N 95°52′W
37 T4 **Commerce City** Colorado, C USA 39°45′N 104°54′W
103 S5 **Commercy** Meuse, NE France 48°46′N 05°36′E
55 W9 **Commewijne** *var.* Commewyne. ◈ *district* NE Surinam
Commewyne *see* Commewijne
15 P8 **Commissaires, Lac des** ◎ Québec, SE Canada
64 A12 **Commissioner's Point** *headland* W Bermuda
9 O7 **Committee Bay** *bay* Nunavut, N Canada
106 D7 **Como** *anc.* Comum. Lombardia, N Italy 45°48′N 09°05′E
63 J19 **Comodoro Rivadavia** Chubut, SE Argentina 45°50′S 67°30′W
106 D6 **Como, Lago di** *var.* Lario, *Eng.* Lake Como, *Ger.* Comer See. ◎ N Italy
Como, Lake *see* Como, Lago di
40 E7 **Comondú** Baja California Sur, NW Mexico 26°01′N 111°50′W
116 F12 **Comorâşte** *Hung.* Komornok. Caraş-Severin, SW Romania 45°13′N 21°34′E
Comores, République Fédérale Islamique des *see* Comoros
155 G24 **Comorin, Cape** *headland* SE India 08°00′N 77°10′E
172 M8 **Comoro Basin** *undersea feature* SW Indian Ocean 14°00′S 44°00′E
172 K14 **Comoro Islands** *island group* W Indian Ocean
172 H13 **Comoros** *off.* Federal Islamic Republic of the Comoros, *Fr.* République Fédérale Islamique des Comores. ◆ *republic* W Indian Ocean
Comoros, Federal Islamic Republic of the *see* Comoros
10 L17 **Comox** Vancouver Island, British Columbia, SW Canada 49°40′N 124°55′W
103 O4 **Compiègne** Oise, N France 49°25′N 02°50′E
Complutum *see* Alcalá de Henares
Compniacum *see* Cognac
40 K12 **Compostela** Nayarit, C Mexico 21°12′N 104°52′W
Compostella *see* Santiago de Compostela
60 L11 **Comprida, Ilha** *island* S Brazil
117 N11 **Comrat** *Rus.* Komrat. S Moldova 46°18′N 28°40′E
25 O11 **Comstock** Texas, SW USA 29°39′N 101°10′W
31 P9 **Comstock Park** Michigan, N USA 43°00′N 85°40′W
193 N3 **Comstock Seamount** *undersea feature* N Pacific Ocean 48°15′N 156°55′W
Comum *see* Como
159 N17 **Cona** Xizang Zizhiqu, W China 27°59′N 91°54′E
76 H14 **Conakry** ● (Guinea) SW Guinea 09°31′N 13°43′W
76 H14 **Conakry** ✈ SW Guinea 09°37′N 13°32′W
Conamara *see* Connemara
Conca *see* Cuenca
25 Q12 **Concan** Texas, SW USA 29°27′N 99°43′W
102 F6 **Concarneau** Finistère, NW France 47°53′N 03°55′W
83 O17 **Conceição** Sofala, C Mozambique 18°47′S 36°18′E
59 K15 **Conceição do Araguaia** Pará, NE Brazil 08°15′S 49°15′W
58 F10 **Conceição do Maú** Roraima, W Brazil 03°35′N 59°52′W
61 D14 **Concepción** *var.* Concepcion. Corrientes, NE Argentina 28°25′S 57°54′W
62 J8 **Concepción** Tucumán, N Argentina 27°20′S 65°35′W
57 O17 **Concepción** Santa Cruz, E Bolivia 16°15′S 62°08′W
62 G13 **Concepción** Bío Bío, C Chile 36°47′S 73°01′W
54 E14 **Concepción** Putumayo, S Colombia 0°03′N 75°35′W
62 O5 **Concepción** *var.* Villa Concepción. Concepción, C Paraguay 23°26′S 57°24′W
62 O5 **Concepción** *off.* Departamento de Concepción. ◈ *department* E Paraguay
Concepción *see* La Concepción
Concepción de la Vega *see* La Vega
41 N9 **Concepción del Oro** Zacatecas, C Mexico 24°38′N 101°25′W
61 D18 **Concepción del Uruguay** Entre Ríos, E Argentina 32°30′S 58°15′W
Concepción, Departamento de *see* Concepción
42 K11 **Concepción, Volcán** ✶ SW Nicaragua 11°31′N 85°37′W
44 J4 **Conception Island** *island* C Bahamas
35 P14 **Conception, Point** *headland* California, W USA 34°27′N 120°28′W
54 H6 **Concha** Zulia, W Venezuela 09°02′N 71°45′W
60 L9 **Conchas** São Paulo, S Brazil 23°00′S 47°58′W
37 U11 **Conchas Dam** New Mexico, SW USA 35°21′N 104°11′W
37 U10 **Conchas Lake** ⊡ New Mexico, SW USA
102 M5 **Conches-en-Ouche** Eure, N France 49°00′N 01°00′E
37 N12 **Concho** Arizona, SW USA 34°28′N 109°33′W
40 J5 **Conchos, Río** ≈ NW Mexico
41 O8 **Conchos, Río** ≈ C Mexico
108 C8 **Concise** Vaud, W Switzerland 46°52′N 06°40′E
35 N8 **Concord** California, W USA 37°58′N 122°01′W
19 O9 **Concord** *state capital* New Hampshire, NE USA 43°10′N 71°32′W
21 R10 **Concord** North Carolina, SE USA 35°25′N 80°34′W
61 D17 **Concordia** Entre Ríos, E Argentina 31°25′S 58°W
60 I13 **Concórdia** Santa Catarina, S Brazil 27°14′S 52°01′W
54 D9 **Concordia** Antioquia, W Colombia 06°03′N 75°57′W
40 J10 **Concordia** Sinaloa, C Mexico 23°18′N 106°02′W
57 I19 **Concordia** Tacna, SW Peru 18°12′S 70°19′W
27 N3 **Concordia** Kansas, C USA 39°35′N 97°39′W
27 S4 **Concordia** Missouri, C USA 38°58′N 93°34′W
167 S7 **Con Cuông** Nghê An, N Vietnam 19°02′N 104°54′E
167 T15 **Côn Đao Sơn** *var.* Con Son. *island* S Vietnam
Condate *see* Rennes, Ille-et-Vilaine, France
Condate *see* St-Claude, Jura, France
Condate *see* Montereau-Faut-Yonne, Seine-St-Denis, France
29 P8 **Conde** South Dakota, N USA 45°08′N 98°07′W
42 J8 **Condega** Estelí, NW Nicaragua 13°19′N 86°26′W
103 P2 **Condé-sur-l'Escaut** Nord, N France 50°27′N 03°36′E
102 K5 **Condé-sur-Noireau** Calvados, N France 48°52′N 00°31′W
Condivincum *see* Nantes
183 P8 **Condobolin** New South Wales, SE Australia 33°04′S 147°08′E
102 L15 **Condom** Gers, S France 43°56′N 00°23′E
32 J11 **Condon** Oregon, NW USA 45°15′N 120°10′W
54 D9 **Condoto** Chocó, W Colombia 05°06′N 76°37′W
23 P7 **Conecuh River** ≈ Alabama/Florida, SE USA
106 H7 **Conegliano** Veneto, NE Italy 45°53′N 12°18′E
61 C19 **Conesa** Buenos Aires, E Argentina 33°36′S 60°21′W
14 F15 **Conestogo** ≈ Ontario, S Canada
Confluentes *see* Koblenz
102 L10 **Confolens** Charente, W France 46°00′N 00°40′E
36 J4 **Confusion Range** ⛰ Utah, W USA
62 N6 **Confuso, Río** ≈ C Paraguay
21 R12 **Congaree River** ≈ South Carolina, SE USA
Công Hoa Xa Hôi Chu Nghia Viêt Nam *see* Vietnam
160 K12 **Congjiang** *var.* Bingmei. Guizhou, S China 25°48′N 108°55′E
79 G18 **Congo** *off.* Republic of the Congo, *Fr.* Moyen-Congo; *prev.* Middle Congo. ◆ *republic* C Africa
79 K19 **Congo** *off.* Democratic Republic of Congo; *prev.* Zaire, Belgian Congo, Congo (Kinshasa). ◆ *republic* C Africa
67 T11 **Congo** *var.* Kongo, *Fr.* Zaire. ≈ C Africa
Congo *see* Zaire (province) Angola
68 G12 **Congo Basin** *drainage basin* W Dem. Rep. Congo
67 Q11 **Congo Canyon** *var.* Congo Seavalley, Congo Submarine Canyon. *undersea feature* E Atlantic Ocean 06°00′S 11°50′E
Congo Cone *see* Congo Fan
Congo/Congo (Kinshasa) *see* Congo (Democratic Republic of)
65 P15 **Congo Fan** *var.* Congo Cone. *undersea feature* E Atlantic Ocean 06°00′S 09°00′E
Congo Seavalley *see* Congo Canyon
Congo Submarine Canyon *see* Congo Canyon
Coni *see* Cuneo
63 H18 **Cónico, Cerro** ▲ SW Argentina 43°12′S 71°42′W
Conimbria/Conimbriga *see* Coimbra
Conjeeveram *see* Kānchīpuram
11 R13 **Conklin** Alberta, C Canada 55°36′N 111°06′W
24 M1 **Conlen** Texas, SW USA 36°16′N 102°10′W
Con, Loch *see* Conn, Lough
Connacht *see* Connaught
97 B17 **Connaught** *var.* Connacht, *Ir.* Chonnacht, Cúige. *cultural region* W Ireland
31 V10 **Conneaut** Ohio, N USA 41°56′N 80°32′W
18 L13 **Connecticut** *off.* State of Connecticut, *also known as* Blue Law State, Constitution State, Land of Steady Habits, Nutmeg State. ◈ *state* NE USA
19 N8 **Connecticut** ≈ Canada/USA
19 O6 **Connecticut Lakes** *lakes* New Hampshire, NE USA
32 K9 **Connell** Washington, NW USA 46°39′N 118°51′W
97 B17 **Connemara** *Ir.* Conamara. *physical region* W Ireland
31 Q14 **Connersville** Indiana, N USA 39°38′N 85°15′W
97 B16 **Conn, Lough** *Ir.* Loch Con. ◎ W Ireland
35 X6 **Connors Pass** *pass* Nevada, W USA
181 X7 **Connors Range** ⛰ Queensland, E Australia
56 E7 **Cononaco, Río** ≈ E Ecuador
29 W13 **Conrad** Iowa, C USA 42°13′N 92°52′W
33 R7 **Conrad** Montana, NW USA 48°10′N 111°58′W
25 W10 **Conroe** Texas, SW USA 30°19′N 95°28′W
25 V10 **Conroe, Lake** ⊡ Texas, SW USA
61 C17 **Conscripto Bernardi** Entre Ríos, E Argentina 31°03′S 59°05′W
59 M20 **Conselheiro Lafaiete** Minas Gerais, SE Brazil 20°40′S 43°48′W
Consentia *see* Cosenza
97 L14 **Consett** N England, United Kingdom 54°50′N 01°53′W
44 B5 **Consolación del Sur** Pinar del Río, W Cuba 22°32′N 83°32′W
Con Son *see* Côn Đao Sơn
11 R15 **Consort** Alberta, SW Canada 51°58′N 110°44′W
Constance *see* Konstanz
108 I6 **Constance, Lake** *Ger.* Bodensee. ◎ C Europe
104 G9 **Constância** Santarém, C Portugal 39°29′N 08°22′W
117 N14 **Constanța** *var.* Küstendje, *Eng.* Constanza, *Ger.* Konstanza, *Turk.* Küstence. Constanța, SE Romania 44°09′N 28°37′E
116 L14 **Constanța** ◈ *county* SE Romania
Constantia *see* Coutances
Constantia *see* Konstanz
104 K13 **Constantina** Andalucía, S Spain 37°54′N 05°36′W
74 L5 **Constantine** *var.* Qacentina, *Ar.* Qoussantina. NE Algeria 36°23′N 06°44′E
39 O14 **Constantine, Cape** *headland* Alaska, USA 58°23′N 158°53′W
Constantinople *see* İstanbul
Constantiola *see* Olteniţa
Constanz *see* Konstanz
Constanza *see* Constanța
62 G13 **Constitución** Maule, C Chile 35°20′S 72°28′W
61 D17 **Constitución** Salto, N Uruguay 31°05′S 57°51′W
Constitution State *see* Connecticut
105 N10 **Consuegra** Castilla-La Mancha, C Spain 39°28′N 03°36′W
181 X9 **Consuelo Peak** ▲ Queensland, E Australia 24°45′S 148°01′E
56 E11 **Contamana** Loreto, N Peru 07°19′S 75°04′W
Contrasto, Colle del *see* Contrasto, Portella del
107 K23 **Contrasto, Portella del** *var.* Colle del Contrasto. *pass* Sicilia, Italy, C Mediterranean Sea
54 G8 **Contratación** Santander, C Colombia 06°18′N 73°27′W
102 M8 **Contres** Loir-et-Cher, C France 47°24′N 01°30′E
107 O17 **Conversano** Puglia, SE Italy 40°58′N 17°07′E
27 U11 **Conway** Arkansas, C USA 35°05′N 92°27′W
19 O8 **Conway** New Hampshire, NE USA 43°58′N 71°05′W
21 U13 **Conway** South Carolina, SE USA 33°51′N 79°04′W
25 N2 **Conway** Texas, SW USA 35°10′N 101°23′W
27 U11 **Conway, Lake** ⊡ Arkansas, C USA
27 N7 **Conway Springs** Kansas, C USA 37°23′N 97°38′W
97 J18 **Conwy** N Wales, United Kingdom 53°17′N 03°51′W
23 T3 **Conyers** Georgia, SE USA 33°40′N 84°01′W
Coo *see* Kos
182 F4 **Coober Pedy** South Australia 29°01′S 134°47′E
181 P2 **Cooinda** Northern Territory, N Australia 12°54′S 132°31′E
182 B6 **Cook** South Australia 30°37′S 130°26′E
29 W4 **Cook** Minnesota, N USA 47°51′N 92°41′W
191 N6 **Cook, Baie de** *bay* Moorea, W French Polynesia
10 J16 **Cook, Cape** *headland* Vancouver Island, British Columbia, SW Canada 50°04′N 127°52′W
37 Q15 **Cookes Peak** ▲ New Mexico, SW USA 32°32′N 107°43′W
20 L8 **Cookeville** Tennessee, S USA 36°10′N 85°30′W
175 P9 **Cook Fracture Zone** *tectonic feature* S Pacific Ocean
Cook, Grand Récif de *see* Cook, Récif de
39 Q12 **Cook Inlet** *inlet* Alaska, USA
191 X2 **Cook Island** *island* Line Islands, E Kiribati
190 J14 **Cook Islands** ◇ *territory in free association with New Zealand* S Pacific Ocean
Cook, Mount *see* Aoraki
187 O15 **Cook, Récif de** *var.* Grand Récif de Cook. *reef* S New Caledonia
14 G14 **Cookstown** Ontario, S Canada 44°12′N 79°39′W
97 F15 **Cookstown** *Ir.* An Chorr Chríochach. C Northern Ireland, United Kingdom 54°39′N 06°45′W
185 K14 **Cook Strait** *var.* Raukawa. *strait* New Zealand
181 W3 **Cooktown** Queensland, NE Australia 15°28′S 145°15′E
183 P6 **Coolabah** New South Wales, SE Australia 31°03′S 146°42′E
182 J11 **Coola Coola Swamp** *wetland* South Australia
183 S7 **Coolah** New South Wales, SE Australia 31°49′S 149°43′E
183 P9 **Coolamon** New South Wales, SE Australia 34°49′S 147°13′E
183 T4 **Coolatai** New South Wales, SE Australia 29°16′S 150°45′E
180 K12 **Coolgardie** Western Australia 31°01′S 121°12′E
36 L14 **Coolidge** Arizona, SW USA 32°58′N 111°29′W
25 U8 **Coolidge** Texas, SW USA 31°45′N 96°39′W
183 Q11 **Cooma** New South Wales, SE Australia 36°16′S 149°09′E
Coomassie *see* Kumasi
183 R6 **Coonabarabran** New South Wales, SE Australia 31°19′S 149°18′E
182 J10 **Coonalpyn** South Australia 35°43′S 139°50′E
183 R6 **Coonamble** New South Wales, SE Australia 30°56′S 148°22′E
Coondapoor *see* Kundāpura
155 G21 **Coonoor** Tamil Nādu, SE India 11°21′N 76°46′E
29 U14 **Coon Rapids** Iowa, C USA 41°52′N 94°40′W
29 V8 **Coon Rapids** Minnesota, N USA 45°12′N 93°18′W
25 V5 **Cooper** Texas, SW USA 33°23′N 95°42′W
181 U9 **Cooper Creek** *var.* Barcoo, Cooper's Creek. *seasonal river* Queensland/South Australia
39 R12 **Cooper Landing** Alaska, USA 60°27′N 149°59′W
21 T14 **Cooper River** ≈ South Carolina, SE USA
Cooper's Creek *see* Cooper Creek
44 H1 **Coopers Town** Great Abaco, N Bahamas 26°46′N 77°27′W
18 J10 **Cooperstown** New York, NE USA 42°43′N 74°56′W
29 P4 **Cooperstown** North Dakota, N USA 47°26′N 98°07′W
31 P9 **Coopersville** Michigan, N USA 43°03′N 85°55′W
182 D7 **Coorabie** South Australia 31°57′S 132°18′E
23 Q3 **Coosa River** ≈ Alabama/Georgia, S USA
32 E14 **Coos Bay** Oregon, NW USA 43°22′N 124°13′W
183 Q9 **Cootamundra** New South Wales, SE Australia 34°41′S 148°03′E
97 E16 **Cootehill** *Ir.* Muinchille. N Ireland 54°04′N 07°05′W
Čop *see* Chop
57 J17 **Copacabana** La Paz, W Bolivia 16°11′S 69°02′W
63 H14 **Copahué, Volcán** ✶ C Chile 37°56′S 71°04′W
41 U16 **Copainalá** Chiapas, SE Mexico 17°04′N 93°13′W
32 F8 **Copalis Beach** Washington, NW USA 47°05′N 124°11′W
42 F6 **Copán** ◈ *department* W Honduras
Copán *see* Copán Ruinas
25 T14 **Copano Bay** *bay* NW Gulf of Mexico
42 F6 **Copán Ruinas** *var.* Copán. Copán, W Honduras 14°52′N 89°10′W
Copenhagen *see* København
107 Q19 **Copertino** Puglia, SE Italy 40°16′N 18°03′E
62 H7 **Copiapó** Atacama, N Chile 27°17′S 70°25′W
62 G8 **Copiapó, Bahía** *bay* N Chile
62 G7 **Copiapó, Río** ≈ N Chile
114 M12 **Çöpköy** Edirne, NW Turkey 41°14′N 26°51′E
182 I5 **Copley** South Australia 30°36′S 138°26′E
106 H9 **Copparo** Emilia-Romagna, C Italy 44°53′N 11°53′E
55 V10 **Coppename Rivier** *var.* Koppename. ≈ C Surinam
25 S9 **Copperas Cove** Texas, SW USA 31°07′N 97°54′W
82 J13 **Copperbelt** ◈ *province* C Zambia
39 S11 **Copper Center** Alaska, USA 61°57′N 145°21′W
8 K8 **Coppermine** ≈ Northwest Territories/Nunavut, N Canada
Coppermine *see* Kugluktuk
39 T11 **Copper River** ≈ Alaska, USA
Copper State *see* Arizona
116 I11 **Copşa Mică** *Ger.* Kleinkopisch, *Hung.* Kiskapus. Sibiu, C Romania 46°06′N 24°15′E
158 J14 **Coqên** Xizang Zizhiqu, W China 31°13′N 85°12′E
Coquilhatville *see* Mbandaka
32 E14 **Coquille** Oregon, NW USA 43°11′N 124°12′W
62 G9 **Coquimbo** Coquimbo, N Chile 30°S 71°18′W
62 G9 **Coquimbo** *off.* Región de Coquimbo. ◈ *region* C Chile
Coquimbo, Región de *see* Coquimbo
116 I15 **Corabia** Olt, S Romania 43°46′N 24°31′E
57 F17 **Coracora** Ayacucho, SW Peru 15°03′S 73°45′W
Cora Droma Rúisc *see* Carrick-on-Shannon
44 K9 **Corail** SW Haiti 18°34′N 73°53′W
183 V4 **Coraki** New South Wales, SE Australia 29°01′S 153°15′E
180 G8 **Coral Bay** Western Australia 23°02′S 113°51′E
23 Y16 **Coral Gables** Florida, SE USA 25°43′N 80°16′W
9 P8 **Coral Harbour** *var.* Salliq. Southampton Island, Nunavut, NE Canada 64°10′N 83°15′W
192 I9 **Coral Sea** *sea* SW Pacific Ocean
174 M7 **Coral Sea Basin** *undersea feature* N Coral Sea
192 H9 **Coral Sea Islands** ◇ *Australian external territory* SW Pacific Ocean
182 M12 **Corangamite, Lake** ◎ Victoria, SE Australia
Corantijn Rivier *see* Courantyne River
18 B14 **Coraopolis** Pennsylvania, NE USA 40°28′N 80°08′W
107 N17 **Corato** Puglia, SE Italy 41°09′N 16°25′E
103 O17 **Corbières** ⛰ S France
103 P8 **Corbigny** Nièvre, C France 47°15′N 03°42′E
21 N7 **Corbin** Kentucky, S USA 36°57′N 84°06′W
104 L14 **Corbones** ≈ SW Spain
Corcaigh *see* Cork
35 R11 **Corcoran** California, W USA 36°06′N 119°33′W
47 T14 **Corcovado, Golfo** *gulf* S Chile
63 G18 **Corcovado, Volcán** ✶ S Chile 43°13′S 72°45′W
104 F3 **Corcubión** Galicia, NW Spain 42°56′N 09°12′W
Corcyra Nigra *see* Korčula
60 Q9 **Cordeiro** Rio de Janeiro, SE Brazil 22°01′S 42°20′W
23 T6 **Cordele** Georgia, SE USA 31°59′N 83°49′W
26 L11 **Cordell** Oklahoma, C USA 35°17′N 98°59′W
103 N14 **Cordes** Tarn, S France 44°03′N 01°57′E
62 O6 **Cordillera** *off.* Departamento de la Cordillera. ◈ *department* C Paraguay
Cordillera *see* Cacaguatique, Cordillera
Cordillera, Departamento de la *see* Cordillera
182 K1 **Cordillo Downs** South Australia 26°44′S 140°37′E
62 K10 **Córdoba** Córdoba, C Argentina 31°25′S 64°11′W
41 R14 **Córdoba** Veracruz-Llave, E Mexico 18°55′N 96°55′W
104 M13 **Córdoba** *var.* Cordoba, *Eng.* Cordova; *anc.* Corduba. Andalucía, SW Spain 37°53′N 04°46′W
62 K11 **Córdoba** *off.* Provincia de Córdoba. ◈ *province* C Argentina
54 D7 **Córdoba** *off.* Departamento de Córdoba. ◈ *province* NW Colombia
104 L13 **Córdoba** ◈ *province* Andalucía, S Spain
Córdoba, Departamento de *see* Córdoba
Córdoba, Provincia de *see* Córdoba
62 K10 **Córdoba, Sierras de** ⛰ C Argentina
23 O3 **Cordova** Alabama, S USA 33°45′N 87°10′W
39 S12 **Cordova** Alaska, USA 60°32′N 145°45′W
Cordova/Cordoba *see* Córdoba
Corduba *see* Córdoba
Corentyne River *see* Courantyne River
Corfu *see* Kérkyra
104 J9 **Coria** Extremadura, W Spain 39°59′N 06°32′W
104 J14 **Coria del Río** Andalucía, S Spain 37°18′N 06°04′W
183 S8 **Coricudgy, Mount** ▲ New South Wales, SE Australia 32°49′S 150°28′E
107 N20 **Corigliano Calabro** Calabria, SW Italy 39°36′N 16°32′E
Corinium/Corinium Dobunorum *see* Cirencester
23 N1 **Corinth** Mississippi, S USA 34°56′N 88°29′W
Corinth *see* Kórinthos
Corinth Canal *see* Dióryga Korinthou
Corinth, Gulf of/Corinthiacus Sinus *see* Korinthiakós Kólpos
Corinthus *see* Kórinthos
42 I9 **Corinto** Chinandega, NW Nicaragua 12°29′N 87°14′W
97 C21 **Cork** *Ir.* Corcaigh. S Ireland 51°54′N 08°06′W
97 C21 **Cork** *Ir.* Corcaigh. *cultural region* SW Ireland
97 C21 **Cork** ✈ Cork, SW Ireland 51°52′N 08°25′W
97 D21 **Cork Harbour** *Ir.* Cuan Chorcaí. *inlet* SW Ireland
107 I23 **Corleone** Sicilia, Italy, C Mediterranean Sea 37°49′N 13°18′E
114 N13 **Çorlu** Tekirdağ, NW Turkey 41°11′N 27°48′E
114 N12 **Çorlu Çayı** ≈ NW Turkey
Cormaiore *see* Courmayeur
11 V13 **Cormorant** Manitoba, C Canada 54°12′N 100°33′W
23 T2 **Cornelia** Georgia, SE USA 34°30′N 83°31′W
60 J10 **Cornélio Procópio** Paraná, S Brazil 23°07′S 50°40′W
55 V9 **Corneliskondre** Sipaliwini, N Surinam 05°21′N 56°10′W
30 J5 **Cornell** Wisconsin, N USA 45°09′N 91°10′W
13 S12 **Corner Brook** Newfoundland, Newfoundland and Labrador, E Canada 48°58′N 57°58′W
Corner Rise Seamounts *see* Corner Seamounts
64 I9 **Corner Seamounts** *var.* Corner Rise Seamounts. *undersea feature* NW Atlantic Ocean 35°30′N 51°30′W
116 M9 **Corneşti** *Rus.* Korneshty. C Moldova 47°23′N 28°00′E
Corneto *see* Tarquinia
Cornhusker State *see* Nebraska
27 X8 **Corning** Arkansas, C USA 36°26′N 90°35′W
35 N5 **Corning** California, W USA 39°54′N 122°12′W
29 U15 **Corning** Iowa, C USA 40°58′N 94°46′W
18 G11 **Corning** New York, NE USA 42°08′N 77°03′W
Corn Islands *see* Maíz, Islas del
107 J14 **Corno Grande** ▲ C Italy 42°26′N 13°29′E
15 N13 **Cornwall** Ontario, SE Canada 45°02′N 74°45′W
97 H25 **Cornwall** *cultural region* SW England, United Kingdom
97 G25 **Cornwall, Cape** *headland* SW England, United Kingdom 50°11′N 05°39′W
54 J4 **Coro** *prev.* Santa Ana de Coro. Falcón, NW Venezuela 11°27′N 69°41′W
57 J18 **Corocoro** La Paz, W Bolivia 17°10′S 68°28′W
57 K17 **Coroico** La Paz, W Bolivia 16°09′S 67°45′W
184 M5 **Coromandel** Waikato, North Island, New Zealand 36°47′S 175°30′E
155 K20 **Coromandel Coast** *coast* E India
184 M5 **Coromandel Peninsula** *peninsula* North Island, New Zealand
184 M6 **Coromandel Range** ⛰ North Island, New Zealand
171 N5 **Coron** Busuanga Island, W Philippines 12°02′N 120°10′E
Coronach *see* A Coruña
35 T15 **Corona** California, W USA 33°52′N 117°34′W
37 T12 **Corona** New Mexico, SW USA 34°15′N 105°36′W
11 U17 **Coronach** Saskatchewan, S Canada 49°07′N 105°33′W
35 U17 **Coronado** California, W USA 32°41′N 117°10′W
43 N15 **Coronado, Bahía de** *bay* S Costa Rica
11 R15 **Coronation** Alberta, SW Canada 52°06′N 111°25′W
8 K7 **Coronation Gulf** *gulf* Nunavut, N Canada
194 I1 **Coronation Island** *island* Antarctica
39 X14 **Coronation Island** *island* Alexander Archipelago, Alaska, USA
61 B18 **Coronda** Santa Fe, C Argentina 31°58′S 60°56′W
63 F14 **Coronel** Bío Bío, C Chile 37°01′S 73°08′W
61 D20 **Coronel Brandsen** *var.* Brandsen. Buenos Aires, E Argentina 35°08′S 58°15′W
62 K4 **Coronel Cornejo** Salta, N Argentina 22°46′S 63°49′W
61 B24 **Coronel Dorrego** Buenos Aires, E Argentina 38°38′S 61°15′W
62 P6 **Coronel Oviedo** Caaguazú, SE Paraguay 25°24′S 56°30′W
61 B23 **Coronel Pringles** Buenos Aires, E Argentina 37°56′S 61°25′W
61 B23 **Coronel Suárez** Buenos Aires, E Argentina 37°30′S 61°52′W
61 E22 **Coronel Vidal** Buenos Aires, E Argentina 37°28′S 57°45′W
55 V9 **Coronie** ◈ *district* NW Surinam
57 G17 **Coropuna, Nevado** ▲ S Peru 15°31′S 72°31′W
Çorovoda *see* Çorovodë
113 L22 **Çorovodë** *var.* Çorovoda. Berat, S Albania 40°29′N 20°15′E
183 P11 **Corowa** New South Wales, SE Australia 36°01′S 146°22′E
42 G1 **Corozal** Corozal, N Belize 18°23′N 88°23′W
54 E6 **Corozal** Sucre, NW Colombia 09°18′N 75°19′W
42 G1 **Corozal** ◈ *district* N Belize
25 T14 **Corpus Christi** Texas, SW USA 27°48′N 97°24′W
25 T14 **Corpus Christi Bay** *inlet* Texas, SW USA
25 R14 **Corpus Christi, Lake** ⊡ Texas, SW USA
63 F16 **Corral** Los Ríos, C Chile 39°55′S 73°30′W
105 O9 **Corral de Almaguer** Castilla-La Mancha, C Spain 39°45′N 03°10′W
104 K6 **Corrales** Castilla y León, N Spain 41°22′N 05°44′W
37 R11 **Corrales** New Mexico, SW USA 35°11′N 106°37′W
Corrán Tuathail *see* Carrauntoohil
106 F9 **Correggio** Emilia-Romagna, C Italy 44°47′N 10°46′E
59 M16 **Corrente** Piauí, E Brazil 10°29′S 45°11′W
59 I19 **Correntes, Rio** ≈ SW Brazil
103 N12 **Corrèze** ◈ *department* C France
97 C17 **Corrib, Lough** *Ir.* Loch Coirib. ◎ W Ireland
61 C14 **Corrientes** Corrientes, NE Argentina 27°29′S 58°42′W
61 D15 **Corrientes** *off.* Provincia de Corrientes. ◈ *province* NE Argentina
44 A5 **Corrientes, Cabo** *headland* W Cuba 21°48′N 84°30′W
40 I13 **Corrientes, Cabo** *headland* SW Mexico 20°25′N 105°42′W
Corrientes, Provincia de *see* Corrientes
61 C16 **Corrientes, Río** ≈ NE Argentina
56 E8 **Corrientes, Río** ≈ Ecuador/Peru
25 W9 **Corrigan** Texas, SW USA 31°00′N 94°49′W
55 U9 **Corriverton** E Guyana 05°55′N 57°09′W
Corriza *see* Korçë
183 Q11 **Corryong** Victoria, SE Australia 36°14′S 147°54′E
103 F2 **Corse** *Eng.* Corsica. ◈ *region* France, C Mediterranean Sea
101 X13 **Corse** *Eng.* Corsica. *island* France, C Mediterranean Sea
103 Y12 **Corse, Cap** *headland* Corse, France, C Mediterranean Sea 43°01′N 09°25′E
103 X15 **Corse-du-Sud** ◈ *department* Corse, France, C Mediterranean Sea
29 P11 **Corsica** South Dakota, N USA 43°25′N 98°24′W
Corsica *see* Corse
25 U7 **Corsicana** Texas, SW USA 32°05′N 96°27′W
103 Y15 **Corte** Corse, France, C Mediterranean Sea 42°18′N 09°08′E
63 G16 **Corte Alto** Los Lagos, S Chile 40°58′S 73°04′W
104 I13 **Cortegana** Andalucía, S Spain 37°55′N 06°49′W
43 N15 **Cortés** *var.* Ciudad Cortés. Puntarenas, SE Costa Rica 08°59′N 83°32′W
42 G5 **Cortés** ◈ *department* NW Honduras
37 P8 **Cortez** Colorado, C USA 37°22′N 108°36′W
Cortez, Sea of *see* California, Golfo de
106 H6 **Cortina d'Ampezzo** Veneto, NE Italy 46°33′N 12°09′E
18 H11 **Cortland** New York, NE USA 42°34′N 76°09′W
31 V11 **Cortland** Ohio, N USA 41°19′N 80°43′W
106 H12 **Cortona** Toscana, C Italy 43°15′N 12°01′E
76 H13 **Corubal, Rio** ≈ E Guinea-Bissau
104 G10 **Coruche** Santarém, C Portugal 38°58′N 08°31′W
Çoruh *see* Rize
137 R11 **Çoruh Nehri** *Geor.* Chorokh, *Rus.* Chorokhi. ≈ Georgia/Turkey
136 K12 **Çorum** *var.* Chorum. Çorum, N Turkey 40°31′N 34°57′E
136 J12 **Çorum** *var.* Chorum. ◈ *province* N Turkey
59 H19 **Corumbá** Mato Grosso do Sul, S Brazil 19°S 57°35′W
14 D16 **Corunna** Ontario, S Canada 42°49′N 82°25′W
Corunna *see* A Coruña
32 F12 **Corvallis** Oregon, NW USA 44°35′N 123°16′W
64 M1 **Corvo** *var.* Ilha do Corvo. *island* Azores, Portugal, NE Atlantic Ocean
Corvo, Ilha do *see* Corvo
31 O16 **Corydon** Indiana, N USA 38°12′N 86°07′W
29 V16 **Corydon** Iowa, C USA 40°45′N 93°19′W
Cos *see* Kos
40 I9 **Cosalá** Sinaloa, C Mexico 24°25′N 106°39′W
41 R15 **Cosamaloapan** *var.* Cosamaloapan de Carpio. Veracruz-Llave, E Mexico 18°23′N 95°50′W
Cosamaloapan de Carpio *see* Cosamaloapan
107 N21 **Cosenza** *anc.* Consentia. Calabria, SW Italy 39°17′N 16°15′E
31 T13 **Coshocton** Ohio, N USA 40°16′N 81°53′W
42 H9 **Cosigüina, Punta** *headland* NW Nicaragua 12°53′N 87°42′W
29 T9 **Cosmos** Minnesota, N USA 44°56′N 94°42′W
103 O8 **Cosne-Cours-sur-Loire** Nièvre, C France 47°25′N 02°56′E
108 B9 **Cossonay** Vaud, W Switzerland 46°37′N 06°28′E
Cossyra *see* Pantelleria
47 R4 **Costa, Cordillera de la** *var.* Cordillera de Venezuela. ⛰ N Venezuela
42 K13 **Costa Rica** *off.* Republic of Costa Rica. ◆ *republic* Central America
Costa Rica, Republic of *see* Costa Rica
43 N15 **Costeña, Fila** ⛰ S Costa Rica
Costermansville *see* Bukavu
116 I14 **Costeşti** Argeş, SW Romania 44°40′N 24°53′E
37 S8 **Costilla** New Mexico, N USA 36°58′N 105°31′W
35 O7 **Cosumnes River** ≈ California, W USA
101 O16 **Coswig** Sachsen, E Germany 51°07′N 13°36′E
101 M14 **Coswig** Sachsen-Anhalt, E Germany 51°53′N 12°26′E
Cosyra *see* Pantelleria
171 Q7 **Cotabato** Mindanao, S Philippines 07°13′N 124°12′E
56 C5 **Cotacachi** ▲ N Ecuador 0°29′N 78°17′W
57 L21 **Cotagaita** Potosí, S Bolivia 20°47′S 65°40′W
103 V15 **Côte d'Azur** *prev.* Nice. ✈ (Nice) Alpes-Maritimes, SE France 43°40′N 07°12′E
Côte d'Ivoire *see* Ivory Coast
Côte d'Ivoire, République de la *see* Ivory Coast
103 R7 **Côte d'Or** ◈ *department* E France
103 R8 **Côte d'Or** *cultural region* C France
Côte Française des Somalis *see* Djibouti
102 J4 **Cotentin** *peninsula* N France
102 G6 **Côtes d'Armor** *prev.* Côtes-du-Nord. ◈ *department* NW France
Côtes-du-Nord *see* Côtes d'Armor
Cöthen *see* Köthen
Côtière, Chaîne *see* Coast Mountains
40 M13 **Cotija** *var.* Cotija de la Paz. Michoacán, SW Mexico 19°49′N 102°39′W
Cotija de la Paz *see* Cotija
77 R16 **Cotonou** *var.* Kotonu. S Benin 06°24′N 02°26′E
77 R16 **Cotonou** ✈ S Benin 06°31′N 02°18′E
56 B6 **Cotopaxi** *prev.* León. ◈ *province* C Ecuador
56 C6 **Cotopaxi** ✶ N Ecuador 0°42′S 78°24′W
Cotrone *see* Crotone
97 L21 **Cotswold Hills** *var.* Cotswolds. *hill range* S England, United Kingdom
Cotswolds *see* Cotswold Hills
32 F13 **Cottage Grove** Oregon, NW USA 43°48′N 123°03′W
21 S14 **Cottageville** South Carolina, SE USA 32°55′N 80°28′W

◆ Country
● Country Capital
◇ Dependent Territory
○ Dependent Territory Capital
◈ Administrative Regions
✈ International Airport
▲ Mountain
⛰ Mountain Range
✶ Volcano
≈ River
◎ Lake
⊡ Reservoir

101 P14 Cottbus Lus. Chośebuz; prev. Kottbus. Brandenburg, E Germany 51°42′N 14°22′E
27 U9 Cotter Arkansas, C USA 36°16′N 92°30′W
106 A9 Cottian Alps Fr. Alpes Cottiennes, It. Alpi Cozie. ▲▲ France/Italy
Cottiennes, Alpes see Cottian Alps
Cotton State, The see Alabama
22 G4 Cotton Valley Louisiana, S USA 32°49′N 93°25′W
36 L12 Cottonwood Arizona, SW USA 34°43′N 112°00′W
32 M10 Cottonwood Idaho, NW USA 46°01′N 116°20′W
29 S9 Cottonwood Minnesota, N USA 44°37′N 95°41′W
25 Q7 Cottonwood Texas, SW USA 32°12′N 99°14′W
27 O5 Cottonwood Falls Kansas, C USA 38°21′N 96°33′W
36 L3 Cottonwood Heights Utah, W USA 40°37′N 111°48′W
29 S10 Cottonwood River ~ Minnesota, N USA
45 O9 Cotuí C Dominican Republic 19°04′N 70°10′W
25 Q13 Cotulla Texas, SW USA 28°27′N 99°15′W
Cotyora see Ordu
102 I11 Coubre, Pointe de la headland W France 45°39′N 01°23′W
18 E12 Coudersport Pennsylvania, NE USA 41°45′N 78°00′W
15 S9 Coudres, Île aux island Québec, SE Canada
182 G11 Couedic, Cape de headland South Australia 36°04′S 136°43′E
Couentrey see Coventry
102 I6 Couesnon ~ NW France
32 H10 Cougar Washington, NW USA 46°03′N 122°18′W
102 L10 Couhé Vienne, W France 46°18′N 00°10′E
32 K8 Coulee City Washington, NW USA 47°36′N 119°18′W
195 Q15 Coulman Island island Antarctica
103 P5 Coulommiers Seine-et-Marne, N France 48°49′N 03°04′E
14 K11 Coulonge ~ Québec, SE Canada
14 K11 Coulonge Est ~ Québec, SE Canada
35 Q9 Coulterville California, W USA 37°41′N 120°10′W
38 M9 Council Alaska, USA 64°54′N 163°40′W
32 M12 Council Idaho, NW USA 44°45′N 116°26′W
29 S15 Council Bluffs Iowa, C USA 41°16′N 95°52′W
27 O5 Council Grove Kansas, C USA 38°41′N 96°29′W
27 O5 Council Grove Lake ⊠ Kansas, C USA
32 G7 Coupeville Washington, NW USA 48°13′N 122°41′W
55 U12 Courantyne River var. Corantijn Rivier, Corentyne River. ~ Guyana/Surinam
99 G21 Courcelles Hainaut, S Belgium 50°28′N 04°23′E
108 C7 Courgenay Jura, NW Switzerland 47°24′N 07°09′E
126 B2 Courland Lagoon Ger. Kurisches Haff, Rus. Kurskiy Zaliv. lagoon Lithuania/Russian Federation
118 B12 Courland Spit Lith. Kuršių Nerija, Rus. Kurshskaya Kosa. spit Lithuania/Russian Federation
106 A6 Courmayeur prev. Cormaiore. Valle d'Aosta, NW Italy 45°48′N 07°00′E
108 D7 Courroux Jura, NW Switzerland 47°22′N 07°23′E
10 K17 Courtenay Vancouver Island, British Columbia, SW Canada 49°40′N 124°58′W
21 W7 Courtland Virginia, NE USA 36°44′N 77°06′W
25 V10 Courtney Texas, SW USA 30°16′N 96°04′W
30 J4 Court Oreilles, Lac ◎ Wisconsin, N USA
Courtrai see Kortrijk
99 H19 Court-Saint-Étienne Walloon Brabant, C Belgium 50°38′N 04°34′E
22 G6 Coushatta Louisiana, S USA 32°00′N 93°20′W
172 I16 Cousin island Inner Islands, NE Seychelles
172 I16 Cousine island Inner Islands, NE Seychelles
102 J4 Coutances anc. Constantia. Manche, N France 49°04′N 01°27′W
102 K12 Coutras Gironde, SW France 45°01′N 00°07′W
45 U14 Couva Trinidad, Trinidad and Tobago 10°25′N 61°27′W
108 B8 Couvet Neuchâtel, W Switzerland 46°57′N 06°41′E
99 H22 Couvin Namur, S Belgium 50°03′N 04°30′E
116 K12 Covasna Ger. Kowasna, Hung. Kovászna. Covasna, E Romania 45°51′N 26°11′E
116 J11 Covasna ◈ county E Romania
14 E12 Cove Island island Ontario, S Canada
34 M5 Covelo California, W USA 39°46′N 123°16′W
97 M20 Coventry anc. Couentrey. C England, United Kingdom 52°25′N 01°30′W
Cove of Cork see Cobh
21 U5 Covesville Virginia, NE USA 37°52′N 78°41′W
104 I8 Covilhã Castelo Branco, E Portugal 40°17′N 07°30′W
23 T3 Covington Georgia, SE USA 33°34′N 83°52′W
31 N13 Covington Indiana, N USA 40°08′N 87°23′W
20 M3 Covington Kentucky, S USA 39°04′N 84°30′W
22 K8 Covington Louisiana, S USA 30°28′N 90°06′W
31 Q13 Covington Ohio, N USA 40°07′N 84°21′W
20 F9 Covington Tennessee, S USA 35°32′N 89°40′W
21 S6 Covington Virginia, NE USA 37°48′N 80°01′W
183 Q8 Cowal, Lake seasonal lake New South Wales, SE Australia
11 W15 Cowan Manitoba, S Canada 51°59′N 100°36′W
18 F12 Cowanesque River ~ New York/Pennsylvania, NE USA
180 L12 Cowan, Lake ◎ Western Australia
15 P13 Cowansville Québec, SE Canada 45°13′N 72°44′W
182 H8 Cowell South Australia 33°43′S 136°53′E
97 M23 Cowes S England, United Kingdom 50°45′N 01°19′W
27 Q10 Coweta Oklahoma, C USA 35°57′N 95°39′W
0 D6 Cowie Seamount undersea feature NE Pacific Ocean 54°15′N 149°30′W
32 G10 Cowlitz River ~ Washington, NW USA
21 Q11 Cowpens South Carolina, SE USA 35°01′N 81°48′W
183 R8 Cowra New South Wales, SE Australia 33°50′S 148°45′E
Coxen Hole see Roatán
59 I19 Coxim Mato Grosso do Sul, S Brazil 18°28′S 54°45′W
59 I19 Coxim, Rio ~ SW Brazil
Coxin Hole see Roatán
153 V17 Cox's Bazar Chittagong, S Bangladesh 21°25′N 91°59′E
76 H14 Coyah Conakry, W Guinea 09°45′N 13°26′W
40 K5 Coyame Chihuahua, N Mexico 29°29′N 105°07′W
24 L9 Coyanosa Draw ~ Texas, SW USA
Coyhaique see Coihaique
42 C7 Coyolate, Río ~ S Guatemala
Coyote State, The see South Dakota
40 I10 Coyotitán Sinaloa, C Mexico 23°48′N 106°37′W
41 O16 Coyuca var. Coyuca de Benítez. Guerrero, S Mexico 17°01′N 100°08′W
41 N15 Coyuca var. Coyuca de Catalán. Guerrero, S Mexico 18°21′N 100°39′W
Coyuca de Benítez/Coyuca de Catalán see Coyuca
29 N15 Cozad Nebraska, C USA 40°52′N 99°58′W
158 L14 Cozhê Xizang Zizhiqu, W China 31°53′N 87°51′E
Cozie, Alpi see Cottian Alps
Cozmeni see Kitsman'
40 E3 Cozón, Cerro ▲ NW Mexico 31°16′N 112°29′W
41 Z12 Cozumel Quintana Roo, E Mexico 20°29′N 86°54′W
41 Z12 Cozumel, Isla island SE Mexico
32 K8 Crab Creek ~ Washington, NW USA
44 H12 Crab Pond Point headland W Jamaica 18°07′N 78°01′W
Cracovia/Cracow see Kraków
83 I25 Cradock Eastern Cape, S South Africa 32°07′S 25°38′E
39 Y14 Craig Prince of Wales Island, Alaska, USA 55°29′N 133°04′W
37 Q3 Craig Colorado, C USA 40°31′N 107°33′W
97 F15 Craigavon C Northern Ireland, United Kingdom 54°28′N 06°25′W
21 T5 Craigsville Virginia, NE USA 38°07′N 79°21′W
101 J21 Crailsheim Baden-Württemberg, S Germany 49°07′N 10°04′E
116 H14 Craiova Dolj, SW Romania 44°19′N 23°49′E
10 K12 Cranberry Junction British Columbia, SW Canada 55°35′N 128°21′W
18 J8 Cranberry Lake ◎ New York, NE USA
11 V13 Cranberry Portage Manitoba, C Canada 54°34′N 101°22′W
11 P17 Cranbrook British Columbia, SW Canada 49°29′N 115°48′W
30 M5 Crandon Wisconsin, N USA 45°34′N 88°54′W
32 K14 Crane Oregon, NW USA 43°24′N 118°35′W
24 M9 Crane Texas, SW USA 31°23′N 102°22′W
Crane see The Crane
25 S8 Cranfills Gap Texas, SW USA 31°46′N 97°49′W
19 O12 Cranston Rhode Island, NE USA 41°46′N 71°26′W
Cranz see Zelenogradsk
59 L15 Craolândia Tocantins, E Brazil 07°17′S 47°23′W
102 J7 Craon Mayenne, NW France 47°52′N 00°57′W
195 V16 Crary, Cape headland Antarctica
Crasna see Kraszna
32 G14 Crater Lake ◎ Oregon, NW USA
33 P14 Craters of the Moon National Monument national park Idaho, NW USA
59 O14 Crateús Ceará, E Brazil 05°10′S 40°39′W
Crathis see Crati
107 N20 Crati anc. Crathis. ~ S Italy
11 U16 Craven Saskatchewan, S Canada 50°44′N 104°50′W
54 I8 Cravo Norte Arauca, E Colombia 06°17′N 70°15′W
28 J12 Crawford Nebraska, C USA 42°40′N 103°24′W
25 T8 Crawford Texas, SW USA 31°31′N 97°26′W
11 O17 Crawford Bay British Columbia, SW Canada 49°39′N 116°44′W
65 M19 Crawford Seamount undersea feature S Atlantic Ocean 40°30′S 10°00′W
31 O13 Crawfordsville Indiana, N USA 40°02′N 86°52′W
23 S9 Crawfordville Florida, SE USA 30°10′N 84°22′W
97 O23 Crawley SE England, United Kingdom 51°07′N 00°12′W
33 S10 Crazy Mountains ▲▲ Montana, NW USA
11 T11 Cree ~ Saskatchewan, C Canada
37 R7 Creede Colorado, C USA 37°51′N 106°55′W
40 I6 Creel Chihuahua, N Mexico 27°45′N 107°36′W
11 S11 Cree Lake ◎ Saskatchewan, C Canada
11 V13 Creighton Saskatchewan, C Canada 54°46′N 101°54′W
29 Q13 Creighton Nebraska, C USA 42°28′N 97°54′W
103 O4 Creil Oise, N France 49°16′N 02°29′E
106 E8 Crema Lombardia, N Italy 45°22′N 09°40′E
106 E8 Cremona Lombardia, N Italy 45°08′N 10°02′E
Creole State see Louisiana
112 M10 Crepaja Hung. Cserépalja. Vojvodina, N Serbia 45°02′N 20°36′E
103 O4 Crépy-en-Valois Oise, N France 49°13′N 02°54′E
112 B10 Cres It. Cherso. Primorje-Gorski Kotar, NW Croatia 44°57′N 14°24′E
112 A11 Cres It. Cherso; anc. Crexa. island W Croatia
32 H14 Crescent Oregon, NW USA 43°27′N 121°40′W
34 K1 Crescent City California, W USA 41°45′N 124°14′W
23 W10 Crescent City Florida, SE USA 29°25′N 81°30′W
167 X10 Crescent Group island group C Paracel Islands
23 W10 Crescent Lake ◎ Florida, SE USA
29 X11 Cresco Iowa, C USA 43°22′N 92°06′W
61 B18 Crespo Entre Ríos, E Argentina 32°05′S 60°20′W
103 R13 Crest Drôme, E France 44°45′N 05°00′E
37 R5 Crested Butte Colorado, C USA 38°52′N 106°59′W
31 S12 Crestline Ohio, N USA 40°47′N 82°44′W
11 O17 Creston British Columbia, SW Canada 49°05′N 116°32′W
29 U15 Creston Iowa, C USA 41°03′N 94°21′W
33 V16 Creston Wyoming, C USA 41°40′N 107°43′W
37 S7 Crestone Peak ▲ Colorado, C USA 37°58′N 105°34′W
23 P8 Crestview Florida, SE USA 30°44′N 86°34′W
121 R10 Cretan Trough undersea feature Aegean Sea, C Mediterranean Sea
29 R16 Crete Nebraska, C USA 40°36′N 96°58′W
Crete see Kríti
103 O5 Créteil Val-de-Marne, N France 48°47′N 02°28′E
Crete, Sea of/Creticum, Mare see Kritikó Pélagos
105 X4 Creus, Cap de headland NE Spain 42°18′N 03°18′E
103 N10 Creuse ◈ department C France
102 L9 Creuse ~ C France
103 T4 Creutzwald Moselle, NE France 49°13′N 06°41′E
105 S12 Crevillent prev. Crevillente. Valenciana, E Spain 38°15′N 00°48′W
Crevillente see Crevillent
97 L18 Crewe C England, United Kingdom 53°05′N 02°27′W
21 V7 Crewe Virginia, NE USA 37°10′N 78°07′W
Crexa see Cres
43 Q15 Cricamola, Río ~ NW Panama
61 K14 Criciúma Santa Catarina, S Brazil 28°39′S 49°23′W
96 J11 Crieff C Scotland, United Kingdom 56°22′N 03°49′W
112 B10 Crikvenica It. Cirquenizza; prev. Cirkvenica, Crjkvenica. Primorje-Gorski Kotar, NW Croatia 45°12′N 14°40′E
Crimea/Crimean Oblast see Krym, Avtonomna Respublika
101 M16 Crimmitschau var. Krimmitschau. Sachsen, E Germany 50°48′N 12°23′E
116 G11 Crișcior Hung. Kristyor. Hunedoara, W Romania 46°09′N 22°54′E
21 Y5 Crisfield Maryland, NE USA 37°58′N 75°51′W
31 P3 Crisp Point headland Michigan, N USA 46°45′N 85°15′W
59 L19 Cristalina Goiás, C Brazil 16°43′S 47°37′W
44 J7 Cristal, Sierra del ▲▲ E Cuba
43 T14 Cristóbal Colón, C Panama 09°18′N 79°52′W
54 F4 Cristóbal Colón, Pico ▲ N Colombia 10°52′N 73°46′W
Cristur/Cristuru Săcuiesc see Cristuru Secuiesc
116 I11 Cristuru Secuiesc prev. Cristur, Cristuru Săcuiesc, Sitaș Cristuru, Ger. Kreutz, Hung. Székelykeresztúr, Szitás-Keresztúr. Harghita, C Romania 46°17′N 25°02′E
116 F10 Crișul Alb var. Weisse Kreisch, Ger. Weisse Körös, Hung. Fehér-Körös. ~ Hungary/Romania
116 F10 Crișul Negru Ger. Schwarze Körös, Hung. Fekete-Körös. ~ Hungary/Romania
116 G10 Crișul Repede var. Schnelle Kreisch, Ger. Schnelle Körös, Hung. Sebes-Körös. ~ Hungary/Romania
117 N10 Criuleni Rus. Kriulyany. C Moldova 47°12′N 29°09′E
Crivadia Vulcanului see Vulcan
Crjkvenica see Crikvenica
113 J17 Crkvice SW Montenegro 42°34′N 18°38′E
113 O17 Crna Gora Alb. Mali i Zi. ▲▲ FYR Macedonia/Serbia
Crna Gora see Montenegro
113 O20 Crna Reka ~ S FYR Macedonia
Crni Drim see Black Drin
109 V10 Črni vrh ▲ NE Slovenia 46°28′N 15°14′E
109 V13 Črnomelj Ger. Tschernembl. SE Slovenia 45°32′N 15°12′E
97 A17 Croagh Patrick Ir. Cruach Phádraig. ▲ W Ireland 53°45′N 09°39′W
112 D9 Croatia off. Republic of Croatia, Ger. Kroatien, SCr. Hrvatska. ◆ republic SE Europe
Croatia, Republic of see Croatia
Croce, Picco di see Wilde Kreuzspitze
15 P8 Croche ~ Québec, SE Canada
169 V7 Crocker, Banjaran var. Crocker Range. ▲▲ East Malaysia
Crocker Range see Crocker, Banjaran
25 V9 Crockett Texas, SW USA 31°21′N 95°30′W
67 V14 Crocodile var. Krokodil. ~ N South Africa
Crocodile see Limpopo
20 I7 Crofton Kentucky, S USA 37°01′N 87°25′W
29 Q12 Crofton Nebraska, C USA 42°43′N 97°30′W
Croia see Krujë
103 R16 Croisette, Cap headland SE France 43°12′N 05°21′E
102 G8 Croisic, Pointe du headland NW France 47°16′N 02°42′W
103 S13 Croix Haute, Col de la pass E France
15 U5 Croix, Pointe à la headland Québec, SE Canada 49°16′N 67°46′W
14 F13 Croker, Cape headland Ontario, S Canada 44°56′N 80°57′W
181 P1 Croker Island island Northern Territory, N Australia
96 I8 Cromarty N Scotland, United Kingdom 57°40′N 04°02′W
99 M21 Crombach Liège, E Belgium 50°14′N 06°07′E
97 Q18 Cromer E England, United Kingdom 52°56′N 01°06′E
185 D22 Cromwell Otago, South Island, New Zealand 45°03′S 169°14′E
185 H16 Cronadun West Coast, South Island, New Zealand 42°03′S 171°52′E
39 O11 Crooked Creek Alaska, USA 61°52′N 158°06′W
44 K5 Crooked Island island SE Bahamas
44 J5 Crooked Island Passage channel SE Bahamas
32 I13 Crooked River ~ Oregon, NW USA
29 R4 Crookston Minnesota, N USA 47°47′N 96°36′W
28 I10 Crooks Tower ▲ South Dakota, N USA 44°09′N 103°55′W
31 T14 Crooksville Ohio, N USA 39°46′N 82°05′W
183 R9 Crookwell New South Wales, SE Australia 34°28′S 149°27′E
14 L14 Crosby Ontario, SE Canada 44°39′N 76°13′W
97 K17 Crosby var. Great Crosby. NW England, United Kingdom 53°30′N 03°02′W
29 U6 Crosby Minnesota, N USA 46°30′N 93°58′W
28 K2 Crosby North Dakota, N USA 48°54′N 103°17′W
25 O5 Crosbyton Texas, SW USA 33°40′N 101°16′W
77 V16 Cross ~ Cameroon/Nigeria
23 U10 Cross City Florida, SE USA 29°37′N 83°08′W
Crossen see Krosno Odrzańskie
27 V14 Crossett Arkansas, C USA 33°08′N 91°58′W
97 K15 Cross Fell ▲ N England, United Kingdom 54°42′N 02°30′W
11 P16 Crossfield Alberta, SW Canada 51°24′N 114°03′W
21 Q12 Cross Hill South Carolina, SE USA 34°18′N 81°58′W
19 U6 Cross Island island Maine, NE USA
11 X13 Cross Lake Manitoba, C Canada 54°38′N 97°35′W
22 F5 Cross Lake ⊠ Louisiana, S USA
36 I12 Crossman Peak ▲ Arizona, SW USA 34°33′N 114°09′W
25 Q7 Cross Plains Texas, SW USA 32°07′N 99°10′W
77 V17 Cross River ◈ state SE Nigeria
20 L9 Crossville Tennessee, S USA 35°57′N 85°02′W
31 S8 Croswell Michigan, N USA 43°16′N 82°37′W
14 K13 Crotch Lake ◎ Ontario, SE Canada
Croton/Crotona see Crotone
107 O21 Crotone var. Cotrone; anc. Croton, Crotona. Calabria, SW Italy 39°05′N 17°07′E
33 V11 Crow Agency Montana, NW USA 45°35′N 107°28′W
183 U7 Crowdy Head headland New South Wales, SE Australia 31°52′S 152°45′E
25 Q4 Crowell Texas, SW USA 33°59′N 99°45′W
183 O6 Crowl Creek seasonal river New South Wales, SE Australia
22 H9 Crowley Louisiana, S USA 30°11′N 92°21′W
35 S9 Crowley, Lake ⊠ California, W USA
27 X10 Crowleys Ridge hill range Arkansas, C USA
31 N11 Crown Point Indiana, N USA 41°25′N 87°22′W
37 P10 Crownpoint New Mexico, SW USA 35°40′N 108°09′W
33 R10 Crow Peak ▲ Montana, NW USA 46°17′N 111°54′W
11 P17 Crowsnest Pass pass Alberta/British Columbia, SW Canada
29 T6 Crow Wing River ~ Minnesota, N USA
97 O22 Croydon SE England, United Kingdom 51°21′N 00°06′W
Crozer, Mount see Finkol, Mount
173 P11 Crozet Basin undersea feature S Indian Ocean 39°00′S 60°00′E
173 O12 Crozet Islands island group French Southern and Antarctic Territories
173 N12 Crozet Plateau var. Crozet Plateaus. undersea feature SW Indian Ocean 46°00′S 51°00′E
Crozet Plateaus see Crozet Plateau
102 E6 Crozon Finistère, NW France 48°14′N 04°31′W
Cruacha Dubha, Na see Macgillycuddy's Reeks
Cruach Phádraig see Croagh Patrick
116 M14 Crucea Constanța, SE Romania 44°30′N 28°18′E
44 E5 Cruces Cienfuegos, C Cuba 22°20′N 80°17′W
107 O20 Crucoli Torretta Calabria, SW Italy 39°26′N 17°03′E
41 P9 Cruillas Tamaulipas, C Mexico 24°43′N 98°26′W
64 K9 Cruiser Tablemount undersea feature E Atlantic Ocean 32°00′N 28°00′W
61 G14 Cruz Alta Rio Grande do Sul, S Brazil 28°38′S 53°38′W
44 G8 Cruz, Cabo headland S Cuba 19°50′N 77°43′W
60 N9 Cruzeiro São Paulo, S Brazil 22°33′S 44°59′W
60 H10 Cruzeiro do Oeste Paraná, S Brazil 23°45′S 53°03′W
59 A15 Cruzeiro do Sul Acre, W Brazil 07°40′S 72°39′W
23 U11 Crystal Bay bay Florida, SE USA NE Gulf of Mexico Atlantic Ocean
182 I8 Crystal Brook South Australia 33°24′S 138°10′E
11 X17 Crystal City Manitoba, S Canada 49°07′N 98°54′W
27 X5 Crystal City Missouri, C USA 38°13′N 90°22′W
25 P13 Crystal City Texas, SW USA 28°43′N 99°51′W
30 M4 Crystal Falls Michigan, N USA 46°06′N 88°20′W
23 Q8 Crystal Lake Florida, SE USA 30°26′N 85°41′W
31 O6 Crystal Lake ◎ Michigan, N USA
23 V11 Crystal River Florida, SE USA 28°54′N 82°35′W
37 Q5 Crystal River ~ Colorado, C USA
22 K6 Crystal Springs Mississippi, S USA 31°59′N 90°21′W
Csaca see Čadca
Csakathurn/Csáktornya see Čakovec
Csap see Chop
Csepén see Čepin
Cserépalja see Crepaja
Csermő see Cermei
Csíkszereda see Miercurea-Ciuc
111 L24 Csongrád Csongrád, SE Hungary 46°42′N 20°09′E
111 L24 Csongrád off. Csongrád Megye. ◈ county SE Hungary
Csongrád Megye see Csongrád
111 H22 Csorna Győr-Moson-Sopron, NW Hungary 47°37′N 17°14′E
Csucsa see Ciucea
111 G25 Csurgó Somogy, SW Hungary 46°16′N 17°09′E
Csurog see Čurug
54 L5 Cúa Miranda, N Venezuela 10°14′N 66°58′W
82 C11 Cuale Malanje, NW Angola 08°22′S 16°10′E
67 T12 Cuando var. Kwando. ~ S Africa
83 E15 Cuando Cubango var. Kuando-Kubango. ◈ province SE Angola
83 E16 Cuangar Cuando Cubango, S Angola 17°34′S 18°39′E
82 D11 Cuango Lunda Norte, NE Angola 09°10′S 17°59′E
82 C10 Cuango Uíge, NW Angola 06°20′S 16°42′E
82 C10 Cuango var. Kwango. ~ Angola/Dem. Rep. Congo see also Kwango
Cuango see Kwango
Cuan, Loch see Strangford Lough
82 C12 Cuanza var. Kwanza. ~ C Angola
82 B11 Cuanza Norte var. Kuanza Norte. ◈ province NE Angola
82 B12 Cuanza Sul var. Kuanza Sul. ◈ province NE Angola
61 E16 Cuareim, Río var. Rio Quaraí. ~ Brazil/Uruguay see also Quaraí, Rio
Cuareim, Río see Quaraí, Rio
83 D15 Cuatir ~ S Angola
40 M7 Cuatro Ciénegas var. Cuatro Ciénegas de Carranza. Coahuila, NE Mexico 27°00′N 102°03′W
Cuatro Ciénegas de Carranza see Cuatro Ciénegas
40 I6 Cuauhtémoc Chihuahua, N Mexico 28°22′N 106°52′W
41 P14 Cuautla Morelos, S Mexico 18°48′N 98°56′W
104 H12 Cuba Beja, S Portugal 38°10′N 07°54′W
27 W6 Cuba Missouri, C USA 38°03′N 91°24′W
37 R10 Cuba New Mexico, SW USA 36°01′N 106°57′W
44 E6 Cuba off. Republic of Cuba. ◆ republic W West Indies
47 O2 Cuba island W West Indies
82 B13 Cubal Benguela, W Angola 12°58′S 14°16′E
83 C15 Cubango var. Kuvango, Port. Vila Artur de Paiva, Vila da Ponte. Huíla, SW Angola 14°27′S 16°18′E
83 D16 Cubango var. Kavango, Kavengo, Kubango, Okavango, Okavanggo. ~ S Africa see also Okavango
Cubango see Okavango
54 H8 Cubará Boyacá, N Colombia 07°01′N 72°07′W
Cuba, Republic of see Cuba
136 I12 Çubuk Ankara, N Turkey 40°13′N 33°02′E
83 D14 Cuchi Cuando Cubango, C Angola 14°40′S 16°58′E
42 C5 Cuchumatanes, Sierra de los ▲▲ W Guatemala
Cuculaya, Rio see Kukalaya, Rio
82 E12 Cucumbi prev. Trás-os-Montes. Lunda Sul, NE Angola 10°13′S 19°04′E
54 G7 Cúcuta var. San José de Cúcuta. Norte de Santander, N Colombia 07°55′N 72°31′W
31 N9 Cudahy Wisconsin, N USA 42°54′N 87°51′W
155 J21 Cuddalore Tamil Nādu, SE India 11°43′N 79°46′E
155 I18 Cuddapah Andhra Pradesh, S India 14°30′N 78°50′E
104 M6 Cuéllar Castilla y León, N Spain 41°24′N 04°19′W
82 D13 Cuemba var. Coemba. Bié, C Angola 12°09′S 18°07′E
56 B8 Cuenca Azuay, S Ecuador 02°54′S 79°W
105 Q9 Cuenca anc. Conca. Castilla-La Mancha, C Spain 40°04′N 02°07′W
105 P9 Cuenca ◈ province Castilla-La Mancha, C Spain
40 L9 Cuencamé var. Cuencamé de Ceniceros. Durango, C Mexico 24°53′N 103°41′W
Cuencamé de Ceniceros see Cuencamé
105 Q8 Cuenca, Serranía de ▲▲ C Spain
Cuera see Chur
105 P5 Cuerda del Pozo, Embalse de la ⊠ N Spain
41 O14 Cuernavaca Morelos, S Mexico 18°57′N 99°15′W
25 T12 Cuero Texas, SW USA 29°06′N 97°19′W
44 I7 Cueto Holguín, E Cuba 20°43′N 75°54′W
41 Q13 Cuetzalán var. Cuetzalán del Progreso. Puebla, S Mexico 20°00′N 97°27′W
Cuetzalán del Progreso see Cuetzalán
105 Q14 Cuevas de Almanzora Andalucía, S Spain 37°19′N 01°52′W
Cuevas de Vinromá see Les Coves de Vinromà
116 H12 Cugir Hung. Kudzsir. Alba, SW Romania 45°48′N 23°25′E
59 H18 Cuiabá prev. Cuyabá. state capital Mato Grosso, SW Brazil 15°32′S 56°05′W
59 H19 Cuiabá, Rio ~ SW Brazil
41 R15 Cuicatlán var. San Juan Bautista Cuicatlán. Oaxaca, SE Mexico 17°49′N 96°59′W
191 W16 Cuidado, Punta headland Easter Island, Chile, E Pacific Ocean 27°08′S 109°18′W
Cúige see Connaught
Cúige Laighean see Leinster
Cúige Mumhan see Munster
Cuihua see Daguan
98 L13 Cuijck Noord-Brabant, SE Netherlands 51°41′N 05°56′E
Cúil an tSúdaire see Portarlington
42 D7 Cuilapa Santa Rosa, S Guatemala 14°16′N 90°18′W
42 B5 Cuilco, Río ~ W Guatemala
Cúil Mhuine see Collooney
Cúil Raithin see Coleraine
83 C14 Cuima Huambo, C Angola 13°16′S 15°39′E
83 E16 Cuito var. Kwito. ~ SE Angola
83 E15 Cuito Cuanavale Cuando Cubango, E Angola 15°01′S 19°07′E
41 N14 Cuitzeo, Lago de ◎ C Mexico
27 W4 Cuivre River ~ Missouri, C USA
Çuka see Çukë
168 L8 Cukai var. Chukai, Kemaman. Terengganu, Peninsular Malaysia 04°15′N 103°25′E
113 L23 Çukë var. Çuka. Vlorë, S Albania 39°50′N 20°01′E
Cularo see Grenoble
33 Y7 Culbertson Montana, NW USA 48°09′N 104°30′W
28 M16 Culbertson Nebraska, C USA 40°13′N 100°50′W
183 P10 Culcairn New South Wales, SE Australia 35°41′S 147°01′E
45 W5 Culebra var. Dewey. E Puerto Rico 18°19′N 65°17′W
45 W6 Culebra, Isla de island E Puerto Rico
37 T8 Culebra Peak ▲ Colorado, C USA 37°07′N 105°11′W
104 J5 Culebra, Sierra de la ▲▲ NW Spain
98 J12 Culemborg Gelderland, C Netherlands 51°57′N 05°17′E
137 V14 Culfa Rus. Dzhul'fa. SW Azerbaijan 38°58′N 45°37′E
183 P4 Culgoa River ~ New South Wales/Queensland, SE Australia
40 I9 Culiacán var. Culiacán Rosales, Culiacán-Rosales. Sinaloa, C Mexico 24°48′N 107°25′W
Culiacán-Rosales/Culiacán Rosales see Culiacán
105 P14 Cúllar-Baza Andalucía, S Spain 37°35′N 02°34′W
105 S10 Cullera Valenciana, E Spain 39°10′N 00°15′W
23 P3 Cullman Alabama, S USA 34°10′N 86°50′W
108 B10 Cully Vaud, W Switzerland 46°58′N 06°46′E
Culm see Chełmno
Culmsee see Chełmża
21 V4 Culpeper Virginia, NE USA 38°28′N 78°00′W
185 I17 Culverden Canterbury, South Island, New Zealand 42°46′S 172°51′E
83 H18 Cum var. Xhumo. Central, C Botswana 21°13′S 24°38′E
55 N5 Cumaná Sucre, NE Venezuela 10°29′N 64°12′W
55 O5 Cumanacoa Sucre, NE Venezuela 10°17′N 63°58′W
54 C13 Cumbal, Nevado de elevation S Colombia
21 O7 Cumberland Kentucky, S USA 36°55′N 83°00′W
21 U2 Cumberland Maryland, NE USA 39°40′N 78°47′W
21 V6 Cumberland Virginia, NE USA 37°31′N 78°16′W
187 P12 Cumberland, Cape var. Cape Nahoi. headland Espiritu Santo, N Vanuatu 14°39′S 166°35′E
11 V14 Cumberland House Saskatchewan, C Canada 53°57′N 102°21′W
23 W8 Cumberland Island island Georgia, SE USA
20 L7 Cumberland, Lake ⊠ Kentucky, S USA
9 R5 Cumberland Peninsula peninsula Baffin Island, Nunavut, NE Canada
2 N9 Cumberland Plateau plateau E USA
30 L1 Cumberland Point headland Michigan, N USA 47°51′N 89°14′W
21 O7 Cumberland River ~ Kentucky/Tennessee, S USA
9 S6 Cumberland Sound inlet Baffin Island, Nunavut, NE Canada
96 I12 Cumbernauld S Scotland, United Kingdom 55°57′N 04°W
97 K15 Cumbria cultural region NW England, United Kingdom
97 K15 Cumbrian Mountains ▲▲ NW England, United Kingdom
23 S2 Cumming Georgia, SE USA 34°12′N 84°08′W
Cummin in Pommern see Kamień Pomorski
182 G9 Cummins South Australia 34°17′S 135°43′E
96 I13 Cumnock W Scotland, United Kingdom 55°32′N 04°28′W
40 G4 Cumpas Sonora, NW Mexico 30°N 109°48′W
136 H16 Çumra Konya, C Turkey 37°34′N 32°38′E
63 G15 Cunco Araucanía, C Chile 38°55′S 72°02′W
54 E9 Cundinamarca off. Departamento de Cundinamarca. ◈ province C Colombia
Cundinamarca, Departamento de see Cundinamarca
41 U15 Cunduacán Tabasco, SE Mexico 18°00′N 93°07′W
83 C16 Cunene ◈ province S Angola
83 A16 Cunene var. Kunene. ~ Angola/Namibia see also Kunene
Cunene see Kunene
106 A9 Cuneo Fr. Coni. Piemonte, NW Italy 44°23′N 07°32′E
83 E15 Cunjamba Cuando Cubango, E Angola 15°22′S 20°07′E
181 V10 Cunnamulla Queensland, E Australia 28°09′S 145°44′E
Čunusavvon see Junosuando
Cuokkarašša see Čohkarášša
106 B7 Cuorgnè Piemonte, NE Italy 45°23′N 07°34′E
96 K11 Cupar E Scotland, United Kingdom 56°19′N 03°01′W
116 L8 Cupcina Rus. Kupchino; prev. Calinisc, Kalinisk. N Moldova 48°07′N 27°22′E
54 C8 Cupica Chocó, W Colombia 06°43′N 77°31′W
54 C8 Cupica, Golfo de gulf W Colombia
112 N13 Ćuprija Serbia, E Serbia 43°57′N 21°21′E
Cura see Villa de Cura
45 S9 Curaçao prev. Dutch West Indies. ◇ Dutch autonomous region S Caribbean Sea
45 P16 Curaçao island Lesser Antilles
56 H13 Curanja, Río ~ E Peru
56 F7 Curaray, Rio ~ Ecuador/Peru
116 K14 Curcani Călărași, SE Romania 44°11′N 26°39′E
182 H4 Curdimurka South Australia 29°27′S 136°56′E
103 P7 Cure ~ C France
173 Y16 Curepipe C Mauritius 20°19′S 57°31′E
55 R6 Curiapo Delta Amacuro, NE Venezuela 10°03′N 63°05′W
Curia Rhaetorum see Chur
62 G12 Curicó Maule, C Chile 35°00′S 71°15′W
Curieta see Krk
172 I15 Curieuse island Inner Islands, NE Seychelles
59 C16 Curitiba Acre, W Brazil 10°08′S 69°00′W
60 K12 Curitiba prev. Curytiba. state capital Paraná, S Brazil 25°25′S 49°25′W
60 J13 Curitibanos Santa Catarina, S Brazil 27°18′S 50°35′W
183 S6 Curlewis New South Wales, SE Australia 31°09′S 150°18′E
182 J6 Curnamona South Australia 31°39′S 139°35′E
83 A15 Curoca ~ SW Angola
183 T6 Currabubula New South Wales, SE Australia 31°17′S 150°43′E
59 Q14 Currais Novos Rio Grande do Norte, E Brazil 06°12′S 36°30′W
35 W7 Currant Nevada, W USA 38°43′N 115°27′W
35 W6 Currant Mountain ▲ Nevada, W USA 38°56′N 115°19′W
44 H2 Current Eleuthera Island, C Bahamas 25°24′N 76°44′W
27 W8 Current River ~ Arkansas/Missouri, C USA
182 M14 Currie Tasmania, SE Australia 39°59′S 143°51′E
21 Y8 Currituck North Carolina, SE USA 36°29′N 76°02′W
21 Y8 Currituck Sound sound North Carolina, SE USA
39 R11 Curry Alaska, USA 62°36′N 150°00′W
Curtbunar see Tervel
116 I13 Curtea de Argeș var. Curtea-de-Arges. Argeș, S Romania 45°06′N 24°40′E
Curtea-de-Arges see Curtea de Argeș
116 E10 Curtici Ger. Kurtitsch, Hung. Kürtös. Arad, W Romania 46°21′N 21°17′E
104 H2 Curtis Galicia, NW Spain 43°09′N 08°10′W
28 M16 Curtis Nebraska, C USA 40°36′N 100°27′W
183 O14 Curtis Group island group Tasmania, SE Australia
181 Y8 Curtis Island island Queensland, SE Australia
58 K11 Curuá, Ilha do island NE Brazil
47 U7 Curuá, Rio ~ N Brazil
59 A14 Curuçá, Rio ~ NW Brazil
112 L9 Čurug Hung. Csurog. Vojvodina, N Serbia 45°30′N 20°02′E
61 D16 Curuzú Cuatiá Corrientes, NE Argentina 29°50′S 58°05′W
59 M19 Curvelo Minas Gerais, SE Brazil 18°45′S 44°27′W
18 E14 Curwensville Pennsylvania, NE USA 40°57′N 78°29′W
30 M3 Curwood, Mount ▲ Michigan, N USA 46°42′N 88°14′W
Curytiba see Curitiba
Curzola see Korčula
42 A10 Cuscatlán ◈ department C El Salvador
57 H15 Cusco var. Cuzco. Cusco, C Peru 13°35′S 72°02′W
57 H15 Cusco off. Departamento de Cusco, var. Cuzco. ◈ department C Peru
Cusco, Departamento de see Cusco
27 O9 Cushing Oklahoma, C USA 36°01′N 96°46′W
25 W8 Cushing Texas, SW USA 31°48′N 94°50′W
40 I6 Cusihuiriachic Chihuahua, N Mexico 28°16′N 106°46′W
103 P10 Cusset Allier, C France 46°08′N 03°27′E
23 S6 Cusseta Georgia, SE USA 32°18′N 84°46′W
28 J10 Custer South Dakota, N USA 43°46′N 103°36′W
Cüstrin see Kostrzyn
33 Q7 Cut Bank Montana, NW USA 48°38′N 112°20′W
Cutch, Gulf of see Kachchh, Gulf of
23 S6 Cuthbert Georgia, SE USA 31°46′N 84°47′W
11 S15 Cut Knife Saskatchewan, S Canada 52°40′N 108°54′W
23 Y16 Cutler Ridge Florida, SE USA 25°34′N 80°21′W

◆ Country
● Country Capital
◇ Dependent Territory
○ Dependent Territory Capital
◈ Administrative Regions
✈ International Airport
▲ Mountain
▲▲ Mountain Range
Volcano
~ River
◎ Lake
⊠ Reservoir

22 K10 **Cut Off** Louisiana, S USA 29°32′N 90°20′W

63 I15 **Cutral-Có** Neuquén, C Argentina 38°56′S 69°13′W

107 O21 **Cutro** Calabria, SW Italy 39°01′N 16°59′E

183 O4 **Cuttaburra Channels** seasonal river New South Wales, SE Australia

154 O12 **Cuttack** Orissa, E India 20°28′N 85°53′E

83 C15 **Cuvelai** Cunene, SW Angola 15°40′S 15°48′E

79 G18 **Cuvette** var. Région de la Cuvette. ◈ province C Congo

Cuvette, Région de la see Cuvette

173 V9 **Cuvier Basin** undersea feature E Indian Ocean

173 U9 **Cuvier Plateau** undersea feature E Indian Ocean

82 B12 **Cuvo** ∽ W Angola

100 H9 **Cuxhaven** Niedersachsen, NW Germany 53°51′N 08°43′E

Cuyabá see Cuiabá

Cuyuni, Río see Cuyuni River

55 S8 **Cuyuni River** var. Río Cuyuni. ∽ Guyana/Venezuela

Cuzco see Cusco

97 K22 **Cwmbran** Wel. Cwmbrân. SW Wales, United Kingdom 51°39′N 03°W

Cwmbrân see Cwmbran

28 K15 **C. W. McConaughy, Lake** ⊠ Nebraska, C USA

81 D20 **Cyangugu** SW Rwanda 02°27′S 29°00′E

110 D11 **Cybinka** Ger. Ziebingen. Lubuskie, W Poland 52°11′N 14°46′E

Cyclades see Kykládes

Cydonia see Chaniá

Cymru see Wales

20 M5 **Cynthiana** Kentucky, S USA 38°22′N 84°18′W

11 S17 **Cypress Hills** ▲▲ Alberta/Saskatchewan, SW Canada

Cypro-Syrian Basin see Cyprus Basin

121 U11 **Cyprus** off. Republic of Cyprus, Gk. Kypros, Turk. Kıbrıs, Kıbrıs Cumhuriyeti. ◆ republic E Mediterranean Sea

84 L14 **Cyprus** Gk. Kypros, Turk. Kıbrıs. island E Mediterranean Sea

121 W11 **Cyprus Basin** var. Cypro-Syrian Basin. undersea feature E Mediterranean Sea 34°00′N 34°00′E

Cyprus, Republic of see Cyprus

Cythera see Kýthira

Cythnos see Kýthnos

110 F9 **Czaplinek** Ger. Tempelburg. Zachodnio-pomorskie, NW Poland 53°33′N 16°14′E

Czarna Woda see Wda

110 G8 **Czarne** Pomorskie, N Poland 53°40′N 17°00′E

110 G10 **Czarnków** Wielkopolskie, C Poland 52°53′N 16°32′E

111 E17 **Czech Republic** Cz. Česká Republika. ◆ republic C Europe

Czegléd see Cegléd

110 G12 **Czempiń** Wielkopolskie, C Poland 52°10′N 16°46′E

Czenstochau see Częstochowa

Czerkow see Čerchov

Czernowitz see Chernivtsi

110 I8 **Czersk** Pomorskie, N Poland 53°48′N 17°58′E

111 J15 **Częstochowa** Ger. Czenstochau, Tschenstochau, Rus. Chenstokhov. Śląskie, S Poland 50°49′N 19°07′E

110 F10 **Człopa** Ger. Schloppe. Zachodnio-pomorskie, NW Poland 53°05′N 16°05′E

110 H8 **Człuchów** Ger. Schlochau. Pomorskie, NW Poland 53°41′N 17°20′E

D

163 V9 **Da'an** var. Dalai. Jilin, NE China 45°28′N 124°18′E

15 S10 **Daaquam** Québec, SE Canada 46°36′N 70°03′W

Daawo, Webi see Dawa Wenz

54 I4 **Dabajuro** Falcón, NW Venezuela 11°00′N 70°41′W

77 N15 **Dabakala** NE Ivory Coast 08°19′N 04°24′W

163 S11 **Daban** var. Bairin Youqi. Nei Mongol Zizhiqu, N China 43°33′N 118°40′E

111 K23 **Dabas** Pest, C Hungary 47°36′N 18°22′E

160 L8 **Daba Shan** ▲▲ C China

Dabba see Daocheng

140 J5 **Dabbāgh, Jabal** ▲ NW Saudi Arabia 27°52′N 35°48′E

54 D8 **Dabeiba** Antioquia, NW Colombia 07°01′N 76°18′W

154 E11 **Dabhoi** Gujarāt, W India 22°08′N 73°28′E

161 P8 **Dabie Shan** ▲▲ C China

76 J13 **Dabola** C Guinea 10°48′N 11°02′W

77 N17 **Dabou** S Ivory Coast 05°20′N 04°23′W

162 M15 **Dabqig** prev. Uxin Qi. Nei Mongol Zizhiqu, N China 38°29′N 108°48′E

110 P8 **Dąbrowa Białostocka** Podlaskie, NE Poland 53°38′N 23°18′E

111 M16 **Dąbrowa Tarnowska** Małopolskie, S Poland 50°10′N 21°E

119 M20 **Dabryn'** Rus. Dobryn'. Homyel'skaya Voblasts', SE Belarus 51°46′N 29°12′E

159 P10 **Dabsan Hu** ⊛ C China

161 Q13 **Dabu** var. Huliao. Guangdong, S China 24°19′N 116°07′E

116 H15 **Dăbuleni** Dolj, SW Romania 43°48′N 24°05′E

152 G9 **Dabwāli** Haryāna, NW India 29°56′N 74°40′E

Dacca see Dhaka

101 L23 **Dachau** Bayern, SE Germany 48°15′N 11°26′E

Dachuan see Dazhou

Dacia Bank see Dacia Seamount

64 M10 **Dacia Seamount** var. Dacia Bank. undersea feature E Atlantic Ocean 31°10′N 13°42′W

37 T3 **Dacono** Colorado, C USA 40°04′N 104°56′W

Đăc Tô see Đăk Tô

Dacura see Dákura

23 W12 **Dade City** Florida, SE USA 28°21′N 82°12′W

152 L10 **Ḍaḍeldhurā** var. Dandeldhura. Far Western, W Nepal 29°12′N 80°31′E

23 Q5 **Dadeville** Alabama, S USA 32°49′N 85°45′W

Dadong see Donggang

103 N15 **Dadou** ∽ S France

154 D12 **Dādra and Nagar Haveli** ◈ union territory W India

149 P14 **Dādu** Sind, SE Pakistan 26°42′N 67°48′E

167 U11 **Da Du Bơloc** Kon Tum, C Vietnam 14°06′N 107°40′E

160 G9 **Dadu He** ∽ C China

163 V15 **Daecheong-do** prev. Taechŏng-do. island NW South Korea

163 Y16 **Daegu** Jap. Taikyū; prev. Taegu. SE South Korea 35°55′N 128°33′E

163 Y15 **Daejeon** Jap. Taiden; prev. Taejŏn. C South Korea 36°20′N 127°28′E

Daerah Istimewa Aceh see Aceh

171 P4 **Daet** Luzon, N Philippines 14°06′N 122°57′E

160 I11 **Dafang** Guizhou, S China 27°07′N 105°40′E

Dafeng see Shanglin

153 W11 **Dafla Hills** ▲▲ NE India

11 U15 **Dafoe** Saskatchewan, S Canada 51°46′N 104°11′W

76 G10 **Dagana** N Senegal 16°28′N 15°35′W

Dagana see Massakory, Chad

Dagana see Dahana, Tajikistan

Dagcagoin see Zoigê

118 K11 **Dagda** SE Latvia 56°06′N 27°36′E

Dagden see Hiiumaa

Dagden-Sund see Soela Väin

127 P16 **Dagestan, Respublika** prev. Dagestanskaya ASSR, Eng. Daghestan. ◈ autonomous republic SW Russian Federation

Dagestanskaya ASSR see Dagestan, Respublika

127 R17 **Dagestanskiye Ogni** Respublika Dagestan, SW Russian Federation 42°09′N 48°08′E

Dagezhen see Fengning

185 A23 **Dagg Sound** sound South Island, New Zealand

Daghestan see Dagestan, Respublika

141 Y8 **Daghmar** NE Oman 23°09′N 59°01′E

Dağliq Quarabağ see Nagorno-Karabakh

Dagö see Hiiumaa

54 D11 **Dagua** Valle del Cauca, W Colombia 03°39′N 76°40′W

160 H11 **Daguan** var. Cuihua. Yunnan, SW China 27°42′N 103°51′E

171 N3 **Dagupan** off. Dagupan City. Luzon, N Philippines 16°05′N 120°21′E

Dagupan City see Dagupan

159 N16 **Dagzê** var. Dêqên. Xizang Zizhiqu, W China 29°38′N 91°15′E

147 Q13 **Dahana** Rus. Dagana, Dakhana. SW Tajikistan 38°03′N 69°51′E

163 V10 **Dahei Shan** ▲▲ N China

163 T7 **Da Hinggan Ling** Eng. Great Khingan Range. ▲▲ NE China

Dahlac Archipelago see Dahlak Archipelago

80 K9 **Dahlak Archipelago** var. Dahlac Archipelago. island group E Eritrea

23 T2 **Dahlonega** Georgia, SE USA 34°31′N 83°59′W

101 O14 **Dahme** Brandenburg, E Germany 52°10′N 13°47′E

100 O13 **Dahme** ∽ E Germany

141 O14 **Dahm, Ramlat** desert NW Yemen

154 E10 **Dāhod** prev. Dohad. Gujarāt, W India 22°48′N 74°18′E

Dahomey see Benin

158 G10 **Dahongliutan** Xinjiang Uygur Zizhiqu, NW China 35°59′N 79°12′E

Dahra see Dara

Dahuaishu see Hongtong

139 R2 **Dahūk** var. Dohuk, Kurd. Dihōk. Dahūk, N Iraq 36°52′N 43°01′E

116 J15 **Daia** Giurgiu, S Romania 44°00′N 25°59′E

165 P12 **Daigo** Ibaraki, Honshū, S Japan 36°43′N 140°22′E

163 O13 **Dai Hai** ⊛ N China

Daihoku see T'aipei

186 M8 **Dai Island** island N Solomon Islands

166 M8 **Daik-u** Bago, SW Burma (Myanmar) 17°46′N 96°40′E

138 H9 **Dā'īl** Dar'ā, S Syria 32°45′N 36°08′E

167 U12 **Đai Lanh** Khanh Hoa, S Vietnam 12°49′N 109°20′E

161 Q13 **Daimao Shan** ▲▲ SE China

105 N11 **Daimiel** Castilla-La Mancha, C Spain 39°04′N 03°37′W

115 F22 **Daimoniá** Pelopónnisos, S Greece 36°38′N 22°54′E

Dainan see Tainan

25 W6 **Daingerfield** Texas, SW USA 33°03′N 94°42′W

Daingin, Bá an see Dingle Bay

159 R13 **Dainkognubma** Xizang Zizhiqu, W China 32°26′N 97°58′E

164 K14 **Daiō-zaki** headland Honshū, SW Japan 34°15′N 136°50′E

Dairbhre see Valencia Island

61 B22 **Daireaux** Buenos Aires, E Argentina 36°34′S 61°40′W

Dairen see Dalian

Dairûṭ see Dayrūṭ

25 X10 **Daisetta** Texas, SW USA 30°06′N 94°38′W

192 G5 **Daitō-jima** island group SW Japan

192 G5 **Daitō Ridge** undersea feature N Philippine Sea 25°30′N 133°00′E

161 N3 **Daixian** var. Dai Xian, Shangguan. Shanxi, C China 39°10′N 112°57′E

Dai Xian see Daixian

Daiyue see Shanyin

161 Q12 **Daiyun Shan** ▲▲ SE China

44 M8 **Dajabón** NW Dominican Republic 19°35′N 71°41′W

160 G8 **Dajin Chuan** ∽ C China

148 J6 **Dak** ⊛ W Afghanistan

76 F11 **Dakar** ● (Senegal) W Senegal 14°44′N 17°27′W

76 F11 **Dakar** ✈ W Senegal 14°42′N 17°27′W

Đak Glây see Đak Glei

167 U10 **Đak Glei** prev. Đak Glây. Kon Tum, C Vietnam 15°05′N 107°42′E

Dakhana see Dahana

153 U16 **Dakhin Shahbazpur Island** island S Bangladesh

Dakhla see Ad Dakhla

76 F7 **Dakhlet Nouâdhibou** ◈ region NW Mauritania

Đak Lap see Kiên Đưc

Đak Nông see Gia Nghia

77 U11 **Dakoro** Maradi, S Niger 14°29′N 06°45′E

29 U12 **Dakota City** Iowa, C USA 42°42′N 94°13′W

29 R13 **Dakota City** Nebraska, C USA 42°25′N 96°25′W

Đakovica see Gjakovë

112 I10 **Đakovo** var. Djakovo, Hung. Diakovár. Osijek-Baranja, E Croatia 45°18′N 18°24′E

Dakshin see Deccan

167 U11 **Đăk Tô** var. Đăc Tô. Kon Tum, C Vietnam 14°35′N 107°55′E

43 N7 **Dákura** var. Dacura. Región Autónoma Atlántico Norte, NE Nicaragua 14°22′N 83°13′W

95 I14 **Dal** Akershus, S Norway 60°19′N 11°16′E

82 E12 **Dala** Lunda Sul, E Angola 11°04′S 20°15′E

108 J8 **Dalaas** Vorarlberg, W Austria 47°08′N 10°03′E

76 I13 **Dalaba** W Guinea 10°47′N 12°12′W

Dalai see Da'an

162 I12 **Dalain Hob** var. Ejin Qi. Nei Mongol Zizhiqu, N China 41°59′N 101°04′E

Dalai Nor see Hulun Nur

163 Q11 **Dalai Nur** salt lake N China

Dala-Jarna see Järna

95 M14 **Dalälven** ∽ C Sweden

136 C16 **Dalaman** Muğla, SW Turkey 36°47′N 28°47′E

136 C16 **Dalaman** ✈ Muğla, SW Turkey 36°37′N 28°51′E

136 D16 **Dalaman Çayı** ∽ SW Turkey

162 K11 **Dalandzadgad** Ömnögovĭ, S Mongolia 43°35′N 104°23′E

95 D17 **Dalane** physical region S Norway

189 Z2 **Dalap-Uliga-Djarrit** var. Delap-Uliga-Darrit, D-U-D. island group Ratak Chain, SE Marshall Islands

94 J12 **Dalarna** prev. Kopparberg. ◈ county C Sweden

94 L13 **Dalarna** prev. Eng. Dalecarlia. cultural region C Sweden

95 P16 **Dalarö** Stockholm, C Sweden 59°07′N 18°25′E

167 U13 **Đa Lat** Lâm Đông, S Vietnam 11°56′N 108°25′E

Dalay see Bayandalay

148 L12 **Dālbandīn** var. Dāl Bandin. Baluchistān, SW Pakistan 28°48′N 64°08′E

95 J17 **Dalbosjön** lake bay S Sweden

181 Y10 **Dalby** Queensland, E Australia 27°11′S 151°12′E

94 D13 **Dale** Hordaland, S Norway 60°35′N 05°48′E

94 C12 **Dale** Sogn Og Fjordane, S Norway 61°22′N 05°24′E

32 K12 **Dale** Oregon, NW USA 44°58′N 118°56′W

25 T11 **Dale** Texas, SW USA 29°56′N 97°34′W

Dalecarlia see Dalarna

21 W4 **Dale City** Virginia, NE USA 38°38′N 77°18′W

20 L8 **Dale Hollow Lake** ⊠ Kentucky/Tennessee, S USA

98 O8 **Dalen** Drenthe, NE Netherlands 52°42′N 06°45′E

95 E15 **Dalen** Telemark, S Norway 59°25′N 07°58′E

166 K14 **Daletme** Chin State, W Burma (Myanmar) 21°44′N 92°48′E

23 Q7 **Daleville** Alabama, S USA 31°18′N 85°42′W

98 M9 **Dalfsen** Overijssel, E Netherlands 52°31′N 06°16′E

24 M1 **Dalhart** Texas, SW USA 36°05′N 102°31′W

13 O13 **Dalhousie** New Brunswick, SE Canada 48°03′N 66°22′W

152 I6 **Dalhousie** Himāchal Pradesh, N India 32°32′N 76°01′E

160 F12 **Dali** var. Xiaguan. Yunnan, SW China 25°34′N 100°11′E

Dali see Idálion

163 U14 **Dalian** var. Dairen, Dalien, Jay Dairen, Lüda, Ta-lien, Rus. Dalny. Liaoning, NE China 38°53′N 121°37′E

105 O15 **Dalías** Andalucía, S Spain 36°49′N 02°50′W

Dalien see Dalian

Dalijan see Delījān

112 J9 **Dalj** Hung. Dalja. Osijek-Baranja, E Croatia 45°29′N 19°00′E

Dalja see Dalj

32 F12 **Dallas** Oregon, NW USA 44°56′N 123°20′W

25 U6 **Dallas** Texas, SW USA 32°47′N 96°48′W

25 T7 **Dallas-Fort Worth** ✈ Texas, SW USA 32°37′N 97°16′W

154 K12 **Dalli Rājhara** var. Dhalli Rajhara. Chhattīsgarh, C India 20°32′N 81°10′E

39 X15 **Dall Island** island Alexander Archipelago, Alaska, USA

38 M12 **Dall Lake** ⊛ Alaska, USA

Dállogilli see Korpilombolo

77 S12 **Dallol Bosso** seasonal river W Niger

141 U7 **Dalmā** island W United Arab Emirates

113 E14 **Dalmacija** Eng. Dalmatia, Ger. Dalmatien, It. Dalmazia. cultural region S Croatia

Dalmatia/Dalmatien/Dalmazia see Dalmacija

123 S15 **Dal'negorsk** Primorskiy Kray, SE Russian Federation 44°27′N 135°30′E

Dalny see Dalian

76 M16 **Daloa** C Ivory Coast 06°56′N 06°28′W

160 J11 **Dalou Shan** ▲▲ S China

181 X7 **Dalrymple Lake** ⊛ Queensland, E Australia

14 H14 **Dalrymple Lake** ⊛ Ontario, S Canada

181 X7 **Dalrymple, Mount** ▲ Queensland, E Australia 21°01′S 148°34′E

93 K20 **Dalsbruk** Fin. Taalintehdas. Länsi-Suomi, W Finland 60°02′N 22°31′E

95 K19 **Dalsjöfors** Västra Götaland, S Sweden 57°43′N 13°05′E

95 J17 **Dals Långed** var. Långed. Västra Götaland, S Sweden 58°54′N 12°20′E

153 O15 **Dāltenganj** prev. Daltonganj. Jhārkhand, N India 24°02′N 84°07′E

23 R2 **Dalton** Georgia, SE USA 34°46′N 84°58′W

Daltonganj see Dāltenganj

195 X14 **Dalton Iceberg Tongue** ice feature Antarctica

92 J1 **Dalvík** Nordhurland Eystra, N Iceland 65°58′N 18°31′W

Dálvvadis see Jokkmokk

35 N8 **Daly City** California, W USA 37°44′N 122°27′W

181 P2 **Daly River** ∽ Northern Territory, N Australia

181 Q3 **Daly Waters** Northern Territory, N Australia 16°21′S 133°22′E

119 F20 **Damachava** var. Damachova, Pol. Domaczewo, Rus. Domachëvo. Brestskaya Voblasts', SW Belarus 51°45′N 23°36′E

Damachova see Damachava

77 W11 **Damagaram Takaya** Zinder, S Niger 14°02′N 09°28′E

154 D12 **Damān** Damān and Diu, W India 20°25′N 72°58′E

154 B12 **Damān and Diu** ◈ union territory W India

75 V7 **Damanhūr** anc. Hermopolis Parva. N Egypt 31°03′N 30°28′E

161 O1 **Damaqun Shan** ▲▲ E China

79 I15 **Damara** Ombella-Mpoko, S Central African Republic 05°00′N 18°45′E

83 D18 **Damaraland** physical region C Namibia

171 S15 **Damar, Kepulauan** var. Baraf Daja Islands, Kepulauan Barat Daya. island group C Indonesia

168 J8 **Damar Laut** Perak, Peninsular Malaysia 04°13′N 100°36′E

171 S15 **Damar, Pulau** island Maluku, E Indonesia

Damas see Dimashq

77 Y12 **Damasak** Borno, NE Nigeria 13°10′N 12°40′E

Damasco see Dimashq

21 Q8 **Damascus** Virginia, NE USA 36°37′N 81°46′W

Damascus see Dimashq

77 X13 **Damaturu** Yobe, NE Nigeria 11°44′N 11°58′E

171 R9 **Damau** Pulau Kaburuang, N Indonesia 03°46′N 126°49′E

143 O5 **Damāvand, Qolleh-ye** ▲ N Iran 35°56′N 52°08′E

82 B10 **Damba** Uíge, NW Angola 06°44′S 15°20′E

114 M12 **Dambaslar** Tekirdağ, NW Turkey 41°13′N 27°13′E

116 J13 **Dâmbovița** prev. Dîmbovița. ◈ county SE Romania

116 J13 **Dâmbovița** prev. Dîmbovița. ∽ S Romania

173 Y15 **D'Ambre, Île** island NE Mauritius

155 K24 **Dambulla** Central Province, C Sri Lanka 07°51′N 80°40′E

44 K9 **Dame-Marie** SW Haiti 18°36′N 74°26′W

44 J9 **Dame Marie, Cap** headland SW Haiti 18°37′N 74°24′W

143 Q4 **Dāmghān** Semnān, N Iran 36°13′N 54°22′E

Damietta see Dumyāt

138 G10 **Dāmiyā** Al Balqā', NW Jordan 32°07′N 35°33′E

146 G11 **Damla** Daşoguz Welaýaty, N Turkmenistan 40°05′N 59°15′E

Dammām see Ad Dammān

100 G12 **Damme** Niedersachsen, NW Germany 52°31′N 08°12′E

153 R15 **Dāmodar** ∽ NE India

154 J9 **Damoh** Madhya Pradesh, C India 23°50′N 79°30′N

77 P15 **Damongo** NW Ghana 09°05′N 01°49′W

138 G7 **Damoûr** var. Ad Dāmūr. W Lebanon 33°36′N 35°30′E

171 N11 **Dampal, Teluk** bay Sulawesi, C Indonesia

180 H7 **Dampier** Western Australia 20°40′S 116°40′E

180 H6 **Dampier Archipelago** island group Western Australia

141 U14 **Damqawt** var. Damqut. E Yemen 16°35′N 52°39′E

159 O13 **Dam Qu** ∽ C China

Damqut see Damqawt

167 R13 **Dâmrei, Chuŏr Phmun** Fr. Chaîne de l'Éléphant. ▲▲ SW Cambodia

108 C7 **Damvant** Jura, NW Switzerland 47°22′N 06°55′E

Damwâld see Damwoude

98 L5 **Damwoude** Fris. Damwâld. Fryslân, N Netherlands 53°18′N 05°59′E

159 N15 **Damxung** var. Gongtang. Xizang Zizhiqu, W China 30°29′N 91°02′E

80 K11 **Danakil Desert** var. Afar Depression, Danakil Plain. desert E Africa

Danakil Plain see Danakil Desert

35 R8 **Dana, Mount** ▲ California, W USA 37°54′N 119°13′W

76 L16 **Danané** W Ivory Coast 07°16′N 08°09′W

167 U10 **Đa Năng** prev. Tourane. Quang Nam-Đa Năng, C Vietnam 16°04′N 108°14′E

160 G9 **Danba** var. Zhanggu, Tib. Rongzhag. Sichuan, C China 30°54′N 101°49′E

Danborg see Daneborg

18 L13 **Danbury** Connecticut, NE USA 41°21′N 73°27′W

25 W12 **Danbury** Texas, SW USA 29°13′N 95°20′W

35 X15 **Danby Lake** ⊛ California, W USA

194 H4 **Danco Coast** physical region Antarctica

82 B11 **Dande** ∽ NW Angola

Dandeldhura see Ḍaḍeldhurā

155 E17 **Dandeli** Karnātaka, W India 15°18′N 74°42′E

183 O12 **Dandenong** Victoria, SE Australia 38°01′S 145°13′E

163 V13 **Dandong** var. Tan-tung; prev. An-tung. Liaoning, NE China 40°10′N 124°23′E

197 Q14 **Daneborg** var. Danborg. ◈ Tunu, N Greenland

25 V12 **Danevang** Texas, SW USA 29°03′N 96°11′W

Dänew see Galkynyş

Danfeng see Shizong

14 L12 **Danford Lake** Québec, SE Canada 45°55′N 76°12′W

19 T4 **Danforth** Maine, NE USA 45°39′N 67°54′W

37 P3 **Danforth Hills** ▲▲ Colorado, C USA

Dangara see Danghara

159 V12 **Dangchang** Gansu, C China 34°01′N 104°19′E

159 P8 **Dangchengwan** var. Subei, Subei Mongolzu Zizhixian. Gansu, N China 39°33′N 94°50′E

82 B10 **Dange** Uíge, NW Angola 07°55′S 15°01′E

Dangerous Archipelago see Tuamotu, Îles

83 E26 **Danger Point** headland SW South Africa 34°37′S 19°20′E

147 Q13 **Danghara** Rus. Dangara. SW Tajikistan 38°05′N 69°14′E

159 P8 **Danghe Nanshan** ▲▲ W China

80 I12 **Dangila** var. Dānglā. Āmara, NW Ethiopia 11°08′N 36°51′E

159 P8 **Dangjin Shankou** pass N China

Dangla see Tanggula Shan, China

Dang La see Tanggula Shankou, China

Dānglā see Dangila, Ethiopia

Dangme Chu see Manās

153 Y11 **Dāngori** Assam, NE India 27°40′N 95°35′E

Dang Raek, Phanom/Dangrek, Chaîne des see Dângrêk, Chuŏr Phnum

167 S11 **Dângrêk, Chuŏr Phnum** var. Phanom Dang Raek, Phanom Dong Rak, Fr. Chaîne des Dangrek. ▲▲ Cambodia/Thailand

42 G3 **Dangriga** prev. Stann Creek. Stann Creek, E Belize 16°59′N 88°13′W

161 P6 **Dangshan** Anhui, E China 34°22′N 116°21′E

33 T15 **Daniel** Wyoming, C USA 42°49′N 110°04′W

83 H22 **Daniëlskuil** Northern Cape, N South Africa 28°11′S 23°33′E

19 N12 **Danielson** Connecticut, NE USA 41°48′N 71°53′W

124 M15 **Danilov** Yaroslavskaya Oblast', W Russian Federation 58°11′N 40°11′E

127 O9 **Danilovka** Volgogradskaya Oblast', SW Russian Federation 50°21′N 44°03′E

Danish West Indies see Virgin Islands (US)

160 L7 **Dan Jiang** ∽ C China

160 M7 **Danjiangkou Shuiku** ⊠ C China

141 W8 **Ḍank** var. Dhank. NW Oman 23°34′N 56°16′E

152 J7 **Dankhar** Himāchal Pradesh, N India 32°08′N 78°12′E

126 L6 **Dankov** Lipetskaya Oblast', W Russian Federation 53°17′N 39°07′E

42 J7 **Danlí** El Paraíso, S Honduras 14°02′N 86°34′W

Danmark see Denmark

Danmarksstraedet see Denmark Strait

95 O14 **Dannemora** Uppsala, C Sweden 60°13′N 17°49′E

18 L6 **Dannemora** New York, NE USA 44°42′N 73°42′W

100 K11 **Dannenberg** Niedersachsen, N Germany 53°05′N 11°06′E

184 N12 **Dannevirke** Manawatu-Wanganui, North Island, New Zealand 40°14′S 176°05′E

21 U8 **Dan River** ∽ Virginia, NE USA

167 P8 **Dan Sai** Loei, C Thailand 17°15′N 101°04′E

18 F10 **Dansville** New York, NE USA 42°34′N 77°40′W

Dantzig see Gdańsk

86 E12 **Danube** Bul. Dunav, Cz. Dunaj, Ger. Donau, Hung. Duna, Rom. Dunărea. ∽ C Europe

Danubian Plain see Dunavska Ravnina

166 L8 **Danubyu** Ayeyarwady, SW Burma (Myanmar) 17°15′N 95°35′E

Danum see Doncaster

19 P11 **Danvers** Massachusetts, NE USA 42°34′N 70°54′W

27 T11 **Danville** Arkansas, C USA 35°03′N 93°22′W

31 N13 **Danville** Illinois, N USA 40°10′N 87°37′W

31 O14 **Danville** Indiana, N USA 39°45′N 86°31′W

29 Y15 **Danville** Iowa, C USA 40°52′N 91°18′W

20 M6 **Danville** Kentucky, S USA 37°40′N 84°49′W

18 G14 **Danville** Pennsylvania, NE USA 40°57′N 76°36′W

21 T6 **Danville** Virginia, NE USA 36°34′N 79°25′W

Danxian/Dan Xian see Danzhou

160 L17 **Danzhou** prev. Danxian, Dan Xian, Nada. Hainan, S China 19°31′N 109°31′E

Danzhou see Yichuan

Danzig see Gdańsk

Danziger Bucht see Danzig, Gulf of

110 J6 **Danzig, Gulf of** var. Gulf of Gdańsk, Ger. Danziger Bucht, Pol. Zakota Gdańska, Rus. Gdan'skaya Bukhta. gulf N Poland

160 F10 **Daocheng** var. Jinzhu, Tib. Dabba. Sichuan, C China 29°05′N 100°14′E

Daojiang see Daoxian

Daokou see Huaxian

104 H7 **Dão, Rio** ∽ N Portugal

Daosa see Dausa

77 Y7 **Dao Timmi** Agadez, NE Niger 20°31′N 13°34′E

160 M13 **Daoxian** var. Daojiang. Hunan, S China 25°30′N 111°37′E

77 Q14 **Dapaong** N Togo 10°52′N 00°12′E

23 N8 **Daphne** Alabama, S USA 30°36′N 87°54′W

171 P7 **Dapitan** Mindanao, S Philippines 08°39′N 123°26′E

159 P9 **Da Qaidam** Qinghai, C China 37°50′N 95°18′E

163 V8 **Daqing** var. Sartu. Heilongjiang, NE China 46°35′N 125°00′E

163 O13 **Daqing Shan** ▲▲ N China

163 T11 **Daqin Tal** var. Naiman Qi. Nei Mongol Zizhiqu, N China 42°51′N 120°41′E

Daqm see Duqm

160 G8 **Da Qu** var. Do Qu. ∽ C China

139 T5 **Dāqūq** var. Tāwūq. At Ta'mím, N Iraq 35°08′N 44°27′E

76 G10 **Dara** var. Dahra. NW Senegal 15°20′N 15°28′W

138 H9 **Dar'ā** var. Der'a, Fr. Déraa. Dar'ā, SW Syria 32°37′N 36°06′E

138 H8 **Dar'ā** off. Muḥāfaẓat Dar'ā, var. Dará, Der'a, Derrá. ◈ governorate S Syria

143 Q12 **Dārāb** Fārs, S Iran 28°52′N 54°25′E

116 K8 **Darabani** Botoşani, NW Romania 48°10′N 26°39′E

Daraj see Dirj

Dar'ā, Muḥāfaẓat see Dar'ā

142 M8 **Dārān** Eşfahān, W Iran 33°00′N 50°27′E

167 U12 **Da Răng, Sông** var. Ba. ∽ S Vietnam

Daraut-Kurgan see Daroot-Korgon

77 W13 **Darazo** Bauchi, E Nigeria 11°01′N 10°27′E

139 S3 **Darband** Arbīl, N Iraq 36°15′N 44°17′E

139 V4 **Darband-i Khān, Sadd** dam NE Iraq

139 N1 **Darbāsīyah** var. Derbisīye. Al Ḥasakah, N Syria 37°06′N 40°42′E

118 C11 **Darbėnai** Klaipėda, NW Lithuania 56°02′N 21°16′E

153 Q13 **Darbhanga** Bihār, N India 26°10′N 85°54′E

38 M9 **Darby, Cape** headland Alaska, USA 64°19′N 162°46′W

112 I9 **Darda** Hung. Dárda. Osijek-Baranja, E Croatia 45°37′N 18°41′E

Dárda see Darda

Dardanë see Kamenicë

27 T11 **Dardanelle** Arkansas, C USA 35°11′N 93°09′W

27 S11 **Dardanelle, Lake** ⊠ Arkansas, C USA

Dardanelles see Çanakkale Boğazı

Dardanelli see Çanakkale

Dardo see Kangding

Dar-el-Beida see Casablanca

136 M14 **Darende** Malatya, C Turkey 38°34′N 37°29′E

81 J22 **Dar es Salaam** Dar es Salaam, E Tanzania 06°51′S 39°18′E

81 J22 **Dar es Salaam** ✈ Pwani, E Tanzania 06°57′S 39°17′E

185 H18 **Darfield** Canterbury, South Island, New Zealand 43°29′S 172°07′E

106 F7 **Darfo** Lombardia, N Italy 45°54′N 10°12′E

80 B10 **Darfur** var. Darfur Massif. cultural region W Sudan

Darfur Massif see Darfur

Darganata/Dargan-Ata see Birata

143 T3 **Dargaz** var. Darreh Gaz; prev. Moḥammadābād. Khorāsān-Razavī, NE Iran 37°28′N 59°08′E

139 U4 **Dargazayn** As Sulaymānīyah, NE Iraq 35°39′N 45°00′E

183 P12 **Dargo** Victoria, SE Australia 37°29′S 147°15′E

162 L6 **Darhan** Darhan Uul, N Mongolia 49°24′N 105°57′E

163 N8 **Darhan** Hentiy, C Mongolia 46°38′N 109°25′E

Darhan see Büreghangay

Darhan Muminggan Lianheqi see Bailingmiao

162 L6 **Darhan Uul** ◈ province N Mongolia

23 W7 **Darien** Georgia, SE USA 31°22′N 81°25′W

43 W16 **Darién** off. Provincia del Darién. ◈ province SE Panama

Darién, Golfo del see Darien, Gulf of

43 X14 **Darien, Gulf of** Sp. Golfo del Darién. gulf S Caribbean Sea

Darien, Isthmus of see Panama, Istmo de

Darién, Provincia del see Darién

42 K9 **Dariense, Cordillera** ▲▲ C Nicaragua

43 W15 **Darién, Serranía del** ▲▲ Colombia/Panama

163 P10 **Darīganga** var. Ovoot. Sühbaatar, SE Mongolia 45°08′N 113°51′E

Dario see Ciudad Darío

Dariorigum see Vannes

Dariv see Darvi

Darj see Dirj

Darjeeling see Dārjiling

153 S12 **Dārjiling** prev. Darjeeling. West Bengal, NE India 27°00′N 88°13′E

Darkehnen see Ozersk

159 S12 **Darlag** var. Gümai. Qinghai, C China 33°43′N 99°42′E

183 T3 **Darling Downs** hill range Queensland, E Australia

28 M2 **Darling, Lake** ⊠ North Dakota, N USA

180 I12 **Darling Range** ▲▲ Western Australia

182 L8 **Darling River** ∽ New South Wales, SE Australia

97 M15 **Darlington** N England, United Kingdom 54°31′N 01°34′W

21 T12 **Darlington** South Carolina, SE USA 34°19′N 79°53′W

30 K9 **Darlington** Wisconsin, N USA 42°41′N 90°08′W

110 G7 **Darłowo** Zachodnio-pomorskie, NW Poland 54°24′N 16°21′E

101 G19 **Darmstadt** Hessen, SW Germany 49°52′N 08°39′E

75 S7 **Darnah** var. Dérna. NE Libya 32°46′N 22°39′E

103 S6 **Darney** Vosges, NE France 48°06′N 05°58′E

182 M7 **Darnick** New South Wales, SE Australia 32°52′S 143°38′E

195 Y6 **Darnley, Cape** cape Antarctica

105 R7 **Daroca** Aragón, NE Spain 41°07′N 01°25′W

147 S11 **Daroot-Korgon** var. Daraut-Kurgan. Oshskaya Oblast', SW Kyrgyzstan 39°35′N 72°13′E

61 A23 **Darragueira** var. Darregueira. Buenos Aires, E Argentina 37°40′S 63°12′W

Darregueira see Darragueira

Darreh Gaz see Dargaz

142 K7 **Darreh Shahr** var. Darreh-ye Shahr. Īlām, W Iran 33°10′N 47°18′E

Darreh-ye Shahr see Darreh Shahr

32 I7 **Darrington** Washington, NW USA 48°15′N 121°36′W

25 P1 **Darrouzett** Texas, SW USA 36°27′N 100°19′W

153 S15 **Darsana** var. Darshana. Khulna, N Bangladesh 23°32′N 88°49′E

Darshana see Darsana

100 M7 **Darss** peninsula NE Germany

100 M7 **Darsser Ort** headland NE Germany 54°28′N 12°31′E

97 J24 **Dart** ∽ SW England, United Kingdom

Dartang see Baqên

97 P22 **Dartford** SE England, United Kingdom 51°27′N 00°13′E

182 L12 **Dartmoor** Victoria, SE Australia 37°56′S 141°18′E

97 I24 **Dartmoor** moorland SW England, United Kingdom

13 Q15 **Dartmouth** Nova Scotia, SE Canada 44°40′N 63°35′W

97 J24 **Dartmouth** SW England, United Kingdom 50°21′N 03°34′W

15 Y6 **Dartmouth** ∽ Québec, SE Canada

183 Q11 **Dartmouth Reservoir** ⊛ Victoria, SE Australia

Dartuch, Cabo see Artrutx, Cap d'

186 C9 **Daru** Western, SW Papua New Guinea 09°05′S 143°10′E

112 G9 **Daruvar** Hung. Daruvár. Bjelovar-Bilogora, NE Croatia 45°34′N 17°12′E

Daruvár see Daruvar

Darvaza see Derweze, Turkmenistan

Darvaza see Darvoza, Uzbekistan

Darvazskiy Khrebet see Darvoz, Qatorkŭhi

Darvel Bay see Lahad Datu, Teluk

Darvel, Teluk see Lahad Datu, Teluk

162 F8 **Darvi** var. Dariv. Govĭ-Altay, W Mongolia 46°20′N 94°11′E

162 F7 **Darvi** var. Bulgan. Hovd, W Mongolia 46°57′N 93°40′E

Darvīshān see Darwēshān

147 O10 **Darvoza** Rus. Darvaza. Jizzax Viloyati, C Uzbekistan 40°59′N 67°19′E

147 R13 **Darvoz, Qatorkŭhi** Rus. Darvazskiy Khrebet. ▲▲ C Tajikistan

148 L9 **Darwēshān**, var. Garmser; prev. Darvīshān. Helmand, S Afghanistan 31°02′N 64°12′E

63 J15 **Darwin** Río Negro, S Argentina 39°13′S 65°41′W

181 O1 **Darwin** prev. Palmerston, Port Darwin. territory capital Northern Territory, N Australia 12°28′S 130°52′E

65 D24 **Darwin** var. Darwin Settlement. East Falkland, Falkland Islands 51°51′S 58°55′W

62 H8 **Darwin, Cordillera** ▲▲ N Chile

Darwin Settlement see Darwin

57 B17 **Darwin, Volcán** Ѫ Galapagos Islands, Ecuador, E Pacific Ocean 0°12′S 91°17′W

149 S8 **Darya Khān** Punjab, E Pakistan 31°47′N 71°10′E

145 O15 **Dar'yalyktakyr, Ravnina** plain S Kazakhstan

143 T11 **Dārzīn** Kermān, S Iran 29°11′N 58°09′E

Dashhowuz see Daşoguz

Dashhowuz Welayaty see Daşoguz Welaýaty

162 K7 **Dashinchilen** var. Süüj. Bulgan, C Mongolia 47°49′N 104°06′E

119 O16 **Dashkawka** Rus. Dashkovka. Mahilyowskaya Voblasts', E Belarus 53°44′N 30°16′E

Dashkhovuz see Daşoguz Welaýaty

Dashkhovuzskiy Velayat see Daşoguz Welaýaty

Dashköpri see Daşköpri

Dashkovka see Dashkawka

148 J15 **Dasht** ∽ SW Pakistan

Dasht-i see Bābūs, Dasht-e

Dashtidzhum see Dashtijum

147 R13 **Dashtijum** Rus. Dashtidzhum. SW Tajikistan 38°06′N 70°11′E

149 W7 **Daska** Punjab, NE Pakistan 32°15′N 74°23′E

146 J16 **Daşköpri** var. Dashköpri, Rus. Tashkepri. Mary Welaýaty, S Turkmenistan 36°15′N 62°37′E

146 H8 **Daşoguz** Rus. Dashkhovuz, Turkm. Dashhowuz; prev. Tashauz. Daşoguz Welaýaty, N Turkmenistan 41°51′N 59°53′E

146 E9 **Daşoguz Welaýaty** var. Dashhowuz Welayaty, Rus. Dashkhovuz, Dashkhovuzskiy Velayat. ◈ province N Turkmenistan

Đa, Sông see Black River

77 R15 **Dassa** var. Dassa-Zoumé. S Benin 07°46′N 02°15′E

Dassa-Zoumé see Dassa

29 U8 **Dassel** Minnesota, N USA 45°06′N 94°18′W

152 H3 **Dastegil Sar** ▲ N India

136 C16 **Datça** Muğla, SW Turkey 36°46′N 27°40′E

165 R4 **Date** Hokkaidō, NE Japan 42°28′N 140°51′E

154 I8 **Datia** prev. Duttia. Madhya Pradesh, C India 25°41′N 78°28′E

Dåtnejaevrie see Tunnsjøen

159 T10 **Datong** var. Datong Huizu Tuzu Zizhixian, Qiaotou. Qinghai, C China 37°01′N 101°33′E

161 N2 Datong var. Tatung, Ta-t'ung. Shanxi, C China 40°09′N 113°17′E
Datong see Tong'an
159 S8 Datong He ≈ C China
Datong Huizu Tuzu Zizhixian see Datong
159 S9 Datong Shan ▲▲ C China
169 O10 Datu, Tanjung headland Indonesia/Malaysia 02°01′N 109°37′E
Datu, Teluk see Lahad Datu, Teluk
Daua see Dawa Wenz
172 H16 Dauban, Mount ▲ Silhouette, NE Seychelles
149 T7 Dāūd Khel Punjab, E Pakistan 32°52′N 71°35′E
119 G15 Daugai Alytus, S Lithuania 54°22′N 24°20′E
Daugava see Western Dvina
118 J11 Daugavpils Ger. Dünaburg; prev. Rus. Dvinsk. SE Latvia 55°53′N 26°34′E
Dauka see Dawkah
Daulatabad see Malāyer
101 D18 Daun Rheinland-Pfalz, W Germany 50°13′N 06°50′E
155 E14 Daund prev. Dhond. Mahārāshtra, W India 18°28′N 74°38′E
166 M12 Daung Kyun island S Burma (Myanmar)
11 W15 Dauphin Manitoba, S Canada 51°09′N 100°05′W
103 S13 Dauphiné cultural region E France
23 N9 Dauphin Island island Alabama, S USA
11 X15 Dauphin River Manitoba, S Canada 51°55′N 98°03′W
77 V12 Daura Katsina, N Nigeria 13°03′N 08°18′E
152 H12 Dausa prev. Daosa. Rājasthān, N India 26°51′N 76°21′E
Dauwa see Dawwah
Dāvaçi see Şabran
155 F18 Dāvangere Karnātaka, W India 14°30′N 75°52′E
171 Q8 Davao off. Davao City. Mindanao, S Philippines 07°06′N 125°36′E
Davao City see Davao
171 Q8 Davao Gulf gulf Mindanao, S Philippines
15 Q11 Daveluyville Québec, SE Canada 46°12′N 72°07′W
29 Z14 Davenport Iowa, C USA 41°31′N 90°35′W
32 L8 Davenport Washington, NW USA 47°39′N 118°09′W
43 P16 David Chiriquí, W Panama 08°26′N 82°26′W
15 O11 David ≈ Québec, SE Canada
29 R15 David City Nebraska, C USA 41°15′N 97°07′W
David-Gorodok see Davyd-Haradok
11 T16 Davidson Saskatchewan, S Canada 51°15′N 105°59′W
21 R10 Davidson North Carolina, SE USA 35°29′N 80°49′W
26 K12 Davidson Oklahoma, C USA 34°15′N 99°06′W
39 S6 Davidson Mountains ▲▲ Alaska, USA
172 M8 Davie Ridge undersea feature W Indian Ocean 17°10′S 41°45′E
182 A1 Davies, Mount ▲ South Australia 26°14′S 129°14′E
35 O7 Davis California, W USA 38°31′N 121°46′W
27 N12 Davis Oklahoma, C USA 34°30′N 97°07′W
195 Y7 Davis Australian research station Antarctica 68°30′S 78°15′E
194 H3 Davis Coast physical region Antarctica
18 C16 Davis, Mount ▲ Pennsylvania, NE USA 39°47′N 79°10′W
24 K9 Davis Mountains ▲▲ Texas, SW USA
195 Z9 Davis Sea sea Antarctica
65 O20 Davis Seamounts undersea feature S Atlantic Ocean
196 M13 Davis Strait strait Baffin Bay/ Labrador Sea
127 U5 Davlekanovo Respublika Bashkortostan, W Russian Federation 54°13′N 55°06′E
108 J9 Davos Rmsch. Tavau. Graubünden, E Switzerland 46°48′N 09°50′E
Davvesiida see Lebesby
119 J20 Davyd-Haradok Pol. Dawidgródek, Rus. David-Gorodok. Brestskaya Voblasts', SW Belarus 52°03′N 27°13′E
163 U12 Dawa Liaoning, NE China 40°55′N 122°02′E
141 O11 Dawāsir, Wādī ad dry watercourse S Saudi Arabia
81 K15 Dawa Wenz var. Daua, Webi Daawo. ≈ E Africa
Dawaymah, Birkat ad see Umm al Baqar, Hawr
167 N10 Dawei var. Tavoy, Htawei. Tanintharyi, S Burma (Myanmar) 14°02′N 98°12′E
119 K14 Dawhinava Rus. Dolginovo. Minskaya Voblasts', N Belarus 54°39′N 27°29′E
Dawidgródek see Davyd-Haradok
141 V12 Dawkah var. Dauka. SW Oman 18°32′N 54°03′E
Dawlat Qaṭar see Qatar
24 M3 Dawn Texas, SW USA 34°54′N 102°10′W
Dawo see Maqên
140 M11 Daws Al Bāḩah, SW Saudi Arabia 20°19′N 41°12′E
10 H5 Dawson var. Dawson City. Yukon Territory, NW Canada 64°04′N 139°24′W
23 S6 Dawson Georgia, SE USA 31°46′N 84°27′W
29 S9 Dawson Minnesota, N USA 44°55′N 96°03′W
Dawson City see Dawson
11 N13 Dawson Creek British Columbia, W Canada 55°45′N 120°07′W
10 H7 Dawson Range ▲▲ Yukon Territory, W Canada
181 Y9 Dawson River ≈ Queensland, E Australia
10 J15 Dawsons Landing British Columbia, SW Canada 51°33′N 127°38′W
20 I7 Dawson Springs Kentucky, S USA 37°10′N 87°41′W
23 S2 Dawsonville Georgia, SE USA 34°28′N 84°07′W
160 G8 Dawu var. Xianshui. Sichuan, C China 30°55′N 101°08′E
Dawu see Maqên
Dawukou see Huinong
141 Y10 Dawwah var. Dauwa. W Oman 20°36′N 58°52′E
102 J15 Dax var. Ax; anc. Aquae Augustae, Aquae Tarbelicae. Landes, SW France 43°43′N 01°03′W
Daxian see Dazhou
Daxiangshan see Gangu
Daxue see Wencheng
160 G9 Daxue Shan ▲▲ C China
Dayan see Lijiang
160 G12 Dayao var. Jinbi. Yunnan, SW China 25°41′N 101°23′E
Dayishan see Gaoyou
Dāykundī see Dāykundī
149 O6 Dāykundī prev. Dāykondī. ◈ province C Afghanistan
183 N12 Daylesford Victoria, SE Australia 37°24′S 144°07′E
35 U10 Daylight Pass pass California, W USA
61 D17 Daymán, Río ≈ N Uruguay
Dayong see Zhangjiajie
Dayr see Ad Dayr
138 G10 Dayr 'Allā var. Deir 'Alla. Al Balqā', N Jordan 32°39′N 36°06′E
139 N4 Dayr az Zawr var. Deir ez Zor. Dayr az Zawr, E Syria 35°12′N 40°12′E
138 M5 Dayr az Zawr off. Muḩāfaẓat Dayr az Zawr, var. Dayr Az-Zor. ◈ governorate E Syria
Dayr az Zawr, Muḩāfaẓat see Dayr az Zawr
Dayr Az-Zor see Dayr az Zawr
75 W9 Dayrūţ var. Dairûṭ. C Egypt 27°34′N 30°48′E
11 Q15 Daysland Alberta, SW Canada 52°53′N 112°19′W
31 R14 Dayton Ohio, N USA 39°46′N 84°12′W
20 L10 Dayton Tennessee, S USA 35°30′N 85°01′W
25 W11 Dayton Texas, SW USA 30°03′N 94°53′W
32 L10 Dayton Washington, NW USA 46°19′N 117°58′W
23 X10 Daytona Beach Florida, SE USA 29°12′N 81°03′W
169 U12 Dayu Borneo, C Indonesia 01°59′S 115°04′E
161 O13 Dayu Ling ▲▲ S China
161 R7 Da Yunhe Eng. Grand Canal. canal E China
161 S11 Dayu Shan island SE China
Dayyer see Bandar-e Dayyer
160 K8 Dazhou prev. Dachuan, Daxian. Sichuan, C China 31°16′N 107°31′E
160 J9 Dazhu var. Zhuyang. Sichuan, C China 30°45′N 107°11′E
161 T13 Dazhuoshui prev. Tachoshui. N Taiwan 24°26′N 121°43′E
160 J9 Dazu var. Longgang. Chongqing Shi, C China 29°47′N 106°30′E
83 H24 De Aar Northern Cape, C South Africa 30°40′S 24°01′E
194 K5 Deacon, Cape headland Antarctica
39 R5 Deadhorse Alaska, USA 70°15′N 148°28′W
33 T12 Dead Indian Peak ▲ Wyoming, C USA 44°36′N 109°45′W
23 R9 Dead Lake ◎ Florida, SE USA
44 J4 Deadman's Cay Long Island, C Bahamas 23°09′N 75°06′W
138 G11 Dead Sea var. Bahret Lut, Lacus Asphaltites, Ar. Al Baḩr al Mayyit, Baḩrat Lūt, Heb. Yam HaMelaḩ. salt lake Israel/ Jordan
28 J9 Deadwood South Dakota, N USA 44°22′N 103°43′W
97 Q22 Deal SE England, United Kingdom 51°14′N 01°23′E
83 I22 Dealesville Free State, C South Africa 28°40′S 25°46′E
161 P10 De'an var. Puting. Jiangxi, S China 29°24′N 115°46′E
62 K9 Deán Funes Córdoba, C Argentina 30°25′S 64°22′W
194 L12 Dean Island island Antarctica
Deanuvuotna see Tanafjorden
31 S10 Dearborn Michigan, N USA 42°16′N 83°13′W
27 R3 Dearborn Missouri, C USA 39°31′N 94°46′W
Deargget see Tārendö
32 K9 Deary Idaho, NW USA 46°46′N 116°33′W
32 M9 Deary Washington, NW USA 46°42′N 116°36′W
10 J10 Dease ≈ British Columbia, W Canada
10 J10 Dease Lake British Columbia, W Canada 58°28′N 130°04′W
35 U11 Death Valley California, W USA 36°25′N 116°50′W
35 U11 Death Valley valley California, W USA
92 M8 Deatnu Fin. Tenojoki, Nor. Tana. ≈ Finland/Norway see also Tana, Tenojoki
Deatnu see Tana
102 L4 Deauville Calvados, N France 49°21′N 00°06′E
117 X7 Debal'tseve Rus. Debal'tsevo. Donets'ka Oblast', SE Ukraine 48°21′N 38°26′E
Debal'tsevo see Debal'tseve
113 M19 Debar Ger. Dibra, Turk. Debre. W FYR Macedonia 41°32′N 20°33′E
39 O9 Debauch Mountain ▲ Alaska, USA 64°31′N 159°52′W
De Behagle see Laï
25 X7 De Berry Texas, SW USA 32°18′N 94°09′W
Debessy see Debesy
127 T2 Debesy prev. Debessy. Udmurtskaya Respublika, NW Russian Federation 57°41′N 53°56′E
111 N16 Dębica Podkarpackie, SE Poland 50°04′N 21°24′E
De Bildt see De Bilt
98 J11 De Bilt var. De Bildt. Utrecht, C Netherlands 52°06′N 05°11′E
123 T9 Debin Magadanskaya Oblast', E Russian Federation 62°18′N 150°42′E
110 N13 Dęblin Rus. Ivangorod. Lubelskie, E Poland 51°34′N 21°50′E
110 D10 Dębno Zachodnio-pomorskie, NW Poland 52°43′N 14°42′E
39 S10 Deborah, Mount ▲ Alaska, USA 63°38′N 147°13′W
33 N8 De Borgia Montana, NW USA 47°23′N 115°24′W
Debra Birhan see Debre Birhan
Debra Marcos see Debre Mark'os
Debra Tabor see Debre Tabor
Debre see Debar
80 J13 Debre Birhan var. Debra Birhan. Āmara, N Ethiopia 09°45′N 39°40′E
111 N22 Debrecen Ger. Debreczin, Rom. Debrețin; prev. Debreczen. Hajdú-Bihar, E Hungary 47°32′N 21°38′E
Debreczen/Debreczin see Debrecen
80 I12 Debre Mark'os var. Debra Marcos. Āmara, N Ethiopia 10°18′N 37°48′E
113 N19 Debrešte SW FYR Macedonia 41°29′N 21°20′E
80 J11 Debre Tabor var. Debra Tabor. Āmara, N Ethiopia 11°46′N 38°06′E
Debrețin see Debrecen
80 J13 Debre Zeyt Oromīya, C Ethiopia 08°41′N 39°00′E
113 L16 Deçan Serb. Dečane; prev. Dečani. W Kosovo 42°33′N 20°18′E
Dečane see Deçan
Dečani see Deçan
23 P2 Decatur Alabama, S USA 34°36′N 86°58′W
23 S3 Decatur Georgia, SE USA 33°46′N 84°18′W
30 L13 Decatur Illinois, N USA 39°50′N 88°57′W
31 Q12 Decatur Indiana, N USA 40°40′N 84°57′W
22 M5 Decatur Mississippi, S USA 32°26′N 89°06′W
29 S14 Decatur Nebraska, C USA 42°00′N 96°19′W
25 S6 Decatur Texas, SW USA 33°14′N 97°35′W
20 H9 Decaturville Tennessee, S USA 35°35′N 88°08′W
103 O13 Decazeville Aveyron, S France 44°34′N 02°18′E
155 H17 Deccan Hind. Dakshin. plateau C India
14 J8 Decelles, Réservoir ▣ Québec, SE Canada
12 K2 Déception Québec, NE Canada 62°06′N 74°36′W
160 G11 Dechang var. Dezhou. Sichuan, C China 27°24′N 102°09′E
111 C15 Děčín Ger. Tetschen. Ústecký Kraj, NW Czech Republic 50°48′N 14°15′E
103 P9 Decize Nièvre, C France 46°51′N 03°25′E
98 I6 De Cocksdorp Noord-Holland, NW Netherlands 53°09′N 04°52′E
29 X11 Decorah Iowa, C USA 43°18′N 91°47′W
Dedeagaç/Dedeagach see Alexandroúpoli
188 C15 Dededo N Guam 13°30′N 144°51′E
98 N9 Dedemsvaart Overijssel, E Netherlands 52°36′N 06°28′E
19 O11 Dedham Massachusetts, NE USA 42°14′N 71°10′W
63 H19 Dedo, Cerro ▲ SW Argentina 44°46′S 71°48′W
77 O13 Dédougou W Burkina 12°29′N 03°25′W
124 G15 Dedovichi Pskovskaya Oblast', W Russian Federation 57°31′N 29°53′E
Dedu see Wudalianchi
155 J24 Deduru Oya ≈ W Sri Lanka
83 N14 Dedza Central, S Malawi 14°20′S 34°24′E
83 N14 Dedza Mountain ▲ C Malawi 14°22′S 34°16′E
96 K9 Dee ≈ NE Scotland, United Kingdom
97 J19 Dee Wel. Afon Dyfrdwy. ≈ England/Wales, United Kingdom
Deep Bay see Chilumba
21 T3 Deep Creek Lake ▣ Maryland, NE USA
36 J4 Deep Creek Range ▲▲ Utah, W USA
27 P10 Deep Fork River ≈ Oklahoma, C USA
14 J11 Deep River Ontario, SE Canada 46°04′N 77°29′W
21 T10 Deep River ≈ North Carolina, SE USA
183 U4 Deepwater New South Wales, SE Australia 29°27′S 151°52′E
31 S14 Deer Creek Lake ◎ Ohio, N USA
23 Z15 Deerfield Beach Florida, SE USA 26°19′N 80°06′W
39 N8 Deering Alaska, USA 66°04′N 162°43′W
38 M16 Deer Island island Alaska, USA
19 S7 Deer Isle island Maine, NE USA
13 S11 Deer Lake Newfoundland and Labrador, SE Canada 49°11′N 57°27′N
99 D18 Deerlijk West-Vlaanderen, W Belgium 50°52′N 03°21′E
33 Q10 Deer Lodge Montana, NW USA 46°24′N 112°43′W
32 L8 Deer Park Washington, NW USA 47°55′N 117°28′W
29 U5 Deer River Minnesota, N USA 47°19′N 93°47′W
Deés see Dej
Defeng see Liping
31 R11 Defiance Ohio, N USA 41°17′N 84°21′W
23 Q8 De Funiak Springs Florida, SE USA 30°43′N 86°07′W
95 L23 Degeberga Skåne, S Sweden 55°48′N 14°06′E
104 H12 Degebe, Ribeira ≈ S Portugal
80 M13 Degeh Bur Sumalē, E Ethiopia 08°08′N 43°35′E
15 U9 Dégelis Québec, SE Canada 47°30′N 68°38′W
77 U17 Degema Rivers, S Nigeria 04°46′N 06°47′E
95 L16 Degerfors Örebro, C Sweden 59°14′N 14°26′E
193 R14 De Gerlache Seamounts undersea feature SE Pacific Ocean
101 N21 Deggendorf Bayern, SE Germany 48°50′N 12°58′E
80 I11 Degoma Āmara, N Ethiopia 12°22′N 37°36′E
De Gordyk see Gorredijk
27 T12 De Gray Lake ▣ Arkansas, C USA
180 J6 De Grey River ≈ Western Australia
126 M10 Degtevo Rostovskaya Oblast', SW Russian Federation 49°12′N 40°39′E
Dehbārez see Rūdān
Deh Bid see Şafāshahr
142 M10 Deh Dasht Kohkīlūyeh va Būyer AḨmad, SW Iran 30°49′N 50°36′E
75 N8 Dehibat SE Tunisia 31°58′N 10°43′E
Dehli see Delhi
142 K8 Dehlorān Īlām, W Iran 32°41′N 47°18′E
147 N13 Dehqonobod Rus. Dekhkanabad. Qashqadaryo Viloyati, S Uzbekistan 38°24′N 66°31′E
152 J9 Dehra Dūn Uttaranchal, N India 30°19′N 78°04′E
153 O14 Dehri Bihār, N India 24°55′N 84°11′E
Deh Shū see Dishū
163 W9 Dehui Jilin, NE China 44°23′N 125°42′E
99 D17 Deinze Oost-Vlaanderen, NW Belgium 50°59′N 03°32′E
Deir 'Alla see Dayr 'Allā
Deir ez Zor see Dayr az Zawr
Deirgeirt, Loch see Derg, Lough
116 H9 Dej Hung. Dés; prev. Deés. Cluj, NW Romania 47°08′N 23°55′E
95 K15 Deje Värmland, C Sweden 59°35′N 13°29′E
171 Y15 De Jongs, Tanjung headland Papua, SE Indonesia 06°56′S 138°32′E
De Jouwer see Joure
30 M10 De Kalb Illinois, N USA 41°55′N 88°45′W
22 M5 De Kalb Mississippi, S USA 32°46′N 88°39′W
25 W5 De Kalb Texas, SW USA 33°30′N 94°34′W
83 G18 Dekar var. D'Kar. Ghanzi, NW Botswana 21°31′S 21°55′E
Dekéleia see Dhekélia
79 K20 Dekese Kasai-Occidental, C Dem. Rep. Congo 03°28′S 21°24′E
Dekhkanabad see Dehqonobod
79 I14 Dékoa Kémo, C Central African Republic 06°17′N 19°07′E
98 H6 De Koog Noord-Holland, NW Netherlands 53°06′N 04°43′E
30 M9 Delafield Wisconsin, N USA 43°03′N 88°22′W
61 C23 De La Garma Buenos Aires, E Argentina 37°58′S 60°25′W
14 K10 Delahey, Lac ◎ Québec, SE Canada
80 E11 Delami Southern Kordofan, C Sudan 11°51′N 30°30′E
23 X11 De Land Florida, SE USA 29°01′N 81°18′W
35 R12 Delano California, W USA 35°46′N 119°15′W
29 V8 Delano Minnesota, N USA 45°03′N 93°46′W
36 K6 Delano Peak ▲ Utah, W USA 38°22′N 112°21′W
Delap-Uliga-Darrit see Dalap-Uliga-Djarrit
Delārām see Dilārām
38 F17 Delarof Islands island group Aleutian Islands, Alaska, USA
30 M9 Delavan Wisconsin, N USA 42°37′N 88°37′W
31 S13 Delaware Ohio, N USA 40°18′N 83°06′W
18 I17 Delaware off. State of Delaware, also known as Blue Hen State, Diamond State, First State. ◈ state NE USA
18 I17 Delaware Bay bay NE USA
24 J8 Delaware Mountains ▲▲ Texas, SW USA
18 I12 Delaware River ≈ NE USA
27 Q3 Delaware River ≈ Kansas, C USA
18 J14 Delaware Water Gap valley New Jersey/Pennsylvania, NE USA
101 G14 Delbrück Nordrhein-Westfalen, W Germany 51°46′N 08°34′E
11 Q15 Delburne Alberta, SW Canada 52°09′N 113°11′W
172 M12 Del Cano Rise undersea feature SW Indian Ocean 45°15′S 44°15′E
113 Q18 Delčevo NE FYR Macedonia 41°57′N 22°45′E
Delcommune, Lac see Nzilo, Lac
98 O10 Delden Overijssel, E Netherlands 52°16′N 06°41′E
183 R12 Delegate New South Wales, SE Australia 37°04′S 148°57′E
De Lemmer see Lemmer
108 D7 Delémont Ger. Delsberg. Jura, NW Switzerland 47°22′N 07°21′E
25 R7 De Leon Texas, SW USA 32°06′N 98°33′W
115 F18 Delfoí Stereá Elláda, C Greece 38°28′N 22°31′E
98 G12 Delft Zuid-Holland, W Netherlands 52°01′N 04°22′E
155 J23 Delft island NW Sri Lanka
98 O5 Delfzijl Groningen, NE Netherlands 53°20′N 06°55′E
0 E9 Delgada Fan undersea feature NE Pacific Ocean 39°15′N 126°00′W
42 F7 Delgado San Salvador, SW El Salvador 13°44′N 89°07′W
82 Q12 Delgado, Cabo headland N Mozambique 10°41′S 40°40′E
162 G8 Delger var. Taygan. Govi-Altay, C Mongolia 46°20′N 97°22′E
163 O9 Delgereh var. Hongor. Dornogovĭ, SE Mongolia 45°49′N 111°20′E
162 J8 Delgerhaan var. Hujirt. Töv, C Mongolia 46°41′N 104°40′E
162 K9 Delgerhangay var. Hashaat. Dundgovĭ, C Mongolia 45°09′N 104°51′E
162 L9 Delgertsogt var. Amardalay. Dundgovĭ, C Mongolia 46°09′N 106°24′E
80 E6 Delgo Northern, N Sudan 20°08′N 30°35′E
159 R10 Delhi var. Delingha. Qinghai, C China 37°19′N 97°22′E
152 I10 Delhi var. Dehli, Hind. Dilli, hist. Shahjahanabad. union territory capital Delhi, N India 28°40′N 77°11′E
22 J5 Delhi Louisiana, S USA 32°28′N 91°29′W
18 J11 Delhi New York, NE USA 42°16′N 74°55′W
152 I10 Delhi ◈ union territory NW India
136 J17 Deli Burnu headland S Turkey 36°43′N 34°55′E
136 J12 Delice Çayı ≈ C Turkey
55 X10 Délices C French Guiana 04°45′N 53°45′W
40 J6 Delicias var. Ciudad Delicias. Chihuahua, N Mexico 28°09′N 105°22′W
143 N7 Delījān var. Dalijan, Dilijan. Markazī, W Iran 34°02′N 50°39′E
112 P12 Deli Jovan ▲▲ E Serbia
Déli-Kárpátok see Carpaţii Meridionalii
8 I8 Déljne prev. Fort Franklin. Northwest Territories, NW Canada 65°10′N 123°30′W
Delingha see Delhi
15 Q7 Delisle Québec, SE Canada 48°39′N 71°42′W
11 T15 Delisle Saskatchewan, S Canada 51°54′N 107°01′W
101 M15 Delitzsch Sachsen, E Germany 51°31′N 12°19′E
33 Q12 Dell Montana, NW USA 44°41′N 112°42′W
24 I7 Dell City Texas, SW USA 31°56′N 105°12′W
103 U7 Delle Territoire-de-Belfort, E France 47°30′N 07°00′E
36 J9 Dellenbaugh, Mount ▲ Arizona, SW USA 36°06′N 113°32′W
29 R11 Dell Rapids South Dakota, N USA 43°50′N 96°42′W
21 Y4 Delmar Maryland, NE USA 38°26′N 75°32′W
18 K11 Delmar New York, NE USA 42°37′N 73°49′W
100 G11 Delmenhorst Niedersachsen, NW Germany 53°03′N 08°38′E
112 C9 Delnice Primorje-Gorski Kotar, NW Croatia 45°24′N 14°49′E
37 R7 Del Norte Colorado, C USA 37°40′N 106°21′W
39 N6 De Long Mountains ▲▲ Alaska, USA
183 P16 Deloraine Tasmania, SE Australia 41°34′S 146°43′E
11 W17 Deloraine Manitoba, S Canada 49°12′N 100°28′W
31 O12 Delphi Indiana, N USA 40°35′N 86°40′W
31 Q12 Delphos Ohio, N USA 40°49′N 84°20′W
23 Z15 Delray Beach Florida, SE USA 26°27′N 80°04′W
25 O12 Del Rio Texas, SW USA 29°23′N 100°56′W
Delsberg see Delémont
94 N11 Delsbo Gävleborg, C Sweden 61°49′N 16°34′E
37 P6 Delta Colorado, C USA 38°44′N 108°04′W
36 K5 Delta Utah, W USA 39°21′N 112°34′W
77 T17 Delta ◈ state S Nigeria
55 Q6 Delta Amacuro off. Territorio Delta Amacuro. ◈ federal district NE Venezuela
Delta Amacuro, Territorio see Delta Amacuro
39 S9 Delta Junction Alaska, USA 64°02′N 145°43′W
23 X11 Deltona Florida, SE USA 28°54′N 81°15′W
183 T5 Delungra New South Wales, SE Australia 29°40′S 150°49′E
162 D6 Delüün var. Rashaant. Bayan-Ölgiy, W Mongolia 47°48′N 90°45′E
154 C12 Delvāda Gujarāt, W India 20°46′N 71°02′E
61 B21 Del Valle Buenos Aires, E Argentina 35°55′S 60°42′W
Delvina see Delvinë
115 C15 Delvinákí var. Dhelvinákion; prev. Pogónion. Ípeiros, W Greece 39°57′N 20°28′E
113 L23 Delvinë var. Delvina, It. Delvino. Vlorë, S Albania 39°56′N 20°07′E
Delvino see Delvinë
116 I7 Delyatyn Ivano-Frankivs'ka Oblast', W Ukraine 48°32′N 24°38′E
127 U5 Dëma ≈ W Russian Federation
105 O5 Demanda, Sierra de la ▲▲ W Spain
39 T5 Demarcation Point headland Alaska, USA 69°40′N 141°19′W
79 K21 Demba Kasai-Occidental, C Dem. Rep. Congo 05°24′S 22°16′E
172 H13 Dembéni Grande Comore, NW Comoros 11°50′S 43°25′E
79 M15 Dembia Mbomou, SE Central African Republic 05°08′N 24°25′E
Dembidollo see Dembī Dolo
80 H13 Dembī Dolo var. Dembidollo. Oromīya, C Ethiopia 08°33′N 34°49′E
152 K6 Demchok var. Dêmqog. China/India 32°30′N 79°42′E see also Dêmqog
152 L6 Demchok var. Dêmqog. disputed region China/India see also Dêmqog
98 I12 De Meern Utrecht, C Netherlands 52°06′N 05°00′E
99 I17 Demer ≈ C Belgium
64 H12 Demerara Plain undersea feature W Atlantic Ocean 10°00′N 48°00′W
64 H12 Demerara Plateau undersea feature W Atlantic Ocean
55 T9 Demerara River ≈ NE Guyana
126 H3 Demidov Smolenskaya Oblast', W Russian Federation 55°15′N 31°30′E
37 Q15 Deming New Mexico, SW USA 32°17′N 107°46′W
32 H6 Deming Washington, NW USA 48°49′N 122°13′W
58 E10 Demini, Rio ≈ NW Brazil
136 D13 Demirci Manisa, W Turkey 39°03′N 28°40′E
113 P19 Demir Kapija prev. Železna Vrata. SE FYR Macedonia 41°25′N 22°15′E
114 N11 Demirköy Kırklareli, NW Turkey 41°48′N 27°49′E
100 N9 Demmin Mecklenburg-Vorpommern, NE Germany 53°53′N 13°03′E
23 O5 Demopolis Alabama, S USA 32°31′N 87°50′W
31 N11 Demotte Indiana, N USA 41°13′N 87°07′W
158 F13 Dêmqog var. Demchok. China/India 32°36′N 79°29′E see also Demchok
152 L6 Dêmqog var. Demchok. disputed region China/India see also Demchok
171 Y13 Demta Papua, E Indonesia 02°19′S 140°06′E
121 K11 Dem'yanka ≈ C Russian Federation
124 H15 Demyansk Novgorodskaya Oblast', W Russian Federation 57°39′N 32°31′E
122 H10 Dem'yanskoye Tyumenskaya Oblast', C Russian Federation 59°39′N 69°15′E
103 P2 Denain Nord, N France 50°19′N 03°24′E
39 S10 Denali Alaska, USA 63°08′N 147°33′W
Denali see McKinley, Mount
81 M14 Denan Sumalē, E Ethiopia 06°40′N 43°31′E
Denau see Denov
97 J18 Denbigh Wel. Dinbych. NE Wales, United Kingdom 53°11′N 03°25′W
97 J18 Denbigh cultural region N Wales, United Kingdom
98 I6 Den Burg Noord-Holland, NW Netherlands 53°03′N 04°47′E
99 F18 Dender Fr. Dendre. ≈ W Belgium
99 F18 Denderleeuw Oost-Vlaanderen, NW Belgium 50°53′N 04°05′E
99 F17 Dendermonde Fr. Termonde. Oost-Vlaanderen, NW Belgium 51°02′N 04°08′E
Dendre see Dender
194 I9 Dendtler Island island Antarctica
98 P10 Denekamp Overijssel, E Netherlands 52°23′N 07°E
77 W12 Dengas Zinder, S Niger 13°15′N 09°43′E
Dêngka see Têwo
Dêngkagoin see Têwo
162 L13 Dengkou var. Bayan Gol. Nei Mongol Zizhiqu, N China 40°15′N 106°59′E
159 Q14 Dêngqên var. Gyamotang. Xizang Zizhiqu, W China 31°28′N 95°28′E
Deng Xian see Dengzhou
160 M7 Dengzhou prev. Deng Xian. Henan, C China 32°48′N 111°59′E
Dengzhou see Penglai
Den Haag see 's-Gravenhage
180 H10 Denham Western Australia 25°56′S 113°35′E
98 N9 Den Ham Overijssel, E Netherlands 52°30′N 06°31′E
44 J12 Denham, Mount ▲ C Jamaica 18°13′N 77°33′W
22 J8 Denham Springs Louisiana, S USA 30°29′N 90°57′W
98 I7 Den Helder Noord-Holland, NW Netherlands 52°54′N 04°45′E
105 T11 Dénia Valenciana, E Spain 38°51′N 00°07′E
189 Q8 Denig W Nauru
183 N10 Deniliquin New South Wales, SE Australia 35°33′S 144°58′E
29 T14 Denison Iowa, C USA 42°00′N 95°22′W
25 U5 Denison Texas, SW USA 33°45′N 96°32′W
144 L8 Denisovka prev. Ordzhonikidze. Kostanay, N Kazakhstan 52°27′N 61°42′E
136 D15 Denizli Denizli, SW Turkey 37°46′N 29°05′E
136 D15 Denizli ◈ province SW Turkey
Denjong see Sikkim
183 S7 Denman New South Wales, SE Australia 32°24′S 150°43′E
195 Y10 Denman Glacier glacier Antarctica
21 R14 Denmark South Carolina, SE USA 33°19′N 81°08′W
95 G23 Denmark off. Kingdom of Denmark, Dan. Danmark; anc. Hafnia. ◆ monarchy N Europe
Denmark, Kingdom of see Denmark
92 H1 Denmark Strait var. Danmarksstraedet. strait Greenland/Iceland
45 T11 Dennery E Saint Lucia 13°55′N 60°53′W
98 I7 Den Oever Noord-Holland, NW Netherlands 52°56′N 05°01′E
147 O13 Denov Rus. Denau. Surkhondaryo Viloyati, S Uzbekistan 38°20′N 67°48′E
169 U17 Denpasar prev. Paloe. Bali, C Indonesia 08°40′S 115°14′E
116 E12 Denta Timiş, W Romania 45°20′N 21°15′E
21 Y3 Denton Maryland, NE USA 38°53′N 75°50′W
25 T6 Denton Texas, SW USA 33°11′N 97°08′W
186 G9 D'Entrecasteaux Islands island group SE Papua New Guinea
37 T4 Denver state capital Colorado, C USA 39°45′N 105°W
37 T4 Denver ✈ Colorado, C USA 39°57′N 104°38′W
24 L6 Denver City Texas, SW USA 32°57′N 102°49′W
152 J9 Deoband Uttar Pradesh, N India 29°41′N 77°40′E
Deoghar see Devghar
163 X15 Deokjeok-gundo prev. Tŏkchŏk-kundo. island group NW South Korea
154 E13 Deolāli Mahārāshtra, W India 19°55′N 73°49′E
154 I10 Deori Madhya Pradesh, C India 23°09′N 78°39′E
153 O12 Deoria Uttar Pradesh, N India 26°31′N 83°48′E
99 A17 De Panne West-Vlaanderen, W Belgium 51°06′N 02°35′E
Departamento del Quindío see Quindío
Departamento de Narino, see Nariño
54 M5 Dependencia Federal off. Territorio Dependencia Federal. ◈ federal dependency N Venezuela
Dependencia Federal, Territorio see Dependencia Federal
30 M7 De Pere Wisconsin, N USA 44°26′N 88°03′W
18 D10 Depew New York, NE USA 42°54′N 78°41′W
99 E17 De Pinte Oost-Vlaanderen, NW Belgium 51°00′N 03°37′E
25 V5 Deport Texas, SW USA 33°31′N 95°19′W
123 Q8 Deputatskiy Respublika Sakha (Yakutiya), NE Russian Federation 69°18′N 139°48′E
Dêqên see Dagzê
27 S13 De Queen Arkansas, C USA 34°02′N 94°20′W
22 G8 De Quincy Louisiana, S USA 30°27′N 93°25′W
81 J20 Dera spring/well S Kenya 02°39′S 39°52′E
Der'a/Derá/Déraa see Dar'ā
149 S10 Dera Ghāzi Khān var. Dera Ghāzikhān. Punjab, C Pakistan 30°01′N 70°37′E
Dera Ghāzikhān see Dera Ghāzi Khān
149 S8 Dera Ismāīl Khān Khyber Pakhtunkhwa, C Pakistan 31°51′N 70°56′E
Đeravica see Gjeravicë
116 L6 Derazhnya Khmel'nyts'ka Oblast', W Ukraine 49°16′N 27°24′E
127 R17 Derbent Respublika Dagestan, SW Russian Federation 42°01′N 48°16′E
147 N13 Derbent Surkhondaryo Viloyati, S Uzbekistan 38°15′N 66°59′E
Derbisīye see Darbāsīyah
79 M15 Derbissaka Mbomou, SE Central African Republic 05°43′N 24°48′E
180 L4 Derby Western Australia 17°18′S 123°37′E
97 M19 Derby C England, United Kingdom 52°55′N 01°30′W
27 N7 Derby Kansas, C USA 37°33′N 97°16′W
97 L18 Derbyshire cultural region C England, United Kingdom
112 O11 Derdap physical region E Serbia
Derelí see Gónnoi
162 L9 Deren var. Tsant. Dundgovĭ, C Mongolia 46°16′N 106°55′E
171 W13 Derew ≈ Papua, E Indonesia
127 R8 Dergachi Saratovskaya Oblast', W Russian Federation 51°15′N 48°58′E
Dergachi see Derhachi
97 C19 Derg, Lough Ir. Loch Deirgeirt. ◎ W Ireland
117 V5 Derhachi Rus. Dergachi. Kharkivs'ka Oblast', E Ukraine 50°09′N 36°11′E
22 G8 De Ridder Louisiana, S USA 30°51′N 93°18′W
137 P16 Derik Mardin, SE Turkey 37°22′N 40°16′E
83 E20 Derm Hardap, C Namibia 23°38′S 18°12′E
Dermentobe see Diirmentobe
27 W14 Dermott Arkansas, C USA 33°31′N 91°26′W
Dérna see Darnah
Dernberg, Cape see Dolphin Head
22 J11 Dernieres, Isles island group Louisiana, S USA
102 I4 Déroute, Passage de la strait Channel Islands/France
Derrá see Dar'ā
81 O16 Derri prev. Dirri. Galguduud, C Somalia 04°15′N 46°31′E
Derry see Londonderry
Dertona see Tortona
Dertosa see Tortosa
80 H8 Derudeb Red Sea, NE Sudan 17°31′N 36°07′E
112 H10 Derventa Republika Srpska, N Bosnia and Herzegovina 44°57′N 17°55′E
183 O16 Derwent Bridge Tasmania, SE Australia 42°10′S 146°13′E
183 O17 Derwent, River ≈ Tasmania, SE Australia
146 F10 Derweze Rus. Darvaza. Ahal Welaýaty, C Turkmenistan 40°10′N 58°27′E
Deržavinsk see Derzhavinsk
145 O9 Derzhavinsk var. Deržavinsk. ◈ Akmola, C Kazakhstan
Dés see Dej
57 J18 Desaguadero Puno, S Peru 16°35′S 69°05′W
57 J18 Desaguadero, Río ≈ Bolivia/Peru
191 W9 Désappointement, Îles du island group Îles Tuamotu, C French Polynesia
27 W11 Des Arc Arkansas, C USA 34°58′N 91°30′W
14 C10 Desbarats Ontario, S Canada 46°20′N 83°52′W
62 H13 Descabezado Grande, Volcán ⛰ C Chile 35°34′S 70°40′W
102 L9 Descartes Indre-et-Loire, C France 46°58′N 00°40′E
11 T13 Deschambault Lake ◎ Saskatchewan, C Canada
Deschnaer Koppe see Velká Deštná
32 I11 Deschutes River ≈ Oregon, NW USA
80 J12 Desē var. Desse, It. Dessie. Āmara, N Ethiopia 11°02′N 39°39′E
63 I20 Deseado, Río ≈ S Argentina
106 F8 Desenzano del Garda Lombardia, N Italy 45°28′N 10°31′E
36 K3 Deseret Peak ▲ Utah, W USA 40°27′N 112°37′W
64 P6 Deserta Grande island Madeira, Portugal, NE Atlantic Ocean
64 P6 Desertas, Ilhas island group Madeira, Portugal, NE Atlantic Ocean
35 X16 Desert Center California, W USA 33°42′N 115°22′W
35 V15 Desert Hot Springs California, W USA 33°57′N 116°33′W
14 K10 Désert, Lac ◎ Québec, SE Canada
36 J2 Desert Peak ▲ Utah, W USA 41°03′N 113°22′W
31 R11 Deshler Ohio, N USA 41°12′N 83°55′W
Deshu see Deh Shū
Desiderii Fanum see St-Dizier
106 D7 Desio Lombardia, N Italy 45°37′N 09°12′E

◆ Country ● Country Capital ◇ Dependent Territory ○ Dependent Territory Capital ◈ Administrative Regions ✈ International Airport ▲ Mountain ▲▲ Mountain Range ⛰ Volcano ≈ River ◎ Lake ▣ Reservoir

115 E15 **Deskáti** *var.* Dheskáti. Dytikí Makedonía, N Greece *39°55′N 21°49′E*
28 L2 **Des Lacs River** ≈ North Dakota, N USA
27 X6 **Desloge** Missouri, C USA *37°52′N 90°31′W*
11 Q12 **Desmarais** Alberta, W Canada *55°58′N 113°56′W*
29 Q10 **De Smet** South Dakota, N USA *44°23′N 97°33′W*
29 V14 **Des Moines** *state capital* Iowa, C USA *41°36′N 93°37′W*
17 N9 **Des Moines River** ≈ C USA
117 P4 **Desna** ≈ Russian Federation/Ukraine
116 G14 **Desnăţui** ≈ S Romania
63 F24 **Desolación, Isla** *island* S Chile
29 V14 **De Soto** Iowa, C USA *41°31′N 94°00′W*
23 Q4 **De Soto Falls** *waterfall* Alabama, S USA
83 I25 **Despatch** Eastern Cape, S South Africa *33°48′S 25°28′E*
105 N12 **Despeñaperros, Desfiladero de** *pass* S Spain
31 N10 **Des Plaines** Illinois, N USA *42°01′N 87°52′W*
115 J21 **Despotikó** *island* Kykládes, Greece, Aegean Sea
112 N12 **Despotovac** Serbia, E Serbia *44°06′N 21°25′E*
101 M14 **Dessau** Sachsen-Anhalt, E Germany *51°51′N 12°15′E*
Desse *see* Desē
99 J16 **Dessel** Antwerpen, N Belgium *51°15′N 05°07′E*
Dessie *see* Desē
Destêrro *see* Florianópolis
23 P9 **Destin** Florida, SE USA *30°23′N 86°30′W*
Deštná *see* Velká Deštná
193 T10 **Desventurados, Islas de los** *island group* W Chile
103 N1 **Desvres** Pas-de-Calais, N France *50°41′N 01°48′E*
116 E12 **Deta** *Ger.* Detta. Timiş, W Romania *45°24′N 21°14′E*
101 H14 **Detmold** Nordrhein-Westfalen, W Germany *51°55′N 08°52′E*
31 S10 **Detroit** Michigan, N USA *42°20′N 83°03′W*
25 W5 **Detroit** Texas, SW USA *33°39′N 95°16′W*
31 S10 **Detroit** ≈ Canada/USA
29 S6 **Detroit Lakes** Minnesota, N USA *46°49′N 95°49′W*
31 S10 **Detroit Metropolitan** ✈ Michigan, N USA *42°12′N 83°16′W*
Detta *see* Deta
167 S10 **Det Udom** Ubon Ratchathani, E Thailand *14°54′N 105°03′E*
111 K20 **Detva** *Hung.* Gyeva. Bankobýstricky Kraj, C Slovakia *48°35′N 19°25′E*
154 G13 **Deūlgaon Rāja** Mahārāshtra, C India *20°04′N 76°08′E*
99 L15 **Deurne** Noord-Brabant, SE Netherlands *51°28′N 05°47′E*
99 H16 **Deurne** ✈ (Antwerpen) Antwerpen, N Belgium *51°10′N 04°28′E*
Deutsch-Brod *see* Havlíčkův Brod
Deutschendorf *see* Poprad
Deutsch-Eylau *see* Iława
109 Y6 **Deutschkreutz** Burgenland, E Austria *47°37′N 16°37′E*
Deutsch Krone *see* Wałcz
Deutschland/Deutschland, Bundesrepublik *see* Germany
109 V9 **Deutschlandsberg** Steiermark, SE Austria *46°52′N 15°13′E*
Deutsch-Südwestafrika *see* Namibia
109 Y3 **Deutsch-Wagram** Niederösterreich, E Austria *48°19′N 16°33′E*
Deux-Ponts *see* Zweibrücken
14 I11 **Deux Rivieres** Ontario, SE Canada *46°13′N 78°16′W*
102 K9 **Deux-Sèvres** ◈ *department* W France
116 G11 **Deva** *Ger.* Diemrich, *Hung.* Déva. Hunedoara, W Romania *45°55′N 22°55′E*
Déva *see* Deva
Deva *see* Chester
Devana *see* Aberdeen
Devana Castra *see* Chester
Devđelija *see* Gevgelija
136 L12 **Deveci Dağları** ▲▲ N Turkey
137 P15 **Devegeçidi Barajī** ▨ SE Turkey
136 K15 **Develi** Kayseri, C Turkey *38°22′N 35°28′E*
98 M11 **Deventer** Overijssel, E Netherlands *52°15′N 06°10′E*
15 O10 **Devenyns, Lac** ◎ Québec, SE Canada
96 K8 **Deveron** ≈ NE Scotland, United Kingdom
153 R14 **Devghar** *prev.* Deoghar. Jhārkhand, NE India
27 R10 **Devil's Den** *plateau* Arkansas, C USA
35 R7 **Devils Gate** *pass* California, W USA
30 J2 **Devils Island** *island* Apostle Islands, Wisconsin, N USA
Devil's Island *see* Diable, Île du
29 P3 **Devils Lake** North Dakota, N USA *48°08′N 98°50′W*
31 R10 **Devils Lake** ◎ Michigan, N USA
29 O3 **Devils Lake** ◎ North Dakota, N USA
35 W13 **Devils Playground** *desert* California, W USA
25 O11 **Devils River** ≈ Texas, SW USA
33 Y12 **Devils Tower** ▲ Wyoming, C USA *44°33′N 104°45′W*
114 I11 **Devin** *prev.* Dovlen. Smolyan, S Bulgaria *41°45′N 24°24′E*
25 R12 **Devine** Texas, SW USA *29°08′N 98°54′W*
152 H13 **Devli** Rājasthān, N India *25°47′N 75°23′E*
Devne *see* Devnya
114 N8 **Devnya** *prev.* Devne. Varna, E Bulgaria *43°15′N 27°35′E*
31 U14 **Devola** Ohio, N USA *39°28′N 81°28′W*
Devoll *see* Devollit, Lumi i
113 M21 **Devollit, Lumi i** *var.* Devoll. ≈ SE Albania
11 Q14 **Devon** Alberta, SW Canada *53°21′N 113°47′W*
97 I23 **Devon** *cultural region* SW England, United Kingdom
197 N10 **Devon Island** *prev.* North Devon Island. *island* Parry Islands, Nunavut, NE Canada
183 O16 **Devonport** Tasmania, SE Australia *41°14′S 146°21′E*
136 H11 **Devrek** Zonguldak, N Turkey *41°14′N 31°57′E*
154 G10 **Dewās** Madhya Pradesh, C India *22°59′N 76°03′E*
De Westerein *see* Zwaagwesteinde
27 P8 **Dewey** Oklahoma, C USA *36°48′N 95°56′W*
Dewey *see* Culebra
98 M8 **De Wijk** Drenthe, NE Netherlands *52°41′N 06°13′E*
27 W12 **De Witt** Arkansas, C USA *34°17′N 91°21′W*
29 Z14 **De Witt** Iowa, C USA *41°49′N 90°32′W*
29 R16 **De Witt** Nebraska, C USA *40°23′N 96°55′W*
97 M17 **Dewsbury** N England, United Kingdom *53°42′N 01°37′W*
161 Q10 **Dexing** Jiangxi, S China *28°51′N 117°36′E*
27 Y8 **Dexter** Missouri, C USA *36°48′N 89°57′W*
37 U14 **Dexter** New Mexico, SW USA *33°12′N 104°25′W*
160 I8 **Deyang** Sichuan, C China *31°08′N 104°23′E*
182 C4 **Dey-Dey, Lake** *salt lake* South Australia
143 S7 **Deyhūk** Yazd, E Iran *33°18′N 57°30′E*
Deynau *see* Galkynyş
Deyyer *see* Bandar-e Dayyer
142 L8 **Dezfūl** *var.* Dizful. Khūzestān, SW Iran *32°23′N 48°28′E*
129 X4 **Dezhneva, Mys** *headland* NE Russian Federation *66°08′N 69°40′W*
161 P4 **Dezhou** Shandong, E China *37°28′N 116°18′E*
Dezhou *see* Dechang
Dezh Shāhpūr *see* Marīvān
Dhaalu Atoll *see* South Nilandhe Atoll
Dhahran *see* Aẓ Ẓahrān
Dhahran Al Khobar *see* Aẓ Ẓahrān al Khubar
153 U14 **Dhaka** *prev.* Dacca. ● (Bangladesh) Dhaka, C Bangladesh *23°42′N 90°22′E*
153 T15 **Dhaka** ◈ *division* C Bangladesh
Dhali *see* Idálion
Dhalli Rajhara *see* Dalli Rājhara
141 O15 **Dhamār** W Yemen *14°31′N 44°25′E*
154 K12 **Dhamtari** Chhattīsgarh, C India *20°43′N 81°36′E*
153 Q15 **Dhanbād** Jhārkhand, NE India *23°48′N 86°27′E*
152 L10 **Dhangaḍhi** *var.* Dhangarhi. Far Western, W Nepal *28°45′N 80°38′E*
Dhangarhi *see* Dhangaḍhi
Dhank *see* Ḍank
153 R12 **Dhankuṭā** Eastern, E Nepal *27°06′N 87°21′E*
152 I6 **Dhaola Dhār** ▲▲ NE India
154 F10 **Dhār** Madhya Pradesh, C India *22°32′N 75°24′E*
153 R12 **Dharān** *var.* Dharan Bazar. Eastern, E Nepal *26°51′N 87°18′E*
Dharan Bazar *see* Dharān
155 H21 **Dhārāpuram** Tamil Nādu, SE India *10°45′N 77°33′E*
155 H20 **Dharmapuri** Tamil Nādu, SE India *12°11′N 78°07′E*
155 H18 **Dharmavaram** Andhra Pradesh, E India *14°27′N 77°44′E*
154 M11 **Dharmjaygarh** Chhattīsgarh, C India *22°27′N 83°16′E*
Dharmsāla *see* Dharmshāla
152 I7 **Dharmshāla** *prev.* Dharmsāla. Himāchal Pradesh, N India *32°14′N 76°24′E*
155 F17 **Dhārwād** *prev.* Dharwar. Karnātaka, SW India *15°30′N 75°04′E*
Dharwar *see* Dhārwād
Dhaulagiri *see* Dhawalāgiri
153 O10 **Dhawalāgiri** *var.* Dhaulagiri. ▲ C Nepal *28°45′N 83°27′E*
81 L18 **Dheere Laaq** *var.* Lak Dera, *It.* Lach Dera. *seasonal river* Kenya/Somalia
121 Q3 **Dhekeleia Sovereign Base Area** *UK military installation* E Cyprus*34°59′N 33°45′E*
121 Q3 **Dhekélia** *Eng.* Dhekelia, *Gk.* Dekéleia. *UK air base* SE Cyprus*35°00′N 33°45′E* *see* Dhekélia
Dhelvinákion *see* Delvináki
113 M22 **Dhëmbelit, Maja e** ▲ S Albania *40°10′N 20°22′E*
154 O12 **Dhenkānāl** Orissa, E India *20°40′N 85°36′E*
Dheskáti *see* Deskáti
138 G11 **Dhībān** Ma'dabā, NW Jordan *31°30′N 35°47′E*
Dhidhimótikhon *see* Didymóteicho
Dhíkti Ori *see* Díkti
138 I12 **Dhirwah, Wādī adh** *dry watercourse* C Jordan
Dhístomon *see* Dístomo
Dhodhekánisos *see* Dodekánisa
Dhodhóni *see* Dodóni
Dhofar *see* Ẓufār
Dhomokós *see* Domokós
Dhond *see* Daund
155 H17 **Dhone** Andhra Pradesh, C India *15°25′N 77°52′E*
154 B11 **Dhorāji** Gujarāt, W India *21°44′N 70°27′E*
Dhráma *see* Dráma
154 C10 **Dhrāngadhra** Gujarāt, W India *22°59′N 71°32′E*
Dhrepanon, Akrotírio *see* Drépano, Akrotírio
153 T13 **Dhuburi** Assam, NE India *26°06′N 89°55′E*
154 F12 **Dhule** *prev.* Dhulia. Mahārāshtra, C India *20°54′N 74°47′E*
Dhulia *see* Dhule
Dhún Dealgan, Cuan *see* Dundalk Bay
Dhún Droma, Cuan *see* Dundrum Bay
Dhún na nGall, Bá *see* Donegal Bay
Dhū Shaykh *see* Qazānīyah
80 Q13 **Dhuudo** Bari, NE Somalia *09°21′N 50°19′E*
81 N15 **Dhuusa Marreeb** *var.* Dusa Marreb, *It.* Dusa Mareb. Galguduud, C Somalia *05°33′N 46°24′E*
115 J24 **Día** *island* SE Greece
55 Y9 **Diable, Île du** *var.* Devil's Island. *island* N French Guiana
15 N12 **Diable, Rivière du** ≈ Québec, SE Canada
35 N8 **Diablo, Mount** ▲ California, W USA *37°52′N 121°57′W*
35 O9 **Diablo Range** ▲▲ California, W USA
24 I8 **Diablo, Sierra** ▲▲ Texas, SW USA
45 O11 **Diablotins, Morne** ▲ N Dominica *15°30′N 61°23′W*
77 N11 **Diafarabé** Mopti, C Mali *14°09′N 05°01′W*
77 N11 **Diaka** ≈ SW Mali
Diakovár *see* Đakovo
76 I12 **Dialakoto** S Senegal *13°21′N 13°19′W*
61 B18 **Diamante** Entre Ríos, E Argentina *32°05′S 60°40′W*
62 I12 **Diamante, Río** ≈ C Argentina
59 M19 **Diamantina** Minas Gerais, SE Brazil *18°17′S 43°37′W*
59 N17 **Diamantina, Chapada** ▲▲ E Brazil
173 U11 **Diamantina Fracture Zone** *tectonic feature* E Indian Ocean
181 T8 **Diamantina River** ≈ Queensland/South Australia
38 D9 **Diamond Head** *headland* O'ahu, Hawai'i, USA *21°15′N 157°48′W*
37 P2 **Diamond Peak** ▲ Colorado, C USA *40°56′N 108°56′W*
35 W5 **Diamond Peak** ▲ Nevada, W USA *39°34′N 115°46′W*
Diamond State *see* Delaware
76 J11 **Diamou** Kayes, SW Mali *14°04′N 11°16′W*
95 I23 **Dianalund** Sjælland, C Denmark *55°32′N 11°30′E*
65 G25 **Diana's Peak** ▲ C Saint Helena
160 M16 **Dianbai** *var.* Shuidong. Guangdong, S China *21°30′N 111°05′E*
160 G13 **Dian Chi** ▨ SW China
106 B10 **Diano Marina** Liguria, NW Italy *43°55′N 08°06′E*
163 V11 **Diaobingshan** *var.* Tiefa. Liaoning, NE China *42°25′N 123°39′E*
77 R13 **Diapaga** E Burkina *12°09′N 01°48′E*
Diarbekr *see* Diyarbakır
107 J15 **Diavolo, Passo del** *pass* C Italy
61 B18 **Díaz** Santa Fe, C Argentina *32°22′S 61°05′W*
141 W6 **Dibā al Ḩiṣn** *var.* Dibāh, Dibba. Ash Shāriqah, NE United Arab Emirates *25°35′N 56°16′E*
139 S3 **Dībaga** Arbīl, N Iraq *35°51′N 43°49′E*
Dibāh *see* Dibā al Ḩiṣn
79 L22 **Dibaya** Kasai-Occidental, S Dem. Rep. Congo *06°31′S 22°57′E*
Dibba *see* Dibā al Ḩiṣn
195 W15 **Dibble Iceberg Tongue** *ice feature* Antarctica
113 L19 **Dibër** ◈ *district* E Albania
83 I20 **Dibete** Central, SE Botswana *23°45′S 26°26′E*
Dibio *see* Dijon
25 W9 **Diboll** Texas, SW USA *31°11′N 94°46′W*
Dibra *see* Debar
153 X11 **Dibrugarh** Assam, NE India *27°29′N 94°49′E*
54 G4 **Dibulla** La Guajira, N Colombia *11°14′N 73°22′W*
25 O5 **Dickens** Texas, SW USA *33°38′N 100°51′W*
19 R2 **Dickey** Maine, NE USA *47°04′N 69°05′W*
30 K9 **Dickeyville** Wisconsin, N USA *42°37′N 90°36′W*
28 K5 **Dickinson** North Dakota, N USA *46°54′N 102°48′W*
0 E6 **Dickins Seamount** *undersea feature* NE Pacific Ocean *54°30′N 137°00′W*
27 O13 **Dickson** Oklahoma, C USA *34°11′N 96°58′W*
20 I9 **Dickson** Tennessee, S USA *36°04′N 87°23′W*
Dicle *see* Tigris
Dicsőszentmárton *see* Târnăveni
98 M12 **Didam** Gelderland, E Netherlands *51°56′N 06°08′E*
163 Y8 **Didao** Heilongjiang, NE China *45°22′N 130°48′E*
76 L12 **Didiéni** Koulikoro, W Mali *13°48′N 08°01′W*
Didimo *see* Dídymo
Didimotiho *see* Didymóteicho
81 K17 **Didimtu** *spring/well* NE Kenya *02°58′N 40°07′E*
67 U9 **Didinga Hills** ▲▲ S Sudan
11 Q16 **Didsbury** Alberta, SW Canada *51°39′N 114°09′W*
152 G11 **Dīdwāna** Rājasthān, N India *27°23′N 74°36′E*
115 G20 **Dídymo** *var.* Didimo. ▲ S Greece *37°28′N 23°12′E*
114 L12 **Didymóteicho** *var.* Dhidhimótikhon, Didimotiho. Anatolikí Makedonía kai Thráki, NE Greece *41°22′N 26°29′E*
103 S13 **Die** Drôme, E France *44°46′N 05°21′E*
77 O13 **Diébougou** SW Burkina *11°00′N 03°12′W*
Diedenhofen *see* Thionville
11 S16 **Diefenbaker, Lake** ▨ Saskatchewan, S Canada
62 H7 **Diego de Almagro** Atacama, N Chile *26°24′S 70°10′W*
63 F23 **Diego de Almagro, Isla** *island* S Chile
61 A20 **Diego de Alvear** Santa Fe, C Argentina *34°25′S 62°10′W*
173 Q7 **Diego Garcia** *island* S British Indian Ocean Territory
Diégo-Suarez *see* Antsirañana
99 M23 **Diekirch** Diekirch, C Luxembourg *49°52′N 06°10′E*
99 L23 **Diekirch** ◈ *district* N Luxembourg
76 K11 **Diéma** Kayes, W Mali *14°30′N 09°12′W*
101 H15 **Diemel** ≈ W Germany
98 I10 **Diemen** Noord-Holland, C Netherlands *52°21′N 04°58′E*
Diemrich *see* Deva
Điên Biên *see* Điên Biên Phu
167 R6 **Điên Biên Phu** *var.* Bien Bien, Điên Biên. Lai Châu, N Vietnam *21°23′N 103°02′E*
167 S7 **Diên Châu** Nghê An, N Vietnam *18°54′N 105°35′E*
99 K18 **Diepenbeek** Limburg, NE Belgium *50°54′N 05°25′E*
98 N11 **Diepenheim** Overijssel, E Netherlands *52°10′N 06°37′E*
98 M10 **Diepenveen** Overijssel, E Netherlands *52°18′N 06°09′E*
100 G12 **Diepholz** Niedersachsen, NW Germany *52°36′N 08°23′E*
102 M3 **Dieppe** Seine-Maritime, N France *49°55′N 01°05′E*
98 M12 **Dieren** Gelderland, E Netherlands *52°03′N 06°06′E*
27 S13 **Dierks** Arkansas, C USA *34°07′N 94°01′W*
99 J17 **Diest** Vlaams Brabant, C Belgium *50°58′N 05°03′E*
108 F7 **Dietikon** Zürich, NW Switzerland *47°24′N 08°25′E*
103 R13 **Dieulefit** Drôme, E France *44°30′N 05°01′E*
103 T5 **Dieuze** Moselle, NE France *48°49′N 06°41′E*
119 H15 **Dieveniškės** Vilnius, SE Lithuania *54°12′N 25°38′E*
98 N7 **Diever** Drenthe, NE Netherlands *52°49′N 06°19′E*
101 F17 **Diez** Rheinland-Pfalz, W Germany *50°22′N 08°01′E*
77 Y12 **Diffa** Diffa, SE Niger *13°19′N 12°37′E*
77 Y10 **Diffa** ◈ *department* SE Niger
99 L25 **Differdange** Luxembourg, SW Luxembourg *49°32′N 05°53′E*
13 O16 **Digby** Nova Scotia, SE Canada *44°37′N 65°47′W*
26 J5 **Dighton** Kansas, C USA *38°28′N 100°28′W*
Dignano d'Istria *see* Vodnjan
103 T14 **Digne** *var.* Digne-les-Bains. Alpes-de-Haute-Provence, SE France *44°05′N 06°14′E*
Digne-les-Bains *see* Digne
Digoel *see* Digul, Sungai
103 Q10 **Digoin** Saône-et-Loire, C France *46°30′N 04°E*
171 Q8 **Digos** Mindanao, S Philippines *06°46′N 125°21′E*
149 Q16 **Digri** Sind, SE Pakistan *25°11′N 69°10′E*
171 Y14 **Digul Barat, Sungai** ≈ Papua, E Indonesia
171 Y15 **Digul, Sungai** *prev.* Digoel. ≈ Papua, E Indonesia
171 Z14 **Digul Timur, Sungai** ≈ Papua, E Indonesia
153 X10 **Dihāng** ≈ NE India
Dihang *see* Brahmaputra
Dihōk *see* Dahūk
81 L17 **Diinsoor** Bay, S Somalia *02°28′N 43°00′E*
144 M14 **Diirmentobe** *Kas.* Dīirmentöbe; *prev.* Dermentobe, Dyurment'yube. Kzyl-Orda, S Kazakhstan *45°46′N 63°42′E*
Dīirmentöbe *see* Diirmentobe
Dijlah *see* Tigris
99 H17 **Dijle** ≈ C Belgium
103 R8 **Dijon** *anc.* Dibio. Côte d'Or, C France *47°21′N 05°04′E*
93 H14 **Dikanäs** Västerbotten, N Sweden *65°15′N 16°00′E*
80 L12 **Dikhil** SW Djibouti *11°08′N 42°19′E*
136 B13 **Dikili** İzmir, W Turkey *39°05′N 26°52′E*
99 B17 **Diksmuide** *var.* Dixmuide, *Fr.* Dixmude. West-Vlaanderen, W Belgium *51°02′N 02°52′E*
122 K7 **Dikson** Krasnoyarskiy Kray, N Russian Federation *73°30′N 80°35′E*
115 K25 **Díkti** *var.* Dhíkti Ori. ▲▲ Kríti, Greece, E Mediterranean Sea
77 Z13 **Dikwa** Borno, NE Nigeria *12°00′N 13°57′E*
81 J15 **Dīla** Southern Nationalities, S Ethiopia *06°19′N 38°16′E*
148 L7 **Dilārām** *prev.* Delārām. Nīmrōz, SW Afghanistan *32°11′N 63°27′E*
99 G18 **Dilbeek** Vlaams Brabant, C Belgium *50°51′N 04°16′E*
171 Q16 **Dili** *var.* Dilli, Dilly. ● (East Timor) N East Timor *08°33′S 125°34′E*
77 Y11 **Dilia** *var.* Dillia. ≈ SE Niger
Dilijan *see* Delījān
167 U13 **Di Linh** Lâm Đông, S Vietnam *11°38′N 108°07′E*
101 G16 **Dillenburg** Hessen, W Germany *50°45′N 08°16′E*
25 Q13 **Dilley** Texas, SW USA *28°40′N 99°10′W*
Dilli *see* Dili, East Timor
Dilli *see* Delhi, India
Dillia *see* Dilia
80 E11 **Dilling** *var.* Ad Dalanj. Southern Kordofan, C Sudan *12°02′N 29°41′E*
101 D20 **Dillingen** Saarland, SW Germany *49°20′N 06°43′E*
Dillingen *see* Dillingen an der Donau
101 J22 **Dillingen an der Donau** *var.* Dillingen. Bayern, S Germany *48°34′N 10°29′E*
39 O13 **Dillingham** Alaska, USA *59°03′N 158°30′W*
33 Q12 **Dillon** Montana, NW USA *45°14′N 112°38′W*
21 T12 **Dillon** South Carolina, SE USA *34°25′N 79°22′W*
31 T13 **Dillon Lake** ▨ Ohio, N USA
Dilly *see* Dili
Dilman *see* Salmās
79 K24 **Dilolo** Katanga, S Dem. Rep. Congo *10°42′S 22°21′E*
115 J20 **Dílos** *island* Kykládes, Greece, Aegean Sea
141 Y11 **Ḑil', Ra's aḑ** *headland* E Oman *19°12′N 57°53′E*
29 R5 **Dilworth** Minnesota, N USA *46°53′N 96°38′W*
138 H7 **Dimashq** *var.* Ash Shām, Esh Sham, *Eng.* Damascus, *Fr.* Damas, *It.* Damasco. ● (Syria) Rīf Dimashq, SW Syria *33°30′N 36°19′E*
138 I7 **Dimashq** ✈ Rīf Dimashq, S Syria *33°30′N 36°19′E*
Dimashq, Muḩāfaẓat *see* Rīf Dimashq
79 L21 **Dimbelenge** Kasai-Occidental, C Dem. Rep. Congo *05°36′S 23°04′E*
77 N16 **Dimbokro** E Ivory Coast *06°43′N 04°46′W*
182 L11 **Dimboola** Victoria, SE Australia *36°29′S 142°03′E*
Dîmboviţa *see* Dâmboviţa
Dimitrov *see* Dymytrov
114 K11 **Dimitrovgrad** Khaskovo, S Bulgaria *42°03′N 25°36′E*
127 R5 **Dimitrovgrad** Ul'yanovskaya Oblast', W Russian Federation *54°14′N 49°37′E*
113 Q15 **Dimitrovgrad** *prev.* Caribrod. Serbia, SE Serbia *43°01′N 22°46′E*
Dimitrovo *see* Pernik
Dimlang *see* Vogel Peak
24 M3 **Dimmitt** Texas, SW USA *34°32′N 102°20′W*
114 F7 **Dimovo** Vidin, NW Bulgaria *43°46′N 22°47′E*
59 A16 **Dimpolis** Acre, W Brazil *09°52′S 71°51′W*
115 O23 **Dimyliá** Ródos, Dodekánisa, Greece, Aegean Sea *36°17′N 27°59′E*
171 Q6 **Dinagat Island** *island* S Philippines
153 S13 **Dinajpur** Rajshahi, NW Bangladesh *25°38′N 88°40′E*
102 I6 **Dinan** Côtes d'Armor, NW France *48°27′N 02°02′W*
99 I21 **Dinant** Namur, S Belgium *50°16′N 04°55′E*
136 E15 **Dinar** Afyon, SW Turkey *38°05′N 30°09′E*
112 F13 **Dinara** ▲ W Croatia *43°49′N 16°42′E*
Dinara *see* Dinaric Alps
102 I5 **Dinard** Ille-et-Vilaine, NW France *48°38′N 02°04′W*
112 F13 **Dinaric Alps** *var.* Dinara. ▲▲ Bosnia and Herzegovina/Croatia
143 N10 **Dīnār, Kūh-e** ▲ C Iran *30°51′N 51°36′E*
Dinbych *see* Denbigh
155 H22 **Dindigul** Tamil Nādu, SE India *10°23′N 78°E*
83 M19 **Dindiza** Gaza, S Mozambique *23°22′S 33°28′E*
79 H21 **Dinga** Bandundu, SW Dem. Rep. Congo *05°00′S 16°29′E*
149 V7 **Dinga** Punjab, E Pakistan *32°38′N 73°45′E*
Dingchang *see* Qinxian
158 L16 **Dinggyê** *var.* Gyangkar. Xizang Zizhiqu, W China *28°18′N 88°06′E*
97 A20 **Dingle** *Ir.* An Daingean. SW Ireland *52°09′N 10°16′W*
97 A20 **Dingle Bay** *Ir.* Bá an Daingin. *bay* SW Ireland
18 I13 **Dingmans Ferry** Pennsylvania, NE USA *41°12′N 74°51′W*
101 N22 **Dingolfing** Bayern, SE Germany *48°37′N 12°28′E*
171 O1 **Dingras** Luzon, N Philippines *18°06′N 120°43′E*
76 J13 **Dinguiraye** N Guinea *11°19′N 10°49′W*
96 I8 **Dingwall** N Scotland, United Kingdom *57°36′N 04°26′W*
159 V10 **Dingxi** Gansu, C China *35°36′N 104°33′E*
Ding Xian *see* Dingzhou
161 Q7 **Dingyuan** Anhui, E China *32°30′N 117°40′E*
161 O3 **Dingzhou** *prev.* Ding Xian. Hebei, E China *38°31′N 114°52′E*
167 U6 **Đinh Lâp** Lang Sơn, N Vietnam *21°33′N 107°03′E*
167 T13 **Đinh Quan** *var.* Tân Phu. Đông Nai, S Vietnam *11°11′N 107°20′E*
100 E13 **Dinkel** ≈ Germany/Netherlands
101 J21 **Dinkelsbühl** Bayern, S Germany *49°06′N 10°18′E*
101 D14 **Dinslaken** Nordrhein-Westfalen, W Germany *51°34′N 06°43′E*
35 R11 **Dinuba** California, W USA *36°32′N 119°23′W*
21 W7 **Dinwiddie** Virginia, NE USA *37°02′N 77°40′W*
98 N13 **Dinxperlo** Gelderland, E Netherlands *51°51′N 06°30′E*
Dio *see* Díon
Diófás *see* Nucet
76 M12 **Dioïla** Koulikoro, W Mali *12°28′N 06°43′W*
115 F14 **Díon** *var.* Dio; *anc.* Dium. *site of ancient city* Kentrikí Makedonía, N Greece
115 G19 **Dióryga Korinthou** *Eng.* Corinth Canal. *canal* S Greece
76 G12 **Diouloulou** SW Senegal *13°00′N 16°34′W*
77 N11 **Dioura** Mopti, W Mali *14°48′N 05°20′W*
76 G11 **Diourbel** W Senegal *14°39′N 16°12′W*
152 L10 **Dipāyal** Far Western, W Nepal *29°09′N 80°46′E*
121 R1 **Dipkarpaz** *Gk.* Rizokarpaso, Rizokárpason. NE Cyprus *35°36′N 34°23′E*
149 R17 **Diplo** Sind, SE Pakistan *24°29′N 69°36′E*
171 P7 **Dipolog** *var.* Dipolog City. Mindanao, S Philippines *08°31′N 123°20′E*
Dipolog City *see* Dipolog
185 C23 **Dipton** Southland, South Island, New Zealand *45°55′S 168°21′E*
77 O10 **Diré** Tombouctou, C Mali *16°12′N 03°31′W*
80 L13 **Dirē Dawa** Dirē Dawa, E Ethiopia *09°35′N 41°53′E*
Dirfis *see* Dírfys
115 H18 **Dírfys** *var.* Dirfis. ▲▲ Évvioa, C Greece
75 N9 **Dirj** *var.* Daraj, Darj. W Libya *30°09′N 10°26′E*
180 G10 **Dirk Hartog Island** *island* Western Australia
77 Y8 **Dirkou** Agadez, NE Niger *18°45′N 13°00′E*
181 X11 **Dirranbandi** Queensland, E Australia *28°37′S 148°13′E*
Dirri *see* Derri
Dirschau *see* Tczew
37 N6 **Dirty Devil River** ≈ Utah, W USA
32 E10 **Disappointment, Cape** *headland* Washington, NW USA *46°16′N 124°06′W*
180 L8 **Disappointment, Lake** *salt lake* Western Australia
183 R12 **Disaster Bay** *bay* New South Wales, SE Australia
44 J11 **Discovery Bay** C Jamaica *18°27′N 77°24′W*
182 K13 **Discovery Bay** *inlet* SE Australia
67 Y15 **Discovery II Fracture Zone** *tectonic feature* SW Indian Ocean
Discovery Seamount/Discovery Seamounts *see* Discovery Tablemounts
65 O19 **Discovery Tablemounts** *var.* Discovery Seamount, Discovery Seamounts. *undersea feature* SW Atlantic Ocean *42°00′S 00°10′E*
108 G9 **Disentis** *Rmsch.* Mustér. Graubünden, S Switzerland *46°43′N 08°52′E*
39 O10 **Dishna River** ≈ Alaska, USA
148 K10 **Dīshū** *var.* Deshu; *prev.* Deh Shū. Helmand, S Afghanistan *30°28′N 63°21′E*
Disko Bugt *see* Qeqertarsuup Tunua
195 X4 **Dismal Mountains** ▲▲ Antarctica
28 M14 **Dismal River** ≈ Nebraska, C USA
Disna *see* Dzisna
99 L19 **Dison** Liège, E Belgium *50°37′N 05°52′E*
153 V12 **Dispur** *state capital* Assam, NE India *26°03′N 91°52′E*
15 R11 **Disraeli** Québec, SE Canada *45°58′N 71°21′W*
115 F18 **Dístomo** *prev.* Dhístomon. Stereá Elláda, C Greece *38°25′N 22°40′E*
Dístos, Límni *see* Dýstos, Límni
59 L18 **Distrito Federal** *Eng.* Federal District. ◈ *federal district* C Brazil
41 P14 **Distrito Federal** ◈ *federal district* S Mexico
54 L4 **Distrito Federal** *off.* Territorio Distrito Federal. ◈ *federal district* N Venezuela
Distrito Federal, Territorio *see* Distrito Federal
116 J10 **Ditrău** *Hung.* Ditró. Harghita, C Romania *46°49′N 25°31′E*
Ditró *see* Ditrău
154 B12 **Diu** Damān and Diu, W India *20°42′N 70°59′E*
Dium *see* Díon
109 S13 **Divača** SW Slovenia *45°40′N 13°58′E*
102 K5 **Dives** ≈ N France
33 Q11 **Divide** Montana, NW USA *45°44′N 112°47′W*
Divin *see* Dzivin
83 N18 **Divinhe** Sofala, E Mozambique *20°41′S 34°46′E*
59 L20 **Divinópolis** Minas Gerais, SE Brazil *20°08′S 44°55′W*
127 N13 **Divnoye** Stavropol'skiy Kray, SW Russian Federation *45°54′N 43°18′E*
76 M17 **Divo** S Ivory Coast *05°50′N 05°22′W*
Divodurum Mediomatricum *see* Metz
137 N13 **Divriği** Sivas, C Turkey *39°23′N 38°06′E*
Diwaniyah *see* Ad Dīwānīyah
14 J10 **Dix Milles, Lac** ◎ Québec, SE Canada
14 M8 **Dix Milles, Lac des** ◎ Québec, SE Canada
Dixmude/Dixmuide *see* Diksmuide
35 N7 **Dixon** California, W USA *38°19′N 121°49′W*
30 L10 **Dixon** Illinois, N USA *41°51′N 89°26′W*
20 I6 **Dixon** Kentucky, S USA *37°30′N 87°39′W*
27 V6 **Dixon** Missouri, C USA *37°59′N 92°05′W*
37 S9 **Dixon** New Mexico, SW USA *36°10′N 105°49′W*
39 Y15 **Dixon Entrance** *strait* Canada/USA
18 D14 **Dixonville** Pennsylvania, NE USA *40°43′N 79°01′W*
137 T13 **Diyadin** Ağrı, E Turkey *39°33′N 43°41′E*
Diyālá, Nahr *see* Sīrvān, Rūdkhāneh-ye
139 V5 **Diyālá, Sirwan Nahr** *var.* Rudkhaneh-ye Sīrvān, Sīrwān. ≈ Iran/Iraq *see also* Sīrvān, Rudkhaneh-ye
137 P15 **Diyarbakır** *var.* Diarbekr; *anc.* Amida. Diyarbakır, SE Turkey *37°55′N 40°14′E*
137 P15 **Diyarbakır** *var.* Diarbekr. ◈ *province* SE Turkey
Dizful *see* Dezfūl
79 F16 **Dja** ≈ SE Cameroon
Djadié *see* Zadié
77 X7 **Djado** Agadez, NE Niger *21°00′N 12°11′E*
77 X6 **Djado, Plateau du** ▲▲ NE Niger
Djailolo *see* Halmahera, Pulau
Djajapura *see* Jayapura
Djakarta *see* Jakarta
Djakovo *see* Đakovo
79 G20 **Djambala** Plateaux, C Congo *02°32′S 14°43′E*
Djambi *see* Jambi
Djambi *see* Hari, Batang
74 M9 **Djanet** E Algeria *28°43′N 08°57′E*
74 M11 **Djanet** *prev.* Fort Charlet. SE Algeria *24°34′N 09°33′E*
Djaul *see* Dyaul Island
Djawa *see* Jawa
Djéblé *see* Jablah
78 I10 **Djédaa** Batha, C Chad *13°31′N 18°34′E*
74 J6 **Djelfa** *var.* El Djelfa. N Algeria *34°43′N 03°14′E*
79 M14 **Djéma** Haut-Mbomou, E Central African Republic *06°04′N 25°20′E*
Djember *see* Jember
Djeneponto *see* Jeneponto
77 N12 **Djenné** *var.* Jenné. Mopti, C Mali *13°55′N 04°31′W*
Djérablous *see* Jarābulus
Djerba *see* Jerba, Île de
79 F15 **Djérem** ≈ C Cameroon
Djevdjelija *see* Gevgelija
77 P11 **Djibo** N Burkina *14°09′N 01°38′W*
80 L12 **Djibouti** *var.* Jibuti. ● (Djibouti) E Djibouti *11°33′N 42°55′E*
80 L12 **Djibouti** *off.* Republic of Djibouti, *var.* Jibuti; *prev.* French Somaliland, French Territory of the Afars and Issas, *Fr.* Côte Française des Somalis, Territoire Français des Afars et des Issas. ◆ *republic* E Africa
80 L12 **Djibouti** ✈ C Djibouti *11°29′N 42°54′E*
Djibouti, Republic of *see* Djibouti
Djidjel/Djidjelli *see* Jijel
Djidji *see* Ivando
55 W10 **Djoemoe** Sipaliwini, C Surinam *04°00′N 55°27′W*
Djokjakarta *see* Yogyakarta
79 K21 **Djoku-Punda** Kasai-Occidental, S Dem. Rep. Congo *05°27′S 20°58′E*
79 K18 **Djolu** Equateur, N Dem. Rep. Congo *0°35′N 22°30′E*
Djombang *see* Jombang
Ďjorče Petrov *see* Đorče Petrov
79 F17 **Djoua** ≈ Congo/Gabon
77 R14 **Djougou** W Benin *09°42′N 01°38′E*
79 F16 **Djoum** Sud, S Cameroon *02°38′N 12°51′E*
78 I8 **Djourab, Erg du** *desert* N Chad
79 P17 **Djugu** Orientale, NE Dem. Rep. Congo *01°55′N 30°31′E*
Djumbir *see* Ďumbier
92 L3 **Djúpivogur** Austurland, SE Iceland *64°40′N 14°18′W*
94 L13 **Djura** Dalarna, C Sweden *60°37′N 15°00′E*
Djurdjevac *see* Đurđevac
D'Kar *see* Dekar
197 U6 **Dmitriya Lapteva, Proliv** *strait* N Russian Federation
126 J7 **Dmitriyev-L'govskiy** Kurskaya Oblast', W Russian Federation *52°08′N 35°09′E*
Dmitriyevsk *see* Makiyivka
126 K3 **Dmitrov** Moskovskaya Oblast', W Russian Federation *56°23′N 37°30′E*
Dmitrovichi *see* Dzmitravichy
126 J6 **Dmitrovsk-Orlovskiy** Orlovskaya Oblast', W Russian Federation *52°28′N 35°01′E*
117 R3 **Dmytrivka** Chernihivs'ka Oblast', N Ukraine *50°56′N 32°57′E*
Dnepr *see* Dnieper
Dneprodzerzhinsk *see* Romaniv
Dneprodzerzhinskoye Vodokhranilishche *see* Dniprodzerzhyns'ke Vodoskhovyshche
Dnepropetrovsk *see* Dnipropetrovs'k
Dnepropetrovskaya Oblast' *see* Dnipropetrovs'ka Oblast'
Dneprorudnoye *see* Dniprorudne
Dneprovskiy Liman *see* Dniprovs'kyy Lyman
Dneprovsko-Bugskiy Kanal *see* Dnyaprowska-Buhski Kanal
Dnestr *see* Dniester
Dnestrovskiy Liman *see* Dnistrovs'kyy Lyman
86 H11 **Dnieper** *Bel.* Dnyapro, *Rus.* Dnepr, *Ukr.* Dnipro. ≈ E Europe
117 P3 **Dnieper Lowland** *Bel.* Prydnyaprowskaya Nizina, *Ukr.* Prydniprovs'ka Nyzovyna. *lowlands* Belarus/Ukraine
116 M8 **Dniester** *Rom.* Nistru, *Rus.* Dnestr, *Ukr.* Dnister; *anc.* Tyras. ≈ Moldova/Ukraine
Dnipro *see* Dnieper
Dniprodzerzhyns'k *see* Romaniv
117 T7 **Dniprodzerzhyns'ke Vodoskhovyshche** *Rus.* Dneprodzerzhinskoye Vodokhranilishche. ▨ C Ukraine
117 U7 **Dnipropetrovs'k** *Rus.* Dnepropetrovsk; *prev.* Yekaterinoslav. Dnipropetrovs'ka Oblast', E Ukraine *48°28′N 35°E*
117 U8 **Dnipropetrovs'k** ✈ Dnipropetrovs'ka Oblast', S Ukraine *48°20′N 35°04′E*
Dnipropetrovs'k *see* Dnipropetrovs'ka Oblast'
117 T7 **Dnipropetrovs'ka Oblast'** *var.* Dnipropetrovs'k, *Rus.* Dnepropetrovskaya Oblast'. ◈ *province* E Ukraine
117 U9 **Dniprorudne** *Rus.* Dneprorudnoye. Zaporiz'ka Oblast', SE Ukraine *47°21′N 35°00′E*
117 Q11 **Dniprovs'kyy Lyman** *Rus.* Dneprovskiy Liman. *bay* S Ukraine
Dnister *see* Dniester
117 O11 **Dnistrovs'kyy Lyman** *Rus.* Dnestrovskiy Liman. *inlet* S Ukraine
124 G14 **Dno** Pskovskaya Oblast', W Russian Federation *57°48′N 29°58′E*
Dnyapro *see* Dnieper
119 H20 **Dnyaprowska-Buhski Kanal** *Rus.* Dneprovsko-Bugskiy Kanal. *canal* SW Belarus
13 O14 **Doaktown** New Brunswick, SE Canada *46°34′N 66°06′W*
78 H13 **Doba** Logone-Oriental, S Chad *08°40′N 16°50′E*
118 E9 **Dobele** *Ger.* Doblen. W Latvia *56°36′N 23°14′E*
101 N16 **Döbeln** Sachsen, E Germany *51°07′N 13°07′E*
171 U12 **Doberai, Jazirah** *Dut.* Vogelkop. *peninsula* Papua, E Indonesia
110 F10 **Dobiegniew** *Ger.* Lubuskie, Woldenberg Neumark. Lubuskie, W Poland *52°58′N 15°43′E*
Doblen *see* Dobele
81 K18 **Dobli** *spring/well* SW Somalia *0°24′N 41°18′E*
112 H11 **Doboj** Republiks Srpska, N Bosnia and Herzegovina *44°45′N 18°03′E*
143 R12 **Doborjī** *var.* Fūrg. Fārs, S Iran *28°16′N 55°13′E*
110 L8 **Dobre Miasto** *Ger.* Guttstadt. Warmińsko-mazurskie, NE Poland *53°59′N 20°25′E*
114 N7 **Dobrich** *Rom.* Bazargic; *prev.* Tolbukhin. Dobrich, NE Bulgaria *43°35′N 27°49′E*
114 N7 **Dobrich** ◈ *province* NE Bulgaria
126 M8 **Dobrinka** Lipetskaya Oblast', W Russian Federation *52°10′N 40°30′E*
126 M7 **Dobrinka** Volgogradskaya Oblast', SW Russian Federation *50°52′N 41°48′E*
Dobrla Vas *see* Eberndorf
111 I15 **Dobrodzień** *Ger.* Guttentag. Opolskie, S Poland *50°43′N 18°24′E*

◆ Country
● Country Capital
◇ Dependent Territory
○ Dependent Territory Capital
◈ Administrative Regions
✈ International Airport
▲ Mountain
▲▲ Mountain Range
Volcano
≈ River
◎ Lake
▨ Reservoir

Dobrogea see Dobruja
117 W7 **Dobropillya** Rus. Dobropol'ye. Donets'ka Oblast', SE Ukraine 48°25′N 37°02′E
Dobropol'ye see Dobropillya
117 P8 **Dobrovelychkivka** Kirovohrads'ka Oblast', C Ukraine 48°22′N 31°12′E
Dobrudja/Dobrudzha see Dobruja
114 O7 **Dobruja** var. Dobrudja, Bul. Dobrudzha, Rom. Dobrogea. physical region Bulgaria/Romania
119 P19 **Dobrush** Homyel'skaya Voblasts', SE Belarus 52°25′N 31°19′E
125 U14 **Dobryanka** Permskiy Kray, NW Russian Federation 58°28′N 56°27′E
117 P2 **Dobryanka** Chernihivs'ka Oblast', N Ukraine 52°03′N 31°09′E
Dobryn' see Dabryn'
21 R8 **Dobson** North Carolina, SE USA 36°25′N 80°45′W
59 N20 **Doce, Rio** ≈ SE Brazil
93 I16 **Docksta** Västernorrland, C Sweden 63°06′N 18°22′E
41 N10 **Doctor Arroyo** Nuevo León, NE Mexico 23°40′N 100°09′W
62 L4 **Doctor Pedro P. Peña** Boquerón, W Paraguay 22°22′S 62°23′W
171 S11 **Dodaga** Pulau Halmahera, E Indonesia 01°06′N 128°10′E
155 G21 **Dodda Betta** ▲ S India 11°28′N 76°44′E
Dodecanese see Dodekánisa
115 M22 **Dodekánisa** var. Nóties Sporádes, Eng. Dodecanese; prev. Dhodhekánisos, Dodekanisos. island group SE Greece
Dodekanisos see Dodekánisa
26 J6 **Dodge City** Kansas, C USA 37°45′N 100°01′W
30 K9 **Dodgeville** Wisconsin, N USA 42°57′N 90°08′W
97 H25 **Dodman Point** headland SW England, United Kingdom 50°13′N 04°47′W
81 J14 **Dodola** Oromīya, C Ethiopia 07°00′N 39°15′E
81 H22 **Dodoma** ● (Tanzania) Dodoma, C Tanzania 06°11′S 35°45′E
81 H22 **Dodoma** ◈ region C Tanzania
115 C16 **Dodóni** var. Dhodhóni. site of ancient city Ípeiros, W Greece
33 U7 **Dodson** Montana, NW USA 48°25′N 108°18′W
25 P3 **Dodson** Texas, SW USA 34°46′N 100°01′W
98 M12 **Doesburg** Gelderland, E Netherlands 52°01′N 06°08′E
98 N12 **Doetinchem** Gelderland, E Netherlands 51°58′N 06°17′E
158 L12 **Dogai Coring** var. Lake Montcalm. ◎ W China
137 N15 **Doğanşehir** Malatya, C Turkey 38°07′N 37°54′E
84 E9 **Dogger Bank** undersea feature C North Sea 55°00′N 03°00′E
23 S10 **Dog Island** island Florida, SE USA
14 C7 **Dog Lake** ◎ Ontario, S Canada
106 B9 **Dogliani** Piemonte, NE Italy 44°33′N 07°55′E
164 H11 **Dōgo** island Oki-shotō, SW Japan
143 N10 **Do Gonbadān** var. Dow Gonbadān, Gonbadān. Kohkīlūyeh va Būyer AḤmad, SW Iran 30°12′N 50°48′E
77 S12 **Dogondoutchi** Dosso, SW Niger 13°36′N 04°03′E
137 T13 **Doğubayazıt** Ağrı, E Turkey 39°33′N 44°07′E
137 P12 **Doğu Karadeniz Dağları** var. Anadolu Dağları. ▲▲ NE Turkey
158 K16 **Dogxung Zangbo** ≈ W China
Doha see Ad Dawḥah
Doha see Ad Dawḥah
Dohad see Dāhod
Dohuk see Dahūk
159 N16 **Doilungdêqên** var. Namka. Xizang Zizhiqu, W China 29°41′N 90°58′E
114 F12 **Doïráni, Límni** var. Limni Doïranis, Bul. Ezero Doyransko. ◎ N Greece
Doire see Londonderry
99 H22 **Doische** Namur, S Belgium 50°09′N 04°43′E
59 P17 **Dois de Julho** ✈ (Salvador) Bahia, NE Brazil 12°04′S 38°58′W
60 H12 **Dois Vizinhos** Paraná, S Brazil 25°47′S 53°03′W
80 H10 **Doka** Gedaref, E Sudan 13°30′N 35°47′E
Doka see Kéita, Bahr
139 T3 **Dokan** var. Dūkān. As Sulaymānīyah, E Iraq 35°55′N 44°58′E
94 H13 **Dokka** Oppland, S Norway 60°49′N 10°04′E
98 L5 **Dokkum** Fryslân, N Netherlands 53°20′N 06°E
98 L5 **Dokkumer Ee** ≈ N Netherlands
76 K13 **Doko** NE Guinea 11°46′N 08°58′W
Dokshitsy see Dokshytsy
118 K13 **Dokshytsy** Rus. Dokshitsy. Vitsyebskaya Voblasts', N Belarus 54°54′N 27°46′E
117 X8 **Dokuchayevs'k** var. Dokuchayevsk. Donets'ka Oblast', SE Ukraine 47°43′N 37°41′E
Dokuchayevsk see Dokuchayevs'k
Dolak, Pulau see Yos Sudarso, Pulau
29 P9 **Doland** South Dakota, N USA 44°51′N 98°06′W
63 J18 **Dolavón** Chaco, S Argentina 43°16′S 65°44′W
15 P6 **Dolbeau** Québec, SE Canada 48°52′N 72°15′W
15 P6 **Dolbeau-Mistassini** Québec, SE Canada 48°54′N 72°13′W
102 I5 **Dol-de-Bretagne** Ille-et-Vilaine, NW France 48°33′N 01°45′W
64 J13 **Doldrums Fracture Zone** tectonic feature W Atlantic Ocean
103 S8 **Dôle** Jura, E France 47°05′N 05°30′E
97 J19 **Dolgellau** NW Wales, United Kingdom 52°45′N 03°54′W
Dolginovo see Dawhinava
Dolgi, Ostrov see Dolgiy, Ostrov
125 U2 **Dolgiy, Ostrov** var. Ostrov Dolgi. island NW Russian Federation
162 J9 **Dölgöön** Övörhangay, C Mongolia 45°57′N 103°14′E
107 C20 **Dolianova** Sardegna, Italy, C Mediterranean Sea 39°23′N 09°08′E
Dolina see Dolyna
123 T13 **Dolinsk** Ostrov Sakhalin, Sakhalinskaya Oblast', SE Russian Federation 47°20′N 142°52′E
Dolinskaya see Dolyns'ka
79 F21 **Dolisie** prev. Loubomo. Niari, S Congo 04°12′S 12°41′E
116 G14 **Dolj** ◈ county SW Romania
98 P5 **Dollard** bay NW Germany
194 J5 **Dolleman Island** island Antarctica
114 K8 **Dolna Oryakhovitsa** Veliko Tŭrnovo, N Bulgaria 43°09′N 25°44′E
114 N9 **Dolni Chiflik** Varna, E Bulgaria 42°59′N 27°43′E
114 I8 **Dolni Dŭbnik** Pleven, N Bulgaria 43°24′N 24°25′E
114 F8 **Dolni Lom** Vidin, NW Bulgaria 43°31′N 22°46′E
Dolnja Lendava see Lendava
129 F14 **Dolnośląskie** ◈ province SW Poland
111 K18 **Dolný Kubín** Hung. Alsókubin. Zilinský Kraj, N Slovakia 49°12′N 19°17′E
106 H8 **Dolo** Veneto, NE Italy 45°25′N 12°06′E
Dolomites/Dolomiti see Dolomitiche, Alpi
106 H6 **Dolomitiche, Alpi** var. Dolomiti, Eng. Dolomites. ▲▲ NE Italy
Dolonnur see Duolun
Doloon see Tsogt-Ovoo
61 E21 **Dolores** Buenos Aires, E Argentina 36°21′S 57°39′W
42 E3 **Dolores** Petén, N Guatemala 16°33′N 89°26′W
171 Q5 **Dolores** Samar, C Philippines 12°01′N 125°27′E
105 S12 **Dolores** Valenciana, E Spain 38°09′N 00°45′W
61 D19 **Dolores** Soriano, SW Uruguay 33°34′S 58°15′W
41 N12 **Dolores Hidalgo** var. Ciudad de Dolores Hidalgo. Guanajuato, C Mexico 21°10′N 100°55′W
8 J7 **Dolphin and Union Strait** strait Northwest Territories/Nunavut, N Canada
65 D23 **Dolphin, Cape** headland East Falkland, Falkland Islands 51°15′S 58°57′W
44 H12 **Dolphin Head** hill W Jamaica
83 B21 **Dolphin Head** var. Cape Dernberg. headland SW Namibia 25°33′S 14°36′E
110 G12 **Dolsk** Ger. Dolzig. Weilkopolskie, C Poland 51°59′N 17°03′E
167 S8 **Đô Lương** Nghê An, N Vietnam 18°51′N 105°19′E
116 I6 **Dolyna** Rus. Dolina. Ivano-Frankivs'ka Oblast', W Ukraine 48°58′N 24°01′E
117 R8 **Dolyns'ka** Rus. Dolinskaya. Kirovohrads'ka Oblast', S Ukraine 48°06′N 32°46′E
Dolzig see Dolsk
Domachëvo/Domaczewo see Damachava
117 P9 **Domanivka** Mykolayivs'ka Oblast', S Ukraine 47°40′N 30°56′E
153 S13 **Domar** Rajshahi, N Bangladesh 26°08′N 88°57′E
108 I9 **Domat/Ems** Graubünden, SE Switzerland 46°50′N 09°28′E
111 A18 **Domažlice** Ger. Taus. Plzeňský Kraj, W Czech Republic 49°26′N 12°54′E
127 X8 **Dombarovskiy** Orenburgskaya Oblast', W Russian Federation 50°53′N 59°18′E
94 G10 **Dombås** Oppland, S Norway 62°04′N 09°07′E
83 M17 **Dombe** Manica, C Mozambique 19°59′S 33°24′E
82 A13 **Dombe Grande** Benguela, C Angola 12°57′S 13°07′E
103 R10 **Dombes** physical region E France
111 I25 **Dombóvár** Tolna, S Hungary 46°24′N 18°09′E
99 D14 **Domburg** Zeeland, SW Netherlands 51°34′N 03°30′E
58 L13 **Dom Eliseu** Pará, NE Brazil 04°02′S 47°31′W
Domel Island see Letsôk-aw Kyun
103 O11 **Dôme, Puy de** ▲ C France 45°46′N 03°00′E
36 H13 **Dome Rock Mountains** ▲▲ Arizona, SW USA
Domesnes, Cape see Kolkasrags
62 G8 **Domeyko** Atacama, N Chile 28°58′S 70°54′W
62 H5 **Domeyko, Cordillera** ▲▲ N Chile
102 K5 **Domfront** Orne, N France 48°35′N 00°39′W
171 X13 **Dom, Gunung** ▲ Papua, E Indonesia 02°41′S 137°00′E
45 X11 **Dominica** off. Commonwealth of Dominica. ◆ republic E West Indies
47 S3 **Dominica** island Dominica
Dominica Channel see Martinique Passage
Dominica, Commonwealth of see Dominica
43 N15 **Dominical** Puntarenas, SE Costa Rica 09°16′N 83°52′W
45 Q8 **Dominican Republic** ◆ republic C West Indies
45 X11 **Dominica Passage** passage E Caribbean Sea
99 K14 **Dommel** ≈ S Netherlands
81 O14 **Domo** Sumalē, E Ethiopia 07°53′N 46°55′E
126 L4 **Domodedovo** ✈ (Moskva) Moskovskaya Oblast', W Russian Federation 55°19′N 37°55′E
106 C6 **Domodossola** Piemonte, NE Italy 46°07′N 08°20′E
115 F17 **Domokós** var. Dhomokós. Stereá Elláda, C Greece 39°07′N 22°18′E
172 I14 **Domoni** Anjouan, SE Comoros 12°15′S 44°39′E
61 G16 **Dom Pedrito** Rio Grande do Sul, S Brazil 31°00′S 54°40′W
Dompoe see Dompu
170 M16 **Dompu** prev. Dompoe. Sumbawa, C Indonesia 08°30′S 118°28′E
Domschale see Domžale
62 H13 **Domuyo, Volcán** ✱ W Argentina 36°36′S 70°22′W
109 U11 **Domžale** Ger. Domschale. C Slovenia 46°09′N 14°33′E
127 O10 **Don** var. Duna, Tanais. ≈ SW Russian Federation
96 K9 **Don** ≈ NE Scotland, United Kingdom
182 M11 **Donald** Victoria, SE Australia 36°27′S 143°03′E
22 J9 **Donaldsonville** Louisiana, S USA 30°06′N 90°59′W
23 S8 **Donalsonville** Georgia, SE USA 31°02′N 84°52′W
Donau see Danube
101 G23 **Donaueschingen** Baden-Württemberg, SW Germany 47°57′N 08°30′E
101 K22 **Donaumoos** wetland S Germany
101 K22 **Donauwörth** Bayern, S Germany 48°43′N 10°46′E
109 U7 **Donawitz** Steiermark, SE Austria 47°23′N 15°00′E
117 X7 **Donbass** industrial region Russian Federation/Ukraine
104 K11 **Don Benito** Extremadura, W Spain 38°57′N 05°52′W
97 M17 **Doncaster** anc. Danum. N England, United Kingdom 53°32′N 01°07′W
44 K12 **Don Christophers Point** headland C Jamaica 18°19′N 76°48′W
55 V9 **Donderkamp** Sipaliwini, NW Surinam 05°18′N 56°22′W
82 B12 **Dondo** Cuanza Norte, NW Angola 09°40′S 14°24′E
171 O12 **Dondo** Sulawesi, N Indonesia 0°54′S 121°33′E
83 N17 **Dondo** Sofala, C Mozambique 19°41′S 34°45′E
155 K26 **Dondra Head** headland S Sri Lanka 05°57′N 80°33′E
Donduşani see Donduşeni
116 M8 **Donduşeni** var. Donduşani, Rus. Dondyushany. N Moldova 48°13′N 27°38′E
Dondyushany see Donduşeni
97 D15 **Donegal** Ir. Dún na nGall. Donegal, NW Ireland 54°39′N 08°06′W
97 D14 **Donegal** Ir. Dún na nGall. cultural region NW Ireland
97 C15 **Donegal Bay** Ir. Bá Dhún na nGall. bay NW Ireland
84 K10 **Donets** ≈ Russian Federation/Ukraine
117 X8 **Donets'k** Rus. Donetsk; prev. Stalino. Donets'ka Oblast', E Ukraine 47°58′N 37°50′E
117 W8 **Donets'k** ✈ Donets'ka Oblast', E Ukraine 48°03′N 37°44′E
Donets'k see Donets'ka Oblast'
117 W8 **Donets'ka Oblast'** var. Donets'k, Rus. Donetskaya Oblast'; prev. Rus. Stalins'kaya Oblast'. ◈ province SE Ukraine
Donetskaya Oblast' see Donets'ka Oblast'
67 P8 **Donga** ≈ Cameroon/Nigeria
157 O13 **Dongchuan** Yunnan, SW China 26°09′N 103°10′E
161 Q14 **Dongchuan Dao** prev. Dongshan Dao. island SE China
99 I14 **Dongen** Noord-Brabant, S Netherlands 51°38′N 04°56′E
160 K17 **Dongfang** var. Basuo. Hainan, S China 19°05′N 108°40′E
163 Z7 **Dongfanghong** Heilongjiang, NE China 46°13′N 133°13′E
163 W11 **Dongfeng** Jilin, NE China 42°39′N 125°33′E
171 N12 **Donggala** Sulawesi, C Indonesia 0°40′S 119°44′E
163 V13 **Donggang** var. Dadong; prev. Donggou. Liaoning, NE China 39°52′N 124°08′E
Donggou see Donggang
161 O14 **Dongguan** Guangdong, S China 23°03′N 113°43′E
167 T9 **Đông Ha** Quang Tri, C Vietnam 16°45′N 107°10′E
163 Y14 **Donghae** prev. Tonghae. NE South Korea 37°26′N 129°09′E
Dong Hai see East China Sea
160 M16 **Donghai Dao** island S China
Dong He see Omon Gol
Donghe see Wangcang
167 T9 **Đông Hơi** Quang Binh, C Vietnam 17°32′N 106°35′E
Donghua see Huating
Donghuang see Xishui
108 H10 **Dongio** Ticino, S Switzerland 46°27′N 08°58′E
Dongkan see Binhai
160 L11 **Dongkou** Hunan, S China 27°06′N 110°35′E
167 S8 **Đông Lê** Quang Binh, C Vietnam 17°52′N 105°49′E
Dongliao see Liaoyuan
Dong-nai see Đông Nai, Sông
167 U13 **Đông Nai, Sông** var. Dong-nai, Dong Noi, Donnai. ≈ S Vietnam
161 N14 **Dongnan Qiuling** plateau SE China
163 Y9 **Dongning** Heilongjiang, NE China 44°01′N 131°03′E
Dong Noi see Đông Nai, Sông
83 C14 **Dongo** Huíla, C Angola 14°35′S 15°51′E
80 E7 **Dongola** var. Donqola, Dunqulah. Northern, N Sudan 19°10′N 30°27′E
79 I17 **Dongou** Likouala, NE Congo 02°05′N 18°E
Đông Phu see Đông Xoai
Dongping see Anhua
Dong Rak, Phanom see Dângrêk, Chuŏr Phnum
Dongshan Dao see Dongchuan Dao
Dongsha Qundao see Tungsha Tao
Dongsheng see Ordos
161 S13 **Dongshi** Jap. Tōsei; prev. Tungshih. N Taiwan 24°13′N 120°54′E
161 R7 **Dongtai** Jiangsu, E China 32°50′N 120°22′E
161 N10 **Dongting Hu** var. Tung-t'ing Hu. ◎ S China
161 P10 **Dongxiang** var. Xiaogang. Jiangxi, S China 28°16′N 116°32′E
167 T13 **Đông Xoai** var. Đông Phu. Sông Be, S Vietnam 11°31′N 106°55′E
161 Q4 **Dongying** Shandong, E China 37°27′N 118°01′E
27 X8 **Doniphan** Missouri, C USA 36°39′N 90°51′W
Donja Łužica see Niederlausitz
10 G7 **Donjek** ≈ Yukon Territory, W Canada
112 E11 **Donji Lapac** Lika-Senj, W Croatia 44°33′N 15°58′E
112 H8 **Donji Miholjac** Osijek-Baranja, NE Croatia 45°45′N 18°10′E
112 P12 **Donji Milanovac** Serbia, E Serbia 44°27′N 22°06′E
112 G12 **Donji Vakuf** var. Srbobran. ◈ Federacija Bosna I Hercegovina, C Bosnia and Herzegovina
98 M6 **Donkerbroek** Fryslân, N Netherlands 52°58′N 06°15′E
167 P11 **Don Muang** ✈ (Krung Thep) Nonthaburi, C Thailand 13°51′N 100°40′E
25 S17 **Donna** Texas, SW USA 26°10′N 98°03′W
15 Q10 **Donnacona** Québec, SE Canada 46°41′N 71°46′W
Donnai see Đông Nai, Sông
29 Y16 **Donnellson** Iowa, C USA 40°38′N 91°33′W
11 O13 **Donnelly** Alberta, W Canada 55°42′N 117°06′W
35 P6 **Donner Pass** Pass California, W USA
101 F19 **Donnersberg** ▲ W Germany 49°37′N 07°54′E
Donoso see Miguel de la Borda
105 P2 **Donostia-San Sebastián** País Vasco, N Spain 43°19′N 01°59′W
115 K21 **Donoúsa** var. Donoússa. island Kykládes, Greece, Aegean Sea
Donoússa see Donoúsa
35 P8 **Don Pedro Reservoir** ⊠ California, W USA
Donqola see Dongola
126 L5 **Donskoy** Tul'skaya Oblast', W Russian Federation 54°02′N 38°27′E
81 L16 **Doolow** Sumalē, E Ethiopia 04°10′N 42°05′E
39 Q7 **Doonerak, Mount** ▲ Alaska, USA 67°54′N 150°33′W
98 J12 **Doorn** Utrecht, C Netherlands 52°02′N 05°21′E
Doornik see Tournai
31 N6 **Door Peninsula** peninsula Wisconsin, N USA
80 P13 **Dooxo Nugaaleed** var. Nogal Valley. valley E Somalia
Do Qu see Da Qu
106 B7 **Dora Baltea** anc. Duria Major. ≈ NW Italy
180 K7 **Dora, Lake** salt lake Western Australia
106 A8 **Dora Riparia** anc. Duria Minor. ≈ NW Italy
Dorbiljin see Emin
Dorbod/Dorbod Mongolzu Zizhixian see Taikang
Dorbod Mongolzu Zizhixian see Taikang
113 N18 **Đorče Petrov** var. Djorče Petrov, Gorče Petrov. N Macedonia 42°01′N 21°21′E
14 F16 **Dorchester** Ontario, S Canada 43°00′N 81°04′W
97 L24 **Dorchester** anc. Durnovaria. S England, United Kingdom 50°43′N 02°26′W
9 P7 **Dorchester, Cape** headland Baffin Island, Nunavut, NE Canada 65°25′N 77°25′W
83 D19 **Dordabis** Khomas, C Namibia 22°57′S 17°39′E
102 L12 **Dordogne** ◈ department SW France
103 N12 **Dordogne** ≈ W France
98 H13 **Dordrecht** var. Dordt, Dort. Zuid-Holland, SW Netherlands 51°48′N 04°40′E
Dordt see Dordrecht
103 P11 **Dore** ≈ C France
11 S13 **Doré Lake** Saskatchewan, C Canada 54°37′N 107°36′W
103 O12 **Dore, Monts** ▲▲ C France
101 M23 **Dorfen** Bayern, SE Germany 48°16′N 12°06′E
107 D18 **Dorgali** Sardegna, Italy, C Mediterranean Sea 40°18′N 09°34′E
159 N11 **Dorgê Co** var. Elsen Nur. ◎ C China
162 E6 **Dörgön** var. Seer. Hovd, W Mongolia 48°18′N 92°37′E
162 F7 **Dörgön Nuur** ◎ NW Mongolia
77 Q12 **Dori** N Burkina 14°03′N 00°02′W
83 E24 **Doring** ≈ S South Africa
101 E16 **Dormagen** Nordrhein-Westfalen, W Germany 51°06′N 06°49′E
103 P4 **Dormans** Marne, N France 49°03′N 03°44′E
108 E6 **Dornach** Solothurn, NW Switzerland 47°29′N 07°37′E
Dorna Watra see Vatra Dornei
108 J7 **Dornbirn** Vorarlberg, W Austria 47°25′N 09°46′E
96 I7 **Dornoch** N Scotland, United Kingdom 57°52′N 04°01′W
96 J7 **Dornoch Firth** inlet N Scotland, United Kingdom
163 P7 **Dornod** ◈ province E Mongolia
163 N10 **Dornogovĭ** ◈ province SE Mongolia
77 P10 **Doro** Tombouctou, S Mali 16°07′N 00°57′W
116 L14 **Dorobanţu** Călăraşi, S Romania 44°15′N 26°55′E
111 J22 **Dorog** Komárom-Esztergom, N Hungary 47°43′N 18°42′E
126 J4 **Dorogobuzh** Smolenskaya Oblast', W Russian Federation 54°56′N 33°16′E
116 K8 **Dorohoi** Botoşani, NE Romania 47°57′N 26°24′E
93 H15 **Dorotea** Västerbotten, N Sweden 64°17′N 16°30′E
Dorpat see Tartu
180 G10 **Dorre Island** island Western Australia
183 U5 **Dorrigo** New South Wales, SE Australia 30°22′S 152°43′E
35 N1 **Dorris** California, W USA 41°58′N 121°54′W
14 H13 **Dorset** Ontario, SE Canada 45°12′N 78°52′W
97 K23 **Dorset** cultural region S England, United Kingdom
101 E14 **Dorsten** Nordrhein-Westfalen, W Germany 51°38′N 06°58′E
Dort see Dordrecht
101 F15 **Dortmund** Nordrhein-Westfalen, W Germany 51°31′N 07°28′E
100 F12 **Dortmund-Ems-Kanal** canal W Germany
136 L17 **Dörtyol** Hatay, S Turkey 36°51′N 36°11′E
Do Rūd see Dow Rūd
79 O15 **Doruma** Orientale, N Dem. Rep. Congo 04°35′N 27°43′E
15 O12 **Dorval** ✈ (Montréal) Québec, SE Canada 45°27′N 73°46′W
162 F7 **Dörvöljin** var. Buga. Dzavhan, W Mongolia 47°42′N 94°53′E
45 T5 **Dos Bocas, Lago** ◎ C Puerto Rico
104 K14 **Dos Hermanas** Andalucía, S Spain 37°16′N 05°55′W
Dospad Dagh see Rhodope Mountains
35 P10 **Dos Palos** California, W USA 37°00′N 120°39′W
114 I11 **Dospat** Smolyan, S Bulgaria 41°39′N 24°10′E
114 H11 **Dospat, Yazovir** ⊠ SW Bulgaria
100 M11 **Dosse** ≈ NE Germany
77 S12 **Dosso** Dosso, SW Niger 13°03′N 03°10′E
77 S12 **Dosso** ◈ department SW Niger
144 G12 **Dossor** Atyrau, SW Kazakhstan 47°31′N 53°01′E
147 O10 **Do'stlik** Jizzax Viloyati, C Uzbekistan 40°37′N 67°59′E
147 V9 **Dostuk** Narynskaya Oblast', C Kyrgyzstan 41°19′N 75°40′E
145 X13 **Dostyk** prev. Druzhba. Almaty, SE Kazakhstan 45°15′N 82°29′E
23 R7 **Dothan** Alabama, S USA 31°13′N 85°23′W
39 T9 **Dot Lake** Alaska, USA 63°39′N 144°10′W
118 F12 **Dotnuva** Kaunas, C Lithuania 55°23′N 23°53′E
99 D19 **Dottignies** Hainaut, W Belgium 50°43′N 03°16′E
103 P2 **Douai** prev. Douay; anc. Duacum. Nord, N France 50°22′N 03°04′E
14 L9 **Douaire, Lac** ◎ Québec, SE Canada
79 D16 **Douala** var. Duala. Littoral, W Cameroon 04°04′N 09°43′E
79 D16 **Douala** ✈ Littoral, W Cameroon 03°57′N 09°48′E
102 F6 **Douarnenez** Finistère, NW France 48°05′N 04°20′W
102 E6 **Douarnenez, Baie de** bay NW France
Douay see Douai
25 O6 **Double Mountain Fork Brazos River** ≈ Texas, SW USA
23 O3 **Double Springs** Alabama, S USA 34°09′N 87°24′W
103 T8 **Doubs** ◈ department E France
108 C8 **Doubs** ≈ France/Switzerland
185 A22 **Doubtful Sound** sound South Island, New Zealand
184 J2 **Doubtless Bay** bay North Island, New Zealand
25 X9 **Doucette** Texas, SW USA 30°48′N 94°25′W
102 K8 **Doué-la-Fontaine** Maine-et-Loire, NW France 47°12′N 00°16′W
77 O11 **Douentza** Mopti, S Mali 14°59′N 02°57′W
65 E24 **Douglas** East Falkland, Falkland Islands
97 I16 **Douglas** ○ (Isle of Man) E Isle of Man 54°09′N 04°28′W
83 H23 **Douglas** Northern Cape, C South Africa 29°04′S 23°47′E
39 X13 **Douglas** Alexander Archipelago, Alaska, USA 58°12′N 134°18′W
37 O17 **Douglas** Arizona, SW USA 31°20′N 109°32′W
23 U7 **Douglas** Georgia, SE USA 31°30′N 82°51′W
33 Y15 **Douglas** Wyoming, C USA 42°48′N 105°23′W
21 O7 **Douglas Cape** headland Alaska, N USA 64°59′N 166°41′W
10 J14 **Douglas Channel** channel British Columbia, W Canada
182 G3 **Douglas Creek** seasonal river South Australia
31 P5 **Douglas Lake** ◎ Michigan, N USA
21 O9 **Douglas Lake** ⊠ Tennessee, S USA
39 Q13 **Douglas, Mount** ▲ Alaska, USA 58°51′N 153°31′W
194 I6 **Douglas Range** ▲▲ Alexander Island, Antarctica
161 S14 **Douliu** prev. Touliu. C Taiwan 23°44′N 120°27′E
103 O2 **Doullens** Somme, N France 50°09′N 02°21′E
Douma see Dūmā
79 F15 **Doumé** Est, E Cameroon 04°14′N 13°27′E
99 E21 **Dour** Hainaut, S Belgium 50°24′N 03°47′E
59 K18 **Dourada, Serra** ▲▲ S Brazil
59 I21 **Dourados** Mato Grosso do Sul, S Brazil 22°09′S 54°52′W
103 N5 **Dourdan** Essonne, N France 48°33′N 01°58′E
104 I6 **Douro** Sp. Duero. ≈ Portugal/Spain see also Duero
Douro see Duero
104 G6 **Douro Litoral** former province N Portugal
Douvres see Dover
102 K15 **Douze** ≈ SW France
183 P17 **Dover** Tasmania, SE Australia 43°19′S 147°01′E
97 Q22 **Dover** Fr. Douvres, Lat. Dubris Portus. SE England, United Kingdom 51°08′N 01°19′E
21 Y3 **Dover** state capital Delaware, NE USA 39°10′N 75°32′W
19 P9 **Dover** New Hampshire, NE USA 43°10′N 70°50′W
18 J14 **Dover** New Jersey, NE USA 40°51′N 74°33′W
31 U12 **Dover** Ohio, N USA 40°31′N 81°28′W
20 H8 **Dover** Tennessee, S USA 36°30′N 87°50′W
97 Q23 **Dover, Strait of** var. Straits of Dover, Fr. Pas de Calais. strait England, United Kingdom/France
Dover, Straits of see Dover, Strait of
Dovlen see Devin
94 G11 **Dovre** Oppland, S Norway 61°59′N 09°16′E
94 G10 **Dovrefjell** plateau S Norway
Dovsk see Dowsk
83 M14 **Dowa** Central, C Malawi 13°40′S 33°55′E
31 O10 **Dowagiac** Michigan, N USA 41°58′N 86°06′W
Dow Gonbadān see Do Gonbadān
148 M2 **Dowlatābād** Fāryāb, N Afghanistan 36°30′N 64°51′E
97 G16 **Down** cultural region SE Northern Ireland, United Kingdom
33 R16 **Downey** Idaho, NW USA 42°25′N 112°06′W
35 P5 **Downieville** California, W USA 39°34′N 120°49′W
97 G16 **Downpatrick** Ir. Dún Pádraig. SE Northern Ireland, United Kingdom 54°20′N 05°43′W
26 M3 **Downs** Kansas, C USA 39°30′N 98°33′W
18 J12 **Downsville** New York, NE USA 42°03′N 74°59′W
142 L7 **Dow Rūd** var. Do Rūd, Durud. Lorestān, W Iran 33°28′N 49°04′E
29 V12 **Dows** Iowa, C USA 42°39′N 93°30′W
119 O17 **Dowsk** Rus. Dovsk. Homyel'skaya Voblasts', SE Belarus 53°09′N 30°28′E
35 Q4 **Doyle** California, W USA 40°00′N 120°06′W
18 I15 **Doylestown** Pennsylvania, NE USA 40°18′N 75°08′W
Doyransko, Ezero see Doïráni, Límni
114 I8 **Doyrentsi** Lovech, N Bulgaria 43°13′N 24°46′E
164 G11 **Dōzen** island Oki-shotō, SW Japan
14 K9 **Dozois, Réservoir** ⊠ Québec, SE Canada
74 D9 **Drâa** seasonal river S Morocco
Drâa, Hammada du see Dra, Hamada du
Drabble see José Enrique Rodó
117 Q5 **Drabiv** Cherkas'ka Oblast', C Ukraine 49°57′N 32°10′E
Drable see José Enrique Rodó
103 S13 **Drac** ≈ E France
Drač/Draç see Durrës
60 I8 **Dracena** São Paulo, S Brazil 21°27′S 51°30′W
98 M6 **Drachten** Fryslân, N Netherlands 53°07′N 06°06′E
92 H11 **Drag** Lapp. Ájluokta. Nordland, C Norway 68°02′N 16°E
116 L14 **Dragalina** Călăraşi, SE Romania 44°26′N 27°19′E
116 I14 **Draganesti-Olt** Olt, S Romania 44°06′N 25°00′E
116 J14 **Drăgăneşti-Vlaşca** Teleorman, S Romania 44°05′N 25°39′E
116 I13 **Drăgăşani** Vâlcea, SW Romania 44°40′N 24°16′E
114 G9 **Dragoman** Sofiya, W Bulgaria 42°32′N 22°56′E
115 L25 **Dragonáda** island SE Greece
Dragonera, Isla see Sa Dragonera
45 T14 **Dragon's Mouths, The** strait Trinidad and Tobago/Venezuela
95 J23 **Dragør** Sjælland, E Denmark 55°36′N 12°42′E
114 F10 **Dragovishtitsa** Kysutendil, W Bulgaria 42°22′N 22°39′E
103 U15 **Draguignan** Var, SE France 43°31′N 06°31′E
74 E9 **Dra, Hamada du** var. Hammada du Drâa, Haut Plateau du Dra. plateau W Algeria
Dra, Haut Plateau du see Dra, Hamada du
119 H19 **Drahichyn** Pol. Drohiczyn Poleski, Rus. Drogichin. Brestskaya Voblasts', SW Belarus 52°11′N 25°10′E
29 N4 **Drake** North Dakota, N USA 47°54′N 100°23′W
83 K23 **Drakensberg** ▲▲ Lesotho/South Africa
194 F3 **Drake Passage** passage Atlantic Ocean/Pacific Ocean
114 L8 **Dralfa** Tŭrgovishte, N Bulgaria 43°17′N 26°25′E
114 I12 **Dráma** var. Dhráma. Anatolikí Makedonía kai Thráki, NE Greece 41°09′N 24°10′E
Dramburg see Drawsko Pomorskie
95 H15 **Drammen** Buskerud, S Norway 59°44′N 10°12′E
95 H15 **Drammensfjorden** fjord S Norway
92 H1 **Drangajökull** ▲ NW Iceland 66°13′N 22°18′W
95 F16 **Drangedal** Telemark, S Norway 59°05′N 09°05′E
92 I2 **Drangsnes** Vestfirdhir, NW Iceland 65°42′N 21°27′W
Drann see Dravinja
109 T10 **Drau** var. Drava, Eng. Drave, Hung. Dráva. ≈ C Europe see also Drava
Drau see Drava
84 I11 **Drava** var. Drau, Eng. Drave, Hung. Dráva. ≈ C Europe see also Drau
Dráva/Drave see Drau/Drava
109 W10 **Dravinja** Ger. Drann. ≈ NE Slovenia
109 V9 **Dravograd** Ger. Unterdrauburg; prev. Spodnji Dravograd. N Slovenia 46°36′N 15°00′E
110 F10 **Drawa** ≈ NW Poland
110 F9 **Drawno** Zachodnio-pomorskie, NW Poland 53°12′N 15°44′E
110 F9 **Drawsko Pomorskie** Ger. Dramburg. Zachodnio-pomorskie, NW Poland 53°32′N 15°48′E
29 R3 **Drayton** North Dakota, N USA 48°34′N 97°10′W
11 P14 **Drayton Valley** Alberta, SW Canada 53°15′N 115°00′W
186 B6 **Dreikikir** East Sepik, NW Papua New Guinea 03°42′S 142°46′E
Dreikirchen see Teiuş
98 N7 **Drenthe** ◈ province NE Netherlands
115 H15 **Drépano, Akrotírio** var. Akrotírio Drepanon. headland N Greece 39°56′N 23°57′E
Drepanum see Trapani
14 D17 **Dresden** Ontario, S Canada 42°34′N 82°09′W
101 O16 **Dresden** Sachsen, E Germany 51°03′N 13°43′E
20 G8 **Dresden** Tennessee, S USA 36°17′N 88°42′W
118 M11 **Dretun'** Vitsyebskaya Voblasts', N Belarus 55°41′N 29°13′E
102 M5 **Dreux** anc. Drocae, Durocasses. Eure-et-Loir, C France 48°44′N 01°23′E
94 I11 **Drevsjø** Hedmark, S Norway 61°52′N 12°01′E
22 K3 **Drew** Mississippi, S USA 33°48′N 90°31′W
110 F10 **Drezdenko** Ger. Driesen. Lubuskie, W Poland 52°51′N 15°50′E
98 J12 **Driebergen** var. Driebergen-Rijsenburg. Utrecht, C Netherlands 52°03′N 05°17′E
Driebergen-Rijsenburg see Driebergen
Driesen see Drezdenko
97 N16 **Driffield** E England, United Kingdom 54°00′N 00°28′W
65 D25 **Driftwood Point** headland East Falkland, Falkland Islands 52°15′S 59°00′W
33 S14 **Driggs** Idaho, NW USA 43°44′N 111°06′W
Drin see Drinit, Lumi i
112 K12 **Drina** ≈ Bosnia and Herzegovina/Serbia
Drin, Gulf of see Drinit, Gjiri i
113 M16 **Drini i Bardhë** Serb. Beli Drim. ≈ Albania/Serbia
113 K18 **Drinit, Gjiri i** var. Pellg i Drinit, Eng. Gulf of Drin. gulf NW Albania
113 L17 **Drinit, Lumi i** var. Drin. ≈ NW Albania
Drinit, Pellg i see Drinit, Gjiri i
Drinit të Zi, Lumi i see Black Drin
113 L22 **Dríno** var. Drino, Drínos Pótamos, Alb. Lumi i Drinos. ≈ Albania/Greece
Drinos, Lumi i/Drínos Pótamos see Dríno
25 S11 **Dripping Springs** Texas, SW USA 30°11′N 98°04′W
25 S15 **Driscoll** Texas, SW USA 27°40′N 97°45′W
22 H5 **Driskill Mountain** ▲ Louisiana, S USA 32°25′N 92°54′W
Drissa see Drysa
94 G10 **Driva** ≈ S Norway
112 E13 **Drniš** It. Šibenik-Knin. Šibenik-Knin, S Croatia 43°51′N 16°10′E
95 H15 **Drøbak** Akershus, S Norway 59°40′N 10°40′E
116 G13 **Drobeta-Turnu Severin** prev. Turnu Severin. Mehedinţi, SW Romania 44°39′N 22°40′E
Drocae see Dreux
116 M8 **Drochia** Rus. Drokiya. N Moldova 48°02′N 27°46′E
97 F17 **Drogheda** Ir. Droichead Átha. NE Ireland 53°43′N 06°21′W
Drogichin see Drahichyn
Drogobych see Drohobych
Drohiczyn Poleski see Drahichyn
116 H6 **Drohobych** Pol. Drohobycz, Rus. Drogobych. L'vivs'ka Oblast', NW Ukraine 49°22′N 23°33′E
Drohobycz see Drohobych
Droichead Átha see Drogheda
Droicheadna Bandan see Bandon
Droichead na Banna see Banbridge
Droim Mór see Dromore
Drokiya see Drochia
103 R13 **Drôme** ◈ department E France
103 S13 **Drôme** ≈ E France
97 G15 **Dromore** Ir. Droim Mór. SE Northern Ireland, United Kingdom 54°25′N 06°09′W
106 A9 **Dronero** Piemonte, NE Italy 44°28′N 07°25′E
102 L12 **Dronne** ≈ SW France
195 T3 **Dronning Fabiolafjella** var. Mount Victor. ▲ Antarctica 72°49′S 33°01′E
195 Q3 **Dronning Maud Land** physical region Antarctica
98 K6 **Dronrijp** Fris. Dronryp. Fryslân, N Netherlands 53°12′N 05°37′E
Dronryp see Dronrijp
98 L9 **Dronten** Flevoland, C Netherlands 52°31′N 05°41′E
Drontheim see Trondheim
102 L13 **Dropt** ≈ SW France
149 T4 **Drosh** Khyber Pakhtunkhwa, NW Pakistan 35°33′N 71°48′E
Drossen see Ośno Lubuskie
Drug see Durg
Drujba see Pitnak
118 I12 **Drūkšiai** ◎ NE Lithuania
Druk-yul see Bhutan
11 Q16 **Drumheller** Alberta, SW Canada 51°28′N 112°42′W
33 Q10 **Drummond** Montana, NW USA 46°39′N 113°12′W
31 R4 **Drummond Island** island Michigan, N USA
Drummond Island see Tabiteuea
21 X7 **Drummond, Lake** ◎ Virginia, NE USA
15 P12 **Drummondville** Québec, SE Canada 45°52′N 72°28′W
39 T11 **Drum, Mount** ▲ Alaska, USA 62°11′N 144°37′W
27 O9 **Drumright** Oklahoma, C USA 35°59′N 96°36′W
99 J14 **Drunen** Noord-Brabant, S Netherlands 51°41′N 05°08′E
Druskienniki see Druskininkai
119 F15 **Druskininkai** Pol. Druskieniki. Alytus, S Lithuania 54°00′N 24°00′E
98 K13 **Druten** Gelderland, SE Netherlands 51°53′N 05°37′E
118 K11 **Druya** Vitsyebskaya Voblasts', NW Belarus 55°47′N 27°27′E
117 S2 **Druzhba** Sums'ka Oblast', NE Ukraine 52°01′N 33°56′E

◆ Country
● Country Capital
◇ Dependent Territory
○ Dependent Territory Capital
◈ Administrative Regions
✈ International Airport
▲ Mountain
▲▲ Mountain Range
✱ Volcano
≈ River
◎ Lake
⊠ Reservoir

Druzhba see Dostyk, Kazakhstan
Druzhba see Pitnak, Uzbekistan
123 R7 **Druzhina** Respublika Sakha (Yakutiya), NE Russian Federation 68°01′N 144°58′E
117 X7 **Druzhkivka** Donets'ka Oblast', E Ukraine 48°38′N 37°31′E
112 E12 **Drvar** Federacija Bosna I Hercegovina, W Bosnia and Herzegovina 44°21′N 16°24′E
113 G15 **Drvenik** Split-Dalmacija, SE Croatia 43°10′N 17°13′E
114 K9 **Dryanovo** Gabrovo, N Bulgaria 42°58′N 25°28′E
26 G7 **Dry Cimarron River** ≈ Kansas/Oklahoma, C USA
12 B11 **Dryden** Ontario, C Canada 49°48′N 92°48′W
24 M11 **Dryden** Texas, SW USA 30°01′N 102°06′W
195 Q14 **Drygalski Ice Tongue** *ice feature* Antarctica
118 L11 **Drysa** *Rus.* Drissa. ≈ N Belarus
23 V17 **Dry Tortugas** *island* Florida, SE USA
79 D15 **Dschang** Ouest, W Cameroon 05°28′N 10°02′E
54 J5 **Duaca** Lara, N Venezuela 10°22′N 69°08′W
Duacum see Douai
Duala see Douala
45 N9 **Duarte, Pico** ▲ C Dominican Republic 19°02′N 70°57′W
140 J5 **Ḑubā** Tabūk, NW Saudi Arabia 27°26′N 35°42′E
Dubai see Dubayy
117 N9 **Dubăsari** *Rus.* Dubossary. NE Moldova 47°16′N 29°07′E
117 N9 **Dubăsari Reservoir** ⊠ NE Moldova
8 M10 **Dubawnt** ≈ Nunavut, NW Canada
8 L9 **Dubawnt Lake** ◎ Northwest Territories/Nunavut, N Canada
30 L6 **Du Bay, Lake** ⊠ Wisconsin, N USA
141 U7 **Dubayy** *Eng.* Dubai. Dubayy, NE United Arab Emirates 25°11′N 55°18′E
141 W7 **Dubayy** *Eng.* Dubai. ✈ Dubayy, NE United Arab Emirates 25°15′N 55°22′E
183 R7 **Dubbo** New South Wales, SE Australia 32°16′S 148°41′E
108 G7 **Dübendorf** Zürich, NW Switzerland 47°23′N 08°37′E
97 F18 **Dublin** *Ir.* Baile Átha Cliath; *anc.* Eblana. ● (Ireland) Dublin, E Ireland 53°20′N 06°15′W
23 U5 **Dublin** Georgia, SE USA 32°32′N 82°54′W
25 R7 **Dublin** Texas, SW USA 32°05′N 98°20′W
97 G18 **Dublin** *Ir.* Baile Átha Cliath; *anc.* Eblana. *cultural region* E Ireland
97 G18 **Dublin Airport** ✈ Dublin, E Ireland 53°25′N 06°18′W
189 V12 **Dublon** *var.* Tonoas. *island* Chuuk Islands, C Micronesia
126 K2 **Dubna** Moskovskaya Oblast', W Russian Federation 56°45′N 37°09′E
111 G19 **Dubňany** *Ger.* Dubnian. Jihomoravský Kraj, SE Czech Republic 48°54′N 17°00′E
Dubnian see Dubňany
111 I19 **Dubnica nad Váhom** *Hung.* Máriatölgyes; *prev.* Dubnicz. Trenčiansky Kraj, W Slovakia 48°58′N 18°10′E
Dubnicz see Dubnica nad Váhom
116 K4 **Dubno** Rivnens'ka Oblast', NW Ukraine 50°28′N 25°40′E
33 R13 **Dubois** Idaho, NW USA 44°10′N 112°13′W
18 D13 **Du Bois** Pennsylvania, NE USA 41°07′N 78°45′W
33 T14 **Dubois** Wyoming, C USA 43°31′N 109°37′W
Dubossary see Dubăsari
127 O10 **Dubovka** Volgogradskaya Oblast', SW Russian Federation 49°10′N 48°49′E
76 H14 **Dubréka** SW Guinea 09°48′N 13°31′W
14 B7 **Dubreuilville** Ontario, S Canada 48°21′N 84°31′W
Dubris Portus see Dover
119 L20 **Dubrova** Homyel'skaya Voblasts', SE Belarus 51°47′N 28°13′E
Dubrovačko-Neretvanska Županija see Dubrovnik-Neretva
126 I5 **Dubrovka** Bryanskaya Oblast', W Russian Federation 53°44′N 33°27′E
113 H16 **Dubrovnik** *It.* Ragusa. Dubrovnik-Neretva, SE Croatia 42°40′N 18°06′E
113 I16 **Dubrovnik** ✈ Dubrovnik-Neretva, SE Croatia 42°34′N 18°17′E
113 F16 **Dubrovnik-Neretva** *off.* Dubrovačko-Neretvanska Županija. ◈ *province* SE Croatia
Dubrovno see Dubrowna
116 L2 **Dubrovytsya** Rivnens'ka Oblast', NW Ukraine 51°34′N 26°37′E
119 O14 **Dubrowna** *Rus.* Dubrovno. Vitsyebskaya Voblasts', N Belarus 54°35′N 30°41′E
29 Z13 **Dubuque** Iowa, C USA 42°30′N 90°40′W
118 E12 **Dubysa** ≈ C Lithuania
Đưc Cơ see Chư Ty
191 V12 **Duc de Gloucester, Îles du** *Eng.* Duke of Gloucester Islands. *island group* C French Polynesia
111 C15 **Duchcov** *Ger.* Dux. Ústecký Kraj, NW Czech Republic 50°37′N 13°45′E
37 N3 **Duchesne** Utah, W USA 40°09′N 110°24′W
191 P17 **Ducie Island** *atoll* E Pitcairn Islands
11 W15 **Duck Bay** Manitoba, S Canada 52°11′N 100°08′W
23 X17 **Duck Key** *island* Florida Keys, Florida, SE USA
11 T14 **Duck Lake** Saskatchewan, S Canada 52°52′N 106°12′W
11 V15 **Duck Mountain** ▲▲ Manitoba, S Canada
20 I9 **Duck River** ≈ Tennessee, S USA
20 M10 **Ducktown** Tennessee, S USA 35°01′N 84°24′W
167 U10 **Đưc Phô** Quang Ngai, C Vietnam 14°56′N 108°55′E
Đưc Tho see Lin Camh
Đưc Trong see Liên Nghia
D-U-D see Dalap-Uliga-Djarrit
153 N15 **Dūddhinagar** *var.* Dūdhi. Uttar Pradesh, N India 24°09′N 83°16′E
99 M25 **Dudelange** *var.* Forge du Sud, *Ger.* Dudelingen. Luxembourg, S Luxembourg 49°28′N 06°05′E
Dudelingen see Dudelange
101 J15 **Duderstadt** Niedersachsen, C Germany 51°31′N 10°16′E
Dūdhi see Dūddhinagar
122 K8 **Dudinka** Krasnoyarskiy Kray, N Russian Federation 69°27′N 86°13′E
97 L20 **Dudley** C England, United Kingdom 52°30′N 02°05′W
154 G13 **Dudna** ≈ C India
76 L16 **Duékoué** W Ivory Coast 05°50′N 05°22′W
104 M5 **Dueñas** Castilla y León, N Spain 41°52′N 04°33′W
104 K4 **Duerna** ≈ NW Spain
105 O6 **Duero** *Port.* Douro. ≈ Portugal/Spain *see also* Douro
Duero see Douro
Duesseldorf see Düsseldorf
21 P12 **Due West** South Carolina, SE USA 34°19′N 82°23′W
195 P11 **Dufek Coast** *physical region* Antarctica
99 H17 **Duffel** Antwerpen, C Belgium 51°06′N 04°30′E
35 S2 **Duffer Peak** ▲ Nevada, W USA 41°40′N 118°45′W
187 Q9 **Duff Islands** *island group* E Solomon Islands
Dufour, Pizzo/Dufour, Punta see Dufour Spitze
108 E12 **Dufour Spitze** *It.* Pizzo Dufour, Punta Dufour. ▲ Italy/Switzerland 45°54′N 07°50′E
112 D9 **Duga Resa** Karlovac, C Croatia 45°25′N 15°30′E
22 H5 **Dugdemona River** ≈ Louisiana, S USA
154 J12 **Duggīpar** Mahārāshtra, C India 21°06′N 80°10′E
112 B13 **Dugi Otok** *var.* Isola Grossa, *It.* Isola Lunga. *island* W Croatia
113 F14 **Dugopolje** Split-Dalmacija, S Croatia 43°35′N 16°35′E
160 L8 **Du He** ≈ C China
54 M11 **Duida, Cerro** ▲ S Venezuela 03°21′N 65°45′W
Duinekerke see Dunkerque
101 E15 **Duisburg** *prev.* Duisburg-Hamborn. Nordrhein-Westfalen, W Germany 51°25′N 06°47′E
Duisburg-Hamborn see Duisburg
99 F14 **Duiveland** *island* SW Netherlands
98 M12 **Duiven** Gelderland, E Netherlands 51°57′N 06°02′E
139 W10 **Dujaylah, Hawr ad** ◎ S Iraq
160 H9 **Dujiangyan** *var.* Guanxian, Guan Xian. Sichuan, C China 31°01′N 103°40′E
81 L18 **Dujuuma** Shabeellaha Hoose, S Somalia 01°04′N 42°37′E
Dūkān see Dokan
39 Z14 **Duke Island** *island* Alexander Archipelago, Alaska, USA
Dukelský Priesmy/ Dukelský Průsmyk see Dukla Pass
Duke of Gloucester Islands see Duc de Gloucester, Îles du
81 F14 **Duk Faiwil** Jonglei, E South Sudan 07°30′N 31°27′E
141 T7 **Dukhān** C Qatar 25°29′N 50°48′E
Dukhan Heights see Dukhān, Jabal
143 N16 **Dukhān, Jabal** *var.* Dukhan Heights. *hill range* S Qatar
127 Q7 **Dukhovnitskoye** Saratovskaya Oblast', W Russian Federation 52°31′N 48°32′E
126 H4 **Dukhovshchina** Smolenskaya Oblast', W Russian Federation 55°15′N 32°22′E
Dukielska, Przełęcz see Dukla Pass
111 N17 **Dukla** Podkarpackie, SE Poland 49°33′N 21°40′E
Duklai Hág see Dukla Pass
111 N18 **Dukla Pass** *Cz.* Dukelský Průsmyk, *Ger.* Dukla-Pass, *Hung.* Duklai Hág, *Pol.* Przełęcz Dukielska, *Slvk.* Dukelský Priesmy. *pass* Poland/Slovakia
Dukla-Pass see Dukla Pass
Dukou see Panzhihua
118 I12 **Dūkštas** Utena, E Lithuania 55°32′N 26°21′E
Dulaan see Herlenbayan-Ulaan
159 R10 **Dulan** *var.* Qagan Us. Qinghai, C China 36°11′N 97°51′E
37 R8 **Dulce** New Mexico, SW USA 36°55′N 107°00′W
43 N16 **Dulce, Golfo** *gulf* S Costa Rica
Dulce, Golfo see Izabal, Lago de
42 K6 **Dulce Nombre de Culmí** Olancho, C Honduras 15°09′N 85°37′W
62 L9 **Dulce, Río** ≈ C Argentina
123 Q9 **Dulgalakh** ≈ NE Russian Federation
114 M8 **Dŭlgopol** Varna, E Bulgaria 43°05′N 27°24′E
153 V14 **Dullabchara** Assam, NE India 24°25′N 92°22′E
20 D3 **Dulles** ✈ (Washington DC)Virginia, NE USA 39°00′N 77°27′W
101 E14 **Dülmen** Nordrhein-Westfalen, W Germany 51°51′N 07°17′E
114 M7 **Dulovo** Silistra, NE Bulgaria 43°51′N 27°10′E
29 W5 **Duluth** Minnesota, N USA 46°47′N 92°06′W
138 H7 **Dūmā** *Fr.* Douma. Rīf Dimashq, SW Syria 33°33′N 36°24′E
171 O8 **Dumagasa Point** *headland* Mindanao, S Philippines 07°01′N 121°54′E
171 P6 **Dumaguete** *var.* Dumaguete City. Negros, C Philippines 09°16′N 123°17′E
Dumaguete City see Dumaguete
168 J10 **Dumai** Sumatera, W Indonesia 01°39′N 101°28′E
183 T4 **Dumaresq River** ≈ New South Wales/Queensland, SE Australia
27 W13 **Dumas** Arkansas, C USA 33°53′N 91°29′W
25 N1 **Dumas** Texas, SW USA 35°51′N 101°57′W
138 I7 **Ḑumayr** Rīf Dimashq, W Syria 33°36′N 36°28′E
96 I12 **Dumbarton** W Scotland, United Kingdom 55°57′N 04°35′W
96 I12 **Dumbarton** *cultural region* C Scotland, United Kingdom
187 Q17 **Dumbéa** Province Sud, S New Caledonia 22°11′S 166°27′E
111 K19 **Ďumbier** *Ger.* Djumbir, *Hung.* Gyömbér. ▲ C Slovakia 48°54′N 19°36′E
116 I11 **Dumbrăveni** *Ger.* Elisabethstedt, *Hung.* Erzsébetváros; *prev.* Ebesfalva, Eppeschdorf, Ibașfalău. Sibiu, C Romania 46°14′N 24°34′E
116 L12 **Dumbrăveni** Vrancea, E Romania 45°31′N 27°09′E
97 J14 **Dumfries** S Scotland, United Kingdom 55°04′N 03°37′W
97 J14 **Dumfries** *cultural region* SW Scotland, United Kingdom
153 R15 **Dumka** Jhārkhand, NE India 24°17′N 87°15′E
Dümmer see Dümmersee
100 G12 **Dümmersee** *var.* Dümmer. ◎ NW Germany
14 J11 **Dumoine** ≈ Québec, SE Canada
14 J10 **Dumoine, Lac** ◎ Québec, SE Canada
195 V16 **Dumont d'Urville** *French research station* Antarctica 66°24′S 139°38′E
195 W15 **Dumont d'Urville Sea** *sea* S Pacific Ocean
14 K11 **Dumont, Lac** ◎ Québec, SE Canada
75 W7 **Dumyāt** *var.* Dumyât, *Eng.* Damietta. N Egypt 31°26′N 31°48′E
Duna see Danube, C Europe
Düna see Western Dvina
Duna see Don, Russian Federation
Dünaburg see Daugavpils
111 J24 **Dunaföldvár** Tolna, C Hungary 46°48′N 18°55′E
Dunaj see Wien, Austria
Dunaj see Danube, C Europe
111 L18 **Dunajec** ≈ S Poland
111 H21 **Dunajská Streda** *Hung.* Dunaszerdahely. Trnavský Kraj, W Slovakia 48°N 17°28′E
Dunapentele see Dunaújváros
Dunărea see Danube
116 M13 **Dunărea Veche, Brațul** ≈ SE Romania
117 N13 **Dunării, Delta** *delta* SE Romania
Dunaszerdahely see Dunajská Streda
111 J23 **Dunaújváros** *prev.* Dunapentele, Sztálinváros. Fejér, C Hungary 47°N 18°55′E
Dunav see Danube
114 J8 **Dunavska Ravnina** *Eng.* Danubian Plain. *lowlands* N Bulgaria
114 G7 **Dunavtsi** Vidin, NW Bulgaria 43°54′N 22°49′E
123 S15 **Dunay** Primorskiy Kray, SE Russian Federation 42°53′N 132°20′E
Dunayevtsy see Dunayivtsi
116 L7 **Dunayivtsi** *Rus.* Dunayevtsy. Khmel'nyts'ka Oblast', NW Ukraine 48°56′N 26°50′E
185 F22 **Dunback** Otago, South Island, New Zealand 45°22′S 170°37′E
10 L17 **Duncan** Vancouver Island, British Columbia, SW Canada 48°46′N 123°10′W
37 O15 **Duncan** Arizona, SW USA 32°43′N 109°06′W
26 M12 **Duncan** Oklahoma, C USA 34°30′N 97°57′W
Duncan Island see Pinzón, Isla
151 Q20 **Duncan Passage** *strait* Andaman Sea/Bay of Bengal
96 K6 **Duncansby Head** *headland* N Scotland, United Kingdom 58°37′N 03°01′W
14 G12 **Dunchurch** Ontario, S Canada 45°36′N 79°54′W
118 D7 **Dundaga** NW Latvia 57°29′N 22°19′E
14 G14 **Dundalk** Ontario, S Canada 44°11′N 80°22′W
97 F16 **Dundalk** *Ir.* Dún Dealgan. Louth, NE Ireland 54°01′N 06°25′W
21 X3 **Dundalk** Maryland, NE USA 39°15′N 76°31′W
97 F16 **Dundalk Bay** *Ir.* Cuan Dhún Dealgan. *bay* NE Ireland
14 G16 **Dundas** Ontario, S Canada 43°16′N 79°55′W
180 L12 **Dundas, Lake** *salt lake* Western Australia
Dundbürd see Batnorov
Dún Dealgan see Dundalk
15 N13 **Dundee** Québec, SE Canada 45°01′N 74°27′W
83 K22 **Dundee** KwaZulu/Natal, E South Africa 28°09′S 30°12′E
96 K11 **Dundee** E Scotland, United Kingdom 56°28′N 03°W
31 R10 **Dundee** Michigan, N USA 41°57′N 83°39′W
25 R5 **Dundee** Texas, SW USA 33°43′N 98°52′W
194 H3 **Dundee Island** *island* Antarctica
162 L9 **Dundgovĭ** ◈ *province* C Mongolia
97 G16 **Dundrum Bay** *Ir.* Cuan Dhún Droma. *inlet* NW Irish Sea
11 T15 **Dundurn** Saskatchewan, S Canada 51°43′N 106°27′W
Dund-Us see Hovd
Dund-Us see Hovd
185 F23 **Dunedin** Otago, South Island, New Zealand 45°52′S 170°31′E
183 R7 **Dunedoo** New South Wales, SE Australia 32°04′S 149°23′E
97 D14 **Dunfanaghy** *Ir.* Dún Fionnachaidh. NW Ireland 55°11′N 07°59′W
96 J12 **Dunfermline** C Scotland, United Kingdom 56°04′N 03°29′W
Dún Fionnachaidh see Dunfanaghy
149 V10 **Dunga Bunga** Punjab, E Pakistan 29°51′N 73°19′E
97 F15 **Dungannon** *Ir.* Dún Geanainn. C Northern Ireland, United Kingdom 54°31′N 06°46′W
Dun Garbháin see Dungarvan
152 F15 **Dūngarpur** Rājasthān, N India 23°50′N 73°43′E
97 E21 **Dungarvan** *Ir.* Dun Garbháin. Waterford, S Ireland 52°05′N 07°37′W
101 N21 **Dungau** *cultural region* SE Germany
Dún Geanainn see Dungannon
97 P23 **Dungeness** *headland* SE England, United Kingdom 50°55′N 00°58′E
63 I23 **Dungeness, Punta** *headland* S Argentina 52°25′S 68°25′W
Dungloe see Dunglow
97 D14 **Dunglow** *var.* Dungloe, *Ir.* An Clochán Liath. Donegal, NW Ireland 54°57′N 08°22′W
183 T7 **Dungog** New South Wales, SE Australia 32°24′S 151°45′E
79 O16 **Dungu** Orientale, NE Dem. Rep. Congo 03°40′N 28°32′E
168 L8 **Dungun** *var.* Kuala Dungun. Terengganu, Peninsular Malaysia 04°47′N 103°26′E
80 I6 **Dungûnab** Red Sea, NE Sudan 21°10′N 37°09′E
15 P13 **Dunham** Québec, SE Canada 45°08′N 72°48′W
Dunheved see Launceston
Dunholme see Durham
163 X10 **Dunhua** Jilin, NE China 43°22′N 128°12′E
159 P8 **Dunhuang** Gansu, N China 40°10′N 94°40′E
182 L12 **Dunkeld** Victoria, SE Australia 37°41′S 142°19′E
103 O1 **Dunkerque** *Eng.* Dunkirk, *Flem.* Duinekerke; *prev.* Dunquerque. Nord, N France 51°06′N 02°34′E
97 K23 **Dunkery Beacon** ▲ SW England, United Kingdom 51°10′N 03°36′W
18 C11 **Dunkirk** New York, NE USA 42°28′N 79°19′W
Dunkirk see Dunkerque
77 P17 **Dunkwa** SW Ghana 05°59′N 01°45′W
97 G18 **Dún Laoghaire** *Eng.* Dunleary; *prev.* Kingstown. E Ireland 53°17′N 06°08′W
29 S14 **Dunlap** Iowa, C USA 41°51′N 95°36′W
20 L10 **Dunlap** Tennessee, S USA 35°22′N 85°23′W
Dunleary see Dún Laoghaire
Dún Mánmhaí see Dunmanway
97 B21 **Dunmanway** *Ir.* Dún Mánmhaí. Cork, SW Ireland 51°43′N 09°07′W
18 I13 **Dunmore** Pennsylvania, NE USA 41°25′N 75°37′W
21 U10 **Dunn** North Carolina, SE USA 35°18′N 78°36′W
Dún na nGall see Donegal
23 V11 **Dunnellon** Florida, SE USA 29°03′N 82°27′W
96 J6 **Dunnet Head** *headland* N Scotland, United Kingdom 58°40′N 03°27′W
29 N14 **Dunning** Nebraska, C USA 41°49′N 100°04′W
65 B24 **Dunnose Head Settlement** West Falkland, Falkland Islands 51°24′S 60°29′W
14 G17 **Dunnville** Ontario, S Canada 42°54′N 79°36′W
Dún Pádraig see Downpatrick
Dunquerque see Dunkerque
Dunqulah see Dongola
96 L12 **Duns** SE Scotland, United Kingdom 55°46′N 02°13′W
29 N2 **Dunseith** North Dakota, N USA 48°48′N 100°03′W
35 N2 **Dunsmuir** California, W USA 41°12′N 122°19′W
97 N21 **Dunstable** *Lat.* Durocobrivae. E England, United Kingdom 51°53′N 00°32′W
185 D21 **Dunstan Mountains** ▲▲ South Island, New Zealand
103 O9 **Dun-sur-Auron** Cher, C France 46°52′N 02°40′E
185 F21 **Duntroon** Canterbury, South Island, New Zealand 44°52′S 170°40′E
149 T10 **Dunyāpur** Punjab, E Pakistan 29°48′N 71°48′E
163 U5 **Duobukur He** ≈ NE China
163 R12 **Duolun** *var.* Dolonnur. Nei Mongol Zizhiqu, N China 42°11′N 116°30′E
167 R14 **Dương Đông** Kiên Giang, S Vietnam 10°15′N 103°58′E
114 G10 **Dupnitsa** *prev.* Marek, Stanke Dimitrov. Kyustendil, W Bulgaria 42°16′N 23°07′E
28 L8 **Dupree** South Dakota, N USA 45°03′N 101°36′W
33 Q7 **Dupuyer** Montana, NW USA 48°13′N 112°34′W
141 Y11 **Duqm** *var.* Daqm. E Oman 19°42′N 57°40′E
63 F23 **Duque de York, Isla** *island* S Chile
181 N4 **Durack Range** ▲▲ Western Australia
136 K10 **Durağan** Sinop, N Turkey 41°26′N 35°03′E
103 S15 **Durance** ≈ SE France
31 R9 **Durand** Michigan, N USA 42°54′N 83°58′W
30 I6 **Durand** Wisconsin, N USA 44°37′N 91°56′W
40 K10 **Durango** *var.* Victoria de Durango. Durango, W Mexico 24°03′N 104°38′W
105 P3 **Durango** País Vasco, N Spain 43°10′N 02°38′W
37 Q8 **Durango** Colorado, C USA 37°13′N 107°51′W
40 J9 **Durango** ◈ *state* C Mexico
114 O7 **Durankulak** *Rom.* Răcari; *prev.* Blatnitsa, Duranulac. Dobrich, NE Bulgaria 43°41′N 28°31′E
22 L4 **Durant** Mississippi, S USA 33°04′N 89°51′W
27 P13 **Durant** Oklahoma, C USA 33°59′N 96°24′W
Duranulac see Durankulak
105 N6 **Duratón** ≈ N Spain
61 E19 **Durazno** *var.* San Pedro de Durazno. Durazno, C Uruguay 33°22′S 56°31′W
61 E19 **Durazno** ◈ *department* C Uruguay
Durazzo see Durrës
83 K23 **Durban** *var.* Port Natal. KwaZulu/Natal, E South Africa 29°51′S 31°E
83 K23 **Durban** ✈ KwaZulu/Natal, E South Africa 29°55′S 31°01′E
118 C9 **Durbe** *Ger.* Durben. W Latvia 56°34′N 21°22′E
Durben see Durbe
99 K21 **Durbuy** Luxembourg, SE Belgium 50°21′N 05°27′E
105 N15 **Dúrcal** Andalucía, S Spain 37°00′N 03°24′W
112 F8 **Đurđevac** *Ger.* Sankt Georgen, *Hung.* Szentgyörgy; *prev.* Djurdjevac, Gjurgjevac. Koprivnica-Kri»zevci, N Croatia 46°02′N 17°03′E
113 K15 **Đurđevica Tara** N Montenegro 43°09′N 19°18′E
97 L24 **Durdle Door** *natural arch* S England, United Kingdom
158 L3 **Düre** Xinjiang Uygur Zizhiqu, W China 46°30′N 88°26′E
101 D16 **Düren** *anc.* Marcodurum. Nordrhein-Westfalen, W Germany 50°48′N 06°30′E
154 K12 **Durg** *prev.* Drug. Chhattīsgarh, C India 21°12′N 81°20′E
153 U13 **Durgapur** Dhaka, N Bangladesh 25°10′N 90°41′E
153 R15 **Durgāpur** West Bengal, NE India 23°30′N 87°20′E
14 F14 **Durham** Ontario, S Canada 44°10′N 80°48′W
97 M14 **Durham** *hist.* Dunholme. N England, United Kingdom 54°47′N 01°34′W
21 U9 **Durham** North Carolina, SE USA 36°N 78°54′W
97 L15 **Durham** *cultural region* N England, United Kingdom
168 J10 **Duri** Sumatera, W Indonesia 01°13′N 101°13′E
Duria Major see Dora Baltea
Duria Minor see Dora Riparia
Durlas see Thurles
141 P8 **Ḑurmā** Ar Riyāḑ, C Saudi Arabia 24°37′N 46°06′E
113 J15 **Durmitor** ▲ N Montenegro
96 H6 **Durness** N Scotland, United Kingdom 58°34′N 04°46′W
109 Y3 **Dürnkrut** Niederösterreich, E Austria 48°28′N 16°50′E
Durnovaria see Dorchester
Durobrivae see Rochester
Durocasses see Dreux
Durocobrivae see Dunstable
Durocortorum see Reims
Durostorum see Silistra
Durovernum see Canterbury
113 K20 **Durrës** *var.* Durrësi, Dursi, *It.* Durazzo, *SCr.* Drač, *Turk.* Draç. Durrës, W Albania 41°20′N 19°26′E
113 K19 **Durrës** ◈ *district* W Albania
Durrësi see Durrës
97 A21 **Dursey Island** *Ir.* Oileán Baoi. *island* SW Ireland
Dursi see Durrës
Duru see Wuchuan
Durud see Dow Rūd
114 P12 **Durusu** İstanbul, NW Turkey 41°18′N 28°41′E
114 O12 **Durusu Gölü** ◎ NW Turkey
138 I9 **Durūz, Jabal ad** ▲ SW Syria 37°00′N 32°30′E
184 K13 **D'Urville Island** *island* C New Zealand
171 X12 **D'Urville, Tanjung** *headland* Papua, E Indonesia 01°26′S 137°52′E
146 H14 **Duşak** *Rus.* Dushak. Ahal Welaýaty, S Turkmenistan 37°15′N 59°57′E
Dusa Mareb/Dusa Marreb see Dhuusa Marreeb
118 I11 **Dusetos** Utena, NE Lithuania 55°44′N 25°49′E
Dushak see Duşak
160 K12 **Dushan** Guizhou, S China 25°50′N 107°36′E
147 P13 **Dushanbe** *var.* Dyushambe; *prev.* Stalinabad, *Taj.* Stalinobod. ● (Tajikistan) W Tajikistan 38°35′N 68°44′E
147 P13 **Dushanbe** ✈ W Tajikistan 38°31′N 68°49′E
137 T9 **Dusheti** *prev.* Dushet'i. E Georgia 42°07′N 44°44′E
Dushet'i see Dusheti
18 H13 **Dushore** Pennsylvania, NE USA 41°30′N 76°23′W
185 A23 **Dusky Sound** *sound* South Island, New Zealand
101 E15 **Düsseldorf** *var.* Duesseldorf. Nordrhein-Westfalen, W Germany 51°14′N 06°49′E
147 P14 **Dŭstí** *Rus.* Dusti. SW Tajikistan 37°22′N 68°41′E
194 I9 **Dustin Island** *island* Antarctica
Dutch East Indies see Indonesia
Dutch Guiana see Surinam
38 L17 **Dutch Harbor** Unalaska Island, Alaska, USA 53°51′N 166°33′W
36 J3 **Dutch Mount** ▲ Utah, W USA 40°16′N 113°56′W
Dutch New Guinea see Papua
Dutch West Indies see Curaçao
83 H20 **Dutlwe** Kweneng, S Botswana 23°58′S 23°56′E
67 V16 **Du Toit Fracture Zone** *tectonic feature* SW Indian Ocean
125 U8 **Dutovo** Respublika Komi, NW Russian Federation 63°45′N 56°38′E
77 V13 **Dutsan Wai** *var.* Dutsen Wai. Kaduna, C Nigeria 10°49′N 08°15′E
77 W13 **Dutse** Jigawa, N Nigeria 11°43′N 09°25′E
Dutsen Wai see Dutsan Wai
Duttia see Datia
14 E17 **Dutton** Ontario, S Canada 42°40′N 81°28′W
36 L7 **Dutton, Mount** ▲ Utah, W USA 38°00′N 112°10′W
162 E7 **Duut** Hovd, W Mongolia 47°28′N 91°52′E
14 K11 **Duval, Lac** ◎ Québec, SE Canada
127 W3 **Duvan** Respublika Bashkortostan, W Russian Federation 55°42′N 57°56′E
138 L9 **Duwaykhilat Satīḩ ar Ruwayshid** *seasonal river* SE Jordan
Dux see Duchcov
160 J13 **Duyang Shan** ▲▲ S China
167 T14 **Duyên Hai** Tra Vinh, S Vietnam 09°39′N 106°28′E
160 K12 **Duyun** Guizhou, S China 26°16′N 107°29′E
136 G11 **Düzce** Düzce, NW Turkey 40°51′N 31°09′E
136 K14 **Düzce** ◈ *province* NW Turkey
Duzdab see Zāhedān
Duzenkyr, Khrebet see Duzkyr, Khrebet
146 I16 **Duzkyr, Khrebet** *prev.* Khrebet Duzenkyr. ▲▲ S Turkmenistan
114 K8 **Dve Mogili** Ruse, N Bulgaria 43°35′N 25°51′E
Dvina Bay see Chëshskaya Guba
Dvinsk see Daugavpils
124 L7 **Dvinskaya Guba** *bay* NW Russian Federation
112 E10 **Dvor** Sisak-Moslavina, C Croatia 45°05′N 16°22′E
117 W5 **Dvorichna** Kharkivs'ka Oblast', E Ukraine 49°52′N 37°43′E
111 F16 **Dvůr Králové nad Labem** *Ger.* Königinhof an der Elbe. Královéhradecký Kraj, N Czech Republic 50°27′N 15°50′E
154 A10 **Dwārka** Gujarāt, W India 22°14′N 68°58′E
30 M12 **Dwight** Illinois, N USA 41°05′N 88°25′W
98 N8 **Dwingeloo** Drenthe, NE Netherlands 52°49′N 06°20′E
33 N10 **Dworshak Reservoir** ⊠ Idaho, NW USA
Dyal see Dyaul Island
Dyanev see Galkynyş
Dyatlovo see Dzyatlava
186 G5 **Dyaul Island** *var.* Djaul, Dyal. *island* NE Papua New Guinea
20 G8 **Dyer** Tennessee, S USA 36°04′N 88°59′W
9 S5 **Dyer, Cape** *headland* Baffin Island, Nunavut, NE Canada 66°37′N 61°13′W
20 F8 **Dyersburg** Tennessee, S USA 36°02′N 89°21′W
29 Y13 **Dyersville** Iowa, C USA 42°29′N 91°07′W
97 I21 **Dyfed** *cultural region* SW Wales, United Kingdom
Dyfrdwy, Afon see Dee
Dyhernfurth see Brzeg Dolny
111 E19 **Dyje** *var.* Thaya. ≈ Austria/Czech Republic *see also* Thaya
Dyje see Thaya
117 T5 **Dykan'ka** Poltavs'ka Oblast', C Ukraine 49°48′N 34°33′E
127 N16 **Dykhtau** ▲ SW Russian Federation 43°01′N 42°56′E
111 A16 **Dyleń** *Ger.* Tillenberg. ▲ NW Czech Republic 49°58′N 12°31′E
110 K9 **Dylewska Góra** ▲ N Poland 53°33′N 19°57′E
117 O4 **Dymer** Kyyivs'ka Oblast', N Ukraine 50°50′N 30°20′E
117 W7 **Dymytrov** *Rus.* Dimitrov. Donets'ka Oblast', SE Ukraine 48°18′N 37°19′E
111 O17 **Dynów** Podkarpackie, SE Poland 49°49′N 22°14′E
29 X13 **Dysart** Iowa, C USA 42°10′N 92°18′W
Dysna see Dzisna
115 H18 **Dýstos, Límni** *var.* Límni Dístos. ◎ Évvoia, C Greece
115 D18 **Dytikí Elláda** *Eng.* Greece West, *var.* Dytikí Ellás. ◈ *region* C Greece
Dytikí Ellás see Dytikí Elláda
115 C14 **Dytikí Makedonía** *Eng.* Macedonia West. ◈ *region* N Greece
Dyurment'yube see Diirmentobe
127 U4 **Dyurtyuli** Respublika Bashkortostan, W Russian Federation 55°31′N 54°49′E
Dyushambe see Dushanbe
162 K7 **Dzaamar** *var.* Bat-Öldziyt. Töv, C Mongolia 48°10′N 104°49′E
Dzaanhushuu see Ihtamir
Dza Chu see Mekong
Dzadgay see Bömbögör
162 H8 **Dzag** Bayanhongor, C Mongolia 46°54′N 99°11′E
Dzalaa see Shinejinst
163 O11 **Dzamїn-Üüd** *var.* Borhoyn Tal. Dornogovĭ, SE Mongolia 43°43′N 111°53′E
172 J14 **Dzaoudzi** E Mayotte 12°48′S 45°18′E
Dzaudzhikau see Vladikavkaz
162 G7 **Dzavhan** ◈ *province* NW Mongolia
162 G7 **Dzavhan Gol** ≈ NW Mongolia
162 G6 **Dzavhanmandal** *var.* Nuga. Dzavhan, W Mongolia 48°17′N 95°07′E
Dzegstey see Ögiynuur
162 E7 **Dzereg** *var.* Altanteel. Hovd, W Mongolia 47°05′N 92°57′E
127 O3 **Dzerzhinsk** Nizhegorodskaya Oblast', W Russian Federation 56°20′N 43°22′E
Dzerzhinsk see Dzyarzhynsk Belarus
Dzerzhinsk see Romaniv
Dzerzhinskiy see Nar'yan-Mar
Dzerzhinskoye see Tokzhaylau
Dzerzhinskoye see Tokzhaylau
Dzerzhyns'k see Romaniv
Dzerzhyns'k see Romaniv
Džetygara see Zhitikara
Dzhailgan see Jayilgan
Dzhalagash see Zhalagash
147 T10 **Dzhalal-Abad** *Kir.* Jalal-Abad. Dzhalal-Abadskaya Oblast', W Kyrgyzstan 40°56′N 73°00′E
147 S9 **Dzhalal-Abadskaya Oblast'** *Kir.* Jalal-Abad Oblasty. ◈ *province* W Kyrgyzstan
Dzhalilabad see Cälilabad
Dzhambeyty see Zhympity
Dzhambul see Taraz
Dzhambulskaya Oblast' see Zhambyl
144 D9 **Dzhanibek** *prev.* Dzhanybek, *Kaz.* Zhänibek. Zapadnyy Kazakhstan, W Kazakhstan 49°27′N 46°51′E
Dzhankel'dy see Jongeldi
117 T12 **Dzhankoy** Avtonomna Respublika Krym, S Ukraine 45°40′N 34°20′E
Dzhansugurov see Zhansugirov
147 R9 **Dzhany-Bazar** *var.* Yangibazar. Dzhalal-Abadskaya Oblast', W Kyrgyzstan 41°40′N 70°49′E
Dzhanybek see Dzhanibek
123 P8 **Dzhardzhan** Respublika Sakha (Yakutiya), NE Russian Federation 68°47′N 123°51′E
Dzharkurgan see Jarqo'rg'on
117 S11 **Dzharylhats'ka Zatoka** *gulf* S Ukraine
Dzhayilgan see Jayilgan
Dzhebel see Jebel
147 T14 **Dzhelandy** SE Tajikistan 37°34′N 72°35′E
147 Y7 **Dzhergalan** *Kir.* Jyrgalan. Issyk-Kul'skaya Oblast', NE Kyrgyzstan 42°37′N 78°56′E
Dzhetysay see Zhetysay
Dzhezkazgan see Zhezkazgan
Dzhigirbent see Jigerbent
Dzhirgatal' see Jirgatol
Dzhizak see Jizzax
Dzhizakskaya Oblast' see Jizzax Viloyati
123 P8 **Dzhugdzhur, Khrebet** ▲▲ E Russian Federation
Dzhul'fa see Culfa
Dzhuma see Juma
Dzhungarskiy Alatau see Zhetysuskiy Alatau
Dzhusaly see Zhosaly
146 J12 **Dzhynlykum, Peski** *desert* E Turkmenistan
110 L9 **Działdowo** Warmińsko-Mazurskie, C Poland 53°13′N 20°12′E
111 L16 **Działoszyce** Świętokrzyskie, C Poland 50°21′N 20°19′E
41 X11 **Dzidzantún** Yucatán, E Mexico
111 G15 **Dzierżoniów** *Ger.* Reichenbach. Dolnośląskie, SW Poland 50°43′N 16°40′E
41 X11 **Dzilam de Bravo** Yucatán, E Mexico 21°24′N 88°52′W
118 L12 **Dzisna** *Rus.* Disna. Vitsyebskaya Voblasts', N Belarus 55°33′N 28°13′E
118 K12 **Dzisna** *Lith.* Dysna, *Rus.* Disna. ≈ Belarus/Lithuania
119 G20 **Dzivin** *Rus.* Divin. Brestskaya Voblasts', SW Belarus 51°58′N 24°33′E
119 M15 **Dzmitravichy** *Rus.* Dmitrovichi. Minskaya Voblasts', C Belarus 53°58′N 29°14′E
Dzogsool see Bayantsagaan
162 I5 **Dzöölön** *var.* Rinchinlhumbe. Hövsgöl, N Mongolia 51°06′N 99°40′E
129 S8 **Dzungaria** *var.* Sungaria, Zungaria. *physical region* W China
Dzungarian Basin see Junggar Pendi
Dzür see Tes
162 J8 **Dzüünbayan-Ulaan** *var.* Bayan-Ulaan. Övörhangay, C Mongolia 46°38′N 102°30′E
Dzüünbulag see Matad, Dornod, Mongolia
Dzüünbulag see Uulbayan, Sühbaatar, Mongolia
162 L8 **Dzuunmod** Töv, C Mongolia 47°45′N 107°00′E
Dzuunmod see Ider
Dzüün Soyonĭ Nuruu see Vostochnyy Sayan
Dzüyl see Tonhil
Dzvina see Western Dvina
119 J16 **Dzyarzhynsk Belarus** *Rus.* Dzerzhinsk; *prev.* Kaydanovo. Minskaya Voblasts', C Belarus 53°41′N 27°09′E
119 H17 **Dzyatlava** *Pol.* Zdzięcioł, *Rus.* Dyatlovo. Hrodzyenskaya Voblasts', W Belarus 53°27′N 25°23′E

E

E see Hubei
Éadan Doire see Edenderry
167 U12 **Ea Drăng** *var.* Ea H'leo. Đắc Lắc, S Vietnam 13°09′N 108°14′E
37 W6 **Eads** Colorado, C USA 38°28′N 102°46′W
37 O13 **Eagar** Arizona, SW USA 34°05′N 109°17′W
39 T8 **Eagle** Alaska, USA 64°47′N 141°12′W
13 S8 **Eagle** ≈ Newfoundland and Labrador, E Canada
10 I3 **Eagle** ≈ Yukon Territory, NW Canada
29 T7 **Eagle Bend** Minnesota, N USA 46°10′N 95°02′W
28 M8 **Eagle Butte** South Dakota, N USA 44°58′N 101°13′W
29 V12 **Eagle Grove** Iowa, C USA 42°39′N 93°54′W
19 R2 **Eagle Lake** Maine, NE USA 47°01′N 68°35′W
25 U11 **Eagle Lake** Texas, SW USA 29°35′N 96°19′W
12 A11 **Eagle Lake** ◎ Ontario, S Canada
35 P3 **Eagle Lake** ◎ California, W USA
19 R3 **Eagle Lake** ◎ Maine, NE USA
29 Y3 **Eagle Mountain** ▲ Minnesota, N USA 47°54′N 90°33′W
25 T6 **Eagle Mountain Lake** ⊠ Texas, SW USA
37 S9 **Eagle Nest Lake** ⊠ New Mexico, SW USA
25 P13 **Eagle Pass** Texas, SW USA 28°44′N 100°31′W
65 C25 **Eagle Passage** *passage* SW Atlantic Ocean
35 Q2 **Eagle Peak** ▲ California, W USA 41°16′N 120°12′W
35 R8 **Eagle Peak** ▲ California, W USA 38°11′N 119°22′W
37 P13 **Eagle Peak** ▲ New Mexico, SW USA 33°39′N 109°36′W
10 I4 **Eagle Plain** Yukon Territory, NW Canada 66°23′N 136°42′W
32 G15 **Eagle Point** Oregon, NW USA 42°28′N 122°48′W
186 P10 **Eagle Point** *headland* SE Papua New Guinea 10°31′S 149°53′E
39 R11 **Eagle River** Alaska, USA 61°18′N 149°38′W
30 M2 **Eagle River** Michigan, N USA 47°24′N 88°18′W
30 L4 **Eagle River** Wisconsin, N USA 45°56′N 89°15′W

◆ Country
● Country Capital
◇ Dependent Territory
○ Dependent Territory Capital
◈ Administrative Regions
✈ International Airport
▲ Mountain
▲▲ Mountain Range
⚲ Volcano
≈ River
◎ Lake
⊠ Reservoir

21 S6 **Eagle Rock** Virginia, NE USA 37°40′N 79°46′W
36 J13 **Eagletail Mountains** ▲▲ Arizona, SW USA
Ea H'leo *see* Ea Drăng
167 U12 **Ea Kar** Đăc Lăc, S Vietnam 12°47′N 108°26′E
Eanjum *see* Anjum
Eanodat *see* Enontekiö
12 B10 **Ear Falls** Ontario, C Canada 50°38′N 93°13′W
27 X10 **Earle** Arkansas, C USA 35°16′N 90°28′W
35 R12 **Earlimart** California, W USA 35°52′N 119°17′W
20 I6 **Earlington** Kentucky, S USA 37°16′N 87°30′W
14 H8 **Earlton** Ontario, S Canada 47°41′N 79°46′W
29 T13 **Early** Iowa, C USA 42°27′N 95°09′W
96 J11 **Earn** ≈ N Scotland, United Kingdom
185 C21 **Earnslaw, Mount** ▲ South Island, New Zealand 44°34′S 168°26′E
24 M4 **Earth** Texas, SW USA 34°13′N 102°24′W
21 P11 **Easley** South Carolina, SE USA 34°49′N 82°36′W
East *see* Est
East Açores Fracture Zone *see* East Azores Fracture Zone
97 P19 **East Anglia** *physical region* E England, United Kingdom
15 Q12 **East Angus** Québec, SE Canada 45°29′N 71°39′W
195 V8 **East Antarctica** *prev.* Greater Antarctica. *physical region* Antarctica
18 E10 **East Aurora** New York, NE USA 42°44′N 78°36′W
East Australian Basin *see* Tasman Basin
East Azerbaijan *see* Āžarbāyjān-e Sharqī
64 L9 **East Azores Fracture Zone** *var.* East Açores Fracture Zone. *tectonic feature* E Atlantic Ocean
22 M11 **East Bay** *bay* Louisiana, S USA
25 V11 **East Bernard** Texas, SW USA 29°32′N 96°04′W
29 V8 **East Bethel** Minnesota, N USA 45°24′N 93°14′W
East Borneo *see* Kalimantan Timur
97 P23 **Eastbourne** SE England, United Kingdom 50°46′N 00°16′E
15 R11 **East-Broughton** Québec, SE Canada 46°14′N 71°05′W
44 M6 **East Caicos** *island* E Turks and Caicos Islands
184 R7 **East Cape** *headland* North Island, New Zealand 37°40′S 178°31′E
174 M4 **East Caroline Basin** *undersea feature* SW Pacific Ocean 04°00′N 146°45′E
192 P4 **East China Sea** *Chin.* Dong Hai. *sea* W Pacific Ocean
97 P19 **East Dereham** E England, United Kingdom 52°41′N 00°55′E
30 J9 **East Dubuque** Illinois, N USA 42°29′N 90°38′W
11 S17 **Eastend** Saskatchewan, S Canada 49°29′N 108°48′W
193 S10 **Easter Fracture Zone** *tectonic feature* E Pacific Ocean
Easter Island *see* Pascua, Isla de
81 J18 **Eastern** ◈ *province* Kenya
153 Q12 **Eastern** ◈ *zone* E Nepal
155 K25 **Eastern** ◈ *province* E Sri Lanka
82 L13 **Eastern** ◈ *province* E Zambia
83 H24 **Eastern Cape** *off.* Eastern Cape Province, *Afr.* Oos-Kaap. ◈ *province* SE South Africa
Eastern Cape Province *see* Eastern Cape
Eastern Desert *see* Sahara el Sharqîya
81 F15 **Eastern Equatoria** ◈ *state* SE South Sudan
Eastern Euphrates *see* Murat Nehri
155 J17 **Eastern Ghats** ▲▲ SE India
186 E7 **Eastern Highlands** ◈ *province* C Papua New Guinea
Eastern Region *see* Ash Sharqīyah
Eastern Sayans *see* Vostochnyy Sayan
Eastern Scheldt *see* Oosterschelde
Eastern Sierra Madre *see* Madre Oriental, Sierra
Eastern Transvaal *see* Mpumalanga
11 W14 **Easterville** Manitoba, C Canada 53°06′N 99°53′W
Easterwâlde *see* Oosterwolde
63 M23 **East Falkland** *var.* Isla Soledad. *island* E Falkland Islands
19 P12 **East Falmouth** Massachusetts, NE USA 41°34′N 70°31′W
East Fayu *see* Fayu
East Flanders *see* Oost-Vlaanderen
39 S6 **East Fork Chandalar River** ≈ Alaska, USA
29 U12 **East Fork Des Moines River** ≈ Iowa/Minnesota, C USA
East Frisian Islands *see* Ostfriesische Inseln
18 K10 **East Glenville** New York, NE USA 42°53′N 73°55′W
29 R4 **East Grand Forks** Minnesota, N USA 47°54′N 97°59′W
97 O23 **East Grinstead** SE England, United Kingdom 51°08′N 00°00′W
18 M12 **East Hartford** Connecticut, NE USA 41°45′N 72°36′W
18 M13 **East Haven** Connecticut, NE USA 41°16′N 72°52′W
173 T9 **East Indiaman Ridge** *undersea feature* E Indian Ocean
129 V16 **East Indies** *island group* SE Asia
East Java *see* Jawa Timur
31 Q6 **East Jordan** Michigan, N USA 45°09′N 85°07′W
East Kalimantan *see* Kalimantan Timur
East Kazakhstan *see* Vostochnyy Kazakhstan
96 I12 **East Kilbride** S Scotland, United Kingdom 55°46′N 04°10′W
25 R7 **Eastland** Texas, SW USA 32°23′N 98°50′W
31 Q9 **East Lansing** Michigan, N USA 42°44′N 84°28′W
35 X11 **East Las Vegas** Nevada, W USA 36°05′N 115°02′W
97 M23 **Eastleigh** S England, United Kingdom 50°58′N 01°22′W
31 V12 **East Liverpool** Ohio, N USA 40°37′N 80°34′W
83 J25 **East London** *Afr.* Oos-Londen; *prev.* Emonti, Port Rex. Eastern Cape, S South Africa 33°S 27°54′E
96 K12 **East Lothian** *cultural region* SE Scotland, United Kingdom
12 I10 **Eastmain** Québec, E Canada 52°11′N 78°27′W
12 J10 **Eastmain** ≈ Québec, C Canada
15 P13 **Eastman** Québec, SE Canada 45°19′N 72°18′W
23 U6 **Eastman** Georgia, SE USA 32°12′N 83°10′W
175 O3 **East Mariana Basin** *undersea feature* W Pacific Ocean
30 K11 **East Moline** Illinois, N USA 41°30′N 90°26′W
186 H7 **East New Britain** ◈ *province* E Papua New Guinea
29 T15 **East Nishnabotna River** ≈ Iowa, C USA
197 V12 **East Novaya Zemlya Trough** *var.* Novaya Zemlya Trough. *undersea feature* W Kara Sea
East Nusa Tenggara *see* Nusa Tenggara Timur
21 X4 **Easton** Maryland, NE USA 38°46′N 76°04′W
18 I14 **Easton** Pennsylvania, NE USA 40°41′N 75°13′W
193 R16 **East Pacific Rise** *undersea feature* E Pacific Ocean 20°00′S 115°00′W
East Pakistan *see* Bangladesh
31 V12 **East Palestine** Ohio, N USA 40°49′N 80°32′W
30 L12 **East Peoria** Illinois, N USA 40°40′N 89°34′W
23 S3 **East Point** Georgia, SE USA 33°40′N 84°26′W
19 U6 **Eastport** Maine, NE USA 44°54′N 66°59′W
27 Z8 **East Prairie** Missouri, C USA 36°46′N 89°23′W
19 O12 **East Providence** Rhode Island, NE USA 41°48′N 71°20′W
20 L11 **East Ridge** Tennessee, S USA 35°00′N 85°15′W
97 N16 **East Riding** *cultural region* N England, United Kingdom
18 F9 **East Rochester** New York, NE USA 43°06′N 77°29′W
30 K15 **East Saint Louis** Illinois, N USA 38°35′N 90°07′W
65 K21 **East Scotia Basin** *undersea feature* SE Scotia Sea
129 Y8 **East Sea** *var.* Sea of Japan, *Rus.* Yapanskoye More. *Sea* NW Pacific Ocean *see also* Japan, Sea of
186 B6 **East Sepik** ◈ *province* NW Papua New Guinea
173 N4 **East Sheba Ridge** *undersea feature* W Arabian Sea 14°30′N 56°15′E
East Siberian Sea *see* Vostochno-Sibirskoye More
18 I14 **East Stroudsburg** Pennsylvania, NE USA 41°00′N 75°10′W
East Tasmanian Rise/East Tasmania Plateau/East Tasmania Rise *see* East Tasman Plateau
192 I12 **East Tasman Plateau** *var.* East Tasmanian Rise, East Tasmania Plateau, East Tasmania Rise. *undersea feature* SW Tasman Sea
64 L7 **East Thulean Rise** *undersea feature* N Atlantic Ocean
171 R16 **East Timor** *var.* Loro Sae; *prev.* Portuguese Timor, Timor Timur. ◆ *country* S Indonesia
21 Y6 **Eastville** Virginia, NE USA 37°22′N 75°58′W
35 R7 **East Walker River** ≈ California/Nevada, W USA
182 D1 **Eateringinna Creek** ≈ South Australia
37 T3 **Eaton** Colorado, C USA 40°31′N 104°42′W
15 Q12 **Eaton** ≈ Québec, SE Canada
11 S16 **Eatonia** Saskatchewan, S Canada 51°13′N 109°22′W
31 Q10 **Eaton Rapids** Michigan, N USA 42°30′N 84°39′W
23 U4 **Eatonton** Georgia, SE USA 33°19′N 83°23′W
32 H9 **Eatonville** Washington, NW USA 46°51′N 122°19′W
30 J6 **Eau Claire** Wisconsin, N USA 44°50′N 91°30′W
12 J7 **Eau Claire, Lac à l'** ◎ Québec, SE Canada
Eau Claire, Lac à L' *see* St. Clair, Lake
30 L6 **Eau Claire River** ≈ Wisconsin, N USA
188 J16 **Eauripik Atoll** *atoll* Caroline Islands, C Micronesia
192 H7 **Eauripik Rise** *undersea feature* W Pacific Ocean 03°00′N 142°00′E
102 K15 **Eauze** Gers, S France 43°52′N 00°06′E
41 P11 **Ébano** San Luis Potosí, C Mexico 22°16′N 98°26′W
97 K21 **Ebbw Vale** SE Wales, United Kingdom 51°48′N 03°13′W
79 E17 **Ebebiyin** NE Equatorial Guinea 02°08′N 11°15′E
95 H22 **Ebeltoft** Midtjylland, C Denmark 56°11′N 10°42′E
109 X5 **Ebenfurth** Niederösterreich, E Austria 47°53′N 16°22′E
18 D14 **Ebensburg** Pennsylvania, NE USA 40°28′N 78°44′W
109 S5 **Ebensee** Oberösterreich, N Austria 47°48′N 13°46′E
101 H20 **Eberbach** Baden-Württemberg, SW Germany 49°28′N 08°58′E
121 U8 **Eber Gölü** *salt lake* C Turkey
109 U9 **Eberndorf** *Slvn.* Dobrla Vas. Kärnten, S Austria 46°33′N 14°35′E
109 R4 **Eberschwang** Oberösterreich, N Austria 48°09′N 13°37′E
100 O11 **Eberswalde-Finow** Brandenburg, E Germany 52°50′N 13°48′E
Ebesfalva *see* Dumbrăveni
165 T4 **Ebetsu** *var.* Ebetu. Hokkaidō, NE Japan 43°08′N 141°37′E
Ebetu *see* Ebetsu
Ebinayon *see* Evinayong
158 I4 **Ebinur Hu** ◎ NW China
138 I3 **Ebla** *Ar.* Tell Mardīkh. *site of ancient city* Idlib, NW Syria
Eblana *see* Dublin
108 H7 **Ebnat** Sankt Gallen, NE Switzerland 47°16′N 09°07′E
107 L18 **Eboli** Campania, S Italy 40°37′N 15°03′E
79 E16 **Ebolowa** Sud, S Cameroon 02°56′N 11°11′E
79 N21 **Ebombo** Kasai-Oriental, C Dem. Rep. Congo 05°42′S 26°07′E
189 T9 **Ebon Atoll** *var.* Epoon. *atoll* Ralik Chain, S Marshall Islands
Ebora *see* Évora
Eboracum *see* York
Eborodunum *see* Yverdon
101 J19 **Ebrach** Bayern, C Germany 49°49′N 10°30′E
109 X5 **Ebreichsdorf** Niederösterreich, E Austria 47°58′N 16°24′E
105 S6 **Ebro** ≈ NE Spain
105 N3 **Ebro, Embalse del** ⊠ N Spain
120 G7 **Ebro Fan** *undersea feature* W Mediterranean Sea
Eburacum *see* York
Ebusus *see* Ibiza
Ebusus *see* Eivissa
99 F20 **Écaussinnes-d'Enghien** Hainaut, SW Belgium 50°34′N 04°10′E
Ecbatana *see* Hamadān
21 Q6 **Eccles** West Virginia, NE USA 37°46′N 81°16′W
115 L14 **Eceabat** Çanakkale, NW Turkey 40°12′N 26°22′E
171 O2 **Echague** Luzon, N Philippines 16°42′N 121°37′E
Ech Cheliff/Ech Chleff *see* Chlef
Echeng *see* Ezhou
115 C18 **Echinádes** *island group* W Greece
114 J12 **Echínos** *var.* Ehinos, Ekhínos. Anatolikí Makedonía kai Thráki, NE Greece 41°16′N 25°00′E
Echizen *see* Takefu
164 J12 **Echizen-misaki** *headland* Honshū, SW Japan 35°59′N 135°57′E
Echmiadzin *see* Vagharshapat
8 J8 **Echo Bay** Northwest Territories, NW Canada 66°04′N 118°W
35 Y11 **Echo Bay** Nevada, W USA 36°19′N 114°27′W
36 L9 **Echo Cliffs** *cliff* Arizona, SW USA
14 C10 **Echo Lake** ◎ Ontario, S Canada
35 Q7 **Echo Summit** ▲ California, W USA 38°47′N 120°06′W
14 L8 **Échouani, Lac** ◎ Québec, SE Canada
99 L17 **Echt** Limburg, SE Netherlands 51°07′N 05°52′E
101 H22 **Echterdingen** ✈ (Stuttgart) Baden-Württemberg, SW Germany 48°40′N 09°13′E
99 N24 **Echternach** Grevenmacher, E Luxembourg 49°49′N 06°25′E
183 N11 **Echuca** Victoria, SE Australia 36°10′S 144°20′E
104 L14 **Ecija** *anc.* Astigi. Andalucía, SW Spain 37°33′N 05°04′W
Eckengraf *see* Viesīte
100 I7 **Eckernförde** Schleswig-Holstein, N Germany 54°28′N 09°49′E
100 J7 **Eckernförder Bucht** *inlet* N Germany
102 L7 **Écommoy** Sarthe, NW France 47°51′N 00°15′E
14 L10 **Écorce, Lac de l'** ◎ Québec, SE Canada
15 Q8 **Écorces, Rivière aux** ≈ Québec, SE Canada
56 C7 **Ecuador** *off.* Republic of Ecuador. ◆ *republic* NW South America
Ecuador, Republic of *see* Ecuador
95 I17 **Ed** Västra Götaland, S Sweden 58°55′N 11°55′E
Ed *see* 'Īdi
98 I9 **Edam** Noord-Holland, C Netherlands 52°30′N 05°02′E
96 K4 **Eday** *island* NE Scotland, United Kingdom
25 S17 **Edcouch** Texas, SW USA 26°17′N 97°57′W
80 C11 **Ed Da'ein** Southern Darfur, W Sudan 11°25′N 26°08′E
80 G11 **Ed Damazin** *var.* Ad Damazīn. Blue Nile, E Sudan 11°45′N 34°20′E
80 G8 **Ed Damer** *var.* Ad Dāmir, Ad Damar. River Nile, NE Sudan 17°37′N 33°59′E
80 E8 **Ed Debba** Northern, N Sudan 18°02′N 30°56′E
80 F10 **Ed Dueim** *var.* Ad Duwaym, Ad Duwēm. White Nile, C Sudan 13°38′N 32°36′E
183 Q16 **Eddystone Point** *headland* Tasmania, SE Australia 41°01′S 148°18′E
97 I25 **Eddystone Rocks** *rocks* SW England, United Kingdom
29 W15 **Eddyville** Iowa, C USA 41°09′N 92°37′W
20 H7 **Eddyville** Kentucky, S USA 37°03′N 88°02′W
98 L12 **Ede** Gelderland, C Netherlands 52°03′N 05°40′E
77 T16 **Ede** Osun, SW Nigeria 07°40′N 04°21′E
79 D16 **Edéa** Littoral, SW Cameroon 03°47′N 10°08′E
111 M20 **Edelény** Borsod-Abaúj-Zemplén, NE Hungary 48°18′N 20°40′E
183 R12 **Eden** New South Wales, SE Australia 37°04′S 149°51′E
21 T8 **Eden** North Carolina, SE USA 36°29′N 79°46′W
25 P9 **Eden** Texas, SW USA 31°13′N 99°51′W
97 K14 **Eden** ≈ NW England, United Kingdom
83 I23 **Edenburg** Free State, C South Africa 29°45′S 25°57′E
185 D24 **Edendale** Southland, South Island, New Zealand 46°18′S 168°48′E
97 E18 **Edenderry** *Ir.* Éadan Doire. Offaly, C Ireland 53°21′N 07°03′W
182 L11 **Edenhope** Victoria, SE Australia 37°04′S 141°15′E
21 X8 **Edenton** North Carolina, SE USA 36°04′N 76°39′W
101 G16 **Eder** ≈ NW Germany
101 H15 **Edersee** ◎ W Germany
114 E13 **Édessa** *var.* Édhessa. Kentrikí Makedonía, N Greece 40°48′N 22°03′E
Edessa *see* Şanlıurfa
Edfu *see* Idfū
29 P16 **Edgar** Nebraska, C USA 40°22′N 97°58′W
19 P13 **Edgartown** Martha's Vineyard, Massachusetts, NE USA 41°23′N 70°30′W
39 X13 **Edgecumbe, Mount** ▲ Baranof Island, Alaska, USA 57°03′N 135°45′W
21 Q13 **Edgefield** South Carolina, SE USA 33°50′N 81°57′W
29 P6 **Edgeley** North Dakota, N USA 46°19′N 98°42′W
28 I11 **Edgemont** South Dakota, N USA 43°18′N 103°49′W
92 O3 **Edgeøya** *island* S Svalbard
27 Q4 **Edgerton** Kansas, C USA 38°45′N 95°00′W
29 S10 **Edgerton** Minnesota, N USA 43°52′N 96°07′W
21 X3 **Edgewood** Maryland, NE USA 39°20′N 76°21′W
25 V6 **Edgewood** Texas, SW USA 32°42′N 95°53′W
Édhessa *see* Édessa
29 V9 **Edina** Minnesota, N USA 44°53′N 93°21′W
27 U2 **Edina** Missouri, C USA 40°10′N 92°10′W
25 S17 **Edinburg** Texas, SW USA 26°18′N 98°10′W
65 M24 **Edinburgh** *var.* Settlement of Edinburgh. ○ (Tristan da Cunha) NW Tristan da Cunha 37°03′S 12°18′W
96 J12 **Edinburgh** ◐ S Scotland, United Kingdom 55°57′N 03°13′W
31 P14 **Edinburgh** Indiana, N USA 39°19′N 86°00′W
96 J12 **Edinburgh** ✈ S Scotland, United Kingdom 55°57′N 03°22′W
116 L8 **Edineț** *var.* Edineți, *Rus.* Yedintsy. NW Moldova 48°10′N 27°18′E
Edineți *see* Edineț
Edingen *see* Enghien
136 B9 **Edirne** *Eng.* Adrianople; *anc.* Adrianopolis, Hadrianopolis. Edirne, NW Turkey 41°40′N 26°34′E
136 B11 **Edirne** ◈ *province* NW Turkey
18 K15 **Edison** New Jersey, NE USA 40°31′N 74°24′W
21 S15 **Edisto Island** South Carolina, SE USA 32°34′N 80°17′W
21 R14 **Edisto River** ≈ South Carolina, SE USA
33 S10 **Edith, Mount** ▲ Montana, NW USA 46°25′N 111°10′W
27 N10 **Edmond** Oklahoma, C USA 35°40′N 97°30′W
32 H8 **Edmonds** Washington, NW USA 47°48′N 122°22′W
11 Q14 **Edmonton** *province capital* Alberta, SW Canada 53°34′N 113°25′W
20 K7 **Edmonton** Kentucky, S USA 36°59′N 85°39′W
11 Q14 **Edmonton** ✈ Alberta, SW Canada 53°22′N 113°43′W
29 P3 **Edmore** North Dakota, N USA 48°22′N 98°26′W
13 N13 **Edmundston** New Brunswick, SE Canada 47°22′N 68°20′W
25 U12 **Edna** Texas, SW USA 29°00′N 96°41′W
39 X14 **Edna Bay** Kosciusko Island, Alaska, USA 55°54′N 133°40′W
77 U16 **Edo** ◈ *state* S Nigeria
106 F6 **Edolo** Lombardia, N Italy 46°13′N 10°20′E
64 L6 **Edoras Bank** *undersea feature* C Atlantic Ocean
96 G7 **Edrachillis Bay** *bay* NW Scotland, United Kingdom
136 B12 **Edremit** Balıkesir, NW Turkey 39°34′N 27°01′E
136 B12 **Edremit Körfezi** *gulf* NW Turkey
95 P14 **Edsbro** Stockholm, C Sweden 59°54′N 18°30′E
95 N18 **Edsbruk** Kalmar, S Sweden 58°01′N 16°30′E
94 M12 **Edsbyn** Gävleborg, C Sweden 61°22′N 15°45′E
11 O14 **Edson** Alberta, SW Canada 53°36′N 116°28′W
62 K13 **Eduardo Castex** La Pampa, C Argentina 35°55′S 64°18′W
58 F12 **Eduardo Gomes** ✈ (Manaus) Amazonas, NW Brazil 05°55′S 35°15′W
Edwardesabad *see* Bannu
67 U9 **Edward, Lake** *var.* Albert Edward Nyanza, Edward Nyanza, Lac Idi Amin, Lake Rutanzige. ◎ Uganda/Dem. Rep. Congo
Edward Nyanza *see* Edward, Lake
22 K5 **Edwards** Mississippi, S USA 32°19′N 90°36′W
25 O10 **Edwards Plateau** *plain* Texas, SW USA
30 J11 **Edwards River** ≈ Illinois, N USA
30 K15 **Edwardsville** Illinois, N USA 38°48′N 89°57′W
195 X4 **Edward VIII Gulf** *bay* Antarctica
195 O13 **Edward VII Peninsula** *peninsula* Antarctica
10 J11 **Edziza, Mount** ▲ British Columbia, W Canada 57°43′N 130°39′W
23 H16 **Edzo** *prev.* Rae-Edzo. Northwest Territories, NW Canada 62°44′N 115°55′W
39 N12 **Eek** Alaska, USA 60°13′N 162°01′W
99 D16 **Eeklo** *var.* Eekloo. Oost-Vlaanderen, NW Belgium 51°11′N 03°34′E
Eekloo *see* Eeklo
39 N12 **Eek River** ≈ Alaska, USA
98 N6 **Eelde** Drenthe, NE Netherlands 53°07′N 06°30′E
34 L5 **Eel River** ≈ California, W USA
31 P12 **Eel River** ≈ Indiana, N USA
Eems *see* Ems
98 O4 **Eemshaven** Groningen, NE Netherlands 53°28′N 06°50′E
98 O5 **Eems Kanaal** *canal* NE Netherlands
98 M11 **Eerbeek** Gelderland, E Netherlands 52°07′N 06°04′E
99 C17 **Eernegem** West-Vlaanderen, W Belgium 51°08′N 03°03′E
99 J15 **Eersel** Noord-Brabant, S Netherlands 51°22′N 05°19′E
Eesti Vabariik *see* Estonia
187 R14 **Efate** *var.* Éfaté, *Fr.* Vaté; *prev.* Sandwich Island. *island* C Vanuatu
Efate *see* Efate
109 S4 **Eferding** Oberösterreich, N Austria 48°18′N 14°00′E
30 M15 **Effingham** Illinois, N USA 39°07′N 88°32′W
117 N15 **Eforie-Nord** Constanța, SE Romania 44°04′N 28°37′E
117 N15 **Eforie-Sud** Constanța, E Romania 44°00′N 28°38′E
Efyrnwy, Afon *see* Vyrnwy
Eg *see* Hentiy
107 G23 **Egadi, Isole** *island group* S Italy
35 X6 **Egan Range** ▲▲ Nevada, W USA
14 K12 **Eganville** Ontario, SE Canada 45°33′N 77°03′W
Ege Denizi *see* Aegean Sea
39 O14 **Egegik** Alaska, USA 58°13′N 157°22′W
111 L21 **Eger** *Ger.* Erlau. Heves, NE Hungary 47°54′N 20°22′E
Eger *see* Cheb, Czech Republic
Eger *see* Ohre, Czech Republic/Germany
173 P8 **Egeria Fracture Zone** *tectonic feature* W Indian Ocean
95 C17 **Egersund** Rogaland, S Norway 58°27′N 06°01′E
108 J7 **Egg** Vorarlberg, NW Austria 47°27′N 09°55′E
101 H14 **Egge-gebirge** ▲▲ C Germany
109 Q4 **Eggelsberg** Oberösterreich, N Austria 48°04′N 13°00′E
109 W2 **Eggenburg** Niederösterreich, NE Austria 48°29′N 15°49′E
101 N22 **Eggenfelden** Bayern, SE Germany 48°24′N 12°45′E
18 J17 **Egg Harbor City** New Jersey, NE USA 39°31′N 74°39′W
65 G25 **Egg Island** *island* W Saint Helena
183 N14 **Egg Lagoon** Tasmania, SE Australia 39°42′S 143°57′E
99 I20 **Éghezèe** Namur, C Belgium 50°36′N 04°55′E
92 L2 **Egilsstadhir** Austurland, E Iceland 65°14′N 14°21′W
Egina *see* Aígina
Egindibulaq *see* Yegindybulak
Egio *see* Aígio
103 N12 **Égletons** Corrèze, C France 45°24′N 02°01′E
98 H9 **Egmond aan Zee** Noord-Holland, NW Netherlands 52°37′N 04°37′E
Egmont *see* Taranaki, Mount
184 J10 **Egmont, Cape** *headland* North Island, New Zealand 39°18′S 173°44′E
Egoli *see* Johannesburg
136 I15 **Eğridir Gölü** ◎ W Turkey
Eğri Palanka *see* Kriva Palanka
95 G23 **Egtved** Syddanmark, C Denmark 55°34′N 09°18′E
123 U5 **Egvekinot** Chukotskiy Avtonomnyy Okrug, NE Russian Federation 66°13′N 178°55′W
75 V9 **Egypt** *off.* Arab Republic of Egypt, *Ar.* Jumhūrīyah Miṣr al 'Arabīyah, *prev.* United Arab Republic; *anc.* Aegyptus. ◆ *republic* NE Africa
30 L17 **Egypt, Lake Of** ⊠ Illinois, N USA
162 I14 **Ehen Hudag** *var.* Alx Youqi. Nei Mongol Zizhiqu, N China 39°12′N 101°40′E
164 F14 **Ehime** *off.* Ehime-ken. ◈ *prefecture* Shikoku, SW Japan
Ehime-ken *see* Ehime
101 I23 **Ehingen** Baden-Württemberg, S Germany 48°16′N 09°43′E
Ehinos *see* Echínos
21 R14 **Ehrhardt** South Carolina, SE USA 33°06′N 81°00′W
108 L7 **Ehrwald** Tirol, W Austria 47°24′N 10°52′E
191 W6 **Eiao** *island* Îles Marquises, NE French Polynesia
105 P2 **Eibar** País Vasco, N Spain 43°11′N 02°28′W
98 O11 **Eibergen** Gelderland, E Netherlands 52°06′N 06°39′E
109 V9 **Eibiswald** Steiermark, SE Austria 46°40′N 15°15′E
109 P8 **Eichham** ▲ SW Austria 47°04′N 12°24′E
101 J15 **Eichsfeld** *hill range* C Germany
101 K21 **Eichstätt** Bayern, SE Germany 48°53′N 11°11′E
100 H8 **Eider** ≈ N Germany
94 E13 **Eidfjord** Hordaland, S Norway 60°26′N 07°05′E
94 D13 **Eidfjorden** *fjord* S Norway
94 F9 **Eidsvåg** Møre og Romsdal, S Norway 62°46′N 08°00′E
95 I14 **Eidsvoll** Akershus, S Norway 60°19′N 11°14′E
92 N2 **Eidsvollfjellet** ▲ NW Svalbard 79°13′N 13°23′E
Eier-Berg *see* Suur Munamägi
101 D18 **Eifel** *plateau* W Germany
108 E9 **Eiger** ▲ C Switzerland 46°33′N 08°02′E
96 G10 **Eigg** *island* W Scotland, United Kingdom
155 D24 **Eight Degree Channel** *channel* India/Maldives
44 G1 **Eight Mile Rock** Grand Bahama Island, N Bahamas 26°28′N 78°43′W
194 J9 **Eights Coast** *physical region* Antarctica
180 K6 **Eighty Mile Beach** *beach* Western Australia
99 L18 **Eijsden** Limburg, SE Netherlands 50°47′N 05°41′E
95 G15 **Eikeren** ◎ S Norway
Eil *see* Eyl
Eilat *see* Elat
183 O12 **Eildon** Victoria, SE Australia 37°17′S 145°57′E
183 O12 **Eildon, Lake** ◎ Victoria, SE Australia
80 E8 **Eilei** Northern Kordofan, C Sudan 16°33′N 30°54′E
101 N15 **Eilenburg** Sachsen, E Germany 51°28′N 12°37′E
Eil Malk *see* Mecherchar
94 H13 **Eina** Oppland, S Norway 60°37′N 10°37′E
138 E12 **Ein Avdat** *prev.* En 'Avedat. *well* S Israel
101 I14 **Einbeck** Niedersachsen, C Germany 51°49′N 09°52′E
99 K15 **Eindhoven** Noord-Brabant, S Netherlands 51°26′N 05°30′E
108 G8 **Einsiedeln** Schwyz, NE Switzerland 47°07′N 08°45′E
Eipel *see* Ipel'
Éire *see* Ireland
Éireann, Muir *see* Irish Sea
Eirik Outer Ridge *see* Eirik Ridge
64 I6 **Eirik Ridge** *var.* Eirik Outer Ridge. *undersea feature* E Labrador Sea
92 I3 **Eiríksjökull** ▲ C Iceland 64°47′N 20°23′W
59 B14 **Eirunepé** Amazonas, N Brazil 06°38′S 69°53′W
99 L17 **Eisden** Limburg, NE Belgium 51°05′N 05°42′E
83 F18 **Eiseb** ≈ Botswana/Namibia
Eisen *see* Yeongcheon
101 J16 **Eisenach** Thüringen, C Germany 50°59′N 10°19′E
Eisenburg *see* Vasvár
109 U6 **Eisenerz** Steiermark, SE Austria 47°33′N 14°53′E
100 Q13 **Eisenhüttenstadt** Brandenburg, E Germany 52°09′N 14°36′E
109 U10 **Eisenkappel** *Slvn.* Železna Kapela. Kärnten, S Austria 46°27′N 14°33′E
Eisenmarkt *see* Hunedoara
109 Y5 **Eisenstadt** Burgenland, E Austria 47°50′N 16°32′E
Eishū *see* Yeongju
119 H15 **Eišiškes** Vilnius, SE Lithuania 54°10′N 24°59′E
101 L15 **Eisleben** Sachsen-Anhalt, C Germany 51°32′N 11°33′E
190 I3 **Eita** Tarawa, W Kiribati 01°21′N 173°05′E
Eitape *see* Aitape
105 V11 **Eivissa** *var.* Iviza, *Cast.* Ibiza; *anc.* Ebusus. Ibiza, Spain, W Mediterranean Sea 38°54′N 01°26′E
Eivissa *see* Ibiza
105 R4 **Ejea de los Caballeros** Aragón, NE Spain 42°07′N 01°09′W
40 E8 **Ejido Insurgentes** Baja California Sur, NW Mexico 25°18′N 111°51′W
Ejin Qi *see* Dalain Hob
Ejmiadzin/Ejmiatsin *see* Vagharshapat
77 P16 **Ejura** C Ghana 07°23′N 01°22′W
41 R16 **Ejutla** *var.* Ejutla de Crespo. Oaxaca, SE Mexico 16°33′N 96°40′W
Ejutla de Crespo *see* Ejutla
33 Y10 **Ekalaka** Montana, NW USA 45°52′N 104°32′W
Ekapa *see* Cape Town
Ekaterinodar *see* Krasnodar
93 L20 **Ekenäs** *Fin.* Tammisaari. Etelä-Suomi, SW Finland 60°00′N 23°30′E
146 B13 **Ekerem** *Rus.* Okarem. Balkan Welaýaty, W Turkmenistan 38°06′N 53°52′E
184 M13 **Eketahuna** Manawatu-Wanganui, North Island, New Zealand 40°41′S 175°40′E
Ekhínos *see* Echínos
Ekiatapskiy Khrebet *see* Ekvyvatapskiy Khrebet
Ekibastuz *see* Yekibastuz
123 R13 **Ekimchan** Amurskaya Oblast', SE Russian Federation 53°04′N 132°56′E
95 O15 **Ekoln** ◎ C Sweden
80 I7 **Ekowit** Red Sea, NE Sudan 18°46′N 37°07′E
95 L19 **Eksjö** Jönköping, S Sweden 57°40′N 15°00′E
93 I15 **Ekträsk** Västerbotten, N Sweden 64°28′N 19°49′E
39 O13 **Ekuk** Alaska, USA 58°48′N 158°25′W
123 U5 **Ekvyvatapskiy Khrebet** *prev.* Ekiatapskiy Khrebet. ▲▲ NE Russian Federation
12 F9 **Ekwan** ≈ Ontario, C Canada
39 O13 **Ekwok** Alaska, USA 59°21′N 157°28′W
166 M6 **Ela** Mandalay, C Burma (Myanmar) 19°37′N 96°15′E
El Aaiun *see* El Ayoun
81 N15 **Ēl Ābrēd** Sumalē, E Ethiopia 05°33′N 45°12′E
115 F22 **Elafónisos** *island* S Greece
115 F22 **Elafonísou, Porthmós** *strait* S Greece
El-Aïoun *see* El Ayoun
El 'Alamein *see* Al 'Alamayn
41 Q12 **El Alazán** Veracruz-Llave, C Mexico 21°06′N 97°43′W
57 J18 **El Alto** *var.* La Paz. ✈ (La Paz) La Paz, W Bolivia 16°31′S 68°07′W
Elam *see* Īlām
El Amparo *see* El Amparo de Apure
54 I8 **El Amparo de Apure** *var.* El Amparo. Apure, C Venezuela 07°07′N 70°47′W
171 R13 **Elara** Pulau Ambelau, E Indonesia 03°49′S 127°10′E
El Araïch/El Araïche *see* Larache
40 D6 **El Arco** Baja California Norte, NW Mexico 28°03′N 113°25′W
El 'Arîsh *see* Al 'Arīsh
115 L25 **Elása** *island* SE Greece
El Asnam *see* Chlef
Elassón *see* Elassóna
115 E15 **Elassóna** *prev.* Elassón. Thessalía, C Greece 39°53′N 22°10′E
105 N2 **El Astillero** Cantabria, N Spain 43°23′N 03°45′W
138 F14 **Elat** *var.* Eilat, Elath. Southern, S Israel 29°33′N 34°57′E
Elat, Gulf of *see* Aqaba, Gulf of
Elath *see* Elat, Israel
Elath *see* Al 'Aqabah, Jordan
115 C17 **Eláti** ▲ Lefkáda, Iónia Nisiá, Greece, C Mediterranean Sea 38°43′N 20°38′E
188 L16 **Elato Atoll** *atoll* Caroline Islands, C Micronesia
80 C7 **El'Atrun** Northern Darfur, NW Sudan 18°11′N 26°40′E
74 H6 **El Ayoun** *var.* El Aaiun, El-Aïoun, La Youne. NE Morocco 34°39′N 02°29′W
137 N14 **Elâzığ** *var.* Elâzig, Elâziz. Elâzığ, E Turkey 38°41′N 39°14′E
137 O14 **Elâzığ** *var.* Elâzig, Elâziz. ◈ *province* C Turkey
Elâzig/Elâziz *see* Elâzığ
23 Q7 **Elba** Alabama, S USA 31°24′N 86°04′W
106 E13 **Elba, Isola d'** *island* Archipelago Toscano, C Italy
123 S13 **El'ban** Khabarovskiy Kray, E Russian Federation 50°03′N 136°34′E
54 F6 **El Banco** Magdalena, N Colombia 09°00′N 74°01′W
El Barco *see* O Barco
104 L8 **El Barco de Ávila** Castilla y León, N Spain 40°21′N 05°31′W
El Barco de Valdeorras *see* O Barco
138 H7 **El Barouk, Jabal** ▲▲ C Lebanon
113 L20 **Elbasan** *var.* Elbasani. Elbasan, C Albania 41°07′N 20°04′E
113 L20 **Elbasan** ◈ *district* C Albania
Elbasani *see* Elbasan
54 K6 **El Baúl** Cojedes, C Venezuela 08°59′N 68°16′W
86 D11 **Elbe** *Cz.* Labe. ≈ Czech Republic/Germany
100 L13 **Elbe-Havel-Kanal** *canal* E Germany
100 K9 **Elbe-Lübeck-Kanal** *canal* N Germany
57 L15 **El Beni** *var.* El Beni. ◈ *department* N Bolivia
El Beni *see* El Beni
138 H7 **El Beqaa** *var.* Al Biqā', Bekaa Valley. *valley* E Lebanon
25 R6 **Elbert** Texas, SW USA 33°15′N 98°58′W
37 R5 **Elbert, Mount** ▲ Colorado, C USA 39°07′N 106°26′W
23 U3 **Elberton** Georgia, SE USA 34°06′N 82°52′W
100 K11 **Elbe-Seiten-Kanal** *canal* N Germany
102 M4 **Elbeuf** Seine-Maritime, N France 49°16′N 01°01′E
Elbing *see* Elbląg
136 M15 **Elbistan** Kahramanmaraş, S Turkey 38°14′N 37°11′E
110 K7 **Elbląg** *var.* Elblag, *Ger.* Elbing. Warmińsko-Mazurskie, NE Poland 54°10′N 19°25′E
43 N10 **El Bluff** Región Autónoma Atlántico Sur, SE Nicaragua 12°00′N 83°40′W
63 H17 **El Bolsón** Río Negro, W Argentina 41°59′S 71°35′W
105 P11 **El Bonillo** Castilla-La Mancha, C Spain 38°57′N 02°32′W
El Bordo *see* Patía
El Boulaida/El Boulaïda *see* Blida
11 T16 **Elbow** Saskatchewan, S Canada 51°07′N 106°30′W
29 S7 **Elbow Lake** Minnesota, N USA 45°59′N 95°58′W
127 N16 **El'brus** *var.* Gora El'brus. ▲ SW Russian Federation 42°29′E 43°21′N
El'brus, Gora *see* El'brus
126 M15 **El'brusskiy** Karachayevo-Cherkesskaya Respublika, SW Russian Federation 43°36′N 42°06′E
81 D14 **El Buhayrat** *var.* Lakes State. ◈ *state* C South Sudan
El Bur *see* Ceel Buur
98 L10 **Elburg** Gelderland, E Netherlands 52°27′N 05°46′E
105 O6 **El Burgo de Osma** Castilla y León, C Spain 41°36′N 03°04′W
Elburz Mountains *see* Alborz, Reshteh-ye Kūhhā-ye
35 V17 **El Cajon** California, W USA 32°46′N 116°52′W
63 H22 **El Calafate** *var.* Calafate. Santa Cruz, S Argentina 50°20′S 72°13′W
55 Q8 **El Callao** Bolívar, E Venezuela 07°18′N 61°48′W
25 U12 **El Campo** Texas, SW USA 29°12′N 96°16′W
54 I7 **El Cantón** Barinas, W Venezuela 07°23′N 71°10′W
35 Q8 **El Capitan** ▲ California, W USA 37°46′N 119°39′W
54 H5 **El Carmelo** Zulia, NW Venezuela 10°20′N 71°48′W
62 J5 **El Carmen** Jujuy, NW Argentina 24°24′S 65°16′W
54 E5 **El Carmen de Bolívar** Bolívar, NW Colombia 09°43′N 75°07′W
55 O8 **El Casabe** Bolívar, SE Venezuela 06°26′N 63°35′W
42 M12 **El Castillo de La Concepción** Río San Juan, SE Nicaragua 11°01′N 84°24′W
El Cayo *see* San Ignacio
35 X17 **El Centro** California, W USA 32°47′N 115°33′W
55 N6 **El Chaparro** Anzoátegui, NE Venezuela 09°12′N 65°03′W
105 S12 **Elche** *Cat.* Elx; *anc.* Ilici, *Lat.* Illicis. Valenciana, E Spain 38°16′N 00°41′W
105 Q12 **Elche de la Sierra** Castilla-La Mancha, C Spain 38°27′N 02°03′W
41 U15 **El Chichónal, Volcán** ⛰ SE Mexico 17°20′N 93°12′W
40 C2 **El Chinero** Baja California Norte, NW Mexico
181 R1 **Elcho Island** *island* Wessel Islands, Northern Territory, N Australia
63 H18 **El Corcovado** Chubut, SW Argentina 43°31′S 71°30′W
105 R12 **Elda** Valenciana, E Spain 38°29′N 00°47′W
100 M10 **Elde** ≈ NE Germany
98 L12 **Elden** Gelderland, E Netherlands 51°57′N 05°53′E
81 J16 **El Der** *spring/well* S Ethiopia 03°55′N 39°48′E
El Dere *see* Ceel Dheere
40 B2 **El Descanso** Baja California Norte, NW Mexico 32°08′N 116°51′W
40 E3 **El Desemboque** Sonora, NW Mexico 30°33′N 112°59′W
54 F5 **El Difícil** *var.* Ariguaní. Magdalena, N Colombia 09°55′N 74°12′W
123 R10 **El'dikan** Respublika Sakha (Yakutiya), NE Russian Federation 60°46′N 135°04′E
El Djazaïr *see* Alger
El Djelfa *see* Djelfa
29 X15 **Eldon** Iowa, C USA 40°55′N 92°13′W

◆ Country
● Country Capital
◇ Dependent Territory
○ Dependent Territory Capital
◈ Administrative Regions
✈ International Airport
▲ Mountain
▲▲ Mountain Range
⛰ Volcano
≈ River
◎ Lake
⊠ Reservoir

27 *U5* **Eldon** Missouri, C USA *38°21′N 92°34′W*
54 *E13* **El Doncello** Caquetá, S Colombia *01°43′N 75°17′W*
29 *W13* **Eldora** Iowa, C USA *42°21′N 93°06′W*
60 *G12* **Eldorado** Misiones, NE Argentina *26°24′S 54°38′W*
40 *I9* **El Dorado** Sinaloa, C Mexico *24°19′N 107°23′W*
27 *U14* **El Dorado** Arkansas, C USA *33°12′N 92°40′W*
30 *M17* **Eldorado** Illinois, N USA *37°48′N 88°26′W*
27 *O6* **El Dorado** Kansas, C USA *37°51′N 96°52′W*
26 *K12* **Eldorado** Oklahoma, C USA *34°28′N 99°39′W*
25 *O9* **Eldorado** Texas, SW USA *30°53′N 100°37′W*
55 *Q8* **El Dorado** Bolívar, E Venezuela *06°45′N 61°37′W*
54 *F10* **El Dorado** ✕ (Bogotá) Cundinamarca, C Colombia *01°15′N 71°52′W*
El Dorado *see* California
27 *O6* **El Dorado Lake** ⊠ Kansas, C USA
27 *S6* **El Dorado Springs** Missouri, C USA *37°53′N 94°01′W*
81 *H18* **Eldoret** Rift Valley, W Kenya *0°31′N 35°17′E*
29 *Z14* **Eldridge** Iowa, C USA *41°39′N 90°34′W*
95 *J21* **Eldsberga** Halland, S Sweden *56°36′N 13°00′E*
25 *R4* **Electra** Texas, SW USA *34°01′N 98°55′W*
37 *Q7* **Electra Lake** ⊠ Colorado, C USA
38 *B8* **'Ele'ele** *var.* Eleele. Kaua'i, Hawaii, USA, C Pacific Ocean *21°54′N 159°35′W*
Eleele *see* 'Ele'ele
Elefantes *see* Lepelle
115 *H19* **Elefsína** *prev.* Elevsís. Attikí, C Greece *38°02′N 23°33′E*
115 *G19* **Eléftheres** *anc.* Eleutherae. *site of ancient city* Attikí/Stereá Elláda, C Greece
114 *I13* **Eleftheroúpoli** *prev.* Elevtheroúpolis. Anatolikí Makedonía kai Thráki, NE Greece *40°55′N 24°15′E*
74 *F10* **El Eglab** ▲▲ SW Algeria
118 *F10* **Eleja** C Latvia *56°24′N 23°41′E*
Elek *see* Yelek
119 *G14* **Elektrėnai** Vilnius, SE Lithuania *54°47′N 24°35′E*
126 *L3* **Elektrostal'** Moskovskaya Oblast', W Russian Federation *55°47′N 38°24′E*
81 *H15* **Elemi Triangle** *disputed region* Kenya/Sudan
114 *K9* **Elena** Veliko Tŭrnovo, N Bulgaria *42°55′N 25°53′E*
54 *G16* **El Encanto** Amazonas, S Colombia *01°45′S 73°12′W*
37 *R14* **Elephant Butte Reservoir** ⊠ New Mexico, SW USA
Éléphant, Chaîne de l' *see* Dâmrei, Chuŏr Phmun
194 *G2* **Elephant Island** *island* South Shetland Islands, Antarctica
Elephant River *see* Olifants
El Escorial *see* San Lorenzo de El Escorial
Élesd *see* Aleşd
114 *F11* **Eleshnitsa** ~ W Bulgaria
137 *S13* **Eleşkirt** Ağrı, E Turkey *39°22′N 42°48′E*
42 *F5* **El Estor** Izabal, E Guatemala *15°37′N 89°22′W*
Eleutherae *see* Eléftheres
44 *I2* **Eleuthera Island** *island* N Bahamas
37 *S5* **Elevenmile Canyon Reservoir** ⊠ Colorado, C USA
27 *W8* **Eleven Point River** ~ Arkansas/Missouri, C USA
Elevsís *see* Elefsína
Elevtheroúpolis *see* Eleftheroúpoli
El Faiyûm *see* Al Fayyūm
80 *B10* **El Fasher** *var.* Al Fāshir. Northern Darfur, W Sudan *13°37′N 25°22′E*
El Fashn *see* Al Fashn
El Ferrol/El Ferrol del Caudillo *see* Ferrol
39 *W13* **Elfin Cove** Chichagof Island, Alaska, USA *58°09′N 136°16′W*
105 *W4* **El Fluvià** ~ NE Spain
40 *H7* **El Fuerte** Sinaloa, W Mexico *26°28′N 108°35′W*
80 *D11* **El Fula** Southern Kordofan, C Sudan *11°44′N 28°20′E*
El Gedaref *see* Gedaref
80 *A10* **El Geneina** *var.* Ajjinena, Al-Genain, Al Junaynah. Western Darfur, W Sudan *13°27′N 22°30′E*
96 *J8* **Elgin** NE Scotland, United Kingdom *57°39′N 03°20′W*
30 *M10* **Elgin** Illinois, N USA *42°02′N 88°16′W*
29 *P14* **Elgin** Nebraska, C USA *41°58′N 98°04′W*
35 *Y9* **Elgin** Nevada, W USA *37°19′N 114°30′W*
28 *L6* **Elgin** North Dakota, N USA *46°24′N 101°51′W*
26 *M12* **Elgin** Oklahoma, C USA *34°46′N 98°17′W*
25 *T10* **Elgin** Texas, SW USA *30°21′N 97°22′W*
123 *R9* **El'ginskiy** Respublika Sakha (Yakutiya), NE Russian Federation *64°27′N 141°57′E*
El Gîza *see* Giza
74 *J8* **El Goléa** *var.* Al Golea. C Algeria *30°35′N 02°59′E*
40 *D2* **El Golfo de Santa Clara** Sonora, NW Mexico *31°48′N 114°40′W*
81 *G18* **Elgon, Mount** ▲ E Uganda *01°07′N 34°29′E*
94 *I10* **Elgpiggen** ▲ S Norway *62°13′N 11°18′E*
105 *T4* **El Grado** Aragón, NE Spain *42°09′N 00°13′E*
40 *L6* **El Guaje, Laguna** ⊠ NE Mexico
54 *H6* **El Guayabo** Zulia, W Venezuela *08°37′N 72°20′W*
77 *O6* **El Guețțâra** *oasis* N Mali
76 *J6* **El Ḩammâmi** *desert* N Mauritania
76 *M5* **El Ḩank** *cliff* N Mauritania
El Haseke *see* Al Ḩasakah
80 *H10* **El Hawata** Gedaref, E Sudan *13°25′N 34°42′E*
El Higo *see* Higos
171 *T16* **Eliase** Pulau Selaru, E Indonesia *08°16′S 130°49′E*
Elías Piña *see* Comendador
25 *R6* **Eliasville** Texas, SW USA *32°55′N 98°46′W*
Elichpur *see* Achalpur
37 *V13* **Elida** New Mexico, SW USA *33°57′N 103°39′W*
115 *F18* **Elikónas** ▲▲ C Greece
67 *T10* **Elila** ~ W Dem. Rep. Congo
39 *N9* **Elim** Alaska, USA *64°37′N 162°15′W*
Elimberrum *see* Auch
Eliocroca *see* Lorca
61 *B16* **Elisa** Santa Fe, C Argentina *30°42′S 61°04′W*
Elisabethstedt *see* Dumbrăveni
Élisabethville *see* Lubumbashi
127 *O13* **Elista** Respublika Kalmykiya, SW Russian Federation *46°18′N 44°09′E*
182 *I9* **Elizabeth** South Australia *34°44′S 138°39′E*
21 *Q3* **Elizabeth** West Virginia, NE USA *39°04′N 81°24′W*
19 *Q9* **Elizabeth, Cape** *headland* Maine, NE USA *43°34′N 70°12′W*
21 *Y8* **Elizabeth City** North Carolina, SE USA *36°18′N 76°16′W*
21 *P8* **Elizabethton** Tennessee, S USA *36°22′N 82°15′W*
30 *M17* **Elizabethtown** Illinois, N USA *37°24′N 88°21′W*
20 *K6* **Elizabethtown** Kentucky, S USA *37°41′N 85°51′W*
18 *L7* **Elizabethtown** New York, NE USA *44°13′N 73°38′W*
21 *U11* **Elizabethtown** North Carolina, SE USA *34°36′N 78°36′W*
18 *G15* **Elizabethtown** Pennsylvania, NE USA *40°08′N 76°36′W*
74 *E6* **El-Jadida** *prev.* Mazagan. W Morocco *33°15′N 08°27′W*
El Jafr *see* Jafr, Qā' al
80 *F11* **El Jebelein** White Nile, E Sudan *12°38′N 32°51′E*
110 *N8* **Ełk** *Ger.* Lyck. Warmińsko-mazurskie, NE Poland *53°51′N 22°20′E*
110 *O8* **Ełk** ~ NE Poland
29 *Y12* **Elkader** Iowa, C USA *42°51′N 91°24′W*
80 *G9* **El Kamlin** Gezira, C Sudan *15°03′N 33°11′E*
33 *N11* **Elk City** Idaho, NW USA *45°50′N 115°28′W*
26 *K10* **Elk City** Oklahoma, C USA *35°24′N 99°24′W*
27 *P7* **Elk City Lake** ⊠ Kansas, C USA
34 *M5* **Elk Creek** California, W USA *39°34′N 122°34′W*
28 *J10* **Elk Creek** ~ South Dakota, N USA
74 *M5* **El Kef** *var.* Al Kāf, Le Kef. NW Tunisia *36°13′N 08°44′E*
74 *F7* **El Kelâa Srarhna** *var.* Kal al Sraghna. C Morocco *32°05′N 07°20′W*
El Kerak *see* Al Karak
11 *P17* **Elkford** British Columbia, SW Canada *49°58′N 114°57′W*
El Khalil *see* Hebron
80 *E7* **El Khandaq** Northern, N Sudan *18°34′N 30°34′E*
El Khârga *see* Al Khārijah
31 *P11* **Elkhart** Indiana, N USA *41°40′N 85°58′W*
26 *H7* **Elkhart** Kansas, C USA *37°00′N 101°51′W*
25 *V8* **Elkhart** Texas, SW USA *31°37′N 95°34′W*
30 *M7* **Elkhart Lake** ◎ Wisconsin, N USA
El Khartûm *see* Khartoum
37 *Q3* **Elkhead Mountains** ▲▲ Colorado, C USA
18 *I12* **Elk Hill** ▲ Pennsylvania, NE USA *41°42′N 75°33′W*
138 *G8* **El Khiyam** *var.* Al Khiyām, Khiam. S Lebanon *33°12′N 35°42′E*
29 *S15* **Elkhorn** Nebraska, C USA *41°17′N 96°13′W*
30 *M9* **Elkhorn** Wisconsin, N USA *42°40′N 88°34′W*
29 *R14* **Elkhorn River** ~ Nebraska, C USA
127 *O16* **El'khotovo** Respublika Severnaya Osetiya, SW Russian Federation *43°18′N 44°17′E*
114 *L10* **Elkhovo** *prev.* Kizilagach. Yambol, E Bulgaria *42°10′N 26°34′E*
21 *R8* **Elkin** North Carolina, SE USA *36°14′N 80°51′W*
21 *S4* **Elkins** West Virginia, NE USA *38°56′N 79°53′W*
195 *X3* **Elkins, Mount** ▲ Antarctica *66°25′S 53°54′E*
14 *G8* **Elk Lake** Ontario, S Canada *47°44′N 80°19′W*
31 *P6* **Elk Lake** ◎ Michigan, N USA
18 *F12* **Elkland** Pennsylvania, NE USA *41°59′N 77°16′W*
35 *W3* **Elko** Nevada, W USA *40°48′N 115°46′W*
11 *R14* **Elk Point** Alberta, SW Canada *53°52′N 110°49′W*
29 *R12* **Elk Point** South Dakota, N USA *42°42′N 96°37′W*
29 *V8* **Elk River** Minnesota, N USA *45°18′N 93°34′W*
20 *J10* **Elk River** ~ Alabama/Tennessee, S USA
21 *R4* **Elk River** ~ West Virginia, NE USA
20 *I7* **Elkton** Kentucky, S USA *36°49′N 87°11′W*
21 *Y2* **Elkton** Maryland, NE USA *39°37′N 75°50′W*
29 *R10* **Elkton** South Dakota, N USA *44°14′N 96°28′W*
20 *I10* **Elkton** Tennessee, S USA *35°01′N 86°51′W*
21 *U5* **Elkton** Virginia, NE USA *38°22′N 78°35′W*
El Kuneitra *see* Al Qunayṭirah
81 *L15* **El Kure** Somali, E Ethiopia *05°37′N 42°05′E*
80 *D12* **El Lagowa** Southern Kordofan, C Sudan *11°23′N 29°10′E*
39 *S12* **Ellamar** Alaska, USA *60°54′N 146°37′W*
Ellás *see* Greece
23 *S6* **Ellaville** Georgia, SE USA *32°14′N 84°18′W*
197 *P9* **Ellef Ringnes Island** *island* Nunavut, N Canada
29 *V10* **Ellendale** Minnesota, N USA *43°53′N 93°19′W*
29 *P7* **Ellendale** North Dakota, N USA *45°57′N 98°33′W*
36 *M6* **Ellen, Mount** ▲ Utah, W USA *38°06′N 110°48′W*
32 *I9* **Ellensburg** Washington, NW USA *47°00′N 124°34′W*
18 *K12* **Ellenville** New York, NE USA *41°43′N 74°24′W*
Ellep *see* Lib
21 *T10* **Ellerbe** North Carolina, SE USA *35°04′N 79°45′W*
197 *P10* **Ellesmere Island** *island* Queen Elizabeth Islands, Nunavut, N Canada
185 *H19* **Ellesmere, Lake** ◎ South Island, New Zealand
97 *K18* **Ellesmere Port** C England, United Kingdom *53°17′N 02°54′W*
31 *O14* **Ellettsville** Indiana, N USA *39°13′N 86°37′W*
99 *E19* **Ellezelles** Hainaut, SW Belgium *50°44′N 03°40′E*
8 *L7* **Ellice** ~ Nunavut, NE Canada
Ellice Islands *see* Tuvalu
Ellichpur *see* Achalpur
21 *W3* **Ellicott City** Maryland, NE USA *39°16′N 76°48′W*
23 *S2* **Ellijay** Georgia, SE USA *34°42′N 84°28′W*
27 *W7* **Ellington** Missouri, C USA *37°14′N 90°58′W*
26 *L5* **Ellinwood** Kansas, C USA *38°21′N 98°34′W*
83 *J24* **Elliot** Eastern Cape, SE South Africa *31°20′S 27°51′E*
14 *D10* **Elliot Lake** Ontario, S Canada *46°24′N 82°38′W*
181 *X6* **Elliot, Mount** ▲ Queensland, E Australia *19°36′S 147°02′E*
21 *T5* **Elliott Knob** ▲ Virginia, NE USA *38°10′N 79°18′W*
26 *K4* **Ellis** Kansas, C USA *38°56′N 99°33′W*
182 *F8* **Elliston** South Australia *33°40′S 134°56′E*
22 *M7* **Ellisville** Mississippi, S USA *31°36′N 89°12′W*
105 *V5* **El Llobregat** ~ NE Spain
96 *L9* **Ellon** NE Scotland, United Kingdom *57°22′N 02°06′W*
Ellore *see* Elūru
21 *S13* **Elloree** South Carolina, SE USA *33°34′N 80°37′W*
26 *M4* **Ellsworth** Kansas, C USA *38°45′N 98°15′W*
19 *S7* **Ellsworth** Maine, NE USA *44°32′N 68°25′W*
30 *I6* **Ellsworth** Wisconsin, N USA *44°44′N 92°29′W*
26 *M11* **Ellsworth, Lake** ⊠ Oklahoma, C USA
194 *K9* **Ellsworth Land** *physical region* Antarctica
194 *L9* **Ellsworth Mountains** ▲▲ Antarctica
101 *J21* **Ellwangen** Baden-Württemberg, S Germany *48°58′N 10°07′E*
18 *B14* **Ellwood City** Pennsylvania, NE USA *40°49′N 80°15′W*
108 *H8* **Elm** Glarus, NE Switzerland *46°55′N 09°09′E*
32 *G9* **Elma** Washington, NW USA *47°00′N 123°24′W*
121 *V13* **El Maḩalla el Kubra** *var.* Al Maḩallah al Kubrá, Mahalla el Kubra. N Egypt *30°59′N 31°10′E*
74 *E9* **El Mahbas** *var.* Mahbés. SW Western Sahara *27°26′N 09°09′W*
63 *H17* **El Maitén** Chubut, W Argentina *42°03′S 71°10′W*
136 *E16* **Elmalı** Antalya, SW Turkey *36°43′N 29°19′E*
80 *G10* **El Manaqil** Gezira, C Sudan *14°12′N 33°01′E*
54 *M12* **El Mango** Amazonas, S Venezuela *01°55′N 66°35′W*
El Manṣûra *see* Al Manṣūrah
55 *P8* **El Manteco** Bolívar, E Venezuela *07°27′N 62°32′W*
29 *O16* **Elm Creek** Nebraska, C USA *40°43′N 99°22′W*
El Mediyya *see* Médéa
77 *V9* **Elméki** Agadez, C Niger *17°52′N 08°07′E*
108 *K7* **Elmen** Tirol, W Austria *47°22′N 10°34′E*
18 *I16* **Elmer** New Jersey, NE USA *39°34′N 75°09′W*
138 *G6* **El Mina** *var.* Al Mīnā'. N Lebanon *34°28′N 35°49′E*
El Minya *see* Al Minyā
14 *F15* **Elmira** Ontario, S Canada *43°35′N 80°34′W*
18 *G11* **Elmira** New York, NE USA *42°06′N 76°50′W*
36 *K13* **El Mirage** Arizona, SW USA *33°36′N 112°19′W*
29 *O7* **Elm Lake** ⊠ South Dakota, N USA
El Moján *see* San Rafael
105 *N7* **El Molar** Madrid, C Spain *40°43′N 03°35′W*
76 *L7* **El Mrâyer** *well* C Mauritania
76 *L5* **El Mreiti** *well* N Mauritania
76 *L8* **El Mreyyé** *desert* E Mauritania
29 *P8* **Elm River** ~ North Dakota/South Dakota, N USA
100 *I9* **Elmshorn** Schleswig-Holstein, N Germany *53°45′N 09°39′E*
80 *D12* **El Muglad** Southern Kordofan, C Sudan *11°02′N 27°44′E*
El Muwaqqar *see* Al Muwaqqar
14 *G14* **Elmvale** Ontario, S Canada *44°34′N 79°53′W*
30 *K12* **Elmwood** Illinois, N USA *40°46′N 89°58′W*
26 *J8* **Elmwood** Oklahoma, C USA *36°37′N 100°31′W*
103 *P17* **Elne** *anc.* Illiberis. Pyrénées-Orientales, S France *42°36′N 02°58′E*
54 *F11* **El Nevado, Cerro** *elevation* C Colombia
171 *N5* **El Nido** Palawan, W Philippines *11°10′N 119°25′E*
62 *I12* **El Nihuil** Mendoza, W Argentina *34°58′S 68°40′W*
75 *W7* **El Nouzha** ✕ (Alexandria) N Egypt *31°06′N 29°58′E*
80 *E10* **El Obeid** *var.* Al Obayyid, Al Ubayyiḑ. Northern Kordofan, C Sudan *13°11′N 30°10′E*
41 *O13* **El Oro** México, S Mexico *19°51′N 100°07′W*
56 *B8* **El Oro** ⬖ *province* SW Ecuador
61 *B19* **Elortondo** Santa Fe, C Argentina *33°42′S 61°37′W*
54 *J8* **Elorza** Apure, C Venezuela *07°02′N 69°30′W*
El Ouâdi *see* El Oued
74 *L7* **El Oued** *var.* Al Oued, El Ouâdi, El Wad. NE Algeria *33°20′N 06°53′E*
36 *L15* **Eloy** Arizona, SW USA *32°47′N 111°33′W*
55 *Q7* **El Palmar** Bolívar, E Venezuela *08°01′N 61°53′W*
40 *K8* **El Palmito** Durango, W Mexico *25°40′N 104°59′W*
55 *P7* **El Pao** Bolívar, E Venezuela *08°03′N 62°40′W*
54 *K5* **El Pao** Cojedes, N Venezuela *09°40′N 68°08′W*
42 *J7* **El Paraíso** El Paraíso, S Honduras *13°51′N 86°31′W*
42 *I7* **El Paraíso** ⬖ *department* SE Honduras
30 *L12* **El Paso** Illinois, N USA *40°44′N 89°01′W*
24 *G8* **El Paso** Texas, SW USA *31°45′N 106°30′W*
24 *G8* **El Paso** ✕ Texas, SW USA *31°48′N 106°24′W*
105 *U7* **El Perelló** Cataluña, NE Spain *40°53′N 00°43′E*
55 *P5* **El Pilar** Sucre, NE Venezuela *10°31′N 63°12′W*
42 *F7* **El Pital, Cerro** ▲ El Salvador/Honduras *14°19′N 89°06′W*
35 *Q9* **El Portal** California, W USA *37°40′N 119°46′W*
40 *J3* **El Porvenir** Chihuahua, N Mexico *31°15′N 105°48′W*
43 *U14* **El Porvenir** Kuna Yala, N Panama *09°33′N 78°56′W*
105 *W6* **El Prat de Llobregat** Cataluña, NE Spain *41°20′N 02°05′E*
42 *H5* **El Progreso** Yoro, NW Honduras *15°25′N 87°49′W*
42 *A2* **El Progreso** *off.* Departamento de El Progreso. ⬖ *department* C Guatemala
El Progreso *see* Guastatoya
El Progreso, Departamento de *see* El Progreso
104 *L9* **El Puente del Arzobispo** Castilla-La Mancha, C Spain *39°48′N 05°10′W*
104 *J15* **El Puerto de Santa María** Andalucía, S Spain *36°36′N 06°13′W*
62 *I8* **El Puesto** Catamarca, NW Argentina *27°57′S 67°37′W*
El Qâhira *see* Cairo
El Qaṣr *see* Al Qaṣr
El Qatrani *see* Al Qaṭrānah
40 *I10* **El Quelite** Sinaloa, C Mexico *23°37′N 106°26′W*
62 *G9* **Elqui, Río** ~ N Chile
El Q'unayṭirah *see* Al Qunayṭirah
El Quneitra *see* Al Qunayṭirah
El Quseir *see* Al Quṣayr
El Quweira *see* Al Quwayrah
141 *O15* **El-Rahaba** ✕ (Ṣan'ā') W Yemen *15°28′N 44°12′E*
42 *M10* **El Rama** Región Autónoma Atlántico Sur, SE Nicaragua *12°09′N 84°15′W*
43 *W16* **El Real** *var.* El Real de Santa María. Darién, SE Panama *08°06′N 77°42′W*
El Real de Santa María *see* El Real
26 *M10* **El Reno** Oklahoma, C USA *35°32′N 95°57′W*
40 *K9* **El Rodeo** Durango, C Mexico *25°12′N 104°35′W*
104 *J13* **El Ronquillo** Andalucía, S Spain *37°43′N 06°09′W*
11 *S16* **Elrose** Saskatchewan, S Canada *51°07′N 107°59′W*
30 *K8* **Elroy** Wisconsin, N USA *43°43′N 90°16′W*
25 *S17* **Elsa** Texas, SW USA *26°17′N 97°59′W*
El Ṣaff *see* Aṣ Ṣaff
40 *J10* **El Salto** Durango, C Mexico *23°47′N 105°22′W*
42 *D8* **El Salvador** *off.* Republica de El Salvador. ◆ *republic* Central America
El Salvador, Republica de *see* El Salvador
54 *K7* **El Samán de Apure** Apure, C Venezuela *07°54′N 68°44′W*
14 *D7* **Elsas** Ontario, S Canada *48°31′N 82°53′W*
40 *F3* **El Sásabe** *var.* Aduana del Sásabe. Sonora, NW Mexico *31°27′N 111°31′W*
Elsass *see* Alsace
40 *J5* **El Sáuz** Chihuahua, N Mexico *29°03′N 106°15′W*
27 *W4* **Elsberry** Missouri, C USA *39°10′N 90°46′W*
45 *P9* **El Seibo** *var.* Santa Cruz de El Seibo, Santa Cruz del Seibo. E Dominican Republic *18°45′N 69°04′W*
42 *B7* **El Semillero Barra Nahualate** Escuintla, SW Guatemala *14°01′N 91°28′W*
Elsene *see* Ixelles
Elsen Nur *see* Dorgê Co
36 *L6* **Elsinore** Utah, W USA *38°40′N 112°09′W*
Elsinore *see* Helsingør
99 *L18* **Elsloo** Limburg, SE Netherlands *50°57′N 05°46′E*
60 *G13* **El Soberbio** Misiones, NE Argentina *27°15′S 54°05′W*
55 *N6* **El Socorro** Guárico, C Venezuela *09°00′N 65°42′W*
54 *L6* **El Sombrero** Guárico, N Venezuela *09°25′N 67°06′W*
98 *L10* **Elspeet** Gelderland, E Netherlands *52°19′N 05°47′E*
98 *L12* **Elst** Gelderland, E Netherlands *51°55′N 05°51′E*
101 *O15* **Elsterwerda** Brandenburg, E Germany *51°27′N 13°32′E*
40 *J4* **El Sueco** Chihuahua, N Mexico *29°53′N 106°24′W*
El Suweida *see* As Suwaydā'
El Suweis *see* Suez
54 *D12* **El Tambo** Cauca, SW Colombia *02°25′N 76°50′W*
175 *T13* **Eltanin Fracture Zone** *tectonic feature* SE Pacific Ocean
105 *X5* **El Ter** ~ NE Spain
184 *K11* **Eltham** Taranaki, North Island, New Zealand *39°26′S 174°25′E*
55 *O6* **El Tigre** Anzoátegui, NE Venezuela *08°55′N 64°15′W*
El Tigrito *see* San José de Guanipa
54 *J5* **El Tocuyo** Lara, N Venezuela *09°48′N 69°51′W*
127 *Q10* **El'ton** Volgogradskaya Oblast', SW Russian Federation *49°07′N 46°50′E*
32 *K10* **Eltopia** Washington, NW USA *46°33′N 118°59′W*
El Toro *see* Mare de Déu del Toro
61 *A18* **El Trébol** Santa Fe, C Argentina *32°12′S 61°40′W*
40 *J13* **El Tuito** Jalisco, SW Mexico *20°19′N 105°22′W*
El Ṭûr *see* Aṭ Ṭūr
161 *S15* **Eluan Bi** *Eng.* Cape Olwanpi; *prev.* Oluan Pi. *headland* S Taiwan *21°57′N 120°48′E*
155 *K16* **Elūru** *prev.* Ellore. Andhra Pradesh, E India *16°45′N 81°10′E*
118 *H13* **Elva** *Ger.* Elwa. Tartumaa, SE Estonia *58°13′N 26°25′E*
37 *R9* **El Vado Reservoir** ⊠ New Mexico, SW USA
43 *S15* **El Valle** Coclé, C Panama *08°39′N 80°08′W*
104 *I11* **Elvas** Portalegre, C Portugal *38°53′N 07°10′W*
54 *K7* **El Venado** Apure, C Venezuela *07°25′N 68°46′W*
105 *V6* **El Vendrell** Cataluña, NE Spain *41°13′N 01°32′E*
94 *I13* **Elverum** Hedmark, S Norway *60°54′N 11°33′E*
42 *I9* **El Viejo** Chinandega, NW Nicaragua *12°39′N 87°11′W*
54 *G7* **El Viejo, Cerro** ▲ C Colombia *07°31′N 72°56′W*
54 *H6* **El Vigía** Mérida, NW Venezuela *08°38′N 71°39′W*
105 *Q4* **El Villar de Arnedo** La Rioja, N Spain *42°19′N 02°05′W*
59 *A14* **Elvira** Amazonas, W Brazil *07°12′S 69°56′W*
Elwa *see* Elva
El Wad *see* El Oued
81 *K17* **El Wak** North Eastern, NE Kenya *02°46′N 40°57′E*
33 *R7* **Elwell, Lake** ⊠ Montana, NW USA
31 *P13* **Elwood** Indiana, N USA *40°16′N 85°50′W*
27 *R3* **Elwood** Kansas, C USA *39°43′N 94°52′W*
29 *N16* **Elwood** Nebraska, C USA *40°35′N 99°51′W*
Elx *see* Elche
97 *O20* **Ely** E England, United Kingdom *52°24′N 00°15′E*
29 *X4* **Ely** Minnesota, N USA *47°54′N 91°52′W*
35 *X6* **Ely** Nevada, W USA *39°15′N 114°53′W*
El Yopal *see* Yopal
31 *T11* **Elyria** Ohio, N USA *41°22′N 82°06′W*
45 *S9* **El Yunque** ▲ E Puerto Rico *18°15′N 65°46′W*
101 *F23* **Elz** ~ SW Germany
187 *R14* **Emae** *island* Shepherd Islands, C Vanuatu
118 *I5* **Emajõgi** *Ger.* Embach. ~ SE Estonia
Emāmrūd *see* Shāhrūd
Emam Saheb *see* Imām Ṣāḩib
Emām Ṣāḩeb *see* Imām Ṣāḩib
Emāmshahr *see* Shāhrūd
95 *M20* **Emån** ~ S Sweden
144 *J11* **Emba** *Kaz.* Embi. Aktyubinsk, W Kazakhstan *48°50′N 58°10′E*
Emba *see* Zhem
Embach *see* Emajõgi
62 *K5* **Embarcación** Salta, N Argentina *23°15′S 64°05′W*
30 *M15* **Embarras River** ~ Illinois, N USA
Embi *see* Emba
81 *I19* **Embu** Eastern, C Kenya *0°32′N 37°28′E*
100 *E10* **Emden** Niedersachsen, NW Germany *53°22′N 07°12′E*
160 *H9* **Emei Shan** ▲ Sichuan, C China *29°32′N 103°21′E*
29 *Q4* **Emerado** North Dakota, N USA *47°55′N 97°21′W*
181 *X8* **Emerald** Queensland, E Australia *23°33′S 148°11′E*
Emerald Isle *see* Montserrat
57 *J15* **Emero, Río** ~ W Bolivia
11 *Y17* **Emerson** Manitoba, S Canada *49°01′N 97°07′W*
29 *T15* **Emerson** Iowa, C USA *41°00′N 95°22′W*
29 *R13* **Emerson** Nebraska, C USA *42°16′N 96°43′W*
36 *M5* **Emery** Utah, W USA *38°54′N 111°16′W*
Emesa *see* Ḩimş
136 *E13* **Emet** Kütahya, W Turkey *39°22′N 29°15′E*
186 *B8* **Emeti** Western, SW Papua New Guinea *07°54′S 143°18′E*
35 *V3* **Emigrant Pass** *pass* Nevada, W USA
78 *I6* **Emi Koussi** ▲ N Chad *19°52′N 18°34′E*
Emilia *see* Emilia-Romagna
41 *V15* **Emiliano Zapata** Chiapas, SE Mexico *17°42′N 91°46′W*
106 *E9* **Emilia-Romagna** *prev.* Emilia; *anc.* Æmilia. ⬖ *region* N Italy
158 *J3* **Emin** *var.* Dorbiljin. Xinjiang Uygur Zizhiqu, NW China *46°30′N 83°42′E*
149 *W8* **Emīnābād** Punjab, E Pakistan *32°02′N 73°51′E*
21 *L5* **Eminence** Kentucky, S USA *38°22′N 85°10′W*
27 *W7* **Eminence** Missouri, C USA *37°09′N 91°22′W*
114 *N9* **Emine, Nos** *headland* E Bulgaria *42°43′N 27°53′E*
158 *I3* **Emin He** ~ NW China
186 *G4* **Emirau Island** *island* N Papua New Guinea
136 *F13* **Emirdağ** Afyon, W Turkey *39°01′N 31°09′E*
83 *K22* **eMkhondo** *prev.* Piet Retief. Mpumalanga, E South Africa *27°00′S 30°49′E* *see also* Piet Retief
95 *M21* **Emmaboda** Kalmar, S Sweden *56°36′N 15°30′E*
118 *E5* **Emmaste** Hiiumaa, W Estonia *58°43′N 22°36′E*
18 *I15* **Emmaus** Pennsylvania, NE USA *40°32′N 75°28′W*
183 *U4* **Emmaville** New South Wales, SE Australia *29°26′S 151°38′E*
108 *E9* **Emme** ~ W Switzerland
98 *L8* **Emmeloord** Flevoland, N Netherlands *52°43′N 05°46′E*
98 *O8* **Emmen** Drenthe, NE Netherlands *52°48′N 06°57′E*
108 *F8* **Emmen** Luzern, C Switzerland *47°03′N 08°14′E*
101 *F23* **Emmendingen** Baden-Württemberg, SW Germany *48°07′N 07°51′E*
98 *P8* **Emmer-Compascuum** Drenthe, NE Netherlands *52°47′N 07°03′E*
101 *D14* **Emmerich** Nordrhein-Westfalen, W Germany *51°49′N 06°16′E*
29 *U12* **Emmetsburg** Iowa, C USA *43°06′N 94°40′W*
32 *M14* **Emmett** Idaho, NW USA *43°52′N 116°30′W*
38 *M10* **Emmonak** Alaska, USA *62°46′N 164°31′W*
Emona *see* Ljubljana
Emonti *see* East London
24 *L12* **Emory Peak** ▲ Texas, SW USA *29°15′N 103°18′W*
40 *F6* **Empalme** Sonora, NW Mexico *27°57′N 110°49′W*
83 *L23* **Empangeni** KwaZulu/Natal, E South Africa *28°45′S 31°54′E*
61 *C14* **Empedrado** Corrientes, NE Argentina *27°59′S 58°47′W*
192 *K3* **Emperor Seamounts** *undersea feature* NW Pacific Ocean *42°00′N 170°00′E*
192 *L3* **Emperor Trough** *undersea feature* N Pacific Ocean
35 *R4* **Empire** Nevada, W USA *40°26′N 119°21′W*
Empire State of the South *see* Georgia
Emplawas *see* Amplawas
106 *F11* **Empoli** Toscana, C Italy *43°43′N 10°57′E*
27 *P5* **Emporia** Kansas, C USA *38°24′N 96°10′W*
21 *W7* **Emporia** Virginia, NE USA *36°42′N 77°33′W*
18 *E13* **Emporium** Pennsylvania, NE USA *41°31′N 78°14′W*
Empty Quarter *see* Ar Rub' al Khālī
100 *E10* **Ems** *Dut.* Eems. ~ NW Germany
100 *F13* **Emsdetten** Nordrhein-Westfalen, NW Germany *52°11′N 07°32′E*
Ems-Hunte Canal *see* Küstenkanal
100 *F10* **Ems-Jade-Kanal** *canal* NW Germany
100 *F11* **Emsland** *cultural region* NW Germany
182 *D3* **Emu Junction** South Australia *28°39′S 132°13′E*
163 *T3* **Emur He** ~ NE China
55 *R8* **Enachu Landing** NW Guyana *06°09′N 60°02′W*
93 *F16* **Enafors** Jämtland, C Sweden *63°17′N 12°24′E*
94 *N11* **Enånger** Gävleborg, C Sweden *61°30′N 17°10′E*
96 *G7* **Enard Bay** *bay* NW Scotland, United Kingdom
Enareträsk *see* Inarijärvi
171 *X14* **Enarotali** Papua, E Indonesia *03°55′S 136°21′E*
En 'Avedat *see* Ein Avdat
165 *T2* **Enbetsu** Hokkaidō, NE Japan *44°44′N 141°47′E*
61 *H16* **Encantadas, Serra das** ▲▲ S Brazil
40 *E7* **Encantado, Cerro** ▲ NW Mexico *26°46′N 112°33′W*
62 *P7* **Encarnación** Itapúa, S Paraguay *27°20′S 55°50′W*
40 *M12* **Encarnación de Díaz** Jalisco, SW Mexico *21°33′N 102°13′W*
77 *O17* **Enchi** SW Ghana *05°53′N 02°48′W*
25 *Q14* **Encinal** Texas, SW USA *28°02′N 99°21′W*
35 *U17* **Encinitas** California, W USA *33°02′N 117°17′W*
25 *S16* **Encino** Texas, SW USA *26°58′N 98°06′W*
54 *H6* **Encontrados** Zulia, NW Venezuela *09°04′N 72°16′W*
182 *I10* **Encounter Bay** *inlet* South Australia
61 *F15* **Encruzilhada** Rio Grande do Sul, S Brazil *28°58′S 55°31′W*
61 *H16* **Encruzilhada do Sul** Rio Grande do Sul, S Brazil *30°30′S 52°32′W*
111 *M20* **Encs** Borsod-Abaúj-Zemplén, NE Hungary *48°21′N 21°09′E*
193 *P3* **Endeavour Seamount** *undersea feature* N Pacific Ocean *48°15′N 129°04′W*
181 *V1* **Endeavour Strait** *strait* Queensland, NE Australia
171 *O16* **Endeh** Flores, S Indonesia *08°48′S 121°37′E*
95 *G23* **Endelave** *island* C Denmark
191 *T4* **Enderbury Island** *atoll* Phoenix Islands, C Kiribati
11 *N16* **Enderby** British Columbia, SW Canada *50°34′N 119°09′W*
195 *W4* **Enderby Land** *physical region* Antarctica
173 *N14* **Enderby Plain** *undersea feature* S Indian Ocean
29 *Q6* **Enderlin** North Dakota, N USA *46°37′N 97°36′W*
Endersdorf *see* Jędrzejów
28 *K16* **Enders Reservoir** ⊠ Nebraska, C USA
18 *H11* **Endicott** New York, NE USA *42°06′N 76°03′W*
39 *P7* **Endicott Mountains** ▲▲ Alaska, USA
118 *I5* **Endla Raba** *wetland* C Estonia
117 *T9* **Enerhodar** Zaporiz'ka Oblast', SE Ukraine *47°30′N 34°40′E*
57 *F14* **Ene, Río** ~ C Peru
189 *N4* **Enewetak Atoll** *var.* Ānewetak, Eniwetok. *atoll* Ralik Chain, W Marshall Islands
114 *L13* **Enez** Edirne, NW Turkey *40°44′N 26°05′E*
21 *W8* **Enfield** North Carolina, SE USA *36°10′N 77°40′W*
186 *B7* **Enga** ⬖ *province* W Papua New Guinea
45 *Q9* **Engaño, Cabo** *headland* E Dominican Republic *18°36′N 68°19′W*
164 *U3* **Engaru** Hokkaidō, NE Japan *44°06′N 143°30′E*
108 *F9* **Engelberg** Unterwalden, C Switzerland *46°51′N 08°25′E*
21 *Y9* **Engelhard** North Carolina, SE USA *35°30′N 76°00′W*
127 *P8* **Engel's** Saratovskaya Oblast', W Russian Federation *51°27′N 46°09′E*
101 *G24* **Engen** Baden-Württemberg, SW Germany *47°52′N 08°46′E*
Engeten *see* Aiud
168 *K15* **Enggano, Pulau** *island* W Indonesia
80 *J8* **Enghershatu** ▲ N Eritrea *16°41′N 38°21′E*
99 *F19* **Enghien** *Dut.* Edingen. Hainaut, SW Belgium *50°42′N 04°03′E*
27 *V12* **England** Arkansas, C USA *34°32′N 91°58′W*
97 *M20* **England** *Lat.* Anglia. ⬖ *national region* England, United Kingdom
14 *H8* **Englehart** Ontario, S Canada *47°50′N 79°52′W*
37 *T4* **Englewood** Colorado, C USA *39°39′N 104°59′W*
31 *O16* **English** Indiana, N USA *38°20′N 86°28′W*
39 *Q13* **English Bay** Alaska, USA *59°21′N 151°55′W*
English Bazar *see* Ingrāj Bāzār
97 *N25* **English Channel** *var.* The Channel, *Fr.* la Manche. *channel* NW Europe
194 *J7* **English Coast** *physical region* Antarctica
105 *S11* **Enguera** Valenciana, E Spain *38°58′N 00°42′W*
118 *E8* **Engure** W Latvia *57°09′N 23°13′E*
118 *E8* **Engures Ezers** ◎ NW Latvia
137 *R9* **Enguri** *Rus.* Inguri. ~ NW Georgia
Engyum *see* Gangi
26 *M9* **Enid** Oklahoma, C USA *36°25′N 97°53′W*
22 *L3* **Enid Lake** ⊠ Mississippi, S USA
189 *Y2* **Enigu** *island* Ratak Chain, SE Marshall Islands
Enikale Strait *see* Kerch Strait
147 *Z8* **Enil'chek** Issyk-Kul'skaya Oblast', E Kyrgyzstan *42°04′N 79°01′E*
115 *F17* **Enipéfs** ~ C Greece
165 *S4* **Eniwa** Hokkaidō, NE Japan *42°53′N 141°14′E*
Eniwetok *see* Enewetak Atoll
Enjiang *see* Yongfeng
Enkeldoorn *see* Chivhu
123 *S11* **Enken, Mys** *prev.* Mys Enkan. *headland* NE Russian Federation *58°29′N 141°27′E*
Enken, Mys *see* Enken, Mys
98 *J8* **Enkhuizen** Noord-Holland, NW Netherlands *52°34′N 05°03′E*
109 *Q4* **Enknach** ~ N Austria
95 *N15* **Enköping** Uppsala, C Sweden *59°38′N 17°05′E*
107 *K24* **Enna** *var.* Castrogiovanni, Henna. Sicilia, Italy, C Mediterranean Sea *37°34′N 14°16′E*
80 *D11* **En Nahud** Southern Kordofan, C Sudan *12°41′N 28°28′E*
138 *F8* **En Nâqoûra** *var.* An Nāqūrah. SW Lebanon *33°06′N 33°30′E*
En Nazira *see* Natzrat
78 *K8* **Ennedi** *plateau* E Chad
101 *E15* **Ennepetal** Nordrhein-Westfalen, W Germany *51°18′N 07°23′E*
183 *P4* **Enngonia** New South Wales, SE Australia *29°19′S 145°52′E*
97 *C19* **Ennis** *Ir.* Inis. Clare, W Ireland *52°50′N 08°59′W*
33 *R11* **Ennis** Montana, NW USA *45°21′N 111°45′W*
25 *U7* **Ennis** Texas, SW USA *32°19′N 96°37′W*
97 *F20* **Enniscorthy** *Ir.* Inis Córthaidh. SE Ireland *52°30′N 06°34′W*
97 *E15* **Enniskillen** *var.* Inniskilling, *Ir.* Inis Ceithleann. SW Northern Ireland, United Kingdom *54°21′N 07°38′W*
97 *B19* **Ennistimon** *Ir.* Inis Díomáin. Clare, W Ireland *52°57′N 09°17′W*
109 *T4* **Enns** Oberösterreich, N Austria *48°13′N 14°28′E*
109 *T4* **Enns** ~ C Austria
93 *O16* **Eno** Itä-Suomi, SE Finland *62°45′N 30°15′E*
24 *M5* **Enochs** Texas, SW USA *33°51′N 102°46′W*
93 *N17* **Enonkoski** Itä-Suomi, E Finland *62°04′N 28°53′E*
92 *K10* **Enontekiö** *Lapp.* Eanodat. Lappi, N Finland *68°25′N 23°40′E*
21 *Q11* **Enoree** South Carolina, SE USA *34°39′N 81°58′W*
21 *P11* **Enoree River** ~ South Carolina, SE USA
18 *M6* **Enosburg Falls** Vermont, NE USA *44°54′N 72°50′W*
171 *N13* **Enrekang** Sulawesi, C Indonesia *03°33′S 119°46′E*
45 *N10* **Enriquillo** SW Dominican Republic *17°57′N 71°13′W*
45 *N9* **Enriquillo, Lago** ◎ SW Dominican Republic
98 *L9* **Ens** Flevoland, N Netherlands *52°39′N 05°49′E*
98 *P11* **Enschede** Overijssel, E Netherlands *52°13′N 06°55′E*
40 *B2* **Ensenada** Baja California Norte, NW Mexico *31°52′N 116°32′W*
101 *E20* **Ensheim** ✕ (Saarbrücken) Saarland, W Germany *49°13′N 07°09′E*
160 *L9* **Enshi** Hubei, C China *30°16′N 109°26′E*
164 *L14* **Enshū-nada** *gulf* SW Japan
23 *O8* **Ensley** Florida, SE USA *30°31′N 87°16′W*
Enso *see* Svetogorsk
81 *F18* **Entebbe** S Uganda *0°07′N 32°30′E*
81 *F18* **Entebbe** ✕ C Uganda *0°04′N 32°29′E*
101 *M18* **Entenbühl** ▲ Czech Republic/Germany *50°09′N 12°10′E*
98 *N10* **Enter** Overijssel, E Netherlands *52°19′N 06°34′E*
23 *Q7* **Enterprise** Alabama, S USA *31°19′N 85°50′W*
32 *L11* **Enterprise** Oregon, NW USA *45°25′N 117°18′W*
36 *J7* **Enterprise** Utah, W USA *37°33′N 113°42′W*
32 *J8* **Entiat** Washington, NW USA *47°39′N 120°15′W*
105 *P15* **Entinas, Punta de las** *headland* S Spain *36°40′N 02°44′W*
108 *F8* **Entlebuch** Luzern, W Switzerland *47°02′N 08°04′E*
108 *F8* **Entlebuch** *valley* C Switzerland
63 *I22* **Entrada, Punta** *headland* S Argentina
103 *O13* **Entraygues-sur-Truyère** Aveyron, S France *44°39′N 02°36′E*
187 *O14* **Entrecasteaux, Récifs d'** *reef* N New Caledonia

◆ Country
● Country Capital
◇ Dependent Territory
○ Dependent Territory Capital
⬖ Administrative Regions
✕ International Airport
▲ Mountain
▲▲ Mountain Range
⩚ Volcano
~ River
◎ Lake
⊠ Reservoir

61 C17 **Entre Ríos** off. Provincia de Entre Ríos. ⬖ province NE Argentina

42 K7 **Entre Ríos, Cordillera** ▲▲ Honduras/Nicaragua

Entre Ríos, Provincia de see Entre Ríos

104 G9 **Entroncamento** Santarém, C Portugal 39°28′N 08°28′W

77 V16 **Enugu** Enugu, S Nigeria 06°24′N 07°24′E

77 U16 **Enugu** ⬖ state SE Nigeria

123 V5 **Enurmino** Chukotskiy Avtonomnyy Okrug, NE Russian Federation 66°46′N 171°40′W

54 E9 **Envigado** Antioquia, W Colombia 06°09′N 75°38′W

59 B15 **Envira** Amazonas, W Brazil 07°12′S 69°59′W

Enyélé see Enyellé

79 I16 **Enyellé** var. Enyélé. Likouala, NE Congo 02°49′N 18°02′E

101 H21 **Enz** ~ SW Germany

165 N13 **Enzan** var. Kōshū. Yamanashi, Honshū, S Japan 35°44′N 138°43′E

104 I2 **Eo** ~ NW Spain

Eochaill see Youghal

Eochaille, Cuan see Youghal Bay

107 K22 **Eolie, Isole** var. Isole Lipari, Eng. Aeolian Islands, Lipari Islands. island group S Italy

189 U12 **Eot** island Chuuk, C Micronesia

Epáno Archánes/Epáno Arkhánai see Archánes

115 G14 **Epanomí** Kentrikí Makedonía, N Greece 40°25′N 22°57′E

98 M10 **Epe** Gelderland, E Netherlands 52°21′N 05°59′E

77 S16 **Epe** Lagos, S Nigeria 06°37′N 04°01′E

79 I17 **Epéna** Likouala, NE Congo 01°28′N 17°29′E

Eperies/Eperjes see Prešov

103 Q4 **Épernay** anc. Sparnacum. Marne, N France 49°02′N 03°58′E

36 L5 **Ephraim** Utah, W USA 39°21′N 111°35′W

18 H15 **Ephrata** Pennsylvania, NE USA 40°09′N 76°08′W

32 J8 **Ephrata** Washington, NW USA 47°19′N 119°33′W

187 R14 **Epi** var. Épi. island C Vanuatu

Épi see Epi

105 R6 **Épila** Aragón, NE Spain 41°34′N 01°19′W

103 T6 **Épinal** Vosges, NE France 48°10′N 06°28′E

Epiphania see Ḩamāh

Epirus see Ípeiros

121 P3 **Episkopí** SW Cyprus 34°37′N 32°53′E

Episkopi Bay see Episkopí, Kólpos

121 P3 **Episkopí, Kólpos** var. Episkopi Bay. bay SE Cyprus

Epitoli see Tshwane

Epoon see Ebon Atoll

Eporedia see Ivrea

Eppeschdorf see Dumbrăveni

101 H21 **Eppingen** Baden-Württemberg, SW Germany 49°09′N 08°54′E

83 E18 **Epukiro** Omaheke, E Namibia 21°40′S 19°09′E

29 Y13 **Epworth** Iowa, C USA 42°27′N 90°55′W

143 O10 **Eqlīd** var. Iqlid. Fārs, C Iran 30°54′N 52°40′E

Equality State see Wyoming

79 J18 **Equateur** off. Région de l' Equateur. ⬖ region N Dem. Rep. Congo

Equateur, Région de l' see Equateur

151 K22 **Equatorial Channel** channel S Maldives

79 B17 **Equatorial Guinea** off. Equatorial Guinea, Republic of. ◆ republic C Africa

Equatorial Guinea, Republic of see Equatorial Guinea

121 V11 **Eratosthenes Tablemount** undersea feature E Mediterranean Sea 33°48′N 32°53′E

Erautini see Johannesburg

136 L12 **Erbaa** Tokat, N Turkey 40°42′N 36°37′E

101 E19 **Erbeskopf** ▲ W Germany 49°43′N 07°04′E

Erbil see Arbīl

121 P2 **Ercan** ✈ (Nicosia) N Cyprus 35°07′N 33°30′E

Ercegnovi see Herceg-Novi

137 T14 **Erçek Gölü** ◎ E Turkey

137 S14 **Erciş** Van, E Turkey 39°02′N 43°21′E

136 K14 **Erciyes Dağı** anc. Argaeus. ▲ C Turkey 38°32′N 35°28′E

111 J22 **Érd** Ger. Hanselbeck. Pest, C Hungary 47°22′N 18°56′E

163 X11 **Erdaobaihe** prev. Baihe. Jilin, NE China 42°24′N 128°09′E

159 O12 **Erdaogou** Qinghai, W China 34°30′N 92°50′E

163 X11 **Erdao Jiang** ▲▲ NE China

Erdăt-Sângeorz see Sângeorgiu de Pădure

136 C11 **Erdek** Balıkesir, NW Turkey 40°24′N 27°47′E

Erdély see Transylvania

Erdélyi-Havasok see Carpaţii Meridionalii

136 J17 **Erdemli** İçel, S Turkey 36°35′N 34°19′E

163 O10 **Erdene** var. Ulaan-Uul. Dornogovĭ, SE Mongolia 44°21′N 111°06′E

162 H9 **Erdene** var. Sangiyn Dalay. Govĭ-Altay, C Mongolia 45°12′N 97°51′E

162 E6 **Erdenebüren** var. Har-Us. Hovd, W Mongolia 48°30′N 91°25′E

162 K9 **Erdenedalay** var. Sangiyn Dalay. Dundgovĭ, C Mongolia 45°59′N 104°58′E

162 G7 **Erdenehayrhan** var. Altan. Dzavhan, W Mongolia 48°05′N 95°48′E

162 J7 **Erdenemandal** var. Öldziyt. Arhangay, C Mongolia 48°30′N 101°25′E

162 K6 **Erdenet** Orhon, N Mongolia 49°01′N 104°07′E

163 Q9 **Erdenetsagaan** var. Chonogol. Sühbaatar, E Mongolia 45°55′N 115°19′E

162 I8 **Erdenetsogt** Bayanhongor, C Mongolia 46°27′N 100°53′E

Erdenetsogt see Bayan-Ovoo

78 K7 **Erdi** plateau NE Chad

78 L7 **Erdi Ma** desert NE Chad

101 M23 **Erding** Bayern, SE Germany 48°18′N 11°54′E

Erdőszáda see Ardusat

Erdőszentgyörgy see Sângeorgiu de Pădure

102 I7 **Erdre** ~ NW France

195 R13 **Erebus, Mount** ⛰ Ross Island, Antarctica 78°11′S 165°09′E

61 H14 **Erechim** Rio Grande do Sul, S Brazil 27°35′S 52°15′W

163 O7 **Ereen Davaanĭ Nuruu** ▲▲ NE Mongolia

163 Q6 **Ereentsav** Dornod, NE Mongolia 49°51′N 115°41′E

136 I16 **Ereğli** Konya, S Turkey 37°30′N 34°02′E

115 A15 **Ereíkoussa** island Iónia Nisiá, Greece, C Mediterranean Sea

163 O11 **Erenhot** var. Erlian. Nei Mongol Zizhiqu, NE China 43°35′N 112°E

104 M6 **Eresma** ~ N Spain

115 K17 **Eresós** var. Eressós. Lésvos, E Greece 39°11′N 25°57′E

Eressós see Eresós

Ereymentaū see Yereymentau

99 K21 **Érezée** Luxembourg, SE Belgium 50°16′N 05°34′E

74 G7 **Erfoud** SE Morocco 31°29′N 04°18′W

101 D16 **Erft** ~ W Germany

101 K16 **Erfurt** Thüringen, C Germany 50°59′N 11°02′E

137 P15 **Ergani** Dıyarbakır, SE Turkey 38°17′N 39°44′E

Ergel see Hatanbulag

Ergene Çayı see Ergene Irmağī

136 C10 **Ergene Irmağī** var. Ergene Çayı. ~ NW Turkey

118 I9 **Ērgli** C Latvia 56°55′N 25°38′E

78 H11 **Erguig, Bahr** ~ SW Chad

163 S5 **Ergun** var. Labudalin; prev. Ergun Youqi. Nei Mongol Zizhiqu, N China 50°13′N 120°09′E

Ergun see Gegan Gol

Ergun He see Argun

Ergun Youqi see Ergun

Ergun Zuoqi see Gegen Gol

160 F12 **Er Hai** ▣ SW China

104 K4 **Eria** ~ NW Spain

80 H8 **Eriba** Kassala, NE Sudan 16°37′N 36°04′E

96 I6 **Eriboll, Loch** inlet NW Scotland, United Kingdom

65 Q18 **Erica Seamount** undersea feature SW Indian Ocean 38°15′S 14°30′E

107 H23 **Erice** Sicilia, Italy, C Mediterranean Sea 38°02′N 12°35′E

104 E10 **Ericeira** Lisboa, C Portugal 38°58′N 09°25′W

96 H10 **Ericht, Loch** ◎ C Scotland, United Kingdom

26 J11 **Erick** Oklahoma, C USA 35°13′N 99°52′W

18 B11 **Erie** Pennsylvania, NE USA 42°07′N 80°04′W

18 E9 **Erie Canal** canal New York, NE USA

Érié, Lac see Erie, Lake

31 T10 **Erie, Lake** Fr. Lac Érié. ◎ Canada/USA

Erigabo see Ceerigaabo

77 N8 **'Erîgât** desert N Mali

Erigavo see Ceerigaabo

92 P2 **Erik Eriksenstretet** strait E Svalbard

11 X15 **Eriksdale** Manitoba, S Canada 50°52′N 98°07′W

189 V6 **Erikub Atoll** var. Ādkup. atoll Ratak Chain, C Marshall Islands

102 G4 **Er, Îles d'** Island group NW France

Erimanthos see Erýmanthos

165 T6 **Erimo** Hokkaidō, NE Japan 42°01′N 143°07′E

165 T6 **Erimo-misaki** headland Hokkaidō, NE Japan 41°57′N 143°12′E

20 H8 **Erin** Tennessee, S USA 36°19′N 87°42′W

96 E9 **Eriskay** island NW Scotland, United Kingdom

Erithraí see Erythrés

80 I9 **Eritrea** off. State of Eritrea, Ērtra. ◆ transitional government E Africa

Eritrea, State of see Eritrea

Erivan see Yerevan

101 D16 **Erkelenz** Nordrhein-Westfalen, W Germany 51°04′N 06°19′E

95 P15 **Erken** ◎ C Sweden

101 K19 **Erlangen** Bayern, S Germany 49°36′N 11°E

160 G9 **Erlang Shan** ▲ C China 29°56′N 102°24′E

Erlau see Eger

109 V5 **Erlauf** ~ NE Austria

181 Q8 **Erldunda Roadhouse** Northern Territory, N Australia 25°13′S 133°13′E

Erlian see Erenhot

27 T15 **Erling, Lake** ▣ Arkansas, USA

109 O8 **Erlsbach** Tirol, W Austria 46°54′N 12°15′E

Ermak see Aksu

98 K10 **Ermelo** Gelderland, C Netherlands 52°18′N 05°38′E

83 K21 **Ermelo** Mpumalanga, NE South Africa 26°32′S 29°59′E

136 H17 **Ermenek** Karaman, S Turkey 36°38′N 32°55′E

Érmihályfalva see Valea lui Mihai

115 G20 **Ermióni** Pelopónnisos, S Greece 37°24′N 23°15′E

115 J20 **Ermoúpoli** var. Hermoupolis; prev. Ermoúpolis. Sýyros, Kykládes, Greece, Aegean Sea 37°26′N 24°55′E

Ermoúpolis see Ermoúpoli

Ernabella see Pukatja

155 G22 **Ernākulam** Kerala, SW India 10°04′N 76°18′E

102 J6 **Ernée** Mayenne, NW France 48°18′N 00°54′W

61 H14 **Ernestina, Barragem** ▣ S Brazil

54 E4 **Ernesto Cortissoz** ✈ (Barranquilla) Atlántico, N Colombia

155 H21 **Erode** Tamil Nādu, SE India 11°21′N 77°43′E

Eroj see Iroj

83 C19 **Erongo** ⬖ district W Namibia

99 F21 **Erquelinnes** Hainaut, S Belgium 50°18′N 04°08′E

74 G7 **Er-Rachidia** var. Ksar al Soule. E Morocco 31°58′N 04°22′W

80 E11 **Er Rahad** var. Ar Rahad. Northern Kordofan, C Sudan 12°43′N 30°39′E

Er Ramle see Ramla

83 O15 **Errego** Zambézia, NE Mozambique 16°02′S 37°11′E

105 Q2 **Errenteria** Cast. Rentería. País Vasco, N Spain 43°17′N 01°54′W

Er Rif/Er Riff see Rif

97 D14 **Errigal Mountain** Ir. An Earagail. ▲ N Ireland 55°03′N 08°09′W

97 A15 **Erris Head** Ir. Ceann Iorrais. headland W Ireland 54°18′N 10°01′W

187 S15 **Erromango** island S Vanuatu

Error Guyot see Error Tablemount

173 O4 **Error Tablemount** var. Error Guyot. undersea feature W Indian Ocean 10°20′N 56°05′E

80 G11 **Er Roseires** Blue Nile, E Sudan 11°52′N 34°23′E

Erseka see Ersekë

113 M22 **Ersekë** var. Erseka, Kolonjë. Korçë, SE Albania 40°19′N 20°39′E

Érsekújvár see Nové Zámky

29 S4 **Erskine** Minnesota, N USA 47°42′N 96°00′W

103 V6 **Erstein** Bas-Rhin, NE France 48°24′N 07°39′E

108 G9 **Erstfeld** Uri, C Switzerland 46°49′N 08°41′E

158 M3 **Ertai** Xinjiang Uygur Zizhiqu, NW China 46°04′N 90°06′E

126 M7 **Ertil'** Voronezhskaya Oblast', W Russian Federation 51°51′N 40°46′E

Ertis see Irtysh, C Asia

Ertis see Irtyshsk, Kazakhstan

158 K2 **Ertix He** Rus. Chërnyy Irtysh. ~ China/Kazakhstan

Ērtra see Eritrea

21 P9 **Erwin** North Carolina, SE USA 35°19′N 78°40′W

Erydropótamos see Erythropótamos

115 E19 **Erýmanthos** var. Erimanthos. ▲ S Greece 37°57′N 21°51′E

115 G19 **Erythrés** prev. Erithraí. Stereá Elláda, C Greece 38°18′N 23°20′E

114 L12 **Erythropótamos** Bul. Byala Reka, var. Erydropótamos. ~ Bulgaria/Greece

160 F12 **Eryuan** var. Yuhu. Yunnan, SW China 26°09′N 100°01′E

109 U6 **Erzbach** ~ W Austria

Erzerum see Erzurum

101 N17 **Erzgebirge** Cz. Krušné Hory, Eng. Ore Mountains. ▲ Czech Republic/Germany see also Krušné Hory

Erzgebirge see Krušné Hory

122 L14 **Erzin** Respublika Tyva, S Russian Federation 50°17′N 95°03′E

137 O13 **Erzincan** var. Erzinjan. Erzincan, E Turkey 39°44′N 39°30′E

137 N13 **Erzincan** var. Erzinjan. ⬖ province NE Turkey

Erzinjan see Erzincan

Erzsébetváros see Dumbrăveni

137 Q13 **Erzurum** prev. Erzerum. Erzurum, NE Turkey 39°57′N 41°17′E

137 Q12 **Erzurum** prev. Erzerum. ⬖ province NE Turkey

186 G9 **Esa'ala** Normanby Island, SE Papua New Guinea 09°45′S 150°47′E

165 T2 **Esashi** Hokkaidō, NE Japan 44°57′N 142°32′E

165 Q9 **Esashi** var. Esasi. Iwate, Honshū, C Japan 39°13′N 141°11′E

165 Q5 **Esasho** Hokkaidō, N Japan

Esasi see Esashi

95 F23 **Esbjerg** Syddtjylland, W Denmark 55°28′N 08°28′E

Esbo see Espoo

36 L7 **Escalante** Utah, W USA 37°46′N 111°36′W

36 M7 **Escalante River** ~ Utah, W USA

14 L12 **Escalier, Réservoir l'** ▣ Québec, SE Canada

40 K7 **Escalón** Chihuahua, N Mexico 26°43′N 104°20′W

104 M8 **Escalona** Castilla-La Mancha, C Spain 40°10′N 04°24′W

23 O8 **Escambia River** ~ Florida, SE USA

31 N5 **Escanaba** Michigan, N USA 45°45′N 87°03′W

31 N4 **Escanaba River** ~ Michigan, N USA

105 R8 **Escandón, Puerto de** pass E Spain

41 W14 **Escárcega** Campache, SE Mexico 18°33′N 90°41′W

171 O1 **Escarpada Point** headland Luzon, N Philippines 18°28′N 122°10′E

23 N8 **Escatawpa River** ~ Alabama/Mississippi, S USA

103 P2 **Escaut** ~ N France

Escaut see Scheldt

99 M25 **Esch-sur-Alzette** Luxembourg, S Luxembourg 49°30′N 05°59′E

101 J15 **Eschwege** Hessen, C Germany 51°10′N 10°03′E

101 D16 **Eschweiler** Nordrhein-Westfalen, W Germany 50°49′N 06°16′E

Esclaves, Grand Lac des see Great Slave Lake

45 O8 **Escocesa, Bahía** bay N Dominican Republic

43 W15 **Escocés, Punta** headland NE Panama 08°50′N 77°37′W

35 U17 **Escondido** California, W USA 33°07′N 117°05′W

42 M10 **Escondido, Río** ~ SE Nicaragua

15 S7 **Escoumins, Rivière des** ~ Québec, SE Canada

37 O13 **Escudilla Mountain** ▲ Arizona, SW USA 33°57′N 109°07′W

40 J11 **Escuinapa** var. Escuinapa de Hidalgo. Sinaloa, C Mexico 22°50′N 105°46′W

Escuinapa de Hidalgo see Escuinapa

42 C6 **Escuintla** Escuintla, S Guatemala 14°17′N 90°46′W

41 V17 **Escuintla** Chiapas, SE Mexico 15°20′N 92°40′W

42 A2 **Escuintla** off. Departamento de Escuintla. ⬖ department S Guatemala

Escuintla, Departamento de see Escuintla

15 W7 **Escuminac** ~ Québec, SE Canada

79 D16 **Eséka** Centre, SW Cameroon 03°40′N 10°48′E

136 I12 **Esenboğa** ✈ (Ankara) Ankara, C Turkey 40°05′N 33°01′E

136 D17 **Eşen Çayı** ~ SW Turkey

146 B13 **Esenguly** Rus. Gasan-Kuli. Balkan Welaýaty, W Turkmenistan 37°29′N 53°57′E

105 T4 **Ésera** ~ NE Spain

143 N8 **Eşfahān** Eng. Isfahan; anc. Aspadana. Eşfahān, C Iran 32°41′N 51°41′E

143 O7 **Eşfahān** off. Ostān-e Eşfahān. ⬖ province C Iran

Eşfahān, Ostān-e see Eşfahān

105 N5 **Esgueva** ~ N Spain

Eshkamesh see Ishkamish

Eshkāshem see Ishkāshim

83 L23 **Eshowe** KwaZulu/Natal, E South Africa 28°53′S 31°28′E

143 T5 **'Eshqābād** Khorāsān, NE Iran 36°00′N 59°01′E

Esh Sham see Rīf Dimashq

Esh Sharā see Ash Sharāh

Esik see Yesik

Esil see Yesil'

Esil see Ishim, Kazakhstan/Russian Federation

183 V2 **Esk** Queensland, E Australia 27°15′S 152°23′E

184 O11 **Eskdale** Hawke's Bay, North Island, New Zealand 39°24′S 176°51′E

Eski Dzhumaya see Tŭrgovishte

92 L2 **Eskifjördhur** Austurland, E Iceland 65°04′N 14°01′W

139 S3 **Eski Kaļak** var. Askī Kalak, Kalak. Arbīl, N Iraq 36°16′N 43°40′E

95 N16 **Eskilstuna** Södermanland, C Sweden 59°22′N 16°31′E

8 H6 **Eskimo Lakes** ◎ Northwest Territories, NW Canada

9 O10 **Eskimo Point** headland Nunavut, E Canada 61°19′N 93°49′W

Eskimo Point see Arviat

139 Q2 **Eski Mosul** Nīnawá, N Iraq 36°31′N 42°45′E

Eski-Nookat see Nookat

136 F12 **Eskişehir** var. Eskishehr. Eskişehir, W Turkey 39°46′N 30°30′E

136 F13 **Eskişehir** var. Eski shehr. ⬖ province NW Turkey

Eskishehr see Eskişehir

104 K5 **Esla** ~ NW Spain

Eslāmābād see Eslāmābād-e Gharb

142 J6 **Eslāmābād-e Gharb** var. Eslāmābād; prev. Harunabad, Shāhābād. Kermānshāhān, W Iran 34°08′N 46°35′E

148 J4 **Eslām Qal'eh** Pash. Islam Qala. Herāt, W Afghanistan 34°41′N 61°03′E

95 K23 **Eslöv** Skåne, S Sweden 55°50′N 13°20′E

143 S12 **Esmā'īlābād** Kermān, S Iran 28°48′N 56°39′E

143 U8 **Esmā'īlābād** Khorāsān, E Iran 35°20′N 60°30′E

136 D14 **Eşme** Uşak, W Turkey 38°26′N 28°59′E

44 G6 **Esmeralda** Camagüey, E Cuba 21°51′N 78°10′W

63 F21 **Esmeralda, Isla** island S Chile

56 B5 **Esmeraldas** Esmeraldas, N Ecuador 0°55′N 79°40′W

56 B5 **Esmeraldas** ⬖ province NW Ecuador

Esna see Isnā

14 B6 **Esnagi Lake** ◎ Ontario, S Canada

143 V14 **Espakeh** Sīstān va Balūchestān, SE Iran 26°54′N 60°09′E

103 O13 **Espalion** Aveyron, S France 44°31′N 02°45′E

España see Spain

14 E11 **Espanola** Ontario, S Canada 46°15′N 81°46′W

37 S10 **Espanola** New Mexico, SW USA 35°59′N 106°04′W

57 C18 **Española, Isla** var. Hood Island. island Galapagos Islands, Ecuador, E Pacific Ocean

104 M13 **Espejo** Andalucía, S Spain 37°40′N 04°34′W

94 C13 **Espeland** Hordaland, S Norway 60°22′N 05°27′E

100 G12 **Espelkamp** Nordrhein-Westfalen, NW Germany 52°22′N 08°37′E

38 M8 **Espenberg, Cape** headland Alaska, USA 66°33′N 163°36′W

180 L13 **Esperance** Western Australia 33°49′S 121°52′E

186 L9 **Esperance, Cape** headland Guadacanal, C Solomon Islands 09°09′S 159°38′E

57 P18 **Esperancita** Santa Cruz, E Bolivia

61 B17 **Esperanza** Santa Fe, C Argentina 31°29′S 61°00′W

40 G6 **Esperanza** Sonora, NW Mexico 27°37′N 109°51′W

24 H9 **Esperanza** Texas, SW USA 31°09′N 105°40′W

194 H3 **Esperanza** Argentinian research station Antarctica 63°29′S 56°53′W

104 E12 **Espichel, Cabo** headland S Portugal 38°25′N 09°15′W

54 E10 **Espinal** Tolima, C Colombia 04°08′N 74°53′W

48 K10 **Espinhaço, Serra do** ▲▲ SE Brazil

104 G6 **Espinho** Aveiro, N Portugal 41°01′N 08°38′W

59 N18 **Espinosa** Minas Gerais, SE Brazil 14°58′S 42°49′W

103 O15 **Espinouse** ▲▲ S France

60 Q8 **Espírito Santo** off. Estado do Espírito Santo. ⬖ state E Brazil

Espírito Santo, Estado do see Espírito Santo

187 P13 **Espiritu Santo** var. Santo. island W Vanuatu

41 Z13 **Espíritu Santo, Bahía del** bay SE Mexico

40 F9 **Espíritu Santo, Isla del** island NW Mexico

41 Y12 **Espita** Yucatán, SE Mexico 21°00′N 88°17′W

15 Y7 **Espoir, Cap d'** headland Québec, SE Canada 48°24′N 64°21′W

Esponsede/Esponsende see Esposende

93 L20 **Espoo** Swe. Esbo. Etelä-Suomi, S Finland 60°10′N 24°42′E

104 G5 **Esposende** var. Esponsede, Esponsende. Braga, N Portugal 41°32′N 08°47′W

83 M18 **Espungabera** Manica, SW Mozambique 20°29′S 32°48′E

63 H17 **Esquel** Chubut, SW Argentina 42°55′S 71°20′W

10 L17 **Esquimalt** Vancouver Island, British Columbia, SW Canada 48°26′N 123°27′W

61 C16 **Esquina** Corrientes, NE Argentina 30°00′S 59°30′W

42 E6 **Esquipulas** Chiquimula, SE Guatemala 14°36′N 89°22′W

42 K9 **Esquipulas** Matagalpa, C Nicaragua 12°30′N 85°55′W

94 I8 **Essandsjøen** ◎ S Norway

74 E7 **Essaouira** prev. Mogador. W Morocco 31°33′N 09°40′W

Esseg see Osijek

Es Semara see Smara

99 G15 **Essen** Antwerpen, N Belgium 51°28′N 04°28′E

101 E15 **Essen** var. Essen an der Ruhr. Nordrhein-Westfalen, W Germany 51°28′N 07°01′E

Essen an der Ruhr see Essen

74 I5 **Es Senia** ✈ (Oran) NW Algeria 35°34′N 00°42′W

55 T8 **Essequibo Islands** island group N Guyana

55 T11 **Essequibo River** ~ C Guyana

14 C18 **Essex** Ontario, S Canada 42°10′N 82°50′W

29 T16 **Essex** Iowa, C USA 40°49′N 95°18′W

97 P21 **Essex** cultural region E England, United Kingdom

31 R8 **Essexville** Michigan, N USA 43°37′N 83°50′W

101 H22 **Esslingen** var. Esslingen am Neckar. Baden-Württemberg, SW Germany 48°45′N 09°19′E

Esslingen am Neckar see Esslingen

103 N6 **Essonne** ⬖ department N France

Es Suweida see As Suwaydā'

79 F16 **Est** Eng. East. ⬖ province SE Cameroon

104 I1 **Estaca de Bares, Punta de** point NW Spain

24 M5 **Estacado, Llano** plain New Mexico/Texas, SW USA

41 P12 **Estación Tamuín** San Luis Potosí, C Mexico 22°00′N 98°44′W

63 K25 **Estados, Isla de los** prev. Eng. Staten Island. island S Argentina

Estado Vargas see Vargas

143 P12 **Eşţahbān** Fārs, S Iran

14 F11 **Estaire** Ontario, S Canada 46°19′N 80°47′W

59 P16 **Estância** Sergipe, E Brazil 11°15′S 37°28′W

37 S12 **Estancia** New Mexico, SW USA 34°45′N 106°03′W

104 G7 **Estarreja** Aveiro, N Portugal 40°45′N 08°35′W

102 M17 **Estats, Pica d'** Sp. Pico d'Estats. ▲ France/Spain 42°39′N 01°24′E

Estats, Pico d' see Estats, Pica d'

83 K23 **Estcourt** KwaZulu/Natal, E South Africa 29°00′S 29°53′E

106 H8 **Este** anc. Ateste. Veneto, NE Italy 45°14′N 11°40′E

42 J9 **Estelí** Estelí, NW Nicaragua 13°05′N 86°21′W

42 J9 **Estelí** ⬖ department NW Nicaragua

105 Q4 **Estella** Bas. Lizarra. Navarra, N Spain 42°41′N 02°02′W

29 R9 **Estelline** South Dakota, N USA 44°34′N 96°54′W

25 P4 **Estelline** Texas, SW USA 34°33′N 100°26′W

104 L14 **Estepa** Andalucía, S Spain 37°17′N 04°52′W

104 L16 **Estepona** Andalucía, S Spain 36°26′N 05°09′W

39 R9 **Ester** Alaska, USA 64°49′N 148°03′W

11 V16 **Esterhazy** Saskatchewan, S Canada 50°40′N 102°02′W

37 S3 **Estes Park** Colorado, C USA 40°22′N 105°31′W

11 V17 **Estevan** Saskatchewan, S Canada 49°07′N 103°05′W

29 T11 **Estherville** Iowa, C USA 43°24′N 94°49′W

21 R15 **Estill** South Carolina, SE USA 32°45′N 81°14′W

103 Q6 **Estissac** Aube, N France 48°17′N 03°51′E

15 T9 **Est, Lac de l'** ◎ Québec, SE Canada

Estland see Estonia

11 S16 **Eston** Saskatchewan, S Canada 51°09′N 198°42′W

118 G5 **Estonia** off. Republic of Estonia, Est. Eesti Vabariik, Ger. Estland, Latv. Igaunija; prev. Estonian SSR, Rus. Estonskaya SSR. ◆ republic NE Europe

Estonian SSR see Estonia

Estonia, Republic of see Estonia

Estonskaya SSR see Estonia

104 E11 **Estoril** Lisboa, W Portugal 38°42′N 09°23′W

59 L14 **Estreito** Maranhão, E Brazil 06°34′S 47°22′W

104 I8 **Estrela, Serra da** ▲▲ C Portugal

40 D3 **Estrella, Punta** headland NW Mexico 30°53′N 114°45′W

104 F10 **Estremadura** cultural and historical region W Portugal

Estremadura see Extremadura

104 H11 **Estremoz** Évora, S Portugal 38°50′N 07°35′W

79 D18 **Estuaire** off. Province de l'Estuaire, var. L'Estuaire. ⬖ province NW Gabon

Estuaire, Province de l' see Estuaire

Eszék see Osijek

111 I22 **Esztergom** Ger. Gran; anc. Strigonium. Komárom-Esztergom, N Hungary 47°47′N 18°44′E

152 K11 **Etah** Uttar Pradesh, N India 27°33′N 78°39′E

189 R17 **Etal Atoll** atoll Mortlock Islands, C Micronesia

99 K24 **Étalle** Luxembourg, SE Belgium 49°41′N 05°36′E

103 N6 **Étampes** Essonne, N France 48°26′N 02°10′E

182 J1 **Etamunbanie, Lake** salt lake South Australia

103 N1 **Étaples** Pas-de-Calais, N France 50°31′N 01°39′E

152 K12 **Etāwah** Uttar Pradesh, N India 26°46′N 79°01′E

15 R10 **Etchemin** ~ Québec, SE Canada

Etchmiadzin see Vagharshapat

40 G7 **Etchojoa** Sonora, NW Mexico 26°54′N 109°37′W

93 L19 **Etelä-Suomi** ⬖ province S Finland

83 B16 **Etengua** Kunene, NW Namibia 17°24′S 13°05′E

99 K25 **Éthe** Luxembourg, SE Belgium 49°34′N 05°32′E

11 W15 **Ethelbert** Manitoba, S Canada 51°30′N 100°22′W

80 H12 **Ethiopia** off. Federal Democratic Republic of Ethiopia; prev. Abyssinia, People's Democratic Republic of Ethiopia. ◆ republic E Africa

Ethiopia, Federal Democratic Republic of see Ethiopia

80 I13 **Ethiopian Highlands** var. Ethiopian Plateau. plateau N Ethiopia

Ethiopian Plateau see Ethiopian Highlands

Ethiopia, People's Democratic Republic of see Ethiopia

34 M2 **Etna** California, W USA 41°25′N 122°53′W

18 B14 **Etna** Pennsylvania, NE USA 40°29′N 79°55′W

94 G12 **Etna** ~ S Norway

107 L24 **Etna, Monte** Eng. Mount Etna. ⛰ Sicilia, Italy, C Mediterranean Sea 37°46′N 15°00′E

Etna, Mount see Etna, Monte

95 C15 **Etne** Hordaland, S Norway 59°40′N 05°55′E

Etoliko see Aitolikó

39 Y14 **Etolin Island** island Alexander Archipelago, Alaska, USA

38 L12 **Etolin Strait** strait Alaska, USA

83 C17 **Etosha Pan** salt lake N Namibia

79 G18 **Etoumbi** Cuvette Ouest, NW Congo 0°01′N 14°57′E

20 M10 **Etowah** Tennessee, S USA 35°19′N 84°31′W

23 S2 **Etowah River** ~ Georgia, SE USA

146 B13 **Etrek** var. Gyzyletrek, Rus. Kizyl-Atrek. Balkan Welaýaty, W Turkmenistan 37°40′N 54°44′E

146 C13 **Etrek** Per. Rūd-e Atrak, Rus. Atrak, Atrek. ~ Iran/Turkmenistan

102 L3 **Étretat** Seine-Maritime, N France 49°46′N 00°23′E

114 H9 **Etropole** Sofiya, W Bulgaria 42°50′N 24°00′E

Etsch see Adige

Et Tafila see Aţ Ţafīlah

99 M23 **Ettelbrück** Diekirch, C Luxembourg 49°51′N 06°06′E

189 V12 **Etten** atoll Chuuk Islands, C Micronesia

99 H14 **Etten-Leur** Noord-Brabant, S Netherlands 51°34′N 04°37′E

76 G7 **Et Tîdra** var. Ile Tîdra. island Dakhlet Nouâdhibou, NW Mauritania

101 G21 **Ettlingen** Baden-Württemberg, SW Germany 48°57′N 08°25′E

102 M2 **Eu** Seine-Maritime, N France 50°01′N 01°24′E

193 W16 **'Eua** prev. Middleburg Island. island Tongatapu Group, SE Tonga

193 W15 **Eua Iki** island Tongatapu Group, S Tonga

Euboea see Évvoia

181 O12 **Eucla** Western Australia 31°41′S 128°51′E

31 U11 **Euclid** Ohio, N USA 41°34′N 81°33′W

27 W14 **Eudora** Arkansas, C USA 33°06′N 91°15′W

27 Q4 **Eudora** Kansas, C USA 38°56′N 95°06′W

182 J9 **Eudunda** South Australia 34°11′S 139°03′E

23 R6 **Eufaula** Alabama, S USA 31°53′N 85°09′W

27 Q11 **Eufaula** Oklahoma, C USA 35°16′N 95°36′W

27 Q11 **Eufaula Lake** var. Eufaula Reservoir. ▣ Oklahoma, C USA

Eufaula Reservoir see Eufaula Lake

32 F13 **Eugene** Oregon, NW USA 44°03′N 123°05′W

40 B6 **Eugenia, Punta** headland NW Mexico 27°48′N 115°03′W

183 Q8 **Eugowra** New South Wales, SE Australia 33°28′S 148°21′E

104 I2 **Eume** ~ NW Spain

104 H2 **Eume, Encoro do** ▣ NW Spain

Eumolpias see Plovdiv

59 O18 **Eunápolis** Bahia, SE Brazil 16°20′S 39°36′W

22 H8 **Eunice** Louisiana, S USA 30°29′N 92°25′W

37 W15 **Eunice** New Mexico, SW USA 32°26′N 103°09′W

99 M19 **Eupen** Liège, E Belgium 50°38′N 06°02′E

130 B10 **Euphrates** Ar. Al-Furāt, Turk. Firat Nehri. ~ SW Asia

138 L3 **Euphrates Dam** dam N Syria

22 M4 **Eupora** Mississippi, S USA 33°32′N 89°16′W

93 K19 **Eura** Länsi-Suomi, SW Finland 61°07′N 22°12′E

93 K19 **Eurajoki** Länsi-Suomi, SW Finland 61°13′N 21°45′E

0-1 **Eurasian Plate** tectonic feature

102 L4 **Eure** ⬖ department N France

102 M4 **Eure** ~ N France

102 M6 **Eure-et-Loir** ⬖ department C France

34 K3 **Eureka** California, W USA 40°47′N 124°12′W

27 P6 **Eureka** Kansas, C USA 37°51′N 96°17′W

33 O6 **Eureka** Montana, NW USA 48°52′N 115°03′W

35 V5 **Eureka** Nevada, W USA 39°31′N 115°58′W

29 O7 **Eureka** South Dakota, N USA 45°46′N 99°37′W

36 L4 **Eureka** Utah, W USA 39°57′N 112°07′W

32 K10 **Eureka** Washington, NW USA 46°21′N 118°41′W

27 S9 **Eureka Springs** Arkansas, C USA 36°25′N 93°45′W

182 K6 **Eurinilla Creek** seasonal river South Australia

183 O11 **Euroa** Victoria, SE Australia 36°46′S 145°35′E

172 M9 **Europa, Île** island W Madagascar

104 L3 **Europa, Picos de** ▲▲ N Spain

104 L16 **Europa Point** headland S Gibraltar 36°07′N 05°20′W

84-85 **Europe** continent

98 F12 **Europoort** Zuid-Holland, W Netherlands 51°59′N 04°08′E

Euskadi see País Vasco

101 D17 **Euskirchen** Nordrhein-Westfalen, W Germany 50°40′N 06°47′E

23 W11 **Eustis** Florida, SE USA 28°51′N 81°41′W

182 M9 **Euston** New South Wales, SE Australia 34°34′S 142°45′E

23 N5 **Eutaw** Alabama, S USA 32°50′N 87°53′W

100 K8 **Eutin** Schleswig-Holstein, N Germany 54°08′N 10°38′E

10 K14 **Eutsuk Lake** ▣ British Columbia, SW Canada

Euxine Sea see Black Sea

83 C16 **Evale** Cunene, SW Angola 16°36′S 15°46′E

37 T3 **Evans** Colorado, C USA 40°22′N 104°41′W

11 P14 **Evansburg** Alberta, SW Canada 53°34′N 114°57′W

29 X13 **Evansdale** Iowa, C USA 42°28′N 92°16′W

183 V4 **Evans Head** New South Wales, SE Australia 29°07′S 153°27′E

12 J11 **Evans, Lac** ◎ Québec, SE Canada

37 S5 **Evans, Mount** ▲ Colorado, C USA 39°15′N 106°10′W

9 Q6 **Evans Strait** strait Nunavut, N Canada

31 N10 **Evanston** Illinois, N USA 42°02′N 87°41′W

33 S17 **Evanston** Wyoming, C USA 41°16′N 110°57′W

14 D11 **Evansville** Manitoulin Island, Ontario, S Canada 45°48′N 82°34′W

31 N16 **Evansville** Indiana, N USA 37°58′N 87°33′W

30 L9 **Evansville** Wisconsin, N USA 42°46′N 89°16′W

25 S8 **Evant** Texas, SW USA 31°28′N 98°09′W

143 P13 **Evaz** Fārs, S Iran 27°48′N 53°58′E

29 W4 **Eveleth** Minnesota, N USA 47°27′N 92°32′W

182 E3 **Evelyn Creek** seasonal river South Australia

181 Q2 **Evelyn, Mount** ▲ Northern Territory, N Australia 13°28′S 132°50′E

122 K10 **Evenkiyskiy Avtonomnyy Okrug** ⬖ autonomous district Krasnoyarskiy Kray, N Russian Federation

183 R13 **Everard, Cape** headland Victoria, SE Australia 37°48′S 149°21′E

182 F6 **Everard, Lake** salt lake South Australia

182 C2 **Everard Ranges** ▲▲ South Australia

153 R11 **Everest, Mount** Chin. Qomolangma Feng, Nep. Sagarmāthā. ▲ China/Nepal 27°59′N 86°57′E

18 E15 **Everett** Pennsylvania, NE USA 40°00′N 78°22′W

32 H7 **Everett** Washington, NW USA 47°59′N 122°12′W

99 E17 **Evergem** Oost-Vlaanderen, NW Belgium 51°07′N 03°43′E

23 X16 **Everglades City** Florida, SE USA 25°51′N 81°22′W

23 Y16 **Everglades, The** wetland Florida, SE USA

23 P7 **Evergreen** Alabama, S USA 31°25′N 86°55′W

37 T4 **Evergreen** Colorado, C USA 39°37′N 105°19′W

Evergreen State see Washington

97 L21 **Evesham** C England, United Kingdom 52°06′N 01°57′W

103 T10 **Évian-les-Bains** Haute-Savoie, E France 46°22′N 06°34′E

93 K16 **Evijärvi** Länsi-Suomi, W Finland 63°22′N 23°30′E

79 D17 **Evinayong** var. Ebinayon, Evinayoung. C Equatorial Guinea 01°28′N 10°17′E

Evinayoung see Evinayong

115 E18 **Évinos** ~ C Greece

95 E17 **Evje** Aust-Agder, S Norway 58°35′N 07°49′E

Evmolpia see Plovdiv

104 H11 **Évora** anc. Ebora, Lat. Liberalitas Julia. Évora, C Portugal 38°34′N 07°54′W

104 G11 **Évora** ⬖ district S Portugal

102 M4 **Évreux** anc. Civitas Eburovicum. Eure, N France 49°02′N 01°10′E

102 K6 **Évron** Mayenne, NW France 48°10′N 00°24′W

114 L13 **Évros** Bul. Maritsa, Turk. Meriç; anc. Hebrus. ~ SE Europe see also Maritsa/Meriç

Évros see Meriç

Évros see Maritsa

115 F21 **Evrótas** ~ S Greece

103 O5 **Évry** Essonne, N France 48°38′N 02°34′E

25 O8 **E. V. Spence Reservoir** ▣ Texas, SW USA

115 I18 **Évvoia** Lat. Euboea. island C Greece

38 D9 **'Ewa Beach** var. Ewa Beach. O'ahu, Hawaii, USA, C Pacific Ocean 21°19′N 158°00′W

Ewa Beach see 'Ewa Beach

32 L9 **Ewan** Washington, NW USA 47°06′N 117°46′W

44 K12 **Ewarton** C Jamaica 18°11′N 77°06′W

81 J18 **Ewaso Ng'iro** var. Nyiro. ~ C Kenya

29 P13 **Ewing** Nebraska, C USA 42°13′N 98°20′W

194 J5 **Ewing Island** island Antarctica

65 P17 **Ewing Seamount** undersea feature E Atlantic Ocean 23°20′S 08°45′E

◆ Country
● Country Capital
◇ Dependent Territory
○ Dependent Territory Capital
⬖ Administrative Regions
✈ International Airport
▲ Mountain
▲▲ Mountain Range
⛰ Volcano
~ River
◎ Lake
▣ Reservoir

158 L6 **Ewirgol** Xinjiang Uygur Zizhiqu, W China 42°56′N 87°39′E
79 G19 **Ewo** Cuvette, W Congo 0°55′S 14°49′E
27 S3 **Excelsior Springs** Missouri, C USA 39°20′N 94°13′W
97 J23 **Exe** SW England, United Kingdom
194 L12 **Executive Committee Range** ▲ Antarctica
14 E16 **Exeter** Ontario, S Canada 43°19′N 81°26′W
97 J24 **Exeter** *anc.* Isca Damnoniorum. SW England, United Kingdom 50°43′N 03°31′W
35 R11 **Exeter** California, W USA 36°17′N 119°08′W
19 P10 **Exeter** New Hampshire, NE USA 42°57′N 70°55′W
Exin *see* Kcynia
29 T14 **Exira** Iowa, C USA 41°36′N 94°55′W
97 J23 **Exmoor** *moorland* SW England, United Kingdom
21 Y6 **Exmore** Virginia, NE USA 37°31′N 75°48′W
180 G8 **Exmouth** Western Australia 22°01′S 114°06′E
97 J24 **Exmouth** SW England, United Kingdom 50°36′N 03°25′W
180 G8 **Exmouth Gulf** *gulf* Western Australia
173 V8 **Exmouth Plateau** *undersea feature* E Indian Ocean
115 J20 **Exompourgo** *ancient monument* Tínos, Kykládes, Greece, Aegean Sea
104 I10 **Extremadura** *var.* Estremadura. ◆ *autonomous community* W Spain
78 F12 **Extrême-Nord** *Eng.* Extreme North. ◆ *province* N Cameroon
Extreme North *see* Extrême-Nord
44 I3 **Exuma Cays** *islets* C Bahamas
44 I3 **Exuma Sound** *sound* C Bahamas
81 H20 **Eyasi, Lake** ◎ N Tanzania
95 F17 **Eydehavn** Aust-Agder, S Norway 58°31′N 08°53′E
96 L12 **Eyemouth** SE Scotland, United Kingdom 55°52′N 02°07′W
96 G7 **Eye Peninsula** *peninsula* NW Scotland, United Kingdom
80 Q13 **Eyl** *It.* Eil. Nugaal, E Somalia 08°03′N 49°49′E
103 N11 **Eymoutiers** Haute-Vienne, C France 45°45′N 01°43′E
Eyo (lower course) *see* Uolo, Río
29 X10 **Eyota** Minnesota, N USA 44°00′N 92°13′W
182 H2 **Eyre Basin, Lake** *salt lake* South Australia
182 I1 **Eyre Creek** *seasonal river* Northern Territory/South Australia
174 L9 **Eyre, Lake** *salt lake* South Australia
185 C22 **Eyre Mountains** ▲ South Island, New Zealand
182 H3 **Eyre North, Lake** *salt lake* South Australia
182 G7 **Eyre Peninsula** *peninsula* South Australia
182 H4 **Eyre South, Lake** *salt lake* South Australia
95 B18 **Eysturoy** *Dan.* Østerø. *island* N Faeroe Islands
61 D20 **Ezeiza** ✈ (Buenos Aires) Buenos Aires, E Argentina 34°49′S 58°30′W
Ezeres *see* Ezeriş
116 F12 **Ezeriş** *Hung.* Ezeres. Caraş-Severin, W Romania 45°21′N 21°55′E
161 O9 **Ezhou** *prev.* Echeng. Hubei, C China 30°23′N 114°52′E
125 R11 **Ezhva** Respublika Komi, NW Russian Federation 61°45′N 50°43′E
136 B12 **Ezine** Çanakkale, NW Turkey 39°46′N 26°20′E
Ezo *see* Hokkaidō
Ezra/Ezraa *see* Izra'

F

191 P7 **Faaa** Tahiti, W French Polynesia 17°32′S 149°36′W
191 P7 **Faaa** ✈ (Papeete) Tahiti, W French Polynesia 17°31′S 149°36′W
95 H24 **Faaborg** *var.* Fåborg. Syddtjylland, C Denmark 55°06′N 10°10′E
151 K19 **Faadhippolhu Atoll** *var.* Fadiffolu, Lhaviyani Atoll. *atoll* N Maldives
191 U10 **Faaite** *atoll* Îles Tuamotu, C French Polynesia
191 Q8 **Faaone** Tahiti, W French Polynesia 17°39′S 149°18′W
24 H8 **Fabens** Texas, SW USA 31°30′N 106°09′W
94 H12 **Fåberg** Oppland, S Norway 61°15′N 10°21′E
Fåborg *see* Faaborg
106 I12 **Fabriano** Marche, C Italy 43°20′N 12°54′E
145 U16 **Fabrichnoye** *prev.* Fabrichnyy. Almaty, SE Kazakhstan 43°12′N 76°19′E
Fabrichnyy *see* Fabrichnoye
54 F10 **Facatativá** Cundinamarca, C Colombia 04°49′N 74°22′W
77 X9 **Fachi** Agadez, C Niger 18°01′N 11°36′E
188 B16 **Facpi Point** *headland* W Guam
18 I13 **Factoryville** Pennsylvania, NE USA 41°34′N 75°45′W
78 K8 **Fada** Borkou-Ennedi-Tibesti, E Chad 17°14′N 21°32′E
77 Q13 **Fada-Ngourma** E Burkina 12°05′N 00°26′E
123 N6 **Faddeya, Zaliv** *bay* N Russian Federation
123 Q5 **Faddeyevskiy, Poluostrov** *island* Novosibirskiye Ostrova, NE Russian Federation
141 W12 **Fadhi** S Oman 17°54′N 55°30′E
Fadiffolu *see* Faadhippolhu Atoll
106 H10 **Faenza** *anc.* Faventia. Emilia-Romagna, N Italy 44°17′N 11°53′E
64 M5 **Faeroe-Iceland Ridge** *undersea feature* NW Norwegian Sea 64°00′N 10°00′W
64 M5 **Faeroe Islands** *Dan.* Færøerne, *Faer.* Føroyar. ◇ *Danish external territory* N Atlantic Ocean
86 C8 **Faeroe Islands** *island group* N Atlantic Ocean
Færøerne *see* Faeroe Islands
64 N6 **Faeroe-Shetland Trough** *undersea feature* NE Atlantic Ocean
104 H6 **Fafe** Braga, N Portugal 41°27′N 08°11′W
80 K13 **Fafen Shet'** E Ethiopia
193 V15 **Fafo** *island* Tongatapu Group, S Tonga
192 I16 **Fagaloa Bay** *bay* Upolu, E Samoa
192 H15 **Fagamālo** Savai'i, N Samoa 13°27′S 172°22′W
116 I12 **Făgăraş** *Ger.* Fogarasch, *Hung.* Fogaras. Braşov, C Romania 45°50′N 24°59′E
191 W10 **Fagatau** *prev.* Fangatau. *atoll* Îles Tuamotu, C French Polynesia
191 X12 **Fagataufa** *prev.* Fangataufa. *island* Îles Tuamotu, SE French Polynesia
95 M20 **Fagerhult** Kalmar, S Sweden 57°07′N 15°40′E
94 G13 **Fagernes** Oppland, S Norway 60°59′N 09°14′E
92 I9 **Fagernes** Troms, N Norway 69°31′N 19°16′E
95 M14 **Fagersta** Västmanland, C Sweden 59°59′N 15°49′E
77 W13 **Faggo** *var.* Foggo. Bauchi, N Nigeria 11°22′N 09°55′E
Faghman *see* Fughmah
Fagibina, Lake *see* Faguibine, Lac
63 J25 **Fagnano, Lago** ◎ S Argentina
99 G22 **Fagne** *hill range* S Belgium
77 N10 **Faguibine, Lac** *var.* Lake Fagibina. ◎ NW Mali
Fahaheel *see* Al Fuḩayḩīl
Fahlun *see* Falun
143 U12 **Fahraj** Kermān, SE Iran 29°00′N 59°00′E
64 P5 **Faial** Madeira, Portugal, NE Atlantic Ocean 32°47′N 16°53′W
64 N2 **Faial** *var.* Ilha do Faial. *island* Azores, Portugal, NE Atlantic Ocean
Faial, Ilha do *see* Faial
108 G10 **Faido** Ticino, S Switzerland 46°30′N 08°48′E
Faifo *see* Hôi An
Failaka Island *see* Faylakah
190 G12 **Faioa, Île** *island* N Wallis and Futuna
181 W8 **Fairbairn Reservoir** ☒ Queensland, E Australia
39 R9 **Fairbanks** Alaska, USA 64°48′N 147°47′W
21 U12 **Fair Bluff** North Carolina, SE USA 34°18′N 79°02′W
31 R14 **Fairborn** Ohio, N USA 39°48′N 84°03′W
23 S3 **Fairburn** Georgia, SE USA 33°34′N 84°34′W
30 M12 **Fairbury** Illinois, N USA 40°45′N 88°30′W
29 Q17 **Fairbury** Nebraska, C USA 40°08′N 97°10′W
29 T9 **Fairfax** Minnesota, N USA 44°31′N 94°43′W
27 O8 **Fairfax** Oklahoma, C USA 36°34′N 96°42′W
21 R14 **Fairfax** South Carolina, SE USA 32°57′N 81°14′W
35 N8 **Fairfield** California, W USA 38°14′N 122°03′W
33 O14 **Fairfield** Idaho, NW USA 43°20′N 114°45′W
30 M16 **Fairfield** Illinois, N USA 38°22′N 88°23′W
29 X15 **Fairfield** Iowa, C USA 41°00′N 91°57′W
33 R8 **Fairfield** Montana, NW USA 47°36′N 111°59′W
31 Q14 **Fairfield** Ohio, N USA 39°21′N 84°34′W
25 U8 **Fairfield** Texas, SW USA 31°43′N 96°10′W
27 T7 **Fair Grove** Missouri, C USA 37°22′N 93°09′W
19 P12 **Fairhaven** Massachusetts, NE USA 41°38′N 70°51′W
23 N8 **Fairhope** Alabama, S USA 30°31′N 87°54′W
96 L4 **Fair Isle** *island* NE Scotland, United Kingdom
185 F20 **Fairlie** Canterbury, South Island, New Zealand 44°06′S 170°50′E
29 U11 **Fairmont** Minnesota, N USA 43°40′N 94°27′W
29 Q16 **Fairmont** Nebraska, C USA 40°37′N 97°36′W
21 S3 **Fairmont** West Virginia, NE USA 39°28′N 80°08′W
31 P13 **Fairmount** Indiana, N USA 40°25′N 85°39′W
18 H10 **Fairmount** New York, NE USA 43°03′N 76°14′W
29 R7 **Fairmount** North Dakota, N USA 46°02′N 96°36′W
37 S5 **Fairplay** Colorado, C USA 39°13′N 106°00′W
18 F9 **Fairport** New York, NE USA 43°06′N 77°26′W
11 O12 **Fairview** Alberta, W Canada 56°03′N 118°28′W
26 L9 **Fairview** Oklahoma, C USA 36°16′N 98°29′W
36 L4 **Fairview** Utah, W USA 39°37′N 111°26′W
35 T6 **Fairview Peak** ▲ Nevada, W USA 39°13′N 118°09′W
188 H14 **Fais** *atoll* Caroline Islands, W Micronesia
149 U8 **Faisalābād** *prev.* Lyallpur. Punjab, NE Pakistan 31°26′N 73°06′E
Faisaliya *see* Fayşalīyah
28 L8 **Faith** South Dakota, N USA 45°01′N 102°02′W
153 N12 **Faizābād** Uttar Pradesh, N India 26°46′N 82°08′E
Faizabad/Faizābād *see* Feizābād
45 S9 **Fajardo** E Puerto Rico 18°20′N 65°39′W
139 R9 **Fajj, Wādī al** *dry watercourse* S Iraq
140 K4 **Fajr, Bi'r** *well* NW Saudi Arabia
191 W11 **Fakahina** *atoll* Îles Tuamotu, C French Polynesia
190 L10 **Fakaofo Atoll** *island* SE Tokelau
191 U10 **Fakarava** *atoll* Îles Tuamotu, C French Polynesia
127 T2 **Fakel** Udmurtskaya Respublika, NW Russian Federation 57°35′N 53°00′E
97 P19 **Fakenham** E England, United Kingdom 52°50′N 00°51′E
171 U13 **Fakfak** Papua, E Indonesia 02°55′S 132°17′E
153 T12 **Fakīragrām** Assam, NE India 26°22′N 90°15′E
114 M10 **Fakiyska Reka** SE Bulgaria
95 J24 **Fakse** Sjælland, SE Denmark 55°16′N 12°08′E
95 J24 **Fakse Bugt** *bay* SE Denmark
95 J24 **Fakse Ladeplads** Sjælland, SE Denmark 55°14′N 12°11′E
163 V11 **Faku** Liaoning, NE China 42°30′N 123°27′E
76 J14 **Falaba** N Sierra Leone 09°54′N 11°22′W
102 K5 **Falaise** Calvados, N France 48°52′N 00°12′W
114 H12 **Falakró** ▲ NE Greece
189 T12 **Falalu** *island* Chuuk, C Micronesia
166 L4 **Falam** Chin State, W Burma (Myanmar) 22°58′N 93°45′E
143 N8 **Falāvarjān** Eşfahān, C Iran 32°33′N 51°28′E
116 M11 **Fălciu** Vaslui, E Romania 46°19′N 28°10′E
54 I4 **Falcón** *off.* Estado Falcón. ◆ *state* NW Venezuela
106 J12 **Falconara Marittima** Marche, C Italy 43°37′N 13°23′E
Falcone, Capo del *see* Falcone, Punta del
107 A16 **Falcone, Punta del** *var.* Capo del Falcone. *headland* Sardegna, Italy, C Mediterranean Sea 40°57′N 8°12′E
Falcón, Estado *see* Falcón
11 Y16 **Falcon Lake** Manitoba, S Canada 49°44′N 95°18′W
Falcon Lake *see* Falcón, Presa/Falcon Reservoir
41 O7 **Falcón, Presa** *var.* Falcon Lake, Falcon Reservoir. ☒ Mexico/USA *see also* Falcon Reservoir
Falcón, Presa *see* Falcon Reservoir
25 Q16 **Falcon Reservoir** *var.* Falcon Lake, Presa Falcón. ☒ Mexico/USA *see also* Falcón, Presa
Falcon Reservoir *see* Falcón, Presa
190 L10 **Fale** *island* Fakaofo Atoll, SE Tokelau
192 F15 **Faleālupo** Savai'i, NW Samoa 13°30′S 172°46′W
190 B10 **Falefatu** *island* Funafuti Atoll, C Tuvalu
192 G15 **Fālelima** Savai'i, NW Samoa 13°30′S 172°41′W
95 N18 **Falerum** Östergötland, S Sweden 58°07′N 16°15′E
Faleshty *see* Făleşti
116 M9 **Făleşti** *Rus.* Faleshty. NW Moldova 47°33′N 27°43′E
25 S15 **Falfurrias** Texas, SW USA 27°17′N 98°10′W
11 O13 **Falher** Alberta, W Canada 55°45′N 117°18′W
Falkenau an der Eger *see* Sokolov
95 J21 **Falkenberg** Halland, S Sweden 56°55′N 12°30′E
Falkenberg *see* Niemodlin
Falkenburg in Pommern *see* Złocieniec
100 N12 **Falkensee** Brandenburg, NE Germany 52°34′N 13°04′E
96 J12 **Falkirk** C Scotland, United Kingdom 56°N 03°48′W
65 I20 **Falkland Escarpment** *undersea feature* SW Atlantic Ocean 50°00′S 45°00′W
63 K24 **Falkland Islands** *var.* Falklands, Islas Malvinas. ◇ *UK dependent territory* SW Atlantic Ocean
47 W14 **Falkland Islands** *island group* SW Atlantic Ocean
65 I20 **Falkland Plateau** *var.* Argentine Rise. *undersea feature* SW Atlantic Ocean 51°00′S 50°00′W
Falklands *see* Falkland Islands
63 M23 **Falkland Sound** *var.* Estrecho de San Carlos. *strait* C Falkland Islands
Falknov nad Ohří *see* Sokolov
115 H21 **Falkonéra** *island* S Greece
95 K18 **Falköping** Västra Götaland, S Sweden 58°10′N 13°31′E
139 U8 **Fallāḩ** Wāsiţ, E Iraq 32°58′N 45°09′E
35 U16 **Fallbrook** California, W USA 33°22′N 117°15′W
189 U12 **Falleallej Pass** *passage* Chuuk Islands, C Micronesia
93 J14 **Fällfors** Västerbotten, N Sweden 65°07′N 20°46′E
194 I6 **Fallières Coast** *physical region* Antarctica
100 I11 **Fallingbostel** Niedersachsen, NW Germany 52°52′N 09°42′E
33 X9 **Fallon** Montana, NW USA 46°49′N 105°07′W
35 S5 **Fallon** Nevada, W USA 39°29′N 118°47′W
19 O12 **Fall River** Massachusetts, NE USA 41°42′N 71°09′W
27 P6 **Fall River Lake** ☒ Kansas, C USA
35 O3 **Fall River Mills** California, W USA 41°00′N 121°28′W
21 W4 **Falls Church** Virginia, NE USA 38°53′N 77°11′W
29 S17 **Falls City** Nebraska, C USA 40°03′N 95°36′W
25 S12 **Falls City** Texas, SW USA 28°58′N 98°01′W
Falluja *see* Al Fallūjah
77 S12 **Falmey** Dosso, SW Niger 12°29′N 02°58′E
45 W10 **Falmouth** Antigua, Antigua and Barbuda 17°02′N 61°47′W
44 J11 **Falmouth** W Jamaica 18°28′N 77°39′W
97 H25 **Falmouth** SW England, United Kingdom 50°08′N 05°04′W
20 M4 **Falmouth** Kentucky, S USA 38°40′N 84°20′W
19 P13 **Falmouth** Massachusetts, NE USA 41°31′N 70°36′W
21 W5 **Falmouth** Virginia, NE USA 38°19′N 77°28′W
189 U12 **Falos** *island* Chuuk, C Micronesia
83 E26 **False Bay** *Afr.* Valsbaai. *bay* SW South Africa
155 K17 **False Divi Point** *headland* E India 15°46′N 80°43′E
38 M16 **False Pass** Unimak Island, Alaska, USA 54°52′N 163°15′W
154 P12 **False Point** *headland* E India 20°23′N 86°52′E
105 U6 **Falset** Cataluña, NE Spain 41°08′N 00°49′E
95 I25 **Falster** *island* SE Denmark
116 K9 **Fălticeni** *Hung.* Falticsén. Suceava, NE Romania 47°27′N 26°20′E
Falticsén *see* Fălticeni
94 M13 **Falun** *var.* Fahlun. Kopparberg, C Sweden 60°36′N 15°36′E
Famagusta *see* Gazimağusa
Famagusta Bay *see* Gazimağusa Körfezi
62 I8 **Famatina** La Rioja, NW Argentina 28°58′S 67°46′W
99 J21 **Famenne** *physical region* SE Belgium
77 X15 **Fan** E Nigeria
76 M12 **Fana** Koulikoro, SW Mali 12°45′N 06°55′W
115 K19 **Fána** *ancient harbour* Chíos, SE Greece
189 V13 **Fanan** *island* Chuuk, C Micronesia
189 U12 **Fanapanges** *island* Chuuk, C Micronesia
115 L20 **Fanári, Akrotírio** *headland* Ikaría, Dodekánisa, Greece, Aegean Sea 37°40′N 26°21′E
45 Q13 **Fancy** Saint Vincent, Saint Vincent and the Grenadines 13°22′N 61°10′W
172 I5 **Fandriana** Fianarantsoa, SE Madagascar 20°14′S 47°21′E
167 O6 **Fang** Chiang Mai, NW Thailand 19°56′N 99°14′E
80 E13 **Fangak** Jonglei, E South Sudan 09°05′N 30°52′E
Fangatau *see* Fagatau
Fangataufa *see* Fagataufa
193 V15 **Fanga Uta** *bay* S Tonga
161 N7 **Fangcheng** Henan, C China 33°18′N 113°03′E
Fangcheng *see* Fangchenggang
160 K15 **Fangchenggang** *var.* Fangcheng Gezu Zizhixian; *prev.* Fangcheng. Guangxi Zhuangzu Zizhiqu, S China 21°49′N 108°21′E
Fangcheng Gezu Zizhixian *see* Fangchenggang
161 S15 **Fangshan** S Taiwan 22°19′N 120°41′E
163 X8 **Fangzheng** Heilongjiang, NE China 45°50′N 128°50′E
Fani *see* Fanit, Lumi i
119 K16 **Fanipal'** *Rus.* Fanipol'. Minskaya Voblasts', C Belarus 53°45′N 27°20′E
Fanipol' *see* Fanipal'
113 D22 **Fanit, Lumi i** *var.* Fani. N Albania
25 T13 **Fannin** Texas, SW USA 28°41′N 97°13′W
Fanning Island *see* Tabuaeran
94 G8 **Fannrem** Sør-Trøndelag, S Norway 63°16′N 09°48′E
106 I11 **Fano** *anc.* Colonia Julia Fanestris, Fanum Fortunae. Marche, C Italy 43°50′N 13°E
95 E23 **Fanø** *island* W Denmark
167 R5 **Fan Si Pan** ▲ N Vietnam 22°18′N 103°36′E
Fanum Fortunae *see* Fano
Fao *see* Al Fāw
141 W7 **Faq'** *var.* Al Faqa. Dubayy, E United Arab Emirates 24°42′N 55°37′E
Farab *see* Farap
185 G16 **Faraday, Mount** ▲ South Island, New Zealand 42°01′S 171°37′E
79 P16 **Faradje** Orientale, NE Dem. Rep. Congo 03°45′N 29°43′E
Faradofay *see* Tôlañaro
172 I7 **Farafangana** Fianarantsoa, SE Madagascar 22°50′S 47°50′E
148 J7 **Farāh** *var.* Farah, Fararud. Farāh, W Afghanistan 32°22′N 62°07′E
148 K7 **Farāh** ◆ *province* W Afghanistan
148 J7 **Farāh Rūd** W Afghanistan
188 K7 **Farallon de Medinilla** *island* C Northern Mariana Islands
188 J2 **Farallon de Pajaros** *var.* Uracas. *island* N Northern Mariana Islands
76 J14 **Faranah** Haute-Guinée, S Guinea 10°02′N 10°44′W
146 K12 **Farap** *Rus.* Farab. Lebap Welaýaty, NE Turkmenistan 39°15′N 63°32′E
Fararud *see* Farāh
140 M13 **Farasān, Jazā'ir** *island group* SW Saudi Arabia
172 I5 **Faratsiho** Antananarivo, C Madagascar 19°24′S 46°57′E
188 K15 **Faraulep Atoll** *atoll* Caroline Islands, C Micronesia
99 H20 **Farciennes** Hainaut, S Belgium 50°26′N 04°33′E
105 O14 **Fardes** S Spain
191 S10 **Fare** Huahine, W French Polynesia 16°42′S 151°01′W
97 M23 **Fareham** S England, United Kingdom 50°51′N 01°10′W
39 P11 **Farewell** Alaska, USA 62°35′N 153°59′W
184 H13 **Farewell, Cape** *headland* South Island, New Zealand 40°30′S 172°39′E
Farewell, Cape *see* Nunap Isua
184 I13 **Farewell Spit** *spit* South Island, New Zealand
95 I17 **Färgelanda** Västra Götaland, S Sweden 58°34′N 11°59′E
Farghona, Wodii/ Farghona Valley *see* Fergana Valley
Farghona Wodiysi *see* Fergana Valley
23 V8 **Fargo** Georgia, SE USA 30°42′N 82°33′W
29 R5 **Fargo** North Dakota, N USA 46°53′N 96°47′W
147 S10 **Farg'ona** *Rus.* Fergana; *prev.* Novyy Margilan. Farg'ona Viloyati, E Uzbekistan 40°28′N 71°44′E
147 R10 **Farg'ona Viloyati** *Rus.* Ferganskaya Oblast'. ◆ *province* E Uzbekistan
29 V10 **Faribault** Minnesota, N USA 44°18′N 93°16′W
152 J11 **Farīdābād** Haryāna, N India 28°26′N 77°190′E
152 H8 **Farīdkot** Punjab, NW India 30°42′N 74°47′E
153 T15 **Faridpur** Dhaka, C Bangladesh 23°29′N 89°50′E
121 P14 **Fārigh, Wādī al** N Libya
172 I4 **Farihy Alaotra** ◎ C Madagascar
94 M11 **Färila** Gävleborg, C Sweden 61°48′N 15°55′E
104 E9 **Farilhões** *island* C Portugal
76 G12 **Farim** NW Guinea-Bissau 12°30′N 15°09′W
Farish *see* Forish
141 T11 **Fāris, Qalamat** *well* SE Saudi Arabia
95 N21 **Färjestaden** Kalmar, S Sweden 56°38′N 16°30′E
149 R2 **Farkhār** Takhār, NE Afghanistan 36°39′N 69°43′E
147 Q14 **Farkhor** *Rus.* Parkhar. SW Tajikistan 37°32′N 69°22′E
116 F12 **Fârliug** *prev.* Fîrliug, *Hung.* Furluk. Caraş-Severin, SW Romania 45°21′N 21°55′E
115 M21 **Farmakonísi** *island* Dodekánisa, Greece, Aegean Sea
30 M13 **Farmer City** Illinois, N USA 40°14′N 88°38′W
31 N14 **Farmersburg** Indiana, N USA 39°14′N 87°21′W
25 U6 **Farmersville** Texas, SW USA 33°09′N 96°21′W
22 H5 **Farmerville** Louisiana, S USA 32°46′N 92°24′W
29 X16 **Farmington** Iowa, C USA 40°37′N 91°43′W
19 Q6 **Farmington** Maine, NE USA 44°40′N 70°09′W
29 V9 **Farmington** Minnesota, N USA 44°39′N 93°09′W
27 X6 **Farmington** Missouri, C USA 37°46′N 90°26′W
19 O9 **Farmington** New Hampshire, NE USA 43°23′N 71°04′W
37 P9 **Farmington** New Mexico, SW USA 36°44′N 108°13′W
36 L2 **Farmington** Utah, W USA 40°58′N 111°53′W
21 W9 **Farmville** North Carolina, SE USA 35°37′N 77°36′W
21 U6 **Farmville** Virginia, NE USA 37°17′N 78°25′W
97 N22 **Farnborough** S England, United Kingdom 51°17′N 00°46′W
97 N22 **Farnham** S England, United Kingdom 51°13′N 00°49′W
10 J7 **Faro** Yukon Territory, W Canada 62°15′N 133°30′W
104 G14 **Faro** Faro, S Portugal 37°01′N 07°56′W
95 Q18 **Fårö** Gotland, SE Sweden 57°55′N 19°10′E
104 G14 **Faro** ◆ *district* S Portugal
78 F13 **Faro** Cameroon/Nigeria
104 G14 **Faro** ✈ Faro, S Portugal 37°02′N 08°01′W
Faro, Punta del *see* Peloro, Capo
95 Q18 **Fårösund** Gotland, SE Sweden 57°51′N 19°02′E
173 N7 **Farquhar Group** *island group* S Seychelles
18 B13 **Farrell** Pennsylvania, NE USA 41°12′N 80°28′W
152 K11 **Farrukhābād** Uttar Pradesh, N India 27°24′N 79°34′E
143 P11 **Fārs** *off.* Ostān-e Fārs; *anc.* Persis. ◆ *province* S Iran
115 F16 **Fársala** Thessalía, C Greece 39°17′N 22°23′E
143 R4 **Fārsīān** Golestān, N Iran
Fars, Khalīj-e *see* Persian Gulf
95 G21 **Farsø** Nordjylland, N Denmark 56°47′N 09°21′E
Fārs, Ostān-e *see* Fārs
95 D18 **Farsund** Vest-Agder, S Norway 58°05′N 06°49′E
141 U14 **Fartak, Ra's** *headland* E Yemen 15°34′N 52°19′E
60 H13 **Fartura, Serra da** ▲ S Brazil
Farvel, Kap *see* Nunap Isua
24 L4 **Farwell** Texas, SW USA 34°23′N 103°03′W
194 I9 **Farwell Island** *island* Antarctica
152 L9 **Far Western** ◆ *zone* W Nepal
148 M3 **Fāryāb** ◆ *province* N Afghanistan
143 P12 **Fasā** Fārs, S Iran 28°55′N 53°39′E
141 U12 **Fasad, Ramlat** *desert* SW Oman
107 P17 **Fasano** Puglia, SE Italy 40°50′N 17°21′E
92 L3 **Fáskrúdhsfjördhur** Austurland, E Iceland 64°55′N 14°01′W
117 O5 **Fastiv** *Rus.* Fastov. Kyyivs'ka Oblast', NW Ukraine 50°08′N 29°59′E
97 B22 **Fastnet Rock** *Ir.* Carraig Aonair. *island* SW Ireland
Fastov *see* Fastiv
190 C9 **Fatato** *island* Funafuti Atoll, C Tuvalu
152 K12 **Fatehgarh** Uttar Pradesh, N India 27°22′N 79°38′E
149 U6 **Fatehjang** Punjab, E Pakistan 33°33′N 72°43′E
152 G11 **Fatehpur** Rājasthān, N India 27°59′N 74°58′E
152 L13 **Fatehpur** Uttar Pradesh, N India 25°56′N 80°55′E
126 J7 **Fatezh** Kurskaya Oblast', W Russian Federation 52°01′N 35°51′E
76 G11 **Fatick** W Senegal 14°19′N 16°27′W
104 G9 **Fátima** Santarém, W Portugal 39°37′N 08°39′W
136 M11 **Fatsa** Ordu, N Turkey 41°02′N 37°31′E
Fatshan *see* Foshan
190 D12 **Fatua, Pointe** *var.* Pointe Nord. *headland* Île Futuna, S Wallis and Futuna
191 X7 **Fatu Hiva** *island* Îles Marquises, NE French Polynesia
Fatunda *see* Fatundu
79 H21 **Fatundu** *var.* Fatunda. Bandundu, W Dem. Rep. Congo 04°08′S 17°13′E
29 O8 **Faulkton** South Dakota, N USA 45°02′N 99°07′W
116 L13 **Făurei** *prev.* Filimon Sirbu. Brăila, SE Romania 45°05′N 27°15′E
92 G12 **Fauske** Nordland, C Norway 67°15′N 15°27′E
11 P13 **Faust** Alberta, W Canada 55°19′N 115°33′W
99 L23 **Fauvillers** Luxembourg, SE Belgium 49°52′N 05°40′E
107 J24 **Favara** Sicilia, Italy, C Mediterranean Sea 37°19′N 13°40′E
Faventia *see* Faenza
107 G23 **Favignana, Isola** *island* Isole Egadi, S Italy
12 D8 **Fawn** Ontario, SE Canada
Faxa Bay *see* Faxaflói
92 H3 **Faxaflói** *Eng.* Faxa Bay. *bay* W Iceland
78 I7 **Faya** *prev.* Faya-Largeau, Largeau. Borkou-Ennedi-Tibesti, N Chad 17°58′N 19°06′E
Faya-Largeau *see* Faya
187 Q16 **Fayaoué** Province des Îles Loyauté, C New Caledonia 20°41′S 166°31′E
138 M5 **Fayḑat** *hill range* E Syria
23 O3 **Fayette** Alabama, S USA 33°40′N 87°49′W
29 X12 **Fayette** Iowa, C USA 42°50′N 91°48′W
22 J6 **Fayette** Mississippi, S USA 31°42′N 91°03′W
27 U4 **Fayette** Missouri, C USA 39°09′N 92°40′W
27 S9 **Fayetteville** Arkansas, C USA 36°04′N 94°10′W
21 U10 **Fayetteville** North Carolina, SE USA 35°03′N 78°53′W
20 J10 **Fayetteville** Tennessee, S USA 35°08′N 86°33′W
25 U11 **Fayetteville** Texas, SW USA 29°52′N 96°40′W
21 R5 **Fayetteville** West Virginia, NE USA 38°03′N 81°09′W
141 R4 **Faylakah** *var.* Failaka Island. *island* E Kuwait
139 T10 **Fayşalīyah** *var.* Faisaliya. Al Qādisīyah, S Iraq 31°48′N 44°36′E
189 P15 **Fayu** *var.* East Fayu. *island* Hall Islands, C Micronesia
152 G8 **Fāzilka** Punjab, NW India 30°26′N 74°04′E
Fdérick *see* Fdérik
76 I6 **Fdérik** *var.* Fdérick, *Fr.* Fort Gouraud. Tiris Zemmour, NW Mauritania 22°40′N 12°41′W
Feabhail, Loch *see* Foyle, Lough
97 B20 **Feale** SW Ireland
21 V12 **Fear, Cape** *headland* Bald Head Island, North Carolina, SE USA 33°50′N 77°57′W
35 O6 **Feather River** California, W USA
185 M14 **Featherston** Wellington, North Island, New Zealand 41°07′S 175°28′E
102 L3 **Fécamp** Seine-Maritime, N France 49°45′N 00°22′E
Fédala *see* Mohammedia
61 D17 **Federación** Entre Ríos, E Argentina 31°00′S 57°55′W
61 D17 **Federal** Entre Ríos, E Argentina 30°55′S 58°45′W
77 T15 **Federal Capital District** ◆ *capital territory* C Nigeria
Federal Capital Territory *see* Australian Capital Territory
Federal District *see* Distrito Federal
21 Y4 **Federalsburg** Maryland, NE USA 38°41′N 75°46′W
74 M6 **Fedjaj, Chott el** *var.* Chott el Fejaj, Shaţţ al Fijāj. *salt lake* C Tunisia
94 B13 **Fedje** *island* S Norway
144 M7 **Fedorovka** Kostanay, N Kazakhstan 51°12′N 52°00′E
127 U6 **Fedorovka** Respublika Bashkortostan, W Russian Federation 53°09′N 55°07′E
Fëdory *see* Fyadory
117 U11 **Fedotova Kosa** *spit* SE Ukraine
189 V13 **Fefan** *atoll* Chuuk Islands, C Micronesia
111 O21 **Fehérgyarmat** Szabolcs-Szatmár-Bereg, E Hungary 47°59′N 22°29′E
Fehér-Körös *see* Crişul Alb
Fehértemplom *see* Bela Crkva
Fehérvölgy *see* Albac
100 L7 **Fehmarn** *island* N Germany
95 H25 **Fehmarn Belt** *Dan.* Femern Bælt, *Ger.* Fehmarnbelt. *strait* Denmark /Germany *see also* Femern Bælt
Fehmarnbelt *see* Fehmarn Belt/Femer Bælt
109 X8 **Fehring** Steiermark, SE Austria 46°56′N 16°00′E
59 B15 **Feijó** Acre, W Brazil 08°07′S 70°27′W
184 M12 **Feilding** Manawatu-Wanganui, North Island, New Zealand 40°15′S 175°34′E
Feira *see* Feira de Santana
59 O17 **Feira de Santana** *var.* Feira. Bahia, E Brazil 12°17′S 38°53′W
109 X7 **Feistritz** SE Austria
Feistritz *see* Ilirska Bistrica
161 P8 **Feixi** *var.* Shangpai; *prev.* Shangpaihe. Anhui, E China 31°40′N 117°08′E
149 S2 **Feizābād** *var.* Faizabad, Faizābād, Feyzābād, Fyzabad; *prev.* Feyzābād. Badakhshān, NE Afghanistan 37°06′N 70°34′E
Fejaj, Chott el *see* Fedjaj, Chott el
111 I23 **Fejér** *off.* Fejér Megye. ◆ *county* W Hungary
Fejér Megye *see* Fejér
95 I24 **Fejø** *island* SE Denmark
136 K15 **Feke** Adana, S Turkey 37°49′N 35°55′E
Feketehalom *see* Codlea
Fekete-Körös *see* Crişul Negru
105 Y9 **Felanitx** Mallorca, Spain, W Mediterranean Sea 39°28′N 03°08′E
109 T3 **Feldaist** N Austria
109 W8 **Feldbach** Steiermark, SE Austria 46°58′N 15°53′E
101 F24 **Feldberg** ▲ SW Germany 47°52′N 08°01′E
116 J12 **Feldioara** *Ger.* Marienburg, *Hung.* Földvár. Braşov, C Romania 45°49′N 25°36′E
108 I7 **Feldkirch** *anc.* Clunia. Vorarlberg, W Austria 47°15′N 09°38′E
109 S9 **Feldkirchen in Kärnten** *Slvn.* Trg. Kärnten, S Austria 46°42′N 14°01′E
Félegyháza *see* Kiskunfélegyháza
192 H16 **Feleolo** ✈ (Āpia) Upolu, C Samoa 13°49′S 171°59′W
104 H6 **Felgueiras** Porto, N Portugal 41°22′N 08°12′W
Felicitas Julia *see* Lisboa
172 J16 **Félicité** *island* Inner Islands, NE Seychelles
151 K20 **Felidhu Atoll** *atoll* C Maldives
41 Y13 **Felipe Carrillo Puerto** Quintana Roo, SE Mexico 19°34′N 88°02′W
97 Q21 **Felixstowe** E England, United Kingdom 51°58′N 01°20′E
103 N11 **Felletin** Creuse, C France 45°53′N 02°12′E
Fellin *see* Viljandi
Felsőbánya *see* Baia Sprie
Felsőmuzslya *see* Mužlja
Felsővisó *see* Vişeu de Sus
35 N10 **Felton** California, W USA 37°03′N 122°04′W
106 H7 **Feltre** Veneto, NE Italy 46°01′N 11°55′E
95 H25 **Femer Bælt** *Dan.* Fehmarn Belt, *Ger.* Fehmarnbelt. *strait* Denmark/Germany *see also* Fehmarn Belt
95 I24 **Femø** *island* SE Denmark
94 I10 **Femunden** ◎ S Norway
104 H2 **Fene** Galicia, NW Spain 43°28′N 08°10′W
14 I14 **Fenelon Falls** Ontario, SE Canada 44°34′N 78°43′W
189 U13 **Feneppi** *atoll* Chuuk Islands, C Micronesia
137 O11 **Fener Burnu** *headland* N Turkey 41°07′N 39°26′E
Fénérive *see* Fenoarivo Atsinanana
115 J14 **Fengári** ▲ Samothráki, E Greece 40°27′N 25°37′E
163 V13 **Fengcheng** *var.* Feng-cheng, Fenghwangcheng. Liaoning, NE China 40°28′N 124°01′E
Fengcheng *see* Lianjiang
Feng-cheng *see* Fengcheng
160 K11 **Fenggang** *var.* Longquan. Guizhou, S China 27°57′N 107°42′E
161 O7 **Feng He** C China
161 S9 **Fenghua** Zhejiang, SE China 29°40′N 121°25′E
Fenghwangcheng *see* Fengcheng
Fengjiaba *see* Wangcang
160 L9 **Fengjie** *var.* Yong'an. Sichuan, C China 31°03′N 109°31′E
160 M14 **Fengkai** *var.* Jiangkou. Guangdong, S China 23°26′N 111°28′E
161 T13 **Fenglin** *Jap.* Hōrin. C Taiwan 23°52′N 121°30′E
161 P1 **Fengning** *prev.* Dagezhen. Hebei, E China 41°12′N 116°37′E
160 E13 **Fengqing** *var.* Fengshan. Yunnan, SW China 24°38′N 99°54′E
161 O6 **Fengqiu** Henan, C China 35°02′N 114°24′E
161 Q2 **Fengrun** Hebei, E China 39°50′N 118°10′E
Fengshan *see* Luoyuan, Fujian, China
Fengshan *see* Fengqing, Yunnan, China
163 T4 **Fengshui Shan** ▲ NE China 52°20′N 123°22′E
161 P14 **Fengshun** Guangdong, S China 23°51′N 116°11′E
Fengtien *see* Shenyang, China
Fengtien *see* Liaoning, China
160 J7 **Fengxian** *var.* Feng Xian; *prev.* Shuangshipu. Shaanxi, C China 33°50′N 106°33′E
Feng Xian *see* Fengxian
Fengxiang *see* Luobei
Fengyizhen *see* Maoxian
163 P13 **Fengzhen** Nei Mongol Zizhiqu, N China 40°25′N 113°09′E
160 M6 **Fen He** C China
153 V15 **Feni** Chittagong, E Bangladesh 23°00′N 91°24′E
186 I6 **Feni Islands** *island group* NE Papua New Guinea
38 H17 **Fenimore Pass** *strait* Aleutian Islands, Alaska, USA
84 B9 **Feni Ridge** *undersea feature* N Atlantic Ocean 53°45′N 18°00′W
Fennern *see* Vändra
30 J9 **Fennimore** Wisconsin, N USA 42°58′N 90°39′W
172 J4 **Fenoarivo Atsinanana** *prev./Fr.* Fénérive. Toamasina, E Madagascar 20°52′S 46°52′E
95 I24 **Fensmark** Sjælland, SE Denmark 55°17′N 11°48′E
97 O19 **Fens, The** *wetland* E England, United Kingdom
31 R9 **Fenton** Michigan, N USA 42°48′N 83°42′W
190 K10 **Fenua Fala** *island* SE Tokelau
190 F12 **Fenuafo'ou, Île** *island* E Wallis and Futuna
190 L10 **Fenua Loa** *island* Fakaofo Atoll, E Tokelau
160 M4 **Fenyang** Shanxi, C China 37°14′N 111°40′E
117 U13 **Feodosiya** *var.* Kefe, *It.* Kaffa; *anc.* Theodosia. Avtonomna Respublika Krym, S Ukraine 45°03′N 35°24′E
94 I10 **Feragen** ◎ S Norway
74 L5 **Fer, Cap de** *headland* NE Algeria 37°05′N 07°10′E
31 O16 **Ferdinand** Indiana, N USA 38°13′N 86°51′W
Ferdinand *see* Montana, Bulgaria
Ferdinand *see* Mihail Kogălniceanu, Romania
Ferdinandsberg *see* Oţelu Roşu
143 T7 **Ferdows** *var.* Firdaus; *prev.* Tūn. Khorāsān-Razavī, E Iran 34°00′N 58°09′E
103 Q5 **Fère-Champenoise** Marne, N France 48°45′N 03°59′E
Ferencz-Jósef Csúcs *see* Gerlachovský štít
107 J16 **Ferentino** Lazio, C Italy 41°40′N 13°16′E
114 L13 **Féres** Anatolikí Makedonía kai Thráki, NE Greece 40°54′N 26°12′E
Fergana *see* Farg'ona
147 S10 **Fergana Valley** *var.* Farghona Valley, *Rus.* Ferganskaya Dolina, *Taj.* Wodii Farghona, *Uzb.* Farghona Wodiysi. *basin* Tajikistan/Uzbekistan
Ferganskaya Dolina *see* Fergana Valley
Ferganskaya Oblast' *see* Farg'ona Viloyati
147 U9 **Ferganskiy Khrebet** ▲ C Kyrgyzstan
14 F15 **Fergus** Ontario, S Canada 43°42′N 80°22′W
29 S6 **Fergus Falls** Minnesota, N USA 46°15′N 96°02′W
186 G9 **Fergusson Island** *var.* Kaluwawa. *island* SE Papua New Guinea
111 K22 **Ferihegy** ✈ (Budapest) Budapest, C Hungary 47°25′N 19°13′E

◆ Country
● Country Capital
◇ Dependent Territory
○ Dependent Territory Capital
◆ Administrative Regions
✈ International Airport
▲ Mountain
▲ Mountain Range
Volcano
River
◎ Lake
☒ Reservoir

113 N17 **Ferizaj** Serb. Uroševac. C Kosovo 42°23′N 21°09′E
77 N14 **Ferkessédougou** N Ivory Coast 09°36′N 05°12′W
109 T10 **Ferlach** Slvn. Borovlje. Kärnten, S Austria 46°31′N 14°18′E
97 E16 **Fermanagh** cultural region SW Northern Ireland, United Kingdom
106 J13 **Fermo** anc. Firmum Picenum. Marche, C Italy 43°09′N 13°44′E
104 J6 **Fermoselle** Castilla y León, N Spain 41°19′N 06°24′W
97 D20 **Fermoy** Ir. Mainistir Fhear Maí. SW Ireland 52°08′N 08°16′W
23 W8 **Fernandina Beach** Amelia Island, Florida, SE USA 30°40′N 81°27′W
57 A17 **Fernandina, Isla** var. Narborough Island. island Galapagos Islands, Ecuador, E Pacific Ocean
47 Y5 **Fernando de Noronha** island E Brazil
Fernando Po/Fernando Póo see Bioco, Isla de
60 J7 **Fernandópolis** São Paulo, S Brazil 20°18′S 50°13′W
104 M13 **Fernán Núñez** Andalucía, S Spain 37°40′N 04°44′W
83 Q14 **Fernão Veloso, Baia de** bay NE Mozambique
34 K3 **Ferndale** California, W USA 40°34′N 124°16′W
32 H6 **Ferndale** Washington, NW USA 48°51′N 122°35′W
11 P17 **Fernie** British Columbia, SW Canada 49°30′N 115°00′W
35 R5 **Fernley** Nevada, W USA 39°35′N 119°15′W
Ferozepore see Fīrozpur
107 N18 **Ferrandina** Basilicata, S Italy 40°30′N 16°25′E
106 G9 **Ferrara** anc. Forum Alieni. Emilia-Romagna, N Italy 44°50′N 11°36′E
120 F9 **Ferrat, Cap** headland NW Algeria 35°52′N 00°24′W
107 D20 **Ferrato, Capo** headland Sardegna, Italy, C Mediterranean Sea 39°18′N 09°37′E
104 G12 **Ferreira do Alentejo** Beja, S Portugal 38°04′N 08°06′W
56 B11 **Ferreñafe** Lambayeque, W Peru 06°42′S 79°45′W
108 C12 **Ferret** Valais, SW Switzerland 45°57′N 07°04′E
102 I13 **Ferret, Cap** headland W France 44°37′N 01°15′W
22 I6 **Ferriday** Louisiana, S USA 31°37′N 91°33′W
Ferro see Hierro
107 D16 **Ferro, Capo** headland Sardegna, Italy, C Mediterranean Sea 41°09′N 09°31′E
104 H2 **Ferrol** var. El Ferrol; prev. El Ferrol del Caudillo. Galicia, NW Spain 43°29′N 08°14′W
56 B12 **Ferrol, Península de** peninsula W Peru
36 M5 **Ferron** Utah, W USA 39°05′N 111°07′W
21 S7 **Ferrum** Virginia, NE USA 36°54′N 80°01′W
23 O8 **Ferry Pass** Florida, SE USA 30°30′N 87°12′W
Ferryville see Menzel Bourguiba
29 S4 **Fertile** Minnesota, N USA 47°32′N 96°16′W
Fertő see Neusiedler See
Ferwerd see Ferwert
98 L5 **Ferwert** Dutch. Ferwerd. Fryslân, N Netherlands 53°21′N 05°47′E
74 G6 **Fès** Eng. Fez. N Morocco 34°06′N 04°57′W
79 I22 **Feshi** Bandundu, SW Dem. Rep. Congo 06°08′S 18°12′E
29 O4 **Fessenden** North Dakota, N USA 47°36′N 99°37′W
Festenberg see Twardogóra
27 X5 **Festus** Missouri, C USA 38°13′N 90°24′W
116 M14 **Fetești** Ialomița, SE Romania 44°22′N 27°51′E
136 D17 **Fethiye** Muğla, SW Turkey 36°37′N 29°08′E
96 M1 **Fetlar** island NE Scotland, United Kingdom
95 I15 **Fetsund** Akershus, S Norway 59°55′N 11°03′E
12 L5 **Feuilles, Lac aux** ◎ Québec, E Canada
12 L5 **Feuilles, Rivière aux** ≈ Québec, E Canada
99 M23 **Feulen** Diekirch, C Luxembourg 49°52′N 06°03′E
103 Q11 **Feurs** Loire, E France 45°44′N 04°14′E
95 F18 **Fevik** Aust-Agder, S Norway 58°22′N 08°40′E
123 R13 **Fevral'sk** Amurskaya Oblast', SE Russian Federation 52°25′N 131°06′E
Feyzābād see Feizābād
Feyẕābād see Feiẕābād
Fez see Fès
97 J19 **Ffestiniog** NW Wales, United Kingdom 52°55′N 03°54′W
Fhóid Duibh, Cuan an see Blacksod Bay
62 I8 **Fiambalá** Catamarca, NW Argentina 27°45′S 67°37′W
172 I6 **Fianarantsoa** Fianarantsoa, C Madagascar 21°27′S 47°05′E
172 H6 **Fianarantsoa** ◈ province SE Madagascar
78 G12 **Fianga** Mayo-Kébbi, SW Chad 09°57′N 15°09′E
Ficce see Fichē
80 J12 **Fichē** It. Ficce. Oromīya, C Ethiopia 09°48′N 38°43′E
101 N17 **Fichtelberg** ▲ Czech Republic/Germany 50°26′N 12°57′E
101 M18 **Fichtelgebirge** ▲▲ SE Germany
101 M19 **Fichtelnaab** ≈ SE Germany
106 E9 **Fidenza** Emilia-Romagna, N Italy 44°52′N 10°04′E
113 K21 **Fier** var. Fieri. Fier, SW Albania 40°44′N 19°34′E
113 K21 **Fier** ◈ district W Albania
Fieri see Fier
Fierza see Fierzë
113 L17 **Fierzë** var. Fierza. Shkodër, N Albania 42°15′N 20°02′E
113 L17 **Fierzës, Liqeni i** ◎ N Albania
108 F10 **Fiesch** Valais, SW Switzerland 46°25′N 08°09′E
106 G11 **Fiesole** Toscana, C Italy 43°50′N 11°18′E
138 G12 **Fīfah** Aṭ Ṭafīlah, W Jordan 30°55′N 35°25′E
96 K11 **Fife** var. Kingdom of Fife. cultural region E Scotland, United Kingdom
Fife, Kingdom of see Fife
96 K11 **Fife Ness** headland E Scotland, United Kingdom 56°16′N 02°35′W
Fifteen Twenty Fracture Zone see Barracuda Fracture Zone
103 N13 **Figeac** Lot, S France 44°37′N 02°01′E
95 N19 **Figeholm** Kalmar, SE Sweden 57°12′N 16°34′E
Figig see Figuig
83 J18 **Figtree** Matabeleland South, SW Zimbabwe 20°24′S 28°21′E
104 F8 **Figueira da Foz** Coimbra, W Portugal 40°09′N 08°51′W
105 X4 **Figueres** Cataluña, E Spain 42°16′N 02°57′E
74 H7 **Figuig** var. Figig. E Morocco 32°09′N 01°13′W
Fijājj, Shaṭṭ al see Fedjaj, Chott el
187 Y15 **Fiji** off. Sovereign Democratic Republic of Fiji, Fij. Viti. ◆ republic SW Pacific Ocean
192 K9 **Fiji** island group SW Pacific Ocean
175 Q8 **Fiji Plate** tectonic feature
Fiji, Sovereign Democratic Republic of see Fiji
105 P14 **Filabres, Sierra de los** ▲▲ SE Spain
83 K18 **Filabusi** Matabeleland South, S Zimbabwe 20°34′S 29°20′E
42 K13 **Filadelfia** Guanacaste, W Costa Rica 10°28′N 85°33′W
111 K20 **Fil'akovo** Hung. Fülek. Banskobýstricky Kraj, C Slovakia 48°15′N 19°53′E
195 N5 **Filchner Ice Shelf** ice shelf Antarctica
14 J11 **Fildegrand** ≈ Québec, SE Canada
33 O15 **Filer** Idaho, NW USA 42°34′N 114°36′W
Filevo see Vŭrbitsa
116 H14 **Filiași** Dolj, SW Romania 44°32′N 23°31′E
115 B16 **Filiátes** Ípeiros, W Greece 39°38′N 20°16′E
115 D21 **Filiatrá** Pelopónnisos, S Greece 37°09′N 21°35′E
107 K22 **Filicudi, Isola** island Isole Eolie, S Italy
141 Y10 **Filim** E Oman 20°37′N 58°11′E
Filimon Sîrbu see Făurei
77 S11 **Filingué** Tillabéri, W Niger 14°21′N 03°22′E
Filiouri see Líssos
114 I13 **Fílippoi** anc. Philippi. site of ancient city Anatolikí Makedonía kai Thráki, NE Greece
95 L15 **Filipstad** Värmland, C Sweden 59°44′N 14°10′E
108 I9 **Filisur** Graubünden, S Switzerland 46°40′N 09°43′E
94 E12 **Fillefjell** ▲▲ S Norway
35 R14 **Fillmore** California, W USA 34°23′N 118°56′W
36 K5 **Fillmore** Utah, W USA 38°57′N 112°19′W
14 J10 **Fils, Lac du** ◎ Québec, SE Canada
Filyos Çayı see Yenice Çayı
Fimbul Ice Shelf see Fimbulisen
195 Q2 **Fimbutheimen** physical region Antarctica
106 G9 **Finale Emilia** Emilia-Romagna, C Italy 44°50′N 11°17′E
106 C10 **Finale Ligure** Liguria, NW Italy 44°11′N 08°22′E
105 P14 **Fiñana** Andalucía, S Spain 37°09′N 02°47′W
21 S6 **Fincastle** Virginia, NE USA 37°30′N 79°54′W
99 M25 **Findel** ✈ (Luxembourg) Luxembourg, C Luxembourg 49°39′N 06°16′E
96 J9 **Findhorn** ≈ N Scotland, United Kingdom
31 R12 **Findlay** Ohio, N USA 41°02′N 83°40′W
18 G11 **Finger Lakes** ◎ New York, NE USA
83 L14 **Fingoè** Tete, NW Mozambique 15°10′S 31°51′E
136 E17 **Finike** Antalya, SW Turkey 36°18′N 30°08′E
102 F6 **Finistère** ◈ department NW France
186 D7 **Finisterre Range** ▲▲ N Papua New Guinea
181 Q8 **Finke** Northern Territory, N Australia 25°37′S 134°35′E
109 S10 **Finkenstein** Kärnten, S Austria 46°34′N 13°53′E
189 Y15 **Finkol, Mount** var. Mount Crozer. ▲ Kosrae, E Micronesia 05°18′N 163°00′E
93 L17 **Finland** off. Republic of Finland, Fin. Suomen Tasavalta, Suomi. ◆ republic N Europe
124 F12 **Finland, Gulf of** Est. Soome Laht, Fin. Suomenlahti, Ger. Finnischer Meerbusen, Rus. Finskiy Zaliv, Swe. Finska Viken. gulf E Baltic Sea
Finland, Republic of see Finland
10 L11 **Finlay** ≈ British Columbia, W Canada
183 O10 **Finley** New South Wales, SE Australia 35°41′S 145°33′E
29 Q4 **Finley** North Dakota, N USA 47°30′N 97°50′W
Finnischer Meerbusen see Finland, Gulf of
92 K9 **Finnmark** ◈ county N Norway
92 K9 **Finnmarksvidda** physical region N Norway
92 I9 **Finnsnes** Troms, N Norway 69°16′N 18°00′E
186 E7 **Finschhafen** Morobe, C Papua New Guinea 06°35′S 147°51′E
94 E13 **Finse** Hordaland, S Norway 60°35′N 07°33′E
Finska Viken/Finskiy Zaliv see Finland, Gulf of
95 M17 **Finspång** Östergötland, S Sweden 58°42′N 15°45′E
108 F10 **Finsteraarhorn** ▲ Switzerland 46°33′N 08°07′E
101 O14 **Finsterwalde** Brandenburg, E Germany 51°38′N 13°43′E
185 A23 **Fiordland** physical region South Island, New Zealand
106 E9 **Fiorenzuola d'Arda** Emilia-Romagna, C Italy 44°57′N 09°53′E
Firat Nehri see Euphrates
Firdaus see Ferdows
18 M14 **Fire Island** island New York, NE USA
106 G11 **Firenze** Eng. Florence; anc. Florentia. Toscana, C Italy 43°47′N 11°15′E
106 G10 **Firenzuola** Toscana, C Italy 44°07′N 11°22′E
14 C6 **Fire River** Ontario, S Canada 48°46′N 83°34′W
Fîrliug see Fârliug
61 B19 **Firmat** Santa Fe, C Argentina 33°29′S 61°29′W
103 Q12 **Firminy** Loire, E France 45°22′N 04°18′E
Firmum Picenum see Fermo
152 J12 **Fīrozābād** Uttar Pradesh, N India 27°09′N 78°24′E
152 G8 **Fīrozpur** var. Ferozepore. Punjab, NW India 30°55′N 74°38′E
First State see Delaware
143 O12 **Fīrūzābād** Fārs, S Iran 28°51′N 52°35′E
Fischamend see Fischamend Markt
109 Y4 **Fischamend Markt** var. Fischamend. Niederösterreich, NE Austria 48°08′N 16°37′E
109 W6 **Fischbacher Alpen** ▲▲ E Austria
Fischhausen see Primorsk
83 D21 **Fish** var. Vis. ≈ S Namibia
83 F24 **Fish** Afr. Vis. ≈ SW South Africa
11 X15 **Fisher Branch** Manitoba, S Canada 51°09′N 97°34′W
11 X15 **Fisher River** Manitoba, S Canada 51°25′N 97°23′W
19 N13 **Fishers Island** island New York, NE USA
37 U8 **Fishers Peak** ▲ Colorado, C USA 37°06′N 104°27′W
9 P9 **Fisher Strait** strait Nunavut, N Canada
97 H21 **Fishguard** Wel. Abergwaun. SW Wales, United Kingdom 51°59′N 04°49′W
19 R2 **Fish River Lake** ◎ Maine, NE USA
194 K6 **Fiske, Cape** headland Antarctica 74°27′S 60°28′W
103 P4 **Fismes** Marne, N France 49°19′N 03°41′E
104 F3 **Fisterra, Cabo** headland NW Spain 42°53′N 09°16′W
19 N11 **Fitchburg** Massachusetts, NE USA 42°34′N 71°48′W
96 L3 **Fitful Head** headland NE Scotland, United Kingdom 59°57′N 01°24′W
95 C14 **Fitjar** Hordaland, S Norway 59°55′N 05°19′E
192 H16 **Fito, Mauga** ▲ Upolu, C Samoa 13°57′S 171°42′W
23 U6 **Fitzgerald** Georgia, SE USA 31°42′N 83°15′W
180 M5 **Fitzroy Crossing** Western Australia 18°10′S 125°40′E
63 G21 **Fitzroy, Monte** var. Cerro Chaltel. ▲ S Argentina 49°18′S 73°06′W
181 Y8 **Fitzroy River** ≈ Queensland, E Australia
180 L5 **Fitzroy River** ≈ Western Australia
14 E12 **Fitzwilliam Island** island Ontario, S Canada
107 J15 **Fiuggi** Lazio, C Italy 41°47′N 13°16′E
Fiume see Rijeka
107 H15 **Fiumicino** Lazio, C Italy 41°46′N 12°13′E
Fiumicino see Leonardo da Vinci
106 E10 **Fivizzano** Toscana, C Italy 44°13′N 10°06′E
79 O21 **Fizi** Sud-Kivu, E Dem. Rep. Congo 04°15′S 28°57′E
Fizuli see Füzuli
92 I11 **Fjällåsen** Norrbotten, N Sweden 67°31′N 20°08′E
95 G20 **Fjerritslev** Nordjylland, N Denmark 57°06′N 09°17′E
F.J.S. see Franz Josef Strauss
95 L16 **Fjugesta** Örebro, C Sweden 59°10′N 14°50′E
Fladstrand see Frederikshavn
37 V5 **Flagler** Colorado, C USA 39°17′N 103°04′W
23 X10 **Flagler Beach** Florida, SE USA 29°28′N 81°07′W
36 L11 **Flagstaff** Arizona, SW USA 35°12′N 111°39′W
65 H24 **Flagstaff Bay** bay N Saint Helena, C Atlantic Ocean
19 P5 **Flagstaff Lake** ◎ Maine, NE USA
94 E13 **Flåm** Sogn Og Fjordane, S Norway 60°51′N 07°06′E
15 O8 **Flamand** ≈ Québec, SE Canada
30 J5 **Flambeau River** ≈ Wisconsin, N USA
97 O16 **Flamborough Head** headland E England, United Kingdom 54°06′N 00°03′W
100 N13 **Fläming** hill range NE Germany
16 H8 **Flaming Gorge Reservoir** ⊞ Utah/Wyoming, NW USA
Flanders see Vlaanderen
Flandre see Vlaanderen
29 R10 **Flandreau** South Dakota, N USA 44°03′N 96°36′W
96 D6 **Flannan Isles** island group NW Scotland, United Kingdom
28 M6 **Flasher** North Dakota, N USA 46°25′N 101°12′W
93 G15 **Flåsjön** ◎ N Sweden
39 O11 **Flat** Alaska, USA 62°27′N 158°00′W
92 H1 **Flateyri** Vestfirdhir, NW Iceland 66°03′N 23°28′W
33 P8 **Flathead Lake** ◎ Montana, NW USA
173 Y15 **Flat Island** Fr. Île Plate. island N Mauritius
25 T11 **Flatonia** Texas, SW USA 29°41′N 97°06′W
185 M14 **Flat Point** headland North Island, New Zealand 41°12′S 176°03′E
27 X6 **Flat River** Missouri, C USA 37°51′N 90°31′W
31 P8 **Flat River** ≈ Michigan, N USA
31 P14 **Flatrock River** ≈ Indiana, N USA
32 E6 **Flattery, Cape** headland Washington, NW USA 48°22′N 124°43′W
64 B12 **Flatts Village** var. The Flatts Village. C Bermuda 32°19′N 64°44′W
108 H7 **Flawil** Sankt Gallen, NE Switzerland 47°25′N 09°12′E
97 N22 **Fleet** S England, United Kingdom 51°16′N 00°50′W
97 K16 **Fleetwood** NW England, United Kingdom 53°55′N 03°02′W
18 H15 **Fleetwood** Pennsylvania, NE USA 40°27′N 75°49′W
95 D18 **Flekkefjord** Vest-Agder, S Norway 58°17′N 06°40′E
21 N5 **Flemingsburg** Kentucky, S USA 38°26′N 83°43′W
18 J15 **Flemington** New Jersey, NE USA 40°30′N 74°51′W
64 I7 **Flemish Cap** undersea feature NW Atlantic Ocean 47°00′N 45°00′W
95 N16 **Flen** Södermanland, C Sweden 59°04′N 16°39′E
100 I6 **Flensburg** Schleswig-Holstein, N Germany 54°47′N 09°26′E
100 J6 **Flensburger Förde** inlet Denmark/Germany
102 K5 **Flers** Orne, N France 48°45′N 00°34′W
95 C14 **Flesland** ✈ (Bergen) Hordaland, S Norway 60°18′N 05°15′E
Flessingue see Vlissingen
21 P10 **Fletcher** North Carolina, SE USA 35°24′N 82°29′W
31 R6 **Fletcher Pond** ◎ Michigan, N USA
102 L15 **Fleurance** Gers, S France 43°50′N 00°39′E
108 B8 **Fleurier** Neuchâtel, W Switzerland 46°55′N 06°37′E
99 H20 **Fleurus** Hainaut, S Belgium 50°28′N 04°33′E
103 N7 **Fleury-les-Aubrais** Loiret, C France 47°55′N 01°55′E
98 K10 **Flevoland** ◈ province C Netherlands
Flickertail State see North Dakota
108 H9 **Flims** Glarus, NE Switzerland 46°50′N 09°16′E
182 F8 **Flinders Island** island Investigator Group, South Australia
183 P14 **Flinders Island** island Furneaux Group, Tasmania, SE Australia
182 I6 **Flinders Ranges** ▲▲ South Australia
181 U5 **Flinders River** ≈ Queensland, NE Australia
11 V13 **Flin Flon** Manitoba, C Canada 54°47′N 101°51′W
97 K18 **Flint** NE Wales, United Kingdom 53°15′N 03°10′W
31 R9 **Flint** Michigan, N USA 43°01′N 83°41′W
97 J18 **Flint** cultural region NE Wales, United Kingdom
27 O7 **Flint Hills** hill range Kansas, C USA
191 Y6 **Flint Island** island Line Islands, E Kiribati
23 S4 **Flint River** ≈ Georgia, SE USA
31 R9 **Flint River** ≈ Michigan, N USA
189 X12 **Flipper Point** headland C Wake Island 19°18′N 166°37′E
94 I13 **Flisa** Hedmark, S Norway 60°36′N 12°02′E
94 J13 **Flisa** ≈ S Norway
122 J5 **Flissingskiy, Mys** headland Novaya Zemlya, NW Russian Federation 76°43′N 69°01′E
Flitsch see Bovec
105 U6 **Flix** Cataluña, NE Spain 41°13′N 00°32′E
95 J19 **Floda** Västra Götaland, S Sweden 57°47′N 12°20′E
101 O16 **Flöha** ≈ E Germany
25 O4 **Flomot** Texas, SW USA 34°13′N 100°58′W
29 V5 **Floodwood** Minnesota, N USA 46°55′N 92°55′W
30 M15 **Flora** Illinois, N USA 38°40′N 88°29′W
103 P14 **Florac** Lozère, S France 44°18′N 03°35′E
23 Q8 **Florala** Alabama, S USA 31°00′N 86°19′W
103 S4 **Florange** Moselle, NE France 49°21′N 06°06′E
Floreana, Isla see Santa María, Isla
23 O2 **Florence** Alabama, S USA 34°48′N 87°40′W
36 L14 **Florence** Arizona, SW USA 33°01′N 111°23′W
37 T6 **Florence** Colorado, C USA 38°20′N 105°06′W
27 O5 **Florence** Kansas, C USA 38°13′N 96°56′W
20 M4 **Florence** Kentucky, S USA 39°00′N 84°37′W
32 E13 **Florence** Oregon, NW USA 43°58′N 124°06′W
21 T12 **Florence** South Carolina, SE USA 34°12′N 79°44′W
25 S9 **Florence** Texas, SW USA 30°50′N 97°47′W
Florence see Firenze
54 E13 **Florencia** Caquetá, S Colombia 01°37′N 75°37′W
99 H21 **Florennes** Namur, S Belgium 50°15′N 04°36′E
Florentia see Firenze
63 J18 **Florentino Ameghino, Embalse** ◎ S Argentina
99 J24 **Florenville** Luxembourg, SE Belgium 49°42′N 05°19′E
42 E3 **Flores** Petén, N Guatemala 16°55′N 89°56′W
61 E19 **Flores** ◈ department S Uruguay
171 O16 **Flores** island Nusa Tenggara, C Indonesia
64 M1 **Flores** island Azores, Portugal, NE Atlantic Ocean
Floreshty see Florești
Flores, Lago de see Petén Itzá, Lago
Flores, Laut see Flores Sea
171 N15 **Flores Sea** Ind. Laut Flores. sea C Indonesia
116 M8 **Florești** Rus. Floreshty. N Moldova 47°52′N 28°19′E
25 S12 **Floresville** Texas, SW USA 29°09′N 98°10′W
59 N14 **Floriano** Piauí, E Brazil 06°45′S 43°W
61 K14 **Florianópolis** prev. Destêrro. state capital Santa Catarina, S Brazil 27°35′S 48°32′W
44 G6 **Florida** Camagüey, C Cuba 21°32′N 78°14′W
61 F19 **Florida** Florida, S Uruguay 34°04′S 56°14′W
61 F19 **Florida** ◈ department S Uruguay
23 U9 **Florida** off. State of Florida, also known as Peninsular State, Sunshine State. ◈ state SE USA
23 Y17 **Florida Bay** bay Florida, SE USA
54 G8 **Floridablanca** Santander, N Colombia 07°04′N 73°06′W
23 Y17 **Florida Keys** island group Florida, SE USA
37 Q16 **Florida Mountains** ▲▲ New Mexico, SW USA
64 D10 **Florida, Straits of** strait Atlantic Ocean/Gulf of Mexico
114 D13 **Flórina** var. Phlórina. Dytikí Makedonía, N Greece 40°48′N 21°26′E
27 X4 **Florissant** Missouri, C USA 38°48′N 90°20′W
94 C11 **Florø** Sogn Og Fjordane, S Norway 61°36′N 05°04′E
115 L22 **Floúda, Akrotírio** headland Astypálaia, Kykládes, Greece, Aegean Sea 36°38′N 26°23′E
21 S7 **Floyd** Virginia, NE USA 36°55′N 80°22′W
25 N4 **Floydada** Texas, SW USA 33°58′N 101°20′W
Flüela Wisshorn see Weisshorn
98 K7 **Fluessen** ◎ N Netherlands
105 S5 **Flúmen** ≈ NE Spain
107 C20 **Flumendosa** ≈ Sardegna, Italy, C Mediterranean Sea
31 R9 **Flushing** Michigan, N USA 43°03′N 83°51′W
Flushing see Vlissingen
25 O6 **Fluvanna** Texas, SW USA 32°54′N 101°06′W
186 B8 **Fly** ≈ Indonesia/Papua New Guinea
194 I10 **Flying Fish, Cape** headland Thurston Island, Antarctica 72°00′S 102°25′W
Flylân see Vlieland
193 Y15 **Foa** island Ha'apai Group, C Tonga
11 U15 **Foam Lake** Saskatchewan, S Canada 51°38′N 103°31′W
113 J14 **Foča** var. Srbinje. SE Bosnia and Herzegovina 43°32′N 18°46′E
116 L12 **Focșani** Vrancea, E Romania 45°45′N 27°13′E
Fogaras/Fogarasch see Făgăraș
107 M16 **Foggia** Puglia, SE Italy 41°28′N 15°31′E
Foggo see Faggo
76 D10 **Fogo** island Ilhas de Sotavento, SW Cape Verde
13 U11 **Fogo Island** island Newfoundland and Labrador, E Canada
109 U7 **Fohnsdorf** Steiermark, SE Austria 47°13′N 14°40′E
100 G7 **Föhr** island NW Germany
104 F14 **Fóia** ▲ S Portugal 37°19′N 08°39′W
14 I10 **Foins, Lac aux** ◎ Québec, SE Canada
103 N17 **Foix** Ariège, S France 42°58′N 01°39′E
126 I5 **Fokino** Bryanskaya Oblast', W Russian Federation 53°22′N 34°22′E
123 S15 **Fokino** Primorskiy Kray, W Russian Federation 42°58′N 132°25′E
Fola, Cnoc see Bloody Foreland
94 E13 **Folarskardnuten** ▲ S Norway 60°34′N 07°18′E
92 G11 **Folda** prev. Foldafjorden. fjord C Norway
Foldafjorden see Folda
93 F14 **Foldereid** Nord-Trøndelag, C Norway 64°58′N 12°09′E
Földvár see Feldioara
115 J22 **Folégandros** island Kykládes, Greece, Aegean Sea
23 O9 **Foley** Alabama, S USA 30°24′N 87°40′W
29 U7 **Foley** Minnesota, N USA 45°39′N 93°54′W
14 E7 **Foleyet** Ontario, S Canada 48°15′N 82°26′W
95 D14 **Folgefonna** glacier S Norway
106 I13 **Foligno** Umbria, C Italy 42°58′N 12°40′E
97 Q23 **Folkestone** SE England, United Kingdom 51°05′N 01°11′E
23 W8 **Folkston** Georgia, SE USA 30°49′N 82°00′W
94 H10 **Folldal** Hedmark, S Norway 62°08′N 10°00′E
25 P1 **Follett** Texas, SW USA 36°25′N 100°08′W
106 F13 **Follonica** Toscana, C Italy 42°55′N 10°45′E
21 T15 **Folly Beach** South Carolina, SE USA 32°39′N 79°56′W
35 O7 **Folsom** California, W USA 38°40′N 121°11′W
116 M12 **Foltești** Galați, E Romania 45°45′N 28°00′E
172 H14 **Fomboni** Mohéli, S Comoros 12°18′S 43°46′E
18 K10 **Fonda** New York, NE USA 42°57′N 74°24′W
11 S10 **Fond-du-Lac** Saskatchewan, C Canada 59°20′N 107°09′W
30 M8 **Fond du Lac** Wisconsin, N USA 43°48′N 88°27′W
11 T10 **Fond-du-Lac** ≈ Saskatchewan, C Canada
190 C9 **Fongafale** var. Funafuti. ● (Tuvalu) Funafuti Atoll, SE Tuvalu 08°31′N 179°11′E
190 G8 **Fongafale** atoll C Tuvalu
107 C18 **Fonni** Sardegna, Italy, C Mediterranean Sea 40°07′N 09°17′E
189 V12 **Fono** island Chuuk, C Micronesia
54 G4 **Fonseca** La Guajira, N Colombia 10°53′N 72°51′W
Fonseca, Golfo de see Fonseca, Gulf of
42 H8 **Fonseca, Gulf of** Sp. Golfo de Fonseca. gulf C Central America
103 O6 **Fontainebleau** Seine-et-Marne, N France 48°24′N 02°42′E
63 G19 **Fontana, Lago** ◎ W Argentina
21 N10 **Fontana Lake** ⊞ North Carolina, SE USA
107 L24 **Fontanarossa** ✈ (Catania) Sicilia, Italy, C Mediterranean Sea 37°28′N 15°04′E
11 N11 **Fontas** ≈ British Columbia, W Canada
58 D12 **Fonte Boa** Amazonas, N Brazil 02°32′S 66°01′W
102 J10 **Fontenay-le-Comte** Vendée, NW France 46°28′N 00°48′W
33 T16 **Fontenelle Reservoir** ⊞ Wyoming, C USA
193 Y14 **Fonualei** island Vava'u Group, N Tonga
111 H24 **Fonyód** Somogy, W Hungary 46°43′N 17°32′E
Foochow see Fuzhou
39 Q10 **Foraker, Mount** ▲ Alaska, USA 62°57′N 151°24′W
187 R14 **Forari** Éfaté, C Vanuatu 17°42′S 168°33′E
103 U4 **Forbach** Moselle, NE France 49°11′N 06°54′E
183 Q8 **Forbes** New South Wales, SE Australia 33°24′S 148°00′E
77 T17 **Forcados** Delta, S Nigeria 05°16′N 05°25′E
103 S14 **Forcalquier** Alpes-de-Haute-Provence, SE France 43°57′N 05°46′E
101 K19 **Forchheim** Bayern, SE Germany 49°43′N 11°07′E
35 R13 **Ford City** California, W USA 35°09′N 119°27′W
94 D11 **Førde** Sogn Og Fjordane, S Norway 61°27′N 05°51′E
31 N4 **Ford River** ≈ Michigan, N USA
183 O4 **Fords Bridge** New South Wales, SE Australia 29°44′S 145°25′E
20 J6 **Fordsville** Kentucky, S USA 37°36′N 86°39′W
27 U13 **Fordyce** Arkansas, C USA 33°49′N 92°23′W
76 I14 **Forécariah** SW Guinea 09°28′N 13°06′W
197 O14 **Forel, Mont** ▲ SE Greenland 66°55′N 36°45′W
11 R17 **Foremost** Alberta, SW Canada 49°30′N 111°34′W
14 D16 **Forest** Ontario, S Canada 43°05′N 82°00′W
22 L5 **Forest** Mississippi, S USA 32°22′N 89°30′W
31 S12 **Forest** Ohio, N USA 40°47′N 83°26′W
29 V11 **Forest City** Iowa, C USA 43°15′N 93°38′W
21 Q10 **Forest City** North Carolina, SE USA 35°19′N 81°52′W
32 G11 **Forest Grove** Oregon, NW USA 45°31′N 123°06′W
183 P17 **Forestier Peninsula** peninsula Tasmania, SE Australia
29 V8 **Forest Lake** Minnesota, N USA 45°16′N 92°59′W
23 S3 **Forest Park** Georgia, SE USA 33°37′N 84°22′W
29 Q3 **Forest River** ≈ North Dakota, N USA
15 T6 **Forestville** Québec, SE Canada 48°45′N 69°04′W
103 Q11 **Forez, Monts du** ▲▲ C France
96 K10 **Forfar** E Scotland, United Kingdom 56°38′N 02°54′W
26 J8 **Forgan** Oklahoma, C USA 36°54′N 100°32′W
Forge du Sud see Dudelange
101 J24 **Forggensee** ◎ S Germany
147 N10 **Forish** Rus. Farish. Jizzax Viloyati, C Uzbekistan 40°33′N 66°52′E
20 F9 **Forked Deer River** ≈ Tennessee, S USA
32 F7 **Forks** Washington, NW USA 47°57′N 124°22′W
92 N2 **Forlandsundet** sound W Svalbard
106 H10 **Forlì** anc. Forum Livii. Emilia-Romagna, N Italy 44°14′N 12°02′E
29 Q7 **Forman** North Dakota, N USA 46°07′N 97°39′W
97 K17 **Formby** NW England, United Kingdom 53°34′N 03°05′W
105 V11 **Formentera** anc. Ophiusa, Lat. Frumentum. island Islas Baleares, Spain, W Mediterranean Sea
Formentor, Cabo de see Formentor, Cap de
105 Y9 **Formentor, Cap de** var. Cabo de Formentor, Cape Formentor. headland Mallorca, Spain, W Mediterranean Sea 39°57′N 03°12′E
Formentor, Cape see Formentor, Cap de
107 J16 **Formia** Lazio, C Italy 41°16′N 13°37′E
62 O7 **Formosa** Formosa, NE Argentina 26°07′S 58°14′W
62 M6 **Formosa** off. Provincia de Formosa. ◈ province NE Argentina
Formosa/Formo'sa see Taiwan
Formosa, Provincia de see Formosa
59 I17 **Formosa, Serra** ▲▲ C Brazil
Formosa Strait see Taiwan Strait
95 H21 **Fornæs** headland C Denmark 56°26′N 10°57′E
25 U6 **Forney** Texas, SW USA 32°45′N 96°28′W
106 E9 **Fornovo di Taro** Emilia-Romagna, C Italy 44°42′N 10°07′E
117 T14 **Foros** Avtonomna Respublika Krym, S Ukraine 44°24′N 33°47′E
Føroyar see Faeroe Islands
96 J8 **Forres** NE Scotland, United Kingdom 57°32′N 03°38′W
27 X11 **Forrest City** Arkansas, C USA 35°01′N 90°48′W
39 Y15 **Forrester Island** island Alexander Archipelago, Alaska, USA
25 N7 **Forsan** Texas, SW USA 32°06′N 101°22′W
181 V5 **Forsayth** Queensland, NE Australia 18°31′S 143°37′E
95 L19 **Forserum** Jönköping, S Sweden 57°42′N 14°28′E
95 K15 **Forshaga** Värmland, C Sweden 59°33′N 13°29′E
93 L19 **Forssa** Etelä-Suomi, S Finland 60°49′N 23°40′E
101 Q14 **Forst** Lus. Baršć Łužyca. Brandenburg, E Germany 51°43′N 14°38′E
183 U7 **Forster-Tuncurry** New South Wales, SE Australia 32°11′S 152°30′E
23 T4 **Forsyth** Georgia, SE USA 33°00′N 83°57′W
27 T8 **Forsyth** Missouri, C USA 36°41′N 93°07′W
33 W10 **Forsyth** Montana, NW USA 46°16′N 106°40′W
149 U11 **Fort Abbās** Punjab, E Pakistan 29°12′N 73°00′E
12 G10 **Fort Albany** Ontario, C Canada 52°15′N 81°35′W
56 L13 **Fortaleza** Pando, N Bolivia 09°48′S 65°29′W
58 P13 **Fortaleza** prev. Ceará. state capital Ceará, NE Brazil 03°45′S 38°35′W
59 D16 **Fortaleza** Rondônia, W Brazil 08°45′S 64°06′W
56 C13 **Fortaleza, Río** ≈ W Peru
Fort-Archambault see Sarh
21 U3 **Fort Ashby** West Virginia, NE USA 39°30′N 78°46′W
96 I9 **Fort Augustus** N Scotland, United Kingdom 57°14′N 04°38′W
Fort-Bayard see Zhanjiang
33 S8 **Fort Benton** Montana, NW USA 47°49′N 110°40′W
35 Q1 **Fort Bidwell** California, W USA 41°50′N 120°07′W
34 L5 **Fort Bragg** California, W USA 39°25′N 123°48′W
31 N16 **Fort Branch** Indiana, N USA 38°15′N 87°34′W
Fort-Bretonnet see Bousso
33 T17 **Fort Bridger** Wyoming, C USA 41°18′N 110°19′W
Fort-Cappolani see Tidjikja
Fort-Carnot see Ikongo
Fort Charlet see Djanet
Fort-Chimo see Kuujjuaq
11 R10 **Fort Chipewyan** Alberta, C Canada 58°42′N 111°08′W
Fort Cobb Lake see Fort Cobb Reservoir
26 L11 **Fort Cobb Reservoir** var. Fort Cobb Lake. ⊞ Oklahoma, C USA
37 T3 **Fort Collins** Colorado, C USA 40°35′N 105°05′W
14 K12 **Fort-Coulonge** Québec, SE Canada 45°50′N 76°45′W
Fort-Crampel see Kaga Bandoro
Fort-Dauphin see Tôlañaro
24 K10 **Fort Davis** Texas, SW USA 30°35′N 103°54′W
37 O10 **Fort Defiance** Arizona, SW USA 35°44′N 109°04′W
45 Q12 **Fort-de-France** prev. Fort-Royal. ○ (Martinique) W Martinique 14°36′N 61°05′W
45 P12 **Fort-de-France, Baie de** bay W Martinique
Fort de Kock see Bukittinggi
23 P6 **Fort Deposit** Alabama, S USA 31°58′N 86°34′W
29 U13 **Fort Dodge** Iowa, C USA 42°30′N 94°10′W
13 S10 **Forteau** Québec, E Canada 51°30′N 56°55′W
106 E11 **Forte dei Marmi** Toscana, C Italy 43°59′N 10°10′E
14 H17 **Fort Erie** Ontario, S Canada 42°55′N 78°56′W
180 H7 **Fortescue River** ≈ Western Australia
19 S2 **Fort Fairfield** Maine, NE USA 46°45′N 67°51′W
Fort-Foureau see Kousséri
12 A11 **Fort Frances** Ontario, S Canada 48°37′N 93°23′W
Fort Franklin see Délı̨ne
23 R7 **Fort Gaines** Georgia, SE USA 31°36′N 85°03′W
37 T8 **Fort Garland** Colorado, C USA 37°22′N 105°24′W
21 P5 **Fort Gay** West Virginia, NE USA 38°06′N 82°35′W
Fort George see La Grande Rivière
Fort George see Chisasibi
27 Q10 **Fort Gibson** Oklahoma, C USA 35°48′N 95°15′W
27 Q9 **Fort Gibson Lake** ⊞ Oklahoma, C USA
8 H7 **Fort Good Hope** var. Rádeyilikóé. Northwest Territories, NW Canada 66°16′N 128°37′W
23 V4 **Fort Gordon** Georgia, SE USA 33°25′N 82°09′W
Fort Gouraud see Fdérik
96 I11 **Forth** ≈ C Scotland, United Kingdom
Fort Hall see Murang'a
24 H8 **Fort Hancock** Texas, SW USA 31°18′N 105°49′W
Fort Hertz see Putao
96 K12 **Forth, Firth of** estuary E Scotland, United Kingdom
14 L14 **Forthton** Ontario, SE Canada 44°43′N 75°31′W
14 M8 **Fortier** ≈ Québec, SE Canada
Fortín General Eugenio Garay see General Eugenio A. Garay
Fort Jameson see Chipata
Fort Johnston see Mangochi
19 R1 **Fort Kent** Maine, NE USA 47°15′N 68°33′W
Fort-Lamy see Ndjamena
23 Z15 **Fort Lauderdale** Florida, SE USA 26°07′N 80°09′W
21 R11 **Fort Lawn** South Carolina, SE USA 34°43′N 80°46′W
8 H10 **Fort Liard** var. Liard. Northwest Territories, W Canada 60°14′N 123°28′W
44 M8 **Fort-Liberté** NE Haiti 19°42′N 71°51′W
21 N9 **Fort Loudoun Lake** ⊞ Tennessee, S USA
37 T3 **Fort Lupton** Colorado, C USA 40°04′N 104°48′W
11 R12 **Fort MacKay** Alberta, C Canada 57°12′N 111°41′W
11 Q17 **Fort Macleod** var. MacLeod. Alberta, SW Canada 49°44′N 113°24′W
29 Y16 **Fort Madison** Iowa, C USA 40°37′N 91°15′W
Fort Manning see Mchinji
25 P9 **Fort McKavett** Texas, SW USA 30°50′N 100°07′W
11 R12 **Fort McMurray** Alberta, C Canada 56°44′N 111°23′W
8 G7 **Fort McPherson** var. McPherson. Northwest Territories, NW Canada 67°29′N 134°50′W
21 R11 **Fort Mill** South Carolina, SE USA 35°00′N 80°57′W
Fort-Millot see Ngouri
37 U3 **Fort Morgan** Colorado, C USA 40°14′N 103°48′W
23 W14 **Fort Myers** Florida, SE USA 26°39′N 81°52′W
23 W15 **Fort Myers Beach** Florida, SE USA 26°27′N 81°57′W
10 M10 **Fort Nelson** British Columbia, W Canada 58°48′N 122°44′W
10 M10 **Fort Nelson** ≈ British Columbia, W Canada
Fort Norman see Tulita
23 Q2 **Fort Payne** Alabama, S USA 34°23′N 85°43′W
33 W7 **Fort Peck** Montana, NW USA 48°00′N 106°28′W
33 V8 **Fort Peck Lake** ⊞ Montana, NW USA
23 Y13 **Fort Pierce** Florida, SE USA 27°28′N 80°20′W
29 N10 **Fort Pierre** South Dakota, N USA 44°21′N 100°22′W

◆ Country
● Country Capital
◇ Dependent Territory
○ Dependent Territory Capital
◈ Administrative Regions
✈ International Airport
▲ Mountain
▲▲ Mountain Range
Volcano
≈ River
◎ Lake
⊞ Reservoir

81 E18 **Fort Portal** SW Uganda 0°39′N 30°17′E
8 J10 **Fort Providence** *var.* Providence. Northwest Territories, W Canada 61°21′N 117°39′W
11 U16 **Fort Qu'Appelle** Saskatchewan, S Canada 50°50′N 103°52′W
Fort-Repoux *see* Akjoujt
8 K10 **Fort Resolution** *var.* Resolution. Northwest Territories, W Canada 61°10′N 113°39′W
33 T13 **Fortress Mountain** ▲ Wyoming, C USA 44°20′N 109°51′W
Fort Rosebery *see* Mansa
Fort Rousset *see* Owando
Fort-Royal *see* Fort-de-France
Fort Rupert *see* Waskaganish
8 H13 **Fort St. James** British Columbia, SW Canada 54°26′N 124°15′W
11 N12 **Fort St. John** British Columbia, W Canada 56°16′N 120°52′W
Fort Sandeman *see* Zhob
11 Q14 **Fort Saskatchewan** Alberta, SW Canada 53°42′N 113°12′W
27 R6 **Fort Scott** Kansas, C USA 37°52′N 94°43′W
12 E6 **Fort Severn** Ontario, C Canada 56°N 87°40′W
31 R12 **Fort Shawnee** Ohio, N USA 40°41′N 84°08′W
144 E14 **Fort-Shevchenko** Mangistau, W Kazakhstan 44°29′N 50°16′E
Fort-Sibut *see* Sibut
8 I10 **Fort Simpson** *var.* Simpson. Northwest Territories, W Canada 61°52′N 121°23′W
8 I10 **Fort Smith** Northwest Territories, W Canada 60°01′N 111°55′W
27 R10 **Fort Smith** Arkansas, C USA 35°23′N 94°24′W
37 T13 **Fort Stanton** New Mexico, SW USA 33°28′N 105°31′W
24 L9 **Fort Stockton** Texas, SW USA 30°54′N 102°54′W
37 U12 **Fort Sumner** New Mexico, SW USA 34°28′N 104°15′W
26 K8 **Fort Supply** Oklahoma, C USA 36°34′N 99°34′W
26 K8 **Fort Supply Lake** ⊠ Oklahoma, C USA
29 O10 **Fort Thompson** South Dakota, N USA 44°01′N 99°22′W
Fort-Trinquet *see* Bîr Mogreïn
105 R12 **Fortuna** Murcia, SE Spain 38°11′N 01°07′W
34 K3 **Fortuna** California, W USA 40°35′N 124°07′W
28 J2 **Fortuna** North Dakota, N USA 48°53′N 103°46′W
23 T5 **Fort Valley** Georgia, SE USA 32°33′N 83°53′W
11 P11 **Fort Vermilion** Alberta, W Canada 58°22′N 115°59′W
Fort Victoria *see* Masvingo
31 P13 **Fortville** Indiana, N USA 39°55′N 85°51′W
23 P9 **Fort Walton Beach** Florida, SE USA 30°24′N 86°37′W
31 P12 **Fort Wayne** Indiana, N USA 41°08′N 85°08′W
96 H10 **Fort William** N Scotland, United Kingdom 56°49′N 05°07′W
25 T6 **Fort Worth** Texas, SW USA 32°44′N 97°19′W
28 M7 **Fort Yates** North Dakota, N USA 46°05′N 100°37′W
39 S7 **Fort Yukon** Alaska, USA 66°35′N 145°05′W
Forum Alieni *see* Ferrara
Forum Julii *see* Fréjus
Forum Livii *see* Forlì
143 Q15 **Forūr-e Bozorg, Jazīreh-ye** *island* S Iran
94 H7 **Fosen** *physical region* S Norway
161 N14 **Foshan** *var.* Fatshan, Fo-shan, Namhoi. Guangdong, S China 23°03′N 113°08′E
Fo-shan *see* Foshan
194 J6 **Fossil Bluff** UK *research station* Antarctica 71°30′S 68°30′W
Fossa Claudia *see* Chioggia
106 B9 **Fossano** Piemonte, NW Italy 44°33′N 07°43′E
99 H21 **Fosses-la-Ville** Namur, S Belgium 50°24′N 04°42′E
32 J12 **Fossil** Oregon, NW USA 45°01′N 120°14′W
Foss Lake *see* Foss Reservoir
106 I11 **Fossombrone** Marche, C Italy 43°42′N 12°48′E
26 K10 **Foss Reservoir** *var.* Foss Lake. ⊠ Oklahoma, C USA
29 S4 **Fosston** Minnesota, N USA 47°34′N 95°45′W
183 O13 **Foster** Victoria, SE Australia 38°40′S 146°15′E
11 T12 **Foster Lakes** ◎ Saskatchewan, C Canada
31 S12 **Fostoria** Ohio, N USA 41°09′N 83°25′W
79 D19 **Fougamou** Ngounié, C Gabon 01°16′S 10°30′E
102 J6 **Fougères** Ille-et-Vilaine, NW France 48°21′N 01°12′W
Fou-hsin *see* Fuxin
27 S14 **Fouke** Arkansas, C USA 33°15′N 93°53′W
96 K2 **Foula** *island* NE Scotland, United Kingdom
65 D24 **Foul Bay** *bay* East Falkland, Falkland Islands
97 P21 **Foulness Island** *island* SE England, United Kingdom
185 F15 **Foulwind, Cape** *headland* South Island, New Zealand 41°45′S 171°28′E
79 E15 **Foumban** Ouest, NW Cameroon 05°43′N 10°50′E
172 H13 **Foumbouni** Grande Comore, NW Comoros 11°49′S 43°30′E
195 N8 **Foundation Ice Stream** *glacier* Antarctica
37 T6 **Fountain** Colorado, C USA 38°40′N 104°42′W
36 L4 **Fountain Green** Utah, W USA 39°37′N 111°37′W
21 P11 **Fountain Inn** South Carolina, SE USA 34°41′N 82°12′W
27 S11 **Fourche LaFave River** ↝ Arkansas, C USA
33 Z13 **Four Corners** Wyoming, C USA 43°04′N 104°08′W
103 Q2 **Fourmies** Nord, N France 50°01′N 04°03′E
38 J17 **Four Mountains, Islands of** *island group* Aleutian Islands, Alaska, USA
173 P17 **Fournaise, Piton de la** Ѫ SE Réunion 21°14′S 55°43′E
14 J8 **Fournière, Lac** ◎ Québec, SE Canada
115 L20 **Foúrnoi** *island* Dodekánisa, Greece, Aegean Sea
64 K13 **Four North Fracture Zone** *tectonic feature* W Atlantic Ocean
Fouron-Saint-Martin *see* Sint-Martens-Voeren
30 L3 **Fourteen Mile Point** *headland* Michigan, N USA 46°59′N 89°07′W
Fou-shan *see* Fushun
76 I13 **Fouta Djallon** *var.* Futa Jallon. ⛰ W Guinea
185 C25 **Foveaux Strait** *strait* S New Zealand
35 Q11 **Fowler** California, W USA 36°35′N 119°40′W
37 U6 **Fowler** Colorado, C USA 38°07′N 104°01′W
31 N12 **Fowler** Indiana, N USA 40°36′N 87°20′W
182 D7 **Fowlers Bay** *bay* South Australia
25 R13 **Fowlerton** Texas, SW USA 28°27′N 98°48′W
142 M3 **Fowman** *var.* Fuman, Fumen. Gīlān, NW Iran 37°15′N 49°19′E
65 C25 **Fox Bay East** West Falkland, Falkland Islands
65 C25 **Fox Bay West** West Falkland, Falkland Islands
14 J14 **Foxboro** Ontario, SE Canada 44°16′N 77°23′W
11 O14 **Fox Creek** Alberta, W Canada 54°25′N 116°57′W
64 G5 **Foxe Basin** *sea* Nunavut, N Canada
64 G5 **Foxe Channel** *channel* Nunavut, N Canada
95 I16 **Foxen** ◎ C Sweden
9 Q7 **Foxe Peninsula** *peninsula* Baffin Island, Nunavut, NE Canada
185 E19 **Fox Glacier** West Coast, South Island, New Zealand 43°28′S 170°00′E
38 L17 **Fox Islands** *island* Aleutian Islands, Alaska, USA
30 M10 **Fox Lake** Illinois, N USA 42°24′N 88°10′W
9 V12 **Fox Mine** Manitoba, C Canada 56°36′N 101°48′W
35 R3 **Fox Mountain** ▲ Nevada, W USA 41°01′N 119°30′W
65 E25 **Fox Point** *headland* East Falkland, Falkland Islands 51°55′S 58°24′W
30 M11 **Fox River** ↝ Illinois/ Wisconsin, N USA
30 L7 **Fox River** ↝ Wisconsin, N USA
184 L13 **Foxton** Manawatu-Wanganui, North Island, New Zealand 40°27′S 175°18′E
11 S16 **Fox Valley** Saskatchewan, S Canada 50°29′N 109°29′W
11 W16 **Foxwarren** Manitoba, S Canada 50°30′N 101°09′W
97 E14 **Foyle, Lough** *Ir.* Loch Feabhail. *inlet* N Ireland
194 H5 **Foyn Coast** *physical region* Antarctica
104 I2 **Foz** Galicia, NW Spain 43°33′N 07°16′W
60 I12 **Foz do Areia, Represa de** ⊠ S Brazil
59 A16 **Foz do Breu** Acre, W Brazil 09°21′S 72°41′W
83 A16 **Foz do Cunene** Namibe, SW Angola 17°11′S 11°52′E
60 G12 **Foz do Iguaçu** Paraná, S Brazil 25°33′S 54°31′W
58 C12 **Foz do Mamoriá** Amazonas, NW Brazil 02°28′S 66°06′W
105 T6 **Fraga** Aragón, NE Spain 41°32′N 00°21′E
44 F5 **Fragoso, Cayo** *island* C Cuba
61 G18 **Fraile Muerto** Cerro Largo, NE Uruguay 32°30′S 54°30′W
99 H21 **Fraire** Namur, S Belgium 50°16′N 04°30′E
99 L21 **Fraiture, Baraque de** *hill* SE Belgium
Frakštát *see* Hlohovec
197 S10 **Fram Basin** *var.* Amundsen Basin. *undersea feature* Arctic Ocean 88°00′N 90°00′E
99 F20 **Frameries** Hainaut, S Belgium 50°25′N 03°41′E
19 O11 **Framingham** Massachusetts, NE USA 42°15′N 71°24′W
60 L7 **Franca** São Paulo, S Brazil 20°33′S 47°27′W
187 O15 **Français, Récif des** *reef* W New Caledonia
107 K14 **Francavilla al Mare** Abruzzo, C Italy 42°25′N 14°16′E
107 P18 **Francavilla Fontana** Puglia, SE Italy 40°32′N 17°35′E
102 M8 **France** *off.* French Republic, *It./Sp.* Francia; *prev.* Gaul, Gaule, *Lat.* Gallia. ◆ *republic* W Europe
45 O8 **Francés Viejo, Cabo** *headland* NE Dominican Republic 19°39′N 69°57′W
79 F19 **Franceville** *var.* Massoukou, Masuku. Haut-Ogooué, E Gabon 01°40′S 13°31′E
79 F19 **Franceville** ✈ Haut-Ogooué, E Gabon 01°38′S 13°24′E
Francfort *see* Frankfurt am Main
103 T8 **Franche-Comté** ◈ *region* E France
Francia *see* France
29 O11 **Francis Case, Lake** ⊠ South Dakota, N USA
60 H12 **Francisco Beltrão** Paraná, S Brazil 26°05′S 53°04′W
Francisco I. Madero *see* Villa Madero
61 A21 **Francisco Madero** Buenos Aires, E Argentina 35°52′S 62°03′W
42 H6 **Francisco Morazán** *prev.* Tegucigalpa. ◈ *department* C Honduras
83 J18 **Francistown** North East, NE Botswana 21°08′S 27°31′E
Franconian Forest *see* Frankenwald
Franconian Jura *see* Fränkische Alb
98 K6 **Franeker** *Fris.* Frentsjer. Fryslân, N Netherlands 53°11′N 05°33′E
Frankenalb *see* Fränkische Alb
101 H16 **Frankenberg** Hessen, C Germany 51°04′N 08°49′E
101 J20 **Frankenhöhe** *hill range* C Germany
31 R8 **Frankenmuth** Michigan, N USA 43°19′N 83°44′W
101 F20 **Frankenstein** *hill* W Germany
Frankenstein/Frankenstein in Schlesien *see* Ząbkowice Śląskie
101 G20 **Frankenthal** Rheinland-Pfalz, W Germany 49°32′N 08°22′E
101 L18 **Frankenwald** *Eng.* Franconian Forest. ⛰ C Germany
44 J12 **Frankfield** C Jamaica 18°08′N 77°22′W
14 J14 **Frankford** Ontario, SE Canada 44°12′N 77°36′W
31 O13 **Frankfort** Indiana, N USA 40°16′N 86°30′W
27 O3 **Frankfort** Kansas, C USA 39°42′N 96°25′W
20 L5 **Frankfort** *state capital* Kentucky, S USA 38°12′N 84°52′W
Frankfort on the Main *see* Frankfurt am Main
Frankfurt *see* Frankfurt am Main, Germany
Frankfurt *see* Słubice, Poland
101 G18 **Frankfurt am Main** *var.* Frankfurt, *Fr.* Francfort; *prev. Eng.* Frankfort on the Main. Hessen, SW Germany 50°07′N 08°41′E
100 Q12 **Frankfurt an der Oder** Brandenburg, E Germany 52°20′N 14°32′E
101 L21 **Fränkische Alb** *var.* Frankenalb, *Eng.* Franconian Jura. ⛰ S Germany
101 I18 **Fränkische Saale** ↝ C Germany
101 L19 **Fränkische Schweiz** *hill range* C Germany
23 R4 **Franklin** Georgia, SE USA 33°15′N 85°06′W
31 P14 **Franklin** Indiana, N USA 39°29′N 86°02′W
20 J7 **Franklin** Kentucky, S USA 36°42′N 86°35′W
22 I9 **Franklin** Louisiana, S USA 29°48′N 91°30′W
29 O17 **Franklin** Nebraska, C USA 40°06′N 98°57′W
21 N10 **Franklin** North Carolina, SE USA 35°12′N 83°23′W
18 C13 **Franklin** Pennsylvania, NE USA 41°24′N 79°49′W
20 J9 **Franklin** Tennessee, S USA 35°55′N 86°52′W
25 U9 **Franklin** Texas, SW USA 31°02′N 96°30′W
21 X7 **Franklin** Virginia, NE USA 36°41′N 76°58′W
21 T4 **Franklin** West Virginia, NE USA 38°39′N 79°21′W
30 M9 **Franklin** Wisconsin, N USA 42°53′N 88°00′W
8 I6 **Franklin Bay** *inlet* Northwest Territories, N Canada
32 K7 **Franklin D. Roosevelt Lake** ⊠ Washington, NW USA
35 W4 **Franklin Lake** ◎ Nevada, W USA
185 B22 **Franklin Mountains** ⛰ South Island, New Zealand
39 R5 **Franklin Mountains** ⛰ Alaska, USA
39 N4 **Franklin, Point** *headland* Alaska, USA 70°54′N 158°48′W
183 O17 **Franklin River** ↝ Tasmania, SE Australia
22 K8 **Franklinton** Louisiana, S USA 30°51′N 90°09′W
21 U9 **Franklinton** North Carolina, SE USA 36°06′N 78°27′W
Frankstadt *see* Frenštát pod Radhoštěm
25 V7 **Frankston** Texas, SW USA 32°03′N 95°30′W
33 U12 **Frannie** Wyoming, C USA 44°57′N 108°37′W
15 U5 **Franquelin** Québec, SE Canada 49°17′N 67°52′W
15 U5 **Franquelin** ↝ Québec, SE Canada
83 C18 **Fransfontein** Kunene, NW Namibia 20°12′S 15°01′E
93 H17 **Fränsta** Västernorrland, C Sweden 62°30′N 16°06′E
122 J3 **Frantsa-Iosifa, Zemlya** *Eng.* Franz Josef Land. *island group* N Russian Federation
185 E18 **Franz Josef Glacier** West Coast, South Island, New Zealand 43°22′S 170°11′E
Franz Josef Land *see* Frantsa-Iosifa, Zemlya
Franz-Josef Spitze *see* Gerlachovský štít
101 L23 **Franz Josef Strauss** *abbrev.* F.J.S.. ✈ (München) Bayern, SE Germany 48°07′N 11°43′E
107 A19 **Frasca, Capo della** *headland* Sardegna, Italy, C Mediterranean Sea 39°46′N 08°27′E
107 I15 **Frascati** Lazio, C Italy 41°48′N 12°41′E
11 N14 **Fraser** ↝ British Columbia, SW Canada
83 G24 **Fraserburg** Western Cape, SW South Africa 31°55′S 21°31′E
96 L8 **Fraserburgh** NE Scotland, United Kingdom 57°42′N 02°20′W
181 Z9 **Fraser Island** *var.* Great Sandy Island. *island* Queensland, E Australia
10 L14 **Fraser Lake** British Columbia, SW Canada 54°00′N 124°45′W
10 L15 **Fraser Plateau** *plateau* British Columbia, SW Canada
184 P10 **Frasertown** Hawke's Bay, North Island, New Zealand 38°58′S 177°25′E
99 E19 **Frasnes-lez-Buissenal** Hainaut, SW Belgium 50°40′N 03°37′E
108 I7 **Frastanz** Vorarlberg, NW Austria 47°13′N 09°38′E
14 B8 **Frater** Ontario, S Canada 47°19′N 84°28′W
Frauenbach *see* Baia Mare
Frauenburg *see* Saldus, Latvia
Frauenburg *see* Frombork, Poland
108 H6 **Frauenfeld** Thurgau, NE Switzerland 47°34′N 08°54′E
109 Z5 **Frauenkirchen** Burgenland, E Austria 47°50′N 16°57′E
61 D19 **Fray Bentos** Río Negro, W Uruguay 33°09′S 58°14′W
61 F19 **Fray Marcos** Florida, S Uruguay 34°13′S 55°43′W
29 S6 **Frazee** Minnesota, N USA 46°42′N 95°40′W
104 M5 **Frechilla** Castilla y León, N Spain 42°08′N 04°50′W
30 I4 **Frederic** Wisconsin, N USA 45°42′N 92°30′W
95 G23 **Fredericia** Syddanmark, C Denmark 55°34′N 09°47′E
21 W3 **Frederick** Maryland, NE USA 39°25′N 77°25′W
26 L12 **Frederick** Oklahoma, C USA 34°24′N 99°03′W
29 P7 **Frederick** South Dakota, N USA 45°49′N 98°31′W
29 X12 **Fredericksburg** Iowa, C USA 42°58′N 92°12′W
25 R10 **Fredericksburg** Texas, SW USA 30°17′N 98°52′W
21 W5 **Fredericksburg** Virginia, NE USA 38°16′N 77°27′W
39 X13 **Frederick Sound** *sound* Alaska, USA
27 X6 **Fredericktown** Missouri, C USA 37°33′N 90°19′W
60 H13 **Frederico Westphalen** Rio Grande do Sul, S Brazil 27°22′S 53°20′W
13 O15 **Fredericton** *province capital* New Brunswick, SE Canada 45°57′N 66°40′W
Frederiksborg Amt *see* Hovedstaden
Frederikshåb *see* Paamiut
95 H19 **Frederikshavn** *prev.* Fladstrand. Nordjylland, N Denmark 57°28′N 10°33′E
95 J22 **Frederikssund** Hovedstaden, E Denmark 55°51′N 12°05′E
45 T9 **Frederiksted** Saint Croix, S Virgin Islands (US) 17°41′N 64°51′W
95 I22 **Frederiksværk** *var.* Frederiksværk og Hanehoved. Hovedstaden, E Denmark 55°58′N 12°02′E
Frederiksværk og Hanehoved *see* Frederiksværk
54 E9 **Fredonia** Antioquia, W Colombia 05°57′N 75°42′W
36 K8 **Fredonia** Arizona, SW USA 36°57′N 112°31′W
27 P7 **Fredonia** Kansas, C USA 37°32′N 95°50′W
18 C11 **Fredonia** New York, NE USA 42°26′N 79°19′W
35 P4 **Fredonyer Pass** *pass* California, W USA
93 I15 **Fredrika** Västerbotten, N Sweden 64°03′N 18°25′E
95 L14 **Fredriksberg** Dalarna, C Sweden 60°07′N 14°23′E
Fredrikshald *see* Halden
Fredrikshamn *see* Hamina
95 H16 **Fredrikstad** Østfold, S Norway 59°12′N 10°57′E
30 K16 **Freeburg** Illinois, N USA 38°25′N 89°54′W
18 K15 **Freehold** New Jersey, NE USA 40°14′N 74°14′W
18 H14 **Freeland** Pennsylvania, NE USA 41°01′N 75°54′W
182 J5 **Freeling Heights** ▲ South Australia 30°09′S 139°24′E
35 Q7 **Freel Peak** ▲ California, W USA 38°52′N 119°52′W
11 Z9 **Freels, Cape** *headland* Newfoundland and Labrador, E Canada 49°16′N 53°30′W
29 Q11 **Freeman** South Dakota, N USA 43°21′N 97°26′W
44 G1 **Freeport** Grand Bahama Island, N Bahamas 26°28′N 78°43′W
30 L10 **Freeport** Illinois, N USA 42°18′N 89°37′W
25 W12 **Freeport** Texas, SW USA 28°57′N 95°21′W
44 G1 **Freeport** ✈ Grand Bahama Island, N Bahamas 26°31′N 78°48′W
25 R14 **Freer** Texas, SW USA 27°52′N 98°37′W
83 I22 **Free State** *off.* Free State Province; *prev.* Orange Free State, *Afr.* Oranje Vrystaat. ◈ *province* C South Africa
Free State *see* Maryland
Free State Province *see* Free State
76 G15 **Freetown** ● (Sierra Leone) W Sierra Leone 08°27′N 13°16′W
172 J16 **Frégate** *island* Inner Islands, NE Seychelles
104 J12 **Fregenal de la Sierra** Extremadura, W Spain 38°10′N 06°39′W
182 C2 **Fregon** South Australia 26°44′S 132°03′E
102 H5 **Fréhel, Cap** *headland* NW France 48°41′N 02°21′W
94 F8 **Frei** Møre og Romsdal, S Norway 63°02′N 07°47′E
101 O16 **Freiberg** Sachsen, E Germany 50°55′N 13°21′E
101 O16 **Freiberger Mulde** ↝ E Germany
Freiburg *see* Freiburg im Breisgau, Germany
Freiburg *see* Fribourg, Switzerland
101 F23 **Freiburg im Breisgau** *var.* Freiburg, *Fr.* Fribourg-en-Brisgau. Baden-Württemberg, SW Germany 48°N 07°52′E
Freiburg in Schlesien *see* Świebodzice
Freie Hansestadt Bremen *see* Bremen
Freie und Hansestadt Hamburg *see* Brandenburg
101 L22 **Freising** Bayern, SE Germany 48°24′N 11°45′E
109 T3 **Freistadt** Oberösterreich, N Austria 48°31′N 14°31′E
Freistadtl *see* Hlohovec
101 O16 **Freital** Sachsen, E Germany 51°00′N 13°40′E
Freiwaldau *see* Jeseník
104 J6 **Freixo de Espada à Cinta** Bragança, N Portugal 41°05′N 06°49′W
103 U15 **Fréjus** *anc.* Forum Julii. Var, SE France 43°26′N 06°44′E
180 I13 **Fremantle** Western Australia 32°07′S 115°44′E
35 N9 **Fremont** California, W USA 37°34′N 122°01′W
31 Q11 **Fremont** Indiana, N USA 41°43′N 84°54′W
29 W15 **Fremont** Iowa, C USA 41°12′N 92°26′W
31 P8 **Fremont** Michigan, N USA 43°28′N 85°56′W
29 R15 **Fremont** Nebraska, C USA 41°25′N 96°30′W
31 S11 **Fremont** Ohio, N USA 41°21′N 83°07′W
33 T14 **Fremont Peak** ▲ Wyoming, C USA 43°07′N 109°37′W
36 M6 **Fremont River** ↝ Utah, W USA
21 O9 **French Broad River** ↝ Tennessee, S USA
21 N5 **Frenchburg** Kentucky, S USA 37°58′N 83°37′W
18 C12 **French Creek** ↝ Pennsylvania, NE USA
32 K15 **Frenchglen** Oregon, NW USA 42°49′N 118°55′W
55 Y10 **French Guiana** *var.* Guiana, Guyane. ◇ *French overseas department* N South America
French Guinea *see* Guinea
31 O15 **French Lick** Indiana, N USA 38°33′N 86°37′W
185 J14 **French Pass** Marlborough, South Island, New Zealand 40°57′S 173°49′E
191 T11 **French Polynesia** ◇ *French overseas territory* S Pacific Ocean
French Republic *see* France
14 F11 **French River** ↝ Ontario, S Canada
French Somaliland *see* Djibouti
173 P12 **French Southern and Antarctic Territories** *Fr.* Terres Australes et Antarctiques Françaises. ◇ *French overseas territory* S Indian Ocean
French Sudan *see* Mali
French Territory of the Afars and Issas *see* Djibouti
French Togoland *see* Togo
74 J6 **Frenda** NW Algeria 35°04′N 01°03′E
111 I18 **Frenštát pod Radhoštěm** *Ger.* Frankstadt. Moravskoslezský Kraj, E Czech Republic 49°33′N 18°10′E
Frentsjer *see* Franeker
76 M17 **Fresco** S Ivory Coast 05°03′N 05°31′W
195 U16 **Freshfield, Cape** *headland* Antarctica
40 L10 **Fresnillo** *var.* Fresnillo de González Echeverría. Zacatecas, C Mexico 23°11′N 102°53′W
Fresnillo de González Echeverría *see* Fresnillo
35 Q10 **Fresno** California, W USA 36°45′N 119°48′W
Freu, Cabo del *see* Freu, Cap des
105 Y9 **Freu, Cap des** *var.* Cabo del Freu. *cape* Mallorca, Spain, W Mediterranean Sea
101 G22 **Freudenstadt** Baden-Württemberg, SW Germany 48°28′N 08°25′E
Freudenthal *see* Bruntál
183 Q17 **Freycinet Peninsula** *peninsula* Tasmania, SE Australia
76 H14 **Fria** W Guinea 10°27′N 13°38′W
83 A17 **Fria, Cape** *headland* NW Namibia 18°32′S 12°00′E
35 Q10 **Friant** California, W USA 36°56′N 119°44′W
62 K8 **Frías** Catamarca, N Argentina 28°41′S 65°00′W
108 D9 **Fribourg** *Ger.* Freiburg. Fribourg, W Switzerland 46°50′N 07°10′E
108 C9 **Fribourg** *Ger.* Freiburg. ◈ *canton* W Switzerland
Fribourg-en-Brisgau *see* Freiburg im Breisgau
32 G7 **Friday Harbor** San Juan Islands, Washington, NW USA 48°31′N 123°01′W
Friedau *see* Ormož
101 K23 **Friedberg** Bayern, S Germany 48°21′N 10°58′E
101 H18 **Friedberg** Hessen, W Germany 50°19′N 08°46′E
Friedeberg Neumark *see* Strzelce Krajeńskie
Friedek-Mistek *see* Frýdek-Místek
Friedland *see* Pravdinsk
101 I24 **Friedrichshafen** Baden-Württemberg, S Germany 47°39′N 09°29′E
Friedrichstadt *see* Jaunjelgava
29 Q16 **Friend** Nebraska, C USA 40°37′N 97°16′W
Friendly Islands *see* Tonga
55 V9 **Friendship** Coronie, N Surinam 05°50′N 56°16′W
30 L7 **Friendship** Wisconsin, N USA 43°58′N 89°48′W
109 T8 **Friesach** Kärnten, S Austria 46°58′N 14°24′E
Friesche Eilanden *see* Frisian Islands
101 F22 **Friesenheim** Baden-Württemberg, SW Germany 48°27′N 07°56′E
Friesische Inseln *see* Frisian Islands
Friesland *see* Fryslân
60 Q10 **Frio, Cabo** *headland* SE Brazil 23°01′S 41°59′W
24 M3 **Friona** Texas, SW USA 34°38′N 102°43′W
42 L12 **Frío, Río** ↝ N Costa Rica
25 R13 **Frio River** ↝ Texas, SW USA
99 M25 **Frisange** Luxembourg, S Luxembourg 49°31′N 06°12′E
Frisches Haff *see* Vistula Lagoon
36 J6 **Frisco Peak** ▲ Utah, W USA 38°31′N 113°17′W
84 F9 **Frisian Islands** *Dut.* Friesche Eilanden, *Ger.* Friesische Inseln. *island group* N Europe
18 L12 **Frissell, Mount** ▲ Connecticut, NE USA 42°01′N 73°25′W
95 J19 **Fristad** Västra Götaland, S Sweden 57°50′N 13°01′E
25 N2 **Fritch** Texas, SW USA 35°38′N 101°36′W
95 J19 **Fritsla** Västra Götaland, S Sweden 57°33′N 12°47′E
101 H16 **Fritzlar** Hessen, C Germany 51°09′N 09°16′E
106 H6 **Friuli-Venezia Giulia** ◈ *region* NE Italy
196 L13 **Frobisher Bay** *inlet* Baffin Island, Nunavut, NE Canada
Frobisher Bay *see* Iqaluit
11 S12 **Frobisher Lake** ◎ Saskatchewan, C Canada
94 G7 **Frohavet** *sound* C Norway
Frohenbruck *see* Veselí nad Lužnicí
109 V7 **Frohnleiten** Steiermark, SE Austria 47°17′N 15°20′E
99 G22 **Froidchapelle** Hainaut, S Belgium 50°10′N 04°18′E
127 O9 **Frolovo** Volgogradskaya Oblast', SW Russian Federation 49°46′N 43°38′E
110 K7 **Frombork** *Ger.* Frauenburg. Warmińsko-Mazurskie, NE Poland 54°21′N 19°40′E
97 L22 **Frome** SW England, United Kingdom 51°15′N 02°22′W
182 I4 **Frome Creek** *seasonal river* South Australia
182 J6 **Frome Downs** South Australia 31°17′S 139°48′E
182 J5 **Frome, Lake** *salt lake* South Australia
Fronicken *see* Wronki
104 H10 **Fronteira** Portalegre, C Portugal 39°03′N 07°39′W
40 M7 **Frontera** Coahuila, NE Mexico 26°55′N 101°27′W
41 U14 **Frontera** Tabasco, SE Mexico 18°32′N 92°39′W
40 G3 **Fronteras** Sonora, NW Mexico 30°51′N 109°33′W
103 Q16 **Frontignan** Hérault, S France 43°27′N 03°45′E
54 D8 **Frontino** Antioquia, NW Colombia 06°46′N 76°10′W
21 V4 **Front Royal** Virginia, NE USA 38°56′N 78°13′W
107 J16 **Frosinone** *anc.* Frusino. Lazio, C Italy 41°38′N 13°22′E
107 K16 **Frosolone** Molise, C Italy 41°34′N 14°25′E
25 U7 **Frost** Texas, SW USA 32°04′N 96°48′W
21 U2 **Frostburg** Maryland, NE USA 39°39′N 78°55′W
23 X13 **Frostproof** Florida, SE USA 27°45′N 81°31′W
Frostviken *see* Kvarnbergsvattnet
95 M15 **Frövi** Örebro, C Sweden 59°28′N 15°24′E
94 F7 **Frøya** *island* W Norway
37 P5 **Fruita** Colorado, C USA 39°10′N 108°42′W
28 J9 **Fruitdale** South Dakota, N USA 44°39′N 103°38′W
23 W11 **Fruitland Park** Florida, SE USA 28°51′N 81°54′W
Frumentum *see* Formentera
147 S11 **Frunze** Batkenskaya Oblast', SW Kyrgyzstan 40°07′N 71°40′E
Frunze *see* Bishkek
117 O9 **Frunzivka** Odes'ka Oblast', SW Ukraine 47°19′N 29°46′E
Frusino *see* Frosinone
108 E9 **Frutigen** Bern, W Switzerland 46°35′N 07°38′E
111 I17 **Frýdek-Místek** *Ger.* Friedek-Mistek. Moravskoslezský Kraj, E Czech Republic 49°40′N 18°22′E
98 K6 **Fryslân** *prev.* Friesland. ◈ *province* N Netherlands
193 V16 **Fua'amotu** Tongatapu, S Tonga 21°15′S 175°08′W
190 A9 **Fuafatu** *island* Funafuti Atoll, C Tuvalu
190 A9 **Fuagea** *island* Funafuti Atoll, C Tuvalu
190 B8 **Fualifeke** *atoll* C Tuvalu
190 A8 **Fualopa** *island* Funafuti Atoll, C Tuvalu
151 K22 **Fuammulah** *var.* Fuammulah, Gnaviyani. *atoll* S Maldives
Fuammulah *see* Fuammulah
161 R11 **Fu'an** Fujian, SE China 27°11′N 119°42′E
Fu-chien *see* Fujian
Fu-chou *see* Fuzhou
164 G13 **Fuchū** *var.* Hutyû. Hiroshima, Honshū, SW Japan 34°35′N 133°12′E
160 M13 **Fuchuan** *var.* Fuyang. Guangxi Zhuangzu Zizhiqu, S China 24°56′N 111°15′E
161 R9 **Fuchun Jiang** *var.* Tsien Tang. ↝ SE China
165 R8 **Fudai** Iwate, Honshū, C Japan 39°59′N 141°50′E
161 S11 **Fuding** *var.* Tongshan. Fujian, SE China 27°21′N 120°10′E
81 J20 **Fudua** *spring/well* S Kenya 02°13′S 39°43′E
104 M16 **Fuengirola** Andalucía, S Spain 36°32′N 04°38′W
104 J12 **Fuente de Cantos** Extremadura, W Spain 38°15′N 06°18′W
104 J11 **Fuente del Maestre** Extremadura, W Spain 38°31′N 06°26′W
104 L12 **Fuente Obejuna** Andalucía, S Spain 38°15′N 05°25′W
104 L6 **Fuentesaúco** Castilla y León, N Spain 41°14′N 05°30′W
62 O3 **Fuerte Olimpo** *var.* Olimpo. Alto Paraguay, NE Paraguay 21°02′S 57°51′W
40 H8 **Fuerte, Río** ↝ C Mexico
64 Q11 **Fuerteventura** *island* Islas Canarias, Spain, NE Atlantic Ocean
141 S14 **Fughmah** *var.* Faghman, Fugma. C Yemen 16°08′N 49°23′E
92 M2 **Fuglehuken** *headland* W Svalbard 78°54′N 10°30′E
Fuglø *see* Fugloy
95 B18 **Fugloy** *Dan.* Fuglø. *island* NE Faeroe Islands
197 T15 **Fugløya Bank** *undersea feature* E Norwegian Sea 71°00′N 19°20′E
Fugma *see* Fughmah
160 E11 **Fugong** Yunnan, SW China 27°00′N 98°48′E
81 K16 **Fugugo** *spring/well* NE Kenya 03°19′N 39°39′E
158 L2 **Fuhai** *var.* Burultokay. Xinjiang Uygur Zizhiqu, NW China 47°15′N 87°39′E
161 P10 **Fu He** ↝ S China
Fuhkien *see* Fujian
100 J9 **Fuhlsbüttel** ✈ (Hamburg) Hamburg, N Germany 53°37′N 09°57′E
101 L14 **Fuhne** ↝ C Germany
Fu-hsin *see* Fuxin
Fujairah *see* Al Fujayrah
164 M14 **Fuji** *var.* Huzi. Shizuoka, Honshū, S Japan 35°08′N 138°39′E
161 Q12 **Fujian** *var.* Fu-chien, Fuhkien, Fukien, Min, Fujian Sheng. ◈ *province* SE China
160 I9 **Fu Jiang** ↝ C China
Fujian Sheng *see* Fujian
164 M14 **Fujieda** *var.* Huzieda. Shizuoka, Honshū, S Japan 34°54′N 138°15′E
Fuji, Mount/Fujiyama *see* Fuji-san
163 Y7 **Fujin** Heilongjiang, NE China 47°12′N 132°01′E
164 M13 **Fujinomiya** *var.* Huzinomiya. Shizuoka, Honshū, S Japan 35°16′N 138°33′E
164 N13 **Fuji-san** *var.* Fujiyama, *Eng.* Mount Fuji. ▲ Honshū, SE Japan 35°23′N 138°44′E
165 N14 **Fujisawa** *var.* Huzisawa. Kanagawa, Honshū, S Japan 35°22′N 139°29′E
165 T3 **Fukagawa** *var.* Hukagawa. Hokkaidō, NE Japan 43°44′N 142°03′E
158 L5 **Fukang** Xinjiang Uygur Zizhiqu, W China 44°07′N 87°55′E
165 P7 **Fukaura** Aomori, Honshū, C Japan 40°38′N 139°55′E
193 W15 **Fukave** *island* Tongatapu Group, S Tonga
Fukien *see* Fujian
164 J13 **Fukuchiyama** *var.* Hukutiyama. Kyōto, Honshū, SW Japan 35°19′N 135°08′E
Fukue *see* Gotō
164 A13 **Fukue-jima** *island* Gotō-rettō, SW Japan
164 K12 **Fukui** *var.* Hukui. Fukui, Honshū, SW Japan 36°03′N 136°12′E
164 K12 **Fukui** *off.* Fukui-ken, *var.* Hukui. ◈ *prefecture* Honshū, SW Japan
Fukui-ken *see* Fukui
164 D13 **Fukuoka** *var.* Hukuoka, *hist.* Najima. Fukuoka, Kyūshū, SW Japan 33°36′N 130°24′E
164 D13 **Fukuoka** *off.* Fukuoka-ken, *var.* Hukuoka. ◈ *prefecture* Kyūshū, SW Japan
Fukuoka-ken *see* Fukuoka
165 Q6 **Fukushima** Hokkaidō, NE Japan 41°27′N 140°14′E
165 Q12 **Fukushima** *off.* Fukushima-ken, *var.* Hukusima. ◈ *prefecture* Honshū, C Japan
Fukushima-ken *see* Fukushima
164 G13 **Fukuyama** *var.* Hukuyama. Hiroshima, Honshū, SW Japan 34°29′N 133°21′E
76 G13 **Fulacunda** C Guinea-Bissau 11°44′N 15°03′W
129 P8 **Fūlādī, Kūh-e** ▲ E Afghanistan 34°38′N 67°32′E
187 Z15 **Fulaga** *island* Lau Group, E Fiji
101 I17 **Fulda** Hessen, C Germany 50°33′N 09°41′E
29 S10 **Fulda** Minnesota, N USA 43°52′N 95°36′W
101 I16 **Fulda** ↝ C Germany
Fülek *see* Fil'akovo
Fuli *see* Jixian
Fulin *see* Hanyuan
160 K10 **Fuling** Chongqing Shi, C China 29°45′N 107°23′E
35 T15 **Fullerton** California, SE USA 33°53′N 117°55′W
29 P15 **Fullerton** Nebraska, C USA 41°21′N 97°58′W
108 M8 **Fulpmes** Tirol, W Austria 47°11′N 11°22′E
20 G8 **Fulton** Kentucky, S USA 36°31′N 88°52′W
23 N2 **Fulton** Mississippi, S USA 34°16′N 88°24′W
27 V4 **Fulton** Missouri, C USA 38°50′N 91°57′W
18 H9 **Fulton** New York, NE USA 43°18′N 76°22′W
Fuman/Fumen *see* Fowman
103 R3 **Fumay** Ardennes, N France 49°58′N 04°42′E
102 M13 **Fumel** Lot-et-Garonne, SW France 44°31′N 00°58′E
190 B10 **Funafara** *atoll* C Tuvalu
190 C9 **Funafuti** ✈ Funafuti Atoll, C Tuvalu 08°30′S 179°12′E
Funafuti *see* Fongafale
190 F8 **Funafuti Atoll** *atoll* C Tuvalu
Funan *see* Fusui
190 B9 **Funangongo** *atoll* C Tuvalu
93 F17 **Funäsdalen** Jämtland, C Sweden 62°33′N 12°33′E
64 O6 **Funchal** Madeira, Portugal, NE Atlantic Ocean 32°40′N 16°55′W
64 P5 **Funchal** ✈ Madeira, Portugal, NE Atlantic Ocean 32°38′N 16°53′W
54 F5 **Fundación** Magdalena, N Colombia 10°31′N 74°09′W
104 I8 **Fundão** *var.* Fundáo. Castelo Branco, C Portugal 40°08′N 07°30′W
Fundáo *see* Fundão
13 O16 **Fundy, Bay of** *bay* Canada/ USA
Fünen *see* Fyn
54 C13 **Fúnes** Nariño, SW Colombia 00°59′N 77°27′W
Fünfkirchen *see* Pécs
83 M19 **Funhalouro** Inhambane, S Mozambique 23°04′S 34°24′E
161 R6 **Funing** Jiangsu, E China 33°43′N 119°47′E
160 I14 **Funing** *var.* Xinhua. Yunnan, SW China 23°39′N 105°41′E
160 M7 **Funiu Shan** ⛰ C China
77 U13 **Funtua** Katsina, N Nigeria 11°31′N 07°19′E
161 R12 **Fuqing** Fujian, SE China 25°40′N 119°23′E
83 M14 **Furancungo** Tete, NW Mozambique 14°51′S 33°39′E
116 I15 **Furculeşti** Teleorman, S Romania 43°51′N 25°07′E
Füred *see* Balatonfüred
165 W4 **Füren-ko** ◎ Hokkaidō, NE Japan
Fürg *see* Doborjī
Furluk *see* Fârliug
Fürmanov/Furmanovka *see* Moyynkum
Furmanovo *see* Zhalpaktal
59 L20 **Furnas, Represa de** ⊠ SE Brazil
183 Q14 **Furneaux Group** *island group* Tasmania, SE Australia
Furnes *see* Veurne
160 J10 **Furong Jiang** ↝ S China
138 I5 **Furqlus** Ḥimṣ, W Syria 34°40′N 37°02′E
100 F12 **Fürstenau** Niedersachsen, NW Germany 52°30′N 07°40′E
109 X8 **Fürstenfeld** Steiermark, SE Austria 47°03′N 16°05′E
101 L23 **Fürstenfeldbruck** Bayern, S Germany 48°10′N 11°16′E

◆ Country ● Country Capital ◇ Dependent Territory ○ Dependent Territory Capital ◈ Administrative Regions ✈ International Airport ▲ Mountain ⛰ Mountain Range Ѫ Volcano ↝ River ◎ Lake ⊠ Reservoir

100 *P12* **Fürstenwalde** Brandenburg, NE Germany *52°22′N 14°04′E*
101 *K20* **Fürth** Bayern, S Germany *49°29′N 10°59′E*
109 *W3* **Furth bei Göttweig** Niederösterreich, NW Austria *48°22′N 15°33′E*
165 *R3* **Furubira** Hokkaidō, NE Japan *43°14′N 140°38′E*
94 *L12* **Furudal** Dalarna, C Sweden *61°10′N 15°07′E*
164 *L12* **Furukawa** *var.* Hida. Gifu, Honshū, SW Japan *36°13′N 137°11′E*
165 *Q10* **Furukawa** *var.* Hurukawa, Ōsaki. Miyagi, Honshū, C Japan *38°36′N 140°57′E*
54 *F10* **Fusagasugá** Cundinamarca, C Colombia *04°22′N 74°21′W*
Fusan *see* Busan
Fushë-Arëzi/Fushë-Arrësi *see* Fushë-Arrëz
113 *L18* **Fushë-Arrëz** *var.* Fushë-Arëzi, Fushë-Arrësi. Shkodër, N Albania *42°05′N 20°01′E*
113 *N16* **Fushë Kosovë** *Serb.* Kosovo Polje. C Kosovo *42°40′N 21°07′E*
Fushë-Kruja *see* Fushë-Krujë
113 *K19* **Fushë-Krujë** *var.* Fushë-Kruja. Durrës, C Albania *41°30′N 19°43′E*
163 *V12* **Fushun** *var.* Fou-shan, Fu-shun. Liaoning, NE China *41°50′N 123°54′E*
Fu-shun *see* Fushun
Fusin *see* Fuxin
108 *G10* **Fusio** Ticino, S Switzerland *46°27′N 08°39′E*
163 *X11* **Fusong** Jilin, NE China *42°20′N 127°17′E*
101 *K24* **Füssen** Bayern, S Germany *47°34′N 10°43′E*
160 *K15* **Fusui** *var.* Xinning; *prev.* Funan. Guangxi Zhuangzu Zizhiqu, S China *22°39′N 107°49′E*
Futa Jallon *see* Fouta Djallon
63 *G18* **Futaleufú** Los Lagos, S Chile *43°14′S 71°50′W*
112 *K10* **Futog** Vojvodina, NW Serbia *45°15′N 19°43′E*
165 *O14* **Futtsu** *var.* Huttu. Chiba, Honshū, S Japan *35°11′N 139°52′E*
187 *S15* **Futuna** *island* S Vanuatu
190 *D12* **Futuna, Île** *island* S Wallis and Futuna
161 *Q11* **Futun Xi** ≈ SE China
160 *L5* **Fuxian** *var.* Fu Xian. Shaanxi, C China *36°03′N 109°19′E*
Fuxian *see* Wafangdian
Fu Xian *see* Fuxian
160 *G13* **Fuxian Hu** ⊠ SW China
163 *U12* **Fuxin** *var.* Fou-hsin, Fu-hsin, Fusin. Liaoning, NE China *41°59′N 121°40′E*
Fuxing *see* Wangmo
161 *P7* **Fuyang** Anhui, E China *32°52′N 115°51′E*
Fuyang *see* Fuchuan
161 *O4* **Fuyang He** ≈ E China
163 *U7* **Fuyu** Heilongjiang, NE China *47°48′N 124°26′E*
163 *Z6* **Fuyuan** Heilongjiang, NE China *48°20′N 134°22′E*
Fuyu/Fu-yü *see* Songyuan
158 *M3* **Fuyun** *var.* Koktokay. Xinjiang Uygur Zizhiqu, NW China *46°58′N 89°30′E*
111 *L22* **Füzesabony** Heves, E Hungary *47°46′N 20°25′E*
161 *R12* **Fuzhou** *var.* Foochow, Fu-chou. *province capital* Fujian, SE China *26°09′N 119°17′E*
161 *P11* **Fuzhou** *prev.* Linchuan. Jiangxi, S China *27°58′N 116°20′E*
137 *W13* **Füzuli** *Rus.* Fizuli. SW Azerbaijan *39°33′N 47°09′E*
119 *I20* **Fyadory** *Rus.* Fëdory. Brestskaya Voblasts', SW Belarus *51°57′N 26°24′E*
95 *G23* **Fyn** *Ger.* Fünen. *island* C Denmark
96 *H12* **Fyne, Loch** *inlet* W Scotland, United Kingdom
95 *E16* **Fyresvatnet** ◎ S Norway
FYR Macedonia/FYROM *see* Macedonia, FYR
Fyzabad *see* Feizābād

G

Gaafu Alifu Atoll *see* North Huvadhu Atoll
81 *O14* **Gaalkacyo** *var.* Galka'yo, *It.* Galcaio. Mudug, C Somalia *06°42′N 47°24′E*
146 *J11* **Gabakly** *Rus.* Kabakly. Lebap Welaýaty, NE Turkmenistan *39°45′N 62°30′E*
114 *H8* **Gabare** Vratsa, NW Bulgaria *43°20′N 23°57′E*
102 *K15* **Gabas** ≈ SW France
Gabasumdo *see* Tongde
35 *T7* **Gabbs** Nevada, W USA *38°51′N 117°55′W*
82 *B12* **Gabela** Cuanza Sul, W Angola *10°50′S 14°21′E*
Gaberones *see* Gaborone
189 *X14* **Gabert** *island* Caroline Islands, E Micronesia
74 *M7* **Gabès** *var.* Qābis. E Tunisia *33°53′N 10°03′E*
74 *M6* **Gabès, Golfe de** *Ar.* Khalīj Qābis. *gulf* E Tunisia
Gablonz an der Neisse *see* Jablonec nad Nisou
Gablös *see* Cavalese
79 *E18* **Gabon** *off.* Gabonese Republic. ◆ *republic* C Africa
Gabonese Republic *see* Gabon
83 *I20* **Gaborone** *prev.* Gaberones. ● (Botswana) South East, SE Botswana *24°42′S 25°50′E*
83 *I20* **Gaborone** ✈ South East, SE Botswana *24°45′S 25°49′E*
104 *K8* **Gabriel y Galán, Embalse de** ⊠ W Spain
143 *U15* **Gābrīk, Rūd-e** ≈ SE Iran
114 *J9* **Gabrovo** Gabrovo, N Bulgaria *42°54′N 25°19′E*
114 *J9* **Gabrovo** ◈ *province* N Bulgaria
76 *H12* **Gabú** *prev.* Nova Lamego. E Guinea-Bissau *12°16′N 14°09′W*
29 *O6* **Gackle** North Dakota, N USA *46°34′N 99°07′W*
113 *I15* **Gacko** Repulika Srpska, S Bosnia and Herzegovina *43°08′N 18°29′E*
155 *F17* **Gadag** Karnātaka, W India *15°25′N 75°37′E*
93 *G15* **Gäddede** Jämtland, C Sweden *64°30′N 14°15′E*
159 *S12* **Gadê** *var.* Kequ; *prev.* Pagqên. Qinghai, C China *33°56′N 99°49′E*
Gades/Gadier/Gadir/Gadire *see* Cádiz
105 *P15* **Gádor, Sierra de** ▲▲ S Spain
149 *S15* **Gadra** Sind, SE Pakistan *25°39′N 70°28′E*
23 *Q3* **Gadsden** Alabama, S USA *34°00′N 86°00′W*
36 *H15* **Gadsden** Arizona, SW USA *32°33′N 114°45′W*
Gadyach *see* Hadyach
124 *J3* **Gadzhiyevo** Murmanskaya Oblast', NW Russian Federation *69°16′N 33°20′E*
79 *H15* **Gadzi** Mambéré-Kadéï, SW Central African Republic *04°46′N 16°42′E*
116 *J13* **Găeşti** Dâmboviţa, S Romania *44°42′N 25°19′E*
107 *J17* **Gaeta** Lazio, C Italy *41°12′N 13°35′E*
107 *J17* **Gaeta, Golfo di** *var.* Gulf of Gaeta. *gulf* C Italy
Gaeta, Gulf of *see* Gaeta, Golfo di
188 *L14* **Gaferut** *atoll* Caroline Islands, W Micronesia
21 *Q10* **Gaffney** South Carolina, SE USA *35°03′N 81°40′W*
Gäfle *see* Gävle
Gäfleborg *see* Gävleborg
74 *M6* **Gafsa** *var.* Qafşah. W Tunisia *34°25′N 08°52′E*
Gafurov *see* Ghafurov
126 *J3* **Gagarin** *prev.* Gzhatsk. Smolenskaya Oblast', W Russian Federation *53°33′N 35°00′E*
147 *O10* **Gagarin** Jizzax Viloyati, C Uzbekistan *40°40′N 68°04′E*
116 *M12* **Găgăuzia** ◈ *cultural region* S Moldavia
101 *G21* **Gaggenau** Baden-Württemberg, SW Germany *48°48′N 08°19′E*
188 *F16* **Gagil Tamil** *var.* Gagil-Tomil. *island* Caroline Islands, W Micronesia
Gagil-Tomil *see* Gagil Tamil
127 *O4* **Gagino** Nizhegorodskaya Oblast', W Russian Federation *55°18′N 45°01′E*
107 *Q19* **Gagliano del Capo** Puglia, SE Italy *39°49′N 18°22′E*
94 *L13* **Gagnef** Dalarna, C Sweden *60°34′N 15°04′E*
76 *M17* **Gagnoa** C Ivory Coast *06°11′N 05°56′W*
13 *N10* **Gagnon** Québec, E Canada *51°56′N 68°16′W*
Gago Coutinho *see* Lumbala N'Guimbo
137 *P8* **Gagra** NW Georgia *43°17′N 40°18′E*
31 *S13* **Gahanna** Ohio, N USA *40°01′N 82°52′W*
143 *R13* **Gahkom** Hormozgān, S Iran *28°14′N 55°48′E*
Gahnpa *see* Ganta
57 *Q19* **Gaíba, Laguna** ◎ E Bolivia
153 *T13* **Gaibandha** *var.* Gaibanda. Rajshahi, NW Bangladesh *25°21′N 89°36′E*
Gaibhlte, Cnoc Mór na n *see* Galtymore Mountain
109 *R9* **Gail** ≈ S Austria
101 *I21* **Gaildorf** Baden-Württemberg, S Germany *48°41′N 10°08′E*
103 *N15* **Gaillac** *var.* Gaillac-sur-Tarn. Tarn, S France *43°54′N 01°54′E*
Gaillac-sur-Tarn *see* Gaillac
Gaillimh *see* Galway
Gaillimhe, Cuan na *see* Galway Bay
109 *Q9* **Gailtaler Alpen** ▲▲ S Austria
63 *J17* **Gaimán** Chaco, S Argentina *43°15′S 65°30′W*
20 *K8* **Gainesboro** Tennessee, S USA *36°20′N 85°41′W*
23 *V10* **Gainesville** Florida, SE USA *29°39′N 82°19′W*
23 *T2* **Gainesville** Georgia, SE USA *34°18′N 83°49′W*
27 *U8* **Gainesville** Missouri, C USA *36°37′N 92°28′W*
25 *T5* **Gainesville** Texas, SW USA *33°39′N 97°08′W*
109 *X5* **Gainfarn** Niederösterreich, NE Austria *47°59′N 16°11′E*
97 *N18* **Gainsborough** E England, United Kingdom *53°24′N 00°48′W*
182 *G6* **Gairdner, Lake** *salt lake* South Australia
Gaissane *see* Gáissát
92 *L8* **Gáissát** *var.* Gaissane. ▲▲ N Norway
43 *T15* **Gaital, Cerro** ▲ C Panama *08°37′N 80°04′W*
21 *W3* **Gaithersburg** Maryland, NE USA *39°08′N 77°13′W*
163 *U13* **Gaizhou** Liaoning, NE China *40°24′N 122°17′E*
Gaizina Kalns *see* Gaiziņkalns
118 *H7* **Gaiziņkalns** *var.* Gaizina Kalns. ▲ E Latvia *56°51′N 25°58′E*
Gajac *see* Villeneuve-sur-Lot
39 *S10* **Gakona** Alaska, USA *62°21′N 145°16′W*
158 *M16* **Gala** Xizang Zizhiqu, China *28°17′N 89°21′E*
Galaassiya *see* Galaosiyo
Ğalāğıl *see* Jalājil
Galam, Pulau *see* Gelam, Pulau
62 *J6* **Galán, Cerro** ▲ NW Argentina *25°54′S 66°45′W*
111 *H21* **Galanta** *Hung.* Galánta. Trnavský Kraj, W Slovakia *48°12′N 17°45′E*
146 *L11* **Galaosiyo** *Rus.* Galaassiya. Buxoro Viloyati, C Uzbekistan *39°53′N 64°25′E*
57 *B17* **Galápagos** *off.* Provincia de Galápagos. ◈ *province* W Ecuador, E Pacific Ocean
193 *P8* **Galapagos Fracture Zone** *tectonic feature* E Pacific Ocean
Galapagos Islands *see* Colón, Archipiélago de
Galápagos, Islas de los *see* Colón, Archipiélago de
Galápagos, Provincia de *see* Galápagos
193 *S9* **Galapagos Rise** *undersea feature* E Pacific Ocean *15°00′S 97°00′W*
96 *K13* **Galashiels** SE Scotland, United Kingdom *55°37′N 02°49′W*
116 *M12* **Galaţi** *Ger.* Galatz. Galaţi, E Romania *45°27′N 28°00′E*
116 *L12* **Galaţi** ◈ *county* E Romania
107 *Q19* **Galatina** Puglia, SE Italy *40°10′N 18°10′E*
107 *Q19* **Galatone** Puglia, SE Italy *40°09′N 18°05′E*
Galatz *see* Galaţi
21 *R8* **Galax** Virginia, NE USA *36°40′N 88°56′W*
146 *J16* **Galaýmor** *Rus.* Kala-i-Mor. Mary Welaýaty, S Turkmenistan *35°40′N 62°28′E*
Galcaio *see* Gaalkacyo
64 *P11* **Gáldar** Gran Canaria, Islas Canarias, NE Atlantic Ocean *28°09′N 15°40′W*
94 *F11* **Galdhøpiggen** ▲ S Norway *61°30′N 08°08′E*
40 *I4* **Galeana** Chihuahua, N Mexico *30°08′N 107°38′W*
41 *O9* **Galeana** Nuevo León, NE Mexico *24°45′N 99°59′W*
60 *P9* **Galeão** ✈ (Rio de Janeiro) Rio de Janeiro, SE Brazil *22°48′S 43°16′W*
171 *R10* **Galela** Pulau Halmahera, E Indonesia *01°52′N 127°48′E*
39 *O9* **Galena** Alaska, USA *64°43′N 156°55′W*
30 *K10* **Galena** Illinois, N USA *42°25′N 90°25′W*
27 *R7* **Galena** Kansas, C USA *37°04′N 94°38′W*
27 *T8* **Galena** Missouri, C USA *36°45′N 93°30′W*
45 *V15* **Galeota Point** *headland* Trinidad, Trinidad and Tobago *10°07′N 60°59′W*
105 *P13* **Galera** Andalucía, S Spain *37°45′N 02°33′W*
45 *Y16* **Galera Point** *headland* Trinidad, Trinidad and Tobago *10°49′N 60°54′W*
56 *A5* **Galera, Punta** *headland* NW Ecuador *0°49′N 80°03′W*
30 *K12* **Galesburg** Illinois, N USA *40°57′N 90°22′W*
30 *J7* **Galesville** Wisconsin, N USA *44°04′N 91°21′W*
18 *F12* **Galeton** Pennsylvania, NE USA *41°43′N 77°38′W*
116 *H9* **Gâlgău** *Hung.* Galgó; *prev.* Gîlgău. Sălaj, NW Romania *47°17′N 23°43′E*
Galgó *see* Gâlgău
Galgóc *see* Hlohovec
81 *N15* **Galguduud** *off.* Gobolka Galguduud. ◈ *region* E Somalia
Galguduud, Gobolka *see* Galguduud
137 *Q9* **Gali** W Georgia *42°40′N 41°39′E*
125 *N14* **Galich** Kostromskaya Oblast', NW Russian Federation *58°21′N 42°21′E*
114 *H7* **Galiche** Vratsa, NW Bulgaria *43°36′N 23°53′E*
104 *H3* **Galicia** *anc.* Gallaecia. ◈ *autonomous community* NW Spain
64 *M8* **Galicia Bank** *undersea feature* E Atlantic Ocean *11°45′W 42°40′N*
Galilee *see* HaGalil
181 *W7* **Galilee, Lake** ◎ Queensland, NE Australia
Galilee, Sea of *see* Tiberias, Lake
106 *E11* **Galileo Galilei** ✈ (Pisa) Toscana, C Italy *43°40′N 10°22′E*
31 *S12* **Galion** Ohio, N USA *40°43′N 82°47′W*
Galka'yo *see* Gaalkacyo
146 *K12* **Galkynyş** *prev. Rus.* Deynau, Dyanev, *Turkm.* Dänew. Lebap Welaýaty, NE Turkmenistan *39°16′N 63°10′E*
80 *H11* **Gallabat** Gedaref, E Sudan *12°57′N 36°10′E*
Gallaecia *see* Galicia
147 *O11* **G'allaorol** Jizzax Viloyati, C Uzbekistan *40°01′N 67°30′E*
106 *C7* **Gallarate** Lombardia, NW Italy *45°39′N 08°47′E*
27 *S2* **Gallatin** Missouri, C USA *39°54′N 93°57′W*
20 *J8* **Gallatin** Tennessee, S USA *36°22′N 86°28′W*
33 *R11* **Gallatin Peak** ▲ Montana, NW USA *45°22′N 111°21′W*
33 *R12* **Gallatin River** ≈ Montana/Wyoming, NW USA
155 *J26* **Galle** *prev.* Point de Galle. Southern Province, SW Sri Lanka *06°04′N 80°12′E*
105 *S5* **Gállego** ≈ NE Spain
193 *Q8* **Gallego Rise** *undersea feature* E Pacific Ocean *02°00′S 115°00′W*
Gallegos *see* Río Gallegos
63 *H23* **Gallegos, Río** ≈ Argentina/Chile
Gallia *see* France
22 *K10* **Galliano** Louisiana, S USA *29°26′N 90°18′W*
114 *G13* **Gallikós** ≈ N Greece
37 *S12* **Gallinas Peak** ▲ New Mexico, SW USA *34°14′N 105°47′W*
54 *H3* **Gallinas, Punta** *headland* NE Colombia *12°27′N 71°44′W*
37 *T11* **Gallinas River** ≈ New Mexico, SW USA
107 *Q19* **Gallipoli** Puglia, SE Italy *40°08′N 18°E*
Gallipoli *see* Gelibolu
Gallipoli Peninsula *see* Gelibolu Yarımadası
31 *T15* **Gallipolis** Ohio, N USA *38°49′N 82°14′W*
92 *J12* **Gällivare** *Lapp.* Váhtjer. Norrbotten, N Sweden *67°08′N 20°39′E*
109 *T4* **Gallneukirchen** Oberösterreich, N Austria *48°22′N 14°25′E*
93 *G17* **Gällö** Jämtland, C Sweden *62°57′N 15°15′E*
105 *Q7* **Gallo** ≈ C Spain
107 *I23* **Gallo, Capo** *headland* Sicilia, Italy, C Mediterranean Sea *38°13′N 13°18′E*
37 *P13* **Gallo Mountains** ▲▲ New Mexico, SW USA
18 *G8* **Galloo Island** *island* New York, NE USA
97 *H15* **Galloway, Mull of** *headland* S Scotland, United Kingdom *54°37′N 04°54′W*
37 *P10* **Gallup** New Mexico, SW USA *35°32′N 108°45′W*
105 *R5* **Gallur** Aragón, NE Spain *41°51′N 01°21′W*
Gâlma *see* Guelma
163 *N9* **Galshar** *var.* Buyant. Hentiy, C Mongolia *46°15′N 110°50′E*
162 *I6* **Galt** *var.* Ider. Hövsgöl, C Mongolia *48°45′N 99°52′E*
35 *O8* **Galt** California, W USA *38°13′N 121°19′W*
74 *C10* **Galtat-Zemmour** C Western Sahara *25°07′N 12°21′W*
95 *G22* **Galten** Midtjylland, C Denmark *56°09′N 09°54′E*
Gålto *see* Kultsjön
97 *D20* **Galtymore Mountain** *Ir.* Cnoc Mór na nGaibhlte. ▲ S Ireland *52°21′N 08°09′W*
97 *D20* **Galty Mountains** *Ir.* Na Gaibhlte. ▲▲ S Ireland
30 *K11* **Galva** Illinois, N USA *41°10′N 90°02′W*
25 *X12* **Galveston** Texas, SW USA *29°17′N 94°48′W*
25 *W11* **Galveston Bay** *inlet* Texas, SW USA
25 *W12* **Galveston Island** *island* Texas, SW USA
61 *B18* **Gálvez** Santa Fe, C Argentina *32°03′S 61°14′W*
97 *C18* **Galway** *Ir.* Gaillimh. W Ireland *53°16′N 09°03′W*
97 *B18* **Galway** *Ir.* Gaillimh. *cultural region* W Ireland
97 *B18* **Galway Bay** *Ir.* Cuan na Gaillimhe. *bay* W Ireland
83 *F18* **Gam** Otjozondjupa, NE Namibia *20°10′S 20°51′E*
164 *L14* **Gamagōri** Aichi, Honshū, SW Japan *34°49′N 137°15′E*
54 *F7* **Gamarra** Cesar, N Colombia *08°21′N 73°46′W*
Gámas *see* Kaamanen
158 *L17* **Gamba** Xizang Zizhiqu, W China *28°13′N 88°32′E*
Gamba *see* Zamtang
77 *P14* **Gambaga** NE Ghana *10°32′N 00°28′W*
80 *G13* **Gambēla** Gambēla Hizboch, W Ethiopia *08°09′N 34°15′E*
81 *H14* **Gambēla Hizboch** ◈ *federal region* W Ethiopia
38 *K10* **Gambell** Saint Lawrence Island, Alaska, USA *63°44′N 171°41′W*
76 *E12* **Gambia** *off.* Republic of The Gambia, The Gambia. ◆ *republic* W Africa
76 *I12* **Gambia** *Fr.* Gambie. ≈ W Africa
64 *K12* **Gambia Plain** *undersea feature* E Atlantic Ocean
Gambia, Republic of The *see* Gambia
Gambia, The *see* Gambia
Gambie *see* Gambia
31 *T13* **Gambier** Ohio, N USA *40°22′N 82°24′W*
191 *Y13* **Gambier, Îles** *island group* E French Polynesia
182 *G10* **Gambier Islands** *island group* South Australia
79 *H19* **Gamboma** Plateaux, E Congo *01°53′S 15°51′E*
79 *G16* **Gamboula** Mambéré-Kadéï, SW Central African Republic *04°09′N 15°12′E*
37 *P10* **Gamerco** New Mexico, SW USA *35°34′N 108°45′W*
137 *V12* **Gamış Dağı** ▲ W Azerbaijan *40°18′N 46°15′E*
Gamlakarleby *see* Kokkola
95 *N18* **Gamleby** Kalmar, S Sweden *57°54′N 16°25′E*
Gammelstad *see* Gammelstaden
93 *J14* **Gammelstaden** *var.* Gammelstad. Norrbotten, N Sweden *65°38′N 22°05′E*
Gammouda *see* Sidi Bouzid
155 *J25* **Gampaha** Western Province, W Sri Lanka *07°05′N 80°00′E*
155 *K25* **Gampola** Central Province, C Sri Lanka *07°10′N 80°34′E*
167 *S5* **Gâm, Sông** ≈ N Vietnam
92 *L7* **Gamvik** Finnmark, N Norway *71°04′N 28°08′E*
150 *H13* **Gan** Addu Atoll, C Maldives
Gan *see* Gansu, China
Gan *see* Jiangxi, China
Ganaane *see* Juba
37 *O10* **Ganado** Arizona, SW USA *35°42′N 109°31′W*
25 *U12* **Ganado** Texas, SW USA *29°02′N 96°30′W*
14 *L14* **Gananoque** Ontario, SE Canada *44°21′N 76°11′W*
Ganāveh *see* Bandar-e Gonāveh
137 *V11* **Gäncä** *Rus.* Gyandzha; *prev.* Kirovabad, Yelisavetpol. W Azerbaijan *40°42′N 46°23′E*
Ganchi *see* Ghonchí
Gand *see* Gent
82 *B13* **Ganda** *var.* Mariano Machado, *Port.* Vila Mariano Machado. Benguela, W Angola *13°02′S 14°40′E*
79 *L22* **Gandajika** Kasai-Oriental, S Dem. Rep. Congo *06°42′S 24°01′E*
153 *O12* **Gandak** *Nep.* Nārāyāni. ≈ India/Nepal
13 *U11* **Gander** Newfoundland and Labrador, SE Canada *48°56′N 54°33′W*
13 *U11* **Gander** ✈ Newfoundland and Labrador, E Canada *49°03′N 54°49′W*
100 *G11* **Ganderkesee** Niedersachsen, NW Germany *53°01′N 08°33′E*
105 *T7* **Gandesa** Cataluña, NE Spain *41°03′N 00°26′E*
154 *B10* **Gāndhīdhām** Gujarāt, W India *23°08′N 70°05′E*
154 *D10* **Gāndhīnagar** *state capital* Gujarāt, W India *23°12′N 72°37′E*
154 *F9* **Gāndhi Sāgar** ◎ C India
105 *T11* **Gandia** *prev.* Gandía. Valenciana, E Spain *38°59′N 00°11′W*
Gandía *see* Gandia
159 *O10* **Gang** Qinghai, W China
152 *G9* **Gangānagar** Rājasthān, NW India *29°54′N 73°56′E*
152 *I12* **Gangāpur** Rājasthān, N India *26°30′N 76°49′E*
153 *S17* **Ganga Sāgar** West Bengal, NE India *21°39′N 88°05′E*
Gangavathi *see* Gangāwati
155 *G17* **Gangāwati** *var.* Gangavathi. Karnātaka, C India *15°26′N 76°35′E*
159 *S9* **Gangca** *var.* Shaliuhe. Qinghai, C China *37°21′N 100°09′E*
158 *H14* **Gangdisê Shan** *Eng.* Kailas Range. ▲▲ W China
103 *Q15* **Ganges** Hérault, S France *43°57′N 03°42′E*
153 *P13* **Ganges** *Ben.* Padma. ≈ Bangladesh/India *see also* Padma
Ganges *see* Padma
Ganges Cone *see* Ganges Fan
173 *S3* **Ganges Fan** *var.* Ganges Cone. *undersea feature* N Bay of Bengal *12°00′N 87°00′E*
153 *U17* **Ganges, Mouths of the** *delta* Bangladesh/India
107 *K23* **Gangi** *anc.* Engyum. Sicilia, Italy, C Mediterranean Sea *37°48′N 14°13′E*
163 *Y14* **Gangneung** *Jap.* Kōryō; *prev.* Kangnŭng. NE South Korea *37°47′N 128°51′E*
152 *K8* **Gangotri** Uttarakhand, N India *30°56′N 79°02′E*
Gangra *see* Çankırı
153 *S11* **Gangtok** *state capital* Sikkim, N India *27°20′N 88°39′E*
159 *W11* **Gangu** *var.* Daxiangshan. Gansu, C China *34°38′N 105°18′E*
163 *U5* **Gan He** ≈ NE China
171 *S12* **Gani** Pulau Halmahera, E Indonesia *0°45′S 128°13′E*
161 *O12* **Gan Jiang** ≈ S China
163 *U11* **Ganjig** *var.* Horqin Zuoyi Houqi. Nei Mongol Zizhiqu, N China *42°53′N 122°22′E*
146 *H15* **Gannaly** Ahal Welaýaty, S Turkmenistan *37°02′N 60°43′E*
163 *U7* **Gannan** Heilongjiang, NE China *47°58′N 123°36′E*
103 *P10* **Gannat** Allier, C France *46°06′N 03°12′E*
33 *T14* **Gannett Peak** ▲ Wyoming, C USA *43°10′N 109°39′W*
29 *O10* **Gannvalley** South Dakota, N USA *44°01′N 98°59′W*
Ganqu *see* Lhünzhub
109 *Y3* **Gänserndorf** Niederösterreich, NE Austria *48°21′N 16°43′E*
Gansos, Lago dos *see* Goose Lake
159 *T9* **Gansu** *var.* Gan, Gansu Sheng, Kansu. ◈ *province* N China
Gansu Sheng *see* Gansu
76 *K16* **Ganta** *var.* Gahnpa. NE Liberia *07°15′N 08°59′W*
182 *H11* **Gantheaume, Cape** *headland* South Australia *36°04′S 137°28′E*
Gantsevichi *see* Hantsavichy
161 *Q6* **Ganyu** *var.* Qingkou. Jiangsu, E China *34°52′N 119°11′E*
144 *D12* **Ganyushkino** Atyrau, SW Kazakhstan *46°38′N 49°12′E*
161 *O12* **Ganzhou** Jiangxi, S China *25°51′N 114°59′E*
Ganzhou *see* Zhangye
77 *Q10* **Gao** Gao, E Mali *16°16′N 00°03′E*
77 *R10* **Gao** ◈ *region* SE Mali
161 *O10* **Gao'an** Jiangxi, S China *28°24′N 115°27′E*
Gaocheng *see* Litang
Gaoleshan *see* Xianfeng
161 *R5* **Gaomi** Shandong, C China *36°23′N 119°45′E*
161 *N5* **Gaoping** Shanxi, C China *35°51′N 112°55′E*
159 *S8* **Gaotai** Gansu, N China *39°22′N 99°44′E*
Gaoth Dobhair *see* Gweedore
77 *O14* **Gaoua** SW Burkina *10°18′N 03°12′W*
76 *I13* **Gaoual** N Guinea *11°44′N 13°14′W*
161 *S14* **Gaoxiong** *var.* Kaohsiung, *Jap.* Takao, Takow. S Taiwan *22°36′N 120°17′E*
161 *S14* **Gaoxiong** ✈ S Taiwan *22°26′N 120°32′E*
161 *R7* **Gaoyou** *var.* Dayishan. Jiangsu, E China *32°48′N 119°26′E*
161 *R7* **Gaoyou Hu** ◎ E China
160 *M15* **Gaozhou** Guangdong, S China *21°56′N 110°49′E*
103 *T13* **Gap** *anc.* Vapincum. Hautes-Alpes, SE France *44°33′N 06°05′E*
146 *E9* **Gaplaňgyr Platosy** *Rus.* Plato Kaplangky. *ridge* Turkmenistan/Uzbekistan
156 *G13* **Gar** *var.* Shiquanhe. Xizang Zizhiqu, W China *32°31′N 80°04′E*
Gar *see* Gar Xincun
Garabekevyul *see* Garabekewül
146 *L13* **Garabekewül** *Rus.* Garabekevyul, Karabekaul. Lebap Welaýaty, E Turkmenistan *38°31′N 64°04′E*
146 *K15* **Garabil Belentligi** *Rus.* Vozvyshennost' Karabil'. ▲▲ S Turkmenistan
146 *A8* **Garabogaz** *Rus.* Bekdash. Balkan Welaýaty, NW Turkmenistan *41°33′N 52°33′E*
146 *B9* **Garabogaz Aylagy** *Rus.* Zaliv Kara-Bogaz-Gol. *bay* NW Turkmenistan
146 *A9* **Garabogazköl** *Rus.* Kara-Bogaz-Gol. Balkan Welaýaty, NW Turkmenistan *41°03′N 52°52′E*
43 *V16* **Garachiné** Darién, SE Panama *08°03′N 78°22′W*
43 *V16* **Garachiné, Punta** *headland* SE Panama *08°05′N 78°23′W*
146 *K12* **Garagan** *Rus.* Karagan. Ahal Welaýaty, C Turkmenistan *38°16′N 57°34′E*
54 *G10* **Garagoa** Boyacá, C Colombia *05°05′N 73°20′W*
146 *A11* **Garagöl'** *Rus.* Karagel'. Balkan Welaýaty, W Turkmenistan *39°24′N 53°13′E*
146 *F12* **Garagum** *var.* Garagumy, Qara Qum, *Eng.* Black Sand Desert, Kara Kum; *prev.* Peski Karakumy. *desert* C Turkmenistan
146 *E12* **Garagum Kanaly** *var.* Kara Kum Canal, *Rus.* Karagumskiy Kanal, Karakumskiy Kanal. *canal* C Turkmenistan
Garagumy *see* Garagum
183 *S4* **Garah** New South Wales, SE Australia *29°07′S 149°37′E*
64 *O11* **Garajonay** ▲ Gomera, Islas Canarias, NE Atlantic Ocean *28°07′N 17°14′W*
114 *M8* **Gara Khitrino** Shumen, NE Bulgaria *43°26′N 26°55′E*
76 *L13* **Garalo** Sikasso, SW Mali *10°58′N 07°26′W*
Garam *see* Hron, Slovakia
146 *L14* **Garamätnyýaz** *Rus.* Karamet-Niyaz. Lebap Welaýaty, E Turkmenistan *37°45′N 64°28′E*
Garamszentkereszt *see* Žiar nad Hronom
77 *Q13* **Garango** S Burkina *11°45′N 00°30′W*
59 *Q15* **Garanhuns** Pernambuco, E Brazil *08°53′S 36°28′W*
188 *H5* **Garapan** Saipan, S Northern Mariana Islands *15°12′S 145°43′E*
Gárasavvon *see* Karesuando
Gárassavon *see* Kaaresuvanto
78 *J13* **Garba** Bamingui-Bangoran, N Central African Republic *09°09′N 20°24′E*
Garba *see* Jiulong
81 *L16* **Garbahaarrey** *It.* Garba Harre. Gedo, SW Somalia *03°14′N 42°18′E*
Garba Harre *see* Garbahaarrey
81 *J18* **Garba Tula** Eastern, C Kenya *0°31′N 38°35′E*
27 *N9* **Garber** Oklahoma, C USA *36°26′N 97°35′W*
34 *L4* **Garberville** California, W USA *40°07′N 123°48′W*
Garbo *see* Lhozhag
100 *I12* **Garbsen** Niedersachsen, N Germany *52°25′N 09°36′E*
60 *K9* **Garça** São Paulo, S Brazil *22°14′S 49°36′W*
104 *L10* **García de Solá, Embalse de** ⊠ C Spain
103 *Q14* **Gard** ◈ *department* S France
103 *Q14* **Gard** ≈ S France
106 *F7* **Garda, Lago di** *var.* Benaco, *Eng.* Lake Garda, *Ger.* Gardasee. ◎ NE Italy
Garda, Lake *see* Garda, Lago di
Gardan Divāl *see* Gardan Dīwāl
149 *Q5* **Gardan Dīwāl** *var.* Gardan Divāl. Wardak, C Afghanistan *34°30′N 68°15′E*
103 *S15* **Gardanne** Bouches-du-Rhône, SE France *43°27′N 05°28′E*
Gardasee *see* Garda, Lago di
100 *L12* **Gardelegen** Sachsen-Anhalt, C Germany *52°31′N 11°25′E*
14 *B10* **Garden** ≈ Ontario, S Canada
23 *X6* **Garden City** Georgia, SE USA *32°06′N 81°09′W*
26 *I6* **Garden City** Kansas, C USA *37°57′N 100°54′W*
27 *S5* **Garden City** Missouri, C USA *38°34′N 94°12′W*
25 *N8* **Garden City** Texas, SW USA *31°51′N 101°30′W*
23 *P3* **Gardendale** Alabama, S USA *33°39′N 86°48′W*
31 *P5* **Garden Island** *island* Michigan, N USA
22 *M11* **Garden Island Bay** *bay* Louisiana, S USA
31 *O5* **Garden Peninsula** *peninsula* Michigan, N USA
Garden State, The *see* New Jersey
95 *I14* **Gardermoen** Akershus, S Norway *60°10′N 11°04′E*
95 *I14* **Gardermoen** ✈ (Oslo) Akershus, S Norway *60°12′N 11°05′E*
Gardeyz/Gardez *see* Gardēz
149 *Q6* **Gardēz** *var.* Gardeyz, Gordiaz; *prev.* Gardīz. Paktiyā, E Afghanistan *33°35′N 69°14′E*
93 *G14* **Gardiken** ◎ N Sweden
19 *Q7* **Gardiner** Maine, NE USA *44°13′N 69°46′W*
33 *S12* **Gardiner** Montana, NW USA *45°02′N 110°42′W*
19 *N13* **Gardiners Island** *island* New York, NE USA
Gardner Island *see* Nikumaroro
19 *T6* **Gardner Lake** ◎ Maine, NE USA
35 *Q6* **Gardnerville** Nevada, W USA *38°55′N 119°44′W*
Gardo *see* Qardho
106 *F7* **Gardone Val Trompia** Lombardia, N Italy *45°40′N 10°11′E*
Garegegasnjárga *see* Karigasniemi
38 *F17* **Gareloi Island** *island* Aleutian Islands, Alaska, USA
Gares *see* Puente la Reina
106 *B10* **Garessio** Piemonte, NE Italy *44°14′N 08°01′E*
32 *M9* **Garfield** Washington, NW USA *47°00′N 117°07′W*
31 *U11* **Garfield Heights** Ohio, N USA *41°25′N 81°36′W*
Gargaliani *see* Gargaliánoi
115 *D21* **Gargaliánoi** *var.* Gargaliani. Pelopónnisos, S Greece *37°04′N 21°38′E*
107 *N15* **Gargàno, Promontorio del** *headland* SE Italy *41°51′N 16°11′E*
108 *J8* **Gargellen** Graubünden, W Switzerland *46°57′N 09°55′E*
93 *I14* **Gargnäs** Västerbotten, N Sweden *65°19′N 18°00′E*
118 *C11* **Gargždai** Klaipėda, W Lithuania *55°42′N 21°24′E*
154 *J13* **Garhchiroli** Mahārāshtra, C India *20°14′N 79°58′E*
153 *O15* **Garhwa** Jhārkhand, N India *24°07′N 83°52′E*
171 *V13* **Gariau** Papua, E Indonesia *03°43′S 134°54′E*
83 *E24* **Garies** Northern Cape, W South Africa *30°30′S 18°00′E*
107 *K17* **Garigliano** ≈ C Italy
81 *K19* **Garissa** Coast, E Kenya *0°27′S 39°39′E*
21 *V11* **Garland** North Carolina, SE USA *34°45′N 78°25′W*
25 *T6* **Garland** Texas, SW USA *32°50′N 96°37′W*
36 *L1* **Garland** Utah, W USA *41°43′N 112°07′W*
106 *D8* **Garlasco** Lombardia, N Italy *45°12′N 08°59′E*
119 *F14* **Garliava** Kaunas, S Lithuania *54°49′N 23°52′E*
Garm *see* Gharm
142 *M9* **Garm, Āb-e** *var.* Rūd-e Khersān. ≈ SW Iran
101 *K25* **Garmisch-Partenkirchen** Bayern, S Germany *47°30′N 11°05′E*
143 *O5* **Garmsār** *prev.* Qishlaq. Semnān, N Iran *35°18′N 52°22′E*
Garmser *see* Darwēshān
29 *V12* **Garner** Iowa, C USA *43°06′N 93°36′W*
21 *U9* **Garner** North Carolina, SE USA *35°42′N 78°36′W*
27 *Q5* **Garnett** Kansas, C USA *38°16′N 95°15′W*
99 *M25* **Garnich** Luxembourg, SW Luxembourg *49°37′N 05°57′E*
182 *M8* **Garnpung, Lake** *salt lake* New South Wales, SE Australia
Garoe *see* Garoowe
Garoet *see* Garut
153 *U13* **Gāro Hills** *hill range* NE India
102 *K13* **Garonne** *anc.* Garumna. ≈ S France
80 *P13* **Garoowe** *var.* Garoe. Nugaal, N Somalia *08°24′N 48°29′E*
78 *F12* **Garoua** *var.* Garua. Nord, N Cameroon *09°17′N 13°22′E*
79 *G14* **Garoua Boulaï** Est, E Cameroon *05°54′N 14°33′E*
77 *O10* **Garou, Lac** ◎ C Mali
95 *L16* **Garphyttan** Örebro, C Sweden *59°18′N 14°54′E*
29 *R11* **Garretson** South Dakota, N USA *43°43′N 96°30′W*
31 *Q11* **Garrett** Indiana, N USA *41°21′N 85°08′W*
33 *Q10* **Garrison** Montana, NW USA *46°32′N 112°46′W*
28 *M4* **Garrison** North Dakota, N USA *47°36′N 101°25′W*
25 *X8* **Garrison** Texas, SW USA *31°49′N 94°29′W*
28 *L4* **Garrison Dam** *dam* North Dakota, N USA
104 *J9* **Garrovillas** Extremadura, W Spain *39°43′N 06°33′W*
Garrygala *see* Magtymguly
8 *L8* **Garry Lake** ◎ Nunavut, N Canada
Gars *see* Gars am Kamp
109 *W3* **Gars am Kamp** *var.* Gars. Niederösterreich, NE Austria *48°35′N 15°40′E*
81 *K20* **Garsen** Coast, S Kenya *02°16′S 40°07′E*
Garshy *see* Garşy
14 *F10* **Garson** Ontario, S Canada *46°33′N 80°51′W*
109 *T5* **Garsten** Oberösterreich, N Austria *48°00′N 14°24′E*
146 *A9* **Garşy** *var.* Garshy, *Rus.* Karshi. Balkan Welaýaty, NW Turkmenistan *40°45′N 52°50′E*
Gartar *see* Qianning
102 *M10* **Gartempe** ≈ C France
Gartog *see* Markam
Garua *see* Garoua
83 *D21* **Garub** Karas, SW Namibia *26°33′S 16°00′E*
Garumna *see* Garonne
169 *P16* **Garut** *prev.* Garoet. Jawa, C Indonesia *07°15′S 107°55′E*
185 *C20* **Garvie Mountains** ▲▲ South Island, New Zealand
110 *N12* **Garwolin** Mazowieckie, E Poland *51°54′N 21°36′E*
25 *U12* **Garwood** Texas, SW USA *29°25′N 96°26′W*
158 *G13* **Gar Xincun** *prev.* Gar. Xizang Zizhiqu, W China *32°04′N 80°01′E*
31 *N11* **Gary** Indiana, N USA *41°36′N 87°21′W*
25 *X7* **Gary** Texas, SW USA *32°00′N 94°21′W*
158 *G13* **Garyarsa** Xizang Zizhiqu, SW China *31°44′N 80°20′E*
158 *G13* **Gar Zangbo** ≈ W China
160 *F8* **Garzê** Sichuan, C China *31°40′N 99°58′E*
54 *E12* **Garzón** Huila, S Colombia *02°14′N 75°37′W*
Gasan-Kuli *see* Esenguly
31 *P13* **Gas City** Indiana, N USA *40°29′N 85°36′W*
102 *K15* **Gascogne** *Eng.* Gascony. *cultural region* S France
26 *V5* **Gasconade River** ≈ Missouri, C USA
Gascony *see* Gascogne
180 *H9* **Gascoyne Junction** Western Australia *25°06′S 115°10′E*
173 *V8* **Gascoyne Plain** *undersea feature* E Indian Ocean
180 *H9* **Gascoyne River** ≈ Western Australia
192 *J11* **Gascoyne Tablemount** *undersea feature* N Tasman Sea *36°30′S 156°30′E*
67 *U6* **Gash** *var.* Nahr al Qāsh. ≈ W Sudan
149 *X3* **Gasherbrum** ▲ NE Pakistan *35°39′N 76°34′E*
Gas Hu *see* Gas Hure Hu
77 *X12* **Gashua** Yobe, NE Nigeria *12°55′N 11°10′E*
159 *N9* **Gas Hure Hu** *var.* Gas Hu. ◎ C China
Gásluokta *see* Kjøpsvik
186 *G7* **Gasmata** New Britain, E Papua New Guinea *06°12′S 150°25′E*
23 *V14* **Gasparilla Island** *island* Florida, SE USA
169 *O13* **Gaspar, Selat** *strait* W Indonesia
15 *Y6* **Gaspé** Québec, SE Canada *48°50′N 64°33′W*
15 *Z6* **Gaspé, Cap de** *headland* Québec, SE Canada *48°45′N 64°10′W*
15 *X6* **Gaspé, Péninsule de** *var.* Péninsule de la Gaspésie. *peninsula* Québec, SE Canada
Gaspésie, Péninsule de la *see* Gaspé, Péninsule de
77 *W15* **Gassol** Taraba, E Nigeria *08°28′N 10°24′E*
Gastein *see* Badgastein
21 *R10* **Gastonia** North Carolina, SE USA *35°14′N 81°12′W*
21 *V8* **Gaston, Lake** ⊠ North Carolina/Virginia, SE USA
115 *D19* **Gastoúni** Dytikí Elláda, S Greece *37°51′N 21°15′E*
63 *I17* **Gastre** Chubut, S Argentina *42°20′S 69°10′W*
Gat *see* Ghāt
105 *P15* **Gata, Cabo de** *cape* S Spain
Gata, Cape *see* Gátas, Akrotíri
105 *T11* **Gata de Gorgos** Valenciana, E Spain *38°45′N 00°06′E*
116 *E12* **Gătaia** *Ger.* Gataja, *Hung.* Gátalja; *prev.* Gáttája. Timiş, W Romania *45°24′N 21°26′E*
Gataja/Gátalja *see* Gătaia
121 *P3* **Gátas, Akrotíri** *var.* Cape Gata. *headland* S Cyprus *34°34′N 33°03′E*
104 *J8* **Gata, Sierra de** ▲▲ W Spain
124 *G13* **Gatchina** Leningradskaya Oblast', NW Russian Federation *59°34′N 30°06′E*
21 *P8* **Gate City** Virginia, NE USA *36°38′N 82°37′W*
97 *M14* **Gateshead** NE England, United Kingdom *54°57′N 01°37′W*
21 *X8* **Gatesville** North Carolina, SE USA *36°24′N 76°46′W*
25 *S8* **Gatesville** Texas, SW USA *31°26′N 97°46′W*

◆ Country ● Country Capital ◇ Dependent Territory ○ Dependent Territory Capital ◈ Administrative Regions ✈ International Airport ▲ Mountain ▲▲ Mountain Range Volcano ≈ River ◎ Lake ⊠ Reservoir

14 L12 **Gatineau** Québec, SE Canada 45°29′N 75°40′W
14 L11 **Gatineau** ≈ Ontario/Québec, SE Canada
21 N9 **Gatlinburg** Tennessee, S USA 35°42′N 83°30′W
Gatooma *see* Kadoma
Gáttája *see* Gătaia
43 T14 **Gatún, Lago** ⊡ C Panama
59 N14 **Gaturiano** Piauí, NE Brazil 06°53′S 41°45′W
97 O22 **Gatwick** ✈ (London) SE England, United Kingdom 51°10′N 00°12′W
187 Y14 **Gau** *prev.* Ngau. *island* C Fiji
187 R12 **Gaua** *var.* Santa Maria. *Island* Banks Island, N Vanuatu
104 L16 **Gaucín** Andalucía, S Spain 36°31′N 05°19′W
Gauhāti *see* Guwāhāti
118 I8 **Gauja** *Ger.* Aa. ≈ Estonia/Latvia
118 I7 **Gaujiena** NE Latvia 57°31′N 26°24′E
94 H9 **Gauldalen** *valley* S Norway
21 R5 **Gauley River** ≈ West Virginia, NE USA
Gaul/Gaule *see* France
99 D19 **Gaurain-Ramecroix** Hainaut, SW Belgium 50°35′N 03°31′E
95 F15 **Gaustatoppen** ▲ S Norway 59°50′N 08°39′E
83 J21 **Gauteng** *off.* Gauteng Province; *prev.* Pretoria-Witwatersrand-Vereeniging. ◈ *province* NE South Africa
Gauteng *see* Johannesburg, South Africa
Gauteng *see* Germiston, South Africa
Gauteng Province *see* Gauteng
137 U11 **Gavarr** *prev.* Kamo. C Armenia 40°21′N 45°07′E
143 P14 **Gāvbandī** Hormozgān, S Iran 27°07′N 53°21′E
115 H25 **Gavdopoúla** *island* SE Greece
115 H26 **Gávdos** *island* SE Greece
102 K16 **Gave de Pau** *var.* Gave-de-Pay. ≈ SW France
Gave-de-Pay *see* Gave de Pau
102 J16 **Gave d'Oloron** ≈ SW France
99 E18 **Gavere** Oost-Vlaanderen, NW Belgium 50°56′N 03°41′E
94 N13 **Gävle** *var.* Gäfle; *prev.* Gefle. Gävleborg, C Sweden 60°41′N 17°09′E
94 M11 **Gävleborg** *var.* Gäfleborg, Gefleborg. ◈ *county* C Sweden
94 O13 **Gävlebukten** *bay* C Sweden
124 L16 **Gavrilov-Yam** Yaroslavskaya Oblast', W Russian Federation 57°19′N 39°52′E
182 I9 **Gawler** South Australia 34°38′S 138°44′E
182 G7 **Gawler Ranges** *hill range* South Australia
Gawso *see* Goaso
162 H11 **Gaxun Nur** ◎ N China
153 P14 **Gaya** Bihār, N India 24°48′N 85°E
77 S13 **Gaya** Dosso, SW Niger 11°52′N 03°28′E
Gaya *see* Kyjov
31 Q6 **Gaylord** Michigan, N USA 45°01′N 84°40′W
29 U9 **Gaylord** Minnesota, N USA 44°33′N 94°13′W
181 Y9 **Gayndah** Queensland, E Australia 25°37′S 151°31′E
125 T12 **Gayny** Komi-Permyatskiy Okrug, NW Russian Federation 60°19′N 54°15′E
Gaysin *see* Haysyn
Gayvorno *see* Hayvoron
138 E11 **Gaza** *Ar.* Ghazzah, *Heb.* 'Azza. NE Gaza Strip 31°30′N 34°E
83 L20 **Gaza** *off.* Província de Gaza. ◈ *province* SW Mozambique
Gaz-Achak *see* Gazojak
147 Q9 **G'azalkent** *Rus.* Gazalkent. Toshkent Viloyati, E Uzbekistan 41°30′N 69°46′E
Gazalkent *see* G'azalkent
Gazandzhyk/Gazanjyk *see* Bereket
77 V12 **Gazaoua** Maradi, S Niger 13°28′N 07°54′E
Gaza, Província de *see* Gaza
138 E11 **Gaza Strip** *Ar.* Qita Ghazzah. *disputed region* SW Asia
136 M16 **Gaziantep** *var.* Gazi Antep; *prev.* Aintab, Antep. Gaziantep, S Turkey 37°04′N 37°21′E
136 M17 **Gaziantep** *var.* Gazi Antep. ◈ *province* S Turkey
Gazi Antep *see* Gaziantep
114 M13 **Gaziköy** Tekirdağ, NW Turkey 40°45′N 27°18′E
121 Q2 **Gazimağusa** *var.* Famagusta, *Gk.* Ammóchostos. E Cyprus 35°07′N 33°57′E
121 Q2 **Gazimağusa Körfezi** *var.* Famagusta Bay, *Gk.* Kólpos Ammóchostos. *bay* E Cyprus
146 K11 **Gazli** Buxoro Viloyati, C Uzbekistan 40°09′N 63°28′E
146 I9 **Gazojak** *Rus.* Gaz-Achak. Lebap Welaýaty, NE Turkmenistan 41°12′N 61°24′E
79 K15 **Gbadolite** Equateur, NW Dem. Rep. Congo 04°14′N 20°59′E
76 K16 **Gbanga** *var.* Gbarnga. N Liberia 07°02′N 09°30′W
Gbarnga *see* Gbanga
77 S14 **Gbéroubouè** *var.* Béroubouay. N Benin 10°35′N 02°47′E
77 W16 **Gboko** Benue, S Nigeria 07°21′N 08°57′E
Gcuwa *see* Butterworth
110 J7 **Gdańsk** *Fr.* Dantzig, *Ger.* Danzig. Pomorskie, N Poland 54°22′N 18°35′E
Gdan'skaya Bukhta/Gdańsk, Gulf of *see* Danzig, Gulf of
Gdańska, Zakota *see* Danzig, Gulf of
Gdingen *see* Gdynia
124 F13 **Gdov** Pskovskaya Oblast', W Russian Federation 58°43′N 27°51′E
110 I6 **Gdynia** *Ger.* Gdingen. Pomorskie, N Poland 54°31′N 18°30′E
26 M10 **Geary** Oklahoma, C USA 35°37′N 98°19′W
Geavvú *see* Kevo
76 H12 **Gêba, Rio** ≈ C Guinea-Bissau
136 E11 **Gebze** Kocaeli, NW Turkey 40°48′N 29°26′E
80 H10 **Gedaref** *var.* Al Qaḑārif, El Gedaref. Gedaref, E Sudan 14°03′N 35°24′E
80 H10 **Gedaref** ◈ *state* E Sudan
80 B11 **Gedid Ras el Fil** Southern Darfur, W Sudan 12°45′N 25°45′E
99 I23 **Gedinne** Namur, SE Belgium 49°57′N 04°55′E
136 E13 **Gediz** Kütahya, W Turkey 39°04′N 29°25′E
136 C14 **Gediz Nehri** ≈ W Turkey
81 N14 **Gedlegubē** Sumalē, E Ethiopia 06°53′N 45°08′E
81 L17 **Gedo** *off.* Gobolka Gedo. ◈ *region* SW Somalia
Gedo, Gobolka *see* Gedo
95 I25 **Gedser** Sjælland, SE Denmark 54°34′N 11°57′E
99 I16 **Geel** *var.* Gheel. Antwerpen, N Belgium 51°10′N 04°59′E
183 N13 **Geelong** Victoria, SE Australia 38°10′S 144°21′E
Ge'e'mu *see* Golmud
99 I14 **Geertruidenberg** Noord-Brabant, S Netherlands 51°43′N 04°52′E
100 H10 **Geeste** ≈ NW Germany
100 J10 **Geesthacht** Schleswig-Holstein, N Germany 53°25′N 10°22′E
183 P17 **Geeveston** Tasmania, SE Australia 43°12′S 146°54′E
Gefle *see* Gävle
Gefleborg *see* Gävleborg
163 S5 **Gegan Gol** *prev.* Ergun, Gen He, Zuoqi. NE China
163 T5 **Gegen Gol** *prev.* Ergun Zuoqi, Genhe. Nei Mongol Zizhiqu, N China 50°48′N 121°30′E
158 G13 **Gê'gyai** Xizang Zizhiqu, W China 32°29′N 81°04′E
77 X12 **Geidam** Yobe, NE Nigeria 12°52′N 11°55′E
11 T11 **Geikie** ≈ Saskatchewan, C Canada
94 F13 **Geilo** Buskerud, S Norway 60°32′N 08°13′E
94 E10 **Geiranger** Møre og Romsdal, S Norway 62°07′N 07°12′E
101 I22 **Geislingen** *var.* Geislingen an der Steige. Baden-Württemberg, SW Germany 48°37′N 09°50′E
Geislingen an der Steige *see* Geislingen
81 F20 **Geita** Mwanza, NW Tanzania 02°52′S 32°12′E
95 G15 **Geithus** Buskerud, S Norway 59°56′N 09°58′E
160 H14 **Gejiu** *var.* Kochiu. Yunnan, S China 23°22′N 103°07′E
Gëkdepe *see* Gökdepe
146 E9 **Geklengkui, Solonchak** *var.* Solonchak Goklenkuy. *salt marsh* NW Turkmenistan
81 D14 **Gel** ≈ C South Sudan
107 K25 **Gela** *prev.* Terranova di Sicilia. Sicilia, Italy, C Mediterranean Sea 37°05′N 14°15′E
81 N14 **Geladī** SE Ethiopia 06°58′N 46°24′E
169 P13 **Gelam, Pulau** *var.* Pulau Galam. *island* N Indonesia
Gelaozu Miaozu Zhizhixian *see* Wuchuan
98 L11 **Gelderland** *prev. Eng.* Guelders. ◈ *province* E Netherlands
98 J13 **Geldermalsen** Gelderland, C Netherlands 51°53′N 05°17′E
101 D14 **Geldern** Nordrhein-Westfalen, W Germany 51°31′N 06°19′E
99 K15 **Geldrop** Noord-Brabant, SE Netherlands 51°25′N 05°34′E
99 L17 **Geleen** Limburg, SE Netherlands 50°57′N 05°49′E
126 K14 **Gelendzhik** Krasnodarskiy Kray, SW Russian Federation 44°34′N 38°06′E
Gelib *see* Jilib
136 B11 **Gelibolu** *Eng.* Gallipoli. Çanakkale, NW Turkey 40°25′N 26°41′E
115 L14 **Gelibolu Yarımadası** *Eng.* Gallipoli Peninsula. *peninsula* NW Turkey
81 O14 **Gellinsor** Galguduud, C Somalia 06°25′N 46°44′E
101 H18 **Gelnhausen** Hessen, C Germany 50°12′N 09°12′E
101 E14 **Gelsenkirchen** Nordrhein-Westfalen, W Germany 51°30′N 07°05′E
83 C20 **Geluk** Hardap, SW Namibia 24°35′S 15°48′E
99 H20 **Gembloux** Namur, Belgium 50°34′N 04°42′E
79 J16 **Gemena** Equateur, NW Dem. Rep. Congo 03°13′N 19°49′E
99 L14 **Gemert** Noord-Brabant, SE Netherlands 51°33′N 05°41′E
136 E11 **Gemlik** Bursa, NW Turkey 40°26′N 29°10′E
Gem of the Mountains *see* Idaho
106 J6 **Gemona del Friuli** Friuli-Venezia Giulia, NE Italy 46°18′N 13°12′E
Gem State *see* Idaho
Genalē Wenz *see* Juba
169 R10 **Genali, Danau** ◎ Borneo, N Indonesia
99 G19 **Genappe** Walloon Brabant, C Belgium 50°39′N 04°27′E
137 P14 **Genç** Bingöl, E Turkey 38°44′N 40°35′E
Genck *see* Genk
98 M9 **Genemuiden** Overijssel, E Netherlands 52°38′N 06°03′E
63 K14 **General Acha** La Pampa, C Argentina 37°25′S 64°38′W
61 C21 **General Alvear** Buenos Aires, E Argentina 36°03′S 60°01′W
62 I12 **General Alvear** Mendoza, W Argentina 34°59′S 67°40′W
61 B20 **General Arenales** Buenos Aires, E Argentina 34°21′S 61°20′W
61 D21 **General Belgrano** Buenos Aires, E Argentina 35°47′S 58°30′W
194 H3 **General Bernardo O'Higgins** *Chilean research station* Antarctica 63°09′S 57°13′W
41 O8 **General Bravo** Nuevo León, NE Mexico 25°47′N 99°04′W
62 M7 **General Capdevila** Chaco, N Argentina 27°25′S 61°30′W
General Carrera, Lago *see* Buenos Aires, Lago
41 N9 **General Cepeda** Coahuila, NE Mexico 25°18′N 101°24′W
63 K15 **General Conesa** Río Negro, E Argentina 40°06′S 64°26′W
61 G18 **General Enrique Martínez** Treinta y Tres, E Uruguay 33°13′S 53°47′W
62 L3 **General Eugenio A. Garay** *var.* Fortín General Eugenio Garay; *prev.* Yrendagüé. Nueva Asunción, NW Paraguay 20°30′S 61°56′W
61 C18 **General Galarza** Entre Ríos, E Argentina 32°43′S 59°24′W
61 E22 **General Guido** Buenos Aires, E Argentina 36°36′S 57°45′W
General José F.Uriburu *see* Zárate
61 E22 **General Juan Madariaga** Buenos Aires, E Argentina 37°00′S 57°09′W
41 O16 **General Juan N Alvarez** ✈ (Acapulco) Guerrero, S Mexico 16°47′N 99°47′W
61 B22 **General La Madrid** Buenos Aires, E Argentina 37°17′S 61°20′W
61 E21 **General Lavalle** Buenos Aires, E Argentina 36°25′S 56°56′W
General Machado *see* Camacupa
62 I8 **General Manuel Belgrano, Cerro** ▲ W Argentina 29°05′S 67°05′W
41 O8 **General Mariano Escobero** ✈ (Monterrey) Nuevo León, NE Mexico 25°47′N 100°00′W
61 B20 **General O'Brien** Buenos Aires, E Argentina 34°54′S 60°45′W
62 K13 **General Pico** La Pampa, C Argentina 35°43′S 63°45′W
62 M7 **General Pinedo** Chaco, N Argentina 27°17′S 61°20′W
61 B20 **General Pinto** Buenos Aires, E Argentina 34°45′S 61°50′W
61 E22 **General Pirán** Buenos Aires, E Argentina 37°16′S 57°46′W
43 N15 **General, Río** ≈ S Costa Rica
63 I15 **General Roca** Río Negro, C Argentina 39°00′S 67°35′W
171 Q8 **General Santos** *off.* General Santos City. Mindanao, S Philippines 06°10′N 125°10′E
General Santos City *see* General Santos
41 O9 **General Terán** Nuevo León, NE Mexico 25°18′N 99°40′W
114 N7 **General Toshevo** *Rom.* I.G.Duca; *prev.* Casim, Kasimköj. Dobrich, NE Bulgaria 43°43′N 28°04′E
61 B20 **General Viamonte** Buenos Aires, E Argentina 35°01′S 61°00′W
61 A20 **General Villegas** Buenos Aires, E Argentina 35°02′S 63°01′W
Gênes *see* Genova
18 E11 **Genesee River** ≈ New York/Pennsylvania, NE USA
30 K11 **Geneseo** Illinois, N USA 41°27′N 90°08′W
18 F10 **Geneseo** New York, NE USA 42°48′N 77°46′W
57 L14 **Geneshuaya, Río** ≈ N Bolivia
23 Q8 **Geneva** Alabama, S USA 31°01′N 85°51′W
30 M10 **Geneva** Illinois, N USA 41°53′N 88°18′W
29 Q16 **Geneva** Nebraska, C USA 40°31′N 97°36′W
18 G10 **Geneva** New York, NE USA 42°52′N 76°58′W
31 U10 **Geneva** Ohio, NE USA 41°48′N 80°53′W
Geneva *see* Genève
108 B10 **Geneva, Lake** *Fr.* Lac de Genève, Lac Léman, le Léman, *Ger.* Genfer See. ◎ France/Switzerland
108 A10 **Genève** *Eng.* Geneva, *Ger.* Genf, *It.* Ginevra. Genève, SW Switzerland 46°13′N 06°09′E
108 A11 **Genève** *Eng.* Geneva, *Ger.* Genf, *It.* Ginevra. ◈ *canton* SW Switzerland
108 A10 **Genève** *var.* Geneva. ✈ Vaud, SW Switzerland 46°13′N 06°06′E
Genève, Lac de *see* Geneva, Lake
Genf *see* Genève
Genfer See *see* Geneva, Lake
Genhe *see* Gegen Gol
Gen He *see* Gegan Gol
Genichesk *see* Heniches'k
104 L14 **Genil** ≈ S Spain
99 K18 **Genk** *var.* Genck. Limburg, NE Belgium 50°58′N 05°30′E
164 C13 **Genkai-nada** *gulf* Kyūshū, SW Japan
107 C19 **Gennargentu, Monti del** ▲▲ Sardegna, Italy, C Mediterranean Sea
99 M14 **Gennep** Limburg, SE Netherlands 51°43′N 05°58′E
30 M10 **Genoa** Illinois, N USA 42°06′N 88°41′W
29 Q15 **Genoa** Nebraska, C USA 41°27′N 97°43′W
Genoa *see* Genova
Genoa, Gulf of *see* Genova, Golfo di
106 D10 **Genova** *Eng.* Genoa; *anc.* Genua, *Fr.* Gênes. Liguria, NW Italy 44°28′N 09°E
106 D10 **Genova, Golfo di** *Eng.* Gulf of Genoa. *gulf* NW Italy
57 C17 **Genovesa, Isla** *var.* Tower Island. *island* Galapagos Islands, Ecuador, E Pacific Ocean
Genshū *see* Wonju
99 E17 **Gent** *Eng.* Ghent, *Fr.* Gand. Oost-Vlaanderen, NW Belgium 51°02′N 03°42′E
169 N16 **Genteng** Jawa, C Indonesia 07°21′S 106°20′E
100 M12 **Genthin** Sachsen-Anhalt, E Germany 52°24′N 12°10′E
27 R9 **Gentry** Arkansas, C USA 36°16′N 94°28′W
Genua *see* Genova
107 I15 **Genzano di Roma** Lazio, C Italy 41°42′N 12°42′E
163 Y17 **Geogeum-do** *prev.* Kōgūm-do. *island* S South Korea
163 Z16 **Geogeum-do** *Jap.* Kyōsai-tō; *prev.* Kōje-do. *island* S South Korea
Geokchay *see* Göyçay
Geok-Tepe *see* Gökdepe
122 I3 **George, Zemlya** *Eng.* George Land. *island* Zemlya Frantsa-Iosifa, N Russian Federation
83 G26 **George** Western Cape, S South Africa 33°57′S 22°28′E
29 S11 **George** Iowa, C USA 43°20′N 96°00′W
13 O5 **George** ≈ Newfoundland and Labrador/Québec, E Canada
George F L Charles *see* Vigie
65 C25 **George Island** *island* S Falkland Islands
183 R10 **George, Lake** ◎ New South Wales, SE Australia
81 E18 **George, Lake** ◎ SW Uganda
23 W10 **George, Lake** ◎ Florida, SE USA
18 L8 **George, Lake** ⊡ New York, NE USA
George Land *see* Georga, Zemlya
Georgenburg *see* Jurbarkas
George River *see* Kangiqsualujjuaq
64 G8 **Georges Bank** *undersea feature* W Atlantic Ocean 41°15′N 67°30′W
185 A21 **George Sound** *sound* South Island, New Zealand
65 F15 **Georgetown** ○ (Ascension Island) NW Ascension Island 17°56′S 14°25′W
181 V5 **Georgetown** Queensland, NE Australia 18°17′S 143°37′E
183 P15 **George Town** Tasmania, SE Australia 41°04′S 146°48′E
44 I4 **George Town** Great Exuma Island, C Bahamas 23°28′N 75°47′W
44 D8 **George Town** *var.* Georgetown. ○ (Cayman Islands) Grand Cayman, SW Cayman Islands 19°16′N 81°23′W
76 H12 **Georgetown** E Gambia 13°33′N 14°49′W
55 T8 **Georgetown** ● (Guyana) N Guyana 06°46′N 58°10′W
168 I7 **George Town** *var.* Penang, Pinang. Pinang, Peninsular Malaysia 05°28′N 100°20′E
45 Y14 **Georgetown** Saint Vincent, Saint Vincent and the Grenadines 13°19′N 61°09′W
21 Y4 **Georgetown** Delaware, NE USA 38°39′N 75°22′W
23 R6 **Georgetown** Georgia, SE USA 31°52′N 85°04′W
20 M5 **Georgetown** Kentucky, S USA 38°13′N 84°30′W
21 T13 **Georgetown** South Carolina, SE USA 33°23′N 79°18′W
25 S10 **Georgetown** Texas, SW USA 30°39′N 97°42′W
55 T8 **Georgetown** ✈ N Guyana 06°46′N 58°10′W
Georgetown *see* George Town
195 U16 **George V Coast** *physical region* Antarctica
194 J7 **George VI Ice Shelf** *ice shelf* Antarctica
194 J6 **George VI Sound** *sound* Antarctica
195 T15 **George V Land** *physical region* Antarctica
25 S14 **George West** Texas, SW USA 28°21′N 98°08′W
137 R9 **Georgia** *off.* Republic of Georgia, *Geor.* Sak'art'velo, *Rus.* Gruzinskaya SSR, Gruziya. ◆ *republic* SW Asia
23 S5 **Georgia** *off.* State of Georgia, *also known as* Empire State of the South, Peach State. ◈ *state* SE USA
14 F12 **Georgian Bay** *lake bay* Ontario, S Canada
Georgia, Republic of *see* Georgia
10 L17 **Georgia, Strait of** *strait* British Columbia, W Canada
Georgi Dimitrov *see* Kostenets
Georgi Dimitrov, Yazovir *see* Koprinka, Yazovir
Georgiu-Dezh *see* Liski
145 W10 **Georgiyevka** Vostochnyy Kazakhstan, E Kazakhstan 49°19′N 81°35′E
Georgiyevka *see* Korday
127 N15 **Georgiyevsk** Stavropol'skiy Kray, SW Russian Federation 44°07′N 43°22′E
100 G13 **Georgsmarienhütte** Niedersachsen, NW Germany 52°13′N 08°02′E
195 O1 **Georg von Neumayer** *German research station* Antarctica 70°41′S 08°18′W
101 M16 **Gera** Thüringen, E Germany 50°51′N 12°13′E
101 K16 **Gera** ≈ C Germany
99 E19 **Geraardsbergen** Oost-Vlaanderen, SW Belgium 50°47′N 03°53′E
115 F21 **Geráki** Pelopónnisos, S Greece 36°56′N 22°46′E
27 W5 **Gerald** Missouri, C USA 38°24′N 91°20′W
47 V8 **Geral de Goiás, Serra** ▲▲ E Brazil
185 G20 **Geraldine** Canterbury, South Island, New Zealand 44°06′S 171°14′E
180 H11 **Geraldton** Western Australia 28°48′S 114°40′E
12 E11 **Geraldton** Ontario, S Canada 49°44′N 86°59′W
60 J12 **Geral, Serra** ▲▲ S Brazil
103 U6 **Gérardmer** Vosges, NE France 48°05′N 06°54′E
Gerasa *see* Jarash
Gerdauen *see* Zheleznodorozhnyy
39 Q11 **Gerdine, Mount** ▲ Alaska, USA 61°40′N 152°21′W
136 H11 **Gerede** Bolu, N Turkey 40°48′N 32°13′E
136 H11 **Gerede Çayı** ≈ N Turkey
148 M8 **Gereshk** Helmand, SW Afghanistan 31°50′N 64°32′E
101 L24 **Geretsried** Bayern, S Germany 47°51′N 11°28′E
105 P14 **Gérgal** Andalucía, S Spain 37°07′N 02°34′W
28 I14 **Gering** Nebraska, C USA 41°49′N 103°39′W
35 R3 **Gerlach** Nevada, W USA 40°38′N 119°21′W
Gerlachfalvi Csúcs/Gerlachovka *see* Gerlachovský štít
111 L18 **Gerlachovský štít** *var.* Gerlachovka, *Ger.* Gerlsdorfer Spitze, *Hung.* Gerlachfalvi Csúcs; *prev.* Stalinov Štít, *Ger.* Franz-Josef Spitze, *Hung.* Ferencz-József Csúcs. ▲ N Slovakia 49°12′N 20°09′E
108 E8 **Gerlafingen** Solothurn, NW Switzerland 47°10′N 07°35′E
Gerlsdorfer Spitze *see* Gerlachovský štít
139 V3 **Germak** As Sulaymānīyah, E Iraq 35°49′N 46°09′E
German East Africa *see* Tanzania
Germanicopolis *see* Çankırı
Germanicum, Mare/German Ocean *see* North Sea
Germanovichi *see* Hyermanavichy
German Southwest Africa *see* Namibia
20 E10 **Germantown** Tennessee, S USA 35°06′N 89°51′W
101 I15 **Germany** *off.* Federal Republic of Germany, Bundesrepublik Deutschland, *Ger.* Deutschland. ◆ *federal republic* N Europe
Germany, Federal Republic of *see* Germany
101 L23 **Germering** Bayern, SE Germany 48°07′N 11°22′E
83 J21 **Germiston** *var.* Gauteng. Gauteng, NE South Africa 26°15′S 28°10′E
Gernika *see* Gernika-Lumo
105 P2 **Gernika-Lumo** *var.* Gernika, Guernica, Guernica y Lumo. País Vasco, N Spain 43°19′N 02°40′W
164 L12 **Gero** Gifu, Honshū, SW Japan 35°48′N 137°15′E
115 F22 **Geroliménas** Pelopónnisos, S Greece 36°28′N 22°25′E
Gerona *see* Girona
99 H21 **Gerpinnes** Hainaut, S Belgium 50°20′N 04°38′E
102 L15 **Gers** ◈ *department* S France
102 L14 **Gers** ≈ S France
Gerunda *see* Girona
158 I13 **Gêrzê** *var.* Luring. Xizang Zizhiqu, W China 32°19′N 84°05′E
136 K10 **Gerze** Sinop, N Turkey 41°48′N 35°13′E
Gesoriacum *see* Boulogne-sur-Mer
Gessoriacum *see* Boulogne-sur-Mer
99 J21 **Gesves** Namur, SE Belgium 50°24′N 05°04′E
93 J20 **Geta** Åland, SW Finland 60°22′N 19°49′E
105 N8 **Getafe** Madrid, C Spain 40°18′N 03°44′W
95 J21 **Getinge** Halland, S Sweden 56°46′N 12°42′E
18 F16 **Gettysburg** Pennsylvania, NE USA 39°49′N 77°13′W
29 N8 **Gettysburg** South Dakota, N USA 45°00′N 99°57′W
194 K12 **Getz Ice Shelf** *ice shelf* Antarctica
137 S15 **Gevaş** Van, SE Turkey 38°16′N 43°05′E
Gevgeli *see* Gevgelija
113 Q20 **Gevgelija** *var.* Đevđelija, Djevdjelija, *Turk.* Gevgeli. SE Macedonia 41°09′N 22°30′E
103 T10 **Gex** Ain, E France 46°21′N 06°02′E
92 I3 **Geysir** *physical region* SW Iceland
136 F11 **Geyve** Sakarya, NW Turkey 40°32′N 30°18′E
80 G10 **Gezira** ◈ *state* E Sudan
109 V3 **Gföhl** Niederösterreich, N Austria 48°30′N 15°27′E
83 H22 **Ghaap Plateau** *Afr.* Ghaapplato. *plateau* C South Africa
Ghaapplato *see* Ghaap Plateau
Ghaba *see* Al Ghābah
138 J8 **Ghāb, Tall** ▲ SE Syria 33°09′N 37°48′E
139 Q9 **Ghadaf, Wādī al** *dry watercourse* C Iraq
Ghadamès *see* Ghadāmis
74 M9 **Ghadāmis** *var.* Ghadamès, Rhadames. W Libya 30°08′N 09°30′E
141 Y10 **Ghadan** E Oman 20°20′N 57°58′E
75 O10 **Ghaddūwah** C Libya 26°36′N 14°26′E
147 Q11 **Ghafurov** *Rus.* Gafurov; *prev.* Sovetabad. NW Tajikistan 40°13′N 69°42′E
153 N12 **Ghāghara** ≈ S Asia
149 P13 **Ghaibi Dero** Sind, SE Pakistan 27°35′N 67°42′E
141 Y10 **Ghalat** E Oman 21°06′N 58°51′E
139 W11 **Ghamūkah, Hawr** ◎ S Iraq
77 P15 **Ghana** *off.* Republic of Ghana. ◆ *republic* W Africa
141 X12 **Ghānah** *spring/well* S Oman 18°35′N 56°34′E
Ghanongga *see* Ranongga
Ghansi/Ghansiland *see* Ghanzi
83 F18 **Ghanzi** *var.* Khanzi. Ghanzi, W Botswana 21°39′S 21°38′E
83 G19 **Ghanzi** *var.* Ghansi, Ghansiland, Khanzi. ◈ *district* C Botswana
67 T14 **Ghanzi** *var.* Knanzi. ≈ Botswana/South Africa
Ghap'an *see* Kapan
138 F13 **Gharandal** Al'Aqabah, SW Jordan 30°12′N 35°18′E
139 U14 **Gharbīyah, Sha'īb al** ≈ S Iraq
Gharbt, Jabal al *see* Liban, Jebel
74 K7 **Ghardaïa** N Algeria 32°30′N 03°44′E
147 R12 **Gharm** *Rus.* Garm. C Tajikistan 39°03′N 70°25′E
149 P17 **Gharo** Sind, SE Pakistan 24°44′N 67°35′E
139 W10 **Gharrāf, Shaṭṭ al** ≈ S Iraq
Gharvān *see* Gharyān
75 O7 **Gharyān** *var.* Gharvān. NW Libya 32°10′N 13°01′E
74 M11 **Ghāt** *var.* Gat. SW Libya 24°58′N 10°11′E
Ghawdex *see* Gozo
141 U8 **Ghayathi** Abū Ẓaby, W United Arab Emirates 23°51′N 53°01′E
Ghazāl, Baḩr al *see* Ghazal, Bahr el
78 H9 **Ghazal, Bahr el** *var.* Soro. *seasonal river* C Chad
80 E13 **Ghazal, Bahr el** *var.* Baḩr al Ghazāl. ≈ N South Sudan
74 H6 **Ghazaouet** NW Algeria 35°08′N 01°50′W
152 J10 **Ghāziābād** Uttar Pradesh, N India 28°42′N 77°28′E
153 O13 **Ghāzīpur** Uttar Pradesh, N India 25°36′N 83°36′E
149 Q6 **Ghaznī** *var.* Ghazni. Ghaznī, E Afghanistan 33°31′N 68°24′E
149 P7 **Ghaznī** ◈ *province* SE Afghanistan
Ghazzah *see* Gaza
Gheel *see* Geel
Ghelizâne *see* Relizane
Ghent *see* Gent
Gheorghe Braţul *see* Sfântu Gheorghe, Braţul
Gheorghe Gheorghiu-Dej *see* Oneşti
116 J10 **Gheorgheni** *prev.* Gheorghieni, Sîn-Miclăuş, *Ger.* Niklasmarkt, *Hung.* Gyergyószentmiklós. Harghita, C Romania 46°43′N 25°36′E
Gheorghieni *see* Gheorgheni
116 H10 **Gherla** *Ger.* Neuschliss, *Hung.* Szamosújvár; *prev.* Armenierstadt. Cluj, NW Romania 47°02′N 23°55′E
Gheweifat *see* Ghuwayfāt
Ghilan *see* Gīlān
107 C18 **Ghilarza** Sardegna, Italy, C Mediterranean Sea 40°09′N 08°50′E
Ghilizane *see* Relizane
Ghimbi *see* Gīmbī
Ghiriş *see* Câmpia Turzii
103 Y15 **Ghisonaccia** Corse, France, C Mediterranean Sea 42°00′N 09°25′E
147 Q11 **Ghonchí** *Rus.* Ganchi. NW Tajikistan 39°57′N 69°10′E
153 T13 **Ghoraghat** Rajshahi, NW Bangladesh 25°18′N 89°20′E
148 J5 **Ghōrīān** *prev.* Ghūrīān. Herāt, W Afghanistan 34°20′N 61°26′E
149 R13 **Ghotki** Sind, SE Pakistan 28°00′N 69°21′E
Ghowr *see* Gōwr
147 T13 **Ghŭdara** *var.* Gudara, *Rus.* Kudara. SE Tajikistan 38°28′N 72°39′E
153 R13 **Ghugri** ≈ N India
147 S14 **Ghund** *Rus.* Gunt. ≈ SE Tajikistan
Ghurābīyah, Sha'īb al *see* Gharbīyah, Sha'īb al
Ghurdaqah *see* Al Ghurdaqah
Ghūrīān *see* Ghōrīān
141 T8 **Ghuwayfāt** *var.* Gheweifat. Abū Ẓaby, W United Arab Emirates 24°06′N 51°40′E
121 O14 **Ghuzayyil, Sabkhat** *salt lake* N Libya
126 J3 **Ghzatsk** Smolenskaya Oblast', W Russian Federation 55°33′N 35°00′E
115 G17 **Giáltra** Évvoia, C Greece 38°21′N 22°58′E
Giamame *see* Jamaame
167 U13 **Gia Nghia** *var.* Đak Nông. Đắc Lắc, S Vietnam 11°58′N 107°42′E
114 F13 **Giannitsá** *var.* Yiannitsá. Kentrikí Makedonía, N Greece 40°49′N 22°24′E
107 F14 **Giannutri, Isola di** *island* Archipelago Toscano, C Italy
96 F13 **Giant's Causeway** *Ir.* Clochán an Aifir. *lava flow* N Northern Ireland, United Kingdom
167 S15 **Gia Rai** Minh Hai, S Vietnam 09°14′N 105°28′E
107 L24 **Giarre** Sicilia, Italy, C Mediterranean Sea 37°44′N 15°12′E
44 I7 **Gibara** Holguín, E Cuba 21°09′N 76°11′W
29 O16 **Gibbon** Nebraska, C USA 40°45′N 98°50′W
32 K11 **Gibbon** Oregon, NW USA 45°40′N 118°22′W
33 P11 **Gibbonsville** Idaho, NW USA 45°33′N 113°55′W
64 A13 **Gibbs Hill** *hill* S Bermuda
92 I9 **Gibostad** Troms, N Norway 69°21′N 18°01′E
104 I14 **Gibraleón** Andalucía, S Spain 37°23′N 06°58′W
104 L16 **Gibraltar** ○ (Gibraltar) S Gibraltar 36°08′N 05°21′W
104 L16 **Gibraltar** ◇ *UK dependent territory* SW Europe
Gibraltar, Détroit de/Gibraltar, Estrecho de *see* Gibraltar, Strait of
104 J17 **Gibraltar, Strait of** *Fr.* Détroit de Gibraltar, *Sp.* Estrecho de Gibraltar. *strait* Atlantic Ocean/Mediterranean Sea
31 S11 **Gibsonburg** Ohio, N USA 41°22′N 83°19′W
30 M13 **Gibson City** Illinois, N USA 40°27′N 88°24′W
180 L8 **Gibson Desert** *desert* Western Australia
10 L17 **Gibsons** British Columbia, SW Canada 49°24′N 123°32′W
149 N12 **Gīdār** Baluchistān, SW Pakistan 28°16′N 66°00′E
155 I17 **Giddalūr** Andhra Pradesh, E India 15°24′N 78°54′E
25 U10 **Giddings** Texas, SW USA 30°12′N 96°59′W
27 Y8 **Gideon** Missouri, C USA 36°27′N 89°55′W
81 I15 **Gīdolē** Southern Nationalities, S Ethiopia 05°31′N 37°26′E
Giebnegáisi *see* Kebnekaise
118 H13 **Giedraičiai** Utena, E Lithuania 55°05′N 25°16′E
103 O7 **Gien** Loiret, C France 47°40′N 02°37′E
101 G17 **Giessen** Hessen, W Germany 50°35′N 08°41′E
98 O6 **Gieten** Drenthe, NE Netherlands 53°00′N 06°43′E
23 Y13 **Gifford** Florida, SE USA 27°40′N 80°24′W
9 O5 **Gifford** ≈ Baffin Island, Nunavut, NE Canada
100 J12 **Gifhorn** Niedersachsen, N Germany 52°28′N 10°33′E
11 P13 **Gift Lake** Alberta, W Canada 55°49′N 115°57′W
164 L13 **Gifu** *var.* Gihu. Gifu, Honshū, SW Japan 35°24′N 136°46′E
164 K13 **Gifu** *off.* Gifu-ken, *var.* Gihu. ◈ *prefecture* Honshū, SW Japan
Gifu-ken *see* Gifu
126 M13 **Gigant** Rostovskaya Oblast', SW Russian Federation 46°29′N 41°18′E
40 E8 **Giganta, Sierra de la** ▲▲ NW Mexico
54 E12 **Gigante** Huila, S Colombia 02°24′N 75°34′W
114 I7 **Gigen** Pleven, N Bulgaria 43°40′N 24°31′E
Giggiga *see* Jijiga
96 G12 **Gigha Island** *island* SW Scotland, United Kingdom
107 E14 **Giglio, Isola del** *island* Archipelago Toscano, C Italy
146 L11 **G'ijduvon** *Rus.* Gizhduvon. Buxoro Viloyati, C Uzbekistan 40°06′N 64°38′E
104 L2 **Gijón** *var.* Xixón. Asturias, NW Spain 43°32′N 05°40′W
81 D20 **Gikongoro** SW Rwanda 02°30′S 29°32′E
36 K14 **Gila Bend** Arizona, SW USA 32°57′N 112°43′W
36 J14 **Gila Bend Mountains** ▲▲ Arizona, SW USA
36 I15 **Gila Mountains** ▲▲ Arizona, SW USA
37 N14 **Gila Mountains** ▲▲ Arizona, SW USA
142 M4 **Gīlān** *off.* Ostān-e Gīlān, *var.* Ghilan, Guilan. ◈ *province* NW Iran
Gīlān, Ostān-e *see* Gīlān
36 L14 **Gila River** ≈ Arizona, SW USA
29 W4 **Gilbert** Minnesota, N USA 47°29′N 92°27′W
Gilbert Islands *see* Tungaru
10 L16 **Gilbert, Mount** ▲ British Columbia, SW Canada 50°49′N 124°03′W
181 U4 **Gilbert River** ≈ Queensland, NE Australia
0 C6 **Gilbert Seamounts** *undersea feature* NE Pacific Ocean 52°50′N 150°10′W
33 S7 **Gildford** Montana, NW USA 48°34′N 110°21′W
83 P15 **Gilé** Zambézia, NE Mozambique 16°10′S 38°17′E
30 K4 **Gile Flowage** ◎ Wisconsin, N USA
182 G7 **Giles, Lake** *salt lake* South Australia
Gilf Kebir Plateau *see* Haḑabat al Jilf al Kabīr
183 R6 **Gilgandra** New South Wales, SE Australia 31°43′S 148°39′E
Gilgău *see* Gâlgău
81 I19 **Gilgil** Rift Valley, SW Kenya 0°29′S 36°19′E
183 S4 **Gil Gil Creek** ≈ New South Wales, SE Australia
149 V3 **Gilgit** Jammu and Kashmir, NE Pakistan 35°54′N 74°20′E
149 V3 **Gilgit** ≈ N Pakistan
11 X11 **Gillam** Manitoba, C Canada 56°25′N 94°45′W
95 J22 **Gilleleje** Hovedstaden, E Denmark 56°05′N 12°17′E
30 K14 **Gillespie** Illinois, N USA 39°07′N 89°49′W
27 W13 **Gillett** Arkansas, C USA 34°07′N 91°22′W
33 X12 **Gillette** Wyoming, C USA 44°17′N 105°30′W
97 P22 **Gillingham** SE England, United Kingdom 51°24′N 00°33′E
195 X6 **Gillock Island** *island* Antarctica
173 O16 **Gillot** ✈ (St-Denis) N Réunion 20°53′S 55°31′E
65 H25 **Gill Point** *headland* E Saint Helena 15°59′S 05°38′W
30 M12 **Gilman** Illinois, N USA 40°44′N 87°58′W
25 W6 **Gilmer** Texas, SW USA 32°44′N 94°58′W
Gilolo *see* Halmahera, Pulau
81 G14 **Gilo Wenz** ≈ SW Ethiopia
35 O10 **Gilroy** California, W USA 37°00′N 121°34′W
123 Q12 **Gilyuy** ≈ SE Russian Federation
99 I14 **Gilze** Noord-Brabant, S Netherlands 51°33′N 04°56′E
165 R16 **Gima** Okinawa, Kume-jima, SW Japan
80 H13 **Gīmbī** *It.* Ghimbi. Oromīya, C Ethiopia 09°13′N 35°39′E
163 Y15 **Gimcheon** *prev.* Kimch'ŏn. C South Korea 36°08′N 128°06′E
163 Z16 **Gimhae** *prev.* Kim Hae. ✈ (Busan) SE South Korea 35°10′N 128°57′E
45 T12 **Gimie, Mount** ▲ C Saint Lucia 13°51′N 61°00′W
11 X16 **Gimli** Manitoba, S Canada 50°39′N 97°00′W
Gimma *see* Jīma
95 O14 **Gimo** Uppsala, C Sweden 60°11′N 18°12′E
102 L15 **Gimone** ≈ S France
Gimpoe *see* Gimpu
171 N12 **Gimpu** *prev.* Gimpoe. Sulawesi, C Indonesia 01°38′S 120°00′E
182 F5 **Gina** South Australia 29°56′S 134°33′E
Ginevra *see* Genève
99 J19 **Gingelom** Limburg, NE Belgium 50°46′N 05°09′E
180 I12 **Gingin** Western Australia 31°22′S 115°51′E
171 Q7 **Gingoog** Mindanao, S Philippines 08°47′N 125°05′E
81 K14 **Ginīr** Oromīya, C Ethiopia 07°12′N 40°43′E
Giohar *see* Jawhar
107 O17 **Gióia del Colle** Puglia, SE Italy 40°47′N 16°56′E
107 M22 **Gioia, Golfo di** *gulf* S Italy
Gíona *see* Gkióna
115 I16 **Gioúra** *island* Vóreies Sporádes, Greece, Aegean Sea
107 O17 **Giovinazzo** Puglia, SE Italy 41°11′N 16°40′E
Gipeswic *see* Ipswich
Gipuzkoa *see* Guipúzcoa
Giran *see* Ilan
30 K14 **Girard** Illinois, N USA 39°27′N 89°46′W
27 R7 **Girard** Kansas, C USA 37°30′N 94°50′W
25 O6 **Girard** Texas, SW USA 33°18′N 100°38′W
54 E10 **Girardot** Cundinamarca, C Colombia 04°19′N 74°47′W
172 M7 **Giraud Seamount** *undersea feature* SW Indian Ocean 09°57′S 46°55′E
83 A15 **Giraul** ≈ SW Angola
96 L9 **Girdle Ness** *headland* NE Scotland, United Kingdom 57°09′N 02°04′W

◆ Country
● Country Capital
◇ Dependent Territory
○ Dependent Territory Capital
◈ Administrative Regions
✈ International Airport
▲ Mountain
▲▲ Mountain Range
Volcano
≈ River
◎ Lake
⊡ Reservoir

137 N11 **Giresun** var. Kerasunt; anc. Cerasus, Pharnacia. Giresun, NE Turkey 40°55′N 38°35′E
137 N12 **Giresun** var. Kerasunt. ◈ province NE Turkey
137 N12 **Giresun Dağları** ▲▲ N Turkey
Girga see Jirjā
Girgeh see Jirjā
Girgenti see Agrigento
153 Q15 **Girīdīh** Jhārkhand, NE India 24°10′N 86°20′E
183 P6 **Girilambone** New South Wales, SE Australia 31°19′S 146°57′E
Girin see Jilin
121 W10 **Girne** Gk. Kerýneia, Kyrenia. N Cyprus 35°20′N 33°20′E
Giron see Kiruna
105 X5 **Girona** var. Gerona; anc. Gerunda. Cataluña, NE Spain 41°59′N 02°49′E
105 W5 **Girona** var. Gerona. ◈ province Cataluña, NE Spain
102 J12 **Gironde** ◈ department SW France
102 J11 **Gironde** estuary SW France
105 V5 **Gironella** Cataluña, NE Spain 42°02′N 01°53′E
103 N15 **Girou** ~ S France
97 H14 **Girvan** W Scotland, United Kingdom 55°14′N 04°53′W
24 M9 **Girvin** Texas, SW USA 31°05′N 102°24′W
184 Q9 **Gisborne** Gisborne, North Island, New Zealand 38°41′S 178°01′E
184 P9 **Gisborne** off. Gisborne District. ◈ unitary authority North Island, New Zealand
Gisborne District see Gisborne
Giseifu see Uijeongbu
Gisenye see Gisenyi
81 D19 **Gisenyi** var. Gisenye. NW Rwanda 01°42′S 29°18′E
95 K20 **Gislaved** Jönköping, S Sweden 57°19′N 13°30′E
103 N4 **Gisors** Eure, N France 49°18′N 01°46′E
Gissar see Hisor
147 P12 **Gissar Range** Rus. Gissarskiy Khrebet. ▲▲ Tajikistan/Uzbekistan
Gissarskiy Khrebet see Gissar Range
99 B16 **Gistel** West-Vlaanderen, W Belgium 51°09′N 02°58′E
108 F9 **Giswil** Obwalden, C Switzerland 46°49′N 08°11′E
115 B16 **Gitánes** ancient monument Ípeiros, W Greece
81 E20 **Gitarama** C Rwanda 02°05′S 29°45′E
81 E20 **Gitega** C Burundi 03°20′S 29°56′E
Githio see Gýtheio
108 H11 **Giubiasco** Ticino, S Switzerland 46°11′N 09°01′E
106 K13 **Giulianova** Abruzzi, C Italy 42°45′N 13°58′E
Giulie, Alpi see Julian Alps
Giumri see Gyumri
116 M13 **Giurgeni** Ialomiţa, SE Romania 44°45′N 27°48′E
116 J15 **Giurgiu** Giurgiu, S Romania 43°54′N 25°58′E
116 J14 **Giurgiu** ◈ county SE Romania
95 F22 **Give** Syddanmark, C Denmark 55°51′N 09°15′E
103 R2 **Givet** Ardennes, N France 50°08′N 04°50′E
103 R11 **Givors** Rhône, E France 45°35′N 04°47′E
83 K19 **Giyani** Limpopo, NE South Africa 23°20′S 30°37′E
80 I13 **Giyon** Oromīya, C Ethiopia 08°31′N 37°56′E
75 W8 **Giza** var. Al Jīzah, El Gîza, Gizeh. N Egypt 30°01′N 31°13′E
75 V8 **Giza, Pyramids of** ancient monument N Egypt
Gizhduvon see G'ijduvon
123 U8 **Gizhiga** Magadanskaya Oblast', E Russian Federation 61°58′N 160°16′E
123 T9 **Gizhiginskaya Guba** bay E Russian Federation
186 K8 **Gizo** Gizo, NW Solomon Islands 08°03′S 156°49′E
110 N7 **Giżycko** Ger. Lötzen. Warmińsko-Mazurskie, NE Poland 54°03′N 21°48′E
Gizymałów see Hrymayliv
113 M17 **Gjakovë** Serb. Đakovica. W Kosovo 42°22′N 20°30′E
94 F12 **Gjende** ◎ S Norway
113 L16 **Gjeravicë** Serb. Đeravica. ▲ S Serbia 42°33′N 20°08′E
95 F17 **Gjerstad** Aust-Agder, S Norway 58°54′N 09°03′E
113 O17 **Gjilan** Serb. Gnjilane. E Kosovo 42°27′N 21°28′E
Gjinokastër see Gjirokastër
113 L23 **Gjirokastër** var. Gjirokastra; prev. Gjinokastër, Gk. Argyrokastron, It. Argirocastro. Gjirokastër, S Albania 40°04′N 20°09′E
113 L22 **Gjirokastër** ◈ district S Albania
Gjirokastra see Gjirokastër
9 N7 **Gjoa Haven** var. Uqsuqtuuq. King William Island, Nunavut, NW Canada 68°38′N 95°57′W
94 H13 **Gjøvik** Oppland, S Norway 60°47′N 10°40′E
113 J22 **Gjuhëzës, Kepi i** headland SW Albania 40°25′N 19°19′E
Gjurgjevac see Đurđevac
115 E18 **Gkióna** var. Giona. ▲ C Greece
121 R3 **Gkréko, Akrotíri** var. Cape Greco, Pidálion. cape E Cyprus
99 I18 **Glabbeek-Zuurbemde** Vlaams Brabant, C Belgium 50°54′N 04°58′E
13 R14 **Glace Bay** Cape Breton Island, Nova Scotia, SE Canada 46°12′N 59°57′W
11 O16 **Glacier** British Columbia, SW Canada 51°12′N 117°33′W
39 W12 **Glacier Bay** inlet Alaska, USA
32 I7 **Glacier Peak** ▲ Washington, NW USA 48°06′N 121°06′W
159 N13 **Gladaindong Feng** ▲ C China 33°24′N 91°00′E
21 Q7 **Glade Spring** Virginia, NE USA 36°47′N 81°46′W
43 W7 **Gladewater** Texas, SW USA 32°32′N 94°57′W
181 Y8 **Gladstone** Queensland, E Australia 23°52′S 151°16′E
182 I8 **Gladstone** South Australia 33°16′S 138°21′E
11 X16 **Gladstone** Manitoba, S Canada 50°12′N 98°56′W
31 O5 **Gladstone** Michigan, N USA 45°51′N 87°01′W
27 R4 **Gladstone** Missouri, C USA 39°12′N 94°33′W
31 Q7 **Gladwin** Michigan, N USA 43°58′N 84°29′W
95 J15 **Glafsfjorden** ◎ C Sweden
92 H2 **Gláma** physical region NW Iceland
94 I12 **Gláma** var. Glommen. ~ S Norway
112 F13 **Glamoč** Federacija Bosna I Hercegovina, NE Boznia and Herzegovina 44°01′N 16°51′E
97 J22 **Glamorgan** cultural region S Wales, United Kingdom
95 G24 **Glamsbjerg** Syddtjylland, C Denmark 55°17′N 10°07′E
171 Q8 **Glan** Mindanao, S Philippines 05°49′N 125°11′E
109 T9 **Glan** ~ SE Austria
101 F19 **Glan** ~ W Germany
95 M17 **Glan** ◎ S Sweden
Glaris see Glarus
108 H9 **Glarner Alpen** Eng. Glarus Alps. ▲▲ E Switzerland
108 H8 **Glarus** Glarus, E Switzerland 47°03′N 09°04′E
108 H9 **Glarus** Fr. Glaris. ◈ canton C Switzerland
Glarus Alps see Glarner Alpen
27 N3 **Glasco** Kansas, C USA 39°21′N 97°50′W
96 I12 **Glasgow** S Scotland, United Kingdom 55°53′N 04°15′W
20 K7 **Glasgow** Kentucky, S USA 37°00′N 85°54′W
27 T4 **Glasgow** Missouri, C USA 39°13′N 92°51′W
33 W7 **Glasgow** Montana, NW USA 48°12′N 106°37′W
21 T6 **Glasgow** Virginia, NE USA 37°37′N 79°27′W
96 I12 **Glasgow** ✈ W Scotland, United Kingdom 55°52′N 04°27′W
11 S14 **Glaslyn** Saskatchewan, S Canada 53°20′N 108°18′W
18 I16 **Glassboro** New Jersey, NE USA 39°40′N 75°05′W
24 L10 **Glass Mountains** ▲▲ Texas, SW USA
97 K23 **Glastonbury** SW England, United Kingdom 51°09′N 02°43′W
Glatz see Kłodzko
101 N16 **Glauchau** Sachsen, E Germany 50°48′N 12°32′E
Glavn'a Morava see Velika Morava
Glavnik see Gllamnik
127 T1 **Glazov** Udmurtskaya Respublika, NW Russian Federation 58°06′N 52°38′E
Głda see Gwda
109 U8 **Gleinalpe** ▲▲ SE Austria
109 W8 **Gleisdorf** Steiermark, SE Austria 47°07′N 15°43′E
Gleiwitz see Gliwice
39 S11 **Glenallen** Alaska, USA 62°06′N 145°33′W
102 F7 **Glénan, Îles** island group NW France
185 G21 **Glenavy** Canterbury, South Island, New Zealand 44°53′S 171°04′E
10 H5 **Glenboyle** Yukon Territory, NW Canada 63°55′N 138°43′W
21 X3 **Glen Burnie** Maryland, NE USA 39°09′N 76°37′W
36 L8 **Glen Canyon** canyon Utah, W USA
36 L8 **Glen Canyon Dam** dam Arizona, SW USA
30 K15 **Glen Carbon** Illinois, N USA 38°45′N 89°58′W
14 E17 **Glencoe** Ontario, S Canada 42°44′N 81°42′W
83 K22 **Glencoe** KwaZulu/Natal, E South Africa 28°10′S 30°15′E
29 U9 **Glencoe** Minnesota, N USA 44°46′N 94°09′W
96 H10 **Glen Coe** valley N Scotland, United Kingdom
36 K13 **Glendale** Arizona, SW USA 33°32′N 112°11′W
35 S15 **Glendale** California, W USA 34°09′N 118°20′W
182 G5 **Glendambo** South Australia 30°59′S 135°45′E
33 Y8 **Glendive** Montana, NW USA 47°08′N 104°42′W
33 Y15 **Glendo** Wyoming, C USA 42°27′N 105°01′W
55 S10 **Glendor Mountains** ▲ C Guyana
182 K12 **Glenelg River** ~ South Australia/Victoria, SE Australia
29 P4 **Glenfield** North Dakota, N USA 47°25′N 98°33′W
25 V12 **Glen Flora** Texas, SW USA 29°22′N 96°12′W
181 P7 **Glen Helen** Northern Territory, N Australia 23°45′S 132°46′E
183 U5 **Glen Innes** New South Wales, SE Australia 29°42′S 151°45′E
31 P6 **Glen Lake** ◎ Michigan, N USA
10 I7 **Glenlyon Peak** ▲ Yukon Territory, W Canada 62°32′N 134°51′W
37 N16 **Glenn, Mount** ▲ Arizona, SW USA 31°55′N 110°00′W
33 N15 **Glenns Ferry** Idaho, NW USA 42°57′N 115°18′W
23 W6 **Glennville** Georgia, SE USA 31°56′N 81°55′W
10 J10 **Glenora** British Columbia, W Canada 57°52′N 131°16′W
182 M11 **Glenorchy** Victoria, SE Australia 36°56′S 142°39′E
183 V5 **Glenreagh** New South Wales, SE Australia 30°04′S 153°00′E
33 X15 **Glenrock** Wyoming, C USA 42°51′N 105°52′W
96 K11 **Glenrothes** E Scotland, United Kingdom 56°11′N 03°09′W
18 L9 **Glens Falls** New York, NE USA 43°18′N 73°38′W
97 D14 **Glenties** Ir. Na Gleannta. Donegal, NW Ireland 54°47′N 08°17′W
28 L5 **Glen Ullin** North Dakota, N USA 46°49′N 101°49′W
21 R4 **Glenville** West Virginia, NE USA 38°57′N 80°51′W
27 T12 **Glenwood** Arkansas, C USA 34°19′N 93°33′W
29 S15 **Glenwood** Iowa, C USA 41°03′N 95°44′W
29 T7 **Glenwood** Minnesota, N USA 45°39′N 95°23′W
36 L5 **Glenwood** Utah, W USA 38°45′N 111°59′W
30 I5 **Glenwood City** Wisconsin, N USA 45°04′N 92°11′W
37 Q4 **Glenwood Springs** Colorado, C USA 39°33′N 107°21′W
108 F10 **Gletsch** Valais, S Switzerland 46°34′N 08°21′E
Glevum see Gloucester
29 U14 **Glidden** Iowa, C USA 42°03′N 94°43′W
112 E9 **Glina** var. Banijska Palanka. Sisak-Moslavina, NE Croatia 45°19′N 16°07′E
94 F11 **Glittertind** ▲ S Norway 61°24′N 08°19′E
111 J16 **Gliwice** Ger. Gleiwitz. Śląskie, S Poland 50°19′N 18°49′E
113 N16 **Gllamnik** Serb. Glavnik. N Kosovo 42°53′N 21°10′E
36 M14 **Globe** Arizona, SW USA 33°24′N 110°47′W
Globino see Hlobyne
108 L9 **Glockturm** ▲ SW Austria 46°54′N 10°42′E
116 L9 **Glodeni** Rus. Glodyany. N Moldova 47°47′N 27°33′E
109 S9 **Glödnitz** Kärnten, S Austria 46°57′N 14°03′E
Glodyany see Glodeni
Glogau see Głogów
109 W6 **Gloggnitz** Niederösterreich, E Austria 47°41′N 15°57′E
110 F13 **Głogów** Ger. Glogau, Glogow. Dolnośląskie, SW Poland 51°40′N 16°04′E
Glogow see Głogów
111 I16 **Głogówek** Ger. Oberglogau. Opolskie, S Poland 50°21′N 17°51′E
92 G12 **Glomfjord** Nordland, C Norway 66°49′N 14°00′E
Glomma see Gláma
Glommen see Gláma
93 I14 **Glommersträsk** Norrbotten, N Sweden 65°17′N 19°40′E
172 I1 **Glorieuses, Îles** Eng. Glorioso Islands. island (to France) N Madagascar
Glorioso Islands see Glorieuses, Îles
65 C25 **Glorious Hill** hill East Falkland, Falkland Islands
38 J12 **Glory of Russia Cape** headland Saint Matthew Island, Alaska, USA 60°36′N 172°57′W
22 J7 **Gloster** Mississippi, S USA 31°12′N 91°01′W
183 U7 **Gloucester** New South Wales, SE Australia 32°01′S 152°00′E
186 F7 **Gloucester** New Britain, E Papua New Guinea 05°30′S 148°30′E
97 L21 **Gloucester** hist. Caer Glou, Lat. Glevum. C England, United Kingdom 51°53′N 02°14′W
19 P10 **Gloucester** Massachusetts, NE USA 42°36′N 70°36′W
21 X6 **Gloucester** Virginia, NE USA 37°26′N 76°33′W
97 K21 **Gloucestershire** cultural region C England, United Kingdom
31 T14 **Glouster** Ohio, N USA 39°30′N 82°04′W
42 H3 **Glovers Reef** reef E Belize
18 K10 **Gloversville** New York, NE USA 43°03′N 74°20′W
110 K12 **Głowno** Łódź, C Poland 51°58′N 19°43′E
111 H16 **Głubczyce** Ger. Leobschütz. Opolskie, S Poland 50°13′N 17°50′E
126 L11 **Glubokiy** Rostovskaya Oblast', SW Russian Federation 48°34′N 40°16′E
145 W9 **Glubokoye** Vostochnyy Kazakhstan, E Kazakhstan 50°08′N 82°16′E
Glubokoye see Hlybokaye
111 H16 **Głuchołazy** Ger. Ziegenhais. Opolskie, S Poland 50°20′N 17°23′E
100 I9 **Glückstadt** Schleswig-Holstein, N Germany 53°47′N 09°26′E
Glukhov see Hlukhiv
Glukhovichi see Hlushkavichy
Glusk/Glussk see Hlusk
Glybokaya see Hlyboka
95 F21 **Glyngøre** Midtjylland, NW Denmark 56°45′N 08°55′E
127 Q9 **Gmelinka** Volgogradskaya Oblast', SW Russian Federation 50°50′N 46°51′E
109 R8 **Gmünd** Kärnten, S Austria 46°56′N 13°32′E
109 U2 **Gmünd** Niederösterreich, N Austria 48°47′N 14°59′E
Gmünd see Schwäbisch Gmünd
109 S5 **Gmunden** Oberösterreich, N Austria 47°56′N 13°48′E
Gmundner See see Traunsee
94 N10 **Gnarp** Gävleborg, C Sweden 62°03′N 17°19′E
109 W8 **Gnas** Steiermark, SE Austria 46°53′N 15°48′E
Gnaviyani see Fuammulah
Gnesen see Gniezno
95 O16 **Gnesta** Södermanland, C Sweden 59°05′N 17°20′E
110 H11 **Gniezno** Ger. Gnesen. Weilkopolskie, C Poland 52°33′N 17°35′E
Gnjilane see Gjilan
95 K20 **Gnosjö** Jönköping, S Sweden 57°22′N 13°44′E
155 E17 **Goa** prev. Old Goa, Vela Goa, Velha Goa. Goa, W India 15°31′N 73°56′E
155 E17 **Goa** var. Old Goa. ◈ state W India
Goabddális see Kåbdalis
42 H7 **Goascorán, Río** ~ El Salvador/Honduras
77 O16 **Goaso** var. Gawso. W Ghana 06°49′N 02°27′W
81 K14 **Goba** Oromīya, C Ethiopia 07°02′N 39°58′E
83 C20 **Gobabed** Erongo, W Namibia 23°36′S 15°03′E
83 E19 **Gobabis** Omaheke, E Namibia 22°25′S 18°58′E
Gobannium see Abergavenny
64 M7 **Goban Spur** undersea feature NW Atlantic Ocean
63 H21 **Gobernador Gregores** Santa Cruz, S Argentina 48°43′S 70°21′W
61 F14 **Gobernador Ingeniero Virasoro** Corrientes, NE Argentina 28°06′S 56°00′W
162 L12 **Gobi** desert China/Mongolia
164 I14 **Gobō** Wakayama, Honshū, SW Japan 33°52′N 135°09′E
Gobolka Awdal see Awdal
Gobolka Sahil see Sahil
Gobolka Sool see Sool
101 D14 **Goch** Nordrhein-Westfalen, W Germany 51°41′N 06°10′E
83 E20 **Gochas** Hardap, S Namibia 24°54′S 18°43′E
155 I14 **Godāvari** var. Godavari. ~ C India
Godavari see Godāvari
155 L16 **Godāvari, Mouths of the** delta E India
15 V5 **Godbout** Québec, SE Canada 49°19′N 67°37′W
15 U5 **Godbout** ~ Québec, SE Canada
15 U5 **Godbout Est** ~ Québec, SE Canada
27 N6 **Goddard** Kansas, C USA 37°39′N 97°34′W
14 E15 **Goderich** Ontario, S Canada 43°43′N 81°43′W
Godhavn see Qeqertarsuaq
154 E10 **Godhra** Gujarāt, W India 22°49′N 73°40′E
Göding see Hodonín
111 K22 **Gödöllő** Pest, N Hungary 47°36′N 19°20′E
62 H11 **Godoy Cruz** Mendoza, W Argentina 32°59′S 68°49′W
11 Y11 **Gods** ~ Manitoba, C Canada
11 X13 **Gods Lake** ◎ Manitoba, C Canada
11 X13 **Gods Lake Narrows** Manitoba, C Canada 54°29′N 94°21′W
Godthaab/Godthåb see Nuuk
Godwin Austen, Mount see K2
Goede Hoop, Kaap de see Good Hope, Cape of
Goedgegun see Nhlangano
Goeie Hoop, Kaap die see Good Hope, Cape of
13 O7 **Goélands, Lac aux** ◎ Québec, SE Canada
98 E13 **Goeree** island SW Netherlands
99 F15 **Goes** Zeeland, SW Netherlands 51°30′N 03°55′E
Goettingen see Göttingen
19 O10 **Goffstown** New Hampshire, NE USA 43°01′N 71°34′W
14 E8 **Gogama** Ontario, S Canada 47°42′N 81°44′W
30 L3 **Gogebic, Lake** ◎ Michigan, N USA
30 K3 **Gogebic Range** hill range Michigan/Wisconsin, N USA
Gogi Lerr see Gogi, Mount
137 V13 **Gogi, Mount** Arm. Gogi Lerr, Az. Küküdağ. ▲ Armenia/Azerbaijan 39°33′N 45°35′E
124 F12 **Gogland, Ostrov** island NW Russian Federation
111 I15 **Gogolin** Opolskie, S Poland 50°28′N 18°04′E
Gogonou see Gogounou
77 S14 **Gogounou** var. Gogonou. N Benin 10°50′N 02°50′E
152 I10 **Gohāna** Haryāna, N India 29°06′N 76°43′E
59 K18 **Goianésia** Goiás, C Brazil 15°21′S 49°02′W
59 K18 **Goiânia** prev. Goyania. state capital Goiás, C Brazil 16°43′S 49°18′W
59 K18 **Goiás** Goiás, C Brazil 15°57′S 50°07′W
59 J18 **Goiás** off. Estado de Goiás; prev. Goiaz, Goyaz. ◈ state C Brazil
Goiás, Estado de see Goiás
Goiaz see Goiás
Goidhoo Atoll see Horsburgh Atoll
159 R14 **Goinsargoin** Xizang Zizhiqu, W China 31°56′N 98°04′E
60 H10 **Goio-Erê** Paraná, SW Brazil 24°08′S 53°07′W
99 I15 **Goirle** Noord-Brabant, S Netherlands 51°31′N 05°04′E
104 H8 **Góis** Coimbra, N Portugal 40°10′N 08°06′W
165 Q8 **Gojōme** Akita, Honshū, NW Japan 39°55′N 140°07′E
149 U9 **Gojra** Punjab, E Pakistan 31°10′N 72°43′E
136 A11 **Gökçeada** var. Imroz Adasī, Gk. Imbros. island NW Turkey
Gökçeada see İmroz
146 F13 **Gökdepe** Rus. Gëkdepe, Geok-Tepe. Ahal Welaýaty, C Turkmenistan 38°05′N 58°08′E
136 I10 **Gökırmak** ~ N Turkey
Goklenkuy, Solonchak see Geklengkui, Solonchak
136 C16 **Gökova Körfezi** gulf SW Turkey
136 K15 **Göksu** ~ S Turkey
136 L15 **Göksun** Kahramanmaraş, C Turkey 38°03′N 36°30′E
136 I17 **Göksu Nehri** ~ S Turkey
83 J16 **Gokwe** Midlands, NW Zimbabwe 18°13′S 28°55′E
94 F13 **Gol** Buskerud, S Norway 60°42′N 08°57′E
153 X12 **Golāghāt** Assam, NE India 26°31′N 93°54′E
110 H10 **Gołańcz** Wielkopolskie, C Poland 52°57′N 17°17′E
138 G8 **Golan Heights** Ar. Al Jawlān, Heb. HaGolan. ▲ SW Syria
Golārā see Ārān-va-Bidgol
Golaya Pristan see Hola Prystan'
143 T11 **Golbāf** Kermān, C Iran 29°51′N 57°44′E
136 M15 **Gölbaşı** Adıyaman, S Turkey 37°46′N 37°40′E
109 P9 **Gölbner** ▲ SW Austria 46°51′N 12°31′E
30 M17 **Golconda** Illinois, N USA 37°20′N 88°29′W
35 T3 **Golconda** Nevada, W USA 40°56′N 117°29′W
136 E11 **Gölcük** Kocaeli, NW Turkey 40°44′N 29°50′E
108 I7 **Goldach** Sankt Gallen, NE Switzerland 47°28′N 09°28′E
110 N7 **Gołdap** Ger. Goldap. Warmińsko-Mazurskie, NE Poland 54°19′N 22°23′E
32 E15 **Gold Beach** Oregon, NW USA 42°25′N 124°27′W
Goldberg see Złotoryja
183 V3 **Gold Coast** cultural region Queensland, E Australia
68 D12 **Gold Coast** coastal region S Ghana
39 R10 **Gold Creek** Alaska, USA 62°48′N 149°40′W
11 O16 **Golden** British Columbia, SW Canada 51°19′N 116°58′W
37 T4 **Golden** Colorado, C USA 39°40′N 105°12′W
184 I13 **Golden Bay** bay South Island, New Zealand
27 R7 **Golden City** Missouri, C USA 37°23′N 94°05′W
32 I11 **Goldendale** Washington, NW USA 45°49′N 120°49′W
Goldener Tisch see Zlatý Stôl
44 L13 **Golden Grove** E Jamaica 17°56′N 76°17′W
14 J12 **Golden Lake** ◎ Ontario, SE Canada
22 K10 **Golden Meadow** Louisiana, S USA 29°22′N 90°15′W
Golden State, The see California
83 K16 **Golden Valley** Mashonaland West, N Zimbabwe 18°11′S 29°50′E
35 U9 **Goldfield** Nevada, W USA 37°42′N 117°15′W
Goldingen see Kuldīga
Goldmarkt see Zlatna
10 K17 **Gold River** Vancouver Island, British Columbia, SW Canada 49°41′N 126°05′W
21 V10 **Goldsboro** North Carolina, SE USA 35°23′N 78°00′W
24 M8 **Goldsmith** Texas, SW USA 31°58′N 102°36′W
25 R8 **Goldthwaite** Texas, SW USA 31°28′N 98°35′W
137 R11 **Göle** Ardahan, NE Turkey 40°47′N 42°36′E
Golema Ada see Ostrovo
114 H9 **Golema Planina** ▲ W Bulgaria
114 F9 **Golemi Vrŭkh** ▲ W Bulgaria 42°41′N 22°38′E
110 D8 **Goleniów** Ger. Gollnow. Zachodnio-pomorskie, NW Poland 53°34′N 14°48′E
143 R3 **Golestān** ◈ province N Iran
35 Q14 **Goleta** California, W USA 34°26′N 119°50′W
43 O16 **Golfito** Puntarenas, SE Costa Rica 08°42′N 83°10′W
25 T13 **Goliad** Texas, SW USA 28°40′N 97°26′W
113 L14 **Golija** ▲▲ SW Serbia
Golinka see Gongbo'gyamda
113 O16 **Goljak** ▲▲ SE Serbia
136 M12 **Gölköy** Ordu, N Turkey 40°42′N 37°37′E
Gollel see Lavumisa
109 X3 **Göllersbach** ~ NE Austria
Gollnow see Goleniów
Golmo see Golmud
159 P10 **Golmud** var. Ge'e'mu, Golmo, Chin. Ko-erh-mu. Qinghai, C China 36°23′N 94°56′E
103 Y14 **Golo** ~ Corse, France, C Mediterranean Sea
Golovanevsk see Holovanivs'k
Golovchin see Halowchyn
39 N9 **Golovin** Alaska, USA 64°33′N 162°54′W
142 M7 **Golpāyegān** var. Gulpaigan. Eşfahān, W Iran 33°23′N 50°18′E
Golshan see Ţabas
Gol'shany see Hal'shany
96 J7 **Golspie** N Scotland, United Kingdom 57°59′N 03°56′W
112 O11 **Golubac** Serbia, NE Serbia 44°38′N 21°36′E
110 J9 **Golub-Dobrzyń** Kujawski-pomorskie, C Poland 53°07′N 19°03′E
145 S7 **Golubovka** Pavlodar, N Kazakhstan 53°07′N 74°11′E
82 B11 **Golungo Alto** Cuanza Norte, NW Angola 09°10′S 14°45′E
114 M8 **Golyama Kamchiya** ~ E Bulgaria
114 L8 **Golyama Reka** ~ N Bulgaria
114 H11 **Golyama Syutkya** ▲ SW Bulgaria 41°55′N 24°03′E
114 I12 **Golyam Perelik** ▲ S Bulgaria 41°37′N 24°34′E
114 I11 **Golyam Persenk** ▲ S Bulgaria 41°50′N 24°33′E
79 P19 **Goma** Nord-Kivu, NE Dem. Rep. Congo 01°36′S 29°08′E
153 N13 **Gomati** var. Gumti. ~ N India
77 X14 **Gombe** Gombe, E Nigeria 10°19′N 11°02′E
67 U10 **Gombe** var. Igombe. ~ E Tanzania
77 Y14 **Gombi** Adamawa, E Nigeria 10°07′N 12°45′E
Gombroon see Bandar-e 'Abbās
Gomel' see Homyel'
Gomel'skaya Oblast' see Homyel'skaya Voblasts'
64 N11 **Gomera** island Islas Canarias, Spain, NE Atlantic Ocean
40 I5 **Gómez Farías** Chihuahua, N Mexico 29°25′N 107°46′W
40 L8 **Gómez Palacio** Durango, C Mexico 25°39′N 103°30′W
158 J13 **Gomo** Xizang Zizhiqu, W China 33°37′N 86°40′E
143 T6 **Gonābād** var. Gunabad. Khorāsān-Razavī, NE Iran 36°30′N 59°18′E
44 L8 **Gonaïves** var. Les Gonaïves. N Haiti 19°26′N 72°41′W
123 Q12 **Gonam** ~ NE Russian Federation
44 L9 **Gonâve, Canal de la** var. Canal de Sud. channel N Caribbean Sea
44 K9 **Gonâve, Golfe de la** gulf N Caribbean Sea
Gonāveh see Bandar-e Gonāveh
44 K9 **Gonâve, Île de la** island C Haiti
Gonbadān see Do Gonbadān
143 Q3 **Gonbad-e Kāvūs** var. Gunbad-i-Qawus. Golestān, N Iran 37°15′N 55°11′E
152 M12 **Gonda** Uttar Pradesh, N India 27°08′N 81°58′E
Gondar see Gonder
80 I11 **Gonder** var. Gondar. Āmara, NW Ethiopia 12°36′N 37°27′E
78 J13 **Gondey** Moyen-Chari, S Chad 09°07′N 19°10′E
154 J12 **Gondia** Mahārāshtra, C India 21°27′N 80°12′E
104 G6 **Gondomar** Porto, NW Portugal 41°10′N 08°35′W
136 C12 **Gönen** Balıkesir, W Turkey 40°06′N 27°39′E
136 C12 **Gönen Çayı** ~ NW Turkey
159 O15 **Gongbo'gyamda** var. Golinka. Xizang Zizhiqu, W China 30°03′N 93°10′E
Gongchang see Longxi
159 N16 **Gonggar** var. Gyixong. Xizang Zizhiqu, W China 29°18′N 90°56′E
160 G9 **Gongga Shan** ▲ C China 29°50′N 101°55′E
159 T10 **Gonghe** var. Qabqa. Qinghai, C China 36°20′N 100°46′E
Gongjiang see Yudu
158 I5 **Gongliu** var. Tokkuztara. Xinjiang Uygur Zizhiqu, NW China 43°29′N 82°16′E
77 W14 **Gongola** ~ E Nigeria
Gongoleh State see Jonglei
183 P5 **Gongolgon** New South Wales, SE Australia 30°19′S 146°57′E
159 Q6 **Gongpoquan** Gansu, N China 41°45′N 100°27′E
Gongquan see Gongxian
Gongtang see Damxung
160 I10 **Gongxian** var. Gongquan, Gong Xian. Sichuan, C China 28°25′N 104°51′E
Gong Xian see Gongxian
157 V10 **Gongzhuling** prev. Huaide. Jilin, NE China 43°30′N 124°48′E
159 S14 **Gonjo** Xizang Zizhiqu, W China 30°51′N 98°16′E
107 B20 **Gonnesa** Sardegna, Italy, C Mediterranean Sea 39°15′N 08°27′E
Gonni/Gónnos see Gónnoi
115 F15 **Gónnoi** var. Gonni, Gónnos; prev. Dereli. Thessalía, C Greece 39°52′N 22°27′E
Gōnoura see Iki
35 O11 **Gonzales** California, W USA 36°30′N 121°26′W
22 J9 **Gonzales** Louisiana, S USA 30°14′N 90°55′W
25 T12 **Gonzales** Texas, SW USA 29°31′N 97°29′W
41 P11 **González** Tamaulipas, C Mexico 22°50′N 98°25′W
21 V6 **Goochland** Virginia, NE USA 37°42′N 77°54′W
195 X14 **Goodenough, Cape** headland Antarctica 66°15′S 126°35′E
186 F9 **Goodenough Island** var. Morata. island SE Papua New Guinea
39 N8 **Goodhope Bay** bay Alaska, USA
83 D26 **Good Hope, Cape of** Afr. Kaap de Goede Hoop, Kaap die Goeie Hoop. headland SW South Africa 34°19′S 18°25′E
10 K10 **Good Hope Lake** British Columbia, W Canada 59°15′N 129°18′W
83 E23 **Goodhouse** Northern Cape, W South Africa 28°54′S 18°13′E
33 O15 **Gooding** Idaho, NW USA 42°56′N 114°42′W
26 H3 **Goodland** Kansas, C USA 39°20′N 101°43′W
173 Y15 **Goodlands** NW Mauritius 20°02′S 57°39′E
20 J8 **Goodlettsville** Tennessee, S USA 36°19′N 86°42′W
39 N13 **Goodnews** Alaska, USA 59°07′N 161°35′W
25 O3 **Goodnight** Texas, SW USA 35°00′N 101°07′W
183 Q4 **Goodooga** New South Wales, SE Australia 29°09′S 147°30′E
29 N4 **Goodrich** North Dakota, N USA 47°24′N 100°07′W
25 W10 **Goodrich** Texas, SW USA 30°36′N 94°57′W
29 X10 **Goodview** Minnesota, N USA 44°04′N 91°42′W
26 H8 **Goodwell** Oklahoma, C USA 36°36′N 101°38′W
97 N17 **Goole** E England, United Kingdom 53°43′N 00°46′W
183 O8 **Goolgowi** New South Wales, SE Australia 34°00′S 145°43′E
182 I10 **Goolwa** South Australia 35°31′S 138°43′E
181 Y11 **Goondiwindi** Queensland, E Australia 28°33′S 150°22′E
98 O11 **Goor** Overijssel, E Netherlands 52°13′N 06°33′E
Goose Bay see Happy Valley-Goose Bay
33 V13 **Gooseberry Creek** ~ Wyoming, C USA
21 S14 **Goose Creek** South Carolina, SE USA 32°58′N 80°01′W
63 M23 **Goose Green** var. Prado del Ganso. East Falkland, Falkland Islands 51°52′S 59°W
16 D8 **Goose Lake** var. Lago dos Gansos. ◎ California/Oregon, W USA
29 Q4 **Goose River** ~ North Dakota, N USA
153 T16 **Gopalganj** Dhaka, S Bangladesh 23°00′N 89°48′E
153 O12 **Gopālganj** Bihār, N India 26°28′N 84°26′E
Gopher State see Minnesota
101 I22 **Göppingen** Baden-Württemberg, SW Germany 48°42′N 09°39′E
110 G13 **Góra** Ger. Guhrau. Dolnośląskie, SW Poland 51°40′N 16°03′E
110 M12 **Góra Kalwaria** Mazowieckie, C Poland 52°00′N 21°14′E
153 O12 **Gorakhpur** Uttar Pradesh, N India 26°45′N 83°23′E
Gora Kyuren see Kürendag
Gorany see Harany
113 J14 **Goražde** Federacija Bosna I Hercegovina, SE Bosnia and Herzegovina 43°39′N 18°58′E
Gorbovichi see Harbavichy
Gorče Petrov see Đorče Petrov
0 E9 **Gorda Ridges** undersea feature NE Pacific Ocean 41°30′N 128°00′W
Gordiaz see Gardēz
78 K12 **Gordil** Vakaga, N Central African Republic 09°37′N 21°42′E
23 U5 **Gordon** Georgia, SE USA 32°52′N 83°19′W
28 K12 **Gordon** Nebraska, C USA 42°48′N 102°12′W
25 R7 **Gordon** Texas, SW USA 32°32′N 98°21′W
28 L13 **Gordon Creek** ~ Nebraska, C USA
63 I25 **Gordon, Isla** island S Chile
183 O17 **Gordon, Lake** ◎ Tasmania, SE Australia
183 O17 **Gordon River** ~ Tasmania, SE Australia
21 V5 **Gordonsville** Virginia, NE USA 38°08′N 78°11′W
78 H13 **Goré** Logone-Oriental, S Chad 07°55′N 16°38′E
80 H13 **Gorē** Oromīya, C Ethiopia 08°08′N 35°33′E
185 D24 **Gore** Southland, South Island, New Zealand 46°06′S 168°58′E
14 D11 **Gore Bay** Manitoulin Island, Ontario, S Canada 45°54′N 82°28′W
25 Q5 **Goree** Texas, SW USA 33°28′N 99°31′W
137 O11 **Görele** Giresun, NE Turkey 41°00′N 39°00′E
19 N6 **Gore Mountain** ▲ Vermont, NE USA 44°55′N 71°47′W
39 R13 **Gore Point** headland Alaska, USA 59°12′N 150°57′W
37 R4 **Gore Range** ▲▲ Colorado, C USA
97 F19 **Gorey** Ir. Guaire. Wexford, SE Ireland 52°40′N 06°18′W
143 R12 **Gorgāb** Kermān, S Iran
143 Q4 **Gorgān** var. Astarabad, Astrabad, Gurgan, prev. Asterābād; anc. Hyrcania. Golestān, N Iran 36°53′N 54°28′E
143 Q4 **Gorgān, Rūd-e** ~ N Iran
76 I10 **Gorgol** ◈ region S Mauritania
106 D12 **Gorgona, Isola di** island Archipelago Toscano, C Italy
19 P8 **Gorham** Maine, NE USA 43°41′N 70°27′W
137 T10 **Gori** C Georgia 42°00′N 44°07′E
98 I13 **Gorinchem** var. Gorkum. Zuid-Holland, C Netherlands 51°50′N 04°59′E
137 V13 **Goris** SE Armenia 39°31′N 46°20′E
124 K16 **Goritsy** Tverskaya Oblast', W Russian Federation 57°09′N 36°44′E
106 J7 **Gorizia** Ger. Görz. Friuli-Venezia Giulia, NE Italy 45°57′N 13°37′E
116 G13 **Gorj** ◈ county SW Romania
109 W12 **Gorjanci** var. Uskočke Planine, Žumberak, Žumberačko Gorje, Ger. Uskokengebirge; prev. Sichelburger Gerbirge. ▲ Croatia/Slovenia Europe see also Žumberačko Gorje
Görkau see Jirkov
Gorki see Horki
Gor'kiy see Nizhniy Novgorod
Gorkum see Gorinchem
95 I23 **Gørlev** Sjælland, E Denmark 55°33′N 11°14′E
111 M17 **Gorlice** Małopolskie, S Poland 49°40′N 21°09′E
101 Q15 **Görlitz** Sachsen, E Germany 51°09′N 14°58′E
Görlitz see Zgorzelec
Gorlovka see Horlivka
25 R7 **Gorman** Texas, SW USA 32°12′N 98°40′W
21 T3 **Gormania** West Virginia, NE USA 39°16′N 79°18′W
Gorna Dzhumaya see Blagoevgrad
114 K8 **Gorna Oryakhovitsa** Veliko Tŭrnovo, N Bulgaria 43°07′N 25°40′E
114 J8 **Gorna Studena** Veliko Tŭrnovo, N Bulgaria 43°26′N 25°21′E
Gornja Mužlja see Mužlja
109 X9 **Gornja Radgona** Ger. Oberradkersburg. NE Slovenia 46°39′N 16°00′E
112 M13 **Gornji Milanovac** Serbia, C Serbia 44°01′N 20°26′E
112 G13 **Gornji Vakuf** var. Uskoplje. Federacija Bosna I Hercegovina, SW Bosnia and Herzegovina 43°55′N 17°34′E
122 J13 **Gorno-Altaysk** Respublika Altay, S Russian Federation 51°59′N 85°56′E
Gorno-Altayskaya Respublika see Altay, Respublika
123 N12 **Gorno-Chuyskiy** Irkutskaya Oblast', C Russian Federation 57°33′N 111°38′E
125 V14 **Gornozavodsk** Permskiy Kray, NW Russian Federation 58°21′N 58°24′E
125 V14 **Gornozavodsk** Ostrov Sakhalin, Sakhalinskaya Oblast', SE Russian Federation 46°34′N 141°52′E
122 I13 **Gornyak** Altayskiy Kray, S Russian Federation 50°58′N 81°24′E
123 O14 **Gornyy** Chitunskaya Oblast', Russian Federation 51°42′N 114°16′E
127 R8 **Gornyy** Saratovskaya Oblast', W Russian Federation 51°42′N 48°26′E
Gornyy Altay see Altay, Respublika
127 O10 **Gornyy Balykley** Volgogradskaya Oblast', SW Russian Federation 49°37′N 45°03′E
80 I13 **Goroch'an** ▲ W Ethiopia 09°09′N 37°16′E
116 J7 **Gorodenka** var. Horodenka. Ivano-Frankivs'ka Oblast', W Ukraine 48°41′N 25°28′E
127 O3 **Gorodets** Nizhegorodskaya Oblast', W Russian Federation 56°36′N 43°27′E
Gorodets see Haradzyets
Gorodeya see Haradzyeya
127 P6 **Gorodishche** Penzenskaya Oblast', W Russian Federation 53°17′N 45°39′E
Gorodishche see Horodyshche
Gorodnya see Horodnya
Gorodok see Haradok
Gorodok/Gorodok Yagellonski see Horodok
126 M13 **Gorodovikovsk** Respublika Kalmykiya, SW Russian Federation 46°07′N 41°56′E
186 D7 **Goroka** Eastern Highlands, C Papua New Guinea 06°02′S 145°22′E
Gorokhov see Horokhiv
127 N3 **Gorokhovets** Vladimirskaya Oblast', W Russian Federation 56°12′N 42°40′E
77 Q11 **Gorom-Gorom** NE Burkina 14°27′N 00°14′W
171 U13 **Gorong, Kepulauan** island group E Indonesia
83 M17 **Gorongosa** Sofala, C Mozambique 18°40′S 34°03′E
171 P11 **Gorontalo** Sulawesi, C Indonesia 0°33′N 123°05′E
171 O11 **Gorontalo** off. Propinsi Gorontalo. ◈ province N Indonesia
Propinsi Gorontalo see Gorontalo
Gorontalo, Teluk see Tomini, Teluk

◆ Country
● Country Capital
◇ Dependent Territory
○ Dependent Territory Capital
◈ Administrative Regions
✈ International Airport
▲ Mountain
▲▲ Mountain Range
Volcano
~ River
◎ Lake
⊠ Reservoir

110 *L7* **Górowo Iławeckie** *Ger.* Landsberg. Warmińsko-Mazurskie, NE Poland 54°18′N 20°30′E
98 *M7* **Gorredijk** *Fris.* De Gordyk. Fryslân, N Netherlands 53°00′N 06°04′E
84 *C14* **Gorringe Ridge** *undersea feature* E Atlantic Ocean 36°40′N 11°35′W
98 *M11* **Gorssel** Gelderland, E Netherlands 52°12′N 06°13′E
109 *T8* **Görtschitz** ≈ S Austria
Goryn *see* Horyn'
145 *S15* **Gory Shu-Ile** *Kaz.* Shū-Ile Taūlary; *prev.* Chu-Iliyskiye Gory. ▲▲ S Kazakhstan
Görz *see* Gorizia
110 *E10* **Gorzów Wielkopolski** *Ger.* Landsberg, Landsberg an der Warthe. Lubuskie, W Poland 52°44′N 15°12′E
146 *B10* **Goşabo** *var.* Goshoba, *Rus.* Koshoba. Balkan Welaýaty, NW Turkmenistan 40°28′N 54°11′E
108 *G9* **Göschenen** Uri, C Switzerland 46°40′N 08°36′E
165 *O11* **Gosen** Niigata, Honshū, C Japan 37°45′N 139°11′E
163 *Y13* **Goseong** *prev.* Kosŏng. SE North Korea 38°41′N 128°14′E
183 *T8* **Gosford** New South Wales, SE Australia 33°25′S 151°18′E
31 *P11* **Goshen** Indiana, N USA 41°34′N 85°49′W
18 *K13* **Goshen** New York, NE USA 41°24′N 74°17′W
Goshoba *see* Goşabo
Goshoba *see* Goşoba
165 *Q7* **Goshogawara** *var.* Gosyogawara. Aomori, Honshū, C Japan 40°47′N 140°24′E
Goshquduq Qum *see* Tosquduq Qumlari
101 *J14* **Goslar** Niedersachsen, C Germany 51°55′N 10°25′E
27 *Y9* **Gosnell** Arkansas, C USA 35°57′N 89°58′W
146 *B10* **Goşoba** *var.* Goshoba, *Rus.* Koshoba. Balkanskiy Velayat, NW Turkmenistan 40°28′N 54°11′E
112 *C11* **Gospić** Lika-Senj, C Croatia 44°32′N 15°21′E
97 *N23* **Gosport** S England, United Kingdom 50°48′N 01°08′W
94 *D9* **Gossa** *island* S Norway
108 *H7* **Gossau** Sankt Gallen, NE Switzerland 47°25′N 09°16′E
99 *G20* **Gosselies** *var.* Goss'lies. Hainaut, S Belgium 50°28′N 04°26′E
77 *P10* **Gossi** Tombouctou, C Mali 15°44′N 01°19′W
Goss'lies *see* Gosselies
113 *N18* **Gostivar** W FYR Macedonia 41°48′N 20°55′E
Gostomel' *see* Hostomel'
110 *G12* **Gostyń** *var.* Gostyn. Wielkopolskie, C Poland 51°52′N 17°00′E
Gostyn *see* Gostyń
110 *K11* **Gostynin** Mazowiesckie, C Poland 52°25′N 19°27′E
Gosyogawara *see* Goshogawara
95 *J18* **Göta Älv** ≈ S Sweden
95 *N17* **Göta kanal** *canal* S Sweden
95 *K18* **Götaland** *cultural region* S Sweden
95 *H17* **Göteborg** *Eng.* Gothenburg. Västra Götaland, S Sweden 57°43′N 11°58′E
77 *X16* **Gotel Mountains** ▲▲ E Nigeria
95 *K17* **Götene** Västra Götaland, S Sweden 58°32′N 13°29′E
Gotera *see* San Francisco
101 *K16* **Gotha** Thüringen, C Germany 50°57′N 10°43′E
29 *N15* **Gothenburg** Nebraska, C USA 40°57′N 100°09′W
Gothenburg *see* Göteborg
77 *R12* **Gothèye** Tillabéri, SW Niger 13°52′N 01°27′E
Gothland *see* Gotland
95 *P19* **Gotland** *var.* Gothland, Gottland. ◐ *county* SE Sweden
95 *O18* **Gotland** *island* SE Sweden
164 *A14* **Gotō** *var.* Hukue; *prev.* Fukue. Nagasaki, Fukue-jima, SW Japan 32°41′N 128°52′E
164 *B13* **Gotō-rettō** *island group* SW Japan
114 *H12* **Gotse Delchev** *prev.* Nevrokop. Blagoevgrad, SW Bulgaria 41°33′N 23°42′E
95 *P17* **Gotska Sandön** *island* SE Sweden
101 *I15* **Göttingen** *var.* Goettingen. Niedersachsen, C Germany 51°33′N 09°55′E
Gottland *see* Gotland
93 *I16* **Gottne** Västernorrland, C Sweden 63°27′N 18°25′E
Gottschee *see* Kočevje
Gottwaldov *see* Zlín
146 *B11* **Goturdepe** *Rus.* Koturdepe. Balkan Welaýaty, W Turkmenistan 39°32′N 53°39′E
108 *I7* **Götzis** Vorarlberg, NW Austria 47°21′N 09°40′E
98 *H12* **Gouda** Zuid-Holland, C Netherlands 52°01′N 04°42′E
76 *I11* **Goudiri** *var.* Goudiry. E Senegal 14°12′N 12°41′W
Goudiry *see* Goudiri
77 *X12* **Goudoumaria** Diffa, S Niger 13°28′N 11°15′E
15 *R9* **Gouffre, Rivière du** ≈ Québec, SE Canada
65 *M19* **Gough Fracture Zone** *tectonic feature* S Atlantic Ocean
65 *M19* **Gough Island** *island* Tristan da Cunha, S Atlantic Ocean
15 *N8* **Gouin, Réservoir** ▣ Québec, SE Canada
14 *B10* **Goulais River** Ontario, S Canada 46°41′N 84°22′W
183 *R9* **Goulburn** New South Wales, SE Australia 34°45′S 149°44′E
183 *O11* **Goulburn River** ≈ Victoria, SE Australia
195 *O10* **Gould Coast** *physical region* Antarctica
Goulimime *see* Guelmime
114 *F13* **Gouménissa** Kentrikí Makedonía, N Greece 40°56′N 22°27′E
77 *O10* **Goundam** Tombouctou, NW Mali 16°27′N 03°39′W
78 *H12* **Goundi** Moyen-Chari, S Chad 09°22′N 17°21′E
78 *G12* **Gounou-Gaya** Mayo-Kébbi, SW Chad 09°37′N 15°30′E
Gourci *see* Goursi
Gourcy *see* Goursi
102 *M13* **Gourdon** Lot, S France 44°45′N 01°22′E
77 *W11* **Gouré** Zinder, SE Niger 13°59′N 10°16′E
102 *G6* **Gourin** Morbihan, NW France 48°07′N 03°37′W
77 *P10* **Gourma-Rharous** Tombouctou, C Mali 16°54′N 01°55′W
103 *N4* **Gournay-en-Bray** Seine-Maritime, N France 49°29′N 01°42′E
78 *J6* **Gouro** Borkou-Ennedi-Tibesti, N Chad 19°26′N 19°36′E
77 *O12* **Goursi** *var.* Gourci, Gourcy. NW Burkina 13°13′N 02°20′W
104 *H8* **Gouveia** Guarda, N Portugal 40°29′N 07°35′W
18 *I7* **Gouverneur** New York, NE USA 44°20′N 75°27′W
99 *L21* **Gouvy** Luxembourg, E Belgium 50°10′N 05°55′E
45 *R14* **Gouyave** *var.* Charlotte Town. NW Grenada 12°10′N 61°44′W
Goverla, Gora *see* Hoverla, Hora
59 *N20* **Governador Valadares** Minas Gerais, SE Brazil 18°51′S 41°57′W
171 *R8* **Governor Generoso** Mindanao, S Philippines 06°36′N 126°06′E
44 *I2* **Governor's Harbour** Eleuthera Island, C Bahamas 25°11′N 76°15′W
162 *F9* **Govĭ-Altay** ◐ *province* SW Mongolia
162 *I10* **Govĭ Altayn Nuruu** ▲▲ S Mongolia
154 *L9* **Govind Ballabh Pant Sāgar** ▣ C India
152 *I7* **Govind Sāgar** ▣ NE India
162 *M8* **Govĭ-Sumber** ◐ *province* C Mongolia
Govurdak *see* Magdanly
18 *D11* **Gowanda** New York, NE USA 42°25′N 78°55′W
148 *J10* **Gowd-e Zereh, Dasht-e** *var.* Guad-i-Zirreh. *marsh* SW Afghanistan
14 *F8* **Gowganda** Ontario, S Canada 47°41′N 80°46′W
14 *G8* **Gowganda Lake** ◎ Ontario, S Canada
148 *M5* **Gōwr** *prev.* Ghowr. ◐ *province* C Afghanistan
29 *U13* **Gowrie** Iowa, C USA 42°16′N 94°17′W
Gowurdak *see* Magdanly
61 *C15* **Goya** Corrientes, NE Argentina 29°10′S 59°15′W
Goyania *see* Goiânia
Goyaz *see* Goiás
137 *X11* **Göyçay** *Rus.* Geokchay. C Azerbaijan 40°38′N 47°44′E
137 *V11* **Göygöl** *prev.* Xanlar, *Rus.* Khanlar. NW Azerbaijan 40°37′N 46°18′E
146 *D10* **Goymat** *Rus.* Koymat. Balkan Welaýaty, NW Turkmenistan 40°23′N 55°45′E
146 *D10* **Goymatdag, Gory** *Rus.* Gory Koymatdag. *hill range* Balkan Welaýaty, NW Turkmenistan
136 *F12* **Göynük** Bolu, NW Turkey 40°24′N 30°45′E
165 *R9* **Goyō-san** ▲ Honshū, C Japan 39°12′N 141°40′E
78 *K11* **Goz Beïda** Ouaddaï, SE Chad 12°06′N 21°22′E
146 *M10* **G'ozg'on** *Rus.* Gazgan. Navoiy Viloyati, C Uzbekistan 40°36′N 65°29′E
158 *H11* **Gozha Co** ◎ W China
121 *O15* **Gozo** *var.* Ghawdex. *island* N Malta
80 *H9* **Gōz Regeb** Kassala, NE Sudan 16°03′N 35°33′E
83 *H25* **Graaff-Reinet** Eastern Cape, S South Africa 32°15′S 24°32′E
Graasten *see* Gråsten
76 *L17* **Grabo** SW Ivory Coast 04°57′N 07°30′W
112 *P11* **Grabovica** Serbia, E Serbia 44°30′N 22°29′E
110 *I13* **Grabów nad Prosną** Wielkopolskie, C Poland 51°30′N 18°06′E
108 *I8* **Grabs** Sankt Gallen, NE Switzerland 47°10′N 09°27′E
112 *D12* **Gračac** Zadar, SW Croatia 44°18′N 15°52′E
112 *I11* **Gračanica** Federacija Bosna I Hercegovina, NE Bosnia and Herzegovina 44°41′N 18°20′E
14 *L11* **Gracefield** Québec, SE Canada 46°06′N 76°03′W
99 *K19* **Grâce-Hollogne** Liège, E Belgium 50°38′N 05°30′E
23 *R8* **Graceville** Florida, SE USA 30°57′N 85°31′W
29 *R8* **Graceville** Minnesota, N USA 45°34′N 96°25′W
42 *G6* **Gracias** Lempira, W Honduras 14°35′N 88°35′W
Gracias *see* Lempira
42 *L5* **Gracias a Dios** ◐ *department* E Honduras
43 *O6* **Gracias a Dios, Cabo de** *headland* Honduras/Nicaragua 15°00′N 83°10′W
64 *O2* **Graciosa** *var.* Ilha Graciosa. *island* Azores, Portugal, NE Atlantic Ocean
64 *Q11* **Graciosa** *island* Islas Canarias, Spain, NE Atlantic Ocean
Graciosa, Ilha *see* Graciosa
112 *I11* **Gradačac** Federacija Bosna I Hercegovina, N Bosnia and Herzegovina 44°51′N 18°24′E
59 *J15* **Gradaús, Serra dos** ▲▲ C Brazil
104 *L3* **Gradefes** Castilla y León, N Spain 42°37′N 05°14′W
Gradiška *see* Bosanska Gradiška
Gradizhsk *see* Hradyz'k
106 *J7* **Grado** Friuli-Venezia Giulia, NE Italy 45°41′N 13°24′E
Grado *see* Grau
113 *P19* **Gradsko** C FYR Macedonia 41°34′N 21°56′E
37 *V11* **Grady** New Mexico, SW USA 34°49′N 103°19′W
Grad Zagreb *see* Zagreb
29 *T12* **Graettinger** Iowa, C USA 43°14′N 94°45′W
101 *M23* **Grafing** Bayern, SE Germany 48°01′N 11°57′E
25 *S6* **Graford** Texas, SW USA 32°56′N 98°15′W
183 *V5* **Grafton** New South Wales, SE Australia 29°41′S 152°55′E
29 *Q3* **Grafton** North Dakota, N USA 48°24′N 97°24′W
21 *S3* **Grafton** West Virginia, NE USA 39°21′N 80°03′W
21 *T9* **Graham** North Carolina, SE USA 36°05′N 79°25′W
25 *R6* **Graham** Texas, SW USA 33°07′N 98°36′W
Graham Bell Island *see* Greem-Bell, Ostrov
10 *I13* **Graham Island** *island* Queen Charlotte Islands, British Columbia, SW Canada
19 *S6* **Graham Lake** ◎ Maine, NE USA
194 *H4* **Graham Land** *physical region* Antarctica
37 *N15* **Graham, Mount** ▲ Arizona, SW USA 32°42′N 109°52′W
Grahamstad *see* Grahamstown
83 *I25* **Grahamstown** *Afr.* Grahamstad. Eastern Cape, S South Africa 33°18′S 26°32′E
Grahovo *see* Bosansko Grahovo
68 *C12* **Grain Coast** *coastal region* S Liberia
169 *S17* **Grajagan, Teluk** *bay* Jawa, S Indonesia
59 *L14* **Grajaú** Maranhão, E Brazil 05°50′S 45°12′W
58 *M13* **Grajaú, Rio** ≈ NE Brazil
110 *O8* **Grajewo** Podlaskie, NE Poland 53°38′N 22°26′E
95 *F24* **Gram** Syddanmark, SW Denmark 55°18′N 09°03′E
103 *N13* **Gramat** Lot, S France 44°45′N 01°45′E
22 *H5* **Grambling** Louisiana, S USA 32°31′N 92°43′W
115 *C14* **Grámmos** ▲▲ Albania/Greece
96 *I9* **Grampian Mountains** ▲▲ C Scotland, United Kingdom
182 *L12* **Grampians, The** ▲▲ Victoria, SE Australia
98 *O9* **Gramsbergen** Overijssel, E Netherlands 52°37′N 06°39′E
113 *L21* **Gramsh** *var.* Gramshi. Elbasan, C Albania 40°52′N 20°12′E
Gramshi *see* Gramsh
Gran *see* Esztergom, Hungary
Gran *see* Hron
54 *F11* **Granada** Meta, C Colombia 03°33′N 73°44′W
42 *J10* **Granada** Granada, SW Nicaragua 11°55′N 85°58′W
105 *N14* **Granada** Andalucía, S Spain 37°13′N 03°41′W
37 *W6* **Granada** Colorado, C USA 38°00′N 102°18′W
42 *J11* **Granada** ◐ *department* SW Nicaragua
105 *N14* **Granada** ◐ *province* Andalucía, S Spain
63 *I21* **Gran Antiplanicie Central** *plain* S Argentina
97 *E17* **Granard** *Ir.* Gránard. C Ireland 53°47′N 07°30′W
Gránard *see* Granard
63 *J20* **Gran Bajo** *basin* S Argentina
63 *J15* **Gran Bajo del Gualicho** *basin* E Argentina
63 *I21* **Gran Bajo de San Julián** *basin* SE Argentina
25 *S7* **Granbury** Texas, SW USA 32°27′N 97°47′W
15 *P12* **Granby** Québec, SE Canada 45°23′N 72°44′W
27 *S8* **Granby** Missouri, C USA 36°55′N 94°14′W
37 *S3* **Granby, Lake** ▣ Colorado, C USA
64 *O12* **Gran Canaria** *var.* Grand Canary. *island* Islas Canarias, Spain, NE Atlantic Ocean
47 *T11* **Gran Chaco** *var.* Chaco. *lowland plain* South America
45 *R14* **Grand Anse** SW Grenada 12°01′N 61°45′W
Grand-Anse *see* Portsmouth
44 *G1* **Grand Bahama Island** *island* N Bahamas
Grand Balé *see* Tui
103 *U7* **Grand Ballon** *Ger.* Ballon de Guebwiller. ▲ NE France 47°53′N 07°06′E
13 *T13* **Grand Bank** Newfoundland, Newfoundland and Labrador, SE Canada 47°06′N 55°48′W
64 *I7* **Grand Banks of Newfoundland** *undersea feature* NW Atlantic Ocean 45°00′N 40°00′W
Grand Bassa *see* Buchanan
77 *N17* **Grand-Bassam** *var.* Bassam. SE Ivory Coast 05°14′N 03°45′W
14 *E16* **Grand Bend** Ontario, S Canada 43°17′N 81°46′W
76 *L17* **Grand-Bérébi** *var.* Grand-Béréby. SW Ivory Coast 04°38′N 06°55′W
Grand-Béréby *see* Grand-Bérébi
45 *X11* **Grand-Bourg** Marie-Galante, SE Guadeloupe 15°53′N 61°19′W
44 *M6* **Grand Caicos** *var.* Middle Caicos. *island* C Turks and Caicos Islands
14 *K12* **Grand Calumet, Île du** *island* Québec, SE Canada
97 *E18* **Grand Canal** *Ir.* An Chanáil Mhór. *canal* C Ireland
Grand Canal *see* Da Yunhe
Grand Canary *see* Gran Canaria
36 *K10* **Grand Canyon** Arizona, SW USA 36°01′N 112°10′W
36 *J9* **Grand Canyon** *canyon* Arizona, SW USA
Grand Canyon State *see* Arizona
44 *D8* **Grand Cayman** *island* SW Cayman Islands
11 *R14* **Grand Centre** Alberta, SW Canada 54°25′N 110°13′W
76 *L17* **Grand Cess** SE Liberia 04°36′N 08°12′W
108 *D12* **Grand Combin** ▲ S Switzerland 45°58′N 07°27′E
32 *K8* **Grand Coulee** Washington, NW USA 47°56′N 119°00′W
32 *J8* **Grand Coulee** *valley* Washington, NW USA
45 *X5* **Grand Cul-de-Sac Marin** *bay* N Guadeloupe
Grand Duchy of Luxembourg *see* Luxembourg
63 *I22* **Grande, Bahía** *bay* S Argentina
11 *N14* **Grande Cache** Alberta, W Canada 53°53′N 119°07′W
103 *U12* **Grande Casse** ▲ E France 45°22′N 06°50′E
Grande Comore *see* Ngazidja
61 *G18* **Grande, Cuchilla** *hill range* E Uruguay
45 *S5* **Grande de Añasco, Río** ≈ W Puerto Rico
Grande de Chiloé, Isla *see* Chiloé, Isla de
58 *J12* **Grande de Gurupá, Ilha** *river island* NE Brazil
57 *K21* **Grande de Lipez, Río** ≈ SW Bolivia
45 *U6* **Grande de Loíza, Río** ≈ E Puerto Rico
45 *T5* **Grande de Manatí, Río** ≈ C Puerto Rico
42 *L9* **Grande de Matagalpa, Río** ≈ C Nicaragua
40 *K12* **Grande de Santiago, Río** *var.* Santiago. ≈ C Mexico
43 *O15* **Grande de Térraba, Río** *var.* Río Térraba. ≈ SE Costa Rica
12 *J9* **Grande Deux, Réservoir la** ▣ Québec, E Canada
60 *O10* **Grande, Ilha** *island* SE Brazil
11 *O13* **Grande Prairie** Alberta, W Canada 55°10′N 118°52′W
74 *I8* **Grand Erg Occidental** *desert* W Algeria
74 *L9* **Grand Erg Oriental** *desert* Algeria/Tunisia
57 *M18* **Grande, Río** ≈ C Bolivia
59 *J20* **Grande, Rio** ≈ S Brazil
2 *F15* **Grande, Rio** *var.* Río Bravo, *Sp.* Río Bravo del Norte, Bravo del Norte. ≈ Mexico/USA
15 *Y7* **Grande-Rivière** Québec, SE Canada 48°27′N 64°37′W
15 *Y6* **Grande Rivière** ≈ Québec, SE Canada
44 *M8* **Grande-Rivière-du-Nord** N Haiti 19°36′N 72°10′W
62 *K9* **Grande, Salina** *var.* Gran Salitral. *salt lake* C Argentina
15 *S7* **Grandes-Bergeronnes** Québec, SE Canada 48°16′N 69°32′W
47 *W6* **Grande, Serra** ▲▲ W Brazil
40 *K4* **Grande, Sierra** ▲▲ N Mexico
103 *S12* **Grandes Rousses** ▲▲ E France
63 *K17* **Grandes, Salinas** *salt lake* E Argentina
45 *Y5* **Grande Terre** *island* E West Indies
15 *X5* **Grande-Vallée** Québec, SE Canada 49°14′N 65°08′W
45 *Y5* **Grande Vigie, Pointe de la** *headland* Grande Terre, N Guadeloupe 16°31′N 61°27′W
13 *N14* **Grand Falls** New Brunswick, SE Canada 47°02′N 67°46′W
13 *T11* **Grand Falls** Newfoundland, Newfoundland and Labrador, SE Canada 48°57′N 55°48′W
24 *L9* **Grandfalls** Texas, SW USA 31°20′N 102°51′W
21 *P9* **Grandfather Mountain** ▲ North Carolina, SE USA 36°06′N 81°48′W
26 *L13* **Grandfield** Oklahoma, C USA 34°15′N 98°40′W
11 *N17* **Grand Forks** British Columbia, SW Canada 49°02′N 118°30′W
29 *R4* **Grand Forks** North Dakota, N USA 47°54′N 97°03′W
31 *O9* **Grand Haven** Michigan, N USA 43°03′N 86°13′W
Grandichi *see* Hrandzichy
29 *P15* **Grand Island** Nebraska, C USA 40°55′N 98°20′W
31 *O3* **Grand Island** *island* Michigan, N USA
22 *K10* **Grand Isle** Louisiana, S USA 29°12′N 90°00′W
65 *A23* **Grand Jason** *island* Jason Islands, NW Falkland Islands
37 *P5* **Grand Junction** Colorado, C USA 39°03′N 108°33′W
20 *F10* **Grand Junction** Tennessee, S USA 35°03′N 89°11′W
14 *J9* **Grand-Lac-Victoria** Québec, SE Canada 47°33′N 77°28′W
14 *J9* **Grand lac Victoria** ◎ Québec, SE Canada
77 *N17* **Grand-Lahou** *var.* Grand Lahu. S Ivory Coast 05°09′N 05°01′W
Grand Lahu *see* Grand-Lahou
37 *S3* **Grand Lake** Colorado, C USA 40°15′N 105°49′W
13 *S11* **Grand Lake** ◎ Newfoundland and Labrador, E Canada
22 *G9* **Grand Lake** ◎ Louisiana, S USA
31 *R5* **Grand Lake** ◎ Michigan, N USA
31 *Q13* **Grand Lake** ▣ Ohio, N USA
27 *R9* **Grand Lake O' The Cherokees** *var.* Lake O' The Cherokees. ▣ Oklahoma, C USA
31 *Q9* **Grand Ledge** Michigan, N USA 42°45′N 84°45′W
102 *I8* **Grand-Lieu, Lac de** ◎ NW France
19 *U6* **Grand Manan Channel** *channel* Canada/USA
13 *O15* **Grand Manan Island** *island* New Brunswick, SE Canada
29 *Y4* **Grand Marais** Minnesota, N USA 47°45′N 90°19′W
15 *P10* **Grand-Mère** Québec, SE Canada 46°36′N 72°41′W
37 *P5* **Grand Mesa** ▲▲ Colorado, C USA
108 *C10* **Grand Muveran** ▲ W Switzerland 46°16′N 07°12′E
104 *G12* **Grândola** Setúbal, S Portugal 38°10′N 08°34′W
Grand Paradis *see* Gran Paradiso
187 *O15* **Grand Passage** *passage* N New Caledonia
77 *R16* **Grand-Popo** S Benin 06°19′N 01°50′E
29 *Z3* **Grand Portage** Minnesota, N USA 48°00′N 89°36′W
25 *T6* **Grand Prairie** Texas, SW USA 32°45′N 97°00′W
11 *W14* **Grand Rapids** Manitoba, C Canada 53°12′N 99°19′W
31 *P9* **Grand Rapids** Michigan, N USA 42°57′N 86°40′W
29 *V5* **Grand Rapids** Minnesota, N USA 47°14′N 93°31′W
14 *L10* **Grand-Remous** Québec, SE Canada 46°36′N 75°53′W
14 *F15* **Grand River** ≈ Ontario, S Canada
31 *P9* **Grand River** ≈ Michigan, N USA
27 *T3* **Grand River** ≈ Missouri, C USA
28 *M7* **Grand River** ≈ South Dakota, N USA
45 *Q11* **Grand' Rivière** N Martinique 14°52′N 61°11′W
32 *F11* **Grand Ronde** Oregon, NW USA 45°03′N 123°43′W
32 *L11* **Grand Ronde River** ≈ Oregon/Washington, NW USA
Grand-Saint-Bernard, Col du *see* Great Saint Bernard Pass
25 *V6* **Grand Saline** Texas, SW USA 32°40′N 95°42′W
55 *X10* **Grand-Santi** W French Guiana 04°19′N 54°24′W
Grandsee *see* Grandson
172 *J16* **Grand Sœur** *island* Les Sœurs, NE Seychelles
108 *B9* **Grandson** *prev.* Grandsee. Vaud, W Switzerland 46°49′N 06°39′E
33 *S14* **Grand Teton** ▲ Wyoming, C USA 43°44′N 110°48′W
31 *P5* **Grand Traverse Bay** *lake bay* Michigan, N USA
45 *N6* **Grand Turk** ○ (Turks and Caicos Islands) Grand Turk Island, S Turks and Caicos Islands 21°24′N 71°08′W
45 *N6* **Grand Turk Island** *island* SE Turks and Caicos Islands
103 *S13* **Grand Veymont** ▲ E France 44°51′N 05°32′E
11 *W15* **Grandview** Manitoba, S Canada 51°11′N 100°41′W
27 *R4* **Grandview** Missouri, C USA 38°53′N 94°31′W
36 *I10* **Grand Wash Cliffs** *cliff* Arizona, SW USA
14 *J8* **Granet, Lac** ◎ Québec, SE Canada
95 *L14* **Grangärde** Dalarna, C Sweden 60°15′N 15°00′E
44 *H12* **Grange Hill** W Jamaica 18°19′N 78°11′W
96 *J12* **Grangemouth** C Scotland, United Kingdom 56°01′N 03°44′W
25 *T10* **Granger** Texas, SW USA 30°43′N 97°26′W
32 *J10* **Granger** Washington, NW USA 46°20′N 120°11′W
33 *T17* **Granger** Wyoming, C USA 41°37′N 109°58′W
Granges *see* Grenchen
95 *L14* **Grängesberg** Dalarna, C Sweden 60°06′N 15°00′E
33 *N11* **Grangeville** Idaho, NW USA 45°55′N 116°07′W
10 *K13* **Granisle** British Columbia, SW Canada 54°55′N 126°14′W
30 *K15* **Granite City** Illinois, N USA 38°42′N 90°09′W
29 *S9* **Granite Falls** Minnesota, N USA 44°48′N 95°33′W
21 *Q9* **Granite Falls** North Carolina, SE USA 35°48′N 81°25′W
36 *K12* **Granite Mountain** ▲ Arizona, SW USA 34°38′N 112°34′W
33 *T12* **Granite Peak** ▲ Montana, NW USA 45°09′N 109°48′W
35 *T2* **Granite Peak** ▲ Nevada, W USA 41°40′N 117°35′W
36 *J3* **Granite Peak** ▲ Utah, W USA 40°09′N 113°18′W
Granite State *see* New Hampshire
107 *H24* **Granitola, Capo** *headland* Sicilia, Italy, C Mediterranean Sea 37°33′N 12°39′E
185 *H15* **Granity** West Coast, South Island, New Zealand 41°37′S 171°53′E
Gran Lago *see* Nicaragua, Lago de
63 *J18* **Gran Laguna Salada** ◎ S Argentina
Gran Malvina *see* West Falkland
95 *L18* **Gränna** Jönköping, S Sweden 58°02′N 14°30′E
105 *W5* **Granollers** *var.* Granollérs. Cataluña, NE Spain 41°37′N 02°18′E
Granollérs *see* Granollers
106 *A7* **Gran Paradiso** *Fr.* Grand Paradis. ▲ NW Italy 45°31′N 07°13′E
Gran Pilastro *see* Hochfeiler
Gran Salitral *see* Grande, Salina
Gran San Bernardo, Passo di *see* Great Saint Bernard Pass
Gran Santiago *see* Santiago
107 *J14* **Gran Sasso d'Italia** ▲▲ C Italy
100 *N11* **Gransee** Brandenburg, NE Germany 53°00′N 13°10′E
28 *L15* **Grant** Nebraska, C USA 40°50′N 101°43′W
27 *R1* **Grant City** Missouri, C USA 40°29′N 94°25′W
97 *N19* **Grantham** E England, United Kingdom 52°55′N 00°39′W
65 *D24* **Grantham Sound** *sound* East Falkland, Falkland Islands
194 *K13* **Grant Island** *island* Antarctica
45 *Z14* **Grantley Adams** ✈ (Bridgetown) SE Barbados 13°04′N 59°29′W
35 *S7* **Grant, Mount** ▲ Nevada, W USA 38°34′N 118°47′W
96 *J9* **Grantown-on-Spey** N Scotland, United Kingdom 57°11′N 03°53′W
35 *W8* **Grant Range** ▲▲ Nevada, W USA
37 *Q11* **Grants** New Mexico, SW USA 35°09′N 107°50′W
30 *I4* **Grantsburg** Wisconsin, N USA 45°47′N 92°40′W
32 *F15* **Grants Pass** Oregon, NW USA 42°26′N 123°20′W
36 *K3* **Grantsville** Utah, W USA 40°36′N 112°27′W
21 *R4* **Grantsville** West Virginia, NE USA 38°55′N 81°07′W
102 *I5* **Granville** Manche, N France 48°50′N 01°35′W
11 *V12* **Granville Lake** ◎ Manitoba, C Canada
25 *V8* **Grapeland** Texas, SW USA 31°29′N 95°28′W
25 *T6* **Grapevine** Texas, SW USA 32°55′N 97°04′W
83 *K20* **Graskop** Mpumalanga, NE South Africa 24°58′S 30°49′E
95 *P14* **Gräsö** Uppsala, C Sweden 60°22′N 18°30′E
93 *I19* **Gräsö** *island* C Sweden
103 *U15* **Grasse** Alpes-Maritimes, SE France 43°42′N 06°52′E
18 *E14* **Grassflat** Pennsylvania, NE USA 41°00′N 78°04′W
33 *U9* **Grassrange** Montana, NW USA 47°02′N 108°48′W
18 *J6* **Grass River** ≈ New York, NE USA
35 *P6* **Grass Valley** California, W USA 39°12′N 121°04′W
183 *N14* **Grassy** Tasmania, SE Australia 40°03′S 144°04′E
28 *K4* **Grassy Butte** North Dakota, N USA 47°20′N 103°13′W
21 *R5* **Grassy Knob** ▲ West Virginia, NE USA 38°04′N 80°31′W
95 *G24* **Gråsten** *var.* Graasten. Syddanmark, SW Denmark 54°55′N 09°37′E
95 *J18* **Grästorp** Västra Götaland, S Sweden 58°20′N 12°40′E
Gratianopolis *see* Grenoble
109 *V8* **Gratwein** Steiermark, SE Austria 47°08′N 15°20′E
Gratz *see* Graz
104 *K2* **Grau** *var.* Grado. Asturias, N Spain 43°23′N 06°04′W
108 *I9* **Graubünden** *Fr.* Grisons, *It.* Grigioni. ◐ *canton* SE Switzerland
Graudenz *see* Grudziądz
103 *N15* **Graulhet** Tarn, S France 43°45′N 01°58′E
105 *T4* **Graus** Aragón, NE Spain 42°11′N 00°21′E
61 *I16* **Gravataí** Rio Grande do Sul, S Brazil 29°55′S 51°00′W
98 *L13* **Grave** Noord-Brabant, SE Netherlands 51°45′N 05°45′E
11 *T17* **Gravelbourg** Saskatchewan, S Canada 49°53′N 106°33′W
103 *N1* **Gravelines** Nord, N France 51°00′N 02°07′E
Graven *see* Grez-Doiceau
14 *H13* **Gravenhurst** Ontario, S Canada 44°55′N 79°22′W
33 *O10* **Grave Peak** ▲ Idaho, NW USA 46°24′N 114°43′W
102 *I11* **Grave, Pointe de** *headland* W France 45°33′N 01°24′W
183 *S4* **Gravesend** New South Wales, SE Australia 29°37′S 150°15′E
97 *P22* **Gravesend** SE England, United Kingdom 51°27′N 00°24′E
107 *N17* **Gravina in Puglia** Puglia, SE Italy 40°48′N 16°25′E
103 *S8* **Gray** Haute-Saône, E France 47°28′N 05°34′E
23 *T4* **Gray** Georgia, SE USA 33°00′N 83°31′W
195 *V16* **Gray, Cape** *headland* Antarctica 67°30′S 143°30′E
32 *F9* **Grayland** Washington, NW USA 46°46′N 124°07′W
39 *N10* **Grayling** Alaska, USA 62°55′N 160°07′W
31 *Q6* **Grayling** Michigan, N USA 44°40′N 84°43′W
32 *F9* **Grays Harbor** *inlet* Washington, NW USA
21 *O5* **Grayson** Kentucky, S USA 38°21′N 82°59′W
37 *S4* **Grays Peak** ▲ Colorado, C USA 39°37′N 105°49′W
30 *M16* **Grayville** Illinois, N USA 38°15′N 87°59′W
109 *V8* **Graz** *prev.* Gratz. Steiermark, SE Austria 47°05′N 15°23′E
104 *L15* **Grazalema** Andalucía, S Spain 36°46′N 05°23′W
113 *P15* **Grdelica** Serbia, SE Serbia 42°54′N 22°05′E
44 *H1* **Great Abaco** *var.* Abaco Island. *island* N Bahamas
Great Admiralty Island *see* Manus Island
Great Alfold *see* Great Hungarian Plain
Great Ararat *see* Büyükağrı Dağı
181 *U8* **Great Artesian Basin** *lowlands* Queensland, C Australia
181 *O12* **Great Australian Bight** *bight* S Australia
64 *E11* **Great Bahama Bank** *undersea feature* E Gulf of Mexico 23°15′N 78°00′W
184 *M4* **Great Barrier Island** *island* N New Zealand
181 *X4* **Great Barrier Reef** *reef* Queensland, NE Australia
18 *L11* **Great Barrington** Massachusetts, NE USA 42°11′N 73°20′W
0 *F10* **Great Basin** *basin* W USA
8 *I8* **Great Bear Lake** *Fr.* Grand Lac de l'Ours. ◎ Northwest Territories, NW Canada
Great Belt *see* Storebælt
26 *L5* **Great Bend** Kansas, C USA 38°22′N 98°47′W
Great Bermuda *see* Bermuda
97 *A20* **Great Blasket Island** *Ir.* An Blascaod Mór. *island* SW Ireland
Great Britain *see* Britain
151 *Q23* **Great Channel** *channel* Andaman Sea/Indian Ocean
166 *J10* **Great Coco Island** *island* SW Burma (Myanmar)
Great Crosby *see* Crosby
21 *X7* **Great Dismal Swamp** *wetland* North Carolina/Virginia, SE USA
33 *V16* **Great Divide Basin** *basin* Wyoming, C USA
181 *W7* **Great Dividing Range** ▲▲ NE Australia
14 *D12* **Great Duck Island** *island* Ontario, S Canada
Great Elder Reservoir *see* Waconda Lake
44 *G8* **Greater Antilles** *island group* West Indies
129 *V16* **Greater Sunda Islands** *var.* Sunda Islands. *island group* Indonesia
184 *I1* **Great Exhibition Bay** *inlet* North Island, New Zealand
44 *H4* **Great Exuma Island** *island* C Bahamas
33 *R8* **Great Falls** Montana, NW USA 47°30′N 111°18′W
21 *R11* **Great Falls** South Carolina, SE USA 34°34′N 80°54′W
84 *F9* **Great Fisher Bank** *undersea feature* C North Sea 57°00′N 04°00′E
Great Glen *see* Mor, Glen
Great Grimsby *see* Grimsby
44 *I4* **Great Guana Cay** *island* C Bahamas
64 *I5* **Great Hellefiske Bank** *undersea feature* N Atlantic Ocean
111 *L24* **Great Hungarian Plain** *var.* Great Alfold, Plain of Hungary, *Hung.* Alföld. *plain* SE Europe
44 *L7* **Great Inagua** *var.* Inagua Islands. *island* S Bahamas
Great Indian Desert *see* Thar Desert
83 *G25* **Great Karoo** *var.* Great Karroo, High Veld, *Afr.* Groot Karoo, Hoë Karoo. *plateau region* S South Africa
Great Karroo *see* Great Karoo
Great Kei *see* Nciba
Great Khingan Range *see* Da Hinggan Ling
14 *E11* **Great La Cloche Island** *island* Ontario, S Canada
183 *P16* **Great Lake** ◎ Tasmania, SE Australia
Great Lake *see* Tônlé Sap
11 *R15* **Great Lakes** *lakes* Ontario, Canada/USA
Great Lakes State *see* Michigan
97 *L20* **Great Malvern** W England, United Kingdom 52°07′N 02°19′W
184 *M5* **Great Mercury Island** *island* N New Zealand
Great Meteor Seamount *see* Great Meteor Tablemount
64 *K10* **Great Meteor Tablemount** *var.* Great Meteor Seamount. *undersea feature* E Atlantic Ocean 30°00′N 28°30′W
31 *Q14* **Great Miami River** ≈ Ohio, N USA
151 *Q24* **Great Nicobar** *island* Nicobar Islands, India, NE Indian Ocean
97 *O19* **Great Ouse** *var.* Ouse. ≈ E England, United Kingdom
183 *Q17* **Great Oyster Bay** *bay* Tasmania, SE Australia
44 *I13* **Great Pedro Bluff** *headland* W Jamaica 17°51′N 77°44′W
21 *T12* **Great Pee Dee River** ≈ North Carolina/South Carolina, SE USA
129 *W9* **Great Plain of China** *plain* E China
0 *F12* **Great Plains** *var.* High Plains. *plains* Canada/USA
37 *W6* **Great Plains Reservoirs** ▣ Colorado, C USA
19 *Q13* **Great Point** *headland* Nantucket Island, Massachusetts, NE USA 41°23′N 70°03′W
68 *I13* **Great Rift Valley** *var.* Rift Valley. *depression* Asia/Africa
81 *I23* **Great Ruaha** ≈ S Tanzania
18 *K10* **Great Sacandaga Lake** ▣ New York, NE USA
108 *C12* **Great Saint Bernard Pass** *Fr.* Col du Grand-Saint-Bernard, *It.* Passo del Gran San Bernardo. *pass* Italy/Switzerland
44 *F1* **Great Sale Cay** *island* N Bahamas
Great Salt Desert *see* Kavīr, Dasht-e
36 *K1* **Great Salt Lake** *salt lake* Utah, W USA
36 *J3* **Great Salt Lake Desert** *plain* Utah, W USA
26 *M8* **Great Salt Plains Lake** ▣ Oklahoma, C USA
75 *T9* **Great Sand Sea** *desert* Egypt/Libya
180 *L6* **Great Sandy Desert** *desert* Western Australia
Great Sandy Desert *see* Ar Rub' al Khālī
Great Sandy Island *see* Fraser Island
187 *Y13* **Great Sea Reef** *reef* Vanua Levu, N Fiji
38 *H17* **Great Sitkin Island** *island* Aleutian Islands, Alaska, USA
8 *J10* **Great Slave Lake** *Fr.* Grand Lac des Esclaves. ◎ Northwest Territories, NW Canada
21 *O10* **Great Smoky Mountains** ▲▲ North Carolina/Tennessee, SE USA
10 *L11* **Great Snow Mountain** ▲ British Columbia, W Canada 57°22′N 124°08′W
Great Socialist People's Libyan Arab Jamahiriya *see* Libya
64 *A12* **Great Sound** *sound* Bermuda, NW Atlantic Ocean
180 *M10* **Great Victoria Desert** *desert* South Australia/Western Australia
194 *H2* **Great Wall** *Chinese research station* South Shetland Islands, Antarctica 61°57′S 58°23′W
19 *T7* **Great Wass Island** *island* Maine, NE USA
97 *Q19* **Great Yarmouth** *var.* Yarmouth. E England, United Kingdom 52°37′N 01°44′E
139 *S1* **Great Zab** *Ar.* Az Zāb al Kabīr, *Kurd.* Zē-i Bādīnān, *Turk.* Büyükzap Suyu. ≈ Iraq/Turkey
95 *I17* **Grebbestad** Västra Götaland, S Sweden 58°42′N 11°15′E
Grebenka *see* Hrebinka
42 *M13* **Grecia** Alajuela, C Costa Rica 10°04′N 84°19′W
61 *E18* **Greco** Río Negro, W Uruguay 32°49′S 57°03′W
Greco, Cape *see* Gkréko, Akrotíri
104 *L8* **Gredos, Sierra de** ▲▲ W Spain
18 *F9* **Greece** New York, NE USA 43°12′N 77°41′W
115 *E17* **Greece** *off.* Hellenic Republic, *Gk.* Ellás; *anc.* Hellas. ◆ *republic* SE Europe
Greece Central *see* Stereá Elláda
Greece West *see* Dytikí Elláda
37 *T3* **Greeley** Colorado, C USA 40°21′N 104°41′W
29 *P14* **Greeley** Nebraska, C USA 41°33′N 98°31′W
122 *K3* **Greem-Bell, Ostrov** *Eng.* Graham Bell Island. *island* Zemlya Frantsa-Iosifa, N Russian Federation
30 *M6* **Green Bay** Wisconsin, N USA 44°32′N 88°W
31 *N6* **Green Bay** *lake bay* Michigan/Wisconsin, N USA

◆ Country
● Country Capital
◇ Dependent Territory
○ Dependent Territory Capital
◐ Administrative Regions
✈ International Airport
▲ Mountain
▲▲ Mountain Range
Volcano
≈ River
◎ Lake
▣ Reservoir

21 *S5* **Greenbrier River** ~ West Virginia, NE USA
29 *S2* **Greenbush** Minnesota, N USA *48°42′N 96°10′W*
183 *R12* **Green Cape** *headland* New South Wales, SE Australia *37°15′S 150°03′E*
31 *O14* **Greencastle** Indiana, N USA *39°38′N 86°51′W*
18 *F16* **Greencastle** Pennsylvania, NE USA *39°47′N 77°43′W*
27 *T2* **Green City** Missouri, C USA *40°16′N 92°57′W*
21 *O9* **Greeneville** Tennessee, S USA *36°10′N 82°50′W*
35 *O11* **Greenfield** California, W USA *36°19′N 121°15′W*
31 *P14* **Greenfield** Indiana, N USA *39°47′N 85°46′W*
29 *U15* **Greenfield** Iowa, C USA *41°18′N 94°27′W*
18 *M11* **Greenfield** Massachusetts, NE USA *42°33′N 72°34′W*
27 *S7* **Greenfield** Missouri, C USA *37°25′N 93°50′W*
31 *S14* **Greenfield** Ohio, N USA *39°21′N 83°22′W*
20 *G8* **Greenfield** Tennessee, S USA *36°09′N 88°48′W*
30 *M9* **Greenfield** Wisconsin, N USA *42°55′N 87°59′W*
27 *T9* **Green Forest** Arkansas, C USA *36°19′N 93°24′W*
37 *T7* **Greenhorn Mountain** ▲ Colorado, C USA *37°50′N 104°59′W*
Green Island *see* Lü Dao
186 *I6* **Green Islands** *var.* Nissan Islands. *island group* NE Papua New Guinea
11 *S14* **Green Lake** Saskatchewan, C Canada *54°15′N 107°51′W*
30 *L8* **Green Lake** ◎ Wisconsin, N USA
197 *O14* **Greenland** *Dan.* Grønland, *Inuit* Kalaallit Nunaat. ◇ *Danish external territory* NE North America
84 *D4* **Greenland** *island* NE North America
197 *R13* **Greenland Plain** *undersea feature* N Greenland Sea
197 *R14* **Greenland Sea** *sea* Arctic Ocean
37 *R4* **Green Mountain Reservoir** ⊠ Colorado, C USA
18 *M8* **Green Mountains** ▲▲ Vermont, NE USA
Green Mountain State *see* Vermont
96 *H12* **Greenock** W Scotland, United Kingdom *55°57′N 04°45′W*
39 *T5* **Greenough, Mount** ▲ Alaska, USA *69°15′N 141°37′W*
186 *A6* **Green River** Sandaun, NW Papua New Guinea *03°54′S 141°08′E*
37 *N5* **Green River** Utah, W USA *39°00′N 110°07′W*
33 *U17* **Green River** Wyoming, C USA *41°33′N 109°27′W*
16 *H9* **Green River** ~ W USA
30 *K11* **Green River** ~ Illinois, N USA
20 *J7* **Green River** ~ Kentucky, C USA
28 *K5* **Green River** ~ North Dakota, N USA
37 *N6* **Green River** ~ Utah, W USA
33 *T16* **Green River** ~ Wyoming, C USA
20 *L7* **Green River Lake** ⊠ Kentucky, S USA
23 *O5* **Greensboro** Alabama, S USA *32°42′N 87°36′W*
23 *U3* **Greensboro** Georgia, SE USA *33°34′N 83°10′W*
21 *T9* **Greensboro** North Carolina, SE USA *36°04′N 79°48′W*
31 *P14* **Greensburg** Indiana, N USA *39°20′N 85°28′W*
26 *K6* **Greensburg** Kansas, C USA *37°36′N 99°17′W*
20 *L7* **Greensburg** Kentucky, S USA *37°14′N 85°30′W*
18 *C15* **Greensburg** Pennsylvania, NE USA *40°18′N 79°32′W*
37 *O13* **Greens Peak** ▲ Arizona, SW USA *34°06′N 109°34′W*
21 *V12* **Green Swamp** *wetland* North Carolina, SE USA
21 *O4* **Greenup** Kentucky, S USA *38°34′N 82°49′W*
36 *M16* **Green Valley** Arizona, SW USA *31°49′N 111°00′W*
76 *K17* **Greenville** *var.* Sino, Sinoe. SE Liberia *05°01′N 09°03′W*
23 *P6* **Greenville** Alabama, S USA *31°49′N 86°37′W*
23 *T8* **Greenville** Florida, SE USA *30°28′N 83°37′W*
23 *S4* **Greenville** Georgia, SE USA *33°03′N 84°42′W*
30 *L15* **Greenville** Illinois, N USA *38°53′N 89°24′W*
20 *I7* **Greenville** Kentucky, S USA *37°11′N 87°11′W*
19 *Q5* **Greenville** Maine, NE USA *45°26′N 69°36′W*
31 *P9* **Greenville** Michigan, N USA *43°10′N 85°15′W*
22 *J4* **Greenville** Mississippi, S USA *33°24′N 91°03′W*
21 *W9* **Greenville** North Carolina, SE USA *35°36′N 77°23′W*
31 *Q13* **Greenville** Ohio, N USA *40°06′N 84°37′W*
19 *O12* **Greenville** Rhode Island, NE USA *41°52′N 71°33′W*
21 *P11* **Greenville** South Carolina, SE USA *34°51′N 82°24′W*
25 *U6* **Greenville** Texas, SW USA *33°09′N 96°07′W*
31 *T12* **Greenwich** Ohio, N USA *41°01′N 82°31′W*
27 *S11* **Greenwood** Arkansas, C USA *35°13′N 94°15′W*
31 *O14* **Greenwood** Indiana, N USA *39°38′N 86°06′W*
22 *K4* **Greenwood** Mississippi, S USA *33°30′N 90°11′W*
21 *P12* **Greenwood** South Carolina, SE USA *34°11′N 82°10′W*
21 *Q12* **Greenwood, Lake** ⊠ South Carolina, SE USA
21 *P11* **Greer** South Carolina, SE USA *34°56′N 82°13′W*
27 *V10* **Greers Ferry Lake** ⊠ Arkansas, C USA
27 *S13* **Greeson, Lake** ⊠ Arkansas, C USA
45 *N8* **Gregorio Luperón** ✈ N Dominican Republic *19°43′N 70°43′W*
29 *O12* **Gregory** South Dakota, N USA *43°11′N 99°26′W*
182 *J3* **Gregory, Lake** *salt lake* South Australia
180 *J9* **Gregory Lake** ◎ Western Australia
181 *V5* **Gregory Range** ▲▲ Queensland, E Australia
Greifenberg/Greifenberg in Pommern *see* Gryfice
Greifenhagen *see* Gryfino
100 *O8* **Greifswald** Mecklenburg-Vorpommern, NE Germany *54°04′N 13°24′E*
100 *O8* **Greifswalder Bodden** *bay* NE Germany
109 *U4* **Grein** Oberösterreich, N Austria *48°14′N 14°50′E*
101 *M17* **Greiz** Thüringen, C Germany *50°40′N 12°11′E*
125 *V14* **Gremyachinsk** Permskiy Kray, NW Russian Federation *58°33′N 57°52′E*
Grenå *see* Grenaa
95 *H21* **Grenaa** *var.* Grenå. Midtjylland, C Denmark *56°25′N 10°53′E*
22 *L3* **Grenada** Mississippi, S USA *33°46′N 89°48′W*
45 *W15* **Grenada** ◆ *commonwealth republic* SE West Indies
47 *S4* **Grenada** *island* Grenada
47 *R4* **Grenada Basin** *undersea feature* W Atlantic Ocean *13°30′N 62°00′W*
22 *L3* **Grenada Lake** ⊠ Mississippi, S USA
45 *Y14* **Grenadines, The** *island group* Grenada/St Vincent and the Grenadines
108 *D7* **Grenchen** *Fr.* Granges. Solothurn, NW Switzerland *47°13′N 07°24′E*
183 *Q9* **Grenfell** New South Wales, SE Australia *33°54′S 148°09′E*
11 *V16* **Grenfell** Saskatchewan, S Canada *50°24′N 102°56′W*
92 *J1* **Grenivík** Nordhurland Eystra, N Iceland *65°57′N 18°10′W*
103 *S12* **Grenoble** *anc.* Cularo, Gratianopolis. Isère, E France *45°11′N 05°42′E*
28 *J2* **Grenora** North Dakota, N USA *48°36′N 103°57′W*
92 *N8* **Grense-Jakobselv** Finnmark, N Norway *69°46′N 30°39′E*
45 *S14* **Grenville** E Grenada *12°07′N 61°37′W*
32 *G11* **Gresham** Oregon, NW USA *45°30′N 122°25′W*
Gresk *see* Hresk
106 *B7* **Gressoney-St-Jean** Valle d'Aosta, NW Italy *45°48′N 07°49′E*
22 *K9* **Gretna** Louisiana, S USA *29°54′N 90°03′W*
21 *T7* **Gretna** Virginia, NE USA *36°57′N 79°21′W*
98 *F13* **Grevelingen** *inlet* S North Sea
100 *F13* **Greven** Nordrhein-Westfalen, NW Germany *52°07′N 07°38′E*
115 *D15* **Grevená** Dytikí Makedonía, N Greece *40°05′N 21°26′E*
101 *D16* **Grevenbroich** Nordrhein-Westfalen, W Germany *51°06′N 06°34′E*
99 *N24* **Grevenmacher** Grevenmacher, E Luxembourg *49°41′N 06°27′E*
99 *M24* **Grevenmacher** ◈ *district* E Luxembourg
100 *K9* **Grevesmülhen** Mecklenburg-Vorpommern, N Germany *53°52′N 11°12′E*
185 *H16* **Grey** ~ South Island, New Zealand
33 *V12* **Greybull** Wyoming, C USA *44°29′N 108°03′W*
33 *U13* **Greybull River** ~ Wyoming, C USA
65 *A24* **Grey Channel** *sound* Falkland Islands
Greyerzer See *see* Gruyère, Lac de la
13 *T10* **Grey Islands** *island group* Newfoundland and Labrador, E Canada
18 *L10* **Greylock, Mount** ▲ Massachusetts, NE USA *42°38′N 73°09′W*
185 *G17* **Greymouth** West Coast, South Island, New Zealand *42°29′S 171°14′E*
181 *U10* **Grey Range** ▲▲ New South Wales/Queensland, E Australia
97 *G18* **Greystones** *Ir.* Na Clocha Liatha. E Ireland *53°08′N 06°05′W*
185 *M14* **Greytown** Wellington, North Island, New Zealand *41°04′S 175°29′E*
83 *K23* **Greytown** KwaZulu/Natal, E South Africa *29°04′S 30°35′E*
Greytown *see* San Juan del Norte
99 *H19* **Grez-Doiceau** *Dut.* Graven. Walloon Brabant, C Belgium *50°43′N 04°41′E*
115 *J19* **Griá, Akrotírio** *headland* Ándros, Kykládes, Greece, Aegean Sea *37°54′N 24°57′E*
127 *N8* **Gribanovskiy** Voronezhskaya Oblast', W Russian Federation *51°27′N 41°53′E*
78 *I13* **Gribingui** ~ N Central African Republic
35 *O6* **Gridley** California, W USA *39°21′N 121°41′W*
83 *G23* **Griekwastad** *var.* Griquatown. Northern Cape, C South Africa *28°50′S 23°16′E*
23 *S4* **Griffin** Georgia, SE USA *33°15′N 84°17′W*
183 *O9* **Griffith** New South Wales, SE Australia *34°18′S 146°04′E*
14 *F13* **Griffith Island** *island* Ontario, S Canada
21 *W10* **Grifton** North Carolina, SE USA *35°22′N 77°26′W*
Grigioni *see* Graubünden
119 *H14* **Grigiškes** Vilnius, SE Lithuania *54°42′N 25°00′E*
117 *N10* **Grigoriopol** C Moldova *47°09′N 29°18′E*
147 *X7* **Grigor'yevka** Issyk-Kul'skaya Oblast', E Kyrgyzstan *42°43′N 77°27′E*
193 *U8* **Grijalva Ridge** *undersea feature* E Pacific Ocean
41 *U15* **Grijalva, Río** *var.* Tabasco. ~ Guatemala/Mexico
98 *N5* **Grijpskerk** Groningen, NE Netherlands *53°15′N 06°18′E*
83 *C22* **Grillenthal** Karas, SW Namibia *26°55′S 15°24′E*
79 *J15* **Grimari** Ouaka, C Central African Republic *05°44′N 20°02′E*
Grimaylov *see* Hrymayliv
99 *G18* **Grimbergen** Vlaams Brabant, C Belgium *50°56′N 04°22′E*
183 *N15* **Grim, Cape** *headland* Tasmania, SE Australia *40°42′S 144°42′E*
100 *N8* **Grimmen** Mecklenburg-Vorpommern, NE Germany *54°06′N 13°03′E*
14 *G16* **Grimsby** Ontario, S Canada *43°12′N 79°35′W*
97 *O17* **Grimsby** *prev.* Great Grimsby. E England, United Kingdom *53°35′N 00°05′W*
92 *J1* **Grímsey** *var.* Grimsey. *island* N Iceland
Grimsey *see* Grímsey
11 *O12* **Grimshaw** Alberta, W Canada *56°11′N 117°37′W*
95 *F18* **Grimstad** Aust-Agder, S Norway *58°20′N 08°35′E*
92 *H4* **Grindavík** Sudurnes, W Iceland *65°57′N 18°10′W*
108 *F9* **Grindelwald** Bern, S Switzerland *46°37′N 08°04′E*
95 *F23* **Grindsted** Syddtjylland, W Denmark *55°46′N 08°56′E*
29 *W14* **Grinnell** Iowa, C USA *41°44′N 92°43′W*
109 *U10* **Grintovec** ▲ N Slovenia *46°21′N 14°31′E*
Griquatown *see* Griekwastad
9 *N4* **Grise Fiord** *var* Aujuittuq. Northwest Territories, Ellesmere Island, N Canada *76°10′N 83°15′W*
182 *H1* **Griselda, Lake** *salt lake* South Australia
Grisons *see* Graubünden
95 *P14* **Grisslehamn** Stockholm, C Sweden *60°04′N 18°50′E*
29 *T15* **Griswold** Iowa, C USA *41°14′N 95°08′W*
102 *M1* **Griz Nez, Cap** *headland* N France *50°51′N 01°34′E*
112 *P13* **Grljan** Serbia, E Serbia *43°52′N 22°18′E*
112 *E11* **Grmeč** ▲▲ NW Bosnia and Herzegovina
99 *H16* **Grobbendonk** Antwerpen, N Belgium *51°12′N 04°41′E*
Grobin *see* Grobiņa
118 *C10* **Grobiņa** *Ger.* Grobin. W Latvia *56°32′N 21°12′E*
83 *K20* **Groblersdal** Mpumalanga, NE South Africa *25°15′S 29°25′E*
83 *G23* **Groblershoop** Northern Cape, W South Africa *28°51′S 22°01′E*
Gródek Jagielloński *see* Horodok
109 *Q6* **Grödig** Salzburg, W Austria *47°42′N 13°06′E*
111 *H15* **Grodków** Opolskie, S Poland *50°42′N 17°23′E*
Grodnenskaya Oblast' *see* Hrodzyenskaya Voblasts'
Grodno *see* Hrodna
110 *L12* **Grodzisk Mazowiecki** Mazowieckie, C Poland *52°09′N 20°38′E*
110 *F12* **Grodzisk Wielkopolski** Wielkopolskie, C Poland *52°13′N 16°21′E*
Grodzyanka *see* Hradzyanka
98 *O12* **Groenlo** Gelderland, E Netherlands *52°02′N 06°36′E*
83 *E22* **Groenrivier** Karas, SE Namibia *27°27′S 18°52′E*
25 *U8* **Groesbeck** Texas, SW USA *31°31′N 96°35′W*
98 *L13* **Groesbeek** Gelderland, SE Netherlands *51°47′N 05°56′E*
102 *G7* **Groix, Îles de** *island group* NW France
110 *M12* **Grójec** Mazowieckie, C Poland *51°51′N 20°52′E*
65 *K15* **Gröll Seamount** *undersea feature* C Atlantic Ocean *12°54′S 33°24′W*
100 *E13* **Gronau** *var.* Gronau in Westfalen. Nordrhein-Westfalen, NW Germany *52°13′N 07°02′E*
Gronau in Westfalen *see* Gronau
93 *F15* **Grong** Nord-Trøndelag, C Norway *64°29′N 12°19′E*
95 *N22* **Grönhögen** Kalmar, S Sweden *56°16′N 16°09′E*
98 *N5* **Groningen** Groningen, NE Netherlands *53°13′N 06°35′E*
55 *W9* **Groningen** Saramacca, N Surinam *05°45′N 55°31′W*
98 *N5* **Groningen** ◈ *province* NE Netherlands
Grønland *see* Greenland
108 *H11* **Grono** Graubünden, S Switzerland *46°15′N 09°07′E*
95 *M20* **Grönskåra** Kalmar, S Sweden *57°04′N 15°45′E*
25 *O2* **Groom** Texas, SW USA *35°12′N 101°06′W*
35 *W9* **Groom Lake** ◎ Nevada, W USA
83 *H25* **Groot** ~ S South Africa
181 *S2* **Groote Eylandt** *island* Northern Territory, N Australia
98 *M6* **Grootegast** Groningen, NE Netherlands *53°11′N 06°12′E*
83 *D17* **Grootfontein** Otjozondjupa, N Namibia *19°32′S 18°05′E*
83 *E22* **Groot Karasberge** ▲▲ S Namibia
Groot Karoo *see* Great Karoo
Groot-Kei *see* Nciba
15 *V6* **Grosses-Roches** Québec, SE Canada *48°55′N 67°06′W*
109 *V2* **Gross-Siegharts** Niederösterreich, N Austria *48°48′N 15°25′E*
45 *T10* **Gros Islet** N Saint Lucia *14°04′N 60°57′W*
44 *L8* **Gros-Morne** NW Haiti *19°45′N 72°46′W*
13 *S11* **Gros Morne** ▲ Newfoundland, Newfoundland and Labrador, E Canada *49°38′N 57°45′W*
103 *R9* **Grosne** ~ C France
45 *S12* **Gros Piton** ▲ SW Saint Lucia *13°48′N 61°04′W*
Grossa, Isola *see* Dugi Otok
Grossbetschkerek *see* Zrenjanin
Grosse Isper *see* Grosse Ysper
Grosse Kokel *see* Târnava Mare
101 *M21* **Grosse Laaber** *var.* Grosse Laber. ~ SE Germany
Grosse Laber *see* Grosse Laaber
Grosse Morava *see* Velika Morava
101 *O15* **Grossenhain** Sachsen, E Germany *51°18′N 13°31′E*
109 *Y4* **Grossenzersdorf** Niederösterreich, NE Austria *48°12′N 16°33′E*
101 *O21* **Grosser Arber** ▲ SE Germany *49°07′N 13°10′E*
101 *K17* **Grosser Beerberg** ▲ C Germany *50°39′N 10°45′E*
101 *G18* **Grosser Feldberg** ▲ W Germany *50°13′N 08°28′E*
109 *O8* **Grosser Löffler** *It.* Monte Lovello. ▲ Austria/Italy *47°02′N 11°56′E*
109 *N8* **Grosser Möseler** *var.* Mesule. ▲ Austria/Italy *47°01′N 11°52′E*
100 *J8* **Grosser Plöner See** ◎ N Germany
101 *O21* **Grosser Rachel** ▲ SE Germany *48°59′N 13°23′E*
Grosser Sund *see* Suur Väin
109 *P8* **Grosses Wiesbachhorn** *var.* Wiesbachhorn. ▲ W Austria *47°09′N 12°44′E*
106 *F13* **Grosseto** Toscana, C Italy *42°45′N 11°07′E*
101 *M22* **Grosse Vils** ~ SE Germany
109 *U4* **Grosse Ysper** *var.* Grosse Isper. ~ N Austria
101 *G19* **Gross-Gerau** Hessen, W Germany *49°55′N 08°28′E*
109 *U3* **Gross Gerungs** Niederösterreich, N Austria *48°33′N 14°58′E*
109 *P8* **Grossglockner** ▲ W Austria *47°05′N 12°39′E*
Grosskanizsa *see* Nagykanizsa
Gross-Karol *see* Carei
Grosskikinda *see* Kikinda
109 *W9* **Grossklein** Steiermark, SE Austria *46°43′N 15°24′E*
Grosskoppe *see* Velká Deštná
Grossmeseritsch *see* Velké Meziříčí
Grossmichel *see* Michalovce
101 *H19* **Grossostheim** Bayern, C Germany *49°54′N 09°03′E*
109 *X7* **Grosspetersdorf** Burgenland, SE Austria *47°15′N 16°19′E*
109 *T5* **Grossraming** Oberösterreich, C Austria *47°54′N 14°34′E*
101 *P14* **Grossräschen** Brandenburg, E Germany *51°34′N 14°00′E*
Grossrauschenbach *see* Revúca
Gross-Sankt-Johannis *see* Suure-Jaani
Gross-Schlatten *see* Abrud
Gross-Skaisgirren *see* Bol'shakovo
Gross-Steffelsdorf *see* Rimavská Sobota
Gross Strehlitz *see* Strzelce Opolskie
109 *O8* **Grossvenediger** ▲ W Austria *47°07′N 12°19′E*
Grosswardein *see* Oradea
Gross Wartenberg *see* Syców
109 *U11* **Grosuplje** C Slovenia *46°00′N 14°36′E*
99 *H17* **Grote Nete** ~ N Belgium
94 *E10* **Grotli** Oppland, S Norway *62°02′N 07°36′E*
19 *N13* **Groton** Connecticut, NE USA *41°20′N 72°03′W*
29 *P8* **Groton** South Dakota, N USA *45°27′N 98°06′W*
107 *P18* **Grottaglie** Puglia, SE Italy *40°32′N 17°26′E*
107 *L17* **Grottaminarda** Campania, S Italy *41°04′N 15°02′E*
106 *K13* **Grottammare** Marche, C Italy *43°00′N 13°52′E*
21 *U5* **Grottoes** Virginia, NE USA *38°16′N 78°49′W*
98 *L6* **Grou** *Dutch.* Grouw. Fryslân, N Netherlands *53°07′N 05°51′E*
13 *N10* **Groulx, Monts** ▲▲ Québec, E Canada
14 *E7* **Groundhog** ~ Ontario, S Canada
36 *J1* **Grouse Creek** Utah, W USA *41°41′N 113°52′W*
36 *J1* **Grouse Creek Mountains** ▲▲ Utah, W USA
Grouw *see* Grou
27 *R8* **Grove** Oklahoma, C USA *36°35′N 94°46′W*
31 *S13* **Grove City** Ohio, N USA *39°52′N 83°05′W*
18 *B13* **Grove City** Pennsylvania, NE USA *41°09′N 80°02′W*
23 *O6* **Grove Hill** Alabama, S USA *31°42′N 87°46′W*
33 *S15* **Grover** Wyoming, C USA *42°48′N 110°57′W*
35 *P13* **Grover City** California, W USA *35°08′N 120°37′W*
25 *Y11* **Groves** Texas, SW USA *29°57′N 93°55′W*
19 *O7* **Groveton** New Hampshire, NE USA *44°35′N 71°28′W*
25 *W9* **Groveton** Texas, SW USA *31°04′N 95°08′W*
36 *J15* **Growler Mountains** ▲▲ Arizona, SW USA
Grozdovo *see* Bratya Daskalovi
127 *P16* **Groznyy** Chechenskaya Respublika, SW Russian Federation *43°20′N 45°43′E*
Grubeshov *see* Hrubieszów
112 *G9* **Grubišno Polje** Bjelovar-Bilogora, NE Croatia *45°42′N 17°09′E*
Grudovo *see* Sredets
110 *J9* **Grudziądz** *Ger.* Graudenz. Kujawsko-pomorskie, C Poland *53°29′N 18°45′E*
25 *R17* **Grulla** *var.* La Grulla. Texas, SW USA *26°15′N 98°37′W*
40 *K14* **Grullo** Jalisco, SW Mexico *19°45′N 104°15′W*
67 *V10* **Grumeti** ~ N Tanzania
95 *K16* **Grums** Värmland, C Sweden *59°22′N 13°11′E*
109 *S5* **Grünau im Almtal** Oberösterreich, N Austria *47°51′N 13°56′E*
101 *H17* **Grünberg** Hessen, W Germany *50°36′N 08°57′E*
Grünberg/Grünberg in Schlesien *see* Zielona Góra
92 *H3* **Grundarfjördhur** Vestfirdhir, W Iceland *64°55′N 23°15′W*
21 *P7* **Grundy** Virginia, NE USA *37°17′N 82°06′W*
29 *W13* **Grundy Center** Iowa, C USA *42°21′N 92°46′W*
Grüneberg *see* Zielona Góra
25 *N1* **Gruver** Texas, SW USA *36°16′N 101°24′W*
108 *C9* **Gruyère, Lac de la** *Ger.* Greyerzer See. ◎ SW Switzerland
108 *C9* **Gruyères** Fribourg, W Switzerland *46°34′N 07°04′E*
118 *E11* **Gruzdīai** Šiauliai, N Lithuania *56°06′N 23°15′E*
Gruzinskaya SSR/Gruziya *see* Georgia
Gryada Akkyr *see* Akgyr Erezi
126 *L7* **Gryazi** Lipetskaya Oblast', W Russian Federation *52°27′N 39°56′E*
124 *M14* **Gryazovets** Vologodskaya Oblast', NW Russian Federation *58°52′N 40°12′E*
111 *M17* **Grybów** Małopolskie, SE Poland *49°35′N 20°54′E*
94 *M13* **Grycksbo** Dalarna, C Sweden *60°40′N 15°30′E*
110 *E8* **Gryfice** *Ger.* Greifenberg, Greifenberg in Pommern. Zachodnio-pomorskie, NW Poland *53°55′N 15°11′E*
110 *D9* **Gryfino** *Ger.* Greifenhagen. Zachodnio-pomorskie, NW Poland *53°15′N 14°30′E*
92 *H9* **Gryllefjord** Troms, N Norway *69°21′N 17°07′E*
95 *L15* **Grythyttan** Örebro, C Sweden *59°52′N 14°31′E*
108 *D10* **Gstaad** Bern, W Switzerland *46°30′N 07°16′E*
43 *P14* **Guabito** Bocas del Toro, NW Panama *09°30′N 82°35′W*
44 *G7* **Guacanayabo, Golfo de** *gulf* S Cuba
40 *I7* **Guachochi** Chihuahua, N Mexico
104 *J11* **Guadajira** ~ SW Spain
104 *M13* **Guadajoz** ~ S Spain
40 *L13* **Guadalajara** Jalisco, C Mexico *20°43′N 103°24′W*
105 *O8* **Guadalajara** *Ar.* Wad Al-Hajarah; *anc.* Arriaca. Castilla-La Mancha, C Spain *40°37′N 03°10′W*
105 *O7* **Guadalajara** ◈ *province* Castilla-La Mancha, C Spain
104 *K12* **Guadalcanal** Andalucía, S Spain *38°06′N 05°49′W*
186 *L10* **Guadalcanal** *off.* Guadalcanal Province. ◈ *province* C Solomon Islands
186 *M9* **Guadalcanal** *island* C Solomon Islands
Guadalcanal Province *see* Guadalcanal
105 *O12* **Guadalén** ~ S Spain
105 *R13* **Guadalentín** ~ SE Spain
104 *K15* **Guadalete** ~ SW Spain
105 *O13* **Guadalimar** ~ S Spain
105 *P12* **Guadalmena** ~ S Spain
104 *L11* **Guadalmez** ~ W Spain
105 *S7* **Guadalope** ~ E Spain
104 *K13* **Guadalquivir** ~ W Spain
104 *J14* **Guadalquivir, Marismas del** *var.* Las Marismas. *wetland* SW Spain
40 *M11* **Guadalupe** Zacatecas, C Mexico *22°47′N 102°30′W*
57 *E16* **Guadalupe** Ica, W Peru *13°59′S 75°49′W*
104 *L10* **Guadalupe** Extremadura, W Spain *39°26′N 05°18′W*
36 *L14* **Guadalupe** Arizona, SW USA *33°20′N 111°57′W*
35 *P13* **Guadalupe** California, W USA *34°55′N 120°34′W*
Guadalupe *see* Canelones
40 *J3* **Guadalupe Bravos** Chihuahua, N Mexico *31°22′N 106°04′W*
40 *A4* **Guadalupe, Isla** *island* NW Mexico
37 *U15* **Guadalupe Mountains** ▲▲ New Mexico/Texas, SW USA
24 *J8* **Guadalupe Peak** ▲ Texas, SW USA *31°53′N 104°51′W*
25 *R11* **Guadalupe River** ~ SW USA
104 *K10* **Guadalupe, Sierra de** ▲▲ W Spain
40 *K9* **Guadalupe Victoria** Durango, C Mexico *24°30′N 104°08′W*
40 *I8* **Guadalupe y Calvo** Chihuahua, N Mexico *26°04′N 106°58′W*
105 *N7* **Guadarrama** Madrid, C Spain *40°40′N 04°06′W*
105 *N7* **Guadarrama** ~ C Spain
104 *M7* **Guadarrama, Puerto de** *pass* C Spain
105 *N9* **Guadarrama, Sierra de** ▲▲ C Spain
105 *Q9* **Guadazaón** ~ C Spain
45 *X10* **Guadeloupe** ◇ *French overseas department* E West Indies
47 *S3* **Guadeloupe** *island group* E West Indies
45 *W10* **Guadeloupe Passage** *passage* E Caribbean Sea
104 *H13* **Guadiana** ~ Portugal/Spain
105 *O13* **Guadiana Menor** ~ S Spain
105 *Q8* **Guadiela** ~ C Spain
105 *O14* **Guadix** Andalucía, S Spain *37°19′N 03°08′W*
Guad-i-Zirreh *see* Gowd-e Zereh, Dasht-e
193 *T12* **Guafo Fracture Zone** *tectonic feature* SE Pacific Ocean
63 *F18* **Guafo, Isla** *island* S Chile
42 *I6* **Guaimaca** Francisco Morazán, C Honduras *14°34′N 86°49′W*
54 *J12* **Guainía** *off.* Comisaría del Guainía. ◈ *province* E Colombia
Guainía, Comisaría del *see* Guainía
54 *K12* **Guainía, Río** ~ Colombia/Venezuela
55 *O9* **Guaiquinima, Cerro** *elevation* SE Venezuela
60 *G10* **Guaíra** Paraná, S Brazil *24°05′S 54°15′W*
60 *L7* **Guaíra** São Paulo, S Brazil *20°17′S 48°21′W*
62 *O7* **Guairá** *off.* Departamento del Guairá. ◈ *department* S Paraguay
Guairá, Departamento del *see* Guairá
Guaire *see* Gorey
63 *F18* **Guaiteca, Isla** *island* S Chile
44 *G6* **Guajaba, Cayo** *headland* C Cuba *21°50′N 77°33′W*
59 *D16* **Guajará-Mirim** Rondônia, W Brazil *10°50′S 65°21′W*
Guajira *see* La Guajira
Guajira, Departamento de La *see* La Guajira
54 *H3* **Guajira, Península de la** *peninsula* N Colombia
42 *J6* **Gualaco** Olancho, C Honduras *15°00′N 86°03′W*
34 *L7* **Gualala** California, W USA *38°45′N 123°33′W*
42 *E5* **Gualán** Zacapa, C Guatemala *15°06′N 89°22′W*
61 *C19* **Gualeguay** Entre Ríos, E Argentina *33°09′S 59°20′W*
61 *D18* **Gualeguaychú** Entre Ríos, E Argentina *33°03′S 58°31′W*
61 *C18* **Gualeguay, Río** ~ E Argentina
63 *K16* **Gualicho, Salina del** *salt lake* E Argentina
188 *B15* **Guam** ◇ *US unincorporated territory* W Pacific Ocean
63 *F19* **Guamblin, Isla** *island* Archipiélago de los Chonos, S Chile
61 *A22* **Guaminí** Buenos Aires, E Argentina *37°01′S 62°28′W*
40 *H8* **Guamúchil** Sinaloa, C Mexico *25°23′N 108°01′W*
54 *H4* **Guana** *var.* Misión de Guana. Zulia, NW Venezuela *11°07′N 72°17′W*
44 *C4* **Guanabacoa** La Habana, W Cuba *23°02′N 82°12′W*
42 *K13* **Guanacaste** *off.* Provincia de Guanacaste. ◈ *province* NW Costa Rica
42 *K12* **Guanacaste, Cordillera de** ▲▲ NW Costa Rica
Guanacaste, Provincia de *see* Guanacaste
40 *J8* **Guanaceví** Durango, C Mexico *25°55′N 105°51′W*
44 *A5* **Guanahacabibes, Golfo de** *gulf* W Cuba
42 *K4* **Guanaja, Isla de** *island* Islas de la Bahía, N Honduras
44 *C4* **Guanajay** La Habana, W Cuba *22°56′N 82°42′W*
41 *N12* **Guanajuato** Guanajuato, C Mexico *21°N 101°19′W*
40 *M12* **Guanajuato** ◈ *state* C Mexico
54 *J6* **Guanare** Portuguesa, N Venezuela *09°04′N 69°45′W*
54 *K7* **Guanare, Río** ~ W Venezuela
54 *J6* **Guanarito** Portuguesa, NW Venezuela *08°43′N 69°12′W*
160 *M3* **Guancen Shan** ▲▲ C China
62 *I9* **Guandacol** La Rioja, W Argentina *29°32′S 68°37′W*
44 *A5* **Guane** Pinar del Río, W Cuba *22°12′N 84°05′W*
161 *N14* **Guangdong** *var.* Guangdong Sheng, Kuang-tung, Kwangtung, Yue. ◈ *province* S China
Guangdong Sheng *see* Guangdong
Guanghua *see* Laohekou
Guangju *see* Gwangju
161 *Q9* **Guangming Ding** ▲ Anhui, China *30°06′N 118°04′E*
160 *I13* **Guangnan** *var.* Liancheng. Yunnan, SW China *24°07′N 104°54′E*
161 *N8* **Guangshui** *prev.* Yinshan. Hubei, C China *31°41′N 113°53′E*
Guangxi *see* Guangxi Zhuangzu Zizhiqu
160 *K14* **Guangxi Zhuangzu Zizhiqu** *var.* Guangxi, Gui, Kuang-hsi, Kwangsi, *Eng.* Kwangsi Chuang Autonomous Region. ◈ *autonomous region* S China
160 *J8* **Guangyuan** *var.* Kuang-yuan, Kwangyuan. Sichuan, C China *32°27′N 105°49′E*
161 *N14* **Guangzhou** *var.* Kuang-chou, Kwangchow, *Eng.* Canton. *province capital* Guangdong, S China *23°11′N 113°19′E*
59 *N19* **Guanhães** Minas Gerais, SE Brazil *18°46′S 42°58′W*
160 *I12* **Guanling** *var.* Guanling Bouyeizu Miaozu Zizhixian. Guizhou, S China *26°00′N 105°40′E*
Guanling Bouyeizu Miaozu Zizhixian *see* Guanling
55 *N5* **Guanta** Anzoátegui, NE Venezuela *10°15′N 64°38′W*
44 *J8* **Guantánamo** Guantánamo, SE Cuba *20°06′N 75°16′W*
44 *J8* **Guantánamo, Bahia de** *Eng.* Guantanamo Bay. *US military base* SE Cuba*20°06′N 75°16′W*
Guantanamo Bay *see* Guantánamo, Bahia de
Guanxian/Guan Xian *see* Dujiangyan
161 *Q6* **Guanyun** *var.* Yishan. Jiangsu, E China *34°18′N 119°14′E*
54 *C12* **Guapí** Cauca, SW Colombia *02°36′N 77°54′W*
43 *N13* **Guápiles** Limón, NE Costa Rica *10°15′N 83°46′W*
61 *I15* **Guaporé** Rio Grande do Sul, S Brazil *28°55′S 51°53′W*
47 *S8* **Guaporé, Rio** *var.* Río Iténez. ~ Bolivia/Brazil *see also* Río Iténez
Guaporé, Rio *see* Iténez, Río
56 *B7* **Guaranda** Bolívar, C Ecuador *01°35′S 78°59′W*
60 *H11* **Guaraniaçu** Paraná, S Brazil *25°05′S 52°52′W*
59 *O20* **Guarapari** Espírito Santo, SE Brazil *20°39′S 40°31′W*
60 *I12* **Guarapuava** Paraná, S Brazil *25°22′S 51°28′W*
60 *J8* **Guararapes** São Paulo, S Brazil *21°16′S 50°37′W*
105 *S4* **Guara, Sierra de** ▲▲ NE Spain
60 *N10* **Guaratinguetá** São Paulo, S Brazil *22°44′S 45°16′W*
104 *I7* **Guarda** Guarda, N Portugal *40°32′N 07°17′W*
104 *I7* **Guarda** ◈ *district* N Portugal
Guardak *see* Magdanly
104 *M3* **Guardo** Castilla y León, N Spain *42°48′N 04°50′W*
104 *K11* **Guareña** Extremadura, W Spain *38°51′N 06°06′W*
60 *J11* **Guaricana, Pico** ▲ S Brazil *25°13′S 48°50′W*
54 *L6* **Guárico** *off.* Estado Guárico. ◈ *state* N Venezuela
Guárico, Estado *see* Guárico
44 *J7* **Guarico, Punta** *headland* E Cuba *20°36′N 74°43′W*
54 *L7* **Guárico, Río** ~ C Venezuela
60 *M10* **Guarujá** São Paulo, SE Brazil *23°50′S 46°27′W*
61 *L22* **Guarulhos** ✈ (São Paulo) São Paulo, S Brazil *23°23′S 46°32′W*
43 *R17* **Guarumal** Veraguas, S Panama *07°48′N 81°15′W*
Guasapa *see* Guasopa
40 *H8* **Guasave** Sinaloa, C Mexico *25°33′N 108°29′W*
54 *I8* **Guasdualito** Apure, C Venezuela *07°15′N 70°40′W*
55 *Q7* **Guasipati** Bolívar, E Venezuela *07°28′N 61°58′W*
186 *I9* **Guasopa** *var.* Guasapa. Woodlark Island, SE Papua New Guinea *09°12′S 152°58′E*
106 *F9* **Guastalla** Emilia-Romagna, C Italy *44°54′N 10°38′E*
42 *D6* **Guastatoya** *var.* El Progreso. El Progreso, C Guatemala *14°51′N 90°01′W*
42 *D5* **Guatemala** *off.* Republic of Guatemala. ◆ *republic* Central America
42 *A2* **Guatemala** *off.* Departamento de Guatemala. ◈ *department* S Guatemala
193 *S7* **Guatemala Basin** *undersea feature* E Pacific Ocean *11°00′N 95°00′W*
Guatemala City *see* Ciudad de Guatemala
Guatemala, Departamento de *see* Guatemala
Guatemala, Republic of *see* Guatemala
45 *V14* **Guatuaro Point** *headland* Trinidad, Trinidad and Tobago *10°19′N 60°58′W*
186 *B8* **Guavi** ~ SW Papua New Guinea
54 *G13* **Guaviare** *off.* Comisaría Guaviare. ◈ *province* S Colombia
Guaviare, Comisaría *see* Guaviare
54 *J11* **Guaviare, Río** ~ E Colombia
61 *E15* **Guaviravi** Corrientes, NE Argentina *29°20′S 56°50′W*
54 *G12* **Guayabero, Río** ~ SW Colombia
45 *U6* **Guayama** E Puerto Rico *17°59′N 66°07′W*
42 *J7* **Guayambre, Río** ~ S Honduras
Guayanas, Macizo de las *see* Guiana Highlands
45 *V6* **Guayanés, Punta** *headland* E Puerto Rico *18°03′N 65°48′W*
42 *J6* **Guayape, Río** ~ C Honduras
56 *B7* **Guayaquil** *var.* Santiago de Guayaquil. Guayas, SW Ecuador *02°13′S 79°54′W*
Guayaquil *see* Simon Bolivar
56 *A8* **Guayaquil, Golfo de** *var.* Gulf of Guayaquil. *gulf* SW Ecuador
Guayaquil, Gulf of *see* Guayaquil, Golfo de
56 *A7* **Guayas** ◈ *province* W Ecuador
62 *N7* **Guaycurú, Río** ~ NE Argentina
40 *F6* **Guaymas** Sonora, NW Mexico *27°56′N 110°54′W*
45 *U5* **Guaynabo** E Puerto Rico *18°19′N 66°05′W*
80 *H12* **Guba** Bīnishangul Gumuz, W Ethiopia *11°11′N 35°21′E*
146 *H8* **Gubadag** *Turkm.* Tel'man; *prev.* Tel'mansk. Daşoguz Welaýaty, N Turkmenistan *42°07′N 59°55′E*
125 *V13* **Gubakha** Permskiy Kray, NW Russian Federation *58°52′N 57°35′E*
106 *I12* **Gubbio** Umbria, C Italy *43°27′N 12°34′E*
100 *Q13* **Guben** *var.* Wilhelm-Pieck-Stadt. Brandenburg, E Germany *51°59′N 14°42′E*
Guben *see* Gubin
110 *D12* **Gubin** *Ger.* Guben. Lubuskie, W Poland *51°59′N 14°43′E*
126 *K8* **Gubkin** Belgorodskaya Oblast', W Russian Federation *51°16′N 37°32′E*
162 *J9* **Guchin-Us** *var.* Arguut. Övörhangay, C Mongolia *45°27′N 102°25′E*
Gudara *see* Ghŭdara
105 *S8* **Gúdar, Sierra de** ▲▲ E Spain
137 *P8* **Gudauta** *prev.* Gudaut'a. NW Georgia *43°07′N 40°35′E*
Gudaut'a *see* Gudauta
94 *G12* **Gudbrandsdalen** *valley* S Norway
95 *G21* **Gudenå** *var.* Gudenaa. ~ C Denmark
Gudenaa *see* Gudenå
127 *P16* **Gudermes** Chechenskaya Respublika, SW Russian Federation *43°23′N 46°06′E*
155 *J18* **Gūdūr** Andhra Pradesh, E India *14°10′N 79°51′E*
146 *B13* **Gudurolum** Balkan Welaýaty, W Turkmenistan *37°28′N 54°30′E*
94 *D13* **Gudvangen** Sogn Og Fjordane, S Norway *60°54′N 06°49′E*
103 *U7* **Guebwiller** Haut-Rhin, NE France *47°55′N 07°13′E*
Guéckédou *see* Guékédou
14 *K8* **Guéguen, Lac** ◎ Québec, SE Canada
76 *J15* **Guékédou** *var.* Guéckédou. Guinée-Forestière, S Guinea *08°33′N 10°08′W*
41 *R16* **Guelatao** Oaxaca, SE Mexico
Guelders *see* Gelderland
78 *G11* **Guélengdeng** Mayo-Kébbi, W Chad *10°55′N 15°31′E*
74 *L5* **Guelma** *var.* Gâlma. NE Algeria *36°29′N 07°25′E*
74 *D8* **Guelmime** *var.* Goulimime. SW Morocco *28°59′N 10°10′W*
14 *G15* **Guelph** Ontario, S Canada *43°34′N 80°16′W*
102 *I7* **Guemené-Penfao** Loire-Atlantique, NW France *47°37′N 01°49′W*
102 *I7* **Guer** Morbihan, NW France *47°54′N 02°07′W*
78 *I11* **Guéra** *off.* Préfecture du Guéra. ◈ *prefecture* S Chad
102 *H8* **Guérande** Loire-Atlantique, NW France *47°20′N 02°25′W*
Guéra, Préfecture du *see* Guéra
78 *K9* **Guéréda** Biltine, E Chad *14°30′N 22°05′E*
103 *N10* **Guéret** Creuse, C France *46°10′N 01°52′E*
Guernica/Guernica y Lumo *see* Gernika-Lumo
33 *Z15* **Guernsey** Wyoming, C USA *42°16′N 104°44′W*
97 *K25* **Guernsey** *island* Channel Islands, NW Europe
76 *J10* **Guérou** Assaba, S Mauritania *16°48′N 11°40′W*
25 *R16* **Guerra** Texas, SW USA *26°54′N 98°53′W*
41 *O15* **Guerrero** ◈ *state* S Mexico

◆ Country
● Country Capital
◇ Dependent Territory
○ Dependent Territory Capital
◈ Administrative Regions
✈ International Airport
▲ Mountain
▲▲ Mountain Range
Volcano
~ River
◎ Lake
⊠ Reservoir

40 D6 **Guerrero Negro** Baja California Sur, NW Mexico 27°56′N 114°04′W
103 P9 **Gueugnon** Saône-et-Loire, C France 46°36′N 04°03′E
76 M17 **Guéyo** S Ivory Coast 05°25′N 06°04′W
107 L15 **Guglionesi** Molise, C Italy 41°54′N 14°54′E
188 K5 **Guguan** island C Northern Mariana Islands
Guhrau see Góra
Gui see Guangxi Zhuangzu Zizhiqu
Guiana see French Guiana
47 V4 **Guiana Basin** undersea feature W Atlantic Ocean 11°00′N 52°00′W
48 G6 **Guiana Highlands** var. Macizo de las Guayanas. ▲▲ N South America
Guiba see Juba
102 I7 **Guichen** Ille-et-Vilaine, NW France 47°57′N 01°47′W
Guichi see Chizhou
61 E18 **Guichón** Paysandú, W Uruguay 32°30′S 57°13′W
77 U12 **Guidan-Roumji** Maradi, S Niger 13°40′N 06°41′E
Guidder see Guider
159 T10 **Guide** var. Heyin. Qinghai, C China 36°06′N 101°25′E
78 F12 **Guider** var. Guidder. Nord, N Cameroon 09°55′N 13°59′E
76 I11 **Guidimaka** ◐ region S Mauritania
77 W12 **Guidimouni** Zinder, S Niger 13°40′N 09°31′E
76 G10 **Guier, Lac de** var. Lac de Guiers. ◎ N Senegal
Guiers, Lac de see Guier, Lac de
160 L14 **Guigang** var. Guixian, Gui Xian. Guangxi Zhuangzu Zizhiqu, S China 23°06′N 109°36′E
76 L16 **Guiglo** W Ivory Coast 06°33′N 07°29′W
54 L5 **Güigüe** Carabobo, N Venezuela 10°05′N 67°48′W
83 M20 **Guijá** Gaza, S Mozambique 24°31′S 33°02′E
42 E7 **Güija, Lago de** ◎ El Salvador/Guatemala
160 L14 **Gui Jiang** var. Gui Shui. ≈ S China
104 K8 **Guijuelo** Castilla y León, N Spain 40°34′N 05°40′W
Guilan see Gīlān
97 N22 **Guildford** SE England, United Kingdom 51°14′N 00°35′W
19 R5 **Guildford** Maine, NE USA 45°10′N 69°22′W
19 O7 **Guildhall** Vermont, NE USA 44°34′N 71°36′W
103 R13 **Guilherand** Ardèche, E France 44°57′N 04°49′E
160 L13 **Guilin** var. Kuei-lin, Kweilin. Guangxi Zhuangzu Zizhiqu, S China 25°15′N 110°16′E
12 J6 **Guillaume-Delisle, Lac** ◎ Québec, NE Canada
103 U13 **Guillestre** Hautes-Alpes, SE France 44°41′N 06°39′E
104 H6 **Guimarães** var. Guimaráes. Braga, N Portugal 41°26′N 08°19′W
Guimarães see Guimarães
58 D11 **Guimarães Rosas, Pico** ▲ NW Brazil
23 N3 **Guin** Alabama, S USA 33°58′N 87°54′W
Güina see Wina
76 I14 **Guinea** off. Republic of Guinea, var. Guinée; prev. French Guinea, People's Revolutionary Republic of Guinea. ◆ republic W Africa
64 N13 **Guinea Basin** undersea feature E Atlantic Ocean 0°00′N 05°00′W
76 E12 **Guinea-Bissau** off. Republic of Guinea-Bissau, Fr. Guinée-Bissau, Port. Guiné-Bissau; prev. Portuguese Guinea. ◆ republic W Africa
Guinea-Bissau, Republic of see Guinea-Bissau
66 K7 **Guinea Fracture Zone** tectonic feature E Atlantic Ocean
64 O13 **Guinea, Gulf of** Fr. Golfe de Guinée. gulf E Atlantic Ocean
Guinea, People's Revolutionary Republic of see Guinea
Guinea, Republic of see Guinea
Guiné-Bissau see Guinea-Bissau
Guinée see Guinea
Guinée-Bissau see Guinea-Bissau
Guinée, Golfe de see Guinea, Gulf of
44 C4 **Güines** La Habana, W Cuba 22°50′N 82°02′W
102 G5 **Guingamp** Côtes d'Armor, NW France 48°34′N 03°09′W
105 P3 **Guipúzcoa** Basq. Gipuzkoa. ◐ province País Vasco, N Spain
44 C5 **Güira de Melena** La Habana, W Cuba 22°47′N 82°33′W
74 G8 **Guir, Hamada du** desert Algeria/Morocco
55 P5 **Güiria** Sucre, NE Venezuela 10°37′N 62°21′W
Gui Shui see Gui Jiang
104 H2 **Guitiriz** Galicia, NW Spain 43°10′N 07°52′W
77 N17 **Guitri** S Ivory Coast 05°31′N 05°14′W
171 Q5 **Guiuan** Samar, C Philippines 11°02′N 125°45′E
Gui Xian/Guixian see Guigang
160 J12 **Guiyang** var. Kuei-Yang, Kuei-yang, Kueyang, Kweiyang; prev. Kweichu. province capital Guizhou, S China 26°33′N 106°45′E
160 J12 **Guizhou** var. Guizhou Sheng, Kuei-chou, Kweichow, Qian. ◐ province S China
Guizhou Sheng see Guizhou
102 J13 **Gujan-Mestras** Gironde, SW France 44°39′N 01°04′W
154 B10 **Gujarāt** var. Gujerat. ◐ state W India
149 V6 **Gujar Khān** Punjab, E Pakistan 33°19′N 73°23′E
Gujerat see Gujarāt
149 V7 **Gujrānwāla** Punjab, NE Pakistan 32°11′N 74°09′E
149 V7 **Gujrāt** Punjab, E Pakistan 32°34′N 74°04′E
146 B8 **Gulandag** Rus. Gory Kulandag. ▲▲ Balkan Welaýaty, W Turkmenistan
159 U9 **Gulang** Gansu, C China 37°31′N 102°55′E
183 R6 **Gulargambone** New South Wales, SE Australia 31°19′S 148°31′E
155 G15 **Gulbarga** Karnātaka, C India 17°22′N 76°47′E
118 J8 **Gulbene** Ger. Alt-Schwanenburg. NE Latvia 57°10′N 26°44′E
147 U10 **Gul'cha** Kir. Gülchö. Oshskaya Oblast', SW Kyrgyzstan 40°16′N 73°27′E
Gülchö see Gul'cha
173 T10 **Gulden Draak Seamount** undersea feature E Indian Ocean 33°45′S 101°00′E
136 J16 **Gülek Boğazı** var. Cilician Gates. pass S Turkey
186 D8 **Gulf** ◐ province S Papua New Guinea
23 O9 **Gulf Breeze** Florida, SE USA 30°21′N 87°09′W
Gulf of Liaotung see Liaodong Wan
23 V13 **Gulfport** Florida, SE USA 27°45′N 82°42′W
22 M9 **Gulfport** Mississippi, S USA 30°22′N 89°06′W
23 O9 **Gulf Shores** Alabama, S USA 30°15′N 87°40′W
183 R7 **Gulgong** New South Wales, SE Australia 32°25′S 149°31′E
160 I11 **Gulin** Sichuan, C China 28°06′N 105°47′E
171 U14 **Gulir** Pulau Kasiui, E Indonesia 04°27′S 131°41′E
Gulistan see Guliston
147 P10 **Guliston** Rus. Gulistan. Sirdaryo Viloyati, E Uzbekistan 40°29′N 68°46′E
163 T6 **Guliya Shan** ▲ NE China 49°42′N 122°22′E
Gulja see Yining
39 S11 **Gulkana** Alaska, USA 62°17′N 145°25′W
11 S17 **Gull Lake** Saskatchewan, S Canada 50°05′N 108°30′W
31 P10 **Gull Lake** ◎ Michigan, N USA
29 T6 **Gull Lake** ◎ Minnesota, N USA
95 L16 **Gullspång** Västra Götaland, S Sweden 58°58′N 14°04′E
136 B15 **Güllük Körfezi** prev. Akbük Limanı. bay W Turkey
152 H5 **Gulmarg** Jammu and Kashmir, NW India 34°04′N 74°25′E
Gulpaigan see Golpāyegān
99 L18 **Gulpen** Limburg, SE Netherlands 50°48′N 05°53′E
Gul'shad see Gul'shat
145 S13 **Gul'shat** var. Gul'shad. Karaganda, E Kazakhstan 46°37′N 74°22′E
81 F17 **Gulu** N Uganda 02°46′N 32°21′E
114 K10 **Gŭlŭbovo** Stara Zagora, C Bulgaria 42°08′N 25°51′E
114 I7 **Gulyantsi** Pleven, N Bulgaria 43°37′N 24°40′E
Gulyaypole see Hulyaipole
Guma see Pishan
Gümai see Darlag
79 K16 **Gumba** Equateur, NW Dem. Rep. Congo 02°58′N 21°23′E
Gumbinnen see Gusev
81 H24 **Gumbiro** Ruvuma, S Tanzania 10°19′S 35°40′E
146 B11 **Gumdag** prev. Kum-Dag. Balkan Welaýaty, W Turkmenistan 39°13′N 54°35′E
77 W12 **Gumel** Jigawa, N Nigeria 12°37′N 09°23′E
105 N5 **Gumiel de Hizán** Castilla y León, N Spain 41°46′N 03°42′W
153 P16 **Gumla** Jhārkhand, N India 23°03′N 84°36′E
Gumma see Gunma
101 F16 **Gummersbach** Nordrhein-Westfalen, W Germany 51°01′N 07°34′E
77 T13 **Gummi** Zamfara, NW Nigeria 12°07′N 05°07′E
Gumpolds see Humpolec
Gumti see Gomati
Gümülcine/Gümüljina see Komotiní
Gümüşane see Gümüşhane
137 O12 **Gümüşhane** var. Gümüşane, Gumushkhane. Gümüşhane, NE Turkey 40°31′N 39°27′E
137 O12 **Gümüşhane** var. Gümüşane, Gumushkhane. ◐ province NE Turkey
Gumushkhane see Gümüşhane
171 V14 **Gumzai** Pulau Kola, E Indonesia 05°27′S 134°38′E
154 H9 **Guna** Madhya Pradesh, C India 24°39′N 77°18′E
Gunabad see Gonābād
Gunan see Qijiang
Gunbad-i-Qawus see Gonbad-e Kāvūs
183 O9 **Gunbar** New South Wales, SE Australia 34°03′S 145°32′E
183 O9 **Gun Creek** seasonal river New South Wales, SE Australia
183 Q10 **Gundagai** New South Wales, SE Australia 35°06′S 148°03′E
79 K17 **Gundji** Equateur, N Dem. Rep. Congo 02°03′N 21°31′E
155 G20 **Gundlupet** Karnātaka, W India 11°48′N 76°42′E
136 G16 **Gündoğmuş** Antalya, S Turkey 36°50′N 32°07′E
137 O14 **Güney Doğu Toroslar** ▲▲ SE Turkey
79 J21 **Gungu** Bandundu, SW Dem. Rep. Congo 05°43′S 19°20′E
127 P17 **Gunib** Respublika Dagestan, SW Russian Federation 42°24′N 46°55′E
112 J11 **Gunja** Vukovar-Srijem, E Croatia 44°53′N 18°51′E
31 P9 **Gun Lake** ◎ Michigan, N USA
165 N12 **Gunma** off. Gunma-ken, var. Gumma. ◐ prefecture Honshū, S Japan
Gunma-ken see Gunma
197 P15 **Gunnbjørn Fjeld** var. Gunnbjørns Bjerge. ▲ C Greenland 69°03′N 29°36′W
Gunnbjørns Bjerge see Gunnbjørn Fjeld
183 S6 **Gunnedah** New South Wales, SE Australia 30°59′S 150°15′E
173 Y15 **Gunner's Quoin** var. Coin de Mire. island N Mauritius
37 R6 **Gunnison** Colorado, C USA 38°33′N 106°55′W
36 L5 **Gunnison** Utah, W USA 39°09′N 111°49′W
37 P5 **Gunnison River** ≈ Colorado, C USA
21 X2 **Gunpowder River** ≈ Maryland, NE USA
Güns see Kőszeg
163 X16 **Gunsan** var. Gunsan, Jap. Gunzan; prev. Kunsan. W South Korea 35°58′N 126°42′E
Gunsan see Gunsan
109 S4 **Gunskirchen** Oberösterreich, N Austria 48°07′N 13°54′E
Gunt see Ghund
155 H17 **Guntakal** Andhra Pradesh, C India 15°11′N 77°24′E
23 Q2 **Guntersville** Alabama, S USA 34°21′N 86°17′W
23 Q2 **Guntersville Lake** ⊠ Alabama, S USA
109 X4 **Guntramsdorf** Niederösterreich, E Austria 48°03′N 16°19′E
155 J16 **Guntūr** var. Guntur. Andhra Pradesh, SE India 16°20′N 80°27′E
168 H10 **Gunungsitoli** Pulau Nias, W Indonesia 01°11′N 97°35′E
155 M14 **Gunupur** Orissa, E India 19°04′N 83°52′E
101 J23 **Günz** ≈ S Germany
Gunzan see Gunsan
101 J22 **Günzburg** Bayern, S Germany 48°26′N 10°18′E
101 K21 **Gunzenhausen** Bayern, S Germany 49°07′N 10°45′E
Guolüezhen see Lingbao
Guovdageaidnu see Kautokeino
161 P7 **Guoyang** Anhui, E China 33°30′N 116°12′E
116 G11 **Gurahonț** Hung. Honctő. Arad, W Romania 46°16′N 22°21′E
Gurahumora see Gura Humorului
116 K9 **Gura Humorului** Ger. Gurahumora. Suceava, NE Romania 47°31′N 26°00′E
146 H8 **Gurbansoltan Eje** prev. Ýylanly, Rus. Il'yaly. Daşoguz Welaýaty, N Turkmenistan 41°57′N 59°42′E
158 K4 **Gurbantünggüt Shamo** desert W China
152 H7 **Gurdāspur** Punjab, N India 32°04′N 75°28′E
27 T13 **Gurdon** Arkansas, C USA 33°55′N 93°09′W
Gurdzhaani see Gurjaani
Gurgan see Gorgān
152 I10 **Gurgaon** Haryāna, N India 28°27′N 77°01′E
59 M15 **Gurguéia, Rio** ≈ NE Brazil
55 Q7 **Guri, Embalse de** ⊠ E Venezuela
137 V10 **Gurjaani** Rus. Gurdzhaani. E Georgia 41°42′N 45°47′E
109 T8 **Gurk** Kärnten, S Austria 46°52′N 14°17′E
109 T9 **Gurk** Slvn. Krka. ≈ S Austria
Gurkfeld see Krško
114 K9 **Gurkovo** prev. Kolupchii. Stara Zagora, C Bulgaria 42°42′N 25°46′E
109 S9 **Gurktaler Alpen** ▲▲ S Austria
146 H8 **Gurlan** Rus. Gurlen. Xorazm Viloyati, W Uzbekistan 41°54′N 60°18′E
Gurlen see Gurlan
83 M16 **Guro** Manica, C Mozambique 17°28′S 33°18′E
136 M14 **Gürün** Sivas, C Turkey 38°44′N 37°15′E
59 K16 **Gurupi** Tocantins, C Brazil 11°44′S 49°01′W
58 L12 **Gurupi, Rio** ≈ NE Brazil
152 E14 **Guru Sikhar** ▲ NW India 24°45′N 72°51′E
162 I8 **Gurvanbulag** var. Höviyn Am. Bayanhongor, C Mongolia 47°08′N 98°41′E
162 K7 **Gurvanbulag** var. Avdzaga. Bulgan, C Mongolia 47°43′N 103°30′E
162 I11 **Gurvantes** var. Urt. Ömnögovĭ, S Mongolia 43°16′N 101°00′E
Gur'yev/Gur'yevskaya Oblast' see Atyrau
77 U13 **Gusau** Zamfara, NW Nigeria 12°18′N 06°27′E
126 C3 **Gusev** Ger. Gumbinnen. Kaliningradskaya Oblast', W Russian Federation 54°36′N 22°14′E
146 J17 **Gushgy** Rus. Kushka. ≈ Mary Welaýaty, S Turkmenistan
Gushiago see Gushiegu
77 Q14 **Gushiegu** var. Gushiago. NE Ghana 09°54′N 00°12′W
165 S17 **Gushikawa** Okinawa, Okinawa, SW Japan 26°21′N 127°50′E
113 L16 **Gusinje** E Montenegro 42°34′N 19°51′E
126 M4 **Gus'-Khrustal'nyy** Vladimirskaya Oblast', W Russian Federation 55°39′N 40°42′E
107 B19 **Guspini** Sardegna, Italy, C Mediterranean Sea 39°33′N 08°39′E
109 X8 **Güssing** Burgenland, SE Austria 47°03′N 16°19′E
109 V6 **Gusswerk** Steiermark, E Austria 47°43′N 15°18′E
92 O2 **Gustav Adolf Land** physical region NE Svalbard
195 X5 **Gustav Bull Mountains** ▲▲ Antarctica
39 W13 **Gustavus** Alaska, USA 58°24′N 135°44′W
92 O1 **Gustav V Land** physical region NE Svalbard
35 P9 **Gustine** California, W USA 37°14′N 121°00′W
25 R8 **Gustine** Texas, SW USA 31°51′N 98°24′W
100 M9 **Güstrow** Mecklenburg-Vorpommern, NE Germany 53°48′N 12°12′E
95 N18 **Gusum** Östergötland, S Sweden 58°15′N 16°30′E
Guta/Gúta see Kolárovo
Gutenstein see Ravne na Koroškem
101 G14 **Gütersloh** Nordrhein-Westfalen, W Germany 51°54′N 08°23′E
27 N10 **Guthrie** Oklahoma, C USA 35°53′N 97°26′W
25 P5 **Guthrie** Texas, SW USA 33°38′N 100°21′W
29 U14 **Guthrie Center** Iowa, C USA 41°40′N 94°30′W
41 Q13 **Gutiérrez Zamora** Veracruz-Llave, E Mexico 20°29′N 97°07′W
Gutta see Kolárovo
29 Y12 **Guttenberg** Iowa, C USA 42°47′N 91°06′W
Guttentag see Dobrodzień
Guttstadt see Dobre Miasto
162 G8 **Guulin** Govĭ-Altay, C Mongolia 46°33′N 97°21′E
153 V12 **Guwāhāti** prev. Gauhāti. Assam, NE India 26°09′N 91°42′E
139 R3 **Guwēr** var. Al Kuwayr, Al Quwayr, Quwair. Arbīl, N Iraq 36°03′N 43°30′E
146 A10 **Guwlumaýak** Rus. Kuuli-Mayak. Balkan Welaýaty, NW Turkmenistan 40°14′N 52°43′E
55 R9 **Guyana** off. Co-operative Republic of Guyana; prev. British Guiana. ◆ republic N South America
Guyana, Co-operative Republic of see Guyana
21 P5 **Guyandotte River** ≈ West Virginia, NE USA
Guyane see French Guiana
Guyi see Sanjiang
26 H8 **Guymon** Oklahoma, C USA 36°42′N 101°30′W
146 K12 **Guynuk** Lebap Welaýaty, NE Turkmenistan 39°18′N 63°00′E
Guyong see Jiangle
21 O9 **Guyot, Mount** ▲ North Carolina/Tennessee, SE USA 35°42′N 83°15′W
183 U5 **Guyra** New South Wales, SE Australia 30°13′S 151°42′E
159 W10 **Guyuan** Ningxia, N China 35°57′N 106°13′E
Guzar see G'uzor
121 P2 **Güzelyurt** Gk. Kólpos Mórfu, Morphou. W Cyprus 35°12′N 33°E
121 N2 **Güzelyurt Körfezi** var. Morfou Bay, Morphou Bay, Gk. Kólpos Mórfou. bay W Cyprus
Guzhou see Rongjiang
40 I3 **Guzmán** Chihuahua, N Mexico 31°13′N 107°27′W
147 N13 **G'uzor** Rus. Guzar. Qashqadaryo Viloyati, S Uzbekistan 38°41′N 66°12′E
119 B14 **Gvardeysk** Ger. Tapaiu. Kaliningradskaya Oblast', W Russian Federation 54°39′N 21°02′E
Gvardeyskoye see Hvardiys'ke
183 R5 **Gwabegar** New South Wales, SE Australia 30°34′S 148°58′E
148 J16 **Gwādar** var. Gwadur. Baluchistān, SW Pakistan 25°09′N 62°21′E
148 J16 **Gwādar East Bay** bay SW Pakistan
148 J16 **Gwādar West Bay** bay SW Pakistan
Gwadur see Gwādar
83 J17 **Gwai** Matabeleland North, W Zimbabwe 19°17′S 27°37′E
154 I7 **Gwalior** Madhya Pradesh, C India 26°16′N 78°12′E
83 J18 **Gwanda** Matabeleland South, SW Zimbabwe 20°56′S 29°E
79 N15 **Gwane** Orientale, N Dem. Rep. Congo 04°40′N 25°51′E
163 X16 **Gwangju** off. Kwangju-gwangyŏksi, var. Guangju, Kwangchu; Jap. Kōshū. SW South Korea 35°09′N 126°53′E
83 J17 **Gwayi** ≈ W Zimbabwe
110 G8 **Gwda** var. Głda, Ger. Küddow. ≈ NW Poland
97 C14 **Gweebarra Bay** Ir. Béal an Bheara. inlet W Ireland
97 D14 **Gweedore** Ir. Gaoth Dobhair. Donegal, NW Ireland 55°03′N 08°14′W
Gwelo see Gweru
97 K21 **Gwent** cultural region S Wales, United Kingdom
83 K17 **Gweru** prev. Gwelo. Midlands, C Zimbabwe 19°27′S 29°49′E
29 Q7 **Gwinner** North Dakota, N USA 46°10′N 97°42′W
77 Y13 **Gwoza** Borno, NE Nigeria 11°07′N 13°40′E
Gwy see Wye
183 R4 **Gwydir River** ≈ New South Wales, SE Australia
97 I19 **Gwynedd** var. Gwyneth. cultural region NW Wales, United Kingdom
Gwyneth see Gwynedd
159 O16 **Gyaca** var. Ngarrab. Xizang Zizhiqu, W China 29°06′N 92°37′E
Gya'gya see Saga
Gyaijêpozhanggê see Zhidoi
Gyaisi see Jiulong
115 M22 **Gyalí** var. Yialí. island Dodekánisa, Greece, Aegean Sea
Gyamotang see Dêngqên
Gyandzha see Gäncä
Gyangkar see Dinggyê
158 M16 **Gyangzê** Xizang Zizhiqu, W China 28°50′N 89°38′E
158 L14 **Gyaring Co** ◎ W China
159 Q12 **Gyaring Hu** ◎ C China
115 I20 **Gyáros** var. Yioúra. island Kykládes, Greece, Aegean Sea
122 J7 **Gyda** Yamalo-Nenetskiy Avtonomnyy Okrug, N Russian Federation 70°55′N 78°34′E
122 J7 **Gydanskiy Poluostrov** Eng. Gyda Peninsula. peninsula N Russian Federation
Gyda Peninsula see Gydanskiy Poluostrov
Gyêgu see Yushu
163 W15 **Gyeonggi-man** prev. Kyŏnggi-man. bay NW South Korea
163 Z16 **Gyeongju** Jap. Keishū; prev. Kyŏngju. SE South Korea 35°49′N 129°09′E
Gyéres see Câmpia Turzii
Gyergyószentmiklós see Gheorgheni
Gyergyótölgyes see Tulgheş
Gyertyámos see Cărpiniş
Gyeva see Detva
Gyigang see Zayü
Gyixong see Gonggar
95 I23 **Gyldenløveshøy** hill range C Denmark
181 Z10 **Gympie** Queensland, E Australia 26°05′S 152°40′E
166 L7 **Gyobingauk** Bago, SW Burma (Myanmar) 18°14′N 95°39′E
111 M23 **Gyomaendrőd** Békés, SE Hungary 46°56′N 20°50′E
Gyömbér see Ďumbier
111 L22 **Gyöngyös** Heves, NE Hungary 47°44′N 19°49′E
111 H22 **Győr** Ger. Raab, Lat. Arrabona. Győr-Moson-Sopron, NW Hungary 47°41′N 17°40′E
111 G22 **Győr-Moson-Sopron** off. Győr-Moson-Sopron Megye. ◐ county NW Hungary
Győr-Moson-Sopron Megye see Győr-Moson-Sopron
11 X15 **Gypsumville** Manitoba, S Canada 51°47′N 98°38′W
12 M4 **Gyrfalcon Islands** island group Northwest Territories, NE Canada
95 N14 **Gysinge** Gävleborg, C Sweden 60°16′N 16°55′E
115 F22 **Gýtheio** var. Githio; prev. Yíthion. Pelopónnisos, S Greece 36°46′N 22°34′E
146 L13 **Gyuichbirleshik** Lebap Welaýaty, E Turkmenistan 38°10′N 64°33′E
111 N24 **Gyula** Rom. Jula. Békés, SE Hungary 46°39′N 21°17′E
Gyulafehérvár see Alba Iulia
Gyulovo see Roza
137 T11 **Gyumri** var. Giumri, Rus. Kumayri; prev. Aleksandropol', Leninakan. W Armenia 40°48′N 43°51′E
146 D13 **Gyunuzyndag, Gora** ▲ Balkan Welaýaty, W Turkmenistan 38°15′N 56°25′E
146 J15 **Gyzylbaydak** Rus. Krasnoye Znamya. Mary Welaýaty, S Turkmenistan 36°51′N 62°24′E
Gyzyletrek see Etrek
146 D10 **Gyzylgaýa** Rus. Kizyl-Kaya. Balkan Welaýaty, NW Turkmenistan 40°37′N 55°15′E
146 A10 **Gyzylsuw** Rus. Kizyl-Su. Balkan Welaýaty, W Turkmenistan 39°49′N 53°00′E
Gyzyrlabat see Serdar
Gzhatsk see Gagarin

H

153 T12 **Ha** W Bhutan 27°17′N 89°22′E
Haabai see Ha'apai Group
99 H17 **Haacht** Vlaams Brabant, C Belgium 50°58′N 04°38′E
109 T4 **Haag** Niederösterreich, NE Austria 48°07′N 14°32′E
194 L8 **Haag Nunataks** ▲ Antarctica
92 N2 **Haakon VII Land** physical region NW Svalbard
98 O11 **Haaksbergen** Overijssel, E Netherlands 52°09′N 06°45′E
99 E14 **Haamstede** Zeeland, SW Netherlands 51°43′N 03°45′E
193 Y15 **Ha'ano** island Ha'apai Group, C Tonga
193 Y15 **Ha'apai Group** var. Haabai. island group C Tonga
93 L15 **Haapajärvi** Oulu, C Finland 63°45′N 25°20′E
93 L17 **Haapamäki** Länsi-Suomi, C Finland 62°11′N 24°32′E
93 L15 **Haapavesi** Oulu, C Finland 64°09′N 25°25′E
191 N7 **Haapiti** Moorea, W French Polynesia 17°33′S 149°52′W
118 F4 **Haapsalu** Ger. Hapsal. Läänemaa, W Estonia 58°58′N 23°32′E
Ha'Arava see 'Arabah, Wādī al
95 G24 **Haarby** var. Hårby. Syddtjylland, C Denmark 55°13′N 10°07′E
98 H10 **Haarlem** prev. Harlem. Noord-Holland, W Netherlands 52°23′N 04°39′E
185 D19 **Haast** West Coast, South Island, New Zealand 43°53′S 169°02′E
185 C20 **Haast** ≈ South Island, New Zealand
185 D20 **Haast Pass** pass South Island, New Zealand
193 W16 **Ha'atua** 'Eau, E Tonga 21°23′S 174°57′W
149 P15 **Hab** ≈ SW Pakistan
141 W7 **Haba** var. Al Haba. Dubayy, NE United Arab Emirates 25°01′N 55°37′E
158 K2 **Habahe** var. Kaba. Xinjiang Uygur Zizhiqu, NW China 48°04′N 86°20′E
141 U13 **Ḥabarūt** var. Habrut. SW Oman 17°19′N 52°45′E
81 J18 **Habaswein** North Eastern, NE Kenya 01°01′N 39°27′E
99 L24 **Habay-la-Neuve** Luxembourg, SE Belgium 49°43′N 05°38′E
139 S8 **Ḥabbānīyah, Buḥayrat** ◎ C Iraq
Habelschwerdt see Bystrzyca Kłodzka
153 V14 **Habiganj** Sylhet, NE Bangladesh 24°23′N 91°25′E
163 Q12 **Habirag** Nei Mongol Zizhiqu, N China 42°18′N 115°40′E
95 L19 **Habo** Västra Götaland, S Sweden 57°55′N 14°05′E
123 V14 **Habomai Islands** island group Kuril'skiye Ostrova, SE Russian Federation
165 S2 **Haboro** Hokkaidō, NE Japan 44°19′N 141°42′E
153 S16 **Habra** West Bengal, NE India 22°39′N 88°17′E
Habrut see Ḥabarūt
143 P17 **Ḥabshān** Abū Ẓaby, C United Arab Emirates 23°51′N 53°34′E
54 E14 **Hacha** Putumayo, S Colombia 0°02′S 75°30′W
165 X13 **Hachijō-jima** island Izu-shotō, SE Japan
164 L12 **Hachiman** Gifu, Honshū, SW Japan 35°46′N 136°57′E
165 P7 **Hachimori** Akita, Honshū, C Japan 40°22′N 139°59′E
165 R7 **Hachinohe** Aomori, Honshū, C Japan 40°30′N 141°29′E
165 X13 **Hachiōji** Tōkyō, Hachijō-jima, SE Japan 35°40′N 139°20′E
137 Y12 **Hacıqabal** prev. Qazimämmäd. SE Azerbaijan 40°03′N 48°56′E
93 G17 **Hackås** Jämtland, C Sweden 62°55′N 14°31′E
18 K14 **Hackensack** New Jersey, NE USA 40°51′N 73°57′W
75 U12 **Ḥaḍabat al Jilf al Kabīr** var. Gilf Kebir Plateau. plateau SW Egypt
Hadama see Nazrēt
141 W13 **Ḥadbaram** S Oman 17°27′N 55°13′E
139 U13 **Ḥaddānīyah** well S Iraq
96 K12 **Haddington** SE Scotland, United Kingdom 55°59′N 02°46′W
141 Z8 **Ḥadd, Ra's al** headland NE Oman 22°28′N 59°58′E
Haded see Xadeed
77 W12 **Hadejia** Jigawa, N Nigeria 12°22′N 10°02′E
77 W12 **Hadejia** ≈ N Nigeria
138 F9 **Hadera** var. Khadera; prev. Ḥadera. Haifa, N Israel 32°26′N 34°55′E
Ḥadera see Hadera
Hadersleben see Haderslev
95 G24 **Haderslev** Ger. Hadersleben. Syddanmark, SW Denmark 55°15′N 09°30′E
151 J21 **Hadhdhunmathi Atoll** atoll S Maldives
141 W17 **Hadīboh** Suquṭrā, SE Yemen 12°38′N 54°05′E
158 K9 **Hadilik** Xinjiang Uygur Zizhiqu, W China 37°51′N 86°10′E
136 H16 **Hadim** Konya, S Turkey 36°58′N 32°27′E
140 K7 **Hadīyah** Al Madīnah, W Saudi Arabia 25°36′N 38°31′E
8 L5 **Hadley Bay** bay Victoria Island, Nunavut, N Canada
167 S6 **Ha Đông** var. Hadong. Ha Tây, N Vietnam 20°58′N 105°46′E
Hadong see Ha Đông
Hadramaut see Ḥaḍramawt
141 R15 **Ḥaḍramawt** Eng. Hadramaut. ▲▲ S Yemen
Hadria see Adria
Hadrianopolis see Edirne
Hadria Picena see Apricena
95 G22 **Hadsten** Midtjylland, C Denmark 56°19′N 10°03′E
95 G21 **Hadsund** Nordjylland, N Denmark 56°43′N 10°08′E
117 S4 **Hadyach** Rus. Gadyach. Poltavs'ka Oblast', NE Ukraine 50°21′N 34°00′E
112 I13 **Hadžići** Federacija Bosna I Hercegovina, SE Bosnia and Herzegovina 43°49′N 18°12′E
163 W14 **Haeju** S North Korea 38°04′N 125°40′E
Haerbin/Haerhpin/Ha-erh-pin see Harbin
141 P5 **Ḥafar al Bāṭin** Ash Sharqīyah, N Saudi Arabia 28°25′N 45°59′E
11 T15 **Hafford** Saskatchewan, S Canada 52°43′N 107°19′W
136 M13 **Hafik** Sivas, N Turkey 39°53′N 37°24′E
149 V8 **Hāfizābād** Punjab, E Pakistan 32°03′N 73°42′E
92 H4 **Hafnarfjörður** Höfudborgarsvæðid, W Iceland 64°03′N 21°57′W
Hafnia see Denmark
Hafnia see København
Hafren see Severn
Hafun see Xaafuun
Hafun, Ras see Xaafuun, Raas
80 G10 **Hag 'Abdullah** Sinnar, E Sudan 13°59′N 33°35′E
81 K18 **Hagadera** North Eastern, E Kenya 0°06′N 40°23′E
138 G8 **HaGalil** Eng. Galilee. ▲ N Israel
14 G10 **Hagar** Ontario, S Canada 46°27′N 80°22′W
155 G18 **Hagari** var. Vedāvati. ≈ W India
188 B16 **Hagåtña**, var. Agaña. ○ (Guam) NW Guam 13°27′N 144°45′E
100 M13 **Hagelberg** hill NE Germany
39 N14 **Hagemeister Island** island Alaska, USA
101 F15 **Hagen** Nordrhein-Westfalen, W Germany 51°22′N 07°27′E
100 K10 **Hagenow** Mecklenburg-Vorpommern, N Germany 53°27′N 11°10′E
10 K15 **Hagensborg** British Columbia, SW Canada 52°24′N 126°24′W
80 I13 **Hägere Hiywet** var. Agere Hiywet, Ambo. Oromiya, C Ethiopia 09°00′N 37°55′E
33 O15 **Hagerman** Idaho, NW USA 42°48′N 114°53′W
37 U14 **Hagerman** New Mexico, SW USA 33°07′N 104°19′W
21 V2 **Hagerstown** Maryland, NE USA 39°39′N 77°44′W
14 G16 **Hagersville** Ontario, S Canada 42°58′N 80°03′W
102 J15 **Hagetmau** Landes, SW France 43°40′N 00°36′W
95 K14 **Hagfors** Värmland, C Sweden 60°03′N 13°45′E
93 G16 **Häggenås** Jämtland, C Sweden 63°24′N 14°53′E
164 E12 **Hagi** Yamaguchi, Honshū, SW Japan 34°25′N 131°22′E
167 S5 **Ha Giang** Ha Giang, N Vietnam 22°50′N 104°58′E
Hagios Evstrátios see Ágios Efstrátios
HaGolan see Golan Heights
103 T4 **Hagondange** Moselle, NE France 49°16′N 06°06′E
97 B18 **Hag's Head** Ir. Ceann Caillí. headland W Ireland 52°56′N 09°29′W
102 I3 **Hague, Cap de la** headland N France 49°43′N 01°56′W
103 V5 **Haguenau** Bas-Rhin, NE France 48°49′N 07°47′E
165 X16 **Hahajima-rettō** island group SE Japan
15 R8 **Há Há, Lac** ◎ Québec, SE Canada
172 H13 **Hahaya** ✈ (Moroni) Grande Comore, NW Comoros
22 K9 **Hahnville** Louisiana, S USA 29°58′N 90°24′W
83 E22 **Haib** Karas, S Namibia 28°12′S 18°19′E
Haibak see Aibak
149 N15 **Haibo** ≈ SW Pakistan
Haibowan see Wuhai
163 U12 **Haicheng** Liaoning, NE China 40°53′N 122°45′E
Haicheng see Haifeng
Haicheng see Haiyuan
Haida see Nový Bor
Haidarabad see Hyderābād
Haidenschaft see Ajdovščina
167 T6 **Hai Dương** Hai Hưng, N Vietnam 20°56′N 106°21′E
138 F9 **Haifa** ◐ district NW Israel
Haifa see Hefa
Haifa, Bay of see Mifrats Hefa
161 P14 **Haifeng** var. Haicheng. Guangdong, S China 22°56′N 115°19′E
Haifong see Hai Phong
161 P3 **Hai He** ≈ E China
Haikang see Leizhou
160 L17 **Haikou** var. Hai-k'ou, Hoihow, Fr. Hoï-Hao. province capital Hainan, S China 20°N 110°17′E
Hai-k'ou see Haikou
140 M6 **Ḥā'il** Ḥā'il, NW Saudi Arabia 27°N 42°50′E
141 N5 **Ḥā'il** off. Minṭaqah Ḥā'il. ◐ province N Saudi Arabia
163 S6 **Hailar He** ≈ NE China
33 P14 **Hailey** Idaho, NW USA 43°31′N 114°18′W
14 H9 **Haileybury** Ontario, S Canada 47°27′N 79°39′W
163 X9 **Hailin** Heilongjiang, NE China 44°37′N 129°24′E
Ḥā'il, Minṭaqah see Ḥā'il
Hailong see Meihekou
93 K14 **Hailuoto** Swe. Karlö. island W Finland
Haima see Haymā'
Haimen see Taizhou
160 M17 **Hainan** var. Hainan Sheng, Qiong. ◐ province S China
160 K17 **Hainan Dao** island S China
Hainan Sheng see Hainan
Hainan Strait see Qiongzhou Haixia
Hainasch see Ainaži
Hainau see Chojnów
99 E20 **Hainaut** ◐ province SW Belgium
Hainburg see Hainburg an der Donau
109 Z4 **Hainburg an der Donau** var. Hainburg. Niederösterreich, NE Austria 48°09′N 16°57′E
39 W12 **Haines** Alaska, USA 59°13′N 135°27′W
32 L12 **Haines** Oregon, NW USA 44°53′N 117°56′W
23 W12 **Haines City** Florida, SE USA 28°06′N 81°37′W
10 H8 **Haines Junction** Yukon Territory, W Canada 60°45′N 137°30′W
109 W4 **Hainfeld** Niederösterreich, NE Austria 48°03′N 15°47′E
101 N16 **Hainichen** Sachsen, E Germany 50°58′N 13°08′E
Hai Ninh see Mong Cai
167 T6 **Hai Phong** var. Haifong, Haiphong. N Vietnam 20°50′N 106°41′E
Haiphong see Hai Phong
161 S12 **Haitan Dao** island SE China
44 K8 **Haiti** off. Republic of Haiti. ◆ republic C West Indies
Haiti, Republic of see Haiti
35 T11 **Haiwee Reservoir** ⊠ California, W USA
80 I7 **Haiya** Red Sea, NE Sudan 18°17′N 36°21′E
159 T10 **Haiyan** var. Sanjiaocheng. Qinghai, W China 36°55′N 100°54′E
160 M13 **Haiyang Shan** ▲ S China
159 V10 **Haiyuan** Ningxia, N China 36°32′N 105°31′E
Hajda see Nový Bor
111 M22 **Hajdú-Bihar** off. Hajdú-Bihar Megye. ◐ county E Hungary
Hajdú-Bihar Megye see Hajdú-Bihar
111 N22 **Hajdúböszörmény** Hajdú-Bihar, E Hungary 47°39′N 21°32′E
111 N22 **Hajdúhadház** Hajdú-Bihar, E Hungary 47°40′N 21°40′E
111 N21 **Hajdúnánás** Hajdú-Bihar, E Hungary 47°50′N 21°26′E
111 N22 **Hajdúszoboszló** Hajdú-Bihar, E Hungary 47°27′N 21°24′E
142 J3 **Ḥājī Ebrāhīm, Kūh-e** ▲ Iran/Iraq 36°53′N 44°56′E
165 O9 **Hajiki-zaki** headland Sado, C Japan 38°19′N 138°28′E
Hajine see Abū Ḥardān
153 P13 **Hājīpur** Bihār, N India 25°41′N 85°13′E
141 N14 **Ḥajjah** W Yemen 15°43′N 43°33′E
139 U11 **Ḥajjama** Al Muthannā, S Iraq 31°24′N 45°20′E
143 R12 **Ḥājjīābād** Hormozgān, C Iran
139 U14 **Ḥajj, Thaqb al** well S Iraq
113 L16 **Hajla** ▲ E Montenegro
110 P10 **Hajnówka** Ger. Hermhausen. Podlaskie, NE Poland 52°45′N 23°32′E
Haka see Hakha
Hakapehi see Punaauia
Hakâri see Hakkâri
138 F12 **HaKatan, HaMakhtesh** prev. HaMakhtesh HaQatan. ≈ S Israel
166 K4 **Hakha** var. Haka. Chin State, W Burma (Myanmar) 22°42′N 93°41′E
Hal see Halle
137 T16 **Hakkâri** var. Çölemerik, Hakâri. Hakkâri, SE Turkey 37°36′N 43°45′E
137 T16 **Hakkâri** var. Hakkari. ◐ province SE Turkey
Hakkari see Hakkâri
92 J12 **Hakkas** Norrbotten, N Sweden 66°53′N 21°36′E
164 J14 **Hakken-zan** ▲ Honshū, SW Japan 34°11′N 135°57′E
165 R7 **Hakkōda-san** ▲ Honshū, C Japan 40°40′N 140°49′E
165 T2 **Hako-dake** ▲ Hokkaidō, NE Japan 44°40′N 142°22′E
165 R5 **Hakodate** Hokkaidō, NE Japan 41°46′N 140°43′E
164 L11 **Hakui** Ishikawa, Honshū, SW Japan 36°55′N 136°46′E
190 B16 **Hakupu** SE Niue 19°06′S 169°50′E
164 L12 **Haku-san** ▲ Honshū, SW Japan 36°07′N 136°45′E
Hakusan see Mattō
149 Q15 **Hāla** Sind, SE Pakistan 25°47′N 68°28′E
138 J3 **Ḥalab** Eng. Aleppo, Fr. Alep; anc. Beroea. Ḥalab, NW Syria 36°14′N 37°10′E
138 J3 **Ḥalab** off. Muḥāfaẓat Ḥalab, var. Aleppo, Halab. ◐ governorate NW Syria
138 J3 **Ḥalab** ✈ Ḥalab, NW Syria 36°12′N 37°10′E
Halab see Ḥalab

◆ Country
● Country Capital
◇ Dependent Territory
○ Dependent Territory Capital
◐ Administrative Regions
✈ International Airport
▲ Mountain
▲▲ Mountain Range
⛰ Volcano
≈ River
◎ Lake
⊠ Reservoir

141 O8 **Ḥalabān** *var.* Halibān. Ar Riyāḍ, C Saudi Arabia *23°29′N 44°20′E*
139 V4 **Ḥalabja** As Sulaymānīyah, NE Iraq *35°11′N 45°59′E*
Ḥalab, Muḥāfaẓat *see* Ḥalab
146 L13 **Halaç** *Rus.* Khalach. Lebap Welaýaty, E Turkmenistan *38°05′N 64°46′E*
190 A16 **Halagigie Point** *headland* W Niue
75 Z11 **Halaib** SE Egypt *22°10′N 36°33′E*
75 Z11 **Hala'ib Triangle** *disputed region* S Egypt / N Sudan
190 G12 **Halalo** Île Uvea, N Wallis and Futuna *13°21′S 176°11′W*
167 U10 **Ha Lam** Quang Nam-Đa Nẵng, C Vietnam *15°42′N 108°24′E*
Halandri *see* Chalándri
141 X13 **Ḥalāniyāt, Juzur al** *var.* Jazā'ir Bin Ghalfān, *Eng.* Kuria Muria Islands. *island group* S Oman
141 W13 **Ḥalānīyāt, Khalīj al** *Eng.* Kuria Muria Bay. *bay* S Oman
Halas *see* Kiskunhalas
38 G11 **Hālawa** *var.* Halawa. Hawaii, USA, C Pacific Ocean *20°13′N 155°46′W*
Halawa *see* Hālawa
38 F9 **Hālawa, Cape** *var.* Cape Halawa. *headland* Moloka'i, Hawai'i, USA *21°09′N 156°43′W*
Cape Halawa *see* Hālawa, Cape
Halban *see* Tsetserleg
101 K14 **Halberstadt** Sachsen-Anhalt, C Germany *51°54′N 11°04′E*
184 M12 **Halcombe** Manawatu-Wanganui, North Island, New Zealand *40°09′S 175°30′E*
95 I16 **Halden** *prev.* Fredrikshald. Østfold, S Norway *59°08′N 11°20′E*
100 L13 **Haldensleben** Sachsen-Anhalt, C Germany *52°18′N 11°25′E*
Háldi *see* Halti
153 S17 **Haldia** West Bengal, NE India *22°04′N 88°02′E*
152 K10 **Haldwāni** Uttarakhand, N India *29°13′N 79°31′E*
163 P9 **Haldzan** Sühbaatar, E Mongolia *46°10′N 112°57′E*
163 P9 **Haldzan** *var.* Hatavch. Sühbaatar, E Mongolia *46°10′N 112°57′E*
38 F10 **Haleakalā** *var.* Haleakala. *crater* Maui, Hawai'i, USA
Haleakala *see* Haleakalā
25 N4 **Hale Center** Texas, SW USA *34°03′N 101°50′W*
99 J18 **Halen** Limburg, NE Belgium *50°35′N 05°08′E*
23 O2 **Haleyville** Alabama, S USA *34°13′N 87°37′W*
77 O17 **Half Assini** SW Ghana *05°03′N 02°57′W*
35 R8 **Half Dome** ▲ California, W USA *37°46′N 119°27′W*
185 C25 **Halfmoon Bay** *var.* Oban. Stewart Island, Southland, New Zealand *46°53′S 168°08′E*
182 E5 **Half Moon Lake** *salt lake* South Australia
163 S8 **Halhgol** *var.* Tsagaannuur. Dornod, E Mongolia *47°30′N 118°45′E*
163 R7 **Halhgol** Dornod, E Mongolia *47°57′N 118°07′E*
Haliacmon *see* Aliákmonas
Halibān *see* Ḥalabān
14 I13 **Haliburton** Ontario, SE Canada *45°03′N 78°20′W*
14 I12 **Haliburton Highlands** *var.* Madawaska Highlands. *hill range* Ontario, SE Canada
13 Q15 **Halifax** *province capital* Nova Scotia, SE Canada *44°38′N 63°35′W*
97 L17 **Halifax** N England, United Kingdom *53°44′N 01°52′W*
21 W8 **Halifax** North Carolina, SE USA *36°19′N 77°37′W*
21 U7 **Halifax** Virginia, NE USA *36°46′N 78°55′W*
13 Q15 **Halifax** ✈ Nova Scotia, SE Canada *44°33′N 63°48′W*
143 T13 **Halīl Rūd** *seasonal river* SE Iran
138 I6 **Ḥalīmah** ▲ Lebanon/Syria *34°12′N 36°37′E*
162 G8 **Haliun** Govi-Altay, W Mongolia *45°55′N 96°06′E*
118 I3 **Haljala** *Ger.* Halljal. Lääne-Virumaa, N Estonia *59°25′N 26°18′E*
39 Q4 **Halkett, Cape** *headland* Alaska, USA *70°48′N 152°11′W*
Halkida *see* Chalkída
96 J6 **Halkirk** N Scotland, United Kingdom *58°30′N 03°29′W*
15 X7 **Hall** ∽ Québec, SE Canada
Hall *see* Schwäbisch Hall
93 H15 **Hälla** Västerbotten, N Sweden *63°56′N 17°20′E*
96 J6 **Halladale** ∽ N Scotland, United Kingdom
95 J21 **Halland** ◆ *county* S Sweden
23 Z15 **Hallandale** Florida, SE USA *25°58′N 80°09′W*
95 K22 **Hallandsås** *physical region* S Sweden
9 P6 **Hall Beach** *var* Sanirajak. Nunavut, N Canada *68°10′N 81°56′W*
99 G19 **Halle** *Fr.* Hal. Vlaams Brabant, C Belgium *50°44′N 04°14′E*
101 M15 **Halle** *var.* Halle an der Saale. Sachsen-Anhalt, C Germany *51°28′N 11°58′E*
Halle an der Saale *see* Halle
35 W3 **Halleck** Nevada, W USA *40°57′N 115°27′W*
95 L15 **Hällefors** Örebro, C Sweden *59°46′N 14°30′E*
95 N16 **Hälleforsnäs** Södermanland, C Sweden *59°10′N 16°30′E*
109 Q6 **Hallein** Salzburg, N Austria *47°41′N 13°06′E*
101 L15 **Halle-Neustadt** Sachsen-Anhalt, C Germany *51°29′N 11°54′E*
25 U12 **Hallettsville** Texas, SW USA *29°27′N 96°57′W*
195 N4 **Halley** *UK research station* Antarctica *75°42′S 26°30′W*
28 L4 **Halliday** North Dakota, N USA *47°19′N 102°19′W*
37 S2 **Halligan Reservoir** ⊠ Colorado, C USA
100 G7 **Halligen** *island group* N Germany
94 G13 **Hallingdal** *valley* S Norway
38 J12 **Hall Island** *island* Alaska, USA
Hall Island *see* Maiana
189 P15 **Hall Islands** *island group* C Micronesia
118 H6 **Halliste** ∽ S Estonia
Halljal *see* Haljala
93 I15 **Hällnäs** Västerbotten, N Sweden *64°20′N 19°41′E*
29 R2 **Hallock** Minnesota, N USA *48°47′N 96°56′W*
9 S6 **Hall Peninsula** *peninsula* Baffin Island, Nunavut, NE Canada
20 F9 **Halls** Tennessee, S USA *35°52′N 89°24′W*
95 M16 **Hallsberg** Örebro, C Sweden *59°05′N 15°07′E*
181 N5 **Halls Creek** Western Australia *18°17′S 127°39′E*
182 L12 **Halls Gap** Victoria, SE Australia *37°09′S 142°30′E*
95 N15 **Hallstahammar** Västmanland, C Sweden *59°37′N 16°13′E*
109 R6 **Hallstatt** Salzburg, W Austria *47°32′N 13°39′E*
109 R6 **Hallstätter See** ◎ C Austria
95 P14 **Hallstavik** Stockholm, C Sweden *60°12′N 18°45′E*
25 X7 **Hallsville** Texas, SW USA *32°31′N 94°30′W*
103 P1 **Halluin** Nord, N France *50°46′N 03°07′E*
171 S12 **Halmahera, Laut** *Eng.* Halmahera Sea. *sea* E Indonesia
171 R11 **Halmahera, Pulau** *prev.* Djailolo, Gilolo, Jailolo. *island* E Indonesia
Halmahera Sea *see* Halmahera, Laut
95 J21 **Halmstad** Halland, S Sweden *56°41′N 12°49′E*
167 T6 **Ha Long** *prev.* Hông Gai, *var.* Hon Gai, Hongay. Quang Ninh, N Vietnam *20°57′N 107°06′E*
119 N15 **Halowchyn** *Rus.* Golovchin. Mahilyowskaya Voblasts', E Belarus *54°04′N 29°55′E*
95 H20 **Hals** Nordjylland, N Denmark *57°00′N 10°19′E*
94 F8 **Halsa** Møre og Romsdal, S Norway *63°04′N 08°13′E*
119 I15 **Hal'shany** *Rus.* Gol'shany. Hrodzyenskaya Voblasts', W Belarus *54°15′N 26°01′E*
Hälsingborg *see* Helsingborg
29 R5 **Halstad** Minnesota, N USA *47°21′N 96°49′W*
27 N6 **Halstead** Kansas, C USA *38°00′N 97°30′W*
99 G15 **Halsteren** Noord-Brabant, S Netherlands *51°32′N 04°16′E*
93 L16 **Halsua** Länsi-Suomi, W Finland *63°28′N 24°10′E*
101 E14 **Haltern** Nordrhein-Westfalen, W Germany *51°45′N 07°10′E*
92 J9 **Halti** *var.* Haltiatunturi, *Lapp.* Háldi. ▲ Finland/Norway *69°18′N 21°19′E*
Haltiatunturi *see* Halti
116 J6 **Halych** Ivano-Frankivs'ka Oblast', W Ukraine *49°08′N 24°44′E*
Halycus *see* Platani
103 P3 **Ham** Somme, N France *49°46′N 03°03′E*
Hama *see* Ḥamāh
164 F12 **Hamada** Shimane, Honshū, SW Japan *34°54′N 132°07′E*
142 L6 **Hamadān** *anc.* Ecbatana. Hamadān, W Iran *34°51′N 48°31′E*
142 L6 **Hamadān** *off.* Ostān-e Hamadān. ◆ *province* W Iran
Hamadān, Ostān-e *see* Hamadān
138 I5 **Ḥamāh** *var.* Hama; *anc.* Epiphania, *Bibl.* Hamath. Ḥamāh, W Syria *35°09′N 36°44′E*
138 I5 **Ḥamāh** *off.* Muḥāfaẓat Ḥamāh, *var.* Hama. ◆ *governorate* C Syria
Ḥamāh, Muḥāfaẓat *see* Ḥamāh
1665 S3 **Hamamasu** Hokkaidō, NE Japan *43°37′N 141°24′E*
164 L14 **Hamamatsu** *var.* Hamamatu. Shizuoka, Honshū, S Japan *34°43′N 137°46′E*
Hamamatu *see* Hamamatsu
165 W14 **Hamanaka** Hokkaidō, NE Japan *43°05′N 145°05′E*
164 L14 **Hamana-ko** ◎ Honshū, S Japan
94 I13 **Hamar** *prev.* Storhammer. Hedmark, S Norway *60°57′N 10°55′E*
141 U10 **Ḥamārīr al Kidan, Qalamat** *well* E Saudi Arabia
164 I12 **Hamasaka** Hyōgo, Honshū, SW Japan *35°37′N 134°27′E*
Hamath *see* Ḥamāh
165 T1 **Hamatonbetsu** Hokkaidō, NE Japan *45°07′N 142°21′E*
155 K26 **Hambantota** Southern Province, SE Sri Lanka *06°07′N 81°07′E*
Hambourg *see* Hamburg
100 J9 **Hamburg** Hamburg, N Germany *53°33′N 10°03′E*
27 V14 **Hamburg** Arkansas, C USA *33°13′N 91°50′W*
29 S16 **Hamburg** Iowa, C USA *40°36′N 95°39′W*
18 D10 **Hamburg** New York, NE USA *42°40′N 78°49′W*
100 I10 **Hamburg** *Fr.* Hambourg. ◆ *state* N Germany
148 K5 **Hamdam Āb, Dasht-e** *Pash.* Dasht-i Hamdamab. ▲▲ W Afghanistan
Hamdamab, Dasht-i *see* Hamdam Āb, Dasht-e
18 M13 **Hamden** Connecticut, NE USA *41°23′N 72°55′W*
140 K6 **Ḥamḍ, Wādī al** *dry watercourse* W Saudi Arabia
93 K18 **Hämeenkyrö** Länsi-Suomi, W Finland *61°39′N 23°10′E*
93 L19 **Hämeenlinna** *Swe.* Tavastehus. Etelä-Suomi, S Finland *61°N 24°25′E*
HaMela h, Yam *see* Dead Sea
Hamelin *see* Hameln
100 I13 **Hameln** *Eng.* Hamelin. Niedersachsen, N Germany *52°07′N 09°22′E*
180 I8 **Hamersley Range** ▲▲ Western Australia
163 Y12 **Hamgyŏng-sanmaek** ▲▲ N North Korea
163 X13 **Hamhŭng** C North Korea *39°53′N 127°31′E*
159 O6 **Hami** *var.* Ha-mi, *Uigh.* Kumul, Qomul. Xinjiang Uygur Zizhiqu, NW China *42°48′N 93°27′E*
Ha-mi *see* Hami
139 X10 **Ḥāmid Amīn** Maysān, E Iraq *32°06′N 46°53′E*
141 W11 **Hamīdān, Khawr** *oasis* SE Saudi Arabia
114 L12 **Hamidiye** Edirne, NW Turkey *41°09′N 26°40′E*
182 L12 **Hamilton** Victoria, SE Australia *37°45′S 142°04′E*
64 B12 **Hamilton** ○ (Bermuda) C Bermuda *32°18′N 64°48′W*
14 G16 **Hamilton** Ontario, S Canada *43°15′N 79°50′W*
184 M7 **Hamilton** Waikato, North Island, New Zealand *37°49′S 175°16′E*
96 I12 **Hamilton** S Scotland, United Kingdom *55°47′N 04°03′W*
23 N3 **Hamilton** Alabama, S USA *34°08′N 87°59′W*
38 M10 **Hamilton** Alaska, USA *62°54′N 163°53′W*
30 J13 **Hamilton** Illinois, N USA *40°24′N 91°20′W*
27 S3 **Hamilton** Missouri, C USA *39°44′N 94°00′W*
33 P10 **Hamilton** Montana, NW USA *46°15′N 114°09′W*
25 S8 **Hamilton** Texas, SW USA *31°42′N 98°08′W*
14 G16 **Hamilton** ✈ Ontario, SE Canada *43°12′N 79°54′W*
64 I6 **Hamilton Bank** *undersea feature* SE Labrador Sea
182 E1 **Hamilton Creek** *seasonal river* South Australia
13 R8 **Hamilton Inlet** *inlet* Newfoundland and Labrador, E Canada
27 T12 **Hamilton, Lake** ⊠ Arkansas, C USA
35 W6 **Hamilton, Mount** ▲ Nevada, W USA *39°15′N 115°30′W*
75 S8 **Ḥamīm, Wādī al** ∽ NE Libya
93 N19 **Hamina** *Swe.* Fredrikshamn. Kymi, S Finland *60°33′N 27°15′E*
11 W16 **Hamiota** Manitoba, S Canada *50°13′N 100°37′W*
152 L13 **Hamīrpur** Uttar Pradesh, N India *25°57′N 80°08′E*
Hamïs Musait *see* Khamīs Mushayṭ
21 T11 **Hamlet** North Carolina, SE USA *34°52′N 79°41′W*
25 P6 **Hamlin** Texas, SW USA *32°52′N 100°07′W*
21 P5 **Hamlin** West Virginia, NE USA *38°16′N 82°07′W*
31 O7 **Hamlin Lake** ◎ Michigan, N USA
101 F14 **Hamm** *var.* Hamm in Westfalen. Nordrhein-Westfalen, W Germany *51°39′N 07°49′E*
Ḥammāmāt, Khalīj al *see* Hammamet, Golfe de
75 N5 **Hammamet, Golfe de** *Ar.* Khalīj al Ḥammāmāt. *gulf* NE Tunisia
139 R3 **Ḥammān al 'Alīl** Nīnawé, N Iraq *36°07′N 43°15′E*
139 X12 **Ḥammār, Hawr al** ◎ SE Iraq
93 J20 **Hammarland** Åland, SW Finland *60°13′N 19°45′E*
93 H16 **Hammarstrand** Jämtland, C Sweden *63°07′N 16°27′E*
93 O17 **Hammaslahti** Itä-Suomi, SE Finland *62°26′N 29°58′E*
99 F17 **Hamme** Oost-Vlaanderen, NW Belgium *51°06′N 04°08′E*
100 H10 **Hamme** ∽ NW Germany
95 G22 **Hammel** Midtjylland, C Denmark *56°15′N 09°53′E*
101 I18 **Hammelburg** Bayern, C Germany *50°06′N 09°50′E*
99 H18 **Hamme-Mille** Walloon Brabant, C Belgium *50°48′N 04°42′E*
100 H10 **Hamme-Oste-Kanal** *canal* NW Germany
93 G16 **Hammerdal** Jämtland, C Sweden *63°34′N 15°19′E*
92 K8 **Hammerfest** Finnmark, N Norway *70°40′N 23°44′E*
101 D14 **Hamminkeln** Nordrhein-Westfalen, W Germany *51°43′N 06°36′E*
Hamm in Westfalen *see* Hamm
26 K10 **Hammon** Oklahoma, C USA *35°37′N 99°22′W*
31 N11 **Hammond** Indiana, N USA *41°35′N 87°30′W*
22 K8 **Hammond** Louisiana, S USA *30°30′N 90°27′W*
99 K20 **Hamoir** Liège, E Belgium *50°28′N 05°35′E*
99 J21 **Hamois** Namur, SE Belgium *50°21′N 05°09′E*
99 K16 **Hamont** Limburg, NE Belgium *51°15′N 05°33′E*
185 F22 **Hampden** Otago, South Island, New Zealand *45°18′S 170°49′E*
19 R6 **Hampden** Maine, NE USA *44°44′N 68°51′W*
97 M23 **Hampshire** *cultural region* S England, United Kingdom
13 O15 **Hampton** New Brunswick, SE Canada *45°30′N 65°50′W*
27 U14 **Hampton** Arkansas, C USA *33°33′N 92°28′W*
29 V12 **Hampton** Iowa, C USA *42°44′N 93°12′W*
19 P10 **Hampton** New Hampshire, NE USA *42°55′N 70°48′W*
21 R14 **Hampton** South Carolina, SE USA *32°52′N 81°06′W*
21 P8 **Hampton** Tennessee, S USA *36°16′N 82°10′W*
21 X7 **Hampton** Virginia, NE USA *37°02′N 76°23′W*
94 L11 **Hamra** Gävleborg, C Sweden *61°40′N 15°00′E*
80 D10 **Hamrat esh Sheikh** Northern Kordofan, C Sudan *14°38′N 27°56′E*
139 S5 **Ḥamrīn, Jabal** ▲ N Iraq
121 P16 **Ħamrun** C Malta *35°53′N 14°28′E*
Ham Thuân Nam *see* Thuân Nam
Hāmūn, Daryācheh-ye *see* Şāberī, Hāmūn-e/Sīstān, Daryācheh-ye
Hamwih *see* Southampton
38 G10 **Hāna** *var.* Hana. Maui, Hawaii, USA, C Pacific Ocean *20°45′N 155°59′W*
Hana *see* Hāna
21 S14 **Hanahan** South Carolina, SE USA *32°55′N 80°01′W*
38 B8 **Hanalei** Kaua'i, Hawaii, USA, C Pacific Ocean *22°12′N 159°30′W*
165 Q9 **Hanamaki** Iwate, Honshū, C Japan *39°25′N 141°04′E*
38 F10 **Hanamanioa, Cape** *headland* Maui, Hawai'i, USA *20°34′N 156°22′W*
190 B16 **Hanan** ✈ (Alofi) SW Niue
101 H18 **Hanau** Hessen, W Germany *50°06′N 08°56′E*
162 M11 **Hanbogd** *var.* Ih Bulag. Ömnögovĭ, S Mongolia *43°04′N 107°42′E*
8 L9 **Hanbury** ∽ Northwest Territories, NW Canada
Hâncești *see* Hîncești
10 M15 **Hanceville** British Columbia, SW Canada *51°54′N 122°56′W*
23 P3 **Hanceville** Alabama, S USA *34°03′N 86°46′W*
Hancewicze *see* Hantsavichy
160 L6 **Hancheng** Shaanxi, C China *35°22′N 110°27′E*
21 V2 **Hancock** Maryland, NE USA *39°42′N 78°10′W*
30 M3 **Hancock** Michigan, N USA *47°07′N 88°34′W*
29 S8 **Hancock** Minnesota, N USA *45°30′N 95°47′W*
18 I12 **Hancock** New York, NE USA *41°57′N 75°15′W*
80 Q12 **Handa** Bari, NE Somalia *10°35′N 51°09′E*
161 O5 **Handan** *var.* Han-tan. Hebei, E China *36°35′N 114°28′E*
95 P16 **Handen** Stockholm, C Sweden *59°12′N 18°09′E*
81 J22 **Handeni** Tanga, E Tanzania *05°25′S 38°04′E*
37 Q7 **Handies Peak** ▲ Colorado, C USA *37°54′N 107°30′W*
111 J19 **Handlová** *Ger.* Krickerhäu, *Hung.* Nyitrabánya; *prev.* Kriegerhaj. Trenčiansky Kraj, C Slovakia *48°45′N 18°45′E*
165 O13 **Haneda** ✈ (Tōkyō) Tōkyō, Honshū, S Japan *35°33′N 139°45′E*
138 F13 **HaNegev** *Eng.* Negev. *desert* S Israel
Hanfeng *see* Kaixian
35 Q11 **Hanford** California, W USA *36°19′N 119°39′W*
191 V16 **Hanga Roa** Easter Island, Chile, E Pacific Ocean *27°09′S 109°26′W*
162 I7 **Hangay** *var.* Hunt. Arhangay, C Mongolia *47°49′N 99°24′E*
162 H7 **Hangayn Nuruu** ▲▲ C Mongolia
Hang-chou/Hangchow *see* Hangzhou
95 K20 **Hånger** Jönköping, S Sweden *57°06′N 13°58′E*
Hangö *see* Hanko
161 R9 **Hangzhou** *var.* Hang-chou, Hangchow. *province capital* Zhejiang, SE China *30°18′N 120°07′E*
162 J4 **Hanh** *var.* Turt. Hövsgöl, N Mongolia *51°30′N 100°40′E*
162 F5 **Hanhöhiy Uul** ▲▲ NW Mongolia
162 K10 **Hanhongor** *var.* Ögöömör. Ömnögovĭ, S Mongolia *43°47′N 104°31′E*
146 I14 **Hanhowuz** *Rus.* Khauz-Khan. Ahal Welaýaty, S Turkmenistan *37°15′N 61°12′E*
146 I14 **Hanhowuz Suw Howdany** *Rus.* Khauzkhanskoye Vodoranilishche. ⊠ S Turkmenistan
137 P15 **Hani** Diyarbakır, SE Turkey *38°26′N 40°23′E*
Hania *see* Chaniá
141 R11 **Ḥanīsh al Kabīr, Jazīrat al** *island* SW Yemen
Hanka, Lake *see* Khanka, Lake
93 M17 **Hankasalmi** Länsi-Suomi, C Finland *62°25′N 26°27′E*
29 R7 **Hankinson** North Dakota, N USA *46°04′N 96°54′W*
93 K20 **Hanko** *Swe.* Hangö. Etelä-Suomi, SW Finland *59°50′N 23°E*
Han-kou/Han-k'ou/Hankow *see* Wuhan
36 M6 **Hanksville** Utah, W USA *38°21′N 110°43′W*
152 K6 **Hanle** Jammu and Kashmir, NW India *32°46′N 79°01′E*
185 I17 **Hanmer Springs** Canterbury, South Island, New Zealand *42°31′S 172°49′E*
11 R16 **Hanna** Alberta, SW Canada *51°38′N 111°56′W*
27 V3 **Hannibal** Missouri, C USA *39°42′N 91°23′W*
180 M3 **Hann, Mount** ▲ Western Australia *15°53′S 125°46′E*
100 I12 **Hannover** *Eng.* Hanover. Niedersachsen, NW Germany *52°23′N 09°43′E*
99 J19 **Hannut** Liège, C Belgium *50°40′N 05°05′E*
95 L22 **Hanöbukten** *bay* S Sweden
167 T6 **Ha Nôi** *Eng.* Hanoi, *Fr.* Hanoï. ● (Vietnam) N Vietnam *21°01′N 105°52′E*
14 F14 **Hanover** Ontario, S Canada *44°10′N 81°03′W*
31 P15 **Hanover** Indiana, N USA *38°42′N 85°28′W*
18 G16 **Hanover** Pennsylvania, NE USA *39°46′N 76°57′W*
21 W6 **Hanover** Virginia, NE USA *37°44′N 77°21′W*
Hanover *see* Hannover
63 G23 **Hanover, Isla** *island* S Chile
Hanselbeck *see* Érd
195 X5 **Hansen Mountains** ▲▲ Antarctica
160 M8 **Han Shui** ∽ C China
152 H10 **Hānsi** Haryāna, NW India *29°06′N 76°01′E*
95 F20 **Hanstholm** Midtjylland, NW Denmark *57°05′N 08°39′E*
Han-tan *see* Handan
158 H6 **Hantengri Feng** *var.* Pik Khan-Tengri. ▲ China/Kazakhstan *42°17′N 80°11′E* *see also* Khan-Tengri, Pik
119 I18 **Hantsavichy** *Pol.* Hancewicze, *Rus.* Gantsevichi. Brestskaya Voblasts', SW Belarus *52°45′N 26°27′E*
9 Q6 **Hantzsch** ∽ Baffin Island, Nunavut, NE Canada
152 G9 **Hanumāngarh** Rājasthān, NW India *29°33′N 74°21′E*
183 O9 **Hanwood** New South Wales, SE Australia *34°19′S 146°03′E*
Hanyang *see* Caidian
Hanyang *see* Wuhan
160 H10 **Hanyuan** *var.* Fulin. Sichuan, C China *29°29′N 102°45′E*
Hanyuan *see* Xihe
160 J7 **Hanzhong** Shaanxi, C China *33°12′N 107°E*
191 W11 **Hao** *atoll* Îles Tuamotu, C French Polynesia
153 S16 **Hāora** *prev.* Howrah. West Bengal, NE India *22°35′N 88°20′E*
78 K8 **Haouach, Ouadi** *dry watercourse* E Chad
92 K13 **Haparanda** Norrbotten, N Sweden *65°49′N 24°05′E*
25 N3 **Happy** Texas, SW USA *34°44′N 101°51′W*
34 M1 **Happy Camp** California, W USA *41°48′N 123°24′W*
13 Q9 **Happy Valley-Goose Bay** *prev.* Goose Bay. Newfoundland and Labrador, E Canada *53°19′N 60°24′W*
Hapsal *see* Haapsalu
152 J10 **Hāpur** Uttar Pradesh, N India *28°43′N 77°47′E*
HaQatan, HaMakhtesh *see* HaKatan, HaMakhtesh
140 I4 **Ḥaql** Tabūk, NW Saudi Arabia *29°18′N 34°58′E*
171 U14 **Har** Pulau Kai Besar, E Indonesia *05°21′S 133°09′E*
Haraat *see* Tsagaandelger
141 R8 **Ḥaraḍ** *var.* Haradh. Ash Sharqīyah, E Saudi Arabia *24°08′N 49°02′E*
Haradh *see* Ḥaraḍ
118 N12 **Haradok** *Rus.* Gorodok. Vitsyebskaya Voblasts', N Belarus *55°28′N 30°00′E*
92 J13 **Harads** Norrbotten, N Sweden *66°04′N 21°04′E*
119 G19 **Haradzyets** *Rus.* Gorodets. Brestskaya Voblasts', SW Belarus *52°12′N 24°40′E*
119 J17 **Haradzyeya** *Rus.* Gorodeya. Minskaya Voblasts', C Belarus *53°19′N 26°32′E*
191 V10 **Haraiki** *atoll* Îles Tuamotu, C French Polynesia
165 Q11 **Haramachi** Fukushima, Honshū, E Japan *37°40′N 140°55′E*
118 M12 **Harany** *Rus.* Gorany. Vitsyebskaya Voblasts', N Belarus *55°25′N 29°03′E*
83 L16 **Harare** *prev.* Salisbury. ● (Zimbabwe) Mashonaland East, NE Zimbabwe *17°47′S 31°04′E*
83 L16 **Harare** ✈ Mashonaland East, NE Zimbabwe *17°51′S 31°06′E*
78 J10 **Haraz-Djombo** Batha, C Chad *14°10′N 19°35′E*
119 O16 **Harbavichy** *Rus.* Gorbovichi. Mahilyowskaya Voblasts', E Belarus *53°49′N 30°42′E*
76 J16 **Harbel** W Liberia *06°19′N 10°20′W*
163 W8 **Harbin** *var.* Haerbin, Ha-erh-pin, Kharbin; *prev.* Haerhpin, Pingkiang, Pinkiang. *province capital* Heilongjiang, NE China *45°45′N 126°41′E*
31 S7 **Harbor Beach** Michigan, N USA *43°50′N 82°39′W*
13 T13 **Harbour Breton** Newfoundland, Newfoundland and Labrador, E Canada *47°29′N 55°50′W*
65 D25 **Harbours, Bay of** *bay* East Falkland, Falkland Islands
Hårby *see* Haarby
36 I13 **Harcuvar Mountains** ▲▲ Arizona, SW USA
108 I7 **Hard** Vorarlberg, NW Austria *47°29′N 09°42′E*
154 H11 **Harda Khas** Madhya Pradesh, C India *22°22′N 77°06′E*
95 D14 **Hardanger** *physical region* S Norway
95 D14 **Hardangerfjorden** *fjord* S Norway
94 E13 **Hardangerjøkulen** *glacier* S Norway
95 E14 **Hardangervidda** *plateau* S Norway
83 D20 **Hardap** ◆ *district* S Namibia
21 R15 **Hardeeville** South Carolina, SE USA *32°18′N 81°04′W*
Hardegarijp *see* Hurdegaryp
98 O9 **Hardenberg** Overijssel, E Netherlands *52°34′N 06°38′E*
183 Q9 **Harden-Murrumburrah** New South Wales, SE Australia *34°33′S 148°22′E*
98 K10 **Harderwijk** Gelderland, C Netherlands *52°21′N 05°37′E*
30 J14 **Hardin** Illinois, N USA *39°10′N 90°38′W*
33 V11 **Hardin** Montana, NW USA *45°44′N 107°35′W*
23 R5 **Harding, Lake** ⊠ Alabama/Georgia, SE USA
20 J6 **Hardinsburg** Kentucky, S USA *37°46′N 86°29′W*
98 I13 **Hardinxveld-Giessendam** Zuid-Holland, C Netherlands *51°52′N 04°49′E*
11 R15 **Hardisty** Alberta, SW Canada *52°42′N 111°22′W*
152 L12 **Hardoi** Uttar Pradesh, N India *27°23′N 80°06′E*
Hardwar *see* Haridwār
23 U4 **Hardwick** Georgia, SE USA *33°03′N 83°13′W*
27 W9 **Hardy** Arkansas, C USA *36°19′N 91°29′W*
94 D10 **Hareid** Møre og Romsdal, S Norway *62°22′N 06°02′E*
8 H7 **Hare Indian** ∽ Northwest Territories, NW Canada
99 D18 **Harelbeke** *var.* Harlebeke. West-Vlaanderen, W Belgium *50°51′N 03°19′E*
Harem *see* Ḥārim
100 E11 **Haren** Niedersachsen, NW Germany *52°47′N 07°16′E*
98 N6 **Haren** Groningen, NE Netherlands *53°10′N 06°37′E*
80 L13 **Hārer** E Ethiopia *09°17′N 42°19′E*
95 P14 **Harg** Uppsala, C Sweden *60°13′N 18°25′E*
Hargeisa *see* Hargeysa
80 M13 **Hargeysa** *var.* Hargeisa. Woqooyi Galbeed, NW Somalia *09°32′N 44°07′E*
116 J10 **Harghita** ◆ *county* NE Romania
25 S17 **Hargill** Texas, SW USA *26°26′N 98°00′W*
162 J8 **Harhorin** Övörhangay, C Mongolia *47°13′N 102°48′E*
159 Q9 **Har Hu** ◎ C China
Hariana *see* Haryāna
141 P15 **Ḥarīb** W Yemen *15°08′N 45°35′E*
168 M12 **Hari, Batang** *prev.* Djambi. ∽ Sumatera, W Indonesia
152 J9 **Haridwār** *prev.* Hardwar. Uttarakhand, N India *29°58′N 78°09′E*
155 F18 **Harihar** Karnātaka, W India *14°33′N 75°44′E*
185 F18 **Harihari** West Coast, South Island, New Zealand *43°09′S 170°35′E*
138 I3 **Ḥārim** *var.* Harem. Idlib, W Syria *36°30′N 36°30′E*
98 F13 **Haringvliet** *channel* SW Netherlands
98 F13 **Haringvlietdam** *dam* SW Netherlands
149 U5 **Haripur** Khyber Pakhtunkhwa, NW Pakistan *34°00′N 73°01′E*
148 J4 **Harīrūd** *var.* Tedzhen, *Turkm.* Tejen. ∽ Afghanistan/Iran *see also* Tejen
Harīrūd *see* Tejen
94 J11 **Härjåhågnen** *Swe.* Härjahågnen, *var.* Härjehågna. ▲ Norway/Sweden *61°43′N 12°07′E*
Härjahågnen *see* Østrehogna
Härjahågnen *see* Härjåhågnen
93 K18 **Harjavalta** Länsi-Suomi, W Finland *61°19′N 22°10′E*
Härjehågna *see* Østrehogna
Härjehågna *see* Härjåhågnen
118 G4 **Harjumaa** *var.* Harju Maakond. ◆ *province* NW Estonia
Harju Maakond *see* Harjumaa
21 X11 **Harkers Island** North Carolina, SE USA *34°42′N 76°33′W*
139 S1 **Harki** Dahūk, N Iraq *37°03′N 43°39′E*
29 T14 **Harlan** Iowa, C USA *41°40′N 95°19′W*
21 O7 **Harlan** Kentucky, S USA *36°50′N 83°19′W*
29 N17 **Harlan County Lake** ⊠ Nebraska, C USA
116 L9 **Hârlău** *var.* Hîrlău. Iași, NE Romania *47°26′N 26°54′E*
Harlebeke *see* Harelbeke
33 U7 **Harlem** Montana, NW USA *48°31′N 108°46′W*
Harlem *see* Haarlem
95 G22 **Harlev** Midtjylland, C Denmark *56°08′N 10°00′E*
98 K6 **Harlingen** *Fris.* Harns. Fryslân, N Netherlands *53°10′N 05°25′E*
25 T17 **Harlingen** Texas, SW USA *26°12′N 97°43′W*
97 O21 **Harlow** E England, United Kingdom *51°47′N 00°07′E*
33 T10 **Harlowton** Montana, NW USA *46°26′N 109°49′W*
94 N11 **Harmånger** Gävleborg, C Sweden *61°55′N 17°19′E*
98 I11 **Harmelen** Utrecht, C Netherlands *52°06′N 04°58′E*
29 X11 **Harmony** Minnesota, N USA *43°33′N 92°00′W*
32 J14 **Harney Basin** *basin* Oregon, NW USA
32 J14 **Harney Lake** ◎ Oregon, NW USA
28 J10 **Harney Peak** ▲ South Dakota, N USA *43°52′N 103°31′W*
93 H17 **Härnösand** *var.* Hernösand. Västernorrland, C Sweden *62°37′N 17°55′E*
Harns *see* Harlingen
105 P4 **Haro** La Rioja, N Spain *42°34′N 02°52′W*
40 F6 **Haro, Cabo** *headland* NW Mexico *27°50′N 110°55′W*
94 D9 **Harøy** *island* S Norway
97 N21 **Harpenden** E England, United Kingdom *51°49′N 00°22′W*
76 L18 **Harper** *var.* Cape Palmas. NE Liberia *04°25′N 07°43′W*
26 M7 **Harper** Kansas, C USA *37°17′N 98°01′W*
32 L13 **Harper** Oregon, NW USA *43°51′N 117°37′W*
25 Q10 **Harper** Texas, SW USA *30°18′N 99°18′W*
35 U13 **Harper Lake** *salt flat* California, W USA
39 T9 **Harper, Mount** ▲ Alaska, USA *64°18′N 143°54′W*
95 J21 **Harplinge** Halland, S Sweden *56°45′N 12°45′E*
36 J13 **Harquahala Mountains** ▲▲ Arizona, SW USA
141 T15 **Ḥarrah** SE Yemen *15°02′N 50°23′E*
12 H11 **Harricana** ∽ Québec, SE Canada
20 M9 **Harriman** Tennessee, S USA *35°57′N 84°33′W*
13 R11 **Harrington Harbour** Québec, E Canada *50°34′N 59°29′W*
64 B12 **Harrington Sound** *bay* Bermuda, NW Atlantic Ocean
96 F8 **Harris** *physical region* NW Scotland, United Kingdom
27 X10 **Harrisburg** Arkansas, C USA *35°33′N 90°43′W*
30 M17 **Harrisburg** Illinois, N USA *37°44′N 88°32′W*
28 I14 **Harrisburg** Nebraska, C USA *41°33′N 103°46′W*
32 F12 **Harrisburg** Oregon, NW USA *44°16′N 123°10′W*
18 G15 **Harrisburg** *state capital* Pennsylvania, NE USA *40°16′N 76°53′W*
182 F6 **Harris, Lake** ◎ South Australia
23 W11 **Harris, Lake** ◎ Florida, SE USA
83 J22 **Harrismith** Free State, E South Africa *28°16′S 29°08′E*
27 T9 **Harrison** Arkansas, C USA *36°13′N 93°07′W*
31 Q7 **Harrison** Michigan, N USA *44°02′N 84°46′W*
28 I12 **Harrison** Nebraska, C USA *42°42′N 103°53′W*
39 Q5 **Harrison Bay** *inlet* Alaska, USA
22 I6 **Harrisonburg** Louisiana, S USA *31°44′N 91°51′W*
21 U4 **Harrisonburg** Virginia, NE USA *38°27′N 78°54′W*
13 R7 **Harrison, Cape** *headland* Newfoundland and Labrador, E Canada *54°55′N 57°48′W*
27 R5 **Harrisonville** Missouri, C USA *38°40′N 94°21′W*
Harris Ridge *see* Lomonosov Ridge
192 M3 **Harris Seamount** *undersea feature* N Pacific Ocean *46°09′N 161°25′W*
96 F8 **Harris, Sound of** *strait* NW Scotland, United Kingdom
31 R6 **Harrisville** Michigan, N USA *44°41′N 83°19′W*
21 R3 **Harrisville** West Virginia, NE USA *39°13′N 81°04′W*
20 M6 **Harrodsburg** Kentucky, S USA *37°45′N 84°51′W*
97 M16 **Harrogate** N England, United Kingdom *54°01′N 01°33′W*
25 Q4 **Harrold** Texas, SW USA *34°05′N 99°02′W*
27 S5 **Harry S. Truman Reservoir** ⊠ Missouri, C USA
100 G13 **Harsewinkel** Nordrhein-Westfalen, W Germany *51°58′N 08°13′E*
116 M14 **Hârşova** *prev.* Hîrşova. Constanţa, SE Romania *44°41′N 27°56′E*
92 H10 **Harstad** Troms, N Norway *68°48′N 16°31′E*
31 O8 **Hart** Michigan, N USA *43°43′N 86°22′W*
24 M4 **Hart** Texas, SW USA *34°23′N 102°07′W*
10 I5 **Hart** ∽ Yukon Territory, NW Canada
83 F23 **Hartbees** ∽ C South Africa
109 X7 **Hartberg** Steiermark, SE Austria *47°18′N 15°58′E*
182 I10 **Hart, Cape** *headland* South Australia *35°54′S 138°01′E*
95 E14 **Hårteigen** ▲ S Norway *60°11′N 07°01′E*
23 Q7 **Hartford** Alabama, S USA *31°06′N 85°42′W*
27 R11 **Hartford** Arkansas, C USA *35°01′N 94°22′W*
18 M12 **Hartford** *state capital* Connecticut, NE USA *41°46′N 72°41′W*
20 J6 **Hartford** Kentucky, S USA *37°26′N 86°57′W*
31 P10 **Hartford** Michigan, N USA *42°12′N 85°54′W*
29 R11 **Hartford** South Dakota, N USA *43°37′N 96°56′W*
30 M8 **Hartford** Wisconsin, N USA *43°19′N 88°25′W*
31 P13 **Hartford City** Indiana, N USA *40°27′N 85°22′W*
29 Q13 **Hartington** Nebraska, C USA *42°37′N 97°15′W*
13 N14 **Hartland** New Brunswick, SE Canada *46°18′N 67°31′W*
97 H23 **Hartland Point** *headland* SW England, United Kingdom *51°01′N 04°33′W*
97 M15 **Hartlepool** N England, United Kingdom *54°41′N 01°13′W*
29 T12 **Hartley** Iowa, C USA *43°10′N 95°28′W*
24 M1 **Hartley** Texas, SW USA *35°52′N 102°24′W*
32 J15 **Hart Mountain** ▲ Oregon, NW USA *42°24′N 119°46′W*
173 U10 **Hartog Ridge** *undersea feature* W Indian Ocean
93 M18 **Hartola** Etelä-Suomi, S Finland *61°34′N 26°04′E*
67 U14 **Harts** *var.* Hartz. ∽ N South Africa
23 P2 **Hartselle** Alabama, S USA *34°26′N 86°56′W*
23 S3 **Hartsfield Atlanta** ✈ Georgia, SE USA *33°38′N 84°24′W*
27 Q11 **Hartshorne** Oklahoma, C USA *34°51′N 95°33′W*
21 S12 **Hartsville** South Carolina, SE USA *34°22′N 80°04′W*
20 K8 **Hartsville** Tennessee, S USA *36°23′N 86°11′W*
27 U7 **Hartville** Missouri, C USA *37°15′N 92°30′W*
23 U2 **Hartwell** Georgia, SE USA *34°21′N 82°55′W*
21 O11 **Hartwell Lake** ⊠ Georgia/South Carolina, SE USA
Hartz *see* Harts
Harunabad *see* Eslāmābād-e Gharb
Har-Us *see* Erdenebüren
162 F6 **Har Us Gol** ◎ Hovd, W Mongolia
162 E6 **Har Us Nuur** ◎ NW Mongolia
30 M10 **Harvard** Illinois, N USA *42°25′N 88°36′W*
29 P16 **Harvard** Nebraska, C USA *40°37′N 98°06′W*
37 R5 **Harvard, Mount** ▲ Colorado, C USA *38°55′N 106°19′W*
31 N11 **Harvey** Illinois, N USA *41°36′N 87°39′W*
29 N4 **Harvey** North Dakota, N USA *47°43′N 99°55′W*
97 Q21 **Harwich** E England, United Kingdom *51°56′N 01°16′E*
152 H10 **Haryāna** *var.* Hariana. ◆ *state* N India
141 Y9 **Ḥaryān, Ṭawī al** *spring/well* NE Oman *21°56′N 58°33′E*
101 J14 **Harz** ▲▲ C Germany
Ḥasakah, Muḥāfaẓat al *see* Al Ḥasakah
165 Q9 **Hasama** Miyagi, Honshū, C Japan *38°42′N 141°09′E*
137 Y13 **Häsänabad** *prev.* 26 Bakı Komissarı. SE Azerbaijan *39°18′N 49°13′E*
136 J15 **Hasan Dağı** ▲ C Turkey *38°09′N 34°15′E*
139 T9 **Ḥasan Ibn Ḥassūn** An Najaf, C Iraq *32°24′N 44°13′E*
149 R6 **Ḥasan Khēl** *var.* Ahmad Khel. Paktiyā, SE Afghanistan *33°46′N 69°37′E*
100 F12 **Hase** ∽ NW Germany
Haselberg *see* Krasnoznamensk
100 F12 **Haselünne** Niedersachsen, NW Germany *52°40′N 07°28′E*
Hashaat *see* Delgerhangay
Hashemite Kingdom of Jordan *see* Jordan
139 V8 **Hāshimah** Wāsiṭ, E Iraq *33°22′N 45°56′E*
142 K3 **Hashtrūd** *var.* Azaran. Āẕarbāyjān-e Khāvarī, N Iran *37°34′N 47°10′E*
141 W13 **Ḥāsik** S Oman *17°22′N 55°18′E*
149 U10 **Hāsilpur** Punjab, E Pakistan *29°42′N 72°40′E*
27 Q10 **Haskell** Oklahoma, C USA *35°49′N 95°40′W*
25 Q6 **Haskell** Texas, SW USA *33°10′N 99°45′W*
114 M11 **Hasköy** Edirne, NW Turkey *41°37′N 26°51′E*
95 L24 **Hasle** Bornholm, E Denmark *55°12′N 14°43′E*
97 N23 **Haslemere** SE England, United Kingdom *51°06′N 00°45′W*
102 I16 **Hasparren** Pyrénées-Atlantiques, SW France *43°23′N 01°18′W*
Hassakeh *see* Al Ḥasakah

◆ Country
● Country Capital
◇ Dependent Territory
○ Dependent Territory Capital
◆ Administrative Regions
✈ International Airport
▲ Mountain
▲▲ Mountain Range
Volcano
∽ River
◎ Lake
⊠ Reservoir

155 G19 **Hassan** Karnātaka, W India 13°01′N 76°03′E
36 J13 **Hassayampa River** ≈ Arizona, SW USA
101 J18 **Hassberge** hill range C Germany
94 N10 **Hassela** Gävleborg, C Sweden 62°06′N 16°45′E
99 J18 **Hasselt** Limburg, NE Belgium 50°56′N 05°20′E
98 M9 **Hasselt** Overijssel, E Netherlands 52°36′N 06°06′E
Hassetché see Al Ḩasakah
101 J18 **Hassfurt** Bayern, C Germany 50°02′N 10°32′E
74 L9 **Hassi Bel Guebbour** E Algeria 28°41′N 06°29′E
74 L8 **Hassi Messaoud** E Algeria 31°41′N 06°10′E
95 K22 **Hässleholm** Skåne, S Sweden 56°09′N 13°45′E
Hasta Colonia/Hasta Pompeia see Asti
183 O13 **Hastings** Victoria, SE Australia 38°18′S 145°12′E
184 O11 **Hastings** Hawke's Bay, North Island, New Zealand 39°39′S 176°51′E
97 P23 **Hastings** SE England, United Kingdom 50°51′N 00°36′E
31 P9 **Hastings** Michigan, N USA 42°38′N 85°17′W
29 W9 **Hastings** Minnesota, N USA 44°44′N 92°51′W
29 P16 **Hastings** Nebraska, C USA 40°35′N 98°23′W
95 K22 **Hästveda** Skåne, S Sweden 56°16′N 13°55′E
92 J8 **Hasvik** Finnmark, N Norway 70°29′N 22°08′E
37 V6 **Haswell** Colorado, C USA 38°27′N 103°09′W
163 N11 **Hatanbulag** var. Ergel. Dornogovĭ, SE Mongolia 43°10′N 109°13′E
Hatansuudal see Bayanlig
Hatavch see Haldzan
136 K17 **Hatay** ◈ province S Turkey
37 R15 **Hatch** New Mexico, SW USA 32°40′N 107°10′W
36 K7 **Hatch** Utah, W USA 37°39′N 112°25′W
20 F9 **Hatchie River** ≈ Tennessee, S USA
116 G12 **Haţeg** Ger. Wallenthal, Hung. Hátszeg; prev. Hatzeg, Hötzing. Hunedoara, SW Romania 45°35′N 22°57′E
165 O17 **Hateruma-jima** island Yaeyama-shotō, SW Japan
183 N8 **Hatfield** New South Wales, SE Australia 33°54′S 143°43′E
162 I5 **Hatgal** Hövsgöl, N Mongolia 50°24′N 100°12′E
153 V16 **Hathazari** Chittagong, SE Bangladesh 22°30′N 91°46′E
141 T13 **Hathūt, Hisā'** oasis NE Yemen
167 R14 **Ha Tiên** Kiên Giang, S Vietnam 10°24′N 104°30′E
167 T8 **Ha Tinh** Ha Tinh, N Vietnam 18°21′N 105°55′E
Ḩatira, Harei see Hatira, Harei
138 F12 **Hatira, Harei** prev. Haré Ḩatira. hill range S Israel
167 R6 **Hat Lot** var. Mai Son. Son La, N Vietnam 21°07′N 104°10′E
45 P16 **Hato Airport** ✈ (Willemstad) Curaçao 12°10′N 68°56′W
54 H9 **Hato Corozal** Casanare, C Colombia 06°08′N 71°45′W
Hato del Volcán see Volcán
45 P9 **Hato Mayor** E Dominican Republic 18°49′N 69°16′W
Hatra see Al Ḩaḑr
Hatria see Adria
Hátszeg see Haţeg
143 R16 **Hattā** Dubayy, NE United Arab Emirates 24°50′N 56°06′E
182 L9 **Hattah** Victoria, SE Australia 34°49′S 142°18′E
98 M9 **Hattem** Gelderland, E Netherlands 52°29′N 06°04′E
21 Z10 **Hatteras** Hatteras Island, North Carolina, SE USA 35°13′N 75°39′W
21 Rr10 **Hatteras, Cape** headland North Carolina, SE USA 35°29′N 75°33′W
21 Z9 **Hatteras Island** island North Carolina, SE USA
64 F10 **Hatteras Plain** undersea feature W Atlantic Ocean 31°00′N 71°00′W
93 G14 **Hattfjelldal** Troms, N Norway 65°37′N 13°58′E
22 M7 **Hattiesburg** Mississippi, S USA 31°20′N 89°17′W
29 Q4 **Hatton** North Dakota, N USA 47°38′N 97°27′W
Hatton Bank see Hatton Ridge
64 L6 **Hatton Ridge** var. Hatton Bank. undersea feature N Atlantic Ocean 59°00′N 17°30′W
191 W6 **Hatutu** island Îles Marquises, NE French Polynesia
111 K22 **Hatvan** Heves, NE Hungary 47°40′N 19°39′E
167 O16 **Hat Yai** var. Ban Hat Yai. Songkhla, SW Thailand 07°01′N 100°27′E
Hatzeg see Haţeg
Hatzfeld see Jimbolia
80 N13 **Haud** plateau Ethiopia/ Somalia
95 D18 **Hauge** Rogaland, S Norway 58°20′N 06°17′E
95 C15 **Haugesund** Rogaland, S Norway 59°24′N 05°17′E
109 X2 **Haugsdorf** Niederösterreich, NE Austria 48°41′N 16°04′E
184 M9 **Hauhungaroa Range** ▲▲ North Island, New Zealand
95 E15 **Haukeligrend** Telemark, S Norway 59°45′N 07°33′E
93 L14 **Haukipudas** Oulu, C Finland 65°11′N 25°21′E
93 M17 **Haukivesi** ◎ SE Finland
93 M17 **Haukivuori** Itä-Suomi, E Finland 62°02′N 27°11′E
Hauptkanal see Havelländ Grosse
187 N10 **Hauraha** Makira-Ulawa, SE Solomon Islands 10°47′S 162°00′E
184 L5 **Hauraki Gulf** gulf North Island, N New Zealand
185 B24 **Hauroko, Lake** ◎ South Island, New Zealand
167 S14 **Hâu, Sông** ≈ S Vietnam
92 N12 **Hautajärvi** Lappi, NE Finland 66°30′N 29°01′E
74 F7 **Haut Atlas** Eng. High Atlas. ▲▲ C Morocco
79 M17 **Haut-Congo** off. Région du Haut-Congo; prev. Haut-Zaïre. ◈ region NE Dem. Rep. Congo
103 Y14 **Haute-Corse** ◈ department Corse, France, C Mediterranean Sea
102 L16 **Haute-Garonne** ◈ department S France
79 K14 **Haute-Kotto** ◈ prefecture E Central African Republic
103 P12 **Haute-Loire** ◈ department C France
103 R6 **Haute-Marne** ◈ department N France
102 M3 **Haute-Normandie** ◈ region N France
15 U6 **Hauterive** Québec, SE Canada 49°11′N 68°16′W
103 T13 **Hautes-Alpes** ◈ department SE France
103 S7 **Haute-Saône** ◈ department E France
103 T10 **Haute-Savoie** ◈ department E France
99 M20 **Hautes Fagnes** Ger. Hohes Venn. ▲▲ E Belgium
102 K16 **Hautes-Pyrénées** ◈ department S France
99 L23 **Haute Sûre, Lac de la** ▣ NW Luxembourg
102 M11 **Haute-Vienne** ◈ department C France
19 S8 **Haut, Isle au** island Maine, NE USA
79 M14 **Haut-Mbomou** ◈ prefecture SE Central African Republic
103 Q2 **Hautmont** Nord, N France 50°15′N 03°55′E
79 F19 **Haut-Ogooué** off. Province du Haut-Ogooué, var. Le Haut-Ogooué. ◈ province SE Gabon
Haut-Ogooué, Le see Haut-Ogooué
Haut-Ogooué, Province du see Haut-Ogooué
103 U7 **Haut-Rhin** ◈ department NE France
74 I6 **Hauts Plateaux** plateau Algeria/Morocco
Haut-Zaïre see Haut-Congo
38 D9 **Hau'ula** var. Hauula. O'ahu, Hawaii, USA, C Pacific Ocean 21°36′N 157°54′W
Hauula see Hau'ula
101 O22 **Hauzenberg** Bayern, SE Germany 48°39′N 13°37′E
30 K13 **Havana** Illinois, N USA 40°18′N 90°03′W
Havana see La Habana
97 N23 **Havant** S England, United Kingdom 50°51′N 00°59′W
35 Y14 **Havasu, Lake** ▣ Arizona/ California, W USA
95 J23 **Havdrup** Sjælland, E Denmark 55°33′N 12°08′E
100 N10 **Havel** ≈ NE Germany
99 J21 **Havelange** Namur, SE Belgium 50°23′N 05°14′E
100 M11 **Havelberg** Sachsen-Anhalt, NE Germany 52°49′N 12°05′E
149 U5 **Haveliān** Khyber Pakhtunkhwa, NW Pakistan 34°05′N 73°14′E
100 N12 **Havelländ Grosse** var. Hauptkanal. canal NE Germany
14 J14 **Havelock** Ontario, SE Canada 44°22′N 77°57′W
185 J14 **Havelock** Marlborough, South Island, New Zealand 41°17′S 173°46′E
21 X11 **Havelock** North Carolina, SE USA 34°52′N 76°54′W
184 O11 **Havelock North** Hawke's Bay, North Island, New Zealand 39°40′S 176°53′E
98 M8 **Havelte** Drenthe, NE Netherlands 52°46′N 06°14′E
27 N6 **Haven** Kansas, C USA 37°54′N 97°46′W
97 H21 **Haverfordwest** SW Wales, United Kingdom 51°50′N 04°57′W
97 P20 **Haverhill** E England, United Kingdom 52°05′N 00°26′E
19 O10 **Haverhill** Massachusetts, NE USA 42°46′N 71°02′W
93 G17 **Haverö** Västernorrland, C Sweden 62°25′N 15°04′E
111 I17 **Havířov** Moravskoslezský Kraj, E Czech Republic 49°47′N 18°30′E
111 E17 **Havlíčkův Brod** Ger. Deutsch-Brod; prev. Německý Brod. Vysočina, C Czech Republic 49°38′N 15°46′E
92 K7 **Havøysund** Finnmark, N Norway 70°59′N 24°39′E
99 F20 **Havré** Hainaut, S Belgium 50°29′N 04°03′E
33 T7 **Havre** Montana, NW USA 48°33′N 109°41′W
Havre see le Havre
13 P11 **Havre-St-Pierre** Québec, E Canada 50°16′N 63°36′W
136 B10 **Havsa** Edirne, NW Turkey 41°32′N 26°49′E
38 D8 **Hawai'i** off. State of Hawai'i, also known as Aloha State, Paradise of the Pacific, var. Hawaii. ◈ state USA, C Pacific Ocean
38 G12 **Hawai'i** var. Hawaii. island Hawaiian Islands, USA, C Pacific Ocean
192 M5 **Hawai'ian Islands** prev. Sandwich Islands. island group Hawaii, USA
192 L5 **Hawaiian Ridge** undersea feature N Pacific Ocean 24°00′N 165°00′W
193 N6 **Hawaiian Trough** undersea feature N Pacific Ocean
29 R12 **Hawarden** Iowa, C USA 43°00′N 96°29′W
Hawash see Āwash
139 P6 **Hawbayn al Gharbīyah** Al Anbār, C Iraq 34°24′N 42°06′E
185 D21 **Hawea, Lake** ◎ South Island, New Zealand
184 K11 **Hawera** Taranaki, North Island, New Zealand 39°36′S 174°16′E
20 J5 **Hawesville** Kentucky, S USA 37°53′N 86°47′W
38 G11 **Hawi** Hawaii, USA, C Pacific Ocean 20°14′N 155°50′W
38 G11 **Hāwī** var. Hawi. Hawaii, USA, C Pacific Ocean 20°13′N 155°49′W
Hawi see Hāwī
96 K13 **Hawick** SE Scotland, United Kingdom 55°24′N 02°49′W
139 S4 **Ḩawījah** At Ta'mím, C Iraq 35°15′N 43°54′E
139 Y10 **Ḩawīzah, Hawr al** ◎ S Iraq
185 E21 **Hawkdun Range** ▲▲ South Island, New Zealand
184 P10 **Hawke Bay** bay North Island, New Zealand
182 I6 **Hawker** South Australia 31°54′S 138°25′E
184 N11 **Hawke's Bay** off. Hawkes Bay Region. ◈ region North Island, New Zealand
149 O16 **Hawkes Bay** bay SE Pakistan
Hawkes Bay Region see Hawke's Bay
15 N12 **Hawkesbury** Ontario, SE Canada 45°36′N 74°38′W
Hawkeye State see Iowa
23 T5 **Hawkinsville** Georgia, SE USA 32°16′N 83°28′W
14 B7 **Hawk Junction** Ontario, S Canada 48°05′N 84°34′W
21 N10 **Haw Knob** ▲ North Carolina/Tennessee, SE USA 35°18′N 84°01′W
21 Q9 **Hawksbill Mountain** ▲ North Carolina, SE USA 35°54′N 81°53′W
33 Z16 **Hawk Springs** Wyoming, C USA 41°48′N 104°17′W
Hawlēr see Arbīl
29 S5 **Hawley** Minnesota, N USA 46°53′N 96°18′W
25 P7 **Hawley** Texas, SW USA 32°36′N 99°47′W
141 R14 **Ḩawrā'** C Yemen 15°39′N 48°21′E
139 P7 **Ḩawrān, Wadi** dry watercourse W Iraq
21 T9 **Haw River** ≈ North Carolina, SE USA
139 U5 **Hawshqūrah** Diyālá, E Iraq 34°34′N 45°33′E
35 S7 **Hawthorne** Nevada, W USA 38°30′N 118°38′W
37 W3 **Haxtun** Colorado, C USA 40°36′N 102°38′W
183 N9 **Hay** New South Wales, SE Australia 34°31′S 144°51′E
11 O10 **Hay** ≈ W Canada
171 S13 **Haya** Pulau Seram, E Indonesia 03°22′S 129°31′E
165 R9 **Hayachine-san** ▲ Honshū, C Japan 39°31′N 141°28′E
103 S4 **Hayange** Moselle, NE France 49°19′N 06°04′E
HaYarden see Jordan
Hayastani Hanrapetut'yun see Armenia
Hayasui-seto see Hōyo-kaikyō
39 N9 **Haycock** Alaska, USA 65°12′N 161°10′W
36 M14 **Hayden** Arizona, SW USA 33°00′N 110°46′W
37 Q3 **Hayden** Colorado, C USA 40°29′N 107°15′W
28 M10 **Hayes** South Dakota, N USA 44°20′N 101°01′W
9 X13 **Hayes** ≈ Manitoba, C Canada
11 P12 **Hayes** ≈ Nunavut, NE Canada
28 M16 **Hayes Center** Nebraska, C USA 40°30′N 101°02′W
39 S10 **Hayes, Mount** ▲ Alaska, USA 63°37′N 146°43′W
21 N11 **Hayesville** North Carolina, SE USA 35°03′N 83°49′W
35 X10 **Hayford Peak** ▲ Nevada, W USA 36°40′N 115°10′W
34 M3 **Hayfork** California, W USA 40°33′N 123°10′W
Hayir, Qasr al see Ḩayr al Gharbī, Qaṣr al
Haylaastay see Sühbaatar
14 I12 **Hay Lake** ◎ Ontario, SE Canada
141 X11 **Haymā'** var. Haima. C Oman 19°59′N 56°20′E
136 H13 **Haymana** Ankara, C Turkey 39°26′N 32°30′E
138 J7 **Ḩaymūr, Jabal** ▲ W Syria
Haynau see Chojnów
22 G4 **Haynesville** Louisiana, S USA 32°57′N 93°08′W
23 P6 **Hayneville** Alabama, S USA 32°13′N 86°34′W
114 M12 **Hayrabolu** Tekirdağ, NW Turkey 41°14′N 27°04′E
136 C10 **Hayrabolu Deresi** ≈ NW Turkey
138 J6 **Ḩayr al Gharbī, Qaṣr al** var. Qasr al Hayir, Qasr al Hir al Gharbi. ruins Ḩimş, C Syria
138 L5 **Ḩayr ash Sharqī, Qaṣr al** var. Qasr al Hir Ash Sharqī. ruins Ḩimş, C Syria
162 J7 **Hayrhan** var. Uubulan. Arhangay, C Mongolia 48°37′N 101°58′E
162 J9 **Hayrhandulaan** var. Mardzad. Övörhangay, C Mongolia 45°58′N 102°06′E
8 J10 **Hay River** Northwest Territories, W Canada 60°51′N 115°42′W
26 K4 **Hays** Kansas, C USA 38°53′N 99°20′W
28 K12 **Hay Springs** Nebraska, C USA 42°40′N 102°41′W
65 H25 **Haystack, The** ▲ NE Saint Helena 15°55′S 05°40′W
27 N7 **Haysville** Kansas, C USA 37°34′N 97°21′W
117 O7 **Haysyn** Rus. Gaysin. Vinnyts'ka Oblast', C Ukraine 48°50′N 29°29′E
27 Y9 **Hayti** Missouri, C USA 36°13′N 89°45′W
29 Q9 **Hayti** South Dakota, N USA 44°40′N 97°22′W
117 O8 **Hayvoron** Rus. Gayvorno. Kirovohrads'ka Oblast', C Ukraine 48°20′N 29°52′E
35 N9 **Hayward** California, W USA 37°40′N 122°07′W
30 J4 **Hayward** Wisconsin, N USA 46°02′N 91°26′W
97 O23 **Haywards Heath** SE England, United Kingdom 51°00′N 00°06′W
146 A11 **Hazar** prev. Rus. Cheleken. Balkan Welaýaty, W Turkmenistan 39°26′N 53°07′E
143 S11 **Hazārān, Kūh-e** var. Kūh-e ā Hazr. ▲ SE Iran 29°26′N 57°15′E
Hazarat Imam see Imām Şāḩib
21 O7 **Hazard** Kentucky, S USA 37°14′N 83°11′W
137 O15 **Hazar Gölü** ◎ C Turkey
153 P15 **Hazārībāg** var. Hazāribāgh. Jhārkhand, N India 24°00′N 85°23′E
Hazāribāgh see Hazārībāg
103 O1 **Hazebrouck** Nord, N France 50°43′N 02°33′E
30 K9 **Hazel Green** Wisconsin, N USA 42°33′N 90°26′W
192 K9 **Hazel Holme Bank** undersea feature S Pacific Ocean 12°49′S 174°30′E
10 K13 **Hazelton** British Columbia, SW Canada 55°15′N 127°38′W
29 N6 **Hazelton** North Dakota, N USA 46°27′N 100°17′W
35 R5 **Hazen** Nevada, W USA 39°33′N 119°02′W
28 L5 **Hazen** North Dakota, N USA 47°18′N 101°37′W
38 L12 **Hazen Bay** bay E Bering Sea
9 N1 **Hazen, Lake** ◎ Nunavut, N Canada
139 S5 **Hazīm, Bi'r** well C Iraq
23 V6 **Hazlehurst** Georgia, SE USA 31°51′N 82°35′W
22 K6 **Hazlehurst** Mississippi, S USA 31°51′N 90°24′W
18 K15 **Hazlet** New Jersey, NE USA 40°24′N 74°10′W
146 J9 **Hazorasp** Rus. Khazarosp. Xorazm Viloyati, W Uzbekistan 41°21′N 61°01′E
147 R13 **Hazratishoh, Qatorkŭhi** var. Khrebet Khazretishi, Rus. Khrebet Khozretishi. ▲▲ S Tajikistan
Hazr, Kūh-e ā see Hazārān, Kūh-e
149 U6 **Hazro** Punjab, E Pakistan 33°55′N 72°33′E
23 R7 **Headland** Alabama, S USA 31°21′N 85°20′W
182 C6 **Head of Bight** headland South Australia 31°33′S 131°05′E
33 N10 **Headquarters** Idaho, NW USA 46°38′N 115°52′W
34 M7 **Healdsburg** California, W USA 38°36′N 122°52′W
27 N13 **Healdton** Oklahoma, C USA 34°13′N 97°29′W
183 O12 **Healesville** Victoria, SE Australia 37°41′S 145°31′E
39 R10 **Healy** Alaska, USA 63°51′N 148°58′W
173 R13 **Heard and McDonald Islands** ◇ Australian external territory S Indian Ocean
173 R13 **Heard Island** island Heard and McDonald Islands, S Indian Ocean
25 U9 **Hearne** Texas, SW USA 30°52′N 96°35′W
12 F12 **Hearst** Ontario, S Canada 49°42′N 83°40′W
194 J5 **Hearst Island** island Antarctica
Heart of Dixie see Alabama
28 L5 **Heart River** ≈ North Dakota, N USA
31 T13 **Heath** Ohio, N USA 40°01′N 82°26′W
183 N11 **Heathcote** Victoria, SE Australia 36°57′S 144°43′E
97 N22 **Heathrow** ✈ (London) SE England, United Kingdom 51°28′N 00°27′W
21 X5 **Heathsville** Virginia, NE USA 37°55′N 76°29′W
27 R11 **Heavener** Oklahoma, C USA 34°53′N 94°36′W
25 R15 **Hebbronville** Texas, SW USA 27°19′N 98°41′W
163 Q13 **Hebei** var. Hebei Sheng, Hopeh, Hopei, Ji; prev. Chihli. ◈ province E China
Hebei Sheng see Hebei
36 M3 **Heber City** Utah, W USA 40°31′N 111°25′W
27 V10 **Heber Springs** Arkansas, C USA 35°30′N 92°01′W
161 N5 **Hebi** Henan, C China 35°57′N 114°08′E
32 F11 **Hebo** Oregon, NW USA 45°10′N 123°55′W
96 F9 **Hebrides, Sea of the** sea NW Scotland, United Kingdom
13 P5 **Hebron** Newfoundland and Labrador, E Canada 58°15′N 62°45′W
31 N11 **Hebron** Indiana, N USA 41°19′N 87°12′W
29 Q17 **Hebron** Nebraska, C USA 40°10′N 97°35′W
28 L5 **Hebron** North Dakota, N USA 46°54′N 102°03′W
138 F11 **Hebron** var. Al Khalil, El Khalil, Heb. Hevron; anc. Kiriath-Arba. S West Bank 31°30′N 35°E
Hebrus see Évros/Maritsa/ Meriç
95 N14 **Heby** Västmanland, C Sweden 59°56′N 16°53′E
10 I14 **Hecate Strait** strait British Columbia, W Canada
41 W12 **Hecelchakán** Campeche, SE Mexico 20°09′N 90°04′W
160 K13 **Hechi** var. Jinchengjiang. Guangxi Zhuangzu Zizhiqu, S China 24°39′N 108°02′E
101 H23 **Hechingen** Baden-Württemberg, S Germany 48°20′N 08°58′E
99 K17 **Hechtel** Limburg, NE Belgium 51°07′N 05°24′E
160 J9 **Hechuan** var. Heyang. Chongqing Shi, C China 30°02′N 106°15′E
29 P7 **Hecla** South Dakota, N USA 45°52′N 98°09′W
9 N1 **Hecla, Cape** headland Nunavut, N Canada 82°00′N 64°00′W
29 T9 **Hector** Minnesota, N USA 44°44′N 94°43′W
93 F17 **Hede** Jämtland, C Sweden 62°25′N 13°33′E
Hede see Sheyang
95 M14 **Hedemora** Dalarna, C Sweden 60°18′N 15°58′E
92 K13 **Hedenäset** Finn. Hietaniemi. Norrbotten, N Sweden 66°12′N 23°40′E
95 G23 **Hedensted** Syddanmark, C Denmark 55°47′N 09°43′E
95 N14 **Hedesunda** Gävleborg, C Sweden 60°25′N 17°00′E
95 N14 **Hedesundafjärden** ◎ C Sweden
25 O3 **Hedley** Texas, SW USA 34°52′N 100°39′W
94 I12 **Hedmark** ◈ county S Norway
165 T16 **Hedo-misaki** headland Okinawa, SW Japan 26°55′N 128°15′E
29 X15 **Hedrick** Iowa, C USA 41°10′N 92°18′W
99 L16 **Heel** Limburg, SE Netherlands 51°12′N 06°01′E
189 Y12 **Heel Point** point Wake Island
98 H9 **Heemskerk** Noord-Holland, W Netherlands 52°31′N 04°40′E
98 M10 **Heerde** Gelderland, E Netherlands 52°24′N 06°02′E
98 L7 **Heerenveen** Fris. It Hearrenfean. Fryslân, N Netherlands 52°57′N 05°55′E
98 I8 **Heerhugowaard** Noord-Holland, NW Netherlands 52°40′N 04°50′E
92 O3 **Heer Land** physical region C Svalbard
99 M18 **Heerlen** Limburg, SE Netherlands 50°55′N 06°E
99 J19 **Heers** Limburg, NE Belgium 50°46′N 05°17′E
Heerwegen see Polkowice
98 K13 **Heesch** Noord-Brabant, S Netherlands 51°44′N 05°32′E
99 K15 **Heeze** Noord-Brabant, SE Netherlands 51°23′N 05°35′E
138 F8 **Hefa** var. Haifa, hist. Caiffa, Caiphas; anc. Sycaminum. Haifa, N Israel 32°49′N 34°59′E
Ḩefa, Mifraz see Mifrats Hefa
161 Q8 **Hefei** var. Hofei, hist. Luchow. province capital Anhui, E China 31°51′N 117°20′E
23 R3 **Heflin** Alabama, S USA 33°39′N 85°35′W
163 X7 **Hegang** Heilongjiang, NE China 47°18′N 130°16′E
164 L10 **Hegura-jima** island SW Japan
Heguri-jima see Heigun-tō
Hei see Heilongjiang
100 H8 **Heide** Schleswig-Holstein, N Germany 54°12′N 09°06′E
101 G20 **Heidelberg** Baden-Württemberg, SW Germany 49°24′N 08°41′E
83 J21 **Heidelberg** Gauteng, NE South Africa 26°31′S 28°21′E
22 M6 **Heidelberg** Mississippi, S USA 31°53′N 88°58′W
Heidenheim see Heidenheim an der Brenz
101 J22 **Heidenheim an der Brenz** var. Heidenheim. Baden-Württemberg, S Germany 48°41′N 10°09′E
109 U2 **Heidenreichstein** Niederösterreich, N Austria 48°53′N 15°07′E
164 F14 **Heigun-tō** var. Heguri-jima. island SW Japan
163 W5 **Heihe** prev. Ai-hun. Heilongjiang, NE China 50°13′N 127°29′E
162 S8 **Hei He** ≈ C China
Hei-ho see Nagqu
83 J22 **Heilbron** Free State, N South Africa 27°17′S 27°58′E
101 H21 **Heilbronn** Baden-Württemberg, SW Germany 49°09′N 09°13′E
Heiligenbeil see Mamonovo
109 Q8 **Heiligenblut** Tirol, W Austria 47°04′N 12°50′E
100 K7 **Heiligenhafen** Schleswig-Holstein, N Germany 54°22′N 10°57′E
Heiligenkreuz see Žiar nad Hronom
101 J15 **Heiligenstadt** Thüringen, C Germany 51°22′N 10°09′E
163 W8 **Heilongjiang** var. Hei, Heilongjiang Sheng, Hei-lung-chiang, Heilungkiang. ◈ province NE China
Heilong Jiang see Amur
Heilongjiang Sheng see Heilongjiang
98 H9 **Heiloo** Noord-Holland, NW Netherlands 52°36′N 04°43′E
Heilsberg see Lidzbark Warmiński
Hei-lung-chiang/ Heilungkiang see Heilongjiang
Heimaæy see Heimaey
92 I4 **Heimaey** var. Heimaæy. island S Iceland
94 H8 **Heimdal** Sør-Trøndelag, S Norway 63°21′N 10°23′E
Heinaste see Ainaži
93 N17 **Heinävesi** Itä-Suomi, E Finland 62°22′N 28°42′E
99 M22 **Heinerscheid** Diekirch, N Luxembourg 50°06′N 06°05′E
98 M10 **Heino** Overijssel, E Netherlands 52°26′N 06°13′E
93 M18 **Heinola** Etelä-Suomi, S Finland 61°13′N 26°05′E
101 C16 **Heinsberg** Nordrhein-Westfalen, W Germany 51°02′N 06°01′E
163 U12 **Heishan** Liaoning, NE China 41°43′N 122°12′E
160 H8 **Heishui** var. Luhua. Sichuan, C China 32°08′N 102°54′E
99 H17 **Heist-op-den-Berg** Antwerpen, C Belgium 51°04′N 04°43′E
Heitō see Pingdong
171 X15 **Heitske** Papua, E Indonesia 07°02′S 138°45′E
Hejanah see Al Hījānah
Hejaz see Al Ḩijāz
160 M14 **He Jiang** ≈ S China
Hejiayan see Lüeyang
158 K6 **Hejing** Xinjiang Uygur Zizhiqu, NW China 42°21′N 86°19′E
Héjjasfalva see Vânători
Heka see Hoika
137 N14 **Hekimhan** Malatya, C Turkey 38°50′N 37°56′E
92 J4 **Hekla** ⩓ S Iceland 63°56′N 19°42′W
Hekou see Yanshan, Jiangxi, China
Hekou see Yajiang, Sichuan, China
110 J6 **Hel** Ger. Hela. Pomorskie, N Poland 54°35′N 18°48′E
Hela see Hel
93 F17 **Helagsfjället** ▲ C Sweden 62°57′N 12°31′E
159 W8 **Helan** var. Xigang. Ningxia, N China 38°33′N 106°21′E
162 K14 **Helan Shan** ▲▲ N China
99 M16 **Helden** Limburg, SE Netherlands 51°20′N 06°00′E
27 X12 **Helena** Arkansas, C USA 34°32′N 90°34′W
33 R10 **Helena** state capital Montana, NW USA 46°36′N 112°02′W
96 H12 **Helensburgh** W Scotland, United Kingdom 56°00′N 04°45′W
184 K5 **Helensville** Auckland, North Island, New Zealand 36°42′S 174°26′E
95 L20 **Helgasjön** ◎ S Sweden
100 G8 **Helgoland** Eng. Heligoland. island NW Germany
Helgoland Bay see Helgoländer Bucht
100 G8 **Helgoländer Bucht** var. Helgoland Bay, Heligoland Bight. bay NW Germany
Heligoland see Helgoland
Heligoland Bight see Helgoländer Bucht
Heliopolis see Baalbek
92 I4 **Hella** Sudhurland, SW Iceland 63°51′N 20°24′W
Hellas see Greece
143 N11 **Ḩelleh, Rūd-e** ≈ S Iran
98 N10 **Hellendoorn** Overijssel, E Netherlands 52°22′N 06°27′E
Hellenic Republic see Greece
121 Q10 **Hellenic Trough** undersea feature Aegean Sea, C Mediterranean Sea 22°00′E 35°30′N
94 E10 **Hellesylt** Møre og Romsdal, S Norway 62°06′N 06°51′E
98 F13 **Hellevoetsluis** Zuid-Holland, SW Netherlands 51°49′N 04°08′E
105 Q12 **Hellín** Castilla-La Mancha, C Spain 38°31′N 01°43′W
115 H19 **Hellinikon** ✈ (Athína) Attikí, C Greece 37°53′N 23°43′E
32 M12 **Hells Canyon** valley Idaho/ Oregon, NW USA
148 L9 **Helmand** ◈ province S Afghanistan
148 K10 **Helmand, Daryā-ye** var. Rūd-e Hīrmand. ≈ Afghanistan/Iran see also Hīrmand, Rūd-e
Helmand, Daryā-ye see Hīrmand, Rūd-e
Helmantica see Salamanca
101 K15 **Helme** ≈ C Germany
99 L15 **Helmond** Noord-Brabant, S Netherlands 51°29′N 05°41′E
96 J7 **Helmsdale** N Scotland, United Kingdom 58°06′N 03°36′W
100 K13 **Helmstedt** Niedersachsen, N Germany 52°14′N 11°01′E
163 Y10 **Helong** Jilin, NE China 42°38′N 129°01′E
36 M4 **Helper** Utah, W USA 39°40′N 110°52′W
100 O10 **Helpter Berge** hill NE Germany
95 J22 **Helsingborg** prev. Hälsingborg. Skåne, S Sweden 56°N 12°48′E
Helsingfors see Helsinki
95 J22 **Helsingør** Eng. Elsinore. Hovedstaden, E Denmark 56°03′N 12°38′E
93 M20 **Helsinki** Swe. Helsingfors. ● (Finland) Etelä-Suomi, S Finland 60°18′N 24°58′E
97 H25 **Helston** SW England, United Kingdom 50°04′N 05°17′W
Heltau see Cisnădie
61 C17 **Helvecia** Santa Fe, C Argentina 31°09′S 60°09′W
97 K15 **Helvellyn** ▲ NW England, United Kingdom 54°31′N 03°00′W
Helvetia see Switzerland
Helwān see Ḩilwān
97 N21 **Hemel Hempstead** E England, United Kingdom 51°46′N 00°28′W
35 U16 **Hemet** California, W USA 33°45′N 116°58′W
28 J13 **Hemingford** Nebraska, C USA 42°18′N 103°02′W
21 T13 **Hemingway** South Carolina, SE USA 33°45′N 79°25′W
92 G13 **Hemnesberget** Nordland, C Norway 66°14′N 13°40′E
25 Y8 **Hemphill** Texas, SW USA 31°21′N 93°50′W
25 V11 **Hempstead** Texas, SW USA 30°06′N 96°06′W
95 P20 **Hemse** Gotland, SE Sweden 57°12′N 18°22′E
94 F13 **Hemsedal** valley S Norway
161 N6 **Henan** var. Henan Sheng, Honan, Yu. ◈ province C China
184 L4 **Hen and Chickens** island group N New Zealand
Henan Mongolzu Zizhixian/Henan Sheng see Yêgainnyin
105 O7 **Henares** ≈ C Spain
165 P7 **Henashi-zaki** headland Honshū, C Japan 40°37′N 139°51′E
102 I16 **Hendaye** Pyrénées-Atlantiques, SW France 43°22′N 01°46′W
136 F11 **Hendek** Sakarya, NW Turkey 40°47′N 30°45′E
61 B21 **Henderson** Buenos Aires, E Argentina 36°18′S 61°43′W
20 I5 **Henderson** Kentucky, S USA 37°50′N 87°35′W
35 X11 **Henderson** Nevada, W USA 36°02′N 114°58′W
21 V8 **Henderson** North Carolina, SE USA 36°20′N 78°26′W
20 G10 **Henderson** Tennessee, S USA 35°27′N 88°40′W
25 W7 **Henderson** Texas, SW USA 32°11′N 94°48′W
30 J12 **Henderson Creek** ≈ Illinois, N USA
186 M9 **Henderson Field** ✈ (Honiara) Guadalcanal, C Solomon Islands 09°28′S 160°02′E
191 O17 **Henderson Island** atoll N Pitcairn Islands
21 O10 **Hendersonville** North Carolina, SE USA 35°19′N 82°28′W
20 J8 **Hendersonville** Tennessee, S USA 36°18′N 86°37′W
143 O14 **Hendorābī, Jazīreh-ye** island S Iran
55 V10 **Hendrik Top** var. Hendriktop. elevation C Surinam
Hendriktop see Hendrik Top
Hendū Kosh see Hindu Kush
14 L12 **Heney, Lac** ◎ Québec, SE Canada
Hengchow see Hengyang
161 S15 **Hengch'un** S Taiwan 22°09′N 120°43′E
159 R16 **Hengduan Shan** ▲▲ SW China
98 N12 **Hengelo** Gelderland, E Netherlands 52°03′N 06°19′E
98 O10 **Hengelo** Overijssel, E Netherlands 52°16′N 06°46′E
Hengnan see Hengyang
161 N11 **Hengshan** Hunan, S China 27°17′N 112°51′E
160 L4 **Hengshan** Shaanxi, C China 37°57′N 109°17′E
161 O4 **Hengshui** Hebei, E China 37°42′N 115°39′E
161 N12 **Hengyang** var. Hengnan, Heng-yang; prev. Hengchow. Hunan, S China 26°55′N 112°34′E
Heng-yang see Hengyang
117 U11 **Heniches'k** Rus. Genichesk. Khersons'ka Oblast', S Ukraine 46°10′N 34°49′E
21 Z4 **Henlopen, Cape** headland Delaware, NE USA 38°48′N 75°06′W
Henna see Enna
94 M10 **Hennan** Gävleborg, C Sweden 62°01′N 15°55′E
102 G7 **Hennebont** Morbihan, NW France 47°48′N 03°17′W
30 L11 **Hennepin** Illinois, N USA 41°14′N 89°21′W
26 M9 **Hennessey** Oklahoma, C USA 36°06′N 97°54′W
100 N12 **Hennigsdorf** var. Hennigsdorf bei Berlin. Brandenburg, NE Germany 52°37′N 13°13′E
Hennigsdorf bei Berlin see Hennigsdorf
19 N9 **Henniker** New Hampshire, NE USA 43°10′N 71°47′W
25 S5 **Henrietta** Texas, SW USA 33°49′N 98°13′W
Henrique de Carvalho see Saurimo
30 L12 **Henry** Illinois, N USA 41°06′N 89°21′W
21 Y7 **Henry, Cape** headland Virginia, NE USA 36°55′N 76°01′W
27 P10 **Henryetta** Oklahoma, C USA 35°26′N 95°58′W
194 M7 **Henry Ice Rise** ice cap Antarctica
9 R5 **Henry Kater, Cape** headland Baffin Island, Nunavut, NE Canada 69°09′N 66°45′W
33 R13 **Henrys Fork** ≈ Idaho, NW USA
14 E15 **Hensall** Ontario, S Canada 43°25′N 81°28′W
100 J9 **Henstedt-Ulzburg** Schleswig-Holstein, N Germany 53°45′N 09°59′E
163 N7 **Hentiy** var. Batshireet, Eg. ◈ province N Mongolia
162 M7 **Hentiyn Nuruu** ▲▲ N Mongolia
183 P10 **Henty** New South Wales, SE Australia 35°33′S 147°03′E
Henzada see Hinthada
Heping see Huishui
101 G19 **Heppenheim** Hessen, W Germany 49°39′N 08°38′E
32 J11 **Heppner** Oregon, NW USA 45°21′N 119°32′W
160 L15 **Hepu** var. Lianzhou. Guangxi Zhuangzu Zizhiqu, S China 21°40′N 109°12′E
Heracleum see Irákleio
92 J2 **Heradhsvötn** ≈ C Iceland
Herakleion see Irákleio
148 K5 **Herāt** var. Herat; anc. Aria. Herāt, W Afghanistan 34°23′N 62°11′E
148 J5 **Herāt** ◈ province W Afghanistan
103 P14 **Hérault** ◈ department S France
103 P15 **Hérault** ≈ S France
11 T16 **Herbert** Saskatchewan, S Canada 50°27′N 107°09′W
185 F22 **Herbert** Otago, South Island, New Zealand 45°14′S 170°48′E
38 J17 **Herbert Island** island Aleutian Islands, Alaska, USA
Herbertshöhe see Kokopo
15 Q7 **Herbertville** Québec, SE Canada 48°23′N 71°42′W
101 G17 **Herborn** Hessen, W Germany 50°40′N 08°18′E
113 I17 **Herceg-Novi** It. Castelnuovo; prev. Ercegnovi. SW Montenegro 42°28′N 18°35′E
11 X10 **Herchmer** Manitoba, C Canada 57°25′N 94°12′W
186 E8 **Hercules Bay** bay E Papua New Guinea
92 K2 **Herdhubreidh** ⩓ C Iceland 65°12′N 16°26′W
42 M13 **Heredia** Heredia, C Costa Rica 10°N 84°06′W
42 M12 **Heredia** off. Provincia de Heredia. ◈ province N Costa Rica
Heredia, Provincia de see Heredia
97 K21 **Hereford** W England, United Kingdom 52°04′N 02°43′W
24 M3 **Hereford** Texas, SW USA 34°49′N 102°25′W
15 Q13 **Hereford, Mont** ▲ Québec, SE Canada 45°04′N 71°38′W
97 K21 **Herefordshire** cultural region W England, United Kingdom
191 U11 **Hereheretue** atoll Îles Tuamotu, C French Polynesia
105 N10 **Herencia** Castilla-La Mancha, C Spain 39°22′N 03°12′W
99 H18 **Herent** Vlaams Brabant, C Belgium 50°54′N 04°40′E
99 I16 **Herentals** var. Herenthals. Antwerpen, N Belgium 51°11′N 04°50′E
Herenthals see Herentals
99 H17 **Herenthout** Antwerpen, N Belgium 51°09′N 04°45′E
95 J23 **Herfølge** Sjælland, E Denmark 55°25′N 12°09′E
100 G13 **Herford** Nordrhein-Westfalen, NW Germany 52°07′N 08°41′E
27 O5 **Herington** Kansas, C USA 38°37′N 96°55′W
108 H7 **Herisau** Fr. Hérisau. Ausser Rhoden, NE Switzerland 47°23′N 09°17′E
Hérisau see Herisau
Héristal see Herstal
99 J18 **Herk-de-Stad** Limburg, NE Belgium 50°57′N 05°12′E
Herkulesbad/ Herkulesfürdő see Băile Herculane
162 M8 **Herlenbayan-Ulaan** var. Dulaan. Hentiy, C Mongolia 47°09′N 108°48′E
Herlen Gol/Herlen He see Kerulen
35 Q4 **Herlong** California, W USA 40°07′N 120°06′W
97 L26 **Herm** island Channel Islands
109 R9 **Hermagor** Slvn. Šmohor. Kärnten, S Austria 46°37′N 13°24′E
29 S7 **Herman** Minnesota, N USA 45°49′N 96°08′W

◆ Country ● Country Capital ◇ Dependent Territory ○ Dependent Territory Capital ◈ Administrative Regions ✈ International Airport ▲ Mountain ▲▲ Mountain Range ⩓ Volcano ≈ River ◎ Lake ▣ Reservoir

96 L1 **Herma Ness** *headland* NE Scotland, United Kingdom 60°51′N 00°55′W
27 V4 **Hermann** Missouri, C USA 38°43′N 91°26′W
181 Q8 **Hermannsburg** Northern Territory, N Australia 23°59′S 132°55′E
Hermannstadt *see* Sibiu
94 E12 **Hermansverk** Sogn Og Fjordane, S Norway 61°11′N 06°52′E
138 H6 **Hermel** *var.* Hirmil. NE Lebanon 34°23′N 36°19′E
Hermhausen *see* Hajnówka
183 P6 **Hermidale** New South Wales, SE Australia 31°36′S 146°42′E
55 X9 **Herminadorp** Sipaliwini, NE Surinam 05°05′N 54°22′W
32 K11 **Hermiston** Oregon, NW USA 45°50′N 119°17′W
27 T6 **Hermitage** Missouri, C USA 37°57′N 93°21′W
186 D4 **Hermit Islands** *island group* N Papua New Guinea
25 O7 **Hermleigh** Texas, SW USA 32°37′N 100°44′W
138 G7 **Hermon, Mount** *Ar.* Jabal ash Shaykh. ▲ S Syria 35°30′N 33°30′E
Hermopolis Parva *see* Damanhûr
28 J10 **Hermosa** South Dakota, N USA 43°49′N 103°12′W
40 F5 **Hermosillo** Sonora, NW Mexico 28°59′N 110°53′W
Hermoupolis *see* Ermoúpoli
111 N20 **Hernád** *var.* Hornád, *Ger.* Kundert. ∽ Hungary/Slovakia
61 C18 **Hernández** Entre Ríos, E Argentina 32°21′S 60°02′W
23 V11 **Hernando** Florida, SE USA 28°54′N 82°22′W
22 L1 **Hernando** Mississippi, S USA 34°49′N 89°59′W
105 Q2 **Hernani** País Vasco, N Spain 43°16′N 01°59′W
99 F19 **Herne** Vlaams Brabant, C Belgium 50°45′N 04°03′E
101 E14 **Herne** Nordrhein-Westfalen, W Germany 51°32′N 07°12′E
95 F22 **Herning** Midtjylland, W Denmark 56°08′N 08°59′E
Hernösand *see* Härnösand
121 U11 **Herodotus Basin** *undersea feature* E Mediterranean Sea
121 Q12 **Herodotus Trough** *undersea feature* C Mediterranean Sea
29 T11 **Heron Lake** Minnesota, N USA 43°48′N 95°18′W
Herowābād *see* Khalkhāl
95 G16 **Herre** Telemark, S Norway 59°06′N 09°34′E
29 N7 **Herreid** South Dakota, N USA 45°49′N 100°04′W
101 H22 **Herrenberg** Baden-Württemberg, S Germany 48°36′N 08°52′E
104 L14 **Herrera** Andalucía, S Spain 37°22′N 04°50′W
43 R17 **Herrera** *off.* Provincia de Herrera. ◈ *province* S Panama
104 L10 **Herrera del Duque** Extremadura, W Spain 39°10′N 05°03′W
104 M4 **Herrera de Pisuerga** Castilla y León, N Spain 42°35′N 04°20′W
Herrera, Provincia de *see* Herrera
41 Z13 **Herrero, Punta** *headland* SE Mexico 19°15′N 87°28′W
183 P16 **Herrick** Tasmania, SE Australia 41°07′S 147°53′E
30 L17 **Herrin** Illinois, N USA 37°48′N 89°01′W
20 M6 **Herrington Lake** ⊠ Kentucky, S USA
95 K18 **Herrljunga** Västra Götaland, S Sweden 58°05′N 13°02′E
103 N16 **Hers** ∽ S France
10 I1 **Herschel Island** *island* Yukon Territory, NW Canada
99 I17 **Herselt** Antwerpen, C Belgium 51°04′N 04°53′E
18 G15 **Hershey** Pennsylvania, NE USA 40°17′N 76°39′W
99 K19 **Herstal** *Fr.* Héristal. Liège, E Belgium 50°40′N 05°38′E
97 O21 **Hertford** E England, United Kingdom 51°48′N 00°05′W
21 X8 **Hertford** North Carolina, SE USA 36°11′N 76°30′W
97 O21 **Hertfordshire** *cultural region* E England, United Kingdom
181 Z9 **Hervey Bay** Queensland, E Australia 25°17′S 152°48′E
101 O14 **Herzberg** Brandenburg, E Germany 51°42′N 13°15′E
99 E18 **Herzele** Oost-Vlaanderen, NW Belgium 50°52′N 03°52′E
101 K20 **Herzogenaurach** Bayern, SE Germany 49°34′N 10°52′E
109 W4 **Herzogenburg** Niederösterreich, NE Austria 48°18′N 15°43′E
Herzogenbusch *see* 's-Hertogenbosch
103 N2 **Hesdin** Pas-de-Calais, N France 50°21′N 02°00′E
160 K14 **Heshan** Guangxi Zhuangzu Zizhiqu, S China 23°45′N 108°58′E
159 X10 **Heshui** *var.* Xihuachi. Gansu, C China 35°42′N 108°06′E
99 M25 **Hespérange** Luxembourg, SE Luxembourg 49°34′N 06°10′E
35 U14 **Hesperia** California, W USA 34°25′N 117°17′W
37 P7 **Hesperus Mountain** ▲ Colorado, C USA 37°27′N 108°05′W
10 J6 **Hess** ∽ Yukon Territory, NW Canada
Hesse *see* Hessen
101 J21 **Hesselberg** ▲ S Germany 49°04′N 10°32′E
95 I22 **Hesselo** *island* E Denmark
101 H17 **Hessen** *Eng./Fr.* Hesse. ◈ *state* C Germany
192 L6 **Hess Tablemount** *undersea feature* C Pacific Ocean 17°49′N 174°15′W
27 N6 **Hesston** Kansas, C USA 38°08′N 97°25′W
93 G15 **Hestkjøltoppen** ▲ C Norway 64°21′N 13°57′E
97 K18 **Heswall** NW England, United Kingdom 53°20′N 03°06′W
153 P12 **Hetaudā** Central, C Nepal
Hétfalu *see* Săcele
28 K7 **Hettinger** North Dakota, N USA 46°00′N 102°38′W
101 L14 **Hettstedt** Sachsen-Anhalt, C Germany 51°39′N 11°31′E
92 P3 **Heuglin, Kapp** *headland* SE Svalbard 78°15′N 22°49′E
163 W17 **Heuksan-jedo** *var.* Hŭksan-gundo. *island group* SW South Korea
187 N10 **Heuru** Makira-Ulawa, SE Solomon Islands 10°13′S 161°25′E
99 J17 **Heusden** Limburg, NE Belgium 51°02′N 05°17′E
98 J13 **Heusden** Noord-Brabant, S Netherlands 51°43′N 05°05′E
102 K3 **Hève, Cap de la** *headland* N France 49°28′N 00°13′W
99 H18 **Heverlee** Vlaams Brabant, C Belgium 50°52′N 04°41′E
111 L22 **Heves** Heves, NE Hungary 47°36′N 20°17′E
111 L22 **Heves** *off.* Heves Megye. ◈ *county* NE Hungary
Heves Megye *see* Heves
Hevron *see* Hebron
45 Y13 **Hewanorra** ✈ (Saint Lucia) S Saint Lucia 13°44′N 60°57′W
Hexian *see* Hezhou
160 L6 **Heyang** Shaanxi, C China 35°14′N 110°02′E
Heyang *see* Hechuan
Heydebrech *see* Kędzierzyn-Kozle
Heydekrug *see* Šilutė
Heyin *see* Guide
97 K16 **Heysham** NW England, United Kingdom 54°02′N 02°54′W
161 O14 **Heyuan** *var.* Yuancheng. Guangdong, S China 23°41′N 114°45′E
182 L12 **Heywood** Victoria, SE Australia 38°09′S 141°38′E
180 K3 **Heywood Islands** *island group* Western Australia
161 O6 **Heze** *var.* Caozhou. Shandong, E China 35°16′N 115°27′E
159 U11 **Hezheng** Gansu, C China 35°29′N 103°36′E
160 M13 **Hezhou** *var.* Babu; *prev.* Hexian. Guangxi Zhuangzu Zizhiqu, S China 24°33′N 11°30′E
159 U11 **Hezuo** Gansu, C China 34°55′N 102°49′E
23 Z16 **Hialeah** Florida, SE USA 25°51′N 80°16′W
27 Q3 **Hiawatha** Kansas, C USA 39°51′N 95°34′W
36 M4 **Hiawatha** Utah, W USA 39°28′N 111°00′W
29 V4 **Hibbing** Minnesota, N USA 47°24′N 92°55′W
183 N17 **Hibbs, Point** *headland* Tasmania, SE Australia 42°37′S 145°15′E
Hibernia *see* Ireland
20 F8 **Hickman** Kentucky, S USA 36°33′N 89°11′W
21 Q9 **Hickory** North Carolina, SE USA 35°44′N 81°20′W
21 Q9 **Hickory, Lake** ◎ North Carolina, SE USA
184 Q7 **Hicks Bay** Gisborne, North Island, New Zealand 37°36′S 178°18′E
25 S8 **Hico** Texas, SW USA 31°58′N 98°01′W
Hida *see* Furukawa
165 T4 **Hidaka** Hokkaidō, NE Japan 42°53′N 142°24′E
164 I12 **Hidaka** Hyōgo, Honshū, SW Japan 35°27′N 134°43′E
165 T5 **Hidaka-sanmyaku** ▲▲ Hokkaidō, NE Japan
41 O6 **Hidalgo** *var.* Villa Hidalgo. Coahuila, NE Mexico 27°46′N 99°54′W
41 N8 **Hidalgo** Nuevo León, NE Mexico 29°59′N 100°27′W
41 O10 **Hidalgo** Tamaulipas, C Mexico 24°16′N 99°28′W
41 O13 **Hidalgo** ◈ *state* C Mexico
40 J7 **Hidalgo del Parral** *var.* Parral. Chihuahua, N Mexico 26°58′N 105°40′W
100 N7 **Hiddensee** *island* NE Germany
80 G6 **Hidiglib, Wadi** ∽ NE Sudan
109 U6 **Hieflau** Salzburg, E Austria 47°36′N 14°34′E
187 P16 **Hienghène** Province Nord, C New Caledonia 20°43′S 164°54′E
Hierosolyma *see* Jerusalem
64 N12 **Hierro** *var.* Ferro. *island* Islas Canarias, Spain, NE Atlantic Ocean
Hietaniemi *see* Hedenäset
164 G13 **Higashi-Hiroshima** *var.* Higasihirosima. Hiroshima, Honshū, SW Japan 34°27′N 132°43′E
164 C12 **Higashi-suidō** *strait* SW Japan
Higasihirosima *see* Higashi-Hiroshima
25 P1 **Higgins** Texas, SW USA 36°06′N 100°01′W
31 P7 **Higgins Lake** ◎ Michigan, N USA
27 S4 **Higginsville** Missouri, C USA 39°04′N 93°43′W
High Atlas *see* Haut Atlas
30 M5 **High Falls Reservoir** ⊠ Wisconsin, N USA
44 K12 **Highgate** C Jamaica 18°16′N 76°53′W
25 X11 **High Island** Texas, SW USA 29°35′N 94°24′W
31 O5 **High Island** *island* Michigan, N USA
30 K15 **Highland** Illinois, N USA 38°44′N 89°40′W
31 N10 **Highland Park** Illinois, N USA 42°10′N 87°48′W
21 O10 **Highlands** North Carolina, SE USA 35°04′N 83°10′W
11 O11 **High Level** Alberta, W Canada 58°31′N 117°08′W
29 O9 **Highmore** South Dakota, N USA 44°29′N 99°26′W
171 N3 **High Peak** ▲ Luzon, N Philippines 15°28′N 120°07′E
High Plains *see* Great Plains
21 S9 **High Point** North Carolina, SE USA 35°58′N 80°00′W
18 J13 **High Point** *hill* New Jersey, NE USA
11 P13 **High Prairie** Alberta, W Canada 55°27′N 116°28′W
11 Q16 **High River** Alberta, SW Canada 50°35′N 113°50′W
21 S9 **High Rock Lake** ⊠ North Carolina, SE USA
23 V9 **High Springs** Florida, SE USA 29°49′N 82°36′W
High Veld *see* Great Karoo
97 J24 **High Willhays** ▲ SW England, United Kingdom 50°39′N 03°58′W
97 N22 **High Wycombe** *prev.* Chepping Wycombe, Chipping Wycombe. SE England, United Kingdom 51°38′N 00°46′W
41 P12 **Higos** *var.* El Higo. Veracruz-Llave, E Mexico 21°48′N 98°25′W
102 I16 **Higuer, Cap** *headland* NE Spain 43°23′N 01°46′W
45 R5 **Higüero, Punta** *headland* W Puerto Rico 18°21′N 67°15′W
45 P9 **Higüey** *var.* Salvaleón de Higüey. E Dominican Republic 18°40′N 68°43′W
190 G11 **Hihifo** ✈ (Matā'utu) Île Uvea, N Wallis and Futuna
81 N16 **Hiiraan** *off.* Gobolka Hiiraan. ◈ *region* C Somalia
Hiiraan, Gobolka *see* Hiiraan
118 E4 **Hiiumaa** *var.* Hiiumaa Maakond. ◈ *province* W Estonia
118 D4 **Hiiumaa** *Ger.* Dagden, *Swe.* Dagö. *island* W Estonia
Hiiumaa Maakond *see* Hiiumaa
Hijanah *see* Al Hījānah
105 S6 **Híjar** Aragón, NE Spain 41°10′N 00°27′W
191 V10 **Hikueru** *atoll* Îles Tuamotu, C French Polynesia
184 K3 **Hikurangi** Northland, North Island, New Zealand 35°37′S 174°16′E
184 Q8 **Hikurangi** ▲ North Island, New Zealand 37°55′S 177°59′E
192 L11 **Hikurangi Trench** *var.* Hikurangi Trough. *undersea feature* SW Pacific Ocean
Hikurangi Trough *see* Hikurangi Trench
190 B15 **Hikutavake** NW Niue
121 Q12 **Hilāl, Ra's al** *headland* N Libya 32°55′N 22°09′E
61 A24 **Hilario Ascasubi** Buenos Aires, E Argentina 39°22′S 62°39′W
101 K17 **Hildburghausen** Thüringen, C Germany 50°26′N 10°44′E
101 E15 **Hilden** Nordrhein-Westfalen, W Germany 51°12′N 06°56′E
100 I13 **Hildesheim** Niedersachsen, N Germany 52°09′N 09°57′E
33 T9 **Hilger** Montana, NW USA 47°15′N 109°18′W
153 S13 **Hili** *var.* Hilli. Rajshahi, NW Bangladesh 25°16′N 89°04′E
Hilla *see* Al Ḥillah
45 O14 **Hillaby, Mount** ▲ N Barbados 13°12′N 59°34′W
95 K19 **Hillared** Västra Götaland, S Sweden 57°37′N 13°10′E
195 R12 **Hillary Coast** *physical region* Antarctica
42 G2 **Hill Bank** Orange Walk, N Belize 17°36′N 88°43′W
33 O14 **Hill City** Idaho, NW USA 43°18′N 115°03′W
26 K3 **Hill City** Kansas, C USA 39°23′N 99°51′W
29 V5 **Hill City** Minnesota, N USA 46°59′N 93°36′W
28 J10 **Hill City** South Dakota, N USA 43°54′N 103°33′W
65 C24 **Hill Cove Settlement** West Falkland, Falkland Islands
98 H10 **Hillegom** Zuid-Holland, W Netherlands 52°18′N 04°35′E
95 J22 **Hillerød** Hovedstaden, E Denmark 55°56′N 12°19′E
36 M7 **Hillers, Mount** ▲ Utah, W USA 37°53′N 110°42′W
Hilli *see* Hili
29 R11 **Hills** Minnesota, N USA 43°31′N 96°21′W
30 L14 **Hillsboro** Illinois, N USA 39°09′N 89°29′W
27 N5 **Hillsboro** Kansas, C USA 38°21′N 97°12′W
27 X5 **Hillsboro** Missouri, C USA 38°13′N 90°33′W
19 N10 **Hillsboro** New Hampshire, NE USA 43°06′N 71°52′W
37 Q14 **Hillsboro** New Mexico, SW USA 32°55′N 107°33′W
29 R4 **Hillsboro** North Dakota, N USA 47°25′N 97°03′W
31 R14 **Hillsboro** Ohio, N USA 39°12′N 83°36′W
32 G11 **Hillsboro** Oregon, NW USA 45°32′N 122°59′W
25 T8 **Hillsboro** Texas, SW USA 32°01′N 97°08′W
30 K8 **Hillsboro** Wisconsin, N USA 43°40′N 90°21′W
23 Y14 **Hillsboro Canal** *canal* Florida, SE USA
45 Y15 **Hillsborough** Carriacou, N Grenada 12°28′N 61°28′W
97 G15 **Hillsborough** E Northern Ireland, United Kingdom 54°27′N 06°06′W
21 U9 **Hillsborough** North Carolina, SE USA 36°04′N 79°06′W
31 Q10 **Hillsdale** Michigan, N USA 41°55′N 84°37′W
183 O8 **Hillston** New South Wales, SE Australia 33°30′S 145°33′E
21 R7 **Hillsville** Virginia, NE USA 36°46′N 80°44′W
96 L2 **Hillswick** NE Scotland, United Kingdom 60°28′N 01°37′W
Hill Tippera *see* Tripura
38 H11 **Hilo** Hawaii, USA, C Pacific Ocean 19°42′N 155°04′W
18 F9 **Hilton** New York, NE USA 43°17′N 77°47′W
14 C10 **Hilton Beach** Ontario, S Canada 46°14′N 83°51′W
21 R16 **Hilton Head Island** South Carolina, SE USA 32°13′N 80°45′W
21 R16 **Hilton Head Island** *island* South Carolina, SE USA
99 J15 **Hilvarenbeek** Noord-Brabant, S Netherlands 51°29′N 05°08′E
98 J11 **Hilversum** Noord-Holland, C Netherlands 52°14′N 05°10′E
75 W8 **Hilwān** *var.* Helwân, Hilwân, Hulwan, Hulwân. N Egypt 29°51′N 31°20′E
Hilwân *see* Hilwān
152 J7 **Himāchal Pradesh** ◈ *state* NW India
Himalaya/Himalaya Shan *see* Himalayas
152 M9 **Himalayas** *var.* Himalaya, *Chin.* Himalaya Shan. ▲▲ S Asia
171 P6 **Himamaylan** Negros, C Philippines 10°04′N 122°52′E
93 K15 **Himanka** Länsi-Suomi, W Finland 64°04′N 23°40′E
Himara *see* Himarë
113 L23 **Himarë** *var.* Himara. Vlorë, S Albania 40°06′N 19°45′E
138 M2 **Ḥimār, Wādī al** *dry watercourse* N Syria
154 D9 **Himatnagar** Gujarāt, W India 23°38′N 73°02′E
109 Y4 **Himberg** Niederösterreich, E Austria 48°05′N 16°27′E
164 I13 **Himeji** *var.* Himezi. Hyōgo, Honshū, SW Japan 34°47′N 134°32′E
164 E14 **Hime-jima** *island* SW Japan
Himezi *see* Himeji
164 L13 **Himi** Toyama, Honshū, SW Japan 36°54′N 136°59′E
109 S9 **Himmelberg** Kärnten, S Austria 46°45′N 14°01′E
138 I5 **Ḥimṣ** *var.* Homs; *anc.* Emesa. Ḥimṣ, C Syria 34°44′N 36°43′E
138 K6 **Ḥimṣ** *off.* Muḥāfazat Hims, *var.* Homs. ◈ *governorate* C Syria
138 I5 **Ḥimṣ, Buḥayrat** *var.* Buhayrat Qattinah. ◎ W Syria
171 R7 **Hinatuan** Mindanao, S Philippines 08°21′N 126°19′E
117 N10 **Hînceşti** *var.* Hânceşti; *prev.* Kotovsk. C Moldova 46°48′N 28°33′E
44 M9 **Hinche** C Haiti 19°07′N 72°00′W
181 X5 **Hinchinbrook Island** *island* Queensland, NE Australia
39 S12 **Hinchinbrook Island** *island* Alaska, USA
97 M19 **Hinckley** C England, United Kingdom 52°33′N 01°21′W
29 V7 **Hinckley** Minnesota, N USA 46°01′N 92°57′W
36 K5 **Hinckley** Utah, W USA 39°21′N 112°39′W
18 J9 **Hinckley Reservoir** ⊠ New York, NE USA
152 I12 **Hindaun** Rājasthān, N India 26°44′N 77°02′E
Hindenburg/Hindenburg in Oberschlesien *see* Zabrze
Hindiya *see* Al Hindīyah
21 O6 **Hindman** Kentucky, S USA 37°20′N 82°58′W
182 L10 **Hindmarsh, Lake** ◎ Victoria, SE Australia
185 G19 **Hinds** Canterbury, South Island, New Zealand 44°01′S 171°33′E
185 G19 **Hinds** ∽ South Island, New Zealand
95 H23 **Hindsholm** *island* C Denmark
149 S4 **Hindu Kush** *Per.* Hendū Kosh. ▲▲ Afghanistan/Pakistan
155 H19 **Hindupur** Andhra Pradesh, E India 13°46′N 77°33′E
11 O12 **Hines Creek** Alberta, W Canada 56°14′N 118°36′W
23 W6 **Hinesville** Georgia, SE USA 31°51′N 81°36′W
154 I12 **Hinganghāt** Mahārāshtra, C India 20°32′N 78°52′E
149 N15 **Hingol** ∽ SW Pakistan
154 H13 **Hingoli** Mahārāshtra, C India 19°45′N 77°08′E
137 R13 **Hınıs** Erzurum, E Turkey 39°22′N 41°44′E
92 O2 **Hinlopenstretet** *strait* N Svalbard
92 G10 **Hinnøya** *Lapp.* Iinnasuolu. *island* C Norway
108 H10 **Hinterrhein** ∽ SW Switzerland
166 L8 **Hinthada** *var.* Henzada. Ayeyarwady, SW Burma (Myanmar) 17°36′N 95°26′E
11 O14 **Hinton** Alberta, SW Canada 53°24′N 117°35′W
26 M10 **Hinton** Oklahoma, C USA 35°28′N 98°21′W
21 R6 **Hinton** West Virginia, NE USA 37°42′N 80°54′W
Hios *see* Chíos
41 N8 **Hipólito** Coahuila, NE Mexico 25°42′N 101°22′W
Hipponium *see* Vibo Valentia
164 B13 **Hirado** Nagasaki, Hirado-shima, SW Japan 33°22′N 129°31′E
164 B13 **Hirado-shima** *island* SW Japan
165 P16 **Hirakubo-saki** *headland* Ishigaki-jima, SW Japan 24°36′N 124°19′E
154 M11 **Hīrākud Reservoir** ⊠ E India
Hir al Gharbi, Qasr al *see* Ḥayr al Gharbī, Qaṣr al
165 Q16 **Hirara** Okinawa, Miyako-jima, SW Japan 24°48′N 125°17′E
Hir Ash Sharqī, Qasr al *see* Ḥayr ash Sharqī, Qaṣr al
164 G12 **Hirata** Shimane, Honshū, SW Japan 35°25′N 132°45′E
136 I13 **Hirfanlı Barajı** ⊠ C Turkey
155 G18 **Hiriyūr** Karnātaka, W India 13°58′N 76°33′E
Hîrlău *see* Hârlău
148 K10 **Hīrmand, Rūd-e** *var.* Daryā-ye Helmand. ∽ Afghanistan/Iran *see also* Helmand, Daryā-ye
Hīrmand, Rūd-e *see* Helmand, Daryā-ye
Hirmil *see* Hermel
165 T5 **Hiroo** Hokkaidō, NE Japan 42°16′N 143°16′E
165 Q7 **Hirosaki** Aomori, Honshū, C Japan 40°34′N 140°28′E
164 G13 **Hiroshima** *var.* Hirosima. Hiroshima, Honshū, SW Japan 34°23′N 132°26′E
164 F13 **Hiroshima** *off.* Hiroshima-ken, *var.* Hirosima. ◈ *prefecture* Honshū, SW Japan
Hiroshima-ken *see* Hiroshima
Hirosima *see* Hiroshima
Hirschberg/Hirschberg im Riesengebirge/Hirschberg in Schlesien *see* Jelenia Góra
103 Q3 **Hirson** Aisne, N France 49°56′N 04°05′E
Hîrşova *see* Hârşova
95 G19 **Hirtshals** Nordjylland, N Denmark 57°34′N 09°58′E
152 H10 **Hisār** Haryāna, NW India 29°10′N 75°45′E
162 K7 **Hishig Öndör** *var.* Maanĭt. Bulgan, C Mongolia 48°17′N 103°29′E
186 E9 **Hisiu** Central, SW Papua New Guinea 09°20′S 146°48′E
147 P13 **Hisor** *Rus.* Gissar. W Tajikistan 38°34′N 68°29′E
Hispalis *see* Sevilla
Hispana/Hispania *see* Spain
44 M7 **Hispaniola** *island* Dominion Republic/Haiti
64 F11 **Hispaniola Basin** *var.* Hispaniola Trough. *undersea feature* SW Atlantic Ocean
Hispaniola Trough *see* Hispaniola Basin
Histonium *see* Vasto
139 R7 **Hīt** Al Anbār, SW Iraq 33°38′N 42°50′E
165 P14 **Hita** Ōita, Kyūshū, SW Japan 33°19′N 130°55′E
165 P12 **Hitachi** *var.* Hitati. Ibaraki, Honshū, S Japan 36°40′N 140°42′E
165 P12 **Hitachiōta** Ibaraki, Honshū, S Japan 36°32′N 140°31′E
Hitati *see* Hitachi
97 O21 **Hitchin** E England, United Kingdom 51°57′N 00°17′W
191 Q7 **Hitiaa** Tahiti, W French Polynesia 17°35′S 149°17′W
164 D15 **Hitoyoshi** *var.* Hitoyosi. Kumamoto, Kyūshū, SW Japan 32°12′N 130°48′E
Hitoyosi *see* Hitoyoshi
94 F7 **Hitra** *prev.* Hitteren. *island* S Norway
Hitteren *see* Hitra
187 Q11 **Hiu** *island* Torres Islands, N Vanuatu
165 O11 **Hiuchiga-take** ▲ Honshū, C Japan 36°57′N 139°18′E
191 X7 **Hiva Oa** *island* Îles Marquises, N French Polynesia
20 M10 **Hiwassee Lake** ⊠ North Carolina, SE USA
20 M10 **Hiwassee River** ∽ SE USA
95 H20 **Hjallerup** Nordjylland, N Denmark 57°10′N 10°10′E
95 M16 **Hjälmaren** *Eng.* Lake Hjalmar. ◎ C Sweden
Hjalmar, Lake *see* Hjälmaren
95 C14 **Hjellestad** Hordaland, S Norway 60°15′N 05°13′E
95 D16 **Hjelmeland** Rogaland, S Norway 59°12′N 06°07′E
94 G10 **Hjerkinn** Oppland, S Norway 62°13′N 09°37′E
95 L18 **Hjo** Västra Götaland, S Sweden 58°18′N 14°17′E
95 G19 **Hjørring** Nordjylland, N Denmark 57°28′N 09°59′E
167 O1 **Hkakabo Razi** ▲ Burma (Myanmar)/China 28°17′N 97°28′E
166 M2 **Hkamti** *var.* Singkaling Hkamti. Sagaing, N Burma (Myanmar) 26°00′N 95°43′E
167 N1 **Hkring Bum** ▲ N Burma (Myanmar) 27°05′N 97°16′E
83 L21 **Hlathikulu** *var.* Hlatikulu. S Swaziland 26°58′S 31°19′E
Hlatikulu *see* Hlathikulu
Hliboka *see* Hlyboka
111 F17 **Hlinsko** *var.* Hlinsko v Čechách. Pardubický Kraj, C Czech Republic 49°46′N 15°54′E
Hlinsko v Čechách *see* Hlinsko
117 S6 **Hlobyne** *Rus.* Globino. Poltavs'ka Oblast', NE Ukraine 49°24′N 33°16′E
111 H20 **Hlohovec** *Ger.* Freistadtl, *Hung.* Galgóc; *prev.* Frakštát. Trnavský Kraj, W Slovakia 48°26′N 17°49′E
83 J23 **Hlotse** *var.* Leribe. NW Lesotho 28°55′S 28°01′E
111 I17 **Hlučín** *Ger.* Hultschin, *Pol.* Hulczyn. Moravskoslezský Kraj, E Czech Republic 49°54′N 18°11′E
117 S2 **Hlukhiv** *Rus.* Glukhov. Sums'ka Oblast', NE Ukraine 51°40′N 33°53′E
119 K21 **Hlushkavichy** *Rus.* Glushkevichi. Homyel'skaya Voblasts', SE Belarus 51°34′N 27°47′E
119 L18 **Hlusk** *Rus.* Glusk, Glussk. Mahilyowskaya Voblasts', E Belarus 52°54′N 28°41′E
116 K8 **Hlyboka** *Ger.* Hliboka, *Rus.* Glybokaya. Chernivets'ka Oblast', W Ukraine 48°04′N 25°56′E
118 K13 **Hlybokaye** *Rus.* Glubokoye. Vitsyebskaya Voblasts', N Belarus 55°08′N 27°41′E
77 Q16 **Ho** SE Ghana 06°36′N 00°28′E
167 S6 **Hoa Binh** Hoa Binh, N Vietnam 20°49′N 105°20′E
83 E20 **Hoachanas** Hardap, C Namibia 23°55′S 18°04′E
Hoai Nhơn *see* Bông Sơn
167 T8 **Hoa Lac** Quang Binh, C Vietnam 17°54′N 106°24′E
167 S5 **Hoang Liên Sơn** ▲▲ N Vietnam
83 B17 **Hoanib** ∽ NW Namibia
33 S15 **Hoback Peak** ▲ Wyoming, C USA 43°04′N 110°34′W
183 P17 **Hobart** *prev.* Hobarton, Hobart Town. *state capital* Tasmania, SE Australia 42°54′S 147°18′E
26 L11 **Hobart** Oklahoma, C USA 35°03′N 99°04′W
183 P17 **Hobart** ✈ Tasmania, SE Australia 42°52′S 147°28′E
Hobarton/Hobart Town *see* Hobart
37 W14 **Hobbs** New Mexico, SW USA 32°42′N 103°08′W
194 L12 **Hobbs Coast** *physical region* Antarctica
23 Z14 **Hobe Sound** Florida, SE USA 27°03′N 80°08′W
Hobicaurikány *see* Uricani
54 E12 **Hobo** Huila, S Colombia 02°34′N 75°28′W
99 G16 **Hoboken** Antwerpen, N Belgium 51°12′N 04°22′E
158 K3 **Hoboksar** *var.* Hoboksar Mongol Zizhixian. Xinjiang Uygur Zizhiqu, NW China 46°48′N 85°42′E
Hoboksar Mongol Zizhixian *see* Hoboksar
95 G21 **Hobro** Nordjylland, N Denmark 56°39′N 09°51′E
21 X10 **Hobucken** North Carolina, SE USA 35°15′N 76°31′W
95 O20 **Hoburgen** *headland* SE Sweden 56°54′N 18°07′E
81 P15 **Hobyo** *It.* Obbia. Mudug, E Somalia 05°16′N 48°24′E
109 R8 **Hochalmspitze** ▲ SW Austria 47°00′N 13°19′E
109 Q4 **Hochburg** Oberösterreich, N Austria 48°10′N 12°57′E
108 F8 **Hochdorf** Luzern, N Switzerland 47°10′N 08°16′E
109 N8 **Hochfeiler** *It.* Gran Pilastro. ▲ Austria/Italy 46°59′N 11°42′E
167 T14 **Hô Chi Minh** *var.* Ho Chi Minh City; *prev.* Saigon. S Vietnam 10°46′N 106°43′E
Ho Chi Minh City *see* Hô Chi Minh
108 I7 **Höchst** Vorarlberg, NW Austria 47°28′N 09°40′E
Höchstadt *see* Höchstadt an der Aisch
101 K19 **Höchstadt an der Aisch** *var.* Höchstadt. Bayern, C Germany 49°43′N 10°48′E
108 L9 **Hochwilde** *It.* L'Altissima. ▲ Austria/Italy 46°45′N 11°00′E
109 S7 **Hochwildstelle** ▲ C Austria 47°21′N 13°53′E
31 T14 **Hocking River** ∽ Ohio, N USA
Hoctúm *see* Hoctún
41 X12 **Hoctún** *var.* Hoctúm. Yucatán, E Mexico 20°48′N 89°14′W
Hodeida *see* Al Ḥudaydah
20 K6 **Hodgenville** Kentucky, S USA 37°34′N 85°45′W
11 T17 **Hodgeville** Saskatchewan, S Canada 50°06′N 106°55′W
76 L9 **Hodh ech Chargui** ◈ *region* E Mauritania
Hodh el Garbi *see* Hodh el Gharbi
76 J10 **Hodh el Gharbi** *var.* Hodh el Garbi. ◈ *region* S Mauritania
111 L25 **Hódmezővásárhely** Csongrád, SE Hungary 46°27′N 20°18′E
74 J6 **Hodna, Chott El** *var.* Chott el-Hodna, *Ar.* Shatt al-Hodna. *salt lake* N Algeria
Hodna, Chott el-/Hodna, Shatt al- *see* Hodna, Chott El
111 G19 **Hodonín** *Ger.* Göding. Jihomoravský Kraj, SE Czech Republic 48°52′N 17°07′E
Hödrögö *see* Nömrög
Hodság/Hodschag *see* Odžaci
39 R7 **Hodzana River** ∽ Alaska, USA
Hoei *see* Huy
99 H19 **Hoeilaart** Vlaams Brabant, C Belgium 50°46′N 04°28′E
Hoë Karoo *see* Great Karoo
98 F12 **Hoek van Holland** *Eng.* Hook of Holland. Zuid-Holland, W Netherlands 52°00′N 04°07′E
98 L11 **Hoenderloo** Gelderland, E Netherlands 52°08′N 05°46′E
99 L18 **Hoensbroek** Limburg, SE Netherlands 50°55′N 05°55′E
163 Y11 **Hoeryŏng** NE North Korea 42°23′N 129°46′E
99 K18 **Hoeselt** Limburg, NE Belgium 50°50′N 05°30′E
98 K11 **Hoevelaken** Gelderland, C Netherlands 52°10′N 05°27′E
Hoey *see* Huy
101 M18 **Hof** Bayern, SE Germany 50°19′N 11°55′E
Höfdhakaupstadhur *see* Skagaströnd
Hofei *see* Hefei
101 G18 **Hofheim am Taunus** Hessen, W Germany 50°04′N 08°27′E
Hofmarkt *see* Odorheiu Secuiesc
92 L3 **Höfn** Austurland, SE Iceland 64°14′N 15°17′W
94 N13 **Hofors** Gävleborg, C Sweden 60°33′N 16°21′E
92 J6 **Hofsjökull** *glacier* C Iceland
92 J1 **Hofsós** Nordhurland Vestra, N Iceland 65°54′N 19°25′W
164 E13 **Hōfu** Yamaguchi, Honshū, SW Japan 34°01′N 131°34′E
92 I4 **Höfudborgarsvædid** ◈ *region* SW Iceland
Hofuf *see* Al Hufūf
95 J22 **Höganäs** Skåne, S Sweden 56°11′N 12°39′E
183 P14 **Hogan Group** *island group* Tasmania, SE Australia
23 R4 **Hogansville** Georgia, SE USA 33°10′N 84°55′W
39 P8 **Hogatza River** ∽ Alaska, USA
28 I14 **Hogback Mountain** ▲ Nebraska, C USA 41°40′N 103°44′W
95 G14 **Høgevarde** ▲ S Norway 60°19′N 09°27′E
Högfors *see* Karkkila
31 P5 **Hog Island** *island* Michigan, N USA
21 Y6 **Hog Island** *island* Virginia, NE USA
Hogoley Islands *see* Chuuk Islands
95 N20 **Högsby** Kalmar, S Sweden 57°10′N 16°03′E
36 K1 **Hogup Mountains** ▲▲ Utah, W USA
101 E17 **Hohe Acht** ▲ W Germany 50°23′N 07°00′E
Hohenelbe *see* Vrchlabí
108 I7 **Hohenems** Vorarlberg, W Austria 47°23′N 09°43′E
Hohenmauth *see* Vysoké Mýto
Hohensalza *see* Inowrocław
Hohenstadt *see* Zábřeh
Hohenstein in Ostpreussen *see* Olsztynek
20 I9 **Hohenwald** Tennessee, S USA 35°33′N 87°31′W
101 L17 **Hohenwarte-Stausee** ⊠ C Germany
Hohes Venn *see* Hautes Fagnes
109 Q8 **Hohe Tauern** ▲▲ W Austria
163 O13 **Hohhot** *var.* Huhehot, Huhohaote, *Mong.* Kukukhoto; *prev.* Kweisui, Kwesui. Nei Mongol Zizhiqu, N China 40°49′N 111°37′E
162 F7 **Hohmorit** *var.* Sayn-Ust. Govĭ-Altay, W Mongolia 47°23′N 94°19′E
103 U6 **Hohneck** ▲ NE France 48°04′N 07°01′E
77 Q16 **Hohoe** E Ghana 07°08′N 00°32′E
164 E12 **Hōhoku** Yamaguchi, Honshū, SW Japan 34°15′N 130°56′E
159 O11 **Hoh Sai Hu** ◎ C China
159 N11 **Hoh Xil Hu** ◎ C China
158 L11 **Hoh Xil Shan** ▲▲ W China
167 U10 **Hôi An** *prev.* Faifo. Quang Nam-Đa Năng, C Vietnam 15°54′N 108°19′E
Hoï-Hao/Hoihow *see* Haikou
159 S11 **Hoika** *prev.* Heka. Qinghai, W China 35°49′N 99°50′E
81 F17 **Hoima** W Uganda 01°25′N 31°22′E
26 L5 **Hoisington** Kansas, C USA 38°31′N 98°46′W
146 D12 **Hojagala** *Rus.* Khodzhakala. Balkan Welaýaty, W Turkmenistan 38°46′N 56°14′E
146 M13 **Hojambaz** *Rus.* Khodzhambas. Lebap Welaýaty, E Turkmenistan 38°11′N 64°33′E
95 H23 **Højby** Syddtjylland, C Denmark 55°20′N 10°27′E
95 F24 **Højer** Syddanmark, SW Denmark 54°57′N 08°43′E
164 E14 **Hōjō** *var.* Hôzyô. Ehime, Shikoku, SW Japan 33°58′N 132°47′E
184 J3 **Hokianga Harbour** *inlet* SE Tasman Sea
185 F17 **Hokitika** West Coast, South Island, New Zealand 42°44′S 170°58′E
165 U4 **Hokkai-dō** ◈ *territory* Hokkaidō, NE Japan
165 T3 **Hokkaidō** *prev.* Ezo, Yeso, Yezo. *island* NE Japan
95 G15 **Hokksund** Buskerud, S Norway 59°45′N 09°55′E
143 S4 **Hokmābād** Khorāsān-Razavī, N Iran 36°37′N 57°34′E
Hokō *see* Pohang
Hoko-guntō/Hoko-shotō *see* Penghu Liedao
Hoktemberyan *see* Armavir
94 F13 **Hol** Buskerud, S Norway 60°36′N 08°18′E
117 R11 **Hola Prystan'** *Rus.* Golaya Pristan. Khersons'ka Oblast', S Ukraine 46°31′N 32°31′E
95 I23 **Holbæk** Sjælland, E Denmark 55°42′N 11°42′E
Holboo *see* Santmargats
183 P10 **Holbrook** New South Wales, SE Australia 35°45′S 147°18′E
37 N11 **Holbrook** Arizona, SW USA 34°54′N 110°09′W
27 S5 **Holden** Missouri, C USA 38°42′N 93°59′W
36 K5 **Holden** Utah, W USA 39°06′N 112°16′W
27 O11 **Holdenville** Oklahoma, C USA 35°05′N 96°25′W
29 O16 **Holdrege** Nebraska, C USA 40°28′N 99°28′W
35 X3 **Hole in the Mountain Peak** ▲ Nevada, W USA 40°54′N 115°06′W
155 G20 **Hole Narsipur** Karnātaka, W India 12°46′N 76°14′E
111 H18 **Holešov** *Ger.* Holleschau. Zlínský Kraj, E Czech Republic 49°20′N 17°35′E
45 N14 **Holetown** *prev.* Jamestown. W Barbados 13°11′N 59°38′W
31 Q12 **Holgate** Ohio, N USA 41°12′N 84°06′W
44 I7 **Holguín** Holguín, SE Cuba 20°51′N 76°16′W
23 V12 **Holiday** Florida, SE USA 28°11′N 82°44′W
163 S9 **Holin Gol** *prev.* Hulingol. Nei Mongol Zizhiqu, N China 45°36′N 119°54′E
39 O12 **Holitna River** ∽ Alaska, USA
94 J13 **Höljes** Värmland, C Sweden 60°54′N 12°34′E
109 X3 **Hollabrunn** Niederösterreich, NE Austria 48°33′N 16°06′E
36 L3 **Holladay** Utah, W USA 40°39′N 111°49′W
11 X16 **Holland** Manitoba, S Canada 49°36′N 98°52′W
31 O9 **Holland** Michigan, N USA 42°47′N 86°06′W
25 T9 **Holland** Texas, SW USA 30°52′N 97°24′W
Holland *see* Netherlands
22 K4 **Hollandale** Mississippi, S USA 33°10′N 90°51′W
Hollandia *see* Jayapura
Hollandsch Diep *see* Hollands Diep
99 H14 **Hollands Diep** *var.* Hollandsch Diep. *channel* SW Netherlands
Holleschau *see* Holešov
25 R5 **Holliday** Texas, SW USA 33°49′N 98°41′W
18 E15 **Hollidaysburg** Pennsylvania, NE USA 40°24′N 78°22′W
21 S6 **Hollins** Virginia, NE USA 37°20′N 79°56′W
26 J12 **Hollis** Oklahoma, C USA 34°42′N 99°56′W
35 O10 **Hollister** California, W USA 36°51′N 121°25′W
27 T8 **Hollister** Missouri, C USA 36°37′N 93°13′W
93 M19 **Hollola** Etelä-Suomi, S Finland 61°N 25°32′E
98 K4 **Hollum** Fryslân, N Netherlands 53°27′N 05°38′E
95 J23 **Höllviken** *prev.* Höllviksnäs. Skåne, S Sweden 55°25′N 12°57′E
Höllviksnäs *see* Höllviken
37 W6 **Holly** Colorado, C USA 38°03′N 102°07′W
31 R9 **Holly** Michigan, N USA 42°47′N 83°37′W
21 S14 **Holly Hill** South Carolina, SE USA 33°19′N 80°24′W
21 W11 **Holly Ridge** North Carolina, SE USA 34°31′N 77°31′W
22 L1 **Holly Springs** Mississippi, S USA 34°47′N 89°25′W
23 Z15 **Hollywood** Florida, SE USA 26°00′N 80°09′W
8 J6 **Holman** Victoria Island, Northwest Territories, N Canada 70°42′N 117°45′W
92 I2 **Hólmavík** Vestfirdhir, NW Iceland 65°42′N 21°43′W
30 J7 **Holmen** Wisconsin, N USA 43°57′N 91°14′W
23 R8 **Holmes Creek** ∽ Alabama/Florida, SE USA
95 H16 **Holmestrand** Vestfold, S Norway 59°29′N 10°20′E
93 J16 **Holmön** *island* N Sweden
95 E22 **Holmsland Klit** *beach* W Denmark
93 J16 **Holmsund** Västerbotten, N Sweden 63°42′N 20°26′E
95 Q18 **Holmudden** *headland* SE Sweden 57°59′N 19°14′E
138 F10 **Holon** *var.* Kholon; *prev.* Ḥolon. Tel Aviv, C Israel 32°01′N 34°46′E
Ḥolon *see* Holon
163 P7 **Hölönbuyr** *var.* Bayan. Dornod, E Mongolia 47°56′N 112°58′E
117 P8 **Holovanivs'k** *Rus.* Golovanevsk. Kirovohrads'ka Oblast', C Ukraine 48°21′N 30°26′E
95 F21 **Holstebro** Midtjylland, W Denmark 56°22′N 08°38′E
95 F23 **Holsted** Syddtjylland, W Denmark 55°30′N 08°54′E

◆ Country
● Country Capital
◇ Dependent Territory
○ Dependent Territory Capital
◈ Administrative Regions
✈ International Airport
▲ Mountain
▲▲ Mountain Range
Volcano
∽ River
◎ Lake
⊠ Reservoir

29 T13 **Holstein** Iowa, C USA 42°29′N 95°32′W
Holsteinborg/ Holsteinsborg/ Holstenborg/Holstensborg see Sisimiut
21 O8 **Holston River** ≈ Tennessee, S USA
31 Q9 **Holt** Michigan, N USA 42°38′N 84°31′W
98 N10 **Holten** Overijssel, E Netherlands 52°16′N 06°25′E
27 P3 **Holton** Kansas, C USA 39°27′N 95°44′W
27 U5 **Holts Summit** Missouri, C USA 38°38′N 92°07′W
35 X17 **Holtville** California, W USA 32°48′N 115°22′W
98 L5 **Holwerd** *Fris.* Holwert. Fryslân, N Netherlands 53°22′N 05°51′E
Holwert see Holwerd
39 O11 **Holy Cross** Alaska, USA 62°12′N 159°46′W
37 R4 **Holy Cross, Mount Of The** ▲ Colorado, C USA 39°28′N 106°28′W
97 I18 **Holyhead** *Wel.* Caer Gybi. NW Wales, United Kingdom 53°19′N 04°38′W
97 H18 **Holy Island** island NW Wales, United Kingdom
96 L12 **Holy Island** island NE England, United Kingdom
37 W3 **Holyoke** Colorado, C USA 40°31′N 102°18′W
18 M11 **Holyoke** Massachusetts, NE USA 42°12′N 72°37′W
101 I14 **Holzminden** Niedersachsen, C Germany 51°49′N 09°27′E
81 G19 **Homa Bay** Nyanza, W Kenya 0°31′S 34°30′E
Homāyūnshahr see Khomeynīshahr
77 P11 **Hombori** Mopti, S Mali 15°13′N 01°39′W
101 E20 **Homburg** Saarland, SW Germany 49°20′N 07°20′E
9 R5 **Home Bay** bay Baffin Bay, Nunavut, NE Canada
Homenau see Humenné
39 Q13 **Homer** Alaska, USA 59°38′N 151°33′W
22 H4 **Homer** Louisiana, S USA 32°47′N 93°03′W
18 H10 **Homer** New York, NE USA 42°38′N 76°10′W
23 V7 **Homerville** Georgia, SE USA 31°02′N 82°45′W
23 Y16 **Homestead** Florida, SE USA 25°28′N 80°28′W
27 O9 **Hominy** Oklahoma, C USA 36°24′N 96°24′W
94 H8 **Hommelvik** Sør-Trøndelag, S Norway 63°24′N 10°48′E
95 C16 **Hommersåk** Rogaland, S Norway 58°55′N 05°51′E
155 H15 **Homnābād** Karnātaka, C India 17°46′N 77°08′E
22 J7 **Homochitto River** ≈ Mississippi, S USA
83 N20 **Homoíne** Inhambane, SE Mozambique 23°51′S 35°04′E
112 O12 **Homoljske Planine** ▲▲ E Serbia
Homonna see Humenné
Homs see Al Khums, Libya
Homs see Ḥimṣ
119 P19 **Homyel'** *Rus.* Gomel'. Homyel'skaya Voblasts', SE Belarus 52°25′N 31°E
118 L12 **Homyel'** Vitsyebskaya Voblasts', N Belarus 55°20′N 28°52′E
119 L19 **Homyel'skaya Voblasts'** *prev. Rus.* Gomel'skaya Oblast'. ◈ province SE Belarus
Honan see Henan, China
Honan see Luoyang, China
164 U4 **Honbetsu** Hokkaidō, NE Japan 43°09′N 143°46′E
Honctő see Gurahonț
54 E9 **Honda** Tolima, C Colombia 05°12′N 74°45′W
83 D24 **Hondeklip** *Afr.* Hondeklipbaai. Northern Cape, W South Africa 30°15′S 17°17′E
Hondeklipbaai see Hondeklip
11 Q13 **Hondo** Alberta, W Canada 54°43′N 113°14′W
25 Q12 **Hondo** Texas, SW USA 29°21′N 99°09′W
42 G1 **Hondo** ≈ Central America
Hondo see Honshū
Hondo see Amakusa
42 G6 **Honduras** *off.* Republic of Honduras. ◆ republic Central America
Honduras, Golfo de see Honduras, Gulf of
42 H4 **Honduras, Gulf of** *Sp.* Golfo de Honduras. gulf W Caribbean Sea
Honduras, Republic of see Honduras
11 V12 **Hone** Manitoba, C Canada 56°13′N 101°12′W
21 P12 **Honea Path** South Carolina, SE USA 34°27′N 82°23′W
95 H14 **Hønefoss** Buskerud, S Norway 60°10′N 10°15′E
31 S12 **Honey Creek** ≈ Ohio, N USA
25 V5 **Honey Grove** Texas, SW USA 33°34′N 95°54′W
35 Q4 **Honey Lake** ◎ California, W USA
102 L4 **Honfleur** Calvados, N France 49°25′N 00°14′E
Hon Gai see Ha Long
161 O8 **Hong'an** *prev.* Huang'an. Hubei, C China 31°20′N 114°43′E
Hongay see Ha Long
Hông Gai see Ha Long
161 O15 **Honghai Wan** bay N South China Sea
Hông Hà, Sông see Red River
161 O7 **Hong He** ≈ C China
161 N9 **Hong Hu** ◎ C China
160 L11 **Hongjiang** Hunan, S China 27°09′N 109°58′E
Hongjiang see Wangcang
161 O15 **Hong Kong** *Chin.* Xianggang. Hong Kong, S China 22°17′N 114°09′E
160 L4 **Hongliu He** ≈ C China
160 L4 **Hongliu He** ≈ C China
159 P8 **Hongliuwan** *var.* Aksay, Aksay Kazakzu Zizhixian. Gansu, N China 39°25′N 94°09′E
159 P7 **Hongliuyuan** Gansu, N China 41°02′N 95°24′E
Hongor see Delgereh
161 S8 **Hongqiao** ✕ (Shanghai) Shanghai Shi, E China 31°28′N 121°08′E
160 K14 **Hongshui He** ≈ S China
160 M5 **Hongtong** *var.* Dahuaishu. Shanxi, C China 36°30′N 111°42′E
164 J15 **Hongū** Wakayama, Honshū, SW Japan 33°50′N 135°42′E
Honguedo, Détroit d' see Honguedo Passage
15 Y5 **Honguedo Passage** *var.* Honguedo Strait, *Fr.* Détroit d'Honguedo. strait Québec, E Canada
Honguedo Strait see Honguedo Passage
Hongwan see Hongwansi
159 S8 **Hongwansi** *var.* Sunan, Sunan Yugurzu Zizhixian; *prev.* Hongwan. Gansu, N China 38°55′N 99°29′E
163 X13 **Hongwŏn** E North Korea 40°03′N 127°54′E
160 H7 **Hongyuan** *var.* Qiongxi; *prev.* Hurama. Sichuan, C China 32°49′N 102°40′E
161 Q7 **Hongze Hu** *var.* Hung-tse Hu. ◎ E China
186 L9 **Honiara** ● (Solomon Islands) Guadalcanal, C Solomon Islands 09°27′S 159°56′E
165 P8 **Honjō** *var.* Honzyô, Yurihonjō. Akita, Honshū, C Japan 39°23′N 140°03′E
93 K18 **Honkajoki** Länsi-Suomi, SW Finland 62°00′N 22°15′E
92 K7 **Honningsvåg** Finnmark, N Norway 70°58′N 25°59′E
95 I19 **Hönö** Västra Götaland, S Sweden 57°42′N 11°39′E
38 G11 **Honoka'a** Hawaii, USA, C Pacific Ocean 20°04′N 155°27′W
38 G11 **Honoka'a** *var.* Honokaa. Hawaii, USA, C Pacific Ocean 20°04′N 155°27′W
Honokaa see Honoka'a
38 D9 **Honolulu** state capital O'ahu, Hawaii, USA, C Pacific Ocean 21°18′N 157°52′W
38 H11 **Honomú** *var.* Honomu. Hawaii, USA, C Pacific Ocean 19°51′N 155°06′W
105 P10 **Honrubia** Castilla-La Mancha, C Spain 39°36′N 02°17′W
164 M12 **Honshū** *var.* Hondo, Honsyû. island SW Japan
Honsyû see Honshū
Honte see Westerschelde
Honzyô see Honjō
8 K8 **Hood** ≈ Nunavut, NW Canada
Hood Island see Española, Isla
32 H11 **Hood, Mount** ▲ Oregon, NW USA 45°22′N 121°41′W
32 H11 **Hood River** Oregon, NW USA 45°44′N 121°31′W
98 H10 **Hoofddorp** Noord-Holland, W Netherlands 52°18′N 04°41′E
99 G15 **Hoogerheide** Noord-Brabant, S Netherlands 51°25′N 04°19′E
98 N8 **Hoogeveen** Drenthe, NE Netherlands 52°44′N 06°30′E
98 O6 **Hoogezand-Sappemeer** Groningen, NE Netherlands 53°10′N 06°47′E
98 J8 **Hoogkarspel** Noord-Holland, NW Netherlands 52°42′N 04°59′E
98 N5 **Hoogkerk** Groningen, NE Netherlands 53°13′N 06°30′E
98 G13 **Hoogvliet** Zuid-Holland, SW Netherlands 51°51′N 04°23′E
26 I8 **Hooker** Oklahoma, C USA 36°51′N 101°12′W
97 E21 **Hook Head** *Ir.* Rinn Duáin. headland SE Ireland 52°07′N 06°55′W
Hook of Holland see Hoek van Holland
Hoolt see Tögrög
39 W13 **Hoonah** Chichagof Island, Alaska, USA 58°05′N 135°21′W
38 L11 **Hooper Bay** Alaska, USA 61°31′N 166°06′W
31 N13 **Hoopeston** Illinois, N USA 40°28′N 87°40′W
95 K22 **Höör** Skåne, S Sweden 55°55′N 13°33′E
98 I9 **Hoorn** Noord-Holland, NW Netherlands 52°38′N 05°04′E
18 L10 **Hoosic River** ≈ New York, NE USA
Hoosier State see Indiana
35 Y11 **Hoover Dam** dam Arizona/Nevada, W USA
Höövör see Baruunbayan-Ulaan
137 Q11 **Hopa** Artvin, NE Turkey 41°23′N 41°28′E
18 J14 **Hopatcong** New Jersey, NE USA 40°55′N 74°39′W
10 M17 **Hope** British Columbia, SW Canada 49°21′N 121°28′W
39 R12 **Hope** Alaska, USA 60°55′N 149°38′W
27 T14 **Hope** Arkansas, C USA 33°40′N 93°36′W
31 P14 **Hope** Indiana, N USA 39°18′N 85°46′W
29 Q5 **Hope** North Dakota, N USA 47°18′N 97°42′W
13 Q7 **Hopedale** Newfoundland and Labrador, NE Canada 55°26′N 60°14′W
Hopeh/Hopei see Hebei
180 K13 **Hope, Lake** salt lake Western Australia
41 X13 **Hopelchén** Campeche, SE Mexico 19°46′N 89°50′W
21 U11 **Hope Mills** North Carolina, SE USA 34°58′N 78°57′W
183 O7 **Hope, Mount** New South Wales, SE Australia 32°49′S 145°55′E
92 P4 **Hopen** island SE Svalbard
197 Q4 **Hope, Point** headland Alaska, USA
12 M3 **Hopes Advance, Cap** cape Québec, NE Canada
182 L10 **Hopetoun** Victoria, SE Australia 35°46′S 142°23′E
83 H23 **Hopetown** Northern Cape, W South Africa 29°37′S 24°05′E
21 W6 **Hopewell** Virginia, NE USA 37°16′N 77°15′W
109 O7 **Hopfgarten im Brixental** Tirol, W Austria 47°28′N 12°14′E
181 N8 **Hopkins Lake** salt lake Western Australia
182 M12 **Hopkins River** ≈ Victoria, SE Australia
20 I7 **Hopkinsville** Kentucky, S USA 36°50′N 87°30′W
34 M6 **Hopland** California, W USA 38°58′N 123°09′W
95 G24 **Hoptrup** Syddanmark, SW Denmark 55°09′N 09°27′E
Hoqin Zuoyi Zhongji see Baokang
32 F9 **Hoquiam** Washington, NW USA 46°58′N 123°53′W
29 R6 **Horace** North Dakota, N USA 46°44′N 96°54′W
117 T14 **Hora Roman-Kosh** ▲ S Ukraine 44°37′N 34°13′E
137 R12 **Horasan** Erzurum, NE Turkey 40°03′N 42°10′E
101 G22 **Horb am Neckar** Baden-Württemberg, S Germany 48°27′N 08°42′E
95 K23 **Hörby** Skåne, S Sweden 55°51′N 13°42′E
43 P16 **Horconcitos** Chiriquí, W Panama 08°20′N 82°10′W
95 C14 **Hordaland** ◈ county S Norway
116 H13 **Horezu** Vâlcea, SW Romania 45°06′N 24°00′E
108 G7 **Horgen** Zürich, N Switzerland 47°16′N 08°36′E
Horgo see Tariat
Hörin see Fenglin
163 O13 **Horinger** Nei Mongol Zizhiqu, N China 40°23′N 111°48′E
Horiult see Bogd
11 U17 **Horizon** Saskatchewan, S Canada 49°33′N 105°05′W
192 K9 **Horizon Bank** undersea feature S Pacific Ocean
192 L10 **Horizon Deep** undersea feature W Pacific Ocean
95 L14 **Hörken** Örebro, S Sweden 60°03′N 14°55′E
119 O15 **Horki** *Rus.* Gorki. Mahilyowskaya Voblasts', E Belarus 54°18′N 31°E
195 O10 **Horlick Mountains** ▲▲ Antarctica
117 X7 **Horlivka** *Rom.* Adâncata, *Rus.* Gorlovka. Donets'ka Oblast', E Ukraine 48°19′N 38°04′E
143 V11 **Ḥormak** Sīstān va Balūchestān, SE Iran 30°00′N 60°50′E
143 R13 **Hormozgān** *off.* Ostān-e Hormozgān. ◈ province S Iran
Hormozgān, Ostān-e see Hormozgān
Hormoz, Tangeh-ye see Hormuz, Strait of
141 W6 **Hormuz, Strait of** *var.* Strait of Ormuz, *Per.* Tangeh-ye Hormoz. strait Iran/Oman
109 W2 **Horn** Niederösterreich, NE Austria 48°40′N 15°40′E
95 M18 **Horn** Östergötland, S Sweden 57°54′N 15°49′E
8 J9 **Horn** ≈ Northwest Territories, NW Canada
Hornád see Hernád
8 I6 **Hornaday** ≈ Northwest Territories, NW Canada
92 H13 **Hornavan** ◎ N Sweden
65 C24 **Hornby Mountains** hill range West Falkland, Falkland Islands
Horn, Cape see Hornos, Cabo de
97 O18 **Horncastle** E England, United Kingdom 53°12′N 00°07′W
95 N14 **Horndal** Dalarna, C Sweden 60°16′N 16°25′E
93 I16 **Hörnefors** Västerbotten, N Sweden 63°37′N 19°54′E
18 F11 **Hornell** New York, NE USA 42°19′N 77°38′W
Horné Nové Mesto see Kysucké Nové Mesto
12 F12 **Hornepayne** Ontario, S Canada 49°14′N 84°48′W
94 D10 **Hornindalsvatnet** ◎ S Norway
101 G22 **Hornisgrinde** ▲ SW Germany 48°37′N 08°13′E
22 M9 **Horn Island** island Mississippi, S USA
Hornja Łužica see Oberlausitz
63 J26 **Hornos, Cabo de** *Eng.* Cape Horn. headland S Chile 55°52′S 67°00′W
117 S10 **Hornostayivka** Khersons'ka Oblast', S Ukraine 47°00′N 33°42′E
183 T9 **Hornsby** New South Wales, SE Australia 33°44′S 151°08′E
97 O16 **Hornsea** E England, United Kingdom 53°54′N 00°10′W
94 O11 **Hornslandet** peninsula C Sweden
95 H22 **Hornslet** Midtjylland, C Denmark 56°19′N 10°20′E
92 O4 **Hornsundtind** ▲ S Svalbard 76°54′N 16°07′E
Horochów see Horokhiv
Horodenka see Gorodenka
117 Q2 **Horodnya** *Rus.* Gorodnya. Chernihivs'ka Oblast', NE Ukraine 51°54′N 31°30′E
116 K6 **Horodok** Khmel'nyts'ka Oblast', W Ukraine 49°10′N 26°34′E
116 H5 **Horodok** *Pol.* Gródek Jagielloński, *Rus.* Gorodok, Gorodok Yagellonski. L'vivs'ka Oblast', NW Ukraine 49°48′N 23°39′E
117 Q6 **Horodyshche** *Rus.* Gorodishche. Cherkas'ka Oblast', C Ukraine 49°19′N 31°27′E
165 T3 **Horokanai** Hokkaidō, NE Japan 44°02′N 142°08′E
116 J4 **Horokhiv** *Pol.* Horochów, *Rus.* Gorokhov. Volyns'ka Oblast', NW Ukraine 50°31′N 24°50′E
165 T4 **Horoshiri-dake** *var.* Horosiri Dake. ▲ Hokkaidō, N Japan 42°43′N 142°41′E
Horosiri Dake see Horoshiri-dake
111 C17 **Hořovice** *Ger.* Horowitz. Střední Čechy, W Czech Republic 49°49′N 13°53′E
Horowitz see Hořovice
Horqin Zuoyi Houqi see Ganjig
Horqin Zuoyi Zhongqi see Bayan Huxu
62 O5 **Horqueta** Concepción, C Paraguay 23°24′S 56°53′W
55 O12 **Horqueta Minas** Amazonas, S Venezuela 02°20′N 63°32′W
95 J20 **Horred** Västra Götaland, S Sweden 57°22′N 12°25′E
151 J19 **Horsburgh Atoll** *var.* Goidhoo Atoll. atoll N Maldives
20 K7 **Horse Cave** Kentucky, S USA 37°10′N 85°54′W
37 V6 **Horse Creek** ≈ Colorado, C USA
27 S6 **Horse Creek** ≈ Missouri, C USA
18 G11 **Horseheads** New York, NE USA 42°10′N 76°49′W
37 P13 **Horse Mount** ▲ New Mexico, SW USA 33°58′N 108°10′W
95 G22 **Horsens** Syddanmark, C Denmark 55°53′N 09°53′E
65 F25 **Horse Pasture Point** headland W Saint Helena 15°57′S 05°46′W
33 N13 **Horseshoe Bend** Idaho, NW USA 43°55′N 116°11′W
36 L13 **Horseshoe Reservoir** ⊡ Arizona, SW USA
64 M9 **Horseshoe Seamounts** undersea feature E Atlantic Ocean 36°30′N 15°00′W
182 L11 **Horsham** Victoria, SE Australia 36°44′S 142°13′E
97 O23 **Horsham** SE England, United Kingdom 51°01′N 00°21′W
99 M15 **Horst** Limburg, SE Netherlands 51°30′N 06°05′E
64 N2 **Horta** Faial, Azores, Portugal, NE Atlantic Ocean 38°32′N 28°39′W
105 S12 **Horta, Cap de l'** *Cast.* Cabo Huertas. headland SE Spain 38°21′N 00°25′W
95 H16 **Horten** Vestfold, S Norway 59°25′N 10°25′E
111 M23 **Hortobágy-Berettyó** ≈ E Hungary
27 Q3 **Horton** Kansas, C USA 39°39′N 95°31′W
8 I7 **Horton** ≈ Northwest Territories, NW Canada
95 I23 **Hørve** Sjælland, E Denmark 55°46′N 11°28′E
95 L22 **Hörvik** Blekinge, S Sweden 56°01′N 14°45′E
Horvot Haluza see Horvot Halutsa
14 E7 **Horwood Lake** ◎ Ontario, S Canada
116 K4 **Horyn'** *Rus.* Goryn. ≈ NW Ukraine
81 I14 **Hosa'ina** *var.* Hosseina, *It.* Hosanna. Southern Nationalities, S Ethiopia 07°38′N 37°58′E
Hosanna see Hosa'ina
101 H18 **Hösbach** Bayern, C Germany 50°00′N 09°12′E
Hose Mountains see Hose, Pegunungan
169 T9 **Hose, Pegunungan** *var.* Hose Mountains. ▲▲ East Malaysia
148 L15 **Hoshāb** Baluchistān, SW Pakistan 26°01′N 63°51′E
154 H10 **Hoshangābād** Madhya Pradesh, C India 22°44′N 77°45′E
116 L4 **Hoshcha** Rivnens'ka Oblast', NW Ukraine 50°37′N 26°38′E
152 I7 **Hoshiārpur** Punjab, NW India 31°30′N 75°59′E
Höshööt see Öldziyt
99 M23 **Hosingen** Diekirch, NE Luxembourg 50°01′N 06°05′E
186 G7 **Hoskins** New Britain, E Papua New Guinea 05°28′S 150°25′E
155 G17 **Hospet** Karnātaka, C India 15°16′N 76°20′E
104 K4 **Hospital de Orbigo** Castilla y León, N Spain 42°27′N 05°53′W
Hospitalet see L'Hospitalet de Llobregat
92 N13 **Hossa** Oulu, E Finland 65°28′N 29°36′E
Hosseina see Hosa'ina
Hosszúmezjő see Câmpulung Moldovenesc
63 I25 **Hoste, Isla** island S Chile
117 O4 **Hostomel'** *Rus.* Gostomel'. Kyyivs'ka Oblast', N Ukraine 50°41′N 30°15′E
155 H20 **Hosūr** Tamil Nādu, SE India 12°45′N 77°51′E
167 N8 **Hot** Chiang Mai, NW Thailand 18°07′N 98°34′E
158 G10 **Hotan** *var.* Khotan, *Chin.* Ho-t'ien. Xinjiang Uygur Zizhiqu, NW China 37°10′N 79°51′E
158 H9 **Hotan He** ≈ NW China
83 G22 **Hotazel** Northern Cape, N South Africa 27°12′S 22°58′E
37 Q5 **Hotchkiss** Colorado, C USA 38°47′N 107°43′W
35 V7 **Hot Creek Range** ▲▲ Nevada, W USA
Hote see Hoti
171 T13 **Hoti** *var.* Hote. Pulau Seram, E Indonesia 02°58′S 130°19′E
Ho-t'ien see Hotan
Hotin see Khotyn
93 H15 **Hoting** Jämtland, C Sweden 64°07′N 16°14′E
162 L14 **Hotong Qagan Nur** ◎ N China
162 J8 **Hotont** Arhangay, C Mongolia 47°21′N 102°27′E
27 T12 **Hot Springs** Arkansas, C USA 34°31′N 93°03′W
28 J11 **Hot Springs** South Dakota, N USA 43°26′N 103°29′W
21 S5 **Hot Springs** Virginia, NE USA 38°00′N 79°50′W
35 Q4 **Hot Springs Peak** ▲ California, W USA 40°23′N 120°06′W
27 T12 **Hot Springs Village** Arkansas, C USA 34°39′N 93°03′W
Hotspur Bank see Hotspur Seamount
65 J16 **Hotspur Seamount** *var.* Hotspur Bank. undersea feature C Atlantic Ocean 18°00′S 35°00′W
8 J8 **Hottah Lake** ◎ Northwest Territories, NW Canada
44 K9 **Hotte, Massif de la** ▲▲ SW Haiti
99 K21 **Hotton** Luxembourg, SE Belgium 50°18′N 05°25′E
Hötzing see Hațeg
187 P17 **Houaïlou** Province Nord, C New Caledonia 21°17′S 165°37′E
74 K5 **Houari Boumediène** ✕ (Alger) N Algeria 36°38′N 03°15′E
167 P6 **Houayxay** *var.* Ban Houayxay. Bokèo, N Laos 20°17′N 100°27′E
103 N5 **Houdan** Yvelines, N France 48°48′N 01°36′E
99 F20 **Houdeng-Goegnies** *var.* Houdeng-Gœgnies. Hainaut, S Belgium 50°29′N 04°10′E
102 K14 **Houeillès** Lot-et-Garonne, SW France 44°15′N 00°02′E
99 L22 **Houffalize** Luxembourg, SE Belgium 50°08′N 05°47′E
30 M3 **Houghton** Michigan, N USA 47°07′N 88°34′W
31 Q7 **Houghton Lake** Michigan, N USA 44°18′N 84°45′W
31 Q7 **Houghton Lake** ◎ Michigan, N USA
19 T3 **Houlton** Maine, NE USA 46°09′N 67°50′W
160 M5 **Houma** Shanxi, C China 35°36′N 11°23′E
193 U16 **Houma** Tongatapu, S Tonga 21°18′S 174°55′W
22 J10 **Houma** Louisiana, S USA 29°35′N 90°44′W
196 V16 **Houma Taloa** headland Tongatapu, S Tonga 21°16′S 175°08′W
77 O13 **Houndé** SW Burkina 11°34′N 03°31′W
102 J12 **Hourtin-Carcans, Lac d'** ◎ SW France
36 J5 **House Range** ▲▲ Utah, W USA
10 K13 **Houston** British Columbia, SW Canada 54°24′N 126°39′W
39 R11 **Houston** Alaska, USA 61°37′N 149°50′W
29 X10 **Houston** Minnesota, N USA 43°45′N 91°34′W
22 M3 **Houston** Mississippi, S USA 33°54′N 89°00′W
27 V7 **Houston** Missouri, C USA 37°19′N 91°59′W
25 W11 **Houston** Texas, SW USA 29°46′N 95°22′W
25 W11 **Houston** ✕ Texas, SW USA 30°03′N 95°18′W
98 J12 **Houten** Utrecht, C Netherlands 52°02′N 05°10′E
99 K17 **Houthalen** Limburg, NE Belgium 51°02′N 05°22′E
99 I22 **Houyet** Namur, SE Belgium 50°10′N 05°00′E
95 H22 **Hov** Midtjylland, C Denmark 55°54′N 10°13′E
95 L17 **Hova** Västra Götaland, S Sweden 58°52′N 14°13′E
162 J10 **Hovd** *var.* Dund-Us. Hovd, W Mongolia 48°06′N 91°22′E
162 E6 **Hovd** *var.* Khovd, Kobdo; *prev.* Jirgalanta. Hovd, W Mongolia 47°59′N 91°41′E
162 E6 **Hovd** *var.* Dund-Us. Hovd, W Mongolia 48°06′N 91°22′E
162 E7 **Hovd** ◈ province W Mongolia
Hovd see Bogd
162 C5 **Hovd Gol** ≈ NW Mongolia
97 O23 **Hove** SE England, United Kingdom 50°49′N 00°11′W
95 I22 **Hovedstaden** *off.* Frederiksborgs Amt. ◈ county E Denmark
29 N8 **Hoven** South Dakota, N USA 45°12′N 99°47′W
116 I8 **Hoverla, Hora** *Rus.* Gora Goverla. ▲ W Ukraine 48°09′N 24°30′E
Höviyn Am see Gurvanbulag
95 M21 **Hovmantorp** Kronoberg, S Sweden 56°47′N 15°08′E
163 N11 **Hövsgöl** Dornogovĭ, SE Mongolia 43°35′N 109°40′E
162 I5 **Hövsgöl** ◈ province N Mongolia
Hovsgol, Lake see Hövsgöl Nuur
162 J5 **Hövsgöl Nuur** *var.* Lake Hovsgol. ◎ N Mongolia
78 L9 **Howa, Ouadi** *var.* Wādi Howar. ≈ Chad/Sudan see also Howar, Wādi
Howa, Ouadi see Howar, Wādi
27 P7 **Howard** Kansas, C USA 37°27′N 96°16′W
29 Q10 **Howard** South Dakota, N USA 43°58′N 97°31′W
25 N10 **Howard Draw** valley Texas, SW USA
29 U8 **Howard Lake** Minnesota, N USA 45°03′N 94°03′W
80 B8 **Howar, Wādi** *var.* Ouadi Howa. ≈ Chad/Sudan see also Howa, Ouadi
Howar, Wādi see Howa, Ouadi
25 U5 **Howe** Texas, SW USA 33°29′N 96°38′W
183 R12 **Howe, Cape** headland New South Wales/Victoria, SE Australia 37°30′S 149°58′E
31 R9 **Howell** Michigan, N USA 42°36′N 83°55′W
28 L9 **Howes** South Dakota, N USA 44°34′N 102°03′W
83 K23 **Howick** KwaZulu/Natal, E South Africa 29°29′S 30°13′E
Howrah see Hāora
167 T9 **Hô Xa** *prev.* Vinh Linh. Quang Tri, C Vietnam 17°02′N 107°03′E
27 W9 **Hoxie** Arkansas, C USA 36°03′N 90°58′W
26 J3 **Hoxie** Kansas, C USA 39°21′N 100°27′W
101 I14 **Höxter** Nordrhein-Westfalen, W Germany 51°46′N 09°22′E
158 K6 **Hoxud** *var.* Tewulike. Xinjiang Uygur Zizhiqu, NW China 42°18′N 86°51′E
96 J5 **Hoy** island N Scotland, United Kingdom
43 S17 **Hoya, Cerro** ▲ S Panama 07°22′N 80°38′W
94 D12 **Høyanger** Sogn Og Fjordane, S Norway 61°13′N 06°05′E
101 P15 **Hoyerswerda** *Lus.* Wojerecy. Sachsen, E Germany 51°27′N 14°18′E
164 R14 **Hōyo-kaikyō** *var.* Hayasui-seto. strait SW Japan
104 J8 **Hoyos** Extremadura, W Spain 40°10′N 06°43′W
29 W4 **Hoyt Lakes** Minnesota, N USA 47°31′N 92°08′W
87 V2 **Hoyvík** Streymoy, N Faeroe Islands
137 O14 **Hozat** Tunceli, E Turkey 39°09′N 39°13′E
Hôzyô see Hōjō
167 N8 **Hpa-an** *var.* Pa-an. Kayin State, S Burma (Myanmar) 16°51′N 97°37′E
167 N8 **Hpapun** *var.* Papun. Kayin State, S Burma (Myanmar) 18°05′N 97°26′E
167 N7 **Hpasawng** *var.* Pasawng. Kayah State, C Burma (Myanmar) 18°50′N 97°16′E
Hpyu see Phyu
111 F16 **Hradec Králové** *Ger.* Königgrätz. Královéhradecký Kraj, N Czech Republic 50°13′N 15°50′E
Hradecký Kraj see Královehradecký Kraj
111 B16 **Hradiště** *Ger.* Burgstadlberg. ▲ NW Czech Republic 50°12′N 13°04′E
117 R6 **Hradyz'k** *Rus.* Gradizhsk. Poltavs'ka Oblast', NE Ukraine 49°14′N 33°07′E
119 M16 **Hradzyanka** *Rus.* Grodzyanka. Mahilyowskaya Voblasts', E Belarus 53°33′N 28°45′E
119 F16 **Hrandzichy** *Rus.* Grandichi. Hrodzyenskaya Voblasts', W Belarus 53°43′N 23°49′E
111 H18 **Hranice** *Ger.* Mährisch-Weisskirchen. Olomoucký Kraj, E Czech Republic 49°34′N 17°45′E
112 I13 **Hrasnica** Federacija Bosna I Hercegovinia, SE Bosnia and Herzegovina 43°48′N 18°19′E
109 V11 **Hrastnik** C Slovenia 46°09′N 15°08′E
137 U12 **Hrazdan** *Rus.* Razdan. C Armenia 40°30′N 44°50′E
137 T12 **Hrazdan** *var.* Zanga, *Rus.* Razdan. ≈ C Armenia
117 R5 **Hrebinka** *Rus.* Grebenka. Poltavs'ka Oblast', NE Ukraine 50°08′N 32°27′E
119 K17 **Hresk** *Rus.* Gresk. Minskaya Voblasts', C Belarus 53°10′N 27°29′E
Hrisoupoli see Chrysoúpoli
119 F16 **Hrodna** *Pol.* Grodno. Hrodzyenskaya Voblasts', W Belarus 53°40′N 23°50′E
119 F16 **Hrodzyenskaya Voblasts'** *prev. Rus.* Grodnenskaya Oblast'. ◈ province W Belarus
111 J21 **Hron** *Ger.* Gran, *Hung.* Garam. ≈ C Slovakia
111 Q14 **Hrubieszów** *Rus.* Grubeshov. Lubelskie, E Poland 50°49′N 23°53′E
112 F13 **Hrvace** Split-Dalmacija, SE Croatia 43°46′N 16°35′E
Hrvatska see Croatia
112 F10 **Hrvatska Kostanjnica** *var.* Kostajnica. Sisak-Moslavina, C Croatia 45°14′N 16°35′E
Hrvatsko Grahovi see Bosansko Grahovo
116 K6 **Hrymayliv** *Pol.* Gízymałów, *Rus.* Grimaylov. Ternopil's'ka Oblast', W Ukraine 49°18′N 26°02′E
167 N4 **Hseni** *var.* Hsenwi. Shan State, E Burma (Myanmar) 23°20′N 97°59′E
Hsenwi see Hseni
Hsia-men see Xiamen
Hsiang-t'an see Xiangtan
Hsi Chiang see Xi Jiang
167 N6 **Hsihseng** Shan State, C Burma (Myanmar) 20°07′N 97°17′E
Hsinchu see Xinzhu
Hsing-K'ai Hu see Khanka, Lake
Hsi-ning/Hsining see Xining
Hsinking see Changchun
Hsin-yang see Xinyang
Hsinying see Xinying
167 N4 **Hsipaw** Shan State, C Burma (Myanmar) 22°32′N 97°12′E
Hsu-chou see Xuzhou
Hsüeh Shan see Xue Shan
Htawei see Dawei
Hu see Shanghai Shi
83 B18 **Huab** ≈ W Namibia
57 M21 **Huacaya** Chuquisaca, S Bolivia 20°45′S 63°42′W
57 J19 **Huachacalla** Oruro, SW Bolivia 18°47′S 68°23′W
159 X9 **Huachi** *var.* Rouyuan, Rouyuanchengzi. Gansu, C China 36°24′N 107°58′E
57 N16 **Huachi, Laguna** ◎ N Bolivia
57 D14 **Huacho** Lima, W Peru 11°05′S 77°36′W
163 Y7 **Huachuan** Heilongjiang, NE China 47°00′S 130°21′E
163 P12 **Huade** Nei Mongol Zizhiqu, N China 41°52′N 113°58′E
163 W10 **Huadian** Jilin, NE China 42°59′N 126°38′E
56 E13 **Huagaruncho, Cordillera** ▲▲ C Peru
Hua Hin see Ban Hua Hin
191 S10 **Huahine** island Îles Sous le Vent, W French Polynesia
Huahua, Rio see Wawa, Río
167 R8 **Huai** ≈ E Thailand
161 Q7 **Huai'an** *var.* Qingjiang. Jiangsu, E China 33°33′N 119°03′E
161 P6 **Huaibei** Anhui, E China 34°00′N 116°48′E
Huaide see Gongzhuling
157 T10 **Huai He** ≈ C China
160 L11 **Huaihua** Hunan, S China 27°36′N 109°57′E
161 N14 **Huaiji** Guangdong, S China 23°54′N 112°12′E
161 O2 **Huailai** *var.* Shacheng. Hebei, E China 40°22′N 115°34′E
161 P7 **Huainan** *var.* Huai-nan, Hwainan. Anhui, E China 32°37′N 116°57′E
Huai-nan see Huainan
161 N2 **Huairen** *var.* Yunzhong. Shanxi, C China 35°28′N 110°29′E
161 O7 **Huaiyang** Henan, C China 33°44′N 114°55′E
161 Q7 **Huaiyin** Jiangsu, E China 33°31′N 119°03′E
167 N16 **Huai Yot** Trang, SW Thailand 07°45′N 99°36′E
41 Q15 **Huajuapan** *var.* Huajuapan de León. Oaxaca, SE Mexico 17°50′N 97°48′W
Huajuapan de León see Huajuapan
41 O9 **Hualahuises** Nuevo León, NE Mexico 24°56′N 99°42′W
36 I11 **Hualapai Mountains** ▲▲ Arizona, SW USA
36 I11 **Hualapai Peak** ▲ Arizona, SW USA 35°04′N 113°54′W
62 J7 **Hualfin** Catamarca, N Argentina 27°15′S 66°53′W
161 T13 **Hualian** *var.* Hualien, Hwalien, *Jap.* Karen. C Taiwan 23°58′N 121°35′E
Hualien see Hualian
56 E10 **Huallaga, Río** ≈ N Peru
56 C11 **Huamachuco** La Libertad, C Peru 07°50′S 78°01′W
41 Q14 **Huamantla** Tlaxcala, S Mexico 19°18′N 97°57′W
82 C13 **Huambo** *Port.* Nova Lisboa. Huambo, C Angola 12°48′S 15°45′E
82 B13 **Huambo** ◈ province C Angola
41 P15 **Huamuxtitlán** Guerrero, S Mexico 17°49′N 98°34′W
163 Y8 **Huanan** Heilongjiang, NE China 46°21′N 130°43′E
63 H17 **Huancache, Sierra** ▲▲ SW Argentina
57 I17 **Huancané** Puno, SE Peru 15°10′S 69°44′W
57 F16 **Huancapi** Ayacucho, C Peru 13°40′S 74°05′W
57 E15 **Huancavelica** Huancavelica, SW Peru 12°45′S 75°03′W
57 E15 **Huancavelica** *off.* Departamento de Huancavelica. ◈ department W Peru
Huancavelica, Departamento de see Huancavelica
57 E14 **Huancayo** Junín, C Peru 12°03′S 75°14′W
57 K20 **Huanchaca, Cerro** ▲ S Bolivia 20°12′S 66°35′W
Huancheng see Huanxian
56 C12 **Huandoy, Nevado** ▲ W Peru 08°48′S 77°33′W
Huang'an see Hong'an
161 O8 **Huangchuan** Henan, C China 32°00′N 115°02′E
161 O9 **Huanggang** Hubei, C China 30°27′N 114°48′E
Huang Hai see Yellow Sea
157 Q8 **Huang He** *var.* Yellow River. ≈ C China
Huanghe see Madoi
161 Q4 **Huanghe Kou** delta E China
Huangheyan see Madoi
160 L5 **Huangling** Shaanxi, C China 35°40′N 109°14′E
161 O9 **Huangpi** Hubei, C China 30°53′N 114°22′E
163 P13 **Huangqi Hai** ◎ N China
161 Q9 **Huangshan** *var.* Tunxi. Anhui, E China 29°43′N 118°20′E
161 O9 **Huangshi** *var.* Huang-shih, Hwangshih. Hubei, C China 30°14′N 115°E
Huang-shih see Huangshi
160 L5 **Huangtu Gaoyuan** plateau C China
61 B22 **Huanguelén** Buenos Aires, E Argentina 37°02′S 61°57′W
161 S10 **Huangyan** Zhejiang, SE China 28°39′N 121°19′E
159 T10 **Huangyuan** Qinghai, C China 36°40′N 101°12′E
159 T10 **Huangzhong** *var.* Lushar. Qinghai, C China 36°31′N 101°32′E
163 W12 **Huanren** *var.* Huanren Manzu Zizhixian. Liaoning, NE China 41°16′N 125°25′E
Huanren Manzu Zizhixian see Huanren
57 F15 **Huanta** Ayacucho, C Peru 12°54′S 74°13′W
56 E13 **Huánuco** Huánuco, C Peru 09°58′S 76°16′W
56 D13 **Huánuco** *off.* Departamento de Huánuco. ◈ department C Peru
Huánuco, Departamento de see Huánuco
57 K19 **Huanuni** Oruro, W Bolivia 18°15′S 66°48′W
159 X9 **Huanxian** *var.* Huancheng. Gansu, C China 36°30′N 107°20′E
161 S12 **Huaping Yu** *prev.* Huap'ing Yu. island N Taiwan
62 H3 **Huara** Tarapacá, N Chile 19°59′S 69°42′W
57 D14 **Huaral** Lima, W Peru 11°31′S 77°10′W
Huarás see Huaraz
56 D13 **Huaraz** *var.* Huarás. Ancash, W Peru 09°31′S 77°32′W
57 I16 **Huari Huari, Río** ≈ S Peru
56 C13 **Huarmey** Ancash, W Peru 10°03′S 78°08′W
40 H4 **Huásabas** Sonora, NW Mexico 29°47′N 109°18′W
56 D8 **Huasaga, Río** ≈ Ecuador/Peru
167 O15 **Hua Sai** Nakhon Si Thammarat, SW Thailand 08°02′N 100°18′E
56 D12 **Huascarán, Nevado** ▲ W Peru 09°01′S 77°27′W
62 G8 **Huasco** Atacama, N Chile 28°30′S 71°15′W
62 G8 **Huasco, Río** ≈ C Chile
159 S11 **Huashixia** Qinghai, W China
40 G7 **Huatabampo** Sonora, NW Mexico 26°49′N 109°40′W
159 W10 **Huating** *var.* Donghua. Gansu, C China 35°13′N 106°39′E
167 S7 **Huatt, Phou** ▲ N Vietnam 19°45′N 104°48′E
41 Q14 **Huatusco** *var.* Huatusco de Chicuellar. Veracruz-Llave, C Mexico 19°13′N 96°57′W
Huatusco de Chicuellar see Huatusco
41 P13 **Huauchinango** Puebla, S Mexico 20°11′N 98°04′W
Huaunta see Wounta
41 R15 **Huautla** *var.* Huautla de Jiménez. Oaxaca, SE Mexico 18°10′N 96°51′W
Huautla de Jiménez see Huautla
161 O5 **Huaxian** *var.* Daokou, Hua Xian. Henan, C China 35°33′N 114°30′E
Hua Xian see Huaxian
Huazangsi see Tianzhu
29 V13 **Hubbard** Iowa, C USA 42°18′N 93°18′W
25 U8 **Hubbard** Texas, SW USA 31°52′N 96°43′W
25 Q6 **Hubbard Creek Lake** ◎ Texas, SW USA
31 R6 **Hubbard Lake** ◎ Michigan, N USA
160 M9 **Hubei** *var.* E, Hubei Sheng, Hupeh, Hupei. ◈ province C China
Hubei Sheng see Hubei
109 P8 **Huben** Tirol, W Austria 46°55′N 12°35′E
31 R13 **Huber Heights** Ohio, N USA 39°50′N 84°07′W
155 F17 **Hubli** Karnātaka, SW India 15°20′N 75°14′E
163 X12 **Huch'ang** N North Korea 41°25′N 127°04′E
97 M18 **Hucknall** C England, United Kingdom 53°02′N 01°11′W

◆ Country
● Country Capital
◇ Dependent Territory
○ Dependent Territory Capital
◈ Administrative Regions
✕ International Airport
▲ Mountain
▲▲ Mountain Range
Volcano
≈ River
◎ Lake
⊡ Reservoir

97 *L17* **Huddersfield** N England, United Kingdom *53°39′N 01°47′W*
95 *O16* **Huddinge** Stockholm, C Sweden *59°15′N 17°57′E*
94 *N11* **Hudiksvall** Gävleborg, C Sweden *61°45′N 17°12′E*
29 *W13* **Hudson** Iowa, C USA *42°24′N 92°27′W*
19 *O11* **Hudson** Massachusetts, NE USA *42°24′N 71°34′W*
31 *Q11* **Hudson** Michigan, N USA *41°51′N 84°21′W*
30 *H6* **Hudson** Wisconsin, N USA *44°59′N 92°43′W*
11 *V14* **Hudson Bay** Saskatchewan, S Canada *52°51′N 102°23′W*
12 *G6* **Hudson Bay** *bay* NE Canada
195 *T16* **Hudson, Cape** *headland* Antarctica *68°15′S 154°00′E*
Hudson, Détroit d' *see* Hudson Strait
27 *Q9* **Hudson, Lake** ⊠ Oklahoma, C USA
18 *K9* **Hudson River** ≈ New Jersey/New York, NE USA
10 *M12* **Hudson's Hope** British Columbia, W Canada *56°03′N 121°59′W*
12 *L2* **Hudson Strait** *Fr.* Détroit d'Hudson. *strait* Northwest Territories/Québec, NE Canada
Ḥudūd ash Shamālīyah, Minṭaqat al *see* Al Ḥudūd ash Shamālīyah
Hudur *see* Xuddur
167 *U9* **Huê** Th,a Thiên-Huê, C Vietnam *16°28′N 107°35′E*
104 *J7* **Huebra** ≈ W Spain
24 *H8* **Hueco Mountains** ▲▲ Texas, SW USA
116 *G10* **Huedin** *Hung.* Bánffyhunyad. Cluj, NW Romania *46°52′N 23°02′E*
40 *J10* **Huehuento, Cerro** ▲ C Mexico *24°04′N 105°42′W*
42 *B5* **Huehuetenango** Huehuetenango, W Guatemala *15°19′N 91°26′W*
42 *B4* **Huehuetenango** *off.* Departamento de Huehuetenango. ◈ *department* W Guatemala
Huehuetenango, Departamento de *see* Huehuetenango
40 *L11* **Huejuquilla** Jalisco, SW Mexico *22°40′N 103°52′W*
41 *P12* **Huejutla** *var.* Huejutla de Reyes. Hidalgo, C Mexico *21°10′N 98°25′W*
Huejutla de Reyes *see* Huejutla
102 *G6* **Huelgoat** Finistère, NW France *48°22′N 03°45′W*
105 *O13* **Huelma** Andalucía, S Spain *37°39′N 03°28′W*
104 *I14* **Huelva** *anc.* Onuba. Andalucía, SW Spain *37°15′N 06°56′W*
104 *I13* **Huelva** ◈ *province* Andalucía, SW Spain
104 *J13* **Huelva** ≈ SW Spain
105 *Q14* **Huercal-Overa** Andalucía, S Spain *37°23′N 01°56′W*
37 *Q9* **Huerfano Mountain** ▲ New Mexico, SW USA *36°25′N 107°50′W*
37 *T7* **Huerfano River** ≈ Colorado, C USA
Huertas, Cabo *see* Horta, Cap de l'
105 *R6* **Huerva** ≈ N Spain
105 *S4* **Huesca** *anc.* Osca. Aragón, NE Spain *42°08′N 00°25′W*
105 *T4* **Huesca** ◈ *province* Aragón, NE Spain
105 *P13* **Huéscar** Andalucía, S Spain *37°39′N 02°32′W*
41 *N15* **Huetamo** *var.* Huetamo de Núñez. Michoacán, SW Mexico *18°36′N 100°54′W*
Huetamo de Núñez *see* Huetamo
105 *P8* **Huete** Castilla-La Mancha, C Spain *40°09′N 02°42′W*
23 *P4* **Hueytown** Alabama, S USA *33°27′N 87°00′W*
28 *L16* **Hugh Butler Lake** ⊠ Nebraska, C USA
181 *V6* **Hughenden** Queensland, NE Australia *20°57′S 144°16′E*
182 *A6* **Hughes** South Australia *30°41′S 129°31′E*
39 *P8* **Hughes** Alaska, USA *66°03′N 154°15′W*
27 *X11* **Hughes** Arkansas, C USA *34°57′N 90°28′W*
25 *W6* **Hughes Springs** Texas, SW USA *33°00′N 94°37′W*
37 *V5* **Hugo** Colorado, C USA *39°08′N 103°28′W*
27 *Q13* **Hugo** Oklahoma, C USA *34°01′N 95°31′W*
27 *Q13* **Hugo Lake** ⊠ Oklahoma, C USA
26 *H7* **Hugoton** Kansas, C USA *37°11′N 101°22′W*
Huhehot/Huhohaote *see* Hohhot
Huhttán *see* Kvikkjokk
161 *R13* **Hui'an** *var.* Luocheng. Fujian, SE China *25°06′N 118°45′E*
184 *O9* **Huiarau Range** ▲▲ North Island, New Zealand
83 *D22* **Huib-Hoch Plateau** *plateau* S Namibia
41 *O13* **Huichapán** Hidalgo, C Mexico *20°24′N 99°40′W*
Huicheng *see* Shexian
163 *W13* **Hŭich'ŏn** C North Korea *40°09′N 126°17′E*
83 *B15* **Huíla** ◈ *province* SW Angola
54 *E12* **Huila** *off.* Departamento del Huila. ◈ *province* S Colombia
Huila, Departamento del *see* Huila
54 *D11* **Huila, Nevado del** *elevation* C Colombia
83 *B15* **Huíla Plateau** *plateau* S Angola
160 *G12* **Huili** Sichuan, C China *26°39′N 102°13′E*
161 *P4* **Huimin** Shandong, E China *37°29′N 117°30′E*
163 *W11* **Huinan** *var.* Chaoyang. Jilin, NE China *42°40′N 126°03′E*
62 *K12* **Huinca Renancó** Córdoba, C Argentina *34°51′S 64°22′W*
159 *V10* **Huining** *var.* Huishi. Gansu, C China *35°42′N 105°01′E*
159 *W8* **Huinong** *var.* Dawukou. Ningxia, N China *39°04′N 106°22′E*
Huishi *see* Huining
160 *J12* **Huishui** *var.* Heping. Guizhou, S China *26°07′N 106°39′E*
102 *L6* **Huisne** ≈ NW France
98 *L12* **Huissen** Gelderland, SE Netherlands *51°57′N 05°57′E*
159 *N11* **Huiten Nur** ◎ C China
93 *K19* **Huittinen** Länsi-Suomi, SW Finland *61°11′N 22°40′E*
41 *O15* **Huitzuco** *var.* Huitzuco de los Figueroa. Guerrero, S Mexico *18°18′N 99°22′W*
Huitzuco de los Figueroa *see* Huitzuco
159 *W11* **Huixian** *var.* Hui Xian. Gansu, C China *33°48′N 106°02′E*
Hui Xian *see* Huixian
41 *V17* **Huixtla** Chiapas, SE Mexico *15°09′N 92°30′W*
160 *H12* **Huize** *var.* Zhongping. Yunnan, SW China *26°28′N 103°18′E*
98 *J10* **Huizen** Noord-Holland, C Netherlands *52°17′N 05°15′E*
161 *O14* **Huizhou** Guangdong, S China *23°02′N 114°28′E*
162 *J6* **Hujirt** Arhangay, C Mongolia *48°49′N 101°20′E*
Hujirt *see* Tsetserleg, Övörhangay, Mongolia
Hujirt *see* Delgerhaan, Töv, Mongolia
Hukagawa *see* Fukagawa
Hŭksan-gundo *see* Heuksan-jedo
Hukue *see* Gotō
Hukui *see* Fukui
83 *G20* **Hukuntsi** Kgalagadi, SW Botswana *23°59′S 21°44′E*
Hukuoka *see* Fukuoka
Hukusima *see* Fukushima
Hukutiyama *see* Fukuchiyama
Hukuyama *see* Fukuyama
163 *W8* **Hulan** Heilongjiang, NE China *45°59′N 126°37′E*
163 *W8* **Hulan He** ≈ NE China
31 *Q4* **Hulbert Lake** ◎ Michigan, N USA
Hulczyn *see* Hlučín
Huliao *see* Dabu
163 *Z8* **Hulin** Heilongjiang, NE China *45°48′N 133°06′E*
Hulingol *see* Holin Gol
14 *L12* **Hull** Québec, SE Canada *45°26′N 75°45′W*
29 *S12* **Hull** Iowa, C USA *43°11′N 96°07′W*
Hull *see* Kingston upon Hull
Hull Island *see* Orona
99 *F16* **Hulst** Zeeland, SW Netherlands *51°17′N 04°03′E*
Hulstay *see* Choybalsan
Hultschin *see* Hlučín
95 *M19* **Hultsfred** Kalmar, S Sweden *57°30′N 15°50′E*
163 *T13* **Huludao** *prev.* Jinxi, Lianshan. Liaoning, NE China *40°46′N 120°47′E*
Hulun *see* Hulun Buir
163 *S6* **Hulun Buir** *var.* Hailar; *prev.* Hulun. Nei Mongol Zizhiqu, N China *49°15′N 119°41′E*
Hu-lun Ch'ih *see* Hulun Nur
163 *Q6* **Hulun Nur** *var.* Hu-lun Ch'ih; *prev.* Dalai Nor. ◎ NE China
Hulwan/Hulwân *see* Hilwān
117 *V8* **Hulyaypole** *Rus.* Gulyaypole. Zaporiz'ka Oblast', SE Ukraine *47°41′N 36°10′E*
163 *V4* **Huma** Heilongjiang, NE China *51°40′N 126°38′E*
45 *V6* **Humacao** E Puerto Rico *18°09′N 65°50′W*
163 *U4* **Huma He** ≈ NE China
62 *J5* **Humahuaca** Jujuy, N Argentina *23°13′S 65°20′W*
59 *E14* **Humaitá** Amazonas, N Brazil *07°33′S 63°01′W*
62 *N7* **Humaitá** Ñeembucú, S Paraguay *27°02′S 58°31′W*
83 *H26* **Humansdorp** Eastern Cape, S South Africa *34°01′S 24°45′E*
27 *S6* **Humansville** Missouri, C USA *37°47′N 93°34′W*
40 *I8* **Humaya, Río** ≈ C Mexico
83 *C16* **Humbe** Cunene, SW Angola *16°37′S 14°52′E*
97 *N17* **Humber** *estuary* E England, United Kingdom
97 *N17* **Humberside** *cultural region* E England, United Kingdom
Humberto *see* Umberto
25 *W11* **Humble** Texas, SW USA *29°58′N 95°15′W*
11 *U15* **Humboldt** Saskatchewan, S Canada *52°13′N 105°09′W*
29 *U12* **Humboldt** Iowa, C USA *42°42′N 94°13′W*
27 *Q6* **Humboldt** Kansas, C USA *37°48′N 95°26′W*
29 *S17* **Humboldt** Nebraska, C USA *40°09′N 95°56′W*
35 *S3* **Humboldt** Nevada, W USA *40°36′N 118°15′W*
20 *G9* **Humboldt** Tennessee, S USA *35°49′N 88°55′W*
34 *K3* **Humboldt Bay** *bay* California, W USA
35 *S4* **Humboldt Lake** ◎ Nevada, W USA
35 *S4* **Humboldt River** ≈ Nevada, W USA
35 *T5* **Humboldt Salt Marsh** *wetland* Nevada, W USA
183 *P11* **Hume, Lake** ◎ New South Wales/Victoria, SE Australia
111 *N19* **Humenné** *Ger.* Homenau, *Hung.* Homonna. Prešovský Kraj, E Slovakia *48°57′N 21°54′E*
29 *V15* **Humeston** Iowa, C USA *40°51′N 93°30′W*
54 *J5* **Humocaro Bajo** Lara, N Venezuela *09°41′N 70°00′W*
29 *Q14* **Humphrey** Nebraska, C USA *41°38′N 97°29′W*
35 *S9* **Humphreys, Mount** ▲ California, W USA *37°11′N 118°39′W*
36 *L11* **Humphreys Peak** ▲ Arizona, SW USA *35°18′N 111°40′W*
111 *E17* **Humpolec** *Ger.* Gumpolds, Humpoletz. Vysočina, C Czech Republic *49°33′N 15°23′E*
Humpoletz *see* Humpolec
93 *K19* **Humppila** Etelä-Suomi, S Finland *60°54′N 23°21′E*
32 *F8* **Humptulips** Washington, NW USA *47°13′N 123°57′W*
42 *H7* **Humuya, Río** ≈ W Honduras
75 *P9* **Hūn** N Libya *29°06′N 15°56′E*
92 *I1* **Húnaflói** *bay* NW Iceland
160 *M11* **Hunan** *var.* Hunan Sheng, Xiang. ◈ *province* S China
Hunan Sheng *see* Hunan
163 *Y10* **Hunchun** Jilin, NE China *42°51′N 130°21′E*
95 *I22* **Hundested** Hovedstaden, E Denmark *55°58′N 11°53′E*
Hundred Mile House *see* 100 Mile House
116 *G12* **Hunedoara** *Ger.* Eisenmarkt, *Hung.* Vajdahunyad. Hunedoara, SW Romania *45°45′N 22°54′E*
116 *G12* **Hunedoara** ◈ *county* W Romania
101 *I17* **Hünfeld** Hessen, C Germany *50°41′N 09°46′E*
Hungarian People's Republic *see* Hungary
111 *H23* **Hungary** *off.* Republic of Hungary, *Ger.* Ungarn, *Hung.* Magyarország, *Rom.* Ungaria, *SCr.* Mađarska, *Ukr.* Uhorshchyna; *prev.* Hungarian People's Republic. ◆ *republic* C Europe
Hungary, Plain of *see* Great Hungarian Plain
Hungary, Republic of *see* Hungary
Hungiy *see* Urgamal
163 *X13* **Hŭngnam** E North Korea *39°50′N 127°36′E*
33 *P8* **Hungry Horse Reservoir** ⊠ Montana, NW USA
Hungt'ou *see* Lan Yu
Hung-tse Hu *see* Hongze Hu
167 *T6* **Hưng Yên** Hai Hưng, N Vietnam *20°38′N 106°05′E*
Hunjiang *see* Baishan
95 *I18* **Hunnebostrand** Västra Götaland, S Sweden *58°26′N 11°19′E*
101 *E19* **Hunsrück** ▲▲ W Germany
97 *P18* **Hunstanton** E England, United Kingdom *52°57′N 00°27′E*
155 *G20* **Hunsūr** Karnātaka, E India *12°18′N 76°15′E*
Hunt *see* Hangay
100 *G12* **Hunte** ≈ NW Germany
29 *Q5* **Hunter** North Dakota, N USA *47°10′N 97°11′W*
25 *S11* **Hunter** Texas, SW USA *29°47′N 98°01′W*
185 *D20* **Hunter** ≈ South Island, New Zealand
183 *N15* **Hunter Island** *island* Tasmania, SE Australia
18 *K11* **Hunter Mountain** ▲ New York, NE USA *42°10′N 74°13′W*
185 *B23* **Hunter Mountains** ▲▲ South Island, New Zealand
183 *S7* **Hunter River** ≈ New South Wales, SE Australia
32 *L7* **Hunters** Washington, NW USA *48°07′N 118°13′W*
185 *F20* **Hunters Hills, The** *hill range* South Island, New Zealand
184 *M12* **Hunterville** Manawatu-Wanganui, North Island, New Zealand *39°55′S 175°34′E*
31 *N16* **Huntingburg** Indiana, N USA *38°18′N 86°57′W*
97 *O20* **Huntingdon** E England, United Kingdom *52°20′N 00°12′W*
18 *E15* **Huntingdon** Pennsylvania, NE USA *40°28′N 78°00′W*
20 *G9* **Huntingdon** Tennessee, S USA *36°00′N 88°25′W*
97 *O20* **Huntingdonshire** *cultural region* C England, United Kingdom
31 *P12* **Huntington** Indiana, N USA *40°52′N 85°30′W*
32 *L13* **Huntington** Oregon, NW USA *44°22′N 117°18′W*
25 *X9* **Huntington** Texas, SW USA *31°16′N 94°34′W*
36 *M5* **Huntington** Utah, W USA *39°19′N 110°57′W*
21 *P5* **Huntington** West Virginia, NE USA *38°25′N 82°27′W*
35 *T16* **Huntington Beach** California, W USA *33°39′N 118°00′W*
35 *W4* **Huntington Creek** ≈ Nevada, W USA
184 *L7* **Huntly** Waikato, North Island, New Zealand *37°34′S 175°09′E*
96 *K8* **Huntly** NE Scotland, United Kingdom *57°25′N 02°48′W*
10 *K8* **Hunt, Mount** ▲ Yukon Territory, NW Canada *61°29′N 129°10′W*
14 *H12* **Huntsville** Ontario, S Canada *45°20′N 79°14′W*
23 *P2* **Huntsville** Alabama, S USA *34°44′N 86°35′W*
27 *S9* **Huntsville** Arkansas, C USA *36°04′N 93°46′W*
27 *U3* **Huntsville** Missouri, C USA *39°27′N 92°31′W*
20 *M8* **Huntsville** Tennessee, S USA *36°25′N 84°30′W*
25 *V10* **Huntsville** Texas, SW USA *30°43′N 95°34′W*
36 *L2* **Huntsville** Utah, W USA *41°16′N 111°47′W*
41 *W12* **Hunucmá** Yucatán, SE Mexico *20°59′N 89°55′W*
149 *W3* **Hunza** ≈ NE Pakistan
Hunza *see* Karīmābād
Hunze *see* Oostermoers Vaart
158 *H4* **Huocheng** *var.* Shuiding. Xinjiang Uygur Zizhiqu, NW China *44°03′N 80°49′E*
161 *N6* **Huojia** Henan, C China *35°14′N 113°38′E*
186 *N14* **Huon** *reef* N New Caledonia
186 *E7* **Huon Peninsula** *headland* C Papua New Guinea *06°24′S 147°50′E*
Huoshao Dao *see* Lü Dao
Huoshao Tao *see* Lan Yu
Hupeh/Hupei *see* Hubei
Hurama *see* Hongyuan
95 *H14* **Hurdalsjøen** *prev.* Hurdalssjøen. ◎ S Norway
Hurdalssjøen *see* Hurdalsjøen
14 *E13* **Hurd, Cape** *headland* Ontario, S Canada *45°12′N 81°43′W*
98 *L5* **Hurdegaryp** *Dutch.* Hardegarijp. Fryslân, N Netherlands *53°13′N 05°57′E*
29 *N4* **Hurdsfield** North Dakota, N USA *47°24′N 99°55′W*
Hüremt *see* Sayhan, Bulgan, Mongolia
Hüremt *see* Taragt, Övörhangay, Mongolia
Hurghada *see* Al Ghurdaqah
67 *V9* **Huri Hills** ▲▲ NW Kenya
37 *P15* **Hurley** New Mexico, SW USA *32°42′N 108°07′W*
30 *K4* **Hurley** Wisconsin, N USA *46°25′N 90°15′W*
21 *Y4* **Hurlock** Maryland, NE USA *38°37′N 75°51′W*
162 *K11* **Hürmen** *var.* Tsoohor. Ömnögovĭ, S Mongolia *43°15′N 104°04′E*
29 *P10* **Huron** South Dakota, N USA *44°19′N 98°13′W*
31 *S6* **Huron, Lake** ◎ Canada/USA
31 *N3* **Huron Mountains** *hill range* Michigan, N USA
36 *J8* **Hurricane** Utah, W USA *37°10′N 113°18′W*
21 *P5* **Hurricane** West Virginia, NE USA *38°25′N 82°01′W*
36 *J8* **Hurricane Cliffs** *cliff* Arizona, SW USA
23 *V6* **Hurricane Creek** ≈ Georgia, SE USA
94 *E12* **Hurrungane** ▲ S Norway *61°25′N 07°48′E*
101 *E16* **Hürth** Nordrhein-Westfalen, W Germany *50°52′N 06°49′E*
Hurukawa *see* Furukawa
185 *I17* **Hurunui** ≈ South Island, New Zealand
95 *F21* **Hurup** Midtjylland, NW Denmark *56°46′N 08°26′E*
117 *T14* **Hurzuf** Avtonomna Respublika Krym, S Ukraine *44°33′N 34°18′E*
Huş *see* Huşi
95 *B19* **Húsavík** *Dan.* Husevig. Sandoy, C Faeroe Islands *65°24′N 06°38′W*
92 *K1* **Húsavík** Nordhurland Eystra, NE Iceland *66°03′N 17°20′W*
Husevig *see* Húsavík
116 *M10* **Huşi** *var.* Huş. Vaslui, E Romania *46°40′N 28°05′E*
95 *L19* **Huskvarna** Jönköping, S Sweden *57°47′N 14°15′E*
39 *P8* **Huslia** Alaska, USA *65°42′N 156°24′W*
Husn *see* Al Ḥuṣn
95 *C15* **Husnes** Hordaland, S Norway *59°52′N 05°46′E*
94 *D8* **Hustadvika** *sea area* S Norway
Husté *see* Khust
100 *H7* **Husum** Schleswig-Holstein, N Germany *54°29′N 09°04′E*
93 *I16* **Husum** Västernorrland, C Sweden *63°21′N 19°12′E*
116 *K6* **Husyatyn** Ternopil's'ka Oblast', W Ukraine *49°04′N 26°10′E*
Huszt *see* Khust
Hutag *see* Hutag-Öndör
162 *K6* **Hutag-Öndör** *var.* Hutag. Bulgan, N Mongolia *49°22′N 102°50′E*
26 *M6* **Hutchinson** Kansas, C USA *38°03′N 97°56′W*
29 *U9* **Hutchinson** Minnesota, N USA *44°53′N 94°22′W*
23 *Y13* **Hutchinson Island** *island* Florida, SE USA
36 *L11* **Hutch Mountain** ▲ Arizona, SW USA *34°49′N 111°22′W*
141 *O14* **Ḥūth** NW Yemen *16°14′N 44°E*
186 *I7* **Hutjena** Buka Island, NE Papua New Guinea *05°19′S 154°40′E*
109 *T8* **Hüttenberg** Kärnten, S Austria *46°58′N 14°33′E*
25 *T10* **Hutto** Texas, SW USA *30°32′N 97°33′W*
Huttu *see* Futtsu
108 *E8* **Huttwil** Bern, W Switzerland *47°06′N 07°48′E*
158 *K5* **Hutubi** Xinjiang Uygur Zizhiqu, NW China *44°10′N 86°51′E*
161 *N4* **Hutuo He** ≈ C China
Hutyû *see* Fuchū
185 *E20* **Huxley, Mount** ▲ South Island, New Zealand *44°02′S 169°42′E*
99 *J20* **Huy** *Dut.* Hoei, Hoey. Liège, E Belgium *50°32′N 05°14′E*
161 *R8* **Huzhou** *var.* Wuxing. Zhejiang, SE China *30°52′N 120°06′E*
Huzi *see* Fuji
Huzieda *see* Fujieda
Huzinomiya *see* Fujinomiya
Huzisawa *see* Fujisawa
92 *I2* **Hvammstangi** Nordhurland Vestra, N Iceland *65°22′N 20°54′W*
92 *K4* **Hvannadalshnúkur** ⛰ S Iceland *64°01′N 16°39′W*
113 *E15* **Hvar** *It.* Lesina. Split-Dalmacija, S Croatia *43°10′N 16°27′E*
113 *F15* **Hvar** *It.* Lesina; *anc.* Pharus. *island* S Croatia
117 *T13* **Hvardiys'ke** *Rus.* Gvardeyskoye. Avtonomna Respublika Krym, S Ukraine *45°08′N 34°01′E*
92 *I4* **Hveragerdhi** Sudhurland, SW Iceland *64°00′N 21°13′W*
95 *E22* **Hvide Sande** Midtjylland, W Denmark *56°00′N 08°08′E*
92 *I3* **Hvitá** ≈ C Iceland
95 *G15* **Hvittingfoss** Buskerud, S Norway *59°28′N 10°00′E*
92 *I4* **Hvolsvöllur** Sudhurland, SW Iceland *63°44′N 20°12′W*
Hwach'ŏn-chŏsuji *see* Paro-ho
Hwainan *see* Huainan
Hwalien *see* Hualian
83 *I16* **Hwange** *prev.* Wankie. Matabeleland North, W Zimbabwe *18°18′S 26°31′E*
Hwang-Hae *see* Yellow Sea
Hwangshih *see* Huangshi
83 *L17* **Hwedza** Mashonaland East, E Zimbabwe *18°35′S 31°35′E*
63 *G20* **Hyades, Cerro** ▲ S Chile *46°57′S 73°09′W*
162 *K6* **Hyalganat** *var.* Selenge. Bulgan, N Mongolia *49°34′N 104°18′E*
19 *Q12* **Hyannis** Massachusetts, NE USA *41°38′N 70°15′W*
28 *L13* **Hyannis** Nebraska, C USA *42°00′N 101°45′W*
162 *F6* **Hyargas Nuur** ◎ NW Mongolia
Hybla/Hybla Major *see* Paternò
39 *Y14* **Hydaburg** Prince of Wales Island, Alaska, USA *55°10′N 132°44′W*
185 *F22* **Hyde** Otago, South Island, New Zealand *45°17′S 170°17′E*
21 *O7* **Hyden** Kentucky, S USA *37°08′N 83°23′W*
18 *K12* **Hyde Park** New York, NE USA *41°46′N 73°52′W*
39 *Z14* **Hyder** Alaska, USA *55°55′N 130°01′W*
155 *I15* **Hyderābād** *var.* Haidarabad. *state capital* Andhra Pradesh, C India *17°22′N 78°26′E*
149 *Q16* **Hyderābād** *var.* Haidarabad. Sind, SE Pakistan *25°26′N 68°22′E*
103 *T16* **Hyères** Var, SE France *43°07′N 06°08′E*
103 *T16* **Hyères, Îles d'** *island group* S France
118 *K12* **Hyermanavichy** *Rus.* Germanovichi. Vitsyebskaya Voblasts', N Belarus *55°24′N 27°48′E*
163 *X12* **Hyesan** NE North Korea *41°18′N 128°13′E*
10 *K8* **Hyland** ≈ Yukon Territory, NW Canada
95 *K20* **Hyltebruk** Halland, S Sweden *57°N 13°14′E*
18 *D16* **Hyndman** Pennsylvania, NE USA *39°49′N 78°42′W*
33 *P14* **Hyndman Peak** ▲ Idaho, NW USA *43°45′N 114°07′W*
164 *I13* **Hyōgo** *off.* Hyōgo-ken. ◈ *prefecture* Honshū, SW Japan
Hyōgo-ken *see* Hyōgo
Hypsas *see* Belice
Hyrcania *see* Gorgān
36 *L1* **Hyrum** Utah, W USA *41°37′N 111°51′W*
93 *N14* **Hyrynsalmi** Oulu, C Finland *64°41′N 28°30′E*
33 *V10* **Hysham** Montana, NW USA *46°16′N 107°14′W*
11 *N13* **Hythe** Alberta, W Canada *55°18′N 119°44′W*
97 *Q23* **Hythe** SE England, United Kingdom *51°05′N 01°04′E*
Hyvinge *see* Hyvinkää
93 *L19* **Hyvinkää** *Swe.* Hyvinge. Etelä-Suomi, S Finland *60°37′N 24°50′E*

I

116 *J9* **Iacobeni** *Ger.* Jakobeny. Suceava, NE Romania *47°24′N 25°20′E*
Iader *see* Zadar
172 *I7* **Iakora** Fianarantsoa, SE Madagascar *23°04′S 46°40′E*
116 *K14* **Ialomiţa** *var.* Jalomitsa. ◈ *county* SE Romania
116 *K14* **Ialomiţa** ≈ SE Romania
117 *N10* **Ialoveni** *Rus.* Yaloveny. C Moldova *46°57′N 28°47′E*
117 *N11* **Ialpug** *var.* Ialpugul Mare, *Rus.* Yalpug. ≈ Moldova/Ukraine
Ialpugul Mare *see* Ialpug
23 *T8* **Iamonia, Lake** ◎ Florida, SE USA
116 *L13* **Ianca** Brăila, SE Romania *45°06′N 27°29′E*
116 *M10* **Iaşi** *Ger.* Jassy. Iaşi, NE Romania *47°08′N 27°38′E*
116 *L9* **Iaşi** *Ger.* Jassy, Yassy. ◈ *county* NE Romania
114 *J13* **Íasmos** Anatolikí Makedonía kai Thráki, NE Greece *41°07′N 25°12′E*
22 *H6* **Iatt, Lake** ⊠ Louisiana, S USA
58 *B11* **Iauretê** Amazonas, NW Brazil *0°37′N 69°10′W*
171 *N3* **Iba** Luzon, N Philippines *15°25′N 119°55′E*
77 *S16* **Ibadan** Oyo, SW Nigeria *07°22′N 04°01′E*
54 *E10* **Ibagué** Tolima, C Colombia *04°27′N 75°14′W*
60 *J10* **Ibaiti** Paraná, S Brazil *23°49′S 50°15′W*
36 *J4* **Ibapah Peak** ▲ Utah, W USA *39°51′N 113°55′W*
Ibar *see* Ibër
165 *P13* **Ibaraki** *off.* Ibaraki-ken. ◈ *prefecture* Honshū, S Japan
Ibaraki-ken *see* Ibaraki
56 *C5* **Ibarra** *var.* San Miguel de Ibarra. Imbabura, N Ecuador *0°23′S 78°08′W*
Ibaşfalău *see* Dumbrăveni
141 *O16* **Ibb** W Yemen *13°55′N 44°10′E*
100 *F13* **Ibbenbüren** Nordrhein-Westfalen, NW Germany *52°17′N 07°43′E*
79 *H16* **Ibenga** ≈ N Congo
113 *M15* **Ibër** *Serb.* Ibar. ≈ C Serbia
57 *I14* **Iberia** Madre de Dios, E Peru *11°21′S 69°36′W*
Iberia *see* Spain
66 *M1* **Iberian Basin** *undersea feature* E Atlantic Ocean *39°00′N 16°00′W*
Iberian Mountains *see* Ibérico, Sistema
84 *D12* **Iberian Peninsula** *physical region* Portugal/Spain
64 *M8* **Iberian Plain** *undersea feature* E Atlantic Ocean *13°30′W 43°45′N*
Ibérica, Cordillera *see* Ibérico, Sistema
105 *P6* **Ibérico, Sistema** *var.* Cordillera Ibérica, *Eng.* Iberian Mountains. ▲▲ NE Spain
12 *K7* **Iberville Lac d'** ◎ Québec, NE Canada
77 *T14* **Ibeto** Niger, W Nigeria *10°30′N 05°07′E*
77 *W15* **Ibi** Taraba, C Nigeria *08°13′N 09°46′E*
105 *S11* **Ibi** Valenciana, E Spain *38°38′N 00°35′W*
59 *L20* **Ibiá** Minas Gerais, SE Brazil *19°30′S 46°31′W*
61 *F15* **Ibicuí, Rio** ≈ S Brazil
61 *C19* **Ibicuy** Entre Ríos, E Argentina *33°44′S 59°10′W*
61 *F16* **Ibirapuitã** ≈ S Brazil
105 *V10* **Ibiza** *var.* Iviza, *Cast.* Eivissa; *anc.* Ebusus. *island* Islas Baleares, Spain, W Mediterranean Sea
Ibiza *see* Eivissa
138 *J4* **Ibn Wardān, Qaşr** *ruins* Ḥamāh, C Syria
Ibo *see* Sassandra
188 *E9* **Ibobang** Babeldaob, N Palau
171 *V13* **Ibonma** Papua, E Indonesia *03°27′S 133°30′E*
59 *N17* **Ibotirama** Bahia, E Brazil *12°13′S 43°12′W*
141 *Y8* **Ibrā** NE Oman *22°45′N 58°30′E*
127 *Q4* **Ibresi** Chuvashskaya Respublika, W Russian Federation *55°22′N 47°04′E*
141 *X8* **ʻIbrī** NW Oman *23°12′N 56°28′E*
164 *C16* **Ibusuki** Kagoshima, Kyūshū, SW Japan *31°15′N 130°40′E*
57 *E16* **Ica** Ica, SW Peru *14°02′S 75°48′W*
57 *E16* **Ica** *off.* Departamento de Ica. ◈ *department* SW Peru
Ica, Departamento de *see* Ica
58 *C11* **Içana** Amazonas, NW Brazil *0°22′N 67°25′W*
Icaria *see* Ikaría
58 *B13* **Içá, Rio** *var.* Río Putumayo. ≈ NW South America *see also* Putumayo, Río
Içá, Rio *see* Putumayo, Río
136 *I17* **İçel** *prev.* Ichili; *prev.* Mersin. ◈ *province* S Turkey
İçel *see* Mersin
92 *I3* **Iceland** *off.* Republic of Iceland, *Dan.* Island, *Icel.* Ísland. ◆ *republic* N Atlantic Ocean
86 *B6* **Iceland** *island* N Atlantic Ocean
64 *L5* **Iceland Basin** *undersea feature* N Atlantic Ocean *61°00′N 19°00′W*
Icelandic Plateau *see* Iceland Plateau
197 *Q15* **Iceland Plateau** *var.* Icelandic Plateau. *undersea feature* S Greenland Sea *12°00′W 69°30′N*
Iceland, Republic of *see* Iceland
155 *E16* **Ichalkaranji** Mahārāshtra, W India *16°42′N 74°28′E*
164 *D15* **Ichifusa-yama** ▲ Kyūshū, SW Japan *32°18′N 131°05′E*
Ichili *see* İçel
164 *K13* **Ichinomiya** *var.* Itinomiya. Aichi, Honshū, SW Japan *35°18′N 136°48′E*
165 *Q9* **Ichinoseki** *var.* Itinoseki. Iwate, Honshū, C Japan *38°56′N 141°08′E*
117 *R3* **Ichnya** Chernihivs'ka Oblast', NE Ukraine *50°52′N 32°24′E*
57 *L17* **Ichoa, Río** ≈ C Bolivia
Iconium *see* Konya
Iculisma *see* Angoulême
39 *U12* **Icy Bay** *inlet* Alaska, USA
39 *N5* **Icy Cape** *headland* Alaska, USA *70°19′N 161°52′W*
39 *W13* **Icy Strait** *strait* Alaska, USA
27 *R13* **Idabel** Oklahoma, C USA *33°54′N 94°50′W*
29 *T13* **Ida Grove** Iowa, C USA *42°21′N 95°28′W*
77 *U16* **Idah** Kogi, S Nigeria *07°06′N 06°45′E*
33 *N13* **Idaho** *off.* State of Idaho, *also known as* Gem of the Mountains, Gem State. ◈ *state* NW USA
33 *N14* **Idaho City** Idaho, NW USA *43°48′N 115°51′W*
33 *R14* **Idaho Falls** Idaho, NW USA *43°28′N 112°01′W*
121 *P2* **Idálion** *var.* Dali, Dhali. C Cyprus *35°00′N 33°25′E*
25 *N5* **Idalou** Texas, SW USA *33°40′N 101°40′W*
104 *I9* **Idanha-a-Nova** Castelo Branco, C Portugal *39°55′N 07°15′W*
101 *E19* **Idar-Oberstein** Rheinland-Pfalz, SW Germany *49°43′N 07°19′E*
118 *J3* **Ida-Virumaa** *var.* Ida-Viru Maakond. ◈ *province* NE Estonia
Ida-Viru Maakond *see* Ida-Virumaa
124 *J8* **Idel'** Respublika Kareliya, NW Russian Federation *64°08′N 34°12′E*
79 *C15* **Idenao** Sud-Ouest, SW Cameroon *04°04′N 09°01′E*
Idensalmi *see* Iisalmi
162 *I6* **Ider** *var.* Dzuunmod. Hövsgöl, C Mongolia *48°09′N 97°22′E*
Ider *see* Galt
75 *X10* **Idfū** *var.* Edfu. SE Egypt *24°55′N 32°52′E*
Ídhi Óros *see* Ídi
Ídhra *see* Ýdra
80 *L10* **ʻĪdi** *var.* Ed. SE Eritrea *13°54′N 41°39′E*
168 *H7* **Idi** Sumatera, W Indonesia *05°00′N 98°00′E*
115 *I25* **Ídi** *var.* Ídhi Óros. ▲▲ Kríti, Greece, E Mediterranean Sea
Idi Amin, Lac *see* Edward, Lake
106 *G10* **Idice** ≈ N Italy
76 *G9* **Idîni** Trarza, W Mauritania *17°58′N 15°40′W*
79 *J21* **Idiofa** Bandundu, SW Dem. Rep. Congo *05°00′S 19°38′E*
39 *O10* **Iditarod River** ≈ Alaska, USA
Idjavuotna *see* Ifjord
95 *M14* **Idkerberget** Dalarna, C Sweden *60°22′N 15°15′E*
138 *I3* **Idlib** Idlib, NW Syria *35°57′N 36°38′E*
138 *I4* **Idlib** *off.* Muḥāfaẓat Idlib. ◈ *governorate* NW Syria
Idlib, Muḥāfaẓat *see* Idlib
Idra *see* Ýdra
94 *J11* **Idre** Dalarna, C Sweden *61°52′N 12°45′E*
Idria *see* Idrija
109 *S11* **Idrija** *It.* Idria. W Slovenia *46°00′N 14°59′E*
101 *G18* **Idstein** Hessen, W Germany *50°10′N 08°16′E*
83 *J25* **Idutywa** Eastern Cape, SE South Africa *32°06′S 28°20′E*
Idzhevan *see* Ijevan
118 *G9* **Iecava** S Latvia *56°36′N 24°10′E*
165 *T16* **Ie-jima** *var.* Ii-shima. *island* Nansei-shotō, SW Japan
99 *B18* **Ieper** *Fr.* Ypres. West-Vlaanderen, W Belgium *50°51′N 02°53′E*
115 *K25* **Ierápetra** Kríti, Greece, E Mediterranean Sea *35°00′N 25°45′E*
115 *G22* **Iérax, Akrotírio** *headland* S Greece *36°45′N 23°06′E*
Ierisós *see* Ierissós
115 *H14* **Ierissós** *var.* Ierisós. Kentrikí Makedonía, N Greece *40°24′N 23°53′E*
116 *I11* **Iernut** *Hung.* Radnót. Mureş, C Romania *46°27′N 24°15′E*
106 *J12* **Iesi** *var.* Jesi. Marche, C Italy *43°33′N 13°16′E*
92 *K9* **Iešjavri** ◎ N Norway
Iesolo *see* Jesolo
188 *K16* **Ifalik Atoll** *atoll* Caroline Islands, C Micronesia
172 *I6* **Ifanadiana** Fianarantsoa, SE Madagascar *21°19′S 47°39′E*
77 *T16* **Ife** Osun, SW Nigeria *07°25′N 04°31′E*
77 *V8* **Iferouâne** Agadez, N Niger *19°05′N 08°24′E*
Iferten *see* Yverdon
92 *L8* **Ifjord** *Lapp.* Idjavuotna. Finnmark, N Norway *70°27′N 27°06′E*
77 *R8* **Ifôghas, Adrar des** *var.* Adrar des Iforas. ▲▲ NE Mali
Iforas, Adrar des *see* Ifôghas, Adrar des
182 *D6* **Ifould lake** *salt lake* South Australia
74 *G6* **Ifrane** C Morocco *33°31′N 05°09′W*
171 *S11* **Iga** Pulau Halmahera, E Indonesia *01°23′N 128°17′E*
81 *G18* **Iganga** SE Uganda *0°34′N 33°27′E*
60 *L7* **Igarapava** São Paulo, S Brazil *20°01′S 47°46′W*
122 *K9* **Igarka** Krasnoyarskiy Kray, N Russian Federation *67°31′N 86°33′E*
Igaunija *see* Estonia
137 *T12* **Iğdir** ◈ *province* NE Turkey
I.G.Duca *see* General Toshevo
Igel *see* Jihlava
94 *N11* **Iggesund** Gävleborg, C Sweden *61°38′N 17°04′E*
39 *P7* **Igikpak, Mount** ▲ Alaska, USA *67°28′N 154°55′W*
39 *P13* **Igiugig** Alaska, USA *59°19′N 155°53′W*
Iglau/Iglawa/Igława *see* Jihlava
107 *B20* **Iglesias** Sardegna, Italy, C Mediterranean Sea *39°20′N 08°34′E*
127 *V4* **Iglino** Respublika Bashkortostan, W Russian Federation *54°51′N 56°29′E*
Igló *see* Spišská Nová Ves
9 *O6* **Igloolik** Nunavut, N Canada *69°24′N 81°55′W*
12 *B11* **Ignace** Ontario, S Canada *49°26′N 91°40′W*
118 *I12* **Ignalina** Utena, E Lithuania *55°20′N 26°10′E*
127 *Q5* **Ignatovka** Ul'yanovskaya Oblast', W Russian Federation *53°56′N 47°40′E*
124 *K12* **Ignatovo** Vologodskaya Oblast', NW Russian Federation *60°47′N 37°51′E*
114 *N11* **İğneada** Kırklareli, NW Turkey *41°54′N 27°58′E*
121 *S7* **İğneada Burnu** *headland* NW Turkey *41°54′N 28°03′E*
Igombe *see* Gombe
115 *B16* **Igoumenítsa** Ípeiros, W Greece *39°30′N 20°16′E*
127 *T2* **Igra** Udmurtskaya Respublika, NW Russian Federation *57°30′N 53°01′E*
122 *H9* **Igrim** Khanty-Mansiyskiy Avtonomnyy Okrug-Yugra, N Russian Federation *63°09′N 64°33′E*
60 *G12* **Iguaçu, Rio** *Sp.* Río Iguazú. ≈ Argentina/Brazil *see also* Iguazú, Río
Iguaçu, Río *see* Iguazú, Río
59 *I22* **Iguaçu, Salto do** *Sp.* Cataratas del Iguazú; *prev.* Victoria Falls. *waterfall* Argentina/Brazil *see also* Iguazú, Cataratas del
Iguaçu, Salto do *see* Iguazú, Cataratas del
41 *O15* **Iguala** *var.* Iguala de la Independencia. Guerrero, S Mexico *18°21′N 99°31′W*
105 *V5* **Igualada** Cataluña, NE Spain *41°35′N 01°37′E*
Iguala de la Independencia *see* Iguala
60 *G12* **Iguazú, Cataratas del** *Port.* Salto do Iguaçu; *prev.* Victoria Falls. *waterfall* Argentina/Brazil *see also* Iguaçu, Salto do
Iguazú, Cataratas del *see* Iguaçu, Salto do
62 *Q6* **Iguazú, Río** *var.* Río Iguaçu. ≈ Argentina/Brazil *see also* Iguaçu, Río
Iguazú, Río *see* Iguaçu, Rio
79 *D19* **Iguéla** *prev.* Iguéla. Ogooué-Maritime, SW Gabon *02°00′S 09°23′E*
Iguéla *see* Iguéla
Iguid, Erg *see* Iguîdi, 'Erg
67 *M5* **Iguîdi, 'Erg** *var.* Erg Iguid. *desert* Algeria/Mauritania
172 *K2* **Iharaña** *prev.* Vohémar. Antsiranana, NE Madagascar *13°22′S 50°00′E*
151 *K18* **Ihavandhippolhu Atoll** *var.* Ihavandiffulu Atoll. *atoll* N Maldives
Ihavandiffulu Atoll *see* Ihavandhippolhu Atoll
Ih Bulag *see* Hanbogd
165 *T16* **Iheya-jima** *island* Nansei-shotō, SW Japan
Ihhayrhan *see* Bayan-Önjüül
163 *N9* **Ihhet** *var.* Bayan. Dornogovĭ, SE Mongolia *46°15′N 110°16′E*
172 *I6* **Ihosy** Fianarantsoa, S Madagascar *22°23′S 46°09′E*
Ihsüüj *see* Bayanchandmanĭ
162 *I7* **Ihtamir** *var.* Dzaanhushuu. Arhangay, C Mongolia *47°36′N 101°06′E*
162 *H6* **Ih-Uul** *var.* Bayan-Uhaa. Dzavhan, C Mongolia *48°41′N 98°46′E*
162 *J6* **Ih-Uul** *var.* Selenge. Hövsgöl, N Mongolia *49°25′N 101°30′E*
93 *L14* **Ii** Oulu, C Finland *65°18′N 25°23′E*
164 *M13* **Iida** Nagano, Honshū, S Japan *35°32′N 137°48′E*
93 *M14* **Iijoki** ≈ C Finland
Iinnasuolu *see* Hinnøya
118 *J4* **Iisaku** *Ger.* Isaak. Ida-Virumaa, NE Estonia *59°06′N 27°19′E*
93 *M16* **Iisalmi** *var.* Idensalmi. Itä-Suomi, C Finland *63°32′N 27°10′E*
Ii-shima *see* Ie-jima
165 *N11* **Iiyama** Nagano, Honshū, S Japan *36°52′N 138°22′E*
77 *S16* **Ijebu-Ode** Ogun, SW Nigeria *06°46′N 03°57′E*
137 *U11* **Ijevan** *Rus.* Idzhevan. N Armenia *40°53′N 45°07′E*
98 *H9* **IJmuiden** Noord-Holland, W Netherlands *52°28′N 04°38′E*
98 *M12* **IJssel** *var.* Yssel. ≈ Netherlands
98 *J8* **IJsselmeer** *prev.* Zuider Zee. ◎ N Netherlands
98 *L9* **IJsselmuiden** Overijssel, E Netherlands *52°34′N 05°55′E*
98 *I12* **IJsselstein** Utrecht, C Netherlands *52°01′N 05°02′E*
61 *G14* **Ijuí** Rio Grande do Sul, S Brazil *28°23′S 53°55′W*
61 *G14* **Ijuí, Rio** ≈ S Brazil
189 *R8* **Ijuw** NE Nauru *0°30′S 166°57′E*
99 *E16* **IJzendijke** Zeeland, SW Netherlands *51°20′N 03°36′E*
99 *A18* **Ijzer** ≈ W Belgium
Ikaahuk *see* Sachs Harbour

◆ Country
● Country Capital
◇ Dependent Territory
○ Dependent Territory Capital
◈ Administrative Regions
✕ International Airport
▲ Mountain
▲▲ Mountain Range
⛰ Volcano
≈ River
◎ Lake
⊠ Reservoir

93 K18 **Ikaalinen** Länsi-Suomi, W Finland 61°46′N 23°05′E
172 I6 **Ikalamavony** Fianarantsoa, SE Madagascar 21°10′S 46°35′E
Ikaluktutiak see Cambridge Bay
185 G16 **Ikamatua** West Coast, South Island, New Zealand 42°16′S 171°42′E
145 P16 **Ikan** prev. Staroikan. Yuzhnyy Kazakhstan, S Kazakhstan 43°09′N 68°34′E
77 U16 **Ikare** Ondo, SW Nigeria 07°36′N 05°52′E
115 L20 **Ikaría** var. Kariot, Nicaria, Nikaria; anc. Icaria. island Dodekánisa, Greece, Aegean Sea
95 F22 **Ikast** Midtjylland, W Denmark 56°09′N 09°10′E
184 O9 **Ikawhenua Range** ▲ North Island, New Zealand
165 U4 **Ikeda** Hokkaidō, NE Japan 42°54′N 143°25′E
164 H14 **Ikeda** Tokushima, Shikoku, SW Japan 34°00′N 133°47′E
77 S16 **Ikeja** Lagos, SW Nigeria 06°36′N 03°16′E
79 L19 **Ikela** Equateur, C Dem. Rep. Congo 01°11′S 23°16′E
114 H10 **Ikhtiman** Sofiya, W Bulgaria 42°26′N 23°49′E
164 C13 **Iki** prev. Gōnoura. Nagasaki, Iki, SW Japan 33°44′N 129°41′E
164 C13 **Iki** island SW Japan
127 O13 **Iki Burul** Respublika Kalmykiya, SW Russian Federation 45°48′N 44°44′E
137 P11 **İkizdere** Rize, NE Turkey 40°47′N 40°34′E
39 P14 **Ikolik, Cape** headland Kodiak Island, Alaska, USA 57°12′N 154°46′W
77 V17 **Ikom** Cross River, SE Nigeria 05°57′N 08°43′E
172 I6 **Ikongo** prev. Fort-Carnot. Fianarantsoa, SE Madagascar 21°52′S 47°27′E
39 P5 **Ikpikpuk River** ⇝ Alaska, USA
190 H1 **Iku** prev. Lone Tree Islet. atoll Tungaru, W Kiribati
164 I12 **Ikuno** Hyōgo, Honshū, SW Japan 35°13′N 134°48′E
190 H16 **Ikurangi** ▲ Rarotonga, S Cook Islands 21°12′S 159°45′W
171 X14 **Ilaga** Papua, E Indonesia 03°54′S 137°30′E
171 O2 **Ilagan** Luzon, N Philippines 17°08′N 121°54′E
142 J7 **Īlām** var. Elam. Īlām, W Iran 33°37′N 46°27′E
153 R12 **Ilām** Eastern, E Nepal 26°52′N 87°58′E
142 J8 **Īlām** off. Ostān-e Īlām. ◆ province W Iran
Īlām, Ostān-e see Īlām
161 T13 **Ilan** Jap. Giran. N Taiwan 24°45′N 121°44′E
146 G9 **Ilanly Obvodnitel'nyy Kanal** canal N Turkmenistan
122 L12 **Ilanskiy** Krasnoyarskiy Kray, S Russian Federation 56°16′N 95°59′E
108 H9 **Ilanz** Graubünden, S Switzerland 46°46′N 09°10′E
77 S16 **Ilaro** Ogun, SW Nigeria 06°52′N 03°01′E
57 I17 **Ilave** Puno, S Peru 16°07′S 69°40′W
110 K8 **Iława** Ger. Deutsch-Eylau. Warmińsko-Mazurskie, NE Poland 53°36′N 19°35′E
121 P16 **Il-Bajja ta' Marsaxlokk** var. Marsaxlokk Bay. bay SE Malta
123 P10 **Ilbenge** Respublika Sakha (Yakutiya), NE Russian Federation 62°52′N 124°13′E
Ile see Ile/Ili He
Ile see Ili He
11 S13 **Île-à-la-Crosse** Saskatchewan, C Canada 55°29′N 108°00′W
79 J21 **Ilebo** prev. Port-Francqui. Kasai-Occidental, W Dem. Rep. Congo 04°19′S 20°32′E
103 N5 **Île-de-France** ◆ region N France
Ilek see Yelek
Ilerda see Lleida
77 T16 **Ilesha** Osun, SW Nigeria 07°35′N 04°49′E
187 Q16 **Îles Loyauté, Province des** ◆ province E New Caledonia
11 X12 **Ilford** Manitoba, C Canada 56°02′N 95°48′W
116 K14 **Ilfov** ◆ county S Romania
97 I23 **Ilfracombe** SW England, United Kingdom 51°12′N 04°10′W
136 I11 **Ilgaz Dağları** ▲ N Turkey
136 G15 **Ilgın** Konya, W Turkey 38°16′N 31°57′E
60 I7 **Ilha Solteira** São Paulo, S Brazil 20°28′S 51°19′W
104 G7 **Ílhavo** Aveiro, N Portugal 40°36′N 08°40′W
59 O18 **Ilhéus** Bahia, E Brazil 14°50′S 39°06′W
129 R7 **Ili** var. Ile, Chin. Ili He, Rus. Reka Ili. ⇝ China/Kazakhstan see also Ili He
116 G11 **Ilia** Hung. Marosillye. Hunedoara, SW Romania 45°57′N 22°40′E
39 P13 **Iliamna** Alaska, USA 59°42′N 154°49′W
39 P13 **Iliamna Lake** ◎ Alaska, USA
137 N13 **İliç** Erzincan, C Turkey 39°27′N 38°34′E
Il'ichevsk see Şärur, Azerbaijan
Il'ichevsk see Illichivs'k, Ukraine
Ilici see Elche
37 V2 **Iliff** Colorado, C USA 40°46′N 103°04′W
171 Q7 **Iligan** off. Iligan City. Mindanao, S Philippines 08°12′N 124°16′E
171 Q7 **Iligan Bay** bay S Philippines
Iligan City see Iligan
158 I5 **Ili He** var. Ili, Kaz. Ile, Rus. Reka Ili. ⇝ China/Kazakhstan see also Ile
Ili He see Ili
56 C6 **Iliniza** ▲ N Ecuador 0°37′S 78°41′W
Ilinski see Il'inskiy
125 U14 **Il'inskiy** var. Ilinski. Permskiy Kray, NW Russian Federation 58°33′N 55°31′E
125 U14 **Il'inskiy** Ostrov Sakhalin, Sakhalinskaya Oblast', SE Russian Federation 47°59′N 142°14′E
18 I10 **Ilion** New York, NE USA 43°01′N 75°02′W
38 E9 **'Ilio Point** var. Ilio Point. headland Moloka'i, Hawai'i, USA 21°13′N 157°15′W
Ilio Point see 'Ilio Point
109 T13 **Ilirska Bistrica** prev. Bistrica, Ger. Feistritz, Illyrisch-Feistritz, It. Villa del Nevoso. SW Slovenia 45°34′N 14°12′E
137 Q16 **Ilısu Barajı** ⊠ SE Turkey
155 G17 **Ilkal** Karnātaka, C India 15°59′N 76°08′E
97 M19 **Ilkeston** C England, United Kingdom 52°59′N 01°18′W
121 O16 **Il-Kullana** headland SW Malta 35°49′N 14°26′E
108 J8 **Ill** ⇝ W Austria
103 U6 **Ill** ⇝ NE France
62 G10 **Illapel** Coquimbo, C Chile 31°40′S 71°13′W
Illaue Fartak Trench see Alula-Fartak Trench
182 C2 **Illbillee, Mount** ▲ South Australia 27°01′S 132°13′E
102 I6 **Ille-et-Vilaine** ◆ department NW France
77 T11 **Illéla** Tahoua, SW Niger 14°25′N 05°10′E
101 J24 **Iller** ⇝ S Germany
101 J23 **Illertissen** Bayern, S Germany 48°13′N 10°08′E
105 X9 **Illes Baleares** ◆ autonomous community E Spain
105 N8 **Illescas** Castilla-La Mancha, C Spain 40°08′N 03°51′W
Ille-sur-la-Têt see Ille-sur-Têt
103 O17 **Ille-sur-Têt** var. Ille-sur-la-Têt. Pyrénées-Orientales, S France 42°40′N 02°37′E
Illiberis see Elne
117 P11 **Illichivs'k** Rus. Il'ichevsk. Odes'ka Oblast', SW Ukraine 46°18′N 30°36′E
Illicis see Elche
102 M6 **Illiers-Combray** Eure-et-Loir, C France 48°18′N 01°15′E
30 K12 **Illinois** off. State of Illinois, also known as Prairie State, Sucker State. ◆ state C USA
30 J13 **Illinois River** ⇝ Illinois, N USA
117 N6 **Illintsi** Vinnyts'ka Oblast', C Ukraine 49°07′N 29°13′E
Illiturgis see Andújar
74 M10 **Illizi** SE Algeria 26°30′N 08°28′E
27 Y7 **Illmo** Missouri, C USA 37°13′N 89°30′W
Illurco see Lorca
Illuro see Mataró
Illyrisch-Feistritz see Ilirska Bistrica
101 K16 **Ilm** ⇝ C Germany
101 K17 **Ilmenau** Thüringen, C Germany 50°40′N 10°55′E
124 H14 **Il'men', Ozero** ◎ NW Russian Federation
57 H18 **Ilo** Moquegua, SW Peru 17°42′S 71°20′W
171 O6 **Iloilo** off. Iloilo City. Panay Island, C Philippines 10°42′N 122°34′E
Iloilo City see Iloilo
112 K10 **Ilok** Hung. Újlak. Vojvodina, NW Serbia 45°12′N 19°22′E
93 O16 **Ilomantsi** Itä-Suomi, SE Finland 62°40′N 30°55′E
42 F8 **Ilopango, Lago de** volcanic lake C El Salvador
77 T15 **Ilorin** Kwara, W Nigeria 08°32′N 04°35′E
117 X8 **Ilovays'k** Rus. Ilovaysk. Donets'ka Oblast', SE Ukraine 47°55′N 38°14′E
Ilovaysk see Ilovays'k
127 O10 **Ilovlya** Volgogradskaya Oblast', SW Russian Federation 49°45′N 44°19′E
127 O10 **Ilovlya** ⇝ SW Russian Federation
121 N15 **Il-Ponta ta' San Dimitri** var. Ras San Dimitri, San Dimitri Point. headland Gozo, NW Malta 36°04′N 14°12′E
126 K14 **Il'skiy** Krasnodarskiy Kray, SW Russian Federation 44°52′N 38°26′E
182 B2 **Iltur** South Australia 27°33′S 130°31′E
171 Y13 **Ilugwa** Papua, E Indonesia 03°42′S 139°09′E
Iluh see Batman
118 I11 **Ilūkste** SE Latvia 55°58′N 26°21′E
171 Y13 **Ilur** Pulau Gorong, E Indonesia 04°00′S 131°25′E
32 F10 **Ilwaco** Washington, NW USA 46°19′N 124°03′W
Il'yaly see Gurbansoltan Eje
Ilyasbaba Burnu see Tekke Burnu
125 U9 **Ilych** ⇝ NW Russian Federation
101 O21 **Ilz** ⇝ SE Germany
111 M14 **Iłża** Radom, SE Poland 51°09′N 21°15′E
164 G13 **Imabari** var. Imaharu. Ehime, Shikoku, SW Japan 34°04′N 132°59′E
Imaharu see Imabari
165 O12 **Imaichi** var. Imaiti. Tochigi, Honshū, S Japan 36°43′N 139°41′E
Imaiti see Imaichi
164 K12 **Imajō** Fukui, Honshū, SW Japan 35°45′N 136°10′E
139 R9 **Imām Ibn Hāshim** Karbalā', C Iraq 32°46′N 43°21′E
149 Q2 **Imām Şāḩib** var. Emam Saheb, Hazarat Imam; prev. Emām Şāḩeb. Kunduz, NE Afghanistan 37°11′N 68°55′E
139 T11 **Imān 'Abd Allāh** Al Qādisīyah, S Iraq 31°36′N 44°34′E
164 F15 **Imano-yama** ▲ Shikoku, SW Japan 32°51′N 132°48′E
164 C13 **Imari** Saga, Kyūshū, SW Japan 33°18′N 129°51′E
Imarssuak Mid-Ocean Seachannel see Imarssuak Seachannel
64 J6 **Imarssuak Seachannel** var. Imarssuak Mid-Ocean Seachannel. channel N Atlantic Ocean
93 N18 **Imatra** Etelä-Suomi, SE Finland 61°14′N 28°50′E
164 K13 **Imazu** Shiga, Honshū, SW Japan 35°25′N 136°00′E
56 C6 **Imbabura** ◆ province N Ecuador
55 R9 **Imbaimadai** W Guyana 05°44′N 60°23′W
61 K14 **Imbituba** Santa Catarina, S Brazil 28°15′S 48°44′W
27 W9 **Imboden** Arkansas, C USA 36°12′N 91°10′W
Imbros see Gökçeada
Imeni 26 Bakinskikh Komissarov see Uzboý
125 N13 **Imeni Babushkina** Vologodskaya Oblast', NW Russian Federation 59°40′N 43°04′E
126 J7 **Imeni Karla Libknekhta** Kurskaya Oblast', W Russian Federation 51°36′N 35°28′E
Imeni Mollanepesa see Mollanepes Adyndaky
Imeni S. A. Niyazova see S.A.Nyýazow Adyndaky
Imeni Sverdlova Rudnik see Sverdlovs'k
188 E9 **Imeong** Babeldaob, N Palau
81 L14 **Īmī** Sumalē, E Ethiopia 06°27′N 42°10′E
115 M21 **Imia** Turk. Kardak. island Dodekánisa, Greece, Aegean Sea
Imishli see İmişli
137 X12 **İmişli** Rus. Imishli. C Azerbaijan 39°54′N 48°04′E
163 X14 **Imjin-gang** ⇝ North Korea/South Korea
35 S3 **Imlay** Nevada, W USA 40°39′N 118°10′W
31 S9 **Imlay City** Michigan, N USA 43°01′N 83°04′W
23 X15 **Immokalee** Florida, SE USA 26°24′N 81°25′W
77 U17 **Imo** ◆ state SE Nigeria
106 G10 **Imola** Emilia-Romagna, N Italy 44°22′N 11°43′E
186 A5 **Imonda** Sandaun, NW Papua New Guinea 03°21′S 141°10′E
Imoschi see Imotski
113 G14 **Imotski** It. Imoschi. Split-Dalmacija, SE Croatia 43°28′N 17°13′E
59 L14 **Imperatriz** Maranhão, NE Brazil 05°32′S 47°28′W
106 B10 **Imperia** Liguria, NW Italy 43°53′N 08°03′E
57 E15 **Imperial** Lima, W Peru 13°04′S 76°21′W
35 X17 **Imperial** California, W USA 32°51′N 115°34′W
28 L16 **Imperial** Nebraska, C USA 40°30′N 101°37′W
24 M9 **Imperial** Texas, SW USA 31°15′N 102°40′W
35 Y17 **Imperial Dam** dam California, W USA
79 I17 **Impfondo** Likouala, NE Congo 01°37′N 18°04′E
153 X14 **Imphāl** state capital Manipur, NE India 24°47′N 93°55′E
103 P9 **Imphy** Nièvre, C France 46°55′N 03°16′E
106 G11 **Impruneta** Toscana, C Italy 43°42′N 11°16′E
115 K15 **İmroz** var. Gökçeada. Çanakkale, NW Turkey 40°06′N 25°50′E
Imroz Adası see Gökçeada
108 L7 **Imst** Tirol, W Austria 47°14′N 10°45′E
40 F3 **Imuris** Sonora, NW Mexico 30°48′N 110°52′W
164 M13 **Ina** Nagano, Honshū, S Japan 35°52′N 137°58′E
65 M18 **Inaccessible Island** island W Tristan da Cunha
115 F20 **Ínachos** ⇝ S Greece
188 H6 **I Naftan, Puntan** headland Saipan, S Northern Mariana Islands
Inagua Islands see Little Inagua
Inagua Islands see Great Inagua
185 H15 **Inangahua** West Coast, South Island, New Zealand 41°51′S 171°58′E
57 I14 **Iñapari** Madre de Dios, E Peru 11°00′S 69°34′W
188 B17 **Inarajan** SE Guam 13°16′N 144°45′E
92 L10 **Inari** Lapp. Anár, Aanaar. Lappi, N Finland 68°54′N 27°06′E
92 L10 **Inarijärvi** Lapp. Aanaarjävri, Swe. Enareträsk. ◎ N Finland
92 L9 **Inarijoki** Lapp. Anárjohka. ⇝ Finland/Norway
Ināu see Ineu
165 P11 **Inawashiro-ko** var. Inawasiro Ko. ◎ Honshū, C Japan
Inawasiro Ko see Inawashiro-ko
105 X9 **Inca** Mallorca, Spain, W Mediterranean Sea 39°43′N 02°54′E
62 H7 **Inca de Oro** Atacama, N Chile 26°45′S 69°54′W
115 J15 **İnce Burnu** cape NW Turkey
136 K9 **İnce Burnu** headland N Turkey 42°06′N 34°57′E
136 I17 **İncekum Burnu** headland S Turkey 36°13′N 33°57′E
163 X15 **Incheon** Jap. Jinsen; prev. Chemulpo, Inch'ŏn. NW South Korea 37°27′N 126°41′E
76 G7 **Inchiri** ◆ region NW Mauritania
161 X15 **Incheon** ✈ (Seoul) NW South Korea 37°37′N 126°42′E
Inch'ŏn see Incheon
83 M17 **Inchope** Manica, C Mozambique 19°09′S 33°54′E
Incoronata see Kornat
103 Y15 **Incudine, Monte** ▲ Corse, France, C Mediterranean Sea 41°52′N 09°13′E
60 M10 **Indaiatuba** São Paulo, S Brazil 23°03′S 47°14′W
93 H17 **Indal** Västernorrland, C Sweden 62°36′N 17°06′E
93 H17 **Indalsälven** ⇝ C Sweden
40 K8 **Inde** Durango, C Mexico 25°55′N 105°10′W
Indefatigable Island see Santa Cruz, Isla
35 S10 **Independence** California, W USA 36°48′N 118°14′W
29 X13 **Independence** Iowa, C USA 42°28′N 91°42′W
27 P7 **Independence** Kansas, C USA 37°13′N 95°43′W
20 M4 **Independence** Kentucky, S USA 38°56′N 84°32′W
27 R4 **Independence** Missouri, C USA 39°04′N 94°27′W
21 R8 **Independence** Virginia, NE USA 36°38′N 81°11′W
30 J7 **Independence** Wisconsin, N USA 44°21′N 91°25′W
197 R12 **Independence Fjord** fjord N Greenland
Independence Island see Malden Island
35 W2 **Independence Mountains** ▲ Nevada, W USA
57 K18 **Independencia** Cochabamba, C Bolivia 17°08′S 66°52′W
57 E16 **Independencia, Bahía de la** bay W Peru
Independencia, Monte see Adam, Mount
116 M12 **Independenţa** Galaţi, SE Romania 45°29′N 27°45′E
Inderagiri see Indragiri, Sungai
144 F11 **Inderbor** prev. Inderborskiy. Atyrau, W Kazakhstan 48°35′N 51°45′E
Inderborskiy see Inderbor
151 I14 **India** off. Republic of India, var. Indian Union, Union of India, Hind. Bhārat. ◆ republic S Asia
India see Indija
18 D14 **Indiana** Pennsylvania, NE USA 40°37′N 79°09′W
31 N13 **Indiana** off. State of Indiana, also known as Hoosier State. ◆ state N USA
31 O14 **Indianapolis** state capital Indiana, N USA 39°46′N 86°09′W
11 O10 **Indian Cabins** Alberta, W Canada 59°51′N 117°06′W
42 G1 **Indian Church** Orange Walk, N Belize 17°47′N 88°39′W
Indian Desert see Thar Desert
11 U16 **Indian Head** Saskatchewan, S Canada 50°32′N 103°41′W
31 O4 **Indian Lake** ◎ Michigan, N USA
18 K9 **Indian Lake** ◎ New York, NE USA
31 R13 **Indian Lake** ⊠ Ohio, N USA
172-173 **Indian Ocean** ocean
29 V15 **Indianola** Iowa, C USA 41°21′N 93°33′W
22 K4 **Indianola** Mississippi, S USA 33°27′N 90°39′W
36 J6 **Indian Peak** ▲ Utah, W USA 38°18′N 113°52′W
23 Y13 **Indian River** lagoon Florida, SE USA
35 W10 **Indian Springs** Nevada, W USA 36°33′N 115°40′W
23 Y14 **Indiantown** Florida, SE USA 27°01′N 80°29′W
Indian Union see India
59 K19 **Indiara** Goiás, S Brazil 17°12′S 50°09′W
India, Republic of see India
India, Union of see India
125 Q4 **Indiga** Nenetskiy Avtonomnyy Okrug, NW Russian Federation 67°40′N 49°01′E
123 R9 **Indigirka** ⇝ NE Russian Federation
112 L10 **Indija** Hung. India; prev. Indjija. Vojvodina, N Serbia 45°03′N 20°04′E
35 V16 **Indio** California, W USA 33°42′N 116°13′W
42 M12 **Indio, Río** ⇝ SE Nicaragua
152 I10 **Indira Gandhi** ✈ (Delhi) Delhi, N India
151 Q23 **Indira Point** headland Andaman and Nicobar Island, India, NE Indian Ocean 6°54′N 93°54′E
Indjija see Indija
129 Q13 **Indo-Australian Plate** tectonic feature
173 N11 **Indomed Fracture Zone** tectonic feature SW Indian Ocean
170 L12 **Indonesia** off. Republic of Indonesia, Ind. Republik Indonesia; prev. Dutch East Indies, Netherlands East Indies, United States of Indonesia. ◆ republic SE Asia
Indonesian Borneo see Kalimantan
Indonesia, Republic of see Indonesia
Indonesia, Republik see Indonesia
Indonesia, United States of see Indonesia
154 G10 **Indore** Madhya Pradesh, C India 22°42′N 75°51′E
168 L11 **Indragiri, Sungai** var. Batang Kuantan, Inderagiri. ⇝ Sumatera, W Indonesia
Indramajoe/Indramaju see Indramayu
169 P15 **Indramayu** prev. Indramajoe, Indramaju. Jawa, C Indonesia 06°22′S 108°20′E
155 K14 **Indrāvati** ⇝ S India
103 N9 **Indre** ◆ department C France
102 M8 **Indre** ⇝ C France
94 D13 **Indre Ålvik** Hordaland, S Norway 60°26′N 06°27′E
102 L8 **Indre-et-Loire** ◆ department C France
Indreville see Châteauroux
152 G3 **Indus** Chin. Yindu He; prev. Yin-tu Ho. ⇝ S Asia
Indus Cone see Indus Fan
173 P3 **Indus Fan** var. Indus Cone. undersea feature N Arabian Sea 16°00′N 66°30′E
149 P17 **Indus, Mouths of the** delta S Pakistan
83 I24 **Indwe** Eastern Cape, SE South Africa 31°28′S 27°20′E
136 I10 **İnebolu** Kastamonu, N Turkey 41°57′N 33°45′E
77 P8 **I-n-Échaï** oasis C Mali
114 M13 **İnecik** Tekirdağ, NW Turkey 40°55′N 27°16′E
136 E12 **İnegöl** Bursa, NW Turkey 40°06′N 29°31′E
Inessa see Biancavilla
116 F10 **Ineu** Hung. Borosjenő; prev. Inău. Arad, W Romania 46°26′N 21°51′E
Ineul/Ineu, Vîrful see Ineu, Vârful
116 J9 **Ineu, Vârful** var. Ineul; prev. Vîrful Ineu. ▲ N Romania 47°31′N 24°52′E
21 P6 **Inez** Kentucky, S USA 37°53′N 82°33′W
74 E8 **Inezgane** ✈ (Agadir) W Morocco 30°35′N 09°27′W
41 T17 **Inferior, Laguna** lagoon S Mexico
40 M15 **Infiernillo, Presa del** ⊠ S Mexico
Infiesto see L'Infiestu
93 L20 **Ingå** Fin. Inkoo. Etelä-Suomi, S Finland 60°01′N 24°05′E
77 U10 **Ingal** var. I-n-Gall. Agadez, C Niger 16°52′N 06°57′E
I-n-Gall see Ingal
99 C18 **Ingelmunster** West-Vlaanderen, W Belgium 50°12′N 03°15′E
79 I18 **Ingende** Equateur, W Dem. Rep. Congo 0°15′S 18°58′E
62 L5 **Ingeniero Guillermo Nueva Juárez** Formosa, N Argentina 23°55′S 61°50′W
63 H16 **Ingeniero Jacobacci** Río Negro, C Argentina 41°18′S 69°35′W
14 F16 **Ingersoll** Ontario, S Canada 43°03′N 80°53′W
Ingettolgoy see Selenge
181 W5 **Ingham** Queensland, NE Australia 18°35′S 146°12′E
146 M11 **Ingichka** Samarqand Viloyati, C Uzbekistan 39°46′N 65°56′E
97 L16 **Ingleborough** ▲ N England, United Kingdom 54°07′N 02°22′W
25 T14 **Ingleside** Texas, SW USA 27°52′N 97°12′W
184 K10 **Inglewood** Taranaki, North Island, New Zealand 39°07′S 174°13′E
35 S15 **Inglewood** California, W USA 33°57′N 118°21′W
101 L21 **Ingolstadt** Bayern, S Germany 48°46′N 11°26′E
33 V9 **Ingomar** Montana, NW USA 46°34′N 107°21′W
13 R14 **Ingonish Beach** Cape Breton Island, Nova Scotia, SE Canada 46°42′N 60°22′W
153 S14 **Ingrāj Bāzār** prev. English Bazar. West Bengal, NE India 25°00′N 88°10′E
25 Q11 **Ingram** Texas, SW USA 30°04′N 99°14′W
195 X7 **Ingrid Christensen Coast** physical region Antarctica
74 K14 **I-n-Guezzam** S Algeria 19°35′N 05°49′E
Ingulets see Inhulets'
Inguri see Enguri
Ingushetia/Ingushetiya, Respublika see Ingushetiya, Respublika
127 O15 **Ingushetiya, Respublika** var. Respublika Ingushetiya, Eng. Ingushetia. ◆ autonomous republic SW Russian Federation
83 N20 **Inhambane** Inhambane, SE Mozambique 23°52′S 35°31′E
83 M20 **Inhambane** off. Província de Inhambane. ◆ province S Mozambique
Inhambane, Província de see Inhambane
83 N17 **Inhaminga** Sofala, C Mozambique 18°24′S 35°00′E
83 N20 **Inharrime** Inhambane, SE Mozambique 24°29′S 35°01′E
83 M18 **Inhassoro** Inhambane, E Mozambique 21°32′S 35°13′E
117 S9 **Inhulets'** Rus. Ingulets. Dnipropetrovs'ka Oblast', E Ukraine 47°43′N 33°16′E
117 R10 **Inhulets'** Rus. Ingulets. ⇝ S Ukraine
105 Q10 **Iniesta** Castilla-La Mancha, C Spain 39°27′N 01°45′W
I-ning see Yining
54 K11 **Inírida, Río** ⇝ E Colombia
Inis see Ennis
Inis Ceithleann see Enniskillen
Inis Córthaidh see Enniscorthy
Inis Díomáin see Ennistimon
97 A17 **Inishbofin** Ir. Inis Bó Finne. island W Ireland
97 B18 **Inisheer** var. Inishere, Ir. Inis Oírr. island W Ireland
Inishere see Inisheer
97 B18 **Inishmaan** Ir. Inis Meáin. island W Ireland
97 A18 **Inishmore** Ir. Árainn. island W Ireland
96 E13 **Inishtrahull** Ir. Inis Trá Tholl. island NW Ireland
97 A17 **Inishturk** Ir. Inis Toirc. island W Ireland
Inkoo see Ingå
185 J16 **Inland Kaikoura Range** ▲ South Island, New Zealand
Inland Sea see Seto-naikai
21 P11 **Inman** South Carolina, SE USA 35°03′N 82°05′W
108 L7 **Inn** ⇝ C Europe
197 O11 **Innaanganeq** var. Kap York. headland NW Greenland 75°54′N 66°27′W
182 K2 **Innamincka** South Australia 27°47′S 140°45′E
92 G12 **Inndyr** Nordland, C Norway 67°01′N 14°00′E
42 G3 **Inner Channel** inlet SE Belize
96 F11 **Inner Hebrides** island group W Scotland, United Kingdom
172 H15 **Inner Islands** var. Central Group. island group NE Seychelles
Inner Mongolia/Inner Mongolian Autonomous Region see Nei Mongol Zizhiqu
108 F7 **Inner-Rhoden** ◆ canton NE Switzerland
96 G8 **Inner Sound** strait NW Scotland, United Kingdom
100 J13 **Innerste** ⇝ C Germany
181 W5 **Innisfail** Queensland, NE Australia 17°29′S 146°03′E
11 Q15 **Innisfail** Alberta, SW Canada 52°01′N 113°59′W
Inniskilling see Enniskillen
39 O11 **Innoko River** ⇝ Alaska, USA
Innsbruch see Innsbruck
108 M7 **Innsbruck** var. Innsbruch. Tirol, W Austria 47°17′N 11°25′E
79 I19 **Inongo** Bandundu, W Dem. Rep. Congo 01°55′S 18°20′E
Inoucdjouac see Inukjuak
Inowrazlaw see Inowrocław
110 I10 **Inowrocław** Ger. Hohensalza; prev. Inowrazlaw. Kujawski-pomorskie, C Poland 52°47′N 18°15′E
57 K18 **Inquisivi** La Paz, W Bolivia 16°55′S 67°10′W
Inrin see Yuanlin
77 O8 **I-n-Sâkâne, 'Erg** desert N Mali
77 O8 **I-n-Sâkâne, 'Erg** desert N Mali
74 J10 **I-n-Salah** var. In Salah. C Algeria 27°11′N 02°31′E
127 O5 **Insar** Respublika Mordoviya, W Russian Federation 53°52′N 44°26′E
189 X15 **Insiaf** Kosrae, E Micronesia
94 L13 **Insjön** Dalarna, C Sweden 60°40′N 15°05′E
Insterburg see Chernyakhovsk
Insula see Lille
116 L13 **Însurăţei** Brăila, SE Romania 44°55′N 27°40′E
125 V6 **Inta** Respublika Komi, NW Russian Federation 66°00′N 60°10′E
77 R9 **I-n-Tebezas** Kidal, E Mali 17°58′N 01°51′E
Interamna see Teramo
Interamna Nahars see Terni
28 L11 **Interior** South Dakota, N USA 43°42′N 101°57′W
108 E9 **Interlaken** Bern, SW Switzerland 46°41′N 07°51′E
29 V2 **International Falls** Minnesota, N USA 48°38′N 93°26′W
167 O7 **Inthanon, Doi** ▲ NW Thailand 18°33′N 98°29′E
42 G7 **Intibucá** ◆ department SW Honduras
42 G8 **Intipucá** La Unión, SE El Salvador 13°10′N 88°03′W
61 B15 **Intiyaco** Santa Fe, C Argentina 28°43′S 60°04′W
116 K12 **Întorsura Buzăului** Ger. Bozau, Hung. Bodzafordulő. Covasna, E Romania 45°40′N 26°02′E
22 H9 **Intracoastal Waterway** inland waterway system Louisiana, S USA
25 V13 **Intracoastal Waterway** inland waterway system Texas, SW USA
108 G11 **Intragna** Ticino, S Switzerland 46°12′N 08°42′E
165 P14 **Inubō-zaki** headland Honshū, S Japan 35°42′N 140°51′E
164 E14 **Inukai** Ōita, Kyūshū, SW Japan 33°05′N 131°37′E
12 I5 **Inukjuak** var. Inoucdjouac; prev. Port Harrison. Québec, NE Canada 58°28′N 77°58′W
63 I24 **Inútil, Bahía** bay S Chile
Inuuvik see Inuvik
11 R8 **Inuvik** var. Inuuvik. Northwest Territories, NW Canada 68°25′N 133°35′W
164 L13 **Inuyama** Aichi, Honshū, SW Japan 35°23′N 136°56′E
56 G13 **Inuya, Río** ⇝ E Peru
125 U13 **In'va** ⇝ NW Russian Federation
96 H11 **Inveraray** W Scotland, United Kingdom 56°13′N 05°05′W
185 C24 **Invercargill** Southland, South Island, New Zealand 46°25′S 168°22′E
183 T5 **Inverell** New South Wales, SE Australia 29°46′S 151°10′E
96 I8 **Invergordon** N Scotland, United Kingdom 57°42′N 04°02′W
11 P16 **Invermere** British Columbia, SW Canada 50°30′N 116°00′W
13 R14 **Inverness** Cape Breton Island, Nova Scotia, SE Canada 46°14′N 61°19′W
96 I8 **Inverness** N Scotland, United Kingdom 57°27′N 04°15′W
23 V11 **Inverness** Florida, SE USA 28°50′N 82°19′W
96 I9 **Inverness** cultural region NW Scotland, United Kingdom
96 K9 **Inverurie** NE Scotland, United Kingdom 57°14′N 02°14′W
182 F8 **Investigator Group** island group South Australia
173 T7 **Investigator Ridge** undersea feature E Indian Ocean 11°30′S 98°10′E
182 H10 **Investigator Strait** strait South Australia
29 R11 **Inwood** Iowa, C USA 43°16′N 96°25′W
123 S10 **Inya** ⇝ E Russian Federation
Inyanga see Nyanga
83 M16 **Inyangani** ▲ NE Zimbabwe 18°22′S 32°57′E
83 J17 **Inyathi** Matabeleland North, SW Zimbabwe 19°39′S 28°54′E
35 T12 **Inyokern** California, W USA 35°37′N 117°48′W
35 T10 **Inyo Mountains** ▲ California, W USA
127 P6 **Inza** Ul'yanovskaya Oblast', W Russian Federation 53°51′N 46°21′E
127 W5 **Inzer** Respublika Bashkortostan, W Russian Federation 54°11′N 57°37′E
127 N7 **Inzhavino** Tambovskaya Oblast', W Russian Federation 52°18′N 42°28′E
115 C16 **Ioánnina** var. Janina, Yannina. Ípeiros, W Greece 39°39′N 20°52′E
164 B17 **Iō-jima** var. Iwojima. island Nansei-shotō, SW Japan
124 L4 **Iokan'ga** ⇝ NW Russian Federation
27 Q6 **Iola** Kansas, C USA 37°55′N 95°24′W
Iolcus see Iolkós
115 G16 **Iolkós** anc. Iolcus. site of ancient city Thessalía, C Greece
Iolotan' see Ýolöten
83 A16 **Iona** Namibe, SW Angola 16°54′S 12°39′E
96 F11 **Iona** island W Scotland, United Kingdom
116 M15 **Ion Corvin** Constanţa, SE Romania 44°07′N 27°50′E
35 P7 **Ione** California, W USA 38°21′N 120°55′W
116 I13 **Ioneşti** Vâlcea, SW Romania 44°52′N 24°12′E
31 Q9 **Ionia** Michigan, N USA 42°59′N 85°04′W
Ionia Basin see Ionian Basin
121 O10 **Ionian Basin** var. Ionia Basin. undersea feature Ionian Sea, C Mediterranean Sea 36°00′N 20°00′E
115 B17 **Iónia Nisiá** var. Iónioi Nísoi, Eng. Ionian Islands. island group W Greece
Ionian Islands see Iónia Nisiá/Iónioi Nísoi
121 O10 **Ionian Sea** Gk. Iónio Pélagos, It. Mar Ionio. sea C Mediterranean Sea
115 B17 **Iónioi Nísoi** Eng. Ionian Islands. ◆ region W Greece
Iónioi Nísoi see Iónia Nisiá
Ionio, Mar/Iónio Pélagos see Ionian Sea
Iordan see Yordon
137 U10 **Iori** var. Qabırrı. ⇝ Azerbaijan/Georgia
Iorrais, Ceann see Erris Head
115 J22 **Íos** var. Nio. island Kykládes, Greece, Aegean Sea
Íos see Chóra
165 U15 **Io-Tori-shima** prev. Tori-shima. island Izu-shotō, SE Japan
115 I20 **Ioulís** prev. Kéa. Tziá, Kykládes, Greece, Aegean Sea 37°40′N 24°19′E
22 G9 **Iowa** Louisiana, S USA 30°12′N 93°00′W
29 V13 **Iowa** off. State of Iowa, also known as Hawkeye State. ◆ state C USA
29 Y14 **Iowa City** Iowa, C USA 41°40′N 91°32′W
29 V13 **Iowa Falls** Iowa, C USA 42°31′N 93°15′W
25 R4 **Iowa Park** Texas, SW USA 33°57′N 98°40′W
29 Y14 **Iowa River** ⇝ Iowa, C USA
119 M19 **Ipa** Rus. Ipa. ⇝ SE Belarus
Ipa see Ipa
59 N20 **Ipatinga** Minas Gerais, SE Brazil 19°32′S 42°30′W
127 N13 **Ipatovo** Stavropol'skiy Kray, SW Russian Federation 45°40′N 42°51′E
115 C16 **Ípeiros** Eng. Epirus. ◆ region W Greece
111 J21 **Ipel'** var. Ipoly, Ger. Eipel. ⇝ Hungary/Slovakia
54 C13 **Ipiales** Nariño, SW Colombia 0°52′N 77°38′W
189 V14 **Ipis** atoll Chuuk Islands, C Micronesia
59 A14 **Ipixuna** Amazonas, W Brazil 06°57′S 71°42′W
168 J8 **Ipoh** Perak, Peninsular Malaysia 04°36′N 101°02′E
Ipoly see Ipel'
187 S15 **Ipota** Erromango, S Vanuatu 18°54′S 169°19′E
79 K14 **Ippy** Ouaka, C Central African Republic 06°17′N 21°13′E
114 L13 **İpsala** Edirne, NW Turkey 40°56′N 26°23′E
Ipsario see Ypsário
183 V3 **Ipswich** Queensland, E Australia 27°38′S 152°40′E
97 Q20 **Ipswich** hist. Gipeswic. E England, United Kingdom 52°05′N 01°08′E
29 O8 **Ipswich** South Dakota, N USA 45°24′N 99°00′W
Iput' see Iputs'
119 P18 **Iputs'** Rus. Iput'. ⇝ Belarus/Russian Federation
9 R7 **Iqaluit** prev. Frobisher Bay. province capital Baffin Island, Nunavut, NE Canada 63°44′N 68°28′W
Iqlid see Eqlid
62 G3 **Iquique** Tarapacá, N Chile 20°15′S 70°08′W
56 G8 **Iquitos** Loreto, N Peru 03°51′S 73°13′W
25 N9 **Iraan** Texas, SW USA 30°52′N 101°52′W
79 K14 **Ira Banda** Haute-Kotto, E Central African Republic 05°57′N 22°05′E
165 P16 **Irabu-jima** island Miyako-shotō, SW Japan
55 Y9 **Iracoubo** N French Guiana 05°28′N 53°15′W
60 H13 **Iraí** Rio Grande do Sul, S Brazil 27°15′S 53°17′W
114 G12 **Irákleia** Kentrikí Makedonía, N Greece 41°09′N 23°16′E
115 J21 **Irákleia** island Kykládes, Greece, Aegean Sea
115 J25 **Irákleio** var. Herakleion, Eng. Candia; prev. Iráklion. Kríti, Greece, E Mediterranean Sea 35°20′N 25°08′E
115 F15 **Irákleio** anc. Heracleum. castle Kentrikí Makedonía, N Greece
115 J25 **Irákleio** ✈ Kríti, Greece, E Mediterranean Sea 35°20′N 25°10′E
Iráklion see Irákleio
143 O7 **Iran** off. Islamic Republic of Iran; prev. Persia. ◆ republic SW Asia
58 F13 **Iranduba** Amazonas, NW Brazil 03°19′S 60°09′W
85 P13 **Iranian Plate** tectonic feature
143 Q9 **Iranian Plateau** var. Plateau of Iran. plateau N Iran
Iran, Islamic Republic of see Iran
Iran Mountains see Iran, Pegunungan
169 U9 **Iran, Pegunungan** var. Iran Mountains. ▲ Indonesia/Malaysia
Iran, Plateau of see Iranian Plateau
143 W13 **Īrānshahr** Sīstān va Balūchestān, SE Iran 27°14′N 60°40′E
55 P5 **Irapa** Sucre, NE Venezuela 10°37′N 62°35′W
41 N13 **Irapuato** Guanajuato, C Mexico 20°40′N 101°23′W
139 R7 **Iraq** off. Republic of Iraq, Ar. 'Irāq. ◆ republic SW Asia
'Irāq see Iraq
Iraq, Republic of see Iraq
60 J12 **Irati** Paraná, S Brazil 25°25′S 50°38′W
105 R3 **Irati** ⇝ N Spain
125 T8 **Irayel'** Respublika Komi, NW Russian Federation 64°28′N 55°20′E
43 N13 **Irazú, Volcán** ⛰ C Costa Rica 09°57′N 83°52′W
Irbenskiy Zaliv/Irbes Šaurums see Irbe Strait
118 D7 **Irbe Strait** Est. Kura Kurk, Latv. Irbes Šaurums, Irbenskiy Zaliv; prev. Est. Irbe Väin. strait Estonia/Latvia
Irbe Väin see Irbe Strait
138 G9 **Irbid** Irbid, N Jordan 32°33′N 35°51′E
138 G9 **Irbid** off. Muḩāfaẓat Irbid. ◆ governorate N Jordan
Irbid, Muḩāfaẓat see Irbid
Irbil see Arbīl
109 S6 **Irdning** Steiermark, SE Austria 47°29′N 14°04′E
79 I18 **Irebu** Equateur, W Dem. Rep. Congo 0°32′S 17°44′E
97 D17 **Ireland** off. Republic of Ireland, Ir. Éire. ◆ republic NW Europe
84 C9 **Ireland** Lat. Hibernia. island Ireland/United Kingdom
64 A12 **Ireland Island North** island W Bermuda
64 A12 **Ireland Island South** island W Bermuda

◆ Country ● Country Capital ◇ Dependent Territory ○ Dependent Territory Capital ◆ Administrative Regions ✈ International Airport ▲ Mountain ▲ Mountain Range ⛰ Volcano ⇝ River ◎ Lake ⊠ Reservoir

Ireland, Republic of *see* Ireland

125 *V15* **Iren'** ≈ NW Russian Federation

185 *A22* **Irene, Mount** ▲ South Island, New Zealand *45°04′S 167°24′E*

Irgalem *see* Yirga 'Alem

Irgiz *see* Yrghyz

Irian *see* New Guinea

Irian Barat *see* Papua

Irian Jaya *see* Papua

Irian, Teluk *see* Cenderawasih, Teluk

78 *K9* **Iriba** Biltine, NE Chad *15°10′N 22°11′E*

127 *X7* **Iriklinskoye Vodokhranilishche** ▣ W Russian Federation

81 *H23* **Iringa** Iringa, C Tanzania *07°49′S 35°39′E*

81 *H23* **Iringa** ⬖ *region* S Tanzania

165 *O16* **Iriomote-jima** *island* Sakishima-shotō, SW Japan

42 *L4* **Iriona** Colón, NE Honduras *15°55′N 85°10′W*

47 *U7* **Iriri** ≈ N Brazil

58 *I13* **Iriri, Rio** ≈ C Brazil

Iris *see* Yeşilırmak

35 *W9* **Irish, Mount** ▲ Nevada, W USA *37°39′N 115°22′W*

97 *H17* **Irish Sea** *Ir.* Muir Éireann. *sea* C British Isles

139 *U12* **Irjal ash Shaykhīyah** Al Muthanná, S Iraq *30°49′N 44°58′E*

147 *U11* **Irkeshtam** Oshskaya Oblast', SW Kyrgyzstan *39°39′N 73°49′E*

122 *M13* **Irkutsk** Irkutskaya Oblast', S Russian Federation *52°18′N 104°15′E*

122 *M12* **Irkutskaya Oblast'** ⬖ *province* S Russian Federation

Irlir, Gora *see* Irlir Tog'i

146 *K8* **Irlir Tog'i** *var.* Gora Irlir. ▲ N Uzbekistan *42°43′N 63°24′E*

Irminger Basin *see* Reykjanes Basin

21 *R12* **Irmo** South Carolina, SE USA *34°05′N 81°10′W*

102 *E6* **Iroise** *sea* NW France

189 *X2* **Iroj** *var.* Eroj. *island* Ratak Chain, SE Marshall Islands

182 *H7* **Iron Baron** South Australia *33°01′S 137°13′E*

14 *C10* **Iron Bridge** Ontario, S Canada *46°16′N 83°12′W*

20 *H10* **Iron City** Tennessee, S USA *35°01′N 87°34′W*

14 *I13* **Irondale** ≈ Ontario, SE Canada

182 *H7* **Iron Knob** South Australia *32°46′S 137°08′E*

30 *M5* **Iron Mountain** Michigan, N USA *45°51′N 88°03′W*

30 *M4* **Iron River** Michigan, N USA *46°05′N 88°38′W*

30 *J3* **Iron River** Wisconsin, N USA *46°34′N 91°22′W*

27 *X6* **Ironton** Missouri, C USA *37°37′N 90°40′W*

31 *S15* **Ironton** Ohio, N USA *38°32′N 82°40′W*

30 *K4* **Ironwood** Michigan, N USA *46°27′N 90°10′W*

12 *H12* **Iroquois Falls** Ontario, S Canada *48°47′N 80°41′W*

31 *N12* **Iroquois River** ≈ Illinois/Indiana, N USA

164 *M15* **Irō-zaki** *headland* Honshū, S Japan *34°36′N 138°49′E*

Irpen' *see* Irpin'

117 *O4* **Irpin'** *Rus.* Irpen'. Kyyivs'ka Oblast', N Ukraine *50°31′N 30°16′E*

117 *O4* **Irpin'** *Rus.* Irpen'. ≈ N Ukraine

141 *Q16* **'Irqah** SW Yemen *13°42′N 47°21′E*

166 *L6* **Irrawaddy** *var.* Ayeyarwady. ≈ W Burma (Myanmar)

Irrawaddy *see* Ayeyarwady

166 *K8* **Irrawaddy, Mouths of the** *delta* SW Burma (Myanmar)

117 *N4* **Irsha** ≈ N Ukraine

116 *H7* **Irshava** Zakarpats'ka Oblast', W Ukraine *48°19′N 23°03′E*

107 *N18* **Irsina** Basilicata, S Italy *40°42′N 16°18′E*

Irtish *see* Yertis

Irtysh *see* Yertis

Irtyshsk *see* Yertis

79 *P17* **Irumu** Orientale, E Dem. Rep. Congo *01°27′N 29°52′E*

105 *Q2* **Irun** *Cast.* Irún. País Vasco, N Spain *43°20′N 01°48′W*

Irún *see* Irun

Iruña *see* Pamplona

105 *Q3* **Irurtzun** Navarra, N Spain *42°55′N 01°50′W*

96 *I13* **Irvine** W Scotland, United Kingdom *55°37′N 04°40′W*

21 *N6* **Irvine** Kentucky, S USA *37°42′N 83°59′W*

25 *T6* **Irving** Texas, SW USA *32°47′N 96°57′W*

20 *K5* **Irvington** Kentucky, S USA *37°52′N 86°16′W*

164 *C15* **Isa** *prev.* Ōkuchi, Ōkuti. Kagoshima, Kyūshū, SW Japan *32°04′N 130°36′E*

Isaak *see* Iisaku

28 *L8* **Isabel** South Dakota, N USA *45°21′N 101°25′W*

186 *L8* **Isabel** *off.* Isabel Province. ⬖ *province* N Solomon Islands

171 *O8* **Isabela** Basilan Island, SW Philippines *06°41′N 122°00′E*

45 *S5* **Isabela** W Puerto Rico *18°30′N 67°02′W*

45 *N8* **Isabela, Cabo** *headland* NW Dominican Republic *19°54′N 71°03′W*

57 *A18* **Isabela, Isla** *var.* Albemarle Island. *island* Galapagos Islands, Ecuador, E Pacific Ocean

40 *I12* **Isabela, Isla** *island* C Mexico

42 *K9* **Isabella, Cordillera** ▲▲ NW Nicaragua

35 *S12* **Isabella Lake** ▣ California, W USA

31 *N2* **Isabelle, Point** *headland* Michigan, N USA *47°20′N 87°56′W*

Isabel Province *see* Isabel

Isabel Segunda *see* Vieques

116 *M13* **Isaccea** Tulcea, E Romania *45°16′N 28°28′E*

92 *H1* **Ísafjarðardjúp** *inlet* NW Iceland

92 *H1* **Ísafjörður** Vestfirdhir, NW Iceland *66°04′N 23°09′W*

164 *C14* **Isahaya** Nagasaki, Kyūshū, SW Japan *32°51′N 130°02′E*

149 *S7* **Isa Khel** Punjab, E Pakistan *32°39′N 71°20′E*

172 *H7* **Isalo** *var.* Massif de L'Isalo. ▲▲ SW Madagascar

79 *K20* **Isandja** Kasai-Occidental, C Dem. Rep. Congo *03°03′S 21°57′E*

187 *R15* **Isangel** Tanna, S Vanuatu *19°34′S 169°17′E*

79 *M18* **Isangi** Orientale, C Dem. Rep. Congo *0°46′N 24°15′E*

101 *L24* **Isar** ≈ Austria/Germany

101 *M23* **Isar-Kanal** *canal* SE Germany

Isbarta *see* Isparta

Isca Damnoniorum *see* Exeter

107 *K18* **Ischia** *var.* Isola d'Ischia; *anc.* Aenaria. Campania, S Italy *40°44′N 13°57′E*

107 *J18* **Ischia, Isola d'** *island* S Italy

54 *B12* **Iscuandé** *var.* Santa Bárbara. Nariño, SW Colombia *02°32′N 78°00′W*

164 *K14* **Ise** Mie, Honshū, SW Japan *34°29′N 136°43′E*

100 *J12* **Ise** ≈ N Germany

95 *I23* **Isefjord** *fjord* E Denmark

Iseghem *see* Izegem

192 *M14* **Iselin Seamount** *undersea feature* S Pacific Ocean *72°30′S 179°00′W*

Isenhof *see* Püssi

106 *E7* **Iseo** Lombardia, N Italy *45°40′N 10°03′E*

103 *U12* **Iseran, Col de l'** *pass* E France

103 *S11* **Isère** ⬖ *department* E France

103 *S12* **Isère** ≈ E France

101 *F15* **Iserlohn** Nordrhein-Westfalen, W Germany *51°23′N 07°42′E*

107 *K16* **Isernia** *var.* Æsernia. Molise, C Italy *41°35′N 14°14′E*

165 *N12* **Isesaki** Gunma, Honshū, S Japan *36°19′N 139°11′E*

129 *Q5* **Iset'** ≈ C Russian Federation

77 *S15* **Iseyin** Oyo, W Nigeria *07°56′N 03°33′E*

Isfahan *see* Eşfahān

147 *Q11* **Isfana** Batkenskaya Oblast', SW Kyrgyzstan *39°51′N 69°31′E*

147 *R11* **Isfara** N Tajikistan *40°06′N 70°34′E*

149 *O4* **Isfi Maidān** Gōwr, N Afghanistan *35°09′N 66°16′E*

92 *O3* **Isfjorden** *fjord* W Svalbard

Isgender *see* Kul'mach

Isha Baydhabo *see* Baydhabo

125 *V11* **Isherim, Gora** ▲ NW Russian Federation *61°06′N 59°09′E*

127 *Q5* **Isheyevka** Ul'yanovskaya Oblast', W Russian Federation *54°27′N 48°18′E*

165 *P16* **Ishigaki** Okinawa, Ishigaki-jima, SW Japan *24°20′N 124°09′E*

165 *P16* **Ishigaki-jima** *island* Sakishima-shotō, SW Japan

165 *R3* **Ishikari-wan** *bay* Hokkaidō, NE Japan

165 *S16* **Ishikawa** *var.* Isikawa. Okinawa, Okinawa, SW Japan *26°25′N 127°47′E*

164 *K11* **Ishikawa** *off.* Ishikawa-ken, *var.* Isikawa. ⬖ *prefecture* Honshū, SW Japan

Ishikawa-ken *see* Ishikawa

122 *H11* **Ishim** Tyumenskaya Oblast', C Russian Federation *56°13′N 69°25′E*

127 *V6* **Ishimbay** Respublika Bashkortostan, W Russian Federation *53°21′N 56°03′E*

145 *O9* **Ishimskoye** Akmola, C Kazakhstan *51°23′N 67°07′E*

165 *Q10* **Ishinomaki** *var.* Isinomaki. Miyagi, Honshū, C Japan *38°26′N 141°17′E*

165 *P13* **Ishioka** *var.* Isioka. Ibaraki, Honshū, S Japan *36°11′N 140°16′E*

149 *Q3* **Ishkamish** *prev.* Eshkamesh. Takhār, NE Afghanistan *36°25′N 69°11′E*

149 *T2* **Ishkāshim** *prev.* Eshkāshem. Badakhshān, NE Afghanistan *36°43′N 71°34′E*

Ishkashim *see* Ishkoshim

Ishkashimskiy Khrebet *see* Ishkoshim, Qatorkūhi

147 *S15* **Ishkoshim** *Rus.* Ishkashim. S Tajikistan *36°46′N 71°35′E*

147 *S15* **Ishkoshim, Qatorkūhi** *Rus.* Ishkashimskiy Khrebet. ▲▲ SE Tajikistan

31 *N4* **Ishpeming** Michigan, N USA *46°29′N 87°40′W*

147 *N11* **Ishtixon** *Rus.* Ishtykhan. Samarqand Viloyati, C Uzbekistan *39°59′N 66°28′E*

Ishtykhan *see* Ishtixon

Ishurdi *see* Iswardi

61 *G17* **Isidoro Noblia** Cerro Largo, NE Uruguay *31°58′S 54°09′W*

102 *J4* **Isigny-sur-Mer** Calvados, N France *49°20′N 01°06′W*

Isikawa *see* Ishikawa

136 *C11* **Işıklar Dağı** ▲▲ NW Turkey

107 *C19* **Isili** Sardegna, Italy, C Mediterranean Sea *39°46′N 09°06′E*

122 *H12* **Isil'kul'** Omskaya Oblast', C Russian Federation *54°52′N 71°07′E*

Isinomaki *see* Ishinomaki

Isioka *see* Ishioka

81 *I18* **Isiolo** Eastern, C Kenya *0°20′N 37°36′E*

79 *O16* **Isiro** Orientale, NE Dem. Rep. Congo *02°51′N 27°47′E*

92 *P2* **Isispynten** *headland* NE Svalbard *79°51′N 26°44′E*

123 *P11* **Isit** Respublika Sakha (Yakutiya), NE Russian Federation *60°53′N 125°32′E*

149 *O2* **Iskabad Canal** *canal* N Afghanistan

147 *Q9* **Iskandar** *Rus.* Iskander. Toshkent Viloyati, E Uzbekistan *41°32′N 69°46′E*

Iskander *see* Iskandar

Iskăr *see* Iskŭr

121 *Q2* **İskele** *var.* Trikomo, *Gk.* Tríkomon. E Cyprus *35°16′N 33°54′E*

136 *K17* **İskenderun** *Eng.* Alexandretta. Hatay, S Turkey *36°34′N 36°10′E*

138 *H2* **İskenderun Körfezi** *Eng.* Gulf of Alexandretta. *gulf* S Turkey

136 *J11* **İskilip** Çorum, N Turkey *40°45′N 34°28′E*

Iski-Nauket *see* Nookat

114 *J11* **Iskra** *prev.* Popovo. Khaskovo, S Bulgaria *41°55′N 25°12′E*

114 *G10* **Iskŭr** *var.* Iskăr. ≈ NW Bulgaria

114 *H10* **Iskŭr, Yazovir** *prev.* Yazovir Stalin. ▣ W Bulgaria

41 *S15* **Isla** Veracruz-Llave, SE Mexico *18°01′N 95°30′W*

119 *J15* **Islach** *Rus.* Isloch'. ≈ C Belarus

104 *H14* **Isla Cristina** Andalucía, S Spain *37°12′N 07°20′W*

Isla de León *see* San Fernando

149 *U6* **Islāmābād** ● (Pakistan) Federal Capital Territory Islāmābād, NE Pakistan *33°40′N 73°08′E*

149 *V6* **Islāmābād** ✈ Federal Capital Territory Islāmābād, NE Pakistan *33°40′N 73°08′E*

Islamabad *see* Anantnāg

149 *R17* **Islāmkot** Sind, SE Pakistan *24°37′N 70°04′E*

23 *Y17* **Islamorada** Florida Keys, Florida, SE USA *24°55′N 80°37′W*

153 *P14* **Islāmpur** Bihār, N India *25°09′N 85°13′E*

Islam Qala *see* Eslām Qal'eh

18 *K16* **Island Beach** *spit* New Jersey, NE USA

19 *S4* **Island Falls** Maine, NE USA *45°59′N 68°16′W*

Island/Ísland *see* Iceland

182 *H6* **Island Lagoon** ◎ South Australia

11 *Y13* **Island Lake** ◎ Manitoba, C Canada

29 *W5* **Island Lake Reservoir** ▣ Minnesota, N USA

33 *R13* **Island Park** Idaho, NW USA *44°27′N 111°21′W*

19 *N6* **Island Pond** Vermont, NE USA *44°48′N 71°51′W*

184 *K2* **Islands, Bay of** *inlet* North Island, New Zealand

103 *R7* **Is-sur-Tille** Côte d'Or, C France *47°34′N 05°03′E*

42 *J3* **Islas de la Bahía** ⬖ *department* N Honduras

65 *L20* **Islas Orcadas Rise** *undersea feature* S Atlantic Ocean

96 *F12* **Islay** *island* SW Scotland, United Kingdom

116 *I15* **Islaz** Teleorman, S Romania *43°44′N 24°45′E*

29 *V7* **Isle** Minnesota, N USA *46°08′N 93°28′W*

102 *M12* **Isle** ≈ W France

97 *I16* **Isle of Man** ◇ *UK crown dependency* NW Europe

21 *X7* **Isle of Wight** Virginia, NE USA *36°54′N 76°41′W*

97 *M24* **Isle of Wight** *cultural region* S England, United Kingdom

191 *Y3* **Isles Lagoon** ◎ Kiritimati, E Kiribati

37 *R11* **Isleta Pueblo** New Mexico, SW USA *34°54′N 106°40′W*

Isloch' *see* Islach

61 *E19* **Ismael Cortinas** Flores, S Uruguay *33°57′S 57°05′W*

Ismailia *see* Al Ismā'īlīya

Ismâ'ilîya *see* Al Ismā'īlīya

Ismailly *see* İsmayıllı

137 *X11* **İsmayıllı** *Rus.* Ismailly. N Azerbaijan *40°47′N 48°09′E*

Ismid *see* İzmit

147 *S12* **Ismoili Somoní, Qullai** *prev.* Qullai Kommunizm. ▲ E Tajikistan

75 *X10* **Isnā** *var.* Esna. SE Egypt *25°16′N 32°30′E*

93 *K18* **Isojoki** Länsi-Suomi, W Finland *62°07′N 22°00′E*

82 *M12* **Isoka** Northern, NE Zambia *10°08′S 32°43′E*

Isola d'Ischia *see* Ischia

Isola d'Istria *see* Izola

Isonzo *see* Soča

15 *U4* **Isoukustouc** ≈ Québec, SE Canada

136 *F15* **İsparta** *var.* Isbarta. Isparta, SW Turkey *37°46′N 30°32′E*

136 *F15* **Isparta** *var.* Isbarta. ⬖ *province* SW Turkey

114 *M7* **Isperikh** *prev.* Kemanlar. Razgrad, N Bulgaria *43°43′N 26°49′E*

107 *L26* **Ispica** Sicilia, Italy, C Mediterranean Sea *36°47′N 14°55′E*

148 *J14* **Ispikān** Baluchistān, SW Pakistan *26°21′N 62°15′E*

137 *Q12* **İspir** Erzurum, NE Turkey *40°29′N 41°02′E*

138 *E12* **Israel** *off.* State of Israel, *var.* Medinat Israel, *Heb.* Yisrael, Yisra'el. ◆ *republic* SW Asia

Israel, State of *see* Israel

Issa *see* Vis

55 *S9* **Issano** C Guyana *05°49′N 59°28′W*

76 *M16* **Issia** SW Ivory Coast *06°33′N 06°33′W*

Issiq Köl *see* Issyk-Kul', Ozero

103 *P11* **Issoire** Puy-de-Dôme, C France *45°33′N 03°15′E*

103 *N9* **Issoudun** *anc.* Uxellodunum. Indre, C France *46°57′N 01°59′E*

81 *H22* **Issuna** Singida, C Tanzania *05°24′S 34°48′E*

Issyk *see* Yesik

Issyk-Kul' *see* Balykchy

147 *X7* **Issyk-Kul', Ozero** *var.* Issiq Köl, *Kir.* Ysyk-Köl. ◎ E Kyrgyzstan

147 *X7* **Issyk-Kul'skaya Oblast'** *Kir.* Ysyk-Köl Oblasty. ⬖ *province* E Kyrgyzstan

149 *Q7* **Īstādeh-ye Moqor, Āb-e-** *var.* Āb-i-Istāda. ◎ SE Afghanistan

136 *D11* **İstanbul** *Bul.* Tsarigrad, *Eng.* Istanbul, *prev.* Constantinople; *anc.* Byzantium. Istanbul, NW Turkey *41°02′N 28°57′E*

114 *P12* **İstanbul** ⬖ *province* NW Turkey

114 *P12* **İstanbul Boğazı** *var.* Bosporus Thracius, *Eng.* Bosphorus, Bosporus, *Turk.* Karadeniz Boğazi. *strait* NW Turkey

Istarska Županija *see* Istra

115 *G19* **Isthmía** Pelopónnisos, S Greece *37°55′N 23°02′E*

115 *G17* **Istiaía** Évvoia, C Greece *38°57′N 23°09′E*

54 *D9* **Istmina** Chocó, W Colombia *05°09′N 76°42′W*

23 *W13* **Istokpoga, Lake** ◎ Florida, SE USA

112 *A9* **Istra** *off.* Istarska Županija. ⬖ *province* NW Croatia

112 *I10* **Istra** *Eng.* Istria, *Ger.* Istrien. *cultural region* NW Croatia

103 *R15* **Istres** Bouches-du-Rhône, SE France *43°30′N 04°59′E*

Istria/Istrien *see* Istra

153 *T15* **Iswardi** *var.* Ishurdi. Rajshahi, W Bangladesh *24°10′N 89°04′E*

127 *V7* **Isyangulovo** Respublika Bashkortostan, W Russian Federation *52°10′N 56°38′E*

62 *O6* **Itá** Central, S Paraguay *25°29′S 57°21′W*

59 *O17* **Itaberaba** Bahia, E Brazil *12°34′S 40°21′W*

59 *M20* **Itabira** *prev.* Presidente Vargas. Minas Gerais, SE Brazil *19°39′S 43°14′W*

59 *O18* **Itabuna** Bahia, E Brazil *14°48′S 39°18′W*

59 *J18* **Itacaiu** Mato Grosso, S Brazil *14°49′S 51°21′W*

58 *G12* **Itacoatiara** Amazonas, N Brazil *03°06′S 58°22′W*

54 *D9* **Itagüí** Antioquia, W Colombia *06°12′N 75°40′W*

60 *D13* **Itá Ibaté** Corrientes, NE Argentina *27°27′S 57°24′W*

60 *G11* **Itaipú, Represa de** ▣ Brazil/Paraguay

58 *H13* **Itaituba** Pará, NE Brazil *04°15′S 55°56′W*

60 *K13* **Itajaí** Santa Catarina, S Brazil *26°50′S 48°39′W*

Italia/Italiana, Republica/Italian Republic, The *see* Italy

Italian Somaliland *see* Somalia

25 *T7* **Italy** Texas, SW USA *32°10′N 96°52′W*

106 *G12* **Italy** *off.* The Italian Republic, *It.* Italia, Repubblica Italiana. ◆ *republic* S Europe

59 *O19* **Itamaraju** Bahia, E Brazil *16°58′S 39°32′W*

59 *C14* **Itamarati** Amazonas, W Brazil *06°13′S 68°17′W*

59 *M19* **Itambé, Pico de** ▲ SE Brazil *18°23′S 43°21′W*

164 *J13* **Itami** ✈ (Ōsaka) Ōsaka, Honshū, SW Japan *34°47′N 135°24′E*

115 *H15* **Ítamos** ▲ N Greece *40°06′N 23°51′E*

153 *W11* **Itānagar** *state capital* Arunāchal Pradesh, NE India *27°02′N 93°38′E*

Itany *see* Litani

59 *N19* **Itaobim** Minas Gerais, SE Brazil *16°34′S 41°27′W*

59 *P15* **Itaparica, Represa de** ▣ E Brazil

58 *M13* **Itapecuru-Mirim** Maranhão, E Brazil *03°24′S 44°20′W*

60 *Q8* **Itaperuna** Rio de Janeiro, SE Brazil *21°14′S 41°51′W*

59 *O18* **Itapetinga** Bahia, E Brazil *15°17′S 40°16′W*

60 *L10* **Itapetininga** São Paulo, S Brazil *23°36′S 48°07′W*

60 *K10* **Itapeva** São Paulo, S Brazil *23°58′S 48°54′W*

47 *W6* **Itapicuru, Rio** ≈ NE Brazil

58 *O13* **Itapipoca** Ceará, E Brazil *03°29′S 39°35′W*

60 *M9* **Itapira** São Paulo, S Brazil *22°25′S 46°46′W*

60 *K8* **Itápolis** São Paulo, S Brazil *21°36′S 48°43′W*

60 *K10* **Itaporanga** São Paulo, S Brazil *23°43′S 49°28′W*

62 *P7* **Itapúa** *off.* Departamento de Itapúa. ⬖ *department* SE Paraguay

Itapúa, Departamento de *see* Itapúa

59 *E15* **Itapuã do Oeste** Rondônia, W Brazil *09°21′S 63°07′W*

61 *E15* **Itaqui** Rio Grande do Sul, S Brazil *29°10′S 56°28′W*

60 *K10* **Itararé** São Paulo, S Brazil *24°07′S 49°16′W*

60 *K10* **Itararé, Rio** ≈ S Brazil

154 *H11* **Itārsi** Madhya Pradesh, C India *22°39′N 77°48′E*

25 *T7* **Itasca** Texas, SW USA *32°09′N 97°09′W*

Itassi *see* Vieille Case

60 *D13* **Itatí** Corrientes, NE Argentina *27°16′S 58°15′W*

60 *K10* **Itatinga** São Paulo, S Brazil *23°08′S 48°36′W*

115 *F18* **Itéas, Kólpos** *gulf* C Greece

57 *N15* **Iténez, Río** *var.* Rio Guaporé. ≈ Bolivia/Brazil *see also* Rio Guaporé

Iténez, Río *see* Guaporé, Rio

54 *H11* **Iteviate, Río** ≈ C Colombia

100 *I13* **Ith** *hill range* C Germany

31 *Q8* **Ithaca** Michigan, N USA *43°17′N 84°36′W*

18 *H11* **Ithaca** New York, NE USA *42°26′N 76°30′W*

115 *C18* **Itháki** *island* Iónia Nísiá, Greece, C Mediterranean Sea

Itháki *see* Vathy

It Hearrenfean *see* Heerenveen

79 *L17* **Itimbiri** ≈ N Dem. Rep. Congo

Itinomiya *see* Ichinomiya

Itinoseki *see* Ichinoseki

39 *Q5* **Itkilik River** ≈ Alaska, USA

164 *M11* **Itoigawa** Niigata, Honshū, C Japan *37°02′N 137°53′E*

15 *R6* **Itomamo, Lac** ◎ Québec, SE Canada

165 *S17* **Itoman** Okinawa, SW Japan *26°05′N 127°40′E*

102 *M5* **Iton** ≈ N France

57 *M16* **Itonamas Río** ≈ NE Bolivia

Itoupé, Mont *see* Sommet Tabulaire

Itseqqortoormiit *see* Ittoqqortoormiit

22 *K4* **Itta Bena** Mississippi, S USA *33°30′N 90°19′W*

107 *B17* **Ittiri** Sardegna, Italy, C Mediterranean Sea *40°36′N 08°34′E*

197 *Q14* **Ittoqqortoormiit** *var.* Itseqqortoormiit, *Dan.* Scoresbysund, *Eng.* Scoresby Sound. Tunu, C Greenland *70°33′N 21°52′W*

60 *M10* **Itu** São Paulo, S Brazil *23°17′S 47°16′W*

54 *D8* **Ituango** Antioquia, NW Colombia *07°07′N 75°46′W*

59 *A14* **Ituí, Rio** ≈ NW Brazil

79 *O20* **Itula** Sud-Kivu, E Dem. Rep. Congo *03°30′S 27°50′E*

59 *K19* **Itumbiara** Goiás, C Brazil *18°25′S 49°15′W*

55 *T9* **Ituni** E Guyana *05°24′N 58°18′W*

41 *X13* **Iturbide** Campeche, SE Mexico *19°41′N 89°29′W*

Ituri *see* Aruwimi

123 *V13* **Iturup, Ostrov** *island* Kuril'skiye Ostrova, SE Russian Federation

60 *L7* **Ituverava** São Paulo, S Brazil *20°22′S 47°48′W*

59 *C15* **Ituxi, Rio** ≈ W Brazil

61 *E14* **Ituzaingó** Corrientes, NE Argentina *27°34′S 56°44′W*

101 *K18* **Itz** ≈ C Germany

100 *I9* **Itzehoe** Schleswig-Holstein, N Germany *53°56′N 09°31′E*

23 *N2* **Iuka** Mississippi, S USA *34°48′N 88°11′W*

60 *I11* **Ivaiporã** Paraná, S Brazil *24°16′S 51°46′W*

60 *I11* **Ivaí, Rio** ≈ S Brazil

92 *L10* **Ivalo** *Lapp.* Avveel, Avvil. Lappi, N Finland *68°34′N 27°29′E*

92 *L10* **Ivalojoki** *Lapp.* Avveel. ≈ N Finland

119 *H20* **Ivanava** *Pol.* Janów, Janów Poleski, *Rus.* Ivanovo. Brestskaya Voblasts', SW Belarus *52°09′N 25°32′E*

79 *F18* **Ivando** *var.* Djidji. ≈ Congo/Gabon

Ivangorod *see* Dęblin

Ivangrad *see* Berane

183 *N7* **Ivanhoe** New South Wales, SE Australia *32°55′S 144°21′E*

29 *S9* **Ivanhoe** Minnesota, N USA *44°27′N 96°15′W*

14 *D8* **Ivanhoe** ≈ Ontario, S Canada

112 *E8* **Ivanić-Grad** Sisak-Moslavina, N Croatia *45°43′N 16°23′E*

117 *T10* **Ivanivka** Khersons'ka Oblast', S Ukraine *46°43′N 34°28′E*

117 *P10* **Ivanivka** Odes'ka Oblast', SW Ukraine *46°57′N 30°26′E*

113 *L14* **Ivanjica** Serbia, C Serbia *43°36′N 20°14′E*

112 *G11* **Ivanjska** *var.* Potkozarje. Republika Srpska, NW Bosnia and Herzegovina *44°54′N 17°04′E*

111 *H21* **Ivanka** ✈ (Bratislava) Bratislavský Kraj, W Slovakia *48°10′N 17°13′E*

117 *O3* **Ivankiv** *Rus.* Ivankov. Kyyivs'ka Oblast', N Ukraine *50°55′N 29°53′E*

Ivankov *see* Ivankiv

39 *O15* **Ivanof Bay** Alaska, USA *55°55′N 159°28′W*

116 *J7* **Ivano-Frankivs'k** *Ger.* Stanislau, *Pol.* Stanisławów, *Rus.* Ivano-Frankovsk; *prev.* Stanislav. Ivano-Frankivs'ka Oblast', W Ukraine *48°55′N 24°45′E*

Ivano-Frankivs'k *see* Ivano-Frankivs'ka Oblast'

116 *I7* **Ivano-Frankivs'ka Oblast'** *var.* Ivano-Frankivs'k, *Rus.* Ivano-Frankovskaya Oblast'; *prev.* Stanislavskaya Oblast'. ⬖ *province* W Ukraine

Ivano-Frankovsk *see* Ivano-Frankivs'k

Ivano-Frankovskaya Oblast' *see* Ivano-Frankivs'ka Oblast'

124 *M16* **Ivanovo** Ivanovskaya Oblast', W Russian Federation *57°02′N 40°58′E*

Ivanovo *see* Ivanava

124 *M16* **Ivanovskaya Oblast'** ⬖ *province* W Russian Federation

35 *X12* **Ivanpah Lake** ◎ California, W USA

112 *E7* **Ivanščica** ▲▲ NE Croatia

127 *R7* **Ivanteyevka** Saratovskaya Oblast', W Russian Federation *52°13′N 49°06′E*

Ivantsevichi/Ivatsevichi *see* Ivatsevichy

116 *I4* **Ivanychi** Volyns'ka Oblast', NW Ukraine *50°37′N 24°22′E*

119 *H18* **Ivatsevichy** *Pol.* Iwacewicze, *Rus.* Ivantsevichi, Ivatsevichi. Brestskaya Voblasts', SW Belarus *52°43′N 25°21′E*

114 *L12* **Ivaylovgrad** Khaskovo, S Bulgaria *41°32′N 26°06′E*

114 *K11* **Ivaylovgrad, Yazovir** ▣ S Bulgaria

122 *G9* **Ivdel'** Sverdlovskaya Oblast', C Russian Federation *60°42′N 60°07′E*

Ivenets *see* Ivyanyets

116 *L12* **Iveşti** Galaţi, E Romania *45°27′N 28°00′E*

Ivgovuotna *see* Lyngen

Ivigtut *see* Ivittuut

59 *I21* **Ivinheima** Mato Grosso do Sul, SW Brazil *22°16′S 53°52′W*

196 *M15* **Ivittuut** *var.* Ivigtut. Kitaa, S Greenland *61°12′N 48°10′W*

Iviza *see* Eivissa\Ibiza

172 *I6* **Ivohibe** Fianarantsoa, SE Madagascar *22°28′S 46°53′E*

Ivoire, Côte d' *see* Ivory Coast

76 *L15* **Ivory Coast** *off.* Republic of the Ivory Coast, *Fr.* Côte d'Ivoire, République de la Côte d'Ivoire. ◆ *republic* W Africa

68 *C12* **Ivory Coast** *Fr.* Côte d'Ivoire. *coastal region* S Ivory Coast

Ivory Coast, Republic of the *see* Ivory Coast

95 *L22* **Ivösjön** ◎ S Sweden

106 *B7* **Ivrea** *anc.* Eporedia. Piemonte, NW Italy *45°28′N 07°52′E*

12 *J2* **Ivujivik** Québec, NE Canada *62°26′N 77°49′W*

119 *J16* **Ivyanyets** *Rus.* Ivenets. Minskaya Voblasts', C Belarus *53°53′N 26°45′E*

Iv'ye *see* Iwye

Iwacewicze *see* Ivatsevichy

165 *R8* **Iwaizumi** Iwate, Honshū, NE Japan *39°48′N 141°46′E*

165 *P12* **Iwaki** Fukushima, Honshū, N Japan *37°01′N 140°52′E*

164 *F13* **Iwakuni** Yamaguchi, Honshū, SW Japan *34°08′N 132°06′E*

165 *S4* **Iwamizawa** Hokkaidō, NE Japan *43°12′N 141°47′E*

165 *R4* **Iwanai** Hokkaidō, NE Japan *42°51′N 140°21′E*

165 *Q10* **Iwanuma** Miyagi, Honshū, C Japan *38°06′N 140°51′E*

164 *L14* **Iwata** Shizuoka, Honshū, S Japan *34°42′N 137°51′E*

165 *R8* **Iwate** Iwate, Honshū, N Japan *40°03′N 141°12′E*

165 *R8* **Iwate** *off.* Iwate-ken. ⬖ *prefecture* Honshū, C Japan

Iwate-ken *see* Iwate

77 *S16* **Iwo** Oyo, SW Nigeria *07°21′N 03°58′E*

Iwojima *see* Iō-jima

119 *I16* **Iwye** *Pol.* Iwje, *Rus.* Iv'ye. Hrodzyenskaya Voblasts', W Belarus *53°56′N 25°46′E*

42 *C4* **Ixcán, Río** ≈ Guatemala/Mexico

99 *G18* **Ixelles** *Dut.* Elsene. Brussels, C Belgium *50°49′N 04°21′E*

57 *J16* **Ixiamas** La Paz, NW Bolivia *13°45′S 68°10′W*

41 *O13* **Ixmiquilpan** *var.* Ixmiquilpán. Hidalgo, C Mexico *20°30′N 99°15′W*

Ixmiquilpán *see* Ixmiquilpan

83 *K23* **Ixopo** KwaZulu/Natal, E South Africa *30°10′S 30°05′E*

Ixtaccíhuatal, Volcán *see* Iztaccíhuati, Volcán

40 *M16* **Ixtapa** Guerrero, S Mexico *17°38′N 101°29′W*

41 *S16* **Ixtepec** Oaxaca, SE Mexico *16°32′N 95°03′W*

40 *K12* **Ixtlán** *var.* Ixtlán del Río. Nayarit, C Mexico *21°02′N 104°21′W*

Ixtlán del Río *see* Ixtlán

122 *H11* **Iyevlevo** Tyumenskaya Oblast', C Russian Federation *57°36′N 67°20′E*

164 *F14* **Iyo** Ehime, Shikoku, SW Japan *33°43′N 132°42′E*

164 *E14* **Iyo-nada** *sea* S Japan

42 *E4* **Izabal** *off.* Departamento de Izabal. ⬖ *department* E Guatemala

Izabal, Departamento de *see* Izabal

42 *F5* **Izabal, Lago de** *prev.* Golfo Dulce. ◎ E Guatemala

143 *O9* **Īzad Khvāst** Fārs, C Iran *31°31′N 52°09′E*

41 *X12* **Izamal** Yucatán, SE Mexico *20°58′N 89°00′W*

127 *Q16* **Izberbash** Respublika Dagestan, SW Russian Federation *42°32′N 47°51′E*

99 *C18* **Izegem** *prev.* Iseghem. West-Vlaanderen, W Belgium *50°55′N 03°13′E*

142 *M9* **Īzeh** Khūzestān, SW Iran *31°48′N 49°49′E*

165 *T16* **Izena-jima** *island* Nansei-shotō, SW Japan

114 *N10* **Izgrev** Burgas, E Bulgaria *42°09′N 27°49′E*

127 *T2* **Izhevsk** *prev.* Ustinov. Udmurtskaya Respublika, NW Russian Federation *56°48′N 53°12′E*

125 *S7* **Izhma** Respublika Komi, NW Russian Federation *64°56′N 53°52′E*

125 *S7* **Izhma** ≈ NW Russian Federation

141 *X8* **Izkī** NE Oman *22°45′N 57°36′E*

Izmail *see* Izmayil

117 *N13* **Izmayil** *Rus.* Izmail. Odes'ka Oblast', SW Ukraine *45°19′N 28°49′E*

136 *B14* **İzmir** *prev.* Smyrna. İzmir, W Turkey *38°25′N 27°10′E*

136 *C14* **İzmir** *prev.* Smyrna. ⬖ *province* W Turkey

136 *E11* **İzmit** *var.* Ismid; *anc.* Astacus. Kocaeli, NW Turkey *40°47′N 29°55′E*

104 *M14* **Iznájar** Andalucía, S Spain *37°17′N 04°16′W*

104 *M14* **Iznajar, Embalse de** ▣ S Spain

105 *N14* **Iznalloz** Andalucía, S Spain *37°23′N 03°31′W*

136 *E11* **İznik** Bursa, NW Turkey *40°27′N 29°43′E*

136 *E12* **İznik Gölü** ◎ NW Turkey

126 *M14* **Izobil'nyy** Stavropol'skiy Kray, SW Russian Federation *45°22′N 41°40′E*

109 *S13* **Izola** *It.* Isola d'Istria. SW Slovenia *45°31′N 13°40′E*

138 *H9* **Izra'** *var.* Ezra, Ezraa. Dar'ā, S Syria *32°52′N 36°15′E*

41 *P14* **Iztaccíhuati, Volcán** *var.* Volcán Ixtaccíhuatal. ⛰ S Mexico *19°07′N 98°37′W*

42 *C7* **Iztapa** Escuintla, SE Guatemala *13°58′N 90°42′W*

Izúcar de Matamoros *see* Matamoros

165 *N14* **Izu-hantō** *peninsula* Honshū, S Japan

Izuhara *see* Tsushima

164 *J14* **Izumiōtsu** Ōsaka, Honshū, SW Japan *34°29′N 135°25′E*

164 *I14* **Izumisano** Ōsaka, Honshū, SW Japan *34°23′N 135°18′E*

164 *G12* **Izumo** Shimane, Honshū, SW Japan *35°22′N 132°46′E*

192 *H5* **Izu Trench** *undersea feature* NW Pacific Ocean

122 *K6* **Izvestiy TsIK, Ostrova** *island* N Russian Federation

114 *G10* **Izvor** Pernik, W Bulgaria *42°27′N 22°53′E*

116 *L5* **Izyaslav** Khmel'nyts'ka Oblast', W Ukraine *50°08′N 26°53′E*

117 *W6* **Izyum** Kharkivs'ka Oblast', E Ukraine *49°12′N 37°19′E*

J

93 *M18* **Jaala** Etelä-Suomi, S Finland *61°04′N 26°30′E*

140 *J5* **Jabal ash Shifā** *desert* NW Saudi Arabia

141 *U8* **Jabal aẓ Ẓannah** *var.* Jebel Dhanna. Abū Ẓaby, W United Arab Emirates *24°10′N 52°36′E*

138 *E11* **Jabalīya** *var.* Jabāliyah. NE Gaza Strip *31°32′N 34°29′E*

Jabāliyah *see* Jabalīya

105 *N11* **Jabalón** ≈ C Spain

154 *J10* **Jabalpur** *prev.* Jubbulpore. Madhya Pradesh, C India *23°10′N 79°59′E*

141 *N15* **Jabal Zuqar, Jazīrat** *var.* Az Zuqur. *island* SW Yemen

Jabat *see* Jabwot

138 *J3* **Jabbūl, Sabkhat al** *sabkha* NW Syria

181 *P1* **Jabiru** Northern Territory, N Australia *12°44′S 132°48′E*

138 *H4* **Jablah** *var.* Jeble, *Fr.* Djéblé. Al Lādhiqīyah, W Syria *35°00′N 36°00′E*

112 *C11* **Jablanac** Lika-Senj, W Croatia *44°43′N 14°54′E*

113 *H14* **Jablanica** Federacija Bosna I Hercegovina, SW Bosnia and Herzegovina *43°39′N 17°43′E*

113 *M20* **Jablanica** *Alb.* Mali i Jabllanicës, *var.* Malet e Jabllanicës. ▲ Albania/FYR Macedonia *see also* Jabllanicës, Mali i

Jabllanicës, Malet e *see* Jablanica/Jabllanicës, Mali i

113 *M20* **Jabllanicës, Mali i**, *Mac.* Jablanica. ▲ Albania/FYR Macedonia *see also* Jablanica

111 *E15* **Jablonec nad Nisou** *Ger.* Gablonz an der Neisse. Liberecký Kraj, N Czech Republic *50°44′N 15°10′E*

Jabłonków/Jablunkau *see* Jablunkov

110 *J9* **Jabłonowo Pomorskie** Kujawski-pomorskie, C Poland *53°24′N 19°08′E*

111 *J17* **Jablunkov** *Ger.* Jablunkau, *Pol.* Jabłonków. Moravskoslezský Kraj, E Czech Republic *49°35′N 18°46′E*

59 *Q15* **Jaboatão** Pernambuco, E Brazil *08°05′S 35°W*

60 *L8* **Jaboticabal** São Paulo, S Brazil *21°15′S 48°17′W*

189 *U7* **Jabwot** *var.* Jabat, Jebat, Jōwat. *island* Ralik Chain, S Marshall Islands

105 *S4* **Jaca** Aragón, NE Spain *42°34′N 00°33′W*

42 *B4* **Jacaltenango** Huehuetenango, W Guatemala *15°39′N 91°46′W*

59 *G14* **Jacaré-a-Canga** Pará, NE Brazil *05°59′S 57°32′W*

60 *N10* **Jacareí** São Paulo, S Brazil *23°18′S 45°55′W*

59 *I18* **Jaciara** Mato Grosso, W Brazil *15°59′S 54°57′W*

59 *E15* **Jaciparaná** Rondônia, W Brazil *09°20′S 64°28′W*

19 *P5* **Jackman** Maine, NE USA *45°35′N 70°14′W*

35 *X1* **Jackpot** Nevada, W USA *41°57′N 114°41′W*

20 *M8* **Jacksboro** Tennessee, S USA *36°19′N 84°11′W*

25 *S6* **Jacksboro** Texas, SW USA *33°13′N 98°11′W*

23 *N7* **Jackson** Alabama, S USA *31°30′N 87°53′W*

35 *P7* **Jackson** California, W USA *38°19′N 120°46′W*

23 *T4* **Jackson** Georgia, SE USA *33°17′N 83°58′W*

21 *O6* **Jackson** Kentucky, S USA *37°32′N 83°24′W*

22 *J8* **Jackson** Louisiana, S USA *30°50′N 91°13′W*

31 *Q10* **Jackson** Michigan, N USA *42°15′N 84°24′W*

29 *T11* **Jackson** Minnesota, N USA *43°38′N 95°00′W*

22 *K5* **Jackson** *state capital* Mississippi, S USA *32°19′N 90°12′W*

27 *Y7* **Jackson** Missouri, C USA *37°23′N 89°40′W*

21 *W8* **Jackson** North Carolina, SE USA *36°24′N 77°25′W*

31 *T15* **Jackson** Ohio, NE USA *39°03′N 82°40′W*

20 *G9* **Jackson** Tennessee, S USA *35°37′N 88°50′W*

33 *S14* **Jackson** Wyoming, C USA *43°28′N 110°45′W*

185 *C19* **Jackson Bay** *bay* South Island, New Zealand

186 *E9* **Jackson Field** ✈ (Port Moresby) Central/National Capital District, S Papua New Guinea *09°28′S 147°12′E*

185 *C20* **Jackson Head** *headland* South Island, New Zealand *43°57′S 168°38′E*

23 *S8* **Jackson, Lake** ◎ Florida, SE USA

33 *S13* **Jackson Lake** ◎ Wyoming, C USA

194 *J6* **Jackson, Mount** ▲ Antarctica *71°43′S 63°45′W*

37 *U3* **Jackson Reservoir** ◎ Colorado, C USA

23 *Q3* **Jacksonville** Alabama, S USA *33°48′N 85°45′W*

27 *V11* **Jacksonville** Arkansas, C USA *34°52′N 92°08′W*

23 *W8* **Jacksonville** Florida, SE USA *30°20′N 81°39′W*

30 *K14* **Jacksonville** Illinois, N USA *39°43′N 90°13′W*

21 *W11* **Jacksonville** North Carolina, SE USA *34°45′N 77°26′W*

25 *W7* **Jacksonville** Texas, SW USA *31°57′N 95°16′W*

23 *X9* **Jacksonville Beach** Florida, SE USA *30°17′N 81°23′W*

44 *L9* **Jacmel** *var.* Jaquemel. S Haiti *18°13′N 72°33′W*

Jacob *see* Nkayi

149 *Q12* **Jacobābād** Sind, SE Pakistan *28°16′N 68°30′E*

55 *T11* **Jacobs Ladder Falls** *waterfall* S Guyana

45 *O11* **Jaco, Pointe** *headland* N Dominica *15°38′N 61°25′W*

15 *Q9* **Jacques-Cartier** ≈ Québec, SE Canada

13 *P11* **Jacques-Cartier, Détroit de** *var.* Jacques-Cartier Passage. *strait* Gulf of St. Lawrence/St. Lawrence River, Canada

15 *W6* **Jacques-Cartier, Mont** ▲ Québec, SE Canada *48°58′N 66°00′W*

Jacques-Cartier Passage *see* Jacques-Cartier, Détroit de

61 *H16* **Jacuí, Rio** ≈ S Brazil

60 *L11* **Jacupiranga** São Paulo, S Brazil *24°42′S 48°00′W*

100 *G10* **Jade** ≈ NW Germany

100 *G10* **Jadebusen** *bay* NW Germany

Jadotville *see* Likasi

Jadransko More/Jadransko Morje *see* Adriatic Sea

105 *O7* **Jadraque** Castilla-La Mancha, C Spain *40°55′N 02°55′W*

95 *I22* **Jægerspris** Hovedstaden, E Denmark *55°52′N 11°59′E*

56 *C10* **Jaén** Cajamarca, N Peru *05°45′S 78°51′W*

105 *N13* **Jaén** Andalucía, SW Spain *37°46′N 03°48′W*

105 *N13* **Jaén** ⬖ *province* Andalucía, S Spain

95 *C17* **Jæren** *physical region* S Norway

155 *J23* **Jaffna** Northern Province, N Sri Lanka *09°42′N 80°03′E*

155 *K23* **Jaffna Lagoon** *lagoon* N Sri Lanka

19 *N10* **Jaffrey** New Hampshire, NE USA *42°46′N 72°00′W*

138 *H13* **Jafr, Qā' al** *var.* El Jafr. *salt pan* S Jordan

152 *J9* **Jagādhri** Haryāna, N India *30°11′N 77°18′E*

118 *H4* **Jägala** *var.* Jägala Jõgi, *Ger.* Jaggowal. ≈ NW Estonia

Jägala Jõgi *see* Jägala

Jagannath *see* Puri

155 *L14* **Jagdalpur** Chhattīsgarh, C India *19°07′N 82°04′E*

◆ Country ● Country Capital ◇ Dependent Territory ○ Dependent Territory Capital ⬖ Administrative Regions ✈ International Airport ▲ Mountain ▲▲ Mountain Range ⛰ Volcano ≈ River ◎ Lake ▣ Reservoir

163 U5 **Jagdaqi** Nei Mongol Zizhiqu, N China 50°26′N 124°03′E
Jägerndorf see Krnov
Jaggowal see Jägala
139 O2 **Jaghjaghah, Nahr** ≈ N Syria
112 N13 **Jagodina** prev. Svetozarevo. Serbia, C Serbia 43°59′N 21°15′E
112 K12 **Jagodnja** ▲▲ W Serbia
101 I20 **Jagst** ≈ SW Germany
155 I14 **Jagtiāl** Andhra Pradesh, C India 18°49′N 78°53′E
61 H18 **Jaguarão** Rio Grande do Sul, S Brazil 32°30′S 53°25′W
61 H18 **Jaguarão, Rio** var. Río Yaguarón. ≈ Brazil/Uruguay
60 K11 **Jaguariaíva** Paraná, S Brazil 24°15′S 49°44′W
44 D5 **Jagüey Grande** Matanzas, W Cuba 22°31′N 81°07′W
153 P14 **Jahānābād** Bihār, N India 25°13′N 84°59′E
Jahra see Al Jahrā'
143 P12 **Jahrom** var. Jahrum. Fārs, S Iran 28°35′N 53°32′E
Jahrum see Jahrom
Jailolo see Halmahera, Pulau
Jainat see Chai Nat
Jainti see Jayanti
152 H12 **Jaipur** prev. Jeypore. state capital Rājasthān, N India 26°54′N 75°47′E
153 T14 **Jaipurhat** var. Joypurhat. Rajshahi, NW Bangladesh 25°04′N 89°06′E
152 D11 **Jaisalmer** Rājasthān, NW India 26°55′N 70°56′E
154 O12 **Jājapur** var. Jajpur, Panikoilli. Orissa, E India 18°54′N 82°36′E
143 R4 **Jājarm** Khorāsān-e Shemālī, NE Iran 36°58′N 56°26′E
112 G12 **Jajce** Federacija Bosna I Hercegovina, W Bosnia and Herzegovina 44°20′N 17°16′E
Jajı see 'Alī Khēl
Jajpur see Jājapur
83 D17 **Jakalsberg** Otjozondjupa, N Namibia 19°23′S 17°28′E
169 O15 **Jakarta** prev. Djakarta, Dut. Batavia. ● (Indonesia) Jawa, C Indonesia 06°08′S 106°45′E
10 I8 **Jakes Corner** Yukon Territory, W Canada 60°18′N 134°00′W
152 H9 **Jākhal** Haryāna, NW India 29°46′N 75°51′E
Jakobeny see Iacobeni
93 K16 **Jakobstad** Fin. Pietarsaari. Länsi-Suomi, W Finland 63°41′N 22°40′E
Jakobstadt see Jēkabpils
113 O18 **Jakupica** ▲▲ C FYR Macedonia
37 W15 **Jal** New Mexico, SW USA 32°07′N 103°10′W
141 P7 **Jalājil** var. Ğalāğıl. Ar Riyāḍ, C Saudi Arabia 25°43′N 45°22′E
149 S5 **Jalālābād** var. Jalalabad, Jelalabad. Nangarhār, E Afghanistan 34°26′N 70°28′E
Jalal-Abad see Dzhalal-Abad, Dzhalal-Abadskaya Oblast', Kyrgyzstan
Jalal-Abad Oblasty see Dzhalal-Abadskaya Oblast'
149 V7 **Jalālpur** Punjab, E Pakistan 32°39′N 74°11′E
149 T11 **Jalālpur Pīrwāla** Punjab, E Pakistan 29°30′N 71°20′E
152 H8 **Jalandhar** prev. Jullundur. Punjab, N India 31°20′N 75°37′E
42 J7 **Jalán, Río** ≈ S Honduras
42 E6 **Jalapa** Jalapa, C Guatemala 14°39′N 89°59′W
42 J7 **Jalapa** Nueva Segovia, NW Nicaragua 13°56′N 86°11′W
42 A3 **Jalapa** off. Departamento de Jalapa. ◐ department SE Guatemala
Jalapa, Departamento de see Jalapa
42 E6 **Jalapa, Río** ≈ SE Guatemala
143 X13 **Jālaq** Sīstān va Balūchestān, SE Iran
93 K17 **Jalasjärvi** Länsi-Suomi, W Finland 62°30′N 22°50′E
149 O8 **Jaldak** Zābul, SE Afghanistan 32°00′N 66°45′E
60 J7 **Jales** São Paulo, S Brazil 20°15′S 50°34′W
154 P11 **Jaleshwar** var. Jaleswar. Orissa, NE India 21°51′N 87°15′E
Jaleswar see Jaleshwar
154 F12 **Jalgaon** Mahārāshtra, C India 21°01′N 75°34′E
139 W12 **Jalībah** Dhī Qār, S Iraq 30°37′N 46°31′E
139 W13 **Jalīb Shahāb** Al Muthanná, S Iraq 30°26′N 46°09′E
77 X15 **Jalingo** Taraba, E Nigeria 08°54′N 11°22′E
40 K13 **Jalisco** ◐ state SW Mexico
154 G13 **Jālna** Mahārāshtra, W India 19°50′N 75°53′N
Jalomitsa see Ialomiţa
105 R5 **Jalón** ≈ N Spain
152 E13 **Jālor** Rājasthān, N India 25°21′N 72°43′E
112 K11 **Jalovik** Serbia, W Serbia 44°37′N 19°48′E
40 L12 **Jalpa** Zacatecas, C Mexico 21°40′N 103°W
153 S12 **Jalpāiguri** West Bengal, NE India 26°43′N 88°24′E
41 O12 **Jalpán** var. Jalpan. Querétaro de Arteaga, C Mexico 21°13′N 99°28′W
Jalpan see Jalpán
67 P2 **Jalta** island N Tunisia
75 S9 **Jālū** var. Jūlā. NE Libya 29°02′N 21°33′E
189 U8 **Jaluit Atoll** var. Jālwōj. atoll Ralik Chain, S Marshall Islands
Jālwōj see Jaluit Atoll
81 L18 **Jamaame** It. Giamame; prev. Margherita. Jubbada Hoose, S Somalia 0°00′N 42°43′E
77 W13 **Jamaare** ≈ NE Nigeria
44 G9 **Jamaica** ◆ commonwealth republic W West Indies
47 P3 **Jamaica** island W West Indies
44 I9 **Jamaica Channel** channel Haiti/Jamaica
153 T14 **Jamalpur** Dhaka, N Bangladesh 24°54′N 89°57′E
153 Q14 **Jamālpur** Bihār, NE India 25°19′N 86°30′E
168 L9 **Jamaluang** var. Jemaluang. Johor, Peninsular Malaysia 02°15′N 103°50′E
59 I14 **Jamanxim, Rio** ≈ C Brazil
56 B8 **Jambeli, Canal de** channel S Ecuador
99 I20 **Jambes** Namur, SE Belgium 50°26′N 04°51′E
168 L12 **Jambi** var. Telanaipura; prev. Djambi. Sumatera, W Indonesia 01°34′S 103°37′E
168 K12 **Jambi** off. Propinsi Jambi, var. Djambi. ◐ province W Indonesia
Jambi, Propinsi see Jambi
Jamdena see Yamdena, Pulau
12 H8 **James Bay** bay Ontario/Québec, E Canada
63 F19 **James, Isla** island Archipiélago de los Chonos, S Chile
181 Q8 **James Ranges** ▲▲ Northern Territory, C Australia
29 P8 **James River** ≈ North Dakota/South Dakota, N USA
21 X7 **James River** ≈ Virginia, NE USA
194 H4 **James Ross Island** island Antarctica
182 I8 **Jamestown** South Australia 33°13′S 138°36′E
65 G25 **Jamestown** ○ (Saint Helena) NW Saint Helena 15°56′S 05°44′W
35 P8 **Jamestown** California, W USA 37°57′N 120°25′W
20 L7 **Jamestown** Kentucky, S USA 36°58′N 85°03′W
18 D11 **Jamestown** New York, NE USA 42°05′N 79°15′W
29 P5 **Jamestown** North Dakota, N USA 46°54′N 98°42′W
20 L8 **Jamestown** Tennessee, S USA 36°24′N 84°58′W
Jamestown see Holetown
15 N10 **Jamet** ≈ Québec, SE Canada
41 Q17 **Jamiltepec** var. Santiago Jamiltepec. Oaxaca, SE Mexico 16°18′N 97°51′W
95 F20 **Jammerbugten** bay Skagerrak, E North Sea
152 H6 **Jammu** prev. Jummoo. state capital Jammu and Kashmir, NW India 32°43′N 74°54′E
152 I5 **Jammu and Kashmir** var. Jammu-Kashmir, Kashmir. ◐ state NW India
149 V4 **Jammu and Kashmīr** disputed region India/Pakistan
Jammu-Kashmir see Jammu and Kashmir
154 B10 **Jāmnagar** prev. Navanagar. Gujarāt, W India 22°28′N 70°06′E
149 S11 **Jāmpur** Punjab, E Pakistan 29°38′N 70°40′E
93 L18 **Jämsä** Länsi-Suomi, C Finland 61°51′N 25°10′E
93 L18 **Jämsänkoski** Länsi-Suomi, C Finland 61°54′N 25°10′E
153 Q16 **Jamshedpur** Jhārkhand, NE India 22°47′N 86°12′E
94 K9 **Jämtland** ◐ county C Sweden
153 Q14 **Jamūi** Bihār, NE India 24°57′N 86°14′E
Jamuna see Brahmaputra
153 T14 **Jamuna Nadi** ≈ N Bangladesh
Jamundá see Nhamundá, Rio
54 D11 **Jamundí** Valle del Cauca, SW Colombia 03°16′N 76°31′W
153 Q12 **Janakpur** Central, C Nepal 26°45′N 85°55′E
59 N18 **Janaúba** Minas Gerais, SE Brazil 15°47′S 43°16′W
58 K11 **Janaucu, Ilha** island NE Brazil
143 Q7 **Jandaq** Eşfahān, C Iran 34°04′N 54°26′E
64 Q11 **Jandia, Punta de** headland Fuerteventura, Islas Canarias, Spain, NE Atlantic Ocean 28°03′N 14°32′W
59 B14 **Jandiatuba, Rio** ≈ NW Brazil
105 N12 **Jándula** ≈ S Spain
29 V10 **Janesville** Minnesota, N USA 44°07′N 93°43′W
30 L9 **Janesville** Wisconsin, N USA 42°42′N 89°02′W
83 N20 **Jangamo** Inhambane, SE Mozambique 24°04′S 35°25′E
155 J14 **Jangaon** Andhra Pradesh, C India 18°47′N 79°25′E
153 S14 **Jangīpur** West Bengal, NE India 24°31′N 88°03′E
Janina see Ioánnina
Janischken see Joniškis
112 J11 **Janja** NE Bosnia and Herzegovina 44°40′N 19°15′E
Jankovac see Jánoshalma
197 Q15 **Jan Mayen** ◇ Norwegian dependency N Atlantic Ocean
84 D5 **Jan Mayen** island N Atlantic Ocean
197 R15 **Jan Mayen Fracture Zone** tectonic feature Greenland Sea/Norwegian Sea
197 R15 **Jan Mayen Ridge** undersea feature Greenland Sea/Norwegian Sea 69°00′N 08°00′W
40 H3 **Janos** Chihuahua, N Mexico 30°50′N 108°10′W
111 K25 **Jánoshalma** SCr. Jankovac. Bács-Kiskun, S Hungary 46°19′N 19°16′E
Janów see Ivanava, Belarus
110 H10 **Janowiec Wielkopolski** Ger. Janowitz. Kujawski-pomorskie, C Poland 52°47′N 17°30′E
Janowitz see Janowiec Wielkopolski
Janow/Janów see Jonava, Lithuania
111 O15 **Janów Lubelski** Lubelski, E Poland 50°42′N 22°24′E
Janów Poleski see Ivanava
83 H25 **Jansenville** Eastern Cape, S South Africa 32°56′S 24°40′E
59 M18 **Januária** Minas Gerais, SE Brazil 15°28′S 44°23′W
Janūbīyah, Al Bādiyah al see Ash Shāmīyah
102 I7 **Janzé** Ille-et-Vilaine, NW France 47°55′N 01°28′W
154 F10 **Jaora** Madhya Pradesh, C India 23°40′N 75°10′E
131 Y9 **Japan** var. Nippon, Jap. Nihon. ◆ monarchy E Asia
129 Y9 **Japan** island group E Asia
192 H4 **Japan Basin** undersea feature N Sea of Japan 40°00′N 135°00′E
129 Y8 **Japan, Sea of** var. East Sea, Rus. Yapanskoye More. sea NW Pacific Ocean see also East Sea
192 H4 **Japan Trench** undersea feature NW Pacific Ocean 37°00′N 143°00′E
Japen see Yapen, Pulau
59 A15 **Japiim** var. Máncio Lima. Acre, W Brazil 08°00′S 73°39′W
58 D12 **Japurá** Amazonas, N Brazil 01°43′S 66°14′W
58 C12 **Japurá, Rio** var. Río Caquetá, Yapurá. ≈ Brazil/Colombia see also Caquetá, Río
Japurá, Rio see Caquetá, Río
43 W17 **Jaqué** Darién, SE Panama 07°31′N 78°09′W
Jaquemel see Jacmel
Jarablos see Jarābulus
138 K2 **Jarābulus** var. Jarablos, Jerablus, Fr. Djérablous. Ḩalab, N Syria 36°51′N 38°02′E
60 K13 **Jaraguá do Sul** Santa Catarina, S Brazil 26°29′S 49°07′W
104 K9 **Jaraicejo** Extremadura, W Spain 39°40′N 05°49′W
104 K9 **Jaráiz de la Vera** Extremadura, W Spain 40°04′N 05°45′W
105 O7 **Jarama** ≈ C Spain
63 J20 **Jaramillo** Santa Cruz, SE Argentina 47°10′S 67°07′W
Jarandilla de la Vega see Jarandilla de la Vera
104 K8 **Jarandilla de la Vera** var. Jarandilla de la Vega. Extremadura, W Spain 40°08′N 05°39′W
149 V9 **Jarānwāla** Punjab, E Pakistan 31°20′N 73°26′E
138 G9 **Jarash** var. Jerash; anc. Gerasa. Irbid, NW Jordan 32°17′N 35°54′E
Jarbah, Jazīrat see Jerba, Île de
94 N13 **Järbo** Gävleborg, C Sweden 60°43′N 16°40′E
Jardan see Yordon
44 F7 **Jardines de la Reina, Archipiélago de los** island group C Cuba
162 I8 **Jargalant** Bayanhongor, C Mongolia 47°14′N 99°43′E
162 K6 **Jargalant** Bulgan, N Mongolia 49°09′N 104°19′E
162 G7 **Jargalant** var. Buyanbat. Govĭ-Altay, W Mongolia 47°00′N 95°57′E
162 I6 **Jargalant** var. Orgil. Hövsgöl, C Mongolia 48°31′N 99°19′E
Jargalant see Battsengel
Jargalant see Bulgan, Bayan-Ölgiy, Mongolia
Jargalant see Biger, Govĭ-Altay, Mongolia
Jarīd, Shaṭṭ al see Jerid, Chott el
58 I11 **Jari, Rio** var. Jary. ≈ N Brazil
141 N7 **Jarīr, Wādī al** dry watercourse C Saudi Arabia
Jarja see Yur'ya
94 L13 **Järna** var. Dala-Jarna. Dalarna, C Sweden 60°31′N 14°22′E
95 O16 **Järna** Stockholm, C Sweden 59°05′N 17°35′E
102 K11 **Jarnac** Charente, W France 45°41′N 00°10′W
110 H12 **Jarocin** Wielkopolskie, C Poland 51°59′N 17°30′E
111 F16 **Jaroměř** Ger. Jermer. Královéhradecký Kraj, N Czech Republic 50°22′N 15°55′E
Jaroslau see Jarosław
111 O16 **Jarosław** Ger. Jaroslau, Rus. Yaroslav. Podkarpackie, SE Poland 50°01′N 22°41′E
93 F16 **Järpen** Jämtland, C Sweden 63°21′N 13°30′E
147 O14 **Jarqo'rg'on** Rus. Dzharkurgan. Surkhondaryo Viloyati, S Uzbekistan 37°31′N 67°20′E
139 P2 **Jarrāh, Wadi** dry watercourse NE Syria
Jars, Plain of see Xiangkhoang, Plateau de
162 K14 **Jartai Yanchi** ◎ N China
59 E16 **Jaru** Rondônia, W Brazil 10°24′S 62°45′W
Jarud Qi see Lubei
118 I4 **Järva-Jaani** Ger. Sankt-Johannis. Järvamaa, N Estonia 59°03′N 25°54′E
118 G5 **Järvakandi** Ger. Jerwakant. Raplamaa, NW Estonia 58°45′N 24°49′E
118 H4 **Järvamaa** var. Järva Maakond. ◐ province N Estonia
Järva Maakond see Järvamaa
93 L19 **Järvenpää** Etelä-Suomi, S Finland 60°29′N 25°06′E
14 G17 **Jarvis** Ontario, S Canada 42°53′N 80°06′W
177 R8 **Jarvis Island** ◇ US unincorporated territory C Pacific Ocean
94 M11 **Järvsö** Gävleborg, C Sweden 61°43′N 16°25′E
Jary see Jari, Rio
112 M9 **Jaša Tomić** Vojvodina, NE Serbia 45°27′N 20°51′E
112 D12 **Jasenice** Zadar, SW Croatia 44°15′N 15°33′E
138 I11 **Jashshat al 'Adlah, Wādī al** dry watercourse C Jordan
77 Q16 **Jasikan** E Ghana 07°24′N 00°28′E
Jāsk see Bandar-e Jāsk
146 F6 **Jasliq** Rus. Zhaslyk. Qoraqalpog'iston Respublikasi, NW Uzbekistan 43°57′N 57°30′E
111 N17 **Jasło** Podkarpackie, SE Poland 49°45′N 21°28′E
11 U16 **Jasmin** Saskatchewan, S Canada 51°11′N 103°34′W
65 A23 **Jason Islands** island group NW Falkland Islands
194 I4 **Jason Peninsula** peninsula Antarctica
31 N15 **Jasonville** Indiana, N USA 39°09′N 87°12′W
11 O15 **Jasper** Alberta, SW Canada 52°55′N 118°05′W
14 L13 **Jasper** Ontario, SE Canada 44°50′N 75°57′W
23 O3 **Jasper** Alabama, S USA 33°49′N 87°16′W
27 T9 **Jasper** Arkansas, C USA 36°00′N 93°11′W
23 U8 **Jasper** Florida, SE USA 30°31′N 82°57′W
31 N16 **Jasper** Indiana, N USA 38°22′N 86°57′W
29 R11 **Jasper** Minnesota, N USA 43°51′N 96°24′W
27 S7 **Jasper** Missouri, C USA 37°20′N 94°18′W
20 K10 **Jasper** Tennessee, S USA 35°04′N 85°36′W
25 Y9 **Jasper** Texas, SW USA 30°55′N 94°00′W
11 O15 **Jasper National Park** national park Alberta/British Columbia, SW Canada
Jassy see Iaşi
113 N14 **Jastrebac** ▲▲ SE Serbia
112 D9 **Jastrebarsko** Zagreb, N Croatia 45°40′N 15°40′E
Jastrow see Jastrowie
110 G9 **Jastrowie** Ger. Jastrow. Wielkopolskie, C Poland 53°25′N 16°48′E
111 J17 **Jastrzębie-Zdrój** Śląskie, S Poland 49°58′N 18°34′E
111 L22 **Jászapáti** Jász-Nagykun-Szolnok, E Hungary 47°30′N 20°10′E
111 L22 **Jászberény** Jász-Nagykun-Szolnok, E Hungary 47°30′N 19°56′E
111 L23 **Jász-Nagykun-Szolnok** off. Jász-Nagykun-Szolnok Megye. ◐ county E Hungary
Jász-Nagykun-Szolnok Megye see Jász-Nagykun-Szolnok
59 J19 **Jataí** Goiás, C Brazil 17°58′S 51°45′W
58 G12 **Jatapu, Serra do** ▲▲ N Brazil
41 W16 **Jatate, Río** ≈ SE Mexico
149 P17 **Jāti** Sind, SE Pakistan 24°20′N 68°18′E
44 F6 **Jatibonico** Sancti Spíritus, C Cuba 21°56′N 79°11′W
169 O16 **Jatiluhur, Danau** ◎ Jawa, S Indonesia
Jativa see Xàtiva
149 S11 **Jatoi** prev. Jattoi. Punjab, E Pakistan 29°29′N 70°58′E
Jattoi see Jatoi
60 L9 **Jaú** São Paulo, S Brazil 22°11′S 48°35′W
58 F11 **Jauaperi, Rio** ≈ N Brazil
99 I19 **Jauche** Walloon Brabant, C Belgium 50°42′N 04°55′E
Jauer see Jawor
Jauf see Al Jawf
149 U7 **Jauharābād** Punjab, E Pakistan 32°16′N 72°17′E
57 E14 **Jauja** Junín, C Peru 11°48′S 75°30′W
41 O10 **Jaumave** Tamaulipas, C Mexico 23°28′N 99°22′W
118 H10 **Jaunjelgava** Ger. Friedrichstadt. S Latvia 56°38′N 25°03′E
Jaunlatgale see Pytalovo
118 I8 **Jaunpiebalga** NE Latvia 57°10′N 26°02′E
118 E9 **Jaunpils** C Latvia 56°45′N 23°03′E
153 N13 **Jaunpur** Uttar Pradesh, N India 25°44′N 82°41′E
29 N8 **Java** South Dakota, N USA 45°29′N 99°54′W
Java see Jawa
105 R9 **Javalambre** ▲ E Spain 40°02′N 01°06′W
173 V7 **Java Ridge** undersea feature E Indian Ocean
59 A14 **Javari, Rio** var. Yavarí. ≈ Brazil/Peru
Javarthushuu see Bayan-Uul
169 Q15 **Java Sea** Ind. Laut Jawa. sea W Indonesia
173 U7 **Java Trench** var. Sunda Trench. undersea feature E Indian Ocean
143 Q10 **Javazm** var. Jowzam. Kermān, C Iran 30°31′N 55°01′E
105 T11 **Jávea** Cat. Xàbia. Valenciana, E Spain 38°48′N 00°10′E
Javhlant see Bayan-Ovoo
63 G20 **Javier, Isla** island S Chile
113 L14 **Javor** ▲▲ Bosnia and Herzegovina/Serbia
111 K20 **Javorie** Hung. Jávoros. ▲ S Slovakia 48°26′N 19°16′E
Jávoros see Javorie
93 J14 **Jävre** Norrbotten, N Sweden 65°07′N 21°31′E
192 E8 **Jawa** Eng. Java; prev. Djawa. island C Indonesia
169 O16 **Jawa Barat** off. Propinsi Jawa Barat, Eng. West Java. ◐ province S Indonesia
Jawa Barat, Propinsi see Jawa Barat
Jawa, Laut see Java Sea
139 R3 **Jawān** Nīnawýa, NW Iraq 35°57′N 43°03′E
169 P16 **Jawa Tengah** off. Propinsi Jawa Tengah, Eng. Central Java. ◐ province S Indonesia
Jawa Tengah, Propinsi see Jawa Tengah
169 R16 **Jawa Timur** off. Propinsi Jawa Timur, Eng. East Java. ◐ province S Indonesia
Jawa Timur, Propinsi see Jawa Timur
81 N17 **Jawhar** var. Jowhar, It. Giohar. Shabeellaha Dhexe, S Somalia 02°37′N 45°30′E
111 F14 **Jawor** Ger. Jauer. Dolnośląskie, SW Poland 51°01′N 16°11′E
Jaworów see Yavoriv
111 J16 **Jaworzno** Śląskie, S Poland 50°13′N 19°11′E
Jaxartes see Syr Darya
27 R9 **Jay** Oklahoma, C USA 36°25′N 94°49′W
Jayabum see Chaiyaphum
Jayanath see Chai Nat
153 T12 **Jayanti** prev. Jainti. West Bengal, NE India 26°45′N 89°40′E
171 X14 **Jaya, Puncak** prev. Puntjak Carstensz, Puntjak Sukarno. ▲ Papua, E Indonesia 04°00′S 137°10′E
171 Z13 **Jayapura** var. Djajapura, Dut. Hollandia; prev. Kotabaru, Sukarnapura. Papua, E Indonesia 02°37′S 140°39′E
Jay Dairen see Dalian
Jayhawker State see Kansas
147 S12 **Jayilgan** Rus. Dzhailgan, Dzhayilgan. C Tajikistan 39°17′N 71°32′E
155 L14 **Jaypur** var. Jeypore, Jeypur. Orissa, E India 18°54′N 82°36′E
25 O6 **Jayton** Texas, SW USA 33°16′N 100°35′W
143 U13 **Jaz Mūrīān, Hāmūn-e** ◎ SE Iran
138 M4 **Jazrah** Ar Raqqah, C Syria 35°56′N 39°02′E
138 G6 **Jbaïl** var. Jebeil, Jubayl, Jubeil; anc. Biblical Gebal, Bybles. W Lebanon 34°00′N 35°45′E
25 O7 **J. B. Thomas, Lake** ⊠ Texas, SW USA
Jdaïdé see Judaydah
35 X12 **Jean** Nevada, W USA 35°45′N 115°20′W
22 I9 **Jeanerette** Louisiana, S USA 29°54′N 91°39′W
44 L8 **Jean-Rabel** NW Haiti 19°48′N 73°05′W
143 T12 **Jebāl Bārez, Kūh-e** ▲▲ SE Iran
Jebat see Jabwot
77 T15 **Jebba** Kwara, W Nigeria 09°04′N 04°50′E
Jebeil see Jbaïl
116 E12 **Jebel** Hung. Széphely; prev. Hung. Zsebely. Timiş, W Romania 45°33′N 21°14′E
146 B11 **Jebel** Rus. Dzhebel. Balkan Welaýaty, W Turkmenistan 39°42′N 54°10′E
Jebel, Bahr el see White Nile
Jebel Dhanna see Jabal aẓ Ẓannah
Jeble see Jablah
163 Y15 **Jecheon** Jap. Teisen; prev. Chech'ŏn. N South Korea 37°06′N 128°15′E
96 K13 **Jedburgh** SE Scotland, United Kingdom 55°29′N 02°34′W
Jedda see Jiddah
111 L15 **Jędrzejów** Ger. Endersdorf. Świętokrzyskie, C Poland 50°39′N 20°18′E
100 K12 **Jeetze** var. Jeetzel. ≈ C Germany
Jeetzel see Jeetze
29 U14 **Jefferson** Iowa, C USA 42°01′N 94°22′W
21 Q8 **Jefferson** North Carolina, SE USA 36°24′N 81°33′W
25 X6 **Jefferson** Texas, SW USA 32°45′N 94°21′W
30 M9 **Jefferson** Wisconsin, N USA 43°01′N 88°48′W
27 U5 **Jefferson City** state capital Missouri, C USA 38°33′N 92°13′W
33 R10 **Jefferson City** Montana, NW USA 46°24′N 112°01′W
21 N9 **Jefferson City** Tennessee, S USA 36°07′N 83°29′W
35 U7 **Jefferson, Mount** ▲ Nevada, W USA 38°49′N 116°54′W
32 H12 **Jefferson, Mount** ▲ Oregon, NW USA 44°40′N 121°48′W
20 L5 **Jeffersontown** Kentucky, S USA 38°11′N 85°33′W
31 P16 **Jeffersonville** Indiana, N USA 38°16′N 85°45′W
33 V15 **Jeffrey City** Wyoming, C USA 42°29′N 107°49′W
77 T13 **Jega** Kebbi, NW Nigeria 12°15′N 04°21′E
Jehol see Chengde
163 X17 **Jeju** Jap. Saishū; prev. Cheju. S South Korea 33°31′N 126°34′E
163 Y17 **Jeju-do** Jap. Saishū; prev. Cheju-do, Quelpart. island S South Korea
163 Y17 **Jeju-haehyeop** Eng. Cheju Strait; prev. Cheju-haehyeop. strait S South Korea
62 P5 **Jejui-Guazú, Río** ≈ E Paraguay
118 I10 **Jēkabpils** Ger. Jakobstadt. S Latvia 56°30′N 25°56′E
23 W7 **Jekyll Island** island Georgia, SE USA
169 R13 **Jelai, Sungai** ≈ Borneo, N Indonesia
Jelalabad see Jalālābād
111 H14 **Jelcz-Laskowice** Dolnośląskie, SW Poland 51°01′N 17°24′E
111 E14 **Jelenia Góra** Ger. Hirschberg, Hirschberg im Riesengebirge, Hirschberg in Riesengebirge, Hirschberg in Schlesien. Dolnośląskie, SW Poland 50°54′N 15°48′E
153 S11 **Jelep La** pass N India
118 F9 **Jelgava** Ger. Mitau. C Latvia 56°38′N 23°47′E
112 L13 **Jelica** ▲▲ C Serbia
20 M8 **Jellico** Tennessee, S USA 36°33′N 84°06′W
95 G23 **Jelling** Syddanmark, C Denmark 55°45′N 09°24′E
169 N9 **Jemaja, Pulau** island W Indonesia
Jemaluang see Jamaluang
99 E20 **Jemappes** Hainaut, S Belgium 50°27′N 03°53′E
169 S17 **Jember** prev. Djember. Jawa, C Indonesia 08°07′S 113°45′E
99 I20 **Jemeppe-sur-Sambre** Namur, S Belgium 50°27′N 04°41′E
37 R10 **Jemez Pueblo** New Mexico, SW USA 35°36′N 106°43′W
158 K2 **Jeminay** var. Tuotiereke. Xinjiang Uygur Zizhiqu, NW China 47°28′N 85°49′E
189 U5 **Jemo Island** atoll Ratak Chain, C Marshall Islands
169 U11 **Jempang, Danau** ◎ Borneo, N Indonesia
101 L16 **Jena** Thüringen, C Germany 50°56′N 11°35′E
22 I6 **Jena** Louisiana, S USA 31°40′N 92°07′W
108 I8 **Jenaz** Graubünden, SE Switzerland 46°56′N 09°43′E
109 N7 **Jenbach** Tirol, W Austria 47°24′N 11°47′E
171 N15 **Jeneponto** prev. Djeneponto. Sulawesi, C Indonesia 05°41′S 119°42′E
138 F9 **Jenin** N West Bank 32°28′N 35°17′E
21 P7 **Jenkins** Kentucky, S USA 37°10′N 82°37′W
27 P9 **Jenks** Oklahoma, C USA 36°01′N 95°58′W
Jenné see Djenné
109 X8 **Jennersdorf** Burgenland, SE Austria 46°57′N 16°08′E
22 H9 **Jennings** Louisiana, S USA 30°13′N 92°39′W
11 N7 **Jenny Lind Island** island Nunavut, N Canada
23 Y13 **Jensen Beach** Florida, SE USA 27°15′N 80°13′W
9 P6 **Jens Munk Island** island Nunavut, NE Canada
163 Y15 **Jeonju** Jap. Zenshū; prev. Chŏnju. SW South Korea 35°51′N 127°08′E
59 O17 **Jequié** Bahia, E Brazil 13°52′S 40°06′W
59 O18 **Jequitinhonha, Rio** ≈ E Brazil
Jerablus see Jarābulus
74 H6 **Jerada** NE Morocco 34°16′N 02°07′W
Jerash see Jarash
75 N7 **Jerba, Île de** var. Djerba, Jazīrat Jarbah. island E Tunisia
44 K9 **Jérémie** SW Haiti 18°39′N 74°11′W
Jeréz see Jerez de García Salinas, Mexico
Jerez see Jeréz de la Frontera, Spain
40 L11 **Jerez de García Salinas** var. Jeréz. Zacatecas, C Mexico 22°40′N 103°00′W
104 J15 **Jerez de la Frontera** var. Jerez; prev. Xeres. Andalucía, SW Spain 36°41′N 06°08′W
104 I12 **Jerez de los Caballeros** Extremadura, W Spain 38°20′N 06°45′W
Jergucati see Jorgucat
138 G10 **Jericho** Ar. Arīḩā, Heb. Yeriho. E West Bank 31°51′N 35°27′E
74 M7 **Jerid, Chott el** var. Shaṭṭ al Jarīd. salt lake SW Tunisia
183 O10 **Jerilderie** New South Wales, SE Australia 35°24′S 145°43′E
Jerischmarkt see Câmpia Turzii
92 K11 **Jerisjärvi** ◎ NW Finland
Jermak see Aksu
Jermentau see Yereymentau
Jermer see Jaroměř
36 K11 **Jerome** Arizona, SW USA 34°45′N 112°06′W
33 O15 **Jerome** Idaho, NW USA 42°43′N 114°31′W
97 L26 **Jersey** island NW Europe
18 K14 **Jersey City** New Jersey, NE USA 40°42′N 74°01′W
18 F13 **Jersey Shore** Pennsylvania, NE USA 41°12′N 77°13′W
30 K14 **Jerseyville** Illinois, N USA 39°07′N 90°19′W
104 K8 **Jerte** ≈ W Spain
138 F10 **Jerusalem** Ar. Al Quds, Al Quds ash Sharīf, Heb. Yerushalayim; anc. Hierosolyma. ● (Israel) Jerusalem, NE Israel 31°47′N 35°13′E
138 G10 **Jerusalem** ◐ district E Israel
183 S10 **Jervis Bay** New South Wales, SE Australia 35°09′S 150°42′E
183 S10 **Jervis Bay Territory** ◐ territory SE Australia
Jerwakant see Järvakandi
109 S10 **Jesenice** Ger. Assling. NW Slovenia 46°26′N 14°01′E
111 H16 **Jeseník** Ger. Freiwaldau. Olomoucký Kraj, E Czech Republic 50°14′N 17°12′E
Jesi see Iesi
106 I8 **Jesolo** var. Iesolo. Veneto, NE Italy 45°32′N 12°37′E
Jesselton see Kota Kinabalu
95 I14 **Jessheim** Akershus, S Norway 60°07′N 11°10′E
153 T15 **Jessore** Khulna, W Bangladesh 23°10′N 89°12′E
23 W6 **Jesup** Georgia, SE USA 31°36′N 81°54′W
41 S15 **Jesús Carranza** Veracruz-Llave, SE Mexico 17°30′N 95°01′W
62 K10 **Jesús María** Córdoba, C Argentina 30°59′S 64°05′W
26 K6 **Jetmore** Kansas, C USA 38°05′N 99°55′W
103 Q2 **Jeumont** Nord, N France 50°18′N 04°06′E
95 H14 **Jevnaker** Oppland, S Norway 60°15′N 10°25′E
Jewe see Jõhvi
25 V9 **Jewett** Texas, SW USA 31°21′N 96°08′W
19 N12 **Jewett City** Connecticut, NE USA 41°36′N 71°58′W
Jeypore see Jaipur, Rājasthān, India
Jeypore/Jeypur see Jaypur, Orissa, India
113 L17 **Jezercës, Maja e** ▲ N Albania 42°27′N 19°49′E
111 B18 **Jezerní Hora** ▲ SW Czech Republic 49°10′N 13°11′E
154 F10 **Jhābua** Madhya Pradesh, C India 22°44′N 74°37′E
152 H14 **Jhālāwār** Rājasthān, N India 24°37′N 76°12′E
Jhang/Jhang Sadar see Jhang Sadr
149 U9 **Jhang Sadr** var. Jhang, Jhang Sadar. Punjab, NE Pakistan 31°16′N 72°19′E
152 J13 **Jhānsi** Uttar Pradesh, N India 25°27′N 78°34′E
153 O16 **Jhārkhand** ◐ state NE India
154 M11 **Jhārsuguda** Orissa, E India 21°56′N 84°04′E
149 V7 **Jhelum** Punjab, NE Pakistan 32°55′N 73°42′E
129 P9 **Jhelum** ≈ E Pakistan
Jhenaida see Jhenaidaha
153 T15 **Jhenaidaha** var. Jhenaida, Jhenida. Khulna, Bangladesh 23°32′N 89°09′E
Jhenaidaha see Jhenida
153 T15 **Jhenida** var. Jhenaidaha. Dhaka, W Bangladesh 23°34′N 89°39′E
jhenida see Jhenaidaha
149 P16 **Jhimpīr** Sind, SE Pakistan 25°00′N 68°01′E
Jhind see Jīnd
149 R16 **Jhudo** Sind, SE Pakistan 24°58′N 69°18′E
Jhumra see Chak Jhumra
152 H11 **Jhunjhunūn** Rājasthān, N India 28°05′N 75°30′E
Ji see Hebei, China
Ji see Jilin, China
Jiading see Xinfeng
153 S14 **Jiāganj** West Bengal, NE India 24°18′N 88°07′E
Jiaji see Qionghai
160 J7 **Jialing Jiang** ≈ C China
163 Y7 **Jiamusi** var. Chia-mu-ssu, Kiamusze. Heilongjiang, NE China 46°46′N 130°19′E
161 O11 **Ji'an** Jiangxi, S China 27°08′N 115°00′E
163 W12 **Ji'an** Jilin, NE China 41°04′N 126°07′E
163 T13 **Jianchang** Liaoning, NE China 40°48′N 119°51′E
Jianchang see Nancheng
Jiancheng see Jianyang
160 F11 **Jianchuan** var. Jinhuan. Yunnan, SW China 26°28′N 99°49′E
158 M4 **Jiangjunmiao** Xinjiang Uygur Zizhiqu, W China 44°42′N 90°06′E
160 K11 **Jiangkou** var. Shuangjiang. Guizhou, S China 27°46′N 108°53′E
Jiangkou see Fengkai
161 Q12 **Jiangle** var. Guyong. Fujian, SE China 26°44′N 117°26′E
161 N15 **Jiangmen** Guangdong, S China 22°35′N 113°02′E
Jiangna see Yanshan
161 Q10 **Jiangshan** Zhejiang, SE China 28°41′N 118°33′E
161 Q7 **Jiangsu** var. Chiang-su, Jiangsu Sheng, Kiangsu, Su. ◐ province E China
Jiangsu see Nanjing
Jiangsu Sheng see Jiangsu
161 O11 **Jiangxi** var. Chiang-hsi, Gan, Jiangxi Sheng, Kiangsi. ◐ province S China
Jiangxi Sheng see Jiangxi
160 I8 **Jiangyou** prev. Zhongba. Sichuan, C China 31°52′N 104°52′E
161 N9 **Jianli** var. Rongcheng. Hubei, C China 29°51′N 112°50′E
161 Q11 **Jian'ou** Fujian, SE China 27°04′N 118°20′E
163 S12 **Jianping** var. Yebaishou. Liaoning, NE China 41°13′N 119°37′E
Jianshe see Baiyü
160 L9 **Jianshi** var. Yezhou. Hubei, C China 30°37′N 109°42′E
Jiantang see Xamgyi'nyilha
129 V11 **Jian Xi** ≈ SE China
161 Q11 **Jianyang** Fujian, SE China 27°20′N 118°01′E
160 I9 **Jianyang** var. Jiancheng. Sichuan, C China 30°22′N 104°31′E
163 X10 **Jiaohe** Jilin, NE China 43°41′N 127°20′E
Jiaojiang see Taizhou
Jiaoxian see Jiaozhou
161 R5 **Jiaozhou** prev. Jiaoxian. Shandong, E China 36°17′N 120°00′E
161 N6 **Jiaozuo** Henan, C China 35°14′N 113°13′E
Jiashan see Mingguang
158 F8 **Jiashi** var. Baren, Payzawat. Xinjiang Uygur Zizhiqu, NW China 39°27′N 76°45′E
154 L9 **Jiāwān** Madhya Pradesh, C India 24°20′N 82°17′E
161 S9 **Jiaxing** Zhejiang, SE China 30°44′N 120°46′E
161 S14 **Jiayi** var. Chia-i, Chiai, Chiayi, Kiayi, Jap. Kagi. C Taiwan 23°29′N 120°27′E
163 X6 **Jiayin** var. Chaoyang. Heilongjiang, NE China 48°51′N 130°24′E
159 R8 **Jiayuguan** Gansu, N China 39°47′N 98°14′E
Jibhalanta see Uliastay
138 M4 **Jibli** Ar Raqqah, C Syria 35°49′N 39°23′E
116 H9 **Jibou** Hung. Zsibó. Sălaj, NW Romania 47°15′N 23°17′E
141 Z9 **Jibsh, Ra's al** headland E Oman 21°20′N 59°23′E
Jibuti see Djibouti
111 E15 **Jičín** Ger. Jitschin. Královéhradecký Kraj, N Czech Republic 50°27′N 15°20′E
140 K10 **Jiddah** Eng. Jedda. (Saudi Arabia) Makkah, W Saudi Arabia 21°34′N 39°13′E
141 W11 **Jiddat al Ḩarāsīs** desert C Oman
Jiesjavrre see Iešjavri
160 M4 **Jiexiu** Shanxi, C China 37°00′N 111°50′E
161 P14 **Jieyang** Guangdong, S China 23°32′N 116°20′E
119 F14 **Jieznas** Kaunas, S Lithuania 54°37′N 24°10′E
Jīfa', Bi'r see Jif'īyah, Bi'r
141 P15 **Jif'īyah, Bi'r** var. Bi'r Jīfa'. well C Yemen
77 W13 **Jigawa** ◐ state N Nigeria
146 J10 **Jigerbent** Rus. Dzhigirbent. Lebap Welaýaty, NE Turkmenistan 40°44′N 61°56′E
44 I7 **Jiguaní** Granma, E Cuba 20°24′N 76°26′W
159 T12 **Jigzhi** var. Chugqênsumdo. Qinghai, C China 33°23′N 101°25′E
Jih-k'a-tse see Xigazê
111 E18 **Jihlava** Ger. Iglau, Pol. Igława. Vysocina, S Czech Republic 49°22′N 15°36′E
111 E18 **Jihlava** var. Igel, Ger. Iglawa. ≈ Vysočina, C Czech Republic
Jihlavský Kraj see Vysočina
111 C18 **Jihočeský Kraj** prev. Budějovický Kraj. ◐ region Czech Republic
111 G19 **Jihomoravský Kraj** prev. Brněnský Kraj. ◐ region SE Czech Republic
74 L5 **Jijel** var. Djidjel; prev. Djidjelli. NE Algeria 36°50′N 05°43′E
116 L9 **Jijia** ≈ N Romania
80 L13 **Jijiga** It. Giggiga. Sumalē, E Ethiopia 09°21′N 42°53′E
105 S12 **Jijona** var. Xixona. Valenciana, E Spain 38°34′N 00°29′W
81 L18 **Jilib** It. Gelib. Jubbada Dhexe, S Somalia 0°18′N 42°48′E
163 W10 **Jilin** var. Chi-lin, Girin, Kirin; prev. Yungki, Yunki. Jilin, NE China 43°46′N 126°32′E
163 W10 **Jilin** var. Chi-lin, Girin, Ji, Jilin Sheng, Kirin. ◐ province NE China
163 W11 **Jilin Hada Ling** ▲▲ NE China
Jilin Sheng see Jilin
163 S4 **Jiliu He** ≈ NE China
105 Q6 **Jiloca** ≈ N Spain
161 T12 **Jilong** var. Keelung, Jap. Kirun, Kirun', prev. Chilung, prev. Sp. Santissima Trinidad. N Taiwan 25°10′N 121°43′E
81 I14 **Jīma** var. Jimma, It. Gimma. Oromīya, C Ethiopia 07°42′N 36°51′E
44 M9 **Jimaní** W Dominican Republic 18°29′N 71°49′W
116 E11 **Jimbolia** Ger. Hatzfeld, Hung. Zsombolya. Timiş, W Romania 45°47′N 20°43′E
104 K16 **Jimena de la Frontera** Andalucía, S Spain 36°27′N 05°28′W
40 K7 **Jiménez** Chihuahua, N Mexico 27°09′N 104°54′W
41 N5 **Jiménez** Coahuila, NE Mexico 29°05′N 100°40′W
41 P9 **Jiménez** var. Santander Jiménez. Tamaulipas, C Mexico 24°11′N 98°29′W
40 L10 **Jiménez del Teul** Zacatecas, C Mexico 23°13′N 103°46′W
77 Y14 **Jimeta** Adamawa, E Nigeria 09°16′N 12°25′E
Jimma see Jīma
158 M5 **Jimsar** Xinjiang Uygur Zizhiqu, NW China 44°05′N 88°48′E
18 I14 **Jim Thorpe** Pennsylvania, NE USA 40°51′N 75°43′W
Jin see Shanxi
Jin see Tianjin Shi

◆ Country
● Country Capital
◇ Dependent Territory
○ Dependent Territory Capital
◐ Administrative Regions
✈ International Airport
▲ Mountain
▲▲ Mountain Range
Volcano
≈ River
◎ Lake
⊠ Reservoir

161 P5 **Jinan** var. Chinan, Chinan, Tsinan. province capital Shandong, E China 36°43′N 116°58′E
Jin'an see Songpan
Jinbi see Dayao
159 T8 **Jinchang** Gansu, N China 38°31′N 102°07′E
161 N5 **Jincheng** Shanxi, C China 35°30′N 112°52′E
Jincheng see Wuding
Jinchengjiang see Hechi
152 I9 **Jīnd** prev. Jhind. Haryāna, NW India 29°29′N 76°22′E
183 Q11 **Jindabyne** New South Wales, SE Australia 36°28′S 148°36′E
163 X17 **Jin-do** Jap. Chin-tō; prev. Chin-do. island SW South Korea
111 O18 **Jindřichův Hradec** Ger. Neuhaus. Jihočeský Kraj, S Czech Republic 49°09′N 15°01′E
Jing see Beijing Shi
Jing see Jinghe, China
159 X10 **Jingchuan** Gansu, C China 35°20′N 107°45′E
161 Q10 **Jingdezhen** Jiangxi, S China 29°18′N 117°18′E
161 O12 **Jinggangshan** Jiangxi, S China 26°36′N 114°11′E
161 P3 **Jinghai** Tianjin Shi, E China 38°53′N 116°45′E
158 I4 **Jinghe** var. Jing. Xinjiang Uygur Zizhiqu, NW China 44°35′N 82°55′E
160 K6 **Jing He** ≈ C China
160 F15 **Jinghong** var. Yunjinghong. Yunnan, SW China 22°03′N 100°56′E
160 M9 **Jingmen** Hubei, C China 30°58′N 112°09′E
163 X10 **Jingpo Hu** ◎ NE China
160 M8 **Jing Shan** ▲▲ C China
159 V9 **Jingtai** var. Yitiaoshan. Gansu, C China 37°12′N 104°06′E
160 J14 **Jingxi** var. Xinjing. Guangxi Zhuangzu Zizhiqu, S China 23°10′N 106°22′E
Jing Xian see Jingzhou, Hunan, China
163 W11 **Jingyu** Jilin, NE China 42°23′N 126°48′E
159 V10 **Jingyuan** var. Wulan. Gansu, C China 36°35′N 104°40′E
160 M9 **Jingzhou** prev. Shashi, Shashih, Shasi. Hubei, C China 30°21′N 112°09′E
160 L12 **Jingzhou** var. Jing Xian, Jingzhou Miaouzu Dongzu Zizhixian, Quyang. Hunan, S China 26°35′N 109°40′E
Jingzhou Miaouzu Dongzu Zizhixian see Jingzhou
163 Z16 **Jinhae** Jap. Chinkai; prev. Chinhae. S South Korea 35°06′N 128°48′E
Jinhe see Jinping
161 R10 **Jinhua** Zhejiang, SE China 29°15′N 119°36′E
Jinhuan see Jianchuan
161 P5 **Jining** Shandong, E China 35°25′N 116°35′E
Jining see Ulan Qab
81 G18 **Jinja** S Uganda 0°27′N 33°14′E
161 R13 **Jinjiang** var. Qingyang. Fujian, SE China 24°53′N 118°36′E
161 O11 **Jin Jiang** ≈ S China
Jinjiang see Chengmai
163 Y16 **Jinju** prev. Chinju, Jap. Shinshū. S South Korea 35°12′N 128°06′E
171 V15 **Jin, Kepulauan** island group E Indonesia
161 R13 **Jinmen Dao** var. Chinmen Tao, Quemoy. island W Taiwan
42 J9 **Jinotega** Jinotega, NW Nicaragua 13°03′N 85°59′W
42 K7 **Jinotega** ◈ department N Nicaragua
42 J11 **Jinotepe** Carazo, SW Nicaragua 11°50′N 86°10′W
160 L13 **Jinping** var. Sanjiang. Guizhou, S China 26°42′N 109°13′E
160 H14 **Jinping** var. Jinhe. Yunnan, SW China 22°47′N 103°12′E
Jinsen see Incheon
160 J11 **Jinsha** Guizhou, S China 27°24′N 106°16′E
160 M10 **Jinshi** Hunan, S China 29°42′N 111°46′E
Jinshi see Xinning
162 I9 **Jinst** var. Bodī. Bayanhongor, C Mongolia 45°25′N 100°33′E
159 R7 **Jinta** Gansu, N China 40°01′N 98°57′E
161 Q12 **Jin Xi** ≈ SE China
Jinxi see Huludao
Jinxian see Jinzhou
161 P6 **Jinxiang** Shandong, E China 35°08′N 116°19′E
161 P8 **Jinzhai** var. Meishan. Anhui, E China 31°42′N 115°47′E
161 N4 **Jinzhong** var. Yuci. Shanxi, C China 37°34′N 112°45′E
163 T12 **Jinzhou** var. Chin-chou, Chinchow; prev. Chinhsien. Liaoning, NE China 41°07′N 121°06′E
163 U14 **Jinzhou** prev. Jinxian. Liaoning, NE China 39°04′N 121°45′E
Jinzhu see Daocheng
138 H12 **Jinz, Qā' al** ◎ C Jordan
47 S8 **Jiparaná, Rio** ≈ W Brazil
56 A7 **Jipijapa** Manabí, W Ecuador 01°23′S 80°35′W
42 F8 **Jiquilisco** Usulután, S El Salvador 13°19′N 88°35′W
Jirgalanta see Hovd
147 S12 **Jirgatol** Rus. Dzhirgatal'. C Tajikistan 39°13′N 71°09′E
75 X10 **Jirjā** var. Girga, Girgeh, Jirjā. C Egypt 26°17′N 31°58′E
Jirjā see Jirjā
111 B15 **Jirkov** Ger. Görkau. Ústecký Kraj, NW Czech Republic 50°30′N 13°27′E
143 T12 **Jīroft** var. Sabzawaran, Sabzvārān. Kermān, SE Iran 28°40′N 57°40′E
81 P14 **Jirriiban** Mudug, E Somalia 07°15′N 48°55′E
160 L11 **Jishou** Hunan, S China 28°20′N 109°43′E
Jisr ash Shadadi see Ash Shadādah
116 I14 **Jitaru** Olt, S Romania 44°27′N 24°32′E
Jitschin see Jičín
116 H14 **Jiu** Ger. Schil, Schyl, Hung. Zsil, Zsily. ≈ S Romania
161 R11 **Jiufeng Shan** ▲▲ SE China
161 P9 **Jiujiang** Jiangxi, S China 29°45′N 115°59′E
161 O10 **Jiuling Shan** ▲▲ S China
160 G10 **Jiulong** var. Garba, Tib. Gyaisi. Sichuan, C China 29°00′N 101°30′E
161 Q13 **Jiulong Jiang** ≈ SE China
161 Q12 **Jiulong Xi** ≈ SE China
159 R8 **Jiuquan** var. Suzhou. Gansu, N China 39°47′N 98°30′E
160 K17 **Jiusuo** Hainan, S China 18°25′N 109°55′E
163 W10 **Jiutai** Jilin, NE China 44°01′N 125°51′E
160 K13 **Jiuwan Dashan** ▲▲ S China
160 I7 **Jiuzhaigou** var. Nongle; prev. Nanping. Sichuan, C China 33°25′N 104°05′E
148 I16 **Jiwani** Baluchistān, SW Pakistan 25°05′N 61°46′E
163 Y8 **Jixi** Heilongjiang, NE China 45°17′N 131°01′E
163 Y7 **Jixian** var. Fuli. Heilongjiang, NE China 46°38′N 131°04′E
160 M5 **Jixian** var. Ji Xian. Shanxi, C China 36°15′N 110°41′E
Ji Xian see Jixian
Jiza see Al Jīzah
141 N13 **Jīzān** var. Qīzān. Jīzān, SW Saudi Arabia 17°50′N 42°50′E
141 N13 **Jīzān** var. Minṭaqat Jīzān. ◈ province SW Saudi Arabia
Jīzān, Minṭaqat see Jīzān
140 K6 **Jizl, Wādī al** dry watercourse W Saudi Arabia
164 H12 **Jizō-zaki** headland Honshū, SW Japan 35°34′N 133°16′E
141 U14 **Jiz', Wādī al** dry watercourse E Yemen
147 O11 **Jizzax** Rus. Dzhizak. Jizzax Viloyati, C Uzbekistan 40°08′N 67°47′E
147 N10 **Jizzax Viloyati** Rus. Dzhizakskaya Oblast'. ◈ province C Uzbekistan
60 I13 **Joaçaba** Santa Catarina, S Brazil 27°08′S 51°30′W
Joal see Joal-Fadiout
76 F11 **Joal-Fadiout** prev. Joal. W Senegal 14°09′N 16°50′W
76 E10 **João Barrosa** Boa Vista, E Cape Verde 16°01′N 22°44′W
João Belo see Xai-Xai
João de Almeida see Chibia
59 Q15 **João Pessoa** prev. Paraíba. state capital Paraíba, E Brazil 07°06′S 34°53′W
25 X7 **Joaquin** Texas, SW USA 31°58′N 94°03′W
62 K6 **Joaquín V. González** Salta, N Argentina 25°06′S 64°07′W
Joazeiro see Juazeiro
Job'urg see Johannesburg
109 O7 **Jochberger Ache** ≈ W Austria
Jo-ch'iang see Ruoqiang
92 K12 **Jock** Norrbotten, N Sweden 66°40′N 22°45′E
42 I5 **Jocón** Yoro, N Honduras 15°17′N 86°55′W
105 O13 **Jódar** Andalucía, S Spain 37°51′N 03°18′W
152 F12 **Jodhpur** Rājasthān, NW India 26°17′N 73°02′E
99 I19 **Jodoigne** Walloon Brabant, C Belgium 50°43′N 04°52′E
93 O16 **Joensuu** Itä-Suomi, SE Finland 62°36′N 29°45′E
37 W4 **Joes** Colorado, C USA 39°36′N 102°40′W
191 Z3 **Joe's Hill** hill Kiritimati, NE Kiribati
165 N11 **Jōetsu** var. Zyôetu. Niigata, Honshū, C Japan 37°09′N 138°13′E
83 M18 **Jofane** Inhambane, S Mozambique 21°16′S 34°21′E
153 R12 **Jogbani** Bihār, NE India 26°23′N 87°16′E
118 I5 **Jõgeva** Ger. Laisholm. Jõgevamaa, E Estonia 58°48′N 26°28′E
118 I4 **Jõgevamaa** off. Jõgeva Maakond. ◈ province E Estonia
Jõgeva Maakond see Jõgevamaa
155 E18 **Jog Falls** Waterfall Karnātaka, W India
143 S4 **Joghatāy** Khorāsān, NE Iran 36°34′N 57°00′E
153 U12 **Jogighopa** Assam, NE India 26°14′N 90°35′E
152 I7 **Jogindarnagar** Himāchal Pradesh, N India 31°51′N 76°47′E
Jogjakarta see Yogyakarta
164 L11 **Jōhana** Toyama, Honshū, SW Japan 36°30′N 136°53′E
83 J21 **Johannesburg** var. Egoli, Erautini, Gauteng, abbrev. Job'urg. Gauteng, NE South Africa 26°10′S 28°02′E
35 T13 **Johannesburg** California, W USA 35°20′N 117°37′W
Johannisburg see Pisz
149 P14 **Johi** Sind, SE Pakistan 26°46′N 67°28′E
55 T13 **Johi Village** S Guyana 01°48′N 58°33′W
45 W10 **John A. Osborne** ✈ (Plymouth) E Montserrat 16°45′N 62°09′W
32 K13 **John Day** Oregon, NW USA 44°25′N 118°57′W
32 I11 **John Day River** ≈ Oregon, NW USA
18 L14 **John F Kennedy** ✈ (New York) Long Island, New York, NE USA 40°39′N 73°45′W
21 V8 **John H. Kerr Reservoir** var. Buggs Island Lake, Kerr Lake. ▣ North Carolina/Virginia, SE USA
37 V6 **John Martin Reservoir** ▣ Colorado, C USA
96 K6 **John o'Groats** N Scotland, United Kingdom 58°38′N 03°03′W
27 P5 **John Redmond Reservoir** ▣ Kansas, C USA
39 Q7 **John River** ≈ Alaska, USA
26 H6 **Johnson** Kansas, C USA 37°33′N 101°46′W
18 M7 **Johnson** Vermont, NE USA 44°39′N 72°40′W
18 D13 **Johnsonburg** Pennsylvania, NE USA 41°28′N 78°37′W
18 H11 **Johnson City** New York, NE USA 42°06′N 75°54′W
21 P8 **Johnson City** Tennessee, S USA 36°18′N 82°21′W
25 R10 **Johnson City** Texas, SW USA 30°17′N 98°27′W
35 S12 **Johnsondale** California, W USA 35°58′N 118°32′W
10 I8 **Johnsons Crossing** Yukon Territory, W Canada 60°30′N 133°15′W
21 T13 **Johnsonville** South Carolina, SE USA 33°50′N 79°26′W
21 Q13 **Johnston** South Carolina, SE USA 33°49′N 81°48′W
192 M6 **Johnston Atoll** ◇ US unincorporated territory C Pacific Ocean
175 Q3 **Johnston Atoll** atoll C Pacific Ocean
30 L17 **Johnston City** Illinois, N USA 37°49′N 88°55′W
180 K12 **Johnston, Lake** salt lake Western Australia
31 S13 **Johnstown** Ohio, N USA 40°08′N 82°39′W
18 D15 **Johnstown** Pennsylvania, NE USA 40°20′N 78°56′W
168 L10 **Johor** var. Johore. ◈ state Peninsular Malaysia
Johor Baharu see Johor Bahru
168 K10 **Johor Bahru** var. Johor Baharu, Johore Bahru. Johor, Peninsular Malaysia 01°29′N 103°44′E
Johore see Johor
Johore Bahru see Johor Bahru
118 K3 **Jõhvi** Ger. Jewe. Ida-Virumaa, NE Estonia 59°21′N 27°25′E
103 P7 **Joigny** Yonne, C France 47°58′N 03°24′E
Joinvile see Joinville
60 K12 **Joinville** var. Joinvile. Santa Catarina, S Brazil 26°20′S 48°55′W
103 R6 **Joinville** Haute-Marne, N France 48°26′N 05°07′E
194 H3 **Joinville Island** island Antarctica
41 O15 **Jojutla** var. Jojutla de Juárez. Morelos, S Mexico 18°38′N 99°10′W
Jojutla de Juárez see Jojutla
92 I12 **Jokkmokk** Lapp. Dálvvadis. Norrbotten, N Sweden 66°35′N 19°57′E
92 L2 **Jökuldalur** ≈ E Iceland
92 K2 **Jökulsá á Fjöllum** ≈ NE Iceland
Jokyakarta see Yogyakarta
30 M11 **Joliet** Illinois, N USA 41°33′N 88°05′W
15 O11 **Joliette** Québec, SE Canada 46°02′N 73°27′W
171 O8 **Jolo** Jolo Island, SW Philippines 06°02′N 121°00′E
94 D11 **Jølstervatnet** ◎ S Norway
169 S16 **Jombang** prev. Djombang. Jawa, S Indonesia 07°33′S 112°14′E
159 R14 **Jomda** Xizang Zizhiqu, W China 31°26′N 98°09′E
118 G13 **Jonava** Ger. Janow, Pol. Janów. Kaunas, C Lithuania 55°05′N 24°19′E
146 L11 **Jondor** Rus. Zhondor. Buxoro Viloyati, C Uzbekistan 39°46′N 64°11′E
159 V11 **Jonê** var. Liulin. Gansu, C China 34°36′N 103°39′E
27 X9 **Jonesboro** Arkansas, C USA 35°50′N 90°42′W
23 S4 **Jonesboro** Georgia, SE USA 33°31′N 84°21′W
30 L17 **Jonesboro** Illinois, N USA 37°25′N 89°19′W
22 H5 **Jonesboro** Louisiana, S USA 32°14′N 92°43′W
21 P8 **Jonesboro** Tennessee, S USA 36°17′N 82°28′W
19 T6 **Jonesport** Maine, NE USA 44°33′N 67°35′W
0 J4 **Jones Sound** channel Nunavut, N Canada
22 I6 **Jonesville** Louisiana, S USA 31°37′N 91°49′W
31 Q10 **Jonesville** Michigan, N USA 41°58′N 84°39′W
21 Q11 **Jonesville** South Carolina, SE USA 34°49′N 81°38′W
146 K10 **Jongeldi** Rus. Dzhankel'dy. Buxoro Viloyati, C Uzbekistan 40°50′N 63°16′E
81 F14 **Jonglei** Jonglei, E South Sudan 06°54′N 31°19′E
81 F14 **Jonglei** var. Gongoleh State. ◈ state E South Sudan
81 F14 **Jonglei Canal** canal E South Sudan
118 F11 **Joniškėlis** Panevėžys, N Lithuania 56°02′N 24°10′E
118 F10 **Joniškis** Ger. Janischken. Šiaulai, N Lithuania 56°15′N 23°36′E
95 L19 **Jönköping** Jönköping, S Sweden 57°45′N 14°10′E
95 K20 **Jönköping** ◈ county S Sweden
15 Q7 **Jonquière** Québec, SE Canada 48°25′N 71°16′W
41 V15 **Jonuta** Tabasco, SE Mexico 18°04′N 92°03′W
102 K12 **Jonzac** Charente-Maritime, W France 45°26′N 00°25′W
27 R7 **Joplin** Missouri, C USA 37°04′N 94°31′W
33 W8 **Jordan** Montana, NW USA 47°18′N 106°54′W
138 H12 **Jordan** off. Hashemite Kingdom of Jordan, Ar. Al Mamlaka al Urdunīya al Hashemīyah, Al Urdunn; prev. Transjordan. ◆ monarchy SW Asia
138 G9 **Jordan** Ar. Urdunn, Heb. HaYarden. ≈ SW Asia
Jordan Lake see B. Everett Jordan Reservoir
111 K17 **Jordanów** Małopolskie, S Poland 49°39′N 19°51′E
32 M15 **Jordan Valley** Oregon, NW USA 42°59′N 117°03′W
138 G9 **Jordan Valley** valley N Israel
57 D15 **Jorge Chávez Internacional** var. Lima. ✈ (Lima) Lima, W Peru 12°07′S 77°01′W
113 L23 **Jorgucat** var. Jergucati, Jorgucati. Gjirokastër, S Albania 39°57′N 20°14′E
Jorgucati see Jorgucat
153 X12 **Jorhāt** Assam, NE India 26°45′N 94°09′E
93 J14 **Jörn** Västerbotten, N Sweden 65°03′N 20°04′E
37 R14 **Jornada Del Muerto** valley New Mexico, SW USA
93 N17 **Joroinen** Itä-Suomi, E Finland 62°11′N 27°50′E
95 C16 **Jørpeland** Rogaland, S Norway 59°01′N 06°04′E
77 W14 **Jos** Plateau, C Nigeria 09°59′N 08°57′E
171 Q8 **Jose Abad Santos** var. Trinidad. Mindanao, S Philippines 05°51′N 125°35′E
61 F19 **José Batlle y Ordóñez** var. Batlle y Ordóñez. Florida, C Uruguay 33°28′S 55°08′W
63 H18 **José de San Martín** Chubut, S Argentina 44°04′S 70°29′W
61 E19 **José Enrique Rodó** var. Rodó, José E.Rodó; prev. Drabble, Drable. Soriano, SW Uruguay 33°43′S 57°33′W
José E.Rodo see José Enrique Rodó
Josefsdorf see Žabalj
44 C4 **José Martí** ✈ (La Habana) Cuidad de La Habana, N Cuba 23°03′N 82°22′W
61 F19 **José Pedro Varela** var. José P.Varela. Lavalleja, S Uruguay 33°30′S 54°28′W
181 N2 **Joseph Bonaparte Gulf** gulf N Australia
37 N11 **Joseph City** Arizona, SW USA 34°56′N 110°18′W
13 O9 **Joseph, Lake** ◎ Newfoundland and Labrador, E Canada
14 G13 **Joseph, Lake** ◎ Ontario, S Canada
186 C6 **Josephstaal** Madang, N Papua New Guinea 04°42′S 144°55′E
José P.Varela see José Pedro Varela
59 J14 **José Rodrigues** Pará, N Brazil 05°45′S 51°20′W
152 K9 **Joshīmath** Uttarakhand, N India 30°33′N 79°35′E
25 T7 **Joshua** Texas, SW USA 32°27′N 97°23′W
35 V15 **Joshua Tree** California, W USA 34°07′N 116°18′W
77 V14 **Jos Plateau** plateau C Nigeria
102 H6 **Josselin** Morbihan, NW France 47°57′N 02°35′W
Jos Sudarso see Yos Sudarso, Pulau
94 E11 **Jostedalsbreen** glacier S Norway
94 F12 **Jotunheimen** ▲▲ S Norway
138 G7 **Joûnié** var. Juniyah. W Lebanon 33°54′N 33°36′E
25 R13 **Jourdanton** Texas, SW USA 28°55′N 98°34′W
98 L7 **Joure** Fris. De Jouwer. Fryslân, N Netherlands 52°58′N 05°48′E
93 M18 **Joutsa** Länsi-Suomi, C Finland 61°46′N 26°09′E
93 N18 **Joutseno** Etelä-Suomi, SE Finland 61°06′N 28°30′E
92 M12 **Joutsijärvi** Lappi, NE Finland 66°40′N 28°00′E
108 A9 **Joux, Lac de** ◎ W Switzerland
Jovakān see Jowkān
44 D5 **Jovellanos** Matanzas, W Cuba 22°49′N 81°11′W
153 V13 **Jowai** Meghālaya, NE India 25°25′N 92°21′E
Jōwat see Jabwot
Jowhar see Jawhar
143 O12 **Jowkān** var. Jovakān. Fārs, S Iran
Jowzam see Javazm
149 N2 **Jowzjān** ◈ province N Afghanistan
Joypurhat see Jaipurhat
Józseffalva see Žabalj
J.Storm Thurmond Reservoir see Clark Hill Lake
45 T6 **Juana Díaz** C Puerto Rico 18°03′N 66°30′W
40 L9 **Juan Aldama** Zacatecas, C Mexico 24°20′N 103°23′W
0 E9 **Juan de Fuca Plate** tectonic feature
32 F7 **Juan de Fuca, Strait of** strait Canada/USA
Juan Fernandez Islands see Juan Fernández, Islas
193 S11 **Juan Fernández, Islas** Eng. Juan Fernandez Islands. island group W Chile
55 O4 **Juangriego** Nueva Esparta, NE Venezuela 11°06′N 63°59′W
56 D11 **Juanjuí** var. Juanjuy. San Martín, N Peru 07°10′S 76°44′W
Juanjuy see Juanjuí
93 N16 **Juankoski** Itä-Suomi, C Finland 63°01′N 28°24′E
Juan Lacaze see Juan L. Lacaze
61 E20 **Juan L. Lacaze** var. Juan Lacaze, Puerto Sauce; prev. Sauce. Colonia, SW Uruguay 34°26′S 57°25′W
62 L5 **Juan Solá** Salta, N Argentina 23°30′S 62°42′W
63 F21 **Juan Stuven, Isla** island S Chile
59 H16 **Juará** Mato Grosso, W Brazil 11°10′S 57°28′W
41 N7 **Juárez** var. Villa Juárez. Coahuila, NE Mexico 27°39′N 100°43′W
40 C2 **Juárez, Sierra de** ▲▲ NW Mexico
59 O15 **Juazeiro** prev. Joazeiro. Bahia, E Brazil 09°25′S 40°30′W
59 P14 **Juazeiro do Norte** Ceará, E Brazil 07°10′S 39°18′W
81 F15 **Juba** var. Jūbā. ● (South Sudan) Central Equatoria, S South Sudan 04°50′N 31°35′E
81 L17 **Juba** Amh. Genalē Wenz, It. Guiba, Som. Ganaane, Webi Jubba. ≈ Ethiopia/Somalia
194 H2 **Jubany** Argentinian research station Antarctica 61°57′S 58°23′W
Jubayl see Jbaïl
81 L18 **Jubbada Dhexe** off. Gobolka Jubbada Dhexe. ◈ region SW Somalia
Jubbada Dhexe, Gobolka see Jubbada Dhexe
81 K18 **Jubbada Hoose** ◈ region SW Somalia
Jubba, Webi see Juba
Jubbulpore see Jabalpur
Jubeil see Jbaïl
74 B9 **Juby, Cap** headland SW Morocco 27°58′N 12°56′W
105 R10 **Júcar** var. Jucar. ≈ C Spain
40 L12 **Juchipila** Zacatecas, C Mexico 21°25′N 103°06′W
41 S16 **Juchitán** var. Juchitán de Zaragosa. Oaxaca, SE Mexico 16°27′N 95°W
Juchitán de Zaragosa see Juchitán
138 G11 **Judaea** cultural region Israel/West Bank
138 F11 **Judaean Hills** Heb. Haré Yehuda. hill range E Israel
138 H8 **Judaydah** Fr. Jdaïdé. Rīf Dimashq, W Syria 33°17′N 36°15′E
139 P11 **Judayyidat Hāmir** Al Anbār, S Iraq 31°50′N 41°50′E
109 U8 **Judenburg** Steiermark, C Austria 47°09′N 14°43′E
33 T8 **Judith River** ≈ Montana, NW USA
27 V11 **Judsonia** Arkansas, C USA 35°16′N 91°38′W
141 P14 **Jufrah, Wādī al** dry watercourse NW Yemen
Jugar see Sêrxü
Jugoslavija see Serbia
42 K10 **Juigalpa** Chontales, S Nicaragua 12°04′N 85°21′W
100 E9 **Juist** island NW Germany
Juisui see Ruisui
59 M21 **Juiz de Fora** Minas Gerais, SE Brazil 21°47′S 43°23′W
62 J5 **Jujuy** off. Provincia de Jujuy. ◈ province N Argentina
Jujuy see San Salvador de Jujuy
Jujuy, Provincia de see Jujuy
92 J11 **Jukkasjärvi** Lapp. Čohkkiras. Norrbotten, N Sweden 67°52′N 20°39′E
Jula see Gyula, Hungary
Jūlā see Jālū, Libya
37 W2 **Julesburg** Colorado, C USA 40°59′N 102°15′W
Julia Beterrae see Béziers
57 I17 **Juliaca** Puno, SE Peru 15°32′S 70°10′W
181 U6 **Julia Creek** Queensland, C Australia 20°40′S 141°49′E
35 V17 **Julian** California, W USA 33°04′N 116°36′W
98 H7 **Julianadorp** Noord-Holland, NW Netherlands 52°53′N 04°43′E
109 S11 **Julian Alps** Ger. Julische Alpen, It. Alpi Giulie, Slvn. Julijske Alpe. ▲▲ Italy/Slovenia
55 V11 **Juliana Top** ▲ C Surinam 03°39′N 56°36′W
Julianehåb see Qaqortoq
Julijske Alpe see Julian Alps
40 J6 **Julimes** Chihuahua, N Mexico 28°29′N 105°21′W
Julio Briga see Bragança
Juliobriga see Logroño
61 G15 **Júlio de Castilhos** Rio Grande do Sul, S Brazil 29°14′S 53°42′W
Juliomagus see Angers
Julische Alpen see Julian Alps
Jullundur see Jalandhar
147 N11 **Juma** Rus. Dzhuma. Samarqand Viloyati, C Uzbekistan 39°43′N 66°37′E
161 O3 **Juma He** ≈ E China
81 L18 **Jumba** prev. Jumboo. Jubbada Hoose, S Somalia 0°12′S 42°34′E
Jumboo see Jumba
35 Y11 **Jumbo Peak** ▲ Nevada, W USA 36°12′N 114°09′W
105 R12 **Jumilla** Murcia, SE Spain 38°28′N 01°19′W
153 N10 **Jumla** Mid Western, NW Nepal 29°22′N 82°13′E
Jummoo see Jammu
Jumna see Yamuna
Jumporn see Chumphon
30 K5 **Jump River** ≈ Wisconsin, N USA
154 B11 **Jūnāgadh** var. Junagarh. Gujarāt, W India 21°32′N 70°32′E
Junagarh see Jūnāgadh
161 Q6 **Junan** var. Shizilu. Shandong, E China 35°11′N 118°47′E
62 G11 **Juncal, Cerro** ▲ C Chile 33°03′S 70°02′W
25 Q10 **Junction** Texas, SW USA 30°31′N 99°48′W
36 K6 **Junction** Utah, W USA 38°14′N 112°13′W
27 O4 **Junction City** Kansas, C USA 39°02′N 96°51′W
32 F13 **Junction City** Oregon, NW USA 44°13′N 123°12′W
60 M10 **Jundiaí** São Paulo, S Brazil 23°10′S 46°54′W
39 X12 **Juneau** state capital Alaska, USA 58°13′N 134°11′W
30 M8 **Juneau** Wisconsin, N USA 43°23′N 88°42′W
105 U6 **Juneda** Cataluña, NE Spain 41°33′N 00°49′E
183 Q9 **Junee** New South Wales, SE Australia 34°51′S 147°33′E
35 R8 **June Lake** California, W USA 37°46′N 119°04′W
Jungbunzlau see Mladá Boleslav
158 L4 **Junggar Pendi** Eng. Dzungarian Basin. basin NW China
99 N24 **Junglinster** Grevenmacher, C Luxembourg 49°43′N 06°15′E
18 F14 **Juniata River** ≈ Pennsylvania, NE USA
61 B20 **Junín** Buenos Aires, E Argentina 34°36′S 61°02′W
57 E14 **Junín** Junín, C Peru 11°11′S 76°00′W
57 F14 **Junín** off. Departamento de Junín. ◈ department C Peru
63 H15 **Junín de los Andes** Neuquén, W Argentina 39°57′S 71°05′W
Junín, Departamento de see Junín
57 D14 **Junín, Lago de** ◎ C Peru
Junīyah see Joûnié
Junkseylon see Phuket
160 I11 **Junlian** Sichuan, C China 28°11′N 104°31′E
25 O11 **Juno** Texas, SW USA 30°09′N 101°07′W
92 J11 **Junosuando** Lapp. Čunusavvon. Norrbotten, N Sweden 67°25′N 22°28′E
93 H16 **Junsele** Västernorrland, C Sweden 63°42′N 16°54′E
Junten see Sunch'ŏn
32 L14 **Juntura** Oregon, NW USA 43°43′N 118°05′W
93 N14 **Juntusranta** Oulu, E Finland 65°12′N 29°30′E
118 H11 **Juodupė** Panevėžys, NE Lithuania 56°07′N 25°37′E
119 H14 **Juozapinės Kalnas** ▲ SE Lithuania 54°29′N 25°27′E
99 K19 **Juprelle** Liège, E Belgium 50°43′N 05°31′E
80 D13 **Jur** ≈ W South Sudan
103 S9 **Jura** ◈ department E France
108 C7 **Jura** ◈ canton NW Switzerland
108 B8 **Jura** var. Jura Mountains. ▲▲ France/Switzerland
96 G12 **Jura** island SW Scotland, United Kingdom
Juraciszki see Yuratsishki
54 C8 **Juradó** Chocó, NW Colombia 07°07′N 77°45′W
Jura Mountains see Jura
96 G12 **Jura, Sound of** strait W Scotland, United Kingdom
139 V15 **Juraybīyāt, Bi'r** well S Iraq
118 E13 **Jurbarkas** Ger. Georgenburg, Jurburg. Tauragė, W Lithuania 55°04′N 22°45′E
99 F20 **Jurbise** Hainaut, SW Belgium 50°33′N 03°54′E
Jurburg see Jurbarkas
118 F9 **Jūrmala** C Latvia 56°57′N 23°42′E
58 D13 **Juruá** Amazonas, NW Brazil 03°08′S 65°59′W
48 F7 **Juruá, Rio** var. Río Yuruá. ≈ Brazil/Peru
59 G16 **Juruena** Mato Grosso, W Brazil 10°32′S 58°38′W
59 G16 **Juruena, Rio** ≈ W Brazil
165 Q6 **Jūsan-ko** ◎ Honshū, C Japan
25 O6 **Justiceburg** Texas, SW USA 32°57′N 101°07′W
Justinianopolis see Kırşehir
62 K11 **Justo Daract** San Luis, C Argentina 33°52′S 65°12′W
59 C14 **Jutaí** Amazonas, W Brazil 05°10′S 68°45′W
58 C13 **Jutaí, Rio** ≈ NW Brazil
100 N13 **Jüterbog** Brandenburg, E Germany 51°58′N 13°06′E
42 E6 **Jutiapa** Jutiapa, S Guatemala 14°18′N 89°52′W
42 A3 **Jutiapa** off. Departamento de Jutiapa. ◈ department SE Guatemala
Jutiapa, Departamento de see Jutiapa
42 J6 **Juticalpa** Olancho, C Honduras 14°39′N 86°12′W
82 I13 **Jutila** North Western, NW Zambia 12°33′S 26°09′E
Jutland see Jylland
84 F8 **Jutland Bank** undersea feature SE North Sea 56°50′N 07°20′E
93 N16 **Juuka** Itä-Suomi, E Finland 63°12′N 29°17′E
93 N17 **Juva** Itä-Suomi, E Finland 61°55′N 27°54′E
Juvavum see Salzburg
44 A6 **Juventud, Isla de la** var. Isla de Pinos, Eng. Isle of Youth; prev. The Isle of the Pines. island W Cuba
161 Q5 **Juxian** var. Chengyang, Ju Xian. Shandong, E China 35°33′N 118°45′E
Ju Xian see Juxian
161 P6 **Juye** Shandong, E China 35°26′N 116°04′E
113 O15 **Južna Morava** Ger. Südliche Morava. ≈ SE Serbia
83 H20 **Jwaneng** Southern, S Botswana 24°35′N 24°45′E
95 I23 **Jyderup** Sjælland, E Denmark 55°40′N 11°25′E
95 F22 **Jylland** Eng. Jutland. peninsula W Denmark
Jyrgalan see Dzhergalan
93 M17 **Jyväskylä** Länsi-Suomi, C Finland 62°08′N 25°47′E

K

38 D9 **Ka'a'awa** var. Kaaawa. O'ahu, Hawaii, USA, C Pacific Ocean 21°33′N 157°47′W
Kaaawa see Ka'a'awa
81 G16 **Kaabong** NE Uganda 03°30′N 34°08′E
Kaaden see Kadaň
Kaafu Atoll see Male' Atoll
55 V9 **Kaaimanston** Sipaliwini, N Surinam 05°06′N 56°04′W
Kaakhka see Kaka
Kaala see Caála
187 O16 **Kaala-Gomen** Province Nord, W New Caledonia 20°40′S 164°24′E
92 L9 **Kaamanen** Lapp. Gámas. Lappi, N Finland 69°05′N 27°16′E
Kaapstad see Cape Town
Kaarasjoki see Karasjok
Kaaresuanto see Karesuando
92 J10 **Kaaresuvanto** Lapp. Gárassavon. Lappi, N Finland 68°28′N 22°29′E
93 K19 **Kaarina** Länsi-Suomi, SW Finland 60°24′N 22°25′E
99 I14 **Kaatsheuvel** Noord-Brabant, S Netherlands 51°39′N 05°02′E
93 N16 **Kaavi** Itä-Suomi, C Finland 62°58′N 28°30′E
Kaba see Habahe
171 O14 **Kabaena, Pulau** island C Indonesia
Kabakly see Gabakly
76 J14 **Kabala** N Sierra Leone 09°40′N 11°36′W
81 E19 **Kabale** SW Uganda 01°15′S 29°58′E
55 U10 **Kabalebo Rivier** ≈ W Surinam
79 N22 **Kabalo** Katanga, SE Dem. Rep. Congo 06°02′S 26°55′E
79 O21 **Kabambare** Maniema, E Dem. Rep. Congo 04°40′S 27°41′E
145 W13 **Kabanbay** Kaz. Qabanbay; prev. Andreyevka, Kaz. Andreevka. Almaty, SE Kazakhstan 45°50′N 80°34′E
145 Q9 **Kabanbay Batyr** prev. Rozhdestvenka. Akmola, C Kazakhstan 50°51′N 71°25′E
187 Y15 **Kabara** prev. Kambara. island Lau Group, E Fiji
Kabardino-Balkaria see Kabardino-Balkarskaya Respublika
126 M15 **Kabardino-Balkarskaya Respublika** Eng. Kabardino-Balkaria. ◈ autonomous republic SW Russian Federation
79 O19 **Kabare** Sud-Kivu, E Dem. Rep. Congo 02°13′S 28°40′E
171 T11 **Kabarei** Papua, E Indonesia 0°01′S 130°58′E
171 P7 **Kabasalan** Mindanao, S Philippines 07°46′N 122°49′E
77 U15 **Kabba** Kogi, S Nigeria 07°48′N 06°07′E
92 I13 **Kåbdalis** Lapp. Goabddális. Norrbotten, N Sweden 66°08′N 20°03′E
138 M6 **Kabd aş Şārim** hill range E Syria
14 B7 **Kabenung Lake** ◎ Ontario, S Canada
29 W3 **Kabetogama Lake** ◎ Minnesota, N USA
Kabia, Pulau see Kabin, Pulau
79 M22 **Kabinda** Kasai-Oriental, SE Dem. Rep. Congo 06°09′S 24°29′E
Kabinda see Cabinda
171 O15 **Kabin, Pulau** var. Pulau Kabia. island W Indonesia
171 P16 **Kabir** Pulau Pantar, S Indonesia 08°15′S 124°12′E
149 T10 **Kabīrwāla** Punjab, E Pakistan 30°24′N 71°51′E
114 M9 **Kableshkovo** Burgas, E Bulgaria 42°65′N 27°34′E
78 I13 **Kabo** Ouham, NW Central African Republic 07°43′N 18°38′E
Kābol see Kābul
83 H14 **Kabompo** North Western, W Zambia 13°36′S 24°10′E
83 H14 **Kabompo** ≈ W Zambia
79 M22 **Kabongo** Katanga, SE Dem. Rep. Congo 07°20′S 25°34′E
120 K11 **Kaboudia, Rass** headland E Tunisia 35°13′N 11°09′E
124 J14 **Kabozha** Novgorodskaya Oblast', W Russian Federation 58°48′N 35°00′E
Kabūd Gonbad see Kalāt
142 L5 **Kabūd Rāhang** Hamadān, W Iran 35°12′N 48°44′E
82 L12 **Kabuko** Northern, NE Zambia 11°31′S 31°16′E
149 Q5 **Kābul** prev. Kābol. ● (Afghanistan) Kābul, E Afghanistan 34°34′N 69°08′E
149 Q5 **Kābul** ; prev. Kābol. ◈ province E Afghanistan
149 Q5 **Kābul** ✈ Kābul, E Afghanistan 34°31′N 69°11′E
149 R5 **Kabul** var. Daryā-ye Kābul. ≈ Afghanistan/Pakistan see also Kābul, Daryā-ye
Kabul see Kābul, Daryā-ye
149 S5 **Kābul, Daryā-ye** var. Kabul. ≈ Afghanistan/Pakistan see also Kabul
Kābul, Daryā-ye see Kabul
79 O25 **Kabunda** Katanga, SE Dem. Rep. Congo 12°21′S 29°14′E
171 R9 **Kaburuang, Pulau** island Kepulauan Talaud, N Indonesia
80 G8 **Kabushiya** River Nile, NE Sudan 16°54′N 33°41′E
83 J14 **Kabwe** Central, C Zambia 14°29′S 28°25′E
186 E7 **Kabwum** Morobe, C Papua New Guinea 06°04′S 147°09′E
113 N17 **Kačanik** Serb. Kačanik. S Kosovo 42°13′N 21°16′E
Kačanik see Kaçanik
118 F13 **Kačerginė** Kaunas, C Lithuania 54°55′N 23°40′E
117 S13 **Kacha** Avtonomna Respublika Krym, S Ukraine 44°46′N 33°33′E
154 A10 **Kachchh, Gulf of** var. Gulf of Cutch, Gulf of Kutch. gulf W India
154 I11 **Kachchhīdhāna** Madhya Pradesh, C India 21°33′N 78°54′E
149 Q11 **Kachchh, Rann of** var. Rann of Kachh, Rann of Kutch. salt marsh India/Pakistan
39 Q13 **Kachemak Bay** bay Alaska, USA
Kachh, Rann of see Kachchh, Rann of
77 V14 **Kachia** Kaduna, C Nigeria 09°52′N 08°00′E
167 N2 **Kachin State** ◈ state N Burma (Myanmar)
Kachiry see Kashyr
137 Q11 **Kaçkar Dağları** ▲▲ NE Turkey
155 C21 **Kadamatt Island** island Lakshadweep, India, N Indian Ocean
111 B15 **Kadaň** Ger. Kaaden. Ústecký Kraj, NW Czech Republic 50°24′N 13°16′E
1667 N11 **Kadan Kyun** prev. King Island. island Mergui Archipelago, S Burma (Myanmar)
187 X15 **Kadavu** prev. Kandavu. island S Fiji
187 X15 **Kadavu Passage** channel S Fiji
79 G16 **Kadéï** ≈ Cameroon/Central African Republic
Kadhimain see Al Kāẓimīyah
Kadijica see Kadiytsa
114 M13 **Kadıköy Barajı** ▣ NW Turkey
182 I8 **Kadina** South Australia 33°59′S 137°43′E
136 H15 **Kadınhanı** Konya, C Turkey 38°15′N 32°14′E
76 M14 **Kadiolo** Sikasso, S Mali 10°30′N 05°43′W
136 L16 **Kadirli** Osmaniye, S Turkey 37°22′N 36°05′E
114 G11 **Kadiytsa** Mac. Kadijica. ▲ Bulgaria/FYR Macedonia 41°48′N 22°58′E
28 L10 **Kadoka** South Dakota, N USA 43°49′N 101°30′W
127 N5 **Kadom** Ryazanskaya Oblast', W Russian Federation 54°35′N 42°27′E
83 K16 **Kadoma** prev. Gatooma. Mashonaland West, C Zimbabwe 18°22′S 29°55′E
80 E12 **Kadugli** Southern Kordofan, S Sudan 11°N 29°44′E
77 V14 **Kaduna** Kaduna, C Nigeria 10°32′N 07°26′E
77 V14 **Kaduna** ◈ state C Nigeria
77 V15 **Kaduna** ≈ N Nigeria
124 K14 **Kaduy** Vologodskaya Oblast', NW Russian Federation 59°10′N 37°11′E
154 E13 **Kadwa** ≈ W India
123 S9 **Kadykchan** Magadanskaya Oblast', E Russian Federation 62°54′N 146°53′E
Kadzharan see K'ajaran
125 T7 **Kadzherom** Respublika Komi, NW Russian Federation 64°42′N 55°51′E
Kadzhi-Say see Bokonbayevo
76 I10 **Kaédi** Gorgol, S Mauritania 16°12′N 13°32′W
78 G12 **Kaélé** Extrême-Nord, N Cameroon 10°05′N 14°28′E
38 C9 **Ka'ena Point** var. Kaena Point. headland O'ahu, Hawai'i, USA 21°34′N 158°16′W
184 J2 **Kaeo** Northland, North Island, New Zealand 35°03′S 173°40′E
163 X14 **Kaesŏng** var. Kaesŏng-si. S North Korea 37°58′N 126°31′E
Kaesŏng-si see Kaesŏng
Kaewieng see Kavieng
79 L24 **Kafakumba** Shaba, S Dem. Rep. Congo 09°39′S 23°43′E
Kafan see Kapan
77 V14 **Kafanchan** Kaduna, C Nigeria 09°32′N 08°18′E
Kaffa see Feodosiya
76 G11 **Kaffrine** C Senegal 14°07′N 15°27′W

◆ Country
● Country Capital
◇ Dependent Territory
○ Dependent Territory Capital
◈ Administrative Regions
✈ International Airport
▲ Mountain
▲▲ Mountain Range
Volcano
≈ River
◎ Lake
▣ Reservoir

Kafiréas, Akrotírio see Ntóro, Kávo
115 I19 **Kafiréos, Stenó** strait Évvoia/Kykládes, Greece, Aegean Sea
Kafirnigan see Kofarnihon
Kafo see Kafu
75 W7 **Kafr ash Shaykh** var. Kafrel Sheik, Kafr el Sheikh. N Egypt 31°07′N 30°56′E
Kafr el Sheikh see Kafr ash Shaykh
81 F17 **Kafu** var. Kafo. ~ W Uganda
83 J15 **Kafue** Lusaka, SE Zambia 15°44′S 28°10′E
83 I14 **Kafue** ~ C Zambia
67 T13 **Kafue Flats** plain C Zambia
164 K12 **Kaga** Ishikawa, Honshū, SW Japan 36°18′N 136°19′E
79 J14 **Kaga Bandoro** prev. Fort-Crampel. Nana-Grébizi, C Central African Republic 06°54′N 19°10′E
81 E18 **Kagadi** W Uganda 0°57′N 30°52′E
38 H17 **Kagalaska Island** island Aleutian Islands, Alaska, USA
Kagan see Kogon
Kaganovichabad see Kolkhozobod
Kagarlyk see Kaharlyk
164 H14 **Kagawa** off. Kagawa-ken. ◐ prefecture Shikoku, SW Japan
Kagawa-ken see Kagawa
154 J13 **Kagaznagar** Andhra Pradesh, C India 19°25′N 79°30′E
93 J14 **Kåge** Västerbotten, N Sweden 64°49′N 21°00′E
81 E19 **Kagera** var. Ziwa Magharibi, Eng. West Lake. ◐ region NW Tanzania
81 E19 **Kagera** var. Akagera. ~ Rwanda/Tanzania see also Akagera
76 L5 **Kâgheț** var. Karet. physical region N Mauritania
Kagi see Jiayi
137 S12 **Kağızman** Kars, NE Turkey 40°08′N 43°07′E
188 I6 **Kagman Point** headland Saipan, S Northern Mariana Islands
164 C16 **Kagoshima** var. Kagosima. Kagoshima, Kyūshū, SW Japan 31°37′N 130°33′E
164 C16 **Kagoshima** off. Kagoshima-ken, var. Kagosima. ◐ prefecture Kyūshū, SW Japan
Kagoshima-ken see Kagoshima
Kagosima see Kagoshima
Kagul see Cahul
Kagul, Ozero see Kahul, Ozero
38 B8 **Kahala Point** headland Kaua'i, Hawai'i, USA 22°08′N 159°17′W
81 F21 **Kahama** Shinyanga, NW Tanzania 03°48′S 32°36′E
117 P5 **Kaharlyk** Rus. Kagarlyk. Kyyivs'ka Oblast', N Ukraine 49°50′N 30°50′E
169 T13 **Kahayan, Sungai** ~ Borneo, C Indonesia
79 I22 **Kahemba** Bandundu, SW Dem. Rep. Congo 07°20′S 19°00′E
185 A23 **Kaherekoau Mountains** ⛰ South Island, New Zealand
143 W14 **Kahīrī** var. Kūhīrī. Sīstān va Balūchestān, SE Iran 26°55′N 61°04′E
101 L16 **Kahla** Thüringen, C Germany 50°49′N 11°33′E
101 G15 **Kahler Asten** ▲ W Germany 51°11′N 08°32′E
149 Q4 **Kahmard, Daryā-ye** prev. Darya-i-surkhab. ~ NE Afghanistan
143 T13 **Kahnūj** Kermān, SE Iran 28°N 57°41′E
27 V1 **Kahoka** Missouri, C USA 40°24′N 91°44′W
38 E10 **Kaho'olawe** var. Kahoolawe. island Hawai'i, USA, C Pacific Ocean
Kahoolawe see Kaho'olawe
136 M16 **Kahramanmaraş** var. Kahraman Maraş, Maraş, Marash. Kahramanmaraş, S Turkey 37°34′N 36°54′E
136 L15 **Kahramanmaraş** var. Kahraman Maraş, Maraş, Marash. ◐ province C Turkey
Kahraman Maraş see Kahramanmaraş
Kahror/Kahror Pakka see Kahror Pakka
149 T11 **Kahror Pakka** var. Kahror, Koror Pacca. Punjab, E Pakistan 29°38′N 71°59′E
137 N15 **Kâhta** Adıyaman, S Turkey 37°48′N 38°35′E
38 D8 **Kahuku** O'ahu, Hawai'i, USA, C Pacific Ocean 21°40′N 157°57′W
38 D8 **Kahuku Point** headland O'ahu, Hawai'i, USA 21°42′N 157°59′W
116 M12 **Kahul, Ozero** var. Lacul Cahul, Rus. Ozero Kagul. ◎ Moldova/Ukraine
143 V11 **Kahūrak** Sīstān va Balūchestān, SE Iran 29°25′N 59°38′E
184 G13 **Kahurangi Point** headland South Island, New Zealand 40°41′S 171°57′E
149 V6 **Kahūta** Punjab, E Pakistan 33°38′N 73°27′E
77 S14 **Kaiama** Kwara, W Nigeria 09°37′N 03°58′E
186 D7 **Kaiapit** Morobe, C Papua New Guinea 06°12′S 146°09′E
185 I18 **Kaiapoi** Canterbury, South Island, New Zealand 43°23′S 172°40′E
36 K9 **Kaibab Plateau** plain Arizona, SW USA
171 U14 **Kai Besar, Pulau** island Kepulauan Kai, E Indonesia
36 L9 **Kaibito Plateau** plain Arizona, SW USA
158 K6 **Kaidu He** var. Karaxahar. ~ NW China
55 S10 **Kaieteur Falls** waterfall C Guyana
161 O6 **Kaifeng** Henan, C China 34°47′N 114°20′E
184 J3 **Kaihu** Northland, North Island, New Zealand 35°47′S 173°39′E
Kaihua see Wenshan
171 U14 **Kai Kecil, Pulau** island Kepulauan Kai, E Indonesia
169 U16 **Kai, Kepulauan** prev. Kei Islands. island group Maluku, SE Indonesia
184 J3 **Kaikohe** Northland, North Island, New Zealand 35°25′S 173°48′E
185 J16 **Kaikoura** Canterbury, South Island, New Zealand 42°22′S 173°40′E
185 J16 **Kaikoura Peninsula** peninsula South Island, New Zealand
Kailas Range see Gangdisê Shan
160 K12 **Kaili** Guizhou, S China 26°34′N 107°58′E
38 F10 **Kailua** Maui, Hawaii, USA, C Pacific Ocean 20°53′N 156°13′W
Kailua see Kalaoa
38 G11 **Kailua-Kona** var. Kona. Hawaii, USA, C Pacific Ocean 19°43′N 155°58′W
186 B7 **Kaim** ~ W Papua New Guinea
171 X14 **Kaima** Papua, E Indonesia 05°36′S 138°39′E
184 M7 **Kaimai Range** ⛰ North Island, New Zealand
114 E13 **Kaïmaktsalán** var. Kajmakčalan. ▲ Greece/FYR Macedonia 40°57′N 21°48′E see also Kajmakčalan
Kaïmaktsalán see Kajmakčalan
185 C20 **Kaimanawa Mountains** ⛰ North Island, New Zealand
118 E4 **Käina** Ger. Keinis; prev. Keina. Hiiumaa, W Estonia 58°50′N 22°49′E
109 V7 **Kainach** ~ SE Austria
164 I14 **Kainan** Tokushima, Shikoku, SW Japan 33°36′N 134°20′E
164 H15 **Kainan** Wakayama, Honshū, SW Japan 34°09′N 135°12′E
147 U7 **Kaindy** Kir. Kayyngdy. Chuyskaya Oblast', N Kyrgyzstan 42°48′N 73°39′E
77 T14 **Kainji Dam** dam W Nigeria
Kainji Lake see Kainji Reservoir
77 T14 **Kainji Reservoir** var. Kainji Lake. ⊠ W Nigeria
186 D8 **Kaintiba** var. Kamina. Gulf, S Papua New Guinea 07°29′S 146°04′E
92 K12 **Kainulasjärvi** Norrbotten, N Sweden 67°00′N 22°31′E
184 K5 **Kaipara Harbour** harbour North Island, New Zealand
152 I10 **Kairāna** Uttar Pradesh, N India 29°24′N 77°10′E
74 M6 **Kairouan** var. Al Qayrawān. E Tunisia 35°46′N 10°11′E
Kaisaria see Kayseri
101 F20 **Kaiserslautern** Rheinland-Pfalz, SW Germany 49°27′N 07°46′E
118 G13 **Kaišiadorys** Kaunas, S Lithuania 54°51′N 24°27′E
184 I2 **Kaitaia** Northland, North Island, New Zealand 35°07′S 173°13′E
185 E24 **Kaitangata** Otago, South Island, New Zealand 46°18′S 169°52′E
152 I9 **Kaithal** Haryāna, NW India 29°47′N 76°26′E
Kaitong see Tongyu
169 N13 **Kait, Tanjung** headland Sumatera, W Indonesia 03°13′S 106°03′E
38 E9 **Kaiwi Channel** channel Hawai'i, USA, C Pacific Ocean
160 K9 **Kaixian** var. Hanfeng. Sichuan, C China 31°13′N 108°25′E
163 V11 **Kaiyuan** var. K'ai-yüan. Liaoning, NE China 42°33′N 124°04′E
160 H14 **Kaiyuan** Yunnan, SW China 23°42′N 103°14′E
K'ai-yüan see Kaiyuan
39 O9 **Kaiyuh Mountains** ⛰ Alaska, USA
93 M15 **Kajaani** Swe. Kajana. Oulu, C Finland 64°17′N 27°46′E
149 N7 **Kajakī, Band-e** ⊠ C Afghanistan
Kajan see Kayan, Sungai
Kajana see Kajaani
137 V13 **K'ajaran** Rus. Kadzharan. SE Armenia 39°10′N 46°09′E
Kajisay see Bokonbayevo
113 O20 **Kajmakčalan** var. Kaïmaktsalán. ▲ S FYR Macedonia 40°57′N 21°48′E see also Kaïmaktsalán
Kajmakčalan see Kaïmaktsalán
Kajnar see Kaynar
149 N6 **Kajrān** Dāykundī, C Afghanistan 33°12′N 65°28′E
149 N5 **Kaj Rūd** ~ C Afghanistan
146 G14 **Kaka** Rus. Kaakhka. Ahal Welaýaty, S Turkmenistan 37°20′N 59°37′E
12 C12 **Kakabeka Falls** Ontario, S Canada 48°24′N 89°40′W
83 F23 **Kakamas** Northern Cape, W South Africa 28°45′S 20°33′E
81 H18 **Kakamega** Western, W Kenya 0°17′N 34°47′E
112 H13 **Kakanj** Federacija Bosna I Hercegovina, C Bosnia and Herzegovina 44°06′N 18°07′E
185 F22 **Kakanui Mountains** ⛰ South Island, New Zealand
184 K11 **Kakaramea** Taranaki, North Island, New Zealand 39°42′S 174°27′E
76 J16 **Kakata** C Liberia 06°35′N 10°19′W
184 M11 **Kakatahi** Manawatu-Wanganui, North Island, New Zealand 39°40′S 175°20′E
113 M23 **Kakavi** Gjirokastër, S Albania 39°55′N 20°19′E
147 O14 **Kakaydi** Surkhondaryo Viloyati, S Uzbekistan 37°37′N 67°30′E
164 F13 **Kake** Hiroshima, Honshū, SW Japan 34°37′N 132°17′E
39 X13 **Kake** Kupreanof Island, Alaska, USA 56°58′N 133°57′W
171 P14 **Kakea** Pulau Wowoni, C Indonesia 04°09′S 123°06′E
164 M14 **Kakegawa** Shizuoka, Honshū, S Japan 34°47′N 138°02′E
165 V16 **Kakeroma-jima** Kagoshima, SW Japan
143 T6 **Kākhak** Khorāsān, E Iran 34°09′N 58°34′E
118 L11 **Kakhanavichy** Rus. Kokhanovichi. Vitsyebskaya Voblasts', N Belarus 55°52′N 28°08′E
39 P13 **Kakhonak** Alaska, USA 59°26′N 154°48′W
117 S10 **Kakhovka** Khersons'ka Oblast', S Ukraine 46°40′N 33°30′E
117 U9 **Kakhovs'ke Vodoskhovyshche** Rus. Kakhovskoye Vodokhranilishche. ⊠ SE Ukraine
Kakhovskoye Vodokhranilishche see Kakhovs'ke Vodoskhovyshche
117 T11 **Kakhovs'kyy Kanal** canal S Ukraine
Kakia see Khakhea
155 L16 **Kākināda** prev. Cocanada. Andhra Pradesh, E India 16°56′N 82°13′E
Käkisalmi see Priozersk
164 I13 **Kakogawa** Hyōgo, Honshū, SW Japan 34°49′N 134°52′E
81 F18 **Kakoge** C Uganda 01°03′N 32°30′E
145 O7 **Kak, Ozero** ◎ N Kazakhstan
Ka-Krem see Malyy Yenisey
Kakshaal-Too, Khrebet see Kokshaal-Tau
39 S5 **Kaktovik** Alaska, USA 70°08′N 143°37′W
165 Q11 **Kakuda** Miyagi, Honshū, C Japan 37°59′N 140°48′E
165 Q8 **Kakunodate** Akita, Honshū, C Japan 39°37′N 140°35′E
Kalaallit Nunaat see Greenland
149 T7 **Kālābāgh** Punjab, E Pakistan 33°00′N 71°35′E
171 Q16 **Kalabahi** Pulau Alor, S Indonesia 08°14′S 124°32′E
188 I5 **Kalabera** Saipan, S Northern Mariana Islands
83 G14 **Kalabo** Western, W Zambia 15°00′S 22°37′E
126 M9 **Kalach** Voronezhskaya Oblast', W Russian Federation 50°24′N 41°00′E
127 N10 **Kalach-na-Donu** Volgogradskaya Oblast', SW Russian Federation 48°45′N 43°29′E
166 K5 **Kaladan** ~ W Burma (Myanmar)
14 K14 **Kaladar** Ontario, SE Canada 44°38′N 77°06′W
38 G13 **Ka Lae** var. South Cape, South Point. headland Hawai'i, USA, C Pacific Ocean 18°54′N 155°40′W
83 G19 **Kalahari Desert** desert Southern Africa
38 B8 **Kalāheo** var. Kalaheo. Kaua'i, Hawaii, USA, C Pacific Ocean 21°55′N 159°31′W
Kalaheo see Kalāheo
Kalaikhum see Qal'aikhum
Kala-i-Mor see Galaýmor
93 K15 **Kalajoki** Oulu, W Finland 64°15′N 24°E
Kalak see Eski Kaļak
Kal al Sraghna see El Kelâa Srarhna
32 G10 **Kalama** Washington, NW USA 46°00′N 122°50′W
Kalámai see Kalámata
115 G14 **Kalamariá** Kentrikí Makedonía, N Greece 40°37′N 22°58′E
115 C15 **Kalamás** var. Thiamis; prev. Thýamis. ~ W Greece
115 E21 **Kalámata** prev. Kalámai. Pelopónnisos, S Greece 37°02′N 22°07′E
148 L16 **Kalamat, Khor** Eng. Kalmat Lagoon. lagoon SW Pakistan
148 L16 **Kalamat, Khor** Eng. Kalmat Lagoon. lagoon SW Pakistan
31 P10 **Kalamazoo** Michigan, N USA 42°17′N 85°35′W
31 P9 **Kalamazoo River** ~ Michigan, N USA
Kalambaka see Kalampáka
117 S13 **Kalamits'ka Zatoka** Rus. Kalamitskiy Zaliv. gulf S Ukraine
Kalamitskiy Zaliv see Kalamits'ka Zatoka
115 H18 **Kálamos** Attikí, C Greece 38°16′N 23°51′E
115 C18 **Kálamos** island Iónioi Nísia, Greece, C Mediterranean Sea
115 D15 **Kalampáka** var. Kalambaka. Thessalía, C Greece 39°43′N 21°36′E
Kalan see Călan, Romania
Kalan see Tunceli, Turkey
117 S11 **Kalanchak** Khersons'ka Oblast', S Ukraine 46°14′N 33°19′E
38 G11 **Kalaoa** var. Kailua. Hawaii, USA, C Pacific Ocean 19°43′N 155°59′W
171 O15 **Kalaotoa, Pulau** island W Indonesia
155 J24 **Kala Oya** ~ NW Sri Lanka
Kalarash see Călărași
93 H17 **Kälarne** Jämtland, C Sweden 63°00′N 16°10′E
143 V15 **Kalar Rūd** ~ SE Iran
169 R9 **Kalasin** var. Muang Kalasin. Kalasin, E Thailand 16°29′N 103°31′E
143 U4 **Kalāt** var. Kabūd Gonbad. Khorāsān, NE Iran 37°02′N 59°46′E
149 O11 **Kālat** var. Kelat, Khelat. Baluchistān, SW Pakistan 29°01′N 66°38′E
Kalāt see Qalāt
115 J14 **Kalathriá, Akrotírio** headland Samothráki, NE Greece 40°24′N 25°34′E
193 W147 **Kalau** island Tongatapu Group, SE Tonga
38 E9 **Kalaupapa** Moloka'i, Hawaii, USA, C Pacific Ocean 21°11′N 156°59′W
127 N13 **Kalaus** ~ SW Russian Federation
Kalávrita see Kalávryta
115 E19 **Kalávryta** var. Kalávrita. Dytikí Elláda, S Greece 38°02′N 22°06′E
141 Y10 **Kalbān** W Oman 20°19′N 58°40′E
180 H11 **Kalbarri** Western Australia 27°43′S 114°08′E
Kalbinskiy Khrebet see Khrebet Kalba
144 G10 **Kaldygayty** ~ W Kazakhstan
136 I12 **Kalecik** Ankara, N Turkey 40°08′N 33°27′E
79 O19 **Kalehe** Sud-Kivu, E Dem. Rep. Congo 02°05′S 28°52′E
79 P22 **Kalemie** prev. Albertville. Katanga, SE Dem. Rep. Congo 05°55′S 29°09′E
166 L4 **Kalemyo** Sagaing, W Burma (Myanmar) 23°11′N 94°03′E
82 H12 **Kalene Hill** North Western, NW Zambia 11°10′S 24°12′E
167 T11 **Kalêng** prev. Phumĭ Kalêng. Stœng Trêng, NE Cambodia 13°57′N 106°17′E
Kale Sultanie see Çanakkale
124 I7 **Kalevala** Respublika Kareliya, NW Russian Federation 65°12′N 31°16′E
166 L4 **Kalewa** Sagaing, C Burma (Myanmar) 23°15′N 94°19′E
Kalgan see Zhangjiakou
39 Q12 **Kalgin Island** island Alaska, USA
180 L12 **Kalgoorlie** Western Australia 30°51′S 121°27′E
Kali see Sārda
115 E17 **Kaliakoúda** ▲ C Greece 38°47′N 21°42′E
114 O8 **Kaliakra, Nos** headland NE Bulgaria 43°22′N 28°28′E
115 F19 **Kaliánoi** Pelopónnisos, S Greece 37°55′N 22°28′E
115 N24 **Kalí Límni** ▲ Kárpathos, SE Greece 35°34′N 27°08′E
79 N20 **Kalima** Maniema, E Dem. Rep. Congo 02°34′S 26°27′E
169 S11 **Kalimantan** Eng. Indonesian Borneo. ◐ geopolitical region Borneo, C Indonesia
169 Q11 **Kalimantan Barat** off. Propinsi Kalimantan Barat, Eng. West Borneo, West Kalimantan. ◐ province N Indonesia
Kalimantan Barat, Propinsi see Kalimantan Barat
169 T13 **Kalimantan Selatan** off. Propinsi Kalimantan Selatan, Eng. South Borneo, South Kalimantan. ◐ province N Indonesia
Kalimantan Selatan, Propinsi see Kalimantan Selatan
169 R12 **Kalimantan Tengah** off. Propinsi Kalimantan Tengah, Eng. Central Borneo, Central Kalimantan. ◐ province N Indonesia
Kalimantan Tengah, Propinsi see Kalimantan Tengah
169 U10 **Kalimantan Timur** off. Propinsi Kalimantan Timur, Eng. East Borneo, East Kalimantan. ◐ province N Indonesia
Kalimantan Timur, Propinsi see Kalimantan Timur
Kálimnos see Kálymnos
153 S12 **Kālimpang** West Bengal, NE India 27°02′N 88°34′E
Kalinin see Tver'
Kalinin see Boldumsaz
Kalininabad see Kalininobod
126 B3 **Kaliningrad** Kaliningradskaya Oblast', W Russian Federation 54°48′N 21°33′E
Kaliningrad see Kaliningradskaya Oblast'
126 A3 **Kaliningradskaya Oblast'** var. Kaliningrad. ◐ province and enclave W Russian Federation
Kalinino see Tashir
147 P14 **Kalininobod** Rus. Kalininabad. SW Tajikistan 37°49′N 68°55′E
127 O8 **Kalininsk** Saratovskaya Oblast', W Russian Federation 51°31′N 44°25′E
Kalininsk see Boldumsaz
Kalinisk see Cupcina
119 M19 **Kalinkavichy** Rus. Kalinkovichi. Homyel'skaya Voblasts', SE Belarus 52°08′N 29°19′E
Kalinkovichi see Kalinkavichy
81 G18 **Kaliro** SE Uganda 0°54′N 33°30′E
Kalisch/Kalish see Kalisz
33 O7 **Kalispell** Montana, NW USA 48°12′N 114°18′W
110 I13 **Kalisz** Ger. Kalisch, Rus. Kalish; anc. Calisia. Wielkopolskie, C Poland 51°46′N 18°04′E
110 F9 **Kalisz Pomorski** Ger. Kallies. Zachodnio-pomorskie, NW Poland 53°55′N 15°55′E
126 M10 **Kalitva** ~ SW Russian Federation
81 F21 **Kaliua** Tabora, C Tanzania 05°03′S 31°48′E
92 K13 **Kalix** Norrbotten, N Sweden 65°51′N 23°14′E
92 K12 **Kalixälven** ~ N Sweden
92 J11 **Kalixfors** Norrbotten, N Sweden 67°45′N 20°20′E
145 T8 **Kalkaman** Kaz. Qalqaman. Pavlodar, NE Kazakhstan 51°57′N 75°58′E
Kalkandelen see Tetovo
181 O4 **Kalkarindji** Northern Territory, N Australia 17°32′S 130°40′E
31 P6 **Kalkaska** Michigan, N USA 44°44′N 85°11′W
93 F16 **Kall** Jämtland, C Sweden 63°31′N 13°16′E
189 X2 **Kallalen** var. Calalen. island Ratak Chain, SE Marshall Islands
118 J5 **Kallaste** Ger. Krasnogor. Tartumaa, SE Estonia 58°40′N 27°12′E
93 N16 **Kallavesi** ◎ SE Finland
115 F17 **Kallídromo** ▲ C Greece
Kallies see Kalisz Pomorski
95 M22 **Kallinge** Blekinge, S Sweden 56°14′N 15°17′E
115 L16 **Kalloní** Lésvos, E Greece 39°14′N 26°16′E
93 F16 **Kallsjön** ◎ C Sweden
95 N21 **Kalmar** var. Calmar. Kalmar, S Sweden 56°40′N 16°22′E
95 M19 **Kalmar** var. Calmar. ◐ county S Sweden
95 N20 **Kalmarsund** strait S Sweden
Kalmat Lagoon see Kalamat, Khor
117 X9 **Kal'mius** ~ E Ukraine
99 H15 **Kalmthout** Antwerpen, N Belgium 51°24′N 04°27′E
Kalmykia/Kalmykiya-Khal'mg Tangch, Respublika see Kalmykiya, Respublika
127 O12 **Kalmykiya, Respublika** var. Respublika Kalmykiya-Khal'mg Tangch, Eng. Kalmykia; prev. Kalmytskaya ASSR. ◐ autonomous republic SW Russian Federation
Kalmytskaya ASSR see Kalmykiya, Respublika
118 F9 **Kalnciems** C Latvia 56°46′N 23°37′E
114 L10 **Kalnitsa** ~ SE Bulgaria
111 J24 **Kalocsa** Bács-Kiskun, S Hungary 46°31′N 19°00′E
114 J9 **Kalofer** Plovdiv, C Bulgaria 42°36′N 25°00′E
38 E10 **Kalohi Channel** channel C Pacific Ocean
83 I16 **Kalomo** Southern, S Zambia 17°02′S 26°29′E
29 X14 **Kalona** Iowa, C USA 41°28′N 91°42′W
115 K22 **Kalotási, Akrotírio** cape Amorgós, Kykládes, Greece, Aegean Sea
152 J8 **Kalpa** Himāchal Pradesh, N India 31°33′N 78°16′E
115 C15 **Kalpáki** Ípeiros, W Greece 39°53′N 20°38′E
155 C22 **Kalpeni Island** island Lakshadweep, India, N Indian Ocean
152 K13 **Kālpi** Uttar Pradesh, N India 26°07′N 79°44′E
158 G7 **Kalpin** Xinjiang Uygur Zizhiqu, NW China 40°35′N 78°52′E
149 P16 **Kalri Lake** ◎ SE Pakistan
143 R5 **Kāl Shūr** ~ N Iran
39 N11 **Kalskag** Alaska, USA 61°32′N 160°15′W
Kalsø see Kalsoy
95 B18 **Kalsoy** Dan. Kalsø. island N Faeroe Islands
39 O9 **Kaltag** Alaska, USA 64°19′N 158°43′W
108 H7 **Kaltbrunn** Sankt Gallen, NE Switzerland 47°11′N 09°00′E
Kaltdorf see Pruszków
77 X14 **Kaltungo** Gombe, E Nigeria 09°49′N 11°22′E
126 K4 **Kaluga** Kaluzhskaya Oblast', W Russian Federation 54°31′N 36°16′E
155 J26 **Kalu Ganga** ~ S Sri Lanka
82 J13 **Kalulushi** Copperbelt, C Zambia 12°50′S 28°03′E
180 M2 **Kalumburu** Western Australia 14°11′S 126°40′E
95 H23 **Kalundborg** Sjælland, E Denmark 55°42′N 11°06′E
82 K11 **Kalungwishi** ~ N Zambia
149 T8 **Kalur Kot** Punjab, E Pakistan 32°08′N 71°20′E
116 I6 **Kalush** Pol. Kałusz. Ivano-Frankivs'ka Oblast', W Ukraine 49°02′N 24°20′E
Kałusz see Kalush
110 N11 **Kałuszyn** Mazowieckie, C Poland 52°12′N 21°43′E
155 J26 **Kalutara** Western Province, SW Sri Lanka 06°35′N 79°59′E
Kaluwawa see Fergusson Island
126 I5 **Kaluzhskaya Oblast'** ◐ province W Russian Federation
119 E14 **Kalvarija** Pol. Kalwaria. Marijampolė, S Lithuania 54°25′N 23°13′E
93 K15 **Kälviä** Länsi-Suomi, W Finland 63°53′N 23°30′E
109 U6 **Kalwang** Steiermark, E Austria 47°25′N 14°48′E
Kalwaria see Kalvarija
154 D13 **Kalyān** Mahārāshtra, W India 19°17′N 73°11′E
124 K16 **Kalyazin** Tverskaya Oblast', W Russian Federation 57°15′N 37°53′E
115 D18 **Kalydón** anc. Calydon. site of ancient city Dytikí Elláda, C Greece
115 M21 **Kálymnos** var. Kálimnos. Kálymnos, Dodekánisa, Greece, Aegean Sea 36°57′N 26°59′E
115 M21 **Kálymnos** var. Kálimnos. island Dodekánisa, Greece, Aegean Sea
117 O5 **Kalynivka** Kyyivs'ka Oblast', N Ukraine 50°14′N 30°16′E
117 N6 **Kalynivka** Vinnyts'ka Oblast', C Ukraine 49°27′N 28°32′E
145 W15 **Kalzhat** prev. Kol'zhat. Almaty, SE Kazakhstan 43°29′N 80°37′E
42 M10 **Kama** var. Cama. Región Autónoma Atlántico Sur, SE Nicaragua 12°06′N 83°55′W
165 R9 **Kamaishi** var. Kamaisi. Iwate, Honshū, C Japan 39°18′N 141°52′E
Kamaisi see Kamaishi
118 H13 **Kamajai** Utena, E Lithuania 55°49′N 25°30′E
Kamajai see Toliejai
149 U9 **Kamālia** Punjab, NE Pakistan 30°44′N 72°39′E
83 I14 **Kamalondo** North Western, NW Zambia 13°42′S 25°38′E
136 I13 **Kaman** Kirşehir, C Turkey 39°22′N 33°43′E
79 O20 **Kamanyola** Sud-Kivu, E Dem. Rep. Congo 02°54′S 29°04′E
141 N14 **Kamarān** island W Yemen
55 R9 **Kamarang** W Guyana 05°49′N 60°38′W
Kāmāreddi/Kamareddy see Rāmāreddi
Kama Reservoir see Kamskoye Vodokhranilishche
148 K13 **Kamarod** Baluchistān, SW Pakistan 27°34′N 63°36′E
171 P14 **Kamaru** Pulau Buton, C Indonesia 05°10′S 123°03′E
77 S13 **Kamba** Kebbi, NW Nigeria 11°50′N 03°44′E
Kambaeng Petch see Kamphaeng Phet
180 L12 **Kambalda** Western Australia 31°15′S 121°33′E
149 P13 **Kambar** var. Qambar. Sind, SE Pakistan 27°35′N 68°03′E
Kambara see Kabara
76 I14 **Kambia** W Sierra Leone 09°09′N 12°53′W
Kambos see Kámpos
79 N25 **Kambove** Katanga, SE Dem. Rep. Congo 10°50′S 26°39′E
Kambryk see Cambrai
123 V10 **Kamchatka** ~ E Russian Federation
Kamchatka see Kamchatka, Poluostrov
Kamchatka Basin see Komandorskaya Basin
123 U10 **Kamchatka, Poluostrov** Eng. Kamchatka. peninsula E Russian Federation
123 V10 **Kamchatskiy Kray** ◐ province E Russian Federation
123 V10 **Kamchatskiy Zaliv** gulf E Russian Federation
114 N9 **Kamchiya** ~ E Bulgaria
114 L9 **Kamchiya, Yazovir** ⊠ E Bulgaria
149 T4 **Kāmdēsh** var. Kamdesh; prev. Kāmdeysh. Nūrestān, E Afghanistan 35°25′N 71°26′E
Kamdesh see Kāmdēsh
Kāmdeysh see Kāmdēsh
Kamenets see Kamyanyets
Kamenets-Podol'skaya Oblast' see Khmel'nyts'ka Oblast'
Kamenets-Podol'skiy see Kam"yanets'-Podil's'kyy
113 Q18 **Kamenica** NE Macedonia 42°03′N 22°34′E
113 O16 **Kamenicë** var. Dardanë, Serb. Kosovska Kamenica. E Kosovo 42°37′N 21°33′E
112 A11 **Kamenjak, Rt** headland NW Croatia
125 O6 **Kamenka** Arkhangel'skaya Oblast', NW Russian Federation 65°55′N 44°01′E
126 6 **Kamenka** Penzenskaya Oblast', W Russian Federation 53°12′N 44°00′E
127 L8 **Kamenka** Voronezhskaya Oblast', W Russian Federation 50°44′N 39°31′E
Kamenka see Taskala
Kamenka see Camenca
Kamenka see Kam"yanka
Kamenka-Bugskaya see Kam"yanka-Buz'ka
Kamenka Dneprovskaya see Kam"yanka-Dniprovs'ka
Kamen Kashirskiy see Kamin'-Kashyrs'kyy
Kamenka-Strumilov see Kam"yanka-Buz'ka
126 L15 **Kamennomostskiy** Respublika Adygeya, SW Russian Federation 44°13′N 40°12′E
126 L11 **Kamenolomni** Rostovskaya Oblast', SW Russian Federation 47°36′N 40°18′E
127 P8 **Kamenskiy** Saratovskaya Oblast', W Russian Federation 50°56′N 45°32′E
Kamenskoye see Romaniv
126 L11 **Kamensk-Shakhtinskiy** Rostovskaya Oblast', SW Russian Federation 48°18′N 40°16′E
101 P15 **Kamenz** Sachsen, E Germany 51°15′N 14°06′E
164 J13 **Kameoka** Kyōto, Honshū, SW Japan 35°02′N 135°35′E
126 M3 **Kameshkovo** Vladimirskaya Oblast', W Russian Federation 56°21′N 41°01′E
164 C11 **Kami-Agata** Nagasaki, Tsushima, SW Japan 34°40′N 129°27′E
33 N10 **Kamiah** Idaho, NW USA 46°13′N 116°01′W
Kamień Koszyrski see Kamin'-Kashyrs'kyy
110 H9 **Kamień Krajeński** Ger. Kamin in Westpreussen. Kujawski-pomorskie, C Poland 53°31′N 17°31′E
111 F15 **Kamienna Góra** Ger. Landeshut, Landeshut in Schlesien. Dolnośląskie, SW Poland 50°48′N 16°00′E
110 D8 **Kamień Pomorski** Ger. Cammin in Pommern. Zachodnio-pomorskie, NW Poland 53°57′N 14°44′E
165 R5 **Kamiiso** Hokkaidō, NE Japan 41°50′N 140°38′E
79 L22 **Kamiji** Kasai-Oriental, S Dem. Rep. Congo 06°39′S 23°27′E
165 T3 **Kamikawa** Hokkaidō, NE Japan 43°51′N 142°47′E
164 B15 **Kami-Koshiki-jima** island SW Japan
79 M23 **Kamina** Katanga, S Dem. Rep. Congo 08°42′S 25°01′E
Kamina see Kaintiba
42 C6 **Kaminaljuyú** ruins Guatemala, C Guatemala
Kamin in Westpreussen see Kamień Krajeński
116 J2 **Kamin'-Kashyrs'kyy** Pol. Kamień Koszyrski, Rus. Kamen Kashirskiy. Volyns'ka Oblast', NW Ukraine 51°39′N 24°59′E
Kaminka Strumiłowa see Kam"yanka-Buz'ka
165 Q5 **Kaminokuni** Hokkaidō, NE Japan 41°48′N 140°05′E
165 P10 **Kaminoyama** Yamagata, Honshū, C Japan 38°10′N 140°16′E
39 Q13 **Kamishak Bay** bay Alaska, USA
165 U4 **Kamishihoro** Hokkaidō, NE Japan 43°14′N 143°18′E
Kamishli see Al Qāmishlī
Kamissar see Kamsar
164 C11 **Kami-Tsushima** Nagasaki, Tsushima, SW Japan 34°40′N 129°27′E
79 O20 **Kamituga** Sud-Kivu, E Dem. Rep. Congo 03°07′S 28°10′E
164 B17 **Kamiyaku** Kagoshima, Yaku-shima, SW Japan 30°24′N 130°32′E
11 N16 **Kamloops** British Columbia, SW Canada 50°39′N 120°24′W
107 G25 **Kamma** Sicilia, Italy, C Mediterranean Sea 36°46′N 12°03′E
192 K4 **Kammu Seamount** undersea feature N Pacific Ocean 32°09′N 173°00′E
109 U11 **Kamnik** Ger. Stein. C Slovenia 46°13′N 14°34′E
Kamniške Alpe see Kamniško-Savinjske Alpe
109 T10 **Kamniško-Savinjske Alpe** var. Kamniške Alpe, Sanntaler Alpen, Ger. Steiner Alpen. ⛰ N Slovenia
Kamo see Gavarr
165 R3 **Kamoenai** var. Kamuenai. Hokkaidō, NE Japan 43°07′N 140°25′E
165 O14 **Kamogawa** Chiba, Honshū, S Japan 35°05′N 140°04′E
149 W8 **Kāmoke** Punjab, E Pakistan 31°58′N 74°15′E
82 L13 **Kamoto** Eastern, E Zambia 13°16′S 32°04′E
109 V3 **Kamp** ~ N Austria
81 F18 **Kampala** ● (Uganda) S Uganda 0°20′N 32°28′E
168 K11 **Kampar, Sungai** ~ Sumatera, W Indonesia
98 L9 **Kampen** Overijssel, E Netherlands 52°33′N 05°55′E
79 N20 **Kampene** Maniema, E Dem. Rep. Congo 03°35′S 26°40′E
29 Q9 **Kampeska, Lake** ◎ South Dakota, N USA
167 O9 **Kamphaeng Phet** var. Kambaeng Petch. Kamphaeng Phet, W Thailand 16°28′N 99°31′E
Kampo see Campo, Cameroon
Kampo see Ntem, Cameroon/Equatorial Guinea
167 S12 **Kâmpóng Cham** prev. Kompong Cham. Kâmpóng Cham, C Cambodia 12°N 105°27′E
167 R12 **Kâmpóng Chhnăng** prev. Kompong. Kâmpóng Chhnăng, C Cambodia 12°15′N 104°40′E
167 R12 **Kâmpóng Khleăng** prev. Kompong Kleang. Siĕmréab, NW Cambodia 13°04′N 104°07′E
Kâmpóng Saôm see Sihanoukville
167 R13 **Kâmpóng Spoe** prev. Kompong Speu. Kâmpóng Spœ, S Cambodia 11°28′N 104°29′E
167 S12 **Kâmpóng Thum** var. Trâpeăng Vêng. Kâmpóng Thum, C Cambodia 12°37′N 104°58′E
167 S12 **Kâmpóng Trâbêk** prev. Phumĭ Kâmpóng Trâbêk, Phum Kompong Trabek. Kâmpóng Thum, C Cambodia 13°06′N 105°16′E
121 O2 **Kámpos** var. Kambos. NW Cyprus 35°03′N 32°44′E
167 R14 **Kâmpôt** Kâmpôt, SW Cambodia 10°37′N 104°11′E
Kamptee see Kāmthi
77 O14 **Kampti** SW Burkina 10°07′N 03°22′W
Kampuchea see Cambodia
Kampuchea, Democratic see Cambodia
Kampuchea, People's Democratic Republic of see Cambodia
169 Q9 **Kampung Sirik** Sarawak, East Malaysia 02°42′N 111°28′E
11 V15 **Kamsack** Saskatchewan, S Canada 51°34′N 101°51′W
76 H13 **Kamsar** var. Kamissar. Guinée-Maritime, W Guinea 10°33′N 14°34′W
127 R4 **Kamskoye Ust'ye** Respublika Tatarstan, W Russian Federation 55°13′N 49°11′E
125 U14 **Kamskoye Vodokhranilishche** var. Kama Reservoir. ⊠ NW Russian Federation
154 I12 **Kāmthi** prev. Kamptee. Mahārāshtra, C India 21°19′N 79°11′E
Kamuela see Waimea
Kamuenai see Kamoenai
165 T5 **Kamui-dake** 🌋 Hokkaidō, NE Japan 42°24′N 142°57′E
165 R3 **Kamui-misaki** headland Hokkaidō, NE Japan 43°20′N 140°20′E
43 O15 **Kámuk, Cerro** ▲ SE Costa Rica 09°15′N 83°01′W
116 K7 **Kam"yanets'-Podil's'kyy** Rus. Kamenets-Podol'skiy. Khmel'nyts'ka Oblast', W Ukraine 48°43′N 26°36′E
117 Q6 **Kam"yanka** Rus. Kamenka. Cherkas'ka Oblast', C Ukraine 49°03′N 32°06′E
116 I5 **Kam"yanka-Buz'ka** prev. Kamenka-Strumilov, Pol. Kaminka Strumiłowa, Rus. Kamenka-Bugskaya. L'vivs'ka Oblast', NW Ukraine 50°04′N 24°21′E
117 T9 **Kam"yanka-Dniprovs'ka** Rus. Kamenka Dneprovskaya. Zaporiz'ka Oblast', SE Ukraine 47°28′N 34°24′E
119 F19 **Kamyanyets** Rus. Kamenets. Brestskaya Voblasts', SW Belarus 52°24′N 23°49′E
118 M13 **Kamyen'** Vitsyebskaya Voblasts', N Belarus 55°01′N 28°53′E
127 P9 **Kamyshin** Volgogradskaya Oblast', SW Russian Federation 50°07′N 45°20′E
127 Q13 **Kamyzyak** Astrakhanskaya Oblast', SW Russian Federation 46°07′N 48°03′E
12 K8 **Kanaaupscow** ~ Québec, C Canada
36 K8 **Kanab** Utah, W USA 37°03′N 112°31′W
36 K9 **Kanab Creek** ~ Arizona/Utah, SW USA
187 Y14 **Kanacea** prev. Kanathea. Taveuni, N Fiji 16°59′S 179°54′E
38 G17 **Kanaga Island** island Aleutian Islands, Alaska, USA
38 G17 **Kanaga Volcano** ▲ Kanaga Island, Alaska, USA 51°55′N 177°09′W
164 N14 **Kanagawa** off. Kanagawa-ken. ◐ prefecture Honshū, S Japan
Kanagawa-ken see Kanagawa
13 Q8 **Kanairiktok** ~ Newfoundland and Labrador, E Canada
Kanaky see New Caledonia
79 K22 **Kananga** prev. Luluabourg. Kasai-Occidental, S Dem. Rep. Congo 05°51′S 22°22′E
Kanara see Karnātaka
36 J7 **Kanarraville** Utah, W USA 37°32′N 113°10′W
127 Q4 **Kanash** Chuvashskaya Respublika, W Russian Federation 55°30′N 47°27′E
Kanathea see Kanacea
21 Q4 **Kanawha River** ~ West Virginia, NE USA
164 L13 **Kanayama** Gifu, Honshū, SW Japan 35°46′N 137°15′E
164 L11 **Kanazawa** Ishikawa, Honshū, SW Japan 36°35′N 136°40′E
166 M4 **Kanbalu** Sagaing, C Burma (Myanmar) 23°10′N 95°31′E
166 L8 **Kanbe** Yangon, SW Burma (Myanmar) 16°40′N 96°01′E
167 O11 **Kanchanaburi** Kanchanaburi, W Thailand 14°02′N 99°32′E
Kanchanjańghā/Kānchenjunga see Kangchenjunga
155 J19 **Kānchīpuram** prev. Conjeeveram. Tamil Nādu, SE India 12°50′N 79°44′E
149 N8 **Kandahār** Per. Qandahār. Kandahār, S Afghanistan 31°36′N 65°48′E

◆ Country
● Country Capital
◇ Dependent Territory
○ Dependent Territory Capital
◐ Administrative Regions
✈ International Airport
▲ Mountain
⛰ Mountain Range
🌋 Volcano
~ River
◎ Lake
⊠ Reservoir

149 N9 **Kandahār** Per. Qandahār. ⬖ province SE Afghanistan
167 S13 **Kândal** var. Ta Khmau. Kândal, S Cambodia 11°30′N 104°59′E
Kandalakša see Kandalaksha
124 I5 **Kandalaksha** var. Kandalakša, Fin. Kantalahti. Murmanskaya Oblast', NW Russian Federation 67°09′N 32°14′E
Kandalaksha Gulf/ Kandalakshskaya Guba see Kandalakshskiy Zaliv
124 K6 **Kandalakshskiy Zaliv** var. Kandalakshskaya Guba, Eng. Kandalaksha Gulf. bay NW Russian Federation
83 G17 **Kandalengoti** var. Kandalengoti. Ngamiland, NW Botswana 19°25′S 22°12′E
Kandalengoti see Kandalengoti
169 U13 **Kandangan** Borneo, C Indonesia 02°50′S 115°15′E
Kandau see Kandava
118 E8 **Kandava** Ger. Kandau. W Latvia 57°02′N 22°48′E
Kandavu see Kadavu
77 R14 **Kandé** var. Kanté. NE Togo 09°55′N 01°01′E
101 F23 **Kandel** ▲ SW Germany 48°03′N 08°00′E
186 C7 **Kandep** Enga, W Papua New Guinea 05°54′S 143°34′E
149 R12 **Kandh Kot** Sind, SE Pakistan 28°15′N 69°18′E
77 S13 **Kandi** N Benin 11°05′N 02°59′E
149 P14 **Kandiāro** Sind, SE Pakistan 27°02′N 68°16′E
136 F11 **Kandıra** Kocaeli, NW Turkey 41°05′N 30°08′E
183 S8 **Kandos** New South Wales, SE Australia 32°52′S 149°58′E
148 M16 **Kandrāch** var. Kanrach. Baluchistān, SW Pakistan 25°26′N 65°28′E
172 I4 **Kandreho** Mahajanga, C Madagascar 17°27′S 46°06′E
186 F7 **Kandrian** New Britain, E Papua New Guinea 06°14′S 149°32′E
Kandukur see Kondukūr
155 K25 **Kandy** Central Province, C Sri Lanka 07°17′N 80°40′E
144 I10 **Kandyagash** Kaz. Qandyaghash; prev. Oktyab'rsk. Aktyubinsk, W Kazakhstan 49°25′N 57°24′E
18 D12 **Kane** Pennsylvania, NE USA 41°39′N 78°47′W
64 I11 **Kane Fracture Zone** tectonic feature NW Atlantic Ocean
Kanëka see Kanëvka
78 G9 **Kanem** off. Préfecture du Kanem. ⬖ prefecture W Chad
Kanem, Préfecture du see Kanem
38 D9 **Kāne'ohe** var. Kaneohe. O'ahu, Hawaii, USA, C Pacific Ocean 21°25′N 157°48′W
Kanestron, Akrotírio see Palioúri, Akrotírio
Kanëv see Kaniv
124 M5 **Kanëvka** var. Kanëka. Murmanskaya Oblast', NW Russian Federation 67°07′N 39°43′E
126 K13 **Kanevskaya** Krasnodarskiy Kray, SW Russian Federation 46°07′N 38°57′E
Kanevskoye Vodokhranilishche see Kanivs'ke Vodoskhovyshche
165 P9 **Kaneyama** Yamagata, Honshū, C Japan 38°54′N 140°20′E
83 G20 **Kang** Kgalagadi, C Botswana 23°41′S 22°50′E
76 L13 **Kangaba** Koulikoro, SW Mali 11°57′N 08°24′W
136 M13 **Kangal** Sivas, C Turkey 39°15′N 37°23′E
Kangān see Bandar-e Kangān
168 J6 **Kangar** Perlis, Peninsular Malaysia 06°28′N 100°10′E
76 L13 **Kangaré** Sikasso, S Mali 11°39′N 08°10′W
182 F10 **Kangaroo Island** island South Australia
93 M17 **Kangasniemi** Itä-Suomi, E Finland 61°58′N 26°37′E
142 K6 **Kangāvar** var. Kangāwar. Kermānshāhān, W Iran 34°29′N 47°55′E
Kangāwar see Kangāvar
153 S11 **Kangchenjunga** var. Kānchenjunga, Nep. Kanchanjańghā. ▲ NE India 27°36′N 88°06′E
160 G9 **Kangding** var. Lucheng, Tib. Dardo. Sichuan, C China 30°03′N 101°56′E
169 U16 **Kangean, Kepulauan** island group S Indonesia
169 T16 **Kangean, Pulau** island Kepulauan Kangean, S Indonesia
67 U8 **Kangen** var. Kengen. ≈ E South Sudan
197 N14 **Kangerlussuaq** Dan. Sondre Strømfjord. ✈ Kitaa, W Greenland 66°59′N 50°28′E
197 Q15 **Kangertittivaq** Dan. Scoresby Sund. fjord E Greenland
167 O2 **Kangfang** Kachin State, N Burma (Myanmar) 26°09′N 98°36′E
163 X12 **Kanggye** N North Korea 40°58′N 126°37′E
197 P15 **Kangikajik** var. Kap Brewster. headland E Greenland 70°10′N 22°00′W
13 N5 **Kangiqsualujjuaq** prev. George River, Port-Nouveau-Québec. Québec, E Canada 58°35′N 65°59′W
12 L2 **Kangiqsujuaq** prev. Maricourt, Wakeham Bay. Québec, NE Canada 61°35′N 72°00′W
12 M4 **Kangirsuk** prev. Bellin, Payne. Québec, E Canada 60°00′N 70°01′W
Kangle see Wanzai
158 M16 **Kangmar** Xizang Zizhiqu, W China 28°34′N 89°40′E
Kangnŭng see Gangneung
79 D18 **Kango** Estuaire, NW Gabon 0°17′N 10°00′E
152 I7 **Kāngra** Himāchal Pradesh, NW India 32°04′N 76°16′E
153 Q16 **Kangsabati Reservoir** ▣ N India
159 O17 **Kangto** ▲ China/India 27°54′N 92°33′E
159 W12 **Kangxian** var. Kang Xian, Zuitai, Zuitaizi. Gansu, C China 33°21′N 105°40′E
Kang Xian see Kangxian
76 M15 **Kani** NW Ivory Coast 08°29′N 06°36′W
166 L4 **Kani** Sagaing, C Burma (Myanmar) 22°24′N 94°55′E
79 M23 **Kaniama** Katanga, S Dem. Rep. Congo 07°32′S 24°11′E
Kanibadam see Konibodom
169 V6 **Kanibongan** Sabah, East Malaysia 06°40′N 117°12′E
185 F17 **Kaniere** West Coast, South Island, New Zealand 42°45′S 171°00′E
185 G17 **Kaniere, Lake** ◎ South Island, New Zealand
188 E17 **Kanifaay** Yap, W Micronesia
125 O4 **Kanin Kamen'** ▲▲ NW Russian Federation
125 N3 **Kanin Nos** Nenetskiy Avtonomnyy Okrug, NW Russian Federation 68°38′N 43°19′E
125 N3 **Kanin Nos, Mys** cape NW Russian Federation
125 O5 **Kanin, Poluostrov** peninsula NW Russian Federation
139 V8 **Kānī Sakht** Wāsiṭ, E Iraq 33°19′N 46°04′E
139 T3 **Kānī Sulaymān** Arbīl, N Iraq 35°54′N 44°35′E
165 Q6 **Kanita** Aomori, Honshū, C Japan 41°04′N 140°36′E
117 Q5 **Kaniv** Rus. Kanëv. Cherkas'ka Oblast', C Ukraine 49°46′N 31°28′E
182 K11 **Kaniva** Victoria, SE Australia 36°25′S 141°13′E
117 Q5 **Kanivs'ke Vodoskhovyshche** Rus. Kanevskoye Vodokhranilishche. ▣ C Ukraine
112 L8 **Kanjiža** Ger. Altkanischa, Hung. Magyarkanizsa, Ókanizsa; prev. Stara Kanjiža. Vojvodina, N Serbia 46°03′N 20°03′E
93 K18 **Kankaanpää** Länsi-Suomi, SW Finland 61°47′N 22°25′E
30 M12 **Kankakee** Illinois, N USA 41°07′N 87°51′W
31 O11 **Kankakee River** ≈ Illinois/ Indiana, N USA
76 K14 **Kankan** E Guinea 10°25′N 09°19′W
154 K13 **Kānker** Chhattīsgarh, C India 20°19′N 81°29′E
76 J10 **Kankossa** Assaba, S Mauritania 15°54′N 11°31′W
169 N12 **Kanmaw Kyun** var. Kisseraing, Kithareng. island Mergui Archipelago, S Burma (Myanmar)
164 F12 **Kanmuri-yama** ▲ Kyūshū, SW Japan 34°28′N 132°03′E
21 R10 **Kannapolis** North Carolina, SE USA 35°30′N 80°36′W
93 L16 **Kannonkoski** Länsi-Suomi, C Finland 62°59′N 25°20′E
93 K15 **Kannus** Länsi-Suomi, W Finland 63°55′N 23°55′E
77 V13 **Kano** Kano, N Nigeria 11°56′N 08°31′E
77 V13 **Kano** ⬖ state N Nigeria
77 V13 **Kano** ✈ Kano, N Nigeria 11°56′N 08°26′E
164 G14 **Kan'onji** var. Kanonzi. Kagawa, Shikoku, SW Japan 34°08′N 133°38′E
Kanonzi see Kan'onji
26 M5 **Kanopolis Lake** ▣ Kansas, C USA
36 K5 **Kanosh** Utah, W USA 38°48′N 112°26′W
169 R9 **Kanowit** Sarawak, East Malaysia 02°03′N 112°15′E
164 C16 **Kanoya** Kagoshima, Kyūshū, SW Japan 31°22′N 130°50′E
152 L13 **Kānpur** Eng. Cawnpore. Uttar Pradesh, N India 26°28′N 80°21′E
Kanrach see Kandrāch
164 I14 **Kansai** ✈ (Ōsaka) Ōsaka, Honshū, SW Japan 34°25′N 135°13′E
27 R9 **Kansas** Oklahoma, C USA 36°14′N 94°46′W
26 L5 **Kansas** off. State of Kansas, also known as Jayhawker State, Sunflower State. ⬖ state C USA
27 R4 **Kansas City** Kansas, C USA 39°07′N 94°38′W
27 R4 **Kansas City** Missouri, C USA 39°06′N 94°35′W
27 R3 **Kansas City** ✈ Missouri, C USA 39°18′N 94°45′W
27 P4 **Kansas River** ≈ Kansas, C USA
122 L14 **Kansk** Krasnoyarskiy Kray, S Russian Federation 56°11′N 95°32′E
Kansu see Gansu
147 V7 **Kant** Chuyskaya Oblast', N Kyrgyzstan 42°54′N 74°47′E
Kantalahti see Kandalaksha
167 N16 **Kantang** var. Ban Kantang. Trang, SW Thailand 07°25′N 99°30′E
115 H25 **Kántanos** Kríti, Greece, E Mediterranean Sea 35°20′N 23°42′E
77 R12 **Kantchari** E Burkina 12°47′N 01°37′E
Kanté see Kandé
Kantemir see Cantemir
126 L9 **Kantemirovka** Voronezhskaya Oblast', W Russian Federation 49°44′N 39°53′E
167 R11 **Kantharalak** Si Sa Ket, E Thailand 14°32′N 104°37′E
Kantipur see Kathmandu
39 Q9 **Kantishna River** ≈ Alaska, USA
191 S3 **Kanton** var. Abariringa, Canton Island; prev. Mary Island. atoll Phoenix Islands, C Kiribati
97 C20 **Kanturk** Ir. Ceann Toirc. Cork, SW Ireland 52°12′N 08°54′W
55 T11 **Kanuku Mountains** ▲▲ S Guyana
165 O12 **Kanuma** Tochigi, Honshū, S Japan 36°34′N 139°44′E
83 H20 **Kanye** Southern, SE Botswana 24°55′S 25°14′E
83 H17 **Kanyu** North-West, C Botswana 20°04′S 24°36′E
166 M7 **Kanyutkwin** Bago, C Burma (Myanmar) 18°19′N 96°30′E
79 M24 **Kanzenze** Katanga, SE Dem. Rep. Congo 10°33′S 25°28′E
193 Y15 **Kao** island Kotu Group, W Tonga
167 Q13 **Kaôh Kŏng** var. Krŏng Kaôh Kŏng. Kaôh Kông, SW Cambodia 11°37′N 102°59′E
Kaohsiung see Gaoxiong
Kaokaona see Kirakira
83 B17 **Kaoko Veld** ▲▲ N Namibia
76 G11 **Kaolack** var. Kaolak. W Senegal 14°09′N 16°08′W
Kaolak see Kaolack
Kaolan see Lanzhou
186 M8 **Kaolo** San Jorge, N Solomon Islands 08°24′S 159°35′E
83 H14 **Kaoma** Western, W Zambia 14°50′S 24°48′E
38 B8 **Kapa'a** var. Kapaa. Kaua'i, Hawaii, USA, C Pacific Ocean 22°04′N 159°19′W
Kapaa see Kapa'a
113 J16 **Kapa Moračka** ▲ C Montenegro 42°53′N 19°01′E
137 V13 **Kapan** Rus. Kafan; prev. Ghap'an. SE Armenia 39°13′N 46°25′E
82 L13 **Kapandashila** Northern, NE Zambia 12°43′S 31°00′E
79 L23 **Kapanga** Katanga, S Dem. Rep. Congo 08°22′S 22°37′E
Kapchagay see Kapshagay
Kapchagayskoye Vodokhranilishche see Vodokhranilishche Kapshagay
99 F15 **Kapelle** Zeeland, SW Netherlands 51°29′N 03°58′E
99 G16 **Kapellen** Antwerpen, N Belgium 51°19′N 04°25′E
95 P15 **Kapellskär** Stockholm, C Sweden 59°43′N 19°03′E
81 H18 **Kapenguria** Rift Valley, W Kenya 01°14′N 35°08′E
109 V6 **Kapfenberg** Steiermark, C Austria 47°27′N 15°18′E
83 J14 **Kapiri Mposhi** Central, C Zambia 13°59′S 28°40′E
149 R4 **Kāpīsā** ⬖ province E Afghanistan
12 G10 **Kapiskau** ≈ Ontario, C Canada
184 K13 **Kapiti Island** island C New Zealand
78 K9 **Kapka, Massif du** ▲▲ E Chad
Kaplamada see Kaubalatmada, Gunung
22 H9 **Kaplan** Louisiana, S USA 30°00′N 92°16′W
Kaplangky, Plato see Gaplaňgyr Platosy
111 D19 **Kaplice** Ger. Kaplitz. Jihočeský Kraj, S Czech Republic 48°42′N 14°27′E
Kaplitz see Kaplice
Kapoche see Capoche
171 T12 **Kapocol** Papua, E Indonesia 01°59′S 130°11′E
167 N14 **Kapoe** Ranong, SW Thailand 09°33′N 98°37′E
Kapoeas see Kapuas, Sungai
81 G15 **Kapoeta** Eastern Equatoria, SE South Sudan 04°50′N 33°35′E
111 I25 **Kapos** ≈ S Hungary
111 H25 **Kaposvár** Somogy, SW Hungary 46°23′N 17°54′E
94 H13 **Kapp** Oppland, S Norway 60°42′N 10°49′E
100 I7 **Kappeln** Schleswig-Holstein, N Germany 54°41′N 09°56′E
Kaproncza see Koprivnica
109 P7 **Kaprun** Salzburg, C Austria 47°15′N 12°48′E
145 U15 **Kapshagay** prev. Kapchagay. Almaty, SE Kazakhstan 43°52′N 77°05′E
Kapstad see Cape Town
Kapsukas see Marijampolė
171 Y13 **Kaptiau** Papua, E Indonesia 02°23′S 139°51′E
119 L19 **Kaptsevichy** Rus. Koptsevichi. Homyel'skaya Voblasts', SE Belarus 52°14′N 28°19′E
Kapuas Hulu, Banjaran/ Kapuas Hulu, Pegunungan see Kapuas Mountains
169 S10 **Kapuas Mountains** Ind. Banjaran Kapuas Hulu, Pegunungan Kapuas Hulu. ▲▲ Indonesia/Malaysia
169 P11 **Kapuas, Sungai** ≈ Borneo, N Indonesia
169 T13 **Kapuas, Sungai** prev. Kapoeas. ≈ Borneo, C Indonesia
182 J9 **Kapunda** South Australia 34°23′S 138°51′E
152 H8 **Kapūrthala** Punjab, N India 31°20′N 75°26′E
12 G12 **Kapuskasing** Ontario, S Canada 49°25′N 82°26′W
14 D6 **Kapuskasing** ≈ Ontario, S Canada
127 P11 **Kapustin Yar** Astrakhanskaya Oblast', SW Russian Federation 48°36′N 45°49′E
82 K11 **Kaputa** Northern, NE Zambia 08°28′S 29°41′E
111 G22 **Kapuvár** Győr-Moson-Sopron, NW Hungary 47°35′N 17°01′E
Kapydzhik, Gora see Qazangödağ
119 J17 **Kapyl'** Rus. Kopyl'. Minskaya Voblasts', C Belarus 53°09′N 27°05′E
43 N9 **Kara** var. Cara. Región Autónoma Atlántico Sur, E Nicaragua 12°50′N 83°35′W
77 R14 **Kara** var. Lama-Kara. NE Togo 09°33′N 01°12′E
77 Q14 **Kara** ≈ N Togo
147 U7 **Kara-Balta** Chuyskaya Oblast', N Kyrgyzstan 42°51′N 73°51′E
144 L7 **Karabalyk** var. Komsomolets, Kaz. Komsomol. Kostanay, N Kazakhstan 53°47′N 61°58′E
144 G11 **Karabau** Kaz. Qarabaū. Atyrau, W Kazakhstan 48°29′N 53°05′E
146 E7 **Karabaur', Uval** Kaz. Korabavur Pastligi, Uzb. Qorabowur Kirlari. physical region Kazakhstan/Uzbekistan
Karabekaul see Garabekewül
Karabil', Vozvyshennost' see Garabil Belentligi
Kara-Bogaz-Gol see Garabogazköl
Kara-Bogaz-Gol, Zaliv see Garabogaz Aylagy
145 R15 **Karaboget** Kaz. Qaraböget. Zhambyl, S Kazakhstan 44°36′N 72°03′E
136 H11 **Karabük** Karabük, NW Turkey 41°12′N 32°36′E
136 H11 **Karabük** ⬖ province NW Turkey
122 L12 **Karabula** Krasnoyarskiy Kray, C Russian Federation 58°01′N 97°17′E
145 V14 **Karabulak** Kaz. Qarabulaq. Taldykorgan, SE Kazakhstan 44°53′N 78°29′E
145 Y11 **Karabulak** Kaz. Qarabulaq. Vostochnyy Kazakhstan, E Kazakhstan 47°34′N 84°40′E
145 Q17 **Karabulak** Kaz. Qarabulaq. Yuzhnyy Kazakhstan, S Kazakhstan 42°31′N 69°47′E
Karabura see Yumin
136 C17 **Kara Burnu** headland SW Turkey 36°34′N 28°00′E
144 K10 **Karabutak** Kaz. Qarabutaq. Aktyubinsk, W Kazakhstan 49°55′N 60°05′E
136 D12 **Karacabey** Bursa, NW Turkey 40°14′N 28°22′E
114 O12 **Karacaköy** İstanbul, NW Turkey 41°24′N 28°21′E
114 M12 **Karacaoğlan** Kırklareli, NW Turkey 41°30′N 27°06′E
Karachay-Cherkessia see Karachayevo-Cherkesskaya Respublika
126 L15 **Karachayevo-Cherkesskaya Respublika** Eng. Karachay-Cherkessia. ⬖ autonomous republic SW Russian Federation
126 M15 **Karachayevsk** Karachayevo-Cherkesskaya Respublika, SW Russian Federation 43°43′N 41°53′E
126 J6 **Karachev** Bryanskaya Oblast', W Russian Federation 53°07′N 35°56′E
149 O16 **Karāchi** Sind, SE Pakistan 24°51′N 67°02′E
149 O16 **Karāchi** ✈ Sind, S Pakistan 24°51′N 67°02′E
Karácsonkő see Piatra-Neamț
155 E15 **Karād** Mahārāshtra, W India 17°19′N 74°15′E
136 H16 **Karadağ** ▲ S Turkey 37°00′N 33°00′E
147 T10 **Karadar'ya** Uzb. Qoradaryo. ≈ Kyrgyzstan/Uzbekistan
Karadeniz see Black Sea
Karadeniz Boğazi see İstanbul Boğazı
146 B13 **Karadepe** Balkan Welaýaty, W Turkmenistan 38°04′N 54°01′E
Karadzhar see Qorajar
Karaferiye see Véroia
Karagan see Garagan
Karaganda see Karagandy
Karaganda see Karagandy
Karagandinskaya Oblast' see Karagandy
145 R10 **Karagandy** Kaz. Qaraghandy; prev. Karaganda. Karaganda, C Kazakhstan 49°53′N 73°07′E
145 R10 **Karagandy** off. Karagandinskaya Oblast', Kaz. Qaraghandy Oblysy; prev. Karaganda. ⬖ province C Kazakhstan
145 T10 **Karagayly** Kaz. Qaraghayly. Karaganda, C Kazakhstan 49°25′N 75°31′E
Karagel' see Garagöl'
123 U9 **Karaginskiy, Ostrov** island E Russian Federation
197 T1 **Karaginskiy Zaliv** bay E Russian Federation
137 P13 **Karagöl Dağları** ▲▲ NE Turkey
Karagumskiy Kanal see Garagum Kanaly
114 L13 **Karahisar** Edirne, NW Turkey 40°47′N 26°34′E
127 V3 **Karaidel'** Respublika Bashkortostan, W Russian Federation 55°50′N 56°55′E
114 L13 **Karaidemir Barajı** ▣ NW Turkey
155 J21 **Kāraikāl** Pondicherry, SE India 10°58′N 79°50′E
155 I22 **Kāraikkudi** Tamil Nādu, SE India 10°04′N 78°46′E
Kara Irtysh see Kara Yertis
143 N5 **Karaj** Alborz, N Iran 35°44′N 51°26′E
168 K8 **Karak** Pahang, Peninsular Malaysia 03°24′N 101°59′E
Karak see Al Karak
147 T11 **Kara-Kabak** Oshskaya Oblast', SW Kyrgyzstan 39°40′N 72°45′E
Kara-Kala see Magtymguly
Karakala see Oqqal'a
Karakalpakstan, Respublika see Qoraqalpog'iston Respublikasi
Karakalpakya see Qoraqalpog'iston
Karakax see Moyu
158 G10 **Karakax He** ≈ NW China
121 X8 **Karakaya Barajı** ▣ C Turkey
171 Q9 **Karakelong, Pulau** island N Indonesia
Karakılısse see Ağrı
Karak, Muḩāfaẓat al see Al Karak
147 X8 **Karakol** var. Karakolka. Issyk-Kul'skaya Oblast', NE Kyrgyzstan 41°30′N 77°18′E
147 Y7 **Karakol** prev. Przheval'sk. Issyk-Kul'skaya Oblast', NE Kyrgyzstan 42°32′N 78°21′E
Kara-Köl see Kara-Kul'
Karakolka see Karakol
149 W2 **Karakoram Highway** road China/Pakistan
149 Z3 **Karakoram Pass** Chin. Karakoram Shankou. pass C Asia
152 I3 **Karakoram Range** ▲▲ C Asia
Karakoram Shankou see Karakoram Pass
Karaköse see Ağrı
145 P14 **Karakoyyn, Ozero** Kaz. Qaraqoyyn. ◎ C Kazakhstan
83 F19 **Karakubis** Ghanzi, W Botswana 22°03′S 20°36′E
147 T9 **Kara-Kul'** Kir. Kara-Köl. Dzhalal-Abadskaya Oblast', W Kyrgyzstan 40°35′N 73°36′E
Karakul' see Qarokŭl, Tajikistan
Karakul' see Qorako'l, Uzbekistan
147 U10 **Kara-Kul'dzha** Oshskaya Oblast', SW Kyrgyzstan 40°32′N 73°50′E
127 T3 **Karakulino** Udmurtskaya Respublika, NW Russian Federation 56°02′N 53°45′E
Karakul', Ozero see Qarokŭl
Kara Kum see Garagum
Kara Kum Canal/ Karakumskiy Kanal see Garagum Kanaly
Karakumy, Peski see Garagum
83 E17 **Karakuwisa** Okavango, NE Namibia 18°56′S 19°40′E
122 M13 **Karam** Irkutskaya Oblast', S Russian Federation 55°07′N 107°21′E
Karamai see Karamay
169 T14 **Karamain, Pulau** island N Indonesia
136 I16 **Karaman** Karaman, S Turkey 37°11′N 33°13′E
136 H16 **Karaman** ⬖ province S Turkey
114 M8 **Karamandere** ≈ NE Bulgaria
158 J4 **Karamay** var. Karamai, Kelamayi; prev. Chin. K'o-la-ma-i. Xinjiang Uygur Zizhiqu, NW China 45°33′N 84°45′E
169 U14 **Karambu** Borneo, N Indonesia 03°48′S 116°06′E
185 H14 **Karamea** West Coast, South Island, New Zealand 41°15′S 172°07′E
185 H14 **Karamea** ≈ South Island, New Zealand
185 G15 **Karamea Bight** gulf South Island, New Zealand
Karamet-Niyaz see Garamätnyýaz
158 K10 **Karamiran He** ≈ NW China
147 S11 **Karamyk** Oshskaya Oblast', SW Kyrgyzstan 39°28′N 71°45′E
169 U17 **Karangasem** Bali, S Indonesia 08°24′S 115°40′E
154 H12 **Kāranja** Mahārāshtra, C India 20°30′N 77°26′E
Karanpur see Karanpura
152 F9 **Karanpura** var. Karanpur. Rājasthān, NW India 29°46′N 73°30′E
Karánsebes/Karansebesch see Caransebeș
145 T14 **Karaoy** Kaz. Qaraoy. Almaty, SE Kazakhstan 45°52′N 74°44′E
144 E10 **Karaozen** Kaz. Ülkenözen; prev. Bol'shoy Uzen'. ≈ Kazakhstan/Russian Federation
114 N7 **Karapelit** Rom. Stejarul. Dobrich, NE Bulgaria 43°40′N 27°33′E
136 I15 **Karapınar** Konya, C Turkey 37°43′N 33°34′E
83 D22 **Karas** ⬖ district S Namibia
147 Y8 **Kara-Say** Issyk-Kul'skaya Oblast', NE Kyrgyzstan 41°34′N 77°56′E
83 E22 **Karasburg** Karas, S Namibia 27°59′S 18°46′E
Kara Sea see Karskoye More
92 K9 **Kárášjohka** var. Karašjokka. ≈ N Norway
Kárášjohka see Karasjok
92 L9 **Karasjok** Fin. Kaarasjoki, Lapp. Kárášjohka. Finnmark, N Norway 69°27′N 25°28′E
Karašjokka see Kárášjohka
Kara Strait see Karskiye Vorota, Proliv
145 N8 **Karasu** Kaz. Qarasū. Kostanay, N Kazakhstan 52°44′N 65°29′E
136 F11 **Karasu** Sakarya, NW Turkey 41°07′N 30°37′E
Kara Su see Mesta/Néstos
Karasubazar see Bilohirs'k
122 I12 **Karasuk** Novosibirskaya Oblast', C Russian Federation 53°41′N 78°04′E
145 U13 **Karatal** Kaz. Qaratal. ≈ SE Kazakhstan
136 K17 **Karataş** Adana, S Turkey 36°32′N 35°22′E
145 Q16 **Karatau** Kaz. Qarataū. Zhambyl, S Kazakhstan 43°09′N 70°28′E
Karatau see Karatau, Khrebet
145 P16 **Karatau, Khrebet** var. Karatau, Kaz. Qarataū. ▲▲ S Kazakhstan
144 G13 **Karaton** Kaz. Qaraton. Atyrau, W Kazakhstan 46°33′N 53°31′E
164 C13 **Karatsu** var. Karatu. Saga, Kyūshū, SW Japan 33°28′N 129°48′E
Karatu see Karatsu
122 K8 **Karaul** Krasnoyarskiy Kray, N Russian Federation 70°07′N 83°12′E
Karaulbazar see Qorowulbozor
Karauzyak see Qorao'zak
115 D16 **Karáva** ▲ C Greece 39°19′N 21°33′E
Karavanke see Karawanken
115 F22 **Karavás** Kýthira, S Greece 36°21′N 22°57′E
113 J20 **Karavastasë, Laguna e** var. Kënet' e Karavastas, Kravasta Lagoon. lagoon W Albania
Karavastas, Kënet' e see Karavastasë, Laguna e
118 I5 **Käravere** Tartumaa, E Estonia 58°25′N 26°29′E
115 L23 **Karavonísia** island Kykládes, Greece, Aegean Sea
169 O15 **Karawang** prev. Krawang. Jawa, C Indonesia 06°13′S 107°16′E
109 T10 **Karawanken** Slvn. Karavanke. ▲▲ Austria/Serbia
Karaxahar see Kaidu He
137 R13 **Karayazı** Erzurum, NE Turkey 39°40′N 42°09′E
145 Y11 **Kara Yertis** Rus. Chërnyy Irtysh prev. Kara Irtysh. ≈ NE Kazakhstan
145 Q12 **Karazhal** Kaz. Qarazhal. Karaganda, C Kazakhstan 48°002′N 70°52′E
139 S9 **Karbalā'** var. Kerbala, Kerbela. Karbalā', S Iraq 32°37′N 44°03′E
94 L11 **Kårböle** Gävleborg, C Sweden 61°59′N 15°16′E
111 M23 **Karcag** Jász-Nagykun-Szolnok, E Hungary 47°22′N 20°51′E
Kardak see Imia
114 N7 **Kardam** Dobrich, NE Bulgaria 43°45′N 28°06′E
Kardamila see Kardámyla
115 L18 **Kardámyla** var. Kardamila, Kardhámila. Chíos, E Greece 38°33′N 26°04′E
Kardeljevo see Ploče
Kardh see Qardho
Kardhámila see Kardámyla
Kardhítsa see Kardítsa
115 E16 **Kardítsa** var. Kardhítsa. Thessalía, C Greece 39°22′N 21°56′E
118 E4 **Kärdla** Ger. Kertel. Hiiumaa, W Estonia 59°00′N 22°42′E
Karelia see Kareliya, Respublika
119 I16 **Karelichy** Pol. Korelicze, Rus. Korelichi. Hrodzyenskaya Voblasts', W Belarus 53°34′N 26°08′E
124 I10 **Kareliya, Respublika** prev. Karel'skaya ASSR, Eng. Karelia. ⬖ autonomous republic NW Russian Federation
Karel'skaya ASSR see Kareliya, Respublika
81 E22 **Karema** Rukwa, W Tanzania 06°50′S 30°25′E
Karen see Hualian
83 I14 **Karenda** Central, C Zambia 14°42′S 26°52′E
Karen State see Kayin State
92 J10 **Karesuando** Fin. Kaaresuanto, Lapp. Gárasavvon. Norrbotten, N Sweden 68°25′N 22°28′E
Karet see Kâgheț
Kareyz-e-Elyās/Kārez Iliās see Kārīz-e Elyās
122 J11 **Kargasok** Tomskaya Oblast', C Russian Federation 59°01′N 80°34′E
122 I12 **Kargat** Novosibirskaya Oblast', C Russian Federation 55°07′N 80°19′E
136 J11 **Kargı** Çorum, N Turkey 41°09′N 34°32′E
152 I5 **Kargil** Jammu and Kashmir, NW India 34°34′N 76°06′E
Kargilik see Yecheng
124 L11 **Kargopol'** Arkhangel'skaya Oblast', NW Russian Federation 61°30′N 38°53′E
110 F12 **Kargowa** Ger. Unruhstadt. Lubuskie, W Poland 52°05′N 15°50′E
77 X13 **Kari** Bauchi, E Nigeria 11°13′N 10°34′E
83 J15 **Kariba** Mashonaland West, N Zimbabwe 16°29′S 28°48′E
83 J16 **Kariba, Lake** ▣ Zambia/ Zimbabwe
165 Q4 **Kariba-yama** ▲ Hokkaidō, NE Japan 42°36′N 139°55′E
83 C19 **Karibib** Erongo, C Namibia 21°56′S 15°51′E
Karies see Karyés
92 L9 **Karigasniemi** Lapp. Garegegasnjárga. Lappi, N Finland 69°24′N 25°52′E
184 J2 **Karikari, Cape** headland North Island, New Zealand 34°47′S 173°24′E
149 W3 **Karīmābād** prev. Hunza. Jammu and Kashmir, NE Pakistan 36°23′N 74°43′E
169 P12 **Karimata, Kepulauan** island group N Indonesia
169 P12 **Karimata, Pulau** island Kepulauan Karimata, N Indonesia
169 O11 **Karimata, Selat** strait W Indonesia
155 I14 **Karīmnagar** Andhra Pradesh, C India 18°28′N 79°09′E
186 C7 **Karimui** Chimbu, C Papua New Guinea 06°19′S 144°48′E
169 Q15 **Karimunjawa, Pulau** island S Indonesia
80 N12 **Karin** Woqooyi Galbeed, N Somalia 10°48′N 45°46′E
Kariot see Ikaría
93 L20 **Karis** Fin. Karjaa. Etelä-Suomi, SW Finland 60°05′N 23°39′E
Káristos see Kárystos
148 J4 **Kārīz-e Elyās** var. Kareyz-e-Elyās, Kārez Iliās. Herāt, NW Afghanistan 35°26′N 61°24′E
Karjaa see Karis
Karkaralinsk see Karkaraly
145 T10 **Karkaraly** prev. Karkaralinsk. Karaganda, E Kazakhstan 49°31′N 75°53′E
186 D6 **Karkar Island** island N Papua New Guinea
143 N7 **Karkas, Kūh-e** ▲ C Iran
142 K8 **Karkheh, Rūd-e** ≈ SW Iran
115 L20 **Karkinágri** var. Karkinagrio. Ikaría, Dodekánisa, Greece, Aegean Sea 37°31′N 26°01′E
Karkinagrio see Karkinágri
117 R12 **Karkinits'ka Zatoka** Rus. Karkinitskiy Zaliv. gulf S Ukraine
Karkinitskiy Zaliv see Karkinits'ka Zatoka
93 L19 **Karkkila** Swe. Högfors. Uusimaa, S Finland 60°32′N 24°10′E
93 M19 **Kärkölä** Etelä-Suomi, S Finland 60°52′N 25°17′E
182 G9 **Karkoo** South Australia 34°03′S 135°45′E
Karkūk see Kirkūk
118 D5 **Kärla** Ger. Kergel. Saaremaa, W Estonia 58°20′N 22°15′E
Karleby see Kokkola
110 F7 **Karlino** Ger. Körlin an der Persante. Zachodinio-pomorskie, NW Poland 54°02′N 15°52′E
137 Q13 **Karlıova** Bingöl, E Turkey 39°16′N 41°01′E
117 U6 **Karlivka** Poltavs'ka Oblast', C Ukraine 49°27′N 35°08′E
Karl-Marx-Stadt see Chemnitz
Karlö see Hailuoto
112 C11 **Karlobag** It. Carlopago. Lika-Senj, W Croatia 44°31′N 15°06′E
112 D9 **Karlovac** Ger. Karlstadt, Hung. Károlyváros. Karlovac, C Croatia 45°29′N 15°31′E
112 C10 **Karlovac** off. Karlovačka Županija. ⬖ province C Croatia
Karlovačka Županija see Karlovac
111 A16 **Karlovarský Kraj** ⬖ W Czech Republic
115 M19 **Karlovási** var. Néon Karlovásion, Néon Karlovasi. Sámos, Dodekánisa, Greece, Aegean Sea 37°47′N 26°40′E
114 J9 **Karlovo** prev. Levskigrad. Plovdiv, C Bulgaria 42°38′N 24°49′E
111 A16 **Karlovy Vary** Ger. Karlsbad; prev. Eng. Carlsbad. Karlovarský Kraj, W Czech Republic 50°13′N 12°51′E
Karlsbad see Karlovy Vary
95 L17 **Karlsborg** Västra Götaland, S Sweden 58°32′N 14°32′E
Karlsburg see Alba Iulia
95 L22 **Karlshamn** Blekinge, S Sweden 56°10′N 14°50′E
95 L16 **Karlskoga** Örebro, C Sweden 59°19′N 14°33′E
95 M22 **Karlskrona** Blekinge, S Sweden 56°11′N 15°39′E
101 G21 **Karlsruhe** var. Carlsruhe. Baden-Württemberg, SW Germany 49°01′N 08°24′E
95 K16 **Karlstad** Värmland, C Sweden 59°22′N 13°36′E
29 R3 **Karlstad** Minnesota, N USA 48°34′N 96°31′W
101 I18 **Karlstadt** Bayern, C Germany 49°58′N 09°46′E
Karlstadt see Karlovac
39 Q14 **Karluk** Kodiak Island, Alaska, USA 57°34′N 154°27′W
Karluk see Qarluq
119 O17 **Karma** Rus. Korma. Homyel'skaya Voblasts', SE Belarus 53°07′N 30°48′E
155 F14 **Karmāla** Mahārāshtra, W India 18°26′N 75°08′E
146 M11 **Karmana** Navoiy Viloyati, C Uzbekistan 40°09′N 65°18′E
138 G8 **Karmi'el** var. Carmiel. Northern, N Israel 32°55′N 35°18′E
95 B16 **Karmøy** island S Norway
152 I9 **Karnāl** Haryāna, N India 29°41′N 76°58′E
153 W15 **Karnaphuli Reservoir** ▣ NE India
155 F17 **Karnātaka** var. Kanara; prev. Maisur, Mysore. ⬖ state W India
25 S13 **Karnes City** Texas, SW USA 28°54′N 97°55′W
109 P9 **Karnische Alpen** It. Alpi Carniche. ▲▲ Austria/Italy
114 M9 **Karnobat** Burgas, E Bulgaria 42°39′N 26°59′E
109 Q9 **Kärnten** off. Land Kärten, Eng. Carinthi, Slvn. Koroška. ⬖ state S Austria
Karnul see Kurnool
83 K16 **Karoi** Mashonaland West, N Zimbabwe 16°50′S 29°40′E
Karol see Carei
Károly-Fehérvár see Alba Iulia
Károlyváros see Karlovac
82 M12 **Karonga** Northern, N Malawi 09°54′S 33°55′E
147 W10 **Karool-Dëbë** Kas. Karool-Döbö; prev. Karool-Tëbë. Narynskaya Oblast', C Kyrgyzstan 40°33′N 75°52′E
Karool-Döbö see Karool-Dëbë
Karool-Tëbë see Karool-Dëbë
182 J9 **Karoonda** South Australia 35°04′S 139°58′E
149 S9 **Karor** var. Koror Lāl Esan. Punjab, E Pakistan 31°15′N 70°58′E
Karosa see Karossa
171 N12 **Karossa** var. Karosa. Sulawesi, C Indonesia 01°38′S 119°21′E
Karpaten see Carpathian Mountains
115 L22 **Karpáthio Pélagos** sea Dodekánisa, Greece, Aegean Sea
115 N24 **Kárpathos** Kárpathos, SE Greece 35°30′N 27°13′E
115 N24 **Kárpathos** It. Scarpanto; anc. Carpathos, Carpathus. island SE Greece
Karpathos Strait see Karpathou, Stenó
115 N24 **Karpathou, Stenó** var. Karpathos Strait, Scarpanto Strait. strait Dodekánisa, Greece, Aegean Sea
Karpaty see Carpathian Mountains
115 E17 **Karpenísi** prev. Karpenísion. Stereá Elláda, C Greece 38°55′N 21°46′E
Karpenísion see Karpenísi
Karpilovka see Aktsyabrski
125 O8 **Karpogory** Arkhangel'skaya Oblast', NW Russian Federation 64°01′N 44°22′E
180 I7 **Karratha** Western Australia 20°44′S 116°52′E
137 S12 **Kars** var. Qars. Kars, NE Turkey 40°35′N 43°05′E
137 S12 **Kars** var. Qars. ⬖ province NE Turkey
145 O12 **Karsakpay** Kaz. Qarsaqbay. Karaganda, C Kazakhstan 47°51′N 66°42′E
93 L15 **Kärsämäki** Oulu, C Finland 63°58′N 25°49′E
Karsau see Kārsava
118 K9 **Kārsava** Ger. Karsau; prev. Rus. Korsovka. E Latvia 56°46′N 27°39′E
Karshi see Garşy, Turkmenistan
Karshi see Qarshi, Uzbekistan
Karshinskaya Step see Qarshi Cho'li
Karshinskiy Kanal see Qarshi Kanali
84 I5 **Karskiye Vorota, Proliv** Eng. Kara Strait. strait N Russian Federation
122 J6 **Karskoye More** Eng. Kara Sea. sea Arctic Ocean
93 L17 **Karstula** Länsi-Suomi, C Finland 62°52′N 24°48′E
127 Q5 **Karsun** Ul'yanovskaya Oblast', W Russian Federation 54°12′N 47°00′E
122 F11 **Kartaly** Chelyabinskaya Oblast', C Russian Federation 53°02′N 60°42′E
18 E13 **Karthaus** Pennsylvania, NE USA 41°06′N 78°03′W
110 I7 **Kartuzy** Pomorskie, NW Poland 54°21′N 18°11′E
165 R8 **Karumai** Iwate, Honshū, C Japan 40°19′N 141°27′E
181 U4 **Karumba** Queensland, NE Australia 17°31′S 140°51′E
142 L10 **Kārūn** var. Rūd-e Kārūn. ≈ SW Iran
92 K13 **Karungi** Norrbotten, N Sweden 66°03′N 23°55′E
92 K13 **Karunki** Lappi, N Finland 66°01′N 24°06′E
Kārūn, Rūd-e see Kārūn
155 H21 **Karūr** Tamil Nādu, SE India 10°58′N 78°03′E
93 K17 **Karvia** Länsi-Suomi, SW Finland 62°07′N 22°34′E
111 J17 **Karviná** Ger. Karwin, Pol. Karwina; prev. Nová Karvinná. Moravskoslezský Krajj, E Czech Republic 49°50′N 18°30′E
155 E17 **Kārwār** Karnātaka, W India 14°50′N 74°09′E
108 M7 **Karwendelgebirge** ▲▲ Austria/Germany
Karwin/Karwina see Karviná
115 I14 **Karyés** var. Karies. Ágion Óros, N Greece 40°15′N 24°15′E

◆ Country
● Country Capital
◇ Dependent Territory
○ Dependent Territory Capital
⬖ Administrative Regions
✈ International Airport
▲ Mountain
▲▲ Mountain Range
Volcano
≈ River
◎ Lake
▣ Reservoir

115 I19 **Kárystos** var. Káristos. Évvoia, C Greece 38°01′N 24°25′E
136 E17 **Kaş** Antalya, SW Turkey 36°12′N 29°38′E
39 Y14 **Kasaan** Prince of Wales Island, Alaska, USA 55°32′N 132°24′W
164 I13 **Kasai** Hyōgo, Honshū, SW Japan 34°56′N 134°49′E
79 K21 **Kasai** var. Cassai, Kassai. ≈ Angola/Dem. Rep. Congo
79 K22 **Kasai-Occidental** off. Région Kasai Occidental. ◐ region S Dem. Rep. Congo
Kasai Occidental, Région see Kasai-Occidental
79 L21 **Kasai-Oriental** off. Région Kasai Oriental. ◐ region C Dem. Rep. Congo
Kasai Oriental, Région see Kasai-Oriental
79 L24 **Kasaji** Katanga, S Dem. Rep. Congo 10°22′S 23°29′E
82 L12 **Kasama** Northern, N Zambia 10°14′S 31°12′E
Kasan see Koson
83 H16 **Kasane** North-West, NE Botswana 17°48′S 20°06′E
81 E23 **Kasanga** Rukwa, W Tanzania 08°27′S 31°10′E
79 G21 **Kasangulu** Bas-Congo, W Dem. Rep. Congo 04°33′S 15°12′E
Kasansay see Kosonsoy
155 E20 **Kāsaragod** Kerala, SW India 12°30′N 74°59′E
Kasargen see Kasari
118 P13 **Kasari** var. Kasari Jõgi, Ger. Kasargen. ≈ W Estonia
Kasari Jõgi see Kasari
8 L11 **Kasba Lake** ◎ Northwest Territories, Nunavut N Canada
Kaschau see Košice
Kaseda see Minamisatsuma
83 I14 **Kasempa** North Western, NW Zambia 13°27′S 25°49′E
79 O24 **Kasenga** Katanga, SE Dem. Rep. Congo 10°22′S 28°37′E
79 P17 **Kasenye** var. Kasenyi. Orientale, NE Dem. Rep. Congo 01°23′N 30°25′E
Kasenyi see Kasenye
79 O19 **Kasese** Maniema, E Dem. Rep. Congo 01°36′S 27°31′E
81 E18 **Kasese** SW Uganda 0°10′N 30°06′E
152 J11 **Kāsganj** Uttar Pradesh, N India 27°48′N 78°38′E
143 U4 **Kashaf Rūd** ≈ NE Iran
143 N7 **Kāshān** Eşfahān, C Iran 33°57′N 51°31′E
126 M10 **Kashary** Rostovskaya Oblast', SW Russian Federation 49°02′N 40°58′E
39 O12 **Kashegelok** Alaska, USA 60°57′N 157°46′W
Kashgar see Kashi
158 E7 **Kashi** Chin. Kaxgar, K'o-shih, Uigh. Kashgar. Xinjiang Uygur Zizhiqu, NW China 39°32′N 75°58′E
164 J14 **Kashihara** var. Kasihara. Nara, Honshū, SW Japan 34°28′N 135°46′E
165 P13 **Kashima-nada** gulf S Japan
124 K15 **Kashin** Tverskaya Oblast', W Russian Federation 57°20′N 37°34′E
152 K10 **Kāshīpur** Uttarakhand, N India 29°13′N 78°58′E
126 L4 **Kashira** Moskovskaya Oblast', W Russian Federation 54°53′N 38°13′E
165 N11 **Kashiwazaki** var. Kasiwazaki. Niigata, Honshū, C Japan 37°22′N 138°33′E
Kashkadar'inskaya Oblast' see Qashqadaryo Viloyati
143 T5 **Kāshmar** var. Turshiz; prev. Solṭānābād, Torshiz. Khorāsān, NE Iran 35°13′N 58°25′E
Kashmir see Jammu and Kashmir
149 R12 **Kashmor** Sind, SE Pakistan 28°24′N 69°42′E
149 S5 **Kashmūnd Ghar** Eng. Kashmund Range. ▲▲ E Afghanistan
Kashmund Range see Kashmūnd Ghar
145 T7 **Kashyr** prev. Kachiry. Pavlodar, NE Kazakhstan 53°07′N 76°08′E
Kasi see Vārānasi
153 O12 **Kasia** Uttar Pradesh, N India 26°45′N 83°55′E
39 N12 **Kasigluk** Alaska, USA 60°54′N 162°31′W
Kasihara see Kashihara
39 R12 **Kasilof** Alaska, USA 60°20′N 151°16′W
Kasimköj see General Toshevo
126 M4 **Kasimov** Ryazanskaya Oblast', W Russian Federation 54°59′N 41°22′E
79 P18 **Kasindi** Nord-Kivu, E Dem. Rep. Congo 0°03′N 29°43′E
82 M12 **Kasitu** ≈ N Malawi
Kasiwazaki see Kashiwazaki
30 L14 **Kaskaskia River** ≈ Illinois, N USA
93 J17 **Kaskinen** Swe. Kaskö. Länsi-Suomi, W Finland 62°23′N 21°10′E
Kaskö see Kaskinen
Kas Kong see Kŏng, Kaôh
11 O17 **Kaslo** British Columbia, SW Canada 49°54′N 116°57′W
Käsmark see Kežmarok
169 T12 **Kasongan** Borneo, C Indonesia 02°01′S 113°21′E
79 N21 **Kasongo** Maniema, E Dem. Rep. Congo 04°22′S 26°42′E
79 H22 **Kasongo-Lunda** Bandundu, SW Dem. Rep. Congo 06°30′S 16°51′E
115 M24 **Kásos** island S Greece
Kasos Strait see Kásou, Stenó
115 M25 **Kásou, Stenó** var. Kasos Strait. strait Dodekánisos/Kríti, Greece, Aegean Sea
137 T10 **K'asp'i** prev. Kaspi. C Georgia 41°54′N 44°25′E
Kaspi see K'asp'i
114 M8 **Kaspichan** Shumen, NE Bulgaria 43°18′N 27°09′E
Kaspīy Mangy Oypaty see Caspian Depression
127 Q16 **Kaspiysk** Respublika Dagestan, SW Russian Federation 42°52′N 47°40′E
Kaspiyskiy see Lagan'
Kaspiyskoye More/Kaspiy Tengizi see Caspian Sea
Kassa see Košice
Kassai see Kasai
80 I9 **Kassala** Kassala, E Sudan 15°24′N 36°25′E
80 H9 **Kassala** ◐ state NE Sudan
115 G15 **Kassándra** prev. Pallíni; anc. Pallene. peninsula NE Greece
115 G15 **Kassándra** headland N Greece 39°58′N 23°22′E
115 H15 **Kassándras, Kólpos** var. Kólpos Toronaíos. gulf N Greece
139 Y11 **Kassārah** Maysān, E Iraq 31°21′N 47°25′E
101 I15 **Kassel** prev. Cassel. Hessen, C Germany 51°19′N 09°30′E
74 M6 **Kasserine** var. Al Qaşrayn. W Tunisia 35°15′N 08°52′E
14 J14 **Kasshabog Lake** ◎ Ontario, SE Canada
139 O5 **Kassīr, Sabkhat al** ◎ E Syria
29 W10 **Kasson** Minnesota, N USA 44°00′N 92°42′W
115 C17 **Kassópeia** Var. Kassópi. site of ancient city Ípeiros, W Greece
Kassópi see Kassópeia
136 I11 **Kastamonu** var. Castamoni, Kastamuni. Kastamonu, N Turkey 41°22′N 33°47′E
136 I10 **Kastamonu** var. Kastamuni. ◐ province N Turkey
Kastamuni see Kastamonu
Kastaneá see Kastaniá
115 E14 **Kastaniá** prev. Kastaneá. Kentrikí Makedonía, N Greece 40°25′N 22°09′E
Kastélli see Kíssamos
Kastellórizon see Megísti
115 N24 **Kástelo, Akrotírio** prev. Akrotírio Kastállou. headland Kárpathos, SE Greece 35°24′N 27°08′E
95 N21 **Kastlösa** Kalmar, S Sweden 56°25′N 16°25′E
115 D14 **Kastoría** Dytikí Makedonía, N Greece 40°33′N 21°15′E
126 K7 **Kastornoye** Kurskaya Oblast', W Russian Federation 51°49′N 38°07′E
115 I21 **Kástro** Sífnos, Kykládes, Greece, Aegean Sea 36°58′N 24°45′E
95 J23 **Kastrup** ✈ (København) København, E Denmark 55°36′N 12°39′E
119 Q17 **Kastsyukovichy** Rus. Kostyukovichi. Mahilyowskaya Voblasts', E Belarus 53°20′N 32°03′E
119 O18 **Kastsyukowka** Rus. Kostyukovka. Homyel'skaya Voblasts', SE Belarus 52°32′N 30°54′E
164 D13 **Kasuga** Fukuoka, Kyūshū, SW Japan 33°31′N 130°27′E
164 L13 **Kasugai** Aichi, Honshū, SW Japan 35°15′N 136°57′E
81 E21 **Kasulu** Kigoma, W Tanzania 04°33′S 30°06′E
164 I12 **Kasumi** Hyōgo, Honshū, SW Japan 35°36′N 134°37′E
127 R17 **Kasumkent** Respublika Dagestan, SW Russian Federation 41°39′N 48°09′E
82 M13 **Kasungu** Central, C Malawi 13°04′S 33°29′E
149 W9 **Kasūr** Punjab, E Pakistan 31°07′N 74°30′E
83 G15 **Kataba** Western, W Zambia 15°28′S 23°25′E
19 R4 **Katahdin, Mount** ▲ Maine, NE USA 45°55′N 68°52′W
79 M20 **Katako-Kombe** Kasai-Oriental, C Dem. Rep. Congo 03°24′S 24°25′E
39 T12 **Katalla** Alaska, USA 60°12′N 144°31′W
Katana see Qaṭanā
79 L24 **Katanga** off. Région du Katanga; prev. Shaba. ◐ region SE Dem. Rep. Congo
122 M11 **Katanga** ≈ C Russian Federation
Katanga, Région du see Katanga
154 J11 **Katāngi** Madhya Pradesh, C India 21°46′N 79°50′E
180 J13 **Katanning** Western Australia 33°45′S 117°33′E
181 P8 **Kata Tjuṯa** var. Mount Olga. ▲ Northern Territory, C Australia 25°20′S 130°47′E
Katawaz see Zarghūn Shahr
151 Q22 **Katchall Island** island Nicobar Islands, India, NE Indian Ocean
115 F14 **Kateríni** Kentrikí Makedonía, N Greece 40°15′N 22°30′E
117 P7 **Katerynopil'** Cherkas'ka Oblast', C Ukraine 49°00′N 30°59′E
166 M3 **Katha** Sagaing, N Burma (Myanmar) 24°11′N 96°20′E
181 P2 **Katherine** Northern Territory, N Australia 14°29′S 132°20′E
154 B11 **Kāthiāwār Peninsula** peninsula W India
153 P11 **Kathmandu** prev. Kantipur. ● (Nepal) Central, C Nepal 27°46′N 85°17′E
152 H7 **Kathua** Jammu and Kashmir, NW India 32°23′N 75°34′E
76 L12 **Kati** Koulikoro, SW Mali 12°41′N 08°04′W
153 R13 **Katihār** Bihār, NE India 25°33′N 87°34′E
184 N7 **Katikati** Bay of Plenty, North Island, New Zealand 37°34′S 175°55′E
83 H16 **Katima Mulilo** Caprivi, NE Namibia 17°31′S 24°20′E
77 N15 **Katiola** C Ivory Coast 08°11′N 05°04′W
191 V10 **Katiu** atoll Îles Tuamotu, C French Polynesia
117 N12 **Katlabuh, Ozero** ◎ SW Ukraine
39 P14 **Katmai, Mount** ▲ Alaska, USA 58°16′N 154°57′W
154 J9 **Katni** Madhya Pradesh, C India 23°47′N 80°29′E
115 D19 **Káto Achaïa** var. Kato Ahaia, Káto Akhaía. Dytikí Elláda, S Greece 38°08′N 21°33′E
Kato Ahaia/Káto Akhaía see Káto Achaïa
121 P2 **Kato Lakatámeia** var. Kato Lakatamia. C Cyprus 35°07′N 33°20′E
Kato Lakatamia see Kato Lakatámeia
79 N22 **Katompi** Katanga, SE Dem. Rep. Congo 06°10′S 26°19′E
83 K14 **Katondwe** Lusaka, C Zambia 15°08′S 30°10′E
114 H12 **Káto Nevrokópi** prev. Káto Nevrokópion. Anatolikí Makedonía kai Thráki, NE Greece 41°21′N 23°51′E
Káto Nevrokópion see Káto Nevrokópi
81 E18 **Katonga** ≈ S Uganda
115 F15 **Káto Ólympos** ▲▲ C Greece
115 D17 **Katoúna** Dytikí Elláda, C Greece 38°47′N 21°07′E
115 E19 **Káto Vlasiá** Dytikí Makedonía, S Greece 38°02′N 21°54′E
111 J16 **Katowice** Ger. Kattowitz. Śląskie, S Poland 50°15′N 19°01′E
153 S15 **Kātoya** West Bengal, NE India 23°39′N 88°11′E
136 E16 **Katrançık Dağı** ▲▲ SW Turkey
95 N16 **Katrineholm** Södermanland, C Sweden 58°59′N 16°15′E
96 I11 **Katrine, Loch** ◎ C Scotland, United Kingdom
77 V12 **Katsina** Katsina, N Nigeria 12°59′N 07°33′E
77 U12 **Katsina** ◐ state N Nigeria
67 P8 **Katsina Ala** ≈ S Nigeria
164 C13 **Katsumoto** Nagasaki, Iki, SW Japan 33°49′N 129°42′E
165 P13 **Katsuta** var. Katuta. Ibaraki, Honshū, S Japan 36°24′N 140°32′E
165 O14 **Katsuura** var. Katuura. Chiba, Honshū, S Japan 35°09′N 140°16′E
164 K12 **Katsuyama** var. Katuyama. Fukui, Honshū, SW Japan 36°00′N 136°30′E
164 H12 **Katsuyama** Okayama, Honshū, SW Japan 35°06′N 133°43′E
Kattakurgan see Kattaqo'rg'on
147 N11 **Kattaqo'rg'on** Rus. Kattakurgan. Samarqand Viloyati, C Uzbekistan 39°56′N 66°11′E
115 O23 **Kattavía** Ródos, Dodekánisa, Greece, Aegean Sea 35°56′N 27°47′E
95 I21 **Kattegat** Dan. Kattegatt. strait N Europe
Kattegatt see Kattegat
95 P19 **Katthammarsvik** Gotland, SE Sweden 57°27′N 18°54′E
Kattowitz see Katowice
122 J13 **Katun'** ≈ S Russian Federation
Katuta see Katsuta
Katuura see Katsuura
Katuyama see Katsuyama
Katwijk see Katwijk aan Zee
98 G11 **Katwijk aan Zee** var. Katwijk. Zuid-Holland, W Netherlands 59°12′N 04°24′E
38 B8 **Kaua'i** var. Kauai. island Hawaiian Islands, Hawai'i, USA, C Pacific Ocean
Kauai see Kaua'i
38 C8 **Kaua'i Channel** var. Kauai Channel. channel Hawai'i, USA, C Pacific Ocean
Kauai Channel see Kaua'i Channel
171 R13 **Kaubalatmada, Gunung** var. Kaplamada. ▲ Pulau Buru, E Indonesia 03°16′S 126°17′E
191 U10 **Kauehi** atoll Îles Tuamotu, C French Polynesia
Kauen see Kaunas
101 K24 **Kaufbeuren** Bayern, S Germany 47°53′N 10°37′E
25 U7 **Kaufman** Texas, SW USA 32°35′N 96°18′W
101 I15 **Kaufungen** Hessen, C Germany 51°16′N 09°39′E
93 K17 **Kauhajoki** Länsi-Suomi, W Finland 62°26′N 22°10′E
93 K16 **Kauhava** Länsi-Suomi, W Finland 63°06′N 23°08′E
30 M7 **Kaukauna** Wisconsin, N USA 44°18′N 88°18′W
92 L11 **Kaukonen** Lappi, N Finland 67°28′N 24°49′E
38 A8 **Kaulakahi Channel** channel Hawai'i, USA, C Pacific Ocean
38 E9 **Kaunakakai** Moloka'i, Hawaii, USA, C Pacific Ocean 21°05′N 157°01′W
38 F12 **Kaunā Point** var. Kauna Point. headland Hawai'i, USA, C Pacific Ocean 19°02′N 155°52′W
Kauna Point see Kaunā Point
118 F13 **Kaunas** Ger. Kauen, Pol. Kowno; prev. Rus. Kovno. Kaunas, C Lithuania 54°54′N 23°57′E
118 F13 **Kaunas** ◐ province C Lithuania
186 C6 **Kaup** East Sepik, NW Papua New Guinea 03°50′S 144°01′E
77 U12 **Kaura Namoda** Zamfara, NW Nigeria 12°43′N 06°17′E
Kaushany see Căuşeni
93 K16 **Kaustinen** Länsi-Suomi, W Finland 63°33′N 23°40′E
99 M23 **Kautenbach** Diekirch, NE Luxembourg 49°57′N 06°01′E
92 K10 **Kautokeino** Lapp. Guovdageaidnu. Finnmark, N Norway 69°N 23°01′E
Kavadar see Kavadarci
113 P19 **Kavadarci** Turk. Kavadar. C Macedonia 41°25′N 22°00′E
Kavaja see Kavajë
113 K20 **Kavajë** It. Cavaia, Kavaja. Tiranë, W Albania 41°11′N 19°33′E
114 M13 **Kavak Çayı** ≈ NW Turkey
Kavakli see Topolovgrad
114 I13 **Kavála** prev. Kavála. Anatolikí Makedonía kai Thráki, NE Greece 40°57′N 24°26′E
114 I13 **Kaválas, Kólpos** gulf Aegean Sea, NE Mediterranean Sea
155 J17 **Kāvali** Andhra Pradesh, E India 15°05′N 80°02′E
Kavála see Kavála
Kavango see Cubango/Okavango
155 C21 **Kavaratti** Lakshadweep, SW India 10°33′N 72°38′E
114 O8 **Kavarna** Dobrich, NE Bulgaria 43°27′N 28°21′E
118 G12 **Kavarskas** Utena, E Lithuania 55°27′N 24°55′E
76 I13 **Kavendou** ▲ C Guinea 10°49′N 12°14′W
Kavengo see Cubango/Okavango
155 F20 **Kāveri** var. Cauvery. ≈ S India
186 G5 **Kavieng** var. Kaewieng. New Ireland, NE Papua New Guinea 04°13′S 152°11′E
83 H16 **Kavimba** North-West, NE Botswana 18°02′S 24°38′E
83 I15 **Kavingu** Southern, S Zambia 15°39′S 26°03′E
143 Q6 **Kavīr, Dasht-e** var. Great Salt Desert. salt pan N Iran
Kavirondo Gulf see Winam Gulf
Kavkaz see Caucasus
95 K23 **Kävlinge** Skåne, S Sweden 55°47′N 13°05′E
82 G12 **Kavungo** Moxico, E Angola 11°31′S 22°59′E
165 Q8 **Kawabe** Akita, Honshū, C Japan 39°39′N 140°14′E
165 R9 **Kawai** Iwate, Honshū, C Japan 39°36′N 141°40′E
38 A8 **Kawaihoa Point** headland Ni'ihau, Hawai'i, USA, C Pacific Ocean 21°47′N 160°12′W
184 K3 **Kawakawa** Northland, North Island, New Zealand 35°23′S 174°06′E
82 I13 **Kawama** North Western, NW Zambia 13°04′S 25°59′E
82 K11 **Kawambwa** Luapula, N Zambia 09°45′S 29°10′E
154 K11 **Kawardha** Chhattīsgarh, C India 21°59′N 81°12′E
14 I14 **Kawartha Lakes** ◎ Ontario, SE Canada
165 O13 **Kawasaki** Kanagawa, Honshū, S Japan 35°32′N 139°41′E
171 R12 **Kawassi** Pulau Obi, E Indonesia 01°32′S 127°25′E
165 R6 **Kawauchi** Aomori, Honshū, C Japan 41°11′N 141°00′E
184 L5 **Kawau Island** island N New Zealand
184 N10 **Kaweka Range** ▲▲ North Island, New Zealand
Kawelecht see Puhja
184 O8 **Kawerau** Bay of Plenty, North Island, New Zealand 38°06′S 176°43′E
184 L8 **Kawhia** Waikato, North Island, New Zealand 38°04′S 174°49′E
184 K8 **Kawhia Harbour** inlet North Island, New Zealand
35 V8 **Kawich Peak** ▲ Nevada, W USA 38°00′N 116°27′W
35 V9 **Kawich Range** ▲▲ Nevada, W USA
14 G12 **Kawigamog Lake** ◎ Ontario, S Canada
171 P9 **Kawio, Kepulauan** island group N Indonesia
167 N9 **Kawkareik** Kayin State, S Burma (Myanmar) 16°33′N 98°18′E
27 O8 **Kaw Lake** ⊠ Oklahoma, C USA
166 M3 **Kawlin** Sagaing, N Burma (Myanmar) 23°48′N 95°41′E
Kawm Umbū see Kom Ombo
Kawthule State see Kayin State
Kaxgar see Kashi
158 D7 **Kaxgar He** ≈ NW China
158 J5 **Kax He** ≈ NW China
77 P12 **Kaya** C Burkina 13°04′N 01°09′W
167 N6 **Kayah State** ◐ state C Burma (Myanmar)
39 T12 **Kayak Island** island Alaska, USA
114 M11 **Kayalıköy Barajı** ⊠ NW Turkey
166 M8 **Kayan** Yangon, SW Burma (Myanmar) 16°54′N 96°35′E
Kayangel Islands see Ngcheangel
155 G23 **Kāyankulam** Kerala, SW India 09°10′N 76°31′E
169 V9 **Kayan, Sungai** prev. Kajan. ≈ Borneo, C Indonesia
144 F14 **Kaydak, Sor** salt flat SW Kazakhstan
Kaydanovo see Dzyarzhynsk Belarus
37 N9 **Kayenta** Arizona, SW USA 36°43′N 110°15′W
76 J11 **Kayes** Kayes, W Mali 14°26′N 11°22′W
76 J11 **Kayes** ◐ region SW Mali
167 N8 **Kayin State** var. Kawthule State, Karen State. ◐ state S Burma (Myanmar)
145 U10 **Kaynar** Kaz. Qaynar, var. Kajnar. Vostochnyy Kazakhstan, E Kazakhstan 49°13′N 77°27′E
Kaynary see Căinari
83 H15 **Kayoya** Western, W Zambia 16°13′S 24°09′E
Kayrakkum see Qayroqqum
Kayrakkumskoye Vodokhranilishche see Qayroqqum, Obanbori
136 K14 **Kayseri** var. Kaisaria; anc. Caesarea Mazaca, Mazaca. Kayseri, C Turkey 38°42′N 35°28′E
136 K14 **Kayseri** var. Kaisaria. ◐ province C Turkey
36 L2 **Kaysville** Utah, W USA 41°10′N 111°55′W
Kayyngdy see Kaindy
14 L11 **Kazabazua** Québec, SE Canada 45°58′N 76°00′W
14 L12 **Kazabazua** ≈ Québec, SE Canada
123 Q7 **Kazach'ye** Respublika Sakha (Yakutiya), NE Russian Federation 70°38′N 135°54′E
Kazakdar'ya see Qozoqdaryo
146 E9 **Kazakhlyshor, Solonchak** var. Solonchak Shorkazakhly. salt marsh NW Turkmenistan
Kazakhskaya SSR/Kazakh Soviet Socialist Republic see Kazakhstan
144 L12 **Kazakhstan** off. Republic of Kazakhstan, var. Kazakstan, Kaz. Qazaqstan, Qazaqstan Respublikasy; prev. Kazakh Soviet Socialist Republic, Rus. Kazakhskaya SSR. ◆ republic C Asia
Kazakhstan, Republic of see Kazakhstan
Kazakh Uplands see Saryarka
Kazakstan see Kazakhstan
Kazalinsk see Kazaly
144 L14 **Kazaly** prev. Kazalinsk. Kzyl-Orda, S Kazakhstan 45°45′N 62°01′E
127 R4 **Kazan'** Respublika Tatarstan, W Russian Federation 55°43′N 49°07′E
8 M10 **Kazan** ≈ Nunavut, NW Canada
127 R4 **Kazan'** ✈ Respublika Tatarstan, W Russian Federation 55°46′N 49°21′E
Kazandzhik see Bereket
117 R8 **Kazanka** Mykolayivs'ka Oblast', S Ukraine 47°49′N 32°50′E
Kazanketken see Qozonketkan
Kazanlik see Kazanlŭk
114 J9 **Kazanlŭk** prev. Kazanlik. Stara Zagora, C Bulgaria 42°38′N 25°24′E
165 Y16 **Kazan-rettō** Eng. Volcano Islands. island group SE Japan
Kazantip, Mys see Kazantyp, Mys
117 V12 **Kazantyp, Mys** prev. Mys Kazantip. headland S Ukraine 45°27′N 35°50′E
147 U9 **Kazarman** Narynskaya Oblast', C Kyrgyzstan 41°21′N 74°03′E
Kazatin see Kozyatyn
Kazbegi see Kazbek
Kazbegi see Q'azbegi
137 T9 **Kazbek** var. Kazbegi, Geor. Mqinvartsveri. ▲ N Georgia 42°43′N 44°28′E
82 M13 **Kazembe** Eastern, NE Zambia 12°06′S 32°45′E
143 N11 **Kāzerūn** Fārs, S Iran 29°41′N 51°38′E
125 R12 **Kazhym** Respublika Komi, NW Russian Federation 60°19′N 51°26′E
Kazi Ahmad see Qāzi Ahmad
136 H16 **Kazımkarabekir** Karaman, S Turkey 37°13′N 32°58′E
111 M20 **Kazincbarcika** Borsod-Abaúj-Zemplén, NE Hungary 48°15′N 20°40′E
119 H17 **Kazlowshchyna** Pol. Kozlowszczyzna, Rus. Kozlovshchina. Hrodzyenskaya Voblasts', W Belarus 53°19′N 25°18′E
119 E14 **Kazlų Rūda** Marijampolė, S Lithuania 54°45′N 23°28′E
144 E9 **Kaztalovka** Zapadnyy Kazakhstan, W Kazakhstan 49°45′N 48°42′E
79 K22 **Kazumba** Kasai-Occidental, S Dem. Rep. Congo 06°25′S 22°02′E
165 Q8 **Kazuno** Akita, Honshū, C Japan 40°14′N 140°48′E
Kazvin see Qazvīn
118 J12 **Kazyany** Rus. Koz'yany. Vitsyebskaya Voblasts', NW Belarus 55°18′N 26°52′E
122 H9 **Kazym** ≈ N Russian Federation
110 H10 **Kcynia** Ger. Exin. Kujawsko-pomorskie, C Poland 53°00′N 17°29′E
Kéa see Tziá
Kéa see Ioulís
38 H11 **Kea'au** var. Keaau. Hawaii, USA, C Pacific Ocean 19°36′N 155°01′W
Keaau see Kea'au
38 F11 **Keāhole Point** var. Keahole Point. headland Hawai'i, USA, C Pacific Ocean 19°43′N 156°03′W
38 G12 **Kealakekua** Hawaii, USA, C Pacific Ocean 19°31′N 155°56′W
38 H11 **Kea, Mauna** ▲ Hawai'i, USA 19°50′N 155°30′W
37 N10 **Keams** Arizona, SW USA 35°47′N 110°09′W
Kéamu see Aneityum
29 O16 **Kearney** Nebraska, C USA 40°42′N 99°06′W
36 L3 **Kearns** Utah, W USA 40°39′N 112°00′W
115 H20 **Kéas, Stenó** strait SE Greece
137 O14 **Keban Barajı** dam C Turkey
137 O14 **Keban Barajı** ⊠ C Turkey
77 S13 **Kebbi** ◐ state NW Nigeria
76 G10 **Kébémèr** NW Senegal 15°24′N 16°25′W
74 M7 **Kebili** var. Qibilī. C Tunisia 33°42′N 09°06′E
138 H4 **Kebir, Nahr el** ≈ NW Syria
80 A10 **Kebkabiya** Northern Darfur, W Sudan 13°39′N 24°05′E
92 I11 **Kebnekaise** Lapp. Giebnegáisi. ▲ N Sweden 68°01′N 18°24′E
81 M14 **K'ebrī Dehar** Sumalē, E Ethiopia 06°43′N 44°15′E
148 K15 **Kech** ≈ SW Pakistan
10 K10 **Kechika** ≈ British Columbia, W Canada
111 K23 **Kecskemét** Bács-Kiskun, C Hungary 46°54′N 19°42′E
168 J6 **Kedah** ◐ state Peninsular Malaysia
118 F12 **Kėdainiai** Kaunas, C Lithuania 55°19′N 24°00′E
152 K8 **Kedārnāth** Uttarakhand, N India 30°44′N 79°03′E
Kedder see Kehra
13 N13 **Kedgwick** New Brunswick, SE Canada 47°38′N 67°21′W
169 R16 **Kediri** Jawa, C Indonesia 07°45′S 112°01′E
171 Y13 **Kedir Sarmi** Papua, E Indonesia 02°00′S 139°01′E
163 V7 **Kedong** Heilongjiang, NE China 48°00′N 126°15′E
76 I12 **Kédougou** SE Senegal 12°35′N 12°09′W
122 I11 **Kedrovyy** Tomskaya Oblast', C Russian Federation 57°31′N 79°45′E
111 H16 **Kędzierzyn-Kozle** Ger. Heydebrech. Opolskie, S Poland 50°20′N 18°12′E
8 H8 **Keele** ≈ Northwest Territories, NW Canada
10 K6 **Keele Peak** ▲ Yukon Territory, NW Canada 63°31′N 130°21′W
Keelung see Jilong
19 N10 **Keene** New Hampshire, NE USA 42°56′N 72°14′W
99 H17 **Keerbergen** Vlaams Brabant, C Belgium 51°01′N 04°39′E
83 E21 **Keetmanshoop** Karas, S Namibia 26°36′S 18°08′E
12 A11 **Keewatin** Ontario, S Canada 49°47′N 94°30′W
29 V4 **Keewatin** Minnesota, N USA 47°24′N 93°04′W
Kefallinía see Kefallonía
115 B18 **Kefallonía** var. Kefallinía. island Iónia Nisiá, Greece, C Mediterranean Sea
115 M22 **Kéfalos** Kos, Dodekánisa, Greece, Aegean Sea 36°44′N 26°58′E
171 Q17 **Kefamenanu** Timor, C Indonesia 09°31′S 124°29′E
Kefar Sava see Kfar Sava
Kefe see Feodosiya
77 V15 **Keffi** Nassarawa, C Nigeria 08°52′N 07°54′E
92 H4 **Keflavík** Sudurnes, W Iceland 64°01′N 22°35′W
92 H4 **Keflavik** ✈ (Reykjavík) Sudurnes, W Iceland 63°58′N 22°37′W
Kegalee see Kegalla
155 J25 **Kegalla** var. Kegalee, Kegalle. Sabaragamuwa Province, C Sri Lanka 07°14′N 80°21′E
Kegalle see Kegalla
Kegayli see Kegeyli
Kegel see Keila
145 W16 **Kegen** Almaty, SE Kazakhstan 42°58′N 79°12′E
146 H7 **Kegeyli** prev. Kegayli. Qoraqalpog'iston Respublikasi, W Uzbekistan 42°46′N 59°49′E
101 F22 **Kehl** Baden-Württemberg, SW Germany 48°34′N 07°49′E
118 H3 **Kehra** Ger. Kedder. Harjumaa, NW Estonia 59°19′N 25°21′E
117 U6 **Kehychivka** Kharkivs'ka Oblast', E Ukraine 49°18′N 35°46′E
97 L17 **Keighley** N England, United Kingdom 53°51′N 01°58′W
Kei Islands see Kai, Kepulauan
Keijō see Seoul
118 G3 **Keila** Ger. Kegel. Harjumaa, NW Estonia 59°18′N 24°29′E
Keilberg see Klínovec
83 F23 **Keimoes** Northern Cape, W South Africa 28°41′S 20°59′E
Keina/Keinis see Käina
Keishū see Gyeongju
77 T11 **Keïta** Tahoua, C Niger 14°45′N 05°40′E
78 J12 **Kéita, Bahr** var. Doka. ≈ S Chad
182 K10 **Keith** South Australia 36°01′S 140°22′E
96 K8 **Keith** NE Scotland, United Kingdom 57°33′N 02°57′W
26 K3 **Keith Sebelius Lake** ⊠ Kansas, C USA
32 G11 **Keizer** Oregon, NW USA 44°59′N 123°01′W
38 A8 **Kekaha** Kaua'i, Hawaii, USA, C Pacific Ocean 21°58′N 159°43′W
147 U10 **Këk-Art** prev. Alaykel', Alay-Kuu. Oshskaya Oblast', SW Kyrgyzstan 40°16′N 74°21′E
147 W10 **Këk-Aygyr** var. Keyaygyr. Narynskaya Oblast', C Kyrgyzstan 40°42′N 75°37′E
147 V9 **Këk-Dzhar** Narynskaya Oblast', C Kyrgyzstan 41°28′N 74°48′E
14 L8 **Kekek** ≈ Québec, SE Canada
185 K15 **Kekerengu** Canterbury, South Island, New Zealand 41°55′S 174°05′E
111 L21 **Kékes** ▲ N Hungary 47°53′N 19°59′E
171 P17 **Kekneno, Gunung** ▲ Timor, S Indonesia
147 S9 **Këk-Tash** Kir. Kök-Tash. Dzhalal-Abadskaya Oblast', W Kyrgyzstan 41°08′N 72°25′E
81 M15 **K'elafo** Sumalē, E Ethiopia 05°36′N 44°12′E
169 U10 **Kelai, Sungai** ≈ Borneo, N Indonesia
Kelamayi see Karamay
Kelang see Klang
168 K7 **Kelantan** ◐ state Peninsular Malaysia
Kelantan see Kelantan, Sungai
168 K7 **Kelantan, Sungai** var. Kelantan. ≈ Peninsular Malaysia
Kelat see Kālat
Këlcyra see Këlcyrë
113 L22 **Këlcyrë** var. Këlcyra. Gjirokastër, S Albania 40°19′N 20°10′E
Kelifskiy Uzboy see Kelif Uzboýy
146 L14 **Kelif Uzboýy** Rus. Kelifskiy Uzboy. salt marsh E Turkmenistan
137 O12 **Kelkit** Gümüşhane, NE Turkey 40°07′N 39°28′E
136 M12 **Kelkit Çayı** ≈ N Turkey
79 G18 **Kéllé** Cuvette-Quest, W Congo 0°04′S 14°33′E
77 W11 **Kellé** Zinder, S Niger 14°10′N 10°10′E
145 P7 **Kellerovka** Severnyy Kazakhstan, N Kazakhstan 53°51′N 69°15′E
8 I5 **Kellett, Cape** headland Banks Island, Northwest Territories, NW Canada 71°57′N 125°55′W
31 S11 **Kelleys Island** island Ohio, N USA
33 N8 **Kellogg** Idaho, NW USA 47°30′N 116°07′W
92 M12 **Kelloselkä** Lappi, N Finland 66°56′N 28°52′E
97 F17 **Kells** Ir. Ceanannas. Meath, E Ireland 53°44′N 06°53′W
118 E12 **Kelmė** Šiaulai, C Lithuania 55°39′N 22°57′E
99 M19 **Kelmis** var. La Calamine. Liège, E Belgium 50°43′N 06°01′E
78 H12 **Kélo** Tandjilé, SW Chad 09°21′N 15°50′E
83 I14 **Kelongwa** North Western, NW Zambia 13°41′S 26°19′E
11 N17 **Kelowna** British Columbia, SW Canada 49°50′N 119°29′W
11 X12 **Kelsey** Manitoba, C Canada 56°02′N 96°31′W
34 M6 **Kelseyville** California, W USA 38°58′N 122°51′W
96 K13 **Kelso** SE Scotland, United Kingdom 55°36′N 02°27′W
32 G10 **Kelso** Washington, NW USA 46°09′N 122°54′W
195 W15 **Keltie, Cape** headland Antarctica
Keltsy see Kielce
168 L9 **Keluang** var. Kluang. Johor, Peninsular Malaysia 02°01′N 103°18′E
168 M11 **Kelume** Pulau Lingga, W Indonesia 0°12′S 104°27′E
11 U15 **Kelvington** Saskatchewan, S Canada 52°10′N 103°30′W
124 J7 **Kem'** Respublika Kareliya, NW Russian Federation 64°55′N 34°18′E
124 I7 **Kem'** ≈ NW Russian Federation
137 O13 **Kemah** Erzincan, E Turkey 39°35′N 39°02′E
137 N13 **Kemaliye** Erzincan, C Turkey 39°16′N 38°29′E
Kemaman see Cukai
Kemanlar see Isperikh
10 K14 **Kemano** British Columbia, SW Canada 53°39′N 127°58′W
Kemarat see Khemmarat
171 P12 **Kembani** Pulau Peleng, N Indonesia 01°32′S 122°57′E
136 F17 **Kemer** Antalya, SW Turkey 36°39′N 30°33′E
122 J12 **Kemerovo** prev. Shcheglovsk. Kemerovskaya Oblast', C Russian Federation 55°25′N 86°05′E
122 K12 **Kemerovskaya Oblast'** ◐ province S Russian Federation
92 L13 **Kemi** Lappi, NW Finland 65°46′N 24°34′E
92 M12 **Kemijärvi** Swe. Kemiträsk. Lappi, N Finland 66°41′N 27°24′E
92 M12 **Kemijärvi** ◎ N Finland
92 L13 **Kemijoki** ≈ NW Finland
147 V7 **Kemin** prev. Bystrovka. Chuyskaya Oblast', N Kyrgyzstan
92 L13 **Keminmaa** Lappi, NW Finland 65°49′N 24°34′E
Kemins Island see Nikumaroro
Kemiö see Kimito
Kemiträsk see Kemijärvi
127 P5 **Kemlya** Respublika Mordoviya, W Russian Federation 54°42′N 45°16′E
99 B18 **Kemmel** West-Vlaanderen, W Belgium 50°42′N 02°51′E
33 S16 **Kemmerer** Wyoming, C USA 41°47′N 110°32′W
121 O15 **Kemmuna** var. Comino. island C Malta
79 I14 **Kémo** ◐ prefecture S Central African Republic
25 U7 **Kemp** Texas, SW USA 32°26′N 96°13′W
93 L14 **Kempele** Oulu, C Finland 64°56′N 25°26′E
101 D15 **Kempen** Nordrhein-Westfalen, W Germany 51°22′N 06°25′E
25 Q5 **Kemp, Lake** ◎ Texas, SW USA
195 W5 **Kemp Land** physical region Antarctica
25 S9 **Kempner** Texas, SW USA 31°03′N 98°01′W
44 H3 **Kemp's Bay** Andros Island, W Bahamas 24°02′N 77°32′W
183 U6 **Kempsey** New South Wales, SE Australia 31°05′S 152°50′E
101 J24 **Kempten** Bayern, S Germany 47°44′N 10°19′E
15 N9 **Kempt, Lac** ◎ Québec, SE Canada
183 P17 **Kempton** Tasmania, SE Australia 42°34′S 147°13′E
154 J9 **Ken** ≈ C India
39 R12 **Kenai** Alaska, USA 60°33′N 151°15′W
0 D5 **Kenai Mountains** ▲▲ Alaska, USA
39 R12 **Kenai Peninsula** peninsula Alaska, USA
21 V11 **Kenansville** North Carolina, SE USA 34°57′N 77°54′W
146 A10 **Kenar** prev. Rus. Ufra. Balkan Welaýaty, NW Turkmenistan 40°00′N 53°05′E
121 U13 **Kenâyis, Râs el-** headland N Egypt 31°13′N 27°53′E
97 K16 **Kendal** NW England, United Kingdom 54°20′N 02°45′W
23 Y16 **Kendall** Florida, SE USA 25°39′N 80°18′W
9 O8 **Kendall, Cape** headland Nunavut, E Canada 63°31′N 87°09′W
18 J15 **Kendall Park** New Jersey, NE USA 40°25′N 74°33′W
31 Q11 **Kendallville** Indiana, N USA 41°24′N 85°10′W
171 P14 **Kendari** Sulawesi, C Indonesia 03°57′S 122°36′E
169 Q13 **Kendawangan** Borneo, C Indonesia 02°32′S 110°13′E
Kendrāpāra see Kendrāparha
154 O12 **Kendrāparha** var. Kendrāpāra. Orissa, E India 20°29′N 86°25′E
154 O11 **Kendujhargarh** prev. Keonjihargarh. Orissa, E India 21°38′N 85°40′E
25 S13 **Kenedy** Texas, SW USA 28°49′N 97°51′W
76 J15 **Kenema** SE Sierra Leone 07°55′N 11°12′W
29 P16 **Kenesaw** Nebraska, C USA 40°37′N 98°39′W
Këneurgench see Köneürgenç
79 H21 **Kenge** Bandundu, SW Dem. Rep. Congo 04°52′S 16°59′E
Kengen see Kangen
167 O5 **Kengtung** Shan State, E Burma (Myanmar) 21°18′N 99°36′E
83 F23 **Kenhardt** Northern Cape, W South Africa 29°19′S 21°08′E
76 J12 **Kéniéba** Kayes, W Mali 12°47′N 11°16′W
Kenimekh see Konimex
169 U7 **Keningau** Sabah, East Malaysia 05°21′N 116°11′E
74 F6 **Kénitra** prev. Port-Lyautey. NW Morocco 34°20′N 06°29′W
21 V9 **Kenly** North Carolina, SE USA 35°39′N 78°16′W
97 B21 **Kenmare** Ir. Neidín. S Ireland 51°53′N 09°35′W
28 L2 **Kenmare** North Dakota, N USA 48°40′N 102°04′W
97 A21 **Kenmare River** Ir. An Ribhéar. inlet NE Atlantic Ocean
18 D10 **Kenmore** New York, NE USA 42°58′N 78°52′W
25 W8 **Kennard** Texas, SW USA 31°21′N 95°10′W
29 N10 **Kennebec** South Dakota, N USA 43°53′N 99°51′W
19 Q7 **Kennebec River** ≈ Maine, NE USA
19 P9 **Kennebunk** Maine, NE USA 43°22′N 70°33′W
39 R13 **Kennedy Entrance** strait Alaska, USA
166 L3 **Kennedy Peak** ▲ W Burma (Myanmar) 23°18′N 93°52′E
22 K9 **Kenner** Louisiana, S USA 29°57′N 90°15′W
180 I8 **Kenneth Range** ▲▲ Western Australia
27 Y9 **Kennett** Missouri, C USA 36°15′N 90°04′W
18 I16 **Kennett Square** Pennsylvania, NE USA 39°50′N 75°40′W
32 K10 **Kennewick** Washington, NW USA 46°12′N 119°08′W
12 E11 **Kenogami** ≈ Ontario, S Canada
15 Q7 **Kénogami, Lac** ◎ Québec, SE Canada
14 G8 **Kenogami Lake** Ontario, S Canada 48°04′N 80°10′W

◆ Country
● Country Capital
◇ Dependent Territory
○ Dependent Territory Capital
◐ Administrative Regions
✈ International Airport
▲ Mountain
▲▲ Mountain Range
Volcano
≈ River
◎ Lake
⊠ Reservoir

14 F7 **Kenogamissi Lake** ◎ Ontario, S Canada
10 I6 **Keno Hill** Yukon Territory, NW Canada 63°54′N 135°18′W
12 A11 **Kenora** Ontario, S Canada 49°47′N 94°26′W
31 N9 **Kenosha** Wisconsin, N USA 42°34′N 87°50′W
13 P14 **Kensington** Prince Edward Island, SE Canada 46°26′N 63°39′W
26 L3 **Kensington** Kansas, C USA 39°46′N 99°01′W
32 I11 **Kent** Oregon, NW USA 45°14′N 120°43′W
24 J9 **Kent** Texas, SW USA 31°03′N 104°13′W
32 H8 **Kent** Washington, NW USA 47°22′N 122°13′W
97 P22 **Kent** *cultural region* SE England, United Kingdom
145 P16 **Kentau** Yuzhnyy Kazakhstan, S Kazakhstan 43°28′N 68°41′E
183 P14 **Kent Group** *island group* Tasmania, SE Australia
31 N12 **Kentland** Indiana, N USA 40°46′N 87°26′W
31 R12 **Kenton** Ohio, N USA 40°39′N 83°36′W
8 K7 **Kent Peninsula** *peninsula* Nunavut, N Canada
115 F14 **Kentrikí Makedonía** *Eng.* Macedonia Central. ◆ *region* N Greece
20 J6 **Kentucky** *off.* Commonwealth of Kentucky, *also known as* Bluegrass State. ◆ *state* C USA
20 H8 **Kentucky Lake** ⊠ Kentucky/Tennessee, S USA
13 P15 **Kentville** Nova Scotia, SE Canada 45°04′N 64°30′W
22 K8 **Kentwood** Louisiana, S USA 30°56′N 90°30′W
31 P9 **Kentwood** Michigan, N USA 42°52′N 85°33′W
81 H17 **Kenya** *off.* Republic of Kenya. ◆ *republic* E Africa
Kenya, Mount *see* Kirinyaga
Kenya, Republic of *see* Kenya
168 L7 **Kenyir, Tasik** *var.* Tasek Kenyir. ◎ Peninsular Malaysia
29 W10 **Kenyon** Minnesota, N USA 44°16′N 92°59′W
29 Y16 **Keokuk** Iowa, C USA 40°24′N 91°22′W
Keonjihargarh *see* Kendujhargarh
Kéos *see* Tziá
29 X16 **Keosauqua** Iowa, C USA 40°43′N 91°58′W
29 X15 **Keota** Iowa, C USA 41°21′N 91°57′W
21 O11 **Keowee, Lake** ⊠ South Carolina, SE USA
124 I7 **Kepa** *var.* Kepe. Respublika Kareliya, NW Russian Federation 65°09′N 32°15′E
Kepe *see* Kepa
189 O13 **Kepirohi Falls** *waterfall* Pohnpei, E Micronesia
185 B22 **Kepler Mountains** ▲▲ South Island, New Zealand
111 I14 **Kępno** Wielkopolskie, C Poland 51°17′N 17°57′E
65 C24 **Keppel Island** *island* N Falkland Islands
Keppel Island *see* Niuatoputapu
65 C23 **Keppel Sound** *sound* N Falkland Islands
136 D12 **Kepsut** Balıkesir, NW Turkey 39°41′N 28°09′E
168 M11 **Kepulauan Riau** *off.* Propinsi Kepulauan Riau. ◆ *province* NW Indonesia
Kequ *see* Gadê
171 V13 **Kerai** Papua, E Indonesia 03°53′S 134°30′E
Kerak *see* Al Karak
155 F22 **Kerala** ◆ *state* S India
165 R16 **Kerama-rettō** *island group* SW Japan
183 N10 **Kerang** Victoria, SE Australia 35°46′S 144°01′E
Kerasunt *see* Giresun
115 H19 **Keratéa** *var.* Keratea. Attikí, C Greece 37°48′N 23°58′E
Keratea *see* Keratéa
93 M19 **Kerava** *Swe.* Kervo. Etelä-Suomi, S Finland 60°25′N 25°10′E
Kerbala/Kerbela *see* Karbalā'
32 F15 **Kerby** Oregon, NW USA 42°10′N 123°39′W
117 W12 **Kerch** *Rus.* Kerch'. Avtonomna Respublika Krym, SE Ukraine 45°22′N 36°30′E
Kerch' *see* Kerch
Kerchens'ka Protska/ Kerchenskiy Proliv *see* Kerch Strait
117 V13 **Kerchens'kyy Pivostriv** *peninsula* S Ukraine
121 V4 **Kerch Strait** *var.* Bosporus Cimmerius, Enikale Strait, *Rus.* Kerchenskiy Proliv, *Ukr.* Kerchens'ka Protska. *strait* Black Sea/Sea of Azov
Kerdilio *see* Kerdýlio
114 H13 **Kerdýlio** *var.* Kerdilio. ▲ N Greece 40°46′N 23°37′E
186 D8 **Kerema** Gulf, S Papua New Guinea 07°59′S 145°46′E
Keremitlik *see* Lyulyakovo
136 I9 **Kerempe Burnu** *headland* N Turkey 42°01′N 33°20′E
80 J9 **Keren** *var.* Cheren. C Eritrea 15°45′N 38°22′E
25 U7 **Kerens** Texas, SW USA 32°07′N 96°13′W
184 M6 **Kerepehi** Waikato, North Island, New Zealand 37°18′S 175°33′E
145 P10 **Kerey, Ozero** ◎ C Kazakhstan
Kergel *see* Kärla
173 Q12 **Kerguelen** *island* C French Southern and Antarctic Territories
173 Q13 **Kerguelen Plateau** *undersea feature* S Indian Ocean
115 C20 **Kerí** Zákynthos, Iónia Nisiá, Greece, C Mediterranean Sea 37°40′N 20°48′E
81 H19 **Kericho** Rift Valley, W Kenya 0°22′S 35°19′E
184 K2 **Kerikeri** Northland, North Island, New Zealand 35°14′S 173°58′E
93 O17 **Kerimäki** Itä-Suomi, E Finland 61°56′N 29°18′E
168 K12 **Kerinci, Gunung** ▲ Sumatera, W Indonesia 02°00′S 101°40′E
Keriya *see* Yutian
158 H9 **Keriya He** ≈ NW China
98 J9 **Kerkbuurt** Noord-Holland, C Netherlands 52°29′N 05°08′E
98 J13 **Kerkdriel** Gelderland, C Netherlands 51°46′N 05°21′E
75 N6 **Kerkenah, Îles de** *var.* Kerkenna Islands, *Ar.* Juzur Qarqannah. *island group* E Tunisia
Kerkenna Islands *see* Kerkenah, Îles de
115 M20 **Kerketévs** ▲ Sámos, Dodekánisa, Greece, Aegean Sea 37°44′N 26°39′E
29 T8 **Kerkhoven** Minnesota, N USA 45°12′N 95°18′W
Kerki *see* Atamyrat
Kerkichi *see* Kerkiçi
146 M14 **Kerkiçi** *Rus.* Kerkichi. Lebap Welaýaty, E Turkmenistan 37°46′N 65°18′E
115 F16 **Kerkíneo** *prehistoric site* Thessalía, C Greece
114 G12 **Kerkíni, Límni** *var.* Límni Kerkinitis. ◎ N Greece
Kerkinitis Límni *see* Kerkíni, Límni
Kérkira *see* Kérkyra
99 M18 **Kerkrade** Limburg, SE Netherlands 50°53′N 06°04′E
Kerkuk *see* Kirkūk
115 B16 **Kérkyra** *var.* Kérkira, *Eng.* Corfu. Kérkyra, Iónia Nisiá, Greece, C Mediterranean Sea 39°37′N 19°56′E
115 B16 **Kerkyra** ✈ Kérkyra, Iónia Nisiá, Greece, C Mediterranean Sea 39°36′N 19°55′E
115 A16 **Kérkyra** *var.* Kérkira, *Eng.* Corfu. *island* Iónia Nisiá, Greece, C Mediterranean Sea
192 K10 **Kermadec Islands** *island group* New Zealand, SW Pacific Ocean
175 R10 **Kermadec Ridge** *undersea feature* SW Pacific Ocean 30°30′S 178°30′W
175 R11 **Kermadec Trench** *undersea feature* SW Pacific Ocean
143 S10 **Kermān** *var.* Kirman; *anc.* Carmana. Kermān, C Iran 30°18′N 57°05′E
143 R11 **Kermān** *off.* Ostān-e Kermān, *var.* Kirman; *anc.* Carmania. ◆ *province* SE Iran
143 U12 **Kermān, Biābān-e** *desert* SE Iran
Kermān, Ostān-e *see* Kermān
142 K6 **Kermānshāh** *var.* Qahremānshahr; *prev.* Bākhtarān. Kermānshāhān, W Iran 34°19′N 47°04′E
143 Q9 **Kermānshāh** Yazd, C Iran 34°19′N 47°04′E
142 J6 **Kermānshāh** *off.* Ostān-e Kermānshāhān; *prev.* Bākhtarān. ◆ *province* W Iran
Kermānshāhān, Ostān-e *see* Kermānshāh
114 L10 **Kermen** Sliven, C Bulgaria 42°30′N 26°12′E
24 L8 **Kermit** Texas, SW USA 31°49′N 103°07′W
21 P6 **Kermit** West Virginia, NE USA 37°51′N 82°24′W
21 S9 **Kernersville** North Carolina, SE USA 36°12′N 80°13′W
35 S12 **Kern River** ≈ California, W USA
35 S12 **Kernville** California, W USA 35°44′N 118°25′W
115 K21 **Kéros** *island* Kykládes, Greece, Aegean Sea
76 K14 **Kérouané** SE Guinea 09°16′N 09°00′W
101 D16 **Kerpen** Nordrhein-Westfalen, W Germany 50°51′N 06°40′E
146 I11 **Kerpichli** Lebap Welaýaty, NE Turkmenistan 40°12′N 61°09′E
24 M1 **Kerrick** Texas, SW USA 36°29′N 102°14′W
Kerr Lake *see* John H. Kerr Reservoir
11 S15 **Kerrobert** Saskatchewan, S Canada 51°56′N 109°09′W
25 Q11 **Kerrville** Texas, SW USA 30°03′N 99°09′W
97 B20 **Kerry** *Ir.* Ciarraí. *cultural region* SW Ireland
21 S11 **Kershaw** South Carolina, SE USA 34°33′N 80°34′W
Kertel *see* Kärdla
95 H23 **Kerteminde** Syddtjylland, C Denmark 55°27′N 10°40′E
163 Q7 **Kerulen** *Chin.* Herlen He, *Mong.* Herlen Gol. ≈ China/ Mongolia
Kervo *see* Kerava
Kerýneia *see* Girne
12 H11 **Kesagami Lake** ◎ Ontario, SE Canada
93 O17 **Kesälahti** Itä-Suomi, SE Finland 61°54′N 29°49′E
136 B11 **Keşan** Edirne, NW Turkey 40°52′N 26°37′E
165 R9 **Kesennuma** Miyagi, Honshū, C Japan 38°55′N 141°35′E
163 V7 **Keshan** Heilongjiang, NE China 48°00′N 125°46′E
30 M6 **Keshena** Wisconsin, N USA 44°54′N 88°37′W
136 I13 **Keskin** Kırıkkale, C Turkey 39°41′N 33°36′E
Késmárk *see* Kežmarok
124 I6 **Kesten'ga** *var.* Kest Enga. Respublika Kareliya, NW Russian Federation 65°53′N 31°47′E
Kest Enga *see* Kesten'ga
98 K12 **Kesteren** Gelderland, C Netherlands 51°55′N 05°34′E
14 H14 **Keswick** Ontario, S Canada 44°15′N 79°26′W
97 K15 **Keswick** NW England, United Kingdom 54°30′N 03°04′W
111 H24 **Keszthely** Zala, SW Hungary 46°47′N 17°16′E
122 K11 **Ket'** ≈ C Russian Federation
77 R17 **Keta** SE Ghana 05°55′N 00°59′E
169 Q12 **Ketapang** Borneo, C Indonesia 01°50′S 109°59′E
127 O12 **Ketchenery** *prev.* Sovetskoye. Respublika Kalmykiya, SW Russian Federation 47°18′N 44°31′E
39 Y14 **Ketchikan** Revillagigedo Island, Alaska, USA 55°21′N 131°39′W
33 O14 **Ketchum** Idaho, NW USA 43°40′N 114°24′W
Kete/Kete Krakye *see* Kete-Krachi
77 Q15 **Kete-Krachi** *var.* Kete, Kete Krakye. E Ghana 07°50′N 00°03′W
98 L9 **Ketelmeer** *channel* E Netherlands
149 P17 **Keti Bandar** Sind, SE Pakistan 23°55′N 67°31′E
77 S16 **Kétou** SE Benin 07°25′N 02°36′E
110 M7 **Kętrzyn** *Ger.* Rastenburg. Warmińsko-Mazurskie, NE Poland 54°05′N 21°24′E
97 N20 **Kettering** C England, United Kingdom 52°24′N 00°44′W
31 R14 **Kettering** Ohio, N USA 39°41′N 84°10′W
18 F13 **Kettle Creek** ≈ Pennsylvania, NE USA
32 L7 **Kettle Falls** Washington, NW USA 48°36′N 118°03′W
14 D16 **Kettle Point** *headland* Ontario, S Canada 43°12′N 82°01′W
29 V6 **Kettle River** ≈ Minnesota, N USA
186 B7 **Ketu** ≈ W Papua New Guinea
18 G10 **Keuka Lake** ◎ New York, NE USA
Keupriya *see* Primorsko
93 L17 **Keuruu** Länsi-Suomi, C Finland 62°15′N 24°34′E
Kevevára *see* Kovin
92 L9 **Kevo** *Lapp.* Geavvú. Lappi, N Finland 69°42′N 27°08′E
44 M6 **Kew** North Caicos, N Turks and Caicos Islands 21°52′N 71°57′W
30 K11 **Kewanee** Illinois, N USA 41°15′N 89°55′W
31 N7 **Kewaunee** Wisconsin, N USA 44°27′N 87°31′W
30 M3 **Keweenaw Bay** ◎ Michigan, N USA
31 N2 **Keweenaw Peninsula** *peninsula* Michigan, N USA
31 N2 **Keweenaw Point** *peninsula* Michigan, N USA
29 N12 **Keya Paha River** ≈ Nebraska/South Dakota, N USA
Keyaygyr *see* Këk-Aygyr
23 Z16 **Key Biscayne** Florida, SE USA 25°41′N 80°09′W
26 G8 **Keyes** Oklahoma, C USA 36°48′N 102°15′W
23 Y17 **Key Largo** Key Largo, Florida, SE USA 25°06′N 80°25′W
21 U3 **Keyser** West Virginia, NE USA 39°25′N 78°59′W
27 O9 **Keystone Lake** ⊠ Oklahoma, C USA
36 L16 **Keystone Peak** ▲ Arizona, SW USA 31°52′N 111°12′W
Keystone State *see* Pennsylvania
21 U7 **Keysville** Virginia, NE USA 37°02′N 78°28′W
27 T3 **Keytesville** Missouri, C USA 39°25′N 92°56′W
23 W17 **Key West** Florida Keys, Florida, SE USA 24°34′N 81°48′W
127 T1 **Kez** Udmurtskaya Respublika, NW Russian Federation 57°55′N 53°42′E
Kezdivásárhely *see* Târgu Secuiesc
122 M12 **Kezhma** Krasnoyarskiy Kray, C Russian Federation 58°57′N 101°00′E
111 L18 **Kežmarok** *Ger.* Käsmark, *Hung.* Késmárk. Prešovský Kraj, E Slovakia 49°09′N 20°25′E
Kfar Saba *see* Kfar Sava
138 F10 **Kfar Sava** *var.* Kfar Saba; *prev.* Kefar Sava. Central, C Israel 32°11′N 34°58′E
83 F20 **Kgalagadi** ◆ *district* SW Botswana
83 I20 **Kgatleng** ◆ *district* SE Botswana
188 F8 **Kgkeklau** Babeldaob, N Palau
125 R6 **Khabarikha** *var.* Chabaricha. Respublika Komi, NW Russian Federation 65°52′N 52°19′E
123 S14 **Khabarovsk** Khabarovskiy Kray, SE Russian Federation 48°32′N 135°08′E
123 R11 **Khabarovskiy Kray** ◆ *territory* E Russian Federation
141 W7 **Khabb** Abū Ẓaby, E United Arab Emirates 24°39′N 55°43′E
Khabour, Nahr al *see* Khābūr, Nahr al
Khabura *see* Al Khābūrah
139 N2 **Khābūr, Nahr al** *var.* Nahr al Khabour. ≈ Syria/Turkey
Khachmas *see* Xaçmaz
80 B12 **Khadari** ≈ W Sudan
Khadera *see* Hadera
141 X12 **Khādhil** *var.* Khudal. SE Oman 18°48′N 56°48′E
155 E14 **Khadki** *prev.* Kirkee. Mahārāshtra, W India 18°34′N 73°52′E
126 L14 **Khadyzhensk** Krasnodarskiy Kray, SW Russian Federation 44°26′N 39°31′E
114 N9 **Khadzhiyska Reka** ≈ E Bulgaria
117 P10 **Khadzhybeys'kyy Lyman** ◎ SW Ukraine
138 K3 **Khafsah** Ḥalab, N Syria 36°16′N 38°03′E
152 M13 **Khāga** Uttar Pradesh, N India 25°47′N 81°05′E
153 Q13 **Khagaria** Bihār, NE India 25°31′N 86°27′E
149 Q13 **Khairpur** Sind, SE Pakistan 27°30′N 68°50′E
122 K13 **Khakasiya, Respublika** *prev.* Khakasskaya Avtonomnaya Oblast', *Eng.* Khakassia. ◆ *autonomous republic* C Russian Federation
Khakassia/Khakasskaya Avtonomnaya Oblast' *see* Khakasiya, Respublika
167 N9 **Kha Khaeng, Khao** ▲ W Thailand 16°13′N 99°03′E
83 G20 **Khakhea** *var.* Kakia. Southern, S Botswana 24°41′S 23°29′E
Khalach *see* Halaç
Khalándrion *see* Chalándri
75 T7 **Khalīj as Sallūm** *Ar.* Gulf of Salûm. *gulf* Egypt/Libya
75 X8 **Khalij as Suways** *var.* Suez, Gulf of. *gulf* NE Egypt
127 W7 **Khalilovo** Orenburgskaya Oblast', W Russian Federation 51°25′N 58°13′E
Khalkabad *see* Xalqobod
142 L3 **Khalkhāl** *prev.* Herowābād. Ardabīl, NW Iran 37°36′N 48°36′E
Khalkidhikí *see* Chalkidikí
Khalkís *see* Chalkída
125 W3 **Khal'mer-Yu** Respublika Komi, NW Russian Federation 68°00′N 64°45′E
119 M14 **Khalopyenichy** *Rus.* Kholopenichi. Minskaya Voblasts', NE Belarus 54°31′N 28°58′E
Khalturin *see* Orlov
141 Y10 **Khalūf** *var.* Al Khaluf. E Oman 20°27′N 57°59′E
154 K10 **Khamaria** Madhya Pradesh, C India 23°07′N 80°54′E
154 D11 **Khambhāt** Gujarāt, W India 22°19′N 72°39′E
154 C12 **Khambhāt, Gulf of** *Eng.* Gulf of Cambay. *gulf* W India
167 U10 **Khâm Đuc** *var.* Phước Sơn. Quang Nam-Đa Năng, C Vietnam 15°28′N 107°49′E
154 G12 **Khāmgaon** Mahārāshtra, C India 20°41′N 76°34′E
141 O14 **Khamir** *var.* Khamr. W Yemen 16°N 43°56′E
141 N12 **Khamis Mushayṭ** *var.* Hamīs Musait. 'Asīr, SW Saudi Arabia 18°19′N 42°41′E
123 P10 **Khampa** Respublika Sakha (Yakutiya), NE Russian Federation 63°43′N 123°02′E
Khamr *see* Khamir
83 C19 **Khan** ≈ W Namibia
149 Q2 **Khānābād** Kunduz, NE Afghanistan 36°42′N 69°08′E
Khân Abou Châmâte/Khan Abou Ech Cham *see* Khān Abū Shāmāt
138 I7 **Khān Abū Shāmāt** *var.* Khân Abou Châmâte, Khan Abou Ech Cham. Rīf Dimashq, W Syria 33°43′N 36°56′E
Khān al Baghdādī *see* Al Baghdādī
Khān al Maḥāwīl *see* Al Maḥāwīl
139 T7 **Khān al Mashāhidah** Baghdād, C Iraq 33°40′N 44°15′E
139 T10 **Khān al Muṣallá** An Najaf, S Iraq 32°09′N 44°20′E
139 U6 **Khānaqīn** Diyālá, E Iraq 34°22′N 45°22′E
139 T11 **Khān ar Ruḥbah** An Najaf, S Iraq 31°42′N 44°18′E
139 P2 **Khān as Sūr** Nīnawá, N Iraq 36°28′N 41°36′E
139 T8 **Khān Āzād** Baghdād, C Iraq 33°08′N 44°21′E
154 N13 **Khandaparha** *prev.* Khandpara. Orissa, E India 20°15′N 85°11′E
Khandpara *see* Khandaparha
149 T2 **Khandūd** *var.* Khandud, Wakhan. Badakhshān, NE Afghanistan 36°57′N 72°19′E
Khandud *see* Khandūd
154 G11 **Khandwa** Madhya Pradesh, C India 21°49′N 76°23′E
123 R10 **Khandyga** Respublika Sakha (Yakutiya), NE Russian Federation 62°39′N 135°30′E
149 T10 **Khānewāl** Punjab, NE Pakistan 30°18′N 71°56′E
149 S10 **Khāngarh** Punjab, E Pakistan 29°57′N 71°14′E
Khanh Hung *see* Soc Trăng
Khaniá *see* Chaniá
Khanka *see* Xonqa
163 Z8 **Khanka, Lake** *var.* Hsing-K'ai Hu, Lake Hanka, *Chin.* Xingkai Hu, *Rus.* Ozero Khanka. ◎ China/Russian Federation
Khanka, Ozero *see* Khanka, Lake
Khankendi *see* Xankändi
123 O9 **Khannya** ≈ NE Russian Federation
144 D10 **Khan Ordasy** *prev.* Urda. Zapadnyy Kazakhstan, W Kazakhstan 48°52′N 47°31′E
149 S12 **Khānpur** Punjab, E Pakistan 28°31′N 70°30′E
138 I4 **Khān Shaykhūn** *var.* Khan Sheikhun. Idlib, NW Syria 35°27′N 36°38′E
Khan Sheikhun *see* Khān Shaykhūn
Khanshyngghys *see* Khrebet Khanshyngys
145 S15 **Khantau** Zhambyl, S Kazakhstan 44°13′N 73°47′E
145 W16 **Khan Tengri, Pik** ▲ SE Kazakhstan 42°17′N 80°11′E
Khan-Tengri, Pik *see* Hantengri Feng
Khanthabouli *see* Savannakhét
127 V8 **Khanty-Mansiysk** *prev.* Ostyako-Voguls'k. Khanty-Mansiyskiy Avtonomnyy Okrug-Yugra, C Russian Federation 61°01′N 69°E
125 V8 **Khanty-Mansiyskiy Avtonomnyy Okrug-Yugra** ◆ *autonomous district* C Russian Federation
139 R4 **Khānūqah** Nīnawýé, C Iraq 35°25′N 43°15′E
138 E11 **Khān Yūnis** *var.* Khān Yūnus. S Gaza Strip 31°21′N 34°18′E
Khān Yūnus *see* Khān Yūnis
Khanzi *see* Ghanzi
139 U5 **Khān Zūr** As Sulaymānīyah, E Iraq 35°03′N 45°08′E
167 N10 **Khao Laem Reservoir** ⊠ W Thailand
123 O14 **Khapcheranga** Zabaykal'skiy Kray, S Russian Federation 49°46′N 112°21′E
127 Q12 **Kharabali** Astrakhanskaya Oblast', SW Russian Federation 47°28′N 47°14′E
153 R16 **Kharagpur** West Bengal, NE India 22°30′N 87°19′E
139 V11 **Kharā'ib 'Abd al Karīm** Al Muthannā, S Iraq 31°07′N 45°33′E
143 Q8 **Kharānaq** Yazd, C Iran 31°54′N 54°21′E
Kharbin *see* Harbin
Kharchi *see* Mārwār
146 H13 **Khardzhagaz** Ahal Welaýaty, C Turkmenistan 37°54′N 60°10′E
154 F11 **Khargon** Madhya Pradesh, C India 21°49′N 75°39′E
149 V7 **Khāriān** Punjab, NE Pakistan 32°52′N 73°52′E
117 V5 **Kharkiv** *Rus.* Khar'kov. Kharkivs'ka Oblast', NE Ukraine 50°N 36°14′E
117 V5 **Kharkiv** ✈ Kharkivs'ka Oblast', E Ukraine 49°54′N 36°20′E
Kharkiv *see* Kharkivs'ka Oblast'
117 U5 **Kharkivs'ka Oblast'** *var.* Kharkiv, *Rus.* Khar'kovskaya Oblast'. ◆ *province* E Ukraine
Khar'kov *see* Kharkiv
Khar'kovskaya Oblast' *see* Kharkivs'ka Oblast'
124 L3 **Kharlovka** Murmanskaya Oblast', NW Russian Federation 68°47′N 37°09′E
114 K11 **Kharmanli** Khaskovo, S Bulgaria 41°56′N 25°54′E
114 K11 **Kharmanliyska Reka** ≈ S Bulgaria
124 M13 **Kharovsk** Vologodskaya Oblast', NW Russian Federation 59°57′N 40°05′E
80 F9 **Khartoum** *var.* El Khartûm, Khartum. ● (Sudan) Khartoum, C Sudan 15°33′N 32°32′E
80 F9 **Khartoum** ◆ *state* NE Sudan
80 F9 **Khartoum** ✈ Khartoum, C Sudan 15°36′N 32°37′E
80 F9 **Khartoum North** Khartoum, C Sudan 15°38′N 32°33′E
117 X8 **Khartsyz'k** *Rus.* Khartsyzsk. Donets'ka Oblast', SE Ukraine 48°01′N 38°10′E
117 X8 **Khartsyz'k** Donets'ka Oblast', E Ukraine 48°01′N 38°10′E
Khartsyzsk *see* Khartsyz'k
Khartum *see* Khartoum
Khasab *see* Al Khaṣab
123 S15 **Khasan** Primorskiy Kray, SE Russian Federation 42°24′N 130°45′E
127 P16 **Khasavyurt** Respublika Dagestan, SW Russian Federation 43°16′N 46°33′E
143 W12 **Khāsh** *prev.* Vāsht. Sīstān va Balūchestān, SE Iran 28°15′N 61°11′E
148 K8 **Khāsh, Dasht-e** *Eng.* Khash Desert. *desert* SW Afghanistan
Khash Desert *see* Khāsh, Dasht-e
Khashim Al Qirba/Khashm al Qirbah *see* Khashm el Girba
80 H9 **Khashm el Girba** *var.* Khashim Al Qirba, Khashm al Qirbah. Kassala, E Sudan 15°00′N 35°59′E
138 G14 **Khashsh, Jabal al** ▲ S Jordan
137 S10 **Khashuri** C Georgia 41°59′N 43°36′E
153 V13 **Khāsi Hills** *hill range* NE India
114 K11 **Khaskovo** Khaskovo, S Bulgaria 41°56′N 25°35′E
114 K11 **Khaskovo** ◆ *province* S Bulgaria
122 M7 **Khatanga** ≈ N Russian Federation
Khatanga, Gulf of *see* Khatangskiy Zaliv
123 N7 **Khatangskiy Zaliv** *var.* Gulf of Khatanga. *bay* N Russian Federation
141 W7 **Khatmat al Malāḥah** N Oman 24°58′N 56°22′E
143 S16 **Khaṭmat al Malāḥah** Ash Shāriqah, E United Arab Emirates
123 V7 **Khatyrka** Chukotskiy Avtonomnyy Okrug, NE Russian Federation 62°03′N 175°09′E
Khauz-Khan *see* Hanhowuz
Khauzkhanskoye Vodoranilishche *see* Hanhowuz Suw Howdany
Khavaling *see* Khovaling
Khavast *see* Xovos
139 W10 **Khawrah, Nahr al** ≈ S Iraq
Khawr Barakah *see* Barka
141 W7 **Khawr Fakkān** *var.* Khor Fakkan. Ash Shāriqah, NE United Arab Emirates 25°22′N 56°19′E
140 L6 **Khaybar** Al Madīnah, NW Saudi Arabia 25°53′N 39°16′E
Khaybar, Kowtal-e *see* Khyber Pass
147 S11 **Khaydarkan** *var.* Khaydarken. Batkenskaya Oblast', SW Kyrgyzstan 39°56′N 71°17′E
Khaydarken *see* Khaydarkan
125 U2 **Khaypudyrskaya Guba** *bay* NW Russian Federation
139 S1 **Khayrūzuk** Arbīl, E Iraq 36°58′N 44°19′E
Khazar, Bahr-e/Khazar, Daryā-ye *see* Caspian Sea
Khazarosp *see* Hazorasp
Khazretishi, Khrebet *see* Hazratishoh, Qatorkŭhi
75 X11 **Khazzān Aswān** *var.* Aswan Dam. *dam* SE Egypt
Khelat *see* Kālat
74 F6 **Khemisset** NW Morocco 33°52′N 06°04′W
167 R10 **Khemmarat** *var.* Kemarat. Ubon Ratchathani, E Thailand 16°03′N 105°11′E
74 L6 **Khenchela** *var.* Khenchla. NE Algeria 35°22′N 07°09′E
Khenchla *see* Khenchela
74 G7 **Khénifra** C Morocco 32°59′N 05°37′W
Khersān, Rūd-e *see* Garm, Āb-e
117 R10 **Kherson** Khersons'ka Oblast', S Ukraine 46°39′N 32°38′E
Kherson *see* Khersons'ka Oblast'
117 S14 **Khersones, Mys** *Rus.* Mys Khersonesskiy. *headland* S Ukraine 44°34′N 33°24′E
Khersonesskiy, Mys *see* Khersones, Mys
117 R10 **Khersons'ka Oblast'** *var.* Kherson, *Rus.* Khersonskaya Oblast'. ◆ *province* S Ukraine
Khersonskaya Oblast' *see* Khersons'ka Oblast'
122 L8 **Kheta** ≈ N Russian Federation
149 U7 **Khewra** Punjab, E Pakistan 32°41′N 73°04′E
Khiam *see* El Khiyam
124 J4 **Khibiny** ▲▲ NW Russian Federation
126 K3 **Khimki** Moskovskaya Oblast', W Russian Federation 55°57′N 37°48′E
147 S12 **Khingov** *Rus.* Obi-Khingou. ≈ C Tajikistan
Khíos *see* Chíos
149 R15 **Khipro** Sind, SE Pakistan 25°50′N 69°24′E
139 S10 **Khirr, Wādī al** *dry watercourse* S Iraq
114 I10 **Khisarya** Plovdiv, C Bulgaria 42°33′N 24°43′E
Khiva/Khiwa *see* Xiva
167 N9 **Khlong Khlung** Kamphaeng Phet, W Thailand 16°15′N 99°41′E
167 N15 **Khlong Thom** Krabi, SW Thailand 07°55′N 99°09′E
167 P12 **Khlung** Chantaburi, S Thailand 12°25′N 102°12′E
Khmel'nik *see* Khmil'nyk
Khmel'nitskaya Oblast' *see* Khmel'nyts'ka Oblast'
Khmel'nitskiy *see* Khmel'nyts'kyy
116 K5 **Khmel'nyts'ka Oblast'** *var.* Khmel'nyts'kyy, *Rus.* Khmel'nitskaya Oblast'; *prev.* Kamenets-Podol'skaya Oblast'. ◆ *province* NW Ukraine
116 L6 **Khmel 'nyts'kyy** *Rus.* Khmel'nitskiy; *prev.* Proskurov. Khmel'nyts'ka Oblast', W Ukraine 49°24′N 26°59′E
Khmel'nyts'kyy *see* Khmel'nyts'ka Oblast'
116 M6 **Khmil'nyk** *Rus.* Khmel'nik. Vinnyts'ka Oblast', C Ukraine 49°36′N 27°59′E
Khobda *see* Kobda
137 R9 **Khobi** W Georgia 42°20′N 41°54′E
119 P15 **Khodasy** *Rus.* Khodosy. Mahilyowskaya Voblasts', E Belarus 53°56′N 31°29′E
116 I6 **Khodoriv** *Pol.* Chodorów, *Rus.* Khodorov. L'vivs'ka Oblast', NW Ukraine 49°20′N 24°19′E
Khodorov *see* Khodoriv
Khodosy *see* Khodasy
Khodzhakala *see* Hojagala
Khodzhambas *see* Hojambaz
Khodzhent *see* Khujand
Khodzheyli *see* Xo'jayli
Khoi *see* Khvoy
Khojend *see* Khujand
Khokand *see* Qo'qon
126 L8 **Khokhol'skiy** Voronezhskaya Oblast', W Russian Federation 51°33′N 38°43′E
167 P10 **Khok Samrong** Lop Buri, C Thailand 15°03′N 100°44′E
124 H15 **Kholm** Novgorodskaya Oblast', W Russian Federation 57°10′N 31°06′E
Kholm *see* Khulm
Kholm *see* Chełm
Kholmech' *see* Kholmyech
123 T13 **Kholmsk** Ostrov Sakhalin, Sakhalinskaya Oblast', SE Russian Federation 46°57′N 142°10′E
119 O19 **Kholmyech** *Rus.* Kholmech'. Homyel'skaya Voblasts', SE Belarus 52°09′N 30°37′E
Kholon *see* Holon
Kholopenichi *see* Khalopyenichy
83 D19 **Khomas** ◆ *district* C Namibia
83 D19 **Khomas Hochland** *var.* Khomasplato. *plateau* C Namibia
Khomasplato *see* Khomas Hochland
Khomein *see* Khomeyn
142 M7 **Khomeyn** *var.* Khomein, Khumain. Markazī, W Iran 33°38′N 50°03′E
143 N8 **Khomeynīshahr** *prev.* Homāyūnshahr. Eṣfahān, C Iran 32°42′N 51°28′E
Khoms *see* Al Khums
Khong Sedone *see* Muang Khôngxédôn
167 Q9 **Khon Kaen** *var.* Muang Khon Kaen. Khon Kaen, E Thailand 16°25′N 102°50′E
Khonqa *see* Xonqa
167 Q9 **Khon San** Khon Kaen, E Thailand 16°40′N 101°51′E
123 R8 **Khonuu** Respublika Sakha (Yakutiya), NE Russian Federation 66°24′N 143°15′E
127 N8 **Khopër** *var.* Khoper. ≈ SW Russian Federation
Khoper *see* Khopër
123 S14 **Khor** Khabarovskiy Kray, SE Russian Federation 47°44′N 134°48′E
143 U9 **Khorāsān-e Jonūbī** *off.* Ostan-e Khorāsān-e Janūbī. ◆ *province* E Iran
143 S3 **Khorāsān-e Shomālī** *off.* Ostan-e Khorāsān-e Shomālī. ◆ *province* NE Iran
Khorat *see* Nakhon Ratchasima
154 O13 **Khordha** *prev.* Khurda. Orissa, E India 20°10′N 85°42′E
125 U4 **Khorey-Ver** Nenetskiy Avtonomnyy Okrug, NW Russian Federation 67°25′N 58°05′E
Khorezmskaya Oblast' *see* Xorazm Viloyati
Khor Fakkan *see* Khawr Fakkān
Khorgos *see* Korgas
123 N13 **Khorinsk** Respublika Buryatiya, S Russian Federation 52°13′N 109°52′E
83 C18 **Khorixas** Kunene, NW Namibia 20°23′S 14°55′E
141 O17 **Khormaksar** *var.* Aden. ✈ ('Adan) SW Yemen 12°56′N 45°00′E
Khormal *see* Khurmāl
Khormuj *see* Khvormūj
Khorog *see* Khorugh
117 S5 **Khorol** Poltavs'ka Oblast', NE Ukraine 49°49′N 33°17′E
142 L7 **Khorramābād** *var.* Khurramabad. Lorestān, W Iran 33°29′N 48°21′E
143 R9 **Khorramdasht** Kermān, C Iran 31°41′N 56°10′E
142 K10 **Khorramshahr** *var.* Khurramshahr, Muhammerah; *prev.* Mohammerah. Khūzestān, SW Iran 30°30′N 48°09′E
147 S14 **Khorugh** *Rus.* Khorog. S Tajikistan 37°30′N 71°31′E
Khorvot Khalutsa *see* Horvot Halutsa
127 Q12 **Khosheutovo** Astrakhanskaya Oblast', SW Russian Federation 47°04′N 47°49′E
149 R6 **Khōst** *prev.* Khowst. Khōst, E Afghanistan 33°22′N 69°57′E
149 S6 **Khōst** *prev.* Khowst. ◆ *province* E Afghanistan
Khotan *see* Hotan
Khotimsk *see* Khotsimsk
Khotin *see* Khotyn
119 R16 **Khotsimsk** *Rus.* Khotimsk. Mahilyowskaya Voblasts', E Belarus 53°24′N 32°35′E
116 K7 **Khotyn** *Rom.* Hotin, *Rus.* Khotin. Chernivets'ka Oblast', W Ukraine 48°29′N 26°30′E
74 F7 **Khouribga** C Morocco 32°55′N 06°51′W
147 Q13 **Khovaling** *Rus.* Khavaling. SW Tajikistan 38°22′N 69°54′E
Khovd *see* Hovd
Khowst *see* Khōst
Khoy *see* Khvoy
119 N20 **Khoyniki** Homyel'skaya Voblasts', SE Belarus 51°54′N 29°58′E
Khozretishi, Khrebet *see* Hazratishoh, Qatorkŭhi
145 V11 **Khrebet Khanshyngys** *Kaz.* Khanshyngghys; *prev.* Khrebet Kanchingiz. ▲▲ E Kazakhstan
145 X10 **Khrebet Kalba** *Kaz.* Qalba Zhotasy; *prev.* Kalbinskiy Khrebet. ▲▲ E Kazakhstan
Khrebet Kanchingiz *see* Khrebet Khanshyngys
Khrebet Ketmen *see* Khrebet Uzynkara
145 Y10 **Khrebet Naryn** *Kaz.* Naryn Zhotasy; *prev.* Narymskiy Khrebet. ▲▲ E Kazakhstan
145 W16 **Khrebet Uzynkara** *prev.* Khrebet Ketmen. ▲▲ SE Kazakhstan
Khrisoúpolis *see* Chrysoúpoli
144 J10 **Khromtau** *Kaz.* Khromtaū. Aktyubinsk, W Kazakhstan 50°14′N 58°22′E
Khromtaū *see* Khromtau
Khrysokhou Bay *see* Chrysochoú, Kólpos
117 O7 **Khrystynivka** Cherkas'ka Oblast', C Ukraine 48°49′N 29°55′E
167 R10 **Khuang Nai** Ubon Ratchathani, E Thailand 15°22′N 104°33′E
Khudal *see* Khādhil
Khudat *see* Xudat
149 W9 **Khudiān** Punjab, E Pakistan 30°59′N 74°19′E
Khudzhand *see* Khujand
83 G21 **Khuis** Kgalagadi, SW Botswana 26°37′S 21°50′E
147 Q11 **Khujand** *var.* Khodzhent, Khojend, *Rus.* Khudzhand; *prev.* Leninabad, *Taj.* Leninobod. N Tajikistan 40°17′N 69°37′E
167 R11 **Khukhan** Si Sa Ket, E Thailand 14°38′N 104°12′E
149 P2 **Khulm** *var.* Tashqurghan; *prev.* Kholm. Balkh, N Afghanistan 36°42′N 67°41′E
153 T16 **Khulna** Khulna, SW Bangladesh 22°48′N 89°32′E
153 T16 **Khulna** ◆ *division* SW Bangladesh
Khumain *see* Khomeyn
Khums *see* Al Khums
149 W2 **Khunjerāb Pass** *pass* China/ Pakistan
Khūnjerāb Pass *see* Kunjirap Daban
153 P16 **Khunti** Jhārkhand, N India 23°02′N 85°19′E
167 N7 **Khun Yuam** Mae Hong Son, NW Thailand 18°54′N 97°54′E
Khurais *see* Khurayş
141 R7 **Khurayş** *var.* Khurais. Ash Sharqīyah, C Saudi Arabia 25°06′N 48°03′E
Khurda *see* Khordha
152 J11 **Khurja** Uttar Pradesh, N India 28°15′N 77°51′E
139 V4 **Khurmāl** *var.* Khormal. As Sulaymānīyah, NE Iraq 35°19′N 46°06′E
Khurramabad *see* Khorramābād
Khurramshahr *see* Khorramshahr
149 U7 **Khushāb** Punjab, NE Pakistan 32°16′N 72°18′E
116 H8 **Khust** *var.* Husté, *Cz.* Chust, *Hung.* Huszt. Zakarpats'ka Oblast', W Ukraine 48°11′N 23°19′E
80 D11 **Khuwei** Southern Kordofan, C Sudan 13°02′N 29°13′E
149 O13 **Khuzdār** Baluchistān, SW Pakistan 27°49′N 66°39′E
142 L9 **Khūzestān** *off.* Ostān-e Khūzestān, *var.* Khuzistan, *prev.* Arabistan; *anc.* Susiana. ◆ *province* SW Iran
Khūzestān, Ostān-e *see* Khūzestān
Khuzistan *see* Khūzestān
Khvājeh Ghār *see* Khwājeh Ghār
127 Q7 **Khvalynsk** Saratovskaya Oblast', W Russian Federation 52°30′N 48°06′E
143 N12 **Khvormūj** *var.* Khormuj. Būshehr, S Iran 28°32′N 51°22′E
142 I2 **Khvoy** *var.* Khoi, Khoy. Āżarbāyjān-e Bākhtarī, NW Iran 38°36′N 45°04′E
Khwajaghar/Khwaja-i-Ghar *see* Khwājeh Ghār
149 R2 **Khwājeh Ghār** *var.* Khwajaghar, Khwaja-i-Ghar; *prev.* Khvājeh Ghār. Takhār, NE Afghanistan 37°08′N 69°24′E
149 U4 **Khyber Pakhtunkhwa** *prev.* North-West Frontier Province. ◆ *province* NW Pakistan
149 S5 **Khyber Pass** *var.* Kowtal-e Khaybar. *pass* Afghanistan/ Pakistan
186 L8 **Kia** Santa Isabel, N Solomon Islands 07°34′S 158°31′E
183 S10 **Kiama** New South Wales, SE Australia 34°41′S 150°49′E
79 O22 **Kiambi** Katanga, SE Dem. Rep. Congo 07°15′S 28°01′E
27 Q12 **Kiamichi Mountains** ▲▲ Oklahoma, C USA
27 Q12 **Kiamichi River** ≈ Oklahoma, C USA
14 M10 **Kiamika, Réservoir** ⊠ Québec, SE Canada
Kiamusze *see* Jiamusi
39 N7 **Kiana** Alaska, USA 66°58′N 160°25′W
Kiangmai *see* Chiang Mai
Kiang-ning *see* Nanjing
Kiangsi *see* Jiangxi
Kiangsu *see* Jiangsu

◆ Country
● Country Capital
◇ Dependent Territory
○ Dependent Territory Capital
◆ Administrative Regions
✈ International Airport
▲ Mountain
▲▲ Mountain Range
Volcano
≈ River
◎ Lake
⊠ Reservoir

93 M14 **Kiantajärvi** ◎ E Finland
115 F19 **Kiáto** prev. Kiáton. Pelopónnisos, S Greece 38°01′N 22°45′E
Kiáton see Kiáto
Kiayi see Jiayi
95 F22 **Kibæk** Midtjylland, W Denmark 56°03′N 08°52′E
67 T9 **Kibali** var. Uele (upper course). ≈ NE Dem. Rep. Congo
79 E20 **Kibangou** Niari, SW Congo 03°27′S 12°21′E
Kibarty see Kybartai
92 M8 **Kiberg** Finnmark, N Norway 70°17′N 30°47′E
79 N20 **Kibombo** Maniema, E Dem. Rep. Congo 03°52′S 25°59′E
81 E20 **Kibondo** Kigoma, NW Tanzania 03°34′S 30°41′E
81 J15 **Kibre Mengist** var. Adola. Oromīya, C Ethiopia 05°50′N 39°06′E
Kıbrıs see Cyprus
Kıbrıs/Kıbrıs Cumhuriyeti see Cyprus
81 E20 **Kibungo** var. Kibungu. SE Rwanda 02°09′S 30°30′E
Kibungu see Kibungo
113 N19 **Kičevo** SW FYR Macedonia 41°31′N 20°57′E
125 P13 **Kichmengskiy Gorodok** Vologodskaya Oblast', NW Russian Federation 60°00′N 45°52′E
30 J8 **Kickapoo River** ≈ Wisconsin, N USA
11 P16 **Kicking Horse Pass** pass Alberta/British Columbia, SW Canada
77 R9 **Kidal** Kidal, C Mali 18°22′N 01°21′E
77 Q8 **Kidal** ◐ region NE Mali
171 Q7 **Kidapawan** Mindanao, S Philippines 07°02′N 125°04′E
97 L20 **Kidderminster** C England, United Kingdom 52°23′N 02°14′W
76 I11 **Kidira** E Senegal 14°28′N 12°13′W
184 O11 **Kidnappers, Cape** headland North Island, New Zealand 41°13′S 175°15′E
100 J8 **Kiel** Schleswig-Holstein, N Germany 54°21′N 10°05′E
111 L15 **Kielce** Rus. Keltsy. Świętokrzyskie, C Poland 50°53′N 20°39′E
100 K7 **Kieler Bucht** bay N Germany
100 J7 **Kieler Förde** inlet N Germany
167 U13 **Kiên Đức** var. Đak Lap. Đắc Lắc, S Vietnam 11°59′N 107°30′E
79 N24 **Kienge** Katanga, SE Dem. Rep. Congo 10°33′S 27°33′E
100 Q12 **Kietz** Brandenburg, NE Germany 52°33′N 14°36′E
Kiev see Kyyiv
Kiev Reservoir see Kyyivs'ke Vodoskhovyshche
76 J10 **Kiffa** Assaba, S Mauritania 16°38′N 11°23′W
115 H19 **Kifisiá** Attikí, C Greece 38°04′N 23°49′E
115 F18 **Kifisós** ≈ C Greece
139 U5 **Kifrī** At Ta'mīm, N Iraq 34°44′N 44°58′E
81 D20 **Kigali** ● (Rwanda) C Rwanda 01°59′S 30°02′E
81 E20 **Kigali** ✈ C Rwanda 01°43′S 30°01′E
137 P13 **Kiğı** Bingöl, E Turkey 39°19′N 40°20′E
81 E21 **Kigoma** Kigoma, W Tanzania 04°52′S 29°36′E
81 E21 **Kigoma** ◐ region W Tanzania
38 F10 **Kihei** var. Kihei. Maui, Hawaii, USA, C Pacific Ocean 20°47′N 156°28′W
93 K17 **Kihniö** Länsi-Suomi, W Finland 62°11′N 23°10′E
118 F6 **Kihnu** var. Kihnu Saar, Ger. Kühnö. island SW Estonia
Kihnu Saar see Kihnu
38 A8 **Kii Landing** Ni'ihau, Hawaii, USA, C Pacific Ocean 21°58′N 160°03′W
93 L14 **Kiiminki** Oulu, C Finland 65°05′N 25°47′E
164 J14 **Kii-Nagashima** var. Nagashima. Mie, Honshū, SW Japan 34°10′N 136°18′E
164 J14 **Kii-sanchi** ▲▲ Honshū, SW Japan
92 L11 **Kiistala** Lappi, N Finland 67°52′N 25°19′E
164 I15 **Kii-suidō** strait S Japan
165 V16 **Kikai-shima** island Nansei-shotō, SW Japan
112 M8 **Kikinda** Ger. Grosskikinda, Hung. Nagykikinda; prev. Velika Kikinda. Vojvodina, N Serbia 45°48′N 20°29′E
Kikládhes see Kykládes
165 Q5 **Kikonai** Hokkaidō, NE Japan 41°40′N 140°25′E
186 C8 **Kikori** Gulf, S Papua New Guinea 07°25′S 144°13′E
186 C8 **Kikori** ≈ W Papua New Guinea
165 O14 **Kikuchi** var. Kikuti. Kumamoto, Kyūshū, SW Japan 33°00′N 130°49′E
Kikuti see Kikuchi
127 N8 **Kikvidze** Volgogradskaya Oblast', SW Russian Federation 50°47′N 42°58′E
14 I10 **Kikwissi, Lac** ◎ Québec, SE Canada
79 I21 **Kikwit** Bandundu, W Dem. Rep. Congo 05°S 18°53′E
95 K15 **Kil** Värmland, C Sweden 59°30′N 13°20′E
94 N12 **Kilafors** Gävleborg, C Sweden 61°13′N 16°34′E
38 B8 **Kilauea** Kaua'i, Hawaii, USA, C Pacific Ocean 22°12′N 159°24′W
38 H12 **Kilauea Caldera** var. Kilauea Caldera. crater Hawai'i, USA, C Pacific Ocean
Kilauea Caldera see Kilauea Caldera
109 V4 **Kilb** Niederösterreich, C Austria 48°06′N 15°21′E
39 O12 **Kilbuck Mountains** ▲▲ Alaska, USA
163 Y12 **Kilchu** NE North Korea 40°58′N 129°22′E
97 F18 **Kilcock** Ir. Cill Choca. Kildare, E Ireland 53°25′N 06°40′W
183 V2 **Kilcoy** Queensland, E Australia 26°58′S 152°30′E
97 F18 **Kildare** Ir. Cill Dara. E Ireland 53°10′N 06°55′W
97 F18 **Kildare** Ir. Cill Dara. cultural region E Ireland
124 K2 **Kil'din, Ostrov** island NW Russian Federation
25 W7 **Kilgore** Texas, SW USA 32°23′N 94°52′W
Kilien Mountains see Qilian Shan
114 K9 **Kilifarevo** Veliko Tŭrnovo, N Bulgaria 43°00′N 25°36′E
81 K20 **Kilifi** Coast, SE Kenya 03°37′S 39°50′E
189 U9 **Kili Island** var. Kōle. island Ralik Chain, S Marshall Islands
149 V2 **Kilik Pass** pass Afghanistan/China
Kilimane see Quelimane
81 I21 **Kilimanjaro** ◐ region E Tanzania
81 I20 **Kilimanjaro** var. Uhuru Peak. ▲ NE Tanzania 03°01′S 37°14′E
Kilimbangara see Kolombangara
Kilinailau Islands see Tulun Islands
81 K23 **Kilindoni** Pwani, E Tanzania 07°56′S 39°40′E
118 H6 **Kilingi-Nõmme** Ger. Kurkund. Pärnumaa, SW Estonia 58°07′N 24°00′E
136 M17 **Kilis** Kilis, S Turkey 36°43′N 37°07′E
136 M16 **Kilis** ◐ province S Turkey
117 N12 **Kiliya** Rom. Chilia-Nouă. Odes'ka Oblast', SW Ukraine 45°30′N 29°16′E
97 B19 **Kilkee** Ir. Cill Chaoi. Clare, W Ireland 52°41′N 09°38′W
97 E19 **Kilkenny** Ir. Cill Chainnigh. Kilkenny, S Ireland 52°39′N 07°15′W
97 E19 **Kilkenny** Ir. Cill Chainnigh. cultural region S Ireland
97 B18 **Kilkieran Bay** Ir. Cuan Chill Chiaráin. bay W Ireland
114 G13 **Kilkís** Kentrikí Makedonía, N Greece 40°59′N 22°55′E
97 C15 **Killala Bay** Ir. Cuan Chill Ala. inlet NW Ireland
11 R15 **Killam** Alberta, SW Canada 52°45′N 111°46′W
183 U3 **Killarney** Queensland, E Australia 28°18′S 152°15′E
11 W17 **Killarney** Manitoba, S Canada 49°12′N 99°40′W
14 E11 **Killarney** Ontario, S Canada 45°58′N 81°27′W
97 B20 **Killarney** Ir. Cill Airne. Kerry, SW Ireland 52°03′N 09°30′W
28 K4 **Killdeer** North Dakota, N USA 47°21′N 102°45′W
28 J4 **Killdeer Mountains** ▲▲ North Dakota, N USA
45 V15 **Killdeer River** ≈ Trinidad, Trinidad and Tobago
25 S9 **Killeen** Texas, SW USA 31°07′N 97°44′W
39 P6 **Killik River** ≈ Alaska, USA
11 T7 **Killinek Island** island Nunavut, NE Canada
Killini see Kyllíni
115 C19 **Killínis, Akrotírio** headland S Greece 37°55′N 21°07′E
97 D15 **Killybegs** Ir. Na Cealla Beaga. NW Ireland 54°38′N 08°27′W
Kilmain see Quelimane
96 I13 **Kilmarnock** W Scotland, United Kingdom 55°37′N 04°30′W
21 X6 **Kilmarnock** Virginia, NE USA 37°42′N 76°22′W
125 S16 **Kil'mez'** Kirovskaya Oblast', NW Russian Federation 56°55′N 51°03′E
127 S2 **Kil'mez'** Udmurtskaya Respublika, NW Russian Federation 57°04′N 51°22′E
125 R16 **Kil'mez'** ≈ NW Russian Federation
67 V11 **Kilombero** ≈ S Tanzania
92 J10 **Kilpisjärvi** Lappi, N Finland 69°03′N 20°50′E
97 B19 **Kilrush** Ir. Cill Rois. Clare, W Ireland 52°39′N 09°29′W
79 O24 **Kilwa** Katanga, SE Dem. Rep. Congo 09°22′S 28°19′E
Kilwa see Kilwa Kivinje
81 J24 **Kilwa Kivinje** var. Kilwa. Lindi, SE Tanzania 08°45′S 39°21′E
81 J24 **Kilwa Masoko** Lindi, SE Tanzania 08°55′S 39°31′E
171 T13 **Kilwo** Pulau Seram, E Indonesia 03°36′S 130°48′E
114 P12 **Kilyos** İstanbul, NW Turkey 41°15′N 29°01′E
37 V8 **Kim** Colorado, C USA 37°12′N 103°22′W
145 O9 **Kima** prev. Kiyma. Akmola, C Kazakhstan 51°37′N 67°31′E
169 U7 **Kimanis, Teluk** bay Sabah, East Malaysia
182 H8 **Kimba** South Australia 33°09′S 136°26′E
28 I15 **Kimball** Nebraska, C USA 41°16′N 103°40′W
29 O11 **Kimball** South Dakota, N USA 43°45′N 98°57′W
79 I21 **Kimbao** Bandundu, SW Dem. Rep. Congo 05°27′S 17°40′E
186 F7 **Kimbe** New Britain, E Papua New Guinea 05°36′S 150°10′E
186 G7 **Kimbe Bay** inlet New Britain, E Papua New Guinea
11 P17 **Kimberley** British Columbia, SW Canada 49°40′N 115°58′W
83 H23 **Kimberley** Northern Cape, C South Africa 28°45′S 24°46′E
180 M4 **Kimberley Plateau** plateau Western Australia
33 P15 **Kimberly** Idaho, NW USA 42°31′N 114°21′W
163 Y12 **Kimch'aek** prev. Sŏngjin. E North Korea 40°42′N 129°13′E
Kimch'ŏn see Gimcheon
Kim Hae see Gimhae
Kími see Kými
93 K20 **Kimito** Swe. Kemiö. Länsi-Suomi, SW Finland 60°10′N 22°45′E
9 R7 **Kimmirut** prev. Lake Harbour. Baffin Island, Nunavut, NE Canada 62°48′N 69°49′W
165 R4 **Kimobetsu** Hokkaidō, NE Japan 42°47′N 140°55′E
115 I21 **Kímolos** island Kykládes, Greece, Aegean Sea
115 I21 **Kímolou Sífnou, Stenó** strait Kykládes, Greece, Aegean Sea
126 L5 **Kimovsk** Tul'skaya Oblast', W Russian Federation 53°59′N 38°34′E
Kimpolung see Câmpulung Moldovenesc
124 K16 **Kimry** Tverskaya Oblast', W Russian Federation 56°52′N 37°21′E
79 H21 **Kimvula** Bas-Congo, SW Dem. Rep. Congo 05°44′S 15°58′E
169 U6 **Kinabalu, Gunung** ▲ East Malaysia 05°52′N 116°08′E
Kinabatangan see Kinabatangan, Sungai
169 V7 **Kinabatangan, Sungai** var. Kinabatangan. ≈ East Malaysia
115 L21 **Kínaros** island Kykládes, Greece, Aegean Sea
11 O15 **Kinbasket Lake** ⊡ British Columbia, SW Canada
96 I7 **Kinbrace** N Scotland, United Kingdom 58°16′N 02°59′W
14 E14 **Kincardine** Ontario, S Canada 44°11′N 81°38′W
96 K10 **Kincardine** cultural region E Scotland, United Kingdom
79 K21 **Kinda** Kasai-Occidental, SE Dem. Rep. Congo 04°48′S 21°50′E
79 M24 **Kinda** Katanga, SE Dem. Rep. Congo 09°20′S 25°06′E
166 L3 **Kindat** Sagaing, N Burma (Myanmar) 23°42′N 94°29′E
109 V6 **Kindberg** Steiermark, C Austria 47°31′N 15°27′E
22 H8 **Kinder** Louisiana, S USA 30°29′N 92°51′W
98 H13 **Kinderdijk** Zuid-Holland, SW Netherlands 51°52′N 04°37′E
97 M17 **Kinder Scout** ▲ C England, United Kingdom 53°25′N 01°52′W
11 S16 **Kindersley** Saskatchewan, S Canada 51°29′N 109°08′W
76 I14 **Kindia** Guinée-Maritime, SW Guinea 10°12′N 12°26′W
64 B11 **Kindley Field** air base E Bermuda
29 R6 **Kindred** North Dakota, N USA 46°39′N 97°01′W
79 N20 **Kindu** prev. Kindu-Port-Empain. Maniema, C Dem. Rep. Congo 02°57′S 25°54′E
Kindu-Port-Empain see Kindu
127 S6 **Kinel'** Samarskaya Oblast', W Russian Federation 53°14′N 50°40′E
125 N15 **Kineshma** Ivanovskaya Oblast', W Russian Federation 57°28′N 42°08′E
King see King William's Town
140 K10 **King Abdul Aziz** ✈ (Makkah) Makkah, W Saudi Arabia 21°44′N 39°08′E
Kingait see Cape Dorset
21 X6 **King and Queen Court House** Virginia, NE USA 37°40′N 76°49′W
King Charles Islands see Kong Karls Land
King Christian IX Land see Kong Christian IX Land
King Christian X Land see Kong Christian X Land
35 O11 **King City** California, W USA 36°12′N 121°09′W
27 R2 **King City** Missouri, C USA 40°03′N 94°31′W
38 M16 **King Cove** Alaska, USA 55°03′N 162°19′W
26 M10 **Kingfisher** Oklahoma, C USA 35°53′N 97°56′W
King Frederik VI Coast see Kong Frederik VI Kyst
King Frederik VIII Land see Kong Frederik VIII Land
65 B24 **King George Bay** bay West Falkland, Falkland Islands
194 G3 **King George Island** var. King George Land. island South Shetland Islands, Antarctica
12 I6 **King George Islands** island group Northwest Territories, C Canada
King George Land see King George Island
124 G13 **Kingisepp** Leningradskaya Oblast', NW Russian Federation 59°23′N 28°37′E
183 N14 **King Island** island Tasmania, SE Australia
10 J15 **King Island** island British Columbia, SW Canada
Kingissepp see Kuressaare
141 Q7 **King Khalid** ✈ (Ar Riyāḍ) Ar Riyāḍ, C Saudi Arabia 25°00′N 46°40′E
35 S2 **King Lear Peak** ▲ Nevada, W USA 41°13′N 118°30′W
195 Y8 **King Leopold and Queen Astrid Land** physical region Antarctica
180 M4 **King Leopold Ranges** ▲▲ Western Australia
36 I11 **Kingman** Arizona, SW USA 35°12′N 114°02′W
26 M6 **Kingman** Kansas, C USA 37°39′N 98°07′W
192 L7 **Kingman Reef** ◇ US territory C Pacific Ocean
79 N20 **Kingombe** Maniema, E Dem. Rep. Congo 02°37′S 26°39′E
182 F5 **Kingoonya** South Australia 30°56′S 135°20′E
194 J10 **King Peninsula** peninsula Antarctica
39 P13 **King Salmon** Alaska, USA 58°41′N 156°39′W
35 Q6 **Kings Beach** California, W USA 39°13′N 120°02′W
35 R11 **Kingsburg** California, W USA 36°30′N 119°33′W
182 I10 **Kingscote** South Australia 35°41′S 137°36′E
King's County see Offaly
194 H2 **King Sejong** South Korean research station Antarctica 61°57′S 58°23′W
183 T9 **Kingsford Smith** ✈ (Sydney) New South Wales, SE Australia 33°58′S 151°09′E
11 P17 **Kingsgate** British Columbia, SW Canada 48°58′N 116°09′W
23 W8 **Kingsland** Georgia, SE USA 30°48′N 81°41′W
29 S13 **Kingsley** Iowa, C USA 42°35′N 95°58′W
97 O19 **King's Lynn** var. Bishop's Lynn, Kings Lynn, Lynn, Lynn Regis. E England, United Kingdom 52°45′N 00°24′E
Kings Lynn see King's Lynn
21 Q10 **Kings Mountain** North Carolina, SE USA 35°15′N 81°20′W
180 K4 **King Sound** sound Western Australia
37 N2 **Kings Peak** ▲ Utah, W USA 40°43′N 110°27′W
21 O8 **Kingsport** Tennessee, S USA 36°32′N 82°33′W
35 R11 **Kings River** ≈ California, W USA
183 P17 **Kingston** Tasmania, SE Australia 42°57′S 147°18′E
14 K14 **Kingston** Ontario, SE Canada 44°14′N 76°30′W
44 K13 **Kingston** ● (Jamaica) E Jamaica 17°58′N 76°48′W
185 C22 **Kingston** Otago, South Island, New Zealand 45°20′S 168°45′E
19 P12 **Kingston** Massachusetts, NE USA 41°59′N 70°43′W
27 S3 **Kingston** Missouri, C USA 39°36′N 94°02′W
18 K12 **Kingston** New York, NE USA 41°55′N 74°00′W
31 S14 **Kingston** Ohio, N USA 39°28′N 82°54′W
19 O13 **Kingston** Rhode Island, NE USA 41°28′N 71°31′W
20 M9 **Kingston** Tennessee, S USA 35°52′N 84°30′W
35 W12 **Kingston Peak** ▲ California, W USA 35°43′N 115°54′W
182 J11 **Kingston Southeast** South Australia 36°51′S 139°53′E
97 N17 **Kingston upon Hull** var. Hull. E England, United Kingdom 53°45′N 00°20′W
97 N22 **Kingston upon Thames** SE England, United Kingdom 51°26′N 00°18′W
45 P14 **Kingstown** ● (Saint Vincent and the Grenadines) Saint Vincent, Saint Vincent and the Grenadines 13°09′N 61°14′W
Kingstown see Dún Laoghaire
21 T13 **Kingstree** South Carolina, SE USA 33°40′N 79°50′W
64 L8 **Kings Trough** undersea feature E Atlantic Ocean 22°00′W 43°48′N
14 C18 **Kingsville** Ontario, S Canada 42°03′N 82°43′W
25 S15 **Kingsville** Texas, SW USA 27°32′N 97°53′W
21 W6 **King William** Virginia, NE USA 37°42′N 77°03′W
9 N7 **King William Island** island Nunavut, N Canada
83 I25 **King William's Town** var. King, Kingwilliamstown. Eastern Cape, S South Africa 32°53′S 27°24′E
Kingwilliamstown see King William's Town
21 T3 **Kingwood** West Virginia, NE USA 39°27′N 79°43′W
136 C13 **Kınık** İzmir, W Turkey 39°05′N 27°25′E
79 G21 **Kinkala** Pool, S Congo 04°18′S 14°49′E
165 R10 **Kinka-san** headland Honshū, C Japan 38°17′N 141°34′E
184 M8 **Kinleith** Waikato, North Island, New Zealand 38°16′S 175°53′E
95 J19 **Kinna** Västra Götaland, S Sweden 57°32′N 12°42′E
96 L8 **Kinnaird Head** var. Kinnairds Head. headland NE Scotland, United Kingdom 58°39′N 03°22′W
Kinnairds Head see Kinnaird Head
95 K20 **Kinnared** Halland, S Sweden 57°01′N 13°04′E
92 L7 **Kinnarodden** headland N Norway 71°07′N 27°40′E
Kinneret, Yam see Tiberias, Lake
155 K24 **Kinniyai** Eastern Province, NE Sri Lanka 08°30′N 81°11′E
93 L16 **Kinnula** Länsi-Suomi, C Finland 63°24′N 25°E
14 I8 **Kinojévis** ≈ Québec, SE Canada
164 I14 **Kino-kawa** ≈ Honshū, SW Japan
11 U11 **Kinoosao** Saskatchewan, C Canada 57°06′N 101°02′W
99 L17 **Kinrooi** Limburg, NE Belgium 51°09′N 05°48′E
96 J11 **Kinross** C Scotland, United Kingdom 56°14′N 03°27′W
96 J11 **Kinross** cultural region C Scotland, United Kingdom
97 C21 **Kinsale** Ir. Cionn tSáile. Cork, SW Ireland 51°42′N 08°32′W
95 D14 **Kinsarvik** Hordaland, S Norway 60°22′N 06°43′E
79 G21 **Kinshasa** prev. Léopoldville. ● Kinshasa, W Dem. Rep. Congo 04°21′S 15°16′E
79 G21 **Kinshasa** off. Ville de Kinshasa, var. Kinshasa City. ◐ region (Dem. Rep. Congo) SW Dem. Rep. Congo
79 G21 **Kinshasa** ✈ Kinshasa, SW Dem. Rep. Congo 04°23′S 15°30′E
Kinshasa City see Kinshasa
117 U9 **Kins'ka** ≈ SE Ukraine
26 K6 **Kinsley** Kansas, C USA 37°55′N 99°26′W
21 W10 **Kinston** North Carolina, SE USA 35°16′N 77°35′W
77 P15 **Kintampo** W Ghana 08°06′N 01°40′W
182 B1 **Kintore, Mount** ▲ South Australia 26°30′S 130°24′E
96 G13 **Kintyre** peninsula W Scotland, United Kingdom
96 G13 **Kintyre, Mull of** headland W Scotland, United Kingdom 55°16′N 05°46′W
166 M4 **Kin-u** Sagaing, C Burma (Myanmar) 22°47′N 95°36′E
12 G8 **Kinushseo** ≈ Ontario, C Canada
11 P13 **Kinuso** Alberta, W Canada 55°19′N 115°23′W
154 I13 **Kinwat** Mahārāshtra, C India 19°37′N 78°12′E
81 F16 **Kinyeti** ▲ S South Sudan 03°56′N 32°52′E
101 I17 **Kinzig** ≈ SW Germany
Kioga, Lake see Kyoga, Lake
26 M8 **Kiowa** Kansas, C USA 37°01′N 98°29′W
27 P12 **Kiowa** Oklahoma, C USA 34°43′N 95°54′W
Kiparissía see Kyparissía
14 H10 **Kipawa, Lac** ◎ Québec, SE Canada
81 G24 **Kipengere Range** ▲▲ SW Tanzania
81 E23 **Kipili** Rukwa, W Tanzania 07°30′S 30°39′E
81 K20 **Kipini** Coast, SE Kenya 02°30′S 40°30′E
11 V16 **Kipling** Saskatchewan, S Canada 50°04′N 102°45′W
38 M13 **Kipnuk** Alaska, USA 59°56′N 164°02′W
97 F18 **Kippure** Ir. Cipiúr. ▲ E Ireland 53°10′N 06°22′W
79 N25 **Kipushi** Katanga, SE Dem. Rep. Congo 11°45′S 27°20′E
187 N10 **Kirakira** var. Kaokaona. Makira-Ulawa, SE Solomon Islands 10°28′S 161°54′E
155 K14 **Kirandul** var. Bailādila. Chhattīsgarh, C India 18°46′N 81°18′E
155 I21 **Kīranūr** Tamil Nādu, SE India 11°37′N 79°10′E
119 N21 **Kiraw** Rus. Kirovo. Homyel'skaya Voblasts', SE Belarus 51°30′N 29°25′E
119 M17 **Kirawsk** Rus. Kirovsk; prev. Startsy. Mahilyowskaya Voblasts', E Belarus 53°16′N 29°29′E
118 F5 **Kirbla** Läänemaa, W Estonia 58°45′N 23°57′E
25 Y9 **Kirbyville** Texas, SW USA 30°39′N 93°53′W
114 M12 **Kırcasalih** Edirne, NW Turkey 41°24′N 26°48′E
109 W8 **Kirchbach** var. Kirchbach in Steiermark. Steiermark, SE Austria 46°55′N 15°40′E
Kirchbach in Steiermark see Kirchbach
108 H7 **Kirchberg** Sankt Gallen, NE Switzerland 47°24′N 09°03′E
109 S5 **Kirchdorf an der Krems** Oberösterreich, N Austria 47°55′N 14°08′E
Kirchheim see Kirchheim unter Teck
101 I22 **Kirchheim unter Teck** var. Kirchheim. Baden-Württemberg, SW Germany 48°39′N 09°28′E
Kirdzhali see Kŭrdzhali
123 N13 **Kirenga** ≈ S Russian Federation
123 N12 **Kirensk** Irkutskaya Oblast', C Russian Federation 57°37′N 107°54′E
Kirghizia see Kyrgyzstan
145 S16 **Kirghiz Range** Rus. Kirgizskiy Khrebet; prev. Alexander Range. ▲▲ Kazakhstan/Kyrgyzstan
Kirghiz SSR see Kyrgyzstan
Kirghiz Steppe see Saryarka
Kirgizskaya SSR see Kyrgyzstan
Kirgizskiy Khrebet see Kirghiz Range
79 I19 **Kiri** Bandundu, W Dem. Rep. Congo 01°29′S 19°00′E
Kiriath-Arba see Hebron
191 R3 **Kiribati** off. Republic of Kiribati. ◆ republic C Pacific Ocean
Kiribati, Republic of see Kiribati
136 L17 **Kırıkhan** Hatay, S Turkey 36°30′N 36°20′E
136 I13 **Kırıkkale** Kırıkkale, C Turkey 39°50′N 33°31′E
136 C10 **Kırıkkale** ◐ province C Turkey
124 L13 **Kirillov** Vologodskaya Oblast', NW Russian Federation 59°52′N 38°24′E
Kirin see Jilin
81 I18 **Kirinyaga** prev. Mount Kenya. ▲ C Kenya 0°02′S 37°19′E
124 H13 **Kirishi** var. Kirisi. Leningradskaya Oblast', NW Russian Federation 59°28′N 32°02′E
164 C16 **Kirishima-yama** ▲ Kyūshū, SW Japan 31°58′N 130°51′E
Kirisi see Kirishi
191 Y2 **Kiritimati** ✈ Kiritimati, E Kiribati 02°00′N 157°30′W
191 Y2 **Kiritimati** prev. Christmas Island. atoll Line Islands, E Kiribati
186 G9 **Kiriwina Island** Eng. Trobriand Island. island SE Papua New Guinea
186 G9 **Kiriwina Islands** var. Trobriand Islands. island group S Papua New Guinea
96 K12 **Kirkcaldy** E Scotland, United Kingdom 56°07′N 03°10′W
97 I14 **Kirkcudbright** S Scotland, United Kingdom 54°50′N 04°03′W
97 I14 **Kirkcudbright** cultural region S Scotland, United Kingdom
Kirkee see Khadki
95 I14 **Kirkenær** Hedmark, S Norway 60°27′N 12°04′E
92 M8 **Kirkenes** Fin. Kirkkoniemi. Finnmark, N Norway 69°43′N 30°02′E
92 J4 **Kirkjubæjarklaustur** Sudhurland, S Iceland 63°46′N 18°03′W
Kirk-Kilissa see Kırklareli
Kirkkoniemi see Kirkenes
93 L20 **Kirkkonummi** Swe. Kyrkslätt. Uusimaa, S Finland 60°06′N 24°20′E
14 G7 **Kirkland Lake** Ontario, S Canada 48°10′N 80°02′W
136 C9 **Kırklareli** prev. Kirk-Kilissa. Kırklareli, NW Turkey 41°45′N 27°12′E
136 I13 **Kırklareli** ◐ province NW Turkey
185 F20 **Kirkliston Range** ▲▲ South Island, New Zealand
14 D10 **Kirkpatrick Lake** ◎ Ontario, S Canada
195 Q11 **Kirkpatrick, Mount** ▲ Antarctica 84°37′S 164°36′E
27 U2 **Kirksville** Missouri, C USA 40°12′N 92°35′W
139 T4 **Kirkūk** var. Karkūk, Kerkuk. At Ta'mīm, N Iraq 35°28′N 44°26′E
139 U7 **Kir Kush** Diyālá, E Iraq 33°42′N 45°15′E
96 K5 **Kirkwall** NE Scotland, United Kingdom 58°59′N 02°58′W
83 H25 **Kirkwood** Eastern Cape, S South Africa 33°23′S 25°19′E
27 X5 **Kirkwood** Missouri, C USA 38°35′N 90°24′W
Kirman see Kermān
Kir Moab/Kir of Moab see Al Karak
126 I5 **Kirov** Kaluzhskaya Oblast', W Russian Federation 54°02′N 34°17′E
125 R14 **Kirov** prev. Vyatka. Kirovskaya Oblast', NW Russian Federation 58°35′N 49°39′E
Kirov see Balpyk Bi/Ust'yevoye
Kirovabad see Gäncä
Kirovabad see Panj, Tajikistan
Kirovakan see Vanadzor
Kirov/Kirova see Kopbirlik, Kazakhstan
Kirovo see Kiraw, Belarus
Kirovo see Beshariq, Uzbekistan
125 R14 **Kirovo-Chepetsk** Kirovskaya Oblast', NW Russian Federation 58°33′N 50°06′E
Kirovogradskaya Oblast'/Kirovohrad see Kirovohrads'ka Oblast'
117 R7 **Kirovohrad** Rus. Kirovograd; prev. Kirovo, Yelizavetgrad, Zinov'yevsk. Kirovohrads'ka Oblast', C Ukraine 48°30′N 31°17′E
117 P7 **Kirovohrads'ka Oblast'** var. Kirovohrad, Rus. Kirovogradskaya Oblast'. ◐ province C Ukraine
Kirovo/Kirovograd see Kirovohrad
124 J4 **Kirovsk** Murmanskaya Oblast', NW Russian Federation 67°37′N 33°38′E
117 X7 **Kirovs'k** Luhans'ka Oblast', E Ukraine 48°40′N 38°39′E
Kirovsk see Kirawsk, Belarus
Kirovsk see Babadaýhan, Turkmenistan
122 E9 **Kirovskaya Oblast'** ◐ province NW Russian Federation
117 U13 **Kirovs'ke** Rus. Kirovskoye. Avtonomna Respublika Krym, S Ukraine 45°13′N 35°12′E
117 X8 **Kirovs'ke** Donets'ka Oblast', E Ukraine 48°12′N 38°20′E
Kirovskiy see Balpyk Bi
Kirovskiy see Ust'yevoye
Kirovskoye see Kyzyl-Adyr
Kirovskoye see Kirovs'ke
146 E11 **Kirpili** Ahal Welaýaty, C Turkmenistan 39°31′N 57°13′E
96 K10 **Kirriemuir** E Scotland, United Kingdom 56°38′N 03°01′W
125 S13 **Kirs** Kirovskaya Oblast', NW Russian Federation 59°22′N 52°20′E
127 N7 **Kirsanov** Tambovskaya Oblast', W Russian Federation 52°40′N 42°48′E
136 J14 **Kırşehir** anc. Justinianopolis. Kırşehir, C Turkey 39°09′N 34°08′E
136 I13 **Kırşehir** ◐ province C Turkey
149 P4 **Kirthar Range** ▲▲ S Pakistan
37 P9 **Kirtland** New Mexico, SW USA 36°43′N 108°21′W
92 J11 **Kiruna** Lapp. Giron. Norrbotten, N Sweden 67°50′N 20°16′E
79 M18 **Kirundu** Orientale, NE Dem. Rep. Congo 0°45′S 25°28′E
Kirun/Kirun' see Jilong
26 L3 **Kirwin Reservoir** ⊡ Kansas, C USA
127 Q4 **Kirya** Chuvashskaya Respublika, W Russian Federation 55°04′N 46°50′E
138 G8 **Kiryat Shmona** prev. Qiryat Shemona. Northern, N Israel 33°13′N 35°35′E
95 M18 **Kisa** Östergötland, S Sweden 58°N 15°39′E
165 P9 **Kisakata** Akita, Honshū, C Japan 39°12′N 139°55′E
Kisalföld see Little Alföld
79 L18 **Kisangani** prev. Stanleyville. Orientale, NE Dem. Rep. Congo 0°30′N 25°14′E
39 N12 **Kisaralik River** ≈ Alaska, USA
165 O14 **Kisarazu** Chiba, Honshū, S Japan 35°23′N 139°57′E
111 I22 **Kisbér** Komárom-Esztergom, NW Hungary 47°30′N 18°00′E
11 V17 **Kisbey** Saskatchewan, S Canada 49°41′N 102°39′W
122 J13 **Kiselevsk** Kemerovskaya Oblast', S Russian Federation 54°00′N 86°38′E
153 R13 **Kishanganj** Bihār, NE India 26°06′N 87°57′E
152 G12 **Kishangarh** Rājasthān, N India 26°33′N 74°52′E
Kishegyes see Mali Iđoš
77 S15 **Kishi** Oyo, W Nigeria 09°01′N 03°53′E
Kishinev see Chişinău
Kishiözen see Saryozen
164 I14 **Kishiwada** var. Kisiwada. Ōsaka, Honshū, SW Japan 34°28′N 135°22′E
143 P14 **Kish, Jazīreh-ye** var. Qey. island S Iran
145 R7 **Kishkenekol'** prev. Kzyltu, Kaz. Qyzyltū. Kokshetau, N Kazakhstan 53°39′N 72°22′E
138 G9 **Kishon, Nahal** prev. Nahal Qishon. ≈ N Israel
152 I6 **Kishtwār** Jammu and Kashmir, NW India 33°20′N 75°49′E
81 H19 **Kisii** Nyanza, SW Kenya 0°40′S 34°47′E
81 J23 **Kisiju** Pwani, E Tanzania 07°25′S 39°20′E
Kisiwada see Kishiwada
Kisjenő see Chişineu-Criş
38 E17 **Kiska Island** island Aleutian Islands, Alaska, USA
Kiskapus see Copşa Mică
111 M22 **Kiskőrei-víztároló** ⊡ E Hungary
Kis-Küküllo see Târnava Mică
111 L24 **Kiskunfélegyháza** var. Félegyháza. Bács-Kiskun, C Hungary 46°42′N 19°52′E
111 K25 **Kiskunhalas** var. Halas. Bács-Kiskun, S Hungary 46°26′N 19°29′E
111 K24 **Kiskunmajsa** Bács-Kiskun, S Hungary 46°30′N 19°46′E
127 N15 **Kislovodsk** Stavropol'skiy Kray, SW Russian Federation 43°55′N 42°45′E
81 L18 **Kismaayo** var. Chisimayu, Kismayu, It. Chisimaio. Jubbada Hoose, S Somalia 0°05′S 42°35′E
Kismayu see Kismaayo
164 M13 **Kiso-sanmyaku** ▲▲ Honshū, S Japan
115 H24 **Kíssamos** prev. Kastélli. Kríti, Greece, E Mediterranean Sea 35°30′N 23°39′E
Kisseraing see Kanmaw Kyun
76 K14 **Kissidougou** Guinée-Forestière, S Guinea 09°15′N 10°08′W
23 X12 **Kissimmee** Florida, SE USA 28°17′N 81°24′W
23 X12 **Kissimmee, Lake** ◎ Florida, SE USA
23 X13 **Kissimmee River** ≈ Florida, SE USA
11 V13 **Kississing Lake** ◎ Manitoba, C Canada
111 L24 **Kistelek** Csongrád, SE Hungary 46°27′N 19°58′E
Kistna see Krishna
111 M23 **Kisújszállás** Jász-Nagykun-Szolnok, E Hungary 47°14′N 20°45′E
164 G12 **Kisuki** var. Unnan. Shimane, Honshū, SW Japan 35°25′N 133°15′E
81 H18 **Kisumu** prev. Port Florence. Nyanza, W Kenya 0°02′N 34°42′E
Kisutzaneustadtl see Kysucké Nové Mesto
111 O20 **Kisvárda** Ger. Kleinwardein. Szabolcs-Szatmár-Bereg, E Hungary 48°13′N 22°03′E
81 J24 **Kiswere** Lindi, SE Tanzania 09°24′S 39°37′E
Kiszucaújhely see Kysucké Nové Mesto
76 K12 **Kita** Kayes, W Mali 13°00′N 09°28′W
197 N14 **Kitaa** ◐ province W Greenland
Kita-Akita see Takanosu
Kitab see Kitob
165 Q4 **Kitahiyama** Hokkaidō, NE Japan 42°25′N 139°55′E
165 P12 **Kitaibaraki** Ibaraki, Honshū, S Japan 36°46′N 140°45′E
165 X16 **Kita-Iō-jima** Eng. San Alessandro. island SE Japan
165 Q9 **Kitakami** Iwate, Honshū, C Japan 39°18′N 141°05′E
165 P11 **Kitakata** Fukushima, Honshū, C Japan 37°38′N 139°52′E
164 D13 **Kitakyūshū** var. Kitakyûsyû. Fukuoka, Kyūshū, SW Japan 33°51′N 130°49′E
Kitakyûsyû see Kitakyūshū
81 H18 **Kitale** Rift Valley, W Kenya 01°01′N 35°01′E
165 U3 **Kitami** Hokkaidō, NE Japan 43°52′N 143°51′E
165 T2 **Kitami-sanchi** ▲▲ Hokkaidō, NE Japan
37 W5 **Kit Carson** Colorado, C USA 38°45′N 102°47′W
180 M12 **Kitchener** Western Australia 31°03′S 124°00′E
14 F16 **Kitchener** Ontario, S Canada 43°28′N 80°27′W
93 O17 **Kitee** Itä-Suomi, SE Finland 62°06′N 30°09′E
81 G16 **Kitgum** N Uganda 03°17′N 32°54′E
Kíthareng see Kanmaw Kyun
Kíthira see Kýthira
Kíthnos see Kýthnos
8 L8 **Kitikmeot** cultural region Nunavut, NE Canada
10 J13 **Kitimat** British Columbia, SW Canada 54°05′N 128°38′W
92 L11 **Kitinen** ≈ N Finland
147 N12 **Kitob** Rus. Kitab. Qashqadaryo Viloyati, S Uzbekistan 39°06′N 66°47′E
116 K7 **Kitsman'** Ger. Kotzman, Rom. Cozmeni, Rus. Kitsman. Chernivets'ka Oblast', W Ukraine 48°30′N 25°50′E
164 E14 **Kitsuki** var. Kituki. Ōita, Kyūshū, SW Japan 33°24′N 131°36′E
18 C14 **Kittanning** Pennsylvania, NE USA 40°48′N 79°28′W
19 P10 **Kittery** Maine, NE USA 43°05′N 70°44′W
92 L11 **Kittilä** Lappi, N Finland 67°39′N 24°53′E
109 Z4 **Kittsee** Burgenland, E Austria 48°06′N 17°03′E
81 J19 **Kitui** Eastern, S Kenya 01°25′S 38°00′E
Kituki see Kitsuki
81 G22 **Kitunda** Tabora, C Tanzania 06°47′S 33°13′E
10 K13 **Kitwanga** British Columbia, SW Canada 55°07′N 128°03′W
82 J13 **Kitwe** var. Kitwe-Nkana. Copperbelt, C Zambia 12°48′S 28°13′E
Kitwe-Nkana see Kitwe
109 O7 **Kitzbühel** Tirol, W Austria 47°27′N 12°23′E
109 O7 **Kitzbüheler Alpen** ▲▲ W Austria
101 J19 **Kitzingen** Bayern, SE Germany 49°45′N 10°11′E
153 Q14 **Kiul** Bihār, NE India 25°10′N 86°06′E
186 A7 **Kiunga** Western, SW Papua New Guinea 06°10′S 141°15′E
93 M16 **Kiuruvesi** Itä-Suomi, C Finland 63°38′N 26°40′E
38 M7 **Kivalina** Alaska, USA 67°44′N 164°32′W
92 L13 **Kivalo** ridge C Finland
9 O10 **Kivalliq** cultural region Nunavut, NE Canada
116 J3 **Kivertsi** Pol. Kiwerce, Rus. Kivertsy. Volyns'ka Oblast', NW Ukraine 50°50′N 25°31′E
Kivertsy see Kivertsi
93 L16 **Kivijärvi** Länsi-Suomi, C Finland 63°09′N 25°04′E
95 L23 **Kivik** Skåne, S Sweden 55°40′N 14°15′E
118 J3 **Kiviõli** Ida-Virumaa, NE Estonia 59°20′N 27°00′E
Kivu, Lac see Kivu, Lake
67 U10 **Kivu, Lake** Fr. Lac Kivu. ◎ Rwanda/Dem. Rep. Congo
186 C9 **Kiwai Island** island SW Papua New Guinea
39 N8 **Kiwalik** Alaska, USA 66°01′N 161°50′W
Kiwerce see Kivertsi
Kiyev see Kyyiv
145 R10 **Kiyevka** Karaganda, C Kazakhstan 50°15′N 71°33′E
Kiyevskaya Oblast' see Kyyivs'ka Oblast'
Kiyevskoye Vodokhranilishche see Kyyivs'ke Vodoskhovyshche
136 D10 **Kiyiköy** Kırklareli, NW Turkey 41°37′N 28°07′E
Kiyma see Kima
125 V13 **Kizel** Permskiy Kray, NW Russian Federation 58°59′N 57°37′E
125 O12 **Kizema** var. Kizëma. Arkhangel'skaya Oblast', NW Russian Federation 61°06′N 44°51′E
Kizëma see Kizema
Kizilagach see Elkhovo

● Country
● Country Capital
◇ Dependent Territory
○ Dependent Territory Capital
◐ Administrative Regions
✈ International Airport
▲ Mountain
▲▲ Mountain Range
Volcano
≈ River
◎ Lake
⊡ Reservoir

136 *H12* **Kızılcahamam** Ankara, N Turkey *40°28′N 32°37′E*
136 *J10* **Kızıl Irmak** ≈ C Turkey
Kizil Kum *see* Kyzyl Kum
137 *P16* **Kızıltepe** Mardin, SE Turkey *37°12′N 40°36′E*
Ki Zil Uzen *see* Qezel Owzan, Rūd-e
127 *Q16* **Kizilyurt** Respublika Dagestan, SW Russian Federation *43°13′N 46°54′E*
127 *Q15* **Kizlyar** Respublika Dagestan, SW Russian Federation *43°51′N 46°39′E*
127 *S3* **Kizner** Udmurtskaya Respublika, NW Russian Federation *56°19′N 51°37′E*
Kizyl-Arvat *see* Serdar
Kizyl-Atrek *see* Etrek
Kizyl-Kaya *see* Gyzylgaýa
Kizyl-Su *see* Gyzylsuw
95 *H16* **Kjerkøy** *island* S Norway
Kjølen *see* Kölen
92 *L7* **Kjøllefjord** Finnmark, N Norway *70°55′N 27°19′E*
92 *H11* **Kjøpsvik** ***Lapp.*** Gásluokta. Nordland, C Norway *68°06′N 16°21′E*
169 *N12* **Klabat, Teluk** *bay* Pulau Bangka, W Indonesia
112 *I12* **Kladanj** ◈ Fedederacijia Bosna I Hercegovina, E Bosnia and Herzegovina
171 *X16* **Kladar** Papua, E Indonesia *08°14′S 137°46′E*
111 *C16* **Kladno** Středočeský, NW Czech Republic *50°10′N 14°05′E*
112 *P11* **Kladovo** Serbia, E Serbia *44°37′N 22°36′E*
167 *P12* **Klaeng** Rayong, S Thailand *12°48′N 101°41′E*
109 *T9* **Klagenfurt** ***Slvn.*** Celovec. Kärnten, S Austria *46°38′N 14°20′E*
118 *B11* **Klaipėda** ***Ger.*** Memel. Klaipeda, NW Lithuania *55°42′N 21°09′E*
118 *C11* **Klaipėda** ◈ *province* W Lithuania
Klaksvig *see* Klaksvík
95 *B18* **Klaksvík** ***Dan.*** Klaksvig. Faeroe Islands *62°13′N 06°34′W*
34 *L2* **Klamath** California, W USA *41°31′N 124°02′W*
32 *H16* **Klamath Falls** Oregon, NW USA *42°14′N 121°47′W*
34 *M1* **Klamath Mountains** ▲▲ California/Oregon, W USA
34 *L2* **Klamath River** ≈ California/Oregon, W USA
168 *K9* **Klang** ***var.*** Kelang; ***prev.*** Port Swettenham. Selangor, Peninsular Malaysia *03°02′N 101°27′E*
94 *J13* **Klarälven** ≈ Norway/ Sweden
111 *B15* **Klášterec nad Ohří** ***Ger.*** Klösterle an der Eger. Ústecky Kraj, NW Czech Republic *50°24′N 13°10′E*
111 *B18* **Klatovy** ***Ger.*** Klattau. Plzeňský Kraj, W Czech Republic *49°24′N 13°16′E*
Klattau *see* Klatovy
Klausenburg *see* Cluj-Napoca
39 *Y14* **Klawock** Prince of Wales Island, Alaska, USA *55°33′N 133°06′W*
98 *P8* **Klazienaveen** Drenthe, NE Netherlands *52°43′N 07°E*
Kleck *see* Klyetsk
110 *H11* **Kłecko** Weilkopolskie, C Poland *52°37′N 17°27′E*
110 *I11* **Kleczew** Wielkopolskie, C Poland *52°22′N 18°12′E*
10 *L15* **Kleena Kleene** British Columbia, SW Canada *51°55′N 124°54′W*
83 *D20* **Klein Aub** Hardap, C Namibia *23°48′S 16°39′E*
Kleine Donau *see* Mosoni-Duna
101 *O14* **Kleine Elster** ≈ E Germany
Kleine Kokel *see* Târnava Mică
99 *I16* **Kleine Nete** ≈ N Belgium
Kleines Ungarisches Tiefland *see* Little Alföld
83 *E22* **Klein Karas** Karas, S Namibia *27°36′S 18°05′E*
Kleinkopisch *see* Copşa Mică
Klein-Marien *see* Väike-Maarja
Kleinschlatten *see* Zlatna
83 *D23* **Kleinsee** Northern Cape, W South Africa *29°43′S 17°03′E*
Kleinwardein *see* Kisvárda
115 *C16* **Kleisoúra** Ípeiros, W Greece *39°21′N 20°52′E*
95 *C17* **Klepp** Rogaland, S Norway *58°46′N 05°39′E*
83 *I22* **Klerksdorp** North-West, N South Africa *26°52′S 26°39′E*
126 *I5* **Kletnya** Bryanskaya Oblast', W Russian Federation *53°25′N 32°58′E*
Kletsk *see* Klyetsk
101 *D14* **Kleve** ***Eng.*** Cleves, ***Fr.*** Clèves; ***prev.*** Cleve. Nordrhein-Westfalen, W Germany *51°47′N 06°11′E*
113 *J16* **Kličevo** C Montenegro *42°45′N 18°58′E*
119 *M16* **Klichaw** ***Rus.*** Klichev. Mahilyowskaya Voblasts', E Belarus *53°29′N 29°21′E*
Klichev *see* Klichaw
119 *Q16* **Klimavichy** ***Rus.*** Klimovichi. Mahilyowskaya Voblasts', E Belarus *53°37′N 31°58′E*
114 *M7* **Kliment** Shumen, NE Bulgaria *43°37′N 27°00′E*
Klimovichi *see* Klimavichy
93 *G14* **Klimpfjäll** Västerbotten, N Sweden *65°05′N 14°50′E*
126 *K3* **Klin** Moskovskaya Oblast', W Russian Federation *56°19′N 36°45′E*
Klina *see* Klinë
113 *M16* **Klinë** ***Serb.*** Klina. W Kosovo *42°38′N 20°35′E*
111 *B15* **Klínovec** ***Ger.*** Keilberg. ▲ NW Czech Republic *50°23′N 12°57′E*
95 *P19* **Klintehamn** Gotland, SE Sweden *57°22′N 18°15′E*
127 *R8* **Klintsovka** Saratovskaya Oblast', W Russian Federation *51°42′N 49°17′E*
126 *H6* **Klintsy** Bryanskaya Oblast', W Russian Federation *52°46′N 32°21′E*
95 *K22* **Klippan** Skåne, S Sweden *56°08′N 13°10′E*
92 *G13* **Klippen** Västerbotten, N Sweden *65°50′N 15°07′E*
121 *P2* **Klírou** W Cyprus *35°01′N 33°11′E*
114 *I9* **Klisura** Plovdiv, C Bulgaria *42°40′N 24°28′E*
95 *F20* **Klitmøller** Midtjylland, NW Denmark *57°01′N 08°29′E*
112 *F11* **Ključ** Federacija Bosna I Hercegovina, NW Bosnia and Herzegovina *44°32′N 16°46′E*
111 *J14* **Kłobuck** Śląskie, S Poland *50°56′N 18°55′E*
110 *J11* **Kłodawa** Wielkopolskie, C Poland *52°14′N 18°55′E*
111 *G16* **Kłodzko** ***Ger.*** Glatz. Dolnośląskie, SW Poland *50°27′N 16°37′E*
95 *I14* **Kløfta** Akershus, S Norway *60°04′N 11°06′E*
112 *P12* **Klokočevac** Serbia, E Serbia *44°19′N 22°11′E*
118 *G3* **Klooga** ***Ger.*** Lodensee. Harjumaa, NW Estonia *59°18′N 24°10′E*
99 *F15* **Kloosterzande** Zeeland, SW Netherlands *51°22′N 04°01′E*
113 *L19* **Klos** ***var.*** Klosi. Dibër, C Albania *41°30′N 20°07′E*
Klosi *see* Klos
Klösterle an der Eger *see* Klášterec nad Ohří
109 *X3* **Klosterneuburg** Niederösterreich, NE Austria *48°19′N 16°20′E*
108 *J9* **Klosters** Graubünden, SE Switzerland *46°54′N 09°52′E*
108 *G7* **Kloten** Zürich, N Switzerland *47°27′N 08°35′E*
108 *G7* **Kloten** ✕ (Zürich) Zürich, N Switzerland *47°25′N 08°36′E*
100 *K12* **Klötze** Sachsen-Anhalt, C Germany *52°37′N 11°09′E*
12 *K3* **Klotz, Lac** ◎ Québec, NE Canada
101 *O15* **Klotzsche** ✕ (Dresden) Sachsen, E Germany *51°06′N 13°44′E*
10 *H7* **Kluane Lake** ◎ Yukon Territory, W Canada
Kluang *see* Keluang
111 *I14* **Kluczbork** ***Ger.*** Kreuzburg, Kreuzburg in Oberschlesien. Opolskie, S Poland *50°59′N 18°13′E*
39 *W12* **Klukwan** Alaska, USA *59°24′N 135°49′W*
Klyastitsy *see* Klyastsitsy
118 *L11* **Klyastsitsy** ***Rus.*** Klyastitsy. Vitsyebskaya Voblasts', N Belarus *55°53′N 28°36′E*
127 *T5* **Klyavlino** Samarskaya Oblast', W Russian Federation *54°21′N 52°12′E*
84 *K9* **Klyaz'in** ≈ W Russian Federation
127 *N3* **Klyaz'ma** ≈ W Russian Federation
119 *J17* **Klyetsk** ***Pol.*** Kleck, ***Rus.*** Kletsk. Minskaya Voblasts', SW Belarus *53°04′N 26°38′E*
147 *S8* **Klyuchevka** Talasskaya Oblast', NW Kyrgyzstan *42°34′N 71°45′E*
123 *V10* **Klyuchevskaya Sopka, Vulkan** ※ E Russian Federation *56°03′N 160°38′E*
95 *D17* **Knaben** Vest-Agder, S Norway *58°46′N 07°04′E*
95 *K21* **Knäred** Halland, S Sweden *56°30′N 13°21′E*
97 *M16* **Knaresborough** N England, United Kingdom *54°01′N 01°35′W*
114 *H8* **Knezha** Vratsa, NW Bulgaria *43°29′N 24°04′E*
25 *O9* **Knickerbocker** Texas, SW USA *31°18′N 100°35′W*
28 *K5* **Knife River** ≈ North Dakota, N USA
10 *K16* **Knight Inlet** *inlet* British Columbia, W Canada
39 *S12* **Knight Island** *island* Alaska, USA
97 *K20* **Knighton** E Wales, United Kingdom *52°20′N 03°01′W*
35 *O7* **Knights Landing** California, W USA *38°47′N 121°43′W*
112 *E13* **Knin** Šibenik-Knin, S Croatia *44°03′N 16°12′E*
25 *Q12* **Knippal** Texas, SW USA
109 *U7* **Knittelfeld** Steiermark, C Austria *47°14′N 14°50′E*
95 *O15* **Knivsta** Uppsala, C Sweden *59°43′N 17°49′E*
113 *P14* **Knjaževac** Serbia, E Serbia *43°34′N 22°16′E*
27 *S4* **Knob Noster** Missouri, C USA *38°47′N 93°33′W*
99 *D15* **Knokke-Heist** West-Vlaanderen, NW Belgium *51°21′N 03°19′E*
95 *H20* **Knøsen** *hill* N Denmark
Knosós *see* Knossos
115 *J25* **Knossos** ***Gk.*** Knosós. *prehistoric site* Kríti, Greece, E Mediterranean Sea
25 *N7* **Knott** Texas, SW USA *32°21′N 101°35′W*
194 *K5* **Knowles, Cape** *headland* Antarctica *71°45′S 60°20′W*
31 *O11* **Knox** Indiana, N USA *41°17′N 86°37′W*
29 *O3* **Knox** North Dakota, N USA *48°19′N 99°43′W*
18 *C13* **Knox** Pennsylvania, NE USA *41°13′N 79°33′W*
189 *X8* **Knox Atoll** ***var.*** Ņadikdik, Narikrik. *atoll* Ratak Chain, SE Marshall Islands
10 *H13* **Knox, Cape** *headland* Graham Island, British Columbia, SW Canada *54°05′N 133°02′W*
25 *P5* **Knox City** Texas, SW USA *33°25′N 99°49′W*
195 *Y11* **Knox Coast** *physical region* Antarctica
31 *T12* **Knox Lake** ⊠ Ohio, N USA
23 *T5* **Knoxville** Georgia, SE USA *32°44′N 83°58′W*
30 *K12* **Knoxville** Illinois, N USA *40°54′N 90°16′W*
29 *W15* **Knoxville** Iowa, C USA *41°19′N 93°06′W*
21 *N9* **Knoxville** Tennessee, S USA *35°58′N 83°55′W*
197 *P11* **Knud Rasmussen Land** *physical region* N Greenland
Knüll *see* Knüllgebirge
101 *I16* **Knüllgebirge** ***var.*** Knüll. ▲▲ C Germany
124 *I5* **Knyazhegubskoye Vodokhranilishche** ◎ NW Russian Federation
Knyazhevo *see* Sredishte
Knyazhitsy *see* Knyazhytsy
119 *O15* **Knyazhytsy** ***Rus.*** Knyazhitsy. Mahilyowskaya Voblasts', E Belarus *54°10′N 30°28′E*
83 *G26* **Knysna** Western Cape, SW South Africa *34°03′S 23°03′E*
Koartac *see* Quaqtaq
169 *N13* **Koba** Pulau Bangka, W Indonesia *02°30′S 106°26′E*
164 *D16* **Kobayashi** ***var.*** Kobayasi. Miyazaki, Kyūshū, SW Japan *32°00′N 130°58′E*
Kobayasi *see* Kobayashi
144 *I10* **Kobda** ***prev.*** Khobda, Novoalekseyevka. Aktyubinsk, W Kazakhstan *50°09′N 55°39′E*
144 *H9* **Kobda** ***Kaz.*** Ülkenqobda; ***prev.*** Bol'shaya Khobda. ≈ Kazakhstan/Russian Federation
Kobdo *see* Hovd
164 *I13* **Kōbe** Hyōgo, Honshū, SW Japan *34°40′N 135°10′E*
Kobelyaki *see* Kobelyaky
117 *T6* **Kobelyaky** ***Rus.*** Kobelyaki. Poltavs'ka Oblast', NE Ukraine *49°10′N 34°13′E*
95 *J22* **København** ***Eng.*** Copenhagen; ***anc.*** Hafnia. ● (Denmark) Sjælland, København, E Denmark *55°43′N 12°34′E*
76 *K10* **Kobenni** Hodh el Gharbi, S Mauritania *15°58′N 09°24′W*
171 *T13* **Kobi** Pulau Seram, E Indonesia *02°56′S 129°53′E*
101 *F17* **Koblenz** ***prev.*** Coblenz, ***Fr.*** Coblence; ***anc.*** Confluentes. Rheinland-Pfalz, W Germany *50°21′N 07°36′E*
108 *F6* **Koblenz** Aargau, N Switzerland *47°34′N 08°16′E*
Kobrin *see* Kobryn
171 *V15* **Kobroor, Pulau** *island* Kepulauan Aru, E Indonesia
119 *G19* **Kobryn** ***Rus.*** Kobrin. Brestskaya Voblasts', SW Belarus *52°13′N 24°21′E*
39 *O7* **Kobuk** Alaska, USA *66°54′N 156°52′W*
39 *O7* **Kobuk River** ≈ Alaska, USA
137 *Q10* **Kobuleti** ***prev.*** K'obulet'i. W Georgia *41°47′N 41°47′E*
K'obulet'i *see* Kobuleti
123 *P10* **Kobyay** Respublika Sakha (Yakutiya), NE Russian Federation *63°36′N 126°33′E*
136 *E11* **Kocaeli** ◈ *province* NW Turkey
113 *P18* **Kočani** NE FYR Macedonia *41°55′N 22°25′E*
112 *K12* **Koceljevo** Serbia, W Serbia *44°28′N 19°49′E*
109 *U12* **Kočevje** ***Ger.*** Gottschee. S Slovenia *45°41′N 14°48′E*
153 *T12* **Koch Bihār** West Bengal, NE India *26°19′N 89°26′E*
Kochchi *see* Cochin/Kochi
122 *M9* **Kochechum** ≈ N Russian Federation
101 *I20* **Kocher** ≈ SW Germany
125 *T13* **Kochevo** Komi-Permyatskiy Okrug, NW Russian Federation *59°37′N 54°16′E*
164 *G14* **Kōchi** ***var.*** Kôti. Kōchi, Shikoku, SW Japan *33°31′N 133°30′E*
164 *G14* **Kōchi** ***off.*** Kōchi-ken, ***var.*** Kôti. ◈ *prefecture* Shikoku, SW Japan
Kōchi-ken *see* Kōchi
Kochiu *see* Gejiu
Kochkor *see* Kochkorka
147 *V8* **Kochkorka** ***Kir.*** Kochkor. Narynskaya Oblast', C Kyrgyzstan *42°09′N 75°42′E*
125 *V5* **Kochmes** Respublika Komi, NW Russian Federation *66°10′N 60°46′E*
127 *P15* **Kochubey** Respublika Dagestan, SW Russian Federation *44°25′N 46°33′E*
115 *I17* **Kochýlas** ▲ Skńyros, Vóreies Sporádes, Greece, Aegean Sea *38°50′N 24°35′E*
110 *O13* **Kock** Lubelskie, E Poland *51°39′N 22°26′E*
81 *J19* **Kodacho** *spring/well* S Kenya *01°52′S 39°22′E*
155 *K24* **Koddiyar Bay** *bay* NE Sri Lanka
39 *Q14* **Kodiak** Kodiak Island, Alaska, USA *57°47′N 152°24′W*
39 *Q14* **Kodiak Island** *island* Alaska, USA
154 *B12* **Kodīnār** Gujarāt, W India *20°44′N 70°46′E*
124 *M9* **Kodino** Arkhangel'skaya Oblast', NW Russian Federation *63°36′N 39°54′E*
122 *M12* **Kodinsk** Krasnoyarskiy Kray, C Russian Federation *58°37′N 99°18′E*
80 *F12* **Kodok** Upper Nile, NE South Sudan *09°51′N 32°07′E*
117 *N8* **Kodyma** Odes'ka Oblast', SW Ukraine *48°05′N 29°09′E*
Koedoes *see* Kudus
99 *B17* **Koekelare** West-Vlaanderen, W Belgium *51°07′N 02°58′E*
Koeln *see* Köln
Koepang *see* Kupang
Ko-erh-mu *see* Golmud
99 *J17* **Koersel** Limburg, NE Belgium *51°04′N 05°17′E*
83 *E21* **Koës** Karas, SE Namibia *25°59′S 19°08′E*
Koetai *see* Mahakam, Sungai
Koetaradja *see* Banda Aceh
36 *I14* **Kofa Mountains** ▲▲ Arizona, SW USA
171 *Y15* **Kofarau** Papua, E Indonesia *07°29′S 140°28′E*
147 *P13* **Kofarnihon** ***Rus.*** Kofarnikhon; ***prev.*** Ordzhonikidzeabad, ***Taj.*** Orjonikidzeobod, Yangi-Bazar. W Tajikistan *38°32′N 68°56′E*
147 *P14* **Kofarnihon** ***Rus.*** Kafirnigan. ≈ SW Tajikistan
Kofarnikhon *see* Kofarnihon
114 *M11* **Kofçaz** Kırklareli, NW Turkey *41°58′N 27°12′E*
115 *J25* **Kófinas** ▲ Kríti, Greece, E Mediterranean Sea *34°58′N 25°03′E*
121 *P3* **Kofínou** ***var.*** Kophinou. S Cyprus *34°49′N 33°24′E*
109 *V8* **Köflach** Steiermark, SE Austria *47°04′N 15°04′E*
77 *Q17* **Koforidua** SE Ghana *06°01′N 00°12′W*
164 *H12* **Kōfu** Tottori, Honshū, SW Japan *35°16′N 133°31′E*
164 *M13* **Kōfu** ***var.*** Kôhu. Yamanashi, Honshū, S Japan *35°41′N 138°33′E*
81 *F22* **Koga** Tabora, C Tanzania *06°08′S 32°20′E*
Kogălniceanu *see* Mihail Kogălniceanu
13 *P6* **Kogaluk** ≈ Newfoundland and Labrador, E Canada
12 *J4* **Kogaluk, Riviére** ≈ Québec, NE Canada
145 *V14* **Kogaly** ***Kaz.*** Qoghaly; ***prev.*** Kugaly. Almaty, SE Kazakhstan *44°30′N 78°40′E*
122 *I10* **Kogalym** Khanty-Mansiyskiy Avtonomnyy Okrug-Yugra, C Russian Federation *62°13′N 74°34′E*
95 *J23* **Køge** Sjælland, E Denmark *55°28′N 12°12′E*
95 *J23* **Køge Bugt** *bay* E Denmark
77 *U16* **Kogi** ◈ *state* C Nigeria
146 *L11* **Kogon** ***Rus.*** Kagan. Buxoro Viloyati, C Uzbekistan *39°47′N 64°29′E*
Kŏgŭm-do *see* Geogeum-do
Kőhalom *see* Rupea
149 *T6* **Kohāt** Khyber Pakhtunkhwa, NW Pakistan *33°37′N 71°30′E*
142 *L10* **Kohgīlūyeh va Bowyer Aḥmad** ***off.*** Ostān-e Kohkīlūyeh va Būyer Aḥmadī, ***var.*** Boyer Ahmadī va Kohkīlūyeh. ◈ *province* SW Iran
118 *G4* **Kohila** ***Ger.*** Koil. Raplamaa, NW Estonia *59°09′N 24°45′E*
153 *X13* **Kohīma** *state capital* Nāgāland, E India *25°40′N 94°08′E*
Koh I Noh *see* Büyükağrı Dağı
Kohkīlūyeh va Būyer Aḥmadī, Ostān-e *see* Kohgīlūyeh va Bowyer Aḥmad
Kohsān *see* Kūhestān
118 *J3* **Kohtla-Järve** Ida-Virumaa, NE Estonia *59°22′N 27°21′E*
Kôhu *see* Kōfu
Kohyl'nyk *see* Cogîlnic
165 *N11* **Koide** Niigata, Honshū, C Japan *37°13′N 138°58′E*
10 *G7* **Koidern** Yukon Territory, W Canada *61°55′N 140°22′W*
76 *J15* **Koidu** E Sierra Leone *08°40′N 11°01′W*
118 *I4* **Koigi** Järvamaa, C Estonia *58°51′N 25°45′E*
Koil *see* Kohila
172 *H13* **Koimbani** Grande Comore, NW Comoros *11°37′S 43°23′E*
139 *T3* **Koi Sanjaq** ***var.*** Koysanjaq, Kūysanjaq. Arbīl, N Iraq *36°05′N 44°38′E*
93 *O16* **Koitere** ◎ E Finland
Koivisto *see* Primorsk
Kŏje-do *see* Geogeum-do
80 *J13* **K'ok'a Hāyk'** ◎ C Ethiopia
Kokand *see* Qo'qon
182 *F6* **Kokatha** South Australia *31°17′S 135°16′E*
146 *M10* **Ko'kcha** ***Rus.*** Kokcha. Buxoro Viloyati, C Uzbekistan *40°30′N 64°58′E*
Kokcha *see* Ko'kcha
Kokchetav *see* Kokshetau
93 *K18* **Kokemäenjoki** ≈ SW Finland
171 *W14* **Kokenau** ***var.*** Kokonau. Papua, E Indonesia *04°38′S 136°24′E*
83 *E22* **Kokerboom** Karas, SE Namibia *28°11′S 19°25′E*
119 *N14* **Kokhanava** ***Rus.*** Kokhanovo. Vitsyebskaya Voblasts', NE Belarus *54°28′N 29°59′E*
Kokhanovichi *see* Kakhanavichy
Kokhanovo *see* Kokhanava
Kök-Janggak *see* Kok-Yangak
93 *K16* **Kokkola** ***Swe.*** Karleby; ***prev. Swe.*** Gamlakarleby. Länsi-Suomi, W Finland *63°50′N 23°10′E*
158 *L3* **Kok Kuduk** *spring/well* N China *46°03′N 87°34′E*
118 *H9* **Koknese** C Latvia *56°38′N 25°27′E*
77 *T13* **Koko** Kebbi, W Nigeria *11°25′N 04°33′E*
186 *E9* **Kokoda** Northern, S Papua New Guinea *08°52′S 147°44′E*
76 *K12* **Kokofata** Kayes, W Mali *12°48′N 09°56′W*
39 *N6* **Kokolik River** ≈ Alaska, USA
31 *O13* **Kokomo** Indiana, N USA *40°29′N 86°07′W*
Kokonau *see* Kokenau
Koko Nor *see* Qinghai, China
Koko Nor *see* Qinghai Hu, China
186 *H6* **Kokopo** ***var.*** Kopopo; ***prev.*** Herbertshöhe. New Britain, E Papua New Guinea *04°18′S 152°17′E*
Kokpekti *see* Kokpekty
Kokpekti *see* Kokpekty
145 *X10* **Kokpekty** ***prev.*** Kokpekti. Vostochnyy Kazakhstan, E Kazakhstan *48°47′N 82°28′E*
145 *X11* **Kokpekty** ***prev.*** Kokpekti. ≈ E Kazakhstan
39 *P9* **Kokrines** Alaska, USA *64°58′N 154°42′W*
39 *P9* **Kokrines Hills** ▲▲ Alaska, USA
145 *P17* **Koksaray** Yuzhnyy Kazakhstan, S Kazakhstan *42°34′N 68°06′E*
147 *X9* **Kokshaal-Tau** ***Rus.*** Khrebet Kakshaal-Too. ▲▲ China/ Kyrgyzstan
145 *P7* **Kokshetau** ***Kaz.*** Kökshetaū; ***prev.*** Kokchetav. Kokshetau, N Kazakhstan *53°18′N 69°25′E*
Kökshetaū *see* Kokshetau
99 *A17* **Koksijde** West-Vlaanderen, W Belgium *51°07′N 02°40′E*
12 *M5* **Koksoak** ≈ Québec, E Canada
83 *K24* **Kokstad** KwaZulu/Natal, E South Africa *30°23′S 29°23′E*
145 *V14* **Koksu** ***Kaz.*** Rūdnīchnyy. Almaty, SE Kazakhstan *44°39′N 78°57′E*
145 *W15* **Koktal** ***Kaz.*** Köktal. Almaty, SE Kazakhstan *44°05′N 79°44′E*
145 *Q12* **Koktas** ≈ C Kazakhstan
Kök-Tash *see* Kĕk-Tash
Koktokay *see* Fuyun
147 *T9* **Kok-Yangak** ***Kir.*** Kök-Janggak. Dzhalal-Abadskaya Oblast', W Kyrgyzstan *41°02′N 73°11′E*
158 *F9* **Kokyar** Xinjiang Uygur Zizhiqu, W China *37°41′N 77°15′E*
149 *O13* **Kolāchi** ***var.*** Kulachi. ≈ SW Pakistan
76 *J15* **Kolahun** N Liberia *08°24′N 10°02′W*
171 *O14* **Kolaka** Sulawesi, C Indonesia *04°04′S 121°38′E*
K'o-la-ma-i *see* Karamay
Kola Peninsula *see* Kol'skiy Poluostrov
155 *H19* **Kolār** Karnātaka, E India *13°10′N 78°10′E*
155 *H19* **Kolār Gold Fields** Karnātaka, E India *12°56′N 78°16′E*
92 *K11* **Kolari** Lappi, NW Finland *67°20′N 23°51′E*
111 *I21* **Kolárovo** ***Ger.*** Gutta; ***prev.*** Guta, ***Hung.*** Gúta. Nitriansky Kraj, SW Slovakia *47°54′N 18°01′E*
113 *K16* **Kolašin** E Montenegro *42°49′N 19°32′E*
Kolāyat *see* Shir Kolāyat
95 *N15* **Kolbäck** Västmanland, C Sweden *59°33′N 16°15′E*
Kolbcha *see* Kowbcha
197 *Q15* **Kolbeinsey Ridge** *undersea feature* Denmark Strait/Norwegian Sea *69°00′N 17°30′W*
Kolberg *see* Kołobrzeg
95 *H15* **Kolbotn** Akershus, S Norway *62°15′N 10°24′E*
111 *N16* **Kolbuszowa** Podkarpackie, SE Poland *50°12′N 22°07′E*
126 *L3* **Kol'chugino** Vladimirskaya Oblast', W Russian Federation *56°19′N 39°24′E*
76 *H12* **Kolda** S Senegal *12°58′N 14°58′W*
95 *G23* **Kolding** Syddanmark, C Denmark *55°29′N 09°30′E*
79 *K20* **Kole** Kasai-Oriental, SW Dem. Rep. Congo *03°30′S 22°28′E*
79 *M17* **Kole** Orientale, N Dem. Rep. Congo *02°08′N 25°25′E*
Kōle *see* Kili Island
84 *F6* **Kölen** ***Nor.*** Kjølen. ▲▲ Norway/Sweden
Kolepom, Pulau *see* Yos Sudarso, Pulau
118 *H3* **Kolga Laht** ***Ger.*** Kolko-Wiek. *bay* N Estonia
125 *Q3* **Kolguyev, Ostrov** *island* NW Russian Federation
155 *E16* **Kolhāpur** Mahārāshtra, SW India *16°42′N 74°13′E*
151 *K21* **Kolhumadulu** ***var.*** Thaa Atoll. *atoll* S Maldives
93 *O16* **Koli** ***var.*** Kolinkylä. Itä-Suomi, E Finland *63°06′N 29°46′E*
39 *O13* **Koliganek** Alaska, USA *59°43′N 157°16′W*
111 *E16* **Kolín** ***Ger.*** Kolin. Střední Čechy, C Czech Republic *50°02′N 15°10′E*
Kolinkylä *see* Koli
190 *E12* **Koliu** Île Futuna, W Wallis and Futuna
118 *E7* **Kolka** NW Latvia *57°44′N 22°34′E*
118 *E7* **Kolkasrags** ***prev. Eng.*** Cape Domesnes. *headland* NW Latvia *57°45′N 22°35′E*
153 *S16* **Kolkata** ***prev.*** Calcutta. *state capital* West Bengal, NE India *22°30′N 88°20′E*
Kolkhozabad *see* Kolkhozobod
147 *P14* **Kolkhozobod** ***Rus.*** Kolkhozabad; ***prev.*** Kaganovichabad, Tugalan. SW Tajikistan *37°33′N 68°34′E*
Kolki/Kołki *see* Kolky
Kolko-Wiek *see* Kolga Laht
116 *K3* **Kolky** ***Pol.*** Kołki, ***Rus.*** Kolki. Volyns'ka Oblast', NW Ukraine *51°05′N 25°40′E*
155 *G20* **Kollegāl** Karnātaka, W India *12°08′N 77°06′E*
98 *M5* **Kollum** Fryslân, N Netherlands *53°17′N 06°09′E*
Kolmar *see* Colmar
101 *E16* **Köln** ***var.*** Koeln, ***Eng./Fr.*** Cologne, ***prev.*** Cöln; ***anc.*** Colonia Agrippina, Oppidum Ubiorum. Nordrhein-Westfalen, W Germany *50°57′N 06°57′E*
110 *N9* **Kolno** Podlaskie, NE Poland *53°24′N 21°57′E*
110 *J12* **Koło** Wielkopolskie, C Poland *52°11′N 18°39′E*
38 *B8* **Kōloa** ***var.*** Koloa. Kaua'i, Hawaii, USA, C Pacific Ocean *21°54′N 159°28′W*
Koloa *see* Kōloa
110 *E7* **Kołobrzeg** ***Ger.*** Kolberg. Zachodnio-pomorskie, NW Poland *54°11′N 15°34′E*
126 *H4* **Kolodnya** Smolenskaya Oblast', W Russian Federation *54°57′N 32°22′E*
190 *E13* **Kolofau, Mont** ※ Île Alofi, S Wallis and Futuna *14°21′S 178°02′W*
125 *O14* **Kologriv** Kostromskaya Oblast', NW Russian Federation *58°49′N 44°22′E*
76 *L12* **Kolokani** Koulikoro, W Mali *13°35′N 08°01′W*
77 *N13* **Koloko** W Burkina *11°06′N 05°18′W*
186 *K8* **Kolombangara** ***var.*** Kilimbangara, Nduke. *island* New Georgia Islands, NW Solomon Islands
Kolomea *see* Kolomyya
126 *L4* **Kolomna** Moskovskaya Oblast', W Russian Federation *55°03′N 38°52′E*
116 *J7* **Kolomyya** ***Ger.*** Kolomea. Ivano-Frankivs'ka Oblast', W Ukraine *48°31′N 25°00′E*
76 *M13* **Kolondiéba** Sikasso, SW Mali *11°04′N 06°55′W*
193 *V15* **Kolonga** Tongatapu, S Tonga *21°07′S 175°05′W*
189 *U16* **Kolonia** ***var.*** Colonia. Pohnpei, E Micronesia *06°57′N 158°12′E*
Kolonja *see* Kolonjë
113 *K21* **Kolonjë** ***var.*** Kolonja. Fier, C Albania *40°49′N 19°37′E*
Kolonjë *see* Ersekë
Kolosjoki *see* Nikel'
Kolotambu *see* Avuavu
193 *U15* **Kolovai** Tongatapu, S Tonga *21°05′S 175°20′W*
Kolozsvár *see* Cluj-Napoca
112 *C9* **Kolpa** ***Ger.*** Kulpa, ***SCr.*** Kupa. ≈ Croatia/Slovenia
122 *J11* **Kolpashevo** Tomskaya Oblast', C Russian Federation *58°21′N 82°44′E*
124 *H13* **Kolpino** Leningradskaya Oblast', NW Russian Federation *59°44′N 30°39′E*
100 *M10* **Kölpinsee** ◎ NE Germany
Kólpos Mórfu *see* Güzelyurt
146 *K8* **Ko'lquduq** ***Rus.*** Kulkuduk. Navoiy Viloyati, N Uzbekistan *42°36′N 63°24′E*
124 *K5* **Kol'skiy Poluostrov** ***Eng.*** Kola Peninsula. *peninsula* NW Russian Federation
127 *T6* **Koltubanovskiy** Orenburgskaya Oblast', W Russian Federation *53°00′N 52°00′E*
112 *L11* **Kolubara** ≈ C Serbia
Kolupchii *see* Gurkovo
110 *K13* **Koluszki** Łódźskie, C Poland *51°44′N 19°50′E*
125 *T6* **Kolva** ≈ NW Russian Federation
93 *E14* **Kolvereid** Nord-Trøndelag, W Norway *64°47′N 11°22′E*
79 *M24* **Kolwezi** Katanga, S Dem. Rep. Congo *10°43′S 25°29′E*
123 *S7* **Kolyma** ≈ NE Russian Federation
Kolyma Lowland *see* Kolymskaya Nizmennost'
Kolyma Range/Kolymskiy, Khrebet *see* Kolymskoye Nagor'ye
123 *S7* **Kolymskaya Nizmennost'** ***Eng.*** Kolyma Lowland. *lowlands* NE Russian Federation
123 *S7* **Kolymskoye** Respublika Sakha (Yakutiya), NE Russian Federation *68°42′N 158°46′E*
123 *U8* **Kolymskoye Nagor'ye** ***var.*** Khrebet Kolymskiy, ***Eng.*** Kolyma Range. ▲▲ E Russian Federation
123 *V5* **Kolyuchinskaya Guba** *bay* NE Russian Federation
Kol'zhat *see* Kalzhat
114 *G8* **Kom** ▲ NW Bulgaria *43°10′N 23°02′E*
80 *I13* **Koma** Oromīya, C Ethiopia *08°19′N 36°48′E*
77 *X12* **Komadugu Gana** ≈ NE Nigeria
164 *M13* **Komagane** Nagano, Honshū, S Japan *35°44′N 137°54′E*
79 *P17* **Komanda** Orientale, NE Dem. Rep. Congo *01°25′N 29°43′E*
197 *U1* **Komandorskaya Basin** ***var.*** Kamchatka Basin. *undersea feature* SW Bering Sea *57°00′N 168°00′E*
125 *Pp9* **Komandorskiye Ostrova** ***Eng.*** Commander Islands. *island group* E Russian Federation
Kománfalva *see* Comăneşti
111 *I22* **Komárno** ***Ger.*** Komorn, ***Hung.*** Komárom. Nitriansky Kraj, SW Slovakia *47°46′N 18°07′E*
111 *I22* **Komárom** Komárom-Esztergom, NW Hungary *47°43′N 18°06′E*
Komárom *see* Komárno
111 *I22* **Komárom-Esztergom** ***off.*** Komárom-Esztergom Megye. ◈ *county* N Hungary
Komárom-Esztergom Megye *see* Komárom-Esztergom
164 *K11* **Komatsu** ***var.*** Komatu. Ishikawa, Honshū, SW Japan *36°25′N 136°27′E*
Komatu *see* Komatsu
83 *D17* **Kombat** Otjozondjupa, N Namibia *19°42′S 17°45′E*
Kombissiguiri *see* Kombissiri
77 *P13* **Kombissiri** ***var.*** Kombissiguiri. C Burkina *12°01′N 01°27′W*
188 *E10* **Komebail Lagoon** *lagoon* N Palau
81 *F20* **Kome Island** *island* N Tanzania
Komeyo *see* Wandai
117 *P10* **Kominternivs'ke** Odes'ka Oblast', SW Ukraine *46°52′N 30°56′E*
125 *R8* **Komi, Respublika** ◈ *autonomous republic* NW Russian Federation
111 *I25* **Komló** Baranya, SW Hungary *46°11′N 18°15′E*
Kommunarsk *see* Alchevs'k
Kommunizm, Qullai *see* Ismoili Somoní, Qullai
186 *B7* **Komo** Southern Highlands, W Papua New Guinea *06°06′S 142°52′E*
170 *M16* **Komodo, Pulau** *island* Nusa Tenggara, S Indonesia
77 *N15* **Komoé** ***var.*** Komoé Fleuve. ≈ E Ivory Coast
Komoé Fleuve *see* Komoé
75 *X11* **Kom Ombo** ***var.*** Kôm Ombo, Kawm Umbū. SE Egypt *24°26′N 32°57′E*
79 *F20* **Komono** Lékoumou, SW Congo *03°15′S 13°14′E*
171 *Y16* **Komoran** Papua, E Indonesia *08°14′S 138°51′E*
171 *Y16* **Komoran, Pulau** *island* E Indonesia
Komorn *see* Komárno
Komornok *see* Comorâşte
Komosolabad *see* Komsomolobod
Komotau *see* Chomutov
114 *K13* **Komotiní** ***var.*** Gümüljina, ***Turk.*** Gümülcine. Anatolikí Makedonía kai Thráki, NE Greece *41°07′N 25°27′E*
113 *K16* **Komovi** ▲▲ E Montenegro
117 *R8* **Kompaniyivka** Kirovohrads'ka Oblast', C Ukraine *48°16′N 32°12′E*
Kompong *see* Kâmpóng Chhnăng
Kompong Cham *see* Kâmpóng Cham
Kompong Kleang *see* Kâmpóng Khleăng
Kompong Som *see* Sihanoukville
Kompong Speu *see* Kâmpóng Spoe
Komrat *see* Comrat
144 *G12* **Komsomol** ***prev.*** Komsomol'skiy. Atyrau, W Kazakhstan *47°18′N 53°37′E*
125 *W4* **Komsomol** ***prev.*** Komsomol'skiy. Respublika Komi, NW Russian Federation *67°33′N 64°00′E*
122 *K14* **Komsomolets, Ostrov** *island* Severnaya Zemlya, N Russian Federation
144 *F13* **Komsomolets, Zaliv** *lake gulf* SW Kazakhstan
Komsomol/Komsomolets *see* Karabalyk, Kostanay, Kazakhstan
147 *Q12* **Komsomolobod** ***Rus.*** Komosolabad. C Tajikistan *38°51′N 69°54′E*
124 *M16* **Komsomol'sk** Ivanovskaya Oblast', W Russian Federation *56°58′N 40°15′E*
117 *S6* **Komsomol's'k** Poltavs'ka Oblast', C Ukraine *49°01′N 33°37′E*
146 *M11* **Komsomol'sk** Navoiy Viloyati, N Uzbekistan *40°14′N 65°10′E*
Komsomol'skiy *see* Komsomol
Komsomol'skiy *see* Komsomol
123 *S13* **Komsomol'sk-na-Amure** Khabarovskiy Kray, SE Russian Federation *50°32′N 136°59′E*
Komsomol'sk-na-Ustyurte *see* Kubla-Ustyurt
144 *K10* **Komsomol'skoye** Aktyubinsk, NW Kazakhstan
127 *Q8* **Komsomol'skoye** Saratovskaya Oblast', W Russian Federation *50°45′N 47°00′E*
145 *P10* **Kon** ≈ C Kazakhstan
Kona *see* Kailua-Kona
124 *K16* **Konakovo** Tverskaya Oblast', W Russian Federation *56°42′N 36°44′E*
Konar *see* Kunar
143 *V15* **Konārak** Sīstān va Balūchestān, SE Iran *25°26′N 60°23′E*
Konarhā *see* Kunar
27 *O11* **Konawa** Oklahoma, C USA *34°57′N 96°45′W*
122 *H10* **Konda** ≈ C Russian Federation
154 *L13* **Kondagaon** Chhattīsgarh, C India *19°38′N 81°41′E*
14 *K10* **Kondiaronk, Lac** ◎ Québec, SE Canada
180 *J13* **Kondinin** Western Australia *32°31′S 118°15′E*
81 *H21* **Kondoa** Dodoma, C Tanzania *04°54′S 35°46′E*
127 *P6* **Kondol'** Penzenskaya Oblast', W Russian Federation *52°49′N 45°03′E*
114 *N10* **Kondolovo** Burgas, E Bulgaria *42°07′N 27°43′E*
171 *Z16* **Kondomirat** Papua, E Indonesia *08°57′S 140°55′E*
124 *J10* **Kondopoga** Respublika Kareliya, NW Russian Federation *62°13′N 34°17′E*
Kondoz *see* Kunduz
155 *J17* **Kondukūr** ***var.*** Kandukur. Andhra Pradesh, E India *15°17′N 79°49′E*
Kondūz *see* Kunduz
187 *P16* **Koné** Province Nord, W New Caledonia *21°04′S 164°51′E*
146 *E13* **Könekesir** Balkan Welaýaty, W Turkmenistan *38°16′N 56°51′E*
146 *G8* **Köneürgenç** ***var.*** Köneürgench, ***Rus.*** Këneurgench; ***prev.*** Kunya-Urgench. Daşoguz Welaýaty, N Turkmenistan *42°21′N 59°09′E*
77 *N15* **Kong** N Ivory Coast *09°10′N 04°33′W*
39 *S5* **Kongakut River** ≈ Alaska, USA
197 *O14* **Kong Christian IX Land** ***Eng.*** King Christian IX Land. *physical region* SE Greenland
197 *P13* **Kong Christian X Land** ***Eng.*** King Christian X Land. *physical region* E Greenland
197 *N13* **Kong Frederik IX Land** *physical region* SW Greenland
197 *Q12* **Kong Frederik VIII Land** ***Eng.*** King Frederik VIII Land. *physical region* NE Greenland
197 *N15* **Kong Frederik VI Kyst** ***Eng.*** King Frederik VI Coast. *physical region* SE Greenland
167 *P13* **Kŏng, Kaôh** ***prev.*** Kas Kong. *island* SW Cambodia
92 *P2* **Kong Karls Land** ***Eng.*** King Charles Islands. *island group* SE Svalbard
81 *G14* **Kong Kong** ≈ E South Sudan
Kongo *see* Congo (river)
83 *G16* **Kongola** Caprivi, NE Namibia *17°47′S 23°24′E*
79 *N21* **Kongolo** Katanga, E Dem. Rep. Congo *05°20′S 26°58′E*
81 *F14* **Kongor** Jonglei, E South Sudan *07°09′N 31°44′E*
197 *Q14* **Kong Oscar Fjord** *fjord* E Greenland
77 *P12* **Kongoussi** N Burkina *13°19′N 01°31′W*
95 *G15* **Kongsberg** Buskerud, S Norway *59°39′N 09°38′E*
92 *Q2* **Kongsøya** *island* Kong Karls Land, E Svalbard
95 *I14* **Kongsvinger** Hedmark, S Norway *60°10′N 12°00′E*
Kongtong *see* Pingliang
167 *T11* **Kông, Tônlé** ***var.*** Xê Kong. ≈ Cambodia/Laos
158 *E8* **Kongur Shan** ▲ NW China *38°39′N 75°21′E*
81 *I22* **Kongwa** Dodoma, C Tanzania *06°13′S 36°28′E*
Kong, Xê *see* Kông, Tônlé
Konia *see* Konya
147 *R11* **Konibodom** ***Rus.*** Kanibadam. N Tajikistan *40°16′N 70°20′E*
111 *K15* **Koniecpol nad Pilicą** Śląskie, S Poland *50°47′N 19°45′E*
Konieh *see* Konya
Königgrätz *see* Hradec Králové
Königinhof an der Elbe *see* Dvůr Králové nad Labem
101 *K23* **Königsbrunn** Bayern, S Germany *48°16′N 10°52′E*
101 *O24* **Königssee** ◎ SE Germany
Königshütte *see* Chorzów
109 *S8* **Königstuhl** ▲ S Austria *46°57′N 13°47′E*
109 *U3* **Königswiesen** Oberösterreich, N Austria *48°25′N 14°48′E*
101 *E17* **Königswinter** Nordrhein-Westfalen, W Germany *50°40′N 07°12′E*
146 *M11* **Konimex** ***Rus.*** Kenimekh. Navoiy Viloyati, N Uzbekistan *40°14′N 65°10′E*
110 *I12* **Konin** ***Ger.*** Kuhnau. Weilkopolskie, C Poland *52°13′N 18°17′E*
Koninkrijk der Nederlanden *see* Netherlands
113 *L24* **Konispol** ***var.*** Konispoli. Vlorë, S Albania *39°40′N 20°10′E*
Konispoli *see* Konispol
115 *C15* **Kónitsa** Ípeiros, W Greece *40°04′N 20°48′E*
Konitz *see* Chojnice
108 *D8* **Köniz** Bern, W Switzerland *46°56′N 07°25′E*

◆ Country ● Country Capital ◇ Dependent Territory ○ Dependent Territory Capital ◈ Administrative Regions ✕ International Airport ▲ Mountain ▲▲ Mountain Range ※ Volcano ≈ River ◎ Lake ⊠ Reservoir

113 H14 **Konjic** ◈ Federacija Bosna I Hercegovina, S Bosnia and Herzegovina
92 J10 **Könkämäälven** ≈ Finland/ Sweden
155 D14 **Konkan** *plain* W India
83 D22 **Konkiep** ≈ S Namibia
76 I14 **Konkouré** ≈ W Guinea
77 O11 **Konna** Mopti, S Mali 14°58′N 03°49′W
186 H6 **Konogaiang, Mount** ▲ New Ireland, NE Papua New Guinea 04°05′S 152°43′E
186 H5 **Konogogo** New Ireland, NE Papua New Guinea 03°25′S 152°09′E
108 E9 **Konolfingen** Bern, W Switzerland 46°53′N 07°36′E
77 P16 **Konongo** C Ghana 06°39′N 01°06′W
186 H5 **Konos** New Ireland, NE Papua New Guinea 03°09′S 151°47′E
124 M12 **Konosha** Arkhangel'skaya Oblast', NW Russian Federation 60°58′N 40°09′E
117 R3 **Konotop** Sums'ka Oblast', NE Ukraine 51°15′N 33°14′E
158 L7 **Konqi He** ≈ NW China
111 L14 **Końskie** Śiętokrzyskie, C Poland 51°12′N 20°23′E
Konstantinovka *see* Kostyantynivka
126 M11 **Konstantinovsk** Rostovskaya Oblast', SW Russian Federation 47°37′N 41°07′E
101 H24 **Konstanz** *var.* Constanz, *Eng.* Constance, *hist.* Kostnitz; *anc.* Constantia. Baden-Württemberg, S Germany 47°40′N 09°10′E
Konstanza *see* Constanța
77 T14 **Kontagora** Niger, W Nigeria 10°25′N 05°29′E
78 E13 **Kontcha** Nord, N Cameroon 08°00′N 12°13′E
99 G17 **Kontich** Antwerpen, N Belgium 51°08′N 04°27′E
93 O16 **Kontiolahti** Itä-Suomi, SE Finland 62°46′N 29°51′E
93 M15 **Kontiomäki** Oulu, C Finland 64°20′N 28°09′E
167 U11 **Kon Tum** *var.* Kontum. Kon Tum, C Vietnam 14°23′N 108°00′E
Kontum *see* Kon Tum
Konur *see* Sulakyurt
136 H15 **Konya** *var.* Konieh, *prev.* Konia; *anc.* Iconium. Konya, C Turkey 37°51′N 32°30′E
136 H15 **Konya** *var.* Konia, Konieh. ◈ *province* C Turkey
151 E15 **Konya Reservoir** *prev.* Shivāji Sāgar. ⊠ W India
145 T13 **Konyrat** *var.* Kounradskiy, *Kaz.* Qongyrat. Karaganda, SE Kazakhstan 46°57′N 75°01′E
145 W15 **Konyrolen** Almaty, SE Kazakhstan 44°16′N 79°18′E
81 I19 **Konza** Eastern, S Kenya 01°44′S 37°07′E
98 I9 **Koog aan den Zaan** Noord-Holland, C Netherlands 52°28′N 04°49′E
182 E7 **Koonibba** South Australia 31°55′S 133°23′E
31 O11 **Koontz Lake** Indiana, N USA 41°25′N 86°24′W
171 U12 **Koor** Papua, E Indonesia 0°21′S 132°28′E
183 R9 **Koorawatha** New South Wales, SE Australia 34°03′S 148°33′E
118 J5 **Koosa** Tartumaa, E Estonia 58°31′N 27°06′E
33 N7 **Kootenai** *var.* Kootenay. ≈ Canada/USA *see also* Kootenay
Kootenai *see* Kootenay
11 P17 **Kootenay** *var.* Kootenai. ≈ Canada/USA *see also* Kootenai
Kootenay *see* Kootenai
83 F24 **Kootjieskolk** Northern Cape, W South Africa 31°16′S 20°21′E
113 M15 **Kopaonik** ▲▲ S Serbia
Kopar *see* Koper
92 K1 **Kópasker** Nordhurland Eystra, N Iceland 66°15′N 16°23′W
92 H4 **Kópavogur** Höfudborgarsvœdid, W Iceland 64°06′N 21°47′W
145 U13 **Kopbirlik** *prev.* Kīrov, Kirova. Almaty, SE Kazakhstan 46°24′N 77°16′E
109 S13 **Koper** *It.* Capodistria; *prev.* Kopar. SW Slovenia 45°32′N 13°43′E
95 C16 **Kopervik** Rogaland, S Norway 59°17′N 05°20′E
Köpetdag Gershi/ Kopetdag, Khrebet *see* Koppeh Dāgh
Kophinou *see* Kofínou
182 G8 **Kopi** South Australia 33°24′S 135°40′E
153 W12 **Kopili** ≈ NE India
95 M15 **Köping** Västmanland, C Sweden 59°31′N 16°00′E
113 K17 **Koplik** *var.* Kopliku. Shkodër, NW Albania 42°12′N 19°26′E
Kopliku *see* Koplik
Kopopo *see* Kokopo
94 I11 **Koppang** Hedmark, S Norway 61°34′N 11°04′E
Kopparberg *see* Dalarna
143 S3 **Koppeh Dāgh** *Rus.* Khrebet Kopetdag, *Turkm.* Köpetdag Gershi. ▲▲ Iran/ Turkmenistan
Koppename *see* Coppename Rivier
95 J15 **Koppom** Värmland, C Sweden 59°42′N 12°07′E
Kopreinitz *see* Koprivnica
114 K9 **Koprinka, Yazovir** *prev.* Yazovir Georgi Dimitrov. ⊠ C Bulgaria
112 F7 **Koprivnica** *Ger.* Kopreinitz, *Hung.* Kaproncza. Koprivnica-Križevci, N Croatia 46°10′N 16°49′E
112 F8 **Koprivnica-Križevci** *off.* Koprivničko-Križevačka Županija. ◈ *province* N Croatia
111 I17 **Kopřivnice** *Ger.* Nesselsdorf. Moravskoslezský Kraj, E Czech Republic 49°36′N 18°09′E
Koprivničko-Križevačka Županija *see* Koprivnica-Križevci
Köprülü *see* Veles
Koptsevichi *see* Kaptsevichy
Kopyl' *see* Kapyl'
119 O14 **Kopys'** Vitsyebskaya Voblasts', NE Belarus 54°19′N 30°18′E
113 M18 **Korab** ▲ Albania/ FYR Macedonia 41°48′N 20°33′E
Korabavur Pastligi *see* Karabaur', Uval
124 M5 **Korabel'noye** Murmanskaya Oblast', NW Russian Federation 67°00′N 41°10′E
81 M14 **K'orahē** Sumalē, E Ethiopia 06°36′N 44°21′E
115 L16 **Kórakas, Akrotírio** *cape* Lésvos, E Greece
112 D9 **Korana** ≈ C Croatia
155 L14 **Korāput** Orissa, E India 18°48′N 82°41′E
Korat *see* Nakhon Ratchasima
167 Q9 **Korat Plateau** *plateau* E Thailand
139 T1 **Kōrāwa, Sar-i** ▲ NE Iraq 37°08′N 44°39′E
154 L11 **Korba** Chhattīsgarh, C India 22°25′N 82°43′E
101 H15 **Korbach** Hessen, C Germany 51°16′N 08°52′E
Korça *see* Korçë
113 M21 **Korçë** *var.* Korça, *Gk.* Korytsa, *It.* Corriza; *prev.* Koritsa. Korçë, SE Albania 40°38′N 20°47′E
113 M21 **Korçë** ◈ *district* SE Albania
113 G15 **Korčula** *It.* Curzola. Dubrovnik-Neretva, S Croatia 42°57′N 17°08′E
113 F15 **Korčula** *It.* Curzola; *anc.* Corcyra Nigra. *island* S Croatia
113 F15 **Korčulanski Kanal** *channel* S Croatia
145 T6 **Korday** *prev.* Georgiyevka. Zhambyl, SE Kazakhstan 43°03′N 74°43′E
142 J5 **Kordestān** *off.* Ostān-e Kordestān, *var.* Kurdestan. ◈ *province* W Iran
Kordestān, Ostān-e *see* Kordestān
143 P4 **Kord Kūy** *var.* Kurd Kui. Golestán, N Iran 36°49′N 54°05′E
163 V13 **Korea Bay** *bay* China/North Korea
Korea, Democratic People's Republic of *see* North Korea
171 T15 **Koreare** Pulau Yamdena, E Indonesia 07°33′S 131°13′E
Korea, Republic of *see* South Korea
163 Z17 **Korea Strait** *Jap.* Chōsen-kaikyō, *Kor.* Taehan-haehyŏp. *channel* Japan/South Korea
Korelichi/Korelicze *see* Karelichy
80 J11 **Korem** Tigrai, N Ethiopia 12°32′N 39°29′E
77 U11 **Korén Adoua** ≈ C Niger
126 I7 **Korenevo** Kurskaya Oblast', W Russian Federation 51°21′N 34°53′E
126 L13 **Korenovsk** Krasnodarskiy Kray, SW Russian Federation 45°28′N 39°25′E
116 L4 **Korets'** *Pol.* Korzec, *Rus.* Korets. Rivnens'ka Oblast', NW Ukraine 50°38′N 27°12′E
Korets *see* Korets'
194 L7 **Korff Ice Rise** *ice cap* Antarctica
145 Q10 **Korgalzhyn** *var.* Kurgal'dzhino, Kurgal'dzhinsky, *Kaz.* Qorghalzhyn. Akmola, C Kazakhstan 50°33′N 69°58′E
145 W15 **Korgas** ; *prev.* Khorgos. Almaty, SE Kazakhstan 44°13′N 80°22′E
92 G13 **Korgen** Troms, N Norway 66°04′N 13°51′E
147 R9 **Korgon-Dëbë** Dzhalal-Abadskaya Oblast', W Kyrgyzstan 41°51′N 70°52′E
76 M14 **Korhogo** N Ivory Coast 09°29′N 05°39′W
115 F19 **Korinthiakós Kólpos** *Eng.* Gulf of Corinth; *anc.* Corinthiacus Sinus. *gulf* C Greece
115 F19 **Kórinthos** *anc.* Corinthus *Eng.* Corinth. Pelopónnisos, S Greece 37°56′N 22°55′E
113 M18 **Koritnik** ▲ S Serbia 42°06′N 20°34′E
Koritsa *see* Korçë
165 P11 **Kōriyama** Fukushima, Honshū, C Japan 37°25′N 140°20′E
136 E16 **Korkuteli** Antalya, SW Turkey 37°07′N 30°11′E
158 K6 **Korla** *Chin.* K'u-erh-lo. Xinjiang Uygur Zizhiqu, NW China 41°48′N 86°10′E
122 J10 **Korliki** Khanty-Mansiyskiy Avtonomnyy Okrug-Yugra, C Russian Federation 61°28′N 82°12′E
Körlin an der Persante *see* Karlino
Korma *see* Karma
14 D8 **Kormak** Ontario, S Canada 47°38′N 83°00′W
Kormakíti, Akrotíri/ Kormakiti, Cape/ Kormakítis *see* Koruçam Burnu
111 G23 **Körmend** Vas, W Hungary 47°02′N 16°35′E
139 T5 **Kōrmōr** Ṣalāḥ ad Dīn, E Iraq 35°06′N 44°47′E
112 C13 **Kornat** *It.* Incoronata. *island* W Croatia
Korneshty *see* Cornești
109 X3 **Korneuburg** Niederösterreich, NE Austria 48°22′N 16°20′E
145 P7 **Korneyevka** Severnyy Kazakhstan, N Kazakhstan 54°01′N 68°30′E
95 I17 **Kornsjø** Østfold, S Norway 58°55′N 11°40′E
77 O11 **Koro** Mopti, S Mali 14°05′N 03°06′W
1873 Y14 **Koro** *island* C Fiji
186 B7 **Koroba** Southern Highlands, W Papua New Guinea 05°46′S 142°48′E
126 K8 **Korocha** Belgorodskaya Oblast', W Russian Federation 50°49′N 37°08′E
136 H12 **Köroğlu Dağları** ▲▲ C Turkey
183 V6 **Korogoro Point** *headland* New South Wales, SE Australia 31°03′S 153°04′E
81 J21 **Korogwe** Tanga, E Tanzania 05°10′S 38°30′E
182 L13 **Koroit** Victoria, SE Australia 38°17′S 142°22′E
187 X15 **Korolevu** Viti Levu, W Fiji 18°12′S 177°44′E
190 I17 **Koromiri** *island* S Cook Islands
171 Q8 **Koronadal** Mindanao, S Philippines 06°23′N 124°54′E
114 G13 **Koróneia, Límni** *var.* Límni Korónia. ◎ N Greece
115 E22 **Koróni** Pelopónnisos, S Greece 36°47′N 21°57′E
Korónia, Límni *see* Koróneia, Límni
110 I9 **Koronowo** *Ger.* Krone an der Brahe. Kujawski-pomorskie,C Poland 53°18′N 17°56′E
117 R2 **Korop** Chernihivs'ka Oblast', N Ukraine 51°35′N 32°57′E
115 H19 **Koropí** Attikí, C Greece 37°54′N 23°52′E
188 C8 **Koror** (Palau) Oreor, N Palau 07°21′N 134°28′E
Koror *see* Oreor
Koror Lāl Esan *see* Karor
Koror Pacca *see* Kahror Pakka
111 L23 **Körös** ≈ E Hungary
Kőrös *see* Križevci
Körösbánya *see* Baia de Criș
187 Y14 **Koro Sea** *sea* C Fiji
Koroška *see* Kärnten
117 N3 **Korosten'** Zhytomyrs'ka Oblast', NW Ukraine 50°56′N 28°39′E
Korostyshev *see* Korostyshiv
117 N4 **Korostyshiv** *Rus.* Korostyshev. Zhytomyrs'ka Oblast', N Ukraine 50°18′N 29°05′E
125 V3 **Korotaikha** ≈ NW Russian Federation
122 J9 **Korotchayevo** Yamalo-Nenetskiy Avtonomnyy Okrug, N Russian Federation 66°00′N 78°11′E
78 I8 **Koro Toro** Borkou-Ennedi-Tibesti, N Chad 16°01′N 18°27′E
39 N16 **Korovin Island** *island* Shumagin Islands, Alaska, USA
187 X14 **Korovou** Viti Levu, W Fiji 17°48′S 178°32′E
93 M17 **Korpilahti** Länsi-Suomi, C Finland 62°02′N 25°34′E
92 K12 **Korpilombolo** *Lapp.* Dállogilli. Norrbotten, N Sweden 66°51′N 23°00′E
123 T13 **Korsakov** Ostrov Sakhalin, Sakhalinskaya Oblast', SE Russian Federation 46°41′N 142°45′E
93 J16 **Korsholm** *Fin.* Mustasaari. Länsi-Suomi, W Finland 63°05′N 21°43′E
95 I23 **Korsør** Sjælland, E Denmark 55°19′N 11°09′E
Korsovka *see* Kārsava
117 P6 **Korsun'-Shevchenkivs'kyy** *Rus.* Korsun'-Shevchenkovskiy. Cherkas'ka Oblast', C Ukraine 49°26′N 31°15′E
Korsun'-Shevchenkovskiy *see* Korsun'-Shevchenkivs'kyy
99 C17 **Kortemark** West-Vlaanderen, W Belgium 51°03′N 03°03′E
99 H18 **Kortenberg** Vlaams Brabant, C Belgium 50°53′N 04°33′E
99 K18 **Kortessem** Limburg, NE Belgium 50°52′N 05°22′E
99 E14 **Kortgene** Zeeland, SW Netherlands 51°34′N 03°48′E
80 F8 **Korti** Northern, N Sudan 18°06′N 31°33′E
99 C18 **Kortrijk** *Fr.* Courtrai. West-Vlaanderen, W Belgium 50°50′N 03°17′E
121 O2 **Koruçam Burnu** *var.* Cape Kormakiti, Kormakítis, *Gk.* Akrotíri Kormakíti. *headland* N Cyprus 35°24′N 32°55′E
183 O13 **Korumburra** Victoria, SE Australia 38°27′S 145°48′E
Koryak Range *see* Koryakskoye Nagor'ye
Koryakskiy Khrebet *see* Koryakskoye Nagor'ye
123 V8 **Koryakskiy Okrug** ◈ *autonomous district* E Russian Federation
123 V7 **Koryakskoye Nagor'ye** *var.* Koryakskiy Khrebet, *Eng.* Koryak Range. ▲▲ NE Russian Federation
125 P11 **Koryazhma** Arkhangel'skaya Oblast', NW Russian Federation 61°16′N 47°07′E
Kōryō *see* Gangneung
Korytsa *see* Korçë
117 Q2 **Koryukivka** Chernihivs'ka Oblast', N Ukraine 51°45′N 32°16′E
Korzec *see* Korets'
115 N21 **Kos** Kos, Dodekánisa, Greece, Aegean Sea 36°53′N 27°19′E
115 M21 **Kos** *It.* Coo; *anc.* Cos. *island* Dodekánisa, Greece, Aegean Sea
125 T12 **Kosa** Komi-Permyatskiy Okrug, NW Russian Federation 59°55′N 54°54′E
125 T13 **Kosa** ≈ NW Russian Federation
164 B12 **Kō-saki** *headland* Nagasaki, Tsushima, SW Japan 34°06′N 129°13′E
163 X13 **Kosan** SE North Korea 38°50′N 127°26′E
119 H18 **Kosava** *Rus.* Kosovo. Brestskaya Voblasts', SW Belarus 52°45′N 25°16′E
Kosch *see* Kose
Koschagyl *see* Kosshagyl
110 G12 **Kościan** *Ger.* Kosten. Wielkopolskie, C Poland 52°05′N 16°38′E
110 I7 **Kościerzyna** Pomorskie, NW Poland 54°07′N 17°55′E
22 L4 **Kosciusko** Mississippi, S USA 33°03′N 89°35′W
Kosciusko, Mount *see* Kosciuszko, Mount
183 R11 **Kosciuszko, Mount** *prev.* Mount Kosciusko. ▲ New South Wales, SE Australia 36°28′S 148°15′E
118 H4 **Kose** *Ger.* Kosch. Harjumaa, NW Estonia 59°11′N 25°10′E
25 U9 **Kosse** Texas, SW USA 31°16′N 96°38′W
114 G6 **Koshava** Vidin, NW Bulgaria 44°03′N 23°00′E
147 U9 **Kosh-Dëbë** *var.* Koshtebë. Narynskaya Oblast', C Kyrgyzstan 41°03′N 74°08′E
K'o-shih *see* Kashi
164 B12 **Koshikijima-rettō** *var.* Kosikizima Rettô. *island group* SW Japan
145 W13 **Koshkarkol', Ozero** ◎ SE Kazakhstan
30 L9 **Koshkonong, Lake** ◎ Wisconsin, N USA
Koshoba *see* Goşabo
Koshoba *see* Goşoba
164 M12 **Kōshoku** *var.* Kôsyoku. Nagano, Honshū, S Japan 36°33′N 138°09′E
Koshtebë *see* Kosh-Dëbë
Kōshū *see* Enzan
Kōshū *see* Gwangju
111 N19 **Košice** *Ger.* Kaschau, *Hung.* Kassa. Košický Kraj, E Slovakia 48°44′N 21°15′E
111 M20 **Košický Kraj** ◈ *region* E Slovakia
Kosikizima Rettô *see* Koshikijima-rettō
153 R12 **Kosi Reservoir** ⊠ E Nepal
116 J8 **Kosiv** Ivano-Frankivs'ka Oblast', W Ukraine 48°19′N 25°04′E
145 O11 **Koskol'** *Kaz.* Qosköl. Karaganda, C Kazakhstan 49°32′N 67°08′E
125 Q9 **Koslan** Respublika Komi, NW Russian Federation 63°27′N 48°52′E
Köslin *see* Koszalin
146 M12 **Koson** *Rus.* Kasan. Qashqadaryo Viloyati, S Uzbekistan 39°04′N 65°35′E
Kosŏng *see* Goseong
147 S9 **Kosonsoy** *Rus.* Kasansay. Namangan Viloyati, E Uzbekistan 41°15′N 71°28′E
113 M16 **Kosovo** *prev.* Autonomous Province of Kosovo and Metohija. ◆ *republic* SE Europe
Kosovo *see* Kosava
Kosovo and Metohija, Autonomous Province of *see* Kosovo
Kosovo Polje *see* Fushë Kosovë
Kosovska Kamenica *see* Kamenicë
Kosovska Mitrovica *see* Mitrovicë
189 X17 **Kosrae** ◈ *state* E Micronesia
189 Y14 **Kosrae** *prev.* Kusaie. *island* Caroline Islands, E Micronesia
109 P6 **Kössen** Tirol, W Austria 47°40′N 12°24′E
144 G12 **Kosshagyl** *prev.* Koschagyl, *Kaz.* Qosshaghyl. Atyrau, W Kazakhstan 46°52′N 53°46′E
76 M16 **Kossou, Lac de** ◎ C Ivory Coast
Kossukavak *see* Krumovgrad
Kostajnica *see* Hrvatska Kostanjnica
Kostamus *see* Kostomuksha
144 M7 **Kostanay** *var.* Kustanay, *Kaz.* Qostanay. Kostanay, N Kazakhstan 53°16′N 63°34′E
144 L8 **Kostanay** *var.* Kostanayskaya Oblast', *Kaz.* Qostanay Oblysy. ◈ *province* N Kazakhstan
Kostanayskaya Oblast' *see* Kostanay
Kosten *see* Kościan
114 H10 **Kostenets** *prev.* Georgi Dimitrov. Sofiya, W Bulgaria 42°15′N 23°48′E
80 F10 **Kosti** White Nile, C Sudan 13°11′N 32°38′E
Kostnitz *see* Konstanz
124 H7 **Kostomuksha** *Fin.* Kostamus. Respublika Kareliya, NW Russian Federation 64°33′N 30°28′E
116 K3 **Kostopil'** *Rus.* Kostopol'. Rivnens'ka Oblast', NW Ukraine 50°20′N 26°29′E
Kostopol' *see* Kostopil'
124 M15 **Kostroma** Kostromskaya Oblast', NW Russian Federation 57°46′N 41°E
125 N14 **Kostroma** ≈ NW Russian Federation
125 N14 **Kostromskaya Oblast'** ◈ *province* NW Russian Federation
110 D11 **Kostrzyn** *Ger.* Cüstrin, Küstrin. Lubuskie, W Poland 52°35′N 14°40′E
110 H11 **Kostrzyn** Wielkopolskie, C Poland 52°23′N 17°13′E
117 X7 **Kostyantynivka** *Rus.* Konstantinovka. Donets'ka Oblast', SE Ukraine
Kostyukovichi *see* Kastsyukovichy
Kostyukovka *see* Kastsyukowka
Kôsyoku *see* Kōshoku
125 U6 **Kos'yu** Respublika Komi, NW Russian Federation 65°39′N 59°01′E
125 U6 **Kos'yu** ≈ NW Russian Federation
110 F7 **Koszalin** *Ger.* Köslin. Zachodnio-pomorskie, NW Poland 54°12′N 16°10′E
111 F22 **Kőszeg** *Ger.* Güns. Vas, W Hungary 47°23′N 16°33′E
152 H13 **Kota** *prev.* Kotah. Rājasthān, N India 25°14′N 75°52′E
Kota Baharu *see* Kota Bharu
Kota Bahru *see* Kota Bharu
169 U13 **Kotabaru** Pulau Laut, C Indonesia 03°15′S 116°15′E
168 K12 **Kota Baru** Sumatera, W Indonesia 01°07′S 101°43′E
Kotabaru *see* Jayapura
168 K6 **Kota Bharu** *var.* Kota Baharu, Kota Bahru. Kelantan, Peninsular Malaysia 06°07′N 102°15′E
Kotaboemi *see* Kotabumi
168 M14 **Kotabumi** *prev.* Kotaboemi. Sumatera, W Indonesia 04°50′S 104°54′E
149 S10 **Kot Addu** Punjab, E Pakistan 30°28′N 70°58′E
Kotah *see* Kota
169 U7 **Kota Kinabalu** *prev.* Jesselton. Sabah, East Malaysia 05°59′N 116°04′E
169 U7 **Kota Kinabalu** ✈ Sabah, East Malaysia 05°59′N 116°04′E
92 M12 **Kotala** Lappi, N Finland 67°01′N 29°00′E
Kotamobagoe *see* Kotamobagu
171 Q11 **Kotamobagu** *prev.* Kotamobagoe. Sulawesi, C Indonesia 0°46′N 124°21′E
155 L14 **Kotapad** *var.* Kotapārh. Orissa, E India 19°10′N 82°23′E
Kotapārh *see* Kotapad
166 N17 **Ko Ta Ru Tao** *island* SW Thailand
169 R13 **Kotawaringin, Teluk** *bay* Borneo, C Indonesia
149 Q13 **Kot Dīji** Sind, SE Pakistan 27°16′N 68°44′E
152 K9 **Kotdwāra** Uttarakhand, N India 29°44′N 78°33′E
125 Q14 **Kotel'nich** Kirovskaya Oblast', NW Russian Federation 58°19′N 48°12′E
127 N12 **Kotel'nikovo** Volgogradskaya Oblast', SW Russian Federation 47°37′N 43°07′E
123 Q6 **Kotel'nyy, Ostrov** *island* Novosibirskiye Ostrova, N Russian Federation
117 T5 **Kotel'va** Poltavs'ka Oblast', C Ukraine 50°04′N 34°46′E
101 M14 **Köthen** *var.* Cöthen. Sachsen-Anhalt, C Germany 51°46′N 11°59′E
Kôti *see* Kōchi
81 G17 **Kotido** NE Uganda 03°03′N 34°07′E
93 N19 **Kotka** Etelä-Suomi, S Finland 60°28′N 26°55′E
125 P11 **Kotlas** Arkhangel'skaya Oblast', NW Russian Federation 61°14′N 46°43′E
38 M10 **Kotlik** Alaska, USA 63°01′N 163°33′W
77 Q17 **Kotoka** ✈ (Accra) S Ghana 05°41′N 00°10′W
Kotonu *see* Cotonou
113 J17 **Kotor** *It.* Cattaro. SW Montenegro 42°25′N 18°47′E
Kotor *see* Kotoriba
112 F7 **Kotoriba** *Hung.* Kotor. Medimurje, N Croatia 46°20′N 16°47′E
113 I17 **Kotorska, Boka** *It.* Bocche di Cattaro. *bay* SW Montenegro
112 H11 **Kotorsko** ◈ Republika Srpska, N Bosnia and Herzegovina
112 G11 **Kotor Varoš** ◈ Republika Srpska, N Bosnia and Herzegovina
Koto Sho/Kotosho *see* Lan Yu
126 M7 **Kotovsk** Tambovskaya Oblast', W Russian Federation 52°39′N 41°31′E
117 O9 **Kotovs'k** *Rus.* Kotovsk. Odes'ka Oblast', SW Ukraine 47°42′N 29°30′E
Kotovsk *see* Hîncești
119 G16 **Kotra** ≈ W Belarus
149 P16 **Kotri** Sind, SE Pakistan 25°22′N 68°18′E
109 Q9 **Kötschach** Kärnten, S Austria 46°41′N 12°57′E
155 K15 **Kottagūdem** Andhra Pradesh, E India 17°36′N 80°40′E
155 F21 **Kottappadi** Kerala, SW India 11°38′N 76°03′E
155 G23 **Kottayam** Kerala, SW India 09°34′N 76°31′E
Kottbus *see* Cottbus
79 K15 **Kotto** ≈ Central African Republic/Dem. Rep. Congo
193 X15 **Kotu Group** *island group* W Tonga
Koturdepe *see* Goturdepe
122 M9 **Kotuy** ≈ N Russian Federation
83 M16 **Kotwa** Mashonaland East, NE Zimbabwe 16°58′S 32°46′E
39 N7 **Kotzebue** Alaska, USA 66°54′N 162°36′W
38 M7 **Kotzebue Sound** *inlet* Alaska, USA
Kotzenan *see* Chocianów
Kotzman *see* Kitsman'
77 R14 **Kouandé** NW Benin 10°20′N 01°42′E
79 J15 **Kouango** Ouaka, S Central African Republic 05°00′N 20°01′E
77 O13 **Koudougou** C Burkina 12°15′N 02°23′W
98 K7 **Koudum** Fryslân, N Netherlands 52°55′N 05°26′E
115 L25 **Koufonísi** *island* SE Greece
115 K21 **Koufonísi** *island* Kykládes, Greece, Aegean Sea
38 M8 **Kougarok Mountain** ▲ Alaska, USA 65°41′N 165°29′W
79 E21 **Kouilou** ◈ *province* SW Congo
79 E20 **Kouilou** ≈ S Congo
167 Q11 **Koŭk Kduŏch** *prev.* Phumĭ Koŭk Kduŏch. Bătdâmbâng, NW Cambodia 13°16′N 103°08′E
121 O3 **Koúklia** SW Cyprus 34°42′N 32°35′E
79 E19 **Koulamoutou** Ogooué-Lolo, C Gabon 01°07′S 12°27′E
76 L12 **Koulikoro** Koulikoro, SW Mali 12°55′N 07°31′W
76 L11 **Koulikoro** ◈ *region* SW Mali
187 P16 **Koumac** Province Nord, W New Caledonia 20°34′S 164°18′E
165 N12 **Koumi** Nagano, Honshū, S Japan 36°06′N 138°27′E
78 I13 **Koumra** Moyen-Chari, S Chad 08°56′N 17°32′E
Kounadougou *see* Koundougou
76 M15 **Kounahiri** C Ivory Coast 07°47′N 05°51′W
76 I12 **Koundâra** Moyenne-Guinée, NW Guinea 12°28′N 13°15′W
77 N13 **Koundougou** *var.* Kounadougou. C Burkina 11°43′N 04°40′W
76 H11 **Koungheul** C Senegal 14°00′N 14°48′W
Kounradskiy *see* Konyrat
25 X10 **Kountze** Texas, SW USA 30°22′N 94°20′W
77 Q13 **Koupéla** C Burkina 12°07′N 00°21′W
77 N13 **Kouri** Sikasso, SW Mali 12°09′N 04°46′W
55 Y9 **Kourou** N French Guiana 05°08′N 52°37′W
114 J12 **Kouroú** ≈ NE Greece
76 K14 **Kouroussa** C Guinea 10°40′N 09°50′W
Kousseir *see* Al Quṣayr
78 G11 **Kousséri** *prev.* Fort-Foureau. Extrême-Nord, NE Cameroon 12°05′N 14°56′E
Kouteifé *see* Al Quṭayfah
76 M13 **Koutiala** Sikasso, S Mali 12°20′N 05°23′W
76 M14 **Kouto** NW Ivory Coast 09°51′N 06°25′W
93 M19 **Kouvola** Etelä-Suomi, S Finland 60°50′N 26°48′E
79 G18 **Kouyou** ≈ C Congo
112 M10 **Kovačica** *Hung.* Antafalva; *prev.* Kovacsicza. Vojvodina, N Serbia 45°08′N 20°36′E
Kovacsicza *see* Kovačica
Kővárhosszúfalu *see* Satulung
Kovászna *see* Covasna
124 I4 **Kovdor** Murmanskaya Oblast', NW Russian Federation 67°32′N 30°27′E
116 J3 **Kovel'** *Pol.* Kowel. Volyns'ka Oblast', NW Ukraine 51°14′N 24°43′E
112 M11 **Kovin** *Hung.* Kevevára; *prev.* Temes-Kubin. Vojvodina, NE Serbia 44°45′N 20°59′E
Kovno *see* Kaunas
127 N3 **Kovrov** Vladimirskaya Oblast', W Russian Federation 56°24′N 41°21′E
127 O5 **Kovylkino** Respublika Mordoviya, W Russian Federation 54°03′N 43°52′E
110 J11 **Kowal** Kujawsko-pomorskie, C Poland 52°31′N 19°09′E
110 J9 **Kowalewo Pomorskie** *Ger.* Schönsee. Kujawsko-pomorskie, N Poland 53°07′N 18°48′E
Kowasna *see* Covasna
119 M16 **Kowbcha** *Rus.* Kolbcha. Mahilyowskaya Voblasts', E Belarus 53°39′N 29°14′E
Koweit *see* Kuwait
Kowel *see* Kovel'
185 F17 **Kowhitirangi** West Coast, South Island, New Zealand 42°54′S 171°01′E
161 O15 **Kowloon** Hong Kong, S China
Kowno *see* Kaunas
159 N7 **Kox Kuduk** *well* NW China
136 D16 **Köyceğiz** Muğla, SW Turkey 36°57′N 28°40′E
125 N6 **Koyda** Arkhangel'skaya Oblast', NW Russian Federation 66°22′N 42°42′E
Koymat *see* Goymat
Koymatdag, Gory *see* Goymatdag, Gory
151 E15 **Koyna Reservoir** ⊠ W India
165 P9 **Koyoshi-gawa** ≈ Honshū, C Japan
Koysanjaq *see* Koi Sanjaq
Koytash *see* Qo'ytosh
146 M14 **Köýtendag** *prev. Rus.* Charshanga, Charshangy, *Turkm.* Charshangngy. Lebap Welaýaty, E Turkmenistan 37°31′N 65°58′E
39 N9 **Koyuk** Alaska, USA 64°55′N 161°09′W
39 N9 **Koyuk River** ≈ Alaska, USA
39 O9 **Koyukuk** Alaska, USA 64°52′N 157°42′W
39 O9 **Koyukuk River** ≈ Alaska, USA
136 J13 **Kozaklı** Nevşehir, C Turkey 39°12′N 34°48′E
136 K16 **Kozan** Adana, S Turkey 37°27′N 35°47′E
115 E14 **Kozáni** Dytikí Makedonía, N Greece 40°19′N 21°48′E
112 F10 **Kozara** ▲▲ NW Bosnia and Herzegovina
Kozarska Dubica *see* Bosanska Dubica
117 P3 **Kozelets'** *Rus.* Kozelets. Chernihivs'ka Oblast', NE Ukraine 50°54′N 31°09′E
Kozelets *see* Kozelets'
117 S6 **Kozel'shchyna** Poltavs'ka Oblast', C Ukraine 49°13′N 33°49′E
126 J5 **Kozel'sk** Kaluzhskaya Oblast', W Russian Federation 54°04′N 35°51′E
151 F21 **Kozhikode** *var.* Calicut. Kerala, SW India 11°17′N 75°49′E *see also* Calicut
Kozhimiz, Gora *see* Kozhymiz, Gora
124 L9 **Kozhozero, Ozero** ◎ NW Russian Federation
125 T7 **Kozhva** Respublika Komi, NW Russian Federation 65°06′N 57°00′E
125 T7 **Kozhva** ≈ NW Russian Federation
125 U6 **Kozhym** Respublika Komi, NW Russian Federation 65°43′N 59°25′E
125 V9 **Kozhymiz, Gora** *prev.* Gora Kozhimiz. ▲ NW Russian Federation 63°13′N 58°54′E
110 N13 **Kozienice** Mazowieckie, C Poland 51°35′N 21°31′E
109 S13 **Kozina** SW Slovenia 45°36′N 13°56′E
114 H7 **Kozloduy** Vratsa, NW Bulgaria 43°48′N 23°42′E
127 Q3 **Kozlovka** Chuvashskaya Respublika, W Russian Federation 55°53′N 48°07′E
Kozlovshchina/ Kozlowszczyzna *see* Kazlowshchyna
127 P3 **Koz'modem'yansk** Respublika Mariy El, W Russian Federation 56°19′N 46°33′E
116 J6 **Kozova** Ternopil's'ka Oblast', W Ukraine 49°25′N 25°09′E
113 P20 **Kožuf** ▲▲ Greece/Macedonia
165 N15 **Kōzu-shima** *island* E Japan
Koz'yany *see* Kazyany
117 N5 **Kozyatyn** *Rus.* Kazatin. Vinnyts'ka Oblast', C Ukraine 49°41′N 28°49′E
77 Q16 **Kpalimé** *var.* Palimé. SW Togo 06°54′N 00°38′E
77 Q16 **Kpandu** E Ghana 07°00′N 00°18′E
99 F15 **Krabbendijke** Zeeland, SW Netherlands 51°25′N 04°07′E
167 N15 **Krabi** *var.* Muang Krabi. Krabi, SW Thailand 08°04′N 98°52′E
167 N13 **Kra Buri** Ranong, SW Thailand 10°25′N 98°48′E
167 S12 **Krâchéh** *prev.* Kratie. Krâchéh, E Cambodia 12°29′N 106°01′E
95 G17 **Kragerø** Telemark, S Norway 58°54′N 09°25′E
112 M13 **Kragujevac** Serbia, C Serbia 44°01′N 20°55′E
Krainburg *see* Kranj
166 N13 **Kra, Isthmus of** *isthmus* Malaysia/Thailand
112 D12 **Krajina** *cultural region* SW Croatia
Krakatau, Pulau *see* Rakata, Pulau
Krakau *see* Kraków
111 L16 **Kraków** *Eng.* Cracow, *Ger.* Krakau; *anc.* Cracovia. Małopolskie, S Poland 50°03′N 19°58′E
100 L9 **Krakower See** ◎ NE Germany
167 Q11 **Krâlănh** Siĕmréab, NW Cambodia 13°35′N 103°27′E
45 Q16 **Kralendijk** ○ Bonaire 12°07′N 68°13′W
112 B10 **Kraljevica** *It.* Porto Re. Primorje-Gorski Kotar, NW Croatia 45°15′N 14°36′E
112 M13 **Kraljevo** *prev.* Rankovićevo. Serbia, C Serbia 43°44′N 20°40′E
111 E16 **Královehradecký Kraj** *prev.* Hradecký Kraj. ◈ *region* N Czech Republic
Kralup an der Moldau *see* Kralupy nad Vltavou
111 C16 **Kralupy nad Vltavou** *Ger.* Kralup an der Moldau. Středočeský Kraj, NW Czech Republic 50°15′N 14°20′E
117 W7 **Kramators'k** *Rus.* Kramatorsk. Donets'ka Oblast', SE Ukraine 48°43′N 37°34′E
Kramatorsk *see* Kramators'k
93 H17 **Kramfors** Västernorrland, C Sweden 62°55′N 17°50′E
Kranéa *see* Kraniá
108 M7 **Kranebitten** ✈ (Innsbruck) Tirol, W Austria 47°18′N 11°21′E
115 D15 **Kraniá** *var.* Kranéa. Dytikí Makedonía, N Greece 39°54′N 21°21′E
115 G20 **Kranídi** Pelopónnisos, S Greece 37°21′N 23°09′E
109 T11 **Kranj** *Ger.* Krainburg. NW Slovenia 46°17′N 14°16′E
115 F16 **Krannón** *battleground* Thessalía, C Greece
Kranz *see* Zelenogradsk
112 D7 **Krapina** Krapina-Zagorje, N Croatia 46°12′N 15°52′E
112 E8 **Krapina** ≈ N Croatia
112 D8 **Krapina-Zagorje** *off.* Krapinsko-Zagorska Županija. ◈ *province* N Croatia
114 L7 **Krapinets** ≈ NE Bulgaria
Krapinsko-Zagorska Županija *see* Krapina-Zagorje
111 I15 **Krapkowice** *Ger.* Krappitz. Opolskie, SW Poland 50°29′N 17°56′E
Krappitz *see* Krapkowice
125 O12 **Krasavino** Vologodskaya Oblast', NW Russian Federation 60°56′N 46°27′E
122 H6 **Krasino** Novaya Zemlya, Arkhangel'skaya Oblast', N Russian Federation 70°45′N 54°16′E
123 S15 **Kraskino** Primorskiy Kray, SE Russian Federation 42°40′N 130°51′E
118 J11 **Krāslava** SE Latvia 55°56′N 27°08′E
119 M14 **Krasnaluki** *Rus.* Krasnoluki. Vitsyebskaya Voblasts', N Belarus 54°37′N 28°50′E
119 P17 **Krasnapollye** *Rus.* Krasnopol'ye. Mahilyowskaya Voblasts', E Belarus 53°20′N 31°24′E
126 L15 **Krasnaya Polyana** Krasnodarskiy Kray, SW Russian Federation 43°40′N 40°13′E
Krasnaya Slabada / Krasnaya Sloboda *see* Chyrvonaya Slabada
119 J15 **Krasnaye** *Rus.* Krasnoye. Minskaya Voblasts', C Belarus 54°14′N 27°05′E
111 O14 **Kraśnik** *Ger.* Kratznick. Lubelskie, E Poland 50°56′N 22°14′E
117 O9 **Krasni Okny** Odes'ka Oblast', SW Ukraine 47°33′N 29°28′E
127 P8 **Krasnoarmeysk** Saratovskaya Oblast', W Russian Federation 51°02′N 45°42′E
Krasnoarmeysk *see* Tayynsha
Krasnoarmeysk *see* Krasnoarmiys'k/Tayynsha
123 T6 **Krasnoarmeyskiy** Chukotskiy Avtonomnyy Okrug, NE Russian Federation 69°30′N 171°44′E
117 W7 **Krasnoarmiys'k** *Rus.* Krasnoarmeysk. Donets'ka Oblast', SE Ukraine 48°17′N 37°14′E
125 P11 **Krasnoborsk** Arkhangel'skaya Oblast', NW Russian Federation 61°31′N 45°57′E
126 K14 **Krasnodar** *prev.* Ekaterinodar, Yekaterinodar. Krasnodarskiy Kray, SW Russian Federation 45°06′N 39°01′E
126 K13 **Krasnodarskiy Kray** ◈ *territory* SW Russian Federation
117 Z7 **Krasnodon** Luhans'ka Oblast', E Ukraine 48°17′N 39°44′E
Krasnogor *see* Kallaste
127 T2 **Krasnogorskoye** Udmurtskaya Respublika, NW Russian Federation 57°42′N 52°29′E
Krasnograd *see* Krasnohrad
Krasnogvardeysk *see* Bulungh'ur
126 M13 **Krasnogvardeyskoye** Stavropol'skiy Kray, SW Russian Federation 45°49′N 41°31′E
Krasnogvardeyskoye *see* Krasnohvardiys'ke
117 U6 **Krasnohrad** *Rus.* Krasnograd. Kharkivs'ka Oblast', E Ukraine 49°22′N 35°28′E
117 S12 **Krasnohvardiys'ke** *Rus.* Krasnogvardeyskoye. Avtonomna Respublika Krym, S Ukraine 45°30′N 34°19′E
123 P14 **Krasnokamensk** Zabaykal'skiy Kray, S Russian Federation 50°03′N 118°01′E
125 U14 **Krasnokamsk** Permskiy Kray, W Russian Federation 58°08′N 55°48′E
127 U8 **Krasnokholm** Orenburgskaya Oblast', W Russian Federation 51°34′N 54°11′E
117 U5 **Krasnokuts'k** *Rus.* Krasnokutsk. Kharkivs'ka Oblast', E Ukraine 50°01′N 35°03′E

◆ Country
● Country Capital
◇ Dependent Territory
○ Dependent Territory Capital
◈ Administrative Regions
✈ International Airport
▲ Mountain
▲▲ Mountain Range
Volcano
≈ River
◎ Lake
⊠ Reservoir

Krasnokutsk see Krasnokuts'k
126 L7 **Krasnolesnyy** Voronezhskaya Oblast', W Russian Federation 51°53′N 39°37′E
Krasnoluki see Krasnaluki
Krasnoosol'skoye Vodokhranilishche see Chervonooskil's'ke Vodoskhovyshche
117 S11 **Krasnoperekops'k** Rus. Krasnoperekopsk. Avtonomna Respublika Krym, S Ukraine 45°56′N 33°47′E
Krasnoperekopsk see Krasnoperekops'k
117 U4 **Krasnopillya** Sums'ka Oblast', NE Ukraine 50°46′N 35°17′E
Krasnopol'ye see Krasnapollye
124 L5 **Krasnoshchel'ye** Murmanskaya Oblast', NW Russian Federation 67°22′N 37°03′E
127 O5 **Krasnoslobodsk** Respublika Mordoviya, W Russian Federation 54°24′N 43°51′E
127 T2 **Krasnoslobodsk** Volgogradskaya Oblast', SW Russian Federation 48°41′N 44°34′E
Krasnostav see Krasnystaw
127 V5 **Krasnousol'skiy** Respublika Bashkortostan, W Russian Federation 53°55′N 56°22′E
125 U12 **Krasnovishersk** Permskiy Kray, NW Russian Federation 60°22′N 57°04′E
Krasnovodsk see Türkmenbaşy
Krasnovodskiy Zaliv see Türkmenbasy Aylagy
146 B10 **Krasnovodskoye Plato** Turkm. Krasnowodsk Platosy. plateau NW Turkmenistan
Krasnowodsk Aylagy see Türkmenbasy Aylagy
Krasnowodsk Platosy see Krasnovodskoye Plato
122 K12 **Krasnoyarsk** Krasnoyarskiy Kray, S Russian Federation 56°05′N 92°46′E
127 X7 **Krasnoyarskiy** Orenburgskaya Oblast', W Russian Federation 51°56′N 59°54′E
122 K11 **Krasnoyarskiy Kray** ⬖ territory C Russian Federation
Krasnoye see Krasnaye
Krasnoye Znamya see Gyzylbaydak
125 R11 **Krasnozatonskiy** Respublika Komi, NW Russian Federation 61°39′N 51°00′E
118 D13 **Krasnoznamensk** prev. Lasdehnen, Ger. Haselberg. Kaliningradskaya Oblast', W Russian Federation 54°57′N 22°28′E
126 K3 **Krasnoznamensk** Moskovskaya Oblast', W Russian Federation 55°40′N 37°05′E
117 R11 **Krasnoznam"yans'kyy Kanal** canal S Ukraine
111 P14 **Krasnystaw** Rus. Krasnostav. Lubelskie, SE Poland 51°N 23°10′E
126 H4 **Krasnyy** Smolenskaya Oblast', W Russian Federation 54°36′N 31°27′E
127 P2 **Krasnyye Baki** Nizhegorodskaya Oblast', W Russian Federation 57°07′N 45°12′E
127 Q13 **Krasnyye Barrikady** Astrakhanskaya Oblast', SW Russian Federation 46°14′N 47°48′E
124 K15 **Krasnyy Kholm** Tverskaya Oblast', W Russian Federation 58°04′N 37°05′E
127 Q8 **Krasnyy Kut** Saratovskaya Oblast', W Russian Federation 50°54′N 46°58′E
Krasnyy Liman see Krasnyy Lyman
117 Y7 **Krasnyy Luch** prev. Krindachevka. Luhans'ka Oblast', E Ukraine 48°09′N 38°52′E
117 X6 **Krasnyy Lyman** Rus. Krasnyy Liman. Donets'ka Oblast', SE Ukraine 49°00′N 37°50′E
127 R3 **Krasnyy Steklovar** Respublika Mariy El, W Russian Federation 56°14′N 48°49′E
127 P8 **Krasnyy Tekstil'shchik** Saratovskaya Oblast', W Russian Federation 51°35′N 45°49′E
127 R13 **Krasnyy Yar** Astrakhanskaya Oblast', SW Russian Federation 46°33′N 48°21′E
Krassóvár see Caraşova
116 L5 **Krasyliv** Khmel'nyts'ka Oblast', W Ukraine 49°38′N 26°59′E
111 O21 **Kraszna** Rom. Crasna. ≈ Hungary/Romania
Kratie see Krâchéh
113 P17 **Kratovo** NE FYR Macedonia 42°04′N 22°08′E
Kratznick see Kraśnik
171 Y13 **Krau** Papua, E Indonesia 03°15′S 140°07′E
167 Q13 **Krâvanh, Chuŏr Phnum** Eng. Cardamom Mountains, Fr. Chaîne des Cardamomes. ▲▲ W Cambodia
Kravasta Lagoon see Karavastasë, Laguna e
Krawang see Karawang
127 Q15 **Kraynovka** Respublika Dagestan, SW Russian Federation 43°58′N 47°24′E
118 D12 **Kražiai** Šiaulai, C Lithuania 55°36′N 22°41′E
27 P11 **Krebs** Oklahoma, C USA 34°55′N 95°43′W
101 D15 **Krefeld** Nordrhein-Westfalen, W Germany 51°20′N 06°34′E
Kreisstadt see Krosno Odrzańskie
115 D17 **Kremastón, Technití Límni** ▣ C Greece
Kremenchug see Kremenchuk
Kremenchugskoye Vodokhranilishche/Kremenchuk Reservoir see Kremenchuts'ke Vodoskhovyshche
117 S6 **Kremenchuk** Rus. Kremenchug. Poltavs'ka Oblast', NE Ukraine 49°04′N 33°27′E
117 R6 **Kremenchuts'ke Vodoskhovyshche** Eng. Kremenchuk Reservoir, Rus. Kremenchugskoye Vodokhranilishche. ▣ C Ukraine
116 K5 **Kremenets'** Pol. Krzemieniec, Rus. Kremenets. Ternopil's'ka Oblast', W Ukraine 50°06′N 25°43′E
Kremennaya see Kreminna
117 X6 **Kreminna** Rus. Kremennaya. Luhans'ka Oblast', E Ukraine 49°03′N 38°15′E
37 R4 **Kremmling** Colorado, C USA 40°03′N 106°23′W
109 V3 **Krems** ≈ NE Austria
Krems see Krems an der Donau
109 W3 **Krems an der Donau** var. Krems. Niederösterreich, N Austria 48°25′N 15°36′E
Kremsier see Kroměříž
109 S4 **Kremsmünster** Oberösterreich, N Austria 48°04′N 14°08′E
38 M17 **Krenitzin Islands** island Aleutian Islands, Alaska, USA
Kresena see Kresna
114 G11 **Kresna** var. Kresena. Blagoevgrad, SW Bulgaria 41°43′N 23°10′E
112 O12 **Krespoljin** Serbia, E Serbia 44°22′N 21°36′E
25 N4 **Kress** Texas, SW USA 34°21′N 101°43′W
123 V6 **Kresta, Zaliv** bay E Russian Federation
115 D20 **Kréstena** prev. Selinoús. Dytikí Elláda, S Greece 37°36′N 21°36′E
124 H14 **Kresttsy** Novgorodskaya Oblast', W Russian Federation 58°15′N 32°28′E
Kretikon Delagos see Kritikó Pélagos
118 C11 **Kretinga** Ger. Krottingen. Klaipėda, NW Lithuania 55°53′N 21°13′E
Kreutz see Cristuru Secuiesc
Kreuz see Križevci, Croatia
Kreuz see Risti, Estonia
Kreuzburg/Kreuzburg in Oberschlesien see Kluczbork
Kreuzingen see Bol'shakovo
108 H6 **Kreuzlingen** Thurgau, NE Switzerland 47°38′N 09°12′E
101 K25 **Kreuzspitze** ▲ S Germany 47°30′N 10°55′E
101 F16 **Kreuztal** Nordrhein-Westfalen, W Germany 50°58′N 08°00′E
119 I15 **Kreva** Rus. Krevo. Hrodzyenskaya Voblasts', W Belarus 54°19′N 26°17′E
Krevo see Kreva
Kría Vrísi see Krýa Vrýsi
79 D16 **Kribi** Sud, SW Cameroon 02°53′N 09°57′E
Krichëv see Krychaw
Krickerhäu/Kriegerhaj see Handlová
109 W6 **Krieglach** Steiermark, E Austria 47°33′N 15°37′E
108 F8 **Kriens** Luzern, W Switzerland 47°03′N 08°17′E
Krievija see Russian Federation
Krimmitschau see Crimmitschau
98 H12 **Krimpen aan den IJssel** Zuid-Holland, SW Netherlands 51°56′N 04°39′E
Krindachevka see Krasnyy Luch
115 G25 **Kríos, Akrotírio** headland Kríti, Greece, E Mediterranean Sea 35°17′N 23°31′E
155 J16 **Krishna** prev. Kistna. ≈ C India
155 H20 **Krishnagiri** Tamil Nādu, SE India 12°33′N 78°11′E
155 K17 **Krishna, Mouths of the** delta SE India
153 S15 **Krishnanagar** West Bengal, N India 23°22′N 88°32′E
155 G20 **Krishnarājāsāgara** var. Paradip. ▣ W India
95 N19 **Kristdala** Kalmar, S Sweden 57°24′N 16°12′E
Kristiania see Oslo
95 E18 **Kristiansand** var. Christiansand. Vest-Agder, S Norway 58°08′N 07°52′E
95 L22 **Kristianstad** Skåne, S Sweden 56°02′N 14°10′E
94 F8 **Kristiansund** var. Christiansund. Møre og Romsdal, S Norway 63°07′N 07°45′E
Kristiinankaupunki see Kristinestad
93 I14 **Kristineberg** Västerbotten, N Sweden 65°07′N 18°36′E
95 L16 **Kristinehamn** Värmland, C Sweden 59°17′N 14°09′E
93 J17 **Kristinestad** Fin. Kristiinankaupunki. Länsi-Suomi, W Finland 62°15′N 21°24′E
Kristyor see Crişcior
115 J25 **Kríti** Eng. Crete. ⬖ region Greece, Aegean Sea
115 J24 **Kríti** Eng. Crete. island Greece, Aegean Sea
115 J23 **Kritikó Pélagos** var. Kretikon Delagos, Eng. Sea of Crete; anc. Mare Creticum. sea Greece, Aegean Sea
Kriulyany see Criuleni
112 I12 **Krivaja** ≈ NE Bosnia and Herzegovina
Krivaja see Mali Iđoš
113 P17 **Kriva Palanka** Turk. Eğri Palanka. NE Macedonia 42°13′N 22°19′E
Krivichi see Kryvichy
114 H8 **Krivodol** Vratsa, NW Bulgaria 43°23′N 23°30′E
126 M10 **Krivorozh'ye** Rostovskaya Oblast', SW Russian Federation 48°51′N 40°49′E
Krivoshin see Kryvoshyn
Krivoy Rog see Kryvyy Rih
112 F7 **Križevci** Ger. Kreuz, Hung. Kőrös. Varaždin, NE Croatia 46°02′N 16°32′E
112 B10 **Krk** It. Veglia. Primorje-Gorski Kotar, NW Croatia 45°01′N 14°36′E
112 B10 **Krk** It. Veglia; anc. Curieta. island NW Croatia
109 V12 **Krka** ≈ SE Slovenia
Krka see Gurk
109 R11 **Krn** ▲ NW Slovenia 46°15′N 13°37′E
111 H16 **Krnov** Ger. Jägerndorf. Moravskoslezský Kraj, E Czech Republic 50°05′N 17°40′E
Kroatien see Croatia
95 G14 **Krøderen** Buskerud, S Norway 60°06′N 09°48′E
95 G14 **Krøderen** ◎ S Norway
Kroi see Krui
95 N17 **Krokek** Östergötland, S Sweden 58°40′N 16°25′E
Krokodil see Crocodile
93 G16 **Krokom** Jämtland, C Sweden 63°20′N 14°30′E
117 S2 **Krolevets'** Rus. Krolevets. Sums'ka Oblast', NE Ukraine 51°34′N 33°24′E
Krolevets see Krolevets'
Królewska Huta see Chorzów
111 H18 **Kroměříž** Ger. Kremsier. Zlínský Kraj, E Czech Republic 49°18′N 17°24′E
98 I9 **Krommenie** Noord-Holland, C Netherlands 52°30′N 04°46′E
126 J6 **Kromy** Orlovskaya Oblast', W Russian Federation 52°41′N 35°45′E
101 L18 **Kronach** Bayern, E Germany 50°14′N 11°19′E
Krone an der Brahe see Koronowo
Krŏng Kaôh Kŏng see Kaôh Kŏng
95 K21 **Kronoberg** ⬖ county S Sweden
123 V10 **Kronotskiy Zaliv** bay E Russian Federation
195 O2 **Kronprinsesse Märtha Kyst** physical region Antarctica
195 V3 **Kronprins Olav Kyst** physical region Antarctica
124 G12 **Kronshtadt** Leningradskaya Oblast', NW Russian Federation 60°01′N 29°42′E
Kronstadt see Braşov
83 I22 **Kroonstad** Free State, C South Africa 27°40′S 27°15′E
123 O12 **Kropotkin** Irkutskaya Oblast', C Russian Federation 58°30′N 115°21′E
126 L14 **Kropotkin** Krasnodarskiy Kray, SW Russian Federation 45°29′N 40°31′E
110 J11 **Krośniewice** Łódzskie, C Poland 52°14′N 19°10′E
111 N17 **Krosno** Ger. Krossen. Podkarpackie, SE Poland 49°40′N 21°46′E
110 E12 **Krosno Odrzańskie** Ger. Crossen, Kreisstadt. Lubuskie, W Poland 52°02′N 15°06′E
Krossen see Krosno
Krotoschin see Krotoszyn
110 H13 **Krotoszyn** Ger. Krotoschin. Wielkopolskie, C Poland 51°43′N 17°24′E
Krottingen see Kretinga
Krousón see Krousónas
115 J25 **Krousónas** prev. Krousón, Kroussón. Kríti, Greece, E Mediterranean Sea 35°14′N 24°59′E
Kroussón see Krousónas
Krraba see Krrabë
113 L20 **Krrabë** var. Krraba. Tiranë, C Albania 41°15′N 19°56′E
113 L17 **Krrabit, Mali i** ▲▲ N Albania
109 W12 **Krško** Ger. Gurkfeld; prev. Videm-Krško. E Slovenia 45°57′N 15°31′E
83 K19 **Kruger National Park** national park Northern, N South Africa
83 J21 **Krugersdorp** Gauteng, NE South Africa 26°06′S 27°46′E
38 D16 **Krugloi Point** headland Agattu Island, Alaska, USA 52°30′N 173°46′E
Krugloye see Kruhlaye
119 N15 **Kruhlaye** Rus. Krugloye. Mahilyowskaya Voblasts', E Belarus 54°15′N 29°48′E
168 L15 **Krui** var. Kroi. Sumatera, SW Indonesia 05°11′S 103°55′E
99 G16 **Kruibeke** Oost-Vlaanderen, N Belgium 51°10′N 04°18′E
83 G25 **Kruidfontein** Western Cape, SW South Africa 32°50′S 21°59′E
99 F15 **Kruiningen** Zeeland, SW Netherlands 51°28′N 04°01′E
Kruja see Krujë
113 L19 **Krujë** var. Kruja, It. Croia. Durrës, C Albania 41°30′N 19°48′E
Krulevshchina/Krulewshchyna see Krulyewshchyzna
118 K13 **Krulyewshchyzna** Rus. Krulevshchina, Krulewshchyna. Vitsyebskaya Voblasts', N Belarus 55°02′N 27°45′E
25 T6 **Krum** Texas, SW USA 33°15′N 97°14′W
101 J23 **Krumbach** Bayern, S Germany 48°12′N 10°21′E
113 M17 **Krumë** Kukës, NE Albania 42°11′N 20°25′E
Krummau see Český Krumlov
114 K12 **Krumovgrad** prev. Kossukavak. Yambol, E Bulgaria 41°27′N 25°40′E
114 K12 **Krumovitsa** ≈ S Bulgaria
114 L10 **Krumovo** Yambol, E Bulgaria 42°16′N 26°25′E
167 O11 **Krung Thep, Ao** var. Bight of Bangkok. bay S Thailand
Krung Thep Mahanakhon see Ao Krung Thep
Krupa/Krupa na Uni see Bosanska Krupa
119 M15 **Krupki** Minskaya Voblasts', C Belarus 54°19′N 29°08′E
95 G24 **Kruså** var. Krusaa. Syddanmark, SW Denmark 54°50′N 09°25′E
Krusaa see Kruså
113 N14 **Kruševac** Serbia, C Serbia 43°37′N 21°20′E
113 N19 **Kruševo** SW FYR Macedonia 41°22′N 21°15′E
111 A15 **Krušné Hory** Eng. Ore Mountains, Ger. Erzgebirge. ▲ Czech Republic/Germany see also Erzgebirge
Krušné Hory see Erzgebirge
39 W13 **Kruzof Island** island Alexander Archipelago, Alaska, USA
114 F13 **Krýa Vrýsi** var. Kría Vrísi. Kentrikí Makedonía, N Greece 40°41′N 22°18′E
119 P16 **Krychaw** Rus. Krichëv. Mahilyowskaya Voblasts', E Belarus 53°42′N 31°43′E
64 K11 **Krylov Seamount** undersea feature E Atlantic Ocean 17°35′N 30°07′W
Krym see Krym, Avtonomna Respublika
117 S13 **Krym, Avtonomna Respublika** var. Krym, Eng. Crimea, Crimean Oblast; prev. Rus. Krymskaya ASSR, Krymskaya Oblast'. ⬖ province SE Ukraine
126 K14 **Krymsk** Krasnodarskiy Kray, SW Russian Federation 44°56′N 38°02′E
Krymskaya ASSR/Krymskaya Oblast' see Krym, Avtonomna Respublika
117 T13 **Kryms'ki Hory** ▲▲ S Ukraine
117 T13 **Kryms'kyy Pivostriv** peninsula S Ukraine
111 M18 **Krynica** Ger. Tannenhof. Małopolskie, S Poland 49°25′N 20°56′E
117 P8 **Kryve Ozero** Odes'ka Oblast', SW Ukraine 47°54′N 30°19′E
119 K14 **Kryvichy** Rus. Krivichi. Minskaya Voblasts', C Belarus 54°43′N 27°17′E
119 I18 **Kryvoshyn** Rus. Krivoshin. Brestskaya Voblasts', SW Belarus 52°52′N 26°08′E
117 S8 **Kryvyy Rih** Rus. Krivoy Rog. Dnipropetrovs'ka Oblast', SE Ukraine 47°53′N 33°24′E
117 N8 **Kryzhopil'** Vinnyts'ka Oblast', C Ukraine 48°22′N 28°51′E
Krzemieniec see Kremenets'
111 J14 **Krzepice** Śląskie, S Poland 50°58′N 18°42′E
110 F10 **Krzyż Wielkopolskie** Wielkopolskie, W Poland 52°52′N 16°03′E
Ksar al Kabir see Ksar-el-Kebir
Ksar al Soule see Er-Rachidia
74 J5 **Ksar El Boukhari** N Algeria 35°55′N 02°47′E
74 G5 **Ksar-el-Kebir** var. Alcázar, Ksar al Kabir, Ksar-el-Kébir, Ar. Al-Kasr al-Kebir, Al-Qsar al-Kbir, Sp. Alcazarquivir. NW Morocco 35°04′N 05°56′W
Ksar-el-Kébir see Ksar-el-Kebir
110 H12 **Książ Wielkopolski** Ger. Xions. Weilkopolskie, W Poland 52°03′N 17°10′E
127 O3 **Kstovo** Nizhegorodskaya Oblast', W Russian Federation 56°07′N 44°12′E
169 T8 **Kuala Belait** W Brunei 04°48′N 114°12′E
Kuala Dungun see Dungun
169 S10 **Kualakeriau** Borneo, C Indonesia
169 S12 **Kualakuayan** Borneo, C Indonesia 02°01′S 112°35′E
168 K8 **Kuala Lipis** Pahang, Peninsular Malaysia 04°11′N 102°00′E
168 K9 **Kuala Lumpur** ● (Malaysia) Kuala Lumpur, Peninsular Malaysia 03°08′N 101°42′E
168 K9 **Kuala Lumpur International** ✈ Selangor, Peninsular Malaysia 02°51′N 101°45′E
Kuala Pelabohan Kelang see Pelabuhan Klang
169 U7 **Kuala Penyu** Sabah, East Malaysia 05°37′N 115°36′E
38 E9 **Kualapu'u** var. Kualapuu. Moloka'i, Hawaii, USA, C Pacific Ocean 21°09′N 157°02′W
Kualapuu see Kualapu'u
168 L7 **Kuala Terengganu** var. Kuala Trengganu. Terengganu, Peninsular Malaysia 05°20′N 103°07′E
168 L11 **Kualatungkal** Sumatera, W Indonesia 0°49′S 103°22′E
171 P11 **Kuandang** Sulawesi, N Indonesia 0°50′N 122°55′E
163 V12 **Kuandian** var. Kuandian Manzu Zizhixian. Liaoning, NE China 40°41′N 124°46′E
Kuandian Manzu Zizhixian see Kuandian
Kuando-Kubango see Cuando Cubango
Kuang-chou see Guangzhou
Kuang-hsi see Guangxi Zhuangzu Zizhiqu
Kuang-tung see Guangdong
Kuang-yuan see Guangyuan
Kuantan, Batang see Indragiri, Sungai
Kuanza Norte see Cuanza Norte
Kuanza Sul see Cuanza Sul
Kuanzhou see Qingjian
Kuba see Quba
Kubango see Cubango/Okavango
141 X8 **Kubārah** NW Oman 23°03′N 56°52′E
93 H16 **Kubbe** Västernorrland, C Sweden 63°31′N 18°04′E
80 A11 **Kubbum** Southern Darfur, W Sudan 11°47′N 23°47′E
124 L13 **Kubenskoye, Ozero** ◎ NW Russian Federation
146 G6 **Kubla-Ustyurt** Rus. Komsomol'sk-na-Ustyurte. Qoraqalpog'iston Respublikasi, NW Uzbekistan 44°06′N 58°14′E
164 G15 **Kubokawa** Kōchi, Shikoku, SW Japan 33°22′N 133°14′E
114 L7 **Kubrat** prev. Balbunar. Razgrad, N Bulgaria 43°48′N 26°31′E
112 O13 **Kučajske Planine** ▲▲ E Serbia
165 T1 **Kuccharo-ko** ◎ Hokkaidō, N Japan
112 O11 **Kučevo** Serbia, NE Serbia 44°29′N 21°42′E
Kuchan see Qūchān
169 Q10 **Kuching** prev. Sarawak. Sarawak, East Malaysia 01°32′N 110°20′E
169 Q10 **Kuching** ✈ Sarawak, East Malaysia 01°32′N 110°20′E
164 B17 **Kuchinoerabu-jima** island Nansei-shotō, SW Japan
Kuchinotsu see Minamishimabara
109 Q6 **Kuchl** Salzburg, NW Austria 47°37′N 13°12′E
148 L9 **Kūchnay Darwēshān** prev. Kūchnay Darweyshān. Helmand, S Afghanistan 31°02′N 64°10′E
Kūchnay Darweyshān see Kūchnay Darwēshān
Kuchurgan see Kuchurhan
117 O9 **Kuchurhan** Rus. Kuchurgan. ≈ NE Ukraine
Kuçova see Kuçovë
113 L21 **Kuçovë** var. Kuçova; prev. Qyteti Stalin. Berat, C Albania 40°48′N 19°55′E
136 D11 **Küçük Çekmece** İstanbul, NW Turkey 41°01′N 28°47′E
164 F14 **Kudamatsu** var. Kudamatu. Yamaguchi, Honshū, SW Japan 34°00′N 131°53′E
Kudamatu see Kudamatsu
Kudara see Ghŭdara
169 V6 **Kudat** Sabah, East Malaysia 06°54′N 116°47′E
Küddow see Gwda
155 G17 **Kūdligi** Karnātaka, W India 14°58′N 76°24′E
Kudowa see Kudowa-Zdrój
111 F16 **Kudowa-Zdrój** Ger. Kudowa. Wałbrzych, SW Poland 50°27′N 16°20′E
117 P9 **Kudryavtsivka** Mykolayivs'ka Oblast', S Ukraine 47°18′N 31°02′E
169 R16 **Kudus** prev. Koedoes. Jawa, C Indonesia 06°46′S 110°48′E
125 T13 **Kudymkar** Permskiy Kray, NW Russian Federation 59°01′N 54°40′E
Kudzsir see Cugir
Kuei-chou see Guizhou
Kuei-lin see Guilin
Kuei-Yang/Kuei-yang see Guiyang
K'u-erh-lo see Korla
Kueyang see Guiyang
Kufa see Al Kūfah
136 E14 **Küfiçayı** ≈ C Turkey
109 O6 **Kufstein** Tirol, W Austria 47°36′N 12°10′E
9 N7 **Kugaaruk** prev. Pelly Bay. Nunavut, N Canada 68°38′N 89°45′W
Kugaly see Kogaly
8 K8 **Kugluktuk** var. Qurlurtuuq; prev. Coppermine. Nunavut, NW Canada 67°49′N 115°12′W
143 Y13 **Kūhak** Sīstān va Balūchestān, SE Iran 27°10′N 63°15′E
143 R9 **Kūhbonān** Kermān, C Iran 31°23′N 56°16′E
148 J5 **Kūhestān** var. Kohsān. Herāt, W Afghanistan 34°40′N 61°11′E
Kūhīrī see Kahīrī
93 N15 **Kuhmo** Oulu, E Finland 64°04′N 29°34′E
93 L18 **Kuhmoinen** Länsi-Suomi, C Finland 61°32′N 25°09′E
Kuhnau see Konin
Kühnö see Kihnu
143 O8 **Kūhpāyeh** Eşfahān, C Iran 32°42′N 52°25′E
167 O12 **Kui Buri** var. Ban Kui Nua. Prachuap Khiri Khan, SW Thailand 12°10′N 99°49′E
Kuibyshev see Kuybyshevskoye Vodokhranilishche
82 D13 **Kuito** Port. Silva Porto. Bié, C Angola 12°21′S 16°55′E
39 X14 **Kuiu Island** island Alexander Archipelago, Alaska, USA
92 L13 **Kuivaniemi** Oulu, C Finland 65°34′N 25°13′E
77 V14 **Kujama** Kaduna, C Nigeria 10°27′N 07°39′E
110 I10 **Kujawsko-pomorskie** ⬖ province C Poland
165 R8 **Kuji** var. Kuzi. Iwate, Honshū, C Japan 40°12′N 141°47′E
Kujto, Ozero see Yushkozerskoye Vodokhranilishche
Kujū-renzan see Kujū-san
164 D14 **Kujū-san** var. Kujū-renzan. ▲ Kyūshū, SW Japan 33°07′N 131°13′E
43 N7 **Kukalaya, Rio** var. Rio Cuculaya, Rio Kukulaya. ≈ NE Nicaragua
113 O16 **Kukavica** var. Vlajna. ▲ SE Serbia 42°46′N 21°58′E
113 M18 **Kukës** var. Kukësi. Kukës, NE Albania 42°03′N 20°25′E
113 L18 **Kukës** ⬖ district NE Albania
Kukësi see Kukës
186 D8 **Kukipi** Gulf, S Papua New Guinea 08°11′S 146°09′E
127 S3 **Kukmor** Respublika Tatarstan, W Russian Federation 56°11′N 50°56′E
Kukong see Shaoguan
39 N6 **Kukpowruk River** ≈ Alaska, USA
38 M6 **Kukpuk River** ≈ Alaska, USA
Küküdağ see Gogi, Mount
Kukukhoto see Hohhot
Kukulaya, Rio see Kukalaya, Rio
189 W12 **Kuku Point** headland NW Wake Island 19°19′N 166°36′E
146 G11 **Kukurtli** Ahal Welaýaty, C Turkmenistan 39°58′N 58°47′E
Kül see Kūl, Rūd-e
114 F7 **Kula** Vidin, NW Bulgaria 43°55′N 22°32′E
112 K9 **Kula** Vojvodina, NW Serbia 45°37′N 19°31′E
136 D14 **Kula** Manisa, W Turkey 38°33′N 28°38′E
149 S8 **Kulāchi** Khyber Pakhtunkhwa, NW Pakistan 31°58′N 70°30′E
Kulachi see Kolāchi
Kulagino see Yesbol
168 L10 **Kulai** Johor, Peninsular Malaysia 01°41′N 103°33′E
114 M7 **Kulak** ≈ NE Bulgaria
153 T11 **Kula Kangri** var. Kulhakangri. ▲ Bhutan/China 28°06′N 90°19′E
144 E13 **Kulaly, Ostrov** island SW Kazakhstan
145 S16 **Kulan** Kaz. Qulan; prev. Lugovoy, Lugovoye. Zhambyl, S Kazakhstan 42°54′N 72°45′E
147 V9 **Kulanak** Narynskaya Oblast', C Kyrgyzstan 41°18′N 75°38′E
Gory Kulandag see Gulandag
153 V14 **Kulaura** Sylhet, NE Bangladesh 24°32′N 92°02′E
118 D9 **Kuldīga** Ger. Goldingen. W Latvia 56°57′N 21°59′E
Kuldja see Yining
Kul'dzhuktau, Gory see QuljuqtovTog'lari
127 N4 **Kulebaki** Nizhegorodskaya Oblast', W Russian Federation 55°25′N 42°31′E
112 E11 **Kulen Vakuf** var. Spasovo. ⬖ Federacija Bosna I Hercegovina, NW Bosnia and Herzegovina
181 Q9 **Kulgera Roadhouse** Northern Territory, N Australia 25°49′S 133°30′E
Kulhakangri see Kula Kangri
127 T1 **Kuliga** Udmurtskaya Respublika, NW Russian Federation 58°14′N 53°49′E
Kulkuduk see Ko'lquduq
118 G4 **Kullamaa** Läänemaa, W Estonia 58°52′N 24°05′E
197 O12 **Kullorsuaq** var. Kuvdlorssuak. ⬖ Kitaa, C Greenland
29 O6 **Kulm** North Dakota, N USA 46°18′N 98°57′W
Kulm see Chełmno
146 D12 **Kul'mach** prev. Turkm. Isgender. Balkan Welaýaty, W Turkmenistan 39°04′N 55°49′E
101 L18 **Kulmbach** Bayern, SE Germany 50°07′N 11°27′E
Kulmsee see Chełmża
147 Q14 **Kŭlob** Rus. Kulyab. SW Tajikistan 37°55′N 68°46′E
92 M13 **Kuloharju** Lappi, N Finland 65°51′N 28°10′E
125 N7 **Kuloy** Arkhangel'skaya Oblast', NW Russian Federation 64°55′N 43°35′E
125 N7 **Kuloy** ≈ NW Russian Federation
137 Q14 **Kulp** Dıyarbakır, SE Turkey 38°32′N 41°01′E
Kulpa see Kolpa
77 P14 **Kulpawn** ≈ N Ghana
143 R13 **Kūl, Rūd-e** var. Kül. ≈ S Iran
144 G12 **Kul'sary** Kaz. Qulsary. Atyrau, W Kazakhstan 46°59′N 54°02′E
153 R15 **Kulti** West Bengal, NE India 23°45′N 86°50′E
93 G14 **Kultsjön** Lapp. Gålto. ◎ N Sweden
136 I14 **Kulu** Konya, W Turkey 39°06′N 33°02′E
123 S9 **Kulu** ≈ E Russian Federation
122 I13 **Kulunda** Altayskiy Kray, S Russian Federation 52°33′N 79°04′E
Kulunda Steppe see Ravnina Kulyndy
Kulundinskaya Ravnina see Ravnina Kulyndy
182 M9 **Kulwin** Victoria, SE Australia 35°04′S 142°37′E
Kulyab see Kŭlob
117 Q3 **Kulykivka** Chernihivs'ka Oblast', N Ukraine 51°23′N 31°39′E
Kum see Qom
164 F14 **Kuma** Ehime, Shikoku, SW Japan 33°36′N 132°53′E
127 P14 **Kuma** ≈ SW Russian Federation
165 O12 **Kumagaya** Saitama, Honshū, S Japan 36°09′N 139°22′E
165 Q5 **Kumaishi** Hokkaidō, NE Japan 42°08′N 139°57′E
169 R13 **Kumai, Teluk** bay Borneo, C Indonesia
127 Y7 **Kumak** Orenburgskaya Oblast', W Russian Federation 51°16′N 60°06′E
164 C14 **Kumamoto** Kumamoto, Kyūshū, SW Japan 32°49′N 130°41′E
164 D15 **Kumamoto** off. Kumamoto-ken. ⬖ prefecture Kyūshū, SW Japan
Kumamoto-ken see Kumamoto
164 J15 **Kumano** Mie, Honshū, SW Japan 33°54′N 136°08′E
Kumanova see Kumanovo
113 O17 **Kumanovo** Turk. Kumanova. N Macedonia 42°08′N 21°43′E
185 G17 **Kumara** West Coast, South Island, New Zealand 42°39′S 171°12′E
180 J8 **Kumarina Roadhouse** Western Australia 24°46′S 119°39′E
153 T15 **Kumarkhali** Khulna, W Bangladesh 23°54′N 89°16′E
77 P16 **Kumasi** prev. Coomassie. C Ghana 06°41′N 01°40′W
Kumayri see Gyumri
79 D15 **Kumba** Sud-Ouest, W Cameroon 04°39′N 09°26′E
114 N13 **Kumbağ** Tekirdağ, NW Turkey 40°51′N 27°26′E
155 J21 **Kumbakonam** Tamil Nādu, SE India 10°59′N 79°24′E
Kum-Dag see Gumdag
165 R16 **Kume-jima** island Nansei-shotō, SW Japan
127 V6 **Kumertau** Respublika Bashkortostan, W Russian Federation 52°48′N 55°48′E
Kumillā see Comilla
35 R4 **Kumiva Peak** ▲ Nevada, W USA 40°24′N 119°16′W
159 N7 **Kum Kuduk** Xinjiang Uygur Zizhiqu, W China 40°15′N 91°55′E
159 N8 **Kum Kuduk** well NW China
Kumkurgan see Qumqo'rg'on
95 M16 **Kumla** Örebro, C Sweden 59°08′N 15°09′E
136 E17 **Kumluca** Antalya, SW Turkey 36°23′N 30°17′E
100 N9 **Kummerower See** ◎ NE Germany
77 X14 **Kumo** Gombe, E Nigeria 10°03′N 11°14′E
145 O13 **Kumola** ≈ C Kazakhstan
167 N1 **Kumon Range** ▲▲ N Burma (Myanmar)
83 F22 **Kums** Karas, SE Namibia 28°07′S 19°40′E
155 E18 **Kumta** Karnātaka, W India 14°25′N 74°24′E
38 H12 **Kumukahi, Cape** headland Hawai'i, USA, C Pacific Ocean 19°31′N 154°48′W
127 Q17 **Kumukh** Respublika Dagestan, SW Russian Federation 42°10′N 47°07′E
Kumul see Hami
158 L6 **Kümüx** Xinjiang Uygur Zizhiqu, W China
127 N9 **Kumylzhenskaya** Volgogradskaya Oblast', SW Russian Federation 49°54′N 42°35′E
141 W6 **Kumzār** N Oman 26°19′N 56°26′E
43 W15 **Kuna de Wargandí** ⬖ special territory NE Panama
149 S4 **Kunar** Per. Konarhā; prev. Konar. ⬖ province E Afghanistan
Kunashiri see Kunashir, Ostrov
123 U14 **Kunashir, Ostrov** var. Kunashiri. island Kuril'skiye Ostrova, SE Russian Federation
43 V14 **Kuna Yala** prev. San Blas. ⬖ special territory NE Panama
118 I3 **Kunda** Lääne-Virumaa, NE Estonia 59°31′N 26°33′E
152 M13 **Kunda** Uttar Pradesh, N India 25°43′N 81°31′E
155 E19 **Kundāpura** var. Coondapoor. Karnātaka, W India 13°39′N 74°41′E
79 O24 **Kundelungu, Monts** ▲▲ S Dem. Rep. Congo
Kundert see Hernád
186 D7 **Kundiawa** Chimbu, W Papua New Guinea 06°00′S 144°57′E
Kundla see Sāvarkundla
Kunduk, Ozero see Sasyk, Ozero
Kunduk, Ozero Sasyk see Sasyk, Ozero
168 L10 **Kundur, Pulau** island W Indonesia
149 Q2 **Kunduz** var. Kondūz, Qondūz; prev. Kondoz, Kundūz. Kunduz, NE Afghanistan 36°49′N 68°50′E
149 Q2 **Kunduz** prev. Kondoz. ⬖ province NE Afghanistan
Kunduz/Kundūz see Kunduz
Kuneitra see Al Qunayţirah
83 B18 **Kunene** ⬖ district NE Namibia
83 A16 **Kunene** var. Cunene. ≈ Angola/Namibia see also Cunene
Kunene see Cunene
Künes see Xinyuan
158 J5 **Künes He** ≈ NW China
95 I19 **Kungälv** Västra Götaland, S Sweden 57°54′N 12°00′E
147 W7 **Kungei Ala-Tau** Rus. Khrebet Kyungëy Ala-Too, Kir. Küngöy Ala-Too. ▲▲ Kazakhstan/Kyrgyzstan
Küngöy Ala-Too see Kungei Ala-Tau
Kungrad see Qo'ng'irot
95 J19 **Kungsbacka** Halland, S Sweden 57°30′N 12°05′E
95 I18 **Kungshamn** Västra Götaland, S Sweden 58°21′N 11°15′E
95 M16 **Kungsör** Västmanland, C Sweden 59°25′N 16°05′E
79 J16 **Kungu** Equateur, NW Dem. Rep. Congo 02°47′N 19°12′E
125 V15 **Kungur** Permskiy Kray, NW Russian Federation 57°24′N 56°56′E
166 L9 **Kungyangon** Yangon, SW Burma (Myanmar) 16°27′N 96°00′E
111 M22 **Kunhegyes** Jász-Nagykun-Szolnok, E Hungary 47°22′N 20°36′E
167 O5 **Kunhing** Shan State, E Burma (Myanmar) 21°17′N 98°26′E
158 D9 **Kunjirap Daban** var. Khūnjerāb Pass. pass China/Pakistan see also Khūnjerāb Pass
Kunjirap Daban see Khunjerāb Pass
Kunlun Mountains see Kunlun Shan
158 H10 **Kunlun Shan** Eng. Kunlun Mountains. ▲▲ NW China
159 P11 **Kunlun Shankou** pass C China
160 G13 **Kunming** var. K'un-ming; prev. Yunnan. province capital Yunnan, SW China 25°04′N 102°41′E
K'un-ming see Kunming
Kunø see Kunoy
95 B18 **Kunoy** Dan. Kunø. island N Faeroe Islands
Kunsan see Gunsan
111 L24 **Kunszentmárton** Jász-Nagykun-Szolnok, E Hungary 46°50′N 20°19′E
111 J23 **Kunszentmiklós** Bács-Kiskun, C Hungary 47°00′N 19°07′E
181 N3 **Kununurra** Western Australia 15°50′S 128°44′E
Kunyang see Pingyang
Kunya-Urgench see Köneürgenç
Kunyé see Pins, Île des
169 T11 **Kunyi** Borneo, C Indonesia 03°23′S 119°20′E
101 I20 **Künzelsau** Baden-Württemberg, S Germany 49°22′N 09°43′E
161 S10 **Kuocang Shan** ▲▲ SE China
Kuolajärvi see Kuoloyarvi
124 H5 **Kuoloyarvi** Finn. Kuolajärvi, var. Luolajarvi. Murmanskaya Oblast', NW Russian Federation 66°58′N 29°13′E
93 N16 **Kuopio** Itä-Suomi, C Finland 62°54′N 27°41′E
93 K17 **Kuortane** Länsi-Suomi, W Finland 62°48′N 23°30′E
93 M18 **Kuortti** Itä-Suomi, E Finland 61°25′N 26°25′E
Kupa see Kolpa
171 P17 **Kupang** prev. Koepang. Timor, C Indonesia 10°13′S 123°38′E
39 Q5 **Kuparuk River** ≈ Alaska, USA
Kupchino see Cupcina
186 E9 **Kupiano** Central, S Papua New Guinea 10°06′S 148°12′E
180 M4 **Kupingarri** Western Australia 16°46′S 125°57′E
122 I12 **Kupino** Novosibirskaya Oblast', C Russian Federation 54°22′N 77°09′E
118 H11 **Kupiškis** Panevėžys, NE Lithuania 55°51′N 24°58′E
114 L13 **Küplü** Edirne, NW Turkey 41°06′N 26°23′E
39 X13 **Kupreanof Island** island Alexander Archipelago, Alaska, USA
39 O16 **Kupreanof Point** headland Alaska, USA 55°34′N 159°36′W
112 G13 **Kupres** ⬖ Federacija Bosna I Hercegovina, SW Bosnia and Herzegovina
117 W5 **Kup"yans'k** Rus. Kupyansk. Kharkivs'ka Oblast', E Ukraine 49°42′N 37°36′E
Kupyansk see Kup"yans'k
117 W5 **Kup"yans'k-Vuzlovyy** Kharkivs'ka Oblast', E Ukraine 49°40′N 37°41′E
158 I6 **Kuqa** Xinjiang Uygur Zizhiqu, NW China 41°43′N 82°58′E

◆ Country
● Country Capital
◇ Dependent Territory
○ Dependent Territory Capital
⬖ Administrative Regions
✈ International Airport
▲ Mountain
▲▲ Mountain Range
Volcano
≈ River
◎ Lake
▣ Reservoir

Kür *see* Kura
137 W11 **Kura** *Az.* Kür, *Geor.* Mtkvari, *Turk.* Kura Nehri. ≈ SW Asia
55 R8 **Kuracki** NW Guyana 06°52′N 60°13′W
Kura Kurk *see* Irbe Strait
147 Q10 **Kurama Range** *Rus.* Kuraminskiy Khrebet. ▲▲ Tajikistan/Uzbekistan
Kuraminskiy Khrebet *see* Kurama Range
Kura Nehri *see* Kura
119 J14 **Kuranyets** *Rus.* Kurenets. Minskaya Voblasts', C Belarus 54°33′N 26°57′E
164 H13 **Kurashiki** *var.* Kurasiki. Okayama, Honshū, SW Japan 34°35′N 133°44′E
154 L10 **Kurasia** Chhattīsgarh, C India 23°11′N 82°16′E
Kurasiki *see* Kurashiki
164 H12 **Kurayoshi** *var.* Kurayosi. Tottori, Honshū, SW Japan 35°27′N 133°52′E
Kurayosi *see* Kurayoshi
163 X6 **Kurbin He** ≈ NE China
Kurchum *see* Kurshim
Kurchum *see* Kurshim
137 X11 **Kürdämir** *Rus.* Kyurdamir. C Azerbaijan 40°21′N 48°08′E
Kurdestan *see* Kordestān
139 S1 **Kurdistan** *cultural region* SW Asia
Kurd Kui *see* Kord Kūy
155 F15 **Kurduvādi** Mahārāshtra, W India 18°06′N 75°31′E
114 J11 **Kŭrdzhali** *var.* Kirdzhali. Kŭrdzhali, S Bulgaria 41°39′N 25°23′E
114 K11 **Kŭrdzhali** ⬖ *province* S Bulgaria
114 J11 **Kŭrdzhali, Yazovir** ⊠ S Bulgaria
164 F13 **Kure** Hiroshima, Honshū, SW Japan 34°15′N 132°33′E
192 K5 **Kure Atoll** *var.* Ocean Island. *atoll* Hawaiian Islands, Hawaii, USA
136 J10 **Küre Dağları** ▲▲ N Turkey
146 C11 **Kürendag** *Rus.* Gora Kyuren. ▲ W Turkmenistan 39°05′N 55°09′E
Kurenets *see* Kuranyets
118 E6 **Kuressaare** *Ger.* Arensburg; *prev.* Kingissepp. Saaremaa, W Estonia 58°17′N 22°29′E
122 K9 **Kureyka** Krasnoyarskiy Kray, N Russian Federation 66°22′N 87°21′E
122 K9 **Kureyka** ≈ N Russian Federation
Kurgal'dzhino/Kurgal'dzhinsky *see* Korgalzhyn
122 G11 **Kurgan** Kurganskaya Oblast', C Russian Federation 55°30′N 65°20′E
126 L14 **Kurganinsk** Krasnodarskiy Kray, SW Russian Federation 44°55′N 40°45′E
122 G11 **Kurganskaya Oblast'** ⬖ *province* C Russian Federation
Kurgan-Tyube *see* Qŭrghonteppa
191 O2 **Kuria** *prev.* Woodle Island. *island* Tungaru, W Kiribati
Kuria Muria Bay *see* Ḩalānīyāt, Khalīj al
Kuria Muria Islands *see* Ḩalānīyāt, Juzur al
153 T13 **Kurigram** Rajshahi, N Bangladesh 25°49′N 89°39′E
93 K17 **Kurikka** Länsi-Suomi, W Finland 62°36′N 22°25′E
192 I3 **Kurile Basin** *undersea feature* NW Pacific Ocean 47°00′N 150°00′E
Kurile Islands *see* Kuril'skiye Ostrova
Kurile-Kamchatka Depression *see* Kurile Trench
192 J3 **Kurile Trench** *var.* Kurile-Kamchatka Depression. *undersea feature* NW Pacific Ocean 47°00′N 155°00′E
127 Q9 **Kurilovka** Saratovskaya Oblast', W Russian Federation 50°39′N 48°02′E
123 U13 **Kuril'sk** *Jap.* Shana. Kuril'skiye Ostrova, Sakhalinskaya Oblats', SE Russian Federation 45°10′N 147°51′E
122 G11 **Kuril'skiye Ostrova** *Eng.* Kurile Islands. *island group* SE Russian Federation
42 M9 **Kurinwas, Río** ≈ E Nicaragua
Kurisches Haff *see* Courland Lagoon
Kurkund *see* Kilingi-Nõmme
126 M4 **Kurlovskiy** Vladimirskaya Oblast', W Russian Federation 55°25′N 40°39′E
80 G12 **Kurmuk** Blue Nile, SE Sudan 10°36′N 34°16′E
Kurna *see* Al Qurnah
155 H17 **Kurnool** *var.* Karnul. Andhra Pradesh, S India 15°51′N 78°01′E
164 M11 **Kurobe** Toyama, Honshū, SW Japan 36°55′N 137°24′E
165 Q7 **Kuroishi** *var.* Kuroisi. Aomori, Honshū, C Japan 40°37′N 140°34′E
Kuroisi *see* Kuroishi
165 O12 **Kuroiso** Tochigi, Honshū, S Japan 36°58′N 140°02′E
165 Q4 **Kuromatsunai** Hokkaidō, NE Japan 42°40′N 140°18′E
164 B17 **Kuro-shima** *island* SW Japan
185 F21 **Kurow** Canterbury, South Island, New Zealand 44°44′S 170°29′E
127 N15 **Kursavka** Stavropol'skiy Kray, SW Russian Federation 44°28′N 42°31′E
118 E11 **Kuršėnai** Šiauliai, N Lithuania 56°00′N 22°56′E
145 X10 **Kurshim** *prev.* Kurchum. Vostochnyy Kazakhstan, E Kazakhstan 48°35′N 83°37′E
145 Y10 **Kurshim** *prev.* Kurchum. ≈ E Kazakhstan
Kurshskaya Kosa/Kuršių Nerija *see* Courland Spit
126 J7 **Kursk** Kurskaya Oblast', W Russian Federation 51°44′N 36°47′E
126 I7 **Kurskaya Oblast'** ⬖ *province* W Russian Federation
Kurskiy Zaliv *see* Courland Lagoon
113 N15 **Kuršumlija** Serbia, S Serbia 43°09′N 21°16′E
137 R15 **Kurtalan** Siirt, SE Turkey 37°58′N 41°36′E
Kurtbunar *see* Tervel
Kurt-Dere *see* Vŭlchidol
Kurtitsch/Kürtös *see* Curtici
145 U15 **Kurtty** ≈ SE Kazakhstan
93 L18 **Kuru** Länsi-Suomi, W Finland 61°51′N 23°46′E
80 C13 **Kuru** ≈ W South Sudan
114 M13 **Kuru Dağı** ▲▲ NW Turkey
158 L7 **Kuruktag** ▲▲ NW China
83 G22 **Kuruman** Northern Cape, N South Africa 27°28′S 23°27′E
67 T14 **Kuruman** ≈ W South Africa
164 D14 **Kurume** Fukuoka, Kyūshū, SW Japan 33°15′N 130°27′E
123 N13 **Kurumkan** Respublika Buryatiya, S Russian Federation 54°13′N 110°21′E
155 J25 **Kurunegala** North Western Province, C Sri Lanka 07°28′N 80°23′E
55 T10 **Kurupukari** C Guyana 04°39′N 58°39′W
125 U10 **Kur"ya** Respublika Komi, NW Russian Federation 61°38′N 57°12′E
144 E15 **Kuryk** *var.* Yeraliyev, *Kaz.* Quryq. Mangistau, SW Kazakhstan 43°12′N 51°43′E
136 B15 **Kuşadası** Aydın, SW Turkey 37°50′N 27°16′E
115 M19 **Kuşadası Körfezi** *gulf* SW Turkey
164 A17 **Kusagaki-guntō** *island* SW Japan
Kusaie *see* Kosrae
145 T12 **Kusak** ≈ C Kazakhstan
Kusary *see* Qusar
167 P7 **Ku Sathan, Doi** ▲ NW Thailand 18°22′N 100°31′E
164 J13 **Kusatsu** *var.* Kusatu. Shiga, Honshū, SW Japan 35°02′N 136°00′E
Kusatu *see* Kusatsu
138 F11 **Kuseifa** Southern, C Israel 31°15′N 35°01′E
136 C12 **Kuş Gölü** ⊛ NW Turkey
126 L12 **Kushchevskaya** Krasnodarskiy Kray, SW Russian Federation 46°35′N 39°40′E
164 D16 **Kushima** *var.* Kusima. Miyazaki, Kyūshū, SW Japan 31°28′N 131°14′E
164 I15 **Kushimoto** Wakayama, Honshū, SW Japan 33°28′N 135°45′E
165 V4 **Kushiro** *var.* Kusiro. Hokkaidō, NE Japan 42°58′N 144°24′E
148 K4 **Kushk** *prev.* Kūshk. Herāt, W Afghanistan 34°55′N 62°20′E
Kushka *see* Serhetabat
Kushka *see* Gushgy/Serhetabat
Kushmurun *see* Kusmuryn
Kushmurun, Ozero *see* Kusmuryn, Ozero
127 U4 **Kushnarenkovo** Respublika Bashkortostan, W Russian Federation 55°07′N 55°24′E
Kushrabat *see* Qo'shrabot
Kushtia *see* Kustia
Kusima *see* Kushima
Kusiro *see* Kushiro
38 M13 **Kuskokwim Bay** *bay* Alaska, USA
39 P11 **Kuskokwim Mountains** ▲▲ Alaska, USA
39 N12 **Kuskokwim River** ≈ Alaska, USA
145 N8 **Kusmuryn** *Kaz.* Qusmuryn; *prev.* Kushmurun. Kostanay, N Kazakhstan 52°27′N 64°31′E
145 N8 **Kusmuryn, Ozero** *Kaz.* Qusmuryn; *prev.* Ozero Kushmurun. ⊛ N Kazakhstan
108 G7 **Küsnacht** Zürich, N Switzerland 47°19′N 08°34′E
165 V4 **Kussharo-ko** *var.* Kussyaro. ⊛ Hokkaidō, NE Japan
Küssnacht *see* Küssnacht am Rigi
108 F8 **Küssnacht am Rigi** *var.* Küssnacht. Schwyz, C Switzerland 47°03′N 08°25′E
Kussyaro *see* Kussharo-ko
Kustanay *see* Kostanay
Küstence/Küstendje *see* Constanţa
100 F11 **Küstenkanal** *var.* Ems-Hunte Canal. *canal* NW Germany
153 T15 **Kustia** *var.* Kushtia. Khulna, W Bangladesh 23°54′N 89°07′E
Küstrin *see* Kostrzyn
171 R11 **Kusu** Pulau Halmahera, E Indonesia 0°51′N 127°41′E
170 L16 **Kuta** Pulau Lombok, S Indonesia 08°53′S 116°15′E
139 T4 **Kutabān** At Ta'mím, N Iraq 35°21′N 44°45′E
136 E13 **Kütahya** *prev.* Kutaia. Kütahya, W Turkey 39°25′N 29°56′E
136 E13 **Kütahya** *var.* Kutaia. ⬖ *province* W Turkey
Kutai *see* Mahakam, Sungai
Kutaia *see* Kütahya
137 R9 **Kutaisi** W Georgia 42°16′N 42°42′E
Kūt al 'Amārah *see* Al Kūt
Kut al Hai/Kūt al Ḩayy *see* Al Ḩayy
Kut al Imara *see* Al Kūt
123 Q11 **Kutana** Respublika Sakha (Yakutiya), NE Russian Federation 59°05′N 131°43′E
Kutaradja/Kutaraja *see* Banda Aceh
165 R4 **Kutchan** Hokkaidō, NE Japan 42°54′N 140°46′E
Kutch, Gulf of *see* Kachchh, Gulf of
Kutch, Rann of *see* Kachchh, Rann of
112 F9 **Kutina** Sisak-Moslavina, NE Croatia 45°29′N 16°45′E
112 H9 **Kutjevo** Požega-Slavonija, NE Croatia 45°26′N 17°54′E
111 E17 **Kutná Hora** *Ger.* Kuttenberg. Střední Čechy, C Czech Republic 49°58′N 15°18′E
110 K12 **Kutno** Łódzkie, C Poland 52°14′N 19°23′E
Kuttenberg *see* Kutná Hora
79 I20 **Kutu** Bandundu, W Dem. Rep. Congo 02°42′S 18°10′E
153 V17 **Kutubdia Island** *island* SE Bangladesh
80 B10 **Kutum** Northern Darfur, W Sudan 14°10′N 24°40′E
147 Y7 **Kuturgu** Issyk-Kul'skaya Oblast', E Kyrgyzstan 42°45′N 78°04′E
12 M5 **Kuujjuaq** *prev.* Fort-Chimo. Québec, E Canada 58°10′N 68°15′W
12 I7 **Kuujjuarapik** Québec, C Canada 55°07′N 78°09′W
12 I7 **Kuujjuarapik** *prev.* Poste-de-la-Baleine. Québec, NE Canada 55°13′N 77°54′W
Kuuli-Mayak *see* Guwlumaýak
118 I6 **Kuulsemägi** ▲ S Estonia
92 N13 **Kuusamo** Oulu, E Finland 65°57′N 29°15′E
93 M19 **Kuusankoski** Etelä-Suomi, S Finland 60°51′N 26°40′E
127 W7 **Kuvandyk** Orenburgskaya Oblast', W Russian Federation 51°27′N 57°18′E
Kuvango *see* Cubango
Kuvasay *see* Quvasoy
Kuvdlorssuak *see* Kullorsuaq
124 I16 **Kuvshinovo** Tverskaya Oblast', W Russian Federation 57°03′N 34°09′E
141 Q4 **Kuwait** *off.* State of Kuwait, *var.* Dawlat al Kuwait, Koweit, Kuweit. ◆ *monarchy* SW Asia
Kuwait *see* Al Kuwayt
Kuwait Bay *see* Kuwayt, Jūn al
Kuwait City *see* Al Kuwayt
Kuwait, Dawlat al *see* Kuwait
Kuwait, State of *see* Kuwait
Kuwajleen *see* Kwajalein Atoll
164 K13 **Kuwana** Mie, Honshū, SW Japan 35°04′N 136°40′E
139 X9 **Kuwayt** Maysān, E Iraq 32°26′N 47°12′E
142 K11 **Kuwayt, Jūn al** *var.* Kuwait Bay. *bay* E Kuwait
Kuweit *see* Kuwait
117 P10 **Kuyal'nyts'kyy Lyman** ⊛ SW Ukraine
122 I12 **Kuybyshev** Novosibirskaya Oblast', C Russian Federation 55°28′N 77°55′E
Kuybyshev *see* Bolgar, Respublika Tatarstan, Russian Federation
Kuybyshev *see* Samara
117 W9 **Kuybysheve** *Rus.* Kuybyshevo. Zaporiz'ka Oblast', SE Ukraine 47°20′N 36°41′E
Kuybyshevo *see* Kuybysheve
Kuybyshev Reservoir *see* Kuybyshevskoye Vodokhranilishche
Kuybyshevskaya Oblast' *see* Samarskaya Oblast'
Kuybyshevskiy *see* Novoishimskiy
127 R4 **Kuybyshevskoye Vodokhranilishche** *var.* Kuibyshev, *Eng.* Kuybyshev Reservoir. ⊠ W Russian Federation
123 S9 **Kuydusun** Respublika Sakha (Yakutiya), NE Russian Federation 63°15′N 143°10′E
125 U16 **Kuyeda** Permskiy Kray, NW Russian Federation 56°23′N 55°19′E
Kūysanjaq *see* Koi Sanjaq
158 J4 **Kuytun** Xinjiang Uygur Zizhiqu, NW China 44°25′N 84°55′E
122 M13 **Kuytun** Irkutskaya Oblast', S Russian Federation 54°18′N 101°28′E
55 S12 **Kuyuwini Landing** S Guyana 02°06′N 59°14′W
Kuzi *see* Kuji
38 M9 **Kuzitrin River** ≈ Alaska, USA
127 P6 **Kuznetsk** Penzenskaya Oblast', W Russian Federation 53°06′N 46°27′E
116 K3 **Kuznetsovs'k** Rivnens'ka Oblast', NW Ukraine 51°21′N 25°51′E
165 R8 **Kuzumaki** Iwate, Honshū, C Japan 40°04′N 141°26′E
95 H24 **Kværndrup** Syddtjylland, C Denmark 55°10′N 10°31′E
92 H9 **Kvaløya** *island* N Norway
92 K8 **Kvalsund** Finnmark, N Norway 70°30′N 23°56′E
94 G11 **Kvam** Oppland, S Norway 61°42′N 09°43′E
127 X7 **Kvarkeno** Orenburgskaya Oblast', W Russian Federation 52°09′N 59°44′E
93 G15 **Kvarnbergsvattnet** *var.* Frostviken. ⊛ N Sweden
112 A11 **Kvarner** *var.* Carnaro, *It.* Quarnero. *gulf* W Croatia
112 B11 **Kvarnerić** *channel* W Croatia
39 O14 **Kvichak Bay** *bay* Alaska, USA
92 H12 **Kvikkjokk** *Lapp.* Huhttán. Norrbotten, N Sweden 66°58′N 17°45′E
95 D17 **Kvina** ≈ S Norway
92 Q1 **Kvitøya** *island* NE Svalbard
95 F16 **Kvitseid** Telemark, S Norway 59°23′N 08°31′E
79 H20 **Kwa** ≈ W Dem. Rep. Congo
77 Q15 **Kwadwokurom** C Ghana 07°49′N 00°15′W
186 M8 **Kwailibesi** Malaita, N Solomon Islands 08°25′S 160°48′E
189 S6 **Kwajalein Atoll** *var.* Kuwajleen. *atoll* Ralik Chain, C Marshall Islands
55 W9 **Kwakoegron** Brokopondo, N Surinam 05°14′N 55°20′W
81 J21 **Kwale** Coast, S Kenya 04°10′S 39°27′E
77 U17 **Kwale** Delta, S Nigeria 05°51′N 06°29′E
79 H20 **Kwamouth** Bandundu, W Dem. Rep. Congo 03°11′S 16°16′E
Kwando *see* Cuando
Kwangchow *see* Guangzhou
Kwangchu *see* Gwangju
Kwangju *see* Gwangju
Kwangju-gwangyŏksi *see* Gwangju
79 H20 **Kwango** *Port.* Cuango. ≈ Angola/Dem. Rep. Congo *see also* Cuango
Kwango *see* Cuango
Kwangsi/Kwangsi Chuang Autonomous Region *see* Guangxi Zhuangzu Zizhiqu
Kwangtung *see* Guangdong
Kwangyuan *see* Guangyuan
81 F17 **Kwania, Lake** ⊛ C Uganda
Kwanza *see* Cuanza
77 S15 **Kwara** ⬖ *state* SW Nigeria
83 K22 **KwaZulu/Natal** *off.* KwaZulu/Natal Province; *prev.* Natal. ⬖ *province* E South Africa
KwaZulu/Natal Province *see* KwaZulu/Natal
Kweichow *see* Guizhou
Kweichu *see* Guiyang
Kweilin *see* Guilin
Kweisui *see* Hohhot
Kweiyang *see* Guiyang
83 K17 **Kwekwe** *prev.* Que Que. Midlands, C Zimbabwe 18°56′S 29°49′E
83 G20 **Kweneng** ⬖ *district* S Botswana
Kwesui *see* Hohhot
39 N12 **Kwethluk** Alaska, USA 60°48′N 161°26′W
39 N12 **Kwethluk River** ≈ Alaska, USA
110 J8 **Kwidzyń** *Ger.* Marienwerder. Pomorskie, N Poland 53°44′N 18°55′E
38 M13 **Kwigillingok** Alaska, USA 59°52′N 163°08′W
186 E9 **Kwikila** Central, S Papua New Guinea 09°51′S 147°43′E
79 I20 **Kwilu** ≈ W Dem. Rep. Congo
Kwito *see* Cuito
171 U12 **Kwoka, Gunung** ▲ Papua, E Indonesia 0°34′S 132°25′E
78 I12 **Kyabé** Moyen-Chari, S Chad 09°28′N 18°54′E
183 O11 **Kyabram** Victoria, SE Australia 36°21′S 145°05′E
166 M9 **Kyaikkami** *prev.* Amherst. Mon State, S Burma (Myanmar) 16°03′N 97°36′E
166 L9 **Kyaiklat** Ayeyarwady, SW Burma (Myanmar) 16°25′N 95°42′E
166 M8 **Kyaikto** Mon State, S Burma (Myanmar) 17°16′N 97°01′E
123 N14 **Kyakhta** Respublika Buryatiya, S Russian Federation 50°25′N 106°13′E
182 G8 **Kyancutta** South Australia 33°10′S 135°33′E
167 T8 **Ky Anh** Ha Tinh, N Vietnam 18°05′N 106°16′E
166 L5 **Kyaukpadaung** Mandalay, C Burma (Myanmar) 20°50′N 95°08′E
Kyaukpyu *see* Kyaunkpyu
166 M5 **Kyaukse** Mandalay, C Burma (Myanmar) 21°33′N 96°06′E
166 L8 **Kyaunggon** Ayeyarwady, SW Burma (Myanmar) 17°04′N 95°12′E
166 J6 **Kyaunkpyu** *var.* Kyaukpyu. Rakhine State, W Burma (Myanmar) 19°27′N 93°33′E
119 E14 **Kybartai** *Pol.* Kibarty. Marijampolė, S Lithuania 54°37′N 22°44′E
152 I7 **Kyelang** Himāchal Pradesh, NW India 32°33′N 77°03′E
111 G19 **Kyjov** *Ger.* Gaya. Jihomoravský Kraj, SE Czech Republic 49°00′N 17°07′E
115 J21 **Kykládes** *var.* Kikládhes, *Eng.* Cyclades. *island group* SE Greece
25 S11 **Kyle** Texas, SW USA 29°59′N 97°52′W
96 G9 **Kyle of Lochalsh** N Scotland, United Kingdom 57°18′N 05°39′W
101 D18 **Kyll** ≈ W Germany
115 F19 **Kyllíni** *var.* Killini. ▲▲ S Greece
115 H18 **Kými** *prev.* Kími. Évvoia, C Greece 38°38′N 24°06′E
93 M19 **Kymijoki** ≈ S Finland
115 H18 **Kýmis, Akrotírio** *headland* Évvoia, C Greece 38°39′N 24°08′E
125 W14 **Kyn** Permskiy Kray, NW Russian Federation 57°48′N 58°38′E
183 N12 **Kyneton** Victoria, SE Australia 37°14′S 144°28′E
81 G17 **Kyoga, Lake** *var.* Lake Kioga. ⊛ C Uganda
164 J12 **Kyōga-misaki** *headland* Honshū, SW Japan 35°46′N 135°13′E
183 V4 **Kyogle** New South Wales, SE Australia 28°37′S 153°00′E
Kyŏnggi-man *see* Gyeonggi-man
Kyŏngju *see* Gyeongju
Kyŏngsŏng *see* Seoul
Kyōsai-tō *see* Geogeum-do
81 F19 **Kyotera** S Uganda 0°38′S 31°34′E
164 J13 **Kyōto** Kyōto, Honshū, SW Japan 35°01′N 135°46′E
164 J13 **Kyōto** *off.* Kyōto-fu, *var.* Kyōto Hu. ⬖ *urban prefecture* Honshū, SW Japan
Kyōto-fu/Kyōto Hu *see* Kyōto
115 D21 **Kyparissía** *var.* Kiparissía. Pelopónnisos, S Greece 37°15′N 21°40′E
115 D20 **Kyparissiakós Kólpos** *gulf* S Greece
Kyperounda *see* Kyperoúnta
121 P3 **Kyperoúnta** *var.* Kyperounda. C Cyprus 34°57′N 33°02′E
Kypros *see* Cyprus
115 H16 **Kyrá Panagía** *island* Vóreies Sporádes, Greece, Aegean Sea
Kyrenia *see* Girne
Kyrenia Mountains *see* Beşparmak Dağları
Kyrgyz Republic *see* Kyrgyzstan
147 U9 **Kyrgyzstan** *off.* Kyrgyz Republic, *var.* Kirghizia; *prev.* Kirgizskaya SSR, Kirghiz SSR, Republic of Kyrgyzstan. ◆ *republic* C Asia
Kyrgyzstan, Republic of *see* Kyrgyzstan
138 F11 **Kyriat Gat** *prev.* Qiryat Gat. Southern, C Israel 31°37′N 34°47′E
100 M11 **Kyritz** Brandenburg, NE Germany 52°56′N 12°24′E
94 G8 **Kyrkseterøra** Sør-Trøndelag, S Norway 63°17′N 09°06′E
Kyrkslätt *see* Kirkkonummi
125 U8 **Kyrta** Respublika Komi, NW Russian Federation 64°03′N 57°41′E
111 J18 **Kysucké Nové Mesto** *prev.* Horné Nové Mesto, *Ger.* Kisutzaneustadtl, Oberneustadtl, *Hung.* Kiszucaújhely. Zílinský Kraj, N Slovakia 49°18′N 18°48′E
117 N12 **Kytay, Ozero** ⊛ SW Ukraine
115 F23 **Kýthira** *var.* Kíthira, *It.* Cerigo, *Lat.* Cythera. Kńythira, S Greece 41°39′N 26°30′E
115 F23 **Kýthira** *var.* Kíthira, *It.* Cerigo, *Lat.* Cythera. *island* S Greece
115 I20 **Kýthnos** Kńythnos, Kykládes, Greece, Aegean Sea 37°24′N 24°28′E
115 I20 **Kýthnos** *var.* Kíthnos, Thermiá, *It.* Termia; *anc.* Cythnos. *island* Kykládes, Greece, Aegean Sea
115 I20 **Kýthnou, Stenó** *strait* Kykládes, Greece, Aegean Sea
Kyungëy Ala-Too, Khrebet *see* Kungei Ala-Tau
Kyurdamir *see* Kürdämir
164 D15 **Kyūshū** *var.* Kyûsyû. *island* SW Japan
192 H6 **Kyushu-Palau Ridge** *var.* Kyusyu-Palau Ridge. *undersea feature* W Pacific Ocean 20°00′N 136°00′E
114 F10 **Kyustendil** *anc.* Pautalia. Kyustendil, W Bulgaria 42°17′N 22°42′E
114 G11 **Kyustendil** ⬖ *province* W Bulgaria
Kyûsyû *see* Kyūshū
Kyusyu-Palau Ridge *see* Kyushu-Palau Ridge
123 P8 **Kyusyur** Respublika Sakha (Yakutiya), NE Russian Federation 70°36′N 127°19′E
183 P10 **Kywong** New South Wales, SE Australia 34°59′S 146°42′E
117 P4 **Kyyiv** *Eng.* Kiev, *Rus.* Kiyev. ● (Ukraine) Kyyivs'ka Oblast', N Ukraine 50°26′N 30°32′E
Kyyiv *see* Kyyivs'ka Oblast'
117 O4 **Kyyivs'ka Oblast'** *var.* Kyyiv, *Rus.* Kiyevskaya Oblast'. ⬖ *province* N Ukraine
117 P3 **Kyyivs'ke Vodoskhovyshche** *Eng.* Kiev Reservoir, *Rus.* Kiyevskoye Vodokhranilishche. ⊠ N Ukraine
93 L16 **Kyyjärvi** Länsi-Suomi, C Finland 63°02′N 24°34′E
122 K14 **Kyzyl** Respublika Tyva, C Russian Federation 51°45′N 94°28′E
147 S8 **Kyzyl-Adyr** *var.* Kirovskoye. Talasskaya Oblast', NW Kyrgyzstan 42°37′N 71°34′E
145 V14 **Kyzylagash** *Kaz.* Qyzylaghash. Almaty, SE Kazakhstan 45°20′N 78°45′E
146 C13 **Kyzylbair** Balkan Welaýaty, W Turkmenistan 38°13′N 55°38′E
Kyzyl-Dzhiik, Pereval *see* Uzbel Shankou
145 S7 **Kyzylkak, Ozero** ⊛ NE Kazakhstan
145 X11 **Kyzylkesek** Vostochnyy Kazakhstan, E Kazakhstan 47°56′N 82°02′E
147 S10 **Kyzyl-Kiya** *Kir.* Kyzyl-Kyya. Batkenskaya Oblast', SW Kyrgyzstan 40°15′N 72°07′E
144 L11 **Kyzylkol', Ozero** ⊛ C Kazakhstan
122 K14 **Kyzyl Kum** *var.* Kizil Kum, Qizil Qum, *Uzb.* Qizilqum. *desert* Kazakhstan/Uzbekistan
Kyzyl-Kyya *see* Kyzyl-Kiya
145 N15 **Kyzylorda** *var.* Kzyl-Orda, Qizil Orda, Qyzylorda; *prev.* Kzylorda, Perovsk. Kyzylorda, S Kazakhstan 44°54′N 65°31′E
144 L14 **Kyzylorda** *off.* Kyzylordinskaya Oblast', *Kaz.* Qyzylorda Oblysy. ⬖ *province* S Kazakhstan
Kyzylordinskaya Oblast' *see* Kyzylorda
Kyzylrabat *see* Qizilravote
Kyzylrabot *see* Qizilrabot
Kyzylsu *see* Kyzyl-Suu
147 X7 **Kyzyl-Suu** *prev.* Pokrovka. Issyk-Kul'skaya Oblast', NE Kyrgyzstan 42°20′N 77°55′E
147 S12 **Kyzyl-Suu** *var.* Kyzylsu. ≈ Kyrgyzstan/Tajikistan
147 X8 **Kyzyl-Tuu** Issyk-Kul'skaya Oblast', E Kyrgyzstan 42°06′N 76°54′E
145 Q12 **Kyzylzhar** *Kaz.* Qyzylzhar. Karaganda, C Kazakhstan 48°22′N 70°00′E
Kzyl-Orda *see* Kyzylorda
Kzylorda *see* Kyzylorda
Kzyltu *see* Kishkenekol'

L

109 X2 **Laa an der Thaya** Niederösterreich, NE Austria 48°44′N 16°23′E
63 K15 **La Adela** La Pampa, SE Argentina 38°57′S 64°02′W
Laagen *see* Numedalslågen
109 S5 **Laakirchen** Oberösterreich, N Austria 47°59′N 13°49′E
Laaland *see* Lolland
104 I11 **La Albuera** Extremadura, W Spain 38°43′N 06°49′W
105 O7 **La Alcarria** *physical region* C Spain
104 K14 **La Algaba** Andalucía, S Spain 37°27′N 06°01′W
105 P9 **La Almarcha** Castilla-La Mancha, C Spain 39°41′N 02°23′W
105 R6 **La Almunia de Doña Godina** Aragón, NE Spain 41°28′N 01°23′W
41 N5 **La Amistad, Presa** ⊠ NW Mexico
118 F4 **Läänemaa** *var.* Lääne Maakond. ⬖ *province* NW Estonia
Lääne Maakond *see* Läänemaa
118 I3 **Lääne-Virumaa** *off.* Lääne-Viru Maakond. ⬖ *province* NE Estonia
Lääne-Viru Maakond *see* Lääne-Virumaa
62 J9 **La Antigua, Salina** *salt lake* W Argentina
99 E17 **Laarne** Oost-Vlaanderen, NW Belgium 51°03′N 03°50′E
80 O13 **Laas Caanood** Sool, N Somalia 08°33′N 47°44′E
41 O9 **La Ascensión** Nuevo León, NE Mexico 24°15′N 99°53′W
80 N12 **Laas Dhaareed** Togdheer, N Somalia 10°12′N 46°09′E
55 O4 **La Asunción** Nueva Esparta, NE Venezuela 11°06′N 63°53′W
Laatokka *see* Ladozhskoye, Ozero
100 I13 **Laatzen** Niedersachsen, NW Germany 52°19′N 09°46′E
38 E9 **La'au Point** *var.* Laau Point. *headland* Moloka'i, Hawai'i, USA 21°06′N 157°18′W
Laau Point *see* La'au Point
42 D6 **La Aurora** ✈ (Ciudad de Guatemala) Guatemala, C Guatemala 14°33′N 90°30′W
74 C9 **Laâyoune** *var.* Aaiún. ● (Western Sahara) NW Western Sahara 27°10′N 13°11′W
126 L14 **Laba** ≈ SW Russian Federation
40 M6 **La Babia** Coahuila, NE Mexico 28°39′N 102°00′W
15 R7 **La Baie** Québec, SE Canada 48°20′N 70°54′W
171 P16 **Labala** Pulau Lomblen, S Indonesia 08°30′S 123°27′E
62 K8 **La Banda** Santiago del Estero, N Argentina 27°44′S 64°14′W
La Banda Oriental *see* Uruguay
104 K4 **La Bañeza** Castilla y León, N Spain 42°18′N 05°54′W
167 T11 **Labăng** *prev.* Phumĭ Labăng. Rôtânôkiri, NE Cambodia 13°51′N 107°01′E
40 M13 **La Barca** Jalisco, SW Mexico 20°20′N 102°33′W
40 K14 **La Barra de Navidad** Jalisco, C Mexico 19°12′N 104°38′W
187 Y13 **Labasa** *prev.* Lambasa. Vanua Levu, N Fiji 16°25′S 179°24′E
102 H8 **la Baule-Escoublac** Loire-Atlantique, NW France 47°17′N 02°24′W
76 I13 **Labé** NW Guinea 11°19′N 12°17′W
Labe *see* Elbe
15 N11 **Labelle** Québec, SE Canada 46°15′N 74°43′W
23 X14 **La Belle** Florida, SE USA 26°45′N 81°26′W
10 H7 **Laberge, Lake** ⊛ Yukon Territory, W Canada
Labes *see* Łobez
Labiau *see* Polessk
112 A10 **Labin** *It.* Albona. Istra, NW Croatia 45°05′N 14°10′E
126 L14 **Labinsk** Krasnodarskiy Kray, SW Russian Federation 44°39′N 40°43′E
105 X5 **La Bisbal d'Empordà** Cataluña, NE Spain 41°58′N 03°02′E
119 P16 **Labkovichy** *Rus.* Lobkovichi. Mahilyowskaya Voblasts', E Belarus 53°50′N 31°45′E
15 S4 **La Blache, Lac de** ⊛ Québec, SE Canada
171 P4 **Labo** Luzon, N Philippines 14°10′N 122°47′E
Laboehanbadjo *see* Labuhanbajo
Laborca *see* Laborec
111 N18 **Laborec** *Hung.* Laborca. ≈ E Slovakia
108 D11 **La Borgne** ≈ S Switzerland
45 T12 **Laborie** SW Saint Lucia 13°45′N 61°00′W
102 J14 **Labouheyre** Landes, SW France 44°12′N 00°55′W
62 L12 **Laboulaye** Córdoba, C Argentina 34°05′S 63°20′W
13 Q7 **Labrador** *cultural region* Newfoundland and Labrador, SW Canada
64 I6 **Labrador Basin** *var.* Labrador Sea Basin. *undersea feature* Labrador Sea 53°00′N 48°00′W
13 N9 **Labrador City** Newfoundland and Labrador, E Canada 52°56′N 66°52′W
13 Q5 **Labrador Sea** *sea* NW Atlantic Ocean
Labrador Sea Basin *see* Labrador Basin
Labrang *see* Xiahe
54 G9 **Labranzagrande** Boyacá, C Colombia 05°34′N 72°34′W
59 D14 **Lábrea** Amazonas, N Brazil 07°20′S 64°46′W
45 U15 **La Brea** Trinidad, Trinidad and Tobago 10°14′N 61°37′W
15 S6 **Labrieville** Québec, SE Canada 49°15′N 69°31′W
102 K14 **Labrit** Landes, SW France 44°03′N 00°29′W
108 C9 **La Broye** ≈ SW Switzerland
103 N15 **Labruguière** Tarn, S France 43°32′N 02°15′E
168 M11 **Labu** Pulau Singkep, W Indonesia 0°34′S 104°24′E
169 T7 **Labuan** *var.* Victoria. Labuan, East Malaysia 05°20′N 115°14′E
169 T7 **Labuan** ⬖ *federal territory* East Malaysia
Labuan *see* Labuan, Pulau
169 T7 **Labuan, Pulau** *var.* Labuan. *island* East Malaysia
Labudalin *see* Ergun
171 N16 **Labuhanbajo** *prev.* Laboehanbadjo. Flores, S Indonesia 08°33′S 119°55′E
168 J9 **Labuhanbilik** Sumatera, N Indonesia 02°30′N 100°10′E
168 G8 **Labuhanhaji** Sumatera, W Indonesia 03°31′N 97°00′E
Labuk *see* Labuk, Sungai
Labuk Bay *see* Labuk, Teluk
169 V7 **Labuk, Sungai** *var.* Labuk. ≈ East Malaysia
169 W6 **Labuk, Teluk** *var.* Labuk Bay, Telukan Labuk. *bay* S Sulu Sea
Labuk, Telukan *see* Labuk, Teluk
166 K9 **Labutta** Ayeyarwady, SW Burma (Myanmar) 16°08′N 94°45′E
122 I8 **Labytnangi** Yamalo-Nenetskiy Avtonomnyy Okrug, N Russian Federation 66°39′N 66°26′E
113 K19 **Laç** *var.* Laci. Lezhë, C Albania 41°37′N 19°37′E
78 F10 **Lac** *off.* Préfecture du Lac. ⬖ *prefecture* W Chad
57 K19 **Lacajahuira, Rio** ≈ W Bolivia
La Calamine *see* Kelmis
62 G11 **La Calera** Valparaíso, C Chile 32°47′S 71°16′W
13 P11 **Lac-Allard** Québec, E Canada 50°37′N 63°26′W
104 L13 **La Campana** Andalucía, S Spain 37°35′N 05°24′W
102 J12 **Lacanau** Gironde, SW France 44°59′N 01°04′W
42 C2 **Lacandón, Sierra del** ▲▲ Guatemala/Mexico
La Cañiza *see* A Cañiza
41 W16 **Lacantún, Río** ≈ SE Mexico
103 Q3 **la Capelle** Aisne, N France 49°58′N 03°55′E
112 K10 **Laćarak** Vojvodina, NW Serbia 45°00′N 19°34′E
62 L11 **La Carlota** Córdoba, C Argentina 33°30′S 63°15′W
104 L13 **La Carlota** Andalucía, S Spain 37°40′N 04°56′W
105 N12 **La Carolina** Andalucía, S Spain 38°15′N 03°37′W
103 O15 **Lacaune** Tarn, S France 43°42′N 02°42′E
15 P7 **Lac-Bouchette** Québec, SE Canada 48°14′N 72°11′W
Laccadive Islands/Laccadive Minicoy and Amindivi Islands, the *see* Lakshadweep
11 Y16 **Lac du Bonnet** Manitoba, S Canada 50°13′N 96°04′W
30 L4 **Lac du Flambeau** Wisconsin, N USA 45°58′N 89°51′W
15 P8 **Lac-Édouard** Québec, SE Canada 47°39′N 72°16′W
42 I4 **La Ceiba** Atlántida, N Honduras 15°45′N 86°29′W
54 E9 **La Ceja** Antioquia, W Colombia 06°02′N 75°30′W
182 J11 **Lacepede Bay** *bay* South Australia
32 G9 **Lacey** Washington, NW USA 47°01′N 122°49′W
103 P12 **la Chaise-Dieu** Haute-Loire, C France 45°19′N 03°41′E
114 G13 **Lachanás** Kentrikí Makedonía, N Greece 40°57′N 23°15′E
124 L11 **Lacha, Ozero** ⊛ NW Russian Federation
103 O8 **la Charité-sur-Loire** Nièvre, C France 47°10′N 02°59′E
103 N9 **la Châtre** Indre, C France 46°35′N 01°59′E
108 C8 **La Chaux-de-Fonds** Neuchâtel, W Switzerland 47°07′N 06°51′E
Lach Dera *see* Dheere Laaq
108 G8 **Lachen** Schwyz, C Switzerland 47°12′N 08°51′E
183 Q8 **Lachlan River** ≈ New South Wales, SE Australia
43 T15 **La Chorrera** Panamá, C Panama 08°51′N 79°46′W
15 V7 **Lac-Humqui** Québec, SE Canada 48°21′N 67°32′W
15 N12 **Lachute** Québec, SE Canada 45°39′N 74°21′W
Lachyn *see* Laçın
Laci *see* Laç
137 W13 **Laçın** *Rus.* Lachyn. SW Azerbaijan 39°36′N 46°34′E
103 S16 **la Ciotat** *anc.* Citharista. Bouches-du-Rhône, SE France 43°10′N 05°36′E
18 D10 **Lackawanna** New York, NE USA 42°49′N 78°49′W
11 Q13 **Lac La Biche** Alberta, SW Canada 54°46′N 111°59′W
Lac la Martre *see* Wha Ti
15 R12 **Lac-Mégantic** *var.* Mégantic. Québec, SE Canada 45°35′N 70°53′W
Lacobriga *see* Lagos
40 G5 **La Colorada** Sonora, NW Mexico 28°49′N 110°32′W
11 Q15 **Lacombe** Alberta, SW Canada 52°30′N 113°42′W
30 L12 **Lacon** Illinois, N USA 41°01′N 89°24′W
43 P16 **La Concepción** *var.* Concepción. Chiriquí, W Panama 08°31′N 82°39′W
54 H5 **La Concepción** Zulia, NW Venezuela 10°48′N 71°46′W
107 C19 **Laconi** Sardegna, Italy, C Mediterranean Sea 39°52′N 09°02′E
19 O9 **Laconia** New Hampshire, NE USA 43°32′N 71°29′W
61 H19 **La Coronilla** Rocha, E Uruguay 33°44′S 53°31′W
La Coruña *see* A Coruña
103 O11 **la Courtine** Creuse, C France 45°42′N 02°18′E
Lac, Préfecture du *see* Lac
102 J16 **Lacq** Pyrénées-Atlantiques, SW France 43°25′N 00°37′W
15 P9 **La Croche** Québec, SE Canada 47°38′N 72°42′W
29 X3 **la Croix, Lac** ⊛ Canada/USA
26 K5 **La Crosse** Kansas, C USA 38°32′N 99°19′W
21 V7 **La Crosse** Virginia, NE USA 36°41′N 78°03′W
32 L9 **La Crosse** Washington, NW USA 46°48′N 117°51′W
30 J7 **La Crosse** Wisconsin, N USA 43°46′N 91°12′W
54 C13 **La Cruz** Nariño, SW Colombia 01°33′N 76°58′W
42 K12 **La Cruz** Guanacaste, NW Costa Rica 11°05′N 85°39′W
40 I10 **La Cruz** Sinaloa, W Mexico 23°53′N 106°53′W
61 F19 **La Cruz** Florida, S Uruguay 33°54′S 56°11′W
42 M9 **La Cruz de Río Grande** Región Autónoma Atlántico Sur, E Nicaragua 13°04′N 84°12′W
54 J4 **La Cruz de Taratara** Falcón, N Venezuela 11°03′N 69°44′W
15 Q10 **Lac-St-Charles** Québec, SE Canada 46°56′N 71°24′W
40 M6 **La Cuesta** Coahuila, NE Mexico 28°45′N 102°26′W
57 A17 **La Cumbra, Volcán** Ѫ Galapagos Islands, Ecuador, E Pacific Ocean 0°21′S 91°30′W
152 J5 **Ladākh Range** ▲▲ NE India
26 I5 **Ladder Creek** ≈ Kansas, C USA
45 X10 **la Désirade** *atoll* E Guadeloupe
Lādhiqīyah, Muḩāfaẓat al *see* Al Lādhiqīyah
Lådik *see* Lødingen
83 F25 **Ladismith** Western Cape, SW South Africa 33°30′S 12°15′E
152 G11 **Lādnūn** Rājasthān, NW India 27°36′N 74°26′E
Ladoga, Lake *see* Ladozhskoye, Ozero
115 E19 **Ládon** ≈ S Greece
54 E9 **La Dorada** Caldas, C Colombia 05°28′N 74°41′W
124 H11 **Ladozhskoye, Ozero** *Eng.* Lake Ladoga, *Fin.* Laatokka. ⊛ NW Russian Federation
37 R12 **Ladron Peak** ▲ New Mexico, SW USA 34°25′N 107°04′W
124 J11 **Ladva-Vetka** Respublika Kareliya, NW Russian Federation 61°18′N 34°24′E
183 Q15 **Lady Barron** Tasmania, SE Australia 40°12′S 148°12′E
14 G9 **Lady Evelyn Lake** ⊛ Ontario, S Canada
23 W11 **Lady Lake** Florida, SE USA 28°55′N 81°55′W
10 L17 **Ladysmith** Vancouver Island, British Columbia, SW Canada 48°55′N 123°45′W

◆ Country
● Country Capital
◇ Dependent Territory
○ Dependent Territory Capital
⬖ Administrative Regions
✈ International Airport
▲ Mountain
▲▲ Mountain Range
Ѫ Volcano
≈ River
⊛ Lake
⊠ Reservoir

83 *J22* **Ladysmith** KwaZulu/Natal, E South Africa *28°34′S 29°47′E*
30 *J5* **Ladysmith** Wisconsin, N USA *45°27′N 91°07′W*
Ladyzhenka *see* Tilekey
186 *E7* **Lae** Morobe, W Papua New Guinea *06°45′S 147°00′E*
189 *R6* **Lae Atoll** *atoll* Ralik Chain, W Marshall Islands
40 *C3* **La Encantada, Cerro de** ▲ NW Mexico *31°03′N 115°25′W*
55 *N11* **La Esmeralda** Amazonas, S Venezuela *03°11′N 65°33′W*
42 *G7* **La Esperanza** Intibucá, SW Honduras *14°19′N 88°09′W*
30 *K8* **La Farge** Wisconsin, N USA *43°36′N 90°39′W*
23 *R5* **Lafayette** Alabama, S USA *32°54′N 85°24′W*
37 *T4* **Lafayette** Colorado, C USA *39°59′N 105°06′W*
23 *R2* **La Fayette** Georgia, SE USA *34°42′N 85°16′W*
31 *O13* **Lafayette** Indiana, N USA *40°25′N 86°52′W*
22 *I9* **Lafayette** Louisiana, S USA *30°13′N 92°01′W*
20 *K8* **Lafayette** Tennessee, S USA *36°31′N 86°01′W*
19 *N7* **Lafayette, Mount** ▲ New Hampshire, NE USA *44°09′N 71°37′W*
La Fe *see* Santa Fé
103 *P3* **la Fère** Aisne, N France *49°41′N 03°20′E*
102 *L6* **la Ferté-Bernard** Sarthe, NW France *48°13′N 00°40′E*
102 *K5* **la Ferté-Macé** Orne, N France *48°35′N 00°21′W*
103 *N7* **la Ferté-St-Aubin** Loiret, C France *47°42′N 01°57′E*
103 *P5* **la Ferté-sous-Jouarre** Seine-et-Marne, N France *48°57′N 03°08′E*
77 *V15* **Lafia** Nassarawa, C Nigeria *08°29′N 08°34′E*
77 *T15* **Lafiagi** Kwara, W Nigeria *08°52′N 05°25′E*
11 *T17* **Lafleche** Saskatchewan, S Canada *49°40′N 106°28′W*
102 *K7* **la Flèche** Sarthe, NW France *47°42′N 00°04′W*
109 *X7* **Lafnitz** ***Hung.*** Lapines. ≋ Austria/Hungary
187 *P17* **La Foa** Province Sud, S New Caledonia *21°46′S 165°49′E*
20 *M8* **La Follette** Tennessee, S USA *36°22′N 84°07′W*
15 *N12* **Lafontaine** Québec, SE Canada *45°52′N 74°01′W*
22 *K10* **Lafourche, Bayou** ≋ Louisiana, S USA
62 *K6* **La Fragua** Santiago del Estero, N Argentina *26°06′S 64°06′W*
54 *H7* **La Fría** Táchira, NW Venezuela *08°13′N 72°15′W*
104 *J7* **La Fuente de San Esteban** Castilla y León, N Spain *40°48′N 06°14′W*
186 *C7* **Lagaip** ≋ W Papua New Guinea
61 *B15* **La Gallareta** Santa Fe, C Argentina *29°34′S 60°23′W*
127 *Q14* **Lagan'** ***prev.*** Kaspiyskiy. Respublika Kalmykiya, SW Russian Federation *45°25′N 47°19′E*
95 *L20* **Lagan** Kronoberg, S Sweden *56°55′N 14°01′E*
95 *K21* **Lågan** ≋ S Sweden
92 *L2* **Lagarfljót** ***var.*** Lögurinn. ◎ E Iceland
37 *R7* **La Garita Mountains** ▲▲ Colorado, C USA
171 *O2* **Lagawe** Luzon, N Philippines *16°46′N 121°06′E*
78 *F13* **Lagdo** Nord, N Cameroon *09°12′N 13°43′E*
78 *F13* **Lagdo, Lac de** ◎ N Cameroon
100 *H13* **Lage** Nordrhein-Westfalen, W Germany *52°00′N 08°48′E*
94 *H12* **Lågen** ≋ S Norway
61 *J14* **Lages** Santa Catarina, S Brazil *27°45′S 50°16′W*
Lágesvuotna *see* Laksefjorden
149 *R4* **Laghmān** ◈ *province* E Afghanistan
74 *J6* **Laghouat** N Algeria *33°49′N 02°59′E*
105 *Q10* **La Gineta** Castilla-La Mancha, C Spain *39°08′N 02°00′W*
115 *E21* **Lagkáda** ***var.*** Langada. Pelopónnisos, S Greece *36°49′N 22°19′E*
114 *G13* **Lagkadás** ***var.*** Langades, Langadhás. Kentrikí Makedonía, N Greece *40°45′N 23°04′E*
115 *E20* **Lagkádia** ***var.*** Langádhia, ***cont.*** Langadia. Pelopónnisos, S Greece *37°40′N 22°01′E*
54 *F6* **La Gloria** Cesar, N Colombia *08°37′N 73°51′W*
41 *O7* **La Gloria** Nuevo León, NE Mexico
92 *N3* **Lågneset** *headland* W Svalbard *77°46′N 13°44′E*
104 *G14* **Lagoa** Faro, S Portugal *37°07′N 08°27′W*
La Goagira *see* La Guajira
Lago Agrio *see* Nueva Loja
61 *I14* **Lagoa Vermelha** Rio Grande do Sul, S Brazil *28°13′S 51°32′W*
137 *V10* **Lagodekhi** SE Georgia *41°49′N 46°15′E*
42 *C7* **La Gomera** Escuintla, S Guatemala *14°05′N 91°03′W*
Lagone *see* Logone
107 *M19* **Lagonegro** Basilicata, S Italy *40°06′N 15°42′E*
63 *G16* **Lago Ranco** Los Ríos, S Chile *40°21′S 72°29′W*
77 *S16* **Lagos** Lagos, SW Nigeria *06°24′N 03°17′E*
104 *F14* **Lagos** ***anc.*** Lacobriga. Faro, S Portugal *37°05′N 08°40′W*
77 *S16* **Lagos** ◈ *state* SW Nigeria
40 *M12* **Lagos de Moreno** Jalisco, SW Mexico *21°21′N 101°55′W*
Lagosta *see* Lastovo
74 *A12* **Lagouira** SW Western Sahara *20°55′N 17°05′W*
92 *O1* **Lågøya** *island* N Svalbard
32 *L11* **La Grande** Oregon, NW USA *45°21′N 118°05′W*
103 *Q14* **la Grande-Combe** Gard, S France *44°13′N 04°01′E*
12 *K9* **La Grande Rivière** ***var.*** Fort George. ≋ Québec, SE Canada
23 *R4* **La Grange** Georgia, SE USA *33°02′N 85°02′W*
31 *P11* **Lagrange** Indiana, N USA *41°38′N 85°25′W*
20 *L5* **La Grange** Kentucky, S USA *38°24′N 85°23′W*
27 *V2* **La Grange** Missouri, C USA *40°00′N 91°31′W*
21 *V10* **La Grange** North Carolina, SE USA *35°18′N 77°47′W*
25 *U11* **La Grange** Texas, SW USA *29°55′N 96°54′W*
105 *N7* **La Granja** Castilla y León, N Spain *40°53′N 04°01′W*
55 *Q9* **La Gran Sabana** *grassland* E Venezuela
54 *H7* **La Grita** Táchira, NW Venezuela *08°09′N 71°58′W*
La Grulla *see* Grulla
15 *R11* **La Guadeloupe** Québec, SE Canada *45°57′N 70°56′W*
65 *L6* **La Guaira** Distrito Federal, N Venezuela *10°35′N 66°52′W*
54 *G4* **La Guajira** ***off.*** Departamento de La Guajira, ***var.*** Guajira, La Goagira. ◈ *province* NE Colombia
188 *I4* **Lagua Lichan, Punta** *headland* Saipan, S Northern Mariana Islands
105 *P4* **Laguardia** ***Basq.*** Biasteri. País Vasco, N Spain *42°32′N 02°31′W*
18 *K14* **La Guardia** ✈ (New York) Long Island, New York, NE USA *40°44′N 73°51′W*
La Guardia/Laguardia *see* A Guarda
La Gudiña *see* A Gudiña
103 *O9* **la Guerche-sur-l'Aubois** Cher, C France *46°55′N 03°00′E*
103 *O13* **Laguiole** Aveyron, S France *44°42′N 02°51′E*
83 *F26* **L'Agulhas** ***var.*** Agulhas. Western Cape, SW South Africa *34°49′S 20°01′E*
61 *K14* **Laguna** Santa Catarina, S Brazil *28°29′S 48°45′W*
37 *Q11* **Laguna** New Mexico, SW USA *35°03′N 107°30′W*
35 *T16* **Laguna Beach** California, W USA *33°32′N 117°46′W*
35 *Y17* **Laguna Dam** *dam* Arizona/California, W USA
40 *L7* **Laguna El Rey** Coahuila, N Mexico
35 *V17* **Laguna Mountains** ▲▲ California, W USA
61 *B17* **Laguna Paiva** Santa Fe, C Argentina *31°21′S 60°40′W*
62 *H3* **Lagunas** Tarapacá, N Chile *21°01′S 69°36′W*
56 *E9* **Lagunas** Loreto, N Peru *05°15′S 75°24′W*
57 *M20* **Lagunillas** Santa Cruz, SE Bolivia *19°38′S 63°39′W*
54 *H6* **Lagunillas** Mérida, NW Venezuela *08°31′N 71°24′W*
44 *C4* **La Habana** ***var.*** Havana. ● (Cuba) Ciudad de La Habana, W Cuba *23°07′N 82°25′W*
169 *W7* **Lahad Datu** Sabah, East Malaysia *05°01′N 118°20′E*
169 *W7* **Lahad Datu, Teluk** ***var.*** Telukan Lahad Datu, Teluk Darvel, Teluk Datu; ***prev.*** Darvel Bay. *bay* Sabah, East Malaysia, C Pacific Ocean
Lahad Datu, Telukan *see* Lahad Datu, Teluk
38 *F10* **Lahaina** Maui, Hawaii, USA, C Pacific Ocean *20°52′N 156°40′W*
168 *L14* **Lahat** Sumatera, W Indonesia *03°46′S 103°32′E*
La Haye *see* 's-Gravenhage
Lahej *see* Laḩij
62 *G9* **La Higuera** Coquimbo, N Chile *29°33′S 71°15′W*
141 *S13* **Lahī, Ḩisā' al** *spring/well* NE Yemen *17°28′N 50°05′E*
141 *O16* **Laḩij** ***var.*** Laḩj, ***Eng.*** Lahej. SW Yemen *13°04′N 44°55′E*
142 *M3* **Lāhījān** Gīlān, NW Iran *37°12′N 50°00′E*
119 *I19* **Lahishyn** ***Pol.*** Lohiszyn, ***Rus.*** Logishin. Brestskaya Voblasts', SW Belarus *52°20′N 25°59′E*
Laḩj *see* Laḩij
101 *F18* **Lahn** ≋ W Germany
Lähn *see* Wleń
95 *J21* **Laholm** Halland, S Sweden *56°30′N 13°05′E*
95 *J21* **Laholmsbukten** *bay* S Sweden
35 *R6* **Lahontan Reservoir** ⊠ Nevada, W USA
149 *W8* **Lahore** Punjab, NE Pakistan *31°36′N 74°18′E*
149 *W8* **Lahore** ✈ Punjab, E Pakistan *31°34′N 74°22′E*
55 *Q6* **La Horqueta** Delta Amacuro, NE Venezuela *09°13′N 62°02′W*
119 *K15* **Lahoysk** ***Rus.*** Logoysk. Minskaya Voblasts', C Belarus *54°12′N 27°53′E*
101 *F22* **Lahr** Baden-Württemberg, S Germany *48°21′N 07°52′E*
93 *M19* **Lahti** ***Swe.*** Lahtis. Etelä-Suomi, S Finland *61°N 25°40′E*
Lahtis *see* Lahti
40 *M14* **La Huacana** Michoacán, SW Mexico *18°56′N 101°52′W*
40 *K14* **La Huerta** Jalisco, SW Mexico *19°29′N 104°40′W*
78 *H12* **Laï** ***prev.*** Behagle, De Behagle. Tandjilé, S Chad *09°22′N 16°14′E*
Laibach *see* Ljubljana
167 *Q5* **Lai Châu** Lai Châu, N Vietnam *22°04′N 103°10′E*
Laichow Bay *see* Laizhou Wan
38 *D9* **Lā'ie** ***var.*** Laie. O'ahu, Hawaii, USA, C Pacific Ocean *21°39′N 157°55′W*
Laie *see* Lā'ie
102 *L5* **l'Aigle** Orne, N France *48°46′N 00°37′E*
103 *Q7* **Laignes** Côte d'Or, C France *47°51′N 04°24′E*
93 *K17* **Laihia** Länsi-Suomi, W Finland *62°58′N 22°00′E*
Laila *see* Laylā
83 *F25* **Laingsburg** Western Cape, SW South Africa *33°12′S 20°51′E*
109 *U2* **Lainsitz** ***Cz.*** Lužnice. ≋ Austria/Czech Republic
96 *I7* **Lairg** N Scotland, United Kingdom *58°02′N 04°23′W*
81 *I17* **Laisamis** Eastern, N Kenya *01°35′N 37°49′E*
Laisberg *see* Leisi
127 *R4* **Laishevo** Respublika Tatarstan, W Russian Federation *55°26′N 49°27′E*
Laisholm *see* Jõgeva
92 *H13* **Laisvall** Norrbotten, N Sweden *66°07′N 17°10′E*
93 *K19* **Laitila** Länsi-Suomi, SW Finland *60°52′N 21°40′E*
161 *P5* **Laiwu** Shandong, E China *36°14′N 117°40′E*
161 *R4* **Laixi** ***var.*** Shuiji. Shandong, E China *36°50′N 120°40′E*
161 *R4* **Laiyang** Shandong, E China *36°58′N 120°40′E*
161 *O3* **Laiyuan** Hebei, E China *39°19′N 114°44′E*
161 *R4* **Laizhou** ***var.*** Ye Xian. Shandong, E China *37°12′N 120°01′E*
161 *Q4* **Laizhou Wan** ***var.*** Laichow Bay. *bay* E China
37 *S8* **La Jara** Colorado, C USA *37°16′N 105°57′W*
61 *I15* **Lajeado** Rio Grande do Sul, S Brazil *29°28′S 52°00′W*
112 *L12* **Lajkovac** Serbia, C Serbia *44°22′N 20°12′E*
111 *K23* **Lajosmizse** Bács-Kiskun, C Hungary *47°02′N 19°31′E*
Lajta *see* Leitha
40 *I6* **La Junta** Chihuahua, N Mexico *28°30′N 107°20′W*
37 *V7* **La Junta** Colorado, C USA *37°59′N 103°34′W*
92 *J13* **Lakaträsk** Norrbotten, N Sweden *66°16′N 21°10′E*
Lak Dera *see* Dheere Laaq
Lakeamu *see* Lakekamu
29 *P12* **Lake Andes** South Dakota, N USA *43°08′N 98°33′W*
22 *H9* **Lake Arthur** Louisiana, S USA *30°04′N 92°40′W*
187 *Z15* **Lakeba** ***prev.*** Lakemba. *island* Lau Group, E Fiji
187 *Z14* **Lakeba Passage** *channel* E Fiji
29 *S10* **Lake Benton** Minnesota, N USA *44°15′N 96°17′W*
23 *V9* **Lake Butler** Florida, SE USA *30°01′N 82°20′W*
183 *P8* **Lake Cargelligo** New South Wales, SE Australia *33°21′S 146°25′E*
22 *G9* **Lake Charles** Louisiana, S USA *30°14′N 93°13′W*
27 *X9* **Lake City** Arkansas, C USA *35°50′N 90°28′W*
37 *Q7* **Lake City** Colorado, C USA *38°01′N 107°18′W*
23 *V9* **Lake City** Florida, SE USA *30°12′N 82°39′W*
29 *U13* **Lake City** Iowa, C USA *42°16′N 94°43′W*
31 *P7* **Lake City** Michigan, N USA *44°22′N 85°12′W*
29 *W9* **Lake City** Minnesota, N USA *44°27′N 92°16′W*
21 *T13* **Lake City** South Carolina, SE USA *33°52′N 79°45′W*
29 *Q7* **Lake City** South Dakota, N USA *45°42′N 97°22′W*
20 *M8* **Lake City** Tennessee, S USA *36°13′N 84°09′W*
10 *L17* **Lake Cowichan** Vancouver Island, British Columbia, SW Canada *48°50′N 124°04′W*
29 *U10* **Lake Crystal** Minnesota, N USA *44°07′N 94°13′W*
25 *T6* **Lake Dallas** Texas, SW USA *33°06′N 97°01′W*
97 *K15* **Lake District** *physical region* NW England, United Kingdom
18 *D10* **Lake Erie Beach** New York, NE USA *42°37′N 79°04′W*
29 *T11* **Lakefield** Minnesota, N USA *43°40′N 95°10′W*
25 *V6* **Lake Fork Reservoir** ◎ Texas, SW USA
30 *M9* **Lake Geneva** Wisconsin, N USA *42°36′N 88°25′W*
18 *L9* **Lake George** New York, NE USA *43°25′N 73°45′W*
Lake Harbour *see* Kimmirut
36 *I12* **Lake Havasu City** Arizona, SW USA *34°26′N 114°20′W*
25 *W12* **Lake Jackson** Texas, SW USA *29°01′N 95°25′W*
186 *D8* **Lakekamu** ***var.*** Lakeamu. ≋ S Papua New Guinea
180 *K13* **Lake King** Western Australia *33°09′S 119°46′E*
23 *V12* **Lakeland** Florida, SE USA *28°03′N 81°57′W*
23 *U7* **Lakeland** Georgia, SE USA *31°02′N 83°04′W*
181 *W4* **Lakeland Downs** Queensland, NE Australia *15°54′S 144°54′E*
11 *P16* **Lake Louise** Alberta, SW Canada *51°26′N 116°10′W*
Lakemba *see* Lakeba
29 *V11* **Lake Mills** Iowa, C USA *43°25′N 93°31′W*
39 *Q10* **Lake Minchumina** Alaska, USA *63°55′N 152°25′W*
Lakemti *see* Nek'emtē
186 *A7* **Lake Murray** Western, SW Papua New Guinea *06°35′S 141°28′E*
31 *R9* **Lake Orion** Michigan, N USA *42°46′N 83°14′W*
190 *B16* **Lakepa** NE Niue *18°59′S 169°48′E*
29 *T11* **Lake Park** Iowa, C USA *43°27′N 95°19′W*
18 *K7* **Lake Placid** New York, NE USA *44°16′N 73°57′W*
18 *K9* **Lake Pleasant** New York, NE USA *43°27′N 74°24′W*
34 *M6* **Lakeport** California, W USA *39°04′N 122°56′W*
29 *Q10* **Lake Preston** South Dakota, N USA *44°21′N 97°22′W*
22 *J5* **Lake Providence** Louisiana, S USA *32°48′N 91°10′W*
185 *E20* **Lake Pukaki** Canterbury, South Island, New Zealand *44°12′S 170°10′E*
183 *Q12* **Lakes Entrance** Victoria, SE Australia *37°52′S 147°58′E*
37 *N12* **Lakeside** Arizona, SW USA *34°09′N 109°58′W*
35 *V17* **Lakeside** California, W USA *32°50′N 116°55′W*
23 *S9* **Lakeside** Florida, SE USA *30°22′N 84°18′W*
28 *K13* **Lakeside** Nebraska, C USA *42°01′N 102°27′W*
32 *E13* **Lakeside** Oregon, NW USA *43°34′N 124°10′W*
21 *W6* **Lakeside** Virginia, NE USA *37°36′N 77°28′W*
Lakes State *see* El Buhayrat
Lake State *see* Michigan
185 *F20* **Lake Tekapo** Canterbury, South Island, New Zealand *44°01′S 170°29′E*
21 *O10* **Lake Toxaway** North Carolina, SE USA *35°06′N 82°57′W*
29 *T13* **Lake View** Iowa, C USA *42°18′N 95°04′W*
32 *I16* **Lakeview** Oregon, NW USA *42°13′N 120°21′W*
25 *O3* **Lakeview** Texas, SW USA *34°38′N 100°36′W*
27 *W14* **Lake Village** Arkansas, C USA *33°20′N 91°19′W*
23 *W12* **Lake Wales** Florida, SE USA *27°54′N 81°35′W*
37 *T4* **Lakewood** Colorado, C USA *39°38′N 105°07′W*
18 *K15* **Lakewood** New Jersey, NE USA *40°04′N 74°11′W*
18 *C11* **Lakewood** New York, NE USA *42°03′N 79°19′W*
31 *T11* **Lakewood** Ohio, N USA *41°28′N 81°48′W*
23 *Y13* **Lakewood Park** Florida, SE USA *27°32′N 80°24′W*
23 *Z14* **Lake Worth** Florida, SE USA *26°37′N 80°03′W*
124 *H11* **Lakhdenpokh'ya** Respublika Kareliya, NW Russian Federation *61°25′N 30°05′E*
152 *L11* **Lakhīmpur** Uttar Pradesh, N India *27°57′N 80°47′E*
154 *J11* **Lakhnādon** Madhya Pradesh, C India *22°34′N 79° 38′E*
Lakhnau *see* Lucknow
154 *A9* **Lakhpat** Gujarāt, W India *23°49′N 68°54′E*
119 *K19* **Lakhva** Brestskaya Voblasts', SW Belarus *52°13′N 27°06′E*
26 *I6* **Lakin** Kansas, C USA *37°57′N 101°16′W*
149 *S7* **Lakki** ***var.*** Lakki Marwat. Khyber Pakhtunkhwa, NW Pakistan *32°35′N 70°58′E*
Lakki Marwat *see* Lakki
115 *F21* **Lakonía** *historical region* S Greece
115 *F22* **Lakonikós Kólpos** *gulf* S Greece
76 *M17* **Lakota** S Ivory Coast *05°50′N 05°40′W*
29 *U11* **Lakota** Iowa, C USA *43°22′N 94°04′W*
29 *P3* **Lakota** North Dakota, N USA *48°02′N 98°20′W*
Lak Sao *see* Ban Lakxao
92 *L8* **Laksefjorden** ***Lapp.*** Lágesvuotna. *fjord* N Norway
92 *K8* **Lakselv** ***Lapp.*** Leavdnja. Finnmark, N Norway *70°02′N 24°57′E*
155 *B21* **Lakshadweep** ***prev.*** the Laccadive Minicoy and Amindivi Islands. ◈ *union territory* India, N Indian Ocean
155 *C22* **Lakshadweep** ***Eng.*** Laccadive Islands. *island group* India, N Indian Ocean
153 *S17* **Lakshmikāntapur** West Bengal, NE India *22°05′N 88°19′E*
112 *G11* **Laktaši** ◈ Republika Srpska, N Bosnia and Herzegovina
149 *V7* **Lāla Mūsa** Punjab, NE Pakistan *32°41′N 74°01′E*
la Laon *see* Laon
114 *M11* **Lalapaşa** Edirne, NW Turkey *41°52′N 26°44′E*
83 *P14* **Lalaua** Nampula, N Mozambique *14°21′S 38°16′E*
105 *S9* **L'Alcora** ***var.*** Alcora. Valenciana, E Spain *40°05′N 00°14′W*
105 *S10* **L'Alcúdia** ***var.*** L'Alcudia. Valenciana, E Spain *39°10′N 00°30′W*
42 *E8* **La Libertad** La Libertad, SW El Salvador *13°28′N 89°20′W**
42 *E3* **La Libertad** Petén, N Guatemala *16°49′N 90°08′W*
42 *H6* **La Libertad** Comayagua, SW Honduras *14°43′N 87°36′W*
40 *E4* **La Libertad** ***var.*** Puerto Libertad. Sonora, NW Mexico *29°52′N 112°39′W*
42 *K10* **La Libertad** Chontales, S Nicaragua *12°12′N 85°10′W*
42 *A9* **La Libertad** ◈ *department* SW El Salvador
56 *B11* **La Libertad** ***off.*** Departamento de La Libertad. ◈ *department* W Peru
La Libertad, Departamento de *see* La Libertad
62 *G11* **La Ligua** Valparaíso, C Chile *31°30′S 71°16′W*
139 *U5* **La'lī Khān** As Sulaymānīyah, E Iraq *34°58′N 45°36′E*
104 *H3* **Lalín** Galicia, NW Spain *42°40′N 08°06′W*
102 *L13* **Lalinde** Dordogne, SW France *44°52′N 00°42′E*
104 *K16* **La Línea** ***var.*** La Línea de la Concepción. Andalucía, S Spain *36°10′N 05°21′W*
La Línea de la Concepción *see* La Línea
152 *J14* **Lalitpur** Uttar Pradesh, N India *24°42′N 78°24′E*
153 *P11* **Lalitpur** Central, C Nepal *27°45′N 85°18′E*
152 *K10* **Lālkua** Uttarachal, N India *29°04′N 79°31′E*
153 *T12* **Lalmanirhat** Rājshāhi, N Bangladesh *25°51′N 89°34′E*
11 *R12* **La Loche** Saskatchewan, C Canada *56°31′N 109°27′W*
102 *M6* **la Loupe** Eure-et-Loir, C France *48°30′N 01°04′E*
99 *G20* **La Louvière** Hainaut, S Belgium *50°29′N 04°15′E*
L'Altissima *see* Hochwilde
104 *L14* **La Luisiana** Andalucía, S Spain *37°30′N 05°14′W*
37 *S14* **La Luz** New Mexico, SW USA *32°58′N 105°56′W*
107 *D16* **la Maddalena** Sardegna, Italy, C Mediterranean Sea *41°13′N 09°25′E*
62 *J7* **La Madrid** Tucumán, N Argentina *27°37′S 65°16′W*
Lama-Kara *see* Kara
15 *S8* **La Malbaie** Québec, SE Canada *47°39′N 70°11′W*
Lamam *see* Xékong
105 *P10* **La Mancha** *physical region* C Spain
la Manche *see* English Channel
187 *R13* **Lamap** Malekula, C Vanuatu *16°26′S 167°47′E*
37 *W6* **Lamar** Colorado, C USA *38°40′N 102°37′W*
27 *S7* **Lamar** Missouri, C USA *37°30′N 94°18′W*
21 *S12* **Lamar** South Carolina, SE USA *34°10′N 80°03′W*
107 *C19* **La Marmora, Punta** ▲ Sardegna, Italy, C Mediterranean Sea *39°58′N 09°20′E*
8 *I9* **La Martre, Lac** ◎ Northwest Territories, NW Canada
56 *D10* **Lamas** San Martín, N Peru *06°28′S 76°31′W*
42 *I5* **La Masica** Atlántida, NW Honduras *15°38′N 87°08′W*
103 *R12* **Lamastre** Ardèche, E France *45°00′N 04°32′E*
La Matepec *see* Santa Ana, Volcán de
44 *I7* **La Maya** Santiago de Cuba, E Cuba *20°11′N 75°40′W*
109 *S5* **Lambach** Oberösterreich, N Austria *48°06′N 13°52′E*
168 *I11* **Lambak** Pulau Pini, W Indonesia *0°08′N 98°36′E*
102 *H5* **Lamballe** Côtes d'Armor, NW France *48°28′N 02°31′W*
79 *D18* **Lambaréné** Moyen-Ogooué, W Gabon *0°41′S 10°13′E*
Lambasa *see* Labasa
56 *B11* **Lambayeque** Lambayeque, W Peru *06°42′S 79°55′W*
56 *A10* **Lambayeque** ***off.*** Departamento de Lambayeque. ◈ *department* NW Peru
Lambayeque, Departamento de *see* Lambayeque
97 *G17* **Lambay Island** ***Ir.*** Reachrainn. *island* E Ireland
186 *G6* **Lambert, Cape** *headland* New Britain, E Papua New Guinea *04°15′S 151°31′E*
195 *W6* **Lambert Glacier** *glacier* Antarctica
29 *T10* **Lamberton** Minnesota, N USA *44°14′N 95°15′W*
27 *X4* **Lambert-Saint Louis** ✈ Missouri, C USA *38°43′N 90°19′W*
31 *R11* **Lambertville** Michigan, N USA *41°46′N 83°37′W*
18 *J15* **Lambertville** New Jersey, NE USA *40°20′N 74°55′W*
171 *N12* **Lambogo** Sulawesi, N Indonesia *0°57′S 120°23′E*
106 *D8* **Lambro** ≋ N Italy
33 *W11* **Lame Deer** Montana, NW USA *45°37′N 106°37′W*
104 *H6* **Lamego** Viseu, N Portugal *41°05′N 07°49′W*
187 *Q14* **Lamen Bay** Épi, C Vanuatu *16°36′S 168°10′E*
45 *X6* **Lamentin** Basse Terre, N Guadeloupe *16°16′N 61°38′W*
Lamentin *see* le Lamentin
182 *K10* **Lameroo** South Australia *35°22′S 140°30′E*
54 *F10* **La Mesa** Cundinamarca, C Colombia *04°37′N 74°30′W*
35 *U17* **La Mesa** California, W USA *32°44′N 117°00′W*
37 *R16* **La Mesa** New Mexico, SW USA *32°03′N 106°41′W*
25 *N6* **Lamesa** Texas, SW USA *32°43′N 101°57′W*
107 *N21* **Lamezia Terme** Calabria, SE Italy *38°54′N 16°13′E*
115 *F17* **Lamía** Stereá Elláda, C Greece *38°54′N 22°27′E*
171 *O8* **Lamitan** Basilan Island, SW Philippines *06°40′N 122°07′E*
187 *Y14* **Lamiti** Gau, C Fiji *18°00′S 179°20′E*
171 *T11* **Lamlam** Papua, E Indonesia *0°03′S 130°46′E*
188 *B16* **Lamlam, Mount** ▲ SW Guam *13°20′N 144°40′E*
109 *Q6* **Lammer** ≋ E Austria
185 *E23* **Lammerlaw Range** ▲▲ South Island, New Zealand
95 *L20* **Lammhult** Kronoberg, S Sweden *57°09′N 14°35′E*
93 *L18* **Lammi** Etelä-Suomi, S Finland *61°06′N 25°00′E*
189 *U11* **Lamoil** *island* Chuuk, C Micronesia
35 *W3* **Lamoille** Nevada, W USA *40°47′N 115°37′W*
18 *M7* **Lamoille River** ≋ Vermont, NE USA
30 *J13* **La Moine River** ≋ Illinois, N USA
171 *P4* **Lamon Bay** *bay* Luzon, N Philippines
29 *V16* **Lamoni** Iowa, C USA *40°37′N 93°56′W*
35 *R13* **Lamont** California, W USA *35°15′N 118°54′W*
27 *N8* **Lamont** Oklahoma, C USA *36°41′N 97°33′W*
54 *E13* **La Montañita** ***var.*** Montañita. Caquetá, S Colombia *01°22′N 75°25′W*
43 *N8* **La Mosquitia** ***var.*** Miskito Coast, ***Eng.*** Mosquito Coast. *coastal region* E Nicaragua
102 *I9* **la Mothe-Achard** Vendée, NW France *46°37′N 01°37′W*
188 *L15* **Lamotrek Atoll** *atoll* Caroline Islands, C Micronesia
29 *P6* **La Moure** North Dakota, N USA *46°21′N 98°17′W*
167 *O8* **Lampang** ***var.*** Muang Lampang. Lampang, NW Thailand *18°16′N 99°30′E*
167 *R9* **Lam Pao Reservoir** ⊠ E Thailand
25 *S9* **Lampasas** Texas, SW USA *31°04′N 98°12′W*
25 *S9* **Lampasas River** ≋ Texas, SW USA
41 *N7* **Lampazos** ***var.*** Lampazos de Naranjo. Nuevo León, NE Mexico *27°00′N 100°28′W*
Lampazos de Naranjo *see* Lampazos
115 *E19* **Lámpeia** Dytikí Elláda, S Greece *37°51′N 21°48′E*
101 *G19* **Lampertheim** Hessen, W Germany *49°36′N 08°28′E*
97 *I20* **Lampeter** SW Wales, United Kingdom *52°08′N 04°04′W*
167 *O7* **Lamphun** ***var.*** Lampun, Muang Lamphun. Lamphun, NW Thailand *18°36′N 99°02′E*
11 *X10* **Lamprey** Manitoba, C Canada *58°18′N 94°06′W*
Lampun *see* Lamphun
168 *M15* **Lampung** ***off.*** Propinsi Lampung. ◈ *province* SW Indonesia
Lampung, Propinsi *see* Lampung
126 *K6* **Lamskoye** Lipetskaya Oblast', W Russian Federation *52°57′N 38°04′E*
81 *K20* **Lamu** Coast, SE Kenya *02°17′S 40°54′E*
43 *N14* **La Muerte, Cerro** ▲ C Costa Rica *09°33′N 83°47′W*
103 *S13* **la Mure** Isère, E France *44°54′N 05°48′E*
37 *S10* **Lamy** New Mexico, SW USA *35°27′N 105°52′W*
119 *J18* **Lan'** ***Rus.*** Lan'. ≋ C Belarus
38 *E10* **Lāna'i** ***var.*** Lanai. *island* Hawai'i, USA, C Pacific Ocean
38 *E10* **Lāna'i City** ***var.*** Lanai City. Lanai, Hawaii, USA, C Pacific Ocean *20°49′N 156°55′W*
Lanai City *see* Lāna'i City
99 *L18* **Lanaken** Limburg, NE Belgium *50°53′N 05°39′E*
171 *Q7* **Lanao, Lake** ***var.*** Lake Sultan Alonto. ◎ Mindanao, S Philippines
96 *J12* **Lanark** S Scotland, United Kingdom *55°38′N 04°25′W*
96 *I13* **Lanark** *cultural region* C Scotland, United Kingdom
104 *L9* **La Nava de Ricomalillo** Castilla-La Mancha, C Spain *39°40′N 04°59′W*
166 *M13* **Lanbi Kyun** ***prev.*** Sullivan Island. *island* Mergui Archipelago, S Burma (Myanmar)
Lancang Jiang *see* Mekong
97 *K17* **Lancashire** *cultural region* N England, United Kingdom
15 *N13* **Lancaster** Ontario, SE Canada *45°10′N 74°31′W*
97 *K16* **Lancaster** NW England, United Kingdom *54°03′N 02°48′W*
35 *T14* **Lancaster** California, W USA *34°42′N 118°08′W*
20 *M6* **Lancaster** Kentucky, S USA *37°35′N 84°34′W*
27 *U1* **Lancaster** Missouri, C USA *40°32′N 92°31′W*
19 *O7* **Lancaster** New Hampshire, NE USA *44°29′N 71°34′W*
18 *D10* **Lancaster** New York, NE USA *42°54′N 78°40′W*
31 *T14* **Lancaster** Ohio, N USA *39°42′N 82°36′W*
18 *H16* **Lancaster** Pennsylvania, NE USA *40°03′N 76°18′W*
21 *R11* **Lancaster** South Carolina, SE USA *34°43′N 80°47′W*
25 *U7* **Lancaster** Texas, SW USA *32°35′N 96°45′W*
21 *X5* **Lancaster** Virginia, NE USA *37°48′N 76°30′W*
30 *J9* **Lancaster** Wisconsin, N USA *42°52′N 90°43′W*
197 *N10* **Lancaster Sound** *sound* Nunavut, N Canada
Lan-chou/Lan-chow/Lanchow *see* Lanzhou
107 *K14* **Lanciano** Abruzzo, C Italy *42°13′N 14°23′E*
111 *O16* **Łańcut** Podkarpackie, SE Poland *50°04′N 22°14′E*
169 *Q11* **Landak, Sungai** ≋ Borneo, N Indonesia
Landao *see* Lantau Island
Landau *see* Landau an der Isar
Landau *see* Landau in der Pfalz
101 *N22* **Landau an der Isar** ***var.*** Landau. Bayern, SE Germany *48°40′N 12°41′E*
101 *F20* **Landau in der Pfalz** ***var.*** Landau. Rheinland-Pfalz, SW Germany *49°12′N 08°07′E*
Land Burgenland *see* Burgenland
108 *K8* **Landeck** Tirol, W Austria *47°09′N 10°35′E*
99 *J19* **Landen** Vlaams Brabant, C Belgium *50°45′N 05°05′E*
33 *U15* **Lander** Wyoming, C USA *42°49′N 108°43′W*
102 *F5* **Landerneau** Finistère, NW France *48°27′N 04°16′W*
95 *K20* **Landeryd** Halland, S Sweden *57°04′N 13°15′E*
102 *J15* **Landes** ◈ *department* SW France
Landeshut/Landeshut in Schlesien *see* Kamienna Góra
105 *R9* **Landete** Castilla-La Mancha, C Spain *39°54′N 01°22′W*
99 *M18* **Landgraaf** Limburg, SE Netherlands *50°55′N 06°04′E*
102 *F5* **Landivisiau** Finistère, NW France *48°31′N 04°03′W*
Land Kärten *see* Kärnten
Land of Enchantment *see* New Mexico
The Land of Opportunity *see* Arkansas
Land of Steady Habits *see* Connecticut
Land of the Midnight Sun *see* Alaska
108 *I8* **Landquart** Graubünden, SE Switzerland *46°58′N 09°35′E*
108 *J9* **Landquart** ≋ Austria/Switzerland
21 *P10* **Landrum** South Carolina, SE USA *35°10′N 82°11′W*
Landsberg *see* Gorzów Wielkopolski, Lubuskie, Poland
Landsberg *see* Górowo Iławeckie, Warmińsko-Mazurskie, NE Poland
101 *K23* **Landsberg am Lech** Bayern, S Germany *48°03′N 10°52′E*
Landsberg an der Warthe *see* Gorzów Wielkopolski
97 *G25* **Land's End** *headland* SW England, United Kingdom *50°02′N 05°41′W*
101 *M22* **Landshut** Bayern, SE Germany *48°32′N 12°09′E*
Landskron *see* Lanškroun
95 *J22* **Landskrona** Skåne, S Sweden *55°52′N 12°52′E*
98 *I10* **Landsmeer** Noord-Holland, C Netherlands *52°26′N 04°55′E*
95 *J19* **Landvetter** ✈ (Göteborg) Västra Götaland, S Sweden *57°39′N 12°22′E*
Landwarów *see* Lentvaris
23 *R5* **Lanett** Alabama, S USA *32°52′N 85°11′W*
108 *C8* **La Neuveville** ***var.*** Neuveville, ***Ger.*** Neuenstadt. Neuchâtel, W Switzerland *47°05′N 07°03′E*
95 *G21* **Langå** ***var.*** Langaa. Midtjylland, C Denmark *56°23′N 09°55′E*
Langaa *see* Langå
158 *G14* **La'nga Co** ◎ W China
Langada *see* Lagkáda
Langades/Langadhás *see* Lagkadás
Langádhia/ *see* Lagkádia
147 *T14* **Langar** ***Rus.*** Lyangar. SE Tajikistan *37°04′N 72°39′E*
146 *M10* **Langar** ***Rus.*** Lyangar. Navoiy Viloyati, C Uzbekistan *40°27′N 65°54′E*
142 *M3* **Langarūd** Gīlān, NW Iran *37°10′N 50°09′E*
11 *V16* **Langbank** Saskatchewan, S Canada *50°01′N 102°16′W*
29 *P2* **Langdon** North Dakota, N USA *48°45′N 98°22′W*
103 *P12* **Langeac** Haute-Loire, C France *45°06′N 03°31′E*
102 *L8* **Langeais** Indre-et-Loire, C France *47°22′N 00°27′E*
80 *I8* **Langeb, Wadi** ≋ NE Sudan
Långed *see* Dals Långed
95 *G25* **Langeland** *island* S Denmark
99 *B18* **Langemark** West-Vlaanderen, W Belgium *50°55′N 02°55′E*
101 *G18* **Langen** Hessen, W Germany *49°58′N 08°40′E*
101 *J22* **Langenau** Baden-Württemberg, S Germany *48°30′N 10°08′E*
11 *V16* **Langenburg** Saskatchewan, S Canada *50°50′N 101°43′W*
108 *L8* **Längenfeld** Tirol, W Austria *47°04′N 10°59′E*
101 *E16* **Langenfeld** Nordrhein-Westfalen, W Germany *51°06′N 06°57′E*
100 *I12* **Langenhagen** Niedersachsen, N Germany *52°26′N 09°45′E*
100 *I12* **Langenhagen** ✈ (Hannover) Niedersachsen, NW Germany *52°28′N 09°40′E*
109 *W3* **Langenlois** Niederösterreich, NE Austria *48°29′N 15°42′E*
108 *E7* **Langenthal** Bern, NW Switzerland *47°13′N 07°48′E*
109 *W6* **Langenwang** Steiermark, E Austria *47°34′N 15°39′E*
109 *X3* **Langenzersdorf** Niederösterreich, E Austria *48°20′N 16°22′E*
100 *F9* **Langeoog** *island* NW Germany
95 *H23* **Langeskov** Syddtjylland, C Denmark *55°22′N 10°36′E*
95 *G16* **Langesund** Telemark, S Norway *59°00′N 09°43′E*
95 *G17* **Langesundsfjorden** *fjord* S Norway
94 *D10* **Langevågen** Møre og Romsdal, S Norway *62°26′N 06°15′E*
161 *P3* **Langfang** Hebei, E China *39°30′N 116°39′E*
94 *E9* **Langfjorden** *fjord* S Norway
29 *Q8* **Langford** South Dakota, N USA *45°36′N 97°48′W*
168 *I10* **Langgapayung** Sumatera, W Indonesia *01°42′N 99°57′E*
106 *E9* **Langhirano** Emilia-Romagna, C Italy *44°37′N 10°16′E*
97 *K14* **Langholm** S Scotland, United Kingdom *55°14′N 03°11′W*
92 *I3* **Langjökull** *glacier* C Iceland
168 *I6* **Langkawi, Pulau** *island* Peninsular Malaysia
166 *M14* **Langkha Tuk, Khao** ▲ SW Thailand *09°19′N 98°39′E*
14 *L8* **Langlade** Québec, SE Canada *48°13′N 75°58′W*
10 *M17* **Langley** British Columbia, SW Canada *49°07′N 122°39′W*
167 *S7* **Lang Mô** Thanh Hoa, N Vietnam *19°36′N 105°30′E*
Langnau *see* Langnau im Emmental
108 *E8* **Langnau im Emmental** ***var.*** Langnau. Bern, W Switzerland *46°57′N 07°47′E*
103 *Q13* **Langogne** Lozère, S France *44°40′N 03°52′E*
102 *K13* **Langon** Gironde, SW France *44°33′N 00°14′W*
La Ngounié *see* Ngounié
92 *G10* **Langøya** *island* C Norway
158 *G14* **Langqên Zangbo** ≋ China/India
Langreo *see* Llangréu
103 *S7* **Langres** Haute-Marne, N France *47°53′N 05°20′E*
103 *R8* **Langres, Plateau de** *plateau* C France
168 *H8* **Langsa** Sumatera, W Indonesia *04°30′N 97°53′E*
93 *H16* **Långsele** Västernorrland, C Sweden *63°11′N 17°05′E*
162 *L12* **Lang Shan** ▲▲ N China
95 *M14* **Långshyttan** Dalarna, C Sweden *60°26′N 16°02′E*
167 *T5* **Lang Sơn** ***var.*** Langson. Lang Sơn, N Vietnam *21°50′N 106°45′E*
Langson *see* Lang Sơn
167 *N14* **Lang Suan** Chumphon, SW Thailand *09°55′N 99°07′E*
93 *J14* **Långträsk** Norrbotten, N Sweden *65°22′N 20°19′E*
25 *N11* **Langtry** Texas, SW USA *29°46′N 101°25′W*
103 *P16* **Languedoc** *cultural region* S France
103 *P15* **Languedoc-Roussillon** ◈ *region* S France
27 *X10* **L'Anguille River** ≋ Arkansas, C USA
93 *I16* **Långviksmon** Västernorrland, N Sweden *63°39′N 18°45′E*
101 *K22* **Langweid** Bayern, S Germany *48°29′N 10°50′E*
160 *J8* **Langzhong** Sichuan, C China *31°46′N 105°55′E*
Lan Hsü *see* Lan Yu
11 *U15* **Lanigan** Saskatchewan, S Canada *51°50′N 105°01′W*
116 *K5* **Lanivtsi** Ternopil's'ka Oblast', W Ukraine *49°52′N 26°05′E*
137 *Y13* **Länkäran** ***Rus.*** Lenkoran'. S Azerbaijan *38°46′N 48°51′E*
102 *L16* **Lannemezan** Hautes-Pyrénées, S France *43°08′N 00°22′E*
102 *G5* **Lannion** Côtes d'Armor, NW France *48°44′N 03°27′W*
14 *M11* **L'Annonciation** Québec, SE Canada *46°22′N 74°51′W*
105 *V5* **L'Anoia** ≋ NE Spain
18 *I15* **Lansdale** Pennsylvania, NE USA *40°14′N 75°13′W*
14 *L14* **Lansdowne** Ontario, SE Canada *44°25′N 76°00′W*
152 *K9* **Lansdowne** Uttarakhand, N India *29°50′N 78°42′E*
30 *M3* **L'Anse** Michigan, N USA *46°45′N 88°27′W*
15 *S7* **L'Anse-St-Jean** Québec, SE Canada *48°14′N 70°13′W*
29 *Y11* **Lansing** Iowa, C USA *43°22′N 91°11′W*
27 *R4* **Lansing** Kansas, C USA *39°15′N 94°54′W*
31 *Q9* **Lansing** *state capital* Michigan, N USA *42°44′N 84°33′W*
93 *K18* **Länsi-Suomi** ◈ *province* W Finland
92 *J12* **Lansjärv** Norrbotten, N Sweden *66°39′N 22°10′E*
111 *G17* **Lanškroun** ***Ger.*** Landskron. Pardubický Kraj, E Czech Republic *49°55′N 16°38′E*
167 *N16* **Lanta, Ko** *island* S Thailand
161 *O15* **Lantau Island** ***Cant.*** Tai Yue Shan, ***Chin.*** Landao. *island* Hong Kong, S China
Lantian *see* Lianyuan
Lan-ts'ang Chiang *see* Mekong

◆ Country
● Country Capital
◇ Dependent Territory
○ Dependent Territory Capital
◈ Administrative Regions
✈ International Airport
▲ Mountain
▲▲ Mountain Range
Volcano
≋ River
◎ Lake
⊠ Reservoir

Lantung, Gulf of see Liaodong Wan
171 O11 Lanu Sulawesi, N Indonesia 01°00′N 121°33′E
107 D19 Lanusei Sardegna, Italy, C Mediterranean Sea 39°55′N 09°31′E
102 H7 Lanvaux, Landes de physical region NW France
163 W8 Lanxi Heilongjiang, NE China 46°18′N 126°15′E
161 R10 Lanxi Zhejiang, SE China 29°12′N 119°27′E
La Nyanga see Nyanga
161 T15 Lan Yu var. Huoshao Tao, Hungt'ou, Lan Hsü, Lanyü, Eng. Orchid Island; prev. Kotosho, Koto Sho, Lan Yü. island SE Taiwan
Lanyü see Lan Yu
64 P11 Lanzarote island Islas Canarias, Spain, NE Atlantic Ocean
159 V10 Lanzhou var. Lan-chou, Lanchow, Lan-chow; prev. Kaolan. province capital Gansu, C China 36°01′N 103°52′E
106 B8 Lanzo Torinese Piemonte, NE Italy 45°18′N 07°26′E
171 O11 Laoag Luzon, N Philippines 18°11′N 120°34′E
171 Q5 Laoang Samar, C Philippines 12°29′N 125°01′E
167 R5 Lao Cai Lao Cai, N Vietnam 22°29′N 104°00′E
Laodicea/Laodicea ad Mare see Al Lādhiqīyah
Laoet see Laut, Pulau
163 T11 Laoha He ≈ NE China
160 M8 Laohekou var. Guanghua. Hubei, C China 32°20′N 111°42′E
Laoi, An see Lee
97 E19 Laois prev. Leix, Queen's County. cultural region C Ireland
163 W12 Lao Ling ▲▲ N China
64 Q11 La Oliva var. Oliva. Fuerteventura, Islas Canarias, Spain, NE Atlantic Ocean 28°36′N 13°53′W
Lao, Loch see Belfast Lough
Laolong see Longchuan
Lao Mangnai see Mangnai
103 P3 Laon var. la Laon; anc. Laudunum. Aisne, N France 49°34′N 03°37′E
Lao People's Democratic Republic see Laos
54 M3 La Orchila, Isla island N Venezuela
64 O11 La Orotava Tenerife, Islas Canarias, Spain, NE Atlantic Ocean 28°23′N 16°32′W
57 E14 La Oroya Junín, C Peru 11°36′S 75°54′W
167 Q7 Laos off. Lao People's Democratic Republic. ◆ republic SE Asia
161 R5 Laoshan Wan bay E China
163 Y10 Laoye Ling ▲▲ NE China
60 J12 Lapa Paraná, S Brazil 25°46′S 49°44′W
103 P10 Lapalisse Allier, C France 46°13′N 03°39′E
54 F9 La Palma Cundinamarca, C Colombia 05°23′N 74°24′W
42 F7 La Palma Chalatenango, N El Salvador 14°19′N 89°10′W
43 W16 La Palma Darién, SE Panama 08°24′N 78°09′W
64 N11 La Palma island Islas Canarias, Spain, NE Atlantic Ocean
104 J14 La Palma del Condado Andalucía, S Spain 37°23′N 06°33′W
61 F18 La Paloma Durazno, C Uruguay 32°54′S 55°36′W
61 G20 La Paloma Rocha, E Uruguay 34°37′S 54°08′W
61 A21 La Pampa off. Provincia de La Pampa. ◈ province C Argentina
La Pampa, Provincia de see La Pampa
55 P8 La Paragua Bolívar, E Venezuela 06°53′N 63°16′W
119 O16 Lapatsichy Rus. Lopatichi. Mahilyowskaya Voblasts', E Belarus 53°34′N 30°53′E
61 C16 La Paz Entre Ríos, E Argentina 30°45′S 59°36′W
62 I11 La Paz Mendoza, C Argentina 33°30′S 67°36′W
57 J18 La Paz var. La Paz de Ayacucho. ● (Bolivia-legislative and administrative capital) La Paz, W Bolivia 16°30′S 68°13′W
42 H6 La Paz La Paz, SW Honduras 14°20′N 87°40′W
40 F9 La Paz Baja California Sur, NW Mexico 24°07′N 110°18′W
61 F20 La Paz Canelones, S Uruguay 34°46′S 56°13′W
57 J16 La Paz ◈ department W Bolivia
42 B9 La Paz ◈ department S El Salvador
42 G7 La Paz ◈ department SW Honduras
La Paz see El Alto, Bolivia
La Paz see Robles, Colombia
La Paz see La Paz Centro
40 F9 La Paz, Bahía de bay NW Mexico
42 I10 La Paz Centro var. La Paz. León, W Nicaragua 12°20′N 86°41′W
La Paz de Ayacucho see La Paz
54 J15 La Pedrera Amazonas, SE Colombia 01°19′S 69°31′W
31 S9 Lapeer Michigan, N USA 43°03′N 83°19′W
40 K6 La Perla Chihuahua, N Mexico 28°18′N 104°34′W
165 T1 La Pérouse Strait Jap. Sōya-kaikyō, Rus. Proliv Laperuza. strait Japan/Russian Federation
63 I14 La Perra, Salitral de salt lake C Argentina
Laperuza, Proliv see La Pérouse Strait
41 Q10 La Pesca Tamaulipas, C Mexico 23°49′N 97°45′W
40 M13 La Piedad Cavadas Michoacán, C Mexico 20°20′N 102°01′W
Lapines see Lafnitz
93 M16 Lapinlahti Itä-Suomi, C Finland 63°21′N 27°25′E
Lápithos see Lapta
22 K9 Laplace Louisiana, S USA 30°04′N 90°28′W
45 X12 La Plaine SE Dominica 15°20′N 61°15′W
173 P16 La Plaine-des-Palmistes C Réunion
92 K11 Lapland Fin. Lappi, Swe. Lappland. cultural region N Europe
28 M8 La Plant South Dakota, N USA 45°06′N 100°40′W
61 D20 La Plata Buenos Aires, E Argentina 34°56′S 57°55′W
54 D12 La Plata Huila, SW Colombia 02°33′N 75°55′W
21 W4 La Plata Maryland, NE USA 38°32′N 76°59′W
La Plata see Sucre
45 U6 la Plata, Río de ≈ C Puerto Rico
105 W4 La Pobla de Lillet Cataluña, NE Spain 42°15′N 01°57′E
105 U4 La Pobla de Segur Cataluña, NE Spain 42°15′N 00°58′E
15 S9 La Pocatière Québec, SE Canada 47°21′N 70°04′W
104 K2 La Pola prev. Pola de Lena. Asturias, N Spain 43°10′N 05°49′W
104 L3 La Pola de Gordón Castilla y León, N Spain 42°50′N 05°38′W
104 L2 La Pola Siero prev. Pola de Siero. Asturias, N Spain 43°24′N 05°39′W
31 O11 La Porte Indiana, N USA 41°36′N 86°43′W
18 H13 Laporte Pennsylvania, NE USA 41°25′N 76°29′W
29 X13 La Porte City Iowa, C USA 42°19′N 92°11′W
62 J8 La Posta Catamarca, C Argentina 27°59′S 65°32′W
40 E8 La Poza Grande Baja California Sur, NW Mexico 25°50′N 112°00′W
93 K16 Lappajärvi Länsi-Suomi, W Finland 63°13′N 23°40′E
93 L16 Lappajärvi ◎ W Finland
93 N18 Lappeenranta Swe. Villmanstrand. Etelä-Suomi, SE Finland 61°04′N 28°15′E
93 J17 Lappfjärd Fin. Lapväärtti. Länsi-Suomi, W Finland 62°14′N 21°30′E
92 L12 Lappi Swe. Lappland. ◈ province N Finland
Lappi/Lappland see Lapland
Lappo see Lapua
61 C23 Laprida Buenos Aires, E Argentina 37°34′S 60°45′W
25 P13 La Pryor Texas, SW USA 28°56′N 99°51′W
136 B11 Lâpseki Çanakkale, NW Turkey 40°22′N 26°42′E
121 P2 Lapta Gk. Lápithos. NW Cyprus 35°20′N 33°11′E
Laptev Sea see Laptevykh, More
122 N6 Laptevykh, More Eng. Laptev Sea. sea Arctic Ocean
93 K16 Lapua Swe. Lappo. Länsi-Suomi, W Finland 62°57′N 23°E
105 P3 La Puebla de Arganzón País Vasco, N Spain 42°45′N 02°49′W
104 L14 La Puebla de Cazalla Andalucía, S Spain 37°14′N 05°18′W
104 M9 La Puebla de Montalbán Castilla-La Mancha, C Spain 39°52′N 04°22′W
54 I6 La Puerta Trujillo, NW Venezuela 09°08′N 70°46′W
Lapurdum see Bayonne
40 E7 La Purísima Baja California Sur, NW Mexico 26°10′N 112°05′W
Lapväärtti see Lappfjärd
110 O10 Łapy Podlaskie, NE Poland 53°N 22°54′E
80 D6 Laqiya Arba'in Northern, NW Sudan 20°01′N 28°01′E
62 J4 La Quiaca Jujuy, N Argentina 22°12′S 65°36′W
107 J14 L'Aquila var. Aquila, Aquila degli Abruzzi. Abruzzo, C Italy 42°21′N 13°24′E
143 Q13 Lār Fārs, S Iran 27°42′N 54°19′E
54 J5 Lara off. Estado Lara. ◈ state NW Venezuela
104 G2 Laracha Galicia, NW Spain 43°14′N 08°34′W
74 G5 Larache var. al Araïch, El Araïch, prev. El Araïch; anc. Lixus. NW Morocco 35°12′N 06°10′W
Lara, Estado see Lara
103 T14 Laragne-Montéglin Hautes-Alpes, SE France 44°21′N 05°46′E
104 M13 La Rambla Andalucía, S Spain 37°37′N 04°44′W
33 Y17 Laramie Wyoming, C USA 41°18′N 105°35′W
33 X15 Laramie Mountains ▲▲ Wyoming, C USA
33 Y16 Laramie River ≈ Wyoming, C USA
60 H12 Laranjeiras do Sul Paraná, S Brazil 25°23′S 52°23′W
Larantoeka see Larantuka
171 P16 Larantuka prev. Larantoeka. Flores, C Indonesia 08°20′S 123°00′E
171 U15 Larat Pulau Larat, E Indonesia 07°07′S 131°46′E
171 U15 Larat, Pulau island Kepulauan Tanimbar, E Indonesia
95 P19 Lärbro Gotland, SE Sweden 57°46′N 18°49′E
106 A9 Larche, Col de pass France/Italy
14 H8 Larder Lake Ontario, S Canada 48°06′N 79°44′W
105 O2 Laredo Cantabria, N Spain 43°23′N 03°22′W
25 Q15 Laredo Texas, SW USA 27°30′N 99°30′W
40 H9 La Reforma Sinaloa, W Mexico 25°05′N 108°03′W
98 N11 Laren Gelderland, E Netherlands 52°12′N 06°22′E
98 J11 Laren Noord-Holland, C Netherlands 52°15′N 05°13′E
102 K13 la Réole Gironde, SW France 44°34′N 00°00′W
La Réunion see Réunion
Largeau see Faya
103 U13 l'Argentière-la-Bessée Hautes-Alpes, SE France 44°49′N 06°34′E
149 O4 Lar Gerd var. Largird. Balkh, N Afghanistan 35°36′N 66°48′E
Largird see Lar Gerd
23 V12 Largo Florida, SE USA 27°55′N 82°47′W
37 Q9 Largo, Canon valley New Mexico, SW USA
44 D6 Largo, Cayo island W Cuba
23 Z17 Largo, Key island Florida Keys, Florida, SE USA
96 H12 Largs W Scotland, United Kingdom 55°48′N 04°50′W
102 I16 la Rhune var. Larrún. ▲ France/Spain 43°19′N 01°36′W see also Larrún
la Rhune see Larrún
la Riege see Ariège
29 Q4 Larimore North Dakota, N USA 47°54′N 97°37′W
107 L15 Larino Molise, C Italy 41°46′N 14°50′E
Lario see Como, Lago di
62 J9 La Rioja La Rioja, NW Argentina 29°26′S 66°50′W
62 I9 La Rioja off. Provincia de la Rioja. ◈ province NW Argentina
105 O4 La Rioja ◈ autonomous community N Spain
La Rioja, Provincia de see La Rioja
115 F16 Lárisa var. Larissa. Thessalía, C Greece 39°38′N 22°27′E
Larissa see Lárisa
149 Q13 Lārkāna var. Larkhana. Sind, SE Pakistan 27°32′N 68°18′E
Larkhana see Lārkāna
Larnaca see Lárnaka
121 Q3 Lárnaka var. Larnaca, Larnax. SE Cyprus 34°55′N 33°39′E
121 Q3 Lárnaka ✈ SE Cyprus 34°52′N 33°38′E
Larnax see Lárnaka
97 G14 Larne Ir. Latharna. E Northern Ireland, United Kingdom 54°51′N 05°49′W
26 L5 Larned Kansas, C USA 38°12′N 99°05′W
104 L3 La Robla Castilla y León, N Spain 42°48′N 05°37′W
104 J10 La Roca de la Sierra Extremadura, W Spain 39°06′N 06°41′W
99 K22 La Roche-en-Ardenne Luxembourg, SE Belgium 50°11′N 05°35′E
102 L11 la Rochefoucauld Charente, W France 45°43′N 00°23′E
102 J10 la Rochelle anc. Rupella. Charente-Maritime, W France 46°09′N 01°07′W
102 I9 la Roche-sur-Yon prev. Bourbon Vendée, Napoléon-Vendée. Vendée, NW France 46°40′N 01°26′W
105 Q10 La Roda Castilla-La Mancha, C Spain 39°13′N 02°10′W
104 L14 La Roda de Andalucía Andalucía, S Spain 37°12′N 04°45′W
45 P9 La Romana E Dominican Republic 18°25′N 69°00′W
11 T13 La Ronge Saskatchewan, C Canada 55°07′N 105°18′W
11 U13 La Ronge, Lac ◎ Saskatchewan, C Canada
22 K10 Larose Louisiana, S USA 29°34′N 90°22′W
42 M7 La Rosita Región Autónoma Atlántico Norte, NE Nicaragua 13°55′N 84°23′W
181 Q3 Larrimah Northern Territory, N Australia 15°30′S 133°12′E
62 N11 Larroque Entre Ríos, E Argentina 33°05′S 59°06′W
105 Q2 Larrún Fr. la Rhune. ▲ France/Spain 43°18′N 01°35′W see also la Rhune
Larrún see la Rhune
195 X6 Lars Christensen Coast physical region Antarctica
39 Q14 Larsen Bay Kodiak Island, Alaska, USA 57°32′N 153°58′W
194 I5 Larsen Ice Shelf ice shelf Antarctica
8 M6 Larsen Sound sound Nunavut, N Canada
La Rúa see A Rúa de Valdeorras
102 K16 Laruns Pyrénées-Atlantiques, SW France 43°00′N 00°25′W
95 G16 Larvik Vestfold, S Norway 59°04′N 10°02′E
La-sa see Lhasa
171 S13 Lasahata Pulau Seram, E Indonesia 02°52′S 128°27′E
Lasahau see Lasihao
37 O6 La Sal Utah, W USA 38°19′N 109°14′W
14 C17 La Salle Ontario, S Canada 42°13′N 83°05′W
30 L11 La Salle Illinois, N USA 41°19′N 89°06′W
45 O9 Las Americas ✈ (Santo Domingo) S Dominican Republic 18°24′N 69°38′W
37 V6 Las Animas Colorado, C USA 38°04′N 103°13′W
108 D10 La Sarine var. Sarine. ≈ SW Switzerland
108 B9 La Sarraz Vaud, W Switzerland 46°40′N 06°32′E
12 H12 La Sarre Québec, SE Canada 48°49′N 79°12′W
54 L3 Las Aves, Islas var. Islas de Aves. island group N Venezuela
55 N7 Las Bonitas Bolívar, C Venezuela 07°50′N 65°40′W
104 K15 Las Cabezas de San Juan Andalucía, S Spain 36°59′N 05°56′W
61 G19 Lascano Rocha, E Uruguay 33°40′S 54°12′W
62 I5 Lascar, Volcán ⛰ N Chile 23°22′S 67°33′W
41 T15 Las Choapas var. Choapas. Veracruz-Llave, SE Mexico 17°51′N 94°00′W
37 R15 Las Cruces New Mexico, SW USA 32°19′N 106°49′W
Lasdehnen see Krasnoznamensk
La Selle see Selle, Pic de la
62 G9 La Serena Coquimbo, C Chile 29°54′S 71°18′W
104 K11 La Serena physical region W Spain
105 V4 La Seu d'Urgell var. La Seu d'Urgell; prev. Seo de Urgel. Cataluña, NE Spain 42°22′N 01°27′E
La Seu d'Urgell see La Seu d'Urgell
103 T16 la Seyne-sur-Mer Var, SE France 43°07′N 05°53′E
61 D21 Las Flores Buenos Aires, E Argentina 36°03′S 59°08′W
62 H9 Las Flores San Juan, W Argentina 30°14′S 69°10′W
11 S14 Lashburn Saskatchewan, S Canada 53°09′N 109°37′W
62 I11 Las Heras Mendoza, W Argentina 32°48′S 68°50′W
148 M8 Lashkar Gāh var. Lash-Kar-Gar'. Helmand, S Afghanistan 31°35′N 64°21′E
Lash-Kar-Gar' see Lashkar Gāh
171 P14 Lasihao var. Lasahau. Pulau Muna, C Indonesia 05°01′S 122°23′E
107 N21 La Sila ▲▲ SW Italy
63 H23 La Silueta, Cerro ▲ S Chile 52°22′S 72°09′W
42 L9 La Sirena Región Autónoma Atlántico Sur, E Nicaragua 12°59′N 84°35′W
110 J13 Łask Łódzkie, C Poland 51°36′N 19°06′E
109 V11 Laško Ger. Tüffer. C Slovenia 46°08′N 15°13′E
63 H14 Las Lajas Neuquén, W Argentina 38°31′S 70°22′W
63 H15 Las Lajas, Cerro ▲ W Argentina 38°49′S 70°42′W
62 M6 Las Lomitas Formosa, N Argentina 24°45′S 60°35′W
41 V16 Las Margaritas Chiapas, SE Mexico 16°15′N 91°58′W
Las Marismas see Guadalquivir, Marismas del
54 M6 Las Mercedes Guárico, N Venezuela 09°08′N 66°27′W
42 F6 Las Minas, Cerro ▲ W Honduras 14°33′N 88°41′W
105 O11 La Solana Castilla-La Mancha, C Spain 38°56′N 03°14′W
45 Q14 La Soufrière ⛰ Saint Vincent, Saint Vincent and the Grenadines 13°20′N 61°11′W
102 M10 la Souterraine Creuse, C France 46°15′N 01°28′E
62 N7 Las Palmas Chaco, N Argentina 27°08′S 58°45′W
43 Q16 Las Palmas Veraguas, W Panama 08°09′N 81°28′W
64 P12 Las Palmas var. Las Palmas de Gran Canaria. Gran Canaria, Islas Canarias, Spain, NE Atlantic Ocean 28°08′N 15°27′W
64 P12 Las Palmas ◈ province Islas Canarias, Spain, NE Atlantic Ocean
64 Q12 Las Palmas ✈ Gran Canaria, Islas Canarias, Spain, NE Atlantic Ocean
Las Palmas de Gran Canaria see Las Palmas
40 D6 Las Palomas Baja California Sur, W Mexico 31°44′N 107°37′W
105 P10 Las Pedroñeras Castilla-La Mancha, C Spain 39°27′N 02°41′W
106 E10 La Spezia Liguria, NW Italy 44°08′N 09°50′E
61 F20 Las Piedras Canelones, S Uruguay 34°42′S 56°14′W
63 J18 Las Plumas Chubut, S Argentina 43°46′S 67°15′W
61 B18 Las Rosas Santa Fe, C Argentina 32°27′S 61°30′W
Lassa see Lhasa
35 O4 Lassen Peak ⛰ California, W USA 40°27′N 121°28′W
194 K6 Lassiter Coast physical region Antarctica
109 V4 Lassnitz ≈ SE Austria
15 O12 L'Assomption Québec, SE Canada 45°48′N 73°27′W
15 N11 L'Assomption ≈ Québec, SE Canada
43 S17 Las Tablas Los Santos, S Panama 07°45′N 80°17′W
Lastarria, Volcán see Azufre, Volcán
37 V4 Last Chance Colorado, C USA 39°41′N 103°34′W
Last Frontier, The see Alaska
11 U16 Last Mountain Lake ◎ Saskatchewan, S Canada
62 H9 Las Tórtolas, Cerro ▲ W Argentina 29°57′S 69°49′W
61 C14 Las Toscas Santa Fe, C Argentina 28°22′S 59°20′W
79 F19 Lastoursville Ogooué-Lolo, E Gabon 0°50′S 12°43′E
113 F16 Lastovo It. Lagosta. island SW Croatia
113 F16 Lastovski Kanal channel SW Croatia
40 E6 Las Tres Vírgenes, Volcán ⛰ NW Mexico 27°27′N 112°34′W
40 F4 Las Trincheras Sonora, NW Mexico 30°21′N 111°27′W
55 N8 Las Trincheras Bolívar, E Venezuela 06°57′N 64°49′W
44 H7 Las Tunas var. Victoria de las Tunas. Las Tunas, E Cuba 20°58′N 76°59′W
La Suisse see Switzerland
40 I5 Las Varas Chihuahua, N Mexico 29°35′N 108°01′W
40 J12 Las Varas Nayarit, C Mexico 21°12′N 105°10′W
62 L10 Las Varillas Córdoba, E Argentina 31°54′S 62°45′W
35 X11 Las Vegas Nevada, W USA 36°09′N 115°10′W
37 T10 Las Vegas New Mexico, SW USA 35°35′N 105°15′W
187 P10 Lata Nendö, Solomon Islands 10°45′S 165°43′E
13 R10 La Tabatière Québec, E Canada 50°51′N 58°59′W
56 C6 Latacunga Cotopaxi, C Ecuador 0°58′S 78°36′W
194 I7 Latady Island island Antarctica
54 E14 La Tagua Putumayo, S Colombia 0°05′S 74°39′W
Latakia see Al Lādhiqīyah
92 J10 Lätäseno ≈ NW Finland
14 H9 Latchford Ontario, S Canada 47°20′N 79°45′W
14 J13 Latchford Bridge Ontario, SE Canada 45°16′N 77°29′W
193 Y14 Late island Vava'u Group, N Tonga
153 P15 Lātehār Jhārkhand, N India 23°48′N 84°28′E
15 R7 Laterrière Québec, SE Canada 48°17′N 71°10′W
102 J13 la Teste Gironde, SW France 44°38′N 01°04′W
25 V8 Latexo Texas, SW USA 31°24′N 95°28′W
18 L10 Latham New York, NE USA 42°45′N 73°45′W
Latharna see Larne
108 B9 La Thielle var. Thièle. ≈ W Switzerland
27 R3 Lathrop Missouri, C USA 39°33′N 94°19′W
107 I16 Latina prev. Littoria. Lazio, C Italy 41°28′N 12°53′E
41 R14 La Tinaja Veracruz-Llave, S Mexico
106 J7 Latisana Friuli-Venezia Giulia, NE Italy 45°47′N 13°01′E
Latium see Lazio
115 K25 Lató site of ancient city Kríti, Greece, E Mediterranean Sea
187 Q17 La Tontouta ✈ (Noumea) Province Sud, S New Caledonia 22°06′S 166°12′E
55 N4 La Tortuga, Isla var. Isla Tortuga. island N Venezuela
108 C10 La Tour-de-Peilz var. La Tour de Peilz. Vaud, SW Switzerland 46°28′N 06°52′E
La Tour de Peilz see La Tour-de-Peilz
103 S11 la Tour-du-Pin Isère, E France 45°34′N 05°25′E
102 J11 la Tremblade Charente-Maritime, W France 45°45′N 01°07′W
102 L10 la Trimouille Vienne, W France 46°27′N 01°02′E
42 J9 La Trinidad Estelí, NW Nicaragua 12°57′N 86°15′W
41 V16 La Trinitaria Chiapas, SE Mexico 16°02′N 92°00′W
45 Q11 la Trinité E Martinique 14°44′N 60°58′W
15 U7 La Trinité-des-Monts Québec, SE Canada 48°07′N 68°31′W
18 C15 Latrobe Pennsylvania, NE USA 40°18′N 79°19′W
183 P13 La Trobe River ≈ Victoria, SE Australia
Lattakia/Lattaquié see Al Lādhiqīyah
171 S13 Latu Pulau Seram, E Indonesia 03°24′S 128°37′E
15 P9 La Tuque Québec, SE Canada 47°26′N 72°47′W
155 G14 Lātūr Mahārāshtra, C India 18°24′N 76°34′E
118 G8 Latvia off. Republic of Latvia, Ger. Lettland, Latv. Latvija, Latvijas Republika; prev. Latvian SSR, Rus. Latviyskaya SSR. ◆ republic NE Europe
Latvian SSR/Latvija/Latvijas Republika/Latviyskaya SSR see Latvia
Latvia, Republic of see Latvia
186 H7 Lau New Britain, E Papua New Guinea 05°46′S 151°21′E
175 R9 Lau Basin undersea feature S Pacific Ocean
101 O15 Lauchhammer Brandenburg, E Germany 51°30′N 13°48′E
105 O3 Laudio var. Llodio. País Vasco, N Spain 43°08′N 02°59′W
Laudunum see Laon
Laudus see St-Lô
Lauenburg/Lauenburg in Pommern see Lębork
101 L20 Lauf an der Pegnitz Bayern, SE Germany 49°31′N 11°16′E
108 D7 Laufen Basel, NW Switzerland 47°26′N 07°31′E
109 P5 Lauffen Salzburg, NW Austria 47°54′N 12°57′E
92 I2 Laugarbakki Nordhurland Vestra, N Iceland 65°18′N 20°51′W
92 I4 Laugarvatn Sudhurland, SW Iceland 64°09′N 20°43′W
31 O3 Laughing Fish Point headland Michigan, N USA 46°31′N 87°01′W
187 Z14 Lau Group island group E Fiji
Lauis see Lugano
93 M17 Laukaa Länsi-Suomi, C Finland 62°27′N 25°58′E
118 D12 Laukuva Tauragė, W Lithuania 55°37′N 22°12′E
Laun see Louny
183 P16 Launceston Tasmania, SE Australia 41°25′S 147°07′E
97 I24 Launceston anc. Dunheved. SW England, United Kingdom 50°38′N 04°21′W
54 C13 La Unión Nariño, SW Colombia 01°35′N 77°09′W
42 H8 La Unión La Unión, SE El Salvador 13°20′N 87°50′W
42 I6 La Unión Olancho, C Honduras 15°02′N 86°40′W
40 M15 La Unión Guerrero, S Mexico 17°58′N 101°49′W
41 Y14 La Unión Quintana Roo, E Mexico 18°00′N 101°48′W
105 S13 La Unión Murcia, SE Spain 37°37′N 00°54′W
54 L7 La Unión Barinas, C Venezuela 08°15′N 67°46′W
42 B10 La Unión ◈ department E El Salvador
38 H11 Laupāhoehoe var. Laupahoehoe. Hawaii, USA, C Pacific Ocean 20°00′N 155°15′W
Laupahoehoe see Laupāhoehoe
101 I23 Laupheim Baden-Württemberg, S Germany 48°13′N 09°54′E
181 W3 Laura Queensland, NE Australia 15°37′S 144°34′E
189 X2 Laura atoll Majuro Atoll, SE Marshall Islands
Laurana see Lovran
54 L8 La Urbana Bolívar, C Venezuela 07°05′N 66°58′W
21 Y4 Laurel Delaware, NE USA 38°33′N 75°34′W
23 V14 Laurel Florida, SE USA 27°07′N 82°27′W
21 W3 Laurel Maryland, NE USA 39°06′N 76°51′W
22 M6 Laurel Mississippi, S USA 31°41′N 89°10′W
33 U11 Laurel Montana, NW USA 45°40′N 108°46′W
29 R13 Laurel Nebraska, C USA 42°25′N 97°04′W
18 H15 Laureldale Pennsylvania, NE USA 40°24′N 75°52′W
18 C16 Laurel Hill ridge Pennsylvania, NE USA
29 T12 Laurens Iowa, C USA 42°51′N 94°51′W
21 P11 Laurens South Carolina, SE USA 34°29′N 82°01′W
Laurentian Highlands see Laurentian Mountains
15 P10 Laurentian Mountains var. Laurentian Highlands, Fr. Les Laurentides. plateau Newfoundland and Labrador/Québec, Canada
15 O12 Laurentides Québec, SE Canada 45°51′N 73°49′W
Laurentides, Les see Laurentian Mountains
107 M19 Lauria Basilicata, S Italy 40°03′N 15°50′E
194 I1 Laurie Island island Antarctica
21 T11 Laurinburg North Carolina, SE USA 34°46′N 79°29′W
30 M2 Laurium Michigan, N USA 47°14′N 88°26′W
Lauru see Choiseul
108 B9 Lausanne It. Losanna. Vaud, SW Switzerland 46°32′N 06°39′E
101 Q16 Lausche var. Luže. ▲ Czech Republic/Germany 50°52′N 14°39′E see also Luže
Lausche see Luže
101 Q16 Lausitzer Bergland var. Lausitzer Gebirge, Cz. Gory Lużyckie, Lužické Hory', Eng. Lusatian Mountains. ▲▲ E Germany
Lausitzer Gebirge see Lausitzer Bergland
Lausitzer Neisse see Neisse
103 T12 Lautaret, Col du pass SE France
63 G15 Lautaro Araucanía, C Chile 38°30′S 71°30′W
101 F21 Lauter ≈ W Germany
108 I7 Lauterach Vorarlberg, NW Austria 47°29′N 09°44′E
101 I17 Lauterbach Hessen, C Germany 50°37′N 09°24′E
108 E9 Lauterbrunnen Bern, C Switzerland 46°36′N 07°52′E
169 U14 Laut Kecil, Kepulauan island group N Indonesia
187 X14 Lautoka Viti Levu, W Fiji 17°36′S 177°28′E
169 O8 Laut, Pulau prev. Laoet. island Borneo, C Indonesia
169 V14 Laut, Pulau island Kepulauan Natuna, W Indonesia
169 U13 Laut, Selat strait Borneo, C Indonesia
168 H8 Laut Tawar, Danau ◎ Sumatera, NW Indonesia
189 V14 Lauvergne Island island Chuuk, C Micronesia
98 M5 Lauwers Meer ◎ N Netherlands
98 M4 Lauwersoog Groningen, NE Netherlands 53°25′N 06°14′E
102 M14 Lauzerte Tarn-et-Garonne, S France 44°15′N 01°08′E
25 U13 Lavaca Bay bay Texas, SW USA
25 U12 Lavaca River ≈ Texas, SW USA
15 O12 Laval Québec, SE Canada 45°32′N 73°44′W
102 J6 Laval Mayenne, NW France 48°04′N 00°46′W
15 T6 Laval ≈ Québec, SE Canada
105 S9 La Vall d'Uixó var. Vall D'Uxó. Valenciana, E Spain 39°49′N 00°15′W
61 F19 Lavalleja ◈ department S Uruguay
15 O12 Lavaltrie Québec, SE Canada 45°56′N 73°14′W
186 M10 Lavanggu Rennell, S Solomon Islands 11°39′S 160°13′E
143 O14 Lāvān, Jazireh-ye island S Iran
109 U8 Lavant ≈ S Austria
118 G5 Lavassaare Ger. Lawassaar. Pärnumaa, SW Estonia 58°29′N 24°22′E
104 L3 La Vecilla de Curueño Castilla y León, N Spain 42°51′N 05°24′W
45 N8 La Vega var. Concepción de la Vega. C Dominican Republic 19°15′N 70°33′W
La Vela see La Vela de Coro
54 J4 La Vela de Coro var. La Vela. Falcón, N Venezuela 11°30′N 69°33′W
103 N17 Lavelanet Ariège, S France 42°56′N 01°50′E
107 M17 Lavello Basilicata, S Italy 41°03′N 15°48′E
36 J8 La Verkin Utah, W USA 37°12′N 113°16′W
26 J8 Laverne Oklahoma, C USA 36°42′N 99°53′W
25 S12 La Vernia Texas, SW USA 29°19′N 98°07′W
93 K18 Lavia Länsi-Suomi, SW Finland 61°36′N 22°34′E
14 I12 Lavieille, Lake ◎ Ontario, SE Canada
94 C12 Lavik Sogn Og Fjordane, S Norway 61°06′N 05°25′E
La Vila Joiosa see Villajoyosa
33 U10 Lavina Montana, NW USA 46°18′N 108°55′W
194 H5 Lavoisier Island island Antarctica
23 U2 Lavonia Georgia, SE USA 34°26′N 83°06′W
103 R13 la Voulte-sur-Rhône Ardèche, E France 44°49′N 04°46′E
123 W5 Lavrentiya Chukotskiy Avtonomnyy Okrug, NE Russian Federation 65°33′N 171°12′W
115 H20 Lávrio prev. Lávrion. Attikí, C Greece 37°43′N 24°03′E
Lávrion see Lávrio
83 L22 Lavumisa prev. Gollel. SE Swaziland 27°18′S 31°55′E
149 T4 Lawarai Pass pass N Pakistan
Lawassaar see Lavassaare
141 P16 Lawdar SW Yemen 13°49′N 45°55′E
25 Q7 Lawn Texas, SW USA 32°07′N 99°45′W
195 Y4 Law Promontory headland Antarctica
77 O14 Lawra NW Ghana 10°40′N 02°49′W
185 E23 Lawrence Otago, South Island, New Zealand 45°53′S 169°43′E
31 P14 Lawrence Indiana, N USA 39°49′N 86°01′W
27 Q4 Lawrence Kansas, C USA 38°58′N 95°15′W
19 O10 Lawrence Massachusetts, NE USA 42°42′N 71°09′W
20 I5 Lawrenceburg Kentucky, S USA 38°02′N 84°53′W
20 I10 Lawrenceburg Tennessee, S USA 35°15′N 87°20′W
23 T3 Lawrenceville Georgia, SE USA 33°57′N 83°59′W
31 N15 Lawrenceville Illinois, N USA 38°43′N 87°40′W
21 V7 Lawrenceville Virginia, NE USA 36°45′N 77°50′W
27 S3 Lawson Missouri, C USA 39°26′N 94°12′W
26 L12 Lawton Oklahoma, C USA 34°35′N 98°20′W
140 I4 Lawz, Jabal al ▲ NW Saudi Arabia 28°45′N 35°20′E
95 L16 Laxå Örebro, C Sweden 59°00′N 14°37′E
125 T5 Laya ≈ NW Russian Federation
57 I19 La Yarada Tacna, SW Peru 18°14′S 70°30′W
141 S15 Layjūn C Yemen 15°27′N 49°16′E
141 Q9 Laylā var. Laila. Ar Riyāḍ, C Saudi Arabia 22°14′N 46°40′E
23 P4 Lay Lake ⊠ Alabama, S USA
45 P14 Layou Saint Vincent, Saint Vincent and the Grenadines 13°11′N 61°16′W
La Youne see El Ayoun
192 L5 Laysan Island island Hawaiian Islands, Hawai'i, USA
36 L2 Layton Utah, W USA 41°03′N 112°00′W
34 L5 Laytonville California, W USA 39°39′N 123°30′W
172 H17 Lazare, Pointe headland Mahé, NE Seychelles 04°46′S 55°28′E
123 T12 Lazarev Khabarovskiy Kray, SE Russian Federation 52°11′N 141°18′E
112 L12 Lazarevac Serbia, C Serbia 44°25′N 20°17′E
65 N22 Lazarev Sea sea Antarctica
40 M15 Lázaro Cárdenas Michoacán, SW Mexico 17°56′N 102°13′W
119 F15 Lazdijai Alytus, S Lithuania 54°13′N 23°33′E
107 H15 Lazio anc. Latium. ◈ region C Italy
111 A16 Lázně Kynžvart Ger. Bad Königswart. Karlovarský Kraj, W Czech Republic 50°00′N 12°40′E
Lazovsk see Singerei
167 R12 Leach Poŭthĭsăt, W Cambodia 12°19′N 103°45′E
27 X9 Leachville Arkansas, C USA 35°56′N 90°15′W
28 I9 Lead South Dakota, N USA 44°21′N 103°45′W
11 S16 Leader Saskatchewan, S Canada 50°55′N 109°31′W
19 S6 Lead Mountain ▲ Maine, NE USA 44°53′N 68°07′W
37 R5 Leadville Colorado, C USA 39°15′N 106°17′W
11 V12 Leaf Rapids Manitoba, C Canada 56°30′N 100°02′W
22 M7 Leaf River ≈ Mississippi, S USA
25 W11 League City Texas, SW USA 29°30′N 95°05′W
92 K8 Leaibevuotna Nor. Olderfjord. Finnmark, N Norway 70°29′N 24°58′E
23 N7 Leakesville Mississippi, S USA 31°09′N 88°33′W
25 Q11 Leakey Texas, SW USA 29°44′N 99°48′W
Leal see Lihula
83 G15 Lealui Western, W Zambia 15°12′S 22°59′E
Leamhcán see Lucan
14 C18 Leamington Ontario, S Canada 42°03′N 82°35′W
Leamington/Leamington Spa see Royal Leamington Spa
Leammi see Lemmenjoki
25 S10 Leander Texas, SW USA 30°34′N 97°51′W
60 F13 Leandro N. Alem Misiones, NE Argentina 27°34′S 55°15′W
97 A20 Leane, Lough Ir. Loch Léin. ◎ SW Ireland
180 G8 Learmonth Western Australia 22°17′S 114°03′E
Leau see Zoutleeuw
L'Eau d'Heure see Plate Taille, Lac de la
190 D12 Leava Île Futuna, S Wallis and Futuna
Leavdnja see Lakselv
27 R3 Leavenworth Kansas, C USA 39°19′N 94°55′W
32 I8 Leavenworth Washington, NW USA 47°36′N 120°39′W
92 L8 Leavvajohka var. Levajok. Finnmark, N Norway 69°57′N 26°18′E
27 R4 Leawood Kansas, C USA 38°57′N 94°37′W
110 H6 Łeba Ger. Leba. Pomorskie, N Poland 54°45′N 17°32′E
110 I6 Łeba Ger. Leba. ≈ N Poland
Leba see Łeba
101 D20 Lebach Saarland, SW Germany 49°25′N 06°54′E
Leba, Jezioro see Łebsko, Jezioro
171 P8 Lebak Mindanao, S Philippines 06°28′N 124°03′E
Lebanese Republic see Lebanon
31 O13 Lebanon Indiana, N USA 40°03′N 86°28′W
20 L6 Lebanon Kentucky, S USA 37°33′N 85°15′W
27 U6 Lebanon Missouri, C USA 37°40′N 92°40′W
19 N9 Lebanon New Hampshire, NE USA 43°40′N 72°15′W
32 G12 Lebanon Oregon, NW USA 44°32′N 122°54′W
18 H15 Lebanon Pennsylvania, NE USA 40°20′N 76°24′W
20 J8 Lebanon Tennessee, S USA 36°11′N 86°19′W
21 P7 Lebanon Virginia, NE USA 36°52′N 82°07′W
138 G6 Lebanon off. Lebanese Republic, Ar. Al Lubnān, Fr. Liban. ◆ republic SW Asia
20 K6 Lebanon Junction Kentucky, S USA 37°49′N 85°43′W
Lebanon, Mount see Liban, Jebel
146 J10 Lebap Lebapskiy Velayat, NE Turkmenistan 41°04′N 61°49′E
Lebapskiy Velayat see Lebap Welaýaty
146 J11 Lebap Welaýaty Rus. Lebapskiy Velayat; prev. Rus. Chardzhevskaya Oblast, Turkm. Chärjew Oblasty. ◈ province E Turkmenistan
Lebasee see Łebsko, Jezioro
99 F17 Lebbeke Oost-Vlaanderen, NW Belgium 51°00′N 04°08′E
35 S14 Lebec California, W USA 34°51′N 118°52′W
Lebedin see Lebedyn

◆ Country
● Country Capital
◇ Dependent Territory
○ Dependent Territory Capital
◈ Administrative Regions
✈ International Airport
▲ Mountain
▲▲ Mountain Range
⛰ Volcano
≈ River
◎ Lake
⊠ Reservoir

123 *Q11* **Lebedinyy** Respublika Sakha (Yakutiya), NE Russian Federation *58°23′N 125°24′E*
126 *L6* **Lebedyan'** Lipetskaya Oblast', W Russian Federation *53°00′N 39°11′E*
117 *T4* **Lebedyn** *Rus.* Lebedin. Sums'ka Oblast', NE Ukraine *50°36′N 34°30′E*
12 *I12* **Lebel-sur-Quévillon** Québec, SE Canada *49°01′N 76°56′W*
92 *L8* **Lebesby** *Lapp.* Davvesiida. Finnmark, N Norway *70°31′N 27°00′E*
102 *M9* **le Blanc** Indre, C France *46°38′N 01°04′E*
79 *L15* **Lebo** Orientale, N Dem. Rep. Congo *04°30′N 23°58′E*
27 *P5* **Lebo** Kansas, C USA *38°22′N 95°50′W*
110 *H6* **Lębork** *var.* Lębórk, *Ger.* Lauenburg, Lauenburg in Pommern. Pomorskie, N Poland *54°32′N 17°43′E*
103 *O17* **le Boulou** Pyrénées-Orientales, S France *42°32′N 02°50′E*
108 *A9* **Le Brassus** Vaud, W Switzerland *46°35′N 06°14′E*
104 *J15* **Lebrija** Andalucía, S Spain *36°55′N 06°04′W*
110 *G6* **Łebsko, Jezioro** *Ger.* Lebasee; *prev.* Jezioro Łeba. ◎ N Poland
63 *F14* **Lebu** Bío Bío, C Chile *37°38′S 73°43′W*
Lebyazh'ye *see* Akku
104 *F6* **Leça da Palmeira** Porto, N Portugal *41°12′N 08°43′W*
103 *U15* **le Cannet** Alpes-Maritimes, SE France *43°35′N 07°E*
Le Cap *see* Cap-Haïtien
103 *P2* **le Cateau-Cambrésis** Nord, N France *50°05′N 03°32′E*
107 *Q18* **Lecce** Puglia, SE Italy *40°23′N 18°11′E*
106 *D7* **Lecco** Lombardia, N Italy *45°51′N 09°23′E*
29 *V10* **Le Center** Minnesota, N USA *44°23′N 93°43′W*
108 *J7* **Lech** Vorarlberg, W Austria *47°14′N 10°10′E*
101 *K22* **Lech** ≈ Austria/Germany
115 *D19* **Lechainá** *var.* Lehena, Lekhainá. Dytikí Elláda, S Greece *37°57′N 21°16′E*
102 *J11* **le Château d'Oléron** Charente-Maritime, W France *45°53′N 01°12′W*
103 *R3* **le Chesne** Ardennes, N France *49°33′N 04°42′E*
103 *R13* **le Cheylard** Ardèche, E France *44°55′N 04°27′E*
108 *K7* **Lechtaler Alpen** ▲▲ W Austria
100 *H6* **Leck** Schleswig-Holstein, N Germany *54°45′N 09°00′E*
14 *L9* **Lecointre, Lac** ◎ Québec, SE Canada
22 *H7* **Lecompte** Louisiana, S USA *31°05′N 92°24′W*
103 *Q9* **le Creusot** Saône-et-Loire, C France *46°48′N 04°27′E*
Lecumberri *see* Lekunberri
110 *P13* **Łęczna** Lubelskie, E Poland *51°20′N 22°52′E*
110 *J12* **Łęczyca** *Ger.* Lentschiza, *Rus.* Lenchitsa. Łódzkie, C Poland *52°04′N 19°10′E*
100 *F10* **Leda** ≈ NW Germany
109 *Y9* **Ledava** ≈ NE Slovenia
99 *F17* **Lede** Oost-Vlaanderen, NW Belgium *50°58′N 03°59′E*
104 *K6* **Ledesma** Castilla y León, N Spain *41°05′N 06°00′W*
45 *Q12* **le Diamant** SW Martinique *14°29′N 61°02′W*
172 *J16* **Le Digue** *island* Inner Islands, NE Seychelles
103 *Q10* **le Donjon** Allier, C France *46°19′N 03°50′E*
102 *M10* **le Dorat** Haute-Vienne, C France *46°14′N 01°05′E*
Ledo Salinarius *see* Lons-le-Saunier
11 *Q14* **Leduc** Alberta, SW Canada *53°17′N 113°30′W*
123 *V7* **Ledyanaya, Gora** ▲ E Russian Federation *61°51′N 171°03′E*
97 *C21* **Lee** *Ir.* An Laoi. ≈ SW Ireland
29 *U5* **Leech Lake** ◎ Minnesota, N USA
26 *K10* **Leedey** Oklahoma, C USA *35°54′N 99°21′W*
97 *M17* **Leeds** N England, United Kingdom *53°50′N 01°35′W*
23 *P4* **Leeds** Alabama, S USA *33°33′N 86°32′W*
29 *O3* **Leeds** North Dakota, N USA *48°19′N 99°43′W*
98 *N6* **Leek** Groningen, NE Netherlands *53°10′N 06°24′E*
99 *K15* **Leende** Noord-Brabant, SE Netherlands *51°21′N 05°34′E*
100 *F10* **Leer** Niedersachsen, NW Germany *53°14′N 07°26′E*
98 *J13* **Leerdam** Zuid-Holland, C Netherlands *51°54′N 05°06′E*
98 *K12* **Leersum** Utrecht, C Netherlands *52°01′N 05°26′E*
23 *W11* **Leesburg** Florida, SE USA *28°48′N 81°52′W*
21 *V3* **Leesburg** Virginia, NE USA *39°09′N 77°34′W*
27 *R4* **Lees Summit** Missouri, C USA *38°55′N 94°21′W*
22 *G7* **Leesville** Louisiana, S USA *31°08′N 93°15′W*
25 *S12* **Leesville** Texas, SW USA *29°22′N 97°45′W*
31 *U13* **Leesville Lake** ⊠ Ohio, N USA
Leesville Lake *see* Smith Mountain Lake
183 *P9* **Leeton** New South Wales, SE Australia *34°33′S 146°24′E*
98 *L6* **Leeuwarden** *Fris.* Ljouwert. Fryslân, N Netherlands *53°15′N 05°48′E*
180 *I14* **Leeuwin, Cape** *headland* Western Australia *34°18′S 115°03′E*
35 *R8* **Lee Vining** California, W USA *37°57′N 119°07′W*
45 *V8* **Leeward Islands** *island group* E West Indies
Leeward Islands *see* Sotavento, Ilhas de
Leeward Islands *see* Vent, Îles Sous le
79 *G20* **Léfini** ≈ SE Congo
115 *C17* **Lefkáda** *prev.* Levkás. Lefkáda, Iónia Nisiá, Greece, C Mediterranean Sea *38°50′N 20°42′E*
115 *B17* **Lefkáda** *It.* Santa Maura, *prev.* Levkás; *anc.* Leucas. *island* Iónia Nisiá, Greece, C Mediterranean Sea
115 *H25* **Lefká Óri** ▲▲ Kríti, Greece, E Mediterranean Sea
115 *B16* **Lefkímmi** *var.* Levkímmi. Kérkyra, Iónia Nisiá, Greece, C Mediterranean Sea *39°26′N 20°05′E*
Lefkosía/Lefkoşa *see* Nicosia
25 *O2* **Lefors** Texas, SW USA *35°26′N 100°48′W*
45 *R12* **le François** E Martinique *14°36′N 60°59′W*
180 *L12* **Lefroy, Lake** *salt lake* Western Australia
Legaceaster *see* Chester
105 *N8* **Leganés** Madrid, C Spain *40°20′N 03°46′W*
Legaspi *see* Legazpi City
Leghorn *see* Livorno
110 *M11* **Legionowo** Mazowieckie, C Poland *52°25′N 20°56′E*
99 *K24* **Léglise** Luxembourg, SE Belgium *49°48′N 05°31′E*
106 *G8* **Legnago** Lombardia, NE Italy *45°13′N 11°18′E*
106 *D7* **Legnano** Veneto, NE Italy *45°36′N 08°54′E*
111 *F14* **Legnica** *Ger.* Liegnitz. Dolnośląskie, SW Poland *51°12′N 16°11′E*
35 *Q9* **Le Grand** California, W USA *37°12′N 120°15′W*
103 *Q15* **le Grau-du-Roi** Gard, S France *43°32′N 04°10′E*
183 *U3* **Legume** New South Wales, SE Australia *28°24′S 152°20′E*
102 *L4* **le Havre** *Eng.* Havre; *prev.* le Havre-de-Grâce. Seine-Maritime, N France *49°30′N 00°06′E*
le Havre-de-Grâce *see* le Havre
Lehena *see* Lechainá
36 *L3* **Lehi** Utah, W USA *40°23′N 111°51′W*
18 *I14* **Lehighton** Pennsylvania, NE USA *40°49′N 75°42′W*
29 *O6* **Lehr** North Dakota, N USA *46°15′N 99°21′W*
38 *A8* **Lehua Island** *island* Hawaiian Islands, Hawai'i, USA
149 *S9* **Leiāh** Punjab, NE Pakistan *30°59′N 70°58′E*
109 *W9* **Leibnitz** Steiermark, SE Austria *46°48′N 15°33′E*
97 *M19* **Leicester** *Lat.* Batae Coritanorum. C England, United Kingdom *52°38′N 01°05′W*
97 *M19* **Leicestershire** *cultural region* C England, United Kingdom
Leicheng *see* Leizhou
98 *H11* **Leiden** *prev.* Leyden; *anc.* Lugdunum Batavorum. Zuid-Holland, W Netherlands *52°09′N 04°30′E*
98 *H11* **Leiderdorp** Zuid-Holland, W Netherlands *52°08′N 04°32′E*
98 *G11* **Leidschendam** Zuid-Holland, W Netherlands *52°05′N 04°24′E*
99 *D18* **Leie** *Fr.* Lys. ≈ Belgium/France
Leifear *see* Lifford
184 *L4* **Leigh** Auckland, North Island, New Zealand *36°17′S 174°48′E*
97 *K17* **Leigh** NW England, United Kingdom *53°30′N 02°33′W*
182 *I5* **Leigh Creek** South Australia *30°27′S 138°23′E*
23 *O2* **Leighton** Alabama, S USA *34°42′N 87°31′W*
97 *M21* **Leighton Buzzard** E England, United Kingdom *51°55′N 00°41′W*
Léim an Bhradáin *see* Leixlip
Léim An Mhadaidh *see* Limavady
Léime, Ceann *see* Loop Head, Ireland
Léime, Ceann *see* Slyne Head, Ireland
101 *G20* **Leimen** Baden-Württemberg, SW Germany *49°21′N 08°40′E*
100 *I13* **Leine** ≈ NW Germany
101 *J15* **Leinefelde** Thüringen, C Germany *51°22′N 10°19′E*
Léin, Loch *see* Leane, Lough
97 *D19* **Leinster** *Ir.* Cúige Laighean. *cultural region* E Ireland
97 *F19* **Leinster, Mount** *Ir.* Stua Laighean. ▲ SE Ireland *52°36′N 06°45′W*
119 *F15* **Leipalingis** Alytus, S Lithuania *54°05′N 23°52′E*
92 *J12* **Leipojärvi** Norrbotten, N Sweden *67°03′N 21°15′E*
31 *R12* **Leipsic** Ohio, N USA *41°06′N 83°58′W*
Leipsic *see* Leipzig
115 *M20* **Leipsoí** *island* Dodekánisa, Greece, Aegean Sea
101 *M15* **Leipzig** *Pol.* Lipsk, *hist.* Leipsic; *anc.* Lipsia. Sachsen, E Germany *51°19′N 12°24′E*
101 *M15* **Leipzig Halle** ✈ Sachsen, E Germany *51°26′N 12°14′E*
104 *G9* **Leiria** *anc.* Collipo. Leiria, C Portugal *39°45′N 08°49′W*
104 *F9* **Leiria** ◐ *district* C Portugal
95 *C15* **Leirvik** Hordaland, S Norway *59°49′N 05°27′E*
118 *E5* **Leisi** *Ger.* Laisberg. Saaremaa, W Estonia *58°33′N 22°41′E*
104 *J3* **Leitariegos, Puerto de** *pass* NW Spain
20 *J6* **Leitchfield** Kentucky, S USA *37°28′N 86°19′W*
109 *Y5* **Leitha** *Hung.* Lajta. ≈ Austria/Hungary
Leitir Ceanainn *see* Letterkenny
Leitmeritz *see* Litoměřice
Leitomischl *see* Litomyšl
97 *D16* **Leitrim** *Ir.* Liatroim. *cultural region* NW Ireland
Leix *see* Laois
97 *F18* **Leixlip** *Eng.* Salmon Leap, *Ir.* Léim an Bhradáin. Kildare, E Ireland *53°23′N 06°32′W*
64 *N8* **Leixões** Porto, N Portugal *41°11′N 08°41′W*
161 *N12* **Leiyang** Hunan, S China *26°23′N 112°49′E*
160 *L16* **Leizhou** *var.* Haikang, Leicheng. Guangdong, S China *20°54′N 110°05′E*
160 *L16* **Leizhou Bandao** *var.* Luichow Peninsula. *peninsula* S China
98 *H13* **Lek** ≈ SW Netherlands
114 *I13* **Lekánis** ▲▲ NE Greece
172 *H13* **Le Kartala** ▲ Grande Comore, NW Comoros
Le Kef *see* El Kef
79 *G20* **Lékéti, Monts de la** ▲▲ S Congo
Lekhainá *see* Lechainá
92 *G11* **Leknes** Nordland, C Norway *68°07′N 13°36′E*
79 *F20* **Lékoumou** ◐ *province* SW Congo
94 *L13* **Leksand** Dalarna, C Sweden *60°44′N 15°E*
124 *H8* **Leksozero, Ozero** ◎ NW Russian Federation
105 *Q3* **Lekunberri** *var.* Lecumberri. Navarra, N Spain *43°00′N 01°54′W*
171 *S11* **Lelai, Tanjung** *headland* Pulau Halmahera, N Indonesia *01°32′N 128°43′E*
45 *Q12* **le Lamentin** *var.* Lamentin. C Martinique *14°37′N 61°01′W*
31 *P6* **Leland** Michigan, N USA *45°01′N 85°44′W*
22 *J4* **Leland** Mississippi, S USA *33°24′N 90°54′W*
95 *J16* **Lelång** *var.* Lelången. ◎ S Sweden
Lelången *see* Lelång
Lel'chitsy *see* Lyel'chytsy
le Léman *see* Geneva, Lake
Leli *see* Tianlin
25 *O3* **Lelia Lake** Texas, SW USA *34°52′N 100°42′W*
113 *I14* **Lelija** ▲ SE Bosnia and Herzegovina *43°25′N 18°31′E*
108 *C8* **Le Locle** Neuchâtel, W Switzerland *47°04′N 06°45′E*
189 *Y14* **Lelu** Kosrae, E Micronesia
Lelu *see* Lelu Island
189 *Y14* **Lelu Island** *var.* Lelu. *island* Kosrae, E Micronesia
55 *W9* **Lelydorp** Wanica, N Surinam *05°36′N 55°04′W*
98 *K9* **Lelystad** Flevoland, C Netherlands *52°30′N 05°26′E*
63 *K25* **Le Maire, Estrecho de** *strait* S Argentina
168 *L10* **Lemang** Pulau Rangsang, W Indonesia *01°04′N 102°44′E*
186 *I7* **Lemankoa** Buka Island, NE Papua New Guinea *05°06′S 154°23′E*
Léman, Lac *see* Geneva, Lake
102 *L6* **le Mans** Sarthe, NW France *48°N 00°12′E*
29 *S12* **Le Mars** Iowa, C USA *42°47′N 96°10′W*
109 *S3* **Lembach im Mühlkreis** Oberösterreich, N Austria *48°28′N 13°53′E*
101 *G23* **Lemberg** ▲ SW Germany *48°09′N 08°47′E*
Lemberg *see* L'viv
Lemdiyya *see* Médéa
121 *P3* **Lemesós** *var.* Limassol. SW Cyprus *34°41′N 33°02′E*
100 *H13* **Lemgo** Nordrhein-Westfalen, W Germany *52°02′N 08°54′E*
33 *P13* **Lemhi Range** ▲▲ Idaho, NW USA
9 *S6* **Lemieux Islands** *island group* Nunavut, NE Canada
171 *O11* **Lemito** Sulawesi, N Indonesia *0°34′N 121°31′E*
92 *L10* **Lemmenjoki** *Lapp.* Leammi. ≈ NE Finland
98 *L7* **Lemmer** *Fris.* De Lemmer. Fryslân, N Netherlands *52°50′N 05°43′E*
28 *L7* **Lemmon** South Dakota, N USA *45°54′N 102°08′W*
36 *M15* **Lemmon, Mount** ▲ Arizona, SW USA *32°26′N 110°47′W*
Lemnos *see* Límnos
31 *O14* **Lemon, Lake** ◎ Indiana, N USA
102 *J5* **le Mont St-Michel** *castle* Manche, N France
35 *Q11* **Lemoore** California, W USA *36°16′N 119°48′W*
189 *T13* **Lemotol Bay** *bay* Chuuk Islands, C Micronesia
45 *Y5* **le Moule** *var.* Moule. Grande Terre, NE Guadeloupe *16°20′N 61°21′W*
Lemovices *see* Limoges
Le Moyen-Ogooué *see* Moyen-Ogooué
12 *M6* **le Moyne, Lac** ◎ Québec, E Canada
93 *L18* **Lempäälä** Länsi-Suomi, W Finland *61°14′N 23°47′E*
42 *E7* **Lempa, Río** ≈ Central America
42 *F7* **Lempira** *prev.* Gracias. ◐ *department* SW Honduras
Lemsalu *see* Limbaži
107 *N17* **Le Murge** ▲▲ SE Italy
125 *V6* **Lemva** ≈ NW Russian Federation
95 *F21* **Lemvig** Midtjylland, W Denmark *56°31′N 08°19′E*
166 *K8* **Lemyethna** Ayeyarwady, SW Burma (Myanmar) *17°36′N 95°08′E*
30 *K10* **Lena** Illinois, N USA *42°22′N 89°49′W*
129 *V4* **Lena** ≈ NE Russian Federation
173 *N13* **Lena Tablemount** *undersea feature* S Indian Ocean *51°06′S 56°54′E*
Lenchitsa *see* Łęczyca
59 *N17* **Lençóis** Bahia, E Brazil *12°36′S 41°24′W*
60 *K9* **Lençóis Paulista** São Paulo, S Brazil *22°35′S 48°51′W*
109 *Y9* **Lendava** *Hung.* Lendva, *Ger.* Unterlimbach; *prev.* Dolnja Lendava. NE Slovenia *46°33′N 16°27′E*
83 *F20* **Lendepas** Hardap, SE Namibia *24°41′S 19°58′E*
124 *H9* **Lendery** *Finn.* Lentiira. Respublika Kareliya, NW Russian Federation *63°20′N 31°18′E*
Lendum *see* Lens
Lendva *see* Lendava
27 *R4* **Lenexa** Kansas, C USA *38°57′N 94°43′W*
109 *Q5* **Lengau** Oberösterreich, N Austria *48°01′N 13°17′E*
145 *Q17* **Lenger** Yuzhnyy Kazakhstan, S Kazakhstan *42°10′N 69°54′E*
Lenghu *see* Lenghuzhen
159 *O9* **Lenghuzhen** *var.* Lenghu. Qinghai, C China *38°50′N 93°25′E*
159 *T9* **Lenglong Ling** ▲ N China *37°40′N 102°13′E*
108 *D7* **Lengnau** Bern, W Switzerland *47°12′N 07°23′E*
95 *M20* **Lenhovda** Kronoberg, S Sweden *57°00′N 15°16′E*
Lenīn *see* Uzynkol', Kazakhstan
Lenin *see* Akdepe, Turkmenistan
Leninabad *see* Khujand
Leninakan *see* Gyumri
Lenina, Pik *see* Lenin Peak
117 *V12* **Lenine** *Rus.* Lenino. Avtonomna Respublika Krym, S Ukraine *45°18′N 35°47′E*
Lenīngor *see* Leninogorsk
Leningrad *see* Sankt-Peterburg
Leningrad *see* Mu'minobod
126 *L13* **Leningradskaya** Krasnodarskiy Kray, SW Russian Federation *46°19′N 39°23′E*
195 *S16* **Leningradskaya** *Russian research station* Antarctica *69°30′S 159°51′E*
124 *H12* **Leningradskaya Oblast'** ◐ *province* NW Russian Federation
Leningradskiy *see* Mu'minobod
Lenino *see* Lyenina, Belarus
Lenino *see* Lenine, Ukraine
Leninobod *see* Khujand
145 *X9* **Leninogorsk** *Kaz.* Lenīngor. Vostochnyy Kazakhstan, E Kazakhstan *50°20′N 83°34′E*
147 *T12* **Lenin Peak** *Rus.* Pik Lenina, *Taj.* Qullai Lenin. ▲ Kyrgyzstan/Tajikistan *39°20′N 72°50′E*
147 *S8* **Leninpol'** Talasskaya Oblast', NW Kyrgyzstan *42°29′N 71°54′E*
Lenin, Qullai *see* Lenin Peak
127 *P11* **Leninsk** Volgogradskaya Oblast', SW Russian Federation *48°41′N 45°18′E*
Leninsk *see* Baykonyr, Kazakhstan
Leninsk *see* Akdepe, Turkmenistan
Leninsk *see* Asaka, Uzbekistan
145 *T8* **Leninskiy** Pavlodar, E Kazakhstan *52°13′N 76°50′E*
122 *I13* **Leninsk-Kuznetskiy** Kemerovskaya Oblast', S Russian Federation *54°42′N 86°16′E*
125 *P15* **Leninskoje** Kirovskaya Oblast', NW Russian Federation *58°19′N 47°03′E*
Leninskoye *see* Uzynkol'
Lenin-Turkmenski *see* Türkmenabat
Leninváros *see* Tiszaújváros
Lenkoran' *see* Länkäran
101 *F15* **Lenne** ≈ W Germany
101 *G16* **Lennestadt** Nordrhein-Westfalen, W Germany *51°07′N 08°04′E*
29 *R11* **Lennox** South Dakota, N USA *43°21′N 96°53′W*
63 *J25* **Lennox, Isla** *Eng.* Lennox Island. *island* S Chile
Lennox Island *see* Lennox, Isla
21 *Q9* **Lenoir** North Carolina, SE USA *35°56′N 81°31′W*
20 *M9* **Lenoir City** Tennessee, S USA *35°48′N 84°15′W*
108 *C7* **Le Noirmont** Jura, NW Switzerland *47°14′N 06°57′E*
14 *L9* **Lenôtre, Lac** ◎ Québec, SE Canada
29 *U15* **Lenox** Iowa, C USA *40°52′N 94°33′W*
103 *O2* **Lens** *anc.* Lendum, Lentium. Pas-de-Calais, N France *50°26′N 02°50′E*
123 *O11* **Lensk** Respublika Sakha (Yakutiya), NE Russian Federation *60°43′N 115°16′E*
111 *F24* **Lenti** Zala, SW Hungary *46°38′N 16°30′E*
Lentia *see* Linz
93 *N14* **Lentiira** Oulu, E Finland *64°22′N 29°52′E*
Lentiira *see* Lendery
107 *L25* **Lentini** *anc.* Leontini. Sicilia, Italy, C Mediterranean Sea *37°17′N 15°00′E*
Lentium *see* Lens
Lentschiza *see* Łęczyca
93 *N15* **Lentua** ◎ E Finland
119 *H14* **Lentvaris** *Pol.* Landwarów. Vilnius, SE Lithuania *24°39′N 24°58′E*
108 *F7* **Lenzburg** Aargau, N Switzerland *47°23′N 08°11′E*
109 *R5* **Lenzing** Oberösterreich, N Austria *47°58′N 13°34′E*
77 *P13* **Léo** SW Burkina *11°07′N 02°08′W*
109 *V7* **Leoben** Steiermark, C Austria *47°23′N 15°06′E*
Leobschütz *see* Głubczyce
44 *L9* **Léogâne** S Haiti *18°32′N 72°37′W*
171 *O11* **Leok** Sulawesi, N Indonesia *01°10′N 121°20′E*
29 *O7* **Leola** South Dakota, N USA *45°41′N 98°58′W*
97 *K20* **Leominster** W England, United Kingdom *52°09′N 02°18′W*
19 *N11* **Leominster** Massachusetts, NE USA *42°29′N 71°43′W*
102 *I15* **Léon** Landes, SW France *43°54′N 01°17′W*
40 *M12* **León** *var.* León de los Aldamas. Guanajuato, C Mexico *21°05′N 101°43′W*
42 *I10* **León** León, NW Nicaragua *12°24′N 86°52′W*
104 *L4* **León** Castilla y León, NW Spain *42°34′N 05°34′W*
29 *V16* **Leon** Iowa, C USA *40°44′N 93°45′W*
42 *I9* **León** ◐ *department* W Nicaragua
104 *K4* **León** ◐ *province* Castilla y León, NW Spain
León *see* Cotopaxi
25 *V9* **Leona** Texas, SW USA *31°09′N 95°58′W*
25 *U5* **Leonard** Texas, SW USA *33°22′N 96°15′W*
107 *H15* **Leonardo da Vinci** *prev.* Fiumicino. ✈ (Roma) Lazio, C Italy *41°48′N 12°15′E*
21 *X5* **Leonardtown** Maryland, NE USA *38°17′N 76°35′W*
25 *Q13* **Leona River** ≈ Texas, SW USA
41 *Z11* **Leona Vicario** Quintana Roo, SE Mexico *20°57′N 87°06′W*
101 *H21* **Leonberg** Baden-Württemberg, SW Germany *48°48′N 09°01′E*
62 *M3* **León, Cerro** ▲ NW Paraguay *20°21′S 60°16′W*
León de los Aldamas *see* León
109 *T4* **Leonding** Oberösterreich, N Austria *48°17′N 14°15′E*
107 *I14* **Leonessa** Lazio, C Italy *42°36′N 12°56′E*
107 *K24* **Leonforte** Sicilia, Italy, C Mediterranean Sea *37°38′N 14°23′E*
183 *O13* **Leongatha** Victoria, SE Australia *38°30′S 145°56′E*
Leonídi *see* Leonídio
115 *F21* **Leonídio** *var.* Leonídi. Pelopónnisos, S Greece *37°11′N 22°50′E*
104 *J4* **León, Montes de** ▲▲ NW Spain
180 *K11* **Leonora** Western Australia *28°52′S 121°16′E*
25 *S8* **Leon River** ≈ Texas, SW USA
Leontini *see* Lentini
Léopold II, Lac *see* Mai-Ndombe, Lac
99 *J17* **Leopoldsburg** Limburg, NE Belgium *51°07′N 05°16′E*
Léopoldville *see* Kinshasa
26 *I5* **Leoti** Kansas, C USA *38°28′N 101°22′W*
116 *M11* **Leova** *Rus.* Leovo. SW Moldova *46°31′N 28°16′E*
Leovo *see* Leova
102 *G8* **le Palais** Morbihan, NW France *47°20′N 03°08′W*
27 *X10* **Lepanto** Arkansas, C USA *35°34′N 90°21′W*
169 *N13* **Lepar, Pulau** *island* W Indonesia
104 *I14* **Lepe** Andalucía, S Spain *37°15′N 07°12′W*
Lepel' *see* Lyepyel'
83 *E25* **Lepelle** *var.* Elefantes; *prev.* Olifants. ≈ SW South Africa
83 *I20* **Lephepe** *var.* Lephephe. Kweneng, SE Botswana *23°20′S 25°50′E*
Lephephe *see* Lephepe
161 *Q10* **Leping** Jiangxi, S China *28°57′N 117°07′E*
Lépontiennes, Alpes/Lepontine, Alpi *see* Lepontine Alps
108 *G10* **Lepontine Alps** *Fr.* Alpes Lépontiennes, *It.* Alpi Lepontine. ▲▲ Italy/Switzerland
79 *G20* **Le Pool** ◐ *province* S Congo
173 *O16* **Le Port** NW Réunion
103 *N1* **le Portel** Pas-de-Calais, N France *50°42′N 01°35′E*
93 *N17* **Leppävirta** Itä-Suomi, C Finland *62°30′N 27°50′E*
45 *Q11* **le Prêcheur** NW Martinique *14°48′N 61°14′W*
145 *V13* **Lepsi** *prev.* Lepsy. Taldykorgan, SE Kazakhstan *46°14′N 78°56′E*
145 *V13* **Lepsi** *prev.* Lepsy. ≈ SE Kazakhstan
Lepsy *see* Lepsi
Le Puglie *see* Puglia
103 *Q12* **le Puy** *prev.* le Puy-en-Velay, *hist.* Anicium, Podium Anicensis. Haute-Loire, C France *45°03′N 03°53′E*
le Puy-en-Velay *see* le Puy
45 *X11* **le Raizet** *var.* Le Raizet. ✈ (Pointe-à-Pitre) Grande Terre, C Guadeloupe *16°16′N 61°31′W*
107 *J24* **Lercara Friddi** Sicilia, Italy, C Mediterranean Sea *37°45′N 13°37′E*
78 *G12* **Léré** Mayo-Kébbi, SW Chad *09°41′N 14°17′E*
Leribe *see* Hlotse
106 *E10* **Lerici** Liguria, NW Italy *44°06′N 09°53′E*
54 *I14* **Lérida** Vaupés, SE Colombia *0°01′S 70°28′W*
105 *U5* **Lérida** ◐ *province* Cataluña, NE Spain
Lérida *see* Lleida
105 *N5* **Lerma** Castilla y León, N Spain *42°02′N 03°46′W*
40 *M13* **Lerma, Río** ≈ C Mexico
Lerna *see* Lérni
115 *F20* **Lérni** *var.* Lerna. *prehistoric site* Pelopónnisos, S Greece
45 *R11* **le Robert** E Martinique *14°41′N 60°57′W*
115 *M21* **Léros** *island* Dodekánisa, Greece, Aegean Sea
30 *L13* **Le Roy** Illinois, N USA *40°21′N 88°45′W*
27 *Q6* **Le Roy** Kansas, C USA *38°04′N 95°37′W*
29 *W11* **Le Roy** Minnesota, N USA *43°30′N 92°30′W*
18 *E10* **Le Roy** New York, NE USA *42°58′N 77°58′W*
Lerrnayin Gharabakh *see* Nagorno-Karabakh
95 *J19* **Lerum** Västra Götaland, S Sweden *57°46′N 12°12′E*
96 *M2* **Lerwick** NE Scotland, United Kingdom *60°09′N 01°09′W*
45 *Y6* **les Abymes** *var.* Abymes. Grande Terre, C Guadeloupe *16°16′N 61°31′W*
les Albères *see* Albères, Chaîne des
102 *M4* **les Andelys** Eure, N France *49°15′N 01°26′E*
45 *Q12* **les Anses-d'Arlets** SW Martinique *14°29′N 61°05′W*
104 *L2* **Les Arriondes** *prev.* Arriondas. Asturias, N Spain *43°23′N 05°11′W*
105 *U6* **Les Borges Blanques** *var.* Borjas Blancas. Cataluña, NE Spain *41°31′N 00°52′E*
Lesbos *see* Lésvos
Les Cayes *see* Cayes
31 *Q4* **Les Cheneaux Islands** *island* Michigan, N USA
105 *T8* **Les Coves de Vinromá** *Cast.* Cuevas de Vinromá. Valenciana, E Spain *40°18′N 00°07′E*
103 *T12* **les Écrins** ▲ E France *44°54′N 06°25′E*
108 *C10* **Le Sépey** Vaud, W Switzerland *46°21′N 07°04′E*
15 *T7* **Les Escoumins** Québec, SE Canada *48°21′N 69°26′W*
Les Gonaïves *see* Gonaïves
160 *H9* **Leshan** Sichuan, C China *29°42′N 103°43′E*
108 *D11* **Les Haudères** Valais, SW Switzerland *46°02′N 07°27′E*
102 *J9* **les Herbiers** Vendée, NW France *46°52′N 01°01′W*
Lesh/Leshi *see* Lezhë
125 *O8* **Leshukonskoye** Arkhangel'skaya Oblast', NW Russian Federation *64°54′N 45°48′E*
Lesina *see* Hvar
107 *M15* **Lesina, Lago di** ◎ SE Italy
114 *K13* **Lesítse** ▲▲ NE Greece
94 *G10* **Lesja** Oppland, S Norway *62°07′N 08°56′E*
95 *L15* **Lesjöfors** Värmland, C Sweden *59°57′N 14°12′E*
111 *O18* **Lesko** Podkarpackie, SE Poland *49°28′N 22°19′E*
113 *O15* **Leskovac** Serbia, SE Serbia *43°00′N 21°58′E*
113 *M22* **Leskovik** *var.* Leskoviku. Korçë, S Albania *40°09′N 20°39′E*
Leskoviku *see* Leskovik
33 *P14* **Leslie** Idaho, NW USA *43°51′N 113°28′W*
31 *Q10* **Leslie** Michigan, N USA *42°27′N 84°25′W*
Leśna/Lesnaya *see* Lyasnaya
Lesnaya *see* Lyasnaya
102 *F5* **Lesneven** Finistère, NW France *48°35′N 04°19′W*
112 *J11* **Lešnica** Serbia, W Serbia *44°40′N 19°18′E*
125 *S13* **Lesnoy** Kirovskaya Oblast', NW Russian Federation *59°49′N 52°07′E*
122 *G10* **Lesnoy** Sverdlovskaya Oblast', C Russian Federation *58°40′N 59°48′E*
122 *K12* **Lesosibirsk** Krasnoyarskiy Kray, C Russian Federation *58°13′N 92°23′E*
83 *J23* **Lesotho** *off.* Kingdom of Lesotho; *prev.* Basutoland. ◆ *monarchy* S Africa
Lesotho, Kingdom of *see* Lesotho
102 *J12* **Lesparre-Médoc** Gironde, SW France *45°18′N 00°57′W*
108 *C8* **Les Ponts-de-Martel** Neuchâtel, W Switzerland *47°00′N 06°45′E*
103 *P1* **Lesquin** ✈ Nord, N France *50°34′N 3°07′E*
102 *I9* **les Sables-d'Olonne** Vendée, NW France *46°30′N 01°47′W*
109 *S7* **Lessach** *var.* Lessachbach. ≈ E Austria
Lessachbach *see* Lessach
45 *W11* **les Saintes** *var.* Îles des Saintes. *island group* S Guadeloupe
74 *L5* **Les Salines** ✈ (Annaba) NE Algeria *36°45′N 07°57′E*
99 *J22* **Lesse** ≈ SE Belgium
95 *M21* **Lessebo** Kronoberg, S Sweden *56°45′N 15°19′E*
Lesser Antarctica *see* West Antarctica
45 *P15* **Lesser Antilles** *island group* E West Indies
137 *T10* **Lesser Caucasus** *Rus.* Malyy Kavkaz. ▲▲ SW Asia
Lesser Khingan Range *see* Xiao Hinggan Ling
11 *P13* **Lesser Slave Lake** ◎ Alberta, W Canada
99 *E19* **Lessines** Hainaut, SW Belgium *50°43′N 05°50′E*
103 *R16* **les Stes-Maries-de-la-Mer** Bouches-du-Rhône, SE France *43°27′N 04°26′E*
14 *G15* **Lester B. Pearson** *var.* Toronto. ✈ (Toronto) Ontario, S Canada *43°59′N 81°30′W*
29 *U9* **Lester Prairie** Minnesota, N USA *44°52′N 94°02′W*
93 *L16* **Lestijärvi** Länsi-Suomi, W Finland *63°29′N 24°41′E*
L'Estuaire *see* Estuaire
29 *U9* **Le Sueur** Minnesota, N USA *44°27′N 93°53′W*
108 *B8* **Les Verrières** Neuchâtel, W Switzerland *46°54′N 06°29′E*
115 *L17* **Lésvos** *anc.* Lesbos. *island* E Greece
110 *G12* **Leszno** *Ger.* Lissa. Wielkopolskie, C Poland *51°51′N 16°35′E*
83 *L20* **Letaba** Northern, NE South Africa *23°44′S 31°29′E*
173 *P17* **Le Tampon** SW Réunion
97 *O21* **Letchworth** E England, United Kingdom *51°58′N 00°14′W*
111 *G25* **Letenye** Zala, SW Hungary *46°25′N 16°44′E*
11 *Q17* **Lethbridge** Alberta, SW Canada *49°43′N 112°48′W*
55 *S11* **Lethem** S Guyana *03°24′N 59°45′W*
83 *H18* **Letiahau** ≈ W Botswana
54 *J18* **Leticia** Amazonas, S Colombia *04°09′N 69°57′W*
171 *S16* **Leti, Kepulauan** *island group* E Indonesia
83 *I18* **Letlhakane** Central, C Botswana *21°26′S 25°36′E*
83 *H20* **Letlhakeng** Kweneng, SE Botswana *24°05′S 25°03′E*
114 *J8* **Letnitsa** Lovech, N Bulgaria *43°19′N 25°02′E*
103 *N1* **le Touquet-Paris-Plage** Pas-de-Calais, N France *50°31′N 01°36′E*
166 *L8* **Letpadan** Bago, SW Burma (Myanmar) *17°46′N 94°45′E*
166 *K6* **Letpan** Rakhine State, W Burma (Myanmar) *19°22′N 94°11′E*
102 *M2* **le Tréport** Seine-Maritime, N France *50°03′N 01°21′E*
166 *M12* **Letsôk-aw Kyun** *var.* Letsutan Island; *prev.* Domel Island. *island* Mergui Archipelago, S Burma (Myanmar)
Letsutan Island *see* Letsôk-aw Kyun
97 *E14* **Letterkenny** *Ir.* Leitir Ceanainn. Donegal, NW Ireland *54°57′N 07°44′W*
Lettland *see* Latvia
116 *M6* **Letychiv** Khmel'nyts'ka Oblast', W Ukraine *49°24′N 27°39′E*
Lëtzebuerg *see* Luxembourg
116 *H14* **Leu** Dolj, SW Romania *44°10′N 24°01′E*
Leucas *see* Lefkáda
103 *P17* **Leucate** Aude, S France *42°55′N 03°03′E*
103 *P17* **Leucate, Étang de** ◎ S France
108 *E10* **Leuk** Valais, SW Switzerland *46°18′N 07°46′E*
108 *E10* **Leukerbad** Valais, SW Switzerland *46°22′N 07°47′E*
Leusden *see* Leusden-Centrum
98 *K11* **Leusden-Centrum** *var.* Leusden. Utrecht, C Netherlands *52°08′N 05°25′E*
Leutensdorf *see* Litvínov
Leutschau *see* Levoča
99 *H18* **Leuven** *Fr.* Louvain, *Ger.* Löwen. Vlaams Brabant, C Belgium *50°53′N 04°42′E*
99 *I20* **Leuze** Namur, C Belgium *50°33′N 04°55′E*
Leuze *see* Leuze-en-Hainaut
99 *E19* **Leuze-en-Hainaut** *var.* Leuze. Hainaut, SW Belgium *50°36′N 03°37′E*
Léva *see* Levice
Levádia *see* Livádeia
Levajok *see* Leavvajohka
36 *L4* **Levan** Utah, W USA *39°33′N 111°51′W*
93 *E16* **Levanger** Nord-Trøndelag, C Norway *63°45′N 11°18′E*
106 *D10* **Levanto** Liguria, W Italy *44°12′N 09°33′E*
107 *H23* **Levanzo, Isola di** *island* Isole Egadi, S Italy
127 *Q17* **Levashi** Respublika Dagestan, SW Russian Federation *42°27′N 47°19′E*
24 *M5* **Levelland** Texas, SW USA *33°35′N 102°23′W*
39 *P13* **Levelock** Alaska, USA *59°07′N 156°51′W*
101 *E16* **Leverkusen** Nordrhein-Westfalen, W Germany *51°02′N 07°E*
111 *J21* **Levice** *Ger.* Lewentz, *Hung.* Léva, Lewenz. Nitriansky Kraj, SW Slovakia *48°14′N 18°38′E*
106 *G6* **Levico Terme** Trentino-Alto Adige, N Italy *46°02′N 11°19′E*
115 *E20* **Levídi** Pelopónnisos, S Greece *37°39′N 22°13′E*
103 *P14* **le Vigan** Gard, S France *43°00′N 03°36′E*
184 *L13* **Levin** Manawatu-Wanganui, North Island, New Zealand *40°38′S 175°17′E*
15 *R10* **Lévis** *var.* Levis. Québec, SE Canada *46°47′N 71°12′W*
Levis *see* Lévis
21 *P6* **Levisa Fork** ≈ Kentucky/Virginia, S USA
115 *L21* **Levítha** *island* Kykládes, Greece, Aegean Sea
18 *L14* **Levittown** Long Island, New York, NE USA *40°42′N 73°29′W*
18 *J15* **Levittown** Pennsylvania, NE USA *40°09′N 74°50′W*
Levkás *see* Lefkáda
Levkímmi *see* Lefkímmi
111 *L19* **Levoča** *Ger.* Leutschau, *Hung.* Locse. Prešovský Kraj, E Slovakia *49°01′N 20°34′E*
Lévrier, Baie du *see* Nouâdhibou, Dakhlet
103 *N9* **Levroux** Indre, C France *47°00′N 01°37′E*
114 *J8* **Levski** Pleven, N Bulgaria *43°21′N 25°11′E*
Levskigrad *see* Karlovo
126 *L6* **Lev Tolstoy** Lipetskaya Oblast', W Russian Federation *53°12′N 39°28′E*
187 *X14* **Levuka** Ovalau, C Fiji *17°42′S 178°50′E*
166 *L6* **Lewe** Mandalay, C Burma (Myanmar) *19°40′N 96°04′E*
Lewentz/Lewenz *see* Levice
97 *O23* **Lewes** SE England, United Kingdom *50°52′N 00°01′E*
21 *Z4* **Lewes** Delaware, NE USA *38°46′N 75°08′W*
29 *Q12* **Lewis And Clark Lake** ⊠ Nebraska/South Dakota, N USA
18 *G14* **Lewisburg** Pennsylvania, NE USA *40°57′N 76°52′W*
20 *J10* **Lewisburg** Tennessee, S USA *35°29′N 86°49′W*
21 *S6* **Lewisburg** West Virginia, NE USA *37°49′N 80°28′W*
96 *F6* **Lewis, Butt of** *headland* NW Scotland, United Kingdom *58°31′N 06°18′W*
96 *F7* **Lewis, Isle of** *island* NW Scotland, United Kingdom
35 *U4* **Lewis, Mount** ▲ Nevada, W USA *40°22′N 116°50′W*
185 *H16* **Lewis Pass** *pass* South Island, New Zealand
33 *P7* **Lewis Range** ▲▲ Montana, NW USA
23 *O3* **Lewis Smith Lake** ⊠ Alabama, S USA
32 *M10* **Lewiston** Idaho, NW USA *46°25′N 117°01′W*
19 *P7* **Lewiston** Maine, NE USA *44°08′N 70°14′W*
29 *X10* **Lewiston** Minnesota, N USA *43°58′N 91°52′W*
18 *D9* **Lewiston** New York, NE USA *43°10′N 79°02′W*
36 *L1* **Lewiston** Utah, W USA *41°58′N 111°52′W*
30 *K13* **Lewistown** Illinois, N USA *40°23′N 90°09′W*
33 *T9* **Lewistown** Montana, NW USA *47°04′N 109°26′W*
27 *T14* **Lewisville** Arkansas, C USA *33°21′N 93°38′W*
25 *T6* **Lewisville** Texas, SW USA *33°00′N 96°57′W*
25 *T6* **Lewisville, Lake** ⊠ Texas, SW USA
Le Woleu-Ntem *see* Woleu-Ntem
23 *U3* **Lexington** Georgia, SE USA *33°51′N 83°04′W*
20 *M5* **Lexington** Kentucky, S USA *38°03′N 84°30′W*
22 *L4* **Lexington** Mississippi, S USA *33°06′N 90°03′W*
27 *S4* **Lexington** Missouri, C USA *39°11′N 93°52′W*
29 *N16* **Lexington** Nebraska, C USA *40°46′N 99°44′W*
20 *S9* **Lexington** North Carolina, SE USA *35°49′N 80°15′W*
27 *N11* **Lexington** Oklahoma, C USA *35°00′N 97°20′W*
21 *R12* **Lexington** South Carolina, SE USA *33°59′N 81°15′W*
20 *G9* **Lexington** Tennessee, S USA *35°39′N 88°24′W*
25 *T10* **Lexington** Texas, SW USA *30°25′N 97°00′W*
21 *T6* **Lexington** Virginia, NE USA *37°47′N 79°27′W*
21 *X5* **Lexington Park** Maryland, NE USA *38°16′N 76°27′W*
Leyden *see* Leiden
102 *J14* **Leyre** ≈ SW France
171 *Q5* **Leyte** *island* C Philippines
171 *Q6* **Leyte Gulf** *gulf* E Philippines
111 *O16* **Leżajsk** Podkarpackie, SE Poland *50°15′N 22°25′E*
Lezha *see* Lezhë
113 *K18* **Lezhë** *var.* Lezha; *prev.* Lesh, Leshi. Lezhë, NW Albania *41°46′N 19°40′E*
113 *K18* **Lezhë** ◐ *district* NW Albania
103 *O16* **Lézignan-Corbières** Aude, S France *43°12′N 02°46′E*
126 *J7* **L'gov** Kurskaya Oblast', W Russian Federation *51°38′N 35°17′E*
159 *P15* **Lhari** Xizang Zizhiqu, W China *30°34′N 93°40′E*
159 *N16* **Lhasa** *var.* La-sa, Lassa. Xizang Zizhiqu, W China *29°41′N 91°10′E*
159 *O15* **Lhasa He** ≈ W China

◆ Country
● Country Capital
◇ Dependent Territory
○ Dependent Territory Capital
◐ Administrative Regions
✈ International Airport
▲ Mountain
▲▲ Mountain Range
⛰ Volcano
≈ River
◎ Lake
⊠ Reservoir

Lhaviyani Atoll see Faadhippolhu Atoll
158 K16 Lhazê var. Quxar. Xizang Zizhiqu, W China 29°07′N 87°32′E
158 K14 Lhazhong Xizang Zizhiqu, W China 31°58′N 86°43′E
168 H7 Lhoksukon Sumatera, W Indonesia 05°04′N 97°19′E
159 Q15 Lhorong var. Zito. Xizang Zizhiqu, W China 30°51′N 95°41′E
105 W6 L'Hospitalet de Llobregat var. Hospitalet. Cataluña, NE Spain 41°21′N 02°06′E
153 R11 Lhotse ▲ China/Nepal 28°00′N 86°55′E
159 N17 Lhozhag var. Garbo. Xizang Zizhiqu, W China 28°21′N 90°47′E
159 O16 Lhünzê var. Xingba. Xizang Zizhiqu, W China 28°25′N 92°30′E
159 N15 Lhünzhub var. Ganqu. Xizang Zizhiqu, W China 30°14′N 91°20′E
167 N8 Li Lamphun, NW Thailand 17°46′N 98°54′E
115 L21 Liádi var. Livádi. island Kykládes, Greece, Aegean Sea
161 P12 Liancheng var. Lianfeng. Fujian, SE China 25°47′N 116°42′E
Liancheng see Lianjiang, Guangdong, China
Liancheng see Qinglong, Guizhou, China
Liancheng see Guangnan, Yunnan, China
Lianfeng see Liancheng
160 K9 Liangping var. Liangshan. Sichuan, C China 30°40′N 107°46′E
Liangshan see Liangping
Liangzhou see Wuwei
161 O9 Liangzi Hu ◎ C China
161 R12 Lianjiang var. Fengcheng. Fujian, SE China 26°14′N 119°33′E
160 L15 Lianjiang var. Liancheng. Guangdong, S China 21°41′N 110°12′E
Lianjiang see Xingguo
161 O13 Lianping var. Yuanshan. Guangdong, S China 24°18′N 114°27′E
Lianshan see Huludao
Lian Xian see Lianzhou
160 M11 Lianyuan prev. Lantian. Hunan, S China 27°51′N 111°44′E
161 Q6 Lianyungang var. Xinpu. Jiangsu, E China 34°38′N 119°12′E
161 N13 Lianzhou var. Linxian; prev. Lian Xian. Guangdong, S China 24°48′N 112°26′E
Lianzhou see Hepu
Liao see Liaoning
161 P5 Liaocheng Shandong, E China 36°31′N 115°59′E
163 U13 Liaodong Bandao var. Liaotung Peninsula. peninsula NE China
163 T13 Liaodong Wan Eng. Gulf of Lantung, Gulf of Liaotung. gulf NE China
163 U11 Liao He ≈ NE China
163 U12 Liaoning var. Liao, Liaoning Sheng, Shengking, hist. Fengtien, Shenking. ◆ province NE China
Liaoning Sheng see Liaoning
Liaotung Peninsula see Liaodong Bandao
163 V12 Liaoyang var. Liao-yang. Liaoning, NE China 41°16′N 123°12′E
Liao-yang see Liaoyang
163 V11 Liaoyuan var. Dongliao, Shuang-liao, Jap. Chengchiatun. Jilin, NE China 42°52′N 125°09′E
163 U12 Liaozhong Liaoning, NE China 41°33′N 122°54′E
Liaqatabad see Piplān
10 M10 Liard ≈ W Canada
Liard see Fort Liard
10 L10 Liard River British Columbia, W Canada 59°23′N 126°05′W
149 O15 Liāri Baluchistān, SW Pakistan 25°43′N 66°28′E
Liatroim see Leitrim
189 S6 Lib var. Ellep. island Ralik Chain, C Marshall Islands
Liban see Lebanon
138 H6 Liban, Jebel Ar. Jabal al Gharbt, Jabal Lubnān, Eng. Mount Lebanon. ▲ C Lebanon
Libau see Liepāja
33 N7 Libby Montana, NW USA 48°25′N 115°33′W
79 I16 Libenge Equateur, NW Dem. Rep. Congo 03°39′N 18°39′E
26 I7 Liberal Kansas, C USA 37°03′N 100°56′W
27 R7 Liberal Missouri, C USA 37°33′N 94°31′W
Liberalitas Julia see Évora
111 D15 Liberec Ger. Reichenberg. Liberecký Kraj, N Czech Republic 50°45′N 15°05′E
111 D15 Liberecký Kraj ◆ region N Czech Republic
42 K12 Liberia Guanacaste, NW Costa Rica 10°36′N 85°26′W
76 K17 Liberia off. Republic of Liberia. ◆ republic W Africa
Liberia, Republic of see Liberia
61 D16 Libertad Corrientes, NE Argentina 30°01′S 57°51′W
61 E20 Libertad San José, S Uruguay 34°38′S 56°39′W
54 I7 Libertad Barinas, NW Venezuela 08°21′N 69°39′W
54 K6 Libertad Cojedes, N Venezuela 09°15′N 68°30′W
62 G12 Libertador off. Región del Libertador General Bernardo O'Higgins. ◆ region C Chile
Libertador General Bernardo O'Higgins, Región del see Libertador
Libertador General San Martín see Ciudad de Libertador General San Martín
20 L6 Liberty Kentucky, S USA 37°19′N 84°58′W
22 J7 Liberty Mississippi, S USA 31°09′N 90°49′W
27 R4 Liberty Missouri, C USA 39°15′N 94°22′W
18 J12 Liberty New York, NE USA 41°48′N 74°45′W
21 T9 Liberty North Carolina, SE USA 35°49′N 79°34′W
Libian Desert see Libyan Desert
99 J23 Libin Luxembourg, SE Belgium 50°01′N 05°13′E
Lībīyah, Aş Şahrā' al see Libyan Desert
160 K13 Libo var. Yuping. Guizhou, S China 25°28′N 107°52′E
Libohova see Libohovë
113 L23 Libohovë var. Libohova. Gjirokastër, S Albania 40°03′N 20°13′E
81 K18 Liboi North Eastern, E Kenya 0°23′N 40°55′E
102 K13 Libourne Gironde, SW France 44°55′N 00°14′W
99 K23 Libramont Luxembourg, SE Belgium 49°55′N 05°21′E
113 M20 Librazhd var. Librazhdi. Elbasan, E Albania 41°10′N 20°22′E
Librazhdi see Librazhd
79 C18 Libreville ● (Gabon) Estuaire, NW Gabon 0°25′N 09°29′E
75 P10 Libya off. Great Socialist People's Libyan Arab Jamahiriya, Ar. Al Jamāhīrīyah al 'Arabīyah al Lībīyah ash Sha'bīyah al Ishtirākīy; prev. Libyan Arab Republic. ◆ Islamic state N Africa
Libyan Arab Republic see Libya
75 T11 Libyan Desert var. Libian Desert, Ar. Aş Şahrā' al Lībīyah. desert N Africa
75 T8 Libyan Plateau var. Aḍ Diffah. plateau Egypt/Libya
62 G12 Licantén Maule, C Chile 35°00′S 72°00′W
107 J25 Licata anc. Phintias. Sicilia, Italy, C Mediterranean Sea 37°07′N 13°57′E
137 P14 Lice Diyarbakır, SE Turkey 38°29′N 40°39′E
Licheng see Lipu
97 L19 Lichfield C England, United Kingdom 52°42′N 01°48′W
83 N14 Lichinga Niassa, N Mozambique 13°19′S 35°13′E
109 V3 Lichtenau Niederösterreich, N Austria 48°29′N 15°24′E
83 I21 Lichtenburg North-West, N South Africa 26°09′S 26°11′E
101 K18 Lichtenfels Bayern, SE Germany 50°09′N 11°04′E
98 O12 Lichtenvoorde Gelderland, E Netherlands 51°59′N 06°34′E
Lichtenwald see Sevnica
99 C17 Lichtervelde West-Vlaanderen, W Belgium 51°02′N 03°09′E
160 L9 Lichuan Hubei, C China 30°20′N 108°56′E
27 V7 Licking Missouri, C USA 37°30′N 91°51′W
20 M4 Licking River ≈ Kentucky, S USA
112 C11 Lički Osik Lika-Senj, C Croatia 44°36′N 15°24′E
Ličko-Senjska Županija see Lika-Senj
107 K19 Licosa, Punta headland S Italy 40°15′N 14°54′E
119 H16 Lida Hrodzyenskaya Voblasts', W Belarus 53°53′N 25°20′E
93 H17 Liden Västernorrland, C Sweden 62°43′N 16°49′E
29 R7 Lidgerwood North Dakota, N USA 46°04′N 97°09′W
Lidhorikion see Lidoríki
95 K21 Lidhult Kronoberg, S Sweden 56°49′N 13°25′E
95 P16 Lidingö Stockholm, C Sweden 59°22′N 18°10′E
95 K17 Lidköping Västra Götaland, S Sweden 58°30′N 13°10′E
Lido di Iesolo see Lido di Jesolo
106 I8 Lido di Jesolo var. Lido di Iesolo. Veneto, NE Italy 45°30′N 12°37′E
107 H15 Lido di Ostia Lazio, C Italy 41°42′N 12°19′E
Lidokhorikion see Lidoríki
115 E18 Lidoríki prev. Lidhorikion, Lidokhorikion. Stereá Elláda, C Greece 38°32′N 22°12′E
110 K9 Lidzbark Warmińsko-Mazurskie, NE Poland 53°15′N 19°49′E
110 L7 Lidzbark Warmiński Ger. Heilsberg. Olsztyn, N Poland 54°08′N 20°35′E
109 U3 Liebenau Oberösterreich, N Austria 48°33′N 14°48′E
181 P7 Liebig, Mount ▲ Northern Territory, C Australia 23°19′S 131°30′E
109 V8 Lieboch Steiermark, SE Austria 47°00′N 15°21′E
108 I8 Liechtenstein off. Principality of Liechtenstein. ◆ principality C Europe
Liechtenstein, Principality of see Liechtenstein
99 F18 Liedekerke Vlaams Brabant, C Belgium 50°51′N 04°05′E
99 K19 Liège Dut. Luik, Ger. Lüttich. Liège, E Belgium 50°38′N 05°35′E
99 K20 Liège Dut. Luik. ◆ province E Belgium
Liegnitz see Legnica
93 O16 Lieksa Itä-Suomi, E Finland 63°20′N 30°E
118 F10 Lielupe ≈ Latvia/Lithuania
118 G9 Lielvārde C Latvia 56°45′N 24°48′E
167 U13 Liên Hương var. Tuy Phong. Binh Thuận, S Vietnam 11°13′N 108°40′E
167 U13 Liên Nghia var. Liên Nghia var. Đưc Trong. Lâm Đông, S Vietnam 11°45′N 108°24′E
Liên Nghia see Liên Nghia
109 P9 Lienz Tirol, W Austria 46°50′N 12°45′E
118 B10 Liepāja Ger. Libau. W Latvia 56°32′N 21°02′E
99 H17 Lier Fr. Lierre. Antwerpen, N Belgium 51°08′N 04°35′E
95 H15 Lierbyen Buskerud, S Norway 59°57′N 10°14′E
99 L21 Lierneux Liège, E Belgium 50°12′N 05°51′E
Lierre see Lier
101 D18 Lieser ≈ W Germany
109 U7 Liesing ≈ E Austria
108 E6 Liestal Basel Landschaft, N Switzerland 47°29′N 07°43′E
Lietuva see Lithuania
Lievenhof see Līvāni
103 O2 Liévin Pas-de-Calais, N France 50°25′N 02°48′E
14 M9 Lièvre, Rivière du ≈ Québec, SE Canada
109 T6 Liezen Steiermark, C Austria 47°34′N 14°12′E
97 E14 Lifford Ir. Leifear. Donegal, NW Ireland 54°50′N 07°29′W
187 Q16 Lifou island Îles Loyauté, E New Caledonia
193 Y15 Lifuka island Ha'apai Group, C Tonga
171 P4 Ligao Luzon, N Philippines 13°16′N 123°30′E
Liger see Loire
42 H2 Lighthouse Reef reef E Belize
183 Q4 Lightning Ridge New South Wales, SE Australia 29°29′S 148°00′E
103 N9 Lignières Cher, C France 46°45′N 02°10′E
103 S5 Ligny-en-Barrois Meuse, NE France 48°42′N 05°22′E
83 P15 Ligonha ≈ NE Mozambique
31 P11 Ligonier Indiana, N USA 41°25′N 85°33′W
81 I25 Ligunga Ruvuma, S Tanzania 10°51′S 37°10′E
106 D9 Ligure, Appennino Eng. Ligurian Mountains. ▲▲ NW Italy
Ligure, Mar see Ligurian Sea
106 C9 Liguria ◆ region NW Italy
Ligurian Mountains see Ligure, Appennino
120 K6 Ligurian Sea Fr. Mer Ligurienne, It. Mar Ligure. sea N Mediterranean Sea
Ligurienne, Mer see Ligurian Sea
186 H5 Lihir Group island group NE Papua New Guinea
38 B8 Līhu'e var. Lihue. Kaua'i, Hawaii, USA 21°59′N 159°23′W
Lihue see Līhu'e
118 F5 Lihula Ger. Leal. Läänemaa, W Estonia 58°44′N 23°49′E
124 I2 Liinakhamari var. Linacmamari. Murmanskaya Oblast', NW Russian Federation 69°40′N 31°27′E
Liivi Laht see Riga, Gulf of
160 F11 Lijiang var. Dayan, Lijiang Naxizu Zizhixian. Yunnan, SW China 26°52′N 100°10′E
Lijiang Naxizu Zizhixian see Lijiang
112 C11 Lika-Senj off. Ličko-Senjska Županija. ◆ province W Croatia
79 N25 Likasi prev. Jadotville. Shaba, SE Dem. Rep. Congo 11°02′S 26°51′E
79 L16 Likati Orientale, N Dem. Rep. Congo 03°28′N 23°45′E
10 M15 Likely British Columbia, SW Canada 52°40′N 121°34′W
153 Y11 Likhapāni Assam, NE India 27°19′N 95°54′E
124 J16 Likhoslavl' Tverskaya Oblast', W Russian Federation 57°08′N 35°27′E
189 U5 Likiep Atoll atoll Ratak Chain, C Marshall Islands
95 D18 Liknes Vest-Agder, S Norway 58°20′N 06°58′E
79 H16 Likouala ◆ province NE Congo
79 H18 Likouala ≈ N Congo
79 H18 Likouala aux Herbes ≈ E Congo
190 B16 Liku E Niue 19°02′S 169°47′E
Likupang, Selat see Bangka, Selat
27 Y8 Lilbourn Missouri, C USA 36°35′N 89°37′W
103 X14 l'Île-Rousse Corse, France, C Mediterranean Sea 42°39′N 08°59′E
109 W5 Lilienfeld Niederösterreich, NE Austria 48°01′N 15°36′E
161 N11 Liling Hunan, S China 27°42′N 113°49′E
95 J18 Lilla Edet Västra Götaland, S Sweden 58°08′N 12°08′E
103 P1 Lille var. l'Isle, Dut. Rijssel, Flem. Ryssel, prev. Lisle; anc. Insula. Nord, N France 50°38′N 03°04′E
95 G24 Lillebælt var. Lille Bælt, Eng. Little Belt. strait S Denmark
Lille Bælt see Lillebælt
102 L3 Lillebonne Seine-Maritime, N France 49°30′N 00°34′E
94 H12 Lillehammer Oppland, S Norway 61°07′N 10°28′E
103 O1 Lillers Pas-de-Calais, N France 50°34′N 02°26′E
95 F18 Lillesand Aust-Agder, S Norway 58°15′N 08°23′E
95 I15 Lillestrøm Akershus, S Norway 59°58′N 11°05′E
93 F18 Lillhärdal Jämtland, C Sweden 61°51′N 14°04′E
21 U10 Lillington North Carolina, SE USA 35°25′N 78°50′W
105 O9 Lillo Castilla-La Mancha, C Spain 39°43′N 03°19′W
10 M16 Lillooet British Columbia, SW Canada 50°41′N 121°59′W
83 M14 Lilongwe ● (Malawi) Central, W Malawi 13°58′S 33°48′E
83 M14 Lilongwe ✈ Central, W Malawi 13°46′S 33°44′E
83 M14 Lilongwe ≈ W Malawi
171 P7 Liloy Mindanao, S Philippines 08°04′N 122°42′E
Lilybaeum see Marsala
182 J7 Lilydale South Australia 32°57′S 140°00′E
183 P16 Lilydale Tasmania, SE Australia 41°17′S 147°13′E
113 J14 Lim ≈ SE Europe
57 D15 Lima ● (Peru) Lima, W Peru 12°06′S 78°W
94 K13 Lima Dalarna, C Sweden 60°55′N 13°19′E
31 R12 Lima Ohio, NE USA 40°43′N 84°06′W
57 D14 Lima ◆ department W Peru
Lima see Jorge Chávez Internacional
137 Y13 Liman prev. Port Il'ic. SE Azerbaijan 38°54′N 48°49′E
111 L17 Limanowa Małopolskie, S Poland 49°43′N 20°25′E
104 G5 Lima, Rio Sp. Limia. ≈ Portugal/Spain see also Limia
Lima, Rio see Limia
168 M11 Limas Pulau Sebangka, W Indonesia 0°09′N 104°31′E
Limassol see Lemesós
97 F14 Limavady Ir. Léim An Mhadaidh. NW Northern Ireland, United Kingdom 55°03′N 06°57′W
63 J14 Limay Mahuida La Pampa, C Argentina 37°09′S 66°40′W
63 H15 Limay, Río ≈ W Argentina
101 N16 Limbach-Oberfrohna Sachsen, E Germany 50°52′N 12°46′E
81 F22 Limba Limba ≈ C Tanzania
107 C17 Limbara, Monte ▲ Sardegna, Italy, C Mediterranean Sea 40°50′N 09°10′E
118 G7 Limbaži Est. Lemsalu. N Latvia 57°33′N 24°46′E
44 M8 Limbé N Haiti 19°44′N 72°25′W
99 L19 Limbourg Liège, E Belgium 50°37′N 05°56′E
99 K17 Limburg ◆ province NE Belgium
99 L16 Limburg ◆ province SE Netherlands
101 F17 Limburg an der Lahn Hessen, W Germany 50°22′N 08°04′E
94 K13 Limedsforsen Dalarna, C Sweden 60°52′N 13°25′E
60 L9 Limeira São Paulo, S Brazil 22°34′S 47°25′W
97 C19 Limerick Ir. Luimneach. Limerick, SW Ireland 52°40′N 08°38′W
97 C20 Limerick Ir. Luimneach. cultural region SW Ireland
19 S2 Limestone Maine, NE USA 46°52′N 67°49′W
25 U9 Limestone, Lake ◎ Texas, SW USA
39 P12 Lime Village Alaska, USA 61°21′N 155°26′W
95 F20 Limfjorden fjord N Denmark
95 J23 Limhamn Skåne, S Sweden 55°34′N 12°57′E
104 H5 Limia Port. Rio Lima. ≈ Portugal/Spain see also Lima,Rio
Limia see Lima, Rio
93 L14 Liminka Oulu, C Finland 64°48′N 25°19′E
Limín Vathéos see Sámos
115 G17 Límni Évvoia, C Greece 38°46′N 23°20′E
115 J15 Límnos anc. Lemnos. island E Greece
102 M11 Limoges anc. Augustoritum Lemovicensium, Lemovices. Haute-Vienne, C France 45°51′N 01°16′E
43 O13 Limón var. Puerto Limón. Limón, E Costa Rica 09°59′N 83°02′W
42 K4 Limón Colón, NE Honduras 15°50′N 85°31′W
37 U5 Limon Colorado, C USA 39°15′N 103°41′W
43 N13 Limón off. Provincia de Limón. ◆ province E Costa Rica
106 A10 Limone Piemonte Piemonte, NE Italy 44°12′N 07°37′E
Limones see Valdéz
Limón, Provincia de see Limón
Limonum see Poitiers
103 N11 Limousin ◆ region C France
103 N16 Limoux Aude, S France 43°03′N 02°13′E
83 J20 Limpopo off. Limpopo Province; prev. Northern, Northern Transvaal. ◆ province NE South Africa
83 L19 Limpopo var. Crocodile. ≈ S Africa
Limpopo Province see Limpopo
160 K17 Limu Ling ▲▲ S China
113 M20 Lin var. Lini. Elbasan, E Albania 41°03′N 20°37′E
Linacmamari see Liinakhamari
62 G13 Linares Maule, C Chile 35°50′S 71°37′W
54 C13 Linares Nariño, SW Colombia 01°24′N 77°30′W
41 O9 Linares Nuevo León, NE Mexico 24°54′N 99°38′W
105 N12 Linares Andalucía, S Spain 38°05′N 03°38′W
107 G15 Linaro, Capo headland C Italy 42°01′N 11°49′E
106 D8 Linate ✈ (Milano) Lombardia, N Italy 45°27′N 09°18′E
167 T8 Lin Camh prev. Đưc Tho. Ha Tinh, N Vietnam 18°30′N 105°36′E
160 F13 Lincang Yunnan, SW China 23°55′N 100°03′E
Lincheng see Lingao
Linchuan see Fuzhou
61 B20 Lincoln Buenos Aires, E Argentina 34°54′S 61°30′W
185 H19 Lincoln Canterbury, South Island, New Zealand 43°37′S 172°30′E
97 N18 Lincoln anc. Lindum, Lindum Colonia. E England, United Kingdom 53°14′N 00°33′W
35 O6 Lincoln California, W USA 38°52′N 121°18′W
30 L13 Lincoln Illinois, N USA 40°09′N 89°21′W
26 M4 Lincoln Kansas, C USA 39°03′N 98°09′W
19 S5 Lincoln Maine, NE USA 45°22′N 68°30′W
27 T5 Lincoln Missouri, C USA 38°23′N 93°19′W
29 R16 Lincoln state capital Nebraska, C USA 40°46′N 96°43′W
32 F11 Lincoln City Oregon, NW USA 44°57′N 124°01′W
167 X10 Lincoln Island island E Paracel Islands
197 Q11 Lincoln Sea sea Arctic Ocean
97 N18 Lincolnshire cultural region E England, United Kingdom
21 R10 Lincolnton North Carolina, SE USA 35°27′N 81°16′W
25 V7 Lindale Texas, SW USA 32°31′N 95°24′W
101 I25 Lindau var. Lindau am Bodensee. Bayern, S Germany 47°33′N 09°41′E
Lindau am Bodensee see Lindau
123 P9 Linde ≈ NE Russian Federation
55 T9 Linden E Guyana 05°58′N 58°12′W
23 O6 Linden Alabama, S USA 32°18′N 87°48′W
20 H9 Linden Tennessee, S USA 35°38′N 87°50′W
25 X6 Linden Texas, SW USA 33°01′N 94°22′W
44 H2 Linden Pindling ✈ New Providence, C Bahamas 25°00′N 77°26′W
18 J16 Lindenwold New Jersey, NE USA 39°47′N 74°58′W
95 M15 Lindesberg Örebro, C Sweden 59°36′N 15°15′E
95 D18 Lindesnes headland S Norway 57°58′N 07°03′E
Líndhos see Líndos
81 K24 Lindi Lindi, SE Tanzania 10°S 39°41′E
81 J24 Lindi ◆ region SE Tanzania
79 N17 Lindi ≈ NE Dem. Rep. Congo
163 V7 Lindian Heilongjiang, NE China 47°15′N 124°51′E
185 E21 Lindis Pass pass South Island, New Zealand
83 J22 Lindley Free State, C South Africa 27°52′S 27°55′E
95 J19 Lindome Västra Götaland, S Sweden 57°34′N 12°05′E
163 S10 Lindong var. Bairin Zuoqi. Nei Mongol Zizhiqu, N China 43°59′N 119°24′E
115 O23 Líndos var. Líndhos. Ródos, Dodekánisa, Greece, Aegean Sea 36°05′N 28°05′E
14 I14 Lindsay Ontario, SE Canada 44°21′N 78°44′W
35 R11 Lindsay California, W USA 36°11′N 119°06′W
33 X8 Lindsay Montana, NW USA 47°13′N 105°10′W
27 N11 Lindsay Oklahoma, C USA 34°50′N 97°37′W
27 N5 Lindsborg Kansas, C USA 38°34′N 97°39′W
95 N21 Lindsdal Kalmar, S Sweden 56°44′N 16°18′E
Lindum/Lindum Colonia see Lincoln
191 W3 Line Islands island group E Kiribati
Linëvo see Linova
160 M5 Linfen var. Lin-fen. Shanxi, C China 36°08′N 111°34′E
Lin-fen see Linfen
104 L2 L'Infiestu prev. Infiesto. Asturias, N Spain 43°21′N 05°21′W
155 F18 Linganamakki Reservoir ⊠ SW India
160 L17 Lingao var. Lincheng. Hainan, S China 19°44′N 109°23′E
171 N3 Lingayen Luzon, N Philippines 16°00′N 120°12′E
160 M6 Lingbao var. Guolüezhen. Henan, C China 34°34′N 110°50′E
94 N12 Lingbo Gävleborg, C Sweden 61°04′N 16°45′E
Lingcheng see Beiliu,Guangxi, China
Lingcheng see Lingshan, Guangxi, China
Lingeh see Bandar-e Lengeh
100 E12 Lingen var. Lingen an der Ems. Niedersachsen, NW Germany 52°31′N 07°19′E
Lingen an der Ems see Lingen
168 M11 Lingga, Kepulauan island group W Indonesia
168 L11 Lingga, Pulau island Kepulauan Lingga, W Indonesia
14 J14 Lingham Lake ◎ Ontario, SE Canada
94 M13 Linghed Dalarna, C Sweden 60°48′N 15°55′E
33 Z15 Lingle Wyoming, C USA 42°07′N 104°21′W
18 G15 Linglestown Pennsylvania, NE USA 40°20′N 76°46′W
160 M12 Lingling prev. Yongzhou, Zhishan. Hunan, S China 26°13′N 111°36′E
79 K18 Lingomo 11 Equateur, NW Dem. Rep. Congo 0°42′N 21°59′E
160 L15 Lingshan var. Lingcheng. Guangxi Zhuangzu Zizhiqu, S China 22°28′N 109°19′E
160 L17 Lingshui var. Lingshui Lizu Zizhixian. Hainan, S China 18°35′N 110°03′E
Lingshui Lizu Zizhixian see Lingshui
155 G16 Lingsugūr Karnātaka, C India 16°13′N 76°33′E
107 L23 Linguaglossa Sicilia, Italy, C Mediterranean Sea 37°51′N 15°06′E
76 H10 Linguère N Senegal 15°24′N 15°06′W
159 W8 Lingwu Ningxia, N China 38°04′N 106°21′E
Lingxi see Yongshun, Hunan, China
Lingxi see Cangnan, Zhejiang, China
Lingxian/Ling Xian see Yanling
163 S12 Lingyuan Liaoning, NE China 41°09′N 119°24′E
163 U4 Linhai Heilongjiang, NE China 51°30′N 124°18′E
161 S10 Linhai var. Taizhou. Zhejiang, SE China 28°54′N 121°08′E
59 O20 Linhares Espírito Santo, SE Brazil 19°22′S 40°04′W
Linhe see Bayannur
Lini see Lin
139 S1 Līnik, Chiyā-ē ▲▲ N Iraq
Linjiang see Shanghang
95 M18 Linköping Östergötland, S Sweden 58°25′N 15°37′E
163 Y8 Linkou Heilongjiang, NE China 45°18′N 130°17′E
118 F11 Linkuva Šiauliai, N Lithuania 56°06′N 23°58′E
27 V5 Linn Missouri, C USA 38°29′N 91°51′W
25 S16 Linn Texas, SW USA 26°32′N 98°06′W
27 T2 Linneus Missouri, C USA 39°53′N 93°10′W
96 H10 Linnhe, Loch inlet W Scotland, United Kingdom
119 G19 Linova Rus. Linëvo. Brestskaya Voblasts', SW Belarus 52°29′N 24°30′E
161 O5 Linqing Shandong, E China 36°51′N 115°42′E
60 K8 Lins São Paulo, S Brazil 21°40′S 49°44′W
93 F17 Linsell Jämtland, C Sweden 62°10′N 14°E
160 J9 Linshui Sichuan, C China 30°24′N 106°54′E
44 K12 Linstead C Jamaica 18°08′N 77°02′W
159 U11 Lintan Gansu, N China 34°43′N 101°27′E
159 V11 Lintao var. Taoyang. Gansu, C China 35°23′N 103°54′E
15 S12 Lintère ≈ Québec, SE Canada
108 H8 Linth ≈ NW Switzerland
108 H8 Linthal Glarus, NE Switzerland 46°59′N 08°57′E
31 N15 Linton Indiana, N USA 39°01′N 87°10′W
29 N6 Linton North Dakota, N USA 46°16′N 100°13′W
163 R11 Linxi Nei Mongol Zizhiqu, N China 43°29′N 117°59′E
159 U11 Linxia var. Linxia Huizu Zizhizhou. Gansu, C China 35°34′N 103°08′E
Linxia Huizu Zizhizhou see Linxia
Linxian see Lianzhou
161 Q6 Linyi Shandong, S China 37°06′N 118°18′E
161 P4 Linyi var. Yishi. Shandong, E China 37°12′N 116°54′E
160 M6 Linyi Shanxi, C China 35°10′N 118°18′E
109 T4 Linz anc. Lentia. Oberösterreich, N Austria 48°19′N 14°18′E
159 S8 Linze var. Shahe; prev. Shahepu. Gansu, N China 39°06′N 100°03′E
44 J13 Lionel Town C Jamaica 17°49′N 77°14′W
103 Q16 Lion, Golfe du Eng. Gulf of Lion, Gulf of Lions; anc. Sinus Gallicus. gulf S France
Lion, Gulf of/Lions, Gulf of see Lion, Golfe du
83 K16 Lions Den Mashonaland West, N Zimbabwe 17°16′S 30°00′E
14 F13 Lion's Head Ontario, S Canada 44°59′N 81°16′W
Lios Ceannúir, Bá see Liscannor Bay
Lios Mór see Lismore
Lios na gCearrbhach see Lisburn
Lios Tuathail see Listowel
79 G17 Liouesso Sangha, N Congo 01°02′N 15°43′E
Liozno see Lyozna
171 O4 Lipa off. Lipa City. Luzon, N Philippines 13°57′N 121°10′E
Lipa City see Lipa
25 S7 Lipan Texas, SW USA 32°31′N 98°03′W
Lipari Islands/Lipari, Isole see Eolie, Isole
107 L22 Lipari, Isola island Isole Eolie, S Italy
116 L8 Lipcani Rus. Lipkany. N Moldova 48°16′N 26°47′E
93 N17 Liperi Itä-Suomi, SE Finland 62°33′N 29°29′E
126 L7 Lipetsk Lipetskaya Oblast', W Russian Federation 52°37′N 39°38′E
126 K6 Lipetskaya Oblast' ◆ province W Russian Federation
57 K22 Lipez, Cordillera de ▲▲ SW Bolivia
110 E10 Lipiany Ger. Lippehne. Zachodnio-pomorskie, W Poland 53°00′N 14°58′E
112 G9 Lipik Požega-Slavonija, NE Croatia 45°24′N 17°08′E
124 L12 Lipin Bor Vologodskaya Oblast', NW Russian Federation 60°12′N 38°04′E
160 L12 Liping var. Defeng. Guizhou, S China 26°16′N 109°08′E
Lipkany see Lipcani
119 H15 Lipnishki Hrodzyenskaya Voblasts', W Belarus 54°00′N 25°37′E
110 J10 Lipno Kujawsko-pomorskie, C Poland 52°52′N 19°11′E
116 F11 Lipova Hung. Lippa. Arad, W Romania 46°05′N 21°42′E
Lipovets see Lypovets'
Lippa see Lipova
101 E14 Lippe ≈ W Germany
Lippehne see Lipiany
101 G14 Lippstadt Nordrhein-Westfalen, W Germany 51°41′N 08°20′E
25 P1 Lipscomb Texas, SW USA 36°14′N 100°16′W
Lipsia/Lipsk see Leipzig
Liptau-Sankt-Nikolaus/Liptószentmiklós see Liptovský Mikuláš
111 K19 Liptovský Mikuláš Ger. Liptau-Sankt-Nikolaus, Hung. Liptószentmiklós. Zílinský Kraj, N Slovakia 49°06′N 19°36′E
183 O13 Liptrap, Cape headland Victoria, SE Australia 38°55′S 145°58′E
160 L13 Lipu var. Licheng. Guangxi Zhuangzu Zizhiqu, S China 24°25′N 110°15′E
81 G17 Lira N Uganda 02°15′N 32°55′E
57 F15 Lircay Huancavelica, C Peru 12°59′S 74°44′W
107 K17 Liri ≈ C Italy
144 M8 Lisakovsk Kostanay, NW Kazakhstan 52°32′N 62°32′E
79 K17 Lisala Equateur, N Dem. Rep. Congo 02°10′N 21°29′E
104 F11 Lisboa Eng. Lisbon; anc. Felicitas Julia, Olisipo. ● (Portugal) Lisboa, W Portugal 38°44′N 09°08′W
104 F10 Lisboa Eng. Lisbon. ◆ district C Portugal
19 N7 Lisbon New Hampshire, NE USA 44°11′N 71°52′W
29 Q6 Lisbon North Dakota, N USA 46°27′N 97°42′W
Lisbon see Lisboa
19 Q8 Lisbon Falls Maine, NE USA 44°00′N 70°03′W
97 G15 Lisburn Ir. Lios na gCearrbhach. E Northern Ireland, United Kingdom 54°31′N 06°03′W
38 L6 Lisburne, Cape headland Alaska, USA 68°52′N 166°13′W
97 B19 Liscannor Bay Ir. Bá Lios Ceannúir. inlet W Ireland
113 Q18 Lisec ▲ E FYR Macedonia 41°46′N 22°30′E
160 F13 Lishe Jiang ≈ SW China
Lishi see Lüliang
163 V10 Lishu Jilin, NE China 43°25′N 124°19′E
161 R10 Lishui Zhejiang, SE China 28°27′N 119°25′E
192 L5 Lisianski Island island Hawaiian Islands, Hawai'i, USA
Lisichansk see Lysychans'k
102 L4 Lisieux anc. Noviomagus. Calvados, N France 49°09′N 00°13′E
126 L8 Liski prev. Georgiu-Dezh. Voronezhskaya Oblast', W Russian Federation 51°00′N 39°36′E
103 N4 l'Isle-Adam Val-d'Oise, N France 49°07′N 02°13′E
Lisle/l'Isle see Lille
103 R15 l'Isle-sur-la-Sorgue Vaucluse, SE France 43°55′N 05°03′E
15 S9 L'Islet Québec, SE Canada 47°07′N 70°18′W
183 V4 Lismore New South Wales, SE Australia 28°48′S 153°12′E
182 M12 Lismore Victoria, SE Australia 37°59′S 143°18′E
97 D20 Lismore Ir. Lios Mór. S Ireland 52°10′N 07°10′W
Lissa see Vis, Croatia
Lissa see Leszno, Poland
98 H11 Lisse Zuid-Holland, W Netherlands 52°15′N 04°33′E
114 K13 Lissos var. Filiouri. ≈ NE Greece
95 D18 Lista peninsula S Norway
95 D18 Listafjorden fjord S Norway
195 R13 Lister, Mount ▲ Antarctica 78°12′S 161°46′E
126 M8 Listopadovka Voronezhskaya Oblast', W Russian Federation 51°54′N 41°08′E
14 F15 Listowel Ontario, S Canada 43°44′N 80°57′W
97 B20 Listowel Ir. Lios Tuathail. Kerry, SW Ireland 52°27′N 09°29′W
160 L14 Litang Guangxi Zhuangzu Zizhiqu, S China 23°09′N 109°08′E
160 F9 Litang var. Gaocheng. Sichuan, C China 30°03′N 100°12′E
160 F10 Litang Qu ≈ C China
55 X12 Litani var. Itany. ≈ French Guiana/Surinam
138 G8 Lītāni, Nahr el var. Nahr al Litant. ≈ C Lebanon
Litant, Nahr al see Lītāni, Nahr el
Litauen see Lithuania
30 K14 Litchfield Illinois, N USA 39°17′N 89°52′W
29 U8 Litchfield Minnesota, N USA 45°09′N 94°31′W
36 K13 Litchfield Park Arizona, SW USA 33°29′N 112°21′W
183 S8 Lithgow New South Wales, SE Australia 33°30′S 150°09′E
115 I26 Líthino, Akrotírio headland Kríti, Greece, E Mediterranean Sea 34°55′N 24°43′E
118 D12 Lithuania off. Republic of Lithuania, Ger. Litauen, Lith. Lietuva, Pol. Litwa, Rus. Litva; prev. Lithuanian SSR, Rus. Litovskaya SSR. ◆ republic NE Europe
Lithuanian SSR see Lithuania
Lithuania, Republic of see Lithuania
109 U11 Litija Ger. Littai. C Slovenia 46°03′N 14°50′E
18 H15 Lititz Pennsylvania, NE USA 40°09′N 76°18′W
115 F15 Litóchoro var. Litohoro, Litókhoron. Kentrikí Makedonía, N Greece 40°06′N 22°30′E
Litohoro/Litókhoron see Litóchoro
111 C15 Litoměřice Ger. Leitmeritz. Ústecký Kraj, NW Czech Republic 50°33′N 14°10′E
111 F17 Litomyšl Ger. Leitomischl. Pardubický Kraj, C Czech Republic 49°54′N 16°18′E
111 G17 Litovel Ger. Littau. Olomoucký Kraj, E Czech Republic 49°42′N 17°05′E
123 S13 Litovko Khabarovskiy Kray, SE Russian Federation 49°22′N 135°10′E
Litovskaya SSR see Lithuania
Littai see Litija
Littau see Litovel
44 G1 Little Abaco var. Abaco Island. island N Bahamas
111 I21 Little Alföld Ger. Kleines Ungarisches Tiefland, Hung. Kisalföld, Slvk. Podunajská Rovina. plain Hungary/Slovakia
151 Q20 Little Andaman island Andaman Islands, India, NE Indian Ocean
26 M5 Little Arkansas River ≈ Kansas, C USA
184 L4 Little Barrier Island island N New Zealand
Little Belt see Lillebælt
38 M11 Little Black River ≈ Alaska, USA
27 O2 Little Blue River ≈ Kansas/Nebraska, C USA
44 D8 Little Cayman island E Cayman Islands
11 X11 Little Churchill ≈ Manitoba, C Canada
166 J10 Little Coco Island island SW Burma (Myanmar)
36 L10 Little Colorado River ≈ Arizona, SW USA
14 E11 Little Current Manitoulin Island, Ontario, S Canada 45°57′N 81°56′W
12 E11 Little Current ≈ Ontario, S Canada
38 L8 Little Diomede Island island Alaska, USA
44 I4 Little Exuma island C Bahamas
29 U7 Little Falls Minnesota, N USA 45°59′N 94°21′W
18 J10 Little Falls New York, NE USA 43°02′N 74°51′W
24 M5 Littlefield Texas, SW USA 33°56′N 102°20′W
29 V3 Littlefork Minnesota, N USA 48°24′N 93°33′W
29 V3 Little Fork River ≈ Minnesota, N USA
11 N16 Little Fort British Columbia, SW Canada 51°27′N 120°15′W
11 Y14 Little Grand Rapids Manitoba, C Canada 52°06′N 95°29′W
97 N23 Littlehampton SE England, United Kingdom 50°48′N 00°33′W
35 T2 Little Humboldt River ≈ Nevada, W USA
44 K6 Little Inagua var. Inagua Islands. island S Bahamas
21 Q4 Little Kanawha River ≈ West Virginia, NE USA
83 F25 Little Karoo plateau S South Africa
39 O16 Little Koniuji Island island Shumagin Islands, Alaska, USA
44 H12 Little London W Jamaica 18°15′N 78°13′W
13 R10 Little Mecatina Fr. Rivière du Petit Mécatina. ≈ Newfoundland and Labrador/Québec, E Canada

◆ Country
● Country Capital
◇ Dependent Territory
○ Dependent Territory Capital
◆ Administrative Regions
✈ International Airport
▲ Mountain
▲▲ Mountain Range
Volcano
≈ River
◎ Lake
⊠ Reservoir

96 F8 **Little Minch, The** *strait* NW Scotland, United Kingdom
27 T13 **Little Missouri River** ≈ Arkansas, USA
28 J7 **Little Missouri River** ≈ NW USA
28 J3 **Little Muddy River** ≈ North Dakota, N USA
151 Q22 **Little Nicobar** *island* Nicobar Islands, India, NE Indian Ocean
27 R6 **Little Osage River** ≈ Missouri, C USA
97 P20 **Little Ouse** ≈ E England, United Kingdom
149 V2 **Little Pamir** *Pash.* Pāmīr-e Khord, *Rus.* Malyy Pamir. ▲▲ Afghanistan/Tajikistan
21 U12 **Little Pee Dee River** ≈ North Carolina/South Carolina, SE USA
27 V10 **Little Red River** ≈ Arkansas, C USA
Little Rhody *see* Rhode Island
185 I19 **Little River** Canterbury, South Island, New Zealand 43°45′S 172°49′E
21 U12 **Little River** South Carolina, SE USA 33°52′N 78°36′W
27 Y9 **Little River** ≈ Arkansas/Missouri, C USA
27 R13 **Little River** ≈ Arkansas/Oklahoma, USA
23 T7 **Little River** ≈ Georgia, SE USA
22 H6 **Little River** ≈ Louisiana, S USA
25 T10 **Little River** ≈ Texas, SW USA
27 V12 **Little Rock** *state capital* Arkansas, C USA 34°45′N 92°17′W
31 N8 **Little Sable Point** *headland* Michigan, N USA 43°38′N 86°32′W
103 U11 **Little Saint Bernard Pass** *Fr.* Col du Petit St-Bernard, *It.* Colle del Piccolo San Bernardo. *pass* France/Italy
36 K7 **Little Salt Lake** ◎ Utah, W USA
180 K8 **Little Sandy Desert** *desert* Western Australia
29 S13 **Little Sioux River** ≈ Iowa, C USA
38 E17 **Little Sitkin Island** *island* Aleutian Islands, Alaska, USA
11 O13 **Little Smoky** Alberta, W Canada 54°35′N 117°06′W
11 O14 **Little Smoky** ≈ Alberta, W Canada
37 P3 **Little Snake River** ≈ Colorado, C USA
64 A12 **Little Sound** *bay* Bermuda, NW Atlantic Ocean
37 T4 **Littleton** Colorado, C USA 39°36′N 105°01′W
19 N7 **Littleton** New Hampshire, NE USA 44°18′N 71°46′W
18 D11 **Little Valley** New York, NE USA 42°15′N 78°47′W
30 M15 **Little Wabash River** ≈ Illinois, N USA
14 D10 **Little White River** ≈ Ontario, S Canada
28 M12 **Little White River** ≈ South Dakota, N USA
25 R5 **Little Wichita River** ≈ Texas, SW USA
142 I4 **Little Zab** *Ar.* Nahraz Zāb aş Şaghīr, *Kurd.* Zē-i Kōya, *Per.* Rūdkhāneh-ye Zāb-e Kūchek. ≈ Iran/Iraq
79 D15 **Littoral** ◐ *province* W Cameroon
Littoria *see* Latina
Litva/Litwa *see* Lithuania
111 B15 **Litvínov** *Ger.* Leutensdorf. Ústecký Kraj, NW Czech Republic 50°38′N 13°30′E
116 M6 **Lityn** Vinnyts'ka Oblast', C Ukraine 49°19′N 28°06′E
Liu-chou/Liuchow *see* Liuzhou
163 W11 **Liuhe** Jilin, NE China 42°15′N 125°49′E
Liujiaxia *see* Yongjing
Liulin *see* Jonê
Liupanshui *see* Lupanshui
83 Q15 **Liúpo** Nampula, NE Mozambique 15°36′S 39°57′E
83 G14 **Liuwa Plain** *plain* W Zambia
160 L13 **Liuzhou** *var.* Liu-chou, Liuchow. Guangxi Zhuangzu Zizhiqu, S China 24°09′N 108°55′E
116 H8 **Livada** *Hung.* Sárköz. Satu Mare, NW Romania 47°52′N 23°04′E
115 J20 **Liváda, Akrotírio** *headland* Tínos, Kykládes, Greece, Aegean Sea 37°36′N 25°15′E
115 F18 **Livádeia** *prev.* Levádia. Stereá Elláda, C Greece 38°24′N 22°51′E
Livádi *see* Liádi
Livanátai *see* Livanátes
115 G18 **Livanátes** *prev.* Livanátai. Stereá Elláda, C Greece 38°43′N 23°03′E
118 I10 **Līvāni** *Ger.* Lievenhof. SE Latvia 56°22′N 26°12′E
65 E25 **Lively Island** *island* SE Falkland Islands
65 D25 **Lively Sound** *sound* SE Falkland Islands
39 R8 **Livengood** Alaska, USA 65°31′N 148°32′W
106 I7 **Livenza** ≈ NE Italy
35 O6 **Live Oak** California, W USA 39°17′N 121°41′W
23 U9 **Live Oak** Florida, SE USA 30°18′N 82°59′W
35 O9 **Livermore** California, W USA 37°40′N 121°46′W
20 I6 **Livermore** Kentucky, S USA 37°31′N 87°08′W
19 Q7 **Livermore Falls** Maine, NE USA 44°30′N 70°09′W
24 J10 **Livermore, Mount** ▲ Texas, SW USA 30°37′N 104°10′W
13 P16 **Liverpool** Nova Scotia, SE Canada 44°03′N 64°43′W
97 K17 **Liverpool** NW England, United Kingdom 53°25′N 02°55′W
183 S7 **Liverpool Range** ▲▲ New South Wales, SE Australia
42 F4 **Livingston** Izabal, E Guatemala 15°50′N 88°44′W
96 J12 **Livingston** C Scotland, United Kingdom 55°51′N 03°31′W
23 N5 **Livingston** Alabama, S USA 32°35′N 88°12′W
35 P9 **Livingston** California, W USA 37°22′N 120°45′W
22 J8 **Livingston** Louisiana, S USA 30°30′N 90°45′W
33 S11 **Livingston** Montana, NW USA 45°40′N 110°33′W
20 L8 **Livingston** Tennessee, S USA 36°22′N 85°20′W
25 W9 **Livingston** Texas, SW USA 30°42′N 94°58′W
83 I16 **Livingstone** *var.* Maramba. Southern, S Zambia 17°51′S 25°48′E
185 B22 **Livingstone Mountains** ▲▲ South Island, New Zealand
80 K13 **Livingstone Mountains** ▲▲ S Tanzania
82 N12 **Livingstonia** Northern, N Malawi 10°29′S 34°06′E
194 G4 **Livingston Island** *island* Antarctica
25 W9 **Livingston, Lake** ⊠ Texas, SW USA
112 F13 **Livno** ◐ Federicija Bosna I Hercegovina, SW Bosnia and Herzegovina
126 K7 **Livny** Orlovskaya Oblast', W Russian Federation 52°25′N 37°42′E
93 M14 **Livojoki** ≈ C Finland
31 R10 **Livonia** Michigan, N USA 42°22′N 83°22′W
106 E11 **Livorno** *Eng.* Leghorn. Toscana, C Italy 43°32′N 10°18′E
Livramento *see* Santana do Livramento
141 U8 **Liwā** *var.* Al Liwā'. *oasis region* S United Arab Emirates
81 I24 **Liwale** Lindi, SE Tanzania 09°46′S 37°56′E
159 W9 **Liwang** Ningxia, N China 36°42′N 106°05′E
83 N15 **Liwonde** Southern, S Malawi 15°01′S 35°15′E
159 V11 **Lixian** *var.* Li Xian. Gansu, C China 34°15′N 105°07′E
160 H8 **Lixian** *var.* Li Xian, Zagunao. Sichuan, C China 31°27′N 103°06′E
Li Xian *see* Lixian
Lixian Jiang *see* Black River
115 B18 **Lixoúri** *prev.* Lixoúrion. Kefallinía, Iónia Nisiá, Greece, C Mediterranean Sea 38°14′N 20°24′E
Lixoúrion *see* Lixoúri
Lixus *see* Larache
33 U15 **Lizard Head Peak** ▲ Wyoming, C USA 42°47′N 109°12′W
97 H25 **Lizard Point** *headland* SW England, United Kingdom 49°57′N 05°12′W
Lizarra *see* Estella
112 L12 **Ljig** Serbia, C Serbia 44°14′N 20°16′E
Ljouwert *see* Leeuwarden
Ljubelj *see* Loibl Pass
109 U11 **Ljubljana** *Ger.* Laibach, *It.* Lubiana; *anc.* Aemona, Emona. ● (Slovenia) C Slovenia 46°03′N 14°29′E
109 T11 **Ljubljana** ✕ C Slovenia 46°14′N 14°26′E
113 N17 **Ljuboten** *Alb.* Luboten. ▲ S Serbia 42°12′N 21°06′E
95 P19 **Ljugarn** Gotland, SE Sweden 57°23′N 18°45′E
84 G7 **Ljungan** ≈ N Sweden
93 F17 **Ljungan** ≈ C Sweden
95 K21 **Ljungby** Kronoberg, S Sweden 56°49′N 13°55′E
95 M17 **Ljungsbro** Östergötland, S Sweden 58°31′N 15°30′E
95 I18 **Ljungskile** Västra Götaland, S Sweden 58°14′N 11°55′E
94 M11 **Ljusdal** Gävleborg, C Sweden 61°50′N 16°10′E
94 M11 **Ljusnan** ≈ C Sweden
94 N12 **Ljusne** Gävleborg, C Sweden 61°11′N 17°07′E
95 P15 **Ljusterö** Stockholm, C Sweden 59°31′N 18°40′E
109 X9 **Ljutomer** *Ger.* Luttenberg. NE Slovenia 46°31′N 16°12′E
63 G15 **Llaima, Volcán** ⛰ S Chile 39°01′S 71°38′W
105 X4 **Llançà** *var.* Llansá. Cataluña, NE Spain 42°23′N 03°08′E
97 J21 **Llandovery** C Wales, United Kingdom 52°01′N 03°47′W
97 J20 **Llandrindod Wells** E Wales, United Kingdom 52°15′N 03°23′W
97 J18 **Llandudno** N Wales, United Kingdom 53°19′N 03°49′W
97 I21 **Llanelli** *prev.* Llanelly. SW Wales, United Kingdom 51°41′N 04°12′W
Llanelly *see* Llanelli
104 M2 **Llanes** Asturias, N Spain 43°25′N 04°46′W
97 K19 **Llangollen** NE Wales, United Kingdom 52°58′N 03°10′W
104 K2 **Llangréu** *var.* Langreo, Sama de Langreo. Asturias, N Spain 43°18′N 05°40′W
25 R10 **Llano** Texas, SW USA 30°49′N 98°42′W
25 Q10 **Llano River** ≈ Texas, SW USA
54 I9 **Llanos** *physical region* Colombia/Venezuela
63 G16 **Llanquihue, Lago** ◎ S Chile
Llansá *see* Llançà
105 U5 **Lleida** *Cast.* Lérida; *anc.* Ilerda. Cataluña, NE Spain 41°38′N 00°35′E
104 K12 **Llerena** Extremadura, W Spain 38°13′N 06°00′W
105 S9 **Llíria** Valenciana, E Spain 39°38′N 00°36′W
105 W4 **Llívia** Cataluña, NE Spain 42°27′N 02°00′E
Llodio *see* Laudio
105 X5 **Lloret de Mar** Cataluña, NE Spain 41°42′N 02°51′E
Llorri *see* Toretta de l'Orrí
10 L11 **Lloyd George, Mount** ▲ British Columbia, W Canada 57°46′N 124°57′W
11 R14 **Lloydminster** Alberta/Saskatchewan, SW Canada 53°18′N 110°00′W
104 K2 **Lluanco** *var.* Luanco. Asturias, N Spain 43°36′N 05°48′W
105 X9 **Llucmajor** Mallorca, Spain, W Mediterranean Sea 39°29′N 02°53′E
36 L6 **Loa** Utah, W USA 38°24′N 111°38′W
169 S8 **Loagan Bunut** ◎ East Malaysia
38 G12 **Loa, Mauna** ▲ Hawai'i, USA 19°28′N 155°39′W
Loanda *see* Luanda
79 J22 **Loange** ≈ S Dem. Rep. Congo
79 E21 **Loango** Kouilou, S Congo 04°38′S 11°50′E
106 B10 **Loano** Liguria, NW Italy 44°07′N 08°15′E
62 H4 **Loa, Río** ≈ N Chile
83 I20 **Lobatse** *var.* Lobatsi. Kgatleng, SE Botswana 25°11′S 25°40′E
Lobatsi *see* Lobatse
101 Q15 **Löbau** Sachsen, E Germany 51°07′N 14°40′E
79 H16 **Lobaye** ◐ *prefecture* SW Central African Republic
79 I16 **Lobaye** ≈ SW Central African Republic
99 G21 **Lobbes** Hainaut, S Belgium 50°21′N 04°16′E
61 D23 **Lobería** Buenos Aires, E Argentina 38°08′S 58°48′W
110 F8 **Łobez** *Ger.* Labes. Zacodniopomorskie, NW Poland 53°38′N 15°39′E
82 A13 **Lobito** Benguela, W Angola 12°20′S 13°34′E
Lobkovichi *see* Labkovichy
Lob Nor *see* Lop Nur
171 V13 **Lobo** Papua, E Indonesia 03°41′S 134°06′E
104 J11 **Lobón** Extremadura, W Spain 38°51′N 06°38′W
61 D20 **Lobos** Buenos Aires, E Argentina 35°11′S 59°08′W
40 E4 **Lobos, Cabo** *headland* NW Mexico 29°53′N 112°43′W
40 F6 **Lobos, Isla** *island* NW Mexico
Lobositz *see* Lovosice
Lobsens *see* Łobżenica
Loburi *see* Lop Buri
110 H9 **Łobżenica** *Ger.* Lobsens. Wielkopolskie, C Poland 53°19′N 17°11′E
108 G11 **Locarno** *Ger.* Luggarus. Ticino, S Switzerland 46°11′N 08°48′E
96 E9 **Lochboisdale** NW Scotland, United Kingdom 57°08′N 07°17′W
98 N11 **Lochem** Gelderland, E Netherlands 52°10′N 06°25′E
102 M8 **Loches** Indre-et-Loire, C France 47°08′N 01°00′E
Loch Garman *see* Wexford
96 H12 **Lochgilphead** W Scotland, United Kingdom 56°02′N 05°27′W
96 H7 **Lochinver** N Scotland, United Kingdom 58°10′N 05°15′W
96 F8 **Lochmaddy** NW Scotland, United Kingdom 57°35′N 07°10′W
96 J10 **Lochnagar** ▲ C Scotland, United Kingdom 56°58′N 03°09′W
99 E17 **Lochristi** Oost-Vlaanderen, NW Belgium 51°07′N 03°49′E
96 H9 **Lochy, Loch** ◎ N Scotland, United Kingdom
182 G8 **Lock** South Australia 33°37′S 135°45′E
97 J14 **Lockerbie** S Scotland, United Kingdom 55°11′N 03°27′W
27 S13 **Lockesburg** Arkansas, C USA 33°58′N 94°10′W
183 P10 **Lockhart** New South Wales, SE Australia 35°15′S 146°43′E
25 S11 **Lockhart** Texas, SW USA 29°54′N 97°41′W
18 F13 **Lock Haven** Pennsylvania, NE USA 41°08′N 77°27′W
25 N4 **Lockney** Texas, SW USA 34°06′N 101°27′W
100 O12 **Löcknitz** ≈ NE Germany
18 E9 **Lockport** New York, NE USA 43°09′N 78°40′W
167 T13 **Lôc Ninh** Sông Be, S Vietnam 11°51′N 106°35′E
107 N23 **Locri** Calabria, SW Italy 38°16′N 16°16′E
Locse *see* Levoča
27 T2 **Locust Creek** ≈ Missouri, C USA
23 P3 **Locust Fork** ≈ Alabama, S USA
27 Q9 **Locust Grove** Oklahoma, C USA 36°12′N 95°10′W
94 E11 **Lodalskåpa** ▲ S Norway 61°47′N 07°10′E
183 N10 **Loddon River** ≈ Victoria, SE Australia
Lodensee *see* Klooga
103 P15 **Lodève** *anc.* Luteva. Hérault, S France 43°44′N 03°19′E
124 I12 **Lodeynoye Pole** Leningradskaya Oblast', NW Russian Federation 60°41′N 33°29′E
33 V11 **Lodge Grass** Montana, NW USA 45°19′N 107°20′W
28 J15 **Lodgepole Creek** ≈ Nebraska/Wyoming, C USA
149 T11 **Lodhrān** Punjab, E Pakistan 29°32′N 71°40′E
106 D8 **Lodi** Lombardia, NW Italy 45°19′N 09°30′E
35 O8 **Lodi** California, W USA 38°07′N 121°17′W
31 T12 **Lodi** Ohio, N USA 41°00′N 82°01′W
92 H10 **Lødingen** *Lapp.* Lådik. Nordland, C Norway 68°25′N 16°00′E
79 L20 **Lodja** Kasai-Oriental, C Dem. Rep. Congo 03°29′S 23°25′E
37 O3 **Lodore, Canyon of** *canyon* Colorado, C USA
105 Q4 **Lodosa** Navarra, N Spain 42°26′N 02°05′W
81 H16 **Lodwar** Rift Valley, NW Kenya 03°06′N 35°38′E
110 K13 **Łódź** *Rus.* Lodz. Łódź, C Poland 51°51′N 19°26′E
110 E12 **Łódzkie** ◐ *province* C Poland
167 P8 **Loei** *var.* Loey, Muang Loei. Loei, C Thailand 17°32′N 101°40′E
98 I11 **Loenen** Utrecht, C Netherlands 52°13′N 05°01′E
167 R9 **Loeng Nok Tha** Yasothon, E Thailand 16°12′N 104°31′E
83 F24 **Loeriesfontein** Northern Cape, W South Africa 30°59′S 19°29′E
Loewoek *see* Luwuk
Loey *see* Loei
76 J16 **Lofa** ≈ N Liberia
109 P6 **Lofer** Salzburg, C Austria 47°37′N 12°42′E
92 F11 **Lofoten** *var.* Lofoten Islands. *island group* C Norway
Lofoten Islands *see* Lofoten
95 N18 **Loftahammar** Kalmar, S Sweden 57°55′N 16°45′E
127 O10 **Log** Volgogradskaya Oblast', SW Russian Federation 49°32′N 43°52′E
77 S12 **Loga** Dosso, SW Niger 13°40′N 03°15′E
29 S14 **Logan** Iowa, C USA 41°38′N 95°47′W
26 K3 **Logan** Kansas, C USA 39°39′N 99°34′W
31 T14 **Logan** Ohio, N USA 39°32′N 82°24′W
36 L1 **Logan** Utah, W USA 41°45′N 111°50′W
21 P6 **Logan** West Virginia, NE USA 37°52′N 82°00′W
35 Y10 **Logandale** Nevada, W USA 36°36′N 114°28′W
19 O11 **Logan International** ✕ (Boston) Massachusetts, NE USA 42°22′N 71°00′W
11 N16 **Logan Lake** British Columbia, SW Canada 50°28′N 120°42′W
23 Q4 **Logan Martin Lake** ⊠ Alabama, S USA
10 G8 **Logan, Mount** ▲ Yukon Territory, W Canada 60°32′N 140°34′W
32 I7 **Logan, Mount** ▲ Washington, NW USA 48°32′N 120°57′W
33 P7 **Logan Pass** *pass* Montana, NW USA
31 O12 **Logansport** Indiana, N USA 40°44′N 86°25′W
22 F6 **Logansport** Louisiana, S USA 31°58′N 94°00′W
149 Q5 **Lōgar** *prev.* Lowgar. ◐ *province* E Afghanistan
67 R11 **Loge** ≈ NW Angola
Logishin *see* Lahishyn
Log na Coille *see* Lugnaquillia Mountain
78 G11 **Logone** *var.* Lagone. ≈ Cameroon/Chad
78 G13 **Logone-Occidental** *off.* Préfecture du Logone-Occidental. ◐ *prefecture* SW Chad
78 H13 **Logone Occidental** ≈ SW Chad
Logone-Occidental, Préfecture du *see* Logone-Occidental
78 G13 **Logone-Oriental** *off.* Préfecture du Logone-Oriental. ◐ *prefecture* SW Chad
78 H13 **Logone Oriental** ≈ SW Chad
Logone Oriental *see* Pendé
Logone-Oriental, Préfecture du *see* Logone-Oriental
L'Ogooué-Ivindo *see* Ogooué-Ivindo
L'Ogooué-Lolo *see* Ogooué-Lolo
L'Ogooué-Maritime *see* Ogooué-Maritime
Logoysk *see* Lahoysk
105 P4 **Logroño** *anc.* Vareia, *Lat.* Juliobriga. La Rioja, N Spain 42°28′N 02°26′W
104 L10 **Logrosán** Extremadura, W Spain 39°21′N 05°29′W
95 G20 **Løgstør** Nordjylland, N Denmark 56°57′N 09°19′E
95 H22 **Løgten** Midtjylland, C Denmark 56°17′N 10°20′E
95 F24 **Løgumkloster** Syddanmark, SW Denmark 55°04′N 08°58′E
Lögurinn *see* Lagarfljót
153 P15 **Lohārdaga** Jhārkhand, N India 23°27′N 84°42′E
152 H10 **Lohāru** Haryāna, N India 28°28′N 75°50′E
101 D15 **Lohausen** ✕ (Düsseldorf) Nordrhein-Westfalen, W Germany 51°18′N 06°51′E
189 O14 **Lohd** Pohnpei, E Micronesia
92 L12 **Lohiniva** Lappi, N Finland 67°09′N 25°04′E
Lohiszyn *see* Lahishyn
93 L20 **Lohja** *var.* Lojo. Etelä-Suomi, S Finland 60°14′N 24°07′E
169 V11 **Lohjanan** Borneo, C Indonesia
25 Q9 **Lohn** Texas, SW USA 31°15′N 99°22′W
100 G12 **Löhne** Niedersachsen, NW Germany 52°40′N 08°13′E
Lohr *see* Lohr am Main
101 I18 **Lohr am Main** *var.* Lohr. Bayern, C Germany 50°00′N 09°30′E
109 T10 **Loibl Pass** *Ger.* Loiblpass, *Slvn.* Ljubelj. *pass* Austria/Slovenia
Loiblpass *see* Loibl Pass
167 N6 **Loikaw** Kayah State, C Burma (Myanmar) 19°40′N 97°17′E
93 K19 **Loimaa** Länsi-Suomi, SW Finland 60°51′N 23°03′E
103 O6 **Loing** ≈ C France
167 R6 **Loi, Phou** ▲ N Laos 20°18′N 103°14′E
102 L7 **Loir** ≈ C France
103 Q11 **Loire** ◐ *department* E France
102 M7 **Loire** *var.* Liger. ≈ C France
102 I7 **Loire-Atlantique** ◐ *department* NW France
103 O7 **Loiret** ◐ *department* C France
102 M8 **Loir-et-Cher** ◐ *department* C France
101 L24 **Loisach** ≈ SE Germany
56 B9 **Loja** Loja, S Ecuador 03°59′S 79°16′W
104 M14 **Loja** Andalucía, S Spain 37°10′N 04°09′W
56 B9 **Loja** ◐ *province* S Ecuador
Lojo *see* Lohja
116 J4 **Lokachi** Volyns'ka Oblast', NW Ukraine 50°44′N 24°39′E
79 M20 **Lokandu** Maniema, C Dem. Rep. Congo 02°34′S 25°44′E
92 M11 **Lokan Tekojärvi** ◎ NE Finland
137 Z11 **Lökbatan** *Rus.* Lokbatan. E Azerbaijan 40°21′N 49°43′E
Lokbatan *see* Lökbatan
99 F17 **Lokeren** Oost-Vlaanderen, NW Belgium 51°06′N 03°59′E
Lokhvitsa *see* Lokhvytsya
117 S4 **Lokhvytsya** *Rus.* Lokhvitsa. Poltavs'ka Oblast', NE Ukraine 50°22′N 33°16′E
81 H17 **Lokichar** Rift Valley, NW Kenya 02°23′N 35°40′E
81 G16 **Lokichokio** Rift Valley, NW Kenya 04°16′N 34°22′E
81 H16 **Lokitaung** Rift Valley, NW Kenya 04°15′N 35°45′E
92 M11 **Lokka** Lappi, N Finland 67°48′N 27°41′E
94 G8 **Løkken Verk** Sør-Trøndelag, S Norway 63°06′N 09°43′E
124 G16 **Loknya** Pskovskaya Oblast', W Russian Federation 56°48′N 30°08′E
77 V15 **Loko** Nassarawa, C Nigeria 08°00′N 07°48′E
77 U15 **Lokoja** Kogi, C Nigeria 07°48′N 06°45′E
81 H17 **Lokori** Rift Valley, W Kenya 01°56′N 36°03′E
77 R16 **Lokossa** S Benin 06°38′N 01°43′E
118 I3 **Loksa** *Ger.* Loxa. Harjumaa, NW Estonia 59°32′N 25°42′E
9 T7 **Loks Land** *island* Nunavut, NE Canada
80 C13 **Lol** ≈ NW South Sudan
76 K15 **Lola** SE Guinea 07°52′N 08°29′W
35 Q5 **Lola, Mount** ▲ California, W USA 39°27′N 120°20′W
81 H20 **Loliondo** Arusha, NE Tanzania 02°03′S 35°46′E
95 H25 **Lolland** *prev.* Laaland. *island* S Denmark
186 G6 **Lolobau Island** *island* E Papua New Guinea
79 E16 **Lolodorf** Sud, SW Cameroon 03°17′N 10°50′E
114 G7 **Lom** *prev.* Lom-Palanka. Montana, NW Bulgaria 43°49′N 23°16′E
114 G7 **Lom** ≈ NW Bulgaria
79 M19 **Lomami** ≈ C Dem. Rep. Congo
57 F17 **Lomas** Arequipa, SW Peru 15°29′S 74°54′W
63 I23 **Lomas, Bahía** *bay* S Chile
61 D20 **Lomas de Zamora** Buenos Aires, E Argentina 34°53′S 58°26′W
61 D20 **Loma Verde** Buenos Aires, E Argentina 35°16′S 58°24′W
180 K4 **Lombadina** Western Australia 16°39′S 122°54′E
106 E6 **Lombardia** *Eng.* Lombardy. ◐ *region* N Italy
Lombardy *see* Lombardia
102 M15 **Lombez** Gers, S France 43°29′N 00°54′E
171 Q16 **Lomblen, Pulau** *island* Nusa Tenggara, S Indonesia
173 W7 **Lombok Basin** *undersea feature* E Indian Ocean 09°50′S 116°00′E
170 L16 **Lombok, Pulau** *island* Nusa Tenggara, C Indonesia
77 Q16 **Lomé** ● (Togo) S Togo 06°08′N 01°13′E
77 Q16 **Lomé** ✕ S Togo 06°08′N 01°13′E
79 L19 **Lomela** Kasai-Oriental, C Dem. Rep. Congo 02°19′S 23°15′E
25 R9 **Lometa** Texas, SW USA 31°13′N 98°23′W
79 F16 **Lomié** Est, SE Cameroon 03°09′N 13°35′E
30 M8 **Lomira** Wisconsin, N USA 43°36′N 88°26′W
95 K23 **Lomma** Skåne, S Sweden 55°41′N 13°05′E
99 J16 **Lommel** Limburg, N Belgium 51°14′N 05°19′E
96 I11 **Lomond, Loch** ◎ C Scotland, United Kingdom
197 R9 **Lomonosov Ridge** *var.* Harris Ridge, *Rus.* Khrebet Homonsova. *undersea feature* Arctic Ocean 88°00′N 140°00′E
Lomonsova, Khrebet *see* Lomonosov Ridge
Lom-Palanka *see* Lom
Lomphat *see* Lumphăt
35 P14 **Lompoc** California, W USA 34°39′N 120°29′W
167 P9 **Lom Sak** *var.* Muang Lom Sak. Phetchabun, C Thailand 16°45′N 101°12′E
110 N9 **Łomża** *Rus.* Lomzha. Podlaskie, NE Poland 53°11′N 22°04′E
Lomzha *see* Łomża
Lonaula *see* Lonāvale
155 D14 **Lonāvale** *prev.* Lonaula. Mahārāshtra, W India 18°45′N 73°27′E
63 G15 **Loncoche** Araucanía, C Chile 39°22′S 72°34′W
63 H14 **Loncopue** Neuquén, W Argentina 38°04′S 70°43′W
99 G17 **Londerzeel** Vlaams Brabant, C Belgium 51°00′N 04°19′E
Londinium *see* London
14 E16 **London** Ontario, S Canada 42°59′N 81°13′W
191 Y2 **London** Kiritimati, E Kiribati 02°00′N 157°28′W
97 O22 **London** *anc.* Augusta, *Lat.* Londinium. ● (United Kingdom) SE England, United Kingdom 51°30′N 00°10′W
21 N7 **London** Kentucky, S USA 37°07′N 84°05′W
31 S13 **London** Ohio, NE USA 39°52′N 83°27′W
25 Q10 **London** Texas, SW USA 30°40′N 99°33′W
97 O22 **London City** ✕ SE England, United Kingdom 51°31′N 00°07′E
97 E14 **Londonderry** *var.* Derry, *Ir.* Doire. NW Northern Ireland, United Kingdom 55°00′N 07°19′W
97 F14 **Londonderry** *cultural region* NW Northern Ireland, United Kingdom
180 M2 **Londonderry, Cape** *cape* Western Australia
63 H25 **Londonderry, Isla** *island* S Chile
43 O7 **Londres, Cayos** *reef* NE Nicaragua
60 I10 **Londrina** Paraná, S Brazil 23°18′S 51°13′W
27 N13 **Lone Grove** Oklahoma, C USA 34°11′N 97°15′W
14 E12 **Lonely Island** *island* Ontario, S Canada
35 T8 **Lone Mountain** ▲ Nevada, W USA 38°01′N 117°28′W
25 V6 **Lone Oak** Texas, SW USA 33°02′N 95°58′W
35 T11 **Lone Pine** California, W USA 36°36′N 118°04′W
Lone Star State *see* Texas
Lone Tree Islet *see* Iku
83 D14 **Longa** Cuando Cubango, C Angola 14°44′S 18°36′E
82 B12 **Longa** ≈ W Angola
83 E15 **Longa** ≈ SE Angola
Long'an *see* Pingwu
163 W11 **Longang Shan** ▲▲ NE China
197 S4 **Longa, Proliv** *Eng.* Long Strait. *strait* NE Russian Federation
44 J13 **Long Bay** *bay* W Jamaica
21 V13 **Long Bay** *bay* North Carolina/South Carolina, E USA
35 T16 **Long Beach** California, W USA 33°46′N 118°11′W
22 M9 **Long Beach** Mississippi, S USA 30°21′N 89°09′W
18 L14 **Long Beach** Long Island, New York, NE USA 40°34′N 73°38′W
32 F9 **Long Beach** Washington, NW USA 46°21′N 124°03′W
18 K16 **Long Beach Island** *island* New Jersey, NE USA
65 M25 **Longbluff** *headland* SW Tristan da Cunha
23 U13 **Longboat Key** *island* Florida, SE USA
18 K15 **Long Branch** New Jersey, NE USA 40°18′N 73°59′W
44 J5 **Long Cay** *island* SE Bahamas
Longcheng *see* Xiaoxian
161 P14 **Longchuan** *var.* Laolong. Guangdong, S China 24°07′N 115°10′E
Longchuan *see* Nanhua
Longchuan Jiang *see* Shweli
32 K12 **Long Creek** Oregon, NW USA 44°40′N 119°07′W
159 W10 **Longde** Ningxia, N China 35°37′N 106°07′E
183 P16 **Longford** Tasmania, SE Australia 41°41′S 147°03′E
97 D17 **Longford** *Ir.* An Longfort. Longford, C Ireland 53°45′N 07°50′W
97 E17 **Longford** *Ir.* An Longfort. *cultural region* C Ireland
Longgang *see* Dazu
161 P1 **Longhua** Hebei, E China 41°18′N 117°44′E
169 U11 **Longiram** Borneo, C Indonesia 0°02′S 115°36′E
44 J4 **Long Island** *island* C Bahamas
12 H8 **Long Island** *island* Nunavut, C Canada
186 D7 **Long Island** *var.* Arop Island. *island* N Papua New Guinea
18 L14 **Long Island** *island* New York, NE USA
Long Island *see* Bermuda
18 M14 **Long Island Sound** *sound* NE USA
163 U7 **Longjiang** Heilongjiang, NE China 47°20′N 123°09′E
160 K13 **Long Jiang** ≈ S China
163 Y10 **Longjing** *var.* Yanji. Jilin, NE China 42°48′N 129°26′E
161 R4 **Longkou** Shandong, E China 37°40′N 120°21′E
12 E11 **Longlac** Ontario, S Canada 49°47′N 86°34′W
19 S1 **Long Lake** ◎ Maine, NE USA
31 O6 **Long Lake** ◎ Michigan, N USA
31 R5 **Long Lake** ◎ Michigan, N USA
29 N6 **Long Lake** ◎ North Dakota, N USA
30 J4 **Long Lake** ⊠ Wisconsin, N USA
99 K23 **Longlier** Luxembourg, SE Belgium 49°51′N 05°27′E
160 I13 **Longlin** *var.* Longlin Gezu Zizhixian, Xinzhou. Guangxi Zhuangzu Zizhiqu, S China 24°46′N 105°19′E
Longlin Gezu Zizhixian *see* Longlin
37 T3 **Longmont** Colorado, C USA 40°09′N 105°07′W
157 P10 **Longnan** *var.* Wudu. Gansu, C China 33°27′N 104°57′E
29 N13 **Long Pine** Nebraska, C USA 42°32′N 99°42′W
Longping *see* Luodian
14 K15 **Long Point** *headland* Ontario, SE Canada 43°56′N 76°53′W
14 F17 **Long Point** *headland* Ontario, S Canada 42°33′N 80°15′W
184 P10 **Long Point** *headland* North Island, New Zealand 39°07′S 177°41′E
30 L2 **Long Point** *headland* Michigan, N USA 47°50′N 89°09′W
14 G17 **Long Point Bay** *lake bay* Ontario, S Canada
29 T7 **Long Prairie** Minnesota, N USA 45°58′N 94°52′W
Longquan *see* Fenggang
Longquan *see* Yanggao
13 S11 **Long Range Mountains** *hill range* Newfoundland and Labrador, E Canada
65 H25 **Long Range Point** *headland* SE Saint Helena 16°00′S 05°41′W
181 V8 **Longreach** Queensland, E Australia 23°31′S 144°18′E
160 H7 **Longriba** Sichuan, C China 32°32′N 102°20′E
160 L10 **Longshan** *var.* Min'an. Hunan, S China 29°25′N 109°28′E
37 S3 **Longs Peak** ▲ Colorado, C USA 40°15′N 105°37′W
Long Strait *see* Longa, Proliv
102 K8 **Longué** Maine-et-Loire, NW France 47°23′N 00°07′W
15 P11 **Longue-Pointe** Québec, E Canada 50°20′N 64°13′W
103 S4 **Longuyon** Meurthe-et-Moselle, NE France 49°25′N 05°37′E
25 W7 **Longview** Texas, SW USA 32°30′N 94°45′W
32 G10 **Longview** Washington, NW USA 46°08′N 122°56′W
65 H25 **Longwood** C Saint Helena
25 P7 **Longworth** Texas, SW USA 32°37′N 100°20′W
103 S3 **Longwy** Meurthe-et-Moselle, NE France 49°31′N 05°46′E
159 V11 **Longxi** *var.* Gongchang. Gansu, C China 35°00′N 104°34′E
Longxian *see* Wengyuan
167 S14 **Long Xuyên** *var.* Longxuyen. An Giang, S Vietnam 10°23′N 105°25′E
Longxuyen *see* Long Xuyên
161 Q13 **Longyan** Fujian, SE China 25°06′N 117°02′E
92 O3 **Longyearbyen** ○ (Svalbard) Spitsbergen, W Svalbard 78°12′N 15°39′E
160 J15 **Longzhou** Guangxi Zhuangzu Zizhiqu, S China 22°22′N 106°46′E
Longzhouping *see* Changyang
100 F12 **Löningen** Niedersachsen, NW Germany 52°43′N 07°42′E
27 V11 **Lonoke** Arkansas, C USA 34°46′N 91°56′W
95 L21 **Lönsboda** Skåne, S Sweden 56°24′N 14°19′E
103 S9 **Lons-le-Saunier** *anc.* Ledo Salinarius. Jura, E France 46°41′N 05°32′E
31 O15 **Loogootee** Indiana, N USA 38°40′N 86°54′W
31 Q9 **Looking Glass River** ≈ Michigan, N USA
21 X11 **Lookout, Cape** *headland* North Carolina, SE USA 34°36′N 76°31′W
39 O6 **Lookout Ridge** *ridge* Alaska, USA
Lookransar *see* Lūnkaransar
181 N11 **Loongana** Western Australia 30°53′S 127°15′E
99 I14 **Loon op Zand** Noord-Brabant, S Netherlands 51°38′N 05°05′E
97 A19 **Loop Head** *Ir.* Ceann Léime. *promontory* W Ireland
109 V4 **Loosdorf** Niederösterreich, NE Austria 48°13′N 15°25′E
158 G10 **Lop** Xinjiang Uygur Zizhiqu, NW China 37°06′N 80°12′E
112 J11 **Lopare** ◐ Republika Srpska, NE Bosnia and Herzegovina
Lopatichi *see* Lapatsichy
127 P7 **Lopatino** Penzenskaya Oblast', W Russian Federation 52°38′N 45°46′E
167 P10 **Lop Buri** *var.* Loburi. Lop Buri, C Thailand 14°49′N 100°37′E
25 R16 **Lopeno** Texas, SW USA 26°42′N 99°06′W
79 C18 **Lopez, Cap** *headland* W Gabon 00°39′S 08°44′E
98 I12 **Lopik** Utrecht, C Netherlands 51°58′N 04°57′E
Lop Nor *see* Lop Nur
158 M7 **Lop Nur** *var.* Lob Nor, Lop Nor, Lo-pu Po. *seasonal lake* NW China
Lopnur *see* Yuli
79 K17 **Lopori** ≈ NW Dem. Rep. Congo
98 O5 **Loppersum** Groningen, NE Netherlands 53°20′N 06°45′E
92 I8 **Lopphavet** *sound* N Norway
Lo-pu Po *see* Lop Nur
Lora *see* Lowrah
182 F3 **Lora Creek** *seasonal river* South Australia
104 K13 **Lora del Río** Andalucía, S Spain 37°39′N 05°32′W
148 M11 **Lora, Hāmūn-i** *wetland* SW Pakistan
31 T11 **Lorain** Ohio, N USA 41°27′N 82°10′W
25 O7 **Loraine** Texas, SW USA 32°24′N 100°42′W
31 R13 **Loramie, Lake** ⊠ Ohio, N USA
105 Q13 **Lorca** *Ar.* Lurka; *anc.* Eliocroca, *Lat.* Illurco. Murcia, S Spain 37°40′N 01°41′W
192 I10 **Lord Howe Island** *island* E Australia
Lord Howe Island *see* Ontong Java Atoll
175 O10 **Lord Howe Rise** *undersea feature* SW Pacific Ocean
192 J10 **Lord Howe Seamounts** *undersea feature* W Pacific Ocean
37 P15 **Lordsburg** New Mexico, SW USA 32°19′N 108°42′W
186 E5 **Lorengau** *var.* Lorungau. Manus Island, N Papua New Guinea 02°01′S 147°15′E
25 N5 **Lorenzo** Texas, SW USA 33°40′N 101°31′W
142 K7 **Lorestān** *off.* Ostān-e Lorestān, *var.* Luristan. ◐ *province* W Iran
Lorestān, Ostān-e *see* Lorestān
57 M17 **Loreto** El Beni, N Bolivia 15°13′S 64°44′W
106 J12 **Loreto** Marche, C Italy 43°25′N 13°37′E
40 F8 **Loreto** Baja California Sur, NW Mexico 25°59′N 111°22′W
40 M11 **Loreto** Zacatecas, C Mexico 22°15′N 102°00′W
56 E9 **Loreto** *off.* Departamento de Loreto. ◐ *department* NE Peru
Loreto, Departamento de *see* Loreto
81 K18 **Lorian Swamp** *swamp* E Kenya
54 E6 **Lorica** Córdoba, NW Colombia 09°14′N 75°50′W
102 G7 **Lorient** *prev.* l'Orient. Morbihan, NW France 47°45′N 03°22′W
l'Orient *see* Lorient
111 K22 **Lőrinci** Heves, NE Hungary 47°46′N 19°40′E
14 G11 **Loring** Ontario, S Canada 45°55′N 79°59′W
33 V6 **Loring** Montana, NW USA 48°49′N 107°48′W
103 R13 **Loriol-sur-Drôme** Drôme, E France 44°46′N 04°51′E
21 U12 **Loris** South Carolina, SE USA 34°03′N 78°53′W
57 I18 **Loriscota, Laguna** ◎ S Peru
183 N13 **Lorne** Victoria, SE Australia 38°33′S 143°57′E
96 G11 **Lorn, Firth of** *inlet* W Scotland, United Kingdom
Loro Sae *see* East Timor
101 F24 **Lörrach** Baden-Württemberg, S Germany 47°38′N 07°40′E
103 T5 **Lorraine** ◐ *region* NE France
Lorungau *see* Lorengau
94 L11 **Los** Gävleborg, C Sweden 61°43′N 15°15′E
35 P14 **Los Alamos** California, W USA 34°44′N 120°16′W
37 S10 **Los Alamos** New Mexico, SW USA 35°52′N 106°17′W
42 F5 **Los Amates** Izabal, E Guatemala 15°14′N 89°06′W
63 G14 **Los Ángeles** Bío Bío, C Chile 37°30′S 72°18′W
35 S15 **Los Angeles** California, W USA 34°03′N 118°15′W
35 S15 **Los Angeles** ✕ California, W USA 33°54′N 118°24′W
35 T13 **Los Angeles Aqueduct** *aqueduct* California, W USA
Losanna *see* Lausanne
63 H20 **Los Antiguos** Santa Cruz, SW Argentina 46°36′S 71°31′W
189 Q16 **Losap Atoll** *atoll* C Micronesia
35 P10 **Los Banos** California, W USA 37°00′N 120°39′W
104 K16 **Los Barrios** Andalucía, S Spain 36°11′N 05°30′W
62 L5 **Los Blancos** Salta, N Argentina 23°36′S 62°35′W
42 L12 **Los Chiles** Alajuela, NW Costa Rica 11°00′N 84°42′W
105 O2 **Los Corrales de Buelna** Cantabria, N Spain 43°15′N 04°04′W
25 T17 **Los Fresnos** Texas, SW USA 26°03′N 97°28′W
35 N9 **Los Gatos** California, W USA 37°13′N 121°58′W

◆ Country
● Country Capital
◇ Dependent Territory
○ Dependent Territory Capital
◐ Administrative Regions
✕ International Airport
▲ Mountain
▲▲ Mountain Range
⛰ Volcano
≈ River
◎ Lake
⊠ Reservoir

127 P10 **Loshchina** Volgogradskaya Oblast', SW Russian Federation 48°58′N 46°14′E
110 O11 **Łosice** Mazowieckie, C Poland 52°13′N 22°42′E
112 B11 **Lošinj** *Ger.* Lussin, *It.* Lussino. *island* W Croatia
Los Jardines *see* Ngetik Atoll
63 G15 **Los Lagos** Los Ríos, C Chile 39°50′S 72°50′W
63 F17 **Los Lagos** *off.* Regíon de los Lagos. ◐ *region* C Chile
los Lagos, Regíon de *see* Los Lagos
Loslau *see* Wodzisław Śląski
64 N11 **Los Llanos de Aridane** *var.* Los Llanos de Aridane. La Palma, Islas Canarias, Spain, NE Atlantic Ocean 28°39′N 17°54′W
Los Llanos de Aridane *see* Los Llanos de Aridane
37 R11 **Los Lunas** New Mexico, SW USA 34°48′N 106°43′W
63 I16 **Los Menucos** Río Negro, C Argentina 40°52′S 68°07′W
40 H8 **Los Mochis** Sinaloa, C Mexico 25°48′N 108°58′W
35 N4 **Los Molinos** California, W USA 40°00′N 122°05′W
104 M9 **Los Navalmorales** Castilla-La Mancha, C Spain 39°43′N 04°38′W
25 S15 **Los Olmos Creek** ≈ Texas, SW USA
Losonc/Losontz *see* Lučenec
167 S5 **Lô, Sông** *var.* Panlong Jiang. ≈ China/Vietnam
44 B5 **Los Palacios** Pinar del Río, W Cuba 22°35′N 83°16′W
104 K14 **Los Palacios y Villafranca** Andalucía, S Spain 37°10′N 05°55′W
37 R12 **Los Pinos Mountains** ▲▲ New Mexico, SW USA
37 R11 **Los Ranchos de Albuquerque** New Mexico, SW USA 35°09′N 106°37′W
40 M14 **Los Reyes** Michoacán, SW Mexico 19°36′N 102°29′W
63 G15 **Los Ríos** ◐ *region* C Chile
56 B7 **Los Ríos** ◐ *province* C Ecuador
64 O11 **Los Rodeos** ✈ (Santa Cruz de Ternerife) Tenerife, Islas Canarias, Spain, NE Atlantic Ocean 28°27′N 16°20′W
54 L4 **Los Roques, Islas** *island group* N Venezuela
43 S17 **Los Santos** Los Santos, S Panama 07°56′N 80°23′W
43 S17 **Los Santos** *off.* Provincia de Los Santos. ◐ *province* S Panama
Los Santos *see* Los Santos de Maimona
104 J12 **Los Santos de Maimona** *var.* Los Santos. Extremadura, W Spain 38°27′N 06°22′W
Los Santos, Provincia de *see* Los Santos
98 P10 **Losser** Overijssel, E Netherlands 52°16′N 06°25′E
96 J8 **Lossiemouth** NE Scotland, United Kingdom 57°43′N 03°18′W
61 B14 **Los Tábanos** Santa Fe, C Argentina 28°27′S 59°57′W
54 J4 **Los Taques** Falcón, N Venezuela 11°50′N 70°16′W
14 G11 **Lost Channel** Ontario, S Canada 45°54′N 80°20′W
54 L5 **Los Teques** Miranda, N Venezuela 10°25′N 67°01′W
35 Q12 **Lost Hills** California, W USA 35°35′N 119°40′W
36 I7 **Lost Peak** ▲ Utah, W USA 37°30′N 113°57′W
33 P11 **Lost Trail Pass** *pass* Montana, NW USA
186 G9 **Losuia** Kiriwina Island, SE Papua New Guinea 08°29′S 151°03′E
62 G10 **Los Vilos** Coquimbo, C Chile 31°56′S 71°35′W
105 N10 **Los Yébenes** Castilla-La Mancha, C Spain 39°35′N 03°52′W
103 N13 **Lot** ◐ *department* S France
103 N13 **Lot** ≈ S France
63 F14 **Lota** Bío Bío, C Chile 37°07′S 73°10′W
81 G15 **Lotagipi Swamp** *wetland* Kenya/Sudan
102 K14 **Lot-et-Garonne** ◐ *department* SW France
83 K21 **Lothair** Mpumalanga, NE South Africa 26°23′S 30°26′E
33 R7 **Lothair** Montana, NW USA 48°28′N 111°15′W
79 L20 **Loto** Kasai-Oriental, C Dem. Rep. Congo 02°48′S 22°30′E
108 E10 **Lötschbergtunnel** *tunnel* Valais, SW Switzerland
25 T9 **Lott** Texas, SW USA 31°12′N 97°02′W
124 H3 **Lotta** *var.* Lutto. ≈ Finland/Russian Federation
184 Q7 **Lottin Point** *headland* North Island, New Zealand 37°26′S 178°07′E
Lötzen *see* Giżycko
Loualaba *see* Lualaba
167 P6 **Louangnamtha** *var.* Luong Nam Tha. Louang Namtha, N Laos 20°55′N 101°24′E
167 Q7 **Louangphabang** *var.* Louangphrabang, Luang Prabang. Louangphabang, N Laos 19°51′N 102°08′E
Louangphrabang *see* Louangphabang
194 H5 **Loubet Coast** *physical region* Antarctica
Loubomo *see* Dolisie
Louch *see* Loukhi
102 H6 **Loudéac** Côtes d'Armor, NW France 48°11′N 02°45′W
160 M11 **Loudi** Hunan, S China 27°51′N 111°59′E
79 F21 **Loudima** Bouenza, S Congo 04°06′S 13°05′E
20 M9 **Loudon** Tennessee, S USA 35°43′N 84°19′W
31 T12 **Loudonville** Ohio, N USA 40°38′N 82°13′W
102 L8 **Loudun** Vienne, W France 47°01′N 00°05′E
102 K7 **Loué** Sarthe, NW France 48°00′N 00°14′W
76 G10 **Louga** NW Senegal 15°36′N 16°15′W
97 M19 **Loughborough** C England, United Kingdom 52°47′N 01°11′W
97 C18 **Loughrea** *Ir.* Baile Locha Riach. Galway, W Ireland 53°12′N 08°34′W
103 S9 **Louhans** Saône-et-Loire, C France 46°38′N 05°12′E
21 P5 **Louisa** Kentucky, S USA 38°06′N 82°37′W
21 V5 **Louisa** Virginia, NE USA 38°02′N 78°00′W
21 V9 **Louisburg** North Carolina, SE USA 36°05′N 78°18′W
25 U12 **Louise** Texas, SW USA 29°07′N 96°22′W
15 P11 **Louiseville** Québec, SE Canada 46°15′N 72°54′W
27 W3 **Louisiana** Missouri, C USA 39°25′N 91°03′W
22 G8 **Louisiana** *off.* State of Louisiana, *also known as* Creole State, Pelican State. ◐ *state* S USA
Louis Trichardt *see* Makhado
23 V4 **Louisville** Georgia, SE USA 33°00′N 82°24′W
30 M15 **Louisville** Illinois, N USA 38°46′N 88°32′W
20 K5 **Louisville** Kentucky, S USA 38°15′N 85°46′W
22 M4 **Louisville** Mississippi, S USA 33°07′N 89°03′W
29 S15 **Louisville** Nebraska, C USA 41°00′N 96°09′W
192 L11 **Louisville Ridge** *undersea feature* S Pacific Ocean
124 J6 **Loukhi** *var.* Louch. Respublika Kareliya, NW Russian Federation 66°05′N 33°04′E
79 H19 **Loukoléla** Cuvette, E Congo 01°04′S 17°10′E
104 G14 **Loulé** Faro, S Portugal 37°08′N 08°02′W
111 C16 **Louny** *Ger.* Laun. Ústecký Kraj, NW Czech Republic 50°22′N 13°50′E
29 O15 **Loup City** Nebraska, C USA 41°16′N 98°58′W
29 P15 **Loup River** ≈ Nebraska, C USA
15 S9 **Loup, Rivière du** ≈ Québec, SE Canada
12 K7 **Loups Marins, Lacs des** ◎ Québec, NE Canada
102 K16 **Lourdes** Hautes-Pyrénées, S France 43°06′N 00°03′W
Lourenço Marques *see* Maputo
104 F11 **Loures** Lisboa, C Portugal 38°50′N 09°10′W
104 F10 **Lourinhã** Lisboa, C Portugal 39°14′N 09°19′W
115 C16 **Loúros** ≈ W Greece
104 G8 **Lousã** Coimbra, N Portugal 40°07′N 08°15′W
Loushanguan *see* Tongzi
160 M10 **Lou Shui** ≈ C China
183 O5 **Louth** New South Wales, SE Australia 30°34′S 145°07′E
97 O18 **Louth** E England, United Kingdom 53°19′N 00°00′E
97 F17 **Louth** *Ir.* Lú. *cultural region* NE Ireland
115 H15 **Loutrá** Kentrikí Makedonía, N Greece 39°55′N 23°37′E
115 G19 **Loutráki** Pelopónnisos, S Greece 37°55′N 22°55′E
Louvain *see* Leuven
99 H19 **Louvain-la Neuve** Walloon Brabant, C Belgium 50°39′N 04°36′E
14 J8 **Louvicourt** Québec, SE Canada 48°04′N 77°22′W
102 M4 **Louviers** Eure, N France 49°13′N 01°11′E
30 K14 **Lou Yaeger, Lake** ⊠ Illinois, N USA
93 J15 **Lövånger** Västerbotten, N Sweden 64°22′N 21°19′E
124 J14 **Lovat'** ≈ NW Russian Federation
113 J17 **Lovćen** ▲ SW Montenegro 42°22′N 18°49′E
114 I8 **Lovech** Lovech, N Bulgaria 43°08′N 24°45′E
114 I9 **Lovech** ◐ *province* N Bulgaria
25 V9 **Lovelady** Texas, SW USA 31°07′N 95°27′W
37 T3 **Loveland** Colorado, C USA 40°24′N 105°04′W
33 U12 **Lovell** Wyoming, C USA 44°50′N 108°23′W
Lovello, Monte *see* Grosser Löffler
35 S4 **Lovelock** Nevada, W USA 40°11′N 118°30′W
106 E7 **Lovere** Lombardia, N Italy 45°51′N 10°06′E
30 L10 **Loves Park** Illinois, N USA 42°19′N 89°03′W
26 M2 **Lovewell Reservoir** ⊠ Kansas, C USA
93 M19 **Loviisa** *Swe.* Lovisa. Etelä-Suomi, S Finland 60°27′N 26°15′E
37 V15 **Loving** New Mexico, SW USA 32°17′N 104°06′W
21 U6 **Lovingston** Virginia, NE USA 37°46′N 78°54′W
37 V14 **Lovington** New Mexico, SW USA 32°56′N 103°21′W
Lovisa *see* Loviisa
111 C15 **Lovosice** *Ger.* Lobositz. Ústecký Kraj, NW Czech Republic 50°30′N 14°02′E
124 K4 **Lovozero** Murmanskaya Oblast', NW Russian Federation 68°00′N 35°03′E
124 K4 **Lovozero, Ozero** ◎ NW Russian Federation
112 B9 **Lovran** *It.* Laurana. Primorje-Gorski Kotar, NW Croatia 45°16′N 14°15′E
116 E11 **Lovrin** *Ger.* Lowrin. Timiș, W Romania 45°58′N 20°49′E
82 E10 **Lóvua** Lunda Norte, NE Angola 07°21′S 20°09′E
82 G12 **Lóvua** Moxico, E Angola 11°33′S 23°35′E
65 D25 **Low Bay** *bay* East Falkland, Falkland Islands
9 P9 **Low, Cape** *headland* Nunavut, E Canada 63°05′N 85°27′W
33 N10 **Lowell** Idaho, NW USA 46°07′N 115°36′W
19 O10 **Lowell** Massachusetts, NE USA 42°38′N 71°19′W
Löwen *see* Leuven
Löwenberg in Schlesien *see* Lwówek Śląski
Lower Austria *see* Niederösterreich
Lower Bann *see* Bann
Lower California *see* Baja California
Lower Danube *see* Niederösterreich
185 L14 **Lower Hutt** Wellington, North Island, New Zealand 41°13′S 174°51′E
39 N11 **Lower Kalskag** Alaska, USA 61°30′N 160°28′W
35 O1 **Lower Klamath Lake** ◎ California, W USA
35 Q2 **Lower Lake** ◎ California/Nevada, W USA
97 E15 **Lower Lough Erne** ◎ SW Northern Ireland, United Kingdom
Lower Lusatia *see* Niederlausitz
Lower Normandy *see* Basse-Normandie
10 K9 **Lower Post** British Columbia, W Canada 59°53′N 128°19′W
29 T4 **Lower Red Lake** ◎ Minnesota, N USA
Lower Rhine *see* Neder Rijn
Lower Saxony *see* Niedersachsen
97 Q19 **Lowestoft** E England, United Kingdom 52°29′N 01°45′E
Lowgar *see* Lōgar
182 H7 **Low Hill** South Australia 32°17′S 136°46′E
110 K12 **Łowicz** Łódzkie, C Poland 52°06′N 19°55′E
33 N13 **Lowman** Idaho, NW USA 44°04′N 115°37′W
149 P8 **Lowrah** *var.* Lora. ≈ SE Afghanistan
Lowrin *see* Lovrin
183 N17 **Low Rocky Point** *headland* Tasmania, SE Australia 42°59′S 145°28′E
18 I8 **Lowville** New York, NE USA 43°47′N 75°29′W
Loxa *see* Loksa
182 K9 **Loxton** South Australia 34°30′S 140°36′E
81 G21 **Loya** Tabora, C Tanzania 04°57′S 33°53′E
30 K6 **Loyal** Wisconsin, N USA 44°45′N 90°30′W
18 G13 **Loyalsock Creek** ≈ Pennsylvania, NE USA
35 Q5 **Loyalton** California, W USA 39°39′N 120°16′W
Lo-yang *see* Luoyang
187 Q16 **Loyauté, Îles** *island group* S New Caledonia
Loyev *see* Loyew
119 O20 **Loyew** *Rus.* Loyev. Homyel'skaya Voblasts', SE Belarus 51°56′N 30°48′E
125 S13 **Loyno** Kirovskaya Oblast', NW Russian Federation 59°44′N 52°42′E
103 P13 **Lozère** ◐ *department* S France
103 Q14 **Lozère, Mont** ▲ S France 44°27′N 03°44′E
112 J11 **Loznica** Serbia, W Serbia 44°32′N 19°13′E
114 L8 **Loznitsa** Razgrad, N Bulgaria 43°22′N 26°36′E
117 V7 **Lozova** *Rus.* Lozovaya. Kharkivs'ka Oblast', E Ukraine 48°54′N 36°23′E
Lozovaya *see* Lozova
105 N7 **Lozoyuela** Madrid, C Spain 40°55′N 03°36′W
Lu *see* Shandong, China
Lú *see* Louth, Ireland
82 F12 **Luacano** Moxico, E Angola 11°19′S 21°30′E
79 N21 **Lualaba** *Fr.* Loualaba. ≈ SE Dem. Rep. Congo
83 H14 **Luampa** Western, NW Zambia 15°02′S 24°27′E
83 H15 **Luampa Kuta** Western, W Zambia 15°22′S 24°40′E
161 P8 **Lu'an** Anhui, E China 31°46′N 116°31′E
Luanco *see* Lluanco
82 A11 **Luanda** *var.* Loanda, *Port.* São Paulo de Loanda. ● Luanda, NW Angola 08°48′S 13°17′E
82 A11 **Luanda** ◐ *province* (Angola) NW Angola
82 A11 **Luanda** ✈ Luanda, NW Angola 08°49′S 13°16′E
82 D12 **Luando** ≈ C Angola
Luang *see* Tapi, Mae Nam
83 G14 **Luanginga** *var.* Luanguinga. ≈ Angola/Zambia
167 N15 **Luang, Khao** ▲ SW Thailand 08°21′N 99°46′E
Luang Prabang *see* Louangphabang
167 P8 **Luang Prabang Range** *Th.* Thiukhaoluang Phrahang. ▲▲ Laos/Thailand
167 N16 **Luang, Thale** *lagoon* S Thailand
Luangua, Rio *see* Luangwa
82 E11 **Luangue** ≈ NE Angola
Luanguinga *see* Luanginga
83 K15 **Luangwa** *var.* Aruângua. Lusaka, C Zambia 15°36′S 30°27′E
83 K14 **Luangwa** *var.* Aruângua, Rio Luangua. ≈ Mozambique/Zambia
161 Q2 **Luan He** ≈ E China
190 G11 **Luaniva, Île** *island* E Wallis and Futuna
161 P2 **Luanping** *var.* Anjiangying. Hebei, E China 40°55′N 117°19′E
82 J13 **Luanshya** Copperbelt, C Zambia 13°09′S 28°24′E
62 K13 **Luan Toro** La Pampa, C Argentina 36°14′S 64°15′W
161 Q2 **Luanxian** *var.* Luan Xian. Hebei, E China 39°46′N 118°46′E
Luan Xian *see* Luanxian
82 J12 **Luapula** ◐ *province* N Zambia
79 O25 **Luapula** ≈ Dem. Rep. Congo/Zambia
104 J2 **Luarca** Asturias, N Spain 43°33′N 06°31′W
169 R10 **Luar, Danau** ◎ Borneo, N Indonesia
79 L25 **Luashi** Katanga, S Dem. Rep. Congo 10°54′S 23°55′E
82 G12 **Luau** *Port.* Vila Teixeira de Sousa. Moxico, NE Angola 10°42′S 22°12′E
79 C16 **Luba** *prev.* San Carlos. Isla de Bioco, NW Equatorial Guinea 03°26′N 08°36′E
42 F4 **Lubaantun** *ruins* Toledo, S Belize
111 P16 **Lubaczów** *var.* Lúbaczów. Podkarpackie, SE Poland 50°10′N 23°08′E
Lubale *see* Lubalo
82 E11 **Lubalo** Lunda Norte, NE Angola 09°02′S 19°11′E
82 E11 **Lubalo** *var.* Lubale. ≈ Angola/Dem. Rep. Congo
118 J9 **Lubāna** E Latvia 56°55′N 29°43′E
Lubānas Ezers *see* Lubāns
171 N4 **Lubang Island** *island* N Philippines
83 B15 **Lubango** *Port.* Sá da Bandeira. Huíla, SW Angola 14°55′S 13°33′E
118 J9 **Lubāns** *var.* Lubānas Ezers. ◎ E Latvia
79 M21 **Lubao** Kasai-Oriental, C Dem. Rep. Congo 05°21′S 25°42′E
110 O13 **Lubartów** *Ger.* Qumälisch. Lublin, E Poland 51°29′N 22°38′E
100 G13 **Lübbecke** Nordrhein-Westfalen, NW Germany 52°18′N 08°37′E
100 O13 **Lübben** Brandenburg, E Germany 51°56′N 13°52′E
101 P14 **Lübbenau** Brandenburg, E Germany 51°52′N 13°57′E
25 N5 **Lubbock** Texas, SW USA 33°35′N 101°51′W
Lubcz *see* Lyubcha
19 U6 **Lubec** Maine, NE USA 44°49′N 67°00′W
100 K9 **Lübeck** Schleswig-Holstein, N Germany 53°52′N 10°41′E
100 K8 **Lübecker Bucht** *bay* N Germany
79 M21 **Lubefu** Kasai-Oriental, C Dem. Rep. Congo 04°43′S 24°25′E
163 T10 **Lubei** *var.* Jarud Qi. Nei Mongol Zizhiqu, N China 44°25′N 121°12′E
111 O14 **Lubelska, Wyżyna** *plateau* SE Poland
110 O13 **Lubelskie** ◐ *province* E Poland
Lubembe *see* Luembe
Lüben *see* Lubin
144 H9 **Lubenka** Zapadnyy Kazakhstan, W Kazakhstan 50°27′N 54°07′E
79 P18 **Lubero** Nord-Kivu, E Dem. Rep. Congo 0°10′S 29°12′E
79 L22 **Lubi** ≈ S Dem. Rep. Congo
Lubiana *see* Ljubljana
110 J11 **Lubień Kujawski** Kujawsko-pomorskie, C Poland 52°25′N 19°10′E
67 T11 **Lubilandji** ≈ S Dem. Rep. Congo
110 F13 **Lubin** *Ger.* Lüben. Dolnośląskie, SW Poland 51°23′N 16°12′E
111 O14 **Lublin** *Rus.* Lyublin. Lubelskie, E Poland 51°15′N 22°33′E
111 J15 **Lubliniec** Śląskie, S Poland 50°41′N 18°41′E
Lubnān, Jabal *see* Liban, Jebel
117 R5 **Lubny** Poltavs'ka Oblast', NE Ukraine 50°00′N 33°00′E
Luboml *see* Lyuboml'
110 G11 **Luboń** *Ger.* Peterhof. Wielkolpolskie, C Poland 52°23′N 16°54′E
Luboten *see* Ljuboten
110 D12 **Lubsko** *Ger.* Sommerfeld. Lubuskie, W Poland 51°47′N 14°57′E
79 N24 **Lubudi** Katanga, SE Dem. Rep. Congo 09°57′S 25°59′E
168 L13 **Lubuklinggau** Sumatera, W Indonesia 03°10′S 102°52′E
79 N25 **Lubumbashi** *prev.* Élisabethville. Shaba, SE Dem. Rep. Congo 11°40′S 27°31′E
83 I14 **Lubungu** Central, C Zambia 14°28′S 26°30′E
110 E12 **Lubuskie** ◐ *province* W Poland
Lubuskie *see* Dobiegniew
79 N18 **Lubutu** Maniema, E Dem. Rep. Congo 0°48′S 26°39′E
Luca *see* Lucca
82 C11 **Lucala** ≈ W Angola
14 E16 **Lucan** Ontario, S Canada 43°10′N 81°22′W
97 F18 **Lucan** *Ir.* Leamhcán. Dublin, E Ireland 53°22′N 06°27′W
Lucanian Mountains *see* Lucano, Appennino
107 M18 **Lucano, Appennino** *Eng.* Lucanian Mountains. ▲▲ S Italy
82 F11 **Lucapa** *var.* Lukapa. Lunda Norte, NE Angola 08°24′S 20°42′E
29 V15 **Lucas** Iowa, C USA 41°01′N 93°26′W
61 C18 **Lucas González** Entre Ríos, E Argentina 32°25′S 59°33′W
65 C25 **Lucas Point** *headland* West Falkland, Falkland Islands 52°10′S 60°22′W
31 S15 **Lucasville** Ohio, N USA 38°52′N 83°00′W
106 F11 **Lucca** *anc.* Luca. Toscana, C Italy 43°50′N 10°30′E
44 H12 **Lucea** W Jamaica 18°26′N 78°11′W
97 H15 **Luce Bay** *inlet* SW Scotland, United Kingdom
22 M8 **Lucedale** Mississippi, S USA 30°55′N 88°35′W
171 O4 **Lucena** *off.* Lucena City. Luzon, N Philippines 13°57′N 121°38′E
104 M14 **Lucena** Andalucía, S Spain 37°25′N 04°29′W
Lucena City *see* Lucena
105 S8 **Lucena del Cid** Valenciana, E Spain 40°07′N 00°15′W
111 D15 **Lučenec** *Ger.* Losontz, *Hung.* Losonc. Banskobystrický Kraj, C Slovakia 48°21′N 19°37′E
Lucentum *see* Alicante
107 M16 **Lucera** Puglia, SE Italy 41°30′N 15°19′E
Lucerna/Lucerne *see* Luzern
Lucerne, Lake of *see* Vierwaldstätter See
40 J4 **Lucero** Chihuahua, N Mexico 30°50′N 106°30′W
123 S14 **Luchegorsk** Primorskiy Kray, SE Russian Federation 46°26′N 134°10′E
105 Q13 **Luchena** ≈ SE Spain
Lucheng *see* Kangding
82 N13 **Lucheringo** *var.* Luchulingo. ≈ N Mozambique
Luchesa *see* Luchosa
Luchin *see* Luchyn
118 N13 **Luchosa** *Rus.* Luchesa. ≈ N Belarus
100 K11 **Lüchow** Mecklenburg-Vorpommern, N Germany 52°57′N 11°10′E
Luchow *see* Hefei
Luchulingo *see* Lucheringo
119 N17 **Luchyn** *Rus.* Luchin. Homyel'skaya Voblasts', SE Belarus 53°01′N 30°01′E
55 U11 **Lucie Rivier** ≈ W Surinam
182 K11 **Lucindale** South Australia 36°57′S 140°20′E
83 A14 **Lucira** Namibe, SW Angola 13°51′S 12°35′E
Łuck *see* Luts'k
101 O14 **Luckau** Brandenburg, E Germany 51°50′N 13°42′E
100 N13 **Luckenwalde** Brandenburg, E Germany 52°05′N 13°11′E
14 E15 **Lucknow** Ontario, S Canada 43°58′N 81°30′W
152 L12 **Lucknow** *var.* Lakhnau. *state capital* Uttar Pradesh, N India 26°50′N 80°54′E
102 J10 **Luçon** Vendée, NW France 46°27′N 01°10′W
44 I7 **Lucrecia, Cabo** *headland* E Cuba 21°00′N 75°34′W
82 F13 **Lucusse** Moxico, E Angola 12°32′S 20°46′E
Lüda *see* Dalian
114 M9 **Luda Kamchiya** ≈ E Bulgaria
161 T14 **Lü Dao** *var.* Huoshao Dao, Lütao, *Eng.* Green Island; *prev.* Lü Tao. *island* SE Taiwan
Ludasch *see* Luduș
114 I10 **Luda Yana** ≈ C Bulgaria
112 F7 **Ludbreg** Varaždin, N Croatia 46°15′N 16°36′E
29 P7 **Ludden** North Dakota, N USA 45°58′N 98°07′W
101 F15 **Lüdenscheid** Nordrhein-Westfalen, W Germany 51°13′N 07°38′E
83 C21 **Lüderitz** *prev.* Angra Pequena. Karas, SW Namibia 26°38′S 15°10′E
152 H8 **Ludhiāna** Punjab, N India 30°56′N 75°52′E
31 O7 **Ludington** Michigan, N USA 43°58′N 86°27′W
97 K20 **Ludlow** W England, United Kingdom 52°20′N 02°28′W
35 W14 **Ludlow** California, W USA 34°43′N 116°07′W
28 J7 **Ludlow** South Dakota, N USA 45°48′N 103°21′W
18 M9 **Ludlow** Vermont, NE USA 43°24′N 72°39′W
114 L7 **Ludogorie** *physical region* NE Bulgaria
23 W6 **Ludowici** Georgia, SE USA 31°42′N 81°44′W
Ludsan *see* Ludza
116 I10 **Luduș** *Ger.* Ludasch, *Hung.* Marosludas. Mureș, C Romania 46°28′N 24°05′E
95 M14 **Ludvika** Dalarna, C Sweden 60°08′N 15°14′E
101 H21 **Ludwigsburg** Baden-Württemberg, SW Germany 48°54′N 09°12′E
100 O13 **Ludwigsfelde** Brandenburg, NE Germany 52°17′N 13°15′E
101 G20 **Ludwigshafen** *var.* Ludwigshafen am Rhein. Rheinland-Pfalz, W Germany 49°29′N 08°24′E
Ludwigshafen am Rhein *see* Ludwigshafen
101 L20 **Ludwigskanal** *canal* SE Germany
100 L10 **Ludwigslust** Mecklenburg-Vorpommern, N Germany 53°19′N 11°29′E
118 K10 **Ludza** *Ger.* Ludsan. E Latvia 56°32′N 27°41′E
79 K21 **Luebo** Kasai-Occidental, SW Dem. Rep. Congo 05°19′S 21°21′E
25 Q6 **Lueders** Texas, SW USA 32°46′N 99°38′W
79 N20 **Lueki** Maniema, C Dem. Rep. Congo 03°25′S 25°50′E
82 F10 **Luembe** *var.* Lubembe. ≈ Angola/Dem. Rep. Congo
82 E13 **Luena** *var.* Lwena, *Port.* Luso. Moxico, E Angola 11°47′S 19°52′E
79 M24 **Luena** Katanga, SE Dem. Rep. Congo 09°28′S 25°45′E
82 K12 **Luena** Northern, NE Zambia 10°40′S 30°21′E
82 F13 **Luena** ≈ E Angola
83 F16 **Luengue** ≈ SE Angola
67 V13 **Luenha** ≈ W Mozambique
83 G15 **Lueti** ≈ Angola/Zambia
160 J7 **Lüeyang** *var.* Hejiayan. Shaanxi, C China 33°12′N 106°31′E
161 P14 **Lufeng** Guangdong, S China 22°59′N 115°40′E
79 N24 **Lufira** ≈ SE Dem. Rep. Congo
79 N25 **Lufira, Lac de Retenue de la** *var.* Lac Tshangalele. ◎ SE Dem. Rep. Congo
25 W8 **Lufkin** Texas, SW USA 31°21′N 94°47′W
82 L11 **Lufubu** ≈ N Zambia
124 G14 **Luga** Leningradskaya Oblast', NW Russian Federation 58°43′N 29°46′E
124 G13 **Luga** ≈ NW Russian Federation
Luganer See *see* Lugano, Lago di
108 H11 **Lugano** *Ger.* Lauis. Ticino, S Switzerland 46°01′N 08°57′E
108 H12 **Lugano, Lago di** *var.* Ceresio, *Ger.* Luganer See. ◎ S Switzerland
Lugansk *see* Luhans'k
187 Q13 **Luganville** Espiritu Santo, C Vanuatu 15°31′S 167°12′E
Lugdunum *see* Lyon
Lugdunum Batavorum *see* Leiden
83 O15 **Lugela** Zambézia, NE Mozambique 16°27′S 36°47′E
83 O16 **Lugela** ≈ C Mozambique
82 P13 **Lugenda, Rio** ≈ N Mozambique
Luggarus *see* Locarno
Lugh Ganana *see* Luuq
97 G19 **Lugnaquillia Mountain** *Ir.* Log na Coille. ▲ E Ireland 52°58′N 06°27′W
106 H10 **Lugo** Emilia-Romagna, N Italy 44°25′N 11°53′E
104 I3 **Lugo** *anc.* Lugus Augusti. Galicia, NW Spain 43°N 07°33′W
104 I3 **Lugo** ◐ *province* Galicia, NW Spain
21 R12 **Lugoff** South Carolina, SE USA 34°13′N 80°41′W
116 F12 **Lugoj** *Ger.* Lugosch, *Hung.* Lugos. Timiș, W Romania 45°41′N 21°56′E
Lugos/Lugosch *see* Lugoj
Lugovoy/Lugovoye *see* Kulan
158 I13 **Lugu** Xizang Zizhiqu, W China 33°26′N 84°10′E
Lugus Augusti *see* Lugo
Luguvallium/Luguvallum *see* Carlisle
117 Y7 **Luhans'k** *Rus.* Lugansk; *prev.* Voroshilovgrad. Luhans'ka Oblast', E Ukraine 48°32′N 39°21′E
117 Y7 **Luhans'k** ✈ Luhans'ka Oblast', E Ukraine 48°25′N 39°24′E
Luhans'k *see* Luhans'ka Oblast'
117 X6 **Luhans'ka Oblast'** *var.* Luhans'k; *prev.* Voroshilovgrad, *Rus.* Voroshilovgradskaya Oblast'. ◐ *province* E Ukraine
161 Q7 **Luhe** Jiangsu, E China 32°20′N 118°52′E
171 S13 **Luhu** Pulau Seram, E Indonesia 03°20′S 127°58′E
Luhua *see* Heishui
160 G8 **Luhuo** *var.* Xindu, *Tib.* Zhaggo. Sichuan, C China 31°18′N 100°39′E
116 M3 **Luhyny** Zhytomyrs'ka Oblast', N Ukraine 51°06′N 28°24′E
83 G15 **Lui** ≈ W Zambia
83 G16 **Luiana** ≈ SE Angola
83 L15 **Luia, Rio** *var.* Ruya. ≈ Mozambique/Zimbabwe
Luichow Peninsula *see* Leizhou Bandao
Luik *see* Liège
82 C13 **Luimbale** Huambo, C Angola 12°15′S 15°19′E
Luimneach *see* Limerick
106 D6 **Luino** Lombardia, N Italy 46°00′N 08°45′E
82 E13 **Luio** ≈ E Angola
92 L11 **Luiro** ≈ NE Finland
79 N25 **Luishia** Katanga, SE Dem. Rep. Congo 11°18′S 27°08′E
59 M19 **Luislândia do Oeste** Minas Gerais, SE Brazil 17°59′S 45°35′W
40 K5 **Luis L. León, Presa** ⊠ N Mexico
45 U5 **Luis Muñoz Marín** *var.* Luis Muñoz Marin. ✈ NE Puerto Rico 18°27′N 66°05′W
Luis Muñoz Marin *see* Luis Muñoz Marín
195 N5 **Luitpold Coast** *physical region* Antarctica
79 K22 **Luiza** Kasai-Occidental, S Dem. Rep. Congo 07°11′S 22°27′E
61 D20 **Luján** Buenos Aires, E Argentina 34°34′S 59°07′W
79 N24 **Lukafu** Katanga, SE Dem. Rep. Congo 10°28′S 27°32′E
Lukapa *see* Lucapa
112 I11 **Lukavac** ◐ Federacija Bosna I Hercegovina, NE Bosnia and Herzegovina
79 I20 **Lukenie** ≈ C Dem. Rep. Congo
114 J11 **Lŭki** Plovdiv, C Bulgaria 40°50′N 24°49′E
79 H19 **Lukolela** Equateur, W Dem. Rep. Congo 01°10′S 17°11′E
Lukoml'skaye, Vozyera *see* Lukomskaye, Vozyera
Lukoml'skoye, Ozero *see* Lukomskaye, Vozyera
119 M14 **Lukomskaye, Vozyera** *Rus.* Ozero Lukoml'skoye; *prev.* Vozyera Lukoml'skaye. ◎ N Belarus
114 I8 **Lukovit** Lovech, N Bulgaria 43°11′N 24°10′E
110 O12 **Łuków** *Ger.* Bogendorf. Lubelskie, E Poland 51°57′N 22°22′E
127 O4 **Lukoyanov** Nizhegorodskaya Oblast', W Russian Federation 55°02′N 44°26′E
Lukransar *see* Lūnkaransar
79 N22 **Lukuga** ≈ SE Dem. Rep. Congo
79 F21 **Lukula** Bas-Congo, SW Dem. Rep. Congo 05°23′S 12°57′E
83 G14 **Lukulu** Western, NW Zambia 14°24′S 23°12′E
189 R17 **Lukunor Atoll** *atoll* Mortlock Islands, C Micronesia
82 J12 **Lukwesa** Luapula, NE Zambia 10°03′S 28°42′E
93 K14 **Luleå** Norrbotten, N Sweden 65°35′N 22°10′E
92 J13 **Luleälven** ≈ N Sweden
136 C10 **Lüleburgaz** Kırklareli, NW Turkey 41°25′N 27°22′E
160 M4 **Lüliang** *var.* Lishi. Shanxi, C China 37°27′N 111°05′E
160 M4 **Lüliang Shan** ▲▲ C China
79 O21 **Lulimba** Maniema, E Dem. Rep. Congo 04°42′S 28°38′E
22 K9 **Luling** Louisiana, S USA 29°55′N 90°22′W
25 T11 **Luling** Texas, SW USA 29°40′N 97°39′W
79 I18 **Lulonga** ≈ NW Dem. Rep. Congo
79 K22 **Lulua** ≈ S Dem. Rep. Congo
Luluabourg *see* Kananga
192 L17 **Luma** Ta'ū, E American Samoa 14°15′S 169°30′W
169 S17 **Lumajang** Jawa, C Indonesia 08°06′S 113°13′E
158 G12 **Lumajangdong Co** ◎ W China
82 G13 **Lumbala Kaquengue** Moxico, E Angola 12°40′S 22°34′E
83 F14 **Lumbala N'Guimbo** *var.* Nguimbo, Gago Coutinho, *Port.* Vila Gago Coutinho. Moxico, E Angola 14°08′S 21°25′E
21 T11 **Lumber River** ≈ North Carolina/South Carolina, SE USA
Lumber State *see* Maine
22 L8 **Lumberton** Mississippi, S USA 31°00′N 89°27′W
21 U11 **Lumberton** North Carolina, SE USA 34°37′N 79°00′W
105 R4 **Lumbier** Navarra, N Spain 42°39′N 01°19′W
83 Q15 **Lumbo** Nampula, NE Mozambique 15°S 40°40′E
124 M4 **Lumbovka** Murmanskaya Oblast', NW Russian Federation 67°41′N 40°31′E
104 J7 **Lumbrales** Castilla y León, N Spain 40°57′N 06°43′W
153 W13 **Lumding** Assam, NE India 25°46′N 93°10′E
82 F12 **Lumege** *var.* Lumeje. Moxico, E Angola 11°30′S 20°57′E
Lumeje *see* Lumege
99 J17 **Lummen** Limburg, NE Belgium 50°58′N 05°12′E
93 J20 **Lumparland** Åland, SW Finland 60°06′N 20°15′E
167 T11 **Lumphăt** *prev.* Lomphat. Rôtânôkiri, NE Cambodia 13°30′N
11 U16 **Lumsden** Saskatchewan, S Canada 50°39′N 104°52′W
185 C23 **Lumsden** Southland, South Island, New Zealand 45°43′S 168°26′E
169 N14 **Lumut, Tanjung** *headland* Sumatera, W Indonesia 03°47′S 105°55′E
157 P4 **Lün** Töv, C Mongolia 47°51′N 105°11′E
116 I13 **Lunca Corbului** Argeș, S Romania 44°41′N 24°46′E
95 K23 **Lund** Skåne, S Sweden 55°42′N 13°10′E
35 X6 **Lund** Nevada, W USA 38°50′N 115°00′W
82 D11 **Lunda Norte** ◐ *province* NE Angola
82 E12 **Lunda Sul** ◐ *province* NE Angola
82 M13 **Lundazi** Eastern, NE Zambia 12°19′S 33°11′E
95 G16 **Lunde** Telemark, S Norway 61°31′N 06°38′E
Lundenburg *see* Břeclav
95 C17 **Lundevatnet** ◎ S Norway
Lundi *see* Runde
97 I23 **Lundy** *island* SW England, United Kingdom
100 J10 **Lüneburg** Niedersachsen, N Germany 53°15′N 10°25′E
100 J11 **Lüneburger Heide** *heathland* NW Germany
103 Q15 **Lunel** Hérault, S France 43°40′N 04°08′E
101 F14 **Lünen** Nordrhein-Westfalen, W Germany 51°37′N 07°31′E
13 P16 **Lunenburg** Nova Scotia, SE Canada 44°23′N 64°21′W
21 V7 **Lunenburg** Virginia, NE USA 36°56′N 78°15′W
103 T5 **Lunéville** Meurthe-et-Moselle, NE France 48°35′N 06°30′E
83 I14 **Lunga** ≈ C Zambia
Lunga, Isola *see* Dugi Otok
158 H12 **Lungdo** Xizang Zizhiqu, W China 33°45′N 82°09′E
158 I14 **Lunggar** Xizang Zizhiqu, W China 31°10′N 84°01′E
76 I15 **Lungi** ✈ (Freetown) W Sierra Leone 08°36′N 13°10′W
Lungkiang *see* Qiqihar
Lungleh *see* Lunglei
153 W15 **Lunglei** *prev.* Lungleh. Mizoram, NE India 22°55′N 92°49′E
158 L15 **Lungsang** Xizang Zizhiqu, W China 29°50′N 88°27′E
82 E13 **Lungué-Bungo** *var.* Lungwebungu. ≈ Angola/Zambia *see also* Lungwebungu
Lungué-Bungo *see* Lungwebungu
83 G14 **Lungwebungu** *var.* Lungué-Bungo. ≈ Angola/Zambia *see also* Lungué-Bungo
Lungwebungu *see* Lungué-Bungo
152 F12 **Lūni** Rājasthān, N India 26°03′N 73°00′E
152 F12 **Lūni** ≈ N India
Luninets *see* Luninyets
35 S7 **Luning** Nevada, W USA 38°29′N 118°10′W
Łuniniec *see* Luninyets
127 P6 **Lunino** Penzenskaya Oblast', W Russian Federation 53°35′N 45°12′E
119 J19 **Luninyets** *Pol.* Łuniniec, *Rus.* Luninets. Brestskaya Voblasts', SW Belarus 52°15′N 26°48′E
152 F10 **Lūnkaransar** *var.* Lookransar, Lukransar. Rājasthān, NW India 28°32′N 73°50′E
119 G17 **Lunna** *Pol.* Łunna. Hrodzyenskaya Voblasts', W Belarus 53°27′N 24°16′E
76 I15 **Lunsar** W Sierra Leone 08°41′N 12°32′W
83 K14 **Lunsemfwa** ≈ C Zambia
158 J6 **Luntai** *var.* Bügür. Xinjiang Uygur Zizhiqu, NW China 41°48′N 84°14′E
98 K11 **Lunteren** Gelderland, C Netherlands 52°05′N 05°38′E
109 U5 **Lunz am See** Niederösterreich, C Austria 47°54′N 15°01′E
163 Y7 **Luobei** *var.* Fengxiang. Heilongjiang, NE China 47°35′N 130°50′E
Luocheng *see* Hui'an, Fujian, China
Luocheng *see* Luoding, Guangdong, China
160 J13 **Luodian** *var.* Longping. Guizhou, S China 25°25′N 106°49′E
160 M15 **Luoding** *var.* Luocheng. Guangdong, S China 22°44′N 111°28′E
161 N7 **Luohe** Henan, C China 33°37′N 114°00′E
160 M6 **Luo He** ≈ C China
160 L5 **Luo He** ≈ C China
Luolajarvi *see* Kuoloyarvi
Luong Nam Tha *see* Louangnamtha
160 L13 **Luoqing Jiang** ≈ S China
161 O8 **Luoshan** Henan, C China 32°12′N 114°30′E
161 O12 **Luoxiao Shan** ▲▲ S China
161 N6 **Luoyang** *var.* Honan, Lo-yang. Henan, C China 34°41′N 112°25′E
161 R12 **Luoyuan** *var.* Fengshan. Fujian, SE China 26°29′N 119°32′E
79 F21 **Luozi** Bas-Congo, W Dem. Rep. Congo 04°57′S 14°08′E
83 J17 **Lupane** Matabeleland North, W Zimbabwe 18°54′S 27°44′E
160 I12 **Lupanshui** *var.* Liupanshui; *prev.* Shuicheng. Guizhou, S China 26°38′N 104°49′E
169 R10 **Lupar, Batang** ≈ East Malaysia
Lupatia *see* Altamura
116 G12 **Lupeni** *Hung.* Lupény. Hunedoara, SW Romania 45°20′N 23°10′E
Lupény *see* Lupeni
82 N13 **Lupiliche** Niassa, N Mozambique 11°36′S 35°15′E
83 E14 **Lupire** Cuando Cubango, E Angola 14°39′S 19°39′E
79 L22 **Luputa** Kasai-Oriental, S Dem. Rep. Congo 07°07′S 23°43′E
121 P16 **Luqa** ✈ (Valletta) S Malta 35°53′N 14°27′E
159 U11 **Luqu** *var.* Ma'ai. Gansu, C China 34°34′N 102°27′E
45 U5 **Luquillo, Sierra de** ▲▲ E Puerto Rico
26 L4 **Luray** Kansas, C USA 39°06′N 98°41′W
21 U4 **Luray** Virginia, NE USA 38°40′N 78°28′W
103 T7 **Lure** Haute-Saône, E France 47°42′N 06°30′E

◆ Country
● Country Capital
◇ Dependent Territory
○ Dependent Territory Capital
◐ Administrative Regions
✈ International Airport
▲ Mountain
▲▲ Mountain Range
⛰ Volcano
≈ River
◎ Lake
⊠ Reservoir

82 D11 **Luremo** Lunda Norte, NE Angola 08°32´S 17°55´E
97 F15 **Lurgan** *Ir.* An Lorgain. S Northern Ireland, United Kingdom 54°28´N 06°20´W
57 K18 **Luribay** La Paz, W Bolivia 17°05´S 67°37´W
Luring *see* Gêrzê
83 Q14 **Lúrio** Nampula, NE Mozambique 13°32´S 40°34´E
83 P14 **Lúrio, Rio** ≈ NE Mozambique
Luristan *see* Lorestān
Lurka *see* Lorca
83 J15 **Lusaka** ● (Zambia) Lusaka, SE Zambia 15°24´S 28°17´E
83 J15 **Lusaka** ◐ *province* C Zambia
83 J15 **Lusaka** ✈ Lusaka, C Zambia 15°10´S 28°22´E
79 L21 **Lusambo** Kasai-Oriental, C Dem. Rep. Congo 04°59´S 23°26´E
186 F8 **Lusancay Islands and Reefs** *island group* SE Papua New Guinea
79 I21 **Lusanga** Bandundu, SW Dem. Rep. Congo 04°55´S 18°40´E
79 N21 **Lusangi** Maniema, E Dem. Rep. Congo 04°39´S 27°10´E
Lusatian Mountains *see* Lausitzer Bergland
Lushar *see* Huangzhong
Lushnja *see* Lushnjë
113 K21 **Lushnjë** *var.* Lushnja. Fier, C Albania 40°54´N 19°43´E
81 J21 **Lushoto** Tanga, E Tanzania 04°48´S 38°20´E
102 L10 **Lusignan** Vienne, W France 46°25´N 00°06´E
33 Z15 **Lusk** Wyoming, C USA 42°45´N 104°27´W
Luso *see* Luena
102 L10 **Lussac-les-Châteaux** Vienne, W France 46°23´N 00°44´E
Lussin/Lussino *see* Lošinj
Lussinpiccolo *see* Mali Lošinj
108 I7 **Lustenau** Vorarlberg, W Austria 47°26´N 09°42´E
Lü Tao *see* Lü Dao
Lütao *see* Lü Dao
Lūt, Baḩrat/Lut, Bahret *see* Dead Sea
22 K9 **Lutcher** Louisiana, S USA 30°02´N 90°42´W
143 T9 **Lūt, Dasht-e** *var.* Kavīr-e Lūt. *desert* E Iran
83 F14 **Lutembo** Moxico, E Angola 13°30´S 21°21´E
Lutetia/Lutetia Parisiorum *see* Paris
Luteva *see* Lodève
14 G15 **Luther Lake** ◎ Ontario, S Canada
186 K8 **Luti** Choiseul, NW Solomon Islands 07°13´S 157°01´E
Lūt, Kavīr-e *see* Lūt, Dasht-e
97 N21 **Luton** E England, United Kingdom 51°53´N 00°25´W
97 N21 **Luton** ✈ (London) SE England, United Kingdom 51°54´N 00°24´W
108 B10 **Lutry** Vaud, SW Switzerland 46°31´N 06°32´E
8 K10 **Łutselk'e** *prev.* Snowdrift. Northwest Territories, W Canada 62°24´N 110°42´W
8 K10 **Lutselk'e** *var.* Snowdrift. ≈ Northwest Territories, NW Canada
29 Y4 **Lutsen** Minnesota, N USA 47°39´N 90°37´W
116 J4 **Luts'k** *Pol.* Łuck, *Rus.* Lutsk. Volyns'ka Oblast', NW Ukraine 50°45´N 25°23´E
Lutsk *see* Luts'k
Luttenberg *see* Ljutomer
Lüttich *see* Liège
83 G25 **Luttig** Western Cape, SW South Africa 32°33´S 22°13´E
Lutto *see* Lotta
82 E13 **Lutuai** Moxico, E Angola 12°38´S 20°06´E
117 Y7 **Lutuhyne** Luhans'ka Oblast', E Ukraine 48°24´N 39°12´E
171 V14 **Lutur, Pulau** *island* Kepulauan Aru, E Indonesia
23 V12 **Lutz** Florida, SE USA 28°09´N 82°27´W
Lutzow-Holm Bay *see* Lützow Holmbukta
195 V2 **Lützow Holmbukta** *var.* Lutzow-Holm Bay. *bay* Antarctica
81 L16 **Luuq** *It.* Lugh Ganana. Gedo, SW Somalia 03°42´N 42°34´E
92 M12 **Luusua** Lappi, NE Finland 66°28´N 27°16´E
23 Q6 **Luverne** Alabama, S USA 31°43´N 86°15´W
29 S11 **Luverne** Minnesota, N USA 43°39´N 96°12´W
79 O22 **Luvua** ≈ SE Dem. Rep. Congo
82 F13 **Luvuei** Moxico, E Angola 13°08´S 21°09´E
81 H24 **Luwego** ≈ S Tanzania
82 K12 **Luwingu** Northern, NE Zambia 10°13´S 29°58´E
171 P12 **Luwuk** *prev.* Loewoek. Sulawesi, C Indonesia 0°56´S 122°47´E
23 N3 **Luxapallila Creek** ≈ Alabama/Mississippi, S USA
99 M25 **Luxembourg** ● (Luxembourg) Luxembourg, S Luxembourg 49°37´N 06°08´E
99 M25 **Luxembourg** *off.* Grand Duchy of Luxembourg, *var.* Lëtzebuerg, Luxemburg. ◆ *monarchy* NW Europe
99 J23 **Luxembourg** ◐ *province* SE Belgium
99 L24 **Luxembourg** ◐ *district* S Luxembourg
31 N6 **Luxemburg** Wisconsin, N USA 44°32´N 87°42´W
Luxemburg *see* Luxembourg
103 U7 **Luxeuil-les-Bains** Haute-Saône, E France 47°49´N 06°22´E
160 E13 **Luxi** *prev.* Mangshi. Yunnan, SW China 24°27´N 98°31´E
82 E10 **Luxico** ≈ Angola/Dem. Rep. Congo
75 X10 **Luxor** *Ar.* Al Uqşur. E Egypt 25°39´N 32°39´E
75 X10 **Luxor** ✈ C Egypt 25°39´N 32°48´E
160 M4 **Luya Shan** ▲▲ C China
102 J15 **Luy de Béarn** ≈ SW France
102 J15 **Luy de France** ≈ SW France
125 P12 **Luza** Kirovskaya Oblast', NW Russian Federation 60°38´N 47°13´E
125 Q12 **Luza** ≈ NW Russian Federation
104 I16 **Luz, Costa de la** *coastal region* SW Spain
111 K20 **Luže** *var.* Lausche. ▲ Czech Republic/Germany 50°51´N 14°40´E *see also* Lausche
Luže *see* Lausche
108 F8 **Luzern** *Fr.* Lucerne, *It.* Lucerna. Luzern, C Switzerland 47°03´N 08°17´E
108 E8 **Luzern** *Fr.* Lucerne. ◐ *canton* C Switzerland
160 L13 **Luzhai** Guangxi Zhuangzu Zizhiqu, S China 24°31´N 109°46´E
118 K12 **Luzhki** Vitsyebskaya Voblasts', N Belarus 55°21´N 27°52´E
160 I10 **Luzhou** Sichuan, C China 28°55´N 105°25´E
Lužická Nisa *see* Neisse
Lužické Hory' *see* Lausitzer Bergland
Lužnice *see* Lainsitz
171 O2 **Luzon** *island* N Philippines
171 N1 **Luzon Strait** *strait* Philippines/Taiwan
Lużyckie, Gory *see* Lausitzer Bergland
116 I5 **L'viv** *Ger.* Lemberg, *Pol.* Lwów, *Rus.* L'vov. L'vivs'ka Oblast', W Ukraine 49°49´N 24°05´E
L'viv *see* L'vivs'ka Oblast'
116 I4 **L'vivs'ka Oblast'** *var.* L'viv, *Rus.* L'vovskaya Oblast'. ◐ *province* NW Ukraine
L'vov *see* L'viv
L'vovskaya Oblast' *see* L'vivs'ka Oblast'
Lwena *see* Luena
Lwów *see* L'viv
110 F11 **Lwówek** *Ger.* Neustadt bei Pinne. Wielkopolskie, C Poland 52°27´N 16°10´E
111 E14 **Lwówek Śląski** *Ger.* Löwenberg in Schlesien. Jelenia Góra, SW Poland 51°06´N 15°35´E
119 I18 **Lyakhavichy** *Rus.* Lyakhovichi. Brestskaya Voblasts', SW Belarus 53°02´N 26°16´E
Lyakhovichi *see* Lyakhavichy
185 B22 **Lyall, Mount** ▲ South Island, New Zealand 45°14´S 167°31´E
Lyallpur *see* Faisalābād
Lyangar *see* Langar
124 H11 **Lyaskelya** Respublika Kareliya, NW Russian Federation 61°42´N 31°06´E
119 I18 **Lyasnaya** *Rus.* Lesnaya. Brestskaya Voblasts', SW Belarus 52°59´N 25°46´E
119 F19 **Lyasnaya** *Pol.* Leśna, *Rus.* Lesnaya. ≈ SW Belarus
124 H15 **Lychkovo** Novgorodskaya Oblast', W Russian Federation 57°55´N 32°24´E
Lyck *see* Ełk
93 I15 **Lycksele** Västerbotten, N Sweden 64°34´N 18°40´E
18 G13 **Lycoming Creek** ≈ Pennsylvania, NE USA
Lycopolis *see* Asyūţ
195 N3 **Lyddan Island** *island* Antarctica
Lydenburg *see* Mashishing
119 L20 **Lyel'chytsy** *Rus.* Lel'chitsy. Homyel'skaya Voblasts', SE Belarus 51°47´N 28°20´E
119 P14 **Lyenina** *Rus.* Lenino. Mahilyowskaya Voblasts', E Belarus 54°25´N 31°08´E
118 L13 **Lyepyel'** *Rus.* Lepel'. Vitsyebskaya Voblasts', N Belarus 54°54´N 28°44´E
25 S17 **Lyford** Texas, SW USA 26°24´N 97°47´W
95 E17 **Lygna** ≈ S Norway
18 G14 **Lykens** Pennsylvania, NE USA 40°33´N 76°42´W
115 E21 **Lykódimo** ▲ S Greece 36°56´N 21°49´E
97 K24 **Lyme Bay** *bay* S England, United Kingdom
97 K24 **Lyme Regis** S England, United Kingdom 50°44´N 02°56´W
110 L7 **Łyna** *Ger.* Alle. ≈ N Poland
29 P12 **Lynch** Nebraska, C USA 42°49´N 98°27´W
20 J10 **Lynchburg** Tennessee, S USA 35°17´N 86°22´W
21 T6 **Lynchburg** Virginia, NE USA 37°24´N 79°09´W
21 T12 **Lynches River** ≈ South Carolina, SE USA
32 H6 **Lynden** Washington, NW USA 48°57´N 122°27´W
182 I5 **Lyndhurst** South Australia 30°19´S 138°20´E
27 Q5 **Lyndon** Kansas, C USA 38°37´N 95°40´W
19 N7 **Lyndonville** Vermont, NE USA 44°31´N 71°58´W
95 D18 **Lyngdal** Vest-Agder, S Norway 58°10´N 07°08´E
92 I9 **Lyngen** *Lapp.* Ivgovuotna. *inlet* Arctic Ocean
95 G17 **Lyngør** Aust-Agder, S Norway 58°38´N 09°05´E
92 I9 **Lyngseidet** Troms, N Norway 69°36´N 20°07´E
19 P11 **Lynn** Massachusetts, NE USA 42°28´N 70°57´W
Lynn *see* King's Lynn
23 R9 **Lynn Haven** Florida, SE USA 30°15´N 85°39´W
11 V11 **Lynn Lake** Manitoba, C Canada 56°51´N 101°01´W
Lynn Regis *see* King's Lynn
118 I13 **Lyntupy** Vitsyebskaya Voblasts', NW Belarus 55°03´N 26°19´E
103 R11 **Lyon** *Eng.* Lyons; *anc.* Lugdunum. Rhône, E France 45°46´N 04°50´E
8 I6 **Lyon, Cape** *headland* Northwest Territories, NW Canada 69°47´N 123°10´W
18 K6 **Lyon Mountain** ▲ New York, NE USA 44°42´N 73°52´W
103 Q11 **Lyonnais, Monts du** ▲▲ C France
65 N25 **Lyon Point** *headland* SE Tristan da Cunha 37°06´S 12°13´W
182 E5 **Lyons** South Australia 30°40´S 133°50´E
37 T3 **Lyons** Colorado, C USA 40°13´N 105°16´W
23 V6 **Lyons** Georgia, SE USA 32°12´N 82°19´W
26 M5 **Lyons** Kansas, C USA 38°22´N 98°13´W
29 R14 **Lyons** Nebraska, C USA 41°56´N 96°28´W
18 G10 **Lyons** New York, NE USA 43°03´N 76°58´W
Lyons *see* Lyon
118 O13 **Lyozna** *Rus.* Liozno. Vitsyebskaya Voblasts', NE Belarus 55°02´N 30°48´E
117 S4 **Lypova Dolyna** Sums'ka Oblast', NE Ukraine 50°36´N 33°50´E
117 N6 **Lypovets'** *Rus.* Lipovets. Vinnyts'ka Oblast', C Ukraine 49°13´N 29°06´E
Lys *see* Leie
111 I18 **Lysá Hora** ▲ E Czech Republic 49°31´N 18°27´E
95 D16 **Lysefjorden** *fjord* S Norway
95 I18 **Lysekil** Västra Götaland, S Sweden 58°16´N 11°26´E
Lýsi *see* Akdoğan
33 V14 **Lysite** Wyoming, C USA 43°16´N 107°42´W
127 P3 **Lyskovo** Nizhegorodskaya Oblast', W Russian Federation 56°04´N 45°01´E
108 D8 **Lyss** Bern, W Switzerland 47°04´N 07°19´E
95 H22 **Lystrup** Midtjylland, C Denmark 56°14´N 10°14´E
125 V14 **Lys'va** Permskiy Kray, NW Russian Federation 58°04´N 57°48´E
117 P6 **Lysyanka** Cherkas'ka Oblast', C Ukraine 49°15´N 30°50´E
117 X6 **Lysychans'k** *Rus.* Lisichansk. Luhans'ka Oblast', E Ukraine 48°52´N 38°27´E
97 K17 **Lytham St Anne's** NW England, United Kingdom 53°45´N 03°01´W
185 I19 **Lyttelton** South Island, New Zealand 43°35´S 172°44´E
10 M17 **Lytton** British Columbia, SW Canada 50°12´N 121°34´W
119 L18 **Lyuban'** Minskaya Voblasts', S Belarus 52°48´N 28°00´E
119 L18 **Lyubanskaye Vodaskhovishcha** ⊞ C Belarus
116 M5 **Lyubar** Zhytomyrs'ka Oblast', N Ukraine 49°54´N 27°48´E
Lyubashëvka *see* Lyubashivka
117 O8 **Lyubashivka** *Rus.* Lyubashëvka. Odes'ka Oblast', SW Ukraine 47°49´N 30°18´E
119 I16 **Lyubcha** *Pol.* Lubcz. Hrodzyenskaya Voblasts', W Belarus 53°45´N 26°04´E
126 L4 **Lyubertsy** Moskovskaya Oblast', W Russian Federation 55°37´N 38°02´E
116 K2 **Lyubeshiv** Volyns'ka Oblast', NW Ukraine 51°46´N 25°33´E
124 M14 **Lyubim** Yaroslavskaya Oblast', NW Russian Federation 58°21´N 40°46´E
114 K11 **Lyubimets** Khaskovo, S Bulgaria 41°51´N 26°03´E
Lyublin *see* Lublin
116 I3 **Lyuboml'** *Pol.* Luboml. Volyns'ka Oblast', NW Ukraine 51°12´N 24°01´E
Lyubotin *see* Lyubotyn
117 U5 **Lyubotyn** *Rus.* Lyubotin. Kharkivs'ka Oblast', E Ukraine 49°57´N 35°57´E
126 I5 **Lyudinovo** Kaluzhskaya Oblast', W Russian Federation 53°52´N 34°28´E
127 T2 **Lyuk** Udmurtskaya Respublika, NW Russian Federation 56°55´N 52°45´E
114 M9 **Lyulyakovo** *prev.* Keremitlik. Burgas, E Bulgaria 42°53´N 27°05´E
119 I18 **Lyusina** *Rus.* Lyusino. Brestskaya Voblasts', SW Belarus 52°38´N 26°31´E
Lyusino *see* Lyusina

M

138 G9 **Ma'ād** Irbid, N Jordan 32°37´N 35°36´E
Ma'ai *see* Luqu
Maalahti *see* Malax
Maale *see* Male'
138 G13 **Ma'ān** Ma'ān, SW Jordan 30°11´N 35°45´E
138 H13 **Ma'ān** *off.* Muḩāfaẓat Ma'ān, *var.* Ma'an, Ma'ān. ◐ *governorate* S Jordan
93 M16 **Maaninka** Itä-Suomi, C Finland 63°10´N 27°19´E
Maanĭt *see* Bayan, Töv, Mongolia
Maanĭt *see* Hishig Öndör, Bulgan, Mongolia
Ma'ān, Muḩāfaẓat *see* Ma'ān
93 N15 **Maanselkä** Oulu, C Finland 63°54´N 28°28´E
161 Q8 **Ma'anshan** Anhui, E China 31°45´N 118°32´E
188 F16 **Maap** *island* Caroline Islands, W Micronesia
118 H3 **Maardu** *Ger.* Maart. Harjumaa, NW Estonia 59°28´N 24°56´E
Ma'aret-en-Nu'man *see* Ma'arrat an Nu'mān
99 K16 **Maarheeze** Noord-Brabant, SE Netherlands 51°19´N 05°37´E
Maarianhamina *see* Mariehamn
138 I4 **Ma'arrat an Nu'mān** *var.* Ma'aret-en-Nu'man, *Fr.* Maarret enn Naamâne. Idlib, NW Syria 35°40´N 36°40´E
Maarret enn Naamâne *see* Ma'arrat an Nu'mān
98 I11 **Maarssen** Utrecht, C Netherlands 52°08´N 05°03´E
Maart *see* Maardu
99 L17 **Maas** *Fr.* Meuse. ≈ W Europe *see also* Meuse
Maas *see* Meuse
99 M15 **Maasbree** Limburg, SE Netherlands 51°22´N 06°03´E
99 L17 **Maaseik** *prev.* Maeseyck. Limburg, NE Belgium 51°05´N 05°48´E
171 Q6 **Maasin** Leyte, C Philippines 10°10´N 124°55´E
99 L17 **Maasmechelen** Limburg, NE Belgium 50°58´N 05°42´E
98 G12 **Maassluis** Zuid-Holland, SW Netherlands 51°55´N 04°15´E
99 L18 **Maastricht** *var.* Maestricht; *anc.* Traiectum ad Mosam, Traiectum Tungorum. Limburg, SE Netherlands 50°51´N 05°42´E
183 N18 **Maatsuyker Group** *island group* Tasmania, SE Australia
Maba *see* Qujiang
83 L20 **Mabalane** Gaza, S Mozambique 23°43´S 32°37´E
25 V7 **Mabank** Texas, SW USA 32°22´N 96°06´W
97 O18 **Mablethorpe** E England, United Kingdom 53°21´N 00°14´E
171 V12 **Maboi** Papua, E Indonesia 01°00´S 134°02´E
83 M19 **Mabote** Inhambane, S Mozambique 22°03´S 34°09´E
32 J10 **Mabton** Washington, NW USA 46°13´N 120°00´W
83 H20 **Mabutsane** Southern, S Botswana 24°24´S 23°34´E
63 G19 **Macá, Cerro** ▲ S Chile 45°07´S 73°11´W
60 Q9 **Macaé** Rio de Janeiro, SE Brazil 22°21´S 41°48´W
82 N13 **Macaloge** Niassa, N Mozambique 12°27´S 35°25´E
Macan *see* Bonerate, Kepulauan
161 N15 **Macao** *Chin.* Aomen, *Port.* Macau. Guangdong, SE China 22°06´N 113°30´E
104 H9 **Mação** Santarém, C Portugal 39°33´N 08°00´W
58 J11 **Macapá** *state capital* Amapá, N Brazil 0°04´N 51°04´W
43 S17 **Macaracas** Los Santos, S Panama 07°46´N 80°31´W
55 P6 **Macare, Caño** ≈ NE Venezuela
55 Q6 **Macareo, Caño** ≈ NE Venezuela
Macarsca *see* Makarska
182 L12 **Macarthur** Victoria, SE Australia 38°04´S 142°02´E
MacArthur *see* Ormoc
56 C7 **Macas** Morona Santiago, SE Ecuador 02°22´S 78°08´W
Macassar *see* Makassar
59 Q14 **Macau** Rio Grande do Norte, E Brazil 05°05´S 36°37´W
Macău *see* Makó, Hungary
Macau *see* Macao
65 E24 **Macbride Head** *headland* East Falkland, Falkland Islands 51°25´S 57°55´W
23 V9 **Macclenny** Florida, SE USA 30°16´N 82°07´W
97 L18 **Macclesfield** C England, United Kingdom 53°16´N 02°07´W
192 F6 **Macclesfield Bank** *undersea feature* N South China Sea 15°50´N 114°20´E
MacCluer Gulf *see* Berau, Teluk
181 N7 **Macdonald, Lake** *salt lake* Western Australia
181 Q7 **Macdonnell Ranges** ▲▲ Northern Territory, C Australia
96 K8 **Macduff** NE Scotland, United Kingdom 57°40´N 02°29´W
104 I6 **Macedo de Cavaleiros** Bragança, N Portugal 41°31´N 06°57´W
Macedonia *see* Macedonia, FYR
Macedonia Central *see* Kentrikí Makedonía
Macedonia East and Thrace *see* Anatolikí Makedonía kai Thráki
113 O19 **Macedonia, FYR** *off.* the Former Yugoslav Republic of Macedonia, *var.* Macedonia, *Mac.* Makedonija, *abbrev.* FYR Macedonia, FYROM. ◆ *republic* SE Europe
Macedonia, the Former Yugoslav Republic of *see* Macedonia, FYR
Macedonia West *see* Dytikí Makedonía
59 Q16 **Maceió** *state capital* Alagoas, E Brazil 09°40´S 35°44´W
76 K15 **Macenta** SE Guinea 08°31´N 09°32´W
106 J12 **Macerata** Marche, C Italy 43°18´N 13°27´E
11 S11 **MacFarlane** ≈ Saskatchewan, C Canada
182 H7 **Macfarlane, Lake** *var.* Lake Mcfarlane. ◎ South Australia
Macgillicuddy's Reeks Mountains *see* Macgillycuddy's Reeks
97 B21 **Macgillycuddy's Reeks** *var.* Macgillicuddy's Reeks Mountains, *Ir.* Na Cruacha Dubha. ▲▲ SW Ireland
11 X16 **MacGregor** Manitoba, S Canada 49°58´N 98°49´W
149 O10 **Mach** Baluchistān, SW Pakistan 29°52´N 67°20´E
56 C6 **Machachi** Pichincha, C Ecuador 0°33´S 78°34´W
83 M19 **Machaila** Gaza, S Mozambique 22°15´S 32°57´E
Machaire Fíolta *see* Magherafelt
Machaire Rátha *see* Maghera
81 I19 **Machakos** Eastern, S Kenya 01°31´S 37°16´E
56 B8 **Machala** El Oro, SW Ecuador 03°20´S 79°57´W
83 J19 **Machaneng** Central, SE Botswana 23°12´S 27°30´E
83 M18 **Machanga** Sofala, E Mozambique 20°56´S 35°04´E
80 G13 **Machar Marshes** *wetland* SE Sudan
102 I8 **Machecoul** Loire-Atlantique, NW France 46°59´N 01°51´W
161 O8 **Macheng** Hubei, C China 31°10´N 115°00´E
155 J16 **Mācherla** Andhra Pradesh, C India 16°29´N 79°25´E
153 O11 **Māchhāpuchhre** ▲ C Nepal 28°30´N 83°57´E
19 T6 **Machias** Maine, NE USA 44°44´N 67°28´W
19 T6 **Machias River** ≈ Maine, NE USA
19 R3 **Machias River** ≈ Maine, NE USA
64 P5 **Machico** Madeira, Portugal, NE Atlantic Ocean 32°43´N 16°47´W
155 K16 **Machilīpatnam** *var.* Bandar Masulipatnam. Andhra Pradesh, E India 16°12´N 81°11´E
54 G5 **Machiques** Zulia, NW Venezuela 10°04´N 72°37´W
57 G15 **Machu Picchu** Cusco, C Peru 13°08´S 72°30´W
83 M20 **Macia** *var.* Vila de Macia. Gaza, S Mozambique 25°02´S 33°08´E
Macías Nguema Biyogo *see* Bioco, Isla de
116 M13 **Măcin** Tulcea, SE Romania 45°15´N 28°09´E
183 T4 **Macintyre River** ≈ New South Wales/Queensland, SE Australia
181 Y7 **Mackay** Queensland, NE Australia 21°10´S 149°10´E
181 O7 **Mackay, Lake** *salt lake* Northern Territory/Western Australia
10 M13 **Mackenzie** British Columbia, W Canada 55°18´N 123°09´W
8 I9 **Mackenzie** ≈ Northwest Territories, NW Canada
195 Y6 **Mackenzie Bay** *bay* Antarctica
10 J1 **Mackenzie Bay** *bay* NW Canada
2 D9 **Mackenzie Delta** *delta* Northwest Territories, NW Canada
197 P8 **Mackenzie King Island** *island* Queen Elizabeth Islands, Northwest Territories, N Canada
8 H8 **Mackenzie Mountains** ▲▲ Northwest Territories, NW Canada
31 Q5 **Mackinac, Straits of** ◎ Michigan, N USA
194 K5 **Mackintosh, Cape** *headland* Antarctica 72°52´S 60°00´W
11 R15 **Macklin** Saskatchewan, S Canada 52°19´N 109°51´W
183 V6 **Macksville** New South Wales, SE Australia 30°39´S 152°54´E
183 V5 **Maclean** New South Wales, SE Australia 29°30´S 153°15´E
83 J24 **Maclear** Eastern Cape, SE South Africa 31°05´S 28°22´E
183 U6 **Macleay River** ≈ New South Wales, SE Australia
MacLeod *see* Fort Macleod
180 G9 **Macleod, Lake** ◎ Western Australia
10 I6 **Macmillan** ≈ Yukon Territory, NW Canada
30 J12 **Macomb** Illinois, N USA 40°27´N 90°40´W
107 B18 **Macomer** Sardegna, Italy, C Mediterranean Sea 40°15´N 08°47´E
82 Q13 **Macomia** Cabo Delgado, NE Mozambique 12°15´S 40°06´E
103 R10 **Mâcon** *anc.* Matisco, Matisco Ædourum. Saône-et-Loire, C France 46°19´N 04°49´E
23 T5 **Macon** Georgia, SE USA 32°49´N 83°41´W
23 N4 **Macon** Mississippi, S USA 33°06´N 88°33´W
27 U3 **Macon** Missouri, C USA 39°44´N 92°27´W
22 J6 **Macon, Bayou** ≈ Arkansas/Louisiana, S USA
82 G13 **Macondo** Moxico, E Angola 12°31´S 23°45´E
83 M16 **Macossa** Manica, C Mozambique 17°51´S 33°54´E
11 T12 **Macoun Lake** ◎ Saskatchewan, C Canada
30 K14 **Macoupin Creek** ≈ Illinois, N USA
Macouria *see* Tonate
83 N18 **Macovane** Inhambane, SE Mozambique 21°30´S 35°07´E
183 N17 **Macquarie Harbour** *inlet* Tasmania, SE Australia
192 J13 **Macquarie Island** *island* New Zealand, SW Pacific Ocean
183 T8 **Macquarie, Lake** *lagoon* New South Wales, SE Australia
183 Q6 **Macquarie Marshes** *wetland* New South Wales, SE Australia
175 O13 **Macquarie Ridge** *undersea feature* SW Pacific Ocean 57°00´S 159°00´E
183 Q6 **Macquarie River** ≈ New South Wales, SE Australia
183 P17 **Macquarie River** ≈ Tasmania, SE Australia
195 V5 **Mac. Robertson Land** *physical region* Antarctica
97 C21 **Macroom** *Ir.* Maigh Chromtha. Cork, SW Ireland 51°54´N 08°57´W
42 G5 **Macuelizo** Santa Bárbara, NW Honduras 15°21´N 88°31´W
182 G2 **Macumba River** ≈ South Australia
57 I16 **Macusani** Puno, S Peru 14°05´S 70°24´W
56 E8 **Macusari, Río** ≈ N Peru
41 U15 **Macuspana** Tabasco, SE Mexico 17°43´N 92°36´W
138 G10 **Ma'dabā** *var.* Mādabā, Madeba; *anc.* Medeba. Ma'dabā, NW Jordan 31°44´N 35°48´E
138 G11 **Ma'dabā** *off.* Muḩāfaẓat Ma'dabā. ◐ *governorate* C Jordan
Mādabā *see* Ma'dabā
172 G2 **Madagascar** *off.* Democratic Republic of Madagascar, *Malg.* Madagasikara; *prev.* Malagasy Republic. ◆ *republic* W Indian Ocean
172 I5 **Madagascar** *island* W Indian Ocean
128 L17 **Madagascar Basin** *undersea feature* W Indian Ocean 27°00´S 53°00´E
Madagascar, Democratic Republic of *see* Madagascar
128 L16 **Madagascar Plain** *undersea feature* W Indian Ocean 19°00´S 52°00´E
67 Y14 **Madagascar Plateau** *var.* Madagascar Ridge, Madagascar Rise, *Rus.* Madagaskarskiy Khrebet. *undersea feature* W Indian Ocean 30°00´S 45°00´E
Madagascar Rise/Madagascar Ridge *see* Madagascar Plateau
Madagasikara *see* Madagascar
Madagaskarskiy Khrebet *see* Madagascar Plateau
64 N2 **Madalena** Pico, Azores, Portugal, NE Atlantic Ocean 38°32´N 28°15´W
77 Y6 **Madama** Agadez, NE Niger 21°54´N 13°43´E
114 J12 **Madan** Smolyan, S Bulgaria 41°29´N 24°56´E
155 I19 **Madanapalle** Andhra Pradesh, E India 13°33´N 78°31´E
186 D7 **Madang** Madang, N Papua New Guinea 05°14´S 145°45´E
186 C6 **Madang** ◐ *province* N Papua New Guinea
146 G7 **Madaniyat** *Rus.* Madeniyet. Qoraqalpog'iston Respublikasi, W Uzbekistan 42°48´N 59°00´E
Madanīyīn *see* Médenine
77 U11 **Madaoua** Tahoua, SW Niger 14°06´N 06°01´E
Madaras *see* Vtáčnik
153 U15 **Madaripur** Dhaka, C Bangladesh 23°09´N 90°11´E
77 U12 **Madarounfa** Maradi, S Niger 13°16´N 07°07´E
Mađarska *see* Hungary
146 B13 **Madau** Balkan Welaýaty, W Turkmenistan 38°11´N 54°46´E
186 H9 **Madau Island** *island* SE Papua New Guinea
19 S1 **Madawaska** Maine, NE USA 47°19´N 68°19´W
14 J13 **Madawaska** ≈ Ontario, SE Canada
Madawaska Highlands *see* Haliburton Highlands
166 M4 **Madaya** Mandalay, C Burma (Myanmar) 22°12´N 96°05´E
107 K17 **Maddaloni** Campania, S Italy 41°03´N 14°23´E
29 O3 **Maddock** North Dakota, N USA 47°57´N 99°31´W
99 I14 **Made** Noord-Brabant, S Netherlands 51°41´N 04°48´E
Madeba *see* Ma'dabā
64 L9 **Madeira** *var.* Ilha de Madeira. *island* Madeira, Portugal, NE Atlantic Ocean
Madeira, Ilha de *see* Madeira
64 O5 **Madeira Islands** *Port.* Região Autoónoma da Madeira. ◐ *autonomous region* Madeira, Portugal, NE Atlantic Ocean
64 L9 **Madeira Plain** *undersea feature* E Atlantic Ocean
Madeira, Região Autoónoma da *see* Madeira Islands
64 L9 **Madeira Ridge** *undersea feature* E Atlantic Ocean 35°30´N 15°45´W
59 F14 **Madeira, Rio** *var.* Río Madera. ≈ Bolivia/Brazil *see also* Madera, Río
Madeira, Rio *see* Madera, Río
101 J25 **Mädelegabel** ▲ Austria/Germany 47°18´N 10°19´E
15 X6 **Madeleine** ≈ Québec, SE Canada
15 X5 **Madeleine, Cap de la** *headland* Québec, SE Canada 49°13´N 65°20´W
13 Q13 **Madeleine, Îles de la** *Eng.* Magdalen Islands. *island group* Québec, E Canada
29 U10 **Madelia** Minnesota, N USA 44°03´N 94°26´W
35 P3 **Madeline** California, W USA 41°02´N 120°28´W
30 K3 **Madeline Island** *island* Apostle Islands, Wisconsin, N USA
137 O15 **Maden** Elazığ, SE Turkey 38°24´N 39°42´E
145 V12 **Madeniyet** Vostochnyy Kazakhstan, E Kazakhstan 47°51´N 78°37´E
Madeniyet *see* Madaniyat
40 H5 **Madera** Chihuahua, N Mexico 29°10´N 108°10´W
35 Q10 **Madera** California, W USA 36°57´N 120°02´W
56 L13 **Madera, Río** *Port.* Rio Madeira. ≈ Bolivia/Brazil *see also* Madeira, Rio
Madera, Río *see* Madeira, Rio
106 D6 **Madesimo** Lombardia, N Italy 46°20´N 09°26´E
141 O14 **Madhāb, Wādī** *dry watercourse* NW Yemen
153 R13 **Madhepura** *prev.* Madhipure. Bihār, NE India 25°56´N 86° 48´E
Madhipure *see* Madhepura
153 Q13 **Madhubani** Bihār, N India 26°21´N 86°05´E
153 Q15 **Madhupur** Jhārkhand, NE India 24°17´N 86°38´E
154 I10 **Madhya Pradesh** *prev.* Central Provinces and Berar. ◐ *state* C India
57 K15 **Madidi, Río** ≈ W Bolivia
155 F20 **Madikeri** *prev.* Mercara. Karnātaka, W India 12°29´N 75°40´E
27 O13 **Madill** Oklahoma, C USA 34°06´N 96°46´W
79 G21 **Madimba** Bas-Congo, SW Dem. Rep. Congo 04°58´S 15°08´E
138 M4 **Ma'din** Ar Raqqah, C Syria 35°45´N 39°36´E
Madīnah, Minṭaqat al *see* Al Madīnah
76 M14 **Madinani** NW Ivory Coast 09°37´N 06°57´W
141 O17 **Madīnat ash Sha'b** *prev.* Al Ittiḩād. SW Yemen 12°52´N 44°55´E
138 K3 **Madīnat ath Thawrah** *var.* Ath Thawrah. Ar Raqqah, N Syria 35°36´N 39°00´E
173 O6 **Madingley Rise** *undersea feature* W Indian Ocean
79 E21 **Madingo-Kayes** Kouilou, S Congo 04°27´S 11°43´E
79 F21 **Madingou** Bouenza, S Congo 04°10´S 13°33´E
Madioen *see* Madiun
23 U8 **Madison** Florida, SE USA 30°27´N 83°24´W
23 T3 **Madison** Georgia, SE USA 33°37´N 83°28´W
31 P15 **Madison** Indiana, N USA 38°44´N 85°22´W
27 P6 **Madison** Kansas, C USA 45´01´N 96´11´W
19 Q6 **Madison** Maine, NE USA 44°48´N 69°52´W
29 S9 **Madison** Minnesota, N USA 45°00´N 96°12´W
22 K5 **Madison** Mississippi, S USA 32°27´N 90°07´W
29 Q14 **Madison** Nebraska, C USA 41°49´N 97°27´W
29 R10 **Madison** South Dakota, N USA 44°00´N 97°06´W
21 V5 **Madison** Virginia, NE USA 38°23´N 78°16´W
21 Q5 **Madison** West Virginia, NE USA 38°03´N 81°50´W
30 L9 **Madison** *state capital* Wisconsin, N USA 43°04´N 89°22´W
21 T6 **Madison Heights** Virginia, NE USA 37°25´N 79°07´W
20 I6 **Madisonville** Kentucky, S USA 37°20´N 87°30´W
20 M10 **Madisonville** Tennessee, S USA 35°31´N 84°21´W
25 V9 **Madisonville** Texas, SW USA 30°58´N 95°56´W
Madisonville *see* Taiohae
169 R16 **Madiun** *prev.* Madioen. Jawa, C Indonesia 07°37´S 111°33´E
Madjene *see* Majene
14 J14 **Madoc** Ontario, SE Canada 44°31´N 77°27´W
Madoera *see* Madura, Pulau
81 J18 **Mado Gashi** North Eastern, E Kenya 0°40´N 39°09´E
159 R11 **Madoi** *var.* Huanghe; *prev.* Huangheyan. Qinghai, C China 34°53´N 98°07´E
189 O13 **Madolenihmw** Pohnpei, E Micronesia
118 I9 **Madona** *Ger.* Modohn. E Latvia 56°51´N 26°10´E
107 J23 **Madonie** ▲▲ Sicilia, Italy, C Mediterranean Sea
141 Y11 **Madrakah, Ra's** *headland* E Oman 18°56´N 57°54´E
32 I12 **Madras** Oregon, NW USA 44°39´N 121°08´W
Madras *see* Chennai
Madras *see* Tamil Nādu
57 H14 **Madre de Dios** *off.* Departamento de Madre de Dios. ◐ *department* E Peru
Madre de Dios, Departamento de *see* Madre de Dios
63 F22 **Madre de Dios, Isla** *island* S Chile
57 J14 **Madre de Dios, Río** ≈ Bolivia/Peru
0 H15 **Madre del Sur, Sierra** ▲▲ S Mexico
41 Q9 **Madre, Laguna** *lagoon* NE Mexico
25 T16 **Madre, Laguna** *lagoon* Texas, SW USA
37 Q12 **Madre Mount** ▲ New Mexico, SW USA 34°18´N 107°54´W
0 H13 **Madre Occidental, Sierra** *var.* Western Sierra Madre. ▲▲ C Mexico
0 H13 **Madre Oriental, Sierra** *var.* Eastern Sierra Madre. ▲▲ C Mexico
41 U17 **Madre, Sierra** *var.* Sierra de Soconusco. ▲▲ Guatemala/Mexico
37 R2 **Madre, Sierra** ▲▲ Colorado/Wyoming, C USA
105 N8 **Madrid** ● (Spain) Madrid, C Spain 40°25´N 03°43´W
29 V14 **Madrid** Iowa, C USA 41°52´N 93°49´W
105 N7 **Madrid** ◐ *autonomous community* C Spain
105 N10 **Madridejos** Castilla-La Mancha, C Spain 39°29´N 03°32´W
104 L7 **Madrigal de las Altas Torres** Castilla y León, N Spain 41°05´N 05°00´W
104 K10 **Madrigalejo** Extremadura, W Spain 39°08´N 05°36´W
34 L3 **Mad River** ≈ California, W USA
42 J8 **Madriz** ◐ *department* NW Nicaragua
104 K10 **Madroñera** Extremadura, W Spain 39°25´N 05°46´W
181 N12 **Madura** Western Australia 31°52´S 127°01´E
Madura *see* Madurai
155 H22 **Madurai** *prev.* Madura, Mathurai. Tamil Nādu, S India 09°55´N 78°07´E
169 S16 **Madura, Pulau** *prev.* Madoera. *island* C Indonesia
169 S16 **Madura, Selat** *strait* C Indonesia
127 Q17 **Madzhalis** Respublika Dagestan, SW Russian Federation 42°12´N 47°46´E
114 K12 **Madzharovo** Khaskovo, S Bulgaria 41°36´N 25°52´E
83 M14 **Madzimoyo** Eastern, E Zambia 13°42´S 32°34´E
165 O12 **Maebashi** *var.* Maebasi, Mayebashi. Gunma, Honshū, S Japan 36°24´N 139°02´E
Maebasi *see* Maebashi
167 O6 **Mae Chan** Chiang Rai, NW Thailand 20°13´N 99°52´E
167 N7 **Mae Hong Son** *var.* Maehongson, Muai To. Mae Hong Son, NW Thailand 19°16´N 97°56´E
Maehongson *see* Mae Hong Son
Mae Nam Khong *see* Mekong
167 Q7 **Mae Nam Nan** ≈ NW Thailand
167 O10 **Mae Nam Tha Chin** ≈ W Thailand
167 P7 **Mae Nam Yom** ≈ W Thailand
37 O3 **Maeser** Utah, W USA 40°28´N 109°35´W
Maeseyck *see* Maaseik
167 N9 **Mae Sot** *var.* Ban Mae Sot. Tak, W Thailand 16°44´N 98°32´E
44 H8 **Maestra, Sierra** ▲▲ E Cuba
Maestricht *see* Maastricht
167 O7 **Mae Suai** *var.* Ban Mae Suai. Chiang Rai, NW Thailand 19°43´N 99°30´E
167 O7 **Mae Tho, Doi** ▲ NW Thailand 18°56´N 99°20´E
172 I4 **Maevatanana** Mahajanga, C Madagascar 16°57´S 46°50´E
187 R13 **Maéwo** *prev.* Aurora. *island* C Vanuatu
171 S11 **Mafa** Pulau Halmahera, E Indonesia 0°01´N 127°50´E
83 I23 **Mafeteng** W Lesotho 29°48´S 27°15´E
99 J21 **Maffe** Namur, SE Belgium 50°21´N 05°19´E
183 P12 **Maffra** Victoria, SE Australia 37°59´S 147°03´E
81 K23 **Mafia** *island* E Tanzania
81 J23 **Mafia Channel** *sea waterway* E Tanzania
83 I21 **Mafikeng** North-West, N South Africa 25°53´S 25°39´E
60 J12 **Mafra** Santa Catarina, S Brazil 26°08´S 49°47´W
104 F10 **Mafra** Lisboa, C Portugal 38°57´N 09°19´W
143 Q17 **Mafraq** Abū Ẓaby, C United Arab Emirates 24°21´N 54°33´E
Mafraq/Muḩāfaẓat al Mafraq *see* Al Mafraq
123 T10 **Magadan** Magadanskaya Oblast', E Russian Federation 59°38´N 150°50´E
123 T9 **Magadanskaya Oblast'** ◐ *province* E Russian Federation

◆ Country ● Country Capital ◇ Dependent Territory ○ Dependent Territory Capital ◐ Administrative Regions ✈ International Airport ▲ Mountain ▲▲ Mountain Range Volcano ≈ River ◎ Lake ⊞ Reservoir

108 G11 **Magadino** Ticino, S Switzerland 46°09′N 08°50′E
63 G23 **Magallanes** *var.* Región de Magallanes y de la Antártica Chilena. ◐ *region* S Chile
Magallanes *see* Punta Arenas
Magallanes, Estrecho de *see* Magellan, Strait of
Magallanes y de la Antártica Chilena, Región de *see* Magallanes
14 I10 **Maganasipi, Lac** ◎ Québec, SE Canada
54 F6 **Magangué** Bolívar, N Colombia 09°14′N 74°46′W
191 Y13 **Magareva** *var.* Mangareva. *island* Îles Tuamotu, SE French Polynesia
77 V12 **Magaria** Zinder, S Niger 13°00′N 08°55′E
186 F10 **Magarida** Central, SW Papua New Guinea 10°10′S 149°21′E
171 O2 **Magat** ≈ Luzon, N Philippines
27 T11 **Magazine Mountain** ▲ Arkansas, C USA 35°10′N 93°38′W
76 I15 **Magburaka** C Sierra Leone 08°44′N 11°57′W
123 Q13 **Magdagachi** Amurskaya Oblast', SE Russian Federation 53°25′N 125°41′E
62 O12 **Magdalena** Buenos Aires, E Argentina 35°05′S 57°30′W
57 M15 **Magdalena** El Beni, N Bolivia 13°22′S 64°07′W
40 F4 **Magdalena** Sonora, NW Mexico 30°38′N 110°59′W
37 Q13 **Magdalena** New Mexico, SW USA 34°07′N 107°14′W
54 F5 **Magdalena** *off.* Departamento del Magdalena. ◐ *province* N Colombia
40 E9 **Magdalena, Bahía** *bay* W Mexico
Magdalena, Departamento del *see* Magdalena
63 G19 **Magdalena, Isla** *island* Archipiélago de los Chonos, S Chile
40 D8 **Magdalena, Isla** *island* NW Mexico
47 P6 **Magdalena, Río** ≈ C Colombia
40 F4 **Magdalena, Río** ≈ NW Mexico
Magdalen Islands *see* Madeleine, Îles de la
147 N14 **Magdanly** *Rus.* Govurdak; *prev.* gowurdak, Guardak. Lebap Welaýaty, E Turkmenistan 37°50′N 66°06′E
100 L13 **Magdeburg** Sachsen-Anhalt, C Germany 52°08′N 11°39′E
22 L6 **Magee** Mississippi, S USA 31°52′N 89°43′W
169 Q16 **Magelang** Jawa, C Indonesia 07°28′S 110°11′E
192 K7 **Magellan Rise** *undersea feature* C Pacific Ocean
63 H24 **Magellan, Strait of** *Sp.* Estrecho de Magallanes. *strait* Argentina/Chile
106 D7 **Magenta** Lombardia, NW Italy 45°28′N 08°52′E
Magerøy *see* Magerøya
92 K7 **Magerøya** *var.* Magerøy, *Lapp.* Máhkarávju. *island* N Norway
164 C17 **Mage-shima** *island* Nansei-shotō, SW Japan
108 G11 **Maggia** Ticino, S Switzerland 46°15′N 08°42′E
108 G10 **Maggia** ≈ SW Switzerland
Maggiore, Lago *see* Maggiore, Lake
106 C6 **Maggiore, Lake** *It.* Lago Maggiore. ◎ Italy/Switzerland
44 I12 **Maggotty** W Jamaica 18°09′N 77°46′W
76 I10 **Maghama** Gorgol, S Mauritania 15°31′N 12°50′W
97 F14 **Maghera** *Ir.* Machaire Rátha. C Northern Ireland, United Kingdom 54°51′N 06°40′W
97 F15 **Magherafelt** *Ir.* Machaire Fíolta. C Northern Ireland, United Kingdom 54°45′N 06°36′W
188 H6 **Magicienne Bay** *bay* Saipan, S Northern Mariana Islands
105 O13 **Magina** ▲ S Spain 37°43′N 03°24′W
81 H24 **Magingo** Ruvuma, S Tanzania 09°57′S 35°23′E
112 H11 **Maglaj** ◐ Federacija Bosna I Hercegovina, N Bosnia and Herzegovina
107 Q19 **Maglie** Puglia, SE Italy 40°07′N 18°18′E
36 L2 **Magna** Utah, W USA 40°42′N 112°06′W
Magnesia *see* Manisa
14 G12 **Magnetawan** ≈ Ontario, S Canada
27 T14 **Magnolia** Arkansas, C USA 33°17′N 93°16′W
22 K7 **Magnolia** Mississippi, S USA 31°08′N 90°27′W
25 V10 **Magnolia** Texas, SW USA 30°12′N 95°46′W
Magnolia State *see* Mississippi
95 J15 **Magnor** Hedmark, S Norway 59°57′N 12°14′E
187 Y14 **Mago** *prev.* Mango. *island* Lau Group, E Fiji
83 L15 **Màgoé** Tete, NW Mozambique 15°50′S 31°42′E
15 Q13 **Magog** Québec, SE Canada 45°16′N 72°09′W
83 J15 **Magoye** Southern, S Zambia 16°00′S 27°34′E
41 Q12 **Magozal** Veracruz-Llave, C Mexico 21°33′N 97°57′W
14 B7 **Magpie** ≈ Ontario, S Canada
11 Q17 **Magrath** Alberta, SW Canada 49°27′N 112°52′W
105 R10 **Magre** ≈ Valenciana, E Spain
76 I9 **Magṭa' Laḥjar** *var.* Magta Lahjar, Magta' Lahjar, Magtá Lahjar. Brakna, SW Mauritania 17°27′N 13°07′W
146 D12 **Magtymguly** *prev.* Garrygala, *Rus.* Kara-Kala. Balkan Welaýaty, W Turkmenistan 38°27′N 56°15′E
83 L20 **Magude** Maputo, S Mozambique 25°02′S 32°40′E
77 Y12 **Magumeri** Borno, NE Nigeria 12°07′N 12°48′E
189 O14 **Magur Islands** *island group* Caroline Islands, C Micronesia
166 L6 **Magway** *var.* Magwe. Magway, W Burma (Myanmar) 20°08′N 94°55′E
166 L6 **Magway** *var.* Magwe. ◐ *division* C Burma (Myanmar)
Magwe *see* Magway
Magyar-Becse *see* Bečej
Magyarkanizsa *see* Kanjiža
Magyarország *see* Hungary
Magyarzsombor *see* Zimbor
142 J4 **Mahābād** *var.* Mehabad; *prev.* Sāūjbulāgh. Āżarbāyjān-e Gharbī, NW Iran 36°44′N 45°44′E
172 H5 **Mahabo** Toliara, W Madagascar 20°22′S 44°39′E
Maha Chai *see* Samut Sakhon
155 D14 **Mahād** Mahārāshtra, W India 18°04′N 73°21′E
81 N17 **Mahadday Weyne** Shabeellaha Dhexe, C Somalia 02°55′N 45°30′E
79 Q17 **Mahagi** Orientale, NE Dem. Rep. Congo 02°16′N 30°59′E
Mahāil *see* Muhāyil
172 I4 **Mahajamba** *seasonal river* NW Madagascar
152 G10 **Mahājan** Rājasthān, NW India 28°47′N 73°50′E
172 I3 **Mahajanga** *var.* Majunga. Mahajanga, NW Madagascar 15°40′S 46°20′E
172 I3 **Mahajanga** ◐ *province* W Madagascar
172 I3 **Mahajanga** ✕ Mahajanga, NW Madagascar 15°40′S 46°20′E
169 U10 **Mahakam, Sungai** *var.* Koetai, Kutai. ≈ Borneo, C Indonesia
83 I19 **Mahalapye** *var.* Mahalatswe. Central, SE Botswana 23°02′S 26°53′E
Mahalatswe *see* Mahalapye
Mahalla el Kubra *see* El Maḥalla el Kubra
171 O13 **Mahalona** Sulawesi, C Indonesia 02°37′S 121°26′E
Mahameru *see* Semeru, Gunung
143 S11 **Māhān** Kermān, E Iran 30°00′N 57°00′E
154 N12 **Mahanādi** ≈ E India
172 J5 **Mahanoro** Toamasina, E Madagascar 19°53′S 48°48′E
153 P13 **Mahārājganj** Bihār, N India 26°07′N 84°31′E
154 G13 **Mahārāshtra** ◐ *state* W India
172 I4 **Mahavavy** *seasonal river* N Madagascar
155 K24 **Mahaweli Ganga** ≈ C Sri Lanka
Mahbés *see* El Mahbas
155 J15 **Mahbūbābād** Andhra Pradesh, E India 17°35′N 80°00′E
155 H16 **Mahbūbnagar** Andhra Pradesh, C India 16°46′N 78°01′E
140 M8 **Mahd adh Dhahab** Al Madīnah, W Saudi Arabia 23°33′N 40°56′E
55 S9 **Mahdia** C Guyana 05°16′N 59°08′W
75 N6 **Mahdia** *var.* Al Mahdīyah, Mehdia. NE Tunisia 35°14′N 11°06′E
155 F20 **Mahe** *Fr.* Mahé; *prev.* Mayyali. Pondicherry, SW India 11°41′N 75°31′E
172 I16 **Mahé** ✕ Mahé, NE Seychelles 04°37′S 55°27′E
172 H16 **Mahé** *island* Inner Islands, NE Seychelles
Mahé *see* Mahe
173 Y17 **Mahebourg** SE Mauritius 20°24′S 57°42′E
152 I11 **Mahendragarh** *prev.* Mohendergarh. Haryāna, N India 28°17′N 76°14′E
152 L10 **Mahendranagar** Far Western, W Nepal 28°58′N 80°13′E
81 I23 **Mahenge** Morogoro, SE Tanzania 08°41′S 36°41′E
185 F22 **Maheno** Otago, South Island, New Zealand 45°10′S 170°51′E
154 D9 **Mahesāna** Gujarāt, W India 23°37′N 72°28′E
154 F11 **Maheshwar** Madhya Pradesh, C India 22°11′N 75°40′E
153 V17 **Maheskhali Island** *var.* Maiskhal Island. *island* SE Bangladesh
151 F14 **Mahi** ≈ N India
184 Q10 **Mahia Peninsula** *peninsula* North Island, New Zealand
119 O16 **Mahilyow** *Rus.* Mogilëv. Mahilyowskaya Voblasts', E Belarus 53°55′N 30°23′E
119 M16 **Mahilyowskaya Voblasts'** *prev. Rus.* Mogilëvskaya Oblast'. ◐ *province* E Belarus
191 P7 **Mahina** Tahiti, W French Polynesia 17°29′S 149°27′W
185 E23 **Mahinerangi, Lake** ◎ South Island, New Zealand
Máhkarávju *see* Magerøya
83 L22 **Mahlabatini** KwaZulu/Natal, E South Africa 28°15′S 31°28′E
166 L5 **Mahlaing** Mandalay, C Burma (Myanmar) 21°03′N 95°44′E
109 X8 **Mahldorf** Steiermark, SE Austria 46°54′N 15°55′E
Mahmūd-e 'Erāqī *see* Maḥmūd-e Rāqī
149 R4 **Maḥmūd-e Rāqī** *var.* Mahmūd-e 'Erāqī. Kāpīsā, NE Afghanistan 35°01′N 69°20′E
Mahmudiya *see* Al Maḥmūdīyah
29 S5 **Mahnomen** Minnesota, N USA 47°19′N 95°58′W
152 K14 **Mahoba** Uttar Pradesh, N India 25°18′N 79°53′E
Mahón *see* Maó
18 D14 **Mahoning Creek Lake** ▦ Pennsylvania, NE USA
105 Q10 **Mahora** Castilla-La Mancha, C Spain 39°13′N 01°44′W
Mähren *see* Moravia
Mährisch-Budwitz *see* Moravské Budějovice
Mährisch-Kromau *see* Moravský Krumlov
Mährisch-Neustadt *see* Uničov
Mährisch-Schönberg *see* Šumperk
Mährisch-Trübau *see* Moravská Třebová
Mährisch-Weisskirchen *see* Hranice
Māh-Shahr *see* Bandar-e Māhshahr
79 N19 **Mahulu** Maniema, E Dem. Rep. Congo 01°04′S 27°10′E
154 C12 **Mahuva** Gujarāt, W India 21°06′N 71°46′E
114 N11 **Mahya Dağı** ▲ NW Turkey 41°47′N 27°34′E
105 T6 **Maials** *var.* Mayals. Cataluña, NE Spain 41°22′N 00°30′E
191 O2 **Maiana** *prev.* Hall Island. *atoll* Tungaru, W Kiribati
191 S11 **Maiao** *var.* Tapuaemanu, Tubuai-Manu. *island* Îles du Vent, W French Polynesia
54 H4 **Maicao** La Guajira, N Colombia 11°23′N 72°16′W
Mai Ceu/Mai Chio *see* Maych'ew
103 U8 **Maîche** Doubs, E France 47°15′N 06°43′E
149 Q5 **Maīdān Shahr** *var.* Maydān Shahr; *prev.* Meydān Shahr. Wardak, E Afghanistan 34°27′N 68°48′E
97 N22 **Maidenhead** S England, United Kingdom 51°32′N 00°44′W
11 S15 **Maidstone** Saskatchewan, S Canada 53°06′N 109°21′W
97 P22 **Maidstone** SE England, United Kingdom 51°17′N 00°31′E
77 Y13 **Maiduguri** Borno, NE Nigeria 11°51′N 13°10′E
108 I8 **Maienfeld** Sankt Gallen, NE Switzerland 47°01′N 09°30′E
116 J12 **Măieruș** *Hung.* Szászmagyarós. Brașov, C Romania 45°55′N 25°30′E
Maigh Chromtha *see* Macroom
Maigh Eo *see* Mayo
55 N9 **Maigualida, Sierra** ▲▲ S Venezuela
154 K9 **Maihar** Madhya Pradesh, C India 24°18′N 80°46′E
154 K11 **Maikala Range** ▲▲ C India
67 T10 **Maiko** ≈ W Dem. Rep. Congo
Mailand *see* Milano
152 L11 **Mailāni** Uttar Pradesh, N India 28°17′N 80°20′E
149 U10 **Māilsi** Punjab, E Pakistan 29°46′N 72°15′E
147 R8 **Maimak** Talasskaya Oblast', NW Kyrgyzstan 42°40′N 71°12′E
Maimāna *see* Maīmanah
148 M3 **Maīmanah** *var.* Maimāna, Maymana; *prev.* Meymaneh. Fāryāb, NW Afghanistan 35°57′N 64°48′E
171 V13 **Maimawa** Papua, E Indonesia 03°21′S 133°36′E
Maimuna *see* Al Maymūnah
101 G18 **Main** ≈ C Germany
115 F22 **Maïna** *ancient monument* Pelopónnisos, S Greece
115 E20 **Maínalo** ▲▲ S Greece
101 L22 **Mainburg** Bayern, SE Germany 48°40′N 11°48′E
Main Camp *see* Banana
14 E12 **Main Channel** *lake channel* Ontario, S Canada
79 I20 **Mai-Ndombe, Lac** *prev.* Lac Léopold II. ◎ W Dem. Rep. Congo
101 K20 **Main-Donau-Kanal** *canal* SE Germany
19 R6 **Maine** *off.* State of Maine, *also known as* Lumber State, Pine Tree State. ◐ *state* NE USA
102 K6 **Maine** *cultural region* NW France
102 J7 **Maine-et-Loire** ◐ *department* NW France
19 Q9 **Maine, Gulf of** *gulf* NE USA
77 X12 **Maïné-Soroa** Diffa, SE Niger 13°14′N 12°00′E
167 N2 **Maingkwan** *var.* Mungkawn. Kachin State, N Burma (Myanmar) 26°20′N 96°37′E
Main Island *see* Bermuda
Mainistir Fhear Maí *see* Fermoy
Mainistirna Búille *see* Boyle
Mainistir na Corann *see* Midleton
Mainistir na Féile *see* Abbeyfeale
96 J5 **Mainland** *island* N Scotland, United Kingdom
96 L2 **Mainland** *island* NE Scotland, United Kingdom
159 P16 **Mainling** *var.* Tungdor. Xizang Zizhiqu, W China 29°12′N 94°06′E
152 K12 **Mainpuri** Uttar Pradesh, N India 27°14′N 79°01′E
103 N5 **Maintenon** Eure-et-Loir, C France 48°35′N 01°34′E
172 H4 **Maintirano** Mahajanga, W Madagascar 18°01′S 44°03′E
93 M15 **Mainua** Oulu, C Finland 64°05′N 27°28′E
101 G18 **Mainz** *Fr.* Mayence. Rheinland-Pfalz, SW Germany 50°00′N 08°16′E
76 I9 **Maio** *var.* Vila do Maio. Maio, S Cape Verde 15°07′N 23°12′W
76 E10 **Maio** *var.* Mayo. *island* Ilhas de Sotavento, SE Cape Verde
62 G12 **Maipo, Río** ≈ C Chile
62 H12 **Maipo, Volcán** Ѫ W Argentina 34°09′S 69°51′W
61 E22 **Maipú** Buenos Aires, E Argentina 36°52′S 57°52′W
62 I11 **Maipú** Mendoza, E Argentina 33°00′S 68°46′W
62 H11 **Maipú** Santiago, C Chile 33°30′S 70°52′W
106 A9 **Maira** ≈ NW Italy
108 I10 **Maira** *It.* Mera. ≈ Italy/Switzerland
153 V12 **Mairābari** Assam, NE India 26°28′N 92°22′E
44 K7 **Maisí** Guantánamo, E Cuba 20°13′N 74°08′W
118 H13 **Maišiagala** Vilnius, SE Lithuania 54°52′N 25°03′E
Maiskhal Island *see* Maheskhali Island
167 N13 **Mai Sombun** Chumphon, SW Thailand 10°49′N 99°13′E
Mai Son *see* Hat Lot
Maisur *see* Mysore, India
Maisur *see* Karnātaka, India
183 T8 **Maitland** New South Wales, SE Australia 32°33′S 151°33′E
182 I9 **Maitland** South Australia 34°21′S 137°42′E
14 F15 **Maitland** ≈ Ontario, S Canada
195 R1 **Maitri** *Indian research station* Antarctica 70°03′S 08°59′E
159 N15 **Maizhokunggar** Xizang Zizhiqu, W China 29°50′N 91°40′E
43 O10 **Maíz, Islas del** *var.* Corn Islands. *island group* SE Nicaragua
164 J12 **Maizuru** Kyōto, Honshū, SW Japan 35°30′N 135°20′E
54 F6 **Majagual** Sucre, N Colombia 08°36′N 74°39′W
41 Z13 **Majahual** Quintana Roo, E Mexico 18°43′N 87°43′W
Mājeej *see* Mejit Island
171 N13 **Majene** *prev.* Madjene. Sulawesi, C Indonesia 03°33′S 118°59′E
43 V15 **Majé, Serranía de** ▲▲ E Panama
112 I11 **Majevica** ▲▲ NE Bosnia and Herzegovina
81 H15 **Majī** Southern Nationalities, S Ethiopia 06°11′N 35°32′E
141 X7 **Majīs** NW Oman 24°25′N 56°34′E
Majorca *see* Mallorca
105 X9 **Major, Puig** ▲ Mallorca, Spain, W Mediterranean Sea 39°50′N 2°50′E
Mājro *see* Majuro Atoll
Majunga *see* Mahajanga
189 Y3 **Majuro** ✕ Majuro Atoll, SE Marshall Islands 07°05′N 171°08′E
189 Y2 **Majuro Atoll** *var.* Mājro. *atoll* Ratak Chain, SE Marshall Islands
189 X2 **Majuro Lagoon** *lagoon* Majuro Atoll, SE Marshall Islands
76 H11 **Maka** C Senegal 13°40′N 14°12′W
79 F20 **Makabana** Niari, SW Congo 03°28′S 12°36′E
38 D9 **Mākaha** *var.* Makaha. O'ahu, Hawaii, USA, C Pacific Ocean 21°28′N 158°13′W
38 B8 **Makahū'ena Point** *var.* Makahuena Point. *headland* Kaua'i, Hawai'i, USA 21°52′N 159°28′W
38 D9 **Makakilo City** O'ahu, Hawaii, USA, C Pacific Ocean 21°21′N 158°05′W
83 H18 **Makalamabedi** Central, C Botswana 20°19′S 23°51′E
Makale *see* Mek'elē
158 K17 **Makalu** *Chin.* Makaru Shan. ▲ China/Nepal 27°53′N 87°09′E
81 G23 **Makampi** Mbeya, S Tanzania 08°00′S 33°17′E
Makanchi *see* Makanshy
145 X12 **Makanshy** *prev.* Makanchi. Vostochnyy Kazakhstan, E Kazakhstan 46°47′N 82°00′E
42 M8 **Makantaka** Región Autónoma Atlántico Norte, NE Nicaragua 13°13′N 84°04′W
190 B16 **Makapu Point** *headland* W Niue 18°59′S 169°56′E
185 C24 **Makarewa** Southland, South Island, New Zealand 46°17′S 168°16′E
117 O4 **Makariv** Kyyivs'ka Oblast', N Ukraine 50°28′N 29°49′E
185 D20 **Makarora** ≈ South Island, New Zealand
123 T13 **Makarov** Ostrov Sakhalin, Sakhalinskaya Oblast', SE Russian Federation 48°24′N 142°37′E
197 R9 **Makarov Basin** *undersea feature* Arctic Ocean
192 I5 **Makarov Seamount** *undersea feature* W Pacific Ocean 29°30′N 153°30′E
113 F15 **Makarska** *It.* Macarsca. Split-Dalmacija, SE Croatia 43°18′N 17°00′E
Makaru Shan *see* Makalu
125 O15 **Makar'yev** Kostromskaya Oblast', NW Russian Federation 57°52′N 43°46′E
82 L11 **Makasa** Northern, NE Zambia 09°42′S 31°54′E
Makasar *see* Makassar
Makasar, Selat *see* Makassar Straits
170 M14 **Makassar** *var.* Macassar, Makasar; *prev.* Ujungpandang. Sulawesi, C Indonesia 05°09′S 119°28′E
192 F7 **Makassar Straits** *Ind.* Makasar Selat. *strait* C Indonesia
144 G12 **Makat** *Kaz.* Maqat. Atyrau, SW Kazakhstan 47°40′N 53°28′E
191 T10 **Makatea** *island* Îles Tuamotu, C French Polynesia
139 U7 **Makātū** Diyālá, E Iraq 33°55′N 45°25′E
172 H6 **Makay** *var.* Massif du Makay. ▲▲ SW Madagascar
Makay, Massif du *see* Makay
114 J12 **Makaza** *pass* Bulgaria/Greece
Makedonija *see* Macedonia, FYR
190 B16 **Makefu** W Niue 18°59′S 169°55′W
191 V10 **Makemo** *atoll* Îles Tuamotu, C French Polynesia
76 I15 **Makeni** C Sierra Leone 08°57′N 12°02′W
Makenzen *see* Orlyak
Makeyevka *see* Makiyivka
127 Q16 **Makhachkala** *prev.* Petrovsk-Port. Respublika Dagestan, SW Russian Federation 42°58′N 47°30′E
83 K19 **Makhado** *prev.* Louis Trichardt. Northern, NE South Africa 23°01′S 29°43′E
144 F11 **Makhambet** Atyrau, W Kazakhstan 47°35′N 51°35′E
Makharadze *see* Ozurgeti
139 W13 **Makhfar al Buṣayyah** Al Muthanná, S Iraq 30°09′N 46°09′E
139 R4 **Makhmūr** Arbīl, N Iraq 35°47′N 43°32′E
138 I11 **Makhrūq, Wadi al** *dry watercourse* E Jordan
139 R4 **Makḥūl, Jabal** ▲▲ C Iraq
141 R13 **Makhyah, Wādī** *dry watercourse* N Yemen
171 V13 **Maki** Papua, E Indonesia 03°00′S 134°10′E
185 G21 **Makikihi** Canterbury, South Island, New Zealand 44°36′S 171°09′E
191 O2 **Makin** *prev.* Pitt Island. *atoll* Tungaru, W Kiribati
81 I20 **Makindu** Eastern, S Kenya 02°15′S 37°49′E
145 Q8 **Makinsk** Akmola, N Kazakhstan 52°40′N 70°28′E
Makira *see* Makira-Ulawa
Makira *see* San Cristobal
187 N10 **Makira-Ulawa** *prev.* Makira. ◐ *province* SE Solomon Islands
117 X8 **Makiyivka** *Rus.* Makeyevka; *prev.* Dmitriyevsk. Donets'ka Oblast', E Ukraine 47°57′N 37°47′E
140 L10 **Makkah** *Eng.* Mecca. Makkah, W Saudi Arabia 21°28′N 39°50′E
140 M10 **Makkah** *var.* Minṭaqat Makkah. ◐ *province* W Saudi Arabia
Makkah, Minṭaqat *see* Makkah
13 R7 **Makkovik** Newfoundland and Labrador, NE Canada 55°06′N 59°07′W
98 K6 **Makkum** Fryslân, N Netherlands 53°03′N 05°25′E
111 M25 **Makó** *Rom.* Macău. Csongrád, SE Hungary 46°14′N 20°28′E
Mako *see* Makung
14 G9 **Makobe Lake** ◎ Ontario, S Canada
79 F18 **Makokou** Ogooué-Ivindo, NE Gabon 0°38′N 12°47′E
81 G23 **Makongolosi** Mbeya, S Tanzania 08°24′S 33°09′E
81 E19 **Makota** SW Uganda 0°37′S 30°12′E
79 G18 **Makoua** Cuvette, C Congo 0°01′S 15°40′E
110 M10 **Maków Mazowiecki** Mazowieckie, C Poland 52°51′N 21°06′E
111 K17 **Maków Podhalański** Małopolskie, S Poland 49°43′N 19°40′E
143 V14 **Makran** *cultural region* Iran/Pakistan
152 G12 **Makrāna** Rājasthān, N India 27°02′N 74°44′E
143 U15 **Makran Coast** *coastal region* SE Iran
119 F20 **Makrany** *Rus.* Mokrany. Brestskaya Voblasts', SW Belarus 51°50′N 24°15′E
Makrinoros *see* Makrynóros
115 H20 **Makrónisosi** *island* Kykládes, Greece, Aegean Sea
115 D17 **Makrynóros** *var.* Makrinoros. ▲▲ C Greece
115 G19 **Makryplági** ▲ C Greece 38°00′N 23°06′E
Maksamaa *see* Maxmo
Maksatha *see* Maksatikha
Maksaticha *see* Maksatikha
124 J15 **Maksatikha** *var.* Maksatha, Maksaticha. Tverskaya Oblast', W Russian Federation 57°49′N 35°46′E
154 G10 **Maksi** Madhya Pradesh, C India 23°20′N 76°36′E
142 I1 **Mākū** Āżarbāyjān-e Gharbī, NW Iran 39°20′N 44°50′E
153 Y11 **Mākum** Assam, NE India 27°28′N 95°28′E
Makun *see* Makung
161 R14 **Makung** *prev.* Mako, Makun. W Taiwan 23°35′N 119°35′E
164 B16 **Makurazaki** Kagoshima, Kyūshū, SW Japan 31°16′N 130°18′E
77 V15 **Makurdi** Benue, C Nigeria 07°42′N 08°36′E
38 L17 **Makushin Volcano** ▲ Unalaska Island, Alaska, USA 53°53′N 166°55′W
83 K16 **Makwiro** Mashonaland West, N Zimbabwe 17°58′S 30°25′E
57 D15 **Mala** Lima, W Peru 12°40′S 76°36′W
93 I14 **Malå** Västerbotten, N Sweden 65°12′N 18°45′E
Mala *see* Mallow, Ireland
Mala *see* Malaita, Solomon Islands
171 P8 **Malabang** Mindanao, S Philippines
155 E21 **Malabār Coast** *coast* SW India
79 C16 **Malabo** *prev.* Santa Isabel. ● (Equatorial Guinea) Isla de Bioco, NW Equatorial Guinea 03°43′N 08°52′E
79 C16 **Malabo** ✕ Isla de Bioco, N Equatorial Guinea 03°44′N 08°51′E
Malaca *see* Málaga
Malacca *see* Melaka
168 I7 **Malacca, Strait of** *Ind.* Selat Malaka. *strait* Indonesia/Malaysia
Malacka *see* Malacky
111 G20 **Malacky** *Hung.* Malacka. Bratislavský Kraj, W Slovakia 48°26′N 17°01′E
33 R16 **Malad City** Idaho, NW USA 42°10′N 112°16′W
117 Q4 **Mala Divytsya** Chernihivs'ka Oblast', N Ukraine 50°40′N 32°13′E
119 J15 **Maladzyechna** *Pol.* Molodeczno, *Rus.* Molodechno. Minskaya Voblasts', C Belarus 54°19′N 26°51′E
190 D12 **Malaee** Île Futuna, N Wallis and Futuna
190 G12 **Mala'etoli** Île Uvea, E Wallis and Futuna
54 G8 **Málaga** Santander, C Colombia 06°44′N 72°45′W
104 M15 **Málaga** *anc.* Malaca. Andalucía, S Spain 36°43′N 04°25′W
37 V15 **Malaga** New Mexico, SW USA 32°10′N 104°04′W
104 L15 **Málaga** ◐ *province* Andalucía, S Spain
104 M15 **Málaga** ✕ Andalucía, S Spain 36°38′N 04°36′W
Malagasy Republic *see* Madagascar
105 N10 **Malagón** Castilla-La Mancha, C Spain 39°10′N 03°51′W
97 G18 **Malahide** *Ir.* Mullach Íde. Dublin, E Ireland 53°27′N 06°09′W
187 N9 **Malaita** *off.* Malaita Province. ◐ *province* N Solomon Islands
187 N8 **Malaita** *var.* Mala. *island* N Solomon Islands
Malaita Province *see* Malaita
80 F13 **Malakal** Upper Nile, NE South Sudan 09°31′N 31°40′E
112 C10 **Mala Kapela** ▲▲ NW Croatia
25 V7 **Malakoff** Texas, SW USA 32°10′N 96°00′W
Malakula *see* Malekula
149 V7 **Malakwāl** *var.* Mālikwāla. Punjab, E Pakistan 32°32′N 73°18′E
186 E7 **Malalamai** Madang, W Papua New Guinea 05°49′S 146°44′E
171 O13 **Malamala** Sulawesi, C Indonesia 03°21′S 120°58′E
169 S17 **Malang** Jawa, C Indonesia 07°59′S 112°45′E
83 O14 **Malanga** Niassa, N Mozambique 13°27′S 36°05′E
Malange *see* Malanje
92 I9 **Malangen** *sound* N Norway
82 C11 **Malanje** *var.* Malange. Malanje, NW Angola 09°34′S 16°25′E
82 C11 **Malanje** *var.* Malange. ◐ *province* N Angola
148 M16 **Malān, Rās** *cape* SW Pakistan
77 S13 **Malanville** NE Benin 11°50′N 03°23′E
Malapane *see* Ozimek
155 F21 **Malappuram** Kerala, SW India 11°00′N 76°02′E
43 T17 **Mala, Punta** *headland* S Panama 07°28′N 79°58′W
148 L15 **Malar** Baluchistān, SW Pakistan 26°19′N 64°55′E
95 N16 **Mälaren** ◎ C Sweden
62 H13 **Malargüe** Mendoza, W Argentina 35°32′S 69°35′W
14 J8 **Malartic** Québec, SE Canada 48°09′N 78°09′W
119 F20 **Malaryta** *Pol.* Maloryta, *Rus.* Malorita. Brestskaya Voblasts', SW Belarus 51°47′N 24°05′E
63 J19 **Malaspina** Chubut, SE Argentina 44°56′S 66°52′W
10 G8 **Malaspina Glacier** *glacier* Yukon Territory, W Canada
39 U12 **Malaspina Glacier** *glacier* Alaska, USA
137 N15 **Malatya** *anc.* Melitene. Malatya, SE Turkey 38°22′N 38°18′E
136 M14 **Malatya** ◐ *province* C Turkey
Malavate *see* Pédima
117 Q7 **Mala Vyska** *Rus.* Malaya Viska. Kirovohrads'ka Oblast', S Ukraine 48°37′N 31°36′E
83 M14 **Malawi** *off.* Republic of Malaŵi; *prev.* Nyasaland, Nyasaland Protectorate. ◆ *republic* S Africa
Malawi, Lake *see* Nyasa, Lake
Malaŵi, Republic of *see* Malawi
93 J17 **Malax** *Fin.* Maalahti. Länsi-Suomi, W Finland 62°55′N 21°30′E
124 H14 **Malaya Vishera** Novgorodskaya Oblast', W Russian Federation 58°52′N 32°12′E
Malaya Viska *see* Mala Vyska
171 Q7 **Malaybalay** Mindanao, S Philippines 08°10′N 125°08′E
142 L6 **Malāyer** *prev.* Daulatabad. Hamadān, W Iran 34°20′N 48°47′E
168 J7 **Malay Peninsula** *peninsula* Malaysia/Thailand
168 L7 **Malaysia** *off.* Malaysia, *var.* Federation of Malaysia; *prev.* the separate territories of Federation of Malaya, Sarawak and Sabah (North Borneo) and Singapore. ◆ *monarchy* SE Asia
Malaysia, Federation of *see* Malaysia
137 R14 **Malazgirt** Muş, E Turkey 39°09′N 42°30′E
15 R8 **Malbaie** ≈ Québec, SE Canada
77 T12 **Malbaza** Tahoua, S Niger 13°57′N 05°32′E
110 J7 **Malbork** *Ger.* Marienburg, Marienburg in Westpreussen. Pomorskie, N Poland 54°01′N 19°03′E
100 N9 **Malchin** Mecklenburg-Vorpommern, N Germany 53°43′N 12°46′E
100 M9 **Malchiner See** ◎ NE Germany
99 D16 **Maldegem** Oost-Vlaanderen, NW Belgium 51°12′N 03°27′E
98 L13 **Malden** Gelderland, SE Netherlands 51°47′N 05°51′E
19 O11 **Malden** Massachusetts, NE USA 42°25′N 71°04′W
27 Y8 **Malden** Missouri, C USA 36°33′N 89°58′W
191 X4 **Malden Island** *prev.* Independence Island. *atoll* E Kiribati
173 Q6 **Maldives** *off.* Maldivian Divehi, Republic of Maldives. ◆ *republic* N Indian Ocean
Maldives, Republic of *see* Maldives
Maldivian Divehi *see* Maldives
97 P21 **Maldon** E England, United Kingdom 51°44′N 00°40′E
61 G20 **Maldonado** Maldonado, S Uruguay 34°57′S 54°59′W
61 G20 **Maldonado** ◐ *department* S Uruguay
41 P17 **Maldonado, Punta** *headland* S Mexico 16°18′N 98°31′W
106 G6 **Malè** Trentino-Alto Adige, N Italy 46°21′N 10°51′E
151 K19 **Male'** *Div.* Maale. ● (Maldives) Male' Atoll, C Maldives 04°10′N 73°29′E
76 K13 **Maléa** *var.* Maléya. NE Guinea 11°46′N 09°43′W
Maléas, Ákra *see* Agriliá, Akrotírio
115 G22 **Maléas, Akrotírio** *headland* S Greece 36°25′N 23°11′E
151 K19 **Male' Atoll** *var.* Kaafu Atoll. *atoll* C Maldives
Malebo, Pool *see* Stanley Pool
154 E12 **Mālegaon** Mahārāshtra, W India 20°33′N 74°32′E
81 F15 **Malek** Jonglei, E South Sudan 06°04′N 31°36′E
187 Q13 **Malekula** *var.* Malakula; *prev.* Mallicolo. *island* W Vanuatu
189 Y15 **Malem** Kosrae, E Micronesia 05°16′N 163°01′E
83 O15 **Malema** Nampula, N Mozambique 14°57′S 37°28′E
79 N23 **Malemba-Nkulu** Katanga, SE Dem. Rep. Congo 08°01′S 26°48′E
124 K9 **Malen'ga** Respublika Kareliya, NW Russian Federation 63°50′N 36°21′E
95 M20 **Målerås** Kalmar, S Sweden 56°55′N 15°34′E
103 O6 **Malesherbes** Loiret, C France 48°18′N 02°25′E
115 G18 **Malesína** Stereá Elláda, E Greece 38°37′N 23°15′E
Maléya *see* Maléa
127 O15 **Malgobek** Respublika Ingushetiya, SW Russian Federation 43°34′N 44°34′E
105 X5 **Malgrat de Mar** Cataluña, NE Spain 41°39′N 02°45′E
80 C9 **Malha** Northern Darfur, W Sudan 15°07′N 26°00′E
139 Q5 **Malḥah** *var.* Malḥāt. Ṣalāḥ ad Dīn, C Iraq 34°44′N 42°41′E
Malḥāt *see* Malḥah
32 K14 **Malheur Lake** ◎ Oregon, NW USA
32 L14 **Malheur River** ≈ Oregon, NW USA
76 I13 **Mali** NW Guinea 12°08′N 12°29′W
77 O9 **Mali** *off.* Republic of Mali, *Fr.* République du Mali; *prev.* French Sudan, Sudanese Republic. ◆ *republic* W Africa
171 Q16 **Maliana** W East Timor 08°57′S 125°25′E
167 O2 **Mali Hka** ≈ N Burma (Myanmar)
Mali Idjoš *see* Mali Iđoš
112 K8 **Mali Iđoš** *var.* Mali Idjoš, *Hung.* Kishegyes; *prev.* Krivaja. Vojvodina, N Serbia 45°43′N 19°40′E
113 M18 **Mali i Sharrit** *Serb.* Šar Planina. ▲▲ FYR Macedonia/Serbia
Mali i Zi *see* Crna Gora
112 K9 **Mali Kanal** *canal* N Serbia
171 P12 **Maliku** Sulawesi, N Indonesia 0°36′S 123°13′E
Malik, Wadi al *see* Milk, Wadi el
Mālikwāla *see* Malakwāl
167 N11 **Mali Kyun** *var.* Tavoy Island. *island* Mergui Archipelago, S Burma (Myanmar)
95 M19 **Målilla** Kalmar, S Sweden 57°24′N 15°49′E
112 B11 **Mali Lošinj** *It.* Lussinpiccolo. Primorje-Gorski Kotar, W Croatia 44°31′N 14°28′E
Malin *see* Malyn
171 P7 **Malindang, Mount** ▲ Mindanao, S Philippines 08°12′N 123°37′E
81 K20 **Malindi** Coast, SE Kenya 03°14′S 40°05′E
Malines *see* Mechelen
96 E13 **Malin Head** *Ir.* Cionn Mhálanna. *headland* NW Ireland 55°37′N 07°37′W
171 O11 **Malino, Gunung** ▲ Sulawesi, N Indonesia 0°44′N 120°45′E
113 M21 **Maliq** *var.* Maliqi. Korçë, SE Albania 40°45′N 20°45′E
Maliqi *see* Maliq
Mali, Republic of *see* Mali
Mali, République du *see* Mali
171 Q8 **Malita** Mindanao, S Philippines 06°13′N 125°39′E
154 G12 **Malkāpur** Mahārāshtra, C India 20°52′N 76°18′E
136 B10 **Malkara** Tekirdağ, NW Turkey 40°54′N 26°54′E
119 J19 **Mal'kavichy** *Rus.* Mal'kovichi. Brestskaya Voblasts', SW Belarus 52°31′N 26°36′E
Malkiye *see* Al Mālikīyah
114 L11 **Malko Sharkovo, Yazovir** ▦ SE Bulgaria
114 N11 **Malko Tŭrnovo** Burgas, E Bulgaria 42°00′N 27°33′E
Mal'kovichi *see* Mal'kavichy
183 R12 **Mallacoota** Victoria, SE Australia 37°34′S 149°45′E
96 G10 **Mallaig** N Scotland, United Kingdom 57°04′N 05°48′W
182 I9 **Mallala** South Australia 34°29′S 138°30′E
75 W9 **Mallawī** *var.* Mallawi. C Egypt 27°44′N 30°50′E
Mallawi *see* Mallawī
105 R5 **Mallén** Aragón, NE Spain 41°53′N 01°25′W
106 F5 **Malles Venosta** *Ger.* Mals im Vinschgau. Trentino-Alto Adige, N Italy 46°40′N 10°37′E
Mallicolo *see* Malekula
109 Q8 **Mallnitz** Salzburg, S Austria 46°58′N 13°09′E
105 W9 **Mallorca** *Eng.* Majorca; *anc.* Baleares Major. *island* Islas Baleares, Spain, W Mediterranean Sea
97 C20 **Mallow** *Ir.* Mala. SW Ireland 52°08′N 08°39′W
93 E15 **Malm** Nord-Trøndelag, C Norway 64°04′N 11°12′E
95 L19 **Malmbäck** Jönköping, S Sweden 57°34′N 14°30′E
92 J12 **Malmberget** *Lapp.* Malmivaara. Norrbotten, N Sweden 67°09′N 20°39′E
99 M20 **Malmédy** Liège, E Belgium 50°26′N 06°02′E
83 E25 **Malmesbury** Western Cape, SW South Africa 33°28′S 18°43′E
Malmivaara *see* Malmberget
95 N16 **Malmköping** Södermanland, C Sweden 59°08′N 16°49′E
95 K23 **Malmö** Skåne, S Sweden 55°36′N 13°E
95 K23 **Malmo** ✕ Skåne, S Sweden 55°33′N 13°23′E
45 Q16 **Malmok** *headland* N Bonaire 12°16′N 68°21′W
95 M18 **Malmslätt** Östergötland, S Sweden 58°25′N 15°30′E
125 R16 **Malmyzh** Kirovskaya Oblast', NW Russian Federation 56°30′N 50°37′E
187 Q13 **Malo** *island* W Vanuatu
126 J7 **Maloarkhangel'sk** Orlovskaya Oblast', W Russian Federation 52°25′N 36°37′E
Maḷoeḷap *see* Maloelap Atoll
189 V6 **Maloelap Atoll** *var.* Maḷoeḷap. *atoll* E Marshall Islands
Maloenda *see* Malunda
108 I10 **Maloja** Graubünden, S Switzerland 46°25′N 09°42′E
82 L12 **Malole** Northern, NE Zambia 10°05′S 31°37′E
171 O3 **Malolos** Luzon, N Philippines 14°51′N 120°49′E
18 K6 **Malone** New York, NE USA 44°51′N 74°18′W
79 K25 **Malonga** Katanga, S Dem. Rep. Congo 10°26′S 23°10′E
111 L17 **Małopolskie** ◐ *province* SE Poland

◆ Country
● Country Capital
◇ Dependent Territory
○ Dependent Territory Capital
◐ Administrative Regions
✕ International Airport
▲ Mountain
▲▲ Mountain Range
Ѫ Volcano
≈ River
◎ Lake
▦ Reservoir

Malorita/Maloryta *see* Malaryta

124 *K9* **Maloshuyka** Arkhangel'skaya Oblast', NW Russian Federation *63°43′N 37°20′E*

114 *G10* **Mal'ovitsa** ▲ W Bulgaria *42°12′N 23°19′E*

145 *V15* **Malovodnoye** Almaty, SE Kazakhstan *43°31′N 77°42′E*

94 *C10* **Måløy** Sogn Og Fjordane, S Norway *61°57′N 05°06′E*

126 *K4* **Maloyaroslavets** Kaluzhskaya Oblast', W Russian Federation *55°03′N 36°31′E*

122 *G7* **Malozemel'skaya Tundra** *physical region* NW Russian Federation

104 *J10* **Malpartida de Cáceres** Extremadura, W Spain *39°26′N 06°30′W*

104 *K9* **Malpartida de Plasencia** Extremadura, W Spain *39°59′N 06°03′W*

106 *C7* **Malpensa** ✈ (Milano) Lombardia, N Italy *45°41′N 08°40′E*

76 *J6* **Malqteïr** *desert* N Mauritania

Mals im Vinschgau *see* Malles Venosta

118 *J10* **Malta** SE Latvia *56°19′N 27°11′E*

33 *V7* **Malta** Montana, NW USA *48°21′N 107°52′W*

120 *M11* **Malta** *off.* Republic of Malta. ◆ *republic* C Mediterranean Sea

109 *R8* **Malta** *var.* Maltabach. ≈ S Austria

120 *M11* **Malta** *island* Malta, C Mediterranean Sea

Maltabach *see* Malta

Malta, Canale di *see* Malta Channel

120 *M11* **Malta Channel** *It.* Canale di Malta. *strait* Italy/Malta

83 *D20* **Maltahöhe** Hardap, SW Namibia *24°50′S 17°00′E*

Malta, Republic of *see* Malta

97 *N16* **Malton** N England, United Kingdom *54°07′N 00°50′W*

171 *R13* **Maluku** *off.* Propinsi Maluku, *Dut.* Molukken, *Eng.* Moluccas. ◈ *province* E Indonesia

171 *R13* **Maluku** *Dut.* Molukken, *Eng.* Moluccas; *prev.* Spice Islands. *island group* E Indonesia

Maluku, Laut *see* Molucca Sea

Maluku, Propinsi *see* Maluku

171 *R11* **Maluku Utara** *off.* Propinsi Maluku Utara. ◈ *province* E Indonesia

Maluku Utara, Propinsi *see* Maluku Utara

77 *V13* **Malumfashi** Katsina, N Nigeria *11°51′N 07°39′E*

171 *N13* **Malunda** *prev.* Maloenda. Sulawesi, C Indonesia *02°58′S 118°52′E*

94 *K13* **Malung** Dalarna, C Sweden *60°40′N 13°45′E*

94 *K13* **Malungsfors** Dalarna, C Sweden *60°43′N 13°34′E*

186 *M8* **Maluu** *var.* Malu'u. Malaita, N Solomon Islands *08°22′S 160°39′E*

Malu'u *see* Maluu

155 *D16* **Mālvan** Mahārāshtra, W India *16°05′N 73°28′E*

Malventum *see* Benevento

27 *U12* **Malvern** Arkansas, C USA *34°21′N 92°50′W*

29 *S15* **Malvern** Iowa, C USA *40°59′N 95°36′W*

44 *I13* **Malvern** ▲ W Jamaica *17°59′N 77°42′W*

Malvina, Isla Gran *see* West Falkland

Malvinas, Islas *see* Falkland Islands

117 *N4* **Malyn** *Rus.* Malin. Zhytomyrs'ka Oblast', N Ukraine *50°46′N 29°14′E*

127 *O11* **Malyye Derbety** Respublika Kalmykiya, SW Russian Federation *47°57′N 44°39′E*

Malyy Kavkaz *see* Lesser Caucasus

123 *Q6* **Malyy Lyakhovskiy, Ostrov** *island* NE Russian Federation

Malyy Pamir *see* Little Pamir

122 *N5* **Malyy Taymyr, Ostrov** *island* Severnaya Zemlya, N Russian Federation

Malyy Uzen' *see* Saryozen

122 *L14* **Malyy Yenisey** *var.* Ka-Krem. ≈ S Russian Federation

127 *S3* **Mamadysh** Respublika Tatarstan, W Russian Federation *55°46′N 51°22′E*

117 *N14* **Mamaia** Constanţa, E Romania *44°13′N 28°37′E*

187 *W14* **Mamanuca Group** *island group* Yasawa Group, W Fiji

146 *L13* **Mamash** Lebap Welaýaty, E Turkmenistan *38°24′N 64°12′E*

79 *O17* **Mambasa** Orientale, NE Dem. Rep. Congo *01°20′N 29°05′E*

171 *X13* **Mamberamo, Sungai** ≈ Papua, E Indonesia

79 *G15* **Mambéré** ≈ SW Central African Republic

79 *G15* **Mambéré-Kadéï** ◈ *prefecture* SW Central African Republic

Mambij *see* Manbij

79 *H18* **Mambili** ≈ W Congo

83 *N18* **Mambone** *var.* Nova Mambone. Inhambane, E Mozambique *20°59′S 35°04′E*

171 *O4* **Mamburao** Mindoro, N Philippines *13°16′N 120°36′E*

172 *I16* **Mamelles** *island* Inner Islands, NE Seychelles

99 *M25* **Mamer** Luxembourg, SW Luxembourg *49°37′N 06°01′E*

102 *L6* **Mamers** Sarthe, NW France *48°21′N 00°22′E*

79 *D15* **Mamfe** Sud-Ouest, W Cameroon *05°46′N 09°18′E*

145 *P6* **Mamlyutka** Severnyy Kazakhstan, N Kazakhstan *54°54′N 68°36′E*

36 *M15* **Mammoth** Arizona, SW USA *32°43′N 110°38′W*

33 *S12* **Mammoth Hot Springs** Wyoming, C USA *44°57′N 110°40′W*

Mamoedjoe *see* Mamuju

119 *A14* **Mamonovo** *Ger.* Heiligenbeil. Kaliningradskaya Oblast', W Russian Federation *54°28′N 19°57′E*

57 *L14* **Mamoré, Rio** ≈ Bolivia/Brazil

76 *I14* **Mamou** W Guinea *10°24′N 12°05′W*

22 *H8* **Mamou** Louisiana, S USA *30°37′N 92°25′W*

172 *I14* **Mamoudzou** ○ (Mayotte) C Mayotte *12°48′S 45°E*

172 *I3* **Mampikony** Mahajanga, N Madagascar *16°03′S 47°39′E*

77 *P16* **Mampong** C Ghana *07°06′N 01°20′W*

110 *M7* **Mamry, Jezioro** *Ger.* Mauersee. ◎ NE Poland

171 *N13* **Mamuju** *prev.* Mamoedjoe. Sulawesi, S Indonesia *02°41′S 118°55′E*

83 *F19* **Mamuno** Ghanzi, W Botswana *22°15′S 20°02′E*

113 *K19* **Mamuras** *var.* Mamurasi, Mamurras. Lezhë, C Albania *41°34′N 19°42′E*

Mamurasi/Mamurras *see* Mamuras

76 *L16* **Man** W Ivory Coast *07°24′N 07°33′W*

55 *X9* **Mana** NW French Guiana *05°40′N 53°49′W*

56 *A6* **Manabí** ◈ *province* W Ecuador

42 *G4* **Manabique, Punta** *var.* Cabo Tres Puntas. *headland* E Guatemala *15°57′N 88°37′W*

54 *G11* **Manacacías, Río** ≈ C Colombia

58 *F13* **Manacapuru** Amazonas, N Brazil *03°16′S 60°37′W*

105 *Y9* **Manacor** Mallorca, Spain, W Mediterranean Sea *39°35′N 03°12′E*

171 *Q11* **Manado** *prev.* Menado. Sulawesi, C Indonesia *01°32′N 124°55′E*

188 *H5* **Managaha** *island* S Northern Mariana Islands

99 *G20* **Manage** Hainaut, S Belgium *50°30′N 04°14′E*

42 *J10* **Managua** ● (Nicaragua) Managua, W Nicaragua *12°08′N 86°15′W*

42 *J10* **Managua** ◈ *department* W Nicaragua

42 *J10* **Managua** ✈ Managua, W Nicaragua *12°07′N 86°11′W*

42 *J10* **Managua, Lago de** *var.* Xolotlán. ◎ W Nicaragua

Manah *see* Bilād Manah

18 *K16* **Manahawkin** New Jersey, NE USA *39°39′N 74°12′W*

184 *K11* **Manaia** Taranaki, North Island, New Zealand *39°33′S 174°07′E*

172 *J6* **Manakara** Fianarantsoa, SE Madagascar *22°09′S 48°E*

152 *J7* **Manāli** Himāchal Pradesh, NW India *32°12′N 77°06′E*

Ma, Nam *see* Sông Ma

Manama *see* Al Manāmah

186 *D6* **Manam Island** *island* N Papua New Guinea

67 *Y13* **Mananara Avaratra** ≈ SE Madagascar

182 *M9* **Manangatang** Victoria, SE Australia *35°04′S 142°53′E*

172 *J6* **Mananjary** Fianarantsoa, SE Madagascar *21°13′S 48°20′E*

76 *L14* **Manankoro** Sikasso, SW Mali *10°33′N 07°25′W*

76 *J12* **Manantali, Lac de** ⊞ W Mali

Manáos *see* Manaus

185 *B23* **Manapouri** Southland, South Island, New Zealand *45°33′S 167°38′E*

185 *B23* **Manapouri, Lake** ◎ South Island, New Zealand

58 *F13* **Manaquiri** Amazonas, NW Brazil *03°27′S 60°37′W*

Manar *see* Mannar

158 *K5* **Manas** Xinjiang Uygur Zizhiqu, NW China *44°16′N 86°12′E*

153 *U12* **Manās** *var.* Dangme Chu. ≈ Bhutan/India

153 *P10* **Manāslu** *var.* Manasalu. ▲ C Nepal *28°33′N 84°33′E*

147 *R8* **Manas, Gora** ▲ Kyrgyzstan/Uzbekistan *42°17′N 71°04′E*

158 *K3* **Manas Hu** ◎ NW China

Manaslu *see* Manāslu

37 *S8* **Manassa** Colorado, C USA *37°10′N 105°56′W*

21 *W4* **Manassas** Virginia, NE USA *38°45′N 77°28′W*

45 *T5* **Manatí** C Puerto Rico *18°26′N 66°29′W*

186 *E8* **Manau** Northern, S Papua New Guinea *08°02′S 148°00′E*

54 *H4* **Manaure** La Guajira, N Colombia *11°46′N 72°28′W*

58 *F12* **Manaus** *prev.* Manáos. *state capital* Amazonas, NW Brazil *03°06′S 60°W*

136 *G17* **Manavgat** Antalya, SW Turkey *36°47′N 31°28′E*

184 *M13* **Manawatu** ≈ North Island, New Zealand

184 *L11* **Manawatu-Wanganui** *off.* Manawatu-Wanganui Region. ◈ *region* North Island, New Zealand

Manawatu-Wanganui Region *see* Manawatu-Wanganui

171 *R7* **Manay** Mindanao, S Philippines *07°12′N 126°29′E*

138 *K2* **Manbij** *var.* Mambij, *Fr.* Membidj. Ḩalab, N Syria *36°32′N 37°55′E*

105 *N13* **Mancha Real** Andalucía, S Spain *37°47′N 03°37′W*

102 *I4* **Manche** ◈ *department* N France

97 *L17* **Manchester** *Lat.* Mancunium. NW England, United Kingdom *53°30′N 02°15′W*

23 *S5* **Manchester** Georgia, SE USA *32°51′N 84°37′W*

29 *Y13* **Manchester** Iowa, C USA *42°28′N 91°27′W*

21 *N7* **Manchester** Kentucky, S USA *37°09′N 83°46′W*

19 *O10* **Manchester** New Hampshire, NE USA *42°59′N 71°26′W*

20 *K10* **Manchester** Tennessee, S USA *35°28′N 86°05′W*

18 *M9* **Manchester** Vermont, NE USA *43°09′N 73°03′W*

97 *L18* **Manchester** ✈ NW England, United Kingdom *53°21′N 02°16′W*

149 *P15* **Manchhar Lake** ◎ SE Pakistan

Man-chou-li *see* Manzhouli

129 *X7* **Manchurian Plain** *plain* NE China

Máncio Lima *see* Japiim

Mancunium *see* Manchester

148 *J15* **Mand** Baluchistān, SW Pakistan *26°06′N 61°58′E*

Mand *see* Mand, Rūd-e

81 *H25* **Manda** Iringa, SW Tanzania *10°30′S 34°37′E*

172 *H6* **Mandabe** Toliara, W Madagascar *21°02′S 44°56′E*

162 *M10* **Mandah** *var.* Töhöm. Dornogovĭ, SE Mongolia *44°25′N 108°18′E*

95 *E18* **Mandal** Vest-Agder, S Norway *58°02′N 07°30′E*

Mandal *see* Arbulag, Hövsgöl, Mongolia

Mandal *see* Batsümber, Töv, Mongolia

166 *L5* **Mandalay** Mandalay, C Burma (Myanmar) *21°57′N 96°04′E*

166 *M6* **Mandalay** ◈ *division* C Burma (Myanmar)

162 *L9* **Mandalgovĭ** Dundgovĭ, C Mongolia *45°47′N 106°18′E*

139 *V7* **Mandalī** Diyālá, E Iraq *33°43′N 45°33′E*

162 *K10* **Mandal-Ovoo** *var.* Sharhulsan. Ömnögovĭ, S Mongolia *44°43′N 104°06′E*

95 *E18* **Mandalselva** ≈ S Norway

163 *P11* **Mandalt** *var.* Sonid Zuoqi. Nei Mongol Zizhiqu, N China *43°49′N 113°36′E*

28 *M5* **Mandan** North Dakota, N USA *46°49′N 100°53′W*

Mandargiri Hill *see* Mandār Hill

153 *R14* **Mandār Hill** *prev.* Mandargiri Hill. Bihār, NE India *24°51′N 87°03′E*

170 *M13* **Mandar, Teluk** *bay* Sulawesi, C Indonesia

107 *C19* **Mandas** Sardegna, Italy, C Mediterranean Sea *39°40′N 09°07′E*

Mandasor *see* Mandsaur

81 *L16* **Mandera** North Eastern, NE Kenya *03°56′N 41°53′E*

33 *V13* **Manderson** Wyoming, C USA *44°13′N 107°55′W*

44 *J12* **Mandeville** C Jamaica *18°02′N 77°31′W*

22 *K9* **Mandeville** Louisiana, S USA *30°21′N 90°04′W*

152 *I7* **Mandi** Himāchal Pradesh, NW India *31°40′N 76°59′E*

76 *K14* **Mandiana** E Guinea *10°37′N 08°39′W*

Mandi Būrewāla *see* Būrewāla

Mandidzudzure *see* Chimanimani

83 *M15* **Mandié** Manica, NW Mozambique *16°27′S 33°28′E*

83 *N14* **Mandimba** Niassa, N Mozambique *14°21′S 35°40′E*

57 *Q19* **Mandioré, Laguna** ◎ E Bolivia

154 *J10* **Mandla** Madhya Pradesh, C India *22°36′N 80°23′E*

83 *M20* **Mandlakazi** *var.* Manjacaze. Gaza, S Mozambique *24°47′S 33°50′E*

95 *E24* **Mandø** *var.* Manø. *island* W Denmark

Mandoúdhion/Mandoudi *see* Mantoúdi

115 *G19* **Mándra** Attikí, C Greece *38°04′N 23°30′E*

172 *I7* **Mandrare** ≈ S Madagascar

114 *M10* **Mandra, Yazovir** *salt lake* SE Bulgaria

107 *L23* **Mandrazzi, Portella** *pass* Sicilia, Italy, C Mediterranean Sea

172 *J3* **Mandritsara** Mahajanga, N Madagascar *15°49′S 48°50′E*

143 *O13* **Mand, Rūd-e** *var.* Mand. ≈ S Iran

154 *F9* **Mandsaur** *prev.* Mandasor. Madhya Pradesh, C India *24°03′N 75°10′E*

154 *F11* **Māndu** Madhya Pradesh, C India *22°22′N 75°24′E*

169 *W8* **Mandul, Pulau** *island* N Indonesia

83 *H15* **Mandundu** Western, W Zambia *16°34′S 22°18′E*

180 *I13* **Mandurah** Western Australia *32°31′S 115°41′E*

107 *P18* **Manduria** Puglia, SE Italy *40°24′N 17°38′E*

155 *G20* **Mandya** Karnātaka, C India *12°34′N 76°55′E*

77 *P12* **Mané** C Burkina *12°59′N 01°21′W*

106 *E8* **Manerbio** Lombardia, NW Italy *45°22′N 10°09′E*

Manevichi *see* Manevychi

116 *K3* **Manevychi** *Pol.* Maniewicze, *Rus.* Manevichi. Volyns'ka Oblast', NW Ukraine *51°18′N 25°29′E*

107 *N16* **Manfredonia** Puglia, SE Italy *41°38′N 15°54′E*

107 *N16* **Manfredonia, Golfo di** *gulf* Adriatic Sea, N Mediterranean Sea

77 *P13* **Manga** C Burkina *11°41′N 01°04′W*

59 *L16* **Mangabeiras, Chapada das** ▲▲ E Brazil

79 *J20* **Mangai** Bandundu, W Dem. Rep. Congo *03°58′S 19°32′E*

190 *L17* **Mangaia** *island group* S Cook Islands

184 *M9* **Mangakino** Waikato, North Island, New Zealand *38°23′S 175°47′E*

116 *M15* **Mangalia** *anc.* Callatis. Constanţa, SE Romania *43°48′N 28°35′E*

78 *J11* **Mangalmé** Guéra, SE Chad *12°26′N 19°37′E*

155 *E19* **Mangalore** Karnātaka, W India *12°54′N 74°51′E*

Mangareva *see* Magareva

83 *I23* **Mangaung** Free State, C South Africa *29°10′S 26°19′E*

Mangaung *see* Bloemfontein

154 *K9* **Mangawān** Madhya Pradesh, C India *24°39′N 81°33′E*

184 *M11* **Mangaweka** Manawatu-Wanganui, North Island, New Zealand *39°49′S 175°47′E*

184 *N11* **Mangaweka** ▲ North Island, New Zealand *39°51′S 176°06′E*

79 *P17* **Mangbwalu** Orientale, NE Dem. Rep. Congo *02°06′N 30°04′E*

101 *L24* **Mangfall** ≈ SE Germany

169 *P13* **Manggar** Pulau Belitung, W Indonesia *02°52′S 108°13′E*

Mangghystaū Ūstirtī *see* Mangystau, Plato

166 *M2* **Mangin Range** ▲▲ N Burma (Myanmar)

139 *R1* **Mangish** Dahūk, N Iraq *37°03′N 43°04′E*

Mangistau *see* Mangystau

146 *H8* **Mang'it** *Rus.* Mangit. Qoraqalpog'iston Respublikasi, W Uzbekistan *42°06′N 60°02′E*

Mangit *see* Mang'it

54 *A13* **Manglares, Cabo** *headland* SW Colombia *01°36′N 79°02′W*

149 *V6* **Mangla Reservoir** ⊞ NE Pakistan

159 *N9* **Mangnai** *var.* Lao Mangnai. Qinghai, C China *37°52′N 91°45′E*

Mango *see* Mago, Fiji

Mango *see* Sansanné-Mango, Togo

Mangoche *see* Mangochi

83 *N14* **Mangochi** *var.* Mangoche; *prev.* Fort Johnston. Southern, SE Malawi *14°30′S 35°15′E*

77 *N14* **Mangodara** SW Burkina *09°49′N 04°22′W*

172 *H6* **Mangoky** ≈ W Madagascar

171 *Q12* **Mangole, Pulau** *island* Kepulauan Sula, E Indonesia

184 *J2* **Mangonui** Northland, North Island, New Zealand *35°00′S 173°30′E*

Mangqystaū Oblysy *see* Mangystau

Mangqystaū Shyghanaghy *see* Mangystau Zaliv

Mangshi *see* Luxi

104 *H7* **Mangualde** Viseu, N Portugal *40°36′N 07°46′W*

61 *H18* **Mangueira, Lagoa** ◎ S Brazil

77 *X6* **Manguéni, Plateau du** ▲ NE Niger

163 *T4* **Mangui** Nei Mongol Zizhiqu, N China *52°02′N 122°13′E*

26 *K11* **Mangum** Oklahoma, C USA *34°52′N 99°30′W*

79 *O18* **Manguredjipa** Nord-Kivu, E Dem. Rep. Congo *0°28′N 28°33′E*

83 *L16* **Mangwendi** Mashonaland East, E Zimbabwe *18°22′S 31°24′E*

Mangyshlak, Plato *see* Mangystau, Plato

Mangyshlakskiy Zaliv *see* Mangystau Zaliv

Mangyshlaskaya *see* Mangystau

144 *F15* **Mangystau** *Kaz.* Mangqystaū Oblysy *prev.* Mangistau; *prev.* Mangyshlaskaya. ◈ *province* SW Kazakhstan

144 *F15* **Mangystau, Plato** *plateau* SW Kazakhstan

144 *E14* **Mangystau Zaliv** *Kaz.* Mangqystaū Shyghanaghy; *prev.* Mangyshlakskiy Zaliv. *gulf* SW Kazakhstan

162 *E7* **Manhan** *var.* Tögrög. Hovd, W Mongolia *47°24′N 92°06′E*

Manhan *see* Alag-Erdene

27 *O4* **Manhattan** Kansas, C USA *39°11′N 96°35′W*

99 *L21* **Manhay** Luxembourg, SE Belgium *50°13′N 05°43′E*

83 *L21* **Manhiça** *prev.* Vila de Manhiça. Maputo, S Mozambique *25°25′S 32°49′E*

83 *L21* **Manhoca** Maputo, S Mozambique *26°49′S 32°36′E*

59 *N20* **Manhuaçu** Minas Gerais, SE Brazil *20°16′S 42°01′W*

117 *W9* **Manhush** *prev.* Pershotravneve. Donets'ka Oblast', E Ukraine *47°03′N 37°20′E*

54 *H10* **Maní** Casanare, C Colombia *04°50′N 72°15′W*

143 *R11* **Mānī** Kermān, C Iran

83 *M17* **Manica** *var.* Vila de Manica. Manica, W Mozambique *18°56′S 32°52′E*

83 *M17* **Manica** *off.* Província de Manica. ◈ *province* W Mozambique

83 *L17* **Manicaland** ◈ *province* E Zimbabwe

Manica, Província de *see* Manica

15 *U5* **Manic Deux, Réservoir** ⊞ Québec, SE Canada

Manich *see* Manych

59 *F14* **Manicoré** Amazonas, N Brazil *05°48′S 61°16′W*

13 *N11* **Manicouagan** Québec, SE Canada *50°40′N 68°46′W*

13 *N11* **Manicouagan** ≈ Québec, SE Canada

15 *U6* **Manicouagan, Péninsule de** *peninsula* Québec, SE Canada

13 *N11* **Manicouagan, Réservoir** ◎ Québec, E Canada

15 *T4* **Manic Trois, Réservoir** ⊞ Québec, SE Canada

79 *M20* **Maniema** *off.* Région du Maniema. ◈ *region* E Dem. Rep. Congo

Maniema, Région du *see* Maniema

Maniewicze *see* Manevychi

160 *F8* **Maniganggo** Sichuan, C China *32°01′N 99°04′E*

11 *Y15* **Manigotagan** Manitoba, S Canada *51°06′N 96°18′W*

153 *R13* **Manihāri** Bihār, N India *25°21′N 87°37′E*

191 *U9* **Manihi** *island* Îles Tuamotu, C French Polynesia

190 *L13* **Manihiki** *atoll* N Cook Islands

175 *U8* **Manihiki Plateau** *undersea feature* C Pacific Ocean

196 *M14* **Maniitsoq** *var.* Manîtsoq, *Dan.* Sukkertoppen. ◈ Kitaa, S Greenland

153 *T15* **Manikganj** Dhaka, C Bangladesh *23°52′N 90°00′E*

152 *M14* **Mānikpur** Uttar Pradesh, N India *25°04′N 81°06′E*

171 *N4* **Manila** *off.* City of Manila. ● (Philippines) Luzon, N Philippines *14°34′N 120°59′E*

27 *Y9* **Manila** Arkansas, C USA *35°52′N 90°10′W*

Manila, City of *see* Manila

189 *N16* **Manila Reef** *reef* W Micronesia

183 *T6* **Manilla** New South Wales, SE Australia *30°44′S 150°43′E*

192 *P6* **Maniloa** *island* Tongatapu Group, S Tonga

123 *U8* **Manily** Krasnoyarskiy Kray, E Russian Federation *62°33′N 165°03′E*

171 *V12* **Manim, Pulau** *island* E Indonesia

168 *I11* **Maninjau, Danau** ◎ Sumatera, W Indonesia

153 *W13* **Manipur** ◈ *state* NE India

153 *X14* **Manipur Hills** *hill range* E India

136 *C14* **Manisa** *var.* Manissa, *prev.* Saruhan; *anc.* Magnesia. Manisa, W Turkey *38°36′N 27°29′E*

136 *C13* **Manisa** *var.* Manissa. ◈ *province* W Turkey

Manissa *see* Manisa

31 *O7* **Manistee** Michigan, N USA *44°14′N 86°19′W*

31 *P7* **Manistee River** ≈ Michigan, N USA

31 *O4* **Manistique** Michigan, N USA *45°57′N 86°15′W*

31 *P4* **Manistique Lake** ◎ Michigan, N USA

11 *W13* **Manitoba** ◈ *province* S Canada

11 *X16* **Manitoba, Lake** ◎ Manitoba, S Canada

11 *X17* **Manitou** Manitoba, S Canada *49°12′N 98°28′W*

31 *N2* **Manitou Island** *island* Michigan, N USA

14 *H11* **Manitou Lake** ◎ Ontario, SE Canada

12 *G15* **Manitoulin Island** *island* Ontario, S Canada

37 *T5* **Manitou Springs** Colorado, C USA *38°51′N 104°56′W*

14 *G12* **Manitouwabing Lake** ◎ Ontario, S Canada

12 *E12* **Manitouwadge** Ontario, S Canada *49°14′N 85°51′W*

12 *G15* **Manitowaning** Manitoulin Island, Ontario, S Canada *45°44′N 81°50′W*

14 *B7* **Manitowik Lake** ◎ Ontario, S Canada

31 *N7* **Manitowoc** Wisconsin, N USA *44°04′N 87°40′W*

Manîtsoq *see* Maniitsoq

139 *O7* **Mānī', Wādī al** *dry watercourse* W Iraq

12 *J14* **Maniwaki** Québec, SE Canada *46°22′N 75°58′W*

171 *W13* **Maniwori** Papua, E Indonesia *02°49′S 136°00′E*

54 *E10* **Manizales** Caldas, W Colombia *05°03′N 75°32′W*

112 *F11* **Manjača** ▲▲ NW Bosnia and Herzegovina

Manjacaze *see* Mandlakazi

180 *J14* **Manjimup** Western Australia *34°18′S 116°14′E*

109 *V4* **Mank** Niederösterreich, C Austria *48°06′N 15°13′E*

79 *I17* **Mankanza** Equateur, NW Dem. Rep. Congo *01°40′N 19°08′E*

153 *N12* **Mankāpur** Uttar Pradesh, N India *27°03′N 82°12′E*

26 *M3* **Mankato** Kansas, C USA *39°48′N 98°13′W*

29 *U10* **Mankato** Minnesota, N USA *44°10′N 94°00′W*

117 *O7* **Man'kivka** Cherkas'ka Oblast', C Ukraine *48°58′N 30°10′E*

76 *M15* **Mankono** C Ivory Coast *08°01′N 06°09′W*

11 *T17* **Mankota** Saskatchewan, S Canada *49°25′N 107°05′W*

155 *K23* **Mankulam** Northern Province, N Sri Lanka *09°07′N 80°27′E*

162 *L10* **Manlay** *var.* Üydzen. Ömnögovĭ, S Mongolia *44°08′N 106°48′E*

39 *Q9* **Manley Hot Springs** Alaska, USA *65°00′N 150°37′W*

18 *H10* **Manlius** New York, NE USA *43°00′N 75°58′W*

105 *W5* **Manlleu** Cataluña, NE Spain *41°59′N 02°17′E*

29 *V11* **Manly** Iowa, C USA *43°17′N 93°12′W*

154 *E13* **Manmād** Mahārāshtra, W India *20°15′N 74°29′E*

182 *J7* **Mannahill** South Australia *32°29′S 139°58′E*

155 *J23* **Mannar** *var.* Manar. Northern Province, NW Sri Lanka *09°01′N 79°53′E*

155 *I24* **Mannar, Gulf of** *gulf* India/Sri Lanka

155 *J23* **Mannar Island** *island* N Sri Lanka

Mannersdorf *see* Mannersdorf am Leithagebirge

109 *Y5* **Mannersdorf am Leithagebirge** *var.* Mannersdorf. Niederösterreich, E Austria *47°59′N 16°36′E*

109 *Y6* **Mannersdorf an der Rabnitz** Burgenland, E Austria *47°25′N 16°32′E*

101 *G20* **Mannheim** Baden-Württemberg, SW Germany *49°29′N 08°29′E*

11 *O12* **Manning** Alberta, W Canada *56°53′N 117°39′W*

29 *T14* **Manning** Iowa, C USA *41°54′N 95°03′W*

28 *K5* **Manning** North Dakota, N USA *47°15′N 102°48′W*

21 *S13* **Manning** South Carolina, SE USA *33°42′N 80°12′W*

191 *Y2* **Manning, Cape** *headland* Kiritimati, NE Kiribati *02°02′N 157°26′W*

21 *S3* **Mannington** West Virginia, NE USA *39°31′N 80°20′W*

182 *A1* **Mann Ranges** ▲▲ South Australia

107 *C19* **Mannu** ≈ Sardegna, Italy, C Mediterranean Sea

11 *R14* **Mannville** Alberta, SW Canada *53°19′N 111°08′W*

76 *J15* **Mano** ≈ Liberia/Sierra Leone

Manø *see* Mandø

61 *F15* **Manoel Viana** Rio Grande do Sul, S Brazil *29°33′S 55°28′W*

39 *O13* **Manokotak** Alaska, USA *59°00′N 158°58′W*

171 *V12* **Manokwari** Papua, E Indonesia *0°53′S 134°05′E*

79 *N22* **Manono** Shaba, SE Dem. Rep. Congo *07°18′S 27°25′E*

25 *T10* **Manor** Texas, SW USA *30°20′N 97°33′W*

97 *D16* **Manorhamilton** *Ir.* Cluainín. Leitrim, NW Ireland *54°18′N 08°10′W*

103 *S15* **Manosque** Alpes-de-Haute-Provence, SE France *43°50′N 05°47′E*

12 *L11* **Manouane, Lac** ◎ Québec, SE Canada

163 *W12* **Manp'o** *var.* Manp'ojin. NW North Korea *41°10′N 126°24′E*

Manp'ojin *see* Manp'o

191 *T4* **Manra** *prev.* Sydney Island. *atoll* Phoenix Islands, C Kiribati

105 *V5* **Manresa** Cataluña, NE Spain *41°43′N 01°50′E*

152 *H9* **Mānsa** Punjab, NW India *30°00′N 75°25′E*

82 *J12* **Mansa** *prev.* Fort Rosebery. Luapula, N Zambia *11°14′S 28°55′E*

76 *G12* **Mansa Konko** C Gambia *13°26′N 15°29′W*

15 *Q11* **Manseau** Québec, SE Canada *46°23′N 71°59′W*

149 *U5* **Mānsehra** Khyber Pakhtunkhwa, NW Pakistan *34°23′N 73°18′E*

9 *Q9* **Mansel Island** *island* Nunavut, NE Canada

183 *O12* **Mansfield** Victoria, SE Australia *37°04′S 146°06′E*

97 *M18* **Mansfield** C England, United Kingdom *53°09′N 01°11′W*

27 *S11* **Mansfield** Arkansas, C USA *35°03′N 94°15′W*

22 *G6* **Mansfield** Louisiana, S USA *32°02′N 93°42′W*

19 *O12* **Mansfield** Massachusetts, NE USA *42°00′N 71°11′W*

31 *T12* **Mansfield** Ohio, N USA *40°45′N 82°31′W*

18 *G12* **Mansfield** Pennsylvania, NE USA *41°46′N 77°02′W*

18 *M7* **Mansfield, Mount** ▲ Vermont, NE USA *44°31′N 72°49′W*

59 *M16* **Mansidão** Bahia, E Brazil *10°46′S 44°04′W*

102 *L11* **Mansle** Charente, W France *45°52′N 00°11′E*

76 *G12* **Mansôa** C Guinea-Bissau *12°08′N 15°18′W*

47 *V8* **Manso, Rio** ≈ C Brazil

Manşūra *see* Al Manşūrah

Mansurabad *see* Mehrān, Rūd-e

56 *A6* **Manta** Manabí, W Ecuador *0°59′S 80°44′W*

56 *A6* **Manta, Bahía de** *bay* W Ecuador

57 *F14* **Mantaro, Río** ≈ C Peru

35 *O8* **Manteca** California, W USA *37°48′N 121°13′W*

54 *J7* **Mantecal** Apure, C Venezuela *07°34′N 69°07′W*

31 *N11* **Manteno** Illinois, N USA *41°15′N 87°49′W*

21 *Y9* **Manteo** Roanoke Island, North Carolina, SE USA *35°54′N 75°42′W*

Mantes-Gassicourt *see* Mantes-la-Jolie

103 *N5* **Mantes-la-Jolie** *prev.* Mantes-Gassicourt, Mantes-sur-Seine; *anc.* Medunta. Yvelines, N France *48°59′N 01°43′E*

Mantes-sur-Seine *see* Mantes-la-Jolie

36 *L5* **Manti** Utah, W USA *39°16′N 111°38′W*

Mantinea *see* Mantíneia

115 *F20* **Mantíneia** *anc.* Mantinea. *site of ancient city* Pelopónnisos, S Greece

59 *M21* **Mantiqueira, Serra da** ▲▲ S Brazil

29 *W10* **Mantorville** Minnesota, N USA *44°04′N 92°45′W*

115 *G17* **Mantoúdi** *var.* Mandoudi; *prev.* Mandoúdhion. Évvoia, C Greece *38°47′N 23°29′E*

Mantoue *see* Mantova

106 *F8* **Mantova** *Eng.* Mantua, *Fr.* Mantoue. Lombardia, NW Italy *45°10′N 10°47′E*

93 *M19* **Mäntsälä** Etelä-Suomi, S Finland *60°38′N 25°21′E*

93 *L17* **Mänttä** Länsi-Suomi, W Finland *62°00′N 24°36′E*

Mantua *see* Mantova

125 *O14* **Manturovo** Kostromskaya Oblast', NW Russian Federation *58°19′N 44°42′E*

93 *M18* **Mäntyharju** Itä-Suomi, SE Finland *61°25′N 26°53′E*

92 *M13* **Mäntyjärvi** Lappi, N Finland *66°00′N 27°35′E*

190 *L16* **Manuae** *island* S Cook Islands

191 *Q10* **Manuae** *atoll* Îles Sous le Vent, W French Polynesia

192 *L16* **Manu'a Islands** *island group* E American Samoa

40 *L5* **Manuel Benavides** Chihuahua, N Mexico *29°07′N 103°52′W*

61 *D21* **Manuel J. Cobo** Buenos Aires, E Argentina *35°49′S 57°54′W*

58 *M12* **Manuel Luís, Recife** *reef* E Brazil

59 *I14* **Manuel Zinho** Pará, N Brazil *07°21′S 54°47′W*

191 *V11* **Manuhagi** *prev.* Manuhangi. *atoll* Îles Tuamotu, C French Polynesia

Manuhangi *see* Manuhagi

185 *E22* **Manuherikia** ≈ South Island, New Zealand

171 *P13* **Manui, Pulau** *island* N Indonesia

Manukau *see* Manurewa

184 *L6* **Manukau Harbour** *harbour* North Island, New Zealand

191 *Z2* **Manulu Lagoon** ◎ Kiritimati, E Kiribati

182 *J7* **Manunda Creek** *seasonal river* South Australia

57 *K15* **Manupari, Río** ≈ N Bolivia

184 *L6* **Manurewa** *var.* Manukau. Auckland, North Island, New Zealand *37°01′S 174°55′E*

57 *K15* **Manurimi, Río** ≈ NW Bolivia

186 *D5* **Manus** ◈ *province* N Papua New Guinea

186 *D5* **Manus Island** *var.* Great Admiralty Island. *island* N Papua New Guinea

171 *T16* **Manuwui** Pulau Babar, E Indonesia *07°47′S 129°39′E*

29 *Q3* **Manvel** North Dakota, N USA *48°07′N 97°15′W*

33 *Z14* **Manville** Wyoming, C USA *42°45′N 104°38′W*

22 *G6* **Many** Louisiana, S USA *31°34′N 93°28′W*

81 *H21* **Manyara, Lake** ◎ NE Tanzania

126 *L12* **Manych** *var.* Manich. ≈ SW Russian Federation

83 *H14* **Manyinga** North Western, NW Zambia *13°28′S 24°18′E*

105 *O11* **Manzanares** Castilla-La Mancha, C Spain *39°N 03°23′W*

44 *H7* **Manzanillo** Granma, E Cuba *20°21′N 77°07′W*

40 *K14* **Manzanillo** Colima, SW Mexico *19°00′N 104°19′W*

40 *K14* **Manzanillo, Bahía** *bay* SW Mexico

37 *S11* **Manzano Mountains** ▲▲ New Mexico, SW USA

37 *R12* **Manzano Peak** ▲ New Mexico, SW USA *34°35′N 106°27′W*

163 *R6* **Manzhouli** *var.* Man-chou-li. Nei Mongol Zizhiqu, N China *49°36′N 117°28′E*

Manzil Bū Ruqaybah *see* Menzel Bourguiba

139 *X9* **Manzilīyah** Maysān, E Iraq *32°26′N 47°01′E*

83 *L21* **Manzini** *prev.* Bremersdorp. C Swaziland *26°30′S 31°22′E*

83 *L21* **Manzini** ✈ (Mbabane) C Swaziland *26°36′S 31°25′E*

78 *G10* **Mao** Kanem, W Chad *14°06′N 15°17′E*

45 *N8* **Mao** NW Dominican Republic *19°37′N 71°04′W*

105 *Z9* **Maó** *Cast.* Mahón, *Eng.* Port Mahon; *anc.* Portus Magonis. Menorca, Spain, W Mediterranean Sea *39°54′N 04°15′E*

Maoemere *see* Maumere

159 *W9* **Maojing** Gansu, N China *36°26′N 106°36′E*

171 *Y14* **Maoke, Pegunungan** *Dut.* Sneeuw-gebergte, *Eng.* Snow Mountains. ▲▲ Papua, E Indonesia

Maol Réidh, Caoc *see* Mweelrea

160 *M15* **Maoming** Guangdong, S China *21°46′N 110°51′E*

160 *H8* **Maoxian** *var.* Mao Xian; *prev.* Fengyizhen. Sichuan, C China *31°42′N 103°48′E*

Mao Xian *see* Maoxian

83 *L19* **Mapai** Gaza, SW Mozambique *22°52′S 32°00′E*

158 *H15* **Mapam Yumco** ◎ W China

83 *I15* **Mapanza** Southern, S Zambia *16°16′S 26°54′E*

54 *J4* **Mapararí** Falcón, N Venezuela *10°52′N 69°27′W*

41 *U17* **Mapastepec** Chiapas, SE Mexico *15°28′N 93°00′W*

169 *V9* **Mapat, Pulau** *island* N Indonesia

171 *Y15* **Mapi** Papua, E Indonesia *07°02′S 139°24′E*

171 *V11* **Mapia, Kepulauan** *island group* E Indonesia

40 *L8* **Mapimí** Durango, C Mexico *25°50′N 103°50′W*

83 *N19* **Mapinhane** Inhambane, SE Mozambique *22°14′S 35°07′E*

55 *N7* **Mapire** Monagas, NE Venezuela *07°48′N 64°40′W*

11 *S17* **Maple Creek** Saskatchewan, S Canada *49°55′N 109°28′W*

31 *Q9* **Maple River** ≈ Michigan, N USA

29 *P7* **Maple River** ≈ North Dakota/South Dakota, N USA

29 *S13* **Mapleton** Iowa, C USA *42°10′N 95°47′W*

29 *U10* **Mapleton** Minnesota, N USA *43°55′N 93°57′W*

29 *R5* **Mapleton** North Dakota, N USA *46°51′N 97°04′W*

32 *F13* **Mapleton** Oregon, NW USA *44°01′N 123°56′W*

36 *L3* **Mapleton** Utah, W USA *40°07′N 111°37′W*

192 *K5* **Mapmaker Seamounts** *undersea feature* N Pacific Ocean *25°00′N 165°00′E*

186 *B6* **Maprik** East Sepik, NW Papua New Guinea *03°38′S 143°02′E*

83 *L21* **Maputo** *prev.* Lourenço Marques. ● (Mozambique) Maputo, S Mozambique *25°58′S 32°35′E*

83 *L21* **Maputo** ◈ *province* S Mozambique

67 *V14* **Maputo** ≈ S Mozambique

83 *L21* **Maputo** ✈ Maputo, S Mozambique *25°47′S 32°36′E*

Maqat *see* Makat

113 *M19* **Maqellarë** Dibër, C Albania *41°36′N 20°29′E*

159 *S12* **Maqên** *var.* Dawo; *prev.* Dawu. Qinghai, C China *34°32′N 100°17′E*

159 *S11* **Maqên Kangri** ▲ C China *34°44′N 99°25′E*

141 *X7* **Maqiz al Kurbá** N Oman *24°13′N 56°48′E*

159 *U12* **Maqu** *var.* Nyinma. Gansu, C China *34°02′N 102°00′E*

104 *M9* **Maqueda** Castilla-La Mancha, C Spain *40°04′N 04°22′W*

82 *B9* **Maquela do Zombo** Uíge, NW Angola *06°06′S 15°12′E*

63 *I16* **Maquinchao** Río Negro, C Argentina *41°19′S 68°47′W*

29 *Z13* **Maquoketa** Iowa, C USA *42°03′N 90°42′W*

29 *Y13* **Maquoketa River** ≈ Iowa, C USA

14 *F13* **Mar** Ontario, S Canada *44°48′N 81°12′W*

95 *F14* **Mår** ◎ S Norway

81 *G19* **Mara** ◈ *region* N Tanzania

58 *D12* **Maraã** Amazonas, NW Brazil *01°48′S 65°21′W*

191 *P8* **Maraa** Tahiti, W French Polynesia *17°44′S 149°34′W*

191 *O8* **Maraa, Pointe** *headland* Tahiti, W French Polynesia *17°44′S 149°34′W*

59 *K14* **Marabá** Pará, NE Brazil *05°23′S 49°10′W*

54 *H5* **Maracaibo** Zulia, NW Venezuela *10°40′N 71°39′W*

Maracaibo, Gulf of *see* Venezuela, Golfo de

54 *H5* **Maracaibo, Lago de** *var.* Lake Maracaibo. *inlet* NW Venezuela

Maracaibo, Lake *see* Maracaibo, Lago de

58 *K10* **Maracá, Ilha de** *island* NE Brazil

59 *H20* **Maracaju, Serra de** ▲▲ S Brazil

58 *I11* **Maracanaquará, Planalto** ▲ NE Brazil

54 *L5* **Maracay** Aragua, N Venezuela *10°15′N 67°36′W*

Marada *see* Marādah

75 *R9* **Marādah** *var.* Marada. N Libya *29°16′N 19°29′E*

77 *U12* **Maradi** Maradi, S Niger *13°30′N 07°05′E*

77 *U11* **Maradi** ◈ *department* S Niger

81 *E21* **Maragarazi** *var.* Muragarazi. ≈ Burundi/Tanzania

Maragha *see* Marāgheh

142 *J3* **Marāgheh** *var.* Maragha. Āžarbāyjān-e Khāvarī, NW Iran *37°21′N 46°14′E*

141 *P7* **Marāh** *var.* Marrāt. Ar Riyāḑ, C Saudi Arabia *25°04′N 45°30′E*

◆ Country ● Country Capital ◇ Dependent Territory ○ Dependent Territory Capital ◈ Administrative Regions ✈ International Airport ▲ Mountain ▲▲ Mountain Range Volcano ≈ River ◎ Lake ⊞ Reservoir

55 N11 Marahuaca, Cerro ▲ S Venezuela 03°37′N 65°25′W
27 R5 Marais des Cygnes River ≈ Kansas/Missouri, C USA
58 L11 Marajó, Baía de bay N Brazil
59 K12 Marajó, Ilha de island N Brazil
191 O2 Marakei atoll Tungaru, W Kiribati
Marakesh see Marrakech
81 I18 Maralal Rift Valley, C Kenya 01°05′N 36°42′E
83 G21 Maralaleng Kgalagadi, S Botswana 25°42′S 22°39′E
145 U8 Maraldy, Ozero ◎ NE Kazakhstan
182 C5 Maralinga South Australia 30°16′S 131°35′E
Máramarossziget see Sighetu Marmației
187 N9 Maramasike var. Small Malaita. island N Solomon Islands
Maramba see Livingstone
194 H3 Marambio Argentinian research station Antarctica 64°22′S 57°18′W
116 H9 Maramureș ◐ county NW Romania
36 L15 Marana Arizona, SW USA 32°24′N 111°12′W
105 P7 Marañchón Castilla-La Mancha, C Spain 41°02′N 02°11′W
142 J2 Marand var. Merend. Āžarbāyjān-e Sharqī, NW Iran 38°25′N 45°40′E
Marandellas see Marondera
58 L13 Maranhão off. Estado do Maranhão. ◐ state E Brazil
104 H10 Maranhão, Barragem do ⊠ C Portugal
Maranhão, Estado do see Maranhão
149 O11 Mārān, Koh-i ▲ SW Pakistan 29°24′N 66°50′E
106 J7 Marano, Laguna di lagoon NE Italy
56 E9 Marañón, Río ≈ N Peru
102 J10 Marans Charente-Maritime, W France 46°19′N 00°58′W
83 M20 Marão Inhambane, S Mozambique 24°15′S 34°09′E
185 B23 Mararoa ≈ South Island, New Zealand
Maraş/Marash see Kahramanmaraş
107 M19 Maratea Basilicata, S Italy 39°57′N 15°44′E
104 G11 Marateca Setúbal, S Portugal 38°34′N 08°40′W
115 B20 Marathiá, Akrotírio headland Zákynthos, Iónia Nisiá, Greece, C Mediterranean Sea 37°39′N 20°49′E
12 E12 Marathon Ontario, S Canada 48°44′N 86°23′W
23 Y17 Marathon Florida Keys, Florida, SE USA 24°42′N 81°05′W
24 L10 Marathon Texas, SW USA 30°10′N 103°14′W
Marathón see Marathónas
115 H19 Marathónas prev. Marathón. Attikí, C Greece 38°09′N 23°57′E
169 W9 Maratua, Pulau island N Indonesia
59 O18 Maraú Bahia, SE Brazil 14°07′S 39°02′W
143 R3 Marāveh Tappeh Golestān, N Iran 37°53′N 55°57′E
24 L11 Maravillas Creek ≈ Texas, SW USA
186 D8 Marawaka Eastern Highlands, C Papua New Guinea 06°56′S 145°54′E
171 Q7 Marawi Mindanao, S Philippines 07°59′N 124°16′E
Mārāzā see Qobustan
Marbat see Mirbāṭ
104 L16 Marbella Andalucía, S Spain 36°31′N 04°50′W
180 J7 Marble Bar Western Australia 21°13′S 119°48′E
36 L9 Marble Canyon canyon Arizona, SW USA
25 S10 Marble Falls Texas, SW USA 30°34′N 98°16′W
27 Y7 Marble Hill Missouri, C USA 37°18′N 89°58′W
33 T15 Marbleton Wyoming, C USA 42°31′N 110°06′W
Marburg see Marburg an der Lahn, Germany
Marburg see Maribor, Slovenia
101 H16 Marburg an der Lahn hist. Marburg. Hessen, W Germany 50°49′N 08°46′E
111 H23 Marcal ≈ W Hungary
42 G7 Marcala La Paz, SW Honduras 14°11′N 88°00′W
111 H24 Marcali Somogy, SW Hungary 46°33′N 17°29′E
83 A16 Marca, Ponta da headland SW Angola 16°31′S 11°42′E
59 I16 Marcelândia Mato Grosso, W Brazil 11°18′S 54°49′W
27 T3 Marceline Missouri, C USA 39°42′N 92°57′W
60 I13 Marcelino Ramos Rio Grande do Sul, S Brazil 27°31′S 51°57′W
55 Y12 Marcel, Mont ▲ S French Guiana 02°32′N 53°00′W
97 O19 March E England, United Kingdom 52°37′N 00°13′E
109 Z3 March var. Morava. ≈ C Europe see also Morava
March see Morava
106 I12 Marche Eng. Marches. ◐ region C Italy
103 N11 Marche cultural region C France
99 J21 Marche-en-Famenne Luxembourg, SE Belgium 50°13′N 05°21′E
104 K14 Marchena Andalucía, S Spain 37°20′N 05°24′W
57 B17 Marchena, Isla var. Bindloe Island. island Galapagos Islands, Ecuador, E Pacific Ocean
Marches see Marche
99 J20 Marchin Liège, E Belgium 50°30′N 05°17′E
181 S1 Marchinbar Island island Wessel Islands, Northern Territory, N Australia
62 L9 Mar Chiquita, Laguna ◎ C Argentina
103 Q10 Marcigny Saône-et-Loire, C France 46°16′N 04°04′E
23 W16 Marco Florida, SE USA 25°56′N 81°43′W
Marcodurum see Düren
59 O15 Marcolândia Pernambuco, E Brazil 07°21′S 40°40′W
106 I8 Marco Polo ✈ (Venezia) Veneto, NE Italy 45°30′N 12°21′E
Marcounda see Markounda
Marcq see Mark
116 M8 Mărculeşti Rus. Markuleshty. N Moldova 47°54′N 28°14′E
29 S12 Marcus Iowa, C USA 42°49′N 95°48′W
39 S11 Marcus Baker, Mount ▲ Alaska, USA 61°26′N 147°45′W
192 I5 Marcus Island var. Minami Tori Shima. island E Japan
18 K8 Marcy, Mount ▲ New York, NE USA 44°06′N 73°55′W
149 T5 Mardān Khyber Pakhtunkhwa, N Pakistan 34°14′N 71°59′E
63 N14 Mar del Plata Buenos Aires, E Argentina 38°S 57°32′W
137 Q16 Mardin Mardin, SE Turkey 37°19′N 40°43′E
137 Q16 Mardin ◐ province SE Turkey
137 Q16 Mardin Dağları ▲▲ SE Turkey
Mardzad see Hayrhandulaan
187 R17 Maré island Îles Loyauté, E New Caledonia
Marea Neagră see Black Sea
105 Z8 Mare de Déu del Toro var. El Toro. ▲ Menorca, Spain, W Mediterranean Sea 39°59′N 04°06′E
181 W4 Mareeba Queensland, NE Australia 17°03′S 145°30′E
96 G8 Maree, Loch ◎ N Scotland, United Kingdom
Mareeq see Mereeg
Marek see Dupnitsa
76 J11 Maréna Kayes, W Mali 14°36′N 10°57′W
190 I2 Marenanuka atoll Tungaru, W Kiribati
29 X14 Marengo Iowa, C USA 41°48′N 92°04′W
102 J11 Marennes Charente-Maritime, W France 45°47′N 01°04′W
107 G23 Marettimo, Isola island Isole Egadi, S Italy
24 K10 Marfa Texas, SW USA 30°19′N 104°03′W
57 P17 Marfil, Laguna ◎ E Bolivia
Marganets see Marhanets'
25 Q4 Margaret Texas, SW USA 34°00′N 99°38′W
180 I14 Margaret River Western Australia 33°58′S 115°10′E
186 C7 Margarima Southern Highlands, W Papua New Guinea 06°00′S 143°23′E
55 N4 Margarita, Isla de island N Venezuela
115 I25 Margarítes Kríti, Greece, E Mediterranean Sea 35°19′N 24°40′E
97 Q22 Margate prev. Mergate. SE England, United Kingdom 51°24′N 01°24′E
23 Z15 Margate Florida, SE USA 26°14′N 80°12′W
Margelan see Marg'ilon
103 P13 Margeride, Montagnes de la ▲▲ C France
Margherita see Jamaame
107 N16 Margherita di Savoia Puglia, SE Italy 41°23′N 16°09′E
Margherita, Lake see Ābaya Hāyk'
81 E18 Margherita Peak Fr. Pic Marguerite. ▲ Uganda/Dem. Rep. Congo 00°28′N 29°58′E
149 O4 Marghī Bāmyān, N Afghanistan 35°10′N 66°26′E
116 G9 Marghita Hung. Margitta. Bihor, NW Romania 47°20′N 22°20′E
Margilan see Marg'ilon
147 S10 Marg'ilon var. Margelan, Rus. Margilan. Farg'ona Viloyati, E Uzbekistan 40°29′N 71°43′E
116 K8 Marginea Suceava, NE Romania 47°49′N 25°47′E
Margitta see Marghita
148 K9 Mārgow, Dasht-e desert SW Afghanistan
99 L18 Margraten Limburg, SE Netherlands 50°49′N 05°49′E
10 M15 Marguerite British Columbia, SW Canada 52°17′N 122°10′W
15 V3 Marguerite ≈ Québec, SE Canada
194 I6 Marguerite Bay bay Antarctica
Marguerite, Pic see Margherita Peak
117 T9 Marhanets' Rus. Marganets. Dnipropetrovs'ka Oblast', E Ukraine 47°35′N 34°37′E
186 B9 Mari Western, SW Papua New Guinea 09°10′S 141°39′E
191 Y12 Maria atoll Groupe Actéon, SE French Polynesia
191 R12 Maria island Îles Australes, SW French Polynesia
40 I12 María Cleofas, Isla island C Mexico
62 H4 María Elena var. Oficina María Elena. Antofagasta, N Chile 22°18′S 69°40′W
95 G21 Mariager Midtjylland, C Denmark 56°39′N 09°59′E
61 C22 María Ignacia Buenos Aires, E Argentina 37°24′S 59°30′W
183 P17 Maria Island island Tasmania, SE Australia
40 H12 María Madre, Isla island C Mexico
40 I12 María Magdalena, Isla island C Mexico
192 H6 Mariana Islands island group Guam/Northern Mariana Islands
175 N3 Mariana Trench var. Challenger Deep. undersea feature W Pacific Ocean 15°00′N 147°30′E
153 X12 Mariāni Assam, NE India 26°39′N 94°18′E
27 X11 Marianna Arkansas, C USA 34°46′N 90°49′W
23 R8 Marianna Florida, SE USA 30°46′N 85°13′W
172 J16 Marianne island Inner Islands, NE Seychelles
95 M19 Mariannelund Jönköping, S Sweden 57°37′N 15°33′E
61 D15 Mariano I. Loza Corrientes, NE Argentina 29°22′S 58°12′W
Mariano Machado see Ganda
111 A16 Mariánské Lázně Ger. Marienbad. Karlovarský Kraj, W Czech Republic 49°57′N 12°43′E
Máriaradna see Radna
33 S7 Marias River ≈ Montana, NW USA
Maria-Theresiopel see Subotica
Máriatölgyes see Dubnica nad Váhom
184 H1 Maria van Diemen, Cape headland North Island, New Zealand 34°27′S 172°38′E
109 V5 Mariazell Steiermark, E Austria 47°47′N 15°20′E
141 P15 Ma'rib W Yemen 15°28′N 45°25′E
95 I25 Maribo Sjælland, S Denmark 54°47′N 11°30′E
109 W9 Maribor Ger. Marburg. NE Slovenia 46°34′N 15°40′E
Marica see Maritsa
35 R13 Maricopa California, W USA 35°03′N 119°24′W
Maricourt see Kangiqsujuaq
81 D15 Maridi Western Equatoria, SW South Sudan 04°55′N 29°30′E
194 M11 Marie Byrd Land physical region Antarctica
193 P14 Marie Byrd Seamount undersea feature N Amundsen Sea 70°00′S 118°00′W
45 X11 Marie-Galante var. Ceyre to the Caribs. island SE Guadeloupe
45 Y6 Marie-Galante, Canal de channel S Guadeloupe
93 J20 Mariehamn Fin. Maarianhamina. Åland, SW Finland 60°05′N 19°55′E
44 C4 Mariel La Habana, W Cuba 23°02′N 82°44′W
99 H22 Mariembourg Namur, S Belgium 50°07′N 04°30′E
Marienbad see Mariánské Lázně
Marienburg see Alūksne, Latvia
Marienburg see Malbork, Poland
Marienburg see Feldioara, Romania
Marienburg in Westpreussen see Malbork
Marienhausen see Viļaka
83 D20 Mariental Hardap, SW Namibia 24°35′S 17°56′E
18 D13 Marienville Pennsylvania, NE USA 41°27′N 79°07′W
Marienwerder see Kwidzyń
58 C12 Marié, Rio ≈ NW Brazil
95 K17 Mariestad Västra Götaland, S Sweden 58°42′N 13°50′E
23 S3 Marietta Georgia, SE USA 33°57′N 84°34′W
31 U14 Marietta Ohio, N USA 39°25′N 81°27′W
27 N13 Marietta Oklahoma, C USA 33°57′N 97°08′W
81 H18 Marigat Rift Valley, W Kenya 0°29′S 35°59′E
103 S16 Marignane Bouches-du-Rhône, SE France 43°25′N 05°12′E
Marignano see Melegnano
45 O11 Marigot NE Dominica 15°32′N 61°18′W
122 K12 Mariinsk Kemerovskaya Oblast', S Russian Federation 56°13′N 87°27′E
127 Q3 Mariinskiy Posad Respublika Mariy El, W Russian Federation 56°07′N 47°44′E
119 E14 Marijampolė prev. Kapsukas. Marijampolė, S Lithuania 54°33′N 23°21′E
Marikostenovo see Marikostinovo
114 G12 Marikostinovo prev. Marikostenovo. Blagoevgrad, SW Bulgaria 41°25′N 23°21′E
60 J9 Marília São Paulo, S Brazil 22°13′S 49°58′W
82 D11 Marimba Malanje, NW Angola 08°18′S 16°58′E
139 T1 Marī Mīlā Arbīl, E Iraq 36°58′N 44°42′E
104 G4 Marín Galicia, NW Spain 42°23′N 08°43′W
35 N10 Marina California, W USA 36°40′N 121°48′W
Mar'ina Gorka see Mar"ina Horka
119 L17 Mar"ina Horka Rus. Mar'ina Gorka. Minskaya Voblasts', C Belarus 53°31′N 28°09′E
171 O4 Marinduque island C Philippines
31 S9 Marine City Michigan, N USA 42°43′N 82°29′W
31 N6 Marinette Wisconsin, N USA 45°06′N 87°38′W
60 I10 Maringá Paraná, S Brazil 23°26′S 51°55′W
83 N16 Maringuè Sofala, C Mozambique 17°57′S 34°23′E
104 F9 Marinha Grande Leiria, C Portugal 39°45′N 08°55′W
107 I15 Marino Lazio, C Italy 41°46′N 12°40′E
59 A15 Mário Lobão Acre, W Brazil 08°21′S 72°58′W
23 O5 Marion Alabama, S USA 32°37′N 87°19′W
27 Y11 Marion Arkansas, C USA 35°12′N 90°12′W
30 L17 Marion Illinois, N USA 37°43′N 88°55′W
31 P13 Marion Indiana, N USA 40°32′N 85°40′W
29 X13 Marion Iowa, C USA 42°01′N 91°36′W
27 O5 Marion Kansas, C USA 38°22′N 97°02′W
20 H6 Marion Kentucky, S USA 37°19′N 88°06′W
21 P9 Marion North Carolina, SE USA 35°43′N 82°00′W
31 S12 Marion Ohio, N USA 40°35′N 83°08′W
21 T12 Marion South Carolina, SE USA 34°11′N 79°23′W
21 Q7 Marion Virginia, NE USA 36°51′N 81°30′W
27 O5 Marion Lake ⊠ Kansas, C USA
21 S13 Marion, Lake ⊠ South Carolina, SE USA
27 S8 Marionville Missouri, C USA 37°00′N 93°38′W
55 N7 Maripa Bolívar, E Venezuela 07°27′N 65°10′W
55 X11 Maripasoula W French Guiana 03°43′N 54°04′W
35 Q9 Mariposa California, W USA 37°28′N 119°59′W
61 G19 Mariscala Lavalleja, S Uruguay 34°03′S 54°47′W
62 M4 Mariscal Estigarribia Boquerón, NW Paraguay 22°03′S 60°39′W
56 C6 Mariscal Sucre var. Quito. ✈ (Quito) Pichincha, C Ecuador 0°21′S 78°37′W
30 K16 Marissa Illinois, N USA 38°15′N 89°45′W
103 U14 Maritime Alps Fr. Alpes Maritimes, It. Alpi Marittime. ▲▲ France/Italy
Maritimes, Alpes see Maritime Alps
Maritime Territory see Primorskiy Kray
114 K11 Maritsa var. Marica, Gk. Évros, Turk. Meriç; anc. Hebrus. ≈ SW Europe see also Évros/Meriç
Maritsa see Simeonovgrad, Bulgaria
Marittime, Alpi see Maritime Alps
Maritzburg see Pietermaritzburg
117 X9 Mariupol' prev. Zhdanov. Donets'ka Oblast', SE Ukraine 47°06′N 37°34′E
55 Q6 Mariusa, Caño ≈ NE Venezuela
142 J5 Marīvān prev. Dezh Shāhpūr. Kordestān, W Iran 35°30′N 46°09′E
127 R3 Mariyets Respublika Mariy El, W Russian Federation 56°31′N 49°48′E
118 G4 Märjamaa Ger. Merjama. Raplamaa, NW Estonia 58°54′N 24°21′E
99 I15 Mark Fr. Marcq. ≈ Belgium/Netherlands
81 N17 Marka var. Merca. Shabeellaha Hoose, S Somalia 01°43′N 44°45′E
145 Z10 Markakol', Ozero Kaz. Marqakōl. ◎ E Kazakhstan
76 M12 Markala Ségou, W Mali 13°38′N 06°07′W
159 S15 Markam var. Gartog. Xizang Zizhiqu, W China 29°40′N 98°33′E
95 K21 Markaryd Kronoberg, S Sweden 56°26′N 13°35′E
142 L7 Markazī off. Ostān-e Markazī. ◐ province W Iran
Markazī, Ostān-e see Markazī
14 F14 Markdale Ontario, S Canada 44°19′N 80°37′W
27 X10 Marked Tree Arkansas, C USA 35°31′N 90°25′W
98 N11 Markelo Overijssel, E Netherlands 52°15′N 06°30′E
98 J9 Markermeer ◎ C Netherlands
97 N20 Market Harborough C England, United Kingdom 52°30′N 00°57′W
97 N18 Market Rasen E England, United Kingdom 53°23′N 00°21′W
123 O10 Markha ≈ NE Russian Federation
12 H16 Markham Ontario, S Canada 43°54′N 79°16′W
25 V12 Markham Texas, SW USA 28°57′N 96°04′W
186 E7 Markham ≈ C Papua New Guinea
195 Q11 Markham, Mount ▲ Antarctica 82°58′S 163°30′E
110 M11 Marki Mazowieckie, C Poland 52°20′N 21°07′E
158 F8 Markit Xinjiang Uygur Zizhiqu, NW China 38°55′N 77°40′E
117 Y5 Markivka Rus. Markovka. Luhans'ka Oblast', E Ukraine 49°34′N 39°35′E
35 Q7 Markleeville California, W USA 38°41′N 119°46′W
98 L8 Marknesse Flevoland, N Netherlands 52°44′N 05°54′E
79 H14 Markounda var. Marcounda. Ouham, NW Central African Republic 07°38′N 17°00′E
Markovka see Markivka
123 U7 Markovo Chukotskiy Avtonomnyy Okrug, NE Russian Federation 64°43′N 170°13′E
127 P8 Marks Saratovskaya Oblast', W Russian Federation 51°40′N 46°44′E
22 K2 Marks Mississippi, S USA 34°15′N 90°16′W
22 I7 Marksville Louisiana, S USA 31°07′N 92°04′W
101 I19 Marktheidenfeld Bayern, C Germany 49°50′N 09°36′E
101 J24 Marktoberdorf Bayern, S Germany 47°45′N 10°36′E
101 M18 Marktredwitz Bayern, E Germany 50°N 12°04′E
Markt-Übelbach see Übelbach
27 V3 Mark Twain Lake ⊠ Missouri, C USA
Markuleshty see Mărculeşti
101 E14 Marl Nordrhein-Westfalen, W Germany 51°38′N 07°06′E
182 E2 Marla South Australia 27°19′S 133°35′E
181 Y8 Marlborough Queensland, E Australia 22°55′S 150°07′E
97 M22 Marlborough S England, United Kingdom 51°25′N 01°45′W
185 I15 Marlborough off. Marlborough District. ◐ unitary authority South Island, New Zealand
Marlborough District see Marlborough
103 P3 Marle Aisne, N France 49°44′N 03°47′E
31 S8 Marlette Michigan, N USA 43°20′N 83°05′W
25 T9 Marlin Texas, SW USA 31°20′N 96°55′W
21 S5 Marlinton West Virginia, NE USA 38°14′N 80°06′W
26 M12 Marlow Oklahoma, C USA 34°39′N 97°57′W
155 E17 Marmagao Goa, W India 15°26′N 73°50′E
Marmanda see Marmande
102 L13 Marmande anc. Marmanda. Lot-et-Garonne, SW France 44°30′N 00°10′E
136 C11 Marmara Balıkesir, NW Turkey 40°36′N 27°34′E
136 D11 Marmara Denizi Eng. Sea of Marmara. sea NW Turkey
114 N13 Marmaraereğlisi Tekirdağ, NW Turkey 40°59′N 27°57′E
Marmara, Sea of see Marmara Denizi
136 C16 Marmaris Muğla, SW Turkey 36°52′N 28°17′E
28 J6 Marmarth North Dakota, N USA 46°17′N 103°55′W
21 Q5 Marmet West Virginia, NE USA 38°12′N 81°31′W
106 H5 Marmolada, Monte ▲ N Italy 46°36′N 11°58′E
104 M13 Marmolejo Andalucía, S Spain 38°03′N 04°10′W
14 J14 Marmora Ontario, SE Canada 44°29′N 77°40′W
39 Q14 Marmot Bay bay Alaska, USA
103 Q4 Marne ◐ department N France
103 Q4 Marne ≈ N France
137 U10 Marneuli prev. Borchalo, Sarvani. S Georgia 41°28′N 44°45′E
78 I13 Maro Moyen-Chari, S Chad 08°25′N 18°46′E
54 L12 Maroa Amazonas, S Venezuela 02°40′N 67°33′W
172 J3 Maroantsetra Toamasina, NE Madagascar 15°23′S 49°44′E
191 W11 Marokau atoll Îles Tuamotu, C French Polynesia
172 J5 Marolambo Toamasina, E Madagascar 20°03′S 48°08′E
172 J2 Maromokotro ▲ N Madagascar
83 L16 Marondera prev. Marandellas. Mashonaland East, NE Zimbabwe 18°11′S 31°33′E
55 X9 Maroni Dut. Marowijne. ≈ French Guiana/Surinam
183 V2 Maroochydore-Mooloolaba Queensland, E Australia 26°36′S 153°04′E
171 N14 Maros Sulawesi, C Indonesia 04°59′S 119°35′E
116 H11 Maros var. Mureş, Mureşul, Ger. Marosch, Mieresch. ≈ Hungary/Romania see also Mureş
Marosch see Maros/Mureş
Marosheviz see Toplița
Marosillye see Ilia
Marosludas see Luduş
Marosújvár/Marosújvárakna see Ocna Mureş
Marosvásárhely see Târgu Mureş
191 V14 Marotiri var. Îlots de Bass, Morotiri. island group Îles Australes, SW French Polynesia
78 G12 Maroua Extrême-Nord, N Cameroon 10°35′N 14°20′E
55 X12 Marouini Rivier ≈ SE Surinam
172 I3 Marovoay Mahajanga, NW Madagascar 16°05′S 46°40′E
55 W9 Marowijne ◐ district NE Surinam
Marowijne see Maroni
Marqakōl see Markakol', Ozero
193 P8 Marquesas Fracture Zone tectonic feature E Pacific Ocean
Marquesas Islands see Marquises, Îles
23 W17 Marquesas Keys island group Florida, SE USA
29 Y12 Marquette Iowa, C USA 43°02′N 91°10′W
31 N3 Marquette Michigan, N USA 46°32′N 87°24′W
103 N1 Marquise Pas-de-Calais, N France 50°49′N 01°42′E
191 X7 Marquises, Îles Eng. Marquesas Islands. island group N French Polynesia
183 Q6 Marra Creek ≈ New South Wales, SE Australia
80 B10 Marra Hills plateau W Sudan
80 B11 Marra, Jebel ▲ W Sudan 12°59′N 24°16′E
74 E7 Marrakech var. Marakesh, Eng. Marrakesh; prev. Morocco. W Morocco 31°39′N 07°58′W
Marrakesh see Marrakech
Marrāt see Marāh
183 N15 Marrawah Tasmania, SE Australia 40°56′S 144°41′E
182 I4 Marree South Australia 29°40′S 138°06′E
81 L17 Marrehan ▲ SW Somalia
83 N17 Marromeu Sofala, C Mozambique 18°18′S 35°58′E
104 J17 Marroquí, Punta headland SW Spain 36°01′N 05°39′W
183 N8 Marrowie Creek seasonal river New South Wales, SE Australia
83 O14 Marrupa Niassa, N Mozambique 13°10′S 37°30′E
182 D1 Marryat South Australia 26°22′S 133°22′E
75 Y10 Marsā al 'Alam var. Marsa 'Alam. SE Egypt 25°03′N 33°44′E
Marsa 'Alam see Marsā al 'Alam
75 R8 Marsá al Burayqah var. Al Burayqah. N Libya 30°21′N 19°37′E
81 J17 Marsabit Eastern, N Kenya 02°20′N 37°59′E
107 H23 Marsala anc. Lilybaeum. Sicilia, Italy, C Mediterranean Sea 37°48′N 12°26′E
75 U7 Marsā Maṭrūḥ var. Matrûh; anc. Paraetonium. NW Egypt 31°21′N 27°15′E
Marsaxlokk Bay see Il-Bajja ta' Marsaxlokk
65 G15 Mars Bay bay Ascension Island, C Atlantic Ocean
101 H15 Marsberg Nordrhein-Westfalen, W Germany 51°28′N 08°51′E
11 R15 Marsden Saskatchewan, S Canada 52°50′N 109°45′W
98 H7 Marsdiep strait NW Netherlands
103 R16 Marseille Eng. Marseilles; anc. Massilia. Bouches-du-Rhône, SE France 43°19′N 05°22′E
Marseille-Marigrane see Provence
30 M11 Marseilles Illinois, N USA 41°19′N 88°42′W
Marseilles see Marseille
76 J16 Marshall W Liberia 06°10′N 10°23′W
39 N11 Marshall Alaska, USA 61°52′N 162°04′W
27 U9 Marshall Arkansas, C USA 35°54′N 92°40′W
31 N14 Marshall Illinois, N USA 39°23′N 87°41′W
31 Q10 Marshall Michigan, N USA 42°16′N 84°57′W
29 S9 Marshall Minnesota, N USA 44°26′N 95°48′W
27 T4 Marshall Missouri, C USA 39°07′N 93°12′W
21 O9 Marshall North Carolina, SE USA 35°48′N 82°43′W
25 X6 Marshall Texas, SW USA 32°33′N 94°22′W
189 S4 Marshall Islands off. Republic of the Marshall Islands. ◆ republic W Pacific Ocean
175 Q3 Marshall Islands island group W Pacific Ocean
Marshall Islands, Republic of the see Marshall Islands
192 K6 Marshall Seamounts undersea feature SW Pacific Ocean 10°00′N 165°00′E
29 W13 Marshalltown Iowa, C USA 42°01′N 92°54′W
19 P12 Marshfield Massachusetts, NE USA 42°04′N 70°40′W
27 T7 Marshfield Missouri, C USA 37°20′N 92°55′W
30 K6 Marshfield Wisconsin, N USA 44°41′N 90°12′W
44 H1 Marsh Harbour Great Abaco, W Bahamas 26°31′N 77°03′W
19 S3 Mars Hill Maine, NE USA 46°31′N 67°51′W
21 P9 Mars Hill North Carolina, SE USA 35°49′N 82°33′W
22 H10 Marsh Island island Louisiana, S USA
21 S11 Marshville North Carolina, SE USA 34°59′N 80°22′W
15 W5 Marsoui Québec, SE Canada 49°12′N 65°58′W
15 R8 Mars, Rivière à ≈ Québec, SE Canada
95 O15 Märsta Stockholm, C Sweden 59°37′N 17°52′E
95 H24 Marstal Syddtjylland, C Denmark 54°52′N 10°32′E
95 I19 Marstrand Västra Götaland, S Sweden 57°54′N 11°31′E
25 U8 Mart Texas, SW USA 31°32′N 96°49′W
Martaban see Mottama
Martaban, Gulf of see Mottama, Gulf of
107 Q19 Martano Puglia, SE Italy 40°12′N 18°19′E
Martapoera see Martapura
169 T13 Martapura prev. Martapoera. Borneo, C Indonesia 03°25′S 114°51′E
99 L23 Martelange Luxembourg, SE Belgium 49°50′N 05°43′E
114 L7 Marten Ruse, N Bulgaria 43°57′N 26°08′E
14 H10 Marten River Ontario, S Canada 46°43′N 79°45′W
11 T15 Martensville Saskatchewan, S Canada 52°15′N 106°42′W
Marteskirch see Târnăveni
Martes Tolosane see Martres-Tolosane
115 K25 Mártha Kríti, Greece, E Mediterranean Sea 35°03′N 25°22′E
183 Q6 Marthaguy Creek ≈ New South Wales, SE Australia
19 P13 Martha's Vineyard island Massachusetts, NE USA
108 C11 Martigny Valais, SW Switzerland 46°06′N 07°04′E
103 R16 Martigues Bouches-du-Rhône, SE France 43°24′N 05°03′E
111 J19 Martin Ger. Sankt Martin, Hung. Turócszentmárton; prev. Turčianský Svätý Martin. Žilinský Kraj, N Slovakia 49°03′N 18°54′E
28 L11 Martin South Dakota, N USA 43°10′N 101°43′W
20 G8 Martin Tennessee, S USA 36°20′N 88°51′W
105 S7 Martín ≈ E Spain
107 P18 Martina Franca Puglia, SE Italy 40°42′N 17°20′E
185 M14 Martinborough Wellington, North Island, New Zealand 41°12′S 175°28′E
25 S11 Martindale Texas, SW USA 29°49′N 97°49′W
35 N8 Martinez California, W USA 38°00′N 122°12′W
23 V3 Martinez Georgia, SE USA 33°31′N 82°04′W
41 Q13 Martínez de La Torre Veracruz-Llave, E Mexico 20°05′N 97°02′W
45 Y12 Martinique ◇ French overseas department E West Indies
1 O15 Martinique island E West Indies
Martinique Channel see Martinique Passage
45 X12 Martinique Passage var. Dominica Channel, Martinique Channel. channel Dominica/Martinique
23 Q5 Martin Lake ⊠ Alabama, S USA
115 G18 Martíno prev. Martínon. Stereá Elláda, C Greece 38°34′N 23°13′E
Martínon see Martíno
194 J11 Martin Peninsula peninsula Antarctica
39 S5 Martin Point headland Alaska, USA 70°06′N 143°04′W
109 V3 Martinsberg Niederösterreich, NE Austria 48°23′N 15°09′E
21 V3 Martinsburg West Virginia, NE USA 39°28′N 77°59′W
31 V13 Martins Ferry Ohio, N USA 40°06′N 80°43′W
Martinskirch see Târnăveni
31 O14 Martinsville Indiana, N USA 39°25′N 86°25′W
21 S8 Martinsville Virginia, NE USA 36°43′N 79°53′W
65 K16 Martin Vaz, Ilhas island group E Brazil
144 I9 Martok prev. Martuk. Aktyubinsk, NW Kazakhstan 50°45′N 56°30′E
184 M12 Marton Manawatu-Wanganui, North Island, New Zealand 40°05′S 175°22′E
105 N13 Martos Andalucía, S Spain 37°44′N 03°58′W
102 M16 Martres-Tolosane var. Martes Tolosane. Haute-Garonne, S France 43°13′N 01°00′E
92 M11 Martti Lappi, NE Finland 67°28′N 28°20′E
Martuk see Martok
137 U12 Martuni E Armenia 40°07′N 45°20′E
58 L11 Marudá Pará, E Brazil 05°25′S 49°04′W
169 V6 Marudu, Teluk bay East Malaysia
149 O8 Ma'rūf Kandahār, SE Afghanistan 31°34′N 67°06′E
164 H13 Marugame Kagawa, Shikoku, SW Japan 34°17′N 133°46′E
185 H16 Maruia ≈ South Island, New Zealand
98 M6 Marum Groningen, NE Netherlands 53°07′N 06°16′E
187 R13 Marum, Mount ▲ Ambrym, C Vanuatu 16°15′S 168°07′E
79 P23 Marungu ▲▲ SE Dem. Rep. Congo
191 Y12 Marutea atoll Groupe Actéon, C French Polynesia
143 O11 Marv Dasht var. Mervdasht. Fārs, S Iran 29°50′N 52°40′E
103 P13 Marvejols Lozère, S France 44°35′N 03°16′E
27 X12 Marvell Arkansas, C USA 34°33′N 90°52′W
36 L6 Marvine, Mount ▲ Utah, W USA 38°40′N 111°38′W
139 Q7 Marwānīyah Al Anbār, C Iraq 33°58′N 42°31′E
152 F13 Mārwār var. Kharchi, Marwar Junction. Rājasthān, N India 25°41′N 73°42′E
Marwar Junction see Mārwār
11 R14 Marwayne Alberta, SW Canada 53°30′N 110°25′W
146 I14 Mary prev. Merv. Mary Welaýaty, S Turkmenistan 37°25′N 61°48′E
Mary see Mary Welaýaty
181 Z9 Maryborough Queensland, E Australia 25°32′S 152°36′E
182 M11 Maryborough Victoria, SE Australia 37°05′S 143°47′E
Maryborough see Port Laoise
83 G23 Marydale Northern Cape, W South Africa 29°25′S 22°06′E
117 W8 Mar"yinka Donets'ka Oblast', E Ukraine 47°57′N 37°27′E
Mary Island see Kanton
21 W4 Maryland off. State of Maryland, also known as America in Miniature, Cockade State, Free State, Old Line State. ◐ state NE USA
Maryland, State of see Maryland
25 P7 Maryneal Texas, SW USA 32°12′N 100°25′W
97 J15 Maryport NW England, United Kingdom 54°45′N 03°28′W
13 U13 Marystown Newfoundland, Newfoundland and Labrador, SE Canada 47°10′N 55°10′W
36 K6 Marysvale Utah, W USA 38°26′N 112°14′W
35 O6 Marysville California, W USA 39°07′N 121°35′W
27 O3 Marysville Kansas, C USA 39°48′N 96°37′W
31 S13 Marysville Michigan, N USA 42°54′N 82°29′W
31 S9 Marysville Ohio, NE USA 40°13′N 83°22′W
32 H7 Marysville Washington, NW USA 48°03′N 122°10′W
27 R2 Maryville Missouri, C USA 40°20′N 94°53′W
21 N9 Maryville Tennessee, S USA 35°45′N 83°59′W
146 I15 Mary Welaýaty var. Mary, Rus. Maryyskiy Velayat. ◐ province S Turkmenistan
Maryyskiy Velayat see Mary Welaýaty
Marzūq see Murzuq
42 J11 Masachapa var. Puerto Masachapa. Managua, W Nicaragua 11°47′N 86°31′W
81 G19 Masai Mara National Reserve reserve C Kenya
81 I21 Masai Steppe grassland NW Tanzania
81 F19 Masaka SW Uganda 0°20′S 31°46′E
169 T15 Masalembo Besar, Pulau island S Indonesia
137 Y13 Masallı Rus. Masally. S Azerbaijan 39°03′N 48°39′E
Masally see Masallı
171 N13 Masamba Sulawesi, C Indonesia 02°33′S 120°20′E
Masampo see Masan
163 Y16 Masan prev. Masampo. S South Korea 35°11′N 128°36′E
Masandam Peninsula see Musandam Peninsula
81 J25 Masasi Mtwara, SE Tanzania 10°43′S 38°48′E
Masawa/Massawa see Mits'iwa
42 J10 Masaya Masaya, W Nicaragua 11°59′N 86°06′W
42 J10 Masaya ◐ department W Nicaragua
171 P5 Masbate Masbate, N Philippines 12°21′N 123°34′E
171 P5 Masbate island C Philippines
74 J6 Mascara var. Mouaskar. NW Algeria 35°20′N 00°09′E
173 O7 Mascarene Basin undersea feature W Indian Ocean 15°00′S 56°00′E
173 O9 Mascarene Islands island group W Indian Ocean
173 N9 Mascarene Plain undersea feature W Indian Ocean 19°00′S 52°00′E
173 O7 Mascarene Plateau undersea feature W Indian Ocean 10°00′S 60°00′E
194 H5 Mascart, Cape headland Adelaide Island, Antarctica
62 J10 Mascasín, Salinas de salt lake C Argentina
40 K13 Mascota Jalisco, C Mexico 20°31′N 104°46′W
15 O12 Mascouche Québec, SE Canada 45°46′N 73°37′W
124 J9 Masel'gskaya Respublika Kareliya, NW Russian Federation 63°09′N 34°22′E
83 J23 Maseru ● (Lesotho) W Lesotho 29°21′S 27°35′E
83 J23 Maseru ✈ W Lesotho 29°27′S 27°37′E
Mashaba see Mashava
160 K14 Mashan var. Baishan. Guangxi Zhuangzu Zizhiqu, S China 23°40′N 108°10′E
83 K17 Mashava prev. Mashaba. Masvingo, SE Zimbabwe 20°03′S 30°29′E
143 U4 Mashhad var. Meshed. Khorāsān-Razavī, NE Iran 36°16′N 59°34′E
165 S3 Mashike Hokkaidō, NE Japan 43°51′N 141°30′E

83 K20 **Mashishing** *prev.* Lydenburg. Mpumalanga, NE South Africa 25°10′S 30°29′E
Mashīz *see* Bardsīr
149 N14 **Mashkai** ∽ SW Pakistan
143 X13 **Māshkel** *var.* Rūd-i Māshkel, Rūd-e Māshkīd. ∽ Iran/Pakistan
148 K12 **Māshkel, Hāmūn-i** *salt marsh* SW Pakistan
Māshkel, Rūd-i/Māshkīd, Rūd-e *see* Māshkel
83 K15 **Mashonaland Central** ◈ *province* N Zimbabwe
83 K16 **Mashonaland East** ◈ *province* NE Zimbabwe
83 J16 **Mashonaland West** ◈ *province* NW Zimbabwe
Mashtagi *see* Maştağa
141 S14 **Masīlah, Wādī al** *dry watercourse* SE Yemen
79 I21 **Masi-Manimba** Bandundu, SW Dem. Rep. Congo 04°47′S 17°54′E
81 F17 **Masindi** W Uganda 01°41′N 31°45′E
81 I19 **Masinga Reservoir** ⊠ S Kenya
Masīra *see* Maşīrah, Jazīrat
Masira, Gulf of *see* Maşīrah, Khalīj
141 Y10 **Maşīrah, Jazīrat** *var.* Masīra. *island* E Oman
141 Y10 **Maşīrah, Khalīj** *var.* Gulf of Masira. *bay* E Oman
Masis *see* Büyükağrı Dağı
79 O19 **Masisi** Nord-Kivu, E Dem. Rep. Congo 01°25′S 28°50′E
Masjed-e Soleymān *see* Masjed Soleymān
142 L9 **Masjed Soleymān** *var.* Masjed-e Soleymān, Masjid-i Sulaiman. Khūzestān, SW Iran 31°59′N 49°18′E
Masjid-i Sulaiman *see* Masjed Soleymān
Maskat *see* Masqaţ
139 Q7 **Maskhān** Al Anbār, C Iraq 33°41′N 42°46′E
141 X8 **Maskin** *var.* Miskin. NW Oman 23°28′N 56°46′E
97 B17 **Mask, Lough** *Ir.* Loch Measca. ◎ W Ireland
114 N10 **Maslen Nos** *headland* E Bulgaria 42°19′N 27°47′E
172 K3 **Masoala, Tanjona** *headland* NE Madagascar 15°59′S 50°13′E
Masohi *see* Amahai
31 Q9 **Mason** Michigan, N USA 42°33′N 84°25′W
31 R14 **Mason** Ohio, N USA 39°21′N 84°18′W
25 Q10 **Mason** Texas, SW USA 30°45′N 99°15′W
21 P4 **Mason** West Virginia, NE USA 39°01′N 82°01′W
185 B25 **Mason Bay** *bay* Stewart Island, New Zealand
30 K13 **Mason City** Illinois, N USA 40°12′N 89°42′W
29 V12 **Mason City** Iowa, C USA 43°09′N 93°12′W
18 B16 **Masontown** Pennsylvania, NE USA 39°49′N 79°53′W
141 Y8 **Masqaţ** *var.* Maskat, *Eng.* Muscat. ● (Oman) NE Oman 23°35′N 58°36′E
106 E10 **Massa** Toscana, C Italy 44°02′N 10°07′E
18 M11 **Massachusetts** *off.* Commonwealth of Massachusetts, *also known as* Bay State, Old Bay State, Old Colony State. ◈ *state* NE USA
19 P11 **Massachusetts Bay** *bay* Massachusetts, NE USA
35 R2 **Massacre Lake** ◎ Nevada, W USA
107 O18 **Massafra** Puglia, SE Italy 40°35′N 17°08′E
108 G11 **Massagno** Ticino, S Switzerland 46°01′N 08°55′E
78 G11 **Massaguet** Chari-Baguirmi, W Chad 12°28′N 15°26′E
Massakori *see* Massakory
78 G10 **Massakory** *var.* Massakori; *prev.* Dagana. Chari-Baguirmi, W Chad 13°02′N 15°43′E
78 H11 **Massalassef** Chari-Baguirmi, SW Chad 11°37′N 17°09′E
106 F13 **Massa Marittima** Toscana, C Italy 43°03′N 10°55′E
82 B11 **Massangano** Cuanza Norte, NW Angola 09°40′S 14°13′E
83 M18 **Massangena** Gaza, S Mozambique 21°34′S 32°57′E
80 K9 **Massawa Channel** *channel* E Eritrea
18 J6 **Massena** New York, NE USA 44°55′N 74°53′W
78 H11 **Massenya** Chari-Baguirmi, SW Chad 11°21′N 16°09′E
10 I13 **Masset** Graham Island, British Columbia, SW Canada 54°00′N 132°09′W
102 L16 **Masseube** Gers, S France 43°26′N 00°33′E
14 E11 **Massey** Ontario, S Canada 46°13′N 82°06′W
103 P12 **Massiac** Cantal, C France 45°16′N 03°13′E
103 P12 **Massif Central** *plateau* C France
Massif de L'Isalo *see* Isalo
Massilia *see* Marseille
31 U12 **Massillon** Ohio, N USA 40°48′N 81°31′W
77 N12 **Massina** Ségou, W Mali 13°58′N 05°24′W
83 N19 **Massinga** Inhambane, SE Mozambique 23°20′S 35°25′E
83 L20 **Massingir** Gaza, SW Mozambique 23°51′S 31°58′E
195 Z10 **Masson Island** *island* Antarctica
Massoukou *see* Franceville
137 Z11 **Maştağa** *Rus.* Mashtagi, Mastaga. E Azerbaijan 40°31′N 50°01′E
Mastanli *see* Momchilgrad
184 M13 **Masterton** Wellington, North Island, New Zealand 40°56′S 175°40′E
18 M14 **Mastic** Long Island, New York, NE USA 40°48′N 72°50′W
149 O10 **Mastung** Baluchistān, SW Pakistan 29°44′N 66°56′E
119 J20 **Mastva** *Rus.* Mostva. ∽ SW Belarus
119 G17 **Masty** *Rus.* Mosty. Hrodzyenskaya Voblasts′, W Belarus 53°25′N 24°32′E
164 F12 **Masuda** Shimane, Honshū, SW Japan 34°40′N 131°50′E
92 J11 **Masugnsbyn** Norrbotten, N Sweden 67°28′N 22°01′E
Masuku *see* Franceville
83 K17 **Masvingo** *prev.* Fort Victoria, Nyanda, Victoria. Masvingo, SE Zimbabwe 20°05′S 30°50′E
83 K18 **Masvingo** *prev.* Victoria. ◈ *province* SE Zimbabwe
138 H5 **Maşyāf** *Fr.* Misiaf. Ḩamāh, C Syria 35°04′N 36°21′E
110 E9 **Maszewo** Zachodniopomorskie, NW Poland 53°29′N 15°01′E
83 I17 **Matabeleland North** ◈ *province* W Zimbabwe
83 J18 **Matabeleland South** ◈ *province* S Zimbabwe
82 O13 **Mataca** Niassa, N Mozambique 12°27′S 36°13′E
14 G8 **Matachewan** Ontario, S Canada 47°58′N 80°37′W
163 Q8 **Matad** *var.* Dzüünbulag. Dornod, E Mongolia 46°48′N 115°21′E
79 F22 **Matadi** Bas-Congo, W Dem. Rep. Congo 05°49′S 13°31′E
25 O4 **Matador** Texas, SW USA 34°01′N 100°50′W
42 J9 **Matagalpa** Matagalpa, C Nicaragua 12°53′N 85°56′W
42 K9 **Matagalpa** ◈ *department* W Nicaragua
12 I12 **Matagami** Québec, S Canada 49°47′N 77°38′W
25 U13 **Matagorda** Texas, SW USA 28°40′N 96°57′W
25 U13 **Matagorda Bay** *inlet* Texas, SW USA
25 U14 **Matagorda Island** *island* Texas, SW USA
25 V13 **Matagorda Peninsula** *headland* Texas, SW USA 28°34′N 96°01′W
191 Q8 **Mataiea** Tahiti, W French Polynesia 17°46′S 149°25′W
191 T9 **Mataiva** *atoll* Îles Tuamotu, C French Polynesia
183 O7 **Matakana** New South Wales, SE Australia 32°59′S 145°53′E
184 N7 **Matakana Island** *island* NE New Zealand
83 C15 **Matala** Huíla, SW Angola 14°45′S 15°02′E
190 G12 **Matala'a Pointe** *headland* Île Uvea, N Wallis and Futuna 13°20′S 176°08′W
155 K25 **Matale** Central Province, C Sri Lanka 07°29′N 80°38′E
190 E12 **Matalesina, Pointe** *headland* Île Alofi, W Wallis and Futuna
76 I10 **Matam** NE Senegal 15°40′N 13°18′W
184 M8 **Matamata** Waikato, North Island, New Zealand 37°49′S 175°45′E
77 V12 **Matamey** Zinder, S Niger 13°27′N 08°27′E
41 N8 **Matamoros** Coahuila, NE Mexico 25°34′N 103°13′W
41 P15 **Matamoros** *var.* Izúcar de Matamoros. Puebla, S Mexico 18°38′N 98°30′W
41 Q8 **Matamoros** Tamaulipas, C Mexico 25°50′N 97°31′W
75 S13 **Ma'ṭan as Sārah** SE Libya 21°45′N 21°55′E
82 J12 **Matanda** Luapula, N Zambia 11°24′S 28°25′E
81 J24 **Matandu** ∽ S Tanzania
15 V6 **Matane** Québec, SE Canada 48°50′N 67°31′W
15 V6 **Matane** ∽ Québec, SE Canada
77 S12 **Matankari** Dosso, SW Niger 13°39′N 04°03′E
39 R11 **Matanuska River** ∽ Alaska, USA
54 G7 **Matanza** Santander, N Colombia 07°22′N 73°02′W
44 D4 **Matanzas** Matanzas, NW Cuba 23°N 81°32′W
15 V7 **Matapédia** ∽ Québec, SE Canada
15 V6 **Matapédia, Lac** ◎ Québec, SE Canada
190 B17 **Mata Point** *headland* SE Niue 19°07′S 169°51′E
190 D12 **Matapu, Pointe** *headland* Île Futuna, W Wallis and Futuna
62 G12 **Mataquito, Río** ∽ C Chile
155 K26 **Matara** Southern Province, S Sri Lanka 05°58′N 80°33′E
115 D18 **Matarágka** *var.* Mataránga. Dytikí Elláda, C Greece 38°32′N 21°28′E
171 K16 **Mataram** Pulau Lombok, C Indonesia 08°36′S 116°07′E
Mataránga *see* Matarágka
181 Q3 **Mataranka** Northern Territory, N Australia 14°55′S 133°03′E
105 W6 **Mataró** *anc.* Illuro. Cataluña, E Spain 41°32′N 02°27′E
184 O8 **Matata** Bay of Plenty, North Island, New Zealand 37°54′S 176°45′E
192 K16 **Matātula, Cape** *headland* Tutuila, W American Samoa 14°15′S 170°35′W
185 D24 **Mataura** Southland, South Island, New Zealand 46°12′S 168°53′E
185 D24 **Mataura** ∽ South Island, New Zealand
Mata Uta *see* Matā'utu
192 H16 **Matāutu** Upolu, C Samoa 13°57′S 171°55′W
190 G11 **Matā'utu** *var.* Mata Uta. ○ (Wallis and Futuna) Île Uvea, Wallis and Futuna 13°22′S 176°12′W
190 G12 **Matā'utu, Baie de** *bay* Île Uvea, Wallis and Futuna
191 P7 **Matavai, Baie de** *bay* Tahiti, W French Polynesia
190 I16 **Matavera** Rarotonga, S Cook Islands 21°13′S 159°44′W
191 V16 **Mataveri** Easter Island, Chile, E Pacific Ocean 27°10′S 109°27′W
191 V17 **Mataveri** ✈ (Easter Island) Easter Island, Chile, E Pacific Ocean 27°10′S 109°27′W
184 P9 **Matawai** Gisborne, North Island, New Zealand 38°23′S 177°31′E
15 O10 **Matawin** ∽ Québec, SE Canada
145 V13 **Matay** Almaty, SE Kazakhstan 45°53′N 78°45′E
14 K8 **Matchi-Manitou, Lac** ◎ Québec, SE Canada
41 O10 **Matehuala** San Luis Potosí, C Mexico 23°40′N 100°40′W
45 V13 **Matelot** Trinidad, Trinidad and Tobago 10°48′N 61°06′W
83 M15 **Matenge** Tete, NW Mozambique 15°22′S 33°47′E
107 O18 **Matera** Basilicata, S Italy 40°39′N 16°35′E
111 O21 **Mátészalka** Szabolcs-Szatmár-Bereg, E Hungary 47°58′N 22°17′E
93 H17 **Matfors** Västernorrland, C Sweden 62°21′N 17°02′E
102 K11 **Matha** Charente-Maritime, W France 45°50′N 00°13′W
0 F15 **Mathematicians Seamounts** *undersea feature* E Pacific Ocean 15°00′N 111°00′W
21 X6 **Mathews** Virginia, NE USA 37°26′N 76°20′W
25 S14 **Mathis** Texas, SW USA 28°05′N 97°49′W
152 J11 **Mathura** *prev.* Muttra. Uttar Pradesh, N India 27°30′N 77°42′E
Mathurai *see* Madurai
171 R7 **Mati** Mindanao, S Philippines 06°58′N 126°11′E
Matianus *see* Orūmīyeh, Daryācheh-ye
Matiara *see* Matiāri
149 Q15 **Matiāri** *var.* Matiara. Sind, SE Pakistan 25°38′N 68°29′E
41 S16 **Matías Romero** Oaxaca, SE Mexico 16°53′N 95°02′W
43 O13 **Matina** Limón, E Costa Rica 10°06′N 83°18′W
14 D10 **Matinenda Lake** ◎ Ontario, S Canada
19 R8 **Matinicus Island** *island* Maine, NE USA
Matisco/Matisco Ædourum *see* Mâcon
113 K19 **Matit, Lumi i** ∽ NW Albania
149 Q16 **Mātli** Sind, SE Pakistan 25°06′N 68°37′E
97 M18 **Matlock** C England, United Kingdom 53°08′N 01°32′W
59 F18 **Mato Grosso** *prev.* Vila Bela da Santissima Trindade. Mato Grosso, W Brazil 14°53′S 59°58′W
59 G17 **Mato Grosso** *off.* Estado de Mato Grosso; *prev.* Matto Grosso. ◈ *state* W Brazil
60 H8 **Mato Grosso do Sul** *off.* Estado de Mato Grosso do Sul. ◈ *state* S Brazil
Mato Grosso do Sul, Estado de *see* Mato Grosso do Sul
Mato Grosso, Estado de *see* Mato Grosso
59 I18 **Mato Grosso, Planalto de** *plateau* C Brazil
83 L21 **Matola** Maputo, S Mozambique 25°57′S 32°27′E
104 G6 **Matosinhos** *prev.* Matozinhos. Porto, NW Portugal 41°11′N 08°42′W
Matou *see* Pingguo
55 Z10 **Matoury** NE French Guiana 04°49′N 52°17′W
Matozinhos *see* Matosinhos
111 L21 **Mátra** ▲▲ N Hungary
141 Y8 **Maṭraḥ** *var.* Mutrah. NE Oman 23°35′N 58°31′E
116 L12 **Mătrașești** Vrancea, E Romania 45°53′N 27°14′E
108 M8 **Matrei am Brenner** Tirol, W Austria 47°09′N 11°28′E
109 P8 **Matrei in Osttirol** Tirol, W Austria 47°04′N 12°31′E
76 I15 **Matru** SW Sierra Leone 07°37′N 12°08′W
Maṭrūḥ *see* Marsā Maṭrūḥ
165 U16 **Matsubara** *var.* Matubara. Kagoshima, Tokuno-shima, SW Japan 32°58′N 129°56′E
161 S12 **Matsu Dao** *var.* Mazu Tao; *prev.* Matsu Tao. *island* NW Taiwan
164 G12 **Matsue** *var.* Matsuye, Matue. Shimane, Honshū, SW Japan 35°27′N 133°04′E
165 Q6 **Matsumae** Hokkaidō, NE Japan 41°27′N 140°04′E
164 M12 **Matsumoto** *var.* Matumoto. Nagano, Honshū, S Japan 36°18′N 137°58′E
164 K14 **Matsusaka** *var.* Matsuzaka, Matusaka. Mie, Honshū, SW Japan 34°33′N 136°31′E
Matsu Tao *see* Matsu Dao
Matsutō *see* Mattō
164 F14 **Matsuyama** *var.* Matuyama. Ehime, Shikoku, SW Japan 33°50′N 132°47′E
Matsuye *see* Matsue
Matsuzaka *see* Matsusaka
164 M14 **Matsuzaki** Shizuoka, Honshū, S Japan 34°43′N 138°45′E
14 F8 **Mattagami** ∽ Ontario, S Canada
14 F8 **Mattagami Lake** ◎ Ontario, S Canada
62 K12 **Mattaldi** Córdoba, C Argentina 34°26′S 64°14′W
21 Y9 **Mattamuskeet, Lake** ◎ North Carolina, SE USA
21 W6 **Mattaponi River** ∽ Virginia, NE USA
14 I11 **Mattawa** Ontario, SE Canada 46°19′N 78°42′W
14 I11 **Mattawa** ∽ Ontario, SE Canada
19 S5 **Mattawamkeag** Maine, NE USA 45°30′N 68°20′W
19 S4 **Mattawamkeag Lake** ◎ Maine, NE USA
108 D11 **Matterhorn** *It.* Monte Cervino. ▲ Italy/Switzerland 45°58′N 07°36′E *see also* Cervino, Monte
32 L12 **Matterhorn** *var.* Sacajawea Peak. ▲ Oregon, NW USA 45°12′N 117°18′W
35 W1 **Matterhorn** ▲ Nevada, W USA 41°48′N 115°22′W
Matterhorn *see* Cervino, Monte
35 R8 **Matterhorn Peak** ▲ California, W USA 38°06′N 119°19′W
109 Y5 **Mattersburg** Burgenland, E Austria 47°45′N 16°24′E
108 E11 **Matter Vispa** ∽ S Switzerland
55 R7 **Matthews Ridge** N Guyana 07°30′N 60°07′W
44 K7 **Matthew Town** Great Inagua, S Bahamas 20°56′N 73°41′W
109 Q4 **Mattighofen** Oberösterreich, NW Austria 48°07′N 13°09′E
107 N16 **Mattinata** Puglia, SE Italy 41°41′N 16°01′E
141 T9 **Maṭṭī, Sabkhat** *salt flat* Saudi Arabia/United Arab Emirates
18 M14 **Mattituck** Long Island, New York, NE USA 40°59′N 72°31′W
164 L11 **Mattō** *var.* Hakusan, Matsutō. Ishikawa, Honshū, SW Japan 36°31′N 136°34′E
Matto Grosso *see* Mato Grosso
30 M14 **Mattoon** Illinois, N USA 39°28′N 88°22′W
57 L16 **Mattos, Río** ∽ C Bolivia
Mattu *see* Metu
169 R9 **Matu** Sarawak, East Malaysia 02°39′N 111°31′E
Matubara *see* Matsubara
57 E14 **Matucana** Lima, W Peru 11°54′S 76°25′W
Matue *see* Matsue
187 Y15 **Matuku** *island* S Fiji
112 B9 **Matulji** Primorje-Gorski Kotar, NW Croatia 45°21′N 14°18′E
Matumoto *see* Matsumoto
55 P5 **Maturín** Monagas, NE Venezuela 09°45′N 63°10′W
Matusaka *see* Matsusaka
Matuyama *see* Matsuyama
126 K11 **Matveyev Kurgan** Rostovskaya Oblast', SW Russian Federation 47°31′N 38°55′E
127 O8 **Matyshevo** Volgogradskaya Oblast', SW Russian Federation 50°53′N 44°09′E
153 O13 **Mau** *var.* Maunāth Bhanjan. Uttar Pradesh, N India 25°57′N 83°33′E
83 O14 **Maúa** Niassa, N Mozambique 13°53′S 37°10′E
102 M17 **Maubermé, Pic de** *var.* Tuc de Moubermé, *Sp.* Pico Mauberme; *prev.* Tuc de Maubermé. ▲ France/Spain 42°48′N 00°54′E *see also* Moubermé, Tuc de
Maubermé, Pic de *see* Moubermé, Tuc de
Mauberme, Pico *see* Maubermé, Pic de/Moubermé, Tuc de
Maubermé, Tuc de *see* Maubermé, Pic de/Moubermé, Tuc de
103 Q2 **Maubeuge** Nord, N France 50°16′N 04°00′E
166 L8 **Maubin** Ayeyarwady, SW Burma (Myanmar) 16°44′N 95°37′E
152 L13 **Maudaha** Uttar Pradesh, N India 25°41′N 80°07′E
183 N9 **Maude** New South Wales, SE Australia 34°30′S 144°20′E
195 P3 **Maudheimvidda** *physical region* Antarctica
65 N22 **Maud Rise** *undersea feature* S Atlantic Ocean
109 Q4 **Mauerkirchen** Oberösterreich, NW Austria 48°11′N 13°08′E
Mauersee *see* Mamry, Jezioro
188 K2 **Maug Islands** *island group* N Northern Mariana Islands
103 Q15 **Mauguio** Hérault, S France 43°37′N 04°01′E
193 N5 **Maui** *island* Hawai'i, USA, C Pacific Ocean
190 M16 **Mauke** *atoll* S Cook Islands
62 G13 **Maule** *var.* Región del Maule. ◈ *region* C Chile
102 J9 **Mauléon** Deux-Sèvres, W France 46°55′N 00°45′W
102 J16 **Mauléon-Licharre** Pyrénées-Atlantiques, SW France 43°14′N 00°51′W
Maule, Región del *see* Maule
62 G13 **Maule, Río** ∽ C Chile
63 G17 **Maullín** Los Lagos, S Chile 41°38′S 73°35′W
31 R11 **Maumee** Ohio, N USA 41°34′N 83°40′W
31 Q12 **Maumee River** ∽ Indiana/Ohio, N USA
27 U11 **Maumelle** Arkansas, C USA 34°51′N 92°24′W
27 T11 **Maumelle, Lake** ⊠ Arkansas, C USA
171 O16 **Maumere** *prev.* Maoemere. Flores, S Indonesia 08°35′S 122°13′E
83 G17 **Maun** North-West, C Botswana 20°01′S 23°28′E
Maunāth Bhanjan *see* Mau
Maunawai *see* Waimea
190 H16 **Maungaroa** ▲ Rarotonga, S Cook Islands 21°13′S 159°48′W
184 K3 **Maungatapere** Northland, North Island, New Zealand 35°46′S 174°10′E
184 K4 **Maungaturoto** Northland, North Island, New Zealand 36°06′S 174°21′E
166 J5 **Maungdaw** *var.* Zullapara. Rakhine State, W Burma (Myanmar) 20°51′N 92°23′E
191 R10 **Maupiti** *var.* Maurua. *island* Îles Sous le Vent, W French Polynesia
152 K14 **Mau Rānīpur** Uttar Pradesh, N India 25°14′N 79°07′E
22 K9 **Maurepas, Lake** ◎ Louisiana, S USA
103 T16 **Maures** ▲▲ SE France
103 O12 **Mauriac** Cantal, C France 45°13′N 02°21′E
Maurice *see* Mauritius
65 J20 **Maurice Ewing Bank** *undersea feature* SW Atlantic Ocean 51°00′S 43°00′W
182 C4 **Maurice, Lake** *salt lake* South Australia
18 I17 **Maurice River** ∽ New Jersey, NE USA
25 Y10 **Mauriceville** Texas, SW USA 30°13′N 93°52′W
98 K12 **Maurik** Gelderland, C Netherlands 51°57′N 05°25′E
76 H8 **Mauritania** *off.* Islamic Republic of Mauritania, *Ar.* Mūrītānīyah. ◆ *republic* W Africa
Mauritania, Islamic Republic of *see* Mauritania
173 W15 **Mauritius** *off.* Republic of Mauritius, *Fr.* Maurice. ◆ *republic* W Indian Ocean
128 M17 **Mauritius** *island* W Indian Ocean
Mauritius, Republic of *see* Mauritius
173 N9 **Mauritius Trench** *undersea feature* W Indian Ocean
102 H6 **Mauron** Morbihan, NW France 48°06′N 02°16′W
103 N13 **Maurs** Cantal, C France 44°45′N 02°12′E
Maurua *see* Maupiti
Maury Mid-Ocean Channel *see* Maury Seachannel
64 L6 **Maury Seachannel** *var.* Maury Mid-Ocean Channel. *undersea feature* N Atlantic Ocean 56°33′N 24°00′W
30 K8 **Mauston** Wisconsin, N USA 43°46′N 90°06′W
109 R8 **Mauterndorf** Salzburg, NW Austria 47°09′N 13°39′E
109 T4 **Mauthausen** Oberösterreich, N Austria 48°13′N 14°30′E
109 Q9 **Mauthen** Kärnten, S Austria 46°39′N 12°58′E
83 F15 **Mavinga** Cuando Cubango, SE Angola 15°44′S 20°21′E
83 M17 **Mavita** Manica, W Mozambique 19°31′S 33°09′E
115 K22 **Mavrópetra, Akrotírio** *headland* Santoríni, Kykládes, Greece, Aegean Sea 36°28′N 25°22′E
115 F16 **Mavrovoúni** ▲ C Greece 39°37′N 22°45′E
184 Q8 **Mawhai Point** *headland* North Island, New Zealand 38°08′S 178°24′E
166 L3 **Mawlaik** Sagaing, C Burma (Myanmar) 23°40′N 94°26′E
Mawlamyaing *see* Mawlamyine
166 M9 **Mawlamyine** *var.* Mawlamyaing, Moulmein. Mon State, S Burma (Myanmar) 16°30′N 97°39′E
166 L8 **Mawlamyinegyunn** *var.* Moulmeingyun. Ayeyarwady, SW Burma (Myanmar) 16°24′N 95°15′E
141 N14 **Mawr, Wādī** *dry watercourse* NW Yemen
195 X5 **Mawson** *Australian research station* Antarctica 67°24′S 63°16′E
195 X5 **Mawson Coast** *physical region* Antarctica
28 M4 **Max** North Dakota, N USA 47°48′N 101°18′W
41 W12 **Maxcanú** Yucatán, SE Mexico 20°35′N 90°00′W
Maxesibebi *see* Mount Ayliff
109 Q5 **Maxglan** ✈ (Salzburg) Salzburg, W Austria 47°46′N 13°00′E
93 K16 **Maxmo** *Fin.* Maksamaa. Länsi-Suomi, W Finland 63°13′N 22°04′E
21 T11 **Maxton** North Carolina, SE USA 34°47′N 79°34′W
25 R8 **May** Texas, SW USA 31°58′N 98°54′W
186 B6 **May** ∽ NW Papua New Guinea
123 R10 **Maya** ∽ E Russian Federation
151 Q19 **Māyābandar** Andaman and Nicobar Islands, India, E Indian Ocean 12°43′N 92°52′E
Mayadin *see* Al Mayādīn
44 L5 **Mayaguana** *island* SE Bahamas
44 L5 **Mayaguana Passage** *passage* SE Bahamas
45 S6 **Mayagüez** W Puerto Rico 18°12′N 67°08′W
45 R6 **Mayagüez, Bahía de** *bay* W Puerto Rico
Mayals *see* Maials
79 G20 **Mayama** Pool, SE Congo 03°50′S 14°52′E
37 V8 **Maya, Mesa De** ▲ Colorado, C USA 37°06′N 103°30′W
143 R4 **Mayamey** Semnān, N Iran 36°50′N 55°50′E
42 F3 **Maya Mountains** *Sp.* Montañas Mayas. ▲▲ Belize/Guatemala
44 I7 **Mayarí** Holguín, E Cuba 20°41′N 75°42′W
Mayas, Montañas *see* Maya Mountains
18 I17 **May, Cape** *headland* New Jersey, NE USA 38°55′N 74°57′W
80 J11 **Maych'ew** *var.* Mai Chio, *It.* Mai Ceu. Tigray, N Ethiopia 12°55′N 39°30′E
138 I2 **Maydān Ikbiz** Ḩalab, N Syria 36°51′N 36°40′E
Maydān Shahr *see* Maīdān Shahr
80 O12 **Maydh** Sanaag, N Somalia 10°57′N 47°07′E
Maydī *see* Mīdī
Mayebashi *see* Maebashi
Mayence *see* Mainz
102 K6 **Mayenne** Mayenne, NW France 48°18′N 00°37′W
102 J6 **Mayenne** ◈ *department* NW France
102 J7 **Mayenne** ∽ N France
36 K12 **Mayer** Arizona, SW USA 34°25′N 112°15′W
22 J4 **Mayersville** Mississippi, S USA 32°54′N 91°04′W
11 P14 **Mayerthorpe** Alberta, SW Canada 53°59′N 115°06′W
21 S12 **Mayesville** South Carolina, SE USA 34°00′N 80°10′W
185 G19 **Mayfield** Canterbury, South Island, New Zealand 43°50′S 171°24′E
33 N14 **Mayfield** Idaho, NW USA 43°24′N 115°56′W
20 G7 **Mayfield** Kentucky, S USA 36°45′N 88°40′W
36 L5 **Mayfield** Utah, W USA 39°06′N 111°42′W
Mayhan *see* Sant
37 T14 **Mayhill** New Mexico, SW USA 32°52′N 105°28′W
Maykain *see* Maykayyn
145 T9 **Maykayyn** *Kaz.* Mayqayyng *prev.* Maykain. Pavlodar, NE Kazakhstan 51°27′N 75°52′E
126 L14 **Maykop** Respublika Adygeya, SW Russian Federation 44°36′N 40°07′E
Maylibash *see* Maylybas
Mayli-Say *see* Mayluu-Suu
147 T9 **Mayluu-Suu** *prev.* Mayli-Say, *Kir.* Mayly-Say. Dzhalal-Abadskaya Oblast', W Kyrgyzstan 41°16′N 72°27′E
144 L14 **Maylybas** *prev.* Maylibash. Kzylorda, S Kazakhstan 45°51′N 62°37′E
Mayly-Say *see* Mayluu-Suu
Maymana *see* Maīmanah
Maymyo *see* Pyin-Oo-Lwin
123 V7 **Mayn** ∽ NE Russian Federation
127 Q5 **Mayna** Ul'yanovskaya Oblast', W Russian Federation 54°04′N 47°20′E
21 N8 **Maynardville** Tennessee, S USA 36°15′N 83°48′W
14 J13 **Maynooth** Ontario, SE Canada 45°14′N 77°54′W
10 I6 **Mayo** Yukon Territory, NW Canada 63°37′N 135°48′W
23 U9 **Mayo** Florida, SE USA 30°03′N 83°10′W
97 B16 **Mayo** *Ir.* Maigh Eo. *cultural region* W Ireland
Mayo *see* Maio
78 G12 **Mayo-Kébbi** *off.* Préfecture du Mayo-Kébbu, *var.* Mayo-Kébi. ◈ *prefecture* SW Chad
Mayo-Kébbu, Préfecture du *see* Mayo-Kébbi
Mayo-Kébi *see* Mayo-Kébbi
79 F19 **Mayoko** Niari, SW Congo 02°19′S 12°47′E
171 P4 **Mayon Volcano** ⛰ Luzon, N Philippines 13°15′N 123°41′E
61 A24 **Mayor Buratovich** Buenos Aires, E Argentina 39°15′S 62°35′W
104 L4 **Mayorga** Castilla y León, N Spain 42°10′N 05°16′W
184 N6 **Mayor Island** *island* NE New Zealand
Mayor Pablo Lagerenza *see* Capitán Pablo Lagerenza
173 I14 **Mayotte** ◇ *French territorial collectivity* E Africa
Mayoumba *see* Mayumba
44 J13 **May Pen** C Jamaica 17°58′N 77°15′W
Mayqayyng *see* Maykayyn
171 O1 **Mayraira Point** *headland* Luzon, N Philippines 18°36′N 120°47′E
109 N8 **Mayrhofen** Tirol, W Austria 47°09′N 11°52′E
186 A6 **May River** East Sepik, NW Papua New Guinea 04°24′S 141°52′E
123 R13 **Mayskiy** Amurskaya Oblast', SE Russian Federation 52°13′N 129°30′E
127 O15 **Mayskiy** Kabardino-Balkarskaya Respublika, SW Russian Federation 43°37′N 44°04′E
145 U9 **Mayskoye** Pavlodar, NE Kazakhstan 50°55′N 78°11′E
18 J17 **Mays Landing** New Jersey, NE USA 39°27′N 74°44′W
21 N4 **Maysville** Kentucky, S USA 38°38′N 83°46′W
27 R2 **Maysville** Missouri, C USA 39°53′N 94°21′W
79 D20 **Mayumba** *var.* Mayoumba. Nyanga, S Gabon 03°23′S 10°38′E
31 S8 **Mayville** Michigan, N USA 43°18′N 83°16′W
18 C11 **Mayville** New York, NE USA 42°15′N 79°32′W
29 Q4 **Mayville** North Dakota, N USA 47°27′N 97°17′W
Mayyali *see* Mahe
Mayyit, Al Baḩr al *see* Dead Sea
83 J15 **Mazabuka** Southern, S Zambia 15°52′S 27°46′E
Mazaca *see* Kayseri
Mazagan *see* El-Jadida
32 I7 **Mazama** Washington, NW USA 48°34′N 120°26′W
103 O15 **Mazamet** Tarn, S France 43°30′N 02°21′E
143 O4 **Māzandarān** *off.* Ostān-e Māzandarān. ◈ *province* N Iran
Māzandarān, Ostān-e *see* Māzandarān
156 F7 **Mazar** Xinjiang Uygur Zizhiqu, NW China 36°28′N 77°00′E
107 H24 **Mazara del Vallo** Sicilia, Italy, C Mediterranean Sea 37°39′N 12°36′E
149 O2 **Mazār-e Sharīf** *var.* Mazār-i Sharif. Balkh, N Afghanistan 36°44′N 67°06′E
Mazār-i Sharif *see* Mazār-e Sharīf
105 R13 **Mazarrón** Murcia, SE Spain 37°36′N 01°19′W
105 R14 **Mazarrón, Golfo de** *gulf* SE Spain
55 S9 **Mazaruni River** ∽ N Guyana
42 B6 **Mazatenango** Suchitepéquez, SW Guatemala 14°31′N 91°30′W
40 I10 **Mazatlán** Sinaloa, C Mexico 23°15′N 106°24′W
36 L12 **Mazatzal Mountains** ▲▲ Arizona, SW USA
118 D10 **Mažeikiai** Telšiai, NW Lithuania 56°19′N 22°22′E
118 D7 **Mazirbe** NW Latvia 57°39′N 22°16′E
40 G5 **Mazocahui** Sonora, NW Mexico 29°32′N 110°09′W
57 I18 **Mazocruz** Puno, S Peru 16°41′S 69°42′W
Mazoe, Rio *see* Mazowe
79 N21 **Mazomeno** Maniema, E Dem. Rep. Congo 04°54′S 27°13′E
159 Q6 **Mazong Shan** ▲ N China 41°40′N 97°10′E
83 L16 **Mazowe** *var.* Rio Mazoe. ∽ Mozambique/Zimbabwe
110 M11 **Mazowieckie** ◈ *province* C Poland
Mazra'a *see* Al Mazra'ah
138 G6 **Mazraat Kfar Debiâne** C Lebanon 34°00′N 35°51′E
118 H7 **Mazsalaca** *Est.* Väike-Salatsi, *Ger.* Salisburg. N Latvia 57°52′N 25°03′E
110 L9 **Mazury** *physical region* NE Poland
Mazu Tao *see* Matsu Dao
119 M20 **Mazyr** *Rus.* Mozyr'. Homyel'skaya Voblasts', SE Belarus 52°04′N 29°15′E
107 K25 **Mazzarino** Sicilia, Italy, C Mediterranean Sea 37°18′N 14°13′E
Mba *see* Ba
83 L21 **Mbabane** ● (Swaziland) NW Swaziland 26°24′S 31°13′E
Mbacké *see* Mbaké
77 N16 **Mbahiakro** E Ivory Coast 07°33′N 04°19′W
79 I16 **Mbaïki** *var.* M'Baiki. Lobaye, SW Central African Republic 03°52′N 17°58′E
M'Baiki *see* Mbaïki
79 F14 **Mbakaou, Lac de** ◎ C Cameroon
76 G11 **Mbaké** *var.* Mbacké. W Senegal 14°47′N 15°54′W
82 L11 **Mbala** *prev.* Abercorn. Northern, NE Zambia 08°50′S 31°23′E
83 J18 **Mbalabala** *prev.* Balla Balla. Matabeleland South, SW Zimbabwe 20°27′S 29°03′E
81 G18 **Mbale** E Uganda 01°04′N 34°12′E
79 E16 **Mbalmayo** *var.* M'Balmayo. Centre, S Cameroon 03°30′N 11°31′E
M'Balmayo *see* Mbalmayo
81 H25 **Mbamba Bay** Ruvuma, S Tanzania 11°15′S 34°44′E
79 I18 **Mbandaka** *prev.* Coquilhatville. Equateur, NW Dem. Rep. Congo 0°07′N 18°12′E
82 B9 **M'Banza Congo** *var.* Mbanza Congo; *prev.* São Salvador, São Salvador do Congo. Dem. Rep. Congo, NW Angola 06°11′S 14°16′E
79 G21 **Mbanza-Ngungu** Bas-Congo, W Dem. Rep. Congo 05°19′S 14°45′E
67 V11 **Mbarangandu** ∽ E Tanzania
81 E19 **Mbarara** SW Uganda 0°36′S 30°40′E
79 L15 **Mbari** ∽ SE Central African Republic
81 I24 **Mbarika Mountains** ▲▲ S Tanzania
78 F13 **Mbé** Nord, N Cameroon 07°51′N 13°36′E
81 J24 **Mbemkuru** *var.* Mbwemkuru. ∽ S Tanzania
Mbengga *see* Beqa
172 H13 **Mbéni** Grande Comore, NW Comoros
83 K18 **Mberengwa** Midlands, S Zimbabwe 20°29′S 29°55′E
81 G24 **Mbeya** Mbeya, SW Tanzania 08°54′S 33°29′E
81 G23 **Mbeya** ◈ *region* S Tanzania
83 J24 **Mbhashe** *prev.* Mbashe. ∽ S South Africa
79 E19 **Mbigou** Ngounié, C Gabon 01°54′S 12°00′E
Mbilua *see* Vella Lavella
79 F19 **Mbinda** Niari, SW Congo 02°07′S 12°52′E
79 D17 **Mbini** W Equatorial Guinea 01°34′N 09°39′E
Mbini *see* Uolo, Río
83 L18 **Mbizi** Masvingo, SE Zimbabwe 21°23′S 30°54′E
81 G23 **Mbogo** Mbeya, W Tanzania 07°24′S 33°26′E
79 N15 **Mboki** Haut-Mbomou, SE Central African Republic 05°18′N 25°52′E
79 G18 **Mbomo** Cuvette, NW Congo 0°25′N 14°42′E
79 L15 **Mbomou** ◈ *prefecture* SE Central African Republic
Mbomou/M'Bomu/Mbomu *see* Bomu
76 F11 **Mbour** W Senegal 14°22′N 16°54′W
76 I10 **Mbout** Gorgol, S Mauritania 16°02′N 12°38′W
79 J14 **Mbrès** *var.* Mbrés. Nana-Grébizi, C Central African Republic 06°40′N 19°46′E
Mbrés *see* Mbrès
79 L22 **Mbuji-Mayi** *prev.* Bakwanga. Kasai-Oriental, S Dem. Rep. Congo 06°05′S 23°30′E
81 H21 **Mbulu** Manyara, N Tanzania 03°45′S 35°33′E
186 E5 **M'bunai** *var.* Bunai. Manus Island, N Papua New Guinea 02°08′S 147°13′E
62 N8 **Mburucuyá** Corrientes, NE Argentina 28°03′S 58°15′W
Mbutha *see* Buca
Mbwemkuru *see* Mbemkuru
81 G21 **Mbwikwe** Singida, C Tanzania 05°19′S 34°09′E
13 O15 **McAdam** New Brunswick, SE Canada 45°34′N 67°20′W
25 O5 **McAdoo** Texas, SW USA 33°41′N 100°58′W
35 V2 **McAfee Peak** ▲ Nevada, W USA 41°31′N 115°57′W
27 P11 **McAlester** Oklahoma, C USA 34°56′N 95°46′W
25 S17 **McAllen** Texas, SW USA 26°12′N 98°14′W
21 S11 **McBee** South Carolina, SE USA 34°30′N 80°12′W
11 N14 **McBride** British Columbia, SW Canada 53°21′N 120°19′W
24 M9 **McCamey** Texas, SW USA 31°08′N 102°13′W
33 R15 **McCammon** Idaho, NW USA 42°38′N 112°10′W
35 X11 **McCarran** ✈ (Las Vegas) Nevada, W USA 36°04′N 115°07′W
39 T11 **McCarthy** Alaska, USA 61°25′N 142°55′W
30 M5 **McCaslin Mountain** *hill* Wisconsin, N USA
25 O2 **McClellan Creek** ∽ Texas, SW USA
21 T14 **McClellanville** South Carolina, SE USA 33°07′N 79°27′W
195 R12 **McClintock, Mount** ▲ Antarctica 80°09′S 156°42′E
35 N2 **McCloud** California, W USA 41°15′N 122°09′W
35 N3 **McCloud River** ∽ California, W USA
35 Q9 **McClure, Lake** ⊠ California, W USA
197 O8 **McClure Strait** *strait* Northwest Territories, N Canada
29 N4 **McClusky** North Dakota, N USA 47°27′N 100°25′W
21 T11 **McColl** South Carolina, SE USA 34°40′N 79°33′W
22 K7 **McComb** Mississippi, S USA 31°14′N 90°27′W
18 E16 **McConnellsburg** Pennsylvania, NE USA 39°56′N 78°00′W
31 T14 **McConnelsville** Ohio, N USA 39°39′N 81°51′W
28 M17 **McCook** Nebraska, C USA 40°12′N 100°38′W
21 P13 **McCormick** South Carolina, SE USA 33°55′N 82°19′W
11 W16 **McCreary** Manitoba, S Canada 50°48′N 99°34′W
27 W11 **McCrory** Arkansas, C USA 35°15′N 91°12′W
25 T10 **McDade** Texas, SW USA 30°15′N 97°15′W
23 O8 **McDavid** Florida, SE USA 30°51′N 87°18′W
35 T1 **McDermitt** Nevada, W USA 41°57′N 117°43′W
23 S4 **McDonough** Georgia, SE USA 33°27′N 84°09′W
36 L12 **McDowell Mountains** ▲▲ Arizona, SW USA
20 H8 **McEwen** Tennessee, S USA 36°06′N 87°37′W
35 R12 **McFarland** California, W USA 35°41′N 119°14′W
Mcfarlane, Lake *see* Macfarlane, Lake
27 P12 **McGee Creek Lake** ⊠ Oklahoma, C USA
27 W13 **McGehee** Arkansas, C USA 33°37′N 91°24′W
35 X5 **Mcgill** Nevada, W USA 39°24′N 114°46′W

◆ Country
● Country Capital
◇ Dependent Territory
○ Dependent Territory Capital
◈ Administrative Regions
✈ International Airport
▲ Mountain
▲▲ Mountain Range
⛰ Volcano
∽ River
◎ Lake
⊠ Reservoir

14 K11 **McGillivray, Lac** ◎ Québec, SE Canada
39 P10 **McGrath** Alaska, USA 62°57′N 155°36′W
25 T8 **McGregor** Texas, SW USA 31°26′N 97°24′W
33 O12 **McGuire, Mount** ▲ Idaho, NW USA 45°10′N 114°36′W
83 M14 **Mchinji** *prev.* Fort Manning. Central, W Malawi 13°48′S 32°55′E
28 M7 **McIntosh** South Dakota, N USA 45°56′N 101°21′W
9 S7 **McKeand** ≈ Baffin Island, Nunavut, NE Canada
191 R4 **McKean Island** *island* Phoenix Islands, C Kiribati
30 J13 **McKee Creek** ≈ Illinois, N USA
18 C15 **Mckeesport** Pennsylvania, NE USA 40°18′N 79°48′W
21 V7 **McKenney** Virginia, NE USA 36°57′N 77°42′W
20 G8 **McKenzie** Tennessee, S USA 36°07′N 88°31′W
185 B20 **McKerrow, Lake** ◎ South Island, New Zealand
39 Q10 **McKinley, Mount** *var.* Denali. ▲ Alaska, USA 63°04′N 151°00′W
39 R10 **McKinley Park** Alaska, USA 63°42′N 149°01′W
34 K3 **McKinleyville** California, W USA 40°56′N 124°06′W
25 U6 **McKinney** Texas, SW USA 33°14′N 96°37′W
26 I5 **McKinney, Lake** ◎ Kansas, C USA
28 M7 **McLaughlin** South Dakota, N USA 45°48′N 100°48′W
25 O2 **McLean** Texas, SW USA 35°13′N 100°36′W
30 M16 **Mcleansboro** Illinois, N USA 38°05′N 88°32′W
11 O13 **McLennan** Alberta, W Canada 55°42′N 116°50′W
14 L9 **McLennan, Lac** ◎ Québec, SE Canada
10 M13 **McLeod Lake** British Columbia, W Canada 55°03′N 123°02′W
8 L6 **M'Clintock Channel** *channel* Nunavut, N Canada
27 N10 **McLoud** Oklahoma, C USA 35°26′N 97°05′W
32 G15 **McLoughlin, Mount** ▲ Oregon, NW USA 42°27′N 122°18′W
37 U15 **McMillan, Lake** ⊠ New Mexico, SW USA
32 G11 **McMinnville** Oregon, NW USA 45°14′N 123°12′W
20 K9 **McMinnville** Tennessee, S USA 35°40′N 85°49′W
195 R13 **McMurdo** *US research station* Antarctica 77°40′S 167°16′E
37 N13 **Mcnary** Arizona, SW USA 34°04′N 109°51′W
24 H9 **McNary** Texas, SW USA 31°15′N 105°46′W
27 N5 **McPherson** Kansas, C USA 38°22′N 97°41′W
McPherson *see* Fort McPherson
23 U6 **McRae** Georgia, SE USA 32°04′N 82°54′W
29 P4 **McVille** North Dakota, N USA 47°45′N 98°10′W
83 J25 **Mdantsane** Eastern Cape, SE South Africa 32°55′S 27°39′E
167 T6 **Me** Ninh Binh, N Vietnam 20°21′N 105°49′E
26 J7 **Meade** Kansas, C USA 37°17′N 100°21′W
39 O5 **Meade River** ≈ Alaska, USA
35 Y11 **Mead, Lake** ⊠ Arizona/Nevada, W USA
24 M5 **Meadow** Texas, SW USA 33°20′N 102°12′W
11 S14 **Meadow Lake** Saskatchewan, C Canada 54°90′N 108°30′W
35 Y10 **Meadow Valley Wash** ≈ Nevada, W USA
22 J7 **Meadville** Mississippi, S USA 31°28′N 90°51′W
18 B12 **Meadville** Pennsylvania, NE USA 41°38′N 80°09′W
14 F14 **Meaford** Ontario, S Canada 44°35′N 80°35′W
Meáin, Inis *see* Inishmaan
104 G8 **Mealhada** Aveiro, N Portugal 40°22′N 08°27′W
13 R8 **Mealy Mountains** ▲▲ Newfoundland and Labrador, E Canada
11 O10 **Meander River** Alberta, W Canada 59°02′N 117°42′W
32 E11 **Meares, Cape** *headland* Oregon, NW USA 45°29′N 123°59′W
47 V6 **Mearim, Rio** ≈ NE Brazil
Measca, Loch *see* Mask, Lough
97 F17 **Meath** *Ir.* An Mhí. *cultural region* E Ireland
11 T14 **Meath Park** Saskatchewan, S Canada 53°25′N 105°18′W
103 O5 **Meaux** Seine-et-Marne, N France 48°47′N 02°54′E
21 T9 **Mebane** North Carolina, SE USA 36°06′N 79°16′W
171 U12 **Mebo, Gunung** ▲ Papua, E Indonesia 01°10′S 133°53′E
94 I8 **Mebonden** Sør-Trøndelag, S Norway 63°13′N 11°00′E
82 A10 **Mebridege** ≈ NW Angola
35 W16 **Mecca** California, W USA 33°34′N 116°04′W
Mecca *see* Makkah
29 Y14 **Mechanicsville** Iowa, C USA 41°54′N 91°15′W
18 L10 **Mechanicville** New York, NE USA 42°54′N 73°41′W
99 H17 **Mechelen** *Eng.* Mechlin, *Fr.* Malines. Antwerpen, C Belgium 51°02′N 04°29′E
188 C8 **Mecherchar** *var.* Eil Malk. *island* Palau Islands, Palau
101 D17 **Mechernich** Nordrhein-Westfalen, W Germany 50°36′N 06°39′E
126 L12 **Mechetinskaya** Rostovskaya Oblast', SW Russian Federation 46°46′N 40°30′E
114 J11 **Mechka** ≈ S Bulgaria
Mechlin *see* Mechelen
61 D23 **Mechongué** Buenos Aires, E Argentina 38°09′S 58°13′W
115 L14 **Mecidiye** Edirne, NW Turkey 40°39′N 26°33′E
101 I24 **Meckenbeuren** Baden-Württemberg, S Germany 47°42′N 09°34′E
100 L8 **Mecklenburger Bucht** *bay* N Germany
100 M10 **Mecklenburgische Seenplatte** *wetland* NE Germany
100 L9 **Mecklenburg-Vorpommern** ⬖ *state* NE Germany
83 Q15 **Meconta** Nampula, NE Mozambique 15°01′S 39°52′E
111 I25 **Mecsek** ▲▲ SW Hungary
83 P14 **Mecubúri** ≈ N Mozambique
83 Q14 **Mecúfi** Cabo Delgado, NE Mozambique 13°20′S 40°32′E
82 O13 **Mecula** Niassa, N Mozambique 12°03′S 37°37′E
168 I8 **Medan** Sumatera, E Indonesia 03°35′N 98°39′E
61 A24 **Médanos** *var.* Medanos. Buenos Aires, E Argentina 38°52′S 62°45′W
61 C19 **Médanos** Entre Ríos, E Argentina 33°28′S 59°07′W
155 K24 **Medawachchiya** North Central Province, N Sri Lanka 08°32′N 80°30′E
106 C8 **Mede** Lombardia, N Italy 45°06′N 08°43′E
74 J5 **Médéa** *var.* El Mediyya, Lemdiyya. N Algeria 36°15′N 02°48′E
Medeba *see* Ma'dabā
54 E8 **Medellín** Antioquia, NW Colombia 06°15′N 75°36′W
100 H9 **Medem** ≈ NW Germany
98 J8 **Medemblik** Noord-Holland, NW Netherlands 52°47′N 05°06′E
75 N7 **Médenine** *var.* Madanīyīn. SE Tunisia 33°23′N 10°30′E
76 G9 **Mederdra** Trarza, SW Mauritania 16°56′N 15°40′W
Medeshamstede *see* Peterborough
42 F4 **Medesto Mendez** Izabal, NE Guatemala 15°54′N 89°13′W
19 O11 **Medford** Massachusetts, NE USA 42°25′N 71°08′W
27 N8 **Medford** Oklahoma, C USA 36°48′N 97°45′W
32 G15 **Medford** Oregon, NW USA 42°20′N 122°52′W
30 K6 **Medford** Wisconsin, N USA 45°08′N 90°22′W
39 P10 **Medfra** Alaska, USA 63°06′N 154°42′W
116 M14 **Medgidia** Constanța, SE Romania 44°15′N 28°16′E
Medgyes *see* Mediaș
43 O5 **Media Luna, Arrecifes de la** *reef* E Honduras
60 G11 **Medianeira** Paraná, S Brazil 25°15′S 54°07′W
29 Y15 **Mediapolis** Iowa, C USA 41°00′N 91°09′W
116 I11 **Mediaș** *Ger.* Mediasch, *Hung.* Medgyes. Sibiu, C Romania 46°10′N 24°20′E
41 S15 **Medias Aguas** Veracruz-Llave, SE Mexico 17°40′N 95°02′W
Mediasch *see* Mediaș
106 G10 **Medicina** Emilia-Romagna, C Italy 44°29′N 11°41′E
33 X16 **Medicine Bow** Wyoming, C USA 41°52′N 106°11′W
37 S2 **Medicine Bow Mountains** ▲▲ Colorado/Wyoming, C USA
33 X16 **Medicine Bow River** ≈ Wyoming, C USA
11 R17 **Medicine Hat** Alberta, SW Canada 50°03′N 110°41′W
26 L7 **Medicine Lodge** Kansas, C USA 37°18′N 98°35′W
26 L7 **Medicine Lodge River** ≈ Kansas/Oklahoma, C USA
112 E7 **Međimurje** *off.* Međimurska Županija. ⬖ *province* N Croatia
Međimurska Županija *see* Međimurje
54 G10 **Medina** Cundinamarca, C Colombia 04°31′N 73°21′W
18 E9 **Medina** New York, NE USA 43°13′N 78°23′W
29 O5 **Medina** North Dakota, N USA 46°53′N 99°18′W
31 T11 **Medina** Ohio, N USA 41°08′N 81°51′W
25 Q11 **Medina** Texas, SW USA 29°46′N 99°14′W
Medina *see* Al Madīnah
105 P6 **Medinaceli** Castilla y León, N Spain 41°10′N 02°26′W
104 L6 **Medina del Campo** Castilla y León, N Spain 41°18′N 04°55′W
104 L5 **Medina de Ríoseco** Castilla y León, N Spain 41°53′N 05°03′W
Médina Gonassé *see* Médina Gounas
76 H12 **Médina Gounas** *var.* Médina Gonassé. S Senegal 13°06′N 13°49′W
25 S12 **Medina River** ≈ Texas, SW USA
104 K16 **Medina Sidonia** Andalucía, S Spain 36°28′N 05°55′W
Medinat Israel *see* Israel
119 H14 **Medininkai** Vilnius, SE Lithuania 54°32′N 25°40′E
153 R16 **Medinīpur** West Bengal, NE India 22°25′N 87°24′E
Mediolanum *see* Saintes, France
Mediolanum *see* Milano, Italy
Mediomatrica *see* Metz
121 Q11 **Mediterranean Ridge** *undersea feature* C Mediterranean Sea 34°00′N 23°00′E
121 O16 **Mediterranean Sea** *Fr.* Mer Méditerranée. *sea* Africa/Asia/Europe
Méditerranée, Mer *see* Mediterranean Sea
79 N17 **Medje** Orientale, NE Dem. Rep. Congo 02°27′N 27°14′E
Medjerda, Oued *see* Mejerda
114 G7 **Medkovets** Montana, NW Bulgaria 43°39′N 23°22′E
93 J15 **Medle** Västerbotten, N Sweden 64°45′N 20°45′E
127 W7 **Mednogorsk** Orenburgskaya Oblast', W Russian Federation 51°24′N 57°37′E
123 W9 **Mednyy, Ostrov** *island* E Russian Federation
102 J12 **Médoc** *cultural region* SW France
159 Q16 **Mêdog** Xizang Zizhiqu, W China 29°26′N 95°26′E
28 J5 **Medora** North Dakota, N USA 46°56′N 103°40′W
79 E17 **Médouneu** Woleu-Ntem, N Gabon 0°58′N 10°50′E
106 I7 **Meduna** ≈ NE Italy
Medunta *see* Mantes-la-Jolie
Medvedica *see* Medveditsa
124 J16 **Medveditsa** *var.* Medvedica. ≈ W Russian Federation
127 O9 **Medveditsa** ≈ SW Russian Federation
112 E8 **Medvednica** ▲▲ NE Croatia
125 R15 **Medvedok** Kirovskaya Oblast', NW Russian Federation 57°23′N 50°01′E
123 S6 **Medvezh'i, Ostrova** *island group* NE Russian Federation
124 J9 **Medvezh'yegorsk** Respublika Kareliya, NW Russian Federation 62°56′N 34°26′E
109 T11 **Medvode** *Ger.* Zwischenwässern. NW Slovenia 46°09′N 14°21′E
126 J4 **Medyn'** Kaluzhskaya Oblast', W Russian Federation 54°59′N 35°52′E
180 J10 **Meekatharra** Western Australia 26°37′S 118°35′E
37 Q4 **Meeker** Colorado, C USA 40°02′N 107°54′W
13 T12 **Meelpaeg Lake** ◎ Newfoundland, Newfoundland and Labrador, E Canada
Meemu Atoll *see* Mulakatholhu
Meenen *see* Menen
101 M16 **Meerane** Sachsen, E Germany 50°50′N 12°28′E
101 D15 **Meerbusch** Nordrhein-Westfalen, W Germany 51°19′N 06°43′E
98 I12 **Meerkerk** Zuid-Holland, C Netherlands 51°55′N 05°00′E
99 L18 **Meerssen** *var.* Mersen. Limburg, SE Netherlands 50°53′N 05°45′E
152 J10 **Meerut** Uttar Pradesh, N India 29°01′N 77°41′E
33 U13 **Meeteetse** Wyoming, C USA 44°10′N 108°53′W
99 K17 **Meeuwen** Limburg, NE Belgium 51°04′N 05°36′E
81 J16 **Mēga** Oromīya, C Ethiopia 04°03′N 38°15′E
81 J16 **Mēga Escarpment** *escarpment* S Ethiopia
Megála Kalívia *see* Megála Kalývia
115 E16 **Megála Kalývia** *var.* Megála Kalívia. Thessalía, C Greece 39°30′N 21°48′E
115 H14 **Megáli Panagiá** *var.* Megáli Panayía. Kentrikí Makedonía, N Greece 40°24′N 23°42′E
Megáli Panayía *see* Megáli Panagiá
Megáli Préspa, Límni *see* Prespa, Lake
114 K12 **Megálo Livádi** ▲ Bulgaria/Greece 41°18′N 25°51′E
115 E20 **Megalópoli** *prev.* Megalópolis. Pelopónnisos, S Greece 37°24′N 22°08′E
Megalópolis *see* Megalópoli
171 U12 **Megamo** Papua, E Indonesia 0°55′S 131°46′E
115 C18 **Meganísi** *island* Iónia Nisiá, Greece, C Mediterranean Sea
Meganom, Mys *see* Mehanom, Mys
Mégantic *see* Lac-Mégantic
15 R12 **Mégantic, Mont** ▲ Québec, SE Canada 45°27′N 71°09′W
115 G19 **Mégara** Attikí, C Greece 38°00′N 23°20′E
25 R5 **Megargel** Texas, SW USA 33°27′N 98°55′W
98 K13 **Megen** Noord-Brabant, S Netherlands 51°49′N 05°34′E
153 U13 **Meghālaya** ⬖ *state* NE India
153 U16 **Meghna Nadi** ≈ S Bangladesh
137 V14 **Meghri** *Rus.* Megri. SE Armenia 38°57′N 46°15′E
115 Q23 **Megísti** *var.* Kastellórizon. *island* SE Greece
Megri *see* Meghri
Mehabad *see* Mahābād
116 F13 **Mehadia** *Hung.* Mehádia. Caraș-Severin, SW Romania 44°53′N 22°20′E
Mehádia *see* Mehadia
92 L7 **Mehamn** Finnmark, N Norway 71°01′N 27°46′E
117 U13 **Mehanom, Mys** *Rus.* Mys Meganom. *headland* S Ukraine 44°48′N 35°04′E
149 P14 **Mehar** Sind, SE Pakistan 27°12′N 67°51′E
180 J8 **Meharry, Mount** ▲ Western Australia 23°17′S 118°48′E
Mehdia *see* Mahdia
116 G14 **Mehedinți** ⬖ *county* SW Romania
153 S15 **Meherpur** Khulna, W Bangladesh 23°47′N 88°40′E
21 W8 **Meherrin River** ≈ North Carolina/Virginia, SE USA
Meheso *see* Mī'ēso
191 T11 **Mehetia** *island* Îles du Vent, W French Polynesia
118 K6 **Mehikoorma** Tartumaa, E Estonia 58°14′N 27°29′E
Me Hka *see* Nmai Hka
143 N5 **Mehrabad** ✕ (Tehrān) Tehrān, N Iran 35°46′N 51°07′E
142 J7 **Mehrān** Īlām, W Iran 33°07′N 46°10′E
143 Q14 **Mehrān, Rūd-e** *prev.* Mansurabad. ≈ W Iran
143 Q9 **Mehrīz** Yazd, C Iran 31°32′N 54°28′E
149 R5 **Mehtar Lām** *var.* Mehtarlām, Meterlam, Methariam, Metharlam. Laghmān, E Afghanistan 34°39′N 70°10′E
Mehtarlām *see* Mehtar Lām
103 N8 **Mehun-sur-Yèvre** Cher, C France 47°09′N 02°15′E
79 G14 **Meiganga** Adamaoua, NE Cameroon 06°31′N 14°07′E
160 H10 **Meigu** *var.* Bapu. Sichuan, C China 28°16′N 103°20′E
163 W11 **Meihekou** *var.* Hailong. Jilin, NE China 42°31′N 125°40′E
99 L15 **Meijel** Limburg, SE Netherlands 51°22′N 05°52′E
Meijiang *see* Ningdu
166 M5 **Meiktila** Mandalay, C Burma (Myanmar) 20°53′N 95°54′E
Meilbhe, Loch *see* Melvin, Lough
108 G7 **Meilen** Zürich, N Switzerland 47°17′N 08°39′E
Meilu *see* Wuchuan
101 J17 **Meiningen** Thüringen, C Germany 50°34′N 10°25′E
108 F9 **Meiringen** Bern, S Switzerland 46°42′N 08°13′E
Meishan *see* Jinzhai
101 O15 **Meissen** *Ger.* Meißen. Sachsen, E Germany 51°10′N 13°28′E
Meißen *see* Meissen
101 I15 **Meissner** ▲ C Germany 51°13′N 09°52′E
99 K25 **Meix-devant-Virton** Luxembourg, SE Belgium 49°36′N 05°27′E
Meixian *see* Meizhou
Meixing *see* Xinjin
161 P13 **Meizhou** *var.* Meixian, Mei Xian. Guangdong, S China 24°21′N 116°05′E
67 P2 **Mejerda** *var.* Oued Medjerda, Wādī Majardah. ≈ Algeria/Tunisia *see also* Medjerda, Oued
42 F7 **Mejicanos** San Salvador, C El Salvador 13°50′N 89°13′W
Méjico *see* Mexico
62 G5 **Mejillones** Antofagasta, N Chile 23°03′S 70°25′W
189 V5 **Mejit Island** *var.* Mājeej. *island* Ratak Chain, NE Marshall Islands
79 F17 **Mékambo** Ogooué-Ivindo, NE Gabon 01°03′N 13°50′E
80 J10 **Mek'elē** *var.* Makale. Tigray, N Ethiopia 13°36′N 39°29′E
74 I10 **Mekerrhane, Sebkha** *var.* Sebkha Meqerghane, Sebkra Mekerrhane. *salt flat* C Algeria
Mekerrhane, Sebkra *see* Mekerrhane, Sebkha
76 G10 **Mékhé** NW Senegal 15°02′N 16°40′W
146 G14 **Mekhinli** Ahal Welaýaty, C Turkmenistan 37°28′N 59°20′E
15 P9 **Mékinac, Lac** ◎ Québec, SE Canada
Meklong *see* Samut Songkhram
74 G6 **Meknès** N Morocco 33°54′N 05°27′W
129 U12 **Mekong** *var.* Lan-ts'ang Chiang, *Cam.* Mékôngk, *Chin.* Lancang Jiang, *Lao.* Mènam Khong, Nam Khong, *Th.* Mae Nam Khong, *Tib.* Dza Chu, *Vtn.* Sông Tiên Giang. ≈ SE Asia
Mékôngk *see* Mekong
167 T15 **Mekong, Mouths of the** *delta* S Vietnam
38 L12 **Mekoryuk** Nunivak Island, Alaska, USA 60°23′N 166°11′W
77 R14 **Mékrou** ≈ N Benin
168 K9 **Melaka** *var.* Malacca. Melaka, Peninsular Malaysia 02°14′N 102°14′E
168 L9 **Melaka** *var.* Malacca. ⬖ *state* Peninsular Malaysia
Melaka, Selat *see* Malacca, Strait of
175 O6 **Melanesia** *island group* W Pacific Ocean
175 P5 **Melanesian Basin** *undersea feature* W Pacific Ocean 0°05′N 160°35′E
171 R9 **Melanguane** Pulau Karakelang, N Indonesia 04°02′N 126°43′E
169 R11 **Melawi, Sungai** ≈ Borneo, N Indonesia
183 N12 **Melbourne** *state capital* Victoria, SE Australia 37°51′S 144°56′E
27 V9 **Melbourne** Arkansas, C USA 36°04′N 91°54′W
23 Y12 **Melbourne** Florida, SE USA 28°04′N 80°36′W
29 W14 **Melbourne** Iowa, C USA 41°57′N 93°07′W
92 G10 **Melbu** Nordland, C Norway 68°31′N 14°50′E
Melchor de Mencos *see* Ciudad Melchor de Mencos
63 F19 **Melchor, Isla** *island* Archipiélago de los Chonos, S Chile
40 M9 **Melchor Ocampo** Zacatecas, C Mexico 24°45′N 101°38′W
14 C11 **Meldrum Bay** Manitoulin Island, Ontario, S Canada 45°55′N 83°06′W
Meleda *see* Mljet
106 D8 **Melegnano** *prev.* Marignano. Lombardia, N Italy 45°22′N 09°19′E
188 F9 **Melekeok** ● Babeldaob, N Palau 07°30′N 134°37′E
112 L9 **Melenci** *Hung.* Melencze. Vojvodina, N Serbia 45°32′N 20°18′E
Melencze *see* Melenci
127 N4 **Melenki** Vladimirskaya Oblast', W Russian Federation 55°21′N 41°37′E
127 V6 **Meleuz** Respublika Bashkortostan, W Russian Federation 52°55′N 55°54′E
12 L6 **Mélèzes, Rivière aux** ≈ Québec, C Canada
78 I11 **Melfi** Guéra, S Chad 11°05′N 17°57′E
107 M17 **Melfi** Basilicata, S Italy 41°00′N 15°33′E
11 U14 **Melfort** Saskatchewan, S Canada 52°52′N 104°38′W
104 H4 **Melgaço** Viana do Castelo, N Portugal 42°07′N 08°15′W
105 N4 **Melgar de Fernamental** Castilla y León, N Spain 42°24′N 04°15′W
74 L6 **Melghir, Chott** *var.* Chott Melrhir. *salt lake* E Algeria
94 H8 **Melhus** Sør-Trøndelag, S Norway 63°17′N 10°18′E
104 H3 **Melide** Galicia, NW Spain 42°54′N 08°01′W
Meligalá *see* Meligalás
115 E21 **Meligalás** *prev.* Meligalá. Pelopónnisos, S Greece 37°13′N 21°58′E
60 L12 **Mel, Ilha do** *island* S Brazil
120 E10 **Melilla** *anc.* Rusaddir, Russadir. Melilla, Spain, N Africa 35°18′N 02°56′W
71 N1 **Melilla** *enclave* Spain, N Africa
63 G18 **Melimoyu, Monte** ▲ S Chile 44°06′S 72°49′W
169 V11 **Melintang, Danau** ◎ Borneo, N Indonesia
117 U7 **Melioratyvne** Dnipropetrovs'ka Oblast', E Ukraine 48°35′N 35°18′E
62 G11 **Melipilla** Santiago, C Chile 33°42′S 71°15′W
115 I25 **Mélissa, Akrotírio** *headland* Kríti, Greece, E Mediterranean Sea 35°06′N 24°33′E
11 W17 **Melita** Manitoba, S Canada 49°16′N 100°59′W
Melita *see* Mljet
Melitene *see* Malatya
107 M23 **Melito di Porto Salvo** Calabria, SW Italy 37°55′N 15°48′E
117 U10 **Melitopol'** Zaporiz'ka Oblast', SE Ukraine 46°49′N 35°23′E
109 V4 **Melk** Niederösterreich, NE Austria 48°14′N 15°21′E
95 K15 **Mellan-Fryken** ◎ C Sweden
99 E17 **Melle** Oost-Vlaanderen, NW Belgium 51°N 03°48′E
100 G13 **Melle** Niedersachsen, NW Germany 52°12′N 08°19′E
95 J17 **Mellerud** Västra Götaland, S Sweden 58°42′N 12°27′E
102 K10 **Melle-sur-Bretonne** Deux-Sèvres, W France 46°13′N 00°07′W
29 P8 **Mellette** South Dakota, N USA 45°07′N 98°29′W
121 O15 **Mellieħa** E Malta 35°58′N 14°21′E
80 B10 **Mellit** Northern Darfur, W Sudan 14°07′N 25°34′E
75 N7 **Mellita** ✕ SE Tunisia 33°47′N 10°51′E
63 G21 **Mellizo Sur, Cerro** ▲ S Chile 48°27′S 73°10′W
100 G9 **Mellum** *island* NW Germany
83 L22 **Melmoth** KwaZulu/Natal, E South Africa 28°35′S 31°25′E
111 D16 **Mělník** *Ger.* Melnik. Středočeský Kraj, NW Czech Republic 50°21′N 14°30′E
122 J12 **Mel'nikovo** Tomskaya Oblast', C Russian Federation 56°35′N 84°11′E
61 G18 **Melo** Cerro Largo, NE Uruguay 32°22′S 54°10′W
Melodunum *see* Melun
Melrhir, Chott *see* Melghir, Chott
183 P7 **Melrose** New South Wales, SE Australia 32°41′S 146°58′E
182 I7 **Melrose** South Australia 32°52′S 138°16′E
29 T7 **Melrose** Minnesota, N USA 45°40′N 94°46′W
33 Q11 **Melrose** Montana, NW USA 45°33′N 112°41′W
37 V12 **Melrose** New Mexico, SW USA 34°25′N 103°37′W
108 I8 **Mels** Sankt Gallen, NE Switzerland 47°03′N 09°26′E
Melsetter *see* Chimanimani
33 V9 **Melstone** Montana, NW USA 46°37′N 107°49′W
101 I16 **Melsungen** Hessen, C Germany 51°08′N 09°33′E
92 L12 **Meltaus** Lappi, NW Finland 66°54′N 25°18′E
97 N19 **Melton Mowbray** C England, United Kingdom 52°46′N 01°04′W
82 Q13 **Meluco** Cabo Delgado, NE Mozambique 12°31′S 39°39′E
103 O5 **Melun** *anc.* Melodunum. Seine-et-Marne, N France 48°32′N 02°40′E
80 F12 **Melut** Upper Nile, NE South Sudan 10°27′N 32°13′E
27 P5 **Melvern Lake** ⊠ Kansas, C USA
11 V16 **Melville** Saskatchewan, S Canada 50°57′N 102°49′W
Melville Bay/Melville Bugt *see* Qimusseriarsuaq
45 O11 **Melville Hall** ✕ (Dominica) NE Dominica 15°33′N 61°19′W
181 O1 **Melville Island** *island* Northern Territory, N Australia
197 O8 **Melville Island** *island* Parry Islands, Northwest Territories, NW Canada
11 W9 **Melville, Lake** ◎ Newfoundland and Labrador, E Canada
9 O7 **Melville Peninsula** *peninsula* Nunavut, NE Canada
Melville Sound *see* Viscount Melville Sound
25 Q9 **Melvin** Texas, SW USA 31°12′N 99°34′W
97 D15 **Melvin, Lough** *Ir.* Loch Meilbhe. ◎ S Northern Ireland, United Kingdom/Ireland
169 S12 **Memala** Borneo, C Indonesia 01°44′S 112°36′E
113 L22 **Memaliaj** Gjirokastër, S Albania 40°21′N 19°56′E
83 Q14 **Memba** Nampula, NE Mozambique 14°07′S 40°33′E
83 Q14 **Memba, Baia de** *inlet* NE Mozambique
Membidj *see* Manbij
Memel *see* Neman, NE Europe
Memel *see* Klaipeda, Lithuania
101 J23 **Memmingen** Bayern, S Germany 47°59′N 10°11′E
27 U1 **Memphis** Missouri, C USA 40°28′N 92°11′W
20 E10 **Memphis** Tennessee, S USA 35°09′N 90°03′W
25 P3 **Memphis** Texas, SW USA 34°43′N 100°34′W
20 E10 **Memphis** ✕ Tennessee, S USA 35°02′N 89°57′W
15 Q13 **Memphrémagog, Lac** *var.* Lake Memphremagog. ◎ Canada/USA *see also* Lake Memphremagog
19 N6 **Memphremagog, Lake** *var.* Lac Memphrémagog. ◎ Canada/USA *see also* Memphrémagog, Lac
117 Q2 **Mena** Chernihivs'ka Oblast', NE Ukraine 51°30′N 32°15′E
27 S12 **Mena** Arkansas, C USA 34°40′N 94°15′W
Menaam *see* Menaldum
Menado *see* Manado
106 D6 **Menaggio** Lombardia, N Italy 46°03′N 09°14′E
29 T6 **Menahga** Minnesota, N USA 46°45′N 95°06′W
77 R10 **Ménaka** Goa, E Mali 15°55′N 02°25′E
98 K5 **Menaldum** *Fris.* Menaam. Fryslân, N Netherlands 53°14′N 05°38′E
Mènam Khong *see* Mekong
74 E7 **Menara** ✕ (Marrakech) C Morocco 31°36′N 08°00′W
25 Q9 **Menard** Texas, SW USA 30°56′N 99°48′W
193 Q12 **Menard Fracture Zone** *tectonic feature* E Pacific Ocean
30 M7 **Menasha** Wisconsin, N USA 44°13′N 88°25′W
Mencezi Garagum *see* Merkezi Garagumy
193 U9 **Mendaña Fracture Zone** *tectonic feature* E Pacific Ocean
169 S13 **Mendawai, Sungai** ≈ Borneo, C Indonesia
103 P13 **Mende** *anc.* Mimatum. Lozère, S France 44°32′N 03°30′E
81 J14 **Mendebo** ▲▲ C Ethiopia
80 J9 **Mendefera** *prev.* Adi Ugri. S Eritrea 14°53′N 38°51′E
197 S7 **Mendeleyev Ridge** *undersea feature* Arctic Ocean
127 T3 **Mendeleyevsk** Respublika Tatarstan, W Russian Federation 55°54′N 52°19′E
101 F15 **Menden** Nordrhein-Westfalen, W Germany 51°26′N 07°47′E
22 L6 **Mendenhall** Mississippi, S USA 31°57′N 89°52′W
38 L13 **Mendenhall, Cape** *headland* Nunivak Island, Alaska, USA 59°45′N 166°10′W
41 P9 **Méndez** *var.* Villa de Méndez. Tamaulipas, C Mexico 25°06′N 98°32′W
80 H13 **Mendī** Oromīya C Ethiopia 09°43′N 35°07′E
186 C7 **Mendi** Southern Highlands, W Papua New Guinea 06°13′S 143°39′E
97 K22 **Mendip Hills** *var.* Mendips. *hill range* S England, United Kingdom
Mendips *see* Mendip Hills
34 L6 **Mendocino** California, W USA 39°18′N 123°48′W
34 J3 **Mendocino, Cape** *headland* California, W USA 40°26′N 124°24′W
0 B8 **Mendocino Fracture Zone** *tectonic feature* NE Pacific Ocean
35 P10 **Mendota** California, W USA 36°44′N 120°24′W
30 L11 **Mendota** Illinois, N USA 41°32′N 89°04′W
30 K8 **Mendota, Lake** ◎ Wisconsin, N USA
62 I11 **Mendoza** Mendoza, W Argentina 33°00′S 68°47′W
62 I12 **Mendoza** *off.* Provincia de Mendoza. ⬖ *province* W Argentina
Mendoza, Provincia de *see* Mendoza
108 H12 **Mendrisio** Ticino, S Switzerland 45°53′N 08°59′E
168 L10 **Mendung** Pulau Mendol, W Indonesia 0°33′N 103°09′E
54 I5 **Mene de Mauroa** Falcón, NW Venezuela 10°39′N 71°04′W
54 I5 **Mene Grande** Zulia, NW Venezuela 09°51′N 70°57′W
136 B14 **Menemen** İzmir, W Turkey 38°34′N 27°03′E
99 C18 **Menen** *var.* Meenen, *Fr.* Menin. West-Vlaanderen, W Belgium 50°48′N 03°07′E
163 Q8 **Menengiyn Tal** *plain* E Mongolia
189 R9 **Meneng Point** *headland* SW Nauru 0°33′S 166°57′E
92 L10 **Menesjärvi** *Lapp.* Menešjávri. Lappi, N Finland 68°39′N 26°22′E
Menešjávri *see* Menesjärvi
107 I24 **Menfi** Sicilia, Italy, C Mediterranean Sea 37°36′N 12°59′E
161 P7 **Mengcheng** Anhui, E China 33°15′N 116°33′E
160 F15 **Menghai** Yunnan, SW China 22°02′N 100°18′E
160 F15 **Mengla** Yunnan, SW China 21°30′N 101°33′E
65 F24 **Menguera Point** *headland* East Falkland, Falkland Islands
160 M13 **Mengzhu Ling** ▲▲ S China
160 H14 **Mengzi** Yunnan, SW China 23°20′N 103°32′E
114 H13 **Meníkio** *var.* Menoíkio. ▲ NE Greece 40°50′N 12°40′E
Menin *see* Menen
182 L7 **Menindee** New South Wales, SE Australia 32°24′S 142°25′E
182 L7 **Menindee Lake** ◎ New South Wales, SE Australia
182 J10 **Meningie** South Australia 35°43′S 139°20′E
103 O5 **Mennecy** Essonne, N France 48°34′N 02°25′E
29 Q12 **Menno** South Dakota, N USA 43°14′N 97°34′W
114 H13 **Menoíkio** ▲▲ NE Greece
Menoíkio *see* Meníkio
31 N5 **Menominee** Michigan, N USA 45°06′N 87°36′W
30 M5 **Menominee River** ≈ Michigan/Wisconsin, N USA
30 M8 **Menomonee Falls** Wisconsin, N USA 43°11′N 88°09′W
30 I6 **Menomonie** Wisconsin, N USA 44°52′N 91°55′W
83 D14 **Menongue** *var.* Vila Serpa Pinto, *Port.* Serpa Pinto. Cuando Cubango, C Angola 14°38′S 17°39′E
120 H8 **Menorca** *Eng.* Minorca; *anc.* Balearis Minor. *island* Islas Baleares, Spain, W Mediterranean Sea
105 S13 **Menor, Mar** *lagoon* SE Spain
39 S10 **Mentasta Lake** ◎ Alaska, USA
39 S10 **Mentasta Mountains** ▲▲ Alaska, USA
168 I13 **Mentawai, Kepulauan** *island group* W Indonesia
168 I12 **Mentawai, Selat** *strait* W Indonesia
168 M12 **Mentok** Pulau Bangka, W Indonesia 02°01′S 105°10′E
103 V15 **Menton** *It.* Mentone. Alpes-Maritimes, SE France 43°47′N 07°30′E
24 K8 **Mentone** Texas, SW USA 31°42′N 103°36′W
Mentone *see* Menton
31 U11 **Mentor** Ohio, N USA 41°40′N 81°20′W
169 U10 **Menyapa, Gunung** ▲ Borneo, N Indonesia 01°04′N 116°01′E
159 T9 **Menyuan** *var.* Menyuan Huizu Zizhixian. Qinghai, C China 37°27′N 101°33′E
Menyuan Huizu Zizhixian *see* Menyuan
74 M5 **Menzel Bourguiba** *var.* Manzil Bū Ruqaybah; *prev.* Ferryville. N Tunisia 37°09′N 09°51′E
136 M15 **Menzelet Barajı** ⊠ C Turkey
127 T4 **Menzelinsk** Respublika Tatarstan, W Russian Federation 55°44′N 53°00′E
180 K11 **Menzies** Western Australia 29°42′S 121°04′E
195 V6 **Menzies, Mount** ▲ Antarctica 73°32′S 61°02′E
40 J6 **Meoqui** Chihuahua, N Mexico 28°18′N 105°30′W
83 N14 **Meponda** Niassa, NE Mozambique 13°20′S 34°53′E
98 M8 **Meppel** Drenthe, NE Netherlands 52°42′N 06°12′E
100 E12 **Meppen** Niedersachsen, NW Germany 52°42′N 07°18′E
Meqerghane, Sebkha *see* Mekerrhane, Sebkha
105 T6 **Mequinenza, Embalse de** ⊠ NE Spain
30 M8 **Mequon** Wisconsin, N USA 43°13′N 87°57′W
Mera *see* Maira
182 D3 **Meramangye, Lake** *salt lake* South Australia
27 W5 **Meramec River** ≈ Missouri, C USA
Meran *see* Merano
168 K13 **Merangin** ≈ Sumatera, W Indonesia
106 G5 **Merano** *Ger.* Meran. Trentino-Alto Adige, N Italy 46°40′N 11°10′E
168 K8 **Merapuh Lama** Pahang, Peninsular Malaysia 04°37′N 101°58′E
106 D7 **Merate** Lombardia, N Italy 45°42′N 09°26′E
169 U13 **Meratus, Pegunungan** ▲▲ Borneo, N Indonesia
171 Y16 **Merauke, Sungai** ≈ Papua, E Indonesia
182 L9 **Merbein** Victoria, SE Australia 34°11′S 142°03′E
99 F21 **Merbes-le-Château** Hainaut, S Belgium 50°19′N 04°09′E
Merca *see* Marka
54 C13 **Mercaderes** Cauca, SW Colombia 01°46′N 77°09′W
Mercara *see* Madikeri
35 P9 **Merced** California, W USA 37°17′N 120°30′W
61 C20 **Mercedes** Buenos Aires, E Argentina 34°42′S 59°30′W
61 D15 **Mercedes** Corrientes, NE Argentina 29°09′S 58°05′W
61 D19 **Mercedes** Soriano, SW Uruguay 33°16′S 58°01′W
25 S17 **Mercedes** Texas, SW USA 26°09′N 97°54′W
Mercedes *see* Villa Mercedes
35 R9 **Merced Peak** ▲ California, W USA 37°34′N 119°30′W
35 P9 **Merced River** ≈ California, W USA
18 B13 **Mercer** Pennsylvania, NE USA 41°14′N 80°14′W
99 G18 **Merchtem** Vlaams Brabant, C Belgium 50°57′N 04°14′E
15 O13 **Mercier** Québec, SE Canada 45°15′N 73°45′W
25 Q9 **Mercury** Texas, SW USA 31°23′N 99°09′W
184 M5 **Mercury Islands** *island group* N New Zealand
19 O9 **Meredith** New Hampshire, NE USA 43°36′N 71°28′W
65 B25 **Meredith, Cape** *var.* Cabo Belgrano. *headland* West Falkland, Falkland Islands 52°15′S 60°40′W
37 V6 **Meredith, Lake** ◎ Colorado, C USA
25 N2 **Meredith, Lake** ⊠ Texas, SW USA
81 O16 **Mereeg** *var.* Mareeq, *It.* Meregh. Galguduud, E Somalia 03°47′N 47°19′E
117 V5 **Merefa** Kharkivs'ka Oblast', E Ukraine 49°49′N 36°05′E
Meregh *see* Mereeg
99 E17 **Merelbeke** Oost-Vlaanderen, NW Belgium 51°00′N 03°45′E
Merend *see* Marand
167 T12 **Méreuch** Môndól Kiri, E Cambodia 13°01′N 107°26′E
Mergate *see* Margate
Mergui *see* Myeik
Mergui Archipelago *see* Myeik Archipelago
114 L12 **Meriç** Edirne, NW Turkey 41°12′N 26°24′E
114 L12 **Meriç** *Bul.* Maritsa, *Gk.* Évros; *anc.* Hebrus. ≈ SE Europe *see also* Évros/Maritsa
41 X12 **Mérida** Yucatán, SW Mexico 20°58′N 89°35′W
104 J11 **Mérida** *anc.* Augusta Emerita. Extremadura, W Spain 38°55′N 06°20′W
54 I6 **Mérida** Mérida, W Venezuela 08°36′N 71°08′W
54 H7 **Mérida** *off.* Estado Mérida. ⬖ *state* W Venezuela
Mérida, Estado *see* Mérida
18 M13 **Meriden** Connecticut, NE USA 41°32′N 72°48′W
22 M5 **Meridian** Mississippi, S USA 32°24′N 88°43′W
25 S8 **Meridian** Texas, SW USA 31°56′N 97°40′W
102 J13 **Mérignac** Gironde, SW France 44°50′N 00°40′W
102 J13 **Mérignac** ✕ (Bordeaux) Gironde, SW France 44°51′N 00°44′W
93 J18 **Merikarvia** Länsi-Suomi, SW Finland 61°51′N 21°30′E
183 R12 **Merimbula** New South Wales, SE Australia 36°52′S 149°51′E
182 L9 **Meringur** Victoria, SE Australia 34°26′S 141°19′E
Merín, Laguna *see* Mirim Lagoon
97 I19 **Merioneth** *cultural region* W Wales, United Kingdom
188 A11 **Merir** *island* Palau Islands, N Palau
188 B17 **Merizo** SW Guam 13°15′N 144°40′E
Merjama *see* Märjamaa
Merke *see* Merki
25 P7 **Merkel** Texas, SW USA 32°28′N 100°00′W
146 E12 **Merkezi Garagumy** *var.* Mencezi Garagum, *Rus.* Tsentral'nyye Nizmennyye Garagumy. *desert* C Turkmenistan
145 S16 **Merki** *prev.* Merke. Zhambyl, S Kazakhstan 42°48′N 73°10′E
119 F15 **Merkinė** Alytus, S Lithuania 54°09′N 24°11′E
99 G16 **Merksem** Antwerpen, N Belgium 51°17′N 04°26′E

◆ Country
● Country Capital
◇ Dependent Territory
○ Dependent Territory Capital
⬖ Administrative Regions
✕ International Airport
▲ Mountain
▲▲ Mountain Range
Volcano
≈ River
◎ Lake
⊠ Reservoir

99 I15 Merksplas Antwerpen, N Belgium 51°22′N 04°54′E
Merkulovichi see Myerkulavichy
119 G15 Merkys ≈ S Lithuania
32 F15 Merlin Oregon, NW USA 42°34′N 123°23′W
61 C20 Merlo Buenos Aires, E Argentina 34°39′S 58°45′W
138 G8 Meron, Harei prev. Haré Meron. ▲ N Israel 35°06′N 33°00′E
74 K6 Merouane, Chott salt lake NE Algeria
80 F7 Merowe Northern, N Sudan 18°29′N 31°49′E
180 J12 Merredin Western Australia 31°31′S 118°18′E
97 I14 Merrick ▲ S Scotland, United Kingdom 55°09′N 04°28′W
32 H16 Merrill Oregon, NW USA 42°00′N 121°37′W
30 L5 Merrill Wisconsin, N USA 45°12′N 89°43′W
31 N11 Merrillville Indiana, N USA 41°28′N 87°19′W
19 O10 Merrimack River ≈ Massachusetts/New Hampshire, NE USA
28 L12 Merriman Nebraska, C USA 42°54′N 101°42′W
11 N17 Merritt British Columbia, SW Canada 50°09′N 120°49′W
23 Y12 Merritt Island Florida, SE USA 28°21′N 80°42′W
23 Y11 Merritt Island island Florida, SE USA
28 M12 Merritt Reservoir ⊠ Nebraska, C USA
183 S7 Merriwa New South Wales, SE Australia 32°09′S 150°24′E
183 O8 Merriwagga New South Wales, SE Australia 33°51′S 145°38′E
22 G8 Merryville Louisiana, S USA 30°45′N 93°32′W
80 K9 Mersa Fat'ma E Eritrea 14°52′N 40°16′E
102 M7 Mer St-Aubin Loir-et-Cher, C France 47°42′N 01°31′E
99 M24 Mersch Luxembourg, C Luxembourg 49°45′N 06°06′E
101 M15 Merseburg Sachsen-Anhalt, C Germany 51°22′N 12°00′E
Mersen see Meerssen
97 K18 Mersey ≈ NW England, United Kingdom
136 J17 Mersin var. İçel. İçel, S Turkey 36°50′N 34°39′E
Mersin see İçel
168 L9 Mersing Johor, Peninsular Malaysia 02°25′N 103°50′E
118 E8 Mērsrags NW Latvia 57°21′N 23°05′E
Merta see Merta City
152 G12 Merta City var. Merta. Rājasthān, N India 26°40′N 74°04′E
152 F12 Merta Road Rājasthān, N India 26°42′N 73°54′E
97 J21 Merthyr Tydfil S Wales, United Kingdom 51°46′N 03°23′W
104 H13 Mértola Beja, S Portugal 37°38′N 07°40′W
144 G14 Mertvyy Kultuk, Sor salt flat SW Kazakhstan
195 V16 Mertz Glacier glacier Antarctica
99 M24 Mertzig Diekirch, C Luxembourg 49°50′N 06°00′E
25 O9 Mertzon Texas, SW USA 31°16′N 100°50′W
103 N4 Méru Oise, N France 49°15′N 02°07′E
81 I18 Meru Eastern, C Kenya 0°03′N 37°38′E
81 I20 Meru, Mount ▲ NE Tanzania 03°12′S 36°45′E
Merv see Mary
Mervdasht see Marv Dasht
136 K11 Merzifon Amasya, N Turkey 40°52′N 35°28′E
101 D20 Merzig Saarland, SW Germany 49°27′N 06°39′E
36 L14 Mesa Arizona, SW USA 33°25′N 111°49′W
29 V4 Mesabi Range ▲▲ Minnesota, N USA
54 H6 Mesa Bolívar Mérida, NW Venezuela 08°30′N 71°38′W
107 Q18 Mesagne Puglia, SE Italy 40°33′N 17°49′E
39 P12 Mesa Mountain ▲ Alaska, USA 60°26′N 155°14′W
115 J25 Mesará lowland Kríti, Greece, E Mediterranean Sea
37 S14 Mescalero New Mexico, SW USA 33°09′N 105°46′W
101 G15 Meschede Nordrhein-Westfalen, W Germany 51°21′N 08°16′E
137 Q12 Mescit Dağları ▲▲ NE Turkey
189 V13 Mesegon island Chuuk, C Micronesia
Meseritz see Międzyrzecz
54 F11 Mesetas Meta, C Colombia 03°14′N 74°09′W
Meshchera Lowland see Meshcherskaya Nizmennost'
Meshcherskaya Nizina see Meshcherskaya Nizmennost'
126 M4 Meshcherskaya Nizmennost' var. Meshcherskaya Nizina, Eng. Meshchera Lowland. basin W Russian Federation
126 J5 Meshchovsk Kaluzhskaya Oblast', W Russian Federation 54°21′N 35°23′E
125 R9 Meshchura Respublika Komi, NW Russian Federation 63°18′N 50°56′E
Meshed see Mashhad
Meshed-i-Sar see Bābolsar
80 E13 Meshra'er Req Warap, W South Sudan 08°30′N 29°27′E
37 R15 Mesilla New Mexico, SW USA 32°15′N 106°49′W
108 H10 Mesocco Ger. Misox. Ticino, S Switzerland 46°18′N 09°13′E
115 D18 Mesolóngi prev. Mesolóngion. Dytikí Elláda, W Greece 38°21′N 21°26′E
Mesolóngion see Mesolóngi
14 E8 Mesomikenda Lake ◎ Ontario, S Canada
61 D15 Mesopotamia var. Mesopotamia Argentina. physical region NE Argentina
Mesopotamia Argentina see Mesopotamia
35 Y10 Mesquite Nevada, W USA 36°47′N 114°04′W
82 Q13 Messalo, Rio var. Mualo. ≈ NE Mozambique
Messana/Messene see Messina
99 L25 Messancy Luxembourg, SE Belgium 49°36′N 05°49′E
107 M23 Messina var. Messana, Messene; anc. Zancle. Sicilia, Italy, C Mediterranean Sea 38°12′N 15°33′E
Messina see Musina
Messina, Strait of see Messina, Stretto di
107 M23 Messina, Stretto di Eng. Strait of Messina. strait SW Italy
115 E21 Messíni Pelopónnisos, S Greece 37°03′N 22°00′E
115 E21 Messinía peninsula S Greece
115 E22 Messiniakós Kólpos gulf S Greece
122 J8 Messoyakha ≈ N Russian Federation
114 H11 Mesta Gk. Néstos, Turk. Kara Su. ≈ Bulgaria/Greece see also Néstos
Mesta see Néstos
Mestghanem see Mostaganem
137 R8 Mest'ia prev. Mestia, var. Mestiya. N Georgia 43°03′N 42°50′E
Mestia see Mest'ia
Mestiya see Mest'ia
115 K18 Mestón, Akrotírio cape Chíos, E Greece
106 H8 Mestre Veneto, NE Italy 45°30′N 12°14′E
59 M16 Mestre, Espigão ▲▲ E Brazil
169 N14 Mesuji ≈ Sumatera, W Indonesia
Mesule see Grosser Möseler
10 J10 Meszah Peak ▲ British Columbia, W Canada 58°31′N 131°28′W
54 G11 Meta off. Departamento del Meta. ◈ province C Colombia
15 Q8 Metabetchouane ≈ Québec, SE Canada
Meta, Departamento del see Meta
9 S7 Meta Incognita Peninsula peninsula Baffin Island, Nunavut, NE Canada
22 K9 Metairie Louisiana, S USA 29°58′N 90°09′W
32 M6 Metaline Falls Washington, NW USA 48°51′N 117°21′W
62 K6 Metán Salta, N Argentina 25°29′S 64°57′W
82 N13 Metangula Niassa, N Mozambique 12°41′S 34°50′E
42 E7 Metapán Santa Ana, NW El Salvador 14°20′N 89°28′W
54 K9 Meta, Río ≈ Colombia/Venezuela
106 I11 Metauro ≈ C Italy
80 H11 Metema Āmara, N Ethiopia 12°53′N 36°10′E
115 D15 Metéora religious building Thessalía, C Greece
65 O20 Meteor Rise undersea feature SW Indian Ocean 46°00′S 05°30′E
186 G5 Meteran New Hanover, NE Papua New Guinea 02°40′S 150°12′E
Meterlam see Mehtar Lām
115 G20 Methanon peninsula S Greece
Metharian/Metharlam see Mehtar Lām
32 J6 Methow River ≈ Washington, NW USA
19 O10 Methuen Massachusetts, NE USA 42°43′N 71°10′W
185 G19 Methven Canterbury, South Island, New Zealand 43°37′S 171°38′E
Metis see Metz
113 G15 Metković Dubrovnik-Neretva, SE Croatia 43°02′N 17°37′E
39 Y14 Metlakatla Annette Island, Alaska, USA 55°07′N 131°34′W
109 V13 Metlika Ger. Möttling. SE Slovenia 45°38′N 15°18′E
109 T8 Metnitz Kärnten, S Austria 46°58′N 14°09′E
27 W12 Meto, Bayou ≈ Arkansas, C USA
168 M15 Metro Sumatera, W Indonesia 05°05′S 105°20′E
30 M17 Metropolis Illinois, N USA 37°09′N 88°43′W
Metropolitan see Santiago
35 N8 Metropolitan Oakland ✈ California, W USA 37°42′N 122°13′W
115 D15 Métsovo prev. Métsovon. Ípeiros, C Greece 39°47′N 21°12′E
Métsovon see Métsovo
23 V5 Metter Georgia, SE USA 32°24′N 82°03′W
99 H21 Mettet Namur, S Belgium 50°19′N 04°43′E
101 D20 Mettlach Saarland, SW Germany 49°28′N 06°37′E
Mettu see Metu
80 H13 Metu var. Mattu, Mettu. Oromīya, C Ethiopia 08°18′N 35°39′E
138 G8 Metula prev. Metulla. Northern, N Israel 33°16′N 35°35′E
Metulla see Metula
169 T10 Metulang Borneo, N Indonesia 01°28′N 114°40′E
103 T4 Metz anc. Divodurum Mediomatricum, Mediomatrica, Metis. Moselle, NE France 49°07′N 06°09′E
101 H22 Metzingen Baden-Württemberg, S Germany 48°31′N 09°16′E
168 G8 Meulaboh Sumatera, W Indonesia 04°10′N 96°09′E
99 D18 Meulebeke West-Vlaanderen, W Belgium 50°57′N 03°18′E
103 U6 Meurthe ≈ NE France
103 S5 Meurthe-et-Moselle ◈ department NE France
103 S4 Meuse ◈ department NE France
84 F10 Meuse Dut. Maas. ≈ W Europe see also Maas
Meuse see Maas
Mexcala, Río see Balsas, Río
25 U8 Mexia Texas, SW USA 31°40′N 96°28′W
58 K11 Mexiana, Ilha island NE Brazil
40 C1 Mexicali Baja California Norte, NW Mexico 32°34′N 115°26′W
Mexicanos, Estados Unidos see Mexico
41 O14 México var. Ciudad de México, Eng. Mexico City. ● (Mexico) México, C Mexico 19°26′N 99°08′W
27 V4 Mexico Missouri, C USA 39°10′N 91°54′W
18 H9 Mexico New York, NE USA 43°27′N 76°14′W
40 L7 Mexico off. United Mexican States, var. Méjico, México, Sp. Estados Unidos Mexicanos. ◆ federal republic N Central America
41 O13 México ◈ state S Mexico
México see Mexico
0 J13 Mexico Basin var. Sigsbee Deep. undersea feature C Gulf of Mexico 25°00′N 92°00′W
Mexico City see México
México, Golfo de see Mexico, Gulf of
44 B4 Mexico, Gulf of Sp. Golfo de México. gulf W Atlantic Ocean
Meyadine see Al Mayādīn
Meydān Shahr see Maīdān Shahr
39 Y14 Meyers Chuck Etolin Island, Alaska, USA 55°44′N 132°15′W
Meymaneh see Maīmanah
143 N7 Meymeh Eşfahān, C Iran 33°29′N 51°09′E
123 V7 Meynypil'gyno Chukotskiy Avtonomnyy Okrug, NE Russian Federation 62°33′N 177°00′E
108 A10 Meyrin Genève, SW Switzerland 46°14′N 06°05′E
166 L7 Mezaligon Ayeyarwady, SW Burma (Myanmar) 17°53′N 95°12′E
41 O15 Mezcala Guerrero, S Mexico 17°55′N 99°34′W
114 H8 Mezdra Vratsa, NW Bulgaria 43°08′N 23°42′E
103 P16 Mèze Hérault, S France 43°26′N 03°37′E
125 O6 Mezen' Arkhangel'skaya Oblast', NW Russian Federation 65°54′N 44°10′E
125 P8 Mezen' ≈ NW Russian Federation
Mezen, Bay of see Mezenskaya Guba
103 Q13 Mézenc, Mont ▲ C France 44°57′N 04°15′E
125 O8 Mezenskaya Guba var. Bay of Mezen. bay NW Russian Federation
Mezha see Myazha
122 H6 Mezhdusharskiy, Ostrov island Novaya Zemlya, N Russian Federation
Mezhëvo see Myezhava
Mezhgor'ye see Mizhhir"ya
117 V8 Mezhova Dnipropetrovs'ka Oblast', E Ukraine 48°15′N 36°44′E
10 J12 Meziadin Junction British Columbia, W Canada 56°06′N 129°15′W
111 G16 Mezileské Sedlo var. Przełęcz Międzyleska. pass Czech Republic/Poland
102 L14 Mézin Lot-et-Garonne, SW France 44°03′N 00°16′E
111 M24 Mezőberény Békés, SE Hungary 46°49′N 21°00′E
111 M25 Mezőhegyes Békés, SE Hungary 46°20′N 20°48′E
111 M25 Mezőkovácsháza Békés, SE Hungary 46°24′N 20°52′E
111 M21 Mezőkövesd Borsod-Abaúj-Zemplén, NE Hungary 47°49′N 20°32′E
Mezőtelegd see Tileagd
111 M23 Mezőtúr Jász-Nagykun-Szolnok, E Hungary 47°N 20°37′E
40 K10 Mezquital Durango, C Mexico 23°31′N 104°19′W
106 G6 Mezzolombardo Trentino-Alto Adige, N Italy 46°13′N 11°08′E
82 L13 Mfuwe Northern, N Zambia 13°00′S 31°45′E
121 O15 Mġarr Gozo, N Malta 36°01′N 14°18′E
126 H6 Mglin Bryanskaya Oblast', W Russian Federation 53°01′N 32°54′E
Mhálanna, Cionn see Malin Head
154 G10 Mhow Madhya Pradesh, C India 22°32′N 75°49′E
Miadziol Nowy see Myadzyel
171 O6 Miagao Panay Island, C Philippines 10°40′N 122°15′E
41 R17 Miahuatlán var. Miahuatlán de Porfirio Díaz. Oaxaca, SE Mexico 16°21′N 96°36′W
Miahuatlán de Porfirio Díaz see Miahuatlán
104 K10 Miajadas Extremadura, W Spain 39°10′N 05°54′W
Miajlar see Myājlār
36 M14 Miami Arizona, SW USA 33°23′N 110°53′W
23 Z16 Miami Florida, SE USA 25°46′N 80°12′W
27 R8 Miami Oklahoma, C USA 36°53′N 94°54′W
25 O2 Miami Texas, SW USA 35°42′N 100°37′W
23 Z16 Miami ✈ Florida, SE USA 25°47′N 80°16′W
23 Z16 Miami Beach Florida, SE USA 25°47′N 80°08′W
23 Y15 Miami Canal canal Florida, SE USA
31 R14 Miamisburg Ohio, N USA 39°38′N 84°17′W
149 U10 Miān Channūn Punjab, E Pakistan 30°24′N 72°27′E
142 J4 Miāndowāb var. Mianduab, Miyāndoāb. Āžarbāyjān-e Gharbī, NW Iran 36°57′N 46°06′E
172 H5 Miandrivazo Toliara, C Madagascar 19°31′S 45°29′E
Mianduab see Miāndowāb
142 K3 Mīāneh var. Miyāneh. Āžarbāyjān-e Sharqī, NW Iran 37°23′N 47°45′E
149 O16 Miāni Hōr lagoon S Pakistan
160 G10 Mianning Sichuan, C China 28°34′N 102°12′E
149 T7 Miānwāli Punjab, NE Pakistan 32°32′N 71°33′E
160 J7 Mianxian var. Mian Xian. Shaanxi, C China 33°12′N 106°36′E
Mian Xian see Mianxian
160 I8 Mianyang Sichuan, C China 31°29′N 104°43′E
Mianyang see Xiantao
161 R3 Miaodao Qundao island group E China
161 S13 Miaoli N Taiwan 24°33′N 120°48′E
122 F11 Miass Chelyabinskaya Oblast', C Russian Federation 55°00′N 59°55′E
110 G8 Miastko Ger. Rummelsburg in Pommern. Pomorskie, N Poland 54°N 16°58′E
Miava see Myjava
11 O15 Mica Creek British Columbia, SW Canada 51°58′N 118°29′W
160 J7 Micang Shan ▲▲ C China
Mi Chai see Nong Khai
111 O19 Michalovce Ger. Grossmichel, Hung. Nagymihály. Košický Kraj, E Slovakia 48°46′N 21°55′E
99 M20 Michel, Baraque hill E Belgium
39 S5 Michelson, Mount ▲ Alaska, USA 69°19′N 144°16′W
45 P9 Miches E Dominican Republic 18°59′N 69°03′W
30 M4 Michigamme, Lake ◎ Michigan, N USA
30 M4 Michigamme Reservoir ⊠ Michigan, N USA
31 N4 Michigamme River ≈ Michigan, N USA
31 O7 Michigan off. State of Michigan, also known as Great Lakes State, Lake State, Wolverine State. ◈ state N USA
31 O11 Michigan City Indiana, N USA 41°43′N 86°52′W
31 O8 Michigan, Lake ◎ N USA
31 P2 Michipicoten Bay lake bay Ontario, N Canada
14 A8 Michipicoten Island island Ontario, S Canada
14 B7 Michipicoten River Ontario, S Canada 47°56′N 84°48′W
Michurin see Tsarevo
126 M6 Michurinsk Tambovskaya Oblast', W Russian Federation 52°56′N 40°31′E
Mico, Punta/Mico, Punto see Monkey Point
42 L10 Mico, Río ≈ SE Nicaragua
45 T12 Micoud SE Saint Lucia 13°49′N 60°54′W
189 N16 Micronesia off. Federated States of Micronesia. ◆ federation W Pacific Ocean
175 P4 Micronesia island group W Pacific Ocean
Micronesia, Federated States of see Micronesia
169 O9 Midai, Pulau island Kepulauan Natuna, W Indonesia
Mid-Atlantic Cordillera see Mid-Atlantic Ridge
65 M17 Mid-Atlantic Ridge var. Mid-Atlantic Cordillera, Mid-Atlantic Rise, Mid-Atlantic Swell. undersea feature Atlantic Ocean 0°00′N 20°00′W
Mid-Atlantic Rise/Mid-Atlantic Swell see Mid-Atlantic Ridge
99 E15 Middelburg Zeeland, SW Netherlands 51°30′N 03°36′E
83 H24 Middelburg Eastern Cape, S South Africa 31°28′S 25°01′E
83 K21 Middelburg Mpumalanga, NE South Africa 25°47′S 29°28′E
95 G23 Middelfart Syddtjylland, C Denmark 55°30′N 09°44′E
98 G13 Middelharnis Zuid-Holland, SW Netherlands 51°45′N 04°10′E
99 B16 Middelkerke West-Vlaanderen, W Belgium 51°12′N 02°51′E
98 I9 Middenbeemster Noord-Holland, C Netherlands 52°33′N 04°55′E
98 I8 Middenmeer Noord-Holland, NW Netherlands 52°48′N 04°58′E
35 Q2 Middle Alkali Lake ◎ California, W USA
193 S6 Middle America Trench undersea feature E Pacific Ocean 15°00′N 95°00′W
151 P19 Middle Andaman island Andaman Islands, India, NE Indian Ocean
Middle Atlas see Moyen Atlas
21 R3 Middlebourne West Virginia, NE USA 39°30′N 80°53′W
23 W9 Middleburg Florida, SE USA 30°03′N 81°55′W
Middleburg Island see 'Eua
Middle Caicos see Grand Caicos
25 N8 Middle Concho River ≈ Texas, SW USA
Middle Congo see Congo (Republic of)
39 R6 Middle Fork Chandalar River ≈ Alaska, USA
39 Q7 Middle Fork Koyukuk River ≈ Alaska, USA
33 O12 Middle Fork Salmon River ≈ Idaho, NW USA
11 T15 Middle Lake Saskatchewan, S Canada 52°31′N 105°16′W
28 L13 Middle Loup River ≈ Nebraska, C USA
185 E22 Middlemarch Otago, South Island, New Zealand 45°30′S 170°07′E
31 T15 Middleport Ohio, N USA 39°00′N 82°03′W
29 U14 Middle Raccoon River ≈ Iowa, C USA
29 R3 Middle River ≈ Minnesota, N USA
21 N8 Middlesboro Kentucky, S USA 36°37′N 83°42′W
97 M15 Middlesbrough N England, United Kingdom 54°35′N 01°14′W
42 G3 Middlesex Stann Creek, C Belize 17°00′N 88°31′W
97 N22 Middlesex cultural region SE England, United Kingdom
13 P15 Middleton Nova Scotia, SE Canada 44°56′N 65°04′W
20 F10 Middleton Tennessee, S USA 35°05′N 88°57′W
30 L9 Middleton Wisconsin, N USA 43°06′N 89°30′W
39 S13 Middleton Island island Alaska, USA
34 M7 Middletown California, W USA 38°44′N 122°39′W
21 Y2 Middletown Delaware, NE USA 39°25′N 75°39′W
18 K15 Middletown New Jersey, NE USA 40°23′N 74°08′W
18 K13 Middletown New York, NE USA 41°27′N 74°25′W
31 R14 Middletown Ohio, N USA 39°33′N 84°19′W
18 G15 Middletown Pennsylvania, NE USA 40°11′N 76°42′W
141 N14 Mīdī var. Maydī. NW Yemen 16°18′N 42°51′E
103 O16 Midi, Canal du canal S France
102 K17 Midi de Bigorre, Pic du ▲ S France 42°57′N 00°08′E
102 K17 Midi d'Ossau, Pic du ▲ SW France 42°51′N 00°27′W
173 R7 Mid-Indian Basin undersea feature N Indian Ocean 10°00′S 80°00′E
173 P7 Mid-Indian Ridge var. Central Indian Ridge. undersea feature C Indian Ocean 12°00′S 66°00′E
103 N14 Midi-Pyrénées ◈ region S France
25 N8 Midkiff Texas, SW USA 31°35′N 101°51′W
14 G13 Midland Ontario, S Canada 44°45′N 79°53′W
31 R8 Midland Michigan, N USA 43°37′N 84°15′W
28 M10 Midland South Dakota, N USA 44°04′N 101°07′W
24 M8 Midland Texas, SW USA 32°N 102°05′W
83 K17 Midlands ◈ province C Zimbabwe
97 D21 Midleton Ir. Mainistir na Corann. SW Ireland 51°55′N 08°10′W
25 T7 Midlothian Texas, SW USA 32°28′N 96°59′W
96 K12 Midlothian cultural region S Scotland, United Kingdom
172 I7 Midongy Atsimo Fianarantsoa, S Madagascar 21°58′S 47°47′E
102 K15 Midou ≈ SW France
192 J6 Mid-Pacific Mountains var. Mid-Pacific Seamounts. undersea feature NW Pacific Ocean 20°00′N 178°00′W
Mid-Pacific Seamounts see Mid-Pacific Mountains
171 Q7 Midsayap Mindanao, S Philippines 07°12′N 124°31′E
95 F21 Midtjylland ◈ region NW Denmark
36 L3 Midway Utah, W USA 40°30′N 111°28′W
192 L5 Midway Islands ◇ US territory C Pacific Ocean
33 X14 Midwest Wyoming, C USA 43°24′N 106°15′W
27 N10 Midwest City Oklahoma, C USA 35°28′N 98°24′W
152 M10 Mid Western ◈ zone W Nepal
98 P5 Midwolda Groningen, NE Netherlands 53°12′N 07°00′E
137 Q16 Midyat Mardin, SE Turkey 37°25′N 41°20′E
114 F8 Midzhur SCr. Midžor. ▲ Bulgaria/Serbia 43°24′N 22°41′E see also Midžor
Midzhur see Midžor
113 Q14 Midžor Bul. Midzhur. ▲ Bulgaria/Serbia 43°24′N 22°40′E see also Midzhur
Midžor see Midzhur
164 K14 Mie off. Mie-ken. ◈ prefecture Honshū, SW Japan
111 L16 Miechów Małopolskie, S Poland 50°21′N 20°01′E
110 F11 Międzychód Ger. Mitteldorf. Wielkopolskie, C Poland 52°36′N 15°53′E
Międzyleska, Przełęcz see Mezileské Sedlo
110 O12 Międzyrzec Podlaski Lubelskie, E Poland 52°N 22°47′E
110 E11 Międzyrzecz Ger. Meseritz. Lubuskie, W Poland 52°26′N 15°33′E
Mie-ken see Mie
102 L16 Miélan Gers, S France 43°26′N 00°19′E
111 N16 Mielec Podkarpackie, SE Poland 50°18′N 21°27′E
95 L21 Mien ◎ S Sweden
161 T12 Mienhua Yü island N Taiwan
41 O8 Mier Tamaulipas, C Mexico 26°28′N 99°10′W
116 J11 Miercurea-Ciuc Ger. Szeklerburg, Hung. Csíkszereda. Harghita, C Romania 46°24′N 25°48′E
Mieresch see Maros/Mureş
104 K2 Mieres del Camín var. Mieres del Camino. Asturias, NW Spain 43°15′N 05°46′W
Mieres del Camino see Mieres del Camín
99 K15 Mierlo Noord-Brabant, SE Netherlands 51°27′N 05°37′E
41 O10 Mier y Noriega Nuevo León, NE Mexico 23°24′N 100°06′W
Mies see Stříbro
80 K13 Mī'ēso var. Meheso, Miesso. Oromīya, C Ethiopia 09°13′N 40°47′E
Miesso see Mī'ēso
110 D10 Mieszkowice Ger. Bärwalde Neumark. Zachodnio-pomorskie, W Poland 52°45′N 14°24′E
18 G14 Mifflinburg Pennsylvania, NE USA 40°55′N 77°03′W
18 F14 Mifflintown Pennsylvania, NE USA 40°34′N 77°24′W
138 F8 Mifrats Hefa Eng. Bay of Haifa; prev. MifrazḤefa. bay N Israel
41 R15 Miguel Alemán, Presa ⊠ SE Mexico
40 L9 Miguel Asua var. Miguel Auza. Zacatecas, C Mexico 24°17′N 103°29′W
Miguel Auza see Miguel Asua
43 S15 Miguel de la Borda var. Donoso. Colón, C Panama 09°09′N 80°20′W
41 N13 Miguel Hidalgo ✈ (Guadalajara) Jalisco, SW Mexico 20°52′N 101°09′W
40 H7 Miguel Hidalgo, Presa ⊠ W Mexico
116 J14 Mihăilești Giurgiu, S Romania 44°20′N 25°54′E
116 M14 Mihail Kogălniceanu var. Kogălniceanu; prev. Caramurat, Ferdinand. Constanța, SE Romania 44°22′N 28°27′E
117 N14 Mihai Viteazu Constanța, SE Romania 44°37′N 28°41′E
136 G12 Mihalıççık Eskişehir, NW Turkey 39°52′N 31°30′E
164 G13 Mihara Hiroshima, Honshū, SW Japan 34°24′N 133°04′E
165 N14 Mihara-yama Ж Miyake-jima, SE Japan 34°43′N 139°23′E
105 S8 Mijares ≈ E Spain
98 I11 Mijdrecht Utrecht, C Netherlands 52°12′N 04°52′E
165 S4 Mikasa Hokkaidō, NE Japan 43°15′N 141°57′E
Mikashevichi see Mikashevichy
119 K19 Mikashevichy Pol. Mikaszewicze, Rus. Mikashevichi. Brestskaya Voblasts', SW Belarus 52°13′N 27°28′E
Mikaszewicze see Mikashevichy
126 L5 Mikhaylov Ryazanskaya Oblast', W Russian Federation 54°12′N 39°03′E
Mikhaylovgrad see Montana
195 Z8 Mikhaylov Island island Antarctica
145 T6 Mikhaylovka Pavlodar, N Kazakhstan 53°49′N 76°31′E
127 N9 Mikhaylovka Volgogradskaya Oblast', SW Russian Federation 50°06′N 43°17′E
Mikhaylovka see Mykhaylivka
81 K24 Mikindani Mtwara, SE Tanzania 10°16′S 40°05′E
93 N18 Mikkeli Swe. Sankt Michel. Itä-Suomi, SE Finland 61°41′N 27°14′E
110 M8 Mikołajki Ger. Nikolaiken. Warmińsko-Mazurskie, NE Poland 53°49′N 21°31′E
Míkonos see Mýkonos
114 I9 Mikre Lovech, N Bulgaria 43°01′N 24°31′E
114 C13 Mikri Préspa, Límni ◎ N Greece
125 P4 Mikulkin, Mys headland NW Russian Federation 67°50′N 46°36′E
81 I23 Mikumi Morogoro, SE Tanzania 07°22′S 37°00′E
125 R10 Mikun' Respublika Komi, NW Russian Federation 62°20′N 50°02′E
164 K13 Mikuni Fukui, Honshū, SW Japan 36°12′N 136°09′E
165 X13 Mikura-jima island E Japan
29 V7 Milaca Minnesota, N USA 45°45′N 93°40′W
62 J10 Milagro La Rioja, C Argentina 31°00′S 66°01′W
56 B7 Milagro Guayas, SW Ecuador 02°11′S 79°36′W
31 P4 Milakokia Lake ◎ Michigan, N USA
30 J1 Milan Illinois, N USA 41°27′N 90°33′W
31 R10 Milan Michigan, N USA 42°05′N 83°40′W
27 T2 Milan Missouri, C USA 40°12′N 93°08′W
37 Q11 Milan New Mexico, SW USA 35°10′N 107°53′W
20 G9 Milan Tennessee, S USA 35°55′N 88°45′W
Milan see Milano
95 F15 Miland Telemark, S Norway 59°57′N 08°48′E
83 N15 Milange Zambézia, NE Mozambique 16°09′S 35°44′E
106 D8 Milano Eng. Milan, Ger. Mailand; anc. Mediolanum. Lombardia, N Italy 45°28′N 09°10′E
25 U10 Milano Texas, SW USA 30°42′N 96°51′W
136 C15 Milas Muğla, SW Turkey 37°17′N 27°46′E
119 K21 Milashavichy Rus. Milashevichi. Homyel'skaya Voblasts', SE Belarus 51°39′N 27°56′E
Milashevichi see Milashavichy
119 I18 Milavidy Rus. Milovidy. Brestskaya Voblasts', SW Belarus 52°54′N 25°51′E
107 L23 Milazzo anc. Mylae. Sicilia, Italy, C Mediterranean Sea 38°13′N 15°15′E
29 R8 Milbank South Dakota, N USA 45°12′N 96°36′W
19 T7 Milbridge Maine, NE USA 44°31′N 67°55′W
100 L11 Milde ≈ C Germany
14 F14 Mildmay Ontario, S Canada 44°03′N 81°07′W
182 L9 Mildura Victoria, SE Australia 34°13′S 142°09′E
137 X12 Mil Düzü Rus. Mil'skaya Ravnina, Mil'skaya Step'. physical region C Azerbaijan
160 H13 Mile var. Miyang. Yunnan, SW China 24°28′N 103°26′E
Mile see Mili Atoll
181 Y10 Miles Queensland, E Australia 26°41′S 150°15′E
25 P8 Miles Texas, SW USA 31°36′N 100°10′W
33 X9 Miles City Montana, NW USA 46°24′N 105°48′W
11 U17 Milestone Saskatchewan, S Canada 50°00′N 104°24′W
107 N22 Mileto Calabria, SW Italy 38°35′N 16°03′E
107 K16 Miletto, Monte ▲ C Italy 41°28′N 14°21′E
18 M13 Milford Connecticut, NE USA 41°12′N 73°01′W
21 Y3 Milford var. Milford City. Delaware, NE USA 38°54′N 75°25′W
29 T11 Milford Iowa, C USA 43°19′N 95°09′W
19 S6 Milford Maine, NE USA 44°57′N 68°37′W
29 R16 Milford Nebraska, C USA 40°46′N 97°03′W
19 O10 Milford New Hampshire, NE USA 42°49′N 71°38′W
18 J13 Milford Pennsylvania, NE USA 41°20′N 74°48′W
25 T7 Milford Texas, SW USA 32°07′N 96°57′W
36 K6 Milford Utah, W USA 38°22′N 112°57′W
Milford see Milford Haven
Milford City see Milford
97 H21 Milford Haven prev. Milford. SW Wales, United Kingdom 51°44′N 05°02′W
27 O4 Milford Lake ⊠ Kansas, C USA
185 B21 Milford Sound Southland, South Island, New Zealand 44°41′S 167°57′E
185 B21 Milford Sound inlet South Island, New Zealand
Milhau see Millau
Milh, Bahr al see Razāzah, Buḩayrat ar
139 T10 Milḩ, Wādī al dry watercourse S Iraq
189 W8 Mili Atoll var. Mile. atoll Ratak Chain, SE Marshall Islands
110 H13 Milicz Dolnośląskie, SW Poland 51°32′N 17°15′E
107 L25 Militello in Val di Catania Sicilia, Italy, C Mediterranean Sea 37°17′N 14°47′E
11 R17 Milk River Alberta, SW Canada 49°10′N 112°06′W
44 J13 Milk River ≈ C Jamaica
33 W7 Milk River ≈ Montana, NW USA
80 D9 Milk, Wadi el var. Wadi al Malik. ≈ C Sudan
99 L14 Mill Noord-Brabant, SE Netherlands 51°42′N 05°46′E
103 P14 Millau var. Milhau; anc. Æmilianum. Aveyron, S France 44°06′N 03°05′E
14 I14 Millbrook Ontario, SE Canada 44°09′N 78°26′W
23 U4 Milledgeville Georgia, SE USA 33°04′N 83°13′W
12 C12 Mille Lacs, Lac des ◎ Ontario, S Canada
29 V6 Mille Lacs Lake ◎ Minnesota, N USA
23 V4 Millen Georgia, SE USA 32°50′N 81°56′W
191 Y5 Millennium Island prev. Caroline Island, Thornton Island. atoll Line Islands, E Kiribati
29 O9 Miller South Dakota, N USA 44°31′N 98°59′W
30 K5 Miller Dam Flowage ⊠ Wisconsin, N USA
39 U12 Miller, Mount ▲ Alaska, USA 60°29′N 142°16′W
126 L10 Millerovo Rostovskaya Oblast', SW Russian Federation 48°57′N 40°26′E
37 N17 Miller Peak ▲ Arizona, SW USA 31°23′N 110°17′W
31 T12 Millersburg Ohio, N USA 40°33′N 81°55′W
18 G15 Millersburg Pennsylvania, NE USA 40°31′N 76°56′W
185 D23 Millers Flat Otago, South Island, New Zealand 45°42′S 169°25′E
25 Q8 Millersview Texas, SW USA 31°26′N 99°44′W
106 B10 Millesimo Piemonte, NE Italy 44°24′N 08°09′E
12 C12 Milles Lacs, Lac des ◎ Ontario, SW Canada
25 Q13 Millett Texas, SW USA 28°33′N 99°10′W
103 N11 Millevaches, Plateau de plateau C France
182 K12 Millicent South Australia 37°29′S 140°01′E
98 M13 Millingen aan den Rijn Gelderland, SE Netherlands 51°52′N 06°02′E
20 E10 Millington Tennessee, S USA 35°20′N 89°54′W
19 R4 Millinocket Maine, NE USA 45°38′N 68°45′W
19 R4 Millinocket Lake ◎ Maine, NE USA
195 Z11 Mill Island island Antarctica
183 T3 Millmerran Queensland, E Australia 27°53′S 151°15′E
109 R9 Millstatt Kärnten, S Austria 46°45′N 13°36′E
97 B19 Milltown Malbay Ir. Sráid na Cathrach. W Ireland 52°51′N 09°23′W
18 J17 Millville New Jersey, NE USA 39°24′N 75°01′W
27 S13 Millwood Lake ⊠ Arkansas, C USA
Milne Bank see Milne Seamounts
186 G10 Milne Bay ◈ province SE Papua New Guinea
64 J8 Milne Seamounts var. Milne Bank. undersea feature N Atlantic Ocean
29 Q6 Milnor North Dakota, N USA 46°15′N 97°27′W
19 R5 Milo Maine, NE USA 45°15′N 69°01′W
115 I22 Mílos island Kykládes, Greece, Aegean Sea
Mílos see Pláka
110 H11 Miłosław Wielkopolskie, C Poland 52°13′N 17°28′E
113 K19 Milot var. Miloti. Lezhë, C Albania 41°42′N 19°43′E
Miloti see Milot
117 Z5 Milove Luhans'ka Oblast', E Ukraine 49°22′N 40°09′E
Milovidy see Milavidy
182 L4 Milparinka New South Wales, SE Australia 29°48′S 141°57′E
35 N9 Milpitas California, W USA 37°25′N 121°54′W
Mil'skaya Ravnina/Mil'skaya Step' see Mil Düzü
14 G15 Milton Ontario, S Canada 43°31′N 79°53′W
185 E24 Milton Otago, South Island, New Zealand 46°08′S 169°59′E
21 Y4 Milton Delaware, NE USA 38°48′N 75°21′W
23 P8 Milton Florida, SE USA 30°37′N 87°02′W
18 G14 Milton Pennsylvania, NE USA 41°01′N 76°49′W
18 L7 Milton Vermont, NE USA 44°37′N 73°04′W
32 K11 Milton-Freewater Oregon, NW USA 45°54′N 118°24′W
97 N21 Milton Keynes SE England, United Kingdom 52°N 00°43′W
27 N3 Miltonvale Kansas, C USA 39°21′N 97°27′W
161 N10 Miluo Hunan, S China 28°52′N 113°00′E
30 M9 Milwaukee Wisconsin, N USA 43°03′N 87°56′W
Milyang see Miryang
Mimatum see Mende
37 Q15 Mimbres Mountains ▲▲ New Mexico, SW USA
182 D2 Mimili South Australia 27°01′S 132°33′E
102 J14 Mimizan Landes, SW France 44°12′N 01°12′W
Mimmaya see Minmaya
79 E19 Mimongo Ngounié, C Gabon 01°36′S 11°44′E
Min see Fujian
35 T7 Mina Nevada, W USA 38°23′N 118°07′W
143 S14 Mīnāb Hormozgān, SE Iran 27°08′N 57°02′E
Mina Baranis see Baranis
149 R9 Mina Bāzār Baluchistān, SW Pakistan 30°58′N 69°11′E
Minami-Awaji see Nandan

◆ Country
● Country Capital
◇ Dependent Territory
○ Dependent Territory Capital
◈ Administrative Regions
✈ International Airport
▲ Mountain
▲▲ Mountain Range
Ж Volcano
≈ River
◎ Lake
⊠ Reservoir

165 X17 **Minami-Iō-jima** *Eng.* San Augustine. *island* SE Japan
165 R5 **Minami-Kayabe** Hokkaidō, NE Japan *41°54′N 140°58′E*
164 B16 **Minamisatsuma** *var.* Kaseda. Kagoshima, Kyūshū, SW Japan *31°25′N 130°17′E*
164 C14 **Minamishimabara** *var.* Kuchinotsu. Nagasaki, Kyūshū, SW Japan *32°36′N 130°11′E*
164 C17 **Minamitane** Kagoshima, Tanega-shima, SW Japan *30°23′N 130°54′E*
Minami Tori Shima *see* Marcus Island
Min'an *see* Longshan
62 J4 **Mina Pirquitas** Jujuy, NW Argentina *22°48′S 66°24′W*
173 O3 **Mīnā' Qābūs** NE Oman
61 F19 **Minas** Lavalleja, S Uruguay *34°20′S 55°15′W*
13 P15 **Minas Basin** *bay* Nova Scotia, SE Canada
61 F17 **Minas de Corrales** Rivera, NE Uruguay *31°35′S 55°20′W*
44 A5 **Minas de Matahambre** Pinar del Río, W Cuba *22°34′N 83°57′W*
104 J13 **Minas de Ríotinto** Andalucía, S Spain *37°40′N 06°36′W*
60 K7 **Minas Gerais** *off.* Estado de Minas Gerais. ◈ *state* E Brazil
Minas Gerais, Estado de *see* Minas Gerais
42 E5 **Minas, Sierra de las** ▲▲ E Guatemala
41 T15 **Minatitlán** Veracruz-Llave, E Mexico *17°59′N 94°32′W*
166 L6 **Minbu** Magway, W Burma (Myanmar) *20°09′N 94°52′E*
149 V10 **Minchinābād** Punjab, E Pakistan *30°10′N 73°40′E*
63 G17 **Minchinmávida, Volcán** ✸ S Chile *42°51′S 72°23′W*
96 G7 **Minch, The** *var.* North Minch. *strait* NW Scotland, United Kingdom
106 F8 **Mincio** *anc.* Mincius. ∽ N Italy
Mincius *see* Mincio
26 M11 **Minco** Oklahoma, C USA *35°18′N 97°56′W*
171 Q7 **Mindanao** *island* S Philippines
Mindanao Sea *see* Bohol Sea
101 J23 **Mindel** ∽ S Germany
101 J23 **Mindelheim** Bayern, S Germany *48°03′N 10°30′E*
Mindello *see* Mindelo
76 C9 **Mindelo** *var.* Mindello; *prev.* Porto Grande. São Vicente, N Cape Verde *16°54′N 25°01′W*
14 I13 **Minden** Ontario, SE Canada *44°54′N 78°41′W*
100 H13 **Minden** *anc.* Minthun. Nordrhein-Westfalen, NW Germany *52°18′N 08°55′E*
22 G5 **Minden** Louisiana, S USA *32°37′N 93°17′W*
29 O16 **Minden** Nebraska, C USA *40°30′N 98°57′W*
35 Q6 **Minden** Nevada, W USA *38°58′N 119°47′W*
182 L8 **Mindona Lake** *seasonal lake* New South Wales, SE Australia
171 O4 **Mindoro** *island* N Philippines
171 N5 **Mindoro Strait** *strait* W Philippines
97 J23 **Minehead** SW England, United Kingdom *51°13′N 03°29′W*
97 E21 **Mine Head** *Ir.* Mionn Ard. *headland* S Ireland *51°58′N 07°36′W*
59 J19 **Mineiros** Goiás, C Brazil *17°34′S 52°33′W*
25 V6 **Mineola** Texas, SW USA *32°39′N 95°29′W*
25 S13 **Mineral** Texas, SW USA *28°32′N 97°54′W*
127 N15 **Mineral'nyye Vody** Stavropol'skiy Kray, SW Russian Federation *44°13′N 43°06′E*
30 K9 **Mineral Point** Wisconsin, N USA *42°54′N 90°09′W*
25 S6 **Mineral Wells** Texas, SW USA *32°48′N 98°06′W*
36 K6 **Minersville** Utah, W USA *38°12′N 112°56′W*
31 U12 **Minerva** Ohio, N USA *40°43′N 81°06′W*
107 N17 **Minervino Murge** Puglia, SE Italy *41°06′N 16°05′E*
103 O16 **Minervois** *physical region* S France
158 I10 **Minfeng** *var.* Niya. Xinjiang Uygur Zizhiqu, NW China *37°07′N 82°43′E*
79 O25 **Minga** Katanga, SE Dem. Rep. Congo *11°06′S 27°57′E*
137 W11 **Mingäçevir** *Rus.* Mingechaur, Mingechevir. C Azerbaijan *40°46′N 47°02′E*
137 W11 **Mingäçevir Su Anbarı** *Rus.* Mingechaurskoye Vodokhranilishche, Mingechevirskoye Vodokhranilishche. ▣ NW Azerbaijan
166 L8 **Mingaladon** ✈ (Yangon) Yangon, SW Burma (Myanmar) *16°55′N 96°11′E*
13 P11 **Mingan** Québec, E Canada *50°19′N 64°02′W*
Mingāora *see* Saīdu
146 K8 **Mingbuloq** *Rus.* Mynbulak. Navoiy Viloyati, N Uzbekistan *42°18′N 62°53′E*
146 K9 **Mingbuloq Botig'I** *Rus.* Vpadina Mynbulak. *depression* N Uzbekistan
Mingechaur/Mingechevir *see* Mingäçevir
Mingechaurskoye Vodokhranilishche/ Mingechevirskoye Vodokhranilishche *see* Mingäçevir Su Anbarı
161 Q7 **Mingguang** *prev.* Jiashan. Anhui, SE China *32°45′N 117°59′E*
166 L4 **Mingin** Sagaing, C Burma (Myanmar) *22°51′N 94°30′E*
105 Q10 **Minglanilla** Castilla-La Mancha, C Spain *39°32′N 01°36′W*
31 V13 **Mingo Junction** Ohio, N USA *40°19′N 80°36′W*
Mingora *see* Saīdu
163 V7 **Mingshui** Heilongjiang, NE China *47°10′N 125°53′E*
Mingtekl Daban *see* Mintaka Pass
Mingu *see* Zhenfeng
83 Q14 **Minguri** Nampula, NE Mozambique *14°30′S 40°37′E*
Mingzhou *see* Suide
159 U10 **Minhe** *var.* Chuankou; *prev.* Minhe Huizu Tuzu Zizhixian, Shangchuankou. Qinghai, C China *36°21′N 102°40′E*
Minhe Huizu Tuzu Zizhixian *see* Minhe
166 L6 **Minhla** Magway, W Burma (Myanmar) *19°58′N 95°03′E*
167 S14 **Minh Lương** Kiên Giang, S Vietnam *09°52′N 105°10′E*
104 G5 **Minho** *former province* N Portugal
104 G5 **Minho, Rio** *Sp.* Miño. ∽ Portugal/Spain *see also* Miño
Minho, Rio *see* Miño
155 C24 **Minicoy Island** *island* SW India
33 P15 **Minidoka** Idaho, NW USA *42°45′N 113°29′W*
118 C11 **Minija** ∽ W Lithuania
180 G9 **Minilya** Western Australia *23°45′S 114°03′E*
14 E8 **Minisinakwa Lake** ◎ Ontario, S Canada
45 T12 **Ministre Point** *headland* S Saint Lucia *13°42′N 60°57′W*
11 V15 **Minitonas** Manitoba, S Canada *52°07′N 101°02′W*
Minius *see* Miño
161 R12 **Min Jiang** ∽ SE China
160 H10 **Min Jiang** ∽ C China
182 H9 **Minlaton** South Australia *34°52′S 137°33′E*
159 S9 **Minle** Gansu, N China
165 Q6 **Minmaya** *var.* Mimmaya. Aomori, Honshū, C Japan *41°10′N 140°24′E*
77 U14 **Minna** Niger, C Nigeria *09°33′N 06°33′E*
165 P16 **Minna-jima** *island* Sakishima-shotō, SW Japan
27 N4 **Minneapolis** Kansas, C USA *39°08′N 97°43′W*
29 U9 **Minneapolis** Minnesota, N USA *44°59′N 93°16′W*
29 V8 **Minneapolis-Saint Paul** ✈ Minnesota, N USA *44°53′N 93°13′W*
11 W16 **Minnedosa** Manitoba, S Canada *50°14′N 99°50′W*
26 J7 **Minneola** Kansas, C USA *37°26′N 100°00′W*
29 S7 **Minnesota** *off.* State of Minnesota, *also known as* Gopher State, New England of the West, North Star State. ◈ *state* N USA
29 S9 **Minnesota River** ∽ Minnesota/South Dakota, N USA
29 V9 **Minnetonka** Minnesota, N USA *44°55′N 93°28′W*
29 O3 **Minnewaukan** North Dakota, N USA *48°04′N 99°14′W*
182 F7 **Minnipa** South Australia *32°52′S 135°07′E*
104 G5 **Miño** *var.* Mino, Minius, *Port.* Rio Minho. ∽ Portugal/Spain *see also* Minho, Rio
Miño *see* Minho, Rio
30 L4 **Minocqua** Wisconsin, N USA *45°53′N 89°42′W*
30 L12 **Minonk** Illinois, N USA *40°54′N 89°01′W*
Minorca *see* Menorca
28 M3 **Minot** North Dakota, N USA *48°15′N 101°19′W*
159 U8 **Minqin** Gansu, N China *38°35′N 103°07′E*
119 J16 **Minsk** ● (Belarus) Minskaya Voblasts', C Belarus *53°52′N 27°34′E*
119 L16 **Minsk** ✈ Minskaya Voblasts', C Belarus *53°52′N 27°58′E*
Minskaya Oblast' *see* Minskaya Voblasts'
119 K16 **Minskaya Voblasts'** *prev. Rus.* Minskaya Oblast'. ◈ *province* C Belarus
119 J16 **Minskaya Wzvyshsha** ▲▲ C Belarus
110 N12 **Mińsk Mazowiecki** *var.* Nowo-Minsk. Mazowieckie, C Poland *52°10′N 21°31′E*
31 Q13 **Minster** Ohio, N USA *40°23′N 84°22′W*
79 F15 **Minta** Centre, C Cameroon *04°34′N 12°54′E*
149 W2 **Mintaka Pass** *Chin.* Mingtekl Daban. *pass* China/Pakistan
115 D20 **Mínthi** ▲▲ S Greece
Minthun *see* Minden
13 O14 **Minto** New Brunswick, SE Canada *46°05′N 66°05′W*
10 H6 **Minto** Yukon Territory, W Canada *62°33′N 136°45′W*
39 R9 **Minto** Alaska, USA *65°07′N 149°22′W*
29 Q3 **Minto** North Dakota, N USA *48°17′N 97°22′W*
12 K6 **Minto, Lac** ◎ Québec, C Canada
195 R16 **Minto, Mount** ▲ Antarctica *71°38′S 169°11′E*
11 U17 **Minton** Saskatchewan, S Canada *49°12′N 104°33′W*
189 R15 **Minto Reef** *atoll* Caroline Islands, C Micronesia
37 R4 **Minturn** Colorado, C USA *39°34′N 106°21′W*
107 J16 **Minturno** Lazio, C Italy *41°15′N 13°47′E*
122 K13 **Minusinsk** Krasnoyarskiy Kray, S Russian Federation *53°37′N 91°49′E*
108 G11 **Minusio** Ticino, S Switzerland *46°11′N 08°47′E*
79 E17 **Minvoul** Woleu-Ntem, N Gabon *02°08′N 12°12′E*
141 R13 **Minwakh** N Yemen *16°55′N 48°04′E*
159 V11 **Minxian** *var.* Min Xian, Minyang. Gansu, C China *34°20′N 104°09′E*
Min Xian *see* Minxian
Minya *see* Al Minyā
Minyang *see* Minxian
31 R6 **Mio** Michigan, N USA *44°40′N 84°09′W*
Mionn Ard *see* Mine Head
158 L5 **Miquan** Xinjiang Uygur Zizhiqu, NW China *44°04′N 87°40′E*
119 I17 **Mir** Hrodzyenskaya Voblasts', W Belarus *53°25′N 26°28′E*
106 H8 **Mira** Veneto, NE Italy *45°25′N 12°07′E*
12 K15 **Mirabel** *var.* Montreal. ✈ (Montréal) Québec, SE Canada *45°27′N 73°47′W*
60 Q8 **Miracema** Rio de Janeiro, SE Brazil *21°24′S 42°10′W*
54 G9 **Miraflores** Boyacá, C Colombia *05°07′N 73°09′W*
40 G10 **Miraflores** Baja California Sur, NW Mexico *23°24′N 109°45′W*
44 L9 **Miragoâne** S Haiti *18°25′N 73°07′W*
155 E16 **Miraj** Mahārāshtra, W India *16°51′N 74°42′E*
61 E23 **Miramar** Buenos Aires, E Argentina *38°15′S 57°50′W*
103 R15 **Miramas** Bouches-du-Rhône, SE France *43°33′N 05°02′E*
102 K12 **Mirambeau** Charente-Maritime, W France *45°23′N 00°33′W*
102 L13 **Miramont-de-Guyenne** Lot-et-Garonne, SW France *44°34′N 00°20′E*
115 L25 **Mirampéllou Kólpos** *gulf* Kríti, Greece, E Mediterranean Sea
158 L8 **Miran** Xinjiang Uygur Zizhiqu, NW China *39°13′N 88°58′E*
54 M5 **Miranda** *off.* Estado Miranda. ◈ *state* N Venezuela
Miranda de Corvo *see* Miranda do Corvo
105 O3 **Miranda de Ebro** La Rioja, N Spain *42°41′N 02°57′W*
104 G8 **Miranda do Corvo** *var.* Miranda de Corvo. Coimbra, N Portugal *40°05′N 08°20′W*
104 J6 **Miranda do Douro** Bragança, N Portugal *41°30′N 06°16′W*
Miranda, Estado *see* Miranda
102 L15 **Mirande** Gers, S France *43°31′N 00°25′E*
104 I6 **Mirandela** Bragança, N Portugal *41°28′N 07°10′W*
25 R15 **Mirando City** Texas, SW USA *27°24′N 99°00′W*
106 G9 **Mirandola** Emilia-Romagna, N Italy *44°52′N 11°04′E*
60 I8 **Mirandópolis** São Paulo, S Brazil *21°10′S 51°03′W*
104 G13 **Mira, Rio** ∽ S Portugal
60 K8 **Mirassol** São Paulo, S Brazil *20°50′S 49°30′W*
104 J3 **Miravalles** ▲ NW Spain *42°52′N 06°45′W*
42 L12 **Miravalles, Volcán** ✸ NW Costa Rica *10°43′N 85°07′W*
141 W13 **Mirbāṭ** *var.* Marbat. S Oman *17°03′N 54°44′E*
44 M9 **Mirebalais** C Haiti *18°51′N 72°08′W*
103 T6 **Mirecourt** Vosges, NE France *48°19′N 06°04′E*
103 N16 **Mirepoix** Ariège, S France *43°05′N 01°51′E*
Mirgorod *see* Myrhorod
139 W10 **Mīr Ḥājī Khalīl** Wāsiṭ, E Iraq *32°11′N 46°19′E*
169 T8 **Miri** Sarawak, East Malaysia *04°23′N 113°59′E*
77 W12 **Miria** Zinder, S Niger *13°39′N 09°15′E*
182 F5 **Mirikata** South Australia *29°56′S 135°13′E*
54 K4 **Mirimire** Falcón, N Venezuela *11°14′N 68°39′W*
61 H18 **Mirim Lagoon** *var.* Lake Mirim, *Sp.* Laguna Merín. *lagoon* Brazil/Uruguay
Mirim, Lake *see* Mirim Lagoon
Mírina *see* Mýrina
172 H14 **Miringoni** Mohéli, S Comoros *12°17′S 93°39′E*
143 W11 **Mīrjāveh** Sīstān va Balūchestān, SE Iran *29°04′N 61°24′E*
195 Z9 **Mirny** *Russian research station* Antarctica *66°25′S 93°09′E*
124 M10 **Mirnyy** Arkhangel'skaya Oblast', NW Russian Federation *62°50′N 40°20′E*
123 O10 **Mirnyy** Respublika Sakha (Yakutiya), NE Russian Federation *62°30′N 113°58′E*
Mironovka *see* Myronivka
110 F9 **Mirosławiec** Zachodnio-pomorskie, NW Poland *53°21′N 16°04′E*
Mirovo *see* Vrattsa
100 N10 **Mirow** Mecklenburg-Vorpommern, N Germany *53°16′N 12°48′E*
152 G6 **Mīrpur** Jammu and Kashmir, NW India *33°06′N 73°49′E*
Mīrpur *see* New Mīrpur
149 P17 **Mīrpur Batoro** Sind, SE Pakistan *24°40′N 68°15′E*
149 Q16 **Mīrpur Khās** Sind, SE Pakistan *25°31′N 69°01′E*
149 P17 **Mīrpur Sakro** Sind, SE Pakistan *24°32′N 67°38′E*
143 T14 **Mīr Shahdād** Hormozgān, S Iran *26°15′N 58°29′E*
Mirtoan Sea *see* Mirtóo Pélagos
115 G21 **Mirtóo Pélagos** *Eng.* Mirtoan Sea; *anc.* Myrtoum Mare. *sea* S Greece
163 Z16 **Miryang** *var.* Milyang, *Jap.* Mitsuō. SE South Korea *35°30′N 128°46′E*
Mirzachirla *see* Murzechirla
164 E14 **Misaki** Ehime, Shikoku, SW Japan *33°22′N 132°04′E*
41 Q13 **Misantla** Veracruz-Llave, E Mexico *19°54′N 96°51′W*
165 R7 **Misawa** Aomori, Honshū, C Japan *40°42′N 141°26′E*
57 G14 **Mishagua, Río** ∽ C Peru
163 Z8 **Mishan** Heilongjiang, NE China *45°30′N 131°53′E*
31 O11 **Mishawaka** Indiana, N USA *41°40′N 86°10′W*
39 N6 **Misheguk Mountain** ▲ Alaska, USA *68°13′N 161°11′W*
165 N14 **Mishima** *var.* Misima. Shizuoka, Honshū, S Japan *35°08′N 138°54′E*
164 E12 **Mi-shima** *island* SW Japan
127 V4 **Mishkino** Respublika Bashkortostan, W Russian Federation *55°31′N 55°57′E*
153 Y10 **Mishmi Hills** *hill range* NE India
161 N11 **Mi Shui** ∽ S China
Misiaf *see* Maṣyāf
107 J23 **Misilmeri** Sicilia, Italy, C Mediterranean Sea *38°03′N 13°27′E*
Misima *see* Mishima
14 C7 **Missinaibi Lake** ◎ Ontario, S Canada
Misión de Guana *see* Guana
60 F13 **Misiones** *off.* Provincia de Misiones. ◈ *province* NE Argentina
62 P8 **Misiones** *off.* Departamento de las Misiones. ◈ *department* S Paraguay
Misiones, Departamento de las *see* Misiones
Misiones, Provincia de *see* Misiones
Misión San Fernando *see* San Fernando
Miskin *see* Maskin
Miskito Coast *see* La Mosquitia
43 O7 **Miskitos, Cayos** *island group* NE Nicaragua
111 M21 **Miskolc** Borsod-Abaúj-Zemplén, NE Hungary *48°05′N 20°46′E*
171 T12 **Misool, Pulau** *island* Maluku, E Indonesia
Misox *see* Mesocco
29 Y3 **Misquah Hills** *hill range* Minnesota, N USA
75 P7 **Miṣrātah** *var.* Misurata. NW Libya *32°23′N 15°06′E*
75 P7 **Miṣrātah, Râs** *headland* N Libya *32°22′N 15°16′E*
14 C7 **Missanabie** Ontario, S Canada *48°18′N 84°04′W*
58 E10 **Missão Catrimani** Roraima, N Brazil *01°26′N 62°05′W*
14 D6 **Missinaibi** ∽ Ontario, S Canada
11 T13 **Missinipe** Saskatchewan, C Canada *55°36′N 104°45′W*
28 M11 **Mission** South Dakota, N USA *43°16′N 100°38′W*
25 S17 **Mission** Texas, SW USA *26°13′N 98°19′W*
12 F10 **Missisa Lake** ◎ Ontario, C Canada
18 M6 **Missisquoi Bay** *lake bay* Canada/USA
14 C10 **Mississagi** ∽ Ontario, S Canada
14 G15 **Mississauga** Ontario, S Canada *43°38′N 79°36′W*
31 P12 **Mississinewa Lake** ▣ Indiana, N USA
31 P12 **Mississinewa River** ∽ Indiana/Ohio, N USA
22 K4 **Mississippi** *off.* State of Mississippi, *also known as* Bayou State, Magnolia State. ◈ *state* SE USA
14 K13 **Mississippi** ∽ Ontario, SE Canada
47 N1 **Mississippi Fan** *undersea feature* N Gulf of Mexico *26°45′N 88°30′W*
14 L13 **Mississippi Lake** ◎ Ontario, SE Canada
22 M10 **Mississippi Delta** *delta* Louisiana, S USA
0 J11 **Mississippi River** ∽ C USA
22 M9 **Mississippi Sound** *sound* Alabama/Mississippi, S USA
33 P9 **Missoula** Montana, NW USA *46°54′N 114°03′W*
27 T5 **Missouri** *off.* State of Missouri, *also known as* Bullion State, Show Me State. ◈ *state* C USA
25 V11 **Missouri City** Texas, SW USA *29°37′N 95°32′W*
0 J10 **Missouri River** ∽ C USA
15 Q6 **Mistassibi** ∽ Québec, SE Canada
15 P6 **Mistassini** ∽ Québec, SE Canada
12 J11 **Mistassini, Lac** ◎ Québec, SE Canada
109 Y3 **Mistelbach an der Zaya** Niederösterreich, NE Austria *48°34′N 16°33′E*
107 L24 **Misterbianco** Sicilia, Italy, C Mediterranean Sea *37°31′N 15°01′E*
95 N19 **Misterhult** Kalmar, S Sweden *57°28′N 16°34′E*
12 K11 **Mistissini** *var.* Baie-du-Poste. Québec, SE Canada *50°20′N 73°50′W*
57 H17 **Misti, Volcán** ✸ S Peru *16°20′S 71°22′W*
Mistras *see* Mystrás
107 K23 **Mistretta** *anc.* Amestratus. Sicilia, Italy, C Mediterranean Sea *37°56′N 14°22′E*
164 F12 **Misumi** Shimane, Honshū, SW Japan *34°47′N 132°00′E*
Misurata *see* Miṣrātah
83 O14 **Mitande** Niassa, N Mozambique *14°06′S 36°03′E*
40 J13 **Mita, Punta de** *headland* C Mexico *20°46′N 105°31′W*
55 W12 **Mitaraka, Massif du** ▲ NE South America *02°18′N 54°31′W*
Mitau *see* Jelgava
181 X9 **Mitchell** Queensland, E Australia *26°29′S 148°00′E*
14 E15 **Mitchell** Ontario, S Canada *43°28′N 81°11′W*
28 I13 **Mitchell** Nebraska, C USA *41°56′N 103°48′W*
32 J12 **Mitchell** Oregon, NW USA *44°34′N 120°09′W*
29 P11 **Mitchell** South Dakota, N USA *43°42′N 98°01′W*
23 P5 **Mitchell Lake** ▣ Alabama, S USA
31 P7 **Mitchell, Lake** ◎ Michigan, N USA
21 P9 **Mitchell, Mount** ▲ North Carolina, SE USA *35°46′N 82°16′W*
181 V3 **Mitchell River** ∽ Queensland, NE Australia
97 D20 **Mitchelstown** *Ir.* Baile Mhistéala. SW Ireland *52°20′N 08°16′W*
14 M9 **Mitchinamécus, Lac** ◎ Québec, SE Canada
Mitèmboni *see* Mitemele, Río
79 D17 **Mitemele, Río** *var.* Mitèmboni, Temboni, Utamboni. ∽ S Equatorial Guinea
149 S12 **Mithān Kot** Punjab, E Pakistan *28°53′N 70°25′E*
149 T7 **Mitha Tiwāna** Punjab, E Pakistan *32°18′N 72°08′E*
149 R17 **Mithi** Sind, SE Pakistan *24°43′N 69°53′E*
Míthimna *see* Míthymna
Mi Tho *see* My Tho
115 L16 **Míthymna** *var.* Míthimna. Lésvos, E Greece *39°20′N 26°12′E*
190 L16 **Mitiaro** *island* S Cook Islands
Mitilíni *see* Mytilíni
15 U7 **Mitis** ∽ Québec, SE Canada
41 R16 **Mitla** Oaxaca, SE Mexico *16°56′N 96°19′W*
165 P13 **Mito** Ibaraki, Honshū, S Japan *36°21′N 140°26′E*
92 N2 **Mitra, Kapp** *headland* W Svalbard *79°07′N 11°11′E*
184 M13 **Mitre** ▲ North Island, New Zealand *40°46′S 175°27′E*
185 B21 **Mitre Peak** ▲ South Island, New Zealand *44°37′S 167°45′E*
39 O15 **Mitrofania Island** *island* Alaska, USA
Mitrovica/Mitrovicë *see* Kosovska Mitrovica, Serbia
Mitrovica/Mitrowitz *see* Sremska Mitrovica, Serbia
113 M16 **Mitrovicë** *Serb.* Mitrovica, Kosovska Mitrovica, Titova Mitrovica. N Kosovo *42°54′N 20°52′E*
172 H12 **Mitsamiouli** Grande Comore, NW Comoros *11°22′S 43°19′E*
172 I3 **Mitsinjo** Mahajanga, NW Madagascar *16°00′S 45°52′E*
80 J9 **Mits'iwa** *var.* Masawa, Massawa. E Eritrea *15°37′N 39°27′E*
172 H13 **Mitsoudjé** Grande Comore, NW Comoros
138 F12 **Mitspe Ramon** *prev.* Mizpe Ramon. Southern, S Israel *30°38′N 34°47′E*
165 T5 **Mitsuishi** Hokkaidō, NE Japan *42°12′N 142°40′E*
165 O11 **Mitsuke** *var.* Mituke. Niigata, Honshū, C Japan *37°30′N 138°54′E*
Mitsuō *see* Miryang
164 C12 **Mitsushima** Nagasaki, Tsushima, SW Japan *34°16′N 129°18′E*
100 G12 **Mittelandkanal** *canal* NW Germany
108 J7 **Mittelberg** Vorarlberg, NW Austria *47°19′N 10°09′E*
Mitteldorf *see* Międzychód
Mittelstadt *see* Baia Sprie
Mitterburg *see* Pazin
109 P7 **Mittersill** Salzburg, NW Austria *47°16′N 12°27′E*
Mittimatalik *see* Pond Inlet
101 N16 **Mittweida** Sachsen, E Germany *50°59′N 12°57′E*
54 J13 **Mitú** Vaupés, SE Colombia *01°07′N 70°05′W*
Mituke *see* Mitsuke
Mitumba, Chaîne des/ Mitumba Range *see* Mitumba, Monts
79 O22 **Mitumba, Monts** *var.* Chaîne des Mitumba, Mitumba Range. ▲▲ E Dem. Rep. Congo
79 N23 **Mitwaba** Katanga, SE Dem. Rep. Congo *08°37′S 27°20′E*
79 E18 **Mitzic** Woleu-Ntem, N Gabon *0°48′N 11°30′E*
82 K11 **Miueru Wantipa, Lake** ◎ N Zambia
165 N14 **Miura** Kanagawa, Honshū, S Japan *35°08′N 139°37′E*
165 Q10 **Miyagi** *off.* Miyagi-ken. ◈ *prefecture* Honshū, C Japan
Miyagi-ken *see* Miyagi
138 M7 **Miyāh, Wādī al** *dry watercourse* E Syria
165 X13 **Miyake** Tōkyō, Miyako-jima, SE Japan *34°35′N 135°33′E*
165 Q16 **Miyake-jima** *island* Sakishima-shotō, SW Japan
165 R8 **Miyako** Iwate, Honshū, C Japan *39°39′N 141°57′E*
164 D16 **Miyakonojō** *var.* Miyakonzyô. Miyazaki, Kyūshū, SW Japan *31°42′N 131°04′E*
Miyakonzyô *see* Miyakonojō
165 Q16 **Miyako-shotō** *island group* SW Japan
144 G11 **Miyaly** Atyrau, W Kazakhstan *48°52′N 53°55′E*
Miyāndoāb *see* Mīāndowāb
Miyāneh *see* Mīāneh
Miyang *see* Mile
164 D16 **Miyazaki** Miyazaki, Kyūshū, SW Japan *31°55′N 131°24′E*
164 D16 **Miyazaki** *off.* Miyazaki-ken. ◈ *prefecture* Kyūshū, SW Japan
Miyazaki-ken *see* Miyazaki
164 J12 **Miyazu** Kyōto, Honshū, SW Japan *35°33′N 135°12′E*
Miyory *see* Myory
164 G12 **Miyoshi** *var.* Miyosi. Hiroshima, Honshū, SW Japan *34°48′N 132°51′E*
Miyosi *see* Miyoshi
Miza *see* Mizë
81 H14 **Mīzan Teferī** Southern Nationalities, S Ethiopia *06°57′N 35°30′E*
Mizda *see* Mizdah
75 O8 **Mizdah** *var.* Mizda. NW Libya *31°26′N 12°59′E*
113 K20 **Mizë** *var.* Miza. Fier, W Albania *40°58′N 19°32′E*
97 A22 **Mizen Head** *Ir.* Carn Uí Néid. *headland* SW Ireland *51°26′N 09°50′W*
116 H7 **Mizhhir"ya** *Rus.* Mezhgor'ye. Zakarpats'ka Oblast', W Ukraine *48°30′N 23°30′E*
160 L4 **Mizhi** Shaanxi, C China *37°50′N 110°03′E*
116 K13 **Mizil** Prahova, SE Romania *45°00′N 26°29′E*
114 H7 **Miziya** Vratsa, NW Bulgaria *43°42′N 23°52′E*
153 W15 **Mizo Hills** *hill range* E India
153 W15 **Mizoram** ◈ *state* NE India
Mizpe Ramon *see* Mitspe Ramon
57 L19 **Mizque** Cochabamba, C Bolivia *17°57′S 65°10′W*
57 M19 **Mizque, Río** ∽ C Bolivia
165 Q9 **Mizusawa** *var.* Ōshū. Iwate, Honshū, C Japan *39°10′N 141°07′E*
95 M18 **Mjölby** Östergötland, S Sweden *58°19′N 15°10′E*
95 G15 **Mjøndalen** Buskerud, S Norway *59°45′N 09°58′E*
95 J19 **Mjörn** ◎ S Sweden
94 I13 **Mjøsa** *var.* Mjøsen. ◎ S Norway
Mjøsen *see* Mjøsa
81 G21 **Mkalama** Singida, C Tanzania *04°09′S 34°35′E*
80 K13 **Mkata** ∽ C Tanzania
83 K14 **Mkushi** Central, C Zambia *13°40′S 29°26′E*
83 L22 **Mkuze** KwaZulu/Natal, E South Africa *27°37′S 32°03′E*
81 J22 **Mkwaja** Tanga, E Tanzania *05°42′S 38°48′E*
111 D16 **Mladá Boleslav** *Ger.* Jungbunzlau. Středočeský Kraj, N Czech Republic *50°26′N 14°55′E*
112 M12 **Mladenovac** Serbia, C Serbia *44°27′N 20°42′E*
114 L11 **Mladinovo** Khaskovo, S Bulgaria *41°57′N 26°13′E*
113 O17 **Mlado Nagoričane** N FYR Macedonia *42°11′N 21°49′E*
Mlanje *see* Mulanje
112 N12 **Mlava** ∽ E Serbia
110 L9 **Mława** Mazowieckie, C Poland *53°07′N 20°23′E*
113 G16 **Mljet** *It.* Meleda; *anc.* Melita. *island* S Croatia
167 S11 **Mlu Prey** *prev.* Phumĭ Mlu Prey. Preăh Vihéar, N Cambodia *13°48′N 105°16′E*
116 K4 **Mlyniv** Rivnens'ka Oblast', NW Ukraine *50°31′N 25°36′E*
83 I21 **Mmabatho** North-West, N South Africa *25°51′S 25°37′E*
83 I19 **Mmashoro** Central, E Botswana *21°56′S 26°39′E*
44 J7 **Moa** Holguín, E Cuba *20°42′N 74°57′W*
76 J15 **Moa** ∽ Guinea/Sierra Leone
37 O6 **Moab** Utah, W USA *38°35′N 109°34′W*
181 V1 **Moa Island** *island* Queensland, NE Australia
187 Y15 **Moala** *island* S Fiji
83 L21 **Moamba** Maputo, SW Mozambique *25°35′S 32°13′E*
79 F19 **Moanda** *var.* Mouanda. Haut-Ogooué, SE Gabon *01°31′S 13°07′E*
83 M15 **Moatize** Tete, NW Mozambique *16°04′S 33°43′E*
79 P22 **Moba** Katanga, E Dem. Rep. Congo *07°03′S 29°52′E*
Mobay *see* Montego Bay
79 K15 **Mobaye** Basse-Kotto, S Central African Republic *04°19′N 21°17′E*
79 K15 **Mobayi-Mbongo** Equateur, NW Dem. Rep. Congo *04°21′N 21°10′E*
25 P2 **Mobeetie** Texas, SW USA *35°33′N 100°25′W*
27 U3 **Moberly** Missouri, C USA *39°25′N 92°26′W*
23 N8 **Mobile** Alabama, S USA *30°42′N 88°03′W*
23 N9 **Mobile Bay** *bay* Alabama, S USA
23 N8 **Mobile River** ∽ Alabama, S USA
29 N8 **Mobridge** South Dakota, N USA *45°32′N 100°25′W*
Mobutu Sese Seko, Lac *see* Albert, Lake
45 N8 **Moca** N Dominican Republic *19°26′N 70°33′W*
83 Q15 **Moçambique** Nampula, NE Mozambique *15°00′S 40°44′E*
Moçâmedes *see* Namibe
167 S6 **Môc Châu** Sơn La, N Vietnam *20°49′N 104°38′E*
187 Z15 **Moce** *island* Lau Group, E Fiji
Mocha *see* Al Mukhā
193 T11 **Mocha Fracture Zone** *tectonic feature* SE Pacific Ocean
63 F14 **Mocha, Isla** *island* C Chile
56 C12 **Moche, Río** ∽ W Peru
167 S14 **Môc Hoa** Long An, S Vietnam *10°46′N 105°56′E*
83 I20 **Mochudi** Kgatleng, SE Botswana *24°25′S 26°07′E*
82 Q13 **Mocímboa da Praia** *var.* Vila de Mocímboa da Praia. Cabo Delgado, N Mozambique *11°17′S 40°21′E*
94 L13 **Mockfjärd** Dalarna, C Sweden *60°30′N 14°57′E*
21 R9 **Mocksville** North Carolina, SE USA *35°53′N 80°33′W*
32 F8 **Moclips** Washington, NW USA *47°11′N 124°13′W*
82 C13 **Môco** *var.* Morro de Môco. ▲ W Angola *12°36′S 15°09′E*
54 D13 **Mocoa** Putumayo, SW Colombia *01°07′N 76°38′W*
60 M8 **Mococa** São Paulo, S Brazil *21°30′S 47°00′W*
Môco, Morro de *see* Môco
40 H8 **Mocorito** Sinaloa, C Mexico *25°24′N 107°55′W*
40 J4 **Moctezuma** Chihuahua, N Mexico *30°10′N 106°28′W*
41 N11 **Moctezuma** San Luis Potosí, C Mexico *22°46′N 101°06′W*
40 G4 **Moctezuma** Sonora, NW Mexico *29°50′N 109°40′W*
41 P12 **Moctezuma, Río** ∽ C Mexico
Mó, Cuan *see* Clew Bay
83 O16 **Mocuba** Zambézia, NE Mozambique *16°50′S 37°02′E*
103 U12 **Modane** Savoie, E France *45°14′N 06°41′E*
106 F9 **Modena** *anc.* Mutina. Emilia-Romagna, N Italy *44°39′N 10°55′E*
36 I7 **Modena** Utah, W USA *37°46′N 113°54′W*
35 O9 **Modesto** California, W USA *37°38′N 121°02′W*
107 L25 **Modica** *anc.* Motyca. Sicilia, Italy, C Mediterranean Sea *36°52′N 14°45′E*
83 J20 **Modimolle** *prev.* Nylstroom. Limpopo, NE South Africa *24°39′N 28°23′E*
79 K17 **Modjamboli** Equateur, N Dem. Rep. Congo *02°27′N 22°03′E*
109 X4 **Mödling** Niederösterreich, NE Austria *48°06′N 16°18′E*
Modohn *see* Madona
Modot *see* Tsenhermandal
171 V14 **Modowi** Papua, E Indonesia *04°05′S 134°39′E*
112 I12 **Modračko Jezero** ▣ NE Bosnia and Herzegovina
112 I10 **Modriča** Republika Srpska, N Bosnia and Herzegovina *44°57′N 18°17′E*
183 O13 **Moe** Victoria, SE Australia *38°11′S 146°18′E*
Moearatewe *see* Muaratewe
Moei, Mae Nam *see* Thaungyin
94 H13 **Moelv** Hedmark, S Norway *60°55′N 10°47′E*
92 I10 **Moen** Troms, N Norway *69°08′N 18°35′E*
Möen *see* Møn, Denmark
Moen *see* Weno, Micronesia
Moena *see* Muna, Pulau
36 M10 **Moenkopi Wash** ∽ Arizona, SW USA
185 F22 **Moeraki Point** *headland* South Island, New Zealand *45°23′S 170°52′E*
99 F16 **Moerbeke** Oost-Vlaanderen, NW Belgium *51°11′N 03°57′E*
99 H14 **Moerdijk** Noord-Brabant, S Netherlands *51°42′N 04°37′E*
Moero, Lac *see* Mweru, Lake
101 D15 **Moers** *var.* Mörs. Nordrhein-Westfalen, W Germany *51°27′N 06°36′E*
Moesi *see* Musi, Air
Moeskroen *see* Mouscron
96 J13 **Moffat** S Scotland, United Kingdom *55°29′N 03°36′W*
185 C22 **Moffat Peak** ▲ South Island, New Zealand *44°57′S 168°10′E*
79 N19 **Moga** Sud-Kivu, E Dem. Rep. Congo *02°16′S 26°54′E*
152 H8 **Moga** Punjab, N India *30°49′N 75°13′E*
Mogadiscio/Mogadishu *see* Muqdisho
Mogador *see* Essaouira
104 J6 **Mogadouro** Bragança, N Portugal *41°20′N 06°43′W*
167 N2 **Mogaung** Kachin State, N Burma (Myanmar) *25°20′N 96°54′E*
110 L13 **Mogielnica** Mazowieckie, C Poland *51°40′N 20°42′E*
Mogilëv *see* Mahilyow
Mogilev-Podol'skiy *see* Mohyliv-Podil's'kyy
Mogilëvskaya Oblast' *see* Mahilyowskaya Voblasts'
110 I11 **Mogilno** Kujawsko-pomorskie, C Poland *52°39′N 17°58′E*
83 Q15 **Mogincual** Nampula, NE Mozambique *15°33′S 40°28′E*
114 E13 **Moglenítsas** ∽ N Greece
106 H8 **Mogliano Veneto** Veneto, NE Italy *45°34′N 12°14′E*
113 M21 **Moglicë** Korçë, SE Albania *40°43′N 20°22′E*
123 O13 **Mogocha** Zabaykal'skiy Kray, S Russian Federation *53°39′N 119°47′E*
122 J11 **Mogochin** Tomskaya Oblast', C Russian Federation *57°42′N 83°24′E*
80 F13 **Mogogh** Jonglei, E South Sudan *08°26′N 31°19′E*
171 U12 **Mogoi** Papua, E Indonesia *01°44′S 133°13′E*
166 M4 **Mogok** Mandalay, C Burma (Myanmar) *22°55′N 96°29′E*
37 P14 **Mogollon Mountains** ▲▲ New Mexico, SW USA
36 M12 **Mogollon Rim** *cliff* Arizona, SW USA
61 E23 **Mogotes, Punta** *headland* E Argentina *38°03′S 57°31′W*
42 J8 **Mogotón** ▲ NW Nicaragua *13°45′N 86°22′W*
104 I14 **Moguer** Andalucía, S Spain *37°15′N 06°52′W*
111 J26 **Mohács** Baranya, SW Hungary *46°N 18°40′E*
185 C20 **Mohaka** ∽ North Island, New Zealand
28 M2 **Mohall** North Dakota, N USA *48°45′N 101°30′W*
Moḥammadābād *see* Dargaz
143 U12 **Moḥammadābād-e Rīgān** Kermān, SE Iran *28°39′N 59°01′E*
74 F6 **Mohammedia** *prev.* Fédala. NW Morocco *33°46′N 07°16′W*
74 F6 **Mohammed V** ✈ (Casablanca) W Morocco *33°07′N 08°28′W*
Mohammerah *see* Khorramshahr
36 H10 **Mohave, Lake** ▣ Arizona/Nevada, W USA
36 I12 **Mohave Mountains** ▲▲ Arizona, SW USA
36 I15 **Mohawk Mountains** ▲▲ Arizona, SW USA
18 J10 **Mohawk River** ∽ New York, NE USA
163 T3 **Mohe** *var.* Xilinji. Heilongjiang, NE China *53°01′N 122°26′E*
95 L20 **Moheda** Kronoberg, S Sweden *57°00′N 14°34′E*
Mohéli *see* Mwali
Mohendergarh *see* Mahendragarh
38 K12 **Mohican, Cape** *headland* Nunivak Island, Alaska, USA *60°12′N 167°25′W*
Mohn *see* Muhu
101 G15 **Möhne** ∽ W Germany
101 G15 **Möhne-Stausee** ▣ W Germany
92 P2 **Mohn, Kapp** *headland* NW Svalbard *79°26′N 25°44′E*
197 S14 **Mohns Ridge** *undersea feature* Greenland Sea/Norwegian Sea *72°30′N 05°00′E*
57 I17 **Moho** Puno, SE Peru *15°21′S 69°32′W*
Mohokare *see* Caledon
95 L17 **Moholm** Västra Götaland, S Sweden *58°37′N 14°04′E*
36 J11 **Mohon Peak** ▲ Arizona, SW USA *34°55′N 113°07′W*
81 J23 **Mohoro** Pwani, E Tanzania *08°09′S 39°10′E*
Mohra *see* Moravice
Mohrungen *see* Morąg
116 M7 **Mohyliv-Podil's'kyy** *Rus.* Mogilev-Podol'skiy. Vinnyts'ka Oblast', C Ukraine *48°29′N 27°49′E*
95 D17 **Moi** Rogaland, S Norway *58°27′N 06°32′E*
Moili *see* Mwali
116 K11 **Moinești** *Hung.* Mojnest. Bacău, E Romania *46°27′N 26°31′E*
Móinteach Mílic *see* Mountmellick
14 J14 **Moira** ∽ Ontario, SE Canada
92 G13 **Mo i Rana** Nordland, C Norway *66°19′N 14°10′E*
153 X14 **Moirāng** Manipur, NE India *24°29′N 93°45′E*
115 J25 **Moíres** Kríti, Greece, E Mediterranean Sea *35°03′N 24°51′E*
118 H6 **Mõisaküla** *Ger.* Moiseküll. Viljandimaa, S Estonia *58°05′N 25°12′E*
Moiseküll *see* Mõisaküla
15 W4 **Moisie** Québec, E Canada *50°12′N 66°06′W*
15 W3 **Moisie** ∽ Québec, SE Canada
102 M14 **Moissac** Tarn-et-Garonne, S France *44°07′N 01°05′E*
78 I13 **Moïssala** Moyen-Chari, S Chad *08°21′N 17°46′E*
55 O7 **Moitaco** Bolívar, E Venezuela *08°00′N 64°22′W*
95 P15 **Möja** Stockholm, C Sweden *59°25′N 18°55′E*
105 Q14 **Mojácar** Andalucía, S Spain *37°09′N 01°50′W*
35 T13 **Mojave** California, W USA *35°03′N 118°10′W*
35 V13 **Mojave Desert** *plain* California, W USA

◆ Country ● Country Capital ◇ Dependent Territory ○ Dependent Territory Capital ◈ Administrative Regions ✈ International Airport ▲ Mountain ▲▲ Mountain Range ✸ Volcano ∽ River ◎ Lake ▣ Reservoir

35 V13 **Mojave River** ≋ California, W USA
60 L9 **Moji-Mirim** var. Moji-Mirim. São Paulo, S Brazil 22°26′S 46°55′W
Moji-Mirim see Moji-Mirim
113 K15 **Mojkovac** E Montenegro 42°57′N 19°34′E
Mojnest see Moinești
Mōka see Mooka
153 Q13 **Mokāma** prev. Mokameh, Mukama. Bihār, N India 25°24′N 85°55′E
79 O25 **Mokambo** Katanga, SE Dem. Rep. Congo 12°23′S 28°21′E
Mokameh see Mokāma
38 D9 **Mōkapu Point** var. Mokapu Point. headland O'ahu, Hawai'i, USA 21°27′N 157°43′W
184 L9 **Mokau** Waikato, North Island, New Zealand 38°42′S 174°37′E
184 L9 **Mokau** ≋ North Island, New Zealand
35 P7 **Mokelumne River** ≋ California, W USA
83 J23 **Mokhotlong** NE Lesotho 29°19′S 29°06′E
Mokil Atoll see Mwokil Atoll
95 N14 **Möklinta** Västmanland, C Sweden 60°04′N 16°34′E
Mokna see Mokra Gora
184 L4 **Mokohinau Islands** island group N New Zealand
153 X12 **Mokokchūng** Nāgāland, NE India 26°20′N 94°30′E
78 F12 **Mokolo** Extrême-Nord, N Cameroon 10°49′N 13°54′E
83 J20 **Mokopane** prev. Potgietersrus. Limpopo, NE South Africa 24°09′S 28°58′E
185 D24 **Mokoreta** ≋ South Island, New Zealand
163 X17 **Mokpo** Jap. Moppo; prev. Mokp'o. SW South Korea 34°50′N 126°26′E
Mokp'o see Mokpo
113 L16 **Mokra Gora** Alb. Mokna. ⛰ S Serbia
Mokrany see Makrany
127 O5 **Moksha** ≋ W Russian Federation
143 X12 **Mok Sukhteh-ye Pāyīn** Sīstān va Balūchestān, SE Iran
Moktama see Mottama
77 T14 **Mokwa** Niger, W Nigeria 09°19′N 05°01′E
99 J16 **Mol** prev. Moll. Antwerpen, N Belgium 51°11′N 05°07′E
107 O17 **Mola di Bari** Puglia, SE Italy 41°03′N 17°05′E
Molai see Moláoi
41 P13 **Molango** Hidalgo, C Mexico 20°48′N 98°44′W
115 F22 **Moláoi** var. Molai. Pelopónnisos, S Greece 36°48′N 22°51′E
41 Z12 **Molas del Norte, Punta** var. Punta Molas. headland SE Mexico 20°34′N 86°43′W
Molas, Punta see Molas del Norte, Punta
105 R11 **Molatón** ▲ C Spain 38°58′N 01°19′W
97 K18 **Mold** NE Wales, United Kingdom 53°10′N 03°08′W
Moldau see Vltava, Czech Republic
Moldau see Moldova
Moldavia see Moldova
Moldavian SSR/Moldavskaya SSR see Moldova
94 E9 **Molde** Møre og Romsdal, S Norway 62°44′N 07°08′E
Moldotau, Khrebet see Moldo-Too, Khrebet
147 V9 **Moldo-Too, Khrebet** prev. Khrebet Moldotau. ⛰ C Kyrgyzstan
116 L9 **Moldova** off. Republic of Moldova, var. Moldavia; prev. Moldavian SSR, Rus. Moldavskaya SSR. ◆ republic SE Europe
116 K9 **Moldova** Eng. Moldavia, Ger. Moldau. former province NE Romania
116 K9 **Moldova** ≋ N Romania
116 F13 **Moldova Nouă** Ger. Neumoldowa, Hung. Újmoldova. Caraş-Severin, SW Romania 44°45′N 21°39′E
Moldova, Republic of see Moldova
116 F13 **Moldova Veche** Ger. Altmoldowa, Hung. Ómoldova. Caraş-Severin, SW Romania 44°45′N 21°13′E
Moldoveanul see Vârful Moldoveanu
83 I20 **Molepolole** Kweneng, SE Botswana 24°25′S 25°30′E
44 L8 **Môle-St-Nicolas** NW Haiti 19°46′N 73°19′W
118 H13 **Molėtai** Utena, E Lithuania 55°14′N 25°25′E
107 O17 **Molfetta** Puglia, SE Italy 41°12′N 16°35′E
171 P11 **Molibagu** Sulawesi, N Indonesia 0°25′N 123°57′E
62 G12 **Molina** Maule, C Chile 35°06′S 71°18′W
105 Q7 **Molina de Aragón** Castilla-La Mancha, C Spain 40°50′N 01°54′W
105 R13 **Molina de Segura** Murcia, SE Spain 38°03′N 01°11′W
30 J11 **Moline** Illinois, N USA 41°30′N 90°31′W
27 P7 **Moline** Kansas, C USA 37°21′N 96°18′W
79 P23 **Moliro** Katanga, SE Dem. Rep. Congo 08°11′S 30°31′E
107 K16 **Molise** ◈ region S Italy
95 K15 **Molkom** Värmland, C Sweden 59°36′N 13°43′E
109 Q9 **Möll** ≋ S Austria
Moll see Mol
146 I14 **Mollanepes Adyndaky** Rus. Imeni Mollanepesa. Mary Welaýaty, S Turkmenistan 37°36′N 61°54′E
95 J22 **Mölle** Skåne, S Sweden 56°15′N 12°19′E
57 H18 **Mollendo** Arequipa, SW Peru 17°02′S 72°01′W
105 U5 **Mollerussa** Cataluña, NE Spain 41°37′N 00°53′E
108 H8 **Mollis** Glarus, NE Switzerland 47°05′N 09°03′E
95 J19 **Mölndal** Västra Götaland, S Sweden 57°39′N 12°05′E
95 J19 **Mölnlycke** Västra Götaland, S Sweden 57°39′N 12°09′E
117 U9 **Molochans'k** Rus. Molochansk. Zaporiz'ka Oblast', SE Ukraine 47°10′N 35°38′E
117 U10 **Molochna** Rus. Molochnaya. ≋ S Ukraine
Molochnaya see Molochna
117 U10 **Molochnyy Lyman** bay N Black Sea
Molodechno/Molodeczno see Maladzyechna
195 V3 **Molodezhnaya** Russian research station Antarctica 67°33′S 46°12′E
124 J14 **Mologa** ≋ NW Russian Federation
38 E9 **Moloka'i** var. Molokai. island Hawaiian Islands, Hawai'i, USA
175 X3 **Molokai Fracture Zone** tectonic feature NE Pacific Ocean
124 K15 **Molokovo** Tverskaya Oblast', W Russian Federation 58°10′N 36°43′E
125 Q14 **Moloma** ≋ NW Russian Federation
183 R8 **Molong** New South Wales, SE Australia 33°07′S 148°52′E
83 H21 **Molopo** seasonal river Botswana/South Africa
115 F17 **Mólos** Stereá Elláda, C Greece 38°48′N 22°39′E
171 O11 **Molosipat** Sulawesi, N Indonesia 0°28′N 121°08′E
Molotov see Severodvinsk, Arkhangel'skaya Oblast', Russian Federation
Molotov see Perm', Permskaya Oblast', Russian Federation
79 G17 **Moloundou** Est, SE Cameroon 02°03′N 15°14′E
103 U5 **Molsheim** Bas-Rhin, NE France 48°33′N 07°30′E
11 X13 **Molson Lake** ◎ Manitoba, C Canada
Moluccas see Maluku
171 Q12 **Molucca Sea** Ind. Laut Maluku. sea E Indonesia
Molukken see Maluku
83 O15 **Molumbo** Zambézia, N Mozambique 15°33′S 36°19′E
171 T15 **Molu, Pulau** island Maluku, E Indonesia
83 P16 **Moma** Nampula, NE Mozambique 16°42′S 39°12′E
171 X14 **Momats** ≋ Papua, E Indonesia
42 J11 **Mombacho, Volcán** ✱ SW Nicaragua 11°49′N 85°58′W
81 K21 **Mombasa** Coast, SE Kenya 04°04′N 39°40′E
81 J21 **Mombasa** ✈ Coast, SE Kenya 04°01′S 39°31′E
Mombetsu see Monbetsu
114 J12 **Momchilgrad** prev. Mastanli. Kŭrdzhali, S Bulgaria 41°33′N 25°25′E
99 F23 **Momignies** Hainaut, S Belgium 50°02′N 04°10′E
54 E6 **Momil** Córdoba, NW Colombia 09°15′N 75°40′W
42 I10 **Momotombo, Volcán** ✱ W Nicaragua 12°25′N 86°33′W
56 B5 **Mompiche, Ensenada de** bay NW Ecuador
79 K18 **Mompono** Equateur, NW Dem. Rep. Congo 0°11′N 21°31′E
54 F6 **Mompós** Bolívar, NW Colombia 09°15′N 74°29′W
95 J24 **Møn** prev. Möen. island SE Denmark
36 L4 **Mona** Utah, W USA 39°49′N 111°52′W
Mona, Canal de la see Mona Passage
96 E8 **Monach Islands** island group NW Scotland, United Kingdom
103 V14 **Monaco** var. Monaco-Ville; anc. Monoecus. ● (Monaco) S Monaco 43°46′N 07°23′E
103 V14 **Monaco** off. Principality of Monaco. ◆ monarchy W Europe
Monaco see München
Monaco Basin see Canary Basin
Monaco, Principality of see Monaco
Monaco-Ville see Monaco
96 I9 **Monadhliath Mountains** ⛰ N Scotland, United Kingdom
55 O6 **Monagas** off. Estado Monagas. ◈ state NE Venezuela
Monagas, Estado see Monagas
97 F16 **Monaghan** Ir. Muineachán. Monaghan, N Ireland 54°15′N 06°58′W
97 E16 **Monaghan** Ir. Muineachán. cultural region N Ireland
43 S16 **Monagrillo** Herrera, S Panama 08°00′N 80°28′W
24 L8 **Monahans** Texas, SW USA 31°35′N 102°54′W
45 Q9 **Mona, Isla** island W Puerto Rico
45 Q9 **Mona Passage** Sp. Canal de la Mona. channel Dominican Republic/Puerto Rico
43 O14 **Mona, Punta** headland E Costa Rica 09°44′N 82°48′W
155 K25 **Monaragala** Uva Province, SE Sri Lanka 06°52′N 81°22′E
33 S9 **Monarch** Montana, NW USA 47°04′N 110°51′W
10 H14 **Monarch Mountain** ▲ British Columbia, SW Canada 51°59′N 125°56′W
Monasterio see Monesterio
Monasterzyska see Monastyrys'ka
Monastir see Bitola
Monastyriska see Monastyrys'ka
117 O7 **Monastyryshche** Cherkas'ka Oblast', C Ukraine 48°59′N 29°47′E
116 J6 **Monastyrys'ka** Pol. Monasterzyska, Rus. Monastyriska. Ternopil's'ka Oblast', W Ukraine 49°05′N 25°10′E
79 E15 **Monatélé** Centre, SW Cameroon 04°16′N 11°12′E
165 U2 **Monbetsu** var. Mombetsu, Monbetu. Hokkaidō, NE Japan 44°23′N 143°22′E
Monbetu see Monbetsu
106 B8 **Moncalieri** Piemonte, NW Italy 45°N 07°41′E
104 G4 **Monção** Viana do Castelo, N Portugal 42°03′N 08°29′W
105 Q5 **Moncayo** ▲ N Spain 41°43′N 01°51′W
105 Q5 **Moncayo, Sierra del** ⛰ N Spain
124 J4 **Monchegorsk** Murmanskaya Oblast', NW Russian Federation 67°56′N 32°47′E
101 D15 **Mönchengladbach** prev. München-Gladbach. Nordrhein-Westfalen, W Germany 51°12′N 06°35′E
104 F14 **Monchique** Faro, S Portugal 37°19′N 08°33′W
104 G14 **Monchique, Serra de** ⛰ S Portugal
21 S14 **Moncks Corner** South Carolina, SE USA 33°12′N 80°00′W
41 N7 **Monclova** Coahuila, NE Mexico 26°55′N 101°25′W
Moncorvo see Torre de Moncorvo
13 P14 **Moncton** New Brunswick, SE Canada 46°04′N 64°50′W
104 F8 **Mondego, Cabo** headland N Portugal 40°10′N 08°58′W
104 G8 **Mondego, Rio** ≋ N Portugal
104 I2 **Mondoñedo** Galicia, NW Spain 43°25′N 07°22′W
99 N25 **Mondorf-les-Bains** Grevenmacher, SE Luxembourg 49°30′N 06°16′E
102 M7 **Mondoubleau** Loir-et-Cher, C France 48°00′N 00°49′E
106 B9 **Mondovì** Piemonte, NW Italy 44°23′N 07°56′E
30 J6 **Mondovi** Wisconsin, N USA 44°34′N 91°40′W
Mondragón see Arrasate
107 J17 **Mondragone** Campania, S Italy 41°07′N 13°53′E
109 R5 **Mondsee** ◎ N Austria
115 G22 **Monemvasiá** var. Monemvasía. Pelopónnisos, S Greece 36°22′N 23°03′E
18 B15 **Monessen** Pennsylvania, NE USA 40°07′N 79°51′W
104 J12 **Monesterio** var. Monasterio. Extremadura, W Spain 38°05′N 06°16′W
14 L8 **Monet** Québec, SE Canada 48°09′N 75°37′W
27 S8 **Monett** Missouri, C USA 36°55′N 93°55′W
27 X9 **Monette** Arkansas, C USA 35°53′N 90°20′W
14 G11 **Monetville** Ontario, S Canada 46°08′N 80°24′W
106 J7 **Monfalcone** Friuli-Venezia Giulia, NE Italy 45°49′N 13°32′E
104 H10 **Monforte** Portalegre, C Portugal 39°03′N 07°26′W
104 I4 **Monforte de Lemos** Galicia, NW Spain 42°32′N 07°30′W
79 L16 **Monga** Orientale, N Dem. Rep. Congo 04°12′N 22°49′E
81 I24 **Monga** Lindi, SE Tanzania 09°05′S 37°51′E
81 F15 **Mongalla** Central Equatoria, S South Sudan 05°12′N 31°42′E
153 U11 **Mongar** E Bhutan 27°16′N 91°07′E
167 U6 **Mong Cai** var. Hai Ninh. Quang Ninh, N Vietnam 21°33′N 107°56′E
180 I11 **Mongers Lake** salt lake Western Australia
186 K8 **Mongga** Kolombangara, NW Solomon Islands 07°51′S 157°00′E
167 O6 **Möng Hpayak** Shan State, E Burma (Myanmar) 20°56′N 100°00′E
Monghyr see Munger
106 B10 **Mongioie** ▲ NW Italy 44°13′N 07°46′E
153 T16 **Mongla** var. Mungla. Khulna, S Bangladesh 22°18′N 89°34′E
188 C15 **Mongmong** C Guam
167 N6 **Möng Nai** Shan State, E Burma (Myanmar) 20°28′N 97°51′E
78 I11 **Mongo** Guéra, C Chad 12°12′N 18°40′E
76 I14 **Mongo** ≋ N Sierra Leone
163 I8 **Mongolia** Mong. Mongol Uls. ◆ republic E Asia
129 V8 **Mongolia, Plateau of** plateau E Mongolia
Mongolküre see Zhaosu
Mongol Uls see Mongolia
79 E17 **Mongomo** E Equatorial Guinea 01°39′N 11°18′E
162 M7 **Möngönmorit** var. Bulag. Töv, C Mongolia 48°09′N 108°33′E
77 Y12 **Mongonu** var. Monguno. Borno, NE Nigeria 12°42′N 13°37′E
Mongora see Saïdu
78 K11 **Mongororo** Ouaddaï, SE Chad 12°03′N 22°26′E
Mongos, Chaîne des see Bongo, Massif des
79 I16 **Mongoumba** Lobaye, SW Central African Republic 03°39′N 18°30′E
Mongrove, Punta see Cayacal, Punta
83 G15 **Mongu** Western, W Zambia 15°13′S 23°09′E
76 I10 **Monguel** Gorgol, SW Mauritania 16°25′N 13°08′W
Monguno see Mongonu
167 N4 **Möng Yai** Shan State, E Burma (Myanmar) 22°25′N 98°02′E
167 O5 **Möng Yang** Shan State, E Burma (Myanmar) 21°52′N 99°31′E
167 N3 **Möng Yu** Shan State, E Burma (Myanmar) 24°00′N 97°57′E
Mönhbulag see Yösöndzüyl
163 O8 **Mönhhaan** var. Bayasgalant. Sühbaatar, E Mongolia 46°55′N 112°11′E
162 E7 **Mönhhayrhan** var. Tsenher. Hovd, W Mongolia 47°07′N 92°04′E
Mönh Sarīdag see Munku-Sardyk, Gora
186 F9 **Moni** ≋ S Papau New Guinea
115 I15 **Moní Megístis Lávras** monastery Kentrikí Makedonía, N Greece
115 F18 **Moní Osíou Loúkas** monastery Stereá Elláda, C Greece
54 F9 **Moniquirá** Boyacá, C Colombia 05°54′N 73°35′W
103 Q12 **Monistrol-sur-Loire** Haute-Loire, C France 45°19′N 04°12′E
35 V7 **Monitor Range** ⛰ Nevada, W USA
115 I14 **Moní Vatopedíou** monastery Kentrikí Makedonía, N Greece
Monkchester see Newcastle upon Tyne
83 N14 **Monkey Bay** Southern, SE Malawi 14°09′S 34°53′E
43 N11 **Monkey Point** var. Punta Mico, Punte Mono, Punto Mico. headland SE Nicaragua 11°37′N 83°39′W
Monkey River see Monkey River Town
42 G3 **Monkey River Town** var. Monkey River. Toledo, SE Belize 16°22′N 88°29′W
14 M13 **Monkland** Ontario, SE Canada 45°11′N 74°51′W
79 J19 **Monkoto** Equateur, NW Dem. Rep. Congo 01°39′S 20°41′E
97 K21 **Monmouth** Wel. Trefynwy. SE Wales, United Kingdom 51°50′N 02°43′W
30 J12 **Monmouth** Illinois, N USA 40°54′N 90°39′W
32 F12 **Monmouth** Oregon, NW USA 44°51′N 123°13′W
97 K21 **Monmouth** cultural region SE Wales, United Kingdom
98 I10 **Monnickendam** Noord-Holland, C Netherlands 52°28′N 05°02′E
77 R15 **Mono** ≋ C Togo
Monoecus see Monaco
35 R8 **Mono Lake** ◎ California, W USA
115 O23 **Monólithos** Ródos, Dodekánisa, Greece, Aegean Sea 36°08′N 27°45′E
19 Q12 **Monomoy Island** island Massachusetts, NE USA
31 O12 **Monon** Indiana, N USA 40°52′N 86°54′W
29 Y12 **Monona** Iowa, C USA 43°03′N 91°23′W
30 L9 **Monona** Wisconsin, N USA 43°03′N 89°18′W
18 B15 **Monongahela** Pennsylvania, NE USA 40°10′N 79°54′W
18 B16 **Monongahela River** ≋ NE USA
107 P17 **Monopoli** Puglia, SE Italy 40°57′N 17°18′E
Mono, Punte see Monkey Point
111 K23 **Monor** Pest, C Hungary 47°21′N 18°27′E
Monostor see Beli Manastir
78 K8 **Monou** Borkou-Ennedi-Tibesti, NE Chad 16°22′N 22°15′E
105 S12 **Monóvar** Cat. Monòver. Valenciana, E Spain 38°26′N 00°50′W
Monòver see Monóvar
105 R7 **Monreal del Campo** Aragón, NE Spain 40°47′N 01°20′W
107 I23 **Monreale** Sicilia, Italy, C Mediterranean Sea 38°05′N 13°17′E
23 T3 **Monroe** Georgia, SE USA 33°47′N 83°42′W
29 W14 **Monroe** Iowa, C USA 41°31′N 93°06′W
22 I5 **Monroe** Louisiana, S USA 32°32′N 92°06′W
31 S10 **Monroe** Michigan, N USA 41°55′N 83°24′W
18 K13 **Monroe** New York, NE USA 41°18′N 74°09′W
21 S11 **Monroe** North Carolina, SE USA 35°00′N 80°35′W
36 L6 **Monroe** Utah, W USA 38°37′N 112°07′W
32 H7 **Monroe** Washington, NW USA 47°51′N 121°58′W
30 L9 **Monroe** Wisconsin, N USA 42°35′N 89°39′W
27 V3 **Monroe City** Missouri, C USA 39°39′N 91°43′W
31 O15 **Monroe Lake** ⊞ Indiana, N USA
23 O7 **Monroeville** Alabama, S USA 31°31′N 87°19′W
18 C15 **Monroeville** Pennsylvania, NE USA 40°24′N 79°44′W
76 J16 **Monrovia** ● (Liberia) W Liberia 06°18′N 10°48′W
76 J16 **Monrovia** ✈ W Liberia 06°22′N 10°50′W
105 T7 **Monroyo** Aragón, NE Spain 40°47′N 00°03′W
99 F20 **Mons** Dut. Bergen. Hainaut, S Belgium 50°28′N 03°58′E
104 I8 **Monsanto** Castelo Branco, C Portugal 40°02′N 07°07′W
106 H8 **Monselice** Veneto, NE Italy 45°15′N 11°47′E
166 M9 **Mon State** ◈ state S Burma (Myanmar)
98 G12 **Monster** Zuid-Holland, W Netherlands 52°01′N 04°10′E
95 N20 **Mönsterås** Kalmar, S Sweden 57°03′N 16°27′E
101 F17 **Montabaur** Rheinland-Pfalz, W Germany 50°25′N 07°48′E
106 G8 **Montagnana** Veneto, NE Italy 45°14′N 11°31′E
35 N1 **Montague** California, W USA 41°43′N 122°31′W
25 S5 **Montague** Texas, SW USA 33°40′N 97°44′W
183 S11 **Montague Island** island New South Wales, SE Australia
39 S12 **Montague Island** island Alaska, USA
39 S13 **Montague Strait** strait N Gulf of Alaska
102 J8 **Montaigu** Vendée, NW France 46°58′N 01°18′W
Montaigu see Scherpenheuvel
105 S7 **Montalbán** Aragón, NE Spain 40°49′N 00°48′W
106 G13 **Montalcino** Toscana, C Italy 43°01′N 11°34′E
104 H5 **Montalegre** Vila Real, N Portugal 41°49′N 07°48′W
114 G8 **Montana** prev. Ferdinand, Mikhaylovgrad. Montana, NW Bulgaria 43°25′N 23°14′E
108 D10 **Montana** Valais, SW Switzerland 46°23′N 07°29′E
39 R11 **Montana** Alaska, USA 62°06′N 150°03′W
114 G8 **Montana** ◈ province NW Bulgaria
33 T9 **Montana** off. State of Montana, also known as Mountain State, Treasure State. ◈ state NW USA
104 J10 **Montánchez** Extremadura, W Spain 39°15′N 06°07′W
Montañita see La Montañita
15 Q8 **Mont-Apica** Québec, SE Canada 47°57′N 71°24′W
104 G10 **Montargil** Portalegre, C Portugal 39°05′N 08°10′W
104 G10 **Montargil, Barragem de** ⊞ C Portugal
103 O7 **Montargis** Loiret, C France 48°N 02°44′E
103 O4 **Montataire** Oise, N France 49°16′N 02°24′E
102 M14 **Montauban** Tarn-et-Garonne, S France 44°01′N 01°20′E
19 N14 **Montauk** Long Island, New York, NE USA 41°01′N 71°58′W
19 N14 **Montauk Point** headland Long Island, New York, NE USA 41°04′N 71°51′W
103 Q7 **Montbard** Côte d'Or, C France 47°35′N 04°25′E
103 U7 **Montbéliard** Doubs, E France 47°31′N 06°49′E
25 W11 **Mont Belvieu** Texas, SW USA 29°51′N 94°53′W
105 U6 **Montblanc** prev. Montblanch. Cataluña, NE Spain 41°23′N 01°10′E
Montblanch see Montblanc
103 Q11 **Montbrison** Loire, E France 45°37′N 04°04′E
Montcalm, Lake see Dogai Coring
103 Q9 **Montceau-les-Mines** Saône-et-Loire, C France 46°40′N 04°19′E
103 U12 **Mont Cenis, Col du** pass E France
102 K15 **Mont-de-Marsan** Landes, SW France 43°54′N 00°30′W
103 O3 **Montdidier** Somme, N France 49°39′N 02°35′E
187 Q17 **Mont-Dore** Province Sud, S New Caledonia 22°18′S 166°34′E
20 K10 **Monteagle** Tennessee, S USA 35°15′N 85°47′W
57 M20 **Monteagudo** Chuquisaca, S Bolivia 19°48′S 63°57′W
41 R16 **Monte Albán** ruins Oaxaca, S Mexico
105 R11 **Montealegre del Castillo** Castilla-La Mancha, C Spain 38°48′N 01°18′W
59 N18 **Monte Azul** Minas Gerais, SE Brazil 15°13′S 42°53′W
14 M12 **Montebello** Québec, SE Canada 45°40′N 74°56′W
106 H7 **Montebelluna** Veneto, NE Italy 45°46′N 12°03′E
60 G13 **Montecarlo** Misiones, NE Argentina 26°38′S 54°45′W
61 D16 **Monte Caseros** Corrientes, NE Argentina 30°15′S 57°39′W
60 J13 **Monte Castelo** Santa Catarina, S Brazil 26°34′S 50°12′W
106 F11 **Montecatini Terme** Toscana, C Italy 43°53′N 10°46′E
42 H7 **Montecillos, Cordillera de** ⛰ W Honduras
62 I12 **Monte Comán** Mendoza, W Argentina 34°35′S 67°53′W
44 M8 **Monte Cristi** var. San Fernando de Monte Cristi. NW Dominican Republic 19°52′N 71°39′W
58 C13 **Monte Cristo** Amazonas, W Brazil 03°14′S 68°00′W
107 E14 **Montecristo, Isola di** island Archipelago Toscano, C Italy
Monte Croce Carnico, Passo di see Plöcken Pass
58 J12 **Monte Dourado** Pará, NE Brazil 0°48′S 52°32′W
40 L11 **Monte Escobedo** Zacatecas, C Mexico 22°19′N 103°30′W
106 I13 **Montefalco** Umbria, C Italy 42°54′N 12°40′E
107 H14 **Montefiascone** Lazio, C Italy 42°33′N 12°01′E
105 N14 **Montefrío** Andalucía, S Spain 37°19′N 04°00′W
44 I11 **Montego Bay** var. Mobay. W Jamaica 18°28′N 77°55′W
Montego Bay see Sangster
104 J8 **Montehermoso** Extremadura, W Spain 40°05′N 06°20′W
104 F10 **Montejunto, Serra de** ▲ C Portugal 39°10′N 09°01′W
Monteleone di Calabria see Vibo Valentia
54 E7 **Montelíbano** Córdoba, NW Colombia 08°02′N 75°29′W
103 R13 **Montélimar** anc. Acunum Acusio, Montilium Adhemari. Drôme, E France 44°33′N 04°45′E
104 K15 **Montellano** Andalucía, S Spain 37°00′N 05°34′W
35 Y2 **Montello** Nevada, W USA 41°18′N 114°10′W
30 L8 **Montello** Wisconsin, N USA 43°47′N 89°20′W
63 J18 **Montemayor, Meseta de** plain SE Argentina
41 O9 **Montemorelos** Nuevo León, NE Mexico 25°10′N 99°52′W
104 G11 **Montemor-o-Novo** Évora, S Portugal 38°38′N 08°13′W
104 G8 **Montemor-o-Velho** var. Montemor-o-Vélho. Coimbra, N Portugal 40°11′N 08°41′W
Montemor-o-Vélho see Montemor-o-Velho
104 H7 **Montemuro, Serra de** ▲ N Portugal 40°59′N 07°59′W
102 K12 **Montendre** Charente-Maritime, W France 45°17′N 00°24′W
61 I15 **Montenegro** Rio Grande do Sul, S Brazil 29°40′S 51°32′W
113 J16 **Montenegro** Serb. Crna Gora. ◆ republic SW Europe
62 G10 **Monte Patria** Coquimbo, N Chile 30°40′S 71°00′W
45 O9 **Monte Plata** E Dominican Republic 18°50′N 69°47′W
83 P14 **Montepuez** Cabo Delgado, N Mozambique 13°09′S 39°00′E
83 P14 **Montepuez** ≋ N Mozambique
106 G13 **Montepulciano** Toscana, C Italy 43°02′N 11°51′E
62 L6 **Monte Quemado** Santiago del Estero, N Argentina 25°48′S 62°52′W
103 O6 **Montereau-Faut-Yonne** anc. Condate. Seine-St-Denis, N France 48°23′N 02°57′E
35 N11 **Monterey** California, W USA 36°36′N 121°53′W
20 L9 **Monterey** Tennessee, S USA 36°09′N 85°16′W
21 T5 **Monterey** Virginia, NE USA 38°24′N 79°36′W
Monterey see Monterrey
35 N10 **Monterey Bay** bay California, W USA
54 D6 **Montería** Córdoba, NW Colombia 08°45′N 75°54′W
57 N18 **Montero** Santa Cruz, C Bolivia 17°20′S 63°15′W
62 J7 **Monteros** Tucumán, C Argentina 27°12′S 65°30′W
104 I5 **Monterrei** Galicia, NW Spain 41°56′N 07°27′W
41 O8 **Monterrey** var. Monterey. Nuevo León, NE Mexico 25°41′N 100°16′W
32 F9 **Montesano** Washington, NW USA 46°58′N 123°37′W
107 M19 **Montesano sulla Marcellana** Campania, S Italy 40°15′N 15°41′E
107 N16 **Monte Sant' Angelo** Puglia, SE Italy 41°43′N 15°58′E
59 O16 **Monte Santo** Bahia, E Brazil 10°25′S 39°18′W
107 D18 **Monte Santu, Capo di** headland Sardegna, Italy, C Mediterranean Sea 40°05′N 09°43′E
59 M19 **Montes Claros** Minas Gerais, SE Brazil 16°45′S 43°52′W
107 K14 **Montesilvano Marina** Abruzzo, C Italy 42°28′N 14°07′E
23 P4 **Montevallo** Alabama, S USA 33°06′N 86°51′W
106 G12 **Montevarchi** Toscana, C Italy 43°32′N 11°34′E
61 F20 **Montevideo** ● (Uruguay) Montevideo, S Uruguay 34°55′S 56°10′W
29 S9 **Montevideo** Minnesota, N USA 44°56′N 95°43′W
37 S7 **Monte Vista** Colorado, C USA 37°33′N 106°08′W
23 T5 **Montezuma** Georgia, SE USA 32°18′N 84°01′W
29 W14 **Montezuma** Iowa, C USA 41°35′N 92°31′W
26 J6 **Montezuma** Kansas, C USA 37°33′N 100°25′W
103 U12 **Montgenèvre, Col de** pass France/Italy
97 K20 **Montgomery** E Wales, United Kingdom 52°38′N 03°05′W
23 Q5 **Montgomery** state capital Alabama, S USA 32°22′N 86°18′W
29 V9 **Montgomery** Minnesota, N USA 44°26′N 93°34′W
18 G13 **Montgomery** Pennsylvania, NE USA 41°08′N 76°52′W
21 Q5 **Montgomery** West Virginia, NE USA 38°07′N 81°19′W
97 K19 **Montgomery** cultural region E Wales, United Kingdom
Montgomery see Sāhīwāl
27 V4 **Montgomery City** Missouri, C USA 38°57′N 91°27′W
35 S8 **Montgomery Pass** pass Nevada, W USA
102 K12 **Montguyon** Charente-Maritime, W France 45°12′N 00°13′W
108 C10 **Monthey** Valais, SW Switzerland 46°15′N 06°56′E
27 V13 **Monticello** Arkansas, C USA 33°38′N 91°49′W
23 T4 **Monticello** Florida, SE USA 30°33′N 83°52′W
23 T8 **Monticello** Georgia, SE USA 33°18′N 83°40′W
30 M13 **Monticello** Illinois, N USA 40°01′N 88°34′W
31 O12 **Monticello** Indiana, N USA 40°45′N 86°46′W
29 Y13 **Monticello** Iowa, C USA 42°14′N 91°11′W
20 L7 **Monticello** Kentucky, S USA 36°50′N 84°50′W
29 V8 **Monticello** Minnesota, N USA 45°19′N 93°45′W
22 K7 **Monticello** Mississippi, S USA 31°33′N 90°06′W
27 V2 **Monticello** Missouri, C USA 40°07′N 91°42′W
18 J12 **Monticello** New York, NE USA 41°39′N 74°41′W
37 O7 **Monticello** Utah, W USA 37°52′N 109°20′W
106 F8 **Montichiari** Lombardia, N Italy 45°24′N 10°27′E
102 M12 **Montignac** Dordogne, SW France 45°24′N 00°54′E
99 G21 **Montignies-le-Tilleul** var. Montigny-le-Tilleul. Hainaut, S Belgium 50°22′N 04°23′E
14 J8 **Montigny, Lac de** ◎ Québec, SE Canada
103 S6 **Montigny-le-Roi** Haute-Marne, N France 48°02′N 05°28′E
Montigny-le-Tilleul see Montignies-le-Tilleul
43 R16 **Montijo** Veraguas, S Panama 07°59′N 80°58′W
104 F11 **Montijo** Setúbal, W Portugal 38°42′N 08°59′W
104 J11 **Montijo** Extremadura, W Spain 38°55′N 06°38′W
Montilium Adhemari see Montélimar
104 M13 **Montilla** Andalucía, S Spain 37°36′N 04°39′W
102 L3 **Montivilliers** Seine-Maritime, N France 49°31′N 00°10′E
15 U7 **Mont-Joli** Québec, SE Canada 48°36′N 68°14′W
14 M10 **Mont-Laurier** Québec, SE Canada 46°33′N 75°31′W
15 X5 **Mont-Louis** Québec, SE Canada 49°15′N 65°46′W
103 N17 **Mont-Louis** var. Mont Louis. Pyrénées-Orientales, S France 42°30′N 02°08′E
103 O10 **Montluçon** Allier, C France 46°21′N 02°37′E
15 R10 **Montmagny** Québec, SE Canada 47°00′N 70°31′W
103 S3 **Montmédy** Meuse, NE France 49°31′N 05°21′E
103 P5 **Montmirail** Marne, N France 48°53′N 03°31′E
15 R9 **Montmorency** ≋ Québec, SE Canada
102 M10 **Montmorillon** Vienne, W France 46°26′N 00°52′E
107 J14 **Montorio al Vomano** Abruzzo, C Italy 42°31′N 13°39′E
104 M13 **Montoro** Andalucía, S Spain 38°00′N 04°21′W
33 S16 **Montpelier** Idaho, NW USA 42°19′N 111°18′W
29 P6 **Montpelier** North Dakota, N USA 46°40′N 98°34′W
18 M7 **Montpelier** state capital Vermont, NE USA 44°16′N 72°32′W
103 Q15 **Montpellier** Hérault, S France 43°37′N 03°52′E
102 L12 **Montpon-Ménestérol** Dordogne, SW France 45°01′N 00°10′E
12 K15 **Montréal** Eng. Montreal. Québec, SE Canada 45°30′N 73°36′W
14 G8 **Montreal** ≋ Ontario, S Canada
Montreal see Mirabel
11 T14 **Montreal Lake** ◎ Saskatchewan, C Canada
14 B9 **Montreal River** Ontario, S Canada 47°13′N 84°36′W
103 N2 **Montreuil** Pas-de-Calais, N France 50°28′N 01°46′E
102 K8 **Montreuil-Bellay** Maine-et-Loire, NW France 47°07′N 00°10′W
108 C10 **Montreux** Vaud, SW Switzerland 46°27′N 06°55′E
108 B9 **Montricher** Vaud, W Switzerland 46°37′N 06°24′E
96 K10 **Montrose** E Scotland, United Kingdom 56°43′N 02°29′W
27 W14 **Montrose** Arkansas, C USA 33°18′N 91°29′W
37 Q6 **Montrose** Colorado, C USA 38°29′N 107°53′W
29 Y16 **Montrose** Iowa, C USA 40°31′N 91°24′W
18 H12 **Montrose** Pennsylvania, NE USA 41°49′N 75°53′W
21 X5 **Montross** Virginia, NE USA 38°04′N 76°51′W
15 O12 **Mont-St-Hilaire** Québec, SE Canada 45°34′N 73°10′W
103 S3 **Mont-St-Martin** Meurthe-et-Moselle, NE France 49°31′N 05°51′E
45 V10 **Montserrat** var. Emerald Isle. ◇ UK dependent territory E West Indies
105 V5 **Montserrat** ▲ NE Spain 41°39′N 01°44′E
104 M7 **Montuenga** Castilla y León, N Spain 41°04′N 04°38′W
99 M19 **Montzen** Liège, E Belgium 50°42′N 05°59′E
37 N8 **Monument Valley** valley Arizona/Utah, SW USA
166 L4 **Monywa** Sagaing, C Burma (Myanmar) 22°05′N 95°12′E
106 D7 **Monza** Lombardia, N Italy 45°35′N 09°16′E
83 J15 **Monze** Southern, S Zambia 16°20′S 27°29′E
105 T5 **Monzón** Aragón, NE Spain 41°54′N 00°12′E
25 T9 **Moody** Texas, SW USA 31°18′N 97°21′W
98 L13 **Mook** Limburg, SE Netherlands 51°45′N 05°52′E
165 O12 **Mooka** var. Mōka. Tochigi, Honshū, S Japan 36°27′N 139°59′E
182 K3 **Moomba** South Australia 28°07′S 140°12′E
14 G13 **Moon** ≋ Ontario, S Canada
Moon see Muhu
181 Y10 **Moonie** Queensland, E Australia 27°46′S 150°22′E
193 O5 **Moonless Mountains** undersea feature E Pacific Ocean 30°40′N 140°00′W
182 L13 **Moonlight Head** headland Victoria, SE Australia 38°47′S 143°12′E
Moon-Sund see Väinameri
182 H8 **Moonta** South Australia 34°03′S 137°36′E
Moor see Mór
180 I12 **Moora** Western Australia 30°23′S 116°05′E
98 H12 **Moordrecht** Zuid-Holland, C Netherlands 51°59′N 04°40′E
33 T9 **Moore** Montana, NW USA 47°00′N 109°40′W
27 N11 **Moore** Oklahoma, C USA 35°21′N 97°30′W
25 R12 **Moore** Texas, SW USA 29°03′N 99°01′W
191 S10 **Moorea** island Îles du Vent, W French Polynesia
21 U3 **Moorefield** West Virginia, NE USA 39°04′N 78°59′W
23 X14 **Moore Haven** Florida, SE USA 26°49′N 81°05′W
180 J11 **Moore, Lake** ◎ Western Australia
19 N7 **Moore Reservoir** ⊞ New Hampshire/Vermont, NE USA
44 G1 **Moores Island** island N Bahamas
21 R10 **Mooresville** North Carolina, SE USA 35°34′N 80°48′W
29 R5 **Moorhead** Minnesota, N USA 46°51′N 96°44′W
22 K4 **Moorhead** Mississippi, S USA 33°27′N 90°30′W
99 F18 **Moorsel** Oost-Vlaanderen, C Belgium 50°58′N 04°06′E
99 C18 **Moorslede** West-Vlaanderen, W Belgium 50°53′N 03°03′E
18 L8 **Moosalamoo, Mount** ▲ Vermont, NE USA 43°55′N 73°03′W
101 M22 **Moosburg in der Isar** Bayern, SE Germany 48°28′N 11°55′E
33 S14 **Moose** Wyoming, C USA 43°38′N 110°42′W
12 H11 **Moose** ≋ Ontario, S Canada
12 H10 **Moose Factory** Ontario, S Canada 51°16′N 80°32′W
19 Q4 **Moosehead Lake** ◎ Maine, NE USA
11 U16 **Moose Jaw** Saskatchewan, S Canada 50°23′N 105°35′W
11 V14 **Moose Lake** Manitoba, C Canada 53°42′N 100°22′W
29 W6 **Moose Lake** Minnesota, N USA 46°28′N 92°46′W
19 P6 **Mooselookmeguntic Lake** ◎ Maine, NE USA
39 R12 **Moose Pass** Alaska, USA 60°28′N 149°21′W
19 P5 **Moose River** ≋ Maine, NE USA
18 J9 **Moose River** ≋ New York, NE USA
11 V16 **Moosomin** Saskatchewan, S Canada 50°09′N 101°41′W
12 H10 **Moosonee** Ontario, SE Canada 51°18′N 80°40′W
19 N12 **Moosup** Connecticut, NE USA 41°42′N 71°51′W
83 N16 **Mopeia** Zambézia, NE Mozambique 17°59′S 35°43′E
83 H18 **Mopipi** Central, C Botswana 21°07′S 24°55′E
Moppo see Mokpo
77 N11 **Mopti** Mopti, C Mali 14°30′N 04°15′W
77 O11 **Mopti** ◈ region S Mali
57 H18 **Moquegua** Moquegua, SE Peru 17°07′S 70°55′W

◆ Country ● Country Capital ◇ Dependent Territory ○ Dependent Territory Capital ◈ Administrative Regions ✈ International Airport ▲ Mountain ⛰ Mountain Range ✱ Volcano ≋ River ◎ Lake ⊞ Reservoir

57 H18 **Moquegua** *off.* Departamento de Moquegua. ◐ *department* S Peru
Moquegua, Departamento de *see* Moquegua
111 I23 **Mór** *Ger.* Moor. Fejér, C Hungary 47°21′N 18°12′E
78 G11 **Mora** Extrême-Nord, N Cameroon 11°02′N 14°07′E
104 G11 **Mora** Évora, S Portugal 38°56′N 08°10′W
105 N9 **Mora** Castilla-La Mancha, C Spain 39°40′N 03°46′W
94 L12 **Mora** Dalarna, C Sweden 61°N 14°30′E
29 V7 **Mora** Minnesota, N USA 45°52′N 93°18′W
37 T10 **Mora** New Mexico, SW USA 35°56′N 105°16′W
113 J17 **Morača** ≈ S Montenegro
152 K10 **Morādābād** Uttar Pradesh, N India 28°50′N 78°45′E
105 U6 **Móra d'Ebre** *var.* Mora de Ebro. Cataluña, NE Spain 41°05′N 00°38′E
Mora de Ebro *see* Móra d'Ebre
105 S8 **Mora de Rubielos** Aragón, NE Spain 40°15′N 00°45′W
172 H4 **Morafenobe** Mahajanga, W Madagascar 17°49′S 44°54′E
110 K8 **Morąg** *Ger.* Mohrungen. Warmińsko-Mazurskie, N Poland 53°55′N 19°56′E
111 L25 **Mórahalom** Csongrád, S Hungary 46°14′N 19°52′E
105 N11 **Moral de Calatrava** Castilla-La Mancha, C Spain 38°50′N 03°34′W
63 G19 **Moraleda, Canal** *strait* SE Pacific Ocean
54 J3 **Morales** Bolívar, N Colombia 08°17′N 73°52′W
54 D12 **Morales** Cauca, SW Colombia 02°46′N 76°44′W
42 F5 **Morales** Izabal, E Guatemala 15°28′N 88°46′W
172 J5 **Moramanga** Toamasina, E Madagascar 18°57′S 48°13′E
27 Q6 **Moran** Kansas, C USA 37°55′N 95°10′W
25 Q7 **Moran** Texas, SW USA 32°33′N 99°10′W
181 X7 **Moranbah** Queensland, NE Australia 22°01′S 148°08′E
44 L13 **Morant Bay** E Jamaica 17°53′N 76°25′W
96 G10 **Morar, Loch** ◎ N Scotland, United Kingdom
Morata *see* Goodenough Island
105 Q12 **Moratalla** Murcia, SE Spain 38°11′N 01°53′W
108 C8 **Morat, Lac de** *Ger.* Murtensee. ◎ W Switzerland
84 I11 **Morava** *var.* March. ≈ C Europe *see also* March
Morava *see* March
Morava *see* Moravia, Czech Republic
Morava *see* Velika Morava, Serbia
29 W15 **Moravia** Iowa, C USA 40°53′N 92°49′W
111 F18 **Moravia** *Cz.* Morava, *Ger.* Mähren. *cultural region* E Czech Republic
111 H17 **Moravice** *Ger.* Mohra. ≈ NE Czech Republic
116 E12 **Moravița** Timiș, SW Romania 45°15′N 21°17′E
111 G17 **Moravská Třebová** *Ger.* Mährisch-Trübau. Pardubický Kraj, C Czech Republic 49°47′N 16°40′E
111 E19 **Moravské Budějovice** *Ger.* Mährisch-Budwitz. Vysočina, C Czech Republic 49°03′N 15°48′E
111 H17 **Moravskoslezský Kraj** *prev.* Ostravský Kraj. ◐ *region* E Czech Republic
111 F19 **Moravský Krumlov** *Ger.* Mährisch-Kromau. Jihomoravský Kraj, SE Czech Republic 48°58′N 16°30′E
96 J8 **Moray** *cultural region* N Scotland, United Kingdom
96 J8 **Moray Firth** *inlet* N Scotland, United Kingdom
42 B10 **Morazán** ◐ *department* NE El Salvador
154 C10 **Morbi** Gujarāt, W India 22°51′N 70°49′E
102 G7 **Morbihan** ◐ *department* NW France
Mörbisch *see* Mörbisch am See
109 Y5 **Mörbisch am See** *var.* Mörbisch. Burgenland, E Austria 47°43′N 16°40′E
95 N21 **Mörbylånga** Kalmar, S Sweden 56°31′N 16°25′E
102 J14 **Morcenx** Landes, SW France 44°04′N 00°55′W
Morcheh Khort *see* Mūrcheh Khvort
163 T5 **Mordaga** Nei Mongol Zizhiqu, N China 51°15′N 120°47′E
11 X17 **Morden** Manitoba, S Canada 49°12′N 98°05′W
Mordovia *see* Mordoviya, Respublika
127 N5 **Mordoviya, Respublika** *prev.* Mordovskaya ASSR, *Eng.* Mordovia, Mordvinia. ◐ *autonomous republic* W Russian Federation
126 M7 **Mordovo** Tambovskaya Oblast', W Russian Federation 52°05′N 40°49′E
Mordovskaya ASSR/ Mordvinia *see* Mordoviya, Respublika
Morea *see* Pelopónnisos
28 K8 **Moreau River** ≈ South Dakota, N USA
97 K16 **Morecambe** NW England, United Kingdom 54°04′N 02°53′W
97 K16 **Morecambe Bay** *inlet* NW England, United Kingdom
183 S4 **Moree** New South Wales, SE Australia 29°29′S 149°53′E
21 N5 **Morehead** Kentucky, S USA 38°11′N 83°27′W
21 X11 **Morehead City** North Carolina, SE USA 34°43′N 76°43′W
27 Y8 **Morehouse** Missouri, C USA 36°51′N 89°41′W
108 E10 **Mörel** Valais, SW Switzerland 46°22′N 08°03′E
54 D13 **Morelia** Caquetá, S Colombia 01°30′N 75°43′W
41 N14 **Morelia** Michoacán, S Mexico 19°40′N 101°11′W
105 T7 **Morella** Valenciana, E Spain 40°37′N 00°06′W
40 I7 **Morelos** Chihuahua, N Mexico 26°37′N 107°37′W
41 O15 **Morelos** ◐ *state* S Mexico
154 H7 **Morena** Madhya Pradesh, C India 26°30′N 78°04′E
104 L12 **Morena, Sierra** ▲▲ S Spain
37 O14 **Morenci** Arizona, SW USA 33°05′N 109°21′W
31 R11 **Morenci** Michigan, N USA 41°43′N 84°13′W
116 J13 **Moreni** Dâmbovița, S Romania 44°59′N 25°39′E
94 D9 **Møre og Romsdal** ◐ *county* S Norway
10 I14 **Moresby Island** *island* Queen Charlotte Islands, British Columbia, SW Canada
183 W2 **Moreton Island** *island* Queensland, E Australia
103 O3 **Moreuil** Somme, N France 49°47′N 02°28′E
35 V7 **Morey Peak** ▲ Nevada, W USA 38°40′N 116°16′W
125 U4 **More-Yu** ≈ NW Russian Federation
103 T9 **Morez** Jura, E France 46°33′N 06°01′E
Morfou Bay/Mórfou, Kólpos *see* Güzelyurt Körfezi
182 J8 **Morgan** South Australia 34°02′S 139°39′E
23 S7 **Morgan** Georgia, SE USA 31°31′N 84°34′W
25 S8 **Morgan** Texas, SW USA 32°01′N 97°36′W
22 J10 **Morgan City** Louisiana, S USA 29°42′N 91°12′W
20 H6 **Morganfield** Kentucky, S USA 37°41′N 87°55′W
35 O10 **Morgan Hill** California, W USA 37°05′N 121°38′W
21 Q9 **Morganton** North Carolina, SE USA 35°44′N 81°43′W
20 J7 **Morgantown** Kentucky, S USA 37°12′N 86°42′W
21 S2 **Morgantown** West Virginia, NE USA 39°38′N 79°57′W
108 B10 **Morges** Vaud, SW Switzerland 46°31′N 06°30′E
Morghāb, Daryā-ye *see* Murgap
Morghāb, Daryā-ye *see* Murghāb, Daryā-ye
96 I9 **Mor, Glen** *var.* Glen Albyn, Great Glen. *valley* N Scotland, United Kingdom
103 T5 **Morhange** Moselle, NE France 48°56′N 06°37′E
158 M5 **Mori** *var.* Mori Kazak Zizhixian. Xinjiang Uygur Zizhiqu, NW China 43°48′N 90°21′E
165 R5 **Mori** Hokkaidō, NE Japan 42°04′N 140°36′E
35 Y6 **Moriah, Mount** ▲ Nevada, W USA 39°16′N 114°10′W
37 S11 **Moriarty** New Mexico, SW USA 34°59′N 106°03′W
54 J12 **Morichal** Guaviare, E Colombia 02°09′N 70°35′W
Mori Kazak Zizhixian *see* Mori
Morin Dawa Daurzu Zizhiqi *see* Nirji
11 Q14 **Morinville** Alberta, SW Canada 53°48′N 113°38′W
165 R8 **Morioka** Iwate, Honshū, C Japan 39°42′N 141°08′E
183 T8 **Morisset** New South Wales, SE Australia 33°07′S 151°32′E
165 Q8 **Moriyoshi-zan** ▲ Honshū, C Japan 39°58′N 140°32′E
92 K13 **Morjärv** Norrbotten, N Sweden 66°03′N 22°45′E
127 R3 **Morki** Respublika Mariy El, W Russian Federation 56°27′N 49°01′E
123 N10 **Morkoka** ≈ NE Russian Federation
102 F5 **Morlaix** Finistère, NW France 48°35′N 03°50′W
95 M20 **Mörlunda** Kalmar, S Sweden 57°19′N 15°52′E
107 N19 **Mormanno** Calabria, SW Italy 39°54′N 15°58′E
36 L11 **Mormon Lake** ◎ Arizona, SW USA
35 Y10 **Mormon Peak** ▲ Nevada, W USA 36°59′N 114°25′W
Mormon State *see* Utah
45 Y5 **Morne-à-l'Eau** Grande Terre, N Guadeloupe 16°20′N 61°31′W
29 Y15 **Morning Sun** Iowa, C USA 41°06′N 91°15′W
193 S12 **Mornington Abyssal Plain** *undersea feature* SE Pacific Ocean 50°00′S 90°00′W
63 F22 **Mornington, Isla** *island* S Chile
181 T4 **Mornington Island** *island* Wellesley Islands, Queensland, N Australia
115 E18 **Mórnos** ≈ C Greece
149 P14 **Moro** Sind, SE Pakistan 26°36′N 67°59′E
32 I11 **Moro** Oregon, NW USA 45°30′N 120°46′W
186 E8 **Morobe** Morobe, C Papua New Guinea 07°46′S 147°35′E
186 E8 **Morobe** ◐ *province* C Papua New Guinea
31 N12 **Morocco** Indiana, N USA 40°57′N 87°27′W
74 E8 **Morocco** *off.* Kingdom of Morocco, *Ar.* Al Mamlakah. ◆ *monarchy* N Africa
Morocco *see* Marrakech
Morocco, Kingdom of *see* Morocco
81 I22 **Morogoro** Morogoro, E Tanzania 06°49′S 37°40′E
81 H24 **Morogoro** ◐ *region* SE Tanzania
171 Q7 **Moro Gulf** *gulf* S Philippines
41 N13 **Moroleón** Guanajuato, C Mexico 20°00′N 101°13′W
172 H6 **Morombe** Toliara, W Madagascar 21°47′S 43°21′E
44 G5 **Morón** Ciego de Ávila, C Cuba 22°08′N 78°39′W
163 N8 **Mörön** Hentiy, C Mongolia 47°21′N 110°21′E
162 I6 **Mörön** Hövsgöl, N Mongolia 49°39′N 100°08′E
54 K5 **Morón** Carabobo, N Venezuela 10°29′N 68°11′W
Morón *see* Morón de la Frontera
56 D8 **Morona, Río** ≈ N Peru
56 C8 **Morona Santiago** ◐ *province* E Ecuador
172 H5 **Morondava** Toliara, W Madagascar 20°19′S 44°17′E
104 K14 **Morón de la Frontera** *var.* Morón. Andalucía, S Spain 37°07′N 05°27′W
172 G13 **Moroni** ● (Comoros) Grande Comore, NW Comoros 11°41′S 43°16′E
171 S10 **Morotai, Pulau** *island* Maluku, E Indonesia
Morotiri *see* Marotiri
81 H17 **Moroto** NE Uganda 02°32′N 34°41′E
Morozov *see* Bratan
126 M11 **Morozovsk** Rostovskaya Oblast', SW Russian Federation 48°21′N 41°54′E
97 L14 **Morpeth** N England, United Kingdom 55°10′N 01°41′W
Morphou *see* Güzelyurt
Morphou Bay *see* Güzelyurt Körfezi
28 I13 **Morrill** Nebraska, C USA 41°57′N 103°55′W
27 U11 **Morrilton** Arkansas, C USA 35°09′N 92°45′W
11 Q16 **Morrin** Alberta, SW Canada 51°40′N 112°45′W
184 M7 **Morrinsville** Waikato, North Island, New Zealand 37°41′S 175°32′E
11 X16 **Morris** Manitoba, S Canada 49°22′N 94°21′W
30 M11 **Morris** Illinois, N USA 41°21′N 88°25′W
29 S8 **Morris** Minnesota, N USA 45°32′N 95°53′W
14 M13 **Morrisburg** Ontario, SE Canada 44°55′N 75°07′W
197 R11 **Morris Jesup, Kap** *headland* N Greenland 83°33′N 32°40′W
182 B1 **Morris, Mount** ▲ South Australia 26°04′S 131°03′E
30 K10 **Morrison** Illinois, N USA 41°48′N 89°58′W
36 K13 **Morristown** Arizona, SW USA 33°48′N 112°34′W
18 J14 **Morristown** New Jersey, NE USA 40°48′N 74°29′W
21 O8 **Morristown** Tennessee, S USA 36°13′N 83°18′W
42 L11 **Morrito** Río San Juan, SW Nicaragua 11°37′N 85°05′W
35 P13 **Morro Bay** California, W USA 35°21′N 120°51′W
95 L22 **Mörrum** Blekinge, S Sweden 56°11′N 14°45′E
83 N16 **Morrumbala** Zambézia, NE Mozambique 17°17′S 35°35′E
83 N20 **Morrumbene** Inhambane, SE Mozambique 23°41′S 35°25′E
95 F21 **Mors** *island* NW Denmark
Mörs *see* Moers
25 N1 **Morse** Texas, SW USA 36°03′N 101°28′W
127 N6 **Morshansk** Tambovskaya Oblast', W Russian Federation 53°27′N 41°46′E
102 L5 **Mortagne-au-Perche** Orne, N France 48°32′N 00°31′E
102 J8 **Mortagne-sur-Sèvre** Vendée, NW France 47°00′N 00°57′W
104 G8 **Mortágua** Viseu, N Portugal 40°24′N 08°14′W
102 J5 **Mortain** Manche, N France 48°39′N 00°51′W
106 C8 **Mortara** Lombardia, N Italy 45°15′N 08°44′E
59 J17 **Mortes, Rio das** ≈ C Brazil
182 M12 **Mortlake** Victoria, SE Australia 38°06′S 142°48′E
Mortlock Group *see* Takuu Islands
189 Q17 **Mortlock Islands** *prev.* Nomoi Islands. *island group* C Micronesia
29 T9 **Morton** Minnesota, N USA 44°33′N 94°58′W
22 L5 **Morton** Mississippi, S USA 32°21′N 89°39′W
24 M5 **Morton** Texas, SW USA 33°40′N 102°45′W
32 H9 **Morton** Washington, NW USA 46°33′N 122°16′W
0 D7 **Morton Seamount** *undersea feature* NE Pacific Ocean 50°15′N 142°45′W
45 U15 **Moruga** Trinidad, Trinidad and Tobago 10°04′N 61°16′W
183 P9 **Morundah** New South Wales, SE Australia 34°57′S 146°18′E
191 X12 **Moruroa** *var.* Mururoa. *atoll* Îles Tuamotu, SE French Polynesia
183 S11 **Moruya** New South Wales, SE Australia 35°55′S 150°04′E
103 Q8 **Morvan** *physical region* C France
185 G21 **Morven** Canterbury, South Island, New Zealand 44°51′S 171°07′E
183 O13 **Morwell** Victoria, SE Australia 38°14′S 146°25′E
125 N6 **Morzhovets, Ostrov** *island* NW Russian Federation
126 J4 **Mosal'sk** Kaluzhskaya Oblast', W Russian Federation 54°30′N 34°55′E
101 H20 **Mosbach** Baden-Württemberg, SW Germany 49°21′N 09°06′E
95 E18 **Mosby** Vest-Agder, S Norway 58°12′N 07°55′E
33 V9 **Mosby** Montana, NW USA 46°58′N 107°53′W
32 M9 **Moscow** Idaho, NW USA 46°43′N 117°00′W
20 F10 **Moscow** Tennessee, S USA 35°04′N 89°27′W
Moscow *see* Moskva
101 D19 **Mosel** *Fr.* Moselle. ≈ W Europe *see also* Moselle
Mosel *see* Moselle
103 T4 **Moselle** ◐ *department* NE France
103 T6 **Moselle** *Ger.* Mosel. ≈ W Europe *see also* Mosel
Moselle *see* Mosel
32 K9 **Moses Lake** ◎ Washington, NW USA
83 I18 **Mosetse** Central, E Botswana 20°40′S 26°38′E
92 H4 **Mosfellsbær** Hofudborgarsvædid, SW Iceland 65°09′N 21°43′W
183 N8 **Mossgiel** New South Wales, SE Australia 33°16′S 144°34′E
185 F23 **Mosgiel** Otago, South Island, New Zealand 45°51′S 170°22′E
124 M11 **Mosha** ≈ NW Russian Federation
81 I20 **Moshi** Kilimanjaro, NE Tanzania 03°21′S 37°19′E
110 G12 **Mosina** Wielkolpolskie, C Poland 52°15′N 16°50′E
30 L6 **Mosinee** Wisconsin, N USA 44°45′N 89°39′W
92 F13 **Mosjøen** Nordland, C Norway 65°49′N 13°12′E
123 S12 **Moskal'vo** Ostrov Sakhalin, Sakhalinskaya Oblast', SE Russian Federation 53°36′N 142°31′E
92 I13 **Moskosel** Norrbotten, N Sweden 65°52′N 19°30′E
126 K4 **Moskovskaya Oblast'** ◐ *province* W Russian Federation
Moskovskiy *see* Moskva
126 J3 **Moskva** *Eng.* Moscow. ● (Russian Federation) Gorod Moskva, W Russian Federation 55°45′N 37°42′E
147 Q14 **Moskva** *Rus.* Moskovskiy; *prev.* Chubek. SW Tajikistan 37°41′N 69°33′E
126 L4 **Moskva** ≈ W Russian Federation
83 I20 **Mosomane** Kgatleng, SE Botswana 24°04′S 26°15′E
Moson and Magyaróvár *see* Mosonmagyaróvár
111 H21 **Mosoni-Duna** *Ger.* Kleine Donau. ≈ NW Hungary
111 H21 **Mosonmagyaróvár** *Ger.* Wieselburg-Ungarisch-Altenburg; *prev.* Moson and Magyaróvár, *Ger.* Wieselburg and Ungarisch-Altenburg. Győr-Moson-Sopron, NW Hungary 47°52′N 17°15′E
Mospino *see* Mospyne
117 X8 **Mospyne** *Rus.* Mospino. Donets'ka Oblast', E Ukraine 47°53′N 38°03′E
54 B12 **Mosquera** Nariño, SW Colombia 02°32′N 78°24′W
37 U10 **Mosquero** New Mexico, SW USA 35°46′N 103°57′W
Mosquito Coast *see* La Mosquitia
31 U11 **Mosquito Creek Lake** ▣ Ohio, N USA
Mosquito Gulf *see* Mosquitos, Golfo de los
23 X11 **Mosquito Lagoon** *wetland* Florida, SE USA
43 N10 **Mosquito, Punta** *headland* E Nicaragua 12°18′N 83°38′W
43 W14 **Mosquito, Punta** *headland* NE Panama 09°06′N 77°52′W
43 Q15 **Mosquitos, Golfo de los** *Eng.* Mosquito Gulf. *gulf* N Panama
95 H16 **Moss** Østfold, S Norway 59°25′N 10°40′E
Mossâmedes *see* Namibe
22 G8 **Moss Bluff** Louisiana, S USA 30°18′N 93°11′W
185 C23 **Mossburn** Southland, South Island, New Zealand 45°40′S 168°15′E
83 G26 **Mosselbaai** *var.* Mosselbai, *Eng.* Mossel Bay. Western Cape, SW South Africa 34°11′S 22°08′E
Mosselbai/Mossel Bay *see* Mosselbaai
79 F20 **Mossendjo** Niari, SW Congo 02°57′S 12°40′E
101 H22 **Mössingen** Baden-Württemberg, S Germany 48°22′N 09°01′E
181 W4 **Mossman** Queensland, NE Australia 16°34′S 145°27′E
59 P14 **Mossoró** Rio Grande do Norte, NE Brazil 05°11′S 37°20′W
23 N9 **Moss Point** Mississippi, S USA 30°24′N 88°31′W
183 S9 **Moss Vale** New South Wales, SE Australia 34°33′S 150°20′E
32 G9 **Mossyrock** Washington, NW USA 46°32′N 122°30′W
111 B15 **Most** *Ger.* Brüx. Ústecký Kraj, NW Czech Republic 50°30′N 13°37′E
162 E7 **Möst** *var.* Ulaantolgoy. Hovd, W Mongolia 46°39′N 92°50′E
121 P16 **Mosta** *var.* Musta. C Malta 35°54′N 14°25′E
74 I5 **Mostaganem** *var.* Mestghanem. NW Algeria 35°54′N 00°05′E
113 H14 **Mostar** Federacija Bosna I Hercegovina, S Bosnia and Herzegovina 43°21′N 17°47′E
61 J17 **Mostardas** Rio Grande do Sul, S Brazil 31°02′S 50°51′W
116 K14 **Mostiștea** ≈ S Romania
Mostva *see* Mastva
Mosty *see* Masty
116 H5 **Mostys'ka** L'vivs'ka Oblast', W Ukraine 49°47′N 23°09′E
Mosul *see* Al Mawșil
95 F15 **Møsvatnet** ◎ S Norway
80 J12 **Mot'a** Āmara, N Ethiopia 11°03′N 38°03′E
79 H16 **Motaba** ≈ N Congo
105 O10 **Mota del Cuervo** Castilla-La Mancha, C Spain 39°30′N 02°52′W
104 L5 **Mota del Marqués** Castilla y León, N Spain 41°38′N 05°11′W
42 F5 **Motagua, Río** ≈ Guatemala/Honduras
119 H19 **Motal'** Brestskaya Voblasts', SW Belarus 52°13′N 25°34′E
95 L17 **Motala** Östergötland, S Sweden 58°34′N 15°05′E
191 X7 **Motane** *island* Îles Marquises, NE French Polynesia
152 K13 **Moth** Uttar Pradesh, N India 25°44′N 78°56′E
Mother of Presidents/ Mother of States *see* Virginia
96 I12 **Motherwell** C Scotland, United Kingdom 55°48′N 04°W
153 P12 **Motīhāri** Bihār, N India 26°40′N 84°55′E
105 Q10 **Motilla del Palancar** Castilla-La Mancha, C Spain 39°34′N 01°55′W
184 N7 **Motiti Island** *island* NE New Zealand
65 E25 **Motley Island** *island* SE Falkland Islands
83 J19 **Motloutse** ≈ E Botswana
41 V17 **Motozintla de Mendoza** Chiapas, SE Mexico 15°21′N 92°14′W
105 N15 **Motril** Andalucía, S Spain 36°45′N 03°30′W
116 G13 **Motru** Gorj, SW Romania 44°49′N 22°56′E
165 Q4 **Motsuta-misaki** *headland* Hokkaidō, NE Japan 42°36′N 139°48′E
28 L6 **Mott** North Dakota, N USA 46°21′N 102°17′W
166 M9 **Mottama** *var.* Martaban, Moktama. Mon State, S Burma (Myanmar) 16°32′N 97°35′E
166 L9 **Mottama, Gulf of** *var.* Gulf of Martaban. *gulf* S Burma (Myanmar)
Möttling *see* Metlika
107 O18 **Mottola** Puglia, SE Italy 40°38′N 17°02′E
184 P8 **Motu** ≈ North Island, New Zealand
185 I14 **Motueka** Tasman, South Island, New Zealand 41°08′S 173°00′E
185 I14 **Motueka** ≈ South Island, New Zealand
Motu Iti *see* Tupai
41 X12 **Motul** *var.* Motul de Felipe Carrillo Puerto. Yucatán, SE Mexico 21°06′N 89°17′W
Motul de Felipe Carrillo Puerto *see* Motul
191 U17 **Motu Nui** *island* Easter Island, Chile, E Pacific Ocean
191 Q10 **Motu One** *var.* Bellingshausen. *atoll* Îles Sous le Vent, W French Polynesia
190 I16 **Motutapu** *island* E Cook Islands
193 V15 **Motu Tapu** *island* Tongatapu Group, S Tonga
184 L5 **Motutapu Island** *island* N New Zealand
Motyca *see* Modica
Mouanda *see* Moanda
Mouaskar *see* Mascara
105 U3 **Moubermé, Tuc de** *Fr.* Pic de Maubermé, *Sp.* Pico Mauberme; *prev.* Tuc de Maubermé. ▲ France/ Spain 42°48′N 00°57′E *see also* Maubermé, Pic de
Moubermé, Tuc de *see* Maubermé, Pic de
45 N7 **Mouchoir Passage** *passage* SE Turks and Caicos Islands
76 I9 **Moudjéria** Tagant, SW Mauritania 17°52′N 12°20′W
108 C9 **Moudon** Vaud, W Switzerland 46°41′N 06°49′E
Mouhoun *see* Black Volta
79 E19 **Mouila** Ngounié, C Gabon 01°50′S 11°02′E
79 K14 **Mouka** Haute-Kotto, C Central African Republic 07°12′N 21°52′E
Moukden *see* Shenyang
183 N10 **Moulamein** New South Wales, SE Australia 35°06′S 144°03′E
Moulamein Creek *see* Billabong Creek
74 F6 **Moulay-Bousselham** NW Morocco 35°00′N 06°22′W
Moule *see* le Moule
80 M11 **Moulhoulé** N Djibouti 12°34′N 43°06′E
103 P9 **Moulins** Allier, C France 46°34′N 03°20′E
Moulmein *see* Mawlamyine
Moulmeingyun *see* Mawlamyinegyunn
74 G6 **Moulouya** *var.* Mulucha, Muluya, Mulwiya. *seasonal river* NE Morocco
23 O2 **Moulton** Alabama, S USA 34°28′N 87°18′W
29 W16 **Moulton** Iowa, C USA 40°41′N 92°40′W
25 T11 **Moulton** Texas, SW USA 29°34′N 97°08′W
23 T7 **Moultrie** Georgia, SE USA 31°10′N 83°47′W
21 S14 **Moultrie, Lake** ▣ South Carolina, SE USA
22 K3 **Mound Bayou** Mississippi, S USA 33°52′N 90°43′W
30 L17 **Mound City** Illinois, N USA 37°06′N 89°09′W
27 R6 **Mound City** Kansas, C USA 38°07′N 94°49′W
27 Q2 **Mound City** Missouri, C USA 40°07′N 95°13′W
29 N7 **Mound City** South Dakota, N USA 45°44′N 100°03′W
78 H13 **Moundou** Logone-Occidental, SW Chad 08°35′N 16°01′E
27 P10 **Mounds** Oklahoma, C USA 35°52′N 96°03′W
21 R2 **Moundsville** West Virginia, NE USA 39°54′N 80°44′W
167 R11 **Moŭng** *prev.* Phumĭ Moŭng. Siĕmréab, NW Cambodia 13°45′N 103°35′E
167 Q12 **Moŭng Roessei** Bătdâmbâng, W Cambodia 12°47′N 103°28′E
Moun Hou *see* Black Volta
8 H8 **Mountain** ≈ Northwest Territories, NW Canada
37 S12 **Mountainair** New Mexico, SW USA 34°31′N 106°14′W
35 V1 **Mountain City** Nevada, W USA 41°48′N 115°58′W
21 Q8 **Mountain City** Tennessee, S USA 36°28′N 81°48′W
27 U7 **Mountain Grove** Missouri, C USA 37°07′N 92°15′W
27 U9 **Mountain Home** Arkansas, C USA 36°19′N 92°24′W
33 N15 **Mountain Home** Idaho, NW USA 43°07′N 115°42′W
25 Q11 **Mountain Home** Texas, SW USA 30°11′N 99°19′W
29 W4 **Mountain Iron** Minnesota, N USA 47°31′N 92°37′W
29 T10 **Mountain Lake** Minnesota, N USA 43°57′N 94°54′W
23 S3 **Mountain Park** Georgia, SE USA 34°04′N 84°24′W
35 W12 **Mountain Pass** *pass* California, W USA
27 T12 **Mountain Pine** Arkansas, C USA 34°34′N 93°10′W
39 Y14 **Mountain Point** Annette Island, Alaska, USA 55°17′N 131°31′W
Mountain State *see* Montana
Mountain State *see* West Virginia
27 V7 **Mountain View** Arkansas, C USA 35°52′N 92°07′W
38 H12 **Mountain View** Hawaii, USA, C Pacific Ocean 19°32′N 155°03′W
27 V10 **Mountain View** Missouri, C USA 37°00′N 91°42′W
38 M11 **Mountain Village** Alaska, USA 62°06′N 163°42′W
21 R8 **Mount Airy** North Carolina, SE USA 36°30′N 80°36′W
83 K24 **Mount Ayliff** *Xh.* Maxesibebi. Eastern Cape, SE South Africa 30°48′S 29°23′E
29 U16 **Mount Ayr** Iowa, C USA 40°42′N 94°14′W
182 J9 **Mount Barker** South Australia 35°06′S 138°52′E
180 J14 **Mount Barker** Western Australia 34°42′S 117°40′E
183 P11 **Mount Beauty** Victoria, SE Australia 36°47′S 147°12′E
14 E16 **Mount Brydges** Ontario, S Canada 42°54′N 81°29′W
31 N16 **Mount Carmel** Illinois, N USA 38°23′N 87°46′W
30 K10 **Mount Carroll** Illinois, N USA 42°05′N 89°59′W
31 S9 **Mount Clemens** Michigan, N USA 42°36′N 82°52′W
185 E19 **Mount Cook** Canterbury, South Island, New Zealand 43°47′S 170°06′E
83 L16 **Mount Darwin** Mashonaland Central, NE Zimbabwe 16°45′S 31°39′E
19 S7 **Mount Desert Island** *island* Maine, NE USA
23 W11 **Mount Dora** Florida, SE USA 28°48′N 81°38′W
182 G5 **Mount Eba** South Australia 30°11′S 135°40′E
25 W8 **Mount Enterprise** Texas, SW USA 31°53′N 94°40′W
182 J4 **Mount Fitton** South Australia 29°55′S 139°26′E
83 J24 **Mount Fletcher** Eastern Cape, SE South Africa 30°41′S 28°30′E
14 F15 **Mount Forest** Ontario, S Canada 43°58′N 80°44′W
182 K12 **Mount Gambier** South Australia 37°47′S 140°49′E
181 W5 **Mount Garnet** Queensland, NE Australia 17°41′S 145°07′E
21 P6 **Mount Gay** West Virginia, NE USA 37°49′N 82°00′W
31 S12 **Mount Gilead** Ohio, N USA 40°33′N 82°49′W
186 C7 **Mount Hagen** Western Highlands, C Papua New Guinea 05°54′S 144°13′E
18 J16 **Mount Holly** New Jersey, NE USA 39°59′N 74°46′W
21 R10 **Mount Holly** North Carolina, SE USA 35°18′N 81°01′W
27 T12 **Mount Ida** Arkansas, C USA 34°32′N 93°38′W
181 T6 **Mount Isa** Queensland, C Australia 20°48′S 139°32′E
21 U4 **Mount Jackson** Virginia, NE USA 38°45′N 78°38′W
18 D12 **Mount Jewett** Pennsylvania, NE USA 41°43′N 78°37′W
18 L13 **Mount Kisco** New York, NE USA 41°12′N 73°42′W
18 B15 **Mount Lebanon** Pennsylvania, NE USA 40°21′N 80°03′W
182 J8 **Mount Lofty Ranges** ▲▲ South Australia
180 J10 **Mount Magnet** Western Australia 28°09′S 117°52′E
184 N7 **Mount Maunganui** Bay of Plenty, North Island, New Zealand 37°39′S 176°11′E
97 E18 **Mountmellick** *Ir.* Móinteach Mílic. Laois, C Ireland 53°07′N 07°20′W
30 L10 **Mount Morris** Illinois, N USA 42°03′N 89°25′W
31 R9 **Mount Morris** Michigan, N USA 43°07′N 83°42′W
18 F10 **Mount Morris** New York, NE USA 42°43′N 77°51′W
18 B16 **Mount Morris** Pennsylvania, NE USA 39°43′N 80°06′W
30 K15 **Mount Olive** Illinois, N USA 39°04′N 89°43′W
21 V10 **Mount Olive** North Carolina, SE USA 35°12′N 78°03′W
21 N4 **Mount Olivet** Kentucky, S USA 38°32′N 84°01′W
29 Y15 **Mount Pleasant** Iowa, C USA 40°57′N 91°33′W
31 Q8 **Mount Pleasant** Michigan, N USA 43°36′N 84°46′W
18 C15 **Mount Pleasant** Pennsylvania, NE USA 40°07′N 79°33′W
21 T14 **Mount Pleasant** South Carolina, SE USA 32°47′N 79°51′W
20 I9 **Mount Pleasant** Tennessee, S USA 35°32′N 87°11′W
25 W6 **Mount Pleasant** Texas, SW USA 33°10′N 94°49′W
36 L4 **Mount Pleasant** Utah, W USA 39°33′N 111°27′W
63 N23 **Mount Pleasant** ✈ (Stanley) East Falkland, Falkland Islands
97 G25 **Mount's Bay** *inlet* SW England, United Kingdom
35 N2 **Mount Shasta** California, W USA 41°18′N 122°19′W
30 J13 **Mount Sterling** Illinois, N USA 39°59′N 90°44′W
21 N5 **Mount Sterling** Kentucky, S USA 38°03′N 83°56′W
18 E15 **Mount Union** Pennsylvania, NE USA 40°21′N 77°51′W
23 V6 **Mount Vernon** Georgia, SE USA 32°10′N 82°35′W
30 L16 **Mount Vernon** Illinois, N USA 38°19′N 88°54′W
20 M6 **Mount Vernon** Kentucky, S USA 37°20′N 84°20′W
27 S7 **Mount Vernon** Missouri, C USA 37°05′N 93°49′W
31 T13 **Mount Vernon** Ohio, N USA 40°23′N 82°29′W
32 K13 **Mount Vernon** Oregon, NW USA 44°22′N 119°07′W
25 W6 **Mount Vernon** Texas, SW USA 33°11′N 95°13′W
32 H7 **Mount Vernon** Washington, NW USA 48°25′N 122°19′W
20 L5 **Mount Washington** Kentucky, S USA 38°03′N 85°33′W
182 F8 **Mount Wedge** South Australia 33°29′S 135°08′E
30 L14 **Mount Zion** Illinois, N USA 39°46′N 88°52′W
181 Y9 **Moura** Queensland, NE Australia 24°34′S 149°57′E
58 F12 **Moura** Amazonas, NW Brazil 01°32′S 61°43′W
104 H12 **Moura** Beja, S Portugal 38°08′N 07°27′W
104 I12 **Mourão** Évora, S Portugal 38°22′N 07°20′W
76 L11 **Mourdiah** Koulikoro, W Mali 14°28′N 07°31′W
78 K7 **Mourdi, Dépression du** *desert lowland* Chad/Sudan
102 J16 **Mourenx** Pyrénées-Atlantiques, SW France 43°24′N 00°37′W
Mourgana *see* Mourgkána
115 C15 **Mourgkána** *var.* Mourgana. ▲ Albania/Greece 39°48′N 20°24′E
97 G16 **Mourne Mountains** *Ir.* Beanna Boirche. ▲▲ SE Northern Ireland, United Kingdom
115 I15 **Moúrtzeflos, Akrotírio** *headland* Límnos, E Greece 40°00′N 25°02′E
99 C19 **Mouscron** *Dut.* Moeskroen. Hainaut, W Belgium 50°44′N 03°14′E
Mouse River *see* Souris River
78 H10 **Moussoro** Kanem, W Chad 13°41′N 16°31′E
103 T11 **Moûtiers** Savoie, E France 45°28′N 06°31′E
172 J14 **Moutsamudou** *var.* Moutsamudou. Anjouan, SE Comoros 12°10′S 44°25′E
Moutsamudou *see* Moutsamudou
74 K11 **Mouydir, Monts de** ▲▲ S Algeria
79 F20 **Mouyondzi** Bouenza, S Congo 03°58′S 13°57′E
115 E16 **Mouzáki** *prev.* Mouzákion. Thessalía, C Greece 39°25′N 21°40′E
Mouzákion *see* Mouzáki
29 S13 **Moville** Iowa, C USA 42°30′N 96°04′W
82 E13 **Moxico** ◐ *province* E Angola
172 I14 **Moya** Anjouan, SE Comoros 12°18′S 44°27′E
40 L12 **Moyahua** Zacatecas, C Mexico 21°18′N 103°09′W
81 J16 **Moyalē** Oromīya, C Ethiopia 03°34′N 38°58′E
76 I15 **Moyamba** W Sierra Leone 08°04′N 12°30′W
74 G7 **Moyen Atlas** *Eng.* Middle Atlas. ▲▲ N Morocco
78 H13 **Moyen-Chari** *off.* Préfecture du Moyen-Chari. ◐ *prefecture* S Chad
Moyen-Chari, Préfecture du *see* Moyen-Chari
Moyen-Congo *see* Congo (Republic of)
83 J24 **Moyeni** *var.* Quthing. SW Lesotho 30°25′S 27°43′E
79 D18 **Moyen-Ogooué** *off.* Province du Moyen-Ogooué, *var.* Le Moyen-Ogooué. ◐ *province* C Gabon
Moyen-Ogooué, Province du *see* Moyen-Ogooué
103 S4 **Moyeuvre-Grande** Moselle, NE France 49°15′N 06°03′E
33 N7 **Moyie Springs** Idaho, NW USA 48°43′N 116°15′W
146 G6 **Mo'ynoq** *Rus.* Muynak. Qoraqalpog'iston Respublikasi, NW Uzbekistan 43°45′N 59°03′E
81 F16 **Moyo** NW Uganda 03°38′N 31°43′E
56 D10 **Moyobamba** San Martín, NW Peru 06°04′S 76°56′W
78 H10 **Moyto** Chari-Baguirmi, W Chad 12°35′N 16°33′E
158 G9 **Moyu** *var.* Karakax. Xinjiang Uygur Zizhiqu, NW China 37°16′N 79°39′E
122 M9 **Moyyero** ≈ N Russian Federation
145 S15 **Moyynkum** *var.* Furmanovka, *Kaz.* Fūrmanov. Zhambyl, S Kazakhstan 44°15′N 72°55′E
145 Q15 **Moyynkum, Peski** *Kaz.* Moyynqum. *desert* S Kazakhstan
Moyynqum *see* Moyynkum, Peski
145 S12 **Moyynty** Karaganda, C Kazakhstan 47°10′N 73°24′E
145 S12 **Moyynty** ≈ Karaganda, C Kazakhstan
Mozambika, Lakandranon' i *see* Mozambique Channel
83 M18 **Mozambique** *off.* Republic of Mozambique; *prev.* People's Republic of Mozambique, Portuguese East Africa. ◆ *republic* S Africa
Mozambique Basin *see* Natal Basin
Mozambique, Canal de *see* Mozambique Channel
83 P17 **Mozambique Channel** *Fr.* Canal de Mozambique, *Mal.* Lakandranon' i Mozambika. *strait* W Indian Ocean
172 L11 **Mozambique Escarpment** *var.* Mozambique Scarp. *undersea feature* SW Indian Ocean 33°00′S 36°30′E
Mozambique, People's Republic of *see* Mozambique
172 L10 **Mozambique Plateau** *var.* Mozambique Rise. *undersea feature* SW Indian Ocean 32°00′S 35°00′E
Mozambique, Republic of *see* Mozambique
Mozambique Rise *see* Mozambique Plateau
Mozambique Scarp *see* Mozambique Escarpment
127 O15 **Mozdok** Respublika Severnaya Osetiya, SW Russian Federation 43°48′N 44°42′E
57 K17 **Mozetenes, Serranías de** ▲▲ C Bolivia
126 J4 **Mozhaysk** Moskovskaya Oblast', W Russian Federation 55°31′N 36°01′E
127 T3 **Mozhga** Udmurtskaya Respublika, NW Russian Federation 56°24′N 52°13′E
Mozyr' *see* Mazyr
79 P22 **Mpala** Katanga, E Dem. Rep. Congo 06°43′S 29°28′E
79 G19 **Mpama** ≈ C Congo
81 E22 **Mpanda** Rukwa, W Tanzania 06°21′S 31°01′E
82 L11 **Mpande** Northern, NE Zambia 09°13′S 31°42′E
83 J18 **Mphoengs** Matabeleland South, SW Zimbabwe 21°04′S 27°56′E
81 F18 **Mpigi** S Uganda 0°14′N 32°19′E
82 L13 **Mpika** Northern, NE Zambia 11°50′S 31°30′E
83 J14 **Mpima** Central, C Zambia 14°25′S 28°34′E
82 J13 **Mpongwe** Copperbelt, C Zambia 13°25′S 28°13′E
82 K11 **Mporokoso** Northern, N Zambia 09°22′S 30°06′E
79 H20 **Mpouya** Plateaux, SE Congo 02°38′S 16°13′E
77 P16 **Mpraeso** C Ghana 06°36′N 00°43′W
82 L11 **Mpulungu** Northern, N Zambia 08°50′S 31°06′E
83 K21 **Mpumalanga** *prev.* Eastern Transvaal, *Afr.* Oos-Transvaal. ◐ *province* NE South Africa
83 D16 **Mpungu** Okavango, N Namibia 17°36′S 18°16′E
81 I22 **Mpwapwa** Dodoma, C Tanzania 06°21′S 36°29′E
Mqinvartsveri *see* Kazbek
110 M8 **Mrągowo** *Ger.* Sensburg. Warmińsko-Mazurskie, NE Poland 53°53′N 21°19′E
127 V6 **Mrakovo** Respublika Bashkortostan, W Russian Federation 52°43′N 56°36′E

◆ Country
● Country Capital
◇ Dependent Territory
○ Dependent Territory Capital
◐ Administrative Regions
✈ International Airport
▲ Mountain
▲▲ Mountain Range
※ Volcano
≈ River
◎ Lake
▣ Reservoir

172 I13 **Mramani** Anjouan, E Comoros 12°18′N 44°39′E
166 K5 **Mrauk-oo** *var.* Mrauk U, Myohaung. Rakhine State, W Burma (Myanmar) 20°35′N 93°12′E
Mrauk U *see* Mrauk-oo
112 F12 **Mrkonjić Grad** ◆ Republika Srpska, W Bosnia and Herzegovina
110 H9 **Mrocza** Kujawsko-pomorskie, C Poland 53°15′N 17°38′E
124 I14 **Msta** NW Russian Federation
Mstislavl' *see* Mstsislaw
119 P15 **Mstsislaw** *Rus.* Mstislavl'. Mahilyowskaya Voblasts', E Belarus 54°01′N 31°43′E
83 J24 **Mthatha** *prev.* Umtata. Eastern Cape, SE South Africa 31°33′S 28°47′E *see also* Umtata
Mtkvari *see* Kura
Mtoko *see* Mutoko
126 K6 **Mtsensk** Orlovskaya Oblast', W Russian Federation 53°17′N 36°34′E
81 K24 **Mtwara** Mtwara, SE Tanzania 10°17′S 40°11′E
81 J25 **Mtwara** ◆ *region* SE Tanzania
104 G14 **Mu** ▲ S Portugal 37°24′N 08°04′W
193 V15 **Mu'a** Tongatapu, S Tonga 21°11′S 175°07′W
Muai To *see* Mae Hong Son
83 P16 **Mualama** Zambézia, NE Mozambique 16°51′S 38°21′E
Mualo *see* Messalo, Rio
79 E22 **Muanda** Bas-Congo, SW Dem. Rep. Congo 05°53′S 12°17′E
Muang Chiang Rai *see* Chiang Rai
167 R6 **Muang Ham** Houaphan, N Laos 20°19′N 104°00′E
167 S8 **Muang Hinboun** Khammouan, C Laos 17°37′N 104°37′E
Muang Kalasin *see* Kalasin
Muang Khammouan *see* Thakhèk
167 S11 **Muang Không** Champasak, S Laos 14°08′N 105°48′E
167 S10 **Muang Khôngxédôn** *var.* Khong Sedone. Salavan, S Laos 15°34′N 105°46′E
Muang Khon Kaen *see* Khon Kaen
167 Q6 **Muang Khoua** Phôngsali, N Laos 21°07′N 102°31′E
Muang Krabi *see* Krabi
Muang Lampang *see* Lampang
Muang Lamphun *see* Lamphun
Muang Loei *see* Loei
Muang Lom Sak *see* Lom Sak
Muang Nakhon Sawan *see* Nakhon Sawan
167 Q6 **Muang Namo** Oudômxai, N Laos 20°58′N 101°46′E
Muang Nan *see* Nan
167 Q6 **Muang Ngoy** Louangphabang, N Laos 20°43′N 102°42′E
167 Q5 **Muang Ou Tai** Phôngsali, N Laos 22°06′N 101°59′E
Muang Pak Lay *see* Pak Lay
Muang Pakxan *see* Pakxan
167 T10 **Muang Pakxong** Champasak, S Laos 15°10′N 106°17′E
167 S9 **Muang Phalan** *var.* Muang Phalane. Savannakhét, S Laos 16°40′N 105°33′E
Muang Phalane *see* Muang Phalan
Muang Phan *see* Phan
Muang Phayao *see* Phayao
Muang Phichit *see* Phichit
167 T9 **Muang Phin** Savannakhét, S Laos 16°31′N 106°01′E
Muang Phitsanulok *see* Phitsanulok
Muang Phrae *see* Phrae
Muang Roi Et *see* Roi Et
Muang Sakon Nakhon *see* Sakon Nakhon
Muang Samut Prakan *see* Samut Prakan
167 P6 **Muang Sing** Louang Namtha, N Laos 21°12′N 101°09′E
Muang Ubon *see* Ubon Ratchathani
Muang Uthai Thani *see* Uthai Thani
167 P7 **Muang Vangviang** Viangchan, C Laos 18°53′N 102°27′E
Muang Xaignabouri *see* Xaignabouli
Muang Xay *see* Oudômxai
167 S9 **Muang Xépôn** *var.* Sepone. Savannakhét, S Laos 16°40′N 106°15′E
168 K10 **Muar** *var.* Bandar Maharani. Johor, Peninsular Malaysia 02°01′N 102°35′E
168 J9 **Muara** Sumatera, W Indonesia 02°18′N 98°54′E
168 L13 **Muarabeliti** Sumatera, W Indonesia 03°13′S 103°00′E
168 K12 **Muarabungo** Sumatera, W Indonesia 01°28′S 102°06′E
168 L13 **Muaraenim** Sumatera, W Indonesia 03°40′S 103°48′E
169 T11 **Muarajuloi** Borneo, C Indonesia 0°12′S 114°03′E
169 U12 **Muarakaman** Borneo, C Indonesia 0°09′S 116°43′E
168 H12 **Muarasigep** Pulau Siberut, W Indonesia 01°01′S 98°48′E
168 L12 **Muaratembesi** Sumatera, W Indonesia 01°40′S 103°08′E
169 T12 **Muaratewe** *var.* Muarateweh; *prev.* Moearatewe. Borneo, C Indonesia 0°58′S 114°52′E
Muarateweh *see* Muaratewe
169 U10 **Muarawahau** Borneo, N Indonesia 01°03′N 116°48′E
138 G13 **Mubārak, Jabal** ▲ S Jordan 29°19′N 35°13′E
153 N13 **Mubārakpur** Uttar Pradesh, N India 26°05′N 83°19′E
Mubarek *see* Muborak
81 F18 **Mubende** SW Uganda 0°35′N 31°24′E
77 Y14 **Mubi** Adamawa, NE Nigeria 10°15′N 13°18′E
146 M12 **Muborak** *Rus.* Mubarek. Qashqadaryo Viloyati, S Uzbekistan 39°17′N 65°10′E
171 U12 **Mubrani** Papua, E Indonesia 0°42′S 133°25′E
67 U12 **Muchinga Escarpment** *escarpment* NE Zambia
127 N7 **Muchkapskiy** Tambovskaya Oblast', W Russian Federation 51°51′N 42°25′E
96 G10 **Muck** *island* W Scotland, United Kingdom
82 Q13 **Mucojo** Cabo Delgado, N Mozambique 12°05′S 40°30′E
82 F12 **Muconda** Lunda Sul, NE Angola 10°37′S 21°19′E
54 I10 **Muco, Río** E Colombia
83 O16 **Mucubela** Zambézia, NE Mozambique 16°51′S 37°48′E
42 J5 **Mucupina, Monte** ▲ N Honduras 15°07′N 86°36′W
136 J14 **Mucur** Kirşehir, C Turkey 39°05′N 34°25′E
143 U8 **Mūd** Khorāsān-e Janūbī, E Iran 32°41′N 59°30′E
163 Y9 **Mudanjiang** *var.* Mu-tan-chiang. Heilongjiang, NE China 44°33′N 129°40′E
163 Y9 **Mudan Jiang** NE China
136 D11 **Mudanya** Bursa, NW Turkey 40°23′N 28°53′E
28 K8 **Mud Butte** South Dakota, N USA 45°00′N 102°51′W
155 G16 **Muddebihāl** Karnātaka, C India 16°26′N 76°07′E
27 P12 **Muddy Boggy Creek** Oklahoma, C USA
36 M6 **Muddy Creek** Utah, W USA
37 V7 **Muddy Creek Reservoir** ⊠ Colorado, C USA
33 W15 **Muddy Gap** Wyoming, C USA 42°21′N 107°27′W
35 Y11 **Muddy Peak** ▲ Nevada, W USA 36°17′N 114°40′W
183 R7 **Mudgee** New South Wales, SE Australia 32°37′S 149°36′E
29 S3 **Mud Lake** ◎ Minnesota, N USA
29 P7 **Mud Lake Reservoir** ⊠ South Dakota, N USA
167 N9 **Mudon** Mon State, S Burma (Myanmar) 16°17′N 97°40′E
81 O14 **Mudug** *off.* Gobolka Mudug. ◆ *region* NE Somalia
81 O14 **Mudug** *var.* Mudugh. *plain* N Somalia
Mudug, Gobolka *see* Mudug
Mudugh *see* Mudug
83 Q15 **Muecate** Nampula, NE Mozambique 14°56′S 39°38′E
82 Q13 **Mueda** Cabo Delgado, NE Mozambique 11°40′S 39°31′E
42 L10 **Muelle de los Bueyes** Región Autónoma Atlántico Sur, SE Nicaragua 12°03′N 84°34′W
Muenchen *see* München
83 M14 **Muende** Tete, NW Mozambique 14°22′S 33°00′E
25 T5 **Muenster** Texas, SW USA 33°39′N 97°22′W
Muenster *see* Münster
43 O6 **Muerto, Cayo** *reef* NE Nicaragua
41 T17 **Muerto, Mar** *lagoon* SE Mexico
64 F11 **Muertos Trough** *undersea feature* N Caribbean Sea
83 H14 **Mufaya Kuta** Western, NW Zambia 14°30′S 24°18′E
82 J13 **Mufulira** Copperbelt, C Zambia 12°33′S 28°16′E
161 O10 **Mufu Shan** ▲ C China
Mugalla *see* Yutian
Mugalzhar Taūlary *see* Mugodzhary, Gory
137 Y12 **Muğan Düzü** *Rus.* Muganskaya Ravnina, Muganskaya Step'. *physical region* S Azerbaijan
Muganskaya Ravnina/ Muganskaya Step' *see* Muğan Düzü
106 K8 **Múggia** Friuli-Venezia Giulia, NE Italy 45°36′N 13°48′E
153 N14 **Mughal Sarāi** Uttar Pradesh, N India 25°18′N 83°07′E
Mughla *see* Muğla
141 W11 **Mughshin** *var.* Muqshin. S Oman 19°26′N 54°38′E
147 S12 **Mughsu** *Rus.* Muksu. C Tajikistan
164 H14 **Mugi** Tokushima, Shikoku, SW Japan 33°39′N 134°24′E
136 C16 **Muğla** *var.* Mughla. Muğla, SW Turkey 37°13′N 28°22′E
136 C16 **Muğla** *var.* Mughla. ◆ *province* SW Turkey
114 K10 **Müglizh** Stara Zagora, C Bulgaria 42°36′N 25°32′E
144 J11 **Mugodzhary, Gory** *Kaz.* Mugalzhar Taūlary. ▲ W Kazakhstan
83 O15 **Mugulama** Zambézia, NE Mozambique 16°01′S 37°33′E
Muḩāfazat Hims *see* Ḩimş
Muḩāfazat Ma'dabā *see* Ma'dabā
139 U9 **Muḩammad** Wāsiţ, E Iraq 32°46′N 45°14′E
139 R8 **Muḩammadīyah** Al Anbār, C Iraq 33°22′N 42°48′E
80 I6 **Muhammad Qol** Red Sea, NE Sudan 20°53′N 37°09′E
75 Y9 **Muḩammad, Râs** *headland* E Egypt 27°45′N 34°18′E
Muhammerah *see* Khorramshahr
Muḩāfazat Al 'Aqabah *see* Al 'Aqabah
140 M12 **Muhāyil** *var.* Mahāil. 'Asīr, SW Saudi Arabia 18°34′N 42°01′E
139 O7 **Muḩaywir** Al Anbār, W Iraq 33°35′N 41°06′E
101 H21 **Mühlacker** Baden-Württemberg, SW Germany 48°57′N 08°51′E
Mühlbach *see* Sebeş
Mühldorf *see* Mühldorf am Inn
101 N23 **Mühldorf am Inn** *var.* Mühldorf. Bayern, SE Germany 48°14′N 12°32′E
101 J15 **Mühlhausen** *var.* Mühlhausen in Thüringen. Thüringen, C Germany 51°13′N 10°28′E
Mühlhausen in Thüringen *see* Mühlhausen
195 Q2 **Mühlig-Hofmannfjella** *Eng.* Mülig-Hofmann Mountains. ▲ Antarctica
93 L14 **Muhos** Oulu, C Finland 64°48′N 26°00′E
138 K6 **Muḩ, Sabkhat al** ◎ C Syria
118 E5 **Muhu** *Ger.* Mohn, Moon. *island* W Estonia
81 F19 **Muhutwe** Kagera, NW Tanzania 01°31′S 31°41′E
Muhu Väin *see* Väinameri
98 J10 **Muiden** Noord-Holland, C Netherlands 52°19′N 05°04′E
193 W15 **Mui Hopohoponga** *headland* Tongatapu, S Tonga 21°09′S 175°02′W
Muinchille *see* Cootehill
Muineachán *see* Monaghan
97 F19 **Muine Bheag** *Eng.* Bagenalstown. Carlow, SE Ireland 52°42′N 06°57′W
56 B5 **Muisne** Esmeraldas, NW Ecuador 0°35′N 79°58′W
83 P14 **Muite** Nampula, NE Mozambique 14°02′S 39°06′E
41 Z11 **Mujeres, Isla** *island* E Mexico
116 G7 **Mukacheve** *Hung.* Munkács, *Rus.* Mukachevo. Zakarpats'ka Oblast', W Ukraine 48°27′N 22°45′E
Mukachevo *see* Mukacheve
169 R9 **Mukah** Sarawak, East Malaysia 02°56′N 112°02′E
Mukalla *see* Al Mukallā
Mukama *see* Mokāma
Mukāshafa/Mukashshafah *see* Mukayshīfah
139 S6 **Mukayshīfah** *var.* Mukāshafa, Mukashshafah. Şalāḩ ad Dīn, N Iraq 34°24′N 43°44′E
167 R9 **Mukdahan** Mukdahan, E Thailand 16°31′N 104°43′E
Mukden *see* Shenyang
165 Y15 **Mukojima-rettō** *Eng.* Parry group. *island group* SE Japan
146 M14 **Mukry** Lebap Welaýaty, E Turkmenistan 37°39′N 65°37′E
Muksu *see* Mughsu
Muktagacha *see* Muktagachha
153 U14 **Muktagachha** *var.* Muktagacha. N Bangladesh 24°46′N 90°16′E
82 K13 **Mukuku** Central, C Zambia 12°10′S 29°50′E
82 K11 **Mukupa Kaoma** Northern, NE Zambia 09°55′S 30°19′E
81 I18 **Mukutan** Rift Valley, W Kenya 01°06′N 36°16′E
83 F16 **Mukwe** Caprivi, NE Namibia 18°01′S 21°24′E
105 R13 **Mula** Murcia, SE Spain 38°02′N 01°29′W
151 K20 **Mulakatholhu** *var.* Meemu Atoll, Mulaku Atoll. *atoll* C Maldives
Mulaku Atoll *see* Mulakatholhu
83 J15 **Mulalika** Lusaka, C Zambia 15°37′S 28°48′E
163 X8 **Mulan** Heilongjiang, NE China 45°57′N 128°00′E
83 N15 **Mulanje** *var.* Mlanje. Southern, S Malawi 16°05′S 35°29′E
40 H5 **Mulatos** Sonora, NW Mexico 28°42′N 108°44′W
23 P3 **Mulberry Fork** Alabama, S USA
39 P12 **Mulchatna River** Alaska, USA
125 W4 **Mul'da** Respublika Komi, NW Russian Federation 67°29′N 63°55′E
101 M14 **Mulde** E Germany
27 R10 **Muldrow** Oklahoma, C USA 35°25′N 94°34′W
40 E7 **Mulegé** Baja California Sur, NW Mexico 26°54′N 112°00′W
108 I10 **Mulegns** Graubünden, S Switzerland 46°30′N 09°36′E
79 M21 **Mulenda** Kasai-Oriental, C Dem. Rep. Congo 04°19′S 24°55′E
24 M4 **Muleshoe** Texas, SW USA 34°13′N 102°43′W
83 O15 **Mulevala** Zambézia, NE Mozambique 16°25′S 37°35′E
183 P5 **Mulgoa Creek** *seasonal river* New South Wales, SE Australia
105 O15 **Mulhacén** *var.* Cerro de Mulhacén. ▲ S Spain 37°07′N 03°11′W
Mulhacén, Cerro de *see* Mulhacén
Mülhausen *see* Mulhouse
101 E24 **Mülheim** Baden-Württemberg, SW Germany 47°50′N 07°37′E
101 E15 **Mülheim** *var.* Mulheim an der Ruhr. Nordrhein-Westfalen, W Germany 51°25′N 06°50′E
Mulheim an der Ruhr *see* Mülheim
103 U7 **Mulhouse** *Ger.* Mülhausen. Haut-Rhin, NE France 47°45′N 07°20′E
160 G11 **Muli** *var.* Qiaowa, Muli Zangzu Zizhixian. Sichuan, C China 27°49′N 101°10′E
171 X15 **Muli** *channel* Papua, E Indonesia
Mülig-Hofmann Mountains *see* Mühlig-Hofmannfjella
163 Y9 **Muling** Heilongjiang, NE China 44°54′N 130°35′E
Muli Zangzu Zizhixian *see* Muli
Mullach Íde *see* Malahide
Mullaitivu *see* Mullaittivu
155 K23 **Mullaittivu** *var.* Mullaitivu. Northern Province, N Sri Lanka 09°15′N 80°48′E
33 N8 **Mullan** Idaho, NW USA 47°28′N 115°48′W
28 M13 **Mullen** Nebraska, C USA 42°02′N 101°01′W
183 Q6 **Mullengudgery** New South Wales, SE Australia 31°42′S 147°24′E
21 Q6 **Mullens** West Virginia, NE USA 37°34′N 81°22′W
Müller-gerbergte *see* Muller, Pegunungan
169 T10 **Muller, Pegunungan** *Dut.* Müller-gerbergte. ▲ Borneo, C Indonesia
31 Q5 **Mullett Lake** ◎ Michigan, N USA
18 J16 **Mullica River** New Jersey, NE USA
25 R8 **Mullin** Texas, SW USA 31°33′N 98°40′W
97 E17 **Mullingar** *Ir.* An Muileann gCearr. C Ireland 53°32′N 07°20′W
21 T12 **Mullins** South Carolina, SE USA 34°12′N 79°15′W
96 G11 **Mull, Isle of** *island* W Scotland, United Kingdom
127 R5 **Mullovka** Ul'yanovskaya Oblast', W Russian Federation 54°13′N 49°19′E
95 K19 **Mullsjö** Västra Götaland, S Sweden 57°56′N 13°55′E
183 V4 **Mullumbimby** New South Wales, SE Australia 28°34′S 153°28′E
83 H15 **Mulobezi** Western, SW Zambia 16°48′S 25°11′E
83 C15 **Mulondo** Huíla, SW Angola 15°41′S 15°09′E
83 G15 **Mulonga Plain** *plain* W Zambia
79 N23 **Mulongo** Katanga, SE Dem. Rep. Congo 07°44′S 26°57′E
149 T10 **Multān** Punjab, E Pakistan 30°12′N 71°30′E
93 L17 **Multia** Länsi-Suomi, C Finland 62°27′N 24°49′E
Mulucha *see* Moulouya
83 J14 **Mulungushi** Central, C Zambia 14°15′S 28°27′E
83 K14 **Mulungwe** Central, C Zambia 13°57′S 29°51′E
Muluya *see* Moulouya
27 N7 **Mulvane** Kansas, C USA 37°28′N 97°14′W
183 O10 **Mulwala** New South Wales, SE Australia 35°59′S 146°00′E
Mulwiya *see* Moulouya
182 K6 **Mulyungarie** South Australia 31°29′S 140°45′E
154 D13 **Mumbai** *prev.* Bombay. *state capital* Mahārāshtra, W India 18°56′N 72°51′E
154 D13 **Mumbai** ✕ Mahārāshtra, W India 19°10′N 72°51′E
83 D14 **Mumbué** Bié, C Angola 13°52′S 17°15′E
186 E8 **Mumeng** Morobe, C Papua New Guinea 06°57′S 146°34′E
171 V12 **Mumi** Papua, E Indonesia 01°33′S 134°09′E
Muminabad/Mŭ'minobod *see* Mu'minobod
147 Q13 **Mu'minobod** *Rus.* Leningradskiy, Muminabad; *prev.* Leningrad. SW Tajikistan 38°03′N 69°50′E
127 Q13 **Mumra** Astrakhanskaya Oblast', SW Russian Federation 45°46′N 47°46′E
41 X12 **Muna** Yucatán, SE Mexico 20°29′N 89°41′W
123 O9 **Muna** NE Russian Federation
152 C12 **Munābāo** Rājasthān, NW India 25°46′N 70°19′E
Munamägi *see* Suur Munamägi
171 O14 **Muna, Pulau** *prev.* Moena. *island* C Indonesia
101 L18 **Münchberg** Bayern, E Germany 50°10′N 11°50′E
101 L23 **München** *var.* Muenchen, *Eng.* Munich, *It.* Monaco. Bayern, SE Germany 48°09′N 11°34′E
München-Gladbach *see* Mönchengladbach
108 E6 **Münchenstein** Basel Landschaft, NW Switzerland 47°31′N 07°38′E
10 L10 **Muncho Lake** British Columbia, W Canada 58°52′N 125°40′W
31 P13 **Muncie** Indiana, N USA 40°11′N 85°22′W
18 G13 **Muncy** Pennsylvania, NE USA 41°10′N 76°46′W
11 Q14 **Mundare** Alberta, SW Canada 53°34′N 112°20′W
25 Q5 **Munday** Texas, SW USA 33°27′N 99°37′W
31 N10 **Mundelein** Illinois, N USA 42°15′N 88°00′W
101 I15 **Münden** Niedersachsen, C Germany 52°16′N 08°54′E
105 Q12 **Mundo** S Spain
82 B12 **Munenga** Cuanza Sul, NW Angola 10°03′S 14°40′E
105 P11 **Munera** Castilla-La Mancha, C Spain 39°03′N 02°29′W
20 E9 **Munford** Tennessee, S USA 35°27′N 89°49′W
20 K7 **Munfordville** Kentucky, S USA 37°17′N 85°55′W
182 D5 **Mungala** South Australia 30°36′S 132°57′E
83 M16 **Mungári** Manica, C Mozambique 17°09′S 33°33′E
79 O16 **Mungbere** Orientale, NE Dem. Rep. Congo 02°38′N 28°30′E
153 Q13 **Munger** *prev.* Monghyr. Bihār, NE India 25°23′N 86°28′E
182 I2 **Mungeranie** South Australia 28°02′S 138°42′E
Mu Nggava *see* Rennell
169 O10 **Munggaresak, Tanjung** *headland* Borneo, N Indonesia 01°57′N 109°19′E
Mungiki *see* Bellona
183 R4 **Mungindi** New South Wales, SE Australia 28°59′S 149°00′E
Mungkawn *see* Maingkwan
Mungla *see* Mongla
82 C13 **Mungo** Huambo, W Angola 11°49′S 16°16′E
188 F16 **Munguuy Bay** *bay* Yap, W Micronesia
82 E13 **Munhango** Bié, C Angola 12°12′S 18°34′E
Munich *see* München
105 S7 **Muniesa** Aragón, NE Spain 41°02′N 00°49′W
31 O4 **Munising** Michigan, N USA 46°24′N 86°39′W
Munkács *see* Mukacheve
95 I17 **Munkedal** Västra Götaland, S Sweden 58°28′N 11°38′E
95 K15 **Munkfors** Värmland, C Sweden 59°50′N 13°35′E
122 M14 **Munku-Sardyk, Gora** *var.* Mönh Sarĭdag. ▲ Mongolia/ Russian Federation 51°45′N 100°22′E
99 E18 **Munkzwalm** Oost-Vlaanderen, NW Belgium 50°53′N 03°44′E
167 R10 **Mun, Mae Nam** E Thailand
153 U15 **Munshiganj** Dhaka, C Bangladesh 23°32′N 90°32′E
108 D8 **Münsingen** Bern, W Switzerland 46°53′N 07°34′E
103 U6 **Munster** Haut-Rhin, NE France 48°03′N 07°09′E
100 J11 **Munster** Niedersachsen, NW Germany 52°59′N 10°07′E
100 F13 **Münster** *var.* Muenster, Münster in Westfalen. Nordrhein-Westfalen, W Germany 51°58′N 07°38′E
108 F10 **Münster** Valais, S Switzerland 46°31′N 08°18′E
97 B20 **Munster** *Ir.* Cúige Mumhan. *cultural region* S Ireland
Münsterberg in Schlesien *see* Ziębice
Münster in Westfalen *see* Münster
100 E13 **Münsterland** *cultural region* NW Germany
100 F13 **Münster-Osnabruck** ✕ Nordrhein-Westfalen, NW Germany 52°08′N 07°41′E
31 R4 **Munuscong Lake** ◎ Michigan, N USA
83 K17 **Munyati** C Zimbabwe
109 R3 **Münzkirchen** Oberösterreich, N Austria 48°29′N 13°37′E
92 K11 **Muodoslompolo** Norrbotten, N Sweden 67°57′N 23°31′E
92 M13 **Muojärvi** ◎ NE Finland
167 S6 **Mương Khên** Hoa Binh, N Vietnam 20°34′N 105°18′E
Muong Sai *see* Oudômxai
167 Q7 **Muong Xiang Ngeun** *var.* Xieng Ngeun. Louangphabang, N Laos 19°43′N 102°09′E
92 K11 **Muonio** Lappi, N Finland 67°58′N 23°40′E
Muonioälv/Muoniojoki *see* Muonionjoki
92 K11 **Muonionjoki** *var.* Muoniojoki, *Swe.* Muonioälv. Finland/Sweden
Muorjek *see* Murjek
83 N17 **Mupa** C Mozambique
83 E16 **Mupini** Okavango, NE Namibia 17°55′S 19°34′E
80 F8 **Muqaddam, Wadi** N Sudan
138 K9 **Muqāţ** Al Mafraq, E Jordan 32°28′N 38°04′E
81 N17 **Muqdisho** *Eng.* Mogadishu, *It.* Mogadiscio. ● (Somalia) Banaadir, S Somalia 02°06′N 45°27′E
81 N17 **Muqdisho** ✕ Banaadir, E Somalia 01°58′N 45°18′E
Muqshin *see* Mughshin
109 T8 **Mur** *SCr.* Mura. C Europe
109 X9 **Mura** NE Slovenia
Mura *see* Mur
137 T14 **Muradiye** Van, E Turkey 39°N 43°44′E
Muragarazi *see* Maragarazi
165 O10 **Murakami** Niigata, Honshū, C Japan 38°13′N 139°28′E
63 G22 **Murallón, Cerro** ▲ S Argentina 49°49′S 73°25′W
81 E20 **Muramvya** C Burundi 03°18′S 29°41′E
81 I19 **Murang'a** *prev.* Fort Hall. Central, SW Kenya 0°43′S 37°10′E
81 H16 **Murangering** Rift Valley, NW Kenya 03°48′N 35°29′E
Murapara *see* Murupara
140 M5 **Murār, Bi'r al** *well* NW Saudi Arabia
125 Q13 **Murashi** Kirovskaya Oblast', NW Russian Federation 59°27′N 48°02′E
103 O12 **Murat** Cantal, C France 45°07′N 02°52′E
114 N12 **Muratlı** Tekirdağ, NW Turkey 41°12′N 27°30′E
137 R14 **Murat Nehri** *var.* Eastern Euphrates; *anc.* Arsanias. NE Turkey
107 D20 **Muravera** Sardegna, Italy, C Mediterranean Sea 39°24′N 09°34′E
165 P10 **Murayama** Yamagata, Honshū, C Japan 38°29′N 140°21′E
121 R13 **Muraysah, Ra's al** *headland* N Libya 31°58′N 25°00′E
104 I6 **Murça** Vila Real, N Portugal 41°24′N 07°28′W
80 Q11 **Murcanyo** Bari, NE Somalia 11°39′N 50°27′E
143 N8 **Mūrcheh Khvort** *var.* Morcheh Khort. Eşfahān, C Iran 33°07′N 51°26′E
185 H15 **Murchison** Tasman, South Island, New Zealand 41°48′S 172°19′E
185 B22 **Murchison Mountains** ▲ South Island, New Zealand
180 I10 **Murchison River** Western Australia
105 R13 **Murcia** Murcia, SE Spain 37°59′N 01°08′W
105 Q13 **Murcia** ◆ *autonomous community* SE Spain
103 O13 **Mur-de-Barrez** Aveyron, S France 44°48′N 02°39′E
182 G8 **Murdinga** South Australia 33°46′S 135°46′E
28 M10 **Murdo** South Dakota, N USA 43°53′N 100°42′W
15 X6 **Murdochville** Québec, SE Canada 48°57′N 65°30′W
109 W9 **Mureck** Steiermark, SE Austria 46°42′N 15°46′E
114 M13 **Mürefte** Tekirdağ, NW Turkey 40°40′N 27°15′E
116 I10 **Mureş** ◆ *county* N Romania
84 J11 **Mureş** Hungary/Romania
Mureş *see* Maros
Mureşul *see* Maros/Mureş
102 M16 **Muret** Haute-Garonne, S France 43°28′N 01°19′E
27 T13 **Murfreesboro** Arkansas, C USA 34°04′N 93°42′W
21 W8 **Murfreesboro** North Carolina, SE USA 36°26′N 77°06′W
20 J9 **Murfreesboro** Tennessee, S USA 35°50′N 86°25′W
Murgab *see* Morghāb, Daryā-ye/Murgap
Murgab *see* Murghob
146 I14 **Murgap** Mary Welaýaty, S Turkmenistan 37°19′N 61°48′E
146 J16 **Murgap** *var.* Deryasy Murgap, Murghab, *Pash.* Daryā-ye Morghāb, *Rus.* Murgab. Afghanistan/ Turkmenistan *see also* Morghāb, Daryā-ye
Murgap *see* Morghāb, Daryā-ye
Murgap, Deryasy *see* Morghāb, Daryā-ye/Murgap
114 H9 **Murgash** ▲ W Bulgaria 42°51′N 23°58′E
Murghab *see* Morghāb, Daryā-ye/Murgap
148 M4 **Murghāb, Daryā-ye** *Rus.* Murgab, Murghab, *Turk.* Murgap, Deryasy Murgap; *prev.* Morghāb, Daryā-ye. Afghanistan/ Turkmenistan *see also* Murgap
147 U13 **Murghob** *Rus.* Murgab. SE Tajikistan 38°11′N 74°E
147 U13 **Murghob** *Rus.* Murgab. SE Tajikistan
181 Z10 **Murgon** Queensland, E Australia 26°08′S 152°04′E
190 I16 **Muri** Rarotonga, S Cook Islands 21°15′S 159°44′W
108 F7 **Muri** Aargau, W Switzerland 47°16′N 08°21′E
108 D8 **Muri** *var.* Muri bei Bern. Bern, W Switzerland 46°55′N 07°30′E
104 K3 **Murias de Paredes** Castilla y León, N Spain 42°51′N 06°11′W
Muri bei Bern *see* Muri
82 F11 **Muriege** Lunda Sul, NE Angola 09°55′S 21°12′E
189 P14 **Murilo Atoll** *atoll* Hall Islands, C Micronesia
Mūrītānīyah *see* Mauritania
100 N10 **Müritz** *var.* Müritzee. ◎ NE Germany
Müritzee *see* Müritz
100 L10 **Müritz-Elde-Wasserstrasse** *canal* N Germany
184 K6 **Muriwai Beach** Auckland, North Island, New Zealand 36°56′S 174°28′E
92 J13 **Murjek** *Lapp.* Muorjek. Norrbotten, N Sweden 66°27′N 20°54′E
124 J3 **Murmansk** Murmanskaya Oblast', NW Russian Federation 68°59′N 33°08′E
124 I4 **Murmanskaya Oblast'** ◆ *province* NW Russian Federation
197 V14 **Murmansk Rise** *undersea feature* SW Barents Sea 71°00′N 37°00′E
124 J3 **Murmashi** Murmanskaya Oblast', NW Russian Federation 68°49′N 32°43′E
126 M5 **Murmino** Ryazanskaya Oblast', W Russian Federation 54°31′N 40°01′E
101 K24 **Murnau** Bayern, SE Germany 47°41′N 11°12′E
103 X16 **Muro, Capo di** *headland* Corse, France, C Mediterranean Sea 41°45′N 08°40′E
107 M18 **Muro Lucano** Basilicata, S Italy 40°48′N 15°33′E
127 N4 **Murom** Vladimirskaya Oblast', W Russian Federation 55°33′N 42°03′E
122 I11 **Muromtsevo** Omskaya Oblast', C Russian Federation 56°18′N 75°15′E
165 R5 **Muroran** Hokkaidō, NE Japan 42°20′N 140°58′E
104 G3 **Muros** Galicia, NW Spain 42°47′N 09°04′W
104 F3 **Muros e Noia, Ría de** *estuary* NW Spain
164 H15 **Muroto** Kōchi, Shikoku, SW Japan 33°16′N 134°10′E
164 H15 **Muroto-zaki** Shikoku, SW Japan
116 L7 **Murovani Kurylivtsi** Vinnyts'ka Oblast', C Ukraine 48°43′N 27°31′E
110 G11 **Murowana Goślina** Wielkolpolskie, W Poland 52°33′N 16°59′E
32 M14 **Murphy** Idaho, NW USA 43°14′N 116°36′W
21 N10 **Murphy** North Carolina, SE USA 35°05′N 84°02′W
35 P8 **Murphys** California, W USA 38°07′N 120°27′W
30 L17 **Murphysboro** Illinois, N USA 37°45′N 89°20′W
29 V15 **Murray** Iowa, C USA 41°03′N 93°56′W
20 H8 **Murray** Kentucky, S USA 36°35′N 88°20′W
182 J10 **Murray Bridge** South Australia 35°10′S 139°17′E
175 X2 **Murray Fracture Zone** *tectonic feature* NE Pacific Ocean
192 H11 **Murray, Lake** ◎ SW Papua New Guinea
21 P12 **Murray, Lake** ⊠ South Carolina, SE USA
10 K8 **Murray, Mount** ▲ Yukon Territory, NW Canada 60°49′N 128°57′W
Murray Range *see* Murray Ridge
173 O3 **Murray Ridge** *var.* Murray Range. *undersea feature* N Arabian Sea 21°45′N 61°50′E
183 N10 **Murray River** SE Australia
182 K10 **Murrayville** Victoria, SE Australia 35°17′S 141°12′E
149 U5 **Murree** Punjab, E Pakistan 33°55′N 73°26′E
101 I21 **Murrhardt** Baden-Württemberg, S Germany 49°00′N 09°34′E
183 O9 **Murrumbidgee River** New South Wales, SE Australia
83 P15 **Murrupula** Nampula, NE Mozambique 15°26′S 38°46′E
183 T7 **Murrurundi** New South Wales, SE Australia 31°47′S 150°51′E
109 X9 **Murska Sobota** *Ger.* Olsnitz. NE Slovenia 46°41′N 16°09′E
154 G12 **Murtajāpur** *prev.* Murtazapur. Mahārāshtra, C India 20°43′N 77°28′E
77 S16 **Murtala Muhammed** ✕ (Lagos) Ogun, SW Nigeria 06°31′N 03°12′E
Murtazapur *see* Murtajāpur
108 C8 **Murten** Neuchâtel, W Switzerland 46°55′N 07°06′E
Murtensee *see* Morat, Lac de
182 L11 **Murtoa** Victoria, SE Australia 36°39′S 142°27′E
92 N13 **Murtovaara** Oulu, E Finland 65°40′N 29°25′E
Murua Island *see* Woodlark Island
155 D14 **Murud** Mahārāshtra, W India 18°27′N 72°56′E
184 O9 **Murupara** *var.* Murapara. Bay of Plenty, North Island, New Zealand 38°27′S 176°41′E
Mururoa *see* Moruroa
Murviedro *see* Sagunto
154 J9 **Murwāra** Madhya Pradesh, N India 23°50′N 80°23′E
183 V4 **Murwillumbah** New South Wales, SE Australia 28°20′S 153°24′E
146 H11 **Murzechirla** *prev.* Mirzachirla. Ahal Welaýaty, C Turkmenistan 39°33′N 60°02′E
Murzuk *see* Murzuq
75 O11 **Murzuq** *var.* Marzūq, Murzuk. SW Libya 25°55′N 13°55′E
Murzuq, Edeyin *see* Murzuq, Idhān
75 N11 **Murzuq, Ḩammādat** *plateau* W Libya
75 O11 **Murzuq, Idhān** *var.* Edeyin Murzuq. *desert* SW Libya
109 W6 **Mürzzuschlag** Steiermark, E Austria 47°35′N 15°41′E
137 Q14 **Muş** *var.* Mush. Muş, E Turkey 38°45′N 41°30′E
137 Q14 **Muş** *var.* Mush. ◆ *province* E Turkey
118 G11 **Mūša** Latvia/Lithuania
186 F9 **Musa** S Papua New Guinea
Mûsa, Gebel *see* Mūsá, Jabal
Musaiyib *see* Al Musayyib
75 X8 **Mūsá, Jabal** *var.* Gebel Mûsa. ▲ NE Egypt 28°33′N 33°51′E
149 R9 **Musā Khel** *var.* Mūsa Khel Bāzār. Baluchistān, SW Pakistan 30°53′N 69°52′E
Mūsa Khel Bāzār *see* Musā Khel
139 Z13 **Mūsá, Khowr-e** *bay* Iraq/ Kuwait
114 H10 **Musala** ▲ W Bulgaria 42°12′N 23°36′E
168 H10 **Musala, Pulau** *island* W Indonesia
83 I15 **Musale** Southern, S Zambia 15°27′S 26°50′E
141 Y9 **Muşalla** NE Oman 22°20′N 58°03′E
141 W6 **Musandam Peninsula** *Ar.* Masandam Peninsula. *peninsula* N Oman
Musay'id *see* Umm Sa'id
Muscat *see* Masqaţ
Muscat and Oman *see* Oman
29 Y14 **Muscatine** Iowa, C USA 41°25′N 91°03′W
Muscat Sīb Airport *see* Seeb
31 O15 **Muscatuck River** Indiana, N USA
30 K8 **Muscoda** Wisconsin, N USA 43°11′N 90°27′W
185 F19 **Musgrave, Mount** ▲ South Island, New Zealand 43°48′S 170°43′E
181 P9 **Musgrave Ranges** ▲ South Australia
Mush *see* Muş
138 H12 **Mushayyish, Qaşr al** *castle* Ma'ān, C Jordan
79 H20 **Mushie** Bandundu, W Dem. Rep. Congo 03°00′S 16°55′E
168 M13 **Musi, Air** *prev.* Moesi. Sumatera, W Indonesia
192 M4 **Musicians Seamounts** *undersea feature* N Pacific Ocean
83 K19 **Musina** *prev.* Messina. Limpopo, NE South Africa 22°18′S 30°02′E
54 D8 **Musinga, Alto** ▲ NW Colombia 06°49′N 76°24′W
29 T2 **Muskeg Bay** *lake bay* Minnesota, N USA
31 O8 **Muskegon** Michigan, N USA 43°13′N 86°15′W
31 O8 **Muskegon Heights** Michigan, N USA 43°12′N 86°14′W
31 P8 **Muskegon River** Michigan, N USA
31 T14 **Muskingum River** Ohio, N USA
95 P16 **Muskö** Stockholm, C Sweden 58°58′N 18°10′E
Muskogean *see* Tallahassee
27 Q10 **Muskogee** Oklahoma, C USA 35°45′N 95°21′W
14 H13 **Muskoka, Lake** ◎ Ontario, S Canada
80 H8 **Musmar** Red Sea, NE Sudan 18°13′N 35°40′E
83 K14 **Musofu** Central, C Zambia 13°31′S 29°02′E
81 G19 **Musoma** Mara, N Tanzania 01°31′S 33°49′E
82 L13 **Musoro** Central, C Zambia 13°21′S 31°04′E
186 F4 **Mussau Island** *island* NE Papua New Guinea
98 P7 **Musselkanaal** Groningen, NE Netherlands 52°55′N 07°01′E
33 V9 **Musselshell River** Montana, NW USA
82 C12 **Mussende** Cuanza Sul, NW Angola 10°33′S 16°02′E
102 L12 **Mussidan** Dordogne, SW France 45°03′N 00°22′E
99 L25 **Musson** Luxembourg, SE Belgium 49°33′N 05°42′E
152 J9 **Mussoorie** Uttarakhand, N India 30°26′N 78°04′E
Musta *see* Mosta
152 M13 **Mustafābād** Uttar Pradesh, N India 25°54′N 81°17′E
136 D12 **Mustafakemalpaşa** Bursa, NW Turkey 40°03′N 28°25′E
Mustafa-Pasha *see* Svilengrad
81 M15 **Mustahīl** Sumalē, E Ethiopia 05°18′N 44°34′E
24 M7 **Mustang Draw** *valley* Texas, SW USA
25 T14 **Mustang Island** *island* Texas, SW USA
Mustasaari *see* Korsholm
Mustér *see* Disentis
63 I19 **Musters, Lago** ◎ S Argentina
45 Y14 **Mustique** *island* C Saint Vincent and the Grenadines
118 I6 **Mustla** Viljandimaa, S Estonia 58°12′N 25°50′E
118 J4 **Mustvee** *Ger.* Tschorna. Jõgevamaa, E Estonia 58°51′N 26°59′E
42 L9 **Musún, Cerro** ▲ NE Nicaragua 13°01′N 85°02′W
183 T7 **Muswellbrook** New South Wales, SE Australia 32°17′S 150°55′E
111 M18 **Muszyna** Małopolskie, SE Poland 49°21′N 20°54′E
75 V10 **Mūţ** *var.* Mut. C Egypt 25°28′N 28°58′E
136 I17 **Mut** İçel, S Turkey 36°38′N 33°27′E
109 V9 **Muta** N Slovenia 46°37′N 15°09′E
190 B15 **Mutalau** N Niue 18°56′S 169°50′E
Mu-tan-chiang *see* Mudanjiang
82 I13 **Mutanda** North Western, NW Zambia 12°24′S 26°13′E
59 O17 **Mutá, Ponta do** *headland* E Brazil 13°54′S 38°54′W
83 L17 **Mutare** *var.* Mutari; *prev.* Umtali. Manicaland, E Zimbabwe 18°55′S 32°36′E
Mutari *see* Mutare
54 D8 **Mutatá** Antioquia, NW Colombia 07°16′N 76°32′W
Mutina *see* Modena
83 L16 **Mutoko** *prev.* Mtoko. Mashonaland East, NE Zimbabwe 17°24′S 32°13′E

◆ Country
● Country Capital
◇ Dependent Territory
○ Dependent Territory Capital
◆ Administrative Regions
✕ International Airport
▲ Mountain
▲ Mountain Range
Volcano
River
◎ Lake
⊠ Reservoir

81 J20 Mutomo Eastern, S Kenya 01°50′S 38°13′E
Mutrah see Maṭraḥ
79 M24 Mutshatsha Katanga, S Dem. Rep. Congo 10°40′S 24°26′E
165 R6 Mutsu var. Mutu. Aomori, Honshū, N Japan 41°18′N 141°11′E
165 R6 Mutsu-wan bay N Japan
108 E6 Muttenz Basel Landschaft, NW Switzerland 47°31′N 07°39′E
185 A26 Muttonbird Islands island group SW New Zealand
Muttra see Mathura
Mutu see Mutsu
83 O15 Mutuáli Nampula, N Mozambique 14°51′S 37°01′E
82 D13 Mutumbo Bié, C Angola 13°10′S 17°22′E
189 Y14 Mutunte, Mount var. Mount Buache. ▲ Kosrae, E Micronesia 05°21′N 163°00′E
155 K24 Mutur Eastern Province, E Sri Lanka 08°27′N 81°15′E
92 L13 Muurola Lappi, NW Finland 66°22′N 25°20′E
162 M14 Mu Us Shadi var. Ordos Desert; prev. Mu Us Shamo. desert N China
Mu Us Shamo see Mu Us Shadi
82 B11 Muxima Bengo, NW Angola 09°33′S 13°58′E
124 I8 Muyezerskiy Respublika Kareliya, NW Russian Federation 63°54′N 32°00′E
81 E20 Muyinga NE Burundi 02°54′S 30°19′E
42 K9 Muy Muy Matagalpa, C Nicaragua 12°43′N 85°35′W
Muynak see Mo'ynoq
79 N22 Muyumba Katanga, SE Dem. Rep. Congo 07°13′S 27°02′E
149 V5 Muzaffarābād Jammu and Kashmir, NE Pakistan 34°23′N 73°34′E
149 S10 Muzaffargarh Punjab, E Pakistan 30°04′N 71°15′E
152 J9 Muzaffarnagar Uttar Pradesh, N India 29°28′N 77°42′E
153 P13 Muzaffarpur Bihār, N India 26°07′N 85°23′E
158 H6 Muzat He ~ W China
83 L15 Muze Tete, NW Mozambique 15°05′S 31°16′E
122 H8 Muzhi Yamalo-Nenetskiy Avtonomnyy Okrug, N Russian Federation 65°25′N 64°28′E
102 H7 Muzillac Morbihan, NW France 47°34′N 02°30′W
Muzkol, Khrebet see Muzqŭl, Qatorkŭhi
112 L9 Mužlja Hung. Felsőmuzslya; prev. Gornja Mužlja. Vojvodina, N Serbia 45°21′N 20°25′E
54 F9 Muzo Boyacá, C Colombia 05°34′N 74°07′W
83 J15 Muzoka Southern, S Zambia 16°39′S 27°18′E
39 Y15 Muzon, Cape headland Dall Island, Alaska, USA 54°39′N 132°41′W
40 M6 Múzquiz Coahuila, NE Mexico 27°54′N 101°30′W
147 U13 Muzqŭl, Qatorkŭhi Rus. Khrebet Muzkol. ▲▲ SE Tajikistan
Muztag see Muztag Feng
158 D8 Muztagata ▲ NW China 38°16′N 75°03′E
158 K10 Muztag Feng var. Muztag. ▲ W China 36°26′N 87°15′E
83 K17 Mvuma prev. Umvuma. Midlands, C Zimbabwe 19°17′S 30°32′E
172 H13 Mwali var. Moili, Fr. Mohéli. island S Comoros
82 L13 Mwanya Eastern, E Zambia 12°40′S 32°15′E
79 N23 Mwanza Katanga, SE Dem. Rep. Congo 07°49′S 26°49′E
81 G20 Mwanza Mwanza, NW Tanzania 02°31′S 32°56′E
81 F20 Mwanza ◆ region N Tanzania
82 M13 Mwase Lundazi Eastern, E Zambia 12°26′S 33°20′E
97 B17 Mweelrea Ir. Caoc Maol Réidh. ▲ W Ireland 53°37′N 09°47′W
79 K21 Mweka Kasai-Occidental, C Dem. Rep. Congo 04°52′S 21°38′E
82 K12 Mwenda Luapula, N Zambia 10°30′S 30°21′E
79 L22 Mwene-Ditu Kasai-Oriental, S Dem. Rep. Congo 07°06′S 23°34′E
83 L18 Mwenezi ~ S Zimbabwe
79 O20 Mwenga Sud-Kivu, E Dem. Rep. Congo 03°00′S 28°28′E
82 K11 Mweru, Lake var. Lac Moero. ◎ Dem. Rep. Congo/Zambia
82 H13 Mwinilunga North Western, NW Zambia 11°44′S 24°24′E
189 V16 Mwokil Atoll prev. Mokil Atoll. atoll Caroline Islands, E Micronesia
Myadel' see Myadzyel
118 J13 Myadzyel Pol. Miadzioł Nowy, Rus. Myadel'. Minskaya Voblasts', N Belarus 54°51′N 26°51′E
152 C12 Myājlār var. Miajlar. Rājasthān, NW India 26°16′N 70°21′E
123 T9 Myakit Magadanskaya Oblast', E Russian Federation 61°23′N 151°58′E
23 W13 Myakka River ~ Florida, SE USA
124 L14 Myaksa Vologodskaya Oblast', NW Russian Federation 58°54′N 38°15′E
183 U8 Myall Lake ◎ New South Wales, SE Australia
166 L7 Myanaung Ayeyarwady, SW Burma (Myanmar) 18°17′N 95°19′E
Myanmar see Burma
166 K8 Myaungmya Ayeyarwady, SW Burma (Myanmar) 16°33′N 94°55′E
Myaydo see Aunglan
118 N11 Myazha Rus. Mezha. Vitsyebskaya Voblasts', NE Belarus 55°41′N 30°25′E
167 N12 Myeik var. Mergui. Tanintharyi, S Burma (Myanmar) 12°26′N 98°34′E
166 M12 Myeik Archipelago var. Mergui Archipelago. island group S Burma (Myanmar)
119 O18 Myerkulavichy Rus. Merkulovichi. Homyel'skaya Voblasts', SE Belarus 52°58′N 30°36′E
119 N14 Myezhava Rus. Mezhëvo. Vitsyebskaya Voblasts', NE Belarus 54°38′N 30°20′E
Myggenaes see Mykines
166 L5 Myingyan Mandalay, C Burma (Myanmar) 21°25′N 95°20′E
167 N12 Myitkyina Kachin State, N Burma (Myanmar) 25°24′N 97°25′E
166 M5 Myittha Mandalay, C Burma (Myanmar) 21°21′N 96°06′E
111 H19 Myjava Hung. Miava. Trenčiansky Kraj, W Slovakia 48°45′N 17°35′E
Myjeldino see Myyëldino
117 U9 Mykhaylivka Rus. Mikhaylovka. Zaporiz'ka Oblast', SE Ukraine 47°16′N 35°14′E
95 A18 Mykines Dan. Myggenaes. island W Faeroe Islands
116 I5 Mykolayiv L'vivs'ka Oblast', W Ukraine 49°34′N 23°58′E
117 Q10 Mykolayiv Rus. Nikolayev. Mykolayivs'ka Oblast', S Ukraine 46°58′N 31°59′E
117 Q10 Mykolayiv ✕ Mykolayivs'ka Oblast', S Ukraine 47°02′N 31°54′E
Mykolayiv see Mykolayivs'ka Oblast'
117 S13 Mykolayivka Avtonomna Respublika Krym, S Ukraine 44°58′N 33°37′E
117 P9 Mykolayivka Odes'ka Oblast', SW Ukraine 47°34′N 30°48′E
117 P9 Mykolayivs'ka Oblast' var. Mykolayiv, Rus. Nikolayevskaya Oblast'. ◆ province S Ukraine
115 J20 Mýkonos Mýkonos, Kykládes, Greece, Aegean Sea 37°27′N 25°20′E
115 K20 Mýkonos var. Míkonos. island Kykládes, Greece, Aegean Sea
125 R7 Myla Respublika Komi, NW Russian Federation 65°24′N 50°51′E
Mylae see Milazzo
93 M19 Myllykoski Etelä-Suomi, S Finland 60°45′N 26°52′E
153 U14 Mymensing var. Mymensingh. Dhaka, N Bangladesh 24°45′N 90°23′E
Mymensingh see Mymensing
93 K19 Mynämäki Länsi-Suomi, SW Finland 60°41′N 22°00′E
145 S14 Mynaral Kaz. Myngaral. Zhambyl, S Kazakhstan 45°25′N 73°37′E
Mynbulak see Mingbuloq
Mynbulak, Vpadina see Mingbuloq Botig'i
Myngaral see Mynaral
Myohaung see Mrauk-oo
163 W13 Myohyang-sanmaek ▲▲ C North Korea
164 M11 Myōkō-san ▲ Honshū, S Japan 36°54′N 138°05′E
83 J15 Myooye Central, C Zambia 15°11′S 27°10′E
118 K12 Myory prev. Miyory. Vitsyebskaya Voblasts', N Belarus 55°39′N 27°39′E
92 J4 Mýrdalsjökull glacier S Iceland
92 G10 Myre Nordland, C Norway 68°54′N 15°04′E
117 S5 Myrhorod Rus. Mirgorod. Poltavs'ka Oblast', NE Ukraine 49°58′N 33°37′E
115 J15 Mýrina var. Mírina. Límnos, SE Greece 39°52′N 25°04′E
117 P5 Myronivka Rus. Mironovka. Kyyivs'ka Oblast', N Ukraine 49°40′N 30°59′E
21 U13 Myrtle Beach South Carolina, SE USA 33°41′N 78°53′W
32 F14 Myrtle Creek Oregon, NW USA 43°01′N 123°19′W
183 P11 Myrtleford Victoria, SE Australia 36°34′S 146°45′E
32 E14 Myrtle Point Oregon, NW USA 43°04′N 124°08′W
115 K25 Mýrtos Kríti, Greece, E Mediterranean Sea 35°00′N 25°34′E
Myrtoum Mare see Mirtóo Pélagos
93 G17 Myrviken Jämtland, C Sweden 62°59′N 14°19′E
95 I15 Mysen Østfold, S Norway 59°33′N 11°20′E
124 L15 Myshkin Yaroslavskaya Oblast', NW Russian Federation 57°47′N 38°28′E
111 K17 Myślenice Małopolskie, S Poland 49°50′N 19°55′E
110 D10 Myślibórz Zachodnio-pomorskie, NW Poland 52°55′N 14°51′E
155 G20 Mysore var. Maisur. Karnātaka, W India 12°18′N 76°37′E
Mysore see Karnātaka
115 F21 Mystrás var. Mistras. Pelopónnisos, S Greece 37°03′N 22°22′E
111 K15 Myszków Śląskie, S Poland 50°36′N 19°20′E
167 T14 My Tho var. Mi Tho. Tiên Giang, S Vietnam 10°21′N 106°21′E
Mytilene see Mytilíni
115 L17 Mytilíni var. Mitilíni; anc. Mytilene. Lésvos, E Greece 39°06′N 26°33′E
126 K3 Mytishchi Moskovskaya Oblast', W Russian Federation 56°00′N 37°51′E
37 N3 Myton Utah, W USA 40°11′N 110°03′W
92 K2 Mývatn ◎ C Iceland
125 T11 Myyëldino var. Myjeldino. Respublika Komi, NW Russian Federation 61°46′N 54°48′E
82 M13 Mzimba Northern, NW Malawi 11°56′S 33°36′E
82 M12 Mzuzu Northern, N Malawi 11°23′S 34°03′E

N

101 M19 Naab ~ SE Germany
98 G12 Naaldwijk Zuid-Holland, W Netherlands 52°00′N 04°13′E
38 G12 Nā'ālehu var. Naalehu. Hawaii, USA, C Pacific Ocean 19°04′N 155°36′W
93 K19 Naantali Swe. Nådendal. Länsi-Suomi, SW Finland 60°28′N 22°05′E
98 J10 Naarden Noord-Holland, C Netherlands 52°18′N 05°10′E
109 U4 Naarn ~ N Austria
97 F18 Naas Ir. An Nás, Nás na Ríogh. Kildare, C Ireland 53°13′N 06°39′W
92 M9 Näätämöjoki Lapp. Njávdám. ~ NE Finland
83 E23 Nababeep var. Nababiep. Northern Cape, W South Africa 29°36′S 17°46′E
Nababiep see Nababeep
Nabadwip see Navadwip
164 J14 Nabari Mie, Honshū, SW Japan 34°37′N 136°05′E
Nabatié see Nabatîyé
138 G8 Nabatîyé var. An Nabaṭīyah at Taḥtā, Nabatié, Nabatiyet et Tahta. SW Lebanon 33°18′N 35°36′E
Nabatiyet et Tahta see Nabatîyé
187 X14 Nabavatu Vanua Levu, N Fiji 16°35′S 178°55′E
190 I2 Nabeina island Tungaru, W Kiribati
127 T4 Naberezhnyye Chelny prev. Brezhnev. Respublika Tatarstan, W Russian Federation 55°43′N 52°21′E
39 T10 Nabesna Alaska, USA 62°22′N 143°00′W
39 T10 Nabesna River ~ Alaska, USA
75 N5 Nabeul var. Nābul. NE Tunisia 36°32′N 10°45′E
152 I9 Nābha Punjab, NW India 30°22′N 76°12′E
171 W13 Nabire Papua, E Indonesia 03°23′S 135°31′E
141 O15 Nabī Shu'ayb, Jabal an ▲ W Yemen 15°24′N 44°04′E
138 F10 Nablus var. Nābulus, Heb. Shekhem; anc. Neapolis, Bibl. Shechem. N West Bank 32°13′N 35°16′E
187 X14 Nabouwalu Vanua Levu, N Fiji 17°00′S 178°43′E
Nābul see Nabeul
Nābulus see Nablus
187 Y13 Nabuna Vanua Levu, N Fiji 16°13′S 179°46′E
83 Q14 Nacala Nampula, NE Mozambique 14°30′S 40°37′E
42 H8 Nacaome Valle, S Honduras 13°30′N 87°31′W
Na Cealla Beaga see Killybegs
Na-Ch'ii see Nagqu
164 J15 Nachikatsuura var. Nachi-Katsuura. Wakayama, Honshū, SE Japan 33°37′N 135°54′E
Nachi-Katsuura see Nachikatsuura
81 J24 Nachingwea Lindi, SE Tanzania 10°21′S 38°46′E
111 F16 Náchod Královéhradecký Kraj, N Czech Republic 50°26′N 16°10′E
Na Clocha Liatha see Greystones
40 G3 Naco Sonora, NW Mexico 31°16′N 109°56′W
25 X8 Nacogdoches Texas, SW USA 31°36′N 94°40′W
40 G4 Nacozari de García Sonora, NW Mexico 30°27′N 109°43′W
Nada see Danzhou
77 O14 Nadawli NW Ghana 10°30′N 02°40′W
104 I3 Nadela Galicia, NW Spain 42°58′N 07°33′W
Nådendal see Naantali
144 M7 Nadezhdinka prev. Nadezhdinskiy. Kostanay, N Kazakhstan 53°46′N 63°44′E
Nadezhdinskiy see Nadezhdinka
Nadgan see Nadqān, Qalamat
187 W14 Nadi prev. Nandi. Viti Levu, W Fiji 17°47′S 177°32′E
187 X14 Nadi prev. Nandi. ✕ Viti Levu, W Fiji 17°46′S 177°28′E
154 D10 Nadiād Gujarāt, W India 22°42′N 72°55′E
Nadikdik see Knox Atoll
116 E11 Nădlac Ger. Nadlak, Hung. Nagylak. Arad, W Romania 46°10′N 20°47′E
Nadlak see Nădlac
74 H6 Nador prev. Villa Nador. NE Morocco 35°10′N 05°22′W
141 S9 Nadqān, Qalamat var. Nadgan. well E Saudi Arabia
111 N22 Nádudvar Hajdú-Bihar, E Hungary 47°36′N 21°09′E
121 O15 Nadur Gozo, N Malta 36°03′N 14°18′E
187 X13 Naduri prev. Nanduri. Vanua Levu, N Fiji 16°26′S 179°08′E
116 I7 Nadvirna Pol. Nadwórna, Rus. Nadvornaya. Ivano-Frankivs'ka Oblast', W Ukraine 48°27′N 24°30′E
124 J8 Nadvoitsy Respublika Kareliya, NW Russian Federation 63°53′N 34°17′E
Nadvornaya/Nadwórna see Nadvirna
122 I9 Nadym Yamalo-Nenetskiy Avtonomnyy Okrug, N Russian Federation 65°25′N 72°40′E
122 I9 Nadym ~ C Russian Federation
186 E7 Nadzab Morobe, C Papua New Guinea 06°36′S 146°46′E
95 C17 Nærbø Rogaland, S Norway 58°40′N 05°39′E
95 I24 Næstved Sjælland, SE Denmark 55°12′N 11°47′E
77 X13 Nafada Gombe, E Nigeria 11°02′N 11°18′E
108 H8 Näfels Glarus, NE Switzerland 47°06′N 09°04′E
115 E18 Náfpaktos var. Návpaktos. Dytikí Elláda, C Greece 38°23′N 21°50′E
115 F20 Náfplio prev. Návplion. Pelopónnisos, S Greece 37°34′N 22°50′E
139 U6 Naft Khāneh Diyālá, E Iraq 34°01′N 45°26′E
149 N13 Nāg Baluchistān, SW Pakistan 27°43′N 65°31′E
171 P4 Naga off. Naga City; prev. Nueva Caceres. Luzon, N Philippines 13°36′N 123°10′E
Nagaarzê see Nagarzê
Naga City see Naga
12 F11 Nagagami ~ Ontario, S Canada
164 F14 Nagahama Ehime, Shikoku, SW Japan 33°36′N 132°29′E
153 X12 Nāga Hills ▲▲ NE India
165 P10 Nagai Yamagata, Honshū, C Japan 38°08′N 140°00′E
Na Gaibhlte see Galty Mountains
39 N16 Nagai Island island Shumagin Islands, Alaska, USA
153 X12 Nāgāland ◆ state NE India
164 M11 Nagano Nagano, Honshū, S Japan 36°39′N 138°11′E
164 M12 Nagano off. Nagano-ken. ◆ prefecture Honshū, S Japan
Nagano-ken see Nagano
165 N11 Nagaoka Niigata, Honshū, C Japan 37°26′N 138°48′E
153 W12 Nagaon prev. Nowgong. Assam, NE India 26°21′N 92°41′E
155 J21 Nāgappattinam var. Negapatam, Negapattinam. Tamil Nādu, SE India 10°45′N 79°50′E
Nagara Nayok see Nakhon Nayok
Nagara Panom see Nakhon Phanom
Nagara Pathom see Nakhon Pathom
Nagara Sridharmaraj see Nakhon Si Thammarat
Nagara Svarga see Nakhon Sawan
155 H16 Nāgārjuna Sāgar ▣ E India
42 I10 Nagarote León, SW Nicaragua 12°15′N 86°35′W
158 M16 Nagarzê var. Nagaarzê. Xizang Zizhiqu, W China 28°57′N 90°26′E
164 C14 Nagasaki Nagasaki, Kyūshū, SW Japan 32°45′N 129°52′E
164 C14 Nagasaki off. Nagasaki-ken. ◆ prefecture Kyūshū, SW Japan
Nagasaki-ken see Nagasaki
Nagashima see Kii-Nagashima
164 E12 Nagato Yamaguchi, Honshū, SW Japan 34°22′N 131°10′E
152 F11 Nāgaur Rājasthān, NW India 27°12′N 73°48′E
154 F10 Nāgda Madhya Pradesh, C India 23°30′N 75°29′E
98 L8 Nagele Flevoland, N Netherlands 52°39′N 05°43′E
155 H24 Nāgercoil Tamil Nādu, SE India 08°11′N 77°30′E
153 X12 Nāginimāra Nāgāland, NE India 26°44′N 94°51′E
Na Gleannta see Glenties
165 T16 Nago Okinawa, Okinawa, SW Japan 26°36′N 127°59′E
154 K9 Nāgod Madhya Pradesh, C India 24°34′N 80°34′E
155 J26 Nagoda Southern Province, S Sri Lanka 06°13′N 80°13′E
101 G22 Nagold Baden-Württemberg, SW Germany 48°33′N 08°43′E
137 V12 Nagorno-Karabakh var. Nagorno- Karabakhskaya Avtonomnaya Oblast, Arm. Lerrnayin Gharabakh, Az. Dağlıq Quarabağ, Rus. Nagornyy Karabakh. former autonomous region SW Azerbaijan
Nagorno- Karabakhskaya Avtonomnaya Oblast see Nagorno-Karabakh
123 Q12 Nagornyy Respublika Sakha (Yakutiya), NE Russian Federation 55°53′N 124°58′E
Nagornyy Karabakh see Nagorno-Karabakh
125 R13 Nagorsk Kirovskaya Oblast', NW Russian Federation 59°18′N 50°49′E
164 K13 Nagoya Aichi, Honshū, SW Japan 35°10′N 136°53′E
154 I12 Nāgpur Mahārāshtra, C India 21°09′N 79°06′E
156 K10 Nagqu Chin. Na-Ch'ii; prev. Hei-ho. Xizang Zizhiqu, W China 31°30′N 91°57′E
152 J8 Nāg Tibba Range ▲▲ N India
45 O8 Nagua NE Dominican Republic 19°25′N 69°49′W
111 H25 Nagyatád Somogy, SW Hungary 46°15′N 17°25′E
Nagybánya see Baia Mare
Nagybecskerek see Zrenjanin
Nagydisznód see Cisnădie
Nagyenyed see Aiud
111 N21 Nagykálló Szabolcs-Szatmár-Bereg, E Hungary 47°50′N 21°47′E
111 G25 Nagykanizsa Ger. Grosskanizsa. Zala, SW Hungary 46°27′N 17°E
Nagykároly see Carei
111 K22 Nagykáta Pest, C Hungary 47°25′N 19°45′E
Nagykikinda see Kikinda
111 K23 Nagykőrös Pest, C Hungary 47°01′N 19°46′E
Nagy-Küküllő see Târnava Mare
Nagylak see Nădlac
Nagymihály see Michalovce
Nagyrőce see Revúca
Nagysomkút see Şomcuta Mare
Nagysurány see Šurany
Nagyszalonta see Salonta
Nagyszeben see Sibiu
Nagyszentmiklós see Sânnicolau Mare
Nagyszöllös see Vynohradiv
Nagyszombat see Trnava
Nagytapolcsány see Topoľčany
Nagyvárad see Oradea
165 S17 Naha Okinawa, Okinawa, SW Japan 26°10′N 127°40′E
152 J8 Nāhan Himāchal Pradesh, NW India 30°33′N 77°18′E
Nahang, Rūd-e see Nihing
138 F8 Nahariya prev. Nahariyya. Northern, N Israel 33°01′N 35°05′E
Nahariyya see Nahariya
142 L6 Nahāvand var. Nehavend. Hamadān, W Iran 34°13′N 48°21′E
101 F19 Nahe ~ SW Germany
Na H-Iarmhidhe see Westmeath
189 O13 Nahnalaud ▲ Pohnpei, E Micronesia
Nahoi, Cape see Cumberland, Cape
Nahtavárr see Nattavaara
63 H16 Nahuel Huapí, Lago ◎ W Argentina
23 W7 Nahunta Georgia, SE USA 31°11′N 81°58′W
40 J6 Naica Chihuahua, N Mexico 27°53′N 105°30′W
11 U15 Naicam Saskatchewan, S Canada 52°26′N 104°30′W
Naiman Qi see Daqin Tal
158 M4 Naimin Bulak spring NW China
13 P6 Nain Newfoundland and Labrador, NE Canada 56°33′N 61°46′W
143 P8 Nā'īn Eşfahān, C Iran 32°52′N 53°05′E
152 K10 Naini Tāl Uttarakhand, N India 29°22′N 79°26′E
154 J11 Nainpur Madhya Pradesh, C India 22°26′N 80°10′E
96 J8 Nairn N Scotland, United Kingdom 57°36′N 03°51′W
96 I8 Nairn cultural region NE Scotland, United Kingdom
81 I19 Nairobi ● (Kenya) Nairobi Area, S Kenya 01°17′S 36°50′E
81 I19 Nairobi ✕ Nairobi Area, S Kenya 01°21′S 37°01′E
82 P13 Nairoto Cabo Delgado, NE Mozambique 12°22′S 39°05′E
118 G3 Naissaar island N Estonia
Naissus see Niš
187 Z14 Naitaba var. Naitauba; prev. Naitamba. island Lau Group, E Fiji
Naitamba/Naitauba see Naitaba
81 I19 Naivasha Rift Valley, SW Kenya 0°44′S 36°26′E
81 H19 Naivasha, Lake ◎ SW Kenya
Najaf see An Najaf
143 N8 Najafābād var. Nejafabad. Eşfahān, C Iran 32°38′N 51°23′E
141 N7 Najd var. Nejd. cultural region C Saudi Arabia
105 O4 Nájera La Rioja, N Spain 42°25′N 02°45′W
105 P4 Najerilla ~ N Spain
163 U7 Naji var. Arun Qi. Nei Mongol Zizhiqu, N China 48°05′N 123°28′E
152 J9 Najībābād Uttar Pradesh, N India 29°37′N 78°19′E
Najima see Fukuoka
163 Y11 Najin NE North Korea 42°13′N 130°16′E
139 T9 Najm al Ḩassūn Bābil, C Iraq 32°24′N 44°13′E
141 O13 Najrān var. Abā as Su'ūd. Najrān, S Saudi Arabia 17°31′N 44°09′E
141 P12 Najrān var. Minṭaqat al Najrān. ◆ province S Saudi Arabia
Najrān, Minṭaqat al see Najrān
165 T2 Nakagawa Hokkaidō, NE Japan 44°49′N 142°04′E
38 F9 Nākālele Point var. Nakalele Point. headland Maui, Hawai'i, USA 21°01′N 156°35′W
164 D13 Nakama Fukuoka, Kyūshū, SW Japan 33°53′N 130°48′E
Nakambé see White Volta
Nakamti see Nek'emtē
164 F15 Nakamura var. Shimanto. Kōchi, Shikoku, SW Japan 33°00′N 132°55′E
186 H7 Nakanai Mountains ▲▲ New Britain, E Papua New Guinea
164 H11 Nakano-shima island Oki-shotō, SW Japan
165 Q6 Nakasato Aomori, Honshū, C Japan 40°58′N 140°26′E
165 T5 Nakasatsunai Hokkaidō, NE Japan 42°42′N 143°09′E
165 W4 Nakashibetsu Hokkaidō, NE Japan 43°31′N 144°58′E
81 F18 Nakasongola C Uganda 01°19′N 32°28′E
165 T1 Nakatonbetsu Hokkaidō, NE Japan 44°58′N 142°18′E
164 L13 Nakatsugawa var. Nakatugawa. Gifu, Honshū, SW Japan 35°30′N 137°29′E
Nakatugawa see Nakatsugawa
Nakdong see Nakdong-gang
163 Y15 Nakdong-gang var. Nakdong, Jap. Rakutō-kō; prev. Naktong-gang. ~ C South Korea
Nakel see Nakło nad Notecią
Nakfa see Nak'fa
80 J8 Nak'fa var. Nakfa. N Eritrea 16°38′N 38°26′E
Nakhichevan' see Naxçıvan
123 S15 Nakhodka Primorskiy Kray, SE Russian Federation 42°46′N 132°48′E
122 J8 Nakhodka Yamalo-Nenetskiy Avtonomnyy Okrug, N Russian Federation 67°48′N 77°48′E
Nakhon Navok see Nakhon Nayok
167 P11 Nakhon Nayok var. Nagara Nayok, Nakhon Navok. Nakhon Nayok, C Thailand 14°15′N 101°12′E
167 O11 Nakhon Pathom var. Nagara Pathom, Nakorn Pathom. Nakhon Pathom, W Thailand 13°49′N 100°06′E
167 R8 Nakhon Phanom var. Nagara Panom. Nakhon Phanom, E Thailand 17°22′N 104°46′E
167 Q10 Nakhon Ratchasima var. Khorat, Korat. Nakhon Ratchasima, E Thailand 15°N 102°06′E
167 O9 Nakhon Sawan var. Muang Nakhon Sawan, Nagara Svarga. Nakhon Sawan, W Thailand 15°42′N 100°06′E
167 N15 Nakhon Si Thammarat var. Nagara Sridharmaraj, Nakhon Sithammaraj. Nakhon Si Thammarat, SW Thailand 08°24′N 99°58′E
Nakhon Sithammaraj see Nakhon Si Thammarat
139 Y11 Nakhrash Al Başrah, SE Iraq 31°13′N 47°24′E
10 I9 Nakina British Columbia, W Canada 59°12′N 132°48′W
110 H9 Nakło nad Notecią Ger. Nakel. Kujawsko-pomorskie, C Poland 53°08′N 17°35′E
39 P13 Naknek Alaska, USA 58°45′N 157°01′W
152 H8 Nakodar Punjab, NW India 31°06′N 75°31′E
82 M11 Nakonde Northern, NE Zambia 09°22′S 32°47′E
Nakorn Pathom see Nakhon Pathom
95 H24 Nakskov Sjælland, SE Denmark 54°50′N 11°10′E
Naktong-gang see Nakdong-gang
81 H18 Nakuru Rift Valley, SW Kenya 0°16′S 36°04′E
81 H19 Nakuru, Lake ◎ Rift Valley, C Kenya
11 O17 Nakusp British Columbia, SW Canada 50°14′N 117°48′W
149 N15 Nāl ~ W Pakistan
162 M7 Nalayh Töv, C Mongolia 47°48′N 107°17′E
153 V12 Nalbāri Assam, NE India 26°36′N 91°49′E
63 G19 Nalcayec, Isla island Archipiélago de los Chonos, S Chile
127 N15 Nal'chik Kabardino-Balkarskaya Respublika, SW Russian Federation 43°30′N 43°39′E
155 I16 Nalgonda Andhra Pradesh, C India 17°04′N 79°15′E
153 S14 Nalhāti West Bengal, NE India 24°19′N 87°53′E
153 U14 Nalitabari Dhaka, N Bangladesh 25°06′N 90°11′E
155 I17 Nallamala Hills ▲▲ E India
136 G12 Nallıhan Ankara, NW Turkey 40°12′N 31°22′E
104 K2 Nalón ~ NW Spain
167 N3 Nalong Kachin State, N Burma (Myanmar) 24°42′N 97°27′E
75 N8 Nālūt NW Libya 31°52′N 10°59′E
171 T14 Nama Pulau Manawoka, E Indonesia 04°07′S 131°22′E
189 Q16 Nama island C Micronesia
83 O16 Namacurra Zambézia, NE Mozambique 17°31′S 37°03′E
188 F9 Namai Bay bay Babeldaob, N Palau
29 W2 Namakan Lake ◎ Canada/USA
143 O6 Namak, Daryācheh-ye marsh N Iran
143 T6 Namak, Kavīr-e salt pan NE Iran
167 O6 Namaklwe Shan State, E Burma (Myanmar) 19°45′N 99°01′E
Namaksār, Kowl-e/ Namakzār, Daryācheh-ye see Namakzar
148 J5 Namakzar Pash. Daryācheh-ye Namakzār, Kowl-e Namaksār. marsh Afghanistan/Iran
171 V15 Namalau Pulau Jursian, E Indonesia 05°50′S 134°43′E
81 I20 Namanga Rift Valley, S Kenya 02°33′S 36°48′E
147 S10 Namangan Namangan Viloyati, E Uzbekistan 40°59′N 71°34′E
Namanganskaya Oblast' see Namangan Viloyati
147 R10 Namangan Viloyati Rus. Namanganskaya Oblast'. ◆ province E Uzbekistan
83 Q14 Namapa Nampula, NE Mozambique 13°43′S 39°48′E
83 C21 Namaqualand physical region S Namibia
81 G18 Namasagali C Uganda 01°02′N 32°58′E
186 H6 Namatanai New Ireland, NE Papua New Guinea 03°40′S 152°26′E
83 I14 Nambala Central, C Zambia 15°04′S 26°56′E
81 J23 Nambanje Lindi, SE Tanzania 08°37′S 38°21′E
183 V2 Nambour Queensland, E Australia 26°40′S 152°52′E
183 V6 Nambucca Heads New South Wales, SE Australia 30°37′S 153°00′E
159 N15 Nam Co ◎ W China
167 R5 Nâm Cum Lai Châu, N Vietnam 22°37′N 103°12′E
Namdik see Namorik Atoll
167 T6 Nam Định Nam Ha, N Vietnam 20°25′N 106°12′E
99 I20 Namêche Namur, SE Belgium 50°29′N 05°02′E
30 J4 Namekagon Lake ◎ Wisconsin, N USA
188 F10 Namekakl Passage passage Babeldaob, N Palau
Namen see Namur
83 P15 Nametil Nampula, NE Mozambique 15°46′S 39°21′E
163 X14 Nam-gang ~ C North Korea
163 Y16 Nam-gang ~ S South Korea
163 Y17 Namhae-do Jap. Nankai-tō. island S South Korea
Namhoi see Foshan
83 C19 Namib Desert desert W Namibia
83 A15 Namibe Port. Moçâmedes, Mossâmedes. Namibe, SW Angola 15°10′S 12°09′E
83 A15 Namibe ◆ province SE Angola
83 C18 Namibia off. Republic of Namibia, var. South West Africa, Afr. Suidwes-Afrika, Ger. Deutsch-Südwestafrika; prev. German Southwest Africa, South-West Africa. ◆ republic S Africa
65 O17 Namibia Plain undersea feature S Atlantic Ocean
Namibia, Republic of see Namibia
165 Q11 Namie Fukushima, Honshū, C Japan 37°29′N 140°58′E
165 Q7 Namioka Aomori, Honshū, C Japan 40°43′N 140°34′E
40 I5 Namiquipa Chihuahua, N Mexico 29°15′N 107°25′W
159 P15 Namjagbarwa Feng ▲ W China 29°39′N 95°00′E
Namka see Doilungdêqên
Nam Khong see Mekong
171 R13 Namlea Pulau Buru, E Indonesia 03°12′S 127°06′E
158 L16 Namling Xizang Zizhiqu, W China 29°40′N 88°58′E
Namnetes see Nantes
167 R8 Nam Ngum ~ C Laos
Namo see Namu Atoll
183 R5 Namoi River ~ New South Wales, SE Australia
189 Q17 Namoluk Atoll atoll Mortlock Islands, C Micronesia
189 O15 Namonuito Atoll atoll Caroline Islands, C Micronesia
189 T9 Namorik Atoll var. Namdik. atoll Ralik Chain, S Marshall Islands
167 Q6 Nam Ou ~ N Laos
32 M14 Nampa Idaho, NW USA 43°32′N 116°33′W
76 M11 Nampala Ségou, W Mali 15°21′N 05°32′W
163 W14 Namp'o SW North Korea 38°46′N 125°25′E
83 P15 Nampula Nampula, NE Mozambique 15°09′S 39°14′E
83 P15 Nampula off. Província de Nampula. ◆ province NE Mozambique
Nampula, Província de see Nampula
163 W13 Namsan-ni NW North Korea 40°25′N 125°01′E
Namslau see Namysłów
93 E15 Namsos Nord-Trøndelag, C Norway 64°28′N 11°31′E
93 F14 Namsskogan Nord-Trøndelag, C Norway 64°57′N 13°04′E
167 O6 Nam Teng ~ E Burma
167 P6 Nam Tha ~ N Laos
123 Q10 Namtsy Respublika Sakha (Yakutiya), NE Russian Federation 62°42′N 129°30′E
167 N4 Namtu Shan State, E Burma (Myanmar) 23°04′N 97°26′E
10 J15 Namu British Columbia, SW Canada 51°46′N 127°49′W
189 T7 Namu Atoll var. Namo. atoll Ralik Chain, C Marshall Islands
187 Y15 Namuka-i-lau island Lau Group, E Fiji
83 O15 Namuli, Mont ▲ NE Mozambique 15°15′S 37°33′E
83 P14 Namuno Cabo Delgado, N Mozambique 13°39′S 38°50′E
99 I20 Namur Dut. Namen. Namur, SE Belgium 50°28′N 04°52′E
99 H21 Namur Dut. Namen. ◆ province S Belgium
83 D17 Namutoni Kunene, N Namibia 18°49′S 16°55′E
163 Y16 Namwon Jap. Nangen; prev. Namwŏn. S South Korea 35°24′N 127°20′E
Namwŏn see Namwon
111 H14 Namysłów Ger. Namslau. Opole, SW Poland 51°03′N 17°41′E
167 P7 Nan var. Muang Nan. Nan, NW Thailand 18°47′N 100°50′E
79 G15 Nana ~ W Central African Republic
165 R5 Nanae Hokkaidō, NE Japan 41°55′N 140°40′E
79 I14 Nana-Grébizi ◆ prefecture N Central African Republic
10 L17 Nanaimo Vancouver Island, British Columbia, SW Canada 49°08′N 123°58′W
38 C9 Nānākuli var. Nanakuli. O'ahu, Hawaii, USA, C Pacific Ocean 21°23′N 158°09′W
79 G15 Nana-Mambéré ◆ prefecture W Central African Republic
161 R13 Nan'an Fujian, SE China 24°57′N 118°22′E
183 U2 Nanango Queensland, E Australia 26°42′S 151°58′E
164 L11 Nanao Ishikawa, Honshū, SW Japan 37°03′N 136°58′E
161 Q14 Nan'ao Dao island S China
164 L10 Nanatsu-shima island SW Japan
56 F8 Nanay, Río ~ NE Peru
160 J8 Nanbu Sichuan, C China 31°19′N 106°02′E
163 X7 Nancha Heilongjiang, NE China 47°09′N 129°17′E
161 P10 Nanchang var. Nan-ch'ang, Nanch'ang-hsien. province capital Jiangxi, S China 28°38′N 115°58′E
Nan-ch'ang see Nanchang
Nanch'ang-hsien see Nanchang
161 P11 Nancheng var. Jianchang. Jiangxi, S China 27°37′N 116°37′E
Nan-ching see Nanjing
160 J9 Nanchong Sichuan, C China 30°47′N 106°03′E
160 J10 Nanchuan Chongqing Shi, C China 29°06′N 107°13′E
103 T5 Nancy Meurthe-et-Moselle, NE France 48°40′N 06°11′E
185 A22 Nancy Sound sound South Island, New Zealand
152 L9 Nanda Devi ▲ NW India 30°27′N 80°00′E
42 J11 Nandaime Granada, SW Nicaragua 11°45′N 86°02′W
160 K13 Nandan var. Minami-Awaji. Guangxi Zhuangzu Zizhiqu, S China 25°03′N 107°31′E
155 H14 Nānded Mahārāshtra, C India 19°11′N 77°21′E
183 S5 Nandewar Range ▲▲ New South Wales, SE Australia
Nandi see Nadi
160 E13 Nanding He ~ China/Vietnam
Nándorhgy see Oţelu Roşu
154 E11 Nandurbār Mahārāshtra, W India 21°22′N 74°18′E
Nanduri see Naduri
155 I17 Nandyāl Andhra Pradesh, E India 15°30′N 78°28′E
161 P11 Nanfeng var. Qincheng. Jiangxi, S China 27°15′N 116°16′E
Nang see Nangxian
79 E15 Nanga Eboko Centre, C Cameroon 04°38′N 12°21′E
Nangah Serawai see Nangaserawai
149 W4 Nanga Parbat ▲ India/Pakistan 35°15′N 74°36′E
169 R11 Nangapinoh Borneo, C Indonesia 0°21′S 111°44′E
149 R5 Nangarhār ◆ province E Afghanistan
169 S11 Nangaserawai var. Nangah Serawai. Borneo, C Indonesia 0°20′S 112°26′E
169 Q12 Nangatayap Borneo, C Indonesia 01°30′S 110°33′E
Nangen see Namwon
103 P5 Nangis Seine-et-Marne, N France 48°36′N 03°02′E
163 X13 Nangnim-sanmaek ▲▲ C North Korea
161 O4 Nangong Hebei, E China 37°22′N 115°20′E
159 Q14 Nangqên var. Xangda. Qinghai, C China 32°05′N 96°28′E
167 Q10 Nang Rong Buri Ram, E Thailand 14°37′N 102°48′E
159 O16 Nangxian var. Nang. Xizang Zizhiqu, W China 29°04′N 93°03′E
Nan Hai see South China Sea
160 L8 Nan He ~ C China
160 F12 Nanhua var. Longchuan. Yunnan, SW China 25°15′N 101°15′E
Naniwa see Ōsaka
155 G20 Nanjangūd Karnātaka, W India 12°07′N 76°40′E

◆ Country
● Country Capital
◇ Dependent Territory
○ Dependent Territory Capital
◆ Administrative Regions
✕ International Airport
▲ Mountain
▲▲ Mountain Range
Ѫ Volcano
~ River
◎ Lake
▣ Reservoir

161 Q8 **Nanjing** var. Nan-ching, Nanking; prev. Chianning, Chian-ning, Kiang-ning, Jiangsu. province capital Jiangsu, E China 32°03′N 118°47′E
Nankai-tō see Namhae-do
161 O12 **Nankang** var. Rongjiang. Jiangxi, S China 25°42′N 114°45′E
Nanking see Nanjing
161 N13 **Nan Ling** ▲ S China
160 L15 **Nanliu Jiang** ~ S China
189 P13 **Nan Madol** ruins Temwen Island, E Micronesia
160 K15 **Nanning** var. Nan-ning; prev. Yung-ning. Guangxi Zhuangzu Zizhiqu, S China 22°50′N 108°19′E
Nan-ning see Nanning
196 M15 **Nanortalik** Kitaa, S Greenland 60°08′M 45°14′W
Nanouki see Aranuka
160 H13 **Nanpan Jiang** ~ S China
152 M11 **Nānpāra** Uttar Pradesh, N India 27°51′N 81°30′E
161 Q12 **Nanping** var. Nan-p'ing; prev. Yenping. Fujian, SE China 26°40′N 118°07′E
Nan-p'ing see Nanping
Nanping see Jiuzhaigou
Nanpu see Pucheng
161 R12 **Nanri Dao** island SE China
165 S16 **Nansei-shotō** Eng. Ryukyu Islands. island group SW Japan
Nansei Syotō Trench see Ryukyu Trench
197 T10 **Nansen Basin** undersea feature Arctic Ocean
197 T10 **Nansen Cordillera** var. Arctic Mid Oceanic Ridge, Nansen Ridge. undersea feature Arctic Ocean 87°00′N 90°00′E
Nansen Ridge see Nansen Cordillera
129 T9 **Nan Shan** ▲ C China
Nansha Qundao see Spratly Islands
12 K3 **Nantais, Lac** ◎ Québec, NE Canada
103 N5 **Nanterre** Hauts-de-Seine, N France 48°53′N 02°13′E
102 I8 **Nantes** Bret. Naoned; anc. Condivincum, Namnetes. Loire-Atlantique, NW France 47°12′N 01°32′W
14 G17 **Nanticoke** Ontario, S Canada 42°49′N 80°04′W
18 H13 **Nanticoke** Pennsylvania, NE USA 41°12′N 76°00′W
21 Y4 **Nanticoke River** ~ Delaware/Maryland, NE USA
11 Q17 **Nanton** Alberta, SW Canada 50°21′N 113°47′W
161 S8 **Nantong** Jiangsu, E China 32°00′N 120°52′E
161 S13 **Nantou** prev. Nant'ou. W Taiwan 23°54′N 120°51′E
Nant'ou see Nantou
103 S10 **Nantua** Ain, E France 46°10′N 05°34′E
19 Q13 **Nantucket** Nantucket Island, Massachusetts, NE USA 41°15′N 70°05′W
19 Q13 **Nantucket Island** island Massachusetts, NE USA
19 Q13 **Nantucket Sound** sound Massachusetts, NE USA
82 P13 **Nantulo** Cabo Delgado, N Mozambique 12°30′S 39°03′E
189 O12 **Nanuh** Pohnpei, E Micronesia
190 D6 **Nanumaga** var. Nanumanga. atoll NW Tuvalu
Nanumanga see Nanumaga
190 D5 **Nanumea Atoll** atoll NW Tuvalu
59 O19 **Nanuque** Minas Gerais, SE Brazil 17°49′S 40°21′W
171 R10 **Nanusa, Kepulauan** island group N Indonesia
163 U4 **Nanweng He** ~ NE China
160 I10 **Nanxi** Sichuan, C China 28°54′N 104°59′E
161 N10 **Nanxian** var. Nan Xian, Nanzhou. Hunan, S China 29°23′N 112°18′E
Nan Xian see Nanxian
161 N7 **Nanyang** var. Nan-yang. Henan, C China 32°59′N 112°29′E
Nan-yang see Nanyang
161 P6 **Nanyang Hu** ◎ E China
165 P10 **Nan'yō** Yamagata, Honshū, C Japan 38°04′N 140°06′E
81 I18 **Nanyuki** Central, C Kenya 0°01′N 37°05′E
160 M8 **Nanzhang** Hubei, C China 31°47′N 111°48′E
Nanzhou see Nanxian
105 T11 **Nao, Cabo de La** headland E Spain 38°43′N 00°13′E
12 M9 **Naococane, Lac** ◎ Québec, E Canada
153 S14 **Naogaon** Rajshahi, NW Bangladesh 24°49′N 88°59′E
Naokot see Naukot
187 R13 **Naone** Maewo, C Vanuatu 15°03′S 168°06′E
Naoned see Nantes
115 E14 **Náousa** Kentrikí Makedonía, N Greece 40°38′N 22°04′E
35 N8 **Napa** California, W USA 38°15′N 122°17′W
39 O11 **Napaimiut** Alaska, USA 61°32′N 158°46′W
39 N12 **Napakiak** Alaska, USA 60°42′N 161°57′W
122 J7 **Napalkovo** Yamalo-Nenetskiy Avtonomnyy Okrug, N Russian Federation 70°06′N 73°43′E
12 I16 **Napanee** Ontario, SE Canada 44°13′N 76°57′W
39 N12 **Napaskiak** Alaska, USA 60°42′N 161°46′W
167 S5 **Na Phác** Cao Bằng, N Vietnam 22°24′N 105°54′E
184 O11 **Napier** Hawke's Bay, North Island, New Zealand 39°30′S 176°55′E
195 X3 **Napier Mountains** ▲ Antarctica
15 O13 **Napierville** Québec, SE Canada 45°12′N 73°25′W
23 W15 **Naples** Florida, SE USA 26°08′N 81°48′W
25 W5 **Naples** Texas, SW USA 33°12′N 94°40′W
Naples see Napoli
160 I14 **Napo** Guangxi Zhuangzu Zizhiqu, S China 23°21′N 105°47′E
56 C6 **Napo** ◆ province NE Ecuador
29 O6 **Napoleon** North Dakota, N USA 46°30′N 99°46′W
31 R11 **Napoleon** Ohio, N USA 41°23′N 84°07′W
Napoléon-Vendée see la Roche-sur-Yon
22 J9 **Napoleonville** Louisiana, S USA 29°55′N 91°01′W
107 K17 **Napoli** Eng. Naples, Ger. Neapel; anc. Neapolis. Campania, S Italy 40°52′N 14°15′E
107 J18 **Napoli, Golfo di** gulf S Italy
57 F7 **Napo, Río** ~ Ecuador/Peru
191 W9 **Napuka** island Îles Tuamotu, C French Polynesia
142 J3 **Naqadeh** Āzarbāyjān-e Bākhtarī, NW Iran 36°57′N 45°24′E
139 U6 **Naqnah** Diyālá, E Iraq 34°13′N 45°33′E
Nar see Nera
164 J14 **Nara** Nara, Honshū, SW Japan 34°41′N 135°49′E
76 L11 **Nara** Koulikoro, W Mali 15°04′N 07°19′W
149 R14 **Nāra Canal** irrigation canal S Pakistan
182 K11 **Naracoorte** South Australia 37°02′S 140°45′E
183 P8 **Naradhan** New South Wales, SE Australia 33°37′S 146°19′E
Naradhivas see Narathiwat
56 B8 **Naranjal** Guayas, W Ecuador 02°43′S 79°38′W
57 Q19 **Naranjos** Santa Cruz, E Bolivia
41 Q12 **Naranjos** Veracruz-Llave, E Mexico 21°21′N 97°41′W
159 Q6 **Naran Sebstein Bulag** spring NW China
164 B14 **Narao** Nagasaki, Nakadōri-jima, SW Japan 32°40′N 129°03′E
155 J16 **Narasaraopet** Andhra Pradesh, E India 16°16′N 80°06′E
158 J5 **Narat** Xinjiang Uygur Zizhiqu, W China 43°20′N 84°02′E
167 P17 **Narathiwat** var. Naradhivas. Narathiwat, SW Thailand 06°25′N 101°48′E
37 V10 **Nara Visa** New Mexico, SW USA 35°35′N 103°06′W
Nārāyāni see Gandak
Narbada see Narmada
Narbo Martius see Narbonne
103 P16 **Narbonne** anc. Narbo Martius. Aude, S France 43°11′N 03°E
Narborough Island see Fernandina, Isla
104 J2 **Narcea** ~ NW Spain
152 J9 **Narendranagar** Uttarakhand, N India 30°10′N 78°21′E
Nares Abyssal Plain see Nares Plain
64 G11 **Nares Plain** var. Nares Abyssal Plain. undersea feature NW Atlantic Ocean 23°30′N 63°00′W
Nares Stræde see Nares Strait
197 P10 **Nares Strait** Dan. Nares Stræde. strait Canada/Greenland
110 O9 **Narew** ~ E Poland
155 F17 **Nargund** Karnātaka, W India 15°43′N 75°23′E
83 D20 **Narib** Hardap, S Namibia 24°11′S 17°46′E
Narikrik see Knox Atoll
Narin Gol see Omon Gol
54 B13 **Nariño** off. Departmento de Nariño. ◆ province SW Colombia
165 P13 **Narita** Chiba, Honshū, S Japan 35°46′N 140°20′E
165 P13 **Narita** ✈ (Tōkyō) Chiba, Honshū, S Japan 35°45′N 140°23′E
Nariya see An Nu'ayrīyah
162 F5 **Nariyn Gol** ~ Mongolia/Russian Federation
162 J8 **Nariynteel** var. Tsagaan-Ovoo. Övörhangay, C Mongolia 45°57′N 101°25′E
152 J8 **Narkanda** Himāchal Pradesh, NW India 31°14′N 77°27′E
92 L13 **Narkaus** Lappi, NW Finland 66°13′N 26°09′E
154 E11 **Narmada** var. Narbada. ~ C India
152 H11 **Narnaul** var. Nārnaul. Haryāna, N India 28°04′N 76°10′E
107 I14 **Narni** Umbria, C Italy 42°31′N 12°31′E
107 J24 **Naro** Sicilia, Italy, C Mediterranean Sea 37°18′N 13°48′E
Narodichi see Narodychi
125 V7 **Narodnaya, Gora** ▲ NW Russian Federation 65°04′N 60°12′E
117 N3 **Narodychi** Rus. Narodichi. Zhytomyrs'ka Oblast', N Ukraine 51°11′N 29°01′E
126 J4 **Naro-Fominsk** Moskovskaya Oblast', W Russian Federation 55°25′N 36°41′E
81 H19 **Narok** Rift Valley, SW Kenya 01°04′S 35°54′E
104 H2 **Narón** Galicia, NW Spain 43°31′N 08°08′W
183 S11 **Narooma** New South Wales, SE Australia 36°16′S 150°08′E
Narova see Narva
Narovlya see Narowlya
149 W8 **Nārowāl** Punjab, E Pakistan 32°04′N 74°54′E
119 N20 **Narowlya** Rus. Narovlya. Homyel'skaya Voblasts', SE Belarus 51°48′N 29°30′E
93 J17 **Närpes** Fin. Närpiö. Länsi-Suomi, W Finland 62°28′N 21°19′E
Närpiö see Närpes
183 S5 **Narrabri** New South Wales, SE Australia 30°21′S 149°48′E
183 P9 **Narrandera** New South Wales, SE Australia 34°46′S 146°32′E
183 Q4 **Narran Lake** ◎ New South Wales, SE Australia
183 Q4 **Narran River** ~ New South Wales/Queensland, SE Australia
180 J13 **Narrogin** Western Australia 32°53′S 117°17′E
183 Q7 **Narromine** New South Wales, SE Australia 32°16′S 148°15′E
21 R6 **Narrows** Virginia, NE USA 37°19′N 80°48′W
196 M15 **Narsarsuaq** ✈ Kitaa, S Greenland 61°07′N 45°03′W
154 I10 **Narsimhapur** Madhya Pradesh, C India 22°58′N 79°15′E
153 U15 **Narsingdi** var. Narsinghdi. Dhaka, C Bangladesh 23°56′N 90°40′E
Narsinghdi see Narsingdi
154 H9 **Narsinghgarh** Madhya Pradesh, C India 23°42′N 77°08′E
163 Q11 **Nart** Nei Mongol Zizhiqu, N China 42°54′N 115°55′E
Nartës, Gjol i/Nartës, Laguna e see Nartës, Liqeni i
113 J22 **Nartës, Liqeni i** var. Gjol i Nartës, Laguna e Nartës. ◎ SW Albania
115 F17 **Narthákí** ▲ C Greece 39°12′N 22°24′E
127 O15 **Nartkala** Kabardino-Balkarskaya Respublika, SW Russian Federation 43°34′N 43°55′E
118 K3 **Narva** Ida-Virumaa, NE Estonia 59°23′N 28°12′E
118 K4 **Narva** prev. Narova. ~ Estonia/Russian Federation
118 J3 **Narva Bay** Est. Narva Laht, Ger. Narwa-Bucht, Rus. Narvskiy Zaliv. bay Estonia/Russian Federation
Narva Laht see Narva Bay
124 F13 **Narva Reservoir** Est. Narva Veehoidla, Rus. Narvskoye Vodokhranilishche. ◙ Estonia/Russian Federation
Narva Veehoidla see Narva Reservoir
92 H10 **Narvik** Nordland, C Norway 68°26′N 17°24′E
Narvskiy Zaliv see Narva Bay
Narvskoye Vodokhranilishche see Narva Reservoir
Narwa-Bucht see Narva Bay
152 I9 **Narwāna** Haryāna, NW India 29°36′N 76°11′E
125 R4 **Nar'yan-Mar** prev. Beloshchel'ye, Dzerzhinskiy. Nenetskiy Avtonomnyy Okrug, NW Russian Federation 67°38′N 53°E
122 J12 **Narym** Tomskaya Oblast', C Russian Federation 58°59′N 81°20′E
Narymskiy Khrebet see Khrebet Naryn
147 W9 **Naryn** Narynskaya Oblast', C Kyrgyzstan 41°24′N 76°E
147 U8 **Naryn** ~ Kyrgyzstan/Uzbekistan
145 W16 **Narynkol** Kaz. Naryngol. Almaty, SE Kazakhstan 42°45′N 80°12′E
Naryn Oblasty see Narynskaya Oblast'
Narynqol see Narynkol
147 V9 **Narynskaya Oblast'** Kir. Naryn Oblasty. ◆ province C Kyrgyzstan
Naryn Zhotasy see Khrebet Naryn
126 J6 **Naryshkino** Orlovskaya Oblast', W Russian Federation 53°00′N 35°41′E
95 L14 **Nås** Dalarna, C Sweden 60°28′N 14°30′E
10 J11 **Nass** ~ British Columbia, SW Canada
92 G13 **Nasafjellet** Lapp. Násávárre. ▲ C Norway 66°29′N 15°23′E
93 H16 **Nasåker** Västernorrland, C Sweden 63°27′N 16°55′E
44 H2 **Nassau** ● (Bahamas) New Providence, N Bahamas 25°03′N 77°21′W
187 Y14 **Nasau** Koro, C Fiji 17°20′S 179°26′E
190 J13 **Nassau** island N Cook Islands
116 I9 **Năsăud** Ger. Nussdorf, Hung. Naszód. Bistrița-Năsăud, N Romania 47°16′N 24°24′E
Násávárre see Nasafjellet
103 P13 **Nasbinals** Lozère, S France 44°40′N 03°03′E
Na Sceirí see Skerries
Nase see Naze
185 E22 **Naseby** Otago, South Island, New Zealand 45°02′S 170°09′E
143 R10 **Naṣerīyeh** Kermān, C Iran
25 X5 **Nash** Texas, SW USA 33°26′N 94°04′W
154 E13 **Nāshik** prev. Nāsik. Mahārāshtra, W India 20°05′N 73°48′E
56 E7 **Nashiño, Río** ~ Ecuador/Peru
29 W12 **Nashua** Iowa, C USA 42°57′N 92°32′W
33 W7 **Nashua** Montana, NW USA 48°06′N 106°16′W
19 O10 **Nashua** New Hampshire, NE USA 42°45′N 71°26′W
27 S13 **Nashville** Arkansas, C USA 33°57′N 93°50′W
23 U7 **Nashville** Georgia, SE USA 31°12′N 83°15′W
30 L16 **Nashville** Illinois, N USA 38°20′N 89°22′W
31 O14 **Nashville** Indiana, N USA 39°13′N 86°15′W
21 V9 **Nashville** North Carolina, SE USA 35°58′N 78°00′W
20 J8 **Nashville** state capital Tennessee, S USA 36°11′N 86°48′W
20 J9 **Nashville** ✈ Tennessee, S USA 36°06′N 86°44′W
64 H10 **Nashville Seamount** undersea feature NW Atlantic Ocean 30°00′N 57°20′W
112 H9 **Našice** Osijek-Baranja, E Croatia 45°29′N 18°05′E
110 M11 **Nasielsk** Mazowieckie, C Poland 52°33′N 20°46′E
93 K18 **Näsijärvi** ◎ SW Finland
Nāsik see Nāshik
80 G13 **Nasir** Upper Nile, NE South Sudan 08°37′N 33°06′E
148 K15 **Nasīrābād** Baluchistān, SW Pakistan 26°15′N 62°32′E
Nasir, Buhayrat/Nâṣir,Buḥeiret see Nasser, Lake
Nâsiri see Ahvāz
Nasiriya see An Nāṣirīyah
Nás na Ríogh see Naas
107 L23 **Naso** Sicilia, Italy, C Mediterranean Sea 38°07′N 14°46′E
Nasratabad see Zābol
77 V15 **Nassarawa** Nassarawa, C Nigeria 08°33′N 07°42′E
23 W8 **Nassau Sound** sound Florida, SE USA
108 L7 **Nassereith** Tirol, W Austria 47°19′N 10°51′E
80 F5 **Nasser, Lake** var. Buhayrat Nasir, Buḥayrat Nāṣir, Buḥeiret Nâṣir. ◎ Egypt/Sudan
95 L19 **Nässjö** Jönköping, S Sweden 57°39′N 14°40′E
99 K22 **Nassogne** Luxembourg, SE Belgium 50°08′N 05°19′E
12 J6 **Nastapoka Islands** island group Northwest Territories, C Canada
93 M19 **Nastola** Etelä-Suomi, S Finland 60°57′N 25°56′E
171 O4 **Nasugbu** Luzon, N Philippines 14°03′N 120°39′E
94 N11 **Näsviken** Gävleborg, C Sweden 61°46′N 16°55′E
Naszód see Năsăud
83 I17 **Nata** Central, NE Botswana 20°11′S 26°10′E
54 E11 **Natagaima** Tolima, C Colombia 03°38′N 75°07′W
59 Q14 **Natal** state capital Rio Grande do Norte, E Brazil 05°46′S 35°15′W
168 I11 **Natal** Sumatera, N Indonesia 0°32′N 99°07′E
Natal see KwaZulu/Natal
173 L10 **Natal Basin** var. Mozambique Basin. undersea feature W Indian Ocean 30°00′S 40°00′E
25 R12 **Natalia** Texas, SW USA 29°11′N 98°51′W
67 W15 **Natal Valley** undersea feature SW Indian Ocean 31°00′S 33°15′E
Natanya see Netanya
143 O7 **Naṭanz** Eṣfahān, C Iran 33°31′N 51°55′E
13 Q11 **Natashquan** Québec, E Canada 50°10′N 61°50′W
13 Q10 **Natashquan** ~ Newfoundland and Labrador/Québec, E Canada
22 J7 **Natchez** Mississippi, S USA 31°34′N 91°24′W
22 G6 **Natchitoches** Louisiana, S USA 31°45′N 93°05′W
108 E10 **Naters** Valais, S Switzerland 46°22′N 08°00′E
Nathanya see Netanya
92 O3 **Nathorst Land** physical region W Svalbard
186 E9 **National Capital District** ◆ province S Papua New Guinea
35 U17 **National City** California, W USA 32°40′N 117°06′W
184 M10 **National Park** Manawatu-Wanganui, North Island, New Zealand 39°11′S 175°22′E
77 R14 **Natitingou** NW Benin 10°21′N 01°26′E
40 B5 **Natividad, Isla** island NW Mexico
165 Q10 **Natori** Miyagi, Honshū, C Japan 38°12′N 140°51′E
18 C14 **Natrona Heights** Pennsylvania, NE USA 40°37′N 79°42′W
81 H20 **Natron, Lake** ◎ Kenya/Tanzania
Natsrat see Natzrat
166 L7 **Nattalin** Bago, C Burma (Myanmar) 18°25′N 95°34′E
92 J12 **Nattavaara** Lapp. Nahtavárr. Norrbotten, N Sweden 66°45′N 20°58′E
109 S3 **Natternbach** Oberösterreich, N Austria 48°26′N 13°44′E
95 M22 **Nättraby** Blekinge, S Sweden 56°12′N 15°30′E
169 P10 **Natuna Besar, Pulau** island Kepulauan Natuna, W Indonesia
Natuna Islands see Natuna, Kepulauan
169 O9 **Natuna, Kepulauan** var. Natuna Islands. island group W Indonesia
169 N9 **Natuna, Laut** Eng. Natuna Sea. sea W Indonesia
Natuna Sea see Natuna, Laut
21 N6 **Natural Bridge** tourist site Kentucky, C USA
173 V11 **Naturaliste Fracture Zone** tectonic feature E Indian Ocean
174 J10 **Naturaliste Plateau** undersea feature E Indian Ocean
138 G9 **Natzrat** var. Natsrat, Ar. En Nazira, Eng. Nazareth; prev. Nazerat. Northern, N Israel 32°42′N 35°18′E
Nau see Nov
103 O14 **Naucelle** Aveyron, S France 44°10′N 02°19′E
83 D20 **Nauchas** Hardap, C Namibia 23°40′S 16°19′E
108 K9 **Nauders** Tirol, W Austria 46°52′N 10°31′E
Naugard see Nowogard
118 F12 **Naujamiestis** Panevėžys, C Lithuania 55°42′N 24°10′E
118 E10 **Naujoji Akmenė** Šiauliai, NW Lithuania 56°20′N 22°57′E
149 R16 **Naukot** var. Naokot. Sind, SE Pakistan 24°52′N 69°27′E
101 L16 **Naumburg** var. Naumburg an der Saale. Sachsen-Anhalt, C Germany 51°09′N 11°48′E
Naumburg am Queis see Nowogrodziec
Naumburg an der Saale see Naumburg
191 W15 **Naunau** ancient monument Easter Island, Chile, E Pacific Ocean
138 G10 **Nā'ūr** 'Ammān, W Jordan 31°52′N 35°50′E
189 Q8 **Nauru** off. Republic of Nauru; prev. Pleasant Island. ◆ republic W Pacific Ocean
175 P5 **Nauru** island W Pacific Ocean
189 Q9 **Nauru International** ✈ S Nauru
Nauru, Republic of see Nauru
Nausari see Navsāri
19 Q12 **Nauset Beach** beach Massachusetts, NE USA
Naushahra see Nowshera
149 P14 **Naushahro Fīroz** Sind, SE Pakistan 26°51′N 68°11′E
Naushara see Nowshera
187 X14 **Nausori** Viti Levu, W Fiji 18°01′S 178°31′E
56 F9 **Nauta** Loreto, N Peru 04°31′S 73°36′W
153 O12 **Nautanwa** Uttar Pradesh, N India 27°26′N 83°25′E
41 R13 **Nautla** Veracruz-Llave, E Mexico 20°15′N 96°45′W
Nauzad see Now Zād
41 N6 **Nava** Coahuila, NE Mexico 28°28′N 100°45′W
Navabad see Navobod
104 L6 **Nava del Rey** Castilla y León, N Spain 41°19′N 05°04′W
153 S15 **Navadwīp** prev. Nabadwip. West Bengal, NE India 23°24′N 88°23′E
104 M9 **Navahermosa** Castilla-La Mancha, C Spain 39°39′N 04°25′W
119 I16 **Navahrudak** Pol. Nowogródek, Rus. Novogrudok. Hrodzyenskaya Voblasts', W Belarus 53°36′N 25°50′E
119 I16 **Navahrudskaye Wzvyshsha** ▲ W Belarus
36 M8 **Navajo Mount** ▲ Utah, W USA 37°00′N 110°52′W
37 Q9 **Navajo Reservoir** ◙ New Mexico, SW USA
104 K9 **Navalmoral de la Mata** Extremadura, W Spain 39°54′N 05°33′W
104 K10 **Navalvillar de Pelea** Extremadura, W Spain 39°05′N 05°27′W
97 F17 **Navan** Ir. An Uaimh. E Ireland 53°39′N 06°41′W
Navanagar see Jāmnagar
118 L12 **Navapolatsk** Rus. Novopolotsk. Vitsyebskaya Voblasts', N Belarus 55°34′N 28°35′E
149 P6 **Nāvar, Dasht-e** Pash. Dasht-i-Nawar. desert C Afghanistan
123 W6 **Navarin, Mys** headland NE Russian Federation 62°18′N 179°06′E
63 J25 **Navarino, Isla** island S Chile
105 Q4 **Navarra** Eng./Fr. Navarre. ◆ autonomous community N Spain
Navarre see Navarra
105 P4 **Navarrete** La Rioja, N Spain 42°26′N 02°34′W
61 C20 **Navarro** Buenos Aires, E Argentina 35°00′S 59°15′W
105 O12 **Navas de San Juan** Andalucía, S Spain 38°11′N 03°19′W
25 V10 **Navasota** Texas, SW USA 30°23′N 96°05′W
25 U9 **Navasota River** ~ Texas, SW USA
44 I9 **Navassa Island** ◇ US unincorporated territory C West Indies
119 L19 **Navasyolki** Rus. Novosëlki. Homyel'skaya Voblasts', SE Belarus 52°24′N 28°33′E
119 H17 **Navayel'nya** Pol. Nowojelnia, Rus. Novoyel'nya. Hrodzyenskaya Voblasts', W Belarus 53°28′N 25°35′E
171 Y13 **Naver** Papua, E Indonesia 03°27′S 139°45′E
118 H5 **Navesti** ~ C Estonia
104 J2 **Navia** Asturias, N Spain 43°33′N 06°43′W
104 J2 **Navia** ~ NW Spain
59 I21 **Naviraí** Mato Grosso do Sul, SW Brazil 23°01′S 54°09′W
126 I6 **Navlya** Bryanskaya Oblast', W Russian Federation 52°47′N 34°28′E
187 X13 **Navoalevu** Vanua Levu, N Fiji 16°22′S 179°28′E
147 R12 **Navobod** Rus. Navabad, Novabad. C Tajikistan 39°00′N 70°06′E
147 P13 **Navobod** Rus. Navabad. W Tajikistan 38°37′N 68°42′E
Navoi see Navoiy
146 M11 **Navoiy** Rus. Navoi. Navoiy Viloyati, C Uzbekistan 40°05′N 65°23′E
Navoiyskaya Oblast' see Navoiy Viloyati
146 K8 **Navoiy Viloyati** Rus. Navoiyskaya Oblast'. ◆ province N Uzbekistan
40 G7 **Navojoa** Sonora, NW Mexico 27°04′N 109°28′W
Navolat see Navolato
40 H9 **Navolato** var. Navolat. Sinaloa, C Mexico 24°46′N 107°42′W
187 Q13 **Navonda** Ambae, C Vanuatu 15°21′S 167°58′E
Návpaktos see Náfpaktos
Návplion see Náfplio
77 P14 **Navrongo** N Ghana 10°51′N 01°03′W
154 D12 **Navsāri** var. Nausari. Gujarāt, W India 20°55′N 72°55′E
187 X15 **Navua** Viti Levu, W Fiji 18°15′S 178°10′E
138 H8 **Nawá** Dar'ā, S Syria 32°53′N 36°03′E
Nawabashah see Nawābshāh
153 S14 **Nawabganj** Rajshahi, NW Bangladesh 24°35′N 88°21′E
153 S14 **Nawābganj** Uttar Pradesh, N India 26°52′N 82°09′E
149 Q15 **Nawābshāh** var. Nawabashah. Sind, S Pakistan 26°15′N 68°26′E
153 P14 **Nawāda** Bihār, N India 24°54′N 85°33′E
152 H11 **Nawalgarh** Rājasthān, N India 27°48′N 75°21′E
Nawāl, Sabkhat an see Noual, Sebkhet en
Nawar, Dasht-i- see Nāvar, Dasht-e
167 N4 **Nawnghkio** var. Nawngkio. Shan State, C Burma (Myanmar) 22°17′N 96°50′E
Nawngkio see Nawnghkio
137 U13 **Naxçıvan** Rus. Nakhichevan'. SW Azerbaijan 39°14′N 45°24′E
160 I10 **Naxi** Sichuan, C China 28°50′N 105°20′E
115 K21 **Náxos** var. Naxos. Náxos, Kykládes, Greece, Aegean Sea 37°07′N 25°24′E
115 K21 **Náxos** island Kykládes, Greece, Aegean Sea
40 J11 **Nayarit** ◆ state C Mexico
187 Y14 **Nayau** island Lau Group, E Fiji
143 S8 **Nāy Band** Yazd, E Iran 32°26′N 57°30′E
165 T2 **Nayoro** Hokkaidō, NE Japan 44°22′N 142°27′E
166 M7 **Nay Pyi Taw** ● (Burma) C Burma (Myanmar) 19°45′N 96°06′E
104 F9 **Nazaré** var. Nazare. Leiria, C Portugal 39°36′N 09°04′W
Nazare see Nazaré
24 M4 **Nazareth** Texas, SW USA 34°32′N 102°06′W
Nazareth see Natzrat
173 O8 **Nazareth Bank** undersea feature W Indian Ocean
40 K9 **Nazas** Durango, C Mexico 25°15′N 104°06′W
57 F16 **Nazca** Ica, S Peru 14°53′S 74°54′W
0 L17 **Nazca Plate** tectonic feature
193 U9 **Nazca Ridge** undersea feature E Pacific Ocean 22°00′S 82°00′W
165 V15 **Naze** var. Nase. Kagoshima, Amami-ōshima, SW Japan 28°21′N 129°30′E
Nazerat see Natzrat
137 R14 **Nazik Gölü** ◎ E Turkey
136 C15 **Nazilli** Aydın, SW Turkey 37°55′N 28°20′E
137 P14 **Nazımiye** Tunceli, E Turkey 39°12′N 39°51′E
Nazinon see Red Volta
10 L15 **Nazko** British Columbia, SW Canada 52°57′N 123°44′W
127 O16 **Nazran'** Respublika Ingushetiya, SW Russian Federation 43°14′N 44°47′E
80 J13 **Nazrēt** var. Adama, Hadama. Oromīya, C Ethiopia 08°31′N 39°20′E
Nazwāh see Nizwá
82 J13 **Nchanga** Copperbelt, C Zambia 12°30′S 27°53′E
82 J11 **Nchelenge** Luapula, N Zambia 09°20′S 28°50′E
Ncheu see Ntcheu
83 J25 **Nciba** Eng. Great Kei; prev. Groot-Kei. ~ S South Africa
Ndaghamcha, Sebkra de see Te-n-Dghâmcha, Sebkhet
81 G21 **Ndala** Tabora, C Tanzania 04°45′S 33°15′E
82 B11 **N'Dalatando** Port. Salazar, Vila Salazar. Cuanza Norte, NW Angola 09°19′S 14°48′E
77 S14 **Ndali** C Benin 09°50′N 02°46′E
81 E18 **Ndeke** SW Uganda 0°11′S 30°04′E
78 J13 **Ndélé** Bamingui-Bangoran, N Central African Republic 08°24′N 20°41′E
79 E19 **Ndendé** Ngounié, S Gabon 02°21′S 11°20′E
79 E20 **Ndindi** Nyanga, S Gabon 03°47′S 11°06′E
78 G11 **Ndjamena** var. N'Djamena; prev. Fort-Lamy. ● (Chad) Chari-Baguirmi, W Chad 12°08′N 15°02′E
78 G11 **Ndjamena** ✈ Chari-Baguirmi, W Chad 12°09′N 15°00′E
N'Djamena see Ndjamena
79 D18 **Ndjolé** Moyen-Ogooué, W Gabon 0°07′S 10°45′E
82 J13 **Ndola** Copperbelt, C Zambia 12°59′S 28°35′E
Ndrhamcha, Sebkha de see Te-n-Dghâmcha, Sebkhet
79 L15 **Ndu** Orientale, N Dem. Rep. Congo 04°36′N 22°49′E
81 H21 **Nduguti** Singida, C Tanzania 04°19′S 34°40′E
186 M9 **Nduindui** Guadalcanal, C Solomon Islands 09°46′S 159°54′E
Nduke see Kolombangara
Ndzouani see Nzwani
115 F16 **Néa Anchíalos** var. Nea Anhialos, Néa Ankhíalos. Thessalía, C Greece 39°16′N 22°49′E
Nea Anhialos/Néa Ankhíalos see Néa Anchíalos
115 H18 **Néa Artáki** Évvoia, C Greece 38°31′N 23°39′E
97 F15 **Neagh, Lough** ◎ E Northern Ireland, United Kingdom
32 F7 **Neah Bay** Washington, NW USA 48°21′N 124°39′W
115 J22 **Nea Kaméni** island Kykládes, Greece, Aegean Sea
182 O8 **Neale, Lake** ◎ Northern Territory, C Australia
182 G3 **Neales River** seasonal river South Australia
115 G14 **Néa Moudanía** var. Néa Moudhaniá. Kentrikí Makedonía, N Greece 40°14′N 23°17′E
Néa Moudhaniá see Néa Moudanía
116 K10 **Neamț** ◆ county NE Romania
Neapel see Napoli
115 D14 **Neápoli** prev. Neápolis. Dytikí Makedonía, N Greece 40°19′N 21°23′E
115 K25 **Neápoli** Kríti, Greece, E Mediterranean Sea 35°15′N 25°37′E
115 G22 **Neápoli** Pelopónnisos, S Greece 36°29′N 23°05′E
Neápolis see Neápoli, Greece
Neapolis see Napoli, Italy
Neapolis see Nablus, West Bank
38 D16 **Near Islands** island group Aleutian Islands, Alaska, USA
97 J21 **Neath** S Wales, United Kingdom 51°40′N 03°48′W
114 H13 **Néa Zíchni** var. Néa Zíkhni; prev. Néa Zíkhna. Kentrikí Makedonía, NE Greece 41°02′N 23°50′E
Néa Zíkhna/Néa Zíkhni see Néa Zíchni
42 C5 **Nebaj** Quiché, W Guatemala 15°25′N 91°05′W
77 P13 **Nebbou** S Burkina 11°22′N 01°49′W
Nebitdag see Balkanabat
54 M13 **Neblina, Pico da** ▲ NW Brazil 0°49′N 66°31′W
124 I13 **Nebolchi** Novgorodskaya Oblast', W Russian Federation 59°08′N 33°19′E
36 L4 **Nebo, Mount** ▲ Utah, W USA 39°47′N 111°46′W
28 L14 **Nebraska** off. State of Nebraska, also known as Blackwater State, Cornhusker State, Tree Planters State. ◆ state C USA
29 S16 **Nebraska City** Nebraska, C USA 40°38′N 95°52′W
107 K23 **Nebrodi, Monti** var. Monti Caronie. ▲ Sicilia, Italy, C Mediterranean Sea
10 L14 **Nechako** ~ British Columbia, SW Canada
29 Q2 **Neche** North Dakota, N USA 48°57′N 97°33′W
25 V8 **Neches** Texas, SW USA 31°51′N 95°28′W
25 W8 **Neches River** ~ Texas, SW USA
101 H20 **Neckar** ~ SW Germany
101 H20 **Neckarsulm** Baden-Württemberg, SW Germany 49°12′N 09°13′E
192 L5 **Necker Island** island C British Virgin Islands
175 U3 **Necker Ridge** undersea feature N Pacific Ocean
61 D23 **Necochea** Buenos Aires, E Argentina 38°34′S 58°42′W
104 H2 **Neda** Galicia, NW Spain 43°29′N 08°09′W
115 E20 **Néda** var. Nédas. ~ S Greece
Nédas see Néda
114 J12 **Nedelino** Smolyan, S Bulgaria 41°27′N 25°05′E
25 Y11 **Nederland** Texas, SW USA 29°58′N 93°59′W
Nederland see Netherlands
98 K12 **Neder Rijn** Eng. Lower Rhine. ~ C Netherlands
99 L16 **Nederweert** Limburg, SE Netherlands 51°17′N 05°45′E
95 G16 **Nedre Tokke** ◎ S Norway
Nedrigaylov see Nedryhayliv
117 S3 **Nedryhayliv** Rus. Nedrigaylov. Sums'ka Oblast', NE Ukraine 50°51′N 33°54′E
98 O11 **Neede** Gelderland, E Netherlands 52°08′N 06°36′E
33 T13 **Needle Mountain** ▲ Wyoming, C USA 44°03′N 109°33′W
35 Y14 **Needles** California, W USA 34°50′N 114°37′W
97 M24 **Needles, The** rocks S England, United Kingdom
62 O7 **Ñeembucú** off. Departamento de Ñeembucú. ◆ department SW Paraguay
Ñeembucú, Departamento de see Ñeembucú
30 M7 **Neenah** Wisconsin, N USA 44°09′N 88°26′W
11 W16 **Neepawa** Manitoba, S Canada 50°14′N 99°29′W
99 K16 **Neerpelt** Limburg, NE Belgium 51°13′N 05°26′E
74 M6 **Nefta** ✈ W Tunisia 34°03′N 08°05′E
126 L15 **Neftegorsk** Krasnodarskiy Kray, SW Russian Federation 44°21′N 39°40′E
127 U3 **Neftekamsk** Respublika Bashkortostan, W Russian Federation 56°07′N 54°13′E
127 O14 **Neftekumsk** Stavropol'skiy Kray, SW Russian Federation 44°45′N 45°00′E
Neftezavodsk see Seýdi
82 C10 **Negage** var. N'Gage. Uíge, NW Angola 07°47′S 15°27′E
Negapatam/Negapattinam see Nāgappattinam
169 T17 **Negara** Bali, Indonesia 08°21′S 114°35′E
169 T13 **Negara** Borneo, C Indonesia 02°40′S 115°05′E
Negara Brunei Darussalam see Brunei
31 N4 **Negaunee** Michigan, N USA 46°30′N 87°36′W
81 J15 **Negēlē** var. Negelli, It. Neghelli. Oromīya, C Ethiopia 05°13′N 39°43′E
Negelli see Negēlē
Negeri Pahang Darul Makmur see Pahang
Negeri Selangor Darul Ehsan see Selangor
168 K9 **Negeri Sembilan** var. Negri Sembilan. ◆ state Peninsular Malaysia
92 P3 **Negerpynten** headland S Svalbard 77°15′N 22°40′E
Negev see HaNegev
Neghelli see Negēlē
116 I12 **Negoiu** var. Negoiul. ▲ S Romania 45°34′N 24°34′E
Negoiul see Negoiu
82 P13 **Negomane** var. Negomano. Cabo Delgado, N Mozambique 11°22′S 38°32′E
Negomano see Negomane
155 J25 **Negombo** Western Province, SW Sri Lanka 07°13′N 79°51′E
191 W11 **Negonego** prev. Nengonengo. atoll Îles Tuamotu, C French Polynesia
Negoreloye see Nyeharelaye
112 P12 **Negotin** Serbia, E Serbia 44°14′N 22°31′E
113 P19 **Negotino** C Macedonia 41°29′N 22°04′E
56 A10 **Negra, Punto** headland NW Peru 06°03′S 81°08′W
104 G3 **Negreira** Galicia, NW Spain 42°54′N 08°46′W
116 L10 **Negrești** Vaslui, E Romania 46°50′N 27°28′E
Negrești see Negrești-Oaș
116 H8 **Negrești-Oaș** Hung. Avasfelsőfalu; prev. Negrești. Satu Mare, NE Romania 47°56′N 23°22′E
44 H12 **Negril** W Jamaica 18°16′N 78°21′W
Negri Sembilan see Negeri Sembilan
63 K15 **Negro, Río** ~ E Argentina
62 N7 **Negro, Río** ~ NE Argentina
57 N17 **Negro, Río** ~ E Bolivia
48 F6 **Negro, Río** ~ N South America
61 E18 **Negro, Río** ~ Brazil/Uruguay
62 O5 **Negro, Río** ~ C Paraguay
Negro, Río see Chixoy, Río, Guatemala/Mexico
Negro, Río see Sico Tinto, Río, Honduras
171 P6 **Negros** island C Philippines
116 M15 **Negru Vodă** Constanța, SE Romania 43°49′N 28°12′E
13 P13 **Neguac** New Brunswick, SE Canada 47°16′N 65°04′W
14 B7 **Negwazu, Lake** ◎ Ontario, S Canada
Négyfalu see Săcele
32 F10 **Nehalem** Oregon, NW USA 45°42′N 123°55′W
32 F10 **Nehalem River** ~ Oregon, NW USA
Nehavend see Nahāvand
143 V9 **Nehbandān** Khorāsān, E Iran 31°00′N 60°00′E
163 V6 **Nehe** Heilongjiang, NE China 48°28′N 124°52′E
193 Y14 **Neiafu** 'Uta Vava'u, N Tonga 18°36′S 173°58′W
45 N9 **Neiba** var. Neyba. SW Dominican Republic 18°31′N 71°25′W
Néid, Carn Uí see Mizen Head
92 M9 **Neiden** Finnmark, N Norway 69°41′N 29°23′E
Neidín see Kenmare
Néifinn see Nephin
103 S10 **Neige, Crêt de la** ▲ E France 46°18′N 05°58′E
173 O16 **Neiges, Piton des** ▲ C Réunion 21°05′S 55°28′E
15 R9 **Neiges, Rivière des** ~ Québec, SE Canada
160 I10 **Neijiang** Sichuan, C China 29°32′N 105°03′E
30 K6 **Neillsville** Wisconsin, N USA 44°34′N 90°36′W
Nei Mongol Zizhiqu/Nei Mongol see Nei Mongol Zizhiqu

◆ Country ● Country Capital ◇ Dependent Territory ○ Dependent Territory Capital ◆ Administrative Regions ✈ International Airport ▲ Mountain ▲ Mountain Range Volcano ~ River ◎ Lake ◙ Reservoir

163 Q10 Nei Mongol Gaoyuan plateau NE China
163 O12 Nei Mongol Zizhiqu var. Nei Mongol, Eng. Inner Mongolia, Inner Mongolian Autonomous Region; prev. Nei Monggol Zizhiqu. ◆ autonomous region N China
161 O4 Neiqiu Hebei, E China 37°22′N 114°34′E
Neiriz see Neyrīz
101 Q16 Neisse Cz. Lužická Nisa Pol. Nisa, Ger. Lausitzer Neisse, Nysa Łużycka. ≈ C Europe
Neisse see Nysa
54 E11 Neiva Huila, S Colombia 02°58′N 75°15′W
160 M7 Neixiang Henan, C China 33°08′N 111°50′E
Nejafabad see Najafābād
11 V9 Nejanilini Lake ◎ Manitoba, C Canada
Nejd see Najd
80 I13 Nek'emtē var. Lakemti, Nakamti. Oromīya, C Ethiopia 09°06′N 36°31′E
126 M9 Nekhayevskaya Volgogradskaya Oblast', SW Russian Federation 50°25′N 41°44′E
30 K7 Nekoosa Wisconsin, N USA 44°19′N 89°54′W
Neksø Bornholm see Nexø
104 H7 Nelas Viseu, N Portugal 40°32′N 07°52′W
124 H16 Nelidovo Tverskaya Oblast', W Russian Federation 56°13′N 32°45′E
29 P13 Neligh Nebraska, C USA 42°07′N 98°01′W
123 R11 Nel'kan Khabarovskiy Kray, E Russian Federation 57°44′N 136°09′E
92 M10 Nellim var. Nellimö, Lapp. Njellim. Lappi, N Finland 68°49′N 28°18′E
Nellimö see Nellim
155 J18 Nellore Andhra Pradesh, E India 14°29′N 80°E
61 B17 Nelson Santa Fe, C Argentina 31°16′S 60°45′W
11 O17 Nelson British Columbia, SW Canada 49°29′N 117°17′W
185 I14 Nelson Nelson, South Island, New Zealand 41°17′S 173°17′E
97 L17 Nelson NW England, United Kingdom 53°51′N 02°13′W
29 P17 Nelson Nebraska, C USA 40°12′N 98°04′W
185 J14 Nelson ◆ unitary authority South Island, New Zealand
11 X12 Nelson ≈ Manitoba, C Canada
183 U8 Nelson Bay New South Wales, SE Australia 32°48′S 152°10′E
182 K13 Nelson, Cape headland Victoria, SE Australia 38°25′S 141°33′E
63 G23 Nelson, Estrecho strait SE Pacific Ocean
11 W12 Nelson House Manitoba, C Canada 55°49′N 98°51′W
30 J4 Nelson Lake ◎ Wisconsin, N USA
31 T14 Nelsonville Ohio, N USA 39°27′N 82°13′W
27 S2 Nelsoon River ≈ Iowa/Missouri, C USA
83 K21 Nelspruit Mpumalanga, NE South Africa 25°28′S 30°58′E
76 L10 Néma Hodh ech Chargui, SE Mauritania 16°32′N 07°12′W
118 D13 Neman Ger. Ragnit. Kaliningradskaya Oblast', W Russian Federation 55°01′N 22°00′E
84 I9 Neman Bel. Nyoman, Ger. Memel, Lith. Nemunas, Pol. Niemen. ≈ NE Europe
Nemausus see Nîmes
115 F19 Neméa Pelopónnisos, S Greece 37°49′N 22°40′E
Německý Brod see Havlíčkův Brod
14 D7 Nemegosenda ≈ Ontario, S Canada
14 D8 Nemegosenda Lake ◎ Ontario, S Canada
119 H14 Nemencinė Vilnius, SE Lithuania 54°50′N 25°29′E
Nemetocenna see Arras
Nemirov see Nemyriv
103 O6 Nemours Seine-et-Marne, N France 48°16′N 02°41′E
Nemunas see Neman
165 W4 Nemuro Hokkaidō, NE Japan 43°20′N 145°35′E
165 W4 Nemuro-hantō peninsula Hokkaidō, NE Japan
165 W3 Nemuro-kaikyō strait Japan/Russian Federation
165 W4 Nemuro-wan bay N Japan
116 H5 Nemyriv Rus. Nemirov. L'vivs'ka Oblast', NW Ukraine 50°08′N 23°28′E
117 N7 Nemyriv Rus. Nemirov. Vinnyts'ka Oblast', C Ukraine 48°58′N 28°50′E
97 D19 Nenagh Ir. An tAonach. Tipperary, C Ireland 52°52′N 08°12′W
39 R9 Nenana Alaska, USA 64°33′N 149°05′W
39 R9 Nenana River ≈ Alaska, USA
187 P10 Nendö var. Swallow Island. island Santa Cruz Islands, E Solomon Islands
97 O19 Nene ≈ E England, United Kingdom
125 R4 Nenetskiy Avtonomnyy Okrug ◆ autonomous district Arkhangel'skaya Oblast', NW Russian Federation
Nengonengo see Negonego
163 V6 Nenjiang Heilongjiang, NE China 49°11′N 125°18′E
163 U6 Nen Jiang var. Nonni. ≈ NE China
189 P16 Neoch atoll Caroline Islands, C Micronesia
115 D18 Neochóri Dytikí Elláda, C Greece 38°23′N 21°14′E
27 Q7 Neodesha Kansas, C USA 37°25′N 95°40′W
29 S14 Neola Iowa, C USA 41°27′N 95°40′W
115 E16 Néo Monastíri var. Néon Monastiri. Thessalía, C Greece 39°22′N 21°55′E
Néon Karlovasi/Néon Karlovásion see Karlovási
Néon Monastiri see Néo Monastíri
27 R8 Neosho Missouri, C USA 36°53′N 94°24′W
27 Q7 Neosho River ≈ Kansas/Oklahoma, C USA
123 N12 Nepa ≈ C Russian Federation
153 N10 Nepal off. Nepal. ◆ monarchy S Asia
Nepal see Nepal
152 M11 Nepalganj Mid Western, SW Nepal 28°04′N 81°37′E
14 L13 Nepean Ontario, SE Canada 45°19′N 75°54′W
36 L4 Nephi Utah, W USA 39°43′N 111°50′W
97 B16 Nephin Ir. Néifinn. ▲ W Ireland 54°00′N 09°21′W
67 T9 Nepoko ≈ NE Dem. Rep. Congo
18 K15 Neptune New Jersey, NE USA 40°10′N 74°03′W
182 G10 Neptune Islands island group South Australia
107 I14 Nera anc. Nar. ≈ C Italy
102 L14 Nérac Lot-et-Garonne, SW France 44°08′N 00°21′E
111 D16 Neratovice Ger. Neratowitz. Středocesky Kraj, C Czech Republic 50°16′N 14°31′E
Neratowitz see Neratovice
123 O13 Nercha ≈ S Russian Federation
123 O13 Nerchinsk Zabaykal'skiy Kray, S Russian Federation 52°01′N 116°25′E
123 P14 Nerchinskiy Zavod Zabaykal'skiy Kray, S Russian Federation 51°13′N 119°25′E
124 M15 Nerekhta Kostromskaya Oblast', NW Russian Federation 57°27′N 40°33′E
118 H10 Nereta S Latvia 56°12′N 25°18′E
106 K13 Nereto Abruzzo, C Italy 42°49′N 13°50′E
113 H15 Neretva ≈ Bosnia and Herzegovina/Croatia
115 C17 Nerikós ruins Lefkáda, Iónia Nísiá, Greece, C Mediterranean Sea
83 F15 Neriquinha Cuando Cubango, SE Angola 15°44′S 21°34′E
118 I13 Neris Bel. Viliya, Pol. Wilia; prev. Pol. Wilja. ≈ Belarus/Lithuania
Neris see Viliya
105 N15 Nerja Andalucía, S Spain 36°45′N 03°35′W
124 L16 Nerl' ≈ W Russian Federation
105 P12 Nerpio Castilla-La Mancha, C Spain 38°08′N 02°18′W
104 J13 Nerva Andalucía, S Spain 37°40′N 06°31′W
98 L4 Nes Fryslân, N Netherlands 53°28′N 05°46′E
94 G13 Nesbyen Buskerud, S Norway 60°36′N 09°35′E
114 M9 Nesebŭr Burgas, E Bulgaria 42°40′N 27°43′E
92 L2 Neskaupstadhur Austurland, E Iceland 65°08′N 13°45′W
92 F13 Nesna Nordland, C Norway 66°11′N 12°54′E
26 K5 Ness City Kansas, C USA 38°27′N 99°54′W
Nesselsdorf see Kopřivnice
108 H7 Nesslau Sankt Gallen, NE Switzerland 47°13′N 09°12′E
96 I9 Ness, Loch ◎ N Scotland, United Kingdom
Nesterov see Zhovkva
114 I12 Néstos Bul. Mesta, Turk. Kara Su. ≈ Bulgaria/Greece see also Mesta
Néstos see Mesta
95 C14 Nesttun Hordaland, S Norway 60°19′N 05°16′E
Nesvizh see Nyasvizh
138 F9 Netanya var. Natanya, Nathanya. Central, C Israel 32°20′N 34°51′E
98 I9 Netherlands off. Kingdom of the Netherlands, var. Holland, Dut. Koninkrijk der Nederlanden, Nederland. ◆ monarchy NW Europe
Netherlands East Indies see Indonesia
Netherlands Guiana see Surinam
Netherlands, Kingdom of the see Netherlands
Netherlands New Guinea see Papua
116 L4 Netishyn Khmel'nyts'ka Oblast', W Ukraine 50°20′N 26°38′E
138 E11 Netivot Southern, S Israel 31°26′N 34°36′E
107 O21 Neto ≈ S Italy
9 Q6 Nettilling Lake ◎ Baffin Island, Nunavut, N Canada
29 V3 Nett Lake ◎ Minnesota, N USA
107 I16 Nettuno Lazio, C Italy 41°27′N 12°40′E
Netum see Noto
41 U16 Netzahualcóyotl, Presa ▣ SE Mexico
Netze see Noteć
Neu Amerika see Puławy
Neubetsche see Novi Bečej
Neubidschow see Nový Bydžov
Neubistritz see Nová Bystřice
100 N9 Neubrandenburg Mecklenburg-Vorpommern, NE Germany 53°33′N 13°16′E
101 K22 Neuburg an der Donau Bayern, S Germany 48°43′N 11°10′E
108 C8 Neuchâtel Ger. Neuenburg. Neuchâtel, W Switzerland 46°59′N 06°55′E
108 C8 Neuchâtel Ger. Neuenburg. ◆ canton W Switzerland
108 C8 Neuchâtel, Lac de Ger. Neuenburger See. ◎ W Switzerland
Neudorf see Spišská Nová Ves
100 L10 Neue Elde canal N Germany
Neuenburg see Neuchâtel
Neuenburg an der Elbe see Nymburk
Neuenburger See see Neuchâtel, Lac de
108 F7 Neuenhof Aargau, N Switzerland 47°27′N 08°17′E
100 H11 Neuenland ✈ (Bremen) Bremen, NW Germany 53°03′N 08°46′E
Neuenstadt see La Neuveville
101 C18 Neuerburg Rheinland-Pfalz, W Germany 50°01′N 06°13′E
99 K24 Neufchâteau Luxembourg, SE Belgium 49°50′N 05°26′E
103 S6 Neufchâteau Vosges, NE France 48°21′N 05°42′E
102 M3 Neufchâtel-en-Bray Seine-Maritime, N France 49°44′N 01°26′E
109 S3 Neufelden Oberösterreich, N Austria 48°27′N 14°01′E
Neugradisk see Nova Gradiška
Neuhaus see Jindřichův Hradec
Neuhäusel see Nové Zámky
108 G6 Neuhausen var. Neuhausen am Rheinfall. Schaffhausen, N Switzerland 47°24′N 08°37′E
Neuhausen am Rheinfall see Neuhausen
101 I17 Neuhof Hessen, C Germany 50°26′N 09°34′E
Neuhof see Zgierz
Neukuhren see Pionerskiy
Neu-Langenburg see Tukuyu
109 W4 Neulengbach Niederösterreich, NE Austria 48°10′N 15°53′E
113 G15 Neum Federacija Bosna I Hercegovina, S Bosnia and Herzegovina 42°57′N 17°33′E
Neumark see Nowy Targ, Małopolskie, Poland
Neumark see Nowe Miasto Lubawskie, Warmińsko-Mazurskie, Poland
Neumarkt see Neumarkt im Hausruckkreis, Oberösterreich, Austria
Neumarkt see Neumarkt am Wallersee, Salzburg, Austria
Neumarkt see Środa Śląska, Dolnośląskie, Poland
Neumarkt see Târgu Secuiesc, Covasna, Romania
Neumarkt see Târgu Mureş
109 Q5 Neumarkt am Wallersee var. Neumarkt. Salzburg, NW Austria 47°55′N 13°16′E
109 R4 Neumarkt im Hausruckkreis var. Neumarkt. Oberösterreich, N Austria 48°16′N 13°40′E
101 L20 Neumarkt in der Oberpfalz Bayern, SE Germany 49°16′N 11°28′E
Neumarktl see Tržič
Neumoldowa see Moldova Nouă
100 J8 Neumünster Schleswig-Holstein, N Germany 54°04′N 09°59′E
109 X5 Neunkirchen var. Neunkirchen am Steinfeld. Niederösterreich, E Austria 47°44′N 16°05′E
101 E20 Neunkirchen Saarland, SW Germany 49°21′N 07°11′E
Neunkirchen am Steinfeld see Neunkirchen
Neuoderberg see Bohumín
63 I15 Neuquén Neuquén, SE Argentina 39°03′S 68°36′W
63 H14 Neuquén off. Provincia de Neuquén. ◆ province W Argentina
Neuquén, Provincia de see Neuquén
63 H14 Neuquén, Río ≈ W Argentina
Neurode see Nowa Ruda
100 N11 Neuruppin Brandenburg, NE Germany 52°56′N 12°49′E
Neusalz an der Oder see Nowa Sól
Neu Sandec see Nowy Sącz
101 K22 Neusäss Bayern, S Germany 48°24′N 10°49′E
Neusatz see Novi Sad
Neuschliss see Gherla
21 N8 Neuse River ≈ North Carolina, SE USA
109 Z5 Neusiedl am See Burgenland, E Austria 47°58′N 16°51′E
111 G22 Neusiedler See Hung. Fertő. ◎ Austria/Hungary
Neusohl see Banská Bystrica
101 D15 Neuss anc. Novaesium, Novesium. Nordrhein-Westfalen, W Germany 51°12′N 06°42′E
Neuss see Nyon
Neustadt see Neustadt bei Coburg, Bayern, Germany
Neustadt see Neustadt an der Aisch, Bayern, Germany
Neustadt see Prudnik, Opole, Poland
Neustadt see Baia Mare, Maramureş, Romania
100 I12 Neustadt am Rübenberge Niedersachsen, N Germany 52°30′N 09°28′E
101 J19 Neustadt an der Aisch var. Neustadt. Bayern, C Germany 49°34′N 10°36′E
Neustadt an der Haardt see Neustadt an der Weinstrasse
101 F20 Neustadt an der Weinstrasse prev. Neustadt an der Haardt, hist. Niewenstat; anc. Nova Civitas. Rheinland-Pfalz, SW Germany 49°21′N 08°09′E
101 K18 Neustadt bei Coburg var. Neustadt. Bayern, C Germany 50°19′N 11°06′E
Neustadt bei Pinne see Lwówek
Neustadt in Oberschlesien see Prudnik
Neustadtl see Novo mesto
Neustadtl in Mähren see Nové Město na Moravě
Neustettin see Szczecinek
108 M8 Neustift im Stubaital var. Stubaital. Tirol, W Austria 47°07′N 11°26′E
100 N10 Neustrelitz Mecklenburg-Vorpommern, NE Germany 53°22′N 13°05′E
Neutitschein see Nový Jičín
Neutra see Nitra
101 J22 Neu-Ulm Bayern, S Germany 48°23′N 10°02′E
Neuveville see La Neuveville
103 N12 Neuvic Corrèze, C France 45°23′N 02°16′E
Neuwarp see Nowe Warpno
100 G9 Neuwerk island NW Germany
101 E17 Neuwied Rheinland-Pfalz, W Germany 50°26′N 07°28′E
Neuzen see Terneuzen
124 H12 Neva ≈ NW Russian Federation
29 V14 Nevada Iowa, C USA 42°01′N 93°27′W
27 R6 Nevada Missouri, C USA 37°51′N 94°22′W
35 R5 Nevada off. State of Nevada, also known as Battle Born State, Sagebrush State, Silver State. ◆ state W USA
35 P6 Nevada City California, W USA 39°15′N 121°02′W
105 O14 Nevada Sierra ▲ S Spain
35 P6 Nevada, Sierra ▲ W USA
62 I13 Nevado, Sierra del ▲ W Argentina
124 G16 Nevel' Pskovskaya Oblast', W Russian Federation 56°01′N 29°54′E
123 T14 Nevel'sk Ostrov Sakhalin, Sakhalinskaya Oblast', SE Russian Federation 46°41′N 141°54′E
123 Q13 Never Amurskaya Oblast', SE Russian Federation 53°58′N 124°04′E
127 Q6 Neverkino Penzenskaya Oblast', W Russian Federation 52°53′N 46°46′E
103 P9 Nevers anc. Noviodunum. Nièvre, C France 47°N 03°09′E
18 J12 Neversink River ≈ New York, NE USA
183 Q6 Nevertire New South Wales, SE Australia 31°52′S 147°42′E
113 H15 Nevesinje ◆ Republika Srpska, S Bosnia and Herzegovina
118 G12 Nevėžis ≈ C Lithuania
138 F11 Neve Zohar prev. Newé Zohar. Southern, E Israel 31°07′N 35°23′E
126 M14 Nevinnomyssk Stavropol'skiy Kray, SW Russian Federation 44°39′N 41°57′E
45 W10 Nevis island Saint Kitts and Nevis
Nevoso, Monte see Veliki Snežnik
Nevrokop see Gotse Delchev
136 J14 Nevşehir var. Nevshehr. Nevşehir, C Turkey 38°38′N 34°43′E
136 J14 Nevşehir var. Nevshehr. ◆ province C Turkey
Nevshehr see Nevşehir
122 G10 Nev'yansk Sverdlovskaya Oblast', C Russian Federation 57°26′N 60°15′E
81 J25 Newala Mtwara, SE Tanzania 10°59′S 39°18′E
31 P16 New Albany Indiana, N USA 38°17′N 85°50′W
22 M2 New Albany Mississippi, S USA 34°29′N 89°00′W
29 Y11 New Albin Iowa, C USA 43°30′N 91°17′W
55 U8 New Amsterdam E Guyana 06°17′N 57°31′W
183 Q4 New Angledool New South Wales, SE Australia 29°06′S 147°54′E
21 Y2 Newark Delaware, NE USA 39°42′N 75°45′W
18 K14 Newark New Jersey, NE USA 40°42′N 74°12′W
18 G10 Newark New York, NE USA 43°01′N 77°04′W
31 T13 Newark Ohio, N USA 40°03′N 82°24′W
Newark see Newark-on-Trent
35 W5 Newark Lake ◎ Nevada, W USA
97 N18 Newark-on-Trent var. Newark. C England, United Kingdom 53°05′N 00°49′W
22 M7 New Augusta Mississippi, S USA 31°12′N 89°03′W
19 P12 New Bedford Massachusetts, NE USA 41°38′N 70°55′W
32 G11 Newberg Oregon, NW USA 45°18′N 122°58′W
21 X10 New Bern North Carolina, SE USA 35°05′N 77°04′W
20 F8 Newbern Tennessee, S USA 36°06′N 89°15′W
31 P4 Newberry Michigan, N USA 46°21′N 85°30′W
21 Q12 Newberry South Carolina, SE USA 34°17′N 81°39′W
18 F15 New Bloomfield Pennsylvania, NE USA 40°24′N 77°08′W
25 X5 New Boston Texas, SW USA 33°27′N 94°25′W
25 S11 New Braunfels Texas, SW USA 29°43′N 98°09′W
31 Q13 New Bremen Ohio, N USA 40°26′N 84°22′W
97 F18 Newbridge Ir. An Droichead Nua. Kildare, C Ireland 53°11′N 06°48′W
18 B14 New Brighton Pennsylvania, NE USA 40°44′N 80°18′W
18 M12 New Britain Connecticut, NE USA 41°37′N 72°45′W
186 G7 New Britain island E Papua New Guinea
192 I8 New Britain Trench undersea feature W Pacific Ocean
18 J15 New Brunswick New Jersey, NE USA 40°29′N 74°27′W
15 V8 New Brunswick Fr. Nouveau-Brunswick. ◆ province SE Canada
18 K13 Newburgh New York, NE USA 41°30′N 74°00′W
97 M22 Newbury S England, United Kingdom 51°25′N 01°20′W
19 P10 Newburyport Massachusetts, NE USA 42°49′N 70°53′W
77 T14 New Bussa Niger, W Nigeria 09°50′N 04°32′E
187 O17 New Caledonia var. Kanaky, Fr. Nouvelle-Calédonie. ◇ French overseas territory SW Pacific Ocean
187 O15 New Caledonia island SW Pacific Ocean
175 O10 New Caledonia Basin undersea feature W Pacific Ocean
183 T8 Newcastle New South Wales, SE Australia 32°55′S 151°46′E
13 O14 Newcastle New Brunswick, SE Canada 47°01′N 65°36′W
14 I15 Newcastle Ontario, SE Canada 43°55′N 78°35′W
83 K22 Newcastle KwaZulu/Natal, E South Africa 27°45′S 29°55′E
97 G16 Newcastle Ir. An Caisleán Nua. SE Northern Ireland, United Kingdom 54°12′N 05°54′W
31 P13 New Castle Indiana, N USA 39°56′N 85°21′W
20 L5 New Castle Kentucky, S USA 38°28′N 85°10′W
27 N11 Newcastle Oklahoma, C USA 35°15′N 97°36′W
18 B13 New Castle Pennsylvania, NE USA 41°00′N 80°22′W
25 R6 Newcastle Texas, SW USA 33°11′N 98°44′W
36 J7 Newcastle Utah, W USA 37°40′N 113°31′W
21 S6 New Castle Virginia, NE USA 37°31′N 80°09′W
33 Z13 Newcastle Wyoming, C USA 43°52′N 104°14′W
97 L14 Newcastle ✈ NE England, United Kingdom 55°03′N 01°42′W
Newcastle see Newcastle upon Tyne
97 L18 Newcastle-under-Lyme C England, United Kingdom 53°N 02°14′W
97 M14 Newcastle upon Tyne var. Newcastle, hist. Monkchester, Lat. Pons Aelii. NE England, United Kingdom 54°59′N 01°35′W
181 Q4 Newcastle Waters Northern Territory, N Australia 17°20′S 133°26′E
Newchwang see Yingkou
18 K13 New City New York, NE USA 41°08′N 73°57′W
31 U13 Newcomerstown Ohio, N USA 40°16′N 81°36′W
18 G15 New Cumberland Pennsylvania, NE USA 40°13′N 76°52′W
21 R1 New Cumberland West Virginia, NE USA 40°30′N 80°35′W
152 I10 New Delhi ● (India) Delhi, N India 28°35′N 77°15′E
11 O17 New Denver British Columbia, SW Canada 49°58′N 117°21′W
28 J9 Newell South Dakota, N USA 44°42′N 103°25′W
21 Q13 New Ellenton South Carolina, SE USA 33°25′N 81°41′W
22 J6 Newellton Louisiana, S USA 32°04′N 91°14′W
28 K6 New England North Dakota, N USA 46°32′N 102°52′W
19 P8 New England cultural region NE USA
New England of the West see Minnesota
183 U5 New England Range ▲ New South Wales, SE Australia
64 G9 New England Seamounts var. Bermuda-New England Seamount Arc. undersea feature W Atlantic Ocean 38°00′N 61°00′W
38 M14 Newenham, Cape headland Alaska, USA 58°39′N 162°10′W
Newé Zohar see Neve Zohar
18 D9 Newfane New York, NE USA 43°16′N 78°40′W
97 M23 New Forest physical region S England, United Kingdom
13 T12 Newfoundland Fr. Terre-Neuve. island Newfoundland and Labrador, SE Canada
13 R9 Newfoundland and Labrador Fr. Terre Neuve. ◆ province E Canada
65 J8 Newfoundland Basin undersea feature NW Atlantic Ocean 45°00′N 40°00′W
64 I8 Newfoundland Ridge undersea feature NW Atlantic Ocean
64 J8 Newfoundland Seamounts undersea feature N Sargasso Sea
18 G16 New Freedom Pennsylvania, NE USA 39°43′N 76°41′W
186 K9 New Georgia island New Georgia Islands, NW Solomon Islands
186 K8 New Georgia Islands island group NW Solomon Islands
186 L8 New Georgia Sound var. The Slot. sound E Solomon Sea
30 L9 New Glarus Wisconsin, N USA 42°50′N 89°38′W
13 Q15 New Glasgow Nova Scotia, SE Canada 45°36′N 62°38′W
New Goa see Panaji
186 A6 New Guinea Dut. Nieuw Guinea, Ind. Irian. island Indonesia/Papua New Guinea
192 H8 New Guinea Trench undersea feature SW Pacific Ocean
32 I6 Newhalem Washington, NW USA 48°40′N 121°18′W
39 P13 Newhalen Alaska, USA 59°43′N 154°54′W
29 X13 Newhall Iowa, C USA 42°00′N 91°58′W
14 F16 New Hamburg Ontario, S Canada 43°24′N 80°37′W
19 N9 New Hampshire off. State of New Hampshire, also known as Granite State. ◆ state NE USA
29 W12 New Hampton Iowa, C USA 43°03′N 92°19′W
186 G5 New Hanover island NE Papua New Guinea
97 P23 Newhaven SE England, United Kingdom 50°48′N 00°00′E
18 M13 New Haven Connecticut, NE USA 41°18′N 72°55′W
31 Q12 New Haven Indiana, N USA 41°02′N 84°59′W
27 W5 New Haven Missouri, C USA 38°34′N 91°15′W
10 K13 New Hazelton British Columbia, SW Canada 55°15′N 127°30′W
New Hebrides see Vanuatu
175 P9 New Hebrides Trench undersea feature N Coral Sea
18 H15 New Holland Pennsylvania, NE USA 40°06′N 76°05′W
22 I9 New Iberia Louisiana, S USA 30°00′N 91°51′W
186 G5 New Ireland ◆ province NE Papua New Guinea
186 G5 New Ireland island NE Papua New Guinea
65 A24 New Island island W Falkland Islands
18 J15 New Jersey off. State of New Jersey, also known as The Garden State. ◆ state NE USA
18 C14 New Kensington Pennsylvania, NE USA 40°33′N 79°45′W
21 W6 New Kent Virginia, NE USA 37°32′N 76°59′W
27 O8 Newkirk Oklahoma, C USA 36°54′N 97°03′W
21 Q9 Newland North Carolina, SE USA 36°04′N 81°50′W
28 L6 New Leipzig North Dakota, N USA 46°21′N 101°54′W
14 H9 New Liskeard Ontario, S Canada 47°31′N 79°41′W
22 G7 Newllano Louisiana, S USA 31°06′N 93°16′W
19 N13 New London Connecticut, NE USA 41°21′N 72°04′W
29 Y15 New London Iowa, C USA 40°55′N 91°24′W
29 T8 New London Minnesota, N USA 45°18′N 94°56′W
27 V3 New London Missouri, C USA 39°34′N 91°24′W
30 M7 New London Wisconsin, N USA 44°25′N 88°44′W
27 Y8 New Madrid Missouri, C USA 36°34′N 89°32′W
180 J8 Newman Western Australia 23°18′S 119°45′E
194 M13 Newman Island island Antarctica
14 H15 Newmarket Ontario, S Canada 44°03′N 79°27′W
97 P20 Newmarket E England, United Kingdom 52°18′N 00°28′E
19 P10 Newmarket New Hampshire, NE USA 43°04′N 70°53′W
21 U4 New Market Virginia, NE USA 38°39′N 78°40′W
21 R2 New Martinsville West Virginia, NE USA 39°39′N 80°52′W
31 U14 New Matamoras Ohio, N USA 39°32′N 81°04′W
32 M12 New Meadows Idaho, NW USA 44°57′N 116°16′W
26 R12 New Mexico off. State of New Mexico, also known as Land of Enchantment, Sunshine State. ◆ state SW USA
149 V6 New Mirpur var. Mirpur. Sind, SE Pakistan 33°11′N 73°46′E
151 N15 New Moore Island Island E India
23 S4 Newnan Georgia, SE USA 33°22′N 84°48′W
183 P17 New Norfolk Tasmania, SE Australia 42°46′S 147°02′E
22 K9 New Orleans Louisiana, S USA 30°00′N 90°01′W
22 K9 New Orleans ✈ Louisiana, S USA 29°59′N 90°17′W
18 K12 New Paltz New York, NE USA 41°44′N 74°04′W
31 U12 New Philadelphia Ohio, N USA 40°29′N 81°27′W
184 K10 New Plymouth Taranaki, North Island, New Zealand 39°04′S 174°06′E
97 M24 Newport S England, United Kingdom 50°42′N 01°18′W
97 K22 Newport SE Wales, United Kingdom 51°35′N 03°W
27 W10 Newport Arkansas, C USA 35°36′N 91°16′W
31 N13 Newport Indiana, N USA 39°52′N 87°24′W
20 M3 Newport Kentucky, S USA 39°05′N 84°27′W
29 W9 Newport Minnesota, N USA 44°52′N 93°00′W
32 F12 Newport Oregon, NW USA 44°39′N 124°04′W
19 O13 Newport Rhode Island, NE USA 41°29′N 71°17′W
21 O9 Newport Tennessee, S USA 35°58′N 83°13′W
19 N6 Newport Vermont, NE USA 44°56′N 72°13′W
32 M7 Newport Washington, NW USA 48°08′N 117°05′W
21 X7 Newport News Virginia, NE USA 36°59′N 76°26′W
97 N20 Newport Pagnell SE England, United Kingdom 52°05′N 00°44′W
23 U12 New Port Richey Florida, SE USA 28°14′N 82°42′W
29 V9 New Prague Minnesota, N USA 44°32′N 93°34′W
44 H3 New Providence island N Bahamas
97 I20 New Quay SW Wales, United Kingdom 52°13′N 04°22′W
97 H24 Newquay SW England, United Kingdom 50°27′N 05°03′W
29 V10 New Richland Minnesota, N USA 43°53′N 93°29′W
15 X7 New-Richmond Québec, SE Canada 48°12′N 65°52′W
31 R15 New Richmond Ohio, N USA 38°57′N 84°16′W
30 I5 New Richmond Wisconsin, N USA 45°09′N 92°31′W
42 G1 New River ≈ N Belize
55 T12 New River ≈ SE Guyana
21 R6 New River ≈ West Virginia, NE USA
42 G1 New River Lagoon ◎ N Belize
22 J8 New Roads Louisiana, S USA 30°42′N 91°26′W
18 L14 New Rochelle New York, NE USA 40°55′N 73°44′W
29 O4 New Rockford North Dakota, N USA 47°40′N 99°08′W
97 P23 New Romney SE England, United Kingdom 50°58′N 00°56′E
97 F20 New Ross Ir. Ros Mhic Thriúin. Wexford, SE Ireland 52°24′N 06°56′W
97 F16 Newry Ir. An tIúr. SE Northern Ireland, United Kingdom 54°11′N 06°20′W
28 M5 New Salem North Dakota, N USA 46°51′N 101°24′W
New Sarum see Salisbury
29 W14 New Sharon Iowa, C USA 41°28′N 92°39′W
New Siberian Islands see Novosibirskiye Ostrova
23 X11 New Smyrna Beach Florida, SE USA 29°01′N 80°55′W
183 O7 New South Wales ◆ state SE Australia
39 O13 New Stuyahok Alaska, USA 59°27′N 157°18′W
21 N8 New Tazewell Tennessee, S USA 36°26′N 83°36′W
152 K9 New Tehri prev. Tehri. Uttarakhand, N India 30°12′N 78°29′E
38 M12 Newtok Alaska, USA 60°56′N 164°37′W
23 S7 Newton Georgia, SE USA 31°18′N 84°20′W
29 W14 Newton Iowa, C USA 41°42′N 93°03′W
27 N6 Newton Kansas, C USA 38°02′N 97°22′W
19 O11 Newton Massachusetts, NE USA 42°19′N 71°10′W
22 M5 Newton Mississippi, S USA 32°19′N 89°09′W
18 J14 Newton New Jersey, NE USA 41°03′N 74°45′W
21 R9 Newton North Carolina, SE USA 35°42′N 81°14′W
25 Y9 Newton Texas, SW USA 30°51′N 93°45′W
97 J24 Newton Abbot SW England, United Kingdom 50°33′N 03°34′W
96 K13 Newton St Boswells SE Scotland, United Kingdom 55°34′N 02°40′W
97 I14 Newton Stewart S Scotland, United Kingdom 54°58′N 04°30′W
92 O2 Newtontoppen ▲ C Svalbard 78°57′N 17°34′E
97 J20 Newtown E Wales, United Kingdom 52°32′N 03°19′W
28 K3 New Town North Dakota, N USA 47°58′N 102°30′W
97 G15 Newtownabbey Ir. Baile na Mainistreach. E Northern Ireland, United Kingdom 54°40′N 05°57′W
97 G15 Newtownards Ir. Baile Nua na hArda. SE Northern Ireland, United Kingdom 54°36′N 05°41′W
29 U10 New Ulm Minnesota, N USA 44°20′N 94°28′W
28 K10 New Underwood South Dakota, N USA 44°05′N 102°46′W
25 V10 New Waverly Texas, SW USA 30°32′N 95°28′W
18 K14 New York New York, NE USA 40°45′N 73°57′W
18 G10 New York ◆ state NE USA
35 X13 New York Mountains ▲ California, W USA
184 K12 New Zealand ◆ commonwealth republic SW Pacific Ocean
95 M24 Nexø var. Neksø Bornholm. E Denmark 55°04′N 15°09′E
125 O15 Neya Kostromskaya Oblast', NW Russian Federation 58°19′N 43°51′E
Neyba see Neiba
143 Q12 Neyrīz var. Neiriz, Niriz. Fārs, S Iran 29°14′N 54°18′E
143 T4 Neyshābūr var. Nishapur. Khorāsān-Razavī, NE Iran 36°15′N 58°47′E
155 J21 Neyveli Tamil Nādu, SE India 11°36′N 79°26′E
Nezhin see Nizhyn
33 N10 Nezperce Idaho, NW USA 46°14′N 116°15′W
22 H8 Nezpique, Bayou ≈ Louisiana, S USA
77 Y13 Ngadda ≈ NE Nigeria
N'Gage see Negage
185 G16 Ngahere West Coast, South Island, New Zealand 42°22′S 171°29′E
77 Z12 Ngala Borno, NE Nigeria 12°19′N 14°11′E
158 K16 Ngamring Xizang Zizhiqu, W China 29°16′N 87°10′E
81 K19 Nganerabeli Plain plain SE Kenya
158 I14 Ngangla Ringco ◎ W China
158 H13 Nganglong Kangri ▲ W China 32°55′N 81°00′E
158 K15 Ngangzê Co ◎ W China
79 F14 Ngaoundéré var. N'Gaoundéré. Adamaoua, N Cameroon 07°20′N 13°35′E
N'Gaoundéré see Ngaoundéré
81 E20 Ngara Kagera, NW Tanzania 02°30′S 30°40′E
188 F8 Ngardmau Bay bay Babeldaob, N Palau
188 F7 Ngaregur island Palau Islands, N Palau
Ngarrab see Gyaca
184 L7 Ngaruawahia Waikato, North Island, New Zealand 37°41′S 175°10′E
184 N11 Ngaruroro ≈ North Island, New Zealand
190 I16 Ngatangiia Rarotonga, S Cook Islands 21°14′S 159°44′W
184 M6 Ngatea Waikato, North Island, New Zealand 37°16′S 175°29′E
166 L8 Ngathainggyaung Ayeyarwady, SW Burma (Myanmar) 17°22′N 95°04′E
Ngatik see Ngetik Atoll
Ngau see Gau
Ngawa see Aba
172 G12 Ngazidja Fr. Grande Comore, var. Njazidja. island NW Comoros
188 C7 Ngcheangel var. Kayangel Islands. island Palau Islands, N Palau
188 E10 Ngchemiangel Babeldaob, N Palau
188 C8 Ngeaur var. Angaur. island Palau Islands, S Palau
188 E10 Ngerkeai Babeldaob, N Palau
188 F9 Ngermechau Babeldaob, N Palau 07°35′N 134°39′E
188 C8 Ngeruktabel prev. Urukthapel. island Palau Islands, S Palau
188 F8 Ngetbong Babeldaob, N Palau 07°37′N 134°35′E
189 T17 Ngetik Atoll var. Ngatik; prev. Los Jardines. atoll Caroline Islands, E Micronesia
188 E10 Ngetkip Babeldaob, N Palau
Nghia Dan see Thai Hoa
83 C16 N'Giva var. Ondjiva, Port. Vila Pereira de Eça. Cunene, S Angola 17°02′S 15°42′E
79 G20 Ngo Plateaux, SE Congo 02°28′S 15°43′E
167 S7 Ngoc Lặc Thanh Hoa, N Vietnam 20°06′N 105°21′E
79 G17 Ngoko ≈ Cameroon/Congo
81 H19 Ngorengore Rift Valley, SW Kenya 01°01′S 35°26′E
159 Q11 Ngoring Hu ◎ C China
Ngorolaka see Banifing
81 H20 Ngorongoro Crater crater N Tanzania
79 D19 Ngounié off. Province de la Ngounié, var. La Ngounié. ◆ province S Gabon
79 D19 Ngounié ≈ Congo/Gabon
Ngounié, Province de la see Ngounié
78 H10 Ngoura var. NGoura. Chari-Baguirmi, W Chad 12°52′N 16°27′E
NGoura see Ngoura
78 G10 Ngouri var. NGouri; prev. Fort-Millot. Lac, W Chad 13°42′N 15°19′E
NGouri see Ngouri
77 Y10 Ngourti Diffa, E Niger 15°22′N 13°13′E
77 Y11 Nguigmi var. N'Guigmi. Diffa, SE Niger 14°17′N 13°07′E
N'Guigmi see Nguigmi
Nguimbo see Lumbala N'Guimbo
188 F15 Ngulu Atoll atoll Caroline Islands, W Micronesia
187 R14 Nguna island C Vanuatu
N'Gunza see Sumbe
169 U17 Ngurah Rai ✈ (Bali) Bali, S Indonesia 08°40′S 115°14′E

◆ Country ● Country Capital ◇ Dependent Territory ○ Dependent Territory Capital ◆ Administrative Regions ✈ International Airport ▲ Mountain ▲ Mountain Range Volcano ≈ River ◎ Lake ▣ Reservoir

77 W12 **Nguru** Yobe, NE Nigeria 12°55′N 10°31′E
Ngwaketze *see* Southern
83 I16 **Ngweze** ≈ S Zambia
83 M17 **Nhamatanda** Sofala, C Mozambique 19°16′S 34°10′E
58 G12 **Nhamundá, Rio** *var.* Jamundá, Yamundá. ≈ N Brazil
60 J7 **Nhandeara** São Paulo, S Brazil 20°40′S 50°03′W
82 D12 **Nharêa** *var.* N'Harea, Nhareia. Bié, W Angola 11°38′S 16°58′E
N'Harea *see* Nharêa
Nhareia *see* Nharêa
167 V12 **Nha Trang** Khanh Hoa, S Vietnam 12°15′N 109°10′E
182 L11 **Nhill** Victoria, SE Australia 36°21′S 141°38′E
83 L22 **Nhlangano** *prev.* Goedgegun. SW Swaziland 27°06′S 31°12′E
181 S1 **Nhulunbuy** Northern Territory, N Australia 12°16′S 136°46′E
77 N10 **Niafounké** Tombouctou, W Mali 15°54′N 03°58′W
31 N5 **Niagara** Wisconsin, N USA 45°45′N 87°57′W
14 H16 **Niagara** ≈ Ontario, S Canada
14 G15 **Niagara Escarpment** *hill range* Ontario, S Canada
14 H16 **Niagara Falls** Ontario, S Canada 43°05′N 79°06′W
18 D9 **Niagara Falls** New York, NE USA 43°06′N 79°04′W
14 H16 **Niagara Falls** *waterfall* Canada/USA
76 K12 **Niagassola** *var.* Nyagassola. Haute-Guinée, NE Guinea 12°24′N 09°03′W
77 R12 **Niamey** ● (Niger) Niamey, SW Niger 13°28′N 02°03′E
77 R12 **Niamey** ✈ Niamey, SW Niger 13°28′N 02°14′E
77 R14 **Niamtougou** N Togo 09°50′N 01°08′E
79 O16 **Niangara** Orientale, NE Dem. Rep. Congo 03°45′N 27°54′E
77 O10 **Niangay, Lac** ◎ E Mali
77 N14 **Niangoloko** SW Burkina 10°15′N 04°53′W
27 U6 **Niangua River** ≈ Missouri, C USA
79 O17 **Nia-Nia** Orientale, NE Dem. Rep. Congo 01°26′N 27°38′E
19 N13 **Niantic** Connecticut, NE USA 41°19′N 72°11′W
163 U7 **Nianzishan** Heilongjiang, NE China 47°31′N 122°53′E
79 E20 **Niari** ◈ *province* SW Congo
168 H10 **Nias, Pulau** *island* W Indonesia
82 O13 **Niassa** *off.* Província do Niassa. ◈ *province* N Mozambique
Niassa, Província do *see* Niassa
191 U10 **Niau** *island* Îles Tuamotu, C French Polynesia
95 G20 **Nibe** Nordjylland, N Denmark 56°59′N 09°39′E
189 Q8 **Nibok** N Nauru 0°31′S 166°55′E
118 C10 **Nīca** W Latvia 56°21′N 21°03′E
Nicaea *see* Nice
42 J9 **Nicaragua** *off.* Republic of Nicaragua. ◆ *republic* Central America
42 K11 **Nicaragua, Lago de** *var.* Cocibolca, Gran Lago, *Eng.* Lake Nicaragua. ◎ S Nicaragua
Nicaragua, Lake *see* Nicaragua, Lago de
64 D11 **Nicaraguan Rise** *undersea feature* NW Caribbean Sea 16°00′N 80°00′W
Nicaragua, Republic of *see* Nicaragua
Nicaria *see* Ikaría
107 N21 **Nicastro** Calabria, SW Italy 38°59′N 16°20′E
103 V15 **Nice** *It.* Nizza; *anc.* Nicaea. Alpes-Maritimes, SE France 43°43′N 07°13′E
Nice *see* Côte d'Azur
Nicephorium *see* Ar Raqqah
12 M9 **Nichicun, Lac** ◎ Québec, E Canada
164 D16 **Nichinan** *var.* Nitinan. Miyazaki, Kyūshū, SW Japan 31°36′N 131°23′E
44 E4 **Nicholas Channel** *channel* N Cuba
Nicholas II Land *see* Severnaya Zemlya
149 U2 **Nicholas Range** *Pash.* Selselehye Kuhe Vākhān, *Taj.* Qatorkŭhi Vakhon. ▲▲ Afghanistan/Tajikistan
20 M6 **Nicholasville** Kentucky, S USA 37°52′N 84°34′W
44 G2 **Nicholls Town** Andros Island, NW Bahamas 25°07′N 78°01′W
21 U12 **Nichols** South Carolina, SE USA 34°13′N 79°09′W
55 U9 **Nickerie** ◈ *district* NW Surinam
55 V9 **Nickerie Rivier** ≈ NW Surinam
151 P22 **Nicobar Islands** *island group* India, E Indian Ocean
116 L9 **Nicolae Bălcescu** Botoşani, NE Romania 47°33′N 26°52′E
15 P11 **Nicolet** Québec, SE Canada 46°13′N 72°37′W
15 Q12 **Nicolet** ≈ Québec, SE Canada
31 Q4 **Nicolet, Lake** ◎ Michigan, N USA
29 U10 **Nicollet** Minnesota, N USA 44°16′N 94°11′W
61 F19 **Nico Pérez** Florida, S Uruguay 33°30′S 55°10′W
Nicopolis *see* Nikopol, Bulgaria
Nicopolis *see* Nikópoli, Greece
121 P2 **Nicosia** *Gk.* Lefkosía, *Turk.* Lefkoşa. ● (Cyprus) C Cyprus 35°10′N 33°23′E
107 K24 **Nicosia** Sicilia, Italy, C Mediterranean Sea 37°45′N 14°24′E
107 N22 **Nicotera** Calabria, SW Italy 38°33′N 15°55′E
42 K13 **Nicoya** Guanacaste, W Costa Rica 10°09′N 85°26′W
42 L14 **Nicoya, Golfo de** *gulf* W Costa Rica
42 L14 **Nicoya, Península de** *peninsula* NW Costa Rica
Nictheroy *see* Niterói
118 B12 **Nida** *Ger.* Nidden. Klaipėda, SW Lithuania 55°20′N 21°00′E
111 L15 **Nida** ≈ S Poland
Nidaros *see* Trondheim
108 D8 **Nidau** Bern, W Switzerland 47°07′N 07°15′E
101 H17 **Nidda** ≈ W Germany
Nidden *see* Nida
95 F17 **Nidelva** ≈ S Norway
108 F9 **Nidwalden** ◈ *canton* C Switzerland
Nidwalden/Unterwalden *see* Nidwalden
110 L9 **Nidzica** *Ger.* Niedenburg. Warmińsko-Mazurskie, NE Poland 53°22′N 20°27′E
100 H6 **Niebüll** Schleswig-Holstein, N Germany 54°47′N 08°51′E
Niedenburg *see* Nidzica
99 N25 **Niederanven** Luxembourg, C Luxembourg 49°39′N 06°15′E
103 V4 **Niederbronn-les-Bains** Bas-Rhin, NE France 48°57′N 07°37′E
Niederdonau *see* Niederösterreich
109 S7 **Niedere Tauern** ▲▲ C Austria
101 P14 **Niederlausitz** *Eng.* Lower Lusatia, *Lus.* Donja Łužica. *physical region* E Germany
109 U5 **Niederösterreich** *off.* Land Niederösterreich, *Eng.* Lower Austria, *Ger.* Niederdonau; *prev.* Lower Danube. ◈ *state* NE Austria
Niederösterreich, Land *see* Niederösterreich
100 G12 **Niedersachsen** *Eng.* Lower Saxony, *Fr.* Basse-Saxe. ◈ *state* NW Germany
79 D17 **Niefang** *var.* Sevilla de Niefang. NW Equatorial Guinea 01°52′N 10°12′E
83 G23 **Niekerkshoop** Northern Cape, W South Africa 29°21′S 22°49′E
99 G17 **Niel** Antwerpen, N Belgium 51°07′N 04°20′E
Niélé *see* Niellé
76 M14 **Niellé** *var.* Niélé. N Ivory Coast 10°12′N 05°38′W
79 O22 **Niemba** Katanga, E Dem. Rep. Congo 05°58′S 28°24′E
111 G15 **Niemcza** *Ger.* Nimptsch. Dolnośląskie, SW Poland 50°45′N 16°52′E
Niemen *see* Neman
92 J13 **Niemisel** Norrbotten, N Sweden 66°00′N 22°00′E
111 H15 **Niemodlin** *Ger.* Falkenberg. Opolskie, SW Poland 50°37′N 17°45′E
76 M13 **Niéna** Sikasso, SW Mali 11°24′N 06°20′W
100 H12 **Nienburg** Niedersachsen, N Germany 52°37′N 09°12′E
100 N13 **Nieplitz** ≈ NE Germany
111 L16 **Niepołomice** Malopolskie, S Poland 50°02′N 20°12′E
101 D14 **Niers** ≈ Germany/Netherlands
101 Q15 **Niesky** *Lus.* Niska. Sachsen, E Germany 51°16′N 14°49′E
Nieśwież *see* Nyasvizh
Nieuport *see* Nieuwpoort
98 O8 **Nieuw-Amsterdam** Drenthe, NE Netherlands 52°43′N 06°52′E
55 W9 **Nieuw Amsterdam** Commewijne, NE Surinam 05°53′N 55°05′W
99 M14 **Nieuw-Bergen** Limburg, SE Netherlands 51°36′N 06°04′E
98 O7 **Nieuw-Buinen** Drenthe, NE Netherlands 52°57′N 06°55′E
98 J12 **Nieuwegein** Utrecht, C Netherlands 52°03′N 05°06′E
98 P6 **Nieuwe Pekela** Groningen, NE Netherlands 53°04′N 06°58′E
98 P5 **Nieuweschans** Groningen, NE Netherlands 53°10′N 07°10′E
Nieuw Guinea *see* New Guinea
98 I11 **Nieuwkoop** Zuid-Holland, C Netherlands 52°09′N 04°46′E
98 M9 **Nieuwleusen** Overijssel, S Netherlands 52°34′N 06°16′E
98 J11 **Nieuw-Loosdrecht** Noord-Holland, C Netherlands 52°12′N 05°08′E
55 U9 **Nieuw Nickerie** Nickerie, NW Surinam 05°56′N 57°W
98 P5 **Nieuwolda** Groningen, NE Netherlands 53°15′N 06°58′E
99 B17 **Nieuwpoort** *var.* Nieuport. West-Vlaanderen, W Belgium 51°08′N 02°45′E
99 G14 **Nieuw-Vossemeer** Noord-Brabant, S Netherlands 51°34′N 04°13′E
98 P7 **Nieuw-Weerdinge** Drenthe, NE Netherlands 52°51′N 07°00′E
40 L10 **Nieves** Zacatecas, C Mexico 24°00′N 102°57′W
64 O11 **Nieves, Pico de las** ▲ Gran Canaria, Islas Canarias, Spain, NE Atlantic Ocean 27°58′N 15°34′W
103 P8 **Nièvre** ◈ *department* C France
Niewenstat *see* Neustadt an der Weinstrasse
136 J15 **Niğde** Niğde, C Turkey 37°58′N 34°42′E
136 J15 **Niğde** ◈ *province* C Turkey
83 J21 **Nigel** Gauteng, NE South Africa 26°25′S 28°28′E
77 V10 **Niger** *off.* Republic of Niger. ◆ *republic* W Africa
77 T14 **Niger** ◈ *state* C Nigeria
67 P8 **Niger** ≈ W Africa
Niger Cone *see* Niger Fan
67 P9 **Niger Delta** *delta* S Nigeria
67 P9 **Niger Fan** *var.* Niger Cone. *undersea feature* E Atlantic Ocean 04°15′N 05°00′E
77 T13 **Nigeria** *off.* Federal Republic of Nigeria. ◆ *federal republic* W Africa
Nigeria, Federal Republic of *see* Nigeria
77 T17 **Niger, Mouths of the** *delta* S Nigeria
Niger, Republic of *see* Niger
185 C24 **Nightcaps** Southland, South Island, New Zealand 45°58′S 168°03′E
14 F7 **Night Hawk Lake** ◎ Ontario, S Canada
65 M19 **Nightingale Island** *island* S Tristan da Cunha, S Atlantic Ocean
38 M12 **Nightmute** Alaska, USA 60°28′N 164°43′W
114 G13 **Nigríta** Kentrikí Makedonía, NE Greece 40°54′N 23°29′E
148 J15 **Nihing** *Per.* Rūd-e Nahang. ≈ Iran/Pakistan
191 V10 **Nihiru** *atoll* Îles Tuamotu, C French Polynesia
Nihommatsu *see* Nihonmatsu
Nihon *see* Japan
165 P11 **Nihonmatsu** *var.* Nihommatsu, Nihonmatu. Fukushima, Honshū, C Japan 37°34′N 140°25′E
Nihonmatu *see* Nihonmatsu
62 I12 **Nihuil, Embalse del** ◎ W Argentina
165 O10 **Niigata** Niigata, Honshū, C Japan 37°55′N 139°01′E
165 O11 **Niigata** *off.* Niigata-ken. ◈ *prefecture* Honshū, C Japan
Niigata-ken *see* Niigata
165 G14 **Niihama** Ehime, Shikoku, SW Japan 33°57′N 133°15′E
38 A8 **Ni'ihau** *var.* Niihau. *island* Hawai'i, USA, C Pacific Ocean
165 X12 **Nii-jima** *island* E Japan
165 H12 **Niimi** Okayama, Honshū, SW Japan 35°00′N 133°27′E
165 O10 **Niitsu** *var.* Niitu. Niigata, Honshū, C Japan 37°48′N 139°09′E
Niitu *see* Niitsu
105 P15 **Nijar** Andalucía, S Spain 36°57′N 02°13′W
98 K11 **Nijkerk** Gelderland, C Netherlands 52°13′N 05°30′E
99 H16 **Nijlen** Antwerpen, N Belgium 51°10′N 04°40′E
98 L13 **Nijmegen** *Ger.* Nimwegen; *anc.* Noviomagus. Gelderland, SE Netherlands 51°50′N 05°52′E
98 N10 **Nijverdal** Overijssel, E Netherlands 52°22′N 06°28′E
190 G16 **Nikao** Rarotonga, S Cook Islands
Nikaria *see* Ikaría
124 I2 **Nikel'** *Finn.* Kolosjoki. Murmanskaya Oblast', NW Russian Federation 69°25′N 30°12′E
171 Q17 **Nikiniki** Timor, S Indonesia 10°S 124°30′E
129 Q15 **Nikitin Seamount** *undersea feature* E Indian Ocean 05°48′S 84°48′E
77 S14 **Nikki** E Benin 09°55′N 03°12′E
Niklasmarkt *see* Gheorgheni
39 P10 **Nikolai** Alaska, USA 63°00′N 154°22′W
Nikolaiken *see* Mikołajki
Nikolainkaupunki *see* Vaasa
Nikolayev *see* Mykolayiv
145 O6 **Nikolayevka** Severnyy Kazakhstan, N Kazakhstan
Nikolayevka *see* Zhetigen
127 P9 **Nikolayevsk** Volgogradskaya Oblast', SW Russian Federation 50°03′N 45°30′E
Nikolayevskaya Oblast' *see* Mykolayivs'ka Oblast'
123 S12 **Nikolayevsk-na-Amure** Khabarovskiy Kray, SE Russian Federation 53°04′N 140°39′E
127 P6 **Nikol'sk** Penzenskaya Oblast', W Russian Federation 53°46′N 46°03′E
125 O13 **Nikol'sk** Vologodskaya Oblast', NW Russian Federation 59°35′N 45°31′E
Nikol'sk *see* Ussuriysk
38 K17 **Nikolski** Umnak Island, Alaska, USA 52°56′N 168°52′W
Nikol'skiy *see* Satpayev
127 V7 **Nikol'skoye** Orenburgskaya Oblast', W Russian Federation 52°01′N 55°48′E
Nikol'sk-Ussuriyskiy *see* Ussuriysk
114 J7 **Nikopol** *anc.* Nicopolis. Pleven, N Bulgaria 43°43′N 24°55′E
117 S9 **Nikopol'** Dnipropetrovs'ka Oblast', SE Ukraine 47°34′N 34°23′E
115 C17 **Nikópoli** *anc.* Nicopolis. *site of ancient city* Ípeiros, W Greece
136 M12 **Niksar** Tokat, N Turkey 40°35′N 36°59′E
143 V14 **Nīkshahr** Sīstān va Balūchestān, SE Iran 26°15′N 60°10′E
113 J16 **Nikšić** C Montenegro 42°47′N 18°56′E
191 R4 **Nikumaroro**; *prev.* Gardner Island. *atoll* Phoenix Islands, C Kiribati
191 P3 **Nikunau** *var.* Nukunau; *prev.* Byron Island. *atoll* Tungaru, W Kiribati
155 G21 **Nilambūr** Kerala, SW India 11°17′N 76°15′E
35 X16 **Niland** California, W USA 33°14′N 115°31′W
80 G8 **Nile** *former province* NW Uganda
67 T3 **Nile** *Ar.* Nahr an Nīl. ≈ N Africa
75 W7 **Nile Delta** *delta* N Egypt
67 T3 **Nile Fan** *undersea feature* E Mediterranean Sea 33°00′N 31°00′E
31 O11 **Niles** Michigan, N USA 41°49′N 86°15′W
31 V11 **Niles** Ohio, N USA 41°10′N 80°46′W
155 F20 **Nīleswaram** Kerala, SW India 12°18′N 75°07′E
14 K10 **Nilgaut, Lac** ◎ Québec, SE Canada
149 O6 **Nīlī** Dāykundī, C Afghanistan 33°43′N 66°07′E
158 I5 **Nilka** Xinjiang Uygur Zizhiqu, NW China 43°46′N 82°33′E
Nīl, Nahr an *see* Nile
93 N16 **Nilsiä** Itä-Suomi, C Finland 63°13′N 28°00′E
154 F9 **Nimach** Madhya Pradesh, C India 24°27′N 74°56′E
152 G14 **Nimbāhera** Rājasthān, N India 24°38′N 74°45′E
76 L15 **Nimba, Monts** *var.* Nimba Mountains. ▲▲ W Africa
Nimba Mountains *see* Nimba, Monts
Nimburg *see* Nymburk
103 Q15 **Nîmes** *anc.* Nemausus, Nismes. Gard, S France 43°49′N 04°20′E
152 H11 **Nīm ka Thāna** Rājasthān, N India 27°42′N 75°50′E
183 R11 **Nimmitabel** New South Wales, SE Australia 36°34′S 149°18′E
Nimptsch *see* Niemcza
195 R11 **Nimrod Glacier** *glacier* Antarctica
148 K8 **Nīmrōz** *var.* Nimroze; *prev.* Chakhānsūr, Nīmrūz. ◈ *province* SW Afghanistan
Nimroze *see* Nīmrōz
Nīmrūz *see* Nīmrōz
81 F16 **Nimule** Eastern Equatoria, S South Sudan 03°35′N 32°03′E
Nimwegen *see* Nijmegen
155 C23 **Nine Degree Channel** *channel* India/Maldives
18 G9 **Ninemile Point** *headland* New York, NE USA 43°31′N 76°22′W
173 S8 **Ninetyeast Ridge** *undersea feature* E Indian Ocean 04°00′S 90°00′E
183 P13 **Ninety Mile Beach** *beach* Victoria, SE Australia
184 I2 **Ninety Mile Beach** *beach* North Island, New Zealand
21 P12 **Ninety Six** South Carolina, SE USA 34°10′N 82°01′W
163 Y9 **Ning'an** Heilongjiang, NE China 44°20′N 129°28′E
161 S9 **Ningbo** *var.* Ning-po, Yin-hsien; *prev.* Ninghsien. Zhejiang, SE China 29°54′N 121°33′E
161 U12 **Ningde** Fujian, SE China 26°48′N 119°33′E
161 P12 **Ningdu** *var.* Meijiang. Jiangxi, S China 26°28′N 115°53′E
Ning'er *see* Pu'er
186 A7 **Ningerum** Western, SW Papua New Guinea 05°40′S 141°10′E
161 R9 **Ningguo** Anhui, E China 30°33′N 118°58′E
161 S9 **Ninghai** Zhejiang, SE China 29°18′N 121°26′E
Ning-hsia *see* Ningxia
Ninghsien *see* Ningbo
160 J15 **Ningming** *var.* Chengzhong. Guangxi Zhuangzu Zizhiqu, S China 22°07′N 106°43′E
160 H11 **Ningnan** *var.* Pisha. Sichuan, C China 26°59′N 102°49′E
Ning-po *see* Ningbo
Ningsia/Ningsia Hui/Ningsia Hui Autonomous Region *see* Ningxia
160 J5 **Ningxia** *off.* Ningxia Huizu Zizhiqu, *var.* Ning-hsia, Ningsia, *Eng.* Ningsia Hui, Ningsia Hui Autonomous Region. ◈ *autonomous region* N China
Ningxia Huizu Zizhiqu *see* Ningxia
159 X10 **Ningxian** *var.* Xinning. Gansu, N China 35°30′N 108°05′E
167 T7 **Ninh Binh** Ninh Binh, N Vietnam 20°14′N 106°00′E
167 V12 **Ninh Hoa** Khanh Hoa, S Vietnam 12°28′N 109°07′E
186 C4 **Ninigo Group** *island group* N Papua New Guinea
39 Q12 **Ninilchik** Alaska, USA 60°03′N 151°40′W
27 N7 **Ninnescah River** ≈ Kansas, C USA
195 U16 **Ninnis Glacier** *glacier* Antarctica
165 R8 **Ninohe** Iwate, Honshū, C Japan 40°16′N 141°18′E
99 F18 **Ninove** Oost-Vlaanderen, C Belgium 50°50′N 04°02′E
171 O4 **Ninoy Aquino** ✈ (Manila) Luzon, N Philippines 14°26′N 121°00′E
Nio *see* Íos
29 P12 **Niobrara** Nebraska, C USA 42°43′N 97°59′W
28 M12 **Niobrara River** ≈ Nebraska/Wyoming, C USA
79 I20 **Nioki** Bandundu, W Dem. Rep. Congo 02°44′S 17°42′E
76 M11 **Niono** Ségou, C Mali 14°18′N 05°59′W
76 K11 **Nioro** *var.* Nioro du Sahel. Kayes, W Mali 15°13′N 09°39′W
76 G11 **Nioro du Rip** SW Senegal 13°44′N 15°48′W
Nioro du Sahel *see* Nioro
102 K10 **Niort** Deux-Sèvres, W France 46°21′N 00°25′W
172 H14 **Nioumachoua** Mohéli, S Comoros 12°21′S 43°43′E
186 C7 **Nipa** Southern Highlands, W Papua New Guinea 06°11′S 143°27′E
11 U14 **Nipawin** Saskatchewan, S Canada 52°23′N 104°01′W
12 D12 **Nipigon** Ontario, S Canada 49°02′N 88°15′W
12 D11 **Nipigon, Lake** ◎ Ontario, S Canada
11 S13 **Nipin** ≈ Saskatchewan, C Canada
14 G11 **Nipissing, Lake** ◎ Ontario, S Canada
35 P13 **Nipomo** California, W USA 35°02′N 120°28′W
Nippon *see* Japan
138 K6 **Niqniqīyah, Jabal an** ▲▲ C Syria
62 I9 **Niquivil** San Juan, W Argentina 30°25′S 68°42′W
171 Y13 **Nirabotong** Papua, E Indonesia 02°35′S 140°08′E
Niriz *see* Neyrīz
163 U7 **Nirji** *var.* Morin Dawa Daurzu Zizhiqi. Nei Mongol Zizhiqu, N China 48°21′N 124°32′E
155 I14 **Nirmal** Andhra Pradesh, C India 19°04′N 78°21′E
153 Q13 **Nirmāli** Bihār, NE India 26°18′N 86°35′E
113 O14 **Niš** *Eng.* Nish, *Ger.* Nisch; *anc.* Naissus. Serbia, SE Serbia 43°21′N 21°53′E
104 H9 **Nisa** Portalegre, C Portugal 39°31′N 07°39′W
Nisa *see* Neisse
141 P4 **Nişab** Al Ḥudūd ash Shamālīyah, N Saudi Arabia 29°11′N 44°43′E
141 Q15 **Nişāb** *var.* Anşāb. SW Yemen 14°24′N 46°47′E
113 P14 **Nišava** *Bul.* Nishava. ≈ Bulgaria/Serbia *see also* Nishava
Nišava *see* Nishava
107 K25 **Niscemi** Sicilia, Italy, C Mediterranean Sea 37°09′N 14°23′E
Nisch/Nish *see* Niš
165 R4 **Niseko** Hokkaidō, NE Japan 42°50′N 140°43′E
Nishapur *see* Neyshābūr
114 G9 **Nishava** *var.* Nišava. ≈ Bulgaria/Serbia *see also* Nišava
Nishava *see* Nišava
118 L11 **Nishcha** ≈ N Belarus
165 C17 **Nishinoomote** Kagoshima, Tanega-shima, SW Japan 30°42′N 130°59′E
165 X15 **Nishino-shima** *Eng.* Rosario. *island* Ogasawara-shotō, SE Japan
165 I13 **Nishiwaki** *var.* Nisiwaki. Hyōgo, Honshū, SW Japan 34°59′N 134°58′E
141 U14 **Nishtūn** SE Yemen 15°47′N 52°08′E
Nisibin *see* Nusaybin
Nisiros *see* Nísyros
Nisiwaki *see* Nishiwaki
Niska *see* Niesky
113 O14 **Niška Banja** Serbia, SE Serbia 43°18′N 22°01′E
12 D6 **Niskibi** ≈ Ontario, C Canada
111 O15 **Nisko** Podkrapackie, SE Poland 50°31′N 22°09′E
10 H7 **Nisling** ≈ Yukon Territory, W Canada
99 H22 **Nismes** Namur, S Belgium 50°04′N 04°31′E
Nismes *see* Nîmes
116 M10 **Nisporeni** *Rus.* Nisporeny. W Moldova 47°04′N 28°10′E
Nisporeny *see* Nisporeni
95 K20 **Nissan** ≈ S Sweden
Nissan Islands *see* Green Islands
95 F16 **Nisser** ◎ S Norway
95 E21 **Nissum Bredning** *inlet* NW Denmark
29 U6 **Nisswa** Minnesota, N USA 46°31′N 94°17′W
Nistru *see* Dniester
115 M22 **Nísyros** *var.* Nisiros. *island* Dodekánisa, Greece, Aegean Sea
118 H8 **Nītaure** C Latvia 57°05′N 25°12′E
60 P10 **Niterói** *prev.* Nictheroy. Rio de Janeiro, SE Brazil 22°54′S 43°06′W
14 F16 **Nith** ≈ Ontario, S Canada
96 J13 **Nith** ≈ S Scotland, United Kingdom
Nitinan *see* Nichinan
111 I21 **Nitra** *Ger.* Neutra, *Hung.* Nyitra. Nitriansky Kraj, SW Slovakia 48°20′N 18°05′E
111 I20 **Nitra** *Ger.* Neutra, *Hung.* Nyitra. ≈ W Slovakia
111 I21 **Nitriansky Kraj** ◈ *region* SW Slovakia
21 Q5 **Nitro** West Virginia, NE USA 38°24′N 81°50′W
Niuatobutabu *see* Niuatoputapu
193 X13 **Niuatoputapu** *var.* Niuatobutabu; *prev.* Keppel Island. *island* N Tonga
193 U15 **Niu'Aunofa** *headland* Tongatapu, S Tonga 21°03′S 175°19′W
Niuchwang *see* Yingkou
190 B16 **Niue** ◇ *self-governing territory in free association with New Zealand* S Pacific Ocean
190 F10 **Niulakita** *var.* Nurakita. *atoll* S Tuvalu
190 E6 **Niutao** *atoll* NW Tuvalu
93 L15 **Nivala** Oulu, C Finland 63°56′N 25°00′E
102 I15 **Nive** ≈ SW France
99 G19 **Nivelles** Walloon Brabant, C Belgium 50°36′N 04°04′E
103 P8 **Nivernais** *cultural region* C France
15 N8 **Niverville, Lac** ◎ Québec, SE Canada
27 T7 **Nixa** Missouri, C USA 37°02′N 93°17′W
35 R5 **Nixon** Nevada, W USA 39°48′N 119°24′W
25 S12 **Nixon** Texas, SW USA 29°16′N 97°45′W
Niya *see* Minfeng
Niyazov *see* Nyýazow
155 H14 **Nizāmābād** Andhra Pradesh, C India 18°40′N 78°05′E
155 H15 **Nizām Sāgar** ◎ C India
125 N16 **Nizhegorodskaya Oblast'** ◈ *province* W Russian Federation
Nizhnegorskiy *see* Nyzhn'ohirs'kyy
127 S4 **Nizhnekamsk** Respublika Tatarstan, W Russian Federation 55°36′N 51°45′E
127 U3 **Nizhnekamskoye Vodokhranilishche** ⊠ W Russian Federation
123 S14 **Nizhneleninskoye** Yevreyskaya Avtonomnaya Oblast', SE Russian Federation 47°50′N 132°30′E
122 L13 **Nizhneudinsk** Irkutskaya Oblast', S Russian Federation 54°48′N 98°51′E
122 I10 **Nizhnevartovsk** Khanty-Mansiyskiy Avtonomnyy Okrug-Yugra, C Russian Federation 60°57′N 76°40′E
123 Q7 **Nizhneyansk** Respublika Sakha (Yakutiya), NE Russian Federation 71°25′N 135°59′E
127 Q11 **Nizhniy Baskunchak** Astrakhanskaya Oblast', SW Russian Federation 48°15′N 46°49′E
127 O6 **Nizhniy Lomov** Penzenskaya Oblast', W Russian Federation 53°32′N 43°39′E
127 P3 **Nizhniy Novgorod** *prev.* Gor'kiy. Nizhegorodskaya Oblast', W Russian Federation 56°17′N 44°E
125 T8 **Nizhniy Odes** Respublika Komi, NW Russian Federation 63°42′N 54°59′E
Nizhniy Pyandzh *see* Panji Poyon
122 G10 **Nizhniy Tagil** Sverdlovskaya Oblast', C Russian Federation 57°57′N 59°51′E
125 T9 **Nizhnyaya-Omra** Respublika Komi, NW Russian Federation 62°46′N 55°54′E
125 P5 **Nizhnyaya Pësha** Nenetskiy Avtonomnyy Okrug, NW Russian Federation 66°54′N 47°37′E
117 Q3 **Nizhyn** *Rus.* Nezhin. Chernihivs'ka Oblast', NE Ukraine 51°03′N 31°54′E
136 M17 **Nizip** Gaziantep, S Turkey 37°02′N 37°47′E
141 X8 **Nizwa** *var.* Nazwāh. NE Oman 23°00′N 57°50′E
Nizza *see* Nice
106 C9 **Nizza Monferrato** Piemonte, NE Italy 44°47′N 08°22′E
Njávdám *see* Näätämöjoki
Njazidja *see* Ngazidja
Njellim *see* Nellim
81 H24 **Njombe** Iringa, S Tanzania 09°20′S 34°47′E
81 G23 **Njombe** ≈ C Tanzania
Njuk, Ozero *see* Nyuk, Ozero
Njuksenica *see* Nyuksenitsa
92 I10 **Njunis** ▲ N Norway 68°47′N 19°24′E
Njurunda *see* Njurundabommen
93 H17 **Njurundabommen** *prev.* Njurunda. Västernorrland, C Sweden 62°15′N 17°24′E
94 N11 **Njutånger** Gävleborg, C Sweden 61°37′N 17°04′E
79 D14 **Nkambe** Nord-Ouest, NW Cameroon 06°35′N 10°44′E
Nkata Bay *see* Nkhata Bay
79 F21 **Nkayi** *prev.* Jacob. Bouenza, S Congo 04°11′S 13°17′E
83 J17 **Nkayi** Matabeleland North, W Zimbabwe 19°00′S 28°54′E
82 N13 **Nkhata Bay** *var.* Nkata Bay. Northern, N Malawi 11°37′S 34°20′E
81 E22 **Nkonde** Kigoma, N Tanzania 06°16′S 30°17′E
79 D15 **Nkongsamba** *var.* N'Kongsamba. Littoral, W Cameroon 04°59′N 09°53′E
N'Kongsamba *see* Nkongsamba
83 E16 **Nkurenkuru** Okavango, N Namibia 17°38′S 18°39′E
77 Q15 **Nkwanta** E Ghana 08°18′N 00°27′E
167 O2 **Nmai Hka** *var.* Me Hka. ≈ N Burma (Myanmar)
Noardwâlde *see* Noordwolde
39 N7 **Noatak** Alaska, USA 67°34′N 162°58′W
39 N7 **Noatak River** ≈ Alaska, USA
164 E15 **Nobeoka** Miyazaki, Kyūshū, SW Japan 32°34′N 131°37′E
27 N11 **Noble** Oklahoma, C USA 35°08′N 97°23′W
31 P13 **Noblesville** Indiana, N USA 40°03′N 86°00′W
165 R5 **Noboribetsu** *var.* Noboribetu. Hokkaidō, NE Japan 42°27′N 141°08′E
Noboribetu *see* Noboribetsu
59 H18 **Nobres** Mato Grosso, W Brazil 14°44′S 56°15′W
107 N21 **Nocera Terinese** Calabria, S Italy 39°03′N 16°10′E
41 Q16 **Nochixtlán** *var.* Asunción Nochixtlán. Oaxaca, SE Mexico 17°29′N 97°17′W
25 S5 **Nocona** Texas, SW USA 33°47′N 97°43′W
63 K21 **Nodales, Bahía de los** *bay* S Argentina
27 Q2 **Nodaway River** ≈ Iowa/Missouri, C USA
27 R8 **Noel** Missouri, C USA 36°33′N 94°29′W
40 H3 **Nogales** Chihuahua, NW Mexico 18°50′N 97°12′W
40 F3 **Nogales** Sonora, NW Mexico 31°17′N 110°53′W
36 M17 **Nogales** Arizona, SW USA 31°20′N 110°55′W
Nogal Valley *see* Dooxo Nugaaleed
102 K15 **Nogaro** Gers, S France 43°46′N 00°01′W
110 J7 **Nogat** ≈ N Poland
164 D12 **Nōgata** Fukuoka, Kyūshū, SW Japan 33°46′N 130°42′E
127 P15 **Nogayskaya Step'** *steppe* SW Russian Federation
102 M6 **Nogent-le-Rotrou** Eure-et-Loir, C France 48°19′N 00°50′E
103 O4 **Nogent-sur-Oise** Oise, N France 49°16′N 02°28′E
103 P6 **Nogent-sur-Seine** Aube, N France 48°30′N 03°31′E
122 L10 **Noginsk** Krasnoyarskiy Kray, N Russian Federation 64°28′N 91°09′E
126 L3 **Noginsk** Moskovskaya Oblast', W Russian Federation 55°51′N 38°23′E
123 T12 **Nogliki** Ostrov Sakhalin, Sakhalinskaya Oblast', SE Russian Federation 51°44′N 143°14′E
164 K12 **Nōgōhaku-san** ▲ Honshū, SW Japan 35°46′N 136°30′E
162 D5 **Nogoonnuur** Bayan-Ölgiy, NW Mongolia 49°31′N 89°48′E
61 C18 **Nogoyá** Entre Ríos, E Argentina 32°25′S 59°50′W
111 K21 **Nógrád** *off.* Nógrád Megye. ◈ *county* N Hungary
Nógrád Megye *see* Nógrád
105 U5 **Noguera Pallaresa** ≈ NE Spain
105 U4 **Noguera Ribagorçana** ≈ NE Spain
101 E19 **Nohfelden** Saarland, SW Germany 49°35′N 07°08′E
38 A8 **Nohili Point** *headland* Kaua'i, Hawai'i, USA 22°03′N 159°48′W
104 G3 **Noia** Galicia, NW Spain 42°48′N 08°52′W
103 N16 **Noire, Montagne** ▲▲ S France
14 J10 **Noire, Rivière** ≈ Québec, SE Canada
15 P12 **Noire, Rivière** ≈ Québec, SE Canada
Noire, Rivi`ere *see* Black River
102 G6 **Noires, Montagnes** ▲▲ NW France
102 H8 **Noirmoutier-en-l'Île** Vendée, NW France 47°00′N 02°15′W
102 H8 **Noirmoutier, Île de** *island* NW France
187 Q10 **Noka** Nendö, E Solomon Islands 10°42′S 165°57′E
83 G17 **Nokaneng** North West, NW Botswana 19°40′S 22°12′E
93 L18 **Nokia** Länsi-Suomi, W Finland 61°29′N 23°30′E
148 K11 **Nok Kundi** Baluchistān, SW Pakistan 28°49′N 62°39′E
30 L14 **Nokomis** Illinois, N USA 39°18′N 89°17′W
30 K5 **Nokomis, Lake** ⊠ Wisconsin, N USA
78 G9 **Nokou** Kanem, W Chad 14°36′N 14°45′E
187 Q12 **Nokuku** Espiritu Santo, W Vanuatu 14°56′S 166°34′E
95 J18 **Nol** Västra Götaland, S Sweden 57°55′N 12°03′E
79 H16 **Nola** Sangha-Mbaéré, SW Central African Republic 03°29′N 16°05′E
25 P7 **Nolan** Texas, SW USA 32°15′N 100°15′W
125 R15 **Nolinsk** Kirovskaya Oblast', NW Russian Federation 57°35′N 49°54′E
Nolsø *see* Nólsoy
95 B19 **Nólsoy** *Dan.* Nolsø. *island* E Faeroe Islands
186 B7 **Nomad** Western, SW Papau New Guinea 06°11′S 142°13′E
164 B16 **Noma-zaki** Kyūshū, SW Japan
40 K10 **Nombre de Dios** Durango, C Mexico 23°51′N 104°14′W
42 I5 **Nombre de Dios, Cordillera** ▲▲ N Honduras
38 M9 **Nome** Alaska, USA 64°30′N 165°24′W
29 Q6 **Nome** North Dakota, N USA 46°39′N 97°49′W
38 M9 **Nome, Cape** *headland* Alaska, USA 64°25′N 165°00′W
162 K11 **Nomgon** *var.* Sangiyn Dalay. Ömnögovĭ, S Mongolia 42°50′N 105°04′E
14 M11 **Nominingue, Lac** ◎ Québec, SE Canada
Nomoi Islands *see* Mortlock Islands
164 B16 **Nomo-zaki** *headland* Kyūshū, SW Japan 32°34′N 129°45′E
162 G6 **Nömrög** *var.* Hödrögö. Dzavhan, N Mongolia 48°51′N 96°48′E
193 X15 **Nomuka** *island* Nomuka Group, C Tonga
193 X15 **Nomuka Group** *island group* W Tonga
189 Q15 **Nomwin Atoll** *atoll* Hall Islands, C Micronesia
8 L10 **Nonacho Lake** ◎ Northwest Territories, NW Canada
Nondaburi *see* Nonthaburi
39 P12 **Nondalton** Alaska, USA 59°58′N 154°51′W
163 V10 **Nong'an** Jilin, NE China 44°25′N 125°10′E
169 P10 **Nong Bua Khok** Nakhon Ratchasima, C Thailand 15°23′N 101°51′E
167 Q9 **Nong Bua Lamphu** Udon Thani, E Thailand 17°11′N 102°27′E
167 R7 **Nông Hèt** Xiangkhoang, N Laos 19°27′N 104°02′E
Nongkaya *see* Nong Khai
167 Q8 **Nong Khai** *var.* Mi Chai, Nongkaya. Nong Khai, E Thailand 17°52′N 102°44′E
Nongle *see* Jiuzhaigou
167 N14 **Nong Met** Surat Thani, SW Thailand 09°27′N 99°09′E
83 L22 **Nongoma** KwaZulu/Natal, E South Africa 27°54′S 31°40′E
167 P9 **Nong Phai** Phetchabun, C Thailand 15°58′N 101°02′E
153 U13 **Nongstoin** Meghālaya, NE India 25°24′N 91°19′E
83 C19 **Nonidas** Erongo, N Namibia 22°36′S 14°40′E
Nonni *see* Nen Jiang
40 I7 **Nonoava** Chihuahua, N Mexico 27°24′N 106°18′W
191 O3 **Nonouti** *prev.* Sydenham Island. *atoll* Tungaru, W Kiribati
167 O11 **Nonthaburi** *var.* Nondaburi, Nontha Buri. Nonthaburi, C Thailand 13°48′N 100°11′E
Nontha Buri *see* Nonthaburi
102 L11 **Nontron** Dordogne, SW France 45°34′N 00°41′E
147 T10 **Nookat** *var.* Iski-Nauket; *prev.* Eski-Nookat. Oshskaya Oblast', SW Kyrgyzstan 40°18′N 72°29′E
181 P1 **Noonamah** Northern Territory, N Australia 12°46′S 131°08′E
28 K2 **Noonan** North Dakota, N USA 48°51′N 102°57′W
Noonu *see* South Miladhunmadulu Atoll
99 E14 **Noord-Beveland** *var.* North Beveland. *island* SW Netherlands
99 J14 **Noord-Brabant** *Eng.* North Brabant. ◈ *province* S Netherlands
98 H7 **Noorder Haaks** *spit* NW Netherlands
98 H9 **Noord-Holland** *Eng.* North Holland. ◈ *province* NW Netherlands
Noordhollandsch Kanaal *see* Noordhollands Kanaal
98 H8 **Noordhollands Kanaal** *var.* Noordhollandsch Kanaal. *canal* NW Netherlands
Noord-Kaap *see* Northern Cape
98 L8 **Noordoostpolder** *island* N Netherlands
45 P16 **Noordpunt** *headland* Curaçao, C Netherlands Antilles 12°21′N 69°08′W
98 I8 **Noord-Scharwoude** Noord-Holland, NW Netherlands 52°42′N 04°48′E
Noordwes *see* North-West
98 G11 **Noordwijk aan Zee** Zuid-Holland, W Netherlands 52°15′N 04°25′E
98 H11 **Noordwijkerhout** Zuid-Holland, W Netherlands 52°16′N 04°30′E
98 M7 **Noordwolde** *Fris.* Noardwâlde. Fryslân, N Netherlands 52°54′N 06°10′E
Noordzee *see* North Sea
98 H10 **Noordzee-Kanaal** *canal* NW Netherlands
93 K18 **Noormarkku** *Swe.* Norrmark. Länsi-Suomi, SW Finland 61°35′N 21°54′E
39 N8 **Noorvik** Alaska, USA 66°50′N 161°01′W
10 J17 **Nootka Sound** *inlet* British Columbia, W Canada
82 A9 **Nóqui** Dem. Rep. Congo, NW Angola 05°54′S 13°30′E
95 L15 **Nora** Örebro, C Sweden 59°31′N 15°02′E
147 Q13 **Norak** *Rus.* Nurek. W Tajikistan 38°23′N 69°14′E
13 I13 **Noranda** Québec, SE Canada 48°16′N 79°03′W
29 W12 **Nora Springs** Iowa, C USA 43°08′N 93°00′W
95 M14 **Norberg** Västmanland, C Sweden 60°04′N 15°56′E
14 K13 **Norcan Lake** ◎ Ontario, SE Canada
197 R12 **Nord** Avannaarsua, N Greenland 81°38′N 12°51′W
78 F13 **Nord** *Eng.* North. ◈ *province* N Cameroon
103 P2 **Nord** ◈ *department* N France
92 P1 **Nordaustlandet** *island* NE Svalbard
95 G24 **Nordborg** *Ger.* Nordburg. Syddanmark, SW Denmark 55°04′N 09°41′E
Nordburg *see* Nordborg
95 F23 **Nordby** Syddtjylland, W Denmark 55°27′N 08°25′E
11 P15 **Nordegg** Alberta, SW Canada 52°27′N 116°06′W
100 E9 **Norden** Niedersachsen, NW Germany 53°36′N 07°12′E

◆ Country
● Country Capital
◇ Dependent Territory
○ Dependent Territory Capital
◈ Administrative Regions
✈ International Airport
▲ Mountain
▲▲ Mountain Range
Volcano
≈ River
◎ Lake
⊠ Reservoir

100 G10 **Nordenham** Niedersachsen, NW Germany 53°30′N 08°29′E
122 M6 **Nordenshel'da, Arkhipelag** island group N Russian Federation
92 O3 **Nordenskiold Land** physical region W Svalbard
100 E9 **Norderney** island NW Germany
100 J9 **Norderstedt** Schleswig-Holstein, N Germany 53°42′N 09°59′E
94 D11 **Nordfjord** fjord S Norway
94 C11 **Nordfjord** physical region S Norway
94 D11 **Nordfjordeid** Sogn og Fjordane, S Norway 61°54′N 06°E
92 G11 **Nordfold** Nordland, C Norway 67°48′N 15°16′E
Nordfriesische Inseln see North Frisian Islands
100 H7 **Nordfriesland** cultural region N Germany
Nordgrønland see Avannaarsua
101 K15 **Nordhausen** Thüringen, C Germany 51°31′N 10°48′E
25 T13 **Nordheim** Texas, SW USA 28°55′N 97°36′W
94 C13 **Nordhordland** physical region S Norway
100 E12 **Nordhorn** Niedersachsen, NW Germany 52°26′N 07°04′E
92 I1 **Nordhurfjördhur** Vestfirdhir, NW Iceland 66°01′N 21°33′W
92 J1 **Nordhurland Eystra** ◐ region N Iceland
92 I2 **Nordhurland Vestra** ◐ region N Iceland
172 H16 **Nord, Île du** island Inner Islands, NE Seychelles
95 F20 **Nordjylland** ◐ region N Denmark
Nordjyllands Amt see Nordjylland
92 K7 **Nordkapp** Eng. North Cape. headland N Norway 25°47′E 71°10′N
92 O1 **Nordkapp** headland N Svalbard 80°31′N 19°58′E
79 N19 **Nord-Kivu** off. Région du Nord Kivu. ◐ region E Dem. Rep. Congo
Nord Kivu, Région du see Nord-Kivu
92 G12 **Nordland** ◐ county C Norway
101 J21 **Nördlingen** Bayern, S Germany 48°49′N 10°28′E
93 I16 **Nordmaling** Västerbotten, N Sweden 63°35′N 19°30′E
95 K15 **Nordmark** Värmland, C Sweden 59°52′N 14°04′E
Nord, Mer du see North Sea
94 F8 **Nordmøre** physical region S Norway
100 I8 **Nord-Ostee-Kanal** canal N Germany
0 J3 **Nordøstrundingen** cape NE Greenland
79 D14 **Nord-Ouest** Eng. North-West. ◐ province NW Cameroon
Nord-Ouest, Territoires du see Northwest Territories
103 N2 **Nord-Pas-de-Calais** ◐ region N France
101 F19 **Nordpfälzer Bergland** ▲▲ W Germany
Nord, Pointe see Fatua, Pointe
187 P16 **Nord, Province** ◐ province C New Caledonia
101 D14 **Nordrhein-Westfalen** Eng. North Rhine-Westphalia, Fr. Rhénanie du Nord-Westphalie. ◐ state W Germany
Nordsee/Nordsjøen/Nordsøen see North Sea
100 H7 **Nordstrand** island N Germany
93 E15 **Nord-Trøndelag** ◐ county C Norway
97 E19 **Nore** Ir. An Fheoir. ~ S Ireland
29 Q14 **Norfolk** Nebraska, C USA 42°01′N 97°25′W
21 X7 **Norfolk** Virginia, NE USA 36°51′N 76°17′W
97 P19 **Norfolk** cultural region E England, United Kingdom
192 K10 **Norfolk Island** ◇ Australian external territory SW Pacific Ocean
175 P9 **Norfolk Ridge** undersea feature W Pacific Ocean
27 U8 **Norfork Lake** ⊡ Arkansas/Missouri, C USA
98 N6 **Norg** Drenthe, NE Netherlands 53°04′N 06°28′E
Norge see Norway
95 D14 **Norheimsund** Hordaland, S Norway 60°22′N 06°09′E
25 S16 **Norias** Texas, SW USA 26°47′N 97°45′W
164 L12 **Norikura-dake** ▲ Honshū, S Japan 36°06′N 137°33′E
122 K8 **Noril'sk** Krasnoyarskiy Kray, N Russian Federation 69°21′N 88°02′E
14 I13 **Norland** Ontario, SE Canada 44°46′N 78°48′W
21 V8 **Norlina** North Carolina, SE USA 36°26′N 78°11′W
30 L13 **Normal** Illinois, N USA 40°30′N 88°59′W
27 N11 **Norman** Oklahoma, C USA 35°13′N 97°27′W
Norman see Tulita
186 G9 **Normanby Island** island SE Papua New Guinea
Normandes, Îles see Channel Islands
58 G9 **Normandia** Roraima, N Brazil 03°57′N 59°39′W
102 L5 **Normandie** Eng. Normandy. cultural region N France
102 J5 **Normandie, Collines de** hill range NW France
Normandy see Normandie
25 V9 **Normangee** Texas, SW USA 31°01′N 96°06′W
21 Q10 **Norman, Lake** ⊡ North Carolina, SE USA
44 K13 **Norman Manley** ✕ (Kingston) E Jamaica 17°55′N 76°46′W
181 U5 **Norman River** ~ Queensland, NE Australia
181 U4 **Normanton** Queensland, NE Australia 17°49′S 141°08′E
8 I8 **Norman Wells** Northwest Territories, NW Canada 65°18′N 126°42′W
12 H12 **Normétal** Québec, S Canada 48°59′N 79°23′W
163 O7 **Norovlin** var. Uldz. Hentiy, NE Mongolia 48°47′N 112°01′E
11 V15 **Norquay** Saskatchewan, S Canada 51°51′N 102°04′W
93 G15 **Norråker** Jämtland, C Sweden 64°25′N 15°40′E
94 N12 **Norrala** Gävleborg, C Sweden 61°22′N 17°04′E
Norra Ny see Stöllet
92 G13 **Norra Storfjället** ▲ N Sweden 65°57′N 15°15′E
92 I13 **Norrbotten** ◐ county N Sweden
94 N11 **Norrdellen** ⊚ C Sweden
95 G23 **Nørre Aaby** var. Nørre Åby. Syddtjylland, C Denmark 55°28′N 09°53′E
Nørre Åby see Nørre Aaby
95 I24 **Nørre Alslev** Sjælland, SE Denmark 54°54′N 11°53′E
95 E23 **Nørre Nebel** Syddtjylland, W Denmark 55°45′N 08°16′E
95 G20 **Nørresundby** Nordjylland, N Denmark 57°05′N 09°55′E
21 N8 **Norris Lake** ⊡ Tennessee, S USA
18 I15 **Norristown** Pennsylvania, NE USA 40°07′N 75°20′W
95 N17 **Norrköping** Östergötland, S Sweden 58°35′N 16°10′E
Norrmark see Noormarkku
94 N13 **Norrsundet** Gävleborg, C Sweden 60°55′N 17°09′E
95 P15 **Norrtälje** Stockholm, C Sweden 59°46′N 18°42′E
180 L12 **Norseman** Western Australia 32°16′S 121°46′E
93 I14 **Norsjö** Västerbotten, N Sweden 64°55′N 19°30′E
95 G16 **Norsjø** ⊚ S Norway
123 R13 **Norsk** Amurskaya Oblast', SE Russian Federation 52°20′N 129°57′E
Norske Havet see Norwegian Sea
187 Q13 **Norsup** Malekula, C Vanuatu 16°05′S 167°24′E
191 V15 **Norte, Cabo** headland Easter Island, Chile, E Pacific Ocean 27°03′S 109°24′W
54 F7 **Norte de Santander** off. Departamento de Norte de Santander. ◐ province N Colombia
Norte de Santander, Departamento de see Norte de Santander
61 E21 **Norte, Punta** headland E Argentina 36°17′S 56°46′W
21 R13 **North** South Carolina, SE USA 33°37′N 81°06′W
North see Nord
18 L10 **North Adams** Massachusetts, NE USA 42°40′N 73°06′W
113 L17 **North Albanian Alps** Alb. Bjeshkët e Namuna, SCr. Prokletije. ▲▲ SE Europe
97 M15 **Northallerton** N England, United Kingdom 54°20′N 01°26′W
180 J12 **Northam** Western Australia 31°40′S 116°40′E
83 J20 **Northam** Northern, N South Africa 24°56′S 27°18′E
1 **North America** continent
1 N12 **North American Basin** undersea feature W Sargasso Sea 30°00′N 60°00′W
0 C5 **North American Plate** tectonic feature
18 M11 **North Amherst** Massachusetts, NE USA 42°24′N 72°31′W
97 N20 **Northampton** C England, United Kingdom 52°14′N 00°54′W
97 M20 **Northamptonshire** cultural region C England, United Kingdom
151 P18 **North Andaman** island Andaman Islands, India, NE Indian Ocean
65 D25 **North Arm** East Falkland, Falkland Islands 52°06′S 59°21′W
21 Q13 **North Augusta** South Carolina, SE USA 33°30′N 81°58′W
173 W8 **North Australian Basin** Fr. Bassin Nord de l' Australie. undersea feature E Indian Ocean
31 R11 **North Baltimore** Ohio, N USA 41°10′N 83°40′W
11 T15 **North Battleford** Saskatchewan, S Canada 52°47′N 108°19′W
14 H11 **North Bay** Ontario, S Canada 46°20′N 79°28′W
12 H6 **North Belcher Islands** island group Belcher Islands, Nunavut, C Canada
29 R15 **North Bend** Nebraska, C USA 41°27′N 96°46′W
32 E14 **North Bend** Oregon, NW USA 43°24′N 124°13′W
96 K12 **North Berwick** SE Scotland, United Kingdom 56°04′N 02°44′W
North Beveland see Noord-Beveland
North Borneo see Sabah
183 P5 **North Bourke** New South Wales, SE Australia 30°03′S 145°56′E
North Brabant see Noord-Brabant
182 F2 **North Branch Neales** seasonal river South Australia
44 M6 **North Caicos** island NW Turks and Caicos Islands
26 L10 **North Canadian River** ~ Oklahoma, C USA
31 U12 **North Canton** Ohio, N USA 40°52′N 81°24′W
13 R13 **North, Cape** headland Cape Breton Island, Nova Scotia, SE Canada 47°06′N 60°24′W
184 I1 **North Cape** headland North Island, New Zealand 34°23′S 173°02′E
186 G5 **North Cape** headland New Ireland, NE Papua New Guinea 02°33′S 150°48′E
North Cape see Nordkapp
18 J17 **North Cape May** New Jersey, NE USA 38°59′N 74°55′W
12 C9 **North Caribou Lake** ⊚ Ontario, C Canada
21 U10 **North Carolina** off. State of North Carolina, also known as Old North State, Tar Heel State, Turpentine State. ◐ state SE USA
North Celebes see Sulawesi Utara
155 J24 **North Central** ◐ province N Sri Lanka
31 S4 **North Channel** lake channel Canada/USA
97 G14 **North Channel** strait Northern Ireland/Scotland, United Kingdom
21 S14 **North Charleston** South Carolina, SE USA 32°53′N 79°59′W
31 N10 **North Chicago** Illinois, N USA 42°19′N 87°50′W
195 Y10 **Northcliffe Glacier** glacier Antarctica
31 Q14 **North College Hill** Ohio, N USA 39°13′N 84°33′W
25 O8 **North Concho River** ~ Texas, SW USA
19 O8 **North Conway** New Hampshire, NE USA 44°03′N 71°06′W
27 V14 **North Crossett** Arkansas, C USA 33°10′N 91°56′W
28 L4 **North Dakota** off. State of North Dakota, also known as Flickertail State, Peace Garden State, Sioux State. ◐ state N USA
North Devon Island see Devon Island
97 O22 **North Downs** hill range SE England, United Kingdom
18 C11 **North East** Pennsylvania, NE USA 42°13′N 79°49′W
83 I18 **North East** ◐ district NE Botswana
65 G15 **North East Bay** bay Ascension Island, C Atlantic Ocean
38 L10 **Northeast Cape** headland Saint Lawrence Island, Alaska, USA 63°16′N 168°50′W
81 J17 **North Eastern** ◐ province Kenya
North East Frontier Agency/North East Frontier Agency of Assam see Arunāchal Pradesh
65 E25 **North East Island** island E Falkland Islands
189 V11 **Northeast Island** island Chuuk, C Micronesia
44 L6 **Northeast Point** headland Great Inagua, S Bahamas 21°18′N 73°01′W
44 K5 **Northeast Point** headland Acklins Island, SE Bahamas 22°43′N 73°50′W
44 L12 **North East Point** headland E Jamaica 18°09′N 76°19′W
191 Z2 **Northeast Point** headland Kiritimati, E Kiribati 10°23′S 105°45′E
44 H2 **Northeast Providence Channel** channel N Bahamas
101 J14 **Northeim** Niedersachsen, C Germany 51°42′N 10°E
29 X14 **North English** Iowa, C USA 41°30′N 92°04′W
138 G8 **Northern** ◐ district N Israel
82 M12 **Northern** ◐ region N Malawi
186 F8 **Northern** ◐ province S Papua New Guinea
155 J22 **Northern** ◐ province N Sri Lanka
80 D7 **Northern** ◐ state N Sudan
82 K12 **Northern** ◐ province NE Zambia
Northern see Limpopo
80 B13 **Northern Bahr el Ghazal** ◐ state NW South Sudan
Northern Border Region see Al Ḥudūd ash Shamālīyah
83 F24 **Northern Cape** off. Northern Cape Province, Afr. Noord-Kaap. ◐ province W South Africa
Northern Cape Province see Northern Cape
190 K14 **Northern Cook Islands** island group N Cook Islands
80 B8 **Northern Darfur** ◐ state NW Sudan
Northern Dvina see Severnaya Dvina
97 F14 **Northern Ireland** var. The Six Counties. cultural region Northern Ireland, United Kingdom
97 F14 **Northern Ireland** var. The Six Counties. ◐ political division Northern Ireland, United Kingdom
80 D9 **Northern Kordofan** ◐ state C Sudan
187 Z14 **Northern Lau Group** island group Lau Group, NE Fiji
188 K3 **Northern Mariana Islands** ◇ US commonwealth territory W Pacific Ocean
Northern Rhodesia see Zambia
Northern Sporades see Vóreies Sporádes
182 D1 **Northern Territory** ◐ territory N Australia
Northern Transvaal see Limpopo
Northern Ural Hills see Severnyye Uvaly
84 I9 **North European Plain** plain N Europe
27 V2 **North Fabius River** ~ Missouri, C USA
65 D24 **North Falkland Sound** sound N Falkland Islands
29 V9 **Northfield** Minnesota, N USA 44°27′N 93°10′W
19 O9 **Northfield** New Hampshire, NE USA 43°26′N 71°34′W
175 Q8 **North Fiji Basin** undersea feature N Coral Sea
97 Q22 **North Foreland** headland SE England, United Kingdom 51°22′N 01°26′E
35 P6 **North Fork American River** ~ California, W USA
39 R7 **North Fork Chandalar River** ~ Alaska, USA
28 K7 **North Fork Grand River** ~ North Dakota/South Dakota, N USA
21 O6 **North Fork Kentucky River** ~ Kentucky, S USA
39 Q7 **North Fork Koyukuk River** ~ Alaska, USA
39 Q10 **North Fork Kuskokwim River** ~ Alaska, USA
26 K11 **North Fork Red River** ~ Oklahoma/Texas, SW USA
26 K3 **North Fork Solomon River** ~ Kansas, C USA
23 W14 **North Fort Myers** Florida, SE USA 26°40′N 81°52′W
31 P5 **North Fox Island** island Michigan, N USA
100 G6 **North Frisian Islands** var. Nordfriesische Inseln. island group N Germany
197 N9 **North Geomagnetic Pole** pole Arctic Ocean
18 M13 **North Haven** Connecticut, NE USA 41°25′N 72°51′W
184 J5 **North Head** headland North Island, New Zealand 36°23′S 174°01′E
18 L6 **North Hero** Vermont, NE USA 44°49′N 73°14′W
35 O7 **North Highlands** California, W USA 38°40′N 121°25′W
North Holland see Noord-Holland
81 I16 **North Horr** Eastern, N Kenya 03°17′N 37°08′E
151 K21 **North Huvadhu Atoll** var. Gaafu Alifu Atoll. atoll S Maldives
65 A24 **North Island** island W Falkland Islands
184 N9 **North Island** island N New Zealand
21 U14 **North Island** island South Carolina, SE USA
31 O11 **North Judson** Indiana, N USA 41°12′N 86°44′W
North Kazakhstan see Severnyy Kazakhstan
31 V10 **North Kingsville** Ohio, N USA 41°54′N 80°41′W
163 Y13 **North Korea** off. Democratic People's Republic of Korea, Kor. Chosŏn-minjujuŭi-inmin-kanghwaguk. ◆ republic E Asia
153 X11 **North Lakhimpur** Assam, NE India 27°10′N 94°00′E
184 J3 **Northland** off. Northland Region. ◐ region North Island, New Zealand
192 K11 **Northland Plateau** undersea feature S Pacific Ocean
Northland Region see Northland
35 X11 **North Las Vegas** Nevada, W USA 36°12′N 115°07′W
31 O11 **North Liberty** Indiana, N USA 41°36′N 86°22′W
29 X14 **North Liberty** Iowa, C USA 41°45′N 91°36′W
27 V12 **North Little Rock** Arkansas, C USA 34°46′N 92°15′W
28 M13 **North Loup River** ~ Nebraska, C USA
151 K18 **North Maalhosmadulu Atoll** var. North Malosmadulu Atoll, Raa Atoll. atoll N Maldives
31 U10 **North Madison** Ohio, N USA 41°48′N 81°03′W
North Malosmadulu Atoll see North Maalhosmadulu Atoll
31 P12 **North Manchester** Indiana, N USA 41°00′N 85°45′W
31 P6 **North Manitou Island** island Michigan, N USA
29 U10 **North Mankato** Minnesota, N USA 44°11′N 94°03′W
23 Z15 **North Miami** Florida, SE USA 25°54′N 80°11′W
151 K18 **North Miladhunmadulu Atoll** var. Shaviyani Atoll. atoll N Maldives
North Minch see Minch, The
23 W15 **North Naples** Florida, SE USA 26°13′N 81°47′W
175 P8 **North New Hebrides Trench** undersea feature N Coral Sea
23 Y15 **North New River Canal** ~ Florida, SE USA
151 K20 **North Nilandhe Atoll** atoll C Maldives
36 L2 **North Ogden** Utah, W USA 41°18′N 111°57′W
North Ossetia see Severnaya Osetiya-Alaniya, Respublika
35 S10 **North Palisade** ▲ California, W USA 37°06′N 118°31′W
189 U11 **North Pass** passage Chuuk Islands, C Micronesia
28 M15 **North Platte** Nebraska, C USA 41°07′N 100°46′W
33 X17 **North Platte River** ~ C USA
65 G14 **North Point** headland Ascension Island, C Atlantic Ocean
172 I16 **North Point** headland Mahé, NE Seychelles 04°23′S 55°28′E
31 S6 **North Point** headland Michigan, N USA 45°01′N 83°16′W
31 R5 **North Point** headland Michigan, N USA 45°21′N 83°30′W
39 S9 **North Pole** Alaska, USA 64°42′N 147°09′W
197 R9 **North Pole** pole Arctic Ocean
23 O4 **Northport** Alabama, S USA 33°13′N 87°34′W
23 W14 **North Port** Florida, SE USA 27°03′N 82°15′W
32 L6 **Northport** Washington, NW USA 48°54′N 117°48′W
32 L12 **North Powder** Oregon, NW USA 45°00′N 117°56′W
29 U13 **North Raccoon River** ~ Iowa, C USA
North Rhine-Westphalia see Nordrhein-Westfalen
97 M16 **North Riding** cultural region N England, United Kingdom
96 G5 **North Rona** island NW Scotland, United Kingdom
96 K4 **North Ronaldsay** island NE Scotland, United Kingdom
36 L2 **North Salt Lake** Utah, W USA 40°51′N 111°54′W
11 P15 **North Saskatchewan** ~ Alberta/Saskatchewan, S Canada
35 X5 **North Schell Peak** ▲ Nevada, W USA 39°25′N 114°34′W
North Scotia Ridge see South Georgia Ridge
86 D10 **North Sea** Dan. Nordsøen, Dut. Noordzee, Fr. Mer du Nord, Ger. Nordsee, Nor. Nordsjøen; prev. German Ocean, Lat. Mare Germanicum. sea NW Europe
35 T6 **North Shoshone Peak** ▲ Nevada, W USA 39°08′N 117°28′W
North Siberian Lowland/North Siberian Plain see Severo-Sibirskaya Nizmennost'
29 R13 **North Sioux City** South Dakota, N USA 42°31′N 96°28′W
96 K4 **North Sound, The** sound N Scotland, United Kingdom
183 T4 **North Star** New South Wales, SE Australia 28°55′S 150°25′E
North Star State see Minnesota
183 V3 **North Stradbroke Island** island Queensland, E Australia
North Sulawesi see Sulawesi Utara
North Sumatra see Sumatera Utara
14 D17 **North Sydenham** ~ Ontario, S Canada
18 H9 **North Syracuse** New York, NE USA 43°07′N 76°07′W
184 K9 **North Taranaki Bight** gulf North Island, New Zealand
12 H9 **North Twin Island** island Nunavut, C Canada
96 E8 **North Uist** island NW Scotland, United Kingdom
97 L14 **Northumberland** cultural region N England, United Kingdom
181 Y7 **Northumberland Isles** island group Queensland, NE Australia
13 Q14 **Northumberland Strait** strait SE Canada
32 G14 **North Umpqua River** ~ Oregon, NW USA
45 Q13 **North Union** Saint Vincent, Saint Vincent and the Grenadines 13°15′N 61°07′W
10 L17 **North Vancouver** British Columbia, SW Canada 49°21′N 123°05′W
18 K9 **Northville** New York, NE USA 43°13′N 74°08′W
97 Q19 **North Walsham** E England, United Kingdom 52°49′N 01°22′E
39 T10 **Northway** Alaska, USA 62°57′N 141°56′W
83 G17 **North-West** ◐ district NW Botswana
83 G21 **North-West** off. North-West Province, Afr. Noordwes. ◐ province N South Africa
North-West see Nord-Ouest
64 I6 **Northwest Atlantic Mid-Ocean Canyon** undersea feature N Atlantic Ocean
180 G8 **North West Cape** cape Western Australia
38 J9 **Northwest Cape** headland Saint Lawrence Island, Alaska, USA 63°46′N 171°45′W
155 J24 **North Western** ◐ province W Sri Lanka
82 H13 **North Western** ◐ province W Zambia
North-West Frontier Province see Khyber Pakhtunkhwa
96 H8 **North West Highlands** ▲▲ N Scotland, United Kingdom
192 J4 **Northwest Pacific Basin** undersea feature NW Pacific Ocean 40°00′N 150°00′E
191 Y2 **Northwest Point** headland Kiritimati, E Kiribati 10°25′S 105°35′E
44 G1 **Northwest Providence Channel** channel N Bahamas
North-West Province see North-West
13 Q8 **North West River** Newfoundland and Labrador, E Canada 53°30′N 60°10′W
8 J9 **Northwest Territories** Fr. Territoires du Nord-Ouest. ◐ territory NW Canada
97 K18 **Northwich** C England, United Kingdom 53°16′N 02°32′W
25 Q5 **North Wichita River** ~ Texas, SW USA
18 J17 **North Wildwood** New Jersey, NE USA 39°00′N 74°45′W
21 R9 **North Wilkesboro** North Carolina, SE USA 36°09′N 81°09′W
19 P8 **North Windham** Maine, NE USA 43°51′N 70°25′W
197 Q6 **Northwind Plain** undersea feature Arctic Ocean
29 V11 **Northwood** Iowa, C USA 43°26′N 93°13′W
29 Q4 **Northwood** North Dakota, N USA 47°43′N 97°34′W
97 M15 **North York Moors** moorland N England, United Kingdom
25 V9 **North Zulch** Texas, SW USA 30°54′N 96°06′W
26 K2 **Norton** Kansas, C USA 39°51′N 99°53′W
31 S13 **Norton** Ohio, N USA 40°25′N 83°04′W
21 P7 **Norton** Virginia, NE USA 36°56′N 82°37′W
39 N9 **Norton Bay** bay Alaska, USA
Norton de Matos see Balombo
31 O9 **Norton Shores** Michigan, N USA 43°10′N 86°15′W
38 M10 **Norton Sound** inlet Alaska, USA
27 Q3 **Nortonville** Kansas, C USA 39°25′N 95°19′W
102 I8 **Nort-sur-Erdre** Loire-Atlantique, NW France 47°27′N 01°30′W
195 N2 **Norvegia, Cape** headland Antarctica 71°16′S 12°25′W
18 L13 **Norwalk** Connecticut, NE USA 41°08′N 73°28′W
29 V14 **Norwalk** Iowa, C USA 41°28′N 93°40′W
31 S11 **Norwalk** Ohio, N USA 41°14′N 82°37′W
19 P7 **Norway** Maine, NE USA 44°13′N 70°30′W
31 N5 **Norway** Michigan, N USA 45°47′N 87°54′W
93 E17 **Norway** off. Kingdom of Norway, Nor. Norge. ◆ monarchy N Europe
11 X13 **Norway House** Manitoba, C Canada 53°59′N 97°50′W
Norway, Kingdom of see Norway
197 R16 **Norwegian Basin** undersea feature NW Norwegian Sea 68°00′N 02°00′W
84 D6 **Norwegian Sea** var. Norske Havet. sea NE Atlantic Ocean
197 S17 **Norwegian Trench** undersea feature NE North Sea 59°00′N 04°30′E
14 F16 **Norwich** Ontario, S Canada 42°57′N 80°37′W
97 Q19 **Norwich** E England, United Kingdom 52°38′N 01°18′E
19 N13 **Norwich** Connecticut, NE USA 41°30′N 72°02′W
18 I11 **Norwich** New York, NE USA 42°31′N 75°31′W
29 U9 **Norwood** Minnesota, N USA 44°46′N 93°55′W
31 Q15 **Norwood** Ohio, N USA 39°07′N 84°27′W
14 H11 **Nosbonsing, Lake** ⊚ Ontario, S Canada
Nösen see Bistrița
165 T1 **Noshappu-misaki** headland Hokkaidō, NE Japan 45°26′N 141°38′E
165 P7 **Noshiro** var. Nosiro; prev. Noshirominato. Akita, Honshū, C Japan 40°11′N 140°02′E
Noshirominato/Nosiro see Noshiro
117 Q3 **Nosivka** Rus. Nosovka. Chernihivs'ka Oblast', NE Ukraine 50°55′N 31°37′E
67 T14 **Nosop** var. Nossob, Nossop. ~ Botswana/Namibia
83 E20 **Nossop** ~ E Namibia
125 S4 **Nosovaya** Nenetskiy Avtonomnyy Okrug, NW Russian Federation 68°12′N 54°33′E
Nosovka see Nosivka
143 V11 **Noṣratābād** Sīstān va Balūchestān, E Iran 29°53′N 59°57′E
95 J18 **Nossebro** Västra Götaland, S Sweden 58°12′N 12°42′E
96 K6 **Noss Head** headland N Scotland, United Kingdom 58°29′N 03°03′W
Nossi-Bé see Be, Nosy
Nossob/Nossop see Nosop
172 J2 **Nosy Be** ✕ Antsiranana, N Madagascar 23°36′S 47°36′E
172 J6 **Nosy Varika** Fianarantsoa, SE Madagascar 20°36′S 48°31′E
14 L10 **Notawassi** ~ Québec, SE Canada
14 M9 **Notawassi, Lac** ⊚ Québec, SE Canada
36 J5 **Notch Peak** ▲ Utah, W USA 39°08′N 113°24′W
110 G10 **Noteć** Ger. Netze. ~ NW Poland
Nóties Sporádes see Dodekánisa
115 J22 **Nótion Aigaíon** Eng. Aegean South. ◐ region E Greece
115 H18 **Nótios Evvoïkós Kólpos** gulf E Greece
115 B16 **Nótio Stenó Kérkyras** strait W Greece
107 L25 **Noto** anc. Netum. Sicilia, Italy, C Mediterranean Sea 36°53′N 15°05′E
164 M10 **Noto** Ishikawa, Honshū, SW Japan 37°18′N 137°11′E
95 G15 **Notodden** Telemark, S Norway 59°35′N 09°18′E
107 L25 **Noto, Golfo di** gulf Sicilia, Italy, C Mediterranean Sea
164 L10 **Noto-hantō** peninsula Honshū, SW Japan
164 L11 **Noto-jima** island SW Japan
13 T11 **Notre Dame Bay** bay Newfoundland, Newfoundland and Labrador, E Canada
15 P6 **Notre-Dame-de-Lorette** Québec, SE Canada 49°05′N 72°24′W
14 L11 **Notre-Dame-de-Pontmain** Québec, SE Canada 46°18′N 75°37′W
15 T8 **Notre-Dame-du-Lac** Québec, SE Canada 47°36′N 68°48′W
15 Q6 **Notre-Dame-du-Rosaire** Québec, SE Canada 48°48′N 71°27′W
15 U8 **Notre-Dame, Monts** ▲▲ Québec, S Canada
77 R16 **Notsé** S Togo 06°59′N 01°12′E
14 G14 **Nottawasaga** ~ Ontario, S Canada
14 G14 **Nottawasaga Bay** lake bay Ontario, S Canada
12 I11 **Nottaway** ~ Québec, SE Canada
23 S1 **Nottely Lake** ⊡ Georgia, SE USA
95 H16 **Nøtterøy** island S Norway
97 M19 **Nottingham** C England, United Kingdom 52°58′N 01°10′W
9 E14 **Nottingham Island** island Nunavut, NE Canada
97 N18 **Nottinghamshire** cultural region C England, United Kingdom
21 V7 **Nottoway** Virginia, NE USA 37°07′N 78°03′W
21 V7 **Nottoway River** ~ Virginia, NE USA
76 G7 **Nouâdhibou** prev. Port-Étienne. Dakhlet Nouâdhibou, W Mauritania 20°54′N 17°01′W
76 G7 **Nouâdhibou** ✕ Dakhlet Nouâdhibou, W Mauritania 20°59′N 17°02′W
76 F7 **Nouâdhibou, Dakhlet** prev. Baie du Lévrier. bay W Mauritania
76 F7 **Nouâdhibou, Râs** prev. Cap Blanc. headland NW Mauritania 20°48′N 17°03′W
76 G9 **Nouakchott** ● (Mauritania) Nouakchott District, SW Mauritania 18°09′N 15°58′W
76 G9 **Nouakchott** ✕ Trarza, SW Mauritania 18°18′N 15°54′W
120 J11 **Noual, Sebkhet en** var. Sabkhat an Nawāl. salt flat C Tunisia
76 G8 **Nouâmghâr** var. Nouamrhar. Dakhlet Nouâdhibou, W Mauritania 19°22′N 16°31′W
Nouamrhar see Nouâmghâr
Nouă Sulița see Novoselytsya
187 Q17 **Nouméa** ○ (New Caledonia) Province Sud, S New Caledonia 22°13′S 166°29′E
79 E15 **Noun** ~ C Cameroon
77 N12 **Nouna** W Burkina 12°44′N 03°54′W
83 H24 **Noupoort** Northern Cape, C South Africa 31°11′S 24°57′E
Nouveau-Brunswick see New Brunswick
Nouveau-Comptoir see Wemindji
15 T4 **Nouvel, Lacs** ⊚ Québec, SE Canada
15 W7 **Nouvelle** Québec, SE Canada 48°07′N 66°16′W
15 W7 **Nouvelle** ~ Québec, SE Canada
Nouvelle-Calédonie see New Caledonia
Nouvelle Écosse see Nova Scotia
103 R3 **Nouzonville** Ardennes, N France 49°49′N 04°45′E
147 Q11 **Nov** Rus. Nau. NW Tajikistan 40°10′N 69°16′E
59 I21 **Nova Alvorada** Mato Grosso do Sul, SW Brazil 21°25′S 54°19′W
Novabad see Navobod
111 D19 **Nová Bystřice** Ger. Neubistritz. Jihočeský Kraj, S Czech Republic 49°N 15°05′E
116 H13 **Novaci** Gorj, SW Romania 45°07′N 23°37′E
Nova Civitas see Neustadt an der Weinstrasse
Novaesium see Neuss
60 H10 **Nova Esperança** Paraná, S Brazil 23°09′S 52°13′W
106 H11 **Novafeltria** Marche, C Italy 43°54′N 12°18′E
60 Q9 **Nova Friburgo** Rio de Janeiro, SE Brazil 22°16′S 42°34′W
82 D12 **Nova Gaia** var. Cambundi-Catembo. Malanje, NE Angola 10°09′S 17°31′E
109 S12 **Nova Gorica** W Slovenia 45°57′N 13°40′E
112 G10 **Nova Gradiška** Ger. Neugradisk, Hung. Újgradiska. Brod-Posavina, NE Croatia 45°15′N 17°23′E
60 K7 **Nova Granada** São Paulo, S Brazil 20°33′S 49°19′W
60 O10 **Nova Iguaçu** Rio de Janeiro, SE Brazil 22°31′S 44°05′W
117 S10 **Nova Kakhovka** Rus. Novaya Kakhovka. Khersons'ka Oblast', SE Ukraine 46°45′N 33°20′E
Nová Karvinná see Karviná
Nova Lamego see Gabú
Nova Lisboa see Huambo
112 C11 **Novalja** Lika-Senj, W Croatia 44°33′N 14°53′E
119 M14 **Novalukoml'** Rus. Novolukoml'. Vitsyebskaya Voblasts', N Belarus 54°40′N 29°09′E
Nova Mambone see Mambone
83 P16 **Nova Nabúri** Zambézia, NE Mozambique 16°47′S 38°55′E
117 Q9 **Nova Odesa** var. Novaya Odessa. Mykolayivs'ka Oblast', S Ukraine 47°19′N 31°45′E
60 H10 **Nova Olímpia** Paraná, S Brazil 23°28′S 53°12′W
61 I15 **Nova Prata** Rio Grande do Sul, S Brazil 28°45′S 51°37′W
14 H12 **Novar** Ontario, S Canada 45°26′N 79°14′W
106 C7 **Novara** anc. Novaria. Piemonte, NW Italy 45°27′N 08°36′E
Novaria see Novara
13 P15 **Nova Scotia** Fr. Nouvelle Écosse. ◐ province SE Canada
0 M9 **Nova Scotia** physical region SE Canada
34 M8 **Novato** California, W USA 38°06′N 122°35′W
192 M7 **Nova Trough** undersea feature W Pacific Ocean
116 L7 **Nova Ushytsya** Khmel'nyts'ka Oblast', W Ukraine 48°50′N 27°16′E
83 M17 **Nova Vanduzi** Manica, C Mozambique 18°54′S 33°18′E
117 U5 **Nova Vodolaha** Rus. Novaya Vodolaga. Kharkivs'ka Oblast', E Ukraine 49°43′N 35°49′E
123 O12 **Novaya Chara** Zabaykal'skiy Kray, S Russian Federation 56°45′N 117°58′E
122 M12 **Novaya Igirma** Irkutskaya Oblast', C Russian Federation 57°08′N 103°52′E
Novaya Kakhovka see Nova Kakhovka
Novaya Kazanka see Zhanakazan
124 I12 **Novaya Ladoga** Leningradskaya Oblast', NW Russian Federation 60°03′N 32°15′E
127 R5 **Novaya Malykla** Ul'yanovskaya Oblast', W Russian Federation 54°13′N 49°55′E
Novaya Odessa see Nova Odesa
123 Q5 **Novaya Sibir', Ostrov** island Novosibirskiye Ostrova, NE Russian Federation
Novaya Vodolaga see Nova Vodolaha
122 I6 **Novaya Zemlya** island group N Russian Federation
Novaya Zemlya Trough see East Novaya Zemlya Trough
114 K10 **Nova Zagora** Sliven, C Bulgaria 42°29′N 26°00′E
105 S12 **Novelda** Valenciana, E Spain 38°24′N 00°45′W
111 H19 **Nové Mesto nad Váhom** Ger. Waagneustadtl, Hung. Vágújhely. Trenčiansky Kraj, W Slovakia 48°46′N 17°50′E
111 F17 **Nové Město na Moravě** Ger. Neustadtl in Mähren. Vysočina, C Czech Republic 49°34′N 16°05′E
Novesium see Neuss
111 I21 **Nové Zámky** Ger. Neuhäusel, Hung. Érsekújvár. Nitriansky Kraj, SW Slovakia 49°00′N 18°10′E
Novgorod see Velikiy Novgorod
Novgorod-Severskiy see Novhorod-Sivers'kyy
122 C7 **Novgorodskaya Oblast'** ◐ province W Russian Federation
117 R8 **Novhorodka** Kirovohrads'ka Oblast', C Ukraine 48°21′N 32°38′E
117 R2 **Novhorod-Sivers'kyy** Rus. Novgorod-Severskiy. Chernihivs'ka Oblast', NE Ukraine 52°00′N 33°15′E
31 R10 **Novi** Michigan, N USA 42°28′N 83°28′W
Novi see Novi Vinodolski
112 L9 **Novi Bečej** prev. Uj-Becse, Vološinovo, Ger. Neubetsche, Hung. Törökbecse. Vojvodina, N Serbia 45°36′N 20°09′E
116 M3 **Novi Bilokorovychi** Rus. Belokorovichi; prev. Bilokorovychi. Zhytomyrs'ka Oblast', N Ukraine 51°07′N 28°02′E
25 Q8 **Novice** Texas, SW USA 32°00′N 99°38′W

112 A9 **Novigrad** Istra, NW Croatia 45°19′N 13°33′E
Novi Grad see Bosanski Novi
114 G9 **Novi Iskŭr** Sofiya-Grad, W Bulgaria 42°46′N 23°19′E
106 C9 **Novi Ligure** Piemonte, NW Italy 44°46′N 08°47′E
99 L22 **Noville** Luxembourg, SE Belgium 50°04′N 05°46′E
194 I10 **Noville Peninsula** peninsula Thurston Island, Antarctica
Noviodunum see Soissons, Aisne, France
Noviodunum see Nevers, Nièvre, France
Noviodunum see Nyon, Vaud, Switzerland
Noviomagus see Lisieux, Calvados, France
Noviomagus see Nijmegen, Netherlands
114 M8 **Novi Pazar** Shumen, NE Bulgaria 43°20′N 27°12′E
113 M15 **Novi Pazar** Turk. Yenipazar. Serbia, S Serbia 43°09′N 20°31′E
112 K10 **Novi Sad** Ger. Neusatz, Hung. Újvidék. Vojvodina, N Serbia 45°16′N 19°49′E
117 T6 **Novi Sanzhary** Poltavs'ka Oblast', C Ukraine 49°21′N 34°18′E
112 H12 **Novi Travnik** prev. Pučarevo. Federacija Bosna I Hercegovina, C Bosnia and Herzegovina 44°12′N 17°39′E
112 B10 **Novi Vinodolski** var. Novi. Primorje-Gorski Kotar, NW Croatia 45°08′N 14°46′E
58 F12 **Novo Airão** Amazonas, N Brazil 02°06′S 61°20′W
Novoalekseyevka see Kobda
127 N9 **Novoanninskiy** Volgogradskaya Oblast', SW Russian Federation 50°31′N 42°43′E
58 F13 **Novo Aripuanã** Amazonas, N Brazil 05°05′S 60°20′W
117 P7 **Novoarkhangel's'k** Kirovohrads'ka Oblast', C Ukraine 48°39′N 30°48′E
117 Y6 **Novoaydar** Luhans'ka Oblast', E Ukraine 49°00′N 39°00′E
117 X9 **Novoazovs'k** Rus. Novoazovsk. Donets'ka Oblast', E Ukraine 47°07′N 38°06′E
123 R14 **Novobureyskiy** Amurskaya Oblast', SE Russian Federation 49°42′N 129°46′E
127 Q3 **Novocheboksarsk** Chuvashskaya Respublika, W Russian Federation 56°07′N 47°33′E
127 R5 **Novocheremshansk** Ul'yanovskaya Oblast', W Russian Federation 54°23′N 50°08′E
126 L12 **Novocherkassk** Rostovskaya Oblast', SW Russian Federation 47°23′N 40°E
127 R6 **Novodevich'ye** Samarskaya Oblast', W Russian Federation 53°33′N 48°51′E
124 M8 **Novodvinsk** Arkhangel'skaya Oblast', NW Russian Federation 64°22′N 40°49′E
Novograd-Volynskiy see Novohrad-Volyns'kyy
Novogrudok see Navahrudak
61 I15 **Novo Hamburgo** Rio Grande do Sul, S Brazil 29°42′S 51°07′W
59 H16 **Novo Horizonte** Mato Grosso, W Brazil 11°19′S 57°11′W
60 K8 **Novo Horizonte** São Paulo, S Brazil 21°27′S 49°14′W
116 M4 **Novohrad-Volyns'kyy** Rus. Novograd-Volynskiy. Zhytomyrs'ka Oblast', N Ukraine 50°34′N 27°32′E
145 O7 **Novoishimskiy** prev. Kuybyshevskiy. Severnyy Kazakhstan, N Kazakhstan 53°15′N 66°51′E
Novokazalinsk see Ayteke Bi
126 M8 **Novokhopersk** Voronezhskaya Oblast', W Russian Federation 51°09′N 41°34′E
127 R6 **Novokuybyshevsk** Samarskaya Oblast', W Russian Federation 53°06′N 49°56′E
122 J13 **Novokuznetsk** prev. Stalinsk. Kemerovskaya Oblast', S Russian Federation 53°45′N 87°12′E
195 R1 **Novolazarevskaya** Russian research station Antarctica 70°42′S 11°31′E
Novolukoml' see Novalukoml'
109 V12 **Novo mesto** Ger. Rudolfswert; prev. Ger. Neustadtl. SE Slovenia 45°49′N 15°09′E
126 K15 **Novomikhaylovskiy** Krasnodarskiy Kray, SW Russian Federation 44°18′N 38°49′E
112 L8 **Novo Miloševo** Vojvodina, N Serbia 45°43′N 20°20′E
Novomirgorod see Novomyrhorod
126 L5 **Novomoskovsk** Tul'skaya Oblast', W Russian Federation 54°05′N 38°23′E
117 U7 **Novomoskovs'k** Rus. Novomoskovsk. Dnipropetrovs'ka Oblast', E Ukraine 48°38′N 35°15′E
117 V8 **Novomykolayivka** Zaporiz'ka Oblast', SE Ukraine 47°58′N 35°54′E
117 Q7 **Novomyrhorod** Rus. Novomirgorod. Kirovohrads'ka Oblast', S Ukraine 48°46′N 31°39′E
127 N8 **Novonikolayevskiy** Volgogradskaya Oblast', SW Russian Federation 50°55′N 42°24′E
127 P10 **Novonikol'skoye** Volgogradskaya Oblast', SW Russian Federation 49°23′N 45°06′E
127 X7 **Novoorsk** Orenburgskaya Oblast', W Russian Federation 51°21′N 59°03′E
126 M13 **Novopokrovskaya** Krasnodarskiy Kray, SW Russian Federation 45°58′N 40°43′E
Novopolotsk see Navapolatsk
117 Y5 **Novopskov** Luhans'ka Oblast', E Ukraine 49°33′N 39°07′E
Novoradomsk see Radomsko
Novo Redondo see Sumbe
127 R8 **Novorepnoye** Saratovskaya Oblast', W Russian Federation 51°04′N 48°34′E
126 K14 **Novorossiysk** Krasnodarskiy Kray, SW Russian Federation 44°50′N 37°38′E
Novorossiyskiy/Novorossiyskoye see Akzhar
124 F15 **Novorzhev** Pskovskaya Oblast', W Russian Federation 57°01′N 29°19′E
Novoselitsa see Novoselytsya
117 S12 **Novoselivs'ke** Avtonomna Respublika Krym, S Ukraine 45°26′N 33°37′E
Novosëlki see Navasyolki
114 G6 **Novo Selo** Vidin, NW Bulgaria 44°08′N 22°48′E
113 M14 **Novo Selo** Serbia, C Serbia 43°39′N 20°54′E
116 K8 **Novoselytsya** Rom. Nouă Sulița, Rus. Novoselitsa. Chernivets'ka Oblast', W Ukraine 48°14′N 26°18′E
127 U7 **Novosergiyevka** Orenburgskaya Oblast', W Russian Federation 52°04′N 53°40′E
126 L11 **Novoshakhtinsk** Rostovskaya Oblast', SW Russian Federation 47°48′N 39°51′E
122 J12 **Novosibirsk** Novosibirskaya Oblast', C Russian Federation 55°04′N 83°05′E
122 J12 **Novosibirskaya Oblast'** ◐ province C Russian Federation
122 M4 **Novosibirskiye Ostrova** Eng. New Siberian Islands. island group N Russian Federation
126 K6 **Novosil'** Orlovskaya Oblast', W Russian Federation 53°00′N 37°59′E
124 G16 **Novosokol'niki** Pskovskaya Oblast', W Russian Federation 56°21′N 30°07′E
127 Q6 **Novospasskoye** Ul'yanovskaya Oblast', W Russian Federation 53°08′N 47°48′E
Novotroickoje see Birlik
127 X8 **Novotroitsk** Orenburgskaya Oblast', W Russian Federation 51°10′N 58°18′E
Novotroitskoye see Brlik, Kazakhstan
Novotroitskoye see Novotroyits'ke, Ukraine
117 T11 **Novotroyits'ke** Rus. Novotroitskoye. Khersons'ka Oblast', S Ukraine 46°21′N 34°21′E
Novoukrainka see Novoukrayinka
117 Q8 **Novoukrayinka** Rus. Novoukrainka. Kirovohrads'ka Oblast', C Ukraine 48°19′N 31°33′E
127 Q5 **Novoul'yanovsk** Ul'yanovskaya Oblast', W Russian Federation 54°10′N 48°19′E
127 W8 **Novoural'sk** Orenburgskaya Oblast', W Russian Federation 51°19′N 56°57′E
Novo-Urgench see Urganch
116 I4 **Novovolyns'k** Rus. Novovolynsk. Volyns'ka Oblast', NW Ukraine 50°46′N 24°09′E
117 S9 **Novovorontsovka** Khersons'ka Oblast', S Ukraine 47°28′N 33°55′E
147 Y7 **Novovoznesenovka** Issyk-Kul'skaya Oblast', E Kyrgyzstan 42°36′N 78°44′E
125 R14 **Novovyatsk** Kirovskaya Oblast', NW Russian Federation 58°30′N 49°42′E
Novoyel'nya see Navayel'nya
117 O6 **Novozhyvotiv** Vinnyts'ka Oblast', C Ukraine 49°16′N 29°31′E
126 H6 **Novozybkov** Bryanskaya Oblast', W Russian Federation 52°36′N 31°58′E
112 F9 **Novska** Sisak-Moslavina, NE Croatia 45°20′N 16°58′E
Nový Bohumín see Bohumín
111 D15 **Nový Bor** Ger. Haida; prev. Bor u České Lípy, Hajda. Liberecký Kraj, N Czech Republic 50°46′N 14°32′E
111 E16 **Nový Bydžov** Ger. Neubidschow. Královéhradecký Kraj, N Czech Republic 50°15′N 15°27′E
119 G18 **Novy Dvor** Rus. Novyy Dvor. Hrodzyenskaya Voblasts', W Belarus 53°48′N 24°34′E
111 I17 **Nový Jičín** Ger. Neutitschein. Moravskoslezský Kraj, E Czech Republic 49°36′N 18°00′E
118 K12 **Novy Pahost** Rus. Novyy Pogost. Vitsyebskaya Voblasts', NW Belarus 55°30′N 27°29′E
Novyy Bug see Novyy Buh
117 R9 **Novyy Buh** Rus. Novyy Bug. Mykolayivs'ka Oblast', S Ukraine 47°40′N 32°30′E
117 Q4 **Novyy Bykiv** Chernihivs'ka Oblast', N Ukraine 50°36′N 31°39′E
Novyy Dvor see Novy Dvor
Novyye Aneny see Anenii Noi
127 P7 **Novyye Burasy** Saratovskaya Oblast', W Russian Federation 52°10′N 46°00′E
Novyy Margilan see Farg'ona
126 K8 **Novyy Oskol** Belgorodskaya Oblast', W Russian Federation 50°43′N 37°55′E
Novyy Pogost see Novy Pahost
127 R2 **Novyy Tor"yal** Respublika Mariy El, W Russian Federation 56°59′N 48°53′E
123 N12 **Novyy Uoyan** Respublika Buryatiya, S Russian Federation 56°06′N 111°27′E
122 J9 **Novyy Urengoy** Yamalo-Nenetskiy Avtonomnyy Okrug, N Russian Federation 66°06′N 76°25′E
Novyy Uzen' see Zhanaozen
111 N16 **Nowa Dęba** Podkarpackie, SE Poland 50°31′N 21°53′E
111 G15 **Nowa Ruda** Ger. Neurode. Dolnośląskie, SW Poland 50°34′N 16°30′E
110 F12 **Nowa Sól** var. Nowasól, Ger. Neusalz an der Oder. Lubuskie, W Poland 51°47′N 15°43′E
Nowasól see Nowa Sól
27 Q8 **Nowata** Oklahoma, C USA 36°42′N 95°36′W
142 M6 **Nowbarān** Markazī, W Iran 35°07′N 49°51′E
110 J8 **Nowe** Kujawski-pomorskie, N Poland 53°40′N 18°44′E
110 K9 **Nowe Miasto Lubawskie** Ger. Neumark. Warmińsko-Mazurskie, NE Poland 53°24′N 19°36′E
110 L13 **Nowe Miasto nad Pilicą** Mazowieckie, C Poland 51°37′N 20°34′E
110 D8 **Nowe Warpno** Ger. Neuwarp. Zachodnio-pomorskie, NW Poland 53°52′N 14°12′E
Nowgong see Nagaon
110 E8 **Nowogard** var. Nowógard, Ger. Naugard. Zachodnio-pomorskie, NW Poland 53°41′N 15°09′E
110 N9 **Nowogród** Podlaskie, NE Poland 53°14′N 21°52′E
Nowogródek see Navahrudak
111 E14 **Nowogrodziec** Ger. Naumburg am Queis. Dolnośląskie, SW Poland 51°12′N 15°24′E
Nowojelnia see Navayel'nya
Nowo-Minsk see Mińsk Mazowiecki
33 V13 **Nowood River** ≈ Wyoming, C USA
Nowo-Święciany see Švenčionėliai
183 S10 **Nowra-Bomaderry** New South Wales, SE Australia 34°51′S 150°41′E
149 T5 **Nowshera** var. Naushahra, Naushara. Khyber Pakhtunkhwa, NE Pakistan 34°00′N 72°00′E
110 J7 **Nowy Dwór Gdański** Ger. Tiegenhof. Pomorskie, N Poland 54°12′N 19°03′E
110 L11 **Nowy Dwór Mazowiecki** Mazowieckie, C Poland 52°26′N 20°43′E
111 M17 **Nowy Sącz** Ger. Neu Sandec. Małopolskie, S Poland 49°36′N 20°42′E
111 L18 **Nowy Targ** Ger. Neumark. Małopolskie, S Poland 49°28′N 20°00′E
110 F11 **Nowy Tomyśl** var. Nowy Tomysl. Wielkopolskie, C Poland 52°18′N 16°07′E
Nowy Tomysl see Nowy Tomyśl
148 M7 **Now Zād** var. Nauzad. Helmand, S Afghanistan 32°22′N 64°32′E
23 N4 **Noxubee River** ≈ Alabama/Mississippi, S USA
122 I10 **Noyabr'sk** Yamalo-Nenetskiy Avtonomnyy Okrug, N Russian Federation 63°08′N 75°19′E
102 L8 **Noyant** Maine-et-Loire, NW France 47°28′N 00°08′W
39 X14 **Noyes Island** island Alexander Archipelago, Alaska, USA
103 O3 **Noyon** Oise, N France 49°35′N 03°E
102 I7 **Nozay** Loire-Atlantique, NW France 47°34′N 01°36′W
82 L12 **Nsando** Northern, NE Zambia 10°22′S 31°14′E
83 N16 **Nsanje** Southern, S Malawi 16°57′S 35°10′E
77 Q17 **Nsawam** SE Ghana 05°47′N 00°19′W
79 E16 **Nsimalen** ✈ Centre, C Cameroon 19°15′N 81°22′E
82 K12 **Nsombo** Northern, NE Zambia 10°35′S 29°58′E
82 H13 **Ntambu** North Western, NW Zambia 12°21′S 25°03′E
83 N14 **Ntcheu** var. Ncheu. Central, S Malawi 14°49′S 34°37′E
79 D17 **Ntem** prev. Campo, Kampo. ≈ Cameroon/Equatorial Guinea
83 I14 **Ntemwa** North Western, NW Zambia 14°03′S 26°13′E
Ntlenyana, Mount see Thabana Ntlenyana
79 I19 **Ntomba, Lac** var. Lac Tumba. ◎ NW Dem. Rep. Congo
115 I19 **Ntóro, Kávo** prev. Akrotírio Kafiréas. cape Évvoia, C Greece
81 E19 **Ntungamo** SW Uganda 0°54′S 30°16′E
81 E18 **Ntusi** SW Uganda 0°05′N 31°13′E
83 H18 **Ntwetwe Pan** salt lake NE Botswana
93 M15 **Nuasjärvi** ◎ C Finland
80 F11 **Nuba Mountains** ▲▲ C Sudan
68 J9 **Nubian Desert** desert NE Sudan
116 G10 **Nucet** Hung. Diófás. Bihor, W Romania 46°28′N 22°35′E
Nu Chiang see Salween
145 U9 **Nuclear Testing Ground** nuclear site Pavlodar, E Kazakhstan
56 E9 **Nucuray, Río** ≈ N Peru
25 R14 **Nueces River** ≈ Texas, SW USA
9 V9 **Nueltin Lake** ◎ Manitoba/Northwest Territories, C Canada
99 K15 **Nuenen** Noord-Brabant, S Netherlands 51°29′N 05°36′E
62 G6 **Nuestra Señora, Bahía** bay N Chile
61 D14 **Nuestra Señora Rosario de Caa Catí** Corrientes, NE Argentina 27°48′S 57°42′W
54 J9 **Nueva Antioquia** Vichada, E Colombia 06°04′N 69°30′W
Nueva Caceres see Naga
41 O7 **Nueva Ciudad Guerrera** Tamaulipas, C Mexico 26°32′N 99°13′W
55 N4 **Nueva Esparta** off. Estado Nueva Esparta. ◐ state NE Venezuela
Nueva Esparta, Estado see Nueva Esparta
44 C5 **Nueva Gerona** Isla de la Juventud, S Cuba 21°49′N 82°49′W
42 H8 **Nueva Guadalupe** San Miguel, E El Salvador 13°30′N 88°21′W
42 M11 **Nueva Guinea** Región Autónoma Atlántico Sur, SE Nicaragua 11°40′N 84°22′W
61 D19 **Nueva Helvecia** Colonia, SW Uruguay 34°16′S 57°53′W
63 J25 **Nueva, Isla** island S Chile
40 M14 **Nueva Italia** Michoacán, SW Mexico 19°01′N 102°06′W
56 D6 **Nueva Loja** var. Lago Agrio. Sucumbíos, NE Ecuador
42 F6 **Nueva Ocotepeque** prev. Ocotepeque. Ocotepeque, W Honduras 14°25′N 89°10′W
61 D19 **Nueva Palmira** Colonia, SW Uruguay 33°53′S 58°25′W
41 N6 **Nueva Rosita** Coahuila, NE Mexico 27°58′N 101°11′W
42 E7 **Nueva San Salvador** prev. Santa Tecla. La Libertad, SW El Salvador 13°40′N 89°18′W
42 J8 **Nueva Segovia** ◐ department NW Nicaragua
Nueva Tabarca see Plana, Isla
Nueva Villa de Padilla see Nuevo Padilla
61 B21 **Nueve de Julio** Buenos Aires, E Argentina 35°29′S 60°52′W
44 H6 **Nuevitas** Camagüey, E Cuba 21°34′N 77°18′W
61 D18 **Nuevo Berlín** Río Negro, W Uruguay 32°59′S 58°03′W
40 I4 **Nuevo Casas Grandes** Chihuahua, N Mexico 30°23′N 107°54′W
43 T14 **Nuevo Chagres** Colón, C Panama 09°14′N 80°05′W
41 W15 **Nuevo Coahuila** Campeche, E Mexico 17°53′N 90°46′W
63 K17 **Nuevo, Golfo** gulf S Argentina
41 O7 **Nuevo Laredo** Tamaulipas, NE Mexico 27°28′N 99°32′W
41 N8 **Nuevo León** ◐ state NE Mexico
41 P10 **Nuevo Padilla** var. Nueva Villa de Padilla. Tamaulipas, C Mexico 24°01′N 98°48′W
56 E6 **Nuevo Rocafuerte** Orellana, E Ecuador 0°59′S 75°27′W
Nuga see Dzavhanmandal
80 O13 **Nugaal** off. Gobolka Nugaal. ◐ region N Somalia
Nugaal, Gobolka see Nugaal
185 E24 **Nugget Point** headland South Island, New Zealand 46°26′S 169°49′E
186 J5 **Nuguria Islands** island group E Papua New Guinea
184 P10 **Nuhaka** Hawke's Bay, North Island, New Zealand 39°03′S 177°43′E
138 M10 **Nuhaydayn, Wādī an** dry watercourse W Iraq
190 E7 **Nui Atoll** atoll W Tuvalu
Nu Jiang see Salween
Nûk see Nuuk
182 G7 **Nukey Bluff** hill South Australia
Nukha see Şǝki
123 T9 **Nukh Yablonevyy, Gora** ▲ E Russian Federation 60°26′N 151°45′E
186 K7 **Nukiki** Choiseul, NW Solomon Islands 06°45′S 156°30′E
186 B6 **Nuku** Sandaun, NW Papua New Guinea 03°48′S 142°23′E
193 W15 **Nuku** island Tongatapu Group, NE Tonga
193 Y16 **Nuku'alofa** ● (Tonga) Tongatapu, S Tonga 21°08′S 175°13′W
193 U15 **Nuku'alofa** Tongatapu, S Tonga 21°09′S 175°14′W
190 G12 **Nukuatea** island N Wallis and Futuna
190 F7 **Nukufetau Atoll** atoll C Tuvalu
190 G12 **Nukuhifala** island E Wallis and Futuna
191 W7 **Nuku Hiva** island Îles Marquises, NE French Polynesia
191 W7 **Nuku Hiva Island** island Îles Marquises, N French Polynesia
190 F9 **Nukulaelae Atoll** var. Nukulailai. atoll E Tuvalu
Nukulailai see Nukulaelae Atoll
190 G11 **Nukuloa** island N Wallis and Futuna
186 L6 **Nukumanu Islands** prev. Tasman Group. island group NE Papua New Guinea
Nukunau see Nikunau
190 J9 **Nukunonu Atoll** island C Tokelau
190 J9 **Nukunonu Village** Nukunonu Atoll, C Tokelau
189 S18 **Nukuoro Atoll** atoll Caroline Islands, S Micronesia
146 H8 **Nukus** Qoraqalpog'iston Respublikasi, W Uzbekistan 42°29′N 59°32′E
190 G11 **Nukutapu** island N Wallis and Futuna
39 O9 **Nulato** Alaska, USA 64°43′N 158°06′W
39 O10 **Nulato Hills** ▲▲ Alaska, USA
105 T9 **Nules** Valenciana, E Spain 39°52′N 00°10′W
Nuling see Sultan Kudarat
182 C6 **Nullarbor** South Australia 31°28′S 130°57′E
180 M11 **Nullarbor Plain** plateau South Australia/Western Australia
163 S12 **Nulu'erhu Shan** ▲▲ N China
77 X14 **Numan** Adamawa, E Nigeria 09°26′N 11°58′E
165 S3 **Numata** Hokkaidō, NE Japan 43°48′N 141°55′E
81 C15 **Numatinna** ≈ W South Sudan
95 F14 **Numedalen** valley S Norway
95 G14 **Numedalslågen** var. Laagen. ≈ S Norway
93 L19 **Nummela** Etelä-Suomi, S Finland 60°21′N 24°20′E
183 O11 **Numurkah** Victoria, SE Australia 36°04′S 145°28′E
196 L16 **Nunap Isua** var. Uummannarsuaq, Dan. Kap Farvel, Eng. Cape Farewell. cape S Greenland
9 N8 **Nunavut** ◐ territory N Canada
54 H9 **Nunchia** Casanare, C Colombia 05°37′N 72°13′W
97 M20 **Nuneaton** C England, United Kingdom 52°32′N 01°28′W
153 W14 **Nungba** Manipur, NE India 24°46′N 93°25′E
38 L12 **Nunivak Island** island Alaska, USA
152 I5 **Nun Kun** ▲ NW India 34°01′N 76°04′E
98 L10 **Nunspeet** Gelderland, E Netherlands 52°21′N 05°45′E
107 C18 **Nuoro** Sardegna, Italy, C Mediterranean Sea 40°20′N 09°20′E
75 R12 **Nuqayy, Jabal** hill range S Libya
54 C9 **Nuquí** Chocó, W Colombia 05°44′N 77°16′W
143 O4 **Nūr** Māzandarān, N Iran 36°32′N 52°00′E
145 Q9 **Nura** ≈ N Kazakhstan
143 N11 **Nūrābād** Fārs, C Iran 30°08′N 51°30′E
Nurakita see Niulakita
Nurata see Nurota
Nuratau, Khrebet see Nurota Tizmasi
136 L17 **Nur Dağları** ▲▲ S Turkey
Nurek see Norak
Nuremberg see Nürnberg
Nūrestān see Nūristān
136 M15 **Nurhak** Kahramanmaraş, S Turkey 37°57′N 37°21′E
182 J9 **Nuriootpa** South Australia 34°28′S 139°00′E
149 S4 **Nūristān** prev. Nūrestān. ◐ province C Afghanistan
127 S5 **Nurlat** Respublika Tatarstan, W Russian Federation 54°26′N 50°48′E
93 N15 **Nurmes** Itä-Suomi, E Finland 63°31′N 29°10′E
101 K20 **Nürnberg** Eng. Nuremberg. Bayern, S Germany 49°27′N 11°05′E
101 K20 **Nürnberg** ✈ Bayern, SE Germany 49°29′N 11°04′E
146 M10 **Nurota** Rus. Nurata. Navoiy Viloyati, C Uzbekistan 40°41′N 65°43′E
147 N10 **Nurota Tizmasi** Rus. Khrebet Nuratau. ▲▲ C Uzbekistan
149 T8 **Nūrpur** Punjab, E Pakistan 31°54′N 71°55′E
183 P6 **Nurri, Mount** hill New South Wales, SE Australia
25 T13 **Nursery** Texas, SW USA 28°55′N 97°05′W
169 V17 **Nusa Tenggara Barat** off. Propinsi Nusa Tenggara Barat, Eng. West Nusa Tenggara. ◐ province S Indonesia
Nusa Tenggara Barat, Propinsi see Nusa Tenggara Barat
171 O16 **Nusa Tenggara Timur** off. Propinsi Nusa Tenggara Timur, Eng. East Nusa Tenggara. ◐ province S Indonesia
Nusa Tenggara Timur, Propinsi see Nusa Tenggara Timur
171 U14 **Nusawulan** Papua, E Indonesia 04°03′S 132°56′E
137 Q16 **Nusaybin** var. Nisibin. Manisa, SE Turkey 37°08′N 41°11′E
39 O14 **Nushagak Bay** bay Alaska, USA
39 O13 **Nushagak Peninsula** headland Alaska, USA 58°39′N 159°03′W
39 O13 **Nushagak River** ≈ Alaska, USA
160 E11 **Nu Shan** ▲▲ SW China
149 N11 **Nushki** Baluchistān, SW Pakistan 29°33′N 66°01′E
Nussdorf see Năsăud
112 J9 **Nuštar** Vukovar-Srijem, E Croatia 45°20′N 18°48′E
99 L18 **Nuth** Limburg, SE Netherlands 50°55′N 05°52′E
100 N13 **Nuthe** ≈ NE Germany
Nutmeg State see Connecticut
39 T10 **Nutzotin Mountains** ▲▲ Alaska, USA
64 I5 **Nuuk** var. Nûk, Dan. Godthaab, Godthåb. ○ (Greenland) Kitaa, SW Greenland 64°15′N 51°35′W
92 L13 **Nuupas** Lappi, NW Finland 66°01′N 26°19′E
191 O7 **Nuupere, Pointe** headland Moorea, W French Polynesia 17°35′S 149°47′W
191 O7 **Nuuroa, Pointe** headland Tahiti, W French Polynesia
Nüürst see Baganuur
Nuwara see Nuwara Eliya
155 K25 **Nuwara Eliya** var. Nuwara. Central Province, S Sri Lanka 06°58′N 80°46′E
182 E7 **Nuyts Archipelago** island group South Australia
83 F17 **Nxaunxau** North West, NW Botswana 18°57′S 21°18′E
39 N12 **Nyac** Alaska, USA 61°00′N 159°56′W
122 H9 **Nyagan'** Khanty-Mansiyskiy Avtonomnyy Okrug-Yugra, N Russian Federation 62°10′N 65°32′E
Nyagassola see Niagassola
Nyagquka see Yajiang
81 I18 **Nyahururu** Central, W Kenya 0°04′N 36°22′E
182 M10 **Nyah West** Victoria, SE Australia 35°14′S 143°18′E
158 M15 **Nyainqêntanglha Feng** ▲ W China 30°20′N 90°28′E
159 N15 **Nyainqêntanglha Shan** ▲▲ W China
80 B11 **Nyala** Southern Darfur, W Sudan 12°01′N 24°50′E
83 M16 **Nyamapanda** Mashonaland East, NE Zimbabwe 16°59′S 32°52′E
81 H25 **Nyamtumbo** Ruvuma, S Tanzania 10°33′S 36°08′E
Nyanda see Masvingo
124 M11 **Nyandoma** Arkhangel'skaya Oblast', NW Russian Federation 61°39′N 40°10′E
83 M16 **Nyanga** prev. Inyanga. Manicaland, E Zimbabwe 18°13′S 32°46′E
79 D20 **Nyanga** off. Province de la Nyanga, var. La Nyanga. ◐ province SW Gabon
79 E20 **Nyanga** ≈ Congo/Gabon
Nyanga, Province de la see Nyanga
81 F20 **Nyantakara** Kagera, NW Tanzania 03°05′S 31°23′E
81 G19 **Nyanza** ◐ province W Kenya
81 E21 **Nyanza-Lac** S Burundi 04°16′S 29°38′E
68 J14 **Nyasa, Lake** var. Lake Malawi; prev. Lago Nyassa. ◎ E Africa
Nyasaland/Nyasaland Protectorate see Malawi
Nyassa, Lago see Nyasa, Lake
119 J17 **Nyasvizh** Pol. Nieśwież, Rus. Nesvizh. Minskaya Voblasts', C Belarus 53°13′N 26°40′E
166 M8 **Nyaunglebin** Bago, SW Burma (Myanmar) 17°59′N 94°44′E
166 M5 **Nyaung-u** Magway, C Burma (Myanmar) 21°03′N 95°44′E
95 H24 **Nyborg** Syddtjylland, C Denmark 55°19′N 10°48′E
95 N21 **Nybro** Kalmar, S Sweden 56°45′N 15°54′E
119 J16 **Nyeharelaye** Rus. Negoreloye. Minskaya Voblasts', C Belarus 53°36′N 27°04′E
195 W3 **Nye Mountains** ▲▲ Antarctica
81 I19 **Nyeri** Central, C Kenya 0°25′S 36°56′E
118 M11 **Nyeshcharda, Vozyera** ◎ N Belarus
92 O2 **Ny-Friesland** physical region N Svalbard
95 L14 **Nyhammar** Dalarna, C Sweden 60°19′N 14°55′E
160 F7 **Nyikog Qu** ≈ C China
83 L14 **Nyimba** Eastern, E Zambia 14°33′S 30°49′E
159 P15 **Nyingchi** var. Bayizhen. Xizang Zizhiqu, W China 29°27′N 94°43′E
159 P15 **Nyingchi** var. Pula. Xizang Zizhiqu, W China 29°34′N 94°33′E
Nyinma see Maqu
111 O21 **Nyírbátor** Szabolcs-Szatmár-Bereg, E Hungary 47°50′N 22°09′E
111 N21 **Nyíregyháza** Szabolcs-Szatmár-Bereg, NE Hungary 47°57′N 21°43′E
Nyiro see Ewaso Ng'iro
Nyitra see Nitra
Nyitrabánya see Handlová
93 K16 **Nykarleby** Fin. Uusikaarlepyy. Länsi-Suomi, W Finland 63°22′N 22°30′E
95 F21 **Nykøbing** Midtjylland, NW Denmark 56°48′N 08°52′E
95 I25 **Nykøbing** Sjælland, SE Denmark 54°47′N 11°53′E
95 I22 **Nykøbing** Sjælland, C Denmark 55°56′N 11°41′E
95 N17 **Nyköping** Södermanland, S Sweden 58°45′N 17°03′E
95 L15 **Nykroppa** Värmland, C Sweden 59°37′N 14°18′E
Nylstroom see Modimolle
183 P7 **Nymagee** New South Wales, SE Australia 32°06′S 146°19′E
183 V5 **Nymboida** New South Wales, SE Australia 29°57′S 152°45′E
183 U5 **Nymboida River** ≈ New South Wales, SE Australia
111 D16 **Nymburk** var. Neuenburg an der Elbe, Ger. Nimburg. Středočesky Kraj, C Czech Republic 50°12′N 15°00′E
95 O16 **Nynäshamn** Stockholm, C Sweden 58°54′N 17°55′E
183 Q6 **Nyngan** New South Wales, SE Australia 31°36′S 147°07′E
Nyoman see Neman
108 A10 **Nyon** Ger. Neuss; anc. Noviodunum. Vaud, SW Switzerland 46°23′N 06°15′E
79 D16 **Nyong** ≈ SW Cameroon
103 S14 **Nyons** Drôme, E France 44°22′N 05°06′E
79 D14 **Nyos, Lac** Eng. Lake Nyos. ◎ NW Cameroon
Nyos, Lake see Nyos, Lac
125 U11 **Nyrob** var. Nyrov. Permskiy Kray, NW Russian Federation 60°41′N 56°42′E
Nyrov see Nyrob
111 H15 **Nysa** Ger. Neisse. Opolskie, S Poland 50°28′N 17°20′E
32 M13 **Nyssa** Oregon, NW USA 43°52′N 116°59′W
Nysa Łużycka see Neisse
Nyslott see Savonlinna
Nystad see Uusikaupunki
95 I25 **Nysted** Sjælland, SE Denmark 54°40′N 11°41′E
125 U14 **Nytva** Permskiy Kray, NW Russian Federation 57°56′N 55°22′E
165 P8 **Nyūdō-zaki** headland Honshū, C Japan 39°59′N 139°40′E
125 P9 **Nyukhcha** Arkhangel'skaya Oblast', NW Russian Federation 63°24′N 46°34′E
124 H8 **Nyuk, Ozero** var. Ozero Njuk. ◎ NW Russian Federation
125 O12 **Nyuksenitsa** var. Njuksenica. Vologodskaya Oblast', NW Russian Federation 60°25′N 44°12′E
79 O22 **Nyunzu** Katanga, SE Dem. Rep. Congo 05°55′S 28°00′E
123 O10 **Nyurba** Respublika Sakha (Yakutiya), NE Russian Federation 63°17′N 118°15′E
123 O11 **Nyuya** Respublika Sakha (Yakutiya), NE Russian Federation 60°33′N 116°10′E
146 K12 **Nyýazow** Rus. Niyazov. Lebap Welaýaty, NE Turkmenistan 39°13′N 63°16′E
117 T10 **Nyzhni Sirohozy** Khersons'ka Oblast', S Ukraine 46°49′N 34°21′E
117 U12 **Nyzhn'ohirs'kyy** Rus. Nizhnegorskiy. Avtonomna Respublika Krym, S Ukraine 45°26′N 34°42′E
NZ see New Zealand
81 G21 **Nzega** Tabora, C Tanzania 04°13′S 33°11′E
76 K15 **Nzérékoré** SE Guinea 07°45′N 08°49′W
82 A10 **N'Zeto** prev. Ambrizete. Zaire, NW Angola 07°14′S 12°52′E
79 M24 **Nzilo, Lac** prev. Lac Delcommune. ◎ SE Dem. Rep. Congo
172 I13 **Nzwani** Fr. Anjouan, var. Ndzouani. island SE Comoros

O

29 O11 **Oacoma** South Dakota, N USA 43°49′N 99°25′W
29 N9 **Oahe Dam** dam South Dakota, N USA
28 M9 **Oahe, Lake** ⊞ North Dakota/South Dakota, N USA
38 C9 **Oa'hu** var. Oahu. island Hawai'ian Islands, Hawai'i, USA
165 V4 **O-Akan-dake** ▲ Hokkaidō, NE Japan 43°26′N 144°09′E
182 K8 **Oakbank** South Australia 33°07′S 140°36′E
19 P13 **Oak Bluffs** Martha's Vineyard, New York, NE USA 41°25′N 70°32′W
36 K4 **Oak City** Utah, W USA 39°22′N 112°19′W
37 R3 **Oak Creek** Colorado, C USA 40°16′N 106°57′W
35 P8 **Oakdale** California, W USA 37°46′N 120°51′W
22 H8 **Oakdale** Louisiana, S USA 30°49′N 92°39′W
29 P7 **Oakes** North Dakota, N USA 46°08′N 98°05′W
22 J4 **Oak Grove** Louisiana, S USA 32°51′N 91°25′W
97 N19 **Oakham** C England, United Kingdom 52°41′N 00°45′W
32 H7 **Oak Harbor** Washington, NW USA 48°17′N 122°38′W
21 R5 **Oak Hill** West Virginia, NE USA 37°59′N 81°09′W
35 N8 **Oakland** California, W USA 37°48′N 122°16′W
29 T15 **Oakland** Iowa, C USA 41°18′N 95°22′W
19 Q7 **Oakland** Maine, NE USA 44°32′N 69°43′W
21 T3 **Oakland** Maryland, NE USA 39°24′N 79°25′W
29 R14 **Oakland** Nebraska, C USA 41°50′N 96°28′W
31 N11 **Oak Lawn** Illinois, N USA 41°43′N 87°45′W
33 P16 **Oakley** Idaho, NW USA 42°13′N 113°54′W
26 I4 **Oakley** Kansas, C USA 39°08′N 100°53′W
31 N10 **Oak Park** Illinois, N USA 41°53′N 87°46′W
11 X16 **Oak Point** Manitoba, S Canada 50°23′N 97°00′W
32 G13 **Oakridge** Oregon, NW USA 43°45′N 122°27′W
20 M9 **Oak Ridge** Tennessee, S USA 36°02′N 84°12′W
184 K10 **Oakura** Taranaki, North Island, New Zealand 39°07′S 173°58′E
22 L7 **Oak Vale** Mississippi, S USA 31°26′N 89°57′W
14 G16 **Oakville** Ontario, S Canada 43°27′N 79°41′W
25 V8 **Oakwood** Texas, SW USA 31°34′N 95°51′W
185 F22 **Oamaru** Otago, South Island, New Zealand 45°10′S 170°51′E
96 F13 **Oa, Mull of** headland W Scotland, United Kingdom 55°35′N 06°20′W
171 O11 **Oan** Sulawesi, N Indonesia 01°16′N 121°25′E
185 J17 **Oaro** Canterbury, South Island, New Zealand 42°29′S 173°30′E
35 X2 **Oasis** Nevada, W USA 41°01′N 114°29′W
195 S15 **Oates Land** physical region Antarctica
183 P17 **Oatlands** Tasmania, SE Australia 42°21′S 147°23′E
36 I11 **Oatman** Arizona, SW USA 35°03′N 114°19′W
41 R16 **Oaxaca** var. Oaxaca de Juárez; prev. Antequera. Oaxaca, SE Mexico 17°04′N 96°41′W
41 Q16 **Oaxaca** ◐ state SE Mexico
Oaxaca de Juárez see Oaxaca
122 I19 **Ob'** ≈ C Russian Federation
145 X9 **Oba** prev. Uba. ≈ E Kazakhstan
14 G9 **Obabika Lake** ◎ Ontario, S Canada
Obagan see Ubagan
118 M12 **Obal'** Rus. Obol'. Vitsyebskaya Voblasts', N Belarus 55°22′N 29°17′E
79 E16 **Obala** Centre, SW Cameroon 04°09′N 11°32′E
14 C6 **Oba Lake** ◎ Ontario, S Canada
164 J12 **Obama** Fukui, Honshū, SW Japan 35°32′N 135°45′E
96 H11 **Oban** W Scotland, United Kingdom 56°25′N 05°29′W
Oban see Halfmoon Bay
Obando see Puerto Inírida
104 I4 **O Barco** var. El Barco, El Barco de Valdeorras, O Barco de Valdeorras. Galicia, NW Spain 42°24′N 07°00′W
O Barco de Valdeorras see O Barco
Obbia see Hobyo
93 J16 **Obbola** Västerbotten, N Sweden 63°41′N 20°16′E
Obbrovazzo see Obrovac
Obchuga see Abchuha
Obdorsk see Salekhard
Óbecse see Bečej
118 I11 **Obeliai** Panevėžys, NE Lithuania 55°57′N 25°47′E
60 F13 **Oberá** Misiones, NE Argentina 27°29′S 55°08′W
108 E8 **Oberburg** Bern, W Switzerland 47°00′N 07°37′E
109 Q9 **Oberdrauburg** Salzburg, S Austria 46°45′N 12°59′E
Oberglogau see Głogówek
109 W4 **Ober Grafendorf** Niederösterreich, NE Austria 48°09′N 15°33′E
101 E15 **Oberhausen** Nordrhein-Westfalen, W Germany 51°27′N 06°50′E
Oberhollabrunn see Tulln
Oberlaibach see Vrhnika
101 Q15 **Oberlausitz** var. Hornja Łužica. physical region E Germany
26 J2 **Oberlin** Kansas, C USA 39°49′N 100°33′W
22 H8 **Oberlin** Louisiana, S USA 30°37′N 92°45′W
31 T11 **Oberlin** Ohio, N USA 41°17′N 82°13′W
103 U5 **Obernai** Bas-Rhin, NE France 48°28′N 07°30′E
109 R4 **Obernberg am Inn** Oberösterreich, N Austria 48°19′N 13°20′E
Oberndorf see Oberndorf am Neckar
101 G23 **Oberndorf am Neckar** var. Oberndorf. Baden-Württemberg, SW Germany 48°18′N 08°32′E
109 Q5 **Oberndorf bei Salzburg** Salzburg, W Austria 47°57′N 12°57′E
Oberneustadtl see Kysucké Nové Mesto
183 S8 **Oberon** New South Wales, SE Australia 33°42′S 149°50′E
109 Q4 **Oberösterreich** off. Land Oberösterreich, Eng. Upper Austria. ◐ state NW Austria

◆ Country
● Country Capital
◇ Dependent Territory
○ Dependent Territory Capital
◐ Administrative Regions
✈ International Airport
▲ Mountain
▲▲ Mountain Range
Volcano
≈ River
◎ Lake
⊞ Reservoir

Oberösterreich, Land *see* Oberösterreich
Oberpahlen *see* Põltsamaa
101 *M19* **Oberpfälzer Wald** ▲ SE Germany
109 *Y6* **Oberpullendorf** Burgenland, E Austria *47°32′N 16°30′E*
Oberradkersburg *see* Gornja Radgona
101 *G18* **Oberursel** Hessen, W Germany *50°12′N 08°34′E*
109 *Q8* **Obervellach** Salzburg, S Austria *46°56′N 13°10′E*
109 *X7* **Oberwart** Burgenland, SE Austria *47°18′N 16°12′E*
Oberwischau *see* Vişeu de Sus
109 *T7* **Oberwölz** *var.* Oberwölz-Stadt. Steiermark, SE Austria *47°12′N 14°20′E*
Oberwölz-Stadt *see* Oberwölz
31 *S13* **Obetz** Ohio, N USA *39°52′N 82°57′W*
Ob', Gulf of *see* Obskaya Guba
58 *H12* **Óbidos** Pará, NE Brazil *01°52′S 55°30′W*
104 *F10* **Óbidos** Leiria, C Portugal *39°21′N 09°09′W*
Obidovichi *see* Abidavichy
147 *Q13* **Obigarm** W Tajikistan *38°42′N 69°34′E*
165 *T2* **Obihiro** Hokkaidō, NE Japan *42°56′N 143°10′E*
Obi-Khingou *see* Khingov
147 *P13* **Obikiik** SW Tajikistan *38°07′N 68°36′E*
Obilić *see* Obiliq
113 *N16* **Obiliq** *Serb.* Obilić. N Kosovo *42°50′N 20°57′E*
127 *O12* **Obil'noye** Respublika Kalmykiya, SW Russian Federation *47°31′N 44°24′E*
20 *F8* **Obion** Tennessee, S USA *36°15′N 89°11′W*
20 *F8* **Obion River** Tennessee, S USA
171 *S12* **Obi, Pulau** *island* Maluku, E Indonesia
165 *S2* **Obira** Hokkaidō, NE Japan *44°01′N 141°39′E*
127 *N11* **Oblivskaya** Rostovskaya Oblast', SW Russian Federation *48°34′N 42°31′E*
123 *R14* **Obluch'ye** Yevreyskaya Avtonomnaya Oblast', SE Russian Federation *48°59′N 131°18′E*
126 *K4* **Obninsk** Kaluzhskaya Oblast', W Russian Federation *55°06′N 36°40′E*
114 *J8* **Obnova** Pleven, N Bulgaria *43°26′N 25°04′E*
79 *N15* **Obo** Haut-Mbomou, E Central African Republic *05°20′N 26°29′E*
159 *T9* **Obo** Qinghai, C China *37°57′N 101°03′E*
80 *M11* **Obock** E Djibouti *11°57′N 43°09′E*
Obol' *see* Obal'
Obolyanka *see* Abalyanka
171 *V13* **Obome** Papua, E Indonesia *03°42′S 133°21′E*
110 *G11* **Oborniki** Wielkolpolskie, W Poland *52°38′N 16°48′E*
79 *G19* **Obouya** Cuvette, C Congo *0°56′S 15°41′E*
126 *J8* **Oboyan'** Kurskaya Oblast', W Russian Federation *51°12′N 36°15′E*
124 *M9* **Obozerskiy** Arkhangel'skaya Oblast', NW Russian Federation *63°26′N 40°20′E*
112 *L11* **Obrenovac** Serbia, N Serbia *44°39′N 20°12′E*
112 *D12* **Obrovac** *It.* Obbrovazzo. Zadar, SW Croatia *44°12′N 15°40′E*
Obrovo *see* Abrova
35 *Q3* **Observation Peak** ▲ California, W USA *40°48′N 120°07′W*
122 *J8* **Obskaya Guba** *Eng.* Gulf of Ob. *gulf* N Russian Federation
173 *N13* **Ob' Tablemount** *undersea feature* S Indian Ocean *50°16′S 51°59′E*
173 *T10* **Ob' Trench** *undersea feature* E Indian Ocean
77 *P16* **Obuasi** S Ghana *06°15′N 01°36′W*
117 *P5* **Obukhiv** *Rus.* Obukhov. Kyyivs'ka Oblast', N Ukraine *50°05′N 30°37′E*
Obukhov *see* Obukhiv
125 *U14* **Obva** NW Russian Federation
108 *F8* **Obwalden** *canton* C Switzerland
117 *V10* **Obytichna Kosa** *spit* SE Ukraine
117 *V10* **Obytichna Zatoka** *gulf* SE Ukraine
114 *N9* **Obzor** Burgas, E Bulgaria *42°52′N 27°53′E*
105 *O3* **Oca** N Spain
23 *W10* **Ocala** Florida, SE USA *29°11′N 82°08′W*
40 *M7* **Ocampo** Coahuila, NE Mexico *27°18′N 102°24′W*
54 *G7* **Ocaña** Norte de Santander, N Colombia *08°16′N 73°21′W*
105 *N9* **Ocaña** Castilla-La Mancha, C Spain *39°57′N 03°30′W*
104 *H4* **O Carballiño** *Cast.* Carballiño. Galicia, NW Spain *42°26′N 08°05′W*
37 *T9* **Ocate** New Mexico, SW USA *36°09′N 105°03′W*
Ocavango *see* Okavango
57 *D14* **Occidental, Cordillera** ▲ W South America
21 *Q6* **Oceana** West Virginia, NE USA *37°41′N 81°37′W*
21 *Z4* **Ocean City** Maryland, NE USA *38°20′N 75°05′W*
18 *J17* **Ocean City** New Jersey, NE USA *39°15′N 74°33′W*
10 *K15* **Ocean Falls** British Columbia, SW Canada *52°24′N 127°42′W*
Ocean Island *see* Banaba
Ocean Island *see* Kure Atoll
64 *J9* **Oceanographer Fracture Zone** *tectonic feature* NW Atlantic Ocean
35 *U17* **Oceanside** California, W USA *33°12′N 117°23′W*
22 *M9* **Ocean Springs** Mississippi, S USA *30°24′N 88°49′W*
Ocean State *see* Rhode Island
25 *O9* **O C Fisher Lake** Texas, SW USA
117 *Q10* **Ochakiv** *Rus.* Ochakov. Mykolayivs'ka Oblast', S Ukraine *46°36′N 31°33′E*
Ochakov *see* Ochakiv
Ochamchira *see* Ochamchire
137 *Q9* **Ochamchire** *Rus.* Ochamchira; *prev.* Och'amch'ire. W Georgia *42°45′N 41°30′E*
Och'amch'ire *see* Ochamchire
Ochansk *see* Okhansk
125 *T15* **Ochër** Permskiy Kray, NW Russian Federation *57°54′N 54°40′E*
115 *I19* **Óchi** ▲ Évvoia, C Greece *38°03′N 24°27′E*
165 *W4* **Ochiishi-misaki** *headland* Hokkaidō, NE Japan *43°10′N 145°29′E*
23 *S9* **Ochlockonee River** Florida/Georgia, SE USA
44 *K12* **Ocho Rios** C Jamaica *18°24′N 77°06′W*
Ochrida *see* Ohrid
Ochrida, Lake *see* Ohrid, Lake
101 *J19* **Ochsenfurt** Bayern, C Germany *49°39′N 10°03′E*
23 *U7* **Ocilla** Georgia, SE USA *31°35′N 83°15′W*
94 *N13* **Ockelbo** Gävleborg, C Sweden *60°51′N 16°46′E*
Ocker *see* Oker
95 *I19* **Öckerö** Västra Götaland, S Sweden *57°43′N 11°39′E*
23 *U6* **Ocmulgee River** Georgia, SE USA
116 *H11* **Ocna Mureş** *Hung.* Marosújvár; *prev.* Ocna Mureşului, *prev. Hung.* Marosújvárakna. Alba, C Romania *46°25′N 23°53′E*
Ocna Mureşului *see* Ocna Mureş
116 *H11* **Ocna Sibiului** *Ger.* Salzburg, *Hung.* Vizakna. Sibiu, C Romania *45°52′N 23°59′E*
116 *H13* **Ocnele Mari** *prev.* Vioara. Vâlcea, S Romania *45°03′N 24°18′E*
116 *L7* **Ocniţa** *Rus.* Oknitsa. N Moldova *48°25′N 27°30′E*
23 *U4* **Oconee, Lake** Georgia, SE USA
23 *U5* **Oconee River** Georgia, SE USA
30 *M9* **Oconomowoc** Wisconsin, N USA *43°06′N 88°29′W*
30 *M6* **Oconto** Wisconsin, N USA *44°55′N 87°52′W*
30 *M6* **Oconto Falls** Wisconsin, N USA *44°52′N 88°06′W*
30 *M6* **Oconto River** Wisconsin, N USA
104 *I3* **O Corgo** Galicia, NW Spain *42°56′N 07°25′W*
41 *V16* **Ocosingo** Chiapas, SE Mexico *17°04′N 92°15′W*
42 *J8* **Ocotal** Nueva Segovia, NW Nicaragua *13°38′N 86°28′W*
42 *F6* **Ocotepeque** *department* W Honduras
Ocotepeque *see* Nueva Ocotepeque
40 *L13* **Ocotlán** Jalisco, SW Mexico *20°21′N 102°42′W*
41 *R16* **Ocotlán** *var.* Ocotlán de Morelos. Oaxaca, SE Mexico *16°49′N 96°49′W*
Ocotlán de Morelos *see* Ocotlán
41 *U16* **Ocozocuautla** Chiapas, SE Mexico *16°46′N 93°22′W*
21 *Y10* **Ocracoke Island** *island* North Carolina, SE USA
102 *I3* **Octeville** Manche, N France *49°37′N 01°39′W*
October Revolution Island *see* Oktyabr'skoy Revolyutsii, Ostrov
43 *R17* **Ocú** Herrera, S Panama *07°55′N 80°43′W*
83 *Q14* **Ocua** Cabo Delgado, NE Mozambique *13°37′S 39°44′E*
Ocumare *see* Ocumare del Tuy
54 *M5* **Ocumare del Tuy** *var.* Ocumare. Miranda, N Venezuela *10°07′N 66°47′W*
77 *P17* **Oda** SE Ghana *05°55′N 00°56′W*
165 *G12* **Ōda** *var.* Oda. Shimane, Honshū, SW Japan *35°10′N 132°29′E*
92 *K3* **Ódadhahraun** *lava flow* C Iceland
165 *Q7* **Ōdate** Akita, Honshū, C Japan *40°18′N 140°34′E*
165 *N14* **Odawara** Kanagawa, Honshū, S Japan *35°15′N 139°08′E*
95 *D14* **Odda** Hordaland, S Norway *60°03′N 06°34′E*
95 *G22* **Odder** Midtjylland, C Denmark *55°59′N 10°10′E*
Oddur *see* Xuddur
29 *T13* **Odebolt** Iowa, C USA *42°18′N 95°15′W*
104 *H14* **Odeleite** Faro, S Portugal *37°02′N 07°29′W*
25 *Q4* **Odell** Texas, SW USA *34°19′N 99°24′W*
25 *T14* **Odem** Texas, SW USA *27°57′N 97°34′W*
104 *F13* **Odemira** Beja, S Portugal *37°35′N 08°38′W*
136 *C14* **Ödemiş** İzmir, SW Turkey *38°11′N 27°58′E*
Ödenburg *see* Sopron
83 *I22* **Odendaalsrus** Free State, C South Africa *27°52′S 26°42′E*
Odenpäh *see* Otepää
95 *H23* **Odense** Syddtjylland, C Denmark *55°24′N 10°23′E*
101 *H19* **Odenwald** ▲ W Germany
84 *H10* **Oder** *Cz./Pol.* Odra. C Europe
Oderberg *see* Bohumín
100 *P11* **Oderbruch** *wetland* Germany/Poland
Oderhaff *see* Szczeciński, Zalew
100 *O11* **Oder-Havel-Kanal** *canal* NE Germany
Oderhellen *see* Odorheiu Secuiesc
100 *P13* **Oder-Spree-Kanal** *canal* NE Germany
Odertal *see* Zdzieszowice
106 *I7* **Oderzo** Veneto, NE Italy *45°48′N 12°33′E*
177 *P10* **Odesa** *Rus.* Odessa. Odes'ka Oblast', SW Ukraine *46°29′N 30°44′E*
24 *M8* **Odessa** Texas, SW USA *31°51′N 102°22′W*
32 *K8* **Odessa** Washington, NW USA *47°19′N 118°41′W*
Odesa *see* Odes'ka Oblast'
95 *L18* **Ödeshög** Östergötland, S Sweden *58°13′N 14°40′E*
117 *O9* **Odes'ka Oblast'** *var.* Odesa, *Rus.* Odesskaya Oblast'. *province* SW Ukraine
Odessa *see* Odesa
Odesskaya Oblast' *see* Odes'ka Oblast'
122 *H12* **Odesskoye** Omskaya Oblast', C Russian Federation *54°15′N 72°45′E*
Odessus *see* Varna
102 *F6* **Odet** NW France
104 *I14* **Odiel** SW Spain
76 *L14* **Odienné** NW Ivory Coast *09°32′N 07°35′W*
171 *O4* **Odiongan** Tablas Island, C Philippines *12°23′N 122°01′E*
Odisha *see* Orissa
116 *L12* **Odobeşti** Vrancea, E Romania *45°46′N 27°06′E*
110 *H13* **Odolanów** *Ger.* Adelnau. Wielkopolskie, C Poland *51°35′N 17°42′E*
167 *R13* **Ôdôngk** Kâmpóng Spoe, S Cambodia *11°48′N 104°45′E*
25 *N6* **O'donnell** Texas, SW USA *32°57′N 101°49′W*
98 *O7* **Odoorn** Drenthe, NE Netherlands *52°52′N 06°49′E*
Odorhei *see* Odorheiu Secuiesc
116 *J11* **Odorheiu Secuiesc** *Ger.* Oderhellen, *Hung.* Vámosudvarhely; *prev.* Odorhei, *Ger.* Hofmarkt. Harghita, C Romania *46°18′N 25°19′E*
Odra *see* Oder
112 *J9* **Odžaci** *Ger.* Hodschag, *Hung.* Hodság. Vojvodina, NW Serbia *45°31′N 19°15′E*
59 *N14* **Oeiras** Piauí, E Brazil *07°00′S 42°07′W*
104 *F11* **Oeiras** Lisboa, C Portugal *38°41′N 09°18′W*
101 *G14* **Oelde** Nordrhein-Westfalen, W Germany *51°49′N 08°09′E*
28 *J11* **Oelrichs** South Dakota, N USA *43°08′N 103°13′W*
101 *M17* **Oelsnitz** Sachsen, E Germany *50°22′N 12°12′E*
Oels/Oels in Schlesien *see* Oleśnica
29 *X12* **Oelwein** Iowa, C USA *42°40′N 91°54′W*
Oeniadae *see* Oiniádes
191 *N17* **Oeno Island** *atoll* Pitcairn Islands, C Pacific Ocean
Oesel *see* Saaremaa
108 *L7* **Oetz** *var.* Ötz. Tirol, W Austria *47°15′N 10°56′E*
137 *P11* **Of** Trabzon, NE Turkey *40°57′N 40°17′E*
30 *K15* **O'Fallon** Illinois, N USA *38°35′N 89°54′W*
27 *W4* **O'Fallon** Missouri, C USA *38°54′N 90°31′W*
107 *N16* **Ofanto** S Italy
97 *D18* **Offaly** *Ir.* Ua Uíbh Fhailí; *prev.* King's County. *cultural region* C Ireland
101 *H18* **Offenbach** *var.* Offenbach am Main. Hessen, W Germany *50°06′N 08°46′E*
Offenbach am Main *see* Offenbach
101 *F22* **Offenburg** Baden-Württemberg, SW Germany *48°28′N 07°57′E*
182 *C2* **Officer Creek** *seasonal river* South Australia
Oficina María Elena *see* María Elena
Oficina Pedro de Valdivia *see* Pedro de Valdivia
115 *K22* **Ofidoússa** *island* Kykládes, Greece, Aegean Sea
Ofiral *see* Sharm ash Shaykh
92 *H10* **Ofotfjorden** *fjord* N Norway
192 *L16* **Ofu** *island* Manua Islands, E American Samoa
165 *R9* **Ōfunato** Iwate, Honshū, C Japan *39°04′N 141°43′E*
165 *P8* **Oga** Akita, Honshū, C Japan *39°56′N 139°47′E*
Ogaadeen *see* Ogaden
165 *Q9* **Ogachi** Akita, Honshū, C Japan *39°03′N 140°26′E*
165 *P9* **Ogachi-tōge** *pass* Honshū, C Japan
81 *N14* **Ogaden** *Som.* Ogaadeen. *plateau* Ethiopia/Somalia
165 *P8* **Oga-hantō** *peninsula* Honshū, C Japan
165 *K13* **Ōgaki** Gifu, Honshū, SW Japan *35°22′N 136°35′E*
28 *L15* **Ogallala** Nebraska, C USA *41°09′N 101°44′W*
168 *M14* **Ogan, Air** Sumatera, W Indonesia
165 *Y15* **Ogasawara-shotō** *Eng.* Bonin Islands. *island group* SE Japan
14 *I9* **Ogascanane, Lac** Québec, SE Canada
165 *R7* **Ogawara-ko** Honshū, C Japan
77 *T15* **Ogbomosho** *var.* Ogmoboso. Oyo, W Nigeria *08°10′N 04°16′E*
29 *U13* **Ogden** Iowa, C USA *42°03′N 94°01′W*
36 *L2* **Ogden** Utah, W USA *41°09′N 111°58′W*
18 *I6* **Ogdensburg** New York, NE USA *44°42′N 75°25′W*
23 *W5* **Ogeechee River** Georgia, SE USA
Oger *see* Ogre
165 *N10* **Ogi** Niigata, Sado, C Japan *37°49′N 138°16′E*
10 *H5* **Ogilvie** Yukon Territory, NW Canada *63°34′N 139°44′W*
10 *H4* **Ogilvie** Yukon Territory, NW Canada
10 *H5* **Ogilvie Mountains** ▲ Yukon Territory, NW Canada
Oginskiy Kanal *see* Ahinski Kanal
162 *J7* **Ögiynuur** *var.* Dzegstey. Arhangay, C Mongolia *47°38′N 102°31′E*
146 *F6* **Og'iyon Sho'rxogi** *wetland* NW Uzbekistan
146 *B10* **Oglanly** Balkan Welaýaty, W Turkmenistan *39°56′N 54°25′E*
23 *T5* **Oglethorpe** Georgia, SE USA *32°17′N 84°03′W*
23 *T2* **Oglethorpe, Mount** ▲ Georgia, SE USA *34°29′N 84°19′W*
106 *F7* **Oglio** *anc.* Ollius. N Italy
Ogmoboso *see* Ogbomosho
103 *T8* **Ognon** E France
123 *R13* **Ogodzha** Amurskaya Oblast', S Russian Federation *52°51′N 132°49′E*
77 *W16* **Ogoja** Cross River, S Nigeria *06°37′N 08°48′E*
12 *C10* **Ogoki** Ontario, S Canada
12 *D11* **Ogoki Lake** Ontario, C Canada
Ögöömör *see* Hanhongor
79 *F19* **Ogooué** Congo/Gabon
79 *E18* **Ogooué-Ivindo** *off.* Province de l'Ogooué-Ivindo, *var.* L'Ogooué-Ivindo. *province* N Gabon
Ogooué-Ivindo, Province de l' *see* Ogooué-Ivindo
79 *E19* **Ogooué-Lolo** *off.* Province de l'Ogooué-Lolo, *var.* L'Ogooué-Lolo. *province* C Gabon
Ogooué-Lolo, Province de l' *see* Ogooué-Lolo
79 *C19* **Ogooué-Maritime** *off.* Province de l'Ogooué-Maritime, *var.* L'Ogooué-Maritime. *province* W Gabon
Ogooué-Maritime, Province de l' *see* Ogooué-Maritime
165 *D14* **Ogōri** Fukuoka, Kyūshū, SW Japan *33°24′N 130°34′E*
114 *H7* **Ogosta** NW Bulgaria
112 *Q9* **Ogražden** *Bul.* Ograzhden. ▲ Bulgaria/FYR Macedonia *see also* Ograzhden
114 *G12* **Ograzhden** *Mac.* Orgražden. ▲ Bulgaria/FYR Macedonia *see also* Orgražden
Ograzhden *see* Ogražden
118 *G9* **Ogre** *Ger.* Oger. C Latvia *56°49′N 24°36′E*
118 *H9* **Ogre** C Latvia
112 *C10* **Ogulin** Karlovac, NW Croatia *45°15′N 15°13′E*
77 *S16* **Ogun** *state* SW Nigeria
Ogurdzhaly, Ostrov *see* OgurjalyAdasy
146 *A12* **OgurjalyAdasy** *Rus.* Ogurdzhaly, Ostrov. *island* W Turkmenistan
77 *U16* **Ogwashi-Uku** Delta, S Nigeria *06°08′N 06°38′E*
185 *B23* **Ohai** Southland, South Island, New Zealand *45°56′S 167°59′E*
147 *Q10* **Ohangaron** *Rus.* Akhangaran. Toshkent Viloyati, E Uzbekistan *40°56′N 69°37′E*
147 *Q10* **Ohangaron** *Rus.* Akhangaran. E Uzbekistan
83 *C16* **Ohangwena** *district* N Namibia
30 *M10* **O'Hare** (Chicago) Illinois, N USA *41°59′N 87°56′W*
165 *R6* **Ōhata** Aomori, Honshū, C Japan *41°23′N 141°09′E*
184 *L13* **Ohau** Manawatu-Wanganui, North Island, New Zealand *40°40′S 175°15′E*
185 *E20* **Ohau, Lake** South Island, New Zealand
Ohcejohka *see* Utsjoki
99 *J20* **Ohey** Namur, SE Belgium *50°26′N 05°07′E*
191 *X15* **O'Higgins, Cabo** *headland* Easter Island, Chile, E Pacific Ocean *27°05′S 109°15′W*
O'Higgins, Lago *see* San Martín, Lago
31 *S12* **Ohio** *off.* State of Ohio, *also known as* Buckeye State. *state* N USA
0 *L10* **Ohio River** N USA
Ohlau *see* Oława
101 *H16* **Ohm** C Germany
193 *W16* **Ohonua** 'Eua, E Tonga *21°20′S 174°57′W*
23 *V5* **Ohoopee River** Georgia, SE USA
100 *L12* **Ohre** *Ger.* Eger. Czech Republic/Germany
Ohri *see* Ohrid
113 *M20* **Ohrid** *Turk.* Ochrida, Ohri. SW FYR Macedonia *41°07′N 20°48′E*
113 *M20* **Ohrid, Lake** *var.* Lake Ochrida, *Alb.* Liqeni i Ohrit, *Mac.* Ohridsko Ezero. Albania/FYR Macedonia
Ohridsko Ezero/Ohrit, Liqeni i *see* Ohrid, Lake
184 *L9* **Ohura** Manawatu-Wanganui, North Island, New Zealand *38°51′S 174°58′E*
58 *J9* **Oiapoque** Amapá, E Brazil *03°54′N 51°46′W*
58 *J10* **Oiapoque, Rio** *var.* Fleuve l'Oyapok, Oyapock. Brazil/French Guiana *see also* Oyapok, Fleuve l'
Oiapoque, Rio *see* Oyapok, Fleuve l'
54 *G8* **Oiba** Santander, C Colombia *06°16′N 73°18′W*
15 *O9* **Oies, Île aux** *island* Québec, SE Canada
92 *L13* **Oijärvi** Oulu, C Finland *65°38′N 26°05′E*
92 *L12* **Oikarainen** Lappi, N Finland *66°30′N 25°46′E*
188 *F10* **Oikuul** Babeldaob, N Palau
18 *C13* **Oil City** Pennsylvania, NE USA *41°25′N 79°42′W*
18 *C12* **Oil Creek** Pennsylvania, NE USA
35 *R13* **Oildale** California, W USA *35°25′N 119°01′W*
Oileán Ciarral *see* Castleisland
Oil Islands *see* Chagos Archipelago
115 *D18* **Oiniádes** *anc.* Oeniadae. *site of ancient city* Dytikí Elláda, W Greece
115 *L18* **Oinoússes** *island* E Greece
Oírr, Inis *see* Inisheer
99 *J15* **Oirschot** Noord-Brabant, S Netherlands *51°30′N 05°18′E*
103 *N4* **Oise** *department* N France
103 *P3* **Oise** N France
99 *J14* **Oisterwijk** Noord-Brabant, S Netherlands *51°35′N 05°12′E*
45 *O14* **Oistins** S Barbados *13°04′N 59°33′W*
165 *E4* **Ōita** Ōita, Kyūshū, SW Japan *33°15′N 131°35′E*
165 *D14* **Ōita** *off.* Ōita-ken. *prefecture* Kyūshū, SW Japan
Ōita-ken *see* Ōita
115 *E17* **Oíti** ▲ C Greece *38°48′N 22°12′E*
165 *S4* **Oiwake** Hokkaidō, NE Japan *42°54′N 141°49′E*
35 *R14* **Ojai** California, W USA *34°25′N 119°15′W*
94 *K13* **Öje** Dalarna, C Sweden *60°49′N 13°54′E*
93 *J14* **Öjebyn** Norrbotten, N Sweden *65°20′N 21°26′E*
165 *B13* **Ojika-jima** *island* SW Japan
40 *K5* **Ojinaga** Chihuahua, N Mexico *29°31′N 104°26′W*
40 *M11* **Ojo Caliente** *var.* Ojocaliente. Zacatecas, C Mexico *22°35′N 102°18′W*
Ojocaliente *see* Ojo Caliente
40 *D6* **Ojo de Liebre, Laguna** *var.* Laguna Scammon, Scammon Lagoon. *lagoon* NW Mexico
62 *I7* **Ojos del Salado, Cerro** ▲ W Argentina *27°04′S 68°34′W*
105 *R7* **Ojos Negros** Aragón, NE Spain *40°43′N 01°30′W*
40 *M12* **Ojuelos de Jalisco** Aguascalientes, C Mexico *21°52′N 101°40′W*
127 *N4* **Oka** W Russian Federation
83 *D19* **Okahandja** Otjozondjupa, C Namibia *21°58′S 16°55′E*
184 *L9* **Okahukura** Manawatu-Wanganui, North Island, New Zealand *38°48′S 175°13′E*
184 *J3* **Okaihau** Northland, North Island, New Zealand *35°19′S 173°45′E*
83 *D18* **Okakarara** Otjozondjupa, N Namibia *20°33′S 17°20′E*
13 *P5* **Okak Islands** *island group* Newfoundland and Labrador, E Canada
10 *M17* **Okanagan** British Columbia, SW Canada
11 *N17* **Okanagan Lake** British Columbia, SW Canada
Ókanizsa *see* Kanjiža
83 *C16* **Okankolo** Oshikoto, N Namibia *17°57′S 16°28′E*
32 *K6* **Okanogan River** Washington, NW USA
83 *D18* **Okaputa** Otjozondjupa, N Namibia *20°09′S 16°56′E*
149 *V9* **Okāra** Punjab, E Pakistan *30°49′N 73°31′E*
26 *M10* **Okarche** Oklahoma, C USA *35°43′N 97°58′W*
Okarem *see* Ekerem
189 *X14* **Okat Harbor** *harbor* Kosrae, E Micronesia
22 *M5* **Okatibbee Creek** Mississippi, S USA
83 *C17* **Okaukuejo** Kunene, N Namibia *19°10′S 15°23′E*
Okavanggo *see* Cubango/Okavango
83 *E17* **Okavango** *district* NW Namibia
83 *G17* **Okavango** *var.* Cubango, Kavango, Kavengo, Kubango, Okavanggo, *Port.* Ocavango. S Africa *see also* Cubango
Okavango *see* Cubango
83 *G17* **Okavango Delta** *wetland* N Botswana
164 *M12* **Okaya** Nagano, Honshū, S Japan *36°03′N 138°00′E*
164 *H13* **Okayama** Okayama, Honshū, SW Japan *34°40′N 133°54′E*
164 *H13* **Okayama** *off.* Okayama-ken. *prefecture* Honshū, SW Japan
Okayama-ken *see* Okayama
164 *L14* **Okazaki** Aichi, Honshū, C Japan *34°58′N 137°10′E*
110 *M12* **Okęcie** (Warszawa) Mazowieckie, C Poland *52°08′N 20°57′E*
23 *Y13* **Okeechobee** Florida, SE USA *27°14′N 80°49′W*
23 *Y14* **Okeechobee, Lake** Florida, SE USA
26 *M9* **Okeene** Oklahoma, C USA *36°07′N 98°19′W*
23 *V8* **Okefenokee Swamp** *wetland* Georgia, SE USA
97 *J24* **Okehampton** SW England, United Kingdom *50°44′N 04°W*
27 *P10* **Okemah** Oklahoma, C USA *35°25′N 96°20′W*
77 *U16* **Okene** Kogi, S Nigeria *07°31′N 06°15′E*
100 *K13* **Oker** *var.* Ocker. NW Germany
101 *J14* **Oker-Stausee** C Germany
123 *T12* **Okha** Ostrov Sakhalin, Sakhalinskaya Oblast', SE Russian Federation *53°33′N 142°55′E*
125 *U15* **Okhansk** *var.* Ochansk. Permskiy Kray, NW Russian Federation *57°44′N 55°20′E*
123 *S10* **Okhotsk** Khabarovskiy Kray, E Russian Federation *59°21′N 143°15′E*
192 *J2* **Okhotsk, Sea of** *sea* NW Pacific Ocean
117 *T4* **Okhtyrka** *Rus.* Akhtyrka. Sums'ka Oblast', NE Ukraine *50°19′N 34°54′E*
83 *E23* **Okiep** Northern Cape, W South Africa *29°39′S 17°53′E*
Oki-guntō *see* Oki-shotō
164 *H11* **Oki-kaikyō** *strait* SW Japan
165 *P16* **Okinawa** Okinawa, SW Japan *26°20′N 127°47′E*
165 *S16* **Okinawa** *off.* Okinawa-ken. *prefecture* Okinawa, SW Japan
165 *S16* **Okinawa** *island* SW Japan
Okinawa-ken *see* Okinawa
165 *U16* **Okinoerabu-jima** *island* Nansei-shotō, SW Japan
164 *F15* **Okino-shima** *island* SW Japan
164 *H11* **Oki-shotō** *var.* Oki-guntō. *island group* SW Japan
77 *T16* **Okitipupa** Ondo, SW Nigeria *06°33′N 04°43′E*
166 *L8* **Okkan** Bago, SW Burma (Myanmar) *17°30′N 95°52′E*
27 *N10* **Oklahoma** *off.* State of Oklahoma, *also known as* The Sooner State. *state* C USA
27 *N11* **Oklahoma City** *state capital* Oklahoma, C USA *35°28′N 97°31′W*
25 *Q4* **Oklaunion** Texas, SW USA *34°07′N 99°07′W*
23 *W10* **Oklawaha River** Florida, SE USA
27 *P10* **Okmulgee** Oklahoma, C USA *35°38′N 95°59′W*
Oknitsa *see* Ocniţa
22 *M3* **Okolona** Mississippi, S USA *34°00′N 88°45′W*
165 *U2* **Okoppe** Hokkaidō, NE Japan *44°27′N 143°06′E*
11 *Q16* **Okotoks** Alberta, SW Canada *50°46′N 113°57′W*
80 *H6* **Oko, Wadi** NE Sudan
79 *G19* **Okoyo** Cuvette, W Congo *01°28′S 15°04′E*
77 *S15* **Okpara** Benin/Nigeria
92 *J8* **Øksfjord** Finnmark, N Norway *70°13′N 22°22′E*
125 *R4* **Oksino** Nenetskiy Avtonomnyy Okrug, NW Russian Federation *67°33′N 52°15′E*
92 *G13* **Oksskolten** ▲ C Norway *66°00′N 14°18′E*
Oksu *see* Oqsu
144 *M8* **Oktaybr'skiy** Kostanay, N Kazakhstan
186 *B7* **Ok Tedi** Western, W Papua New Guinea
Oktemberyan *see* Armavir
166 *M7* **Oktwin** Bago, C Burma (Myanmar) *18°47′N 96°21′E*
127 *R6* **Oktyabr'sk** Samarskaya Oblast', W Russian Federation *53°13′N 48°36′E*
Oktyab'rsk *see* Kandyagash
125 *N12* **Oktyabr'skiy** Arkhangel'skaya Oblast', NW Russian Federation *61°03′N 43°16′E*
122 *E10* **Oktyabr'skiy** Kamchatskiy Kray, E Russian Federation *52°35′N 156°18′E*
127 *T5* **Oktyabr'skiy** Respublika Bashkortostan, W Russian Federation *54°28′N 53°29′E*
127 *O11* **Oktyabr'skiy** Volgogradskaya Oblast', SW Russian Federation *48°00′N 43°35′E*
Oktyabr'skiy *see* Aktsyabrski
127 *V7* **Oktyabr'skoye** Orenburgskaya Oblast', W Russian Federation *52°22′N 55°39′E*
122 *M5* **Oktyabr'skoy Revolyutsii, Ostrov** *Eng.* October Revolution Island. *island* Severnaya Zemlya, N Russian Federation
Ōkuchi *see* Isa
124 *I14* **Okulovka** *var.* Okulovka. Novgorodskaya Oblast', W Russian Federation *58°24′N 33°16′E*
Okulovka *see* Okulovka
165 *Q4* **Okushiri-tō** *var.* Okusiri Tô. *island* NE Japan
Okusiri Tô *see* Okushiri-tō
77 *S15* **Okuta** Kwara, W Nigeria *09°18′N 03°09′E*
Ôkuti *see* Isa
83 *F19* **Okwa** *var.* Chapman's. Botswana/Namibia
123 *T10* **Ola** Magadanskaya Oblast', E Russian Federation *59°36′N 151°18′E*
27 *T11* **Ola** Arkansas, C USA *35°01′N 93°13′W*
Ola *see* Ala
35 *T11* **Olacha Peak** ▲ California, W USA *36°15′N 118°07′W*
92 *J1* **Ólafsfjördhur** Nordhurland Eystra, N Iceland *66°04′N 18°36′W*
92 *H3* **Ólafsvík** Vesturland, W Iceland *64°52′N 23°45′W*
Oláhbrettye *see* Bretea-Română
Oláhszentgyőrgy *see* Sângeorz-Băi
Oláh-Toplicza *see* Topliţa
118 *F9* **Olaine** C Latvia *56°47′N 23°56′E*
35 *T11* **Olancha** California, W USA *36°16′N 118°00′W*
42 *J5* **Olanchito** Yoro, C Honduras *15°30′N 86°34′W*
42 *J6* **Olancho** *department* E Honduras
95 *O20* **Öland** *island* S Sweden
95 *O19* **Ölands norra udde** *headland* S Sweden *57°21′N 17°06′E*
95 *N22* **Ölands södra udde** *headland* S Sweden *56°12′N 16°26′E*
182 *K7* **Olary** South Australia *32°18′S 140°16′E*
27 *R4* **Olathe** Kansas, C USA *38°52′N 94°50′W*
61 *C22* **Olavarría** Buenos Aires, E Argentina *36°57′S 60°20′W*
92 *O2* **Olav V Land** *physical region* C Svalbard
111 *H14* **Oława** *Ger.* Ohlau. Dolnośląskie, SW Poland *50°57′N 17°18′E*
107 *D17* **Olbia** *prev.* Terranova Pausania. Sardegna, Italy, C Mediterranean Sea *40°55′N 09°30′E*
44 *G5* **Old Bahama Channel** *channel* Bahamas/Cuba
Old Bay State/Old Colony State *see* Massachusetts
10 *H2* **Old Crow** Yukon Territory, NW Canada *67°34′N 139°55′W*
Old Dominion *see* Virginia
Oldeberkeap *see* Oldeberkoop
98 *M7* **Oldeberkoop** *Fris.* Oldeberkeap. Fryslân, N Netherlands *52°55′N 06°07′E*
98 *L10* **Oldebroek** Gelderland, E Netherlands *52°27′N 05°54′E*
98 *L8* **Oldemarkt** Overijssel, N Netherlands *52°49′N 05°58′E*
94 *E11* **Olden** Sogn Og Fjordane, C Norway *61°52′N 06°44′E*
100 *G10* **Oldenburg** Niedersachsen, NW Germany *53°09′N 08°13′E*
100 *K8* **Oldenburg** *var.* Oldenburg in Holstein. Schleswig-Holstein, N Germany *54°17′N 10°55′E*
Oldenburg in Holstein *see* Oldenburg
98 *P10* **Oldenzaal** Overijssel, E Netherlands *52°19′N 06°53′E*
Olderfjord *see* Leaibevuotna
18 *J8* **Old Forge** New York, NE USA *43°42′N 74°59′W*
Old Goa *see* Goa
97 *L17* **Oldham** NW England, United Kingdom *53°36′N 02°W*
39 *Q14* **Old Harbor** Kodiak Island, Alaska, USA *57°12′N 153°18′W*
44 *J13* **Old Harbour** C Jamaica *17°56′N 77°06′W*
97 *C22* **Old Head of Kinsale** *Ir.* An Seancheann. *headland* SW Ireland *51°37′N 08°33′W*
20 *J8* **Old Hickory Lake** Tennessee, S USA
Old Line State *see* Maryland
Old North State *see* North Carolina
81 *I17* **Ol Doinyo Lengeyo** ▲ C Kenya
11 *Q16* **Olds** Alberta, SW Canada *51°50′N 114°06′W*
19 *O7* **Old Speck Mountain** ▲ Maine, NE USA *44°34′N 70°55′W*
19 *S6* **Old Town** Maine, NE USA *44°55′N 68°39′W*
11 *T17* **Old Wives Lake** Saskatchewan, S Canada
162 *J7* **Öldziyt** *var.* Höshööt. Arhangay, C Mongolia *48°06′N 102°34′E*
162 *I8* **Öldziyt** *var.* Ulaan-Uul. Bayanhongor, C Mongolia *46°03′N 100°52′E*
162 *L10* **Öldziyt** *var.* Rashaant. Dundgovĭ, C Mongolia *44°54′N 106°32′E*
162 *K8* **Öldziyt** *var.* Sangiyn Dalay. Övörhangay, C Mongolia *46°35′N 103°18′E*
Öldziyt *see* Erdenemandal, Arhangay, Mongolia
Öldziyt *see* Sayhandulaan, Dornogovĭ, Mongolia
188 *H6* **Oleai** *var.* San Jose. Saipan, S Northern Mariana Islands
18 *E11* **Olean** New York, NE USA *42°04′N 78°24′W*
110 *O7* **Olecko** *Ger.* Treuburg. Warmińsko-Mazurskie, NE Poland *54°02′N 22°29′E*
106 *C7* **Oleggio** Piemonte, NE Italy *45°36′N 08°37′E*
123 *P11* **Olëkma** Amurskaya Oblast', SE Russian Federation *57°00′N 120°27′E*
123 *P12* **Olëkma** C Russian Federation
123 *P11* **Olëkminsk** Respublika Sakha (Yakutiya), NE Russian Federation *60°25′N 120°25′E*
117 *W7* **Oleksandrivka** Donets'ka Oblast', E Ukraine *48°42′N 36°56′E*
117 *R7* **Oleksandrivka** *Rus.* Aleksandrovka. Kirovohrads'ka Oblast', C Ukraine *48°59′N 32°14′E*
117 *Q9* **Oleksandrivka** Mykolayivs'ka Oblast', S Ukraine *47°42′N 31°17′E*
117 *S7* **Oleksandriya** *Rus.* Aleksandriya. Kirovohrads'ka Oblast', C Ukraine *48°42′N 33°07′E*
93 *B20* **Ølen** Hordaland, S Norway *59°36′N 05°48′E*
124 *J4* **Olenegorsk** Murmanskaya Oblast', NW Russian Federation *68°06′N 33°15′E*
123 *N9* **Olenëk** Respublika Sakha (Yakutiya), NE Russian Federation *68°28′N 112°18′E*
123 *N9* **Olenëk** NE Russian Federation
123 *O7* **Olenëkskiy Zaliv** *bay* N Russian Federation
124 *K6* **Olenitsa** Murmanskaya Oblast', NW Russian Federation *66°27′N 35°21′E*
102 *I11* **Oléron, Île d'** *island* W France
111 *H14* **Oleśnica** *Ger.* Oels, Oels in Schlesien. Dolnośląskie, SW Poland *51°13′N 17°20′E*
111 *I15* **Olesno** *Ger.* Rosenberg. Opolskie, S Poland *50°53′N 18°23′E*
116 *M3* **Olevs'k** *Rus.* Olevsk. Zhytomyrs'ka Oblast', N Ukraine *51°12′N 27°38′E*
Olevsk *see* Olevs'k
123 *S15* **Ol'ga** Primorskiy Kray, SE Russian Federation *43°41′N 135°06′E*
Olga, Mount *see* Kata Tjuṯa
92 *P2* **Olgastretet** *strait* E Svalbard
162 *D5* **Ölgiy** Bayan-Ölgiy, W Mongolia *48°57′N 89°59′E*
95 *F23* **Ølgod** Syddtjylland, W Denmark *55°44′N 08°37′E*
104 *H14* **Olhão** Faro, S Portugal *37°01′N 07°50′W*
93 *L14* **Olhava** Oulu, C Finland *65°28′N 25°25′E*
105 *V5* **Oliana** Cataluña, NE Spain *42°04′N 01°19′E*
112 *B12* **Olib** *It.* Ulbo. *island* W Croatia
83 *B16* **Olifa** Kunene, NW Namibia *17°25′S 14°27′E*
83 *E20* **Olifants** *var.* Elephant River. E Namibia
Olifants *see* Lepelle
83 *I20* **Olifants Drift** *var.* Oliphants Drift. Kgatleng, SE Botswana *24°13′S 26°52′E*
83 *G22* **Olifantshoek** Northern Cape, N South Africa *27°56′S 22°45′E*
188 *L15* **Olimarao Atoll** *atoll* Caroline Islands, C Micronesia
Ólimbos *see* Ólympos
Olimpo *see* Fuerte Olimpo
59 *Q15* **Olinda** Pernambuco, E Brazil *08°S 34°51′W*
Olinthos *see* Ólynthos
Oliphants Drift *see* Olifants Drift
Olisipo *see* Lisboa
Olita *see* Alytus
105 *Q4* **Olite** Navarra, N Spain *42°29′N 01°40′W*
62 *K10* **Oliva** Córdoba, C Argentina *32°03′S 63°34′W*
105 *T11* **Oliva** Valenciana, E Spain *38°55′N 00°09′W*
Oliva *see* La Oliva
104 *I12* **Oliva de la Frontera** Extremadura, W Spain *38°17′N 06°54′W*
Olivares *see* Olivares de Júcar
62 *H9* **Olivares, Cerro de** ▲ N Chile *30°25′S 69°52′W*
105 *P9* **Olivares de Júcar** *var.* Olivares. Castilla-La Mancha, C Spain *39°45′N 02°21′W*
22 *L1* **Olive Branch** Mississippi, S USA *34°58′N 89°49′W*
21 *O5* **Olive Hill** Kentucky, S USA *38°18′N 83°10′W*
35 *O6* **Olivehurst** California, W USA *39°05′N 121°33′W*
104 *G7* **Oliveira de Azeméis** Aveiro, N Portugal *40°49′N 08°29′W*
104 *I11* **Olivenza** Extremadura, W Spain *38°41′N 07°06′W*
11 *N17* **Oliver** British Columbia, SW Canada *49°10′N 119°37′W*
103 *N7* **Olivet** Loiret, C France *47°53′N 01°53′E*
29 *Q12* **Olivet** South Dakota, N USA *43°14′N 97°40′W*
29 *T9* **Olivia** Minnesota, N USA *44°46′N 94°59′W*
185 *C20* **Olivine Range** ▲ South Island, New Zealand
108 *H10* **Olivone** Ticino, S Switzerland *46°32′N 08°55′E*
Ölkeyek *see* Ol'keyyek
144 *L11* **Ol'keyyek** *Kaz.* Ölkeyek; *prev.* Ul'kayak. C Kazakhstan

Country · Country Capital · Dependent Territory · Dependent Territory Capital · Administrative Regions · International Airport · ▲ Mountain · ▲ Mountain Range · Volcano · River · Lake · Reservoir

127 O9 **Ol'khovka** Volgogradskaya Oblast', SW Russian Federation 49°54′N 44°36′E
111 K16 **Olkusz** Małopolskie, S Poland 50°18′N 19°33′E
22 I6 **Olla** Louisiana, S USA 31°54′N 92°14′W
62 I4 **Ollagüe, Volcán** *var.* Oyahue, Volcán Oyahue. 🌋 N Chile 21°25′S 68°10′W
189 U13 **Ollan** *island* Chuuk, C Micronesia
188 F7 **Ollei** Babeldaob, N Palau 07°43′N 134°37′E
Ollius *see* Oglio
108 C10 **Ollon** Vaud, W Switzerland 46°19′N 07°00′E
147 Q10 **Olmaliq** *Rus.* Almalyk. Toshkent Viloyati, E Uzbekistan 40°51′N 69°39′E
104 M6 **Olmedo** Castilla y León, N Spain 41°17′N 04°41′W
56 B10 **Olmos** Lambayeque, W Peru 06°00′S 79°43′W
Olmütz *see* Olomouc
30 M15 **Olney** Illinois, N USA 38°43′N 88°05′W
25 R5 **Olney** Texas, SW USA 33°22′N 98°45′W
95 L22 **Olofström** Blekinge, S Sweden 56°16′N 14°33′E
187 N9 **Olomburi** Malaita, N Solomon Islands 09°00′S 161°09′E
111 H17 **Olomouc** *Ger.* Olmütz, *Pol.* Ołomuniec. Olomoucký Kraj, E Czech Republic 49°36′N 17°13′E
111 H18 **Olomoucký Kraj** ◈ *region* E Czech Republic
Ołomuniec *see* Olomouc
122 D7 **Olonets** Respublika Kareliya, NW Russian Federation 60°58′N 33°01′E
171 N3 **Olongapo** *off.* Olongapo City. Luzon, N Philippines 14°52′N 120°16′E
Olongapo City *see* Olongapo
102 J16 **Oloron-Ste-Marie** Pyrénées-Atlantiques, SW France 43°12′N 00°35′W
192 L16 **Olosega** *island* Manua Islands, E American Samoa
105 W4 **Olot** Cataluña, NE Spain 42°11′N 02°30′E
146 K12 **Olot** *Rus.* Alat. Buxoro Viloyati, C Uzbekistan 39°22′N 63°42′E
112 I12 **Olovo** Federacija Bosna I Hercegovina, E Bosnia and Herzegovina 44°08′N 18°35′E
123 O14 **Olovyannaya** Zabaykal'skiy Kray, S Russian Federation 50°59′N 115°24′E
123 T7 **Oloy** ≈ NE Russian Federation
101 F16 **Olpe** Nordrhein-Westfalen, W Germany 51°02′N 07°51′E
109 N8 **Olperer** ▲ SW Austria 47°03′N 11°36′E
Olshanka *see* Vil'shanka
Ol'shany *see* Al'shany
Olsnitz *see* Murska Sobota
98 M10 **Olst** Overijssel, E Netherlands 52°19′N 06°06′E
110 L8 **Olsztyn** *Ger.* Allenstein. Warmińsko-Mazurskie, N Poland 53°46′N 20°28′E
110 L8 **Olsztynek** *Ger.* Hohenstein in Ostpreussen. Warmińsko-Mazurskie, N Poland 53°35′N 20°17′E
116 I14 **Olt** ◈ *county* SW Romania
116 I14 **Olt** *var.* Oltul, *Ger.* Alt. ≈ S Romania
108 E7 **Olten** Solothurn, NW Switzerland 47°22′N 07°55′E
116 K14 **Oltenița** *prev. Eng.* Oltenitsa; *anc.* Constantiola. Călărași, SE Romania 44°05′N 26°40′E
Oltenitsa *see* Oltenița
116 H14 **Olteț** ≈ S Romania
24 M4 **Olton** Texas, SW USA 34°10′N 102°07′W
137 R12 **Oltu** Erzurum, NE Turkey 40°34′N 41°59′E
Oltul *see* Olt
146 G7 **Oltynko'l** Qoraqalpog'iston Respublikasi, NW Uzbekistan 43°04′N 58°51′E
Oluan Pi *see* Eluan Bi
Ólubló *see* Stará L'ubovňa
137 R11 **Olur** Erzurum, NE Turkey 40°49′N 42°08′E
104 L15 **Olvera** Andalucía, S Spain 36°56′N 05°15′W
Ol'viopol' *see* Pervomays'k
Olwanpi, Cape *see* Eluan Bi
115 D20 **Olympía** Dytikí Elláda, S Greece 37°39′N 21°36′E
32 G9 **Olympia** *state capital* Washington, NW USA 47°02′N 122°54′W
182 H5 **Olympic Dam** South Australia 30°25′S 136°56′E
32 F7 **Olympic Mountains** ▲▲ Washington, NW USA
121 O3 **Ólympos** *var.* Troodos, *Eng.* Mount Olympus. ▲ C Cyprus 34°55′N 32°49′E
115 F15 **Ólympos** *var.* Ólimbos, *Eng.* Mount Olympus. ▲ N Greece 40°04′N 22°24′E
115 L17 **Ólympos** ▲ Lésvos, E Greece 39°03′N 26°20′E
16 C5 **Olympus, Mount** ▲ Washington, NW USA 47°48′N 123°42′W
Olympus, Mount *see* Ólympos
115 G14 **Ólynthos** *var.* Olinthos; *anc.* Olynthus. *site of ancient city* Kentrikí Makedonía, N Greece
Olynthus *see* Ólynthos
117 Q3 **Olyshivka** Chernihivs'ka Oblast', N Ukraine 51°13′N 31°19′E
123 W8 **Olyutorskiy, Mys** *headland* E Russian Federation 59°56′N 170°22′E
123 V8 **Olyutorskiy Zaliv** *bay* E Russian Federation
186 M10 **Om** ≈ W Papua New Guinea
129 S6 **Om'** ≈ N Russian Federation
158 I13 **Oma** Xizang Zizhiqu, W China 32°30′N 83°14′E
165 R6 **Ōma** Aomori, Honshū, C Japan 41°31′N 140°54′E
125 P6 **Oma** ≈ NW Russian Federation
164 M12 **Ōmachi** *var.* Ōmati. Nagano, Honshū, S Japan 36°30′N 137°51′E
165 Q8 **Ōmagari** Akita, Honshū, C Japan 39°29′N 140°29′E
97 E15 **Omagh** *Ir.* An Ómaigh. W Northern Ireland, United Kingdom 54°36′N 07°18′W
29 S15 **Omaha** Nebraska, C USA 41°14′N 95°57′W
83 E19 **Omaheke** ◈ *district* W Namibia
141 W10 **Oman** *off.* Sultanate of Oman, *Ar.* Salṭanat 'Umān; *prev.* Muscat and Oman. ◆ *monarchy* SW Asia
129 O10 **Oman Basin** *var.* Bassin d'Oman. *undersea feature* N Indian Ocean 23°20′N 63°00′E
Oman, Bassin d' *see* Oman Basin
129 N10 **Oman, Gulf of** *Ar.* Khalīj 'Umān. *gulf* N Arabian Sea
Oman, Sultanate of *see* Oman
184 J3 **Omapere** Northland, North Island, New Zealand 35°32′S 173°24′E
185 E20 **Omarama** Canterbury, South Island, New Zealand 44°29′S 169°57′E
112 F11 **Omarska** ◈ Republika Srpska, NW Bosnia and Herzegovina
83 C18 **Omaruru** Erongo, NW Namibia 21°28′S 15°56′E
83 C19 **Omaruru** ≈ W Namibia
83 E17 **Omatako** ≈ NE Namibia
Ōmati *see* Ōmachi
83 E18 **Omawewozonyanda** Omaheke, E Namibia 21°30′S 19°34′E
165 R6 **Ōma-zaki** *headland* Honshū, C Japan 41°32′N 140°53′E
Omba *see* Ambae
Ombai *see* Alor, Pulau
83 C16 **Ombalantu** Omusati, N Namibia 17°33′S 14°58′E
79 H15 **Ombella-Mpoko** ◈ *prefecture* S Central African Republic
Ombetsu *see* Onbetsu
83 B17 **Ombombo** Kunene, NW Namibia 18°43′S 13°53′E
79 D19 **Omboué** Ogooué-Maritime, W Gabon 01°38′S 09°20′E
106 G13 **Ombrone** ≈ C Italy
80 F9 **Omdurman** *var.* Umm Durmān. Khartoum, C Sudan 15°37′N 32°29′E
165 N13 **Ōme** Tōkyō, Honshū, S Japan 35°48′N 139°17′E
106 C6 **Omegna** Piemonte, NE Italy 45°54′N 08°25′E
183 P12 **Omeo** Victoria, SE Australia 37°09′S 147°36′E
138 F11 **Omer** Southern, C Israel 31°16′N 34°51′E
41 P16 **Ometepec** Guerrero, S Mexico 16°39′N 98°23′W
42 K11 **Ometepe, Isla de** *island* S Nicaragua
Om Hager *see* Om Ḥajer
80 I10 **Om Ḥajer** *var.* Om Hager. SW Eritrea 14°19′N 36°46′E
165 J13 **Ōmihachiman** Shiga, Honshū, SW Japan 35°08′N 136°04′E
10 L12 **Omineca Mountains** ▲▲ British Columbia, W Canada
113 F14 **Omiš** *It.* Almissa. Split-Dalmacija, S Croatia 43°27′N 16°41′E
112 B10 **Omišalj** Primorje-Gorski Kotar, NW Croatia 45°10′N 14°33′E
83 D19 **Omitara** Khomas, C Namibia 22°18′S 18°01′E
41 O16 **Omitlán, Río** ≈ S Mexico
39 X14 **Ommaney, Cape** *headland* Baranof Island, Alaska, USA 56°10′N 134°40′W
98 N9 **Ommen** Overijssel, E Netherlands 52°31′N 06°25′E
163 N7 **Ömnödelger** *var.* Bayanbulag. Hentiy, C Mongolia 47°54′N 109°51′E
162 K11 **Ömnögovĭ** ◈ *province* S Mongolia
191 X7 **Omoa** Fatu Hira, NE French Polynesia 10°30′S 138°41′E
Omo Botego *see* Omo Wenz
Ómoldova *see* Moldova Veche
123 T7 **Omolon** Chukotskiy Avtonomnyy Okrug, NE Russian Federation 65°11′N 160°33′E
123 T7 **Omolon** ≈ NE Russian Federation
123 Q8 **Omoloy** ≈ NE Russian Federation
162 I12 **Omon Gol** *Chin.* Dong He, *var.* Narin Gol. ≈ N China
165 P8 **Omono-gawa** ≈ Honshū, C Japan
81 I14 **Omo Wenz** *var.* Omo Botego. ≈ Ethiopia/Kenya
122 H12 **Omsk** Omskaya Oblast', C Russian Federation 55°N 73°22′E
122 H11 **Omskaya Oblast'** ◈ *province* C Russian Federation
165 U2 **Ōmu** Hokkaidō, NE Japan 44°36′N 142°55′E
110 M9 **Omulew** ≈ NE Poland
116 J12 **Omul, Vârful** *prev.* Vîrful Omu. ▲ C Romania 45°24′N 25°26′E
83 D16 **Omundaungilo** Ohangwena, N Namibia 17°28′S 16°39′E
164 C14 **Ōmura** Nagasaki, Kyūshū, SW Japan 32°56′N 129°58′E
83 B17 **Omusati** ◈ *district* N Namibia
164 C14 **Ōmuta** Fukuoka, Kyūshū, SW Japan 33°01′N 130°27′E
125 S14 **Omutninsk** Kirovskaya Oblast', NW Russian Federation 58°37′N 52°08′E
Omu, Vîrful *see* Omul, Vârful
29 V7 **Onamia** Minnesota, N USA 46°04′N 93°40′W
21 Y5 **Onancock** Virginia, NE USA 37°42′N 75°45′W
14 E10 **Onaping Lake** ◎ Ontario, S Canada
30 M12 **Onarga** Illinois, N USA 40°39′N 88°00′W
15 R6 **Onatchiway, Lac** ◎ Québec, SE Canada
29 S14 **Onawa** Iowa, C USA 42°01′N 96°06′W
165 U5 **Onbetsu** *var.* Ombetsu. Hokkaidō, NE Japan 42°52′N 143°54′E
83 B16 **Oncócua** Cunene, SW Angola 16°37′S 13°23′E
105 S9 **Onda** Valenciana, E Spain 39°58′N 00°17′W
111 N18 **Ondava** ≈ NE Slovakia
Ondjiva *see* N'Giva
77 T16 **Ondo** Ondo, SW Nigeria 07°07′N 04°50′E
77 T16 **Ondo** ◈ *state* SW Nigeria
163 N8 **Öndörhaan** *var.* Undur Khan; *prev.* Tsetsen Khan. Hentiy, E Mongolia 47°21′N 110°42′E
162 M9 **Öndörshil** *var.* Böhöt. Dundgovĭ, C Mongolia 45°13′N 108°12′E
162 L8 **Öndörshireet** *var.* Bayshint. Töv, C Mongolia 47°22′N 105°04′E
162 I7 **Öndör-Ulaan** *var.* Teel. Arhangay, C Mongolia 48°01′N 100°30′E
83 D18 **Ondundazongonda** Otjozondjupa, N Namibia 20°28′S 18°00′E
151 K21 **One and Half Degree Channel** *channel* S Maldives
187 Z15 **Oneata** *island* Lau Group, E Fiji
124 L9 **Onega** Arkhangel'skaya Oblast', NW Russian Federation 63°54′N 37°59′E
124 L9 **Onega** ≈ NW Russian Federation
Onega Bay *see* Onezhskaya Guba
Onega, Lake *see* Onezhskoye Ozero
18 I10 **Oneida** New York, NE USA 43°05′N 75°39′W
20 M8 **Oneida** Tennessee, S USA 36°30′N 84°30′W
18 H9 **Oneida Lake** ◎ New York, NE USA
29 P13 **O'Neill** Nebraska, C USA 42°28′N 98°38′W
123 V12 **Onekotan, Ostrov** *island* Kuril'skiye Ostrova, SE Russian Federation
23 P3 **Oneonta** Alabama, S USA 33°57′N 86°28′W
18 J11 **Oneonta** New York, NE USA 42°27′N 75°03′W
190 I16 **Oneroa** *island* S Cook Islands
116 K11 **Onești** *Hung.* Onyest; *prev.* Gheorghe Gheorghiu-Dej. Bacău, E Romania 46°14′N 26°46′E
193 V15 **Onevai** *island* Tongatapu Group, S Tonga
108 A11 **Onex** Genève, SW Switzerland 46°12′N 06°04′E
124 K8 **Onezhskaya Guba** *Eng.* Onega Bay. *bay* NW Russian Federation
122 D7 **Onezhskoye Ozero** *Eng.* Lake Onega. ◎ NW Russian Federation
83 C16 **Ongandjera** Omusati, N Namibia 17°49′S 15°06′E
184 N12 **Ongaonga** Hawke's Bay, North Island, New Zealand 39°57′S 176°21′E
Ongi *see* Sayhan-Ovoo, Dundgovĭ, Mongolia
Ongi *see* Uyanga
163 W14 **Ongjin** SW North Korea 37°56′N 125°22′E
155 J17 **Ongole** Andhra Pradesh, E India 15°33′N 80°03′E
Ongon *see* Bürd
Ongtüstik Qazaqstan Oblysy *see* Yuzhnyy Kazakhstan
99 I21 **Onhaye** Namur, S Belgium 50°15′N 04°51′E
166 M8 **Onhne** Bago, SW Burma (Myanmar) 17°02′N 96°28′E
137 S9 **Oni** N Georgia 42°36′N 43°13′E
29 N9 **Onida** South Dakota, N USA 44°42′N 100°03′W
164 F15 **Onigajō-yama** ▲ Shikoku, SW Japan 33°10′N 132°37′E
172 H7 **Onilahy** ≈ S Madagascar
77 U16 **Onitsha** Anambra, S Nigeria 06°09′N 06°48′E
164 K12 **Ōno** Fukui, Honshū, SW Japan 35°59′N 136°30′E
164 I13 **Ono** Hyōgo, Honshū, SW Japan 34°52′N 134°55′E
187 K15 **Ono** *island* SW Fiji
164 E13 **Onoda** Yamaguchi, Honshū, SW Japan 34°00′N 131°11′E
187 Z16 **Ono-i-lau** *island* SE Fiji
164 D13 **Ōnojō** *var.* Ōnozyô. Fukuoka, Kyūshū, SW Japan 33°34′N 130°29′E
163 O7 **Onon Gol** ≈ N Mongolia
Ononte *see* Orontes
55 N6 **Onoto** Anzoátegui, NE Venezuela 09°36′N 65°12′W
191 O3 **Onotoa** *prev.* Clerk Island. *atoll* Tungaru, W Kiribati
Ōnozyô *see* Ōnojō
83 E23 **Onseepkans** Northern Cape, W South Africa 28°44′S 19°18′E
104 F4 **Ons, Illa de** *island* NW Spain
180 H7 **Onslow** Western Australia 21°42′S 115°08′E
21 W11 **Onslow Bay** *bay* North Carolina, E USA
98 P6 **Onstwedde** Groningen, NE Netherlands 53°01′N 07°04′E
164 C16 **On-take** ▲ Kyūshū, SW Japan 31°35′N 130°39′E
35 T15 **Ontario** California, W USA 34°03′N 117°39′W
32 M13 **Ontario** Oregon, NW USA 44°01′N 116°57′W
12 D10 **Ontario** ◈ *province* S Canada
11 P14 **Ontario, Lake** ◎ Canada/USA
0 L9 **Ontario Peninsula** *peninsula* Canada/USA
Onteniente *see* Ontinyent
105 S11 **Ontinyent** *var.* Onteniente. Valenciana, E Spain 38°49′N 00°37′W
93 N15 **Ontojärvi** ◎ E Finland
30 L3 **Ontonagon** Michigan, N USA 46°52′N 89°18′W
30 L3 **Ontonagon River** ≈ Michigan, N USA
186 M7 **Ontong Java Atoll** *prev.* Lord Howe Island. *atoll* N Solomon Islands
175 N5 **Ontong Java Rise** *undersea feature* W Pacific Ocean 01°00′N 157°00′E
Onuba *see* Huelva
55 W9 **Onverwacht** Para, N Surinam 05°36′N 55°12′W
Onyest *see* Onești
Oodeypore *see* Udaipur
182 J7 **Oodla Wirra** South Australia 32°52′S 139°05′E
182 F2 **Oodnadatta** South Australia 27°34′S 135°27′E
182 C5 **Ooldea** South Australia 30°29′S 131°50′E
27 Q8 **Oologah Lake** ⊠ Oklahoma, C USA
Oos-Kaap *see* Eastern Cape
Oos-Londen *see* East London
99 E17 **Oostakker** Oost-Vlaanderen, NW Belgium 51°06′N 03°46′E
99 D15 **Oostburg** Zeeland, SW Netherlands 51°20′N 03°30′E
98 K9 **Oostelijk-Flevoland** *polder* C Netherlands
99 B16 **Oostende** *Eng.* Ostend, *Fr.* Ostende. West-Vlaanderen, NW Belgium 51°13′N 02°55′E
99 B16 **Oostende** ✈ West-Vlaanderen, NW Belgium 51°12′N 02°55′E
98 L12 **Oosterbeek** Gelderland, SE Netherlands 51°59′N 05°51′E
99 I14 **Oosterhout** Noord-Brabant, S Netherlands 51°38′N 04°51′E
98 O6 **Oostermoers Vaart** *var.* Hunze. ≈ NE Netherlands
99 F14 **Oosterschelde** *Eng.* Eastern Scheldt. *inlet* SW Netherlands
99 E14 **Oosterscheldedam** *dam* SW Netherlands
98 M7 **Oosterwolde** *Fris.* Easterwâlde. Fryslân, N Netherlands 53°01′N 06°15′E
98 I9 **Oosthuizen** Noord-Holland, NW Netherlands 52°34′N 05°00′E
99 H16 **Oostmalle** Antwerpen, N Belgium 51°18′N 04°44′E
Oos-Transvaal *see* Mpumalanga
99 E15 **Oost-Souburg** Zeeland, SW Netherlands 51°28′N 03°36′E
99 E17 **Oost-Vlaanderen** *Eng.* East Flanders. ◈ *province* NW Belgium
98 J5 **Oost-Vlieland** Fryslân, N Netherlands 53°19′N 05°02′E
98 F12 **Oostvoorne** Zuid-Holland, SW Netherlands 51°55′N 04°06′E
Ootacamund *see* Udagamandalam
98 O10 **Ootmarsum** Overijssel, E Netherlands 52°25′N 06°55′E
10 K14 **Ootsa Lake** ⊠ British Columbia, SW Canada
Ooty *see* Udagamandalam
114 L8 **Opaka** Tŭrgovishte, N Bulgaria 43°26′N 26°12′E
79 M18 **Opala** Orientale, C Dem. Rep. Congo 0°40′S 24°20′E
125 Q13 **Oparino** Kirovskaya Oblast', NW Russian Federation 59°52′N 48°14′E
14 H8 **Opasatica, Lac** ◎ Québec, SE Canada
112 B9 **Opatija** *It.* Abbazia. Primorje-Gorski Kotar, NW Croatia 45°18′N 14°15′E
111 N15 **Opatów** Šuiętokrzyskie, C Poland 50°45′N 21°27′E
111 I17 **Opava** *Ger.* Troppau. Moravskoslezský Kraj, E Czech Republic 49°56′N 17°53′E
111 H16 **Opava** *Ger.* Oppa. ≈ NE Czech Republic
Ópazova *see* Stara Pazova
Ópécska *see* Pecica
14 E8 **Opeepeesway Lake** ◎ Ontario, S Canada
23 R5 **Opelika** Alabama, S USA 32°39′N 85°22′W
22 I8 **Opelousas** Louisiana, S USA 30°31′N 92°04′W
186 G6 **Open Bay** *bay* New Britain, E Papua New Guinea
14 I12 **Opeongo Lake** ◎ Ontario, SE Canada
99 K17 **Opglabbeek** Limburg, NE Belgium 51°04′N 05°39′E
33 W6 **Opheim** Montana, NW USA 48°50′N 106°24′W
39 P10 **Ophir** Alaska, USA 63°08′N 156°31′W
Ophiusa *see* Formentera
79 N18 **Opienge** Orientale, E Dem. Rep. Congo 0°15′N 27°25′E
185 G20 **Opihi** ≈ South Island, New Zealand
12 J9 **Opinaca** ≈ Québec, C Canada
12 J10 **Opinaca, Réservoir** ⊠ Québec, E Canada
117 T5 **Opishnya** *Rus.* Oposhnya. Poltavs'ka Oblast', NE Ukraine 49°58′N 34°37′E
98 I8 **Opmeer** Noord-Holland, NW Netherlands 52°43′N 04°56′E
77 V17 **Opobo** Akwa Ibom, S Nigeria 04°36′N 07°37′E
124 F16 **Opochka** Pskovskaya Oblast', W Russian Federation 56°42′N 28°40′E
110 L13 **Opoczno** Łodzkie, C Poland 51°24′N 20°18′E
111 I15 **Opole** *Ger.* Oppeln. Opolskie, S Poland 50°40′N 17°56′E
111 H15 **Opolskie** ◈ *province* S Poland
Opornyy *see* Borankul
104 G4 **O Porriño** *var.* Porriño. Galicia, NW Spain 42°10′N 08°38′W
Oporto *see* Porto
Oposhnya *see* Opishnya
184 P8 **Opotiki** Bay of Plenty, North Island, New Zealand 38°02′S 177°18′E
23 Q7 **Opp** Alabama, S USA 31°16′N 86°14′W
Oppa *see* Opava
94 G9 **Oppdal** Sør-Trøndelag, S Norway 62°36′N 09°41′E
Oppeln *see* Opole
107 N23 **Oppido Mamertina** Calabria, SW Italy 38°17′N 15°58′E
Oppidum Ubiorum *see* Köln
94 F12 **Oppland** ◈ *county* S Norway
118 J12 **Opsa** Vitsyebskaya Voblasts', NW Belarus 55°32′N 26°50′E
26 I8 **Optima Lake** ⊠ Oklahoma, C USA
184 J11 **Opunake** Taranaki, North Island, New Zealand 39°27′S 173°52′E
191 N6 **Opunohu, Baie d'** *bay* Moorea, W French Polynesia
83 B17 **Opuwo** Kunene, NW Namibia 18°03′S 13°54′E
146 H6 **Oqqal'a** *var.* Akkala, *Rus.* Karakala. Qoraqalpog'iston Respublikasi, NW Uzbekistan 43°43′N 59°25′E
147 V13 **Oqsu** *Rus.* Oksu. ≈ SE Tajikistan
147 P14 **Oqtogh, Qatorkŭhi** *Rus.* Khrebet Aktau. ▲▲ SW Tajikistan
146 M11 **Oqtosh** *Rus.* Aktash. Samarqand Viloyati, C Uzbekistan 39°23′N 65°46′E
147 N11 **Oqtov Tizmasi** *var.* Khrebet Aktau. ▲▲ C Uzbekistan
30 J12 **Oquawka** Illinois, N USA 40°56′N 90°56′W
144 J10 **Or'** *Kaz.* Or. ≈ Kazakhstan/Russian Federation
36 M15 **Oracle** Arizona, SW USA 32°36′N 110°46′W
147 N13 **O'radaryo** *Rus.* Uradar'ya. ≈ S Uzbekistan
116 F9 **Oradea** *prev.* Oradea Mare, *Ger.* Grosswardein, *Hung.* Nagyvárad. Bihor, NW Romania 47°03′N 21°56′E
Oradea Mare *see* Oradea
Orahovac *see* Rahovec
112 H9 **Orahovica** Virovitica-Podravina, NE Croatia 45°33′N 17°54′E
152 K13 **Orai** Uttar Pradesh, N India 26°00′N 79°26′E
92 K12 **Orajärvi** Lappi, NW Finland 66°54′N 24°04′E
138 F9 **Or'Akiva** *prev.* Or 'Aqiva. Haifa, N Israel 32°40′N 34°58′E
Oral *see* Ural'sk
74 I5 **Oran** *var.* Ouahran, Wahran. NW Algeria 35°42′N 00°37′W
183 R8 **Orange** New South Wales, SE Australia 33°16′S 149°06′E
103 R14 **Orange** *anc.* Arausio. Vaucluse, SE France 44°06′N 04°52′E
25 Y10 **Orange** Texas, SW USA 30°05′N 93°43′W
21 V5 **Orange** Virginia, NE USA 38°14′N 78°07′W
21 R13 **Orangeburg** South Carolina, SE USA 33°28′N 80°53′W
58 J9 **Orange, Cabo** *headland* NE Brazil 04°24′N 51°33′W
29 S12 **Orange City** Iowa, C USA 43°00′N 96°03′W
Orange Cone *see* Orange Fan
172 J10 **Orange Fan** *var.* Orange Cone. *undersea feature* SW Indian Ocean 32°00′S 12°00′E
Orange Free State *see* Free State
25 S14 **Orange Grove** Texas, SW USA 27°57′N 97°56′W
18 K13 **Orange Lake** New York, NE USA 41°32′N 74°06′W
23 V10 **Orange Lake** ◎ Florida, SE USA
Orange Mouth/Orangemund *see* Oranjemund
23 W9 **Orange Park** Florida, SE USA 30°10′N 81°42′W
83 E23 **Orange River** *Afr.* Oranjerivier. ≈ S Africa
14 G15 **Orangeville** Ontario, S Canada 43°55′N 80°06′W
36 M5 **Orangeville** Utah, W USA 39°14′N 111°03′W
42 G1 **Orange Walk** Orange Walk, N Belize 18°06′N 88°30′W
42 F1 **Orange Walk** ◈ *district* NW Belize
100 N11 **Oranienburg** Brandenburg, NE Germany 52°46′N 13°15′E
98 O7 **Oranjekanaal** *canal* NE Netherlands
83 D23 **Oranjemund** *var.* Orangemund; *prev.* Orange Mouth. Karas, SW Namibia 28°33′S 16°28′E
Oranjerivier *see* Orange River
45 N16 **Oranjestad** ○ (Aruba) W Aruba 12°31′N 70°W
Oranje Vrystaat *see* Free State
Orany *see* Varėna
83 H18 **Orapa** Central, C Botswana 21°16′S 25°22′E
Or 'Aqiva *see* Or'Akiva
112 I10 **Orašje** ◈ Federacija Bosna I Herecegovina, N Bosnia and Herzegovina
116 G11 **Orăștie** *Ger.* Broos, *Hung.* Szászváros. Hunedoara, W Romania 45°50′N 23°11′E
Orașul Stalin *see* Brașov
111 K18 **Orava** *Hung.* Árva, *Pol.* Orawa. ≈ N Slovakia
Oravainen *see* Oravais
93 K16 **Oravais** *Fin.* Oravainen. Länsi-Suomi, W Finland 63°18′N 22°25′E
Oravicabánya *see* Oravița
116 F13 **Oravița** *Ger.* Orawitza, *Hung.* Oravicabánya. Caraș-Severin, SW Romania 45°02′N 21°43′E
Orawa *see* Orava
185 B24 **Orawia** Southland, South Island, New Zealand 46°03′S 167°49′E
Orawitza *see* Oravița
103 P16 **Orb** ≈ S France
106 C9 **Orba** ≈ NW Italy
158 H12 **Orba Co** ◎ W China
108 B9 **Orbe** Vaud, W Switzerland 46°42′N 06°28′E
107 G14 **Orbetello** Toscana, C Italy 42°28′N 11°15′E
104 K3 **Orbigo** ≈ NW Spain
183 Q12 **Orbost** Victoria, SE Australia 37°44′S 148°28′E
95 O14 **Örbyhus** Uppsala, C Sweden 60°15′N 17°43′E
194 I1 **Orcadas** *Argentinian research station* South Orkney Islands, Antarctica 60°37′S 44°48′W
105 P12 **Orcera** Andalucía, S Spain 38°20′N 02°36′W
33 P9 **Orchard Homes** Montana, NW USA 46°52′N 114°01′W
37 P5 **Orchard Mesa** Colorado, C USA 39°02′N 108°33′W
18 D10 **Orchard Park** New York, NE USA 42°46′N 78°44′W
Orchid Island *see* Lan Yu
115 G18 **Orchómenos** *var.* Orhomenos, Orkhómenos, *prev.* Skripón; *anc.* Orchomenus. Stereá Elláda, C Greece 38°29′N 22°58′E
Orchomenus *see* Orchómenos
106 B7 **Orco** ≈ NW Italy
103 R8 **Or, Côte d'** *physical region* C France
29 O14 **Ord** Nebraska, C USA 41°36′N 98°55′W
119 O15 **Ordats'** *Rus.* Ordat'. Mahilyowskaya Voblasts', E Belarus 54°10′N 30°42′E
36 K8 **Orderville** Utah, W USA 37°16′N 112°38′W
104 H2 **Ordes** Galicia, NW Spain 43°04′N 08°25′W
35 V14 **Ord Mountain** ▲ California, W USA 34°41′N 116°46′W
163 N14 **Ordos** *prev.* Dongsheng. Nei Mongol Zizhiqu, N China 39°51′N 110°00′E
Ordos Desert *see* Mu Us Shadi
188 B16 **Ordot** C Guam
137 N11 **Ordu** *anc.* Cotyora. Ordu, N Turkey 41°N 37°52′E
136 M11 **Ordu** ◈ *province* N Turkey
137 V14 **Ordubad** SW Azerbaijan 38°55′N 46°00′E
Orduña *see* Urduña
37 U6 **Ordway** Colorado, C USA 38°13′N 103°45′W
117 T9 **Ordzhonikidze** Dnipropetrovs'ka Oblast', E Ukraine 47°39′N 34°08′E
Ordzhonikidze *see* Denisovka, Kazakhstan
Ordzhonikidze *see* Vladikavkaz, Russian Federation
Ordzhonikidze *see* Yenakiyeve, Ukraine
Ordzhonikidzeabad *see* Kofarnihon
55 U9 **Orealla** E Guyana 05°13′N 57°17′W
113 G15 **Orebić** *It.* Sabbioncello. Dubrovnik-Neretva, S Croatia 42°58′N 17°12′E
95 M16 **Örebro** Örebro, C Sweden 59°18′N 15°12′E
95 L16 **Örebro** ◈ *county* C Sweden
25 W6 **Ore City** Texas, SW USA 32°48′N 94°43′W
30 L10 **Oregon** Illinois, N USA 42°00′N 89°19′W
27 Q2 **Oregon** Missouri, C USA 39°59′N 95°08′W
31 R11 **Oregon** Ohio, N USA 41°38′N 83°29′W
32 H13 **Oregon** *off.* State of Oregon, *also known as* Beaver State, Sunset State, Valentine State, Webfoot State. ◈ *state* NW USA
32 G11 **Oregon City** Oregon, NW USA 45°21′N 122°36′W
Oregon, State of *see* Oregon
95 P14 **Öregrund** Uppsala, C Sweden 60°19′N 18°30′E
Orekhov *see* Orikhiv
126 L3 **Orekhovo-Zuyevo** Moskovskaya Oblast', W Russian Federation 55°46′N 39°01′E
Orekhovsk *see* Arekhawsk
126 J6 **Orël** Orlovskaya Oblast', W Russian Federation 52°57′N 36°06′E
Orel *see* Oril'
56 E11 **Orellana** Loreto, N Peru 06°53′S 75°10′W
56 E6 **Orellana** ◈ *province* NE Ecuador
104 L11 **Orellana, Embalse de** ⊠ W Spain
36 L3 **Orem** Utah, W USA 40°18′N 111°42′W
Ore Mountains *see* Erzgebirge/Krušné Hory
127 V7 **Orenburg** *prev.* Chkalov. Orenburgskaya Oblast', W Russian Federation 51°46′N 55°12′E
127 V7 **Orenburg** ✈ Orenburgskaya Oblast', W Russian Federation 51°54′N 55°15′E
127 T7 **Orenburgskaya Oblast'** ◈ *province* W Russian Federation
Orense *see* Ourense
188 C8 **Oreor** *var.* Koror. *island* N Palau
185 B24 **Orepuki** Southland, South Island, New Zealand 46°17′S 167°45′E
114 L12 **Orestiáda** *prev.* Orestiás. Anatolikí Makedonía kai Thráki, NE Greece 41°30′N 26°31′E
Orestiás *see* Orestiáda
Öresund/Øresund *see* Sound, The
185 C23 **Oreti** ≈ South Island, New Zealand
184 L5 **Orewa** Auckland, North Island, New Zealand 36°34′S 174°43′E
65 A25 **Orford, Cape** *headland* West Falkland, Falkland Islands 52°00′S 61°04′W
44 B5 **Órganos, Sierra de los** ▲▲ W Cuba
37 R15 **Organ Peak** ▲ New Mexico, SW USA 32°17′N 106°35′W
105 N9 **Orgaz** Castilla-La Mancha, C Spain 39°39′N 03°52′W
Orgeyev *see* Orhei
Orgil *see* Jargalant
105 O15 **Orgiva** *var.* Orjiva. Andalucía, S Spain 36°54′N 03°25′W
163 O10 **Örgön** *var.* Senj. Dornogovĭ, SE Mongolia 44°34′N 110°58′E
Örgön *see* Bayangovĭ
Ogražden *see* Ograzhden
117 N9 **Orhei** *var.* Orheiu, *Rus.* Orgeyev. N Moldova 47°25′N 28°48′E
Orheiu *see* Orhei
105 R3 **Orhi** *var.* Orhy, Pico de Orhy, Pic d'Orhy. ▲ France/Spain 42°55′N 01°01′W *see also* Orhy
Orhi *see* Orhy
Orhomenos *see* Orchómenos
162 K6 **Orhon** ◈ *province* N Mongolia
162 L6 **Orhon Gol** ≈ N Mongolia
102 J16 **Orhy** *var.* Orhi, Pico de Orhy, Pic d'Orhy. ▲ France/Spain 43°00′N 01°00′W *see also* Orhi
Orhy *see* Orhi
Orhy, Pic d'/Orhy, Pico de *see* Orhi/Orhy
34 L2 **Orick** California, W USA 41°16′N 124°03′W
32 L6 **Orient** Washington, NW USA 48°51′N 118°14′W
48 D6 **Oriental, Cordillera** ▲▲ Bolivia/Peru
48 D6 **Oriental, Cordillera** ▲▲ C Colombia
57 H16 **Oriental, Cordillera** ▲▲ C Peru
63 M15 **Oriente** Buenos Aires, E Argentina 38°45′S 60°37′W
105 R12 **Orihuela** Valenciana, E Spain 38°05′N 00°56′W
117 V9 **Orikhiv** *Rus.* Orekhov. Zaporiz'ka Oblast', SE Ukraine 47°32′N 35°48′E
113 K22 **Orikum** *var.* Orikumi. Vlorë, SW Albania 40°20′N 19°28′E
Orikumi *see* Orikum
117 V6 **Oril'** *Rus.* Orel. ≈ E Ukraine
14 H14 **Orillia** Ontario, S Canada 44°36′N 79°26′W
93 M19 **Orimattila** Etelä-Suomi, S Finland 60°48′N 25°40′E
33 Y15 **Orin** Wyoming, C USA 42°39′N 105°10′W
47 R4 **Orinoco, Río** ≈ Colombia/Venezuela
186 C9 **Oriomo** Western, SW Papua New Guinea 08°53′S 143°13′E
30 K11 **Orion** Illinois, N USA 41°21′N 90°22′W
29 Q5 **Oriska** North Dakota, N USA 46°54′N 97°46′W
153 P17 **Orissa** *var.* Odisha. ◈ *state* NE India
Orissaar *see* Orissaare
118 E5 **Orissaare** *Ger.* Orissaar. Saaremaa, W Estonia 58°34′N 23°05′E
107 B19 **Oristano** Sardegna, Italy, C Mediterranean Sea 39°54′N 08°35′E
107 A19 **Oristano, Golfo di** *gulf* Sardegna, Italy, C Mediterranean Sea
54 D13 **Orito** Putumayo, SW Colombia 0°49′N 76°57′W
93 L18 **Orivesi** Häme, W Finland 61°39′N 24°21′E
93 N17 **Orivesi** ◎ Länsi-Suomi, SE Finland
58 H12 **Oriximiná** Pará, NE Brazil 01°45′S 55°50′W
41 Q14 **Orizaba** Veracruz-Llave, E Mexico 18°51′N 97°08′W
41 Q14 **Orizaba, Volcán Pico de** *var.* Citlaltépetl. ▲ S Mexico 19°00′N 97°15′W
95 I16 **Ørje** Østfold, S Norway 59°28′N 11°40′E
113 I16 **Orjen** ▲▲ Bosnia and Herzegovina/Montenegro
Orjiva *see* Orgiva
Orjonikidzeobod *see* Kofarnihon
94 G8 **Orkanger** Sør-Trøndelag, S Norway 63°17′N 09°52′E
94 G8 **Orkdalen** *valley* S Norway
95 K22 **Örkelljunga** Skåne, S Sweden 56°17′N 13°20′E
Orkhaniye *see* Botevgrad
Orkhómenos *see* Orchómenos
94 H9 **Orkla** ≈ S Norway
Orkney *see* Orkney Islands
65 J22 **Orkney Deep** *undersea feature* Scotia Sea/Weddell Sea
96 J4 **Orkney Islands** *var.* Orkney, Orkneys. *island group* N Scotland, United Kingdom
Orkneys *see* Orkney Islands
24 K8 **Orla** Texas, SW USA 31°48′N 103°55′W
35 N5 **Orland** California, W USA 39°43′N 122°12′W
23 X11 **Orlando** Florida, SE USA 28°32′N 81°23′W
23 X12 **Orlando** ✈ Florida, SE USA 28°24′N 81°16′W
107 K23 **Orlando, Capo d'** *headland* Sicilia, Italy, C Mediterranean Sea 38°10′N 14°44′E
Orlau *see* Orlová
103 N6 **Orléanais** *cultural region* C France
103 N7 **Orléans** *anc.* Aurelianum. Loiret, C France 47°54′N 01°53′E
34 L2 **Orleans** California, W USA 41°16′N 123°36′W
19 Q12 **Orleans** Massachusetts, NE USA 41°48′N 69°57′W
15 R10 **Orléans, Île d'** *island* Québec, SE Canada
Orléansville *see* Chlef
111 F16 **Orlice** *Ger.* Adler. ≈ NE Czech Republic
122 L13 **Orlik** Respublika Buryatiya, S Russian Federation 52°32′N 99°36′E
125 Q14 **Orlov** *prev.* Khalturin. Kirovskaya Oblast', NW Russian Federation 58°34′N 48°57′E
111 I17 **Orlová** *Ger.* Orlau, *Pol.* Orłowa. Moravskoslezský Kraj, E Czech Republic 49°50′N 18°21′E
Orlov, Mys *see* Orlovskiy, Mys
126 I6 **Orlovskaya Oblast'** ◈ *province* W Russian Federation
124 M5 **Orlovskiy, Mys** *var.* Mys Orlov. *headland* NW Russian Federation 67°14′N 41°17′E
Orłowa *see* Orlová
103 O5 **Orly** ✈ (Paris) Essonne, N France 48°43′N 02°24′E
119 G16 **Orlya** Hrodzyenskaya Voblasts', W Belarus 53°30′N 24°59′E
114 M7 **Orlyak** *prev.* Makenzen, Trubchular, *Rom.* Trupcilar. Dobrich, NE Bulgaria 43°39′N 27°21′E
148 L16 **Ormāra** Baluchistān, SW Pakistan 25°14′N 64°36′E
171 P5 **Ormoc** *off.* Ormoc City, *var.* MacArthur. Leyte, C Philippines 11°02′N 124°35′E
Ormoc City *see* Ormoc
23 X10 **Ormond Beach** Florida, SE USA 29°16′N 81°04′W
109 X10 **Ormož** *Ger.* Friedau. NE Slovenia 46°24′N 16°09′E
14 J13 **Ormsby** Ontario, SE Canada 44°52′N 77°45′W
97 K17 **Ormskirk** NW England, United Kingdom 53°35′N 02°54′W
Ormsö *see* Vormsi
15 N13 **Ormstown** Québec, SE Canada 45°08′N 73°57′W
Ormuz, Strait of *see* Hormuz, Strait of
103 T8 **Ornans** Doubs, E France 47°06′N 06°06′E
102 K5 **Orne** ◈ *department* N France
102 K5 **Orne** ≈ N France
92 G12 **Ørnes** Nordland, C Norway 66°51′N 13°43′E
110 L7 **Orneta** Warmińsko-Mazurskie, NE Poland 54°07′N 20°10′E
95 P16 **Ornö** Stockholm, C Sweden 59°03′N 18°28′E
37 Q3 **Orno Peak** ▲ Colorado, C USA 40°06′N 107°06′W

◆ Country
● Country Capital
◇ Dependent Territory
○ Dependent Territory Capital
◈ Administrative Regions
✈ International Airport
▲ Mountain
▲▲ Mountain Range
🌋 Volcano
≈ River
◎ Lake
⊠ Reservoir

93 I16 **Örnsköldsvik** Västernorrland, C Sweden 63°16′N 18°45′E

163 X13 **Oro** E North Korea 39°59′N 127°27′E

45 T6 **Orocovis** C Puerto Rico 18°13′N 66°22′W

54 H10 **Orocué** Casanare, E Colombia 04°51′N 71°21′W

77 N13 **Orodara** SW Burkina 11°00′N 04°54′W

105 S4 **Oroel, Peña de** ▲ N Spain 42°30′N 00°31′W

33 N10 **Orofino** Idaho, NW USA 46°28′N 116°15′W

162 I9 **Orog Nuur** ◎ S Mongolia

35 U14 **Oro Grande** California, W USA 34°36′N 117°19′W

37 S15 **Orogrande** New Mexico, SW USA 32°24′N 106°04′W

191 Q7 **Orohena, Mont** ⛩ Tahiti, W French Polynesia 17°37′S 149°27′W

Orolaunum *see* Arlon

Orol Dengizi *see* Aral Sea

189 S15 **Oroluk Atoll** *atoll* Caroline Islands, C Micronesia

80 J13 **Oromīya** *var.* Oromo. ◈ C Ethiopia

Oromo *see* Oromīya

13 O15 **Oromocto** New Brunswick, SE Canada 45°50′N 66°28′W

191 S4 **Orona** *prev.* Hull Island. *atoll* Phoenix Islands, C Kiribati

191 V17 **Orongo** *ancient monument* Easter Island, Chile, E Pacific Ocean

138 I3 **Orontes** *var.* Ononte, Nahr el Aassi, *Ar.* Nahr al 'Aṣī. ≈ SW Asia

104 L9 **Oropesa** Castilla-La Mancha, C Spain 39°55′N 05°10′W

Oropesa *see* Oropesa del Mar

105 T8 **Oropesa del Mar** *var.* Oropesa, Orpesa, *Cat.* Orpes. Valenciana, E Spain 40°06′N 00°07′E

Oropeza *see* Cochabamba

Oroqen Zizhiqi *see* Alihe

171 P7 **Oroquieta** *var.* Oroquieta City. Mindanao, S Philippines 08°27′N 123°46′E

Oroquieta City *see* Oroquieta

40 J8 **Oro, Río del** ≈ C Mexico

59 O14 **Orós, Açude** ⊠ E Brazil

107 D18 **Orosei, Golfo di** *gulf* Tyrrhenian Sea, C Mediterranean Sea

111 M24 **Orosháza** Békés, SE Hungary 46°33′N 20°40′E

Orosirá Rodhópis *see* Rhodope Mountains

111 I22 **Oroszlány** Komárom-Esztergom, W Hungary 47°28′N 18°16′E

188 B16 **Orote Peninsula** *peninsula* W Guam

123 T9 **Orotukan** Magadanskaya Oblast', E Russian Federation 62°18′N 150°46′E

35 O5 **Oroville** California, W USA 39°29′N 121°35′W

32 K6 **Oroville** Washington, NW USA 48°56′N 119°25′W

35 O5 **Oroville, Lake** ⊠ California, W USA

0 G15 **Orozco Fracture Zone** *tectonic feature* E Pacific Ocean

Orpes *see* Oropesa del Mar

Orpesa *see* Oropesa del Mar

64 I7 **Orphan Knoll** *undersea feature* NW Atlantic Ocean 51°00′N 47°00′W

29 V3 **Orr** Minnesota, N USA 48°03′N 92°48′W

95 M21 **Orrefors** Kalmar, S Sweden 56°48′N 15°45′E

182 I7 **Orroroo** South Australia 32°46′S 138°38′E

31 T12 **Orrville** Ohio, N USA 40°50′N 81°45′W

94 L12 **Orsa** Dalarna, C Sweden 61°07′N 14°40′E

Orschowa *see* Orşova

Orschütz *see* Orzyc

119 O14 **Orsha** Vitsyebskaya Voblasts', NE Belarus 54°30′N 30°26′E

127 Q2 **Orshanka** Respublika Mariy El, W Russian Federation 56°54′N 47°54′E

108 C11 **Orsières** Valais, SW Switzerland 46°00′N 07°09′E

127 X8 **Orsk** Orenburgskaya Oblast', W Russian Federation 51°13′N 58°35′E

116 F13 **Orşova** *Ger.* Orschowa, *Hung.* Orsova. Mehedinţi, SW Romania 44°42′N 22°22′E

94 D10 **Ørsta** Møre og Romsdal, S Norway 62°12′N 06°09′E

95 O15 **Örsundsbro** Uppsala, C Sweden 59°45′N 17°19′E

136 D16 **Ortaca** Muğla, SW Turkey 36°49′N 28°43′E

83 I21 **O.R. Tambo** ✈ (Johannesburg) Gauteng, NE South Africa 26°08′S 28°01′E

107 M16 **Orta Nova** Puglia, SE Italy 41°20′N 15°43′E

136 I17 **Orta Toroslar** ⛰ S Turkey

54 E11 **Ortega** Tolima, W Colombia 03°57′N 75°11′W

104 H1 **Ortegal, Cabo** *headland* NW Spain 43°46′N 07°54′W

Ortelsburg *see* Szczytno

102 J15 **Orthez** Pyrénées-Atlantiques, SW France 43°29′N 00°46′W

60 J10 **Ortigueira** Paraná, S Brazil 24°10′S 50°55′W

104 H1 **Ortigueira** Galicia, NW Spain 43°40′N 07°50′W

106 H5 **Ortisei** *Ger.* Sankt-Ulrich. Trentino-Alto Adige, N Italy 46°35′N 11°42′E

40 F6 **Ortiz** Sonora, NW Mexico 28°18′N 110°40′W

54 L5 **Ortiz** Guárico, N Venezuela 09°37′N 67°20′W

Ortler *see* Ortles

106 F5 **Ortles** *Ger.* Ortler. ▲ N Italy 46°29′N 10°33′E

107 K14 **Ortona** Abruzzo, C Italy 42°21′N 14°24′E

57 K14 **Ortón, Río** ≈ N Bolivia

29 R8 **Ortonville** Minnesota, N USA 45°18′N 96°26′W

147 W8 **Orto-Tokoy** Issyk-Kul'skaya Oblast', NE Kyrgyzstan 42°20′N 76°03′E

93 I15 **Örträsk** Västerbotten, N Sweden 64°10′N 19°00′E

100 J12 **Örtze** ≈ NW Germany

Oruba *see* Aruba

142 I3 **Orūmīyeh** *var.* Rizaiyeh, Urmia, Urmiyeh; *prev.* Reẕā'īyeh. Āžarbāyjān-e Gharbī, NW Iran 37°33′N 45°06′E

142 J3 **Orūmīyeh, Daryācheh-ye** *var.* Matianus, Sha Hi, Urumi Yeh, *Eng.* Lake Urmia; *prev.* Daryācheh-ye Reẕā'īyeh. ◎ NW Iran

57 K19 **Oruro** Oruro, W Bolivia 17°58′S 67°06′W

57 J19 **Oruro** ◈ *department* W Bolivia

95 I18 **Orust** *island* S Sweden

Orūzgān *see* Uruzgān

106 H13 **Orvieto** *anc.* Velsuna. Umbria, C Italy 42°43′N 12°06′E

194 K7 **Orville Coast** *physical region* Antarctica

114 H7 **Oryakhovo** Vratsa, NW Bulgaria 43°44′N 23°58′E

Oryokko *see* Yalu

117 R5 **Orzhytsya** Poltavs'ka Oblast', C Ukraine 49°48′N 32°40′E

110 M9 **Orzyc** *Ger.* Orschütz. ≈ NE Poland

110 N8 **Orzysz** *Ger.* Arys. Warmińsko-Mazurskie, NE Poland 53°49′N 21°54′E

98 K13 **Oss** Noord-Brabant, S Netherlands 51°46′N 05°32′E

94 I10 **Os** Hedmark, S Norway 62°29′N 11°14′E

125 U15 **Osa** Permskiy Kray, NW Russian Federation 57°16′N 55°22′E

115 F15 **Óssa** ⛰ C Greece

104 H11 **Ossa** ▲ S Portugal 38°43′N 07°33′W

29 W11 **Osage** Iowa, C USA 43°16′N 92°48′W

27 U5 **Osage Beach** Missouri, C USA 38°09′N 92°37′W

27 P5 **Osage City** Kansas, C USA 38°37′N 95°49′W

27 U7 **Osage Fork River** ≈ Missouri, C USA

27 U5 **Osage River** ≈ Missouri, C USA

164 J13 **Ōsaka** *hist.* Naniwa. Ōsaka, Honshū, SW Japan 34°38′N 135°28′E

164 I13 **Ōsaka** *off.* Ōsaka-fu, *var.* Ōsaka Hu. ◈ *urban prefecture* Honshū, SW Japan

Ōsaka-fu/Ōsaka Hu *see* Ōsaka

145 R10 **Osakarovka** Karaganda, C Kazakhstan 50°32′N 72°39′E

Ōsaki *see* Furukawa

29 T7 **Osakis** Minnesota, N USA 45°51′N 95°08′W

43 N16 **Osa, Península de** *peninsula* S Costa Rica

60 M10 **Osasco** São Paulo, S Brazil 23°32′S 46°46′W

27 R5 **Osawatomie** Kansas, C USA 38°30′N 94°57′W

26 L3 **Osborne** Kansas, C USA 39°26′N 98°42′W

173 S8 **Osborn Plateau** *undersea feature* E Indian Ocean

95 L21 **Osby** Skåne, S Sweden 56°24′N 14°00′E

Osca *see* Huesca

92 N2 **Oscar II Land** *physical region* W Svalbard

27 Y10 **Osceola** Arkansas, C USA 35°43′N 89°58′W

29 V15 **Osceola** Iowa, C USA 41°01′N 93°45′W

27 S6 **Osceola** Missouri, C USA 38°01′N 93°41′W

29 Q15 **Osceola** Nebraska, C USA 41°09′N 97°28′W

101 N15 **Oschatz** Sachsen, E Germany 51°17′N 13°10′E

100 K13 **Oschersleben** Sachsen-Anhalt, C Germany 52°02′N 11°14′E

31 R7 **Oscoda** Michigan, N USA 44°25′N 83°19′W

Ösel *see* Saaremaa

94 H6 **Osen** Sør-Trøndelag, S Norway 64°17′N 10°29′E

94 I12 **Osensjøen** ◎ S Norway

164 A14 **Ōse-zaki** Fukue-jima, SW Japan

147 T10 **Osh** Oshskaya Oblast', SW Kyrgyzstan 40°34′N 72°46′E

83 C16 **Oshakati** Oshana, N Namibia 17°46′S 15°43′E

83 C16 **Oshana** ◈ *district* N Namibia

14 H15 **Oshawa** Ontario, SE Canada 43°54′N 78°50′W

165 R10 **Oshika-hantō** *peninsula* Honshū, C Japan

83 C16 **Oshikango** Ohangwena, N Namibia 17°29′S 15°54′E

83 C17 **Oshikoto** *var.* Otjikoto. ◈ *district* N Namibia

165 P5 **Ō-shima** *island* NE Japan

165 N14 **Ō-shima** *island* S Japan

165 Q5 **Oshima-hantō** ⛰ Hokkaidō, NE Japan

83 D17 **Oshivelo** Oshikoto, N Namibia 18°37′S 17°10′E

28 K14 **Oshkosh** Nebraska, C USA 41°25′N 102°21′W

30 M7 **Oshkosh** Wisconsin, N USA 44°01′N 88°32′W

Oshmyany *see* Ashmyany

Osh Oblasty *see* Oshskaya Oblast'

77 T16 **Oshogbo** *var.* Osogbo. Osun, W Nigeria 07°42′N 04°31′E

147 S11 **Oshskaya Oblast'** *Kir.* Osh Oblasty. ◈ *province* SW Kyrgyzstan

Ōshū *see* Mizusawa

Oshun *see* Osun

79 J20 **Oshwe** Bandundu, C Dem. Rep. Congo 03°24′S 19°32′E

Osiek *see* Osijek

112 I9 **Osijek** *prev.* Osiek, Osjek, *Ger.* Esseg, *Hung.* Eszék. Osijek-Baranja, E Croatia 45°33′N 18°41′E

112 I9 **Osijek-Baranja** *off.* Osječko-Baranjska Županija. ◈ *province* E Croatia

106 J12 **Osimo** Marche, C Italy 43°28′N 13°29′E

122 M12 **Osinovka** Irkutskaya Oblast', C Russian Federation 56°19′N 101°55′E

Osintorf *see* Asintorf

112 N11 **Osipaonica** Serbia, NE Serbia 44°34′N 21°00′E

Osipenko *see* Berdyans'k

Osipovichi *see* Asipovichy

Osječko-Baranjska Županija *see* Osijek-Baranja

Osjek *see* Osijek

29 W15 **Oskaloosa** Iowa, C USA 41°17′N 92°38′W

27 Q4 **Oskaloosa** Kansas, C USA 39°14′N 95°21′W

95 N20 **Oskarshamn** Kalmar, S Sweden 57°16′N 16°25′E

95 J21 **Oskarström** Halland, S Sweden 56°48′N 13°00′E

14 M8 **Oskélanéo** Québec, SE Canada 48°06′N 75°12′W

Öskemen *see* Ust'-Kamenogorsk

117 W5 **Oskil** *Rus.* Oskil. ≈ Russian Federation/Ukraine

Oskil *see* Oskil

93 D20 **Oslo** *prev.* Christiania, Kristiania. ● (Norway) Oslo, S Norway 59°54′N 10°44′E

93 D20 **Oslo** ◈ *county* S Norway

93 D21 **Oslofjorden** *fjord* S Norway

155 G15 **Osmānābād** Mahārāshtra, C India 18°09′N 76°06′E

136 J11 **Osmancık** Çorum, N Turkey 40°58′N 34°50′E

136 L16 **Osmaniye** Osmaniye, S Turkey 37°04′N 36°15′E

136 L16 **Osmaniye** ◈ *province* S Turkey

95 O16 **Ösmo** Stockholm, C Sweden 58°58′N 17°55′E

118 E3 **Osmussaar** *island* W Estonia

100 G13 **Osnabrück** Niedersachsen, NW Germany 52°09′N 07°42′E

110 D11 **Ośno Lubuskie** *Ger.* Drossen. Lubuskie, W Poland 52°28′N 14°51′E

Osogbo *see* Oshogbo

113 P19 **Osogov Mountains** *var.* Osogovske Planine, Osogovski Planina, *Mac.* Osogovski Planini. ⛰ Bulgaria/FYR Macedonia

Osogovske Planine/Osogovski Planina/Osogovski Planini *see* Osogov Mountains

165 R6 **Osore-zan** ▲ Honshū, C Japan 41°18′N 141°06′E

Oşorhei *see* Târgu Mureş

61 J16 **Osório** Rio Grande do Sul, S Brazil 29°53′S 50°17′W

63 G16 **Osorno** Los Lagos, C Chile 40°39′S 73°05′W

104 M4 **Osorno** Castilla y León, N Spain 42°24′N 04°22′W

11 N17 **Osoyoos** British Columbia, SW Canada 49°02′N 119°31′W

95 C14 **Osøyro** Hordaland, S Norway 60°11′N 05°30′E

54 J6 **Ospino** Portuguesa, N Venezuela 09°17′N 69°26′W

23 X6 **Ossabaw Island** *island* Georgia, SE USA

23 X6 **Ossabaw Sound** *sound* Georgia, SE USA

183 O16 **Ossa, Mount** ▲ Tasmania, SE Australia 41°55′S 146°03′E

104 H11 **Ossa, Serra d'** ⛰ SE Portugal

77 U16 **Osse** ≈ S Nigeria

30 J6 **Osseo** Wisconsin, N USA 44°33′N 91°13′W

109 S9 **Ossiacher See** ◎ S Austria

18 K13 **Ossining** New York, NE USA 41°10′N 73°50′W

123 V9 **Ossora** Krasnoyarskiy Kray, E Russian Federation 59°16′N 163°02′E

124 I15 **Ostashkov** Tverskaya Oblast', W Russian Federation 57°08′N 33°10′E

100 H9 **Oste** ≈ NW Germany

Ostee *see* Baltic Sea

Ostend/Ostende *see* Oostende

117 P3 **Oster** Chernihivs'ka Oblast', N Ukraine 50°57′N 30°55′E

95 O14 **Österbybruk** Uppsala, C Sweden 60°13′N 17°55′E

95 M19 **Österbymo** Östergotland, S Sweden 57°49′N 15°15′E

94 K12 **Österdalälven** ≈ C Sweden

94 I12 **Østerdalen** *valley* S Norway

95 L18 **Östergötland** ◈ *county* S Sweden

100 H10 **Osterholz-Scharmbeck** Niedersachsen, NW Germany 53°13′N 08°46′E

Östermark *see* Teuva

Östermyra *see* Seinäjoki

Østerø *see* Eysturoy

101 J14 **Osterode am Harz** Niedersachsen, C Germany 51°43′N 10°15′E

Osterode/Osterode in Ostpreussen *see* Ostróda

Osterøy *see* Osterøyni

94 C13 **Osterøyni** *prev.* Osterøy. *island* S Norway

Österreich *see* Austria

93 G16 **Östersund** Jämtland, C Sweden 63°10′N 14°44′E

95 N14 **Östervåla** Västmanland, C Sweden 60°10′N 17°13′E

101 H22 **Ostfildern** Baden-Württemberg, SW Germany 48°43′N 09°16′E

95 H16 **Østfold** ◈ *county* S Norway

100 E9 **Ostfriesische Inseln** *Eng.* East Frisian Islands. *island group* NW Germany

100 F10 **Ostfriesland** *historical region* NW Germany

95 P14 **Östhammar** Uppsala, C Sweden 60°15′N 18°25′E

Ostia Aterni *see* Pescara

106 G8 **Ostiglia** Lombardia, N Italy 45°04′N 11°09′E

95 J14 **Östmark** Värmland, C Sweden 60°15′N 12°45′E

95 K22 **Östra Ringsjön** ◎ S Sweden

111 I17 **Ostrava** Moravskoslezský Kraj, E Czech Republic 49°50′N 18°15′E

Ostravský Kraj *see* Moravskoslezský Kraj

94 J11 **Østrehogna** *Swe.* Härjahågnen, Härjehågna. ▲ Norway/Sweden 61°43′N 12°07′E

110 K8 **Ostróda** *Ger.* Osterode, Osterode in Ostpreussen. Warmińsko-Mazurskie, NE Poland 53°42′N 19°59′E

Ostrog/Ostróg *see* Ostroh

126 L8 **Ostrogozhsk** Voronezhskaya Oblast', W Russian Federation 50°52′N 39°00′E

116 L4 **Ostroh** *Pol.* Ostróg, *Rus.* Ostrog. Rivnens'ka Oblast', NW Ukraine 50°20′N 26°29′E

110 N9 **Ostrołęka** *Ger.* Wiesenhof, *Rus.* Ostrolenka. Mazowieckie, C Poland 53°06′N 21°34′E

Ostrolenka *see* Ostrołęka

111 A16 **Ostrov** *Ger.* Schlackenwerth. Karlovarský Kraj, W Czech Republic 50°18′N 12°56′E

124 F15 **Ostrov** *Latv.* Austrava. Pskovskaya Oblast', W Russian Federation 57°21′N 28°18′E

Ostrovets *see* Ostrowiec Świętokrzyski

113 M21 **Ostrovicës, Mali i** ▲ SE Albania 40°36′N 20°25′E

165 Z2 **Ostrov Iturup** *island* NE Russian Federation

124 M4 **Ostrovnoy** Murmanskaya Oblast', NW Russian Federation 68°00′N 39°40′E

114 L7 **Ostrovo** *prev.* Golema Ada. Razgrad, N Bulgaria 43°40′N 26°37′E

125 N15 **Ostrovskoye** Kostromskaya Oblast', NW Russian Federation 57°46′N 42°18′E

Ostrów *see* Ostrów Wielkopolski

Ostrowiec *see* Ostrowiec Świętokrzyski

111 M14 **Ostrowiec Świętokrzyski** *var.* Ostrowiec, *Rus.* Ostrovets. Świętokrzyskie, C Poland 50°55′N 21°23′E

110 P13 **Ostrów Lubelski** Lubelskie, E Poland 51°29′N 22°57′E

110 N10 **Ostrów Mazowiecka** *var.* Ostrów Mazowiecki. Mazowieckie, NE Poland 52°49′N 21°53′E

Ostrów Mazowiecki *see* Ostrów Mazowiecka

Ostrowo *see* Ostrów Wielkopolski

110 H13 **Ostrów Wielkopolski** *var.* Ostrów, *Ger.* Ostrowo. Wielkopolskie, C Poland 51°40′N 17°47′E

Ostryna *see* Astryna

110 I13 **Ostrzeszów** Wielkopolskie, C Poland 51°25′N 17°55′E

107 P18 **Ostuni** Puglia, SE Italy 40°44′N 17°35′E

Ostyako-Voguls'k *see* Khanty-Mansiysk

114 I9 **Osŭm** ≈ N Bulgaria

Osum *see* Osumit, Lumi i

164 C17 **Ōsumi-hantō** ⛰ Kyūshū, SW Japan

164 C17 **Ōsumi-kaikyō** *strait* SW Japan

113 L22 **Osumit, Lumi i** *var.* Osum. ≈ SE Albania

77 T16 **Osun** *var.* Oshun. ◈ *state* SW Nigeria

104 L14 **Osuna** Andalucía, S Spain 37°14′N 05°06′W

60 J8 **Osvaldo Cruz** São Paulo, S Brazil 21°49′S 50°52′W

Osveya *see* Asvyeya

18 J7 **Oswegatchie River** ≈ New York, NE USA

27 Q7 **Oswego** Kansas, C USA 37°11′N 95°10′W

18 H9 **Oswego** New York, NE USA 43°27′N 76°13′W

97 K19 **Oswestry** W England, United Kingdom 52°51′N 03°06′W

111 J16 **Oświęcim** *Ger.* Auschwitz. Małopolskie, S Poland 50°02′N 19°11′E

185 E22 **Otago** *off.* Otago Region. ◈ *region* South Island, New Zealand

185 F23 **Otago Peninsula** *peninsula* South Island, New Zealand

Otago Region *see* Otago

165 F13 **Ōtake** Hiroshima, Honshū, SW Japan 34°13′N 132°12′E

184 L13 **Otaki** Wellington, North Island, New Zealand 40°46′S 175°08′E

93 M15 **Otanmäki** Oulu, C Finland 64°07′N 27°04′E

145 T15 **Otar** Zhambyl, SE Kazakhstan 43°30′N 75°13′E

165 R4 **Otaru** Hokkaidō, NE Japan 43°14′N 140°59′E

185 C24 **Otatara** Southland, South Island, New Zealand 46°26′S 168°18′E

185 C24 **Otautau** Southland, South Island, New Zealand 46°10′S 168°01′E

93 M18 **Otava** Itä-Suomi, E Finland 61°37′N 27°07′E

111 B18 **Otava** *Ger.* Wottawa. ≈ SW Czech Republic

56 C6 **Otavalo** Imbabura, N Ecuador 0°13′N 78°15′W

83 D17 **Otavi** Otjozondjupa, N Namibia 19°35′S 17°25′E

165 P12 **Ōtawara** Tochigi, Honshū, S Japan 36°52′N 140°01′E

83 B16 **Otchinjau** Cunene, SW Angola 16°31′S 13°54′E

116 F12 **Oţelu Roşu** *Ger.* Ferdinandsberg, *Hung.* Nándorhgy. Caras-Severin, SW Romania 45°30′N 22°22′E

185 E21 **Otematata** Canterbury, South Island, New Zealand 44°37′S 170°12′E

118 I6 **Otepää** *Ger.* Odenpäh. Valgamaa, SE Estonia 58°01′N 26°30′E

144 G14 **Otes** *Kaz.* Say-Ötesh; *prev.* Say-Utës. Mangistau, SW Kazakhstan 44°20′N 53°32′E

162 H7 **Otgon** *var.* Buyant. Dzavhan, C Mongolia 47°14′N 97°14′E

32 K9 **Othello** Washington, NW USA 46°49′N 119°10′W

83 K23 **oThongathi** *prev.* Tongaat, *var.* uThongathi. KwaZulu/Natal, E South Africa 29°35′S 31°07′E *see also* Tongaat

115 A15 **Othonoí** *island* Iónia Nisiá, Greece, C Mediterranean Sea

Othris *see* Óthrys

115 F17 **Óthrys** *var.* Othris. ⛰ C Greece

77 Q14 **Oti** ≈ N Togo

40 K10 **Otinapa** Durango, C Mexico 24°01′N 104°58′W

185 G17 **Otira** West Coast, South Island, New Zealand 42°52′S 171°33′E

37 V3 **Otis** Colorado, C USA 40°09′N 102°57′W

12 L10 **Otish, Monts** ⛰ Québec, E Canada

83 C17 **Otjikondo** Kunene, N Namibia 19°50′S 15°23′E

Otjikoto *see* Oshikoto

83 E18 **Otjinene** Omaheke, NE Namibia 21°10′S 18°43′E

83 D18 **Otjiwarongo** Otjozondjupa, N Namibia 20°29′S 16°36′E

83 D18 **Otjosondu** *var.* Otjosundu. Otjozondjupa, C Namibia 21°19′S 17°51′E

Otjosundu *see* Otjosondu

83 D18 **Otjozondjupa** ◈ *district* C Namibia

112 C11 **Otočac** Lika-Senj, W Croatia 44°52′N 15°13′E

Otog Qi *see* Ulan

112 J10 **Otok** Vukovar-Srijem, E Croatia 45°10′N 18°52′E

116 K14 **Otopeni** ✈ (Bucureşti) Ilfov, S Romania 44°34′N 26°09′E

184 L8 **Otorohanga** Waikato, North Island, New Zealand 38°10′S 175°14′E

12 D9 **Otoskwin** ≈ Ontario, C Canada

165 G14 **Ōtoyo** Kōchi, Shikoku, SW Japan 33°45′N 133°42′E

95 E16 **Otra** ≈ S Norway

107 R19 **Otranto** Puglia, SE Italy 40°08′N 18°28′E

Otranto, Canale d' *see* Otranto, Strait of

107 Q18 **Otranto, Strait of** *It.* Canale d'Otranto. *strait* Albania/Italy

111 H18 **Otrokovice** *Ger.* Otrokowitz. Zlínský Kraj, E Czech Republic 49°13′N 17°33′E

Otrokowitz *see* Otrokovice

31 P10 **Otsego** Michigan, N USA 42°27′N 85°42′W

31 Q6 **Otsego Lake** ◎ Michigan, N USA

18 I11 **Otselic River** ≈ New York, NE USA

164 J14 **Ōtsu** *var.* Ôtu. Shiga, Honshū, SW Japan 35°03′N 135°49′E

94 G11 **Otta** Oppland, S Norway 61°46′N 09°33′E

189 U13 **Otta** *island* Chuuk, C Micronesia

94 F11 **Otta** ≈ S Norway

189 U13 **Otta Pass** *passage* Chuuk Islands, C Micronesia

95 J22 **Ottarp** Skåne, S Sweden 55°55′N 12°55′E

14 L12 **Ottawa** ● (Canada) Ontario, SE Canada 45°24′N 75°41′W

30 L11 **Ottawa** Illinois, N USA 41°21′N 88°50′W

27 Q5 **Ottawa** Kansas, C USA 38°35′N 95°16′W

31 R12 **Ottawa** Ohio, N USA 41°01′N 84°03′W

14 L12 **Ottawa** *var.* Uplands. ✈ Ontario, SE Canada 45°19′N 75°39′W

14 M12 **Ottawa** *Fr.* Outaouais. ≈ Ontario/Québec, SE Canada

9 R10 **Ottawa Islands** *island group* Nunavut, C Canada

18 L8 **Otter Creek** ≈ Vermont, NE USA

36 L6 **Otter Creek Reservoir** ⊠ Utah, W USA

98 L11 **Otterlo** Gelderland, E Netherlands 52°06′N 05°46′E

94 D9 **Otterøya** *island* S Norway

29 S6 **Otter Tail Lake** ◎ Minnesota, N USA

29 R7 **Otter Tail River** ≈ Minnesota, C USA

95 H23 **Otterup** Syddtjylland, C Denmark 55°31′N 10°25′E

99 H19 **Ottignies** Wallon Brabant, C Belgium 50°40′N 04°34′E

101 L23 **Ottobrunn** Bayern, SE Germany 48°02′N 11°40′E

29 X15 **Ottumwa** Iowa, C USA 41°00′N 92°24′W

Ôtu *see* Ōtsu

83 B16 **Otuazuma** Kunene, NW Namibia 17°52′S 13°16′E

77 V16 **Oturkpo** Benue, S Nigeria 07°12′N 08°06′E

193 Y15 **Otu Tolu Group** *island group* SE Tonga

182 M13 **Otway, Cape** *headland* Victoria, SE Australia 38°52′S 143°31′E

63 H24 **Otway, Seno** *inlet* S Chile

Ötz *see* Oetz

108 L8 **Ötztaler Ache** ≈ W Austria

108 L9 **Ötztaler Alpen** *It.* Alpi Venoste. ⛰ SW Austria

27 T12 **Ouachita, Lake** ⊠ Arkansas, C USA

27 R11 **Ouachita Mountains** ⛰ Arkansas/Oklahoma, C USA

27 U13 **Ouachita River** ≈ Arkansas/Louisiana, C USA

Ouadaï *see* Ouaddaï

76 J7 **Ouadâne** *var.* Ouadane. Adrar, C Mauritania 20°57′N 11°35′W

78 K13 **Ouadda** Haute-Kotto, N Central African Republic 08°02′N 22°22′E

78 J10 **Ouaddaï** *off.* Préfecture du Ouaddaï, *var.* Ouadaï, Wadai. ◈ *prefecture* SE Chad

Ouaddaï, Préfecture du *see* Ouaddaï

77 P13 **Ouagadougou** *var.* Wagadugu. ● (Burkina) C Burkina 12°20′N 01°32′W

77 P13 **Ouagadougou** ✈ C Burkina 12°21′N 01°27′W

77 O12 **Ouahigouya** NW Burkina 13°31′N 02°20′W

Ouahran *see* Oran

79 J14 **Ouaka** ◈ *prefecture* C Central African Republic

79 J15 **Ouaka** ≈ S Central African Republic

Oualam *see* Ouallam

76 M9 **Oualâta** *var.* Oualata. Hodh ech Chargui, SE Mauritania 17°18′N 07°00′W

77 R11 **Ouallam** *var.* Oualam. Tillabéri, W Niger 14°23′N 02°09′E

172 H14 **Ouanani** Mohéli, S Comoros 12°19′S 93°98′E

55 Z10 **Ouanary** E French Guiana 04°11′N 51°40′W

78 L13 **Ouanda Djallé** Vakaga, NE Central African Republic 08°53′N 22°47′E

79 N14 **Ouando** Haut-Mbomou, SE Central African Republic 05°57′N 25°57′E

79 L15 **Ouango** Mbomou, S Central African Republic 04°19′N 22°30′E

77 N14 **Ouangolodougou** *var.* Wangolodougou. N Ivory Coast 09°58′N 05°09′W

172 I13 **Ouani** Anjouan, SE Comoros

79 M15 **Ouara** ≈ E Central African Republic

76 K7 **Ouarâne** *desert* C Mauritania

15 O11 **Ouareau** ≈ Québec, SE Canada

74 K7 **Ouargla** *var.* Wargla. NE Algeria 32°N 05°16′E

74 F8 **Ouarzazate** S Morocco 30°54′N 06°55′W

77 Q11 **Ouatagouna** Gao, E Mali 15°06′N 00°41′E

74 G6 **Ouazzane** *var.* Ouezzane, *Ar.* Wazan, Wazzan. N Morocco 34°52′N 05°35′W

Oubangui *see* Ubangi

Oubangui-Chari *see* Central African Republic

Oubangui-Chari, Territoire de l' *see* Central African Republic

Oubari, Edeyen d' *see* Awbāri, Idhān

98 G13 **Oud-Beijerland** Zuid-Holland, SW Netherlands 51°50′N 04°25′E

98 F13 **Ouddorp** Zuid-Holland, SW Netherlands 51°49′N 03°55′E

77 P9 **Oudeïka** *oasis* C Mali

98 G13 **Oude Maas** ≈ SW Netherlands

99 E18 **Oudenaarde** *Fr.* Audenarde. Oost-Vlaanderen, SW Belgium 50°50′N 03°37′E

99 H14 **Oudenbosch** Noord-Brabant, S Netherlands 51°35′N 04°32′E

98 P6 **Oude Pekela** Groningen, NE Netherlands 53°06′N 07°00′E

Ouderkerk *see* Ouderkerk aan den Amstel

98 I10 **Ouderkerk aan den Amstel** *var.* Ouderkerk. Noord-Holland, C Netherlands 52°18′N 04°54′E

98 I6 **Oudeschild** Noord-Holland, NW Netherlands 53°01′N 04°51′E

99 G14 **Oude-Tonge** Zuid-Holland, SW Netherlands 51°40′N 04°13′E

98 I12 **Oudewater** Utrecht, C Netherlands 52°02′N 04°54′E

Oudjda *see* Oujda

Oudkerk *see* Aldtsjerk

167 Q6 **Oudômxai** *var.* Muang Xay, Muong Sai, Xai. Oudômxai, N Laos 20°41′N 102°00′E

102 J7 **Oudon** ≈ NW France

98 I9 **Oudorp** Noord-Holland, NW Netherlands 52°39′N 04°47′E

83 G25 **Oudtshoorn** Western Cape, SW South Africa 33°35′S 22°14′E

99 I16 **Oud-Turnhout** Antwerpen, N Belgium 51°19′N 05°01′E

74 F7 **Oued-Zem** C Morocco 32°53′N 06°30′W

187 P16 **Ouégoa** Province Nord, C New Caledonia 20°22′S 164°25′E

76 L13 **Ouéléssébougou** *var.* Ouolossébougou. Koulikoro, SW Mali 11°58′N 07°51′W

77 N16 **Ouéllé** E Ivory Coast 07°18′N 04°01′W

77 R16 **Ouémé** ≈ C Benin

77 O13 **Ouessa** S Burkina 11°02′N 02°44′W

102 D5 **Ouessant, Île d'** *Eng.* Ushant. *island* NW France

79 H17 **Ouésso** Sangha, NW Congo 01°38′N 16°03′E

79 D15 **Ouest** *Eng.* West. ◈ *province* W Cameroon

190 G11 **Ouest, Baie del'** *bay* Îles Wallis, E Wallis and Futuna

15 Y7 **Ouest, Pointe de l'** *headland* Québec, SE Canada 48°08′N 64°57′W

Ouezzane *see* Ouazzane

99 K20 **Ouffet** Liège, E Belgium 50°30′N 05°31′E

79 H14 **Ouham** ◈ *prefecture* NW Central African Republic

78 I13 **Ouham** ≈ Central African Republic/Chad

79 G14 **Ouham-Pendé** ◈ *prefecture* W Central African Republic

77 R16 **Ouidah** *Eng.* Whydah, Wida. S Benin 06°23′N 02°08′E

74 H6 **Oujda** *Ar.* Oudjda, Ujda. NE Morocco 34°45′N 01°53′W

76 I7 **Oujeft** Adrar, C Mauritania 20°05′N 13°00′W

93 L15 **Oulainen** Oulu, C Finland 64°14′N 24°50′E

Ould Yanja *see* Ould Yenjé

76 J10 **Ould Yenjé** *var.* Ould Yanja. Guidimaka, S Mauritania 15°33′N 11°43′W

93 L14 **Oulu** *Swe.* Uleåborg. Oulu, C Finland 65°01′N 25°28′E

93 M14 **Oulu** *Swe.* Uleåborg. ◈ *province* N Finland

93 L15 **Oulujärvi** *Swe.* Uleträsk. ◎ C Finland

93 M14 **Oulujoki** *Swe.* Uleälv. ≈ C Finland

93 L14 **Oulunsalo** Oulu, C Finland 64°55′N 25°19′E

106 A8 **Oulx** Piemonte, NE Italy 45°05′N 06°41′E

78 J9 **Oum-Chalouba** Borkou-Ennedi-Tibesti, NE Chad 15°48′N 20°46′E

76 M16 **Oumé** C Ivory Coast 06°25′N 05°23′W

74 F7 **Oum er Rbia** ≈ C Morocco

78 J10 **Oum-Hadjer** Batha, E Chad 13°18′N 19°41′E

92 K10 **Ounasjoki** ≈ N Finland

78 J7 **Ounianga Kébir** Borkou-Ennedi-Tibesti, N Chad 19°06′N 20°29′E

Ouolossébougou *see* Ouéléssébougou

Oup *see* Auob

99 K19 **Oupeye** Liège, E Belgium 50°42′N 05°38′E

99 N21 **Our** ≈ NW Europe

37 Q7 **Ouray** Colorado, C USA 38°01′N 107°40′W

103 R7 **Ource** ≈ C France

104 G9 **Ourém** Santarém, C Portugal 39°40′N 08°32′W

104 H4 **Ourense** *Cast.* Orense, *Lat.* Aurium. Galicia, NW Spain 42°20′N 07°52′W

104 I4 **Ourense** *Cast.* Orense. ◈ *province* Galicia, NW Spain

59 O15 **Ouricuri** Pernambuco, E Brazil 07°51′S 40°05′W

60 J9 **Ourinhos** São Paulo, S Brazil 22°59′S 49°52′W

104 G13 **Ourique** Beja, S Portugal 37°38′N 08°13′W

59 M20 **Ouro Preto** Minas Gerais, NE Brazil 20°25′S 43°30′W

Ours, Grand Lac de l' *see* Great Bear Lake

99 K20 **Ourthe** ≈ E Belgium

165 Q9 **Ōu-sanmyaku** ⛰ Honshū, C Japan

97 M17 **Ouse** ≈ N England, United Kingdom

Ouse *see* Great Ouse

102 H7 **Oust** ≈ NW France

Outaouais *see* Ottawa

15 T4 **Outardes Quatre, Réservoir** ⊠ Québec, SE Canada

15 T5 **Outardes, Rivière aux** ≈ Québec, SE Canada

96 E8 **Outer Hebrides** *var.* Western Isles. *island group* NW Scotland, United Kingdom

30 K3 **Outer Island** *island* Apostle Islands, Wisconsin, N USA

35 S16 **Outer Santa Barbara Passage** *passage* California, SW USA

83 C18 **Outjo** Kunene, N Namibia 20°08′S 16°08′E

11 T16 **Outlook** Saskatchewan, S Canada 51°30′N 107°03′W

93 N16 **Outokumpu** Itä-Suomi, E Finland 62°43′N 29°05′E

96 M2 **Out Skerries** *island group* NE Scotland, United Kingdom

187 Q16 **Ouvéa** *island* Îles Loyauté, NE New Caledonia

103 S14 **Ouvèze** ≈ SE France

182 L9 **Ouyen** Victoria, SE Australia 35°07′S 142°19′E

39 Q14 **Ouzinkie** Kodiak Island, Alaska, USA 57°54′N 152°27′W

137 O13 **Ovacık** Tunceli, E Turkey 39°23′N 39°13′E

106 C9 **Ovada** Piemonte, NE Italy 44°41′N 08°39′E

187 X14 **Ovalau** *island* C Fiji

62 G9 **Ovalle** Coquimbo, N Chile 30°33′S 71°16′W

83 C17 **Ovamboland** *physical region* N Namibia

54 L10 **Ovana, Cerro** ▲ S Venezuela 04°41′N 66°54′W

104 G7 **Ovar** Aveiro, N Portugal 40°52′N 08°38′W

114 L10 **Ovcharitsa, Yazovir** ⊠ SE Bulgaria

54 E6 **Ovejas** Sucre, NW Colombia 09°32′N 75°14′W

101 E16 **Overath** Nordrhein-Westfalen, W Germany 50°55′N 07°16′E

98 F13 **Overflakkee** *island* SW Netherlands

99 H19 **Overijse** Vlaams Brabant, C Belgium 50°46′N 04°32′E

98 N10 **Overijssel** ◈ *province* E Netherlands

98 M9 **Overijssels Kanaal** *canal* E Netherlands

92 K13 **Överkalix** Norrbotten, N Sweden 66°19′N 22°49′E

27 R4 **Overland Park** Kansas, C USA 38°57′N 94°41′W

99 L14 **Overloon** Noord-Brabant, SE Netherlands 51°35′N 05°54′E

99 K16 **Overpelt** Limburg, NE Belgium 51°13′N 05°24′E

35 Y10 **Overton** Nevada, W USA 36°32′N 114°25′W

25 W7 **Overton** Texas, SW USA 32°16′N 94°58′W

92 K13 **Övertorneå** Norrbotten, N Sweden 66°22′N 23°40′E

95 N18 **Överum** Kalmar, S Sweden 57°58′N 16°20′E

92 G13 **Överuman** ◎ N Sweden

117 P11 **Ovidiopol'** Odes'ka Oblast', SW Ukraine 46°15′N 30°27′E

116 M14 **Ovidiu** Constanţa, SE Romania 44°16′N 28°34′E

45 N10 **Oviedo** SW Dominican Republic 17°47′N 71°22′W

104 K2 **Oviedo** *anc.* Asturias. Asturias, NW Spain 43°21′N 05°50′W

104 K2 **Oviedo** ✈ Asturias, N Spain 43°21′N 05°50′W

Ovilava *see* Wels

118 D7 **Oviši** W Latvia 57°34′N 21°43′E

146 K10 **Ovminzatovo Tog'lari** *Rus.* Gory Auminzatau. ⛰ N Uzbekistan

Övögdiy *see* Telmen

Ovoot *see* Darīganga

157 O4 **Övörhangay** ◈ *province* C Mongolia

94 E12 **Øvre Årdal** Sogn Og Fjordane, S Norway 61°18′N 07°48′E

95 J14 **Övre Fryken** ◎ C Sweden

92 J11 **Övre Soppero** *Lapp.* Badje-Sohppar. Norrbotten, N Sweden 68°07′N 21°40′E

117 N3 **Ovruch** Zhytomyrs'ka Oblast', N Ukraine 51°20′N 58°50′E

Övt *see* Bat-Öldziy

185 E24 **Owaka** Otago, South Island, New Zealand 46°27′S 169°42′E

79 H18 **Owando** *prev.* Fort Rousset. Cuvette, C Congo 0°29′S 15°55′E

164 J14 **Owase** Mie, Honshū, SW Japan 34°04′N 136°11′E

27 P9 **Owasso** Oklahoma, C USA 36°16′N 95°51′W

29 V10 **Owatonna** Minnesota, N USA 44°04′N 93°13′W

173 O4 **Owen Fracture Zone** *tectonic feature* W Arabian Sea

185 H15 **Owen, Mount** ▲ South Island, New Zealand 41°32′S 172°33′E

185 H15 **Owen River** Tasman, South Island, New Zealand 41°40′S 172°28′E

44 D8 **Owen Roberts** ✈ Grand Cayman, Cayman Islands 19°15′N 81°22′W

20 I6 **Owensboro** Kentucky, S USA 37°46′N 87°07′W

35 T11 **Owens Lake** *salt flat* California, W USA

14 F14 **Owen Sound** Ontario, S Canada 44°34′N 80°56′W

14 F13 **Owen Sound** ◎ Ontario, S Canada

35 T10 **Owens River** ≈ California, W USA

186 F9 **Owen Stanley Range** ⛰ S Papua New Guinea

27 V5 **Owensville** Missouri, C USA 38°21′N 91°30′W

20 M4 **Owenton** Kentucky, S USA 38°33′N 84°50′W

77 U17 **Owerri** Imo, S Nigeria 05°19′N 07°07′E

184 M10 **Owhango** Manawatu-Wanganui, North Island, New Zealand 39°01′S 175°22′E

21 N5 **Owingsville** Kentucky, S USA 38°09′N 83°46′W

77 T16 **Owo** Ondo, SW Nigeria 07°10′N 05°31′E

◆ Country ● Country Capital ◇ Dependent Territory ○ Dependent Territory Capital ◈ Administrative Regions ✈ International Airport ▲ Mountain ⛰ Mountain Range ⛩ Volcano ≈ River ◎ Lake ⊠ Reservoir

31 R9 **Owosso** Michigan, N USA 43°00′N 84°10′W
35 V1 **Owyhee** Nevada, W USA 41°57′N 116°07′W
32 L14 **Owyhee, Lake** ◎ Oregon, NW USA
32 L15 **Owyhee River** Idaho/Oregon, NW USA
92 K1 **Öxarfjördhur** *var.* Axarfjördhur. *fjord* N Iceland
94 K12 **Oxberg** Dalarna, C Sweden 61°07′N 14°10′E
11 V17 **Oxbow** Saskatchewan, S Canada 49°16′N 102°12′W
95 O17 **Oxelösund** Södermanland, S Sweden 58°40′N 17°10′E
185 H18 **Oxford** Canterbury, South Island, New Zealand 43°18′S 172°10′E
97 M21 **Oxford** *Lat.* Oxonia. S England, United Kingdom 51°46′N 01°15′W
23 Q3 **Oxford** Alabama, S USA 33°36′N 85°50′W
22 L2 **Oxford** Mississippi, S USA 34°23′N 89°30′W
29 N16 **Oxford** Nebraska, C USA 40°15′N 99°37′W
18 I11 **Oxford** New York, NE USA 42°21′N 75°39′W
21 U8 **Oxford** North Carolina, SE USA 36°22′N 78°37′W
31 Q14 **Oxford** Ohio, N USA 39°30′N 84°45′W
18 H16 **Oxford** Pennsylvania, NE USA 39°46′N 75°57′W
11 X12 **Oxford House** Manitoba, C Canada 54°55′N 95°13′W
29 Y13 **Oxford Junction** Iowa, C USA 41°58′N 90°57′W
11 X12 **Oxford Lake** ◎ Manitoba, C Canada
97 M21 **Oxfordshire** *cultural region* S England, United Kingdom
Oxia *see* Oxyá
41 X12 **Oxkutzcab** Yucatán, SE Mexico 20°18′N 89°26′W
35 R15 **Oxnard** California, W USA 34°12′N 119°10′W
Oxonia *see* Oxford
14 I12 **Oxtongue** Ontario, SE Canada
Oxus *see* Amu Darya
115 E15 **Oxyá** *var.* Oxia. ▲ C Greece 39°46′N 21°56′E
164 L11 **Oyabe** Toyama, Honshū, SW Japan 36°42′N 136°52′E
Oyahue/Oyahue, Volcán *see* Ollagüe, Volcán
165 O12 **Oyama** Tochigi, Honshū, S Japan 36°19′N 139°46′E
47 U5 **Oyapock** E French Guiana
Oyapock *see* Oiapoque, Rio/Oyapok, Fleuve l'
55 Z10 **Oyapok, Baie de L'** *bay* Brazil/French Guiana South America W Atlantic Ocean
55 Z11 **Oyapok, Fleuve l'** *var.* Rio Oiapoque, Oyapock. Brazil/French Guiana *see also* Oiapoque, Rio
Oyapok, Fleuve l' *see* Oiapoque, Rio
79 E17 **Oyem** Woleu-Ntem, N Gabon 01°34′N 11°31′E
11 R16 **Oyen** Alberta, SW Canada 51°20′N 110°28′W
95 I15 **Øyeren** ◎ S Norway
Oygon *see* Tüdevtey
96 I7 **Oykel** N Scotland, United Kingdom
123 R9 **Oymyakon** Respublika Sakha (Yakutiya), NE Russian Federation 63°28′N 142°22′E
79 H19 **Oyo** Cuvette, C Congo 01°17′S 16°00′E
77 S15 **Oyo** Oyo, W Nigeria 07°51′N 03°57′E
77 S15 **Oyo** ❖ *state* SW Nigeria
56 D13 **Oyón** Lima, C Peru 10°39′S 76°44′W
103 S10 **Oyonnax** Ain, E France 46°16′N 05°39′E
146 L10 **Oyoqog'itma** *Rus.* Ayakagytma. Buxoro Viloyati, C Uzbekistan 40°37′N 64°26′E
146 M9 **Oyoqquduq** *Rus.* Ayakkuduk. Navoiy Viloyati, N Uzbekistan 41°16′N 65°12′E
32 F9 **Oysterville** Washington, NW USA 46°33′N 124°03′W
95 D14 **Øystese** Hordaland, S Norway 60°23′N 06°13′E
145 S16 **Oytal** Zhambyl, S Kazakhstan 42°54′N 73°21′E
147 U10 **Oy-Tal** Oshskaya Oblast', SW Kyrgyzstan 40°23′N 74°04′E
147 T10 **Oy-Tal** SW Kyrgyzstan
145 Q15 **Oyyk** *prev.* Uyuk. Zhambyl, S Kazakhstan 43°46′N 70°55′E
144 H10 **Oyyl** *prev.* Uil. Aktyubinsk, W Kazakhstan 49°06′N 54°41′E
144 H10 **Oyyl** *prev.* Uil. W Kazakhstan
Ozarichi *see* Azarychy
23 R7 **Ozark** Alabama, S USA 31°27′N 85°38′W
27 S10 **Ozark** Arkansas, C USA 35°30′N 93°50′W
27 T8 **Ozark** Missouri, C USA 37°01′N 93°12′W
27 T8 **Ozark Plateau** *plain* Arkansas/Missouri, C USA
27 T6 **Ozarks, Lake of the** ⊠ Missouri, C USA
192 L10 **Ozbourn Seamount** *undersea feature* W Pacific Ocean 26°00′S 174°49′W
111 L20 **Ózd** Borsod-Abaúj-Zemplén, NE Hungary 48°15′N 20°18′E
112 D11 **Ozeblin** ▲ C Croatia 44°37′N 15°52′E
123 V11 **Ozernovskiy** Kamchatskiy Kray, E Russian Federation 51°28′N 156°32′E
144 M7 **Ozërnoye** *var.* Ozërnyy. Kostanay, N Kazakhstan 53°29′N 63°14′E
124 J15 **Ozërnyy** Tverskaya Oblast', W Russian Federation 57°55′N 33°45′E
Ozërnyy *see* Ozërnoye
Ozero Azhbulat *see* Ozero Ul'ken Azhibolat
Ozero Segozero *see* Segozerskoye Vodokhranilishche
115 D18 **Ozerós, Límni** ◎ W Greece
145 T7 **Ozero Ul'ken Azhibolat** *prev.* Ozero Azhbulat. ◎ NE Kazakhstan
122 G11 **Ozërsk** Chelyabinskaya Oblast', C Russian Federation 55°44′N 60°59′E
119 D14 **Ozersk** *prev.* Darkehnen, *Ger.* Angerapp. Kaliningradskaya Oblast', W Russian Federation 54°23′N 21°59′E
126 L4 **Ozery** Moskovskaya Oblast', W Russian Federation 54°51′N 38°37′E
Özgön *see* Uzgen
107 C17 **Ozieri** Sardegna, Italy, C Mediterranean Sea 40°35′N 09°01′E
111 I15 **Ozimek** *Ger.* Malapane. Opolskie, SW Poland 50°41′N 18°16′E
127 R8 **Ozinki** Saratovskaya Oblast', W Russian Federation 51°16′N 49°45′E
25 O10 **Ozona** Texas, SW USA 30°43′N 101°13′W
Ozorkov *see* Ozorków
110 J12 **Ozorków** *Rus.* Ozorkov. Łódźz, C Poland 52°00′N 19°17′E
164 F14 **Ōzu** Ehime, Shikoku, SW Japan 33°30′N 132°33′E
137 R10 **Ozurgeti** *prev.* Makharadze, Ozurget'i. W Georgia 41°57′N 42°01′E
Ozurget'i *see* Ozurgeti

P

99 J17 **Paal** Limburg, NE Belgium 51°03′N 05°08′E
196 M14 **Paamiut** *var.* Pâmiut, *Dan.* Frederikshåb. S Greenland 61°59′N 49°40′W
Pa-an *see* Hpa-an
101 L22 **Paar** SE Germany
83 E26 **Paarl** Western Cape, SW South Africa 33°45′S 18°58′E
93 L15 **Paavola** Oulu, C Finland 64°34′N 25°15′E
96 E8 **Pabbay** *island* NW Scotland, United Kingdom
153 T15 **Pabna** Rajshahi, W Bangladesh 24°02′N 89°15′E
109 U4 **Pabneukirchen** Oberösterreich, N Austria 48°19′N 14°49′E
118 H13 **Pabradė** *Pol.* Podbrodzie. Vilnius, SE Lithuania 54°58′N 25°43′E
56 L13 **Pacahuaras, Río** N Bolivia
Pacaraima, Sierra/Pacaraim, Serra *see* Pakaraima Mountains
56 B11 **Pacasmayo** La Libertad, W Peru 07°27′S 79°33′W
42 D6 **Pacaya, Volcán de** S Guatemala 14°19′N 90°36′W
115 K23 **Pacheía** *var.* Pachía. *island* Kykládes, Greece, Aegean Sea
Pachía *see* Pacheía
107 L26 **Pachino** Sicilia, Italy, C Mediterranean Sea 36°43′N 15°06′E
56 F12 **Pachitea, Río** C Peru
154 I11 **Pachmarhi** Madhya Pradesh, C India 22°36′N 78°18′E
121 P3 **Páchna** *var.* Pakhna. SW Cyprus 34°47′N 32°48′E
115 H25 **Páchnes** ▲ Kríti, Greece, E Mediterranean Sea 35°19′N 24°00′E
54 F9 **Pacho** Cundinamarca, C Colombia 05°09′N 74°08′W
154 F12 **Pāchora** Mahārāshtra, C India 20°52′N 75°28′E
41 P13 **Pachuca** *var.* Pachuca de Soto. Hidalgo, C Mexico 20°05′N 98°46′W
Pachuca de Soto *see* Pachuca
27 W5 **Pacific** Missouri, C USA 38°28′N 90°44′W
192 L14 **Pacific-Antarctic Ridge** *undersea feature* S Pacific Ocean 62°00′S 157°00′W
32 F8 **Pacific Beach** Washington, NW USA 47°09′N 124°12′W
35 N10 **Pacific Grove** California, W USA 36°35′N 121°54′W
29 S15 **Pacific Junction** Iowa, C USA 41°01′N 95°48′W
192-193 **Pacific Ocean** *ocean*
129 Z10 **Pacific Plate** *tectonic feature*
113 J15 **Pačir** ▲ N Montenegro 43°19′N 19°07′E
182 L5 **Packsaddle** New South Wales, SE Australia 30°42′S 141°55′E
32 H9 **Packwood** Washington, NW USA 46°37′N 121°38′W
Padalung *see* Phatthalung
168 J12 **Padang** Sumatera, W Indonesia 01°S 100°21′E
168 L9 **Padang Endau** Pahang, Peninsular Malaysia 02°38′N 103°37′E
Padangpandjang *see* Padangpanjang
168 I11 **Padangpanjang** *prev.* Padangpandjang. Sumatera, W Indonesia 0°30′S 100°26′E
168 I10 **Padangsidempuan** *prev.* Padangsidimpoean. Sumatera, W Indonesia 01°23′N 99°15′E
Padangsidimpoean *see* Padangsidempuan
124 I9 **Padany** Respublika Kareliya, NW Russian Federation 63°18′N 33°20′E
93 M18 **Padasjoki** Etelä-Suomi, S Finland 61°20′N 25°21′E
57 M22 **Padcaya** Tarija, S Bolivia 21°52′S 64°46′W
101 H14 **Paderborn** Nordrhein-Westfalen, NW Germany 51°43′N 08°45′E
Padeşul/Padeş, Vîrful *see* Padeş, Vârful
116 F12 **Padeş, Vârful** *var.* Padeşul; *prev.* Vîrful Padeş. ▲ W Romania 45°39′N 22°19′E
112 L10 **Padinska Skela** Serbia, N Serbia 44°58′N 20°25′E
153 S14 **Padma** *var.* Ganges. Bangladesh/India *see also* Ganges
Padma *see* Brahmaputra
Padma *see* Ganges
106 H8 **Padova** *Eng.* Padua; *anc.* Patavium. Veneto, NE Italy 45°24′N 11°52′E
82 A10 **Padrão, Ponta do** *headland* NW Angola 06°06′S 12°18′E
25 T16 **Padre Island** *island* Texas, SW USA
104 G3 **Padrón** Galicia, NW Spain 42°44′N 08°40′W
118 K13 **Padsvillye** *Rus.* Podsvil'ye. Vitsyebskaya Voblasts', N Belarus 55°09′N 27°58′E
182 K11 **Padthaway** South Australia 36°39′S 140°30′E
Padua *see* Padova
20 G7 **Paducah** Kentucky, S USA 37°03′N 88°36′W
25 P4 **Paducah** Texas, SW USA 34°01′N 100°18′W
105 N15 **Padul** Andalucía, S Spain 37°02′N 03°37′W
191 P8 **Paea** Tahiti, W French Polynesia 17°41′S 149°35′W
185 L14 **Paekakariki** Wellington, North Island, New Zealand 41°00′S 174°58′E
163 X11 **Paektu-san** *var.* Baitou Shan. ▲ China/North Korea 42°00′N 128°03′W
Paengnyŏng *see* Baengnyong-do
184 M7 **Paeroa** Waikato, North Island, New Zealand 37°23′S 175°39′E
54 D12 **Páez** Cauca, SW Colombia 02°37′N 76°00′W
121 O3 **Páfos** *var.* Paphos. W Cyprus 34°46′N 32°26′E
121 O3 **Páfos** ✈ SW Cyprus 34°46′N 32°25′E
83 L19 **Pafúri** Gaza, SW Mozambique 22°27′S 31°21′E
112 C12 **Pag** *It.* Pago. Lika-Senj, SW Croatia 44°26′N 15°01′E
112 B11 **Pag** *It.* Pago. *island* Zadar, C Croatia
171 P7 **Pagadian** Mindanao, S Philippines 07°47′N 123°22′E
168 J13 **Pagai Selatan, Pulau** *island* Kepulauan Mentawai, W Indonesia
168 J13 **Pagai Utara, Pulau** *island* Kepulauan Mentawai, W Indonesia
188 K4 **Pagan** *island* C Northern Mariana Islands
115 G16 **Pagasitikós Kólpos** *gulf* E Greece
36 L8 **Page** Arizona, SW USA 36°54′N 111°28′W
29 Q5 **Page** North Dakota, N USA 47°09′N 97°33′W
118 D13 **Pagėgiai** *Ger.* Pogegen. Tauragė, SW Lithuania 55°08′N 21°54′E
21 S11 **Pageland** South Carolina, SE USA 34°46′N 80°23′W
81 G16 **Pager** NE Uganda
149 Q5 **Paghmān** Kābul, E Afghanistan 34°33′N 68°55′E
Pago *see* Pag
188 C16 **Pago Bay** *bay* E Guam, W Pacific Ocean
115 M20 **Pagóndas** *var.* Pagóndhas. Sámos, Dodekánisa, Greece, Aegean Sea 37°41′N 26°50′E
Pagóndhas *see* Pagóndas
192 J16 **Pago Pago** ○ (American Samoa) Tutuila, W American Samoa 14°16′S 170°43′W
37 R8 **Pagosa Springs** Colorado, C USA 37°13′N 107°01′W
Pagqên *see* Gadê
38 H12 **Pāhala** *var.* Pahala. Hawaii, USA, C Pacific Ocean 19°12′N 155°28′W
168 K8 **Pahang** *var.* Negeri Pahang Darul Makmur. ❖ *state* Peninsular Malaysia
Pahang *see* Pahang, Sungai
168 L8 **Pahang, Sungai** *var.* Pahang, Sungei Pahang. Peninsular Malaysia
149 S8 **Pahārpur** Khyber Pakhtunkhwa, NW Pakistan 32°06′N 71°00′E
185 B24 **Pahia Point** *headland* South Island, New Zealand 46°19′S 167°42′E
184 M13 **Pahiatua** Manawatu-Wanganui, North Island, New Zealand 40°30′S 175°49′E
38 H12 **Pāhoa** *var.* Pahoa. Hawaii, USA, C Pacific Ocean 19°29′N 154°56′W
23 Y14 **Pahokee** Florida, SE USA 26°49′N 80°40′W
35 X9 **Pahranagat Range** ▲▲ Nevada, W USA
35 W11 **Pahrump** Nevada, W USA 36°11′N 115°58′W
Pahsien *see* Chongqing
35 V9 **Pahute Mesa** ▲▲ Nevada, W USA
167 N7 **Pai** Mae Hong Son, NW Thailand 19°24′N 98°26′E
38 F10 **Pa'ia** *var.* Paia. Maui, Hawaii, USA, C Pacific Ocean 20°54′N 156°22′W
Paia *see* Pa'ia
Pai-ch'eng *see* Baicheng
118 H4 **Paide** *Ger.* Weissenstein. Järvamaa, N Estonia 58°55′N 25°36′E
97 J24 **Paignton** SW England, United Kingdom 50°26′N 03°34′W
184 K3 **Paihia** Northland, North Island, New Zealand 35°18′S 174°06′E
93 M18 **Päijänne** ◎ S Finland
114 F13 **Páïko** ▲▲ N Greece
57 M17 **Paila, Río** C Bolivia
167 Q12 **Pailĭn** Bătdâmbâng, W Cambodia 12°51′N 102°34′E
Pailing *see* Chun'an
54 F6 **Pailitas** Cesar, N Colombia 08°58′N 73°38′W
38 F9 **Pailolo Channel** *channel* Hawai'i, USA, C Pacific Ocean
93 K19 **Paimio** *Swe.* Pemar. Länsi-Suomi, SW Finland 60°27′N 22°42′E
165 O16 **Paimi-saki** *var.* Yaeme-saki. *headland* Iriomote-jima, SW Japan 24°18′N 123°40′E
102 G5 **Paimpol** Côtes d'Armor, NW France 48°47′N 03°03′W
168 J12 **Painan** Sumatera, W Indonesia 01°22′S 100°33′E
63 G23 **Paine, Cerro** ▲ S Chile 51°01′S 72°57′W
31 U11 **Painesville** Ohio, N USA 41°43′N 81°15′W
31 S14 **Paint Creek** Ohio, N USA
36 L10 **Painted Desert** *desert* Arizona, SW USA
Paint Hills *see* Wemindji
30 M4 **Paint River** Michigan, N USA
25 P8 **Paint Rock** Texas, SW USA 31°32′N 99°56′W
21 O6 **Paintsville** Kentucky, S USA 37°48′N 82°48′W
Paisance *see* Piacenza
96 I12 **Paisley** W Scotland, United Kingdom 55°50′N 04°26′W
32 I15 **Paisley** Oregon, NW USA 42°40′N 120°31′W
105 O3 **País Vasco** *Basq.* Euskadi, *Eng.* The Basque Country, *Sp.* Provincias Vascongadas. ❖ *autonomous community* N Spain
56 A9 **Paita** Piura, NW Peru 05°11′S 81°09′W
169 V6 **Paitan, Teluk** *bay* Sabah, East Malaysia
104 H7 **Paiva, Rio** N Portugal
92 K12 **Pajala** Norrbotten, N Sweden 67°12′N 23°19′E
104 K3 **Pajares, Puerto de** *pass* NW Spain
54 G9 **Pajarito** Boyacá, C Colombia 05°18′N 72°43′W
54 G4 **Pajaro** La Guajira, S Colombia 11°41′N 72°37′W
Pakanbaru *see* Pekanbaru
Pākaur *see* Pākur
55 Q10 **Pakaraima Mountains** *var.* Serra Pacaraim, Sierra Pacaraima. ▲▲ N South America
167 P10 **Pak Chong** Nakhon Ratchasima, C Thailand 14°38′N 101°22′E
123 V8 **Pakhachi** Krasnoyarskiy Kray, E Russian Federation 60°36′N 168°59′E
Pakhna *see* Páchna
189 U16 **Pakin Atoll** *atoll* Caroline Islands, E Micronesia
149 Q12 **Pakistan** *off.* Islamic Republic of Pakistan, *var.* Islami Jamhuriya e Pakistan. ◆ *republic* S Asia
Pakistan, Islamic Republic of *see* Pakistan
Pakistan, Islami Jamhuriya e *see* Pakistan
167 P8 **Pak Lay** *var.* Muang Pak Lay. Xaignabouli, C Laos 18°06′N 101°21′E
Paknam *see* Samut Prakan
166 L5 **Pakokku** Magway, C Burma (Myanmar) 21°20′N 95°05′E
110 I10 **Pakość** *Ger.* Pakosch. Kujawski-pomorskie, C Poland 52°47′N 18°03′E
Pakosch *see* Pakość
149 V10 **Pākpattan** Punjab, E Pakistan 30°20′N 73°27′E
167 O15 **Pak Phanang** *var.* Ban Pak Phanang. Nakhon Si Thammarat, SW Thailand 08°20′N 100°10′E
112 G9 **Pakrac** *Hung.* Pakrácz. Požega-Slavonija, NE Croatia 45°26′N 17°09′E
Pakrácz *see* Pakrac
118 F11 **Pakruojis** Šiaulai, N Lithuania 56°N 23°51′E
111 J24 **Paks** Tolna, S Hungary 46°38′N 18°51′E
Pak Sane *see* Pakxan
Paksé *see* Pakxé
167 Q10 **Pak Thong Chai** Nakhon Ratchasima, C Thailand 14°43′N 102°01′E
Paktīā *see* Paktiyā
149 Q7 **Paktīkā** ❖ *province* SE Afghanistan
149 R6 **Paktiyā** *prev.* Paktīā. ❖ *province* SE Afghanistan
171 N12 **Pakuli** Sulawesi, C Indonesia 01°14′S 119°55′E
153 S14 **Pākur** *var.* Pākaur. Jharkhand, N India 24°48′N 87°14′E
81 F17 **Pakwach** NW Uganda 02°28′N 31°28′E
167 R8 **Pakxan** *var.* Muang Pakxan, Pak Sane. Bolikhamxai, C Laos 18°27′N 103°38′E
167 S10 **Pakxé** *var.* Paksé. Champasak, S Laos 15°09′N 105°49′E
78 G12 **Pala** Mayo-Kébbi, SW Chad 09°22′N 14°54′E
61 A17 **Palacios** Santa Fe, C Argentina 30°43′S 61°37′W
25 V13 **Palacios** Texas, SW USA 28°42′N 96°13′W
105 X5 **Palafrugell** Cataluña, NE Spain 41°55′N 03°10′E
107 L24 **Palagonia** Sicilia, Italy, C Mediterranean Sea 37°20′N 14°45′E
113 E17 **Palagruža** *It.* Pelagosa. *island* SW Croatia
115 G20 **Palaiá Epídavros** Pelopónnisos, S Greece 37°38′N 23°09′E
121 P3 **Palaichóri** *var.* Palekhori. C Cyprus 34°55′N 33°06′E
115 H25 **Palaiochóra** Kríti, Greece, E Mediterranean Sea 35°14′N 23°37′E
115 A15 **Palaiolastrítsa** *religious building* Kérkyra, Iónia Nisiá, Greece, C Mediterranean Sea
115 J19 **Palaiópoli** Ándros, Kykládes, Greece, Aegean Sea 37°49′N 24°49′E
103 N5 **Palaiseau** Essonne, N France 48°41′N 02°14′E
154 N11 **Pāla Laharha** Orissa, E India 21°25′N 85°18′E
83 G19 **Palamakoloi** Ghanzi, C Botswana 23°10′S 22°22′E
115 E16 **Palamás** Thessalía, C Greece 39°28′N 22°05′E
105 X5 **Palamós** Cataluña, NE Spain 41°51′N 03°06′E
118 J5 **Palamuse** *Ger.* Sankt-Bartholomäi. Jõgevamaa, E Estonia 58°41′N 26°35′E
183 Q14 **Palana** Tasmania, SE Australia 39°48′S 147°54′E
123 U9 **Palana** Krasnoyarskiy Kray, E Russian Federation 59°05′N 159°59′E
118 C11 **Palanga** *Ger.* Polangen. Klaipėda, NW Lithuania 05°54′N 21°05′E
143 V10 **Palangān, Kūh-e** ▲▲ E Iran
Palangkaraja *see* Palangkaraya
169 T12 **Palangkaraya** *prev.* Palangkaraja. Borneo, C Indonesia 02°16′S 113°55′E
155 H22 **Palani** Tamil Nādu, SE India 10°30′N 77°24′E
Palanka *see* Bačka Palanka
154 D9 **Pālanpur** Gujarāt, W India 24°12′N 72°29′E
Palantia *see* Palencia
83 I19 **Palapye** Central, SE Botswana 22°37′S 27°06′E
155 J19 **Pālār** SE India
104 H3 **Palas de Rei** Galicia, NW Spain 42°52′N 07°51′W
123 T9 **Palatka** Magadanskaya Oblast', E Russian Federation 60°09′N 150°33′E
23 W10 **Palatka** Florida, SE USA 29°39′N 81°38′W
188 B9 **Palau** *var.* Belau. ◆ *republic* W Pacific Ocean
Palau *see* Palau Islands
129 Y14 **Palau Islands** *var.* Palau. *island group* N Palau
192 G16 **Palauli Bay** *bay* Savai'i, C Samoa, C Pacific Ocean
167 N11 **Palaw** Tanintharyi, S Burma (Myanmar) 12°57′N 98°39′E
170 M6 **Palawan** *island* W Philippines
171 N6 **Palawan Passage** *passage* W Philippines
192 E7 **Palawan Trough** *undersea feature* S South China Sea 07°00′N 115°00′E
155 H23 **Pālayankottai** Tamil Nādu, SE India 08°42′N 77°46′E
107 L25 **Palazzola Acreide** *anc.* Acrae. Sicilia, Italy, C Mediterranean Sea 37°04′N 14°54′E
118 G3 **Paldiski** *prev.* Baltiski, *Eng.* Baltic Port, *Ger.* Baltischport. Harjumaa, NW Estonia 59°22′N 24°08′E
112 I13 **Pale** Republika Srpska, SE Bosnia and Herzegovina 43°49′N 18°35′E
Palekhori *see* Palaichóri
168 L13 **Palembang** Sumatera, W Indonesia 02°59′S 104°45′E
63 G18 **Palena** Los Lagos, S Chile 43°40′S 71°50′W
63 G18 **Palena, Río** S Chile
104 M5 **Palencia** *anc.* Palantia, Pallantia. Castilla y León, NW Spain 42°23′N 04°32′W
104 M3 **Palencia** ❖ *province* Castilla y León, N Spain
35 X15 **Palen Dry Lake** ◎ California, W USA
41 V15 **Palenque** Chiapas, SE Mexico 17°32′N 91°59′W
41 V15 **Palenque** *var.* Ruinas de Palenque. *ruins* Chiapas, SE Mexico
45 O9 **Palenque, Punta** *headland* S Dominican Republic 18°13′N 70°08′W
Palenque, Ruinas de *see* Palenque
Palerme *see* Palermo
107 I23 **Palermo** *Fr.* Palerme; *anc.* Panhormus, Panormus. Sicilia, Italy, C Mediterranean Sea 38°08′N 13°23′E
25 V8 **Palestine** Texas, SW USA 31°45′N 93°39′W
25 V7 **Palestine, Lake** ⊠ Texas, SW USA
107 I15 **Palestrina** Lazio, C Italy 41°49′N 12°53′E
166 K5 **Paletwa** Chin State, W Burma (Myanmar) 21°25′N 92°49′E
155 G21 **Pālghāt** *var.* Palakkad. Kerala, SW India 10°46′N 76°42′E *see also* Palakkad
152 F13 **Pāli** Rājasthān, N India 25°48′N 73°21′E
167 N16 **Palian** Trang, SW Thailand
189 O12 **Palikir** ● (Micronesia) Pohnpei, E Micronesia 06°58′N 158°13′E
Palimé *see* Kpalimé
107 L19 **Palinuro, Capo** *headland* S Italy 40°02′N 15°16′E
115 H15 **Palioúri, Akrotírio** *var.* Akrotírio Kanestron. *headland* N Greece 39°55′N 23°45′E
33 R14 **Palisades Reservoir** ⊠ Idaho, NW USA
99 J23 **Paliseul** Luxembourg, SE Belgium 49°55′N 05°09′E
154 C11 **Pālitāna** Gujarāt, W India 21°30′N 71°50′E
118 F4 **Palivere** Läänemaa, W Estonia 58°59′N 23°58′E
41 V14 **Palizada** Campeche, SE Mexico 18°15′N 92°03′W
93 L18 **Pälkäne** Länsi-Suomi, W Finland 61°22′N 24°16′E
155 J22 **Palk Strait** *strait* India/Sri Lanka
155 J23 **Pallai** Northern Province, NW Sri Lanka 09°35′N 80°20′E
Pallantia *see* Palencia
106 C6 **Pallanza** Piemonte, NE Italy 45°57′N 08°32′E
127 Q9 **Pallasovka** Volgogradskaya Oblast', SW Russian Federation 50°06′N 46°52′E
Pallene/Pallíni *see* Kassándra
185 L15 **Palliser Bay** *bay* North Island, New Zealand
185 L15 **Palliser, Cape** *headland* North Island, New Zealand 41°37′S 175°16′E
191 U9 **Palliser, Îles** *island group* Îles Tuamotu, C French Polynesia
82 Q12 **Palma** Cabo Delgado, N Mozambique 10°46′S 40°30′E
105 X9 **Palma** *var.* Palma de Mallorca. Mallorca, Spain, W Mediterranean Sea 39°35′N 02°39′E
105 X9 **Palma** ✈ Mallorca, Spain, W Mediterranean Sea
105 X10 **Palma, Badia de** *bay* Mallorca, Spain, W Mediterranean Sea
104 L13 **Palma del Río** Andalucía, S Spain 37°42′N 05°16′W
Palma de Mallorca *see* Palma
107 J25 **Palma di Montechiaro** Sicilia, Italy, C Mediterranean Sea 37°12′N 13°46′E
106 J7 **Palmanova** Friuli-Venezia Giulia, NE Italy 45°54′N 13°20′E
54 J7 **Palmarito** Apure, C Venezuela 07°36′N 70°08′W
43 N15 **Palmar Sur** Puntarenas, SE Costa Rica 08°54′N 83°27′W
60 I12 **Palmas** Paraná, S Brazil 26°29′S 52°00′W
59 K16 **Palmas** *var.* Palmas do Tocantins. Tocantins, C Brazil 10°24′S 48°19′W
76 L18 **Palmas, Cape** *Fr.* Cap des Palmès. *headland* SW Ivory Coast 04°18′N 07°31′W
Palmas do Tocantins *see* Palmas
54 D11 **Palmaseca** ✈ (Cali) Valle del Cauca, SW Colombia 03°31′N 76°27′W
107 B21 **Palmas, Golfo di** *gulf* Sardegna, Italy, C Mediterranean Sea
44 I7 **Palma Soriano** Santiago de Cuba, E Cuba 20°10′N 76°00′W
23 Y12 **Palm Bay** Florida, SE USA 28°01′N 80°35′W
35 T14 **Palmdale** California, W USA 34°34′N 118°07′W
61 H14 **Palmeira das Missões** Rio Grande do Sul, S Brazil 27°54′S 53°20′W
82 A11 **Palmeirinhas, Ponta das** *headland* NW Angola 09°04′S 13°02′E
39 R11 **Palmer** Alaska, USA 61°36′N 149°06′W
19 N11 **Palmer** Massachusetts, NE USA 42°09′N 72°19′W
25 U7 **Palmer** Texas, SW USA 32°25′N 96°40′W
194 H4 **Palmer** *US research station* Antarctica 64°37′S 64°01′W
15 R11 **Palmer** Québec, SE Canada
37 T5 **Palmer Lake** Colorado, C USA 39°07′N 104°55′W
194 J6 **Palmer Land** *physical region* Antarctica
14 F15 **Palmerston** Ontario, SE Canada 43°51′N 80°49′W
185 F22 **Palmerston** Otago, South Island, New Zealand 45°27′S 170°42′E
190 K15 **Palmerston** *island* S Cook Islands
Palmerston *see* Darwin
184 M12 **Palmerston North** Manawatu-Wanganui, North Island, New Zealand 40°20′S 175°52′E
23 V13 **Palmetto** Florida, SE USA 27°31′N 82°34′W
The Palmetto State *see* South Carolina
107 M22 **Palmi** Calabria, SW Italy 38°21′N 15°51′E
54 D11 **Palmira** Valle del Cauca, W Colombia 03°33′N 76°17′W
56 F8 **Palmira, Río** N Peru
61 D19 **Palmitas** Soriano, SW Uruguay 33°27′S 57°48′W
Palmnicken *see* Yantarnyy
35 V15 **Palm Springs** California, W USA 33°48′N 116°33′W
27 V2 **Palmyra** Missouri, C USA 39°48′N 91°31′W
18 G10 **Palmyra** New York, NE USA 43°02′N 77°13′W
18 G15 **Palmyra** Pennsylvania, NE USA 40°18′N 76°35′W
21 V5 **Palmyra** Virginia, NE USA 37°53′N 78°17′W
Palmyra *see* Tudmur
192 L7 **Palmyra Atoll** ◇ *US privately owned unincorporated territory* C Pacific Ocean
154 P12 **Palmyras Point** *headland* E India 20°46′N 87°00′E
35 N9 **Palo Alto** California, W USA 37°26′N 122°08′W
25 O1 **Palo Duro Creek** Texas, SW USA
Paloe *see* Denpasar, Bali, C Indonesia
Paloe *see* Palu
168 L9 **Paloh** Johor, Peninsular Malaysia 02°10′N 103°11′E
80 F12 **Paloich** Upper Nile, NE South Sudan 10°29′N 32°31′E
40 I3 **Palomas** Chihuahua, N Mexico 31°45′N 107°38′W
107 I15 **Palombara Sabina** Lazio, C Italy 42°04′N 12°45′E
105 S13 **Palos, Cabo de** *headland* SE Spain 37°38′N 00°42′W
104 I14 **Palos de la Frontera** Andalucía, S Spain 37°14′N 06°53′W
60 G11 **Palotina** Paraná, S Brazil 24°16′S 53°49′W
32 M9 **Palouse** Washington, NW USA 46°54′N 117°04′W
32 L9 **Palouse River** Washington, NW USA
35 Y16 **Palo Verde** California, W USA 33°25′N 114°43′W
57 E16 **Palpa** Ica, W Peru 14°35′S 75°09′W
95 M16 **Pålsboda** Örebro, C Sweden 59°04′N 15°21′E
93 M15 **Paltamo** Oulu, C Finland 64°25′N 27°50′E
171 N12 **Palu** *prev.* Paloe. Sulawesi, C Indonesia 0°54′S 119°52′E
137 P14 **Palu** Elazığ, E Turkey 38°43′N 39°56′E
152 I11 **Palwal** Haryāna, N India 28°15′N 77°18′E
123 U6 **Palyavaam** NE Russian Federation
77 Q13 **Pama** SE Burkina 11°13′N 00°46′E
172 J14 **Pamandzi** ✈ (Mamoudzou) Petite-Terre, E Mayotte
Pamangkat *see* Pemangkat
143 R11 **Pā Mazār** Kermān, C Iran
83 N19 **Pambarra** Inhambane, SE Mozambique 21°57′S 35°06′E
171 X12 **Pamdai** Papua, E Indonesia 01°58′S 137°19′E
103 N16 **Pamiers** Ariège, S France 43°07′N 01°37′E
147 T14 **Pamir** *var.* Daryā-ye Pāmīr, *Taj.* Dar"yoi Pomir. Afghanistan/Tajikistan *see also* Pāmīr, Daryā-ye
Pamir *see* Pāmīr, Daryā-ye
149 U1 **Pāmīr, Daryā-ye** *var.* Pamir, *Taj.* Dar"yoi Pomir. Afghanistan/Tajikistan *see also* Pamir
Pāmīr, Daryā-ye *see* Pamir
Pāmīr-e Khord *see* Little Pamir
Pamir/Pāmīr, Daryā-ye *see* Pamirs
129 Q8 **Pamirs** *Pash.* Daryā-ye Pāmīr, *Rus.* Pamir. ▲▲ C Asia
Pâmiut *see* Paamiut
21 X10 **Pamlico River** North Carolina, SE USA
21 Y10 **Pamlico Sound** *sound* North Carolina, SE USA
25 O2 **Pampa** Texas, SW USA 35°32′N 100°58′W
Pampa Aullagas, Lago *see* Poopó, Lago
61 B21 **Pampa Húmeda** *grassland* E Argentina
56 A10 **Pampa las Salinas** *salt lake* NW Peru
57 F15 **Pampas** Huancavelica, C Peru 12°22′S 74°53′W
62 K13 **Pampas** *plain* C Argentina
55 O4 **Pampatar** Nueva Esparta, NE Venezuela 11°03′N 63°51′W
Pampeluna *see* Pamplona
104 H8 **Pampilhosa da Serra** *var.* Pampilhosa de Serra. Coimbra, N Portugal 40°03′N 07°58′W
173 Y15 **Pamplemousses** N Mauritius 20°06′S 57°34′E
54 G7 **Pamplona** Norte de Santander, N Colombia 07°24′N 72°38′W
105 Q3 **Pamplona** *Basq.* Iruña, *prev.* Pampeluna; *anc.* Pompaelo. Navarra, N Spain 42°49′N 01°39′W
114 I11 **Pamporovo** *prev.* Vasil Kolarov. Smolyan, S Bulgaria 41°39′N 24°45′E
136 D15 **Pamukkale** Denizli, W Turkey 37°51′N 29°13′E
21 W5 **Pamunkey River** Virginia, NE USA
152 K5 **Pamzal** Jammu and Kashmir, NW India 34°17′N 78°50′E
30 L14 **Pana** Illinois, N USA 39°23′N 89°04′W
41 Y11 **Panabá** Yucatán, SE Mexico 21°20′N 88°16′W
35 Y8 **Panaca** Nevada, W USA 37°47′N 114°24′W
115 E19 **Panachaikó** ▲▲ S Greece
14 F11 **Panache Lake** ◎ Ontario, S Canada
114 I10 **Panagyurishte** Pazardzhik, C Bulgaria 42°30′N 24°11′E
168 M16 **Panaitan, Pulau** *island* S Indonesia
115 D18 **Panaitolikó** ▲▲ C Greece
155 E17 **Panaji** *var.* Pangim, Panjim, New Goa. *state capital* Goa, W India 15°31′N 73°52′E
43 T15 **Panamá** *var.* Ciudad de Panama, *Eng.* Panama City. ● (Panama) Panamá, C Panama 08°57′N 79°33′W
43 T14 **Panama** *off.* Republic of Panama. ◆ *republic* Central America
43 U14 **Panamá** *off.* Provincia de Panamá. ❖ *province* E Panama
43 U15 **Panamá, Bahía de** *bay* N Gulf of Panama
193 T7 **Panama Basin** *undersea feature* E Pacific Ocean 05°00′N 83°30′W
43 T15 **Panama Canal** *canal* E Panama
23 R9 **Panama City** Florida, SE USA 30°09′N 85°39′W
43 T14 **Panama City** ✈ Panamá, C Panama 09°02′N 79°24′W
Panama City *see* Panamá
23 Q9 **Panama City Beach** Florida, SE USA 30°10′N 85°48′W
43 T17 **Panamá, Golfo de** *var.* Gulf of Panama. *gulf* S Panama
Panama, Gulf of *see* Panamá, Golfo de
Panama, Isthmus of *see* Panama, Istmo de
43 T15 **Panama, Istmo de** *Eng.* Isthmus of Panama; *prev.* Isthmus of Darien. *isthmus* E Panama
Panamá, Provincia de *see* Panamá
Panama, Republic of *see* Panama
35 U11 **Panamint Range** ▲▲ California, W USA
107 L22 **Panarea, Isola** *island* Isole Eolie, S Italy
106 G9 **Panaro** N Italy
171 P5 **Panay Island** *island* C Philippines
35 W7 **Pancake Range** ▲▲ Nevada, W USA
112 M11 **Pančevo** *Ger.* Pantschowa, *Hung.* Pancsova. Vojvodina, N Serbia 44°53′N 20°40′E
113 M15 **Pančićev Vrh** ▲ SW Serbia 43°16′N 20°49′E
116 L12 **Panciu** Vrancea, E Romania 45°54′N 27°08′E
116 F10 **Pâncota** *Hung.* Pankota; *prev.* Pîncota. Arad, W Romania 46°20′N 21°45′E
Pancsova *see* Pančevo
83 N20 **Panda** Inhambane, SE Mozambique 24°02′S 34°45′E
171 X12 **Pandaidori, Kepulauan** *island group* E Indonesia
25 N11 **Pandale** Texas, SW USA 30°09′N 101°34′W
169 P12 **Pandang Tikar, Pulau** *island* N Indonesia
61 F20 **Pan de Azúcar** Maldonado, S Uruguay 34°45′S 55°14′W
118 H11 **Pandėlys** Panevėžys, NE Lithuania 56°04′N 25°18′E
155 F15 **Pandharpur** Mahārāshtra, W India 17°42′N 75°24′E
182 J1 **Pandie Pandie** South Australia 26°06′S 139°26′E
171 O12 **Pandiri** Sulawesi, C Indonesia 01°32′S 120°47′E
61 F20 **Pando** Canelones, S Uruguay 34°44′S 55°58′W
57 J14 **Pando** ❖ *department* N Bolivia
192 K9 **Pandora Bank** *undersea feature* W Pacific Ocean
95 G20 **Pandrup** Nordjylland, N Denmark 57°14′N 09°42′E
79 J15 **Pandu** Equateur, NW Dem. Rep. Congo 05°03′N 19°14′E
153 V12 **Pandu** Assam, NE India 26°08′N 91°37′E
Paneas *see* Bāniyās
59 F15 **Panelas** Mato Grosso, W Brazil 09°06′S 60°41′W
118 G12 **Panevėžys** Panevėžys, C Lithuania 55°44′N 24°21′E
118 G11 **Panevėžys** ❖ *province* NW Lithuania
Panfilov *see* Zharkent
127 N9 **Panfilovo** Volgogradskaya Oblast', SW Russian Federation 50°25′N 42°55′E
79 N17 **Panga** Orientale, N Dem. Rep. Congo 01°52′N 26°18′E
193 Y15 **Pangai** Lifuka, C Tonga 19°50′S 174°23′W
114 H13 **Pangaío** ▲▲ N Greece
79 G20 **Pangala** Pool, S Congo 03°26′S 14°38′E
81 J22 **Pangani** Tanga, E Tanzania 05°27′S 39°00′E
81 I21 **Pangani** NE Tanzania
186 K8 **Panggoe** Choiseul, NW Solomon Islands 07°00′S 157°05′E
79 N20 **Pangi** Maniema, E Dem. Rep. Congo 03°12′S 26°39′E
Pangim *see* Panaji
168 H8 **Pangkalanbrandan** Sumatera, W Indonesia 04°00′N 98°15′E
Pangkalanbun *see* Pangkalanbuun
169 R13 **Pangkalanbuun** *var.* Pangkalanbun. Borneo, C Indonesia 02°43′S 111°38′E

◆ Country
● Country Capital
◇ Dependent Territory
○ Dependent Territory Capital
❖ Administrative Regions
✈ International Airport
▲ Mountain
▲▲ Mountain Range
Volcano
River
◎ Lake
⊠ Reservoir

169 N12 **Pangkalpinang** Pulau Bangka, W Indonesia 02°05′S 106°09′E
11 U17 **Pangman** Saskatchewan, S Canada 49°37′N 104°33′W
Pang-Nga *see* Phang-Nga
9 S6 **Pangnirtung** Baffin Island, Nunavut, NE Canada 66°05′N 65°45′W
152 K6 **Pangong Tso** *var.* Bangong Co. ◎ China/India *see also* Bangong Co
Pangong Tso *see* Banggong Co
36 K7 **Panguitch** Utah, W USA 37°49′N 112°26′W
186 J7 **Panguna** Bougainville Island, NE Papua New Guinea 06°22′S 155°20′E
171 N8 **Pangutaran Group** *island group* Sulu Archipelago, SW Philippines
25 N2 **Panhandle** Texas, SW USA 35°21′N 101°24′W
Panhormus *see* Palermo
171 W14 **Paniai, Danau** ◎ Papua, E Indonesia
79 L21 **Pania-Mutombo** Kasai-Oriental, C Dem. Rep. Congo 05°09′S 23°49′E
187 P16 **Panié, Mont** ▲ C New Caledonia 20°33′S 164°41′E
Panikoilli *see* Jājapur
152 I10 **Pānīpat** Haryāna, N India 29°18′N 77°00′E
147 Q14 **Panj** *Rus.* Pyandzh; *prev.* Kirovabad. SW Tajikistan 37°39′N 69°55′E
147 P15 **Panj** *Rus.* Pyandzh. ≈ Afghanistan/Tajikistan
149 O5 **Panjāb** Bāmyān, C Afghanistan 34°21′N 67°00′E
147 O12 **Panjakent** *Rus.* Pendzhikent. W Tajikistan 39°28′N 67°33′E
148 L14 **Panjgūr** Baluchistān, SW Pakistan 26°58′N 64°05′E
Panjim *see* Panaji
163 U12 **Panjin** Liaoning, NE China 41°11′N 122°05′E
147 P14 **Panji Poyon** *Rus.* Nizhniy Pyandzh. SW Tajikistan 37°14′N 68°32′E
149 Q4 **Panjshayr** *prev.* Panjshīr. ≈ E Afghanistan
149 S4 **Panjshīr** ◐ *province* NE Afghanistan
Panjshīr *see* Panjshayr
Pankota *see* Pâncota
77 W14 **Pankshin** Plateau, C Nigeria 09°21′N 09°27′E
163 Y10 **Pan Ling** ▲▲ N China
Panlong Jiang *see* Lô, Sông
154 J9 **Panna** Madhya Pradesh, C India 24°43′N 80°11′E
99 M16 **Panningen** Limburg, SE Netherlands 51°20′N 05°59′E
149 R13 **Pāno Āqil** Sind, SE Pakistan 27°55′N 69°18′E
121 P3 **Páno Léfkara** S Cyprus 34°52′N 33°18′E
121 O3 **Páno Panagiá** *var.* Pano Panayia. W Cyprus 34°55′N 32°38′E
Pano Panayia *see* Páno Panagiá
Panopolis *see* Akhmīm
29 U14 **Panora** Iowa, C USA 41°41′N 94°21′W
60 I8 **Panorama** São Paulo, S Brazil 21°22′S 51°51′W
115 I24 **Pánormos** Kríti, Greece, E Mediterranean Sea 35°24′N 24°42′E
Panormus *see* Palermo
163 W11 **Panshi** Jilin, NE China 42°56′N 126°02′E
59 H19 **Pantanal** *var.* Pantanalmato-Grossense. *swamp* SW Brazil
Pantanalmato-Grossense *see* Pantanal
61 H16 **Pântano Grande** Rio Grande do Sul, S Brazil 30°12′S 52°24′W
171 Q16 **Pantar, Pulau** *island* Kepulauan Alor, S Indonesia
21 X9 **Pantego** North Carolina, SE USA 35°34′N 76°39′E
107 G25 **Pantelleria** *anc.* Cossyra, Cosyra. Sicilia, Italy, C Mediterranean Sea 36°47′N 12°00′E
107 G25 **Pantelleria, Isola di** *island* SW Italy
Pante Makasar/Pante Macassar/Pante Makassar *see* Ponte Macassar
152 K10 **Pantnagar** Uttarakhand, N India 29°00′N 79°28′E
115 A15 **Pantokrátoras** ▲ Kérkyra, Iónia Nisiá, Greece, C Mediterranean Sea 39°45′N 19°51′E
Pantschowa *see* Pančevo
41 P11 **Pánuco** Veracruz-Llave, E Mexico 22°01′N 98°13′W
41 P11 **Pánuco, Río** ≈ C Mexico
160 I12 **Panxian** Guizhou, S China 25°45′N 104°39′E
168 I10 **Panyabungan** Sumatera, N Indonesia 0°55′N 99°30′E
77 W14 **Panyam** Plateau, C Nigeria 09°28′N 09°13′E
157 N13 **Panzhihua** *prev.* Dukou, Tu-k'ou. Sichuan, C China 26°35′N 101°41′E
79 I22 **Panzi** Bandundu, SW Dem. Rep. Congo 07°10′S 17°55′E
42 E5 **Panzós** Alta Verapaz, E Guatemala 15°21′N 89°40′W
Pao-chi/Paoki *see* Baoji
Pao-king *see* Shaoyang
107 N20 **Paola** Calabria, SW Italy 39°21′N 16°03′E
121 P16 **Paola** E Malta 35°52′N 14°30′E
27 R5 **Paola** Kansas, C USA 38°34′N 94°54′W
31 O15 **Paoli** Indiana, N USA 38°35′N 86°25′W
187 R14 **Paonangisu** Éfaté, C Vanuatu 17°33′S 168°23′E
171 S13 **Paoni** *var.* Pauni. Pulau Seram, E Indonesia 02°48′S 129°03′E
37 Q5 **Paonia** Colorado, C USA 38°52′N 107°35′W
191 O7 **Paopao** Moorea, W French Polynesia 17°28′S 149°48′W
Pao-shan *see* Baoshan
Pao-ting *see* Baoding
Pao-t'ou/Paotow *see* Baotou
79 H14 **Paoua** Ouham-Pendé, W Central African Republic 07°22′N 16°25′E
Pap *see* Pop
111 H23 **Pápa** Veszprém, W Hungary 47°20′N 17°29′E
42 J12 **Papagayo, Golfo de** *gulf* NW Costa Rica
38 H11 **Pāpa'ikou** *var.* Papaikou. Hawaii, USA, C Pacific Ocean 19°45′N 155°06′W
41 R15 **Papaloapan, Río** ≈ S Mexico
184 L6 **Papakura** Auckland, North Island, New Zealand 37°03′S 174°57′E
41 Q13 **Papantla** *var.* Papantla de Olarte. Veracruz-Llave, E Mexico 20°30′N 97°21′W
Papantla de Olarte *see* Papantla
191 P8 **Papara** Tahiti, W French Polynesia 17°45′S 149°33′W
184 K4 **Paparoa** Northland, North Island, New Zealand 36°06′S 174°12′E
185 G16 **Paparoa Range** ▲▲ South Island, New Zealand
115 K20 **Pápas, Akrotírio** *headland* Ikaría, Dodekánisa, Greece, Aegean Sea 37°31′N 25°58′E
96 L2 **Papa Stour** *island* NE Scotland, United Kingdom
184 L6 **Papatoetoe** Auckland, North Island, New Zealand 36°58′S 174°52′E
185 E25 **Papatowai** Otago, South Island, New Zealand 46°33′S 169°33′E
96 K4 **Papa Westray** *island* NE Scotland, United Kingdom
191 T10 **Papeete** ○ (French Polynesia) Tahiti, W French Polynesia 17°32′S 149°34′W
100 F11 **Papenburg** Niedersachsen, NW Germany 53°04′N 07°24′E
98 H13 **Papendrecht** Zuid-Holland, SW Netherlands 51°50′N 04°42′E
191 Q7 **Papenoo** Tahiti, W French Polynesia 17°29′S 149°25′W
191 Q7 **Papenoo Rivière** ≈ Tahiti, W French Polynesia
191 N7 **Papetoai** Moorea, W French Polynesia 17°29′S 149°52′W
92 L3 **Papey** *island* E Iceland
Paphos *see* Páfos
40 H5 **Papigochic, Río** ≈ NW Mexico
118 E10 **Papilė** Šiaulai, NW Lithuania 56°08′N 22°51′E
29 S15 **Papillion** Nebraska, C USA 41°09′N 96°02′W
15 T5 **Papinachois** ≈ Québec, SE Canada
171 X13 **Papua** *var.* Irian Barat, West Irian, West New Guinea, West Papua; *prev.* Dutch New Guinea, Irian Jaya, Netherlands New Guinea. ◐ *province* E Indonesia
Papua and New Guinea, Territory of *see* Papua New Guinea
170 V10 **Papua Barat** *off.* Propinsi Irian Jaya Barat, *Eng.* West Irian Jaya. ◐ *province* E Indonesia
186 C9 **Papua, Gulf of** *gulf* S Papua New Guinea
186 C8 **Papua New Guinea** *off.* Independent State of Papua New Guinea; *prev.* Territory of Papua and New Guinea. ◆ *commonwealth republic* NW Melanesia
Papua New Guinea, Independent State of *see* Papua New Guinea
192 H8 **Papua Plateau** *undersea feature* N Coral Sea
112 G9 **Papuk** ▲▲ NE Croatia
Papun *see* Hpapun
42 L14 **Paquera** Puntarenas, W Costa Rica 09°52′N 84°56′W
58 I13 **Pará** *off.* Estado do Pará. ◐ *state* NE Brazil
55 V9 **Para** ◐ *district* N Surinam
Pará *see* Belém
180 I8 **Paraburdoo** Western Australia 23°07′S 117°40′E
57 E16 **Paracas, Península de** *peninsula* W Peru
59 L19 **Paracatu** Minas Gerais, NE Brazil 17°14′S 46°52′W
192 E6 **Paracel Islands** ◇ *disputed territory* SE Asia
182 I6 **Parachilna** South Australia 31°09′S 138°23′E
149 R6 **Pārachinār** Khyber Pakhtunkhwa, NW Pakistan 33°56′N 70°04′E
112 N13 **Paraćin** Serbia, C Serbia 43°51′N 21°25′E
Paradip *see* Krishnarājāsāgara
14 K8 **Paradis** Québec, SE Canada 48°13′N 76°36′W
39 N11 **Paradise** *var.* Paradise Hill. Alaska, USA 62°28′N 160°09′W
35 O5 **Paradise** California, W USA 39°42′N 121°39′W
35 X11 **Paradise** Nevada, W USA 36°05′N 115°10′W
Paradise Hill *see* Paradise
37 R11 **Paradise Hills** New Mexico, SW USA 35°12′N 106°42′W
Paradise of the Pacific *see* Hawai'i
36 L13 **Paradise Valley** Arizona, SW USA 33°31′N 111°56′W
35 T2 **Paradise Valley** Nevada, W USA 41°30′N 117°30′W
115 O22 **Paradisi** ✈ (Ródos) Ródos, Dodekánisa, Greece, Aegean Sea 36°24′N 28°08′E
154 P12 **Pārādwīp** Orissa, E India 20°17′N 86°42′E
Pará, Estado do *see* Pará
Paraetonium *see* Marsā Maṭrūḥ
117 R4 **Parafiyivka** Chernihivs'ka Oblast', N Ukraine 50°53′N 32°40′E
36 K7 **Paragonah** Utah, W USA 37°53′N 112°46′W
27 X9 **Paragould** Arkansas, C USA 36°02′N 90°30′W
47 X8 **Paraguaçu** *var.* Paraguassú. ≈ E Brazil
60 J9 **Paraguaçu Paulista** São Paulo, S Brazil 22°22′S 50°35′W
54 H4 **Paraguaipoa** Zulia, NW Venezuela 11°21′N 71°58′W
62 O6 **Paraguarí** Paraguarí, S Paraguay 25°36′S 57°06′W
62 O7 **Paraguarí** *off.* Departamento de Paraguarí. ◐ *department* S Paraguay
Paraguarí, Departamento de *see* Paraguarí
57 O16 **Paraguá, Río** ≈ NE Bolivia
55 O8 **Paragua, Río** ≈ SE Venezuela
Paraguassú *see* Paraguaçu
62 N5 **Paraguay** ◆ *republic* C South America
47 U10 **Paraguay** *var.* Río Paraguay. ≈ C South America
Paraguay, Río *see* Paraguay
Parahiba/Parahyba *see* Paraíba
59 P15 **Paraíba** *off.* Estado da Paraíba; *prev.* Parahiba, Parahyba. ◐ *state* E Brazil
Paraíba *see* João Pessoa
60 P9 **Paraíba do Sul, Rio** ≈ SE Brazil
Paraíba, Estado da *see* Paraíba
Parainen *see* Pargas
43 N14 **Paraíso** Cartago, C Costa Rica 09°51′N 83°50′W
41 U14 **Paraíso** Tabasco, SE Mexico 18°26′N 93°10′W
57 O17 **Paraiso, Río** ≈ E Bolivia
Parajd *see* Praid
77 S14 **Parakou** C Benin 09°23′N 02°40′E
115 F20 **Paralía Tyrou** Pelopónnisos, S Greece 37°17′N 22°50′E
121 Q2 **Paralímni** E Cyprus 35°02′N 34°00′E
115 G18 **Paralímni, Límni** ◎ C Greece
55 W8 **Paramaribo** ● (Surinam) Paramaribo, N Surinam 05°52′N 55°14′W
55 W9 **Paramaribo** ◐ *district* N Surinam
55 W9 **Paramaribo** ✈ Paramaribo, N Surinam 05°52′N 55°14′W
Paramithiá *see* Paramythiá
56 C13 **Paramonga** Lima, W Peru 10°42′S 77°50′W
123 V12 **Paramushir, Ostrov** *island* SE Russian Federation
115 C16 **Paramythiá** *var.* Paramithiá. Ípeiros, W Greece 39°28′N 20°31′E
62 M10 **Paraná** Entre Ríos, E Argentina 31°48′S 60°29′W
60 H11 **Paraná** *off.* Estado do Paraná. ◐ *state* S Brazil
47 U11 **Paraná** *var.* Alto Paraná. ≈ C South America
Paraná, Estado do *see* Paraná
60 K12 **Paranaguá** Paraná, S Brazil 25°32′S 48°36′W
59 J20 **Paranaíba, Rio** ≈ E Brazil
61 C19 **Paraná Ibicuy, Río** ≈ E Argentina
59 H15 **Paranaíta** Mato Grosso, W Brazil 09°35′S 57°01′W
60 H9 **Paranapanema, Rio** ≈ S Brazil
60 K11 **Paranapiacaba, Serra do** ▲▲ S Brazil
60 H9 **Paranavaí** Paraná, S Brazil 23°02′S 52°36′W
143 N5 **Parandak** Markazī, W Iran 35°19′N 50°40′E
114 I12 **Paranésti** *var.* Paranestio. Anatolikí Makedonía kai Thráki, NE Greece 41°16′N 24°31′E
Paranestio *see* Paranésti
191 W11 **Paraoa** *atoll* Îles Tuamotu, C French Polynesia
184 L13 **Paraparaumu** Wellington, North Island, New Zealand 40°55′S 175°01′E
57 N20 **Parapeti, Río** ≈ SE Bolivia
54 L10 **Paraque, Cerro** ▲ W Venezuela 06°00′S 67°00′W
154 I11 **Parāsiya** Madhya Pradesh, C India 22°11′N 78°50′E
115 M23 **Paraspóri, Akrotírio** *headland* Kárpathos, SE Greece 35°54′N 27°15′E
60 O10 **Parati** Rio de Janeiro, SE Brazil 23°15′S 44°42′W
59 K14 **Parauapebas** Pará, N Brazil 06°03′S 49°48′W
103 Q10 **Paray-le-Monial** Saône-et-Loire, C France 46°27′N 04°07′E
Parbatsar *see* Parvatsar
154 G13 **Parbhani** Mahārāshtra, C India 19°16′N 76°51′E
100 L10 **Parchim** Mecklenburg-Vorpommern, N Germany 53°26′N 11°51′E
Parchwitz *see* Prochowice
110 P13 **Parczew** Lubelskie, E Poland 51°40′N 23°E
60 L8 **Pardo, Rio** ≈ S Brazil
111 E16 **Pardubice** *Ger.* Pardubitz. Pardubický Kraj, C Czech Republic 50°01′N 15°47′E
111 E17 **Pardubický Kraj** ◐ *region* N Czech Republic
Pardubitz *see* Pardubice
119 F16 **Parechcha** *Pol.* Porzecze, *Rus.* Porech'ye. Hrodzyenskaya Voblasts', W Belarus 53°53′N 24°08′E
59 F17 **Parecis, Chapada dos** *var.* Serra dos Parecis. ▲▲ W Brazil
Parecis, Serra dos *see* Parecis, Chapada dos
104 M4 **Paredes de Nava** Castilla y León, N Spain 42°09′N 04°42′W
189 U12 **Parem** *island* Chuuk, C Micronesia
189 O12 **Parem Island** *island* E Micronesia
184 I1 **Parengarenga Harbour** *inlet* North Island, New Zealand
15 N8 **Parent** Québec, SE Canada 47°55′N 74°36′W
102 J14 **Parentis-en-Born** Landes, SW France 44°22′N 01°04′W
Parenzo *see* Poreč
185 G20 **Pareora** Canterbury, South Island, New Zealand 44°28′S 171°12′E
171 N14 **Parepare** Sulawesi, C Indonesia 04°S 119°40′E
115 B16 **Párga** Ípeiros, W Greece 39°18′N 20°19′E
93 K20 **Pargas** *Swe.* Parainen. Länsi-Suomi, SW Finland 60°18′N 22°20′E
64 O5 **Pargo, Ponta do** *headland* Madeira, Portugal, NE Atlantic Ocean 32°48′N 17°17′W
Paria, Golfo de *see* Paria, Gulf of
55 N6 **Pariaguán** Anzoátegui, NE Venezuela 08°51′N 64°43′W
45 X17 **Paria, Gulf of** *var.* Golfo de Paria. *gulf* Trinidad and Tobago/Venezuela
57 I15 **Pariamanu, Río** ≈ E Peru
36 L8 **Paria River** ≈ Utah, W USA
Parichi *see* Parychy
40 M14 **Paricutín, Volcán** ⛰ C Mexico 19°25′N 102°20′W
43 P16 **Parida, Isla** *island* SW Panama
55 T8 **Parika** NE Guyana 06°51′N 58°25′W
93 O18 **Parikkala** Etelä-Suomi, SE Finland 61°33′N 29°34′E
58 E10 **Parima, Serra** *var.* Sierra Parima. ▲ Brazil/Venezuela *see also* Parima, Sierra
55 N11 **Parima, Sierra** *var.* Serra Parima. ▲ Brazil/Venezuela *see also* Parima, Serra
57 F17 **Parinacochas, Laguna** ◎ SW Peru
56 A9 **Pariñas, Punta** *headland* NW Peru 04°45′S 81°22′W
58 H12 **Parintins** Amazonas, N Brazil 02°38′S 56°45′W
103 O5 **Paris** *anc.* Lutetia, Lutetia Parisiorum, Parisii. ● (France) Paris, N France 48°52′N 02°19′E
191 Y2 **Paris** Kiritimati, E Kiribati 01°55′N 157°30′W
27 S11 **Paris** Arkansas, C USA 35°17′N 93°46′W
33 S16 **Paris** Idaho, NW USA 42°14′N 111°24′W
31 N14 **Paris** Illinois, N USA 39°36′N 87°42′W
20 M5 **Paris** Kentucky, S USA 38°13′N 84°15′W
27 V3 **Paris** Missouri, C USA 39°28′N 92°00′W
20 H8 **Paris** Tennessee, S USA 36°19′N 88°20′W
25 V5 **Paris** Texas, SW USA 33°41′N 95°33′W
Parisii *see* Paris
43 S16 **Parita** Herrera, S Panama 08°01′N 80°30′W
43 S16 **Parita, Bahía de** *bay* S Panama
93 K18 **Parkano** Länsi-Suomi, W Finland 62°03′N 23°E
Parkan/Párkány *see* Štúrovo
27 N6 **Park City** Kansas, C USA 37°48′N 97°19′W
36 L3 **Park City** Utah, W USA 40°39′N 111°30′W
36 I12 **Parker** Arizona, SW USA 34°07′N 114°16′W
23 R9 **Parker** Florida, SE USA 30°07′N 85°36′W
29 R11 **Parker** South Dakota, N USA 43°24′N 97°08′W
35 Z14 **Parker Dam** California, W USA 34°17′N 114°08′W
29 W13 **Parkersburg** Iowa, C USA 42°34′N 92°47′W
21 Q3 **Parkersburg** West Virginia, NE USA 39°17′N 81°33′W
29 T7 **Parkers Prairie** Minnesota, N USA 46°09′N 95°19′W
171 P8 **Parker Volcano** ⛰ Mindanao, S Philippines 06°09′N 124°52′E
181 W13 **Parkes** New South Wales, SE Australia 33°10′S 148°10′E
30 K4 **Park Falls** Wisconsin, N USA 45°57′N 90°25′W
Parkhar *see* Farkhor
14 E16 **Parkhill** Ontario, S Canada 43°11′N 81°39′W
29 T5 **Park Rapids** Minnesota, N USA 46°55′N 95°03′W
29 Q3 **Park River** North Dakota, N USA 48°24′N 97°44′W
29 Q11 **Parkston** South Dakota, N USA 43°24′N 97°58′W
10 L17 **Parksville** Vancouver Island, British Columbia, SW Canada 49°13′N 124°13′W
37 S3 **Parkview Mountain** ▲ Colorado, C USA 40°19′N 106°08′W
105 N8 **Parla** Madrid, C Spain 40°13′N 03°48′W
29 S8 **Parle, Lac qui** ⊠ Minnesota, N USA
155 G14 **Parli Vaijnāth** Mahārāshtra, C India 18°53′N 76°36′E
106 F9 **Parma** Emilia-Romagna, N Italy 44°50′N 10°20′E
31 T11 **Parma** Ohio, N USA 41°24′N 81°43′W
Parnahyba *see* Parnaíba
58 N13 **Parnaíba** *var.* Parnahyba. Piauí, E Brazil 02°58′S 41°46′W
65 J14 **Parnaíba Ridge** *undersea feature* C Atlantic Ocean
58 N13 **Parnaíba, Rio** ≈ NE Brazil
115 F18 **Parnassós** ▲▲ C Greece
185 J17 **Parnassus** Canterbury, South Island, New Zealand 42°41′S 173°18′E
182 H10 **Parndana** South Australia 35°48′S 137°13′E
115 H19 **Párnitha** ▲▲ C Greece
Parnon *see* Párnonas
115 F21 **Párnonas** *var.* Parnon. ▲▲ S Greece
118 G5 **Pärnu** *Ger.* Pernau, *Latv.* Pērnava; *prev. Rus.* Pernov. Pärnumaa, SW Estonia 58°24′N 24°32′E
118 G6 **Pärnu** *var.* Parnu Jõgi, *Ger.* Pernau. ≈ SW Estonia
118 G5 **Pärnu-Jaagupi** *Ger.* Sankt-Jakobi. Pärnumaa, SW Estonia 58°36′N 24°30′E
Parnu Jõgi *see* Pärnu
118 G5 **Pärnu Laht** *Ger.* Pernauer Bucht. *bay* SW Estonia
118 F5 **Pärnumaa** *var.* Pärnu Maakond. ◐ *province* SW Estonia
Pärnu Maakond *see* Pärnumaa
153 T11 **Paro** W Bhutan 27°23′N 89°31′E
153 T11 **Paro** ✈ (Thimphu) W Bhutan 27°23′N 89°31′E
185 G17 **Paroa** West Coast, South Island, New Zealand 42°31′S 171°10′E
163 X14 **Paro-ho** *var.* Hwach'ŏn-chŏsuji; *prev.* P'aro-ho. ⊠ N South Korea
P'aro-ho *see* Paro-ho
115 J21 **Pároikiá** *prev.* Páros. Páros, Kykládes, Greece, Aegean Sea 37°04′N 25°06′E
183 N6 **Paroo River** *seasonal river* New South Wales/Queensland, SE Australia
Paropamisus Range *see* Sefīd Kūh, Selseleh-ye
Paropamisus Range *see* Sefīd Kūh, Selseleh-ye
115 J21 **Páros** *island* Kykládes, Greece, Aegean Sea
Páros *see* Pároikiá
36 K7 **Parowan** Utah, W USA 37°50′N 112°49′W
103 U13 **Parpaillon** ▲▲ SE France
108 I9 **Parpan** Graubünden, S Switzerland 46°46′N 09°32′E
62 G13 **Parral** Maule, C Chile 36°08′S 71°52′W
Parral *see* Hidalgo del Parral
183 T9 **Parramatta** New South Wales, SE Australia 33°49′S 150°59′E
21 Y6 **Parramore Island** *island* Virginia, NE USA
40 M8 **Parras** *var.* Parras de la Fuente. Coahuila, NE Mexico 25°26′N 102°07′W
Parras de la Fuente *see* Parras
42 M14 **Parrita** Puntarenas, S Costa Rica 09°30′N 84°20′W
Parry group *see* Mukojima-rettō
14 G13 **Parry Island** *island* Ontario, S Canada
197 O9 **Parry Islands** *island group* Nunavut, NW Canada
14 G12 **Parry Sound** Ontario, S Canada 45°21′N 80°03′W
110 F7 **Parsęta** *Ger.* Persante. ≈ NW Poland
28 L3 **Parshall** North Dakota, N USA 47°57′N 102°07′W
27 Q7 **Parsons** Kansas, C USA 37°20′N 95°15′W
20 H9 **Parsons** Tennessee, S USA 35°39′N 88°07′W
21 T3 **Parsons** West Virginia, NE USA 39°06′N 79°43′W
Parsonstown *see* Birr
100 P11 **Parsteiner See** ◎ NE Germany
107 I24 **Partanna** Sicilia, Italy, C Mediterranean Sea 37°43′N 12°54′E
108 J8 **Partenen** Graubünden, E Switzerland 46°58′N 10°01′E
102 K9 **Parthenay** Deux-Sèvres, W France 46°39′N 00°13′W
95 J19 **Partille** Västra Götaland, S Sweden 57°43′N 12°12′E
107 I23 **Partinico** Sicilia, Italy, C Mediterranean Sea 38°03′N 13°07′E
111 I20 **Partizánske** *prev.* Šimonovany, *Hung.* Simony. Trenčiansky Kraj, W Slovakia 48°35′N 18°23′E
58 H11 **Paru de Oeste, Rio** ≈ N Brazil
182 K9 **Paruna** South Australia 34°45′S 140°43′E
58 I11 **Paru, Rio** ≈ N Brazil
Parvān *see* Parwān
155 M14 **Pārvatipuram** Andhra Pradesh, E India 17°01′N 81°47′E
152 G12 **Parvatsar** *prev.* Parbatsar. Rājasthān, N India 26°52′N 74°49′E
149 Q5 **Parwān** *prev.* Parvān. E Afghanistan
158 I15 **Paryang** Xizang Zizhiqu, W China 30°04′N 83°28′E
119 M18 **Parychy** *Rus.* Parichi. Homyel'skaya Voblasts', SE Belarus 52°48′N 29°25′E
83 J21 **Parys** Free State, C South Africa 26°55′S 27°28′E
35 T15 **Pasadena** California, W USA 34°09′N 118°09′W
25 W11 **Pasadena** Texas, SW USA 29°41′N 95°13′W
56 B8 **Pasaje** El Oro, SW Ecuador 03°23′S 79°50′W
137 T9 **Pasanauri** *prev.* P'asanauri. N Georgia 42°21′N 44°40′E
P'asanauri *see* Pasanauri
168 I13 **Pasapuat** Pulau Pagai Utara, W Indonesia 02°36′S 99°58′E
Pasawng *see* Hpasawng
114 L13 **Paşayiğit** Edirne, NW Turkey 40°58′N 26°38′E
23 N9 **Pascagoula** Mississippi, S USA 30°21′N 88°32′W
22 M8 **Pascagoula River** ≈ Mississippi, S USA
116 F12 **Paşcani** *Hung.* Páskán. Iaşi, NE Romania 47°14′N 26°46′E
109 T4 **Pasching** Oberösterreich, N Austria 48°16′N 14°10′E
32 K10 **Pasco** Washington, NW USA 46°13′N 119°06′W
56 E13 **Pasco** *off.* Departamento de Pasco. ◐ *department* C Peru
Pasco, Departamento de *see* Pasco
191 N11 **Pascua, Isla de** *var.* Rapa Nui, Easter Island. *island* E Pacific Ocean
63 G21 **Pascua, Río** ≈ S Chile
103 N1 **Pas-de-Calais** ◐ *department* N France
100 P10 **Pasewalk** Mecklenburg-Vorpommern, NE Germany 53°31′N 13°59′E
11 T10 **Pasfield Lake** ◎ Saskatchewan, C Canada
Pa-shih Hai-hsia *see* Bashi Channel
Pashkeni *see* Bolyarovo
Pashmakli *see* Smolyan
153 X10 **Pāsighāt** Arunāchel Pradesh, NE India 28°08′N 95°13′E
137 Q12 **Pasinler** Erzurum, NE Turkey 39°59′N 41°41′E
Pasi Oloy, Qatorkŭhi *see* Zaalayskiy Khrebet
42 E3 **Pasión, Río de la** ≈ N Guatemala
168 J12 **Pasirganting** Sumatera, W Indonesia 02°04′S 100°51′E
Pasirpangarayan *see* Bagansiapiapi
168 K6 **Pasir Puteh** *var.* Pasir Putih. Kelantan, Peninsular Malaysia 05°50′N 102°24′E
Pasir Putih *see* Pasir Puteh
169 R9 **Pasir, Tanjung** *headland* East Malaysia 02°24′N 111°12′E
95 N20 **Påskallavik** Kalmar, S Sweden 57°10′N 16°25′E
Páskán *see* Paşcani
Paskevicha, Zaliv *see* Tushchybas, Zaliv
110 K7 **Pasłęk** *Ger.* Preußisch Holland. Warmińsko-Mazurskie, NE Poland 54°03′N 19°40′E
110 K7 **Pasłęka** *Ger.* Passarge. ≈ N Poland
148 K16 **Pasni** Baluchistān, SW Pakistan 25°13′N 63°30′E
63 I18 **Paso de Indios** Chubut, S Argentina 43°52′S 69°06′W
54 L7 **Paso del Caballo** Guárico, N Venezuela 08°19′N 67°08′W
61 E15 **Paso de los Libres** Corrientes, NE Argentina 29°43′S 57°09′W
61 E18 **Paso de los Toros** Tacuarembó, C Uruguay 32°45′S 56°30′W
Pasoeroean *see* Pasuruan
35 P12 **Paso Robles** California, W USA 35°37′N 120°42′W
15 Y7 **Paspébiac** Québec, SE Canada 48°03′N 65°10′W
11 U14 **Pasquia Hills** ▲▲ Saskatchewan, S Canada
149 W7 **Pasrūr** Punjab, E Pakistan 32°12′N 74°42′E
30 M1 **Passage Island** *island* Michigan, N USA
65 B24 **Passage Islands** *island group* W Falkland Islands
8 K5 **Passage Point** *headland* Banks Island, Northwest Territories, NW Canada 73°31′N 115°12′W
Passarge *see* Pasłęka
115 C15 **Passarón** *ancient monument* Ípeiros, W Greece
Passarowitz *see* Požarevac
101 O22 **Passau** Bayern, SE Germany 48°34′N 13°28′E
22 M9 **Pass Christian** Mississippi, S USA 30°19′N 89°15′W
107 L26 **Passero, Capo** *headland* Sicilia, Italy, C Mediterranean Sea 36°40′N 15°09′E
171 P5 **Passi** Panay Island, C Philippines 11°05′N 122°37′E
61 H14 **Passo Fundo** Rio Grande do Sul, S Brazil 28°16′S 52°20′W
60 H13 **Passo Fundo, Barragem de** ⊠ S Brazil
61 H15 **Passo Real, Barragem de** ⊠ S Brazil
59 L20 **Passos** Minas Gerais, NE Brazil 20°45′S 46°38′W
167 X10 **Passu Keah** *island* S Paracel Islands
118 J13 **Pastavy** *Pol.* Postawy, *Rus.* Postavy. Vitsyebskaya Voblasts', NW Belarus 55°07′N 26°50′E
56 D7 **Pastaza** ◐ *province* E Ecuador
56 D9 **Pastaza, Río** ≈ Ecuador/Peru
61 A21 **Pasteur** Buenos Aires, E Argentina 35°10′S 62°14′W
15 V3 **Pasteur** ≈ Québec, SE Canada
147 Q12 **Pastigav** *Rus.* Pastigov. W Tajikistan 39°27′N 69°16′E
Pastigov *see* Pastigav
54 C13 **Pasto** Nariño, SW Colombia 01°12′N 77°17′W
38 M10 **Pastol Bay** *bay* Alaska, USA
37 O8 **Pastora Peak** ▲ Arizona, SW USA 36°48′N 109°10′W
105 O8 **Pastrana** Castilla-La Mancha, C Spain 40°24′N 02°55′W
169 S16 **Pasuruan** *prev.* Pasoeroean. Jawa, C Indonesia 07°38′S 112°44′E
118 F11 **Pasvalys** Panevėžys, N Lithuania 56°03′N 24°24′E
111 K21 **Pásztó** Nógrád, N Hungary 47°57′N 19°41′E
189 U12 **Pata** *var.* Patta. *atoll* Chuuk Islands, C Micronesia
36 M16 **Patagonia** Arizona, SW USA 31°32′N 110°45′W
63 H20 **Patagonia** *physical region* Argentina/Chile
Patalung *see* Phatthalung
154 D9 **Pātan** Gujarāt, W India 23°51′N 72°11′E
154 J10 **Pātan** Madhya Pradesh, C India 23°19′N 79°41′E
171 S11 **Patani** Pulau Halmahera, E Indonesia 0°19′N 128°46′E
Patani *see* Pattani
15 V7 **Patapédia Est** ≈ Québec, SE Canada
116 K13 **Pătâriagele** *prev.* Pătîriagele. Buzău, SE Romania 45°19′N 26°21′E
Patavium *see* Padova
182 I5 **Patawarta Hill** ▲ South Australia 30°57′S 138°42′E
182 L10 **Patchewollock** Victoria, SE Australia 35°24′S 142°11′E
184 K11 **Patea** Taranaki, North Island, New Zealand 39°48′S 174°35′E
184 K11 **Patea** ≈ North Island, New Zealand
77 U15 **Pategi** Kwara, C Nigeria 08°39′N 05°46′E
81 K20 **Pate Island** *var.* Patta Island. *island* SE Kenya
105 S10 **Paterna** Valenciana, E Spain 39°30′N 00°24′W
109 R9 **Paternion** *Slvn.* Špatrjan. Kärnten, S Austria 46°40′N 13°43′E
107 L24 **Paternò** *anc.* Hybla, Hybla Major. Sicilia, Italy, C Mediterranean Sea 37°34′N 14°55′E
32 J7 **Pateros** Washington, NW USA 48°01′N 119°55′W
18 J14 **Paterson** New Jersey, NE USA 40°55′N 74°12′W
32 J10 **Paterson** Washington, NW USA 45°56′N 119°37′W
185 C25 **Paterson Inlet** *inlet* Stewart Island, New Zealand
98 N6 **Paterswolde** Drenthe, NE Netherlands 53°07′N 06°32′E
152 H7 **Pathānkot** Himāchal Pradesh, N India 32°16′N 75°43′E
166 K8 **Pathein** *var.* Bassein. Ayeyarwady, SW Burma (Myanmar) 16°46′N 94°45′E
33 W15 **Pathfinder Reservoir** ⊠ Wyoming, C USA
167 O11 **Pathum Thani** *var.* Patumdhani, Prathum Thani. Pathum Thani, C Thailand 14°03′N 100°29′E
54 C12 **Patía** *var.* El Bordo. Cauca, SW Colombia 02°07′N 76°57′W
152 I9 **Patiāla** *var.* Puttiala. Punjab, NW India 30°21′N 76°27′E
54 B12 **Patía, Río** ≈ SW Colombia
188 D15 **Pati Point** *headland* NE Guam 13°36′N 144°39′E
Pătîriagele *see* Pătâriagele
56 C13 **Pativilca** Lima, W Peru 10°44′S 77°45′W
166 M1 **Patkai Bum** *var.* Patkai Range. ▲▲ Burma (Myanmar)/India
Patkai Range *see* Patkai Bum
115 L20 **Pátmos** Pátmos, Dodekánisa, Greece, Aegean Sea 37°18′N 26°32′E
115 L20 **Pátmos** *island* Dodekánisa, Greece, Aegean Sea
153 P13 **Patna** *var.* Azimabad. *state capital* Bihār, N India 25°36′N 85°11′E
154 M12 **Patnāgarh** Orissa, E India 20°42′N 83°12′E
171 O5 **Patnongon** Panay Island, C Philippines 10°56′N 122°03′E
137 S13 **Patnos** Ağrı, E Turkey 39°14′N 42°52′E
60 H12 **Pato Branco** Paraná, S Brazil 26°20′S 52°40′W
31 O16 **Patoka Lake** ◎ Indiana, N USA
92 L9 **Patoniva** *Lapp.* Buoddobohki. Lappi, N Finland 69°44′N 27°01′E
113 K21 **Patos** *var.* Patosi. Fier, SW Albania 40°40′N 19°37′E
Patos *see* Patos de Minas
59 K19 **Patos de Minas** *var.* Patos. Minas Gerais, NE Brazil 18°35′S 46°32′W
Patosi *see* Patos
61 I17 **Patos, Lagoa dos** *lagoon* S Brazil
62 J9 **Patquía** La Rioja, C Argentina 30°02′S 66°54′W
115 E19 **Pátra** *Eng.* Patras; *prev.* Pátrai. Dytikí Elláda, S Greece 38°14′N 21°45′E
115 D18 **Patraïkós Kólpos** *gulf* S Greece
Pátrai/Patras *see* Pátra
92 G2 **Patreksfjördhur** Vestfirdhir, W Iceland 65°33′N 23°54′W
24 M7 **Patricia** Texas, SW USA 32°34′N 102°00′W
63 F21 **Patricio Lynch, Isla** *island* S Chile
Patta *see* Pata
Patta Island *see* Pate Island
167 O16 **Pattani** *var.* Patani. Pattani, SW Thailand 06°50′N 101°20′E
167 P12 **Pattaya** Chon Buri, S Thailand 12°57′N 100°53′E
19 S4 **Patten** Maine, NE USA 45°58′N 68°27′W
35 O9 **Patterson** California, W USA 37°27′N 121°07′W
22 J10 **Patterson** Louisiana, S USA 29°41′N 91°18′W
35 R7 **Patterson, Mount** ▲ California, W USA 38°27′N 119°16′W
31 P4 **Patterson, Point** *headland* Michigan, N USA 45°58′N 85°39′W
107 L23 **Patti** Sicilia, Italy, C Mediterranean Sea 38°08′N 14°58′E
107 L23 **Patti, Golfo di** *gulf* Sicilia, Italy
93 L14 **Pattijoki** Oulu, W Finland 64°41′N 24°40′E
193 Q4 **Patton Escarpment** *undersea feature* E Pacific Ocean
27 S2 **Pattonsburg** Missouri, C USA 40°03′N 94°08′W
0 D6 **Patton Seamount** *undersea feature* NE Pacific Ocean 54°40′N 150°30′W
10 J12 **Pattullo, Mount** ▲ British Columbia, W Canada 56°18′N 129°43′W
153 U16 **Patuakhali** *var.* Patukhali. Barisal, S Bangladesh 22°20′N 90°20′E
42 M5 **Patuca, Río** ≈ E Honduras
Patukhali *see* Patuakhali
Patumdhani *see* Pathum Thani
40 M14 **Pátzcuaro** Michoacán, SW Mexico 19°30′N 101°38′W
42 C6 **Patzicía** Chimaltenango, S Guatemala 14°38′N 90°52′W
102 K16 **Pau** Pyrénées-Atlantiques, SW France 43°18′N 00°22′W
102 J12 **Pauillac** Gironde, SW France 45°12′N 00°44′W
166 L5 **Pauk** Magway, W Burma (Myanmar) 21°25′N 94°30′E
8 I6 **Paulatuk** Northwest Territories, NW Canada 69°23′N 124°W
42 K5 **Paulayá, Río** ≈ NE Honduras
22 M6 **Paulding** Mississippi, S USA 32°01′N 89°01′W
31 Q12 **Paulding** Ohio, N USA 41°08′N 84°34′W
29 S12 **Paullina** Iowa, C USA 42°58′N 95°41′W
59 P15 **Paulo Afonso** Bahia, E Brazil 09°21′S 38°14′W
38 M16 **Pauloff Harbor** *var.* Pavlor Harbour. Sanak Island, Alaska, USA 54°26′N 162°43′W
27 N12 **Pauls Valley** Oklahoma, C USA 34°46′N 97°14′W
166 L7 **Paungde** Bago, C Burma (Myanmar) 18°30′N 95°30′E
Pauni *see* Paoni
152 K9 **Pauri** Uttaranchal, N India 30°08′N 78°48′E
Pautalia *see* Kyustendil
142 J5 **Pāveh** Kermānshāhān, NW Iran 35°02′N 46°15′E
114 I9 **Pavel Banya** Stara Zagora, C Bulgaria 42°35′N 25°19′E
126 L5 **Pavelets** Ryazanskaya Oblast', W Russian Federation 53°47′N 39°22′E
106 D8 **Pavia** *anc.* Ticinum. Lombardia, N Italy 45°10′N 09°10′E
118 C9 **Pāvilosta** W Latvia 56°52′N 21°12′E
125 P14 **Pavino** Kostromskaya Oblast', NW Russian Federation 59°10′N 46°09′E
114 J8 **Pavlikeni** Veliko Tŭrnovo, N Bulgaria 43°14′N 25°20′E
145 T8 **Pavlodar** Pavlodar, NE Kazakhstan 52°21′N 76°59′E
145 S9 **Pavlodar** *off.* Pavlodarskaya Oblast', *Kaz.* Pavlodar Oblysy. ◐ *province* NE Kazakhstan
Pavlodar Oblysy/Pavlodarskaya Oblast' *see* Pavlodar
Pavlograd *see* Pavlohrad
117 U7 **Pavlohrad** *Rus.* Pavlograd. Dnipropetrovs'ka Oblast', E Ukraine 48°32′N 35°50′E
Pavlor Harbour *see* Pauloff Harbor
145 R9 **Pavlovka** Akmola, C Kazakhstan 51°22′N 72°35′E
127 V4 **Pavlovka** Respublika Bashkortostan, W Russian Federation 55°28′N 56°36′E
127 Q7 **Pavlovka** Ul'yanovskaya Oblast', W Russian Federation 52°40′N 47°08′E
127 N3 **Pavlovo** Nizhegorodskaya Oblast', W Russian Federation 55°59′N 43°03′E
126 L9 **Pavlovsk** Voronezhskaya Oblast', W Russian Federation 50°26′N 40°08′E
126 L13 **Pavlovskaya** Krasnodarskiy Kray, SW Russian Federation 46°06′N 39°52′E
117 S7 **Pavlysh** Kirovohrads'ka Oblast', C Ukraine 48°54′N 33°20′E

106 *F10* **Pavullo nel Frignano** Emilia-Romagna, C Italy *44°19′N 10°52′E*
27 *P8* **Pawhuska** Oklahoma, C USA *36°42′N 96°21′W*
21 *U13* **Pawleys Island** South Carolina, SE USA *33°27′N 79°07′W*
30 *K14* **Pawnee** Illinois, N USA *39°35′N 89°34′W*
27 *O9* **Pawnee** Oklahoma, C USA *36°21′N 96°50′W*
37 *U2* **Pawnee Buttes** ▲ Colorado, C USA *40°49′N 103°58′W*
29 *S17* **Pawnee City** Nebraska, C USA *40°06′N 96°09′W*
26 *K5* **Pawnee River** ⇝ Kansas, C USA
167 *N6* **Pawn, Nam** ⇝ C Burma (Myanmar)
31 *O10* **Paw Paw** Michigan, N USA *42°12′N 86°09′W*
31 *O10* **Paw Paw Lake** Michigan, N USA *42°12′N 86°16′W*
19 *O12* **Pawtucket** Rhode Island, NE USA *41°52′N 71°22′W*
Pax Augusta *see* Badajoz
115 *I25* **Paximádia** *island* SE Greece
Pax Julia *see* Beja
115 *B16* **Paxoí** *island* Iónia Nisiá, Greece, C Mediterranean Sea
39 *S10* **Paxson** Alaska, USA *62°58′N 145°27′W*
147 *O11* **Paxtakor** Jizzax Viloyati, C Uzbekistan *40°21′N 67°54′E*
30 *M13* **Paxton** Illinois, N USA *40°27′N 88°06′W*
124 *J11* **Pay** Respublika Kareliya, NW Russian Federation *61°10′N 34°24′E*
166 *M8* **Payagyi** Bago, SW Burma (Myanmar) *17°28′N 96°32′E*
108 *C9* **Payerne** *Ger.* Peterlingen. Vaud, W Switzerland *46°49′N 06°57′E*
32 *M13* **Payette** Idaho, NW USA *44°04′N 116°55′W*
32 *M13* **Payette River** ⇝ Idaho, NW USA
125 *V2* **Pay-Khoy, Khrebet** ▲▲ NW Russian Federation
Payne *see* Kangirsuk
12 *K4* **Payne, Lac** ◎ Québec, NE Canada
29 *T8* **Paynesville** Minnesota, N USA *45°22′N 94°42′W*
169 *S8* **Payong, Tanjung** *cape* East Malaysia
Payo Obispo *see* Chetumal
61 *D18* **Paysandú** Paysandú, W Uruguay *32°21′S 58°05′W*
61 *D17* **Paysandú** ◆ *department* W Uruguay
102 *I7* **Pays de la Loire** ◆ *region* NW France
36 *L12* **Payson** Arizona, SW USA *34°13′N 111°19′W*
36 *L4* **Payson** Utah, W USA *40°02′N 111°43′W*
125 *W4* **Payyer, Gora** ▲ NW Russian Federation *66°49′N 64°33′E*
Payzawat *see* Jiashi
137 *Q11* **Pazar** Rize, NE Turkey *41°10′N 40°53′E*
136 *F10* **Pazarbaşı Burnu** *headland* NW Turkey *41°12′N 30°18′E*
136 *M16* **Pazarcık** Kahramanmaraş, S Turkey *37°31′N 37°19′E*
114 *I10* **Pazardzhik** *prev.* Tatar Pazardzhik. Pazardzhik, SW Bulgaria *42°11′N 24°21′E*
64 *H11* **Pazardzhik** ◆ *province* C Bulgaria
54 *H9* **Paz de Ariporo** Casanare, E Colombia *05°54′N 71°52′W*
112 *A10* **Pazin** *Ger.* Mitterburg, *It.* Pisino. Istra, NW Croatia *45°14′N 13°56′E*
42 *D7* **Paz, Río** ⇝ El Salvador/Guatemala
113 *O18* **Pčinja** ⇝ N Macedonia
193 *V15* **Pea** Tongatapu, S Tonga *21°10′S 175°14′W*
27 *O6* **Peabody** Kansas, C USA *38°10′N 97°06′W*
11 *O12* **Peace** ⇝ Alberta/British Columbia, W Canada
Peace Garden State *see* North Dakota
11 *Q10* **Peace Point** Alberta, C Canada *59°11′N 112°12′W*
11 *O12* **Peace River** Alberta, W Canada *56°15′N 117°18′W*
23 *W13* **Peace River** ⇝ Florida, SE USA
11 *N17* **Peachland** British Columbia, SW Canada *49°49′N 119°48′W*
36 *J10* **Peach Springs** Arizona, SW USA *35°33′N 113°27′W*
Peach State *see* Georgia
23 *S4* **Peachtree City** Georgia, SE USA *33°24′N 84°36′W*
189 *Y13* **Peacock Point** *point* SE Wake Island
97 *M18* **Peak District** *physical region* C England, United Kingdom
183 *Q7* **Peak Hill** New South Wales, SE Australia *32°39′S 148°12′E*
65 *G15* **Peak, The** ▲ C Ascension Island
105 *O13* **Peal de Becerro** Andalucía, S Spain *37°55′N 03°08′W*
189 *X11* **Peale Island** *island* N Wake Island
37 *O6* **Peale, Mount** ▲ Utah, W USA *38°26′N 109°13′W*
39 *O4* **Peard Bay** *bay* Alaska, USA
23 *Q7* **Pea River** ⇝ Alabama/Florida, S USA
25 *W11* **Pearland** Texas, SW USA *29°33′N 95°17′W*
38 *D9* **Pearl City** O'ahu, Hawaii, USA, C Pacific Ocean *21°24′N 157°58′W*
38 *D9* **Pearl Harbor** *inlet* O'ahu, Hawai'i, USA, C Pacific Ocean
Pearl Islands *see* Perlas, Archipiélago de las
Pearl Lagoon *see* Perlas, Laguna de
22 *M5* **Pearl River** ⇝ Louisiana/Mississippi, S USA
25 *Q13* **Pearsall** Texas, SW USA *28°54′N 99°07′W*
23 *U7* **Pearson** Georgia, SE USA *31°18′N 82°51′W*
25 *P4* **Pease River** ⇝ Texas, SW USA
12 *F7* **Peawanuck** Ontario, C Canada *54°55′N 85°31′W*
12 *E8* **Peawanuk** ⇝ Ontario, S Canada
83 *P16* **Pebane** Zambézia, NE Mozambique *17°14′S 38°10′E*
65 *C23* **Pebble Island** *island* N Falkland Islands
65 *C23* **Pebble Island Settlement** Pebble Island, N Falkland Islands *51°20′S 59°40′W*
Peć *see* Pejë
25 *R8* **Pecan Bayou** ⇝ Texas, SW USA
22 *H10* **Pecan Island** Louisiana, S USA *29°39′N 92°26′W*
60 *L12* **Peças, Ilha das** *island* S Brazil
30 *L10* **Pecatonica River** ⇝ Illinois/Wisconsin, N USA
108 *G10* **Peccia** Ticino, S Switzerland *46°24′N 08°39′E*
Pechenegi *see* Pechenihy
Pechenezhskoye Vodokhranilishche *see* Pecheniz'ke Vodoskhovyshche
124 *I2* **Pechenga** *Fin.* Petsamo. Murmanskaya Oblast', NW Russian Federation *69°34′N 31°14′E*
117 *V5* **Pechenihy** *Rus.* Pechenegi. Kharkivs'ka Oblast', E Ukraine *49°49′N 36°57′E*
117 *V5* **Pecheniz'ke Vodoskhovyshche** *Rus.* Pechenezhskoye Vodokhranilishche. ▣ E Ukraine
125 *U7* **Pechora** Respublika Komi, NW Russian Federation *65°09′N 57°09′E*
125 *R6* **Pechora** ⇝ NW Russian Federation
Pechora Bay *see* Pechorskaya Guba
Pechora Sea *see* Pechorskoye More
125 *S3* **Pechorskaya Guba** *Eng.* Pechora Bay. *bay* NW Russian Federation
122 *H7* **Pechorskoye More** *Eng.* Pechora Sea. *sea* NW Russian Federation
116 *E11* **Pecica** *Ger.* Petschka, *Hung.* Ópécska. Arad, W Romania *46°09′N 21°06′E*
24 *K8* **Pecos** Texas, SW USA *31°25′N 103°30′W*
25 *N11* **Pecos River** ⇝ New Mexico/Texas, SW USA
111 *I25* **Pécs** *Ger.* Fünfkirchen, *Lat.* Sopianae. Baranya, SW Hungary *46°05′N 18°11′E*
43 *T17* **Pedasí** Los Santos, S Panama *07°36′N 80°04′W*
Pedde *see* Pedja
183 *O17* **Pedder, Lake** ◎ Tasmania, SE Australia
44 *M10* **Pedernales** SW Dominican Republic *18°02′N 71°41′W*
55 *Q5* **Pedernales** Delta Amacuro, NE Venezuela *09°58′N 62°15′W*
25 *R10* **Pedernales River** ⇝ Texas, SW USA
62 *H6* **Pedernales, Salar de** *salt lake* N Chile
Pedhoulas *see* Pedoulás
55 *X11* **Pédima** *var.* Malavate. SW French Guiana *03°15′N 54°08′W*
182 *F1* **Pedirka** South Australia *26°41′S 135°11′E*
171 *S11* **Pediwang** Pulau Halmahera, E Indonesia *01°29′N 127°57′E*
118 *I5* **Pedja** *var.* Pedja Jõgi, *Ger.* Pedde. ⇝ E Estonia
Pedja Jõgi *see* Pedja
121 *O3* **Pedoulás** *var.* Pedhoulas. W Cyprus *34°58′N 32°51′E*
59 *N18* **Pedra Azul** Minas Gerais, NE Brazil *16°02′S 41°17′W*
104 *I3* **Pedrafita, Porto de** *var.* Puerto de Piedrafita. *pass* NW Spain
76 *E9* **Pedra Lume** Sal, NE Cape Verde *16°47′N 22°54′W*
43 *P16* **Pedregal** Chiriquí, W Panama *09°04′N 79°25′W*
54 *J4* **Pedregal** Falcón, N Venezuela *11°04′N 70°08′W*
40 *L9* **Pedriceña** Durango, C Mexico *25°08′N 103°46′W*
60 *L11* **Pedro Barros** São Paulo, S Brazil *24°12′S 47°22′W*
39 *Q13* **Pedro Bay** Alaska, USA *59°47′N 154°06′W*
62 *H4* **Pedro de Valdivia** *var.* Oficina Pedro de Valdivia. Antofagasta, N Chile *22°33′S 69°38′W*
62 *P4* **Pedro Juan Caballero** Amambay, E Paraguay *22°34′S 55°41′W*
63 *L15* **Pedro Luro** Buenos Aires, E Argentina *39°30′S 62°38′W*
105 *O10* **Pedro Muñoz** Castilla-La Mancha, C Spain *39°25′N 02°56′W*
155 *J22* **Pedro, Point** *headland* NW Sri Lanka *09°54′N 80°08′E*
182 *K9* **Peebinga** South Australia *34°56′S 140°56′E*
96 *J13* **Peebles** SE Scotland, United Kingdom *55°40′N 03°15′W*
31 *S15* **Peebles** Ohio, N USA *38°57′N 83°23′W*
96 *J12* **Peebles** *cultural region* SE Scotland, United Kingdom
18 *K13* **Peekskill** New York, NE USA *41°17′N 73°54′W*
97 *I16* **Peel** W Isle of Man *54°13′N 04°04′W*
8 *G7* **Peel** ⇝ Northwest Territories/Yukon Territory, NW Canada
8 *K5* **Peel Point** *headland* Victoria Island, Northwest Territories, NW Canada *73°22′N 114°33′W*
8 *M5* **Peel Sound** *passage* Nunavut, N Canada
100 *N9* **Peene** ⇝ NE Germany
99 *K17* **Peer** Limburg, NE Belgium *51°08′N 05°29′E*
14 *H14* **Pefferlaw** Ontario, S Canada *44°18′N 79°11′W*
185 *I18* **Pegasus Bay** *bay* South Island, New Zealand
121 *O3* **Pégeia** *var.* Peyia. SW Cyprus *34°52′N 32°24′E*
109 *V7* **Peggau** Steiermark, SE Austria *47°10′N 15°20′E*
101 *L19* **Pegnitz** Bayern, SE Germany *49°45′N 11°33′E*
101 *L19* **Pegnitz** ⇝ SE Germany
105 *T11* **Pego** Valenciana, E Spain *38°51′N 00°08′W*
Pegu *see* Bago
Pegu *see* Bago
189 *N13* **Pehleng** Pohnpei, E Micronesia
114 *M12* **Pehlivanköy** Kırklareli, NW Turkey *41°21′N 26°55′E*
77 *R14* **Péhonko** C Benin *10°14′N 01°57′E*
61 *B21* **Pehuajó** Buenos Aires, E Argentina *35°48′S 61°53′W*
Pei-ching *see* Beijing/Beijing Shi
100 *J13* **Peine** Niedersachsen, C Germany *52°19′N 10°14′E*
Pei-p'ing *see* Beijing/Beijing Shi
Peipsi Järv/Peipus-See *see* Peipus, Lake
118 *J5* **Peipus, Lake** *Est.* Peipsi Järv, *Ger.* Peipus-See, *Rus.* Chudskoye Ozero. ◎ Estonia/Russian Federation
115 *H19* **Peiraías** *prev.* Piraiévs, *Eng.* Piraeus. Attikí, C Greece *37°57′N 23°42′E*
Peisern *see* Pyzdry
60 *I8* **Peixe, Rio do** ⇝ S Brazil
59 *I16* **Peixoto de Azevedo** Mato Grosso, W Brazil *10°18′S 55°03′W*
168 *O11* **Pejantan, Pulau** *island* W Indonesia
113 *L16* **Pejë** *Serb.* Peć. W Kosovo *42°40′N 20°19′E*
112 *N11* **Pek** ⇝ E Serbia
Pèk *see* Phônsaven
169 *Q16* **Pekalongan** Jawa, C Indonesia *06°54′S 109°37′E*
168 *K11* **Pekanbaru** *var.* Pakanbaru. Sumatera, W Indonesia *0°31′N 101°27′E*
30 *L12* **Pekin** Illinois, N USA *40°34′N 89°38′W*
Peking *see* Beijing/Beijing Shi
Pelabohan Kelang/Pelabuhan Kelang *see* Pelabuhan Klang
168 *J9* **Pelabuhan Klang** *var.* Kuala Pelabohan Kelang, Pelabohan Kelang, Pelabuhan Kelang, Port Klang, Port Swettenham. Selangor, Peninsular Malaysia *02°57′N 101°24′E*
120 *L11* **Pelagie, Isole** *island group* SW Italy
Pelagosa *see* Palagruža
22 *L5* **Pelahatchie** Mississippi, S USA *32°19′N 89°48′W*
169 *T14* **Pelaihari** *var.* Pleihari. Borneo, C Indonesia *03°48′S 114°45′E*
103 *U14* **Pelat, Mont** ▲ SE France *44°16′N 06°46′E*
116 *F12* **Peleaga, Vârful** *prev.* Vîrful Peleaga. ▲ W Romania *45°23′N 22°52′E*
Peleaga, Vîrful *see* Peleaga, Vârful
123 *O11* **Peleduy** Respublika Sakha (Yakutiya), NE Russian Federation *59°39′N 112°36′E*
14 *C18* **Pelee Island** *island* Ontario, S Canada
45 *Q11* **Pelée, Montagne** ▲ N Martinique *14°47′N 61°10′W*
14 *D18* **Pelee, Point** *headland* Ontario, S Canada *41°56′N 82°30′W*
171 *P12* **Pelei** Pulau Peleng, N Indonesia *01°26′S 123°27′E*
Peleliu *see* Beliliou
171 *P12* **Peleng, Pulau** *island* Kepulauan Banggai, N Indonesia
23 *T7* **Pelham** Georgia, SE USA *31°07′N 84°09′W*
111 *E18* **Pelhřimov** *Ger.* Pilgram. Vysočina, C Czech Republic *49°26′N 15°14′E*
39 *W13* **Pelican** Chichagof Island, Alaska, USA *57°52′N 136°05′W*
191 *Z3* **Pelican Lagoon** ◎ Kiritimati, E Kiribati
29 *U6* **Pelican Lake** ◎ Minnesota, N USA
29 *V3* **Pelican Lake** ◎ Minnesota, N USA
30 *L5* **Pelican Lake** ◎ Wisconsin, N USA
44 *G1* **Pelican Point** Grand Bahama Island, N Bahamas *26°39′N 78°09′W*
83 *B19* **Pelican Point** *headland* W Namibia *22°55′S 14°25′E*
29 *S6* **Pelican Rapids** Minnesota, N USA *46°34′N 96°04′W*
Pelican State *see* Louisiana
11 *U13* **Pelikan Narrows** Saskatchewan, C Canada *55°11′N 102°51′W*
115 *L18* **Pelinaío** ▲ Chíos, E Greece *38°31′N 26°01′E*
Pelinnaeum *see* Pelinnaío
115 *E16* **Pelinnaío** *anc.* Pelinnaeum. *ruins* Thessalía, C Greece
113 *N20* **Pelister** ▲ SW FYR Macedonia *41°00′N 21°12′E*
113 *G15* **Pelješac** *peninsula* S Croatia
92 *M12* **Pelkosenniemi** Lappi, NE Finland *67°06′N 27°30′E*
29 *W15* **Pella** Iowa, C USA *41°24′N 92°55′W*
114 *F13* **Pélla** *site of ancient city* Kentrikí Makedonía, N Greece
23 *Q3* **Pell City** Alabama, S USA *33°35′N 86°17′W*
61 *A22* **Pellegrini** Buenos Aires, E Argentina *36°16′S 63°07′W*
92 *K12* **Pello** Lappi, NW Finland *66°47′N 24°E*
100 *G7* **Pellworm** *island* N Germany
10 *H6* **Pelly** ⇝ Yukon Territory, NW Canada
Pelly Bay *see* Kugaaruk
10 *I8* **Pelly Mountains** ▲▲ Yukon Territory, W Canada
Pélmonostor *see* Beli Manastir
37 *P13* **Pelona Mountain** ▲ New Mexico, SW USA *33°40′N 108°06′W*
Peloponnese/Peloponnesus *see* Pelopónnisos
115 *E20* **Pelopónnisos** *Eng.* Peloponnese. ◆ *region* S Greece
115 *E20* **Pelopónnisos** *var.* Morea, *Eng.* Peloponnese; *anc.* Peloponnesus. *peninsula* S Greece
107 *L23* **Peloritani, Monti** *anc.* Pelorus and Neptunius. ▲▲ Sicilia, Italy, C Mediterranean Sea
107 *M22* **Peloro, Capo** *var.* Punta del Faro. *headland* S Italy *38°15′N 15°39′E*
Pelorus and Neptunius *see* Peloritani, Monti
61 *H17* **Pelotas** Rio Grande do Sul, S Brazil *31°45′S 52°20′W*
61 *I14* **Pelotas, Rio** ⇝ S Brazil
92 *K10* **Peltovuoma** *Lapp.* Bealdovuopmi. Lappi, N Finland *68°23′N 24°12′E*
19 *R4* **Pemadumcook Lake** ◎ Maine, NE USA
169 *Q16* **Pemalang** Jawa, C Indonesia *06°53′S 109°07′E*
169 *P10* **Pemangkat** *var.* Pamangkat. Borneo, C Indonesia *01°11′N 109°00′E*
Pemar *see* Paimio
168 *I9* **Pematangsiantar** Sumatera, W Indonesia *02°59′N 99°01′E*
83 *Q14* **Pemba** *prev.* Port Amelia, Porto Amélia. Cabo Delgado, NE Mozambique *13°S 40°35′E*
81 *J22* **Pemba** ◆ *region* E Tanzania
81 *K21* **Pemba** *island* E Tanzania
83 *Q14* **Pemba, Baia de** *inlet* NE Mozambique
81 *J21* **Pemba Channel** *channel* E Tanzania
180 *J14* **Pemberton** Western Australia *34°27′S 116°09′E*
10 *M16* **Pemberton** British Columbia, SW Canada *50°19′N 122°49′W*
29 *Q2* **Pembina** North Dakota, N USA *48°58′N 97°14′W*
11 *P15* **Pembina** ⇝ Alberta, SW Canada
29 *Q2* **Pembina** ⇝ Canada/USA
171 *X16* **Pembre** Papua, E Indonesia *07°49′S 138°01′E*
14 *K12* **Pembroke** Ontario, SE Canada *45°49′N 77°08′W*
97 *H21* **Pembroke** SW Wales, United Kingdom *51°41′N 04°55′W*
23 *W6* **Pembroke** Georgia, SE USA *32°09′N 81°35′W*
21 *U11* **Pembroke** North Carolina, SE USA *34°40′N 79°12′W*
21 *R7* **Pembroke** Virginia, NE USA *37°19′N 80°38′W*
97 *H21* **Pembroke** *cultural region* SW Wales, United Kingdom
Pembuang, Sungai *see* Seruyan, Sungai
43 *S15* **Peña Blanca, Cerro** ▲ C Panama *08°39′N 80°39′W*
104 *K8* **Peña de Francia, Sierra de la** ▲▲ W Spain
104 *G6* **Penafiel** *var.* Peñafiel. Porto, N Portugal *41°12′N 08°17′W*
105 *N6* **Peñafiel** Castilla y León, N Spain *41°36′N 04°07′W*
Peñafiel *see* Penafiel
Peñagolosa *see* Penyagolosa
105 *N7* **Peñalara, Pico de** ▲ C Spain *40°52′N 03°55′W*
171 *X16* **Penambo, Banjaran** *var.* Banjaran Tama Abu, Penambo Range. ▲▲ Indonesia/Malaysia
Penambo Range *see* Penambo, Banjaran
41 *O10* **Peña Nevada, Cerro** ▲ C Mexico *23°46′N 99°52′W*
Penang *see* Pinang, Pulau, Peninsular Malaysia
Penang *see* Pinang
Penang *see* George Town
60 *J8* **Penápolis** São Paulo, S Brazil *21°23′S 50°02′W*
104 *L7* **Peñaranda de Bracamonte** Castilla y León, N Spain *40°54′N 05°13′W*
105 *S8* **Peñarroya** ▲ E Spain *40°24′N 00°42′W*
104 *L12* **Peñarroya-Pueblonuevo** Andalucía, S Spain *38°21′N 05°18′W*
97 *K22* **Penarth** S Wales, United Kingdom *51°27′N 03°11′W*
104 *K1* **Peñas, Cabo de** *headland* N Spain *43°39′N 05°52′W*
63 *F20* **Penas, Golfo de** *gulf* S Chile
Pen-ch'i *see* Benxi
79 *H14* **Pendé** *var.* Logone Oriental. ⇝ Central African Republic/Chad
76 *I14* **Pendembu** E Sierra Leone *09°06′N 12°12′W*
29 *R13* **Pender** Nebraska, C USA *42°06′N 96°42′W*
Penderma *see* Bandırma
32 *K11* **Pendleton** Oregon, NW USA *45°40′N 118°47′W*
32 *M7* **Pend Oreille, Lake** ◎ Idaho, NW USA
32 *M7* **Pend Oreille River** ⇝ Idaho/Washington, NW USA
Pendzhikent *see* Panjakent
Peneius *see* Pineiós
104 *G8* **Penela** Coimbra, N Portugal *40°02′N 08°23′W*
14 *G13* **Penetanguishene** Ontario, S Canada *44°45′N 79°55′W*
151 *H15* **Penganga** ⇝ C India
P'engchia Yu *see* Pengjia Yu
79 *M21* **Penge** Kasai-Oriental, C Dem. Rep. Congo *05°29′S 24°38′E*
Penghu Archipelago/P'enghu Ch'üntao/Penghu Islands *see* Penghu Liedao
161 *R14* **Penghu Liedao** *var.* P'enghu Ch'üntao, Penghu Islands, P'enghu Liehtao, *Eng.* Penghu Archipelago, Pescadores, *Jap.* Hoko-guntō, Hoko-shotō. *island group* W Taiwan
P'enghu Liehtao *see* Penghu Liedao
161 *S14* **Penghu Shuidao** *var.* Pescadores Channel, P'enghu Shuitao. *channel* W Taiwan
P'enghu Shuitao *see* Penghu Shuidao
161 *T12* **Pengjia Yu** *prev.* P'engchia Yu. *island* N Taiwan
161 *R4* **Penglai** *var.* Dengzhou. Shandong, E China *37°50′N 120°45′E*
Peng-pu *see* Bengbu
Penhsihu *see* Benxi
Penibético, Sistema *see* Béticos, Sistemas
104 *F10* **Peniche** Leiria, W Portugal *39°21′N 09°23′W*
169 *U17* **Penida, Nusa** *island* S Indonesia
Peninsular State *see* Florida
105 *T8* **Peñíscola** *var.* Peñíscola. Valenciana, E Spain *40°22′N 00°24′E*
40 *M13* **Pénjamo** Guanajuato, C Mexico *20°26′N 101°44′W*
Penki *see* Benxi
102 *F7* **Penmarch, Pointe de** *headland* NW France *47°46′N 04°34′W*
107 *L15* **Penna, Punta della** *headland* C Italy *42°10′N 14°43′E*
107 *K14* **Penne** Abruzzo, C Italy *42°28′N 13°57′E*
Penner *see* Penneru
155 *J18* **Penneru** *var.* Penner. ⇝ C India
182 *I10* **Penneshaw** South Australia *35°45′S 137°57′E*
18 *C14* **Penn Hills** Pennsylvania, NE USA *40°28′N 79°53′W*
Penninae, Alpes/Pennine, Alpi *see* Pennine Alps
108 *D11* **Pennine Alps** *Fr.* Alpes Pennines, *It.* Alpi Pennine, *Lat.* Alpes Penninae. ▲▲ Italy/Switzerland
Pennine Chain *see* Pennines
97 *L15* **Pennines** *var.* Pennine Chain. ▲▲ N England, United Kingdom
Pennines, Alpes *see* Pennine Alps
21 *O8* **Pennington Gap** Virginia, NE USA *36°45′N 83°01′W*
18 *I16* **Penns Grove** New Jersey, NE USA *39°42′N 75°27′W*
18 *I16* **Pennsville** New Jersey, NE USA *39°37′N 75°29′W*
18 *E14* **Pennsylvania** *off.* Commonwealth of Pennsylvania, *also known as* Keystone State. ◆ *state* NE USA
18 *G10* **Penn Yan** New York, NE USA *42°39′N 77°02′W*
124 *H16* **Peno** Tverskaya Oblast', W Russian Federation *56°55′N 32°44′E*
19 *R7* **Penobscot Bay** *bay* Maine, NE USA
19 *S5* **Penobscot River** ⇝ Maine, NE USA
182 *K12* **Penola** South Australia *37°24′S 140°50′E*
40 *K9* **Peñón Blanco** Durango, C Mexico *25°12′N 100°50′W*
182 *E7* **Penong** South Australia *31°57′S 133°01′E*
43 *S16* **Penonomé** Coclé, C Panama *08°29′N 80°22′W*
190 *L13* **Penrhyn** *atoll* N Cook Islands
192 *M9* **Penrhyn Basin** *undersea feature* C Pacific Ocean
183 *S9* **Penrith** New South Wales, SE Australia *33°45′S 150°48′E*
97 *K15* **Penrith** NW England, United Kingdom *54°40′N 02°44′W*
23 *O9* **Pensacola** Florida, SE USA *30°25′N 87°13′W*
23 *O9* **Pensacola Bay** *bay* Florida, SE USA
195 *N7* **Pensacola Mountains** ▲▲ Antarctica
182 *L12* **Penshurst** Victoria, SE Australia *37°54′S 142°19′E*
187 *R13* **Pentecost** *Fr.* Pentecôte. *island* C Vanuatu
15 *V4* **Pentecôte** ⇝ Québec, SE Canada
Pentecôte *see* Pentecost
15 *V4* **Pentecôte, Lac** ◎ Québec, SE Canada
8 *H15* **Penticton** British Columbia, SW Canada *49°29′N 119°38′W*
96 *J6* **Pentland Firth** *strait* N Scotland, United Kingdom
96 *J12* **Pentland Hills** *hill range* S Scotland, United Kingdom
171 *Q12* **Penu** Pulau Taliabu, E Indonesia *01°43′S 125°09′E*
155 *H18* **Penukonda** Andhra Pradesh, E India *14°04′N 77°38′E*
166 *L7* **Penwegon** Bago, C Burma (Myanmar) *18°14′N 96°34′E*
24 *M8* **Penwell** Texas, SW USA *31°45′N 102°32′W*
105 *S8* **Penyagolosa** *var.* Peñagolosa. ▲ E Spain *40°10′N 00°15′W*
97 *J21* **Pen y Fan** ▲ SE Wales, United Kingdom *51°52′N 03°25′W*
97 *L16* **Pen-y-ghent** ▲ N England, United Kingdom *54°11′N 02°15′W*
127 *O6* **Penza** Penzenskaya Oblast', W Russian Federation *53°11′N 45°E*
97 *G25* **Penzance** SW England, United Kingdom *50°08′N 05°33′W*
127 *N6* **Penzenskaya Oblast'** ◆ *province* W Russian Federation
123 *U7* **Penzhina** ⇝ E Russian Federation
123 *U9* **Penzhinskaya Guba** *bay* E Russian Federation
Penzig *see* Pieńsk
36 *K13* **Peoria** Arizona, SW USA *33°34′N 112°14′W*
30 *L12* **Peoria** Illinois, N USA *40°42′N 89°35′W*
30 *L12* **Peoria Heights** Illinois, N USA *40°45′N 89°34′W*
31 *N11* **Peotone** Illinois, N USA *41°19′N 87°47′W*
18 *J11* **Pepacton Reservoir** ▣ New York, NE USA
76 *I15* **Pepel** W Sierra Leone *08°39′N 13°04′W*
30 *I6* **Pepin, Lake** ▣ Minnesota/Wisconsin, N USA
99 *L20* **Pepinster** Liège, E Belgium *50°34′N 05°49′E*
113 *L20* **Peqin** *var.* Peqini. Elbasan, C Albania *41°03′N 19°46′E*
Peqini *see* Peqin
40 *D7* **Pequeña, Punta** *headland* NW Mexico *26°13′N 112°34′W*
168 *J8* **Perak** ◆ *state* Peninsular Malaysia
105 *R7* **Perales del Alfambra** Aragón, NE Spain *40°38′N 01°00′W*
115 *C15* **Pérama** *var.* Perama. Ípeiros, W Greece *39°42′N 20°51′E*
Perama *see* Pérama
92 *M13* **Perä-Posio** Lappi, NE Finland *66°10′N 27°56′E*
15 *Z6* **Percé** Québec, SE Canada *48°32′N 64°14′W*
15 *Z6* **Percé, Rocher** *island* Québec, S Canada
102 *L5* **Perche, Collines de** ▲ N France
109 *X4* **Perchtoldsdorf** Niederösterreich, NE Austria *48°06′N 16°16′E*
180 *L6* **Percival Lakes** *lakes* Western Australia
105 *T3* **Perdido, Monte** ▲ NE Spain *42°41′N 00°01′E*
23 *O8* **Perdido River** ⇝ Alabama/Florida, S USA
Perece Vela Basin *see* West Mariana Basin
116 *G7* **Perechyn** Zakarpats'ka Oblast', W Ukraine *48°45′N 22°28′E*
54 *E10* **Pereira** Risaralda, W Colombia *04°47′N 75°46′W*
60 *I7* **Pereira Barreto** São Paulo, S Brazil *20°37′S 51°07′W*
59 *G15* **Pereirinha** Pará, N Brazil *08°18′S 57°30′W*
127 *N10* **Perelazovskiy** Volgogradskaya Oblast', SW Russian Federation *49°10′N 42°30′E*
127 *S7* **Perelyub** Saratovskaya Oblast', W Russian Federation *51°52′N 50°19′E*
31 *P7* **Pere Marquette River** ⇝ Michigan, N USA
Peremyshl *see* Przemyśl
116 *I5* **Peremyshlyany** L'vivs'ka Oblast', W Ukraine *49°42′N 24°33′E*
Pereshchepino *see* Pereshchepyne
116 *L9* **Pereshchepyne** *Rus.* Pereshchepino. Dnipropetrovs'ka Oblast', E Ukraine *48°59′N 35°22′E*
124 *L16* **Pereslavl'-Zalesskiy** Yaroslavskaya Oblast', W Russian Federation *56°42′N 38°45′E*
117 *Y7* **Pereval's'k** Luhans'ka Oblast', E Ukraine *48°28′N 38°54′E*
127 *U7* **Perevolotskiy** Orenburgskaya Oblast', W Russian Federation *51°54′N 54°05′E*
Pereyaslav-Khmel'nitskiy *see* Pereyaslav-Khmel'nyts'kyy
117 *Q5* **Pereyaslav-Khmel'nyts'kyy** *Rus.* Pereyaslav-Khmel'nitskiy. Kyyivs'ka Oblast', N Ukraine *50°05′N 31°28′E*
109 *U4* **Perg** Oberösterreich, N Austria *48°15′N 14°38′E*
61 *B19* **Pergamino** Buenos Aires, E Argentina *33°56′S 60°38′W*
106 *G6* **Pergine Valsugana** *Ger.* Persen. Trentino-Alto Adige, N Italy *46°04′N 11°13′E*
29 *S6* **Perham** Minnesota, N USA *46°35′N 95°34′W*
93 *L16* **Perho** Länsi-Suomi, W Finland *63°15′N 24°25′E*
116 *E11* **Periam** *Ger.* Perjamosch, *Hung.* Perjámos. Timiş, W Romania *46°02′N 20°54′E*
15 *Q6* **Péribonca** ⇝ Québec, SE Canada
12 *L11* **Péribonca, Lac** ◎ Québec, SE Canada
15 *Q6* **Péribonca, Petite Rivière** ⇝ Québec, SE Canada
15 *Q7* **Péribonka** Québec, SE Canada *48°45′N 72°01′W*
40 *I9* **Pericos** Sinaloa, C Mexico *25°03′N 107°42′W*
169 *Q10* **Perigi** Borneo, C Indonesia
102 *L12* **Périgueux** *anc.* Vesuna. Dordogne, SW France *45°12′N 00°41′E*
54 *G5* **Perijá, Serranía de** ▲▲ Columbia/Venezuela
115 *H17* **Peristéra** *island* Vóreies Sporádes, Greece, Aegean Sea
63 *H20* **Perito Moreno** Santa Cruz, S Argentina *46°35′S 71°W*
155 *G22* **Periyāl** *var.* Periyār. ⇝ SW India
Periyār *see* Periyāl
155 *G23* **Periyār Lake** ◎ S India
Perjámos/Perjamosch *see* Periam
27 *O9* **Perkins** Oklahoma, C USA *35°58′N 97°01′W*
116 *L7* **Perkivtsi** Chernivets'ka Oblast', W Ukraine *48°28′N 26°48′E*
43 *U15* **Perlas, Archipiélago de las** *Eng.* Pearl Islands. *island group* SE Panama
43 *O10* **Perlas, Cayos de** *reef* SE Nicaragua
43 *N9* **Perlas, Laguna de** *Eng.* Pearl Lagoon. *lagoon* E Nicaragua
43 *N10* **Perlas, Punta de** *headland* E Nicaragua *12°22′N 83°30′W*
100 *L11* **Perleberg** Brandenburg, N Germany *53°04′N 11°52′E*
Perlepe *see* Prilep
168 *I6* **Perlis** ◆ *state* Peninsular Malaysia
125 *U14* **Perm'** *prev.* Molotov. Permskiy Kray, NW Russian Federation *58°01′N 56°10′E*
113 *M22* **Përmet** *var.* Përmeti, Prëmet. Gjirokastër, S Albania *40°12′N 20°24′E*
Përmeti *see* Përmet
125 *U15* **Permskiy Kray** ◆ *province* NW Russian Federation
59 *P15* **Pernambuco** *off.* Estado de Pernambuco. ◆ *state* E Brazil
Pernambuco *see* Recife
Pernambuco Abyssal Plain *see* Pernambuco Plain
Pernambuco, Estado de *see* Pernambuco
47 *Y6* **Pernambuco Plain** *var.* Pernambuco Abyssal Plain. *undersea feature* E Atlantic Ocean *07°30′S 27°00′W*
65 *K15* **Pernambuco Seamounts** *undersea feature* C Atlantic Ocean
182 *H6* **Pernatty Lagoon** *salt lake* South Australia
Pernau *see* Pärnu
Pernauer Bucht *see* Pärnu Laht
Pērnava *see* Pärnu
114 *G9* **Pernik** *prev.* Dimitrovo. Pernik, W Bulgaria *42°36′N 23°02′E*
114 *G10* **Pernik** ◆ *province* W Bulgaria
93 *K20* **Perniö** *Swe.* Bjärnå. Länsi-Suomi, SW Finland *60°13′N 23°10′E*
109 *X5* **Pernitz** Niederösterreich, E Austria *47°54′N 15°58′E*
Pernov *see* Pärnu
103 *O3* **Péronne** Somme, N France *49°56′N 02°57′E*
14 *L8* **Péronne, Lac** ◎ Québec, SE Canada
106 *A8* **Perosa Argentina** Piemonte, NE Italy *45°02′N 07°10′E*
41 *Q14* **Perote** Veracruz-Llave, E Mexico *19°32′N 97°16′W*
Pérouse *see* Perugia
191 *W15* **Pérouse, Bahía de la** *bay* Easter Island, Chile, E Pacific Ocean
Perovsk *see* Kyzylorda
103 *O17* **Perpignan** Pyrénées-Orientales, S France *42°41′N 02°53′E*
113 *M20* **Përrenjas** *var.* Përrenjasi, Prenjas, Prenjasi. Elbasan, E Albania *41°04′N 20°34′E*
Përrenjasi *see* Përrenjas
92 *O2* **Perriertoppen** ▲ C Svalbard *79°10′N 17°01′E*
25 *S6* **Perrin** Texas, SW USA *32°59′N 98°03′W*
23 *Y16* **Perrine** Florida, SE USA *25°36′N 80°21′W*
37 *S12* **Perro, Laguna del** ◎ New Mexico, SW USA
102 *G5* **Perros-Guirec** Côtes d'Armor, NW France *48°49′N 03°28′W*
23 *T9* **Perry** Florida, SE USA *30°07′N 83°34′W*
23 *T5* **Perry** Georgia, SE USA *32°27′N 83°43′W*
29 *U14* **Perry** Iowa, C USA *41°50′N 94°06′W*
18 *E10* **Perry** New York, NE USA *42°43′N 78°00′W*
27 *N9* **Perry** Oklahoma, C USA *36°17′N 97°18′W*
27 *Q3* **Perry Lake** ▣ Kansas, C USA
31 *R11* **Perrysburg** Ohio, N USA *41°33′N 83°37′W*
25 *O1* **Perryton** Texas, SW USA *36°23′N 100°48′W*
39 *O15* **Perryville** Alaska, USA *55°55′N 159°08′W*
27 *U11* **Perryville** Arkansas, C USA *35°00′N 92°48′W*
27 *Y6* **Perryville** Missouri, C USA *37°43′N 89°51′W*
Persante *see* Parsęta
Persen *see* Pergine Valsugana
Pershay *see* Pyarshai
117 *V7* **Pershotravens'k** Dnipropetrovs'ka Oblast', E Ukraine *48°19′N 36°22′E*
Pershotravneve *see* Manhush
Persia *see* Iran
141 *T5* **Persian Gulf** *var.* Gulf, The, *Ar.* Khalīj al 'Arabī, *Per.* Khalīj-e Fars. *gulf* SW Asia *see also* Persian Gulf
141 *T5* **Persian Gulf** *var.* The Gulf, *Ar.* Khalīj al 'Arabī, *Per.* Khalīj-e Fars. *Gulf* SW Asia *see also* Gulf, The
Persis *see* Fārs
95 *K22* **Perstorp** Skåne, S Sweden *56°08′N 13°23′E*
137 *O14* **Pertek** Tunceli, C Turkey *38°53′N 39°19′E*
183 *P16* **Perth** Tasmania, SE Australia *41°39′S 147°11′E*
180 *I13* **Perth** *state capital* Western Australia *31°58′S 115°49′E*
14 *L13* **Perth** Ontario, SE Canada *44°54′N 76°15′W*
96 *J11* **Perth** C Scotland, United Kingdom *56°24′N 03°28′W*
96 *J10* **Perth** *cultural region* C Scotland, United Kingdom
180 *I12* **Perth** ✈ Western Australia *31°51′S 116°06′E*
173 *V10* **Perth Basin** *undersea feature* SE Indian Ocean *28°30′S 110°00′E*
103 *S15* **Pertuis** Vaucluse, SE France *43°42′N 05°30′E*
103 *Y16* **Pertusato, Capo** *headland* Corse, France, C Mediterranean Sea *41°22′N 09°10′E*
30 *L11* **Peru** Illinois, N USA *41°18′N 89°09′W*
31 *P12* **Peru** Indiana, N USA *40°45′N 86°04′W*
57 *E13* **Peru** *off.* Republic of Peru. ◆ *republic* W South America
Peru *see* Beru
193 *T9* **Peru Basin** *undersea feature* E Pacific Ocean *15°00′S 85°00′W*
193 *U8* **Peru-Chile Trench** *undersea feature* E Pacific Ocean *20°00′S 73°00′W*
112 *F13* **Perućko Jezero** ◎ S Croatia
106 *H13* **Perugia** *Fr.* Pérouse; *anc.* Perusia. Umbria, C Italy *43°06′N 12°24′E*
Perugia, Lake of *see* Trasimeno, Lago
61 *D15* **Perugorría** Corrientes, NE Argentina *29°21′S 58°35′W*
60 *M11* **Peruíbe** São Paulo, S Brazil *24°18′S 47°01′W*
155 *B21* **Perumalpār** *reef* India, N Indian Ocean
Peru, Republic of *see* Peru
Perusia *see* Perugia
99 *D20* **Péruwelz** Hainaut, SW Belgium *50°30′N 03°35′E*
137 *R15* **Pervari** Siirt, SE Turkey *37°55′N 42°32′E*
127 *O4* **Pervomaysk** Nizhegorodskaya Oblast', W Russian Federation *54°52′N 43°49′E*
117 *X7* **Pervomays'k** Luhans'ka Oblast', E Ukraine *48°38′N 38°36′E*
117 *P8* **Pervomays'k** *prev.* Ol'viopol'. Mykolayivs'ka Oblast', S Ukraine *48°02′N 30°51′E*
117 *S12* **Pervomays'ke** Avtonomna Respublika Krym, S Ukraine *45°43′N 33°49′E*
127 *V7* **Pervomayskiy** Orenburgskaya Oblast', W Russian Federation *51°32′N 54°58′E*
126 *M6* **Pervomayskiy** Tambovskaya Oblast', W Russian Federation *53°15′N 40°20′E*
117 *V6* **Pervomays'kyy** Kharkivs'ka Oblast', E Ukraine *49°24′N 36°12′E*
122 *F10* **Pervoural'sk** Sverdlovskaya Oblast', C Russian Federation *56°58′N 59°50′E*
123 *V11* **Pervyy Kuril'skiy Proliv** *strait* E Russian Federation
99 *I19* **Perwez** Walloon Brabant, C Belgium *50°39′N 04°49′E*
106 *I11* **Pesaro** *anc.* Pisaurum. Marche, C Italy *43°55′N 12°53′E*
35 *N9* **Pescadero** California, W USA *37°15′N 122°23′W*
Pescadores *see* Penghu Liedao
Pescadores Channel *see* Penghu Shuidao
107 *K14* **Pescara** *anc.* Aternum, Ostia Aterni. Abruzzo, C Italy *42°28′N 14°13′E*
107 *K15* **Pescara** ⇝ C Italy
106 *F11* **Pescia** Toscana, C Italy *43°54′N 10°41′E*
108 *C8* **Peseux** Neuchâtel, W Switzerland *46°59′N 06°53′E*
125 *P6* **Pesha** ⇝ NW Russian Federation
149 *T5* **Peshāwar** Khyber Pakhtunkhwa, N Pakistan *34°01′N 71°33′E*
149 *T6* **Peshāwar** ✈ Khyber Pakhtunkhwa, N Pakistan *34°01′N 71°40′E*

◆ Country ● Country Capital ◇ Dependent Territory ○ Dependent Territory Capital ◆ Administrative Regions ✈ International Airport ▲ Mountain ▲▲ Mountain Range ⛰ Volcano ⇝ River ◎ Lake ▣ Reservoir

113 M19 **Peshkopi** *var.* Peshkopia, Peshkopija. Dibër, NE Albania 41°40′N 20°25′E
Peshkopia/Peshkopija *see* Peshkopi
114 I11 **Peshtera** Pazardzhik, C Bulgaria 42°02′N 24°18′E
31 N6 **Peshtigo** Wisconsin, N USA 45°04′N 87°43′W
31 N6 **Peshtigo River** ≈ Wisconsin, N USA
Peski *see* Pyaski
125 S13 **Peskovka** Kirovskaya Oblast', NW Russian Federation 59°04′N 52°17′E
103 S8 **Pesmes** Haute-Saône, E France 47°17′N 05°33′E
104 H6 **Peso da Régua** *var.* Pêso da Regua. Vila Real, N Portugal 41°10′N 07°47′W
40 F5 **Pesqueira** Sonora, NW Mexico 29°22′N 110°58′W
102 J13 **Pessac** Gironde, SW France 44°46′N 00°42′W
111 J23 **Pest** *off.* Pest Megye. ◈ *county* C Hungary
Pest Megye *see* Pest
124 J14 **Pestovo** Novgorodskaya Oblast', W Russian Federation 58°37′N 35°48′E
40 M15 **Petacalco, Bahía** *bay* W Mexico
Petach-Tikva *see* Petah Tikva
138 F10 **Petah Tikva** *var.* Petach-Tikva, Petah Tiqva, Petakh Tikva; *prev.* Petah Tiqwa. Tel Aviv, C Israel 32°05′N 34°53′E
Petah Tiqwa *see* Petah Tikva
93 L17 **Petäjävesi** Länsi-Suomi, C Finland 62°17′N 25°10′E
Petakh Tikva/Petah Tiqva *see* Petah Tikva
22 M7 **Petal** Mississippi, S USA 31°21′N 89°15′W
115 I19 **Petalioí** *island* C Greece
115 H19 **Petalión, Kólpos** *gulf* E Greece
115 J19 **Pétalo** ▲ Ándros, Kykládes, Greece, Aegean Sea 37°51′N 24°50′E
34 M8 **Petaluma** California, W USA 38°15′N 122°37′W
99 L25 **Pétange** Luxembourg, SW Luxembourg 49°33′N 05°53′E
54 M5 **Petare** Miranda, N Venezuela 10°31′N 66°50′W
41 N16 **Petatlán** Guerrero, S Mexico 17°31′N 101°16′W
83 L14 **Petauke** Eastern, E Zambia 14°12′S 31°16′E
14 J12 **Petawawa** Ontario, SE Canada 45°54′N 77°18′W
14 J11 **Petawawa** ≈ Ontario, SE Canada
Petchaburi *see* Phetchaburi
42 D2 **Petén** *off.* Departamento del Petén. ◈ *department* N Guatemala
Petén, Departamento del *see* Petén
42 D2 **Petén Itzá, Lago** *var.* Lago de Flores. ◎ N Guatemala
30 K7 **Petenwell Lake** ⊠ Wisconsin, N USA
14 D6 **Peterbell** Ontario, S Canada 48°34′N 83°19′W
182 I7 **Peterborough** South Australia 32°59′S 138°51′E
14 I14 **Peterborough** Ontario, SE Canada 44°19′N 78°20′W
97 N20 **Peterborough** *prev.* Medeshamstede. E England, United Kingdom 52°35′N 00°15′W
19 N10 **Peterborough** New Hampshire, NE USA 42°51′N 71°54′W
96 L8 **Peterhead** NE Scotland, United Kingdom 57°30′N 01°46′W
Peterhof *see* Luboń
Peter I øy *see* Peter I Øy
193 Q14 **Peter I Øy** ◇ *Norwegian dependency* Antarctica
194 H9 **Peter I Øy** *var.* Peter I øy. *island* Antarctica
97 M14 **Peterlee** N England, United Kingdom 54°45′N 01°18′W
Peterlingen *see* Payerne
197 P14 **Petermann Bjerg** ▲ C Greenland 73°16′N 27°59′W
11 S12 **Peter Pond Lake** ◎ Saskatchewan, C Canada
39 X13 **Petersburg** Mytkof Island, Alaska, USA 56°43′N 132°51′W
30 K13 **Petersburg** Illinois, N USA 40°01′N 89°52′W
31 N16 **Petersburg** Indiana, N USA 38°30′N 87°16′W
29 Q3 **Petersburg** North Dakota, N USA 47°59′N 97°59′W
25 N5 **Petersburg** Texas, SW USA 33°52′N 101°36′W
21 V7 **Petersburg** Virginia, NE USA 37°14′N 77°24′W
21 T4 **Petersburg** West Virginia, NE USA 39°01′N 79°09′W
100 H12 **Petershagen** Nordrhein-Westfalen, NW Germany 52°22′N 08°58′E
55 S9 **Peters Mine** *var.* Peter's Mine. N Guyana 06°13′N 59°18′W
107 O21 **Petilia Policastro** Calabria, SW Italy 39°07′N 16°48′E
44 M9 **Pétionville** S Haiti 18°29′N 72°16′W
45 X6 **Petit-Bourg** Basse Terre, C Guadeloupe 16°12′N 61°36′W
15 Y5 **Petit-Cap** Québec, SE Canada 49°00′N 64°26′W
45 Y6 **Petit Cul-de-Sac Marin** *bay* C Guadeloupe
44 M9 **Petite-Rivière-de-l'Artibonite** C Haiti 19°10′N 72°30′W
173 X16 **Petite Rivière Noire, Piton de la** ▲ C Mauritius
15 R9 **Petite-Rivière-St-François** Québec, SE Canada 47°18′N 70°34′W
44 L9 **Petit-Goâve** S Haiti 18°27′N 72°51′W
Petitjean *see* Sidi-Kacem
13 N10 **Petit Lac Manicouagan** ◎ Québec, E Canada
19 T7 **Petit Manan Point** *headland* Maine, NE USA 44°23′N 67°54′W
Petit Mécatina, Rivière du *see* Little Mecatina
11 N10 **Petitot** ≈ Alberta/British Columbia, W Canada
45 S12 **Petit Piton** ▲ SW Saint Lucia 13°49′N 61°03′W
Petit-Popo *see* Aného
Petit St-Bernard, Col du *see* Little Saint Bernard Pass
13 O8 **Petitsikapau Lake** ◎ Newfoundland and Labrador, E Canada
92 L11 **Petkula** Lappi, N Finland 67°41′N 26°44′E
41 X12 **Peto** Yucatán, SE Mexico 20°09′N 88°55′W
62 G10 **Petorca** Valparaíso, C Chile 32°18′S 70°49′W
31 Q5 **Petoskey** Michigan, N USA 45°51′N 88°03′W
138 G14 **Petra** *archaeological site* Ma'ān, W Jordan
Petra *see* Wādī Mūsā
115 F14 **Pétras, Sténa** *pass* N Greece
123 S16 **Petra Velikogo, Zaliv** *bay* SE Russian Federation
Petrel *see* Petrer
14 K15 **Petre, Point** *headland* Ontario, SE Canada 43°49′N 77°07′W
105 S12 **Petrer** *var.* Petrel. Valenciana, E Spain 38°28′N 00°46′W
125 U11 **Petretsovo** Permskiy Kray, NW Russian Federation 61°22′N 57°21′E
114 G12 **Petrich** Blagoevgrad, SW Bulgaria 41°25′N 23°12′E
187 P15 **Petrie, Récif** *reef* N New Caledonia
37 N11 **Petrified Forest** *prehistoric site* Arizona, SW USA
Petrikau *see* Piotrków Trybunalski
Petrikov *see* Pyetrykaw
116 H12 **Petrila** *Hung.* Petrilla. Hunedoara, W Romania 45°27′N 23°25′E
Petrilla *see* Petrila
112 E9 **Petrinja** Sisak-Moslavina, C Croatia 45°27′N 16°14′E
Petroaleksandrovsk *see* To'rtkok'l
Petrőcz *see* Bački Petrovac
124 G12 **Petrodvorets** *Fin.* Pietarhovi. Leningradskaya Oblast', NW Russian Federation 59°53′N 29°52′E
Petrograd *see* Sankt-Peterburg
Petrokov *see* Piotrków Trybunalski
54 G6 **Petrólea** Norte de Santander, NE Colombia 08°30′N 72°35′W
14 D16 **Petrolia** Ontario, S Canada 42°54′N 82°07′W
25 S4 **Petrolia** Texas, SW USA 34°00′N 98°13′W
59 O15 **Petrolina** Pernambuco, E Brazil 09°22′S 40°30′W
45 T6 **Petrona, Punta** *headland* C Puerto Rico 17°57′N 66°23′W
Petropavl *see* Petropavlovsk
117 V7 **Petropavlivka** Dnipropetrovs'ka Oblast', E Ukraine 48°28′N 36°28′E
145 P6 **Petropavlovsk** *Kaz.* Petropavl. Severnyy Kazakhstan, N Kazakhstan 54°47′N 69°06′E
123 V11 **Petropavlovsk-Kamchatskiy** Kamchatskiy Kray, E Russian Federation 53°03′N 158°43′E
60 P9 **Petrópolis** Rio de Janeiro, SE Brazil 22°30′S 43°28′W
116 H12 **Petroşani** *var.* Petroşeni, *Ger.* Petroschen, *Hung.* Petrozsény. Hunedoara, W Romania 45°25′N 23°22′E
Petroschen/Petroşeni *see* Petroşani
Petroskoi *see* Petrozavodsk
112 N12 **Petrovac** Serbia, E Serbia 42°22′N 21°25′E
Petrovac *see* Bosanski Petrovac
113 J17 **Petrovac na Moru** S Montenegro 42°11′N 19°00′E
Petrovac/Petrovácz *see* Bački Petrovac
117 S8 **Petrove** Kirovohrads'ka Oblast', C Ukraine 48°22′N 33°12′E
113 O18 **Petrovec** C FYR Macedonia 41°57′N 21°37′E
Petrovgrad *see* Zrenjanin
127 P7 **Petrovsk** Saratovskaya Oblast', W Russian Federation 52°20′N 45°23′E
Petrovsk-Port *see* Makhachkala
127 P9 **Petrov Val** Volgogradskaya Oblast', SW Russian Federation 50°10′N 45°16′E
124 J11 **Petrozavodsk** *Fin.* Petroskoi. Respublika Kareliya, NW Russian Federation 61°46′N 34°19′E
Petrozsény *see* Petroşani
83 D20 **Petrusdal** Hardap, C Namibia 23°42′S 17°23′E
117 T7 **Petrykivka** Dnipropetrovs'ka Oblast', E Ukraine 48°44′N 34°42′E
Petsamo *see* Pechenga
Petschka *see* Pecica
Pettau *see* Ptuj
109 S5 **Pettenbach** Oberösterreich, C Austria 47°58′N 14°03′E
25 S13 **Pettus** Texas, SW USA 28°34′N 97°49′W
122 G12 **Petukhovo** Kurganskaya Oblast', C Russian Federation 55°04′N 67°49′E
Petuna *see* Songyuan
109 R4 **Peuerbach** Oberösterreich, N Austria 48°19′N 13°45′E
62 G12 **Peumo** Libertador, C Chile 34°20′S 71°12′W
123 T6 **Pevek** Chukotskiy Avtonomnyy Okrug, NE Russian Federation 69°41′N 170°19′E
27 X5 **Pevely** Missouri, C USA 38°16′N 90°24′W
Peyia *see* Pégeia
102 J15 **Peyrehorade** Landes, SW France 43°33′N 01°05′W
124 J14 **Peza** ≈ NW Russian Federation
103 P16 **Pézenas** Hérault, S France 43°28′N 03°25′E
111 H20 **Pezinok** *Ger.* Bösing, *Hung.* Bazin. Bratislavský Kraj, W Slovakia 48°17′N 17°15′E
101 L22 **Pfaffenhofen an der Ilm** Bayern, SE Germany 48°31′N 11°30′E
108 G7 **Pfäffikon** Schwyz, C Switzerland 47°11′N 08°46′E
101 F20 **Pfälzer Wald** *hill range* W Germany
101 N22 **Pfarrkirchen** Bayern, SE Germany 48°25′N 12°56′E
101 G21 **Pforzheim** Baden-Württemberg, SW Germany 48°53′N 08°42′E
101 H24 **Pfullendorf** Baden-Württemberg, S Germany 47°55′N 09°16′E
108 K8 **Pfunds** Tirol, W Austria 46°56′N 10°30′E
101 G19 **Pfungstadt** Hessen, W Germany 49°48′N 08°36′E
83 L20 **Phalaborwa** Limpopo, NE South Africa 23°59′S 31°04′E
152 E11 **Phalodi** Rājasthān, NW India 27°06′N 72°22′E
152 E12 **Phalsund** Rājasthān, NW India 26°22′N 71°56′E
155 E15 **Phaltan** Mahārāshtra, W India 18°01′N 74°31′E
167 O7 **Phan** *var.* Muang Phan. Chiang Rai, NW Thailand 19°34′N 99°44′E
167 O14 **Phangan, Ko** *island* SW Thailand
166 M15 **Phang-Nga** *var.* Pang-Nga, Phangnga. Phangnga, SW Thailand 08°29′N 98°31′E
Phangnga *see* Phang-Nga
Phan Rang/Phanrang *see* Phan Rang-Thap Cham
167 V13 **Phan Rang-Thap Cham** *var.* Phanrang, Phan Rang, Phan Rang Thap Cham. Ninh Thuân, S Vietnam 11°34′N 109°00′E
167 U13 **Phan Ri** Binh Thuân, S Vietnam 11°11′N 108°31′E
167 U13 **Phan Thiêt** Binh Thuân, S Vietnam 10°56′N 108°06′E
Pharnacia *see* Giresun
25 S17 **Pharr** Texas, SW USA 26°11′N 98°10′W
Pharus *see* Hvar
167 N16 **Phatthalung** *var.* Padalung, Patalung. Phatthalung, SW Thailand 07°38′N 100°04′E
167 O7 **Phayao** *var.* Muang Phayao. Phayao, NW Thailand 19°10′N 99°55′E
11 U10 **Phelps Lake** ◎ Saskatchewan, C Canada
21 X9 **Phelps Lake** ◎ North Carolina, SE USA
23 R5 **Phenix City** Alabama, S USA 32°28′N 85°00′W
Phet Buri *see* Phetchaburi
167 O11 **Phetchaburi** *var.* Bejraburi, Petchaburi, Phet Buri. Phetchaburi, SW Thailand 13°05′N 99°58′E
167 O9 **Phichit** *var.* Bichitra, Muang Phichit, Pichit. Phichit, C Thailand 16°29′N 100°21′E
22 M5 **Philadelphia** Mississippi, S USA 32°45′N 89°06′W
18 I7 **Philadelphia** New York, NE USA 44°10′N 75°40′W
18 I16 **Philadelphia** Pennsylvania, NE USA 40°N 75°10′W
18 I16 **Philadelphia** ✈ Pennsylvania, NE USA 39°51′N 75°13′W
Philadelphia *see* 'Amman
28 L10 **Philip** South Dakota, N USA 44°02′N 101°39′W
99 H22 **Philippeville** Namur, S Belgium 50°12′N 04°33′E
Philippeville *see* Skikda
21 S3 **Philippi** West Virginia, NE USA 39°08′N 80°03′W
Philippi *see* Fílippoi
195 Y9 **Philippi Glacier** *glacier* Antarctica
192 G6 **Philippine Basin** *undersea feature* W Pacific Ocean 17°00′N 132°00′E
129 X12 **Philippine Plate** *tectonic feature*
171 O5 **Philippines** *off.* Republic of the Philippines. ◆ *republic* SE Asia
129 X13 **Philippines** *island group* W Pacific Ocean
171 P3 **Philippine Sea** *sea* W Pacific Ocean
Philippines, Republic of the *see* Philippines
192 F6 **Philippine Trench** *undersea feature* W Philippine Sea
83 H23 **Philippolis** Free State, C South Africa 30°16′S 25°16′E
Philippopolis *see* Plovdiv
Philippopolis *see* Shahbā', Syria
45 V9 **Philipsburg** ○ Sint Maarten 17°58′N 63°02′W
33 P10 **Philipsburg** Montana, NW USA 46°19′N 113°17′W
39 R6 **Philip Smith Mountains** ▲▲ Alaska, USA
152 H8 **Phillaur** Punjab, N India 31°02′N 75°50′E
183 N13 **Phillip Island** *island* Victoria, SE Australia
25 N2 **Phillips** Texas, SW USA 35°39′N 101°21′W
30 K5 **Phillips** Wisconsin, N USA 45°42′N 90°23′W
26 K3 **Phillipsburg** Kansas, C USA 39°45′N 99°19′W
18 I14 **Phillipsburg** New Jersey, NE USA 40°39′N 75°09′W
21 S7 **Philpott Lake** ⊠ Virginia, NE USA
Phintias *see* Licata
167 P9 **Phitsanulok** *var.* Bisnulok, Muang Phitsanulok, Pitsanulok. Phitsanulok, C Thailand 16°49′N 100°15′E
Phlórina *see* Flórina
Phnom Penh *see* Phnum Penh
167 S13 **Phnum Penh** *var.* Phnom Penh. ● (Cambodia) Phnum Penh, S Cambodia 11°35′N 104°55′E
167 S11 **Phnum Tbêng Meanchey** Preăh Vihéar, N Cambodia 13°45′N 104°58′E
36 K13 **Phoenix** *state capital* Arizona, SW USA 33°27′N 112°04′W
Phoenix Island *see* Rawaki
191 R3 **Phoenix Islands** *island group* C Kiribati
18 I15 **Phoenixville** Pennsylvania, NE USA 40°07′N 75°31′W
83 K22 **Phofung** *var.* Mont-aux-Sources. ▲ N Lesotho 28°47′S 28°52′E
167 Q10 **Phon** Khon Kaen, E Thailand 15°47′N 102°35′E
167 Q5 **Phôngsali** *var.* Phong Saly. Phôngsali, N Laos 21°40′N 102°04′E
Phong Saly *see* Phôngsali
Phônhông *see* Ban Phônhông
167 R7 **Phônsaven** *var.* Pèk, Xieng Khouang; *prev.* Xiangkhoang. Xiangkhoang, N Laos 19°19′N 103°23′E
167 R5 **Phô Rang** *var.* Bao Yèn. Lao Cai, N Vietnam 22°12′N 104°27′E
Phort Láirge, Cuan *see* Waterford Harbour
Phou Louang *see* Annamite Mountains
167 N10 **Phra Chedi Sam Ong** Kanchanaburi, W Thailand 15°18′N 98°26′E
167 O8 **Phrae** *var.* Muang Phrae, Prae. Phrae, NW Thailand 18°07′N 100°09′E
Phra Nakhon Si Ayutthaya *see* Ayutthaya
167 M14 **Phra Thong, Ko** *island* SW Thailand
Phu Cŭơng *see* Thu Dâu Môt
166 M15 **Phuket** *var.* Bhuket, Puket, *Mal.* Ujung Salang; *prev.* Junkseylon, Salang. Phuket, SW Thailand 07°52′N 98°22′E
166 M15 **Phuket** ✈ Phuket, SW Thailand 08°03′N 98°16′E
166 M15 **Phuket, Ko** *island* SW Thailand
154 N12 **Phulabāni** *prev.* Phulbani. Orissa, E India 20°30′N 84°18′E
Phulbani *see* Phulabāni
167 U9 **Phu Lôc** Th,a Thiên-Huê, C Vietnam 16°13′N 107°53′E
167 R13 **Phumĭ Chŏâm** Kâmpóng Spœ, SW Cambodia 11°42′N 103°58′E
Phumĭ Kalêng *see* Kalêng
Phumĭ Kâmpóng Trâbêk *see* Kâmpóng Trâbêk
Phumĭ Koŭk Kduŏch *see* Koŭk Kduŏch
Phumĭ Labăng *see* Labăng
Phumĭ Mlu Prey *see* Mlu Prey
Phumĭ Moŭng *see* Moŭng
Phumĭ Prâmaôy *see* Prâmaôy
Phumĭ Samĭt *see* Samĭt
Phumĭ Sâmraông *see* Sâmraông
Phumĭ Siĕmbok *see* Siĕmbok
Phumĭ Thalabârĭvăt *see* Thalabârĭvăt
Phumĭ Veal Renh *see* Veal Renh
Phumĭ Yeay Sên *see* Yeay Sên
Phum Kompong Trabek *see* Kâmpóng Trâbêk
Phum Samrong *see* Sâmraông
167 V11 **Phu My** Binh Đinh, C Vietnam 14°07′N 109°05′E
Phung Hiêp *see* Tân Hiêp
153 T12 **Phuntsholing** SW Bhutan 26°52′N 89°26′E
167 V13 **Phư ơ c Dân** Ninh Thuân, S Vietnam 11°28′N 108°53′E
167 R15 **Phươc Long** Minh Hai, S Vietnam 09°27′N 105°25′E
Phươc Sơn *see* Khâm Đức
167 R14 **Phu Quôc, Đao** *var.* Phu Quoc Island. *island* S Vietnam
Phu Quoc Island *see* Phu Quôc, Đao
167 S6 **Phu Tho** Vinh Phu, N Vietnam 21°23′N 105°13′E
Phu Vinh *see* Tra Vinh
166 M7 **Phyu** *var.* Hpyu, Pyu. Bago, C Burma (Myanmar) 18°29′N 96°28′E
189 T13 **Piaanu Pass** *passage* Chuuk Islands, C Micronesia
106 E8 **Piacenza** *Fr.* Paisance; *anc.* Placentia. Emilia-Romagna, N Italy 45°02′N 09°42′E
107 K14 **Pianella** Abruzzo, C Italy 42°23′N 14°04′E
107 M15 **Pianosa, Isola** *island* Archipelago Toscano, C Italy
171 U13 **Piar** Papua, E Indonesia 02°49′S 132°46′E
45 U14 **Piarco** *var.* Port of Spain. ✈ (Port-of-Spain) Trinidad, Trinidad and Tobago 10°36′N 61°21′W
110 M12 **Piaseczno** Mazowieckie, C Poland 52°03′N 21°00′E
116 I15 **Piatra** Teleorman, S Romania 43°49′N 25°10′E
116 L10 **Piatra-Neamţ** *Hung.* Karácsonkő. Neamţ, NE Romania 46°54′N 26°23′E
Piauhy *see* Piauí
59 N15 **Piauí** *off.* Estado do Piauí; *prev.* Piauhy. ◈ *state* E Brazil
Piauí, Estado do *see* Piauí
106 I7 **Piave** ≈ NE Italy
107 K24 **Piazza Armerina** *var.* Chiazza. Sicilia, Italy, C Mediterranean Sea 37°23′N 14°22′E
81 G14 **Pibor** *Amh.* Pībor Wenz. ≈ Ethiopia/South Sudan
81 G14 **Pibor Post** Jonglei, E South Sudan 06°50′N 33°06′E
Pībor Wenz *see* Pibor
Pibrans *see* Příbram
36 K11 **Picacho Butte** ▲ Arizona, SW USA 35°12′N 112°44′W
40 D4 **Picachos, Cerro** ▲ NW Mexico 29°15′N 114°04′W
103 O4 **Picardie** *Eng.* Picardy. ◈ *region* N France
Picardy *see* Picardie
22 L8 **Picayune** Mississippi, S USA 30°31′N 89°40′W
Piccolo San Bernardo, Colle di *see* Little Saint Bernard Pass
PicdeBälaitous *see* Balaïtous
62 K5 **Pichanal** Salta, N Argentina 23°18′S 64°10′W
147 P12 **Pichandar** W Tajikistan 38°44′N 68°51′E
27 R8 **Picher** Oklahoma, C USA 36°59′N 94°49′W
62 G12 **Pichilemu** Libertador, C Chile 34°25′S 72°00′W
40 F9 **Pichilingue** Baja California Sur, NW Mexico 24°20′N 110°17′W
56 B6 **Pichincha** ◈ *province* N Ecuador
56 C6 **Pichincha** ▲ N Ecuador 0°12′S 78°39′W
Pichit *see* Phichit
41 U15 **Pichucalco** Chiapas, SE Mexico 17°32′N 93°07′W
22 L5 **Pickens** Mississippi, S USA 32°52′N 89°58′W
21 O11 **Pickens** South Carolina, SE USA 34°53′N 82°42′W
14 G11 **Pickerel** ≈ Ontario, S Canada
14 H15 **Pickering** Ontario, S Canada 43°50′N 79°03′W
97 N16 **Pickering** N England, United Kingdom 54°14′N 00°47′W
31 S13 **Pickerington** Ohio, N USA 39°52′N 82°45′W
12 C10 **Pickle Lake** Ontario, C Canada 51°30′N 90°10′W
29 P12 **Pickstown** South Dakota, N USA 43°02′N 98°31′W
25 V6 **Pickton** Texas, SW USA 33°01′N 95°19′W
23 N1 **Pickwick Lake** ⊠ S USA
64 N2 **Pico** *var.* Ilha do Pico. *island* Azores, Portugal, NE Atlantic Ocean
63 J19 **Pico de Salamanca** Chubut, SE Argentina 45°26′S 67°26′W
1 P9 **Pico Fracture Zone** *tectonic feature* NW Atlantic Ocean
Pico, Ilha do *see* Pico
59 O14 **Picos** Piauí, E Brazil 07°05′S 41°24′W
63 I20 **Pico Truncado** Santa Cruz, SE Argentina 46°45′S 68°00′W
183 S9 **Picton** New South Wales, SE Australia 34°12′S 150°36′E
14 K15 **Picton** Ontario, SE Canada 43°59′N 77°09′W
185 K14 **Picton** Marlborough, South Island, New Zealand 41°18′S 174°00′E
63 H15 **Picún Leufú, Arroyo** ≈ SW Argentina
Pidálion *see* Gkréko, Akrotíri
155 K25 **Pidurutalagala** ▲ S Sri Lanka 07°03′N 80°47′E
116 K6 **Pidvolochys'k** Ternopil's'ka Oblast', W Ukraine 49°31′N 26°09′E
107 K16 **Piedimonte Matese** Campania, S Italy 41°20′N 14°30′E
27 X7 **Piedmont** Missouri, C USA 37°09′N 90°42′W
21 P11 **Piedmont** South Carolina, SE USA 34°42′N 82°27′W
17 S12 **Piedmont** *escarpment* E USA
Piedmont *see* Piemonte
31 U13 **Piedmont Lake** ⊠ Ohio, N USA
104 M11 **Piedrabuena** Castilla-La Mancha, C Spain 39°02′N 04°10′W
Piedrafita, Puerto de *see* Pedrafita, Porto de
104 L8 **Piedrahita** Castilla y León, N Spain 40°27′N 05°20′W
41 N6 **Piedras Negras** *var.* Ciudad Porfirio Díaz. Coahuila, NE Mexico 28°40′N 100°32′W
61 E21 **Piedras, Punta** *headland* E Argentina 35°27′S 57°04′W
57 I14 **Piedras, Río de las** ≈ E Peru
111 J16 **Piekary Śląskie** Śląskie, S Poland 50°24′N 18°58′E
93 M17 **Pieksämäki** Itä-Suomi, E Finland 62°18′N 27°10′E
109 V5 **Pielach** ≈ NE Austria
93 M16 **Pielavesi** Itä-Suomi, C Finland 63°14′N 26°45′E
93 M16 **Pielavesi** ◎ C Finland
93 N16 **Pielinen** *var.* Pielisjärvi. ◎ E Finland
Pielisjärvi *see* Pielinen
106 A8 **Piemonte** *Eng.* Piedmont. ◈ *region* NW Italy
111 L18 **Pieniny** ▲▲ S Poland
111 E14 **Pieńsk** *Ger.* Penzig. Dolnośląskie, SW Poland 51°14′N 15°03′E
29 Q13 **Pierce** Nebraska, C USA 42°12′N 97°31′W
11 R14 **Pierceland** Saskatchewan, C Canada
115 E14 **Piéria** ▲▲ N Greece
29 N10 **Pierre** *state capital* South Dakota, N USA 44°22′N 100°21′W
102 K16 **Pierrefitte-Nestalas** Hautes-Pyrénées, S France 42°57′N 00°04′W
103 R14 **Pierrelatte** Drôme, E France 44°22′N 04°40′E
15 P11 **Pierreville** Québec, SE Canada 46°05′N 72°48′W
15 O7 **Pierriche** ≈ Québec, SE Canada
111 H20 **Piešt'any** *Ger.* Pistyan, *Hung.* Pöstyén. Tranavský Kraj, W Slovakia 48°37′N 17°48′E
109 X5 **Piesting** ≈ E Austria
Pietarhovi *see* Petrodvorets
Pietari *see* Sankt-Peterburg
Pietarsaari *see* Jakobstad
83 K23 **Pietermaritzburg** *var.* Maritzburg. KwaZulu/Natal, E South Africa 29°35′S 30°23′E
Pietersburg *see* Polokwane
107 K24 **Pietraperzia** Sicilia, Italy, C Mediterranean Sea 37°25′N 14°08′E
107 N22 **Pietra Spada, Passo della** *pass* SW Italy
Piet Retief *see* eMkhondo
116 J10 **Pietrosul, Vârful** *prev.* Vîrful Pietrosu. ▲ N Romania 47°06′N 25°09′E
106 I6 **Pieve di Cadore** Veneto, NE Italy 46°27′N 12°22′E
14 C18 **Pigeon Bay** *lake bay* Ontario, S Canada
27 X8 **Piggott** Arkansas, C USA 36°22′N 90°11′W
83 L21 **Piggs Peak** NW Swaziland 25°58′S 31°17′E
Pigs, Bay of *see* Cochinos, Bahía de
61 A23 **Pigüé** Buenos Aires, E Argentina 37°38′S 62°27′W
41 O12 **Piguícas** ▲ C Mexico 21°08′N 99°37′W
193 W15 **Piha Passage** *passage* S Tonga
Pihkva Järv *see* Pskov, Lake
93 N18 **Pihlajavesi** ◎ SE Finland
93 J18 **Pihlava** Länsi-Suomi, SW Finland 61°33′N 21°36′E
93 L16 **Pihtipudas** Länsi-Suomi, C Finland 63°20′N 25°37′E
40 L14 **Pihuamo** Jalisco, SW Mexico 19°20′N 103°21′W
189 U11 **Piis Moen** *var.* Pis. *atoll* Chuuk Islands, C Micronesia
41 U17 **Pijijiapán** Chiapas, SE Mexico 15°42′N 93°12′W
98 G12 **Pijnacker** Zuid-Holland, W Netherlands 52°01′N 04°26′E
42 H5 **Pijol, Pico** ▲ NW Honduras 15°07′N 87°39′W
Pikaar *see* Bikar Atoll
124 I13 **Pikalevo** Leningradskaya Oblast', NW Russian Federation 59°33′N 34°04′E
188 M15 **Pikelot** *island* Caroline Islands, C Micronesia
30 M5 **Pike River** ≈ Wisconsin, N USA
37 T5 **Pikes Peak** ▲ Colorado, C USA 38°51′N 105°06′W
21 P6 **Pikeville** Kentucky, S USA 37°29′N 82°33′W
20 L9 **Pikeville** Tennessee, S USA 35°35′N 85°11′W
Pikinni *see* Bikini Atoll
79 H18 **Pikounda** Sangha, C Congo 0°30′N 16°44′E
110 G9 **Piła** *Ger.* Schneidemühl. Wielkopolskie, C Poland 53°09′N 16°44′E
62 N6 **Pilagá, Riacho** ≈ NE Argentina
61 D20 **Pilar** Buenos Aires, E Argentina 34°28′S 58°55′W
62 N7 **Pilar** *var.* Villa del Pilar. Ñeembucú, S Paraguay 26°55′S 58°20′W
62 N6 **Pilcomayo, Rio** ≈ C South America
147 R12 **Pildon** *Rus.* Pil'don. C Tajikistan 39°10′N 71°00′E
Piles *see* Pylés
Pilgram *see* Pelhřimov
152 L10 **Pīlībhīt** Uttar Pradesh, N India 28°37′N 79°48′E
110 M13 **Pilica** ≈ C Poland
115 G16 **Pílio** ▲▲ C Greece
111 J22 **Pilisvörösvár** Pest, N Hungary 47°38′N 18°55′E
65 G15 **Pillar Bay** *bay* Ascension Island, C Atlantic Ocean
183 P17 **Pillar, Cape** *headland* Tasmania, SE Australia 43°13′S 147°58′E
Pillau *see* Baltiysk
183 R5 **Pilliga** New South Wales, SE Australia 30°22′S 148°53′E
44 H8 **Pilón** Granma, E Cuba 19°54′N 77°20′W
Pilos *see* Pýlos
11 W17 **Pilot Mound** Manitoba, S Canada 49°12′N 98°49′W
21 S8 **Pilot Mountain** North Carolina, SE USA 36°23′N 80°28′W
39 O14 **Pilot Point** Alaska, USA 57°33′N 157°34′W
25 T5 **Pilot Point** Texas, SW USA 33°24′N 96°57′W
32 K11 **Pilot Rock** Oregon, NW USA 45°28′N 118°49′W
38 M11 **Pilot Station** Alaska, USA 61°56′N 162°52′W
Pilsen *see* Plzeň
111 K18 **Pilsko** ▲ N Slovakia 49°31′N 19°21′E
Pilten *see* Piltene
118 D8 **Piltene** *Ger.* Pilten. W Latvia 57°14′N 21°41′E
111 M16 **Pilzno** Podkarpackie, SE Poland 49°58′N 21°18′E
Pilzno *see* Plzeň
37 N14 **Pima** Arizona, SW USA 32°49′N 109°50′W
58 H13 **Pimenta** Pará, N Brazil 04°32′S 56°17′W
59 F16 **Pimenta Bueno** Rondônia, W Brazil 11°40′S 61°14′W
56 B11 **Pimentel** Lambayeque, W Peru 06°51′S 79°53′W
105 S6 **Pina** Aragón, NE Spain 41°28′N 00°31′W
119 I20 **Pina** ≈ SW Belarus
40 E2 **Pinacate, Sierra del** ▲ NW Mexico 31°49′N 113°30′W
63 H22 **Pináculo, Cerro** ▲ S Argentina 50°46′S 72°07′W
191 X11 **Pinaki** *atoll* Îles Tuamotu, E French Polynesia
37 N15 **Pinaleno Mountains** ▲▲ Arizona, SW USA
171 P4 **Pinamalayan** Mindoro, N Philippines 13°00′N 121°30′E
169 Q10 **Pinang** Borneo, C Indonesia 0°36′N 109°11′W
168 J7 **Pinang** *var.* Penang. ◈ *state* Peninsular Malaysia
Pinang *see* Pinang, Pulau, Peninsular Malaysia
Pinang *see* George Town
168 J7 **Pinang, Pulau** *var.* Penang, Pinang; *prev.* Prince of Wales Island. *island* Peninsular Malaysia
44 B5 **Pinar del Río** Pinar del Río, W Cuba 22°24′N 83°42′W
114 N11 **Pınarhisar** Kırklareli, NW Turkey 41°37′N 27°32′E
171 O3 **Pinatubo, Mount** ⛰ Luzon, N Philippines 15°08′N 120°21′E
11 Y16 **Pinawa** Manitoba, S Canada 50°09′N 95°52′W
11 Q17 **Pincher Creek** Alberta, SW Canada 49°31′N 113°53′W
30 L16 **Pinckneyville** Illinois, N USA 38°04′N 89°22′W
Pîncota *see* Pâncota
111 L15 **Pińczów** Świętokrzyskie, C Poland 50°30′N 20°30′E
149 U7 **Pind Dādan Khān** Punjab, E Pakistan 32°36′N 73°07′E
Píndhos/Píndhos Óros *see* Píndos
149 V8 **Pindi Bhattiān** Punjab, E Pakistan 31°54′N 73°20′E
149 U6 **Pindi Gheb** Punjab, E Pakistan 33°16′N 72°21′E
115 D15 **Píndos** *var.* Píndhos Óros, *Eng.* Pindus Mountains; *prev.* Píndhos. ▲▲ C Greece
Pindus Mountains *see* Píndos
18 J16 **Pine Barrens** *physical region* New Jersey, NE USA
27 V12 **Pine Bluff** Arkansas, C USA 34°15′N 92°00′W
23 X11 **Pine Castle** Florida, SE USA 28°28′N 81°22′W
29 V7 **Pine City** Minnesota, N USA 45°49′N 92°55′W
181 P2 **Pine Creek** Northern Territory, N Australia 13°51′S 131°51′E
35 V4 **Pine Creek** ≈ Nevada, W USA
18 F13 **Pine Creek** ≈ Pennsylvania, NE USA
27 Q13 **Pine Creek Lake** ⊠ Oklahoma, C USA
33 T15 **Pinedale** Wyoming, C USA 42°52′N 109°51′W
11 X15 **Pine Dock** Manitoba, S Canada 51°34′N 96°47′W
11 Y16 **Pine Falls** Manitoba, S Canada 50°29′N 96°12′W
35 R10 **Pine Flat Lake** ⊠ California, W USA
125 N8 **Pinega** Arkhangel'skaya Oblast', NW Russian Federation 64°40′N 43°24′E
125 N8 **Pinega** ≈ NW Russian Federation
15 N12 **Pine Hill** Québec, SE Canada 45°44′N 74°30′W
11 T12 **Pinehouse Lake** ◎ Saskatchewan, C Canada
21 T10 **Pinehurst** North Carolina, SE USA 35°12′N 79°28′W
115 D19 **Pineiós** ≈ S Greece
115 E16 **Pineiós** *var.* Piniós; *anc.* Peneius. ≈ C Greece
29 W10 **Pine Island** Minnesota, N USA 44°12′N 92°39′W
23 V15 **Pine Island** *island* Florida, SE USA
194 K10 **Pine Island Glacier** *glacier* Antarctica
25 X9 **Pineland** Texas, SW USA 31°15′N 93°58′W
23 V13 **Pinellas Park** Florida, SE USA 27°50′N 82°42′W
10 M13 **Pine Pass** *pass* British Columbia, W Canada
8 J10 **Pine Point** Northwest Territories, W Canada 60°52′N 114°30′W
28 K12 **Pine Ridge** South Dakota, N USA 43°01′N 102°33′W
29 U6 **Pine River** Minnesota, N USA 46°43′N 94°24′W
31 Q8 **Pine River** ≈ Michigan, N USA
30 M4 **Pine River** ≈ Wisconsin, N USA
106 A8 **Pinerolo** Piemonte, NE Italy 44°56′N 07°21′E
115 I15 **Pínes, Akrotírio** *var.* Akrotírio Pínnes. *headland* N Greece 40°06′N 24°19′E
25 W6 **Pines, Lake O' the** ⊠ Texas, SW USA
Pines, The Isle of the *see* Juventud, Isla de la
Pine Tree State *see* Maine
21 N7 **Pineville** Kentucky, S USA 36°47′N 83°43′W
22 H7 **Pineville** Louisiana, S USA 31°19′N 92°25′W
27 R8 **Pineville** Missouri, C USA 36°36′N 94°23′W
21 R10 **Pineville** North Carolina, SE USA 35°04′N 80°53′W
21 Q6 **Pineville** West Virginia, NE USA 37°35′N 81°34′W
33 V8 **Piney Buttes** *physical region* Montana, NW USA
163 W9 **Ping'an** Jilin, NE China 44°36′N 127°13′E
160 H14 **Pingbian** *var.* Pingbian Miaozu Zizhixian, Yuping. Yunnan, SW China 22°51′N 103°28′E
Pingbian Miaozu Zizhixian *see* Pingbian
157 S9 **Pingdingshan** Henan, C China 33°52′N 113°20′E
161 S14 **Pingdong** *Jap.* Heitō; *prev.* P'ingtung. S Taiwan 22°40′N 120°30′E
161 R4 **Pingdu** Shandong, E China 36°50′N 119°55′E
189 W16 **Pingelap Atoll** *atoll* Caroline Islands, E Micronesia
160 K14 **Pingguo** *var.* Matou. Guangxi Zhuangzu Zizhiqu, S China 23°24′N 107°30′E
161 Q13 **Pinghe** *var.* Xiaoxi. Fujian, SE China 24°30′N 117°19′E
P'ing-hsiang *see* Pingxiang
161 N10 **Pingjiang** Hunan, S China 28°44′N 113°33′E
Pingkiang *see* Harbin
160 L8 **Pingli** Shaanxi, C China 32°27′N 109°21′E
159 W10 **Pingliang** *var.* Kongtong, P'ing-liang. Gansu, C China 35°27′N 106°38′E
P'ing-liang *see* Pingliang
159 W8 **Pingluo** Ningxia, N China 38°55′N 106°31′E
Pingma *see* Tiandong
167 O7 **Ping, Mae Nam** ≈ W Thailand
161 Q1 **Pingquan** Hebei, E China 41°02′N 118°35′E
29 P5 **Pingree** North Dakota, N USA 47°07′N 98°54′W
Pingsiang *see* Pingxiang
P'ingtung *see* Pingdong
160 I8 **Pingwu** *var.* Long'an. Sichuan, C China 32°33′N 104°32′E
160 J15 **Pingxiang** Guangxi Zhuangzu Zizhiqu, S China 22°03′N 106°44′E
161 O11 **Pingxiang** *var.* P'ing-hsiang; *prev.* Pingsiang. Jiangxi, S China 27°42′N 113°50′E
Pingxiang *see* Tongwei
161 S11 **Pingyang** *var.* Kunyang. Zhejiang, SE China 27°46′N 120°37′E
161 P5 **Pingyi** Shandong, E China 35°30′N 117°38′E
161 P5 **Pingyin** Shandong, E China 36°18′N 116°24′E
60 H13 **Pinhalzinho** Santa Catarina, S Brazil 26°53′S 52°57′W
60 I12 **Pinhão** Paraná, S Brazil 25°46′S 51°32′W
61 H17 **Pinheiro Machado** Rio Grande do Sul, S Brazil 31°34′S 53°22′W
104 I7 **Pinhel** Guarda, N Portugal 40°47′N 07°03′W
Piniós *see* Pineiós
168 I11 **Pini, Pulau** *island* Kepulauan Batu, W Indonesia
109 Y7 **Pinka** ≈ SE Austria
109 X7 **Pinkafeld** Burgenland, SE Austria 47°23′N 16°08′E
Pinkiang *see* Harbin
10 M12 **Pink Mountain** British Columbia, W Canada 57°10′N 122°36′W
166 M3 **Pinlebu** Sagaing, N Burma (Myanmar) 24°02′N 95°21′E
38 J12 **Pinnacle Island** *island* Alaska, USA
180 I12 **Pinnacles, The** *tourist site* Western Australia
182 K10 **Pinnaroo** South Australia 35°17′S 140°54′E
Pinne *see* Pniewy
100 I9 **Pinneberg** Schleswig-Holstein, N Germany 53°40′N 09°49′E
Pínnes, Akrotírio *see* Pínes, Akrotírio
Pinos, Isla de *see* Juventud, Isla de la
35 R14 **Pinos, Mount** ▲ California, W USA 34°48′N 119°09′W
105 R12 **Pinoso** Valenciana, E Spain 38°25′N 01°02′W
105 N14 **Pinos-Puente** Andalucía, S Spain 37°16′N 03°46′W
41 Q17 **Pinotepa Nacional** *var.* Santiago Pinotepa Nacional. Oaxaca, SE Mexico 16°20′N 98°02′W
114 F13 **Pínovo** ▲ N Greece 41°06′N 22°19′E
187 R17 **Pins, Île des** *var.* Kunyé. *island* E New Caledonia

◆ Country ● Country Capital ◇ Dependent Territory ○ Dependent Territory Capital ◈ Administrative Regions ✈ International Airport ▲ Mountain ▲▲ Mountain Range ⛰ Volcano ≈ River ◎ Lake ⊠ Reservoir

119 I20 Pinsk Pol. Pińsk. Brestskaya Voblasts', SW Belarus 52°07′N 26°07′E
14 D18 Pins, Pointe aux headland Ontario, S Canada 42°14′N 81°53′W
57 B16 Pinta, Isla var. Abingdon. island Galapagos Islands, Ecuador, E Pacific Ocean
125 Q12 Pinyug Kirovskaya Oblast', NW Russian Federation 60°12′N 47°45′E
57 B17 Pinzón, Isla var. Duncan Island. island Galapagos Islands, Ecuador, E Pacific Ocean
35 Y8 Pioche Nevada, W USA 37°57′N 114°30′W
106 F13 Piombino Toscana, C Italy 42°54′N 10°30′E
0 C9 Pioneer Fracture Zone tectonic feature NE Pacific Ocean
122 L5 Pioner, Ostrov island Severnaya Zemlya, N Russian Federation
118 A13 Pionerskiy Ger. Neukuhren. Kaliningradskaya Oblast', W Russian Federation 54°57′N 20°16′E
110 N13 Pionki Mazowieckie, C Poland 51°30′N 21°27′E
184 L9 Piopio Waikato, North Island, New Zealand 38°27′S 175°00′E
110 K13 Piotrków Trybunalski Ger. Petrikau, Rus. Petrokov. Łodzkie, C Poland 51°25′N 19°42′E
152 F12 Pipār Road Rājasthān, N India 26°25′N 73°29′E
115 I16 Pipéri island Vóreies Sporádes, Greece, Aegean Sea
29 S10 Pipestone Minnesota, N USA 44°00′N 96°19′W
12 C9 Pipestone ≈ Ontario, C Canada
61 E21 Pipinas Buenos Aires, E Argentina 35°32′S 57°20′W
149 T7 Piplān prev. Liaqatabad. Punjab, E Pakistan 32°17′N 71°24′E
15 R5 Pipmuacan, Réservoir ⊠ Québec, SE Canada
Piqan see Shanshan
31 R13 Piqua Ohio, N USA 40°08′N 84°14′W
105 P5 Piqueras, Puerto de pass N Spain
60 H11 Piquiri, Rio ≈ S Brazil
60 L9 Piracicaba São Paulo, S Brazil 22°45′S 47°40′W
Piraeus/Piraiévs see Peiraías
60 K10 Piraju São Paulo, S Brazil 23°12′S 49°24′W
60 K9 Pirajuí São Paulo, S Brazil 21°58′S 49°27′W
63 G21 Pirámide, Cerro ▲ S Chile 49°06′S 73°32′W
Piramiva see Pyramíva
109 R13 Piran It. Pirano. SW Slovenia 45°35′N 13°35′E
62 N6 Piranė Formosa, N Argentina 25°42′S 59°06′W
59 J18 Piranhas Goiás, S Brazil 16°24′S 51°51′W
Pirano see Piran
142 I4 Pirānshahr Āžarbāyjān-e Gharbī, NW Iran 36°41′N 45°08′E
59 M19 Pirapora Minas Gerais, NE Brazil 17°20′S 44°54′W
60 I9 Pirapòzinho São Paulo, S Brazil 22°17′S 51°31′W
61 G19 Pirarajá Lavalleja, S Uruguay 33°44′S 54°45′W
60 L9 Pirassununga São Paulo, S Brazil 21°58′S 47°23′W
45 V6 Pirata, Monte ▲ E Puerto Rico 18°06′N 65°33′W
60 I13 Piratuba Santa Catarina, S Brazil 27°26′S 51°47′W
114 I9 Pirdop prev. Strednogorie. Sofiya, W Bulgaria 42°44′N 24°09′E
191 P7 Pirea Tahiti, W French Polynesia
59 K18 Pirenópolis Goiás, S Brazil 15°48′S 49°00′W
153 S13 Pirganj Rajshahi, NW Bangladesh 25°51′N 88°25′E
Pirgi see Pyrgí
Pírgos see Pýrgos
61 F20 Piriápolis Maldonado, S Uruguay 34°51′S 55°15′W
114 G11 Pirin ▲▲ SW Bulgaria
Pirineos see Pyrenees
58 N13 Piripiri Piauí, E Brazil 04°15′S 41°46′W
118 H4 Pirita var. Pirita Jõgi. ≈ NW Estonia
Pirita Jõgi see Pirita
54 J6 Píritu Portuguesa, N Venezuela 09°21′N 69°16′W
93 L18 Pirkkala Länsi-Suomi, W Finland 61°27′N 23°47′E
101 F20 Pirmasens Rheinland-Pfalz, SW Germany 49°12′N 07°37′E
101 P16 Pirna Sachsen, E Germany 50°57′N 13°56′E
Piroe see Piru
113 Q15 Pirot Serbia, SE Serbia 43°12′N 22°34′E
152 H6 Pīr Panjāl Range ▲▲ NE India
43 W16 Pirre, Cerro ▲ SE Panama 07°54′N 77°42′W
137 Y11 Pirsaat Rus. Pirsagat. ≈ E Azerbaijan
Pirsagat see Pirsaat
143 V11 Pīr Shūrān, Selseleh-ye ▲▲ SE Iran
92 M12 Pirttikoski Lappi, N Finland 66°20′N 27°08′E
Pirttikylä see Pörtom
171 R13 Piru prev. Piroe. Pulau Seram, E Indonesia 03°01′S 128°10′E
Piryatin see Pyryatyn
Pis see Piis Moen
106 F11 Pisa var. Pisae. Toscana, C Italy 43°43′N 10°23′E
Pisae see Pisa
189 V12 Pisar atoll Chuuk Islands, C Micronesia
Pisaurum see Pesaro
14 M10 Piscatosine, Lac ◎ Québec, SE Canada
109 W7 Pischeldorf Steiermark, SE Austria 47°11′N 15°48′E
Pischk see Simeria
107 L19 Pisciotta Campania, S Italy 40°07′N 15°13′E
57 E16 Pisco Ica, SW Peru 13°46′S 76°12′W
116 G9 Pişcolt Hung. Piskolt. Satu Mare, NW Romania 47°35′N 22°18′E
57 E16 Pisco, Río ≈ E Peru
111 C18 Písek Budějovický Kraj, S Czech Republic 49°19′N 14°07′E
31 R14 Pisgah Ohio, N USA 39°19′N 84°22′W
Pisha see Ningnan
158 F9 Pishan var. Guma. Xinjiang Uygur Zizhiqu, NW China 37°36′N 78°45′E
117 N8 Pishchanka Vinnyts'ka Oblast', C Ukraine 48°12′N 28°52′E
113 K21 Pishë Fier, SW Albania 40°40′N 19°22′E
143 X14 Pīshīn Sīstān va Balūchestān, SE Iran 26°05′N 61°46′E
149 O9 Pishīn Khyber Pakhtunkhwa, NW Pakistan 30°33′N 67°01′E
149 N11 Pishin Lora var. Psein Lora, Pash. Pseyn Bowr. ≈ SW Pakistan
Pishma see Pizhma
Pishpek see Bishkek
171 O14 Pising Pulau Kabaena, C Indonesia 05°07′S 121°50′E
Pisino see Pazin
Piski see Simeria
Piskolt see Pişcolt
147 Q9 Piskom Rus. Pskem. ≈ E Uzbekistan
Piskom Tizmasi see Pskemskiy Khrebet
35 P13 Pismo Beach California, W USA 35°08′N 120°38′W
77 P12 Pissila C Burkina 13°07′N 00°51′W
62 H8 Pissis, Monte ▲ N Argentina 27°45′S 68°43′W
41 X12 Piste Yucatán, E Mexico 20°40′N 88°34′W
107 O18 Pisticci Basilicata, S Italy 40°23′N 16°33′E
106 F11 Pistoia anc. Pistoria, Pistoriæ. Toscana, C Italy 43°57′N 10°53′E
32 E15 Pistol River Oregon, NW USA 42°13′N 124°23′W
Pistoria/Pistoriæ see Pistoia
15 U5 Pistuacanis ≈ Québec, SE Canada
Pistyan see Piešt'any
104 M5 Pisuerga ≈ N Spain
110 N8 Pisz Ger. Johannisburg. Warmińsko-Mazurskie, NE Poland 53°37′N 21°49′E
76 I13 Pita NW Guinea 11°05′N 12°15′W
54 D12 Pitalito Huila, S Colombia 01°51′N 76°01′W
60 I11 Pitanga Paraná, S Brazil 24°45′S 51°43′W
182 M9 Pitarpunga Lake salt lake New South Wales, SE Australia
193 P10 Pitcairn Island island S Pitcairn Islands
193 P10 Pitcairn Islands ◇ UK dependent territory C Pacific Ocean
93 J14 Piteå Norrbotten, N Sweden 65°19′N 21°30′E
92 I13 Piteälven ≈ N Sweden
116 I13 Piteşti Argeş, S Romania 44°53′N 24°49′E
Pithagorio see Pythagóreio
180 I12 Pithara Western Australia 30°31′S 116°38′E
103 N6 Pithiviers Loiret, C France 48°10′N 02°15′E
152 L9 Pithorāgarh Uttarakhand, N India 29°35′N 80°12′E
188 B16 Piti W Guam 13°28′N 144°42′E
106 G13 Pitigliano Toscana, C Italy 42°38′N 11°40′E
40 F3 Pitiquito Sonora, NW Mexico 30°39′N 112°00′W
Pitkäranta see Pitkyaranta
38 M11 Pitkas Point Alaska, USA 62°01′N 163°17′W
124 H11 Pitkyaranta Fin. Pitkäranta. Respublika Kareliya, NW Russian Federation 61°34′N 31°27′E
96 J10 Pitlochry C Scotland, United Kingdom 56°47′N 03°48′W
18 I16 Pitman New Jersey, NE USA 39°43′N 75°06′W
146 I9 Pitnak var. Drujba, Rus. Druzhba. Xorazm Viloyati, W Uzbekistan 41°14′N 61°13′E
112 G8 Pitomača Virovitica-Podravina, NE Croatia 45°57′N 17°14′E
35 O2 Pit River ≈ California, W USA
63 G15 Pitrufquén Araucanía, S Chile 38°59′S 72°40′W
Pitsanulok see Phitsanulok
Pitschen see Byczyna
Pitsunda see Bich'vinta
109 X6 Pitten ≈ E Austria
10 J14 Pitt Island island British Columbia, W Canada
Pitt Island see Makin
22 M3 Pittsboro Mississippi, S USA 33°55′N 89°20′W
21 T9 Pittsboro North Carolina, SE USA 35°46′N 79°12′W
27 R7 Pittsburg Kansas, C USA 37°24′N 94°42′W
25 W6 Pittsburg Texas, SW USA 33°00′N 94°58′W
18 B14 Pittsburgh Pennsylvania, NE USA 40°26′N 80°W
30 J14 Pittsfield Illinois, N USA 39°36′N 90°48′W
19 R6 Pittsfield Maine, NE USA 44°46′N 69°22′W
18 L11 Pittsfield Massachusetts, NE USA 42°27′N 73°15′W
183 U3 Pittsworth Queensland, E Australia 27°43′S 151°36′E
62 I8 Pituil La Rioja, NW Argentina 28°33′S 67°24′W
56 A10 Piura Piura, NW Peru 05°11′S 80°41′W
56 A9 Piura off. Departamento de Piura. ◆ department NW Peru
Piura, Departamento de see Piura
35 S13 Piute Peak ▲ California, W USA 35°27′N 118°24′W
113 J15 Piva ≈ NW Montenegro
117 V5 Pivdenne Kharkivs'ka Oblast', E Ukraine 49°52′N 36°04′E
117 P8 Pivdennyy Buh Rus. Yuzhnyy Bug. ≈ S Ukraine
54 F5 Pivijay Magdalena, N Colombia 10°31′N 74°36′W
109 T13 Pivka prev. Šent Peter, Ger. Sankt Peter, It. San Pietro del Carso. SW Slovenia 45°41′N 14°12′E
117 U13 Pivnichno-Kryms'kyy Kanal canal S Ukraine
113 J15 Pivsko Jezero ◎ NW Montenegro
111 M18 Piwniczna Małopolskie, S Poland 49°26′N 20°43′E
35 R12 Pixley California, W USA 35°58′N 119°18′W
125 Q15 Pizhma var. Pishma. ≈ NW Russian Federation
13 U13 Placentia Newfoundland, Newfoundland and Labrador, SE Canada 47°12′N 53°58′W
Placentia see Piacenza
13 U13 Placentia Bay inlet Newfoundland, Newfoundland and Labrador, SE Canada
171 P5 Placer Masbate, N Philippines 11°54′N 123°54′E
35 P7 Placerville California, W USA 38°42′N 120°48′W
44 F5 Placetas Villa Clara, C Cuba 22°18′N 79°40′W
113 Q18 Plačkovica ▲▲ E Macedonia
36 L2 Plain City Utah, W USA 41°18′N 112°05′W
22 G4 Plain Dealing Louisiana, S USA 32°54′N 93°42′W
31 O14 Plainfield Indiana, N USA 39°42′N 86°18′W
18 K14 Plainfield New Jersey, NE USA 40°37′N 74°25′W
33 O8 Plains Montana, NW USA 47°27′N 114°52′W
24 L6 Plains Texas, SW USA 33°12′N 102°50′W
29 X10 Plainview Minnesota, N USA 44°10′N 92°10′W
29 Q13 Plainview Nebraska, C USA 42°21′N 97°47′W
25 N4 Plainview Texas, SW USA 34°12′N 101°43′W
26 K4 Plainville Kansas, C USA 39°13′N 99°18′W
115 I22 Pláka var. Mílos. Mílos, Kykládes, Greece, Aegean Sea 36°44′N 24°25′E
115 J15 Pláka, Akrotírio headland Límnos, E Greece 40°02′N 25°25′E
113 N19 Plakenska Planina ▲▲ SW Macedonia
44 K5 Plana Cays islets SE Bahamas
105 S12 Plana, Isla var. Nueva Tabarca. island E Spain
59 L18 Planaltina Goiás, S Brazil 15°35′S 47°28′W
83 O14 Planalto Moçambicano plateau N Mozambique
112 N10 Plandište Vojvodina, NE Serbia 45°13′N 21°07′E
100 N13 Plane ≈ NE Germany
54 E6 Planeta Rica Córdoba, NW Colombia 08°24′N 75°39′W
29 P11 Plankinton South Dakota, N USA 43°43′N 98°28′W
30 M11 Plano Illinois, N USA 41°39′N 88°32′W
25 U6 Plano Texas, SW USA 33°01′N 96°42′W
23 W12 Plant City Florida, SE USA 28°01′N 82°06′W
22 J9 Plaquemine Louisiana, S USA 30°17′N 91°13′W
104 K9 Plasencia Extremadura, W Spain 40°02′N 06°05′W
110 P7 Płaska Podlaskie, NE Poland 53°55′N 23°18′E
112 C10 Plaški Karlovac, C Croatia 45°04′N 15°21′E
113 Q19 Plasnica SW FYR Macedonia 41°28′N 21°07′E
13 N14 Plaster Rock New Brunswick, SE Canada 46°55′N 67°24′W
107 J24 Platani anc. Halycus. ≈ Sicilia, Italy, C Mediterranean Sea
115 G17 Plataniá Thessalía, C Greece 39°09′N 23°15′E
115 G24 Plátanos Kriti, Greece, E Mediterranean Sea 35°27′N 23°34′E
65 H18 Plata, Río de la var. River Plate. estuary Argentina/ Uruguay
77 V15 Plateau ◆ state C Nigeria
79 G19 Plateaux var. Région des Plateaux. ◆ province C Congo
Plateaux, Région des see Plateaux
Plate, Île see Flat Island
92 P1 Platen, Kapp headland NE Svalbard 80°30′N 22°46′E
Plate, River see Plata, Río de la
99 G22 Plate Taille, Lac de la var. L'Eau d'Heure. ◎ SE Belgium
Plathe see Płoty
39 N13 Platinum Alaska, USA 59°01′N 161°49′W
54 F5 Plato Magdalena, N Colombia 09°47′N 74°47′W
29 O11 Platte South Dakota, N USA 43°20′N 98°51′W
27 R3 Platte City Missouri, C USA 39°22′N 94°47′W
Plattensee see Balaton
27 R3 Platte River ≈ Iowa/ Missouri, USA
29 Q15 Platte River ≈ Nebraska, C USA
37 T3 Platteville Colorado, C USA 40°13′N 104°49′W
30 K9 Platteville Wisconsin, N USA 42°44′N 90°27′W
101 N21 Plattling Bayern, SE Germany 48°45′N 12°52′E
27 R3 Plattsburg Missouri, C USA 39°33′N 94°27′W
18 L6 Plattsburgh New York, NE USA 44°42′N 73°29′W
29 S15 Plattsmouth Nebraska, C USA 41°00′N 95°52′W
101 M17 Plauen var. Plauen im Vogtland. Sachsen, E Germany 50°31′N 12°08′E
Plauen im Vogtland see Plauen
100 M10 Plauer See ◎ NE Germany
113 L16 Plav E Montenegro 42°36′N 19°57′E
118 I10 Plaviņas Ger. Stockmannshof. S Latvia 56°37′N 25°40′E
126 K5 Plavsk Tul'skaya Oblast', W Russian Federation 53°42′N 37°21′E
41 Z12 Playa del Carmen Quintana Roo, E Mexico 20°37′N 87°04′W
40 J12 Playa Los Corchos Nayarit, SW Mexico 21°91′N 105°28′W
37 P16 Playas Lake ◎ New Mexico, SW USA
41 S15 Playa Vicenté Veracruz-Llave, SE Mexico 17°42′N 95°01′W
Plây Cu see Plei Ku
28 L3 Plaza North Dakota, N USA 48°00′N 102°00′W
63 I15 Plaza Huincul Neuquén, C Argentina 38°55′S 69°14′W
36 L3 Pleasant Grove Utah, W USA 40°21′N 111°44′W
29 V14 Pleasant Hill Iowa, C USA 41°34′N 93°31′W
27 R4 Pleasant Hill Missouri, C USA 38°47′N 94°16′W
Pleasant Island see Nauru
36 K13 Pleasant, Lake ⊠ Arizona, SW USA
19 P8 Pleasant Mountain ▲ Maine, NE USA 44°01′N 70°47′W
27 R5 Pleasanton Kansas, C USA 38°09′N 94°43′W
25 R12 Pleasanton Texas, SW USA 28°58′N 98°28′W
185 G20 Pleasant Point Canterbury, South Island, New Zealand 44°16′S 171°09′E
19 R5 Pleasant River ≈ Maine, NE USA
18 J17 Pleasantville New Jersey, NE USA 39°22′N 74°31′W
103 N12 Pléaux Cantal, C France 45°08′N 02°10′E
111 B19 Plechý var. Plöckenstein. ▲ Austria/Czech Republic 48°45′N 13°50′E
Pleebo see Plibo
Pleihari see Pelaihari
167 U11 Plei Ku prev. Plây Cu. Gia Lai, C Vietnam 13°57′N 108°01′E
101 M16 Pleisse ≈ E Germany
Plencia see Plentzia
184 O7 Plenty, Bay of bay North Island, New Zealand
33 Y6 Plentywood Montana, NW USA 48°46′N 104°33′W
105 O2 Plentzia var. Plencia. País Vasco, N Spain 43°25′N 02°56′W
102 H5 Plérin Côtes d'Armor, NW France 48°33′N 02°46′W
124 M10 Plesetsk Arkhangel'skaya Oblast', NW Russian Federation 62°41′N 40°14′E
Pleshchenitsy see Plyeshchanitsy
Pleskau see Pskov
Pleskauer See see Pskov, Lake
Pleskava see Pskov
112 E8 Pleso International ✕ (Zagreb) Zagreb, NW Croatia 45°45′N 16°00′E
Pless see Pszczyna
15 Q11 Plessisville Québec, SE Canada 46°14′N 71°46′W
110 H12 Pleszew Wielkopolskie, C Poland 51°54′N 17°47′E
12 L10 Plétipi, Lac ◎ Québec, SE Canada
101 F15 Plettenberg Nordrhein-Westfalen, W Germany 51°13′N 07°52′E
114 I8 Pleven prev. Plevna. Pleven, N Bulgaria 43°25′N 24°36′E
114 I8 Pleven ◆ province N Bulgaria
Plevlja/Plevlje see Pljevlja
Plevna see Pleven
Plezzo see Bovec
Pliberk see Bleiburg
76 L17 Plibo var. Pleebo. SE Liberia 04°38′N 07°41′W
121 R11 Pliny Trench undersea feature C Mediterranean Sea
118 K13 Plisa Rus. Plissa. Vitsyebskaya Voblasts', N Belarus 55°13′N 27°57′E
Plissa see Plisa
112 D11 Plitvica Selo Lika-Senj, W Croatia 44°53′N 15°36′E
112 D11 Plješevica ▲▲ C Croatia
113 K14 Pljevlja prev. Plevlja, Plevlje. N Montenegro 43°21′N 19°21′E
Ploça see Ploçë
Plocce see Ploče
113 K22 Ploçë var. Ploça. Vlorë, SW Albania 40°24′N 19°41′E
113 G15 Ploče It. Plocce; prev. Kardeljevo. Dubrovnik-Neretva, SE Croatia 43°02′N 17°25′E
110 K11 Płock Ger. Plozk. Mazowieckie, C Poland 52°32′N 19°40′E
109 Q10 Plöcken Pass Ger. Plöckenpass, It. Passo di Monte Croce Carnico. pass SW Austria
Plöckenpass see Plöcken Pass
Plöckenstein see Plechý
99 B19 Ploegsteert Hainaut, W Belgium 50°45′N 02°52′E
102 H6 Ploërmel Morbihan, NW France 47°57′N 02°24′W
Ploeşti see Ploieşti
116 K13 Ploieşti prev. Ploeşti. Prahova, SE Romania 44°56′N 26°03′E
115 L17 Plomári prev. Plomárion. Lésvos, E Greece 38°58′N 26°24′E
Plomárion see Plomári
103 O12 Plomb du Cantal ▲ C France 45°03′N 02°48′E
183 V6 Plomer, Point headland New South Wales, SE Australia 31°19′S 153°00′E
100 J8 Plön Schleswig-Holstein, N Germany 54°10′N 10°25′E
110 L11 Płońsk Mazowieckie, C Poland 52°38′N 20°23′E
119 J20 Plotnitsa Brestskaya Voblasts', SW Belarus 52°03′N 26°39′E
110 E8 Płoty Ger. Plathe. Zachodnio-pomorskie, NW Poland 53°48′N 15°16′E
102 G7 Plouay Morbihan, NW France 47°54′N 03°14′W
111 D15 Ploučnice Ger. Polzen. ≈ NE Czech Republic
114 I10 Plovdiv prev. Eumolpias; anc. Evmolpia, Philippopolis, Lat. Trimontium. Plovdiv, C Bulgaria 42°09′N 24°47′E
114 I11 Plovdiv ◆ province C Bulgaria
30 L6 Plover Wisconsin, N USA 44°30′N 89°33′W
Plozk see Płock
27 U11 Plumerville Arkansas, C USA 35°09′N 92°38′W
19 P10 Plum Island island Massachusetts, NE USA
32 M9 Plummer Idaho, NW USA 47°19′N 116°54′W
83 J18 Plumtree Matabeleland South, SW Zimbabwe 20°30′S 27°50′E
118 D11 Plungė Telšiai, W Lithuania 55°55′N 21°53′E
113 J15 Plužine NW Montenegro 43°08′N 18°49′E
119 K14 Plyeshchanitsy Rus. Pleshchenitsy. Minskaya Voblasts', N Belarus 54°25′N 27°50′E
97 I24 Plymouth SW England, United Kingdom 50°23′N 04°10′W
31 O11 Plymouth Indiana, N USA 41°20′N 86°19′W
19 P12 Plymouth Massachusetts, NE USA 41°57′N 70°40′W
19 N8 Plymouth New Hampshire, NE USA 43°43′N 71°39′W
21 X9 Plymouth North Carolina, SE USA 35°53′N 76°46′W
30 M8 Plymouth Wisconsin, N USA 43°48′N 87°58′W
Plymouth ○ (Montserrat) see Brades
97 J20 Plynlimon ▲ C Wales, United Kingdom 52°27′N 03°48′W
124 G14 Plyussa Pskovskaya Oblast', W Russian Federation 58°27′N 29°21′E
111 B17 Plzeň Ger. Pilsen, Pol. Pilzno. Plzeňský Kraj, W Czech Republic 49°45′N 13°23′E
111 B17 Plzeňský Kraj ◆ region W Czech Republic
110 F11 Pniewy Ger. Pinne. Wielkolpolskie, W Poland 52°31′N 16°14′E
77 P13 Pô S Burkina 11°11′N 01°10′W
106 D8 Po ≈ N Italy
42 M13 Poás, Volcán ⛰ NW Costa Rica 10°12′N 84°12′W
77 S16 Pobè S Benin 07°00′N 02°41′E
123 S8 Pobeda, Gora ▲ NE Russian Federation 65°28′N 145°44′E
Pobeda Peak see Pobedy, Pik/Tomur Feng
147 Z7 Pobedy, Pik Chin. Tomür Feng. ▲ China/Kyrgyzstan 42°02′N 80°02′E see also Tomür Feng
Pobedy, Pik see Tomür Feng
110 H11 Pobiedziska Ger. Pudewitz. Wielkolpolskie, C Poland 52°30′N 17°19′E
Po, Bocche del see Po, Foci del
27 W9 Pocahontas Arkansas, C USA 36°15′N 91°00′W
29 U12 Pocahontas Iowa, C USA 42°44′N 94°40′W
33 Q15 Pocatello Idaho, NW USA 42°52′N 112°27′W
167 S13 Pochentong ✕ (Phnum Penh) Phnum Penh, S Cambodia 11°24′N 104°52′E
126 I6 Pochep Bryanskaya Oblast', W Russian Federation 52°56′N 33°20′E
126 H4 Pochinok Smolenskaya Oblast', W Russian Federation 54°21′N 32°29′E
41 R17 Pochutla var. San Pedro Pochutla. Oaxaca, SE Mexico 15°45′N 96°30′W
62 I6 Pocitos, Salar var. Salar Quiróm. salt lake NW Argentina
101 O22 Pocking Bayern, SE Germany 48°22′N 13°17′E
186 I10 Pocklington Reef reef SE Papua New Guinea
59 P15 Poço da Cruz, Açude ⊠ E Brazil
27 R11 Pocola Oklahoma, C USA 35°13′N 94°28′W
21 Y5 Pocomoke City Maryland, NE USA 38°04′N 75°34′W
59 L21 Poços de Caldas Minas Gerais, NE Brazil 21°48′S 46°33′W
124 H14 Podberez'ye Novgorodskaya Oblast', NW Russian Federation 58°42′N 31°22′E
Podbrodzie see Pabrade
125 U8 Podcher'ye Respublika Komi, NW Russian Federation 63°55′N 57°34′E
111 E16 Poděbrady Ger. Podiebrad. Středočeský Kraj, C Czech Republic 50°10′N 15°06′E
126 L9 Podgorenskiy Voronezhskaya Oblast', W Russian Federation 50°22′N 39°43′E
113 J17 Podgorica prev. Titograd. ● S Montenegro 42°25′N 19°16′E
113 K17 Podgorica ✕ S Montenegro 42°22′N 19°16′E
109 T13 Podgrad SW Slovenia 45°31′N 14°09′E
Podiebrad see Poděbrady
116 M5 Podil's'ka Vysochina plateau W Ukraine
Podium Anicensis see le Puy
122 L11 Podkamennaya Tunguska Eng. Stony Tunguska. ≈ C Russian Federation
111 N17 Podkarpackie ◆ province SW Poland
Pod Klošter see Arnoldstein
110 P9 Podlaskie ◆ province Mazowieckie, C Poland
127 Q8 Podlesnoye Saratovskaya Oblast', W Russian Federation 51°51′N 47°03′E
126 K4 Podol'sk Moskovskaya Oblast', W Russian Federation 55°24′N 37°30′E
76 H10 Podor N Senegal 16°40′N 14°57′W
125 P12 Podosinovets Kirovskaya Oblast', NW Russian Federation 60°15′N 47°06′E
124 I12 Podporozh'ye Leningradskaya Oblast', NW Russian Federation 60°52′N 34°00′E
Podravska Slatina see Slatina
112 J13 Podromanlja Republika Srpska, SE Bosnia and Herzegovina 43°55′N 18°46′E
Podsvil'ye see Padsvillye
116 L9 Podu Iloaiei prev. Podul Iloaiei. Iași, NE Romania 47°13′N 27°16′E
113 N15 Podujevë Serb. Podujevo. N Kosovo 42°56′N 21°13′E
Podujevo see Podujevë
Podul Iloaiei see Podu Iloaiei
Podunajská Rovina see Little Alföld
124 M12 Podyuga Arkhangel'skaya Oblast', NW Russian Federation 61°04′N 40°46′E
56 A9 Poechos, Embalse ◎ NW Peru
55 W10 Poeketi Sipaliwini, E Surinam
100 L8 Poel island N Germany
83 M20 Poelela, Lagoa ◎ S Mozambique
Poerwodadi see Purwodadi
Poerwokerto see Purwokerto
Poerwordjo see Purworejo
Poetovio see Ptuj
83 E23 Pofadder Northern Cape, W South Africa 29°09′S 19°25′E
106 I9 Po, Foci del var. Bocche del Po. ≈ NE Italy
116 E12 Pogăniș ≈ W Romania
Pogegen see Pagėgiai
106 G12 Poggibonsi Toscana, C Italy 43°28′N 11°09′E
107 I14 Poggio Mirteto Lazio, C Italy 42°17′N 12°42′E
109 V4 Pöggstall Niederösterreich, N Austria 48°19′N 15°10′E
116 L13 Pogoanele Buzău, SE Romania 44°55′N 27°00′E
Pogónion see Delvináki
113 M21 Pogradec var. Pogradeci. Korçë, SE Albania 40°54′N 20°40′E
Pogradeci see Pogradec
123 S15 Pogranichnyy Primorskiy Kray, SE Russian Federation 44°18′N 131°33′E
38 M16 Pogromni Volcano ▲ Unimak Island, Alaska, USA 54°34′N 164°41′W
163 Z15 Pohang Jap. Hokō; prev. P'ohang. E South Korea 36°02′N 129°20′E
P'ohang see Pohang
15 T9 Pohénégamook, Lac ◎ Québec, SE Canada
93 L20 Pohja Swe. Pojo. Etelä-Suomi, SW Finland 60°07′N 23°30′E
Pohjanlahti see Bothnia, Gulf of
189 U16 Pohnpei ◆ state E Micronesia
189 O12 Pohnpei ✕ Pohnpei, E Micronesia
189 O12 Pohnpei prev. Ponape Ascension Island. island E Micronesia
111 F19 Pohořelice Ger. Pohrlitz. Jihomoravský Kraj, SE Czech Republic 48°58′N 16°30′E
109 V10 Pohorje Ger. Bacher. ▲▲ N Slovenia
117 N6 Pohrebyshche Vinnyts'ka Oblast', C Ukraine 49°31′N 29°16′E
Pohrlitz see Pohořelice
161 P9 Po Hu ⊠ E China
116 G15 Poiana Mare Dolj, S Romania 43°55′N 23°02′E
Poictiers see Poitiers
127 N6 Poim Penzenskaya Oblast', W Russian Federation 53°03′N 43°11′E
159 N15 Poindo Xizgang Zizhiqu, W China 29°58′N 91°20′E
195 Y13 Poinsett, Cape headland Antarctica 65°35′S 113°00′E
29 R9 Poinsett, Lake ◎ South Dakota, N USA
22 I10 Point Au Fer Island island Louisiana, S USA
39 X14 Point Baker Prince of Wales Island, Alaska, USA 56°19′N 133°31′W
25 U13 Point Comfort Texas, SW USA 28°40′N 96°33′W
Point de Galle see Galle
44 K10 Pointe à Gravois headland SW Haiti 18°00′N 73°53′W
22 L10 Pointe a la Hache Louisiana, S USA 29°34′N 89°48′W
45 Y6 Pointe-à-Pitre Grande Terre, C Guadeloupe 16°14′N 61°32′W
15 U7 Pointe-au-Père Québec, SE Canada 48°31′N 68°27′W
15 V5 Pointe-aux-Anglais Québec, SE Canada 49°34′N 67°09′W
45 T10 Pointe Du Cap headland N Saint Lucia 14°06′N 60°56′W
79 E21 Pointe-Noire Kouilou, S Congo 04°46′S 11°53′E
45 X6 Pointe Noire Basse Terre, W Guadeloupe 16°14′N 61°47′W
79 E21 Pointe-Noire ✕ Kouilou, S Congo 04°45′S 11°55′E
45 U15 Point Fortin Trinidad, Trinidad and Tobago 10°12′N 61°41′W
38 M6 Point Hope Alaska, USA 68°21′N 166°48′W
39 N5 Point Lay Alaska, USA 69°42′N 162°57′W
18 B16 Point Marion Pennsylvania, NE USA 39°44′N 79°53′W
18 K16 Point Pleasant New Jersey, NE USA 40°04′N 74°00′W
21 P4 Point Pleasant West Virginia, NE USA 38°53′N 82°07′W
45 R14 Point Salines ✕ (St. George's) SW Grenada 12°00′N 61°47′W
102 L9 Poitiers prev. Poictiers; anc. Limonum. Vienne, W France 46°35′N 00°19′E
102 K9 Poitou cultural region W France
102 K10 Poitou-Charentes ◆ region W France
103 N3 Poix-de-Picardie Somme, N France 49°47′N 01°58′E
Pojo see Pohja
37 S10 Pojoaque New Mexico, SW USA 35°52′N 106°01′W
152 E11 Pokaran Rājasthān, NW India 26°55′N 71°55′E
183 R4 Pokataroo New South Wales, SE Australia 29°37′S 148°43′E
119 P18 Pokats' Rus. Pokot'. ≈ SE Belarus
29 V5 Pokegama Lake ◎ Minnesota, N USA
184 L6 Pokeno Waikato, North Island, New Zealand 37°15′S 175°01′E
153 O11 Pokharā Western, C Nepal 28°14′N 84°E
127 T6 Pokhvistnevo Samarskaya Oblast', W Russian Federation 53°38′N 52°07′E
55 W10 Pokigron Sipaliwini, C Surinam 04°31′N 55°23′W
92 L10 Pokka Lapp. Bohkká. Lappi, N Finland 68°11′N 25°45′E
79 N16 Poko Orientale, NE Dem. Rep. Congo 03°08′N 26°52′E
Pokot' see Pokats'
Po-ko-to Shan see Bogda Shan
147 S7 Pokrovka Talasskaya Oblast', NW Kyrgyzstan 42°45′N 71°33′E
Pokrovka see Kyzyl-Suu
117 V8 Pokrovs'ke Rus. Pokrovskoye. Dnipropetrovs'ka Oblast', E Ukraine 47°58′N 36°15′E
Pokrovskoye see Pokrovs'ke
Pola see Pula
37 N10 Polacca Arizona, SW USA 35°49′N 110°21′W
Pola de Laviana see Pola de Llaviana
Pola de Lena see La Pola
104 L2 Pola de Llaviana var. Pola de Laviana. Asturias, N Spain 43°15′N 05°33′W
Pola de Siero see La Pola Siero
191 Y3 Poland Kiritimati, E Kiribati 01°52′N 157°33′W
110 H12 Poland off. Republic of Poland, var. Polish Republic, Pol. Polska, Rzeczpospolita Polska; prev. Pol. Polska Rzeczpospolita Ludowa, The Polish People's Republic. ◆ republic C Europe
Poland, Republic of see Poland
Polangen see Palanga
110 G7 Polanów Ger. Pollnow. Zachodnio-pomorskie, NW Poland 54°07′N 16°38′E
136 H13 Polatlı Ankara, C Turkey 39°34′N 32°08′E
118 L12 Polatsk Rus. Polotsk. Vitsyebskaya Voblasts', N Belarus 55°29′N 28°47′E
110 F8 Połczyn-Zdrój Ger. Bad Polzin. Zachodnio-pomorskie, NW Poland 53°44′N 16°02′E
Pol-e-'Alam see Pul-e-'Alam
Polekhatum see Pulhatyn
Pol-e Khomrī see Pul-e Khumrī
197 S10 Pole Plain undersea feature Arctic Ocean
Pol-e-Safid see Pol-e Sefid
143 P5 Pol-e Sefid var. Pol-e-Safid, Pul-i-Sefid. Māzandarān, N Iran 36°05′N 53°01′E
118 B13 Polessk Ger. Labiau. Kaliningradskaya Oblast', W Russian Federation 54°52′N 21°06′E
Polesskoye see Polis'ke
171 N13 Polewali Sulawesi, C Indonesia 03°26′S 119°23′E
114 G11 Polezhan ▲ SW Bulgaria 41°42′N 23°28′E
78 F13 Poli Nord, N Cameroon 09°31′N 13°10′E
Poli see Pólis
107 M19 Policastro, Golfo di gulf S Italy
110 D8 Police Ger. Politz. Zachodnio-pomorskie, NW Poland 53°34′N 14°34′E
172 I17 Police, Pointe headland Mahé, NE Seychelles 04°48′S 55°31′E
115 L17 Polichnítos var. Polihnitos, Políkhnitos. Lésvos, E Greece 39°04′N 26°10′E
Poligiros see Polýgyros
107 P17 Polignano a Mare Puglia, SE Italy 40°59′N 17°13′E
103 S9 Poligny Jura, E France 46°51′N 05°42′E
Polihnitos see Polichnítos
Polikastro/Políkastron see Polýkastro
Políkhnitos see Polichnítos
171 O3 Polillo Islands island group N Philippines
109 Q9 Polinik ▲ SW Austria 46°54′N 13°10′E
115 J15 Políochni var. Polýochni. site of ancient city Límnos, E Greece
121 O2 Pólis var. Poli. W Cyprus 35°02′N 32°27′E
Polish People's Republic, The see Poland
Polish Republic see Poland
117 O3 Polis'ke Rus. Polesskoye. Kyyivs'ka Oblast', N Ukraine 51°16′N 29°27′E
107 N22 Polistena Calabria, SW Italy 38°25′N 16°05′E
Politz see Police
Políyiros see Polýgyros
29 V14 Polk City Iowa, C USA 41°46′N 93°42′W
110 F13 Polkowice Ger. Heerwegen. Dolnośląskie, W Poland 51°32′N 16°06′E
155 G22 Pollāchi Tamil Nādu, SE India 10°38′N 77°00′E
109 W7 Pöllau Steiermark, SE Austria 47°18′N 15°46′E
189 T13 Polle atoll Chuuk Islands, C Micronesia
105 X9 Pollença Mallorca, Spain, W Mediterranean Sea 39°52′N 03°01′E
Pollnow see Polanów
29 N7 Pollock South Dakota, N USA 45°53′N 100°15′W
92 L8 Polmak Finnmark, N Norway 70°01′N 28°04′E
30 L10 Polo Illinois, N USA 41°59′N 89°34′W
193 V15 Poloa island Tongatapu Group, N Tonga
42 E5 Polochic, Río ≈ C Guatemala
Pologi see Polohy
117 V9 Polohy Rus. Pologi. Zaporiz'ka Oblast', SE Ukraine 47°30′N 36°18′E
83 K20 Polokwane prev. Pietersburg. Limpopo, NE South Africa 23°54′S 29°23′E
14 M10 Polonais, Lac des ◎ Québec, SE Canada
61 G20 Polonio, Cabo headland E Uruguay 34°22′S 53°46′W
155 K24 Polonnaruwa North Central Province, C Sri Lanka 07°56′N 81°02′E
116 L5 Polonne Rus. Polonnoye. Khmel'nyts'ka Oblast', NW Ukraine 50°10′N 27°30′E
Polonnoye see Polonne
Polotsk see Polatsk
Polovinka see Ugleural'skiy
109 T7 Pöls var. Pölsbach. ≈ E Austria
Pölsbach see Pöls
Polska/Polska, Rzeczpospolita/Polska Rzeczpospolita Ludowa see Poland
114 L10 Polski Gradets Stara Zagora, C Bulgaria 42°12′N 26°06′E
114 K8 Polski Trŭmbesh Ruse, N Bulgaria 43°22′N 25°38′E
33 P8 Polson Montana, NW USA 47°41′N 114°09′W

◆ Country
● Country Capital
◇ Dependent Territory
○ Dependent Territory Capital
◆ Administrative Regions
✕ International Airport
▲ Mountain
▲▲ Mountain Range
⛰ Volcano
≈ River
◎ Lake
⊠ Reservoir

117 T6 **Poltava** Poltavs'ka Oblast', NE Ukraine 49°33'N 34°32'E
Poltava *see* Poltavs'ka Oblast'
117 R5 **Poltavs'ka Oblast'** *var.* Poltava, *Rus.* Poltavskaya Oblast'. ◈ *province* NE Ukraine
Poltavskaya Oblast' *see* Poltavs'ka Oblast'
Poltoratsk *see* Aşgabat
118 I5 **Põltsamaa** *Ger.* Oberpahlen. Jõgevamaa, E Estonia 58°40'N 26°00'E
118 I4 **Põltsamaa** *var.* Põltsamaa Jõgi. ≈ C Estonia
Põltsamaa Jõgi *see* Põltsamaa
122 I8 **Poluy** ≈ N Russian Federation
118 J6 **Põlva** *Ger.* Pölwe. Põlvamaa, SE Estonia 58°04'N 27°06'E
93 N16 **Polvijärvi** Itä-Suomi, SE Finland 62°53'N 29°20'E
Pölwe *see* Põlva
115 I22 **Polýaigos** *island* Kykládes, Greece, Aegean Sea
115 I22 **Polyaígou Folégandrou, Stenó** *strait* Kykládes, Greece, Aegean Sea
124 J3 **Polyarnyy** Murmanskaya Oblast', NW Russian Federation 69°10'N 33°21'E
125 W5 **Polyarnyy Ural** ▲▲ NW Russian Federation
115 G14 **Polýgyros** *var.* Poligiros, Políyiros. Kentrikí Makedonía, N Greece 40°21'N 23°27'E
114 F13 **Polýkastro** *var.* Polikastro; *prev.* Políkastron. Kentrikí Makedonía, N Greece 41°01'N 22°33'E
193 O9 **Polynesia** *island group* C Pacific Ocean
Polyóchni *see* Políochni
41 Y13 **Polyuc** Quintana Roo, E Mexico
109 V10 **Polzela** C Slovenia 46°18'N 15°04'E
Polzen *see* Ploučnice
56 D12 **Pomabamba** Ancash, C Peru 08°48'S 77°30'W
185 D23 **Pomahaka** ≈ South Island, New Zealand
106 F12 **Pomarance** Toscana, C Italy 43°19'N 10°53'E
104 G9 **Pombal** Leiria, C Portugal 39°55'N 08°38'W
76 D9 **Pombas** Santo Antão, NW Cape Verde 17°09'N 25°02'W
83 N19 **Pomene** Inhambane, SE Mozambique 22°57'S 35°34'E
110 G8 **Pomerania** *cultural region* Germany/Poland
110 D7 **Pomeranian Bay** *Ger.* Pommersche Bucht, *Pol.* Zatoka Pomorska. *bay* Germany/Poland
31 T15 **Pomeroy** Ohio, N USA 39°01'N 82°01'W
32 L10 **Pomeroy** Washington, NW USA 46°28'N 117°36'W
117 Q8 **Pomichna** Kirovohrads'ka Oblast', C Ukraine 48°07'N 31°25'E
186 H7 **Pomio** New Britain, E Papua New Guinea 05°31'S 151°30'E
Pomir, Dar"yoi *see* Pamir/Pāmīr, Daryā-ye
27 T6 **Pomme de Terre Lake** ⊠ Missouri, C USA
29 S8 **Pomme de Terre River** ≈ Minnesota, N USA
Pommersche Bucht *see* Pomeranian Bay
35 T15 **Pomona** California, W USA 34°03'N 117°45'W
114 N9 **Pomorie** Burgas, E Bulgaria 42°32'N 27°39'E
Pomorska, Zatoka *see* Pomeranian Bay
110 H8 **Pomorskie** ◈ *province* N Poland
125 Q4 **Pomorskiy Proliv** *strait* NW Russian Federation
125 T10 **Pomozdino** Respublika Komi, NW Russian Federation 62°11'N 54°13'E
Pompaelo *see* Pamplona
23 Z15 **Pompano Beach** Florida, SE USA 26°14'N 80°06'W
107 K18 **Pompei** Campania, S Italy 40°45'N 14°27'E
33 V10 **Pompeys Pillar** Montana, NW USA 45°58'N 107°55'W
Ponape Ascension Island *see* Pohnpei
29 R13 **Ponca** Nebraska, C USA 42°35'N 96°42'W
27 O8 **Ponca City** Oklahoma, C USA 36°41'N 97°04'W
45 T6 **Ponce** C Puerto Rico 18°01'N 66°36'W
23 X10 **Ponce de Leon Inlet** *inlet* Florida, SE USA
22 K8 **Ponchatoula** Louisiana, S USA 30°26'N 90°26'W
26 M8 **Pond Creek** Oklahoma, C USA 36°40'N 97°48'W
155 J20 **Pondicherry** *var.* Puduchcheri, *Fr.* Pondichéry. Pondicherry, SE India 11°59'N 79°50'E
151 I20 **Pondicherry** *var.* Puduchcheri, *Fr.* Pondichéry. ◈ *union territory* India
Pondichéry *see* Pondicherry
197 N11 **Pond Inlet** *var.* Mittimatalik. Baffin Island, Nunavut, NE Canada 72°37'N 77°56'W
187 P16 **Ponérihouen** Province Nord, C New Caledonia 21°04'S 165°24'E
104 J4 **Ponferrada** Castilla y León, NW Spain 42°33'N 06°35'W
184 N13 **Pongaroa** Manawatu-Wanganui, North Island, New Zealand 40°36'S 176°08'E
167 Q12 **Pong Nam Ron** Chantaburi, S Thailand 12°55'N 102°15'E
81 C14 **Pongo** ≈ W South Sudan
152 I7 **Pong Reservoir** ⊠ N India
111 N14 **Poniatowa** Lubelskie, E Poland 51°11'N 22°05'E
167 R12 **Pônley** Kâmpóng Chhnăng, C Cambodia 12°26'N 104°25'E
155 I20 **Ponnaiyār** ≈ SE India
11 Q15 **Ponoka** Alberta, SW Canada 52°42'N 113°33'W
127 U6 **Ponomarevka** Orenburgskaya Oblast', W Russian Federation 53°16'N 54°10'E
169 Q17 **Ponorogo** Jawa, C Indonesia 07°51'S 111°30'E
122 F6 **Ponoy** ≈ NW Russian Federation
102 K11 **Pons** Charente-Maritime, W France 45°31'N 00°31'W
Pons *see* Ponts
Pons Aelii *see* Newcastle upon Tyne
Pons Vetus *see* Pontevedra
99 G20 **Pont-à-Celles** Hainaut, S Belgium 50°31'N 04°21'E
102 K16 **Pontacq** Pyrénées-Atlantiques, SW France 43°11'N 00°06'W
64 P3 **Ponta Delgada** São Miguel, Azores, Portugal, NE Atlantic Ocean 37°29'N 25°40'W
64 P3 **Ponta Delgado** ✕ São Miguel, Azores, Portugal, NE Atlantic Ocean 37°28'N 25°40'W
64 N2 **Ponta do Pico** ▲ Pico, Azores, Portugal, NE Atlantic Ocean 38°28'N 28°25'W
60 J11 **Ponta Grossa** Paraná, S Brazil 25°07'S 50°09'W
103 S5 **Pont-à-Mousson** Meurthe-et-Moselle, NE France 48°55'N 06°03'E
103 T9 **Pontarlier** Doubs, E France 46°54'N 06°20'E
106 G11 **Pontassieve** Toscana, C Italy 43°46'N 11°28'E
102 L4 **Pont-Audemer** Eure, N France 49°22'N 00°31'E
22 K9 **Pontchartrain, Lake** ◎ Louisiana, S USA
102 I8 **Pontchâteau** Loire-Atlantique, NW France 47°26'N 02°04'W
103 R10 **Pont-de-Vaux** Ain, E France 46°25'N 04°57'E
104 G4 **Ponteareas** Galicia, NW Spain 42°11'N 08°29'W
106 J6 **Pontebba** Friuli-Venezia Giulia, NE Italy 46°32'N 13°18'E
104 G4 **Ponte Caldelas** Galicia, NW Spain 42°23'N 08°30'W
107 J16 **Pontecorvo** Lazio, C Italy 41°27'N 13°40'E
104 G5 **Ponte da Barca** Viana do Castelo, N Portugal 41°48'N 08°25'W
104 G5 **Ponte de Lima** Viana do Castelo, N Portugal 41°46'N 08°35'W
106 F11 **Pontedera** Toscana, C Italy 43°40'N 10°38'E
104 H10 **Ponte de Sor** Portalegre, C Portugal 39°15'N 08°01'W
104 H2 **Pontedeume** Galicia, NW Spain 43°22'N 08°09'W
106 F6 **Ponte di Legno** Lombardia, N Italy 46°16'N 10°31'E
11 T17 **Ponteix** Saskatchewan, S Canada 49°43'N 107°22'W
171 Q16 **Ponte Macassar** *var.* Pante Macassar, Pante Makasar, Pante Makassar. W East Timor 09°11'S 124°27'E
59 N20 **Ponte Nova** Minas Gerais, NE Brazil 20°25'S 42°54'W
59 G18 **Pontes e Lacerda** Mato Grosso, W Brazil 15°14'S 59°21'W
104 G4 **Pontevedra** *anc.* Pons Vetus. Galicia, NW Spain 42°25'N 08°39'W
104 G3 **Pontevedra** ◈ *province* Galicia, NW Spain
104 G4 **Pontevedra, Ría de** *estuary* NW Spain
30 M12 **Pontiac** Illinois, N USA 40°54'N 88°36'W
31 R9 **Pontiac** Michigan, N USA 42°38'N 83°17'W
169 P11 **Pontianak** Borneo, C Indonesia 00°05'S 109°16'E
107 I16 **Pontino, Agro** *plain* C Italy
Pontisarae *see* Pontoise
102 H6 **Pontivy** Morbihan, NW France 48°04'N 02°58'W
102 F6 **Pont-l'Abbé** Finistère, NW France 47°52'N 04°14'W
103 N4 **Pontoise** *anc.* Briva Isarae, Cergy-Pontoise, Pontisarae. Val-d'Oise, N France 49°03'N 02°05'E
11 W13 **Ponton** Manitoba, C Canada 54°36'N 99°02'W
102 J5 **Pontorson** Manche, N France 48°33'N 01°31'W
22 M2 **Pontotoc** Mississippi, S USA 34°15'N 89°00'W
25 R9 **Pontotoc** Texas, SW USA 30°52'N 98°57'W
106 E10 **Pontremoli** Toscana, C Italy 44°24'N 09°55'E
108 J10 **Pontresina** Graubünden, S Switzerland 46°29'N 09°52'E
105 U5 **Ponts** *var.* Pons. Cataluña, NE Spain 41°55'N 01°12'E
103 R14 **Pont-St-Esprit** Gard, S France 44°15'N 04°37'E
97 K21 **Pontypool** *Wel.* Pontypŵl. SE Wales, United Kingdom 51°43'N 03°02'W
97 J22 **Pontypridd** S Wales, United Kingdom 51°37'N 03°22'W
Pontypŵl *see* Pontypool
43 R17 **Ponuga** Veraguas, SE Panama 07°50'N 80°58'W
184 L6 **Ponui Island** *island* N New Zealand
119 K14 **Ponya** ≈ N Belarus
107 I17 **Ponza, Isola di** *island* Isole Ponziane, S Italy
107 I17 **Ponziane, Isole** *island* C Italy
182 F7 **Poochera** South Australia 32°45'S 134°51'E
97 L24 **Poole** S England, United Kingdom 50°43'N 01°59'W
25 S6 **Poolville** Texas, SW USA 33°00'N 97°55'W
Poona *see* Pune
182 M8 **Pooncarie** New South Wales, SE Australia 33°26'S 142°37'E
183 N6 **Poopelloe Lake** *seasonal lake* New South Wales, SE Australia
57 K19 **Poopó** Oruro, C Bolivia 18°23'S 66°58'W
57 K19 **Poopó, Lago** *var.* Lago Pampa Aullagas. ◎ W Bolivia
184 L3 **Poor Knights Islands** *island* N New Zealand
39 P10 **Poorman** Alaska, USA 64°05'N 155°34'W
182 E3 **Pootnoura** South Australia 28°31'S 134°09'E
147 R10 **Pop** *Rus.* Pap. Namangan Viloyati, E Uzbekistan 40°49'N 71°06'E
117 X7 **Popasna** *Rus.* Popasnaya. Luhans'ka Oblast', E Ukraine 48°38'N 38°24'E
Popasnaya *see* Popasna
54 D12 **Popayán** Cauca, SW Colombia 02°27'N 76°32'W
99 B18 **Poperinge** West-Vlaanderen, W Belgium 50°52'N 02°44'E
123 N7 **Popigay** Krasnoyarskiy Kray, N Russian Federation 71°54'N 110°45'E
123 N7 **Popigay** ≈ N Russian Federation
117 O5 **Popil'nya** Zhytomyrs'ka Oblast', N Ukraine 49°57'N 29°24'E
182 K8 **Popiltah Lake** *seasonal lake* New South Wales, SE Australia
33 X7 **Poplar** Montana, NW USA 48°06'N 105°12'W
11 Y14 **Poplar** ≈ Manitoba, C Canada
27 X8 **Poplar Bluff** Missouri, C USA 36°45'N 90°23'W
33 X6 **Poplar River** ≈ Montana, NW USA
41 P14 **Popocatépetl** ⛰ S Mexico 18°59'N 98°37'W
79 H21 **Popokabaka** Bandundu, SW Dem. Rep. Congo 05°42'S 16°35'E
107 J15 **Popoli** Abruzzo, C Italy 42°09'N 13°51'E
186 F9 **Popondetta** Northern, S Papua New Guinea 08°45'S 148°15'E
112 F9 **Popovača** Sisak-Moslavina, NE Croatia 45°35'N 16°37'E
114 L8 **Popovo** Tŭrgovishte, N Bulgaria 43°20'N 26°14'E
Popovo *see* Iskra
Popper *see* Poprad
30 M5 **Popple River** ≈ Wisconsin, N USA
111 L19 **Poprad** *Ger.* Deutschendorf, *Hung.* Poprád. Prešovský Kraj, E Slovakia 49°04'N 20°16'E
111 L18 **Poprad** *Ger.* Popper, *Hung.* Poprád. ≈ Poland/Slovakia
111 L19 **Poprad-Tatry** ✕ (Poprad) Prešovský Kraj, E Slovakia 49°04'N 20°21'E
21 X7 **Poquoson** Virginia, NE USA 37°08'N 76°21'W
149 O15 **Porāli** ≈ SW Pakistan
184 N12 **Porangahau** Hawke's Bay, North Island, New Zealand 40°19'S 176°36'E
59 K17 **Porangatu** Goiás, C Brazil 13°28'S 49°14'W
119 G18 **Porazava** *Pol.* Porozow, *Rus.* Porozovo. Hrodzyenskaya Voblasts', W Belarus 52°56'N 24°22'E
154 A11 **Porbandar** Gujarāt, W India 21°40'N 69°40'E
10 I13 **Porcher Island** *island* British Columbia, SW Canada
104 M13 **Porcuna** Andalucía, S Spain 37°52'N 04°12'W
14 F7 **Porcupine** Ontario, S Canada 48°31'N 81°07'W
64 M6 **Porcupine Bank** *undersea feature* N Atlantic Ocean
11 V15 **Porcupine Hills** ▲▲ Manitoba/Saskatchewan, S Canada
30 L3 **Porcupine Mountains** *hill range* Michigan, N USA
64 M7 **Porcupine Plain** *undersea feature* E Atlantic Ocean 16°00'W 49°00'N
8 G7 **Porcupine River** ≈ Canada/USA
106 I7 **Pordenone** *anc.* Portenau. Friuli-Venezia Giulia, NE Italy 45°58'N 12°39'E
54 H9 **Pore** Casanare, E Colombia 05°42'N 71°59'W
112 A9 **Poreč** *It.* Parenzo. Istra, NW Croatia 45°16'N 13°36'E
60 I9 **Porecatu** Paraná, S Brazil 22°46'S 51°22'W
Porech'ye *see* Parechcha
127 P4 **Poretskoye** Chuvashskaya Respublika, W Russian Federation 55°12'N 46°20'E
77 Q13 **Porga** N Benin 11°04'N 00°58'E
186 B7 **Porgera** Enga, W Papua New Guinea 05°32'S 143°08'E
93 K18 **Pori** *Swe.* Björneborg. Länsi-Suomi, SW Finland 61°28'N 21°50'E
185 L14 **Porirua** Wellington, North Island, New Zealand 41°08'S 174°51'E
92 I12 **Porjus** *Lapp.* Bårjås. Norrbotten, N Sweden 66°55'N 19°55'E
124 G14 **Porkhov** Pskovskaya Oblast', W Russian Federation 57°46'N 29°27'E
55 O4 **Porlamar** Nueva Esparta, NE Venezuela 10°57'N 63°51'W
102 I8 **Pornic** Loire-Atlantique, NW France 47°07'N 02°07'W
186 B7 **Poroma** Southern Highlands, W Papua New Guinea 06°15'S 143°34'E
123 T13 **Poronaysk** Ostrov Sakhalin, Sakhalinskaya Oblast', SE Russian Federation 49°15'N 143°00'E
115 G20 **Póros** Póros, S Greece 37°30'N 23°27'E
115 C19 **Póros** Kefallinía, Iónia Nisiá, Greece, C Mediterranean Sea 38°09'N 20°46'E
115 G20 **Póros** *island* S Greece
81 G24 **Poroto Mountains** ▲▲ SW Tanzania
112 B10 **Porozina** Primorje-Gorski Kotar, NW Croatia 45°07'N 14°17'E
Porozovo/Porozow *see* Porazava
195 X15 **Porpoise Bay** *bay* Antarctica
65 G15 **Porpoise Point** *headland* NE Ascension Island 07°54'S 14°22'W
65 C25 **Porpoise Point** *headland* East Falkland, Falkland Islands 52°20'S 59°18'W
108 C6 **Porrentruy** Jura, NW Switzerland 47°25'N 07°06'E
106 F10 **Porretta Terme** Emilia-Romagna, C Italy 44°10'N 11°01'E
Porriño *see* O Porriño
92 L7 **Porsangenfjorden** *Lapp.* Porsáŋgguvuotna. *fjord* N Norway
92 K8 **Porsangerhalvøya** *peninsula* N Norway
Porsáŋgguvuotna *see* Porsangenfjorden
95 G16 **Porsgrunn** Telemark, S Norway 59°08'N 09°38'E
136 E13 **Porsuk Çayı** ≈ C Turkey
Porsy *see* Boldumsaz
57 N18 **Portachuelo** Santa Cruz, C Bolivia 17°21'S 63°24'W
182 I9 **Port Adelaide** South Australia 34°49'S 138°31'E
97 F15 **Portadown** *Ir.* Port An Dúnáin. S Northern Ireland, United Kingdom 54°26'N 06°27'W
31 P10 **Portage** Michigan, N USA 42°12'N 85°34'W
18 D15 **Portage** Pennsylvania, NE USA 40°23'N 78°40'W
30 K8 **Portage** Wisconsin, N USA 43°33'N 89°29'W
30 M3 **Portage Lake** ◎ Michigan, N USA
11 X16 **Portage la Prairie** Manitoba, S Canada 49°58'N 98°20'W
31 R11 **Portage River** ≈ Ohio, N USA
27 Y8 **Portageville** Missouri, C USA 36°25'N 89°42'W
28 L2 **Portal** North Dakota, N USA 48°57'N 102°33'W
10 L17 **Port Alberni** Vancouver Island, British Columbia, SW Canada 49°11'N 124°49'W
14 E15 **Port Albert** Ontario, S Canada 43°51'N 81°42'W
104 I10 **Portalegre** *anc.* Ammaia, Amoea. Portalegre, E Portugal 39°17'N 07°25'W
104 H10 **Portalegre** ◈ *district* C Portugal
37 V12 **Portales** New Mexico, SW USA 34°11'N 103°19'W
39 X14 **Port Alexander** Baranof Island, Alaska, USA 56°15'N 134°39'W
83 I25 **Port Alfred** Eastern Cape, S South Africa 33°31'S 26°55'E
10 J16 **Port Alice** Vancouver Island, British Columbia, SW Canada 50°23'N 127°24'W
22 J8 **Port Allen** Louisiana, S USA 30°27'N 91°12'W
Port Amelia *see* Pemba
Port An Dúnáin *see* Portadown
32 G7 **Port Angeles** Washington, NW USA 48°06'N 123°26'W
44 L12 **Port Antonio** NE Jamaica 18°10'N 76°27'W
115 D16 **Pórta Panagiá** *religious building* Thessalía, C Greece
25 T14 **Port Aransas** Texas, SW USA 27°49'N 97°03'W
97 E18 **Portarlington** *Ir.* Cúil an tSúdaire. Laois/Offaly, C Ireland 53°10'N 07°11'W
183 P17 **Port Arthur** Tasmania, SE Australia 43°09'S 147°51'E
25 Y11 **Port Arthur** Texas, SW USA 29°55'N 93°56'W
96 G12 **Port Askaig** W Scotland, United Kingdom 55°51'N 06°06'W
182 I7 **Port Augusta** South Australia 32°29'S 137°44'E
44 M9 **Port-au-Prince** ● (Haiti) C Haiti 18°33'N 72°20'W
22 I8 **Port Barre** Louisiana, S USA 30°33'N 91°57'W
Port-Bergé *see* Boriziny
151 Q19 **Port Blair** Andaman and Nicobar Islands, SE India 11°40'N 92°44'E
25 X12 **Port Bolivar** Texas, SW USA 29°21'N 94°45'W
105 X4 **Portbou** Cataluña, NE Spain 42°26'N 03°10'E
77 N17 **Port Bouet** ✕ (Abidjan) SE Ivory Coast 05°17'N 03°55'W
182 I8 **Port Broughton** South Australia 33°39'S 137°55'E
14 F17 **Port Burwell** Ontario, S Canada 42°39'N 80°47'W
12 G17 **Port Burwell** Québec, NE Canada 60°25'N 64°49'W
182 M13 **Port Campbell** Victoria, SE Australia 38°37'S 143°00'E
15 V4 **Port-Cartier** Québec, SE Canada 50°00'N 66°55'W
185 F23 **Port Chalmers** Otago, South Island, New Zealand 45°46'S 170°37'E
23 W14 **Port Charlotte** Florida, SE USA 27°00'N 82°07'W
38 L9 **Port Clarence** Alaska, USA 65°15'N 166°51'W
10 I13 **Port Clements** Graham Island, British Columbia, SW Canada 53°37'N 132°12'W
31 S11 **Port Clinton** Ohio, N USA 41°30'N 82°56'W
14 H17 **Port Colborne** Ontario, S Canada 42°51'N 79°16'W
15 Y7 **Port-Daniel** Québec, SE Canada 48°10'N 64°58'W
Port Darwin *see* Darwin
183 O17 **Port Davey** *headland* Tasmania, SE Australia 43°19'S 145°54'E
44 K8 **Port-de-Paix** NW Haiti 19°56'N 72°52'W
181 W4 **Port Douglas** Queensland, NE Australia 16°33'S 145°27'E
10 J13 **Port Edward** British Columbia, SW Canada 54°11'N 130°16'W
83 K24 **Port Edward** KwaZulu/Natal, SE South Africa 31°03'S 30°14'E
58 J12 **Portel** Pará, NE Brazil 01°58'S 50°45'W
104 H12 **Portel** Évora, S Portugal 38°18'N 07°42'W
14 E14 **Port Elgin** Ontario, S Canada 44°26'N 81°22'W
45 Y14 **Port Elizabeth** Bequia, Saint Vincent and the Grenadines 13°01'N 61°15'W
83 I26 **Port Elizabeth** Eastern Cape, S South Africa 33°58'S 25°36'E
96 G13 **Port Ellen** W Scotland, United Kingdom 55°37'N 06°12'W
Portenau *see* Pordenone
97 H16 **Port Erin** SW Isle of Man 54°05'N 04°47'W
45 Q13 **Porter Point** *headland* Saint Vincent, Saint Vincent and the Grenadines 13°22'N 61°10'W
185 G18 **Porters Pass** *pass* South Island, New Zealand
83 E25 **Porterville** Western Cape, SW South Africa 33°03'S 19°00'E
35 R12 **Porterville** California, W USA 36°03'N 119°03'W
Port-Étienne *see* Nouâdhibou
182 L13 **Port Fairy** Victoria, SE Australia 38°24'S 142°13'E
184 M4 **Port Fitzroy** Great Barrier Island, Auckland, NE New Zealand 36°10'S 175°21'E
Port Florence *see* Kisumu
Port Francqui *see* Ilebo
79 C18 **Port-Gentil** Ogooué-Maritime, W Gabon 00°40'S 08°50'E
182 I7 **Port Germein** South Australia 33°02'S 138°01'E
22 J6 **Port Gibson** Mississippi, S USA 31°57'N 90°58'W
39 Q13 **Port Graham** Alaska, USA 59°21'N 151°49'W
77 U17 **Port Harcourt** Rivers, S Nigeria 04°43'N 07°02'E
10 J16 **Port Hardy** Vancouver Island, British Columbia, SW Canada 50°41'N 127°30'W
Port Harrison *see* Inukjuak
13 R14 **Port Hawkesbury** Cape Breton Island, Nova Scotia, SE Canada 45°36'N 61°22'W
180 I6 **Port Hedland** Western Australia 20°23'S 118°40'E
39 O15 **Port Heiden** Alaska, USA 56°54'N 158°40'W
97 I19 **Porthmadog** *var.* Portmadoc. NW Wales, United Kingdom 52°55'N 04°08'W
14 I15 **Port Hope** Ontario, SE Canada 43°58'N 78°18'W
13 S9 **Port Hope Simpson** Newfoundland and Labrador, E Canada 52°30'N 56°18'W
65 C24 **Port Howard Settlement** West Falkland, Falkland Islands
31 T9 **Port Huron** Michigan, N USA 42°58'N 82°25'W
107 K17 **Portici** Campania, S Italy 40°48'N 14°20'E
Port-Iliç *see* Liman
104 G14 **Portimão** *var.* Vila Nova de Portimão. Faro, S Portugal 37°08'N 08°32'W
25 T17 **Port Isabel** Texas, SW USA 26°04'N 97°13'W
18 J13 **Port Jervis** New York, NE USA 41°22'N 74°39'W
55 S7 **Port Kaituma** NW Guyana 07°42'N 59°52'W
126 K12 **Port Katon** Rostovskaya Oblast', SW Russian Federation 46°52'N 38°46'E
183 S9 **Port Kembla** New South Wales, SE Australia 34°30'S 150°54'E
182 F8 **Port Kenny** South Australia 33°09'S 134°38'E
Port Klang *see* Pelabuhan Klang
Port Láirge *see* Waterford
183 S8 **Portland** New South Wales, SE Australia 33°24'S 150°00'E
182 L13 **Portland** Victoria, SE Australia 38°21'S 141°38'E
184 K4 **Portland** Northland, North Island, New Zealand 35°48'S 174°19'E
31 Q13 **Portland** Indiana, N USA 40°25'N 84°58'W
19 P8 **Portland** Maine, NE USA 43°41'N 70°16'W
31 Q9 **Portland** Michigan, N USA 42°51'N 84°52'W
29 Q4 **Portland** North Dakota, N USA 47°28'N 97°22'W
32 G11 **Portland** Oregon, NW USA 45°31'N 122°41'W
20 J8 **Portland** Tennessee, S USA 36°34'N 86°31'W
25 T14 **Portland** Texas, SW USA 27°52'N 97°19'W
32 G11 **Portland** ✕ Oregon, NW USA 45°36'N 122°34'W
182 L13 **Portland Bay** *bay* Victoria, SE Australia
44 K13 **Portland Bight** *bay* S Jamaica
97 L24 **Portland Bill** *var.* Bill of Portland. *headland* S England, United Kingdom 50°31'N 02°28'W
Portland, Bill of *see* Portland Bill
183 P15 **Portland, Cape** *headland* Tasmania, SE Australia 40°46'S 147°58'E
10 J12 **Portland Inlet** *inlet* British Columbia, W Canada
184 P11 **Portland Island** *island* E New Zealand
65 F15 **Portland Point** *headland* SW Ascension Island
44 J13 **Portland Point** *headland* C Jamaica 17°42'N 77°10'W
103 P16 **Port-la-Nouvelle** Aude, S France 43°01'N 03°04'E
Portlaoighise *see* Port Laoise
97 E18 **Port Laoise** *var.* Portlaoise, *Ir.* Portlaoighise; *prev.* Maryborough. C Ireland 53°02'N 07°17'W
Portlaoise *see* Port Laoise
25 U13 **Port Lavaca** Texas, SW USA 28°36'N 96°39'W
182 G9 **Port Lincoln** South Australia 34°43'S 135°49'E
39 Q14 **Port Lions** Kodiak Island, Alaska, USA 57°55'N 152°48'W
76 I15 **Port Loko** W Sierra Leone 08°50'N 12°50'W
65 E24 **Port Louis** East Falkland, Falkland Islands 51°31'S 58°07'W
45 Y5 **Port-Louis** Grande Terre, N Guadeloupe 16°25'N 61°32'W
173 X16 **Port Louis** ● (Mauritius) NW Mauritius 20°10'S 57°30'E
Port Louis *see* Scarborough
Port-Lyautey *see* Kénitra
182 K12 **Port MacDonnell** South Australia 38°04'S 140°40'E
183 U7 **Port Macquarie** New South Wales, SE Australia 31°26'S 152°55'E
Portmadoc *see* Porthmadog
Port Mahon *see* Maó
44 K12 **Port Maria** C Jamaica 18°22'N 76°54'W
10 K16 **Port McNeill** Vancouver Island, British Columbia, SW Canada 50°34'N 127°06'W
13 P11 **Port-Menier** Île d'Anticosti, Québec, E Canada 49°49'N 64°19'W
39 N15 **Port Moller** Alaska, USA 56°00'N 160°31'W
44 L13 **Port Morant** E Jamaica 17°53'N 76°20'W
44 K13 **Portmore** C Jamaica 17°58'N 76°52'W
186 D9 **Port Moresby** ● (Papua New Guinea) Central/National Capital District, SW Papua New Guinea 09°28'S 147°12'E
Port Natal *see* Durban
25 Y11 **Port Neches** Texas, SW USA 29°59'N 93°57'W
182 G9 **Port Neill** South Australia 34°06'S 136°19'E
15 S6 **Portneuf** ≈ Québec, SE Canada
15 R6 **Portneuf, Lac** ◎ Québec, SE Canada
83 D23 **Port Nolloth** Northern Cape, W South Africa 29°17'S 16°51'E
18 J17 **Port Norris** New Jersey, NE USA 39°13'N 75°00'W
Port-Nouveau-Québec *see* Kangiqsualujjuaq
104 G6 **Porto** *Eng.* Oporto; *anc.* Portus Cale. Porto, NW Portugal 41°09'N 08°37'W
104 G6 **Porto** *var.* Pôrto. ◈ *district* N Portugal
104 G6 **Porto** ✕ Porto, W Portugal 41°09'N 08°37'W
Pôrto *see* Porto
61 I16 **Porto Alegre** *var.* Pôrto Alegre. *state capital* Rio Grande do Sul, S Brazil 30°03'S 51°10'W
Porto Alexandre *see* Tombua
82 B12 **Porto Amboim** Cuanza Sul, NW Angola 10°47'S 13°43'E
Porto Amélia *see* Pemba
Porto Bello *see* Portobelo
43 T14 **Portobelo** *var.* Porto Bello, Puerto Bello. Colón, N Panama 09°33'N 79°37'W
60 G10 **Pôrto Camargo** Paraná, S Brazil 23°23'S 53°47'W
25 U13 **Port O'Connor** Texas, SW USA 28°26'N 96°26'W
Pôrto de Mós *see* Porto de Moz
58 J12 **Porto de Moz** *var.* Pôrto de Mós. Pará, NE Brazil 01°45'S 52°15'W
64 O5 **Porto do Moniz** Madeira, Portugal, NE Atlantic Ocean
59 H16 **Porto dos Gaúchos** Mato Grosso, W Brazil 11°32'S 57°16'W
Porto Edda *see* Sarandë
107 J24 **Porto Empedocle** Sicilia, Italy, C Mediterranean Sea 37°18'N 13°32'E
59 H20 **Porto Esperança** Mato Grosso do Sul, SW Brazil 19°36'S 57°24'W
106 E13 **Portoferraio** Toscana, C Italy 42°49'N 10°18'E
96 G6 **Port of Ness** NW Scotland, United Kingdom 58°29'N 06°15'W
45 U14 **Port-of-Spain** ● (Trinidad and Tobago) Trinidad, Trinidad and Tobago 10°39'N 61°30'W
Port of Spain *see* Piarco
103 X15 **Porto, Golfe de** *gulf* Corse, France, C Mediterranean Sea
Porto Grande *see* Mindelo
106 I7 **Portogruaro** Veneto, NE Italy 45°46'N 12°50'E
35 P5 **Portola** California, W USA 39°48'N 120°28'W
187 Q13 **Port-Olry** Espiritu Santo, C Vanuatu 15°03'S 167°04'E
93 J17 **Pörtom** *Fin.* Pirttikylä. Länsi-Suomi, W Finland 62°42'N 21°40'E
Port Omna *see* Portumna
59 G21 **Porto Murtinho** Mato Grosso do Sul, SW Brazil 21°42'S 57°52'W
59 K16 **Porto Nacional** Tocantins, C Brazil 10°41'S 48°19'W
77 S16 **Porto-Novo** ● (Benin) S Benin 06°29'N 02°37'E
23 X10 **Port Orange** Florida, SE USA 29°06'N 80°59'W
32 G8 **Port Orchard** Washington, NW USA 47°32'N 122°38'W
Porto Re *see* Kraljevica
32 E15 **Port Orford** Oregon, NW USA 42°45'N 124°30'W
Porto Rico *see* Puerto Rico
106 J13 **Porto San Giorgio** Marche, C Italy 43°10'N 13°47'E
107 F14 **Porto San Stefano** Toscana, C Italy 42°26'N 11°09'E
64 P5 **Porto Santo** *var.* Vila Baleira. Porto Santo, Madeira, Portugal, NE Atlantic Ocean 33°04'N 16°20'W
64 Q5 **Porto Santo** ✕ Porto Santo, Madeira, Portugal, NE Atlantic Ocean 33°04'N 16°20'W
64 P5 **Porto Santo** *var.* Ilha do Porto Santo. *island* Madeira, Portugal, NE Atlantic Ocean
Porto Santo, Ilha do *see* Porto Santo
60 H9 **Porto São José** Paraná, S Brazil 22°43'S 53°10'W
59 O19 **Porto Seguro** Bahia, E Brazil 16°25'S 39°07'W
107 B17 **Porto Torres** Sardegna, Italy, C Mediterranean Sea 40°50'N 08°23'E
59 J23 **Porto União** Santa Catarina, S Brazil 26°15'S 51°04'W
103 Y16 **Porto-Vecchio** Corse, France, C Mediterranean Sea 41°35'N 09°17'E
59 E15 **Porto Velho** *var.* Velho. *state capital* Rondônia, W Brazil 08°45'S 63°54'W
56 A6 **Portoviejo** *var.* Puertoviejo. Manabí, W Ecuador 01°03'S 80°31'W
185 B26 **Port Pegasus** *bay* Stewart Island, New Zealand
14 H15 **Port Perry** Ontario, SE Canada 44°08'N 78°57'W
183 N12 **Port Phillip Bay** *harbour* Victoria, SE Australia
182 I8 **Port Pirie** South Australia 33°11'S 138°01'E
96 G9 **Portree** N Scotland, United Kingdom 57°26'N 06°12'W
Port Rex *see* East London
Port Rois *see* Portrush
44 K13 **Port Royal** E Jamaica 17°55'N 76°52'W
21 R15 **Port Royal** South Carolina, SE USA 32°22'N 80°41'W
21 R15 **Port Royal Sound** *inlet* South Carolina, SE USA
97 F14 **Portrush** *Ir.* Port Rois. N Northern Ireland, United Kingdom 55°12'N 06°40'W
Port Said *see* Būr Saʻīd
23 R9 **Port Saint Joe** Florida, SE USA 29°49'N 85°18'W
23 Y11 **Port Saint John** Florida, SE USA 28°28'N 80°46'W
103 R16 **Port-St-Louis-du-Rhône** Bouches-du-Rhône, SE France 43°22'N 04°48'E
44 K10 **Port Salut** SW Haiti 18°04'N 73°55'W
65 E24 **Port Salvador** *inlet* East Falkland, Falkland Islands
65 D24 **Port San Carlos** East Falkland, Falkland Islands 51°30'S 58°59'W
13 S10 **Port Saunders** Newfoundland, Newfoundland and Labrador, SE Canada 50°40'N 57°17'W
83 K24 **Port Shepstone** KwaZulu/Natal, E South Africa 30°44'S 30°28'E
45 O11 **Portsmouth** *var.* Grand-Anse. NW Dominica 15°34'N 61°27'W
97 N24 **Portsmouth** S England, United Kingdom 50°48'N 01°05'W
19 P10 **Portsmouth** New Hampshire, NE USA 43°04'N 70°47'W
31 S15 **Portsmouth** Ohio, N USA 38°43'N 83°00'W
21 X7 **Portsmouth** Virginia, NE USA 36°50'N 76°18'W
14 E17 **Port Stanley** Ontario, S Canada 42°39'N 81°12'W
Port Stanley *see* Stanley
65 B25 **Port Stephens** *inlet* West Falkland, Falkland Islands
65 B25 **Port Stephens Settlement** West Falkland, Falkland Islands
97 F14 **Portstewart** *Ir.* Port Stíobhaird. N Northern Ireland, United Kingdom 55°11'N 06°43'W
Port Stíobhaird *see* Portstewart
83 K24 **Port St. Johns** Eastern Cape, SE South Africa 31°37'S 29°32'E
80 I7 **Port Sudan** Red Sea, NE Sudan 19°37'N 37°14'E
22 L10 **Port Sulphur** Louisiana, S USA 29°28'N 89°41'W
Port Swettenham *see* Klang/Pelabuhan Klang
97 J22 **Port Talbot** S Wales, United Kingdom 51°36'N 03°47'W
92 L11 **Porttipahdan Tekojärvi** ⊠ N Finland
32 G7 **Port Townsend** Washington, NW USA 48°07'N 122°45'W
104 H9 **Portugal** *off.* Portuguese Republic. ◆ *republic* SW Europe
105 O2 **Portugalete** País Vasco, N Spain 43°19'N 03°01'W
54 J6 **Portuguesa** *off.* Estado Portuguesa. ◈ *state* N Venezuela
Portuguesa, Estado *see* Portuguesa
Portuguese East Africa *see* Mozambique
Portuguese Guinea *see* Guinea-Bissau
Portuguese Republic *see* Portugal
Portuguese Timor *see* East Timor
Portuguese West Africa *see* Angola
97 D18 **Portumna** *Ir.* Port Omna. Galway, W Ireland 53°06'N 08°13'W
Portus Cale *see* Porto
Portus Magnus *see* Almería
Portus Magonis *see* Maó
103 P17 **Port-Vendres** *var.* Port Vendres. Pyrénées-Orientales, S France 42°31'N 03°06'E
182 H9 **Port Victoria** South Australia 34°34'S 137°31'E
187 Q14 **Port-Vila** *var.* Vila. ● (Vanuatu) Éfaté, C Vanuatu 17°45'S 168°21'E
Port Vila *see* Bauer Field
182 I9 **Port Wakefield** South Australia 34°13'S 138°10'E
31 N8 **Port Washington** Wisconsin, N USA 43°23'N 87°54'W
57 J14 **Porvenir** Pando, NW Bolivia 11°15'S 68°43'W
63 I24 **Porvenir** Magallanes, S Chile 53°18'S 70°22'W
61 D18 **Porvenir** Paysandú, W Uruguay 32°23'S 57°59'W
93 M19 **Porvoo** *Swe.* Borgå. Etelä-Suomi, S Finland 60°25'N 25°40'E
Porzecze *see* Parechcha
104 M10 **Porzuna** Castilla-La Mancha, C Spain 39°10'N 04°10'W
61 E14 **Posadas** Misiones, NE Argentina 27°27'S 55°52'W
104 L13 **Posadas** Andalucía, S Spain 37°48'N 05°06'W
Poschega *see* Požega
108 J11 **Poschiavino** ≈ Italy/Switzerland
108 J10 **Poschiavo** *Ger.* Puschlav. Graubünden, S Switzerland 46°19'N 10°02'E
112 D12 **Posedarje** Zadar, SW Croatia 44°12'N 15°27'E
Posen *see* Poznań
124 L14 **Poshekhon'ye** Yaroslavskaya Oblast', W Russian Federation 58°31'N 39°07'E
92 M13 **Posio** Lappi, NE Finland 66°06'N 28°16'E
Poskam *see* Zepu
Posnania *see* Poznań
1713 O12 **Poso** Sulawesi, C Indonesia 01°23'S 120°45'E
171 O12 **Poso, Danau** ◎ Sulawesi, C Indonesia
137 R10 **Posof** Ardahan, NE Turkey 41°30'N 42°33'E
25 R6 **Possum Kingdom Lake** ⊠ Texas, SW USA
25 N6 **Post** Texas, SW USA 33°14'N 101°24'W
Postavy/Postawy *see* Pastavy
Poste-de-la-Baleine *see* Kuujjuarapik
99 M17 **Posterholt** Limburg, SE Netherlands 51°07'N 06°02'E
83 G22 **Postmasburg** Northern Cape, N South Africa 28°20'S 23°05'E
Pôsto Diuarum *see* Campo de Diauarum
59 I16 **Pôsto Jacaré** Mato Grosso, W Brazil 12°S 53°27'W
109 T12 **Postojna** *Ger.* Adelsberg, *It.* Postumia. SW Slovenia 45°48'N 14°12'E
Postumia *see* Postojna
29 X12 **Postville** Iowa, C USA 43°04'N 91°34'W
Pöstyén *see* Piešťany
113 G14 **Posušje** Federacija Bosna I Hercegovina, SW Bosnia and Herzegovina 43°28'N 17°20'E
171 O16 **Pota** Flores, C Indonesia 08°21'S 120°50'E
115 G23 **Potamós** Antikýthira, S Greece 35°33'N 23°17'E

◆ Country
● Country Capital
◇ Dependent Territory
○ Dependent Territory Capital
◈ Administrative Regions
✕ International Airport
▲ Mountain
▲▲ Mountain Range
⛰ Volcano
≈ River
◎ Lake
⊠ Reservoir

55 S9 **Potaru River** ≈ C Guyana
83 I21 **Potchefstroom** North-West, N South Africa 26°42′S 27°06′E
27 R11 **Poteau** Oklahoma, C USA 35°03′N 94°36′W
25 R12 **Poteet** Texas, SW USA 29°02′N 98°34′W
115 G14 **Poteídaia** *site of ancient city* Kentrikí Makedonía, N Greece
Potentia *see* Potenza
107 M18 **Potenza** *anc.* Potentia. Basilicata, S Italy 40°40′N 15°50′E
185 A24 **Poteriteri, Lake** ◎ South Island, New Zealand
104 M2 **Potes** Cantabria, N Spain 43°10′N 04°41′W
Potgietersrus *see* Mokopane
25 S12 **Poth** Texas, SW USA 29°04′N 98°04′W
32 J9 **Potholes Reservoir** ⊠ Washington, NW USA
137 Q9 **Poti** *prev.* P'ot'i. W Georgia 42°10′N 41°42′E
P'ot'i *see* Poti
77 X13 **Potiskum** Yobe, NE Nigeria 11°38′N 11°07′E
Potkozarje *see* Ivanjska
32 M9 **Potlatch** Idaho, NW USA 46°55′N 116°51′W
33 N9 **Pot Mountain** ▲ Idaho, NW USA 46°44′N 115°24′W
113 H14 **Potoci** Federacija Bosna I Hercegovina, S Bosnia and Herzegovina 43°24′N 17°52′E
21 V3 **Potomac River** ≈ NE USA
57 L20 **Potosí** Potosí, S Bolivia 19°35′S 65°51′W
42 H9 **Potosí** Chinandega, NW Nicaragua 12°58′N 87°30′W
27 W6 **Potosi** Missouri, C USA 37°57′N 90°49′W
57 K21 **Potosí** ◈ *department* SW Bolivia
62 H7 **Potrerillos** Atacama, N Chile 26°30′S 69°25′W
42 H5 **Potrerillos** Cortés, NW Honduras 15°10′N 87°58′W
62 H8 **Potro, Cerro del** ▲ N Chile 28°22′S 69°34′W
100 N12 **Potsdam** Brandenburg, NE Germany 52°24′N 13°04′E
18 J7 **Potsdam** New York, NE USA 44°40′N 74°58′W
109 X5 **Pottendorf** Niederösterreich, E Austria 47°55′N 16°23′E
109 X5 **Pottenstein** Niederösterreich, E Austria 47°58′N 16°07′E
18 I15 **Pottstown** Pennsylvania, NE USA 40°15′N 75°39′W
18 H14 **Pottsville** Pennsylvania, NE USA 40°40′N 76°10′W
155 L25 **Pottuvil** Eastern Province, SE Sri Lanka 06°53′N 81°49′E
149 U6 **Potwar Plateau** *plateau* NE Pakistan
102 J7 **Pouancé** Maine-et-Loire, W France 47°46′N 01°11′W
15 R6 **Poulin de Courval, Lac** ◎ Québec, SE Canada
18 L9 **Poultney** Vermont, NE USA 43°31′N 73°12′W
187 O16 **Poum** Province Nord, W New Caledonia 20°15′S 164°03′E
59 L21 **Pouso Alegre** Minas Gerais, NE Brazil 22°13′S 45°56′W
192 I16 **Poutasi** Upolu, SE Samoa 14°00′S 171°43′W
167 R12 **Poŭthĭsăt** *prev.* Pursat. Poŭthĭsăt, W Cambodia 12°32′N 103°55′E
167 R12 **Poŭthĭsăt, Stœng** *prev.* Pursat. ≈ W Cambodia
102 J9 **Pouzauges** Vendée, NW France 46°47′N 00°54′W
Po, Valle del *see* Po Valley
106 F8 **Po Valley** *It.* Valle del Po. *valley* N Italy
111 I19 **Považská Bystrica** *Ger.* Waagbistritz, *Hung.* Vágbeszterce. Trenčiansky Kraj, W Slovakia 49°07′N 18°26′E
124 J10 **Povenets** Respublika Kareliya, NW Russian Federation 62°50′N 34°47′E
184 Q9 **Poverty Bay** *inlet* North Island, New Zealand
112 K12 **Povlen** ▲▲ W Serbia
104 G6 **Póvoa de Varzim** Porto, NW Portugal 41°22′N 08°46′W
127 N8 **Povorino** Voronezhskaya Oblast', W Russian Federation 51°10′N 42°16′E
Povungnituk *see* Puvirnituq
Rivière de Povungnituk *see* Puvirnituq, Riviere de
14 H11 **Powassan** Ontario, S Canada 46°05′N 79°21′W
35 U17 **Poway** California, W USA 32°57′N 117°02′W
33 W14 **Powder River** Wyoming, C USA 43°01′N 106°57′W
33 Y10 **Powder River** ≈ Montana/Wyoming, NW USA
32 L12 **Powder River** ≈ Oregon, NW USA
33 W13 **Powder River Pass** *pass* Wyoming, C USA
33 U12 **Powell** Wyoming, C USA 44°45′N 108°45′W
65 I22 **Powell Basin** *undersea feature* NW Weddell Sea
36 M8 **Powell, Lake** ◎ Utah, W USA
37 R4 **Powell, Mount** ▲ Colorado, C USA 39°25′N 106°20′W
10 L17 **Powell River** British Columbia, SW Canada 49°54′N 124°34′W
31 N5 **Powers** Michigan, N USA 45°40′N 87°29′W
28 K2 **Powers Lake** North Dakota, N USA 48°33′N 102°37′W
21 V6 **Powhatan** Virginia, NE USA 37°33′N 77°56′W
31 V13 **Powhatan Point** Ohio, N USA 39°49′N 80°49′W
97 J20 **Powys** *cultural region* E Wales, United Kingdom
187 P17 **Poya** Province Nord, C New Caledonia 21°19′S 165°07′E
161 P10 **Poyang Hu** ◎ S China
30 L7 **Poygan, Lake** ◎ Wisconsin, N USA
109 Y2 **Poysdorf** Niederösterreich, NE Austria 48°40′N 16°38′E
112 N11 **Požarevac** *Ger.* Passarowitz. Serbia, NE Serbia 44°37′N 21°11′E
41 Q13 **Poza Rica** *var.* Poza Rica de Hidalgo. Veracruz-Llave, E Mexico 20°34′N 97°26′W
Poza Rica de Hidalgo *see* Poza Rica
112 L13 **Požega** *prev.* Slavonska Požega, *Ger.* Poschega, *Hung.* Pozsega. Požega-Slavonija, NE Croatia 45°19′N 17°42′E
112 H9 **Požega-Slavonija** *off.* Požeško-Slavonska Županija. ◈ *province* NE Croatia
Požeško-Slavonska Županija *see* Požega-Slavonija
125 U13 **Pozhva** Komi-Permyatskiy Okrug, NW Russian Federation 59°07′N 56°04′E
110 G11 **Poznań** *Ger.* Posen, Posnania. Wielkolpolskie, C Poland 52°24′N 16°56′E
105 O13 **Pozo Alcón** Andalucía, S Spain 37°43′N 02°55′W
62 H3 **Pozo Almonte** Tarapacá, N Chile 20°16′S 69°50′W
104 L12 **Pozoblanco** Andalucía, S Spain 38°23′N 04°48′W
105 Q11 **Pozo Cañada** Castilla-La Mancha, C Spain 38°49′N 01°45′W
62 N5 **Pozo Colorado** Presidente Hayes, C Paraguay 23°26′S 58°51′W
63 J20 **Pozos, Punta** *headland* S Argentina 47°55′S 65°46′W
Pozsega *see* Požega
Pozsony *see* Bratislava
55 N5 **Pozuelos** Anzoátegui, NE Venezuela 10°11′N 64°39′W
107 L26 **Pozzallo** Sicilia, Italy, C Mediterranean Sea 36°44′N 14°51′E
107 K17 **Pozzuoli** *anc.* Puteoli. Campania, S Italy 40°49′N 14°07′E
77 P17 **Pra** ≈ S Ghana
111 C19 **Prachatice** *Ger.* Prachatitz. Jihočeský Kraj, S Czech Republic 49°01′N 14°02′E
Prachatitz *see* Prachatice
167 P11 **Prachin Buri** *var.* Prachinburi. Prachin Buri, C Thailand 14°05′N 101°23′E
Prachinburi *see* Prachin Buri
Prachuab Girikhand *see* Prachuap Khiri Khan
167 O12 **Prachuap Khiri Khan** *var.* Prachuab Girikhand. Prachuap Khiri Khan, SW Thailand 11°50′N 99°49′E
111 H16 **Praděd** *Ger.* Altvater. ▲ NE Czech Republic 50°06′N 17°14′E
54 D11 **Pradera** Valle del Cauca, SW Colombia 03°23′N 76°11′W
103 O17 **Prades** Pyrénées-Orientales, S France 42°36′N 02°22′E
59 O19 **Prado** Bahia, SE Brazil 17°13′S 39°15′W
54 E11 **Prado** Tolima, C Colombia 03°45′N 74°55′W
Prado del Ganso *see* Goose Green
Prae *see* Phrae
95 I24 **Præstø** Sjælland, SE Denmark 55°08′N 12°03′E
Prag/Praga/Prague *see* Praha
27 O10 **Prague** Oklahoma, C USA 35°29′N 96°40′W
111 D16 **Praha** *Eng.* Prague, *Ger.* Prag, *Pol.* Praga. ● (Czech Republic) Středočeský Kraj, NW Czech Republic 50°06′N 14°26′E
116 J13 **Prahova** ◈ *county* SE Romania
116 J13 **Prahova** ≈ S Romania
76 E10 **Praia** ● (Cape Verde) Santiago, S Cape Verde 14°55′N 23°31′W
83 M21 **Praia do Bilene** Gaza, S Mozambique 25°18′S 33°10′E
83 M20 **Praia do Xai-Xai** Gaza, S Mozambique 25°04′S 33°43′E
116 J10 **Praid** *Hung.* Parajd. Harghita, C Romania 46°33′N 25°06′E
26 J3 **Prairie Dog Creek** ≈ Kansas/Nebraska, C USA
30 J9 **Prairie du Chien** Wisconsin, N USA 43°02′N 91°08′W
27 S9 **Prairie Grove** Arkansas, C USA 35°58′N 94°19′W
31 P10 **Prairie River** ≈ Michigan, N USA
Prairie State *see* Illinois
25 V11 **Prairie View** Texas, SW USA 30°05′N 95°59′W
167 Q10 **Prakhon Chai** Buri Ram, E Thailand 14°36′N 103°04′E
109 R4 **Pram** ≈ N Austria
167 Q12 **Prâmaôy** *prev.* Phumĭ Prâmaôy. Poŭthĭsăt, W Cambodia 12°13′N 103°05′E
109 S4 **Prambachkirchen** Oberösterreich, N Austria 48°18′N 13°50′E
118 H2 **Prangli** *island* N Estonia
154 J13 **Prānhita** ≈ C India
172 I15 **Praslin** *island* Inner Islands, NE Seychelles
115 O23 **Prasonísi, Akrotírio** *cape* Ródos, Dodekánisa, Greece, Aegean Sea
111 I14 **Praszka** Opolskie, S Poland 51°05′N 18°29′E
Pratas Island *see* Tungsha Tao
119 M18 **Pratasy** *Rus.* Protasy. Homyel'skaya Voblasts', SE Belarus 52°47′N 29°05′E
167 Q10 **Prathai** Nakhon Ratchasima, E Thailand 15°31′N 102°42′E
Prathet Thai *see* Thailand
Prathum Thani *see* Pathum Thani
63 F21 **Prat, Isla** *island* S Chile
106 G11 **Prato** Toscana, C Italy 43°53′N 11°05′E
103 O17 **Prats-de-Mollo-la-Preste** Pyrénées-Orientales, S France 42°25′N 02°28′E
26 L6 **Pratt** Kansas, C USA 37°40′N 98°45′W
108 E6 **Pratteln** Basel Landschaft, NW Switzerland 47°32′N 07°42′E
193 O2 **Pratt Seamount** *undersea feature* N Pacific Ocean 56°09′N 142°30′W
23 P5 **Prattville** Alabama, S USA 32°27′N 86°27′W
Praust *see* Pruszcz Gdański
119 B14 **Pravdinsk** *Ger.* Friedland. Kaliningradskaya Oblast', W Russian Federation 54°26′N 21°01′E
104 K2 **Pravia** Asturias, N Spain 43°30′N 06°06′W
118 L12 **Prazaroki** *Rus.* Prozoroki. Vitsyebskaya Voblasts', N Belarus 55°18′N 28°13′E
Prázsmár *see* Prejmer
167 S11 **Preăh Vihéar** Preăh Vihéar, N Cambodia 13°57′N 104°48′E
116 J12 **Predeal** *Hung.* Predeál. Brașov, C Romania 45°30′N 25°31′E
109 S8 **Predlitz** Steiermark, SE Austria 47°04′N 13°54′E
11 V15 **Preeceville** Saskatchewan, S Canada 51°58′N 102°40′W
Preenkuln *see* Priekule
102 K6 **Pré-en-Pail** Mayenne, NW France 48°27′N 00°15′W
109 T4 **Pregarten** Oberösterreich, N Austria 48°21′N 14°31′E
54 H7 **Pregonero** Táchira, NW Venezuela 08°02′N 71°35′W
118 J10 **Preiļi** *Ger.* Preli. SE Latvia 56°17′N 26°52′E
116 J12 **Prejmer** *Ger.* Tartlau, *Hung.* Prázsmár. Brașov, S Romania 45°42′N 25°49′E
113 J16 **Prekornica** ▲▲ C Montenegro
Preli *see* Preiļi
Prëmet *see* Përmet
100 M12 **Premnitz** Brandenburg, NE Germany 52°33′N 12°22′E
25 S15 **Premont** Texas, SW USA 27°21′N 98°07′W
113 H14 **Prenj** ▲▲ S Bosnia and Herzegovina
Prenjas/Prenjasi *see* Përrenjas
22 L7 **Prentiss** Mississippi, S USA 31°36′N 89°52′W
Preny *see* Prienai
100 O10 **Prenzlau** Brandenburg, NE Germany 53°19′N 13°52′E
123 N11 **Preobrazhenka** Irkutskaya Oblast', C Russian Federation 60°01′N 108°00′E
166 J9 **Preparis Island** *island* SW Burma (Myanmar)
Prerau *see* Přerov
111 H18 **Přerov** *Ger.* Prerau. Olomoucký Kraj, E Czech Republic 49°27′N 17°27′E
Preschau *see* Prešov
14 M14 **Prescott** Ontario, SE Canada 44°43′N 75°33′W
36 K12 **Prescott** Arizona, SW USA 34°33′N 112°26′W
27 T13 **Prescott** Arkansas, C USA 33°49′N 93°25′W
32 L10 **Prescott** Washington, NW USA 46°17′N 118°21′W
30 H6 **Prescott** Wisconsin, N USA 44°46′N 92°45′W
185 A24 **Preservation Inlet** *inlet* South Island, New Zealand
112 O7 **Preševo** Serbia, SE Serbia 42°20′N 21°38′E
29 N10 **Presho** South Dakota, N USA 43°54′N 100°03′W
58 M13 **Presidente Dutra** Maranhão, E Brazil 05°17′S 44°30′W
60 I8 **Presidente Epitácio** São Paulo, S Brazil 21°45′S 52°07′W
62 N5 **Presidente Hayes** *off.* Departamento de Presidente Hayes. ◈ *department* C Paraguay
Presidente Hayes, Departamento de *see* Presidente Hayes
60 I9 **Presidente Prudente** São Paulo, S Brazil 22°09′S 51°24′W
Presidente Stroessner *see* Ciudad del Este
Presidente Vargas *see* Itabira
60 I8 **Presidente Venceslau** São Paulo, S Brazil 21°52′S 51°51′W
193 O10 **President Thiers Seamount** *undersea feature* C Pacific Ocean 24°39′S 145°50′W
24 J11 **Presidio** Texas, SW USA 29°33′N 104°22′W
Preslav *see* Veliki Preslav
111 M19 **Prešov** *var.* Preschau, *Ger.* Eperies, *Hung.* Eperjes. Prešovský Kraj, E Slovakia 49°N 21°14′E
111 M19 **Prešovský Kraj** ◈ *region* E Slovakia
113 N20 **Prespa, Lake** *Alb.* Liqen i Prespës, *Gk.* Límni Megáli Préspa, Limni Prespa, *Mac.* Prespansko Ezero, *Serb.* Prespansko Jezero. ◎ SE Europe
Prespa, Limni/Prespansko Ezero/Prespansko Jezero/Prespës, Liqen i *see* Prespa, Lake
19 S2 **Presque Isle** Maine, NE USA 46°40′N 68°01′W
18 B11 **Presque Isle** *headland* Pennsylvania, NE USA 42°09′N 80°06′W
Pressburg *see* Bratislava
77 P17 **Prestea** SW Ghana 05°22′N 02°07′W
111 B17 **Přeštice** *Ger.* Pschestitz. Plzeňský Kraj, W Czech Republic 49°36′N 13°19′E
97 K17 **Preston** NW England, United Kingdom 53°46′N 02°42′W
23 S6 **Preston** Georgia, SE USA 32°03′N 84°32′W
33 R16 **Preston** Idaho, NW USA 42°06′N 111°52′W
29 Z13 **Preston** Iowa, C USA 42°03′N 90°24′W
29 X11 **Preston** Minnesota, N USA 43°41′N 92°06′W
21 O6 **Prestonsburg** Kentucky, S USA 37°40′N 82°46′W
96 I13 **Prestwick** W Scotland, United Kingdom 55°31′N 04°39′W
83 I45 **Pretoria** *var.* Epitoli, Tshwane. ● Gauteng, NE South Africa 25°41′S 28°12′E *see also* Tshwane
Pretoria-Witwatersrand-Vereeniging *see* Gauteng
Pretusha *see* Pretushë
113 M21 **Pretushë** *var.* Pretusha. Korçë, SE Albania 40°50′N 20°45′E
Preussisch Eylau *see* Bagrationovsk
Preußisch Holland *see* Pasłęk
Preussisch-Stargard *see* Starogard Gdański
115 C17 **Préveza** Ípeiros, W Greece 38°59′N 20°44′E
37 V3 **Prewitt Reservoir** ⊠ Colorado, C USA
167 S13 **Prey Vêng** Prey Vêng, S Cambodia 11°30′N 105°20′E
Priaral'skiye Karakumy, Peski *see* Priaral'skiy Karakum
144 M12 **Priaral'skiy Karakum** *prev.* Priaral'skiye Karakumy, Peski. *desert* SW Kazakhstan
123 P14 **Priargunsk** Zabaykal'skiy Kray, S Russian Federation 50°25′N 119°12′E
38 K14 **Pribilof Islands** *island group* Alaska, USA
113 K14 **Priboj** Serbia, W Serbia 43°34′N 19°33′E
111 C17 **Příbram** *Ger.* Pibrans. Středočeský Kraj, W Czech Republic 49°41′N 14°02′E
36 M4 **Price** Utah, W USA 39°35′N 110°49′W
37 N5 **Price River** ≈ Utah, W USA
23 N8 **Prichard** Alabama, S USA 30°44′N 88°04′W
25 R8 **Priddy** Texas, SW USA 31°39′N 98°30′W
105 P8 **Priego** Castilla-La Mancha, C Spain 40°26′N 02°19′W
104 M14 **Priego de Córdoba** Andalucía, S Spain 37°27′N 04°12′W
118 C10 **Priekule** *Ger.* Preenkuln. SW Latvia 56°26′N 21°36′E
118 C12 **Priekulė** *Ger.* Prökuls. Klaipėda, W Lithuania 55°36′N 21°16′E
119 F14 **Prienai** *Pol.* Preny. Kaunas, S Lithuania 54°37′N 23°56′E
83 G23 **Prieska** Northern Cape, C South Africa 29°40′S 22°45′E
32 M7 **Priest Lake** ⊠ Idaho, NW USA
32 M7 **Priest River** Idaho, NW USA 48°10′N 117°02′W
104 M3 **Prieta, Peña** ▲ N Spain 43°01′N 04°42′W
40 J10 **Prieto, Cerro** ▲ C Mexico 24°10′N 105°21′W
111 J19 **Prievidza** *var.* Priewitz, *Ger.* Priwitz, *Hung.* Privigye. Trenčiansky Kraj, W Slovakia 48°47′N 18°35′E
Priewitz *see* Prievidza
112 F10 **Prijedor** ◈ Republika Srpska, NW Bosnia and Herzegovina
113 K14 **Prijepolje** Serbia, W Serbia 43°24′N 19°39′E
Prikaspiyskaya Nizmennost' *see* Caspian Depression
113 O19 **Prilep** *Turk.* Perlepe. S FYR Macedonia 41°21′N 21°34′E
108 B9 **Prilly** Vaud, SW Switzerland 46°32′N 06°38′E
Priluki *see* Pryluky
62 L10 **Primero, Río** ≈ C Argentina
29 S12 **Primghar** Iowa, C USA 43°05′N 95°37′W
112 B9 **Primorje-Gorski Kotar** *off.* Primorsko-Goranska Županija. ◈ *province* NW Croatia
118 A13 **Primorsk** *Ger.* Fischhausen. Kaliningradskaya Oblast', W Russian Federation 54°45′N 20°00′E
124 G12 **Primorsk** *Fin.* Koivisto. Leningradskaya Oblast', NW Russian Federation 60°20′N 28°39′E
123 S14 **Primorskiy Kray** *prev. Eng.* Maritime Territory. ◈ *territory* SE Russian Federation
114 N10 **Primorsko** *prev.* Keupriya. Burgas, E Bulgaria 42°15′N 27°45′E
126 K13 **Primorsko-Akhtarsk** Krasnodarskiy Kray, SW Russian Federation 46°03′N 38°44′E
Primorsko-Goranska Županija *see* Primorje-Gorski Kotar
Primorsk/Primorskoye *see* Prymors'k
113 D14 **Primošten** Šibenik-Knin, S Croatia 43°34′N 15°57′E
11 R13 **Primrose Lake** ◎ Saskatchewan, C Canada
11 T14 **Prince Albert** Saskatchewan, S Canada 53°09′N 105°43′W
83 G25 **Prince Albert** Western Cape, SW South Africa 33°13′S 22°03′E
8 J5 **Prince Albert Peninsula** *peninsula* Victoria Island, Northwest Territories, NW Canada
8 J6 **Prince Albert Sound** *inlet* Northwest Territories, N Canada
J5 8 **Prince Alfred, Cape** *headland* Northwest Territories, NW Canada
9 P6 **Prince Charles Island** *island* Nunavut, NE Canada
195 W6 **Prince Charles Mountains** ▲▲ Antarctica
Prince-Édouard, Île-du *see* Prince Edward Island
172 M13 **Prince Edward Fracture Zone** *tectonic feature* SW Indian Ocean
13 P14 **Prince Edward Island** *Fr.* Île-du Prince-Édouard. ◈ *province* SE Canada
13 Q14 **Prince Edward Island** *Fr.* Île-du Prince-Édouard. *island* SE Canada
173 M12 **Prince Edward Islands** *island group* S South Africa
21 X4 **Prince Frederick** Maryland, NE USA 38°32′N 76°35′W
10 M14 **Prince George** British Columbia, SW Canada 53°55′N 122°49′W
21 W6 **Prince George** Virginia, NE USA 37°13′N 77°13′W
197 O8 **Prince Gustaf Adolf Sea** *sea* Nunavut, N Canada
197 Q3 **Prince of Wales, Cape** *headland* Alaska, USA 65°39′N 168°12′W
181 V1 **Prince of Wales Island** *island* Queensland, E Australia
8 L5 **Prince of Wales Island** *island* Queen Elizabeth Islands, Nunavut, NW Canada
39 Y14 **Prince of Wales Island** *island* Alexander Archipelago, Alaska, USA
Prince of Wales Island *see* Pinang, Pulau
8 J5 **Prince of Wales Strait** *strait* Northwest Territories, N Canada
197 O8 **Prince Patrick Island** *island* Parry Islands, Northwest Territories, NW Canada
9 N5 **Prince Regent Inlet** *channel* Nunavut, N Canada
10 J13 **Prince Rupert** British Columbia, SW Canada 54°18′N 130°17′W
Prince's Island *see* Príncipe
21 Y5 **Princess Anne** Maryland, NE USA 38°12′N 75°42′W
Princess Astrid Coast *see* Prinsesse Astrid Kyst
181 W2 **Princess Charlotte Bay** *bay* Queensland, NE Australia
195 W7 **Princess Elizabeth Land** *physical region* Antarctica
10 J14 **Princess Royal Island** *island* British Columbia, SW Canada
45 U15 **Princes Town** Trinidad, Trinidad and Tobago 10°16′N 61°23′W
11 N17 **Princeton** British Columbia, SW Canada 49°25′N 120°35′W
30 L11 **Princeton** Illinois, N USA 41°22′N 89°27′W
31 N16 **Princeton** Indiana, N USA 38°21′N 87°33′W
29 Z14 **Princeton** Iowa, C USA 41°40′N 90°21′W
20 H7 **Princeton** Kentucky, S USA 37°06′N 87°52′W
29 V8 **Princeton** Minnesota, N USA 45°34′N 93°34′W
27 S1 **Princeton** Missouri, C USA 40°22′N 93°37′W
18 J15 **Princeton** New Jersey, NE USA 40°21′N 74°39′W
21 R6 **Princeton** West Virginia, NE USA 37°23′N 81°06′W
39 S12 **Prince William Sound** *inlet* Alaska, USA
67 P9 **Príncipe** *var.* Príncipe Island, *Eng.* Prince's Island. *island* N Sao Tome and Principe
Príncipe Island *see* Príncipe
32 I13 **Prineville** Oregon, NW USA 44°19′N 120°50′W
28 J11 **Pringle** South Dakota, N USA 43°34′N 103°34′W
25 N1 **Pringle** Texas, SW USA 35°55′N 101°28′W
99 H14 **Prinsenbeek** Noord-Brabant, S Netherlands 51°36′N 04°42′E
98 L6 **Prinses Margriet Kanaal** *canal* N Netherlands
195 R1 **Prinsesse Astrid Kyst** *Eng.* Princess Astrid Coast. *physical region* Antarctica
195 T2 **Prinsesse Ragnhild Kyst** *physical region* Antarctica
195 U2 **Prins Harald Kyst** *physical region* Antarctica
92 N2 **Prins Karls Forland** *island* W Svalbard
43 N8 **Prinzapolka** Región Autónoma Atlántico Norte, NE Nicaragua 13°19′N 83°35′W
42 L8 **Prinzapolka, Río** ≈ NE Nicaragua
122 H9 **Priob'ye** Khanty-Mansiyskiy Avtonomnyy Okrug-Yugra, N Russian Federation 62°25′N 65°36′E
104 H1 **Prior, Cabo** *headland* NW Spain 43°33′N 08°21′W
29 V9 **Prior Lake** Minnesota, N USA 44°42′N 93°25′W
124 H11 **Priozersk** *Fin.* Käkisalmi. Leningradskaya Oblast', NW Russian Federation 61°02′N 30°07′E
119 J20 **Pripet** *Bel.* Prypyats', *Ukr.* Pryp"yat'. ≈ Belarus/Ukraine
119 J20 **Pripet Marshes** *wetland* Belarus/Ukraine
113 N16 **Prishtinë** *Serb.* Priština. C Kosovo 42°40′N 21°10′E
126 J8 **Pristen'** Kurskaya Oblast', W Russian Federation 51°15′N 36°47′E
Priština *see* Prishtinë
100 M10 **Pritzwalk** Brandenburg, NE Germany 53°10′N 12°11′E
103 R13 **Privas** Ardèche, E France 44°45′N 04°35′E
107 I16 **Priverno** Lazio, C Italy 41°28′N 13°11′E
Privigye *see* Prievidza
112 C12 **Privlaka** Zadar, SW Croatia 44°15′N 15°07′E
124 M15 **Privolzhsk** Ivanovskaya Oblast', NW Russian Federation 57°24′N 41°16′E
127 P7 **Privolzhskaya Vozvyshennost'** *var.* Volga Uplands. ▲▲ W Russian Federation
127 P8 **Privolzhskoye** Saratovskaya Oblast', W Russian Federation 51°08′N 45°57′E
Priwitz *see* Prievidza
127 N13 **Priyutnoye** Respublika Kalmykiya, SW Russian Federation 46°08′N 43°33′E
113 M17 **Prizren** S Kosovo 42°14′N 20°46′E
107 I24 **Prizzi** Sicilia, Italy, C Mediterranean Sea 37°44′N 13°26′E
113 P18 **Probištip** NE FYR Macedonia 42°00′N 22°06′E
169 S16 **Probolinggo** Jawa, C Indonesia 07°45′S 113°12′E
Probstberg *see* Wyszków
111 F14 **Prochowice** *Ger.* Parchwitz. Dolnośląskie, SW Poland 51°15′N 16°22′E
29 W5 **Proctor** Minnesota, N USA 46°46′N 92°13′W
25 R8 **Proctor** Texas, SW USA 31°57′N 98°25′W
25 R8 **Proctor Lake** ⊠ Texas, SW USA
155 I18 **Proddatūr** Andhra Pradesh, E India 14°45′N 78°34′E
104 H9 **Proença-a-Nova** *var.* Proença a Nova. Castelo Branco, C Portugal 39°45′N 07°56′W
Proença a Nova *see* Proença-a-Nova
99 I21 **Profondeville** Namur, SE Belgium 50°22′N 04°52′E
41 W11 **Progreso** Yucatán, SE Mexico 21°14′N 89°41′W
123 R14 **Progress** Amurskaya Oblast', SE Russian Federation 49°40′N 129°30′E
127 O15 **Prokhladnyy** Kabardino-Balkarskaya Respublika, SW Russian Federation 43°48′N 44°02′E
Prokletije *see* North Albanian Alps
Prökuls *see* Priekulė
113 O15 **Prokuplje** Serbia, SE Serbia 43°15′N 21°35′E
124 H14 **Proletariy** Novgorodskaya Oblast', W Russian Federation 58°24′N 31°40′E
126 M12 **Proletarsk** Rostovskaya Oblast', SW Russian Federation 46°42′N 41°48′E
127 N13 **Proletarskoye Vodokhranilishche** *salt lake* SW Russian Federation
Prome *see* Pyay
60 J8 **Promissão** São Paulo, S Brazil 21°33′S 49°51′W
60 J8 **Promissão, Represa de** ⊠ S Brazil
125 V4 **Promyshlennyy** Respublika Komi, NW Russian Federation 67°36′N 64°E
119 O16 **Pronya** ≈ E Belarus
10 M11 **Prophet River** British Columbia, W Canada 58°07′N 122°39′W
30 K11 **Prophetstown** Illinois, N USA 41°40′N 89°56′W
Propinsi Irian Jaya Barat *see* Papua Barat
Propinsi Kepulauan Riau *see* Kepulauan Riau
59 P16 **Propriá** Sergipe, E Brazil 10°15′S 36°51′W
103 X16 **Propriano** Corse, France, C Mediterranean Sea 41°41′N 08°54′E
Prościejów *see* Prostějov
Proskurov *see* Khmel 'nyts'kyy
114 H12 **Prosotsáni** Anatolikí Makedonía kai Thráki, NE Greece 41°11′N 23°59′E
171 Q7 **Prosperidad** Mindanao, S Philippines 08°36′N 125°54′E
32 J10 **Prosser** Washington, NW USA 46°12′N 119°46′W
Prossnitz *see* Prostějov
111 G18 **Prostějov** *Ger.* Prossnitz, *Pol.* Prościejów. Olomoucký Kraj, E Czech Republic 49°29′N 17°08′E
117 V8 **Prosyana** Dnipropetrovs'ka Oblast', E Ukraine 48°07′N 36°22′E
111 L16 **Proszowice** Malopolskie, S Poland 50°12′N 20°15′E
Protasy *see* Pratasy
172 J11 **Protea Seamount** *undersea feature* SW Indian Ocean 36°50′S 18°05′E
115 D21 **Próti** *island* S Greece
114 N8 **Provadiya** Varna, E Bulgaria 43°10′N 27°29′E
103 T14 **Provence** *cultural region* SE France
103 S15 **Provence** *prev.* Marseille-Marigrane. ✈ (Marseille) Bouches-du-Rhône, SE France 43°25′N 05°15′E
103 T14 **Provence-Alpes-Côte d'Azur** ◈ *region* SE France
20 H6 **Providence** Kentucky, S USA 37°23′N 87°47′W
19 N12 **Providence** *state capital* Rhode Island, NE USA 41°50′N 71°26′W
36 L1 **Providence** Utah, W USA 41°42′N 111°49′W
Providence *see* Fort Providence
Providence *see* Providence Atoll
67 X10 **Providence Atoll** *var.* Providence. *atoll* S Seychelles
14 D12 **Providence Bay** Manitoulin Island, Ontario, S Canada 45°39′N 82°16′W
23 R6 **Providence Canyon** *valley* Alabama/Georgia, S USA
22 I5 **Providence, Lake** ◎ Louisiana, S USA
35 X13 **Providence Mountains** ▲▲ California, W USA
44 L6 **Providenciales** *island* W Turks and Caicos Islands
19 Q12 **Provincetown** Massachusetts, NE USA 42°01′N 70°10′W
103 P5 **Provins** Seine-et-Marne, N France 48°34′N 03°18′E
36 L3 **Provo** Utah, W USA 40°14′N 111°39′W
11 R15 **Provost** Alberta, SW Canada 52°24′N 110°16′W
112 G13 **Prozor** Federacija Bosna I Hercegovina, SW Bosnia and Herzegovina 43°46′N 17°38′E
Prozoroki *see* Prazaroki
60 I11 **Prudentópolis** Paraná, S Brazil 25°12′S 50°58′W
39 R5 **Prudhoe Bay** Alaska, USA 70°16′N 148°18′W
39 R4 **Prudhoe Bay** *bay* Alaska, USA
111 H16 **Prudnik** *Ger.* Neustadt, Neustadt in Oberschlesien. Opole, SW Poland 50°20′N 17°34′E
119 J16 **Prudy** Minskaya Voblasts', C Belarus 53°47′N 26°32′E
101 D18 **Prüm** Rheinland-Pfalz, W Germany 50°15′N 06°27′E
101 D18 **Prüm** ≈ W Germany
Prusa *see* Bursa
110 J7 **Pruszcz Gdański** *Ger.* Praust. Pomorskie, N Poland 54°16′N 18°36′E
110 M12 **Pruszków** *Ger.* Kaltdorf. Mazowieckie, C Poland 52°09′N 20°49′E
116 K8 **Prut** *Ger.* Pruth. ≈ E Europe
Pruth *see* Prut
108 L8 **Prutz** Tirol, W Austria 47°07′N 10°42′E
Pružana *see* Pruzhany
119 G19 **Pruzhany** *Pol.* Pružana. Brestskaya Voblasts', SW Belarus 52°33′N 24°28′E
124 I11 **Pryazha** Respublika Kareliya, NW Russian Federation 61°42′N 33°39′E
117 U10 **Pryazovs'ke** Zaporiz'ka Oblast', SE Ukraine 46°43′N 35°39′E
Prychornomor'ska Nyzovyna *see* Black Sea Lowland
Prydniprovs'ka Nyzovyna/Prydnyaprowskaya Nizina *see* Dnieper Lowland
195 Y7 **Prydz Bay** *bay* Antarctica
117 R4 **Pryluky** *Rus.* Priluki. Chernihivs'ka Oblast', NE Ukraine 50°35′N 32°23′E
117 V10 **Prymors'k** *Rus.* Primorsk; *prev.* Primorskoye. Zaporiz'ka Oblast', SE Ukraine 46°44′N 36°19′E
117 U13 **Prymors'kyy** Avtonomna Respublika Krym, S Ukraine 45°09′N 35°33′E
27 Q9 **Pryor** Oklahoma, C USA 36°19′N 95°19′W
33 U11 **Pryor Creek** ≈ Montana, NW USA
Pryp"yat'/Prypyats' *see* Pripet
110 M10 **Przasnysz** Mazowieckie, C Poland 53°01′N 20°51′E
111 K14 **Przedbórz** Łodzkie, S Poland 51°04′N 19°51′E
111 P17 **Przemyśl** *Rus.* Peremyshl. Podkarpackie, C Poland 49°47′N 22°47′E
111 O16 **Przeworsk** Podkarpackie, SE Poland 50°04′N 22°30′E
Przheval'sk *see* Karakol
110 L13 **Przysucha** Mazowieckie, SE Poland 51°22′N 20°36′E
115 H18 **Psachná** *var.* Psahna, Psakhná. Évvoia, C Greece 38°35′N 23°39′E
Psahna/Psakhná *see* Psachná
115 K18 **Psará** *island* E Greece
115 I16 **Psathoúra** *island* Vóreies Sporádes, Greece, Aegean Sea
Pschestitz *see* Přeštice
Psein Lora *see* Pishin Lora
117 S5 **Psel** *Rus.* Psël. ≈ Russian Federation/Ukraine
Psël *see* Psel
115 M21 **Psérimos** *island* Dodekánisa, Greece, Aegean Sea
Pseyn Bowr *see* Pishin Lora
Pskem *see* Piskom
147 R8 **Pskemskiy Khrebet** *Uzb.* Piskom Tizmasi. ▲▲ Kyrgyzstan/Uzbekistan
124 F14 **Pskov** *Ger.* Pleskau, *Latv.* Pleskava. Pskovskaya Oblast', W Russian Federation 58°32′N 31°15′E
118 K6 **Pskov, Lake** *Est.* Pihkva Järv, *Ger.* Pleskauer See, *Rus.* Pskovskoye Ozero. ◎ Estonia/Russian Federation
124 F15 **Pskovskaya Oblast'** ◈ *province* W Russian Federation
Pskovskoye Ozero *see* Pskov, Lake
112 G9 **Psunj** ▲▲ NE Croatia
111 J17 **Pszczyna** *Ger.* Pless. Śląskie, S Poland 49°59′N 18°54′E
Ptačnik/Ptacsnik *see* Vtáčnik
115 D17 **Ptéri** ▲ C Greece 39°08′N 21°32′E
Ptich' *see* Ptsich
115 E14 **Ptolemaïda** *prev.* Ptolemaïs. Dytikí Makedonía, N Greece 40°34′N 21°42′E
Ptolemaïs *see* Ptolemaïda, Greece
Ptolemaïs *see* 'Akko, Israel
119 M19 **Ptsich** *Rus.* Ptich'. Homyel'skaya Voblasts', SE Belarus 52°11′N 28°49′E
119 M18 **Ptsich** *Rus.* Ptich'. ≈ SE Belarus
109 X10 **Ptuj** *Ger.* Pettau; *anc.* Poetovio. NE Slovenia 46°26′N 15°54′E
61 A23 **Puán** Buenos Aires, E Argentina 37°35′S 62°45′W
192 H15 **Pu'apu'a** Savai'i, C Samoa 13°32′S 172°09′W
192 G15 **Puava, Cape** *headland* Savai'i, NW Samoa
Pubao *see* Baingoin
56 F12 **Pucallpa** Ucayali, C Peru 08°21′S 74°33′W
57 J17 **Pucarani** La Paz, NW Bolivia 16°25′S 68°29′W
Pučarevo *see* Novi Travnik
157 U12 **Pucheng** Shaanxi, SE China 35°00′N 109°34′E
160 L6 **Pucheng** *var.* Nanpu. Fujian, C China 27°59′N 118°31′E
125 N16 **Puchezh** Ivanovskaya Oblast', W Russian Federation 56°58′N 41°08′E
111 I19 **Púchov** *Hung.* Puhó. Trenčiansky Kraj, W Slovakia 49°08′N 18°15′E
116 J13 **Pucioasa** Dâmbovița, S Romania 45°04′N 25°23′E
110 I6 **Puck** Pomorskie, N Poland 54°43′N 18°24′E
30 L8 **Puckaway Lake** ◎ Wisconsin, N USA
63 G15 **Pucón** Araucanía, S Chile 39°18′S 71°52′W
93 M14 **Pudasjärvi** Oulu, C Finland 65°20′N 27°02′E
148 L8 **Pūdeh Tal, Shelleh-ye** ≈ SW Afghanistan
127 S1 **Pudem** Udmurtskaya Respublika, NW Russian Federation 58°18′N 52°08′E
Pudewitz *see* Pobiedziska
124 K11 **Pudozh** Respublika Kareliya, NW Russian Federation 61°48′N 36°30′E
97 M17 **Pudsey** N England, United Kingdom 53°48′N 01°40′W
Puduchcheri *see* Pondicherry
151 H21 **Pudukkottai** Tamil Nādu, SE India 10°23′N 78°47′E
171 Z13 **Pue** Papua, E Indonesia 02°42′S 140°36′E
41 P14 **Puebla** *var.* Puebla de Zaragoza. Puebla, S Mexico 19°02′N 98°13′W
41 P15 **Puebla** ◈ *state* S Mexico
104 L11 **Puebla de Alcocer** Extremadura, W Spain 38°59′N 05°14′W
Puebla de Don Fabrique *see* Puebla de Don Fadrique
105 P13 **Puebla de Don Fadrique** *var.* Puebla de Don Fabrique. Andalucía, S Spain 37°58′N 02°25′W
104 J11 **Puebla de la Calzada** Extremadura, W Spain 38°54′N 06°38′W
104 J5 **Puebla de Sanabria** Castilla y León, N Spain 42°04′N 06°38′W
Puebla de Trives *see* A Pobla de Trives
Puebla de Zaragoza *see* Puebla
37 T6 **Pueblo** Colorado, C USA 38°15′N 104°37′W
37 N10 **Pueblo Colorado Wash** *valley* Arizona, SW USA
61 C16 **Pueblo Libertador** Corrientes, NE Argentina 30°13′S 59°23′W
40 J10 **Pueblo Nuevo** Durango, C Mexico 23°24′N 105°21′W
42 J8 **Pueblo Nuevo** Estelí, NW Nicaragua 13°21′N 86°30′W
54 J3 **Pueblo Nuevo** Falcón, N Venezuela 11°59′N 69°57′W

◆ Country
● Country Capital
◇ Dependent Territory
○ Dependent Territory Capital
◈ Administrative Regions
✈ International Airport
▲ Mountain
▲▲ Mountain Range
⋀ Volcano
≈ River
◎ Lake
⊠ Reservoir

42 B6 Pueblo Nuevo Tiquisate var. Tiquisate. Escuintla, SW Guatemala 14°16′N 91°21′W
41 Q11 Pueblo Viejo, Laguna de lagoon E Mexico
63 J14 Puelches La Pampa, C Argentina 38°08′S 65°56′W
104 L14 Puente-Genil Andalucía, S Spain 37°23′N 04°45′W
105 Q3 Puente la Reina Bas. Gares. Navarra, N Spain 42°40′N 01°49′W
104 L12 Puente Nuevo, Embalse de ▣ S Spain
57 D14 Puente Piedra Lima, W Peru 11°49′S 77°01′W
160 F14 Pu'er var. Ning'er. Yunnan, SW China 23°09′N 100°58′E
45 V6 Puerca, Punta headland E Puerto Rico 18°13′N 65°36′W
37 R12 Puerco, Rio ≈ New Mexico, SW USA
57 J17 Puerto Acosta La Paz, W Bolivia 15°33′S 69°15′W
63 G19 Puerto Aisén Aisén, S Chile 45°24′S 72°42′W
41 R17 Puerto Ángel Oaxaca, SE Mexico 15°39′N 96°29′W
Puerto Argentino see Stanley
41 T17 Puerto Arista Chiapas, SE Mexico 15°55′N 93°47′W
43 O16 Puerto Armuelles Chiriquí, SW Panama 08°19′N 82°51′W
Puerto Arrecife see Arrecife
54 D14 Puerto Asís Putumayo, SW Colombia 0°31′N 76°31′W
54 L9 Puerto Ayacucho Amazonas, SW Venezuela 05°45′N 67°37′W
57 C18 Puerto Ayora Galapagos Islands, Ecuador, E Pacific Ocean 0°45′S 90°19′W
57 C18 Puerto Baquerizo Moreno var. Baquerizo Moreno. Galapagos Islands, Ecuador, E Pacific Ocean 0°54′S 89°37′W
42 G4 Puerto Barrios Izabal, E Guatemala 15°42′N 88°34′W
Puerto Bello see Portobelo
54 F8 Puerto Berrío Antioquia, C Colombia 06°28′N 74°28′W
54 F9 Puerto Boyaca Boyacá, C Colombia 05°58′N 74°36′W
54 K4 Puerto Cabello Carabobo, N Venezuela 10°29′N 68°02′W
43 N7 Puerto Cabezas var. Bilwi. Región Autónoma Atlántico Norte, NE Nicaragua 14°05′N 83°22′W
54 L9 Puerto Carreño Vichada, E Colombia 06°08′N 67°30′W
54 E4 Puerto Colombia Atlántico, N Colombia 10°59′N 74°57′W
42 H4 Puerto Cortés Cortés, NW Honduras 15°50′N 87°55′W
54 J4 Puerto Cumarebo Falcón, N Venezuela 11°29′N 69°21′W
Puerto de Cabras see Puerto del Rosario
55 Q5 Puerto de Hierro Sucre, NE Venezuela 10°40′N 62°03′W
64 O11 Puerto de la Cruz Tenerife, Islas Canarias, Spain, NE Atlantic Ocean 28°24′N 16°33′W
64 Q11 Puerto del Rosario var. Puerto de Cabras. Fuerteventura, Islas Canarias, Spain, NE Atlantic Ocean 28°29′N 13°52′W
63 J20 Puerto Deseado Santa Cruz, SE Argentina 47°46′S 65°53′W
40 F8 Puerto Escondido Baja California Sur, NW Mexico 25°48′N 111°20′W
41 R17 Puerto Escondido Oaxaca, SE Mexico 15°48′N 96°57′W
60 G12 Puerto Esperanza Misiones, NE Argentina 26°01′S 54°39′W
54 H10 Puerto Gaitán Meta, C Colombia 04°20′N 72°10′W
Puerto Gallegos see Río Gallegos
60 G12 Puerto Iguazú Misiones, NE Argentina 25°39′S 54°35′W
56 F12 Puerto Inca Huánuco, N Peru 09°22′S 74°54′W
54 L11 Puerto Inírida var. Obando. Guainía, E Colombia 03°48′N 67°54′W
42 K13 Puerto Jesús Guanacaste, NW Costa Rica 10°08′N 85°26′W
41 Z11 Puerto Juárez Quintana Roo, SE Mexico 21°06′N 86°46′W
55 N5 Puerto La Cruz Anzoátegui, NE Venezuela 10°14′N 64°40′W
54 E14 Puerto Leguízamo Putumayo, S Colombia 0°14′N 74°45′W
43 N5 Puerto Lempira Gracias a Dios, E Honduras 15°14′N 83°48′W
Puerto Libertad see La Libertad
54 I11 Puerto Limón Meta, E Colombia 04°00′N 71°09′W
54 D13 Puerto Limón Putumayo, SW Colombia 01°02′N 76°30′W
Puerto Limón see Limón
105 N11 Puertollano Castilla-La Mancha, C Spain 38°41′N 04°07′W
63 K17 Puerto Lobos Chubut, SE Argentina 42°00′S 64°58′W
54 I3 Puerto López La Guajira, N Colombia 11°54′N 71°21′W
105 Q14 Puerto Lumbreras Murcia, SE Spain 37°35′N 01°49′W
41 V17 Puerto Madero Chiapas, SE Mexico 14°44′N 92°25′W
63 K17 Puerto Madryn Chubut, S Argentina 42°45′S 65°02′W
Puerto Magdalena see Bahía Magdalena
57 J15 Puerto Maldonado Madre de Dios, E Peru 12°37′S 69°11′W
Puerto Masachapa see Masachapa
Puerto México see Coatzacoalcos
63 G17 Puerto Montt Los Lagos, C Chile 41°28′S 72°57′W
41 Z12 Puerto Morelos Quintana Roo, SE Mexico 20°47′N 86°54′W
54 L10 Puerto Nariño Vichada, E Colombia 04°57′N 67°51′W
63 H23 Puerto Natales Magallanes, S Chile 51°42′S 72°28′W
43 X15 Puerto Obaldía Kuna Yala, NE Panama 08°38′N 77°26′W
44 H6 Puerto Padre Las Tunas, E Cuba 21°13′N 76°35′W
54 L9 Puerto Páez Apure, C Venezuela 06°10′N 67°30′W
40 E3 Puerto Peñasco Sonora, NW Mexico 31°20′N 113°35′W
55 N5 Puerto Píritu Anzoátegui, NE Venezuela 10°04′N 65°00′W
45 N8 Puerto Plata var. San Felipe de Puerto Plata. N Dominican Republic 19°46′N 70°42′W
Puerto Presidente Stroessner see Ciudad del Este
171 N6 Puerto Princesa off. Puerto Princesa City. Palawan, W Philippines 09°48′N 118°43′E
Puerto Princesa City see Puerto Princesa
Puerto Príncipe see Camagüey
Puerto Quellón see Quellón
60 F13 Puerto Rico Misiones, NE Argentina 26°48′S 54°59′W
57 K14 Puerto Rico Pando, N Bolivia 11°07′S 67°32′W
54 E12 Puerto Rico Caquetá, S Colombia 01°54′N 75°13′W
45 U5 Puerto Rico off. Commonwealth of Puerto Rico; prev. Porto Rico. ◇ US commonwealth territory C West Indies
64 F11 Puerto Rico island C West Indies
Puerto Rico, Commonwealth of see Puerto Rico
64 G11 Puerto Rico Trench undersea feature NE Caribbean Sea
54 I8 Puerto Rondón Arauca, E Colombia 06°16′N 71°05′W
Puerto San José see San José
63 J21 Puerto San Julián var. San Julián. Santa Cruz, SE Argentina 49°14′S 67°41′W
63 I22 Puerto Santa Cruz var. Santa Cruz. Santa Cruz, SE Argentina 50°05′S 68°31′W
Puerto Sauce see Juan L. Lacaze
57 Q20 Puerto Suárez Santa Cruz, E Bolivia 18°59′S 57°47′W
54 D13 Puerto Umbría Putumayo, SW Colombia 0°52′N 76°36′W
40 J13 Puerto Vallarta Jalisco, SW Mexico 20°36′N 105°15′W
63 G16 Puerto Varas Los Lagos, C Chile 41°20′S 73°00′W
42 M13 Puerto Viejo Heredia, NE Costa Rica 10°27′N 84°00′W
Puertoviejo see Portoviejo
57 B18 Puerto Villamil var. Villamil. Galapagos Islands, Ecuador, E Pacific Ocean 0°57′S 91°00′W
54 F8 Puerto Wilches Santander, N Colombia 07°22′N 73°53′W
63 H20 Pueyrredón, Lago var. Lago Cochrane. ◎ S Argentina
127 R7 Pugachëv Saratovskaya Oblast', W Russian Federation 52°06′N 48°50′E
127 T3 Pugachëvo Udmurtskaya Respublika, NW Russian Federation 56°38′N 53°03′E
32 H8 Puget Sound sound Washington, NW USA
107 O17 Puglia var. Le Puglie, Eng. Apulia. ◐ region SE Italy
107 N17 Puglia, Canosa di anc. Canusium. Puglia, SE Italy 41°13′N 16°04′E
118 I6 Puhja Ger. Kawelecht. Tartumaa, SE Estonia 58°20′N 26°19′E
Puhó see Púchov
105 V4 Puigcerdà Cataluña, NE Spain 42°25′N 01°53′E
Puigmal see Puigmal d'Err
103 N17 Puigmal d'Err var. Puigmal. ▲ S France 42°24′N 02°07′E
76 I16 Pujehun S Sierra Leone 07°23′N 11°44′W
Puka see Pukë
185 E20 Pukaki, Lake ◎ South Island, New Zealand
38 F10 Pukalani Maui, Hawaii, USA, C Pacific Ocean 20°50′N 156°20′W
190 J13 Pukapuka atoll N Cook Islands
191 X9 Pukapuka atoll Îles Tuamotu, E French Polynesia
Pukari Neem see Purekkari Neem
191 X11 Pukarua var. Pukaruha. atoll Îles Tuamotu, E French Polynesia
Pukaruha see Pukarua
14 A7 Pukaskwa ≈ Ontario, S Canada
11 V12 Pukatawagan Manitoba, C Canada 55°46′N 101°14′W
191 X16 Pukatikei, Maunga ▲ Easter Island, Chile, E Pacific Ocean
182 C1 Pukatja var. Ernabella. South Australia 26°18′S 132°13′E
163 Y12 Pukch'ŏng E North Korea 40°13′N 128°20′E
113 L18 Pukë var. Puka. Shkodër, N Albania 42°03′N 19°53′E
184 L6 Pukekohe Auckland, North Island, New Zealand 37°12′S 174°54′E
184 L7 Pukemiro Waikato, North Island, New Zealand 37°37′S 175°02′E
190 D12 Puke, Mont ▲ Île Futuna, W Wallis and Futuna
Puket see Phuket
185 C20 Puketeraki Range ⛰ South Island, New Zealand
184 N13 Puketoi Range ⛰ North Island, New Zealand
185 F21 Pukeuri Junction Otago, South Island, New Zealand 45°01′S 171°01′E
119 L16 Pukhavichy Rus. Pukhovichi. Minskaya Voblasts', C Belarus 53°32′N 28°15′E
Pukhovichi see Pukhavichy
124 M10 Puksoozero Arkhangel'skaya Oblast', NW Russian Federation 62°37′N 40°29′E
112 A10 Pula It. Pola; prev. Pulj. Istra, NW Croatia 44°53′N 13°51′E
Pula see Nyingchi
163 U14 Pulandian var. Xinjin. Liaoning, NE China 39°25′N 121°58′E
163 T14 Pulandian Wan bay NE China
189 O15 Pulap Atoll atoll Caroline Islands, C Micronesia
18 H9 Pulaski New York, NE USA 43°34′N 76°06′W
20 I10 Pulaski Tennessee, S USA 35°11′N 87°00′W
21 R7 Pulaski Virginia, NE USA 37°03′N 80°47′W
171 Y14 Pulau, Sungai ≈ Papua, E Indonesia
110 N13 Puławy Ger. Neu Amerika. Lubelskie, E Poland 51°25′N 21°57′E
149 R5 Pul-e-'Alam prev. Pol-e-'Alam. Lōgar, E Afghanistan 33°59′N 69°02′E
149 Q3 Pul-e Khumrī prev. Pol-e Khomrī. Baghlān, NE Afghanistan 35°55′N 68°45′E
146 I16 Pulhatyn Rus. Polekhatum; prev. Pul'-I-Khatum. Ahal Welaýaty, S Turkmenistan 36°01′N 61°08′E
101 E16 Pulheim Nordrhein-Westfalen, W Germany 51°00′N 06°48′E
155 J19 Pulicat Lake lagoon SE India
Pul'-I-Khatum see Pulhatyn
Pul-i-Sefid see Pol-e Sefīd
Pulj see Pula
109 W2 Pulkau ≈ NE Austria
93 L15 Pulkkila Oulu, C Finland 64°15′N 25°53′E
122 C7 Pulkovo ✈ (Sankt-Peterburg) Leningradskaya Oblast', NW Russian Federation 60°06′N 30°23′E
32 M9 Pullman Washington, NW USA 46°43′N 117°10′W
108 B10 Pully Vaud, SW Switzerland 46°31′N 06°40′E
40 F7 Púlpita, Punta headland NW Mexico 26°30′N 111°28′W
110 M10 Pułtusk Mazowieckie, C Poland 52°41′N 21°04′E
158 H10 Pulu Xinjiang Uygur Zizhiqu, W China 36°10′N 81°29′E
137 P13 Pülümür Tunceli, E Turkey 39°30′N 39°54′E
189 N16 Pulusuk island Caroline Islands, C Micronesia
189 N16 Puluwat Atoll atoll Caroline Islands, C Micronesia
25 N11 Pumpville Texas, SW USA 29°55′N 101°43′W
191 P7 Punaauia var. Hakapehi. Tahiti, W French Polynesia 17°38′S 149°37′W
56 B8 Puná, Isla island SW Ecuador
185 G16 Punakaiki West Coast, South Island, New Zealand 42°07′S 171°21′E
153 T11 Punakha C Bhutan 27°38′N 89°50′E
57 L18 Punata Cochabamba, C Bolivia 17°32′S 65°50′W
155 E14 Pune prev. Poona. Mahārāshtra, W India 18°32′N 73°52′E
83 M17 Pungoè, Rio var. Púnguè, Pungwe. ≈ C Mozambique
21 X10 Pungo River ≈ North Carolina, SE USA
Púnguè/Pungwe see Pungoè, Rio
79 N19 Punia Maniema, E Dem. Rep. Congo 01°28′S 26°25′E
62 H8 Punilla, Sierra de la ⛰ W Argentina
161 P14 Puning Guangdong, S China 23°24′N 116°14′E
62 G10 Punitaqui Coquimbo, C Chile 30°50′S 71°29′W
149 T9 Punjab prev. West Punjab, Western Punjab. ◐ province E Pakistan
152 H8 Punjab state NW India
129 Q9 Punjab Plains plain N India
93 O17 Punkaharju var. Punkasalmi. Itä-Suomi, E Finland 61°45′N 29°21′E
Punkasalmi see Punkaharju
57 I17 Puno Puno, SE Peru 15°53′S 70°03′W
57 H17 Puno off. Departamento de Puno. ◐ department S Peru
Puno, Departamento de see Puno
61 B24 Punta Alta Buenos Aires, E Argentina 38°54′S 62°01′W
63 H24 Punta Arenas prev. Magallanes. Magallanes, S Chile 53°10′S 70°56′W
45 T6 Punta, Cerro de ▲ C Puerto Rico 18°10′N 66°36′W
43 T15 Punta Chame Panamá, C Panama 08°39′N 79°42′W
57 G17 Punta Colorada Arequipa, SW Peru 16°17′S 72°31′W
40 F9 Punta Coyote Baja California Sur, NW Mexico
62 G8 Punta de Díaz Atacama, N Chile 28°03′S 70°36′W
61 G20 Punta del Este Maldonado, S Uruguay 34°59′S 54°58′W
63 K17 Punta Delgada Chubut, SE Argentina 42°46′S 63°40′W
55 O5 Punta de Mata Monagas, NE Venezuela 09°48′N 63°38′W
55 O4 Punta de Piedras Nueva Esparta, NE Venezuela 10°57′N 64°06′W
42 F4 Punta Gorda Toledo, SE Belize 16°07′N 88°47′W
43 N11 Punta Gorda Región Autónoma Atlántico Sur, SE Nicaragua 11°31′N 83°46′W
23 W14 Punta Gorda Florida, SE USA 26°55′N 82°03′W
42 M11 Punta Gorda, Río ≈ SE Nicaragua
62 H6 Punta Negra, Salar de salt lake N Chile
40 D5 Punta Prieta Baja California Norte, NW Mexico 28°56′N 114°11′W
42 L13 Puntarenas Puntarenas, W Costa Rica 09°58′N 84°50′W
42 L13 Puntarenas off. Provincia de Puntarenas. ◐ province W Costa Rica
Puntarenas, Provincia de see Puntarenas
80 P13 Puntland cultural region NE Somalia
54 J4 Punto Fijo Falcón, N Venezuela 11°42′N 70°13′W
105 S4 Puntón de Guara ▲ N Spain 42°18′N 00°13′W
18 D14 Punxsutawney Pennsylvania, NE USA 40°55′N 78°57′W
93 M14 Puolanka Oulu, C Finland 64°51′N 27°42′E
57 J17 Pupuya, Nevado ▲ W Bolivia 15°04′S 69°01′W
Puqi see Chibi
57 F16 Puquio Ayacucho, S Peru 14°44′S 74°07′W
122 J9 Pur ≈ N Russian Federation
186 D7 Purari ≈ S Papua New Guinea
27 N11 Purcell Oklahoma, C USA 35°00′N 97°21′W
11 O16 Purcell Mountains ⛰ British Columbia, SW Canada
105 P14 Purchena Andalucía, S Spain 37°21′N 02°21′W
27 S8 Purdy Missouri, C USA 36°49′N 93°55′W
118 I2 Purekkari Neem prev. Pukari Neem. headland N Estonia 59°33′N 24°49′E
37 U7 Purgatoire River ≈ Colorado, C USA
Purgstall see Purgstall an der Erlauf
109 V5 Purgstall an der Erlauf var. Purgstall. Niederösterreich, NE Austria 48°01′N 15°08′E
154 O13 Puri var. Jagannath. Orissa, E India 19°52′N 85°49′E
Puriramya see Buriram
109 X4 Purkersdorf Niederösterreich, NE Austria 48°13′N 16°12′E
98 I9 Purmerend Noord-Holland, C Netherlands 52°30′N 04°56′E
151 G16 Pūrna ≈ C India
Purnea see Pūrnia
153 R13 Pūrnia prev. Purnea. Bihār, NE India 25°47′N 87°28′E
Pursat see Poŭthĭsăt, Stœ̆ng, W Cambodia
Pursat see Poŭthĭsăt, Poŭthĭsăt, W Cambodia
Purulia see Puruliya
150 L13 Puruliya prev. Purulia. West Bengal, NE India 23°20′N 86°24′E
47 G7 Purus, Rio var. Río Purús. ≈ Brazil/Peru
186 C9 Purutu Island island SW Papua New Guinea
93 N17 Puruvesi ◎ SE Finland
22 L7 Purvis Mississippi, S USA 31°08′N 89°24′W
114 J11 Pŭrvomay prev. Borisovgrad. Plovdiv, C Bulgaria 42°06′N 25°13′E
169 R16 Purwodadi prev. Poerwodadi. Jawa, C Indonesia 07°05′S 110°53′E
169 P16 Purwokerto prev. Poerwokerto. Jawa, C Indonesia 07°25′S 109°14′E
169 P16 Purworejo prev. Poerworedjo. Jawa, C Indonesia 07°45′S 110°04′E
20 H8 Puryear Tennessee, S USA 36°25′N 88°21′W
154 H13 Pusad Mahārāshtra, C India 19°56′N 77°40′E
Pusan see Busan
Pusan-gwangyŏksi see Busan
168 H7 Pusatgajo, Pegunungan ⛰ Sumatera, NW Indonesia
Puschlav see Poschiavo
124 G13 Pushkin prev. Tsarskoye Selo. Leningradskaya Oblast', NW Russian Federation 59°42′N 30°24′E
126 L3 Pushkino Moskovskaya Oblast', W Russian Federation 55°57′N 37°45′E
127 Q8 Pushkino Saratovskaya Oblast', W Russian Federation 51°09′N 47°00′E
Pushkino see Biläsuvar
111 M22 Püspökladány Hajdú-Bihar, E Hungary 47°20′N 21°05′E
118 J3 Püssi Ger. Isenhof. Ida-Virumaa, NE Estonia 59°22′N 27°04′E
116 I5 Pustomyty L'vivs'ka Oblast', W Ukraine 49°43′N 23°55′E
124 F16 Pustoshka Pskovskaya Oblast', W Russian Federation 56°21′N 29°16′E
Pusztakalán see Călan
167 N1 Putao prev. Fort Hertz. Kachin State, N Burma (Myanmar) 27°22′N 97°24′E
184 M8 Putaruru Waikato, North Island, New Zealand 38°03′S 175°48′E
Puteoli see Pozzuoli
161 R12 Putian Fujian, SE China 25°32′N 119°02′E
107 O17 Putignano Puglia, SE Italy 40°51′N 17°08′E
Puting see De'an
Putivl' see Putyvl'
41 Q16 Putla var. Putla de Guerrero. Oaxaca, SE Mexico 17°01′N 97°56′W
Putla de Guerrero see Putla
19 N12 Putnam Connecticut, NE USA 41°56′N 71°52′W
25 Q7 Putnam Texas, SW USA 32°22′N 99°11′W
18 M10 Putney Vermont, NE USA 42°59′N 72°30′W
111 L20 Putnok Borsod-Abaúj-Zemplén, NE Hungary 48°18′N 20°25′E
Putorana, Gory/Putorana Mountains see Putorana, Plato
122 L8 Putorana, Plato var. Gory Putorana, Eng. Putorana Mountains. ⛰ N Russian Federation
168 K9 Putrajaya ● (Malaysia) Kuala Lumpur, Peninsular Malaysia 02°57′N 101°42′E
62 H2 Putre Arica y Parinacota, N Chile 18°11′S 69°30′W
155 J24 Puttalam North Western Province, W Sri Lanka 08°02′N 79°55′E
155 J24 Puttalam Lagoon lagoon W Sri Lanka
99 H17 Putte Antwerpen, C Belgium 51°04′N 04°39′E
94 E10 Puttegga ▲ S Norway 62°13′N 07°40′E
98 K11 Putten Gelderland, C Netherlands 52°15′N 05°36′E
100 K7 Puttgarden Schleswig-Holstein, N Germany 54°30′N 11°13′E
Puttiala see Patiāla
101 D20 Püttlingen Saarland, SW Germany 49°16′N 06°52′E
54 D14 Putumayo off. Intendencia del Putumayo. ◐ province S Colombia
Putumayo, Intendencia del see Putumayo
48 E7 Putumayo, Río var. Içá, Rio. ≈ NW South America see also Içá, Rio
Putumayo, Río see Içá, Rio
169 P11 Putus, Tanjung headland Borneo, N Indonesia 0°27′S 109°04′E
116 J8 Putyla Chernivets'ka Oblast', W Ukraine 47°59′N 25°04′E
117 S3 Putyvl' Rus. Putivl'. Sums'ka Oblast', NE Ukraine 51°21′N 33°53′E
93 M18 Puula ◎ SE Finland
93 N18 Puumala Itä-Suomi, E Finland 61°31′N 28°12′E
118 I5 Puurmani Ger. Talkhof. Jõgevamaa, E Estonia 58°36′N 26°17′E
99 G17 Puurs Antwerpen, N Belgium 51°05′N 04°17′E
38 F10 Pu'u 'Ula'ula var. Red Hill. ▲ Maui, Hawai'i, USA 20°42′N 156°16′W
38 A8 Pu'uwai var. Puuwai. Ni'ihau, Hawaii, USA, C Pacific Ocean 21°54′N 160°11′W
12 J4 Puvirnituq prev. Povungnituk. Québec, NE Canada 60°10′N 77°20′W
12 J3 Puvirnituq, Riviere de prev. Rivière de Povungnituk. ≈ Québec, NE Canada
32 H8 Puyallup Washington, NW USA 47°11′N 122°17′W
161 O5 Puyang Henan, C China 35°40′N 115°00′E
103 O11 Puy-de-Dôme ◐ department C France
103 N15 Puylaurens Tarn, S France 43°33′N 02°01′E
102 M13 Puy-l'Evêque Lot, S France 44°31′N 01°10′E
103 N17 Puymorens, Col de pass S France
56 C7 Puyo Pastaza, C Ecuador 01°30′S 77°58′W
185 A24 Puysegur Point headland South Island, New Zealand 46°09′S 166°38′E
148 J8 Pūzak, Hāmūn-e Pash. Hāmūn-i-Puzak. ◎ SW Afghanistan
Puzak, Hāmūn-i- see Pūzak, Hāmūn-e
81 J23 Pwani Eng. Coast. ◐ region E Tanzania
79 O23 Pweto Katanga, SE Dem. Rep. Congo 08°28′S 28°52′E
97 I19 Pwllheli NW Wales, United Kingdom 52°54′N 04°23′W
189 O14 Pwok Pohnpei, E Micronesia
122 I9 Pyakupur ≈ N Russian Federation
124 M6 Pyalitsa Murmanskaya Oblast', NW Russian Federation 66°17′N 39°56′E
124 K10 Pyal'ma Respublika Kareliya, NW Russian Federation 62°24′N 35°56′E
Pyandzh see Panj
166 L9 Pyapon Ayeyarwady, SW Burma (Myanmar) 16°15′N 95°40′E
119 J15 Pyarshai Rus. Pershay. Minskaya Voblasts', C Belarus 54°02′N 26°41′E
122 K8 Pyasina ≈ N Russian Federation
119 G17 Pyaski Rus. Peski; prev. Pyeski. Hrodzyenskaya Voblasts', W Belarus 53°21′N 24°38′E
114 I10 Pyasŭchnik, Yazovir ▣ C Bulgaria
Pyatikhatki see P"yatykhatky
117 S7 P"yatykhatky Rus. Pyatikhatki. Dnipropetrovs'ka Oblast', E Ukraine 48°23′N 33°43′E
166 M6 Pyawbwe Mandalay, C Burma (Myanmar) 20°39′N 96°04′E
166 L7 Pyay var. Prome, Pye. Bago, C Burma (Myanmar) 18°50′N 95°14′E
127 T3 Pychas Udmurtskaya Respublika, NW Russian Federation 56°30′N 52°33′E
Pye see Pyay
166 K6 Pyechin Chin State, W Burma (Myanmar) 20°01′N 93°36′E
163 X15 Pyeongtaek prev. P'yŏngt'aek. NW South Korea 37°00′N 127°04′E
Pyeski see Pyaski
119 L19 Pyetrykaw Rus. Petrikov. Homyel'skaya Voblasts', SE Belarus 52°08′N 28°30′E
93 O17 Pyhäjärvi ◎ SE Finland
93 M16 Pyhäjärvi ◎ C Finland
93 L15 Pyhäjoki Oulu, W Finland 64°28′N 24°15′E
93 L15 Pyhäjoki ≈ W Finland
93 M15 Pyhäntä Oulu, C Finland 64°07′N 26°19′E
93 M16 Pyhäsalmi Oulu, C Finland 63°38′N 26°E
93 O17 Pyhäselkä ◎ SE Finland
93 M19 Pyhtää Swe. Pyttis. Etelä-Suomi, S Finland 60°29′N 26°40′E
166 M5 Pyin-Oo-Lwin var. Maymyo. Mandalay, C Burma (Myanmar) 22°03′N 96°30′E
115 N24 Pylés var. Piles. Kárpathos, SE Greece 35°31′N 27°08′E
115 D21 Pýlos var. Pilos. Pelopónnisos, S Greece 36°55′N 21°42′E
18 B12 Pymatuning Reservoir ▣ Ohio/Pennsylvania, NE USA
P'yŏngt'aek see Pyeongtaek
163 V14 P'yŏngyang var. P'yŏngyang-si, Eng. Pyongyang. ● (North Korea) SW North Korea 39°04′N 125°46′E
P'yŏngyang-si see P'yŏngyang
35 Q4 Pyramid Lake ◎ Nevada, W USA
37 P15 Pyramid Mountains ⛰ New Mexico, SW USA
37 R5 Pyramid Peak ▲ Colorado, C USA 39°04′N 106°57′W
115 D17 Pyramíva var. Piramiva. ▲ C Greece 39°08′N 21°18′E
Pyrenaei Montes see Pyrenees
86 B12 Pyrenees Fr. Pyrénées, Sp. Pirineos; anc. Pyrenaei Montes. ⛰ SW Europe
102 J16 Pyrénées-Atlantiques ◐ department SW France
103 N17 Pyrénées-Orientales ◐ department S France
115 L19 Pyrgí var. Pirgi. Chíos, E Greece 38°13′N 26°01′E
115 D20 Pýrgos var. Pírgos. Dytikí Elláda, S Greece 37°40′N 21°27′E
Pyritz see Pyrzyce
115 E19 Pýrros ≈ S Greece
117 R4 Pyryatyn Rus. Piryatin. Poltavs'ka Oblast', NE Ukraine 50°14′N 32°31′E
110 D9 Pyrzyce Ger. Pyritz. Zachodnio-pomorskie, NW Poland 53°09′N 14°53′E
124 F15 Pytalovo Latv. Abrene; prev. Jaunlatgale. Pskovskaya Oblast', W Russian Federation 57°06′N 27°55′E
115 M20 Pythagóreio var. Pithagorio. Sámos, Dodekánisa, Greece, Aegean Sea 37°42′N 26°57′E
14 L11 Pythonga, Lac ◎ Québec, SE Canada
Pyttis see Pyhtää
Pyu see Phyu
166 M8 Pyuntaza Bago, SW Burma (Myanmar) 17°51′N 96°44′E
153 N11 Pyuthān Mid Western, W Nepal 28°09′N 82°50′E
110 H12 Pyzdry Ger. Peisern. Wielkopolskie, C Poland 52°10′N 17°42′E

Q

138 H13 Qā' al Jafr ◎ S Jordan
197 O11 Qaanaaq var. Qânâq, Dan. Thule. ◐ Avannaarsua, N Greenland
Qabanbay see Kabanbay
138 G7 Qabb Eliâs E Lebanon 33°46′N 35°49′E
Qabil see Al Qābil
Qabırrı see Iori
Qābis see Gabès
Qābis, Khalīj see Gabès, Golfe de
Qabqa see Gonghe
141 S14 Qabr Hūd C Yemen 16°02′N 49°36′E
Qacentina see Constantine
Qādes see Qādis
148 L4 Qādis prev. Qādes. Bādghīs, NW Afghanistan 34°48′N 63°26′E
139 T11 Qādisīyah Al Qādisīyah, S Iraq 31°43′N 44°28′E
143 O4 Qā'emshahr prev. 'Alīābad, Shāhī. Māzandarān, N Iran 36°31′N 52°49′E
143 U7 Qā'en var. Qain, Qāyen. Khorāsān-Razavī, E Iran 33°43′N 59°07′E
141 U13 Qafa spring/well SW Oman 17°46′N 52°55′E
Qafṣah see Gafsa
163 Q12 Qagan Nur var. Xulun Hobot Qagan, Zhengxiangbai Qi. Nei Mongol Zizhiqu, N China 42°10′N 114°57′E
163 V9 Qagan Nur ◎ NE China
163 Q11 Qagan Nur ◎ N China
Qagan Us see Dulan
158 H13 Qagcaka Xizang Zizhiqu, W China 32°32′N 81°52′E
Qagchêng see Xiangcheng
Qahremānshahr see Kermānshāh
159 Q10 Qaidam He ≈ C China
156 L8 Qaidam Pendi basin C China
Qain see Qā'en
Qala Āhangarān see Chaghcharān
139 U3 Qalā Diza var. Qal 'at Dīzah. As Sulaymānīyah, NE Iraq 36°11′N 45°07′E
Qal'ah Sālih see Qal'at Ṣāliḥ
149 N4 Qal'ah Shahr Pash. Qala Shāhar; prev. Qal'eh Shahr. Sar-e Pul, N Afghanistan 35°34′N 65°38′E
148 L4 Qal'ah-ye Now var. Qala Nau; prev. Qal'eh-ye Now. Bādghīs, NW Afghanistan 35°N 63°08′E
147 R13 Qal'aikhum Rus. Kalaikhum. S Tajikistan 38°28′N 70°49′E
Qala Nau see Qal'ah-ye Now
141 V17 Qalansīyah Suquṭrā, W Yemen 12°40′N 53°30′E
Qala Panja see Qal'eh-ye Panjeh
Qala Shāhar see Qal'ah Shahr
149 O8 Qalāt Per. Kalāt. Zābul, S Afghanistan 32°10′N 66°54′E
139 W9 Qal'at Aḥmad Maysān, E Iraq 32°24′N 46°46′E
141 N11 Qal'at Bīshah 'Asīr, SW Saudi Arabia 19°59′N 42°38′E
138 H4 Qal'at Burzay Ḥamāh, W Syria 35°37′N 36°16′E
Qal 'at Dīzah see Qalā Diza
139 W9 Qal'at Ḥuṣayn Maysān, E Iraq 32°19′N 46°46′E
139 V10 Qal'at Majnūnah Al Qādisīyah, S Iraq 31°39′N 45°44′E
139 X11 Qal'at Ṣāliḥ var. Qal'ah Sālih. Maysān, E Iraq 31°30′N 47°24′E
139 V10 Qal'at Sukkar Dhī Qār, SE Iraq 31°52′N 46°05′E
Qalba Zhotasy see Khrebet Kalba
143 Q12 Qal'eh Bīābān Fārs, S Iran
Qal'eh Shahr see Qal'ah Shahr
Qal'eh-ye Now see Qal'ah-ye Now
149 T2 Qal'eh-ye Panjeh var. Qala Panja. Badakhshān, NE Afghanistan 36°56′N 72°15′E
Qalqaman see Kalkaman
Qamanittuaq see Baker Lake
Qamar Bay see Qamar, Ghubbat al
141 U14 Qamar, Ghubbat al Eng. Qamar Bay. bay Oman/Yemen
141 V13 Qamar, Jabal al ⛰ SW Oman
147 N12 Qamashi Qashqadaryo Viloyati, S Uzbekistan 38°52′N 66°30′E
Qambar see Kambar
159 R14 Qamdo Xizang Zizhiqu, W China 31°09′N 97°09′E
75 R7 Qaminis NE Libya 31°48′N 20°04′E
Qamishly see Al Qāmishlī
Qânâq see Qaanaaq
Qandahār see Kandahār
80 Q11 Qandala Bari, NE Somalia 11°30′N 50°00′E
Qandyaghash see Kandyagash
138 L2 Qanṭārī Ar Raqqah, N Syria 36°24′N 39°16′E
Qapiciğ Dağı see Qazangödağ
158 H5 Qapqal var. Qapqal Xibe Zizhixian. Xinjiang Uygur Zizhiqu, NW China 43°46′N 81°09′E
Qapqal Xibe Zizhixian see Qapqal
Qapshagay Böyeni see Vodokhranilishche Kapshagay
Qapugtang see Zadoi
196 M15 Qaqortoq Dan. Julianehåb. ◐ Kitaa, S Greenland
139 T4 Qara Anjīr At Ta'mīm, N Iraq 35°30′N 44°37′E
Qarabāgh see Qarah Bāgh
Qarabaū see Karabau
Qaraböget see Karaboget
Qarabulaq see Karabulak
Qarabutaq see Karabutak
Qaraghandy/Qaraghandy Oblysy see Karagandy
Qaraghayly see Karagayly
139 U4 Qara Gol As Sulaymānīyah, NE Iraq 35°21′N 45°38′E
75 U8 Qārah var. Qâra. NW Egypt 29°34′N 26°28′E
Qārah see Qārah
148 J4 Qarah Bāgh var. Qarabāgh. Herāt, NW Afghanistan 35°06′N 61°33′E
138 G7 Qaraoun, Lac de var. Buḥayrat al Qir'awn. ◎ S Lebanon
Qaraoy see Karaoy
Qaraqoyyn see Karakoyyn, Ozero
Qara Qum see Garagum
Qarasū see Karasu
Qaratal see Karatal
Qarataū see Karatau, Khrebet, Kazakhstan
Qarataū see Karatau, Zhambyl, Kazakhstan
Qaraton see Karaton
Qarazhal see Karazhal
80 P13 Qardho var. Kardh, It. Gardo. Bari, N Somalia 09°34′N 49°30′E
142 M6 Qareh Chāy ≈ N Iran
142 K2 Qareh Sū ≈ NW Iran
Qariateïne see Al Qaryatayn
Qarkilik see Ruoqiang
147 O13 Qarluq Rus. Karluk. Surkhondaryo Viloyati, S Uzbekistan 38°17′N 67°39′E
147 U12 Qarokŭl Rus. Karakul'. E Tajikistan 39°07′N 73°33′E
147 T12 Qarokŭl Rus. Ozero Karakul'. ◎ E Tajikistan
Qarqan see Qiemo
158 K9 Qarqan He ≈ NW China
Qarqannah, Juzur see Kerkenah, Îles de
149 O1 Qarqīn Jowzjān, N Afghanistan 37°25′N 66°03′E
Qars see Kars
Qarsaqbay see Karsakpay
146 M12 Qarshi Rus. Karshi; prev. Bek-Budi. Qashqadaryo Viloyati, S Uzbekistan 38°54′N 65°48′E
146 L12 Qarshi Cho'li Rus. Karshinskaya Step. grassland S Uzbekistan
146 M13 Qarshi Kanali Rus. Karshinskiy Kanal. canal Turkmenistan/Uzbekistan
Qaryatayn see Al Qaryatayn
Qāsh, Nahr al see Gash
146 M12 Qashqadaryo Viloyati Rus. Kashkadar'inskaya Oblast'. ◐ province S Uzbekistan
Qasigianguit see Qasigiannguit
197 N13 Qasigiannguit var. Qasigianguit, Dan. Christianshåb. ◐ Kitaa, C Greenland
Qasim, Mintaqat see Al Qaṣīm
75 V10 Qaṣr al Farāfirah var. Qasr Farâfra. W Egypt 27°00′N 27°59′E
139 P8 Qaṣr 'Amīj Al Anbār, C Iraq 33°30′N 41°52′E
139 R9 Qaṣr Darwīshāh Karbalā', C Iraq 32°36′N 43°27′E
142 J6 Qaṣr-e Shīrīn Kermānshāhān, W Iran 34°32′N 45°36′E
Qasr Farâfra see Qaṣr al Farāfirah
Qassim see Al Qaṣīm
141 O16 Qa'ṭabah SW Yemen 13°51′N 44°42′E
138 H7 Qaṭanā var. Katana. Rīf Dimashq, S Syria 33°27′N 36°04′E
143 N15 Qatar off. State of Qatar, Ar. Dawlat Qaṭar. ◆ monarchy SW Asia
Qatar, State of see Qatar
Qatrana see Al Qaṭrānah
143 Q12 Qaṭrūyeh Fārs, S Iran 29°08′N 54°42′E
Qattara Depression/Qaṭṭārah, Munkhafaḍ al see Qaṭṭārah, Munkhafaḍ al
75 U8 Qaṭṭārah, Munkhafaḍ al var. Monkhafad el Qaṭṭâra var. Munkhafaḍ al Qaṭṭārah, Eng. Qattara Depression. desert NW Egypt
Qaṭṭâra, Monkhafad el see Qaṭṭārah, Munkhafaḍ al
Qattinah, Buhayrat see Ḥimṣ, Buḥayrat
Qausuittuq see Resolute
Qaydār see Qeydār
Qāyen see Qā'en
Qaynar see Kaynar
147 Q11 Qayroqqum Rus. Kayrakkum. NW Tajikistan 40°16′N 69°46′E
147 Q10 Qayroqqum, Obanbori Rus. Kayrakkumskoye Vodokhranilishche. ▣ NW Tajikistan
137 V13 Qazangödağ Rus. Gora Kapydzhik, Turk. Qapiciğ Dağı. ▲ SW Azerbaijan 39°18′N 46°00′E
139 U7 Qazānīyah var. Dhū Shaykh. Diyālá, E Iraq 33°39′N 45°33′E
Qazaqstan/Qazaqstan Respublikasy see Kazakhstan
137 T9 Q'azbegi Rus. Kazbegi; prev. Qazbegi. NE Georgia 42°39′N 44°36′E
Qazbegi see Q'azbegi
149 P15 Qāzi Ahmad var. Kazi Ahmad. Sind, SE Pakistan 26°19′N 68°08′E
Qazris see Cáceres
Qazimämmäd see Hacıqabal
142 M4 Qazvīn var. Kazvin. Qazvīn, N Iran 36°16′N 50°E
142 M5 Qazvīn ◐ province N Iran

◆ Country
● Country Capital
◇ Dependent Territory
○ Dependent Territory Capital
◐ Administrative Regions
✈ International Airport
▲ Mountain
⛰ Mountain Range
Volcano
≈ River
◎ Lake
▣ Reservoir

187 Z13 **Qelelevu Lagoon** lagoon NE Fiji
Qena see Qinā
113 L23 **Qeparo** Vlorë, S Albania 40°04′N 19°49′E
Qeqertarsuaq see Qeqertarsuaq
197 N13 **Qeqertarsuaq** var. Qeqertarssuaq, Dan. Godhavn. ◆ Kitaa, S Greenland
196 M13 **Qeqertarsuaq** island W Greenland
197 N13 **Qeqertarsuup Tunua** Dan. Disko Bugt. inlet W Greenland
Qerveh see Qorveh
143 S14 **Qeshm** Hormozgān, S Iran 26°58′N 56°17′E
143 R14 **Qeshm** var. Jazīreh-ye Qeshm, Qeshm Island. island S Iran
Qeshm Island/Qeshm, Jazīreh-ye see Qeshm
Qey see Kīsh, Jazīreh-ye
142 L4 **Qeydār** var. Qaydār. Zanjān, NW Iran 36°50′N 47°40′E
142 K5 **Qezel Owzan, Rūd-e** var. Ki Zil Uzen, Qi Zil Uzun. NW Iran
Qian see Guizhou
161 Q2 **Qian'an** Heilongjiang, E China 45°00′N 124°00′E
161 R10 **Qiandao Hu** prev. Xin'anjiang Shuiku. SE China
Qiandaohu see Chun'an
Qian Gorlo/Qian Gorlos/Qian Gorlos Mongolzu Zizhixian/Quianguozhen see Qianguo
163 V9 **Qianguo** var. Qian Gorlo, Qian Gorlos, Qian Gorlos Mongolzu Zizhixian, Quianguozhen. Jilin, NE China 45°08′N 124°48′E
161 N9 **Qianjiang** Hubei, C China 30°23′N 112°58′E
160 K10 **Qianjiang** Sichuan, C China 29°30′N 108°45′E
160 L14 **Qian Jiang** S China
160 G9 **Qianning** var. Gartar. Sichuan, C China 30°27′N 101°24′E
163 U13 **Qian Shan** ▲ NE China
160 H10 **Qianwei** var. Yujin. Sichuan, C China 29°15′N 103°52′E
160 J11 **Qianxi** Guizhou, S China 27°00′N 106°01′E
Qiaotou see Datong
Qiaowa see Muli
159 Q7 **Qiaowan** Gansu, N China 40°37′N 96°40′E
Qibili see Kebili
158 K9 **Qiemo** var. Qarqan. Xinjiang Uygur Zizhiqu, NW China 38°09′N 85°30′E
160 J10 **Qijiang** var. Gunan. Chongqing Shi, C China 29°01′N 106°40′E
159 N5 **Qijiaojing** Xinjiang Uygur Zizhiqu, NW China 43°29′N 91°35′E
Qike see Xunke
9 N5 **Qikiqtaaluk** cultural region Nunavut, N Canada
9 R5 **Qikiqtarjuaq** prev. Broughton Island. Nunavut, NE Canada 67°35′N 63°55′W
149 P9 **Qila Saifullāh** Baluchistān, SW Pakistan 30°45′N 68°08′E
159 S9 **Qilian** var. Babao. Qinghai, C China 38°09′N 100°08′E
159 N8 **Qilian Shan** var. Kilien Mountains. ▲ N China
197 O11 **Qimusseriarsuaq** Dan. Melville Bugt, Eng. Melville Bay. bay NW Greenland
75 X10 **Qinā** var. Qena; anc. Caene, Caenepolis. E Egypt 26°12′N 32°49′E
159 W11 **Qin'an** Gansu, C China 34°49′N 105°50′E
Qincheng see Nanfeng
Qing see Qinghai
163 W7 **Qing'an** Heilongjiang, NE China 46°53′N 127°29′E
159 X10 **Qingcheng** var. Xifeng. Gansu, C China 35°46′N 107°35′E
161 R5 **Qingdao** var. Ching-Tao, Ch'ing-tao, Tsingtao, Tsintao, Ger. Tsingtau. Shandong, E China 36°31′N 120°55′E
163 V8 **Qinggang** Heilongjiang, NE China 46°41′N 126°05′E
Qinggil see Qinghe
159 P11 **Qinghai** var. Chinghai, Koko Nor, Qing, Qinghai Sheng, Tsinghai. ◆ province C China
159 S10 **Qinghai Hu** var. Ch'ing Hai, Tsing Hai, Mong. Koko Nor. C China
Qinghai Sheng see Qinghai
158 M3 **Qinghe** var. Qinggil. Xinjiang Uygur Zizhiqu, NW China 46°42′N 90°19′E
160 L4 **Qingjian** var. Kuanzhou; prev. Xiuyan. Shaanxi, C China 37°10′N 110°09′E
160 L9 **Qing Jiang** C China
Qingjiang see Huai'an
Qingkou see Ganyu
160 I12 **Qinglong** var. Liancheng. Guizhou, S China 25°49′N 105°10′E
161 Q2 **Qinglong** Hebei, E China 40°24′N 118°57′E
Qingshan see Wudalianchi
159 R12 **Qingshuihe** Qinghai, C China 33°47′N 97°10′E
Qingyang see Jinjiang
161 N14 **Qingyuan** Guangdong, S China 23°42′N 113°02′E
163 V11 **Qingyuan** var. Qingyuan Manzu Zizhixian. Liaoning, NE China 42°08′N 124°55′E
Qingyuan see Weiyuan
Qingyuan see Shandan
Qingyuan Manzu Zizhixian see Qingyuan
158 L13 **Qingzang Gaoyuan** var. Xizang Gaoyuan, Eng. Plateau of Tibet. plateau W China
161 Q4 **Qingzhou** prev. Yidu. Shandong, E China 36°41′N 118°29′E
157 R9 **Qin He** C China
161 Q2 **Qinhuangdao** Hebei, E China 39°57′N 119°31′E
160 K7 **Qin Ling** ▲ C China
161 N5 **Qinxian** var. Dingchang, Qin Xian. Shanxi, C China 36°46′N 112°42′E
Qin Xian see Qinxian
161 N6 **Qinyang** Henan, C China 35°05′N 112°56′E
160 K15 **Qinzhou** Guangxi Zhuangzu Zizhiqu, S China 22°09′N 108°36′E
Qiong see Hainan
160 L17 **Qionghai** prev. Jiaji. Hainan, S China 19°12′N 110°26′E
160 H9 **Qionglai** Sichuan, C China 30°24′N 103°28′E
160 H8 **Qionglai Shan** ▲ C China
Qiongxi see Hongyuan
160 L17 **Qiongzhou Haixia** var. Hainan Strait. strait S China
163 U7 **Qiqihar** var. Ch'i-ch'i-ha-erh, Tsitsihar; prev. Lungkiang. Heilongjiang, NE China 47°23′N 124°E
Qir see Qīr-va-Kārzīn
158 H10 **Qira** Xinjiang Uygur Zizhiqu, NW China 37°05′N 80°45′E
Qir'awn, Buḥayrat al see Qaraoun, Lac de
143 P12 **Qīr-va-Kārzīn** var. Qir. Fārs, S Iran 28°27′N 53°04′E
Qiryat Gat see Kyriat Gat
Qiryat Shemona see Kiryat Shmona
Qishlaq see Garmsār
141 U14 **Qishn** SE Yemen 15°29′N 51°44′E
Qishon, Naḥal see Kishon, Nahal
Qita Ghazzah see Gaza Strip
156 K5 **Qitai** Xinjiang Uygur Zizhiqu, NW China 44°N 89°34′E
163 Y8 **Qitaihe** Heilongjiang, NE China 45°45′N 130°53′E
141 W12 **Qitbīt, Wādī** dry watercourse S Oman
161 O5 **Qixian** var. Qi Xian, Zhaoge. Henan, C China 35°35′N 114°10′E
Qi Xian see Qixian
Qīzān see Jīzān
Qizil Orda see Kyzylorda
Qizil Qum/Qizilqum see Kyzyl Kum
147 V14 **Qizilrabot** Rus. Kyzylrabot. SE Tajikistan 37°29′N 74°44′E
146 J10 **Qizilravote** Rus. Kyzylrabat. Buxoro Viloyati, C Uzbekistan 40°35′N 62°09′E
Qi Zil Uzun see Qezel Owzan, Rūd-e
139 S4 **Qizil Yār** At Ta'mím, N Iraq 35°26′N 44°12′E
164 J12 **Qkutango-hantō** peninsula Honshū, SW Japan
137 Y11 **Qobustan** Rus. Mărăză. E Azerbaijan 40°32′N 48°56′E
Qoghaly see Kogaly
Qogir Feng see K2
143 N6 **Qom** var. Kum, Qum. Qom, N Iran 34°43′N 50°54′E
143 N6 **Qom** ◆ province N Iran
Qomisheh see Shahreẓā
Qomolangma Feng see Everest, Mount
142 M7 **Qom, Rūd-e** C Iran
Qomsheh see Shahreẓā
Qomul see Hami
Qondūz see Kunduz
146 G7 **Qo'ng'irot** Rus. Kungrad. Qoraqalpog'iston Respublikasi, NW Uzbekistan 43°01′N 58°49′E
Qongyrat see Konyrat
Qoqek see Tacheng
147 R10 **Qo'qon** var. Khokand, Rus. Kokand. Farg'ona Viloyati, E Uzbekistan 40°34′N 70°55′E
Qorabowur Kirlari see Karabaur', Uval
Qoradaryo see Karadar'ya
146 G6 **Qorajar** Rus. Karadzhar. Qoraqalpog'iston Respublikasi, NW Uzbekistan 43°34′N 58°35′E
146 K12 **Qorako'l** Rus. Karakul'. Buxoro Viloyati, C Uzbekistan 39°27′N 63°45′E
146 H7 **Qorao'zak** Rus. Karauzyak. Qoraqalpog'iston Respublikasi, NW Uzbekistan 43°07′N 60°03′E
146 E5 **Qoraqalpog'iston** Rus. Karakalpakya. Qoraqalpog'iston Respublikasi, NW Uzbekistan 44°45′N 56°06′E
146 G7 **Qoraqalpog'iston Respublikasi** Rus. Respublika Karakalpakstan. ◆ autonomous republic NW Uzbekistan
Qorghalzhyn see Korgalzhyn
138 H6 **Qornet es Saouda** ▲ NE Lebanon 36°06′N 34°06′E
146 L12 **Qorowulbozor** Rus. Karaulbazar. Buxoro Viloyati, C Uzbekistan 39°28′N 64°49′E
142 K5 **Qorveh** var. Qerveh, Qurveh. Kordestān, W Iran 35°09′N 47°48′E
147 N11 **Qo'shrabot** Rus. Kushrabat. Samarqand Viloyati, C Uzbekistan 40°15′N 66°40′E
Qosköl see Koskol'
Qosshaghyl see Kosshagyl
Qostanay/Qostanay Oblysy see Kostanay
143 P12 **Qoṭbābād** Fārs, S Iran 28°52′N 53°40′E
143 R13 **Qoṭbābād** Hormozgān, S Iran 27°49′N 56°00′E
138 H6 **Qoubaïyât** var. Al Qubayyāt. N Lebanon 37°00′N 34°30′E
Qoussantîna see Constantine
Qowowuyag see Cho Oyu
147 O11 **Qo'ytosh** Rus. Koytash. Jizzax Viloyati, C Uzbekistan 40°13′N 67°19′E
146 G7 **Qozonketkan** Rus. Kazanketken. Qoraqalpog'iston Respublikasi, W Uzbekistan 42°59′N 59°21′E
146 H6 **Qozoqdaryo** Rus. Kazakdar'ya. Qoraqalpog'iston Respublikasi, NW Uzbekistan 43°26′N 59°47′E
19 N11 **Quabbin Reservoir** Massachusetts, NE USA
100 F12 **Quakenbrück** Niedersachsen, NW Germany 52°41′N 07°57′E
18 I15 **Quakertown** Pennsylvania, NE USA 40°26′N 75°17′W
182 M10 **Quambatook** Victoria, SE Australia 35°52′S 143°28′E
25 Q4 **Quanah** Texas, SW USA 34°17′N 99°46′W
167 V10 **Quang Ngai** var. Quangngai, Quang Nghia. Quang Ngai, C Vietnam 15°09′N 108°50′E
Quangngai see Quang Ngai
Quang Nghia see Quang Ngai
167 T9 **Quang Tri** var. Triêu Hai. Quang Tri, C Vietnam 16°46′N 107°11′E
Quanjiang see Suichuan
Quan Long see Ca Mau
152 L4 **Quanshuigou** China/India 35°40′N 79°28′E
161 R13 **Quanzhou** var. Ch'uan-chou, Tsinkiang; prev. Chin-chiang. Fujian, SE China 24°56′N 118°31′E
160 M12 **Quanzhou** Guangxi Zhuangzu Zizhiqu, S China 25°59′N 111°02′E
11 V16 **Qu'Appelle** Saskatchewan, S Canada
12 M3 **Quaqtaq** prev. Koartac. Québec, NE Canada 60°50′N 69°30′W
61 E16 **Quaraí** Rio Grande do Sul, S Brazil 30°38′S 56°25′W
59 H24 **Quaraí, Rio** Sp. Río Cuareim. Brazil/Uruguay see also Cuareim, Río
Quaraí, Rio see Cuareim, Río
171 N13 **Quarles, Pegunungan** ▲ Sulawesi, C Indonesia
Quarnero see Kvarner
107 C20 **Quartu Sant' Elena** Sardegna, Italy, C Mediterranean Sea 39°15′N 09°12′E
29 X13 **Quasqueton** Iowa, C USA 42°23′N 91°45′W
173 X16 **Quatre Bornes** W Mauritius 20°15′S 57°28′E
172 I17 **Quatre Bornes** Mahé, NE Seychelles
137 X10 **Quba** Rus. Kuba. N Azerbaijan 41°22′N 48°30′E
Qubba see Ba'qūbah
143 T3 **Qūchān** var. Kuchan. Khorāsān-Razavī, NE Iran 37°12′N 58°28′E
183 R10 **Queanbeyan** New South Wales, SE Australia 35°24′S 149°17′E
15 Q10 **Québec** var. Quebec. province capital Québec, SE Canada 46°50′N 71°15′W
14 K10 **Québec** var. Quebec. ◆ province SE Canada
61 D17 **Quebracho** Paysandú, W Uruguay 31°58′S 57°53′W
101 K14 **Quedlinburg** Sachsen-Anhalt, C Germany 51°48′N 11°09′E
138 H10 **Queen Alia** ✕ ('Ammān) 'Ammān, C Jordan
10 L16 **Queen Bess, Mount** ▲ British Columbia, SW Canada 51°15′N 124°29′W
10 I14 **Queen Charlotte** British Columbia, SW Canada 53°18′N 132°04′W
65 B24 **Queen Charlotte Bay** bay West Falkland, W Falkland Islands
10 H14 **Queen Charlotte Islands** Fr. Îles de la Reine-Charlotte. island group British Columbia, SW Canada
10 I15 **Queen Charlotte Sound** sea area British Columbia, W Canada
10 J16 **Queen Charlotte Strait** strait British Columbia, W Canada
27 U1 **Queen City** Missouri, C USA 40°24′N 92°34′W
25 X5 **Queen City** Texas, SW USA 33°09′N 94°09′W
197 O9 **Queen Elizabeth Islands** Fr. Îles de la Reine-Élisabeth. island group Nunavut, N Canada
195 Y10 **Queen Mary Coast** physical region Antarctica
65 N24 **Queen Mary's Peak** ▲ C Tristan da Cunha
196 M8 **Queen Maud Gulf** gulf Arctic Ocean
195 P11 **Queen Maud Mountains** ▲ Antarctica
Queen's County see Laois
181 U7 **Queensland** ◆ state N Australia
192 I9 **Queensland Plateau** undersea feature N Coral Sea
183 O16 **Queenstown** Tasmania, SE Australia 42°06′S 145°33′E
185 C22 **Queenstown** Otago, South Island, New Zealand 45°01′S 168°44′E
83 I24 **Queenstown** Eastern Cape, S South Africa 31°52′S 26°50′E
Queenstown see Cobh
32 F8 **Queets** Washington, NW USA 47°31′N 124°19′W
61 D18 **Queguay Grande, Río** W Uruguay
59 O16 **Queimadas** Bahia, E Brazil 10°59′S 39°38′W
82 D11 **Quela** Malanje, NW Angola 09°18′S 17°07′E
83 O16 **Quelimane** var. Kilimane, Kilmain, Quilimane. Zambézia, NE Mozambique 17°53′S 36°51′E
63 G18 **Quellón** var. Puerto Quellón. Los Lagos, S Chile 43°05′S 73°38′W
Quelpart see Jeju-do
37 P12 **Quemado** New Mexico, SW USA 34°18′N 108°29′W
25 O12 **Quemado** Texas, SW USA 28°58′N 100°36′W
44 K7 **Quemado, Punta de** headland E Cuba 20°13′N 74°07′W
Quemoy see Jinmen Dao
62 K13 **Quemú Quemú** La Pampa, E Argentina 36°03′S 63°36′W
155 E17 **Quepem** Goa, W India 15°13′N 74°03′E
42 M14 **Quepos** Puntarenas, S Costa Rica 09°28′N 84°10′W
Que Que see Kwekwe
61 D23 **Quequén** Buenos Aires, E Argentina 38°30′S 58°44′W
61 D23 **Quequén Grande, Río** E Argentina
61 C23 **Quequén Salado, Río** E Argentina
Quera see Chur
41 N13 **Querétaro** Querétaro de Arteaga, C Mexico 20°36′N 100°24′W
40 F4 **Querobabi** Sonora, NW Mexico 30°02′N 111°02′W
42 M13 **Quesada** var. Ciudad Quesada, San Carlos. Alajuela, N Costa Rica 10°19′N 84°26′W
105 O13 **Quesada** Andalucía, S Spain 37°52′N 03°05′W
161 O7 **Queshan** Henan, C China 32°48′N 114°03′E
10 M15 **Quesnel** British Columbia, SW Canada 52°59′N 122°30′W
37 S9 **Questa** New Mexico, SW USA 36°41′N 105°37′W
102 H7 **Questembert** Morbihan, NW France 47°39′N 02°24′W
57 K22 **Quetena, Río** SW Bolivia
149 O10 **Quetta** Baluchistān, SW Pakistan 30°15′N 67°E
Quetzalcoalco see Coatzacoalcos
Quetzaltenango see Quezaltenango
56 B6 **Quevedo** Los Ríos, C Ecuador 01°02′S 79°27′W
42 B6 **Quezaltenango** var. Quetzaltenango. Quezaltenango, W Guatemala 14°50′N 91°30′W
42 A2 **Quezaltenango** off. Departamento de Quezaltenango, var. Quetzaltenango. ◆ department SW Guatemala
Quezaltenango, Departamento de see Quezaltenango
42 E6 **Quezaltepeque** Chiquimula, SE Guatemala 14°38′N 89°25′W
170 M6 **Quezon** Palawan, W Philippines 09°13′N 118°01′E
161 P5 **Qufu** Shandong, E China 35°37′N 117°05′E
82 B12 **Quibala** Cuanza Sul, NW Angola 10°44′S 14°58′E
82 B11 **Quibaxe** var. Quibaxi. Cuanza Norte, NW Angola 08°30′S 14°36′E
Quibaxi see Quibaxe
54 D9 **Quibdó** Chocó, W Colombia 05°40′N 76°38′W
102 G7 **Quiberon** Morbihan, NW France 47°30′N 03°07′W
102 G7 **Quiberon, Baie de** bay NW France
54 J5 **Quíbor** Lara, N Venezuela 09°55′N 69°35′W
42 C4 **Quiché** off. Departamento del Quiché. ◆ department W Guatemala
Quiché, Departamento del see Quiché
99 E21 **Quiévrain** Hainaut, S Belgium 50°25′N 03°41′E
40 I9 **Quila** Sinaloa, C Mexico 24°24′N 107°11′W
83 B14 **Quilengues** Huíla, SW Angola 14°09′S 14°04′E
Quilimane see Quelimane
57 G15 **Quillabamba** Cusco, C Peru 12°49′S 72°41′W
57 L18 **Quillacollo** Cochabamba, C Bolivia 17°26′S 66°16′W
62 H4 **Quillagua** Antofagasta, N Chile 21°33′S 69°32′W
103 N17 **Quillan** Aude, S France 42°52′N 02°11′E
11 U15 **Quill Lakes** Saskatchewan, S Canada
62 G11 **Quillota** Valparaíso, C Chile 32°54′S 71°16′W
155 G23 **Quilon** var. Kollam. Kerala, SW India 08°57′N 76°37′E see also Kollam
181 V9 **Quilpie** Queensland, C Australia 26°39′S 144°15′E
149 O4 **Quil-Qala** Bāmyān, N Afghanistan 35°13′N 67°02′E
62 L7 **Quimilí** Santiago del Estero, C Argentina 27°35′S 62°25′W
57 O19 **Quimome** Santa Cruz, E Bolivia 17°45′S 61°15′W
102 F6 **Quimper** anc. Quimper Corentin. Finistère, NW France 48°00′N 04°05′W
Quimper Corentin see Quimper
102 G7 **Quimperlé** Finistère, NW France 47°52′N 03°33′W
32 F8 **Quinault** Washington, NW USA 47°27′N 123°53′W
32 F8 **Quinault River** Washington, NW USA
35 P5 **Quincy** California, W USA 39°56′N 120°56′W
23 S8 **Quincy** Florida, SE USA 30°35′N 84°34′W
30 I13 **Quincy** Illinois, N USA 39°56′N 91°24′W
19 O11 **Quincy** Massachusetts, NE USA 42°15′N 71°00′W
32 J9 **Quincy** Washington, NW USA 47°13′N 119°51′W
54 E10 **Quindío** off. Departamento del Quindío. ◆ province C Colombia
54 E10 **Quindío, Nevado del** ▲ C Colombia 04°42′N 75°25′W
62 J10 **Quines** San Luis, C Argentina 32°15′S 65°46′W
39 N13 **Quinhagak** Alaska, USA 59°45′N 161°55′W
76 G13 **Quinhámel** W Guinea-Bissau 11°52′N 15°52′W
Qui Nhon/Quinhon see Quy Nhơn
Quinindé see Rosa Zárate
25 U6 **Quinlan** Texas, SW USA 32°54′N 96°08′W
61 H17 **Quinta** Rio Grande do Sul, S Brazil 32°05′S 52°18′W
105 O10 **Quintanar de la Orden** Castilla-La Mancha, C Spain 39°36′N 03°03′W
41 X13 **Quintana Roo** ◆ state SE Mexico
105 S6 **Quinto** Aragón, NE Spain 41°25′N 00°31′W
108 G10 **Quinto** Ticino, S Switzerland 46°32′N 08°44′E
27 Q11 **Quinton** Oklahoma, C USA 35°07′N 95°22′W
62 K12 **Quinto, Río** C Argentina
82 A10 **Quinzau** Dem. Rep. Congo, NW Angola 06°50′S 12°48′E
14 H8 **Quinze, Lac des** Québec, SE Canada
83 B15 **Quipungo** Huíla, C Angola 14°49′S 14°29′E
62 G13 **Quirihue** Bío Bío, C Chile 36°15′S 72°35′W
82 D12 **Quirima** Malanje, NW Angola 10°51′S 18°06′E
183 T6 **Quirindi** New South Wales, SE Australia 31°29′S 150°40′E
55 P5 **Quiriquire** Monagas, NE Venezuela 09°59′N 63°14′W
14 D10 **Quirke Lake** Ontario, S Canada
61 B21 **Quiroga** Buenos Aires, E Argentina 35°18′S 61°22′W
104 I4 **Quiroga** Galicia, NW Spain 42°28′N 07°15′W
Quiróm, Salar see Pocitos, Salar
56 B9 **Quiroz, Río** NW Peru
82 Q13 **Quissanga** Cabo Delgado, NE Mozambique 12°24′S 40°33′E
83 M20 **Quissico** Inhambane, S Mozambique 24°42′S 34°44′E
25 O4 **Quitaque** Texas, SW USA 34°22′N 101°03′W
82 Q13 **Quiterajo** Cabo Delgado, NE Mozambique 11°37′S 40°22′E
23 T6 **Quitman** Georgia, SE USA 30°46′N 83°33′W
22 M6 **Quitman** Mississippi, S USA 32°02′N 88°43′W
25 V6 **Quitman** Texas, SW USA 32°37′N 95°26′W
56 C6 **Quito** ● (Ecuador) Pichincha, N Ecuador 0°14′S 78°30′W
Quito see Mariscal Sucre
58 P13 **Quixadá** Ceará, E Brazil 04°57′S 39°04′W
83 Q15 **Quixaxe** Nampula, NE Mozambique 15°15′S 40°07′E
161 N13 **Qujiang** var. Maba. Guangdong, S China 24°47′N 113°34′E
160 J9 **Qu Jiang** C China
161 R10 **Qu Jiang** SE China
160 H12 **Qujing** Yunnan, SW China 25°39′N 103°52′E
Qulan see Kulan
Qulin Gol see Chaor He
146 L10 **QuljuqtovTog'lari** Rus. Gory Kul'dzhuktau. ▲ C Uzbekistan
Qulsary see Kul'sary
Qulyndy Zhazyghy see Ravnina Kulyndy
Qum see Qom
Qumälisch see Lubartów
159 P11 **Qumar He** C China
159 Q12 **Qumarlêb** var. Yuegai; prev. Yuegaitan. Qinghai, C China 34°06′N 95°54′E
Qumisheh see Shahreẓā
147 O14 **Qumqo'rg'on** Rus. Kumkurgan. Surkhondaryo Viloyati, S Uzbekistan 37°54′N 67°31′E
Qunaytirah/Qunayṭirah, Muḥāfaẓat al see Al Qunayṭirah
189 V12 **Quoi** island Chuuk, C Micronesia
9 N8 **Quoich** Nunavut, NE Canada
83 E26 **Quoin Point** headland SW South Africa 34°48′S 19°39′E
182 I7 **Quorn** South Australia 32°22′S 138°03′E
Qurein see Al Kuwayt
147 P14 **Qŭrghonteppa** Rus. Kurgan-Tyube. SW Tajikistan 37°51′N 68°42′E
Qurlurtuuq see Kugluktuk
Qurveh see Qorveh
Quryq see Kuryk
Qusair see Al Quṣayr
137 X10 **Qusar** Rus. Kusary. NE Azerbaijan 41°26′N 48°27′E
Quṣayr see Al Quṣayr
Quseir see Al Quṣayr
142 I2 **Qūshchī** Āzarbāyjān-e Gharbi, N Iran 37°59′N 45°05′E
Qusmuryn see Kusmuryn, Ozero
Qusmuryn see Kushmurun, Kostanay, Kazakhstan
Quṭayfah/Qutayfe/Quteife see Al Quṭayfah
Quthing see Moyeni
147 S10 **Quvasoy** Rus. Kuvasay. Farg'ona Viloyati, E Uzbekistan 40°17′N 71°53′E
Quwair see Guwēr
Quxar see Lhazê
Qu Xian see Quzhou
159 N16 **Qüxü** var. Xoi. Xizang Zizhiqu, W China 29°25′N 90°48′E
Quyang see Jingzhou
167 V11 **Quy Nhơn** var. Quinhon, Qui Nhon. Bình Định, C Vietnam 13°47′N 109°11′E
161 R10 **Quzhou** var. Qu Xian. Zhejiang, SE China 28°55′N 118°54′E
Qyteti Stalin see Kuçovë
Qyzylaghash see Kyzylagash
Qyzylorda see Kyzylorda
Qyzyltū see Kishkenekol'
Qyzylzhar see Kyzylzhar

R

Raa Atoll see North Maalhosmadulu Atoll
109 R4 **Raab** Oberösterreich, N Austria 48°19′N 13°40′E
109 X8 **Raab** Hung. Rába. Austria/Hungary see also Rába
Raab see Rába
Raab see Győr
109 V2 **Raabs an der Thaya** Niederösterreich, E Austria 48°51′N 15°28′E
93 L14 **Raahe** Swe. Brahestad. Oulu, W Finland 64°42′N 24°31′E
98 M10 **Raalte** Overijssel, E Netherlands 52°23′N 06°16′E
99 I14 **Raamsdonksveer** Noord-Brabant, S Netherlands 51°42′N 04°54′E
92 L12 **Raanujärvi** Lappi, NW Finland 66°39′N 24°40′E
96 G9 **Raasay** island NW Scotland, United Kingdom
118 H3 **Raasiku** Ger. Rasik. Harjumaa, NW Estonia 59°22′N 25°11′E
112 B11 **Rab** It. Arbe. Primorje-Gorski Kotar, NW Croatia 44°46′N 14°46′E
112 B11 **Rab** It. Arbe. island NW Croatia
171 N16 **Raba** Sumbawa, S Indonesia 08°27′S 118°45′E
111 G22 **Rába** Ger. Raab. Austria/Hungary see also Raab
Rába see Raab
112 A10 **Rabac** Istra, NW Croatia 45°03′N 14°09′E
104 I2 **Rábade** Galicia, NW Spain 43°07′N 07°37′W
80 F10 **Rabak** White Nile, C Sudan 13°12′N 32°44′E
186 G9 **Rabaraba** Milne Bay, SE Papua New Guinea 10°00′S 149°50′E
102 K16 **Rabastens-de-Bigorre** Hautes-Pyrénées, S France 43°23′N 00°10′E
121 O16 **Rabat** W Malta 35°51′N 14°25′E
74 F6 **Rabat** var. al Dar al Baida. ● (Morocco) NW Morocco 34°02′N 06°51′W
Rabat see Victoria
186 H6 **Rabaul** New Britain, E Papua New Guinea 04°13′S 152°11′E
Rabbah Ammon/Rabbath Ammon see 'Ammān
28 K8 **Rabbit Creek** South Dakota, N USA
14 H10 **Rabbit Lake** Ontario, S Canada
187 Y14 **Rabi** prev. Rambi. island N Fiji
140 K9 **Rābigh** Makkah, W Saudi Arabia 22°51′N 39°E
42 D5 **Rabinal** Baja Verapaz, C Guatemala 15°05′N 90°26′W
168 G9 **Rabi, Pulau** island NW Indonesia, East Indies
111 L17 **Rabka** Małopolskie, S Poland 49°38′N 20°E
155 F16 **Rabkavi** Karnātaka, W India 16°40′N 75°03′E
Râbnița see Rîbnița
109 Y6 **Rabnitz** E Austria
124 J7 **Rabocheostrovsk** Respublika Kareliya, NW Russian Federation 64°58′N 34°46′E
23 U1 **Rabun Bald** ▲ Georgia, SE USA 34°58′N 83°18′W
75 S11 **Rabyānah** SE Libya 24°07′N 21°58′E
75 S11 **Rabyānah, Ramlat** var. Rebiana Sand Sea, Ṣaḥrā' Rabyānah. desert SE Libya
Rabyānah, Ṣaḥrā' see Rabyānah, Ramlat
116 L11 **Răcăciuni** Bacău, E Romania 46°20′N 27°00′E
Racaka see Riwoqê
107 J24 **Racalmuto** Sicilia, Italy, C Mediterranean Sea 37°25′N 13°44′E
116 J14 **Răcari** Dâmbovița, SE Romania 44°37′N 25°43′E
Răcari see Durankulak
116 F13 **Răcășdia** Hung. Rakasd. Caraș-Severin, SW Romania 44°58′N 21°36′E
106 B9 **Racconigi** Piemonte, NE Italy 44°45′N 07°41′E
31 T15 **Raccoon Creek** Ohio, N USA
13 V13 **Race, Cape** headland Newfoundland, Newfoundland and Labrador, E Canada 46°40′N 53°05′W
22 K10 **Raceland** Louisiana, S USA 29°43′N 90°36′W
19 Q12 **Race Point** headland Massachusetts, NE USA 42°03′N 70°14′W
167 S14 **Rach Gia** Kiên Giang, S Vietnam 10°01′N 105°05′E
167 S14 **Rach Gia, Vinh** bay S Vietnam
76 J8 **Rachid** Tagant, C Mauritania 18°48′N 11°41′W
110 L10 **Raciąż** Mazowieckie, C Poland 52°46′N 20°04′E
111 I16 **Racibórz** Ger. Ratibor. Śląskie, S Poland 50°05′N 18°10′E
31 N9 **Racine** Wisconsin, N USA 42°42′N 87°50′W
14 D7 **Racine Lake** Ontario, S Canada
111 J23 **Ráckeve** Pest, C Hungary 47°10′N 18°58′E
Rácz-Becse see Bečej
141 O15 **Radā'** var. Ridā'. W Yemen 14°24′N 44°49′E
113 O15 **Radan** ▲ SE Serbia 42°59′N 21°31′E
63 J19 **Rada Tilly** Chubut, SE Argentina 45°54′S 67°33′W
116 K8 **Rădăuți** Ger. Radautz, Hung. Rádóc. Suceava, N Romania 47°49′N 25°58′E
116 L8 **Rădăuți-Prut** Botoșani, NE Romania 48°14′N 26°47′E
Radautz see Rădăuți
Radbusa see Radbuza
111 A17 **Radbuza** Ger. Radbusa. SE Czech Republic
20 K6 **Radcliff** Kentucky, S USA 37°50′N 85°57′W
139 O2 **Radd, Wādī ar** dry watercourse N Syria
95 H16 **Råde** Østfold, S Norway 59°21′N 10°53′E
109 V11 **Radeče** Ger. Ratschach. C Slovenia 46°01′N 15°10′E
Radein see Radenci
116 J4 **Radekhiv** Pol. Radziechów, Rus. Radekhov. L'vivs'ka Oblast', W Ukraine 50°17′N 24°39′E
Radekhov see Radekhiv
109 X9 **Radenci** Ger. Radein; prev. Radinci. NE Slovenia 46°36′N 16°02′E
109 S9 **Radenthein** Kärnten, S Austria 46°48′N 13°42′E
Rádeyilikóé see Fort Good Hope
21 R7 **Radford** Virginia, NE USA 37°07′N 80°34′W
154 C9 **Rādhanpur** Gujarāt, W India 23°52′N 71°49′E
Radinci see Radenci
127 Q6 **Radishchevo** Ul'yanovskaya Oblast', W Russian Federation 52°49′N 47°54′E
12 I9 **Radisson** Québec, E Canada 53°47′N 77°35′W
11 P16 **Radium Hot Springs** British Columbia, SW Canada 50°39′N 116°09′W
116 F11 **Radna** Hung. Máriaradna. Arad, W Romania 46°05′N 21°41′E
Rádnávrre see Randijaure
114 K10 **Radnevo** Stara Zagora, C Bulgaria 42°17′N 25°58′E
97 J20 **Radnor** cultural region E Wales, United Kingdom
Radnót see Iernut
Rádóc see Rădăuți
101 H24 **Radolfzell am Bodensee** Baden-Württemberg, S Germany 47°43′N 08°58′E
110 M13 **Radom** Mazowieckie, C Poland 51°23′N 21°08′E
116 I14 **Radomirești** Olt, S Romania 44°06′N 25°00′E
111 K14 **Radomsko** Rus. Novoradomsk. Łódzkie, C Poland 51°04′N 19°25′E
117 N4 **Radomyshl'** Zhytomyrs'ka Oblast', N Ukraine 50°30′N 29°16′E
113 P19 **Radoviš** prev. Radovište. E Macedonia 41°39′N 22°26′E
Radovište see Radoviš
Radøy see Radøyni
94 B13 **Radøyni** prev. Radøy. island S Norway
109 R7 **Radstadt** Salzburg, NW Austria 47°24′N 13°31′E
182 E8 **Radstock, Cape** headland South Australia 33°11′S 134°18′E
109 U10 **Raduha** ▲ N Slovenia 46°24′N 14°46′E
119 G15 **Radun'** Hrodzyenskaya Voblasts', W Belarus 54°03′N 25°00′E
126 M3 **Raduzhnyy** Vladimirskaya Oblast', W Russian Federation 55°59′N 40°15′E
118 F11 **Radviliškis** Šiauliai, N Lithuania 55°48′N 23°32′E
11 U17 **Radville** Saskatchewan, S Canada 49°28′N 104°19′W
140 K7 **Raḍwā, Jabal** ▲ W Saudi Arabia 24°31′N 38°21′E
111 P16 **Radymno** Podkarpackie, SE Poland 49°57′N 22°49′E
116 J5 **Radyvyliv** Rivnens'ka Oblast', NW Ukraine 50°07′N 25°12′E
Radziechów see Radekhiv
110 I11 **Radziejów** Kujawsko-pomorskie, C Poland 52°36′N 18°33′E
110 O12 **Radzyń Podlaski** Lubelskie, E Poland 51°48′N 22°37′E
8 J7 **Rae** Nunavut, NW Canada
152 M13 **Rāe Bareli** Uttar Pradesh, N India 26°14′N 81°14′E
Rae-Edzo see Edzo
21 T11 **Raeford** North Carolina, SE USA 34°59′N 79°15′W
99 M19 **Raeren** Liège, E Belgium 50°42′N 06°06′E
9 N7 **Rae Strait** strait Nunavut, N Canada
184 L11 **Raetihi** Manawatu-Wanganui, North Island, New Zealand 39°29′S 175°16′E
Raevavae see Raivavae
Rafa see Rafah
62 M10 **Rafaela** Santa Fe, E Argentina 31°16′S 61°25′W
54 E5 **Rafael Núñez** ✕ (Cartagena) Bolívar, NW Colombia 10°27′N 75°31′W
138 E11 **Rafah** var. Rafa, Rafaḥ, Heb. Rafiaḥ, Raphiah. SW Gaza Strip 31°18′N 34°15′E
79 L15 **Rafaï** Mbomou, SE Central African Republic 05°01′N 23°51′E
141 O4 **Rafḥah** Al Ḥudūd ash Shamālīyah, N Saudi Arabia 29°41′N 43°29′E
Rafiaḥ see Rafah
143 R10 **Rafsanjān** Kermān, C Iran 30°25′N 56°E
80 B13 **Raga** Western Bahr el Ghazal, W South Sudan 08°28′N 25°41′E
19 S8 **Ragged Island** island Maine, NE USA
44 I5 **Ragged Island Range** island group S Bahamas
184 L7 **Raglan** Waikato, North Island, New Zealand 37°48′S 174°54′E
22 G8 **Ragley** Louisiana, S USA 30°31′N 93°13′W
Ragnit see Neman
107 K25 **Ragusa** Sicilia, Italy, C Mediterranean Sea 36°56′N 14°42′E
Ragusa see Dubrovnik
Ragusavecchia see Cavtat
171 P14 **Raha** Pulau Muna, C Indonesia 04°50′S 122°43′E
119 N17 **Rahachow** Rus. Rogachëv. Homyel'skaya Voblasts', SE Belarus 53°03′N 30°03′E
67 U6 **Rahad** var. Nahr ar Rahad. W Sudan
Rahad, Nahr ar see Rahad
Rahaeng see Tak
138 F11 **Rahat** Southern, C Israel 31°20′N 34°43′E
140 L8 **Rahaṭ, Ḥarrat** lava flow W Saudi Arabia
149 S12 **Rahīmyār Khān** Punjab, SE Pakistan 28°27′N 70°21′E
95 I14 **Råholt** Akershus, S Norway 60°16′N 11°10′E
113 M17 **Rahovec** Serb. Orahovac. W Kosovo 42°24′N 20°40′E
191 S10 **Raiatea** island Îles Sous le Vent, W French Polynesia
155 H16 **Rāichūr** Karnātaka, C India 16°15′N 77°20′E
Raidestos see Tekirdağ
153 S13 **Raiganj** West Bengal, NE India 25°38′N 88°11′E
154 M11 **Raigarh** Chhattīsgarh, C India 21°53′N 83°28′E
183 O16 **Railton** Tasmania, SE Australia 41°24′S 146°28′E
36 L8 **Rainbow Bridge** natural arch Utah, W USA
23 Q3 **Rainbow City** Alabama, S USA 33°57′N 86°02′W
11 N11 **Rainbow Lake** Alberta, W Canada 58°30′N 119°24′W
21 R5 **Rainelle** West Virginia, NE USA 37°57′N 80°46′W
32 G10 **Rainier** Oregon, NW USA 46°05′N 122°55′W
32 H9 **Rainier, Mount** Washington, NW USA 46°51′N 121°45′W
23 Q2 **Rainsville** Alabama, S USA 34°29′N 85°51′W
12 B11 **Rainy Lake** Canada/USA
12 A11 **Rainy River** Ontario, C Canada 48°44′N 94°33′W
Raippaluoto see Replot
154 K12 **Raipur** Chhattīsgarh, C India 21°16′N 81°42′E
154 H10 **Raisen** Madhya Pradesh, C India 23°21′N 77°49′E
15 N13 **Raisin** Ontario, SE Canada
31 R11 **Raisin, River** Michigan, N USA
191 U13 **Raivavae** var. Raevavae. Îles Australes, SW French Polynesia
149 W9 **Rāiwind** Punjab, E Pakistan 31°14′N 74°10′E
171 T12 **Raja Ampat, Kepulauan** island group E Indonesia
155 L16 **Rājahmundry** Andhra Pradesh, E India 17°05′N 81°42′E
155 I18 **Rājampet** Andhra Pradesh, E India 14°09′N 79°10′E
Rajang see Rajang, Batang
169 S9 **Rajang, Batang** var. Rajang. East Malaysia
149 S11 **Rājanpur** Punjab, E Pakistan 29°05′N 70°25′E
155 H23 **Rājapālaiyam** Tamil Nādu, SE India 09°26′N 77°36′E

◆ Country
● Country Capital
◇ Dependent Territory
○ Dependent Territory Capital
◆ Administrative Regions
✕ International Airport
▲ Mountain
▲ Mountain Range
Volcano
River
Lake
Reservoir

152 E12 Rājasthān ◆ state NW India
153 T15 Rajbari Dhaka, C Bangladesh 23°47'N 89°39'E
153 R12 Rajbiraj Eastern, E Nepal 26°34'N 86°52'E
154 G9 Rājgarh Madhya Pradesh, C India 24°01'N 76°42'E
152 H10 Rājgarh Rājasthān, NW India 28°38'N 75°21'E
153 P14 Rājgīr Bihār, N India 25°01'N 85°26'E
110 O8 Rajgród Podlaskie, NE Poland 53°43'N 22°40'E
154 L12 Rājim Chhattīsgarh, C India 20°57'N 81°58'E
112 C11 Rajinac, Mali ▲ W Croatia 44°47'N 15°04'E
154 B10 Rājkot Gujarāt, W India 22°18'N 70°47'E
153 R14 Rājmahal Jhārkhand, NE India 25°03'N 87°49'E
153 Q14 Rājmahāl Hills hill range N India
154 K12 Rāj Nāndgaon Chhattīsgarh, C India 21°06'N 81°02'E
152 I8 Rājpura Punjab, NW India 30°29'N 76°40'E
153 S14 Rajshahi prev. Rampur Boalia. Rajshahi, W Bangladesh 24°24'N 88°40'E
153 S13 Rajshahi ◆ division NW Bangladesh
190 K13 Rakahanga atoll N Cook Islands
185 H19 Rakaia Canterbury, South Island, New Zealand 43°45'S 172°02'E
185 G19 Rakaia ⤳ South Island, New Zealand
152 H3 Rakaposhi ▲ N India 36°06'N 74°31'E
Rakasd see Răcăşdia
169 N15 Rakata, Pulau var. Pulau Krakatau. island S Indonesia
141 U10 Rakbah, Qalamat ar well SE Saudi Arabia
166 K6 Rakhine State var. Arakan State. ◆ state W Burma (Myanmar)
116 I8 Rakhiv Zakarpats'ka Oblast', W Ukraine 48°05'N 24°15'E
141 V13 Rakhyūt SW Oman 16°41'N 53°09'E
192 K9 Rakiraki Viti Levu, W Fiji 17°22'S 178°10'E
126 J8 Rakitnoye Belgorodskaya Oblast', W Russian Federation 50°50'N 35°51'E
Rakka see Ar Raqqah
118 I4 Rakke Lääne-Virumaa, NE Estonia 58°58'N 26°14'E
95 I16 Rakkestad Østfold, S Norway 59°25'N 11°17'E
110 F12 Rakoniewice Ger. Rakwitz. Wielkopolskie, C Poland 52°09'N 16°10'E
Rakonitz see Rakovník
83 H18 Rakops Central, C Botswana 21°01'S 24°20'E
111 C16 Rakovník Ger. Rakonitz. Středočeský Kraj, W Czech Republic 50°07'N 13°44'E
114 J10 Rakovski Plovdiv, C Bulgaria 42°16'N 24°58'E
Rakutō-kō see Nakdong-gang
118 I3 Rakvere Ger. Wesenberg. Lääne-Virumaa, N Estonia 59°21'N 26°20'E
Rakwitz see Rakoniewice
22 L6 Raleigh Mississippi, S USA 32°01'N 89°30'W
21 U9 Raleigh state capital North Carolina, SE USA 35°46'N 78°38'W
21 Y11 Raleigh Bay bay North Carolina, SE USA
21 U9 Raleigh-Durham ✕ North Carolina, SE USA 35°54'N 78°45'W
189 S6 Ralik Chain island group Ralik Chain, W Marshall Islands
25 N5 Ralls Texas, SW USA 33°40'N 101°23'W
18 G13 Ralston Pennsylvania, NE USA 41°29'N 76°57'W
141 O16 Ramādah W Yemen 13°35'N 43°50'E
Ramadi see Ar Ramādī
105 N2 Ramales de la Victoria Cantabria, N Spain 43°15'N 03°28'W
138 F10 Ramallah C West Bank 31°55'N 35°12'E
61 C19 Ramallo Buenos Aires, E Argentina 33°30'S 60°01'W
155 H20 Rāmanagaram Karnātaka, E India 12°45'N 77°16'E
155 I23 Rāmanāthapuram Tamil Nādu, SE India 09°23'N 78°53'E
154 N12 Rāmapur Orissa, E India 21°48'N 84°00'E
155 I14 Rāmāreddi var. Kāmāreddi, Kamareddy. Andhra Pradesh, C India 18°19'N 78°23'E
138 F10 Ramat Gan Tel Aviv, W Israel 32°04'N 34°48'E
103 T6 Rambervillers Vosges, NE France 48°15'N 06°50'E
Rambi see Rabi
103 N5 Rambouillet Yvelines, N France 48°39'N 01°50'E
186 E5 Rambutyo Island island N Papua New Guinea
153 Q12 Ramechhāp Central, C Nepal 27°20'N 86°05'E
183 R12 Rame Head headland Victoria, SE Australia 37°48'S 149°30'E
126 L4 Ramenskoye Moskovskaya Oblast', W Russian Federation 55°31'N 38°24'E
124 J15 Rameshki Tverskaya Oblast', W Russian Federation 57°21'N 36°05'E
153 P14 Rāmgarh Jhārkhand, N India 23°37'N 85°32'E
152 D11 Rāmgarh Rājasthān, NW India 27°29'N 70°38'E
142 M9 Rāmhormoz var. Ram Hormuz, Ramuz. Khūzestān, SW Iran 31°15'N 49°38'E
Ram Hormuz see Rāmhormoz
Ram, Jebel see Ramm, Jabal
138 F10 Ramla var. Ramle, Ramleh, Ar. Er Ramle. Central, C Israel 31°56'N 34°52'E
Ramle/Ramleh see Ramla
138 F14 Ramm, Jabal var. Jebel Ram. ▲ SW Jordan 29°34'N 35°24'E
152 K10 Rāmnagar Uttarakhand, N India 29°23'N 79°07'E
95 N15 Ramnäs Västmanland, C Sweden 59°46'N 16°16'E
Râmnicul-Sărat see Râmnicu Sărat
116 L12 Râmnicu Sărat prev. Râmnicul-Sărat, Rîmnicu-Sărat. Buzău, E Romania 45°24'N 27°06'E
116 I13 Râmnicu Vâlcea prev. Rîmnicu Vîlcea. Vâlcea, C Romania 45°04'N 24°32'E
Ramokgwebana see Ramokgwebane
83 J18 Ramokgwebane var. Ramokgwebana. Central, NE Botswana 20°38'S 27°40'E
126 L7 Ramon' Voronezhskaya Oblast', W Russian Federation 51°51'N 39°18'E
35 V17 Ramona California, W USA 33°02'N 116°52'W
56 A10 Ramón, Laguna ◎ NW Peru
14 G7 Ramore Ontario, S Canada 48°26'N 80°19'W
40 M11 Ramos San Luis Potosí, C Mexico 22°48'N 101°55'W
41 N8 Ramos Arizpe Coahuila, NE Mexico 25°35'N 100°59'W
40 J9 Ramos, Río de ⤳ C Mexico
83 J21 Ramotswa South East, S Botswana 24°56'S 25°50'E
39 R8 Rampart Alaska, USA 65°30'N 150°10'W
8 H8 Ramparts ⤳ Northwest Territories, NW Canada
152 K10 Rāmpur Uttar Pradesh, N India 28°48'N 79°03'E
154 F9 Rāmpura Madhya Pradesh, C India 24°30'N 75°32'E
Rampur Boalia see Rajshahi
166 K6 Ramree Island island W Burma (Myanmar)
141 W6 Rams var. Ar Rams. Ra's al Khaymah, NE United Arab Emirates 25°52'N 56°01'E
143 N4 Rāmsar prev. Sakhtsar. Māzandarān, N Iran 36°55'N 50°39'E
93 H16 Ramsele Västernorrland, N Sweden 63°33'N 16°35'E
21 T9 Ramseur North Carolina, SE USA 35°43'N 79°39'W
97 I16 Ramsey NE Isle of Man 54°19'N 04°24'W
97 I16 Ramsey Bay bay NE Isle of Man
14 E9 Ramsey Lake ◎ Ontario, S Canada
97 Q22 Ramsgate SE England, United Kingdom 51°20'N 01°25'E
94 M10 Ramsjö Gävleborg, C Sweden 62°10'N 15°40'E
154 I12 Rāmtek Mahārāshtra, C India 21°28'N 79°28'E
Ramtha see Ar Ramthā
Ramuz see Rāmhormoz
118 G12 Ramygala Panevėžys, C Lithuania 55°30'N 24°18'E
152 H14 Rāna Pratāp Sāgar ◎ N India
169 V7 Ranau Sabah, East Malaysia 05°56'N 116°43'E
168 L14 Ranau, Danau ◎ Sumatera, W Indonesia
62 H12 Rancagua Libertador, C Chile 34°10'S 70°45'W
99 G22 Rance Hainaut, S Belgium 50°09'N 04°16'E
102 H6 Rance ⤳ NW France
60 J9 Rancharia São Paulo, S Brazil 22°13'S 50°53'W
153 P15 Rānchi Jhārkhand, N India 23°22'N 85°20'E
61 D21 Ranchos Buenos Aires, E Argentina 35°32'S 58°22'W
37 S9 Ranchos De Taos New Mexico, SW USA 36°21'N 105°36'W
63 G16 Ranco, Lago ◎ C Chile
95 C16 Randaberg Rogaland, S Norway 59°00'N 05°38'E
29 U7 Randall Minnesota, N USA 46°05'N 94°30'W
107 L23 Randazzo Sicilia, Italy, C Mediterranean Sea 37°52'N 14°57'E
95 G21 Randers Midtjylland, C Denmark 56°28'N 10°03'E
92 I12 Randijaure Lapp. Rádnávrre. ◎ N Sweden
21 T9 Randleman North Carolina, SE USA 35°49'N 79°48'W
19 O11 Randolph Massachusetts, NE USA 42°09'N 71°02'W
29 Q13 Randolph Nebraska, C USA 42°25'N 97°05'W
36 M1 Randolph Utah, W USA 41°40'N 111°10'W
100 P9 Randow ⤳ NE Germany
95 H14 Randsfjorden ◎ S Norway
92 K13 Råneå Norrbotten, N Sweden 65°52'N 22°17'E
92 G12 Ranelva ⤳ C Norway
94 F15 Ranemsletta Nord-Trøndelag, C Norway 64°36'N 11°55'E
76 H10 Ranérou C Senegal 15°17'N 14°00'W
Råneš see Ringvassøya
185 E22 Ranfurly Otago, South Island, New Zealand 45°07'S 170°06'E
167 P17 Rangae Narathiwat, SW Thailand 06°15'N 101°45'E
153 V16 Rangamati Chittagong, SE Bangladesh 22°40'N 92°10'E
184 I2 Ranganu Bay bay North Island, New Zealand
19 P6 Rangeley Maine, NE USA 44°58'N 70°37'W
37 O4 Rangely Colorado, C USA 40°05'N 108°48'W
25 R7 Ranger Texas, SW USA 32°28'N 98°40'W
14 C9 Ranger Lake Ontario, S Canada 46°51'N 83°34'W
14 C9 Ranger Lake ◎ Ontario, S Canada
153 V12 Rangia Assam, NE India 26°26'N 91°38'E
185 I18 Rangiora Canterbury, South Island, New Zealand 43°19'S 172°34'E
191 T9 Rangiroa atoll Îles Tuamotu, W French Polynesia
184 N9 Rangitaiki ⤳ North Island, New Zealand
185 F19 Rangitata ⤳ South Island, New Zealand
184 M12 Rangitikei ⤳ North Island, New Zealand
184 L6 Rangitoto Island island N New Zealand
Rangkasbitoeng see Rangkasbitung
169 N16 Rangkasbitung prev. Rangkasbitoeng. Jawa, SW Indonesia 06°21'S 106°12'E
167 P9 Rang, Khao ▲ C Thailand 16°13'N 99°03'E
147 V13 Rangkŭl Rus. Rangkul'. SE Tajikistan 38°30'N 74°24'E
Rangkul' see Rangkŭl
Rangoon see Yangon
153 T13 Rangpur Rajshahi, N Bangladesh 25°46'N 89°20'E
155 F18 Rānibennur Karnātaka, W India 14°36'N 75°39'E
153 R15 Rāniganj West Bengal, NE India 23°34'N 87°13'E
149 Q13 Rānīpur Sind, SE Pakistan 27°17'N 68°34'E
Rāniyah see Rānya
25 N9 Rankin Texas, SW USA 31°14'N 101°56'W
9 O9 Rankin Inlet Nunavut, C Canada 62°52'N 92°14'W
183 P8 Rankins Springs New South Wales, SE Australia 33°51'S 146°16'E
Rankovićevo see Kraljevo
108 I7 Rankweil Vorarlberg, W Austria 47°17'N 09°40'E
Rann see Brežice
127 T8 Ranneye Orenburgskaya Oblast', W Russian Federation 51°28'N 52°29'E
96 I10 Rannoch, Loch ◎ C Scotland, United Kingdom
191 U17 Rano Kau var. Rano Kao. crater Easter Island, Chile, E Pacific Ocean
167 N14 Ranong Ranong, SW Thailand 09°59'N 98°40'E
186 J8 Ranongga var. Ghanongga. island NW Solomon Islands
191 W16 Rano Raraku ancient monument Easter Island, Chile, E Pacific Ocean
171 V12 Ransiki Papua, E Indonesia 01°27'S 134°12'E
92 K12 Rantajärvi Norrbotten, N Sweden 66°45'N 23°39'E
93 N17 Rantasalmi Itä-Suomi, SE Finland 62°02'N 28°22'E
169 U13 Rantau Borneo, C Indonesia 02°56'S 115°09'E
168 L10 Rantau, Pulau var. Pulau Tebingtinggi. island W Indonesia
171 N13 Rantepao Sulawesi, C Indonesia 02°58'S 119°58'E
30 M13 Rantoul Illinois, N USA 40°19'N 88°08'W
93 L15 Rantsila Oulu, C Finland 64°31'N 25°40'E
92 L13 Ranua Lappi, NW Finland 65°55'N 26°34'E
139 T3 Rānya var. Rāniyah. As Sulaymānīyah, NE Iraq 36°15'N 44°53'E
157 X3 Raohe Heilongjiang, NE China 46°49'N 134°00'E
74 H9 Raoui, Erg er desert W Algeria
193 O10 Rapa island Îles Australes, S French Polynesia
191 V14 Rapa Iti island Îles Australes, SW French Polynesia
106 D10 Rapallo Liguria, NW Italy 44°21'N 09°13'E
Rapa Nui see Pascua, Isla de
Raphiah see Rafah
21 V5 Rapidan River ⤳ Virginia, NE USA
28 J10 Rapid City South Dakota, N USA 44°05'N 103°14'W
15 P8 Rapide-Blanc Québec, SE Canada 47°48'N 72°57'W
14 I8 Rapide-Deux Québec, SE Canada 47°56'N 78°33'W
118 K6 Räpina Ger. Rappin. Põlvamaa, SE Estonia 58°06'N 27°27'E
118 G4 Rapla Ger. Rappel. Raplamaa, NW Estonia 59°00'N 24°46'E
118 G4 Raplamaa var. Rapla Maakond. ◆ province NW Estonia
Rapla Maakond see Raplamaa
21 X6 Rappahannock River ⤳ Virginia, NE USA
Rappel see Rapla
108 G7 Rapperswil Sankt Gallen, NE Switzerland 47°14'N 08°50'E
Rappin see Räpina
153 N12 Rāpti ⤳ N India
57 K16 Rápulo, Río ⤳ E Bolivia
Raqqah/Raqqah, Muḩāfaẓat al see Ar Raqqah
18 J8 Raquette Lake ◎ New York, NE USA
18 J6 Raquette River ⤳ New York, NE USA
191 V10 Raraka atoll Îles Tuamotu, C French Polynesia
191 V10 Raroia atoll Îles Tuamotu, C French Polynesia
190 H15 Rarotonga ✕ Rarotonga, S Cook Islands, C Pacific Ocean 21°15'S 159°45'W
190 H16 Rarotonga island S Cook Islands, C Pacific Ocean
147 P12 Rarz W Tajikistan 39°23'N 68°43'E
Ras al'Ain see Ra's al 'Ayn
139 N2 Ra's al 'Ayn var. Ras al'Ain. Al Ḩasakah, N Syria 36°52'N 40°05'E
138 H3 Ra's al Basīṭ Al Lādhiqīyah, W Syria 35°57'N 35°55'E
Ra's al-Hafğī see Ra's al Khafjī
141 R5 Ra's al Khafjī var. Ra's al-Hafğī. Ash Sharqīyah, NE Saudi Arabia 28°22'N 48°30'E
Ras al-Khaimah/Ras al Khaimah see Ra's al Khaymah
143 R15 Ra's al Khaymah var. Ras al Khaimah. Ra's al Khaymah, NE United Arab Emirates 25°44'N 55°55'E
143 R15 Ra's al Khaymah var. Ras al-Khaimah. ✕ Ra's al Khaymah, NE United Arab Emirates 25°37'N 55°51'E
138 G13 Ra's an Naqb Ma'ān, S Jordan 30°00'N 35°29'E
61 B26 Rasa, Punta headland E Argentina 40°50'S 62°15'W
171 V12 Rasawi Papua, E Indonesia 02°04'S 134°02'E
Râşcani see Rîşcani
80 J10 Ras Dashen Terara ▲ N Ethiopia 13°12'N 38°09'E
Rasdhoo Atoll see Rasdu Atoll
151 K19 Rasdu Atoll var. Rasdhoo Atoll. atoll C Maldives
118 E12 Raseiniai Kaunas, C Lithuania 55°23'N 23°06'E
75 X8 Ra's Ghārib var. Râs Ghârib. E Egypt 28°16'N 33°01'E
Râs Ghârib see Ra's Ghārib
162 J6 Rashaant Hövsgöl, N Mongolia 49°08'N 101°27'E
Rashaant see Delüün, Bayan-Ölgiy, Mongolia
Rashaant see Öldziyt, Dundgovĭ, Mongolia
75 V7 Rashīd Eng. Rosetta. N Egypt 31°25'N 30°25'E
139 Y11 Rashīd Al Baṣrah, E Iraq 31°15'N 47°31'E
142 M3 Rasht var. Resht. Gīlān, NW Iran 37°18'N 49°38'E
139 S2 Ŗashwan Arbīl, N Iraq 36°28'N 43°54'E
Rasik see Raasiku
113 M15 Raška Serbia, C Serbia 43°18'N 20°37'E
119 P15 Rasna Rus. Ryasna. Mahilyowskaya Voblasts', E Belarus 54°01'N 31°12'E
116 J12 Râşnov prev. Rîşno, Rozsnyó, Hung. Barcarozsnyó. Braşov, C Romania 45°35'N 25°27'E
118 L11 Rasony Rus. Rossony. Vitsyebskaya Voblasts', N Belarus 55°53'N 28°50'E
Ra's Shamrah see Ugarit
127 N7 Rasskazovo Tambovskaya Oblast', W Russian Federation 52°42'N 41°45'E
119 O16 Rasta ⤳ E Belarus
Rastadt see Rastatt
Rastâne see Ar Rastān
141 S6 Ra's Tannūrah Eng. Ras Tanura. Ash Sharqīyah, NE Saudi Arabia 26°44'N 50°04'E
Ras Tanura see Ra's Tannūrah
101 G21 Rastatt var. Rastadt. Baden-Württemberg, SW Germany 48°51'N 08°13'E
Rastenburg see Kętrzyn
149 V7 Rasūlnagar Punjab, E Pakistan 32°20'N 73°51'E
189 U6 Ratak Chain island group Ratak Chain, E Marshall Islands
119 K15 Ratamka Rus. Ratomka. Minskaya Voblasts', C Belarus 53°56'N 27°21'E
93 G17 Ratän Jämtland, C Sweden 62°28'N 14°35'E
152 G11 Ratangarh Rājasthān, NW India 28°02'N 74°39'E
Rat Buri see Ratchaburi
167 O11 Ratchaburi var. Rat Buri. Ratchaburi, W Thailand 13°30'N 99°50'E
29 W15 Rathbun Lake ▣ Iowa, C USA
Ráth Caola see Rathkeale
166 K5 Rathedaung Rakhine State, W Burma (Myanmar) 20°30'N 92°48'E
100 M12 Rathenow Brandenburg, NE Germany 52°37'N 12°21'E
97 C19 Rathkeale Ir. Ráth Caola. Limerick, SW Ireland 52°32'N 08°56'W
96 F13 Rathlin Island Ir. Reachlainn. island N Northern Ireland, United Kingdom
97 C20 Ráth Luirc Ir. An Ráth. Cork, SW Ireland 52°22'N 08°44'W
Ratibor see Racibórz
Ratisbon/Ratisbona/Ratisbonne see Regensburg
Rätische Alpen see Rhaetian Alps
38 E17 Rat Island island Aleutian Islands, Alaska, USA
38 E17 Rat Islands island group Aleutian Islands, Alaska, USA
154 F10 Ratlām prev. Rutlam. Madhya Pradesh, C India 23°23'N 75°04'E
155 D15 Ratnāgiri Mahārāshtra, W India 17°00'N 73°20'E
155 K26 Ratnapura Sabaragamuwa Province, S Sri Lanka 06°41'N 80°25'E
Ratne see Ratno
116 J2 Ratno var. Ratne. Volyns'ka Oblast', NW Ukraine 51°40'N 24°33'E
Ratomka see Ratamka
37 U8 Raton New Mexico, SW USA 36°54'N 104°27'W
139 O7 Ratqah, Wādī ar dry watercourse W Iraq
Ratschach see Radeče
167 O16 Rattaphum Songkhla, SW Thailand 07°07'N 100°16'E
26 L6 Rattlesnake Creek ⤳ Kansas, C USA
94 L13 Rättvik Dalarna, C Sweden 60°53'N 15°12'E
100 K9 Ratzeburg Mecklenburg-Vorpommern, N Germany 53°41'N 10°48'E
100 K9 Ratzeburger See ◎ N Germany
10 J10 Ratz, Mount ▲ British Columbia, SW Canada 57°22'N 132°17'W
61 D22 Rauch Buenos Aires, E Argentina 36°45'S 59°05'W
41 U16 Raudales Chiapas, SE Mexico
Raudhatain see Ar Rawḑatayn
Raudnitz an der Elbe see Roudnice nad Labem
92 K1 Raufarhöfn Nordhurland Eystra, NE Iceland 66°27'N 15°58'W
94 H13 Raufoss Oppland, S Norway 60°44'N 10°39'E
Raukawa see Cook Strait
184 Q8 Raukumara ▲ North Island, New Zealand 37°46'S 178°07'E
192 K11 Raukumara Plain undersea feature N Coral Sea
184 P8 Raukumara Range ▲ North Island, New Zealand
Rāulakela see Rāurkela
95 F15 Rauland Telemark, S Norway 59°41'N 07°57'E
93 J19 Rauma Swe. Raumo. Länsi-Suomi, SW Finland 61°09'N 21°30'E
94 F10 Rauma ⤳ S Norway
Raumo see Rauma
118 H8 Rauna C Latvia 57°19'N 25°34'E
169 T17 Raung, Gunung ▲ Jawa, S Indonesia 08°00'S 114°07'E
154 N11 Rāurkela var. Rāulakela, Rourkela. Orissa, E India 22°13'N 84°53'E
95 J22 Raus Skåne, S Sweden 56°01'N 12°48'E
165 W3 Rausu Hokkaidō, NE Japan 44°00'N 145°06'E
165 W3 Rausu-dake ▲ Hokkaidō, NE Japan 44°06'N 145°04'E
116 M9 Răut var. Răuţel. ⤳ C Moldova
93 M17 Rautalampi Itä-Suomi, C Finland 62°37'N 26°48'E
93 N16 Rautavaara Itä-Suomi, C Finland 63°30'N 28°19'E
Răuţel see Răut
93 O18 Rautjärvi Etelä-Suomi, SE Finland 61°21'N 29°20'E
Rautu see Sosnovo
191 V11 Ravahere atoll Îles Tuamotu, C French Polynesia
107 J25 Ravanusa Sicilia, Italy, C Mediterranean Sea 37°16'N 13°59'E
143 S9 Rāvar Kermān, C Iran 31°15'N 56°51'E
147 Q11 Ravat Batkenskaya Oblast', SW Kyrgyzstan 39°54'N 70°06'E
18 K11 Ravena New York, NE USA 42°28'N 73°49'W
106 H10 Ravenna Emilia-Romagna, N Italy 44°28'N 12°15'E
29 O15 Ravenna Nebraska, C USA 41°01'N 98°54'W
31 U11 Ravenna Ohio, N USA 41°09'N 81°14'W
101 I24 Ravensburg Baden-Württemberg, S Germany 47°47'N 09°37'E
181 W4 Ravenshoe Queensland, NE Australia 17°29'S 145°28'E
180 K13 Ravensthorpe Western Australia 33°37'S 120°03'E
21 Q4 Ravenswood West Virginia, NE USA 38°57'N 81°45'W
149 U9 Rāvi ⤳ India/Pakistan
112 C9 Ravna Gora Primorje-Gorski Kotar, NW Croatia 45°20'N 14°54'E
109 U10 Ravne na Koroškem Ger. Gutenstein. N Slovenia 46°33'N 14°57'E
145 T7 Ravnina Kulyndy prev. Kulunda Steppe, Kaz. Qulyndy Zhazyghy, Rus. Kulundinskaya Ravnina. grassland Kazakhstan/Russian Federation
139 P6 Rāwah Al Anbār, W Iraq 34°32'N 41°54'E
191 T4 Rawaki prev. Phoenix Island. atoll Phoenix Islands, C Kiribati
149 U6 Rāwalpindi Punjab, NE Pakistan 33°38'N 73°06'E
110 L13 Rawa Mazowiecka Łódzkie, C Poland 51°47'N 20°16'E
139 T2 Rawāndiz var. Rawandoz, Rawāndūz. Arbīl, N Iraq 36°38'N 44°32'E
Rawandoz/Rawāndūz see Rawāndiz
171 U12 Rawas Papua, E Indonesia 01°07'S 132°12'E
139 O4 Rawḑah ◎ E Syria
110 G13 Rawicz Ger. Rawitsch. Wielkopolskie, C Poland 51°37'N 16°51'E
Rawitsch see Rawicz
180 M11 Rawlinna Western Australia 31°01'S 125°36'E
33 W16 Rawlins Wyoming, C USA 41°47'N 107°14'W
63 K17 Rawson Chubut, SE Argentina 43°22'S 65°01'W
159 R16 Rawu Xizang Zizhiqu, W China 29°30'N 96°42'E
153 P12 Raxaul Bihār, N India 26°58'N 84°51'E
28 K3 Ray North Dakota, N USA 48°19'N 103°11'W
169 S11 Raya, Bukit ▲ Borneo, C Indonesia 0°40'S 112°40'E
155 I18 Rāyachoti Andhra Pradesh, E India 14°03'N 78°43'E
Rāyadrug see Rāyagarha
Rāyagada see Rāyagarha
155 M14 Rāyagarha prev. Rāyagada. var. Rāyadrug. Orissa, E India 19°10'N 83°28'E
138 H7 Rayak var. Rayaq, Riyāq. E Lebanon 33°51'N 36°03'E
Rayaq see Rayak
139 T2 Rāyat Arbīl, E Iraq 36°39'N 44°56'E
169 N12 Raya, Tanjung cape Pulau Bangka, W Indonesia
13 R13 Ray, Cape headland Newfoundland, Newfoundland and Labrador, E Canada 47°38'N 59°15'W
123 Q13 Raychikhinsk Amurskaya Oblast', SE Russian Federation 49°47'N 129°19'E
127 U5 Rayevskiy Respublika Bashkortostan, W Russian Federation 54°04'N 54°58'E
11 Q17 Raymond Alberta, SW Canada 49°30'N 112°41'W
22 K6 Raymond Mississippi, S USA 32°15'N 90°25'W
32 F9 Raymond Washington, NW USA 46°41'N 123°43'W
183 T8 Raymond Terrace New South Wales, SE Australia 32°47'S 151°45'E
25 T17 Raymondville Texas, SW USA 26°30'N 97°48'W
11 U16 Raymore Saskatchewan, S Canada 51°24'N 104°34'W
39 Q8 Ray Mountains ▲ Alaska, USA
22 H9 Rayne Louisiana, S USA 30°13'N 92°15'W
41 O12 Rayón San Luis Potosí, C Mexico 21°54'N 99°33'W
40 G4 Rayón Sonora, NW Mexico 29°45'N 110°33'W
167 P12 Rayong Rayong, S Thailand 12°42'N 101°17'E
25 T5 Ray Roberts, Lake ◎ Texas, SW USA
18 E15 Raystown Lake ▣ Pennsylvania, NE USA
141 V13 Raysūt SW Oman 16°58'N 54°02'E
27 R4 Raytown Missouri, C USA 39°00'N 94°27'W
22 I5 Rayville Louisiana, S USA 32°29'N 91°45'W
142 L5 Razan Hamadān, W Iran 35°22'N 48°58'E
139 S9 Razāzah, Buḩayrat ar var. Baḩr al Milḩ. ◎ C Iraq
114 L9 Razboyna ▲ E Bulgaria 42°54'N 26°31'E
Razdan see Hrazdan
Razdolnoye see Rozdol'ne
Razelm, Lacul see Razim, Lacul
139 U2 Razga As Sulaymānīyah, E Iraq 36°25'N 45°06'E
114 L8 Razgrad Razgrad, N Bulgaria 43°33'N 26°31'E
114 L8 Razgrad ◆ province NE Bulgaria
117 N13 Razim, Lacul prev. Lacul Razelm. lagoon NW Black Sea
114 G11 Razlog Blagoevgrad, SW Bulgaria 41°53'N 23°28'E
118 K10 Rāznas Ezers ◎ SE Latvia
102 E6 Raz, Pointe du headland NW France 48°06'N 04°52'W
Reachlainn see Rathlin Island
Reachrainn see Lambay Island
97 N22 Reading S England, United Kingdom 51°28'N 00°59'W
18 H15 Reading Pennsylvania, NE USA 40°20'N 75°55'W
48 C7 Real, Cordillera ▲ C Ecuador
62 K12 Realicó La Pampa, C Argentina 35°02'S 64°14'W
25 R15 Realitos Texas, SW USA 27°26'N 98°31'W
108 G9 Realp Uri, C Switzerland 46°36'N 08°32'E
167 Q12 Reăng Kesei Bătdâmbâng, W Cambodia 12°57'N 103°15'E
191 Y11 Reao atoll Îles Tuamotu, E French Polynesia
Reate see Rieti
Greater Antarctica see East Antarctica
180 L11 Rebecca, Lake ◎ Western Australia
Rebiana Sand Sea see Rabyānah, Ramlat
124 H8 Reboly Finn. Repola. Respublika Kareliya, NW Russian Federation 63°51'N 30°49'E
165 S1 Rebun Rebun-tō, NE Japan 45°19'N 141°02'E
165 S1 Rebun-tō island NE Japan
106 J12 Recanati Marche, C Italy 43°23'N 13°34'E
Rechitsa see Rechytsa
109 Y7 Rechnitz Burgenland, SE Austria 47°19'N 16°26'E
119 J20 Rechytsa Rus. Rechitsa. Brestskaya Voblasts', SW Belarus 51°51'N 26°48'E
119 O19 Rechytsa Rus. Rechitsa. Homyel'skaya Voblasts', SE Belarus 52°22'N 30°23'E
59 Q15 Recife prev. Pernambuco. state capital Pernambuco, E Brazil 08°06'S 34°53'W
83 I26 Recife, Cape Afr. Kaap Recife. headland S South Africa 34°03'S 25°37'E
Recife, Kaap see Recife, Cape
172 I16 Récifs, Îles aux island Inner Islands, NE Seychelles
101 E14 Recklinghausen Nordrhein-Westfalen, W Germany 51°37'N 07°12'E
100 M8 Recknitz ⤳ NE Germany
99 K23 Recogne Luxembourg, SE Belgium 49°56'N 05°20'E
61 C15 Reconquista Santa Fe, C Argentina 29°08'S 59°38'W
195 O6 Recovery Glacier glacier Antarctica
59 G15 Recreio Mato Grosso, W Brazil 08°13'S 58°15'W
27 X9 Rector Arkansas, C USA 36°15'N 90°17'W
110 E9 Recz Ger. Reetz Neumark. Zachodnio-pomorskie, NW Poland 53°16'N 15°32'E
99 L24 Redange var. Redange-sur-Attert. Diekirch, W Luxembourg 49°46'N 05°53'E
Redange-sur-Attert see Redange
18 C13 Redbank Creek ⤳ Pennsylvania, NE USA
13 S9 Red Bay Québec, E Canada 51°40'N 56°37'W
23 N2 Red Bay Alabama, S USA 34°26'N 88°08'W
35 N4 Red Bluff California, W USA 40°09'N 122°14'W
24 J8 Red Bluff Reservoir ◎ New Mexico/Texas, SW USA
30 K16 Red Bud Illinois, N USA 38°12'N 89°59'W
30 J5 Red Cedar River ⤳ Wisconsin, N USA
11 R17 Redcliff Alberta, SW Canada 50°06'N 110°48'W
83 K17 Redcliff Midlands, C Zimbabwe 19°00'S 29°49'E
182 L9 Red Cliffs Victoria, SE Australia 34°21'S 142°12'E
29 P17 Red Cloud Nebraska, C USA 40°05'N 98°31'W
22 L8 Red Creek ⤳ Mississippi, S USA
11 P15 Red Deer Alberta, SW Canada 52°15'N 113°48'W
11 Q16 Red Deer ⤳ Alberta, SW Canada
39 O11 Red Devil Alaska, USA 61°45'N 157°18'W
35 N3 Redding California, W USA 40°33'N 122°26'W
97 L20 Redditch W England, United Kingdom 52°19'N 01°56'W
29 P9 Redfield South Dakota, N USA 44°51'N 98°31'W
24 J12 Redford Texas, SW USA 29°31'N 104°19'W
45 V13 Redhead Trinidad, Trinidad and Tobago 10°44'N 60°58'W
182 I8 Red Hill South Australia 33°34'S 138°13'E
Red Hill see Pu'u 'Ula'ula
26 K7 Red Hills hill range Kansas, C USA
13 T12 Red Indian Lake ◎ Newfoundland, Newfoundland and Labrador, E Canada
124 J16 Redkino Tverskaya Oblast', W Russian Federation 56°41'N 36°07'E
12 A10 Red Lake Ontario, C Canada 51°00'N 93°55'W
36 I10 Red Lake salt flat Arizona, SW USA
29 S4 Red Lake Falls Minnesota, N USA 47°52'N 96°16'W
29 R4 Red Lake River ⤳ Minnesota, N USA
35 U15 Redlands California, W USA 34°03'N 117°10'W
18 G16 Red Lion Pennsylvania, NE USA 39°53'N 76°36'W
33 U11 Red Lodge Montana, NW USA 45°11'N 109°15'W
32 H13 Redmond Oregon, NW USA 44°16'N 121°10'W
36 L5 Redmond Utah, W USA 39°00'N 111°51'W
32 H8 Redmond Washington, NW USA 47°40'N 122°07'W
Rednitz see Regnitz
29 T15 Red Oak Iowa, C USA 41°00'N 95°10'W
18 K12 Red Oaks Mill New York, NE USA 41°39'N 73°52'W
102 I7 Redon Ille-et-Vilaine, NW France 47°39'N 02°05'W
45 W10 Redonda island SW Antigua and Barbuda
104 G4 Redondela Galicia, NW Spain 42°17'N 08°36'W
104 H11 Redondo Évora, S Portugal 38°38'N 07°32'W
39 Q12 Redoubt Volcano ▲ Alaska, USA 60°29'N 152°44'W
11 Y16 Red River ⤳ Canada/USA
129 U12 Red River var. Yuan, Chin. Yuan Jiang, Vtn. Sông Hông Hà. ⤳ China/Vietnam
25 W4 Red River ⤳ S USA
22 H7 Red River ⤳ Louisiana, S USA
30 M6 Red River ⤳ Wisconsin, N USA
Red Rock, Lake see Red Rock Reservoir
29 W14 Red Rock Reservoir var. Lake Red Rock. ▣ Iowa, C USA
80 H7 Red Sea ◆ state NE Sudan
75 Y9 Red Sea var. Sinus Arabicus. sea Africa/Asia
21 T11 Red Springs North Carolina, SE USA 34°49'N 79°10'W
8 I9 Redstone ⤳ Northwest Territories, NW Canada
11 V17 Redvers Saskatchewan, S Canada 49°31'N 101°33'W
77 P13 Red Volta var. Nazinon, Fr. Volta Rouge. ⤳ Burkina/Ghana
11 Q14 Redwater Alberta, SW Canada 53°57'N 113°06'W
28 M16 Red Willow Creek ⤳ Nebraska, C USA
29 W9 Red Wing Minnesota, N USA 44°33'N 92°31'W
35 N9 Redwood City California, W USA 37°29'N 122°13'W
29 T9 Redwood Falls Minnesota, N USA 44°33'N 95°07'W
31 P7 Reed City Michigan, N USA 43°52'N 85°30'W
28 K6 Reeder North Dakota, N USA 46°03'N 102°55'W
35 R11 Reedley California, W USA 36°35'N 119°27'W
33 T11 Reedpoint Montana, NW USA 45°41'N 109°33'W
30 K8 Reedsburg Wisconsin, N USA 43°33'N 90°03'W
32 E13 Reedsport Oregon, NW USA 43°42'N 124°06'W
187 Q9 Reef Islands island group Santa Cruz Islands, E Solomon Islands
185 H16 Reefton West Coast, South Island, New Zealand 42°07'S 171°53'E
20 F8 Reelfoot Lake ◎ Tennessee, S USA
97 D17 Ree, Lough Ir. Loch Rí. ◎ C Ireland
Reengus see Ringas
35 U4 Reese River ⤳ Nevada, W USA
98 M8 Reest ⤳ E Netherlands
Reetz Neumark see Recz
Reevhtse see Røssvatnet
137 N13 Refahiye Erzincan, C Turkey 39°54'N 38°45'E
23 N4 Reform Alabama, S USA 33°22'N 88°01'W
95 K20 Reftele Jönköping, S Sweden 57°10'N 13°34'E
25 T14 Refugio Texas, SW USA 28°19'N 97°18'W
110 E8 Rega ⤳ NW Poland
Regar see Tursunzoda
101 O21 Regen Bayern, SE Germany 48°57'N 13°10'E
101 M20 Regen ⤳ SE Germany
101 M21 Regensburg Eng. Ratisbon, Fr. Ratisbonne, hist. Ratisbona; anc. Castra Regina, Reginum. Bayern, SE Germany 49°01'N 12°06'E
101 M21 Regenstauf Bayern, SE Germany 49°06'N 12°07'E
148 M10 Rēgestān var. Registan prev. Rīgestān. desert region S Afghanistan
74 I10 Reggane C Algeria 26°46'N 00°09'E
98 N9 Regge ⤳ E Netherlands
Reggio see Reggio nell'Emilia
Reggio Calabria see Reggio di Calabria
107 M23 Reggio di Calabria var. Reggio Calabria, Gk. Rhegion; anc. Regium, Rhegium. Calabria, SW Italy 38°06'N 15°39'E
Reggio Emilia see Reggio nell'Emilia
106 F9 Reggio nell'Emilia var. Reggio Emilia, abbrev. Reggio; anc. Regium Lepidum. Emilia-Romagna, N Italy 44°42'N 10°37'E
116 I10 Reghin Ger. Sächsisch-Reen, Hung. Szászrégen; prev. Reghinul Săsesc, Ger. Sächsisch-Regen. Mureş, C Romania 46°46'N 24°41'E
Reghinul Săsesc see Reghin
11 U16 Regina province capital Saskatchewan, S Canada 50°25'N 104°39'W
55 Z10 Régina E French Guiana 04°20'N 52°07'W
11 U16 Regina ✕ Saskatchewan, S Canada 50°21'N 104°43'W
11 U16 Regina Beach Saskatchewan, S Canada 50°44'N 105°03'W
Reginum see Regensburg
Région du Haut-Congo see Haut-Congo
Registan see Rēgestān
60 L11 Registro São Paulo, S Brazil 24°30'S 47°50'W
Regium see Reggio di Calabria
Regium Lepidum see Reggio nell'Emilia
101 K19 Regnitz var. Rednitz. ⤳ SE Germany
40 K10 Regocijo Durango, W Mexico 23°35'N 105°11'W
104 H12 Reguengos de Monsaraz Évora, S Portugal 38°25'N 07°32'W
101 M18 Rehau Bayern, E Germany 50°15'N 12°03'E
83 D19 Rehoboth Hardap, C Namibia 23°18'S 17°03'E
21 Z4 Rehoboth Beach Delaware, NE USA 38°42'N 75°03'W

138 F10 **Rehovot** ; prev. Reẖovot. Central, C Israel 31°54′N 34°49′E
Reẖovot see Rehovot
81 J20 **Rei** spring/well S Kenya 03°24′S 39°18′E
Reichenau see Rychnov nad Kněžnou
Reichenau see Bogatynia, Poland
101 M17 **Reichenbach** var. Reichenbach im Vogtland. Sachsen, E Germany 50°36′N 12°18′E
Reichenbach see Dzierżoniów
Reichenbach im Vogtland see Reichenbach
Reichenberg see Liberec
181 O11 **Reid** Western Australia 30°49′S 128°24′E
23 V6 **Reidsville** Georgia, SE USA 32°05′N 82°07′W
21 T8 **Reidsville** North Carolina, SE USA 36°21′N 79°39′W
Reifnitz see Ribnica
97 O22 **Reigate** SE England, United Kingdom 51°14′N 00°13′W
Reikjavik see Reykjavík
102 I10 **Ré, Île de** island W France
37 N15 **Reiley Peak** ▲ Arizona, SW USA 32°24′N 110°09′W
103 Q4 **Reims** Eng. Rheims; anc. Durocortorum, Remi. Marne, N France 49°16′N 04°01′E
63 G23 **Reina Adelaida, Archipiélago** island group S Chile
45 O16 **Reina Beatrix** ✈ (Oranjestad) C Aruba 12°30′N 69°57′W
108 F7 **Reinach** Aargau, W Switzerland 47°16′N 08°12′E
108 E6 **Reinach** Basel Landschaft, NW Switzerland 47°30′N 07°36′E
64 O11 **Reina Sofía** ✈ (Tenerife) Tenerife, Islas Canarias, Spain, NE Atlantic Ocean
29 W13 **Reinbeck** Iowa, C USA 42°19′N 92°36′W
100 J10 **Reinbek** Schleswig-Holstein, N Germany 53°31′N 10°15′E
11 U12 **Reindeer** ≈ Saskatchewan, C Canada
11 U11 **Reindeer Lake** ◎ Manitoba/Saskatchewan, C Canada
Reine-Charlotte, Îles de la see Queen Charlotte Islands
Reine-Élisabeth, Îles de la see Queen Elizabeth Islands
94 F13 **Reineskarvet** ▲ S Norway 60°38′N 07°48′E
184 H1 **Reinga, Cape** headland North Island, New Zealand 34°24′S 172°40′E
105 N3 **Reinosa** Cantabria, N Spain 43°01′N 04°09′W
109 R8 **Reisseck** ▲ S Austria 46°57′N 13°21′E
21 W3 **Reisterstown** Maryland, NE USA 39°27′N 76°46′W
Reisui see Yeosu
98 N5 **Reitdiep** ≈ NE Netherlands
191 V10 **Reitoru** atoll Îles Tuamotu, C French Polynesia
95 M17 **Rejmyre** Östergötland, S Sweden 58°49′N 15°55′E
Reka see Rijeka
Reka Ili see Ile/Ili He
Rekarne see Tumbo
Rekhovot see Rehovot
8 K9 **Reliance** Northwest Territories, C Canada 62°45′N 109°08′W
33 U16 **Reliance** Wyoming, C USA 41°42′N 109°13′W
74 I5 **Relizane** var. Ghelîzâne, Ghilizane. NW Algeria 35°45′N 00°33′E
182 I7 **Remarkable, Mount** ▲ South Australia 32°46′S 138°08′E
54 E8 **Remedios** Antioquia, N Colombia 07°02′N 74°42′W
43 Q16 **Remedios** Veraguas, W Panama 08°13′N 81°48′W
42 D8 **Remedios, Punta** headland SW El Salvador 13°31′N 89°48′W
Remi see Reims
99 N25 **Remich** Grevenmacher, SE Luxembourg 49°33′N 06°23′E
99 J19 **Remicourt** Liège, E Belgium 50°40′N 05°19′E
14 H8 **Rémigny, Lac** ◎ Québec, SE Canada
55 Z10 **Rémire** NE French Guiana 04°52′N 52°16′W
127 N13 **Remontnoye** Rostovskaya Oblast', SW Russian Federation 46°35′N 43°38′E
171 U14 **Remoon** Pulau Kur, E Indonesia 05°18′S 131°59′E
99 L20 **Remouchamps** Liège, E Belgium 50°29′N 05°43′E
103 R15 **Remoulins** Gard, S France 43°56′N 04°34′E
173 X16 **Rempart, Mont du** hill W Mauritius
101 E15 **Remscheid** Nordrhein-Westfalen, W Germany 51°10′N 07°11′E
29 S12 **Remsen** Iowa, C USA 42°48′N 95°58′W
94 I12 **Rena** Hedmark, S Norway 61°08′N 11°21′E
94 I11 **Renåa** ≈ S Norway
Renaix see Ronse
118 H7 **Rencēni** N Latvia 57°43′N 25°25′E
118 D9 **Renda** W Latvia 57°04′N 22°18′E
107 N20 **Rende** Calabria, SW Italy 39°19′N 16°10′E
99 K21 **Rendeux** Luxembourg, SE Belgium 50°15′N 05°28′E
Rendina see Rentína
30 L16 **Rend Lake** ⊠ Illinois, N USA
186 K9 **Rendova** island New Georgia Islands, NW Solomon Islands
100 I8 **Rendsburg** Schleswig-Holstein, N Germany 54°18′N 09°40′E
108 B9 **Renens** Vaud, SW Switzerland 46°32′N 06°36′E
14 K12 **Renfrew** Ontario, SE Canada 45°28′N 76°44′W
96 I12 **Renfrew** cultural region SW Scotland, United Kingdom
168 L11 **Rengat** Sumatera, W Indonesia 0°26′S 102°38′E
153 W12 **Rengma Hills** ▲▲ NE India
62 H12 **Rengo** Libertador, C Chile 34°24′S 70°50′W
116 M12 **Reni** Odes'ka Oblast', SW Ukraine 45°30′N 28°18′E
80 F11 **Renk** Upper Nile, NE South Sudan 11°48′N 32°49′E
93 L19 **Renko** Etelä-Suomi, S Finland 60°52′N 24°16′E
98 L12 **Renkum** Gelderland, SE Netherlands 51°58′N 05°43′E
182 K9 **Renmark** South Australia 34°12′S 140°43′E
186 L10 **Rennell** var. Mu Nggava. island S Solomon Islands
186 M9 **Rennell and Bellona** prev. Central. ◈ province S Solomon Islands
181 Q4 **Renner Springs Roadhouse** Northern Territory, N Australia 18°12′S 133°48′E
102 I6 **Rennes** Bret. Roazon; anc. Condate. Ille-et-Vilaine, NW France 48°08′N 01°40′W
195 S16 **Rennick Glacier** glacier Antarctica
11 Y16 **Rennie** Manitoba, S Canada 49°51′N 95°28′W
35 Q5 **Reno** Nevada, W USA 39°32′N 119°49′W
106 H10 **Reno** ≈ N Italy
35 Q5 **Reno-Cannon** ✈ Nevada, W USA 39°26′N 119°42′W
83 F24 **Renoster** ≈ SW South Africa
15 T5 **Renouard, Lac** ◎ Québec, SE Canada
18 F13 **Renovo** Pennsylvania, NE USA 41°19′N 77°42′W
161 O3 **Renqiu** Hebei, E China 38°49′N 116°02′E
160 I9 **Renshou** Sichuan, C China 30°02′N 104°09′E
31 N12 **Rensselaer** Indiana, N USA 40°57′N 87°09′W
18 L11 **Rensselaer** New York, NE USA 42°38′N 73°44′W
Rentería see Errenteria
115 E17 **Rentína** var. Rendina. Thessalía, C Greece 39°04′N 21°58′E
29 T9 **Renville** Minnesota, N USA 44°48′N 95°13′W
77 O13 **Réo** W Burkina 12°20′N 02°28′W
15 O12 **Repentigny** Québec, SE Canada 45°42′N 73°28′W
146 K13 **Repetek** Lebap Welaýaty, E Turkmenistan 38°40′N 63°12′E
93 J16 **Replot** Fin. Raippaluoto. island W Finland
Repola see Reboly
Reppen see Rzepin
Reps see Rupea
27 T7 **Republic** Missouri, C USA 37°07′N 93°28′W
32 K7 **Republic** Washington, NW USA 48°39′N 118°44′W
27 N3 **Republican River** ≈ Kansas/Nebraska, C USA
9 O7 **Repulse Bay** Northwest Terretories, N Canada 66°35′N 86°20′W
56 F9 **Requena** Loreto, NE Peru 05°05′S 73°52′W
105 R10 **Requena** Valenciana, E Spain 39°29′N 01°08′W
103 O14 **Réquista** Aveyron, S France 44°00′N 02°31′E
136 M12 **Reşadiye** Tokat, N Turkey 40°24′N 37°19′E
Reschenpass see Resia, Passo di
Reschitza see Reşiţa
113 N20 **Resen** Turk. Resne. SW FYR Macedonia 41°07′N 21°00′E
60 J11 **Reserva** Paraná, S Brazil 24°40′S 50°52′W
11 V15 **Reserve** Saskatchewan, S Canada 52°24′N 102°37′W
37 P13 **Reserve** New Mexico, SW USA 33°42′N 108°45′W
Reshetilovka see Reshetylivka
117 S6 **Reshetylivka** Rus. Reshetilovka. Poltavs'ka Oblast', NE Ukraine 49°34′N 34°05′E
Resht see Rasht
106 F5 **Resia, Passo di** Ger. Reschenpass. pass Austria/Italy
Resicabánya see Reşiţa
62 N7 **Resistencia** Chaco, NE Argentina 27°27′S 58°56′W
116 F12 **Reşiţa** Ger. Reschitza, Hung. Resicabánya. Caraş-Severin, W Romania 45°14′N 21°58′E
Resne see Resen
197 N9 **Resolute** Inuit Qausuittuq. Cornwallis Island, Nunavut, N Canada 74°41′N 94°54′W
Resolution see Fort Resolution
9 T7 **Resolution Island** island Nunavut, NE Canada
185 A23 **Resolution Island** island SW New Zealand
15 W7 **Restigouche** Québec, SE Canada 48°02′N 66°42′W
11 W17 **Reston** Manitoba, S Canada 49°33′N 101°03′W
14 H11 **Restoule Lake** ◎ Ontario, S Canada
54 F10 **Restrepo** Meta, C Colombia 04°20′N 73°29′W
42 B6 **Retalhuleu** Retalhuleu, SW Guatemala 14°31′N 91°40′W
42 A1 **Retalhuleu** off. Departamento de Retalhuleu. ◈ department SW Guatemala
Retalhuleu, Departamento de see Retalhuleu
97 N18 **Retford** C England, United Kingdom 53°18′N 00°52′W
103 Q3 **Rethel** Ardennes, N France 49°31′N 04°22′E
Rethimno/Réthimnon see Réthymno
115 I25 **Réthymno** prev. Rethimno, Réthimnon. Kríti, Greece, E Mediterranean Sea 35°21′N 24°29′E
Retiche, Alpi see Rhaetian Alps
99 J16 **Retie** Antwerpen, N Belgium 51°18′N 05°05′E
111 J21 **Rétság** Nógrád, N Hungary 47°57′N 19°08′E
109 W2 **Retz** Niederösterreich, NE Austria 48°46′N 15°58′E
173 N15 **Réunion** off. La Réunion. ◇ French overseas department W Indian Ocean
128 L17 **Réunion** island W Indian Ocean
105 U6 **Reus** Cataluña, E Spain 41°10′N 01°06′E
108 F7 **Reuss** ≈ NW Switzerland
99 J15 **Reusel** Noord-Brabant, S Netherlands 51°21′N 05°10′E
Reuţel see Ciuhuru
101 H22 **Reutlingen** Baden-Württemberg, S Germany 48°30′N 09°13′E
108 L7 **Reutte** Tirol, W Austria 47°30′N 10°44′E
99 M16 **Reuver** Limburg, SE Netherlands 51°17′N 06°05′E
28 K7 **Reva** South Dakota, N USA 45°30′N 103°03′W
Reval/Revel see Tallinn
124 J4 **Revda** Murmanskaya Oblast', NW Russian Federation 67°57′N 34°29′E
122 F6 **Revda** Sverdlovskaya Oblast', C Russian Federation 56°48′N 59°42′E
103 N16 **Revel** Haute-Garonne, S France 43°27′N 01°59′E
11 O16 **Revelstoke** British Columbia, SW Canada 51°02′N 118°12′W
43 N13 **Reventazón, Río** ≈ E Costa Rica
106 G9 **Revere** Lombardia, N Italy 45°03′N 11°07′E
39 Y14 **Revillagigedo Island** island Alexander Archipelago, Alaska, USA
193 R7 **Revillagigedo Islands** Mexico
103 R3 **Revin** Ardennes, N France 49°57′N 04°39′E
92 O3 **Revnosa** headland C Svalbard 78°03′N 18°52′E
Revolyutsii, Pik see Revolyutsiya, Qullai
147 T13 **Revolyutsiya, Qullai** Rus. Pik Revolyutsii. ▲ SE Tajikistan 38°40′N 72°26′E
111 L19 **Revúca** Ger. Grossrauschenbach, Hung. Nagyrőce. Banskobystrický Kraj, C Slovakia 48°40′N 20°10′E
154 K9 **Rewa** Madhya Pradesh, C India 24°32′N 81°18′E
152 I11 **Rewāri** Haryāna, N India 28°14′N 76°38′E
33 R14 **Rexburg** Idaho, NW USA 43°49′N 111°47′W
78 G13 **Rey Bouba** Nord, NE Cameroon 08°40′N 14°11′E
92 L3 **Reydharfjördhur** Austurland, E Iceland 65°02′N 14°12′W
57 K16 **Reyes** El Beni, NW Bolivia 14°17′S 67°18′W
34 L8 **Reyes, Point** headland California, W USA 37°59′N 123°01′W
54 B12 **Reyes, Punta** headland SW Colombia 02°44′N 78°08′W
136 L17 **Reyhanlı** Hatay, S Turkey 36°16′N 36°35′E
43 U16 **Rey, Isla del** island Archipiélago de las Perlas, SE Panama
92 H2 **Reykhólar** Vestfirdhir, W Iceland 65°28′N 22°12′W
92 K2 **Reykjahlídh** Nordhurland Eystra, NE Iceland 65°37′N 16°54′W
197 O16 **Reykjanes Basin** var. Irminger Basin. undersea feature N Atlantic Ocean 62°30′N 33°30′W
197 N17 **Reykjanes Ridge** undersea feature N Atlantic Ocean 62°00′N 27°00′W
92 H4 **Reykjavík** var. Reikjavik. ● (Iceland) Höfudhborgarsvaedhi, W Iceland 64°08′N 21°54′W
18 D13 **Reynoldsville** Pennsylvania, NE USA 41°04′N 78°51′W
41 P8 **Reynosa** Tamaulipas, C Mexico 26°03′N 98°19′W
Reẕā'īyeh see Orūmīyeh
Reẕā'īyeh, Daryācheh-ye see Orūmīyeh, Daryācheh-ye
102 I8 **Rezé** Loire-Atlantique, NW France 47°10′N 01°36′W
118 K10 **Rēzekne** Ger. Rositten; prev. Rus. Rezhitsa. SE Latvia 56°31′N 27°22′E
Rezhitsa see Rēzekne
117 N9 **Rezina** NE Moldova 47°44′N 28°58′E
114 N11 **Rezovo** Turk. Rezve. Burgas, E Bulgaria 42°00′N 28°00′E
114 N11 **Rezovska Reka** Turk. Rezve Deresi. ≈ Bulgaria/Turkey see also Rezve Deresi
Rezovska Reka see Rezve Deresi
Rezve see Rezovo
114 N11 **Rezve Deresi** Bul. Rezovska Reka. ≈ Bulgaria/Turkey see also Rezovska Reka
Rezve Deresi see Rezovska Reka
Rhadames see Ghadāmis
Rhaedestus see Tekirdağ
108 J10 **Rhaetian Alps** Fr. Alpes Rhétiques, Ger. Rätische Alpen, It. Alpi Retiche. ▲▲ C Europe
108 I8 **Rhätikon** ▲▲ C Europe
101 G14 **Rheda-Wiedenbrück** Nordrhein-Westfalen, W Germany 51°51′N 08°17′E
98 M12 **Rheden** Gelderland, E Netherlands 52°01′N 06°03′E
Rhegion/Rhegium see Reggio di Calabria
Rheims see Reims
Rhein see Rhine
101 E17 **Rheinbach** Nordrhein-Westfalen, W Germany 50°37′N 06°57′E
100 F13 **Rheine** var. Rheine in Westfalen. Nordrhein-Westfalen, NW Germany 52°17′N 07°27′E
Rheine in Westfalen see Rheine
Rheinfeld see Rheinfelden
101 F24 **Rheinfelden** Baden-Württemberg, S Germany 47°34′N 07°46′E
108 E6 **Rheinfelden** var. Rheinfeld. Aargau, N Switzerland 47°33′N 07°47′E
101 E17 **Rheinisches Schiefergebirge** var. Rhine State Uplands, Eng. Rhenish Slate Mountains. ▲▲ W Germany
101 D18 **Rheinland-Pfalz** Eng. Rhineland-Palatinate, Fr. Rhénanie-Palatinat. ◈ state W Germany
101 G18 **Rhein Main** ✈ (Frankfurt am Main) Hessen, W Germany 50°03′N 08°33′E
Rhénanie du Nord-Westphalie see Nordrhein-Westfalen
Rhénanie-Palatinat see Rheinland-Pfalz
98 K12 **Rhenen** Utrecht, C Netherlands 52°01′N 06°02′E
Rhenish Slate Mountains see Rheinisches Schiefergebirge
Rhétiques, Alpes see Rhaetian Alps
100 N10 **Rhin** ≈ NE Germany
Rhin see Rhine
84 F10 **Rhine** Dut. Rijn, Fr. Rhin, Ger. Rhein. ≈ W Europe
30 L5 **Rhinelander** Wisconsin, N USA 45°39′N 89°23′W
Rhineland-Palatinate see Rheinland-Pfalz
Rhine State Uplands see Rheinisches Schiefergebirge
100 N11 **Rhinkanal** canal NE Germany
81 F17 **Rhino Camp** NW Uganda 02°58′N 31°24′E
74 D7 **Rhir, Cap** headland W Morocco 30°40′N 09°54′W
106 D7 **Rho** Lombardia, N Italy 45°32′N 09°02′E
19 N12 **Rhode Island** off. State of Rhode Island and Providence Plantations, also known as Little Rhody, Ocean State. ◈ state NE USA
19 O13 **Rhode Island** island Rhode Island, NE USA
19 O13 **Rhode Island Sound** sound Maine/Rhode Island, NE USA
Rhodes see Ródos
Rhode-Saint-Genèse see Sint-Genesius-Rode
84 L14 **Rhodes Basin** undersea feature E Mediterranean Sea 35°55′N 28°30′E
Rhodesia see Zimbabwe
114 I12 **Rhodope Mountains** var. Rodhópi Óri, Bul. Rhodope Planina, Rodopi, Gk. Orosirá Rodhópis, Turk. Dospad Dagh. ▲▲ Bulgaria/Greece
Rhodope Planina see Rhodope Mountains
101 I18 **Rhön** ▲▲ C Germany
103 Q10 **Rhône** ◈ department E France
86 C12 **Rhône** ≈ France/Switzerland
103 R12 **Rhône-Alpes** ◈ region E France
98 G13 **Rhoon** Zuid-Holland, SW Netherlands 51°52′N 04°25′E
96 G9 **Rhum** var. Rum. island W Scotland, United Kingdom
Rhuthun see Ruthin
97 J18 **Rhyl** NE Wales, United Kingdom 53°19′N 03°28′W
59 K18 **Rialma** Goiás, S Brazil 15°22′S 49°35′W
104 L3 **Riaño** Castilla y León, N Spain 42°59′N 05°00′W
105 O9 **Riansáres** ≈ C Spain
152 H6 **Riāsi** Jammu and Kashmir, NW India 33°03′N 74°51′E
168 K10 **Riau** off. Propinsi Riau. ◈ province W Indonesia
Riau Archipelago see Riau, Kepulauan
168 M11 **Riau, Kepulauan** var. Riau Archipelago, Dut. Riouw-Archipel. island group W Indonesia
Riau, Propinsi see Riau
105 O6 **Riaza** Castilla y León, N Spain 41°17′N 03°29′W
105 N6 **Riaza** ≈ N Spain
81 K17 **Riba** spring/well NE Kenya 01°56′N 40°38′E
104 H4 **Ribadavia** Galicia, NW Spain 42°17′N 08°08′W
104 J2 **Ribadeo** Galicia, NW Spain 43°32′N 07°04′W
104 L2 **Ribadesella** var. Ribeseya. Asturias, N Spain 43°27′N 05°04′W
104 G10 **Ribatejo** former province C Portugal
83 P15 **Ribáuè** Nampula, N Mozambique 14°56′S 38°19′E
97 K17 **Ribble** ≈ NW England, United Kingdom
95 F23 **Ribe** Syddtjylland, W Denmark 55°20′N 08°47′E
Ribeira see Sanata Uxía de Ribeira
64 O5 **Ribeira Brava** Madeira, Portugal, NE Atlantic Ocean 32°39′N 17°04′W
64 P3 **Ribeira Grande** São Miguel, Azores, Portugal, NE Atlantic Ocean 37°34′N 25°32′W
60 L8 **Ribeirão Preto** São Paulo, S Brazil 21°09′S 47°48′W
60 L11 **Ribeira, Rio** ≈ S Brazil
107 I24 **Ribera** Sicilia, Italy, C Mediterranean Sea 37°31′N 13°16′E
57 L14 **Riberalta** El Beni, N Bolivia 11°01′S 66°04′W
105 W4 **Ribes de Freser** Cataluña, NE Spain 42°18′N 02°11′E
Ribeseya see Ribadesella
30 L6 **Rib Mountain** ▲ Wisconsin, N USA 44°55′N 89°41′W
109 U12 **Ribnica** Ger. Reifnitz. S Slovenia 45°46′N 14°40′E
117 N9 **Rîbniţa** var. Râbniţa, Rus. Rybnitsa. NE Moldova 47°46′N 29°01′E
100 M8 **Ribnitz-Damgarten** Mecklenburg-Vorpommern, NE Germany 54°14′N 12°25′E
111 D16 **Říčany** Ger. Ritschan. Středočesky Kraj, W Czech Republic 49°59′N 14°40′E
29 U7 **Rice** Minnesota, N USA 45°42′N 94°10′W
30 J5 **Rice Lake** Wisconsin, N USA 45°33′N 91°43′W
14 E8 **Rice Lake** ◎ Ontario, S Canada
14 I15 **Rice Lake** ◎ Ontario, SE Canada
23 V3 **Richard B. Russell Lake** ⊠ Georgia, SE USA
25 U6 **Richardson** Texas, SW USA 32°55′N 96°44′W
11 R11 **Richardson** ≈ Alberta, C Canada
10 I3 **Richardson Mountains** ▲▲ Yukon Territory, NW Canada
185 C21 **Richardson Mountains** ▲▲ South Island, New Zealand
42 F3 **Richardson Peak** ▲ SE Belize 16°34′N 88°46′W
76 G10 **Richard Toll** N Senegal 16°28′N 15°44′W
28 L5 **Richardton** North Dakota, N USA 46°52′N 102°19′W
14 F13 **Rich, Cape** headland Ontario, S Canada 44°42′N 80°37′W
102 L8 **Richelieu** Indre-et-Loire, C France 47°01′N 00°18′E
33 P15 **Richfield** Idaho, NW USA 43°03′N 114°11′W
36 K5 **Richfield** Utah, W USA 38°45′N 112°05′W
18 J10 **Richfield Springs** New York, NE USA 42°52′N 74°57′W
18 M6 **Richford** Vermont, NE USA 44°59′N 72°37′W
27 R6 **Rich Hill** Missouri, C USA 38°06′N 94°22′W
13 P14 **Richibucto** New Brunswick, SE Canada 46°42′N 64°54′W
108 G8 **Richisau** Glarus, NE Switzerland 47°00′N 08°54′E
23 S6 **Richland** Georgia, SE USA 32°05′N 84°40′W
27 U6 **Richland** Missouri, C USA 37°51′N 92°24′W
25 U8 **Richland** Texas, SW USA 31°55′N 96°25′W
32 K10 **Richland** Washington, NW USA 46°17′N 119°16′W
30 K8 **Richland Center** Wisconsin, N USA 43°22′N 90°24′W
21 W11 **Richlands** North Carolina, SE USA 34°52′N 77°33′W
21 Q7 **Richlands** Virginia, NE USA 37°05′N 81°47′W
25 R9 **Richland Springs** Texas, SW USA 31°16′N 98°56′W
183 S8 **Richmond** New South Wales, SE Australia 33°36′S 150°44′E
10 L17 **Richmond** British Columbia, SW Canada 49°07′N 123°09′W
14 L13 **Richmond** Ontario, SE Canada 45°12′N 75°49′W
15 Q12 **Richmond** Québec, SE Canada 45°39′N 72°07′W
185 I14 **Richmond** Tasman, South Island, New Zealand 41°25′S 173°04′E
35 N8 **Richmond** California, W USA 37°57′N 122°22′W
31 Q14 **Richmond** Indiana, N USA 39°50′N 84°51′W
20 M6 **Richmond** Kentucky, S USA 37°45′N 84°19′W
27 S4 **Richmond** Missouri, C USA 39°15′N 93°59′W
25 V11 **Richmond** Texas, SW USA 29°36′N 95°48′W
36 L1 **Richmond** Utah, W USA 41°55′N 111°51′W
21 W6 **Richmond** state capital Virginia, NE USA 37°33′N 77°28′W
14 H15 **Richmond Hill** Ontario, S Canada 43°51′N 79°24′W
185 J15 **Richmond Range** ▲▲ South Island, New Zealand
27 S12 **Rich Mountain** ▲ Arkansas, C USA 34°37′N 94°17′W
31 S13 **Richwood** Ohio, N USA 40°25′N 83°18′W
21 R5 **Richwood** West Virginia, NE USA 38°13′N 80°31′W
104 K5 **Ricobayo, Embalse de** ⊠ NW Spain
Ricomagus see Riom
Ridā' see Radā'
127 T5 **Ridder** Respublika Tatarstan, W Russian Federation 54°34′N 52°27′E
98 H13 **Ridderkerk** Zuid-Holland, SW Netherlands 51°52′N 04°35′E
33 N16 **Riddle** Idaho, NW USA 42°07′N 116°09′W
32 F14 **Riddle** Oregon, NW USA 42°57′N 123°21′W
14 L13 **Rideau** ≈ Ontario, SE Canada
35 T12 **Ridgecrest** California, W USA 35°37′N 117°40′W
18 L13 **Ridgefield** Connecticut, NE USA 41°16′N 73°30′W
22 K5 **Ridgeland** Mississippi, S USA 32°25′N 90°07′W
21 R15 **Ridgeland** South Carolina, SE USA 32°30′N 80°59′W
20 F8 **Ridgely** Tennessee, S USA 36°15′N 89°29′W
14 D17 **Ridgetown** Ontario, S Canada 42°27′N 81°52′W
21 R12 **Ridgeway** South Carolina, SE USA 34°17′N 80°56′W
Ridgeway see Ridgway
18 D13 **Ridgway** var. Ridgeway. Pennsylvania, NE USA 41°24′N 78°40′W
11 W16 **Riding Mountain** ▲▲ Manitoba, S Canada
Ried see Ried im Innkreis
109 R4 **Ried im Innkreis** var. Ried. Oberösterreich, NW Austria 48°13′N 13°29′E
109 X8 **Riegersburg** Steiermark, SE Austria 47°03′N 15°52′E
108 E6 **Riehen** Basel-Stadt, NW Switzerland 47°35′N 07°39′E
92 J9 **Riehppegáisá** var. Rieppe. ▲ N Norway 69°38′N 21°31′E
99 K18 **Riemst** Limburg, NE Belgium 50°49′N 05°36′E
Rieppe see Riehppegáisá
101 O15 **Riesa** Sachsen, E Germany 51°18′N 13°18′E
63 H24 **Riesco, Isla** island S Chile
107 K25 **Riesi** Sicilia, Italy, C Mediterranean Sea 37°17′N 14°05′E
83 F25 **Riet** ≈ SW South Africa
83 I23 **Riet** ≈ SW South Africa
118 D11 **Rietavas** Telšiai, W Lithuania 55°43′N 21°56′E
83 F19 **Rietfontein** Omaheke, E Namibia 21°58′S 20°58′E
107 I14 **Rieti** anc. Reate. Lazio, C Italy 42°24′N 12°51′E
84 D14 **Rif** var. Riff, Er Rif, Er Riff. ▲▲ N Morocco
138 I8 **Rīf Dimashq** off. Muḩāfaẓat Dimashq, var. Damascus, Ar. Ash Sham, Ash Shām, Damasco, Esh Sham, Fr. Damas. ◈ governorate S Syria
Riff see Rif
37 Q4 **Rifle** Colorado, C USA 39°30′N 107°46′W
31 R7 **Rifle River** ≈ Michigan, N USA
81 H18 **Rift Valley** ◈ province Kenya
Rift Valley see Great Rift Valley
118 F9 **Rīga** Eng. Riga. ● C Latvia 56°57′N 24°08′E
Rigaer Bucht see Riga, Gulf of
118 F6 **Riga, Gulf of** Est. Liivi Laht, Ger. Rigaer Bucht, Latv. Rīgas Jūras Līcis, Rus. Rizhskiy Zaliv; prev. Est. Riia Laht. gulf Estonia/Latvia
Rīgas Jūras Līcis see Riga, Gulf of
15 N12 **Rigaud** ≈ Ontario/Québec, SE Canada
33 R14 **Rigby** Idaho, NW USA 43°40′N 111°54′W
Rīgestān see Rēgestān
32 M11 **Riggins** Idaho, NW USA 45°24′N 116°18′W
13 R8 **Rigolet** Newfoundland and Labrador, NE Canada 51°10′N 58°25′W
78 G9 **Rig-Rig** Kanem, W Chad 14°16′N 14°21′E
118 F4 **Riguldi** Läänemaa, W Estonia 59°07′N 23°34′E
Riia Laht see Riga, Gulf of
93 L19 **Riihimäki** Etelä-Suomi, S Finland 60°45′N 24°45′E
195 U2 **Riiser-Larsen Peninsula** peninsula Antarctica
65 P22 **Riiser-Larsen Sea** sea Antarctica
Riisser Larsen Ice Shelf see Riiser-Larsenisen
40 D2 **Riíto** Sonora, NW Mexico 32°06′N 114°57′W
112 B9 **Rijeka** Ger. Sankt Veit am Flaum, It. Fiume, Slvn. Reka; anc. Tarsatica. Primorje-Gorski Kotar, NW Croatia 45°20′N 14°26′E
99 I14 **Rijen** Noord-Brabant, S Netherlands 51°35′N 04°55′E
99 H15 **Rijkevorsel** Antwerpen, N Belgium 51°23′N 04°43′E
Rijn see Rhine
98 G11 **Rijnsburg** Zuid-Holland, W Netherlands 52°12′N 04°27′E
Rijssel see Lille
98 N10 **Rijssen** Overijssel, E Netherlands 52°19′N 06°30′E
98 G12 **Rijswijk** Eng. Ryswick. Zuid-Holland, W Netherlands 52°03′N 04°20′E
92 I10 **Riksgränsen** Norrbotten, N Sweden 68°24′N 18°15′E
165 U4 **Rikubetsu** Hokkaidō, NE Japan 43°30′N 143°43′E
165 R9 **Rikuzen-Takata** Iwate, Honshū, C Japan 39°03′N 141°38′E
27 O4 **Riley** Kansas, C USA 39°18′N 96°49′W
99 I17 **Rillaar** Vlaams Brabant, C Belgium 50°58′N 04°58′E
Rí, Loch see Ree, Lough
114 G11 **Rilska Reka** ≈ W Bulgaria
77 T12 **Rima** ≈ N Nigeria
141 N7 **Rimah, Wādī ar** var. Wādī ar Rummah. dry watercourse C Saudi Arabia
Rimaszombat see Rimavská Sobota
191 R12 **Rimatara** island Îles Australes, SW French Polynesia
111 L20 **Rimavská Sobota** Ger. Gross-Steffelsdorf, Hung. Rimaszombat. Bankobystrický Kraj, C Slovakia 48°24′N 20°01′E
11 Q15 **Rimbey** Alberta, SW Canada 52°39′N 114°10′W
95 P15 **Rimbo** Stockholm, C Sweden 59°44′N 18°21′E
95 M18 **Rimforsa** Östergötland, S Sweden 58°06′N 15°40′E
106 I11 **Rimini** anc. Ariminum. Emilia-Romagna, N Italy 44°03′N 12°33′E
Rîmnicu-Sărat see Râmnicu Sărat
Rîmnicu Vîlcea see Râmnicu Vâlcea
149 Y3 **Rimo Muztāgh** ▲▲ India/Pakistan
15 U7 **Rimouski** Québec, SE Canada 48°26′N 68°32′W
158 M16 **Rinbung** Xizang Zizhiqu, W China 29°15′N 89°40′E
Rinchinlhumbe see Dzöölön
62 I5 **Rincón, Cerro** ▲ N Chile 24°01′S 67°19′W
104 M15 **Rincón de la Victoria** Andalucía, S Spain 36°43′N 04°18′W
Rincón del Bonete, Lago Artificial de see Río Negro, Embalse del
105 Q4 **Rincón de Soto** La Rioja, N Spain 42°15′N 01°50′W
94 G8 **Rindal** Møre og Romsdal, S Norway 63°02′N 09°09′E
115 J20 **Ríneia** island Kykládes, Greece, Aegean Sea
152 H11 **Rīngas** prev. Reengus, Rīngus. Rājasthān, N India 27°18′N 75°27′E
95 H24 **Ringe** Syddtjylland, C Denmark 55°14′N 10°30′E
94 H11 **Ringebu** Oppland, S Norway 61°31′N 10°09′E
Ringen see Rõngu
186 K8 **Ringgi** Kolombangara, NW Solomon Islands 08°03′S 157°08′E
23 R1 **Ringgold** Georgia, SE USA 34°55′N 85°06′W
22 G5 **Ringgold** Louisiana, S USA 32°19′N 93°16′W
25 S5 **Ringgold** Texas, SW USA 33°47′N 97°56′W
95 E22 **Ringkøbing** Midtjylland, W Denmark 56°04′N 08°22′E
95 E22 **Ringkøbing Fjord** fjord W Denmark
33 S10 **Ringling** Montana, NW USA 46°15′N 110°48′W
27 N13 **Ringling** Oklahoma, C USA 34°12′N 97°35′W
94 H13 **Ringsaker** Hedmark, S Norway 60°54′N 10°45′E
95 I23 **Ringsted** Sjælland, E Denmark 55°28′N 11°48′E
Rīngus see Rīngas
92 I9 **Ringvassøya** Lapp. Ráneš. island N Norway
18 K13 **Ringwood** New Jersey, NE USA 41°06′N 74°15′W
Rinn Duáin see Hook Head
100 H13 **Rinteln** Niedersachsen, NW Germany 52°10′N 09°04′E
115 E18 **Río** Dytikí Elláda, S Greece 38°18′N 21°48′E
Rio see Rio de Janeiro
56 C7 **Riobamba** Chimborazo, C Ecuador 01°44′S 78°40′W
60 P9 **Rio Bonito** Rio de Janeiro, SE Brazil 22°42′S 42°38′W
59 C16 **Rio Branco** state capital Acre, W Brazil 09°59′S 67°49′W
61 H18 **Río Branco** Cerro Largo, NE Uruguay 32°32′S 53°28′W
Rio Branco, Território de see Roraima
41 P8 **Río Bravo** Tamaulipas, C Mexico 25°57′N 98°03′W
63 G16 **Río Bueno** Los Ríos, C Chile 40°20′S 72°55′W
55 P5 **Río Caribe** Sucre, NE Venezuela 10°43′N 63°06′W
54 M5 **Río Chico** Miranda, N Venezuela 10°18′N 66°00′W
63 H18 **Río Cisnes** Aisén, S Chile 44°29′S 71°15′W
60 L9 **Rio Claro** São Paulo, S Brazil 22°19′S 47°35′W
45 V14 **Rio Claro** Trinidad, Trinidad and Tobago 10°18′N 61°11′W
54 J5 **Río Claro** Lara, N Venezuela 09°54′N 69°23′W
63 K15 **Rio Colorado** Río Negro, E Argentina 39°01′S 64°05′W
62 K11 **Río Cuarto** Córdoba, C Argentina 33°06′S 64°20′W
60 P10 **Rio de Janeiro** var. Rio. state capital Rio de Janeiro, SE Brazil 22°53′S 43°17′W
60 P9 **Rio de Janeiro** off. Estado do Rio de Janeiro. ◈ state SE Brazil
Rio de Janeiro, Estado do see Rio de Janeiro
43 R17 **Río de Jesús** Veraguas, S Panama 07°58′N 81°01′W
34 K3 **Rio Dell** California, W USA 40°30′N 124°07′W
60 K13 **Rio do Sul** Santa Catarina, S Brazil 27°15′S 49°37′W
63 I23 **Río Gallegos** var. Gallegos, Puerto Gallegos. Santa Cruz, S Argentina 51°40′S 69°21′W
63 J24 **Río Grande** Tierra del Fuego, S Argentina 53°45′S 67°46′W
61 I18 **Rio Grande** var. São Pedro do Rio Grande do Sul. Rio Grande do Sul, S Brazil 32°03′S 52°08′W
40 L10 **Río Grande** Zacatecas, C Mexico 23°50′N 103°20′W
42 J9 **Río Grande** León, NW Nicaragua 12°59′N 86°34′W
45 V5 **Río Grande** E Puerto Rico 18°23′N 65°51′W
24 I9 **Rio Grande** ≈ Texas, SW USA
25 R17 **Rio Grande City** Texas, SW USA 26°24′N 98°50′W
59 P14 **Rio Grande do Norte** off. Estado do Rio Grande do Norte. ◈ state E Brazil
Rio Grande do Norte, Estado do see Rio Grande do Norte
61 G15 **Rio Grande do Sul** off. Estado do Rio Grande do Sul. ◈ state S Brazil
Rio Grande do Sul, Estado do see Rio Grande do Sul
65 M17 **Rio Grande Fracture Zone** tectonic feature C Atlantic Ocean
65 J18 **Rio Grande Gap** undersea feature S Atlantic Ocean
Rio Grande Plateau see Rio Grande Rise
65 J18 **Rio Grande Rise** var. Rio Grande Plateau. undersea feature SW Atlantic Ocean 31°00′S 35°00′W
54 G4 **Ríohacha** La Guajira, N Colombia 11°23′N 72°47′W
43 S16 **Río Hato** Coclé, C Panama 08°21′N 80°10′W
25 T17 **Rio Hondo** Texas, SW USA 26°14′N 97°34′W
56 D10 **Rioja** San Martín, N Peru 06°02′S 77°10′W
41 Y11 **Río Lagartos** Yucatán, SE Mexico 21°35′N 88°08′W
103 P11 **Riom** anc. Ricomagus. Puy-de-Dôme, C France 45°54′N 03°06′E
104 F10 **Rio Maior** Santarém, C Portugal 39°20′N 08°55′W
103 O12 **Riom-ès-Montagnes** Cantal, C France 45°15′N 02°39′E
60 J12 **Rio Negro** Paraná, S Brazil 26°06′S 49°46′W
63 I15 **Río Negro** off. Provincia de Río Negro. ◈ province C Argentina
61 D18 **Río Negro** ◈ department W Uruguay
47 V12 **Río Negro, Embalse del** var. Lago Artificial de Rincón del Bonete. ⊠ C Uruguay
Río Negro, Provincia de see Río Negro
107 M17 **Rionero in Vulture** Basilicata, S Italy 40°55′N 15°40′E
137 S9 **Rioni** ≈ W Georgia
105 P12 **Riópar** Castilla-La Mancha, C Spain 38°31′N 02°27′W
61 H16 **Rio Pardo** Rio Grande do Sul, S Brazil 29°41′S 52°25′W
37 R11 **Rio Rancho Estates** New Mexico, SW USA 35°14′N 106°40′W
42 L11 **Río San Juan** ◈ department S Nicaragua
54 E9 **Ríosucio** Caldas, W Colombia 05°26′N 75°44′W
54 C7 **Ríosucio** Chocó, NW Colombia 07°25′N 77°05′W
62 K10 **Río Tercero** Córdoba, C Argentina 32°15′S 64°08′W
42 K5 **Río Tinto, Sierra** ▲▲ NE Honduras
54 J5 **Río Tocuyo** Lara, N Venezuela 10°18′N 70°00′W
Riouw-Archipel see Riau, Kepulauan
59 J19 **Rio Verde** Goiás, C Brazil 17°50′S 50°55′W
41 O12 **Río Verde** var. Rioverde. San Luis Potosí, C Mexico 21°58′N 100°W
Rioverde see Río Verde
35 O8 **Rio Vista** California, W USA 38°09′N 121°42′W
112 M11 **Ripanj** Serbia, N Serbia 44°37′N 20°30′E
106 J13 **Ripatransone** Marche, C Italy 43°00′N 13°45′E
22 M2 **Ripley** Mississippi, S USA 34°43′N 88°57′W
31 R15 **Ripley** Ohio, N USA 38°45′N 83°51′W
20 F9 **Ripley** Tennessee, S USA 35°43′N 89°30′W
21 Q4 **Ripley** West Virginia, NE USA 38°49′N 81°44′W

◆ Country
● Country Capital
◇ Dependent Territory
○ Dependent Territory Capital
◈ Administrative Regions
✈ International Airport
▲ Mountain
▲▲ Mountain Range
⁂ Volcano
≈ River
◎ Lake
⊠ Reservoir

105 W4 **Ripoll** Cataluña, NE Spain 42°12′N 02°12′E
97 M16 **Ripon** N England, United Kingdom 54°07′N 01°31′W
30 M7 **Ripon** Wisconsin, N USA 43°52′N 88°48′W
107 L24 **Riposto** Sicilia, Italy, C Mediterranean Sea 37°44′N 15°13′E
99 L14 **Rips** Noord-Brabant, SE Netherlands 51°31′N 05°49′E
54 D9 **Risaralda** *off.* Departamento de Risaralda. ◐ *province* C Colombia
Risaralda, Departamento de *see* Risaralda
116 L8 **Rîşcani** *var.* Răşcani, *Rus.* Ryshkany. NW Moldova 47°55′N 27°31′E
152 J9 **Rishikesh** Uttarakhand, N India 30°06′N 78°16′E
165 S1 **Rishiri-tō** *var.* Risiri Tô. *island* NE Japan
165 S1 **Rishiri-yama** ⛰ Rishiri-tō, NE Japan 45°11′N 141°11′E
25 R7 **Rising Star** Texas, SW USA 32°06′N 98°57′W
31 Q15 **Rising Sun** Indiana, N USA 38°58′N 84°53′W
Risiri Tô *see* Rishiri-tō
102 L4 **Risle** ↝ N France
Rîşno *see* Râşnov
27 V13 **Rison** Arkansas, C USA 33°58′N 92°11′W
95 G17 **Risør** Aust-Agder, S Norway 58°44′N 09°15′E
92 H10 **Risøyhamn** Nordland, C Norway 69°00′N 15°37′E
101 I23 **Riss** ↝ S Germany
118 G4 **Risti** *Ger.* Kreuz. Läänemaa, W Estonia 59°01′N 24°01′E
15 V8 **Ristigouche** ↝ Québec, SE Canada
93 N18 **Ristiina** Itä-Suomi, E Finland 61°32′N 27°15′E
93 N14 **Ristijärvi** Oulu, C Finland 64°30′N 28°15′E
188 C14 **Ritidian Point** *headland* N Guam 13°39′N 144°51′E
Ritschan *see* Říčany
35 R9 **Ritter, Mount** ▲ California, W USA 37°40′N 119°10′W
31 T12 **Rittman** Ohio, N USA 40°58′N 81°46′W
32 L9 **Ritzville** Washington, NW USA 47°07′N 118°22′W
Riva *see* Riva del Garda
61 A21 **Rivadavia** Buenos Aires, E Argentina 35°29′S 62°59′W
106 F7 **Riva del Garda** *var.* Riva. Trentino-Alto Adige, N Italy 45°54′N 10°50′E
106 B8 **Rivarolo Canavese** Piemonte, W Italy 45°21′N 07°42′E
42 K11 **Rivas** Rivas, SW Nicaragua 11°26′N 85°50′W
42 J11 **Rivas** ◐ *department* SW Nicaragua
103 R11 **Rive-de-Gier** Loire, E France 45°31′N 04°36′E
61 A22 **Rivera** Buenos Aires, E Argentina 37°13′S 63°14′W
61 F16 **Rivera** Rivera, NE Uruguay 30°54′S 55°31′W
61 F17 **Rivera** ◐ *department* NE Uruguay
35 P9 **Riverbank** California, W USA 37°43′N 120°59′W
76 K17 **River Cess** SW Liberia 05°28′N 09°32′W
28 M4 **Riverdale** North Dakota, N USA 47°29′N 101°22′W
30 I6 **River Falls** Wisconsin, N USA 44°52′N 92°38′W
11 T16 **Riverhurst** Saskatchewan, S Canada 50°52′N 106°49′W
183 O10 **Riverina** *physical region* New South Wales, SE Australia
80 G8 **River Nile** ◐ *state* NE Sudan
61 F19 **Rivero, Isla** *island* Archipiélago de los Chonos, S Chile
11 W16 **Rivers** Manitoba, S Canada 50°02′N 100°14′W
77 U17 **Rivers** ◐ *state* S Nigeria
185 D23 **Riversdale** Southland, South Island, New Zealand 45°54′S 168°44′E
83 F26 **Riversdale** Western Cape, SW South Africa 34°05′S 21°15′E
35 U15 **Riverside** California, W USA 33°58′N 117°25′W
25 W9 **Riverside** Texas, SW USA 30°51′N 95°24′W
37 U3 **Riverside Reservoir** ☐ Colorado, C USA
10 K15 **Rivers Inlet** British Columbia, SW Canada 51°43′N 127°19′W
10 K15 **Rivers Inlet** *inlet* British Columbia, SW Canada
11 X15 **Riverton** Manitoba, S Canada 51°00′N 97°00′W
185 C24 **Riverton** Southland, South Island, New Zealand 46°20′S 168°02′E
30 L13 **Riverton** Illinois, N USA 39°50′N 89°31′W
36 L3 **Riverton** Utah, W USA 40°32′N 111°57′W
33 V15 **Riverton** Wyoming, C USA 43°01′N 108°22′W
14 G10 **River Valley** Ontario, S Canada 46°36′N 80°09′W
13 P14 **Riverview** New Brunswick, SE Canada 46°03′N 64°47′W
103 O17 **Rivesaltes** Pyrénées-Orientales, S France 42°46′N 02°48′E
36 H11 **Riviera** Arizona, SW USA 35°06′N 114°36′W
25 S15 **Riviera** Texas, SW USA 27°15′N 97°48′W
23 Z14 **Riviera Beach** Florida, SE USA 26°46′N 80°03′W
15 Q10 **Rivière-à-Pierre** Québec, SE Canada 46°59′N 72°12′W
15 T9 **Rivière-Bleue** Québec, SE Canada 47°26′N 69°02′W
15 T8 **Rivière-du-Loup** Québec, SE Canada 47°49′N 69°32′W
173 Y15 **Rivière du Rempart** NE Mauritius 20°06′S 57°41′E
45 R12 **Rivière-Pilote** S Martinique 14°29′N 60°54′W
173 O17 **Rivière St-Etienne, Pointe de la** *headland* SW Réunion
13 S10 **Rivière-St-Paul** Québec, E Canada 51°26′N 57°52′W
Rivière Sèche *see* Bel Air
116 K4 **Rivne** *Pol.* Równe, *Rus.* Rovno. Rivnens'ka Oblast', NW Ukraine 50°37′N 26°16′E
Rivne *see* Rivnens'ka Oblast'
116 K3 **Rivnens'ka Oblast'** *var.* Rivne, *Rus.* Rovenskaya Oblast'. ◐ *province* NW Ukraine
106 B8 **Rivoli** Piemonte, NW Italy 45°04′N 07°31′E
159 Q14 **Riwoqê** *var.* Racaka. Xizang Zizhiqu, W China 31°10′N 96°25′E
99 H19 **Rixensart** Walloon Brabant, C Belgium 50°43′N 04°32′E
Riyadh/Riyāḍ, Minṭaqat ar *see* Ar Riyāḍ
Riyāq *see* Rayak
Rizaiyeh *see* Orūmīyeh
137 P11 **Rize** Rize, NE Turkey 41°03′N 40°33′E
137 P11 **Rize** *prev.* Çoruh. ◐ *province* NE Turkey
161 R5 **Rizhao** Shandong, E China 35°23′N 119°32′E
Rizhskiy Zaliv *see* Riga, Gulf of
Rizokarpaso/Rizokárpason *see* Dipkarpaz
107 O21 **Rizzuto, Capo** *headland* S Italy 38°54′N 17°05′E
95 F15 **Rjukan** Telemark, S Norway 59°54′N 08°33′E
95 D16 **Rjuven** ▲▲ S Norway
76 H9 **Rkiz** Trarza, W Mauritania 16°50′N 15°20′W
115 Q23 **Ro** *prev.* Ágios Geórgios. *island* SE Greece
95 H14 **Roa** Oppland, S Norway 60°16′N 10°38′E
105 N5 **Roa** Castilla y León, N Spain 41°42′N 03°55′W
45 T9 **Road Town** ○ (British Virgin Islands) Tortola, C British Virgin Islands 18°28′N 64°39′W
96 F6 **Roag, Loch** *inlet* NW Scotland, United Kingdom
37 O5 **Roan Cliffs** *cliff* Colorado/Utah, W USA
21 P9 **Roan High Knob** *var.* Roan Mountain. ▲ North Carolina/Tennessee, SE USA 36°09′N 82°07′W
Roan Mountain *see* Roan High Knob
103 Q10 **Roanne** *anc.* Rodunma. Loire, E France 46°03′N 04°04′E
23 R4 **Roanoke** Alabama, S USA 33°09′N 85°22′W
21 S7 **Roanoke** Virginia, NE USA 37°16′N 79°57′W
21 Z9 **Roanoke Island** *island* North Carolina, SE USA
21 W8 **Roanoke Rapids** North Carolina, SE USA 36°27′N 77°39′W
21 X9 **Roanoke River** ↝ North Carolina/Virginia, SE USA
37 O4 **Roan Plateau** *plain* Utah, W USA
37 R5 **Roaring Fork River** ↝ Colorado, C USA
25 O5 **Roaring Springs** Texas, SW USA 33°54′N 100°51′W
42 J4 **Roatán** *var.* Coxen Hole, Coxin Hole. Islas de la Bahía, N Honduras 16°19′N 86°33′W
42 I4 **Roatán, Isla de** *island* Islas de la Bahía, N Honduras
Roat Kampuchea *see* Cambodia
Roazon *see* Rennes
143 T7 **Robāṭ-e Chāh Gonbad** Yazd, E Iran 33°24′N 57°43′E
143 R7 **Robāṭ-e Khān** Yazd, C Iran 33°24′N 56°04′E
143 T7 **Robāṭ-e Khvosh Āb** Yazd, E Iran
143 R8 **Robāṭ-e Posht-e Bādām** Yazd, NE Iran 33°01′N 55°34′E
143 Q8 **Robāṭ-e Rīzāb** Yazd, C Iran
175 S8 **Robbie Ridge** *undersea feature* W Pacific Ocean
21 T10 **Robbins** North Carolina, SE USA 35°25′N 79°35′W
183 N15 **Robbins Island** *island* Tasmania, SE Australia
21 N10 **Robbinsville** North Carolina, SE USA 35°18′N 83°49′W
182 J12 **Robe** South Australia 37°11′S 139°48′E
21 W9 **Robersonville** North Carolina, SE USA 35°49′N 77°15′W
45 V10 **Robert L. Bradshaw** ✕ (Basseterre) Saint Kitts, Saint Kitts and Nevis 17°16′N 62°43′W
25 P8 **Robert Lee** Texas, SW USA 31°50′N 100°30′W
35 V5 **Roberts Creek Mountain** ▲ Nevada, W USA 39°52′N 116°16′W
93 J15 **Robertsfors** Västerbotten, N Sweden 64°12′N 20°50′E
27 R11 **Robert S. Kerr Reservoir** ☐ Oklahoma, C USA
38 L12 **Roberts Mountain** ▲ Nunivak Island, Alaska, USA 60°01′N 166°15′W
83 F26 **Robertson** Western Cape, SW South Africa 33°48′S 19°53′E
194 H4 **Robertson Island** *island* Antarctica
76 J16 **Robertsport** W Liberia 06°45′N 11°15′W
182 J8 **Robertstown** South Australia 34°00′S 139°04′E
Robert Williams *see* Caála
15 P7 **Roberval** Québec, SE Canada 48°31′N 72°16′W
31 N15 **Robinson** Illinois, N USA 39°00′N 87°44′W
193 U11 **Róbinson Crusoe, Isla** *island* Islas Juan Fernández, Chile, E Pacific Ocean
180 J9 **Robinson Range** ▲▲ Western Australia
182 M9 **Robinvale** Victoria, SE Australia 34°37′S 142°45′E
105 P11 **Robledo** Castilla-La Mancha, C Spain 38°45′N 02°27′W
54 G5 **Robles** *var.* La Paz, Robles La Paz. Cesar, N Colombia 10°24′N 73°11′W
Robles La Paz *see* Robles
11 V15 **Roblin** Manitoba, S Canada 51°15′N 101°20′W
11 S17 **Robsart** Saskatchewan, S Canada 49°22′N 109°15′W
11 N15 **Robson, Mount** ▲ British Columbia, SW Canada 53°09′N 119°16′W
25 T14 **Robstown** Texas, SW USA 27°47′N 97°40′W
25 P6 **Roby** Texas, SW USA 32°42′N 100°23′W
104 E11 **Roca, Cabo da** *cape* C Portugal
Rocadas *see* Xangongo
41 S14 **Roca Partida, Punta** *headland* C Mexico 18°43′N 95°11′W
47 X6 **Rocas, Atol das** *island* E Brazil
107 L18 **Roccadaspide** *var.* Rocca d'Aspide. Campania, S Italy 40°25′N 15°12′E
Rocca d'Aspide *see* Roccadaspide
107 K15 **Roccaraso** Abruzzo, C Italy 41°49′N 14°01′E
106 H10 **Rocca San Casciano** Emilia-Romagna, C Italy 44°06′N 11°51′E
106 G13 **Roccastrada** Toscana, C Italy 43°00′N 11°09′E
61 G20 **Rocha** Rocha, E Uruguay 34°30′S 54°22′W
61 G19 **Rocha** ◐ *department* E Uruguay
97 L17 **Rochdale** NW England, United Kingdom 53°38′N 02°09′W
102 L11 **Rochechouart** Haute-Vienne, C France 45°49′N 00°49′E
99 J22 **Rochefort** Namur, SE Belgium 50°10′N 05°13′E
102 J11 **Rochefort** *var.* Rochefort sur Mer. Charente-Maritime, W France 45°57′N 00°58′W
Rochefort sur Mer *see* Rochefort
125 N10 **Rochegda** Arkhangel'skaya Oblast', NW Russian Federation 62°37′N 43°21′E
30 L10 **Rochelle** Illinois, N USA 41°54′N 89°03′W
25 Q9 **Rochelle** Texas, SW USA 31°13′N 99°10′W
15 V3 **Rochers Ouest, Rivière aux** ↝ Québec, SE Canada
97 O22 **Rochester** *anc.* Durobrivae. SE England, United Kingdom 51°24′N 00°30′E
31 O12 **Rochester** Indiana, N USA 41°03′N 86°13′W
29 W10 **Rochester** Minnesota, N USA 44°01′N 92°28′W
19 O9 **Rochester** New Hampshire, NE USA 43°18′N 70°58′W
18 F9 **Rochester** New York, NE USA 43°09′N 77°37′W
25 P5 **Rochester** Texas, SW USA 33°19′N 99°51′W
31 S9 **Rochester Hills** Michigan, N USA 42°39′N 83°04′W
Rocheuses, Montagnes/Rockies *see* Rocky Mountains
64 M6 **Rockall** *island* N Atlantic Ocean, United Kingdom
64 L6 **Rockall Bank** *undersea feature* N Atlantic Ocean
84 B8 **Rockall Rise** *undersea feature* N Atlantic Ocean 59°00′N 14°00′W
84 C9 **Rockall Trough** *undersea feature* N Atlantic Ocean 57°00′N 12°00′W
35 U2 **Rock Creek** ↝ Nevada, W USA
25 T10 **Rockdale** Texas, SW USA 30°39′N 96°58′W
195 N12 **Rockefeller Plateau** *plateau* Antarctica
30 K11 **Rock Falls** Illinois, N USA 41°46′N 89°41′W
23 Q5 **Rockford** Alabama, S USA 32°53′N 86°11′W
30 L10 **Rockford** Illinois, N USA 42°16′N 89°06′W
15 Q12 **Rock Forest** Québec, SE Canada 45°21′N 71°58′W
11 T17 **Rockglen** Saskatchewan, S Canada 49°11′N 105°57′W
181 Y8 **Rockhampton** Queensland, E Australia 23°31′S 150°31′E
21 R11 **Rock Hill** South Carolina, SE USA 34°55′N 81°01′W
180 I13 **Rockingham** Western Australia 32°16′S 115°21′E
21 T11 **Rockingham** North Carolina, SE USA 34°56′N 79°47′W
30 J11 **Rock Island** Illinois, N USA 41°30′N 90°34′W
25 U12 **Rock Island** Texas, SW USA 29°31′N 96°33′W
14 C10 **Rock Lake** Ontario, S Canada 46°25′N 83°49′W
29 O2 **Rock Lake** North Dakota, N USA 48°45′N 99°12′W
14 I12 **Rock Lake** ◎ Ontario, SE Canada
14 M12 **Rockland** Ontario, SE Canada 45°33′N 75°16′W
19 R7 **Rockland** Maine, NE USA 44°08′N 69°06′W
182 L11 **Rocklands Reservoir** ☐ Victoria, SE Australia
35 O7 **Rocklin** California, W USA 38°48′N 121°13′W
23 R3 **Rockmart** Georgia, SE USA 34°00′N 85°02′W
31 N16 **Rockport** Indiana, N USA 37°53′N 87°04′W
27 Q1 **Rock Port** Missouri, C USA 40°26′N 95°30′W
25 T14 **Rockport** Texas, SW USA 28°02′N 97°04′W
32 I7 **Rockport** Washington, NW USA 48°28′N 121°36′W
29 S11 **Rock Rapids** Iowa, C USA 43°25′N 96°10′W
30 K11 **Rock River** ↝ Illinois/Wisconsin, N USA
44 I3 **Rock Sound** Eleuthera Island, C Bahamas 24°52′N 76°10′W
25 P11 **Rocksprings** Texas, SW USA 30°02′N 100°14′W
33 U17 **Rock Springs** Wyoming, C USA 41°35′N 109°12′W
55 T9 **Rockstone** C Guyana 05°58′N 58°33′W
29 S12 **Rock Valley** Iowa, C USA 43°12′N 96°17′W
31 N14 **Rockville** Indiana, N USA 39°45′N 87°15′W
21 W3 **Rockville** Maryland, NE USA 39°05′N 77°10′W
25 U6 **Rockwall** Texas, SW USA 32°56′N 96°27′W
29 U13 **Rockwell City** Iowa, C USA 42°24′N 94°37′W
31 S10 **Rockwood** Michigan, N USA 42°04′N 83°15′W
20 M9 **Rockwood** Tennessee, S USA 35°52′N 84°41′W
25 Q8 **Rockwood** Texas, SW USA 31°29′N 99°23′W
37 U6 **Rocky Ford** Colorado, C USA 38°03′N 103°45′W
14 D9 **Rocky Island Lake** ◎ Ontario, S Canada
21 V9 **Rocky Mount** North Carolina, SE USA 35°56′N 77°48′W
21 S7 **Rocky Mount** Virginia, NE USA 37°00′N 79°53′W
33 Q8 **Rocky Mountain** ▲ Montana, NW USA 47°45′N 112°46′W
11 P15 **Rocky Mountain House** Alberta, SW Canada 52°24′N 114°52′W
37 T3 **Rocky Mountain National Park** *national park* Colorado, C USA
2 E12 **Rocky Mountains** *var.* Rockies, *Fr.* Montagnes Rocheuses. ▲▲ Canada/USA
42 H1 **Rocky Point** *headland* NE Belize 18°21′N 88°04′W
83 A17 **Rocky Point** *headland* NW Namibia 19°01′S 12°27′E
95 F14 **Rødberg** Buskerud, S Norway 60°16′N 09°00′E
95 I25 **Rødby** Sjælland, SE Denmark 54°42′N 11°24′E
95 I25 **Rødbyhavn** Sjælland, SE Denmark 54°39′N 11°24′E
13 T10 **Roddickton** Newfoundland, Newfoundland and Labrador, SE Canada 50°51′N 56°03′W
95 F23 **Rødding** Syddanmark, SW Denmark 55°22′N 09°04′E
95 M22 **Rödeby** Blekinge, S Sweden 56°16′N 15°35′E
98 N6 **Roden** Drenthe, NE Netherlands 53°08′N 06°26′E
62 H9 **Rodeo** San Juan, W Argentina 30°12′S 69°06′W
103 O14 **Rodez** *anc.* Segodunum. Aveyron, S France 44°21′N 02°34′E
Rodholívos *see* Rodolívos
Rodhópi Óri *see* Rhodope Mountains
Ródhos/Rodi *see* Ródos
107 N15 **Rodi Garganico** Puglia, SE Italy 41°54′N 15°51′E
101 N20 **Roding** Bayern, SE Germany 49°12′N 12°30′E
113 J19 **Rodinit, Kepi i** *headland* W Albania 41°35′N 19°27′E
116 I9 **Rodnei, Munţii** ▲▲ N Romania
184 L4 **Rodney, Cape** *headland* North Island, New Zealand 36°16′S 174°48′E
38 L9 **Rodney, Cape** *headland* Alaska, USA 64°39′N 166°24′W
124 M16 **Rodniki** Ivanovskaya Oblast', W Russian Federation 57°04′N 41°45′E
119 Q16 **Rodnya** Mahilyowskaya Voblasts', E Belarus 53°31′N 32°07′E
Rodó *see* José Enrique Rodó
114 H13 **Rodolívos** *var.* Rodholívos. Kentrikí Makedonía, NE Greece 40°55′N 24°00′E
Rodopi *see* Rhodope Mountains
115 O22 **Ródos** *var.* Ródhos, *Eng.* Rhodes, *It.* Rodi. Ródos, Dodekánisa, Greece, Aegean Sea 36°26′N 28°14′E
115 O22 **Ródos** *var.* Ródhos, *Eng.* Rhodes, *It.* Rodi; *anc.* Rhodos. *island* Dodekánisa, Greece, Aegean Sea
Rodosto *see* Tekirdağ
59 A14 **Rodrigues** Amazonas, W Brazil 06°50′S 73°45′W
173 P8 **Rodrigues** *var.* Rodriquez. *island* E Mauritius
Rodriquez *see* Rodrigues
Rodunma *see* Roanne
180 I7 **Roebourne** Western Australia 20°49′S 117°04′E
83 J20 **Roedtan** Limpopo, NE South Africa 24°37′S 29°05′E
98 H11 **Roelofarendsveen** Zuid-Holland, W Netherlands 52°12′N 04°37′E
Roepat *see* Rupat, Pulau
Roer *see* Rur
99 M16 **Roermond** Limburg, SE Netherlands 51°12′N 06°00′E
99 C18 **Roeselare** *Fr.* Roulers; *prev.* Rousselaere. West-Vlaanderen, W Belgium 50°57′N 03°08′E
9 P8 **Roes Welcome Sound** *strait* Nunavut, N Canada
Roeteng *see* Ruteng
Rofreit *see* Rovereto
Rogachëv *see* Rahachow
57 L15 **Rogagua, Laguna** ◎ NW Bolivia
95 C16 **Rogaland** ◐ *county* S Norway
25 Y9 **Roganville** Texas, SW USA 30°49′N 93°54′W
109 W11 **Rogaška Slatina** *Ger.* Rohitsch-Sauerbrunn; *prev.* Rogatec-Slatina. E Slovenia 46°13′N 15°38′E
Rogatec-Slatina *see* Rogaška Slatina
112 J13 **Rogatica** Republika Srpska, SE Bosnia and Herzegovina 43°50′N 18°55′E
Rogatin *see* Rohatyn
93 F17 **Rogen** ◎ C Sweden
27 S9 **Rogers** Arkansas, C USA 36°19′N 94°07′W
29 P5 **Rogers** North Dakota, N USA 47°03′N 98°12′W
25 T9 **Rogers** Texas, SW USA 30°53′N 97°10′W
31 R5 **Rogers City** Michigan, N USA 45°25′N 83°49′W
Roger Simpson Island *see* Abemama
35 T14 **Rogers Lake** *salt flat* California, W USA
21 Q8 **Rogers, Mount** ▲ Virginia, NE USA 36°39′N 81°32′W
33 O16 **Rogerson** Idaho, NW USA 42°11′N 114°36′W
11 O16 **Rogers Pass** *pass* British Columbia, SW Canada
21 O8 **Rogersville** Tennessee, S USA 36°26′N 83°01′W
99 L16 **Roggel** Limburg, SE Netherlands 51°16′N 05°55′E
Roggeveen *see* Roggewein, Cabo
193 R10 **Roggeveen Basin** *undersea feature* E Pacific Ocean 31°30′S 95°30′W
191 X16 **Roggewein, Cabo** *var.* Roggeveen. *headland* Easter Island, Chile, E Pacific Ocean 27°07′S 109°15′W
103 Y13 **Rogliano** Corse, France, C Mediterranean Sea 42°58′N 09°25′E
107 N21 **Rogliano** Calabria, SW Italy 39°09′N 16°18′E
92 G12 **Rognan** Nordland, C Norway 67°04′N 15°21′E
100 K10 **Rögnitz** ↝ N Germany
Rogozhina/Rogozhinë *see* Rrogozhinë
110 G10 **Rogoźno** Wielkopolskie, C Poland 52°46′N 16°58′E
32 E15 **Rogue River** ↝ Oregon, NW USA
116 I6 **Rohatyn** *Rus.* Rogatin. Ivano-Frankivs'ka Oblast', W Ukraine 49°25′N 24°35′E
189 O14 **Rohi** Pohnpei, E Micronesia
Rohitsch-Sauerbrunn *see* Rogaška Slatina
149 Q13 **Rohri** Sind, SE Pakistan 27°39′N 68°57′E
152 I10 **Rohtak** Haryāna, N India 28°57′N 76°38′E
Roi Ed *see* Roi Et
167 R9 **Roi Et** *var.* Muang Roi Et, Roi Ed. Roi Et, E Thailand 16°05′N 103°38′E
191 U9 **Roi Georges, Îles du** *island group* Îles Tuamotu, C French Polynesia
153 Y10 **Roing** Arunāchal Pradesh, NE India 28°06′N 95°46′E
118 E7 **Roja** NW Latvia 57°31′N 22°44′E
61 B20 **Rojas** Buenos Aires, E Argentina 34°10′S 60°45′W
149 R12 **Rojhān** Punjab, E Pakistan 28°39′N 70°00′E
41 Q12 **Rojo, Cabo** *headland* C Mexico 21°33′N 97°19′W
45 Q10 **Rojo, Cabo** *headland* W Puerto Rico 17°57′N 67°10′W
168 K10 **Rokan Kiri, Sungai** ↝ Sumatera, W Indonesia
118 I11 **Rokiškis** Panevėžys, NE Lithuania 55°58′N 25°35′E
165 R7 **Rokkasho** Aomori, Honshū, C Japan 40°59′N 141°22′E
111 B17 **Rokycany** *Ger.* Rokytzan. Plzeňský Kraj, W Czech Republic 49°45′N 13°36′E
117 P6 **Rokytne** Kyyivs'ka Oblast', N Ukraine 49°40′N 30°29′E
116 L3 **Rokytne** Rivnens'ka Oblast', NW Ukraine 51°19′N 27°09′E
Rokytzan *see* Rokycany
158 L11 **Rola Co** ◎ W China
29 V13 **Roland** Iowa, C USA 42°10′N 93°30′W
95 D15 **Røldal** Hordaland, S Norway 59°52′N 06°49′E
98 O7 **Rolde** Drenthe, NE Netherlands 52°58′N 06°39′E
29 O2 **Rolette** North Dakota, N USA 48°39′N 99°50′W
27 V6 **Rolla** Missouri, C USA 37°56′N 91°47′W
29 O2 **Rolla** North Dakota, N USA 48°51′N 99°37′W
108 A10 **Rolle** Vaud, W Switzerland 46°27′N 06°19′E
181 X8 **Rolleston** Queensland, E Australia 24°30′S 148°36′E
185 H19 **Rolleston** Canterbury, South Island, New Zealand 43°34′S 172°24′E
185 G18 **Rolleston Range** ▲▲ South Island, New Zealand
14 H8 **Rollet** Québec, SE Canada 47°56′N 79°14′W
22 J4 **Rolling Fork** Mississippi, S USA 32°54′N 90°52′W
20 L6 **Rolling Fork** ↝ Kentucky, S USA
14 J11 **Rolphton** Ontario, SE Canada 46°09′N 77°43′W
Röm *see* Rømø
181 X10 **Roma** Queensland, E Australia 26°37′S 148°54′E
107 I15 **Roma** *Eng.* Rome. ● (Italy) Lazio, C Italy 41°53′N 12°30′E
95 P19 **Roma** Gotland, SE Sweden 57°31′N 18°28′E
21 T14 **Romain, Cape** *headland* South Carolina, SE USA 33°00′N 79°21′W
13 P11 **Romaine** ↝ Newfoundland and Labrador/Québec, E Canada
25 R17 **Roma Los Saenz** Texas, SW USA 26°24′N 99°01′W
114 H8 **Roman** Vratsa, NW Bulgaria 43°09′N 23°56′E
116 L10 **Roman** *Hung.* Románvásár. Neamţ, NE Romania 46°46′N 26°56′E
64 M13 **Romanche Fracture Zone** *tectonic feature* E Atlantic Ocean
61 C15 **Romang** Santa Fe, C Argentina 29°30′S 59°46′W
171 R15 **Romang, Pulau** *var.* Pulau Roma. *island* Kepulauan Damar, E Indonesia
171 R15 **Romang, Selat** *strait* Nusa Tenggara, S Indonesia
116 J11 **Romania** *Bul.* Rumŭniya, *Ger.* Rumänien, *Hung.* Románia, *Rom.* România, *SCr.* Rumunjska, *Ukr.* Rumuniya, *prev.* Republica Socialistă România, Roumania, Rumania, Socialist Republic of Romania, *prev.Rom.* Romînia. ◆ *republic* SE Europe
România, Republica Socialistă *see* Romania
Romania, Socialist Republic of *see* Romania
117 T7 **Romaniv** *Rus.* Dneprodzerzhinsk, *prev.* Dniprodzerzhyns'k, *prev.* Kamenskoye. Dnipropetrovs'ka Oblast', E Ukraine 48°30′N 34°35′E
117 X7 **Romaniv** *Rus.* Dzerzhinsk; *prev.* Dzerzhyns'k. Donets'ka Oblast', SE Ukraine 48°21′N 37°50′E
116 M5 **Romaniv** *prev.* Dzerzhyns'k. Zhytomyrs'ka Oblast', N Ukraine 50°07′N 27°56′E
23 W16 **Romano, Cape** *headland* Florida, SE USA 25°51′N 81°40′W
44 G5 **Romano, Cayo** *island* C Cuba
123 O13 **Romanovka** Respublika Buryatiya, S Russian Federation 53°10′N 112°34′E
127 N8 **Romanovka** Saratovskaya Oblast', W Russian Federation 51°45′N 42°45′E
108 I6 **Romanshorn** Thurgau, NE Switzerland 47°34′N 09°23′E
103 R12 **Romans-sur-Isère** Drôme, E France 45°03′N 05°03′E
189 U12 **Romanum** *island* Chuuk, C Micronesia
Románvásár *see* Roman
39 S5 **Romanzof Mountains** ▲▲ Alaska, USA
Roma, Pulau *see* Romang, Pulau
103 S4 **Rombas** Moselle, NE France 49°15′N 06°04′E
23 R2 **Rome** Georgia, SE USA 34°01′N 85°02′W
18 I9 **Rome** New York, NE USA 43°13′N 75°28′W
Rome *see* Roma
31 S9 **Romeo** Michigan, N USA 42°48′N 83°00′W
Römerstadt *see* Rýmařov
103 P5 **Romilly-sur-Seine** Aube, N France 48°31′N 03°44′E
Romînia *see* Romania
146 L11 **Romiton** *Rus.* Rometan. Buxoro Viloyati, C Uzbekistan 39°56′N 64°21′E
21 U3 **Romney** West Virginia, NE USA 39°21′N 78°44′W
117 S4 **Romny** Sums'ka Oblast', NE Ukraine 50°45′N 33°30′E
95 E24 **Rømø** *Ger.* Röm. *island* SW Denmark
117 S5 **Romodan** Poltavs'ka Oblast', NE Ukraine 50°00′N 33°20′E
127 P5 **Romodanovo** Respublika Mordoviya, W Russian Federation 54°25′N 45°24′E
Romorantin *see* Romorantin-Lanthenay
103 N8 **Romorantin-Lanthenay** *var.* Romorantin. Loir-et-Cher, C France 47°22′N 01°44′E
94 F9 **Romsdal** *physical region* S Norway
94 F10 **Romsdalen** *valley* S Norway
94 E9 **Romsdalsfjorden** *fjord* S Norway
33 P8 **Ronan** Montana, NW USA 47°31′N 114°06′W
59 M14 **Roncador** Maranhão, E Brazil 05°48′S 45°08′W
186 M7 **Roncador Reef** *reef* N Solomon Islands
59 J17 **Roncador, Serra do** ▲▲ C Brazil
21 S6 **Ronceverte** West Virginia, NE USA 37°45′N 80°27′W
107 H14 **Ronciglione** Lazio, C Italy 42°16′N 12°15′E
104 L15 **Ronda** Andalucía, S Spain 36°45′N 05°10′W
94 G11 **Rondane** ▲▲ S Norway
104 L15 **Ronda, Serranía de** ▲▲ S Spain
95 H22 **Rønde** Midtjylland, C Denmark 56°18′N 10°28′E
Ronde, Île *see* Round Island
Rōndik *see* Rongrik Atoll
59 E16 **Rondônia** *off.* Estado de Rondônia; *prev.* Território de Rondônia. ◐ *state* W Brazil
Rondônia, Estado de *see* Rondônia
Rondônia, Território de *see* Rondônia
59 I18 **Rondonópolis** Mato Grosso, W Brazil 16°29′S 54°37′W
94 G11 **Rondslottet** ▲ S Norway 61°54′N 09°48′E
95 P20 **Ronehamn** Gotland, SE Sweden 57°10′N 18°30′E
160 L13 **Rong'an** *var.* Chang'an, Rongan. Guangxi Zhuangzu Zizhiqu, S China 25°14′N 109°20′E
Rongan *see* Rong'an
Rongcheng *see* Rongxian, Guangxi, China
Rongcheng *see* Jianli, Hubei, China
189 R4 **Rongelap Atoll** *var.* Rōnlap. *atoll* Ralik Chain, NW Marshall Islands
Rongerik *see* Rongrik Atoll
160 K12 **Rongjiang** *var.* Guzhou. Guizhou, S China 25°59′N 108°27′E
160 L13 **Rong Jiang** ↝ S China
Rongjiang *see* Nankang
Rong, Kas *see* Rŭng, Kaôh
167 P8 **Rong Kwang** Phrae, NW Thailand 18°19′N 100°18′E
189 T4 **Rongrik Atoll** *var.* Rōndik, Rongerik. *atoll* Ralik Chain, N Marshall Islands
189 X2 **Rongrong** *island* SE Marshall Islands
160 L13 **Rongshui** *var.* Rongshui Miaozu Zizhixian. Guangxi Zhuangzu Zizhiqu, S China 25°05′N 109°09′E
Rongshui Miaozu Zizhixian *see* Rongshui
118 I6 **Rõngu** *Ger.* Ringen. Tartumaa, SE Estonia 58°10′N 26°17′E
Rongwo *see* Tongren
160 L15 **Rongxian** *var.* Rongzhou; *prev.* Rongcheng. Guangxi Zhuangzu Zizhiqu, S China 22°52′N 110°33′E
Rongzhag *see* Danba
Rongzhou *see* Rongxian
Roniu, Mont *see* Rooniu, Mont
189 N13 **Ronkiti** Pohnpei, E Micronesia 06°48′N 158°10′E
Rōnlap *see* Rongelap Atoll
95 L24 **Rønne** Bornholm, E Denmark 55°07′N 14°43′E
95 M22 **Ronneby** Blekinge, S Sweden 56°12′N 15°18′E
194 J7 **Ronne Entrance** *inlet* Antarctica
194 L6 **Ronne Ice Shelf** *ice shelf* Antarctica
99 E19 **Ronse** *Fr.* Renaix. Oost-Vlaanderen, SW Belgium 50°45′N 03°36′E
30 K14 **Roodhouse** Illinois, N USA 39°28′N 90°22′W
83 C19 **Rooibank** Erongo, W Namibia 23°04′S 14°34′E
Rooke Island *see* Umboi Island
65 N24 **Rookery Point** *headland* NE Tristan da Cunha 37°03′S 12°15′W
191 R8 **Rooniu, Mont** *prev.* Mont Roniu. ⛰ Tahiti, W French Polynesia 17°49′S 149°12′W
171 V13 **Roon, Pulau** *island* E Indonesia
173 V7 **Roo Rise** *undersea feature* E Indian Ocean
152 J9 **Roorkee** Uttarakhand, N India 29°51′N 77°54′E
99 H15 **Roosendaal** Noord-Brabant, S Netherlands 51°32′N 04°29′E
25 P10 **Roosevelt** Texas, SW USA 30°28′N 100°06′W
37 N3 **Roosevelt** Utah, W USA 40°18′N 109°59′W
47 T8 **Roosevelt** ↝ W Brazil
195 O13 **Roosevelt Island** *island* Antarctica
10 L10 **Roosevelt, Mount** ▲ British Columbia, W Canada 58°28′N 125°22′W
11 P17 **Roosville** British Columbia, SW Canada 48°59′N 115°03′W
29 X10 **Root River** ↝ Minnesota, N USA
Ropar *see* Rūpnagar
111 N16 **Ropczyce** Podkarpackie, SE Poland 50°04′N 21°31′E
181 Q3 **Roper Bar** Northern Territory, N Australia 14°45′S 134°30′E
24 M5 **Ropesville** Texas, SW USA 33°24′N 102°09′W
102 K14 **Roquefort** Landes, SW France 44°01′N 00°18′W
61 C21 **Roque Pérez** Buenos Aires, E Argentina 35°25′S 59°24′W
58 E10 **Roraima** *off.* Estado de Roraima; *prev.* Território de Rio Branco, Território de Roraima. ◐ *state* N Brazil
Roraima, Estado de *see* Roraima
58 F9 **Roraima, Mount** ▲ N South America 05°10′N 60°36′W
Roraima, Território de *see* Roraima
94 I9 **Røros** Sør-Trøndelag, S Norway 62°37′N 11°25′E
108 I7 **Rorschach** Sankt Gallen, NE Switzerland 47°28′N 09°30′E
93 E14 **Rørvik** Nord-Trøndelag, C Norway 64°54′N 11°15′E
119 G17 **Ros'** *Rus.* Ross'. Hrodzyenskaya Voblasts', W Belarus 53°21′N 24°24′E
185 F17 **Ross** West Coast, South Island, New Zealand 42°54′S 170°52′E
119 G17 **Ros'** *Rus.* Ross'. ↝ W Belarus
10 J7 **Ross** ↝ Yukon Territory, W Canada
117 O6 **Ros'** ↝ N Ukraine
44 K7 **Rosa, Lake** ◎ Great Inagua, S Bahamas
32 M9 **Rosalia** Washington, NW USA 47°14′N 117°22′W
191 W15 **Rosalia, Punta** *headland* Easter Island, Chile, E Pacific Ocean 27°04′S 109°19′W
45 P12 **Rosalie** E Dominica 15°22′N 61°15′W
35 T14 **Rosamond** California, W USA 34°51′N 118°09′W
35 S14 **Rosamond Lake** *salt flat* California, W USA
96 H8 **Ross and Cromarty** *cultural region* N Scotland, United Kingdom
61 B18 **Rosario** Santa Fe, C Argentina 32°56′S 60°39′W
40 J11 **Rosario** Sinaloa, C Mexico 23°00′N 105°51′W
40 G6 **Rosario** Sonora, NW Mexico 27°53′N 109°18′W
62 O6 **Rosario** San Pedro, C Paraguay 24°26′S 57°06′W
61 E20 **Rosario** Colonia, SW Uruguay 34°20′S 57°26′W
54 H5 **Rosario** Zulia, NW Venezuela 10°18′N 72°19′W
Rosario *see* Nishino-shima
Rosario *see* Rosarito
40 B4 **Rosario, Bahía del** *bay* NW Mexico
62 K6 **Rosario de la Frontera** Salta, N Argentina 25°50′S 65°00′W
61 C18 **Rosario del Tala** Entre Ríos, E Argentina 32°20′S 59°10′W
61 F16 **Rosário do Sul** Rio Grande do Sul, S Brazil 30°15′S 54°55′W
59 H18 **Rosário Oeste** Mato Grosso, W Brazil 14°50′S 56°25′W
40 D5 **Rosarito** Baja California Norte, NW Mexico 28°27′N 113°58′W
40 B1 **Rosarito** *var.* Rosario. Baja California Norte, NW Mexico 32°25′N 117°04′W
40 F7 **Rosarito** Baja California Sur, NW Mexico 26°28′N 111°41′W
104 L9 **Rosarito, Embalse del** ☐ W Spain
107 N22 **Rosarno** Calabria, SW Italy 38°29′N 15°59′E
56 B5 **Rosa Zárate** *var.* Quinindé. Esmeraldas, SW Ecuador 0°14′N 79°28′W
Roscianum *see* Rossano
29 O8 **Roscoe** South Dakota, N USA 45°24′N 99°19′W
25 P7 **Roscoe** Texas, SW USA 32°27′N 100°32′W
102 F5 **Roscoff** Finistère, NW France 48°43′N 04°00′W
Ros Comáin *see* Roscommon
97 C17 **Roscommon** *Ir.* Ros Comáin. C Ireland 53°38′N 08°11′W
31 Q7 **Roscommon** Michigan, N USA 44°30′N 84°35′W
97 C17 **Roscommon** *Ir.* Ros Comáin. *cultural region* C Ireland
Ros. Cré *see* Roscrea
97 D19 **Roscrea** *Ir.* Ros. Cré. C Ireland 52°57′N 07°47′W
14 H13 **Rosseau** Ontario, S Canada 45°15′N 79°38′W
45 X12 **Roseau** *prev.* Charlotte Town. ● (Dominica) SW Dominica 15°17′N 61°23′W
29 S2 **Roseau** Minnesota, N USA 48°51′N 95°45′W
173 Y16 **Rose Belle** SE Mauritius 20°24′S 57°36′E
183 O16 **Rosebery** Tasmania, SE Australia 41°51′S 145°33′E
21 U11 **Roseboro** North Carolina, SE USA 34°58′N 78°31′W
25 T9 **Rosebud** Texas, SW USA 31°04′N 96°58′W
33 W10 **Rosebud Creek** ↝ Montana, NW USA
32 F14 **Roseburg** Oregon, NW USA 43°13′N 123°21′W
22 J3 **Rosedale** Mississippi, S USA 33°51′N 91°01′W
99 H21 **Rosée** Namur, S Belgium 50°15′N 04°43′E
55 U8 **Rose Hall** E Guyana 06°14′N 57°30′W
173 X16 **Rose Hill** W Mauritius 20°14′S 57°29′E
80 H12 **Roseires, Reservoir** *var.* Lake Rusayris. ☐ E Sudan
Rosenau *see* Rožnov pod Radhoštěm
Rosenau *see* Rožňava

◆ Country ● Country Capital ◇ Dependent Territory ○ Dependent Territory Capital ◐ Administrative Regions ✕ International Airport ▲ Mountain ▲▲ Mountain Range ⛰ Volcano ↝ River ◎ Lake ☐ Reservoir

25 V11 Rosenberg Texas, SW USA 29°33′N 95°48′W
Rosenberg see Olesno, Poland
Rosenberg see Ružomberok, Slovakia
100 I10 Rosengarten Niedersachsen, N Germany 53°24′N 09°54′E
101 M24 Rosenheim Bayern, S Germany 47°51′N 12°08′E
Rosenhof see Zilupe
105 X4 Roses Cataluña, NE Spain 42°15′N 03°11′E
105 X4 Roses, Golf de gulf NE Spain
107 K14 Roseto degli Abruzzi Abruzzo, C Italy 42°39′N 14°01′E
11 S16 Rosetown Saskatchewan, S Canada 51°34′N 107°59′W
Rosetta see Rashîd
35 O7 Roseville California, W USA 38°44′N 121°16′W
30 J12 Roseville Illinois, N USA 40°42′N 90°40′W
29 V8 Roseville Minnesota, N USA 45°00′N 93°09′W
29 R7 Rosholt South Dakota, N USA 45°51′N 96°42′W
106 F12 Rosignano Marittimo Toscana, C Italy 43°24′N 10°28′E
116 I14 Roşiori de Vede Teleorman, S Romania 44°06′N 25°00′E
114 K8 Rositsa N Bulgaria
Rositten see Rēzekne
95 J23 Roskilde Sjælland, E Denmark 55°39′N 12°07′E
Ros Láir see Rosslare
126 H5 Roslavl' Smolenskaya Oblast', W Russian Federation 54°N 32°57′E
32 I8 Roslyn Washington, NW USA 47°13′N 120°52′W
99 K14 Rosmalen Noord-Brabant, S Netherlands 51°43′N 05°21′E
Ros Mhic Thriúin see New Ross
113 P19 Rosoman C FYR Macedonia 41°31′N 21°55′E
102 F6 Rosporden Finistère, NW France 47°58′N 03°54′W
Ross' see Ros'
107 O20 Rossano anc. Roscianum. Calabria, SW Italy 39°35′N 16°38′E
22 L5 Ross Barnett Reservoir Mississippi, S USA
11 W16 Rossburn Manitoba, S Canada 50°42′N 100°49′W
14 H13 Rosseau, Lake Ontario, S Canada
186 I10 Rossel Island prev. Yela Island. island SE Papua New Guinea
195 P12 Ross Ice Shelf ice shelf Antarctica
13 P16 Rossignol, Lake Nova Scotia, SE Canada
83 C19 Rössing Erongo, W Namibia 22°31′S 14°52′E
195 Q14 Ross Island island Antarctica
Rossitten see Rybachiy
Rossiyskaya Federatsiya see Russian Federation
11 N17 Rossland British Columbia, SW Canada 49°03′N 117°49′W
97 F20 Rosslare Ir. Ros Láir. Wexford, SE Ireland 52°16′N 06°23′W
97 F20 Rosslare Harbour Wexford, SE Ireland 52°15′N 06°20′W
101 M14 Rosslau Sachsen-Anhalt, E Germany 51°52′N 12°15′E
76 G10 Rosso Trarza, SW Mauritania 16°36′N 15°50′W
103 X14 Rosso, Cap headland Corse, France, C Mediterranean Sea 42°25′N 08°22′E
93 H16 Rossön Jämtland, C Sweden 63°54′N 16°21′E
97 K21 Ross-on-Wye W England, United Kingdom 51°55′N 02°34′W
Rossony see Rasony
126 L9 Rossosh' Voronezhskaya Oblast', W Russian Federation 50°10′N 39°34′E
181 Q7 Ross River Northern Territory, N Australia 23°36′S 134°30′E
10 J7 Ross River Yukon Territory, W Canada 61°57′N 132°26′W
195 O15 Ross Sea sea Antarctica
92 G13 Røssvatnet Lapp. Reevhtse. C Norway
23 R1 Rossville Georgia, SE USA 34°59′N 85°22′W
Rostak see Ar Rustāq
143 P14 Rostāq Hormozgān, S Iran 26°48′N 53°50′E
117 N5 Rostavytsya N Ukraine
11 T15 Rosthern Saskatchewan, S Canada 52°40′N 106°20′W
100 M8 Rostock Mecklenburg-Vorpommern, NE Germany 54°05′N 12°08′E
124 L16 Rostov Yaroslavskaya Oblast', W Russian Federation 57°11′N 39°19′E
Rostov see Rostov-na-Donu
126 L12 Rostov-na-Donu var. Rostov, Eng. Rostov-on-Don. Rostovskaya Oblast', SW Russian Federation 47°16′N 39°45′E
Rostov-on-Don see Rostov-na-Donu
126 L10 Rostovskaya Oblast' ◈ province SW Russian Federation
93 J14 Rosvik Norrbotten, N Sweden 65°26′N 21°48′E
23 S3 Roswell Georgia, SE USA 34°01′N 84°21′W
37 U14 Roswell New Mexico, SW USA 33°23′N 104°31′W
94 K12 Rot Dalarna, C Sweden 61°16′N 14°04′E
101 I23 Rot S Germany
104 J15 Rota Andalucía, S Spain 36°39′N 06°20′W
188 K9 Rota island S Northern Mariana Islands
25 P6 Rotan Texas, SW USA 32°51′N 100°28′W
Rotcher Island see Tamana
100 I11 Rotenburg Niedersachsen, NW Germany 53°06′N 09°25′E
Rotenburg see Rotenburg an der Fulda
101 I16 Rotenburg an der Fulda var. Rotenburg. Thüringen, C Germany 51°00′N 09°43′E
101 L18 Roter Main E Germany
101 K20 Roth Bayern, SE Germany 49°15′N 11°06′E
101 G16 Rothaargebirge ▲▲ W Germany
Rothenburg see Rothenburg ob der Tauber
101 J20 Rothenburg ob der Tauber var. Rothenburg. Bayern, S Germany 49°23′N 10°10′E
194 H6 Rothera UK research station Antarctica 67°28′S 68°31′W
185 I17 Rotherham Canterbury, South Island, New Zealand 42°42′S 172°56′E
97 M17 Rotherham N England, United Kingdom 53°26′N 01°20′W
96 H12 Rothesay W Scotland, United Kingdom 55°49′N 05°03′W
108 E7 Rothrist Aargau, N Switzerland 47°18′N 07°54′E
194 H6 Rothschild Island island Antarctica
171 P17 Roti, Pulau island S Indonesia
95 H14 Rotnes Akershus, S Norway 60°08′N 10°45′E
183 O8 Roto New South Wales, SE Australia 33°04′S 145°27′E
184 N8 Rotoiti, Lake North Island, New Zealand
Rotomagus see Rouen
107 N19 Rotondella Basilicata, S Italy 40°12′N 16°30′E
103 X15 Rotondo, Monte ▲ Corse, France, C Mediterranean Sea 42°15′N 09°03′E
185 I15 Rotoroa, Lake South Island, New Zealand
184 N8 Rotorua Bay of Plenty, North Island, New Zealand 38°10′S 176°14′E
184 N8 Rotorua, Lake North Island, New Zealand
101 N22 Rott SE Germany
108 F10 Rotten SW Switzerland
109 T6 Rottenmann Steiermark, E Austria 47°31′N 14°18′E
98 H12 Rotterdam Zuid-Holland, SW Netherlands 51°55′N 04°30′E
18 K10 Rotterdam New York, NE USA 42°46′N 73°57′W
95 M21 Rottnen S Sweden
98 N4 Rottumeroog island Waddeneilanden, NE Netherlands
98 N4 Rottumerplaat island Waddeneilanden, NE Netherlands
101 G23 Rottweil Baden-Württemberg, S Germany 48°10′N 08°38′E
191 O7 Rotui, Mont Moorea, W French Polynesia 17°30′S 149°50′W
103 P1 Roubaix Nord, N France 50°42′N 03°10′E
111 C15 Roudnice nad Labem Ger. Raudnitz an der Elbe. Ústecký Kraj, NW Czech Republic 50°25′N 14°14′E
102 M4 Rouen anc. Rotomagus. Seine-Maritime, N France 49°26′N 01°05′E
171 X13 Rouffaer Reserves reserve Papua, E Indonesia
15 N10 Rouge, Rivière Québec, SE Canada
20 J6 Rough River Kentucky, S USA
20 J6 Rough River Lake Kentucky, S USA
Rouhaïbé see Ar Ruḩaybah
102 K11 Rouillac Charente, W France 45°46′N 00°04′W
Roulers see Roeselare
Roumania see Romania
173 Y15 Round Island var. Île Ronde. island NE Mauritius
14 J12 Round Lake Ontario, SE Canada
35 U7 Round Mountain Nevada, W USA 38°42′N 117°04′W
25 R10 Round Mountain Texas, SW USA 30°25′N 98°20′W
183 U5 Round Mountain ▲ New South Wales, SE Australia 30°22′S 152°13′E
25 S10 Round Rock Texas, SW USA 30°30′N 97°40′W
33 U10 Roundup Montana, NW USA 46°27′N 108°32′W
55 Y10 Roura NE French Guiana 04°44′N 52°16′W
Rourkela see Räurkela
96 J4 Rousay island N Scotland, United Kingdom
Rousselaere see Roeselare
103 O17 Roussillon cultural region S France
15 V7 Routhierville Québec, SE Canada 48°09′N 67°07′W
99 K25 Rouvroy Luxembourg, SE Belgium 49°33′N 05°28′E
14 I7 Rouyn-Noranda Québec, SE Canada 48°16′N 79°03′W
Rouyuan see Huachi
Rouyuanchengzi see Huachi
92 L12 Rovaniemi Lappi, N Finland 66°29′N 25°40′E
106 E7 Rovato Lombardia, N Italy 45°34′N 10°03′E
125 N11 Rovdino Arkhangel'skaya Oblast', NW Russian Federation 61°36′N 42°28′E
Roven'ki see Roven'ky
117 Y8 Roven'ky var. Roven'ki. Luhans'ka Oblast', E Ukraine 48°05′N 39°20′E
Rovenskaya Oblast' see Rivnens'ka Oblast'
Rovenskaya Sloboda see Rovyenskaya Slabada
106 G7 Rovereto Ger. Rofreit. Trentino-Alto Adige, N Italy 45°53′N 11°03′E
167 S12 Rôviĕng Tbong Preăh Vihéar, N Cambodia 13°18′N 105°06′E
Rovigno see Rovinj
106 H8 Rovigo Veneto, NE Italy 45°04′N 11°48′E
112 A10 Rovinj It. Rovigno. Istra, NW Croatia 45°06′N 13°39′E
54 E10 Rovira Tolima, C Colombia 04°15′N 75°15′W
Rovno see Rivne
127 P9 Rovnoye Saratovskaya Oblast', W Russian Federation 50°43′N 46°03′E
82 Q12 Rovuma, Rio var. Ruvuma. Mozambique/Tanzania see also Ruvuma
Rovuma, Rio see Ruvuma
119 O19 Rovyenskaya Slabada Rus. Rovenskaya Sloboda. Homyel'skaya Voblasts', SE Belarus 52°13′N 30°19′E
183 R5 Rowena New South Wales, SE Australia 29°51′S 148°55′E
21 T11 Rowland North Carolina, SE USA 34°32′N 79°17′W
9 P5 Rowley Baffin Island, Nunavut, NE Canada
9 P6 Rowley Island island Nunavut, NE Canada
173 W8 Rowley Shoals reef NW Australia
Równe see Rivne
171 O4 Roxas Mindoro, N Philippines 12°36′N 121°29′E
171 P5 Roxas City Panay Island, C Philippines 11°33′N 122°43′E
21 U8 Roxboro North Carolina, SE USA 36°24′N 79°00′W
185 D23 Roxburgh Otago, South Island, New Zealand 45°32′S 169°18′E
96 K13 Roxburgh cultural region SE Scotland, United Kingdom
182 H5 Roxby Downs South Australia 30°29′S 136°56′E
95 M17 Roxen S Sweden
25 V5 Roxton Texas, SW USA 33°33′N 95°43′W
15 P12 Roxton-Sud Québec, SE Canada 45°30′N 72°35′W
33 U8 Roy Montana, NW USA 47°19′N 108°55′W
37 U10 Roy New Mexico, SW USA 35°56′N 104°12′W
97 E17 Royal Canal Ir. An Chanáil Ríoga. canal C Ireland
30 L1 Royale, Isle island Michigan, N USA
37 S6 Royal Gorge valley Colorado, C USA
97 M20 Royal Leamington Spa var. Leamington, Leamington Spa. C England, United Kingdom 52°18′N 01°31′W
97 O23 Royal Tunbridge Wells var. Tunbridge Wells. SE England, United Kingdom 51°08′N 00°16′E
24 L9 Royalty Texas, SW USA 31°21′N 102°51′W
102 J11 Royan Charente-Maritime, W France 45°37′N 01°01′W
65 B24 Roy Cove Settlement West Falkland, Falkland Islands 51°32′S 60°23′W
103 O3 Roye Somme, N France 49°42′N 02°46′E
95 H15 Røyken Buskerud, S Norway 59°47′N 10°21′E
93 F14 Røyrvik Nord-Trøndelag, C Norway 64°53′N 13°30′E
25 U6 Royse City Texas, SW USA 32°58′N 96°19′W
97 O21 Royston E England, United Kingdom 52°05′N 00°01′W
23 U2 Royston Georgia, SE USA 34°17′N 83°06′W
114 L10 Roza prev. Gyulovo. Yambol, E Bulgaria 42°29′N 26°30′E
113 L16 Rožaje E Montenegro 42°51′N 20°11′E
110 M10 Różan Mazowieckie, C Poland 52°36′N 21°27′E
117 O10 Rozdil'na Odes'ka Oblast', SW Ukraine 46°51′N 30°03′E
117 S12 Rozdol'ne Rus. Razdolnoye. Avtonomna Respublika Krym, S Ukraine 45°45′N 33°27′E
Rozhdestvenka see Kabanbay Batyr
116 I6 Rozhnyativ Ivano-Frankivs'ka Oblast', W Ukraine 48°58′N 24°07′E
116 J3 Rozhyshche Volyns'ka Oblast', NW Ukraine 50°54′N 25°16′E
Roznau am Radhost see Rožnov pod Radhoštěm
111 L19 Rožňava Ger. Rosenau, Hung. Rozsnyó. Košický Kraj, E Slovakia 48°41′N 20°32′E
116 K10 Roznov Neamţ, NE Romania 46°47′N 26°33′E
111 I18 Rožnov pod Radhoštěm Ger. Rosenau, Roznau am Radhost. Zlínský Kraj, E Czech Republic 49°28′N 18°09′E
Rózsahegy see Ružomberok
Rozsnyó see Râşnov, Romania
Rozsnyó see Rožňava, Slovakia
113 K18 Rranxë Shkodër, NW Albania 41°58′N 19°27′E
113 L18 Rrëshen var. Rresheni, Rrshen. Lezhë, C Albania 41°46′N 19°54′E
Rresheni see Rrëshen
Rrogozhina see Rrogozhinë
113 K20 Rrogozhinë var. Rogozhina, Rogozhinë, Rrogozhina. Tiranë, W Albania 41°04′N 19°40′E
Rrshen see Rrëshen
112 O13 Rtanj ▲ E Serbia 43°45′N 21°54′E
127 O7 Rtishchevo Saratovskaya Oblast', W Russian Federation 52°16′N 43°46′E
184 N12 Ruahine Range var. Ruarine. ▲▲ North Island, New Zealand
185 L14 Ruamahanga North Island, New Zealand
Ruanda see Rwanda
184 M10 Ruapehu, Mount North Island, New Zealand 39°15′S 175°33′E
185 C25 Ruapuke Island island SW New Zealand
Ruarine see Ruahine Range
184 O9 Ruatahuna Bay of Plenty, North Island, New Zealand 38°38′S 176°56′E
184 Q8 Ruatoria Gisborne, North Island, New Zealand 37°54′S 178°18′E
184 K4 Ruawai Northland, North Island, New Zealand 36°08′S 174°04′E
15 N8 Ruban Québec, SE Canada
81 I22 Rubeho Mountains ▲▲ C Tanzania
165 U3 Rubeshibe Hokkaidō, NE Japan 43°49′N 143°37′E
Rubezhnoye see Rubizhne
113 L18 Rubik Lezhë, C Albania 41°46′N 19°48′E
54 H7 Rubio Táchira, W Venezuela 07°42′N 72°23′W
117 X6 Rubizhne Rus. Rubezhnoye. Luhans'ka Oblast', E Ukraine 49°01′N 38°22′E
81 F20 Rubondo Island island N Tanzania
122 I13 Rubtsovsk Altayskiy Kray, S Russian Federation 51°34′N 81°11′E
39 P9 Ruby Alaska, USA 64°44′N 155°29′W
35 W3 Ruby Dome ▲ Nevada, W USA 40°35′N 115°25′W
35 W4 Ruby Lake Nevada, W USA
35 W4 Ruby Mountains ▲▲ Nevada, W USA
33 Q12 Ruby Range ▲▲ Montana, NW USA
118 C10 Rucava SW Latvia 56°09′N 21°10′E
143 S13 Rūdān var. Dehbārez. Hormozgān, S Iran 27°30′N 57°10′E
Rudelstadt see Ciechanowiec
Rudensk see Rudzyensk
119 G14 Rūdiškės Vilnius, S Lithuania 54°31′N 24°49′E
95 H24 Rudkøbing Syddtjylland, C Denmark 54°57′N 10°43′E
125 S13 Rudnichnyy Kirovskaya Oblast', NW Russian Federation 59°37′N 52°28′E
Rūdnichnyy see Koksu
Rudnik see Rudnyy
126 H4 Rudnya Smolenskaya Oblast', W Russian Federation 54°55′N 31°10′E
127 O8 Rudnya Volgogradskaya Oblast', SW Russian Federation 50°54′N 44°27′E
144 M7 Rudnyy var. Rudny. Kostanay, N Kazakhstan 53°N 63°05′E
122 K3 Rudol'fa, Ostrov island Zemlya Frantsa-Iosifa, NW Russian Federation
Rudolf, Lake see Turkana, Lake
Rudolfswert see Novo mesto
101 L17 Rudolstadt Thüringen, C Germany 50°44′N 11°20′E
31 Q4 Rudyard Michigan, N USA 46°15′N 84°36′W
33 S7 Rudyard Montana, NW USA 48°33′N 110°37′W
119 K16 Rudzyensk Rus. Rudensk. Minskaya Voblasts', C Belarus 53°36′N 27°52′E
104 L6 Rueda Castilla y León, N Spain 41°24′N 04°58′W
114 F10 Ruen ▲ Bulgaria/FYR Macedonia 42°10′N 22°31′E
80 G10 Rufa'a Gezira, C Sudan 14°49′N 33°21′E
102 L10 Ruffec Charente, W France 46°01′N 00°10′E
21 R14 Ruffin South Carolina, SE USA 33°00′N 80°48′W
81 J23 Rufiji E Tanzania
61 A20 Rufino Santa Fe, C Argentina 34°16′S 62°45′W
76 F11 Rufisque W Senegal 14°44′N 17°18′W
83 K14 Rufunsa Lusaka, C Zambia 15°02′S 29°35′E
118 J9 Rugāji E Latvia 57°01′N 27°07′E
161 R7 Rugao Jiangsu, E China 32°27′N 120°35′E
97 M20 Rugby C England, United Kingdom 52°22′N 01°18′W
29 N3 Rugby North Dakota, N USA 48°24′N 100°00′W
100 N7 Rügen headland NE Germany 54°25′N 13°21′E
Ruhaybeh see Ar Ruḩaybah
81 E19 Ruhengeri NW Rwanda 01°39′S 29°16′E
Ruhja see Rūjiena
100 M10 Ruhner Berg hill N Germany
118 F7 Ruhnu var. Ruhnu Saar, Swe. Runö. island SW Estonia
Ruhnu Saar see Ruhnu
101 G15 Ruhr W Germany
91 W6 Ruhr Valley industrial region W Germany
161 S11 Rui'an var. Rui an. Zhejiang, SE China 27°51′N 120°39′E
Rui an see Rui'an
161 P10 Ruichang Jiangxi, S China 29°46′N 115°37′E
24 J11 Ruidosa Texas, SW USA 30°00′N 104°40′W
37 S14 Ruidoso New Mexico, SW USA 33°19′N 105°40′W
161 P12 Ruijin Jiangxi, S China 25°52′N 116°01′E
160 D13 Ruili Yunnan, SW China 24°04′N 97°49′E
98 N8 Ruinen Drenthe, NE Netherlands 52°46′N 06°19′E
99 D17 Ruiselede West-Vlaanderen, W Belgium 51°03′N 03°21′E
161 T13 Ruisui prev. Juisui. C Taiwan 23°43′N 121°28′E
64 P5 Ruivo de Santana, Pico ▲ Madeira, Portugal, NE Atlantic Ocean 32°46′N 16°57′W
40 J12 Ruiz Nayarit, SW Mexico 22°00′N 105°09′W
54 E10 Ruiz, Nevado del W Colombia 04°53′N 75°22′W
138 J9 Rujaylah, Ḩarrat ar salt lake N Jordan
Rujen see Rūjiena
118 H7 Rūjiena Est. Ruhja, Ger. Rujen. N Latvia 57°54′N 25°22′E
79 I18 Ruki W Dem. Rep. Congo
81 E22 Rukwa ◈ region SW Tanzania
81 F23 Rukwa, Lake SE Tanzania
25 P6 Rule Texas, SW USA 33°10′N 99°53′W
22 K3 Ruleville Mississippi, S USA 33°43′N 90°33′W
Rum see Rhum
112 K10 Ruma Vojvodina, N Serbia 45°02′N 19°51′E
Rumadiya see Ar Ramādī
141 Q7 Rumāḩ Ar Riyāḑ, C Saudi Arabia 25°35′N 47°09′E
Rumaitha see Ar Rumaythah
Rumania/Rumänien see Romania
Rumänisch-Sankt-Georgen see Sângeorz-Băi
139 Y13 Rumaylah Al Başrah, SE Iraq 30°16′N 47°22′E
139 P2 Rumaylah, Wādī dry watercourse NE Syria
171 U13 Rumbati Papua, E Indonesia 02°44′S 132°04′E
81 E14 Rumbek El Buhayrat, C South Sudan 06°50′N 29°42′E
Rumburg see Rumburk
111 D14 Rumburk Ger. Rumburg. Ústecký Kraj, NW Czech Republic 50°58′N 14°35′E
44 J4 Rum Cay island C Bahamas
99 M26 Rumelange Luxembourg, S Luxembourg 49°28′N 06°02′E
99 D20 Rumes Hainaut, SW Belgium 50°33′N 03°19′E
19 P7 Rumford Maine, NE USA 44°31′N 70°31′W
110 I6 Rumia Pomorskie, N Poland 54°36′N 18°21′E
113 J17 Rumija ▲ S Montenegro
103 T11 Rumilly Haute-Savoie, E France 45°52′N 05°57′E
139 O6 Rūmiyah Al Anbār, W Iraq 34°28′N 41°17′E
Rummah, Wādī ar see Rimah, Wādī ar
Rummelsburg in Pommern see Miastko
165 S3 Rumoi Hokkaidō, NE Japan 43°57′N 141°40′E
82 M12 Rumphi var. Rumpi. Northern, N Malawi 11°00′S 33°51′E
Rumpi see Rumphi
29 V7 Rum River Minnesota, N USA
188 F16 Rumung island Caroline Islands, W Micronesia
Rumuniya/Rumŭniya/Rumunjska see Romania
185 G16 Runanga West Coast, South Island, New Zealand 42°25′S 171°15′E
184 P7 Runaway, Cape headland North Island, New Zealand 37°33′S 177°59′E
97 K18 Runcorn C England, United Kingdom 53°20′N 02°44′W
118 K10 Rundāni var. Rundāni. E Latvia 56°19′N 27°51′E
Rundāni see Rundāni
83 L18 Runde var. Lundi. SE Zimbabwe
83 E16 Rundu var. Runtu. Okavango, NE Namibia 17°55′S 19°45′E
93 I16 Rundvik Västerbotten, N Sweden 63°31′N 19°22′E
81 G20 Runere Mwanza, N Tanzania 03°06′S 33°18′E
25 S13 Runge Texas, SW USA 28°52′N 97°42′W
167 Q13 Rŭng, Kaôh prev. Kas Rong. island SW Cambodia
79 O16 Rungu Orientale, NE Dem. Rep. Congo 03°11′N 27°52′E
81 F23 Rungwa Rukwa, W Tanzania 07°18′S 31°40′E
81 G22 Rungwa Singida, C Tanzania 06°54′S 33°33′E
94 M14 Runn C Sweden
24 M4 Running Water Draw valley New Mexico/Texas, SW USA
Runö see Ruhnu
Runtu see Rundu
189 V12 Ruo island Caroline Islands, C Micronesia
158 L9 Ruoqiang var. Jo-ch'iang. Uigh. Charkhlik, Charkhliq, Qarkilik. Xinjiang Uygur Zizhiqu, NW China 38°59′N 88°08′E
159 S7 Ruo Shui N China
92 L8 Ruostekfielbmá var. Rustefjelbma Finnmark. Finnmark, N Norway 70°25′N 28°10′E
93 L18 Ruovesi Länsi-Suomi, W Finland 61°59′N 24°05′E
112 B9 Rupa Primorje-Gorski Kotar, NW Croatia 45°29′N 14°15′E
182 M11 Rupanyup Victoria, SE Australia 36°38′S 142°37′E
168 K9 Rupat, Pulau prev. Roepat. island W Indonesia
168 K10 Rupat, Selat strait Sumatera, W Indonesia
116 J11 Rupea Ger. Reps, Hung. Kőhalom; prev. Cohalm. Braşov, C Romania 46°02′N 25°13′E
99 G17 Rupel N Belgium
Rupella see la Rochelle
33 P15 Rupert Idaho, NW USA 42°37′N 113°40′W
21 R5 Rupert West Virginia, NE USA 37°57′N 80°40′W
Rupert House see Waskaganish
12 J10 Rupert, Rivière de Québec, C Canada
152 I8 Rūpnagar var. Ropar. Punjab, India
194 M13 Ruppert Coast physical region Antarctica
100 N11 Ruppiner Kanal canal NE Germany
55 S11 Rupununi River S Guyana
101 D16 Rur Dut. Roer. Germany/Netherlands
58 H13 Rurópolis Presidente Medici Pará, N Brazil 04°05′S 55°26′W
191 S12 Rurutu island Îles Australes, SW French Polynesia
Rusaddir see Melilla
83 L17 Rusape Manicaland, E Zimbabwe 18°32′S 32°07′E
Rusayris, Lake see Roseires, Reservoir
Ruschuk/Rusçuk see Ruse
114 K7 Ruse var. Ruschuk, Rustchuk, Turk. Rusçuk. Ruse, N Bulgaria 43°50′N 25°59′E
109 W10 Ruše NE Slovenia 46°31′N 15°30′E
114 L7 Ruse ◈ province N Bulgaria
114 K7 Rusenski Lom N Bulgaria
97 G17 Rush Ir. An Ros. Dublin, E Ireland 53°32′N 06°06′W
161 S4 Rushan var. Xiacun. Shandong, E China 36°55′N 121°26′E
Rushan see Rŭshon
Rushanskiy Khrebet see Rushon, Qatorkŭhi
29 V7 Rush City Minnesota, N USA 45°41′N 92°56′W
37 V5 Rush Creek Colorado, C USA
29 X10 Rushford Minnesota, N USA 43°48′N 91°45′W
154 N13 Rushikulya E India
14 D8 Rush Lake Ontario, S Canada
30 M7 Rush Lake Wisconsin, N USA
28 J10 Rushmore, Mount ▲ South Dakota, N USA 43°52′N 103°27′W
147 S13 Rŭshon Rus. Rushan. S Tajikistan 37°58′N 71°31′E
147 S14 Rushon, Qatorkŭhi Rus. Rushanskiy Khrebet. ▲▲ SE Tajikistan
26 M12 Rush Springs Oklahoma, C USA 34°46′N 97°57′W
45 V15 Rushville Trinidad, Trinidad and Tobago 10°07′N 61°03′W
30 J13 Rushville Illinois, N USA 40°07′N 90°33′W
28 K12 Rushville Nebraska, C USA 42°41′N 102°28′W
183 O11 Rushworth Victoria, SE Australia 36°36′S 145°03′E
25 W8 Rusk Texas, SW USA 31°49′N 95°11′W
93 I14 Ruskele Västerbotten, N Sweden 64°49′N 18°55′E
118 C12 Rusnė Klaipėda, W Lithuania 55°18′N 21°19′E
114 M10 Rusokastrenska Reka E Bulgaria
Russadir see Melilla
109 X3 Russbach NE Austria
11 V16 Russell Manitoba, S Canada 50°47′N 101°17′W
184 K2 Russell Northland, North Island, New Zealand 35°17′S 174°07′E
26 L4 Russell Kansas, C USA 38°54′N 98°51′W
21 O4 Russell Kentucky, S USA 38°30′N 82°43′W
20 L7 Russell Springs Kentucky, S USA 37°02′N 85°03′W
23 O2 Russellville Alabama, S USA 34°30′N 87°43′W
27 T11 Russellville Arkansas, C USA 35°17′N 93°06′W
20 J7 Russellville Kentucky, S USA 36°50′N 86°54′W
101 G18 Rüsselsheim Hessen, W Germany 50°00′N 08°25′E
Russia see Russian Federation
Russian America see Alaska
122 J11 Russian Federation off. Russian Federation, var. Russia, Latv. Krievija, Rus. Rossiyskaya Federatsiya. ◆ republic Asia/Europe
Russian Federation see Russian Federation
39 N11 Russian Mission Alaska, USA 61°48′N 161°23′W
34 M7 Russian River California, W USA
122 J5 Russkaya Gavan' Novaya Zemlya, Arkhangel'skaya Oblast', N Russian Federation 76°13′N 62°48′E
122 J5 Russkiy, Ostrov island N Russian Federation
109 Y5 Rust Burgenland, E Austria 47°48′N 16°42′E
Rustaq see Ar Rustāq
137 U10 Rustavi prev. Rust'avi. SE Georgia 41°36′N 45°00′E
Rust'avi see Rustavi
21 T7 Rustburg Virginia, NE USA 37°17′N 79°07′W
Rustchuk see Ruse
Rustefjelbma Finnmark see Ruostekfielbmá
83 I21 Rustenburg North-West, N South Africa 25°40′S 27°15′E
22 H5 Ruston Louisiana, S USA 32°31′N 92°38′W
81 E21 Rutana SE Burundi 04°01′S 30°01′E
62 I4 Rutana, Volcán N Chile 22°43′S 67°52′W
Rutanzige, Lake see Edward, Lake
Rutba see Ar Ruṭbah
104 M14 Rute Andalucía, S Spain 37°20′N 04°23′W
171 N16 Ruteng prev. Roeteng. Flores, C Indonesia 08°35′S 120°28′E
194 L8 Rutford Ice Stream ice feature Antarctica
35 X6 Ruth Nevada, W USA 39°15′N 115°00′W
101 G15 Rüthen Nordrhein-Westfalen, W Germany 51°30′N 08°28′E
14 D17 Rutherford Ontario, S Canada 42°39′N 82°06′W
21 Q10 Rutherfordton North Carolina, SE USA 35°23′N 81°57′W
97 J18 Ruthin Wel. Rhuthun. NE Wales, United Kingdom 53°05′N 03°18′W
108 G7 Rüti Zürich, N Switzerland 47°16′N 08°51′E
Rutlam see Ratlām
18 M9 Rutland Vermont, NE USA 43°37′N 72°59′W
97 N19 Rutland cultural region C England, United Kingdom
21 N8 Rutledge Tennessee, S USA 36°16′N 83°31′W
158 G12 Rutog var. Rutög, Rutok. Xizang Zizhiqu, W China 33°27′N 79°43′E
Rutok see Rutog
79 P19 Rutshuru Nord-Kivu, E Dem. Rep. Congo 01°11′S 29°28′E
98 L8 Rutten Flevoland, N Netherlands 52°49′N 05°44′E
127 Q17 Rutul Respublika Dagestan, SW Russian Federation 41°35′N 47°30′E
93 L14 Ruukki Oulu, C Finland 64°40′N 25°35′E
98 N11 Ruurlo Gelderland, E Netherlands 52°04′N 06°27′E
143 S15 Ru'ūs al Jibāl cape Oman/United Arab Emirates
138 I7 Ru'ūs aţ Ţiwāl, Jabal ▲▲ W Syria
81 H23 Ruvuma ◈ region SE Tanzania
81 I25 Ruvuma var. Rio Rovuma. Mozambique/Tanzania see also Rovuma, Rio
Ruvuma see Rovuma, Rio
Ruwais see Ar Ruways
138 M9 Ruwayshid, Wadi ar dry watercourse NE Jordan
141 Z10 Ruways, Ra's ar headland E Oman 20°58′N 59°00′E
79 P18 Ruwenzori ▲▲ Dem. Rep. Congo/Uganda
141 Y8 Ruwi NE Oman 23°33′N 58°31′E
114 F9 Ruy ▲ Bulgaria/Serbia 42°52′N 22°35′E
Ruya see Luia, Rio
81 E20 Ruyigi E Burundi 03°28′S 30°19′E
127 P5 Ruzayevka Respublika Mordoviya, W Russian Federation 54°04′N 44°56′E
119 G18 Ruzhany Brestskaya Voblasts', SW Belarus 52°52′N 24°53′E
114 I10 Rŭzhevo Konare Plovdiv, C Bulgaria 42°16′N 24°58′E
Ruzhin see Ruzhyn
114 G7 Ruzhintsi Vidin, NW Bulgaria 43°38′N 22°50′E
161 N6 Ruzhou Henan, C China 34°10′N 112°51′E
117 N5 Ruzhyn Rus. Ruzhin. Zhytomyrs'ka Oblast', N Ukraine 49°42′N 29°01′E
111 K19 Ružomberok Ger. Rosenberg, Hung. Rózsahegy. Zilinský Kraj, N Slovakia 49°04′N 19°19′E
111 C16 Ruzyně ✈ (Praha) Praha, C Czech Republic
81 D19 Rwanda off. Rwandese Republic; prev. Ruanda. ◆ republic C Africa
Rwandese Republic see Rwanda
95 G22 Ry Midtjylland, C Denmark 56°06′N 09°46′E
Ryasna see Rasna
126 L5 Ryazan' Ryazanskaya Oblast', W Russian Federation 54°37′N 39°37′E
126 L5 Ryazanskaya Oblast' ◈ province W Russian Federation
126 M6 Ryazhsk Ryazanskaya Oblast', W Russian Federation 53°42′N 40°09′E
118 B13 Rybachiy Ger. Rossitten. Kaliningradskaya Oblast', W Russian Federation 55°09′N 20°49′E
124 J2 Rybachiy, Poluostrov peninsula NW Russian Federation
Rybach'ye see Balykchy
124 L15 Rybinsk prev. Andropov. Yaroslavskaya Oblast', W Russian Federation 58°03′N 38°53′E
124 K14 Rybinskoye Vodokhranilishche Eng. Rybinsk Reservoir, Rybinsk Sea. W Russian Federation
Rybinsk Reservoir/Rybinsk Sea see Rybinskoye Vodokhranilishche
111 I16 Rybnik Śląskie, S Poland 50°05′N 18°31′E
Rybnitsa see Rîbniţa
111 F16 Rychnov nad Kněžnou Ger. Reichenau. Královéhradecký Kraj, N Czech Republic 50°10′N 16°17′E
110 I12 Rychwał Wielkopolskie, C Poland 52°04′N 18°10′E
11 O13 Rycroft Alberta, W Canada 55°45′N 118°42′W
95 L21 Ryd Kronoberg, S Sweden 56°27′N 14°44′E
95 L20 Rydaholm Jönköping, S Sweden 56°57′N 14°19′E
194 I8 Rydberg Peninsula peninsula Antarctica
97 P23 Rye SE England, United Kingdom 50°57′N 00°42′E
33 T10 Ryegate Montana, NW USA 46°21′N 109°12′W
35 S3 Rye Patch Reservoir Nevada, W USA
95 D15 Ryfylke physical region S Norway
95 H16 Rygge Østfold, S Norway 59°22′N 10°45′E
110 N13 Ryki Lubelskie, E Poland 51°38′N 21°57′E
Rykovo see Yenakiyeve
126 I7 Ryl'sk Kurskaya Oblast', W Russian Federation 51°34′N 34°41′E
183 S8 Rylstone New South Wales, SE Australia 32°48′S 149°58′E
111 H17 Rýmařov Ger. Römerstadt. Moravskoslezský Kraj, E Czech Republic 49°56′N 17°15′E
144 E11 Ryn-Peski desert W Kazakhstan
165 N10 Ryōtsu var. Ryôtu. Niigata, Sado, C Japan 38°06′N 138°28′E
Ryôtu see Ryōtsu
110 K10 Rypin Kujawsko-pomorskie, C Poland 53°03′N 19°25′E
Ryshkany see Rîşcani
Ryssel see Lille
Ryswick see Rijswijk
95 M24 Rytterknægten hill E Denmark
Ryukyu Islands see Nansei-shotō
192 G5 Ryukyu Trench var. Nansei Syotō Trench. undersea feature S East China Sea 24°45′N 128°00′E
110 D11 Rzepin Ger. Reppen. Lubuskie, W Poland 52°20′N 14°48′E
111 N16 Rzeszów Podkarpackie, SE Poland 50°03′N 22°01′E
124 I16 Rzhev Tverskaya Oblast', W Russian Federation 56°17′N 34°22′E
Rzhishchev see Rzhyshchiv
117 P5 Rzhyshchiv Rus. Rzhishchev. Kyyivs'ka Oblast', N Ukraine 49°58′N 31°02′E

S

138 E11 Sa'ad Southern, W Israel 31°27′N 34°31′E
109 P7 Saalach W Austria
101 L14 Saale C Germany
101 L17 Saalfeld var. Saalfeld an der Saale. Thüringen, C Germany 50°39′N 11°22′E
Saalfeld see Zalewo
Saalfeld an der Saale see Saalfeld
108 C8 Saane W Switzerland
101 D19 Saar Fr. Sarre. France/Germany
101 E20 Saarbrücken Fr. Sarrebruck. Saarland, SW Germany 49°13′N 07°01′E
Saarburg see Sarrebourg
118 D6 Sääre var. Sjar. Saaremaa, W Estonia 57°57′N 21°53′E
Saare see Saaremaa
118 D5 Saaremaa off. Saare Maakond. ◈ province W Estonia
118 E6 Saaremaa Ger. Oesel, Ösel; prev. Saare. island W Estonia
Saare Maakond see Saaremaa
92 L12 Saarenkylä Lappi, N Finland 66°31′N 25°51′E
Saargemund see Sarreguemines
93 L17 Saarijärvi Länsi-Suomi, C Finland 62°42′N 25°16′E
Saar in Mähren see Žďár nad Sázavou
92 M10 Saariselkä Lapp. Suoločielgi. Lappi, N Finland 68°27′N 27°29′E
92 L10 Saariselkä hill range NE Finland
101 D20 Saarland Fr. Sarre. ◈ state SW Germany
Saarlautern see Saarlouis

101 D20 **Saarlouis** prev. Saarlautern. Saarland, SW Germany 49°19′N 06°45′E
108 E11 **Saaser Vispa** S Switzerland
137 X12 **Saatlı** Rus. Saatly. C Azerbaijan 39°57′N 48°24′E
Saatly see Saatlı
Saaz see Žatec
45 V9 **Saba** island Sint Maarten
138 J7 **Sab' Ābār** var. Sab'a Biyar, Sa'b Bi'ār. Ḥimṣ, C Syria 33°46′N 37°41′E
Sab'a Biyar see Sab' Ābār
112 K11 **Šabac** Serbia, W Serbia 44°45′N 19°42′E
105 W5 **Sabadell** Cataluña, E Spain 41°33′N 02°07′E
164 K12 **Sabae** Fukui, Honshū, SW Japan 36°00′N 136°12′E
169 V7 **Sabah** prev. British North Borneo, North Borneo. ◆ state East Malaysia
168 J8 **Sabak** var. Sabak Bernam. Selangor, Peninsular Malaysia 03°45′N 100°59′E
Sabak Bernam see Sabak
38 D16 **Sabak, Cape** headland Agattu Island, Alaska, USA 52°21′N 173°43′E
81 J20 **Sabaki** S Kenya
142 L2 **Sabalān, Kuhhā-ye** ▲ NW Iran 38°21′N 47°47′E
154 H7 **Sabalgarh** Madhya Pradesh, C India 26°18′N 77°28′E
44 E4 **Sabana, Archipiélago de** island group C Cuba
42 H7 **Sabanagrande** var. Sabana Grande. Francisco Morazán, S Honduras 13°48′N 87°15′W
Sabana Grande see Sabanagrande
54 E5 **Sabanalarga** Atlántico, N Colombia 10°38′N 74°55′W
41 W14 **Sabancuy** Campeche, SE Mexico 18°58′N 91°11′W
45 N8 **Sabaneta** NW Dominican Republic 19°30′N 71°21′W
54 J4 **Sabaneta** Falcón, N Venezuela 11°17′N 70°00′W
188 H4 **Sabaneta, Puntan** prev. Ushi Point. headland Saipan, S Northern Mariana Islands 15°17′N 145°49′E
171 X14 **Sabang** Papua, E Indonesia 04°33′S 138°42′E
116 L10 **Săbăoani** Neamţ, NE Romania 47°01′N 26°51′E
155 J26 **Sabaragamuwa** ◆ province C Sri Lanka
Sabaria see Szombathely
154 D10 **Sābarmati** NW India
171 S10 **Sabatai** Pulau Morotai, E Indonesia 02°04′N 128°23′E
141 Q15 **Sab'atayn, Ramlat as** desert C Yemen
107 I16 **Sabaudia** Lazio, C Italy 41°17′N 13°02′E
57 J19 **Sabaya** Oruro, S Bolivia 19°09′S 68°21′W
Sa'b Bi'ār see Sab' Ābār
Sabbioncello see Orebić
148 I8 **Şāberī, Hāmūn-e** var. Daryācheh-ye Hāmun, Daryācheh-ye Sīstān. ◎ Afghanistan/Iran see also Sīstān, Daryācheh-ye
Şāberī, Hāmūn-e see Sīstān, Daryācheh-ye
27 P2 **Sabetha** Kansas, C USA 39°54′N 95°48′W
75 P10 **Sabhā** C Libya 27°02′N 14°26′E
67 V13 **Sabi** var. Save. Mozambique/Zimbabwe see also Save
Sabi see Save
118 E8 **Sabile** Ger. Zabeln. NW Latvia 57°03′N 22°33′E
31 R14 **Sabina** Ohio, N USA 39°29′N 83°38′W
40 I3 **Sabinal** Chihuahua, N Mexico 30°59′N 107°29′W
25 Q12 **Sabinal** Texas, SW USA 29°19′N 99°28′W
25 Q11 **Sabinal River** Texas, SW USA
105 S4 **Sabiñánigo** Aragón, NE Spain 42°31′N 00°22′W
41 N6 **Sabinas** Coahuila, NE Mexico 27°52′N 101°04′W
41 O8 **Sabinas Hidalgo** Nuevo León, NE Mexico 26°29′N 100°09′W
41 N6 **Sabinas, Río** NE Mexico
22 F9 **Sabine Lake** ◎ Louisiana/Texas, S USA
92 O3 **Sabine Land** physical region C Svalbard
25 W7 **Sabine River** Louisiana/Texas, SW USA
137 X12 **Sabirabad** C Azerbaijan 40°00′N 48°27′E
Sabkha see As Sabkhah
171 O4 **Sablayan** Mindoro, N Philippines 12°48′N 120°48′E
13 P16 **Sable, Cape** headland Newfoundland and Labrador, SE Canada 43°21′N 65°40′W
23 X17 **Sable, Cape** headland Florida, SE USA 25°12′N 81°06′W
13 R16 **Sable Island** island Nova Scotia, SE Canada
14 L11 **Sables, Lac des** ◎ Québec, SE Canada
14 E10 **Sables, Rivière aux** Ontario, S Canada
102 K7 **Sable-sur-Sarthe** Sarthe, NW France 47°49′N 00°19′W
125 U7 **Sablya, Gora** ▲ NW Russian Federation 64°46′N 58°52′E
77 U14 **Sabon Birnin Gwari** Kaduna, C Nigeria 10°43′N 06°39′E
77 V11 **Sabon Kafi** Zinder, C Niger 14°37′N 08°46′E
104 I6 **Sabor, Rio** N Portugal
14 J8 **Sabourin, Lac** ◎ Québec, SE Canada
137 Y10 **Şabran** prev. Dăvăçi. NE Azerbaijan 41°15′N 48°58′E
102 J14 **Sabres** Landes, SW France 44°07′N 00°46′W
195 X13 **Sabrina Coast** physical region Antarctica
140 M11 **Sabt al Ulāyā** 'Asīr, SW Saudi Arabia 19°33′N 41°58′E
104 I8 **Sabugal** Guarda, N Portugal 40°20′N 07°05′W
29 Z13 **Sabula** Iowa, C USA 42°04′N 90°10′W
141 N13 **Şabyā** Jīzān, SW Saudi Arabia 17°50′N 42°50′E
Sabzawar see Sabzevār
Sabzawaran see Jīroft
143 S4 **Sabzevār** var. Sabzawar. Khorāsān-Razavi, NE Iran 36°13′N 57°38′E
Sabzvārān see Jīroft
Sacajawea Peak see Matterhorn
82 C9 **Sacandica** Uíge, NW Angola 06°01′S 15°57′E
42 A2 **Sacatepéquez** off. Departamento de Sacatepéquez. ◆ department S Guatemala
Sacatepéquez, Departamento de see Sacatepéquez
104 F11 **Sacavém** Lisboa, W Portugal 38°47′N 09°06′W
29 T13 **Sac City** Iowa, C USA 42°25′N 94°59′W
105 P8 **Sacedón** Castilla-La Mancha, C Spain 40°29′N 02°44′W
116 J12 **Săcele** Ger. Vierdörfer, Hung. Négyfalu; prev. Ger. Sieben Dörfer, Hung. Hétfalu. Braşov, C Romania 45°36′N 25°40′E
163 Y16 **Sacheon** Jap. Sansenhō; prev. Sach'ŏn, Samch'ŏnpŏ. S South Korea 34°55′N 128°07′E
12 C7 **Sachigo** Ontario, C Canada
12 C8 **Sachigo Lake** Ontario, C Canada 53°52′N 92°16′W
12 C8 **Sachigo Lake** ◎ Ontario, C Canada
Sach'ŏn see Sacheon
101 O15 **Sachsen** Eng. Saxony, Fr. Saxe. ◆ state E Germany
101 K14 **Sachsen-Anhalt** Eng. Saxony-Anhalt. ◆ state C Germany
109 R9 **Sachsenburg** Salzburg, S Austria 46°49′N 13°23′E
Sachsenfeld see Žalec
8 I5 **Sachs Harbour** var. Ikaahuk. Banks Island, Northwest Territories, N Canada 72°N 125°14′W
Sächsisch-Reen/Sächsisch-Regen see Reghin
18 H8 **Sackets Harbor** New York, NE USA 43°57′N 76°06′W
13 P14 **Sackville** New Brunswick, SE Canada 45°54′N 64°23′W
19 P9 **Saco** Maine, NE USA 43°32′N 70°25′W
19 P8 **Saco River** Maine/New Hampshire, NE USA
35 O7 **Sacramento** state capital California, W USA 38°35′N 121°30′W
37 T14 **Sacramento Mountains** ▲ New Mexico, SW USA
35 N6 **Sacramento River** California, W USA
35 N5 **Sacramento Valley** valley California, W USA
36 I10 **Sacramento Wash** valley Arizona, SW USA
105 N15 **Sacratif, Cabo** headland S Spain 36°41′N 03°30′W
116 F9 **Săcueni** prev. Săcuieni, Hung. Székelyhid. Bihor, W Romania 47°20′N 22°05′E
Săcuieni see Săcueni
105 R4 **Sádaba** Aragón, NE Spain 42°15′N 01°16′W
Sá da Bandeira see Lubango
138 I6 **Şadad** Ḥimṣ, W Syria 34°19′N 36°52′E
141 O13 **Şa'dah** NW Yemen 16°59′N 43°45′E
167 O16 **Sadao** Songkhla, SW Thailand 06°39′N 100°30′E
142 L8 **Sadd-e Dez, Daryācheh-ye** ◎ W Iran
19 S3 **Saddleback Mountain** hill Maine, NE USA
19 P6 **Saddleback Mountain** ▲ Maine, NE USA 44°57′N 70°27′W
141 W13 **Sadh** S Oman 17°11′N 55°08′E
76 J11 **Sadiola** Kayes, W Mali 13°48′N 11°47′W
149 R12 **Sādiqābād** Punjab, E Pakistan 28°16′N 70°10′E
153 Y10 **Sadiya** Assam, NE India 27°49′N 95°38′E
139 W9 **Sa'dīyah, Hawr as** ◎ E Iraq
Sado see Sadoga-shima
165 N9 **Sadoga-shima** var. Sado. island C Japan
104 F12 **Sado, Rio** S Portugal
114 I8 **Sadovets** Pleven, N Bulgaria 43°19′N 24°21′E
114 J11 **Sadovo** Plovdiv, C Bulgaria 42°07′N 24°56′E
127 O11 **Sadovoye** Respublika Kalmykiya, SW Russian Federation 47°51′N 44°34′E
105 W9 **Sa Dragonera** var. Isla Dragonera. island Islas Baleares, Spain, W Mediterranean Sea
105 P9 **Saelices** Castilla-La Mancha, C Spain 39°55′N 02°49′W
Saena Julia see Siena
Saetabicula see Alzira
114 O12 **Safaalan** Tekirdağ, NW Turkey 41°26′N 28°07′E
Safad see Tsefat
Şafāqis see Sfax
143 P10 **Şafāshahr** var. Deh Bīd. Fārs, C Iran 30°50′N 53°50′E
192 I16 **Safata Bay** bay Upolu, Samoa, C Pacific Ocean
Safed see Tsefat
139 X11 **Şaffāf, Ḩawr aş** marshy lake S Iraq
95 J16 **Säffle** Värmland, C Sweden 59°08′N 12°55′E
37 N15 **Safford** Arizona, SW USA 32°46′N 109°41′W
74 E7 **Safi** W Morocco 32°19′N 09°14′W
126 I4 **Safonovo** Smolenskaya Oblast', W Russian Federation 55°05′N 33°12′E
136 H11 **Safranbolu** Karabük, NW Turkey 41°16′N 32°41′E
139 Y13 **Safwān** Al Başrah, SE Iraq 30°06′N 47°44′E
158 J16 **Saga** var. Gya'gya. Xizang Zizhiqu, W China 29°22′N 85°19′E
164 C14 **Saga** Saga, Kyūshū, SW Japan 33°14′N 130°16′E
164 C13 **Saga** off. Saga-ken. ◆ prefecture Kyūshū, SW Japan
165 P10 **Sagae** Yamagata, Honshū, C Japan 38°22′N 140°12′E
166 L3 **Sagaing** Sagaing, C Burma (Myanmar) 21°55′N 95°56′E
166 L5 **Sagaing** ◆ division N Burma (Myanmar)
Saga-ken see Saga
165 N13 **Sagamihara** Kanagawa, Honshū, S Japan 35°34′N 139°22′E
165 N14 **Sagami-nada** inlet SW Japan
Sagan see Żagań
29 Y3 **Saganaga Lake** ◎ Minnesota, N USA
155 F18 **Sāgar** Karnātaka, W India 14°09′N 75°02′E
154 I9 **Sāgar** prev. Saugor. Madhya Pradesh, C India 23°53′N 78°46′E
15 S8 **Sagard** Québec, SE Canada 48°01′N 70°03′W
Sagarmāthā see Everest, Mount
Sagebrush State see Nevada
143 V11 **Sāghand** Yazd, C Iran 32°33′N 55°12′E
19 N14 **Sag Harbor** Long Island, New York, NE USA 40°59′N 72°15′W
Saghez see Saqqez
31 R8 **Saginaw** Michigan, N USA 43°25′N 83°57′W
31 R8 **Saginaw Bay** lake bay Michigan, N USA
Sagiz see Sagyz
64 H6 **Saglek Bank** undersea feature W Labrador Sea
13 P5 **Saglek Bay** bay SW Labrador Sea
Saglouc/Sagluk see Salluit
103 X15 **Sagonne, Golfe de** gulf Corse, France, C Mediterranean Sea
105 P13 **Sagra** ▲ S Spain 37°59′N 02°33′W
104 F14 **Sagres** Faro, S Portugal 37°01′N 08°56′W
37 S7 **Saguache** Colorado, C USA 38°05′N 106°05′W
44 J7 **Sagua de Tánamo** Holguín, E Cuba 20°38′N 75°14′W
44 E5 **Sagua la Grande** Villa Clara, C Cuba 22°48′N 80°06′W
15 R7 **Saguenay** Québec, SE Canada
74 C9 **Saguia al Hamra** var. As Saqia al Hamra. N Western Sahara
105 S9 **Sagunto** Cat. Sagunt, Ar. Murviedro; anc. Saguntum. Valenciana, E Spain 39°40′N 00°17′W
Sagunt/Saguntum see Sagunto
144 H11 **Sagyz** prev. Sagiz. Atyrau, W Kazakhstan 48°12′N 54°56′E
138 H10 **Saḩāb** 'Ammān, NW Jordan 31°52′N 36°00′E
54 E6 **Sahagún** Córdoba, NW Colombia 08°58′N 75°30′W
104 L4 **Sahagún** Castilla y León, N Spain 42°23′N 05°02′W
141 X8 **Şaḩam** N Oman 24°06′N 56°52′E
68 F9 **Sahara** desert Libya/Algeria
Sahara el Gharbîya see Şaḩrā' al Gharbīyah
75 X9 **Sahara el Sharqîya** var. Aş Şaḩrā' ash Sharqīyah, Eng. Arabian Desert, Eastern Desert. desert E Egypt
Saharan Atlas see Atlas Saharien
152 J9 **Sahāranpur** Uttar Pradesh, N India 29°58′N 77°33′E
64 L10 **Saharan Seamounts** var. Saharian Seamounts. undersea feature E Atlantic Ocean 25°00′N 20°00′W
Saharian Seamounts see Saharan Seamounts
153 Q13 **Saharsa** Bihār, NE India 25°54′N 86°36′E
67 O7 **Sahel** physical region C Africa
153 R14 **Sāhibganj** Jhārkhand, NE India 25°15′N 87°40′E
139 Q7 **Sahilīyah** Al Anbār, C Iraq 33°43′N 42°42′E
138 H4 **Şāḩilīyah, Jibāl as** ▲ NW Syria
114 M13 **Şahin** Tekirdağ, NW Turkey 41°01′N 26°51′E
149 U9 **Sāhīwāl** prev. Montgomery. Punjab, E Pakistan 30°40′N 73°05′E
149 U8 **Sāhīwāl** Punjab, E Pakistan 31°57′N 72°22′E
141 W11 **Şaḩmah, Ramlat as** desert C Oman
75 U9 **Şaḩrā' al Gharbīyah** var. Sahara el Gharbîya, Eng. Western Desert. desert C Egypt
139 T13 **Şaḩrā' al Ḩijārah** desert S Iraq
40 H5 **Sahuaripa** Sonora, NW Mexico 29°02′N 109°14′W
36 M16 **Sahuarita** Arizona, SW USA 31°24′N 110°55′W
40 L13 **Sahuayo** var. Sahuayo de José María Morelos; prev. Sahuayo de Porfirio Díaz. Michoacán, SW Mexico 20°05′N 102°42′W
Sahuayo de Díaz/Sahuayo de José María Morelos/Sahuayo de Porfirio Díaz see Sahuayo
173 W8 **Sahul Shelf** undersea feature N Timor Sea
167 P17 **Sai Buri** Pattani, SW Thailand 06°42′N 101°37′E
74 I6 **Saïda** NW Algeria 34°50′N 00°10′E
138 G7 **Saïda** var. Şaydā, Sayida; anc. Sidon. W Lebanon 33°20′N 35°24′E
Sa'īdābād see Sīrjān
80 B13 **Sa'īd Bundas** Western Bahr el Ghazal, W South Sudan 08°24′N 24°53′E
186 E7 **Saidor** Madang, N Papua New Guinea 05°38′S 146°28′E
153 S13 **Saidpur** var. Syedpur. Rajshahi, NW Bangladesh 25°48′N 89°E
149 U5 **Saïdu** var. Mingora, Mongora; prev. Mingāora. Khyber Pakhtunkhwa, N Pakistan 34°45′N 72°21′E
108 C7 **Saignelégier** Jura, NW Switzerland 47°18′N 07°03′E
164 H11 **Saigō** Shimane, Dōgo, SW Japan 36°12′N 133°18′E
Saigon see Hô Chi Minh
163 P11 **SaihanTal** var. Sonid Youqi. Nei Mongol Zizhiqu, N China 42°45′N 112°36′E
162 I12 **Saihan Toroi** Nei Mongol Zizhiqu, N China 41°44′N 100°29′E
Sai Hun see Syr Darya
92 M11 **Saija** Lappi, NE Finland 67°07′N 28°46′E
164 G14 **Saijō** Ehime, Shikoku, SW Japan 33°55′N 133°10′E
164 E15 **Saiki** Ōita, Kyūshū, SW Japan 32°57′N 131°52′E
93 N18 **Saimaa** ◎ SE Finland
93 N18 **Saimaa Canal** Fin. Saimaan Kanava, Rus. Saymenskiy Kanal. canal Finland/Russian Federation
Saimaan Kanava see Saimaa Canal
40 L10 **Sain Alto** Zacatecas, C Mexico 23°36′N 103°14′W
96 L12 **St Abb's Head** headland SE Scotland, United Kingdom 55°54′N 02°07′W
11 Y16 **St. Adolphe** Manitoba, S Canada 49°39′N 96°55′W
103 O15 **St-Affrique** Aveyron, S France 43°57′N 02°52′E
15 Q10 **St-Agapit** Québec, SE Canada 46°22′N 71°37′W
97 O21 **St Albans** anc. Verulamium. E England, United Kingdom 51°46′N 00°21′W
18 L6 **Saint Albans** Vermont, NE USA 44°49′N 73°07′W
21 Q5 **Saint Albans** West Virginia, NE USA 38°21′N 81°47′W
St. Alban's Head see St Aldhelm's Head
11 Q14 **St. Albert** Alberta, SW Canada 53°38′N 113°38′W
97 M24 **St Aldhelm's Head** var. St. Alban's Head. headland S England, United Kingdom 50°34′N 02°04′W
15 O11 **St-Alexis-des-Monts** Québec, SE Canada 46°30′N 73°08′W
103 P2 **St-Amand-les-Eaux** Nord, N France 50°27′N 03°25′E
103 O9 **St-Amand-Montrond** var. St-Amand-Mont-Rond. Cher, C France 46°43′N 02°29′E
173 P16 **St-André** NE Réunion
14 M12 **St-André-Avellin** Québec, SE Canada 45°45′N 75°04′W
Saint-André, Cap see Vilanandro, Tanjona
102 K12 **St-André-de-Cubzac** Gironde, SW France 45°01′N 00°26′W
96 K11 **St Andrews** E Scotland, United Kingdom 56°20′N 02°49′W
23 Q9 **Saint Andrews Bay** bay Florida, SE USA
23 W7 **Saint Andrew Sound** sound Georgia, SE USA
Saint Anna Trough see Svyataya Anna Trough
44 J11 **St. Ann's Bay** C Jamaica 18°26′N 77°12′W
13 T10 **St. Anthony** Newfoundland and Labrador, SE Canada 51°22′N 55°34′W
33 R13 **Saint Anthony** Idaho, NW USA 43°56′N 111°38′W
182 M11 **Saint Arnaud** Victoria, SE Australia 36°39′S 143°15′E
185 I15 **St.Arnaud Range** ▲ South Island, New Zealand
13 R10 **St-Augustin** Québec, E Canada 51°13′N 58°39′W
23 X9 **Saint Augustine** Florida, SE USA 29°54′N 81°19′W
97 H24 **St Austell** SW England, United Kingdom 50°21′N 04°47′W
103 T4 **St-Avold** Moselle, NE France 49°06′N 06°43′E
103 N17 **St-Barthélemy** ▲ S France
102 L17 **St-Béat** Haute-Garonne, S France 42°55′N 00°39′E
97 I15 **St Bees Head** headland NW England, United Kingdom 54°30′N 03°39′W
173 P16 **St-Benoit** E Réunion
103 T13 **St-Bonnet** Hautes-Alpes, SE France 44°41′N 06°04′E
St.Botolph's Town see Boston
97 G21 **St Brides Bay** inlet SW Wales, United Kingdom
102 H5 **St-Brieuc** Côtes d'Armor, NW France 48°31′N 02°45′W
102 H5 **St-Brieuc, Baie de** bay NW France
102 L7 **St-Calais** Sarthe, NW France 47°55′N 00°48′E
15 Q10 **St-Casimir** Québec, SE Canada 46°40′N 72°05′W
14 H16 **St. Catharines** Ontario, S Canada 43°10′N 79°15′W
45 R14 **St. Catherine, Mount** ▲ N Grenada 12°10′N 61°41′W
64 C11 **St Catherine Point** headland E Bermuda
23 X6 **Saint Catherines Island** island Georgia, SE USA
97 M24 **St Catherine's Point** headland S England, United Kingdom 50°34′N 01°17′W
103 N13 **St-Céré** Lot, S France 44°52′N 01°53′E
108 A10 **St. Cergue** Vaud, W Switzerland 46°25′N 06°10′E
103 R11 **St-Chamond** Loire, E France 45°29′N 04°32′E
33 S16 **Saint Charles** Idaho, NW USA 42°05′N 111°23′W
27 X4 **Saint Charles** Missouri, C USA 38°48′N 90°29′W
103 P13 **St-Chély-d'Apcher** Lozère, S France 44°51′N 03°16′E
Saint Christopher and Nevis, Federation of see Saint Kitts and Nevis
Saint Christopher-Nevis see Saint Kitts and Nevis
31 S9 **Saint Clair** Michigan, N USA 42°49′N 82°29′W
183 O17 **St. Clair, Lake** ◎ Tasmania, SE Australia
14 C17 **St. Clair, Lake** var. Lac à L'Eau Claire. ◎ Canada/USA
31 S10 **Saint Clair Shores** Michigan, N USA 42°30′N 82°53′W
103 S10 **St-Claude** anc. Condate. Jura, E France 46°23′N 05°52′E
45 X6 **St-Claude** Basse Terre, SW Guadeloupe 16°02′N 61°42′W
23 X12 **Saint Cloud** Florida, SE USA 28°15′N 81°15′W
29 U8 **Saint Cloud** Minnesota, N USA 45°34′N 94°10′W
45 T9 **Saint Croix** island S Virgin Islands (US)
30 J4 **Saint Croix Flowage** ◫ Wisconsin, N USA
19 T5 **Saint Croix River** Canada/USA
29 W7 **Saint Croix River** Minnesota/Wisconsin, N USA
45 S14 **St.David's** SE Grenada 12°01′N 61°40′W
97 H21 **St David's** SW Wales, United Kingdom 51°53′N 05°16′W
97 G21 **St David's Head** headland SW Wales, United Kingdom 51°54′N 05°19′W
64 C12 **St David's Island** island E Bermuda
173 O16 **St-Denis** ○ (Réunion) NW Réunion 20°55′S 14°34′E
103 U6 **St-Dié** Vosges, NE France 48°17′N 06°57′E
103 R5 **St-Dizier** anc. Desiderii Fanum. Haute-Marne, N France 48°39′N 05°00′E
15 N11 **St-Donat** Québec, SE Canada 46°19′N 74°15′W
15 N11 **Ste-Adèle** Québec, SE Canada 45°58′N 74°10′W
15 N11 **Ste-Agathe-des-Monts** Québec, SE Canada 46°03′N 74°19′W
11 Y16 **Ste. Anne** Manitoba, S Canada 49°40′N 96°40′W
45 R12 **Ste-Anne** Grande Terre, E Guadeloupe 16°13′N 61°23′W
45 Y6 **Ste-Anne** SE Martinique 14°26′N 60°53′W
15 Q10 **Ste-Anne** Québec, SE Canada
172 I16 **Sainte Anne** island Inner Islands, NE Seychelles
15 W6 **Ste-Anne-des-Monts** Québec, SE Canada 49°07′N 66°29′W
14 M10 **Ste-Anne-du-Lac** Québec, SE Canada 46°51′N 75°20′W
15 S10 **Ste-Apolline** Québec, SE Canada 46°47′N 70°15′W
15 R10 **Ste-Claire** Québec, SE Canada 46°30′N 70°40′W
15 Q10 **Ste-Croix** Québec, SE Canada 46°36′N 71°42′W
108 B8 **Ste. Croix** Vaud, SW Switzerland 46°50′N 06°31′E
103 P14 **Ste-Énimie** Lozère, S France 44°21′N 03°26′E
27 Y6 **Sainte Genevieve** Missouri, C USA 37°57′N 90°01′W
103 S12 **St-Egrève** Isère, E France 45°15′N 05°41′E
39 T12 **Saint Elias, Cape** headland Kayak Island, Alaska, USA 59°48′N 144°36′W
39 U11 **Saint Elias, Mount** ▲ Alaska, USA 60°18′N 140°57′W
10 G8 **Saint Elias Mountains** ▲ Canada/USA
55 Y10 **St-Élie** N French Guiana 04°50′N 53°21′W
103 O10 **St-Eloy-les-Mines** Puy-de-Dôme, C France 46°07′N 02°50′E
15 R10 **Ste-Marie** Québec, SE Canada 46°28′N 71°00′W
45 Q11 **Ste-Marie** NE Martinique 14°47′N 61°00′W
173 P16 **Ste-Marie** NE Réunion
103 U6 **Ste-Marie-aux-Mines** Haut-Rhin, NE France 48°16′N 07°12′E
Sainte Marie, Cap see Vohimena, Tanjona
102 L8 **Ste-Maure-de-Touraine** Indre-et-Loire, C France 47°06′N 00°38′E
103 R4 **Ste-Menehould** Marne, NE France 49°06′N 04°54′E
Ste-Perpétue see Ste-Perpétue-de-l'Islet
15 S9 **Ste-Perpétue-de-l'Islet** var. Ste-Perpétue. Québec, SE Canada 47°02′N 69°58′W
45 X11 **Ste-Rose** Basse Terre, N Guadeloupe 16°20′N 61°42′W
173 P16 **Ste-Rose** E Réunion
11 W15 **Ste. Rose du Lac** Manitoba, S Canada 51°04′N 99°31′W
102 J11 **Saintes** anc. Mediolanum. Charente-Maritime, W France 45°45′N 00°37′W
45 X7 **Saintes, Canal des** channel SW Guadeloupe
Saintes, Îles des see les Saintes
173 P16 **Ste-Suzanne** N Réunion
15 P10 **Ste-Thècle** Québec, SE Canada 46°48′N 72°31′W
103 Q12 **St-Étienne** Loire, E France 45°26′N 04°23′E
102 M4 **St-Étienne-du-Rouvray** Seine-Maritime, N France 49°22′N 01°07′E
Saint Eustatius see Sint Eustatius
14 M11 **Ste-Véronique** Québec, SE Canada 46°30′N 74°58′W
15 P7 **St-Félicien** Québec, SE Canada 48°38′N 72°29′W
15 O11 **St-Félix-de-Valois** Québec, SE Canada 46°10′N 73°26′W
103 Y14 **St-Florent** Corse, France, C Mediterranean Sea 42°41′N 09°19′E
103 Y14 **St-Florent, Golfe de** gulf Corse, France, C Mediterranean Sea
103 P6 **St-Florentin** Yonne, C France 48°00′N 03°46′E
103 N9 **St-Florent-sur-Cher** Cher, C France 47°00′N 02°13′E
103 P12 **St-Flour** Cantal, C France 45°02′N 03°05′E
26 H2 **Saint Francis** Kansas, C USA 39°45′N 101°31′W
83 H26 **St. Francis, Cape** headland S South Africa 34°11′S 24°45′E
27 X10 **Saint Francis River** Arkansas/Missouri, C USA
22 J8 **Saint Francisville** Louisiana, S USA 30°46′N 91°22′W
45 Y6 **St-François** Grande Terre, E Guadeloupe 16°15′N 61°17′W
15 Q12 **St-François** Québec, SE Canada
27 X7 **Saint Francois Mountains** ▲ Missouri, C USA
St-Gall see Saint Gall/Saint Gall/St.Gallen
St-Gall/Saint Gall/St. Gallen see Sankt Gallen
102 L16 **St-Gaudens** Haute-Garonne, S France 43°07′N 00°43′E
15 R12 **St-Gédéon** Québec, SE Canada 45°51′N 70°36′W
181 X10 **Saint George** Queensland, E Australia 28°05′S 148°40′E
64 B12 **St George** N Bermuda 32°24′N 64°42′W
38 K15 **Saint George** Saint George Island, Alaska, USA 56°34′N 169°30′W
21 S14 **Saint George** South Carolina, SE USA 33°12′N 80°34′W
36 J8 **Saint George** Utah, W USA 37°06′N 113°35′W
13 R12 **St. George, Cape** headland Newfoundland and Labrador, E Canada 48°26′N 59°17′W
186 I6 **St. George, Cape** headland New Ireland, NE Papua New Guinea 04°49′S 152°52′E
38 J15 **Saint George Island** island Pribilof Islands, Alaska, USA
23 S10 **Saint George Island** island Florida, SE USA
99 J19 **Saint-Georges** Liège, E Belgium 50°36′N 05°20′E
15 R11 **St-Georges** Québec, SE Canada 46°08′N 70°40′W
55 Z11 **St-Georges** E French Guiana 03°55′N 51°49′W
45 R14 **St. George's** ● (Grenada) SW Grenada 12°04′N 61°45′W
13 R12 **St. George's Bay** inlet Newfoundland and Labrador, E Canada
97 G21 **Saint George's Channel** channel Ireland/Wales, United Kingdom
186 H6 **St. George's Channel** channel NE Papua New Guinea
64 B11 **St George's Island** island E Bermuda
99 I21 **Saint-Gérard** Namur, S Belgium 50°20′N 04°47′E
St-Germain see St-Germain-en-Laye
15 P12 **St-Germain-de-Grantham** Québec, SE Canada 45°49′N 72°32′W
103 N5 **St-Germain-en-Laye** var. St-Germain. Yvelines, N France 48°53′N 02°04′E
102 H8 **St-Gildas, Pointe du** headland NW France 47°09′N 02°25′W
103 R15 **St-Gilles** Gard, S France 43°41′N 04°24′E
102 I9 **St-Gilles-Croix-de-Vie** Vendée, NW France 46°41′N 01°55′W
173 O16 **St-Gilles-les-Bains** W Réunion 21°02′S 55°14′E
102 M16 **St-Girons** Ariège, S France 42°58′N 01°07′E
Saint Gotthard see Szentgotthárd
108 G9 **St. Gotthard Tunnel** tunnel Ticino, S Switzerland
97 H22 **St Govan's Head** headland SW Wales, United Kingdom 51°35′N 04°55′W
34 M7 **Saint Helena** California, W USA 38°29′N 122°30′W
65 F24 **Saint Helena** ◇ UK dependent territory C Atlantic Ocean
67 O12 **Saint Helena** island C Atlantic Ocean
65 M16 **Saint Helena Fracture Zone** tectonic feature C Atlantic Ocean
34 M7 **Saint Helena, Mount** ▲ California, W USA 38°40′N 122°39′W
21 S15 **Saint Helena Sound** inlet South Carolina, SE USA
31 Q7 **Saint Helen, Lake** ◎ Michigan, N USA
183 Q16 **Saint Helens** Tasmania, SE Australia 41°21′S 148°15′E
97 K18 **St Helens** NW England, United Kingdom 53°28′N 02°44′W
32 G10 **Saint Helens** Oregon, NW USA 45°54′N 122°50′W
32 H10 **Saint Helens, Mount** ▲ Washington, NW USA 46°24′N 121°49′W
97 L26 **St Helier** ○ (Jersey) S Jersey, Channel Islands 49°12′N 02°07′W
15 S9 **St-Hilarion** Québec, SE Canada 47°34′N 70°24′W
99 K22 **Saint-Hubert** Luxembourg, SE Belgium 50°02′N 05°23′E
15 P12 **St-Hyacinthe** Québec, SE Canada 45°38′N 72°57′W
St.Iago de la Vega see Spanish Town
31 Q4 **Saint Ignace** Michigan, N USA 45°53′N 84°44′W
15 O10 **St-Ignace-du-Lac** Québec, SE Canada 46°43′N 73°49′W
12 D12 **St. Ignace Island** island Ontario, S Canada
108 C7 **St. Imier** Bern, W Switzerland 47°09′N 06°55′E
97 G25 **St Ives** SW England, United Kingdom 50°12′N 05°29′W
29 U10 **Saint James** Minnesota, N USA 44°00′N 94°36′W
10 I15 **St. James, Cape** headland Graham Island, British Columbia, SW Canada 51°57′N 131°04′W
15 O13 **St-Jean** var. St-Jean-sur-Richelieu. Québec, SE Canada 45°15′N 73°16′W
55 X9 **St-Jean** NW French Guiana 05°25′N 54°05′W
Saint-Jean-d'Acre see Akko
102 K11 **St-Jean-d'Angély** Charente-Maritime, W France 45°57′N 00°31′W
103 N7 **St-Jean-de-Braye** Loiret, C France 47°54′N 01°58′E
102 I16 **St-Jean-de-Luz** Pyrénées-Atlantiques, SW France 43°24′N 01°40′W
103 T12 **St-Jean-de-Maurienne** Savoie, E France 45°17′N 06°21′E
102 I9 **St-Jean-de-Monts** Vendée, NW France 46°45′N 02°00′W
103 Q14 **St-Jean-du-Gard** Gard, S France 44°06′N 03°49′E
15 Q7 **St-Jean, Lac** ◎ Québec, SE Canada
102 I16 **St-Jean-Pied-de-Port** Pyrénées-Atlantiques, SW France 43°10′N 01°14′W
15 S9 **St-Jean-Port-Joli** Québec, SE Canada 47°13′N 70°16′W
St-Jean-sur-Richelieu see St-Jean
15 N12 **St-Jérôme** Québec, SE Canada 45°47′N 74°01′W
25 T5 **Saint Jo** Texas, SW USA 33°42′N 97°33′W
13 O15 **St. John** New Brunswick, SE Canada 45°16′N 66°03′W
26 L6 **Saint John** Kansas, C USA 37°59′N 98°44′W
19 Q2 **Saint John** Fr. Saint-John. Canada/USA
76 K16 **Saint John** C Liberia
45 T9 **Saint John** island C Virgin Islands (US)
Saint-John see Saint John
22 I6 **Saint John, Lake** ◎ Louisiana, S USA
45 W10 **St John's** ● (Antigua and Barbuda) Antigua, Antigua and Barbuda 17°06′N 61°50′W
13 V12 **St. John's** province capital Newfoundland and Labrador, E Canada 47°34′N 52°41′W
37 O12 **Saint Johns** Arizona, SW USA 34°28′N 109°22′W
31 Q9 **Saint Johns** Michigan, N USA 43°01′N 84°31′W
13 V12 **St. John's** ✕ Newfoundland and Labrador, E Canada 47°22′N 52°45′W
23 X11 **Saint Johns River** Florida, SE USA
103 Q11 **St-Just-St-Rambert** Loire, E France 45°30′N 04°13′E
45 N13 **St. Joseph** W Dominica 15°24′N 61°26′W
173 P17 **St-Joseph** S Réunion
22 J6 **Saint Joseph** Louisiana, S USA 31°56′N 91°14′W
31 O10 **Saint Joseph** Michigan, N USA 42°05′N 86°30′W
27 R3 **Saint Joseph** Missouri, C USA 39°46′N 94°49′W
20 I10 **Saint Joseph** Tennessee, S USA 35°02′N 87°29′W
22 R9 **Saint Joseph Bay** bay Florida, SE USA
15 R11 **St-Joseph-de-Beauce** Québec, SE Canada 46°20′N 70°52′W
12 C10 **St. Joseph, Lake** ◎ Ontario, C Canada
31 Q11 **Saint Joseph River** N USA
14 C11 **Saint Joseph's Island** island Ontario, S Canada
15 N11 **St-Jovite** Québec, SE Canada 46°07′N 74°35′W
St Julian's see San Giljan
St.Julien see St-Julien-en-Genevois
103 T10 **St-Julien-en-Genevois** var. St-Julien. Haute-Savoie, E France 46°07′N 06°06′E
102 M11 **St-Junien** Haute-Vienne, C France 45°52′N 00°54′E
96 D8 **St Kilda** island NW Scotland, United Kingdom
45 V10 **Saint Kitts** island Saint Kitts and Nevis
45 U10 **Saint Kitts and Nevis** off. Federation of Saint Christopher and Nevis, var. Saint Christopher-Nevis. ◆ commonwealth republic E West Indies
11 X16 **St. Laurent** Manitoba, S Canada 50°20′N 97°55′W
St-Laurent see St-Laurent-du-Maroni
55 X9 **St-Laurent-du-Maroni** var. St-Laurent. NW French Guiana 05°29′N 54°03′W
St-Laurent, Fleuve see St. Lawrence
102 J12 **St-Laurent-Médoc** Gironde, SW France 45°11′N 00°50′W
15 N12 **St. Lawrence** Fr. Fleuve St-Laurent. Canada/USA
13 Q12 **St. Lawrence, Gulf of** gulf NW Atlantic Ocean
38 K10 **Saint Lawrence Island** island Alaska, USA
14 M14 **Saint Lawrence River** Canada/USA
99 L25 **Saint-Léger** Luxembourg, SE Belgium 49°36′N 05°39′E
13 N14 **St. Léonard** New Brunswick, SE Canada 47°10′N 67°55′W
15 P11 **St-Léonard** Québec, SE Canada 46°06′N 72°18′W
173 O17 **St-Leu** W Réunion 21°09′S 55°17′E
102 J4 **St-Lô** anc. Briovera, Laudus. Manche, N France 49°07′N 01°08′W
11 T15 **St. Louis** Saskatchewan, S Canada 52°50′N 105°43′W
103 V7 **St-Louis** Haut-Rhin, NE France 47°35′N 07°34′E
173 O17 **St-Louis** S Réunion
76 G10 **Saint Louis** NW Senegal 15°59′N 16°30′W
27 X4 **Saint Louis** Missouri, C USA 38°38′N 90°15′W
29 W5 **Saint Louis River** Minnesota, N USA
103 T7 **St-Loup-sur-Semouse** Haute-Saône, E France 47°53′N 06°15′E
15 O12 **St-Luc** Québec, SE Canada 45°19′N 73°18′W
45 X13 **Saint Lucia** ◆ commonwealth republic SE West Indies
47 S3 **Saint Lucia** island SE West Indies
83 L22 **St. Lucia, Cape** headland E South Africa 28°29′S 32°26′E
45 Y13 **Saint Lucia Channel** channel Martinique/Saint Lucia
23 Y14 **Saint Lucie Canal** canal Florida, SE USA
23 Z13 **Saint Lucie Inlet** inlet Florida, SE USA
96 L2 **St Magnus Bay** bay N Scotland, United Kingdom
102 K10 **St-Maixent-l'École** Deux-Sèvres, W France 46°24′N 00°13′W
11 Y16 **St. Malo** Manitoba, S Canada 49°16′N 96°58′W
102 I5 **St-Malo** Ille-et-Vilaine, NW France 48°39′N 02°00′W
102 H4 **St-Malo, Golfe de** gulf NW France
44 L9 **St-Marc** C Haiti 19°08′N 72°41′W
44 L9 **St-Marc, Canal de** channel W Haiti
103 S12 **St-Marcellin-le-Mollard** Isère, E France 45°12′N 05°18′E
55 Y12 **Saint-Marcel, Mont** ▲ S French Guiana 2°32′N 53°00′E
96 K5 **St Margaret's Hope** NE Scotland, United Kingdom 58°50′N 02°57′W
32 M9 **Saint Maries** Idaho, NW USA 47°19′N 116°37′W
23 T9 **Saint Marks** Florida, SE USA 30°09′N 84°12′W
108 D11 **St. Martin** Valais, SW Switzerland 46°09′N 07°27′E
Saint Martin see Sint Maarten
31 O5 **Saint Martin Island** island Michigan, N USA
22 I9 **Saint Martinville** Louisiana, S USA 30°09′N 91°51′W
185 E20 **St. Mary, Mount** ▲ South Island, New Zealand 44°16′S 169°42′E
186 E8 **St. Mary, Mount** ▲ S Papua New Guinea 08°06′S 147°00′E
182 I6 **Saint Mary Peak** ▲ South Australia 31°25′S 138°39′E
183 Q16 **Saint Marys** Tasmania, SE Australia 41°34′S 148°13′E
14 E16 **St. Marys** Ontario, S Canada 43°15′N 81°08′W

◆ Country
● Country Capital
◇ Dependent Territory
○ Dependent Territory Capital
◆ Administrative Regions
✕ International Airport
▲ Mountain
▲ Mountain Range
Volcano
River
◎ Lake
◫ Reservoir

38 M11 **Saint Marys** Alaska, USA 62°03′N 163°10′W
23 W8 **Saint Marys** Georgia, SE USA 30°44′N 81°30′W
27 P4 **Saint Marys** Kansas, C USA 39°09′N 96°00′W
31 Q4 **Saint Marys** Ohio, N USA 40°31′N 84°22′W
21 R3 **Saint Marys** West Virginia, NE USA 39°24′N 81°13′W
23 W8 **Saint Marys River** ≈ Florida/Georgia, SE USA
31 Q4 **Saint Marys River** ≈ Michigan, N USA
102 D6 **St-Mathieu, Pointe** headland NW France 48°17′N 04°56′W
38 J12 **Saint Matthew Island** island Alaska, USA
21 R13 **Saint Matthews** South Carolina, SE USA 33°40′N 80°44′W
St.Matthew's Island see Zadetkyi Kyun
186 G4 **St.Matthias Group** island group NE Papua New Guinea
108 C11 **St. Maurice** Valais, SW Switzerland 46°09′N 07°28′E
15 P9 **St-Maurice** ≈ Québec, SE Canada
102 J13 **St-Médard-en-Jalles** Gironde, SW France 44°54′N 00°43′W
39 N10 **Saint Michael** Alaska, USA 63°28′N 162°02′W
15 N10 **St-Michel-des-Saints** Québec, SE Canada 46°39′N 73°54′W
103 S5 **St-Mihiel** Meuse, NE France 48°57′N 05°33′E
108 J10 **St. Moritz** Ger. Sankt Moritz, Rmsch. San Murezzan. Graubünden, SE Switzerland 46°30′N 09°51′E
102 H8 **St-Nazaire** Loire-Atlantique, NW France 47°17′N 02°12′W
Saint Nicholas see São Nicolau
Saint-Nicolas see Sint-Niklaas
103 N1 **St-Omer** Pas-de-Calais, N France 50°45′N 02°15′E
102 J11 **Saintonge** cultural region W France
15 S9 **St-Pacôme** Québec, SE Canada 47°22′N 69°56′W
15 S10 **St-Pamphile** Québec, SE Canada 46°57′N 69°46′W
15 S9 **St-Pascal** Québec, SE Canada 47°32B 69°48′W
14 J11 **St-Patrice, Lac** ◎ Québec, SE Canada
11 R14 **St. Paul** Alberta, SW Canada 54°00′N 111°18′W
173 O16 **St-Paul** NW Réunion
38 K14 **Saint Paul** Saint Paul Island, Alaska, USA 57°08′N 170°13′W
29 V8 **Saint Paul** state capital Minnesota, N USA 45°N 93°10′W
29 P15 **Saint Paul** Nebraska, C USA 41°13′N 98°26′W
21 P7 **Saint Paul** Virginia, NE USA 36°53′N 82°18′W
77 Q17 **Saint Paul, Cape** headland S Ghana 05°44′N 00°55′E
103 O17 **St-Paul-de-Fenouillet** Pyrénées-Orientales, S France 42°49′N 02°29′E
65 K14 **Saint Paul Fracture Zone** tectonic feature E Atlantic Ocean
38 J14 **Saint Paul Island** island Pribilof Islands, Alaska, USA
102 J15 **St-Paul-les-Dax** Landes, SW France 43°45′N 01°01′W
21 U11 **Saint Pauls** North Carolina, SE USA 34°45′N 78°56′W
Saint Paul's Bay see San Pawl il Bahar
191 R16 **St Paul's Point** headland Pitcairn Island, Pitcairn Islands
29 U10 **Saint Peter** Minnesota, N USA 44°21′N 93°58′W
97 L26 **St Peter Port** ○ (Guernsey) C Guernsey, Channel Islands 49°28′N 02°33′W
23 V13 **Saint Petersburg** Florida, SE USA 27°47′N 82°37′W
Saint Petersburg see Sankt-Peterburg
23 V13 **Saint Petersburg Beach** Florida, SE USA 27°43′N 82°43′W
173 P17 **St-Philippe** SE Réunion 21°21′S 55°46′E
45 Q11 **St-Pierre** NW Martinique 14°44′N 61°11′W
173 O17 **St-Pierre** SW Réunion
13 S13 **St-Pierre and Miquelon** Fr. Îles St-Pierre et Miquelon. ◇ French territorial collectivity NE North America
15 P11 **St-Pierre, Lac** ◎ Québec, SE Canada
102 F5 **St-Pol-de-Léon** Finistère, NW France 48°42′N 04°00′W
103 O2 **St-Pol-sur-Ternoise** Pas-de-Calais, N France 50°22′N 02°21′E
St. Pons see St-Pons-de-Thomières
103 O16 **St-Pons-de-Thomières** var. St. Pons. Hérault, S France 43°28′N 02°48′E
103 P10 **St-Pourçain-sur-Sioule** Allier, C France 46°19′N 03°16′E
15 S11 **St-Prosper** Québec, SE Canada 46°14′N 70°28′W
103 P3 **St-Quentin** Aisne, N France 49°51′N 03°17′E
15 R10 **St-Raphaël** Québec, SE Canada 46°47′N 70°46′W
103 U15 **St-Raphaël** Var, SE France 43°26′N 06°46′E
15 Q10 **St-Raymond** Québec, SE Canada 46°53′N 71°49′W
33 O9 **Saint Regis** Montana, NW USA 47°18′N 115°06′W
18 J7 **Saint Regis River** ≈ New York, NE USA
103 R15 **St-Rémy-de-Provence** Bouches-du-Rhône, SE France 43°48′N 04°49′E
102 M9 **St-Savin** Vienne, W France 46°34′N 00°53′E
Saint-Sébastien,Cap see Anorontany, Tanjona
23 X7 **Saint Simons Island** island Georgia, SE USA
191 Y2 **Saint Stanislas Bay** bay Kiritimati, E Kiribati
13 O15 **St. Stephen** New Brunswick, SE Canada 45°12′N 67°18′W
39 X12 **Saint Terese** Alaska, USA 58°28′N 134°46′W
14 E17 **St. Thomas** Ontario, S Canada 42°46′N 81°12′W
29 Q2 **Saint Thomas** North Dakota, N USA 48°37′N 97°28′W
45 T9 **Saint Thomas** island W Virgin Islands (US)
Saint Thomas see São Tomé, Sao Tome and Principe
Saint Thomas see Charlotte Amalie, Virgin Islands (US)
15 P10 **St-Tite** Québec, SE Canada 46°42′N 72°32′W
Saint-Trond see Sint-Truiden
103 U16 **St-Tropez** Var, SE France 43°16′N 06°39′E
Saint Ubes see Setúbal
102 L3 **St-Valéry-en-Caux** Seine-Maritime, N France 49°53′N 00°42′E
103 Q9 **St-Vallier** Saône-et-Loire, C France 46°39′N 04°19′E
106 B7 **St-Vincent** Valle d'Aosta, NW Italy 45°47′N 07°42′E
45 Q14 **Saint Vincent** island N Saint Vincent and the Grenadines
Saint Vincent see São Vicente
45 W14 **Saint Vincent and the Grenadines** ◆ commonwealth republic SE West Indies
Saint-Vincent, Cap see Ankaboa, Tanjona
Saint Vincent, Cape see São Vicente, Cabo de
102 I15 **St-Vincent-de-Tyrosse** Landes, SW France 43°39′N 01°16′W
182 I9 **Saint Vincent, Gulf** gulf South Australia
23 R10 **Saint Vincent Island** island Florida, SE USA
45 T12 **Saint Vincent Passage** passage Saint Lucia/Saint Vincent and the Grenadines
183 N18 **Saint Vincent, Point** headland Tasmania, SE Australia 43°19′S 145°50′E
Saint-Vith see Sankt-Vith
11 S14 **St. Walburg** Saskatchewan, S Canada 53°38′N 109°12′W
St Wolfgangsee see Wolfgangsee
102 M11 **St-Yrieix-la-Perche** Haute-Vienne, C France 45°31′N 01°12′E
Saint Yves see Setúbal
188 H5 **Saipan** island ● (Northern Mariana Islands) S Northern Mariana Islands
188 H6 **Saipan Channel** channel S Northern Mariana Islands
188 H6 **Saipan International** ✈ Saipan, S Northern Mariana Islands
74 G6 **Sais** ✈ (Fès) C Morocco 33°58′N 04°48′W
Saishū see Jeju-do
Saishū see Jeju
102 J16 **Saison** ≈ SW France
169 R10 **Sai, Sungai** ≈ Borneo, N Indonesia
165 N13 **Saitama** off. Saitama-ken. ◈ prefecture Honshū, S Japan
Saitama see Urawa
Saitama-ken see Saitama
Saiyid Abid see Sayyid 'Abīd
57 J19 **Sajama, Nevado** ▲ W Bolivia 17°57′S 68°51′W
141 V13 **Sājir, Ras** headland S Oman 16°42′N 53°40′E
111 M20 **Sajószentpéter** Borsod-Abaúj-Zemplén, NE Hungary 48°13′N 20°43′E
83 F24 **Sak** ≈ SW South Africa
81 J18 **Saka** Coast, E Kenya 0°11′S 39°27′E
167 P11 **Sa Kaeo** Prachin Buri, C Thailand 13°47′N 102°03′E
164 J14 **Sakai** Ōsaka, Honshū, SW Japan 34°35′N 135°28′E
164 H14 **Sakaide** Kagawa, Shikoku, SW Japan 34°19′N 133°50′E
164 H12 **Sakaiminato** Tottori, Honshū, SW Japan 35°34′N 133°12′E
140 M3 **Sakākah** Al Jawf, NW Saudi Arabia 29°56′N 40°10′E
28 L4 **Sakakawea, Lake** ⊠ North Dakota, N USA
12 J9 **Sakami, Lac** ◎ Québec, C Canada
79 O26 **Sakania** Katanga, SE Dem. Rep. Congo 12°44′S 28°34′E
146 K12 **Sakar** Lebap Welaýaty, E Turkmenistan 38°57′N 63°46′E
172 H7 **Sakaraha** Toliara, SW Madagascar 22°54′S 44°31′E
146 I14 **Sakarçäge** var. Sakarchäge, Rus. Sakar-Chaga. Mary Welaýaty, C Turkmenistan 37°40′N 61°33′E
Sakar-Chaga/Sakarchäge see Sakarçäge
Sak'art'velo see Georgia
136 F11 **Sakarya** ◈ province NW Turkey
136 F12 **Sakarya Nehri** ≈ NW Turkey
165 P9 **Sakata** Yamagata, Honshū, C Japan 38°54′N 139°51′E
123 P9 **Sakha (Yakutiya), Respublika** var. Respublika Yakutiya, Eng. Yakutia. ◈ autonomous republic NE Russian Federation
Sakhalin see Sakhalin, Ostrov
192 I3 **Sakhalin, Ostrov** var. Sakhalin. island SE Russian Federation
123 U12 **Sakhalinskaya Oblast'** ◈ province SE Russian Federation
123 T12 **Sakhalinskiy Zaliv** gulf E Russian Federation
Sakhnovshchina see Sakhnovshchyna
117 U6 **Sakhnovshchyna** Rus. Sakhnovshchina. Kharkivs'ka Oblast', E Ukraine 49°08′N 35°52′E
Sakhon Nakhon see Sakon Nakhon
Sakhtsar see Rāmsar
137 W10 **Şäki** Rus. Sheki; prev. Nukha. NW Azerbaijan 41°09′N 47°10′E
Saki see Saky
118 E13 **Šakiai** Ger. Schaken. Marijampolė, S Lithuania 54°57′N 23°04′E
165 O16 **Sakishima-shotō** var. Sakisima Syotô. island group SW Japan
Sakisima Syotô see Sakishima-shotō
Sakiz see Saqqez
Sakiz-Adasi see Chíos
155 F19 **Sakleshpur** Karnātaka, E India 12°58′N 75°45′E
167 S9 **Sakon Nakhon** var. Muang Sakon Nakhon, Sakhon Nakhon. Sakon Nakhon, E Thailand 17°10′N 104°08′E
149 P15 **Sakrand** Sind, SE Pakistan 26°06′N 68°20′E
83 F24 **Sak River** Afr. Sakrivier. Northern Cape, W South Africa 30°49′S 20°24′E
Sakrivier see Sak River
Saksaul'skiy see Saksaul'skoye
144 K13 **Saksaul'skoye** var. Saksaul'skiy, Kaz. Sekseüil. Kzylorda, S Kazakhstan 47°07′N 61°06′E
95 I25 **Sakskøbing** Sjælland, SE Denmark 54°48′N 11°39′E
165 N12 **Saku** Nagano, Honshū, S Japan 36°17′N 138°29′E
117 S13 **Saky** Rus. Saki. Avtonomna Respublika Krym, S Ukraine 45°09′N 33°36′E
76 E9 **Sal** island Ilhas de Barlavento, NE Cape Verde
127 N12 **Sal** ≈ SW Russian Federation
111 I21 **Sal'a** Hung. Sellye, Vágsellye. Nitriansky Kraj, SW Slovakia 48°09′N 17°51′E
95 N15 **Sala** Västmanland, C Sweden 59°55′N 16°38′E
15 N13 **Salaberry-de-Valleyfield** var. Valleyfield. Québec, SE Canada 45°15′N 74°07′W
118 G7 **Salacgrīva** Est. Salatsi. N Latvia 57°45′N 24°21′E
107 M18 **Sala Consilina** Campania, S Italy 40°23′N 15°35′E
40 C2 **Salada, Laguna** ◎ NW Mexico
61 D14 **Saladas** Corrientes, NE Argentina 28°15′S 58°40′W
61 C21 **Saladillo** Buenos Aires, E Argentina 35°40′S 59°50′W
61 B16 **Saladillo, Río** ≈ C Argentina
25 T9 **Salado** Texas, SW USA 30°57′N 97°32′W
63 J16 **Salado, Arroyo** ≈ SE Argentina
61 D21 **Salado, Río** ≈ E Argentina
62 J12 **Salado, Río** ≈ C Argentina
41 N7 **Salado, Río** ≈ NE Mexico
37 Q12 **Salado, Rio** ≈ New Mexico, SW USA
143 N6 **Salafchegān** var. Sarafjagān. Quom, N Iran 34°28′N 50°28′E
77 Q15 **Salaga** C Ghana 08°31′N 00°37′W
192 G5 **Sala'ilua** Savai'i, W Samoa 13°39′S 172°33′W
116 G9 **Sălaj** ◈ county NW Romania
83 H20 **Salajwe** Kweneng, SE Botswana 23°40′S 24°46′E
78 H9 **Salal** Kanem, W Chad 14°48′N 17°12′E
80 I6 **Salala** Red Sea, NE Sudan 21°17′N 36°16′E
141 V13 **Şalālah** SW Oman 17°01′N 54°04′E
42 D5 **Salamá** Baja Verapaz, C Guatemala 15°06′N 90°18′W
42 J6 **Salamá** Olancho, C Honduras 14°48′N 86°34′W
62 G10 **Salamanca** Coquimbo, C Chile 31°47′S 70°58′W
41 N13 **Salamanca** Guanajuato, C Mexico 20°34′N 101°12′W
104 K7 **Salamanca** anc. Helmantica, Salmantica. Castilla y León, NW Spain 40°58′N 05°40′W
18 D11 **Salamanca** New York, NE USA 42°09′N 78°43′W
104 J7 **Salamanca** ◈ province Castilla y León, W Spain
63 J19 **Salamanca, Pampa de** plain S Argentina
78 J12 **Salamat** off. Préfecture du Salamat. ◈ prefecture SE Chad
78 I12 **Salamat, Bahr** ≈ S Chad
Salamat, Préfecture du see Salamat
54 F5 **Salamina** Magdalena, N Colombia 10°30′N 74°48′W
115 G19 **Salamína** var. Salamís. Salamína, C Greece 37°58′N 23°29′E
115 G19 **Salamína** island C Greece
Salamís see Salamína
138 I5 **Salamīyah** var. As Salamīyah. Ḩamāh, W Syria 35°01′N 37°02′E
31 P12 **Salamonie Lake** ⊠ Indiana, N USA
31 P12 **Salamonie River** ≈ Indiana, N USA
Salang see Phuket
192 I16 **Salani** Upolu, SE Samoa 14°00′S 171°35′W
118 C11 **Salantai** Klaipėda, NW Lithuania 56°05′N 21°36′E
104 K2 **Salas** Asturias, N Spain 43°25′N 06°15′W
105 O5 **Salas de los Infantes** Castilla y León, N Spain 42°02′N 03°17′W
102 M16 **Salat** ≈ S France
189 V13 **Salat** island Chuuk, C Micronesia
169 Q16 **Salatiga** Jawa, C Indonesia 07°15′S 110°34′E
189 V13 **Salat Pass** passage W Pacific Ocean
Salatsi see Salacgrīva
167 T10 **Salavan** var. Saravan, Saravane. Salavan, S Laos 15°43′N 106°26′E
127 V6 **Salavat** Respublika Bashkortostan, W Russian Federation 53°20′N 55°54′E
56 C12 **Salaverry** La Libertad, N Peru 08°14′S 78°55′W
171 T12 **Salawati, Pulau** island E Indonesia
193 R10 **Sala y Gomez** island Chile, E Pacific Ocean
Sala y Gomez Fracture Zone see Sala y Gomez Ridge
193 S10 **Sala y Gomez Ridge** var. Sala y Gomez Fracture Zone. tectonic feature SE Pacific Ocean
61 A22 **Salazar** Buenos Aires, E Argentina 36°20′S 62°11′W
54 G7 **Salazar** Norte de Santander, N Colombia 07°46′N 72°46′W
Salazar see N'Dalatando
173 P16 **Salazie** C Réunion 21°02′S 55°33′E
103 N8 **Salbris** Loir-et-Cher, C France 47°25′N 02°02′E
57 G15 **Salcantay, Nevado** ▲ C Peru 13°21′S 72°31′W
45 O8 **Salcedo** N Dominican Republic 19°26′N 70°25′W
39 S9 **Salcha River** ≈ Alaska, USA
119 H15 **Šalčininkai** Vilnius, SE Lithuania 54°20′N 25°26′E
Saldae see Béjaïa
54 E11 **Saldaña** Tolima, C Colombia 03°57′N 75°01′W
104 M4 **Saldaña** Castilla y León, N Spain 42°31′N 04°44′W
83 E25 **Saldanha** Western Cape, SW South Africa 33°00′S 17°56′E
Salduba see Zaragoza
61 B23 **Saldungaray** Buenos Aires, E Argentina 38°15′S 61°45′W
118 D9 **Saldus** Ger. Frauenburg. W Latvia 56°40′N 22°29′E
183 P13 **Sale** Victoria, SE Australia 38°06′S 147°06′E
74 F6 **Salé** NW Morocco 34°07′N 06°40′W
74 F6 **Salé** ✈ (Rabat) W Morocco 34°09′N 06°30′W
Salehābād see Andīmeshk
170 M16 **Saleh, Teluk** bay Nusa Tenggara, S Indonesia
122 H8 **Salekhard** prev. Obdorsk. Yamalo-Nenetskiy Avtonomnyy Okrug, N Russian Federation 66°33′N 66°35′E
192 H16 **Sālelologa** Savai'i, C Samoa 13°42′S 172°10′W
155 H21 **Salem** Tamil Nādu, SE India 11°38′N 78°08′E
27 V9 **Salem** Arkansas, C USA 36°21′N 91°49′W
30 L15 **Salem** Illinois, N USA 38°37′N 88°57′W
31 P15 **Salem** Indiana, N USA 38°38′N 86°06′W
19 P11 **Salem** Massachusetts, NE USA 42°30′N 70°51′W
27 V6 **Salem** Missouri, C USA 37°39′N 91°32′W
18 I16 **Salem** New Jersey, NE USA 39°33′N 75°26′W
31 U12 **Salem** Ohio, N USA 40°52′N 80°51′W
32 G12 **Salem** state capital Oregon, NW USA 44°57′N 123°01′W
29 Q11 **Salem** South Dakota, N USA 43°43′N 97°23′W
36 L4 **Salem** Utah, W USA 40°03′N 111°40′W
21 S7 **Salem** Virginia, NE USA 37°16′N 80°00′W
21 R3 **Salem** West Virginia, NE USA 39°15′N 80°32′W
107 H23 **Salemi** Sicilia, Italy, C Mediterranean Sea 37°48′N 12°48′E
Salemy see As Sālimī
94 K12 **Sälen** Dalarna, C Sweden 61°11′N 13°14′E
107 Q18 **Salentina, Campi** Puglia, SE Italy 40°23′N 18°01′E
107 Q18 **Salentina, Penisola** peninsula SE Italy
107 L18 **Salerno** anc. Salernum. Campania, S Italy 40°40′N 14°44′E
107 L18 **Salerno, Golfo di** Eng. Gulf of Salerno. gulf S Italy
Salerno, Gulf of see Salerno, Golfo di
Salernum see Salerno
97 K17 **Salford** NW England, United Kingdom 53°30′N 02°16′W
Salgir see Salhyr
111 K21 **Salgótarján** Nógrád, N Hungary 48°07′N 19°47′E
59 O15 **Salgueiro** Pernambuco, E Brazil 08°04′S 39°05′W
94 C13 **Salhus** Hordaland, S Norway 60°30′N 05°15′E
117 T12 **Salhyr** Rus. Salgir. ≈ S Ukraine
171 Q9 **Salibabu, Pulau** island N Indonesia
37 S6 **Salida** Colorado, C USA 38°29′N 105°57′W
102 J15 **Salies-de-Béarn** Pyrénées-Atlantiques, SW France 43°28′N 00°55′W
136 C14 **Salihli** Manisa, W Turkey 38°29′N 28°08′E
119 K18 **Salihorsk** Rus. Soligorsk. Minskaya Voblasts', S Belarus 52°48′N 27°32′E
119 K18 **Salihorskaye Vodaskhovishcha** ⊠ C Belarus
83 N14 **Salima** Central, C Malawi 13°44′S 34°21′E
166 L5 **Salin** Magway, W Burma (Myanmar) 20°30′N 94°40′E
27 N4 **Salina** Kansas, C USA 38°53′N 97°36′W
36 L5 **Salina** Utah, W USA 38°57′N 111°54′W
41 S17 **Salina Cruz** Oaxaca, SE Mexico 16°11′N 95°12′W
107 L22 **Salina, Isola** island Isole Eolie, S Italy
44 J5 **Salina Point** headland Acklins Island, SE Bahamas 22°10′N 74°16′W
56 A7 **Salinas** Guayas, W Ecuador 02°15′S 80°58′W
40 M11 **Salinas** var. Salinas de Hidalgo. San Luis Potosí, C Mexico 22°36′N 101°41′W
45 T6 **Salinas** C Puerto Rico 17°57′N 66°18′W
35 O10 **Salinas** California, W USA 36°41′N 121°40′W
Salinas, Cabo de see Salines, Cap de ses
Salinas de Hidalgo see Salinas
82 A13 **Salinas, Ponta das** headland W Angola 12°50′S 12°57′E
45 O10 **Salinas, Punta** headland S Dominican Republic 18°11′N 70°32′W
Salinas, Río see Chixoy, Río
35 O11 **Salinas River** ≈ California, W USA
22 H6 **Saline Lake** ◎ Louisiana, S USA
25 R17 **Salineno** Texas, SW USA 26°29′N 99°06′W
27 V14 **Saline River** ≈ Arkansas, C USA
30 M17 **Saline River** ≈ Illinois, N USA
105 X10 **Salines, Cap de ses** var. Cabo de Salinas. headland Mallorca, Spain, W Mediterranean Sea 39°15′N 03°03′E
Salisburg see Mazsalaca
45 O12 **Salisbury** var. Baroui. W Dominica 15°26′N 61°27′W
97 M23 **Salisbury** var. New Sarum. S England, United Kingdom 51°05′N 01°48′W
21 Y4 **Salisbury** Maryland, NE USA 38°22′N 75°37′W
27 T3 **Salisbury** Missouri, C USA 39°25′N 92°48′W
21 S9 **Salisbury** North Carolina, SE USA 35°40′N 80°28′W
Salisbury see Harare
9 Q7 **Salisbury Island** island Nunavut, NE Canada
Salisbury, Lake see Bisina, Lake
97 L23 **Salisbury Plain** plain S England, United Kingdom
21 R14 **Salkehatchie River** ≈ South Carolina, SE USA
138 I9 **Şalkhad** As Suwaydā', SW Syria 32°29′N 36°42′E
92 M12 **Salla** Lappi, NE Finland 66°50′N 28°40′E
Sállan see Sørøya
103 U11 **Sallanches** Haute-Savoie, E France 45°55′N 06°37′E
105 V5 **Sallent** Cataluña, NE Spain 41°48′N 01°52′E
Salliq see Coral Harbour
61 A22 **Salliqueló** Buenos Aires, E Argentina 36°45′S 62°55′W
27 R10 **Sallisaw** Oklahoma, C USA 35°27′N 94°49′W
80 I7 **Sallom** Red Sea, NE Sudan 19°17′N 37°02′E
12 J2 **Salluit** prev. Saglouc, Sagluk. Québec, NE Canada 62°10′N 75°40′W
Sallyana see Şalyān
13 S11 **Sally's Cove** Newfoundland and Labrador, E Canada 49°43′N 58°00′W
139 W9 **Salmān Bin 'Arāzah** Maysān, E Iraq 32°33′N 46°36′E
Salmantica see Salamanca
142 I2 **Salmās** prev. Dilman, Shāpūr. Āzarbāyjān-e Gharbī, NW Iran 38°13′N 44°50′E
124 I11 **Salmi** Respublika Kareliya, NW Russian Federation 61°21′N 31°55′E
33 P12 **Salmon** Idaho, NW USA 45°10′N 113°54′W
11 N16 **Salmon Arm** British Columbia, SW Canada 50°41′N 119°18′W
192 L5 **Salmon Bank** undersea feature N Pacific Ocean 26°55′N 176°28′W
Salmon Leap see Leixlip
34 L2 **Salmon Mountains** ▲▲ California, W USA
14 J15 **Salmon Point** headland Ontario, SE Canada 43°51′N 77°15′W
33 N11 **Salmon River** ≈ Idaho, NW USA
18 K6 **Salmon River** ≈ New York, NE USA
33 N12 **Salmon River Mountains** ▲▲ Idaho, NW USA
18 I9 **Salmon River Reservoir** ⊠ New York, NE USA
93 K19 **Salo** Länsi-Suomi, SW Finland 60°23′N 23°10′E
106 F7 **Salò** Lombardia, N Italy 45°37′N 10°30′E
Salona/Salonae see Solin
103 S15 **Salon-de-Provence** Bouches-du-Rhône, SE France 43°39′N 05°05′E
Salonica/Salonika see Thessaloníki
115 I14 **Salonikiós, Akrotírio** var. Akrotírio Salonikós. headland Thásos, E Greece 40°34′N 24°39′E
Salonikós, Akrotírio see Salonikiós, Akrotírio
116 F10 **Salonta** Hung. Nagyszalonta. Bihor, W Romania 46°49′N 21°40′E
104 I9 **Salor** ≈ W Spain
105 U6 **Salou** Cataluña, NE Spain 41°05′N 01°08′E
76 H11 **Saloum** ≈ C Senegal
42 H4 **Sal, Punta** headland NW Honduras 15°55′N 87°36′W
92 N3 **Salpynten** headland W Svalbard 78°12′N 12°11′E
138 I3 **Salqīn** Idlib, W Syria 36°09′N 36°27′E
93 F14 **Salsbruket** Nord-Trøndelag, C Norway 64°49′N 11°48′E
126 M13 **Sal'sk** Rostovskaya Oblast', SW Russian Federation 46°30′N 41°31′E
107 J25 **Salso** ≈ Sicilia, Italy, C Mediterranean Sea
107 K25 **Salso** ≈ Sicilia, Italy, C Mediterranean Sea
106 E9 **Salsomaggiore Terme** Emilia-Romagna, N Italy 44°49′N 09°58′E
Salt see As Salţ
62 J6 **Salta** Salta, NW Argentina 24°47′S 65°23′W
62 K6 **Salta** off. Provincia de Salta. ◈ province N Argentina
Salta, Provincia de see Salta
97 I24 **Saltash** SW England, United Kingdom 50°26′N 04°14′W
24 I8 **Salt Basin** basin Texas, SW USA
11 V16 **Saltcoats** Saskatchewan, S Canada 51°06′N 102°12′W
30 L13 **Salt Creek** ≈ Illinois, N USA
24 J9 **Salt Draw** ≈ Texas, SW USA
97 F21 **Saltee Islands** island group SE Ireland
92 G12 **Saltfjorden** inlet C Norway
24 I8 **Salt Flat** Texas, SW USA 31°43′N 105°05′W
27 N8 **Salt Fork Arkansas River** ≈ Oklahoma, C USA
31 T13 **Salt Fork Lake** ⊠ Ohio, N USA
26 J11 **Salt Fork Red River** ≈ Oklahoma/Texas, C USA
95 J23 **Saltholm** island E Denmark
41 N8 **Saltillo** Coahuila, NE Mexico 25°30′N 101°W
182 L5 **Salt Lake** salt lake New South Wales, SE Australia
37 V15 **Salt Lake** ◎ New Mexico, SW USA
36 K2 **Salt Lake City** state capital Utah, W USA 40°45′N 111°54′W
61 C20 **Salto** Buenos Aires, E Argentina 34°18′S 60°17′W
61 D17 **Salto** Salto, N Uruguay 31°23′S 57°58′W
61 E17 **Salto** ◈ department N Uruguay
107 I14 **Salto** ≈ C Italy
62 Q6 **Salto del Guairá** Canindeyú, E Paraguay 24°06′S 54°22′W
61 D17 **Salto Grande, Embalse de** var. Lago de Salto Grande. ⊠ Argentina/Uruguay
Salto Grande, Lago de see Salto Grande, Embalse de
35 W16 **Salton Sea** ◎ California, W USA
60 I12 **Salto Santiago, Represa de** ⊠ S Brazil
149 U7 **Salt Range** ▲▲ E Pakistan
36 M13 **Salt River** ≈ Arizona, SW USA
20 L5 **Salt River** ≈ Kentucky, S USA
27 V3 **Salt River** ≈ Missouri, C USA
95 F17 **Saltrød** Aust-Agder, S Norway 58°28′N 08°49′E
95 P16 **Saltsjöbaden** Stockholm, C Sweden 59°15′N 18°20′E
92 G12 **Saltstraumen** Nordland, C Norway 67°16′N 14°42′E
21 Q7 **Saltville** Virginia, NE USA 36°52′N 81°48′W
Saluces/Saluciae see Saluzzo
21 Q12 **Saluda** South Carolina, SE USA 34°00′N 81°47′W
21 X6 **Saluda** Virginia, NE USA 37°36′N 76°36′W
21 Q12 **Saluda River** ≈ South Carolina, SE USA
Salûm see As Sallūm
152 F14 **Sālūmbar** Rājasthān, N India 24°16′N 74°04′E
Salûm, Gulf of see Khalīj as Sallūm
171 O11 **Salumpaga** Sulawesi, N Indonesia 01°18′N 120°58′E
155 M14 **Sālūr** Andhra Pradesh, E India 18°31′N 83°16′E
55 Y9 **Salut, Îles du** island group N French Guiana
106 A9 **Saluzzo** Fr. Saluces; anc. Saluciae. Piemonte, NW Italy 44°39′N 07°29′E
63 F23 **Salvación, Bahía** bay S Chile
59 P17 **Salvador** prev. São Salvador. state capital Bahia, E Brazil 12°58′S 38°29′W
65 E24 **Salvador** East Falkland, Falkland Islands 51°28′S 58°22′W
22 K10 **Salvador, Lake** ◎ Louisiana, S USA
Salvaleón de Higüey see Higüey
104 F10 **Salvaterra de Magos** Santarém, C Portugal 39°01′N 08°47′W
41 N13 **Salvatierra** Guanajuato, C Mexico 20°14′N 100°52′W
105 P3 **Salvatierra** Basq. Agurain. País Vasco, N Spain 42°52′N 02°23′W
Salwa/Salwah see As Salwā
166 M7 **Salween** Bur. Thanlwin, Chin. Nu Chiang, Nu Jiang. ≈ SE Asia
137 Y12 **Salyan** Rus. Sal'yany. SE Azerbaijan 39°36′N 48°57′E
153 N11 **Şalyān** var. Sallyana. Mid Western, W Nepal 28°22′N 82°10′E
Sal'yany see Salyan
21 O6 **Salyersville** Kentucky, S USA 37°43′N 83°06′W
109 V6 **Salza** ≈ E Austria
109 Q7 **Salzach** ≈ Austria/Germany
109 Q6 **Salzburg** anc. Juvavum. Salzburg, N Austria 47°48′N 13°03′E
109 O8 **Salzburg** off. Land Salzburg. ◈ state C Austria
Salzburg see Ocna Sibiului
Salzburg Alps see Salzburger Kalkalpen
109 Q7 **Salzburger Kalkalpen** Eng. Salzburg Alps. ▲▲ C Austria
Salzburg, Land see Salzburg
100 J13 **Salzgitter** prev. Watenstedt-Salzgitter. Niedersachsen, C Germany 52°07′N 10°24′E
101 G14 **Salzkotten** Nordrhein-Westfalen, W Germany 51°40′N 08°36′E
100 K11 **Salzwedel** Sachsen-Anhalt, N Germany 52°51′N 11°10′E
152 D11 **Sām** Rājasthān, NW India 26°50′N 70°30′E
Šamac see Bosanski Šamac
54 G9 **Samacá** Boyacá, C Colombia 05°28′N 73°33′W
40 I7 **Samachique** Chihuahua, N Mexico 27°17′N 107°28′W
141 Y8 **Şamad** NE Oman 22°47′N 58°12′E
Sama de Langreo see Sama, Spain
Samaden see Samedan
57 M19 **Samaipata** Santa Cruz, C Bolivia 18°08′S 63°53′W
Samakhixai see Attapu
Samakov see Samokov
42 B6 **Samalá, Río** ≈ SW Guatemala
40 J3 **Samalayuca** Chihuahua, N Mexico 31°25′N 106°30′W
155 L16 **Sāmalkot** Andhra Pradesh, E India 17°03′N 82°15′E
45 P8 **Samaná** var. Santa Bárbara de Samaná. E Dominican Republic 19°14′N 69°20′W
45 P8 **Samaná, Bahía de** bay E Dominican Republic
44 K4 **Samana Cay** island SE Bahamas
136 K17 **Samandağı** Hatay, S Turkey 36°07′N 35°55′E
149 P3 **Samangān** ◈ province N Afghanistan
Samangān see Aibak
165 T5 **Samani** Hokkaidō, NE Japan 42°07′N 142°57′E
54 C13 **Samaniego** Nariño, SW Colombia 01°22′N 77°35′W
171 Q5 **Samar** island C Philippines
127 S6 **Samara** prev. Kuybyshev. Samarskaya Oblast', W Russian Federation 53°15′N 50°15′E
127 T7 **Samara** ≈ W Russian Federation
127 S6 **Samara** ✈ Samarskaya Oblast', W Russian Federation 53°11′N 50°27′E
117 V7 **Samara** ≈ E Ukraine
186 G10 **Samarai** Milne Bay, SE Papua New Guinea 10°36′S 150°39′E
Samarang see Semarang
123 T14 **Samarga** Khabarovskiy Kray, SE Russian Federation 47°43′N 139°08′E
138 G9 **Samarian Hills** hill range N Israel
54 L9 **Samariapo** Amazonas, C Venezuela 05°16′N 67°43′W
169 V11 **Samarinda** Borneo, C Indonesia 0°30′S 117°09′E
Samarkand see Samarqand
Samarkandskaya Oblast' see Samarqand Viloyati
Samarkandski/Samarkandskoye see Temirtau
Samarobriva see Amiens
147 N11 **Samarqand** Rus. Samarkand. Samarqand Viloyati, C Uzbekistan 39°40′N 66°56′E
146 M11 **Samarqand Viloyati** Rus. Samarkandskaya Oblast'. ◈ province C Uzbekistan
139 S6 **Sāmarrā'** Şalāḩ ad Dīn, C Iraq 34°13′N 43°52′E
127 R7 **Samarskaya Oblast'** prev. Kuybyshevskaya Oblast'. ◈ province W Russian Federation
153 Q13 **Samastīpur** Bihār, N India 25°52′N 85°47′E
76 L14 **Samatiguila** NW Ivory Coast 09°51′N 07°36′W
Samawa see As Samāwah
137 Y11 **Şamaxı** Rus. Shemakha. E Azerbaijan 40°38′N 48°34′E
79 K18 **Samba** Equateur, NW Dem. Rep. Congo 0°13′N 21°17′E
79 N21 **Samba** Maniema, E Dem. Rep. Congo 04°41′S 26°23′E
152 H6 **Samba** Jammu and Kashmir, NW India 32°32′N 75°08′E
169 W10 **Sambaliung, Pegunungan** ▲▲ Borneo, N Indonesia
154 M11 **Sambalpur** Orissa, E India 21°28′N 84°04′E
67 X12 **Sambao** ≈ W Madagascar
169 Q10 **Sambas, Sungai** ≈ Borneo, N Indonesia
172 K2 **Sambava** Antsiranana, NE Madagascar 14°16′S 50°10′E
152 J10 **Sambhal** Uttar Pradesh, N India 28°35′N 78°34′E
152 H12 **Sāmbhar Salt Lake** ◎ N India
107 N21 **Sambiase** Calabria, SW Italy 38°58′N 16°16′E
116 H5 **Sambir** Rus. Sambor. L'vivs'ka Oblast', NW Ukraine 49°31′N 23°10′E
82 C13 **Sambo** Huambo, C Angola 13°07′S 16°06′E
Sambor see Sambir
61 E21 **Samborombón, Bahía** bay NE Argentina
99 H20 **Sambre** ≈ Belgium/France
43 V16 **Sambú, Río** ≈ SE Panama
163 Z14 **Samcheok** Jap. Sanchoku; prev. Samch'ŏk. NE South Korea 37°21′N 129°12′E
Samch'ŏk see Samcheok
Samch'ŏnpŏ see Sacheon
81 I21 **Same** Kilimanjaro, NE Tanzania 04°04′S 37°41′E
108 J10 **Samedan** Ger. Samaden. Graubünden, S Switzerland 46°31′N 09°51′E
82 K12 **Samfya** Luapula, N Zambia 11°22′S 29°34′E
141 W13 **Samḩān, Jabal** ▲▲ SW Oman
115 C18 **Sámi** Kefallonía, Iónia Nisiá, Greece, C Mediterranean Sea 38°15′N 20°39′E
56 F10 **Samiria, Río** ≈ N Peru
Samirum see Semīrom
167 Q13 **Samĭt** prev. Phumĭ Samĭt. Kaôh Kông, SW Cambodia 10°54′N 103°09′E
137 V11 **Şämkir** Rus. Shamkhor. NW Azerbaijan 40°51′N 46°03′E
167 S7 **Sam, Nam** Vtn. Sông Chu. ≈ Laos/Vietnam
Samnān see Semnān
Sam Neua see Xam Nua
75 P10 **Samnū** C Libya 27°19′N 15°01′E
192 H15 **Samoa** off. Independent State of Samoa, var. Sāmoa; prev. Western Samoa. ◆ monarchy W Polynesia
192 L9 **Sāmoa** island group C Pacific Ocean
Sāmoa see Samoa
175 T9 **Samoa Basin** undersea feature W Pacific Ocean
Samoa, Independent State of see Samoa
112 D8 **Samobor** Zagreb, N Croatia 45°48′N 15°38′E
114 H10 **Samokov** var. Samakov. Sofiya, W Bulgaria 42°19′N 23°34′E
111 H21 **Šamorín** Ger. Sommerein, Hung. Somorja. Trnavský Kraj, W Slovakia 48°01′N 17°18′E
115 M19 **Sámos** prev. Limín Vathéos. Sámos, Dodekánisa, Greece, Aegean Sea 37°45′N 26°58′E
115 M20 **Sámos** island Dodekánisa, Greece, Aegean Sea
Samosch see Szamos
168 I9 **Samosir, Pulau** island W Indonesia
Samothrace see Samothráki
115 K14 **Samothráki** Samothráki, NE Greece 40°28′N 25°31′E
115 J14 **Samothráki** anc. Samothrace. island NE Greece
115 A15 **Samothráki** island Iónia Nisiá, Greece, C Mediterranean Sea
Samotschin see Szamocin
Sampê see Xiangcheng
169 S13 **Sampit** Borneo, C Indonesia 02°30′S 112°30′E
169 S12 **Sampit, Sungai** ≈ Borneo, N Indonesia
Sampoku see Sanpoku
186 H7 **Sampun** New Britain, E Papua New Guinea 05°19′S 152°06′E
79 N24 **Sampwe** Katanga, SE Dem. Rep. Congo 09°17′S 27°22′E
167 R11 **Sâmraông** prev. Phumĭ Sâmraông, Phum Samrong. Siĕmréab, NW Cambodia 14°11′N 103°31′E
25 X8 **Sam Rayburn Reservoir** ⊠ Texas, SW USA
167 Q6 **Sam Sao, Phou** ▲▲ Laos/Thailand
95 H22 **Samsø** island E Denmark
95 H23 **Samsø Bælt** channel E Denmark
167 T7 **Sâm Sơn** Thanh Hoa, N Vietnam 19°44′N 105°53′E
136 L11 **Samsun** anc. Amisus. Samsun, N Turkey 41°17′N 36°22′E
136 K11 **Samsun** ◈ province N Turkey
137 R9 **Samt'redia** prev. Samtredia. W Georgia 42°09′N 42°20′E
Samtredia see Samt'redia

◆ Country
● Country Capital
◇ Dependent Territory
○ Dependent Territory Capital
◈ Administrative Regions
✈ International Airport
▲ Mountain
▲▲ Mountain Range
✱ Volcano
≈ River
◎ Lake
⊠ Reservoir

59 E15 **Samuel, Represa de** ⊠ W Brazil
167 O14 **Samui, Ko** *island* SW Thailand
Samundari *see* Samundri
149 U9 **Samundri** *var.* Samundari. Punjab, E Pakistan 31°04′N 72°58′E
137 X10 **Samur** ≈ Azerbaijan/ Russian Federation
137 Y11 **Samur-Abşeron Kanalı** *Rus.* Sam ur-Apsheronskiy Kanal. *canal* E Azerbaijan
Sam ur-Apsheronskiy Kanal *see* Samur-Abşeron Kanalı
167 O11 **Samut Prakan** *var.* Muang Samut Prakan, Paknam. Samut Prakan, C Thailand 13°36′N 100°36′E
167 O11 **Samut Sakhon** *var.* Maha Chai, Samut Sakorn, Tha Chin. Samut Sakhon, C Thailand 13°31′N 100°15′E
Samut Sakorn *see* Samut Sakhon
167 O11 **Samut Songkhram** *prev.* Meklong. Samut Songkhram, SW Thailand 13°25′N 100°01′E
77 N12 **San** Ségou, C Mali 13°21′N 04°57′W
111 O15 **San** ≈ SE Poland
141 O15 **Şan'ā'** *Eng.* Sana. ● (Yemen) W Yemen 15°24′N 44°14′E
112 F11 **Sana** ≈ NW Bosnia and Herzegovina
80 O12 **Sanaag** *off.* Gobolka Sanaag. ◈ *region* N Somalia
Sanaag, Gobolka *see* Sanaag
114 J8 **Sanadinovo** Pleven, N Bulgaria 43°33′N 25°00′E
195 P1 **Sanae** *South African research station* Antarctica 70°19′S 01°31′W
139 Y10 **Sanāf, Hawr as** ◎ S Iraq
79 E15 **Sanaga** ≈ C Cameroon
54 D12 **San Agustín** Huila, SW Colombia 01°53′N 76°14′W
171 R8 **San Agustin, Cape** *headland* Mindanao, S Philippines 06°17′N 126°12′E
37 Q13 **San Agustin, Plains of** *plain* New Mexico, SW USA
38 M16 **Sanak Islands** *island* Aleutian Islands, Alaska, USA
San Alessandro *see* Kita-Iō-jima
193 U10 **San Ambrosio, Isla** *Eng.* San Ambrosio Island. *island* W Chile
San Ambrosio Island *see* San Ambrosio, Isla
171 Q12 **Sanana** Pulau Sanana, E Indonesia 02°04′S 125°58′E
171 Q12 **Sanana, Pulau** *island* Maluku, E Indonesia
142 K5 **Sanandaj** *prev.* Sinneh. Kordestān, W Iran 35°18′N 47°01′E
35 P8 **San Andreas** California, W USA 38°10′N 120°40′W
2 C13 **San Andreas Fault** *fault* W USA
54 G8 **San Andrés** Santander, C Colombia 06°52′N 72°53′W
61 C20 **San Andrés de Giles** Buenos Aires, E Argentina 34°27′S 59°27′W
37 R14 **San Andres Mountains** ▲▲ New Mexico, SW USA
41 S15 **San Andrés Tuxtla** *var.* Tuxtla. Veracruz-Llave, E Mexico 18°28′N 95°15′W
25 P8 **San Angelo** Texas, SW USA 31°28′N 100°26′W
107 A20 **San Antioco, Isola di** *island* W Italy
42 F4 **San Antonio** Toledo, S Belize 16°13′N 89°02′W
62 G11 **San Antonio** Valparaíso, C Chile 33°35′S 71°38′W
188 H6 **San Antonio** Saipan, S Northern Mariana Islands
37 R13 **San Antonio** New Mexico, SW USA 33°53′N 106°52′W
25 R12 **San Antonio** Texas, SW USA 29°25′N 98°30′W
54 M11 **San Antonio** Amazonas, S Venezuela 03°31′N 66°47′W
54 I7 **San Antonio** Barinas, C Venezuela 07°24′N 71°28′W
55 O5 **San Antonio** Monagas, NE Venezuela 10°03′N 63°45′W
25 S12 **San Antonio** ✈ Texas, SW USA 29°31′N 98°11′W
San Antonio *see* San Antonio del Táchira
San Antonio Abad *see* Sant Antoni de Portmany
25 U13 **San Antonio Bay** *inlet* Texas, SW USA
61 E22 **San Antonio, Cabo** *headland* E Argentina 36°45′S 56°40′W
44 A5 **San Antonio, Cabo de** *headland* W Cuba 21°51′N 84°58′W
105 T11 **San Antonio, Cabo de** *headland* E Spain 38°50′N 00°09′E
54 H7 **San Antonio de Caparo** Táchira, W Venezuela 07°34′N 71°28′W
62 J5 **San Antonio de los Cobres** Salta, NE Argentina 24°10′S 66°17′W
54 H7 **San Antonio del Táchira** *var.* San Antonio. Táchira, W Venezuela 07°48′N 72°28′W
35 T15 **San Antonio, Mount** ▲ California, W USA 34°18′N 117°37′W
63 K16 **San Antonio Oeste** Río Negro, E Argentina 40°45′S 64°58′W
25 T13 **San Antonio River** ≈ Texas, SW USA
54 J5 **Sanare** Lara, N Venezuela 09°45′N 69°39′W
103 T16 **Sanary-sur-Mer** Var, SE France 43°07′N 05°48′E
104 G3 **Sanata Uxía de Ribeira** *var.* Ribeira. Galicia, NW Spain 42°33′N 09°01′W
25 X8 **San Augustine** Texas, SW USA 31°32′N 94°09′W
San Augustine *see* Minami-Iō-jima
141 T13 **Sanāw** *var.* Sanaw. NE Yemen 18°N 51°E
41 O11 **San Bartolo** San Luis Potosí, C Mexico 22°20′N 100°05′W
107 L16 **San Bartolomeo in Galdo** Campania, S Italy 41°24′N 15°01′E
106 K13 **San Benedetto del Tronto** Marche, C Italy 42°57′N 13°53′E
42 E3 **San Benito** Petén, N Guatemala 16°56′N 89°53′W
25 T17 **San Benito** Texas, SW USA 26°07′N 97°37′W
54 E6 **San Benito Abad** Sucre, N Colombia 08°56′N 75°02′W
35 P11 **San Benito Mountain** ▲ California, W USA 36°21′N 120°37′W
35 O10 **San Benito River** ≈ California, W USA
108 H10 **San Bernardino** Graubünden, S Switzerland 46°21′N 09°13′E
35 U15 **San Bernardino** California, W USA 34°06′N 117°15′W
35 U15 **San Bernardino Mountains** ▲▲ California, W USA
62 H11 **San Bernardo** Santiago, C Chile 33°37′S 70°45′W
40 J8 **San Bernardo** Durango, C Mexico 25°58′N 105°27′W
164 G12 **Sanbe-san** ▲ Kyūshū, SW Japan 35°09′N 132°36′E
San Bizenti-Barakaldo *see* San Vicente de Barakaldo
40 J12 **San Blas** Nayarit, C Mexico 21°35′N 105°20′W
40 H8 **San Blas** Sinaloa, C Mexico 26°05′N 108°44′W
San Blas *see* Kuna Yala
43 U14 **San Blas, Archipiélago de** *island group* NE Panama
23 Q10 **San Blas, Cape** *headland* Florida, SE USA 29°39′N 85°21′W
43 V14 **San Blas, Cordillera de** ▲▲ NE Panama
62 J8 **San Blas de los Sauces** Catamarca, NW Argentina 28°18′S 67°12′W
106 G8 **San Bonifacio** Veneto, NE Italy 45°22′N 11°14′E
29 S12 **Sanborn** Iowa, C USA 43°10′N 95°39′W
40 M7 **San Buenaventura** Coahuila, NE Mexico 27°04′N 101°32′W
105 S5 **San Caprasio** ▲ N Spain 41°45′N 00°26′W
62 G13 **San Carlos** Bío Bío, C Chile 36°25′S 71°58′W
40 E9 **San Carlos** Baja California Sur, NW Mexico 24°52′N 112°15′W
41 N5 **San Carlos** Coahuila, NE Mexico 29°00′N 100°51′W
41 P9 **San Carlos** Tamaulipas, C Mexico 24°36′N 98°42′W
42 L12 **San Carlos** Río San Juan, S Nicaragua 11°06′N 84°46′W
43 T16 **San Carlos** Panamá, C Panama 08°29′N 79°58′W
171 N3 **San Carlos** *off.* San Carlos City. Luzon, N Philippines 15°57′N 120°18′E
61 G20 **San Carlos** Maldonado, S Uruguay 34°46′S 54°58′W
36 M14 **San Carlos** Arizona, SW USA 33°21′N 110°27′W
54 K5 **San Carlos** Cojedes, N Venezuela 09°39′N 68°35′W
San Carlos *see* Quesada, Costa Rica
San Carlos *see* Luba, Equatorial Guinea
61 B17 **San Carlos Centro** Santa Fe, C Argentina 31°45′S 61°05′W
171 P6 **San Carlos City** Negros, C Philippines 10°34′N 123°24′E
San Carlos City *see* San Carlos
San Carlos de Ancud *see* Ancud
63 H16 **San Carlos de Bariloche** Río Negro, SW Argentina 41°08′S 71°15′W
61 B21 **San Carlos de Bolívar** Buenos Aires, E Argentina 36°15′S 61°06′W
54 H6 **San Carlos del Zulia** Zulia, W Venezuela 09°01′N 71°58′W
54 L12 **San Carlos de Río Negro** Amazonas, S Venezuela 01°54′N 67°54′W
San Carlos, Estrecho de *see* Falkland Sound
36 M14 **San Carlos Reservoir** ⊠ Arizona, SW USA
42 M12 **San Carlos, Río** ≈ N Costa Rica
65 D24 **San Carlos Settlement** East Falkland, Falkland Islands
61 C23 **San Cayetano** Buenos Aires, E Argentina 38°20′S 59°37′W
103 O8 **Sancergues** Cher, C France 47°19′N 02°53′E
158 G7 **Sanchakou** Xinjiang Uygur Zizhiqu, NW China 39°56′N 78°28′E
Sanchoku *see* Samcheok
41 O12 **San Ciro** San Luis Potosí, C Mexico 21°40′N 99°50′W
105 P10 **San Clemente** Castilla-La Mancha, C Spain 39°24′N 02°25′W
35 T16 **San Clemente** California, W USA 33°25′N 117°36′W
61 E21 **San Clemente del Tuyú** Buenos Aires, E Argentina 36°22′S 56°43′W
35 S17 **San Clemente Island** *island* Channel Islands, California, W USA
103 O9 **Sancoins** Cher, C France 46°49′N 03°00′E
61 B16 **San Cristóbal** Santa Fe, C Argentina 30°20′S 61°14′W
44 B4 **San Cristóbal** Pinar del Río, W Cuba 22°43′N 83°03′W
45 O9 **San Cristóbal** *var.* Benemérita de San Cristóbal. S Dominican Republic 18°27′N 70°07′W
54 H7 **San Cristóbal** Táchira, W Venezuela 07°46′N 72°15′W
187 N10 **San Cristobal** *var.* Makira. *island* SE Solomon Islands
San Cristóbal *see* San Cristóbal de Las Casas
41 U16 **San Cristóbal de Las Casas** *var.* San Cristóbal. Chiapas, SE Mexico 16°44′N 92°40′W
187 N10 **San Cristobal, Isla** *var.* Chatham Island. *island* Galapagos Islands, Ecuador, E Pacific Ocean
42 D5 **San Cristóbal Verapaz** Alta Verapaz, C Guatemala 15°21′N 90°22′W
44 F6 **Sancti Spíritus** Sancti Spíritus, C Cuba 21°54′N 79°27′W
103 O11 **Sancy, Puy de** ▲ C France 45°33′N 02°48′E
95 D15 **Sand** Rogaland, S Norway 59°28′N 06°16′E
169 W7 **Sandakan** Sabah, East Malaysia 05°52′N 118°04′E
182 K9 **Sandalwood** South Australia 34°51′S 140°13′E
Sandalwood Island *see* Sumba, Pulau
94 D11 **Sandane** Sogn Og Fjordane, S Norway 61°47′N 06°14′E
114 G12 **Sandanski** *prev.* Sveti Vrach. Blagoevgrad, SW Bulgaria 41°36′N 23°19′E
Sandaohezi *see* Shawan
76 J11 **Sandaré** Kayes, W Mali 14°36′N 10°22′W
95 J19 **Sandared** Västra Götaland, S Sweden 57°43′N 12°47′E
94 N12 **Sandarne** Gävleborg, C Sweden 61°15′N 17°10′E
186 B5 **Sandaun** *prev.* West Sepik. ◈ *province* NW Papua New Guinea
96 K4 **Sanday** *island* NE Scotland, United Kingdom
31 P15 **Sand Creek** ≈ Indiana, N USA
95 H15 **Sande** Vestfold, S Norway 59°34′N 10°13′E
95 H16 **Sandefjord** Vestfold, S Norway 59°10′N 10°15′E
77 O15 **Sandégué** E Ivory Coast 07°59′N 03°33′W
77 P14 **Sandema** N Ghana 10°42′N 01°17′W
37 O11 **Sanders** Arizona, SW USA 35°13′N 109°21′W
24 M11 **Sanderson** Texas, SW USA 30°08′N 102°25′W
23 U4 **Sandersville** Georgia, SE USA 32°58′N 82°48′W
92 H4 **Sandgerdhi** Sudurnes, SW Iceland 64°01′N 22°42′W
28 K14 **Sand Hills** ▲▲ Nebraska, C USA
25 S14 **Sandia** Texas, SW USA 27°59′N 97°52′W
35 T17 **San Diego** California, W USA 32°43′N 117°09′W
25 S14 **San Diego** Texas, SW USA 27°47′N 98°15′W
136 F14 **Sandıklı** Afyon, W Turkey 38°28′N 30°17′E
152 L12 **Sandila** Uttar Pradesh, N India 27°05′N 80°37′E
San Dimitri Point *see* Il-Ponta ta' San Dimitri
San Dimitri, Ras *see* Il-Ponta ta' San Dimitri
168 J13 **Sanding, Selat** *strait* W Indonesia
30 J3 **Sand Island** *island* Apostle Islands, Wisconsin, N USA
95 C16 **Sandnes** Rogaland, S Norway 58°51′N 05°45′E
92 F13 **Sandnessjøen** Nordland, C Norway 66°00′N 12°37′E
Sandø *see* Sandoy
79 L24 **Sandoa** Katanga, S Dem. Rep. Congo 09°41′S 22°56′E
111 N15 **Sandomierz** *Rus.* Sandomir. Świętokrzyskie, C Poland 50°42′N 21°45′E
Sandomir *see* Sandomierz
54 C13 **Sandoná** Nariño, SW Colombia 01°18′N 77°28′W
106 I7 **San Donà di Piave** Veneto, NE Italy 45°38′N 12°34′E
124 K14 **Sandovo** Tverskaya Oblast', W Russian Federation 58°26′N 36°30′E
Sandoway *see* Thandwe
97 M24 **Sandown** S England, United Kingdom 50°40′N 01°11′W
95 B19 **Sandoy** *Dan.* Sandø. *island* C Faeroe Islands
39 N16 **Sand Point** Popof Island, Alaska, USA 55°20′N 160°30′W
32 M7 **Sandpoint** Idaho, NW USA 48°16′N 116°33′W
65 N24 **Sand Point** *headland* E Tristan da Cunha
31 R7 **Sand Point** *headland* Michigan, N USA 43°54′N 83°24′W
93 H14 **Sandsele** Västerbotten, N Sweden 65°16′N 17°40′E
10 I14 **Sandspit** Moresby Island, British Columbia, SW Canada 53°14′N 131°50′W
27 P9 **Sand Springs** Oklahoma, C USA 36°08′N 96°06′W
29 W7 **Sandstone** Minnesota, N USA 46°07′N 92°51′W
36 K15 **Sand Tank Mountains** ▲▲ Arizona, SW USA
31 S8 **Sandusky** Michigan, N USA 43°26′N 82°50′W
31 S11 **Sandusky** Ohio, N USA 41°27′N 82°42′W
31 S12 **Sandusky River** ≈ Ohio, N USA
83 D22 **Sandverhaar** Karas, S Namibia 26°50′S 17°25′E
95 L24 **Sandvig** Bornholm, E Denmark 55°15′N 14°45′E
95 H15 **Sandvika** Akershus, S Norway 59°54′N 10°29′E
94 N13 **Sandviken** Gävleborg, C Sweden 60°38′N 16°50′E
30 M11 **Sandwich** Illinois, N USA 41°39′N 88°37′W
Sandwich Island *see* Efate
Sandwich Islands *see* Hawai'ian Islands
153 V16 **Sandwip** *island* SE Bangladesh
11 U12 **Sandy Bay** Saskatchewan, C Canada 55°31′N 102°14′W
183 N16 **Sandy Cape** *headland* Tasmania, SE Australia 41°27′S 144°43′E
36 L3 **Sandy City** Utah, W USA 40°36′N 111°53′W
31 U12 **Sandy Creek** ≈ Ohio, N USA
21 O5 **Sandy Hook** Kentucky, S USA 38°05′N 83°09′W
18 K15 **Sandy Hook** *headland* New Jersey, NE USA 40°27′N 73°59′W
Sandykachi/Sandykgachy *see* Sandykgaçy
146 J15 **Sandykaçy** *var.* Sandykgachy. Maryyskiy Velayat, S Turkmenistan 36°34′N 62°28′E
Sandykgachy *see* Sandykgaçy
146 J15 **Sandykgaçy** *var.* Sandykgachy, *Rus.* Sandykachi. Mary Welaýaty, S Turkmenistan 36°34′N 62°28′E
146 L13 **Sandykly Gumy** *Rus.* Peski Sandykly. *desert* E Turkmenistan
Sandykly, Peski *see* Sandykly Gumy
11 Q13 **Sandy Lake** Alberta, W Canada 55°50′N 113°30′W
12 B8 **Sandy Lake** Ontario, C Canada 53°00′N 93°25′W
12 B8 **Sandy Lake** ◎ Ontario, C Canada
23 S3 **Sandy Springs** Georgia, SE USA 33°57′N 84°23′W
24 H8 **San Elizario** Texas, SW USA 31°35′N 106°16′W
99 L25 **Sanem** Luxembourg, SW Luxembourg 49°33′N 05°56′E
42 K5 **San Esteban** Olancho, C Honduras 15°19′N 85°52′W
105 O6 **San Esteban de Gormaz** Castilla y León, N Spain 41°34′N 03°13′W
40 E5 **San Esteban, Isla** *island* NW Mexico
San Eugenio/San Eugenio del Cuareim *see* Artigas
62 H11 **San Felipe** *var.* San Felipe de Aconcagua. Valparaíso, C Chile 32°45′S 70°42′W
40 D3 **San Felipe** Baja California Norte, NW Mexico 31°03′N 114°52′W
40 N12 **San Felipe** Guanajuato, C Mexico 21°30′N 101°15′W
54 K5 **San Felipe** Yaracuy, NW Venezuela 10°25′N 68°40′W
44 B5 **San Felipe, Cayos de** *island group* W Cuba
San Felipe de Aconcagua *see* San Felipe
San Felipe de Puerto Plata *see* Puerto Plata
37 R11 **San Felipe Pueblo** New Mexico, SW USA 35°25′N 106°27′W
San Feliú de Guixols *see* Sant Feliu de Guíxols
193 T10 **San Félix, Isla** *Eng.* San Felix Island. *island* W Chile
San Felix Island *see* San Félix, Isla
40 C4 **San Fernando** *var.* Misión San Fernando. Baja California Norte, NW Mexico 29°58′N 115°14′W
41 P9 **San Fernando** Tamaulipas, C Mexico 24°50′N 98°10′W
171 N2 **San Fernando** Luzon, N Philippines 16°45′N 120°21′E
171 O3 **San Fernando** Luzon, N Philippines 15°01′N 120°41′E
104 J16 **San Fernando** *prev.* Isla de León. Andalucía, S Spain 36°28′N 06°12′W
45 U14 **San Fernando** Trinidad, Trinidad and Tobago 10°17′N 61°27′W
35 S15 **San Fernando** California, W USA 34°16′N 118°26′W
54 L7 **San Fernando** *var.* San Fernando de Apure. Apure, C Venezuela 07°54′N 67°28′W
San Fernando de Apure *see* San Fernando
54 L11 **San Fernando de Atabapo** Amazonas, S Venezuela 04°00′N 67°42′W
62 L8 **San Fernando del Valle de Catamarca** *var.* Catamarca. Catamarca, NW Argentina 28°28′S 65°46′W
San Fernando de Monte Cristi *see* Monte Cristi
41 P9 **San Fernando, Río** ≈ C Mexico
23 X11 **Sanford** Florida, SE USA 28°48′N 81°16′W
19 P9 **Sanford** Maine, NE USA 43°26′N 70°46′W
21 T10 **Sanford** North Carolina, SE USA 35°29′N 79°10′W
25 N2 **Sanford** Texas, SW USA 35°42′N 101°31′W
39 T10 **Sanford, Mount** ▲ Alaska, USA 62°21′N 144°12′W
42 G8 **San Francisco** *var.* Gotera, San Francisco Gotera. Morazán, E El Salvador 13°41′N 88°06′W
43 R16 **San Francisco** Veraguas, C Panama 08°19′N 80°59′W
171 N2 **San Francisco** *var.* Aurora. Luzon, N Philippines 13°22′N 122°31′E
35 L8 **San Francisco** California, W USA 37°47′N 122°25′W
54 H5 **San Francisco** Zulia, NW Venezuela 10°36′N 71°39′W
34 M8 **San Francisco** ✈ California, W USA 37°37′N 122°23′W
35 N9 **San Francisco Bay** *bay* California, W USA
61 C24 **San Francisco de Bellocq** Buenos Aires, E Argentina 38°42′S 60°01′W
40 I6 **San Francisco de Borja** Chihuahua, N Mexico 27°57′N 106°42′W
42 J6 **San Francisco de la Paz** Olancho, C Honduras 14°55′N 86°14′W
40 J7 **San Francisco del Oro** Chihuahua, N Mexico 26°52′N 105°50′W
40 M12 **San Francisco del Rincón** Jalisco, SW Mexico 21°00′N 101°51′W
45 O8 **San Francisco de Macorís** C Dominican Republic 19°19′N 70°15′W
San Francisco de Satipo *see* Satipo
San Francisco Gotera *see* San Francisco
San Francisco Telixtlahuaca *see* Telixtlahuaca
107 K23 **San Fratello** Sicilia, Italy, C Mediterranean Sea 38°00′N 14°35′E
San Fructuoso *see* Tacuarembó
82 C12 **Sanga** Cuanza Sul, NW Angola 11°10′S 15°27′E
56 C5 **San Gabriel** Carchi, N Ecuador 00°35′N 77°48′W
159 S15 **Sa'ngain** Xizang Zizhiqu, W China 30°47′N 98°45′E
154 E13 **Sangamner** Mahārāshtra, W India 19°37′N 74°18′E
152 H12 **Sāngāner** Rājasthān, N India 26°48′N 75°48′E
Sangan, Koh-i- *see* Sangān, Kūh-e
149 N6 **Sangān, Kūh-e** *Pash.* Koh-i-Sangan. ▲ C Afghanistan
123 P10 **Sangar** Respublika Sakha (Yakutiya), NE Russian Federation 63°48′N 127°37′E
169 V11 **Sangasanga** Borneo, C Indonesia 0°36′S 117°12′E
103 N1 **Sangatte** Pas-de-Calais, N France 50°56′N 01°41′E
107 B19 **San Gavino Monreale** Sardegna, Italy, C Mediterranean Sea 39°33′N 08°47′E
57 D16 **Sangayan, Isla** *island* W Peru
30 L14 **Sangchris Lake** ⊠ Illinois, N USA
171 N16 **Sangeang, Pulau** *island* S Indonesia
116 I10 **Sângeorgiu de Pădure** *prev.* Erdăt-Sângeorz, Singeorgiu de Pădure, *Hung.* Erdőszentgyörgy. Mureş, C Romania 46°27′N 24°50′E
116 I9 **Sângeorz-Băi** *var.* Singeroz Băi, *Ger.* Rumänisch-Sankt-Georgen, *Hung.* Oláhszentgyörgy; *prev.* Singeorz-Băi. Bistriţa-Năsăud, N Romania 47°24′N 24°40′E
35 R10 **Sanger** California, W USA 36°42′N 119°33′W
25 T5 **Sanger** Texas, SW USA 33°21′N 97°10′W
Sângerei *see* Sîngerei
101 L15 **Sangerhausen** Sachsen-Anhalt, C Germany 51°29′N 11°18′E
45 S6 **San Germán** W Puerto Rico 18°05′N 67°02′W
San Germano *see* Cassino
161 N2 **Sanggan He** ≈ E China
169 Q11 **Sanggau** Borneo, C Indonesia 0°08′N 110°35′E
79 G17 **Sangha** ◈ *province* N Congo
79 H16 **Sangha** ≈ Central African Republic/Congo
79 G16 **Sangha-Mbaéré** ◈ *prefecture* SW Central African Republic
149 Q15 **Sānghar** Sind, SE Pakistan 26°10′N 68°59′E
115 F22 **Sangiás** ▲ S Greece 36°39′N 22°24′E
Sangihe, Kepulauan *see* Sangir, Kepulauan
171 Q9 **Sangihe, Pulau** *var.* Sangir. *island* N Indonesia
54 G8 **San Gil** Santander, C Colombia 06°35′N 73°08′W
121 P16 **San Giljan** *var.* St Julian's. N Malta 35°55′N 14°29′E
106 F12 **San Gimignano** Toscana, C Italy 43°30′N 11°00′E
148 M8 **Sangīn** *var.* Sangin. Helmand, S Afghanistan 32°03′N 64°50′E
Sangin *see* Sangīn
107 O21 **San Giovanni in Fiore** Calabria, SW Italy 39°15′N 16°42′E
107 M16 **San Giovanni Rotondo** Puglia, SE Italy 41°43′N 15°44′E
106 G12 **San Giovanni Valdarno** Toscana, C Italy 43°34′N 11°31′E
Sangir *see* Sangihe, Pulau
171 Q10 **Sangir, Kepulauan** *var.* Kepulauan Sangihe. *island group* N Indonesia
Sangiyn Dalay *see* Erdenedalay, Dundgovĭ, Mongolia
Sangiyn Dalay *see* Erdene, Govĭ-Altay, Mongolia
Sangiyn Dalay *see* Nomgon, Ömnögovĭ, Mongolia
Sangiyn Dalay *see* Öldziyt, Övörhangay, Mongolia
163 Y15 **Sangju** *Jap.* Shōshū. C South Korea 36°26′N 128°09′E
167 R11 **Sângkha** Surin, E Thailand 14°36′N 103°43′E
169 W10 **Sangkulirang** Borneo, N Indonesia 01°00′N 117°56′E
169 W10 **Sangkulirang, Teluk** *bay* Borneo, N Indonesia
155 E16 **Sāngli** Mahārāshtra, W India 16°55′N 74°37′E
79 E16 **Sangmélima** Sud, S Cameroon 02°57′N 11°56′E
35 V15 **San Gorgonio Mountain** ▲ California, W USA 34°06′N 116°50′W
37 T8 **Sangre de Cristo Mountains** ▲▲ Colorado/ New Mexico, C USA
61 A20 **San Gregorio** Santa Fe, C Argentina 34°18′S 62°02′W
61 F18 **San Gregorio de Polanco** Tacuarembó, C Uruguay 32°37′S 55°50′W
45 V14 **Sangre Grande** Trinidad, Trinidad and Tobago 10°35′N 61°08′W
159 N16 **Sangri** Xizang Zizhiqu, W China 29°17′N 92°01′E
152 H9 **Sangrūr** Punjab, NW India 30°16′N 75°52′E
44 I11 **Sangster** *off.* Sir Donald Sangster International Airport, *var.* Montego Bay. ✈ (Montego Bay) W Jamaica 18°30′N 77°54′W
59 G17 **Sangue, Rio do** ≈ W Brazil
105 R4 **Sangüesa** *Bas.* Zangoza. Navarra, N Spain 42°34′N 01°17′W
61 C16 **San Gustavo** Entre Ríos, E Argentina 30°41′S 59°23′W
Sangyuan *see* Wuqiao
40 C6 **San Hipólito, Punta** *headland* NW Mexico 26°57′N 114°00′W
23 W15 **Sanibel** Sanibel Island, Florida, SE USA 26°27′N 82°01′W
23 V15 **Sanibel Island** *island* Florida, SE USA
60 F13 **San Ignacio** Misiones, NE Argentina 27°15′S 55°32′W
42 F2 **San Ignacio** *prev.* Cayo, El Cayo. Cayo, W Belize 17°09′N 89°02′W
57 L16 **San Ignacio** El Beni, N Bolivia 14°54′S 65°35′W
57 O18 **San Ignacio** Santa Cruz, E Bolivia 16°23′S 60°59′W
42 M14 **San Ignacio** *var.* San Ignacio de Acosta. San José, W Costa Rica 09°46′N 84°10′W
40 E6 **San Ignacio** Baja California Sur, NW Mexico 27°18′N 112°51′W
40 J10 **San Ignacio** Sinaloa, W Mexico 23°55′N 106°25′W
56 B9 **San Ignacio** Cajamarca, N Peru 05°09′S 79°00′W
San Ignacio de Acosta *see* San Ignacio
40 D7 **San Ignacio, Laguna** *lagoon* W Mexico
12 I6 **Sanikiluaq** Belcher Islands, Nunavut, C Canada 55°20′N 77°50′W
171 O3 **San Ildefonso Peninsula** *peninsula* Luzon, N Philippines
Saniquillie *see* Sanniquellie
Sanirajak *see* Hall Beach
61 D20 **San Isidro** Buenos Aires, E Argentina 34°28′S 58°31′W
43 N14 **San Isidro** *var.* San Isidro de El General. San José, SE Costa Rica 09°28′N 83°42′W
San Isidro de El General *see* San Isidro
54 E5 **San Jacinto** Bolívar, N Colombia 09°53′N 75°06′W
35 U16 **San Jacinto** California, W USA 33°47′N 116°58′W
35 V15 **San Jacinto Peak** ▲ California, W USA 33°48′N 116°40′W
61 F14 **San Javier** Misiones, NE Argentina 27°50′S 55°06′W
61 C16 **San Javier** Santa Fe, C Argentina 30°35′S 59°59′W
105 S13 **San Javier** Murcia, SE Spain 37°49′N 00°50′W
61 D18 **San Javier** Río Negro, W Uruguay 32°41′S 58°08′W
61 C16 **San Javier, Río** ≈ C Argentina
160 L12 **Sanjiang** *var.* Guyi, Sanjiang Dongzu Zizhixian. Guangxi Zhuangzu Zizhiqu, S China 25°46′N 109°26′E
Sanjiang *see* Jinping, Guizhou
Sanjiang Dongzu Zizhixian *see* Sanjiang
Sanjiaocheng *see* Haiyan
165 N11 **Sanjō** *var.* Sanzyô. Niigata, Honshū, C Japan 37°39′N 139°00′E
57 M15 **San Joaquín** El Beni, N Bolivia 13°06′S 64°46′W
55 O6 **San Joaquín** Anzoátegui, NE Venezuela 09°21′N 64°30′W
35 O9 **San Joaquin River** ≈ California, W USA
35 P10 **San Joaquin Valley** *valley* California, W USA
61 A18 **San Jorge** Santa Fe, C Argentina 31°50′S 61°50′W
40 D3 **San Jorge, Bahía de** *bay* NW Mexico
63 J19 **San Jorge, Golfo** *var.* Gulf of San Jorge. *gulf* S Argentina
San Jorge, Gulf of *see* San Jorge, Golfo
San Jorge, Isla de *see* Weddell Island
61 F14 **San José** Misiones, NE Argentina 27°46′S 55°47′W
57 P19 **San José** *var.* San José de Chiquitos. Santa Cruz, E Bolivia 14°13′S 68°05′W
42 M14 **San José** ● (Costa Rica) San José, C Costa Rica 09°55′N 84°05′W
42 C7 **San José** *var.* Puerto San José. Escuintla, S Guatemala 14°00′N 90°50′W
40 G6 **San José** Sonora, NW Mexico 27°32′N 110°09′W
188 K8 **San Jose** Tinian, S Northern Mariana Islands 15°00′S 145°38′E
105 U11 **San José** Eivissa, Spain, W Mediterranean Sea 38°55′N 01°18′E
35 N9 **San Jose** California, W USA 37°18′N 121°53′W
54 H5 **San José** Zulia, NW Venezuela 10°02′N 72°24′W
42 M14 **San José** *off.* Provincia de San José. ◈ *province* W Costa Rica
61 E19 **San José** ◈ *department* S Uruguay
42 M13 **San José** ✈ Alajuela, C Costa Rica 10°03′N 84°12′W
San José *see* San José del Guaviare, Colombia
San Jose *see* Oleai
San Jose *see* Sant Josep de sa Talaia, Ibiza, Spain
San José *see* San José de Mayo, Uruguay
171 O3 **San Jose City** Luzon, N Philippines 15°49′N 120°57′E
San José de Chiquitos *see* San José
San José de Cúcuta *see* Cúcuta
61 D16 **San José de Feliciano** Entre Ríos, E Argentina 30°26′S 58°46′W
55 O6 **San José de Guanipa** *var.* El Tigrito. Anzoátegui, NE Venezuela 08°54′N 64°10′W
62 I9 **San José de Jáchal** San Juan, W Argentina 30°15′S 68°46′W
40 G10 **San José del Cabo** Baja California Sur, NW Mexico 23°01′N 109°40′W
54 G12 **San José del Guaviare** *var.* San José. Guaviare, S Colombia 02°34′N 72°38′W
61 E20 **San José de Mayo** *var.* San José. San José, S Uruguay 34°20′S 56°42′W
54 I10 **San José de Ocuné** Vichada, E Colombia 04°10′N 70°21′W
41 O9 **San José de Raíces** Nuevo León, NE Mexico 24°32′N 100°15′W
63 K17 **San José, Golfo** *gulf* E Argentina
40 F9 **San José, Isla** *island* NW Mexico
43 U16 **San José, Isla** *island* SE Panama
25 U14 **San Jose Island** *island* Texas, SW USA
San José, Provincia de *see* San José
62 I10 **San Juan** San Juan, W Argentina 31°37′S 68°27′W
45 N9 **San Juan** *var.* San Juan de la Maguana. C Dominican Republic 18°49′N 71°12′W
57 E17 **San Juan** Ica, S Peru 15°22′S 75°07′W
45 U5 **San Juan** ○ (Puerto Rico) NE Puerto Rico 18°28′N 66°06′W
62 H10 **San Juan** *off.* Provincia de San Juan. ◈ *province* W Argentina
San Juan *see* San Juan de los Morros
62 O7 **San Juan Bautista** Misiones, S Paraguay 26°40′S 57°08′W
35 O10 **San Juan Bautista** California, W USA 36°50′N 121°34′W
San Juan Bautista *see* Villahermosa
San Juan Bautista Cuicatlán *see* Cuicatlán
San Juan Bautista Tuxtepec *see* Tuxtepec
79 C17 **San Juan, Cabo** *headland* S Equatorial Guinea 01°09′N 09°25′E
San Juan de Alicante *see* Sant Joan d'Alacant
54 H7 **San Juan de Colón** Táchira, NW Venezuela 08°02′N 72°17′W
40 L9 **San Juan de Guadalupe** Durango, C Mexico 25°12′N 100°50′W
San Juan de la Maguana *see* San Juan
54 G4 **San Juan del Cesar** La Guajira, N Colombia 10°45′N 73°00′W
40 L15 **San Juan de Lima, Punta** *headland* SW Mexico 18°34′N 103°40′W
42 I8 **San Juan de Limay** Estelí, NW Nicaragua 13°10′N 86°36′W
43 N12 **San Juan del Norte** *var.* Greytown. Río San Juan, SE Nicaragua 10°58′N 83°40′W
54 K4 **San Juan de los Cayos** Falcón, N Venezuela 11°11′N 68°27′W
40 M12 **San Juan de los Lagos** Jalisco, C Mexico 21°15′N 102°15′W
54 L5 **San Juan de los Morros** *var.* San Juan. Guárico, N Venezuela 09°53′N 67°23′W
40 K9 **San Juan del Río** Durango, C Mexico 25°12′N 100°50′W
41 O13 **San Juan del Río** Querétaro de Arteaga, C Mexico 20°24′N 100°00′W
42 J11 **San Juan del Sur** Rivas, SW Nicaragua 11°16′N 85°51′W
54 M9 **San Juan de Manapiare** Amazonas, S Venezuela 05°15′N 66°05′W
40 E7 **San Juanico** Baja California Sur, NW Mexico
40 D7 **San Juanico, Punta** *headland* NW Mexico 26°01′N 112°17′W
32 G6 **San Juan Islands** *island group* Washington, NW USA
40 I6 **San Juanito** Chihuahua, N Mexico
40 I12 **San Juanito, Isla** *island* C Mexico
37 R8 **San Juan Mountains** ▲▲ Colorado, C USA
54 E5 **San Juan Nepomuceno** Bolívar, NW Colombia 09°57′N 75°06′W
44 E5 **San Juan, Pico** ▲ C Cuba 21°58′N 80°10′W
San Juan, Provincia de *see* San Juan
191 W15 **San Juan, Punta** *headland* Easter Island, Chile, E Pacific Ocean 27°03′S 109°22′W
42 M12 **San Juan, Río** ≈ Costa Rica/Nicaragua
41 S15 **San Juan, Río** ≈ SE Mexico
37 O8 **San Juan River** ≈ Colorado/Utah, W USA
San Julián *see* Puerto San Julián
61 B17 **San Justo** Santa Fe, C Argentina 30°47′S 60°32′W
109 W5 **Sankt Aegyd am Neuwalde** Niederösterreich, E Austria 47°51′N 15°34′E
109 U9 **Sankt Andrä** *Slvn.* Šent Andraž. Kärnten, S Austria 46°46′N 14°49′E
Sankt Andrä *see* Szentendre
Sankt Anna *see* Sântana
108 K8 **Sankt Anton-am-Arlberg** Vorarlberg, W Austria 47°08′N 10°11′E
101 E16 **Sankt Augustin** Nordrhein-Westfalen, W Germany 50°46′N 07°10′E
Sankt-Bartholomäi *see* Palamuse
101 F24 **Sankt Blasien** Baden-Württemberg, SW Germany 47°43′N 08°09′E
109 R3 **Sankt Florian am Inn** Oberösterreich, N Austria 48°24′N 13°27′E
108 I7 **Sankt Gallen** *var.* St. Gallen, *Eng.* Saint Gall, *Fr.* St-Gall. Sankt Gallen, NE Switzerland 47°25′N 09°23′E
108 H8 **Sankt Gallen** *var.* St.Gallen, *Eng.* Saint Gall, *Fr.* St-Gall. ◈ *canton* NE Switzerland
108 J8 **Sankt Gallenkirch** Vorarlberg, W Austria 47°00′N 10°59′E
109 Q5 **Sankt Georgen** Salzburg, N Austria 47°59′N 12°57′E
Sankt Georgen *see* Đurđevac
Sankt-Georgen *see* Sfântu Gheorghe
109 R6 **Sankt Gilgen** Salzburg, NW Austria 47°46′N 13°21′E
Sankt Gotthard *see* Szentgotthárd
101 E20 **Sankt Ingbert** Saarland, SW Germany 49°17′N 07°07′E
Sankt-Jakobi *see* Viru-Jaagupi, Lääne-Virumaa, Estonia
Sankt-Jakobi *see* Pärnu-Jaagupi, Pärnumaa, Estonia
Sankt Johann *see* Sankt Johann in Tirol
109 T7 **Sankt Johann am Tauern** Steiermark, E Austria 47°20′N 14°27′E
109 Q7 **Sankt Johann im Pongau** Salzburg, NW Austria 47°22′N 13°13′E
109 P6 **Sankt Johann in Tirol** *var.* Sankt Johann. Tirol, W Austria 47°32′N 12°26′E
Sankt-Johannis *see* Järva-Jaani
108 L8 **Sankt Leonhard** Tirol, W Austria 47°05′N 10°53′E
Sankt Margarethen *see* Sankt Margarethen im Burgenland
109 Y5 **Sankt Margarethen im Burgenland** *var.* Sankt Margarethen. Burgenland, E Austria 47°49′N 16°38′E
Sankt Martin *see* Martin
109 X8 **Sankt Martin an der Raab** Burgenland, SE Austria 46°59′N 16°12′E
109 U7 **Sankt Michael in Obersteiermark** Steiermark, SE Austria 47°21′N 14°59′E
Sankt Michel *see* Mikkeli
Sankt Moritz *see* St. Moritz
108 E11 **Sankt Niklaus** Valais, S Switzerland 46°09′N 07°48′E

◆ Country ● Country Capital ◇ Dependent Territory ○ Dependent Territory Capital ◈ Administrative Regions ✈ International Airport ▲ Mountain ▲▲ Mountain Range ※ Volcano ≈ River ◎ Lake ⊠ Reservoir

109 S7 **Sankt Nikolai** var. Sankt Nikolai im Sölktal. Steiermark, SE Austria 47°18′N 14°04′E
Sankt Nikolai im Sölktal see Sankt Nikolai
109 U9 **Sankt Paul** var. Sankt Paul im Lavanttal. Kärnten, S Austria 46°42′N 14°53′E
Sankt Paul im Lavanttal see Sankt Paul
Sankt Peter see Pivka
109 W9 **Sankt Peter am Ottersbach** Steiermark, SE Austria 46°49′N 15°48′E
124 J13 **Sankt-Peterburg** prev. Leningrad, Petrograd, Eng. Saint Petersburg, Fin. Pietari. Leningradskaya Oblast', NW Russian Federation 59°55′N 30°25′E
100 H8 **Sankt Peter-Ording** Schleswig-Holstein, N Germany 54°18′N 08°37′E
109 V4 **Sankt Pölten** Niederösterreich, N Austria 48°14′N 15°38′E
109 W7 **Sankt Ruprecht** var. Sankt Ruprecht an der Raab. Steiermark, SE Austria 47°10′N 15°41′E
Sankt Ruprecht an der Raab see Sankt Ruprecht
Sankt-Ulrich see Ortisei
109 T4 **Sankt Valentin** Niederösterreich, C Austria 48°11′N 14°33′E
Sankt Veit am Flaum see Rijeka
109 T9 **Sankt Veit an der Glan** Slvn. St. Vid. Kärnten, S Austria 46°47′N 14°22′E
99 M21 **Sankt-Vith** var. Saint-Vith. Liège, E Belgium 50°17′N 06°07′E
101 E20 **Sankt Wendel** Saarland, SW Germany 49°28′N 07°10′E
109 R6 **Sankt Wolfgang** Salzburg, NW Austria 47°43′N 13°30′E
79 K21 **Sankuru** ≈ C Dem. Rep. Congo
40 D8 **San Lázaro, Cabo** headland NW Mexico 24°46′N 112°15′W
137 O16 **Şanlıurfa** prev. Sanli Urfa, Urfa; anc. Edessa. şanlıurfa, S Turkey 37°08′N 38°45′E
137 O16 **Şanlıurfa** prev. Urfa. ◈ province SE Turkey
Sanli Urfa see Şanlıurfa
137 O16 **Şanlıurfa Yaylası** plateau SE Turkey
61 B18 **San Lorenzo** Santa Fe, C Argentina 32°45′S 60°45′W
57 M21 **San Lorenzo** Tarija, S Bolivia 21°25′S 64°45′W
56 C5 **San Lorenzo** Esmeraldas, N Ecuador 01°15′N 78°51′W
42 H8 **San Lorenzo** Valle, S Honduras 13°24′N 87°27′W
56 A6 **San Lorenzo, Cabo** headland W Ecuador 0°57′S 80°49′W
105 N8 **San Lorenzo de El Escorial** var. El Escorial. Madrid, C Spain 40°36′N 04°07′W
40 E5 **San Lorenzo, Isla** island NW Mexico
57 C14 **San Lorenzo, Isla** island W Peru
63 G20 **San Lorenzo, Monte** ▲ S Argentina 47°40′S 72°12′W
40 I9 **San Lorenzo, Río** ≈ C Mexico
104 J15 **Sanlúcar de Barrameda** Andalucía, S Spain 36°46′N 06°21′W
104 J14 **Sanlúcar la Mayor** Andalucía, S Spain 37°24′N 06°13′W
40 F11 **San Lucas** Baja California Sur, NW Mexico 22°50′N 109°52′W
40 E6 **San Lucas** var. Cabo San Lucas. Baja California Sur, NW Mexico 27°14′N 112°15′W
40 G11 **San Lucas, Cabo** var. San Lucas Cape. headland NW Mexico 22°52′N 109°53′W
San Lucas Cape see San Lucas, Cabo
62 J11 **San Luis** San Luis, C Argentina 33°18′S 66°18′W
42 E4 **San Luis** Petén, NE Guatemala 16°16′N 89°27′W
42 M7 **San Luis** Región Autónoma Atlántico Norte, NE Nicaragua 13°59′N 84°10′W
36 H15 **San Luis** Arizona, SW USA 32°27′N 114°45′W
37 T8 **San Luis** Colorado, C USA 37°09′N 105°24′W
54 J4 **San Luis** Falcón, N Venezuela 11°09′N 69°39′W
62 J11 **San Luis** off. Provincia de San Luis. ◈ province C Argentina
41 N12 **San Luis de la Paz** Guanajuato, C Mexico 21°15′N 100°33′W
40 K8 **San Luis del Cordero** Durango, C Mexico 25°25′N 104°09′W
40 D4 **San Luis, Isla** island NW Mexico
42 E6 **San Luis Jilotepeque** Jalapa, SE Guatemala 14°40′N 89°42′W
57 M16 **San Luis, Laguna de** ◎ NW Bolivia
35 P13 **San Luis Obispo** California, W USA 35°17′N 120°40′W
37 R7 **San Luis Peak** ▲ Colorado, C USA 37°59′N 106°55′W
41 N11 **San Luis Potosí** San Luis Potosí, C Mexico 22°10′N 100°57′W
41 N11 **San Luis Potosí** ◈ state C Mexico
San Luis, Provincia de see San Luis
35 O10 **San Luis Reservoir** ⊠ California, W USA
40 D2 **San Luis Río Colorado** var. San Luis Río Colorado. Sonora, NW Mexico 32°26′N 114°48′W
San Luis Río Colorado see San Luis Río Colorado
37 S8 **San Luis Valley** basin Colorado, C USA
107 C19 **Sanluri** Sardegna, Italy, C Mediterranean Sea 39°34′N 08°54′E
61 D23 **San Manuel** Buenos Aires, E Argentina 37°47′S 58°50′W
36 M15 **San Manuel** Arizona, SW USA 32°36′N 110°37′W
106 F11 **San Marcello Pistoiese** Toscana, C Italy 44°03′N 10°46′E
107 N20 **San Marco Argentano** Calabria, SW Italy 39°31′N 16°07′E
54 E6 **San Marcos** Sucre, N Colombia 08°38′N 75°10′W
42 M14 **San Marcos** San José, C Costa Rica 09°39′N 84°00′W
42 B5 **San Marcos** San Marcos, W Guatemala 14°58′N 91°48′W
42 F6 **San Marcos** Ocotepeque, SW Honduras 14°23′N 88°57′W
41 O16 **San Marcos** Guerrero, S Mexico 16°45′N 99°22′W
25 S11 **San Marcos** Texas, SW USA 29°54′N 97°57′W
42 A5 **San Marcos** off. Departamento de San Marcos. ◈ department W Guatemala
San Marcos de Arica see Arica
San Marcos, Departamento de see San Marcos
40 E6 **San Marcos, Isla** island NW Mexico
106 H11 **San Marino** ● (San Marino) C San Marino 43°54′N 12°27′E
106 I11 **San Marino** off. Republic of San Marino. ◆ republic S Europe
San Marino, Republic of see San Marino
62 I11 **San Martín** Mendoza, C Argentina 33°05′S 68°28′W
54 F11 **San Martín** Meta, C Colombia 03°43′N 73°42′W
56 D11 **San Martín** off. Departamento de San Martín. ◈ department C Peru
194 I5 **San Martín** Argentinian research station Antarctica 68°18′S 67°03′W
63 H16 **San Martín de los Andes** Neuquén, W Argentina 40°11′S 71°22′W
San Martín, Departamento de see San Martín
104 M8 **San Martín de Valdeiglesias** Madrid, C Spain 40°21′N 04°24′W
63 G21 **San Martín, Lago** var. Lago O'Higgins. ◎ S Argentina
106 H6 **San Martino di Castrozza** Trentino-Alto Adige, N Italy 46°16′N 11°50′E
57 N16 **San Martín, Río** ≈ N Bolivia
San Martín Texmelucan see Texmelucan
35 N9 **San Mateo** California, W USA 37°33′N 122°19′W
55 O6 **San Mateo** Anzoátegui, NE Venezuela 09°48′N 64°36′W
42 B4 **San Mateo Ixtatán** Huehuetenango, W Guatemala 15°50′N 91°30′W
57 Q18 **San Matías** Santa Cruz, E Bolivia 16°20′S 58°24′W
63 K16 **San Matías, Golfo** var. Gulf of San Matías. gulf E Argentina
San Matías, Gulf of see San Matías, Golfo
15 O8 **Sanmaur** Québec, SE Canada 47°52′N 73°47′W
161 T10 **Sanmen Wan** bay E China
160 M6 **Sanmenxia** var. Shan Xian. Henan, C China 34°46′N 111°17′E
Sânmiclăuş Mare see Sânnicolau Mare
61 D14 **San Miguel** Corrientes, NE Argentina 28°02′S 57°41′W
57 L16 **San Miguel** El Beni, N Bolivia 16°43′S 61°06′W
42 G8 **San Miguel** San Miguel, SE El Salvador 13°27′N 88°11′W
40 L6 **San Miguel** Coahuila, N Mexico 29°10′N 101°28′W
40 J9 **San Miguel** var. San Miguel de Cruces. Durango, C Mexico 24°25′N 105°55′W
43 U16 **San Miguel** Panamá, SE Panama 08°27′N 78°51′W
35 P12 **San Miguel** California, W USA 35°45′N 120°42′W
42 B9 **San Miguel** ◈ department E El Salvador
41 N13 **San Miguel de Allende** Guanajuato, C Mexico 20°56′N 100°48′W
San Miguel de Cruces see San Miguel
San Miguel de Ibarra see Ibarra
61 D21 **San Miguel del Monte** Buenos Aires, E Argentina 35°26′S 58°50′W
62 J7 **San Miguel de Tucumán** var. Tucumán. Tucumán, N Argentina 26°47′S 65°15′W
43 V16 **San Miguel, Golfo de** gulf S Panama
35 P15 **San Miguel Island** island California, W USA
42 L11 **San Miguelito** Río San Juan, S Nicaragua 11°22′N 84°54′W
43 T15 **San Miguelito** Panamá, C Panama 08°58′N 79°31′W
57 N18 **San Miguel, Río** ≈ E Bolivia
56 D6 **San Miguel, Río** ≈ Colombia/Ecuador
40 I7 **San Miguel, Río** ≈ N Mexico
42 G8 **San Miguel, Volcán de** ⛰ SE El Salvador 13°27′N 88°18′W
161 Q12 **Sanming** Fujian, SE China 26°11′N 117°37′E
106 F11 **San Miniato** Toscana, C Italy 43°40′N 10°53′E
San Murezzan see St. Moritz
Sannär see Sennar
107 M15 **Sannicandro Garganico** Puglia, SE Italy 41°50′N 15°32′E
40 H6 **San Nicolás** Sonora, NW Mexico 28°31′N 109°24′W
61 C19 **San Nicolás de los Arroyos** Buenos Aires, E Argentina 33°20′S 60°13′W
35 R16 **San Nicolas Island** island Channel Islands, California, W USA
Sânnicolaul-Mare see Sânnicolau Mare
116 E11 **Sânnicolau Mare** var. Sânnicolaul-Mare, Hung. Nagyszentmiklós; prev. Sânmiclăuş Mare, Sînnicolau Mare. Timiş, W Romania 46°05′N 20°38′E
123 Q6 **Sannikova, Proliv** strait NE Russian Federation
76 K16 **Sanniquellie** var. Saniquillie. NE Liberia 07°24′N 08°45′W
165 R7 **Sannohe** Aomori, Honshū, C Japan 40°23′N 141°16′E
Sanntaler Alpen see Kamniško-Savinjske Alpe
111 O17 **Sanok** Podkarpackie, SE Poland 49°31′N 22°14′E
54 E5 **San Onofre** Sucre, NW Colombia 09°45′N 75°33′W
57 K21 **San Pablo** Potosí, S Bolivia 21°43′S 66°38′W
171 O4 **San Pablo** off. San Pablo City. Luzon, N Philippines 14°04′N 121°16′E
San Pablo Balleza see Balleza
35 N8 **San Pablo Bay** bay California, W USA
San Pablo City see San Pablo
40 C6 **San Pablo, Punta** headland NW Mexico 27°12′N 114°30′W
43 R16 **San Pablo, Río** ≈ C Panama
171 P4 **San Pascual** Burias Island, C Philippines 13°06′N 122°59′E
121 Q16 **San Pawl il Baħar** Eng. Saint Paul's Bay. E Malta 35°57′N 14°24′E
61 C19 **San Pedro** Buenos Aires, E Argentina 33°43′S 59°45′W
62 K5 **San Pedro** Jujuy, N Argentina 24°12′S 64°55′W
60 G13 **San Pedro** Misiones, NE Argentina 26°38′S 54°12′W
42 H1 **San Pedro** Corozal, NE Belize 17°58′N 87°55′W
76 M17 **San-Pédro** S Ivory Coast 04°45′N 06°37′W
40 L8 **San Pedro** var. San Pedro de las Colonias. Coahuila, NE Mexico 25°47′N 102°57′W
62 O5 **San Pedro** San Pedro, SE Paraguay 24°08′S 57°08′W
62 O6 **San Pedro** off. Departamento de San Pedro. ◈ department C Paraguay
44 G6 **San Pedro** ≈ C Cuba
77 N16 **San Pedro** ✕ (Yamoussoukro) C Ivory Coast 06°49′N 05°14′W
San Pedro see San Pedro del Pinatar
42 D5 **San Pedro Carchá** Alta Verapaz, C Guatemala 15°30′N 90°12′W
35 S16 **San Pedro Channel** channel California, W USA
62 I5 **San Pedro de Atacama** Antofagasta, N Chile 22°52′S 68°10′W
San Pedro de Durazno see Durazno
40 G5 **San Pedro de la Cueva** Sonora, NW Mexico 29°17′N 109°47′W
San Pedro de las Colonias see San Pedro
56 B11 **San Pedro de Lloc** La Libertad, NW Peru 07°26′S 79°31′W
105 S13 **San Pedro del Pinatar** var. San Pedro. Murcia, SE Spain 37°50′N 00°47′W
45 P9 **San Pedro de Macorís** SE Dominican Republic 18°30′N 69°18′W
San Pedro, Departamento de see San Pedro
40 C3 **San Pedro Mártir, Sierra** ▲▲ NW Mexico
San Pedro Pochutla see Pochutla
42 D2 **San Pedro, Río** ≈ Guatemala/Mexico
40 K10 **San Pedro, Río** ≈ C Mexico
104 J10 **San Pedro, Sierra de** ▲▲ W Spain
42 G5 **San Pedro Sula** Cortés, NW Honduras 15°26′N 88°01′W
San Pedro Tapanatepec see Tapanatepec
62 I4 **San Pedro, Volcán** ⛰ N Chile 21°46′S 68°13′W
106 E7 **San Pellegrino Terme** Lombardia, N Italy 45°53′N 09°42′E
25 T16 **San Perlita** Texas, SW USA 26°30′N 97°38′W
San Pietro see Supetar
San Pietro del Carso see Pivka
107 A20 **San Pietro, Isola di** island W Italy
32 K7 **Sanpoil River** ≈ Washington, NW USA
165 O9 **Sanpoku** var. Sampoku. Niigata, Honshū, C Japan 38°32′N 139°33′E
40 C3 **San Quintín** Baja California Norte, NW Mexico 30°28′N 115°58′W
40 B3 **San Quintín, Bahía de** bay NW Mexico
40 B3 **San Quintín, Cabo** headland NW Mexico 30°22′N 116°01′W
62 I12 **San Rafael** Mendoza, W Argentina 34°44′S 68°15′W
41 N9 **San Rafael** Nuevo León, NE Mexico 25°01′N 100°33′W
34 M8 **San Rafael** California, W USA 37°58′N 122°31′W
37 Q11 **San Rafael** New Mexico, SW USA 35°03′N 107°52′W
54 H4 **San Rafael** var. El Moján. Zulia, NW Venezuela 10°58′N 71°45′W
42 J8 **San Rafael del Norte** Jinotega, NW Nicaragua 13°12′N 86°06′W
42 J10 **San Rafael del Sur** Managua, SW Nicaragua 11°51′N 86°24′W
36 M5 **San Rafael Knob** ▲ Utah, W USA 38°46′N 110°45′W
35 Q14 **San Rafael Mountains** ▲▲ California, W USA
42 M13 **San Ramón** Alajuela, C Costa Rica 10°04′N 84°31′W
57 E14 **San Ramón** Junín, C Peru 11°08′S 75°18′W
61 F19 **San Ramón** Canelones, S Uruguay 34°18′S 55°55′W
62 K5 **San Ramón de la Nueva Orán** Salta, N Argentina 23°08′S 64°20′W
57 O16 **San Ramón, Río** ≈ E Bolivia
106 B11 **San Remo** Liguria, NW Italy 43°48′N 07°47′E
54 J3 **San Román, Cabo** headland NW Venezuela 12°10′N 70°01′W
61 C15 **San Roque** Corrientes, NE Argentina 28°35′S 58°45′W
188 I4 **San Roque** Saipan, S Northern Mariana Islands 15°15′S 145°47′E
104 K16 **San Roque** Andalucía, S Spain 36°13′N 05°23′W
25 R9 **San Saba** Texas, SW USA 31°13′N 98°44′W
25 Q9 **San Saba River** ≈ Texas, SW USA
61 D17 **San Salvador** Entre Ríos, E Argentina 31°38′S 58°30′W
42 F7 **San Salvador** ● (El Salvador) San Salvador, SW El Salvador 13°42′N 89°12′W
42 A10 **San Salvador** ◈ department C El Salvador
44 K4 **San Salvador** prev. Watlings Island. island E Bahamas
42 F8 **San Salvador** ✕ La Paz, S El Salvador 13°27′N 89°04′W
62 J5 **San Salvador de Jujuy** var. Jujuy. Jujuy, N Argentina 24°10′S 65°20′W
42 F7 **San Salvador, Volcán de** ⛰ C El Salvador 13°58′N 89°14′W
77 Q14 **Sansanné-Mango** var. Mango. N Togo 10°21′N 00°28′E
45 S5 **San Sebastián** W Puerto Rico 18°21′N 67°00′W
63 J24 **San Sebastián, Bahía** bay S Argentina
Sansenhō see Sacheon
106 H12 **Sansepolcro** Toscana, C Italy 43°35′N 12°12′E
107 M16 **San Severo** Puglia, SE Italy 41°41′N 15°23′E
112 F11 **Sanski Most** ◈ Federacija Bosna I Hercegovina, NW Bosnia and Herzegovina
171 W12 **Sansundi** Papua, E Indonesia 0°42′S 135°48′E
162 K9 **Sant** var. Mayhan. Övörhangay, C Mongolia 46°02′N 104°00′E
104 K11 **Santa Amalia** Extremadura, W Spain 39°00′N 06°01′W
60 F13 **Santa Ana** Misiones, NE Argentina 27°22′S 55°34′W
57 L16 **Santa Ana** El Beni, N Bolivia 13°43′S 65°37′W
42 E7 **Santa Ana** Santa Ana, NW El Salvador 13°59′N 89°34′W
40 F4 **Santa Ana** Sonora, NW Mexico 30°31′N 111°08′W
35 T16 **Santa Ana** California, W USA 33°45′N 117°52′W
55 N6 **Santa Ana** Nueva Esparta, NE Venezuela 09°15′N 64°39′W
42 A9 **Santa Ana** ◈ department NW El Salvador
Santa Ana de Coro see Coro
35 U16 **Santa Ana Mountains** ▲▲ California, W USA
42 E7 **Santa Ana, Volcán de** var. La Matepec. ⛰ W El Salvador 13°49′N 89°36′W
42 G6 **Santa Bárbara** Santa Bárbara, W Honduras 14°56′N 88°11′W
40 J7 **Santa Barbara** Chihuahua, N Mexico 26°46′N 105°46′W
35 Q14 **Santa Barbara** California, W USA 34°24′N 119°40′W
54 L11 **Santa Bárbara** Amazonas, S Venezuela 03°55′N 67°06′W
54 I7 **Santa Bárbara** Barinas, W Venezuela 07°48′N 71°10′W
42 F5 **Santa Bárbara** ◈ department NW Honduras
Santa Bárbara see Iscuandé
35 Q15 **Santa Barbara Channel** channel California, W USA
Santa Bárbara de Samaná see Samaná
35 R16 **Santa Barbara Island** island Channel Islands, California, W USA
54 E5 **Santa Catalina** Bolívar, N Colombia 10°36′N 75°17′W
43 R15 **Santa Catalina** Ngöbe Bugle, W Panama 08°46′N 81°18′W
104 G2 **Santa Catalina de Armada** Galicia, NW Spain 43°02′N 08°49′W
35 T17 **Santa Catalina, Gulf of** gulf California, W USA
40 F8 **Santa Catalina, Isla** island NW Mexico
35 S16 **Santa Catalina Island** island Channel Islands, California, W USA
41 N8 **Santa Catarina** Nuevo León, NE Mexico 25°39′N 100°30′W
60 H13 **Santa Catarina** off. Estado de Santa Catarina. ◈ state S Brazil
Santa Catarina de Tepehuanes see Tepehuanes
Santa Catarina, Estado de see Santa Catarina
60 L13 **Santa Catarina, Ilha de** island S Brazil
45 Q16 **Santa Catherina** Curaçao 12°07′N 68°46′W
44 E5 **Santa Clara** Villa Clara, C Cuba 22°25′N 78°01′W
35 N9 **Santa Clara** California, W USA 37°20′N 121°57′W
36 J8 **Santa Clara** Utah, W USA 37°07′N 113°39′W
Santa Clara see Santa Clara de Olimar
61 F18 **Santa Clara de Olimar** var. Santa Clara. Cerro Largo, NE Uruguay 32°50′S 54°54′W
61 A17 **Santa Clara de Saguier** Santa Fe, C Argentina 31°21′S 61°50′W
Santa Coloma see Santa Coloma de Gramenet
105 X5 **Santa Coloma de Farners** var. Santa Coloma de Farnés. Cataluña, NE Spain 41°52′N 02°39′E
Santa Coloma de Farnés see Santa Coloma de Farners
Santa Coloma de Gramanet see Santa Coloma de Gramenet
105 W6 **Santa Coloma de Gramenet** var. Santa Coloma; prev. Santa Coloma de Gramanet. Cataluña, NE Spain 41°28′N 02°14′E
Santa Comba see Uaco Cungo
104 H8 **Santa Comba Dão** Viseu, N Portugal 40°23′N 08°07′W
82 C10 **Santa Cruz** Uíge, NW Angola 06°56′S 16°25′E
57 N19 **Santa Cruz** var. Santa Cruz de la Sierra. Santa Cruz, C Bolivia 17°49′S 63°11′W
62 G12 **Santa Cruz** Libertador, C Chile 34°38′S 71°27′W
42 K13 **Santa Cruz** Guanacaste, W Costa Rica 10°15′N 85°35′W
44 I12 **Santa Cruz** W Jamaica 18°03′N 77°43′W
64 P6 **Santa Cruz** Madeira, Portugal, NE Atlantic Ocean 32°43′N 16°47′W
35 N10 **Santa Cruz** California, W USA 36°58′N 122°01′W
63 H20 **Santa Cruz** off. Provincia de Santa Cruz. ◈ province S Argentina
57 O18 **Santa Cruz** ◈ department E Bolivia
Santa Cruz see Puerto Santa Cruz
Santa Cruz see Viru-Viru
Santa Cruz Barillas see Barillas
59 O18 **Santa Cruz Cabrália** Bahia, E Brazil 16°17′S 39°03′W
Santa Cruz de El Seibo see El Seibo
64 N11 **Santa Cruz de la Palma** La Palma, Islas Canarias, Spain, NE Atlantic Ocean 28°41′N 17°46′W
Santa Cruz de la Sierra see Santa Cruz
105 O9 **Santa Cruz de la Zarza** Castilla-La Mancha, C Spain 39°59′N 03°10′W
42 C5 **Santa Cruz del Quiché** Quiché, W Guatemala 15°02′N 91°06′W
105 N8 **Santa Cruz del Retamar** Castilla-La Mancha, C Spain 40°08′N 04°14′W
Santa Cruz del Seibo see El Seibo
44 G7 **Santa Cruz del Sur** Camagüey, C Cuba 20°44′N 78°00′W
105 O11 **Santa Cruz de Mudela** Castilla-La Mancha, C Spain 38°37′N 03°27′W
64 Q11 **Santa Cruz de Tenerife** Tenerife, Islas Canarias, Spain, NE Atlantic Ocean 28°28′N 16°15′W
64 P11 **Santa Cruz de Tenerife** ◈ province Islas Canarias, Spain, NE Atlantic Ocean
60 K9 **Santa Cruz do Rio Pardo** São Paulo, S Brazil 22°52′S 49°37′W
61 H15 **Santa Cruz do Sul** Rio Grande do Sul, S Brazil 29°42′S 52°25′W
57 C17 **Santa Cruz, Isla** var. Indefatigable Island, Isla Chávez. island Galapagos Islands, Ecuador, E Pacific Ocean
40 F8 **Santa Cruz, Isla** island NW Mexico
35 Q15 **Santa Cruz Island** island California, W USA
187 Q10 **Santa Cruz Islands** island group E Solomon Islands
Santa Cruz, Provincia de see Santa Cruz
63 I22 **Santa Cruz, Río** ≈ S Argentina
36 L15 **Santa Cruz River** ≈ Arizona, SW USA
61 C17 **Santa Elena** Entre Ríos, E Argentina 30°58′S 59°47′W
42 F2 **Santa Elena** Cayo, W Belize 17°08′N 89°04′W
25 R16 **Santa Elena** Texas, SW USA 26°43′N 98°30′W
56 A7 **Santa Elena, Bahía de** bay W Ecuador
55 R10 **Santa Elena de Uairén** Bolívar, E Venezuela 04°40′N 61°03′W
42 K12 **Santa Elena, Península** peninsula NW Costa Rica
56 A7 **Santa Elena, Punta** headland W Ecuador 02°11′S 81°00′W
104 L11 **Santa Eufemia** Andalucía, S Spain 38°36′N 04°54′W
107 N21 **Santa Eufemia, Golfo di** gulf S Italy
105 S4 **Santa Eulalia de Gállego** Aragón, NE Spain 42°16′N 00°46′W
105 V11 **Santa Eulalia del Río** Ibiza, Spain, W Mediterranean Sea 39°00′N 01°33′E
61 B17 **Santa Fe** Santa Fe, C Argentina 31°36′S 60°47′W
44 C6 **Santa Fé** var. La Fe. Isla de la Juventud, W Cuba 21°45′N 82°45′W
43 R16 **Santa Fé** Veraguas, C Panama 08°29′N 80°50′W
105 N14 **Santa Fe** Andalucía, S Spain 37°11′N 03°43′W
37 S10 **Santa Fe** state capital New Mexico, SW USA 35°41′N 105°56′W
61 B15 **Santa Fe** off. Provincia de Santa Fe. ◈ province C Argentina
Santa Fe see Bogotá
Santa Fe de Bogotá see Bogotá
60 J7 **Santa Fé do Sul** São Paulo, S Brazil 20°13′S 50°56′W
57 B18 **Santa Fe, Isla** var. Barrington Island. island Galapagos Islands, Ecuador, E Pacific Ocean
Santa Fe, Provincia de see Santa Fe
23 V9 **Santa Fe River** ≈ Florida, SE USA
59 M15 **Santa Filomena** Piauí, E Brazil 09°06′S 45°52′W
40 G10 **Santa Genoveva** ▲ NW Mexico 23°07′N 109°56′W
153 S14 **Santahar** Rajshahi, NW Bangladesh 24°45′N 89°03′E
60 G11 **Santa Helena** Paraná, S Brazil 24°53′S 54°19′W
54 J5 **Santa Inés** Lara, N Venezuela 10°37′N 69°18′W
63 G24 **Santa Inés, Isla** island S Chile
62 J13 **Santa Isabel** La Pampa, C Argentina 36°11′S 66°59′W
43 U14 **Santa Isabel** Colón, N Panama 09°31′N 79°12′W
186 L8 **Santa Isabel** var. Bughotu. island N Solomon Islands
Santa Isabel see Malabo
58 D11 **Santa Isabel do Rio Negro** Amazonas, NW Brazil 0°40′S 64°56′W
61 C15 **Santa Lucia** Corrientes, NE Argentina 28°58′S 59°05′W
57 I17 **Santa Lucía** Puno, S Peru 15°45′S 70°34′W
61 F20 **Santa Lucía** var. Santa Lucia. Canelones, S Uruguay 34°26′S 56°25′W
42 B6 **Santa Lucía Cotzumalguapa** Escuintla, SW Guatemala 14°20′N 91°00′W
107 L23 **Santa Lucia del Mela** Sicilia, Italy, C Mediterranean Sea 38°08′N 15°17′E
35 O11 **Santa Lucia Range** ▲▲ California, W USA
40 D9 **Santa Margarita, Isla** island NW Mexico
62 J7 **Santa María** Catamarca, N Argentina 26°51′S 66°02′W
61 G15 **Santa Maria** Rio Grande do Sul, S Brazil 29°41′S 53°48′W
35 P13 **Santa Maria** California, W USA 34°56′N 120°25′W
64 Q4 **Santa Maria** ✕ Santa Maria, Azores, Portugal, NE Atlantic Ocean
64 P3 **Santa Maria** island Azores, Portugal, NE Atlantic Ocean
Santa Maria see Gaua
Santa María Asunción Tlaxiaco see Tlaxiaco
40 G9 **Santa María, Bahía** bay W Mexico
83 L21 **Santa Maria, Cabo de** headland S Mozambique 26°05′S 32°58′E
104 G15 **Santa Maria, Cabo de** headland S Portugal 36°57′N 07°55′W
44 J4 **Santa Maria, Cape** headland Long Island, C Bahamas 23°40′N 75°20′W
107 J17 **Santa Maria Capua Vetere** Campania, S Italy 41°05′N 14°15′E
104 G7 **Santa Maria da Feira** Aveiro, N Portugal 40°55′N 08°32′W
59 M17 **Santa Maria da Vitória** Bahia, E Brazil 13°26′S 44°09′W
55 N9 **Santa María de Erebato** Bolívar, SE Venezuela 05°09′N 64°50′W
55 N6 **Santa María de Ipire** Guárico, C Venezuela 08°51′N 65°21′W
Santa María del Buen Aire see Buenos Aires
40 J8 **Santa María del Oro** Durango, C Mexico 25°57′N 105°22′W
41 N12 **Santa María del Río** San Luis Potosí, C Mexico 21°48′N 100°42′W
Santa Maria di Castellabate see Castellabate
107 Q20 **Santa Maria di Leuca, Capo** headland SE Italy 39°48′N 18°21′E
108 K10 **Santa Maria-im-Munstertal** Graubünden, SE Switzerland 46°36′N 10°25′E
57 B18 **Santa María, Isla** var. Isla Floreana, Charles Island. island Galapagos Islands, Ecuador, E Pacific Ocean
40 J3 **Santa María, Laguna de** ◎ N Mexico
61 G16 **Santa Maria, Rio** ≈ S Brazil
43 R16 **Santa María, Río** ≈ C Panama
36 J12 **Santa Maria River** ≈ Arizona, SW USA
107 G15 **Santa Marinella** Lazio, C Italy 42°01′N 11°51′E
54 F4 **Santa Marta** Magdalena, N Colombia 11°14′N 74°13′W
104 J11 **Santa Marta** Extremadura, W Spain 38°37′N 06°39′W
54 F4 **Santa Marta, Sierra Nevada de** ▲▲ NE Colombia
Santa Maura see Lefkáda
35 S15 **Santa Monica** California, W USA 34°01′N 118°29′W
116 F10 **Sântana** Ger. Sankt Anna, Hung. Újszentanna; prev. Sîntana. Arad, W Romania 46°20′N 21°30′E
61 F16 **Santana, Coxilha de** hill range S Brazil
61 H16 **Santana da Boa Vista** Rio Grande do Sul, S Brazil 30°52′S 53°03′W
61 F16 **Santana do Livramento** prev. Livramento. Rio Grande do Sul, S Brazil 30°52′S 55°30′W
105 N2 **Santander** Cantabria, N Spain 43°28′N 03°48′W
54 F8 **Santander** off. Departamento de Santander. ◈ province C Colombia
Santander, Departamento de see Santander
Santander Jiménez see Jiménez
Sant'Andrea see Svetac
107 B20 **Sant'Antioco** Sardegna, Italy, C Mediterranean Sea 39°03′N 08°28′E
105 V11 **Sant Antoni de Portmany** Cas. San Antonio Abad. Ibiza, Spain, W Mediterranean Sea 38°58′N 01°18′E
105 Y10 **Santanyí** Mallorca, Spain, W Mediterranean Sea 39°22′N 03°07′E
104 J13 **Santa Olalla del Cala** Andalucía, S Spain 37°54′N 06°13′W
35 R15 **Santa Paula** California, W USA 34°21′N 119°03′W
36 L4 **Santaquin** Utah, W USA 39°58′N 111°46′W
58 I12 **Santarém** Pará, N Brazil 02°26′S 54°41′W
104 G10 **Santarém** anc. Scalabis. Santarém, W Portugal 39°14′N 08°40′W
104 G10 **Santarém** ◈ district C Portugal
44 F4 **Santaren Channel** channel W Bahamas
54 K10 **Santa Rita** Vichada, E Colombia 04°51′N 68°27′W
188 B16 **Santa Rita** SW Guam
42 H5 **Santa Rita** Cortés, NW Honduras 15°10′N 87°54′W
40 E9 **Santa Rita** Baja California Sur, NW Mexico 27°29′N 100°33′W
54 H5 **Santa Rita** Zulia, NW Venezuela 10°35′N 71°30′W
59 I19 **Santa Rita de Araguaia** Goiás, S Brazil 17°17′S 53°13′W
59 M16 **Santa Rita de Cassia** var. Cássia. Bahia, E Brazil 11°03′S 44°16′W
61 D14 **Santa Rosa** Corrientes, NE Argentina 28°18′S 58°04′W
62 K13 **Santa Rosa** La Pampa, C Argentina 36°38′S 64°15′W
61 G14 **Santa Rosa** Rio Grande do Sul, S Brazil 27°50′S 54°29′W
58 E10 **Santa Rosa** Roraima, N Brazil 03°41′N 62°29′W
56 B8 **Santa Rosa** El Oro, SW Ecuador 03°29′S 79°57′W
57 I16 **Santa Rosa** Puno, S Peru 14°38′S 70°45′W
34 M7 **Santa Rosa** California, W USA 38°27′N 122°42′W
37 U11 **Santa Rosa** New Mexico, SW USA 34°54′N 104°43′W
55 O6 **Santa Rosa** Anzoátegui, NE Venezuela 09°37′N 64°20′W
42 A3 **Santa Rosa** off. Departamento de Santa Rosa. ◈ department SE Guatemala
Santa Rosa see Santa Rosa de Copán
63 J15 **Santa Rosa, Bajo de** basin E Argentina
42 F6 **Santa Rosa de Copán** var. Santa Rosa. Copán, W Honduras 14°48′N 88°43′W
54 E8 **Santa Rosa de Osos** Antioquia, C Colombia 06°40′N 75°27′W
Santa Rosa, Departamento de see Santa Rosa
35 Q15 **Santa Rosa Island** island California, W USA
23 O9 **Santa Rosa Island** island Florida, SE USA
40 E6 **Santa Rosalía** Baja California Sur, NW Mexico 27°20′N 112°20′W
54 K6 **Santa Rosalía** Portuguesa, NW Venezuela 09°02′N 69°01′W
188 C15 **Santa Rosa, Mount** ▲ NE Guam
35 V16 **Santa Rosa Mountains** ▲▲ California, W USA
35 T2 **Santa Rosa Range** ▲▲ Nevada, W USA
62 M8 **Santa Sylvina** Chaco, N Argentina 27°49′S 61°09′W
Santa Tecla see Nueva San Salvador
61 B19 **Santa Teresa** Santa Fe, C Argentina 33°30′S 60°45′W
59 O20 **Santa Teresa** Espírito Santo, SE Brazil 19°51′S 40°49′W
61 E21 **Santa Teresita** Buenos Aires, E Argentina 36°32′S 56°41′W
61 H19 **Santa Vitória do Palmar** Rio Grande do Sul, S Brazil 33°32′S 53°25′W
35 Q14 **Santa Ynez River** ≈ California, W USA
Sant Carles de la Rápida see Sant Carles de la Ràpita
105 U7 **Sant Carles de la Ràpita** var. Sant Carles de la Rápida. Cataluña, NE Spain 40°37′N 00°36′E
105 W5 **Sant Celoni** Cataluña, NE Spain 41°39′N 02°25′E
35 U17 **Santee** California, W USA 32°50′N 116°58′W
21 T13 **Santee River** ≈ South Carolina, SE USA
40 K15 **San Telmo, Punta** headland SW Mexico 18°19′N 103°30′W
107 O17 **Santeramo in Colle** Puglia, SE Italy 40°47′N 16°45′E
107 M23 **San Teresa di Riva** Sicilia, Italy, C Mediterranean Sea 38°00′N 15°25′E
105 X5 **Sant Feliu de Guíxols** var. San Feliú de Guixols. Cataluña, NE Spain 41°47′N 03°02′E
105 W6 **Sant Feliu de Llobregat** Cataluña, NE Spain 41°22′N 02°00′E
106 C7 **Santhià** Piemonte, NE Italy 45°21′N 08°11′E
61 F15 **Santiago** Rio Grande do Sul, S Brazil 29°11′S 54°52′W
62 H11 **Santiago** var. Gran Santiago. ● (Chile) Santiago, C Chile 33°30′S 70°40′W
45 N8 **Santiago** var. Santiago de los Caballeros. N Dominican Republic 19°27′N 70°42′W
40 G10 **Santiago** Baja California Sur, NW Mexico 23°32′N 109°47′W
41 O8 **Santiago** Nuevo León, NE Mexico 25°22′N 100°09′W
43 R16 **Santiago** Veraguas, S Panama 08°06′N 80°59′W
57 E16 **Santiago** Ica, SW Peru 14°14′S 75°44′W
62 H11 **Santiago** off. Región Metropolitana de Santiago, var. Metropolitan. ◈ region C Chile
76 D10 **Santiago** var. São Tiago. island Ilhas de Sotavento, S Cape Verde
62 H11 **Santiago** ✕ Santiago, C Chile 33°27′S 70°40′W
104 G3 **Santiago** ✕ Galicia, NW Spain
Santiago see Santiago de Cuba, Cuba
Santiago see Grande de Santiago, Río, Mexico
Santiago see Santiago de Compostela
42 B6 **Santiago Atitlán** Sololá, SW Guatemala 14°39′N 91°12′W
43 Q16 **Santiago, Cerro** ▲ W Panama 08°27′N 81°42′W
104 G3 **Santiago de Compostela** var. Santiago, Eng. Compostella; anc. Campus Stellae. Galicia, NW Spain 42°52′N 08°33′W
44 I8 **Santiago de Cuba** var. Santiago. Santiago de Cuba, E Cuba 20°01′N 75°51′W
Santiago de Guayaquil see Guayaquil
62 K8 **Santiago del Estero** Santiago del Estero, C Argentina 27°51′S 64°16′W
61 A15 **Santiago del Estero** off. Provincia de Santiago del Estero. ◈ province N Argentina
Santiago del Estero, Provincia de see Santiago del Estero
40 J8 **Santiago de los Caballeros** Sinaloa, W Mexico 25°33′N 107°22′W
Santiago de los Caballeros see Santiago, Dominican Republic
Santiago de los Caballeros see Ciudad de Guatemala, Guatemala
42 F8 **Santiago de María** Usulután, SE El Salvador 13°28′N 88°28′W
104 F12 **Santiago do Cacém** Setúbal, S Portugal 38°01′N 08°42′W
40 J12 **Santiago Ixcuintla** Nayarit, C Mexico 21°50′N 105°11′W
Santiago Jamiltepec see Jamiltepec
24 L11 **Santiago Mountains** ▲▲ Texas, SW USA
40 J9 **Santiago Papasquiaro** Durango, C Mexico 25°00′N 105°27′W
Santiago Pinotepa Nacional see Pinotepa Nacional

◆ Country
● Country Capital
◇ Dependent Territory
○ Dependent Territory Capital
◈ Administrative Regions
✕ International Airport
▲ Mountain
▲▲ Mountain Range
⛰ Volcano
≈ River
◎ Lake
⊠ Reservoir

Santiago, Región Metropolitana de see Santiago
56 C8 **Santiago, Río** ≈ N Peru
40 M10 **San Tiburcio** Zacatecas, C Mexico 24°08′N 101°29′W
105 N2 **Santillana** Cantabria, N Spain 43°24′N 04°06′W
54 I5 **San Timoteo** Zulia, NW Venezuela 09°50′N 71°05′W
Santi Quaranta see Sarandë
Santissima Trinidad see Jilong
105 O12 **Santisteban del Puerto** Andalucía, S Spain 38°15′N 03°11′W
105 S12 **Sant Joan d'Alacant** *Cast.* San Juan de Alicante. Valenciana, E Spain 38°26′N 00°27′W
105 U7 **Sant Jordi, Golf de** *gulf* NE Spain
105 U11 **Sant Josep de sa Talaia** *var.* San Jose. Ibiza, Spain, W Mediterranean Sea 38°55′N 1°18′E
162 G6 **Santmargats** *var.* Holboo. Dzavhan, W Mongolia 48°35′N 95°25′E
105 T8 **Sant Mateu** Valenciana, E Spain 40°28′N 00°10′E
25 S7 **Santo** Texas, SW USA 32°35′N 98°06′W
Santo see Espiritu Santo
60 M10 **Santo Amaro, Ilha de** *island* SE Brazil
61 G14 **Santo Ângelo** Rio Grande do Sul, S Brazil 28°17′S 54°15′W
76 C9 **Santo Antão** *island* Ilhas de Barlavento, N Cape Verde
60 J10 **Santo Antônio da Platina** Paraná, S Brazil 23°20′S 50°05′W
58 C13 **Santo Antônio do Içá** Amazonas, N Brazil 03°05′S 67°56′W
57 Q18 **Santo Corazón, Río** ≈ E Bolivia
44 E5 **Santo Domingo** Villa Clara, C Cuba 22°35′N 80°15′W
45 O9 **Santo Domingo** *prev.* Ciudad Trujillo. ● (Dominican Republic) SE Dominican Republic 18°30′N 69°57′W
40 E8 **Santo Domingo** Baja California Sur, NW Mexico 25°34′N 112°00′W
40 M10 **Santo Domingo** San Luis Potosí, C Mexico 23°18′N 101°42′W
42 L10 **Santo Domingo** Chontales, S Nicaragua 12°15′N 84°59′W
105 P4 **Santo Domingo de la Calzada** La Rioja, N Spain 42°26′N 02°57′W
56 B6 **Santo Domingo de los Colorados** Pichincha, NW Ecuador 0°13′S 79°09′W
Santo Domingo Tehuantepec see Tehuantepec
55 O6 **San Tomé** Anzoátegui, NE Venezuela 08°58′N 64°08′W
San Tomé de Guayana see Ciudad Guayana
105 R13 **Santomera** Murcia, SE Spain 38°03′N 01°05′W
105 O2 **Santoña** Cantabria, N Spain 43°27′N 03°28′W
Santorin see Santoríni
115 K22 **Santoríni** *var.* Santorin, *prev.* Thíra; *anc.* Thera. *island* Kykládes, Greece, Aegean Sea
60 M10 **Santos** São Paulo, S Brazil 23°56′S 46°22′W
65 J17 **Santos Plateau** *undersea feature* SW Atlantic Ocean 25°00′S 43°00′W
104 G6 **Santo Tirso** Porto, N Portugal 41°20′N 08°25′W
40 B2 **Santo Tomás** Baja California Norte, NW Mexico 31°32′N 116°26′W
42 L10 **Santo Tomás** Chontales, S Nicaragua 12°04′N 85°02′W
42 G5 **Santo Tomás de Castilla** Izabal, E Guatemala 15°40′N 88°36′W
40 B2 **Santo Tomás, Punta** *headland* NW Mexico 31°30′N 116°40′W
57 H16 **Santo Tomás, Río** ≈ C Peru
57 B18 **Santo Tomás, Volcán** ⛰ Galapagos Islands, Ecuador, E Pacific Ocean 0°46′S 91°01′W
61 F14 **Santo Tomé** Corrientes, NE Argentina 28°31′S 56°03′W
Santo Tomé de Guayana see Ciudad Guayana
98 H10 **Santpoort** Noord-Holland, W Netherlands 52°26′N 04°38′E
Santurce see Santurtzi
105 O2 **Santurtzi** *var.* Santurce, Santurzi. País Vasco, N Spain 43°20′N 03°03′W
Santurzi see Santurtzi
63 G20 **San Valentín, Cerro** ▲ S Chile 46°36′S 73°17′W
42 F8 **San Vicente** San Vicente, C El Salvador 13°38′N 88°42′W*
40 C2 **San Vicente** Baja California Norte, NW Mexico 31°20′N 116°15′W
188 H6 **San Vicente** Saipan, S Northern Mariana Islands
42 B9 **San Vicente** ◐ *department* E El Salvador
104 I10 **San Vicente de Alcántara** Extremadura, W Spain 39°21′N 07°07′W
105 N2 **San Vicente de Barakaldo** *var.* Baracaldo, *Basq.* San Bizenti-Barakaldo. País Vasco, N Spain 43°17′N 02°59′W
57 E15 **San Vicente de Cañete** *var.* Cañete. Lima, W Peru 13°06′S 76°23′W
104 M2 **San Vicente de la Barquera** Cantabria, N Spain 43°23′N 04°24′W
54 E12 **San Vicente del Caguán** Caquetá, S Colombia 02°07′N 74°47′W
42 F8 **San Vicente, Volcán de** ⛰ C El Salvador 13°34′N 88°50′W
43 O15 **San Vito** Puntarenas, SE Costa Rica 08°49′N 82°58′W
106 I7 **San Vito al Tagliamento** Friuli-Venezia Giulia, NE Italy 45°54′N 12°55′E
107 H23 **San Vito, Capo** *headland* Sicilia, Italy, C Mediterranean Sea 38°11′N 12°41′E
107 P18 **San Vito dei Normanni** Puglia, SE Italy 40°40′N 17°42′E
160 L17 **Sanya** *var.* Ya Xian. Hainan, S China 18°25′N 109°27′E
83 J16 **Sanyati** ≈ N Zimbabwe
25 Q16 **San Ygnacio** Texas, SW USA 27°04′N 99°26′W
160 L6 **Sanyuan** Shaanxi, C China 34°40′N 108°56′E
123 P11 **Sanyyakhtakh** Respublika Sakha (Yakutiya), NE Russian Federation 60°34′N 124°09′E
146 J15 **S. A.Nyýazow Adyndaky** *Rus.* Imeni S. A. Niyazova. Maryyskiy Velayat, S Turkmenistan 36°44′N 62°23′E
82 C10 **Sanza Pombo** Uíge, NW Angola 07°20′S 16°00′E
Sanzyô see Sanjō
104 G14 **São Bartolomeu de Messines** Faro, S Portugal 37°12′N 08°16′W
60 M10 **São Bernardo do Campo** São Paulo, S Brazil 23°45′S 46°34′W
61 F15 **São Borja** Rio Grande do Sul, S Brazil 28°35′S 56°01′W
104 H14 **São Brás de Alportel** Faro, S Portugal 37°09′N 07°55′W
60 M10 **São Caetano do Sul** São Paulo, S Brazil 23°37′S 46°34′W
60 L9 **São Carlos** São Paulo, S Brazil 22°02′S 47°53′W
59 P16 **São Cristóvão** Sergipe, E Brazil 10°59′S 37°10′W
61 F15 **São Fancisco de Assis** Rio Grande do Sul, S Brazil 29°32′S 55°07′W
58 K13 **São Félix** Pará, NE Brazil 06°43′S 51°56′W
São Félix see São Félix do Araguaia
59 J16 **São Félix do Araguaia** *var.* São Félix. Mato Grosso, W Brazil 11°36′S 50°40′W
59 J14 **São Félix do Xingu** Pará, NE Brazil 06°38′S 51°59′W
60 Q9 **São Fidélis** Rio de Janeiro, SE Brazil 21°37′S 41°40′W
76 D10 **São Filipe** Fogo, S Cape Verde 14°52′N 24°29′W
60 K12 **São Francisco do Sul** Santa Catarina, S Brazil 26°17′S 48°39′W
60 K12 **São Francisco, Ilha de** *island* S Brazil
59 P16 **São Francisco, Rio** ≈ E Brazil
61 G16 **São Gabriel** Rio Grande do Sul, S Brazil 30°17′S 54°17′W
60 P10 **São Gonçalo** Rio de Janeiro, SE Brazil 22°48′S 43°03′W
81 H23 **Sao Hill** Iringa, S Tanzania 08°19′S 35°11′E
60 R9 **São João da Barra** Rio de Janeiro, SE Brazil 21°39′S 41°04′W
104 G7 **São João da Madeira** Aveiro, N Portugal 40°52′N 08°28′W
58 M12 **São João de Cortes** Maranhão, E Brazil 02°30′S 44°27′W
59 M21 **São João del Rei** Minas Gerais, NE Brazil 21°08′S 44°15′W
59 N15 **São João do Piauí** Piauí, E Brazil 08°21′S 42°14′W
59 N14 **São João dos Patos** Maranhão, E Brazil 06°29′S 43°44′W
61 C11 **São Joaquim** Amazonas, NW Brazil 0°08′S 67°10′W
61 J14 **São Joaquim** Santa Catarina, S Brazil 28°20′S 49°55′W
60 L7 **São Joaquim da Barra** São Paulo, S Brazil 20°36′S 47°50′W
64 N2 **São Jorge** *island* Azores, Portugal, NE Atlantic Ocean
61 K14 **São José** Santa Catarina, S Brazil 27°34′S 48°39′W
60 M8 **São José do Rio Pardo** São Paulo, S Brazil 21°37′S 46°52′W
60 K8 **São José do Rio Preto** São Paulo, S Brazil 20°50′S 49°20′W
60 N10 **São Jose dos Campos** São Paulo, S Brazil 23°07′S 45°52′W
61 I17 **São Lourenço do Sul** Rio Grande do Sul, S Brazil 31°25′S 52°00′W
58 M12 **São Luís** *state capital* Maranhão, NE Brazil 02°34′S 44°16′W
58 F11 **São Luís** Roraima, N Brazil 01°11′N 60°15′W
58 M12 **São Luís, Ilha de** *island* NE Brazil
61 F14 **São Luiz Gonzaga** Rio Grande do Sul, S Brazil 28°24′S 54°58′W
São Mandol see São Manuel, Rio
47 U8 **São Manuel** ≈ C Brazil
59 H15 **São Manuel, Rio** *var.* São Mandol, Teles Pirés. ≈ C Brazil
58 C11 **São Marcelino** Amazonas, NW Brazil 0°53′N 67°16′W
58 N12 **São Marcos, Baía de** *bay* N Brazil
59 O20 **São Mateus** Espírito Santo, SE Brazil 18°44′S 39°53′W
60 J12 **São Mateus do Sul** Paraná, S Brazil 25°58′S 50°29′W
64 P3 **São Miguel** *island* Azores, Portugal, NE Atlantic Ocean
60 G13 **São Miguel d'Oeste** Santa Catarina, S Brazil 26°45′S 53°34′W
45 P9 **Saona, Isla** *island* SE Dominican Republic
172 H12 **Saondzou** ▲ Grande Comore, NW Comoros
103 R10 **Saône** ≈ E France
103 Q9 **Saône-et-Loire** ◐ *department* C France
76 D9 **São Nicolau** *Eng.* Saint Nicholas. *island* Ilhas de Barlavento, N Cape Verde
60 M10 **São Paulo** *state capital* São Paulo, S Brazil 23°33′S 46°39′W
60 K9 **São Paulo** *off.* Estado de São Paulo. ◐ *state* S Brazil
São Paulo de Loanda see Luanda
São Paulo, Estado de see São Paulo
São Pedro do Rio Grande do Sul see Rio Grande
104 H7 **São Pedro do Sul** Viseu, N Portugal 40°46′N 07°58′W
64 K13 **São Pedro e São Paulo** *undersea feature* C Atlantic Ocean 01°25′N 28°54′W
59 M14 **São Raimundo das Mangabeiras** Maranhão, E Brazil 07°00′S 45°30′W
59 Q14 **São Roque, Cabo de** *headland* E Brazil 05°29′S 35°16′W
São Salvador see Salvador, Brazil
São Salvador/São Salvador do Congo see M'Banza Congo, Angola
60 N10 **São Sebastião, Ilha de** *island* S Brazil
83 N19 **São Sebastião, Ponta** *headland* C Mozambique 22°09′S 35°33′E
104 F13 **São Teotónio** Beja, S Portugal 37°30′N 08°41′W
São Tiago see Santiago
79 B18 **São Tomé** ● (Sao Tome and Principe) São Tomé, S Sao Tome and Principe 0°22′N 06°41′E
79 B18 **São Tomé** ✈ São Tomé, S Sao Tome and Principe 0°24′N 06°39′E
79 B18 **São Tomé** *Eng.* Saint Thomas. *island* S Sao Tome and Principe
79 B17 **Sao Tome and Principe** *off.* Democratic Republic of Sao Tome and Principe. ◆ *republic* E Atlantic Ocean
Sao Tome and Principe, Democratic Republic of see Sao Tome and Principe
74 H9 **Saoura, Oued** ≈ NW Algeria
60 M10 **São Vicente** *Eng.* Saint Vincent. São Paulo, S Brazil 23°55′S 46°25′W
64 O5 **São Vicente** Madeira, Portugal, NE Atlantic Ocean 32°48′N 17°03′W
76 C9 **São Vicente** *Eng.* Saint Vincent. *island* Ilhas de Barlavento, N Cape Verde
104 F14 **São Vicente, Cabo de** *Eng.* Cape Saint Vincent, *Port.* Cabode São Vicente. *cape* S Portugal
São Vicente, Cabo de see São Vicente, Cabo de
Sápai see Sápes
Sapaleri, Cerro see Zapaleri, Cerro
Saparoea see Saparua
171 S13 **Saparua** *prev.* Saparoea. Pulau Saparau, C Indonesia 03°35′S 128°37′E
168 L11 **Sapat** Sumatera, W Indonesia 0°18′S 103°18′E
77 U17 **Sapele** Delta, S Nigeria 05°54′N 05°43′E
23 X7 **Sapelo Island** *island* Georgia, SE USA
23 X7 **Sapelo Sound** *sound* Georgia, SE USA
114 K13 **Sápes** *var.* Sápai. Anatolikí Makedonía kai Thráki, NE Greece 41°02′N 25°44′E
Sapiéntza see Sapiénza
115 D22 **Sapiénza** *var.* Sapiéntza. *island* S Greece
138 F12 **Sapir** *prev.* Sappir. Southern, S Israel 30°43′N 35°11′E
61 I15 **Sapiranga** Rio Grande do Sul, S Brazil 29°39′S 50°58′W
115 K13 **Sápka** ▲▲ NE Greece
105 X9 **Sa Pobla** Mallorca, Spain, W Mediterranean Sea 39°46′N 03°03′E
56 D11 **Saposoa** San Martín, N Peru 06°53′S 76°45′W
119 F16 **Sapotskin** *Pol.* Sopockinie, *Rus.* Sapotskino, Sopotskin. Hrodzyenskaya Voblasts', W Belarus 53°50′N 23°39′E
77 P13 **Sapoui** *var.* Sapouy. S Burkina 11°34′N 01°44′W
Sapouy see Sapoui
Sappir see Sapir
165 S4 **Sapporo** Hokkaidō, NE Japan 43°05′N 141°21′E
107 M19 **Sapri** Campania, S Italy 40°05′N 15°36′E
169 T16 **Sapudi, Pulau** *island* S Indonesia
27 P9 **Sapulpa** Oklahoma, C USA 36°00′N 96°06′W
142 J4 **Saqqez** *var.* Saghez, Sakiz, Saqqiz. Kordestān, NW Iran 36°31′N 46°16′E
Saqqiz see Saqqez
139 U8 **Sarābādī** Wāsiṭ, E Iraq 33°00′N 44°52′E
167 P10 **Sara Buri** *var.* Saraburi. Saraburi, C Thailand 14°32′N 100°53′E
Saraburi see Sara Buri
Sarafjagān see Salafchegān
24 K9 **Saragosa** Texas, SW USA 31°03′N 103°39′W
Saragossa see Zaragoza
Saragt see Sarahs
56 B8 **Saraguro** Loja, S Ecuador 03°42′S 79°18′W
146 I15 **Sarahs** *var.* Saragt, *Rus.* Serakhs. Ahal Welaýaty, S Turkmenistan 36°33′N 61°10′E
126 M6 **Sarai** Ryazanskaya Oblast', W Russian Federation 53°43′N 39°59′E
Sarāi see Sarāy
154 M12 **Saraipāli** Chhattīsgarh, C India 21°21′N 83°01′E
149 T9 **Sarāi Sidhu** Punjab, E Pakistan 30°35′N 72°02′E
93 M15 **Säräisniemi** Oulu, C Finland 64°25′N 26°50′E
113 I14 **Sarajevo** ● (Bosnia and Herzegovina) Federacija Bosna I Hercegovina, SE Bosnia and Herzegovina 43°53′N 18°24′E
112 I13 **Sarajevo** ✈ Federacija Bosna I Hercegovina, C Bosnia and Herzegovina 43°49′N 18°21′E
143 V4 **Sarakhs** Khorāsān-Razavī, NE Iran 36°30′N 61°00′E
115 H17 **Sarakíniko, Akrotírio** *headland* Évvoia, C Greece 38°46′N 23°43′E
115 I18 **Sarakinó** *island* Vóreies Sporádes, Greece, Aegean Sea
127 V7 **Saraktash** Orenburgskaya Oblast', W Russian Federation 51°46′N 56°23′E
30 L15 **Sara, Lake** ▣ Illinois, N USA
23 N8 **Saraland** Alabama, S USA 30°49′N 88°04′W
55 V9 **Saramacca** ◐ *district* N Surinam
55 V10 **Saramacca Rivier** ≈ C Surinam
166 M2 **Saramati** ▲ N Burma (Myanmar) 25°46′N 95°01′E
145 R10 **Saran'** *Kaz.* Saran. Karaganda, C Kazakhstan 49°47′N 73°02′E
18 K7 **Saranac Lake** New York, NE USA 44°18′N 74°06′W
18 K7 **Saranac River** ≈ New York, NE USA
Saranda see Sarandë
113 L23 **Sarandë** *var.* Saranda, *It.* Porto Edda; *prev.* Santi Quaranta. Vlorë, S Albania 39°53′N 20°E
61 H14 **Sarandi** Rio Grande do Sul, S Brazil 27°57′S 52°58′W
61 F19 **Sarandí del Yí** Durazno, C Uruguay 33°18′S 55°38′W
61 F19 **Sarandí Grande** Florida, S Uruguay 33°43′S 56°19′W
171 Q8 **Sarangani Islands** *island group* S Philippines
127 P5 **Saransk** Respublika Mordoviya, W Russian Federation 54°11′N 45°10′E
115 C14 **Sarantáporos** ≈ N Greece
114 H9 **Sarantsi** Sofiya, W Bulgaria 42°43′N 23°46′E
127 T3 **Sarapul** Udmurtskaya Respublika, NW Russian Federation 56°26′N 53°52′E
Sarāqeb see Sarāqib
138 I3 **Sarāqib** *Fr.* Saraqeb. Idlib, N Syria 35°52′N 36°48′E
54 J5 **Sarare** Lara, N Venezuela 09°47′N 69°10′W
55 O10 **Sarariña** Amazonas, S Venezuela 04°10′N 64°31′W
143 S10 **Sar Ashk** Kermān, C Iran
23 V13 **Sarasota** Florida, SE USA 27°20′N 82°31′W
117 O11 **Sarata** Odes'ka Oblast', SW Ukraine 46°01′N 29°40′E
116 I10 **Sărăţel** *Hung.* Szeretfalva. Bistriţa-Năsăud, N Romania 47°02′N 24°24′E
25 X10 **Saratoga** Texas, SW USA 30°15′N 94°31′W
18 K10 **Saratoga Springs** New York, NE USA 43°04′N 73°47′W
127 P8 **Saratov** Saratovskaya Oblast', W Russian Federation 51°33′N 45°58′E
127 P8 **Saratovskaya Oblast'** ◐ *province* W Russian Federation
127 Q7 **Saratovskoye Vodokhranilishche** ▣ W Russian Federation
143 X13 **Sarāvān** Sīstān va Balūchestān, SE Iran 27°11′N 62°35′E
Saravan/Saravane see Salavan
169 S9 **Sarawak** ◐ *state* East Malaysia
Sarawak see Kuching
139 U6 **Sarāy** *var.* Sarāi. Diyālá, E Iraq 34°06′N 45°06′E
136 D10 **Saray** Tekirdağ, NW Turkey 41°27′N 27°56′E
76 J12 **Saraya** SE Senegal 12°50′N 11°45′W
143 W14 **Sarbāz** Sīstān va Balūchestān, SE Iran 26°38′N 61°13′E
143 U8 **Sarbīsheh** Khorāsān-e Janūbī, E Iran 32°35′N 59°50′E
111 J24 **Sárbogárd** Fejér, C Hungary 46°54′N 18°36′E
Şărcad see Sarkad
27 S7 **Sarcoxie** Missouri, C USA 37°04′N 94°07′W
152 L11 **Sārda** *Nep.* Kali. ≈ India/Nepal
152 G10 **Sardārshahr** Rājasthān, NW India 28°30′N 74°30′E
107 C18 **Sardegna** *Eng.* Sardinia. ◐ *region* Italy, C Mediterranean Sea
107 A18 **Sardegna** *Eng.* Sardinia. *island* Italy, C Mediterranean Sea
42 K13 **Sardinal** Guanacaste, NW Costa Rica 10°30′N 85°38′W
54 G7 **Sardinata** Norte de Santander, N Colombia 08°07′N 72°47′W
Sardinia see Sardegna
120 K8 **Sardinia-Corsica Trough** *undersea feature* Tyrrhenian Sea, C Mediterranean Sea
22 L2 **Sardis** Mississippi, S USA 34°25′N 89°55′W
22 L2 **Sardis Lake** ▣ Mississippi, S USA
27 P12 **Sardis Lake** ▣ Oklahoma, C USA
92 H12 **Sarek** ▲▲ N Sweden
92 H11 **Sarektjåhkkå** ▲ N Sweden 67°28′N 17°56′E
Sar-e Pol see Sar-e Pul
Sar-e Pol see Sar-e Pol-e Ẕahāb
142 J6 **Sar-e Pol-e Ẕahāb** *var.* Sar-e Pol, Sar-i Pul. Kermānshāhān, W Iran 34°28′N 45°52′E
149 N3 **Sar-e Pul** *var.* Sar-i-Pul; *prev.* Sar-e Pol. Sar-e Pul, N Afghanistan 36°16′N 65°55′E
149 O3 **Sar-e Pul** ◐ *province* N Afghanistan
Sarera, Teluk see Cenderawasih, Teluk
147 T13 **Sarez, Kŭli** *Rus.* Sarezskoye Ozero. ◎ SE Tajikistan
Sarezskoye Ozero see Sarez, Kŭli
64 G10 **Sargasso Sea** *sea* W Atlantic Ocean
149 U8 **Sargodha** Punjab, NE Pakistan 32°06′N 72°48′E
78 I13 **Sarh** *prev.* Fort-Archambault. Moyen-Chari, S Chad 09°08′N 18°22′E
143 P4 **Sārī** *var.* Sari, Sāri. Māzandarān, N Iran 36°37′N 53°05′E
115 N23 **Saría** *island* SE Greece
Sariasiya see Sariosiyo
40 F3 **Saric** Sonora, NW Mexico 31°08′N 111°22′W
188 K6 **Sarigan** *island* C Northern Mariana Islands
136 D14 **Sarıgöl** Manisa, SW Turkey 38°16′N 28°41′E
139 T6 **Sārihah** At Ta'mīm, E Iraq 34°34′N 44°38′E
137 R12 **Sarıkamış** Kars, NE Turkey 40°18′N 42°36′E
169 R9 **Sarikei** Sarawak, East Malaysia 02°07′N 111°30′E
147 U12 **Sarikol Range** *Rus.* Sarykol'skiy Khrebet. ▲▲ China/Tajikistan
181 Y7 **Sarina** Queensland, NE Australia 21°34′S 149°12′E
Sarine see La Sarine
105 S5 **Sariñena** Aragón, NE Spain 41°47′N 00°10′W
147 O13 **Sariosiyo** *Rus.* Sariasiya. Surkhondaryo Viloyati, S Uzbekistan 38°25′N 67°51′E
Sar-i-Pul see Sar-e Pul, Afghanistan
Sar-i Pul see Sar-e Pol-e Ẕahāb, Iran
Sariqamish Kŭli see Sarygamyş Köli
149 V1 **Sarī Qūl** *Rus.* Ozero Zurkul', *Taj.* Zŭrkŭl. ◎ Afghanistan/Tajikistan *see also* Zŭrkŭl
Sarī Qūl see Zŭrkŭl
75 Q12 **Sarīr Tibistī** *var.* Serir Tibesti. *desert* S Libya
25 S15 **Sarita** Texas, SW USA 27°14′N 97°48′W
163 W14 **Sariwŏn** SW North Korea 38°30′N 125°52′E
114 P12 **Sarıyer** İstanbul, NW Turkey 41°11′N 29°03′E
97 L26 **Sark** *Fr.* Sercq. *island* Channel Islands
111 N24 **Sarkad** *Rom.* Şărcad. Békés, SE Hungary 46°44′N 21°25′E
145 W14 **Sarkand** *Kaz.* Sarqan. Almaty, SW Kazakhstan 45°24′N 79°55′E
152 D11 **Sarkāri Tala** Rājasthān, NW India 27°39′N 70°52′E
136 G15 **Şarkikaraağaç** *var.* Şarki Karaağaç. Isparta, SW Turkey 38°04′N 31°22′E
Şarki Karaağaç see Şarkikaraağaç
136 L13 **Şarkışla** Sivas, C Turkey 39°21′N 36°27′E
136 C11 **Şarköy** Tekirdağ, NW Turkey 40°37′N 27°07′E
Sárköz see Livada
Sarlat see Sarlat-la-Canéda
102 M13 **Sarlat-la-Canéda** *var.* Sarlat. Dordogne, SW France 44°54′N 01°12′E
109 S3 **Sarleinsbach** Oberösterreich, N Austria 48°33′N 13°55′E
Şarma see Ash Sharmah
171 Y12 **Sarmi** Papua, E Indonesia 01°51′S 138°45′E
63 I19 **Sarmiento** Chubut, S Argentina 45°38′S 69°07′W
63 H25 **Sarmiento, Monte** ▲ S Chile 54°28′S 70°49′W
94 J11 **Särna** Dalarna, C Sweden 61°40′N 13°10′E
108 F8 **Sarnen** Obwalden, C Switzerland 46°54′N 08°15′E
108 F9 **Sarner See** ◎ C Switzerland
14 D16 **Sarnia** Ontario, S Canada 42°58′N 82°23′W
116 L3 **Sarny** Rivnens'ka Oblast', NW Ukraine 51°20′N 26°35′E
171 O13 **Saroako** Sulawesi, C Indonesia 02°31′S 121°18′E
118 L13 **Sarochyna** *Rus.* Sorochino. Vitsyebskaya Voblasts', N Belarus 55°12′N 28°45′E
168 L12 **Sarolangun** Sumatera, W Indonesia 02°17′S 102°39′E
165 U3 **Saroma** Hokkaidō, NE Japan 44°01′N 143°43′E
165 V3 **Saroma-ko** ◎ Hokkaidō, NE Japan
Saronic Gulf see Saronikós Kólpos
115 H20 **Saronikós Kólpos** *Eng.* Saronic Gulf. *gulf* S Greece
106 D7 **Saronno** Lombardia, N Italy 45°38′N 09°02′E
136 B11 **Saros Körfezi** *gulf* NW Turkey
111 N20 **Sárospatak** Borsod-Abaúj-Zemplén, NE Hungary 48°18′N 21°30′E
127 O4 **Sarov** *prev.* Sarova. Respublika Mordoviya, SW Russian Federation 54°39′N 43°09′E
Sarova see Sarov
127 P12 **Sarpa** Respublika Kalmykiya, SW Russian Federation 47°00′N 45°42′E
127 P12 **Sarpa, Ozero** ◎ SW Russian Federation
Šar Planina see Mali i Sharrit
95 I16 **Sarpsborg** Østfold, S Norway 59°16′N 11°07′E
139 U5 **Sarqalā** At Ta'mīm, N Iraq
Sarqan see Sarkand
103 U4 **Sarralbe** Moselle, NE France 49°02′N 07°01′E
Sarre see Saar, France/Germany
Sarre see Saarland, Germany
103 U5 **Sarrebourg** *Ger.* Saarburg. Moselle, NE France 48°43′N 07°03′E
Sarrebruck see Saarbrücken
103 U4 **Sarreguemines** *prev.* Saargemund. Moselle, NE France 49°06′N 07°04′E
104 I3 **Sarria** Galicia, NW Spain 42°47′N 07°25′W
105 S8 **Sarrión** Aragón, NE Spain 40°09′N 00°49′W
42 F4 **Sarstoon** *Sp.* Río Sarstún. ≈ Belize/Guatemala
Sarstún, Río see Sarstoon
123 Q9 **Sartang** ≈ NE Russian Federation
103 X16 **Sartène** Corse, France, C Mediterranean Sea 41°38′N 08°58′E
102 K7 **Sarthe** ◐ *department* NW France
102 K7 **Sarthe** ≈ N France
115 H15 **Sárti** Kentrikí Makedonía, N Greece 40°05′N 24°E
Sartu see Daqing
165 T1 **Sarufutsu** Hokkaidō, NE Japan 45°20′N 142°03′E
Saruhan see Manisa
152 G9 **Sarūpsar** Rājasthān, NW India 29°25′N 73°50′E
137 U13 **Şärur** *prev.* Il'ichevsk. SW Azerbaijan 39°30′N 44°59′E
Sarvani see Marneuli
111 G23 **Sárvár** Vas, W Hungary 47°15′N 16°59′E
143 P11 **Sarvestān** Fārs, S Iran 29°16′N 53°13′E
171 W12 **Sarwon** Papua, E Indonesia 0°58′S 136°08′E
145 P17 **Saryagash** *Kaz.* Saryaghash. Yuzhnyy Kazakhstan, S Kazakhstan 41°29′N 69°10′E
Saryaghash see Saryagash
145 R9 **Saryarka** *Eng.* Kazakh Uplands, Kirghiz Steppe. *uplands* C Kazakhstan
147 W8 **Sary-Bulak** Narynskaya Oblast', C Kyrgyzstan 41°56′N 75°44′E
147 U10 **Sary-Bulak** Oshskaya Oblast', SW Kyrgyzstan 40°49′N 73°44′E
117 S14 **Sarych, Mys** *headland* S Ukraine 44°23′N 33°44′E
147 Z7 **Sary-Dzhaz** *var.* Aksu He. ≈ China/Kyrgyzstan *see also* Aksu He
Sary-Dzhaz see Aksu He
146 F8 **Sarygamyş Köli** *Rus.* Sarykamyshkoye Ozero, *Uzb.* Sariqamish Kŭli. *salt lake* Kazakhstan/Uzbekistan
144 G13 **Sarykamys** *Kaz.* Saryqamys. Mangistau, SW Kazakhstan 45°58′N 53°30′E
Sarykamyshkoye Ozero see Sarygamyş Köli
145 N7 **Sarykol'** *prev.* Uritskiy. Kustanay, N Kazakhstan 53°19′N 65°34′E
Sarykol'skiy Khrebet see Sarikol Range
144 M10 **Sarykopa, Ozero** ◎ C Kazakhstan
145 V15 **Saryozek** *Kaz.* Saryözek. Almaty, SE Kazakhstan 44°22′N 77°57′E
144 E10 **Saryozen** *Kaz.* Kishiözen; *prev.* Malyy Uzen'. ≈ Kazakhstan/Russian Federation
Saryqamys see Sarykamys
145 S13 **Saryshagan** *Kaz.* Saryshaghan. Karaganda, SE Kazakhstan 46°05′N 73°38′E
Saryshaghan see Saryshagan
145 O13 **Sarysu** ≈ S Kazakhstan
147 T11 **Sary-Tash** Oshskaya Oblast', SW Kyrgyzstan 39°44′N 73°14′E
145 T12 **Saryterek** Karaganda, C Kazakhstan 47°46′N 74°06′E
Saryyazynskoye Vodokhranilishche see Saryýazy Suw Howdany
146 J15 **Saryýazy Suw Howdany** *Rus.* Saryyazynskoye Vodokhranilishche. ▣ S Turkmenistan
145 T14 **Saryyesik-Atyrau, Peski** *desert* E Kazakhstan
106 E10 **Sarzana** Liguria, NW Italy 44°07′N 09°59′E
188 B17 **Sasalaguan, Mount** ▲ S Guam
153 O14 **Sasarām** Bihār, N India 24°58′N 84°01′E
186 M8 **Sasari, Mount** ▲ Santa Isabel, N Solomon Islands 08°09′S 159°32′E
164 C13 **Sasebo** Nagasaki, Kyūshū, SW Japan 33°10′N 129°42′E
14 I9 **Saseginaga, Lac** ◎ Québec, SE Canada
Saseno see Sazan
11 R13 **Saskatchewan** ◐ *province* SW Canada
11 U14 **Saskatchewan** ≈ Manitoba/Saskatchewan, C Canada
11 T15 **Saskatoon** Saskatchewan, S Canada 52°10′N 106°40′W
11 T15 **Saskatoon** ✈ Saskatchewan, S Canada 52°15′N 107°05′W
123 N7 **Saskylakh** Respublika Sakha (Yakutiya), NE Russian Federation 71°56′N 114°07′E
42 L7 **Saslaya, Cerro** ▲ N Nicaragua 13°52′N 85°06′W
38 G17 **Sasmik, Cape** *headland* Tanaga Island, Alaska, USA 51°36′N 177°55′W
119 N19 **Sasnovy Bor** *Rus.* Sosnovyy Bor. Homyel'skaya Voblasts', SE Belarus 52°32′N 29°35′E
127 N5 **Sasovo** Ryazanskaya Oblast', W Russian Federation 54°19′N 41°54′E
25 S12 **Saspamco** Texas, SW USA 29°13′N 98°18′W
109 W9 **Sass** *var.* Sassbach. ≈ SE Austria
76 M17 **Sassandra** S Ivory Coast 04°58′N 06°08′W
76 M17 **Sassandra** *var.* Ibo, Sassandra Fleuve. ≈ S Ivory Coast
Sassandra Fleuve see Sassandra
107 B17 **Sassari** Sardegna, Italy, C Mediterranean Sea 40°44′N 08°33′E
Sassbach see Sass
98 H11 **Sassenheim** Zuid-Holland, W Netherlands 52°14′N 04°31′E
Sassmacken see Valdemārpils
100 O7 **Sassnitz** Mecklenburg-Vorpommern, NE Germany 54°32′N 13°39′E
99 E16 **Sas van Gent** Zeeland, SW Netherlands 51°13′N 03°48′E
145 W12 **Sasykkol', Ozero** ◎ E Kazakhstan
117 O12 **Sasyk, Ozero** *Rus.* Ozero Sasyk Kunduk, *var.* Ozero Kunduk. ◎ SW Ukraine
76 J12 **Satadougou** Kayes, SW Mali 12°40′N 11°25′W
164 C17 **Sata-misaki** Kyūshū, SW Japan
26 I7 **Satanta** Kansas, C USA 37°23′N 102°00′W
155 E15 **Sātāra** Mahārāshtra, W India 17°41′N 73°59′E
192 G15 **Sātaua** Savai'i, NW Samoa 13°26′S 172°40′W
188 M16 **Satawal** *island* Caroline Islands, C Micronesia
189 R17 **Satawan Atoll** *atoll* Mortlock Islands, C Micronesia
Sätbaev see Satpayev
23 Y12 **Satellite Beach** Florida, SE USA 28°10′N 80°35′W
95 M14 **Säter** Dalarna, C Sweden 60°21′N 15°45′E
Sathmar see Satu Mare
23 V7 **Satilla River** ≈ Georgia, SE USA
57 F14 **Satipo** *var.* San Francisco de Satipo. Junín, C Peru 11°19′S 74°37′W
122 F11 **Satka** Chelyabinskaya Oblast', C Russian Federation 55°08′N 58°54′E
153 T16 **Satkhira** Khulna, SW Bangladesh 22°43′N 89°06′E
146 J13 **Şatlyk** *Rus.* Shatlyk. Mary Welaýaty, C Turkmenistan 37°55′N 61°00′E
154 K9 **Satna** *prev.* Sutna. Madhya Pradesh, C India 24°33′N 80°50′E
103 R11 **Satolas** ✈ (Lyon) Rhône, E France 45°44′N 05°01′E
111 N20 **Sátoraljaújhely** Borsod-Abaúj-Zemplén, NE Hungary 48°24′N 21°39′E
145 O12 **Satpayev** *Kaz.* Sätbaev; *prev.* Nikol'skiy. Karaganda, C Kazakhstan 47°59′N 67°27′E
154 G11 **Sātpura Range** ▲▲ C India
165 Q10 **Satsuma-Sendai** Miyagi, Honshū, C Japan 38°16′N 140°52′E
Satsuma-Sendai see Sendai
167 P12 **Sattahip** *var.* Ban Sattahip, Ban Sattahipp. Chon Buri, S Thailand 12°36′N 100°56′E
92 L11 **Sattanen** Lappi, NE Finland 67°31′N 26°35′E
Satul see Satun
116 H9 **Satulung** *Hung.* Kővárhosszúfalu. Maramureş, N Romania 47°34′N 23°26′E
Satul-Vechi see Staro Selo
116 G8 **Satu Mare** *Ger.* Sathmar, *Hung.* Szatmárnémeti. Satu Mare, NW Romania 47°46′N 22°55′E
116 G8 **Satu Mare** ◐ *county* NW Romania
167 N16 **Satun** *var.* Satul, Setul. Satun, SW Thailand 06°40′N 100°01′E
192 G16 **Satupa'iteau** Savai'i, W Samoa 13°46′S 172°26′W
Sau see Sava
14 F14 **Sauble** ≈ Ontario, S Canada
14 F13 **Sauble Beach** Ontario, S Canada 44°36′N 81°15′W
61 C16 **Sauce** Corrientes, NE Argentina 30°05′S 58°46′W
Sauce see Juan L. Lacaze
36 K15 **Sauceda Mountains** ▲▲ Arizona, SW USA
61 C17 **Sauce de Luna** Entre Ríos, E Argentina 31°15′S 59°09′W
63 L15 **Sauce Grande, Río** ≈ E Argentina
40 K6 **Saucillo** Chihuahua, N Mexico 28°01′N 105°17′W
95 D15 **Sauda** Rogaland, S Norway 59°38′N 06°23′E
145 Q16 **Saudakent** *Kaz.* Saūdakent; *prev.* Baykadam, *Kaz.* Bayqadam. Zhambyl, S Kazakhstan 43°49′N 69°56′E
92 J2 **Saudhárkrókur** Nordhurland Vestra, N Iceland 65°45′N 19°39′W
141 P9 **Saudi Arabia** *off.* Kingdom of Saudi Arabia, Al 'Arabiyah as Su'ūdiyah, *Ar.* Al Mamlakah al 'Arabiyah as Su'ūdiyah. ◆ *monarchy* SW Asia
Saudi Arabia, Kingdom of see Saudi Arabia
101 D19 **Sauer** *var.* Sûre. ≈ NW Europe *see also* Sûre
Sauer see Sûre
101 F15 **Sauerland** *forest* W Germany
14 F14 **Saugeen** ≈ Ontario, S Canada
18 K12 **Saugerties** New York, NE USA 42°04′N 73°55′W
Saugor see Sāgar
10 K15 **Saugstad, Mount** ▲ British Columbia, SW Canada 52°12′N 126°35′W
Sāūjbulāgh see Mahābād
102 J11 **Saujon** Charente-Maritime, W France 45°40′N 00°54′W
29 T7 **Sauk Centre** Minnesota, N USA 45°44′N 94°57′W
30 L8 **Sauk City** Wisconsin, N USA 43°16′N 89°43′W
29 U7 **Sauk Rapids** Minnesota, N USA 45°35′N 94°09′W
55 Y11 **Saül** C French Guiana 03°37′N 53°12′W
103 O7 **Sauldre** ≈ C France
101 I23 **Saulgau** Baden-Württemberg, SW Germany 48°03′N 09°28′E
103 Q8 **Saulieu** Côte d'Or, C France 47°15′N 04°15′E
118 G8 **Saulkrasti** C Latvia 57°14′N 24°25′E
15 S6 **Sault-aux-Cochons, Rivière du** ≈ Québec, SE Canada
31 Q4 **Sault Sainte Marie** Michigan, N USA 46°29′N 84°22′W
12 F14 **Sault Ste. Marie** Ontario, S Canada 46°30′N 84°17′W
145 P7 **Saumalkol'** *prev.* Volodarskoye. Severnyy Kazakhstan, N Kazakhstan 53°19′N 68°05′E
190 E13 **Sauma, Pointe** *headland* Île Alofi, W Wallis and Futuna 14°21′S 177°58′W
171 T16 **Saumlaki** *var.* Saumlakki. Pulau Yamdena, E Indonesia 07°53′S 131°18′E
Saumlakki see Saumlaki
15 R12 **Saumon, Rivière au** ≈ Québec, SE Canada
102 K8 **Saumur** Maine-et-Loire, NW France 47°16′N 00°04′W
185 F23 **Saunders, Cape** *headland* South Island, New Zealand 45°53′S 170°40′E
195 N13 **Saunders Coast** *physical region* Antarctica
65 B23 **Saunders Island** *island* NW Falkland Islands
65 C24 **Saunders Island Settlement** Saunders Island, NW Falkland Islands 51°22′S 60°05′W
82 F11 **Saurimo** *Port.* Henrique de Carvalho, Vila Henrique de Carvalho. Lunda Sul, NE Angola 09°39′S 20°24′E
55 S11 **Sauriwaunawa** S Guyana 03°10′N 59°51′W
82 D12 **Sautar** Malanje, NW Angola 11°10′S 18°26′E
45 S13 **Sauteurs** N Grenada 12°14′N 61°38′W
102 K13 **Sauveterre-de-Guyenne** Gironde, SW France 44°43′N 00°02′W
119 O14 **Sava** Mahilyowskaya Voblasts', E Belarus 54°22′N 30°49′E
42 J5 **Savá** Colón, N Honduras 15°30′N 86°16′W
84 H11 **Sava** *Eng.* Save, *Ger.* Sau, *Hung.* Száva. ≈ SE Europe
33 Y8 **Savage** Montana, NW USA 47°28′N 104°17′W
183 N16 **Savage River** Tasmania, SE Australia 41°34′S 145°15′E
77 R15 **Savalou** S Benin 07°59′N 01°58′E
30 K10 **Savanna** Illinois, N USA 42°05′N 90°09′W
23 X6 **Savannah** Georgia, SE USA 32°02′N 81°01′W
27 R2 **Savannah** Missouri, C USA 39°57′N 94°49′W
20 H10 **Savannah** Tennessee, S USA 35°12′N 88°15′W
21 O12 **Savannah River** ≈ Georgia/South Carolina, SE USA
167 S9 **Savannakhét** *var.* Khanthabouli. Savannakhét, S Laos 16°38′N 104°49′E
44 H12 **Savanna-La-Mar** W Jamaica 18°13′N 78°08′W
12 B10 **Savant Lake** ◎ Ontario, S Canada

◆ Country
● Country Capital
◇ Dependent Territory
○ Dependent Territory Capital
◐ Administrative Regions
✈ International Airport
▲ Mountain
▲▲ Mountain Range
⛰ Volcano
≈ River
◎ Lake
▣ Reservoir

155 *F17* **Savanūr** Karnātaka, W India *14°58′N 75°19′E*
93 *J16* **Sävar** Västerbotten, N Sweden *63°52′N 20°33′E*
Savaria *see* Szombathely
154 *C11* **Sāvarkundla** *var.* Kundla. Gujarāt, W India *21°21′N 71°20′E*
116 *F11* **Săvârşin** *Hung.* Soborsin; *prev.* Săvirşin. Arad, W Romania *46°00′N 22°15′E*
136 *C13* **Savaştepe** Balıkesir, W Turkey *39°20′N 27°38′E*
147 *P11* **Savat** *Rus.* Savat. Sirdaryo Viloyati, E Uzbekistan *40°03′N 68°35′E*
Savat *see* Savat
Sávdijári *see* Skaulo
77 *R15* **Savè** SE Benin *08°04′N 02°29′E*
83 *N18* **Save** Inhambane, E Mozambique *21°07′S 34°35′E*
102 *L16* **Save** ≈ S France
83 *L17* **Save** *var.* Sabi. ≈ Mozambique/Zimbabwe *see also* Sabi
Save *see* Sava
Save *see* Sabi
142 *M6* **Sāveh** Markazī, W Iran *35°00′N 50°22′E*
116 *L8* **Săveni** Botoşani, NE Romania *47°57′N 26°52′E*
103 *N16* **Saverdun** Ariège, S France *43°15′N 01°34′E*
103 *U5* **Saverne** *var.* Zabern; *anc.* Tres Tabernae. Bas-Rhin, NE France *48°45′N 07°22′E*
106 *B9* **Savigliano** Piemonte, NW Italy *44°39′N 07°39′E*
Savigsivik *see* Savissivik
109 *U10* **Savinja** ≈ N Slovenia
106 *H11* **Savio** ≈ C Italy
Săvirşin *see* Săvârşin
197 *O11* **Savissivik** *var.* Savigsivik. ◈ Avannaarsua, N Greenland
93 *N18* **Savitaipale** Etelä-Suomi, SE Finland *61°12′N 27°43′E*
113 *J15* **Šavnik** C Montenegro *42°57′N 19°04′E*
108 *I9* **Savognin** Graubünden, S Switzerland *46°34′N 09°35′E*
103 *T12* **Savoie** ◈ *department* E France
106 *C10* **Savona** Liguria, NW Italy *44°18′N 08°29′E*
93 *N17* **Savonlinna** *Swe.* Nyslott. Itä-Suomi, E Finland *61°51′N 28°56′E*
93 *N17* **Savonranta** Itä-Suomi, E Finland *62°10′N 29°10′E*
38 *K10* **Savoonga** Saint Lawrence Island, Alaska, USA *63°40′N 170°29′W*
30 *M13* **Savoy** Illinois, N USA *40°03′N 88°15′W*
117 *O8* **Savran'** Odes'ka Oblast', SW Ukraine *48°07′N 30°00′E*
137 *R11* **Şavşat** Artvin, NE Turkey *41°15′N 42°30′E*
95 *L19* **Sävsjö** Jönköping, S Sweden *57°25′N 14°40′E*
Savu, Kepulauan *see* Sawu, Kepulauan
92 *M11* **Savukoski** Lappi, NE Finland *67°17′N 28°14′E*
Savu, Pulau *see* Sawu, Pulau
187 *Y14* **Savusavu** Vanua Levu, N Fiji *16°48′S 179°20′E*
171 *O17* **Savu Sea** *Ind.* Laut Sawu. *sea* S Indonesia
83 *H17* **Savute** North-West, N Botswana *18°33′S 24°06′E*
139 *N7* **Şawāb Uqlat** *well* W Iraq
138 *M7* **Sawāb, Wādī as** *dry watercourse* W Iraq
152 *H13* **Sawāi Mādhopur** Rājasthān, N India *26°00′N 76°22′E*
Sawakin *see* Suakin
167 *R8* **Sawang Daen Din** Sakon Nakhon, E Thailand *17°28′N 103°27′E*
167 *O8* **Sawankhalok** *var.* Swankalok. Sukhothai, NW Thailand *17°19′N 99°50′E*
165 *P13* **Sawara** Chiba, Honshū, S Japan *35°52′N 140°31′E*
37 *R5* **Sawatch Range** ▲▲ Colorado, C USA
141 *N12* **Sawdā', Jabal** ▲ SW Saudi Arabia *18°15′N 42°26′E*
75 *P9* **Sawdā', Jabal as** ▲▲ C Libya
Sawdirī *see* Sodiri
97 *F14* **Sawel Mountain** ▲ C Northern Ireland, United Kingdom *54°49′N 07°04′W*
75 *X10* **Sawhāj** *var.* Sawhāj, *var.* Sohâg, Suliag. C Egypt *26°28′N 31°44′E*
Sawhāj *see* Sawhāj
77 *O15* **Sawla** N Ghana *09°14′N 02°26′W*
141 *X12* **Şawqirah** *var.* Suqrah. S Oman *18°16′N 56°34′E*
141 *X12* **Şawqirah, Dawḩat** *var.* Ghubbat Sawqirah, Sukra Bay, Suqrah Bay. *bay* S Oman
Sawqirah, Ghubbat *see* Şawqirah, Dawḩat
183 *V5* **Sawtell** New South Wales, SE Australia *30°22′S 153°04′E*
138 *K7* **Şawt, Wādī aş** *dry watercourse* S Syria
171 *O17* **Sawu, Kepulauan** *var.* Kepulauan Savu. *island group* S Indonesia
Sawu, Laut *see* Savu Sea
171 *O17* **Sawu, Pulau** *var.* Pulau Sawu. *island* Kepulauan Sawu, S Indonesia
105 *S12* **Sax** Valenciana, E Spain *38°33′N 00°49′W*
Saxe *see* Sachsen
108 *C11* **Saxon** Valais, SW Switzerland *46°07′N 07°09′E*
Saxony *see* Sachsen
Saxony-Anhalt *see* Sachsen-Anhalt
77 *R12* **Say** Niamey, SW Niger *13°08′N 02°20′E*
15 *V7* **Sayabec** Québec, SE Canada *48°33′N 67°42′W*
Sayaboury *see* Xaignabouli
145 *U12* **Sayak** *Kaz.* Sayaq. Karaganda, E Kazakhstan *46°54′N 77°17′E*
57 *D14* **Sayán** Lima, W Peru *11°10′S 77°08′W*
129 *T6* **Sayanskiy Khrebet** ▲▲ S Russian Federation
Sayaq *see* Sayak
146 *K13* **Saýat** *Rus.* Sayat. Lebap Welaýaty, E Turkmenistan *38°44′N 63°51′E*
42 *D3* **Sayaxché** Petén, N Guatemala *16°34′N 90°14′W*
Şaydā/Sayida *see* Saïda
162 *J7* **Sayhan** *var.* Hüremt. Bulgan, C Mongolia *48°40′N 102°33′E*
163 *N10* **Sayhandulaan** *var.* Öldziyt. Dornogovĭ, SE Mongolia *44°42′N 109°10′E*
162 *K9* **Sayhan-Ovoo** *var.* Ongi. Dundgovĭ, C Mongolia *45°27′N 103°58′E*
141 *T15* **Sayḩūt** E Yemen *15°18′N 51°16′E*
29 *U14* **Saylorville Lake** ⊠ Iowa, C USA
Saymenskiy Kanal *see* Saimaa Canal
163 *N10* **Saynshand** Dornogovĭ, SE Mongolia *44°51′N 110°07′E*
Saynshand *see* Sevrey
Sayn-Ust *see* Hohmorĭt
Say-Ötesh *see* Otes
138 *J7* **Şayqal, Baḩr** ⊚ S Syria
Sayrab *see* Sayrob
158 *H4* **Sayram Hu** ⊚ NW China
26 *K11* **Sayre** Oklahoma, C USA *35°18′N 99°38′W*
18 *H12* **Sayre** Pennsylvania, NE USA *41°57′N 76°30′W*
18 *K15* **Sayreville** New Jersey, NE USA *40°27′N 74°19′W*
147 *N13* **Sayrob** *Rus.* Sayrab. Surkhondaryo Viloyati, S Uzbekistan *38°03′N 66°54′E*
40 *L13* **Sayula** Jalisco, SW Mexico *19°52′N 103°36′W*
141 *R14* **Say'ūn** *var.* Saywūn. C Yemen *15°53′N 48°32′E*
Say-Utës *see* Otes
10 *K16* **Sayward** Vancouver Island, British Columbia, SW Canada *50°20′N 126°01′W*
Saywūn *see* Say'ūn
Sayyāl *see* As Sayyāl
139 *U8* **Sayyid 'Abīd** *var.* Saiyid Abid. Wāsiţ, E Iraq *32°51′N 45°07′E*
113 *J22* **Sazan** *var.* Ishulli i Sazanit, *It.* Saseno. *island* SW Albania
Sazanit, Ishulli i *see* Sazan
Sazau/Sazawa *see* Sázava
111 *E17* **Sázava** *var.* Sazau, *Ger.* Sazawa. ≈ C Czech Republic
124 *J14* **Sazonovo** Vologodskaya Oblast', NW Russian Federation *59°04′N 35°10′E*
102 *G6* **Scaër** Finistère, NW France *48°00′N 03°40′W*
97 *J15* **Scafell Pike** ▲ NW England, United Kingdom *54°26′N 03°10′W*
Scalabis *see* Santarém
96 *M2* **Scalloway** N Scotland, United Kingdom *60°10′N 01°17′W*
38 *M11* **Scammon Bay** Alaska, USA *61°50′N 165°34′W*
Scammon Lagoon/ Scammon, Laguna *see* Ojo de Liebre, Laguna
84 *F7* **Scandinavia** *geophysical region* NW Europe
Scania *see* Skåne
96 *K5* **Scapa Flow** *sea basin* N Scotland, United Kingdom
107 *K26* **Scaramia, Capo** *headland* Sicilia, Italy, C Mediterranean Sea *36°46′N 14°29′E*
14 *H15* **Scarborough** Ontario, SE Canada *43°46′N 79°14′W*
45 *Z16* **Scarborough** *prev.* Port Louis. Tobago, Trinidad and Tobago *11°11′N 60°45′W*
97 *N16* **Scarborough** N England, United Kingdom *54°17′N 00°24′W*
185 *I17* **Scargill** Canterbury, South Island, New Zealand *42°57′S 172°57′E*
96 *E7* **Scarp** *island* NW Scotland, United Kingdom
Scarpanto *see* Kárpathos
Scarpanto Strait *see* Karpathou, Stenó
107 *G25* **Scauri** Sicilia, Italy, C Mediterranean Sea *36°45′N 12°06′E*
Scealg, Bá na *see* Ballinskelligs Bay
Scebeli *see* Shebeli
100 *K10* **Schaale** ≈ N Germany
100 *K9* **Schaalsee** ⊚ N Germany
99 *G18* **Schaerbeek** Brussels, C Belgium *50°52′N 04°21′E*
108 *G6* **Schaffhausen** *Fr.* Schaffhouse. Schaffhausen, N Switzerland *47°42′N 08°38′E*
108 *G6* **Schaffhausen** *Fr.* Schaffhouse. ◈ *canton* N Switzerland
Schaffhouse *see* Schaffhausen
98 *I8* **Schagen** Noord-Holland, NW Netherlands *52°47′N 04°47′E*
Schaken *see* Šakiai
98 *M10* **Schalkhaar** Overijssel, E Netherlands *52°16′N 06°10′E*
109 *R3* **Schärding** Oberösterreich, N Austria *48°27′N 13°26′E*
100 *G9* **Scharhörn** *island* NW Germany
Schässburg *see* Sighişoara
Schaulen *see* Šiauliai
30 *M10* **Schaumburg** Illinois, N USA *42°01′N 88°04′W*
Schebschi Mountains *see* Shebshi Mountains
98 *P6* **Scheemda** Groningen, NE Netherlands *53°10′N 06°58′E*
100 *I10* **Scheessel** Niedersachsen, NW Germany *53°11′N 09°33′E*
13 *N8* **Schefferville** Québec, E Canada *54°50′N 67°W*
Schelde *see* Scheldt
99 *D18* **Scheldt** *Dut.* Schelde, *Fr.* Escaut. ≈ W Europe
35 *X5* **Schell Creek Range** ▲▲ Nevada, W USA
18 *K10* **Schenectady** New York, NE USA *42°48′N 73°57′W*
99 *I17* **Scherpenheuvel** *Fr.* Montaigu. Vlaams Brabant, C Belgium *51°00′N 04°57′E*
98 *K11* **Scherpenzeel** Gelderland, C Netherlands *52°07′N 05°30′E*
25 *S12* **Schertz** Texas, SW USA *29°33′N 98°16′W*
98 *G11* **Scheveningen** Zuid-Holland, W Netherlands *52°07′N 04°18′E*
98 *G12* **Schiedam** Zuid-Holland, SW Netherlands *51°55′N 04°25′E*
99 *M24* **Schieren** Diekirch, NE Luxembourg *49°50′N 06°06′E*
98 *M4* **Schiermonnikoog** *Fris.* Skiermûntseach. Fryslân, N Netherlands *53°28′N 06°09′E*
98 *M4* **Schiermonnikoog** *Fris.* Skiermûntseach. *island* Waddeneilanden, N Netherlands
99 *K14* **Schijndel** Noord-Brabant, S Netherlands *51°37′N 05°27′E*
Schil *see* Jiu
99 *H16* **Schilde** Antwerpen, N Belgium *51°14′N 04°35′E*
Schillen *see* Zhilino
103 *V5* **Schiltigheim** Bas-Rhin, NE France *48°38′N 07°47′E*
106 *G7* **Schio** Veneto, NE Italy *45°42′N 11°21′E*
98 *H10* **Schiphol** ✈ (Amsterdam) Noord-Holland, C Netherlands *52°18′N 04°48′E*
Schippenbeil *see* Sępopol
Schiria *see* Şiria
Schivelbein *see* Świdwin
115 *D22* **Schíza** *island* S Greece
175 *U3* **Schjetman Reef** *reef* Antarctica
Schlackenwerth *see* Ostrov
109 *R7* **Schladming** Steiermark, SE Austria *47°24′N 13°42′E*
Schlan *see* Slaný
Schlanders *see* Silandro
100 *I7* **Schlei** *inlet* N Germany
101 *D17* **Schleiden** Nordrhein-Westfalen, W Germany *50°31′N 06°30′E*
Schlelau *see* Szydłowiec
100 *I7* **Schleswig** Schleswig-Holstein, N Germany *54°31′N 09°34′E*
29 *T13* **Schleswig** Iowa, C USA *42°10′N 95°27′W*
100 *H8* **Schleswig-Holstein** ◈ *state* N Germany
Schlettstadt *see* Sélestat
108 *F7* **Schlieren** Zürich, N Switzerland *47°23′N 08°27′E*
Schlochau *see* Człuchów
Schloppe *see* Człopa
101 *I18* **Schlüchtern** Hessen, C Germany *50°19′N 09°27′E*
101 *J17* **Schmalkalden** Thüringen, C Germany *50°42′N 10°26′E*
109 *W2* **Schmida** ≈ NE Austria
65 *P19* **Schmidt-Ott Seamount** *var.* Schmitt-Ott Seamount, Schmitt-Ott Tablemount. *undersea feature* SW Indian Ocean *39°37′S 13°00′E*
Schmiegel *see* Śmigiel
Schmitt-Ott Seamount/ Schmitt-Ott Tablemount *see* Schmidt-Ott Seamount
15 *V3* **Schmon** ≈ Québec, SE Canada
101 *M18* **Schneeberg** ▲ W Germany *50°03′N 11°51′E*
Schneeberg *see* Veliki Snežnik
Schnee-Eifel *see* Schneifel
Schneekoppe *see* Sněžka
Schneidemühl *see* Piła
101 *D18* **Schneifel** *var.* Schnee-Eifel. *plateau* W Germany
Schnelle Körös/Schnelle Kreisch *see* Crişul Repede
100 *I11* **Schneverdingen** *var.* Schneverdingen (Wümme). Niedersachsen, NW Germany *53°07′N 09°48′E*
Schneverdingen (Wümme) *see* Schneverdingen
Schoden *see* Skuodas
45 *Q12* **Schœlcher** W Martinique *14°37′N 61°08′W*
18 *K10* **Schoharie** New York, NE USA *42°40′N 74°20′W*
18 *K11* **Schoharie Creek** ≈ New York, NE USA
115 *J21* **Schoinoússa** *island* Kykládes, Greece, Aegean Sea
100 *L13* **Schönebeck** Sachsen-Anhalt, C Germany *52°01′N 11°45′E*
Schöneck *see* Skarszewy
100 *O12* **Schönefeld** ✈ (Berlin) Berlin, NE Germany *52°23′N 13°29′E*
101 *K24* **Schongau** Bayern, S Germany *47°49′N 10°54′E*
100 *K13* **Schöningen** Niedersachsen, C Germany *52°07′N 10°58′E*
Schönlanke *see* Trzcianka
Schönsee *see* Kowalewo Pomorskie
31 *P10* **Schoolcraft** Michigan, N USA *42°05′N 85°39′W*
98 *O8* **Schoonebeek** Drenthe, NE Netherlands *52°39′N 06°57′E*
98 *I12* **Schoonhoven** Zuid-Holland, C Netherlands *51°57′N 04°°51′E*
98 *H8* **Schoorl** Noord-Holland, NW Netherlands *52°42′N 04°40′E*
Schooten *see* Schoten
101 *F24* **Schopfheim** Baden-Württemberg, SW Germany *47°39′N 07°49′E*
101 *I21* **Schorndorf** Baden-Württemberg, S Germany *48°48′N 09°31′E*
100 *F10* **Schortens** Niedersachsen, NW Germany *53°31′N 07°57′E*
99 *H16* **Schoten** *var.* Schooten. Antwerpen, N Belgium *51°15′N 04°30′E*
183 *Q17* **Schouten Island** *island* Tasmania, SE Australia
186 *C5* **Schouten Islands** *island group* NW Papua New Guinea
98 *E13* **Schouwen** *island* SW Netherlands
Schreiberhau *see* Szklarska Poręba
109 *U2* **Schrems** Niederösterreich, E Austria *48°48′N 15°05′E*
101 *L22* **Schrobenhausen** Bayern, SE Germany *48°33′N 11°14′E*
18 *L8* **Schroon Lake** ⊚ New York, NE USA
108 *J8* **Schruns** Vorarlberg, W Austria *47°04′N 09°54′E*
Schubin *see* Szubin
25 *U11* **Schulenburg** Texas, SW USA *29°40′N 96°54′W*
Schuls *see* Scuol
108 *E8* **Schüpfheim** Luzern, C Switzerland *47°02′N 07°23′E*
35 *S6* **Schurz** Nevada, W USA *38°55′N 118°48′W*
101 *I24* **Schussen** ≈ S Germany
Schüttenhofen *see* Sušice
29 *R15* **Schuyler** Nebraska, C USA *41°25′N 97°04′W*
18 *L10* **Schuylerville** New York, NE USA *43°05′N 73°34′W*
101 *K20* **Schwabach** Bayern, SE Germany *49°20′N 11°02′E*
Schwabenalb *see* Schwäbische Alb
101 *I23* **Schwäbische Alb** *var.* Schwabenalb, *Eng.* Swabian Jura. ▲▲ S Germany
101 *I22* **Schwäbisch Gmünd** *var.* Gmünd. Baden-Württemberg, SW Germany *48°49′N 09°48′E*
101 *I21* **Schwäbisch Hall** *var.* Hall. Baden-Württemberg, SW Germany *49°07′N 09°45′E*
101 *H16* **Schwalm** ≈ C Germany
109 *V9* **Schwanberg** Steiermark, SE Austria *46°46′N 15°12′E*
108 *H8* **Schwanden** Glarus, E Switzerland *47°02′N 09°04′E*
101 *M20* **Schwandorf** Bayern, SE Germany *49°20′N 12°07′E*
109 *S5* **Schwanenstadt** Oberösterreich, NW Austria *48°03′N 13°47′E*
169 *S11* **Schwaner, Pegunungan** ▲▲ Borneo, N Indonesia
109 *W5* **Schwarza** ≈ E Austria
109 *P9* **Schwarzach** ≈ S Austria
101 *M20* **Schwarzach** *Cz.* Černice. ≈ Czech Republic/Germany
Schwarzach *see* Schwarzach im Pongau
109 *Q7* **Schwarzach im Pongau** *var.* Schwarzach. Salzburg, NW Austria *47°19′N 13°09′E*
Schwarzawa *see* Svratka
101 *N14* **Schwarze Elster** ≈ E Germany
Schwarze Körös *see* Crişul Negru
108 *D9* **Schwarzenburg** Bern, W Switzerland *46°51′N 07°28′E*
83 *D21* **Schwarzrand** ▲▲ S Namibia
101 *G23* **Schwarzwald** *Eng.* Black Forest. ▲▲ SW Germany
Schwarzwasser *see* Wda
39 *P7* **Schwatka Mountains** ▲▲ Alaska, USA
109 *N7* **Schwaz** Tirol, W Austria *47°21′N 11°44′E*
109 *Y4* **Schwechat** Niederösterreich, NE Austria *48°09′N 16°29′E*
109 *Y4* **Schwechat** ✈ (Wien) Wien, E Austria *48°04′N 16°31′E*
100 *P11* **Schwedt** Brandenburg, NE Germany *53°04′N 14°16′E*
101 *D19* **Schweich** Rheinland-Pfalz, SW Germany *49°49′N 06°44′E*
Schweidnitz *see* Świdnica
101 *J18* **Schweinfurt** Bayern, SE Germany *50°03′N 10°13′E*
Schweiz *see* Switzerland
100 *L9* **Schwerin** Mecklenburg-Vorpommern, N Germany *53°38′N 11°25′E*
Schwerin *see* Skwierzyna
100 *L9* **Schweriner See** ⊚ N Germany
Schwertberg *see* Świecie
101 *F15* **Schwerte** Nordrhein-Westfalen, W Germany *51°27′N 07°34′E*
Schwiebus *see* Świebodzin
100 *P13* **Schwielochsee** ⊚ NE Germany
Schwihau *see* Švihov
Schwiz *see* Schwyz
108 *G8* **Schwyz** *var.* Schwiz. Schwyz, C Switzerland *47°02′N 08°39′E*
108 *G8* **Schwyz** *var.* Schwiz. ◈ *canton* C Switzerland
14 *J11* **Schyan** ≈ Québec, SE Canada
Schyl *see* Jiu
107 *I24* **Sciacca** Sicilia, Italy, C Mediterranean Sea *37°31′N 13°05′E*
Sciasciamana *see* Shashemenē
107 *L26* **Scicli** Sicilia, Italy, C Mediterranean Sea *36°48′N 14°43′E*
97 *F25* **Scilly, Isles of** *island group* SW England, United Kingdom
111 *H17* **Ścinawa** *Ger.* Steinau an der Elbe. Dolnośląskie, SW Poland *51°22′N 16°27′E*
Scio *see* Chíos
31 *S14* **Scioto River** ≈ Ohio, N USA
36 *L5* **Scipio** Utah, W USA *39°15′N 112°06′W*
33 *X6* **Scobey** Montana, NW USA *48°47′N 105°25′W*
183 *T7* **Scone** New South Wales, SE Australia *32°02′S 150°51′E*
Scoresby Sound/ Scoresbysund *see* Ittoqqortoormiit
Scoresby Sund *see* Kangertittivaq
Scorno, Punta dello *see* Caprara, Punta
34 *K3* **Scotia** California, W USA *40°34′N 124°07′W*
47 *Y14* **Scotia Plate** *tectonic feature*
47 *V15* **Scotia Ridge** *undersea feature* S Atlantic Ocean
194 *H2* **Scotia Sea** *sea* SW Atlantic Ocean
29 *Q12* **Scotland** South Dakota, N USA *43°09′N 97°43′W*
25 *R5* **Scotland** Texas, SW USA *33°37′N 98°27′W*
96 *H11* **Scotland** ◈ *national region* Scotland, U K
21 *W8* **Scotland Neck** North Carolina, SE USA *36°07′N 77°25′W*
195 *R13* **Scott Base** *NZ research station* Antarctica *77°52′S 167°18′E*
10 *J16* **Scott, Cape** *headland* Vancouver Island, British Columbia, SW Canada *50°43′N 128°24′W*
26 *I5* **Scott City** Kansas, C USA *38°28′N 100°55′W*
27 *Y7* **Scott City** Missouri, C USA *37°13′N 89°31′W*
195 *R14* **Scott Coast** *physical region* Antarctica
18 *C15* **Scottdale** Pennsylvania, NE USA *40°05′N 79°35′W*
195 *Y11* **Scott Glacier** *glacier* Antarctica
195 *Q17* **Scott Island** *island* Antarctica
26 *L11* **Scott, Mount** ▲ Oklahoma, USA *34°52′N 98°34′W*
32 *G15* **Scott, Mount** ▲ Oregon, NW USA *42°53′N 122°06′W*
34 *M1* **Scott River** ≈ California, W USA
28 *I13* **Scottsbluff** Nebraska, C USA *41°52′N 103°40′W*
23 *Q2* **Scottsboro** Alabama, S USA *34°40′N 86°01′W*
31 *P15* **Scottsburg** Indiana, N USA *38°42′N 85°47′W*
183 *P16* **Scottsdale** Tasmania, SE Australia *41°13′S 147°30′E*
36 *L13* **Scottsdale** Arizona, SW USA *33°31′N 111°54′W*
45 *O12* **Scotts Head Village** *var.* Cachacrou. S Dominica *15°12′N 61°22′W*
192 *L14* **Scott Shoal** *undersea feature* S Pacific Ocean
20 *K7* **Scottsville** Kentucky, S USA *36°45′N 86°11′W*
29 *U14* **Scranton** Iowa, C USA *42°01′N 94°33′W*
18 *I13* **Scranton** Pennsylvania, NE USA *41°25′N 75°40′W*
186 *B6* **Screw** ≈ NW Papua New Guinea
29 *R14* **Scribner** Nebraska, C USA *41°40′N 96°40′W*
Scrobesbyrig' *see* Shrewsbury
14 *I14* **Scugog** ≈ Ontario, SE Canada
14 *I14* **Scugog, Lake** ⊚ Ontario, SE Canada
97 *N17* **Scunthorpe** E England, United Kingdom *53°35′N 00°39′W*
108 *K9* **Scuol** *Ger.* Schuls. Graubünden, E Switzerland *46°51′N 10°21′E*
Scupi *see* Skopje
Scutari *see* Shkodër
113 *K17* **Scutari, Lake** *Alb.* Liqeni i Shkodrës, *SCr.* Skadarsko Jezero. ⊚ Albania/ Montenegro
Scyros *see* Skýros
Scythopolis *see* Beit She'an
138 *E11* **Sderot** *prev.* Sederot. Southern, S Israel *31°31′N 34°35′E*
25 *U13* **Seadrift** Texas, SW USA *28°25′N 96°42′W*
21 *Y4* **Seaford** *var.* Seaford City. Delaware, NE USA *38°39′N 75°35′W*
Seaford City *see* Seaford
14 *E15* **Seaforth** Ontario, S Canada *43°33′N 81°25′W*
24 *M6* **Seagraves** Texas, SW USA *32°56′N 102°33′W*
11 *X9* **Seal** ≈ Manitoba, C Canada
182 *M10* **Sea Lake** Victoria, SE Australia *35°34′S 142°51′E*
83 *G26* **Seal, Cape** *headland* S South Africa *34°06′S 23°18′E*
65 *D26* **Sea Lion Islands** *island group* SE Falkland Islands
19 *S8* **Seal Island** *island* Maine, NE USA
25 *V11* **Sealy** Texas, SW USA *29°46′N 96°09′W*
35 *X12* **Searchlight** Nevada, W USA *35°27′N 114°54′W*
27 *V11* **Searcy** Arkansas, C USA *35°14′N 91°43′W*
19 *R7* **Searsport** Maine, NE USA *44°28′N 68°54′W*
35 *N10* **Seaside** California, W USA *36°36′N 121°51′W*
32 *F10* **Seaside** Oregon, NW USA *45°57′N 123°55′W*
18 *K16* **Seaside Heights** New Jersey, NE USA *39°56′N 74°03′W*
32 *H8* **Seattle** Washington, NW USA *47°35′N 122°20′W*
32 *H9* **Seattle-Tacoma** ✈ Washington, NW USA *47°04′N 122°27′W*
185 *J16* **Seaward Kaikoura Range** ▲▲ South Island, New Zealand
42 *J9* **Sébaco** Matagalpa, W Nicaragua *12°51′N 86°08′W*
19 *P8* **Sebago Lake** ⊚ Maine, NE USA
169 *S13* **Sebangan, Teluk** *bay* Borneo, C Indonesia
Sebaste/Sebastia *see* Sivas
23 *Y12* **Sebastian** Florida, SE USA *27°55′N 80°31′W*
40 *C5* **Sebastían Vizcaíno, Bahía** *bay* NW Mexico
19 *R6* **Sebasticook Lake** ⊚ Maine, NE USA
34 *M7* **Sebastopol** California, W USA *38°22′N 122°50′W*
Sebastopol *see* Sevastopol'
169 *W8* **Sebatik, Pulau** *island* N Indonesia
19 *R5* **Sebec Lake** ⊚ Maine, NE USA
76 *K12* **Sébékoro** Kayes, W Mali *13°00′N 09°03′W*
Sebenico *see* Šibenik
40 *G6* **Seberi, Cerro** ▲ NW Mexico *27°49′N 110°18′W*
116 *H11* **Sebeş** *Ger.* Mühlbach, *Hung.* Szászsebes; *prev.* Sebeşu Săsesc. Alba, W Romania *45°58′N 23°34′E*
Sebes-Körös *see* Crişul Repede
Sebeşu Săsesc *see* Sebeş
31 *R8* **Sebewaing** Michigan, N USA *43°43′N 83°27′W*
124 *F16* **Sebezh** Pskovskaya Oblast', W Russian Federation *56°19′N 28°31′E*
137 *N12* **Şebinkarahisar** Giresun, N Turkey *40°19′N 38°25′E*
116 *F11* **Sebiş** *Hung.* Borossebes. Arad, W Romania *46°21′N 22°09′E*
Sebkra Azz el Matti *see* Azzel Matti, Sebkha
19 *Q4* **Seboomook Lake** ⊚ Maine, NE USA
74 *G6* **Sebou** *var.* Sebu. ≈ N Morocco
20 *I6* **Sebree** Kentucky, S USA *37°34′N 87°30′W*
23 *X13* **Sebring** Florida, SE USA *27°30′N 81°26′W*
Sebta *see* Ceuta
Sebu *see* Sebou
169 *U13* **Sebuku, Pulau** *island* N Indonesia
169 *W8* **Sebuku, Teluk** *bay* Borneo, N Indonesia
106 *F10* **Secchia** ≈ N Italy
10 *L17* **Sechelt** British Columbia, SW Canada *49°25′N 123°37′W*
56 *C12* **Sechin, Río** ≈ W Peru
56 *A10* **Sechura, Bahía de** *bay* NW Peru
185 *A22* **Secretary Island** *island* SW New Zealand
155 *I15* **Secunderābād** *var.* Sikandarabad. Andhra Pradesh, C India *17°30′N 78°33′E*
57 *L17* **Sécure, Río** ≈ C Bolivia
118 *D10* **Seda** Telšiai, NW Lithuania *56°10′N 22°04′E*
27 *T5* **Sedalia** Missouri, C USA *38°42′N 93°15′W*
103 *R3* **Sedan** Ardennes, N France *49°42′N 04°56′E*
27 *P7* **Sedan** Kansas, C USA *37°07′N 96°11′W*
105 *N3* **Sedano** Castilla y León, N Spain *42°43′N 03°43′W*
104 *H10* **Seda, Ribeira de** *stream* C Portugal
185 *K15* **Seddon** Marlborough, South Island, New Zealand *41°42′S 174°05′E*
185 *H15* **Seddonville** West Coast, South Island, New Zealand *41°35′S 171°59′E*
143 *U7* **Sedeh** Khorāsān-e Janūbī, E Iran *33°18′N 59°12′E*
Sederot *see* Sderot
65 *B23* **Sedge Island** *island* NW Falkland Islands
76 *G12* **Sédhiou** SW Senegal *12°39′N 15°33′W*
11 *U16* **Sedley** Saskatchewan, S Canada *50°06′N 103°51′W*
Sedlez *see* Siedlce
117 *Q2* **Sedniv** Chernihivs'ka Oblast', N Ukraine *51°39′N 31°34′E*
36 *L11* **Sedona** Arizona, SW USA *34°52′N 111°45′W*
Sedunum *see* Sion
118 *F12* **Šeduva** Šiaulai, N Lithuania *55°45′N 23°46′E*
141 *Y8* **Seeb** *var.* Muscat Sīb Airport. ✈ (Masqaţ) NE Oman *23°36′N 58°27′E*
Seeb *see* As Sīb
108 *M7* **Seefeld-in-Tirol** Tirol, W Austria *47°19′N 11°16′E*
83 *E22* **Seeheim Noord** Karas, S Namibia *26°50′S 17°45′E*
Seeland *see* Sjælland
195 *N9* **Seelig, Mount** ▲ Antarctica *81°45′S 102°15′W*
Seenu Atoll *see* Addu Atoll
Seeonee *see* Seoni
Seer *see* Dörgön
102 *L5* **Sées** Orne, N France *48°36′N 00°11′E*
101 *J14* **Seesen** Niedersachsen, C Germany *51°54′N 10°11′E*
Seesker Höhe *see* Szeska Góra
100 *J10* **Seevetal** Niedersachsen, N Germany *53°24′N 10°01′E*
109 *V6* **Seewiesen** Steiermark, E Austria *47°37′N 15°16′E*
136 *J13* **Şefaatli** *var.* Kızılkoca. Yozgat, C Turkey *39°32′N 34°45′E*
143 *V9* **Sefīdābeh** Khorāsān-e Janūbī, E Iran *31°05′N 60°30′E*
149 *N3* **Sefīd, Darya-ye** *Pash.* Āb-i-safed. ≈ N Afghanistan
148 *K5* **Sefīd Kūh, Selseleh-ye** *Eng.* Paropamisus Range. ▲ W Afghanistan *34°00′N 61°40′E*
148 *K5* **Sefīd Kūh, Selseleh-ye** *Eng.* Paropamisus Range. ▲▲ W Afghanistan
142 *M4* **Sefīd, Rūd-e** ≈ NW Iran
74 *G6* **Sefrou** N Morocco *33°51′N 04°49′W*
185 *E19* **Sefton, Mount** ▲ South Island, New Zealand *43°43′S 169°58′E*
171 *S13* **Segaf, Kepulauan** *island group* E Indonesia
169 *W7* **Segama, Sungai** ≈ East Malaysia
168 *L9* **Segamat** Johor, Peninsular Malaysia *02°30′N 102°48′E*
77 *S13* **Ségbana** NE Benin *10°56′N 03°42′E*
Segestica *see* Sisak
Segesvár *see* Sighişoara
171 *T12* **Seget** Papua, E Indonesia *01°21′S 131°04′E*
Segewold *see* Sigulda
124 *J9* **Segezha** Respublika Kareliya, NW Russian Federation *63°39′N 34°24′E*
Seghedin *see* Szeged
Segna *see* Senj
107 *I16* **Segni** Lazio, C Italy *41°41′N 13°02′E*
Segodunum *see* Rodez
105 *S9* **Segorbe** Valenciana, E Spain *39°51′N 00°30′W*
76 *M12* **Ségou** *var.* Segu. Ségou, C Mali *13°26′N 06°12′W*
76 *M12* **Ségou** ◈ *region* SW Mali
54 *E8* **Segovia** Antioquia, N Colombia *07°08′N 74°39′W*
105 *N7* **Segovia** Castilla y León, C Spain *40°57′N 04°07′W*
104 *M6* **Segovia** ◈ *province* Castilla y León, N Spain
Segoviao Wangkí *see* Coco, Río
124 *J9* **Segozerskoye Vodokhranilishche** *prev.* Ozero Segozero. ⊚ NW Russian Federation
102 *J7* **Segré** Maine-et-Loire, NW France *47°41′N 00°51′W*
105 *U5* **Segre** ≈ NE Spain
Segu *see* Ségou
38 *I17* **Seguam Island** *island* Aleutian Islands, Alaska, USA
38 *I17* **Seguam Pass** *strait* Aleutian Islands, Alaska, USA
77 *Y7* **Séguédine** Agadez, NE Niger *20°12′N 13°03′E*
76 *M15* **Séguéla** W Ivory Coast *07°58′N 06°44′W*
25 *S11* **Seguin** Texas, SW USA *29°34′N 97°58′W*
38 *E17* **Segula Island** *island* Aleutian Islands, Alaska, USA
62 *K10* **Segundo, Río** ≈ C Argentina
105 *Q12* **Segura** ≈ S Spain
105 *P13* **Segura , Sierra de** ▲▲ S Spain
83 *G18* **Sehithwa** North-West, N Botswana *20°28′S 22°43′E*
154 *H10* **Sehore** Madhya Pradesh, C India *23°12′N 77°08′E*
186 *G9* **Sehulea** Normanby Island, S Papua New Guinea *09°55′S 151°10′E*
149 *P15* **Sehwān** Sind, SE Pakistan *26°26′N 67°52′N*
109 *V8* **Seiersberg** Steiermark, SE Austria *47°01′N 15°22′E*
26 *L9* **Seiling** Oklahoma, C USA *36°09′N 98°55′W*
103 *S9* **Seille** ≈ E France
99 *J20* **Seilles** Namur, SE Belgium *50°31′N 05°12′E*
93 *K17* **Seinäjoki** *Swe.* Östermyra. Länsi-Suomi, W Finland *62°45′N 22°55′E*
12 *B12* **Seine** ≈ Ontario, S Canada
102 *M4* **Seine** ≈ N France
102 *K4* **Seine, Baie de la** *bay* N France
Seine, Banc de la *see* Seine Seamount
103 *O5* **Seine-et-Marne** ◈ *department* N France
102 *L3* **Seine-Maritime** ◈ *department* N France
84 *B14* **Seine Plain** *undersea feature* E Atlantic Ocean *34°00′N 12°15′W*
84 *B15* **Seine Seamount** *var.* Banc de la Seine. *undersea feature* E Atlantic Ocean *33°45′N 14°25′W*
102 *E6* **Sein, Île de** *island* NW France
171 *Y14* **Seinma** Papua, E Indonesia *04°10′S 138°54′E*
Seisbierrum *see* Sexbierum
109 *U5* **Seitenstetten Markt** Niederösterreich, C Austria *48°03′N 14°41′E*
Seiyo *see* Uwa
Seiyu *see* Chŏnju
95 *H22* **Sejerø** *island* E Denmark
110 *P7* **Sejny** Podlaskie, NE Poland *54°09′N 23°21′E*
163 *X15* **Sejong City** ● (South Korea) E South Korea *36°29′N 127°16′E*
81 *G20* **Seke** Shinyanga, N Tanzania *03°16′S 33°31′E*
164 *L13* **Seki** Gifu, Honshū, SW Japan *35°30′N 136°54′E*
161 *U12* **Sekibi-sho** *island* China/ Japan/Taiwan
165 *U3* **Sekihoku-tōge** *pass* Hokkaidō, NE Japan
Sekondi *see* Sekondi-Takoradi
77 *P17* **Sekondi-Takoradi** *var.* Sekondi. S Ghana *04°55′N 01°45′W*
80 *J11* **Sek'ot'a** Āmara, N Ethiopia *12°41′N 39°05′E*
Sekseūil *see* Saksaul'skoye
32 *I9* **Selah** Washington, NW USA *46°39′N 120°31′W*
168 *J8* **Selangor** *var.* Negeri Selangor Darul Ehsan. ◈ *state* Peninsular Malaysia
Selânik *see* Thessaloníki
167 *R10* **Selaphum** Roi Et, E Thailand *16°00′N 103°54′E*
171 *T16* **Selaru, Pulau** *island* Kepulauan Tanimbar, E Indonesia
171 *U13* **Selassi** Papua, E Indonesia *03°16′S 132°50′E*
168 *J7* **Selatan, Selat** *strait* Peninsular Malaysia
168 *K10* **Selatpanjang** Pulau Rantau, W Indonesia *01°00′N 102°44′E*
39 *N8* **Selawik** Alaska, USA *66°36′N 160°00′W*
39 *N8* **Selawik Lake** ⊚ Alaska, USA
171 *N14* **Selayar, Selat** *strait* Sulawesi, C Indonesia
95 *C14* **Selbjørnsfjorden** *fjord* S Norway
94 *H8* **Selbusjøen** ⊚ S Norway
97 *M17* **Selby** N England, United Kingdom *53°49′N 01°06′W*
29 *N8* **Selby** South Dakota, N USA *45°30′N 100°01′W*
21 *Z4* **Selbyville** Delaware, NE USA *38°28′N 75°12′W*
136 *B15* **Selçuk** *var.* Akıncılar. İzmir, SW Turkey *37°56′N 27°25′E*
39 *Q13* **Seldovia** Alaska, USA *59°26′N 151°42′W*
107 *M18* **Sele** *anc.* Silarius. ≈ S Italy
83 *J19* **Selebi-Phikwe** Central, E Botswana *21°58′S 27°48′E*
42 *B5* **Selegua, Río** ≈ W Guatemala
129 *X7* **Selemdzha** ≈ SE Russian Federation
129 *U7* **Selenga** *Mong.* Selenge Mörön. ≈ Mongolia/ Russian Federation
79 *I19* **Selenge** Bandundu, W Dem. Rep. Congo *01°58′S 18°11′E*
162 *K6* **Selenge** *var.* Ingettolgoy. Bulgan, N Mongolia *49°27′N 103°59′E*
162 *L6* **Selenge** ◈ *province* N Mongolia
Selenge *see* Hyalganat, Bulgan, Mongolia
Selenge *see* Ih-Uul, Hövsgöl, Mongolia
Selenge Mörön *see* Selenga
123 *N14* **Selenginsk** Respublika Buryatiya, S Russian Federation *52°00′N 106°40′E*
Selenica *see* Selenicë
113 *K22* **Selenicë** *var.* Selenica. Vlorë, SW Albania *40°32′N 19°38′E*
123 *Q8* **Selennyakh** ≈ NE Russian Federation
100 *J8* **Selenter See** ⊚ N Germany
Sele Sound *see* Soela Väin
103 *U6* **Sélestat** *Ger.* Schlettstadt. Bas-Rhin, NE France *48°16′N 07°28′E*
Seleucia *see* Silifke
92 *I4* **Selfoss** Sudhurland, SW Iceland *63°56′N 20°59′W*
28 *M7* **Selfridge** North Dakota, N USA *46°01′N 100°52′W*
76 *I15* **Seli** ≈ N Sierra Leone
76 *I11* **Sélibabi** *var.* Sélibaby. Guidimaka, S Mauritania *15°14′N 12°11′W*
Sélibaby *see* Sélibabi
Selidovka/Selidovo *see* Selydove
124 *I15* **Seliger, Ozero** ⊚ W Russian Federation
36 *J11* **Seligman** Arizona, SW USA *35°20′N 112°56′W*
27 *S8* **Seligman** Missouri, C USA *36°31′N 93°56′W*
80 *E6* **Selima Oasis** *oasis* N Sudan
76 *L13* **Sélingué, Lac de** ⊠ S Mali
Selinoús *see* Kréstena
18 *G14* **Selinsgrove** Pennsylvania, NE USA *40°47′N 76°51′W*
Selishche *see* Syelishcha
124 *I16* **Selizharovo** Tverskaya Oblast', W Russian Federation *56°50′N 33°24′E*
94 *C10* **Selje** Sogn Og Fjordane, S Norway *62°02′N 05°22′E*
11 *X16* **Selkirk** Manitoba, S Canada *50°10′N 96°52′W*
96 *K13* **Selkirk** SE Scotland, United Kingdom *55°36′N 02°48′W*
96 *K13* **Selkirk** *cultural region* SE Scotland, United Kingdom
11 *O16* **Selkirk Mountains** ▲▲ British Columbia, SW Canada
193 *T11* **Selkirk Rise** *undersea feature* SE Pacific Ocean
115 *F21* **Sellasía** Pelopónnisos, S Greece *37°14′N 22°24′E*
44 *M9* **Selle, Pic de la** *var.* La Selle. ▲ SE Haiti *18°18′N 71°55′W*
102 *M8* **Selles-sur-Cher** Loir-et-Cher, C France *47°16′N 01°31′E*
36 *K16* **Sells** Arizona, SW USA *31°54′N 111°52′W*
Sellye *see* Sal'a
23 *P5* **Selma** Alabama, S USA *32°24′N 87°01′W*
35 *Q11* **Selma** California, W USA *36°33′N 119°37′W*
20 *G10* **Selmer** Tennessee, S USA *35°10′N 88°34′W*
173 *N17* **Sel, Pointe au** *headland* W Réunion
Selselehye Kuhe Vākhān *see* Nicholas Range

◆ Country
● Country Capital
◇ Dependent Territory
○ Dependent Territory Capital
◈ Administrative Regions
✈ International Airport
▲ Mountain
▲▲ Mountain Range
Volcano
≈ River
⊚ Lake
⊠ Reservoir

127 S2 **Selty** Udmurtskaya Respublika, NW Russian Federation 57°19′N 52°09′E
Selukwe *see* Shurugwi
62 L9 **Selva** Santiago del Estero, N Argentina 29°46′S 62°02′W
11 T9 **Selwyn Lake** ◎ Northwest Territories/Saskatchewan, C Canada
10 K6 **Selwyn Mountains** ⛰ Yukon Territory, NW Canada
181 T6 **Selwyn Range** ⛰ Queensland, C Australia
117 W8 **Selydove** *var.* Selidovka, *Rus.* Selidovo. Donets'ka Oblast', SE Ukraine 48°06′N 37°16′E
Selzaete *see* Zelzate
Seman *see* Semanit, Lumi i
168 M15 **Semangka, Teluk** *bay* Sumatera, SW Indonesia
113 D22 **Semanit, Lumi i** *var.* Seman. ≈ W Albania
169 Q16 **Semarang** *var.* Samarang. Jawa, C Indonesia 06°58′S 110°29′E
169 Q10 **Sematan** Sarawak, East Malaysia 01°50′N 109°44′E
171 P17 **Semau, Pulau** *island* S Indonesia
169 V8 **Sembakung, Sungai** ≈ Borneo, N Indonesia
79 G17 **Sembé** Sangha, NW Congo 01°38′N 14°35′E
169 S13 **Sembulu, Danau** ◎ Borneo, N Indonesia
Semendria *see* Smederevo
117 R1 **Semenivka** Chernihivs'ka Oblast', N Ukraine 52°10′N 32°37′E
117 S6 **Semenivka** *Rus.* Semenovka. Poltavs'ka Oblast', NE Ukraine 49°36′N 33°10′E
127 O3 **Semenov** Nizhegorodskaya Oblast', W Russian Federation 56°47′N 44°27′E
Semenovka *see* Semenivka
169 S17 **Semeru, Gunung** *var.* Mahameru. ▲ Jawa, S Indonesia 08°01′S 112°53′E
145 V9 **Semey** *prev.* Semipalatinsk. Vostochnyy Kazakhstan, E Kazakhstan 50°26′N 80°16′E
Semezhevo *see* Syemyezhava
126 L7 **Semiluki** Voronezhskaya Oblast', W Russian Federation 51°46′N 39°00′E
33 W16 **Seminoe Reservoir** ⊠ Wyoming, C USA
27 O11 **Seminole** Oklahoma, C USA 35°13′N 96°40′W
24 M6 **Seminole** Texas, SW USA 32°43′N 102°39′W
23 S8 **Seminole, Lake** ⊠ Florida/Georgia, SE USA
Semiozernoye *see* Auliyekol'
Semipalatinsk *see* Semey
143 O9 **Semīrom** *var.* Samirom. Eşfahān, C Iran 31°20′N 51°50′E
38 F17 **Semisopochnoi Island** *island* Aleutian Islands, Alaska, USA
169 R11 **Semitau** Borneo, C Indonesia 0°30′N 111°59′E
81 E18 **Semliki** ≈ Uganda/Dem. Rep. Congo
143 P5 **Semnān** *var.* Samnān. Semnān, N Iran 35°37′N 53°21′E
143 Q5 **Semnān** *off.* Ostān-e Semnān. ◐ *province* N Iran
Semnān, Ostān-e *see* Semnān
99 K24 **Semois** ≈ SE Belgium
108 E8 **Sempacher See** ◎ C Switzerland
Sena *see* Vila de Sena
30 L12 **Senachwine Lake** ◎ Illinois, N USA
59 O14 **Senador Pompeu** Ceará, E Brazil 05°30′S 39°25′W
Sena Gallica *see* Senigallia
59 C15 **Sena Madureira** Acre, W Brazil 09°05′S 68°41′W
155 L25 **Senanayake Samudra** ◎ E Sri Lanka
83 G15 **Senanga** Western, SW Zambia 16°09′S 23°16′E
27 Y9 **Senath** Missouri, C USA 36°07′N 90°09′W
22 L2 **Senatobia** Mississippi, S USA 34°37′N 89°58′W
164 C16 **Sendai** *var.* Satsuma-Sendai. Kagoshima, Kyūshū, SW Japan 31°49′N 130°17′E
165 Q11 **Sendai-wan** *bay* E Japan
101 J23 **Senden** Bayern, S Germany 48°18′N 10°04′E
154 F11 **Sendhwa** Madhya Pradesh, C India 21°38′N 75°04′E
111 H21 **Senec** *Ger.* Wartberg, *Hung.* Szenc; *prev.* Szempcz. Bratislavský Kraj, W Slovakia 48°14′N 17°24′E
27 P3 **Seneca** Kansas, C USA 39°50′N 96°04′W
27 R8 **Seneca** Missouri, C USA 36°50′N 94°36′W
32 K13 **Seneca** Oregon, NW USA 44°06′N 118°57′W
21 O11 **Seneca** South Carolina, SE USA 34°41′N 82°57′W
18 G11 **Seneca Lake** ◎ New York, NE USA
31 U13 **Senecaville Lake** ◎ Ohio, N USA
76 G11 **Senegal** *off.* Republic of Senegal, *Fr.* Sénégal. ◆ *republic* W Africa
76 H9 **Senegal** *Fr.* Sénégal. ≈ W Africa
Senegal, Republic of *see* Senegal
31 O4 **Seney Marsh** *wetland* Michigan, N USA
101 P14 **Senftenberg** Brandenburg, E Germany 51°31′N 14°01′E
82 L11 **Senga Hill** Northern, NE Zambia 09°26′S 31°12′E
158 G13 **Sênggê Zangbo** ≈ W China
171 Z13 **Senggi** Papua, E Indonesia 03°26′S 140°46′E
127 R5 **Sengiley** Ul'yanovskaya Oblast', W Russian Federation 53°54′N 48°51′E
63 I19 **Senguerr, Río** ≈ S Argentina
83 J16 **Sengwa** ≈ C Zimbabwe
Senia *see* Senj
111 H19 **Senica** *Ger.* Senitz, *Hung.* Szenice. Trnavský Kraj, W Slovakia 48°40′N 17°22′E
Seniça *see* Sjenica
106 J11 **Senigallia** *anc.* Sena Gallica. Marche, C Italy 43°43′N 13°13′E
136 F15 **Senirkent** Isparta, SW Turkey 38°07′N 30°34′E
Senitz *see* Senica
112 C10 **Senj** *Ger.* Zengg, *It.* Segna; *anc.* Senia. Lika-Senj, NW Croatia 44°58′N 14°55′E
Senj *see* Örgön
92 H9 **Senja** *prev.* Senjen. *island* N Norway
Senjen *see* Senja
161 U12 **Senkaku-shotō** *island group* SW Japan
137 R12 **Şenkaya** Erzurum, NE Turkey 40°33′N 42°17′E
83 I16 **Senkobo** Southern, S Zambia 17°38′S 25°58′E
103 O4 **Senlis** Oise, N France 49°13′N 02°33′E
Senmonorom *see* Sênmônoŭrôm
167 T12 **Sênmônoŭrôm** *var.* Senmonorom. Môndól Kiri, E Cambodia 12°27′N 107°12′E
80 G10 **Sennar** *var.* Sannār. Sinnar, C Sudan 13°31′N 33°38′E
Senno *see* Syanno
Senones *see* Sens
109 W11 **Senovo** E Slovenia 46°01′N 15°24′E
103 P6 **Sens** *anc.* Agendicum, Senones. Yonne, C France 48°12′N 03°17′E
Sensburg *see* Mrągowo
167 S11 **Sên, Stœng** ≈ C Cambodia
42 F7 **Sensuntepeque** Cabañas, NE El Salvador 13°52′N 88°38′W
112 L8 **Senta** *Hung.* Zenta. Vojvodina, N Serbia 45°57′N 20°04′E
Šent Andraž *see* Sankt Andrä
171 Y13 **Sentani, Danau** ◎ Papua, E Indonesia
28 J5 **Sentinel Butte** ▲ North Dakota, N USA 46°52′N 103°50′W
10 M13 **Sentinel Peak** ▲ British Columbia, W Canada 54°51′N 122°02′W
59 N16 **Sento Sé** Bahia, E Brazil 09°51′S 41°56′W
Šent Peter *see* Pivka
Št. Vid *see* Sankt Veit an der Glan
Seo de Urgel *see* La Seu d'Urgell
163 X17 **Seogwipo** *prev.* Sŏgwip'o. S South Korea 33°14′N 126°33′E
154 I7 **Seondha** Madhya Pradesh, C India 26°09′N 78°47′E
163 Y17 **Seongsan** *prev.* Sŏngsan. S South Korea
154 J11 **Seoni** *prev.* Seonee. Madhya Pradesh, C India 22°06′N 79°36′E
163 X14 **Seoul** *Jap.* Keijō; *prev.* Kyŏngsŏng, Sŏul. ● (South Korea) NW South Korea 37°30′N 126°58′E
83 I17 **Sepako** Central, NE Botswana 19°50′S 26°29′E
184 I13 **Separation Point** *headland* South Island, New Zealand 40°46′S 172°58′E
169 V10 **Sepasu** Borneo, N Indonesia 0°44′N 117°38′E
186 B6 **Sepik** ≈ Indonesia/Papua New Guinea
Sepone *see* Muang Xépôn
110 M7 **Sępopol** *Ger.* Schippenbeil. Warmińsko-Mazurskie, N Poland 54°16′N 21°09′E
116 F10 **Şepreuş** *Hung.* Seprős. Arad, W Romania 46°34′N 21°44′E
Seprős *see* Şepreuş
Şepşi-Sângeorz/Sepsiszentgyörgy *see* Sfântu Gheorghe
15 W4 **Sept-Îles** Québec, SE Canada 50°11′N 66°19′W
105 N6 **Sepúlveda** Castilla y León, N Spain 41°18′N 03°45′W
104 K8 **Sequeros** Castilla y León, N Spain 40°31′N 06°04′W
104 L5 **Sequillo** ≈ NW Spain
32 G7 **Sequim** Washington, NW USA 48°04′N 123°06′W
35 S11 **Sequoia National Park** *national park* California, W USA
137 Q14 **Şerafettin Dağları** ⛰ E Turkey
127 N10 **Serafimovich** Volgogradskaya Oblast', SW Russian Federation 49°34′N 42°43′E
171 Q10 **Serai** Sulawesi, N Indonesia 01°45′N 124°58′E
99 K19 **Seraing** Liège, E Belgium 50°37′N 05°31′E
Sêraitang *see* Baima
Serakhs *see* Sarahs
171 W13 **Serami** Papua, E Indonesia 02°11′S 136°46′E
171 R13 **Seram, Laut** *Eng.* Ceram Sea. *sea* E Indonesia
Serampore/Serampur *see* Shrīrāmpur
171 S13 **Seram, Pulau** *var.* Serang, *Eng.* Ceram. *island* Maluku, E Indonesia
169 N15 **Serang** Jawa, C Indonesia 06°07′S 106°09′E
Serang *see* Seram, Pulau
169 P9 **Serasan, Pulau** *island* Kepulauan Natuna, W Indonesia
169 P9 **Serasan, Selat** *strait* Indonesia/Malaysia
112 M13 **Serbia** *off.* Federal Republic of Serbia; *prev.* Yugoslavia, *SCr.* Jugoslavija. ◆ *federal republic* SE Europe
112 M12 **Serbia** *Ger.* Serbien, *Serb.* Srbija. ◐ *republic* Serbia
Serbia, Federal Republic of *see* Serbia
Serbien *see* Serbia
Sercq *see* Sark
146 D12 **Serdar** *prev. Rus.* Gyzyrlabat, Kizyl-Arvat. Balkan Welaýaty, W Turkmenistan 39°02′N 56°15′E
Serdica *see* Sofiya
Serdobol' *see* Sortavala
127 O7 **Serdobsk** Penzenskaya Oblast', W Russian Federation 52°30′N 44°16′E
145 X9 **Serebryansk** Vostochnyy Kazakhstan, E Kazakhstan 49°44′N 83°16′E
123 Q12 **Serebryanyy Bor** Respublika Sakha (Yakutiya), NE Russian Federation 56°40′N 124°46′E
111 H20 **Sered'** *Hung.* Szered. Trnavský Kraj, W Slovakia 48°19′N 17°45′E
117 S1 **Seredyna-Buda** Sums'ka Oblast', NE Ukraine 52°09′N 34°00′E
118 E13 **Seredžius** Tauragė, C Lithuania 55°04′N 23°24′E
136 I14 **Şereflikoçhisar** Ankara, C Turkey 38°56′N 33°31′E
106 D7 **Seregno** Lombardia, N Italy 45°39′N 09°12′E
103 P7 **Serein** ≈ C France
168 K9 **Seremban** Negeri Sembilan, Peninsular Malaysia 02°42′N 101°54′E
81 H20 **Serengeti Plain** *plain* N Tanzania
82 K13 **Serenje** Central, E Zambia 13°12′S 30°15′E
Seres *see* Sérres
116 J5 **Seret** ≈ W Ukraine
Seret/Sereth *see* Siret
115 I21 **Serfopoúla** *island* Kykládes, Greece, Aegean Sea
127 P4 **Sergach** Nizhegorodskaya Oblast', W Russian Federation 55°31′N 45°29′E
29 S13 **Sergeant Bluff** Iowa, C USA 42°24′N 96°19′W
163 P7 **Sergelen** Dornod, NE Mongolia 48°31′N 114°01′E
Sergelen *see* Tuvshinshiree
168 H8 **Sergeulangit, Pegunungan** ⛰ Sumatera, NW Indonesia
122 L5 **Sergeya Kirova, Ostrova** *island* N Russian Federation
Sergeyevichi *see* Syarhyeyevichy
145 O7 **Sergeyevka** Severnyy Kazakhstan, N Kazakhstan 53°53′N 67°25′E
Sergiopol *see* Ayagoz
59 P16 **Sergipe** *off.* Estado de Sergipe. ◐ *state* E Brazil
Sergipe, Estado de *see* Sergipe
126 L3 **Sergiyev Posad** Moskovskaya Oblast', W Russian Federation 56°21′N 38°10′E
124 K5 **Sergozero, Ozero** ◎ NW Russian Federation
146 J17 **Serhetabat** *prev. Rus.* Gushgy, Kushka. Mary Welaýaty, S Turkmenistan 35°19′N 62°17′E
169 Q10 **Serian** Sarawak, East Malaysia 01°10′N 110°35′E
115 I21 **Sérifos** *anc.* Seriphos. *island* Kykládes, Greece, Aegean Sea
115 I21 **Sérifou, Stenó** *strait* SE Greece
136 F16 **Serik** Antalya, SW Turkey 36°55′N 31°06′E
106 E7 **Serio** ≈ N Italy
Seriphos *see* Sérifos
Serir Tibesti *see* Sarīr Tībistī
Serkog *see* Sêrtar
127 S5 **Sernovodsk** Samarskaya Oblast', W Russian Federation 53°56′N 51°16′E
127 R2 **Sernur** Respublika Mariy El, W Russian Federation 56°55′N 49°09′E
110 M11 **Serock** Mazowieckie, C Poland 52°30′N 21°03′E
61 B18 **Serodino** Santa Fe, C Argentina 32°33′S 60°52′W
Seroei *see* Serui
105 P14 **Serón** Andalucía, S Spain 37°20′N 02°28′W
99 E14 **Serooskerke** Zeeland, SW Netherlands 51°42′N 03°52′E
105 T6 **Serós** Cataluña, NE Spain 41°27′N 00°24′E
122 G10 **Serov** Sverdlovskaya Oblast', C Russian Federation 59°42′N 60°32′E
83 I19 **Serowe** Central, SE Botswana 22°26′S 26°44′E
104 H13 **Serpa** Beja, S Portugal 37°56′N 07°36′W
Serpa Pinto *see* Menongue
182 A4 **Serpentine Lakes** *salt lake* South Australia
45 T15 **Serpent's Mouth, The** *Sp.* Boca de la Serpiente. *strait* Trinidad and Tobago/Venezuela
Serpiente, Boca de la *see* Serpent's Mouth, The
126 K4 **Serpukhov** Moskovskaya Oblast', W Russian Federation 54°54′N 37°26′E
104 I10 **Serra de São Mamede** ▲ C Portugal 39°18′N 07°19′W
60 K13 **Serra do Mar** ⛰ S Brazil
Sérrai *see* Sérres
107 N22 **Serra San Bruno** Calabria, SW Italy 38°32′N 16°18′E
103 S14 **Serres** Hautes-Alpes, SE France 44°26′N 05°42′E
114 H13 **Sérres** *var.* Seres; *prev.* Sérrai. Kentrikí Makedonía, NE Greece 41°03′N 23°33′E
62 J9 **Serrezuela** Córdoba, C Argentina 30°38′S 65°26′W
59 O16 **Serrinha** Bahia, E Brazil 11°38′S 38°56′W
59 M19 **Sêrro** *var.* Sêrro. Minas Gerais, NE Brazil 18°38′S 43°22′W
Sêrro *see* Serro
Sert *see* Siirt
104 H9 **Sertã** *var.* Sertá. Castelo Branco, C Portugal 39°48′N 08°05′W
Sertá *see* Sertã
60 L8 **Sertãozinho** São Paulo, S Brazil 21°04′S 47°55′W
160 F7 **Sêrtar** *var.* Sêrkog. Sichuan, C China 32°18′N 100°18′E
124 G12 **Sertolovo** Leningradskaya Oblast', NW Russian Federation 60°08′N 30°06′E
171 W13 **Serui** *prev.* Seroei. Papua, E Indonesia 01°53′S 136°15′E
83 J19 **Serule** Central, E Botswana 21°58′S 27°20′E
169 S12 **Seruyan, Sungai** *var.* Sungai Pembuang. ≈ Borneo, N Indonesia
115 E14 **Sérvia** Dytikí Makedonía, N Greece 40°12′N 22°01′E
160 E7 **Sêrxü** *var.* Jugar. Sichuan, C China 32°54′N 98°06′E
123 R13 **Seryshevo** Amurskaya Oblast', SE Russian Federation 51°03′N 128°16′E
Sesana *see* Sežana
169 V8 **Sesayap, Sungai** ≈ Borneo, N Indonesia
Sesdlets *see* Siedlce
79 N17 **Sese** Orientale, N Dem. Rep. Congo 02°13′N 25°52′E
81 F18 **Sese Islands** *island group* S Uganda
83 H16 **Sesheke** *var.* Sesheko. Western, SE Zambia 17°28′S 24°20′E
Sesheko *see* Sesheke
106 C8 **Sesia** *anc.* Sessites. ≈ NW Italy
104 F11 **Sesimbra** Setúbal, S Portugal 38°26′N 09°06′W
115 N22 **Sesklió** *island* Dodekánisa, Greece, Aegean Sea
30 L16 **Sesser** Illinois, N USA 38°05′N 89°03′W
Sessites *see* Sesia
106 G11 **Sesto Fiorentino** Toscana, C Italy 43°50′N 11°12′E
106 E7 **Sesto San Giovanni** Lombardia, N Italy 45°32′N 09°14′E
106 A8 **Sestriere** Piemonte, NE Italy 45°00′N 06°54′E
106 D10 **Sestri Levante** Liguria, NW Italy 44°16′N 09°22′E
107 C20 **Sestu** Sardegna, Italy, C Mediterranean Sea 39°15′N 09°06′E
112 E8 **Sesvete** Zagreb, N Croatia 45°50′N 16°03′E
118 G12 **Šeta** Kaunas, C Lithuania 55°17′N 24°16′E
Setabis *see* Xàtiva
165 Q4 **Setana** Hokkaidō, NE Japan 42°27′N 139°52′E
103 Q16 **Sète** *prev.* Cette. Hérault, S France 43°24′N 03°42′E
58 J11 **Sete Ilhas** Amapá, NE Brazil 01°06′N 52°06′W
59 L20 **Sete Lagoas** Minas Gerais, NE Brazil 19°29′S 44°15′W
60 G10 **Sete Quedas, Ilha das** *island* S Brazil
92 I10 **Setermoen** Troms, N Norway 68°51′N 18°20′E
95 E17 **Setesdal** *valley* S Norway
43 W16 **Setetule, Cerro** ▲ SE Panama 07°51′N 77°37′W
21 Q5 **Seth** West Virginia, NE USA 38°06′N 81°40′W
Setia *see* Sezze
74 K5 **Sétif** *var.* Stif. N Algeria 36°11′N 05°24′E
164 L5 **Seto** Aichi, Honshū, SW Japan 35°14′N 137°06′E
164 G13 **Seto-naikai** *Eng.* Inland Sea. *sea* S Japan
165 V16 **Setouchi** *var.* Setoushi. Kagoshima, Amami-Ō-shima, SW Japan 44°19′N 142°58′E
Setoushi *see* Setouchi
74 F6 **Settat** W Morocco 33°03′N 07°37′W
79 D20 **Setté Cama** Ogooué-Maritime, SW Gabon 02°32′S 09°46′E
11 W13 **Setting Lake** ◎ Manitoba, C Canada
97 L16 **Settle** N England, United Kingdom 54°04′N 02°17′W
189 Y12 **Settlement** E Wake Island 19°17′N 166°38′E
104 F11 **Setúbal** *Eng.* Saint Ubes, Saint Yves. Setúbal, W Portugal 38°31′N 08°54′W
104 F11 **Setúbal** ◐ *district* S Portugal
104 F12 **Setúbal, Baía de** *bay* W Portugal
Setul *see* Satun
12 B10 **Seul, Lac** ◎ Ontario, S Canada
103 R8 **Seurre** Côte d'Or, C France 47°00′N 05°09′E
137 U11 **Sevan** C Armenia 40°32′N 44°56′E
137 V12 **Sevana Lich** *Eng.* Lake Sevan, *Rus.* Ozero Sevan. ◎ E Armenia
Sevan, Lake/Sevan, Ozero *see* Sevana Lich
77 N11 **Sévaré** Mopti, C Mali 14°32′N 04°06′W
117 S14 **Sevastopol'** *Eng.* Sebastopol. Avtonomna Respublika Krym, S Ukraine 44°36′N 33°33′E
25 R14 **Seven Sisters** Texas, SW USA 27°57′N 98°34′W
10 K13 **Seven Sisters Peaks** ▲ British Columbia, SW Canada 54°57′N 128°10′W
99 M15 **Sevenum** Limburg, SE Netherlands 51°25′N 06°01′E
103 P14 **Séverac-le-Château** Aveyron, S France 44°18′N 03°03′E
14 H13 **Severn** ≈ Ontario, S Canada
97 L21 **Severn** *Wel.* Hafren. ≈ England/Wales, United Kingdom
125 O11 **Severnaya Dvina** *var.* Northern Dvina. ≈ NW Russian Federation
127 N16 **Severnaya Osetiya-Alaniya, Respublika** *Eng.* North Ossetia; *prev.* Respublika Severnaya Osetiya, Severo-Osetinskaya SSR. ◐ *autonomous republic* SW Russian Federation
Severnaya Osetiya, Respublika *see* Severnaya Osetiya-Alaniya, Respublika
122 M5 **Severnaya Zemlya** *var.* Nicholas II Land. *island group* N Russian Federation
127 T5 **Severnoye** Orenburgskaya Oblast', W Russian Federation 54°03′N 52°31′E
35 S3 **Severn Troughs Range** ⛰ Nevada, W USA
125 W3 **Severnyy** Respublika Komi, NW Russian Federation 67°38′N 64°13′E
144 I13 **Severnyy Chink Ustyurta** ⛰ W Kazakhstan
125 Q13 **Severnyye Uvaly** *var.* Northern Ural Hills. *hill range* NW Russian Federation
145 O6 **Severnyy Kazakhstan** *off.* Severo-Kazakhstanskaya Oblast', *var.* North Kazakhstan, *Kaz.* Soltüstik Qazaqstan Oblysy. ◐ *province* N Kazakhstan
122 I6 **Severnyy, Ostrov** NW Russian Federation
125 V9 **Severnyy Ural** ⛰ NW Russian Federation
Severo-Alichurskiy Khrebet *see* Alichuri Shimolí, Qatorkŭhi
123 N12 **Severobaykal'sk** Respublika Buryatiya, S Russian Federation 55°39′N 109°17′E
Severodonetsk *see* Syeverodonets'k
124 M8 **Severodvinsk** *prev.* Molotov, Sudostroy. Arkhangel'skaya Oblast', NW Russian Federation 64°32′N 39°50′E
Severo-Kazakhstanskaya Oblast' *see* Severnyy Kazakhstan
123 U11 **Severo-Kuril'sk** Sakhalinskaya Oblast', SE Russian Federation 50°38′N 155°57′E
124 J3 **Severomorsk** Murmanskaya Oblast', NW Russian Federation 69°00′N 33°16′E
Severo-Osetinskaya SSR *see* Severnaya Osetiya-Alaniya, Respublika
122 M7 **Severo-Sibirskaya Nizmennost'** *var.* North Siberian Plain, *Eng.* North Siberian Lowland. *lowlands* N Russian Federation
122 G10 **Severoural'sk** Sverdlovskaya Oblast', C Russian Federation 60°09′N 59°58′E
122 L11 **Severo-Yeniseyskiy** Krasnoyarskiy Kray, C Russian Federation 60°29′N 93°13′E
122 J12 **Seversk** Tomskaya Oblast', C Russian Federation 53°37′N 84°47′E
126 M11 **Severskiy Donets** *Ukr.* Sivers'kyy Donets'. ≈ Russian Federation/Ukraine *see also* Sivers'kyy Donets'
Severskiy Donets *see* Sivers'kyy Donets'
92 M9 **Sevettijärvi** Lappi, N Finland 69°31′N 28°40′E
36 M5 **Sevier Bridge Reservoir** ⊠ Utah, W USA
36 J4 **Sevier Desert** *plain* Utah, W USA
36 J5 **Sevier Lake** ◎ Utah, W USA
21 N9 **Sevierville** Tennessee, S USA 35°53′N 83°34′W
104 J14 **Sevilla** *Eng.* Seville; *anc.* Hispalis. Andalucía, SW Spain 37°24′N 05°59′W
104 J13 **Sevilla** ◐ *province* Andalucía, SW Spain
Sevilla de Niefang *see* Niefang
43 O16 **Sevilla, Isla** *island* SW Panama
Seville *see* Sevilla
114 J9 **Sevlievo** Gabrovo, N Bulgaria 43°01′N 25°06′E
Sevluš/Sevlyush *see* Vynohradiv
109 V11 **Sevnica** *Ger.* Lichtenwald. E Slovenia 46°00′N 15°20′E
162 J11 **Sevrey** *var.* Saynshand. Ömnögovĭ, S Mongolia 43°30′N 102°08′E
126 I7 **Sevsk** Bryanskaya Oblast', W Russian Federation 52°03′N 34°31′E
76 J15 **Sewa** ≈ E Sierra Leone
39 R12 **Seward** Alaska, USA 60°06′N 149°26′W
29 R15 **Seward** Nebraska, C USA 40°52′N 97°06′W
197 Q3 **Seward Peninsula** *peninsula* Alaska, USA
Seward's Folly *see* Alaska
62 H12 **Sewell** Libertador, C Chile 34°05′S 70°25′W
98 K5 **Sexbierum** *Fris.* Seisbierrum. Fryslân, N Netherlands 53°13′N 05°28′E
11 O13 **Sexsmith** Alberta, W Canada 55°18′N 118°45′W
41 W13 **Seybaplaya** Campeche, SE Mexico 19°39′N 90°36′W
173 N6 **Seychelles** *off.* Republic of Seychelles. ◆ *republic* W Indian Ocean
67 Z9 **Seychelles** *island group* NE Seychelles
173 N6 **Seychelles Bank** *var.* Le Banc des Seychelles. *undersea feature* W Indian Ocean 04°45′S 55°30′E
Seychelles, Le Banc des *see* Seychelles Bank
Seychelles, Republic of *see* Seychelles
172 H17 **Seychellois, Morne** ▲ Mahé, NE Seychelles
92 L2 **Seydhisfjördhur** Austurland, E Iceland 65°15′N 14°00′W
146 J12 **Seýdi** *Rus.* Seydi; *prev.* Neftezavodsk. Lebap Welaýaty, E Turkmenistan 39°31′N 62°53′E
136 G16 **Seydişehir** Konya, SW Turkey 37°25′N 31°51′E
136 J13 **Seyfe Gölü** ◎ C Turkey
Seyhan *see* Adana
136 K16 **Seyhan Barajı** ⊠ S Turkey
136 K17 **Seyhan Nehri** ≈ S Turkey
136 F13 **Seyitgazi** Eskişehir, W Turkey 39°27′N 30°42′E
126 J7 **Seym** ≈ W Russian Federation
117 S3 **Seym** ≈ N Ukraine
123 T9 **Seymchan** Magadanskaya Oblast', E Russian Federation 62°54′N 152°27′E
114 N12 **Seymen** Tekirdağ, NW Turkey 41°06′N 27°56′E
183 O11 **Seymour** Victoria, SE Australia 37°01′S 145°10′E
83 I25 **Seymour** Eastern Cape, S South Africa 32°33′S 26°46′E
29 W16 **Seymour** Iowa, C USA 40°40′N 93°07′W
27 U7 **Seymour** Missouri, C USA 37°09′N 92°46′W
25 Q5 **Seymour** Texas, SW USA 33°36′N 99°16′W
114 M12 **Şeytan Deresi** ≈ NW Turkey
109 S12 **Sežana** *It.* Sesana. SW Slovenia 45°42′N 13°52′E
103 P5 **Sézanne** Marne, N France 48°43′N 03°41′E
107 I16 **Sezze** *anc.* Setia. Lazio, C Italy 41°29′N 13°04′E
Sfákia *see* Chóra Sfakíon
115 D21 **Sfaktiría** *island* S Greece
116 J11 **Sfântu Gheorghe** *Ger.* Sankt-Georgen, *Hung.* Sepsiszentgyörgy; *prev.* Şepşi-Sângeorz, Sfîntu Gheorghe. Covasna, C Romania 45°52′N 25°49′E
117 N13 **Sfântu Gheorghe, Braţul** *var.* Gheorghe Braţul. ≈ E Romania
75 N6 **Sfax** *Ar.* Şafāqis. E Tunisia 34°45′N 10°45′E
75 N6 **Sfax** ✈ E Tunisia 34°43′N 10°37′E
Sfîntu Gheorghe *see* Sfântu Gheorghe
98 H13 **'s-Gravendeel** Zuid-Holland, SW Netherlands 51°48′N 04°36′E
98 F11 **'s-Gravenhage** *var.* Den Haag, *Eng.* The Hague, *Fr.* La Haye. ● (Netherlands-seat of government) Zuid-Holland, W Netherlands 52°07′N 04°17′E
98 G12 **'s-Gravenzande** Zuid-Holland, W Netherlands 52°00′N 04°10′E
Shaan/Shaanxi Sheng *see* Shaanxi
159 X11 **Shaanxi** *var.* Shaan, Shaanxi Sheng, Shan-hsi, Shenshi, Shensi. ◐ *province* C China
Shaartuz *see* Shahrtuz
Shaba *see* Katanga
Shabani *see* Zvishavane
81 N17 **Shabeellaha Dhexe** *off.* Gobolka Shabeellaha Dhexe. ◐ *region* E Somalia
Shabeellaha Dhexe, Gobolka *see* Shabeellaha Dhexe
81 L17 **Shabeellaha Hoose** *off.* Gobolka Shabeellaha Hoose. ◐ *region* S Somalia
Shabeellaha Hoose, Gobolka *see* Shabeellaha Hoose
Shabeelle, Webi *see* Shebeli
114 O7 **Shabla** Dobrich, NE Bulgaria 43°33′N 28°31′E
114 O7 **Shabla, Nos** *headland* NE Bulgaria 43°30′N 28°36′E
13 N9 **Shabogama Lake** ◎ Newfoundland and Labrador, E Canada
79 N20 **Shabunda** Sud-Kivu, E Dem. Rep. Congo 02°42′S 27°20′E
141 Q15 **Shabwah** C Yemen 15°09′N 46°46′E
158 F8 **Shache** *var.* Yarkant. Xinjiang Uygur Zizhiqu, NW China 38°27′N 77°16′E
Shacheng *see* Huailai
195 R12 **Shackleton Coast** *physical region* Antarctica
195 Z10 **Shackleton Ice Shelf** *ice shelf* Antarctica
Shaddādī *see* Ash Shadādah
28 K7 **Shadehill Reservoir** ⊠ South Dakota, N USA
122 G11 **Shadrinsk** Kurganskaya Oblast', C Russian Federation 56°08′N 63°18′E
31 O12 **Shafer, Lake** ⊠ Indiana, N USA
35 R13 **Shafter** California, W USA 35°27′N 119°15′W
24 J11 **Shafter** Texas, SW USA 29°49′N 104°18′W
97 L23 **Shaftesbury** S England, United Kingdom 51°01′N 02°12′W
185 F22 **Shag** ≈ South Island, New Zealand
145 V9 **Shagan** ≈ E Kazakhstan
39 O11 **Shageluk** Alaska, USA 62°40′N 159°33′W
122 K14 **Shagonar** Respublika Tyva, S Russian Federation 51°31′N 93°06′E
185 F22 **Shag Point** *headland* South Island, New Zealand 45°28′S 170°50′E
144 J12 **Shagyray, Plato** *plain* SW Kazakhstan
Shāhābād *see* Eslāmābād-e Gharb
168 K9 **Shah Alam** Selangor, Peninsular Malaysia 03°02′N 101°31′E
117 O12 **Shahany, Ozero** ◎ SW Ukraine
138 H9 **Shahbā'** *anc.* Philippopolis. As Suwaydā', S Syria 32°50′N 36°38′E
Shahbān *see* Ad Dayr
149 P17 **Shāh Bandar** Sind, SE Pakistan 23°59′N 67°54′E
149 P13 **Shāhdād Kot** Sind, SW Pakistan 27°49′N 67°49′E
143 T10 **Shāhdād, Namakzār-e** *salt pan* E Iran
149 Q15 **Shāhdādpur** Sind, SE Pakistan 25°56′N 68°40′E
154 K10 **Shahdol** Madhya Pradesh, C India 23°19′N 81°26′E
161 N7 **Sha He** ≈ C China
Shahe *see* Linze
Shahepu *see* Linze
153 N13 **Shāhganj** Uttar Pradesh, N India 26°03′N 82°41′E
152 C11 **Shāhgarh** Rājasthān, NW India 27°08′N 69°56′E
Sha Hi *see* Orūmīyeh, Daryācheh-ye
Shāhī *see* Qā'emshahr
Shahjahanabad *see* Delhi
152 L11 **Shāhjahānpur** Uttar Pradesh, N India 27°53′N 79°55′E
149 U7 **Shāhpur** Punjab, E Pakistan 32°15′N 72°32′E
Shāhpur *see* Shāhpur Chākar
152 G13 **Shāhpura** Rājasthān, N India 25°38′N 75°01′E
149 Q15 **Shāhpur Chākar** *var.* Shāhpur. Sind, SE Pakistan 26°11′N 68°44′E
148 M5 **Shahrak** Gōwr, C Afghanistan 34°09′N 64°16′E
143 Q11 **Shahr-e Bābak** Kermān, C Iran 30°08′N 55°04′E
143 N8 **Shahr-e Kord** *var.* Shahr Kord. Chahār Maḩall va Bakhtīārī, C Iran 32°20′N 50°52′E
143 O9 **Shahreẕā** *var.* Qomisheh, Qumisheh, Shahriza; *prev.* Qomsheh. Eşfahān, C Iran 32°01′N 51°51′E
147 S10 **Shahrikhon** *Rus.* Shakhrikhan. Andijon Viloyati, E Uzbekistan 40°42′N 72°03′E
147 P11 **Shahriston** *Rus.* Shakhristan. NW Tajikistan 39°45′N 68°47′E
Shahriza *see* Shahreẕā
Shahr-i-Zabul *see* Zābol
Shahr Kord *see* Shahr-e Kord
147 P14 **Shahrtuz** *Rus.* Shaartuz. SW Tajikistan 37°13′N 68°05′E
143 Q4 **Shāhrūd** *prev.* Emāmrūd, Emāmshahr. Semnān, N Iran 36°30′N 55°E
Shahsavār/Shahsawar *see* Tonekābon
Shaikh Ābid *see* Shaykh 'Ābid
Shaikh Fāris *see* Shaykh Fāris
Shaikh Najm *see* Shaykh Najm
138 K5 **Shā'ir, Jabal** ▲ C Syria 34°51′N 37°49′E
154 G10 **Shājāpur** Madhya Pradesh, C India 23°27′N 76°21′E
80 J8 **Shakal, Ras** *headland* NE Sudan 18°04′N 38°34′E
83 G17 **Shakawe** North West, NW Botswana 18°25′S 21°53′E
Shakhdarinskiy Khrebet *see* Shokhdara, Qatorkŭhi
Shakhrikhan *see* Shahrikhon
Shakhrisabz *see* Sharixon
Shakhristan *see* Shahriston
Shakhtërsk *see* Zuhres
145 R10 **Shakhtinsk** Karaganda, C Kazakhstan 49°40′N 72°37′E
126 L11 **Shakhty** Rostovskaya Oblast', SW Russian Federation 47°45′N 40°14′E
127 P2 **Shakhun'ya** Nizhegorodskaya Oblast', W Russian Federation 57°42′N 46°36′E
77 S15 **Shaki** Oyo, W Nigeria 08°37′N 03°25′E
81 J15 **Shakiso** Oromīya, C Ethiopia 05°33′N 38°48′E
29 V9 **Shakopee** Minnesota, N USA 44°48′N 93°31′W
165 R3 **Shakotan-misaki** *headland* Hokkaidō, NE Japan 43°22′N 140°28′E
39 N9 **Shaktoolik** Alaska, USA 64°19′N 161°05′W
81 J14 **Shala Hāyk'** ◎ C Ethiopia
124 M10 **Shalakusha** Arkhangel'skaya Oblast', NW Russian Federation 62°16′N 40°16′E
145 U8 **Shalday** Pavlodar, NE Kazakhstan 51°57′N 78°51′E
127 P16 **Shali** Chechenskaya Respublika, SW Russian Federation 43°03′N 45°55′E
141 W12 **Shalīm** *var.* Shelim. S Oman 18°07′N 55°39′E
Shaliuhe *see* Gangca
144 K12 **Shalkar** *var.* Chelkar. Aktyubinsk, W Kazakhstan 47°50′N 59°29′E
144 F9 **Shalkar, Ozero** *prev.* Chelkar Ozero. ◎ W Kazakhstan
21 V12 **Shallotte** North Carolina, SE USA 33°58′N 78°21′W
25 N5 **Shallowater** Texas, SW USA 33°41′N 102°00′W
124 K11 **Shal'skiy** Respublika Kareliya, NW Russian Federation 61°45′N 36°02′E
160 F9 **Shaluli Shan** ⛰ C China
81 F22 **Shama** ≈ C Tanzania
11 Z11 **Shamattawa** Manitoba, C Canada 55°52′N 92°05′W
12 F8 **Shamattawa** ≈ Ontario, C Canada
Shām, Bādiyat ash *see* Syrian Desert
Shamiya *see* Ash Shāmīyah
141 X8 **Shām, Jabal ash** *var.* Jebel Sham. ▲ NW Oman 23°21′N 57°08′E
Sham, Jebel *see* Shām, Jabal ash
Shamkhor *see* Şämkir
18 G14 **Shamokin** Pennsylvania, NE USA 40°47′N 76°33′W
25 P2 **Shamrock** Texas, SW USA 35°12′N 100°15′W
Shana *see* Kuril'sk
Sha'nabī, Jabal ash *see* Chambi, Jebel
139 Y12 **Shanāwah** Al Başrah, E Iraq 30°57′N 47°25′E
Shancheng *see* Taining
159 T8 **Shandan** *var.* Qingyuan. Gansu, N China 38°50′N 101°08′E
Shandi *see* Shendi
161 Q5 **Shandong** *var.* Lu, Shandong Sheng, Shantung. ◐ *province* E China
161 R4 **Shandong Bandao** *var.* Shantung Peninsula. *peninsula* E China
Shandong Sheng *see* Shandong
139 U8 **Shandrūkh** Diyālá, E Iraq 33°20′N 45°19′E
83 J17 **Shangani** ≈ W Zimbabwe
161 O15 **Shangchuan Dao** *island* S China
Shangchuankou *see* Minhe
163 P12 **Shangdu** Nei Mongol Zizhiqu, N China 41°32′N 113°33′E
161 O11 **Shanggao** *var.* Aoyang. Jiangxi, S China 28°16′N 114°55′E
Shangguan *see* Daixian
161 S8 **Shanghai** *var.* Shang-hai. Shanghai Shi, E China 31°14′N 121°28′E
161 S8 **Shanghai Shi** *var.* Hu, Shanghai. ◐ *municipality* E China
161 P13 **Shanghang** *var.* Linjiang. Fujian, SE China 25°03′N 116°25′E
160 K14 **Shanglin** *var.* Dafeng. Guangxi Zhuangzu Zizhiqu, S China 23°26′N 108°32′E
160 L7 **Shangluo** *prev.* Shangxian, Shangzhou. Shaanxi, C China 33°51′N 109°55′E
83 G15 **Shangombo** Western, W Zambia 16°28′S 22°10′E
Shangpai/Shangpaihe *see* Feixi
161 O6 **Shangqiu** *var.* Zhuji. Henan, C China 34°24′N 115°37′E
161 Q10 **Shangrao** Jiangxi, S China 28°27′N 117°57′E
Shangxian *see* Shangluo
161 S9 **Shangyu** *var.* Baiguan. Zhejiang, SE China 30°03′N 120°52′E
163 X9 **Shangzhi** Heilongjiang, NE China 45°13′N 127°59′E
Shangzhou *see* Shangluo
Shanhe *see* Zhengning
163 W9 **Shanhetun** Heilongjiang, NE China 44°42′N 127°12′E
Shan-hsi *see* Shaanxi, China
Shan-hsi *see* Shanxi, China
159 O6 **Shankou** Xinjiang Uygur Zizhiqu, W China 42°02′N 94°08′E
184 M13 **Shannon** Manawatu-Wanganui, North Island, New Zealand 40°32′S 175°24′E
97 C17 **Shannon** *Ir.* An tSionainn. ≈ W Ireland
97 B19 **Shannon** ✈ W Ireland 52°42′N 08°57′W
167 N6 **Shan Plateau** *plateau* E Burma (Myanmar)
158 M6 **Shanshan** *var.* Piqan. Xinjiang Uygur Zizhiqu, NW China 42°53′N 90°18′E
Shansi *see* Shanxi
167 N5 **Shan State** ◐ *state* E Burma (Myanmar)
Shantar Islands *see* Shantarskiye Ostrova
123 S12 **Shantarskiye Ostrova** *Eng.* Shantar Islands. *island group* E Russian Federation

◆ Country ● Country Capital ◇ Dependent Territory ○ Dependent Territory Capital ◐ Administrative Regions ✈ International Airport ▲ Mountain ⛰ Mountain Range 🌋 Volcano ≈ River ◎ Lake ⊠ Reservoir

161 Q14 **Shantou** *var.* Shan-t'ou, Swatow. Guangdong, S China 23°23′N 116°39′E
Shan-t'ou *see* Shantou
Shantung *see* Shandong
Shantung Peninsula *see* Shandong Bandao
163 O14 **Shanxi** *var.* Jin, Shan-hsi, Shansi, Shanxi Sheng. ◆ *province* C China
161 P6 **Shanxian** *var.* Shan Xian. Shandong, E China 34°51′N 116°09′E
Shan Xian *see* Sanmenxia
Shan Xian *see* Shanxian
Shanxi Sheng *see* Shanxi
160 L7 **Shanyang** Shaanxi, C China 33°35′N 109°48′E
161 N13 **Shanyin** *var.* Daiyue. Shanxi, C China E Asia 39°30′N 112°56′E
161 O13 **Shaoguan** *var.* Shao-kuan, *Cant.* Kukong; *prev.* Ch'u-chiang. Guangdong, S China 24°57′N 113°38′E
Shao-kuan *see* Shaoguan
161 Q11 **Shaowu** Fujian, SE China 27°24′N 117°26′E
161 S9 **Shaoxing** Zhejiang, SE China 30°02′N 120°35′E
160 M12 **Shaoyang** *var.* Tangdukou. Hunan, S China 26°54′N 111°14′E
160 M11 **Shaoyang** *var.* Baoqing, Shao-yang; *prev.* Pao-king. Hunan, S China 27°13′N 111°31′E
Shao-yang *see* Shaoyang
96 K5 **Shapinsay** *island* NE Scotland, United Kingdom
125 S4 **Shapkina** NW Russian Federation
Shāpūr *see* Salmās
158 M4 **Shaqiuhe** Xinjiang Uygur Zizhiqu, W China 45°00′N 88°52′E
139 T2 **Shaqlāwa** *var.* Shaqlāwah. Arbīl, E Iraq 36°24′N 44°21′E
Shaqlāwah *see* Shaqlāwa
138 I8 **Shaqqā** As Suwaydā', S Syria 32°53′N 36°42′E
141 P7 **Shaqrā'** Ar Riyāḍ, C Saudi Arabia 25°11′N 45°08′E
Shaqrā *see* Shuqrah
145 W10 **Shar** *var.* Charsk. Vostochnyy Kazakhstan, E Kazakhstan 49°33′N 81°03′E
149 O6 **Sharan** Dāykundī, SE Afghanistan 33°28′N 66°19′E
149 Q7 **Sharan** *var.* Zareh Sharan. Paktīkā, E Afghanistan 33°08′N 68°47′E
Sharaqpur *see* Sharqpur
145 U8 **Sharbakty** *Kaz.* Sharbaqty; *prev.* Shcherbakty. Pavlodar, E Kazakhstan 52°28′N 78°00′E
Sharbaqty *see* Sharbakty
141 X12 **Sharbatāt** S Oman 17°57′N 56°14′E
Sharbatāt, Ra's *see* Sharbithāt, Ras
141 X12 **Sharbithāt, Ras** *var.* Ra's Sharbatāt. *headland* S Oman 17°55′N 56°30′E
14 K14 **Sharbot Lake** Ontario, SE Canada 44°45′N 76°46′W
145 P17 **Shardara** *var.* Chardara. Yuzhnyy Kazakhstan, S Kazakhstan 41°15′N 68°01′E
Shardara Dalasy *see* Step' Shardara
145 P17 **Shardarinskoye Vodokhranilishche** *prev.* Chardarinskoye Vodokhranilishche. S Kazakhstan
162 F8 **Sharga** Govĭ-Altay, W Mongolia 46°16′N 95°32′E
Sharga *see* Tsagaan-Uul
116 M7 **Sharhorod** Vinnyts'ka Oblast', C Ukraine 48°46′N 28°05′E
Sharhulsan *see* Mandal-Ovoo
165 V3 **Shari** Hokkaidō, NE Japan 43°54′N 144°42′E
Shari *see* Chari
139 T6 **Shārī, Buḩayrat** C Iraq
147 N12 **Sharixon** *Rus.* Shakhrisabz. Qashqadaryo Viloyati, S Uzbekistan 39°01′N 66°45′E
Sharjah *see* Ash Shāriqah
118 K12 **Sharkawshchyna** *var.* Sharkowshchyna, *Pol.* Szarkowszczyzna, *Rus.* Sharkovshchina. Vitsyebskaya Voblasts', NW Belarus 55°27′N 27°28′E
180 G9 **Shark Bay** *bay* Western Australia
141 Y9 **Sharkh** E Oman 21°20′N 59°04′E
Sharkovshchina/Sharkowshchyna *see* Sharkawshchyna
127 U6 **Sharlyk** Orenburgskaya Oblast', W Russian Federation 52°52′N 54°45′E
75 Y9 **Sharm ash Shaykh** *var.* Ofiral, Sharm el Sheikh. E Egypt 27°51′N 34°16′E
Sharm el Sheikh *see* Sharm ash Shaykh
18 B13 **Sharon** Pennsylvania, NE USA 41°12′N 80°28′W
26 H4 **Sharon Springs** Kansas, C USA 38°54′N 101°46′W
31 Q14 **Sharonville** Ohio, N USA 39°16′N 84°24′W
Sharourah *see* Sharūrah
29 O10 **Sharpe, Lake** South Dakota, N USA
Sharqī, Al Jabal ash/Sharqi, Jebel esh *see* Anti-Lebanon
Sharqīyah, Al Minṭaqah ash *see* Ash Sharqīyah
138 I6 **Sharqīyat an Nabk, Jabal** ▲ W Syria
149 W8 **Sharqpur** *var.* Sharaqpur. Punjab, E Pakistan 31°29′N 74°08′E
141 Q13 **Sharūrah** *var.* Sharourah. Najrān, S Saudi Arabia 17°29′N 47°05′E
125 O14 **Shar'ya** Kostromskaya Oblast', NW Russian Federation 58°22′N 45°30′E
145 W15 **Sharyn** *prev.* Charyn. Almaty, SE Kazakhstan 43°48′N 79°22′E
145 V15 **Sharyn** *var.* Charyn. SE Kazakhstan
122 K13 **Sharypovo** Krasnoyarskiy Kray, C Russian Federation 55°33′N 89°12′E
83 J18 **Shashe** Central, NE Botswana 21°25′S 27°28′E
83 J18 **Shashe** *var.* Shashi. Botswana/Zimbabwe
81 J14 **Shashemenē** *var.* Shashemenne, Shashhamana, *It.* Sciasciamana. Oromīya, C Ethiopia 07°16′N 38°38′E
Shashemenne/Shashhamana *see* Shashemenē
Shashi *see* Shashe
Shashi/Sha-shih/Shasi *see* Jingzhou, Hubei
35 N3 **Shasta Lake** California, W USA
35 N2 **Shasta, Mount** ▲ California, W USA 41°24′N 122°11′W
127 O4 **Shatki** Nizhegorodskaya Oblast', W Russian Federation 55°09′N 44°04′E
Shatlyk *see* Şatlyk
Shatra *see* Ash Shaṭrah
119 K17 **Shatsk** Minskaya Voblasts', C Belarus 53°25′N 27°41′E
127 N5 **Shatsk** Ryazanskaya Oblast', W Russian Federation 54°02′N 41°38′E
26 J9 **Shattuck** Oklahoma, C USA 36°16′N 99°52′W
145 P16 **Shauil'dir** *prev.* Shaul'der. Yuzhnyy Kazakhstan, S Kazakhstan 42°45′N 68°21′E
Shaul'der *see* Shauil'dir
11 S17 **Shaunavon** Saskatchewan, S Canada 49°49′N 108°25′W
Shavat *see* Shovot
Shaviyani Atoll *see* North Miladhunmadulu Atoll
158 K4 **Shawan** *var.* Sandaohezi. Xinjiang Uygur Zizhiqu, NW China 44°21′N 85°37′E
14 G12 **Shawanaga** Ontario, S Canada 45°29′N 80°16′W
30 M6 **Shawano** Wisconsin, N USA 44°46′N 88°38′W
30 M6 **Shawano Lake** Wisconsin, N USA
15 P10 **Shawinigan** *prev.* Shawinigan Falls. Québec, SE Canada 46°33′N 72°45′W
Shawinigan Falls *see* Shawinigan
15 P10 **Shawinigan-Sud** Québec, SE Canada 46°30′N 72°43′W
138 J5 **Shawmarīyah, Jabal ash** ▲ C Syria
27 O11 **Shawnee** Oklahoma, C USA 35°20′N 96°55′W
14 K12 **Shawville** Québec, SE Canada 45°37′N 76°31′W
145 Q16 **Shayan** *var.* Chayan. Yuzhnyy Kazakhstan, S Kazakhstan 42°59′N 69°22′E
Shaykh *see* Ash Shakk
139 W9 **Shaykh 'Ābid** *var.* Shaikh Ābid. Wāsiṭ, E Iraq 32°40′N 46°09′E
139 Y10 **Shaykh Fāris** *var.* Shaikh Fāris. Maysān, E Iraq 32°06′N 47°39′E
139 T7 **Shaykh Ḩātim** Baghdād, E Iraq 33°29′N 44°15′E
Shaykh, Jabal ash *see* Hermon, Mount
139 X10 **Shaykh Najm** *var.* Shaikh Najm. Maysān, E Iraq 32°04′N 46°54′E
139 W9 **Shaykh Sa'd** Maysān, E Iraq 32°35′N 46°16′E
147 T14 **Shazud** SE Tajikistan 37°45′N 72°22′E
119 N18 **Shchadryn** *Rus.* Shchedrin. Homyel'skaya Voblasts', SE Belarus 52°53′N 29°33′E
119 H18 **Shchara** SW Belarus
Shchedrin *see* Shchadryn
Shcheglovsk *see* Kemerovo
126 K5 **Shchëkino** Tul'skaya Oblast', W Russian Federation 53°57′N 37°33′E
125 S7 **Shchel'yayur** Respublika Komi, NW Russian Federation 65°19′N 53°27′E
Shcherbakty *see* Sharbakty
126 K7 **Shchigry** Kurskaya Oblast', W Russian Federation 51°53′N 36°49′E
Shchitkovichi *see* Shchytkavichy
117 Q2 **Shchors** Chernihivs'ka Oblast', N Ukraine 51°49′N 31°58′E
117 T8 **Shchors'k** Dnipropetrovs'ka Oblast', E Ukraine 48°20′N 34°07′E
Shchuchin *see* Shchuchyn
145 Q7 **Shchuchinsk** *prev.* Shchuchye. Akmola, N Kazakhstan 52°57′N 70°10′E
Shchuchye *see* Shchuchinsk
119 G16 **Shchuchyn** *Pol.* Szczuczyn Nowogródzki, *Rus.* Shchuchin. Hrodzyenskaya Voblasts', W Belarus 53°36′N 24°45′E
119 K17 **Shchytkavichy** *Rus.* Shchitkovichi. Minskaya Voblasts', C Belarus 53°13′N 27°59′E
122 J13 **Shebalino** Respublika Altay, S Russian Federation 51°16′N 85°41′E
126 J9 **Shebekino** Belgorodskaya Oblast', W Russian Federation 50°25′N 36°55′E
Shebelē Wenz, Wabē *see* Shebeli
81 L14 **Shebeli** *Amh.* Wabē Shebelē Wenz, *It.* Scebeli, *Som.* Webi Shabeelle. Ethiopia/Somalia
113 M20 **Shebenikut, Maja e** ▲ E Albania 41°13′N 20°27′E
Sheberghān *see* Shibirghān
144 F14 **Shebir** Mangistau, SW Kazakhstan 44°52′N 52°01′E
31 N8 **Sheboygan** Wisconsin, N USA 43°46′N 87°44′W
77 X15 **Shebshi Mountains** *var.* Schebschi Mountains. ▲ E Nigeria
Shechem *see* Nablus
Shedadi *see* Ash Shadādah
13 P14 **Shediac** New Brunswick, SE Canada 46°13′N 64°35′W
126 L15 **Shedok** Krasnodarskiy Kray, SW Russian Federation 44°12′N 40°49′E
Sheekh *see* Shiikh
38 M11 **Sheenjek River** Alaska, USA
96 D13 **Sheep Haven** *Ir.* Cuan na gCaorach. *inlet* N Ireland
35 X10 **Sheep Range** ▲ Nevada, W USA
98 M13 **'s-Heerenberg** Gelderland, E Netherlands 51°52′N 06°15′E
97 P22 **Sheerness** SE England, United Kingdom 51°27′N 00°45′E
13 Q15 **Sheet Harbour** Nova Scotia, SE Canada 44°56′N 62°31′W
185 H18 **Sheffield** Canterbury, South Island, New Zealand 43°22′S 172°01′E
97 M18 **Sheffield** N England, United Kingdom 53°23′N 01°30′W
23 O2 **Sheffield** Alabama, S USA 34°46′N 87°42′W
29 V12 **Sheffield** Iowa, C USA 42°53′N 93°13′W
25 N10 **Sheffield** Texas, SW USA 30°42′N 101°49′W
63 H22 **Shehuen, Río** S Argentina
Shekhem *see* Nablus
149 V8 **Shekhūpura** Punjab, NE Pakistan 31°42′N 74°08′E
Sheki *see* Şäki
124 L14 **Sheksna** Vologodskaya Oblast', NW Russian Federation 59°11′N 38°32′E
123 T5 **Shelagskiy, Mys** *headland* NE Russian Federation 70°04′N 170°39′E
27 V3 **Shelbina** Missouri, C USA 39°41′N 92°02′W
13 P16 **Shelburne** Nova Scotia, SE Canada 43°47′N 65°20′W
14 G14 **Shelburne** Ontario, S Canada 44°04′N 80°12′W
33 R7 **Shelby** Montana, NW USA 48°30′N 111°52′W
21 Q10 **Shelby** North Carolina, SE USA 35°15′N 81°34′W
31 S12 **Shelby** Ohio, N USA 40°52′N 82°39′W
30 L14 **Shelbyville** Illinois, N USA 39°24′N 88°47′W
31 P14 **Shelbyville** Indiana, N USA 39°31′N 85°46′W
20 L5 **Shelbyville** Kentucky, S USA 38°13′N 85°12′W
27 V2 **Shelbyville** Missouri, C USA 39°48′N 92°01′W
20 J10 **Shelbyville** Tennessee, S USA 35°29′N 86°30′W
25 X8 **Shelbyville** Texas, SW USA 31°42′N 94°03′W
30 L14 **Shelbyville, Lake** Illinois, N USA
29 S12 **Sheldon** Iowa, C USA 43°10′N 95°51′W
38 M11 **Sheldons Point** Alaska, USA 62°31′N 165°03′W
145 V15 **Shelek** *prev.* Chilik. Almaty, SE Kazakhstan 43°35′N 78°12′E
145 V15 **Shelek** *prev.* Chilik. SE Kazakhstan
Shelekhov Gulf *see* Shelikhova, Zaliv
123 U9 **Shelikhova, Zaliv** *Eng.* Shelekhov Gulf. *gulf* E Russian Federation
39 P14 **Shelikof Strait** *strait* Alaska, USA
Shelim *see* Shalīm
11 T14 **Shellbrook** Saskatchewan, S Canada 53°14′N 106°24′W
28 L3 **Shell Creek** North Dakota, N USA
Shellif *see* Chelif, Oued
22 I10 **Shell Keys** *island group* Louisiana, S USA
30 I4 **Shell Lake** Wisconsin, N USA 45°44′N 91°56′W
29 W12 **Shell Rock** Iowa, C USA 42°42′N 92°34′W
185 C26 **Shelter Point** *headland* Stewart Island, New Zealand 47°04′S 168°13′E
18 L13 **Shelton** Connecticut, NE USA 41°19′N 73°06′W
32 G8 **Shelton** Washington, NW USA 47°13′N 123°06′W
Shemakha *see* Şamaxı
145 W9 **Shemonaikha** Vostochnyy Kazakhstan, E Kazakhstan 50°38′N 81°55′E
127 Q4 **Shemursha** Chuvashskaya Respublika, W Russian Federation 54°57′N 47°27′E
38 D16 **Shemya Island** *island* Aleutian Islands, Alaska, USA
29 T16 **Shenandoah** Iowa, C USA 40°46′N 95°23′W
21 U4 **Shenandoah** Virginia, NE USA 38°26′N 78°34′W
21 U4 **Shenandoah Mountains** *ridge* West Virginia, NE USA
21 V3 **Shenandoah River** West Virginia, NE USA
77 W15 **Shendam** Plateau, C Nigeria 08°52′N 09°30′E
80 G8 **Shendi** *var.* Shandī. River Nile, NE Sudan 16°41′N 33°22′E
76 I15 **Shenge** SW Sierra Leone 07°54′N 12°54′W
146 L10 **Shengeldi** *Rus.* Chingildi. Navoiy Viloyati, N Uzbekistan 40°59′N 64°13′E
145 U15 **Shengel'dy** Almaty, SE Kazakhstan 44°04′N 77°31′E
113 K18 **Shëngjin** *var.* Shëngjini. Lezhë, NW Albania 41°49′N 19°34′E
Shëngjini *see* Shëngjin
Shengking *see* Liaoning
Sheng Xian/Shengxian *see* Shengzhou
161 S9 **Shengzhou** *var.* Shengxian, Sheng Xian. Zhejiang, SE China 29°36′N 120°42′E
Shenking *see* Liaoning
125 N11 **Shenkursk** Arkhangel'skaya Oblast', NW Russian Federation 62°10′N 42°58′E
160 L3 **Shenmu** Shaanxi, C China 38°49′N 110°27′E
113 L19 **Shën Noj i Madh** ▲ C Albania 41°23′N 20°07′E
160 L8 **Shennong Ding** ▲ C China 31°24′N 110°16′E
Shenshi/Shensi *see* Shaanxi
163 V12 **Shenyang** *Chin.* Shen-yang, *Eng.* Moukden, Mukden; *prev.* Fengtien. *province capital* Liaoning, NE China 41°50′N 123°26′E
Shen-yang *see* Shenyang
161 O15 **Shenzhen** Guangdong, S China 22°39′N 114°02′E
154 G8 **Sheopur** Madhya Pradesh, C India 25°41′N 76°42′E
116 L5 **Shepetivka** *Rus.* Shepetovka. Khmel'nyts'ka Oblast', NW Ukraine 50°12′N 27°01′E
Shepetovka *see* Shepetivka
25 W10 **Shepherd** Texas, SW USA 30°30′N 95°00′W
187 R14 **Shepherd Islands** *island group* C Vanuatu
20 K5 **Shepherdsville** Kentucky, S USA 38°00′N 85°42′W
183 O11 **Shepparton** Victoria, SE Australia 36°25′S 145°26′E
97 P22 **Sheppey, Isle of** *island* SE England, United Kingdom
Sherabad *see* Sherobod
9 O4 **Sherard, Cape** *headland* Nunavut, N Canada 74°36′N 80°10′W
97 L23 **Sherborne** S England, United Kingdom 50°58′N 02°30′W
76 H16 **Sherbro Island** *island* SW Sierra Leone
15 Q12 **Sherbrooke** Québec, SE Canada 45°23′N 71°55′W
29 T11 **Sherburn** Minnesota, N USA 43°39′N 94°43′W
78 H6 **Sherda** Borkou-Ennedi-Tibesti, N Chad 20°04′N 16°48′E
80 G7 **Shereik** River Nile, N Sudan 18°44′N 33°37′E
126 K3 **Sheremet'yevo** ✈ (Moskva) Moskovskaya Oblast', W Russian Federation 56°05′N 37°10′E
153 P14 **Sherghāti** Bihār, N India 24°35′N 84°51′E
27 U12 **Sheridan** Arkansas, C USA 34°18′N 92°22′W
33 W12 **Sheridan** Wyoming, C USA 44°47′N 106°59′W
182 G8 **Sheringa** South Australia 33°51′S 135°13′E
25 U5 **Sherman** Texas, SW USA 33°39′N 96°35′W
194 J10 **Sherman Island** *island* Antarctica
19 S4 **Sherman Mills** Maine, NE USA 45°51′N 68°23′W
29 O15 **Sherman Reservoir** Nebraska, C USA
147 N14 **Sherobod** *Rus.* Sherabad. Surkhondaryo Viloyati, S Uzbekistan 37°43′N 66°59′E
147 O13 **Sherobod** *Rus.* Sherabad. S Uzbekistan
153 T14 **Sherpur** Dhaka, N Bangladesh 25°00′N 90°01′E
37 T4 **Sherrelwood** Colorado, C USA 39°49′N 105°00′W
99 J14 **'s-Hertogenbosch** *Fr.* Bois-le-Duc, *Ger.* Herzogenbusch. Noord-Brabant, S Netherlands 51°41′N 05°19′E
28 M2 **Sherwood** North Dakota, N USA 48°55′N 101°36′W
11 Q14 **Sherwood Park** Alberta, SW Canada 53°34′N 113°04′W
56 F13 **Sheshea, Río** E Peru
143 T5 **Sheshtamad** Khorāsān-Razavī, NE Iran 36°03′N 57°45′E
29 S10 **Shetek, Lake** Minnesota, N USA
96 M2 **Shetland Islands** *island group* NE Scotland, United Kingdom
144 F14 **Shetpe** Mangistau, SW Kazakhstan 44°06′N 52°03′E
154 C11 **Shetrunji** W India
Shevchenko *see* Aktau
117 W5 **Shevchenkove** Kharkivs'ka Oblast', E Ukraine 49°40′N 37°13′E
81 H14 **Shewa Gīmīra** Southern Nationalities, S Ethiopia 07°12′N 35°49′E
161 Q9 **Shexian** *var.* Huicheng, She Xian. Anhui, E China 29°53′N 118°27′E
She Xian *see* Shexian
161 R6 **Sheyang** *prev.* Hede. Jiangsu, E China 33°49′N 120°13′E
29 O4 **Sheyenne** North Dakota, N USA 47°49′N 99°08′W
29 P4 **Sheyenne River** North Dakota, N USA
96 G7 **Shiant Islands** *island group* NW Scotland, United Kingdom
123 U12 **Shiashkotan, Ostrov** *island* Kuril'skiye Ostrova, SE Russian Federation
31 R9 **Shiawassee River** Michigan, N USA
141 R14 **Shibām** C Yemen 15°49′N 48°24′E
Shibarghān *see* Shibirghān
165 O10 **Shibata** *var.* Sibata. Niigata, Honshū, C Japan 37°57′N 139°20′E
Shiberghan/Shiberghān *see* Shibirghān
Shibh Jazirat Sīnā' *see* Sinai
75 W8 **Shibīn al Kawm** *var.* Shibîn el Kôm. N Egypt 30°33′N 31°00′E
Shibîn el Kôm *see* Shibīn al Kawm
149 N2 **Shibirghān** *var.* Shibarghān, Shiberghan, Shiberghān; *prev.* Sheberghān. Jowzjān, N Afghanistan 36°41′N 65°45′E
143 O13 **Shīb, Kūh-e** ▲ S Iran
12 D8 **Shibogama Lake** Ontario, C Canada
Shibotsu-jima *see* Zelënyy, Ostrov
164 B16 **Shibushi** Kagoshima, Kyūshū, SW Japan 31°27′N 131°05′E
189 U13 **Shichiyo Islands** *island group* Chuuk, C Micronesia
Shickshock Mountains *see* Chic-Chocs, Monts
shiderti *see* Shiderty
Shiderti *see* Shiderty
145 S8 **Shiderty** *prev.* Shiderti. Pavlodar, NE Kazakhstan 51°40′N 74°50′E
145 S9 **Shiderty** *prev.* Shiderti. N Kazakhstan
96 G10 **Shiel, Loch** N Scotland, United Kingdom
164 J13 **Shiga** *off.* Shiga-ken, *var.* Siga. ◆ *prefecture* Honshū, SW Japan
Shiga-ken *see* Shiga
Shigatse *see* Xigazê
141 U13 **Shiḩan** *oasis* NE Yemen
Shih-chia-chuang/Shihmen *see* Shijiazhuang
158 K4 **Shihezi** Xinjiang Uygur Zizhiqu, NW China 44°21′N 85°59′E
Shiichi *see* Shyichy
80 N12 **Shiikh** *prev.* Sheekh. Togdheer, N Somalia 10°01′N 45°21′E
113 K19 **Shijak** *var.* Shijaku. Durrës, W Albania 41°21′N 19°34′E
Shijaku *see* Shijak
161 O4 **Shijiazhuang** *var.* Shih-chia-chuang; *prev.* Shihmen. *province capital* Hebei, E China 38°04′N 114°28′E
165 R5 **Shikabe** Hokkaidō, NE Japan 42°03′N 140°45′E
149 Q13 **Shikārpur** Sind, S Pakistan 27°59′N 68°39′E
127 Q7 **Shikhany** Saratovskaya Oblast', W Russian Federation 52°07′N 47°13′E
189 V12 **Shiki Islands** *island group* Chuuk, C Micronesia
164 G14 **Shikoku** *var.* Sikoku. *island* SW Japan
192 H5 **Shikoku Basin** *var.* Sikoku Basin. *undersea feature* N Philippine Sea 28°00′N 137°00′E
164 G14 **Shikoku-sanchi** ▲ Shikoku, SW Japan
165 X4 **Shikotan, Ostrov** *Jap.* Shikotan-tō. *island* NE Russian Federation
Shikotan-tō *see* Shikotan, Ostrov
165 R4 **Shikotsu-ko** *var.* Sikotu Ko. Hokkaidō, NE Japan
81 N15 **Shilabo** Sumalē, E Ethiopia 06°05′N 44°48′E
127 X7 **Shil'da** Orenburgskaya Oblast', W Russian Federation 51°46′N 59°48′E
139 V3 **Shilēr, Āw-e** E Iraq
153 S12 **Shiliguri** *prev.* Siliguri. West Bengal, NE India 26°46′N 88°24′E
Shiliu *see* Changjiang
129 V7 **Shilka** S Russian Federation
18 H15 **Shillington** Pennsylvania, NE USA 40°18′N 75°57′W
153 V13 **Shillong** *state capital* Meghālaya, NE India 25°37′N 91°54′E
126 M5 **Shilovo** Ryazanskaya Oblast', W Russian Federation 54°18′N 40°53′E
164 C14 **Shimabara** *var.* Simabara. Nagasaki, Kyūshū, SW Japan 32°48′N 130°20′E
164 C14 **Shimabara-wan** *bay* SW Japan
164 F12 **Shimane** *off.* Shimane-ken, *var.* Simane. ◆ *prefecture* Honshū, SW Japan
164 G11 **Shimane-hantō** *peninsula* Honshū, SW Japan
Shimane-ken *see* Shimane
123 Q13 **Shimanovsk** Amurskaya Oblast', SE Russian Federation 52°00′N 127°36′E
Shimanto *see* Nakamura
Shimbir Berris *see* Shimbiris
80 O12 **Shimbiris** *var.* Shimbir Berris. ▲ N Somalia 10°43′N 47°10′E
165 T4 **Shimizu** Hokkaidō, NE Japan 42°58′N 142°54′E
164 M14 **Shimizu** *var.* Simizu. Shizuoka, Honshū, S Japan 35°01′N 138°29′E
152 I8 **Shimla** *prev.* Simla. *state capital* Himāchal Pradesh, N India 31°07′N 77°09′E
165 N14 **Shimoda** *var.* Simoda. Shizuoka, Honshū, S Japan 34°40′N 138°55′E
165 O13 **Shimodate** *var.* Simodate. Ibaraki, Honshū, S Japan 36°20′N 140°00′E
155 F18 **Shimoga** Karnātaka, W India 13°56′N 75°31′E
164 C15 **Shimo-jima** *island* SW Japan
164 B15 **Shimo-Koshiki-jima** *island* SW Japan
81 J21 **Shimoni** Coast, S Kenya 04°40′S 39°22′E
164 D13 **Shimonoseki** *var.* Simonoseki, *hist.* Akamagaseki, Bakan. Yamaguchi, Honshū, SW Japan 33°57′N 130°54′E
124 G14 **Shimsk** Novgorodskaya Oblast', NW Russian Federation 58°12′N 30°43′E
141 W7 **Shināş** N Oman 24°45′N 56°24′E
148 J6 **Shīndand** *prev.* Shīndand. Herāt, W Afghanistan 33°19′N 62°09′E
Shīndand *see* Shīndand
Shinei *see* Xinying
162 H10 **Shinejinst** *var.* Dzalaa. Bayanhongor, C Mongolia 44°29′N 99°19′E
25 T12 **Shiner** Texas, SW USA 29°25′N 97°10′W
167 N1 **Shingbwiyang** Kachin State, N Burma (Myanmar) 26°40′N 96°14′E
Shingozha *see* Shynkozha
164 J15 **Shingū** *var.* Singû. Wakayama, Honshū, SW Japan 33°41′N 135°57′E
14 F8 **Shining Tree** Ontario, S Canada 47°36′N 81°12′W
165 P9 **Shinjō** *var.* Sinzyô. Yamagata, Honshū, C Japan 38°47′N 140°17′E
96 I7 **Shin, Loch** N Scotland, United Kingdom
21 S3 **Shinnston** West Virginia, NE USA 39°22′N 80°19′W
138 I6 **Shinshār** *Fr.* Chinnchâr. Ḩimş, W Syria 34°36′N 36°45′E
Shinshū *see* Jinju
165 T4 **Shintoku** Hokkaidō, NE Japan 43°03′N 142°50′E
81 G20 **Shinyanga** Shinyanga, NW Tanzania 03°40′S 33°25′E
81 G20 **Shinyanga** ◆ *region* N Tanzania
165 Q10 **Shiogama** *var.* Siogama. Miyagi, Honshū, C Japan 38°19′N 141°00′E
164 M12 **Shiojiri** *var.* Sioziri. Nagano, Honshū, S Japan 36°08′N 137°58′E
164 I15 **Shiono-misaki** *headland* Honshū, SW Japan 33°25′N 135°45′E
165 Q12 **Shioya-zaki** *headland* Honshū, C Japan 37°00′N 140°57′E
114 J9 **Shipchenski Prokhod** *pass* C Bulgaria
160 G14 **Shiping** Yunnan, SW China 23°45′N 102°23′E
13 P13 **Shippagan** *var.* Shippegan. New Brunswick, SE Canada 47°45′N 64°44′W
Shippegan *see* Shippagan
18 F15 **Shippensburg** Pennsylvania, NE USA 40°03′N 77°31′W
37 P9 **Shiprock** New Mexico, SW USA 36°47′N 108°41′W
37 O9 **Ship Rock** ▲ New Mexico, SW USA 36°41′N 108°50′W
15 R6 **Shipshaw** Québec, SE Canada
123 V10 **Shipunskiy, Mys** *headland* E Russian Federation 53°04′N 159°57′E
160 K7 **Shiquan** Shaanxi, C China 33°05′N 108°15′E
Shiquanhe *see* Gar
122 K13 **Shira** Respublika Khakasiya, S Russian Federation 54°35′N 89°58′E
Shirajganj Ghat *see* Sirajganj
165 P12 **Shirakawa** *var.* Sirakawa. Fukushima, Honshū, C Japan 37°07′N 140°11′E
164 M13 **Shirane-san** ▲ Honshū, S Japan 35°39′N 138°13′E
165 U14 **Shiranuka** Hokkaidō, NE Japan 42°57′N 144°01′E
195 N12 **Shirase Coast** *physical region* Antarctica
165 U3 **Shirataki** Hokkaidō, NE Japan 43°55′N 143°14′E
143 O11 **Shīrāz** *var.* Shīrāz. Fārs, S Iran 29°38′N 52°34′E
83 N15 **Shire** *var.* Chire. Malawi/Mozambique
Shiree *see* Tsagaanhayrhan
Shireet *see* Bayandelger
165 W3 **Shiretoko-hantō** *headland* Hokkaidō, NE Japan 44°06′N 145°07′E
165 W3 **Shiretoko-misaki** *headland* Hokkaidō, NE Japan 44°20′N 145°19′E
127 N5 **Shiringushi** Respublika Mordoviya, W Russian Federation 53°50′N 42°49′E
148 M3 **Shīrīn Tagāb** Fāryāb, N Afghanistan 36°49′N 65°01′E
149 N2 **Shīrīn Tagāb** N Afghanistan
165 R6 **Shiriya-zaki** *headland* Honshū, C Japan 41°24′N 141°27′E
144 I12 **Shirkala, Gryada** *plain* W Kazakhstan
152 F11 **Shir Kolāyat** *var.* Kolāyat. Rājasthān, NW India 27°56′N 73°02′E
165 P10 **Shiroishi** *var.* Siroisi. Miyagi, Honshū, C Japan 38°00′N 140°38′E
Shirokoye *see* Shyroke
165 O10 **Shirone** *var.* Sirone. Niigata, Honshū, C Japan 37°46′N 139°00′E
164 L12 **Shirotori** Gifu, Honshū, SW Japan 35°53′N 136°52′E
197 T1 **Shirshov Ridge** *undersea feature* W Bering Sea
Shirshütür/Shirshyutyur, Peski *see* Şirşütür Gumy
143 T3 **Shīrvān** *var.* Shirwān. Khorāsān, NE Iran 37°25′N 57°55′E
Shirwa, Lake *see* Chilwa, Lake
Shirwān *see* Shīrvān
159 N5 **Shisanjianfang** Xinjiang Uygur Zizhiqu, W China 43°10′N 91°15′E
38 M16 **Shishaldin Volcano** ▲ Unimak Island, Alaska, USA 54°45′N 163°58′W
Shishchitsy *see* Shyshchytsy
83 G16 **Shishikola** North West, N Botswana 18°09′S 23°08′E
38 M8 **Shishmaref** Alaska, USA 66°15′N 166°04′W
Shisur *see* Ash Shişar
164 L13 **Shitara** Aichi, Honshū, SW Japan 35°06′N 137°33′E
152 D12 **Shiv** Rājasthān, NW India 26°11′N 71°14′E
Shivāji Sāgar *see* Konya Reservoir
154 H8 **Shivpuri** Madhya Pradesh, C India 25°28′N 77°41′E
36 J9 **Shivwits Plateau** *plain* Arizona, SW USA
Shiwalik Range *see* Siwalik Range
160 M8 **Shiyan** Hubei, C China 32°31′N 110°45′E
145 O15 **Shiyeli** *prev.* Chiili. Kzylorda, S Kazakhstan 44°13′N 66°46′E
Shizilu *see* Junan
160 H13 **Shizong** *var.* Danfeng. Yunnan, SW China 24°53′N 104′E
165 R10 **Shizugawa** Miyagi, Honshū, NE Japan 38°40′N 141°26′E
165 T5 **Shizunai** Hokkaidō, NE Japan 42°20′N 142°24′E
165 M14 **Shizuoka** *var.* Sizuoka. Shizuoka, Honshū, S Japan 34°59′N 138°20′E
164 M13 **Shizuoka** *off.* Shizuoka-ken, *var.* Sizuoka. ◆ *prefecture* Honshū, S Japan
Shizuoka-ken *see* Shizuoka
Shklov *see* Shklow
119 N15 **Shklow** *Rus.* Shklov. Mahilyowskaya Voblasts', E Belarus 54°13′N 30°18′E
113 K18 **Shkodër** *var.* Shkodra, *It.* Scutari, *SCr.* Skadar. Shkodër, NW Albania 42°03′N 19°31′E
113 K17 **Shkodër** ◆ *district* NW Albania
Shkodra *see* Shkodër
Shkodrës, Liqeni i *see* Scutari, Lake
113 L20 **Shkumbinit, Lumi i** *var.* Shkumbî, Shkumbin. C Albania
Shkumbî/Shkumbin *see* Shkumbinit, Lumi i
Shligigh, Cuan *see* Sligo Bay
122 L4 **Shmidta, Ostrov** *island* Severnaya Zemlya, N Russian Federation
183 S10 **Shoalhaven River** New South Wales, SE Australia
11 W16 **Shoal Lake** Manitoba, S Canada 50°28′N 100°36′W
31 O15 **Shoals** Indiana, N USA 38°40′N 86°47′W
164 I13 **Shōdo-shima** *island* SW Japan
Shōka *see* Zhanghua
122 M5 **Shokal'skogo, Proliv** *strait* N Russian Federation
147 T14 **Shokhdara, Qatorkŭhi** *Rus.* Shakhdarinskiy Khrebet. ▲ SE Tajikistan
145 T15 **Shokpar** *Kaz.* Shoqpar; *prev.* Chokpar. Zhambyl, S Kazakhstan 43°49′N 74°25′E
145 P15 **Sholakkorgan** *var.* Chulakkurgan. Yuzhnyy Kazakhstan, S Kazakhstan 43°45′N 69°10′E
145 N9 **Sholaksay** Kostanay, N Kazakhstan 51°45′N 64°45′E
Sholāpur *see* Solāpur
Sholdaneshty *see* Şoldăneşti
145 W15 **Shonzhy** *prev.* Chundzha. Almaty, SE Kazakhstan 43°32′N 79°28′E
Shoqpar *see* Shokpar
155 G21 **Shoranūr** Kerala, SW India 10°53′N 76°06′E
155 G16 **Shorāpur** Karnātaka, C India 16°34′N 76°48′E
147 O14 **Sho'rchi** *Rus.* Shurchi. Surkhondaryo Viloyati, S Uzbekistan 37°58′N 67°40′E
30 M11 **Shorewood** Illinois, N USA 41°31′N 88°12′W
Shorkazakhly, Solonchak *see* Kazakhlyshor, Solonchak
145 Q9 **Shortandy** Akmola, C Kazakhstan 51°45′N 71°01′E
149 O2 **Shōr Tappeh** *var.* Shortepa, Shor Tepe; *prev.* Shūr Tappeh. Balkh, N Afghanistan 37°22′N 66°49′E
Shortepa/Shor Tepe *see* Shōr Tappeh
186 J7 **Shortland Island** *var.* Alu. *island* Shortland Islands, NW Solomon Islands
Shosambetsu *see* Shosanbetsu
165 S2 **Shosanbetsu** *var.* Shosambetsu. Hokkaidō, NE Japan 44°31′N 141°47′E
33 O15 **Shoshone** Idaho, NW USA 42°56′N 114°24′W
35 T6 **Shoshone Mountains** ▲ Nevada, W USA
33 U12 **Shoshone River** Wyoming, C USA
83 I19 **Shoshong** Central, SE Botswana 23°02′S 26°31′E
33 V14 **Shoshoni** Wyoming, C USA 43°13′N 108°06′W
Shōshū *see* Sangju
117 S2 **Shostka** Sums'ka Oblast', NE Ukraine 51°52′N 33°30′E
185 C21 **Shotover** South Island, New Zealand
146 H9 **Shovot** *Rus.* Shavat. Xorazm Viloyati, W Uzbekistan 41°41′N 60°13′E
37 N12 **Show Low** Arizona, SW USA 34°15′N 110°01′W
Show Me State *see* Missouri
125 O4 **Shoyna** Nenetskiy Avtonomnyy Okrug, NW Russian Federation 67°50′N 44°09′E
124 M11 **Shozhma** Arkhangel'skaya Oblast', NW Russian Federation 61°57′N 40°10′E
117 Q7 **Shpola** Cherkas'ka Oblast', N Ukraine 49°00′N 31°27′E
Shqipëria/Shqipërisë, Republika e *see* Albania
22 G5 **Shreveport** Louisiana, S USA 32°32′N 93°45′W
97 K19 **Shrewsbury** *hist.* Scrobesbyrig'. W England, United Kingdom 52°43′N 02°45′W
152 D11 **Shri Mohangarh** *prev.* Sri Mohangorh. Rājasthān, NW India 27°17′N 71°18′E
153 S16 **Shrīrāmpur** *prev.* Serampore, Serampur. West Bengal, NE India 22°44′N 88°20′E
97 K19 **Shropshire** *cultural region* W England, United Kingdom
113 N17 **Shtime** *Serb.* Štimlje. C Kosovo 42°27′N 21°03′E
145 S16 **Shu** *Kaz.* Shū. Zhambyl, SE Kazakhstan 43°34′N 73°41′E
129 Q7 **Shu** *Kaz.* Shū; *prev.* Chu. Kazakhstan/Kyrgyzstan
160 G13 **Shuangbai** *var.* Tuodian. Yunnan, SW China 24°45′N 101°38′E
163 W9 **Shuangcheng** Heilongjiang, NE China 45°20′N 126°21′E
Shuangcheng *see* Zherong
160 E14 **Shuangjiang** *var.* Weiyuan. Yunnan, SW China 23°28′N 99°43′E
Shuangjiang *see* Jiangkou
Shuangjiang *see* Tongdao
163 U10 **Shuangliao** *var.* Zhengjiatun. Jilin, NE China 43°31′N 123°32′E
Shuang-liao *see* Liaoyuan
Shuangshipu *see* Fengxian
163 Y7 **Shuangyashan** *var.* Shuang-ya-shan. Heilongjiang, NE China 46°37′N 131°10′E
Shuang-ya-shan *see* Shuangyashan
Shu'aymiah *see* Shu'aymīyah
141 W12 **Shu'aymīyah** *var.* Shu'aymiah. S Oman 17°55′N 55°39′E
Shubarkuduk *see* Shubarkudyk
144 I10 **Shubarkudyk** *prev.* Shubarkuduk, *Kaz.* Shubarqudyq. Aktyubinsk, W Kazakhstan 49°09′N 56°31′E
Shubarqudyq *see* Shubarkudyk
145 N12 **Shubar-Tengiz, Ozero** C Kazakhstan
39 S5 **Shublik Mountains** ▲ Alaska, USA
Shubrā al Khaymah *see* Shubrâ el Kheima
121 U13 **Shubrâ el Kheima** *var.* Shubrā al Khaymah. N Egypt 30°06′N 31°15′E
158 E8 **Shufu** *var.* Tuokezhake. Xinjiang Uygur Zizhiqu, NW China 39°18′N 75°43′E
147 S14 **Shughnon, Qatorkŭhi** *Rus.* Shugnanskiy Khrebet. ▲ SE Tajikistan
Shugnanskiy Khrebet *see* Shughnon, Qatorkŭhi
161 Q6 **Shu He** E China
Shuicheng *see* Lupanshui
Shuiding *see* Huocheng
Shuidong *see* Dianbai
Shuiji *see* Laixi
Shū-Ile Taūlary *see* Gory Shu-Ile
Shuilocheng *see* Zhuanglang
Shuiluo *see* Zhuanglang
149 T10 **Shujāābād** Punjab, E Pakistan 29°53′N 71°23′E
Shū, Kazakhstan *see* Shu
Shū, Kazakhstan/Kyrgyzstan *see* Shu
163 W9 **Shulan** Jilin, NE China 44°28′N 126°57′E
158 E8 **Shule** Xinjiang Uygur Zizhiqu, NW China 39°19′N 76°06′E
Shuleh *see* Shule He
159 Q8 **Shule He** *var.* Shuleh, Sulo. C China
30 K9 **Shullsburg** Wisconsin, N USA 42°37′N 90°12′W
Shulu *see* Xinji
39 N16 **Shumagin Islands** *island group* Alaska, USA
146 G7 **Shumanay** Qoraqalpog'iston Respublikasi, W Uzbekistan 42°42′N 58°56′E
114 M8 **Shumen** Shumen, NE Bulgaria 43°17′N 26°57′E
114 M8 **Shumen** ◆ *province* NE Bulgaria

◆ Country
● Country Capital
◇ Dependent Territory
○ Dependent Territory Capital
◆ Administrative Regions
✈ International Airport
▲ Mountain
▲ Mountain Range
Volcano
River
Lake
Reservoir

127 P4 **Shumerlya** Chuvashskaya Respublika, W Russian Federation 55°31′N 46°24′E
122 G11 **Shumikha** Kurganskaya Oblast', C Russian Federation 55°12′N 63°09′E
118 M12 **Shumilina** *Rus.* Shumilino. Vitsyebskaya Voblasts', NE Belarus 55°18′N 29°37′E
Shumilino *see* Shumilina
123 V11 **Shumshu, Ostrov** *island* SE Russian Federation
116 K5 **Shums'k** Ternopil's'ka Oblast', W Ukraine 50°06′N 26°04′E
Shūnan *see* Tokuyama
39 O7 **Shungnak** Alaska, USA 66°53′N 157°08′W
Shunsen *see* Chuncheon
Shuoxian *see* Shuozhou
161 N3 **Shuozhou** *var.* Shuoxian. Shanxi, C China 39°20′N 112°25′E
141 P16 **Shuqrah** *var.* Shaqrā. SW Yemen 13°26′N 45°44′E
Shurab *see* Shŭrob
Shurchi *see* Sho'rchi
147 R11 **Shŭrob** *Rus.* Shurab. NW Tajikistan 40°02′N 70°31′E
143 T10 **Shūr, Rūd-e** ≋ E Iran
Shūr Tappeh *see* Shōr Tappeh
83 K17 **Shurugwi** *prev.* Selukwe. Midlands, C Zimbabwe 19°40′S 30°00′E
142 L8 **Shūsh** *anc.* Susa, *Bibl.* Shushan. Khūzestān, SW Iran 32°12′N 48°20′E
Shushan *see* Shūsh
142 L9 **Shūshtar** *var.* Shustar, Shushter. Khūzestān, SW Iran 32°03′N 48°51′E
Shushter/Shustar *see* Shūshtar
141 T9 **Shuṭfah, Qalamat** *well* E Saudi Arabia
139 V9 **Shuwayjah, Hawr ash** *var.* Hawr as Suwayqiyah. ◎ E Iraq
124 M16 **Shuya** Ivanovskaya Oblast', W Russian Federation 56°51′N 41°24′E
39 Q14 **Shuyak Island** *island* Alaska, USA
166 M4 **Shwebo** Sagaing, C Burma (Myanmar) 22°35′N 95°42′E
166 L7 **Shwedaung** Bago, W Burma (Myanmar) 18°44′N 95°12′E
166 M7 **Shwegyin** Bago, SW Burma (Myanmar) 17°56′N 96°59′E
167 N4 **Shweli** *Chin.* Longchuan Jiang. ≋ Burma (Myanmar)/China
166 M6 **Shwemyo** Mandalay, C Burma (Myanmar) 20°04′N 96°13′E
145 S14 **Shyganak** *var.* Čiganak, Chiganak, *Kaz.* Shyghanaq. Zhambyl, SE Kazakhstan 45°10′N 73°55′E
Shyghanaq *see* Shyganak
Shyghys Qazagastan Oblysy *see* Vostochnyy Kazakhstan
Shyghys Qongyrat *see* Shygys Konyrat
145 T12 **Shygys Konyrat** , *Kaz.* Shyghys Qongyrat. Karaganda, C Kazakhstan 47°01′N 75°05′E
119 M19 **Shyichy** *Rus.* Shiichi. Homyel'skaya Voblasts', SE Belarus 52°15′N 29°14′E
145 Q17 **Shymkent** *prev.* Chimkent. Yuzhnyy Kazakhstan, S Kazakhstan 42°19′N 69°36′E
144 H9 **Shyngghyrlau** *prev.* Chingirlau. Zapadnyy Kazakhstan, W Kazakhstan 51°10′N 53°44′E
144 G9 **Shyngyrlau** *prev.* Utva. ≋ NW Kazakhstan
145 W11 **Shynkozha** *prev.* Shingozha. Vostochnyy Kazakhstan, E Kazakhstan 47°46′N 80°38′E
152 J5 **Shyok** Jammu and Kashmir, NW India 34°13′N 78°12′E
117 S9 **Shyroke** *Rus.* Shirokoye. Dnipropetrovs'ka Oblast', E Ukraine 47°41′N 33°16′E
117 O9 **Shyryayeve** Odes'ka Oblast', SW Ukraine 47°21′N 30°11′E
117 S5 **Shyshaky** Poltavs'ka Oblast', C Ukraine 49°54′N 34°00′E
119 K17 **Shyshchytsy** *Rus.* Shishchitsy. Minskaya Voblasts', C Belarus 53°13′N 27°33′E
149 Y3 **Siachen Muztāgh** ▲▲ NE Pakistan
Siadehan *see* Tākestān
148 M13 **Siāhān Range** ▲▲ W Pakistan
142 I1 **Sīāh Chashmeh** *var.* Chālderān. Āzarbāyjān-e Gharbī, N Iran 39°02′N 44°22′E
149 W7 **Siālkot** Punjab, NE Pakistan 32°29′N 74°35′E
186 E7 **Sialum** Morobe, C Papua New Guinea 06°02′S 147°37′E
Siam *see* Thailand
Siam, Gulf of *see* Thailand, Gulf of
Sian *see* Xi'an
Siang *see* Brahmaputra
Siangtan *see* Xiangtan
169 N8 **Siantan, Pulau** *island* Kepulauan Anambas, W Indonesia
54 H11 **Siare, Río** ≋ C Colombia
171 R6 **Siargao Island** *island* S Philippines
186 F72 **Siassi** Umboi Island, C Papua New Guinea 05°34′S 147°50′E
115 D14 **Siátista** Dytikí Makedonía, N Greece 40°16′N 21°34′E
166 K4 **Siatlai** Chin State, W Burma (Myanmar) 22°05′N 93°36′E
171 P6 **Siaton** Negros, C Philippines 09°03′N 123°03′E
171 P6 **Siaton Point** *headland* Negros, C Philippines 09°03′N 123°00′E
118 F11 **Šiauliai** *Ger.* Schaulen. Šiauliai, N Lithuania 55°55′N 23°21′E
118 E11 **Šiauliai** ⬖ *province* N Lithuania
171 Q10 **Siau, Pulau** *island* N Indonesia
83 J15 **Siavonga** Southern, SE Zambia 16°33′S 28°42′E
Siazan' *see* Siyäzän
Sibah *see* As Sībah
107 N20 **Sibari** Calabria, S Italy 39°45′N 16°26′E
Sibata *see* Shibata
127 X6 **Sibay** Respublika Bashkortostan, W Russian Federation 52°40′N 58°39′E
93 M19 **Sibbo** *Fin.* Sipoo. Etelä-Suomi, S Finland 60°22′N 25°20′E
112 D13 **Šibenik** *It.* Sebenico. Šibenik-Knin, S Croatia 43°43′N 15°54′E
Sibenik *see* Šibenik-Knin
112 E13 **Šibenik-Knin** *off.* Šibenska Županija, *var.* Sibenik. ⬖ *province* S Croatia
Šibenik-Knin *see* Drniš
Šibenska Županija *see* Šibenik-Knin
Siberia *see* Sibir'
Siberoet *see* Siberut, Pulau
168 H12 **Siberut, Pulau** *prev.* Siberoet. *island* Kepulauan Mentawai, W Indonesia
168 I12 **Siberut, Selat** *strait* W Indonesia
149 P11 **Sibi** Baluchistān, SW Pakistan 29°31′N 67°54′E
186 B9 **Sibidiri** Western, SW Papua New Guinea 08°58′S 142°14′E
123 N10 **Sibir'** *var.* Siberia. *physical region* NE Russian Federation
79 F20 **Sibiti** Lékoumou, S Congo 03°41′S 13°20′E
81 G21 **Sibiti** ≋ C Tanzania
116 I12 **Sibiu** *Ger.* Hermannstadt, *Hung.* Nagyszeben. Sibiu, C Romania 45°48′N 24°09′E
116 I11 **Sibiu** ⬖ *county* C Romania
29 S11 **Sibley** Iowa, C USA 43°24′N 95°45′W
169 R9 **Sibu** Sarawak, East Malaysia 02°18′N 111°49′E
42 G2 **Sibun** ≋ E Belize
79 I15 **Sibut** *prev.* Fort-Sibut. Kémo, S Central African Republic 05°44′N 19°07′E
171 P4 **Sibuyan Island** *island* C Philippines
189 U1 **Sibylla Island** *island* N Marshall Islands
11 N16 **Sicamous** British Columbia, SW Canada 50°49′N 118°52′W
Sichelburger Gerbirge *see* Gorjanci
167 N14 **Sichon** *var.* Ban Sichon, Si Chon. Nakhon Si Thammarat, SW Thailand 09°03′N 99°51′E
Si Chon *see* Sichon
160 H9 **Sichuan** *var.* Chuan, Sichuan Sheng, Ssu-ch'uan, Szechuan, Szechwan. ⬖ *province* C China
160 I9 **Sichuan Pendi** *basin* C China
Sichuan Sheng *see* Sichuan
103 S16 **Sicie, Cap** *headland* SE France 43°03′N 05°50′E
107 J24 **Sicilia** *Eng.* Sicily; *anc.* Trinacria. ⬖ *region* Italy, C Mediterranean Sea
107 M24 **Sicilia** *Eng.* Sicily; *anc.* Trinacria. *island* Italy, C Mediterranean Sea
Sicilian Channel *see* Sicily, Strait of
107 H24 **Sicily, Strait of** *var.* Sicilian Channel. *strait* C Mediterranean Sea
42 K5 **Sico Tinto, Río** *var.* Río Negro. ≋ NE Honduras
57 H16 **Sicuani** Cusco, S Peru 14°21′S 71°13′W
112 J10 **Šid** Vojvodina, NW Serbia 45°07′N 19°13′E
115 A15 **Sidári** Kérkyra, Iónia Nisiá, Greece, C Mediterranean Sea 39°47′N 19°43′E
169 Q11 **Sidas** Borneo, C Indonesia 0°24′N 109°46′E
98 O5 **Siddeburen** Groningen, NE Netherlands 53°15′N 06°52′E
154 D9 **Siddhapur** *prev.* Siddhpur, Sidhpur. Gujarāt, W India 23°57′N 72°28′E
Siddhpur *see* Siddhapur
155 I15 **Siddipet** Andhra Pradesh, C India 18°10′N 78°54′E
77 N14 **Sidéradougou** SW Burkina 10°39′N 04°16′W
107 N23 **Siderno** Calabria, SW Italy 38°18′N 16°19′E
Siders *see* Sierre
154 L9 **Sidhi** Madhya Pradesh, C India 24°24′N 81°54′E
Sidhirókastron *see* Sidirókastro
Sidhpur *see* Siddhapur
75 U7 **Sîdi Barrâni** NW Egypt 31°38′N 25°58′E
74 I6 **Sidi Bel Abbès** *var.* Sidi bel Abbès, Sidi-Bel-Abbès. NW Algeria 35°12′N 00°43′W
74 E7 **Sidi-Bennour** W Morocco 32°39′N 08°28′W
74 M6 **Sidi Bouzid** *var.* Gammouda, Sīdī Bu Zayd. C Tunisia 35°05′N 09°20′E
Sīdī Bu Zayd *see* Sidi Bouzid
74 D8 **Sidi-Ifni** SW Morocco 29°33′N 10°04′W
74 G6 **Sidi-Kacem** *prev.* Petitjean. N Morocco 34°21′N 05°46′W
114 G12 **Sidirókastro** *prev.* Sidhirókastron. Kentrikí Makedonía, NE Greece 41°14′N 23°23′E
194 L12 **Sidley, Mount** ▲ Antarctica 76°39′S 124°48′W
29 S16 **Sidney** Iowa, C USA 40°45′N 95°39′W
33 Y7 **Sidney** Montana, NW USA 47°42′N 104°10′W
28 J15 **Sidney** Nebraska, C USA 41°09′N 102°57′W
18 I11 **Sidney** New York, NE USA 42°18′N 75°21′W
31 R13 **Sidney** Ohio, N USA 40°16′N 84°09′W
23 T2 **Sidney Lanier, Lake** ⊠ Georgia, SE USA
Sidon *see* Saïda
122 J9 **Sidorovsk** Yamalo-Nenetskiy Avtonomnyy Okrug, N Russian Federation 66°34′N 82°12′E
Sidra *see* Surt
Sidra/Sidra, Gulf of *see* Surt, Khalīj, N Libya
Siebenbürgen *see* Transylvania
Sieben Dörfer *see* Săcele
110 O12 **Siedlce** *Ger.* Sedlez, *Rus.* Sesdlets. Mazowieckie, C Poland 52°10′N 22°18′E
101 E16 **Sieg** ≋ W Germany
101 F16 **Siegen** Nordrhein-Westfalen, W Germany 50°53′N 08°02′E
109 X4 **Sieghartskirchen** Niederösterreich, E Austria 48°13′N 16°01′E
167 S12 **Siĕmbok** *prev.* Phumĭ Siĕmbok. Stœng Trêng, N Cambodia 13°28′N 105°59′E
110 O11 **Siemiatycze** Podlaskie, NE Poland 52°27′N 22°52′E
167 T11 **Siĕmpang** Stœng Trêng, NE Cambodia 14°07′N 106°24′E
167 R11 **Siĕmréab** *prev.* Siemreap. Siĕmréab, NW Cambodia 13°21′N 103°50′E
Siemreap *see* Siĕmréab
106 G12 **Siena** *Fr.* Sienne; *anc.* Saena Julia. Toscana, C Italy 43°20′N 11°20′E
Sienne *see* Siena
92 K12 **Sieppijärvi** Lappi, NW Finland 67°09′N 23°58′E
110 J13 **Sieradz** Sieradz, C Poland 51°36′N 18°42′E
110 K10 **Sierpc** Mazowieckie, C Poland 52°51′N 19°44′E
24 I9 **Sierra Blanca** Texas, SW USA 31°10′N 105°22′W
37 S14 **Sierra Blanca Peak** ▲ New Mexico, SW USA 33°22′N 105°48′W
35 P5 **Sierra City** California, W USA 39°34′N 120°35′W
63 I16 **Sierra Colorada** Río Negro, S Argentina 40°37′S 67°48′W
63 J16 **Sierra Grande** Río Negro, E Argentina 41°34′S 65°21′W
76 G15 **Sierra Leone** *off.* Republic of Sierra Leone. ◆ *republic* W Africa
64 M13 **Sierra Leone Basin** *undersea feature* E Atlantic Ocean 05°00′N 17°00′W
66 K8 **Sierra Leone Fracture Zone** *tectonic feature* E Atlantic Ocean
Sierra Leone, Republic of *see* Sierra Leone
Sierra Leone Ridge *see* Sierra Leone Rise
64 L13 **Sierra Leone Rise** *var.* Sierra Leone Ridge, Sierra Leone Schwelle. *undersea feature* E Atlantic Ocean 05°30′N 21°00′W
Sierra Leone Schwelle *see* Sierra Leone Rise
40 L7 **Sierra Mojada** Coahuila, NE Mexico 27°13′N 103°42′W
37 N16 **Sierra Vista** Arizona, SW USA 31°33′N 110°18′W
108 D10 **Sierre** *Ger.* Siders. Valais, SW Switzerland 46°18′N 07°33′E
36 L16 **Sierrita Mountains** ▲▲ Arizona, SW USA
Siete Moai *see* Ahu Akivi
76 M15 **Sifié** W Ivory Coast 07°59′N 06°55′W
115 I21 **Sífnos** *anc.* Siphnos. *island* Kykládes, Greece, Aegean Sea
115 I21 **Sífnou, Stenó** *strait* SE Greece
Siga *see* Shiga
103 P16 **Sigean** Aude, S France 43°02′N 02°58′E
Sighet *see* Sighetu Marmaţiei
Sighetul Marmaţiei *see* Sighetu Marmaţiei
116 I8 **Sighetu Marmaţiei** *var.* Sighet, Sighetul Marmaţiei, *Hung.* Máramarossziget. Maramureş, N Romania 47°56′N 23°53′E
116 I11 **Sighişoara** *Ger.* Schässburg, *Hung.* Segesvár. Mureş, C Romania 46°12′N 24°48′E
168 G7 **Sigli** Sumatera, W Indonesia 05°21′N 95°56′E
92 J1 **Siglufjördhur** Nordhurland Vestra, N Iceland 66°09′N 18°56′W
101 H23 **Sigmaringen** Baden-Württemberg, S Germany 48°04′N 09°12′E
101 N20 **Signalberg** ▲ SE Germany 49°30′N 12°34′E
36 I13 **Signal Peak** ▲ Arizona, SW USA 33°20′N 114°03′W
Signan *see* Xi'an
194 H1 **Signy** *UK research station* South Orkney Islands, Antarctica 60°27′S 45°35′W
29 X15 **Sigourney** Iowa, C USA 41°19′N 92°12′W
115 K17 **Sígri, Akrotírio** *headland* Lésvos, E Greece 39°12′N 25°49′E
Sigsbee Deep *see* Mexico Basin
47 N2 **Sigsbee Escarpment** *undersea feature* N Gulf of Mexico 26°00′N 92°30′W
56 C8 **Sigsig** Azuay, S Ecuador 03°04′S 78°50′W
95 O15 **Sigtuna** Stockholm, C Sweden 59°36′N 17°44′E
42 H6 **Siguatepeque** Comayagua, W Honduras 14°39′N 87°48′W
105 P7 **Sigüenza** Castilla-La Mancha, C Spain 41°04′N 02°38′W
105 R4 **Sigües** Aragón, NE Spain 42°39′N 01°00′W
76 K13 **Siguiri** NE Guinea 11°26′N 09°08′W
118 G8 **Sigulda** *Ger.* Segewold. C Latvia 57°08′N 24°51′E
167 Q14 **Sihanoukville** *var.* Kâmpóng Saôm; *prev.* Kompong Som. Kâmpóng Saôm, SW Cambodia 10°38′N 103°30′E
108 G8 **Sihlsee** ◎ NW Switzerland
93 K18 **Siikainen** Länsi-Suomi, SW Finland 61°52′N 21°49′E
93 M16 **Siilinjärvi** Itä-Suomi, C Finland 63°05′N 27°40′E
137 R15 **Siirt** *var.* Sert; *anc.* Tigranocerta. Siirt, SE Turkey 37°56′N 41°56′E
137 R15 **Siirt** *var.* Sert. ⬖ *province* SE Turkey
187 N8 **Sikaiana** *var.* Stewart Islands. *island group* W Solomon Islands
Sikandarabad *see* Secunderābād
152 J11 **Sikandra Rao** Uttar Pradesh, N India 27°42′N 78°21′E
10 M11 **Sikanni Chief** British Columbia, W Canada 57°16′N 122°44′W
10 M11 **Sikanni Chief** ≋ British Columbia, W Canada
152 H11 **Sīkar** Rājasthān, N India 27°33′N 75°12′E
76 M13 **Sikasso** Sikasso, S Mali 11°21′N 05°43′W
76 L13 **Sikasso** ⬖ *region* SW Mali
167 N3 **Sikaw** Kachin State, C Burma (Myanmar) 23°50′N 97°04′E
83 H14 **Sikelenge** Western, W Zambia 14°51′S 24°13′E
27 Y7 **Sikeston** Missouri, C USA 36°52′N 89°35′W
93 J14 **Sikfors** Norrbotten, N Sweden 65°29′N 21°17′E
123 T14 **Sikhote-Alin', Khrebet** ▲▲ SE Russian Federation
Siking *see* Xi'an
115 J22 **Síkinos** *island* Kykládes, Greece, Aegean Sea
153 S11 **Sikkim** *Tib.* Denjong. ⬖ *state* N India
111 I26 **Siklós** Baranya, SW Hungary 45°51′N 18°18′E
Sikoku *see* Shikoku
Sikoku Basin *see* Shikoku Basin
83 G14 **Sikongo** Western, W Zambia 15°03′S 22°07′E
Sikotu Ko *see* Shikotsu-ko
Sikouri/Sikoúrion *see* Sykoúrio
123 P8 **Siktyakh** Respublika Sakha (Yakutiya), NE Russian Federation 69°45′N 124°42′E
118 D12 **Šilalė** Tauragė, W Lithuania 55°29′N 22°10′E
106 G5 **Silandro** *Ger.* Schlanders. Trentino-Alto Adige, N Italy 46°39′N 10°55′E
41 N12 **Silao** Guanajuato, C Mexico 20°56′N 101°28′W
Silarius *see* Sele
153 W14 **Silchar** Assam, NE India 24°49′N 92°48′E
108 G9 **Silenen** Uri, C Switzerland 46°49′N 08°39′E
21 T9 **Siler City** North Carolina, SE USA 35°43′N 79°27′W
33 U11 **Silesia** Montana, NW USA 45°32′N 108°52′W
110 F13 **Silesia** *physical region* SW Poland
74 K12 **Silet** S Algeria 22°45′N 04°51′E
Sileti *see* Silety
Siletitengiz *see* Siletyteniz, Ozero
145 R8 **Silety** *prev.* Sileti. ≋ N Kazakhstan
145 R7 **Siletyteniz, Ozero** *Kaz.* Siletitengiz. ◎ N Kazakhstan
172 H16 **Silhouette** *island* Inner Islands, SE Seychelles
136 I17 **Silifke** *anc.* Seleucia. İçel, S Turkey 36°22′N 33°57′E
Siliguri *see* Shiliguri
156 J10 **Siling Co** ◎ W China
Silinhot *see* Xilinhot
192 G14 **Silisili, Mauga** ▲ Savai'i, C Samoa 13°37′S 172°26′W
114 M6 **Silistra** *var.* Silistria; *anc.* Durostorum. Silistra, NE Bulgaria 44°06′N 27°17′E
114 M7 **Silistra** ⬖ *province* NE Bulgaria
Silistria *see* Silistra
136 D10 **Silivri** İstanbul, NW Turkey 41°05′N 28°15′E
94 L13 **Siljan** ◎ C Sweden
95 G22 **Silkeborg** Midtjylland, C Denmark 56°10′N 09°34′E
108 M8 **Sill** ≋ W Austria
105 S10 **Silla** Valenciana, E Spain 39°22′N 00°25′W
62 H3 **Sillajguay, Cordillera** ▲ N Chile 19°45′S 68°39′W
118 K3 **Sillamäe** *Ger.* Sillamäggi. Ida-Virumaa, NE Estonia 59°23′N 27°45′E
Sillamäggi *see* Sillamäe
Sillein *see* Žilina
109 P9 **Sillian** Tirol, W Austria 46°45′N 12°25′E
112 B10 **Šilo** Primorje-Gorski Kotar, NW Croatia 45°09′N 14°39′E
27 R9 **Siloam Springs** Arkansas, C USA 36°11′N 94°32′W
25 X10 **Silsbee** Texas, SW USA 30°21′N 94°10′W
143 W15 **Sīlūp, Rūd-e** ≋ SE Iran
118 C12 **Šilutė** *Ger.* Heydekrug. Klaipėda, W Lithuania 55°20′N 21°30′E
137 Q15 **Silvan** Dıyarbakır, SE Turkey 38°08′N 41°E
108 J10 **Silvaplana** Graubünden, S Switzerland 46°27′N 09°45′E
Silva Porto *see* Kuito
58 M12 **Silva, Recife do** *reef* E Brazil
154 D12 **Silvassa** Dādra and Nagar Haveli, W India 20°13′N 73°03′E
29 X4 **Silver Bay** Minnesota, N USA 47°17′N 91°15′W
37 P15 **Silver City** New Mexico, SW USA 32°47′N 108°16′W
18 D10 **Silver Creek** New York, NE USA 42°32′N 79°10′W
37 N12 **Silver Creek** ≋ Arizona, SW USA
27 P4 **Silver Lake** Kansas, C USA 39°06′N 95°51′W
32 I14 **Silver Lake** Oregon, NW USA 43°07′N 121°04′W
35 T9 **Silver Peak Range** ▲▲ Nevada, W USA
21 W3 **Silver Spring** Maryland, NE USA 39°00′N 77°01′W
Silver State *see* Colorado
Silver State *see* Nevada
37 Q7 **Silverton** Colorado, C USA 37°48′N 107°39′W
18 K16 **Silverton** New Jersey, NE USA 40°00′N 74°09′W
32 G11 **Silverton** Oregon, NW USA 45°00′N 122°46′W
25 N4 **Silverton** Texas, SW USA 34°28′N 101°18′W
104 G14 **Silves** Faro, S Portugal 37°11′N 08°26′W
54 D12 **Silvia** Cauca, SW Colombia 02°37′N 76°24′W
108 J9 **Silvrettagruppe** ▲▲ Austria/Switzerland
Sily-Vajdej *see* Vulcan
108 L7 **Silz** Tirol, W Austria 47°17′N 11°00′E
172 I13 **Sima** Anjouan, SE Comoros 12°11′S 44°18′E
Simabara *see* Shimabara
83 H15 **Simakando** Western, W Zambia 16°43′S 24°46′E
Simane *see* Shimane
119 L20 **Simanichy** *Rus.* Simonichi. Homyel'skaya Voblasts', SE Belarus 51°53′N 28°05′E
160 F14 **Simao** Yunnan, SW China 22°30′N 101°06′E
153 P12 **Simarā** Central, C Nepal 27°14′N 85°00′E
14 I8 **Simard, Lac** ◎ Québec, SE Canada
136 D13 **Simav** Kütahya, W Turkey 39°05′N 28°59′E
136 D13 **Simav Çayı** ≋ NW Turkey
79 L18 **Simba** Orientale, N Dem. Rep. Congo 0°46′N 22°54′E
186 C7 **Simbai** Madang, N Papua New Guinea 05°12′S 144°33′E
Simbirsk *see* Ul'yanovsk
14 F17 **Simcoe** Ontario, S Canada 42°50′N 80°19′W
14 H14 **Simcoe, Lake** ◎ Ontario, S Canada
80 J11 **Sīmēn** ▲▲ N Ethiopia
114 K11 **Simeonovgrad** *prev.* Maritsa. Khaskovo, S Bulgaria 42°03′N 25°36′E
116 G11 **Simeria** *Ger.* Pischk, *Hung.* Piski. Hunedoara, W Romania 45°51′N 23°00′E
107 L24 **Simeto** ≋ Sicilia, Italy, C Mediterranean Sea
168 G9 **Simeulue, Pulau** *island* NW Indonesia
117 T13 **Simferopol'** Avtonomna Respublika Krym, S Ukraine 44°55′N 33°06′E
117 T13 **Simferopol'** ✈ Avtonomna Respublika Krym, S Ukraine 44°55′N 34°04′E
Simi *see* Sými
152 M9 **Simikot** Far Western, NW Nepal 30°02′N 81°49′E
54 F7 **Simití** Bolívar, N Colombia 07°57′N 73°57′W
114 G11 **Simitla** Blagoevgrad, SW Bulgaria 41°57′N 23°06′E
35 S15 **Simi Valley** California, W USA 34°16′N 118°47′W
Simizu *see* Shimizu
Simla *see* Shimla
Şimlăul Silvaniei/Şimleul Silvaniei *see* Şimleu Silvaniei
116 G9 **Şimleu Silvaniei** *Hung.* Szilágysomlyó; *prev.* Şimlăul Silvaniei, Şimleul Silvaniei. Sălaj, NW Romania 47°12′N 22°49′E
Simmer *see* Simmerbach
101 E19 **Simmerbach** *var.* Simmer. ≋ W Germany
101 F18 **Simmern** Rheinland-Pfalz, W Germany 50°00′N 07°30′E
22 I7 **Simmesport** Louisiana, S USA 30°58′N 91°48′W
119 F14 **Simnas** Alytus, S Lithuania 54°23′N 23°40′E
92 L13 **Simo** Lappi, NW Finland 65°40′N 25°04′E
Simoda *see* Shimoda
Simodate *see* Shimodate
92 M13 **Simojärvi** ◎ N Finland
92 L13 **Simojoki** ≋ NW Finland
41 U15 **Simojovel** *var.* Simojovel de Allende. Chiapas, SE Mexico 17°14′N 92°40′W
Simojovel de Allende *see* Simojovel
56 B7 **Simon Bolivar** *var.* Guayaquil. ✈ (Quayaquil) Guayas, W Ecuador 02°16′S 79°54′W
54 L5 **Simon Bolívar** ✈ (Caracas) Vargas, N Venezuela 10°33′N 66°54′W
Simonichi *see* Simanichy
14 M12 **Simon, Lac** ◎ Québec, SE Canada
Simonoseki *see* Shimonoseki
Šimonovany *see* Partizánske
Simonstad *see* Simon's Town
83 E26 **Simon's Town** *var.* Simonstad. Western Cape, SW South Africa 34°12′S 18°26′E
Simony *see* Partizánske
Simpeln *see* Simplon
99 M18 **Simpelveld** Limburg, SE Netherlands 50°50′N 05°59′E
108 E11 **Simplon** *var.* Simpeln. Valais, SW Switzerland 46°13′N 08°01′E
108 E11 **Simplon Pass** *pass* S Switzerland
106 C6 **Simplon Tunnel** *tunnel* Italy/Switzerland
Simpson *see* Fort Simpson
182 G1 **Simpson Desert** *desert* Northern Territory/South Australia
10 J9 **Simpson Peak** ▲ British Columbia, W Canada 59°43′N 131°29′W
9 N7 **Simpson Peninsula** *peninsula* Nunavut, NE Canada
21 P11 **Simpsonville** South Carolina, SE USA 34°44′N 82°15′W
95 L23 **Simrishamn** Skåne, S Sweden 55°34′N 14°20′E
123 U13 **Simushir, Ostrov** *island* Kuril'skiye Ostrova, SE Russian Federation
168 G9 **Sinabang** Sumatera, W Indonesia 02°27′N 96°24′E
81 N15 **Sina Dhaqa** Galguduud, C Somalia 05°21′N 46°21′E
75 X8 **Sinai** *var.* Sinai Peninsula, *Ar.* Shibh Jazirat Sīnā', Sīnā. *physical region* NE Egypt
116 J12 **Sinaia** Prahova, SE Romania 45°20′N 25°33′E
188 B16 **Sinajana** C Guam 13°28′N 144°45′E
40 H8 **Sinaloa** ⬖ *state* C Mexico
54 H4 **Sinamaica** Zulia, NW Venezuela 11°06′N 71°52′W
163 X14 **Sinan-ni** SE North Korea 38°37′N 127°43′E
Sīnā/Sinai Peninsula *see* Sinai
Sīnāwan *see* Sīnāwin
75 N8 **Sīnāwin** *var.* Sīnāwan. NW Libya 31°00′N 10°37′E
83 J16 **Sinazongwe** Southern, S Zambia 17°14′S 27°27′E
166 L6 **Sinbaungwe** Magway, W Burma (Myanmar) 19°44′N 95°10′E
166 L5 **Sinbyugyun** Magway, W Burma (Myanmar) 20°38′N 94°40′E
54 E6 **Since** Sucre, NW Colombia 09°14′N 75°08′W
54 E6 **Sincelejo** Sucre, NW Colombia 09°17′N 75°23′W
23 U4 **Sinclair, Lake** ⊠ Georgia, SE USA
10 M14 **Sinclair Mills** British Columbia, SW Canada 54°03′N 121°37′W
154 I8 **Sind** ≋ N India
Sind *see* Sindh
95 H19 **Sindal** Nordjylland, N Denmark 57°29′N 10°13′E
171 P7 **Sindañgan** Mindanao, S Philippines 08°09′N 122°59′E
79 D19 **Sindara** Ngounié, W Gabon 01°07′S 10°41′E
152 E13 **Sindari** *prev.* Sindri. Rājasthān, N India 25°32′N 71°58′E
114 N8 **Sindel** Varna, E Bulgaria 43°07′N 27°35′E
101 H22 **Sindelfingen** Baden-Württemberg, SW Germany 48°43′N 09°E
155 G16 **Sindgi** Karnātaka, C India 17°01′N 76°22′E
149 Q14 **Sindh** *prev.* Sind. ⬖ *province* SE Pakistan
118 G5 **Sindi** *Ger.* Zintenhof. Pärnumaa, SW Estonia 58°28′N 24°41′E
136 C13 **Sındırgı** Balıkesir, W Turkey 39°13′N 28°10′E
77 N14 **Sindou** SW Burkina 10°35′N 05°04′W
Sindri *see* Sindari
149 T9 **Sind Sāgar Doāb** *desert* E Pakistan
126 M11 **Sinegorskiy** Rostovskaya Oblast', SW Russian Federation 48°01′N 40°52′E
123 S9 **Sinegor'ye** Magadanskaya Oblast', E Russian Federation 62°04′N 150°33′E
114 O12 **Sinekli** İstanbul, NW Turkey 41°13′N 28°13′E
104 F12 **Sines** Setúbal, S Portugal 37°58′N 08°52′W
104 F12 **Sines, Cabo de** *headland* S Portugal 37°57′N 08°55′W
92 L12 **Sinettä** Lappi, NW Finland 66°39′N 25°25′E
186 H6 **Sinewit, Mount** ▲ New Britain, C Papua New Guinea 04°42′S 151°58′E
80 G11 **Singa** *var.* Sinja, Sinjah. Sinnar, E Sudan 13°11′N 33°55′E
78 J12 **Singako** Moyen-Chari, S Chad 09°52′N 19°31′E
Singan *see* Xi'an
168 K10 **Singapore** ● (Singapore) S Singapore 01°17′N 103°48′E
168 L10 **Singapore** *off.* Republic of Singapore. ◆ *republic* SE Asia
Singapore, Republic of *see* Singapore
169 U17 **Singaraja** Bali, C Indonesia 08°06′S 115°04′E
167 O10 **Sing Buri** *var.* Singhaburi. Sing Buri, C Thailand 14°56′N 100°21′E
101 H24 **Singen** Baden-Württemberg, S Germany 47°46′N 08°50′E
Sîngeorgiu de Pădure *see* Sângeorgiu de Pădure
Sîngeorz-Băi/Singeroz Băi *see* Sângeorz-Băi
116 M9 **Sîngerei** *var.* Sângerei; *prev.* Lazovsk. N Moldova 47°38′N 28°08′E
Singhaburi *see* Sing Buri
81 H21 **Singida** Singida, C Tanzania 04°45′S 34°48′E
81 G22 **Singida** ⬖ *region* C Tanzania
Singidunum *see* Beograd
Singkaling Hkamti *see* Hkamti
171 N14 **Singkang** Sulawesi, C Indonesia 04°09′S 119°58′E
168 J11 **Singkarak, Danau** ◎ Sumatera, W Indonesia
169 N10 **Singkawang** Borneo, C Indonesia 0°57′N 108°57′E
168 M11 **Singkep, Pulau** *island* Kepulauan Lingga, W Indonesia
168 H9 **Singkilbaru** Sumatera, W Indonesia 02°18′N 97°47′E
183 T7 **Singleton** New South Wales, SE Australia 32°38′S 151°00′E
Singora *see* Songkhla
Singû *see* Shingū
Sining *see* Xining
107 D17 **Siniscola** Sardegna, Italy, C Mediterranean Sea 40°34′N 09°42′E
113 F14 **Sinj** Split-Dalmacija, SE Croatia 43°41′N 16°37′E
Sinjajevina *see* Sinjavina
139 P3 **Sinjār** Nīnawýa, NW Iraq 36°20′N 41°51′E
139 P2 **Sinjār, Jabal** ▲▲ N Iraq
Sinja/Sinjah *see* Singa
113 K15 **Sinjavina** *var.* Sinjajevina. ▲▲ C Montenegro
80 I7 **Sinkat** Red Sea, NE Sudan 18°52′N 36°51′E
Sinkiang/Sinkiang Uighur Autonomous Region *see* Xinjiang Uygur Zizhiqu
Sînmartin *see* Târnăveni
163 V13 **Sinmi-do** *island* NW North Korea
101 I18 **Sinn** ≋ C Germany
Sinnamarie *see* Sinnamary
55 Y9 **Sinnamary** *var.* Sinnamarie. N French Guiana 05°23′N 53°00′W
80 G11 **Sinnar** ⬖ *state* E Sudan
Sinneh *see* Sanandaj
18 E13 **Sinnemahoning Creek** ≋ Pennsylvania, NE USA
Sînnicolau Mare *see* Sânnicolau Mare
Sinoe, Lacul *see* Sinoie, Lacul
Sinoia *see* Chinhoyi
117 N14 **Sinoie, Lacul** *prev.* Lacul Sinoe. *lagoon* SE Romania
59 H16 **Sinop** Mato Grosso, W Brazil 11°38′S 55°27′W
136 K10 **Sinop** *anc.* Sinope. Sinop, N Turkey 42°02′N 35°09′E
136 J10 **Sinop** ⬖ *province* N Turkey
136 K10 **Sinop Burnu** *headland* N Turkey 42°02′N 35°12′E
Sinope *see* Sinop
Sino/Sinoe *see* Greenville
163 Y12 **Sinp'o** E North Korea 40°01′N 128°10′E
101 H20 **Sinsheim** Baden-Württemberg, SW Germany 49°15′N 08°53′E
Sîntana *see* Sântana
169 R11 **Sintang** Borneo, C Indonesia 0°03′N 111°31′E
99 F14 **Sint Annaland** Zeeland, SW Netherlands 51°36′N 04°07′E
98 L5 **Sint Annaparochie** *Fris.* Sint Anne. Fryslân, N Netherlands 53°20′N 05°46′E
Sint Anne *see* Sint Annaparochie
45 V9 **Sint Eustatius** *Eng.* Saint Eustatius. *island* Sint Maarten
99 G19 **Sint-Genesius-Rode** *Fr.* Rhode-Saint-Genèse. Vlaams Brabant, C Belgium 50°45′N 04°21′E
99 F16 **Sint-Gillis-Waas** Oost-Vlaanderen, N Belgium 51°14′N 04°08′E
99 H17 **Sint-Katelijne-Waver** Antwerpen, C Belgium 51°05′N 04°31′E
99 E18 **Sint-Lievens-Houtem** Oost-Vlaanderen, NW Belgium 50°55′N 03°52′E
45 V9 **Sint Maarten** *Eng.* Saint Martin. ◇ *Dutch autonomous region* NE Caribbean Sea
99 F14 **Sint Maartensdijk** Zeeland, SW Netherlands 51°33′N 04°05′E
99 L19 **Sint-Martens-Voeren** *Fr.* Fouron-Saint-Martin. Limburg, NE Belgium 50°46′N 05°49′E
99 J14 **Sint-Michielsgestel** Noord-Brabant, S Netherlands 51°38′N 05°21′E
Sîn-Miclăuş *see* Gheorgheni
45 O16 **Sint Nicholaas** S Aruba 12°25′N 69°52′W
99 F16 **Sint-Niklaas** *Fr.* Saint-Nicolas. Oost-Vlaanderen, N Belgium 51°10′N 04°09′E
99 K14 **Sint-Oedenrode** Noord-Brabant, S Netherlands 51°34′N 05°28′E
25 T14 **Sinton** Texas, SW USA 28°02′N 97°33′W
99 G14 **Sint Philipsland** Zeeland, SW Netherlands 51°37′N 04°11′E
99 G19 **Sint-Pieters-Leeuw** Vlaams Brabant, C Belgium 50°47′N 04°16′E
104 E11 **Sintra** *prev.* Cintra. Lisboa, W Portugal 38°48′N 09°22′W
99 J18 **Sint-Truiden** *Fr.* Saint-Trond. Limburg, NE Belgium 50°48′N 05°13′E
99 H14 **Sint Willebrord** Noord-Brabant, S Netherlands 51°33′N 04°35′E
163 V13 **Sinŭiju** W North Korea 40°08′N 124°33′E
80 P13 **Sinujiif** Nugaal, NE Somalia 08°33′N 49°05′E
Sinus Aelaniticus *see* Aqaba, Gulf of
Sinus Gallicus *see* Lion, Golfe du
Sinyang *see* Xinyang
Sinyavka *see* Sinyawka
119 I18 **Sinyawka** *Rus.* Sinyavka. Minskaya Voblasts', SW Belarus 52°57′N 26°29′E
Sinying *see* Xinying
Sinyukha *see* Synyukha
Sinzyô *see* Shinjō
111 I24 **Sió** ≋ W Hungary
171 O7 **Siocon** Mindanao, S Philippines 07°37′N 122°09′E
111 I24 **Siófok** Somogy, Hungary 46°54′N 18°03′E
Siogama *see* Shiogama
83 G15 **Sioma** Western, SW Zambia 16°39′S 23°36′E
108 D11 **Sion** *Ger.* Sitten; *anc.* Sedunum. Valais, SW Switzerland 46°15′N 07°23′E
103 O11 **Sioule** ≋ C France
29 S12 **Sioux Center** Iowa, C USA 43°04′N 96°10′W
29 R13 **Sioux City** Iowa, C USA 42°30′N 96°24′W
29 R11 **Sioux Falls** South Dakota, N USA 43°33′N 96°45′W
12 B11 **Sioux Lookout** Ontario, S Canada 49°27′N 94°06′W
29 T12 **Sioux Rapids** Iowa, C USA 42°53′N 95°09′W
Sioux State *see* North Dakota
Sioziri *see* Shiojiri
171 P6 **Sipalay** Negros, C Philippines 09°46′N 122°25′E
55 V11 **Sipaliwini** ⬖ *district* S Surinam
45 U15 **Siparia** Trinidad, Trinidad and Tobago 10°08′N 61°31′W
Siphnos *see* Sífnos
163 V11 **Siping** *var.* Ssu-p'ing, Szeping; *prev.* Ssu-p'ing-chieh. Jilin, NE China 43°09′N 124°22′E
11 X12 **Sipiwesk** Manitoba, C Canada 55°28′N 97°16′W
11 W13 **Sipiwesk Lake** ◎ Manitoba, C Canada
195 O11 **Siple Coast** *physical region* Antarctica
194 K12 **Siple Island** *island* Antarctica
194 K13 **Siple, Mount** ▲ Siple Island, Antarctica 73°25′S 126°24′W
Sipoo *see* Sibbo
112 G12 **Šipovo** Republika Srpska, W Bosnia and Herzegovina 44°16′N 17°05′E
23 O4 **Sipsey River** ≋ Alabama, S USA
168 I13 **Sipura, Pulau** *island* W Indonesia
0 G16 **Siqueiros Fracture Zone** *tectonic feature* E Pacific Ocean
42 L10 **Siquia, Río** ≋ SE Nicaragua
43 N13 **Siquirres** Limón, E Costa Rica 10°05′N 83°30′W
54 J5 **Siquisique** Lara, N Venezuela 10°36′N 69°45′W
155 G19 **Sīra** Karnātaka, W India 13°46′N 76°54′E
95 D16 **Sira** ≋ S Norway
167 P12 **Si Racha** *var.* Ban Si Racha, Si Racha. Chon Buri, S Thailand 13°10′N 100°57′E
Si Racha *see* Si Racha
107 L25 **Siracusa** *Eng.* Syracuse. Sicilia, Italy, C Mediterranean Sea 37°04′N 15°17′E
153 T14 **Sirajganj** *var.* Shirajganj Ghat. Rajshahi, C Bangladesh 24°27′N 89°42′E
Sirakawa *see* Shirakawa
11 N14 **Sir Alexander, Mount** ▲ British Columbia, W Canada 54°00′N 120°33′W
137 O12 **Şiran** Gümüşhane, NE Turkey 40°12′N 39°07′E
77 Q12 **Sirba** ≋ E Burkina
143 O17 **Şīr Banī Yās** *island* W United Arab Emirates
95 D17 **Sirdalsvatnet** ◎ S Norway
Sir Darya/Sirdaryo *see* Syr Darya
147 P10 **Sirdaryo** Sirdaryo Viloyati, E Uzbekistan 40°46′N 68°34′E
147 O11 **Sirdaryo Viloyati** *Rus.* Syrdar'inskaya Oblast'. ⬖ *province* E Uzbekistan
Sir Donald Sangster International Airport *see* Sangster
181 S3 **Sir Edward Pellew Group** *island group* Northern Territory, NE Australia
116 K8 **Siret** *Ger.* Sereth, *Hung.* Szeret. Suceava, N Romania 47°55′N 26°05′E
116 K8 **Siret** *var.* Siretul, *Ger.* Sereth, *Rus.* Seret. ≋ Romania/Ukraine
Siretul *see* Siret
140 K3 **Sirḥān, Wādī as** *dry watercourse* Jordan/Saudi Arabia
152 I8 **Sirhind** Punjab, N India 30°39′N 76°28′E

116 F11 **Şiria** *Ger.* Schiria. Arad, W Romania 46°16′N 21°38′E
Siria *see* Syria
143 S14 **Sīrīk** Hormozgān, SE Iran 26°32′N 57°07′E
167 P8 **Sirikit Reservoir** ◎ N Thailand
58 K12 **Sirituba, Ilha** *island* NE Brazil
143 R11 **Sīrjān** *prev.* Sa'īdābād. Kermān, S Iran 29°29′N 55°39′E
182 H9 **Sir Joseph Banks Group** *island group* South Australia
92 K11 **Sirkka** Lappi, N Finland 67°49′N 24°48′E
Sirna *see* Sýrna
137 R16 **Şırnak** Şırnak, SE Turkey 37°33′N 42°27′E
137 S16 **Şırnak** ◆ *province* SE Turkey
Siroisi *see* Shiroishi
155 J14 **Sironcha** Mahārāshtra, C India 18°51′N 80°03′E
Sirone *see* Shirone
Síros *see* Sýros
Sirotino *see* Sirotsina
118 M12 **Sirotsina** *Rus.* Sirotino. Vitsyebskaya Voblasts', N Belarus 55°23′N 29°37′E
152 H9 **Sirsa** Haryāna, NW India 29°32′N 75°04′E
173 Y17 **Sir Seewoosagur Ramgoolam** ✕ (port Louis) SE Mauritius
155 E18 **Sirsi** Karnātaka, W India 14°46′N 74°49′E
146 K12 **Şirşütür Gumy** *var.* Shirshütür, *Rus.* Peski Shirshyutyur. *desert* E Turkmenistan
Sirte *see* Surt
182 A2 **Sir Thomas, Mount** ▲ South Australia 27°09′S 129°49′E
Sirti, Gulf of *see* Surt, Khalīj
137 Y12 **Şirvan** *prev.* Äli-Bayramlı. SE Azerbaijan 39°57′N 48°54′E
142 J5 **Sīrvān, Rūdkhāneh-ye** *var.* Nahr Diyālá, Sirwan. ⟿ Iran/Iraq *see also* Diyālá, Nahr
Sīrvān, Rudkhaneh-ye *see* Diyālá, Sirwan Nahr
118 H13 **Širvintos** Vilnius, SE Lithuania 55°01′N 24°58′E
Sīrwān *see* Diyālá, Nahr/ Sīrvān, Rudkhaneh-ye
11 N15 **Sir Wilfrid Laurier, Mount** ▲ British Columbia, SW Canada 52°45′N 119°51′W
14 M10 **Sir-Wilfrid, Mont** ▲ Québec, SE Canada 46°57′N 75°33′W
Sisačko-Moslavačka Županija *see* Sisak-Moslavina
112 E9 **Sisak** *var.* Siscia, *Ger.* Sissek, *Hung.* Sziszek; *anc.* Segestica. Sisak-Moslavina, C Croatia 45°28′N 16°21′E
167 R10 **Si Sa Ket** *var.* Sisaket, Sri Saket. Si Sa Ket, E Thailand 15°08′N 104°18′E
Sisaket *see* Si Sa Ket
112 E9 **Sisak-Moslavina** *off.* Sisačko-Moslavačka Županija. ◆ *province* C Croatia
167 O8 **Si Satchanalai** Sukhothai, NW Thailand
Siscia *see* Sisak
83 G22 **Sishen** Northern Cape, NW South Africa 27°47′S 22°59′E
137 V13 **Sisian** SE Armenia 39°31′N 46°03′E
197 N13 **Sisimiut** *var.* Holsteinborg, Holsteinsborg, Holstenborg, Holstensborg. Kitaa, S Greenland 67°07′N 53°42′W
30 M1 **Siskiwit Bay** *lake bay* Michigan, N USA
34 L1 **Siskiyou Mountains** ▲▲ California/Oregon, W USA
Sisŏphŏn *see* Bântéay Méan Choăy
108 E7 **Sissach** Basel Landschaft, NW Switzerland 47°28′N 07°48′E
186 B5 **Sissano** Sandaun, NW Papua New Guinea 03°02′S 142°01′E
Sissek *see* Sisak
29 R7 **Sisseton** South Dakota, N USA 45°39′N 97°03′W
143 W9 **Sīstān, Daryācheh-ye** *var.* Daryācheh-ye Hāmūn, Hāmūn-e Şāberī. ◎ Afghanistan/Iran *see also* Şāberī, Hāmūn-e
Sīstān, Daryācheh-ye *see* Şāberī, Hāmūn-e
143 V12 **Sīstān va Balūchestān** *off.* Ostān-e Sīstān va Balūchestān, *var.* Balūchestān va Sīstān. ◆ *province* SE Iran
Sīstān va Balūchestān, Ostān-e *see* Sīstān va Balūchestān
103 T14 **Sisteron** Alpes-de-Haute-Provence, SE France 44°12′N 05°55′E
32 H13 **Sisters** Oregon, NW USA 44°17′N 121°33′W
65 G15 **Sisters Peak** ▲ N Ascension Island 07°56′S 14°23′W
21 R3 **Sistersville** West Virginia, NE USA 39°33′N 81°00′W
Sistova *see* Svishtov
Sitakund *see* Sitakunda
153 V16 **Sitakunda** *var.* Sitakund. Chittagong, SE Bangladesh 22°35′N 91°40′E
153 P12 **Sītāmarhi** Bihār, N India 26°36′N 85°30′E
152 L11 **Sītāpur** Uttar Pradesh, N India 27°33′N 80°40′E
Sitaş Cristuru *see* Cristuru Secuiesc
115 L25 **Siteía** *var.* Sitía. Kríti, Greece, E Mediterranean Sea 35°13′N 26°06′E
105 V6 **Sitges** Cataluña, NE Spain 41°14′N 01°49′E
115 H15 **Sithoniá' Atavyros** *peninsula* NE Greece
Sitía *see* Siteía
54 F4 **Sitionuevo** Magdalena, N Colombia 10°46′N 74°43′W
39 X13 **Sitka** Baranof Island, Alaska, USA 57°03′N 135°19′W
39 Q15 **Sitkinak Island** *island* Trinity Islands, Alaska, USA
Sittang *see* Sittoung
99 L17 **Sittard** Limburg, SE Netherlands 51°N 05°52′E
Sitten *see* Sion
108 H7 **Sitter** ⟿ NW Switzerland
109 U10 **Sittersdorf** Kärnten, S Austria 46°31′N 14°34′E
166 M7 **Sittoung** *var.* Sittang. ⟿ S Burma (Myanmar)
166 K6 **Sittwe** *var.* Akyab. Rakhine State, W Burma (Myanmar) 22°09′N 92°51′E
42 L8 **Siuna** Región Autónoma Atlántico Norte, NE Nicaragua 13°44′N 84°46′W
153 R15 **Siuri** West Bengal, NE India 23°54′N 87°32′E
Siut *see* Asyūţ
123 Q13 **Sivaki** Amurskaya Oblast', SE Russian Federation 52°39′N 126°43′E
136 M13 **Sivas** *anc.* Sebastia, Sebaste. Sivas, C Turkey 39°44′N 37°01′E
136 M13 **Sivas** ◆ *province* C Turkey
137 O15 **Siverek** Şanlıurfa, S Turkey 37°46′N 39°19′E
117 X6 **Sivers'k** Donets'ka Oblast', E Ukraine 48°52′N 38°07′E
124 G13 **Siverskiy** Leningradskaya Oblast', NW Russian Federation 59°21′N 30°01′E
117 X6 **Sivers'kyy Donets'** *Rus.* Severskiy Donets. ⟿ Russian Federation/Ukraine *see also* Severskiy Donets
Sivers'kyy Donets' *see* Severskiy Donets
125 W5 **Sivomaskinskiy** Respublika Komi, NW Russian Federation 66°42′N 62°33′E
136 G13 **Sivrihisar** Eskişehir, W Turkey 39°29′N 31°32′E
99 F22 **Sivry** Hainaut, S Belgium 50°10′N 04°11′E
123 V9 **Sivuchiy, Mys** *headland* E Russian Federation 56°45′N 163°13′E
Siwa *see* Sīwah
75 U9 **Sīwah** *var.* Siwa. NW Egypt 29°11′N 25°32′E
152 J9 **Siwalik Range** *var.* Shiwalik Range. ▲▲ India/Nepal
153 O13 **Siwān** Bihār, N India 26°14′N 84°21′E
43 O14 **Sixaola, Río** ⟿ Costa Rica/ Panama
Six Counties, The *see* Northern Ireland
103 T16 **Six-Fours-les-Plages** Var, SE France 43°05′N 05°50′E
161 Q7 **Sixian** *var.* Si Xian. Anhui, E China 33°29′N 117°53′E
Si Xian *see* Sixian
22 J9 **Six Mile Lake** ◎ Louisiana, S USA
139 V3 **Siyāh Gūz** As Sulaymānīyah, E Iraq 35°49′N 45°45′E
155 L25 **Siyambalanduwa** Uva Province, SE Sri Lanka 06°54′N 81°32′E
137 Y10 **Siyäzän** *Rus.* Siazan'. NE Azerbaijan 41°05′N 49°05′E
Sizebolu *see* Sozopol
Sizuoka *see* Shizuoka
95 I24 **Sjælland** ◆ *region* SE Denmark
95 I24 **Sjælland** *Eng.* Zealand, *Ger.* Seeland. *island* E Denmark
Sjar *see* Sääre
Sjars *see* Sääre
113 L15 **Sjenica** *Turk.* Seniça. Serbia, SW Serbia 43°16′N 20°01′E
94 G11 **Sjoa** ⟿ S Norway
95 K23 **Sjöbo** Skåne, S Sweden 55°37′N 13°45′E
94 E9 **Sjøholt** Møre og Romsdal, S Norway 62°29′N 06°50′E
92 O1 **Sjuøyane** *island group* N Svalbard
Skadar *see* Shkodër
Skadarsko Jezero *see* Scutari, Lake
117 R11 **Skadovs'k** Khersons'ka Oblast', S Ukraine 46°07′N 32°53′E
95 I24 **Skælskør** Sjælland, E Denmark 55°16′N 11°18′E
92 I2 **Skagaströnd** *prev.* Höfdhakaupstadhur. Nordhurland Vestra, N Iceland 65°49′N 20°18′W
95 H19 **Skagen** Nordjylland, N Denmark 57°44′N 10°37′E
Skagerak *see* Skagerrak
95 L16 **Skagern** ◎ C Sweden
197 T17 **Skagerrak** *var.* Skagerak. *channel* N Europe
94 G12 **Skaget** ▲ S Norway 61°19′N 09°07′E
32 H7 **Skagit River** ⟿ Washington, NW USA
39 W12 **Skagway** Alaska, USA 59°27′N 135°18′W
92 K8 **Skaidi** Finnmark, N Norway 70°26′N 24°31′E
115 F21 **Skála** Pelopónnisos, S Greece 36°51′N 22°39′E
116 K6 **Skalat** *Pol.* Skałat. Ternopil's'ka Oblast', W Ukraine 49°27′N 25°59′E
95 J22 **Skälderviken** *inlet* Denmark/ Sweden
92 I12 **Skalka** *Lapp.* Skalkká. ◎ N Sweden
Skalkká *see* Skalka
114 I12 **Skaloti** Anatolikí Makedonía kai Thrakí, NE Greece 41°24′N 24°16′E
95 G22 **Skanderborg** Midtjylland, C Denmark 56°02′N 09°57′E
95 K22 **Skåne** *prev. Eng.* Scania. ◆ *county* S Sweden
75 N6 **Skanès** ✕ (Sousse) E Tunisia 35°36′N 10°56′E
95 C15 **Skånevik** Hordaland, S Norway 59°43′N 06°35′E
95 M18 **Skänninge** Östergötland, S Sweden 58°24′N 15°05′E
95 J23 **Skanör med Falsterbo** Skåne, S Sweden 55°24′N 12°48′E
115 H17 **Skantzoúra** *island* Vóreies Sporádes, Greece, Aegean Sea
95 K18 **Skara** Västra Götaland, S Sweden 58°23′N 13°25′E
95 M17 **Skärblacka** Östergötland, S Sweden 58°34′N 15°54′E
95 J18 **Skärhamn** Västra Götaland, S Sweden 57°59′N 11°33′E
95 I14 **Skarnes** Hedmark, S Norway 60°14′N 11°41′E
119 M21 **Skarodnaye** *Rus.* Skorodnoye. Homyel'skaya Voblasts', SE Belarus 51°38′N 28°50′E
110 I8 **Skarszewy** *Ger.* Schöneck. Pomorskie, NW Poland 54°04′N 18°25′E
111 M14 **Skarżysko-Kamienna** Świętokrzyskie, C Poland 51°07′N 20°52′E
95 K16 **Skattkärr** Värmland, C Sweden 59°25′N 13°42′E
118 D12 **Skaudvilė** Tauragė, SW Lithuania 55°25′N 22°33′E
92 J12 **Skaulo** *Lapp.* Sávdijári. Norrbotten, N Sweden 67°21′N 21°03′E
111 K17 **Skawina** Małopolskie, S Poland 49°59′N 19°49′E
10 K12 **Skeena** ⟿ British Columbia, SW Canada
10 J11 **Skeena Mountains** ▲▲ British Columbia, W Canada
97 O18 **Skegness** E England, United Kingdom 53°10′N 00°21′E
92 J4 **Skeidharársandur** *coast* S Iceland
93 J15 **Skellefteå** Västerbotten, N Sweden 64°45′N 20°58′E
93 I14 **Skellefteälven** ⟿ N Sweden
93 J15 **Skelleftehamn** Västerbotten, N Sweden 64°41′N 21°13′E
25 O2 **Skellytown** Texas, SW USA 35°34′N 101°10′W
95 J19 **Skene** Västra Götaland, S Sweden 57°30′N 12°34′E
97 G17 **Skerries** *Ir.* Na Sceirí. Dublin, E Ireland 53°35′N 06°07′W
95 H15 **Ski** Akershus, S Norway 59°43′N 10°50′E
115 G17 **Skíathos** Skíathos, Vóreies Sporádes, Greece, Aegean Sea 39°10′N 23°30′E
115 G17 **Skíathos** *island* Vóreies Sporádes, Greece, Aegean Sea
27 P9 **Skiatook** Oklahoma, C USA 36°22′N 96°00′W
27 P9 **Skiatook Lake** ⊠ Oklahoma, C USA
97 B22 **Skibbereen** *Ir.* An Sciobairín. Cork, SW Ireland 51°33′N 09°15′W
92 I9 **Skibotn** Troms, N Norway 69°22′N 20°18′E
119 F16 **Skidal'** *Rus.* Skidel'. Hrodzyenskaya Voblasts', W Belarus 53°35′N 24°15′E
97 K15 **Skiddaw** ▲ NW England, United Kingdom 54°37′N 03°07′W
Skidel' *see* Skidal'
25 T14 **Skidmore** Texas, SW USA 28°13′N 97°40′W
95 G16 **Skien** Telemark, S Norway 59°14′N 09°37′E
Skiermûntseach *see* Schiermonnikoog
110 L12 **Skierniewice** Łódzkie, C Poland 51°58′N 20°10′E
74 L5 **Skikda** *prev.* Philippeville. NE Algeria 36°51′N 07°E
30 M16 **Skillet Fork** ⟿ Illinois, N USA
95 L19 **Skillingaryd** Jönköping, S Sweden 57°27′N 14°05′E
115 B19 **Skinári, Akrotírio** *headland* Iónia Nisiá, Greece 37°55′N 20°57′E
95 M15 **Skinnskatteberg** Västmanland, C Sweden 59°50′N 15°41′E
182 M12 **Skipton** Victoria, SE Australia 37°44′S 143°21′E
97 L16 **Skipton** N England, United Kingdom 53°57′N 02°W
Skiropoula *see* Skyropoúla
Skíros *see* Skýros
95 F21 **Skive** Midtjylland, NW Denmark 56°34′N 09°02′E
94 F11 **Skjåk** Oppland, S Norway 61°52′N 08°21′E
95 F22 **Skjern** Midtjylland, W Denmark 55°57′N 08°30′E
95 F22 **Skjern Å** *var.* Skjern Aa. ⟿ W Denmark
Skjern Aa *see* Skjern Å
92 G12 **Skjerstad** Nordland, C Norway 67°14′N 15°00′E
92 J8 **Skjervøy** Troms, N Norway 70°03′N 20°56′E
92 I10 **Skjold** Troms, N Norway 69°03′N 19°18′E
111 I17 **Skoczów** Śląskie, S Poland 49°49′N 18°45′E
109 T11 **Škofja Loka** *Ger.* Bischoflack. NW Slovenia 46°12′N 14°16′E
94 N12 **Skog** Gävleborg, C Sweden 61°10′N 16°49′E
95 K16 **Skoghall** Värmland, C Sweden 59°20′N 13°30′E
31 N10 **Skokie** Illinois, N USA 42°01′N 87°43′W
116 H6 **Skole** L'vivs'ka Oblast', W Ukraine 49°04′N 23°29′E
115 D19 **Skóllis** ▲ S Greece 37°58′N 21°33′E
167 S13 **Skon** Kâmpóng Cham, C Cambodia 12°56′N 104°36′E
115 H17 **Skópelos** Skópelos, Vóreies Sporádes, Greece, Aegean Sea 39°07′N 23°43′E
115 H17 **Skópelos** *island* Vóreies Sporádes, Greece, Aegean Sea
126 L5 **Skopin** Ryazanskaya Oblast', W Russian Federation 53°46′N 39°37′E
113 N18 **Skopje** *var.* Üsküb, *Turk.* Üsküp, *prev.* Skoplje; *anc.* Scupi. ● (FYR Macedonia) N FYR Macedonia 42°N 21°28′E
113 O18 **Skopje** ✕ N FYR Macedonia 41°58′N 21°35′E
Skoplje *see* Skopje
110 I8 **Skórcz** *Ger.* Skurz. Pomorskie, N Poland 53°46′N 18°43′E
Skorodnoye *see* Skarodnaye
93 H16 **Skorped** Västernorrland, C Sweden 63°23′N 17°55′E
95 G21 **Skørping** Nordjylland, N Denmark 56°50′N 09°55′E
95 K18 **Skövde** Västra Götaland, S Sweden 58°24′N 13°52′E
123 Q13 **Skovorodino** Amurskaya Oblast', SE Russian Federation 54°03′N 123°47′E
19 Q6 **Skowhegan** Maine, NE USA 44°46′N 69°41′W
11 W15 **Skownan** Manitoba, S Canada 51°55′N 99°34′W
94 H13 **Skreia** Oppland, S Norway 60°37′N 11°00′E
Skripón *see* Orchómenos
118 H9 **Skrīveri** S Latvia 56°39′N 25°08′E
118 J11 **Skrudaliena** SE Latvia 55°50′N 26°42′E
118 D9 **Skrunda** W Latvia 56°39′N 22°01′E
95 C16 **Skudeneshavn** Rogaland, S Norway 59°10′N 05°16′E
95 C16 **Skudnesfjorden** S Norway
83 L20 **Skukuza** Mpumalanga, NE South Africa 25°01′S 31°35′E
97 B22 **Skull** *Ir.* An Scoil. SW Ireland 51°32′N 09°34′W
22 L3 **Skuna River** ⟿ Mississippi, S USA
29 X15 **Skunk River** ⟿ Iowa, C USA
Skuø *see* Skúvoy
118 C10 **Skuodas** *Ger.* Schoden, *Pol.* Szkudy. Klaipėda, NW Lithuania 56°16′N 21°30′E
95 K23 **Skurup** Skåne, S Sweden 55°28′N 13°30′E
Skurz *see* Skórcz
114 H8 **Skŭt** ⟿ NW Bulgaria
94 O13 **Skutskär** Uppsala, C Sweden 60°39′N 17°25′E
95 B19 **Skúvoy** *Dan.* Skuø. *island* C Faeroe Islands
Skvira *see* Skvyra
117 O5 **Skvyra** *Rus.* Skvira. Kyyivs'ka Oblast', N Ukraine 49°44′N 29°42′E
39 Q11 **Skwentna** Alaska, USA 61°56′N 151°03′W
110 E11 **Skwierzyna** *Ger.* Schwerin. Lubuskie, W Poland 52°37′N 15°27′E
96 G9 **Skye, Isle of** *island* NW Scotland, United Kingdom
36 K13 **Sky Harbor** ✕ (Phoenix) Arizona, SW USA 32°26′N 112°00′W
32 I8 **Skykomish** Washington, NW USA 47°40′N 121°20′W
Skylge *see* Terschelling
63 F19 **Skyring, Peninsula** *peninsula* S Chile
63 H24 **Skyring, Seno** *inlet* S Chile
115 H17 **Skyropoúla** *var.* Skiropoula. *island* Vóreies Sporádes, Greece, Aegean Sea
115 I17 **Skýros** *var.* Skíros. Skńyros, Vóreies Sporádes, Greece, Aegean Sea 38°55′N 24°34′E
115 I17 **Skýros** *var.* Skíros; *anc.* Scyros. *island* Vóreies Sporádes, Greece, Aegean Sea
118 J12 **Slabodka** *Rus.* Slobodka. Vitsyebskaya Voblasts', NW Belarus 55°41′N 27°11′E
95 I23 **Slagelse** Sjælland, E Denmark 55°25′N 11°22′E
93 I14 **Slagnäs** Norrbotten, N Sweden 65°36′N 18°10′E
39 T10 **Slana** Alaska, USA 62°46′N 144°00′W
97 F20 **Slaney** *Ir.* An tSláine. ⟿ SE Ireland
116 J13 **Slănic** Prahova, SE Romania 45°14′N 25°58′E
116 K11 **Slănic Moldova** Bacău, E Romania 46°12′N 26°23′E
113 H16 **Slano** Dubrovnik-Neretva, SE Croatia 42°47′N 17°54′E
124 F13 **Slantsy** Leningradskaya Oblast', NW Russian Federation 59°06′N 28°00′E
111 C16 **Slaný** *Ger.* Schlan. Střední Čechy, NW Czech Republic 50°14′N 14°05′E
111 K16 **Śląskie** ◆ *province* S Poland
12 C10 **Slate Falls** Ontario, S Canada 51°11′N 91°32′W
27 T4 **Slater** Missouri, C USA 39°13′N 93°04′W
112 H9 **Slatina** *Hung.* Szlatina; *prev.* Podravska Slatina. Virovitica-Podravina, NE Croatia 45°40′N 17°46′E
116 I14 **Slatina** Olt, S Romania 44°27′N 24°21′E
25 N5 **Slaton** Texas, SW USA 33°26′N 101°38′W
95 H14 **Slattum** Akershus, S Norway 60°00′N 10°55′E
11 R10 **Slave** ⟿ Alberta/Northwest Territories, C Canada
68 E12 **Slave Coast** *coastal region* W Africa
11 P13 **Slave Lake** Alberta, SW Canada 55°17′N 114°46′W
122 I13 **Slavgorod** Altayskiy Kray, S Russian Federation 52°55′N 78°46′E
Slavgorod *see* Slawharad
Slavonia *see* Slavonija
112 G9 **Slavonija** *Eng.* Slavonia, *Ger.* Slawonien, *Hung.* Szlavonia, Szlavonország. *cultural region* NE Croatia
112 H10 **Slavonski Brod** *Ger.* Brod, *Hung.* Bród; *prev.* Brod, Brod na Savi. Brod-Posavina, NE Croatia 45°09′N 18°00′E
112 G10 **Slavonski Brod-Posavina** *off.* Brodsko-Posavska Županija, *var.* Brod-Posavina. ◆ *province* NE Croatia
116 L4 **Slavuta** Khmel'nyts'ka Oblast', NW Ukraine 50°18′N 26°52′E
117 P2 **Slavutych** Chernihivs'ka Oblast', N Ukraine 51°31′N 30°47′E
123 R15 **Slavyanka** Primorskiy Kray, SE Russian Federation 42°46′N 131°19′E
114 J8 **Slavyanovo** Pleven, N Bulgaria 43°28′N 24°52′E
Slavyansk *see* Slov"yans'k
126 K14 **Slavyansk-na-Kubani** Krasnodarskiy Kray, SW Russian Federation 45°16′N 38°09′E
119 N20 **Slawharad** *Rus.* Slavgorod. Mahilyowskaya Voblasts', E Belarus 53°27′N 31°00′E
110 G7 **Sławno** Zachodnio-pomorskie, NW Poland 54°23′N 16°43′E
Slawonien *see* Slavonija
29 S10 **Slayton** Minnesota, N USA 43°59′N 95°45′W
97 N18 **Sleaford** E England, United Kingdom 52°59′N 00°28′W
97 A20 **Slea Head** *Ir.* Ceann Sléibhe. *headland* SW Ireland 52°05′N 10°25′W
96 G9 **Sleat, Sound of** *strait* NW Scotland, United Kingdom
Sledyuki *see* Slyedzyuki
12 I5 **Sleeper Islands** *island group* Nunavut, C Canada
31 O6 **Sleeping Bear Point** *headland* Michigan, N USA 44°54′N 86°02′W
29 T10 **Sleepy Eye** Minnesota, N USA 44°18′N 94°43′W
39 O11 **Sleetmute** Alaska, USA 61°42′N 157°10′W
Sléibhe, Ceann *see* Slea Head
Slēmānī *see* As Sulaymānīyah
195 O5 **Slessor Glacier** *glacier* Antarctica
22 L9 **Slidell** Louisiana, S USA 30°16′N 89°46′W
18 K12 **Slide Mountain** ▲ New York, NE USA 42°00′N 74°23′W
98 I13 **Sliedrecht** Zuid-Holland, C Netherlands 51°50′N 04°46′E
121 P16 **Sliema** N Malta 35°54′N 14°31′E
97 G16 **Slieve Donard** ▲ SE Northern Ireland, United Kingdom 54°10′N 05°57′W
Sligeach *see* Sligo
97 D16 **Sligo** *Ir.* Sligeach. Sligo, NW Ireland 54°17′N 08°28′W
97 C16 **Sligo** *Ir.* Sligeach. *cultural region* NW Ireland
97 C15 **Sligo Bay** *Ir.* Cuan Shligigh. *inlet* NW Ireland
18 B13 **Slippery Rock** Pennsylvania, NE USA 41°02′N 80°02′W
95 P19 **Slite** Gotland, SE Sweden 57°37′N 18°46′E
114 L9 **Sliven** *var.* Slivno. Sliven, C Bulgaria 42°42′N 26°21′E
114 L10 **Sliven** ◆ *province* C Bulgaria
114 G9 **Slivnitsa** Sofiya, W Bulgaria 42°51′N 23°01′E
Slivno *see* Sliven
114 L7 **Slivo Pole** Ruse, N Bulgaria 43°57′N 26°15′E
29 S13 **Sloan** Iowa, C USA 42°13′N 96°13′W
35 X12 **Sloan** Nevada, W USA 35°56′N 115°13′W
Slobodka *see* Slabodka
125 R14 **Slobodskoy** Kirovskaya Oblast', NW Russian Federation 58°43′N 50°12′E
Slobodzeya *see* Slobozia
117 O10 **Slobozia** *Rus.* Slobodzeya. E Moldova 46°45′N 29°42′E
116 L14 **Slobozia** Ialomiţa, SE Romania 44°34′N 27°23′E
98 O5 **Slochteren** Groningen, NE Netherlands 53°13′N 06°48′E
119 H17 **Slonim** *Pol.* Słonim. Hrodzyenskaya Voblasts', W Belarus 53°06′N 25°19′E
Słonim *see* Slonim
98 K7 **Sloter Meer** ◎ N Netherlands
Slot, The *see* New Georgia Sound
97 N22 **Slough** S England, United Kingdom 51°31′N 00°36′W
111 J20 **Slovakia** *off.* Slovenská Republika, *Ger.* Slowakei, *Hung.* Szlovákia, *Slvk.* Slovensko. ◆ *republic* C Europe
Slovak Ore Mountains *see* Slovenské rudohorie
Slovechna *see* Slavyechna
109 S12 **Slovenia** *off.* Republic of Slovenia, *Ger.* Slowenien, *Slvn.* Slovenija. ◆ *republic* SE Europe
Slovenia, Republic of *see* Slovenia
Slovenija *see* Slovenia
109 V10 **Slovenj Gradec** *Ger.* Windischgraz. N Slovenia 46°29′N 15°05′E
109 W10 **Slovenska Bistrica** *Ger.* Windischfeistritz. NE Slovenia 46°21′N 15°27′E
Slovenská Republika *see* Slovakia
109 W10 **Slovenske Konjice** E Slovenia 46°21′N 15°28′E
111 K20 **Slovenské rudohorie** *Eng.* Slovak Ore Mountains, *Ger.* Slowakisches Erzgebirge, Ungarisches Erzgebirge. ▲▲ C Slovakia
Slovensko *see* Slovakia
117 Y7 **Slov"yanoserbs'k** Luhans'ka Oblast', E Ukraine 48°41′N 39°00′E
117 W6 **Slov"yans'k** *Rus.* Slavyansk. Donets'ka Oblast', E Ukraine 48°51′N 37°38′E
Slowakei *see* Slovakia
Slowakisches Erzgebirge *see* Slovenské rudohorie
Slowenien *see* Slovenia
110 D11 **Słubice** *Ger.* Frankfurt. Lubuskie, W Poland 52°20′N 14°35′E
119 K19 **Sluch** *Rus.* Sluch'. ⟿ C Belarus
116 L4 **Sluch** ⟿ NW Ukraine
99 D16 **Sluis** Zeeland, SW Netherlands 51°18′N 03°22′E
112 D10 **Slunj** *Hung.* Szluin. Karlovac, C Croatia 45°06′N 15°35′E
110 I11 **Słupca** Wielkopolskie, C Poland 52°17′N 17°52′E
110 G6 **Słupia** *Ger.* Stolpe. ⟿ NW Poland
110 G6 **Słupsk** *Ger.* Stolp. Pomorskie, N Poland 54°28′N 17°01′E
119 K18 **Slutsk** Minskaya Voblasts', S Belarus 53°02′N 27°32′E
119 O16 **Slyedzyuki** *Rus.* Sledyuki. Mahilyowskaya Voblasts', E Belarus 53°35′N 30°22′E
97 A17 **Slyne Head** *Ir.* Ceann Léime. *headland* W Ireland 53°25′N 10°11′W
27 U14 **Smackover** Arkansas, C USA 33°21′N 92°43′W
95 L20 **Småland** *cultural region* S Sweden
95 K20 **Smålandsstenar** Jönköping, S Sweden 57°10′N 13°24′E
Small Malaita *see* Maramasike
13 O8 **Smallwood Reservoir** ◎ Newfoundland and Labrador, S Canada
119 N14 **Smalyany** *Rus.* Smolyany. Vitsyebskaya Voblasts', NE Belarus 54°36′N 30°04′E
119 L15 **Smalyavichy** *Rus.* Smolevichi. Minskaya Voblasts', C Belarus 54°02′N 28°05′E
74 C9 **Smara** *var.* Es Semara. N Western Sahara 26°45′N 11°44′W
119 I14 **Smarhon'** *Pol.* Smorgonie, *Rus.* Smorgon'. Hrodzyenskaya Voblasts', W Belarus 54°29′N 26°24′E
112 M11 **Smederevo** *Ger.* Semendria. Serbia, N Serbia 44°41′N 20°56′E
112 M12 **Smederevska Palanka** Serbia, C Serbia 44°24′N 20°56′E
95 M14 **Smedjebacken** Dalarna, C Sweden 60°08′N 15°25′E
116 L13 **Smeeni** Buzău, SE Romania 45°00′N 26°52′E
Smela *see* Smila
107 D16 **Smeralda, Costa** *cultural region* Sardegna, Italy, C Mediterranean Sea
111 J22 **Śmigiel** *Ger.* Schmiegel. Wielkopolskie, C Poland 52°02′N 16°33′E
117 Q6 **Smila** *Rus.* Smela. Cherkas'ka Oblast', C Ukraine 49°15′N 31°54′E
98 N7 **Smilde** Drenthe, NE Netherlands 52°57′N 06°28′E
11 S16 **Smiley** Saskatchewan, S Canada 51°40′N 109°24′W
25 T12 **Smiley** Texas, SW USA 29°16′N 97°38′W
Smilten *see* Smiltene
118 I8 **Smiltene** *Ger.* Smilten. N Latvia 57°25′N 25°53′E
123 T13 **Smirnykh** Ostrov Sakhalin, Sakhalinskaya Oblast', SE Russian Federation 49°43′N 142°48′E
11 Q13 **Smith** Alberta, W Canada 55°06′N 113°57′W
39 P4 **Smith Bay** *bay* Alaska, NW USA
12 I3 **Smith, Cape** *headland* Québec, NE Canada 60°50′N 78°06′W
26 L3 **Smith Center** Kansas, C USA 39°46′N 98°46′W
10 K13 **Smithers** British Columbia, SW Canada 54°45′N 127°10′W
21 V10 **Smithfield** North Carolina, SE USA 35°30′N 78°21′W
36 L1 **Smithfield** Utah, W USA 41°50′N 111°49′W
21 X7 **Smithfield** Virginia, NE USA 36°41′N 76°38′W
12 I3 **Smith Island** *island* Nunavut, C Canada
Smith Island *see* Sumisu-jima
20 H7 **Smithland** Kentucky, S USA 37°06′N 88°24′W
21 T7 **Smith Mountain Lake** *var.* Leesville Lake. ⊠ Virginia, NE USA
34 L1 **Smith River** California, W USA 41°54′N 124°09′W
33 R9 **Smith River** ⟿ Montana, NW USA
14 L13 **Smiths Falls** Ontario, SE Canada 44°54′N 76°01′W
33 N13 **Smiths Ferry** Idaho, NW USA 44°19′N 116°04′W
20 K7 **Smiths Grove** Kentucky, S USA 37°01′N 86°14′W
183 N15 **Smithton** Tasmania, SE Australia 40°54′S 145°06′E
18 L14 **Smithtown** Long Island, New York, NE USA 40°52′N 73°13′W
20 K9 **Smithville** Tennessee, S USA 35°59′N 85°49′W
25 T11 **Smithville** Texas, SW USA 30°04′N 97°32′W
Šmohor *see* Hermagor
35 Q4 **Smoke Creek Desert** *desert* Nevada, W USA
11 O14 **Smoky** ⟿ Alberta, W Canada
182 E7 **Smoky Bay** South Australia 32°22′S 133°57′E
183 V6 **Smoky Cape** *headland* New South Wales, SE Australia 30°54′S 153°06′E
26 L4 **Smoky Hill River** ⟿ Kansas, C USA
26 L4 **Smoky Hills** *hill range* Kansas, C USA
11 Q14 **Smoky Lake** Alberta, SW Canada 54°08′N 112°26′W
94 E8 **Smøla** *island* W Norway
126 H4 **Smolensk** Smolenskaya Oblast', W Russian Federation 54°48′N 32°08′E
126 H4 **Smolenskaya Oblast'** ◆ *province* W Russian Federation
Smolensk-Moscow Upland *see* Smolensko-Moskovskaya Vozvyshennost'
126 J3 **Smolensko-Moskovskaya Vozvyshennost'** *var.* Smolensk-Moscow Upland. ▲▲ W Russian Federation
Smolevichi *see* Smalyavichy
115 C15 **Smólikas** *var.* Smolikás. ▲ W Greece 40°06′N 20°54′E
114 I12 **Smolyan** *prev.* Pashmakli. Smolyan, S Bulgaria 41°34′N 24°42′E
114 I12 **Smolyan** ◆ *province* S Bulgaria
Smolyany *see* Smalyany
33 S15 **Smoot** Wyoming, C USA 42°37′N 110°55′W
12 G12 **Smooth Rock Falls** Ontario, S Canada 49°17′N 81°37′W
Smorgon'/Smorgonie *see* Smarhon'
95 K23 **Smygehamn** Skåne, S Sweden 55°19′N 13°25′E
194 I7 **Smyley Island** *island* Antarctica
21 Y3 **Smyrna** Delaware, NE USA 39°18′N 75°36′W
23 S3 **Smyrna** Georgia, SE USA 33°52′N 84°30′W
20 J9 **Smyrna** Tennessee, S USA 36°00′N 86°30′W
Smyrna *see* İzmir
97 I16 **Snaefell** ▲ C Isle of Man 54°15′N 04°29′W
92 H3 **Snaefellsjökull** ▲ W Iceland 64°51′N 23°51′W
92 J3 **Snækollur** ▲ C Iceland 64°38′N 19°18′W
10 J4 **Snake** ⟿ Yukon Territory, NW Canada
29 O8 **Snake Creek** ⟿ South Dakota, N USA
183 P13 **Snake Island** *island* Victoria, SE Australia
35 Y6 **Snake Range** ▲▲ Nevada, W USA
32 K10 **Snake River** ⟿ NW USA
29 V6 **Snake River** ⟿ Minnesota, N USA
28 L12 **Snake River** ⟿ Nebraska, C USA
33 Q14 **Snake River Plain** *plain* Idaho, NW USA
93 F15 **Snåsa** Nord-Trøndelag, C Norway 64°16′N 12°25′E
21 O8 **Sneedville** Tennessee, S USA 36°31′N 83°13′W
98 K6 **Sneek** *Fris.* Snits. Fryslân, N Netherlands 53°02′N 05°40′E
Sneeuw-gebergte *see* Maoke, Pegunungan
95 F22 **Snejbjerg** Midtjylland, C Denmark 56°08′N 08°55′E
122 K9 **Snezhnogorsk** Krasnoyarskiy Kray, N Russian Federation 68°06′N 87°37′E
124 J3 **Snezhnogorsk** Murmanskaya Oblast', NW Russian Federation 69°12′N 33°20′E
Snezhnoye *see* Snizhne
111 G15 **Sněžka** *Ger.* Schneekoppe, *Pol.* Śnieżka. ▲ N Czech Republic/Poland 50°42′N 15°55′E
110 N8 **Śniardwy, Jezioro** *Ger.* Spirdingsee. ◎ NE Poland
Sniečkus *see* Visaginas
Śnieżka *see* Sněžka
117 R10 **Snihurivka** Mykolayivs'ka Oblast', S Ukraine 47°05′N 32°48′E
116 I5 **Snilov** ✕ (L'viv) L'vivs'ka Oblast', W Ukraine 49°45′N 23°59′E
111 O19 **Snina** *Hung.* Szinna. Prešovský Kraj, E Slovakia 49°N 22°10′E
Snits *see* Sneek
117 Y8 **Snizhne** *Rus.* Snezhnoye. Donets'ka Oblast', SE Ukraine 48°01′N 38°46′E
94 G10 **Snøhetta** *var.* Snohetta. ▲ S Norway 62°22′N 09°08′E
92 G12 **Snøtinden** ▲ C Norway 66°39′N 13°50′E
97 I18 **Snowdon** ▲ NW Wales, United Kingdom 53°04′N 04°04′W
97 I18 **Snowdonia** ▲▲ NW Wales, United Kingdom
Snowdrift *see* Lutselk'e
Snowdrift *see* Lutselk'e
37 N12 **Snowflake** Arizona, SW USA 34°30′N 110°04′W
21 Y5 **Snow Hill** Maryland, NE USA 38°11′N 75°23′W
21 W10 **Snow Hill** North Carolina, SE USA 35°26′N 77°39′W
194 H3 **Snowhill Island** *island* Antarctica
11 V13 **Snow Lake** Manitoba, C Canada 54°56′N 100°02′W
37 R5 **Snowmass Mountain** ▲ Colorado, C USA 39°07′N 107°04′W
18 M10 **Snow, Mount** ▲ Vermont, NE USA 42°56′N 72°52′W
34 M5 **Snow Mountain** ▲ California, W USA 39°44′N 123°01′W
Snow Mountains *see* Maoke, Pegunungan
33 N7 **Snowshoe Peak** ▲ Montana, NW USA 48°15′N 115°44′W
182 I8 **Snowtown** South Australia 33°49′S 138°13′E
36 K1 **Snowville** Utah, W USA 41°59′N 112°42′W
35 X3 **Snow Water Lake** ◎ Nevada, W USA
183 Q11 **Snowy Mountains** ▲▲ New South Wales/Victoria, SE Australia
183 Q12 **Snowy River** ⟿ New South Wales/Victoria, SE Australia
44 K5 **Snug Corner** Acklins Island, SE Bahamas 22°31′N 73°51′W
167 T13 **Snuŏl** Krâchéh, E Cambodia 12°04′N 106°26′E
116 J7 **Snyatyn** Ivano-Frankivs'ka Oblast', W Ukraine 48°30′N 25°50′E
26 L12 **Snyder** Oklahoma, C USA 34°37′N 98°56′W
25 O6 **Snyder** Texas, SW USA 32°43′N 100°54′W
172 H3 **Soalala** Mahajanga, W Madagascar 16°05′S 45°21′E
172 J4 **Soanierana-Ivongo** Toamasina, E Madagascar 16°53′S 49°35′E
171 R11 **Soasiu** *var.* Tidore. Pulau Tidore, E Indonesia 0°40′N 127°25′E
54 G8 **Soatá** Boyacá, C Colombia 06°23′N 72°40′W
172 I5 **Soavinandriana** Antananarivo, C Madagascar 19°09′S 46°43′E
77 V13 **Soba** Kaduna, C Nigeria 10°58′N 08°06′E
163 Y16 **Sobaek-sanmaek** ▲▲ S South Korea
80 F13 **Sobat** ⟿ NE South Sudan
171 Z14 **Sobger, Sungai** ⟿ Papua, E Indonesia
171 V13 **Sobiei** Papua, E Indonesia 02°31′S 134°30′E
126 M3 **Sobinka** Vladimirskaya Oblast', W Russian Federation 56°00′N 39°55′E
127 S7 **Sobolevo** Orenburgskaya Oblast', W Russian Federation 51°57′N 51°42′E
Soborsin *see* Săvârşin
164 D15 **Sobo-san** ▲ Kyūshū, SW Japan 32°50′N 131°16′E
111 G14 **Sobótka** Dolnośląskie, SW Poland 50°53′N 16°48′E
59 O15 **Sobradinho** Bahia, E Brazil 09°33′S 40°56′W
Sobradinho, Barragem de *see* Sobradinho, Represa de
59 O16 **Sobradinho, Represa de** *var.* Barragem de Sobradinho. ⊠ E Brazil
58 O13 **Sobral** Ceará, E Brazil 03°45′S 40°20′W
105 T4 **Sobrarbe** *physical region* NE Spain
109 R10 **Soča** *It.* Isonzo. ⟿ Italy/ Slovenia
110 L11 **Sochaczew** Mazowieckie, C Poland 52°15′N 20°15′E
126 L15 **Sochi** Krasnodarskiy Kray, SW Russian Federation 43°35′N 39°46′E
114 G13 **Sochós** *var.* Sohos, Sokhós. Kentrikí Makedonía, N Greece 40°49′N 23°23′E
191 R11 **Société, Archipel de la** *var.* Archipel de Tahiti, Îles de la Société, *Eng.* Society Islands. *island group* W French Polynesia
Société, Îles de la/Society Islands *see* Société, Archipel de la
21 T11 **Society Hill** South Carolina, SE USA 34°28′N 79°54′W
175 W9 **Society Ridge** *undersea feature* C Pacific Ocean
62 I5 **Socompa, Volcán** ▲ N Chile 24°18′S 68°03′W
Soconusco, Sierra de *see* Madre, Sierra
54 G8 **Socorro** Santander, C Colombia 06°30′N 73°16′W
37 R13 **Socorro** New Mexico, SW USA 33°58′N 106°55′W
Socotra *see* Suquṭrā
167 S14 **Soc Trăng** *var.* Khanh Hung. Soc Trăng, S Vietnam 09°36′N 105°58′E
105 P10 **Socuéllamos** Castilla-La Mancha, C Spain 39°18′N 02°48′W
35 W13 **Soda Lake** *salt flat* California, W USA

◆ Country ● Country Capital ◇ Dependent Territory ○ Dependent Territory Capital ◈ Administrative Regions ✕ International Airport ▲ Mountain ▲▲ Mountain Range Volcano ⟿ River ◎ Lake ⊠ Reservoir

92 L11 **Sodankylä** Lappi, N Finland 67°26′N 26°35′E
Sodari see Sodiri
33 R15 **Soda Springs** Idaho, NW USA 42°39′N 111°36′W
Soddo/Soddu see Sodo
20 L10 **Soddy Daisy** Tennessee, S USA 35°14′N 85°11′W
95 N14 **Söderfors** Uppsala, C Sweden 60°23′N 17°14′E
94 N12 **Söderhamn** Gävleborg, C Sweden 61°19′N 17°10′E
95 N17 **Söderköping** Östergötland, S Sweden 58°28′N 16°20′E
95 N17 **Södermanland** ◐ county C Sweden
95 O16 **Södertälje** Stockholm, C Sweden 59°11′N 17°39′E
80 D10 **Sodiri** var. Sawdirī, Sodari. Northern Kordofan, C Sudan 14°23′N 29°06′E
81 I14 **Sodo** var. Soddo, Soddu. Southern Nationalities, S Ethiopia 06°49′N 37°43′E
95 M19 **Södra Vi** Kalmar, S Sweden 57°45′N 15°45′E
18 G9 **Sodus Point** headland New York, NE USA 43°16′N 76°59′W
171 Q17 **Soe** prev. Soë. Timor, C Indonesia 09°51′S 124°29′E
Soebang see Subang
Soekaboemi see Sukabumi
169 N15 **Soekarno-Hatta** ✈ (Jakarta) Jawa, S Indonesia
Soëla-Sund see Soela Väin
118 E5 **Soela Väin** prev. Eng. Sele Sound, Ger. Dagden-Sund, Soëla-Sund. strait W Estonia
Soemba see Sumba, Pulau
Soembawa see Sumbawa
Soemenep see Sumenep
Soengaipenoeh see Sungaipenuh
Soerabaja see Surabaya
Soerakarta see Surakarta
101 G14 **Soest** Nordrhein-Westfalen, W Germany 51°34′N 08°06′E
98 J11 **Soest** Utrecht, C Netherlands 52°10′N 05°20′E
100 F11 **Soeste** 〰 NW Germany
98 J11 **Soesterberg** Utrecht, C Netherlands 52°07′N 05°17′E
115 E16 **Sofádes** var. Sofádhes. Thessalía, C Greece 39°20′N 22°06′E
Sofádhes see Sofádes
83 N18 **Sofala** Sofala, C Mozambique 20°04′S 34°43′E
83 N17 **Sofala** ◐ province C Mozambique
83 N18 **Sofala, Baia de** bay C Mozambique
172 J3 **Sofia** seasonal river NW Madagascar
Sofia see Sofiya
115 G19 **Sofikó** Pelopónnisos, S Greece 37°46′N 23°04′E
Sofi-Kurgan see Sopu-Korgon
114 G10 **Sofiya** var. Sophia, Eng. Sofia, Lat. Serdica. ● (Bulgaria) Sofiya-Grad, W Bulgaria 42°42′N 23°20′E
114 H9 **Sofiya** ◐ province W Bulgaria
114 G9 **Sofiya** ✈ Sofiya-Grad, W Bulgaria 42°42′N 23°26′E
114 G9 **Sofiya, Grad** ◐ municipality W Bulgaria
Sofiyevka see Sofiyivka
117 S8 **Sofiyivka** Rus. Sofiyevka. Dnipropetrovs'ka Oblast', E Ukraine 48°04′N 33°55′E
123 R13 **Sofiysk** Khabarovskiy Kray, SE Russian Federation 52°20′N 133°37′E
123 R12 **Sofiysk** Khabarovskiy Kray, SE Russian Federation 51°32′N 139°46′E
124 I6 **Sofporog** Respublika Kareliya, NW Russian Federation 65°48′N 31°30′E
115 L23 **Sofraná** prev. Záfora. island Kykládes, Greece, Aegean Sea
165 Y14 **Sōfu-gan** island Izu-shotō, SE Japan
156 K10 **Sog** Xizang Zizhiqu, W China 31°52′N 93°40′E
54 G9 **Sogamoso** Boyacá, C Colombia 05°43′N 72°56′W
136 I11 **Soğanlı Çayı** 〰 N Turkey
94 E12 **Sogn** physical region S Norway
Sogndal see Sogndalsfjøra
94 E12 **Sogndalsfjøra** var. Sogndal. Sogn Og Fjordane, S Norway 61°13′N 07°05′E
95 E18 **Søgne** Vest-Agder, S Norway 58°05′N 07°49′E
94 D12 **Sognefjorden** fjord NE North Sea
94 C12 **Sogn Og Fjordane** ◐ county S Norway
162 I11 **Sogo Nur** ◎ N China
159 T12 **Sogruma** Qinghai, W China 32°32′N 100°52′E
Sŏgwip'o see Seogwipo
Sohâg see Sawhāj
Sohar see Şuḩār
64 H9 **Sohm Plain** undersea feature NW Atlantic Ocean
100 H7 **Soholmer Au** 〰 N Germany
Sohos see Sochós
Sohrau see Żory
99 F20 **Soignies** Hainaut, SW Belgium 50°35′N 04°04′E
159 R15 **Soila** Xizang Zizhiqu, W China 30°40′N 97°07′E
103 P4 **Soissons** anc. Augusta Suessionum, Noviodunum. Aisne, N France 49°23′N 03°20′E
164 H13 **Sōja** Okayama, Honshū, SW Japan 34°40′N 133°42′E
152 F13 **Sojat** Rājasthān, N India 25°53′N 73°45′E
163 W13 **Sŏjosŏn-man** inlet W North Korea
116 I4 **Sokal'** Rus. Sokal. L'vivs'ka Oblast', NW Ukraine 50°29′N 24°17′E
163 Y14 **Sokcho** prev. Sokch'o. N South Korea 38°07′N 128°34′E
Sokch'o see Sokcho
136 B15 **Söke** Aydın, SW Turkey 37°46′N 27°24′E
189 N12 **Sokehs Island** island E Micronesia
79 M24 **Sokele** Katanga, SE Dem. Rep. Congo 09°54′S 24°38′E
147 R11 **Sokh** Uzb. Sūkh. 〰 Kyrgyzstan/Uzbekistan
Sokh see So'x
Sokhós see Sochós
137 Q8 **Sokhumi** Rus. Sukhumi. NW Georgia 43°02′N 41°01′E
113 O14 **Sokobanja** Serbia, E Serbia 43°39′N 21°51′E
77 R15 **Sokodé** C Togo 08°58′N 01°10′E
123 T10 **Sokol** Magadanskaya Oblast', E Russian Federation 59°51′N 150°56′E
124 M13 **Sokol** Vologodskaya Oblast', NW Russian Federation 59°26′N 40°09′E
110 P9 **Sokółka** Podlaskie, NE Poland 53°24′N 23°31′E
76 M11 **Sokolo** Ségou, W Mali 14°43′N 06°02′W
111 A16 **Sokolov** Ger. Falkenau an der Eger; prev. Falknov nad Ohří. Karlovarský Kraj, W Czech Republic 50°10′N 12°38′E
111 O16 **Sokołów Małopolski** Podkarpackie, SE Poland 50°12′N 22°07′E
110 O11 **Sokołów Podlaski** Mazowieckie, C Poland 52°26′N 22°14′E
76 G11 **Sokone** W Senegal 13°53′N 16°22′W
77 T12 **Sokoto** Sokoto, NW Nigeria 13°05′N 05°16′E
77 T12 **Sokoto** ◐ state NW Nigeria
77 S12 **Sokoto** 〰 NW Nigeria
Sokotra see Suquṭrā
147 U7 **Sokuluk** Chuyskaya Oblast', N Kyrgyzstan 42°53′N 74°19′E
116 L7 **Sokyryany** Chernivets'ka Oblast', W Ukraine 48°28′N 27°25′E
95 C16 **Sola** Rogaland, S Norway 58°53′N 05°36′E
187 R12 **Sola** Vanua Lava, N Vanuatu 13°51′S 167°34′E
95 C17 **Sola** ✈ (Stavanger) Rogaland, S Norway 58°54′N 05°36′E
81 H18 **Solai** Rift Valley, W Kenya 0°02′N 36°03′E
152 I8 **Solan** Himāchal Pradesh, N India 30°54′N 77°06′E
185 A25 **Solander Island** island SW New Zealand
Solano see Bahía Solano
155 F15 **Solāpur** var. Sholāpur. Mahārāshtra, W India 17°43′N 75°54′E
93 H16 **Solberg** Västernorrland, C Sweden 63°48′N 17°40′E
116 K9 **Solca** Ger. Solka. Suceava, N Romania 47°40′N 25°50′E
105 O16 **Sol, Costa del** coastal region S Spain
106 F5 **Solda** Ger. Sulden. Trentino-Alto Adige, N Italy 46°33′N 10°35′E
117 N9 **Şoldăneşti** Rus. Sholdaneshty. N Moldova 47°49′N 28°45′E
Soldau see Wkra
108 L8 **Sölden** Tirol, W Austria 46°58′N 11°01′E
27 P3 **Soldier Creek** 〰 Kansas, C USA
39 R12 **Soldotna** Alaska, USA 60°29′N 151°03′W
110 I10 **Solec Kujawski** Kujawsko-pomorskie, C Poland 53°04′N 18°09′E
61 B16 **Soledad** Santa Fe, C Argentina 30°38′S 60°52′W
55 E4 **Soledad** Atlántico, N Colombia 10°54′N 74°48′W
35 O11 **Soledad** California, W USA 36°25′N 121°19′W
55 O7 **Soledad** Anzoátegui, NE Venezuela 08°10′N 63°36′W
61 H15 **Soledade** Rio Grande do Sul, S Brazil 28°50′S 52°30′W
Isla Soledad see East Falkland
103 Y15 **Solenzara** Corse, France, C Mediterranean Sea 41°55′N 09°24′E
Soleure see Solothurn
94 C12 **Solheim** Hordaland, S Norway 60°54′N 05°30′E
125 N14 **Soligalich** Kostromskaya Oblast', NW Russian Federation 59°05′N 42°15′E
Soligorsk see Salihorsk
97 L20 **Solihull** C England, United Kingdom 52°25′N 01°45′W
125 U13 **Solikamsk** Permskiy Kray, NW Russian Federation 59°37′N 56°46′E
127 V8 **Sol'-Iletsk** Orenburgskaya Oblast', W Russian Federation 51°09′N 55°05′E
57 G17 **Solimana, Nevado** ▲ S Peru 15°24′S 72°49′W
58 E13 **Solimões, Rio** 〰 C Brazil
113 E14 **Solin** It. Salona; anc. Salonae. Split-Dalmacija, S Croatia 43°33′N 16°29′E
101 E15 **Solingen** Nordrhein-Westfalen, W Germany 51°10′N 07°05′E
Solka see Solca
93 H16 **Sollefteå** Västernorrland, C Sweden 63°09′N 17°15′E
95 O15 **Sollentuna** Stockholm, C Sweden 59°26′N 17°56′E
105 X9 **Sóller** Mallorca, Spain, W Mediterranean Sea 39°46′N 02°42′E
94 L13 **Sollerön** Dalarna, C Sweden 60°55′N 14°34′E
101 I14 **Solling** hill range C Germany
95 O16 **Solna** Stockholm, C Sweden 59°22′N 17°58′E
126 K3 **Solnechnogorsk** Moskovskaya Oblast', W Russian Federation 56°07′N 37°04′E
123 R10 **Solnechnyy** Khabarovskiy Kray, SE Russian Federation 50°41′N 136°42′E
123 S13 **Solnechnyy** Respublika Sakha (Yakutiya), NE Russian Federation 60°13′N 137°42′E
Solo see Surakarta
107 L17 **Solofra** Campania, S Italy 40°49′N 14°48′E
168 J11 **Solok** Sumatera, W Indonesia 0°45′S 100°42′E
42 C6 **Sololá** Sololá, W Guatemala 14°46′N 91°09′W
42 A2 **Sololá** off. Departamento de Sololá. ◐ department SW Guatemala
Sololá, Departamento de see Sololá
81 J16 **Sololo** Eastern, N Kenya 03°31′N 38°39′E
42 C4 **Soloma** Huehuetenango, W Guatemala 15°38′N 91°25′W
38 M9 **Solomon** Alaska, USA 64°33′N 164°26′W
27 N4 **Solomon** Kansas, C USA 38°55′N 97°22′W
187 N9 **Solomon Islands** prev. British Solomon Islands Protectorate. ◆ commonwealth republic W Solomon Islands N Melanesia W Pacific Ocean
186 L7 **Solomon Islands** island group Papua New Guinea/Solomon Islands
26 M3 **Solomon River** 〰 Kansas, C USA
186 H8 **Solomon Sea** sea W Pacific Ocean
31 U11 **Solon** Ohio, N USA 41°23′N 81°26′W
117 T8 **Solone** Dnipropetrovs'ka Oblast', E Ukraine 48°12′N 34°49′E
171 P16 **Solor, Kepulauan** island group S Indonesia
126 M4 **Solotcha** Ryazanskaya Oblast', W Russian Federation 54°43′N 39°50′E
108 D7 **Solothurn** Fr. Soleure. Solothurn, NW Switzerland 47°13′N 07°32′E
108 D7 **Solothurn** Fr. Soleure. ◐ canton NW Switzerland
124 J7 **Solovetskiye Ostrova** island group NW Russian Federation
105 V5 **Solsona** Cataluña, NE Spain 42°00′N 01°31′E
113 E14 **Šolta** It. Solta. island S Croatia
Soltānābād see Kāshmar
142 L4 **Soltānīyeh** Zanjān, NW Iran 36°24′N 48°50′E
100 I11 **Soltau** Niedersachsen, NW Germany 52°59′N 09°50′E
124 G14 **Sol'tsy** Novgorodskaya Oblast', W Russian Federation 58°09′N 30°23′E
Soltüstik Qazaqstan Oblysy see Severnyy Kazakhstan
Solun see Thessaloníki
113 O19 **Solunska Glava** ▲ C FYR Macedonia 41°43′N 21°24′E
95 L22 **Sölvesborg** Blekinge, S Sweden 56°04′N 14°35′E
97 J15 **Solway Firth** inlet England/Scotland, United Kingdom
82 I13 **Solwezi** North Western, NW Zambia 12°11′S 26°23′E
165 Q11 **Sōma** Fukushima, Honshū, C Japan 37°49′N 140°52′E
136 C13 **Soma** Manisa, W Turkey 39°10′N 27°36′E
Somali see Sumalē
81 O15 **Somalia** off. Somali Democratic Republic, Som. Jamuuriyada Demuqraadiga Soomaaliyeed, Soomaaliya; prev. Italian Somaliland, Somaliland Protectorate. ◆ republic E Africa
173 N6 **Somali Basin** undersea feature W Indian Ocean 0°00′N 52°00′E
Somali Democratic Republic see Somalia
80 N12 **Somaliland** ◐ disputed territory N Somalia
Somaliland Protectorate see Somalia
67 Y8 **Somali Plain** undersea feature W Indian Ocean 01°00′N 51°30′E
112 J8 **Sombor** Hung. Zombor. Vojvodina, NW Serbia 45°46′N 19°07′E
99 H20 **Sombreffe** Namur, S Belgium 50°32′N 04°39′E
40 L10 **Sombrerete** Zacatecas, C Mexico 23°38′N 103°40′W
45 V8 **Sombrero** island N Anguilla
151 Q21 **Sombrero Channel** channel Nicobar Islands, India
116 H9 **Şomcuta Mare** Hung. Nagysomkút; prev. Somcuţa Mare. Maramureş, N Romania 47°29′N 23°30′E
Somcuţa Mare see Şomcuta Mare
167 R9 **Somdet** Kalasin, E Thailand 16°41′N 103°44′E
99 L15 **Someren** Noord-Brabant, SE Netherlands 51°23′N 05°42′E
93 L19 **Somero** Länsi-Suomi, SW Finland 60°37′N 23°30′E
33 P7 **Somers** Montana, NW USA 48°04′N 114°16′W
64 A12 **Somerset** var. Somerset Village. W Bermuda 32°18′N 64°53′W
37 Q5 **Somerset** Colorado, C USA 38°55′N 107°27′W
20 M7 **Somerset** Kentucky, S USA 37°05′N 84°36′W
19 O12 **Somerset** Massachusetts, NE USA 41°46′N 71°07′W
97 K23 **Somerset** cultural region SW England, United Kingdom
Somerset East see Somerset-Oos
64 A12 **Somerset Island** island W Bermuda
197 N9 **Somerset Island** island Queen Elizabeth Islands, Nunavut, NW Canada
Somerset Nile see Victoria Nile
83 I25 **Somerset-Oos** var. Somerset East. Eastern Cape, S South Africa 32°44′S 25°35′E
Somerset Village see Somerset
83 E26 **Somerset-Wes** var. Somerset West. Western Cape, SW South Africa 34°05′S 18°51′E
Somerset West see Somerset-Wes
Somers Islands see Bermuda
18 J17 **Somers Point** New Jersey, NE USA 39°18′N 74°34′W
19 P9 **Somersworth** New Hampshire, NE USA 43°15′N 70°52′W
36 H15 **Somerton** Arizona, SW USA 32°36′N 114°42′W
18 J14 **Somerville** New Jersey, NE USA 40°34′N 74°36′W
20 F10 **Somerville** Tennessee, S USA 35°14′N 89°24′W
25 U10 **Somerville** Texas, SW USA 30°21′N 96°31′W
25 T10 **Somerville Lake** ⊠ Texas, SW USA
Someş/Somesch/Someşul see Szamos
103 N2 **Somme** ◐ department N France
103 N2 **Somme** 〰 N France
95 L18 **Sommen** Jönköping, S Sweden 58°07′N 14°58′E
95 M18 **Sommen** ◎ S Sweden
101 K16 **Sömmerda** Thüringen, C Germany 51°10′N 11°07′E
Sommerein see Šamorín
Sommerfeld see Lubsko
55 Y11 **Sommet Tabulaire** var. Mont Itoupé. ▲ S French Guiana
111 H25 **Somogy** off. Somogy Megye. ◐ county SW Hungary
Somogy Megye see Somogy
Somorja see Šamorín
105 N7 **Somosierra, Puerto de** pass N Spain
187 Y14 **Somosomo** Taveuni, N Fiji 16°46′S 179°57′W
42 I9 **Somotillo** Chinandega, NW Nicaragua 13°01′N 86°53′W
42 I8 **Somoto** Madriz, NW Nicaragua 13°29′N 86°36′W
110 I11 **Sompolno** Wielkopolskie, C Poland 52°24′N 18°30′E
102 J17 **Somport** var. Puerto de Somport, Sp. Somport; anc. Summus Portus. pass France/Spain see also Somport
99 K15 **Son** Noord-Brabant, S Netherlands 51°32′N 05°34′E
95 H15 **Son** Akershus, S Norway 59°32′N 10°42′E
154 L9 **Son** var. Sone. 〰 C India
43 R16 **Soná** Veraguas, W Panama 08°00′N 81°20′W
Sonag see Zêkog
Sonapur see Subarnapur
95 G24 **Sønderborg** Ger. Sonderburg. Syddanmark, SW Denmark 54°55′N 09°48′E
Sonderburg see Sønderborg
Sønderjyllands Amt see Syddanmark
101 K15 **Sondershausen** Thüringen, C Germany 51°22′N 10°52′E
Søndre Strømfjord see Kangerlussuaq
106 E6 **Sondrio** Lombardia, N Italy 46°11′N 09°52′E
Sone see Son
Sonepur see Subarnapur
57 K22 **Sonequera** ▲ S Bolivia 22°06′S 67°10′W
167 V12 **Sông Câu** Phu Yên, C Vietnam 13°26′N 109°12′E
167 R15 **Sông Đôc** Minh Hai, S Vietnam 09°03′N 104°51′E
81 H25 **Songea** Ruvuma, S Tanzania 10°42′S 35°39′E
163 X10 **Songhua Hu** ◎ NE China
163 Y7 **Songhua Jiang** var. Sungari. 〰 NE China
161 S8 **Songjiang** Shanghai Shi, E China 31°01′N 121°14′E
Sŏngjin see Kimch'aek
167 O16 **Songkhla** var. Songkla, Mal. Singora. Songkhla, SW Thailand 07°12′N 100°35′E
Songkla see Songkhla
163 T13 **Song Ling** ▲▲ NE China
129 U12 **Sông Ma** Laos Ma, Nam. 〰 Laos/Vietnam
163 W14 **Songnim** SW North Korea 38°43′N 125°40′E
82 B10 **Songo** Uíge, NW Angola 07°30′S 14°56′E
83 M15 **Songo** Tete, NW Mozambique 15°36′S 32°45′E
79 F21 **Songololo** Bas-Congo, SW Dem. Rep. Congo 05°40′S 14°05′E
160 H7 **Songpan** var. Jin'an, Tib. Sungpu. Sichuan, C China 32°49′N 103°39′E
Sŏngsan see Seongsan
161 R11 **Songxi** Fujian, SE China 27°33′N 118°46′E
160 M6 **Songxian** var. Song Xian. Henan, C China 34°11′N 112°04′E
Song Xian see Songxian
161 R10 **Songyang** var. Xiping; prev. Songyin. Zhejiang, SE China 28°29′N 119°27′E
Songyin see Songyang
163 V9 **Songyuan** var. Fu-yü, Petuna; prev. Fuyu. Jilin, NE China 45°10′N 124°52′E
Sonid Youqi see Saihan Tal
Sonid Zuoqi see Mandalt
152 I10 **Sonīpat** Haryāna, N India 29°00′N 77°01′E
93 M15 **Sonkajärvi** Itä-Suomi, C Finland 63°40′N 27°30′E
167 R6 **Sơn La** Sơn La, N Vietnam 21°20′N 103°55′E
149 O16 **Sonmiāni** Baluchistān, S Pakistan 25°24′N 66°37′E
149 O16 **Sonmiāni Bay** bay S Pakistan
101 K18 **Sonneberg** Thüringen, C Germany 50°22′N 11°10′E
101 N24 **Sonntagshorn** ▲ Austria/Germany 47°40′N 12°42′E
Sonoita see Sonoyta
40 E3 **Sonoita, Rio** var. Río Sonoyta. 〰 Mexico/USA
35 N7 **Sonoma** California, W USA 38°16′N 122°28′W
35 T3 **Sonoma Peak** ▲ Nevada, W USA 40°50′N 117°34′W
35 P8 **Sonora** California, W USA 37°58′N 120°22′W
25 O10 **Sonora** Texas, SW USA 30°34′N 100°39′W
40 F5 **Sonora** ◐ state NW Mexico
35 X17 **Sonoran Desert** var. Desierto de Altar. desert Mexico/USA see also Altar, Desierto de
40 G5 **Sonora, Río** 〰 NW Mexico
40 E2 **Sonoyta** var. Sonoita. Sonora, NW Mexico 31°49′N 112°50′W
Sonoyta, Río see Sonoita, Rio
142 K6 **Sonqor** var. Sunqur. Kermānshāhān, W Iran 34°45′N 47°39′E
105 N9 **Sonseca** var. Sonseca con Casalgordo. Castilla-La Mancha, C Spain 39°40′N 03°59′W
Sonseca con Casalgordo see Sonseca
54 E9 **Sonsón** Antioquia, W Colombia 05°45′N 75°18′W
42 E7 **Sonsonate** Sonsonate, W El Salvador 13°44′N 89°43′W
42 A9 **Sonsonate** ◐ department SW El Salvador
188 A10 **Sonsorol Islands** island group S Palau
112 J9 **Sonta** Hung. Szond; prev. Szonta. Vojvodina, NW Serbia 45°34′N 19°06′E
167 S6 **Sơn Tây** var. Sontay. Ha Tây, N Vietnam 21°06′N 105°32′E
Sontay see Sơn Tây
101 J25 **Sonthofen** Bayern, S Germany 47°31′N 10°16′E
Soochow see Suzhou
80 O13 **Sool** off. Gobolka Sool. ◐ region N Somalia
Soomaaliya/Soomaaliyeed, Jamuuriyada Demuqraadiga see Somalia
Soome Laht see Finland, Gulf of
23 V5 **Soperton** Georgia, SE USA 32°22′N 82°35′W
167 S6 **Sop Hao** Houaphan, N Laos 20°33′N 104°25′E
Sophia see Sofiya
171 S10 **Sopi** Pulau Morotai, E Indonesia 02°36′N 128°32′E
Sopianae see Pécs
171 U13 **Sopinusa** Papua, E Indonesia 03°31′S 132°55′E
81 B14 **Sopo** 〰 W South Sudan
Sopockinie/Sopotskin/Sopotskino see Sapotskin
114 I9 **Sopot** Plovdiv, C Bulgaria 42°39′N 24°43′E
110 I7 **Sopot** Ger. Zoppot. Pomorskie, N Poland 54°26′N 18°33′E
167 O8 **Sop Prap** var. Ban Sop Prap. Lampang, NW Thailand 17°55′N 99°20′E
111 G22 **Sopron** Ger. Ödenburg. Győr-Moson-Sopron, NW Hungary 47°40′N 16°35′E
147 U11 **Sopu-Korgon** var. Sofi-Kurgan. Oshskaya Oblast', SW Kyrgyzstan 40°03′N 73°30′E
152 H5 **Sopur** Jammu and Kashmir, NW India 34°19′N 74°30′E
107 J15 **Sora** Lazio, C Italy 41°43′N 13°37′E
154 N13 **Sorada** Orissa, E India 19°46′N 84°29′E
93 H17 **Söråker** Västernorrland, C Sweden 62°32′N 17°32′E
57 J17 **Sorata** La Paz, W Bolivia 15°47′S 68°38′W
Sorau/Sorau in der Niederlausitz see Żary
105 Q14 **Sorbas** Andalucía, S Spain 37°06′N 02°06′W
94 N11 **Sördellen** ◎ C Sweden
Sord/Sórd Choluim Chille see Swords
15 O11 **Sorel** Québec, SE Canada 46°03′N 73°06′W
183 P17 **Sorell** Tasmania, SE Australia 42°49′S 147°34′E
183 O17 **Sorell, Lake** ◎ Tasmania, SE Australia
106 E8 **Soresina** Lombardia, N Italy 45°17′N 09°51′E
95 D14 **Sørfjorden** fjord S Norway
94 N11 **Sörforsa** Gävleborg, C Sweden 61°45′N 17°00′E
103 R14 **Sorgues** Vaucluse, SE France 44°N 04°52′E
136 K13 **Sorgun** Yozgat, C Turkey 39°49′N 35°10′E
105 P5 **Soria** Castilla y León, N Spain 41°47′N 02°26′W
105 P6 **Soria** ◐ province Castilla y León, N Spain
61 D19 **Soriano** Soriano, SW Uruguay 33°25′S 58°21′W
61 D19 **Soriano** ◐ department SW Uruguay
92 O4 **Sørkapp** headland SW Svalbard 76°34′N 16°33′E
143 T5 **Sorkh, Kūh-e** ▲▲ NE Iran
95 I23 **Sorø** Sjælland, E Denmark 55°26′N 11°34′E
Soro see Ghazal, Bahr el
116 M8 **Soroca** Rus. Soroki. N Moldova 48°10′N 28°18′E
60 L10 **Sorocaba** São Paulo, S Brazil 23°29′S 47°27′W
Sorochino see Sarochyna
127 T7 **Sorochinsk** Orenburgskaya Oblast', W Russian Federation 52°26′N 53°10′E
Soroki see Soroca
188 H15 **Sorol** atoll Caroline Islands, W Micronesia
171 T12 **Sorong** Papua, E Indonesia 0°49′S 131°16′E
81 G17 **Soroti** C Uganda 01°42′N 33°37′E
Sørøy see Sørøya
92 J8 **Sørøya** var. Sørøy, Lapp. Sállan. island N Norway
104 G11 **Sorraia, Rio** 〰 C Portugal
92 I10 **Sørreisa** Troms, N Norway 69°08′N 18°09′E
107 K18 **Sorrento** anc. Surrentum. Campania, S Italy 40°37′N 14°23′E
104 H10 **Sor, Ribeira de** stream C Portugal
195 T3 **Sør Rondane** Eng. Sor Rondane Mountains. ▲▲ Antarctica
Sor Rondane Mountains see Sør Rondane
93 H14 **Sorsele** Västerbotten, N Sweden 65°31′N 17°34′E
107 B17 **Sorso** Sardegna, Italy, C Mediterranean Sea 40°46′N 08°33′E
171 P4 **Sorsogon** Luzon, N Philippines 12°57′N 124°04′E
105 U4 **Sort** Cataluña, NE Spain 42°25′N 01°07′E
124 H11 **Sortavala** prev. Serdobol'. Respublika Kareliya, NW Russian Federation 61°45′N 30°37′E
107 L25 **Sortino** Sicilia, Italy, C Mediterranean Sea 37°10′N 15°02′E
92 G10 **Sortland** Nordland, C Norway 68°44′N 15°25′E
94 G9 **Sør-Trøndelag** ◐ county S Norway
95 I15 **Sørumsand** Akershus, S Norway 59°58′N 11°13′E
118 D6 **Sõrve Säär** headland SW Estonia 57°54′N 22°02′E
95 K22 **Sösdala** Skåne, S Sweden 56°00′N 13°36′E
105 R4 **Sos del Rey Católico** Aragón, NE Spain 42°30′N 01°13′W
93 F15 **Sösjöfjällen** ▲ C Sweden 63°51′N 13°15′E
126 K7 **Sosna** 〰 W Russian Federation
62 H12 **Sosneado, Cerro** ▲ W Argentina 34°44′S 69°52′W
125 S9 **Sosnogorsk** Respublika Komi, NW Russian Federation 63°33′N 53°55′E
124 J8 **Sosnovets** Respublika Kareliya, NW Russian Federation 64°25′N 34°23′E
Sosnovets see Sosnowiec
127 Q3 **Sosnovka** Chuvashskaya Respublika, W Russian Federation 56°18′N 47°14′E
125 S16 **Sosnovka** Kirovskaya Oblast', NW Russian Federation 56°15′N 51°20′E
124 M6 **Sosnovka** Murmanskaya Oblast', NW Russian Federation 66°28′N 40°31′E
126 M6 **Sosnovka** Tambovskaya Oblast', W Russian Federation 53°14′N 41°19′E
124 H12 **Sosnovo** Fin. Rautu. Leningradskaya Oblast', NW Russian Federation 60°30′N 30°13′E
127 V3 **Sosnovyy Bor** Respublika Bashkortostan, W Russian Federation 55°51′N 57°09′E
Sosnovyy Bor see Sasnovy Bor
111 J16 **Sosnowiec** Ger. Sosnowitz, Rus. Sosnovets. Śląskie, S Poland 50°16′N 19°07′E
Sosnowitz see Sosnowiec
117 R2 **Sosnytsya** Chernihivs'ka Oblast', N Ukraine 51°31′N 32°30′E
109 V10 **Šoštanj** N Slovenia 46°23′N 15°03′E
122 G10 **Sos'va** Sverdlovskaya Oblast', C Russian Federation 59°13′N 61°58′E
54 D12 **Sotará, Volcán** 🌋 S Colombia 02°04′N 76°40′W
76 D10 **Sotavento, Ilhas de** var. Leeward Islands. island group S Cape Verde
93 N15 **Sotkamo** Oulu, C Finland 64°06′N 28°30′E
109 W11 **Sotla** 〰 E Slovenia
41 P10 **Soto la Marina** Tamaulipas, C Mexico 23°44′N 98°10′W
41 P10 **Soto la Marina, Río** 〰 C Mexico
95 B14 **Sotra** island S Norway
41 X12 **Sotuta** Yucatán, SE Mexico 20°34′N 89°00′W
79 F17 **Souanké** Sangha, NW Congo 02°03′N 14°02′E
76 M17 **Soubré** S Ivory Coast 05°50′N 06°35′W
115 H24 **Soúda** var. Soúdha, Eng. Suda. Kríti, Greece, E Mediterranean Sea 35°29′N 24°04′E
Soúdha see Soúda
Soueida see As Suwaydā'
114 L12 **Souflí** prev. Souflíon. Anatolikí Makedonía kai Thráki, NE Greece 41°12′N 26°18′E
Souflíon see Souflí
45 S11 **Soufrière** W Saint Lucia 13°51′N 61°03′W
45 X6 **Soufrière** 🌋 Basse Terre, S Guadeloupe 16°03′N 61°39′W
102 M13 **Souillac** Lot, S France 44°53′N 01°29′E
173 Y17 **Souillac** S Mauritius 20°31′S 57°31′E
74 M5 **Souk Ahras** NE Algeria 36°14′N 08°00′E
Souk el Arba du Rharb/Souk-el-Arba-du-Rharb/Souk-el-Arba-el-Rhab see Souk-el-Arba-Rharb
74 E6 **Souk-el-Arba-Rharb** var. Souk el Arba du Rharb, Souk-el-Arba-du-Rharb, Souk-el-Arba-el-Rhab. NW Morocco 34°38′N 06°00′W
Soukhné see As Sukhnah
Sŏul see Seoul
102 J11 **Soulac-sur-Mer** Gironde, SW France 45°31′N 01°06′W
99 L19 **Soumagne** Liège, E Belgium 50°36′N 05°48′E
18 M14 **Sound Beach** Long Island, New York, NE USA 40°56′N 72°58′W
95 J22 **Sound, The** Dan. Øresund, Swe. Öresund. strait Denmark/Sweden
115 H20 **Soúnio, Akrotírio** headland C Greece 37°39′N 24°01′E
138 F8 **Soûr** var. Şūr; anc. Tyre. SW Lebanon 33°18′N 35°30′E
Sources, Mont-aux- see Phofung
104 G8 **Soure** Coimbra, N Portugal 40°04′N 08°38′W
11 W17 **Souris** Manitoba, S Canada 49°38′N 100°17′W
13 Q14 **Souris** Prince Edward Island, SE Canada 46°22′N 62°16′W
28 L2 **Souris River** var. Mouse River. 〰 Canada/USA
25 X10 **Sour Lake** Texas, SW USA 30°08′N 94°24′W
115 F17 **Soúrpi** Thessalía, C Greece 39°07′N 22°55′E
104 H11 **Sousel** Portalegre, C Portugal 38°57′N 07°40′W
75 N6 **Sousse** var. Sūsah. NE Tunisia 35°46′N 10°38′E
14 H11 **South** 〰 Ontario, S Canada
South see Sud
83 G23 **South Africa** off. Republic of South Africa, Afr. Suid-Afrika. ◆ republic S Africa
South Africa, Republic of see South Africa
46-47 **South America** continent
2 J17 **South American Plate** tectonic feature
97 M23 **Southampton** hist. Hamwih, Lat. Clausentum. S England, United Kingdom 50°54′N 01°23′W
19 N14 **Southampton** Long Island, New York, NE USA 40°52′N 72°22′W
9 P8 **Southampton Island** island Nunavut, NE Canada
151 P20 **South Andaman** island Andaman Islands, India, NE Indian Ocean
13 Q6 **South Aulatsivik Island** island Newfoundland and Labrador, E Canada
182 E4 **South Australia** ◐ state S Australia
South Australian Abyssal Plain see South Australian Plain
192 G11 **South Australian Basin** undersea feature SW Indian Ocean 38°00′S 126°00′E
173 X12 **South Australian Plain** var. South Australian Abyssal Plain. undersea feature SE Indian Ocean
37 R13 **South Baldy** ▲ New Mexico, SW USA 33°59′N 107°11′W
23 Y14 **South Bay** Florida, SE USA 26°39′N 80°43′W
14 E12 **South Baymouth** Manitoulin Island, Ontario, S Canada 45°33′N 82°01′W
30 L10 **South Beloit** Illinois, N USA 42°29′N 89°02′W
31 O11 **South Bend** Indiana, N USA 41°40′N 86°15′W
25 R6 **South Bend** Texas, SW USA 32°58′N 98°39′W
32 F9 **South Bend** Washington, NW USA 46°38′N 123°48′W
South Beveland see Zuid-Beveland
South Borneo see Kalimantan Selatan
21 U7 **South Boston** Virginia, NE USA 36°42′N 78°58′W
182 F2 **South Branch Neales** seasonal river South Australia
21 U3 **South Branch Potomac River** 〰 West Virginia, NE USA
185 H19 **Southbridge** Canterbury, South Island, New Zealand 43°49′S 172°17′E
19 N12 **Southbridge** Massachusetts, NE USA 42°03′N 72°00′W
183 P17 **South Bruny Island** island Tasmania, SE Australia
18 L7 **South Burlington** Vermont, NE USA 44°27′N 73°08′W
44 M6 **South Caicos** island S Turks and Caicos Islands
South Cape see Ka Lae
23 V3 **South Carolina** off. State of South Carolina, also known as The Palmetto State. ◐ state SE USA
South Carpathians see Carpaţii Meridionalii
South Celebes see Sulawesi Selatan
21 Q5 **South Charleston** West Virginia, NE USA 38°22′N 81°42′W
192 D7 **South China Basin** undersea feature SE South China Sea 15°00′N 115°00′E
169 R8 **South China Sea** Chin. Nan Hai, Ind. Laut Cina Selatan, Vtn. Biên Đông. sea SE Asia
33 Z10 **South Dakota** off. State of South Dakota, also known as The Coyote State, Sunshine State. ◐ state N USA
23 X10 **South Daytona** Florida, SE USA 29°09′N 81°01′W
37 R10 **South Domingo Pueblo** New Mexico, SW USA 35°28′N 106°24′W
97 N23 **South Downs** hill range SE England, United Kingdom
83 I21 **South East** ◐ district SE Botswana
65 H15 **South East Bay** bay Ascension Island, C Atlantic Ocean
183 O17 **South East Cape** headland Tasmania, SE Australia 43°36′S 146°52′E
38 K10 **Southeast Cape** headland Saint Lawrence Island, Alaska, USA 62°56′N 169°39′W
South-East Celebes see Sulawesi Tenggara
192 G12 **Southeast Indian Ridge** undersea feature Indian Ocean/Pacific Ocean 50°00′S 110°00′E
Southeast Island see Tagula Island
193 P13 **Southeast Pacific Basin** var. Belling Hausen Mulde. undersea feature SE Pacific Ocean 60°00′S 115°00′W
65 H15 **South East Point** headland SE Ascension Island
183 O14 **South East Point** headland Victoria, S Australia 39°10′S 146°21′E
44 L5 **Southeast Point** headland Mayaguana, SE Bahamas 22°15′N 72°44′W
191 Z3 **South East Point** headland Kiritimati, NE Kiribati 01°42′N 157°10′W
South-East Sulawesi see Sulawesi Tenggara
11 U12 **Southend** Saskatchewan, C Canada 56°20′N 103°14′W
97 P22 **Southend-on-Sea** E England, United Kingdom 51°33′N 00°43′E
83 H20 **Southern** var. Bangwaketse, Ngwaketze. ◐ district SE Botswana
138 E13 **Southern** ◐ district S Israel
83 N15 **Southern** ◐ region S Malawi
155 J26 **Southern** ◐ province S Sri Lanka
83 I15 **Southern** ◐ province S Zambia
185 E19 **Southern Alps** ▲▲ South Island, New Zealand
190 K15 **Southern Cook Islands** island group S Cook Islands
180 K12 **Southern Cross** Western Australia 31°17′S 119°15′E
80 A12 **Southern Darfur** ◐ state W Sudan
186 B7 **Southern Highlands** ◐ province W Papua New Guinea
11 V11 **Southern Indian Lake** ◎ Manitoba, C Canada
80 E11 **Southern Kordofan** ◐ state C Sudan
187 Z15 **Southern Lau Group** island group Lau Group, SE Fiji
81 I15 **Southern Nationalities** ◐ region S Ethiopia
173 S13 **Southern Ocean** ocean
21 T10 **Southern Pines** North Carolina, SE USA 35°10′N 79°23′W
96 I13 **Southern Uplands** ▲ S Scotland, United Kingdom
Southern Urals see Yuzhnyy Ural
183 P16 **South Esk River** 〰 Tasmania, SE Australia
11 U16 **Southey** Saskatchewan, S Canada 50°53′N 104°27′W
27 V2 **South Fabius River** 〰 Missouri, C USA
31 S10 **Southfield** Michigan, N USA 42°28′N 83°12′W
192 K10 **South Fiji Basin** undersea feature S Pacific Ocean 26°00′S 175°00′E
97 Q22 **South Foreland** headland SE England, United Kingdom 51°08′N 01°24′E
35 P7 **South Fork American River** 〰 California, W USA
28 K7 **South Fork Grand River** 〰 South Dakota, N USA

◆ Country
● Country Capital
◇ Dependent Territory
○ Dependent Territory Capital
◐ Administrative Regions
✈ International Airport
▲ Mountain
▲▲ Mountain Range
🌋 Volcano
〰 River
◎ Lake
⊠ Reservoir

35 *T12* **South Fork Kern River** ≈ California, W USA
39 *Q7* **South Fork Koyukuk River** ≈ Alaska, USA
39 *Q11* **South Fork Kuskokwim River** ≈ Alaska, USA
26 *H2* **South Fork Republican River** ≈ C USA
26 *L3* **South Fork Solomon River** ≈ Kansas, C USA
31 *P5* **South Fox Island** *island* Michigan, N USA
20 *G8* **South Fulton** Tennessee, S USA *36°28′N 88°53′W*
195 *U10* **South Geomagnetic Pole** *pole* Antarctica
65 *J20* **South Georgia** *island* South Georgia and the South Sandwich Islands, SW Atlantic Ocean
65 *K21* **South Georgia and the South Sandwich Islands** ◇ *UK Dependent Territory* SW Atlantic Ocean
47 *Y14* **South Georgia Ridge** *var.* North Scotia Ridge. *undersea feature* SW Atlantic Ocean *54°00′S 40°00′W*
181 *Q1* **South Goulburn Island** *island* Northern Territory, N Australia
153 *U16* **South Hatia Island** *island* SE Bangladesh
31 *O10* **South Haven** Michigan, N USA *42°24′N 86°16′W*
21 *V7* **South Hill** Virginia, NE USA *36°43′N 78°07′W*
South Holland *see* Zuid-Holland
21 *P8* **South Holston Lake** ⊠ Tennessee/Virginia, S USA
175 *N1* **South Honshu Ridge** *undersea feature* W Pacific Ocean
26 *M6* **South Hutchinson** Kansas, C USA *38°01′N 97°56′W*
151 *K21* **South Huvadhu Atoll** *atoll* S Maldives
173 *U14* **South Indian Basin** *undersea feature* Indian Ocean/Pacific Ocean *60°00′S 120°00′E*
11 *W11* **South Indian Lake** Manitoba, C Canada *56°48′N 98°56′W*
81 *I17* **South Island** *island* NW Kenya
185 *C20* **South Island** *island* S New Zealand
65 *B23* **South Jason** *island* Jason Islands, NW Falkland Islands
South Kalimantan *see* Kalimantan Selatan
South Kazakhstan *see* Yuzhnyy Kazakhstan
163 *X15* **South Korea** *off.* Republic of Korea, *Kor.* Taehan Min'guk. ◆ *republic* E Asia
35 *Q6* **South Lake Tahoe** California, W USA *38°56′N 119°57′W*
25 *N6* **Southland** Texas, SW USA *33°16′N 101°31′W*
185 *B23* **Southland** *off.* Southland Region. ◐ *region* South Island, New Zealand
Southland Region *see* Southland
29 *N15* **South Loup River** ≈ Nebraska, C USA
151 *K19* **South Maalhosmadulu Atoll** *atoll* N Maldives
14 *E15* **South Maitland** ≈ Ontario, S Canada
192 *E8* **South Makassar Basin** *undersea feature* E Java Sea
31 *O6* **South Manitou Island** *island* Michigan, N USA
151 *K18* **South Miladhunmadulu Atoll** *var.* Noonu. *atoll* N Maldives
21 *X8* **South Mills** North Carolina, SE USA *36°28′N 76°18′W*
8 *H9* **South Nahanni** ≈ Northwest Territories, NW Canada
39 *P13* **South Naknek** Alaska, USA *58°39′N 157°01′W*
14 *M13* **South Nation** ≈ Ontario, SE Canada
44 *F9* **South Negril Point** *headland* W Jamaica *18°14′N 78°21′W*
151 *K20* **South Nilandhe Atoll** *var.* Dhaalu Atoll. *atoll* C Maldives
36 *L2* **South Ogden** Utah, W USA *41°09′N 111°58′W*
18 *M14* **Southold** Long Island, New York, NE USA *41°03′N 72°24′W*
194 *H1* **South Orkney Islands** *island group* Antarctica
137 *S9* **South Ossetia** *former autonomous region* SW Georgia
South Pacific Basin *see* Southwest Pacific Basin
19 *P7* **South Paris** Maine, NE USA *44°14′N 70°33′W*
189 *U13* **South Pass** *passage* Chuuk Islands, C Micronesia
33 *U15* **South Pass** *pass* Wyoming, C USA
20 *K10* **South Pittsburg** Tennessee, S USA *35°00′N 85°42′W*
28 *K15* **South Platte River** ≈ Colorado/Nebraska, C USA
31 *T16* **South Point** Ohio, N USA *38°25′N 82°35′W*
65 *G15* **South Point** *headland* S Ascension Island
31 *R6* **South Point** *headland* Michigan, N USA *44°51′N 83°17′W*
South Point *see* Ka Lae
195 *Q9* **South Pole** *pole* Antarctica
183 *P17* **Southport** Tasmania, SE Australia *43°26′S 146°57′E*
97 *K17* **Southport** NW England, United Kingdom *53°39′N 03°01′W*
21 *V12* **Southport** North Carolina, SE USA *33°55′N 78°00′W*
19 *P8* **South Portland** Maine, NE USA *43°38′N 70°14′W*
14 *H12* **South River** Ontario, S Canada *45°50′N 79°23′W*
21 *U11* **South River** ≈ North Carolina, SE USA
96 *K5* **South Ronaldsay** *island* NE Scotland, United Kingdom
36 *L2* **South Salt Lake** Utah, W USA *40°42′N 111°52′W*
65 *L21* **South Sandwich Islands** *island group* SW Atlantic Ocean
65 *K21* **South Sandwich Trench** *undersea feature* SW Atlantic Ocean *56°30′S 25°00′W*
11 *S16* **South Saskatchewan** ≈ Alberta/Saskatchewan, S Canada
65 *I21* **South Scotia Ridge** *undersea feature* S Scotia Sea
11 *V10* **South Seal** ≈ Manitoba, C Canada
194 *G4* **South Shetland Islands** *island group* Antarctica
65 *H22* **South Shetland Trough** *undersea feature* Atlantic Ocean/Pacific Ocean *61°00′S 59°30′W*
97 *M14* **South Shields** NE England, United Kingdom *55°N 01°25′W*
29 *R13* **South Sioux City** Nebraska, C USA *42°28′N 96°24′W*
192 *J9* **South Solomon Trench** *undersea feature* W Pacific Ocean
183 *V3* **South Stradbroke Island** *island* Queensland, E Australia
South Sulawesi *see* Sulawesi Selatan
South Sumatra *see* Sumatera Selatan
81 *E15* **South Sudan** *off.* Republic of South Sudan ◆ *republic* E Africa
184 *K11* **South Taranaki Bight** *bight* SE Tasman Sea
South Tasmania Plateau *see* Tasman Plateau
36 *M15* **South Tucson** Arizona, SW USA *32°11′N 110°56′W*
12 *H9* **South Twin Island** *island* Nunavut, C Canada
South Tyrol *see* Trentino-Alto Adige
96 *E9* **South Uist** *island* NW Scotland, United Kingdom
South-West *see* Sud-Ouest
South-West Africa/South West Africa *see* Namibia
65 *F15* **South West Bay** *bay* Ascension Island, C Atlantic Ocean
183 *N18* **South West Cape** *headland* Tasmania, SE Australia *43°34′S 146°01′E*
185 *B26* **South West Cape** *headland* Stewart Island, New Zealand *47°15′S 167°28′E*
38 *J10* **Southwest Cape** *headland* Saint Lawrence Island, Alaska, USA *63°19′N 171°27′W*
Southwest Indian Ocean Ridge *see* Southwest Indian Ridge
173 *N11* **Southwest Indian Ridge** *var.* Southwest Indian Ocean Ridge. *undersea feature* SW Indian Ocean *43°00′S 40°00′E*
192 *L10* **Southwest Pacific Basin** *var.* South Pacific Basin. *undersea feature* SE Pacific Ocean *40°00′S 150°00′W*
44 *H2* **Southwest Point** *headland* Great Abaco, N Bahamas *25°50′N 77°12′W*
191 *X3* **South West Point** *headland* Kiritimati, NE Kiribati *01°53′N 157°34′E*
65 *G25* **South West Point** *headland* SW Saint Helena *16°00′S 05°48′W*
25 *P5* **South Wichita River** ≈ Texas, SW USA
97 *Q20* **Southwold** E England, United Kingdom *52°15′N 01°36′E*
19 *Q12* **South Yarmouth** Massachusetts, NE USA *41°38′N 70°09′W*
116 *J10* **Sovata** *Hung.* Szováta. Mureș, C Romania *46°36′N 25°04′E*
107 *N22* **Soverato** Calabria, SW Italy *38°40′N 16°31′E*
121 *O4* **Sovereign Base Area** *uk military installation* S Cyprus
Sovetabad *see* Ghafurov
126 *C2* **Sovetsk** *Ger.* Tilsit. Kaliningradskaya Oblast', W Russian Federation *53°04′N 21°52′E*
125 *Q15* **Sovetsk** Kirovskaya Oblast', NW Russian Federation *57°37′N 49°02′E*
127 *N10* **Sovetskaya** Rostovskaya Oblast', SW Russian Federation *49°00′N 42°09′E*
Sovetskoye *see* Ketchenery
146 *I15* **Sovet"yab** *prev.* Sovet"yap. Ahal Welaýaty, S Turkmenistan *36°29′N 61°13′E*
Sovet"yap *see* Sovet"yab
117 *U12* **Sovyets'kyy** Avtonomna Respublika Krym, S Ukraine *45°20′N 34°54′E*
83 *I18* **Sowa** *var.* Sua. Central, NE Botswana *20°33′S 26°18′E*
83 *I18* **Sowa Pan** *var.* Sua Pan. *salt lake* NE Botswana
83 *J21* **Soweto** Gauteng, NE South Africa *26°08′S 27°54′E*
147 *R11* **So'x** *Rus.* Sokh. Farg'ona Viloyati, E Uzbekistan *39°56′N 71°10′E*
Sōya-kaikyō *see* La Pérouse Strait
165 *T1* **Sōya-misaki** *headland* Hokkaidō, NE Japan *45°31′N 141°55′E*
125 *N7* **Soyana** ≈ NW Russian Federation
146 *A8* **Soye, Mys** *var.* Mys Suz. *headland* NW Turkmenistan *41°47′N 52°27′E*
82 *A10* **Soyo** Dem. Rep. Congo, NW Angola *06°07′S 12°18′E*
80 *J10* **Soyra** ▲ C Eritrea *14°46′N 39°29′E*
145 *P15* **Sozak** *Kaz.* Sozaq; *prev.* Suzak. Yuzhnyy Kazakhstan, S Kazakhstan *44°09′N 68°28′E*
Sozaq *see* Sozak
119 *P16* **Sozh** ≈ NE Europe
114 *N10* **Sozopol** *prev.* Sizebolu; *anc.* Apollonia. Burgas, E Bulgaria *42°25′N 27°42′E*
99 *L20* **Spa** Liège, E Belgium *50°29′N 05°52′E*
194 *I7* **Spaatz Island** *island* Antarctica
144 *M14* **Space Launching Centre** *space station* Kzylorda, S Kazakhstan
105 *O7* **Spain** *off.* Kingdom of Spain, *Sp.* España; *anc.* Hispania, Iberia, *Lat.* Hispana. ◆ *monarchy* SW Europe
Spain, Kingdom of *see* Spain
Spalato *see* Split
97 *O19* **Spalding** E England, United Kingdom *52°49′N 00°06′W*
14 *D11* **Spanish** Ontario, S Canada *46°12′N 82°21′W*
36 *L3* **Spanish Fork** Utah, W USA *40°09′N 111°40′W*
64 *B12* **Spanish Point** *headland* C Bermuda *32°18′N 64°49′W*
14 *E9* **Spanish River** ≈ Ontario, S Canada
44 *K13* **Spanish Town** *hist.* St.Iago de la Vega. C Jamaica *18°N 76°57′W*
Spánta, Akrotírio *see* Spátha, Akrotírio
35 *Q5* **Sparks** Nevada, W USA *39°32′N 119°45′W*
Sparnacum *see* Épernay
95 *N16* **Sparreholm** Södermanland, C Sweden *59°04′N 16°51′E*
23 *U4* **Sparta** Georgia, SE USA *33°16′N 82°58′W*
30 *K16* **Sparta** Illinois, N USA *38°07′N 89°42′W*
31 *P9* **Sparta** Michigan, N USA *43°09′N 85°42′W*
21 *R8* **Sparta** North Carolina, SE USA *36°30′N 81°07′W*
20 *L9* **Sparta** Tennessee, S USA *35°55′N 85°30′W*
30 *I7* **Sparta** Wisconsin, N USA *43°57′N 90°50′W*
Sparta *see* Spárti
21 *Q11* **Spartanburg** South Carolina, SE USA *34°56′N 81°57′W*
115 *F21* **Spárti** *Eng.* Sparta. Pelopónnisos, S Greece *37°05′N 22°25′E*
107 *B21* **Spartivento, Capo** *headland* Sardegna, Italy, C Mediterranean Sea *38°52′N 08°50′E*
11 *P17* **Sparwood** British Columbia, SW Canada *49°45′N 114°45′W*
126 *I4* **Spas-Demensk** Kaluzhskaya Oblast', W Russian Federation *54°22′N 34°16′E*
126 *M4* **Spas-Klepiki** Ryazanskaya Oblast', W Russian Federation *55°08′N 40°15′E*
Spasovo *see* Kulen Vakuf
123 *R15* **Spassk-Dal'niy** Primorskiy Kray, SE Russian Federation *44°34′N 132°52′E*
126 *M5* **Spassk-Ryazanskiy** Ryazanskaya Oblast', W Russian Federation *54°25′N 40°21′E*
115 *H19* **Spáta** Attikí, C Greece *37°58′N 23°55′E*
121 *Q11* **Spátha, Akrotírio** *var.* Akrotírio Spánta. *headland* Kríti, Greece, E Mediterranean Sea *35°42′N 23°44′E*
Špatrjan *see* Paternion
28 *I9* **Spearfish** South Dakota, N USA *44°29′N 103°51′W*
25 *O1* **Spearman** Texas, SW USA *36°12′N 101°13′W*
65 *C25* **Speedwell Island** *island* S Falkland Islands
65 *C25* **Speedwell Island Settlement** S Falkland Islands *52°13′S 59°41′W*
65 *G25* **Speery Island** *island* S Saint Helena
45 *N14* **Speightstown** NW Barbados *13°15′N 59°39′W*
106 *I13* **Spello** Umbria, C Italy *43°00′N 12°41′E*
39 *R12* **Spenard** Alaska, USA *61°09′N 150°03′W*
Spence Bay *see* Taloyoak
31 *O14* **Spencer** Indiana, N USA *39°18′N 86°46′W*
29 *T12* **Spencer** Iowa, C USA *43°09′N 95°07′W*
29 *P12* **Spencer** Nebraska, C USA *42°52′N 98°42′W*
21 *S9* **Spencer** North Carolina, SE USA *35°41′N 80°26′W*
20 *L9* **Spencer** Tennessee, S USA *35°46′N 85°27′W*
21 *Q4* **Spencer** West Virginia, NE USA *38°48′N 81°22′W*
30 *K6* **Spencer** Wisconsin, N USA *44°46′N 90°17′W*
182 *G10* **Spencer, Cape** *headland* South Australia *35°17′S 136°52′E*
39 *V13* **Spencer, Cape** *headland* Alaska, USA *58°12′N 136°39′W*
182 *H9* **Spencer Gulf** *gulf* South Australia
18 *F9* **Spencerport** New York, NE USA *43°11′N 77°48′W*
31 *Q12* **Spencerville** Ohio, N USA *40°42′N 84°21′W*
115 *E17* **Spercheiáda** *var.* Sperhiada, Sperkhiás. Stereá Elláda, C Greece *38°54′N 22°07′E*
115 *E17* **Spercheiós** ≈ C Greece
Sperhiada *see* Spercheiáda
95 *G14* **Sperillen** ◎ S Norway
Sperkhiás *see* Spercheiáda
101 *I18* **Spessart** *hill range* C Germany
Spétsai *see* Spétses
115 *G21* **Spétses** *prev.* Spétsai. Spétses, S Greece *37°16′N 23°09′E*
115 *G21* **Spétses** *island* S Greece
96 *J8* **Spey** ≈ NE Scotland, United Kingdom
101 *G20* **Speyer** *Eng.* Spires; *anc.* Civitas Nemetum, Spira. Rheinland-Pfalz, SW Germany *49°18′N 08°26′E*
101 *G20* **Speyerbach** ≈ W Germany
107 *N20* **Spezzano Albanese** Calabria, SW Italy *39°40′N 16°17′E*
Spice Islands *see* Maluku
100 *F9* **Spiekeroog** *island* NW Germany
109 *W9* **Spielfeld** Steiermark, SE Austria *46°43′N 15°36′E*
65 *N21* **Spiess Seamount** *undersea feature* S Atlantic Ocean *53°00′S 02°00′W*
108 *E9* **Spiez** Bern, W Switzerland *46°42′N 07°41′E*
98 *G13* **Spijkenisse** Zuid-Holland, SW Netherlands *51°52′N 04°19′E*
39 *T6* **Spike Mountain** ▲ Alaska, USA *67°42′N 141°39′W*
115 *I25* **Spíli** Kríti, Greece, E Mediterranean Sea *35°12′N 24°33′E*
108 *D10* **Spillgerten** ▲ W Switzerland *46°34′N 07°25′E*
118 *F9* **Spilve** ✈ (Rīga) C Latvia *56°55′N 24°03′E*
107 *N17* **Spinazzola** Puglia, SE Italy *40°58′N 16°06′E*
149 *O9* **Spīn Bōldak** *prev.* Spīn Būldak. Kandahār, S Afghanistan *31°01′N 66°23′E*
Spīn Būldak *see* Spīn Bōldak
Spira *see* Speyer
Spirdingsee *see* Śniardwy, Jezioro
Spires *see* Speyer
29 *T11* **Spirit Lake** Iowa, C USA *43°25′N 95°06′W*
29 *T11* **Spirit Lake** ◎ Iowa, C USA
11 *N13* **Spirit River** Alberta, W Canada *55°46′N 118°51′W*
11 *S14* **Spiritwood** Saskatchewan, S Canada *53°18′N 107°33′W*
27 *R11* **Spiro** Oklahoma, C USA *35°14′N 94°37′W*
111 *L19* **Spišská Nová Ves** *Ger.* Neudorf, Zipser Neudorf, *Hung.* Igló. Košický Kraj, E Slovakia *48°58′N 20°35′E*
137 *T11* **Spitak** NW Armenia *40°51′N 44°17′E*
92 *O2* **Spitsbergen** *island* NW Svalbard
Spittal *see* Spittal an der Drau
109 *R9* **Spittal an der Drau** *var.* Spittal. Kärnten, S Austria *46°48′N 13°30′E*
109 *V3* **Spitz** Niederösterreich, NE Austria *48°24′N 15°22′E*
94 *D9* **Spjelkavik** Møre og Romsdal, S Norway *62°28′N 06°22′E*
25 *W10* **Splendora** Texas, SW USA *30°13′N 95°09′W*
113 *E14* **Split** *It.* Spalato. Split-Dalmacija, S Croatia *43°31′N 16°27′E*
113 *E14* **Split** ✈ Split-Dalmacija, S Croatia *43°33′N 16°19′E*
113 *E14* **Split-Dalmacija** *off.* Splitsko-Dalmatinska Županija. ◐ *province* S Croatia
11 *X12* **Split Lake** ◎ Manitoba, C Canada
Splitsko-Dalmatinska Županija *see* Split-Dalmacija
108 *H10* **Splügen** Graubünden, S Switzerland *46°33′N 09°18′E*
Spodnji Dravograd *see* Dravograd
25 *P12* **Spofford** Texas, SW USA *29°10′N 100°24′W*
118 *J11* **Špoģi** SE Latvia *56°03′N 26°47′E*
32 *L8* **Spokane** Washington, NW USA *47°40′N 117°26′W*
32 *L8* **Spokane River** ≈ Washington, NW USA
106 *I13* **Spoleto** Umbria, C Italy *42°44′N 12°44′E*
30 *I4* **Spooner** Wisconsin, N USA *45°51′N 91°49′W*
30 *K12* **Spoon River** ≈ Illinois, N USA
21 *W5* **Spotsylvania** Virginia, NE USA *38°12′N 77°35′W*
32 *L8* **Sprague** Washington, NW USA *47°19′N 117°55′W*
170 *J5* **Spratly Island** *island* SW Spratly Islands
192 *E6* **Spratly Islands** *Chin.* Nansha Qundao. ◇ *disputed territory* SE Asia
32 *J12* **Spray** Oregon, NW USA *44°30′N 119°38′W*
112 *I11* **Spreča** ≈ N Bosnia and Herzegovina
100 *P13* **Spree** ≈ E Germany
100 *P13* **Spreewald** *wetland* NE Germany
101 *P14* **Spremberg** Brandenburg, E Germany *51°34′N 14°22′E*
25 *W11* **Spring** Texas, SW USA *30°03′N 95°24′W*
31 *Q10* **Spring Arbor** Michigan, N USA *42°12′N 84°33′W*
83 *E23* **Springbok** Northern Cape, W South Africa *29°44′S 17°56′E*
18 *I15* **Spring City** Pennsylvania, NE USA *40°10′N 75°33′W*
20 *L9* **Spring City** Tennessee, S USA *35°41′N 84°51′W*
36 *L4* **Spring City** Utah, W USA *39°28′N 111°30′W*
35 *W3* **Spring Creek** Nevada, W USA *40°45′N 115°40′W*
27 *S9* **Springdale** Arkansas, C USA *36°11′N 94°07′W*
31 *Q14* **Springdale** Ohio, N USA *39°17′N 84°29′W*
100 *I13* **Springe** Niedersachsen, N Germany *52°13′N 09°33′E*
37 *U9* **Springer** New Mexico, SW USA *36°21′N 104°35′W*
37 *W7* **Springfield** Colorado, C USA *37°24′N 102°36′W*
23 *W5* **Springfield** Georgia, SE USA *32°21′N 81°20′W*
30 *K14* **Springfield** *state capital* Illinois, N USA *39°48′N 89°39′W*
20 *L6* **Springfield** Kentucky, S USA *37°42′N 85°18′W*
18 *M12* **Springfield** Massachusetts, NE USA *42°06′N 72°32′W*
29 *T10* **Springfield** Minnesota, N USA *44°15′N 94°58′W*
27 *T7* **Springfield** Missouri, C USA *37°13′N 93°18′W*
31 *R13* **Springfield** Ohio, N USA *39°55′N 83°49′W*
32 *G13* **Springfield** Oregon, NW USA *44°03′N 123°01′W*
29 *Q12* **Springfield** South Dakota, N USA *42°51′N 97°54′W*
20 *J8* **Springfield** Tennessee, S USA *36°30′N 86°54′W*
18 *M9* **Springfield** Vermont, NE USA *43°18′N 72°27′W*
30 *K14* **Springfield, Lake** ⊠ Illinois, N USA
55 *T8* **Spring Garden** NE Guyana *06°58′N 58°34′W*
30 *K8* **Spring Green** Wisconsin, N USA *43°10′N 90°02′W*
29 *X11* **Spring Grove** Minnesota, N USA *43°33′N 91°38′W*
13 *P15* **Springhill** Nova Scotia, SE Canada *45°40′N 64°04′W*
23 *V12* **Spring Hill** Florida, SE USA *28°28′N 82°36′W*
27 *R4* **Spring Hill** Kansas, C USA *38°44′N 94°49′W*
22 *G4* **Springhill** Louisiana, S USA *33°01′N 93°27′W*
20 *I9* **Spring Hill** Tennessee, S USA *35°46′N 86°55′W*
21 *U10* **Spring Lake** North Carolina, SE USA *35°10′N 78°58′W*
24 *M4* **Springlake** Texas, SW USA *34°13′N 102°18′W*
35 *W11* **Spring Mountains** ▲▲ Nevada, W USA
65 *B24* **Spring Point** West Falkland, Falkland Islands *51°49′S 60°27′W*
27 *W9* **Spring River** ≈ Arkansas/Missouri, C USA
27 *S7* **Spring River** ≈ Missouri/Oklahoma, C USA
83 *J21* **Springs** Gauteng, NE South Africa *26°16′S 28°26′E*
185 *H16* **Springs Junction** West Coast, South Island, New Zealand *42°21′S 172°11′E*
181 *X8* **Springsure** Queensland, E Australia *24°09′S 148°06′E*
29 *W11* **Spring Valley** Minnesota, N USA *43°41′N 92°23′W*
18 *K13* **Spring Valley** New York, NE USA *41°10′N 73°58′W*
29 *N12* **Springview** Nebraska, C USA *42°49′N 99°45′W*
18 *D11* **Springville** New York, NE USA *42°27′N 78°52′W*
36 *L3* **Springville** Utah, W USA *40°10′N 111°36′W*
Sprottau *see* Szprotawa
15 *V4* **Sproule, Pointe** *headland* Québec, SE Canada *49°47′N 67°02′W*
11 *Q14* **Spruce Grove** Alberta, SW Canada *53°36′N 113°55′W*
21 *T4* **Spruce Knob** ▲ West Virginia, NE USA *38°40′N 79°37′W*
35 *X3* **Spruce Mountain** ▲ Nevada, W USA *40°33′N 114°46′W*
21 *P9* **Spruce Pine** North Carolina, SE USA *35°55′N 82°03′W*
98 *G13* **Spui** ≈ SW Netherlands
107 *O19* **Spulico, Capo** *headland* S Italy *39°57′N 16°38′E*
25 *O5* **Spur** Texas, SW USA *33°28′N 100°51′W*
97 *O17* **Spurn Head** *headland* E England, United Kingdom *53°34′N 00°06′E*
99 *H20* **Spy** Namur, S Belgium *50°29′N 04°43′E*
95 *I15* **Spydeberg** Østfold, S Norway *59°36′N 11°04′E*
185 *J17* **Spy Glass Point** *headland* South Island, New Zealand *42°33′S 173°31′E*
10 *L17* **Squamish** British Columbia, SW Canada *49°41′N 123°11′W*
19 *O8* **Squam Lake** ◎ New Hampshire, NE USA
19 *S2* **Squa Pan Mountain** ▲ Maine, NE USA *46°36′N 68°09′W*
39 *N16* **Squaw Harbor** Unga Island, Alaska, USA *55°12′N 160°41′W*
14 *E11* **Squaw Island** *island* Ontario, S Canada
107 *O22* **Squillace, Golfo di** *gulf* S Italy
107 *Q18* **Squinzano** Puglia, SE Italy *40°26′N 18°03′E*
Sráid na Cathrach *see* Milltown Malbay
167 *S11* **Srâlau** Stœ̆ng Trêng, N Cambodia *14°03′N 105°46′E*
Srath an Urláir *see* Stranorlar
112 *G10* **Srbac** ◐ Republika Srpska, N Bosnia and Herzegovina
Srbija *see* Serbia
Srbinje *see* Foča
112 *K9* **Srbobran** *var.* Bácsszenttamás, *Hung.* Szenttamás. Vojvodina, N Serbia *45°33′N 19°46′E*
Srbobran *see* Donji Vakuf
167 *R13* **Srê Âmběl** Kaôh Kông, SW Cambodia *11°07′N 103°46′E*
112 *K13* **Srebrenica** Republika Srpska, E Bosnia and Herzegovina *44°04′N 19°18′E*
112 *I11* **Srebrenik** Federacija Bosna I Hercegovina, NE Bosnia and Herzegovina *44°42′N 18°30′E*
114 *K10* **Sredets** *prev.* Syulemeshlii. Stara Zagora, C Bulgaria *42°16′N 25°40′E*
114 *M10* **Sredets** *prev.* Grudovo. ◐ Burgas, E Bulgaria
114 *M10* **Sredetska Reka** ≈ SE Bulgaria
123 *U9* **Sredinnyy Khrebet** ▲▲ E Russian Federation
114 *N7* **Sredishte** *Rom.* Beibunar; *prev.* Knyazhevo. Dobrich, NE Bulgaria *43°51′N 27°30′E*
114 *I10* **Sredna Gora** ▲▲ C Bulgaria
123 *R7* **Srednekolymsk** Respublika Sakha (Yakutiya), NE Russian Federation *67°28′N 153°52′E*
126 *K7* **Srednerusskaya Vozvyshennost'** *Eng.* Central Russian Upland. ▲▲ W Russian Federation
122 *L9* **Srednesibirskoye Ploskogor'ye** *var.* Central Siberian Uplands, *Eng.* Central Siberian Plateau. ▲▲ N Russian Federation
125 *V13* **Sredniy Ural** ▲▲ NW Russian Federation
167 *T12* **Srê Khtŭm** Môndól Kiri, E Cambodia *12°10′N 106°52′E*
110 *G12* **Śrem** Wielkopolskie, C Poland *52°07′N 17°00′E*
112 *K10* **Sremska Mitrovica** *prev.* Mitrovica, *Ger.* Mitrowitz. Vojvodina, NW Serbia *44°58′N 19°37′E*
167 *R11* **Srêng, Stœ̆ng** ≈ NW Cambodia
167 *R11* **Srê Noy** Siĕmréab, NW Cambodia *13°47′N 104°03′E*
Srepok, Sông *see* Srêpôk, Tônle
167 *T12* **Srêpôk, Tônle** *var.* Sông Srepok. ≈ Cambodia/Vietnam
123 *P13* **Sretensk** Zabaykal'skiy Kray, S Russian Federation *52°14′N 117°33′E*
169 *R10* **Sri Aman** Sarawak, East Malaysia *01°13′N 111°25′E*
117 *R4* **Sribne** Chernihivs'ka Oblast', N Ukraine *50°40′N 32°55′E*
Sri Jayawardanapura *see* Sri Jayewardenapura Kotte
155 *I25* **Sri Jayewardenapura Kotte** *var.* Sri Jayawardanapura. ● (Sri Lanka: legislative) Western Province, W Sri Lanka *06°54′N 79°58′E*
155 *M14* **Srīkākulam** Andhra Pradesh, E India *18°18′N 83°54′E*
155 *I25* **Sri Lanka** *off.* Democratic Socialist Republic of Sri Lanka; *prev.* Ceylon. ◆ *republic* S Asia
130 *F14* **Sri Lanka** *island* S Asia
Sri Lanka, Democratic Socialist Republic of *see* Sri Lanka
153 *V14* **Srimangal** Sylhet, E Bangladesh *24°19′N 91°40′E*
Sri Mohangorh *see* Shri Mohangarh
152 *H5* **Srīnagar** *state capital* Jammu and Kashmir, N India *34°07′N 74°50′E*
167 *N10* **Srinagarind Reservoir** ◎ W Thailand
155 *F19* **Sringeri** Karnātaka, W India *13°26′N 75°13′E*
155 *K25* **Sri Pada** *Eng.* Adam's Peak. ▲ S Sri Lanka *06°49′N 80°25′E*
Sri Saket *see* Si Sa Ket
111 *G14* **Sroda Śląska** *Ger.* Neumarkt. Dolnośląskie, SW Poland *51°10′N 16°30′E*
110 *H12* **Środa Wielkopolska** Wielkopolskie, C Poland *52°13′N 17°17′E*
Srpska Kostajnica *see* Bosanska Kostajnica
113 *G14* **Srpska, Republika** ◐ *republic* Bosnia and Herzegovina
Srpski Brod *see* Bosanski Brod
Ssu-ch'uan *see* Sichuan
Ssu-p'ing/Ssu-p'ing-chieh *see* Siping
Stablo *see* Stavelot
99 *G15* **Stabroek** Antwerpen, N Belgium *51°21′N 04°22′E*
Stackeln *see* Strenči
96 *I5* **Stack Skerry** *island* N Scotland, United Kingdom
100 *I9* **Stade** Niedersachsen, NW Germany *53°36′N 09°29′E*
94 *C10* **Stadlandet** *peninsula* S Norway
109 *R5* **Stadl-Paura** Oberösterreich, NW Austria *48°05′N 13°52′E*
119 *L20* **Stadolichy** *Rus.* Stodolichi. Homyel'skaya Voblasts', SE Belarus *51°44′N 28°30′E*
98 *P7* **Stadskanaal** Groningen, NE Netherlands *53°N 06°55′E*
101 *H16* **Stadtallendorf** Hessen, C Germany *50°49′N 09°01′E*
101 *K23* **Stadtbergen** Bayern, S Germany *48°21′N 10°50′E*
108 *G7* **Stäfa** Zürich, NE Switzerland *47°14′N 08°45′E*
95 *K23* **Staffanstorp** Skåne, S Sweden *55°38′N 13°13′E*
101 *K18* **Staffelstein** Bayern, C Germany *50°05′N 11°00′E*
97 *L19* **Stafford** C England, United Kingdom *52°48′N 02°07′W*
26 *L6* **Stafford** Kansas, C USA *37°57′N 98°36′W*
21 *W4* **Stafford** Virginia, NE USA *38°26′N 77°27′W*
97 *L19* **Staffordshire** *cultural region* C England, United Kingdom
19 *N12* **Stafford Springs** Connecticut, NE USA *41°57′N 72°18′W*
115 *H14* **Stágira** Kentrikí Makedonía, N Greece *40°31′N 23°46′E*
118 *G7* **Staicele** N Latvia *57°52′N 24°48′E*
Ștaierdorf-Anina *see* Anina
109 *V8* **Stainz** Steiermark, SE Austria *46°55′N 15°18′E*
Stájerlakanina *see* Anina
117 *Y7* **Stakhanov** Luhans'ka Oblast', E Ukraine *48°30′N 38°42′E*
108 *E11* **Stalden** Valais, SW Switzerland *46°12′N 07°55′E*
15 *S8* **St-Alexandre** Québec, SE Canada *47°39′N 69°36′W*
Stalin *see* Varna
Stalinabad *see* Dushanbe
Stalingrad *see* Volgograd
Staliniri *see* Tskhinvali
Stalino *see* Donets'k
Stalinobod *see* Dushanbe
Stalinov Štít *see* Gerlachovský štít
Stalinsk *see* Novokuznetsk
Stalins'kaya Oblast' *see* Donets'ka Oblast'
Stalinski Zaliv *see* Varnenski Zaliv
Stalin, Yazovir *see* Iskŭr, Yazovir
111 *N15* **Stalowa Wola** Podkarpackie, SE Poland *50°35′N 22°02′E*
114 *I11* **Stamboliyski** Plovdiv, C Bulgaria *42°09′N 24°32′E*
15 *Q7* **St-Ambroise** Québec, SE Canada *48°35′N 71°19′W*
97 *N19* **Stamford** E England, United Kingdom *52°39′N 00°32′W*
18 *L14* **Stamford** Connecticut, NE USA *41°03′N 73°32′W*
25 *P6* **Stamford** Texas, SW USA *32°55′N 99°49′W*
25 *Q6* **Stamford, Lake** ⊠ Texas, SW USA
108 *I10* **Stampa** Graubünden, SE Switzerland *46°21′N 09°35′E*
Stampalia *see* Astypálaia
27 *T14* **Stamps** Arkansas, C USA *33°22′N 93°30′W*
92 *G11* **Stamsund** Nordland, C Norway *68°07′N 13°50′E*
27 *R2* **Stanberry** Missouri, C USA *40°12′N 94°33′W*
195 *O3* **Stancomb-Wills Glacier** *glacier* Antarctica
83 *K21* **Standerton** Mpumalanga, E South Africa *26°57′S 29°14′E*
31 *R7* **Standish** Michigan, N USA *43°59′N 83°58′W*
20 *M6* **Stanford** Kentucky, S USA *37°30′N 84°40′W*
33 *S9* **Stanford** Montana, NW USA *47°08′N 110°15′W*
95 *P19* **Stånga** Gotland, SE Sweden *57°16′N 18°30′E*
94 *I13* **Stange** Hedmark, S Norway *60°40′N 11°05′E*
83 *L23* **Stanger** KwaZulu/Natal, E South Africa *29°20′S 31°18′E*
Stanimaka *see* Asenovgrad
Stanislau *see* Ivano-Frankivs'k
35 *P8* **Stanislaus River** ≈ California, W USA
Stanislav *see* Ivano-Frankivs'k
Stanislavskaya Oblast' *see* Ivano-Frankivs'ka Oblast'
Stanisławów *see* Ivano-Frankivs'k
Stanke Dimitrov *see* Dupnitsa
183 *O15* **Stanley** Tasmania, SE Australia *40°48′S 145°18′E*
65 *E24* **Stanley** *var.* Port Stanley, Puerto Argentino. ○ (Falkland Islands) East Falkland, Falkland Islands *51°45′S 57°56′W*
33 *O13* **Stanley** Idaho, NW USA *44°12′N 114°58′W*
28 *L3* **Stanley** North Dakota, N USA *48°19′N 102°23′W*
21 *U4* **Stanley** Virginia, NE USA *38°34′N 78°30′W*
30 *J6* **Stanley** Wisconsin, N USA *44°58′N 90°54′W*
79 *G21* **Stanley Pool** *var.* Pool Malebo. ◎ Congo/Dem. Rep. Congo
155 *H20* **Stanley Reservoir** ⊠ S India
Stanleyville *see* Kisangani
42 *G3* **Stann Creek** ◐ *district* SE Belize
Stann Creek *see* Dangriga
123 *Q12* **Stanovoy Khrebet** ▲▲ SE Russian Federation
108 *F8* **Stans** Nidwalden, C Switzerland *46°57′N 08°23′E*
97 *O21* **Stansted** ✈ (London) Essex, E England, United Kingdom *51°53′N 00°16′E*
183 *U4* **Stanthorpe** Queensland, E Australia *28°35′S 151°52′E*
21 *N6* **Stanton** Kentucky, S USA *37°51′N 83°51′W*
31 *Q8* **Stanton** Michigan, N USA *43′19′N 85′04′W*
29 *Q14* **Stanton** Nebraska, C USA *41°57′N 97°13′W*
28 *L5* **Stanton** North Dakota, N USA *47°19′N 101°22′W*
25 *N7* **Stanton** Texas, SW USA *32°07′N 101°47′W*
32 *H7* **Stanwood** Washington, NW USA *48°14′N 122°22′W*
117 *Y7* **Stanychno-Luhans'ke** Luhans'ka Oblast', E Ukraine *48°39′N 39°30′E*
108 *K7* **Stanzach** Tirol, W Austria *47°24′N 10°36′E*
98 *M9* **Staphorst** Overijssel, E Netherlands *52°38′N 06°12′E*
14 *D18* **Staples** Ontario, S Canada *42°09′N 82°34′W*
29 *T6* **Staples** Minnesota, N USA *46°21′N 94°47′W*
28 *M14* **Stapleton** Nebraska, C USA *41°29′N 100°40′W*
25 *S8* **Star** Texas, SW USA *31°27′N 98°16′W*
111 *M14* **Starachowice** Świętokrzyskie, C Poland *51°04′N 21°02′E*
Stara Kanjiža *see* Kanjiža
111 *M18* **Stará L'ubovňa** *Ger.* Altlublau, *Hung.* Ólubló. Prešovský Kraj, E Slovakia *49°19′N 20°40′E*
112 *L10* **Stara Pazova** *Ger.* Altpasua, *Hung.* Ópazova. Vojvodina, N Serbia *44°59′N 20°10′E*
Stara Planina *see* Balkan Mountains
114 *L9* **Stara Reka** ≈ C Bulgaria
116 *M5* **Stara Synyava** Khmel'nyts'ka Oblast', W Ukraine *49°39′N 27°39′E*
116 *I2* **Stara Vyzhivka** Volyns'ka Oblast', NW Ukraine *51°27′N 24°25′E*
Staraya Belitsa *see* Staraya Byelitsa
119 *M14* **Staraya Byelitsa** *Rus.* Staraya Belitsa. Vitsyebskaya Voblasts', NE Belarus *54°42′N 29°38′E*
127 *R5* **Staraya Mayna** Ul'yanovskaya Oblast', W Russian Federation *54°36′N 48°57′E*
119 *O18* **Staraya Rudnya** Homyel'skaya Voblasts', SE Belarus *52°50′N 30°17′E*
124 *H14* **Staraya Russa** Novgorodskaya Oblast', W Russian Federation *57°59′N 31°18′E*
114 *K10* **Stara Zagora** *Lat.* Augusta Trajana. Stara Zagora, C Bulgaria *42°26′N 25°39′E*
114 *K10* **Stara Zagora** ◐ *province* C Bulgaria
29 *S8* **Starbuck** Minnesota, N USA *45°36′N 95°31′W*
191 *W4* **Starbuck Island** *prev.* Volunteer Island. *island* E Kiribati
27 *V13* **Star City** Arkansas, C USA *33°56′N 91°52′W*
112 *F13* **Staretina** ▲▲ W Bosnia and Herzegovina
Stargard in Pommern *see* Stargard Szczeciński
110 *E9* **Stargard Szczeciński** *Ger.* Stargard in Pommern. Zachodnio-pomorskie, NW Poland *53°20′N 15°02′E*
187 *N10* **Star Harbour** *harbour* San Cristobal, SE Solomon Islands
Stari Bečej *see* Bečej
113 *F15* **Stari Grad** *It.* Cittavecchia. Split-Dalmacija, S Croatia *43°11′N 16°36′E*
124 *J16* **Staritsa** Tverskaya Oblast', W Russian Federation *56°28′N 34°51′E*
23 *V9* **Starke** Florida, SE USA *29°56′N 82°07′W*
22 *M4* **Starkville** Mississippi, S USA *33°27′N 88°49′W*
186 *B7* **Star Mountains** *Ind.* Pegunungan Sterren. ▲▲ Indonesia/Papua New Guinea
101 *L23* **Starnberg** Bayern, SE Germany *48°00′N 11°19′E*
101 *L24* **Starnberger See** ◎ SE Germany
Starobel'sk *see* Starobil's'k
117 *X8* **Starobesheve** Donets'ka Oblast', E Ukraine *47°45′N 38°01′E*
117 *Y6* **Starobil's'k** *Rus.* Starobel'sk. Luhans'ka Oblast', E Ukraine *49°16′N 38°56′E*
119 *K18* **Starobin** *var.* Starobyn. Minskaya Voblasts', S Belarus *52°44′N 27°28′E*
Starobyn *see* Starobin
126 *H6* **Starodub** Bryanskaya Oblast', W Russian Federation *52°30′N 32°56′E*
110 *I8* **Starogard Gdański** *Ger.* Preussisch-Stargard. Pomorskie, N Poland *53°57′N 18°29′E*
Staroikan *see* Ikan
Starokonstantinov *see* Starokostyantyniv
116 *L5* **Starokostyantyniv** *Rus.* Starokonstantinov. Khmel'nyts'ka Oblast', NW Ukraine *49°43′N 27°13′E*
126 *K12* **Starominskaya** Krasnodarskiy Kray, SW Russian Federation *46°31′N 39°03′E*
114 *L7* **Staro Selo** *Rom.* Satul-Vechi; *prev.* Star-Smil. Silistra, NE Bulgaria *43°58′N 26°32′E*
126 *K12* **Staroshcherbinovskaya** Krasnodarskiy Kray, SW Russian Federation *46°36′N 38°42′E*

◆ Country
● Country Capital
◇ Dependent Territory
○ Dependent Territory Capital
◐ Administrative Regions
✈ International Airport
▲ Mountain
▲▲ Mountain Range
Volcano
≈ River
◎ Lake
⊠ Reservoir

127 V6 **Starosubkhangulovo** Respublika Bashkortostan, W Russian Federation 53°05′N 57°22′E
35 S4 **Star Peak** ▲ Nevada, W USA 40°31′N 118°09′W
15 T8 **St-Arsène** Québec, SE Canada 47°55′N 69°21′W
Star-Smil *see* Staro Selo
97 J25 **Start Point** *headland* SW England, United Kingdom 50°13′N 03°38′W
Startsy *see* Kirawsk
Starum *see* Stavoren
119 L18 **Staryya Darohi** *Rus.* Staryye Dorogi. Minskaya Voblasts', S Belarus 53°02′N 28°16′E
Staryye Dorogi *see* Staryya Darohi
127 T2 **Staryye Zyattsy** Udmurtskaya Respublika, NW Russian Federation 57°22′N 52°42′E
117 U13 **Staryy Krym** Avtonomna Respublika Krym, S Ukraine 45°03′N 35°06′E
126 K8 **Staryy Oskol** Belgorodskaya Oblast', W Russian Federation 51°21′N 37°52′E
116 H6 **Staryy Sambir** L'vivs'ka Oblast', W Ukraine 49°27′N 23°00′E
101 L14 **Stassfurt** *var.* Staßfurt. Sachsen-Anhalt, C Germany 51°51′N 11°35′E
Staßfurt *see* Stassfurt
111 M15 **Staszów** Świętokrzyskie, C Poland 50°33′N 21°07′E
29 W13 **State Center** Iowa, C USA 42°01′N 93°09′W
18 E14 **State College** Pennsylvania, NE USA 40°48′N 77°52′W
18 K15 **Staten Island** *island* New York, NE USA
Staten Island *see* Estados, Isla de los
23 U8 **Statenville** Georgia, SE USA 30°42′N 83°00′W
23 W5 **Statesboro** Georgia, SE USA 32°28′N 81°47′W
States, The *see* United States of America
21 R9 **Statesville** North Carolina, SE USA 35°46′N 80°54′W
95 G16 **Stathelle** Telemark, S Norway 59°01′N 09°40′E
30 K15 **Staunton** Illinois, N USA 39°00′N 89°47′W
21 T5 **Staunton** Virginia, NE USA 38°10′N 79°05′W
95 C16 **Stavanger** Rogaland, S Norway 58°58′N 05°43′E
99 L21 **Stavelot** *Dut.* Stablo. Liège, E Belgium 50°24′N 05°56′E
95 G16 **Stavern** Vestfold, S Norway 58°58′N 10°01′E
Stavers Island *see* Vostok Island
98 J7 **Stavoren** *Fris.* Starum. Fryslân, N Netherlands 52°52′N 05°22′E
115 K21 **Stavrí, Akrotírio** *var.* Akrotírio Stavrós. *headland* Naxos, Kykládes, Greece, Aegean Sea 37°12′N 25°32′E
126 M14 **Stavropol'** *prev.* Voroshilovsk. Stavropol'skiy Kray, SW Russian Federation 45°02′N 41°58′E
Stavropol' *see* Tol'yatti
126 M14 **Stavropol'skaya Vozvyshennost'** ▲▲ SW Russian Federation
126 M14 **Stavropol'skiy Kray** ◆ *territory* SW Russian Federation
115 H14 **Stavrós** Kentrikí Makedonía, N Greece 40°39′N 23°43′E
115 J24 **Stavrós, Akrotírio** *headland* Kríti, Greece, E Mediterranean Sea 35°25′N 24°57′E
Stavrós, Akrotírio *see* Stavrí, Akrotírio
114 I12 **Stavroúpoli** *prev.* Stavroúpolis. Anatolikí Makedonía kai Thráki, NE Greece 41°12′N 24°45′E
Stavroúpolis *see* Stavroúpoli
117 O6 **Stavyshche** Kyyivs'ka Oblast', N Ukraine 49°23′N 30°10′E
182 M11 **Stawell** Victoria, SE Australia 37°06′S 142°52′E
110 N9 **Stawiski** Podlaskie, NE Poland 53°22′N 22°08′E
14 G14 **Stayner** Ontario, S Canada 44°25′N 80°05′W
14 D17 **St. Clair** ∽ Canada/USA
37 R3 **Steamboat Springs** Colorado, C USA 40°28′N 106°51′W
15 U4 **Ste-Anne, Lac** ◎ Québec, SE Canada
20 M8 **Stearns** Kentucky, S USA 36°39′N 84°27′W
39 N10 **Stebbins** Alaska, USA 63°30′N 162°15′W
15 U7 **Ste-Blandine** Québec, SE Canada 48°22′N 68°27′W
108 K7 **Steeg** Tirol, W Austria 47°15′N 10°18′E
27 Y9 **Steele** Missouri, C USA 36°04′N 89°49′W
29 N5 **Steele** North Dakota, N USA 46°51′N 99°55′W
194 J5 **Steele Island** *island* Antarctica
30 K16 **Steeleville** Illinois, N USA 38°00′N 89°39′W
27 W6 **Steelville** Missouri, C USA 37°57′N 91°21′W
99 G14 **Steenbergen** Noord-Brabant, S Netherlands 51°35′N 04°19′E
Steenkool *see* Bintuni
11 O10 **Steen River** Alberta, W Canada 59°37′N 117°17′W
98 M8 **Steenwijk** Overijssel, N Netherlands 52°47′N 06°07′E
65 A23 **Steeple Jason** *island* Jason Islands, NW Falkland Islands
174 J8 **Steep Point** *headland* Western Australia 26°09′S 113°11′E
116 L9 **Ştefăneşti** Botoşani, NE Romania 47°44′N 27°15′E
Stefanie, Lake *see* Ch'ew Bahir
8 L5 **Stefansson Island** *island* Nunavut, N Canada
117 O10 **Ştefan Vodă** *Rus.* Suvorovo. SE Moldova 46°33′N 29°39′E
63 H18 **Steffen, Cerro** ▲ S Chile 44°27′S 71°42′W
108 D9 **Steffisburg** Bern, C Switzerland 46°47′N 07°38′E
95 J24 **Stege** Sjælland, SE Denmark 54°59′N 12°18′E
116 G10 **Ştei** *Hung.* Vaskohsziklás. Bihor, W Romania 46°34′N 22°28′E
Steier *see* Steyr
Steierdorf/Steierdorf-Anina *see* Anina
109 T7 **Steiermark** *off.* Land Steiermark, *Eng.* Styria. ◆ *state* C Austria
Steiermark, Land *see* Steiermark
101 J19 **Steigerwald** *hill range* C Germany
99 L17 **Stein** Limburg, SE Netherlands 50°58′N 05°45′E
Stein *see* Stein an der Donau
Stein *see* Kamnik, Slovenia
108 M8 **Steinach** Tirol, W Austria 47°07′N 11°30′E
Steinamanger *see* Szombathely
109 W3 **Stein an der Donau** *var.* Stein. Niederösterreich, NE Austria 48°25′N 15°35′E
Steinau an der Elbe *see* Ścinawa
11 Y16 **Steinbach** Manitoba, S Canada 49°32′N 96°40′W
Steiner Alpen *see* Kamniško-Savinjske Alpe
99 L24 **Steinfort** Luxembourg, W Luxembourg 49°39′N 05°55′E
100 H12 **Steinhuder Meer** ◎ NW Germany
93 E15 **Steinkjer** Nord-Trøndelag, C Norway 64°01′N 11°29′E
Stejarul *see* Karapelit
99 F16 **Stekene** Oost-Vlaanderen, NW Belgium 51°13′N 04°04′E
83 E26 **Stellenbosch** Western Cape, SW South Africa 33°56′S 18°51′E
98 F13 **Stellendam** Zuid-Holland, SW Netherlands 51°48′N 04°01′E
39 T12 **Steller, Mount** ▲ Alaska, USA 60°36′N 142°49′W
103 Y14 **Stello, Monte** ▲ Corse, France, C Mediterranean Sea 42°49′N 09°24′E
106 F5 **Stelvio, Passo dello** *pass* Italy/Switzerland
15 S7 **Ste-Maguerite Nord-Est** ∽ Québec, SE Canada
15 V4 **Ste-Marguerite, Pointe** *headland* Québec, SE Canada 50°01′N 66°43′W
12 J14 **Ste-Marie, Lac** ⊠ Québec, S Canada
103 R3 **Stenay** Meuse, NE France 49°29′N 05°12′E
100 L12 **Stendal** Sachsen-Anhalt, C Germany 52°36′N 11°52′E
118 E8 **Stende** NW Latvia 57°09′N 22°33′E
182 H10 **Stenhouse Bay** South Australia 35°15′S 136°58′E
95 J23 **Stenløse** Hovedstaden, E Denmark 55°47′N 12°13′E
95 L19 **Stensjön** Jönköping, S Sweden 57°36′N 14°42′E
95 K18 **Stenstorp** Västra Götaland, S Sweden 58°15′N 13°45′E
95 I18 **Stenungsund** Västra Götaland, S Sweden 58°05′N 11°49′E
Stepanakert *see* Xankändi
137 T11 **Step'anavan** N Armenia 41°00′N 44°27′E
100 K9 **Stepenitz** ∽ N Germany
29 O10 **Stephan** South Dakota, N USA 44°12′N 99°25′W
29 R3 **Stephen** Minnesota, N USA 48°27′N 96°54′W
27 T14 **Stephens** Arkansas, C USA 33°25′N 93°04′W
184 J13 **Stephens, Cape** *headland* D'Urville Island, Marlborough, SW New Zealand 40°42′S 173°56′E
21 V3 **Stephens City** Virginia, NE USA 39°03′N 78°10′W
182 L6 **Stephens Creek** New South Wales, SE Australia 31°51′S 141°30′E
184 K13 **Stephens Island** *island* C New Zealand
31 N5 **Stephenson** Michigan, N USA 45°27′N 87°36′W
13 S12 **Stephenville** Newfoundland, Newfoundland and Labrador, SE Canada 48°33′N 58°34′W
25 S7 **Stephenville** Texas, SW USA 32°12′N 98°13′W
Step' Nardara *see* Step' Shardara
145 R8 **Stepnogorsk** Akmola, C Kazakhstan 52°04′N 72°18′E
127 O15 **Stepnoye** Stavropol'skiy Kray, SW Russian Federation 44°18′N 44°34′E
145 Q8 **Stepnyak** Akmola, N Kazakhstan 52°52′N 70°49′E
145 P17 **Step' Shardara** *Kaz.* Shardara Dalasy; *prev.* Step' Nardara. *grassland* S Kazakhstan
192 J17 **Steps Point** *headland* Tutuila, W American Samoa 14°23′S 170°46′W
115 F17 **Stereá Elláda** *Eng.* Greece Central *var.* Stereá Ellás. ◆ *region* C Greece
Stereá Ellás *see* Stereá Elláda
83 J24 **Sterkspruit** Eastern Cape, SE South Africa 30°31′S 27°22′E
127 U6 **Sterlibashevo** Respublika Bashkortostan, W Russian Federation 53°19′N 55°12′E
39 R12 **Sterling** Alaska, USA 60°32′N 150°51′W
37 V3 **Sterling** Colorado, C USA 40°37′N 103°12′W
30 K11 **Sterling** Illinois, N USA 41°47′N 89°42′W
26 M5 **Sterling** Kansas, C USA 38°12′N 98°12′W
25 O8 **Sterling City** Texas, SW USA 31°50′N 101°00′W
31 S9 **Sterling Heights** Michigan, N USA 42°34′N 83°01′W
21 W3 **Sterling Park** Virginia, NE USA 39°00′N 77°24′W
37 V2 **Sterling Reservoir** ⊠ Colorado, C USA
22 I5 **Sterlington** Louisiana, S USA 32°42′N 92°05′W
127 U6 **Sterlitamak** Respublika Bashkortostan, W Russian Federation 53°39′N 56°00′E
Sternberg *see* Šternberk
111 H17 **Šternberk** *Ger.* Sternberg. Olomoucký Kraj, E Czech Republic 49°45′N 17°20′E
141 V17 **Stēroh** Suquţrā, S Yemen 12°21′N 53°50′E
Sterren, Pegunungan *see* Star Mountains
110 G11 **Stęszew** Wielkopolskie, C Poland 52°16′N 16°41′E
Stettin *see* Szczecin
Stettiner Haff *see* Szczeciński, Zalew
11 Q15 **Stettler** Alberta, SW Canada 52°21′N 112°40′W
31 V13 **Steubenville** Ohio, N USA 40°21′N 80°37′W
97 O21 **Stevenage** E England, United Kingdom 51°55′N 00°14′W
23 Q1 **Stevenson** Alabama, S USA 34°52′N 85°50′W
32 H11 **Stevenson** Washington, NW USA 45°43′N 121°54′W
182 E1 **Stevenson Creek** *seasonal river* South Australia
39 Q13 **Stevenson Entrance** *strait* Alaska, USA
30 L6 **Stevens Point** Wisconsin, N USA 44°32′N 89°33′W
39 R8 **Stevens Village** Alaska, USA 66°01′N 149°02′W
33 P10 **Stevensville** Montana, NW USA 46°30′N 114°05′W
93 E25 **Stevns Klint** *headland* E Denmark 55°15′N 12°25′E
10 J12 **Stewart** British Columbia, W Canada 55°58′N 129°52′W
10 J6 **Stewart** ∽ Yukon Territory, NW Canada
10 I6 **Stewart Crossing** Yukon Territory, NW Canada 63°22′N 136°37′W
63 H25 **Stewart, Isla** *island* S Chile
185 B25 **Stewart Island** *island* S New Zealand
Stewart Islands *see* Sikaiana
181 W6 **Stewart, Mount** ▲ Queensland, E Australia 20°11′S 145°29′E
10 H6 **Stewart River** Yukon Territory, NW Canada 63°17′N 139°24′W
27 R3 **Stewartsville** Missouri, C USA 39°45′N 94°30′W
11 S16 **Stewart Valley** Saskatchewan, S Canada 50°34′N 107°47′W
29 W10 **Stewartville** Minnesota, N USA 43°51′N 92°29′W
Steyerlak-Anina *see* Anina
109 T5 **Steyr** *var.* Steier. Oberösterreich, N Austria 48°02′N 14°26′E
109 T5 **Steyr** ∽ NW Austria
15 T7 **St-Fabien** Québec, SE Canada 48°19′N 68°51′W
15 R11 **St-François, Lac** ◎ Québec, SE Canada
83 E25 **St. Helena Bay** *bay* SW South Africa
15 T8 **St-Hubert** Québec, SE Canada 47°46′N 69°15′W
29 P11 **Stickney** South Dakota, N USA 43°24′N 98°23′W
98 L5 **Stiens** Fryslân, N Netherlands 53°15′N 05°45′E
Stif *see* Sétif
27 Q11 **Stigler** Oklahoma, C USA 35°16′N 95°08′W
107 N18 **Stigliano** Basilicata, S Italy 40°24′N 16°13′E
95 N17 **Stigtomta** Södermanland, C Sweden 58°48′N 16°47′E
10 I11 **Stikine** ∽ British Columbia, W Canada
Stilida/Stilís *see* Stylída
95 G22 **Stilling** Midtjylland, C Denmark 56°04′N 10°00′E
29 W8 **Stillwater** Minnesota, N USA 45°03′N 92°48′W
27 O9 **Stillwater** Oklahoma, C USA 36°07′N 97°03′W
35 S5 **Stillwater Range** ▲▲ Nevada, W USA
18 I8 **Stillwater Reservoir** ⊠ New York, NE USA
107 O22 **Stilo, Punta** *headland* S Italy 38°27′N 16°36′E
27 R10 **Stilwell** Oklahoma, C USA 35°48′N 94°37′W
Stimlje *see* Shtime
25 N1 **Stinnett** Texas, SW USA 35°49′N 101°27′W
113 P18 **Štip** E FYR Macedonia 41°45′N 22°10′E
Stira *see* Stýra
96 J12 **Stirling** C Scotland, United Kingdom 56°07′N 03°57′W
96 I12 **Stirling** *cultural region* C Scotland, United Kingdom
180 J14 **Stirling Range** ▲▲ Western Australia
15 R8 **St-Jean** ∽ Québec, SE Canada
93 E16 **Stjørdalshalsen** Nord-Trøndelag, C Norway 63°27′N 10°57′E
83 L22 **St. Lucia** KwaZulu/Natal, E South Africa 28°22′N 32°25′E
Stochód *see* Stokhid
101 H24 **Stockach** Baden-Württemberg, S Germany 47°51′N 09°01′E
25 S12 **Stockdale** Texas, SW USA 29°14′N 97°57′W
109 X3 **Stockerau** Niederösterreich, NE Austria 48°24′N 16°13′E
93 H20 **Stockholm** ● (Sweden) Stockholm, C Sweden 59°17′N 18°03′E
95 O15 **Stockholm** ◆ *county* C Sweden
Stockmannshof *see* Pļaviņas
97 L18 **Stockport** NW England, United Kingdom 53°25′N 02°10′W
65 K15 **Stocks Seamount** *undersea feature* C Atlantic Ocean 11°42′S 33°48′W
35 O8 **Stockton** California, W USA 37°56′N 121°19′W
26 L3 **Stockton** Kansas, C USA 39°27′N 99°17′W
27 S6 **Stockton** Missouri, C USA 37°43′N 93°49′W
30 K3 **Stockton Island** *island* Apostle Islands, Wisconsin, N USA
27 S7 **Stockton Lake** ⊠ Missouri, C USA
97 M15 **Stockton-on-Tees** *var.* Stockton on Tees. N England, United Kingdom 54°34′N 01°19′W
Stockton on Tees *see* Stockton-on-Tees
24 M10 **Stockton Plateau** *plain* Texas, SW USA
28 M16 **Stockville** Nebraska, C USA 40°33′N 100°20′W
93 H17 **Stöde** Västernorrland, C Sweden 62°27′N 16°34′E
Stodolichi *see* Stadolichy
113 M19 **Stogovo Karaorman** ▲▲ W FYR Macedonia
Stoke *see* Stoke-on-Trent
97 L19 **Stoke-on-Trent** *var.* Stoke. C England, United Kingdom 53°N 02°10′W
182 M15 **Stokes Point** *headland* Tasmania, SE Australia 40°09′S 143°55′E
116 J2 **Stokhid** *Pol.* Stochód, *Rus.* Stokhod. ∽ NW Ukraine
Stokhod *see* Stokhid
92 I4 **Stokkseyri** Sudhurland, SW Iceland 63°49′N 21°00′W
92 G10 **Stokmarknes** Nordland, C Norway 68°34′N 14°55′E
Stol *see* Veliki Krš
113 H15 **Stolac** Federacija Bosna I Hercegovina, S Bosnia and Herzegovina 43°04′N 17°58′E
Stolbce *see* Stowbtsy
101 D16 **Stolberg** *var.* Stolberg im Rheinland. Nordrhein-Westfalen, W Germany 50°45′N 06°15′E
Stolberg im Rheinland *see* Stolberg
123 P6 **Stolbovoy, Ostrov** *island* NE Russian Federation
Stolbtsy *see* Stowbtsy
119 J20 **Stolin** Brestskaya Voblasts', SW Belarus 51°53′N 26°51′E
95 K14 **Stöllet** *var.* Norra Ny. Värmland, C Sweden 60°24′N 13°15′E
Stolp *see* Słupsk
Stolpe *see* Słupia
Stolpmünde *see* Ustka
115 F15 **Stómio** Thessalía, C Greece 39°51′N 22°45′E
14 J11 **Stonecliffe** Ontario, SE Canada 46°12′N 77°58′W
96 L10 **Stonehaven** NE Scotland, United Kingdom 56°59′N 02°14′W
97 M23 **Stonehenge** *ancient monument* Wiltshire, S England, United Kingdom
23 T3 **Stone Mountain** ▲ Georgia, SE USA 33°48′N 84°10′W
11 X16 **Stonewall** Manitoba, S Canada 50°08′N 97°20′W
21 S3 **Stonewood** West Virginia, NE USA 39°15′N 80°18′W
14 D17 **Stoney Point** Ontario, S Canada 42°18′N 82°32′W
92 H10 **Stonglandseidet** Troms, N Norway 69°03′N 17°06′E
65 N25 **Stonybeach Bay** *bay* Tristan da Cunha, SE Atlantic Ocean
35 N5 **Stony Creek** ∽ California, W USA
65 N25 **Stonyhill Point** *headland* S Tristan da Cunha
14 I14 **Stony Lake** ◎ Ontario, SE Canada
11 Q14 **Stony Plain** Alberta, SW Canada 53°31′N 114°04′W
21 R9 **Stony Point** North Carolina, SE USA 35°51′N 81°04′W
18 G8 **Stony Point** *headland* New York, NE USA 43°50′N 76°18′W
11 T10 **Stony Rapids** Saskatchewan, C Canada 59°14′N 105°48′W
39 P11 **Stony River** Alaska, USA 61°48′N 156°37′W
Stony Tunguska *see* Podkamennaya Tunguska
12 G10 **Stooping** ∽ Ontario, C Canada
100 I9 **Stör** ∽ N Germany
95 M15 **Storå** Örebro, S Sweden 59°44′N 15°10′E
95 J16 **Stora Gla** ◎ C Sweden
95 I16 **Stora Le** *Nor.* Store Le. ◎ Norway/Sweden
92 I12 **Stora Lulevatten** ◎ N Sweden
92 H13 **Storavan** ◎ N Sweden
93 I20 **Storby** Åland, SW Finland 60°12′N 19°33′E
94 E10 **Stordalen** Møre og Romsdal, S Norway 62°22′N 07°00′E
95 H23 **Storebælt** *var.* Store Bælt, *Eng.* Great Belt, Storebelt. *channel* Baltic Sea/Kattegat
Store Bælt *see* Storebælt
Storebelt *see* Storebælt
95 M19 **Storebro** Kalmar, S Sweden 57°36′N 15°30′E
95 J24 **Store Heddinge** Sjælland, SE Denmark 55°19′N 12°24′E
Store Le *see* Stora Le
93 E16 **Støren** Sør-Trøndelag, S Norway 63°02′N 10°16′E
92 O4 **Storfjorden** *fjord* S Norway
95 L15 **Storfors** Värmland, C Sweden 59°33′N 14°16′E
92 G13 **Storforshei** Nordland, C Norway 66°25′N 14°25′E
Storhammer *see* Hamar
93 F16 **Storlien** Jämtland, C Sweden 63°18′N 12°10′E
183 P17 **Storm Bay** *inlet* Tasmania, SE Australia
29 T12 **Storm Lake** Iowa, C USA 42°38′N 95°12′W
29 S13 **Storm Lake** ◎ Iowa, C USA
96 G7 **Stornoway** NW Scotland, United Kingdom 58°13′N 06°23′W
Storojineţ *see* Storozhynets'
92 P1 **Storøya** *island* NE Svalbard
125 S10 **Storozhevsk** Respublika Komi, NW Russian Federation 61°56′N 52°18′E
Storozhinets *see* Storozhynets'
116 K8 **Storozhynets'** *Ger.* Storozynetz, *Rom.* Storojineţ, *Rus.* Storozhinets. Chernivets'ka Oblast', W Ukraine 48°11′N 25°42′E
Storozynetz *see* Storozhynets'
92 H11 **Storriten** *Lapp.* Stuorrarijjda. ▲ C Norway 68°09′N 17°12′E
19 N12 **Storrs** Connecticut, NE USA 41°48′N 72°15′W
94 I11 **Storsjøen** ◎ S Norway
94 N13 **Storsjön** ◎ C Sweden
93 F16 **Storsjön** ◎ C Sweden
92 J9 **Storslett** Troms, N Norway 69°45′N 21°03′E
94 H11 **Storsølnkletten** ▲ S Norway 61°52′N 11°32′E
92 I9 **Storsteinnes** Troms, N Norway 69°13′N 19°14′E
Storstrøms Amt *see* Sjælland
93 J14 **Storsund** Norrbotten, N Sweden 65°36′N 20°40′E
94 J9 **Storsylen** *Swe.* Sylarna. ▲ Norway/Sweden 63°00′N 12°14′E
92 H11 **Stortoppen** ▲ N Sweden 67°33′N 17°27′E
93 H14 **Storuman** Västerbotten, N Sweden 65°05′N 17°10′E
93 H14 **Storuman** ◎ N Sweden
94 N13 **Storvik** Gävleborg, C Sweden 60°37′N 16°30′E
95 O14 **Storvreta** Uppsala, C Sweden 59°58′N 17°42′E
100 L10 **Störwasserstrasse** *canal* N Germany
29 V13 **Story City** Iowa, C USA 42°10′N 93°36′W
11 V17 **Stoughton** Saskatchewan, S Canada 49°40′N 103°01′W
19 O11 **Stoughton** Massachusetts, NE USA 42°07′N 71°06′W
30 L9 **Stoughton** Wisconsin, N USA 42°56′N 89°12′W
97 L23 **Stour** ∽ E England, United Kingdom
97 P21 **Stour** ∽ S England, United Kingdom
27 T5 **Stover** Missouri, C USA 38°26′N 92°59′W
95 G21 **Støvring** Nordjylland, N Denmark 56°53′N 09°52′E
119 J17 **Stowbtsy** *Pol.* Stołbce, *Rus.* Stolbtsy. Minskaya Voblasts', C Belarus 53°29′N 26°44′E
25 X11 **Stowell** Texas, SW USA 29°47′N 94°22′W
97 P20 **Stowmarket** E England, United Kingdom 52°05′N 00°54′E
114 N8 **Stozher** Dobrich, NE Bulgaria 43°27′N 27°49′E
97 E14 **Strabane** *Ir.* An Srath Bán. W Northern Ireland, United Kingdom 54°49′N 07°27′W
121 S11 **Strabo Trench** *undersea feature* C Mediterranean Sea
27 T7 **Strafford** Missouri, C USA 37°16′N 93°07′W
183 N17 **Strahan** Tasmania, SE Australia 42°10′S 145°18′E
111 C18 **Strakonice** *Ger.* Strakonitz. Jihočeský Kraj, S Czech Republic 49°14′N 13°55′E
Strakonitz *see* Strakonice
100 N8 **Stralsund** Mecklenburg-Vorpommern, NE Germany 54°18′N 13°06′E
99 L16 **Stramproy** Limburg, SE Netherlands 51°12′N 05°43′E
83 E26 **Strand** Western Cape, SW South Africa 34°06′S 18°50′E
94 E10 **Stranda** Møre og Romsdal, S Norway 62°18′N 06°56′E
97 G15 **Strangford Lough** *Ir.* Loch Cuan. *inlet* E Northern Ireland, United Kingdom
95 N16 **Strängnäs** Södermanland, C Sweden 59°22′N 17°02′E
97 E14 **Stranorlar** *Ir.* Srath an Urláir. NW Ireland 54°48′N 07°46′W
97 H14 **Stranraer** S Scotland, United Kingdom 54°54′N 05°02′W
11 U16 **Strasbourg** Saskatchewan, S Canada 51°05′N 104°58′W
103 V5 **Strasbourg** *Ger.* Strassburg; *anc.* Argentoratum. Bas-Rhin, NE France 48°35′N 07°45′E
109 T8 **Strassburg** Kärnten, S Austria 46°54′N 14°21′E
37 U4 **Strasburg** Colorado, C USA 39°42′N 104°13′W
29 N7 **Strasburg** North Dakota, N USA 46°07′N 100°10′W
31 U12 **Strasburg** Ohio, N USA 40°35′N 81°31′W
21 U3 **Strasburg** Virginia, NE USA 38°59′N 78°21′W
117 N10 **Strășeni** *var.* Strasheny. C Moldova 47°07′N 28°37′E
Strasheny *see* Strășeni
Strassburg *see* Strasbourg, France
Strassburg *see* Aiud, Romania
99 M25 **Strassen** Luxembourg, S Luxembourg 49°37′N 06°05′E
109 R5 **Strasswalchen** Salzburg, C Austria 47°59′N 13°19′E
14 F16 **Stratford** Ontario, S Canada 43°22′N 81°00′W
184 K10 **Stratford** Taranaki, North Island, New Zealand 39°20′S 174°16′E
35 Q11 **Stratford** California, W USA 36°10′N 119°47′W
29 V13 **Stratford** Iowa, C USA 42°16′N 93°55′W
27 O12 **Stratford** Oklahoma, C USA 34°48′N 96°57′W
25 N1 **Stratford** Texas, SW USA 36°21′N 102°05′W
30 K6 **Stratford** Wisconsin, N USA 44°53′N 90°13′W
Stratford *see* Stratford-upon-Avon
97 M20 **Stratford-upon-Avon** *var.* Stratford. C England, United Kingdom 52°12′N 01°41′W
183 O17 **Strathgordon** Tasmania, SE Australia 42°49′S 146°04′E
11 Q16 **Strathmore** Alberta, SW Canada 51°05′N 113°20′W
35 R11 **Strathmore** California, W USA 36°07′N 119°04′W
14 E16 **Strathroy** Ontario, S Canada 42°57′N 81°40′W
96 I6 **Strathy Point** *headland* N Scotland, United Kingdom 58°36′N 04°04′W
37 W4 **Stratton** Colorado, C USA 39°16′N 102°34′W
19 P6 **Stratton** Maine, NE USA 45°08′N 70°25′W
18 M10 **Stratton Mountain** ▲ Vermont, NE USA 43°05′N 72°55′W
101 N21 **Straubing** Bayern, SE Germany 48°53′N 12°35′E
100 O12 **Strausberg** Brandenburg, E Germany 52°34′N 13°52′E
32 K13 **Strawberry Mountain** ▲ Oregon, NW USA 44°18′N 118°43′W
29 X12 **Strawberry Point** Iowa, C USA 42°40′N 91°31′W
36 M3 **Strawberry Reservoir** ⊠ Utah, W USA
36 M4 **Strawberry River** ∽ Utah, W USA
25 R7 **Strawn** Texas, SW USA 32°33′N 98°30′W
113 P17 **Straža** ▲ Bulgaria/FYR Macedonia 42°16′N 22°13′E
111 I19 **Strážov** *Hung.* Sztrazsó. ▲ NW Slovakia 48°59′N 18°29′E
182 F7 **Streaky Bay** South Australia 32°49′S 134°13′E
182 E7 **Streaky Bay** *bay* South Australia
30 L12 **Streator** Illinois, N USA 41°07′N 88°50′W
Streckenbach *see* Świdnik
Strednogorie *see* Pirdop
111 C17 **Středočeský Kraj** ◆ *region* C Czech Republic
29 O6 **Streeter** North Dakota, N USA 46°37′N 99°23′W
25 U8 **Streetman** Texas, SW USA 31°52′N 96°19′W
116 G13 **Strehaia** Mehedinţi, SW Romania 44°37′N 23°10′E
Strehlen *see* Strzelin
114 I10 **Strelcha** Pazardzhik, C Bulgaria 42°28′N 24°21′E
122 L12 **Strelka** Krasnoyarskiy Kray, C Russian Federation 58°05′N 92°54′E
124 L6 **Strel'na** ∽ NW Russian Federation
118 H7 **Strenči** *Ger.* Stackeln. N Latvia 57°38′N 25°42′E
15 V6 **St-René-de-Matane** Québec, SE Canada 48°42′N 67°22′W
108 K8 **Strengen** Tirol, W Austria 47°07′N 10°25′E
106 C6 **Stresa** Piemonte, NE Italy 45°52′N 08°32′E
Streshin *see* Streshyn
119 N18 **Streshyn** *Rus.* Streshin. Homyel'skaya Voblasts', SE Belarus 52°43′N 30°07′E
95 B18 **Streymoy** *Dan.* Strømø. *island* N Faeroe Islands
95 G23 **Strib** Syddtjylland, C Denmark 55°33′N 09°47′E
111 A17 **Stříbro** *Ger.* Mies. Plzeňský Kraj, W Czech Republic 49°44′N 12°55′E
186 B7 **Strickland** ∽ SW Papua New Guinea
Striegau *see* Strzegom
Strigonium *see* Esztergom
98 H13 **Strijen** Zuid-Holland, SW Netherlands 51°45′N 04°34′E
63 H21 **Strobel, Lago** ◎ S Argentina
61 B25 **Stroeder** Buenos Aires, E Argentina 40°11′S 62°35′W
115 C20 **Strofádes** *island* Iónia Nisiá, Greece, C Mediterranean Sea
Strofilia *see* Strofyliá
115 G17 **Strofyliá** *var.* Strofilia. Évvoia, C Greece 38°49′N 23°25′E
100 O10 **Strom** ∽ NE Germany
107 L22 **Stromboli** ☆ Isola Stromboli, SW Italy 38°48′N 15°13′E
107 L22 **Stromboli, Isola** *island* Isole Eolie, S Italy
96 H9 **Stromeferry** N Scotland, United Kingdom 57°20′N 05°35′W
96 J5 **Stromness** N Scotland, United Kingdom 58°57′N 03°18′W
Strømø *see* Streymoy
94 N11 **Strömsbruk** Gävleborg, C Sweden 61°52′N 17°19′E
29 Q15 **Stromsburg** Nebraska, C USA 41°06′N 97°36′W
95 K21 **Strömsnäsbruk** Kronoberg, S Sweden 56°35′N 13°45′E
95 I17 **Strömstad** Västra Götaland, S Sweden 58°56′N 11°11′E
93 G16 **Strömsund** Jämtland, C Sweden 63°51′N 15°35′E
93 G15 **Ströms Vattudal** *valley* N Sweden
27 V14 **Strong** Arkansas, C USA 33°06′N 92°19′W
Strongilí *see* Strongylí
107 O21 **Strongoli** Calabria, SW Italy 39°17′N 17°03′E
31 T11 **Strongsville** Ohio, N USA 41°18′N 81°50′W
115 Q23 **Strongylí** *var.* Strongili. *island* SE Greece
96 K5 **Stronsay** *island* NE Scotland, United Kingdom
97 L21 **Stroud** C England, United Kingdom 51°46′N 02°15′W
27 O10 **Stroud** Oklahoma, C USA 35°45′N 96°39′W
18 I14 **Stroudsburg** Pennsylvania, NE USA 40°59′N 75°12′W
95 F21 **Struer** Midtjylland, W Denmark 56°29′N 08°37′E
113 M20 **Struga** SW FYR Macedonia 41°11′N 20°40′E
Strugi-Kranyse *see* Strugi-Krasnyye
124 G14 **Strugi-Krasnyye** *var.* Strugi-Kranyse. Pskovskaya Oblast', W Russian Federation 58°19′N 29°09′E
114 G11 **Struma** *Gk.* Strymónas. ∽ Bulgaria/Greece *see also* Strymónas
Struma *see* Strymónas
97 G21 **Strumble Head** *headland* SW Wales, United Kingdom 52°01′N 05°05′W
Strumeshnitsa *see* Strumica
113 Q19 **Strumica** E FYR Macedonia 41°27′N 22°39′E
113 Q19 **Strumica** *Bulg.* Strumeshnitsa. ∽ Bulgaria/FYR Macedonia
114 G11 **Strumyani** Blagoevgrad, SW Bulgaria 41°41′N 23°13′E
31 V12 **Struthers** Ohio, N USA 41°03′N 80°36′W
114 I10 **Stryama** ∽ C Bulgaria
114 G13 **Strymónas** *Bul.* Struma. ∽ Bulgaria/Greece *see also* Struma
Strymónas *see* Struma
115 H14 **Strymonikós Kólpos** *gulf* N Greece
116 I6 **Stryy** L'vivs'ka Oblast', NW Ukraine 49°16′N 23°51′E
116 H6 **Stryy** ∽ W Ukraine
111 F14 **Strzegom** *Ger.* Striegau. Wałbrzych, SW Poland 50°59′N 16°20′E
110 E10 **Strzelce Krajeńskie** *Ger.* Friedeberg Neumark. Lubuskie, W Poland 52°52′N 15°30′E
111 I15 **Strzelce Opolskie** *Ger.* Gross Strehlitz. Opolskie, SW Poland 50°31′N 18°19′E
182 K3 **Strzelecki Creek** *seasonal river* South Australia
182 J3 **Strzelecki Desert** *desert* South Australia
111 G15 **Strzelin** *Ger.* Strehlen. Dolnośląskie, SW Poland 50°48′N 17°03′E
110 I11 **Strzelno** Kujawsko-pomorskie, C Poland 52°38′N 18°11′E
111 N17 **Strzyżów** Podkarpackie, SE Poland 49°52′N 21°46′E
15 S8 **St-Siméon** Québec, SE Canada 47°50′N 69°55′W
Stua Laighean *see* Leinster, Mount
23 Y13 **Stuart** Florida, SE USA 27°12′N 80°15′W
29 U14 **Stuart** Iowa, C USA 41°30′N 94°19′W
29 O13 **Stuart** Nebraska, C USA 42°36′N 99°08′W
21 S8 **Stuart** Virginia, NE USA 36°38′N 80°19′W
10 L13 **Stuart** ∽ British Columbia, SW Canada
39 N10 **Stuart Island** *island* Alaska, USA
10 L13 **Stuart Lake** ◎ British Columbia, SW Canada
185 B22 **Stuart Mountains** ▲▲ South Island, New Zealand
182 F3 **Stuart Range** *hill range* South Australia
Stubaital *see* Neustift im Stubaital
95 I24 **Stubbekøbing** Sjælland, SE Denmark 54°53′N 12°04′E
45 P14 **Stubbs** Saint Vincent, Saint Vincent and the Grenadines 13°08′N 61°09′W
109 V6 **Stübming** ∽ E Austria
114 J11 **Studen Kladenets, Yazovir** ⊠ S Bulgaria
185 G21 **Studholme** Canterbury, South Island, New Zealand 44°44′S 171°08′E
Stuhlweissenberg *see* Székesfehérvár
Stuhm *see* Sztum
12 C7 **Stull Lake** ◎ Ontario, C Canada
Stuorrarijjda *see* Storriten
126 L4 **Stupino** Moskovskaya Oblast', W Russian Federation 54°54′N 38°06′E
27 U4 **Sturgeon** Missouri, C USA 39°13′N 92°16′W
14 G10 **Sturgeon** ∽ Ontario, S Canada
31 N6 **Sturgeon Bay** Wisconsin, N USA 44°51′N 87°21′W
14 G11 **Sturgeon Falls** Ontario, S Canada 46°22′N 79°57′W
12 C11 **Sturgeon Lake** ◎ Ontario, S Canada
30 M3 **Sturgeon River** ∽ Michigan, N USA
20 H6 **Sturgis** Kentucky, S USA 37°33′N 87°58′W
31 P11 **Sturgis** Michigan, N USA 41°48′N 85°25′W
28 J9 **Sturgis** South Dakota, N USA 44°24′N 103°30′W
112 D10 **Šturlić** ◆ Federacija Bosna I Hercegovina, NW Bosnia and Herzegovina
111 J22 **Štúrovo** *Hung.* Párkány; *prev.* Parkan. Nitriansky Kraj, SW Slovakia 47°49′N 18°40′E
182 L4 **Sturt, Mount** *hill* New South Wales, SE Australia
181 P4 **Sturt Plain** *plain* Northern Territory, N Australia
181 T9 **Sturt Stony Desert** *desert* South Australia
83 J25 **Stutterheim** Eastern Cape, S South Africa 32°35′S 27°26′E
101 H21 **Stuttgart** Baden-Württemberg, SW Germany 48°47′N 09°12′E
27 W12 **Stuttgart** Arkansas, C USA 34°30′N 91°32′W
92 H2 **Stykkishólmur** Vesturland, W Iceland 65°04′N 22°43′W
115 F17 **Stylída** *var.* Stilida, Stilís. Stereá Elláda, C Greece 38°55′N 22°37′E
116 K2 **Styr** *Rus.* Styr'. ∽ Belarus/Ukraine
115 I19 **Stýra** *var.* Stira. Évvoia, C Greece 38°10′N 24°13′E
Styria *see* Steiermark
15 Y5 **St-Yvon** Québec, SE Canada 49°09′N 64°51′W
Su *see* Jiangsu
Sua *see* Sowa
171 Q17 **Suai** W East Timor 09°19′S 125°16′E
54 G9 **Suaita** Santander, C Colombia 06°07′N 73°30′W
80 I7 **Suakin** *var.* Sawakin. Red Sea, NE Sudan 19°06′N 37°17′E
161 T13 **Su'ao** *Jap.* Suō. N Taiwan 24°33′N 121°48′E
Suao *see* Suau
Sua Pan *see* Sowa Pan
40 G6 **Suaqui Grande** Sonora, NW Mexico 28°22′N 109°52′W
61 A16 **Suardi** Santa Fe, C Argentina 30°32′S 61°58′W
54 D11 **Suárez** Cauca, SW Colombia 02°55′N 76°41′W
186 G10 **Suau** *var.* Suao. Suaul Island, SE Papua New Guinea 10°39′S 150°03′E
118 G12 **Subačius** Panevėžys, NE Lithuania 55°46′N 24°45′E
168 K9 **Subang** *prev.* Soebang. Jawa, C Indonesia 06°32′S 107°45′E
169 O16 **Subang** ✕ (Kuala Lumpur) Pahang, Peninsular Malaysia
129 S10 **Subansiri** ∽ NE India
154 M12 **Subarnapur** *prev.* Sonapur, Sonepur. Orissa, E India 20°50′N 83°58′E
118 I11 **Subate** SE Latvia 56°00′N 25°54′E
139 N5 **Subaykhān** Dayr az Zawr, E Syria 34°52′N 40°35′E
Subei/Subei Mongolzu Zizhixian *see* Dangchengwan
169 P9 **Subi Besar, Pulau** *island* Kepulauan Natuna, W Indonesia
Subiyah *see* Aş Şubayḩiyah
26 I7 **Sublette** Kansas, C USA 37°28′N 100°52′W
112 K8 **Subotica** *Ger.* Maria-Theresiopel, *Hung.* Szabadka. Vojvodina, N Serbia 46°06′N 19°41′E
116 K9 **Suceava** *Ger.* Suczawa, *Hung.* Szucsava. Suceava, NE Romania 47°41′N 26°16′E
116 J9 **Suceava** ◆ *county* NE Romania
116 K9 **Suceava** *Ger.* Suczawa. ∽ N Romania
112 E12 **Sućevići** Zadar, SW Croatia 44°13′N 16°04′E
111 K17 **Sucha Beskidzka** Małopolskie, S Poland 49°44′N 19°36′E
111 M14 **Suchedniów** Świętokrzyskie, C Poland 51°01′N 20°49′E
42 A2 **Suchitepéquez** *off.* Departamento de Suchitepéquez. ◆ *department* SW Guatemala
Suchitepéquez, Departamento de *see* Suchitepéquez
Su-chou *see* Suzhou
Suchow *see* Xuzhou, Jiangsu, China
Suchow *see* Suzhou, Jiangsu, China
97 D17 **Suck** ∽ C Ireland

◆ Country
● Country Capital
◇ Dependent Territory
○ Dependent Territory Capital
◆ Administrative Regions
✕ International Airport
▲ Mountain
▲▲ Mountain Range
☆ Volcano
∽ River
◎ Lake
⊠ Reservoir

Sucker State *see* Illinois
186 *F9* **Suckling, Mount** ▲ S Papua New Guinea *09°36′S 149°00′E*
57 *L19* **Sucre** *hist.* Chuquisaca, La Plata. ● (Bolivia-legal capital) Chuquisaca, S Bolivia *18°53′S 65°25′W*
54 *E6* **Sucre** Santander, N Colombia *08°50′N 74°22′W*
56 *A7* **Sucre** Manabí, W Ecuador *01°21′S 80°27′W*
54 *E6* **Sucre** *off.* Departamento de Sucre. ⬖ *province* N Colombia
55 *O5* **Sucre** *off.* Estado Sucre. ⬖ *state* NE Venezuela
Sucre, Departamento de *see* Sucre
Sucre, Estado *see* Sucre
56 *D6* **Sucumbíos** ⬖ *province* NE Ecuador
113 *G15* **Sućuraj** Split-Dalmacija, S Croatia *43°07′N 17°10′E*
58 *K10* **Sucuriju** Amapá, NE Brazil *01°31′N 50°W*
Suczawa *see* Suceava
79 *E16* **Sud** *Eng.* South. ⬖ *province* S Cameroon
124 *K13* **Suda** ≈ NW Russian Federation
Suda *see* Soúda
117 *U13* **Sudak** Avtonomna Respublika Krym, S Ukrainę *44°52′N 34°57′E*
24 *M4* **Sudan** Texas, SW USA *34°04′N 102°32′W*
80 *C10* **Sudan** *off.* Republic of Sudan, *Ar.* Jumhuriyat as-Sudan; *prev.* Anglo-Egyptian Sudan. ◆ *republic* N Africa
Sudanese Republic *see* Mali
Sudan, Jumhuriyat as- *see* Sudan
Sudan, Republic of *see* Sudan
14 *F10* **Sudbury** Ontario, S Canada *46°29′N 81°W*
97 *P20* **Sudbury** E England, United Kingdom *52°04′N 00°43′E*
Sud, Canal de *see* Gonâve, Canal de la
80 *E13* **Sudd** *swamp region* C South Sudan
100 *K10* **Sude** ≈ N Germany
Suderø *see* Sudhuroy
Sudest Island *see* Tagula Island
111 *E15* **Sudeten** *var.* Sudetes, Sudetic Mountains, *Cz./Pol.* Sudety. ▲▲ Czech Republic/ Poland
Sudetes/Sudetic Mountains/Sudety *see* Sudeten
92 *G1* **Sudhureyri** Vestfirdhir, NW Iceland *66°08′N 23°31′W*
92 *J4* **Sudhurland** ⬖ *region* S Iceland
95 *B19* **Sudhuroy** *Dan.* Suderø. *island* S Faeroe Islands
124 *M15* **Sudislavl'** Kostromskaya Oblast', NW Russian Federation *57°55′N 41°45′E*
Südkarpaten *see* Carpații Meridionalii
79 *N20* **Sud-Kivu** *off.* Région Sud Kivu. ⬖ *region* E Dem. Rep. Congo
Sud Kivu, Région *see* Sud-Kivu
Südliche Morava *see* Južna Morava
100 *E12* **Süd-Nord-Kanal** *canal* NW Germany
126 *M3* **Sudogda** Vladimirskaya Oblast', W Russian Federation *55°58′N 40°57′E*
Sudostroy *see* Severodvinsk
79 *C15* **Sud-Ouest** *Eng.* South-West. ⬖ *province* W Cameroon
173 *X17* **Sud Ouest, Pointe** *headland* SW Mauritius *20°27′S 57°18′E*
187 *P17* **Sud, Province** ⬖ *province* S New Caledonia
92 *H4* **Sudurnes** ⬖ *region* SW Iceland
126 *J8* **Sudzha** Kurskaya Oblast', W Russian Federation *51°12′N 35°19′E*
81 *D15* **Sue** ≈ W South Sudan
105 *S10* **Sueca** Valenciana, E Spain *39°13′N 00°19′W*
114 *I10* **Sŭedinenie** Plovdiv, C Bulgaria *42°14′N 24°36′E*
Suero *see* Alzira
75 *X8* **Suez** *Ar.* As Suways, El Suweis. NE Egypt *29°59′N 32°33′E*
75 *W7* **Suez Canal** *Ar.* Qanāt as Suways. *canal* NE Egypt
Suez, Gulf of *see* Khalīj as Suways
11 *R17* **Suffield** Alberta, SW Canada *50°15′N 111°05′W*
21 *X7* **Suffolk** Virginia, NE USA *36°44′N 76°37′W*
97 *P20* **Suffolk** *cultural region* E England, United Kingdom
142 *J2* **Şūfīān** Āžarbāyjān-e Sharqī, N Iran *38°15′N 45°59′E*
31 *N12* **Sugar Creek** ≈ Illinois, N USA
30 *L13* **Sugar Creek** ≈ Illinois, N USA
31 *R3* **Sugar Island** *island* Michigan, N USA
25 *V11* **Sugar Land** Texas, SW USA *29°37′N 95°37′W*
19 *P6* **Sugarloaf Mountain** ▲ Maine, NE USA *45°01′N 70°18′W*
65 *G24* **Sugar Loaf Point** *headland* N Saint Helena *15°54′S 05°43′W*
136 *G16* **Suğla Gölü** ◎ SW Turkey
123 *T8* **Sugoy** ≈ E Russian Federation
158 *F7* **Sugun** Xinjiang Uygur Zizhiqu, W China *39°46′N 76°45′E*
147 *U11* **Sugut, Gora** ▲ SW Kyrgyzstan *39°52′N 73°36′E*
169 *V6* **Sugut, Sungai** ≈ East Malaysia
159 *O9* **Suhai Hu** ◎ C China
162 *K14* **Suhait** Nei Mongol Zizhiqu, N China *39°29′N 105°11′E*
141 *X7* **Şuḩār** *var.* Sohar. N Oman *24°20′N 56°43′E*
113 *M17* **Suharekë** *Serb.* Suva Reka. S Kosovo *42°23′N 20°50′E*
162 *L6* **Sühbaatar** Selenge, N Mongolia *50°12′N 106°14′E*
163 *P8* **Sühbaatar** *var.* Haylaastay. Sühbaatar, E Mongolia *46°44′N 113°51′E*
163 *P9* **Sühbaatar** ⬖ *province* E Mongolia
101 *K17* **Suhl** Thüringen, C Germany *50°37′N 10°43′E*
108 *F7* **Suhr** Aargau, N Switzerland *47°23′N 08°05′E*
Sui'an *see* Zhangpu
Suicheng *see* Suixi
161 *O12* **Suichuan** *var.* Quanjiang. Jiangxi, S China *26°26′N 114°34′E*
Suid-Afrika *see* South Africa
160 *L4* **Suide** *var.* Mingzhou. Shaanxi, C China *37°30′N 110°10′E*
Suidwes-Afrika *see* Namibia
163 *Y9* **Suifenhe** Heilongjiang, NE China *44°22′N 131°12′E*
Suigen *see* Suwon
163 *W8* **Suihua** Heilongjiang, NE China *46°40′N 127°00′E*
Súilí, Loch *see* Swilly, Lough
161 *Q6* **Suining** Jiangsu, E China *33°54′N 117°58′E*
160 *I9* **Suining** Sichuan, C China *30°31′N 105°33′E*
103 *Q4* **Suippes** Marne, N France *49°08′N 04°31′E*
97 *E20* **Suir** *Ir.* An tSiúir. ≈ S Ireland
165 *J13* **Suita** Ōsaka, Honshū, SW Japan *34°39′N 135°27′E*
160 *L16* **Suixi** *var.* Suicheng. Guangdong, S China *21°23′N 110°14′E*
Sui Xian *see* Suizhou
163 *T13* **Suizhong** Liaoning, NE China *40°19′N 120°22′E*
161 *N8* **Suizhou** *prev.* Sui Xian. Hubei, C China *31°46′N 113°20′E*
149 *P17* **Sujāwal** Sind, SE Pakistan *24°36′N 68°06′E*
169 *O16* **Sukabumi** *prev.* Soekaboemi. Jawa, C Indonesia *06°55′S 106°56′E*
169 *Q12* **Sukadana, Teluk** *bay* Borneo, W Indonesia
165 *P11* **Sukagawa** Fukushima, Honshū, C Japan *37°16′N 140°20′E*
Sukarnapura *see* Jayapura
Sukarno, Puntjak *see* Jaya, Puncak
Sŭkh *see* Sokh
114 *N8* **Sukha Reka** ≈ NE Bulgaria
114 *J8* **Sukhindol** Veliko Turnovo, N Bulgaria *43°11′N 24°10′E*
126 *J5* **Sukhinichi** Kaluzhskaya Oblast', W Russian Federation *54°06′N 35°22′E*
Sukhne *see* As Sukhnah
129 *Q4* **Sukhona** *var.* Tot'ma. ≈ NW Russian Federation
167 *O8* **Sukhothai** *var.* Sukotai. Sukhothai, W Thailand *17°00′N 99°51′E*
Sukhumi *see* Sokhumi
Sukkertoppen *see* Maniitsoq
149 *Q13* **Sukkur** Sind, SE Pakistan *27°45′N 68°46′E*
Sukotai *see* Sukhothai
Sukra Bay *see* Şawqirah, Dawḩat
125 *V15* **Suksun** Permskiy Kray, NW Russian Federation *57°10′N 57°27′E*
165 *F15* **Sukumo** Kōchi, Shikoku, SW Japan *32°55′N 132°42′E*
94 *B12* **Sula** *island* S Norway
125 *Q5* **Sula** ≈ NW Russian Federation
117 *R5* **Sula** ≈ N Ukraine
42 *H6* **Sulaco, Río** ≈ NW Honduras
Sulaimaniya *see* As Sulaymānīyah
149 *S10* **Sulaimān Range** ▲▲ C Pakistan
127 *Q16* **Sulak** Respublika Dagestan, SW Russian Federation *43°19′N 47°28′E*
127 *Q16* **Sulak** ≈ SW Russian Federation
171 *Q13* **Sula, Kepulauan** *island group* C Indonesia
136 *I12* **Sulakyurt** *var.* Konur. Kırıkkale, N Turkey *40°10′N 33°42′E*
171 *P17* **Sulamu** Timor, S Indonesia *09°57′S 123°33′E*
96 *F5* **Sula Sgeir** *island* NW Scotland, United Kingdom
171 *N13* **Sulawesi** *Eng.* Celebes. *island* C Indonesia
Sulawesi, Laut *see* Celebes Sea
171 *N14* **Sulawesi Selatan** *off.* Propinsi Sulawesi Selatan, *Eng.* South Celebes, South Sulawesi. ⬖ *province* C Indonesia
Sulawesi Selatan, Propinsi *see* Sulawesi Selatan
171 *P12* **Sulawesi Tengah** *off.* Propinsi Sulawesi Tengah, *Eng.* Central Celebes, Central Sulawesi. ⬖ *province* N Indonesia
Sulawesi Tengah, Propinsi *see* Sulawesi Tengah
171 *O14* **Sulawesi Tenggara** *off.* Propinsi Sulawesi Tenggara, *Eng.* South-East Celebes, South-East Sulawesi. ⬖ *province* C Indonesia
Sulawesi Tenggara, Propinsi *see* Sulawesi Tenggara
171 *P11* **Sulawesi Utara** *off.* Propinsi Sulawesi Utara, *Eng.* North Celebes, North Sulawesi. ⬖ *province* N Indonesia
Sulawesi Utara, Propinsi *see* Sulawesi Utara
139 *T5* **Sulaymān Beg** At Ta'mím, N Iraq
95 *D15* **Suldalsvatnet** ◎ S Norway
Sulden *see* Solda
110 *E12* **Sulechów** *Ger.* Züllichau. Lubuskie, W Poland *52°05′N 15°37′E*
110 *E11* **Sulęcin** Lubuskie, W Poland *52°29′N 15°06′E*
77 *U14* **Suleja** Niger, C Nigeria *09°15′N 07°10′E*
111 *K14* **Sulejów** Łodzkie, S Poland *51°21′N 19°57′E*
96 *I5* **Sule Skerry** *island* N Scotland, United Kingdom
Suliag *see* Sawhāj
76 *J16* **Sulima** S Sierra Leone *06°59′N 11°34′W*
117 *O13* **Sulina** Tulcea, SE Romania *45°07′N 29°40′E*
117 *N13* **Sulina, Braţul** ≈ SE Romania
100 *H12* **Sulingen** Niedersachsen, NW Germany *52°40′N 08°48′E*
Sulisjielmmá *see* Sulitjelma
92 *H12* **Suliskongen** ▲ C Norway *67°10′N 16°16′E*
92 *H12* **Sulitjelma** *Lapp.* Sulisjielmmá. Nordland, C Norway *67°10′N 16°05′E*
56 *A9* **Sullana** Piura, NW Peru *04°54′S 80°42′W*
23 *N3* **Sulligent** Alabama, S USA *33°54′N 88°07′W*
30 *M14* **Sullivan** Illinois, N USA *39°36′N 88°36′W*
31 *N15* **Sullivan** Indiana, N USA *39°05′N 87°24′W*
27 *W5* **Sullivan** Missouri, C USA *38°12′N 91°09′W*
Sullivan Island *see* Lanbi Kyun
96 *M1* **Sullom Voe** NE Scotland, United Kingdom *60°24′N 01°09′W*
103 *O7* **Sully-sur-Loire** Loiret, C France *47°46′N 02°21′E*
Sulmo *see* Sulmona
107 *K15* **Sulmona** *anc.* Sulmo. Abruzzo, C Italy *42°03′N 13°56′E*
Sulo *see* Shule He
114 *M11* **Süloğlu** Edirne, NW Turkey *41°46′N 26°55′E*
22 *G9* **Sulphur** Louisiana, S USA *30°14′N 93°22′W*
27 *O12* **Sulphur** Oklahoma, C USA *34°31′N 96°58′W*
28 *K9* **Sulphur Creek** ≈ South Dakota, N USA
24 *M5* **Sulphur Draw** ≈ Texas, SW USA
25 *W5* **Sulphur River** ≈ Arkansas/ Texas, SW USA
25 *V6* **Sulphur Springs** Texas, SW USA *33°09′N 95°36′W*
24 *M6* **Sulphur Springs Draw** ≈ Texas, SW USA
14 *D8* **Sultan** Ontario, S Canada *47°34′N 82°45′W*
Sultānābād *see* Arāk
Sultan Alonto, Lake *see* Lanao, Lake
136 *G15* **Sultan Dağları** ▲▲ C Turkey
114 *N13* **Sultanköy** Tekirdağ, NW Turkey *41°01′N 27°58′E*
171 *Q7* **Sultan Kudarat** *var.* Nuling. Mindanao, S Philippines *07°20′N 124°16′E*
152 *M13* **Sultānpur** Uttar Pradesh, N India *26°15′N 82°04′E*
171 *O9* **Sulu Archipelago** *island group* SW Philippines
192 *F7* **Sulu Basin** *undersea feature* SE South China Sea *08°00′N 121°30′E*
Sülüktü *see* Sulyukta
Sulu, Laut *see* Sulu Sea
169 *X6* **Sulu Sea** *var.* Laut Sulu. *sea* SW Philippines
145 *O15* **Sulutobe** *Kaz.* Sulūtöbe. Kzylorda, S Kazakhstan *44°31′N 66°17′E*
Sulūtöbe *see* Sulutobe
147 *Q11* **Sulyukta** *Kir.* Sülüktü. Batkenskaya Oblast', SW Kyrgyzstan *39°57′N 69°31′E*
Sulz *see* Sulz am Neckar
101 *G22* **Sulz am Neckar** *var.* Sulz. Baden-Württemberg, SW Germany *48°22′N 08°37′E*
101 *L20* **Sulzbach-Rosenberg** Bayern, SE Germany *49°30′N 11°43′E*
195 *N13* **Sulzberger Bay** *bay* Antarctica
Sumail *see* Summēl
81 *M14* **Sumalē** *var.* Somali. ⬖ E Ethiopia
113 *F15* **Sumartin** Split-Dalmacija, S Croatia *43°17′N 16°52′E*
32 *H6* **Sumas** Washington, NW USA *49°00′N 122°15′W*
168 *J10* **Sumatera** *Eng.* Sumatra. *island* W Indonesia
168 *J12* **Sumatera Barat** *off.* Propinsi Sumatera Barat, *Eng.* West Sumatra. ⬖ *province* W Indonesia
Sumatera Barat, Propinsi *see* Sumatera Barat
168 *L13* **Sumatera Selatan** *off.* Propinsi Sumatera Selatan, *Eng.* South Sumatra. ⬖ *province* W Indonesia
Sumatera Selatan, Propinsi *see* Sumatera Selatan
168 *H10* **Sumatera Utara** *off.* Propinsi Sumatera Utara, *Eng.* North Sumatra. ⬖ *province* W Indonesia
Sumatera Utara, Propinsi *see* Sumatera Utara
Sumatra *see* Sumatera
Šumava *see* Bohemian Forest
Sumayl *see* Summēl
139 *U7* **Sumayr al Muḩammad** Diyālá, E Iraq *33°34′N 45°06′E*
171 *N17* **Sumba, Pulau** *Eng.* Sandalwood Island; *prev.* Soemba. *island* Nusa Tenggara, C Indonesia
146 *D12* **Sumbar** ≈ W Turkmenistan
192 *E9* **Sumbawa** *prev.* Soembawa. *island* Nusa Tenggara, C Indonesia
170 *L16* **Sumbawabesar** Sumbawa, S Indonesia *08°30′S 117°25′E*
81 *F23* **Sumbawanga** Rukwa, W Tanzania *07°57′S 31°37′E*
82 *B12* **Sumbe** *var.* N'Gunza, *Port.* Novo Redondo. Cuanza Sul, W Angola *11°13′S 13°53′E*
96 *M3* **Sumburgh Head** *headland* NE Scotland, United Kingdom *59°51′N 01°16′W*
111 *H23* **Sümeg** Veszprém, W Hungary *47°01′N 17°13′E*
80 *C12* **Sumeih** Southern Darfur, S Sudan *09°50′N 27°39′E*
169 *T16* **Sumenep** *prev.* Soemenep. Pulau Madura, C Indonesia *07°01′S 113°51′E*
Sumgait *see* Sumqayıt, Azerbaijan
Sumgait *see* Sumqayıtçay, Azerbaijan
165 *Y14* **Sumisu-jima** *Eng.* Smith Island. *island* SE Japan
139 *Q2* **Summēl** *var.* Sumail, Sumayl. Dahūk, N Iraq *36°52′N 42°51′E*
31 *O5* **Summer Island** *island* Michigan, N USA
32 *H15* **Summer Lake** ◎ Oregon, NW USA
11 *N17* **Summerland** British Columbia, SW Canada *49°35′N 119°45′W*
13 *P14* **Summerside** Prince Edward Island, SE Canada *46°24′N 63°46′W*
21 *R5* **Summersville** West Virginia, NE USA *38°17′N 80°52′W*
21 *R5* **Summersville Lake** ⊠ West Virginia, NE USA
21 *S13* **Summerton** South Carolina, SE USA *33°36′N 80°21′W*
23 *R2* **Summerville** Georgia, SE USA *34°28′N 85°21′W*
21 *S14* **Summerville** South Carolina, SE USA *33°01′N 80°10′W*
39 *R10* **Summit** Alaska, USA *63°21′N 148°50′W*
35 *V6* **Summit Mountain** ▲ Nevada, W USA *39°23′N 116°25′W*
37 *R8* **Summit Peak** ▲ Colorado, C USA *37°21′N 106°42′W*
Summus Portus *see* Somport, Col du
29 *X12* **Sumner** Iowa, C USA *42°51′N 92°05′W*
22 *K3* **Sumner** Mississippi, S USA *33°58′N 90°22′W*
185 *H17* **Sumner, Lake** ◎ South Island, New Zealand
37 *U12* **Sumner, Lake** ⊠ New Mexico, SW USA
111 *G17* **Šumperk** *Ger.* Mährisch-Schönberg. Olomoucký Kraj, E Czech Republic *49°58′N 17°00′E*
42 *F7* **Sumpul, Río** ≈ El Salvador/ Honduras
137 *Z11* **Sumqayıt** *Rus.* Sumgait. E Azerbaijan *40°33′N 49°41′E*
137 *Y11* **Sumqayıtçay** *Rus.* Sumgait. ≈ E Azerbaijan
147 *R9* **Sumsar** Dzhalal-Abadskaya Oblast', W Kyrgyzstan *41°12′N 71°16′E*
117 *S3* **Sums'ka Oblast'** *var.* Sumy, *Rus.* Sumskaya Oblast'. ⬖ *province* NE Ukraine
Sumskaya Oblast' *see* Sums'ka Oblast'
124 *J8* **Sumskiy Posad** Respublika Kareliya, NW Russian Federation *64°12′N 35°22′E*
21 *S12* **Sumter** South Carolina, SE USA *33°54′N 80°22′W*
117 *T3* **Sumy** Sums'ka Oblast', NE Ukraine *50°54′N 34°49′E*
Sumy *see* Sums'ka Oblast'
159 *Q15* **Sumzom** Xizang Zizhiqu, W China *29°45′N 96°14′E*
125 *R15* **Suna** Kirovskaya Oblast', NW Russian Federation *57°53′N 50°04′E*
124 *I10* **Suna** ≈ NW Russian Federation
165 *S3* **Sunagawa** Hokkaidō, NE Japan *43°30′N 141°55′E*
153 *V13* **Sunamganj** Sylhet, NE Bangladesh *25°04′N 91°24′E*
163 *W14* **Sunan** ✕ (P'yŏngyang) SW North Korea *39°12′N 125°40′E*
Sunan/Sunan Yugurzu Zizhixian *see* Hongwansi
19 *N9* **Sunapee Lake** ◎ New Hampshire, NE USA
139 *P4* **Sunaysilah** *salt marsh* N Iraq
20 *M8* **Sunbright** Tennessee, S USA *36°12′N 84°39′W*
33 *R6* **Sunburst** Montana, NW USA *48°51′N 111°54′W*
183 *N12* **Sunbury** Victoria, SE Australia *37°36′S 114°45′E*
21 *X8* **Sunbury** North Carolina, SE USA *36°27′N 76°34′W*
18 *G14* **Sunbury** Pennsylvania, NE USA *40°51′N 76°47′W*
61 *A17* **Sunchales** Santa Fe, C Argentina *30°58′S 61°35′W*
163 *Y16* **Suncheon** *Jap.* Junten, *prev.* Sunch'ŏn. S South Korea *34°56′N 127°29′E*
Sunch'ŏn *see* Suncheon
36 *K13* **Sun City** Arizona, SW USA *33°36′N 112°16′W*
19 *O9* **Suncook** New Hampshire, NE USA *43°07′N 71°25′W*
161 *P5* **Suncun** *prev.* Xinwen. Shandong, E China *35°49′N 117°36′E*
Sunda Islands *see* Greater Sunda Islands
33 *Z12* **Sundance** Wyoming, C USA *44°24′N 104°22′W*
153 *T17* **Sundarbans** *wetland* Bangladesh/India
154 *M11* **Sundargarh** Orissa, E India *22°07′N 84°02′E*
129 *U15* **Sunda Shelf** *undersea feature* S South China Sea *05°00′N 107°00′E*
Sunda Trench *see* Java Trench
129 *U17* **Sunda Trough** *undersea feature* E Indian Ocean *08°50′S 109°30′E*
95 *O16* **Sundbyberg** Stockholm, C Sweden *59°22′N 17°58′E*
97 *M14* **Sunderland** *var.* Wearmouth. NE England, United Kingdom *54°55′N 01°23′W*
101 *F15* **Sundern** Nordrhein-Westfalen, W Germany *51°19′N 08°00′E*
136 *F12* **Sündiken Dağları** ▲▲ C Turkey
24 *M5* **Sundown** Texas, SW USA *33°27′N 102°29′W*
11 *P16* **Sundre** Alberta, SW Canada *51°49′N 114°46′W*
14 *H12* **Sundridge** Ontario, S Canada *45°45′N 79°25′W*
93 *H17* **Sundsvall** Västernorrland, C Sweden *62°22′N 17°20′E*
26 *H4* **Sunflower, Mount** ▲ Kansas, C USA *39°01′N 102°02′W*
Sunflower State *see* Kansas
169 *N14* **Sungaibuntu** Sumatera, SW Indonesia *04°04′S 105°37′E*
168 *K12* **Sungaidareh** Sumatera, W Indonesia *0°58′S 101°30′E*
167 *P17* **Sungai Kolok** *var.* Sungai Ko-Lok. Narathiwat, SW Thailand *06°02′N 101°58′E*
Sungai Ko-Lok *see* Sungai Kolok
168 *K12* **Sungaipenuh** *prev.* Soengaipenoeh. Sumatera, W Indonesia *02°S 101°28′E*
169 *P11* **Sungaipinyuh** Borneo, C Indonesia *0°16′N 109°06′E*
Sungari *see* Songhua Jiang
Sungaria *see* Dzungaria
Sungei Pahang *see* Pahang, Sungai
167 *O8* **Sung Men** Phrae, NW Thailand *17°59′N 100°07′E*
83 *M15* **Sungo** Tete, NW Mozambique *16°31′S 33°58′E*
Sungpu *see* Songpan
168 *M13* **Sungsang** Sumatera, W Indonesia *02°22′S 104°50′E*
114 *M9* **Sungurlare** Burgas, E Bulgaria *42°47′N 26°46′E*
136 *J12* **Sungurlu** Çorum, N Turkey *40°10′N 34°23′E*
112 *F9* **Sunja** Sisak-Moslavina, C Croatia *45°21′N 16°33′E*
153 *Q12* **Sun Koshī** ≈ E Nepal
94 *F9* **Sunndalen** *valley* S Norway
94 *F9* **Sunndalsøra** Møre og Romsdal, S Norway *62°39′N 08°37′E*
95 *K15* **Sunne** Värmland, C Sweden *59°52′N 13°05′E*
95 *O15* **Sunnersta** Uppsala, C Sweden *59°46′N 17°40′E*
94 *C11* **Sunnfjord** *physical region* S Norway
95 *C15* **Sunnhordland** *physical region* S Norway
94 *D10* **Sunnmøre** *physical region* S Norway
37 *N4* **Sunnyside** Utah, W USA *39°33′N 110°23′W*
32 *J10* **Sunnyside** Washington, NW USA *46°01′N 119°58′W*
35 *N9* **Sunnyvale** California, W USA *37°22′N 122°02′W*
30 *L8* **Sun Prairie** Wisconsin, N USA *43°12′N 89°12′W*
Sunqur *see* Sonqor
25 *N1* **Sunray** Texas, SW USA *36°01′N 101°49′W*
22 *I8* **Sunset** Louisiana, S USA *30°24′N 92°04′W*
25 *S5* **Sunset** Texas, SW USA *33°24′N 97°45′W*
Sunset State *see* Oregon
181 *Z10* **Sunshine Coast** *cultural region* Queensland, E Australia
Sunshine State *see* Florida
Sunshine State *see* New Mexico
Sunshine State *see* South Dakota
123 *O10* **Suntar** Respublika Sakha (Yakutiya), NE Russian Federation *62°10′N 117°34′E*
39 *R10* **Suntrana** Alaska, USA *63°51′N 148°51′W*
148 *J15* **Suntsar** Baluchistān, SW Pakistan *25°30′N 62°03′E*
163 *W15* **Sunwi-do** *island* SW North Korea
163 *W6* **Sunwu** Heilongjiang, NE China *49°29′N 127°15′E*
77 *O16* **Sunyani** W Ghana *07°22′N 02°18′W*
Suō *see* Su'ao
93 *M17* **Suolahti** Länsi-Suomi, C Finland *62°32′N 25°51′E*
Suoločielgi *see* Saariselkä
Suomenlahti *see* Finland, Gulf of
Suomen Tasavalta/Suomi *see* Finland
93 *N14* **Suomussalmi** Oulu, E Finland *64°54′N 29°05′E*
165 *E13* **Suō-nada** *sea* SW Japan
93 *M17* **Suonenjoki** Itä-Suomi, C Finland *62°36′N 27°07′E*
167 *S13* **Suŏng** Kâmpóng Cham, C Cambodia *11°53′N 105°41′E*
124 *I10* **Suoyarvi** Respublika Kareliya, NW Russian Federation *62°02′N 32°24′E*
Supanburi *see* Suphan Buri
57 *D14* **Supe** Lima, W Peru *10°49′S 77°40′W*
15 *V7* **Supérieur, Lac** ◎ Québec, SE Canada
Supérieur, Lac *see* Superior, Lake
36 *M14* **Superior** Arizona, SW USA *33°17′N 111°06′W*
33 *O9* **Superior** Montana, NW USA *47°11′N 114°53′W*
29 *P17* **Superior** Nebraska, C USA *40°01′N 98°04′W*
30 *I3* **Superior** Wisconsin, N USA *46°42′N 92°04′W*
41 *S17* **Superior, Laguna** *lagoon* S Mexico
31 *N2* **Superior, Lake** *Fr.* Lac Supérieur. ◎ Canada/USA
36 *L13* **Superstition Mountains** ▲▲ Arizona, SW USA
113 *F14* **Supetar** *It.* San Pietro. Split-Dalmacija, S Croatia *43°22′N 16°34′E*
167 *O10* **Suphan Buri** *var.* Supanburi. Suphan Buri, W Thailand *14°29′N 100°10′E*
171 *V12* **Supiori, Pulau** *island* E Indonesia
188 *K2* **Supply Reef** *reef* N Northern Mariana Islands
195 *O7* **Support Force Glacier** *glacier* Antarctica
137 *R10* **Supsa** *prev.* Sup'sa. ≈ W Georgia
Sup'sa *see* Supsa
Sūq 'Abs *see* 'Abs
139 *W12* **Sūq ash Shuyūkh** Dhī Qār, SE Iraq *30°53′N 46°28′E*
138 *H4* **Şuqaylibīyah** Ḩamāh, W Syria *35°21′N 36°24′E*
161 *Q6* **Suqian** Jiangsu, E China *33°57′N 118°18′E*
Suqrah *see* Şawqirah
Suqrah Bay *see* Şawqirah, Dawḩat
141 *V16* **Suquṭrā** *var.* Sokotra, *Eng.* Socotra. *island* SE Yemen
141 *Z8* **Şūr** NE Oman *22°32′N 59°33′E*
Şūr *see* Soûr
127 *P5* **Sura** Penzenskaya Oblast', W Russian Federation *53°23′N 45°03′E*
127 *P4* **Sura** ≈ W Russian Federation
149 *N12* **Sūrāb** Baluchistān, SW Pakistan *28°28′N 66°15′E*
Surabaja *see* Surabaya
192 *E8* **Surabaya** *prev.* Surabaja, Soerabaja. Jawa, C Indonesia *07°14′S 112°45′E*
95 *N15* **Surahammar** Västmanland, C Sweden *59°43′N 16°13′E*
169 *Q16* **Surakarta** *Eng.* Solo; *prev.* Soerakarta. Jawa, S Indonesia *07°32′S 110°50′E*
Surakhany *see* Suraxanı
137 *S10* **Surami** C Georgia *41°59′N 43°36′E*
143 *X13* **Sūrān** Sīstān va Balūchestān, SE Iran *27°18′N 61°58′E*
111 *I21* **Šurany** *Hung.* Nagysurány. Nitriansky Kraj, SW Slovakia *48°05′N 18°10′E*
154 *D12* **Sūrat** Gujarāt, W India *21°10′N 72°54′E*
Suratdhani *see* Surat Thani
152 *G9* **Sūratgarh** Rājasthān, NW India *29°20′N 73°59′E*
167 *N14* **Surat Thani** *var.* Suratdhani. Surat Thani, SW Thailand *09°09′N 99°20′E*
119 *Q16* **Suraw** *Rus.* Surov. ≈ E Belarus
137 *Z11* **Suraxanı** *Rus.* Surakhany. E Azerbaijan *40°25′N 49°59′E*
141 *Y11* **Surayr** E Oman *19°56′N 57°47′E*
138 *K2* **Suraysāt** Ḩalab, N Syria *36°42′N 38°01′E*
118 *O12* **Surazh** Vitsyebskaya Voblasts', NE Belarus *55°25′N 30°44′E*
126 *H6* **Surazh** Bryanskaya Oblast', W Russian Federation *53°04′N 32°29′E*
191 *V17* **Sur, Cabo** *headland* Easter Island, Chile, E Pacific Ocean *27°11′S 109°26′W*
112 *L11* **Surčin** Serbia, N Serbia *44°48′N 20°19′E*
116 *H9* **Surduc** *Hung.* Szurduk. Sălaj, NW Romania *47°13′N 23°20′E*
113 *P16* **Surdulica** Serbia, SE Serbia *42°43′N 22°10′E*
99 *L24* **Sûre** *var.* Sauer. ≈ W Europe *see also* Sauer
Sûre *see* Sauer
154 *C10* **Surendranagar** Gujarāt, W India *22°44′N 71°43′E*
18 *K16* **Surf City** New Jersey, NE USA *39°21′N 74°24′W*
183 *V3* **Surfers Paradise** Queensland, E Australia *27°54′S 153°18′E*
21 *U13* **Surfside Beach** South Carolina, SE USA *33°36′N 78°58′W*
102 *J10* **Surgères** Charente-Maritime, W France *46°07′N 00°44′W*
122 *H10* **Surgut** Khanty-Mansiyskiy Avtonomnyy Okrug-Yugra, C Russian Federation *61°13′N 73°28′E*
122 *K10* **Surgutikha** Krasnoyarskiy Kray, N Russian Federation *64°44′N 87°13′E*
98 *M6* **Surhuisterveen** *Fris.* Surhusterfean. Fryslân, N Netherlands *53°11′N 06°10′E*
Surhusterfean *see* Surhuisterveen
105 *V5* **Súria** Cataluña, NE Spain *41°50′N 01°45′E*
143 *P10* **Sūrīān** Fārs, S Iran
155 *J15* **Suriāpet** Andhra Pradesh, C India *17°10′N 79°42′E*
171 *Q6* **Surigao** Mindanao, S Philippines *09°43′N 125°31′E*
167 *R10* **Surin** Surin, E Thailand *14°53′N 103°29′E*
55 *U11* **Surinam** *off.* Republic of Suriname, *var.* Suriname; *prev.* Dutch Guiana, Netherlands Guiana. ◆ *republic* N South America
Suriname *see* Surinam
Suriname, Republic of *see* Surinam
Sūrīya/Sūrīyah, Al-Jumhūrīyah al-'Arabīyah as- *see* Syria
Surkhab, Darya-i- *see* Kahmard, Daryā-ye
Surkhandar'inskaya Oblast' *see* Surxondaryo Viloyati
Surkhandar'ya *see* Surxondaryo
Surkhet *see* Birendranagar
147 *R12* **Surkhob** ≈ C Tajikistan
137 *P11* **Sürmene** Trabzon, NE Turkey *40°56′N 40°03′E*
Surov *see* Suraw
127 *N11* **Surovikino** Volgogradskaya Oblast', SW Russian Federation *48°39′N 42°46′E*
35 *N11* **Sur, Point** *headland* California, W USA *36°18′N 121°54′W*
187 *N15* **Surprise, Île** *island* N New Caledonia
61 *E22* **Sur, Punta** *headland* E Argentina *50°59′S 69°10′W*
Surrentum *see* Sorrento
28 *M3* **Surrey** North Dakota, N USA *48°13′N 101°05′W*
97 *O22* **Surrey** *cultural region* SE England, United Kingdom
21 *X7* **Surry** Virginia, NE USA *37°08′N 81°34′W*
108 *F8* **Sursee** Luzern, W Switzerland *47°11′N 08°07′E*
127 *P6* **Sursk** Penzenskaya Oblast', W Russian Federation *53°06′N 45°46′E*
127 *P5* **Surskoye** Ul'yanovskaya Oblast', W Russian Federation *54°28′N 46°47′E*
75 *P8* **Surt** *var.* Sidra, Sirte. N Libya *31°13′N 16°35′E*
95 *I19* **Surte** Västra Götaland, S Sweden *57°49′N 12°01′E*
75 *Q8* **Surt, Khalīj** *Eng.* Gulf of Sidra, Gulf of Sirti, Sidra. *gulf* N Libya
92 *I5* **Surtsey** *island* S Iceland
137 *N17* **Suruç** Şanlıurfa, S Turkey *36°58′N 38°24′E*
168 *L13* **Surulangun** Sumatera, W Indonesia *02°35′S 102°47′E*
147 *P13* **Surxondaryo** *Rus.* Surkhandar'ya. ≈ Tajikistan/Uzbekistan
147 *N13* **Surxondaryo Viloyati** *Rus.* Surkhandar'inskaya Oblast'. ⬖ *province* S Uzbekistan
Süs *see* Susch
106 *A8* **Susa** Piemonte, NE Italy *45°10′N 07°01′E*
165 *E12* **Susa** Yamaguchi, Honshū, SW Japan *34°35′N 131°34′E*
Susa *see* Shūsh
113 *E16* **Sušac** *It.* Cazza. *island* SW Croatia
Sūsah *see* Sousse
164 *G14* **Susaki** Kōchi, Shikoku, SW Japan *33°22′N 133°13′E*
165 *I15* **Susami** Wakayama, Honshū, SW Japan *33°32′N 135°32′E*
142 *K9* **Sūsangerd** *var.* Susangird. Khūzestān, SW Iran *31°40′N 48°06′E*
Susangird *see* Sūsangerd
35 *P4* **Susanville** California, W USA *40°25′N 120°39′W*
108 *J9* **Susch** *var.* Süs. Graubünden, SE Switzerland *46°45′N 10°04′E*
137 *N12* **Suşehri** Sivas, N Turkey *40°11′N 38°06′E*
Susiana *see* Khūzestān
111 *B18* **Sušice** *Ger.* Schüttenhofen. Plzeňský Kraj, W Czech Republic *49°14′N 13°32′E*
39 *R11* **Susitna** Alaska, USA *61°32′N 150°30′W*
39 *R11* **Susitna River** ≈ Alaska, USA
127 *Q3* **Suslonger** Respublika Mariy El, W Russian Federation *56°18′N 48°16′E*
105 *N14* **Suspiro del Moro, Puerto del** *pass* S Spain
18 *H16* **Susquehanna River** ≈ New York/Pennsylvania, NE USA
13 *O15* **Sussex** New Brunswick, SE Canada *45°43′N 65°32′W*
18 *J13* **Sussex** New Jersey, NE USA *41°12′N 74°34′W*
21 *W7* **Sussex** Virginia, NE USA *36°54′N 77°16′W*
97 *O23* **Sussex** *cultural region* S England, United Kingdom
183 *S10* **Sussex Inlet** New South Wales, SE Australia *35°10′S 150°35′E*
99 *L17* **Susteren** Limburg, SE Netherlands *51°04′N 05°50′E*
10 *K12* **Sustut Peak** ▲ British Columbia, W Canada *56°25′N 126°34′W*
123 *S9* **Susuman** Magadanskaya Oblast', E Russian Federation *62°46′N 148°08′E*
188 *H6* **Susupe** ● (Northern Mariana Islands-judicial capital) Saipan, S Northern Mariana Islands
136 *D12* **Susurluk** Balıkesir, NW Turkey *39°55′N 28°10′E*
114 *M13* **Susuzmüsellim** Tekirdağ, NW Turkey *41°04′N 27°03′E*
136 *F15* **Sütçüler** Isparta, SW Turkey *37°31′N 31°00′E*
116 *L13* **Şuțești** Brăila, SE Romania *45°13′N 27°27′E*
83 *F25* **Sutherland** Western Cape, SW South Africa *32°24′S 20°40′E*
28 *L15* **Sutherland** Nebraska, C USA *41°09′N 101°07′W*
96 *I7* **Sutherland** *cultural region* N Scotland, United Kingdom
185 *B21* **Sutherland Falls** *waterfall* South Island, New Zealand
32 *F14* **Sutherlin** Oregon, NW USA *43°23′N 123°18′W*
149 *V10* **Sutlej** ≈ India/Pakistan
Sutna *see* Satna
35 *P7* **Sutter Creek** California, W USA *38°22′N 120°49′W*
39 *R11* **Sutton** Alaska, USA *61°42′N 148°53′W*
29 *Q16* **Sutton** Nebraska, C USA *40°36′N 97°52′W*
21 *R4* **Sutton** West Virginia, NE USA *38°41′N 80°43′W*
12 *F8* **Sutton** ≈ Ontario, C Canada
97 *M19* **Sutton Coldfield** C England, United Kingdom *52°34′N 01°48′W*
21 *R4* **Sutton Lake** ⊠ West Virginia, NE USA
15 *P13* **Sutton, Monts** *hill range* Québec, SE Canada
12 *F8* **Sutton Ridges** ▲▲ Ontario, C Canada
165 *Q4* **Suttsu** Hokkaidō, NE Japan *42°46′N 140°12′E*
39 *P15* **Sutwik Island** *island* Alaska, USA
Süüj *see* Dashinchilen
118 *H5* **Suure-Jaani** *Ger.* Gross-Sankt-Johannis. Viljandimaa, S Estonia *58°34′N 25°28′E*
118 *J7* **Suur Munamägi** *var.* Munamägi, *Ger.* Eier-Berg. ▲ SE Estonia *57°42′N 27°03′E*
118 *F5* **Suur Väin** *Ger.* Grosser Sund. *strait* W Estonia
147 *U8* **Suusamyr** Chuyskaya Oblast', C Kyrgyzstan *42°07′N 73°55′E*
187 *X14* **Suva** ● (Fiji) Viti Levu, W Fiji *18°08′S 178°27′E*
187 *X15* **Suva** ✕ Viti Levu, C Fiji *18°01′S 178°30′E*
113 *N18* **Suva Gora** ▲▲ W FYR Macedonia
118 *H11* **Suvainiškis** Panevėžys, NE Lithuania *56°09′N 25°15′E*
Suvalkai/Suvalki *see* Suwałki
113 *P15* **Suva Planina** ▲▲ SE Serbia
Suva Reka *see* Suharekë
126 *K5* **Suvorov** Tul'skaya Oblast', W Russian Federation *54°08′N 36°33′E*
117 *N12* **Suvorove** Odes'ka Oblast', SW Ukraine *45°35′N 28°58′E*
114 *M8* **Suvorovo** Varna, E Bulgaria *43°19′N 27°26′E*
Suvorovo *see* Ştefan Vodă
Suwaik *see* As Suwayq
Suwaira *see* Aş Şuwayrah
110 *O7* **Suwałki** *Lith.* Suvalkai, *Rus.* Suvalki. Podlaskie, NE Poland *54°06′N 22°56′E*
167 *R10* **Suwannaphum** Roi Et, E Thailand *15°36′N 103°46′E*
23 *V8* **Suwannee River** ≈ Florida/ Georgia, SE USA
Şuwār *see* Aş Şuwār
190 *K14* **Suwarrow** *atoll* N Cook Islands
143 *R16* **Suwaydān** *var.* Sweiham. Abū Ẓaby, E United Arab Emirates *24°30′N 55°19′E*
Suwaydá/Suwaydā', Muḩāfaẓat as *see* As Suwaydā'
Suwayqiyah, Hawr as *see* Shuwayjah, Hawr ash
Suways, Qanāt as *see* Suez Canal
Suweida *see* As Suwaydā'
Suweon *see* Suwon
163 *X15* **Suwon** *var.* Suweon; *prev.* Suwŏn, *Jap.* Suigen. NW South Korea *37°17′N 127°03′E*
Suwŏn *see* Suwon
Su Xian *see* Suzhou
143 *R14* **Sūzā** Hormozgān, S Iran *26°50′N 56°05′E*
Suzak *see* Sozak
165 *K14* **Suzaka** Mie, Honshū, SW Japan *34°52′N 136°37′E*
165 *N12* **Suzaka** Nagano, Honshū, S Japan *36°38′N 138°20′E*
126 *M3* **Suzdal'** Vladimirskaya Oblast', W Russian Federation *56°27′N 40°29′E*
161 *P7* **Suzhou** *var.* Su Xian. Anhui, E China *33°38′N 117°02′E*
161 *R8* **Suzhou** *var.* Soochow, Su-chou, Suchow; *prev.* Wuhsien. Jiangsu, E China *31°23′N 120°34′E*
Suzhou *see* Jiuquan
163 *V12* **Suzi He** ≈ NE China
Suz, Mys *see* Soye, Mys
165 *M10* **Suzu** Ishikawa, Honshū, SW Japan *37°24′N 137°12′E*
165 *M10* **Suzu-misaki** *headland* Honshū, SW Japan *37°31′N 137°19′E*
Svågälv *see* Svågan
94 *M10* **Svågan** *var.* Svågälv. ≈ C Sweden
Svalava/Svaljava *see* Svalyava

◆ Country
● Country Capital
◇ Dependent Territory
○ Dependent Territory Capital
⬖ Administrative Regions
✕ International Airport
▲ Mountain
▲▲ Mountain Range
Volcano
≈ River
◎ Lake
⊠ Reservoir

92 O2 **Svalbard** ◇ *Norwegian dependency* Arctic Ocean
92 J2 **Svalbardhseyri** Nordhurland Eystra, N Iceland 65°43′N 18°03′W
95 K22 **Svalöv** Skåne, S Sweden 55°55′N 13°06′E
116 H7 **Svalyava** *Cz.* Svalava, Svaljava, *Hung.* Szolyva. Zakarpats'ka Oblast', W Ukraine 48°33′N 23°00′E
92 O2 **Svanbergfjellet** ▲ C Svalbard 78°40′N 18°10′E
95 M24 **Svaneke** Bornholm, E Denmark 55°07′N 15°08′E
95 L22 **Svängsta** Blekinge, S Sweden 56°16′N 14°46′E
95 J16 **Svanskog** Värmland, C Sweden 59°10′N 12°34′E
95 L16 **Svartå** Örebro, C Sweden 59°13′N 14°07′E
95 L15 **Svartälven** ≈ C Sweden
92 G12 **Svartisen** *glacier* C Norway
117 X6 **Svatove** *Rus.* Svatovo. Luhans'ka Oblast', E Ukraine 49°24′N 38°11′E
Svatovo *see* Svatove
Sväty Kríž nad Hronom *see* Žiar nad Hronom
167 Q11 **Svay Chék, Stœng** ≈ Cambodia/Thailand
167 S13 **Svay Riĕng** Svay Riĕng, S Cambodia 11°05′N 105°48′E
92 O3 **Sveagruva** Spitsbergen, W Svalbard 77°53′N 16°42′E
95 K23 **Svedala** Skåne, S Sweden 55°30′N 13°15′E
118 H12 **Svėdesai** Utena, NE Lithuania 55°42′N 25°22′E
93 G18 **Sveg** Jämtland, C Sweden 62°02′N 14°20′E
118 C12 **Švėkšna** Klaipėda, W Lithuania 55°31′N 21°37′E
94 C11 **Svelgen** Sogn Og Fjordane, S Norway 61°47′N 05°18′E
95 H15 **Svelvik** Vestfold, S Norway 59°37′N 10°24′E
118 I13 **Švenčionėliai** *Pol.* Nowo-Święciany. Vilnius, SE Lithuania 55°10′N 26°00′E
118 I13 **Švenčionys** *Pol.* Swięciany. Vilnius, SE Lithuania 55°08′N 26°08′E
95 H24 **Svendborg** Syddtjylland, C Denmark 55°04′N 10°38′E
95 K19 **Svenljunga** Västra Götaland, S Sweden 57°30′N 13°05′E
92 P2 **Svenskøya** *island* E Svalbard
93 G17 **Svenstavik** Jämtland, C Sweden 62°40′N 14°24′E
95 G20 **Svenstrup** Nordjylland, N Denmark 56°58′N 09°52′E
118 H12 **Šventoji** ≈ C Lithuania
117 Z8 **Sverdlovs'k** *Rus.* Sverdlovsk; *prev.* Imeni Sverdlova Rudnik. Luhans'ka Oblast', E Ukraine 48°05′N 39°37′E
Sverdlovsk *see* Yekaterinburg
127 W2 **Sverdlovskaya Oblast'** ◐ *province* C Russian Federation
122 K6 **Sverdrupa, Ostrov** *island* N Russian Federation
Sverige *see* Sweden
113 D15 **Svetac** *prev.* Sveti Andrea, *It.* Sant'Andrea. *island* SW Croatia
Sveti Andrea *see* Svetac
Sveti Nikola *see* Sveti Nikole
113 O18 **Sveti Nikole** *prev.* Sveti Nikola. C FYR Macedonia 41°54′N 21°55′E
Sveti Vrach *see* Sandanski
123 T14 **Svetlaya** Primorskiy Kray, SE Russian Federation 46°33′N 138°20′E
126 B2 **Svetlogorsk** Kaliningradskaya Oblast', W Russian Federation 54°56′N 20°09′E
122 K9 **Svetlogorsk** Krasnoyarskiy Kray, N Russian Federation 66°51′N 88°29′E
Svetlogorsk *see* Svyetlahorsk
127 N14 **Svetlograd** Stavropol'skiy Kray, SW Russian Federation 45°20′N 42°53′E
Svetlovodsk *see* Svitlovods'k
119 A14 **Svetlyy** *Ger.* Zimmerbude. Kaliningradskaya Oblast', W Russian Federation 54°42′N 20°07′E
127 Y8 **Svetlyy** Orenburgskaya Oblast', W Russian Federation 50°34′N 60°42′E
127 P7 **Svetlyy** Saratovskaya Oblast', W Russian Federation 51°42′N 45°40′E
124 G11 **Svetogorsk** *Fin.* Enso. Leningradskaya Oblast', NW Russian Federation 61°06′N 28°52′E
Svetozarevo *see* Jagodina
111 B18 **Švihov** *Ger.* Schwihau. Plzeňský Kraj, W Czech Republic 49°31′N 13°18′E
112 E13 **Svilaja** ▲▲ SE Croatia
112 N12 **Svilajnac** Serbia, C Serbia 44°15′N 21°12′E
114 L11 **Svilengrad** *prev.* Mustafa-Pasha. Khaskovo, S Bulgaria 41°45′N 26°14′E
Svinecea Mare, Munte *see* Svinecea Mare, Vârful
116 F13 **Svinecea Mare, Vârful** *var.* Munte Svinecea Mare. ▲ SW Romania 44°47′N 22°10′E
Svinø *see* Svínoy
95 B18 **Svínoy** *Dan.* Svinø. *island* NE Faeroe Islands
147 N14 **Svintsovyy Rudnik** *Turkm.* Swintsowyy Rudnik. Lebap Welaýaty, E Turkmenistan 37°54′N 66°25′E
118 I13 **Svir** *Rus.* Svir'. Minskaya Voblasts', NW Belarus 54°51′N 26°24′E
124 I12 **Svir'** *canal* NW Russian Federation
Svir', Ozero *see* Svir, Vozyera
119 I14 **Svir, Vozyera** *Rus.* Ozero Svir'. ⊛ C Belarus
114 J7 **Svishtov** *prev.* Sistova. Veliko Tŭrnovo, N Bulgaria 43°37′N 25°20′E
119 F18 **Svislach** *Pol.* Świsłocz, *Rus.* Svisloch'. Hrodzyenskaya Voblasts', W Belarus 53°02′N 24°06′E
119 M17 **Svislach** *Rus.* Svisloch'. Mahilyowskaya Voblasts', E Belarus 53°26′N 28°59′E
119 L17 **Svislach** *Rus.* Svisloch'. ≈ E Belarus
Svisloch' *see* Svislach
111 F17 **Svitavy** *Ger.* Zwittau. Pardubický Kraj, C Czech Republic 49°45′N 16°27′E
117 S6 **Svitlovods'k** *Rus.* Svetlovodsk. Kirovohrads'ka Oblast', C Ukraine 49°05′N 33°15′E
Svizzera *see* Switzerland
123 Q13 **Svobodnyy** Amurskaya Oblast', SE Russian Federation 51°24′N 128°05′E
114 G9 **Svoge** Sofiya, W Bulgaria 42°58′N 23°20′E
92 G11 **Svolvær** Nordland, C Norway 68°15′N 14°40′E
111 F18 **Svratka** *Ger.* Schwarzawa. ≈ SE Czech Republic
113 P14 **Svrljig** Serbia, E Serbia 43°26′N 22°07′E
197 U10 **Svyataya Anna Trough** *var.* Saint Anna Trough. *undersea feature* N Kara Sea
124 M4 **Svyatoy Nos, Mys** *headland* NW Russian Federation 68°07′N 39°49′E
119 N18 **Svyetlahorsk** *Rus.* Svetlogorsk. Homyel'skaya Voblasts', SE Belarus 52°38′N 29°46′E
Swabian Jura *see* Schwäbische Alb
97 P19 **Swaffham** E England, United Kingdom 52°39′N 00°40′E
23 V5 **Swainsboro** Georgia, SE USA 32°36′N 82°19′W
83 C19 **Swakop** ≈ W Namibia
83 C19 **Swakopmund** Erongo, W Namibia 22°40′S 14°34′E
97 M15 **Swale** ≈ N England, United Kingdom
Swallow Island *see* Nendö
99 M16 **Swalmen** Limburg, SE Netherlands 51°13′N 06°02′E
12 G8 **Swan** ≈ Ontario, C Canada
97 L24 **Swanage** S England, United Kingdom 50°37′N 01°59′W
182 M10 **Swan Hill** Victoria, SE Australia 35°23′S 143°37′E
11 P13 **Swan Hills** Alberta, W Canada 54°41′N 116°20′W
65 D24 **Swan Island** *island* C Falkland Islands
Swankalok *see* Sawankhalok
29 U10 **Swan Lake** ⊛ Minnesota, N USA
21 Y10 **Swanquarter** North Carolina, SE USA 35°24′N 76°20′W
182 J9 **Swan Reach** South Australia 34°39′S 139°35′E
11 V15 **Swan River** Manitoba, S Canada 52°06′N 101°17′W
183 P17 **Swansea** Tasmania, SE Australia 42°09′S 148°03′E
97 J22 **Swansea** *Wel.* Abertawe. S Wales, United Kingdom 51°38′N 03°57′W
21 R13 **Swansea** South Carolina, SE USA 33°47′N 81°06′W
19 S7 **Swans Island** *island* Maine, NE USA
28 L17 **Swanson Lake** ⊠ Nebraska, C USA
31 R11 **Swanton** Ohio, N USA 41°35′N 83°53′W
110 G11 **Swarzędz** Poznań, W Poland 52°24′N 17°05′E
Swatow *see* Shantou
83 L22 **Swaziland** *off.* Kingdom of Swaziland. ◆ *monarchy* S Africa
Swaziland, Kingdom of *see* Swaziland
93 G18 **Sweden** *off.* Kingdom of Sweden, *Swe.* Sverige. ◆ *monarchy* N Europe
Sweden, Kingdom of *see* Sweden
Swedru *see* Agona Swedru
25 V12 **Sweeny** Texas, SW USA 29°02′N 95°42′W
33 R6 **Sweetgrass** Montana, NW USA 48°58′N 111°58′W
32 G12 **Sweet Home** Oregon, NW USA 44°24′N 122°44′W
25 T12 **Sweet Home** Texas, SW USA 29°21′N 97°04′W
27 T4 **Sweet Springs** Missouri, C USA 38°57′N 93°24′W
20 M10 **Sweetwater** Tennessee, S USA 35°36′N 84°27′W
25 P7 **Sweetwater** Texas, SW USA 32°27′N 100°25′W
33 V15 **Sweetwater River** ≈ Wyoming, C USA
Sweiham *see* Suwaydān
83 F26 **Swellendam** Western Cape, SW South Africa 34°01′S 20°26′E
111 G15 **Świdnica** *Ger.* Schweidnitz. Wałbrzych, SW Poland 50°51′N 16°29′E
111 O14 **Świdnik** *Ger.* Streckenbach. Lubelskie, E Poland 51°14′N 22°41′E
110 F8 **Świdwin** *Ger.* Schivelbein. Zachodnio-pomorskie, NW Poland 53°47′N 15°44′E
111 F15 **Świebodzice** *Ger.* Freiburg in Schlesien, Swiebodzice. Wałbrzych, SW Poland 50°54′N 16°23′E
110 E11 **Świebodzin** *Ger.* Schwiebus. Lubuskie, W Poland 52°15′N 15°31′E
Święciany *see* Švenčionys
110 I9 **Świecie** *Ger.* Schwertberg. Kujawsko-pomorskie, C Poland 53°24′N 18°24′E
111 L15 **Świętokrzyskie** ◐ *province* S Poland
11 T16 **Swift Current** Saskatchewan, S Canada 50°17′N 107°49′W
98 K9 **Swifterbant** Flevoland, C Netherlands 52°36′N 05°33′E
183 Q12 **Swifts Creek** Victoria, SE Australia 37°17′S 147°41′E
96 E13 **Swilly, Lough** *Ir.* Loch Súilí. *inlet* N Ireland
97 M22 **Swindon** S England, United Kingdom 51°34′N 01°47′W
Swinemünde *see* Świnoujście
110 D8 **Świnoujście** *Ger.* Swinemünde. Zachodnio-pomorskie, NW Poland 53°54′N 14°13′E
Swintsowyy Rudnik *see* Svintsovyy Rudnik
Świsłocz *see* Svislach
Swiss Confederation *see* Switzerland
108 E9 **Switzerland** *off.* Swiss Confederation, *Fr.* La Suisse, *Ger.* Schweiz, *It.* Svizzera; *anc.* Helvetia. ◆ *federal republic* C Europe
97 F17 **Swords** *Ir.* Sord, Sórd Choluim Chille. Dublin, E Ireland 53°28′N 06°13′W
18 H13 **Swoyersville** Pennsylvania, NE USA 41°18′N 75°48′W
124 I10 **Syamozero, Ozero** ⊛ NW Russian Federation
124 M13 **Syamzha** Vologodskaya Oblast', NW Russian Federation 60°02′N 41°09′E
118 N13 **Syanno** *Rus.* Senno. Vitsyebskaya Voblasts', NE Belarus 54°49′N 29°43′E
119 K16 **Syarhyeyevichy** *Rus.* Sergeyevichi. Minskaya Voblasts', C Belarus 53°30′N 27°45′E
124 I12 **Syas'stroy** Leningradskaya Oblast', NW Russian Federation 60°05′N 32°37′E
Sycaminum *see* Hefa
30 M10 **Sycamore** Illinois, N USA 41°59′N 88°41′W
126 J3 **Sychëvka** Smolenskaya Oblast', W Russian Federation 55°52′N 34°19′E
111 H14 **Syców** *Ger.* Gross Wartenberg. Dolnosląskie, SW Poland 51°18′N 17°42′E
95 F24 **Syddanmark** ◐ *region* SW Denmark
14 E17 **Sydenham** ≈ Ontario, S Canada
Sydenham Island *see* Nonouti
183 T9 **Sydney** *state capital* New South Wales, SE Australia 33°55′S 151°10′E
13 R14 **Sydney** Cape Breton Island, Nova Scotia, SE Canada 46°10′N 60°10′W
Sydney Island *see* Manra
13 R14 **Sydney Mines** Cape Breton Island, Nova Scotia, SE Canada 46°14′N 60°19′W
Syedpur *see* Saidpur
119 K18 **Syelishcha** *Rus.* Selishche. Minskaya Voblasts', C Belarus 53°01′N 27°25′E
119 J18 **Syemyezhava** *Rus.* Semezhevo. Minskaya Voblasts', C Belarus 52°58′N 27°00′E
Syene *see* Aswān
117 X6 **Syeverodonets'k** *Rus.* Severodonetsk. Luhans'ka Oblast', E Ukraine 48°59′N 38°28′E
161 T6 **Sÿiao Shan** *island* SE China
100 H11 **Syke** Niedersachsen, NW Germany 52°55′N 08°49′E
94 D10 **Sykkylven** Møre og Romsdal, S Norway 62°23′N 06°35′E
Sykoúri *see* Sykoúrio
115 F15 **Sykoúrio** *var.* Sikouri, Sykoúri; *prev.* Sikoúrion. Thessalía, C Greece 39°46′N 22°35′E
125 R11 **Syktyvkar** *prev.* Ust'-Sysol'sk. Respublika Komi, NW Russian Federation 61°42′N 50°45′E
23 Q4 **Sylacauga** Alabama, S USA 33°10′N 86°15′W
Sylarna *see* Storsylen
153 V14 **Sylhet** Sylhet, NE Bangladesh 24°53′N 91°51′E
153 V13 **Sylhet** ◐ *division* NE Bangladesh
100 G6 **Sylt** *island* NW Germany
21 O10 **Sylva** North Carolina, SE USA 35°23′N 83°13′W
125 V15 **Sylva** ≈ NW Russian Federation
23 W5 **Sylvania** Georgia, SE USA 32°45′N 81°38′W
31 R11 **Sylvania** Ohio, N USA 41°43′N 83°42′W
11 Q15 **Sylvan Lake** Alberta, SW Canada 52°18′N 114°02′W
33 T13 **Sylvan Pass** *pass* Wyoming, C USA
23 T7 **Sylvester** Georgia, SE USA 31°31′N 83°50′W
25 P6 **Sylvester** Texas, SW USA 32°42′N 100°15′W
10 L11 **Sylvia, Mount** ▲ British Columbia, W Canada 58°03′N 124°26′W
122 K11 **Sym** ≈ C Russian Federation
115 N22 **Sými** *var.* Simi. *island* Dodekánisa, Greece, Aegean Sea
117 U8 **Synel'nykove** Dnipropetrovs'ka Oblast', E Ukraine 48°19′N 35°32′E
125 U6 **Synya** Respublika Komi, NW Russian Federation 65°21′N 58°01′E
117 P7 **Synyukha** *Rus.* Sinyukha. ≈ S Ukraine
195 V2 **Syowa** *Japanese research station* Antarctica 68°58′S 40°07′E
26 H6 **Syracuse** Kansas, C USA 38°00′N 101°43′W
29 S16 **Syracuse** Nebraska, C USA 40°39′N 96°11′W
18 H10 **Syracuse** New York, NE USA 43°03′N 76°09′W
Syracuse *see* Siracusa
Syrdar'inskaya Oblast' *see* Sirdaryo Viloyati
Syrdariya *see* Syr Darya
144 L14 **Syr Darya** *var.* Sai Hun, Sir Darya, Syrdarya, *Kaz.* Syrdariya, *Rus.* Syrdar'ya, *Uzb.* Sirdaryo; *anc.* Jaxartes. ≈ C Asia
Syrdarya *see* Syr Darya
138 J6 **Syria** *off.* Syrian Arab Republic, *var.* Siria, Syrie, *Ar.* Al-Jumhūrīyah al-'Arabīyah as-Sūrīyah, Sūrīya. ◆ *republic* SW Asia
Syrian Arab Republic *see* Syria
138 L9 **Syrian Desert** *Ar.* Al Hamad, Bādiyat ash Shām. *desert* SW Asia
Syrie *see* Syria
115 L22 **Sýrna** *var.* Sirna. *island* Kykládes, Greece, Aegean Sea
115 I20 **Sýros** *var.* Síros. *island* Kykládes, Greece, Aegean Sea
93 M18 **Sysmä** Etelä-Suomi, S Finland 61°28′N 25°37′E
125 R12 **Sysola** ≈ NW Russian Federation
Syulemeshlii *see* Sredets
127 S2 **Syumsi** Udmurtskaya Respublika, NW Russian Federation 57°07′N 51°35′E
114 K10 **Syuyutliyka** ≈ C Bulgaria
Syvash, Zaliv *see* Syvash, Zatoka
117 U12 **Syvash, Zatoka** *Rus.* Zaliv Syvash. *inlet* S Ukraine
127 Q6 **Syzran'** Samarskaya Oblast', W Russian Federation 53°10′N 48°23′E
Szabadka *see* Subotica
111 N21 **Szabolcs-Szatmár-Bereg** *off.* Szabolcs-Szatmár-Bereg Megye. ◐ *county* E Hungary
Szabolcs-Szatmár-Bereg Megye *see* Szabolcs-Szatmár-Bereg
110 G10 **Szamocin** *Ger.* Samotschin. Wielkopolskie, C Poland 53°02′N 17°04′E
116 H8 **Szamos** *var.* Someş, Someşul, *Ger.* Samosch, Somesch. ≈ Hungary/Romania
Szamosújvár *see* Gherla
110 G11 **Szamotuły** Poznań, W Poland 52°35′N 16°36′E
Szarkowszczyzna *see* Sharkawshchyna
111 M24 **Szarvas** Békés, SE Hungary 46°51′N 20°35′E
Szászmagyarós *see* Măieruş
Szászrégen *see* Reghin
Szászsebes *see* Sebeş
Szászváros *see* Orăştie
Szatmárrnémeti *see* Satu Mare
Száva *see* Sava
111 P15 **Szczebrzeszyn** Lubelskie, E Poland 50°43′N 23°00′E
110 D9 **Szczecin** *Eng./Ger.* Stettin. Zachodnio-pomorskie, NW Poland 53°25′N 14°32′E
110 G8 **Szczecinek** *Ger.* Neustettin. Zachodnio-pomorskie, NW Poland 53°43′N 16°40′E
110 D8 **Szczeciński, Zalew** *var.* Stettiner Haff, *Ger.* Oderhaff. *bay* Germany/Poland
111 K15 **Szczekociny** Śląskie, S Poland 50°38′N 19°46′E
110 N8 **Szczuczyn** Podlaskie, NE Poland 53°34′N 22°17′E
Szczuczyn Nowogródzki *see* Shchuchyn
110 M8 **Szczytno** *Ger.* Ortelsburg. Warmińsko-Mazurskie, NE Poland 53°34′N 21°E
Szechuan/Szechwan *see* Sichuan
111 K21 **Szécsény** Nógrád, N Hungary 48°07′N 19°30′E
111 L25 **Szeged** *Ger.* Szegedin, *Rom.* Seghedin. Csongrád, SE Hungary 46°17′N 20°06′E
Szegedin *see* Szeged
111 N23 **Szeghalom** Békés, SE Hungary 47°01′N 21°09′E
Székelyhid *see* Săcueni
Székelykeresztúr *see* Cristuru Secuiesc
111 I23 **Székesfehérvár** *Ger.* Stuhlweissenberg; *anc.* Alba Regia. Fejér, W Hungary 47°13′N 18°24′E
Szeklerburg *see* Miercurea-Ciuc
Szekler Neumarkt *see* Târgu Secuiesc
111 J25 **Szekszárd** Tolna, S Hungary 46°21′N 18°41′E
Szempcz/Szenc *see* Senec
Szenice *see* Senica
Szentágota *see* Agnita
111 J22 **Szentendre** *Ger.* Sankt Andrä. Pest, N Hungary 47°40′N 19°02′E
111 L24 **Szentes** Csongrád, SE Hungary 46°40′N 20°17′E
111 F23 **Szentgotthárd** *Eng.* Saint Gotthard, *Ger.* Sankt Gotthard. Vas, W Hungary 46°57′N 16°18′E
Szentgyörgy *see* Đurđevac
Szenttamás *see* Srbobran
Széphely *see* Jebel
Szeping *see* Siping
Szered *see* Sered'
111 N21 **Szerencs** Borsod-Abaúj-Zemplén, NE Hungary 48°10′N 21°11′E
Szeret *see* Siret
Szeretfalva *see* Sărăţel
110 N7 **Szeska Góra** *var.* Szeskie Wygórza, *Ger.* Seesker Höhe. *hill* NE Poland
Szeskie Wygórza *see* Szeska Góra
111 H25 **Szigetvár** Baranya, SW Hungary 46°01′N 17°50′E
Szilágysomlyó *see* Şimleu Silvaniei
Szinna *see* Snina
Sziszek *see* Sisak
Szitás-Keresztúr *see* Cristuru Secuiesc
111 E15 **Szklarska Poręba** *Ger.* Schreiberhau. Dolnośląskie, SW Poland 50°50′N 15°30′E
Szkudy *see* Skuodas
Szlatina *see* Slatina
Szlavonia/Szlavonország *see* Slavonija
Szlovákia *see* Slovakia
Szluin *see* Slunj
111 L23 **Szolnok** Jász-Nagykun-Szolnok, C Hungary 47°11′N 20°12′E
Szolyva *see* Svalyava
111 G23 **Szombathely** *Ger.* Steinamanger; *anc.* Sabaria, Savaria. Vas, W Hungary 47°14′N 16°38′E
Szond/Szonta *see* Sonta
Szováta *see* Sovata
110 F13 **Szprotawa** *Ger.* Sprottau. Lubuskie, W Poland 51°33′N 15°32′E
Sztálinváros *see* Dunaújváros
Sztrazsó *see* Strážov
110 J8 **Sztum** *Ger.* Stuhm. Pomorskie, N Poland 53°54′N 19°01′E
110 H10 **Szubin** *Ger.* Schubin. Kujawsko-pomorskie, C Poland 53°04′N 17°49′E
Szucsava *see* Suceava
Szurduk *see* Surduc
111 M14 **Szydłowiec** *Ger.* Schlelau. Mazowieckie, C Poland 51°14′N 20°50′E

T

Taalintehdas *see* Dalsbruk
171 O4 **Taal, Lake** ⊛ Luzon, NW Philippines
95 J23 **Taastrup** *var.* Tåstrup. Sjælland, E Denmark 55°39′N 12°19′E
111 I24 **Tab** Somogy, W Hungary 46°45′N 18°01′E
171 P4 **Tabaco** Luzon, N Philippines 13°22′N 123°42′E
186 G4 **Tabalo** Mussau Island, NE Papua New Guinea 01°22′S 149°37′E
104 K5 **Tábara** Castilla y León, N Spain 41°49′N 05°57′W
186 H5 **Tabar Islands** *island group* NE Papua New Guinea
Tabariya, Bahrat *see* Tiberias, Lake
143 S7 **Ţabas** *var.* Golshan. Yazd, C Iran 33°37′N 56°54′E
43 P15 **Tabasará, Serranía de** ▲▲ W Panama
41 U15 **Tabasco** ◐ *state* SE Mexico
Tabasco *see* Grijalva, Río
127 Q2 **Tabashino** Respublika Mariy El, W Russian Federation 57°00′N 47°47′E
58 B13 **Tabatinga** Amazonas, N Brazil 04°14′S 69°44′W
74 G9 **Tabelbala** W Algeria 29°22′N 03°01′W
11 Q17 **Taber** Alberta, SW Canada 49°48′N 112°09′W
171 V15 **Taberfane** Pulau Trangan, E Indonesia 06°14′S 134°08′E
95 L19 **Taberg** Jönköping, S Sweden 57°42′N 14°05′E
191 O3 **Tabiteuea** *prev.* Drummond Island. *atoll* Tungaru, W Kiribati
171 O5 **Tablas Island** *island* C Philippines
184 Q10 **Table Cape** *headland* North Island, New Zealand 39°07′S 178°00′E
13 S13 **Table Mountain** ▲ Newfoundland, Newfoundland and Labrador, E Canada 47°39′N 59°15′W
173 P17 **Table, Pointe de la** *headland* SE Réunion 21°19′S 55°49′E
27 S8 **Table Rock Lake** ⊠ Arkansas/Missouri, C USA
36 K14 **Table Top** ▲ Arizona, SW USA 32°45′N 112°07′W
186 D8 **Tabletop, Mount** ▲ C Papua New Guinea 06°51′S 146°00′E
111 D18 **Tábor** Jihočeský Kraj, S Czech Republic 49°25′N 14°41′E
123 R7 **Tabor** Respublika Sakha (Yakutiya), NE Russian Federation 71°14′N 150°23′E
29 S15 **Tabor** Iowa, C USA 40°54′N 95°40′W
81 F21 **Tabora** Tabora, W Tanzania 05°04′S 32°49′E
81 F21 **Tabora** ◐ *region* C Tanzania
21 U12 **Tabor City** North Carolina, SE USA 34°09′N 78°52′W
147 Q10 **Taboshar** NW Tajikistan 40°37′N 69°33′E
76 L18 **Tabou** *var.* Tabu. S Ivory Coast 04°28′N 07°20′W
142 J2 **Tabrīz** *var.* Tebriz; *anc.* Tauris. Āžarbāyjān-e Sharqī, NW Iran 38°05′N 46°18′E
Tabu *see* Tabou
191 W1 **Tabuaeran** *prev.* Fanning Island. *atoll* Line Islands, E Kiribati
171 O2 **Tabuk** Luzon, N Philippines 17°26′N 121°25′E
140 J4 **Tabūk** Tabūk, NW Saudi Arabia 28°25′N 36°34′E
140 J5 **Tabūk** *off.* Minţaqat Tabūk. ◐ *province* NW Saudi Arabia
Tabūk, Minţaqat *see* Tabūk
187 Q13 **Tabwemasana, Mount** ▲ Espiritu Santo, W Vanuatu 15°22′S 166°44′E
95 O15 **Täby** Stockholm, C Sweden 59°29′N 18°04′E
41 N14 **Tacámbaro** Michoacán, SW Mexico 19°12′N 101°27′W
42 A5 **Tacaná, Volcán** ⩓ Guatemala/Mexico 15°07′N 92°06′W
43 X16 **Tacarcuna, Cerro** ▲ SE Panama 08°08′N 77°15′W
Tachau *see* Tachov
158 J3 **Tacheng** *var.* Qoqek. Xinjiang Uygur Zizhiqu, NW China 46°45′N 82°55′E
54 H7 **Táchira** *off.* Estado Táchira. ◐ *state* W Venezuela
Táchira, Estado *see* Táchira
Tachoshui *see* Dazhuoshui
111 A17 **Tachov** *Ger.* Tachau. Plvenský Kraj, W Czech Republic 49°48′N 12°38′E
171 Q5 **Tacloban** *off.* Tacloban City. Leyte, C Philippines 11°15′N 125°E
Tacloban City *see* Tacloban
57 I19 **Tacna** Tacna, SE Peru 18°S 70°15′W
57 H18 **Tacna** *off.* Departamento de Tacna. ◐ *department* S Peru
Tacna, Departamento de *see* Tacna
32 H8 **Tacoma** Washington, NW USA 47°15′N 122°27′W
18 L11 **Taconic Range** ▲▲ NE USA
62 L6 **Taco Pozo** Formosa, N Argentina 25°35′S 63°15′W
57 M20 **Tacsara, Cordillera de** ▲▲ S Bolivia
61 F17 **Tacuarembó** *prev.* San Fructuoso. Tacuarembó, C Uruguay 31°42′S 56°W
61 E18 **Tacuarembó** ◐ *department* C Uruguay
61 F17 **Tacuarembó, Río** ≈ C Uruguay
83 I14 **Taculi** North Western, NW Zambia 14°17′S 26°51′E
171 Q8 **Tacurong** Mindanao, S Philippines 06°42′N 124°40′E
77 V8 **Tadek** ≈ NW Niger
74 J9 **Tademaït, Plateau du** *plateau* C Algeria
187 R17 **Tadine** Province des Îles Loyauté, E New Caledonia 21°33′S 167°54′E
80 M11 **Tadjoura, Golfe de** *Eng.* Gulf of Tajura. *inlet* E Djibouti
80 L11 **Tadjourah** E Djibouti 11°47′N 42°51′E
Tadmor/Tadmur *see* Tudmur
11 W10 **Tadoule Lake** ⊛ Manitoba, C Canada
15 S8 **Tadoussac** Québec, SE Canada 48°09′N 69°43′W
155 H18 **Tādpatri** Andhra Pradesh, E India 14°55′N 77°59′E
Tadzhikabad *see* Tojikobod
Tadzhikistan *see* Tajikistan
163 Y14 **Taebaek-sanmaek** *prev.* T'aebaek-sanmaek. ▲▲ E South Korea
T'aebaek-sanmaek *see* Taebaek-sanmaek
Taechŏng-do *see* Daecheong-do
163 X13 **Taedong-gang** ≈ C North Korea
Taegu *see* Daegu
Taegu-gwangyŏksi *see* Daegu
Taehan-haehyŏp *see* Korea Strait
Taehan Min'guk *see* South Korea
Taejŏn *see* Daejeon
Taejŏn-gwangyŏksi *see* Daejeon
193 Z13 **Tafahi** *island* N Tonga
105 Q4 **Tafalla** Navarra, N Spain 42°32′N 01°41′W
77 W7 **Tafassâsset, Ténéré du** *desert* N Niger
75 M12 **Tafassâsset, Oued** ≈ SE Algeria
55 U11 **Tafelberg** ▲ S Surinam 03°55′N 56°09′W
97 J21 **Taff** ≈ SE Wales, United Kingdom
Tafila/Ţafīlah, Muḩāfaẓat aṭ *see* Aṭ Ţafīlah
77 N15 **Tafiré** N Ivory Coast 09°04′N 05°10′W
142 M6 **Tafresh** Markazī, W Iran 34°40′N 50°00′E
143 Q9 **Taft** Yazd, C Iran 31°45′N 54°14′E
35 R13 **Taft** California, W USA 35°08′N 119°27′W
25 T14 **Taft** Texas, SW USA 27°58′N 97°24′W
143 W12 **Taftān, Kūh-e** ▲ SE Iran 28°38′N 61°06′E
35 R13 **Taft Heights** California, W USA 35°06′N 119°29′W
189 Y14 **Tafunsak** Kosrae, E Micronesia 05°21′N 162°58′E
192 G16 **Tāga** Savai'i, SW Samoa 13°46′S 172°31′W
149 O6 **Tagāb** Dāikondī, E Afghanistan 33°53′N 66°23′E
39 O8 **Tagagawik River** ≈ Alaska, USA
165 Q10 **Tagajō** *var.* Tagazyô. Miyagi, Honshū, C Japan 38°18′N 140°58′E
126 K12 **Taganrog** Rostovskaya Oblast', SW Russian Federation 47°10′N 38°55′E
126 K12 **Taganrog, Gulf of** *Rus.* Taganrogskiy Zaliv, *Ukr.* Tahanroz'ka Zatoka. *gulf* Russian Federation/Ukraine
Taganrogskiy Zaliv *see* Taganrog, Gulf of
76 J8 **Tagant** ◐ *region* C Mauritania
148 M14 **Tagas** Baluchistān, SW Pakistan 27°09′N 64°36′E
171 O4 **Tagaytay** Luzon, N Philippines 14°04′N 120°55′E
Tagazyô *see* Tagajō
171 P6 **Tagbilaran** *var.* Tagbilaran City. Bohol, C Philippines 09°41′N 123°54′E
Tagbilaran City *see* Tagbilaran
106 B10 **Taggia** Liguria, NW Italy 43°51′N 07°48′E
77 V9 **Taghouaji, Massif de** ▲ C Niger 17°13′N 08°37′E
107 J15 **Tagliacozzo** Lazio, C Italy 42°03′N 13°15′E
106 J7 **Tagliamento** ≈ NE Italy
149 N3 **Tagow Bāy** *var.* Bai. Sar-e Pul, N Afghanistan 35°41′N 66°01′E
146 H9 **Tagta** *var.* Tahta, *Rus.* Takhta. Daşoguz Welaýaty, N Turkmenistan 41°40′N 59°51′E
146 J16 **Tagtabazar** *var.* Takhtabazar. Mary Welaýaty, S Turkmenistan 35°57′N 62°49′E
59 L17 **Taguatinga** Tocantins, C Brazil 12°16′S 46°25′W
186 I10 **Tagula** Tagula Island, SE Papua New Guinea 11°21′S 153°11′E
186 I11 **Tagula Island** *prev.* Southeast Island, Sudest Island. *island* SE Papua New Guinea
171 Q7 **Tagum** Mindanao, S Philippines 07°22′N 125°51′E
54 C7 **Tagún, Cerro** *elevation* Colombia/Panama
105 P7 **Tagus** *Port.* Rio Tejo, *Sp.* Río Tajo. ≈ Portugal/Spain
64 M9 **Tagus Plain** *undersea feature* E Atlantic Ocean 37°30′N 12°00′W
191 S10 **Tahaa** *island* Îles Sous le Vent, W French Polynesia
191 U10 **Tahanea** *atoll* Îles Tuamotu, C French Polynesia
Tahanroz'ka Zatoka *see* Taganrog, Gulf of
74 K12 **Tahat** ▲ SE Algeria 23°15′N 05°34′E
163 U4 **Tahe** Heilongjiang, NE China 52°21′N 124°42′E
Tahilt *see* Tsogt
191 T10 **Tahiti** *island* Îles du Vent, W French Polynesia
Tahiti, Archipel de *see* Société, Archipel de la
118 E4 **Tahkuna Nina** *headland* W Estonia 59°06′N 22°35′E
148 K12 **Tāhlāb** ≈ W Pakistan
148 K12 **Tāhlāb, Dasht-i** *desert* SW Pakistan
27 R10 **Tahlequah** Oklahoma, C USA 35°57′N 94°58′W
35 Q6 **Tahoe City** California, W USA 39°09′N 120°09′W
35 P6 **Tahoe, Lake** ⊛ California/Nevada, W USA
25 N6 **Tahoka** Texas, SW USA 33°10′N 101°47′W
32 F8 **Taholah** Washington, NW USA 47°19′N 124°17′W
77 T11 **Tahoua** Tahoua, W Niger 14°53′N 05°18′E
77 T11 **Tahoua** ◐ *department* W Niger
31 P3 **Tahquamenon Falls** *waterfall* Michigan, N USA
31 P4 **Tahquamenon River** ≈ Michigan, N USA
139 V10 **Taḩrīr** Al Qādisīyah, S Iraq 31°58′N 45°34′E
10 K17 **Tahsis** Vancouver Island, British Columbia, SW Canada 49°42′N 126°31′W
75 W9 **Ţahţā** *var.* Ţahta. C Egypt 26°47′N 31°31′E
Tahta *see* Tagta
136 L15 **Tahtalı Dağları** ▲▲ C Turkey
57 I14 **Tahuamanu, Río** ≈ Bolivia/Peru
56 F13 **Tahuanía, Río** ≈ E Peru
191 X7 **Tahuata** *island* Îles Marquises, NE French Polynesia
76 L17 **Taï** SW Ivory Coast 05°52′N 07°28′W
161 P5 **Tai'an** Shandong, E China 36°13′N 117°12′E
191 R8 **Taiarapu, Presqu'île de** *peninsula* Tahiti, W French Polynesia
Taibad *see* Tāybād
160 K7 **Taibai Shan** ▲ C China 33°57′N 107°31′E
105 Q12 **Taibilla, Sierra de** ▲▲ S Spain
Taibus Qi *see* Baochang
Taichū *see* Taizhong
T'aichung *see* Taizhong
Taiden *see* Daejeon
161 T14 **Taidong** *Jap.* Taitō; *prev.* T'aitung. S Taiwan 22°43′N 121°10′E
185 E23 **Taieri** ≈ South Island, New Zealand
115 E21 **Taïgetos** ▲▲ S Greece
161 N4 **Taihang Shan** ▲▲ C China
184 M11 **Taihape** Manawatu-Wanganui, North Island, New Zealand 39°41′S 175°47′E
161 O7 **Taihe** Anhui, E China 33°14′N 115°35′E
161 O12 **Taihe** *var.* Chengjiang. Jiangxi, S China 26°47′N 114°52′E
Taihoku *see* T'aipei
161 P9 **Taihu** Anhui, E China 30°22′N 116°20′E
161 R8 **Tai Hu** ⊛ E China
159 O9 **Taikang** *var.* Dorbod, Dorbod Mongolzu Zizhixian. Heilongjiang, NE China 46°50′N 124°25′E
161 O6 **Taikang** Henan, C China 34°01′N 114°59′E
165 T5 **Taiki** Hokkaidō, NE Japan 42°29′N 143°15′E
166 L8 **Taikkyi** Yangon, SW Burma (Myanmar) 17°16′N 95°55′E
Taikyū *see* Daegu
163 U8 **Tailai** Heilongjiang, NE China 46°25′N 123°25′E
168 I12 **Taileleo** Pulau Siberut, W Indonesia 01°45′S 99°06′E
182 J10 **Tailem Bend** South Australia 35°20′S 139°34′E
96 I8 **Tain** N Scotland, United Kingdom 57°49′N 04°04′W
161 S14 **Tainan** *prev.* Dainan, T'ainan. S Taiwan 23°01′N 120°05′E
115 E22 **Taínaro, Akrotírio** *cape* S Greece
161 Q11 **Taining** *var.* Shancheng. Fujian, SE China 26°55′N 117°13′E
191 W7 **Taiohae** *prev.* Madisonville. Nuku Hiva, NE French Polynesia 08°55′S 140°04′W
161 T13 **T'aipei** *Jap.* Taihoku; *prev.* Daihoku. ● (Taiwan) N Taiwan 25°02′N 121°28′E
168 J7 **Taiping** Perak, Peninsular Malaysia 04°54′N 100°42′E
Taiping *see* Chongzuo
163 S8 **Taiping Ling** ▲ NE China 47°27′N 120°27′E
165 Q4 **Taisei** Hokkaidō, NE Japan 42°13′N 139°52′E
165 G12 **Taisha** Shimane, Honshū, SW Japan 35°23′N 132°40′E
109 R4 **Taiskirchen** Oberösterreich, NW Austria 48°15′N 13°33′E
63 F20 **Taitao, Peninsula de** *peninsula* S Chile
Taitō *see* Taidong
T'aitung *see* Taidong
92 M13 **Taivalkoski** Oulu, E Finland 65°35′N 28°20′E
93 K19 **Taivassalo** Länsi-Suomi, SW Finland 60°35′N 21°36′E
161 T14 **Taiwan** *off.* Republic of China, *var.* Formosa, Formo'sa. ◆ *republic* E Asia
192 F5 **Taiwan** *var.* Formosa. *island* E Asia
Taiwan *see* Taizhong
T'aiwan Haihsia/Taiwan Haixia *see* Taiwan Strait
Taiwan Shan *see* Chungyang Shanmo
161 R13 **Taiwan Strait** *var.* Formosa Strait, *Chin.* T'aiwan Haihsia, Taiwan Haixia. *strait* China/Taiwan
161 N4 **Taiyuan** *var.* T'ai-yuan, T'ai-yüan; *prev.* Yangku. *province capital* Shanxi, C China 37°48′N 112°33′E
T'ai-yuan/T'ai-yüan *see* Taiyuan
161 S13 **Taizhong** *Jap.* Taichū; *prev.* T'aichung, Taiwan. C Taiwan 24°09′N 120°40′E
161 R7 **Taizhou** Jiangsu, E China 32°36′N 119°52′E
161 S10 **Taizhou** *var.* Jiaojiang; *prev.* Haimen. Zhejiang, SE China 28°36′N 121°19′E
Taizhou *see* Linhai
141 O16 **Ta'izz** SW Yemen 13°36′N 44°04′E
141 O16 **Ta'izz** ✕ SW Yemen 13°40′N 44°10′E
75 P12 **Tajarhī** SW Libya 24°21′N 14°28′E
147 P13 **Tajikistan** *off.* Republic of Tajikistan, *Rus.* Tadzhikistan, *Taj.* Jumhurii Tojikiston; *prev.* Tajik S.S.R. ◆ *republic* C Asia
Tajikistan, Republic of *see* Tajikistan
Tajik S.S.R *see* Tajikistan
165 O11 **Tajima** Fukushima, Honshū, C Japan 37°10′N 139°46′E
Tajoe *see* Tayu
Tajo, Río *see* Tagus
42 B5 **Tajumulco, Volcán** ▲ W Guatemala 15°04′N 91°50′W
105 P7 **Tajuña** ≈ C Spain
Tajura, Gulf of *see* Tadjoura, Golfe de
167 O9 **Tak** *var.* Rahaeng. Tak, W Thailand 16°51′N 99°08′E
189 U4 **Taka Atoll** *var.* Tōke. *atoll* Ratak Chain, N Marshall Islands
165 P12 **Takahagi** Ibaraki, Honshū, S Japan 36°42′N 140°42′E
165 H13 **Takahashi** *var.* Takahasi. Okayama, Honshū, SW Japan 34°48′N 133°38′E
Takahasi *see* Takahashi
189 P12 **Takaieu Island** *island* E Micronesia
184 I13 **Takaka** Tasman, South Island, New Zealand 40°52′S 172°49′E
170 M14 **Takalar** Sulawesi, C Indonesia 05°28′S 119°24′E
165 H13 **Takamatsu** *var.* Takamatu. Kagawa, Shikoku, SW Japan 34°19′N 133°59′E
Takamatu *see* Takamatsu

◆ Country
● Country Capital
◇ Dependent Territory
○ Dependent Territory Capital
◐ Administrative Regions
✕ International Airport
▲ Mountain
▲▲ Mountain Range
⩓ Volcano
≈ River
⊛ Lake
⊠ Reservoir

165 D14 **Takamori** Kumamoto, Kyūshū, SW Japan 32°50′N 131°08′E
165 D16 **Takanabe** Miyazaki, Kyūshū, SW Japan 32°13′N 131°31′E
170 M16 **Takan, Gunung** ▲ Pulau Sumba, S Indonesia 08°52′S 117°32′E
165 Q7 **Takanosu** *var.* Kita-Akita. Akita, Honshū, C Japan 40°13′N 140°23′E
Takao *see* Gaoxiong
165 L11 **Takaoka** Toyama, Honshū, SW Japan 36°44′N 137°02′E
184 N12 **Takapau** Hawke's Bay, North Island, New Zealand 40°01′S 176°21′E
191 U9 **Takapoto** *atoll* Îles Tuamotu, C French Polynesia
184 L5 **Takapuna** Auckland, North Island, New Zealand 36°48′S 174°46′E
165 J3 **Takarazuka** Hyōgo, Honshū, SW Japan 34°49′N 135°21′E
191 U9 **Takaroa** *atoll* Îles Tuamotu, C French Polynesia
165 N12 **Takasaki** Gunma, Honshū, S Japan 36°20′N 139°00′E
164 L12 **Takayama** Gifu, Honshū, SW Japan 36°09′N 137°16′E
164 K12 **Takefu** *var.* Echizen, Takehu. Fukui, Honshū, SW Japan 35°55′N 136°11′E
Takehu *see* Takefu
164 C14 **Takeo** Saga, Kyūshū, SW Japan 33°13′N 130°00′E
Takeo *see* Takêv
164 C17 **Take-shima** *island* Nansei-shotō, SW Japan
142 M5 **Tākestān** *var.* Takistan; *prev.* Siadehan. Qazvin, N Iran 36°02′N 49°40′E
164 D14 **Taketa** Ōita, Kyūshū, SW Japan 33°00′N 131°23′E
167 R13 **Takêv** *prev.* Takeo. Takêv, S Cambodia 10°59′N 104°47′E
167 O10 **Tak Fah** Nakhon Sawan, C Thailand
139 T13 **Takhādīd** *well* S Iraq
149 R3 **Takhār** ◈ *province* NE Afghanistan
Takhiatash *see* Taxiatosh
Ta Khmau *see* Kândal
Takhta *see* Tagta
Takhtabazar *see* Tagtabazar
145 O8 **Takhtabrod** Severnyy Kazakhstan, N Kazakhstan 52°35′N 67°37′E
Takhtakupyr *see* Taxtako'pir
142 M8 **Takht-e Shāh, Kūh-e** ▲▲ C Iran
77 V12 **Takiéta** Zinder, S Niger 13°43′N 08°33′E
8 J8 **Takijuq Lake** ◎ Nunavut, NW Canada
165 S3 **Takikawa** Hokkaidō, NE Japan 43°35′N 141°54′E
165 U3 **Takinoue** Hokkaidō, NE Japan 44°10′N 143°09′E
Takistan *see* Tākestān
185 B23 **Takitimu Mountains** ▲▲ South Island, New Zealand
Takkaze *see* Tekezē
165 R7 **Takko** Aomori, Honshū, C Japan 40°19′N 141°11′E
10 L13 **Takla Lake** ◎ British Columbia, SW Canada
Takla Makan Desert *see* Taklimakan Shamo
158 H9 **Taklimakan Shamo** *Eng.* Takla Makan Desert. *desert* NW China
167 T12 **Takôk** Môndól Kiri, E Cambodia 12°37′N 106°30′E
39 P10 **Takotna** Alaska, USA 62°59′N 156°03′W
Takow *see* Gaoxiong
123 O12 **Taksimo** Respublika Buryatiya, S Russian Federation 56°18′N 114°53′E
164 C13 **Taku** Saga, Kyūshū, SW Japan 33°19′N 130°06′E
10 I10 **Taku** 〰 British Columbia, W Canada
166 M15 **Takua Pa** *var.* Ban Takua Pa. Phangnga, SW Thailand 08°55′N 98°20′E
77 W16 **Takum** Taraba, E Nigeria 07°16′N 10°00′E
191 V10 **Takume** *atoll* Îles Tuamotu, C French Polynesia
190 L16 **Takutea** *island* S Cook Islands
186 K6 **Takuu Islands** *prev.* Mortlock Group. *island group* NE Papua New Guinea
119 L18 **Tal'** Minskaya Voblasts', S Belarus 52°52′N 27°58′E
40 L13 **Tala** Jalisco, C Mexico 20°39′N 103°45′W
61 F19 **Tala** Canelones, S Uruguay 34°24′S 55°45′W
Talabriga *see* Aveiro, Portugal
Talabriga *see* Talavera de la Reina, Spain
119 N14 **Talachyn** *Rus.* Tolochin. Vitsyebskaya Voblasts', NE Belarus 54°25′N 29°42′E
149 U7 **Talagang** Punjab, E Pakistan 32°55′N 72°29′E
105 V11 **Talaiassa** ▲ Ibiza, Spain, W Mediterranean Sea 38°55′N 1°17′E
155 J23 **Talaimannar** Northern Province, NW Sri Lanka 09°05′N 79°43′E
117 R3 **Talalayivka** Chernihivs'ka Oblast', N Ukraine 50°51′N 33°09′E
43 O15 **Talamanca, Cordillera de** ▲▲ S Costa Rica
56 A9 **Talara** Piura, NW Peru 04°31′S 81°17′W
104 L11 **Talarrubias** Extremadura, W Spain 39°03′N 05°14′W
147 S8 **Talas** Talasskaya Oblast', NW Kyrgyzstan 42°29′N 72°21′E
147 S8 **Talas** 〰 NW Kyrgyzstan
186 G7 **Talasea** New Britain, E Papua New Guinea 05°20′S 150°01′E
Talas Oblasty *see* Talasskaya Oblast'
147 S8 **Talasskaya Oblast'** *Kir.* Talas Oblasty. ◈ *province* NW Kyrgyzstan
147 S8 **Talasskiy Alatau, Khrebet** ▲▲ Kazakhstan/Kyrgyzstan
77 U12 **Talata Mafara** Zamfara, NW Nigeria 12°33′N 06°01′E
171 R9 **Talaud, Kepulauan** *island group* E Indonesia
104 M9 **Talavera de la Reina** *anc.* Caesarobriga, Talabriga. Castilla-La Mancha, C Spain 39°58′N 04°50′W
104 J11 **Talavera la Real** Extremadura, W Spain 38°53′N 06°46′W
186 F7 **Talawe, Mount** ▲ New Britain, C Papua New Guinea 05°30′S 148°24′E
23 S5 **Talbotton** Georgia, SE USA 32°40′N 84°32′W
183 R7 **Talbragar River** 〰 New South Wales, SE Australia
62 G13 **Talca** Maule, C Chile 35°28′S 71°42′W
62 F13 **Talcahuano** Bío Bío, C Chile 36°43′S 73°07′W
154 N12 **Tālcher** Orissa, E India 20°57′N 85°13′E
25 W5 **Talco** Texas, SW USA 33°21′N 95°06′W
145 V14 **Taldykorgan** *Kaz.* Taldyqorghan; *prev.* Taldy-Kurgan. Taldykorgan, SE Kazakhstan 45°N 78°23′E
Taldy-Kurgan/Taldyqorghan *see* Taldykorgan
147 Y7 **Taldy-Suu** Issyk-Kul'skaya Oblast', E Kyrgyzstan 42°49′N 78°33′E
147 U10 **Taldy-Suu** Oshskaya Oblast', SW Kyrgyzstan 40°33′N 73°52′E
Tal-e Khosravī *see* Yāsūj
193 Y15 **Taleki Tonga** *island* Otu Tolu Group, C Tonga
193 Y15 **Taleki Vavu'u** *island* Otu Tolu Group, C Tonga
102 J13 **Talence** Gironde, SW France 44°49′N 00°35′W
145 U16 **Talgar** *Kaz.* Talghar. Almaty, SE Kazakhstan 43°17′N 77°15′E
Talghar *see* Talgar
171 Q12 **Taliabu, Pulau** *island* Kepulauan Sula, C Indonesia
115 L22 **Taliarós, Akrotírio** *headland* Astypálaia, Kykládes, Greece, Aegean Sea 36°31′N 26°18′E
Ta-lien *see* Dalian
27 Q12 **Talihina** Oklahoma, C USA 34°45′N 95°03′W
Talimardzhan *see* Tollimarjon
137 T12 **T'alin** *Rus.* Talin; *prev.* Verin T'alin. W Armenia 40°23′N 43°51′E
Talin *see* T'alin
81 E15 **Tali Post** Central Equatoria, S South Sudan 05°55′N 30°44′E
Taliq-an *see* Tāloqān
Taliş Dağları *see* Talish Mountains
142 L2 **Talish Mountains** *Az.* Taliş Dağları, *Per.* Kūhhā-ye Ṭavālesh, *Rus.* Talyshskiye Gory. ▲▲ Azerbaijan/Iran
170 M16 **Taliwang** Sumbawa, C Indonesia 08°45′S 116°55′E
119 L17 **Tal'ka** Minskaya Voblasts', C Belarus 53°22′N 28°21′E
39 R11 **Talkeetna** Alaska, USA 62°19′N 150°06′W
39 R11 **Talkeetna Mountains** ▲▲ Alaska, USA
Talkhof *see* Puurmani
92 H2 **Tálknafjördhur** Vestfirdhir, W Iceland 65°38′N 23°51′W
139 Q3 **Tall 'Abṭah** Nīnawá, N Iraq 35°52′N 42°40′E
138 M2 **Tall Abyaḍ** *var.* Tell Abiad. Ar Raqqah, N Syria 36°42′N 38°56′E
23 Q4 **Talladega** Alabama, S USA 33°26′N 86°06′W
139 Q2 **Tall 'Afar** Nīnawýa, N Iraq 36°22′N 42°27′E
23 S8 **Tallahassee** *prev.* Muskogean. *state capital* Florida, SE USA 30°26′N 84°17′W
22 L2 **Tallahatchie River** 〰 Mississippi, S USA
Tall al Abyaḍ *see* At Tall al Abyaḍ
139 W12 **Tall al Laḥm** Dhī Qār, S Iraq 30°46′N 46°22′E
183 P11 **Tallangatta** Victoria, SE Australia 36°15′S 147°13′E
23 R4 **Tallapoosa River** 〰 Alabama/Georgia, S USA
103 T13 **Tallard** Hautes-Alpes, SE France 44°30′N 06°04′E
139 Q3 **Tall ash Sha'īr** Nīnawá, N Iraq 36°11′N 42°26′E
23 Q5 **Tallassee** Alabama, S USA 32°32′N 85°53′W
139 R4 **Tall 'Azbah** Nīnawýa, NW Iraq 35°47′N 43°13′E
138 I5 **Tall Bīsah** Ḥimṣ, W Syria 34°50′N 36°44′E
139 R3 **Tall Ḥassūnah** Al Anbār, N Iraq 36°05′N 43°10′E
139 Q2 **Tall Ḥuqnah** *var.* Tell Huqnah. Nīnawá, N Iraq 36°33′N 42°34′E
Tallin *see* Tallinn
118 G3 **Tallinn** *Ger.* Reval, *Rus.* Tallin; *prev.* Revel. ● (Estonia) Harjumaa, NW Estonia 59°26′N 24°42′E
118 H3 **Tallinn** ✈ Harjumaa, NW Estonia 59°23′N 24°52′E
138 H5 **Tall Kalakh** *var.* Tell Kalakh. Ḥimṣ, C Syria 34°40′N 36°18′E
139 R2 **Tall Kayf** Nīnawýa, NW Iraq 36°30′N 43°08′E
Tall Kūchak *see* Tall Kūshik
139 P2 **Tall Kūshik** *var.* Tall Kūchak. Al Ḥasakah, E Syria 36°48′N 42°01′E
31 U12 **Tallmadge** Ohio, N USA 41°06′N 81°26′W
22 J5 **Tallulah** Louisiana, S USA 32°22′N 91°12′W
139 Q2 **Tall 'Uwaynāt** Nīnawýa, NW Iraq 36°43′N 42°18′E
139 Q2 **Tall Ẓāhir** Nīnawá, N Iraq 36°51′N 42°29′E
122 J13 **Tal'menka** Altayskiy Kray, S Russian Federation 53°55′N 83°26′E
122 K8 **Talnakh** Krasnoyarskiy Kray, N Russian Federation 69°26′N 88°27′E
117 P7 **Tal'ne** *Rus.* Tal'noye. Cherkas'ka Oblast', C Ukraine 48°55′N 30°40′E
Tal'noye *see* Tal'ne
80 E12 **Talodi** Southern Kordofan, C Sudan 10°40′N 30°25′E
188 B16 **Talofofo** SE Guam 13°21′N 144°45′E
188 B16 **Talofofo Bay** *bay* SE Guam
26 L9 **Taloga** Oklahoma, C USA 36°02′N 98°58′W
123 T10 **Talon** Magadanskaya Oblast', E Russian Federation 59°47′N 148°46′E
14 H11 **Talon, Lake** ◎ Ontario, S Canada
149 R2 **Tāloqān** *var.* Taliq-an. Takhār, NE Afghanistan 36°44′N 69°33′E
126 M8 **Talovaya** Voronezhskaya Oblast', W Russian Federation 51°07′N 40°46′E
9 N6 **Taloyoak** *prev.* Spence Bay. Nunavut, N Canada 69°30′N 93°25′W
25 Q8 **Talpa** Texas, SW USA 31°46′N 99°42′W
40 K13 **Talpa de Allende** Jalisco, C Mexico 20°22′N 104°51′W
23 S9 **Talquin, Lake** ⊠ Florida, SE USA
Talsen *see* Talsi
Talshand *see* Chandmanĭ
118 E8 **Talsi** *Ger.* Talsen. NW Latvia 57°14′N 22°35′E
143 V11 **Tal Sīāh** Sīstān va Balūchestān, SE Iran 28°19′N 57°43′E
62 G6 **Taltal** Antofagasta, N Chile 25°22′S 70°27′W
8 K10 **Taltson** 〰 Northwest Territories, NW Canada
168 K11 **Taluk** Sumatera, W Indonesia 0°32′S 101°35′E
92 J8 **Talvik** Finnmark, N Norway 70°02′N 22°59′E
182 M7 **Talyawalka Creek** 〰 New South Wales, SE Australia
Talyshskiye Gory *see* Talish Mountains
29 W14 **Tama** Iowa, C USA 41°58′N 92°34′W
Tama Abu, Banjaran *see* Penambo, Banjaran
169 U9 **Tamabo, Banjaran** ▲▲ East Malaysia
190 B16 **Tamakautoga** SW Niue 19°05′S 169°55′W
127 N7 **Tamala** Penzenskaya Oblast', W Russian Federation 52°32′N 43°18′E
77 P15 **Tamale** C Ghana 09°21′N 00°54′W
191 P3 **Tamana** *prev.* Rotcher Island. *atoll* Tungaru, W Kiribati
74 K12 **Tamanrasset** *var.* Tamenghest. S Algeria 22°49′N 05°32′E
74 J13 **Tamanrasset** *wadi* Algeria/Mali
166 M2 **Tamanthi** Sagaing, N Burma (Myanmar) 25°17′N 95°18′E
97 I24 **Tamar** 〰 SW England, United Kingdom
Tamar *see* Tudmur
54 H9 **Támara** Casanare, C Colombia 05°51′N 72°09′W
54 F7 **Tamar, Alto de** ▲ C Colombia 07°25′N 74°28′W
173 X16 **Tamarin** E Mauritius 20°20′S 57°22′E
105 T5 **Tamarite de Litera** *var.* Tararite de Llitera. Aragón, NE Spain 41°52′N 00°25′E
111 I24 **Tamási** Tolna, S Hungary 46°39′N 18°17′E
Tamatave *see* Toamasina
41 O9 **Tamaulipas** ◈ *state* C Mexico
41 P10 **Tamaulipas, Sierra de** ▲▲ C Mexico
56 F12 **Tamaya, Río** 〰 E Peru
40 I9 **Tamazula** Durango, C Mexico 24°43′N 106°33′W
40 L14 **Tamazula** Jalisco, C Mexico 19°41′N 103°18′W
Tamazulápam *see* Tamazulapán
41 Q15 **Tamazulapán** *var.* Tamazulápam. Oaxaca, SE Mexico 17°41′N 97°33′W
41 P12 **Tamazunchale** San Luis Potosí, C Mexico 21°17′N 98°46′W
76 H11 **Tambacounda** SE Senegal 13°44′N 13°43′W
83 M16 **Tambara** Manica, C Mozambique 16°42′S 34°14′E
77 T13 **Tambawel** Sokoto, NW Nigeria 12°24′N 04°42′E
186 M9 **Tambea** Guadalcanal, C Solomon Islands 09°19′S 159°42′E
169 N10 **Tambelan, Kepulauan** *island group* W Indonesia
57 E15 **Tambo de Mora** Ica, W Peru 13°30′S 76°08′W
170 L16 **Tambora, Gunung** 🌋 Sumbawa, S Indonesia 08°16′S 117°59′E
61 E17 **Tambores** Paysandú, W Uruguay 31°50′S 56°17′W
57 F14 **Tambo, Río** 〰 C Peru
56 F7 **Tamboryacu, Río** 〰 N Peru
126 M7 **Tambov** Tambovskaya Oblast', W Russian Federation 52°43′N 41°28′E
126 L6 **Tambovskaya Oblast'** ◈ *province* W Russian Federation
104 H3 **Tambre** 〰 NW Spain
169 V7 **Tambunan** Sabah, East Malaysia 05°40′N 116°22′E
81 C15 **Tambura** Western Equatoria, SW South Sudan 05°38′N 27°30′E
Tamchaket *see* Tâmchekkeṭ
76 J9 **Tâmchekkeṭ** *var.* Tamchaket. Hodh el Gharbi, S Mauritania 17°23′N 10°37′W
167 T7 **Tam Điệp** Ninh Binh, N Vietnam 20°09′N 105°54′E
Tamdybulak *see* Tomdibuloq
54 H8 **Tame** Arauca, C Colombia 06°27′N 71°42′W
104 H6 **Tâmega, Rio** *Sp.* Río Támega. 〰 Portugal/Spain
Támega, Río *see* Tâmega, Rio
115 H20 **Tamélos, Akrotírio** *headland* Tziá, Kykládes, Greece, Aegean Sea 37°31′N 24°16′E
Tamenghest *see* Tamanrasset
77 V8 **Tamgak, Adrar** ▲ C Niger 19°10′N 08°39′E
76 I13 **Tamgue** ▲ NW Guinea 12°14′N 12°18′W
41 Q12 **Tamiahua** Veracruz-Llave, E Mexico 21°15′N 97°27′W
41 Q12 **Tamiahua, Laguna de** *lagoon* E Mexico
23 Y16 **Tamiami Canal** *canal* Florida, SE USA
188 F17 **Tamil Harbor** *harbour* Yap, W Micronesia
155 H21 **Tamil Nādu** *prev.* Madras. ◈ *state* SE India
99 H20 **Tamines** Namur, S Belgium 50°27′N 04°37′E
116 E12 **Tamiš** *Ger.* Temesch, *Hung.* Temes. 〰 Romania/Serbia
167 U10 **Tam Ky** Quang Nam-ƒa Năng, C Vietnam 15°32′N 108°30′E
Tammerfors *see* Tampere
Tammisaari *see* Ekenäs
95 N14 **Tämnaren** ◎ C Sweden
191 Q7 **Tamotoe, Passe** *passage* Tahiti, W French Polynesia
23 V12 **Tampa** Florida, SE USA 27°57′N 82°27′W
23 V12 **Tampa** ✈ Florida, SE USA 27°57′N 82°29′W
23 V13 **Tampa Bay** *bay* Florida, SE USA
93 L18 **Tampere** *Swe.* Tammerfors. Länsi-Suomi, W Finland 61°30′N 23°45′E
41 Q11 **Tampico** Tamaulipas, C Mexico 22°18′N 97°52′W
171 P14 **Tampo** Pulau Muna, C Indonesia 04°38′S 122°40′E
167 V11 **Tam Quan** Binh Đinh, C Vietnam 14°34′N 109°00′E
162 J13 **Tamsag Muchang** Nei Mongol Zizhiqu, N China 40°28′N 102°34′E
Tamsal *see* Tamsalu
118 I4 **Tamsalu** *Ger.* Tamsal. Lääne-Virumaa, NE Estonia 59°10′N 26°07′E
109 S8 **Tamsweg** Salzburg, SW Austria 47°08′N 13°49′E
188 C15 **Tamuning** NW Guam 13°29′N 144°47′E
183 T6 **Tamworth** New South Wales, SE Australia 31°07′S 150°54′E
97 M19 **Tamworth** C England, United Kingdom 52°39′N 01°40′W
81 K19 **Tana** *Finn.* Tenojoki, *Lapp.* Deatnu. 〰 SE Kenya *see also* Deatnu, Tenojoki
Tana *see* Deatnu/Tana
164 I15 **Tanabe** Wakayama, Honshū, SW Japan 33°43′N 135°22′E
92 L8 **Tana Bru** Finnmark, N Norway 70°11′N 28°06′E
39 T10 **Tanacross** Alaska, USA 63°30′N 143°21′W
92 L7 **Tanafjorden** *Lapp.* Deanuvuotna. *fjord* N Norway
38 G17 **Tanaga Island** *island* Aleutian Islands, Alaska, USA
38 G17 **Tanaga Volcano** ▲ Tanaga Island, Alaska, USA 51°53′N 178°08′W
107 M18 **Tanagro** 〰 S Italy
80 H11 **T'ana Hāyk'** *var.* Lake Tana. ◎ NW Ethiopia
168 H11 **Tanahbela, Pulau** *island* Kepulauan Batu, W Indonesia
171 H15 **Tanahjampea, Pulau** *island* W Indonesia
168 H11 **Tanahmasa, Pulau** *island* Kepulauan Batu, W Indonesia
Tanais *see* Don
152 L10 **Tanakpur** Uttarakhand, N India 29°04′N 80°06′E
Tana, Lake *see* T'ana Hāyk'
181 P5 **Tanami Desert** *desert* Northern Territory, N Australia
167 T14 **Tân An** Long An, S Vietnam 10°32′N 106°24′E
39 Q9 **Tanana** Alaska, USA 65°12′N 152°00′W
Tananarive *see* Antananarivo
39 Q9 **Tanana River** 〰 Alaska, USA
95 C16 **Tananger** Rogaland, S Norway 58°55′N 05°34′E
188 H5 **Tanapag** Saipan, S Northern Mariana Islands 15°14′S 145°45′E
188 H5 **Tanapag, Puetton** *bay* Saipan, S Northern Mariana Islands
106 C9 **Tanaro** 〰 N Italy
163 Y12 **Tanch'ŏn** E North Korea 40°22′N 128°49′E
40 M14 **Tancitaro, Cerro** 🌋 C Mexico 19°16′N 102°25′W
153 N12 **Tānda** Uttar Pradesh, N India 26°33′N 82°39′E
77 O15 **Tanda** E Ivory Coast 07°48′N 03°10′W
116 L14 **Ţăndărei** Ialomiţa, SE Romania 44°39′N 27°40′E
63 N14 **Tandil** Buenos Aires, E Argentina 37°18′S 59°10′W
78 H12 **Tandjilé** *off.* Préfecture du Tandjilé. ◈ *prefecture* SW Chad
Tandjilé, Préfecture du *see* Tandjilé
Tandjoeng *see* Tanjung
Tandjoengkarang *see* Bandar Lampung
Tandjoengpandan *see* Tanjungpandan
Tandjoengpinang *see* Tanjungpinang
Tandjoengredeb *see* Tanjungredeb
149 Q16 **Tando Allāhyār** Sind, SE Pakistan 25°28′N 68°44′E
149 Q17 **Tando Bāgo** Sind, SE Pakistan 24°48′N 68°59′E
149 Q16 **Tando Muhammad Khān** Sind, SE Pakistan 25°07′N 68°35′E
182 L7 **Tandou Lake** *seasonal lake* New South Wales, SE Australia
94 L11 **Tandsjöborg** Gävleborg, C Sweden 61°40′N 14°40′E
155 H15 **Tāndūr** Andhra Pradesh, C India 17°16′N 77°37′E
164 C17 **Tanega-shima** *island* Nansei-shotō, SW Japan
165 R7 **Taneichi** Iwate, Honshū, C Japan 40°23′N 141°42′E
Tanen Taunggyi *see* Tane Range
167 N8 **Tane Range** *Bur.* Tanen Taunggyi. ▲▲ W Thailand
111 P15 **Tanew** 〰 SE Poland
21 W2 **Taneytown** Maryland, NE USA 39°39′N 77°10′W
74 H12 **Tanezrouft** *desert* Algeria/Mali
138 L7 **Ţanf, Jabal aţ** ▲ SE Syria 33°32′N 38°43′E
81 J21 **Tanga** Tanga, E Tanzania 05°07′S 39°05′E
81 I22 **Tanga** ◈ *region* E Tanzania
153 T14 **Tangail** Dhaka, C Bangladesh 24°15′N 89°55′E
186 I5 **Tanga Islands** *island group* NE Papua New Guinea
155 K26 **Tangalla** Southern Province, S Sri Lanka 06°02′N 80°47′E
Tanganyika and Zanzibar *see* Tanzania
68 J13 **Tanganyika, Lake** ◎ E Africa
56 E7 **Tangarana, Río** 〰 N Peru
191 V16 **Tangaroa, Maunga** 🌋 Easter Island, Chile, E Pacific Ocean
Tangdukou *see* Shaoyang
74 G5 **Tanger** *var.* Tangiers, Tangier, *Fr./Ger.* Tangerk, *Sp.* Tánger; *anc.* Tingis. NW Morocco 35°49′N 05°49′W
169 N15 **Tangerang** Jawa, C Indonesia 06°14′S 106°36′E
Tangerk *see* Tanger
100 M12 **Tangermünde** Sachsen-Anhalt, C Germany 52°35′N 11°57′E
159 O12 **Tanggulashan** *var.* Togton Heyan, Tuotuoheyan. Qinghai, C China 34°13′N 92°25′E
156 K10 **Tanggula Shan** *var.* Dangla, Tangla Range. ▲▲ W China
159 N13 **Tanggula Shan** ▲ W China 33°18′N 91°10′E
156 K10 **Tanggula Shankou** *Tib.* Dang La. *pass* W China
161 N7 **Tanghe** Henan, C China 32°40′N 112°53′E
149 T5 **Tāngi** Khyber Pakhtunkhwa, NW Pakistan 34°18′N 71°42′E
Tangier *see* Tanger
21 Y5 **Tangier Island** *island* Virginia, NE USA
Tangiers *see* Tanger
22 K8 **Tangipahoa River** 〰 Louisiana, S USA
Tangla Range *see* Tanggula Shan
156 I10 **Tangra Yumco** *var.* Tangro Tso. ◎ W China
Tangro Tso *see* Tangra Yumco
157 T7 **Tangshan** *var.* T'ang-shan. Hebei, E China 39°39′N 118°15′E
T'ang-shan *see* Tangshan
77 R14 **Tanguiéta** NW Benin 10°35′N 01°19′E
163 X7 **Tangwang He** 〰 NE China
163 X7 **Tangyuan** Heilongjiang, NE China 46°45′N 129°52′E
167 S14 **Tân Hiệp** *var.* Phung Hiệp. Cần Thơ, S Vietnam 09°50′N 105°48′E
92 M11 **Tanhua** Lappi, N Finland 67°31′N 27°30′E
171 U16 **Tanimbar, Kepulauan** *island group* Maluku, E Indonesia
167 N12 **Tanintharyi** *var.* Tenasserim. Tanintharyi, S Burma (Myanmar) 12°05′N 99°00′E
167 N11 **Tanintharyi** *var.* Tenasserim. ◈ *division* S Burma (Myanmar)
139 U4 **Tānjarō** 〰 E Iraq
129 T15 **Tanjong Piai** *headland* Peninsular Malaysia
Tanjore *see* Thanjāvūr
169 U12 **Tanjung** *prev.* Tandjoeng. Borneo, C Indonesia 02°08′S 115°23′E
169 W9 **Tanjungbatu** Borneo, N Indonesia 02°19′N 118°03′E
Tanjungkarang/Tanjungkarang-Telukbetung *see* Bandar Lampung
169 N13 **Tanjungpandan** *prev.* Tandjoengpandan. Pulau Belitung, W Indonesia 02°44′S 107°36′E
168 M10 **Tanjungpinang** *prev.* Tandjoengpinang. Pulau Bintan, W Indonesia 0°55′N 104°28′E
169 V9 **Tanjungredeb** *var.* Tanjungredep; *prev.* Tandjoengredeb. Borneo, C Indonesia 02°09′N 117°29′E
Tanjungredep *see* Tanjungredeb
149 S8 **Tānk** Khyber Pakhtunkhwa, NW Pakistan 32°14′N 70°29′E
187 S15 **Tanna** *island* S Vanuatu
93 F17 **Tännäs** Jämtland, C Sweden 62°27′N 12°40′E
Tannenhof *see* Krynica
108 K7 **Tannheim** Tirol, W Austria 47°30′N 10°32′E
Tannu-Tuva *see* Tyva, Respublika
171 Q12 **Tano** Pulau Taliabu, E Indonesia 01°51′S 124°55′E
77 O17 **Tano** 〰 S Ghana
152 D10 **Tanot** Rājasthān, NW India 27°44′N 70°17′E
77 V11 **Tanout** Zinder, C Niger 14°58′N 08°54′E
Tân Phu *see* Đinh Quan
41 P12 **Tanquián** San Luis Potosí, C Mexico 21°38′N 98°39′W
77 R13 **Tansarga** E Burkina 11°51′N 01°51′E
167 T13 **Tan Son Nhat** ✈ (Hô Chi Minh) Tây Ninh, S Vietnam 10°52′N 106°38′E
75 V8 **Ţanţā** *var.* Tanta, Tantā, Tantâ. N Egypt 30°42′N 31°00′E
74 D9 **Tan-Tan** SW Morocco 28°30′N 11°11′W
41 P12 **Tantoyuca** Veracruz-Llave, E Mexico 21°21′N 98°12′W
152 J12 **Tāntpur** Uttar Pradesh, N India 26°51′N 77°29′E
Tan-tung *see* Dandong
38 M12 **Tanunak** Alaska, USA 60°35′N 165°15′W
166 L5 **Ta-nyaung** Magway, W Burma (Myanmar) 20°49′N 94°40′E
167 S5 **Tân Yên** Tuyên Quang, N Vietnam 22°08′N 104°58′E
81 F22 **Tanzania** *off.* United Republic of Tanzania, *Swa.* Jamhuri ya Muungano wa Tanzania; *prev.* German East Africa, Tanganyika and Zanzibar. ◆ *republic* E Africa
Tanzania, Jamhuri ya Muungano wa *see* Tanzania
Tanzania, United Republic of *see* Tanzania
Tao'an *see* Taonan
163 T8 **Tao'er He** 〰 NE China
159 U11 **Tao He** 〰 C China
163 U9 **Taonan** *var.* Tao'an. Jilin, NE China 45°20′N 122°46′E
T'aon-an *see* Baicheng
Taongi *see* Bokaak Atoll
107 M23 **Taormina** *anc.* Tauromenium. Sicilia, Italy, C Mediterranean Sea 37°54′N 15°18′E
37 S9 **Taos** New Mexico, SW USA 36°24′N 105°35′W
Taoudenit *see* Taoudenni
77 O6 **Taoudenni** *var.* Taoudenit. Tombouctou, N Mali 22°46′N 03°54′W
74 G6 **Taounate** N Morocco 34°33′N 04°39′N
Taoyang *see* Lintao
161 S13 **Taoyuan** *Jap.* Tōen; *prev.* T'aoyüan. N Taiwan 25°00′N 121°15′E
118 I3 **Tapa** *Ger.* Taps. Lääne-Virumaa, NE Estonia 59°15′N 26°E
41 V17 **Tapachula** Chiapas, SE Mexico 14°53′N 92°18′W
Tapaiu *see* Gvardeysk
59 H14 **Tapajós, Rio** *var.* Tapajóz. 〰 NW Brazil
Tapajóz *see* Tapajós, Rio
61 C21 **Tapalqué** *var.* Tapalquén. Buenos Aires, E Argentina 36°21′S 60°01′W
Tapalquén *see* Tapalqué
Tapanahoni *see* Tapanahony Rivier
55 W11 **Tapanahony Rivier** *var.* Tapanahoni. 〰 E Surinam
41 T16 **Tapanatepec** *var.* San Pedro Tapanatepec. Oaxaca, SE Mexico 16°23′N 94°09′W
185 D23 **Tapanui** Otago, South Island, New Zealand 45°55′S 169°16′E
59 E14 **Tapauá** Amazonas, N Brazil 05°42′S 64°15′W
47 R7 **Tapauá, Rio** 〰 W Brazil
185 I14 **Tapawera** Tasman, South Island, New Zealand 41°24′S 172°50′E
61 I16 **Tapes** Rio Grande do Sul, S Brazil 30°40′S 51°25′W
76 K16 **Tapeta** C Liberia 06°36′N 08°52′W
154 H11 **Tāpi** *prev.* Tāpti. 〰 W India
104 J2 **Tapia de Casariego** Asturias, N Spain 43°34′N 06°56′W
56 F10 **Tapiche, Río** 〰 N Peru
167 N15 **Tapi, Mae Nam** *var.* Luang. 〰 SW Thailand
186 E8 **Tapini** Central, S Papua New Guinea 08°16′S 146°09′E
Tapirapecó, Serra *see* Tapirapecó, Sierra
55 N13 **Tapirapecó, Sierra** *Port.* Serra Tapirapecó. ▲▲ Brazil/Venezuela
77 R13 **Tapoa** 〰 Benin/Niger
188 H5 **Tapochau, Mount** ▲ Saipan, S Northern Mariana Islands
111 H24 **Tapolca** Veszprém, W Hungary 46°54′N 17°29′E
21 X5 **Tappahannock** Virginia, NE USA 37°55′N 76°54′W
31 U13 **Tappan Lake** ⊠ Ohio, N USA
165 Q6 **Tappi-zaki** *headland* Honshū, C Japan 41°15′N 140°19′E
Taps *see* Tapa
Tāpti *see* Tāpi
Tapuaemanu *see* Maiao
185 J16 **Tapuaenuku** ▲ South Island, New Zealand 42°00′S 173°39′E
171 N8 **Tapul Group** *island group* Sulu Archipelago, SW Philippines
58 E11 **Tapurmcuará** *var.* Tapuruquara. Amazonas, NW Brazil 0°17′S 65°00′W
Tapuruquara *see* Tapurmcuará
192 J17 **Taputapu, Cape** *headland* Tutuila, W American Samoa 14°20′S 170°51′W
141 W13 **Ţāqah** S Oman 17°02′N 54°23′E
139 T3 **Taqtaq** Arbīl, N Iraq 35°54′N 44°36′E
61 J15 **Taquara** Rio Grande do Sul, S Brazil 29°36′S 50°46′W
59 H19 **Taquari, Rio** 〰 C Brazil
60 L8 **Taquaritinga** São Paulo, S Brazil 21°22′S 48°29′W
122 I11 **Tara** Omskaya Oblast', C Russian Federation 56°54′N 74°17′E
83 I16 **Tara** Southern, S Zambia 16°56′S 26°50′E
113 J15 **Tara** 〰 Montenegro
112 K13 **Tara** ▲▲ W Serbia
77 W15 **Taraba** ◈ *state* E Nigeria
77 X15 **Taraba** 〰 E Nigeria
75 O7 **Ţarābulus** *var.* Ţarābulus al Gharb, *Eng.* Tripoli. ● (Libya) NW Libya 32°54′N 13°11′E
75 O7 **Tarābulus** ✈ NW Libya 32°37′N 13°07′E
Ţarābulus al Gharb *see* Ţarābulus
Tarābulus/Ţarābulus ash Shām *see* Tripoli
105 O7 **Taracena** Castilla-La Mancha, C Spain 40°39′N 03°08′W
117 N12 **Taraclia** *Rus.* Tarakilya. S Moldova 45°55′N 28°40′E
139 V10 **Tarād al Kahf** Dhī Qār, SE Iraq 31°58′N 45°58′E
183 R10 **Tarago** New South Wales, SE Australia 35°04′S 149°40′E
162 J8 **Taragt** *var.* Hüremt. Övörhangay, C Mongolia 46°18′N 102°27′E
169 V8 **Tarakan** Borneo, C Indonesia 03°20′N 117°38′E
169 V9 **Tarakan, Pulau** *island* N Indonesia
Tarakilya *see* Taraclia
165 P16 **Tarama-jima** *island* Sakishima-shotō, SW Japan
184 K10 **Taranaki** *off.* Taranaki Region. ◈ *region* North Island, New Zealand
184 K10 **Taranaki, Mount** *var.* Egmont. 🌋 North Island, New Zealand 39°16′S 174°04′E
Taranaki Region *see* Taranaki
105 O9 **Tarancón** Castilla-La Mancha, C Spain 40°01′N 03°01′W
188 M15 **Tarang Reef** *reef* C Micronesia
96 E7 **Taransay** *island* NW Scotland, United Kingdom
107 P18 **Taranto** *var.* Tarentum. Puglia, SE Italy 40°30′N 17°11′E
107 O19 **Taranto, Golfo di** *Eng.* Gulf of Taranto. *gulf* S Italy
Taranto, Gulf of *see* Taranto, Golfo di
62 G3 **Tarapacá** *off.* Región de Tarapacá. ◈ *region* N Chile
Tarapacá, Región de *see* Tarapacá
187 N9 **Tarapaina** Maramasike Island, N Solomon Islands 09°28′S 161°24′E
56 D10 **Tarapoto** San Martín, N Peru 06°31′S 76°23′W
138 M6 **Ţaraq an Na'jah** *hill range* E Syria
138 M6 **Ţaraq Sidāwī** *hill range* E Syria
103 Q11 **Tarare** Rhône, E France 45°54′N 04°26′E
Tararite de Llitera *see* Tamarite de Litera
184 M13 **Tararua Range** ▲▲ North Island, New Zealand
151 Q22 **Tarāsa Dwīp** *island* Nicobar Islands, India, NE Indian Ocean
103 Q15 **Tarascon** Bouches-du-Rhône, SE France 43°48′N 04°39′E
102 M17 **Tarascon-sur-Ariège** Ariège, S France 42°51′N 01°35′E
117 P6 **Tarashcha** Kyyivs'ka Oblast', N Ukraine 49°34′N 30°31′E
57 L18 **Tarata** Cochabamba, C Bolivia 17°35′S 66°04′W
57 I18 **Tarata** Tacna, SW Peru 17°30′S 70°00′W
190 H2 **Taratai** *atoll* Tungaru, W Kiribati
59 B15 **Tarauacá** Acre, W Brazil 08°06′S 70°45′W
59 B15 **Tarauacá, Rio** 〰 NW Brazil
191 Q8 **Taravao** Tahiti, W French Polynesia 17°44′S 149°19′W
191 R8 **Taravao, Baie de** *bay* Tahiti, W French Polynesia
191 Q8 **Taravao, Isthme de** *isthmus* Tahiti, W French Polynesia
103 X16 **Taravo** 〰 Corse, France, C Mediterranean Sea
190 J3 **Tarawa** ✈ Tarawa, W Kiribati 0°53′S 169°32′E
190 H2 **Tarawa** *atoll* Tungaru, W Kiribati
184 N10 **Tarawera** Hawke's Bay, North Island, New Zealand 39°03′S 176°34′E
184 N8 **Tarawera, Lake** ◎ North Island, New Zealand
184 N8 **Tarawera, Mount** ▲ North Island, New Zealand 38°13′S 176°29′E
105 S8 **Tarayuela** ▲ N Spain 40°28′N 00°22′W
145 R16 **Taraz** *prev.* Aulie Ata, Auliye-Ata, Dzhambul, Zhambyl. Zhambyl, S Kazakhstan 42°55′N 71°27′E
105 Q5 **Tarazona** Aragón, NE Spain 41°54′N 01°44′W
105 Q10 **Tarazona de la Mancha** Castilla-La Mancha, C Spain 39°16′N 01°55′W
145 X12 **Tarbagatay, Khrebet** ▲▲ China/Kazakhstan
96 J8 **Tarbat Ness** *headland* N Scotland, United Kingdom 57°51′N 03°48′W
149 U5 **Tarbela Reservoir** ⊠ N Pakistan
96 H12 **Tarbert** W Scotland, United Kingdom 55°52′N 05°26′W
96 F7 **Tarbert** NW Scotland, United Kingdom 57°54′N 06°48′W
102 K16 **Tarbes** *anc.* Bigorra. Hautes-Pyrénées, S France 43°14′N 00°04′E
21 W9 **Tarboro** North Carolina, SE USA 35°54′N 77°34′W
Tarca *see* Torysa
106 J6 **Tarcento** Friuli-Venezia Giulia, NE Italy 46°13′N 13°13′E
182 F5 **Tarcoola** South Australia 30°44′S 134°34′E
105 S5 **Tardienta** Aragón, NE Spain 41°58′N 00°31′W
102 L11 **Tardoire** 〰 W France
183 U7 **Taree** New South Wales, SE Australia 31°56′S 152°29′E
92 K12 **Tärendö** *Lapp.* Deargget. Norrbotten, N Sweden 67°10′N 22°40′E
Tarentum *see* Taranto
74 C9 **Tarfaya** SW Morocco 27°56′N 12°55′W
116 J13 **Târgovişte** *prev.* Tîrgovişte. Dâmboviţa, S Romania 44°54′N 25°29′E
Tărgovište *see* Tŭrgovishte
116 M12 **Târgu Bujor** *prev.* Tîrgu Bujor. Galaţi, E Romania 45°52′N 27°55′E
116 H13 **Târgu Cărbuneşti** *prev.* Tîrgu. Gorj, SW Romania 44°57′N 23°32′E
116 L9 **Târgu Frumos** *prev.* Tîrgu Frumos. Iaşi, NE Romania 47°12′N 27°00′E
116 H13 **Targu Jiu** *prev.* Tîrgu Jiu. Gorj, W Romania 45°03′N 23°20′E
116 H9 **Târgu Lăpuş** *prev.* Tîrgu Lăpuş. Maramureş, N Romania 47°28′N 23°54′E
Târgul-Neamţ *see* Târgu-Neamţ
Târgul-Săcuiesc *see* Târgu Secuiesc
116 I10 **Târgu Mureş** *prev.* Oşorhei, Tîrgu Mures, *Ger.* Neumarkt, *Hung.* Marosvásárhely. Mureş, C Romania 46°33′N 24°36′E
116 K9 **Târgu-Neamţ** *var.* Târgul-Neamţ; *prev.* Tîrgu-Neamţ. Neamţ, NE Romania 47°12′N 26°25′E
116 K11 **Târgu Ocna** *Hung.* Aknavásár; *prev.* Tîrgu Ocna. Bacău, E Romania 46°17′N 26°37′E
116 K11 **Târgu Secuiesc** *Ger.* Neumarkt, Szekler Neumarkt, *Hung.* Kezdivásárhely; *prev.* Chezdi-Oşorheiu, Târgul-Săcuiesc, Tîrgu Secuiesc. Covasna, E Romania 46°00′N 26°08′E
145 X10 **Targyn** Vostochnyy Kazakhstan, E Kazakhstan 49°32′N 82°47′E
Tar Heel State *see* North Carolina
186 C7 **Tari** Southern Highlands, W Papua New Guinea 05°52′S 142°58′E
162 J6 **Tarialan** *var.* Badrah. Hövsgöl, N Mongolia 49°33′N 101°58′E
162 I7 **Tariat** *var.* Horgo. Arhangay, C Mongolia 48°06′N 99°52′E
143 P17 **Ţarīf** Abū Ẓaby, C United Arab Emirates 24°02′N 53°47′E
104 K16 **Tarifa** Andalucía, S Spain 36°01′N 05°36′W
84 C14 **Tarifa, Punta de** *headland* SW Spain 36°01′N 05°39′W
57 M21 **Tarija** Tarija, S Bolivia 21°33′S 64°42′W
57 M21 **Tarija** ◈ *department* S Bolivia
141 R14 **Tarīm** C Yemen 16°N 48°50′E
Tarim Basin *see* Tarim Pendi

◆ Country
● Country Capital
◇ Dependent Territory
○ Dependent Territory Capital
◈ Administrative Regions
✈ International Airport
▲ Mountain
▲▲ Mountain Range
🌋 Volcano
〰 River
◎ Lake
⊠ Reservoir

81 G19 **Tarime** Mara, N Tanzania *01°20′S 34°24′E*
129 S8 **Tarim He** ≈ NW China
159 H8 **Tarim Pendi** *Eng.* Tarim Basin. *basin* NW China
149 N7 **Tarīn Kōt** *var.* Terinkot; *prev.* Tarīn Kowt. Uruzgān, C Afghanistan *32°38′N 65°52′E*
Tarīn Kowt *see* Tarīn Kōt
171 O12 **Taripa** Sulawesi, C Indonesia *01°51′S 120°46′E*
117 Q12 **Tarkhankut, Mys** *headland* S Ukraine *45°20′N 32°32′E*
27 Q1 **Tarkio** Missouri, C USA *40°25′N 95°24′W*
122 J9 **Tarko-Sale** Yamalo-Nenetskiy Avtonomnyy Okrug, N Russian Federation *64°55′N 77°34′E*
77 P17 **Tarkwa** S Ghana *05°16′N 01°59′W*
171 O3 **Tarlac** Luzon, N Philippines *15°29′N 120°34′E*
95 F22 **Tarm** Midtjylland, W Denmark *55°55′N 08°32′E*
57 E14 **Tarma** Junín, C Peru *11°28′S 75°41′W*
103 N15 **Tarn** ◈ *department* S France
102 M15 **Tarn** ≈ S France
111 L22 **Tarna** ≈ C Hungary
92 G13 **Tärnaby** Västerbotten, N Sweden *65°44′N 15°20′E*
149 P8 **Tarnak Rūd** ≈ SE Afghanistan
116 J11 **Târnava Mare** *Ger.* Grosse Kokel, *Hung.* Nagy-Küküllő; *prev.* Tîrnava Mare. ≈ S Romania
116 I11 **Târnava Mică** *Ger.* Kleine Kokel, *Hung.* Kis-Küküllő; *prev.* Tirnava Mică. ≈ C Romania
116 I11 **Târnăveni** *Ger.* Marteskirch, Martinskirch, *Hung.* Dicsőszentmárton; *prev.* Sînmartin, Tîrnăveni. Mureş, C Romania *46°20′N 24°17′E*
102 L14 **Tarn-et-Garonne** ◈ *department* S France
111 P18 **Tarnica** ▲ SE Poland *49°05′N 22°43′E*
111 N15 **Tarnobrzeg** Podkarpackie, SE Poland *50°35′N 21°40′E*
125 N12 **Tarnogskiy Gorodok** Vologodskaya Oblast', NW Russian Federation *60°28′N 43°45′E*
Tarnopol *see* Ternopil'
111 M16 **Tarnów** Małopolskie, S Poland *50°01′N 20°59′E*
Tarnowice/Tarnowitz *see* Tarnowskie Góry
111 J16 **Tarnowskie Góry** *var.* Tarnowice, Tarnowskie Gory, *Ger.* Tarnowitz. Śląskie, S Poland *50°27′N 18°52′E*
95 N14 **Tärnsjö** Västmanland, C Sweden *60°10′N 16°57′E*
186 K7 **Taro** Choiseul, NW Solomon Islands *07°00′S 156°57′E*
106 E9 **Taro** ≈ NW Italy
186 I6 **Taron** New Ireland, NE Papua New Guinea *04°22′S 153°04′E*
74 E8 **Taroudannt** *var.* Taroudant. SW Morocco *30°31′N 08°50′W*
Taroudant *see* Taroudannt
23 V12 **Tarpon, Lake** ◎ Florida, SE USA
23 V12 **Tarpon Springs** Florida, SE USA *28°09′N 82°45′W*
107 G14 **Tarquinia** *anc.* Tarquinii, *hist.* Corneto. Lazio, C Italy *42°23′N 11°45′E*
Tarquinii *see* Tarquinia
Tarraco *see* Tarragona
76 D10 **Tarrafal** Santiago, S Cape Verde *15°16′N 23°45′W*
105 V6 **Tarragona** *anc.* Tarraco. Cataluña, E Spain *41°07′N 01°15′E*
105 T7 **Tarragona** ◈ *province* Cataluña, NE Spain
183 O17 **Tarraleah** Tasmania, SE Australia *42°11′S 146°29′E*
23 P3 **Tarrant City** Alabama, S USA *33°34′N 86°45′W*
185 D21 **Tarras** Otago, South Island, New Zealand *44°48′S 169°25′E*
Tarrasa *see* Terrassa
105 U5 **Tàrrega** *var.* Tarrega. Cataluña, NE Spain *41°39′N 01°09′E*
21 W9 **Tar River** ≈ North Carolina, SE USA
Tarsatica *see* Rijeka
136 J17 **Tarsus** İçel, S Turkey *36°52′N 34°52′E*
62 K4 **Tartagal** Salta, N Argentina *22°32′S 63°50′W*
137 V12 **Tärtär** *Rus.* Terter. ≈ SW Azerbaijan
102 J15 **Tartas** Landes, SW France *43°52′N 00°45′W*
Tartlau *see* Prejmer
Tartous/Tartouss *see* Ţarţūs
118 J5 **Tartu** *Ger.* Dorpat; *prev. Rus.* Yurev, Yur'ev. Tartumaa, SE Estonia *58°20′N 26°44′E*
118 I5 **Tartumaa** *off.* Tartu Maakond. ◈ *province* E Estonia
Tartu Maakond *see* Tartumaa
138 H5 **Ţarţūs** *Fr.* Tartouss; *anc.* Tortosa. Ţarţūs, W Syria *34°55′N 35°52′E*
138 H5 **Ţarţūs** *off.* Muḩāfaẓat Ţarţūs, *var.* Tartous, Tartus. ◈ *governorate* W Syria
Ţarţūs, Muḩāfaẓat *see* Ţarţūs
164 C16 **Tarumizu** Kagoshima, Kyūshū, SW Japan *31°30′N 130°40′E*
126 K4 **Tarusa** Kaluzhskaya Oblast', W Russian Federation *54°45′N 37°10′E*
117 N11 **Tarutyne** Odes'ka Oblast', SW Ukraine *46°11′N 29°09′E*
162 I7 **Tarvagatyn Nuruu** ▲▲ N Mongolia
106 J6 **Tarvisio** Friuli-Venezia Giulia, NE Italy *46°31′N 13°33′E*
Tarvisium *see* Treviso
57 O16 **Tarvo, Río** ≈ E Bolivia
14 G8 **Tarzwell** Ontario, S Canada *48°00′N 79°58′W*
40 K5 **Tasajera, Sierra de la** ▲▲ N Mexico
145 S13 **Tasaral** Karaganda, C Kazakhstan *46°17′N 73°54′E*
145 N15 **Tasboget** *Kaz.* Tasböget; *prev.* Tasbuget. Kzylorda, S Kazakhstan *44°46′N 65°38′E*
Tasböget *see* Tasboget
Tasbuget *see* Tasboget
108 E11 **Tasch** Valais, SW Switzerland *46°04′N 07°43′E*
Tasek Kenyir *see* Kenyir, Tasik
122 J14 **Tashanta** Respublika Altay, S Russian Federation *49°42′N 89°15′E*
Tashauz *see* Daşoguz
Tashi Chho Dzong *see* Thimphu
153 U11 **Tashigang** E Bhutan *27°19′N 91°33′E*
137 T11 **Tashir** *prev.* Kalinino. N Armenia *41°07′N 44°16′E*
143 Q11 **Ţashk, Daryācheh-ye** ◎ C Iran
Tashkent *see* Toshkent
Tashkentskaya Oblast' *see* Toshkent Viloyati
Tashkepri *see* Daşköpri
Tash-Kömür *see* Tash-Kumyr
147 S9 **Tash-Kumyr** *Kir.* Tash-Kömür. Dzhalal-Abadskaya Oblast', W Kyrgyzstan *41°22′N 72°09′E*
127 T7 **Tashla** Orenburgskaya Oblast', W Russian Federation *51°42′N 52°33′E*
Tashqurghan *see* Khulm
122 J13 **Tashtagol** Kemerovskaya Oblast', S Russian Federation *52°49′N 88°00′E*
95 H24 **Tåsinge** *island* C Denmark
12 M5 **Tasiujaq** Québec, E Canada *58°43′N 69°58′W*
144 F8 **Taskala** *prev.* Kamenka. Zapadnyy Kazakhstan, NW Kazakhstan *51°06′N 51°16′E*
77 W11 **Tasker** Zinder, C Niger *15°06′N 10°42′E*
145 W12 **Taskesken** Vostochnyy Kazakhstan, E Kazakhstan *47°15′N 80°45′E*
136 J10 **Taşköprü** Kastamonu, N Turkey *41°30′N 34°12′E*
Taskuduk, Peski *see* Tosquduq Qumlari
186 G5 **Taskul** New Ireland, NE Papua New Guinea *02°34′S 150°25′E*
137 S13 **Taşlıçay** Ağrı, E Turkey *39°37′N 43°23′E*
185 H14 **Tasman** *off.* Tasman District. ◈ *unitary authority* South Island, New Zealand
192 J12 **Tasman Basin** *var.* East Australian Basin. *undersea feature* S Tasman Sea
185 I14 **Tasman Bay** *inlet* South Island, New Zealand
Tasman District *see* Tasman
192 I13 **Tasman Fracture Zone** *tectonic feature* S Indian Ocean
185 E19 **Tasman Glacier** *glacier* South Island, New Zealand
Tasman Group *see* Nukumanu Islands
183 N15 **Tasmania** *prev.* Van Diemen's Land. ◈ *state* SE Australia
183 Q16 **Tasmania** *island* SE Australia
185 H14 **Tasman Mountains** ▲▲ South Island, New Zealand
183 P17 **Tasman Peninsula** *peninsula* Tasmania, SE Australia
192 I11 **Tasman Plain** *undersea feature* W Tasman Sea
192 I12 **Tasman Plateau** *var.* South Tasmania Plateau. *undersea feature* SW Tasman Sea
192 I11 **Tasman Sea** *sea* SW Pacific Ocean
116 G9 **Tăşnad** *Ger.* Trestenberg, Trestendorf, *Hung.* Tasnád. Satu Mare, NW Romania *47°30′N 22°33′E*
136 L11 **Taşova** Amasya, N Turkey *40°45′N 36°20′E*
77 T10 **Tassara** Tahoua, W Niger *16°40′N 05°34′E*
12 K4 **Tassialouc, Lac** ◎ Québec, C Canada
Tassili du Hoggar *see* Tassili Ta-n-Ahaggar
74 L11 **Tassili-n-Ajjer** *plateau* E Algeria
74 K14 **Tassili Ta-n-Ahaggar** *var.* Tassili du Hoggar, Tassili ta-n-Ahaggar. *plateau* S Algeria
Tassili ta-n-Ahaggar *see* Tassili Ta-n-Ahaggar
59 M15 **Tasso Fragoso** Maranhão, E Brazil *08°22′S 45°53′W*
Tåstrup *see* Taastrup
145 O9 **Tasty-Taldy** Akmola, C Kazakhstan *50°47′N 66°31′E*
143 W10 **Tāsūkī** Sīstān va Balūchestān, SE Iran
111 I22 **Tata** *Ger.* Totis. Komárom-Esztergom, NW Hungary *47°39′N 18°19′E*
74 E8 **Tata** SW Morocco *29°38′N 08°04′W*
Tataaihoa, Pointe *see* Vénus, Pointe
111 I22 **Tatabánya** Komárom-Esztergom, NW Hungary *47°33′N 18°23′E*
191 X10 **Tatakoto** *atoll* Îles Tuamotu, E French Polynesia
75 N7 **Tataouine** *var.* Taţāwīn. SE Tunisia *32°48′N 10°27′E*
55 O5 **Tataracual, Cerro** ▲ NE Venezuela *10°13′N 64°20′W*
117 O12 **Tatarbunary** Odes'ka Oblast', SW Ukraine *45°50′N 29°37′E*
119 M17 **Tatarka** Mahilyowskaya Voblasts', E Belarus *53°15′N 28°50′E*
Tatar Pazardzhik *see* Pazardzhik
122 I12 **Tatarsk** Novosibirskaya Oblast', C Russian Federation *55°08′N 75°58′E*
Tatarskaya ASSR *see* Tatarstan, Respublika
123 T13 **Tatarskiy Proliv** *Eng.* Tatar Strait. *strait* SE Russian Federation
127 R4 **Tatarstan, Respublika** *prev.* Tatarskaya ASSR. ◈ *autonomous republic* W Russian Federation
Tatar Strait *see* Tatarskiy Proliv
Taţāwīn *see* Tataouine
171 N12 **Tate** Sulawesi, N Indonesia *0°12′S 119°44′E*
141 N11 **Tathlīth** 'Asīr, S Saudi Arabia *19°38′N 43°32′E*
141 O11 **Tathlīth, Wādī** *dry watercourse* S Saudi Arabia
183 R11 **Tathra** New South Wales, SE Australia *36°46′S 149°58′E*
127 P8 **Tatishchevo** Saratovskaya Oblast', W Russian Federation *51°43′N 45°35′E*
39 S12 **Tatitlek** Alaska, USA *60°49′N 146°29′W*
10 L15 **Tatla Lake** British Columbia, SW Canada *51°54′N 124°39′W*
121 Q2 **Tatlısu** *Gk.* Akanthoú. N Cyprus *35°21′N 33°45′E*
11 Z10 **Tatnam, Cape** *headland* Manitoba, C Canada *57°16′N 91°03′W*
111 K18 **Tatra Mountains** *Ger.* Tatra, *Hung.* Tátra, *Pol./Slvk.* Tatry. ▲▲ Poland/Slovakia
Tatra/Tátra *see* Tatra Mountains
Tatry *see* Tatra Mountains
164 I13 **Tatsuno** *var.* Tatuno. Hyōgo, Honshū, SW Japan *34°54′N 134°30′E*
Tatti *see* Tatty
145 S16 **Tatty** *prev.* Tatti. Zhambyl, S Kazakhstan *43°11′N 73°22′E*
60 L10 **Tatuí** São Paulo, S Brazil *23°21′S 47°49′W*
37 V14 **Tatum** New Mexico, SW USA *33°15′N 103°19′W*
25 X7 **Tatum** Texas, SW USA *32°19′N 94°31′W*
Ta-t'ung/Tatung *see* Datong
Tatuno *see* Tatsuno
137 R14 **Tatvan** Bitlis, SE Turkey *38°31′N 42°15′E*
95 C16 **Tau** Rogaland, S Norway *59°04′N 05°55′E*
192 L17 **Ta'ū** *var.* Tau. *island* Manua Islands, E American Samoa
193 W15 **Tau** *island* Tongatapu Group, N Tonga
59 O14 **Tauá** Ceará, E Brazil *06°04′S 40°26′W*
60 N10 **Taubaté** São Paulo, S Brazil *23°S 45°36′W*
101 I19 **Tauber** ≈ SW Germany
101 I19 **Tauberbischofsheim** Baden-Württemberg, C Germany *49°37′N 09°39′E*
Tauchik *see* Taushyk
191 W10 **Tauere** *atoll* Îles Tuamotu, C French Polynesia
101 H17 **Taufstein** ▲ C Germany *50°31′N 09°18′E*
190 I17 **Taukoka** *island* SE Cook Islands
145 T15 **Taukum, Peski** *desert* SE Kazakhstan
184 L10 **Taumarunui** Manawatu-Wanganui, North Island, New Zealand *38°52′S 175°14′E*
59 A15 **Taumaturgo** Acre, W Brazil *08°54′S 72°48′W*
27 X6 **Taum Sauk Mountain** ▲ Missouri, C USA *37°34′N 90°43′W*
83 H22 **Taung** North-West, N South Africa *27°32′S 24°48′E*
166 L6 **Taungdwingyi** Magway, C Burma (Myanmar) *20°01′N 95°20′E*
166 M6 **Taunggyi** Shan State, C Burma (Myanmar) *20°47′N 97°00′E*
166 M7 **Taungoo** Bago, C Burma (Myanmar) *18°57′N 96°26′E*
166 L5 **Taungtha** Mandalay, C Burma (Myanmar) *21°16′N 95°25′E*
Taungup *see* Toungup
149 S9 **Taunsa** Punjab, E Pakistan *30°43′N 70°41′E*
97 K23 **Taunton** SW England, United Kingdom *51°01′N 03°06′W*
19 O12 **Taunton** Massachusetts, NE USA *41°54′N 71°03′W*
101 F18 **Taunus** ▲▲ W Germany
101 G18 **Taunusstein** Hessen, W Germany *50°09′N 08°09′E*
184 N9 **Taupo** Waikato, North Island, New Zealand *38°42′S 176°05′E*
184 M9 **Taupo, Lake** ◎ North Island, New Zealand
109 R8 **Taurach** *var.* Taurachbach. ≈ E Austria
Taurachbach *see* Taurach
118 D12 **Tauragė** *Ger.* Tauroggen. Tauragė, SW Lithuania *55°16′N 22°17′E*
118 D13 **Tauragė** ◈ *province* Lithuania
54 G10 **Tauramena** Casanare, C Colombia *05°02′N 72°43′W*
184 N7 **Tauranga** Bay of Plenty, North Island, New Zealand *37°42′S 176°09′E*
15 O10 **Taureau, Réservoir** ▣ Québec, SE Canada
107 N22 **Taurianova** Calabria, SW Italy *38°22′N 16°01′E*
Tauris *see* Tabrīz
184 I2 **Tauroa Point** *headland* North Island, New Zealand *35°09′S 173°02′E*
Tauroggen *see* Tauragė
Tauromenium *see* Taormina
Taurus Mountains *see* Toros Dağları
Taus *see* Domažlice
144 E14 **Taushyk** *Kaz.* Taūshyq; *prev.* Tauchik. Mangistau, SW Kazakhstan *44°17′N 51°22′E*
Taūshyq *see* Taushyk
105 R5 **Tauste** Aragón, NE Spain *41°55′N 01°15′W*
191 V16 **Tautara, Motu** *island* Easter Island, Chile, E Pacific Ocean
191 R8 **Tautira** Tahiti, W French Polynesia *17°45′S 149°10′W*
Tauz *see* Tovuz
Tavālesh, Kūhhā-ye *see* Talish Mountains
136 D15 **Tavas** Denizli, SW Turkey *37°33′N 29°04′E*
Tavastehus *see* Hämeenlinna
Tavau *see* Davos
122 G10 **Tavda** Sverdlovskaya Oblast', C Russian Federation *58°01′N 65°07′E*
122 G10 **Tavda** ≈ C Russian Federation
105 T11 **Tavernes de la Valldigna** Valenciana, E Spain *39°03′N 00°13′W*
81 I20 **Taveta** Coast, S Kenya *03°23′S 37°40′E*
187 Y14 **Taveuni** *island* N Fiji
147 R13 **Tavildara** *Rus.* Tavil'dara, Tovil'-Dora. C Tajikistan *38°42′N 70°27′E*
Tavin *see* Adaatsag
104 H14 **Tavira** Faro, S Portugal *37°07′N 07°39′W*
97 I24 **Tavistock** SW England, United Kingdom *50°33′N 04°08′W*
Tavoy *see* Dawei
Tavoy Island *see* Mali Kyun
115 E16 **Tavropoú, Techníti Límni** ▣ C Greece
136 E13 **Tavşanlı** Kütahya, NW Turkey *39°34′N 29°28′E*
187 X14 **Tavua** Viti Levu, W Fiji *17°27′S 177°51′E*
97 J23 **Taw** ≈ SW England, United Kingdom
185 L14 **Tawa** Wellington, North Island, New Zealand *41°10′S 174°50′E*
25 V6 **Tawakoni, Lake** ▣ Texas, SW USA
153 V11 **Tawang** Arunāchal Pradesh, NE India *27°34′N 91°54′E*
169 R17 **Tawang, Teluk** *bay* Jawa, S Indonesia
31 R7 **Tawas Bay** ◎ Michigan, N USA
31 R7 **Tawas City** Michigan, N USA *44°16′N 83°33′W*
169 V8 **Tawau** Sabah, East Malaysia *04°16′N 117°54′E*
141 U10 **Ţawīl, Qalamat aţ** *well* SE Saudi Arabia
171 N9 **Tawitawi** *island* Tawitawi Group, SW Philippines
Ţawkar *see* Tokar
Tawŭq *see* Dāqūq
Tawzar *see* Tozeur
41 O15 **Taxco** *var.* Taxco de Alarcón. Guerrero, S Mexico *18°32′N 99°37′W*
Taxco de Alarcón *see* Taxco
146 H8 **Taxiatosh** *Rus.* Takhiatash. Qoraqalpog'iston Respublikasi, W Uzbekistan *42°27′N 59°27′E*
158 D9 **Taxkorgan** *var.* Taxkorgan Tajik Zizhixian. Xinjiang Uygur Zizhiqu, NW China *37°43′N 75°13′E*
Taxkorgan Tajik Zizhixian *see* Taxkorgan
146 H7 **Taxtako'pir** *Rus.* Takhtakupyr. Qoraqalpog'iston Respublikasi, NW Uzbekistan *43°04′N 60°23′E*
96 J10 **Tay** ≈ C Scotland, United Kingdom
143 V6 **Tāybād** *var.* Taibad, Tāyybād, Tayyebāt. Khorāsān-Razavī, NE Iran *34°48′N 60°46′E*
Taybert at Turkz *see* Ţayyibah at Turkī
124 J3 **Taybola** Murmanskaya Oblast', NW Russian Federation *68°30′N 33°18′E*
81 M16 **Tayeeglow** Bakool, C Somalia *04°01′N 44°25′E*
96 K11 **Tay, Firth of** *inlet* E Scotland, United Kingdom
122 J12 **Tayga** Kemerovskaya Oblast', S Russian Federation *56°02′N 85°26′E*
Taygan *see* Delger
123 T9 **Taygonos, Mys** *headland* E Russian Federation *60°36′N 160°09′E*
96 I11 **Tay, Loch** ◎ C Scotland, United Kingdom
11 N12 **Taylor** British Columbia, W Canada *56°09′N 120°43′W*
29 O14 **Taylor** Nebraska, C USA *41°47′N 99°23′W*
18 I13 **Taylor** Pennsylvania, NE USA *41°22′N 75°41′W*
25 T10 **Taylor** Texas, SW USA *30°34′N 97°24′W*
37 Q11 **Taylor, Mount** ▲ New Mexico, SW USA *35°14′N 107°36′W*
37 R5 **Taylor Park Reservoir** ▣ Colorado, C USA
37 R6 **Taylor River** ≈ Colorado, C USA
21 P11 **Taylors** South Carolina, SE USA *34°55′N 82°18′W*
20 L5 **Taylorsville** Kentucky, S USA *38°01′N 85°21′W*
21 R6 **Taylorsville** North Carolina, SE USA *35°56′N 81°10′W*
30 L14 **Taylorville** Illinois, N USA *39°33′N 89°17′W*
140 K5 **Taymā'** Tabūk, NW Saudi Arabia *27°39′N 38°32′E*
122 M10 **Taymura** ≈ C Russian Federation
123 O7 **Taymylyr** Respublika Sakha (Yakutiya), NE Russian Federation *72°32′N 121°54′E*
122 L7 **Taymyr, Ozero** ◎ N Russian Federation
122 M6 **Taymyr, Poluostrov** *peninsula* N Russian Federation
122 L8 **Taymyrskiy (Dolgano-Nenetskiy) Avtonomnyy Okrug** ◈ *autonomous district* Krasnoyarskiy Kray, N Russian Federation
167 S13 **Tây Ninh** Tây Ninh, S Vietnam *11°21′N 106°07′E*
122 L12 **Tayshet** Irkutskaya Oblast', S Russian Federation *55°51′N 98°04′E*
162 G8 **Tayshir** *var.* Tsagaan-Olom. Govi-Altay, C Mongolia *46°42′N 96°30′E*
171 N5 **Taytay** Palawan, W Philippines *10°49′N 119°30′E*
169 Q16 **Tayu** *prev.* Tajoe. Jawa, C Indonesia *06°32′S 111°02′E*
Tayybād/Tayyebāt *see* Tāybād
138 L5 **Ţayyibah** *var.* At Taybé. Ḩimş, C Syria *35°13′N 38°51′E*
138 I4 **Ţayyibat at Turkī** *var.* Taybert at Turkz. Ḩamāh, W Syria *35°16′N 36°55′E*
145 P7 **Tayynsha** *prev.* Krasnoarmeysk. Severnyy Kazakhstan, N Kazakhstan *53°52′N 69°51′E*
122 J10 **Taz** ≈ N Russian Federation
74 G6 **Taza** NE Morocco *34°13′N 04°06′W*
139 T4 **Tāza Khurmātū** At Ta'mīm, E Iraq *35°18′N 44°22′E*
165 Q8 **Tazawa-ko** ◎ Honshū, C Japan
21 N8 **Tazewell** Tennessee, S USA *36°27′N 83°34′W*
21 Q7 **Tazewell** Virginia, NE USA *37°08′N 81°34′W*
75 S11 **Tāzirbū** SE Libya *25°43′N 21°16′E*
39 S11 **Tazlina Lake** ◎ Alaska, USA
122 J8 **Tazovskiy** Yamalo-Nenetskiy Avtonomnyy Okrug, N Russian Federation *67°33′N 78°21′E*
137 U10 **Tbilisi** *Eng.* Tiflis. ● (Georgia) SE Georgia *41°41′N 44°55′E*
137 T10 **Tbilisi** ✈ S Georgia *41°43′N 44°49′E*
79 E14 **Tchabal Mbabo** ▲ NW Cameroon *07°12′N 12°16′E*
Tchad *see* Chad
Tchad, Lac *see* Chad, Lake
77 S15 **Tchaourou** E Benin *08°58′N 02°40′E*
79 E20 **Tchibanga** Nyanga, S Gabon *02°49′S 11°00′E*
Tchien *see* Zwedru
77 Z6 **Tchigaï, Plateau du** ▲ NE Niger
77 V9 **Tchighozérine** Agadez, C Niger *17°15′N 07°48′E*
77 T10 **Tchin-Tabaradene** Tahoua, W Niger *15°57′N 05°49′E*
78 G13 **Tcholliré** Nord, NE Cameroon *08°48′N 14°00′E*
Tchongking *see* Chongqing
22 K4 **Tchula** Mississippi, S USA *33°10′N 90°13′W*
110 I7 **Tczew** *Ger.* Dirschau. Pomorskie, N Poland *54°05′N 18°46′E*
116 I10 **Teaca** *Ger.* Tekendorf, *Hung.* Teke; *prev. Ger.* Teckendorf. Bistriţa-Năsăud, N Romania *46°55′N 24°30′E*
40 J11 **Teacapán** Sinaloa, C Mexico *22°33′N 105°44′W*
190 A10 **Teafuafou** *island* Funafuti Atoll, C Tuvalu
25 U8 **Teague** Texas, SW USA *31°37′N 96°16′W*
191 R9 **Teahupoo** Tahiti, W French Polynesia *17°51′S 149°15′W*
190 H15 **Te Aiti Point** *headland* Rarotonga, S Cook Islands *21°11′S 159°47′W*
65 D24 **Teal Inlet** East Falkland, Falkland Islands *51°34′S 58°25′W*
185 B22 **Te Anau** Southland, South Island, New Zealand *45°25′S 167°45′E*
185 B22 **Te Anau, Lake** ◎ South Island, New Zealand
41 U15 **Teapa** Tabasco, SE Mexico *17°36′N 92°57′W*
184 Q7 **Te Araroa** Gisborne, North Island, New Zealand *37°37′S 178°21′E*
184 M7 **Te Aroha** Waikato, North Island, New Zealand *37°32′S 175°58′E*
Teate *see* Chieti
190 A9 **Te Ava Fuagea** *channel* Funafuti Atoll, SE Tuvalu
190 B8 **Te Ava I Te Lape** *channel* Funafuti Atoll, SE Tuvalu
190 B9 **Te Ava Pua Pua** *channel* Funafuti Atoll, SE Tuvalu
184 M8 **Te Awamutu** Waikato, North Island, New Zealand *38°00′S 177°18′E*
171 X12 **Teba** Papua, E Indonesia *01°27′S 137°54′E*
104 L15 **Teba** Andalucía, S Spain *36°59′N 04°54′W*
126 M15 **Teberda** Karachayevo-Cherkesskaya Respublika, SW Russian Federation *43°28′N 41°45′E*
74 M6 **Tébessa** NE Algeria *35°21′N 08°06′E*
62 O7 **Tebicuary, Río** ≈ S Paraguay
168 L13 **Tebingtinggi** Sumatera, W Indonesia *03°33′S 103°00′E*
168 I8 **Tebingtinggi** Sumatera, N Indonesia *03°20′N 99°08′E*
Tebingtinggi, Pulau *see* Rantau, Pulau
Tebriz *see* Tabrīz
137 U9 **T'ebulos Mta** *Rus.* Gora Tebulosmta. ▲ Georgia/Russian Federation *42°33′N 45°21′E*
Tebulos Mta *see* T'ebulos Mta
Tebulosmta, Gora *see* T'ebulos Mta
41 Q14 **Tecamachalco** Puebla, S Mexico *18°52′N 97°44′W*
40 B1 **Tecate** Baja California Norte, NW Mexico *32°33′N 116°38′W*
136 M13 **Tecer Dağları** ▲ C Turkey
103 O17 **Tech** ≈ S France
77 P16 **Techiman** W Ghana *07°35′N 01°56′W*
117 N15 **Techirghiol** Constanţa, SE Romania *44°03′N 28°37′E*
74 A12 **Techla** *var.* Techlé. SW Western Sahara *21°39′N 14°57′W*
Techlé *see* Techla
63 H18 **Tecka, Sierra de** ▲▲ SW Argentina
Teckendorf *see* Teaca
40 K13 **Tecolotlán** Jalisco, SW Mexico *20°10′N 104°07′W*
40 K14 **Tecomán** Colima, SW Mexico *18°53′N 103°54′W*
35 V12 **Tecopa** California, W USA *35°51′N 116°14′W*
40 G5 **Tecoripa** Sonora, NW Mexico *28°38′N 109°58′W*
41 N16 **Tecpan** *var.* Tecpan de Galeana. Guerrero, S Mexico *17°12′N 100°39′W*
Tecpan de Galeana *see* Tecpan
40 J11 **Tecuala** Nayarit, C Mexico *22°24′N 105°30′W*
116 L12 **Tecuci** Galaţi, E Romania *45°50′N 27°27′E*
31 R10 **Tecumseh** Michigan, N USA *42°00′N 83°57′W*
29 S16 **Tecumseh** Nebraska, C USA *40°22′N 96°12′W*
27 O11 **Tecumseh** Oklahoma, C USA *35°15′N 96°56′W*
Tedzhen *see* Harīrūd/Tejen
Tedzhen *see* Tejen
146 H15 **Tedzhenstroy** *Turkm.* Tejenstroy. Ahal Welaýaty, S Turkmenistan *36°57′N 60°49′E*
Teel *see* Öndör-Ulaan
97 L15 **Tees** ≈ N England, United Kingdom
14 E15 **Teeswater** Ontario, S Canada *44°00′N 81°17′W*
190 A10 **Tefala** *island* Funafuti Atoll, C Tuvalu
58 D13 **Tefé** Amazonas, N Brazil *03°24′S 64°45′W*
74 K11 **Tefedest** ▲ S Algeria
136 E16 **Tefenni** Burdur, SW Turkey *37°19′N 29°45′E*
58 D13 **Tefé, Rio** ≈ NW Brazil
169 P16 **Tegal** Jawa, C Indonesia *06°52′S 109°07′E*
100 O12 **Tegel** ✈ (Berlin) Berlin, NE Germany *52°33′N 13°16′E*
99 M15 **Tegelen** Limburg, SE Netherlands *51°20′N 06°09′E*
101 L24 **Tegernsee** ◎ SE Germany
107 M18 **Teggiano** Campania, S Italy *40°25′N 15°28′E*
77 U14 **Tegina** Niger, C Nigeria *10°06′N 06°10′E*
Tegucigalpa *see* Central District
Tegucigalpa *see* Toncontín
Tegucigalpa *see* Francisco Morazán
77 U9 **Teguidda-n-Tessoumt** Agadez, C Niger *17°27′N 06°40′E*
64 Q11 **Teguise** Lanzarote, Islas Canarias, Spain, NE Atlantic Ocean *29°04′N 13°38′W*
122 K12 **Tegul'det** Tomskaya Oblast', C Russian Federation *57°16′N 87°58′E*
35 S13 **Tehachapi** California, W USA *35°07′N 118°27′W*
35 S13 **Tehachapi Mountains** ▲▲ California, W USA
Tehama *see* Tihāmah
Teheran *see* Tehrān
77 O14 **Téhini** NE Ivory Coast *09°36′N 03°40′W*
143 N5 **Tehrān** *var.* Teheran. ● (Iran) Tehrān, N Iran *35°44′N 51°27′E*
143 N6 **Tehrān** *off.* Ostān-e Tehrān, *var.* Tehran. ◈ *province* N Iran
Tehrān, Ostān-e *see* Tehrān
Tehri *see* Tikamgarh
Tehri *see* New Tehri
41 Q15 **Tehuacán** Puebla, S Mexico *18°29′N 97°24′W*
41 S17 **Tehuantepec** *var.* Santo Domingo Tehuantepec. Oaxaca, SE Mexico *16°18′N 95°14′W*
41 S17 **Tehuantepec, Golfo de** *var.* Gulf of Tehuantepec. *gulf* S Mexico
Tehuantepec, Gulf of *see* Tehuantepec, Golfo de
Tehuantepec, Isthmus of *see* Tehuantepec, Istmo de
41 T16 **Tehuantepec, Istmo de** *var.* Isthmus of Tehuantepec. *isthmus* SE Mexico
0 I16 **Tehuantepec Ridge** *undersea feature* E Pacific Ocean *13°30′N 98°00′W*
41 S16 **Tehuantepec, Río** ≈ SE Mexico
191 W10 **Tehuata** *atoll* Îles Tuamotu, C French Polynesia
64 O11 **Teide, Pico del** ▲ Gran Canaria, Islas Canarias, Spain, NE Atlantic Ocean *28°16′N 16°39′W*
97 I21 **Teifi** ≈ SW Wales, United Kingdom
80 B9 **Teiga Plateau** *plateau* W Sudan
97 J24 **Teignmouth** SW England, United Kingdom *50°34′N 03°29′W*
Teisen *see* Jecheon
116 H11 **Teiuş** *Ger.* Dreikirchen, *Hung.* Tövis. Alba, C Romania *46°12′N 23°40′E*
169 U17 **Tejakula** Bali, C Indonesia *08°09′S 115°19′E*
146 H14 **Tejen** *Rus.* Tedzhen. Ahal Welaýaty, S Turkmenistan *37°24′N 60°29′E*
146 I15 **Tejen** *Per.* Harīrūd, *Rus.* Tedzhen. ≈ Afghanistan/Iran *see also* Harīrūd
Tejen *see* Harīrūd
Tejenstroy *see* Tedzhenstroy
35 S14 **Tejon Pass** *pass* California, W USA
Tejo, Rio *see* Tagus
41 O14 **Tejupilco** *var.* Tejupilco de Hidalgo. México, S Mexico *18°55′N 100°10′W*
Tejupilco de Hidalgo *see* Tejupilco
184 P7 **Te Kaha** Bay of Plenty, North Island, New Zealand *37°45′S 177°42′E*
29 S14 **Tekamah** Nebraska, C USA *41°46′N 96°13′W*
184 I1 **Te Kao** Northland, North Island, New Zealand *34°40′S 172°57′E*
185 F20 **Tekapo** ≈ South Island, New Zealand
185 F19 **Tekapo, Lake** ◎ South Island, New Zealand
184 P9 **Te Karaka** Gisborne, North Island, New Zealand *38°30′S 177°52′E*
184 L7 **Te Kauwhata** Waikato, North Island, New Zealand *37°22′S 175°07′E*
41 X12 **Tekax** *var.* Tekax de Álvaro Obregón. Yucatán, SE Mexico *20°07′N 89°10′W*
Tekax de Álvaro Obregón *see* Tekax
136 A14 **Teke Burnu** *headland* W Turkey *38°06′N 26°35′E*
114 M12 **Teke Deresi** ≈ NW Turkey
146 D10 **Tekedzhik, Gory** *hill range* NW Turkmenistan
145 V14 **Tekeli** Almaty, SE Kazakhstan *44°50′N 78°47′E*
145 R7 **Teke, Ozero** ◎ N Kazakhstan
158 I5 **Tekes** Xinjiang Uygur Zizhiqu, NW China *43°15′N 81°43′E*
145 W16 **Tekes** Almaty, SE Kazakhstan *42°40′N 80°01′E*
Tekes *see* Tekes He
158 H5 **Tekes He** *Rus.* Tekes. ≈ China/Kazakhstan
Teke/Tekendorf *see* Teaca
80 I10 **Tekezē** *var.* Takkaze. ≈ Eritrea/Ethiopia
Tekhtin *see* Tsyakhtsin
136 C10 **Tekirdağ** *It.* Rodosto; *anc.* Bisanthe, Raidestos, Rhaedestus. Tekirdağ, NW Turkey *40°59′N 27°31′E*
136 C10 **Tekirdağ** ◈ *province* NW Turkey
155 N14 **Tekkali** Andhra Pradesh, E India *18°37′N 84°15′E*
115 K15 **Tekke Burnu** *Turk.* İlyasbaba Burnu. *headland* NW Turkey *40°03′N 26°12′E*
137 Q13 **Tekman** Erzurum, NE Turkey *39°39′N 41°31′E*
32 M9 **Tekoa** Washington, NW USA *47°13′N 117°05′W*
190 H16 **Te Kou** ▲ Rarotonga, S Cook Islands *21°14′S 159°46′W*
Tekrit *see* Tikrīt
171 P12 **Teku** Sulawesi, N Indonesia *0°46′S 123°25′E*
184 L9 **Te Kuiti** Waikato, North Island, New Zealand *38°21′S 175°10′E*
42 H4 **Tela** Atlántida, NW Honduras *15°46′N 87°25′W*
138 F12 **Telalim** Southern, S Israel *30°58′N 34°47′E*
Telanaipura *see* Jambi
137 U10 **Telavi** *prev.* T'elavi. E Georgia *41°55′N 45°29′E*
T'elavi *see* Telavi
138 F10 **Tel Aviv** ◈ *district* W Israel
Tel Aviv-Jaffa *see* Tel Aviv-Yafo
138 F10 **Tel Aviv-Yafo** *var.* Tel Aviv-Jaffa. Tel Aviv, C Israel *32°05′N 34°46′E*
111 E18 **Telč** *Ger.* Teltsch. Vysočina, C Czech Republic *49°10′N 15°28′E*
186 B6 **Telefomin** Sandaun, NW Papua New Guinea *05°08′S 141°31′E*
10 J10 **Telegraph Creek** British Columbia, W Canada *57°56′N 131°10′W*
190 B10 **Telele** *island* Funafuti Atoll, C Tuvalu
60 J11 **Telêmaco Borba** Paraná, S Brazil *24°20′S 50°44′W*
95 E15 **Telemark** ◈ *county* S Norway
62 J13 **Telén** La Pampa, C Argentina *36°20′S 65°31′W*
Teleneshty *see* Teleneşti
116 M9 **Teleneşti** *Rus.* Teleneshty. C Moldova *47°35′N 28°20′E*
104 J4 **Teleno, El** ▲ NW Spain *42°19′N 06°21′W*
116 I15 **Teleorman** ◈ *county* S Romania
116 I14 **Teleorman** ≈ S Romania
25 V5 **Telephone** Texas, SW USA *33°48′N 96°00′W*
35 U11 **Telescope Peak** ▲ California, W USA *36°09′N 117°03′W*
Teles Pirés *see* São Manuel, Rio
97 L19 **Telford** W England, United Kingdom *52°42′N 02°28′W*
108 L7 **Telfs** Tirol, W Austria *47°19′N 11°05′E*
42 I9 **Telica** León, NW Nicaragua *12°30′N 86°52′W*
42 J6 **Telica, Río** ≈ C Honduras
76 I13 **Télimélé** W Guinea *10°45′N 13°02′W*
43 O14 **Telire, Río** ≈ Costa Rica/Panama
114 I8 **Telish** *prev.* Azizie. Pleven, N Bulgaria *43°20′N 24°15′E*
41 R16 **Telixtlahuaca** *var.* San Francisco Telixtlahuaca. Oaxaca, SE Mexico *17°18′N 96°54′W*
10 K13 **Telkwa** British Columbia, SW Canada *54°39′N 126°51′W*
25 P4 **Tell** Texas, SW USA *34°18′N 100°20′W*
Tell Abiad *see* Tall Abyaḑ
Tell Abiad/Tell Abyad *see* At Tall al Abyaḑ
31 O16 **Tell City** Indiana, N USA *37°56′N 86°47′W*
38 M9 **Teller** Alaska, USA *65°15′N 166°21′W*
Tell Huqnah *see* Tall Ḩuqnah
155 F20 **Tellicherry** *var.* Thalashsheri, Thalassery. Kerala, SW India *11°44′N 75°29′E see also* Thalassery
20 M10 **Tellico Plains** Tennessee, S USA *35°19′N 84°18′W*
Tell Kalakh *see* Tall Kalakh
Tell Mardikh *see* Ebla
54 E11 **Tello** Huila, C Colombia *03°06′N 75°08′W*
Tell Shedadi *see* Ash Shadādah
37 Q7 **Telluride** Colorado, C USA *37°56′N 107°48′W*
117 X9 **Tel'manove** Donets'ka Oblast', E Ukraine *47°24′N 38°03′E*
Tel'man/Tel'mansk *see* Gubadag
162 H6 **Telmen** *var.* Övögdiy. Dzavhan, C Mongolia *48°38′N 97°39′E*
162 H6 **Telmen Nuur** ◎ NW Mongolia
Teloekbetoeng *see* Bandar Lampung
41 O15 **Teloloapán** Guerrero, S Mexico *18°21′N 99°52′W*
Telo Martius *see* Toulon
Telposiz, Gora *see* Telpoziz, Gora
125 V8 **Telpoziz, Gora** *prev.* Gora Telposiz. ▲ NW Russian Federation *63°52′N 59°15′E*
Telschen *see* Telšiai
63 J17 **Telsen** Chubut, S Argentina *42°27′S 66°59′W*
118 D11 **Telšiai** *Ger.* Telschen. Telšiai, NW Lithuania *55°59′N 22°21′E*
118 D11 **Telšiai** ◈ *province* NW Lithuania
Teltsch *see* Telč
Telukbetung *see* Bandar Lampung
168 H10 **Telukdalam** Pulau Nias, W Indonesia *0°34′N 97°47′E*
14 H9 **Temagami** Ontario, S Canada *47°03′N 79°47′W*
14 G9 **Temagami, Lake** ◎ Ontario, S Canada
190 H16 **Te Manga** ▲ Rarotonga, S Cook Islands *21°13′S 159°45′W*
191 W12 **Tematangi** *prev.* Tematagi. *atoll* Îles Tuamotu, S French Polynesia
Tematagi *see* Tematangi
41 X11 **Temax** Yucatán, SE Mexico *21°10′N 88°53′W*
171 E14 **Tembagapura** Papua, E Indonesia *04°10′S 137°19′E*
129 U5 **Tembenchi** ≈ N Russian Federation
55 P6 **Temblador** Monagas, NE Venezuela *08°59′N 62°44′W*
105 N9 **Tembleque** Castilla-La Mancha, C Spain *39°41′N 03°30′W*
Temboni *see* Mitemele, Río
35 U16 **Temecula** California, W USA *33°29′N 117°09′W*
168 K7 **Temengor, Tasik** ◎ Peninsular Malaysia
112 L9 **Temerin** Vojvodina, N Serbia *45°25′N 19°54′E*
Temeschburg/Temeschwar *see* Timişoara
Temes-Kubin *see* Kovin
Temes/Temesch *see* Tamiš

◆ Country
● Country Capital
◇ Dependent Territory
○ Dependent Territory Capital
◈ Administrative Regions
✈ International Airport
▲ Mountain
▲▲ Mountain Range
※ Volcano
≈ River
◎ Lake
▣ Reservoir

Temesvár/Temeswar *see* Timișoara
Teminaboean *see* Teminabuan
171 U12 **Teminabuan** *prev.* Teminaboean. Papua, E Indonesia 01°30´S 131°59´E
145 P17 **Temirlan** *prev.* Temirlanovka. Yuzhnyy Kazakhstan, S Kazakhstan 42°36´N 69°17´E
Temirlanovka *see* Temirlan
145 R10 **Temirtau** *prev.* Samarkandski, Samarkandskoye. Karaganda, C Kazakhstan 50°05´N 72°55´E
14 H10 **Témiscaming** Québec, SE Canada 46°40´N 79°04´W
Témiscamingue, Lac *see* Timiskaming, Lake
15 T8 **Témiscouata, Lac** Québec, SE Canada
127 N5 **Temnikov** Respublika Mordoviya, W Russian Federation 54°39´N 43°09´E
191 Y13 **Temoe** *island* Îles Gambier, E French Polynesia
183 Q9 **Temora** New South Wales, SE Australia 34°28´S 147°33´E
40 H7 **Témoris** Chihuahua, W Mexico 27°16´N 108°15´W
40 I5 **Temósachic** Chihuahua, N Mexico 28°55´N 107°42´W
187 Q10 **Temotu** *var.* Temotu Province. ❖ *province* E Solomon Islands
Temotu Province *see* Temotu
36 L14 **Tempe** Arizona, SW USA 33°24´N 111°54´W
Tempelburg *see* Czaplinek
107 C17 **Tempio Pausania** Sardegna, Italy, C Mediterranean Sea 40°55´N 09°07´E
42 K12 **Tempisque, Río** NW Costa Rica
25 T9 **Temple** Texas, SW USA 31°06´N 97°22´W
100 O12 **Templehof** ✈ (Berlin) Berlin, NE Germany 52°28´N 13°24´E
97 D19 **Templemore** *Ir.* An Teampall Mór. Tipperary, C Ireland 52°48´N 07°50´W
100 O11 **Templin** Brandenburg, NE Germany 53°07´N 13°31´E
41 P12 **Tempoal** *var.* Tempoal de Sánchez. Veracruz-Llave, E Mexico 21°32´N 98°23´W
Tempoal de Sánchez *see* Tempoal
41 P13 **Tempoal, Río** C Mexico
83 E14 **Tempué** Moxico, C Angola 13°36´S 18°56´E
126 J14 **Temryuk** Krasnodarskiy Kray, SW Russian Federation 45°15´N 37°26´E
99 G17 **Temse** Oost-Vlaanderen, N Belgium 51°08´N 04°13´E
63 F15 **Temuco** Araucanía, C Chile 38°45´S 72°37´W
185 G20 **Temuka** Canterbury, South Island, New Zealand 44°14´S 171°17´E
189 P13 **Temwen Island** *island* E Micronesia
56 C6 **Tena** Napo, C Ecuador 01°00´S 77°48´W
41 W13 **Tenabo** Campeche, E Mexico 20°02´N 90°12´W
Tenaghau *see* Aola
25 X7 **Tenaha** Texas, SW USA 31°56´N 94°14´W
39 X13 **Tenake** Chichagof Island, Alaska, USA 57°46´N 135°13´W
155 K16 **Tenāli** Andhra Pradesh, E India 16°13´N 80°36´E
Tenan *see* Cheonan
41 O14 **Tenancingo** *var.* Tenencingo de Degollado. México, S Mexico 18°57´N 99°39´W
191 X12 **Tenararo** *island* Groupe Actéon, SE French Polynesia
Tenasserim *see* Tanintharyi
Tenasserim *see* Tanintharyi
98 O5 **Ten Boer** Groningen, NE Netherlands 53°16´N 06°42´E
97 I21 **Tenby** SW Wales, United Kingdom 51°41´N 04°43´W
80 K11 **Tendaho** Āfar, NE Ethiopia 11°39´N 40°59´E
103 V14 **Tende** Alpes Maritimes, SE France 44°04´N 07°34´E
151 Q20 **Ten Degree Channel** *strait* Andaman and Nicobar Islands, India, E Indian Ocean
80 F11 **Tendelti** White Nile, E Sudan 13°01´N 31°55´E
76 G8 **Te-n-Dghâmcha, Sebkhet** *var.* Sebkha de Ndrhamcha, Sebkra de Ndaghamcha. *salt lake* W Mauritania
165 P10 **Tendō** Yamagata, Honshū, C Japan 38°22´N 140°22´E
74 H7 **Tendrara** NE Morocco 33°06´N 01°58´W
117 Q11 **Tendrivs'ka Kosa** *spit* S Ukraine
117 Q11 **Tendrivs'ka Zatoka** *gulf* S Ukraine
Tenencingo de Degollado *see* Tenancingo
77 N11 **Ténenkou** Mopti, C Mali 14°28´N 04°55´W
77 W9 **Ténéré** *physical region* C Niger
77 W9 **Ténére, Erg du** *desert* C Niger
64 O11 **Tenerife** *island* Islas Canarias, Spain, NE Atlantic Ocean
74 J5 **Ténès** NW Algeria 36°35´N 01°18´E
170 M15 **Tengah, Kepulauan** *island group* C Indonesia
Tengcheng *see* Tengxian
169 V11 **Tenggarong** Borneo, C Indonesia 0°23´S 117°00´E
162 J15 **Tengger Shamo** *desert* N China
168 L8 **Tenggul, Pulau** *island* Peninsular Malaysia
Tengiz Köl *see* Teniz, Ozero
76 M14 **Tengréla** *var.* Tingréla. N Ivory Coast 10°26´N 06°20´W
160 M14 **Tengxian** *var.* Tengcheng, Tengxian, Teng Xian. Guangxi Zhuangzu Zizhiqu, S China 23°24´N 110°49´E
Tengxian *see* Tengxian
Teng Xian *see* Tengxian
194 H2 **Teniente Rodolfo Marsh** *Chilean research station* South Shetland Islands, Antarctica 61°57´S 58°23´W
32 G9 **Tenino** Washington, NW USA 46°51´N 122°51´W
145 P9 **Teniz, Ozero** *Kaz.* Tengiz Köl. *salt lake* C Kazakhstan
112 I9 **Tenja** Osijek-Baranja, E Croatia 45°30´N 18°45´E
188 B16 **Tenjo, Mount** ▲ W Guam
155 H23 **Tenkāsi** Tamil Nādu, SE India 08°58´N 77°22´E
79 N24 **Tenke** Katanga, SE Dem. Rep. Congo 10°34´S 26°12´E
Tenke *see* Tinca
123 Q7 **Tenkeli** Respublika Sakha (Yakutiya), NE Russian Federation 70°09´N 140°39´E
27 R10 **Tenkiller Ferry Lake** Oklahoma, C USA
77 Q13 **Tenkodogo** S Burkina 11°54´N 00°19´W
181 Q5 **Tennant Creek** Northern Territory, C Australia 19°40´S 134°16´E
20 G9 **Tennessee** *off.* State of Tennessee, *also known as* The Volunteer State. ❖ *state* SE USA
37 R5 **Tennessee Pass** *pass* Colorado, C USA
20 H10 **Tennessee River** S USA
23 N2 **Tennessee Tombigbee Waterway** *canal* Alabama/Mississippi, S USA
99 K22 **Tenneville** Luxembourg, SE Belgium 50°05´N 05°31´E
92 M11 **Tenniöjoki** NE Finland
92 L9 **Tenojoki** *Lapp.* Deatnu, *Nor.* Tana. Finland/Norway *see also* Deatnu, Tana
Tenojoki *to see* Tana
169 U7 **Tenom** Sabah, East Malaysia 05°07´N 115°57´E
Tenos *see* Tínos
41 V15 **Tenosique** *var.* Tenosique de Pino Suárez. Tabasco, SE Mexico 17°30´N 91°24´W
Tenosique de Pino Suárez *see* Tenosique
22 I6 **Tensas River** Louisiana, S USA
23 O8 **Tensaw River** Alabama, S USA
74 E7 **Tensift** *seasonal river* W Morocco
171 O12 **Tentena** *var.* Tenteno. Sulawesi, C Indonesia 01°46´S 120°40´E
Tenteno *see* Tentena
183 U4 **Tenterfield** New South Wales, SE Australia 29°04´S 152°02´E
23 X16 **Ten Thousand Islands** *island group* Florida, SE USA
60 H9 **Teodoro Sampaio** São Paulo, S Brazil 22°30´S 52°13´W
59 N19 **Teófilo Otoni** *var.* Theophilo Ottoni. Minas Gerais, NE Brazil 17°52´S 41°31´W
116 K5 **Teofipol'** Khmel'nyts'ka Oblast', W Ukraine 50°00´N 26°22´E
Teohatu *see* Toahotu
41 P14 **Teotihuacán** *ruins* México, S Mexico
Teotilán *see* Teotitlán del Camino
41 Q15 **Teotitlán del Camino** *var.* Teotilán. Oaxaca, S Mexico 18°10´N 97°08´W
190 G12 **Tepa** Île Uvea, E Wallis and Futuna 13°19´S 176°09´W
191 P8 **Tepaee, Récif** *reef* Tahiti, W French Polynesia
40 L14 **Tepalcatepec** Michoacán, SW Mexico 19°11´N 102°50´W
190 A16 **Tepa Point** *headland* SW Niue 19°07´S 169°56´E
40 L13 **Tepatitlán** *var.* Tepatitlán de Morelos. Jalisco, SW Mexico 20°50´N 102°46´W
Tepatitlán de Morelos *see* Tepatitlán
40 J9 **Tepehuanes** *var.* Santa Catarina de Tepehuanes. Durango, C Mexico 25°22´N 105°42´W
Tepelena *see* Tepelenë
113 L22 **Tepelenë** *var.* Tepelena, *It.* Tepeleni. Gjirokastër, S Albania 40°18´N 20°00´E
Tepeleni *see* Tepelenë
40 K12 **Tepic** Nayarit, C Mexico 21°30´N 104°55´W
111 C15 **Teplice** *Ger.* Teplitz; *prev.* Teplice-Šanov, Teplitz-Schönau. Ústecký Kraj, NW Czech Republic 50°38´N 13°49´E
Teplice-Šanov/Teplitz/Teplitz-Schönau *see* Teplice
117 O7 **Teplyk** Vinnyts'ka Oblast', C Ukraine 48°40´N 29°46´E
123 R10 **Teplyy Klyuch** Respublika Sakha (Yakutiya), NE Russian Federation 62°46´N 137°01´E
40 E5 **Tepoca, Cabo** *headland* NW Mexico 29°19´N 112°24´W
191 W9 **Tepoto** *island* Îles du Désappointement, C French Polynesia
92 L11 **Tepsa** Lappi, N Finland 67°34´N 25°36´E
190 B8 **Tepuka** *atoll* Funafuti Atoll, C Tuvalu
184 N7 **Te Puke** Bay of Plenty, North Island, New Zealand 37°48´S 176°19´E
40 L13 **Tequila** Jalisco, SW Mexico 20°52´N 103°48´W
41 O13 **Tequisquiapan** Querétaro de Arteaga, C Mexico 20°34´N 99°52´W
77 Q12 **Téra** Tillabéri, W Niger 14°01´N 00°45´E
104 J5 **Tera** NW Spain
191 V1 **Teraina** *prev.* Washington Island. *atoll* Line Islands, E Kiribati
81 F15 **Terakeka** Central Equatoria, S South Sudan 05°26´N 31°45´E
107 J14 **Teramo** *anc.* Interamna. Abruzzi, C Italy 42°40´N 13°43´E
98 P7 **Ter Apel** Groningen, NE Netherlands 52°52´N 07°05´E
104 H11 **Tera, Ribeira de** S Portugal
185 K14 **Terawhiti, Cape** *headland* North Island, New Zealand 41°17´S 174°36´E
98 N12 **Terborg** Gelderland, E Netherlands 51°55´N 06°22´E
137 P13 **Tercan** Erzincan, NE Turkey 39°47´N 40°23´E
64 O2 **Terceira** ✈ Terceira, Azores, Portugal, NE Atlantic Ocean 38°43´N 27°13´W
64 O2 **Terceira** *var.* Ilha Terceira. *island* Azores, Portugal, NE Atlantic Ocean
Terceira, Ilha *see* Terceira
116 K6 **Terebovlya** Ternopil's'ka Oblast', W Ukraine 49°18´N 25°44´E
127 O15 **Terek** SW Russian Federation
Terekhovka *see* Tsyerakhowka
147 R9 **Terek-Say** Dzhalal-Abadskaya Oblast', W Kyrgyzstan 41°28´N 71°06´E
145 Z10 **Terekty** *prev.* Alekseevka, Alekseyevka. Vostochnyy Kazakhstan, E Kazakhstan 48°25´N 85°38´E
168 L7 **Terengganu** *var.* Trengganu. ❖ *state* Peninsular Malaysia
127 X7 **Terensay** Orenburgskaya Oblast', W Russian Federation 51°35´N 59°28´E
58 N13 **Teresina** *var.* Therezina. *state capital* Piauí, NE Brazil 05°09´S 42°46´W
60 P9 **Teresópolis** Rio de Janeiro, SE Brazil 22°25´S 42°59´W
110 P12 **Terespol** Lubelskie, E Poland 52°05´N 23°37´E
191 V16 **Terevaka, Maunga** Easter Island, Chile, E Pacific Ocean 27°05´S 109°23´W
103 P3 **Tergnier** Aisne, N France 49°39´N 03°18´E
43 O14 **Teribe, Río** NW Panama
124 K3 **Teriberka** Murmanskaya Oblast', NW Russian Federation 69°10´N 35°18´E
Terinkot *see* Tarīn Kōt
Terisaqqan *see* Tersakkan
24 K12 **Terlingua** Texas, SW USA 29°18´N 103°36´W
24 K11 **Terlingua Creek** Texas, SW USA
62 K7 **Termas de Río Hondo** Santiago del Estero, N Argentina 27°29´S 64°52´W
136 M11 **Terme** Samsun, N Turkey 41°12´N 37°00´E
Termez *see* Termiz
Termia *see* Kýthnos
107 J23 **Termini Imerese** *anc.* Thermae Himerenses. Sicilia, Italy, C Mediterranean Sea 37°59´N 13°42´E
41 V14 **Términos, Laguna de** *lagoon* SE Mexico
77 X10 **Termit-Kaoboul** Zinder, C Niger 15°34´N 11°31´E
147 O14 **Termiz** *Rus.* Termez. Surkhondaryo Viloyati, S Uzbekistan 37°17´N 67°12´E
107 L15 **Termoli** Molise, C Italy 42°00´N 14°58´E
Termonde *see* Dendermonde
98 P5 **Termunten** Groningen, NE Netherlands 53°18´N 07°02´E
171 R11 **Ternate** Pulau Ternate, E Indonesia 0°48´N 127°23´E
109 T5 **Ternberg** Oberösterreich, N Austria 47°57´N 14°22´E
99 E15 **Terneuzen** *var.* Neuzen. Zeeland, SW Netherlands 51°20´N 03°50´E
123 T14 **Terney** Primorskiy Kray, SE Russian Federation 45°03´N 136°43´E
107 I14 **Terni** *anc.* Interamna Nahars. Umbria, C Italy 42°34´N 12°38´E
109 X6 **Ternitz** Niederösterreich, E Austria 47°43´N 16°02´E
117 V7 **Ternivka** Dnipropetrovs'ka Oblast', E Ukraine 48°30´N 36°05´E
116 K6 **Ternopil'** *Pol.* Tarnopol, *Rus.* Ternopol'. Ternopil's'ka Oblast', W Ukraine 49°32´N 25°38´E
Ternopil' *see* Ternopil's'ka Oblast'
116 I6 **Ternopil's'ka Oblast'** *var.* Ternopil', *Rus.* Ternopol'skaya Oblast'. ❖ *province* NW Ukraine
Ternopol' *see* Ternopil'
Ternopol'skaya Oblast' *see* Ternopil's'ka Oblast'
123 U13 **Terpeniya, Mys** *headland* Ostrov Sakhalin, SE Russian Federation 48°37´N 144°40´E
Térraba, Río *see* Grande de Térraba, Río
10 J13 **Terrace** British Columbia, W Canada 54°31´N 128°32´W
12 D12 **Terrace Bay** Ontario, S Canada 48°47´N 87°06´W
107 I16 **Terracina** Lazio, C Italy 41°18´N 13°13´E
93 F14 **Terråk** Troms, N Norway 65°03´N 12°22´E
26 M13 **Terral** Oklahoma, C USA 33°55´N 97°54´W
107 B19 **Terralba** Sardegna, Italy, C Mediterranean Sea 39°47´N 08°35´E
Terranova di Sicilia *see* Gela
Terranova Pausania *see* Olbia
105 W5 **Terrassa** *Cast.* Tarrasa. Cataluña, E Spain 41°34´N 02°01´E
15 O12 **Terrebonne** Québec, SE Canada 45°42´N 73°37´W
22 J11 **Terrebonne Bay** *bay* Louisiana, SE USA
31 N14 **Terre Haute** Indiana, N USA 39°27´N 87°24´W
25 U6 **Terrell** Texas, SW USA 32°44´N 96°16´W
Terre Neuve *see* Newfoundland and Labrador
33 Q14 **Terreton** Idaho, NW USA 43°49´N 112°25´W
103 T7 **Territoire-de-Belfort** ❖ *department* E France
33 X9 **Terry** Montana, NW USA 46°46´N 105°16´W
28 J9 **Terry Peak** ▲ South Dakota, N USA 44°19´N 103°49´W
136 H14 **Tersakan Gölü** C Turkey
145 O10 **Tersakkan** *Kaz.* Terisaqqan. C Kazakhstan
98 J4 **Terschelling** *Fris.* Skylge. *island* Waddeneilanden, N Netherlands
78 H10 **Tersef** Chari-Baguirmi, C Chad 12°55´N 16°49´E
147 X8 **Terskey Ala-Too, Khrebet** ▲▲ Kazakhstan/Kyrgyzstan
Terter *see* Tärtär
105 R8 **Teruel** *anc.* Turba. Aragón, E Spain 40°21´N 01°06´W
105 R7 **Teruel** ❖ *province* Aragón, E Spain
114 M7 **Tervel** *prev.* Kurtbunar, *Rom.* Curtbunar. Dobrich, NE Bulgaria 43°45´N 27°25´E
93 M16 **Tervo** Itä-Suomi, C Finland 62°57´N 26°48´E
92 L13 **Tervola** Lappi, NW Finland 66°04´N 24°49´E
Tervueren *see* Tervuren
99 H18 **Tervuren** *var.* Tervueren. Vlaams Brabant, C Belgium 50°48´N 04°28´E
162 G5 **Tes** *var.* Dzür. Dzavhan, W Mongolia 49°37´N 95°46´E
112 H11 **Tešanj** Federacija Bosna I Hercegovina, N Bosnia and Herzegovina 44°37´N 18°00´E
Teschen *see* Cieszyn
83 M19 **Tesenane** Inhambane, S Mozambique 22°48´S 34°02´E
80 I9 **Teseney** *var.* Tessenei. W Eritrea 15°05´N 36°42´E
39 P5 **Teshekpuk Lake** Alaska, USA
162 K6 **Teshig** Bulgan, N Mongolia 49°51´N 102°45´E
165 T2 **Teshio** Hokkaidō, NE Japan 44°49´N 141°46´E
165 T2 **Teshio-sanchi** ▲▲ Hokkaidō, NE Japan
14 L7 **Tessier, Lac** Québec, SE Canada
Těšín *see* Cieszyn
Tesiyn Gol *see* Tes-Khem
129 T7 **Tes-Khem** *var.* Tesiyn Gol. Mongolia/Russian Federation
112 H11 **Teslić** Republika Srpska, N Bosnia and Herzegovina 44°35´N 17°50´E
10 I9 **Teslin** Yukon Territory, W Canada 60°12´N 132°44´W
10 I8 **Teslin** British Columbia/Yukon Territory, W Canada
77 Q8 **Tessalit** Kidal, NE Mali 20°12´N 00°58´E
77 V12 **Tessaoua** Maradi, S Niger 13°46´N 07°55´E
99 J17 **Tessenderlo** Limburg, NE Belgium 51°05´N 05°04´E
Tessenei *see* Teseney
Tessin *see* Ticino
97 M23 **Test** S England, United Kingdom
Testama *see* Tõstamaa
55 P4 **Testigos, Islas los** *island group* N Venezuela
37 S10 **Tesuque** New Mexico, SW USA 35°45´N 105°55´W
103 O17 **Têt** *var.* Tet. S France
Tet *see* Têt
54 G5 **Tetas, Cerro de las** ▲ NW Venezuela 09°58´N 73°00´W
83 M15 **Tete** Tete, NW Mozambique 16°14´S 33°34´E
83 M15 **Tete** *off.* Província de Tete. ❖ *province* NW Mozambique
11 N15 **Tête Jaune Cache** British Columbia, SW Canada 52°52´N 119°22´W
184 O8 **Te Teko** Bay of Plenty, North Island, New Zealand 38°03´S 176°48´E
186 K9 **Tetepare** *island* New Georgia Islands, NW Solomon Islands
Tete, Província de *see* Tete
Teterev *see* Teteriv
116 M5 **Teteriv** *Rus.* Teterev. N Ukraine
100 M9 **Teterow** Mecklenburg-Vorpommern, NE Germany 53°47´N 12°34´E
114 I9 **Teteven** Lovech, N Bulgaria 42°54´N 24°18´E
191 T10 **Tetiaroa** *atoll* Îles du Vent, W French Polynesia
105 P14 **Tetica de Bacares** ▲ S Spain 37°15´N 02°24´W
Tetiyev *see* Tetiyiv
117 O6 **Tetiyiv** *Rus.* Tetiyev. Kyyivs'ka Oblast', N Ukraine 49°21´N 29°40´E
39 T10 **Tetlin** Alaska, USA 63°08´N 142°31´W
33 R8 **Teton River** Montana, NW USA
74 G5 **Tétouan** *var.* Tetouan, Tetuán. N Morocco 35°33´N 05°22´W
Tetova/Tetovë *see* Tetovo
114 L7 **Tetovo** Razgrad, N Bulgaria 43°49´N 26°21´E
113 N18 **Tetovo** *Alb.* Tetova, Tetovë, *Turk.* Kalkandelen. NW FYR Macedonia 42°01´N 20°58´E
115 E20 **Tetrázio** ▲ S Greece
Tetschen *see* Děčín
Tetuán *see* Tétouan
191 Q8 **Tetufera, Mont** ▲ Tahiti, W French Polynesia 17°40´S 149°26´W
127 R4 **Tetyushi** Respublika Tatarstan, W Russian Federation 54°55´N 48°46´E
108 I7 **Teufen** Ausser Rhoden, NE Switzerland 47°24´N 09°24´E
40 L12 **Teul** *var.* Teul de Gonzáles Ortega. Zacatecas, C Mexico 21°30´N 103°28´W
107 B21 **Teulada** Sardegna, Italy, C Mediterranean Sea 38°58´N 08°46´E
Teul de Gonzáles Ortega *see* Teul
11 X16 **Teulon** Manitoba, S Canada 50°20´N 97°14´W
42 I7 **Teupasenti** El Paraíso, S Honduras 14°13´N 86°42´W
165 S2 **Teuri-tō** *island* NE Japan
100 G13 **Teutoburger Wald** *Eng.* Teutoburg Forest. *hill range* NW Germany
Teutoburg Forest *see* Teutoburger Wald
93 K17 **Teuva** *Swe.* Östermark. Länsi-Suomi, W Finland 62°29´N 21°45´E
107 H15 **Tevere** *Eng.* Tiber. C Italy
Teverya *see* Tverya
96 K13 **Teviot** SE Scotland, United Kingdom
Tevli *see* Tewli
122 H11 **Tevriz** Omskaya Oblast', C Russian Federation 57°30´N 72°13´E
185 B24 **Te Waewae Bay** *bay* South Island, New Zealand
97 L21 **Tewkesbury** C England, United Kingdom 51°59´N 02°09´W
119 F19 **Tewli** *Rus.* Tevli. Brestskaya Voblasts', SW Belarus 52°20´N 24°15´E
159 U12 **Têwo** *var.* Dêngka; *prev.* Dêngkagoin. Gansu, C China 34°05´N 103°15´E
Tewulike *see* Hoxud
25 U12 **Texana, Lake** Texas, SW USA
27 S14 **Texarkana** Arkansas, C USA 33°26´N 94°02´W
25 X5 **Texarkana** Texas, SW USA 33°26´N 94°03´W
25 N9 **Texas** *off.* State of Texas, *also known as* Lone Star State. ❖ *state* S USA
25 W12 **Texas City** Texas, SW USA 29°23´N 94°55´W
41 P14 **Texcoco** México, C Mexico 19°32´N 98°52´W
98 I6 **Texel** *island* Waddeneilanden, NW Netherlands
26 H8 **Texhoma** Oklahoma, C USA 36°30´N 101°46´W
25 N1 **Texhoma** Texas, SW USA 36°30´N 101°46´W
37 W12 **Texico** New Mexico, SW USA 34°23´N 103°03´W
24 L1 **Texline** Texas, SW USA 36°22´N 103°01´W
41 P14 **Texmelucan** *var.* San Martín Texmelucan. Puebla, S Mexico 19°46´N 98°53´W
27 O13 **Texoma, Lake** Oklahoma/Texas, C USA
25 N9 **Texon** Texas, SW USA 31°13´N 101°42´W
83 J23 **Teyateyaneng** NW Lesotho 29°04´S 27°51´E
124 M16 **Teykovo** Ivanovskaya Oblast', W Russian Federation 56°49´N 40°31´E
124 M16 **Teza** W Russian Federation
41 Q13 **Teziutlán** Puebla, S Mexico 19°49´N 97°22´W
153 W12 **Tezpur** Assam, NE India 26°39´N 92°47´E
Thaa Atoll *see* Kolhumadulu
9 N10 **Tha-Anne** Nunavut, NE Canada
83 K23 **Thabana Ntlenyana** *var.* Thabantshonyana, Mount Ntlenyana. ▲ E Lesotho 29°26´S 29°16´E
Thabantshonyana *see* Thabana Ntlenyana
83 J23 **Thaba Putsoa** ▲ C Lesotho 29°48´S 27°46´E
167 Q8 **Tha Bo** Nong Khai, E Thailand 17°52´N 102°34´E
103 T12 **Thabor, Pic du** ▲ E France 45°07´N 06°34´E
Tha Chin *see* Samut Sakhon
166 M7 **Thagaya** Bago, C Burma (Myanmar) 19°19´N 96°16´E
Thai, Ao *see* Thailand, Gulf of
167 T6 **Thai Binh** Thai Binh, N Vietnam 20°27´N 106°20´E
167 S7 **Thai Hoa** *var.* Nghia Dan. Nghê An, N Vietnam 19°21´N 105°26´E
167 P9 **Thailand** *off.* Kingdom of Thailand, *Th.* Prathet Thai; *prev.* Siam. ◆ *monarchy* SE Asia
167 P13 **Thailand, Gulf of** *var.* Gulf of Siam, *Th.* Ao Thai, *Vtn.* Vinh Thai Lan. *gulf* SE Asia
Thailand, Kingdom of *see* Thailand
Thai Lan, Vinh of *see* Thailand, Gulf of
167 T6 **Thai Nguyên** Bắc Thai, N Vietnam 21°36´N 105°50´E
167 S8 **Thakhèk** *var.* Muang Khammouan. Khammouan, C Laos 17°25´N 104°51´E
153 S13 **Thakurgaon** Rajshahi, NW Bangladesh 26°05´N 88°34´E
149 S6 **Thal** Khyber Pakhtunkhwa, NW Pakistan 33°24´N 70°32´E
167 S11 **Thalabârivât** *prev.* Phumĭ Thalabârivăt. Stœng Trêng, N Cambodia 13°34´N 105°57´E
166 M15 **Thalang** Phuket, SW Thailand 08°00´N 98°21´E
Thalashsheri *see* Tellicherry/Thalassery
167 Q10 **Thalat Khae** Nakhon Ratchasima, C Thailand 15°15´N 102°24´E
109 Q5 **Thalgau** Salzburg, NW Austria 47°49´N 13°19´E
108 G7 **Thalwil** Zürich, NW Switzerland 47°17´N 08°35´E
83 I20 **Thamaga** Kweneng, SE Botswana 24°41´S 25°31´E
Thamarid *see* Thamarīt
141 V13 **Thamarīt** *var.* Thamarid, Thumrayt. SW Oman 17°39´N 54°02´E
141 P16 **Thamar, Jabal** ▲ SW Yemen 13°46´N 45°32´E
184 M6 **Thames** Waikato, North Island, New Zealand 37°10´S 175°33´E
14 D17 **Thames** Ontario, S Canada
97 O22 **Thames** S England, United Kingdom
184 M6 **Thames, Firth of** *gulf* North Island, New Zealand
14 D17 **Thamesville** Ontario, S Canada 42°33´N 81°58´W
141 S13 **Thamūd** N Yemen 17°18´N 49°57´E
167 N9 **Thanbyuzayat** Mon State, S Burma (Myanmar) 15°58´N 97°44´E
166 K7 **Thandwe** *var.* Sandoway. Rakhine State, W Burma (Myanmar) 18°28´N 94°20´E
152 I9 **Thānesar** Haryāna, NW India 29°58´N 76°48´E
167 T7 **Thanh Hoa** Thanh Hoa, N Vietnam 19°49´N 105°48´E
Thanintari Taungdan *see* Bilauktaung Range
155 I21 **Thanjāvūr** *prev.* Tanjore. Tamil Nādu, SE India 10°46´N 79°09´E
Thanlwin *see* Salween
103 U7 **Thann** Haut-Rhin, NE France 47°51´N 07°04´E
167 O16 **Tha Nong Phrom** Phatthalung, SW Thailand 07°24´N 100°04´E
167 N13 **Thap Sakae** *var.* Thap Sakau. Prachuap Khiri Khan, SW Thailand 11°30´N 99°35´E
Thap Sakau *see* Thap Sakae
98 L10 **'t Harde** Gelderland, E Netherlands 52°25´N 05°53´E
152 D11 **Thar Desert** *var.* Great Indian Desert, Indian Desert. *desert* India/Pakistan
181 V10 **Thargomindah** Queensland, C Australia 28°00´S 143°47´E
150 D11 **Thar Pārkar** *desert* SE Pakistan
139 S7 **Tharthār al Furāt, Qanāt ath** *canal* C Iraq
139 R7 **Tharthār, Buḩayrat ath** C Iraq
139 R5 **Tharthār, Wādī ath** *dry watercourse* N Iraq
167 N13 **Tha Sae** Chumphon, SW Thailand
167 N15 **Tha Sala** Nakhon Si Thammarat, SW Thailand 08°43´N 99°54´E
114 I13 **Thásos** Thásos, E Greece 40°47´N 24°43´E
115 I14 **Thásos** *island* E Greece
37 N14 **Thatcher** Arizona, SW USA 32°47´N 109°46´W
167 T5 **Thât Khê** *var.* Tràng Dinh. Lang Sơn, N Vietnam 22°15´N 106°26´E
166 M8 **Thaton** Mon State, S Burma (Myanmar) 16°56´N 97°20´E
167 S9 **That Phanom** Nakhon Phanom, E Thailand 16°52´N 104°41´E
167 R10 **Tha Tum** Surin, E Thailand 15°18´N 103°39´E
103 P16 **Thau, Bassin de** *var.* Étang de Thau. S France
Thau, Étang de *see* Thau, Bassin de
166 L3 **Thaungdut** Sagaing, N Burma (Myanmar) 24°26´N 94°45´E
167 O8 **Thaungyin** *Th.* Mae Nam Moei. Burma (Myanmar)/Thailand
167 R8 **Tha Uthen** Nakhon Phanom, E Thailand 17°32´N 104°34´E
109 W2 **Thaya** *var.* Dyje. Austria/Czech Republic *see also* Dyje
Thaya *see* Dyje
27 V8 **Thayer** Missouri, C USA 36°31´N 91°34´W
166 L6 **Thayetmyo** Magway, C Burma (Myanmar) 19°20´N 95°10´E
33 S15 **Thayne** Wyoming, C USA 42°54´N 111°01´W
166 M5 **Thazi** Mandalay, C Burma (Myanmar) 20°50´N 96°04´E
Thebes *see* Thíva
44 L5 **The Carlton** *var.* Abraham Bay. Mayaguana, SE Bahamas 22°21´N 72°56´W
45 O14 **The Crane** *var.* Crane. S Barbados 13°06´N 59°27´W
32 I11 **The Dalles** Oregon, NW USA 45°36´N 121°10´W
28 M14 **Thedford** Nebraska, C USA 41°59´N 100°32´W
The Flatts Village *see* Flatts Village
The Hague *see* 's-Gravenhage
Theiss *see* Tisa/Tisza
8 M9 **Thelon** Northwest Territories, N Canada
11 V15 **Theodore** Saskatchewan, S Canada 51°25´N 103°01´W
23 N8 **Theodore** Alabama, S USA 30°33´N 88°10´W
36 L13 **Theodore Roosevelt Lake** Arizona, SW USA
Theodosia *see* Feodosiya
Theophilo Ottoni *see* Teófilo Otoni
11 V13 **The Pas** Manitoba, C Canada 53°49´N 101°09´W
31 T14 **The Plains** Ohio, N USA 39°22´N 82°07´W
Thera *see* Santoríni
172 H17 **Thérèse, Île** *island* Inner Islands, NE Seychelles
Therezina *see* Teresina
115 L20 **Thérma** Ikaría, Dodekánisa, Greece, Aegean Sea 37°37´N 26°18´E
Thermae Himerenses *see* Termini Imerese
Thermae Pannonicae *see* Baden
Thermaic Gulf/Thermaicus Sinus *see* Thermaïkós Kólpos
121 Q8 **Thermaïkós Kólpos** *Eng.* Thermaic Gulf; *anc.* Thermaicus Sinus. *gulf* N Greece
Thermiá *see* Kýthnos
115 L17 **Thermís** Lésvos, E Greece 39°08´N 26°32´E
115 E18 **Thérmo** Dytikí Elláda, C Greece 38°32´N 21°42´E
33 V14 **Thermopolis** Wyoming, C USA 43°39´N 108°12´W
183 P10 **The Rock** New South Wales, SE Australia 35°18´S 147°07´E
195 O5 **Theron Mountains** ▲▲ Antarctica
The Sooner State *see* Oklahoma
115 G18 **Thespiés** Stereá Elláda, C Greece 38°18´N 23°08´E
115 E16 **Thessalía** *Eng.* Thessaly. ❖ *region* C Greece
14 C10 **Thessalon** Ontario, S Canada 46°15´N 83°34´W
115 G14 **Thessaloníki** *Eng.* Salonica, Salonika, *SCr.* Solun, *Turk.* Selânik. Kentrikí Makedonía, N Greece 40°38´N 22°58´E
115 G14 **Thessaloníki** ✈ Kentrikí Makedonía, N Greece 40°30´N 22°58´E
Thessaly *see* Thessalía
84 B12 **Theta Gap** *undersea feature* E Atlantic Ocean 12°40´W 43°30´N
97 P20 **Thetford** E England, United Kingdom 52°25´N 00°45´E
15 R11 **Thetford-Mines** Québec, SE Canada 46°07´N 71°16´W
113 K17 **Theth** *var.* Thethi. Shkodër, N Albania 42°25´N 19°45´E
Thethi *see* Theth
99 L20 **Theux** Liège, E Belgium 50°33´N 05°48´E
45 V9 **The Valley** ○ (Anguilla) E Anguilla 18°13´N 63°00´W
27 N10 **The Village** Oklahoma, C USA 35°33´N 97°33´W
The Volunteer State *see* Tennessee
25 W10 **The Woodlands** Texas, SW USA 30°09´N 95°27´E
Thiamis *see* Kalamás
Thian Shan *see* Tien Shan
Thibet *see* Xizang Zizhiqu
22 J9 **Thibodaux** Louisiana, S USA 29°48´N 90°49´W
29 S3 **Thief Lake** Minnesota, N USA
29 S3 **Thief River** Minnesota, C USA
29 S3 **Thief River Falls** Minnesota, N USA 48°07´N 96°10´W
Thièle *see* La Thielle
32 G14 **Thielsen, Mount** ▲ Oregon, NW USA 43°09´N 122°04´W
Thielt *see* Tielt
106 G7 **Thiene** Veneto, NE Italy 45°43´N 11°29´E
Thienen *see* Tienen
103 P11 **Thiers** Puy-de-Dôme, C France 45°51´N 03°33´E
76 F11 **Thiès** W Senegal 14°49´N 16°52´W
81 I19 **Thika** Central, S Kenya 01°03´S 37°05´E
Thikombia *see* Cikobia
151 K18 **Thiladhunmathi Atoll** *var.* Tiladummati Atoll. *atoll* N Maldives
Thimbu *see* Thimphu
153 T11 **Thimphu** *var.* Thimbu; *prev.* Tashi Chho Dzong. ● (Bhutan) W Bhutan 27°28´N 89°37´E
92 H2 **Thingeyri** Vestfirdhir, NW Iceland 65°52´N 23°28´W
92 I3 **Thingvellir** Sudhurland, SW Iceland 64°15´N 21°06´W
187 Q17 **Thio** Province Sud, C New Caledonia 21°37´S 166°13´E
103 T4 **Thionville** *Ger.* Diedenhofen. Moselle, NE France 49°22´N 06°11´E
77 O12 **Thiou** NW Burkina 13°42´N 02°34´W
115 K22 **Thíra** Santoríni, Kykládes, Greece, Aegean Sea 36°25´N 25°26´E
Thíra *see* Santoríni
115 J22 **Thirasía** *island* Kykládes, Greece, Aegean Sea
97 M16 **Thirsk** N England, United Kingdom 54°07´N 01°17´W
14 F12 **Thirty Thousand Islands** *island group* Ontario, S Canada
95 F20 **Thisted** Midtjylland, NW Denmark 56°58´N 08°42´E
Thistil Fjord *see* Thistilfjördhur
92 L1 **Thistilfjördhur** *var.* Thistil Fjord. *fjord* NE Iceland
182 G9 **Thistle Island** *island* South Australia
Thithia *see* Cicia
Thiukhaoluang Phrahang *see* Luang Prabang Range
115 G18 **Thíva** *Eng.* Thebes; *prev.* Thívai. Stereá Elláda, C Greece 38°19´N 23°19´E
Thívai *see* Thíva
102 M12 **Thiviers** Dordogne, SW France 45°24´N 00°54´E
92 J4 **Thjórsá** C Iceland
9 N10 **Thlewiaza** Nunavut, NE Canada
8 L10 **Thoa** Northwest Territories, NW Canada
99 G14 **Tholen** Zeeland, SW Netherlands 51°31´N 04°13´E
99 F14 **Tholen** *island* SW Netherlands
26 L10 **Thomas** Oklahoma, C USA 35°44´N 98°45´W
21 T3 **Thomas** West Virginia, NE USA 39°09´N 79°28´W
27 U3 **Thomas Hill Reservoir** Missouri, C USA
23 S5 **Thomaston** Georgia, SE USA 32°53´N 84°19´W
19 R7 **Thomaston** Maine, NE USA 44°06´N 69°10´W
25 T12 **Thomaston** Texas, SW USA 28°56´N 97°07´W
23 O6 **Thomasville** Alabama, S USA 31°54´N 87°42´W
23 T8 **Thomasville** Georgia, SE USA 30°49´N 83°57´W
21 S9 **Thomasville** North Carolina, SE USA 35°52´N 80°04´W
35 N5 **Thomes Creek** California, W USA
11 W12 **Thompson** Manitoba, C Canada 55°45´N 97°54´W
29 R4 **Thompson** North Dakota, N USA 47°45´N 97°07´W
0 F8 **Thompson** Alberta/British Columbia, SW Canada
33 O8 **Thompson Falls** Montana, NW USA 47°36´N 115°20´W
29 Q10 **Thompson, Lake** South Dakota, N USA
34 M3 **Thompson Peak** ▲ California, W USA 41°00´N 123°01´W
27 S2 **Thompson River** Missouri, C USA
185 A22 **Thompson Sound** *sound* South Island, New Zealand
8 J5 **Thomsen** Banks Island, Northwest Territories, NW Canada
23 V4 **Thomson** Georgia, SE USA 33°28´N 82°30´W
103 T10 **Thonon-les-Bains** Haute-Savoie, E France 46°22´N 06°30´E
103 O15 **Thoré** *var.* Thore. S France
Thore *see* Thoré
37 P11 **Thoreau** New Mexico, SW USA 35°24´N 108°13´W
Thorenburg *see* Turda
92 J3 **Thórisvatn** C Iceland
92 P2 **Thor, Kapp** *headland* S Svalbard 76°25´N 25°01´E
92 I4 **Thorlákshöfn** Sudhurland, SW Iceland 63°52´N 21°24´W
Thorn *see* Toruń
25 T10 **Thorndale** Texas, SW USA 30°36´N 97°12´W
14 H10 **Thorne** Ontario, S Canada 46°38´N 79°04´W
97 J14 **Thornhill** S Scotland, United Kingdom 55°13´N 03°46´W
25 U8 **Thornton** Texas, SW USA 31°24´N 96°34´W
Thornton Island *see* Millennium Island
14 H16 **Thorold** Ontario, S Canada 43°07´N 79°15´W
32 I9 **Thorp** Washington, NW USA 47°03´N 120°40´W
Thorshavn *see* Tórshavn
195 S3 **Thorshavnheiane** *physical region* Antarctica
92 L1 **Thórshöfn** Nordhurland Eystra, NE Iceland 66°09´N 15°18´W
Thospitis *see* Van Gölü
167 S14 **Thôt Nôt** Cần Thơ, S Vietnam 10°17´N 105°31´E
102 K8 **Thouars** Deux-Sèvres, W France 46°59´N 00°13´W
153 X14 **Thoubal** Manipur, NE India 24°40´N 94°00´E
102 K9 **Thouet** W France
Thoune *see* Thun
18 H7 **Thousand Islands** *island* Canada/USA
35 S15 **Thousand Oaks** California, W USA 34°10´N 118°50´W
114 L12 **Thrace** *cultural region* SE Europe
114 J13 **Thracian Sea** *Gk.* Thrakikó Pélagos; *anc.* Thracium Mare. *sea* Greece/Turkey
Thracium Mare/Thrakikó Pélagos *see* Thracian Sea

◆ Country
● Country Capital
◇ Dependent Territory
○ Dependent Territory Capital
❖ Administrative Regions
✈ International Airport
▲ Mountain
▲▲ Mountain Range
Volcano
River
Lake
Reservoir

Thrá Lí, Bá see Tralee Bay
33 R11 Three Forks Montana, NW USA 45°53′N 111°34′W
162 M8 Three Gorges Dam dam Hubei, C China
160 L9 Three Gorges Reservoir ⊠ C China
11 Q16 Three Hills Alberta, SW Canada 51°43′N 113°15′W
183 N15 Three Hummock Island island Tasmania, SE Australia
184 H1 Three Kings Islands island group N New Zealand
175 P10 Three Kings Rise undersea feature W Pacific Ocean
77 O18 Three Points, Cape headland S Ghana 04°43′N 02°03′W
31 P10 Three Rivers Michigan, N USA 41°56′N 85°37′W
25 S13 Three Rivers Texas, SW USA 28°27′N 98°10′W
83 G24 Three Sisters Northern Cape, SW South Africa 31°51′S 23°04′E
32 H13 Three Sisters ▲ Oregon, NW USA 44°08′N 121°46′W
187 N10 Three Sisters Islands island group SE Solomon Islands
25 Q6 Throckmorton Texas, SW USA 33°11′N 99°12′W
180 M10 Throssell, Lake salt lake Western Australia
115 K25 Thryptís var. Thrýptis. ▲ Kriti, Greece, E Mediterranean Sea 35°06′N 25°51′E
167 U14 Thuận Nam prev. Ham Thuận Nam. Bình Thuận, S Vietnam 10°49′N 107°49′E
167 T13 Thu Dâu Môt var. Phu Cuông. Sông Be, S Vietnam 10°58′N 106°40′E
167 S6 Thu Do ✈ (Ha Nôi) Ha Nôi, N Vietnam 21°13′N 105°46′E
99 G21 Thuin Hainaut, S Belgium 50°21′N 04°18′E
149 Q12 Thul Sind, SE Pakistan 28°14′N 68°50′E
Thule see Qaanaaq
83 J18 Thuli var. Tuli. ≈ S Zimbabwe
Thumrayt see Thamarīt
108 D9 Thun Fr. Thoune. Bern, W Switzerland 46°46′N 07°38′E
12 C12 Thunder Bay Ontario, S Canada 48°27′N 89°12′W
30 M1 Thunder Bay lake bay S Canada
31 R6 Thunder Bay lake bay Michigan, N USA
31 R6 Thunder Bay River ≈ Michigan, N USA
27 N11 Thunderbird, Lake ⊠ Oklahoma, C USA
28 L8 Thunder Butte Creek ≈ South Dakota, N USA
108 E9 Thuner See ◎ C Switzerland
167 N15 Thung Song var. Cha Mai. Nakhon Si Thammarat, SW Thailand 08°10′N 99°41′E
108 H7 Thur ≈ N Switzerland
108 G6 Thurgau Fr. Thurgovie. ◐ canton NE Switzerland
Thurgovie see Thurgau
Thuringe see Thüringen
108 J7 Thüringen Vorarlberg, W Austria 47°12′N 09°48′E
101 J17 Thüringen Eng. Thuringia, Fr. Thuringe. ◐ state C Germany
101 J17 Thüringer Wald Eng. Thuringian Forest. ▲▲ C Germany
Thuringia see Thüringen
Thuringian Forest see Thüringer Wald
97 D19 Thurles Ir. Durlas. S Ireland 52°41′N 07°49′W
21 W2 Thurmont Maryland, NE USA 39°36′N 77°22′W
Thurø see Thurø By
95 H24 Thurø By var. Thurø. Syddtjylland, C Denmark 55°03′N 10°43′E
14 M12 Thurso Québec, SE Canada 45°36′N 75°13′W
96 J6 Thurso N Scotland, United Kingdom 58°35′N 03°32′W
194 I10 Thurston Island island Antarctica
108 I9 Thusis Graubünden, S Switzerland 46°40′N 09°27′E
Thýamis see Kalamás
95 E21 Thyborøn var. Tyborøn. Midtjylland, W Denmark 56°40′N 08°12′E
195 U3 Thyer Glacier glacier Antarctica
115 L20 Thýmaina island Dodekánisa, Greece, Aegean Sea
83 N15 Thyolo var. Cholo. Southern, S Malawi 16°03′S 35°11′E
183 O16 Tia New South Wales, SE Australia 31°14′S 151°51′E
54 H5 Tía Juana Zulia, NW Venezuela 10°18′N 71°24′W
Tiancheng see Chongyang
160 J14 Tiandong var. Pingma. Guangxi Zhuangzu Zizhiqu, S China 23°37′N 107°06′E
161 O3 Tianjin var. Tientsin. Tianjin Shi, E China 39°13′N 117°06′E
Tianjin see Tianjin Shi
161 P3 Tianjin Shi var. Jin, Tianjin, T'ien-ching, Tientsin. ◐ municipality E China
159 S10 Tianjun var. Xinyuan. Qinghai, C China 37°16′N 99°03′E
160 J13 Tianlin var. Leli. Guangxi Zhuangzu Zizhiqu, S China 24°27′N 106°03′E
Tian Shan see Tien Shan
159 W11 Tianshui Gansu, C China 34°33′N 105°51′E
150 I7 Tianshuihai Xinjiang Uygur Zizhiqu, W China 35°17′N 79°30′E
161 S10 Tiantai Zhejiang, SE China 29°11′N 121°01′E
160 J14 Tianyang var. Tianzhou. Guangxi Zhuangzu Zizhiqu, S China 23°50′N 106°52′E
Tianzhou see Tianyang
159 U9 Tianzhu var. Huazangsi, Tianzhu Zangzu Zizhixian. Gansu, C China 37°01′N 103°04′E
Tianzhu Zangzu Zizhixian see Tianzhu
191 Q7 Tiarei Tahiti, W French Polynesia 17°32′S 149°20′W
74 J6 Tiaret var. Tihert. NW Algeria 35°20′N 01°20′E
77 N17 Tiassalé S Ivory Coast 05°54′N 04°50′W
192 I16 Ti'avea Upolu, SE Samoa 13°58′S 171°30′W
Tiba see Chiba
60 J11 Tibagi var. Tibaji. Paraná, S Brazil 24°29′S 50°29′W
60 J10 Tibagi, Rio var. Rio Tibají. ≈ S Brazil
Tibaji see Tibagi
Tibají, Rio see Tibagi, Rio
139 Q9 Tibal, Wādī dry watercourse S Iraq
54 G9 Tibaná Boyacá, C Colombia 05°19′N 73°25′W
79 F14 Tibati Adamaoua, N Cameroon 06°25′N 12°33′E
76 K15 Tibé, Pic de ▲ SE Guinea 08°39′N 08°58′W
Tiber see Tevere, Italy
Tiber see Tivoli, Italy
Tiberias see Tverya
138 G8 Tiberias, Lake var. Chinnereth, Sea of Bahr Tabariya, Sea of Galilee, Ar. Bahrat Tabariya, Heb. Yam Kinneret. ◎ N Israel
67 Q5 Tibesti var. Tibesti Massif, Ar. Tibistī. ▲▲ N Africa
Tibesti Massif see Tibesti
Tibet see Xizang Zizhiqu
Tibetan Autonomous Region see Xizang Zizhiqu
Tibet, Plateau of see Qingzang Gaoyuan
Tibistī see Tibesti
14 K7 Tiblemont, Lac ◎ Québec, SE Canada
139 X9 Ţīb, Nahr aţ ≈ S Iraq
Tibnī see At Tibnī
182 L4 Tibooburra New South Wales, SE Australia 29°24′S 142°01′E
95 L18 Tibro Västra Götaland, S Sweden 58°25′N 14°11′E
40 E5 Tiburón, Isla var. Isla del Tiburón. island NW Mexico
Tiburón, Isla del see Tiburón, Isla
23 W14 Tice Florida, SE USA 26°40′N 81°49′W
Tichau see Tychy
114 L8 Ticha, Yazovir ⊠ NE Bulgaria
76 K9 Tichît var. Tichitt. Tagant, C Mauritania 18°26′N 09°31′W
Tichitt see Tichît
108 G11 Ticino Fr./Ger. Tessin. ◐ canton S Switzerland
106 D8 Ticino ≈ Italy/Switzerland
108 H11 Ticino Ger. Tessin. ≈ SW Switzerland
Ticinum see Pavia
41 X12 Ticul Yucatán, SE Mexico 20°22′N 89°30′W
95 K18 Tidaholm Västra Götaland, S Sweden 58°12′N 13°55′E
Tidjikdja see Tidjikja
76 J8 Tidjikja var. Tidjikdja; prev. Fort-Cappolani. Tagant, C Mauritania 18°31′N 11°24′W
Tidore see Soasiu
171 R11 Tidore, Pulau island E Indonesia
Tidra, Ile see Et Tidra
77 N16 Tiébissou var. Tiebissou. C Ivory Coast 07°10′N 05°10′W
Tiebissou see Tiébissou
Tiefa see Diaobingshan
108 I9 Tiefencastel Graubünden, S Switzerland 46°40′N 09°33′E
Tiegenhof see Nowy Dwór Gdański
T'ieh-ling see Tieling
98 K13 Tiel Gelderland, C Netherlands 51°53′N 05°26′E
163 W7 Tieli Heilongjiang, NE China 46°57′N 128°01′E
163 V11 Tieling var. T'ieh-ling. Liaoning, NE China 42°19′N 123°52′E
152 L4 Tielongtan China/India 35°10′N 79°32′E
99 D17 Tielt var. Thielt. West-Vlaanderen, W Belgium 51°00′N 03°20′E
T'ien-ching see Tianjin Shi
99 I18 Tienen var. Thienen, Fr. Tirlemont. Vlaams Brabant, C Belgium 50°48′N 04°56′E
Tiên Giang, Sông see Mekong
147 X9 Tien Shan Chin. Thian Shan, Tian Shan, T'ien Shan, Rus. Tyan'-Shan'. ▲▲ C Asia
Tientsin see Tianjin
167 U6 Tiên Yên Quang Ninh, N Vietnam 21°19′N 107°24′E
95 O14 Tierp Uppsala, C Sweden 60°20′N 17°30′E
62 H7 Tierra Amarilla Atacama, N Chile 27°28′S 70°17′W
37 R9 Tierra Amarilla New Mexico, SW USA 36°42′N 106°31′W
41 R15 Tierra Blanca Veracruz-Llave, E Mexico 18°28′N 96°21′W
41 O16 Tierra Colorada Guerrero, S Mexico 17°10′N 99°30′W
63 J17 Tierra Colorada, Bajo de la basin SE Argentina
63 I25 Tierra del Fuego off. Provincia de la Tierra del Fuego. ◐ province S Argentina
63 J24 Tierra del Fuego island Argentina/Chile
Tierra del Fuego, Provincia de la see Tierra del Fuego
54 D7 Tierralta Córdoba, NW Colombia 08°10′N 76°04′W
104 K9 Tiétar ≈ W Spain
60 L10 Tietê São Paulo, S Brazil 23°04′S 47°41′W
60 J8 Tietê, Rio ≈ S Brazil
32 I9 Tieton Washington, NW USA 46°41′N 120°43′W
32 J6 Tiffany Mountain ▲ Washington, NW USA 48°40′N 119°55′W
31 S12 Tiffin Ohio, N USA 41°06′N 83°10′W
31 Q11 Tiffin River ≈ Ohio, N USA
Tiflis see Tbilisi
23 U7 Tifton Georgia, SE USA 31°27′N 83°31′W
171 R13 Tifu Pulau Buru, E Indonesia 03°46′S 126°36′E
38 L17 Tigalda Island island Aleutian Islands, Alaska, USA
115 I15 Tigáni, Akrotírio headland Límnos, E Greece 39°50′N 25°03′E
169 V6 Tiga Tarok Sabah, East Malaysia 06°57′N 117°07′E
117 O10 Tighina Rus. Bendery; prev. Bender. E Moldova 46°51′N 29°28′E
145 X9 Tigiretskiy Khrebet ▲▲ E Kazakhstan
79 F14 Tignère Adamaoua, N Cameroon 07°24′N 12°35′E
13 P14 Tignish Prince Edward Island, SE Canada 46°58′N 64°03′W
186 M10 Tigoa var. Tinggoa. Rennell, S Solomon Islands 11°39′S 160°13′E
Tigranocerta see Siirt
80 I11 Tigray ◐ federal region N Ethiopia
41 O11 Tigre, Cerro del ▲ C Mexico 23°06′N 99°13′W
56 F8 Tigre, Río ≈ N Peru
139 X10 Tigris Ar. Dijlah, Turk. Dicle. ≈ Iraq/Turkey
76 G9 Tiguent Trarza, SW Mauritania 17°15′N 16°00′W
74 M10 Tiguentourine E Algeria 27°59′N 09°16′E
77 V10 Tiguidit, Falaise de ridge C Niger
141 N13 Tihāmah var. Tehama. plain Saudi Arabia/Yemen
Tihert see Tiaret
Ti-hua/Tihwa see Ürümqi
41 Q13 Tihuatlán Veracruz-Llave, E Mexico 20°44′N 97°30′W
40 B1 Tijuana Baja California Norte, NW Mexico 32°32′N 117°01′W
42 E2 Tikal Petén, N Guatemala 17°11′N 89°36′W
154 I9 Tīkamgarh prev. Tehri. Madhya Pradesh, C India 24°44′N 78°50′E
158 L7 Tikanlik Xinjiang Uygur Zizhiqu, NW China 40°34′N 87°37′E
77 P12 Tikaré N Burkina 13°16′N 01°39′W
39 O12 Tikchik Lakes lakes Alaska, USA
191 T9 Tikehau atoll Îles Tuamotu, C French Polynesia
191 V9 Tikei island Îles Tuamotu, C French Polynesia
126 L13 Tikhoretsk Krasnodarskiy Kray, SW Russian Federation 45°51′N 40°07′E
124 I13 Tikhvin Leningradskaya Oblast', NW Russian Federation 59°37′N 33°30′E
193 P9 Tiki Basin undersea feature S Pacific Ocean
76 K13 Tikinsso ≈ NE Guinea
Tikirarjuaq see Whale Cove
184 Q8 Tikitiki Gisborne, North Island, New Zealand 37°49′S 178°23′E
79 D16 Tiko Sud-Ouest, SW Cameroon 04°02′N 09°19′E
139 S6 Tikrīt var. Tekrit. Şalāḩ ad Dīn, N Iraq 34°36′N 43°42′E
124 I8 Tiksha Respublika Kareliya, NW Russian Federation 64°07′N 32°31′E
124 I6 Tikshozero, Ozero ◎ NW Russian Federation
123 P7 Tiksi Respublika Sakha (Yakutiya), NE Russian Federation 71°40′N 128°47′E
Tiladummati Atoll see Thiladhunmathi Atoll
42 A6 Tilapa San Marcos, SW Guatemala 14°31′N 92°11′W
42 L13 Tilarán Guanacaste, NW Costa Rica 10°28′N 84°57′W
99 J14 Tilburg Noord-Brabant, S Netherlands 51°34′N 05°05′E
14 D17 Tilbury Ontario, S Canada 42°15′N 82°26′W
182 K4 Tilcha South Australia 29°37′S 140°52′E
Tilcha Creek see Callabonna Creek
29 Q14 Tilden Nebraska, C USA 42°03′N 97°49′W
25 R13 Tilden Texas, SW USA 28°27′N 98°43′W
14 H10 Tilden Lake Ontario, S Canada 46°35′N 79°36′W
116 G9 Tileagd Hung. Mezőtelegd. Bihor, W Romania 47°03′N 22°11′E
145 P9 Tilekey prev. Ladyzhenka. Akmola, C Kazakhstan 50°58′N 68°44′E
77 Q8 Tilemsi, Vallée de ≈ C Mali
123 V8 Tilichiki Krasnoyarskiy Kray, E Russian Federation 60°25′N 165°55′E
Tiligul see Tilihul
Tiligul'skiy Liman see Tilihul's'kyy Lyman
117 P9 Tilihul Rus. Tiligul. ≈ SW Ukraine
117 P10 Tilihul's'kyy Lyman Rus. Tiligul'skiy Liman. ◎ S Ukraine
Tilimsen see Tlemcen
Tilio Martius see Toulon
77 R11 Tillabéri var. Tillabéry. Tillabéri, W Niger 14°13′N 01°27′E
77 R11 Tillabéri ◐ department SW Niger
Tillabéry see Tillabéri
32 F11 Tillamook Oregon, NW USA 45°28′N 123°50′W
32 E11 Tillamook Bay inlet Oregon, NW USA
151 Q22 Tillanchāng Dwīp island Nicobar Islands, India, NE Indian Ocean
95 N15 Tillberga Västmanland, C Sweden 59°41′N 16°37′E
Tillenberg see Dyleň
21 S10 Tillery, Lake ⊠ North Carolina, SE USA
77 T10 Tillia Tahoua, W Niger 16°13′N 04°51′E
23 N8 Tillmans Corner Alabama, S USA 30°35′N 88°10′W
14 F17 Tillsonburg Ontario, S Canada 42°53′N 80°44′W
115 N22 Tílos island Dodekánisa, Greece, Aegean Sea
183 N5 Tilpa New South Wales, SE Australia 30°56′S 144°24′E
Tilsit see Sovetsk
31 N13 Tilton Illinois, N USA 40°06′N 87°39′W
126 K7 Tim Kurskaya Oblast', W Russian Federation 51°39′N 37°11′E
54 D12 Timaná Huila, S Colombia 01°58′N 75°55′W
Timan Ridge see Timanskiy Kryazh
125 Q6 Timanskiy Kryazh Eng. Timan Ridge. ridge NW Russian Federation
185 G20 Timaru Canterbury, South Island, New Zealand 44°23′S 171°15′E
127 S6 Timashevo Samarskaya Oblast', W Russian Federation 53°22′N 51°13′E
126 K13 Timashevsk Krasnodarskiy Kray, SW Russian Federation 45°37′N 38°57′E
Timbaki/Timbákion see Tympáki
22 K10 Timbalier Bay bay Louisiana, S USA
22 K11 Timbalier Island island Louisiana, S USA
76 L10 Timbedgha var. Timbédra. Hodh ech Chargui, SE Mauritania 16°17′N 08°14′W
Timbédra see Timbedgha
32 G10 Timber Oregon, NW USA 45°42′N 123°19′W
181 O3 Timber Creek Northern Territory, N Australia 15°35′S 130°21′E
28 M8 Timber Lake South Dakota, N USA 45°25′N 101°01′W
54 D12 Timbío Cauca, SW Colombia 02°20′N 76°40′W
54 C12 Timbiquí Cauca, SW Colombia 02°43′N 77°45′W
83 O17 Timbue, Ponta headland C Mozambique 18°49′S 36°22′E
Timbuktu see Tombouctou
169 W8 Timbun Mata, Pulau island E Malaysia
77 P8 Timétrine var. Ti-n-Kâr. oasis C Mali
Timfi see Týmfi
Timfristos see Tymfristós
77 V9 Timia Agadez, C Niger 18°07′N 08°49′E
171 X14 Timika Papua, E Indonesia 04°39′S 137°15′E
74 I9 Timimoun C Algeria 29°18′N 00°21′E
Timiris, Cap see Timirist, Râs
76 F8 Timirist, Râs var. Cap Timiris. headland NW Mauritania 19°18′N 16°28′W
145 O7 Timiryazevo Severnyy Kazakhstan, N Kazakhstan 53°45′N 66°33′E
116 E11 Timiş ◐ county SW Romania
14 H9 Timiskaming, Lake Fr. Lac Témiscamingue. ◎ Ontario/Québec, SE Canada
116 E11 Timişoara Ger. Temeschwar, Temeswar, Hung. Temesvár; prev. Temeschburg. Timiş, W Romania 45°46′N 21°17′E
116 E11 Timişoara ✈ Timiş, SW Romania 45°50′N 21°21′E
Timkovichi see Tsimkavichy
77 U8 Ti-m-Meghsoï ≈ NW Niger
100 K8 Timmerdorfer Strand Schleswig-Holstein, N Germany 53°59′N 10°50′E
14 F7 Timmins Ontario, S Canada 48°09′N 80°01′W
21 S12 Timmonsville South Carolina, SE USA 34°07′N 79°56′W
30 K5 Timms Hill ▲ Wisconsin, N USA 45°27′N 90°12′W
112 P12 Timok ≈ E Serbia
58 N13 Timon Maranhão, E Brazil 05°08′S 42°52′W
171 Q17 Timor Sea sea E Indian Ocean
Timor Timur see East Timor
Timor Trench see Timor Trough
192 G8 Timor Trough var. Timor Trench. undersea feature NE Timor Sea
61 A21 Timote Buenos Aires, E Argentina 35°22′S 62°13′W
54 I6 Timotes Mérida, NW Venezuela 08°57′N 70°46′W
25 X8 Timpson Texas, SW USA 31°54′N 94°24′W
123 Q11 Timpton ≈ NE Russian Federation
93 H17 Timrå Västernorrland, C Sweden 62°29′N 17°20′E
20 J10 Tims Ford Lake ⊠ Tennessee, S USA
168 L7 Timur, Banjaran ▲▲ Peninsular Malaysia
171 Q8 Tinaca Point headland Mindanao, S Philippines 05°35′N 125°18′E
54 K5 Tinaco Cojedes, N Venezuela 09°44′N 68°28′W
64 Q11 Tinajo Lanzarote, Islas Canarias, Spain, NE Atlantic Ocean 29°03′N 13°41′W
187 P10 Tinakula island Santa Cruz Islands, E Solomon Islands
54 K5 Tinaquillo Cojedes, N Venezuela 09°57′N 68°20′W
116 F10 Tinca Hung. Tenke. Bihor, W Romania 46°46′N 21°58′E
155 J20 Tindivanam Tamil Nādu, SE India 12°15′N 79°41′E
74 E9 Tindouf W Algeria 27°43′N 08°09′W
74 E9 Tindouf, Sebkha de salt lake W Algeria
104 J2 Tineo Asturias, N Spain 43°20′N 06°25′W
77 R9 Ti-n-Essako Kidal, E Mali 18°30′N 02°27′E
Tinggoa see Tigoa
183 T5 Tingha New South Wales, SE Australia 29°56′S 151°13′E
Tingis see Tanger
Tinglett see Tinglev
95 F24 Tinglev Ger. Tinglett. Syddanmark, SW Denmark 54°57′N 09°15′E
56 E12 Tingo María Huánuco, C Peru 09°10′S 76°00′W
Tingréla see Tengréla
158 K16 Tingri var. Xégar. Xizang Zizhiqu, W China 28°40′N 87°04′E
95 M21 Tingsryd Kronoberg, S Sweden 56°30′N 15°E
95 P19 Tingstäde Gotland, SE Sweden 57°45′N 18°36′E
62 H12 Tinguiririca, Volcán ※ C Chile 34°52′S 70°24′W
94 F9 Tingvoll Møre og Romsdal, S Norway 62°55′N 08°13′E
188 K8 Tinian island S Northern Mariana Islands
Ti-n-Kâr see Timétrine
Tinnevelly see Tirunelveli
95 G15 Tinnoset Telemark, S Norway 59°43′N 09°03′E
95 F15 Tinnsjå prev. Tinnsjø, var. Tinnsjö. ◎ S Norway see also Tinnsjø
Tinnsjø see Tinnsjå
Tinnsjö see Tinnsjå
Tino see Chino
115 J20 Tínos Tínos, Kykládes, Greece, Aegean Sea 37°33′N 25°08′E
115 J20 Tínos anc. Tenos. island Kykládes, Greece, Aegean Sea
153 R14 Tinpahar Jhārkhand, NE India 25°00′N 87°43′E
153 X11 Tinsukia Assam, NE India 27°28′N 95°20′E
76 K10 Tintâne Hodh el Gharbi, S Mauritania 16°25′N 10°08′W
62 L7 Tintina Santiago del Estero, N Argentina 27°00′S 62°45′W
182 K10 Tintinara South Australia 35°54′S 140°04′E
104 I14 Tinto ≈ SW Spain
77 S8 Ti-n-Zaouâtene Kidal, NE Mali 19°56′N 02°45′E
Tiobraid Árann see Tipperary
28 K3 Tioga North Dakota, N USA 48°24′N 102°56′W
18 G12 Tioga Pennsylvania, NE USA 41°54′N 77°07′W
25 T5 Tioga Texas, SW USA 33°28′N 96°55′W
35 Q8 Tioga Pass pass California, W USA
18 G12 Tioga River ≈ New York/Pennsylvania, NE USA
Tioman Island see Tioman, Pulau
168 M9 Tioman, Pulau var. Tioman Island. island Peninsular Malaysia
18 C12 Tionesta Pennsylvania, NE USA 41°31′N 79°30′W
18 D12 Tionesta Creek ≈ Pennsylvania, NE USA
168 J13 Tiop Pulau Pagai Selatan, W Indonesia 03°12′S 100°21′E
18 H11 Tioughnioga River ≈ New York, NE USA
74 J5 Tipasa var. Tipaza. N Algeria 36°35′N 02°27′E
Tipaza see Tipasa
42 J10 Tipitapa Managua, W Nicaragua 12°08′N 86°04′W
31 R13 Tipp City Ohio, N USA 39°57′N 84°10′W
31 O12 Tippecanoe River ≈ Indiana, N USA
97 D20 Tipperary Ir. Tiobraid Árann. S Ireland 52°29′N 08°10′W
97 D19 Tipperary Ir. Tiobraid Árann. cultural region S Ireland
35 R12 Tipton California, W USA 36°02′N 119°19′W
31 P13 Tipton Indiana, N USA 40°19′N 86°00′W
29 Y14 Tipton Iowa, C USA 41°46′N 91°07′W
27 U5 Tipton Missouri, C USA 38°39′N 92°46′W
36 I10 Tipton, Mount ▲ Arizona, SW USA 35°32′N 114°11′W
20 F8 Tiptonville Tennessee, S USA 36°21′N 89°30′W
12 E12 Tip Top Mountain ▲ Ontario, S Canada 48°18′N 86°06′W
155 G19 Tiptūr Karnātaka, W India 13°17′N 76°31′E
Tiquisate see Pueblo Nuevo Tiquisate
58 L13 Tiracambu, Serra do ▲▲ E Brazil
Tirana see Tiranë
113 K19 Tirana Rinas ✈ Durrës, W Albania 41°25′N 19°41′E
113 L20 Tiranë var. Tirana. ● (Albania) Tiranë, C Albania 41°20′N 19°50′E
113 K20 Tiranë ◐ district W Albania
140 I5 Tirān, Jazīrat island Egypt/Saudi Arabia
106 F6 Tirano Lombardia, N Italy 46°13′N 10°10′E
182 I2 Tirari Desert desert South Australia
117 O10 Tiraspol Rus. Tiraspol'. E Moldova 46°50′N 29°35′E
Tiraspol' see Tiraspol
184 M8 Tirau Waikato, North Island, New Zealand 37°59′S 175°44′E
136 C14 Tire İzmir, SW Turkey 38°04′N 27°45′E
137 O11 Tirebolu Giresun, N Turkey 41°01′N 38°49′E
96 F11 Tiree island W Scotland, United Kingdom
Tîrgovişte see Târgovişte
Tîrgu see Târgu Cărbuneşti
Tîrgu Bujor see Târgu Bujor
Tîrgu Frumos see Târgu Frumos
Tîrgu Jiu see Târgu Jiu
Tîrgu Lăpuş see Târgu Lăpuş
Tîrgu Mures see Târgu Mureş
Tîrgu-Neamţ see Târgu-Neamţ
Tîrgu Ocna see Târgu Ocna
Tîrgu Secuiesc see Târgu Secuiesc
149 T3 Tirich Mir ▲ NW Pakistan 36°12′N 71°51′E
76 J5 Tiris Zemmour ◐ region N Mauritania
Tirlemont see Tienen
127 W5 Tirlyanskiy Respublika Bashkortostan, W Russian Federation 54°09′N 58°32′E
Tîrnava Mare see Târnava Mare
Tîrnava Mică see Târnava Mică
Tîrnăveni see Târnăveni
Tírnavos see Týrnavos
Tirnovo see Veliko Tŭrnovo
154 J11 Tirodi Madhya Pradesh, C India 21°40′N 79°44′E
108 K8 Tirol off. Land Tirol, var. Tyrol, It. Tirolo. ◐ state W Austria
Tirol, Land see Tirol
Tirolo see Tirol
Tirreno, Mare see Tyrrhenian Sea
107 B19 Tirso ≈ Sardegna, Italy, C Mediterranean Sea
95 H22 Tirstrup ✈ (Århus) Århus, C Denmark 56°17′N 10°36′E
155 I21 Tiruchchirāppalli prev. Trichinopoly. Tamil Nādu, SE India 10°50′N 78°43′E
155 H23 Tirunelveli var. Tinnevelly. Tamil Nādu, SE India 08°45′N 77°43′E
155 J19 Tirupati Andhra Pradesh, E India 13°39′N 79°25′E
155 I20 Tiruppattūr Tamil Nādu, SE India 12°28′N 78°31′E
155 H21 Tiruppur Tamil Nādu, SW India 11°05′N 77°20′E
Tiruvantapuram see Thiruvanathapuram/Trivandrum
155 I20 Tiruvannāmalai Tamil Nādu, SE India 12°13′N 79°07′E
112 L10 Tisa Ger. Theiss, Hung. Tisza, Rus. Tissa, Ukr. Tysa. ≈ SE Europe see also Tisza
Tisa see Tisza
Tischnowitz see Tišnov
11 U14 Tisdale Saskatchewan, S Canada 52°51′N 104°01′W
27 O13 Tishomingo Oklahoma, C USA 34°15′N 96°41′W
95 M17 Tisnaren ◎ S Sweden
111 F18 Tišnov Ger. Tischnowitz. Jihomoravský Kraj, SE Czech Republic 49°22′N 16°24′E
Tissa see Tisa/Tisza
74 J6 Tissemsilt N Algeria 35°37′N 01°48′E
153 S12 Tista ≈ NE India
112 L8 Tisza Ger. Theiss, Rom./Slvn./SCr. Tisa, Rus. Tissa, Ukr. Tysa. ≈ SE Europe see also Tisa
Tisza see Tisa
111 L23 Tiszaföldvár Jász-Nagykun-Szolnok, E Hungary 47°00′N 20°16′E
111 M22 Tiszafüred Jász-Nagykun-Szolnok, E Hungary 47°38′N 20°45′E
111 L23 Tiszakécske Bács-Kiskun, C Hungary 46°56′N 20°04′E
111 M21 Tiszaújváros prev. Leninváros. Borsod-Abaúj-Zemplén, NE Hungary 47°56′N 21°03′E
111 N21 Tiszavasvári Szabolcs-Szatmár-Bereg, NE Hungary 47°56′N 21°21′E
57 I17 Titicaca, Lake ◎ Bolivia/Peru
190 H17 Titikaveka Rarotonga, S Cook Islands 21°16′S 159°45′W
154 M13 Titilāgarh var. Titlagarh. Orissa, E India 20°18′N 83°09′E
168 K8 Titiwangsa, Banjaran ▲▲ Peninsular Malaysia
Titlagarh see Titilāgarh
Titograd see Podgorica
Titose see Chitose
Titova Mitrovica see Mitrovicë
Titovo Užice see Užice
113 M18 Titov Vrv ▲ NW FYR Macedonia 41°58′N 20°49′E
94 F7 Titran Sør-Trøndelag, S Norway 63°40′N 08°20′E
31 Q8 Tittabawassee River ≈ Michigan, N USA
116 J13 Titu Dâmboviţa, S Romania 44°40′N 25°32′E
79 M16 Titule Orientale, N Dem. Rep. Congo 03°20′N 25°23′E
23 X11 Titusville Florida, SE USA 28°37′N 80°50′W
18 C12 Titusville Pennsylvania, NE USA 41°36′N 79°39′W
76 G11 Tivaouane W Senegal 14°59′N 16°50′W
113 I17 Tivat SW Montenegro 42°25′N 18°43′E
14 E14 Tiverton Ontario, S Canada 44°15′N 81°31′W
97 J23 Tiverton SW England, United Kingdom 50°54′N 03°30′W
19 O12 Tiverton Rhode Island, NE USA 41°38′N 71°10′W
107 I15 Tivoli anc. Tiber. Lazio, C Italy 41°58′N 12°45′E
25 U13 Tivoli Texas, SW USA 28°26′N 96°54′W
141 Z8 Ţīwī NE Oman 22°43′N 59°20′E
41 Y11 Tizimín Yucatán, SE Mexico 21°10′N 88°09′W
74 K5 Tizi Ouzou var. Tizi-Ouzou. N Algeria 36°44′N 04°06′E
Tizi-Ouzou see Tizi Ouzou
74 D8 Tiznit SW Morocco 29°43′N 09°39′W
95 F23 Tjæreborg Syddtjylland, W Denmark 55°28′N 08°35′E
113 I14 Tjentište Republika Srpska, SE Bosnia and Herzegovina 43°23′N 18°42′E
98 L7 Tjeukemeer ◎ N Netherlands
Tjiamis see Ciamis
Tjiandjoer see Cianjur
Tjilatjap see Cilacap
Tjirebon see Cirebon
95 I18 Tjörn island S Sweden
92 O3 Tjuvfjorden fjord S Svalbard
Tkvarcheli see T'q'varcheli
40 L8 Tlahualilo Durango, N Mexico 26°06′N 103°25′W
41 P14 Tlalnepantla México, C Mexico 19°34′N 99°12′W
41 Q13 Tlapacoyán Veracruz-Llave, E Mexico 19°58′N 97°13′W
41 P16 Tlapa de Comonfort Guerrero, S Mexico 17°33′N 98°33′W
40 L13 Tlaquepaque Jalisco, C Mexico 20°36′N 103°19′W
Tlascala see Tlaxcala
41 P14 Tlaxcala var. Tlascala, Tlaxcala de Xicohténcatl. Tlaxcala, C Mexico 19°17′N 98°16′W
41 P14 Tlaxcala ◐ state S Mexico
Tlaxcala de Xicohténcatl see Tlaxcala
41 P14 Tlaxco var. Tlaxco de Morelos. Tlaxcala, S Mexico 19°38′N 98°06′W
Tlaxco de Morelos see Tlaxco
41 Q16 Tlaxiaco var. Santa María Asunción Tlaxiaco. Oaxaca, S Mexico 17°18′N 97°42′W
74 I6 Tlemcen var. Tilimsen, Tlemsen. NW Algeria 34°53′N 01°21′W
Tlemsen see Tlemcen
138 L4 Tlété Ouâte Rharbi, Jebel ▲ N Syria
116 J7 Tlumach Ivano-Frankivs'ka Oblast', W Ukraine 48°53′N 25°00′E
127 P17 Tlyarata Respublika Dagestan, SW Russian Federation 42°10′N 46°30′E
116 K10 Toaca, Vârful prev. Vîrful Toaca. ▲ NE Romania 46°58′N 25°55′E
Toaca, Vîrful see Toaca, Vârful
191 Q8 Toahotu prev. Teohatu. Tahiti, W French Polynesia
187 R13 Toak Ambrym, C Vanuatu 16°21′S 168°16′E
172 J4 Toamasina prev./Fr. Tamatave. Toamasina, E Madagascar 18°10′S 49°23′E
172 J4 Toamasina ◐ province E Madagascar
172 J4 Toamasina ✈ Toamasina, E Madagascar 18°10′S 49°23′E
21 X6 Toano Virginia, NE USA 37°22′N 76°46′W
191 U10 Toau atoll Îles Tuamotu, C French Polynesia
45 T6 Toa Vaca, Embalse ⊠ C Puerto Rico
62 K13 Toay La Pampa, C Argentina 36°43′S 64°22′W
159 R14 Toba Xizang Zizhiqu, W China 31°17′N 97°37′E
164 K14 Toba Mie, Honshū, SW Japan 34°29′N 136°51′E
168 I9 Toba, Danau ◎ Sumatera, W Indonesia
45 Y16 Tobago island NE Trinidad and Tobago
149 Q9 Toba Kākar Range ▲▲ NW Pakistan
105 Q12 Tobarra Castilla-La Mancha, C Spain 38°36′N 01°41′W
149 U9 Toba Tek Singh Punjab, E Pakistan 30°54′N 72°30′E
171 R11 Tobelo Pulau Halmahera, E Indonesia 01°45′N 127°59′E
14 E12 Tobermory Ontario, S Canada 45°15′N 81°39′W
96 G10 Tobermory W Scotland, United Kingdom 56°37′N 06°12′W
165 S4 Tōbetsu Hokkaidō, NE Japan 43°12′N 141°28′E
180 M6 Tobin Lake ◎ Western Australia
11 U14 Tobin Lake ◎ Saskatchewan, C Canada
35 T4 Tobin, Mount ▲ Nevada, W USA 40°25′N 117°28′W
165 O9 Tobi-shima island C Japan
169 N13 Toboali Pulau Bangka, W Indonesia 03°00′S 106°30′E
Tobol see Tobyl
122 H11 Tobol'sk Tyumenskaya Oblast', C Russian Federation 58°15′N 68°12′E
Tobruch/Tobruk see Ţubruq
125 R3 Tobseda Nenetskiy Avtonomnyy Okrug, NW Russian Federation 68°37′N 52°24′E
144 M8 Tobyl prev. Tobol. Kustanay, N Kazakhstan 52°42′N 62°36′E
144 L8 Tobyl prev. Tobol. ≈ Kazakhstan/Russian Federation
125 Q6 Tobysh ≈ NW Russian Federation
54 F10 Tocaima Cundinamarca, C Colombia 04°30′N 74°38′W
59 K16 Tocantins off. Estado do Tocantins. ◐ state C Brazil
Tocantins, Estado do see Tocantins
59 K15 Tocantins, Rio ≈ N Brazil
23 T2 Toccoa Georgia, SE USA 34°34′N 83°19′W
165 O12 Tochigi off. Tochigi-ken, var. Totigi. ◐ prefecture Honshū, S Japan
Tochigi-ken see Tochigi
165 O11 Tochio var. Totio. Niigata, Honshū, C Japan 37°27′N 139°00′E
95 J15 Töcksfors Värmland, C Sweden 59°30′N 11°49′E
42 J5 Tocoa Colón, N Honduras 15°40′N 86°01′W
62 H4 Tocopilla Antofagasta, N Chile 22°06′S 70°08′W
62 J4 Tocorpuri, Cerro de ▲ Bolivia/Chile 22°26′S 67°53′W
183 O10 Tocumwal New South Wales, SE Australia 35°53′S 145°35′E
54 K4 Tocuyo de la Costa Falcón, NW Venezuela 11°04′N 68°23′W
152 H13 Toda Rāisingh Rājasthān, N India 26°02′N 75°35′E
106 H13 Todi Umbria, C Italy 42°47′N 12°25′E
108 G9 Tödi ▲ NE Switzerland 46°52′N 08°53′E
171 T12 Todlo Papua, E Indonesia 0°46′S 130°50′E
165 S9 Todoga-saki headland Honshū, C Japan 39°33′N 142°02′E
59 P17 Todos os Santos, Baía de bay E Brazil
40 F10 Todos Santos Baja California Sur, NW Mexico 23°28′N 110°14′W
40 B2 Todos Santos, Bahía de bay NW Mexico
Toeban see Tuban
Toekang Besi Eilanden see Tukangbesi, Kepulauan
Toeloengagoeng see Tulungagung
Tōen see Taoyuan
185 D25 Toetoes Bay bay South Island, New Zealand
11 Q14 Tofield Alberta, SW Canada 53°22′N 112°39′W
10 K17 Tofino Vancouver Island, British Columbia, SW Canada 49°05′N 125°51′W
189 X17 Tofol Kosrae, E Micronesia
95 J20 Tofta Halland, S Sweden 57°10′N 12°19′E
95 H15 Tofte Buskerud, S Norway 59°31′N 10°33′E
95 F24 Toftlund Syddanmark, SW Denmark 55°12′N 09°04′E
193 X15 Tofua island Ha'apai Group, C Tonga
187 Q12 Toga island Torres Islands, N Vanuatu
80 N13 Togdheer off. Gobolka Togdheer. ◐ region NW Somalia
Togdheer, Gobolka see Togdheer
164 L11 Togi Ishikawa, Honshū, SW Japan 37°06′N 136°44′E
39 N13 Togiak Alaska, USA 59°03′N 160°31′W
171 O11 Togian, Kepulauan island group C Indonesia
77 Q15 Togo off. Togolese Republic; prev. French Togoland. ◆ republic W Africa
Togolese Republic see Togo

◆ Country
● Country Capital
◇ Dependent Territory
○ Dependent Territory Capital
◐ Administrative Regions
✈ International Airport
▲ Mountain
▲▲ Mountain Range
※ Volcano
≈ River
◎ Lake
⊠ Reservoir

162 F8 **Tögrög** Govĭ-Altay, SW Mongolia *45°51′N 95°04′E*
162 F8 **Tögrög** *var.* Hoolt. Övörhangay, C Mongolia *45°31′N 103°06′E*
Tögrög *see* Manhan
159 N12 **Togton He** *var.* Tuotuo He. C China
Togton Heyan *see* Tanggulashan
Toguzak *see* Togyzak
144 L7 **Togyzak** *prev.* Toguzak. Kazakhstan/Russian Federation
37 P10 **Tohatchi** New Mexico, SW USA *35°51′N 108°45′W*
191 O7 **Tohiea, Mont** Moorea, W French Polynesia *17°33′S 149°48′W*
137 N14 **Tohma Çayı** C Turkey
93 O17 **Tohmajärvi** Itä-Suomi, SE Finland *62°12′N 30°19′E*
93 L16 **Toholampi** Länsi-Suomi, W Finland *63°46′N 24°15′E*
Töhöm *see* Mandah
23 X12 **Tohopekaliga, Lake** Florida, SE USA
164 M14 **Toi** Shizuoka, Honshū, S Japan *34°55′N 138°45′E*
190 B15 **Toi** N Niue *18°57′S 169°51′W*
93 L19 **Toijala** Länsi-Suomi, SW Finland *61°09′N 23°51′E*
171 P12 **Toima** Sulawesi, N Indonesia *0°48′S 122°21′E*
164 D17 **Toi-misaki** Kyūshū, SW Japan
171 Q17 **Toineke** Timor, S Indonesia *10°06′S 124°22′E*
Toirc, Inis *see* Inishturk
35 U6 **Toiyabe Range** ▲▲ Nevada, W USA
Tojikiston, Jumhurii *see* Tajikistan
147 R12 **Tojikobod** *Rus.* Tadzhikabad. C Tajikistan *39°08′N 70°54′E*
164 G12 **Tōjō** Hiroshima, Honshū, SW Japan *34°54′N 133°15′E*
39 T10 **Tok** Alaska, USA *63°20′N 142°59′W*
164 K13 **Tōkai** Aichi, Honshū, SW Japan *35°01′N 136°51′E*
111 N21 **Tokaj** Borsod-Abaúj-Zemplén, NE Hungary *48°08′N 21°25′E*
165 N11 **Tōkamachi** Niigata, Honshū, C Japan *37°08′N 138°44′E*
185 D25 **Tokanui** Southland, South Island, New Zealand *46°33′S 169°02′E*
80 I7 **Tokar** *var.* Ţawkar. Red Sea, NE Sudan *18°27′N 37°41′E*
136 L12 **Tokat** Tokat, N Turkey *40°20′N 36°35′E*
136 L12 **Tokat** ◈ *province* N Turkey
Tŏkchŏk-kundo *see* Deokjeok-gundo
Tōke *see* Taka Atoll
190 J9 **Tokelau** ◇ *NZ overseas territory* W Polynesia
Tőketerebes *see* Trebišov
Tokhtamyshbek *see* Tŭkhtamish
24 M6 **Tokio** Texas, SW USA *33°09′N 102°31′W*
Tokio *see* Tōkyō
189 W11 **Toki Point** *point* NW Wake Island
Tokkuztara *see* Gongliu
117 V9 **Tokmak** *var.* Velykyy Tokmak. Zaporiz'ka Oblast', SE Ukraine *47°13′N 35°43′E*
Tokmak *see* Tomok
184 Q8 **Tokomaru Bay** Gisborne, North Island, New Zealand *38°10′S 178°18′E*
184 M8 **Tokoroa** Waikato, North Island, New Zealand *38°14′S 175°52′E*
76 K14 **Tokounou** C Guinea *09°43′N 09°46′W*
38 M12 **Toksook Bay** Alaska, USA *60°33′N 165°01′W*
Toksu *see* Xinhe
Toksum *see* Toksun
158 L6 **Toksun** *var.* Toksum. Xinjiang Uygur Zizhiqu, NW China *42°47′N 88°38′E*
147 T8 **Toktogul** Talasskaya Oblast', NW Kyrgyzstan *41°51′N 72°56′E*
147 T9 **Toktogul'skoye Vodokhranilishche** W Kyrgyzstan
Toktomush *see* Tŭkhtamish
193 Y14 **Toku** *island* Vava'u Group, N Tonga
165 U16 **Tokunoshima** Kagoshima, Tokuno-shima, SW Japan
165 U16 **Tokuno-shima** *island* Nansei-shotō, SW Japan
164 I14 **Tokushima** *var.* Tokusima. Tokushima, Shikoku, SW Japan *34°04′N 134°28′E*
164 H14 **Tokushima** *off.* Tokushima-ken, *var.* Tokusima. ◈ *prefecture* Shikoku, SW Japan
Tokushima-ken *see* Tokushima
Tokusima *see* Tokushima
164 E13 **Tokuyama** *var.* Shūnan. Yamaguchi, Honshū, SW Japan *34°04′N 131°48′E*
165 N13 **Tōkyō** *var.* Tokio. ● (Japan) Tōkyō, Honshū, S Japan *35°40′N 139°45′E*
165 O13 **Tōkyō** *off.* Tōkyō-to. ◈ *capital district* Honshū, S Japan
Tōkyō-to *see* Tōkyō
145 T12 **Tokyrau** C Kazakhstan
149 O3 **Tokzār** *Pash.* Tukzār. Sar-e Pul, N Afghanistan *35°47′N 66°28′E*
145 W13 **Tokzhaylau** *prev.* Dzerzhinskoye. Almaty, SE Kazakhstan *45°49′N 81°04′E*
145 W13 **Tokzhaylau** *var.* Dzerzhinskoye. Taldykorgan, SE Kazakhstan *45°49′N 81°04′E*
189 U12 **Tol** *atoll* Chuuk Islands, C Micronesia
184 Q9 **Tolaga Bay** Gisborne, North Island, New Zealand *38°22′S 178°17′E*
172 I7 **Tôlañaro** *prev.* Faradofay, Fort-Dauphin. Toliara, SE Madagascar
162 D6 **Tolbo** Bayan-Ölgiy, W Mongolia *48°22′N 90°22′E*
Tolbukhin *see* Dobrich
60 G11 **Toledo** Paraná, S Brazil *24°45′S 53°41′W*
54 G8 **Toledo** Norte de Santander, N Colombia *07°16′N 72°28′W*
105 N9 **Toledo** *anc.* Toletum. Castilla-La Mancha, C Spain *39°52′N 04°02′W*
30 M14 **Toledo** Illinois, N USA *39°16′N 88°15′W*
29 W13 **Toledo** Iowa, C USA *42°00′N 92°34′W*
31 R11 **Toledo** Ohio, N USA *41°40′N 83°33′W*
32 F12 **Toledo** Oregon, NW USA *44°37′N 123°56′W*
32 G9 **Toledo** Washington, NW USA *46°27′N 122°49′W*
42 F3 **Toledo** ◈ *district* S Belize
104 M9 **Toledo** ◈ *province* Castilla-La Mancha, C Spain
25 Y7 **Toledo Bend Reservoir** Louisiana/Texas, SW USA
104 M10 **Toledo, Montes de** ▲▲ C Spain
106 J12 **Tolentino** Marche, C Italy *43°08′N 13°17′E*
Toletum *see* Toledo
94 H10 **Tolga** Hedmark, S Norway *62°25′N 11°00′E*
158 J3 **Toli** Xinjiang Uygur Zizhiqu, NW China *45°55′N 83°33′E*
172 H7 **Toliara** *var.* Toliary; *prev.* Tuléar. Toliara, SW Madagascar *23°20′S 43°41′E*
172 H7 **Toliara** ◈ *province* SW Madagascar
Toliary *see* Toliara
118 H11 **Toliejai** *prev.* Kamajai. Panevėžys, NE Lithuania *55°16′N 25°30′E*
54 D11 **Tolima** *off.* Departamento del Tolima. ◈ *province* C Colombia
Tolima, Departamento del *see* Tolima
171 N11 **Tolitoli** Sulawesi, C Indonesia *01°05′N 120°50′E*
95 K22 **Tollarp** Skåne, S Sweden *55°55′N 14°00′E*
100 N9 **Tollense** NE Germany
100 N10 **Tollensesee** NE Germany
36 K13 **Tolleson** Arizona, SW USA *33°25′N 112°15′W*
146 M13 **Tollimarjon** *Rus.* Talimardzhan. Qashqadaryo Viloyati, S Uzbekistan *38°22′N 65°31′E*
Tolmein *see* Tolmin
106 J6 **Tolmezzo** Friuli-Venezia Giulia, NE Italy *46°27′N 13°01′E*
109 S11 **Tolmin** *Ger.* Tolmein, *It.* Tolmino. W Slovenia *46°12′N 13°39′E*
Tolmino *see* Tolmin
111 J25 **Tolna** *Ger.* Tolnau. Tolna, S Hungary *46°26′N 18°47′E*
111 I24 **Tolna** *off.* Tolna Megye. ◈ *county* SW Hungary
Tolna Megye *see* Tolna
Tolnau *see* Tolna
79 I20 **Tolo** Bandundu, W Dem. Rep. Congo *02°57′S 18°35′E*
Tolochin *see* Talachyn
190 D12 **Toloke** Île Futuna, W Wallis and Futuna
30 M13 **Tolono** Illinois, N USA *39°59′N 88°16′W*
105 Q3 **Tolosa** País Vasco, N Spain *43°09′N 02°04′W*
Tolosa *see* Toulouse
171 O13 **Tolo, Teluk** *bay* Sulawesi, C Indonesia
39 R9 **Tolovana River** Alaska, USA
123 U10 **Tolstoy, Mys** *headland* E Russian Federation *59°12′N 155°04′E*
63 G15 **Toltén** Araucanía, C Chile *39°13′S 73°15′W*
63 G15 **Toltén, Río** S Chile
54 E6 **Tolú** Sucre, NW Colombia *09°32′N 75°34′W*
41 O14 **Toluca** *var.* Toluca de Lerdo. México, S Mexico *19°20′N 99°40′W*
Toluca de Lerdo *see* Toluca
41 O14 **Toluca, Nevado de** C Mexico *19°05′N 99°45′W*
127 R6 **Tol'yatti** *prev.* Stavropol'. Samarskaya Oblast', W Russian Federation *53°32′N 49°27′E*
77 O12 **Toma** NW Burkina *12°46′N 02°51′W*
30 K7 **Tomah** Wisconsin, N USA *43°59′N 90°31′W*
30 L5 **Tomahawk** Wisconsin, N USA *45°27′N 89°40′W*
117 T8 **Tomakivka** Dnipropetrovs'ka Oblast', E Ukraine *47°47′N 34°45′E*
165 S4 **Tomakomai** Hokkaidō, NE Japan *42°38′N 141°32′E*
165 S2 **Tomamae** Hokkaidō, NE Japan *44°18′N 141°38′E*
104 G9 **Tomar** Santarém, W Portugal *39°36′N 08°25′W*
123 T13 **Tomari** Ostrov Sakhalin, Sakhalinskaya Oblast', SE Russian Federation *47°47′N 142°09′E*
115 C16 **Tómaros** ▲ W Greece *39°31′N 20°45′E*
Tomaschow *see* Tomaszów Mazowiecki
Tomaschow *see* Tomaszów Lubelski
61 E16 **Tomás Gomensoro** Artigas, N Uruguay *30°28′S 57°28′W*
117 N7 **Tomashpil'** Vinnyts'ka Oblast', C Ukraine *48°32′N 28°31′E*
Tomaszów *see* Tomaszów Mazowiecki
111 P15 **Tomaszów Lubelski** *Ger.* Tomaschow. Lubelskie, E Poland *50°29′N 23°23′E*
Tomaszów Mazowiecka *see* Tomaszów Mazowiecki
110 L13 **Tomaszów Mazowiecki** *var.* Tomaszów Mazowiecka; *prev.* Tomaszów, *Ger.* Tomaschow. Łódzkie, C Poland *51°33′N 20°E*
40 J13 **Tomatlán** Jalisco, C Mexico *19°53′N 105°18′W*
81 F15 **Tombe** Jonglei, E South Sudan *05°52′N 31°40′E*
23 N4 **Tombigbee River** Alabama/Mississippi, S USA
82 A10 **Tomboco** Dem. Rep. Congo, NW Angola *06°50′S 13°20′E*
77 O10 **Tombouctou** *Eng.* Timbuktu. Tombouctou, N Mali *16°47′N 03°03′W*
77 N9 **Tombouctou** ◈ *region* W Mali
37 N16 **Tombstone** Arizona, SW USA *31°42′N 110°04′W*
83 A15 **Tombua** *Port.* Porto Alexandre. Namibe, SW Angola *15°49′S 11°53′E*
83 J19 **Tom Burke** Limpopo, NE South Africa *23°07′S 28°01′E*
146 L9 **Tomdibuloq** *Rus.* Tamdybulak. Navoiy Viloyati, N Uzbekistan *41°48′N 64°33′E*
146 L9 **Tomditov-Tog'lari** ▲▲ N Uzbekistan
62 G13 **Tomé** Bío Bío, C Chile *36°38′S 72°57′W*
58 L12 **Tomé-Açu** Pará, NE Brazil *02°25′S 48°09′W*
95 L23 **Tomelilla** Skåne, S Sweden *55°33′N 14°00′E*
105 O10 **Tomelloso** Castilla-La Mancha, C Spain *39°09′N 03°01′W*
14 H10 **Tomiko Lake** Ontario, S Canada
77 N12 **Tominian** Ségou, C Mali *13°18′N 04°39′W*
Tomini, Gulf of *see* Tomini, Teluk
171 N12 **Tomini, Teluk** *var.* Gulf of Tomini; *prev.* Teluk Gorontalo. *bay* Sulawesi, C Indonesia
165 Q11 **Tomioka** Fukushima, Honshū, C Japan *37°19′N 140°57′E*
113 G14 **Tomislavgrad** Federacija Bosna I Hercegovina, SW Bosnia and Herzegovina *43°43′N 17°15′E*
181 O9 **Tomkinson Ranges** ▲▲ South Australia/Western Australia
123 Q11 **Tommot** Respublika Sakha (Yakutiya), NE Russian Federation *58°57′N 126°24′E*
171 Q11 **Tomohon** Sulawesi, N Indonesia *01°19′N 124°49′E*
147 V7 **Tomok** *prev.* Tokmak. Chuyskaya Oblast', N Kyrgyzstan *42°50′N 75°18′E*
54 K9 **Tomo, Río** E Colombia
113 L21 **Tomorrit, Mali i** ▲ S Albania *40°43′N 20°12′E*
11 S17 **Tompkins** Saskatchewan, S Canada *50°03′N 108°49′W*
20 K8 **Tompkinsville** Kentucky, S USA *36°43′N 85°41′W*
171 N11 **Tompo** Sulawesi, N Indonesia *0°56′N 120°16′E*
180 I8 **Tom Price** Western Australia *22°48′S 117°49′E*
122 J12 **Tomsk** Tomskaya Oblast', C Russian Federation *56°30′N 85°05′E*
122 I11 **Tomskaya Oblast'** ◈ *province* C Russian Federation
18 K16 **Toms River** New Jersey, NE USA *39°56′N 74°09′W*
Tom Steed Lake *see* Tom Steed Reservoir
26 L12 **Tom Steed Reservoir** *var.* Tom Steed Lake. Oklahoma, C USA
171 U13 **Tomu** Papua, E Indonesia *02°07′S 133°01′E*
158 H6 **Tomür Feng** *var.* Pobeda Peak, *Rus.* Pik Pobedy. ▲ China/Kyrgyzstan *42°02′N 80°07′E* *see also* Pobedy, Pik
Tomür Feng *see* Pobedy, Pik
189 N13 **Tomworoahlang** Pohnpei, E Micronesia
41 U17 **Tonalá** Chiapas, SE Mexico *16°08′N 93°41′W*
106 F6 **Tonale, Passo del** *pass* N Italy
164 I11 **Tonami** Toyama, Honshū, SW Japan *36°40′N 136°55′E*
58 C12 **Tonantins** Amazonas, W Brazil *02°58′S 67°30′W*
32 K6 **Tonasket** Washington, NW USA *48°41′N 119°27′W*
55 Y9 **Tonate** *var.* Macouria. N French Guiana *05°00′N 52°28′W*
18 D10 **Tonawanda** New York, NE USA *43°00′N 78°51′W*
42 I7 **Toncontín** *prev.* Tegucigalpa. ● (Honduras) Francisco Morazán, SW Honduras *14°04′N 87°11′W*
42 H7 **Toncontín** ✈ Central District, C Honduras *14°03′N 87°20′W*
171 Q11 **Tondano** Sulawesi, C Indonesia *01°19′N 124°56′E*
104 H7 **Tondela** Viseu, N Portugal *40°31′N 08°05′W*
95 F24 **Tønder** *Ger.* Tondern. Syddanmark, SW Denmark *54°57′N 08°53′E*
Tondern *see* Tønder
143 N4 **Tonekābon** *var.* Shahsawar, Tonkābon; *prev.* Shahsavār. Māzandarān, N Iran *36°40′N 51°25′E*
Tonezh *see* Tonyezh
193 Y14 **Tonga** *off.* Kingdom of Tonga, *var.* Friendly Islands. ◆ *monarchy* SW Pacific Ocean
175 R9 **Tonga** *island group* SW Pacific Ocean
Tongaat *see* oThongathi
Tonga, Kingdom of *see* Tonga
161 Q13 **Tong'an** *var.* Datong, Tong an. Fujian, SE China *24°43′N 118°07′E*
Tong an *see* Tong'an
27 Q4 **Tonganoxie** Kansas, C USA *39°06′N 95°05′W*
39 Y13 **Tongass National Forest** *reserve* Alaska, USA
193 Y16 **Tongatapu** ✈ Tongatapu, S Tonga *21°10′S 175°10′W*
193 Y16 **Tongatapu** *island* Tongatapu Group, S Tonga
193 Y16 **Tongatapu Group** *island group* S Tonga
175 S9 **Tonga Trench** *undersea feature* S Pacific Ocean
161 N8 **Tongbai Shan** ▲▲ C China
161 P8 **Tongcheng** Anhui, E China *31°16′N 117°00′E*
160 L6 **Tongchuan** Shaanxi, C China *35°10′N 109°03′E*
160 L12 **Tongdao** *var.* Tongdao Dongzu Zizhixian; *prev.* Shuangjiang. Hunan, S China *26°06′N 109°46′E*
Tongdao Dongzu Zizhixian *see* Tongdao
159 T11 **Tongde** *var.* Gabasumdo. Qinghai, C China *35°13′N 100°39′E*
99 K19 **Tongeren** *Fr.* Tongres. Limburg, NE Belgium *50°47′N 05°28′E*
Tonghae *see* Donghae
160 G13 **Tonghai** *var.* Xiushan. Yunnan, SW China *24°06′N 102°45′E*
163 X8 **Tonghe** Heilongjiang, NE China *46°00′N 128°45′E*
163 W11 **Tonghua** Jilin, NE China *41°45′N 125°50′E*
163 Z6 **Tongjiang** Heilongjiang, NE China *47°39′N 132°29′E*
163 Y13 **Tongjosŏn-man** *prev.* Broughton Bay. *bay* E North Korea
163 V7 **Tongken He** NE China
167 T7 **Tongking, Gulf of** *Chin.* Beibu Wan, *Vtn.* Vinh Băc Bô. *gulf* China/Vietnam
163 U10 **Tongliao** Nei Mongol Zizhiqu, N China *43°37′N 122°15′E*
161 Q9 **Tongling** Anhui, E China *30°55′N 117°50′E*
161 R9 **Tonglu** Zhejiang, SE China *29°50′N 119°38′E*
187 R14 **Tongoa** *island* Shepherd Islands, S Vanuatu
62 G9 **Tongoy** Coquimbo, C Chile *30°16′S 71°31′W*
160 L11 **Tongren** *var.* Rongwo. Guizhou, S China *27°44′N 109°10′E*
159 T11 **Tongren** *var.* Rongwo. Qinghai, C China *35°31′N 101°58′E*
Tongres *see* Tongeren
153 U11 **Tongsa** *var.* Tongsa Dzong. C Bhutan *27°33′N 90°30′E*
Tongsa Dzong *see* Tongsa
Tongshan *see* Fuding, Fujian, China
Tongshan *see* Xuzhou, Jiangsu, China
Tongshi *see* Wuzhishan
159 P12 **Tongtian He** *var.* Zhi Qu. C China
96 I6 **Tongue** N Scotland, United Kingdom *58°30′N 04°25′W*
44 H3 **Tongue of the Ocean** *strait* C Bahamas
33 X10 **Tongue River** Montana, NW USA
33 W11 **Tongue River Resevoir** Montana, NW USA
159 V11 **Tongwei** *var.* Pingxiang. Gansu, C China *35°09′N 105°15′E*
159 W9 **Tongxin** Ningxia, N China *37°00′N 105°41′E*
163 U9 **Tongyu** *var.* Kaitong. Jilin, NE China *44°49′N 123°08′E*
160 J11 **Tongzi** *var.* Loushanguan. Guizhou, S China *28°08′N 106°49′E*
162 F8 **Tonhil** *var.* Dzüyl. Govĭ-Altay, SW Mongolia *46°09′N 93°55′E*
40 G5 **Tónichi** Sonora, NW Mexico *28°37′N 109°34′W*
81 D14 **Tonj** Warap, W South Sudan *07°18′N 28°41′E*
152 H13 **Tonk** Rājasthān, N India *26°10′N 75°50′E*
Tonkābon *see* Tonekābon
27 N8 **Tonkawa** Oklahoma, C USA *36°40′N 97°18′W*
167 Q12 **Tônlé Sap** *Eng.* Great Lake. W Cambodia
102 L14 **Tonneins** Lot-et-Garonne, SW France *44°21′N 00°21′E*
103 Q7 **Tonnerre** Yonne, C France *47°50′N 04°00′E*
Tonoas *see* Dublon
35 U8 **Tonopah** Nevada, W USA *38°04′N 117°13′W*
164 H13 **Tonoshō** Okayama, Shōdo-shima, SW Japan *34°29′N 134°10′E*
43 S17 **Tonosí** Los Santos, S Panama *07°23′N 80°26′W*
95 H16 **Tønsberg** Vestfold, S Norway *59°16′N 10°25′E*
39 T11 **Tonsina** Alaska, USA *61°39′N 145°10′W*
95 D17 **Tonstad** Vest-Agder, S Norway *58°40′N 06°42′E*
193 X15 **Tonumea** *island* Nomuka Group, W Tonga
137 O11 **Tonya** Trabzon, NE Turkey *40°52′N 39°17′E*
119 K20 **Tonyezh** *Rus.* Tonezh. Homyel'skaya Voblasts', SE Belarus *51°50′N 27°48′E*
36 L3 **Tooele** Utah, W USA *40°32′N 112°18′W*
122 L13 **Toora-Khem** Respublika Tyva, S Russian Federation *52°25′N 96°01′E*
183 O5 **Toorale East** New South Wales, SE Australia *30°29′S 145°25′E*
83 H25 **Toorberg** ▲ S South Africa *32°02′S 24°02′E*
118 G5 **Tootsi** Pärnumaa, SW Estonia *58°34′N 24°43′E*
183 U3 **Toowoomba** Queensland, E Australia *27°35′S 151°54′E*
27 Q4 **Topeka** *state capital* Kansas, C USA *39°03′N 95°41′W*
122 J12 **Topki** Kemerovskaya Oblast', S Russian Federation *55°12′N 85°40′E*
111 M18 **Topľa** *Hung.* Toplya. NE Slovakia
Toplicza *see* Toplița
116 J10 **Toplița** *Ger.* Töplitz, *Hung.* Maroshevíz; *prev.* Toplița Română, *Hung.* Oláh-Toplicza, Toplicza. Harghita, C Romania *45°56′N 25°20′E*
Toplița Română/Töplitz *see* Toplița
Toplya *see* Topľa
111 I20 **Topoľčany** *Hung.* Nagytapolcsány. Nitriansky Kraj, W Slovakia *48°33′N 18°10′E*
40 G8 **Topolobampo** Sinaloa, C Mexico *25°36′N 109°04′W*
116 I13 **Topoloveni** Argeș, S Romania *44°49′N 25°02′E*
114 L11 **Topolovgrad** *prev.* Kavakli. Khaskovo, S Bulgaria *42°06′N 26°20′E*
Topolya *see* Bačka Topola
32 J10 **Toppenish** Washington, NW USA *46°22′N 120°18′W*
181 P4 **Top Springs Roadhouse** Northern Territory, N Australia *16°37′S 131°49′E*
189 U11 **Tora** *island* Chuuk, C Micronesia
Toraigh *see* Tory Island
189 U11 **Tora Island Pass** *passage* Chuuk Islands, C Micronesia
143 U5 **Torbat-e Ḩeydarīyeh** *var.* Turbat-i-Haidari. Khorāsān-Razavī, NE Iran *35°18′N 59°12′E*
143 V5 **Torbat-e Jām** *var.* Turbat-i-Jam. Khorāsān-Razavī, NE Iran *35°16′N 60°36′E*
39 Q11 **Torbert, Mount** ▲ Alaska, USA *61°30′N 152°15′W*
31 P6 **Torch Lake** Michigan, N USA
Törcsvár *see* Bran
Torda *see* Turda
104 L6 **Tordesillas** Castilla y León, N Spain *41°30′N 05°00′W*
92 K13 **Töre** Norrbotten, N Sweden *65°55′N 22°40′E*
95 L17 **Töreboda** Västra Götaland, S Sweden *58°41′N 14°07′E*
95 J21 **Torekov** Skåne, S Sweden *56°25′N 12°39′E*
92 O3 **Torell Land** *physical region* SW Svalbard
105 U4 **Toretta de l'Orrí** *var.* Llorri; *prev.* Tossal de l'Orrí. ▲ NE Spain *42°24′N 01°15′E*
144 M14 **Toretum** Kyzylorda, S Kazakhstan *45°38′N 63°20′E*
117 Y8 **Torez** Donets'ka Oblast', SE Ukraine *48°00′N 38°38′E*
101 N14 **Torgau** Sachsen, E Germany *51°34′N 13°01′E*
145 R8 **Torgay** *Kaz.* Torghay; *prev.* Turgay. Akmola, W Kazakhstan *51°46′N 72°45′E*
145 N10 **Torgay** *prev.* Turgay. C Kazakhstan
Torgay Üstirti *see* Turgayskaya Stolovaya Strana
Torghay *see* Torgay
95 N22 **Torhamn** Blekinge, S Sweden *56°04′N 15°49′E*
99 C17 **Torhout** West-Vlaanderen, W Belgium *51°04′N 03°06′E*
106 B8 **Torino** *Eng.* Turin. Piemonte, NW Italy *45°03′N 07°39′E*
Tori-shima *see* Īo-Tori-shima
81 F16 **Torit** Eastern Equatoria, S South Sudan *04°27′N 32°31′E*
186 H6 **Toriu** New Britain, E Papua New Guinea *04°39′S 151°42′E*
148 M4 **Torkestān, Selseleh-ye Band-e** *var.* Bandi-i Turkistan. ▲▲ NW Afghanistan
104 L7 **Tormes** W Spain
Tornacum *see* Tournai
Torneå *see* Tornio
92 K12 **Torneälven** *var.* Torniojoki, *Fin.* Tornionjoki. Finland/Sweden
92 I11 **Torneträsk** N Sweden
13 O4 **Torngat Mountains** ▲▲ Newfoundland and Labrador, NE Canada
24 H8 **Tornillo** Texas, SW USA *31°26′N 106°06′W*
92 K13 **Tornio** *Swe.* Torneå. Lappi, NW Finland *65°50′N 24°18′E*
Torniojoki/Tornionjoki *see* Torneälven
61 B23 **Tornquist** Buenos Aires, E Argentina *38°08′S 62°15′W*
104 L6 **Toro** Castilla y León, N Spain *41°31′N 05°24′W*
62 H9 **Toro, Cerro del** ▲ N Chile *29°10′S 69°43′W*
77 R12 **Torodi** Tillabéri, SW Niger *13°05′N 01°46′E*
Törökbecse *see* Novi Bečej
186 J7 **Torokina** Bougainville Island, NE Papua New Guinea *06°12′S 155°04′E*
111 L23 **Törökszentmiklós** Jász-Nagykun-Szolnok, E Hungary *47°11′N 20°26′E*
42 G7 **Torola, Río** El Salvador/Honduras
Toronaíos, Kólpos *see* Kassándras, Kólpos
14 H15 **Toronto** *province capital* Ontario, S Canada *43°42′N 79°25′W*
31 V12 **Toronto** Ohio, N USA *40°27′N 80°36′W*
Toronto *see* Lester B. Pearson
27 P6 **Toronto Lake** Kansas, C USA
35 V16 **Toro Peak** ▲ California, W USA *33°31′N 116°25′W*
124 H16 **Toropets** Tverskaya Oblast', W Russian Federation *56°29′N 31°37′E*
81 G18 **Tororo** E Uganda *0°42′N 34°12′E*
136 H16 **Toros Dağları** *Eng.* Taurus Mountains. ▲▲ S Turkey
183 N13 **Torquay** Victoria, SE Australia *38°21′S 144°18′E*
97 J24 **Torquay** SW England, United Kingdom *50°28′N 03°30′W*
104 M5 **Torquemada** Castilla y León, N Spain *42°02′N 04°17′W*
35 S16 **Torrance** California, W USA *33°50′N 118°20′W*
104 G12 **Torrão** Setúbal, S Portugal *38°18′N 08°13′W*
104 H8 **Torre, Alto da** ▲ C Portugal *40°21′N 07°31′W*
107 K18 **Torre Annunziata** Campania, S Italy *40°45′N 14°27′E*
105 T8 **Torreblanca** Valenciana, E Spain *40°14′N 00°12′E*
104 L15 **Torrecilla** ▲ S Spain *36°38′N 04°54′W*
105 P4 **Torrecilla en Cameros** La Rioja, N Spain *42°18′N 02°33′W*
105 N13 **Torredelcampo** Andalucía, S Spain *37°45′N 03°52′W*
107 K17 **Torre del Greco** Campania, S Italy *40°46′N 14°22′E*
104 I6 **Torre de Moncorvo** *var.* Moncorvo, Tôrre de Moncorvo. Bragança, N Portugal *41°10′N 07°03′W*
104 J9 **Torrejoncillo** Extremadura, W Spain *39°54′N 06°28′W*
105 O8 **Torrejón de Ardoz** Madrid, C Spain *40°27′N 03°29′W*
105 N7 **Torrelaguna** Madrid, C Spain *40°50′N 03°33′W*
105 N2 **Torrelavega** Cantabria, N Spain *43°21′N 04°03′W*
107 M16 **Torremaggiore** Puglia, SE Italy *41°42′N 15°17′E*
104 M15 **Torremolinos** Andalucía, S Spain *36°38′N 04°30′W*
182 I6 **Torrens, Lake** *salt lake* South Australia
105 S10 **Torrent** *Cas.* Torrente, *var.* Torrent de l'Horta. Valenciana, E Spain *39°27′N 00°28′W*
Torrent de l'Horta/Torrente *see* Torrent
40 L8 **Torreón** Coahuila, NE Mexico *25°47′N 103°21′W*
105 R13 **Torre-Pacheco** Murcia, SE Spain *37°43′N 00°57′W*
106 A8 **Torre Pellice** Piemonte, NE Italy *44°49′N 07°12′E*
105 O13 **Torreperogil** Andalucía, S Spain *38°02′N 03°17′W*
61 J15 **Torres** Rio Grande do Sul, S Brazil *29°20′S 49°43′W*
Torrès, Îles *see* Torres Islands
187 Q11 **Torres Islands** *Fr.* Îles Torrès. *island group* N Vanuatu
104 G9 **Torres Novas** Santarém, C Portugal *39°28′N 08°32′W*
181 V1 **Torres Strait** *strait* Australia/Papua New Guinea
104 F10 **Torres Vedras** Lisboa, C Portugal *39°05′N 09°15′W*
105 S13 **Torrevieja** Valenciana, E Spain *37°59′N 00°40′W*
186 B6 **Torricelli Mountains** ▲▲ NW Papua New Guinea
96 G8 **Torridon, Loch** *inlet* NW Scotland, United Kingdom
106 D9 **Torriglia** Liguria, NW Italy *44°31′N 09°08′E*
104 M9 **Torrijos** Castilla-La Mancha, C Spain *39°59′N 04°18′W*
18 L12 **Torrington** Connecticut, NE USA *41°48′N 73°07′W*
33 Z15 **Torrington** Wyoming, C USA *42°04′N 104°10′W*
Torröjen *see* Torrön
94 F16 **Torrön** *prev.* Torröjen. C Sweden
105 N15 **Torrox** Andalucía, S Spain *36°45′N 03°58′W*
94 N13 **Torsåker** Gävleborg, C Sweden *60°31′N 16°30′E*
95 N21 **Torsås** Kalmar, S Sweden *56°24′N 16°00′E*
95 J14 **Torsby** Värmland, C Sweden *60°07′N 13°E*
95 N16 **Torshälla** Södermanland, C Sweden *59°25′N 16°28′E*
95 B19 **Tórshavn** *Dan.* Thorshavn. ○ Faeroe Islands *62°02′N 06°47′W*
Torshiz *see* Kāshmar
146 I9 **To'rtkok'l** *var.* Tŭrtkŭl, *Rus.* Turtkul'; *prev.* Petroaleksandrovsk. Qoraqalpog'iston Respublikasi, W Uzbekistan *41°35′N 61°E*
Tortoise Islands *see* Colón, Archipiélago de
45 T9 **Tortola** *island* C British Virgin Islands
106 D9 **Tortona** *anc.* Dertona. Piemonte, NW Italy *44°54′N 08°52′E*
107 L23 **Tortorici** Sicilia, Italy, C Mediterranean Sea *38°02′N 14°49′E*
105 U7 **Tortosa** *anc.* Dertosa. Cataluña, E Spain *40°49′N 00°31′E*
Tortosa *see* Ţarţūs
105 U7 **Tortosa, Cap** *cape* E Spain
44 L8 **Tortue, Île de la** *var.* Tortuga Island. *island* N Haiti
55 Y10 **Tortue, Montagne** ▲▲ C French Guiana
Tortuga, Isla *see* La Tortuga, Isla
Tortuga Island *see* Tortue, Île de la
54 C11 **Tortugas, Golfo** *gulf* W Colombia
45 T5 **Tortuguero, Laguna** *lagoon* N Puerto Rico
137 Q12 **Tortum** Erzurum, NE Turkey *40°20′N 41°36′E*
Torugart, Pereval *see* Turugart Shankou
137 O12 **Torul** Gümüşhane, NE Turkey *40°35′N 39°18′E*
110 J10 **Toruń** *Ger.* Thorn. Toruń, Kujawsko-pomorskie, C Poland *53°02′N 18°36′E*
95 K20 **Torup** Halland, S Sweden *56°57′N 13°04′E*
118 I6 **Tõrva** *Ger.* Törwa. Valgamaa, S Estonia *58°00′N 25°54′E*
Törwa *see* Tõrva
96 D13 **Tory Island** *Ir.* Toraigh. *island* NW Ireland
111 N19 **Torysa** *Hung.* Tarca. NE Slovakia
Törzburg *see* Bran
124 J16 **Torzhok** Tverskaya Oblast', W Russian Federation *57°04′N 34°55′E*
164 F15 **Tosa-Shimizu** *var.* Tosasimizu. Kōchi, Shikoku, SW Japan *32°47′N 132°58′E*
Tosasimizu *see* Tosa-Shimizu
164 G15 **Tosa-wan** *bay* SW Japan
83 H21 **Tosca** North-West, N South Africa *25°51′S 23°56′E*
106 F12 **Toscana** *Eng.* Tuscany. ◈ *region* C Italy
107 E14 **Toscano, Archipelago** *Eng.* Tuscan Archipelago. *island group* C Italy
106 G10 **Tosco-Emiliano, Appennino** *Eng.* Tuscan-Emilian Mountains. ▲▲ C Italy
Tōsei *see* Dongshi
165 N15 **To-shima** *island* Izu-shotō, SE Japan
147 Q9 **Toshkent** *Eng./Rus.* Tashkent. ● Toshkent Viloyati, E Uzbekistan *41°19′N 69°17′E*
147 Q9 **Toshkent** ✈ Toshkent Viloyati, E Uzbekistan *41°13′N 69°15′E*
147 P9 **Toshkent Viloyati** *Rus.* Tashkentskaya Oblast'. ◈ *province* E Uzbekistan
124 H13 **Tosno** Leningradskaya Oblast', NW Russian Federation *59°34′N 30°48′E*
159 Q10 **Toson Hu** C China
162 H6 **Tosontsengel** Dzavhan, NW Mongolia *48°42′N 98°14′E*
162 J6 **Tosontsengel** *var.* Tsengel. Hövsgöl, N Mongolia *49°29′N 101°09′E*
146 I8 **Tosquduq Qumlari** *var.* Goshquduq Qum, Taskuduk, Peski. *desert* W Uzbekistan
Tossal de l'Orrí *see* Toretta de l'Orrí
61 A15 **Tostado** Santa Fe, C Argentina *29°15′S 61°45′W*
118 F6 **Tõstamaa** *Ger.* Testama. Pärnumaa, SW Estonia *58°20′N 23°59′E*
100 I10 **Tostedt** Niedersachsen, NW Germany *53°16′N 09°42′E*
136 J11 **Tosya** Kastamonu, N Turkey *41°02′N 34°02′E*
95 F15 **Totak** S Norway
105 R13 **Totana** Murcia, SE Spain *37°45′N 01°30′W*
94 H13 **Toten** *physical region* S Norway
83 G18 **Toteng** North-West, C Botswana *20°25′S 23°00′E*
102 M3 **Tôtes** Seine-Maritime, N France *49°40′N 01°02′E*
Totigi *see* Tochigi
Totio *see* Tochio
Totis *see* Tata
189 U13 **Totiw** *island* Chuuk, C Micronesia
125 N13 **Tot'ma** *var.* Totma. Vologodskaya Oblast', NW Russian Federation *59°58′N 42°42′E*
Tot'ma *see* Sukhona
55 V9 **Totness** Coronie, N Surinam *05°53′N 56°19′W*
42 C5 **Totonicapán** Totonicapán, W Guatemala *14°58′N 91°12′W*
42 A2 **Totonicapán** *off.* Departamento de Totonicapán. ◈ *department* W Guatemala
Totonicapán, Departamento de *see* Totonicapán
61 B18 **Totoras** Santa Fe, C Argentina *32°35′S 61°11′W*
187 Y15 **Totoya** *island* S Fiji
183 Q7 **Tottenham** New South Wales, SE Australia *32°16′S 147°23′E*
164 I12 **Tottori** Tottori, Honshū, SW Japan *35°29′N 134°14′E*
164 H12 **Tottori** *off.* Tottori-ken. ◈ *prefecture* Honshū, SW Japan
Tottori-ken *see* Tottori
76 I6 **Touâjîl** Tiris Zemmour, N Mauritania *22°03′N 12°40′W*
76 L15 **Touba** W Ivory Coast *08°17′N 07°41′W*
76 G11 **Touba** W Senegal *14°55′N 15°53′W*
74 E7 **Toubkal, Jbel** ▲ W Morocco *31°00′N 07°50′W*
32 K10 **Touchet** Washington, NW USA *46°03′N 118°40′W*
103 P7 **Toucy** Yonne, C France *47°45′N 03°18′E*
77 O12 **Tougan** W Burkina *13°06′N 03°03′W*
74 L7 **Touggourt** NE Algeria *33°08′N 06°04′E*
77 Q12 **Tougouri** N Burkina *13°22′N 00°25′W*
76 J13 **Tougué** NW Guinea *11°29′N 11°48′W*
76 K12 **Toukoto** Kayes, W Mali *13°27′N 09°52′W*
103 S5 **Toul** Meurthe-et-Moselle, NE France *48°41′N 05°54′E*
76 L16 **Toulépleu** *var.* Toulobli. W Ivory Coast *06°37′N 08°27′W*
Touliu *see* Douliu
15 U3 **Toulnustouc** Québec, SE Canada
Toulobli *see* Toulépleu
103 T16 **Toulon** *anc.* Telo Martius, Tilio Martius. Var, SE France *43°07′N 05°56′E*
30 K12 **Toulon** Illinois, N USA *41°05′N 89°54′W*
102 M15 **Toulouse** *anc.* Tolosa. Haute-Garonne, S France *43°37′N 01°25′E*
102 M15 **Toulouse** ✈ Haute-Garonne, S France *43°38′N 01°19′E*
77 N16 **Toumodi** C Ivory Coast *06°34′N 05°01′W*
74 G9 **Tounassine, Hamada** *hill range* W Algeria
Toungoo *see* Taungoo
166 K7 **Toungup** *var.* Taungup. Rakhine State, W Burma (Myanmar) *18°50′N 94°14′E*
102 L8 **Touraine** *cultural region* C France
Tourane *see* Đa Năng
103 P1 **Tourcoing** Nord, N France *50°44′N 03°10′E*
104 F2 **Touriñán, Cabo** *headland* NW Spain *43°02′N 09°20′W*
76 J6 **Tourine** Tiris Zemmour, N Mauritania *22°23′N 11°50′W*
102 J3 **Tourlaville** Manche, N France *49°38′N 01°34′W*
99 D19 **Tournai** *var.* Tournay, *Dut.* Doornik; *anc.* Tornacum. Hainaut, SW Belgium *50°36′N 03°24′E*
102 L16 **Tournay** Hautes-Pyrénées, S France *43°10′N 00°16′E*
Tournay *see* Tournai
103 R12 **Tournon** Ardèche, E France *45°05′N 04°49′E*
103 R9 **Tournus** Saône-et-Loire, C France *46°33′N 04°53′E*
59 Q14 **Touros** Rio Grande do Norte, E Brazil *05°10′S 35°29′W*
102 L8 **Tours** *anc.* Caesarodunum, Turoni. Indre-et-Loire, C France *47°22′N 00°40′E*
183 Q17 **Tourville, Cape** *headland* Tasmania, SE Australia *42°09′S 148°20′E*
44 M9 **Toussaint Louverture** ✈ E Haiti *18°38′N 72°13′W*
162 L8 **Töv** ◈ *province* C Mongolia
54 H7 **Tovar** Mérida, NW Venezuela *08°22′N 71°50′W*
126 L5 **Tovarkovskiy** Tul'skaya Oblast', W Russian Federation *53°41′N 38°18′E*
Tovil'-Dora *see* Tavildara
Tövis *see* Teiuș
137 V11 **Tovuz** *Rus.* Tauz. W Azerbaijan *40°58′N 45°41′E*
165 R7 **Towada** Aomori, Honshū, C Japan *40°35′N 141°13′E*
184 K3 **Towai** Northland, North Island, New Zealand *35°29′S 174°06′E*
18 H12 **Towanda** Pennsylvania, NE USA *41°45′N 76°25′W*
29 W4 **Tower** Minnesota, N USA *47°48′N 92°16′W*
171 N12 **Towera** Sulawesi, N Indonesia *0°29′S 120°01′E*
Tower Island *see* Genovesa, Isla
180 M13 **Tower Peak** ▲ Western Australia *33°23′S 123°27′E*
35 U11 **Towne Pass** *pass* California, W USA
29 N3 **Towner** North Dakota, N USA *48°20′N 100°27′W*
33 R10 **Townsend** Montana, NW USA *46°19′N 111°31′W*
181 X6 **Townsville** Queensland, NE Australia *19°24′S 146°53′E*
Towoeti Meer *see* Towuti, Danau

◆ Country
● Country Capital
◇ Dependent Territory
○ Dependent Territory Capital
◈ Administrative Regions
✈ International Airport
▲ Mountain
▲▲ Mountain Range
Volcano
River
Lake
Reservoir

148 K4 **Towraghoudī** Herāt, NW Afghanistan 35°13′N 62°19′E
21 X3 **Towson** Maryland, NE USA 39°25′N 76°36′W
171 O13 **Towuti, Danau** *Dut.* Towoeti Meer. ◎ Sulawesi, C Indonesia
Toxkan He *see* Ak-say
24 K9 **Toyah** Texas, SW USA 31°18′N 103°47′W
165 R4 **Tōya-ko** ◎ Hokkaidō, NE Japan
164 L11 **Toyama** Toyama, Honshū, SW Japan 36°41′N 137°13′E
164 L11 **Toyama** *off.* Toyama-ken. ◈ *prefecture* Honshū, SW Japan
Toyama-ken *see* Toyama
164 L11 **Toyama-wan** *bay* W Japan
164 H15 **Tōyo** Kōchi, Shikoku, SW Japan 33°22′N 134°18′E
Toyohara *see* Yuzhno-Sakhalinsk
164 L14 **Toyohashi** *var.* Toyohasi. Aichi, Honshū, SW Japan 34°46′N 137°22′E
Toyohasi *see* Toyohashi
164 L14 **Toyokawa** Aichi, Honshū, SW Japan 34°47′N 137°24′E
164 I14 **Toyooka** Hyōgo, Honshū, SW Japan 35°35′N 134°48′E
164 L13 **Toyota** Aichi, Honshū, SW Japan 35°04′N 137°09′E
165 T1 **Toyotomi** Hokkaidō, NE Japan 45°07′N 141°45′E
147 Q10 **To'ytepa** *Rus.* Toytepa. Toshkent Viloyati, E Uzbekistan 41°04′N 69°22′E
Toytepa *see* To'ytepa
74 M6 **Tozeur** *var.* Tawzar. W Tunisia 34°00′N 08°09′E
39 Q8 **Tozi, Mount** ▲ Alaska, USA 65°45′N 151°01′W
137 Q9 **T'q'varcheli** *Rus.* Tkvarcheli; *prev.* Tqvarch'eli. NW Georgia 42°51′N 41°42′E
Tqvarch'eli *see* T'q'varcheli
Trâblous *see* Tripoli
137 O11 **Trabzon** *Eng.* Trebizond; *anc.* Trapezus. Trabzon, NE Turkey 41°N 39°43′E
137 O11 **Trabzon** *Eng.* Trebizond. ◈ *province* NE Turkey
13 P13 **Tracadie** New Brunswick, SE Canada 47°32′N 64°57′W
Trachenberg *see* Żmigród
15 O11 **Tracy** Québec, SE Canada 45°59′N 73°07′W
35 O8 **Tracy** California, W USA 37°43′N 121°27′W
29 S10 **Tracy** Minnesota, N USA 44°14′N 95°37′W
20 K10 **Tracy City** Tennessee, S USA 35°15′N 85°44′W
106 D7 **Tradate** Lombardia, N Italy 45°43′N 08°57′E
84 F6 **Traena Bank** *undersea feature* E Norwegian Sea 66°15′N 09°45′E
29 W13 **Traer** Iowa, C USA 42°11′N 92°28′W
104 J16 **Trafalgar, Cabo de** *headland* SW Spain 36°10′N 06°03′W
Traiectum ad Mosam/ Traiectum Tungorum *see* Maastricht
Tráigh Mhór *see* Tramore
11 O17 **Trail** British Columbia, SW Canada 49°94′N 117°39′W
58 B11 **Traíra, Serra do** ▲▲ NW Brazil
109 V5 **Traisen** Niederösterreich, NE Austria 48°03′N 15°37′E
109 W4 **Traisen** 〰 NE Austria
109 X4 **Traiskirchen** Niederösterreich, NE Austria 48°01′N 16°18′E
Trajani Portus *see* Civitavecchia
Trajectum ad Rhenum *see* Utrecht
119 H14 **Trakai** *Ger.* Traken, *Pol.* Troki. Vilnius, SE Lithuania 54°39′N 24°58′E
Traken *see* Trakai
97 B20 **Tralee** *Ir.* Trá Lí. SW Ireland 52°16′N 09°42′W
97 A20 **Tralee Bay** *Ir.* Bá Thrá Lí. *bay* SW Ireland
Trá Lí *see* Tralee
Trälleborg *see* Trelleborg
Tralles Aydin *see* Aydın
61 J16 **Tramandaí** Rio Grande do Sul, S Brazil 30°01′S 50°11′W
108 C7 **Tramelan** Bern, W Switzerland 47°13′N 07°07′E
Trá Mhór *see* Tramore
97 E20 **Tramore** *Ir.* Tráigh Mhór, Trá Mhór. Waterford, S Ireland 52°10′N 07°10′W
95 L18 **Tranås** Jönköping, S Sweden 58°03′N 15°00′E
62 J7 **Trancas** Tucumán, N Argentina 26°11′S 65°20′W
104 I7 **Trancoso** Guarda, N Portugal 40°46′N 07°21′W
95 H22 **Tranebjerg** Midtjylland, C Denmark 55°51′N 10°36′E
95 K19 **Tranemo** Västra Götaland, S Sweden 57°30′N 13°20′E
167 N16 **Trang** Trang, S Thailand 07°33′N 99°36′E
171 V15 **Trangan, Pulau** *island* Kepulauan Aru, E Indonesia
Trâng Dinh *see* Thât Khê
183 Q7 **Trangie** New South Wales, SE Australia 32°01′S 147°58′E
94 K12 **Trängslet** Dalarna, C Sweden 61°22′N 13°43′E
107 N16 **Trani** Puglia, SE Italy 41°17′N 16°25′E
61 F17 **Tranqueras** Rivera, NE Uruguay 31°13′S 55°45′W
63 G17 **Tranqui, Isla** *island* S Chile
39 V6 **Trans-Alaska pipeline** *oil pipeline* Alaska, USA
195 Q10 **Transantarctic Mountains** ▲▲ Antarctica
Transcarpathian Oblast *see* Zakarpats'ka Oblast'
122 E9 **Trans-Siberian Railway** *railway* Russian Federation
Transilvania *see* Transylvania
Transilvaniei, Alpi *see* Carpaţii Meridionalii
Transjordan *see* Jordan
172 L11 **Transkei Basin** *undersea feature* SW Indian Ocean 35°30′S 29°00′E
117 O10 **Transnistria** *cultural region* E Moldavia
Transsylvanische Alpen/ Transylvanian Alps *see* Carpaţii Meridionalii
94 K12 **Transtrand** Dalarna, C Sweden 61°06′N 13°19′E
116 G10 **Transylvania** *Eng.* Ardeal, Transilvania, *Ger.* Siebenbürgen, *Hung.* Erdély. *cultural region* NW Romania
167 S14 **Tra Ôn** Vinh Long, S Vietnam 09°58′N 105°58′E
107 H23 **Trapani** *anc.* Drepanum. Sicilia, Italy, C Mediterranean Sea 38°02′N 12°32′E
Trâpeăng Vêng *see* Kâmpóng Thum
Trapezus *see* Trabzon
114 L9 **Trapoklovo** Sliven, C Bulgaria 42°40′N 26°36′E
183 P13 **Traralgon** Victoria, SE Australia 38°15′S 146°36′E
76 H9 **Trarza** ◈ *region* SW Mauritania
Trasimenischersee *see* Trasimeno, Lago
106 H12 **Trasimeno, Lago** *Eng.* Lake of Perugia, *Ger.* Trasimenischersee. ◎ C Italy
95 J20 **Träslövsläge** Halland, S Sweden 57°02′N 12°18′E
Trás-os-Montes *see* Cucumbi
104 I6 **Trás-os-Montes e Alto Douro** *former province* N Portugal
167 Q12 **Trat** *var.* Bang Phra. Trat, S Thailand 12°16′N 102°30′E
Trá Tholl, Inis *see* Inishtrahull
Traù *see* Trogir
109 T4 **Traun** Oberösterreich, N Austria 48°14′N 14°15′E
109 S5 **Traun** 〰 N Austria
Traun, Lake *see* Traunsee
101 N23 **Traunreut** Bayern, SE Germany 47°58′N 12°36′E
109 S5 **Traunsee** *var.* Gmundner See, *Eng.* Lake Traun. ◎ N Austria
Trautenau *see* Trutnov
21 P11 **Travelers Rest** South Carolina, SE USA 34°58′N 82°26′W
182 L8 **Travellers Lake** *seasonal lake* New South Wales, SE Australia
31 P6 **Traverse City** Michigan, N USA 44°45′N 85°37′W
29 R7 **Traverse, Lake** ◎ Minnesota/South Dakota, N USA
185 I16 **Travers, Mount** ▲ South Island, New Zealand 42°01′S 172°46′E
11 P17 **Travers Reservoir** ⊠ Alberta, SW Canada
167 T14 **Tra Vinh** *var.* Phu Vinh. Tra Vinh, S Vietnam 09°57′N 106°20′E
25 S10 **Travis, Lake** ⊠ Texas, SW USA
112 H12 **Travnik** Federacija Bosna I Hercegovina, C Bosnia and Herzegovina 44°14′N 17°40′E
109 V11 **Trbovlje** *Ger.* Trifail. C Slovenia 46°10′N 15°03′E
23 V13 **Treasure Island** Florida, SE USA 27°46′N 82°46′W
Treasure State *see* Montana
186 I8 **Treasury Islands** *island group* NW Solomon Islands
106 D9 **Trebbia** *anc.* Trebia. 〰 NW Italy
100 N8 **Trebel** 〰 NE Germany
103 O16 **Trèbes** Aude, S France 43°12′N 02°26′E
Trebia *see* Trebbia
111 F18 **Třebíč** *Ger.* Trebitsch. Vysočina, C Czech Republic 49°13′N 15°52′E
113 I16 **Trebinje** Republika Srpska, S Bosnia and Herzegovina 42°42′N 18°19′E
Trebišnica *see* Trebišnjica
113 H16 **Trebišnjica** *var.* Trebišnica. 〰 S Bosnia and Herzegovina
111 N20 **Trebišov** *Hung.* Tőketerebes. Košický Kraj, E Slovakia 48°37′N 21°44′E
Trebitsch *see* Třebíč
Trebizond *see* Trabzon
Trebnitz *see* Trzebnica
109 V12 **Trebnje** SE Slovenia 45°54′N 15°01′E
111 D19 **Třeboň** *Ger.* Wittingau. Jihočeský Kraj, S Czech Republic 49°00′N 14°46′E
104 J15 **Trebujena** Andalucía, S Spain 36°52′N 06°11′W
100 I7 **Treene** 〰 N Germany
Tree Planters State *see* Nebraska
109 S9 **Treffen** Kärnten, S Austria 46°40′N 13°51′E
Trefynwy *see* Monmouth
102 G5 **Tréguier** Côtes d'Armor, NW France 48°50′N 03°12′W
61 G18 **Treinta y Tres** Treinta y Tres, E Uruguay 33°16′S 54°17′W
61 F18 **Treinta y Tres** ◈ *department* E Uruguay
122 F11 **Trëkhgornyy** Chelyabinskaya Oblast', C Russian Federation 54°42′N 58°25′E
114 F9 **Treklyanska Reka** 〰 W Bulgaria
102 K8 **Trélazé** Maine-et-Loire, NW France 47°27′N 00°28′W
63 K17 **Trelew** Chubut, SE Argentina 43°13′S 65°15′W
95 K23 **Trelleborg** *var.* Trälleborg. Skåne, S Sweden 55°22′N 13°10′E
113 P15 **Trem** ▲ SE Serbia 43°10′N 22°12′E
15 N11 **Tremblant, Mont** ▲ Québec, SE Canada 46°13′N 74°34′W
99 H17 **Tremelo** Vlaams Brabant, C Belgium 51°N 04°34′E
107 M15 **Tremiti, Isole** *island group* SE Italy
30 K12 **Tremont** Illinois, N USA 40°30′N 89°31′W
36 L1 **Tremonton** Utah, W USA 41°42′N 112°09′W
105 U4 **Tremp** Cataluña, NE Spain 42°09′N 00°53′E
30 J7 **Trempealeau** Wisconsin, N USA 44°00′N 91°25′W
15 P8 **Trenche** 〰 Québec, SE Canada
15 O7 **Trenche, Lac** ◎ Québec, SE Canada
111 I20 **Trenčiansky Kraj** ◈ *region* W Slovakia
111 I19 **Trenčín** *Ger.* Trentschin, *Hung.* Trencsén. Trenčiansky Kraj, W Slovakia 48°54′N 18°03′E
Trencsén *see* Trenčín
Trengganu *see* Terengganu
Trengganu, Kuala *see* Kuala Terengganu
61 A21 **Trenque Lauquen** Buenos Aires, E Argentina 36°01′S 62°47′W
14 J14 **Trent** 〰 Ontario, SE Canada
97 N18 **Trent** 〰 C England, United Kingdom
Trent *see* Trento
106 F5 **Trentino-Alto Adige** *Eng.* South Tyrol, *Ger.* Trentino-Südtirol; *prev.* Venezia Tridentina. ◈ *region* N Italy
Trentino-Südtirol *see* Trentino-Alto Adige
106 G6 **Trento** *Eng.* Trent, *Ger.* Trient; *anc.* Tridentum. Trentino-Alto Adige, N Italy 46°05′N 11°08′E
14 J15 **Trenton** Ontario, SE Canada 44°07′N 77°34′W
23 V10 **Trenton** Florida, SE USA 29°36′N 82°49′W
23 R1 **Trenton** Georgia, SE USA 34°52′N 85°27′W
31 S10 **Trenton** Michigan, N USA 42°08′N 83°10′W
27 S2 **Trenton** Missouri, C USA 40°04′N 93°37′W
28 M17 **Trenton** Nebraska, C USA 40°10′N 101°00′W
18 J15 **Trenton** *state capital* New Jersey, NE USA 40°13′N 74°45′W
21 W10 **Trenton** North Carolina, SE USA 35°03′N 77°20′W
20 G9 **Trenton** Tennessee, S USA 35°59′N 88°59′W
36 L1 **Trenton** Utah, W USA 41°53′N 111°57′W
Trentschin *see* Trenčín
Treptow an der Rega *see* Trzebiatów
61 C23 **Tres Arroyos** Buenos Aires, E Argentina 38°22′S 60°17′W
61 J15 **Três Cachoeiras** Rio Grande do Sul, S Brazil 29°21′S 49°48′W
106 E7 **Trescore Balneario** Lombardia, N Italy 45°43′N 09°52′E
41 V17 **Tres Cruces, Cerro** ▲ SE Mexico 15°28′N 92°27′W
57 K18 **Tres Cruces, Cordillera** ▲▲ W Bolivia
113 N18 **Treska** 〰 NW FYR Macedonia
113 I14 **Treskavica** ▲▲ SE Bosnia and Herzegovina
59 J20 **Três Lagoas** Mato Grosso do Sul, SW Brazil 20°46′S 51°43′W
40 H12 **Tres Marías, Islas** *island group* C Mexico
59 M19 **Três Marias, Represa** ⊠ SE Brazil
63 F20 **Tres Montes, Península** *headland* S Chile 46°49′S 75°29′W
105 O3 **Trespaderne** Castilla y León, N Spain 42°47′N 03°24′W
60 G13 **Três Passos** Rio Grande do Sul, S Brazil 27°33′S 53°55′W
61 A23 **Tres Picos, Cerro** ▲ E Argentina 38°10′S 61°54′W
63 G17 **Tres Picos, Cerro** ▲ SW Argentina 42°22′S 71°51′W
60 I12 **Três Pinheiros** Paraná, S Brazil 25°25′S 51°57′W
59 M21 **Três Pontas** Minas Gerais, SE Brazil 21°33′S 45°18′W
Tres Puntas, Cabo *see* Manabique, Punta
60 P9 **Três Rios** Rio de Janeiro, SE Brazil 22°06′S 43°15′W
Tres Tabernae *see* Saverne
Trestenberg/Trestendorf *see* Tăşnad
41 R15 **Tres Valles** Veracruz-Llave, SE Mexico 18°14′N 96°03′W
94 H12 **Tretten** Oppland, S Norway 61°19′N 10°19′E
Treuburg *see* Olecko
101 K21 **Treuchtlingen** Bayern, S Germany 48°57′N 10°55′E
100 N13 **Treuenbrietzen** Brandenburg, E Germany 52°06′N 12°52′E
63 H17 **Trevelín** Chubut, SW Argentina 43°02′S 71°27′W
Treves/Trèves *see* Trier
106 I13 **Trevi** Umbria, C Italy 42°52′N 12°46′E
106 E7 **Treviglio** Lombardia, N Italy 45°32′N 09°35′E
104 J4 **Trevinca, Peña** ▲ NW Spain 42°10′N 06°49′W
105 P3 **Treviño** Castilla y León, N Spain 42°45′N 02°41′W
106 I7 **Treviso** *anc.* Tarvisium. Veneto, NE Italy 45°40′N 12°15′E
97 G24 **Trevose Head** *headland* SW England, United Kingdom 50°33′N 05°03′W
Trg *see* Feldkirchen in Kärnten
183 P17 **Triabunna** Tasmania, SE Australia 42°33′S 147°55′E
21 W4 **Triangle** Virginia, NE USA 38°30′N 77°17′W
83 L18 **Triangle** Masvingo, SE Zimbabwe 20°58′S 31°28′E
115 L23 **Tría Nisía** *island* Kykládes, Greece, Aegean Sea
Triberg *see* Triberg im Schwarzwald
101 G23 **Triberg im Schwarzwald** *var.* Triberg. Baden-Württemberg, SW Germany 48°07′N 08°13′E
153 P11 **Tribhuvan** ✈ (Kathmandu) Central, C Nepal
54 C9 **Tribugá, Golfo de** *gulf* W Colombia
181 W4 **Tribulation, Cape** *headland* Queensland, NE Australia 16°14′S 145°48′E
108 M8 **Tribulaun** ▲ SW Austria 46°59′N 11°18′E
11 U17 **Tribune** Saskatchewan, S Canada 49°16′N 103°50′W
26 H5 **Tribune** Kansas, C USA 38°27′N 101°46′W
107 N18 **Tricarico** Basilicata, S Italy 40°37′N 16°09′E
107 Q19 **Tricase** Puglia, SE Italy 39°56′N 18°21′E
Trichinopoly *see* Tiruchchirāppalli
115 D18 **Trichonída, Límni** ◎ C Greece
155 G22 **Trichūr** *var.* Thrissur. Kerala, SW India 10°32′N 76°14′E *see also* Thrissur
Tricorno *see* Triglav
183 O8 **Trida** New South Wales, SE Australia 33°02′S 145°03′E
35 S1 **Trident Peak** ▲ Nevada, W USA 41°52′N 118°22′W
Tridentum/Trient *see* Trento
109 T6 **Trieben** Steiermark, SE Austria 47°29′N 14°30′E
101 D19 **Trier** *Eng.* Treves, *Fr.* Trèves; *anc.* Augusta Treverorum. Rheinland-Pfalz, SW Germany 49°45′N 06°39′E
106 K7 **Trieste** *Slvn.* Trst. Friuli-Venezia Giulia, NE Italy 45°39′N 13°45′E
Trieste, Golfo di/Triest, Golf von *see* Trieste, Gulf of
106 J8 **Trieste, Gulf of** *Cro.* Tršćanski Zaljev, *Ger.* Golf von Triest, *It.* Golfo di Trieste, *Slvn.* Tržaški Zaliv. *gulf* S Europe
109 W4 **Triesting** 〰 W Austria
Triêu Hai *see* Quang Tri
Trifail *see* Trbovlje
116 L9 **Trifeşti** Iaşi, NE Romania 47°30′N 27°31′E
109 S10 **Triglav** *It.* Tricorno. ▲ NW Slovenia 46°22′N 13°40′E
104 I14 **Trigueros** Andalucía, S Spain 37°24′N 06°50′W
115 E16 **Tríkala** *prev.* Trikkala. Thessalía, C Greece 39°33′N 21°46′E
115 E17 **Trikeriótis** 〰 C Greece
Trikkala *see* Tríkala
Trikomo/Tríkomon *see* İskele
97 F17 **Trim** *Ir.* Baile Átha Troim. Meath, E Ireland 53°34′N 06°47′W
108 E7 **Trimbach** Solothurn, NW Switzerland 47°22′N 07°53′E
109 Q5 **Trimmelkam** Oberösterreich, N Austria 48°02′N 12°55′E
29 U11 **Trimont** Minnesota, N USA 43°45′N 94°42′W
Trimontium *see* Plovdiv
Trinacria *see* Sicilia
155 K24 **Trincomalee** *var.* Trinkomali. Eastern Province, NE Sri Lanka 08°34′N 81°13′E
65 K16 **Trindade, Ilha da** *island* Brazil, W Atlantic Ocean
47 Y9 **Trindade Spur** *undersea feature* SW Atlantic Ocean 21°00′S 35°00′W
111 J17 **Třinec** *Ger.* Trzynietz. Moravskoslezský Kraj, E Czech Republic 49°41′N 18°39′E
57 M16 **Trinidad** El Beni, N Bolivia 14°52′S 64°54′W
54 H9 **Trinidad** Casanare, E Colombia 05°25′N 71°39′W
44 E6 **Trinidad** Sancti Spíritus, C Cuba 21°48′N 80°00′W
61 E19 **Trinidad** Flores, S Uruguay 33°35′S 56°54′W
37 U8 **Trinidad** Colorado, C USA 37°11′N 104°31′W
45 Y17 **Trinidad** *island* C Trinidad and Tobago
Trinidad *see* Jose Abad Santos
45 Y16 **Trinidad and Tobago** *off.* Republic of Trinidad and Tobago. ◆ *republic* SE West Indies
Trinidad and Tobago, Republic of *see* Trinidad and Tobago
63 F22 **Trinidad, Golfo** *gulf* S Chile
61 B24 **Trinidad, Isla** *island* E Argentina
107 N16 **Trinitapoli** Puglia, SE Italy 41°22′N 16°06′E
55 X10 **Trinité, Montagnes de la** ▲▲ C French Guiana
25 W9 **Trinity** Texas, SW USA 30°57′N 95°22′W
13 U12 **Trinity Bay** *inlet* Newfoundland, Newfoundland and Labrador, E Canada
39 P15 **Trinity Islands** *island group* Alaska, USA
35 N2 **Trinity Mountains** ▲▲ California, W USA
35 S4 **Trinity Peak** ▲ Nevada, W USA 40°13′N 118°43′W
35 S5 **Trinity Range** ▲▲ Nevada, W USA
35 N2 **Trinity River** 〰 California, W USA
25 V8 **Trinity River** 〰 Texas, SW USA
Trinkomali *see* Trincomalee
173 Y15 **Triolet** NW Mauritius 20°05′S 57°32′E
107 O20 **Trionto, Capo** *headland* S Italy 39°37′N 16°46′E
Tripití, Ákra *see* Trypití, Akrotírio
115 F20 **Trípoli** *prev.* Trípolis. Pelopónnisos, S Greece 37°31′N 22°22′E
138 G6 **Tripoli** *var.* Tarābulus, Ţarābulus ash Shām, Trâblous; *anc.* Tripolis. N Lebanon 34°30′N 35°42′E
29 X12 **Tripoli** Iowa, C USA 42°48′N 92°15′W
Tripoli *see* Ţarābulus
Trípolis *see* Trípoli, Greece
Tripolis *see* Tripoli, Lebanon
29 Q12 **Tripp** South Dakota, N USA 43°12′N 97°57′W
153 V15 **Tripura** *var.* Hill Tippera. ◈ *state* NE India
108 K8 **Trisanna** 〰 W Austria
100 H8 **Trischen** *island* NW Germany
65 M24 **Tristan da Cunha** ◇ *dependency of Saint Helena* SE Atlantic Ocean
67 P15 **Tristan da Cunha** *island* SE Atlantic Ocean
65 L18 **Tristan da Cunha Fracture Zone** *tectonic feature* S Atlantic Ocean
167 S14 **Tri Tôn** An Giang, S Vietnam 10°26′N 105°01′E
167 W10 **Triton Island** *island* S Paracel Islands
155 G24 **Trivandrum** *var.* Thiruvanathapuram, Tiruvantapuram. *state capital* Kerala, SW India 08°30′N 76°57′E
111 H20 **Trnava** *Ger.* Tyrnau, *Hung.* Nagyszombat. Trnavský Kraj, W Slovakia 48°22′N 17°36′E
111 H20 **Trnavský Kraj** ◈ *region* W Slovakia
Trnovo *see* Veliko Tŭrnovo
Trobriand Island *see* Kiriwina Island
Trobriand Islands *see* Kiriwina Islands
11 Q16 **Trochu** Alberta, SW Canada 51°48′N 113°12′W
109 U7 **Trofaiach** Steiermark, SE Austria 47°25′N 15°01′E
93 F14 **Trofors** Troms, N Norway 65°31′N 13°19′E
113 E14 **Trogir** *It.* Traù. Split-Dalmacija, S Croatia 43°32′N 16°13′E
112 F13 **Troglav** ▲ Bosnia and Herzegovina/Croatia 44°00′N 16°36′E
107 M16 **Troia** Puglia, SE Italy 41°21′N 15°19′E
107 K24 **Troina** Sicilia, Italy, C Mediterranean Sea 37°47′N 14°37′E
173 O16 **Trois-Bassins** W Réunion 21°05′S 55°18′E
101 E17 **Troisdorf** Nordrhein-Westfalen, W Germany 50°49′N 07°09′E
74 H5 **Trois Fourches, Cap des** *headland* NE Morocco 35°27′N 02°58′W
15 T8 **Trois-Pistoles** Québec, SE Canada 48°08′N 69°10′W
99 L21 **Trois-Ponts** Liège, E Belgium 50°22′N 05°52′E
15 P11 **Trois-Rivières** Québec, SE Canada 46°21′N 72°34′W
55 Y12 **Trois Sauts** S French Guiana 02°15′N 52°52′W
99 M22 **Troisvierges** Diekirch, N Luxembourg 50°07′N 06°00′E
122 F11 **Troitsk** Chelyabinskaya Oblast', S Russian Federation 54°04′N 61°31′E
125 T9 **Troitsko-Pechorsk** Respublika Komi, NW Russian Federation 62°39′N 56°06′E
127 V7 **Troitskoye** Orenburgskaya Oblast', W Russian Federation 52°23′N 56°24′E
Troki *see* Trakai
94 F9 **Trolla** ▲ S Norway 62°41′N 09°47′E
95 J18 **Trollhättan** Västra Götaland, S Sweden 58°17′N 12°20′E
94 G9 **Trollheimen** ▲▲ S Norway
94 E9 **Trolltindane** ▲ S Norway 62°30′N 07°43′E
58 H11 **Trombetas, Rio** 〰 NE Brazil
128 L16 **Tromelin, Île** *island* N Réunion
92 I9 **Troms** ◈ *county* N Norway
92 I9 **Tromsø** *Fin.* Tromssa. Troms, N Norway 69°39′N 19°01′E
84 F5 **Tromsøflaket** *undersea feature* W Barents Sea 18°30′E 71°30′N
Tromssa *see* Tromsø
94 H10 **Tron** ▲ S Norway 62°12′N 10°46′E
35 U12 **Trona** California, W USA 35°46′N 117°21′W
63 G16 **Tronador, Cerro** ▲ S Chile 41°12′S 71°51′W
94 H8 **Trondheim** *Ger.* Drontheim; *prev.* Nidaros, Trondhjem. Sør-Trøndelag, S Norway 63°25′N 10°24′E
94 H7 **Trondheimsfjorden** *fjord* S Norway
Trondhjem *see* Trondheim
107 J14 **Tronto** 〰 C Italy
121 P3 **Troódos** *var.* Troodos Mountains. ▲▲ C Cyprus
Troodos *see* Ólympos
Troodos Mountains *see* Troódos
96 I13 **Troon** W Scotland, United Kingdom 55°32′N 04°41′W
107 M22 **Tropea** Calabria, SW Italy 38°40′N 15°52′E
36 L7 **Tropic** Utah, W USA 37°37′N 112°04′W
64 L10 **Tropic Seamount** *var.* Banc du Tropique. *undersea feature* E Atlantic Ocean 23°50′N 20°40′W
Tropique, Banc du *see* Tropic Seamount
Tropoja *see* Tropojë
113 L17 **Tropojë** *var.* Tropoja. Kukës, N Albania 42°25′N 20°09′E
Troppau *see* Opava
95 O16 **Trosa** Södermanland, C Sweden 58°54′N 17°35′E
118 H12 **Troškūnai** Utena, E Lithuania 55°36′N 24°55′E
101 G23 **Trossingen** Baden-Württemberg, SW Germany 48°04′N 08°37′E
117 T4 **Trostyanets'** *Rus.* Trostyanets. Sums'ka Oblast', NE Ukraine 50°30′N 34°59′E
117 N7 **Trostyanets'** *Rus.* Trostyanets. Vinnyts'ka Oblast', C Ukraine 48°35′N 29°10′E
Trostyanets *see* Trostyanets'
116 L11 **Trotuş** 〰 E Romania
44 M8 **Trou-du-Nord** N Haiti 19°34′N 71°57′W
25 W7 **Troup** Texas, SW USA 32°08′N 95°07′W
8 I10 **Trout** 〰 Northwest Territories, NW Canada
33 N8 **Trout Creek** Montana, NW USA 47°51′N 115°40′W
32 H10 **Trout Lake** Washington, NW USA 45°59′N 121°33′W
12 B9 **Trout Lake** ◎ Ontario, S Canada
33 T12 **Trout Peak** ▲ Wyoming, C USA 44°36′N 109°33′W
102 L4 **Trouville** Calvados, N France 49°21′N 00°07′E
97 L22 **Trowbridge** S England, United Kingdom 51°20′N 02°13′W
23 Q6 **Troy** Alabama, S USA 31°48′N 85°58′W
27 Q3 **Troy** Kansas, C USA 39°45′N 95°06′W
27 W4 **Troy** Missouri, C USA 38°59′N 90°59′W
18 L10 **Troy** New York, NE USA 42°43′N 73°37′W
21 S10 **Troy** North Carolina, SE USA 35°23′N 79°54′W
31 R13 **Troy** Ohio, N USA 40°02′N 84°12′W
25 T9 **Troy** Texas, SW USA 31°12′N 97°18′W
114 I9 **Troyan** Lovech, N Bulgaria 42°52′N 24°42′E
114 I9 **Troyanski Prokhod** *pass* N Bulgaria
145 N6 **Troyebratskiy** Severnyy Kazakhstan, N Kazakhstan 54°25′N 66°03′E
103 Q6 **Troyes** *anc.* Augustobona Tricassium. Aube, N France 48°18′N 04°04′E
117 X5 **Troyits'ke** Luhans'ka Oblast', E Ukraine 49°55′N 38°18′E
35 W7 **Troy Peak** ▲ Nevada, W USA 38°18′N 115°27′W
113 G15 **Trpanj** Dubrovnik-Neretva, S Croatia 43°00′N 17°18′E
Tršćanski Zaljev *see* Trieste, Gulf of
Trst *see* Trieste
113 N14 **Trstenik** Serbia, C Serbia 43°38′N 21°01′E
126 I6 **Trubchevsk** Bryanskaya Oblast', W Russian Federation 52°33′N 33°45′E
Trubchular *see* Orlyak
37 S10 **Truchas Peak** ▲ New Mexico, SW USA 35°57′N 105°38′W
143 P16 **Trucial Coast** *physical region* C United Arab Emirates
Trucial States *see* United Arab Emirates
35 Q6 **Truckee** California, W USA 39°18′N 120°10′W
35 R5 **Truckee River** 〰 Nevada, W USA
127 Q13 **Trudfront** Astrakhanskaya Oblast', SW Russian Federation 45°56′N 47°42′E
14 I9 **Truite, Lac à la** ◎ Québec, SE Canada
42 K4 **Trujillo** Colón, NE Honduras 15°59′N 85°54′W
56 C12 **Trujillo** La Libertad, NW Peru 08°04′S 79°02′W
104 K10 **Trujillo** Extremadura, W Spain 39°28′N 05°53′W
54 I6 **Trujillo** Trujillo, NW Venezuela 09°20′N 70°38′W
54 I6 **Trujillo** *off.* Estado Trujillo. ◈ *state* W Venezuela
Trujillo, Estado *see* Trujillo
Truk *see* Chuuk
Truk Islands *see* Chuuk Islands
29 U10 **Truman** Minnesota, N USA 43°49′N 94°26′W
27 X10 **Trumann** Arkansas, C USA 35°40′N 90°30′W
36 J9 **Trumbull, Mount** ▲ Arizona, SW USA 36°22′N 113°09′W
114 F9 **Trŭn** Pernik, W Bulgaria 42°51′N 22°37′E
183 Q8 **Trundle** New South Wales, SE Australia 32°55′S 147°43′E
129 U13 **Trung Phân** *physical region* S Vietnam
Trupcilar *see* Orlyak
13 Q15 **Truro** Nova Scotia, SE Canada 45°24′N 63°18′W
97 H25 **Truro** SW England, United Kingdom 50°16′N 05°03′W
25 P5 **Truscott** Texas, SW USA 33°43′N 99°48′W
116 K9 **Truşeşti** Botoşani, NE Romania 47°45′N 27°01′E
116 H6 **Truskavets'** L'vivs'ka Oblast', W Ukraine 49°15′N 23°30′E
95 H22 **Trustrup** Midtjylland, C Denmark 56°20′N 10°46′E
10 M11 **Trutch** British Columbia, W Canada 57°42′N 123°00′W
37 Q14 **Truth Or Consequences** New Mexico, SW USA 33°07′N 107°15′W
111 F15 **Trutnov** *Ger.* Trautenau. Královéhradecký Kraj, N Czech Republic 50°34′N 15°55′E
103 P13 **Truyère** 〰 C France
114 K9 **Tryavna** Lovech, N Bulgaria 42°52′N 25°30′E
28 M14 **Tryon** Nebraska, C USA 41°33′N 100°57′W
115 J16 **Trypití, Akrotírio** *var.* Ákra Tripití. *headland* Ágios Efstrátios, E Greece 39°28′N 24°58′E
94 J12 **Trysil** Hedmark, S Norway 61°18′N 12°16′E
94 I11 **Trysilelva** 〰 S Norway
112 D10 **Tržac** Federacija Bosna I Hercegovina, NW Bosnia and Herzegovina 44°58′N 15°48′E
Tržaški Zaliv *see* Trieste, Gulf of
110 G10 **Trzcianka** *Ger.* Schönlanke. Pila, Wielkopolskie, C Poland 53°02′N 16°24′E
110 E7 **Trzebiatów** *Ger.* Treptow an der Rega. Zachodnio-pomorskie, NW Poland 54°04′N 15°14′E
111 G14 **Trzebnica** *Ger.* Trebnitz. Dolnośląskie, SW Poland 51°19′N 17°03′E
109 T10 **Tržič** *Ger.* Neumarktl. NW Slovenia 46°22′N 14°17′E
Trzynietz *see* Třinec
83 G21 **Tsabong** *var.* Tshabong. Kgalagadi, SW Botswana 26°03′S 22°27′E
162 G7 **Tsagaanchuluut** Dzavhan, C Mongolia 47°06′N 96°40′E
162 M8 **Tsagaandelger** *var.* Haraat. Dundgovĭ, C Mongolia 46°30′N 107°39′E
Tsagaanders *see* Bayantümen
162 G7 **Tsagaanhayrhan** *var.* Shiree. Dzavhan, W Mongolia 47°30′N 96°48′E
Tsagaannuur *see* Halhgol
Tsagaan-Olom *see* Tayshir
Tsagaan-Ovoo *see* Nariynteel
Tsagaantüngi *see* Altantsögts
162 H6 **Tsagaan-Uul** *var.* Sharga. Hövsgöl, N Mongolia 49°33′N 98°36′E
162 J5 **Tsagaan-Üür** *var.* Bulgan. Hövsgöl, N Mongolia 50°30′N 101°28′E
127 P12 **Tsagan Aman** Respublika Kalmykiya, SW Russian Federation 47°37′N 46°43′E
23 V11 **Tsala Apopka Lake** ◎ Florida, SE USA
Tsamkong *see* Zhanjiang
Tsangpo *see* Brahmaputra
Tsant *see* Deren
Tsao *see* Tsau
172 I4 **Tsaratanana** Mahajanga, C Madagascar 16°46′S 47°40′E
114 N10 **Tsarevo** *prev.* Michurin. Burgas, E Bulgaria 42°10′N 27°51′E
Tsarigrad *see* İstanbul
Tsaritsyn *see* Volgograd
114 K7 **Tsar Kaloyan** Ruse, N Bulgaria 43°36′N 26°14′E
Tsarskoye Selo *see* Pushkin
117 T7 **Tsarychanka** Dnipropetrovs'ka Oblast', E Ukraine 48°56′N 34°29′E
83 H21 **Tsatsu** Southern, S Botswana 25°21′S 24°45′E
83 G17 **Tsau** *var.* Tsao. North-West, NW Botswana 20°08′S 22°29′E
81 J20 **Tsavo** Coast, S Kenya 02°59′S 38°28′E
83 E21 **Tsawisis** Karas, S Namibia 26°18′S 18°09′E
Tschakathurn *see* Čakovec
Tschaslau *see* Čáslav
Tschenstochau *see* Częstochowa
Tschernembl *see* Črnomelj
28 K6 **Tschida, Lake** ⊠ North Dakota, N USA
Tschorna *see* Mustvee
162 G8 **Tseel** Govĭ-Altay, SW Mongolia 45°45′N 95°54′E
138 G8 **Tsefat** *var.* Safed, *Ar.* Safad; *prev.* Zefat. Northern, N Israel 32°57′N 35°27′E
126 M13 **Tselina** Rostovskaya Oblast', SW Russian Federation 46°31′N 41°01′E
Tselinograd *see* Astana
Tselinogradskaya Oblast *see* Akmola
Tsengel *see* Tosontsengel
162 J8 **Tsenher** *var.* Altan-Ovoo. Arhangay, C Mongolia 47°24′N 101°51′E
Tsenher *see* Mönhhayrhan
163 N8 **Tsenhermandal** *var.* Modot. Hentiy, C Mongolia 47°45′N 109°03′E
Tsentral'nyye Nizmennyye Garagumy *see* Merkezi Garagumy
83 E21 **Tses** Karas, S Namibia 25°58′S 18°08′E
Tseshevlya *see* Tsyeshawlya
162 E7 **Tsetseg** *var.* Tsetsegnuur. Hovd, W Mongolia 46°30′N 93°16′E
Tsetsegnuur *see* Tsetseg
Tsetsen Khan *see* Öndörhaan
162 J8 **Tsetserleg** Arhangay, C Mongolia 47°29′N 101°19′E
162 H6 **Tsetserleg** *var.* Halban. Hövsgöl, N Mongolia 49°30′N 97°33′E
162 J8 **Tsetserleg** *var.* Hujirt. Övörhangay, C Mongolia 46°50′N 102°38′E
77 R16 **Tsévié** S Togo 06°25′N 01°13′E
Tshabong *see* Tsabong
83 G20 **Tshane** Kgalagadi, SW Botswana 24°05′S 21°54′E
Tshangalele, Lac *see* Lufira, Lac de Retenue de la
83 H17 **Tshauxaba** Central, C Botswana 19°56′S 25°09′E
79 F21 **Tshela** Bas-Congo, W Dem. Rep. Congo 04°56′S 13°02′E
79 K22 **Tshibala** Kasai-Occidental, S Dem. Rep. Congo 06°53′S 22°01′E
79 J22 **Tshikapa** Kasai-Occidental, SW Dem. Rep. Congo 06°23′S 20°47′E
79 L22 **Tshilenge** Kasai Oriental , S Dem. Rep. Congo 06°17′S 23°48′E
79 L24 **Tshimbalanga** Katanga, S Dem. Rep. Congo 09°42′S 23°04′E
79 L22 **Tshimbulu** Kasai-Occidental, S Dem. Rep. Congo 06°27′S 22°54′E
Tshiumbe *see* Chiumbe
79 M21 **Tshofa** Kasai-Oriental, C Dem. Rep. Congo 05°13′S 25°13′E
79 K18 **Tshuapa** 〰 C Dem. Rep. Congo
83 J21 **Tshwane** *var.* Epitoli; *prev.* Pretoria. ● Gauteng, NE South Africa 25°41′S 28°12′E *see also* Pretoria
114 G7 **Tsibritsa** 〰 NW Bulgaria
Tsien Tang *see* Fuchun Jiang
114 I12 **Tsigansko Gradishte** ▲ Bulgaria/Greece 41°24′N 24°41′E
Tsihombe *see* Tsiombe
8 H7 **Tsiigehtchic** *prev.* Arctic Red River. Northwest Territories, NW Canada 67°24′N 133°40′W
125 Q7 **Tsil'ma** 〰 NW Russian Federation
119 J17 **Tsimkavichy** *Rus.* Timkovichi. Minskaya Voblasts', C Belarus 53°04′N 26°59′E
126 M11 **Tsimlyansk** Rostovskaya Oblast', SW Russian Federation 47°39′N 42°05′E
127 N11 **Tsimlyanskoye Vodokhranilishche** *var.* Tsimlyansk Vodoskhovshche, *Eng.* Tsimlyansk Reservoir. ⊠ SW Russian Federation
Tsimlyansk Reservoir *see* Tsimlyanskoye Vodokhranilishche
Tsimlyansk Vodoskhovshche *see* Tsimlyanskoye Vodokhranilishche
Tsinan *see* Jinan
Tsinghai *see* Qinghai, China
Tsing Hai *see* Qinghai Hu, China
Tsingtao/Tsingtau *see* Qingdao
Tsingyuan *see* Baoding
Tsinkiang *see* Quanzhou
Tsintao *see* Qingdao
83 D17 **Tsintsabis** Oshikoto, N Namibia 18°45′S 17°51′E
172 H8 **Tsiombe** *var.* Tsihombe. Toliara, S Madagascar
123 O13 **Tsipa** 〰 S Russian Federation
172 H5 **Tsiribihina** 〰 W Madagascar
172 I5 **Tsiroanomandidy** Antananarivo, C Madagascar 18°44′S 46°02′E
189 U13 **Tsis** *island* Chuuk, C Micronesia
Tsitsihar *see* Qiqihar
127 Q3 **Tsivil'sk** Chuvashskaya Respublika, W Russian Federation 55°51′N 47°30′E
137 T9 **Tskhinvali** *prev.* Staliniri, Ts'khinvali. C Georgia 42°12′N 43°58′E
119 J19 **Tsna** 〰 SW Belarus
124 I15 **Tsna** *var.* Zna. 〰 W Russian Federation

◆ Country
● Country Capital
◇ Dependent Territory
○ Dependent Territory Capital
◈ Administrative Regions
✈ International Airport
▲ Mountain
▲▲ Mountain Range
Volcano
〰 River
◎ Lake
⊠ Reservoir

162 G9 Tsogt var. Tahilt. Govi-Altay, W Mongolia 45°20′N 96°42′E
162 K10 Tsogt-Ovoo var. Doloon. Ömnögovĭ, S Mongolia 44°28′N 105°22′E
162 L10 Tsogttsetsiy var. Baruunsuu. Ömnögovĭ, S Mongolia 43°46′N 105°28′E
114 M9 Tsonevo, Yazovir prev. Yazovir Georgi Traykov. ⊠ NE Bulgaria
Tsoohor see Hürmen
164 K14 Tsu var. Tu. Mie, Honshū, SW Japan 34°41′N 136°30′E
165 O10 Tsubame var. Tubame. Niigata, Honshū, C Japan 37°40′N 138°56′E
165 V3 Tsubetsu Hokkaidō, NE Japan 43°43′N 144°01′E
165 O13 Tsuchiura var. Tutiura. Ibaraki, Honshū, S Japan 36°05′N 140°11′E
165 Q6 Tsugaru-kaikyō strait N Japan
164 E14 Tsukumi var. Tukumi. Ōita, Kyūshū, SW Japan 33°00′N 131°51′E
Tsul-Ulaan see Bayannuur
Tsul-Ulaan see Bayanuur
83 D17 Tsumeb Oshikoto, N Namibia 19°13′S 17°42′E
83 F17 Tsumkwe Otjozondjupa, NE Namibia 19°37′S 20°30′E
164 D15 Tsuno Miyazaki, Kyūshū, SW Japan 32°43′N 131°32′E
164 D12 Tsuno-shima island SW Japan
164 K12 Tsuruga var. Turuga. Fukui, Honshū, SW Japan 35°38′N 136°01′E
164 H12 Tsurugi-san ▲ Shikoku, SW Japan 33°50′N 134°04′E
165 P9 Tsuruoka var. Turuoka. Yamagata, Honshū, C Japan 38°44′N 139°48′E
164 C12 Tsushima prev. Izuhara. Nagasaki, Tsushima, SW Japan 34°11′N 129°16′E
164 C12 Tsushima var. Tsushima-tō, Tusima. island group SW Japan
Tsushima-tō see Tsushima
164 H12 Tsuyama var. Tuyama. Okayama, Honshū, SW Japan 35°04′N 134°01′E
83 G19 Tswaane Ghanzi, W Botswana 22°21′S 21°52′E
119 N16 Tsyakhtsin Rus. Tekhtin. Mahilyowskaya Voblasts', E Belarus 53°51′N 29°44′E
119 P19 Tsyerakhowka Rus. Terekhovka. Homyel'skaya Voblasts', SE Belarus 52°13′N 31°24′E
119 I17 Tsyeshawlya Rus. Cheshevlya, Tseshevlya. Brestskaya Voblasts', SW Belarus 53°14′N 25°49′E
Tsyurupinsk see Tsyurupyns'k
117 R10 Tsyurupyns'k Rus. Tsyurupinsk. Khersons'ka Oblast', S Ukraine 46°35′N 32°43′E
Tu see Tsu
186 C7 Tua ≈ C Papua New Guinea
Tuaim see Tuam
184 L6 Tuakau Waikato, North Island, New Zealand 37°16′S 174°56′E
97 C17 Tuam Ir. Tuaim. Galway, W Ireland 53°31′N 08°50′W
185 K14 Tuamarina Marlborough, South Island, New Zealand 41°27′S 174°00′E
Tuamotu, Archipel des see Tuamotu, Îles
193 Q9 Tuamotu Fracture Zone tectonic feature E Pacific Ocean
191 W9 Tuamotu, Îles var. Archipel des Tuamotu, Dangerous Archipelago, Tuamotu Islands. island group N French Polynesia
Tuamotu Islands see Tuamotu, Îles
175 X10 Tuamotu Ridge undersea feature C Pacific Ocean
167 R5 Tuân Giao Lai Châu, N Vietnam 21°34′N 103°24′E
171 O2 Tuao Luzon, N Philippines 17°42′N 121°25′E
190 B15 Tuapa NW Niue 18°57′S 169°59′W
43 N7 Tuapi Región Autónoma Atlántico Norte, NE Nicaragua 14°10′N 83°20′W
126 K15 Tuapse Krasnodarskiy Kray, SW Russian Federation 44°08′N 39°07′E
169 U6 Tuaran Sabah, East Malaysia 06°12′N 116°12′E
104 I6 Tua, Rio ≈ N Portugal
192 H15 Tuasivi Savai'i, C Samoa 13°38′S 172°08′W
185 B24 Tuatapere Southland, South Island, New Zealand 46°09′S 167°43′E
36 M9 Tuba City Arizona, SW USA 36°08′N 111°14′W
138 H11 Ṭūbah, Qaṣr aṭ castle 'Ammān, C Jordan
Tubame see Tsubame
169 R16 Tuban prev. Toeban. Jawa, C Indonesia 06°55′S 112°01′E
141 O16 Tuban, Wādī dry watercourse SW Yemen
61 K14 Tubarão Santa Catarina, S Brazil 28°29′S 49°00′W
98 O10 Tubbergen Overijssel, E Netherlands 52°25′N 06°46′E
Tubeke see Tubize
101 H22 Tübingen var. Tuebingen. Baden-Württemberg, SW Germany 48°32′N 09°04′E
127 W6 Tubinskiy Respublika Bashkortostan, W Russian Federation 52°48′N 58°18′E
99 G19 Tubize Dut. Tubeke. Walloon Brabant, C Belgium 50°43′N 04°14′E
76 J16 Tubmanburg NW Liberia 06°50′N 10°53′W
75 T7 Ṭubruq Eng. Tobruk, It. Tobruch. NE Libya 32°05′N 23°59′E
191 T13 Tubuai island Îles Australes, SW French Polynesia
Tubuai, Îles/Tubuai Islands see Australes, Îles
Tubuai-Manu see Maiao
40 F3 Tubutama Sonora, NW Mexico 30°51′N 111°31′W
54 K4 Tucacas Falcón, N Venezuela 10°50′N 68°22′W
59 P16 Tucano Bahia, E Brazil 10°52′S 38°48′W
57 P19 Tucavaca, Río ≈ E Bolivia
110 H8 Tuchola Kujawsko-pomorskie, C Poland 53°36′N 17°50′E
111 M17 Tuchów Małopolskie, S Poland 49°53′N 21°04′E
23 S3 Tucker Georgia, SE USA 33°53′N 84°10′W
27 W10 Tuckerman Arkansas, C USA 35°43′N 91°12′W
64 B12 Tucker's Town E Bermuda 32°20′N 64°42′W
Tuckum see Tukums
36 M15 Tucson Arizona, SW USA 32°14′N 111°01′W
62 J7 Tucumán off. Provincia de Tucumán. ◈ province N Argentina
Tucumán see San Miguel de Tucumán
Tucumán, Provincia de see Tucumán
37 V11 Tucumcari New Mexico, SW USA 35°10′N 103°43′W
58 H13 Tucuraré Pará, N Brazil 05°15′S 55°49′W
55 Q6 Tucupita Delta Amacuro, NE Venezuela 09°02′N 62°04′W
58 K13 Tucuruí, Represa de ⊠ NE Brazil
110 F9 Tuczno Zachodnio-pomorskie, NW Poland 53°12′N 16°08′E
Tuddo see Tudu
105 Q5 Tudela Basq. Tutera; anc. Tutela. Navarra, N Spain 42°04′N 01°37′W
104 M6 Tudela de Duero Castilla y León, N Spain 41°35′N 04°34′W
162 G6 Tüdevtey var. Oygon. Dzavhan, N Mongolia 48°57′N 96°33′E
138 K6 Tudmur var. Tadmur, Tamar, Gk. Palmyra, Bibl. Tadmor. Ḥimṣ, C Syria 34°36′N 38°15′E
118 J4 Tudu Ger. Tuddo. Lääne-Virumaa, NE Estonia 59°12′N 26°52′E
Tuebingen see Tübingen
122 J14 Tuekta Respublika Altay, S Russian Federation 50°51′N 85°52′E
104 I5 Tuela, Rio ≈ N Portugal
153 X12 Tuensang Nāgāland, NE India 26°16′N 94°45′E
136 L15 Tufanbeyli Adana, C Turkey 38°15′N 36°13′E
Tuffer see Laško
186 F9 Tufi Northern, S Papua New Guinea 09°08′S 149°20′E
193 O3 Tufts Plain undersea feature N Pacific Ocean
Tugalan see Kolkhozobod
67 V14 Tugela ≈ SE South Africa
21 P6 Tug Fork ≈ S USA
39 P15 Tugidak Island island Trinity Islands, Alaska, USA
171 O2 Tuguegarao Luzon, N Philippines 17°37′N 121°48′E
123 S12 Tugur Khabarovskiy Kray, SE Russian Federation 53°43′N 137°00′E
161 P4 Tuhai He ≈ E China
104 G4 Tui Galicia, NW Spain 42°02′N 08°37′W
77 O13 Tui var. Grand Balé. ≈ W Burkina
57 J16 Tuichi, Río ≈ W Bolivia
64 Q11 Tuineje Fuerteventura, Islas Canarias, Spain, NE Atlantic Ocean 28°18′N 14°03′W
43 X16 Tuira, Río ≈ SE Panama
Tuisarkan see Tūysarkān
Tujiabu see Yongxiu
127 W5 Tukan Respublika Bashkortostan, W Russian Federation 53°58′N 57°29′E
171 P14 Tukangbesi, Kepulauan Dut. Toekang Besi Eilanden. island group C Indonesia
147 V13 Tŭkhtamish Rus. Toktomush; prev. Tokhtamyshbek. SE Tajikistan 37°51′N 74°41′E
184 O12 Tukituki ≈ North Island, New Zealand
Tu-k'ou see Panzhihua
121 P12 Tūkrah NE Libya 32°32′N 20°35′E
8 H6 Tuktoyaktuk Northwest Territories, NW Canada 69°27′N 133°W
168 I9 Tuktuk Pulau Samosir, W Indonesia 02°32′N 98°43′E
Tukumi see Tsukumi
118 E9 Tukums Ger. Tuckum. W Latvia 56°58′N 23°12′E
81 G24 Tukuyu prev. Neu-Langenburg. Mbeya, S Tanzania 09°14′S 33°39′E
Tukzār see Tokzār
41 O13 Tula var. Tula de Allende. Hidalgo, C Mexico 20°01′N 99°21′W
41 O11 Tula Tamaulipas, C Mexico 22°59′N 99°43′W
126 K5 Tula Tul'skaya Oblast', W Russian Federation 54°11′N 37°39′E
Tulach Mhór see Tullamore
Tula de Allende see Tula
186 M9 Tulaghi var. Tulagi. Florida Islands, C Solomon Islands 09°04′S 160°09′E
Tulagi see Tulaghi
159 N10 Tulagt Ar Gol ≈ W China
41 P13 Tulancingo Hidalgo, C Mexico 20°34′N 98°25′W
35 R11 Tulare California, W USA 36°12′N 119°21′W
29 P9 Tulare South Dakota, N USA 44°43′N 98°29′W
35 Q12 Tulare Lake Bed salt flat California, W USA
37 S14 Tularosa New Mexico, SW USA 33°04′N 106°01′W
37 P13 Tularosa Mountains ▲▲ New Mexico, SW USA
37 S15 Tularosa Valley basin New Mexico, SW USA
83 E25 Tulbagh Western Cape, SW South Africa 33°17′S 19°09′E
56 C5 Tulcán Carchi, N Ecuador 0°44′N 77°43′W
117 N13 Tulcea Tulcea, E Romania 45°11′N 28°49′E
117 N13 Tulcea ◈ county SE Romania
Tul'chin see Tul'chyn
117 N7 Tul'chyn Rus. Tul'chin. Vinnyts'ka Oblast', C Ukraine 48°40′N 28°49′E
Tuléar see Toliara
35 O1 Tulelake California, W USA 41°57′N 121°30′W
116 J10 Tulgheş Hung. Gyergyótölgyes. Harghita, C Romania 46°57′N 25°46′E
Tuli see Thuli
25 N4 Tulia Texas, SW USA 34°32′N 101°46′W
8 I9 Tulita prev. Fort Norman, Norman. Northwest Territories, NW Canada 64°55′N 125°25′W
20 J10 Tullahoma Tennessee, S USA 35°21′N 86°12′W
183 N12 Tullamarine ✈ (Melbourne) Victoria, SE Australia 37°40′S 144°46′E
183 Q7 Tullamore New South Wales, SE Australia 32°39′S 147°35′E
97 E18 Tullamore Ir. Tulach Mhór. Offaly, C Ireland 53°16′N 07°30′W
103 N12 Tulle anc. Tutela. Corrèze, C France 45°16′N 01°46′E
109 X3 Tulln var. Oberhollabrunn. Niederösterreich, NE Austria 48°20′N 16°02′E
109 W4 Tulln ≈ NE Austria
22 H6 Tullos Louisiana, S USA 31°48′N 92°19′W
97 F19 Tullow Ir. An Tullach. Carlow, SE Ireland 52°48′N 06°44′W
181 W5 Tully Queensland, NE Australia 18°03′S 145°56′E
124 J3 Tuloma ≈ NW Russian Federation
27 P9 Tulsa Oklahoma, C USA 36°09′N 96°W
153 N11 Tulsipur Mid Western, W Nepal 28°01′N 82°22′E
126 K6 Tul'skaya Oblast' ◈ province W Russian Federation
126 L14 Tul'skiy Respublika Adygeya, SW Russian Federation 44°26′N 40°12′E
186 E5 Tulu Manus Island, N Papua New Guinea 01°58′S 146°50′E
54 D10 Tuluá Valle del Cauca, W Colombia 04°01′N 76°16′W
116 M12 Tuluceşti Galaţi, E Romania 45°35′N 28°01′E
39 N12 Tuluksak Alaska, USA 61°06′N 160°57′W
41 Z12 Tulum, Ruinas de ruins Quintana Roo, SE Mexico
169 R17 Tulungagung prev. Toeloengagoeng. Jawa, C Indonesia 08°03′S 111°54′E
186 J6 Tulun Islands var. Kilinailau Islands; prev. Carteret Islands. island group NE Papua New Guinea
126 M4 Tuma Ryazanskaya Oblast', W Russian Federation 55°09′N 40°27′E
54 B12 Tumaco Nariño, SW Colombia 01°51′N 78°46′W
54 B12 Tumaco, Bahía de bay SW Colombia
Tuman-gang see Tumen
42 L8 Tuma, Río ≈ N Nicaragua
95 O16 Tumba Stockholm, C Sweden 59°12′N 17°49′E
Tumba, Lac see Ntomba, Lac
169 S12 Tumbangsenamang Borneo, C Indonesia 01°17′S 112°21′E
183 Q10 Tumbarumba New South Wales, SE Australia 35°47′S 148°03′E
56 A8 Tumbes Tumbes, NW Peru 03°33′S 80°27′W
56 A9 Tumbes off. Departamento de Tumbes. ◈ department NW Peru
Tumbes, Departamento de see Tumbes
19 P5 Tumbledown Mountain ▲ Maine, NE USA 45°27′N 70°28′W
11 N13 Tumbler Ridge British Columbia, W Canada 55°06′N 120°51′W
95 N16 Tumbo prev. Rekarne. Västmanland, C Sweden 59°25′N 16°04′E
167 Q12 Tumbŏt, Phnum ▲ W Cambodia 12°23′N 102°57′E
182 G9 Tumby Bay South Australia 34°22′S 136°05′E
163 Y10 Tumen Jilin, NE China 42°56′N 129°47′E
163 Y11 Tumen Chin. Tumen Jiang, Kor. Tuman-gang, Rus. Tumyn'tszyan. ≈ E Asia
Tumen Jiang see Tumen
55 Q8 Tumeremo Bolívar, E Venezuela 07°17′N 61°30′W
155 G19 Tumkūr Karnātaka, W India 13°20′N 77°06′E
96 I10 Tummel ≈ C Scotland, United Kingdom
188 B15 Tumon Bay bay W Guam
77 P14 Tumu NW Ghana 10°55′N 01°59′W
58 I10 Tumuc-Humac Mountains var. Serra Tumucumaque. ▲▲ N South America
Tumucumaque, Serra see Tumuc-Humac Mountains
183 Q10 Tumut New South Wales, SE Australia 35°20′S 148°14′E
158 F7 Tumxuk var. Urad Qianqi. Xinjiang Uygur Zizhiqu, NW China 78°40′N 39°54′E
Tumyn'tszyan see Tumen
Tün see Ferdows
45 U14 Tunapuna Trinidad, Trinidad and Tobago 10°38′N 61°23′W
60 K11 Tunas Paraná, S Brazil 24°57′S 49°05′W
Tunbridge Wells see Royal Tunbridge Wells
114 L11 Tunca Nehri Bul. Tundzha. ≈ Bulgaria/Turkey see also Tundzha
Tunca Nehri see Tundzha
137 O14 Tunceli var. Kalan. Tunceli, E Turkey 39°07′N 39°34′E
137 O14 Tunceli ◈ province C Turkey
152 J12 Tūndla Uttar Pradesh, N India 27°13′N 78°14′E
81 I25 Tunduru Ruvuma, S Tanzania 11°08′S 37°21′E
114 L10 Tundzha Turk. Tunca Nehri. ≈ Bulgaria/Turkey see also Tunca Nehri
Tundzha see Tunca Nehri
162 I6 Tünel var. Bulag. Hövsgöl, N Mongolia 49°51′N 100°41′E
155 H17 Tungabhadra ≈ S India
155 F17 Tungabhadra Reservoir ◎ S India
191 P2 Tungaru prev. Gilbert Islands. island group W Kiribati
171 P7 Tungawan Mindanao, S Philippines 07°33′N 122°22′E
Tungdor see Mainling
T'ung-shan see Xuzhou
161 Q16 Tungsha Tao Chin. Dongsha Qundao, Eng. Pratas Island. island S Taiwan
Tungshih see Dongshi
8 H9 Tungsten Northwest Territories, W Canada 62°N 128°09′W
Tung-t'ing Hu see Dongting Hu
56 A13 Tungurahua ◈ province C Ecuador
95 F14 Tunhovdfjorden ◎ S Norway
22 K2 Tunica Mississippi, S USA 34°40′N 90°22′W
75 N5 Tunis var. Tūnis. ● (Tunisia) NE Tunisia 36°53′N 10°10′E
75 N5 Tunis, Golfe de Ar. Khalīj Tūnis. gulf NE Tunisia
75 N6 Tunisia off. Tunisian Republic, Ar. Al Jumhūrīyah at Tūnisīyah, Fr. République Tunisienne. ◆ republic N Africa
Tunisian Republic see Tunisia
Tunisienne, République see Tunisia
Tūnisīyah, Al Jumhūrīyah at see Tunisia
Tūnis, Khalīj see Tunis, Golfe de
54 G9 Tunja Boyacá, C Colombia 05°33′N 73°23′W
93 F14 Tunnsjøen Lapp. Dåtnejaevrie. ◎ C Norway
39 N12 Tuntutuliak Alaska, USA 60°21′N 162°40′W
197 P14 Tunu ◈ province E Greenland
147 U8 Tunuk Chuyskaya Oblast', C Kyrgyzstan 42°11′N 73°55′E
13 Q6 Tunungayualok Island island Newfoundland and Labrador, E Canada
62 H11 Tunuyán Mendoza, W Argentina 33°35′S 69°00′W
62 I11 Tunuyán, Río ≈ W Argentina
Tunxi see Huangshan
Tuodian see Shuangbai
Tuoji see Zhongba
Tuokezhake see Shufu
35 P9 Tuolumne River ≈ California, W USA
Tuong Buong see Tương Đương
167 R7 Tương Đương var. Tuong Buong. Nghê An, N Vietnam 19°15′N 104°30′E
160 I13 Tuoniang Jiang ≈ S China
Tuotiereke see Jeminay
Tuotuo He see Togton He
Tuotuoheyan see Tanggulashan
Tüp see Tyup
60 J9 Tupã São Paulo, S Brazil 21°57′S 50°28′W
191 S10 Tupai var. Motu Iti. atoll Îles Sous le Vent, W French Polynesia
61 G15 Tupanciretã Rio Grande do Sul, S Brazil 29°06′S 53°48′W
22 M2 Tupelo Mississippi, S USA 34°15′N 88°42′W
59 K18 Tupiraçaba Goiás, S Brazil 14°33′S 48°40′W
57 L21 Tupiza Potosí, S Bolivia 21°27′S 65°45′W
144 D14 Tupkaragan, Mys prev. Mys Tyub-Karagan. headland SW Kazakhstan 44°40′N 50°19′E
11 N13 Tupper British Columbia, W Canada 55°30′N 119°59′W
18 J8 Tupper Lake ◎ New York, NE USA
146 J10 Tuproqqal'a Khorazm Viloyati, W Uzbekistan 40°52′N 62°00′E
146 J10 Tuproqqal'a Rus. Turpakkla. Xorazm Viloyati, W Uzbekistan 40°52′N 62°00′E
62 H11 Tupungato, Volcán ⩚ W Argentina 33°27′S 69°42′W
163 T9 Tuquan Nei Mongol Zizhiqu, N China 45°21′N 121°36′E
54 C13 Túquerres Nariño, SW Colombia 01°06′N 77°37′W
153 U13 Tura Meghālaya, NE India 25°33′N 90°14′E
122 M10 Tura Krasnoyarskiy Kray, N Russian Federation 64°20′N 100°17′E
122 G10 Tura ≈ C Russian Federation
140 M10 Turabah Makkah, W Saudi Arabia 22°00′N 42°00′E
55 O8 Turagua, Cerro ▲ C Venezuela 06°59′N 64°34′W
184 L12 Turakina Manawatu-Wanganui, North Island, New Zealand 40°03′S 175°13′E
185 K15 Turakirae Head headland North Island, New Zealand 41°26′S 174°54′E
186 B8 Turama ≈ S Papua New Guinea
122 K13 Turan Respublika Tyva, S Russian Federation 52°11′N 93°40′E
184 M10 Turangi Waikato, North Island, New Zealand 39°01′S 175°47′E
146 F11 Turan Lowland var. Turan Plain, Kaz. Turan Oypaty, Rus. Turanskaya Nizmennost', Turk. Turan Pesligi, Uzb. Turon Pasttekisligi. plain C Asia
Turan Oypaty/Turan Pesligi/Turan Plain/Turanskaya Nizmennost' see Turan Lowland
Turan Pasttekisligi see Turan Lowland
138 K7 Ṭurāq al 'Ilab hill range S Syria
119 K20 Turaw Rus. Turov. Homyel'skaya Voblasts', SE Belarus 52°04′N 27°44′E
140 L2 Ṭurayf Al Ḥudūd ash Shamālīyah, NW Saudi Arabia 31°43′N 38°40′E
Turba see Teruel
54 E5 Turbaco Bolívar, N Colombia 10°20′N 75°25′W
148 K15 Turbat Baluchistān, SW Pakistan 26°02′N 62°56′E
Turbat-i-Haidari see Torbat-e Ḥeydarīyeh
Turbat-i-Jam see Torbat-e Jām
54 D7 Turbo Antioquia, NW Colombia 08°06′N 76°44′W
Turčianský Svätý Martin see Martin
116 H10 Turda Ger. Thorenburg, Hung. Torda. Cluj, NW Romania 46°35′N 23°50′E
142 M7 Ṭūreh Markazī, W Iran
191 X12 Tureia atoll Îles Tuamotu, SE French Polynesia
110 I12 Turek Wielkopolskie, C Poland 52°01′N 18°30′E
93 L19 Turenki Etelä-Suomi, SW Finland 60°55′N 24°38′E
Turfan see Turpan
Turgay see Torgay
Turgay see Torgay
144 M8 Turgayskaya Stolovaya Strana Kaz. Torgay Üstirti. plateau Kazakhstan/Russian Federation
Turgel see Türi
114 L8 Türgovishte prev. Eski Dzhumaya, Tărgovište. Türgovishte, N Bulgaria 43°15′N 26°34′E
114 L8 Türgovishte ◈ province N Bulgaria
136 C14 Turgutlu Manisa, W Turkey 38°30′N 27°43′E
136 L12 Turhal Tokat, N Turkey 40°23′N 36°05′E
118 H4 Türi Ger. Turgel. Järvamaa, N Estonia 58°48′N 25°28′E
105 S9 Turia ≈ E Spain
58 M12 Turiaçu Maranhão, E Brazil 01°40′S 45°22′W
Turin see Torino
116 J2 Turiya Pol. Turja, Rus. Tur'ya; prev. Tur"ya. ≈ NW Ukraine
116 I3 Turiys'k Volyns'ka Oblast', NW Ukraine 51°05′N 24°31′E
Turja see Turiya
116 H6 Turka L'vivs'ka Oblast', W Ukraine 49°07′N 23°01′E
81 H16 Turkana, Lake var. Lake Rudolf. ◎ N Kenya
Turkestan see Turkistan
147 Q12 Turkestan Range Rus. Turkestanskiy Khrebet. ▲▲ C Asia
Turkestanskiy Khrebet see Turkestan Range
111 M23 Túrkeve Jász-Nagykun-Szolnok, E Hungary 47°06′N 20°42′E
25 O4 Turkey Texas, SW USA 34°23′N 100°54′W
136 H14 Turkey off. Republic of Turkey, Turk. Türkiye Cumhuriyeti. ◆ republic SW Asia
181 N4 Turkey Creek Western Australia 16°54′S 128°12′E
26 M9 Turkey Creek ≈ Oklahoma, C USA
37 T9 Turkey Mountains ▲▲ New Mexico, SW USA
Turkey, Republic of see Turkey
29 X11 Turkey River ≈ Iowa, C USA
127 N7 Turki Saratovskaya Oblast', W Russian Federation 52°00′N 43°16′E
121 O1 Turkish Republic of Northern Cyprus ◇ disputed territory Cyprus
145 P16 Turkistan prev. Turkestan. Yuzhnyy Kazakhstan, S Kazakhstan 43°18′N 68°18′E
Turkistan, Bandi-i see Torkestān, Selseleh-ye Band-e
Türkiye Cumhuriyeti see Turkey
146 K12 Türkmenabat prev. Rus. Chardzhev, Chardzhou, Chardzhui, Lenin-Turkmenski, Turkm. Chärjew. Lebap Welaýaty, E Turkmenistan 39°07′N 63°30′E
146 A11 Türkmen Aylagy Rus. Turkmenskiy Zaliv. lake gulf W Turkmenistan
Turkmenbashi see Türkmenbaşy
146 A10 Türkmenbaşy Rus. Turkmenbashi; prev. Krasnovodsk. Balkan Welaýaty, W Turkmenistan 40°N 53°04′E
146 A10 Türkmenbaşy Aylagy prev. Rus. Krasnovodskiy Zaliv, Turkm. Krasnowodsk Aylagy. lake Gulf W Turkmenistan
146 J14 Türkmengala Rus. Turkmen-kala; prev. Turkmen-Kala. Mary Welaýaty, S Turkmenistan 37°25′N 62°19′E
146 G13 Turkmenistan; prev. Turkmenskaya Soviet Socialist Republic. ◆ republic C Asia
Turkmen-kala/Turkmen-Kala see Türkmengala
Turkmenskaya Soviet Socialist Republic see Turkmenistan
Turkmenskiy Zaliv see Türkmen Aylagy
136 L16 Türkoğlu Kahramanmaraş, S Turkey 37°24′N 36°49′E
44 L6 Turks and Caicos Islands ◇ UK dependent territory N West Indies
64 G10 Turks and Caicos Islands UK dependent territory N West Indies
45 N6 Turks Islands island group SE Turks and Caicos Islands
93 K19 Turku Swe. Åbo. Länsi-Suomi, SW Finland 60°27′N 22°17′E
81 H17 Turkwel seasonal river NW Kenya
27 P9 Turley Oklahoma, C USA 36°14′N 95°58′W
35 P9 Turlock California, W USA 37°29′N 120°52′W
118 I12 Turmantas Utena, NE Lithuania 55°41′N 26°27′E
Turmberg see Wieżyca
54 L5 Turmero Aragua, N Venezuela South America 10°14′N 66°40′W
184 N13 Turnagain, Cape headland North Island, New Zealand 40°30′S 176°36′E
Turnau see Turnov
42 H2 Turneffe Islands island group E Belize
18 M11 Turners Falls Massachusetts, NE USA 42°36′N 72°31′W
11 P16 Turner Valley Alberta, SW Canada 50°43′N 114°19′W
99 I16 Turnhout Antwerpen, N Belgium 51°19′N 04°57′E
109 V5 Türnitz Niederösterreich, E Austria 47°56′N 15°26′E
11 S12 Turnor Lake ◎ Saskatchewan, C Canada
111 E15 Turnov Ger. Turnau. Liberecký Kraj, N Czech Republic 50°36′N 15°10′E
Tŭrnovo see Veliko Tŭrnovo
116 I15 Turnu Măgurele var. Turnu-Măgurele. Teleorman, S Romania 43°44′N 24°53′E
Turnu Severin see Drobeta-Turnu Severin
Turócszentmárton see Martin
Turoni see Tours
Turov see Turaw
Turpakkla see Tuproqqal'a
158 M6 Turpan var. Turfan. Xinjiang Uygur Zizhiqu, NW China 42°55′N 89°06′E
Turpan Depression see Turpan Pendi
158 M6 Turpan Pendi Eng. Turpan Depression. depression NW China
158 M5 Turpan Zhan Xinjiang Uygur Zizhiqu, W China 43°10′N 89°06′E
Turpentine State see North Carolina
44 H8 Turquino, Pico ▲ E Cuba 19°54′N 76°55′W
27 Y10 Turrell Arkansas, C USA 35°22′N 90°13′W
43 N14 Turrialba Cartago, E Costa Rica 09°56′N 83°40′W
96 K8 Turriff NE Scotland, United Kingdom 57°32′N 02°28′W
139 V7 Tursāq Diyālá, E Iraq 33°27′N 45°47′E
Turshiz see Kāshmar
Tursunzade see Tursunzoda
147 P13 Tursunzoda Rus. Tursunzade; prev. Regar. W Tajikistan 38°30′N 68°10′E
Turt see Hanh
Tŭrtkŭl/Turtkul' see To'rtko'l
29 O9 Turtle Creek ≈ South Dakota, N USA
30 K4 Turtle Flambeau Flowage ⊠ Wisconsin, N USA
11 S14 Turtleford Saskatchewan, S Canada 53°21′N 108°48′W
28 M4 Turtle Lake North Dakota, N USA 47°31′N 100°53′W
92 K12 Turtola Lappi, NW Finland 66°39′N 23°55′E
122 M10 Turu ≈ N Russian Federation
Turuga see Tsuruga
147 V10 Turugart Pass pass China/Kyrgyzstan
158 E7 Turugart Shankou var. Pereval Torugart. pass China/Kyrgyzstan
122 K9 Turukhan ≈ N Russian Federation
122 K9 Turukhansk Krasnoyarskiy Kray, N Russian Federation 65°50′N 87°48′E
139 N3 Turumbah well NE Syria
Turuoka see Tsuruoka
Turush see Turysh
60 K7 Turvo, Rio ≈ S Brazil
Tur"ya see Turiya
144 H14 Turysh prev. Turush. Mangistau, SW Kazakhstan 45°24′N 56°02′E
23 O4 Tuscaloosa Alabama, S USA 33°13′N 87°34′W
23 O4 Tuscaloosa, Lake ◎ Alabama, S USA
Tuscan Archipelago see Toscano, Archipelago
Tuscan-Emilian Mountains see Tosco-Emiliano, Appennino
Tuscany see Toscana
35 V2 Tuscarora Nevada, W USA 41°16′N 116°13′W
18 F15 Tuscarora Mountain ridge Pennsylvania, NE USA
30 M14 Tuscola Illinois, N USA 39°46′N 88°19′W
25 P7 Tuscola Texas, SW USA 32°12′N 99°48′W
23 O2 Tuscumbia Alabama, S USA 34°43′N 87°42′W
92 O4 Tusenøyane island group S Svalbard
144 K13 Tushchybas, Zaliv prev. Zaliv Paskevicha. lake gulf SW Kazakhstan
Tusima see Tsushima
171 Y15 Tusirah Papua, E Indonesia 06°46′S 140°19′E
23 Q5 Tuskegee Alabama, S USA 32°25′N 85°41′W
94 E8 Tustna island S Norway
39 R12 Tustumena Lake ◎ Alaska, USA
110 K13 Tuszyn Łódzkie, C Poland 51°36′N 19°31′E
137 S13 Tutak Ağrı, E Turkey 39°34′N 42°48′E
185 C20 Tutamoe Range ▲▲ North Island, New Zealand
Tutasev see Tutayev
124 L15 Tutayev var. Tutasev. Yaroslavskaya Oblast', W Russian Federation 57°51′N 39°29′E
Tutela see Tulle, France
Tutela see Tudela, Spain
Tutera see Tudela
155 H23 Tuticorin Tamil Nādu, SE India 08°48′N 78°10′E
113 L15 Tutin Serbia, S Serbia 43°00′N 20°20′E
184 O10 Tutira Hawke's Bay, North Island, New Zealand 39°14′S 176°53′E
Tutiura see Tsuchiura
122 K10 Tutonchny Krasnoyarskiy Kray, N Russian Federation 64°12′N 93°52′E
114 L6 Tutrakan Silistra, NE Bulgaria 44°03′N 26°38′E
29 N5 Tuttle North Dakota, N USA 47°07′N 99°58′W
26 M11 Tuttle Oklahoma, C USA 35°17′N 97°48′W
27 O3 Tuttle Creek Lake ⊠ Kansas, C USA
101 H23 Tuttlingen Baden-Württemberg, S Germany 47°59′N 08°49′E
171 R16 Tutuala East Timor 08°23′S 127°12′E
192 K17 Tutuila island W American Samoa
83 I18 Tutume Central, E Botswana 20°26′S 27°02′E
39 N7 Tututalak Mountain ▲ Alaska, USA 67°51′N 161°27′W
22 K3 Tutwiler Mississippi, S USA 34°00′N 90°25′W
162 L8 Tuul Gol ≈ N Mongolia
93 O16 Tuupovaara Itä-Suomi, E Finland 62°30′N 30°40′E
Tuva see Tyva, Respublika
190 E7 Tuvalu prev. Ellice Islands. ◆ commonwealth republic SW Pacific Ocean
Tuvinskaya ASSR see Tyva, Respublika
163 O9 Tuvshinshiree var. Sergelen. Sühbaatar, E Mongolia 46°12′N 111°48′E
141 P9 Ṭuwayq, Jabal ▲▲ C Saudi Arabia
138 H13 Ṭuwayyil ash Shihāq desert S Jordan
11 U16 Tuxford Saskatchewan, S Canada 50°33′N 105°32′W
167 U12 Tu Xoay Đắc Lắc, S Vietnam 12°18′N 107°33′E
40 L14 Tuxpan Jalisco, C Mexico 19°33′N 103°21′W
40 J12 Tuxpan Nayarit, C Mexico 21°57′N 105°12′W
41 Q12 Tuxpán var. Tuxpán de Rodríguez Cano. Veracruz-Llave, E Mexico 20°58′N 97°23′W
Tuxpán de Rodríguez Cano see Tuxpán
41 R15 Tuxtepec var. San Juan Bautista Tuxtepec. Oaxaca, S Mexico 18°02′N 96°05′W
41 U16 Tuxtla var. Tuxtla Gutiérrez. Chiapas, SE Mexico 16°44′N 93°03′W
Tuxtla see San Andrés Tuxtla
Tuxtla Gutiérrez see Tuxtla
Tuyama see Tsuyama
167 T5 Tuyên Quang Tuyên Quang, N Vietnam 21°48′N 105°18′E
167 U13 Tuy Hoa Binh Thuân, S Vietnam 11°03′N 108°12′E
167 V12 Tuy Hoa Phu Yên, S Vietnam 13°02′N 109°15′E
127 U5 Tuymazy Respublika Bashkortostan, W Russian Federation 54°36′N 53°40′E
Tuy Phong see Liên Hương
142 L6 Tūysarkān var. Tuisarkan, Tuyserkān. Hamadān, W Iran 34°31′N 48°30′E
Tuyserkān see Tūysarkān
Tuyuk see Tuyyk
145 W16 Tuyyk Kaz. Tuyyq; prev. Tuyuk. Taldykorgan, SE Kazakhstan 43°07′N 79°24′E
Tuyyq see Tuyyk
136 I14 Tuz Gölü ◎ C Turkey
125 Q15 Tuzha Kirovskaya Oblast', NW Russian Federation 57°37′N 48°02′E
113 K17 Tuzi S Montenegro 42°22′N 19°21′E
139 T5 Ṭūz Khurmātū At Ta'mím, N Iraq 34°56′N 44°38′E
112 I11 Tuzla Federacija Bosna I Hercegovina, NE Bosnia and Herzegovina 44°33′N 18°40′E
117 N15 Tuzla Constanţa, SE Romania 43°58′N 28°38′E
137 T12 Tuzluca Iğdır, E Turkey 40°02′N 43°39′E
95 J20 Tvååker Halland, S Sweden 57°04′N 12°25′E
95 F17 Tvedestrand Aust-Agder, S Norway 58°36′N 08°55′E
124 J16 Tver' prev. Kalinin. Tverskaya Oblast', W Russian Federation 56°53′N 35°52′E
126 I15 Tverskaya Oblast' ◈ province W Russian Federation
124 I15 Tvertsa ≈ W Russian Federation
138 G9 Tverya var. Tiberias; prev. Teverya. Northern, N Israel 32°48′N 35°32′E
95 F16 Tvietsund Telemark, S Norway 59°00′N 08°34′E
110 H13 Twardogóra Ger. Festenberg. Dolnośląskie, SW Poland 51°21′N 17°27′E
14 J14 Tweed Ontario, SE Canada 44°29′N 77°19′W
96 K13 Tweed ≈ England/Scotland, United Kingdom
98 O7 Tweede-Exloërmond Drenthe, NE Netherlands 52°55′N 06°55′E
183 V3 Tweed Heads New South Wales, SE Australia 28°10′S 153°32′E
98 M11 Twello Gelderland, E Netherlands 52°14′N 06°07′E
35 W15 Twentynine Palms California, W USA 34°08′N 116°03′W
25 P9 Twin Buttes Reservoir ⊠ Texas, SW USA
33 O15 Twin Falls Idaho, NW USA 42°34′N 114°28′W
39 N13 Twin Hills Alaska, USA 59°06′N 160°21′W
11 O11 Twin Lakes Alberta, W Canada 57°47′N 117°30′W
33 O12 Twin Peaks ▲ Idaho, NW USA 44°37′N 114°24′W
185 I14 Twins, The ▲ South Island, New Zealand 41°14′S 172°38′E
29 S5 Twin Valley Minnesota, N USA 47°15′N 96°15′W
100 G11 Twistringen Niedersachsen, NW Germany 52°48′N 08°39′E
185 E20 Twizel Canterbury, South Island, New Zealand 44°04′S 171°12′E
29 X5 Two Harbors Minnesota, N USA 47°01′N 91°40′W
11 R14 Two Hills Alberta, SW Canada 53°40′N 111°43′W
31 N7 Two Rivers Wisconsin, N USA 44°10′N 87°33′W
116 H8 Tyachiv Zakarpats'ka Oblast', W Ukraine 48°02′N 23°35′E
Tyan'-Shan' see Tien Shan
166 L3 Tyao ≈ Burma (Myanmar)/India
117 R6 Tyasmyn ≈ N Ukraine
23 X6 Tybee Island Georgia, SE USA 32°00′N 80°51′W
Tyborøn see Thyborøn
111 J16 Tychy Ger. Tichau. Śląskie, S Poland 50°12′N 19°01′E
111 O16 Tyczyn Podkarpackie, SE Poland 49°58′N 22°03′E
94 I8 Tydal Sør-Trøndelag, S Norway 63°01′N 11°36′E
115 H24 Tyflós ≈ Kríti, Greece, E Mediterranean Sea
21 S3 Tygart Lake ⊠ West Virginia, NE USA
123 Q13 Tygda Amurskaya Oblast', SE Russian Federation 53°07′N 126°12′E
21 Q11 Tyger River ≈ South Carolina, SE USA
32 I11 Tygh Valley Oregon, NW USA 45°15′N 121°12′W
94 F12 Tyin ◎ S Norway

◆ Country
● Country Capital
◇ Dependent Territory
○ Dependent Territory Capital
◈ Administrative Regions
✈ International Airport
▲ Mountain
▲▲ Mountain Range
⩚ Volcano
≈ River
◎ Lake
⊠ Reservoir

29 S10 **Tyler** Minnesota, N USA *44°16′N 96°07′W*
25 W7 **Tyler** Texas, SW USA *32°21′N 95°18′W*
25 W7 **Tyler, Lake** ⊠ Texas, SW USA
22 K7 **Tylertown** Mississippi, S USA *31°07′N 90°08′W*
117 P10 **Tylihuls'kyy Lyman** ◎ SW Ukraine
Tylos *see* Bahrain
115 C15 **Týmfi** *var.* Timfi. ▲ W Greece *39°58′N 20°51′E*
115 E17 **Tymfristós** *var.* Timfristos. ▲ C Greece *38°57′N 21°49′E*
115 J25 **Tympáki** *var.* Timbaki; *prev.* Timbákion. Kríti, Greece, E Mediterranean Sea *35°04′N 24°47′E*
123 Q12 **Tynda** Amurskaya Oblast', SE Russian Federation *55°09′N 124°44′E*
29 Q12 **Tyndall** South Dakota, N USA *42°57′N 97°52′W*
97 L14 **Tyne** ≈ N England, United Kingdom
97 M14 **Tynemouth** NE England, United Kingdom *55°01′N 01°24′W*
97 L14 **Tyneside** *cultural region* NE England, United Kingdom
94 H10 **Tynset** Hedmark, S Norway *61°45′N 10°49′E*
39 Q12 **Tyonek** Alaska, USA *61°04′N 151°08′W*
Tyôsi *see* Chōshi
Tyras *see* Dniester
Tyras *see* Bilhorod-Dnistrovs'kyy
Tyre *see* Soûr
95 G14 **Tyrifjorden** ◎ S Norway
95 K22 **Tyringe** Skåne, S Sweden *56°09′N 13°35′E*
123 R13 **Tyrma** Khabarovskiy Kray, SE Russian Federation *50°00′N 132°04′E*
Tyrnau *see* Trnava
115 F15 **Týrnavos** *var.* Tírnavos. Thessalía, C Greece *39°45′N 22°18′E*
127 N16 **Tyrnyauz** Kabardino-Balkarskaya Respublika, SW Russian Federation *43°19′N 42°55′E*
Tyrol *see* Tirol
18 E14 **Tyrone** Pennsylvania, NE USA *40°41′N 78°12′W*
97 E15 **Tyrone** *cultural region* W Northern Ireland, United Kingdom
Tyros *see* Bahrain
182 M10 **Tyrrell, Lake** *salt lake* Victoria, SE Australia
84 H14 **Tyrrhenian Basin** *undersea feature* Tyrrhenian Sea, C Mediterranean Sea *39°30′N 13°00′E*
120 L8 **Tyrrhenian Sea** *It.* Mare Tirreno. *sea* N Mediterranean Sea
94 J12 **Tyrsil** ≈ Hedmark, S Norway
Tysa *see* Tisa/Tisza
116 J7 **Tysmenytsya** Ivano-Frankivs'ka Oblast', W Ukraine *48°54′N 24°50′E*
95 C14 **Tysnesøya** *island* S Norway
95 C14 **Tysse** Hordaland, S Norway *60°23′N 05°46′E*
95 D14 **Tyssedal** Hordaland, S Norway *60°07′N 06°36′E*
95 O17 **Tystberga** Södermanland, C Sweden *58°51′N 17°15′E*
118 E12 **Tytuvėnai** Šiaulai, C Lithuania *55°36′N 23°14′E*
Tyub-Karagan, Mys *see* Tupkaragan, Mys
147 V8 **Tyugel'-Say** Narynskaya Oblast', C Kyrgyzstan *41°57′N 74°40′E*
122 H11 **Tyukalinsk** Omskaya Oblast', C Russian Federation *55°56′N 72°02′E*
127 V7 **Tyul'gan** Orenburgskaya Oblast', W Russian Federation *52°27′N 56°08′E*
122 G11 **Tyumen'** Tyumenskaya Oblast', C Russian Federation *57°11′N 65°29′E*
122 H11 **Tyumenskaya Oblast'** ◐ *province* C Russian Federation
147 Y7 **Tyup** *Kir.* Tüp. Issyk-Kul'skaya Oblast', NE Kyrgyzstan *42°44′N 78°18′E*
122 L14 **Tyva, Respublika** *prev.* Tannu-Tuva, Tuva, Tuvinskaya ASSR. ◐ *autonomous republic* C Russian Federation
117 N7 **Tyvriv** Vinnyts'ka Oblast', C Ukraine *49°01′N 28°28′E*
97 J21 **Tywi** ≈ S Wales, United Kingdom
97 I19 **Tywyn** W Wales, United Kingdom *52°35′N 04°06′W*
83 K20 **Tzaneen** Limpopo, NE South Africa *23°50′S 30°09′E*
Tzekung *see* Zigong
115 I20 **Tziá** *prev.* Kéa, Kéos; *anc.* Ceos. *island* Kykládes, Greece, Aegean Sea
41 X12 **Tzucacab** Yucatán, SE Mexico *20°04′N 89°03′W*

U

82 B12 **Uaco Cungo** *var.* Waku Kungo, *Port.* Santa Comba. Cuanza Sul, C Angola *11°21′S 15°04′E*
UAE *see* United Arab Emirates
191 X7 **Ua Huka** *island* Îles Marquises, NE French Polynesia
58 E10 **Uaiacás** Roraima, N Brazil *03°28′N 63°13′W*
Uamba *see* Wamba
Uanle Uen *see* Wanlaweyn
191 W7 **Ua Pu** *island* Îles Marquises, NE French Polynesia
81 L17 **Uar Garas** *spring/well* SW Somalia *01°19′N 41°22′E*
58 G12 **Uatumã, Rio** ≈ C Brazil
Ua Uíbh Fhailí *see* Offaly
58 C11 **Uaupés, Rio** *var.* Río Vaupés. ≈ Brazil/Colombia *see also* Vaupés, Río
Uaupés, Rio *see* Vaupés, Río
Uba *see* Oba
145 N6 **Ubagan** *Kaz.* Obagan. ≈ Kazakhstan/Russian Federation
186 G7 **Ubai** New Britain, E Papua New Guinea *05°38′S 150°45′E*
79 J15 **Ubangi** *Fr.* Oubangui. ≈ C Africa
Ubangi-Shari *see* Central African Republic
116 M3 **Ubarts'** *Ukr.* Ubort'. ≈ Belarus/Ukraine *see also* Ubort'
Ubarts' *see* Ubort'
54 F9 **Ubaté** Cundinamarca, C Colombia *05°20′N 73°50′W*
60 N10 **Ubatuba** São Paulo, S Brazil *23°26′S 45°04′W*
149 R12 **Ubauro** Sind, SE Pakistan *28°08′N 69°43′E*
171 Q6 **Ubay** Bohol, C Philippines *10°02′N 124°29′E*
103 U14 **Ubaye** ≈ SE France
Ubayid, Wadi al *see* Ubayyiḍ, Wādī al
139 N8 **Ubaylah** Al Anbār, W Iraq *33°06′N 40°13′E*
139 O10 **Ubayyiḍ, Wādī al** *var.* Wadi al Ubayid. *dry watercourse* SW Iraq
98 L13 **Ubbergen** Gelderland, E Netherlands *51°49′N 05°54′E*
164 E13 **Ube** Yamaguchi, Honshū, SW Japan *33°57′N 131°15′E*
105 O13 **Ubeda** Andalucía, S Spain *38°01′N 03°22′W*
109 V7 **Übelbach** *var.* Markt-Übelbach. Steiermark, SE Austria *47°13′N 15°15′E*
59 L20 **Uberaba** Minas Gerais, SE Brazil *19°47′S 47°57′W*
57 Q19 **Uberaba, Laguna** ◎ E Bolivia
59 K19 **Uberlândia** Minas Gerais, SE Brazil *18°17′S 48°17′W*
101 H24 **Überlingen** Baden-Württemberg, S Germany *47°46′N 09°10′E*
77 U16 **Ubiaja** Edo, S Nigeria *06°39′N 06°23′E*
104 K3 **Ubiña, Peña** ▲ NW Spain *43°01′N 05°58′W*
57 H17 **Ubinas, Volcán** ⛰ S Peru *16°16′S 70°49′W*
Ubol Rajadhani/Ubol Ratchathani *see* Ubon Ratchathani
167 P9 **Ubolratna Reservoir** ⊠ C Thailand
167 S10 **Ubon Ratchathani** *var.* Muang Ubon, Ubol Rajadhani, Ubol Ratchathani, Udon Ratchathani. Ubon Ratchathani, E Thailand *15°15′N 104°50′E*
119 L20 **Ubort'** *Bel.* Ubarts'. ≈ Belarus/Ukraine *see also* Ubarts'
Ubort' *see* Ubarts'
104 K15 **Ubrique** Andalucía, S Spain *36°42′N 05°27′W*
Ubsu-Nur, Ozero *see* Uvs Nuur
79 M18 **Ubundu** Orientale, C Dem. Rep. Congo *0°24′S 25°30′E*
146 J13 **Üçajy** *var.* Üchajy, *Rus.* Uch-Adzhi. Mary Welaýaty, C Turkmenistan *38°06′N 62°44′E*
137 X11 **Ucar** *Rus.* Udzhary. C Azerbaijan *40°31′N 47°40′E*
56 G13 **Ucayali** *off.* Departamento de Ucayali. ◐ *department* E Peru
Ucayali, Departamento de *see* Ucayali
56 F10 **Ucayali, Río** ≈ C Peru
Uccle *see* Ukkel
Uch-Adzhi/Üchajy *see* Üçajy
127 X4 **Uchaly** Respublika Bashkortostan, W Russian Federation *54°19′N 59°33′E*
Ucharal *see* Usharal
164 C17 **Uchinoura** Kagoshima, Kyūshū, SW Japan *31°16′N 131°04′E*
165 R5 **Uchiura-wan** *bay* NW Pacific Ocean
Uchkuduk *see* Uchquduq
147 S9 **Uchqo'rg'on** *Rus.* Uchkurghan. Namangan Viloyati, E Uzbekistan *41°06′N 72°04′E*
146 K8 **Uchquduq** *Rus.* Uchkuduk. Navoiy Viloyati, N Uzbekistan *42°12′N 63°27′E*
Uchsay *see* Uchsoy
146 G6 **Uchsoy** *Rus.* Uchsay. Qoraqalpog'iston Respublikasi, NW Uzbekistan *43°51′N 58°51′E*
Uchtagan Gumy/Uchtagan, Peski *see* Uçtagan Gumy
123 R11 **Uchur** ≈ E Russian Federation
100 O10 **Uckermark** *cultural region* E Germany
10 K17 **Ucluelet** Vancouver Island, British Columbia, SW Canada *48°55′N 123°34′W*
146 D10 **Uçtagan Gumy** *var.* Uchtagan Gumy, *Rus.* Peski Uchtagan. *desert* NW Turkmenistan
122 M13 **Uda** ≈ S Russian Federation
123 R12 **Uda** ≈ E Russian Federation
123 N6 **Udachnyy** Respublika Sakha (Yakutiya), NE Russian Federation *66°27′N 112°18′E*
155 G21 **Udagamandalam** *var.* Ooty, Udhagamandalam; *prev.* Ootacamund. Tamil Nādu, SW India *11°28′N 76°42′E*
152 F14 **Udaipur** *prev.* Oodeypore. Rājasthān, N India *24°35′N 73°41′E*
Udayadhani *see* Uthai Thani
143 N16 **'Udayd, Khawr al** *var.* Khor al Udeid. *inlet* Qatar/Saudi Arabia
112 D11 **Udbina** Lika-Senj, W Croatia *44°33′N 15°46′E*
95 I18 **Uddevalla** Västra Götaland, S Sweden *58°20′N 11°56′E*
Uddjaur *see* Uddjaure
92 H13 **Uddjaure** *var.* Uddjaur. ◎ N Sweden
Udeid, Khor al *see* 'Udayd, Khawr al
99 K14 **Uden** Noord-Brabant, SE Netherlands *51°40′N 05°37′E*
Uden *see* Udenhout
99 J14 **Udenhout** *var.* Uden. Noord-Brabant, S Netherlands *51°37′N 05°09′E*
155 H14 **Udgīr** Mahārāshtra, C India *18°23′N 77°06′E*
Udhagamandalam *see* Udagamandalam
152 H6 **Udhampur** Jammu and Kashmir, NW India *32°55′N 75°07′E*
139 X14 **'Udhaybah, 'Uqlat al** *well* S Iraq
106 J7 **Udine** *anc.* Utina. Friuli-Venezia Giulia, NE Italy *46°05′N 13°10′E*
175 T14 **Udintsev Fracture Zone** *tectonic feature* S Pacific Ocean
Udipi *see* Udupi
Udmurtia *see* Udmurtskaya Respublika
127 S2 **Udmurtskaya Respublika** *Eng.* Udmurtia. ◐ *autonomous republic* NW Russian Federation
124 J15 **Udomlya** Tverskaya Oblast', W Russian Federation *57°53′N 34°59′E*
Udon Ratchathani *see* Ubon Ratchathani
167 Q8 **Udon Thani** *var.* Ban Mak Khaeng, Udorndhani. Udon Thani, N Thailand *17°25′N 102°45′E*
Udorndhani *see* Udon Thani
189 U12 **Udot** *atoll* Chuuk Islands, C Micronesia
123 S12 **Udskaya Guba** *bay* E Russian Federation
123 R12 **Udskoye** Khabarovskiy Kray, SE Russian Federation *54°32′N 134°26′E*
155 E19 **Udupi** *var.* Udipi. Karnātaka, SW India *13°18′N 74°46′E*
Udzhary *see* Ucar
100 O9 **Uecker** ≈ NE Germany
100 P9 **Ueckermünde** Mecklenburg-Vorpommern, NE Germany *53°43′N 14°03′E*
164 M12 **Ueda** *var.* Uyeda. Nagano, Honshū, S Japan *36°27′N 138°13′E*
79 L16 **Uele** *var.* Welle. ≈ NE Dem. Rep. Congo
123 W5 **Uelen** Chukotskiy Avtonomnyy Okrug, NE Russian Federation *66°01′N 169°52′W*
Uele (upper course) *see* Kibali, Dem. Rep. Congo
Uele (upper course) *see* Uolo, Río, Equatorial Guinea/Gabon
100 J11 **Uelzen** Niedersachsen, N Germany *52°58′N 10°34′E*
164 J14 **Ueno** Mie, Honshū, SW Japan *34°45′N 136°08′E*
127 V4 **Ufa** Respublika Bashkortostan, W Russian Federation *54°46′N 56°02′E*
127 V4 **Ufa** ≈ W Russian Federation
Ufra *see* Kenar
83 C18 **Ugab** ≈ C Namibia
118 D8 **Ugāle** NW Latvia *57°16′N 21°58′E*
81 F17 **Uganda** *off.* Republic of Uganda. ◆ *republic* E Africa
Uganda, Republic of *see* Uganda
138 G4 **Ugarit** *Ar.* Ra's Shamrah. *site of ancient city* Al Lādhiqīyah, NW Syria
39 O14 **Ugashik** Alaska, USA *57°30′N 157°24′W*
107 Q19 **Ugento** Puglia, SE Italy *39°53′N 18°09′E*
105 O15 **Ugíjar** Andalucía, S Spain *36°58′N 03°03′W*
103 T11 **Ugine** Savoie, E France *45°45′N 06°25′E*
123 R13 **Uglegorsk** Amurskaya Oblast', S Russian Federation *51°40′N 128°05′E*
Ugleural'sk *see* Ugleural'skiy
125 V13 **Ugleural'skiy** *prev.* Polovinka, Ugleural'sk. Permskiy Kray, NW Russian Federation *58°57′N 57°37′E*
124 L15 **Uglich** Yaroslavskaya Oblast', W Russian Federation *57°33′N 38°23′E*
126 I4 **Ugra** ≈ W Russian Federation
147 V9 **Ugyut** Narynskaya Oblast', C Kyrgyzstan *41°22′N 74°49′E*
111 H19 **Uherské Hradiště** *Ger.* Ungarisch-Hradisch. Zlínský Kraj, E Czech Republic *49°05′N 17°26′E*
111 H19 **Uherský Brod** *Ger.* Ungarisch-Brod. Zlínský Kraj, E Czech Republic *49°01′N 17°40′E*
111 B17 **Úhlava** *Ger.* Angel. ≈ W Czech Republic
Uhorshchyna *see* Hungary
31 T13 **Uhrichsville** Ohio, N USA *40°23′N 81°21′W*
Uhuru Peak *see* Kilimanjaro
96 G8 **Uig** N Scotland, United Kingdom *57°35′N 06°22′W*
82 B10 **Uíge** *Port.* Carmona, Vila Marechal Carmona. Uíge, NW Angola *07°37′S 15°02′E*
82 B10 **Uíge** ◐ *province* N Angola
193 Y15 **Uiha** *island* Ha'apai Group, C Tonga
189 U13 **Uijec** *island* Chuuk, C Micronesia
163 X14 **Uijeongbu** *Jap.* Giseifu; *prev.* Ŭijŏngbu. NW South Korea *37°42′N 127°02′E*
Ŭijŏngbu *see* Uijeongbu
Uil *see* Oyyl
36 M3 **Uinta Mountains** ▲▲ Utah, W USA
83 C18 **Uis** Erongo, NW Namibia *21°08′S 14°49′E*
83 I25 **Uitenhage** Eastern Cape, S South Africa *33°44′S 25°27′E*
98 H9 **Uitgeest** Noord-Holland, W Netherlands *52°32′N 04°43′E*
98 I11 **Uithoorn** Noord-Holland, C Netherlands *52°14′N 04°50′E*
98 O4 **Uithuizen** Groningen, NE Netherlands *53°24′N 06°40′E*
98 O4 **Uithuizermeeden** Groningen, NE Netherlands *53°25′N 06°43′E*
189 R6 **Ujae Atoll** *var.* Wūjae. *atoll* Ralik Chain, W Marshall Islands
Ujain *see* Ujjain
111 I16 **Ujazd** Opolskie, S Poland *50°22′N 18°20′E*
Új-Becse *see* Novi Bečej
Ujda *see* Oujda
189 N5 **Ujelang Atoll** *var.* Wujlān. *atoll* Ralik Chain, W Marshall Islands
111 N21 **Újfehértó** Szabolcs-Szatmár-Bereg, E Hungary *47°48′N 21°40′E*
Újgradiska *see* Nova Gradiška
164 J13 **Uji** *var.* Uzi. Kyōto, Honshū, SW Japan *34°54′N 135°48′E*
81 E21 **Ujiji** Kigoma, W Tanzania *04°55′S 29°39′E*
154 G10 **Ujjain** *prev.* Ujain. Madhya Pradesh, C India *23°11′N 75°50′E*
Újlak *see* Ilok
'Ujmān *see* 'Ajmān
Újmoldova *see* Moldova Nouă
Újszentanna *see* Sântana
Ujungpandang *see* Makassar
Ujung Salang *see* Phuket
Újvidék *see* Novi Sad
UK *see* United Kingdom
154 E11 **Ukāi Reservoir** ⊠ W India
81 G19 **Ukara Island** *island* N Tanzania
'Ukash, Wādī *see* 'Akāsh, Wādī
81 F19 **Ukerewe Island** *island* N Tanzania
139 S9 **Ukhayḍir** Al Anbār, C Iraq *32°28′N 43°36′E*
153 X13 **Ukhrul** Manipur, NE India *25°08′N 94°24′E*
125 S9 **Ukhta** Respublika Komi, NW Russian Federation *63°31′N 53°48′E*
34 L6 **Ukiah** California, W USA *39°07′N 123°14′W*
32 K12 **Ukiah** Oregon, NW USA *45°06′N 118°57′W*
99 G18 **Ukkel** *Fr.* Uccle. Brussels, C Belgium *50°47′N 04°19′E*
118 G13 **Ukmergė** *Pol.* Wiłkomierz. Vilnius, C Lithuania *55°16′N 24°46′E*
Ukraina *see* Ukraine
116 L6 **Ukraine** *off.* Ukraine, *Rus.* Ukraina, *Ukr.* Ukrayina; *prev.* Ukrainian Soviet Socialist Republic, Ukrainskay S.S.R. ◆ *republic* SE Europe
Ukraine *see* Ukraine
Ukrainian Soviet Socialist Republic *see* Ukraine
Ukrainskay S.S.R/ Ukrayina *see* Ukraine
82 B13 **Uku** Cuanza Sul, NW Angola *11°25′S 14°18′E*
164 B13 **Uku-jima** *island* Gotō-rettō, SW Japan
83 F20 **Ukwi** Kgalagadi, SW Botswana *23°41′S 20°26′E*
118 M13 **Ula** *Rus.* Ulla. Vitsyebskaya Voblasts', N Belarus *55°14′N 29°15′E*
136 C16 **Ula** Muğla, SW Turkey *37°08′N 28°25′E*
118 M13 **Ula** *Rus.* Ulla. ≈ N Belarus
162 L7 **Ulaanbaatar** *Eng.* Ulan Bator; *prev.* Urga. ● (Mongolia) Töv, C Mongolia *47°55′N 106°57′E*
Ulaan-Ereg *see* Bayanmönh
162 E5 **Ulaangom** Uvs, NW Mongolia *49°56′N 92°06′E*
162 D5 **Ulaanhus** *var.* Bilüü. Bayan-Ölgiy, W Mongolia *48°54′N 89°40′E*
Ulaantolgoy *see* Möst
Ulaan-Uul *see* Öldziyt, Bayanhongor, Mongolia
Ulaan-Uul *see* Erdene, Dornogovĭ, Mongolia
162 M14 **Ulan** *var.* Otog Qi. Nei Mongol Zizhiqu, N China *39°05′N 107°58′E*
159 R10 **Ulan** *var.* Xireg; *prev.* Xiligou. Qinghai, C China *36°59′N 98°21′E*
Ulan Bator *see* Ulaanbaatar
162 L13 **Ulan Buh Shamo** *desert* N China
Ulanhad *see* Chifeng
163 T8 **Ulanhot** Nei Mongol Zizhiqu, N China *46°02′N 122°E*
127 Q14 **Ulan Khol** Respublika Kalmykiya, SW Russian Federation *45°27′N 46°48′E*
163 P13 **Ulan Qab** *var.* Jining. Nei Mongol Zizhiqu, N China *40°59′N 113°08′E*
162 M13 **Ulansuhai Nur** ◎ N China
123 N14 **Ulan-Ude** *prev.* Verkhneudinsk. Respublika Buryatiya, S Russian Federation *51°55′N 107°40′E*
159 N12 **Ulan Ul Hu** ◎ C China
187 N9 **Ulawa Island** *island* SE Solomon Islands
138 J7 **'Ulayyānīyah, Bi'r al** *var.* Al Hilbeh. *well* S Syria
123 S12 **Ul'banskiy Zaliv** *strait* E Russian Federation
Ulbo *see* Olib
113 J18 **Ulcinj** S Montenegro *41°56′N 19°14′E*
Uldz *see* Norovlin
Uleåborg *see* Oulu
Uleälv *see* Oulujoki
95 G16 **Ulefoss** Telemark, S Norway *59°17′N 09°15′E*
Uleträsk *see* Oulujärvi
113 L19 **Ulëz** *var.* Ulëza. Dibër, C Albania *41°42′N 19°52′E*
Ulëza *see* Ulëz
95 F22 **Ulfborg** Midtjylland, W Denmark *56°16′N 08°21′E*
98 N13 **Ulft** Gelderland, E Netherlands *51°53′N 06°23′E*
162 G7 **Uliastay** *prev.* Jibhalanta. Dzavhan, W Mongolia *47°47′N 96°53′E*
188 F8 **Ulimang** Babeldaob, N Palau
67 T10 **Ulindi** ≈ W Dem. Rep. Congo
188 H14 **Ulithi Atoll** *atoll* Caroline Islands, W Micronesia
112 N10 **Uljma** Vojvodina, NE Serbia *45°04′N 21°08′E*
Ul'kayak *see* Ol'keyyek
145 Q7 **Ul'ken-Karaoy, Ozero** *prev.* Ul'ken-Karoy, Ozero. ◎ N Kazakhstan
Ul'ken-Karoy, Ozero *see* Ul'ken-Karaoy, Ozero
Ülkenözen *see* Karaozen
Ülkenqobda *see* Kobda
104 G3 **Ulla** ≈ NW Spain
Ulla *see* Ula
183 S10 **Ulladulla** New South Wales, SE Australia *35°21′S 150°25′E*
153 T14 **Ullapara** Rajshahi, W Bangladesh *24°20′N 89°34′E*
96 H7 **Ullapool** N Scotland, United Kingdom *57°54′N 05°10′W*
95 J20 **Ullared** Halland, S Sweden *57°07′N 12°45′E*
105 T7 **Ulldecona** Cataluña, NE Spain *40°36′N 00°27′E*
92 I9 **Ullsfjorden** *fjord* N Norway
97 K15 **Ullswater** ◎ NW England, United Kingdom
101 I22 **Ulm** Baden-Württemberg, S Germany *48°24′N 09°59′E*
33 R8 **Ulm** Montana, NW USA *47°27′N 111°32′W*
183 V5 **Ulmarra** New South Wales, SE Australia *29°37′S 153°06′E*
116 K13 **Ulmeni** Buzău, C Romania *45°08′N 26°43′E*
116 K14 **Ulmeni** Călărași, S Romania *44°08′N 26°43′E*
42 L7 **Ulmukhuás** Región Autónoma Atlántico Norte, NE Nicaragua *14°20′N 84°30′W*
188 C8 **Ulong** *var.* Aulong. *island* Palau Islands, N Palau
83 N14 **Ulonguè** *var.* Ulongwé. Tete, NW Mozambique *14°34′S 34°21′E*
Ulongwé *see* Ulonguè
95 K19 **Ulricehamn** Västra Götaland, S Sweden *57°47′N 13°25′E*
98 N5 **Ulrum** Groningen, NE Netherlands *53°24′N 06°20′E*
163 Z16 **Ulsan** *Jap.* Urusan. SE South Korea *35°33′N 129°19′E*
94 D10 **Ulsteinvik** Møre og Romsdal, S Norway *62°21′N 05°53′E*
97 D15 **Ulster** ◐ *province* Northern Ireland, United Kingdom/Ireland
171 Q10 **Ulu** Pulau Siau, N Indonesia *02°46′N 125°22′E*
123 Q11 **Ulu** Respublika Sakha (Yakutiya), NE Russian Federation *60°18′N 127°27′E*
42 H5 **Ulúa, Río** ≈ NW Honduras
136 D12 **Ulubat Gölü** ◎ NW Turkey
136 E12 **Uludağ** ▲ NW Turkey *40°08′N 29°13′E*
158 D7 **Ulugqat** Xinjiang Uygur Zizhiqu, W China *39°45′N 74°10′E*
136 J16 **Ulukışla** Niğde, S Turkey *37°33′N 34°29′E*
189 O15 **Ulul** *island* Caroline Islands, C Micronesia
83 L22 **Ulundi** KwaZulu/Natal, E South Africa *28°18′S 31°26′E*
158 M3 **Ulungur He** ≈ NW China
158 K2 **Ulungur Hu** ◎ NW China
181 P8 **Uluru** *var.* Ayers Rock. *monolith* Northern Territory, C Australia
97 K16 **Ulverston** NW England, United Kingdom *54°13′N 03°08′W*
183 O16 **Ulverstone** Tasmania, SE Australia *41°09′S 146°10′E*
94 D13 **Ulvik** Hordaland, S Norway *60°34′N 06°53′E*
93 J18 **Ulvila** Länsi-Suomi, W Finland *61°26′N 21°55′E*
117 O8 **Ul'yanovka** Kirovohrads'ka Oblast', C Ukraine *48°18′N 30°15′E*
127 Q5 **Ul'yanovsk** *prev.* Simbirsk. Ul'yanovskaya Oblast', W Russian Federation *54°17′N 48°21′E*
127 Q5 **Ul'yanovskaya Oblast'** ◐ *province* W Russian Federation
Ul'yanovskiy *see* Botakara
Ul'yanovskiy Kanal *see* Ul'yanow Kanali
146 M13 **Ul'yanow Kanali** *Rus.* Ul'yanovskiy Kanal. *canal* Turkmenistan/Uzbekistan
Ulyshylanshyq *see* Uly-Zhylanshyk
26 H6 **Ulysses** Kansas, C USA *37°36′N 101°23′W*
145 O12 **Ulytau, Gory** ▲▲ C Kazakhstan
145 N11 **Uly-Zhylanshyk** *Kaz.* Ulyshylanshyq. ≈ C Kazakhstan
112 A9 **Umag** *It.* Umago. Istra, NW Croatia *45°25′N 13°32′E*
Umago *see* Umag
41 W12 **Umán** Yucatán, SE Mexico *20°51′N 89°43′W*
117 O7 **Uman'** *Rus.* Uman. Cherkas'ka Oblast', C Ukraine *48°45′N 30°10′E*
189 V13 **Uman** *atoll* Chuuk Islands, C Micronesia
Uman *see* Uman'
Umanak/Umanaq *see* Uummannaq
'Umān, Khalīj *see* Oman, Gulf of
'Umān, Salṭanat *see* Oman
154 K10 **Umaria** Madhya Pradesh, C India *23°34′N 80°49′E*
149 R16 **Umarkot** Sind, SE Pakistan *25°22′N 69°48′E*
188 B17 **Umatac** SW Guam *13°17′N 144°40′E*
188 A17 **Umatac Bay** *bay* SW Guam
139 S6 **Umayqah** Ṣalāḥ ad Dīn, C Iraq *34°32′N 43°45′E*
124 J5 **Umba** Murmanskaya Oblast', NW Russian Federation *66°39′N 34°24′E*
138 I8 **Umbāshī, Khirbat al** *ruins* As Suwaydā', S Syria
80 A12 **Umbelasha** ≈ W South Sudan
106 H12 **Umbertide** Umbria, C Italy *43°16′N 12°21′E*
61 B17 **Umberto** *var.* Humberto. Santa Fe, C Argentina *30°52′S 61°19′W*
186 E7 **Umboi Island** *var.* Rooke Island. *island* C Papua New Guinea
124 J4 **Umbozero, Ozero** ◎ NW Russian Federation
106 H13 **Umbria** ◐ *region* C Italy
Umbrian-Machigian Mountains *see* Umbro-Marchigiano, Appennino
106 I12 **Umbro-Marchigiano, Appennino** *Eng.* Umbrian-Machigian Mountains. ▲▲ C Italy
93 J16 **Umeå** Västerbotten, N Sweden *63°50′N 20°15′E*
93 H14 **Umeälven** ≈ N Sweden
39 Q5 **Umiat** Alaska, USA *69°22′N 152°09′W*
83 K23 **Umlazi** KwaZulu/Natal, E South Africa *29°58′S 30°50′E*
139 X10 **Umm al Baqar, Hawr** *var.* Birkat ad Dawaymah. *spring* S Iraq
139 Q5 **Umm al Faṭūr** *var.* Umm al Tūz. Ṣalāḥ ad Dīn, C Iraq *34°53′N 42°42′E*
141 U12 **Umm al Ḥayt, Wādī** *var.* Wādī Amilḥayt. *seasonal river* SW Oman
Umm al Qaiwain *see* Umm al Qaywayn
143 R15 **Umm al Qaywayn** *var.* Umm al Qaiwain. Umm al Qaywayn, NE United Arab Emirates *25°43′N 55°55′E*
Umm al Tūz *see* Umm al Faṭūr
138 J3 **Umm 'Āmūd** Ḥalab, N Syria *35°57′N 37°39′E*
141 Y10 **Umm ar Ruṣāṣ** *var.* Umm Ruṣayṣ. W Oman *20°26′N 58°48′E*
141 X9 **Umm as Samīn** *salt flat* C Oman
141 V9 **Umm az Zumūl** *oasis* E Saudi Arabia
80 A9 **Umm Buru** Western Darfur, W Sudan *15°01′N 23°36′E*
80 A12 **Umm Dafag** Southern Darfur, W Sudan *10°28′N 23°20′E*
Umm Durmān *see* Omdurman
138 F9 **Umm el Fahm** Haifa, N Israel *32°30′N 35°06′E*
80 F9 **Umm Inderab** Northern Kordofan, C Sudan *15°12′N 31°54′E*
80 C10 **Umm Keddada** Northern Darfur, W Sudan *13°36′N 26°42′E*
140 J7 **Umm Lajj** Tabūk, W Saudi Arabia *25°02′N 37°19′E*
138 L10 **Umm Maḥfur** ≈ N Jordan
139 Y13 **Umm Qaṣr** Al Baṣrah, SE Iraq *30°02′N 47°55′E*
Umm Ruṣayṣ *see* Umm ar Ruṣāṣ
80 F11 **Umm Ruwaba** *var.* Umm Ruwābah, Um Ruwāba. Northern Kordofan, C Sudan *12°54′N 31°13′E*
Umm Ruwābah *see* Umm Ruwaba
143 N16 **Umm Sa'īd** *var.* Musay'īd. S Qatar *24°57′N 51°32′E*
139 Y10 **Umm Sawān, Hawr** ◎ S Iraq
138 K10 **Umm Ṭuways, Wādī** *dry watercourse* N Jordan
38 J17 **Umnak Island** *island* Aleutian Islands, Alaska, USA
32 F13 **Umpqua River** ≈ Oregon, NW USA
82 D13 **Umpulo** Bié, C Angola *12°43′S 17°42′E*
154 I12 **Umred** Mahārāshtra, C India *20°54′N 79°19′E*
Um Ruwāba *see* Umm Ruwaba
Umtali *see* Mutare
Umtata *see* Mthatha
77 V17 **Umuahia** Abia, SW Nigeria *05°30′N 07°33′E*
60 H10 **Umuarama** Paraná, S Brazil *23°45′S 53°20′W*
Umvuma *see* Mvuma
83 K18 **Umzingwani** ≈ S Zimbabwe
112 D11 **Una** ≈ Bosnia and Herzegovina/Croatia
112 E12 **Unac** ≈ W Bosnia and Herzegovina
23 T6 **Unadilla** Georgia, SE USA *32°15′N 83°44′W*
18 I10 **Unadilla River** ≈ New York, NE USA
59 L18 **Unaí** Minas Gerais, SE Brazil *16°24′S 46°49′W*
39 N10 **Unalakleet** Alaska, USA *63°52′N 160°47′W*
38 K17 **Unalaska Island** *island* Aleutian Islands, Alaska, USA
185 I16 **Una, Mount** ▲ South Island, New Zealand *42°12′S 172°34′E*
82 N13 **Unango** Niassa, N Mozambique *12°45′S 35°28′E*
Unao *see* Unnāo
92 L12 **Unari** Lappi, N Finland *67°07′N 25°37′E*
141 O6 **'Unayzah** *var.* Anaiza. Al Qaṣīm, C Saudi Arabia *26°03′N 44°00′E*
138 L10 **'Unayzah, Jabal** ▲ Jordan/Saudi Arabia *32°09′N 39°11′E*
Unci *see* Almería
57 K19 **Uncía** Potosí, C Bolivia *18°30′S 66°29′W*
37 Q7 **Uncompahgre Peak** ▲ Colorado, C USA *38°04′N 107°27′W*
37 P6 **Uncompahgre Plateau** *plain* Colorado, C USA
95 L17 **Unden** ◎ S Sweden
28 M4 **Underwood** North Dakota, N USA *47°25′N 101°09′W*
171 T13 **Undur** Pulau Seram, E Indonesia *03°41′S 130°38′E*
Undur Khan *see* Öndörhaan
126 H6 **Unecha** Bryanskaya Oblast', W Russian Federation *52°51′N 32°38′E*
39 N16 **Unga** Unga Island, Alaska, USA *55°14′N 160°34′W*
Ungaria *see* Hungary
183 P8 **Ungarie** New South Wales, SE Australia *33°39′S 146°54′E*
Ungarisch-Brod *see* Uherský Brod
Ungarisches Erzgebirge *see* Slovenské rudohorie
Ungarisch-Hradisch *see* Uherské Hradiště
Ungarn *see* Hungary
12 M4 **Ungava Bay** *bay* Québec, E Canada
12 J2 **Ungava, Péninsule d'** *peninsula* Québec, SE Canada
Ungeny *see* Ungheni
116 M9 **Ungheni** *Rus.* Ungeny. W Moldova *47°13′N 27°48′E*
Unguja *see* Zanzibar
146 G10 **Üngüz Angyrsyndaky Garagum** *Rus.* Zaunguzskiye Garagumy. *desert* N Turkmenistan
146 H11 **Unguz, Solonchakovyye Vpadiny** *salt marsh* C Turkmenistan
Ungvár *see* Uzhhorod
60 I12 **União da Vitória** Paraná, S Brazil *26°13′S 51°05′W*
111 G17 **Uničov** *Ger.* Mährisch-Neustadt. Olomoucký Kraj, E Czech Republic *49°48′N 17°05′E*
110 J12 **Uniejów** Łódzkie, C Poland *51°58′N 18°46′E*
112 A11 **Unije** *island* W Croatia
38 L16 **Unimak Island** *island* Aleutian Islands, Alaska, USA
38 L16 **Unimak Pass** *strait* Aleutian Islands, Alaska, USA
62 J12 **Unión** San Luis, C Argentina *35°09′S 65°55′W*
27 W5 **Union** Missouri, C USA *38°27′N 91°01′W*
32 L12 **Union** Oregon, NW USA *45°12′N 117°51′W*
21 Q11 **Union** South Carolina, SE USA *34°42′N 81°37′W*
21 R6 **Union** West Virginia, NE USA *37°36′N 80°34′W*
61 B25 **Unión, Bahía** *bay* E Argentina
31 Q13 **Union City** Indiana, N USA *40°12′N 84°50′W*
31 Q10 **Union City** Michigan, N USA *42°03′N 85°06′W*
18 C12 **Union City** Pennsylvania, NE USA *41°54′N 79°51′W*
20 G8 **Union City** Tennessee, S USA *36°26′N 89°03′W*
32 G14 **Union Creek** Oregon, NW USA *42°54′N 122°26′W*
83 G25 **Uniondale** Western Cape, SW South Africa *33°40′S 23°07′E*
40 K13 **Unión de Tula** Jalisco, SW Mexico *19°58′N 104°16′W*
30 M9 **Union Grove** Wisconsin, N USA *42°39′N 88°03′W*
45 Y15 **Union Island** *island* S Saint Vincent and the Grenadines
Union of Myanmar *see* Burma
46 K5 **Union Reefs** *reef* SW Mexico
0 D7 **Union Seamount** *undersea feature* NE Pacific Ocean *49°35′N 132°45′W*
23 Q6 **Union Springs** Alabama, S USA *32°08′N 85°43′W*
20 H6 **Uniontown** Kentucky, S USA *37°46′N 87°55′W*
18 C16 **Uniontown** Pennsylvania, NE USA *39°54′N 79°44′W*
27 T1 **Unionville** Missouri, C USA *40°28′N 93°00′W*
141 V8 **United Arab Emirates** *Ar.* Al Imārāt al 'Arabīyah al Muttaḥidah, *abbrev.* UAE; *prev.* Trucial States. ◆ *federation* SW Asia
United Arab Republic *see* Egypt
97 H14 **United Kingdom** *off.* United Kingdom of Great Britain and Northern Ireland, *abbrev.* UK. ◆ *monarchy* NW Europe
United Kingdom of Great Britain and Northern Ireland *see* United Kingdom
United Mexican States *see* Mexico
United Provinces *see* Uttar Pradesh
16 L10 **United States of America** *off.* United States of America, *var.* America, The States, *abbrev.* U.S., USA. ◆ *federal republic* North America
United States of America *see* United States of America
124 J10 **Unitsa** Respublika Kareliya, NW Russian Federation *62°31′N 34°31′E*
11 S15 **Unity** Saskatchewan, S Canada *52°27′N 109°10′W*
Unity State *see* Wahda
105 Q8 **Universales, Montes** ▲▲ C Spain
27 X4 **University City** Missouri, C USA *38°40′N 90°19′W*
187 Q13 **Unmet** Malekula, C Vanuatu *16°09′S 167°16′E*
101 F15 **Unna** Nordrhein-Westfalen, W Germany *51°32′N 07°41′E*
Unnan *see* Kisuki
152 L12 **Unnão** *prev.* Unao. Uttar Pradesh, N India *26°32′N 80°30′E*
187 R15 **Unpongkor** Erromango, S Vanuatu *18°48′S 169°01′E*
Unruhstadt *see* Kargowa
96 M1 **Unst** *island* NE Scotland, United Kingdom
101 K16 **Unstrut** ≈ C Germany
Unterdrauburg *see* Dravograd
Unterlimbach *see* Lendava
101 L23 **Unterschleissheim** Bayern, SE Germany *48°16′N 11°34′E*
101 H24 **Untersee** ◎ Germany/Switzerland
100 O10 **Unterueckersee** ◎ NE Germany
Unterwalden *former canton see* Nidwalden, Obwalden
55 N12 **Unturán, Sierra de** ▲▲ Brazil/Venezuela
159 N11 **Unuli Horog** Qinghai, W China *35°10′N 91°50′E*
136 M11 **Ünye** Ordu, W Turkey *41°08′N 37°14′E*
Unza *see* Unzha
125 O14 **Unzha** *var.* Unza. ≈ NW Russian Federation
79 E17 **Uolo, Río** *var.* Eyo (lower course), Mbini, Uele (upper course), Woleu; *prev.* Benito. ≈ Equatorial Guinea/Gabon
55 Q10 **Uonán** Bolívar, SE Venezuela *04°33′N 62°10′W*
161 T12 **Uotsuri-shima** *island* China/Japan/Taiwan
165 M11 **Uozu** Toyama, Honshū, SW Japan *36°50′N 137°25′E*
42 L12 **Upala** Alajuela, NW Costa Rica *10°52′N 85°W*
55 P7 **Upata** Bolívar, E Venezuela *08°02′N 62°25′W*
79 M23 **Upemba, Lac** ◎ SE Dem. Rep. Congo
145 R11 **Upenskoye** *prev.* Uspenskiy. Karaganda, C Kazakhstan *48°45′N 72°46′E*
197 O12 **Upernavik** *var.* Upernivik. Kitaa, C Greenland *73°06′N 55°42′W*
Upernivik *see* Upernavik
83 F22 **Upington** Northern Cape, W South Africa *28°28′S 21°14′E*
Uplands *see* Ottawa
192 I16 **'Upolu** *island* SE Samoa
38 G11 **'Upolu Point** *var.* Upolu Point. *headland* Hawai'i, USA, C Pacific Ocean *20°15′N 155°51′W*
Upper Austria *see* Oberösterreich
Upper Bann *see* Bann
14 M13 **Upper Canada Village** *tourist site* Ontario, SE Canada
18 I16 **Upper Darby** Pennsylvania, NE USA *39°57′N 75°15′W*
28 L2 **Upper Des Lacs Lake** ⊠ North Dakota, N USA
185 L14 **Upper Hutt** Wellington, North Island, New Zealand *41°06′S 175°06′E*
29 X11 **Upper Iowa River** ≈ Iowa, C USA
32 H15 **Upper Klamath Lake** ◎ Oregon, NW USA
34 M6 **Upper Lake** California, W USA *39°07′N 122°53′W*
35 Q1 **Upper Lake** ◎ California, W USA
10 K9 **Upper Liard** Yukon Territory, W Canada *60°01′N 128°59′W*
97 E16 **Upper Lough Erne** ◎ SW Northern Ireland, United Kingdom
80 F12 **Upper Nile** ◐ *state* NE South Sudan

◆ Country
● Country Capital
◇ Dependent Territory
○ Dependent Territory Capital
◐ Administrative Regions
✈ International Airport
▲ Mountain
▲▲ Mountain Range
⛰ Volcano
≈ River
◎ Lake
⊠ Reservoir

29 T3 **Upper Red Lake** ◎ Minnesota, N USA
31 S12 **Upper Sandusky** Ohio, N USA 40°49′N 83°16′W
Upper Volta *see* Burkina
95 O15 **Upplands Väsby** *var.* Upplandsväsby. Stockholm, C Sweden 59°29′N 18°04′E
Upplandsväsby *see* Upplands Väsby
95 O15 **Uppsala** Uppsala, C Sweden 59°52′N 17°38′E
95 O14 **Uppsala** ◈ *county* C Sweden
38 J12 **Upright Cape** *headland* Saint Matthew Island, Alaska, USA 60°19′N 172°15′W
20 K6 **Upton** Kentucky, S USA 37°25′N 85°53′W
33 Y13 **Upton** Wyoming, C USA 44°06′N 104°37′W
141 N7 **'Uqlat aş Şuqūr** Al Qaşīm, W Saudi Arabia 25°51′N 42°13′E
Uqsuqtuuq *see* Gjoa Haven
Uqturpan *see* Wushi
54 C7 **Urabá, Golfo de** *gulf* NW Colombia
Uracas *see* Farallon de Pajaros
uradqianqi *see* Wulashan, N China
Uradar'ya *see* O'radaryo
Urad Qianqi *see* Xishanzui, N China
165 U5 **Urahoro** Hokkaidō, NE Japan 42°47′N 143°41′E
165 T5 **Urakawa** Hokkaidō, NE Japan 42°11′N 142°42′E
Ural *see* Zhayyk
183 T6 **Uralla** New South Wales, SE Australia 30°39′S 151°30′E
Ural Mountains *see* Ural'skiye Gory
144 F8 **Ural'sk** *Kaz.* Oral. Zapadnyy Kazakhstan, NW Kazakhstan 51°12′N 51°17′E
Ural'skaya Oblast' *see* Zapadnyy Kazakhstan
127 W5 **Ural'skiye Gory** *var.* Ural'skiy Khrebet, *Eng.* Ural Mountains. ⛰ Kazakhstan/Russian Federation
Ural'skiy Khrebet *see* Ural'skiye Gory
138 I3 **Urām aş Şughrá** Ḩalab, N Syria 36°10′N 36°55′E
183 P10 **Urana** New South Wales, SE Australia 35°22′S 146°16′E
11 S10 **Uranium City** Saskatchewan, C Canada 59°30′N 108°46′W
58 F10 **Uraricoera** Roraima, N Brazil 03°26′N 60°54′W
47 S5 **Uraricoera, Rio** ≈ N Brazil
Ura-Tyube *see* Üroteppa
165 O13 **Urawa** *var.* Saitama. Saitama, Honshū, S Japan 35°52′N 139°40′E
122 H10 **Uray** Khanty-Mansiyskiy Avtonomnyy Okrug-Yugra, C Russian Federation 60°07′N 64°38′E
141 R7 **'Uray'irah** Ash Sharqīyah, E Saudi Arabia 25°59′N 48°52′E
30 M13 **Urbana** Illinois, N USA 40°06′N 88°12′W
31 R13 **Urbana** Ohio, N USA 40°04′N 83°46′W
29 V14 **Urbandale** Iowa, C USA 41°37′N 93°42′W
106 I11 **Urbania** Marche, C Italy 43°40′N 12°33′E
106 I11 **Urbino** Marche, C Italy 43°45′N 12°38′E
57 H16 **Urcos** Cusco, S Peru 13°40′S 71°38′W
105 N10 **Urda** Castilla-La Mancha, C Spain 39°25′N 03°43′W
Urda *see* Khan Ordasy
Urdgol *see* Chandmanĭ
105 O3 **Urduña** *var.* Orduña. País Vasco, N Spain 43°00′N 03°00′W
Urdunn *see* Jordan
Urdzhar *see* Urzhar
97 L16 **Ure** ≈ N England, United Kingdom
119 K18 **Urechcha** *Rus.* Urech'ye. Minskaya Voblasts', S Belarus 52°57′N 27°54′E
Urech'ye *see* Urechcha
127 P2 **Uren'** Nizhegorodskaya Oblast', W Russian Federation 57°30′N 45°48′E
122 J9 **Urengoy** Yamalo-Nenetskiy Avtonomnyy Okrug, N Russian Federation 65°52′N 78°42′E
184 K10 **Urenui** Taranaki, North Island, New Zealand 38°59′S 174°25′E
187 Q12 **Ureparapara** *island* Banks Islands, N Vanuatu
40 G5 **Ures** Sonora, NW Mexico 29°26′N 110°24′W
Urfa *see* Şanlıurfa
Urga *see* Ulaanbaatar
162 F6 **Urgamal** *var.* Hungiy. Dzavhan, W Mongolia 48°31′N 94°15′E
146 H9 **Urganch** *Rus.* Urgench; *prev.* Novo-Urgench. Xorazm Viloyati, W Uzbekistan 41°40′N 60°32′E
Urgench *see* Urganch
136 J14 **Ürgüp** Nevşehir, C Turkey 38°39′N 34°55′E
147 O12 **Urgut** Samarqand Viloyati, C Uzbekistan 39°26′N 67°15′E
158 K3 **Urho** Xinjiang Uygur Zizhiqu, W China 46°05′N 84°51′E
152 G5 **Uri** Jammu and Kashmir, NW India 34°05′N 74°03′E
108 G9 **Uri** ◈ *canton* C Switzerland
54 F11 **Uribe** Meta, C Colombia 03°01′N 74°33′W
54 H4 **Uribia** La Guajira, N Colombia 11°45′N 72°19′W
116 G12 **Uricani** *Hung.* Hobicaurikány. Hunedoara, SW Romania 45°18′N 23°03′E
57 M21 **Uriondo** Tarija, S Bolivia 21°43′S 64°40′W
40 I7 **Urique** Chihuahua, N Mexico 27°16′N 107°51′W
40 I7 **Urique, Río** ≈ N Mexico
56 E9 **Urituyacu, Río** ≈ N Peru
Uritskiy *see* Sarykol'
98 K8 **Urk** Flevoland, N Netherlands 52°40′N 05°35′E
136 B14 **Urla** İzmir, W Turkey 38°19′N 26°47′E
116 K13 **Urlaţi** Prahova, SE Romania 44°59′N 26°15′E
127 V4 **Urman** Respublika Bashkortostan, W Russian Federation 54°53′N 56°52′E
147 P12 **Urmetan** W Tajikistan 39°27′N 68°13′E
Urmia *see* Orūmīyeh
Urmia, Lake *see* Orūmīyeh, Daryācheh-ye
Urmiyeh *see* Orūmīyeh
Uroševac *see* Ferizaj
147 P11 **Üroteppa** *Rus.* Ura-Tyube. NW Tajikistan 39°55′N 68°57′E
54 D8 **Urrao** Antioquia, W Colombia 06°16′N 76°10′W
Ursat'yevskaya *see* Xovos
Urt *see* Gurvantes
127 X7 **Urtazym** Orenburgskaya Oblast', W Russian Federation 52°12′N 58°48′E
59 K18 **Uruaçu** Goiás, C Brazil 14°38′S 49°06′W
40 M14 **Uruapan** *var.* Uruapan del Progreso. Michoacán, SW Mexico 19°26′N 102°04′W
Uruapan del Progreso *see* Uruapan
57 G15 **Urubamba, Cordillera** ⛰ C Peru
57 G14 **Urubamba, Río** ≈ C Peru
58 G12 **Urucará** Amazonas, N Brazil 02°30′S 57°45′W
61 E16 **Uruguaiana** Rio Grande do Sul, S Brazil 29°45′S 57°05′W
Uruguai, Rio *see* Uruguay
61 E18 **Uruguay** *off.* Oriental Republic of Uruguay; *prev.* La Banda Oriental. ◆ *republic* E South America
61 E15 **Uruguay** *var.* Rio Uruguai, Río Uruguay. ≈ E South America
Uruguay, Oriental Republic of *see* Uruguay
Uruguay, Río *see* Uruguay
Urukthapel *see* Ngeruktabel
Urumchi *see* Ürümqi
Urumi Yeh *see* Orūmīyeh, Daryācheh-ye
158 L5 **Ürümqi** *var.* Tihwa, Urumchi, Urumqi, Urumtsi, Wu-lu-k'o-mu-shi, Wu-lu-mu-ch'i; *prev.* Ti-hua. Xinjiang Uygur Zizhiqu, NW China 43°52′N 87°31′E
Urumtsi *see* Ürümqi
Urundi *see* Burundi
183 V6 **Urunga** New South Wales, SE Australia 30°33′S 152°58′E
188 C15 **Uruno Point** *headland* NW Guam 13°37′N 144°50′E
123 U13 **Urup, Ostrov** *island* Kuril'skiye Ostrova, SE Russian Federation
141 P11 **'Uruq al Mawārid** *desert* S Saudi Arabia
Urusan *see* Ulsan
127 T5 **Urussu** Respublika Tatarstan, W Russian Federation 54°34′N 53°23′E
184 K10 **Uruti** Taranaki, North Island, New Zealand 38°57′S 174°32′E
57 K19 **Uru Uru, Lago** ◎ W Bolivia
55 P9 **Uruyén** Bolívar, SE Venezuela 05°40′N 62°26′W
149 O7 **Uruzgān** ; *prev.* Orūzgān. Uruzgān, C Afghanistan 32°58′N 66°39′E
149 N6 **Uruzgān** *prev.* Orūzgān. ◈ *province* C Afghanistan
165 T3 **Uryū-gawa** ≈ Hokkaidō, NE Japan
165 T2 **Uryū-ko** ◎ Hokkaidō, NE Japan
127 N8 **Uryupinsk** Volgogradskaya Oblast', SW Russian Federation 50°51′N 41°59′E
145 X12 **Urzhar** *prev.* Urdzhar. Vostochnyy Kazakhstan, E Kazakhstan 47°06′N 81°33′E
125 R16 **Urzhum** Kirovskaya Oblast', NW Russian Federation 57°09′N 49°56′E
116 K13 **Urziceni** Ialomiţa, SE Romania 44°43′N 26°39′E
164 E14 **Usa** Ōita, Kyūshū, SW Japan 33°31′N 131°22′E
125 T6 **Usa** ≈ NW Russian Federation
136 E14 **Uşak** *prev.* Ushak. Uşak, W Turkey 38°42′N 29°25′E
136 D14 **Uşak** *var.* Ushak. ◈ *province* W Turkey
83 C19 **Usakos** Erongo, W Namibia 22°01′S 15°32′E
81 J21 **Usambara Mountains** ⛰ NE Tanzania
81 G23 **Usangu Flats** *wetland* SW Tanzania
65 D24 **Usborne, Mount** ▲ East Falkland, Falkland Islands 51°35′S 58°57′W
100 O8 **Usedom** *island* NE Germany
99 M24 **Useldange** Diekirch, C Luxembourg 49°47′N 05°59′E
119 L16 **Usha** ≈ C Belarus
Ushachi *see* Ushachy
118 L13 **Ushachy** *Rus.* Ushachi. Vitsyebskaya Voblasts', N Belarus 55°11′N 28°37′E
Ushak *see* Uşak
122 L4 **Ushakova, Ostrov** *island* Severnaya Zemlya, N Russian Federation
Ushant *see* Ouessant, Île d'
145 W13 **Usharal** *prev.* Ucharal. Almaty, E Kazakhstan 46°08′N 80°55′E
164 B15 **Ushibuka** *var.* Usibuka. Kumamoto, Shimo-jima, SW Japan 32°12′N 130°00′E
Ushi Point *see* Sabaneta, Puntan
145 V14 **Ushtobe** *Kaz.* Üshtöbe. Almaty, SE Kazakhstan 45°15′N 77°59′E
Üshtöbe *see* Ushtobe
63 I25 **Ushuaia** Tierra del Fuego, S Argentina 54°48′S 68°19′W
39 R10 **Usibelli** Alaska, USA 63°54′N 148°41′W
Usibuka *see* Ushibuka
186 D7 **Usino** Madang, N Papua New Guinea 05°40′S 145°31′E
125 U6 **Usinsk** Respublika Komi, NW Russian Federation 66°01′N 57°37′E
97 K22 **Usk** *Wel.* Wysg. ≈ SE Wales, United Kingdom
Uskočke Planine/Uskokengebirge *see* Gorjanci
Uskoplje *see* Gornji Vakuf
Üsküb/Üsküp *see* Skopje
114 M11 **Üsküpdere** Kırklareli, NW Turkey 41°41′N 27°21′E
126 L7 **Usman'** Lipetskaya Oblast', W Russian Federation 52°04′N 39°41′E
118 D8 **Usmas Ezers** ◎ NW Latvia
125 U13 **Usol'ye** Permskiy Kray, NW Russian Federation 59°27′N 56°33′E
41 T16 **Uspanapa, Río** ≈ SE Mexico
Uspenskiy *see* Upenskoye
103 O11 **Ussel** Corrèze, C France 45°33′N 02°18′E
163 Z6 **Ussuri** *var.* Usuri, Wusuri, *Chin.* Wusuli Jiang. ≈ China/Russian Federation
123 S15 **Ussuriysk** *prev.* Nikol'sk, Nikol'sk-Ussuriyskiy, Voroshilov. Primorskiy Kray, SE Russian Federation 43°48′N 131°59′E
136 J10 **Usta Burnu** *headland* N Turkey 41°58′N 34°30′E
149 P13 **Usta Muhammad** Baluchistān, SW Pakistan 28°07′N 68°00′E
123 V11 **Ust'-Bol'sheretsk** Kamchatskiy Kray, E Russian Federation 52°48′N 156°12′E
127 N9 **Ust'-Buzulukskaya** Volgogradskaya Oblast', SW Russian Federation 50°12′N 42°06′E
111 C16 **Ustecký Kraj** ◈ *region* NW Czech Republic
108 G7 **Uster** Zürich, NE Switzerland 47°21′N 08°49′E
107 I22 **Ustica, Isola d'** *island* S Italy
122 M11 **Ust'-Ilimsk** Irkutskaya Oblast', C Russian Federation 57°57′N 102°30′E
111 C15 **Ústí nad Labem** *Ger.* Aussig. Ústecký Kraj, NW Czech Republic 50°41′N 14°04′E
111 F17 **Ústí nad Orlicí** *Ger.* Wildenschwert. Pardubický Kraj, C Czech Republic 49°58′N 16°24′E
Ustinov *see* Izhevsk
113 J14 **Ustiprača** ◈ Republika Srpska, SE Bosnia and Herzegovina
122 H11 **Ust'-Ishim** Omskaya Oblast', C Russian Federation 57°42′N 70°58′E
110 G6 **Ustka** *Ger.* Stolpmünde. Pomorskie, N Poland 54°35′N 16°50′E
123 V9 **Ust'-Kamchatsk** Kamchatskiy Kray, E Russian Federation 56°14′N 162°28′E
145 X9 **Ust'-Kamenogorsk** *Kaz.* Öskemen. Vostochnyy Kazakhstan, E Kazakhstan 49°58′N 82°36′E
123 T10 **Ust'-Khayryuzovo** Krasnoyarskiy Kray, E Russian Federation 57°07′N 156°37′E
122 I14 **Ust'-Koksa** Respublika Altay, S Russian Federation 50°15′N 85°45′E
125 S11 **Ust'-Kulom** Respublika Komi, NW Russian Federation 61°42′N 53°42′E
123 Q8 **Ust'-Kuyga** Respublika Sakha (Yakutiya), NE Russian Federation 69°59′N 135°27′E
126 L14 **Ust'-Labinsk** Krasnodarskiy Kray, SW Russian Federation 44°40′N 40°46′E
123 R10 **Ust'-Maya** Respublika Sakha (Yakutiya), NE Russian Federation 60°27′N 134°28′E
123 R9 **Ust'-Nera** Respublika Sakha (Yakutiya), NE Russian Federation 64°28′N 143°01′E
123 P12 **Ust'-Nyukzha** Amurskaya Oblast', S Russian Federation 56°30′N 121°32′E
123 O7 **Ust'-Olenëk** Respublika Sakha (Yakutiya), NE Russian Federation 73°03′N 119°34′E
123 T9 **Ust'-Omchug** Magadanskaya Oblast', E Russian Federation 61°07′N 149°17′E
122 M13 **Ust'-Ordynskiy** Irkutskaya Oblast', S Russian Federation 52°50′N 104°42′E
125 N8 **Ust'-Pinega** Arkhangel'skaya Oblast', NW Russian Federation 64°09′N 41°55′E
122 K8 **Ust'-Port** Krasnoyarskiy Kray, N Russian Federation 69°42′N 84°25′E
114 L11 **Ustrem** *prev.* Vakav. Yambol, E Bulgaria 42°01′N 26°28′E
111 O18 **Ustrzyki Dolne** Podkarpackie, SE Poland 49°26′N 22°36′E
Ust'-Sysol'sk *see* Syktyvkar
125 R7 **Ust'-Tsil'ma** Respublika Komi, NW Russian Federation 65°25′N 52°09′E
Ust Urt *see* Ustyurt Plateau
125 O11 **Ust'ya** ≈ NW Russian Federation
124 K6 **Ust'ye Varzugi** Murmanskaya Oblast', NW Russian Federation 66°16′N 36°47′E
123 V10 **Ust'yevoye** *prev.* Kirovskiy. Kamchatskiy Kray, E Russian Federation 54°06′N 155°48′E
117 R8 **Ustynivka** Kirovohrads'ka Oblast', C Ukraine 47°58′N 32°32′E
144 H15 **Ustyurt Plateau** *var.* Ust Urt, *Uzb.* Ustyurt Platosi. *plateau* Kazakhstan/Uzbekistan
Ustyurt Platosi *see* Ustyurt Plateau
124 K14 **Ustyuzhna** Vologodskaya Oblast', NW Russian Federation 58°50′N 36°25′E
158 J4 **Usu** Xinjiang Uygur Zizhiqu, NW China 44°27′N 84°37′E
171 O13 **Usu** Sulawesi, C Indonesia 02°34′S 120°58′E
164 E14 **Usuki** Ōita, Kyūshū, SW Japan 33°07′N 131°48′E
42 G8 **Usulután** Usulután, SE El Salvador 13°20′N 88°26′W
42 B9 **Usulután** ◈ *department* SE El Salvador
41 W16 **Usumacinta, Río** ≈ Guatemala/Mexico
Usumbura *see* Bujumbura
Usuri *see* Ussuri
U.S./USA *see* United States of America
171 W14 **Uta** Papua, E Indonesia 04°28′S 136°03′E
36 K5 **Utah** *off.* State of Utah, *also known as* Beehive State, Mormon State. ◈ *state* W USA
36 L3 **Utah Lake** ◎ Utah, W USA
Utaidhani *see* Uthai Thani
93 M14 **Utajärvi** Oulu, C Finland 64°45′N 26°25′E
Utamboni *see* Mitemele, Río
Utaradit *see* Uttaradit
165 T3 **Utashinai** *var.* Utasinai. Hokkaidō, NE Japan 43°32′N 142°03′E
Utasinai *see* Utashinai
193 Y14 **'Uta Vava'u** *island* Vava'u Group, N Tonga
37 V9 **Ute Creek** ≈ New Mexico, SW USA
118 H12 **Utena** Utena, E Lithuania 55°30′N 25°34′E
118 H12 **Utena** ◈ *province* Lithuania
37 V10 **Ute Reservoir** ▣ New Mexico, SW USA
167 O10 **Uthai Thani** *var.* Muang Uthai Thani, Udayadhani, Utaidhani. Uthai Thani, W Thailand 15°22′N 100°03′E
149 O15 **Uthal** Baluchistān, SW Pakistan 25°53′N 66°37′E
uThongathi *see* oThongathi
18 I10 **Utica** New York, NE USA 43°06′N 75°15′W
105 R10 **Utiel** Valenciana, E Spain 39°33′N 01°13′W
11 O13 **Utikuma Lake** ◎ Alberta, W Canada
42 I4 **Utila, Isla de** *island* Islas de la Bahía, N Honduras
Utina *see* Udine
59 O17 **Utinga** Bahia, E Brazil 12°05′S 41°07′W
Utirik *see* Utrik Atoll
95 M22 **Utlängan** *island* S Sweden
117 U11 **Utlyuts'kyy Lyman** *bay* S Ukraine
95 P16 **Utö** Stockholm, C Sweden 58°55′N 18°19′E
25 Q12 **Utopia** Texas, SW USA 29°30′N 99°31′W
98 J11 **Utrecht** *Lat.* Trajectum ad Rhenum. Utrecht, C Netherlands 52°06′N 05°07′E
83 K22 **Utrecht** KwaZulu/Natal, E South Africa 27°40′S 30°20′E
98 I11 **Utrecht** ◈ *province* C Netherlands
104 K14 **Utrera** Andalucía, S Spain 37°10′N 05°47′W
189 V4 **Utrik Atoll** *var.* Utirik, Utrōk, Utrōnk. *atoll* Ratak Chain, N Marshall Islands
Utrōk/Utrōnk *see* Utrik Atoll
95 B16 **Utsira** *island* SW Norway
92 L8 **Utsjoki** *var.* Ohcejohka. Lappi, N Finland 69°54′N 27°01′E
165 O12 **Utsunomiya** *var.* Utunomiya. Tochigi, Honshū, S Japan 36°36′N 139°53′E
127 P13 **Utta** Respublika Kalmykiya, SW Russian Federation 46°22′N 46°03′E
167 O8 **Uttaradit** *var.* Utaradit. Uttaradit, N Thailand 17°38′N 100°05′E
152 J9 **Uttarakhand** ◈ *state* N India
152 J8 **Uttarkāshi** Uttarakhand, N India 30°45′N 78°19′E
152 K11 **Uttar Pradesh** *prev.* United Provinces, United Provinces of Agra and Oudh. ◈ *state* N India
45 T5 **Utuado** C Puerto Rico 18°17′N 66°41′W
158 K3 **Utubulak** Xinjiang Uygur Zizhiqu, W China 46°50′N 86°15′E
39 N5 **Utukok River** ≈ Alaska, USA
Utunomiya *see* Utsunomiya
187 P10 **Utupua** *island* Santa Cruz Islands, E Solomon Islands
Utva *see* Shyngyrlau
189 Y15 **Utwe** Kosrae, E Micronesia
189 X15 **Utwe Harbor** *harbour* Kosrae, E Micronesia
Uubulan *see* Hayrhan
163 O8 **Uulbayan** *var.* Dzüünbulag. Sühbaatar, E Mongolia 46°30′N 112°22′E
118 G6 **Uulu** Pärnumaa, SW Estonia 58°15′N 24°32′E
197 N13 **Uummannaq** *var.* Umanak, Umanaq. ◈ Kitaa, C Greenland
Uummannarsuaq *see* Nunap Isua
162 E4 **Üüreg Nuur** ◎ NW Mongolia
Uusikaarlepyy *see* Nykarleby
93 J19 **Uusikaupunki** *Swe.* Nystad. Länsi-Suomi, SW Finland 60°48′N 21°25′E
127 S2 **Uva** Udmurtskaya Respublika, NW Russian Federation 56°41′N 52°15′E
155 K25 **Uva** ◈ *province* SE Sri Lanka
113 L14 **Uvac** ≈ W Serbia
25 Q12 **Uvalde** Texas, SW USA 29°14′N 99°49′W
119 O18 **Uvaravichy** *Rus.* Uvarovichi. Homyel'skaya Voblasts', SE Belarus 52°36′N 30°44′E
54 J11 **Uvá, Río** ≈ E Colombia
Uvarovichi *see* Uvaravichy
127 N7 **Uvarovo** Tambovskaya Oblast', W Russian Federation 51°58′N 42°13′E
122 H10 **Uvat** Tyumenskaya Oblast', C Russian Federation 59°11′N 68°37′E
190 G12 **Uvea, Île** *island* N Wallis and Futuna
81 E21 **Uvinza** Kigoma, W Tanzania 05°08′S 30°23′E
79 O20 **Uvira** Sud-Kivu, E Dem. Rep. Congo 03°24′S 29°05′E
162 E5 **Uvs** ◈ *province* NW Mongolia
162 F5 **Uvs Nuur** *var.* Ozero Ubsu-Nur. ◎ Mongolia/Russian Federation
164 F14 **Uwa** *var.* Seiyo. Ehime, Shikoku, SW Japan 33°22′N 132°29′E
164 F14 **Uwajima** *var.* Uwazima. Ehime, Shikoku, SW Japan 33°13′N 132°32′E
80 B5 **'Uwaynāt, Jabal al** *var.* Jebel Uweinat. ▲ Libya/Sudan 21°51′N 25°01′E
Uwazima *see* Uwajima
Uweinat, Jebel *see* 'Uwaynāt, Jabal al
14 H14 **Uxbridge** Ontario, S Canada 44°07′N 79°07′W
Uxellodunum *see* Issoudun
Uxin Qi *see* Dabqig, N China
41 X12 **Uxmal, Ruinas** *ruins* Yucatán, SE Mexico
129 Q5 **Uy** ≈ Kazakhstan/Russian Federation
144 K15 **Uyaly** Kzylorda, S Kazakhstan 44°22′N 61°16′E
123 R8 **Uyandina** ≈ NE Russian Federation
162 J8 **Uyanga** *var.* Ongi. Övörhangay, C Mongolia 46°30′N 102°18′E
Üydzen *see* Manlay
Uyeda *see* Ueda
122 K5 **Uyedineniya, Ostrov** *island* N Russian Federation
77 V17 **Uyo** Akwa Ibom, S Nigeria 05°00′N 07°57′E
162 D8 **Üyönch** Hovd, W Mongolia 46°04′N 92°05′E
Uyuk *see* Oyyk
141 V13 **'Uyūn** SW Oman 17°19′N 53°50′E
57 K20 **Uyuni** Potosí, W Bolivia 20°27′S 66°48′W
57 J20 **Uyuni, Salar de** *wetland* SW Bolivia
146 I9 **Uzbekistan** *off.* Republic of Uzbekistan. ◆ *republic* C Asia
Uzbekistan, Republic of *see* Uzbekistan
158 D8 **Uzbel Shankou** *Rus.* Pereval Kyzyl-Dzhiik. *pass* China/Tajikistan
146 B11 **Uzboý** *prev. Rus.* Imeni 26 Bakinskikh Komissarov, *Turkm.* 26 Baku Komissarlary Adyndaky. Balkan Welaýaty, W Turkmenistan 39°24′N 54°04′E
119 J17 **Uzda** Minskaya Voblasts', C Belarus 53°29′N 27°10′E
103 N12 **Uzerche** Corrèze, C France 45°24′N 01°35′E
103 R14 **Uzès** Gard, S France 44°00′N 04°25′E
147 T10 **Uzgen** *Kir.* Özgön. Oshskaya Oblast', SW Kyrgyzstan 40°42′N 73°17′E
117 O3 **Uzh** ≈ N Ukraine
Uzhgorod *see* Uzhhorod
116 G7 **Uzhhorod** *Rus.* Uzhgorod; *prev.* Ungvár. Zakarpats'ka Oblast', W Ukraine 48°36′N 22°19′E
Uzi *see* Uji
112 K13 **Užice** *prev.* Titovo Užice. Serbia, W Serbia 43°52′N 19°51′E
Uzin *see* Uzyn
126 L5 **Uzlovaya** Tul'skaya Oblast', W Russian Federation 54°01′N 38°15′E
108 H7 **Uznach** Sankt Gallen, NE Switzerland 47°12′N 09°00′E
Uzunagach *see* Uzynagash
136 B10 **Uzunköprü** Edirne, NW Turkey 41°18′N 26°40′E
118 D11 **Užventis** Šiaulai, C Lithuania 55°49′N 22°38′E
117 P5 **Uzyn** *Rus.* Uzin. Kyyivs'ka Oblast', N Ukraine 49°52′N 30°27′E
145 U16 **Uzynagash** *prev.* Uzunagach. Almaty, SE Kazakhstan 43°08′N 76°20′E
145 N7 **Uzynkol'** *prev.* Lenīn, Leninskoye. Kustanay, N Kazakhstan 54°05′N 65°23′E

V

Vääksy *see* Asikkala
83 H23 **Vaal** ≈ C South Africa
93 M14 **Vaala** Oulu, C Finland 64°34′N 26°49′E
93 N19 **Vaalimaa** Etelä-Suomi, SE Finland 60°34′N 27°49′E
99 M19 **Vaals** Limburg, SE Netherlands 50°46′N 06°01′E
93 J16 **Vaasa** *Swe.* Vasa; *prev.* Nikolainkaupunki. Länsi-Suomi, W Finland 63°07′N 21°39′E
98 L10 **Vaassen** Gelderland, E Netherlands 52°18′N 05°59′E
118 G11 **Vabalninkas** Panevėžys, NE Lithuania 55°59′N 24°45′E
Vabkent *see* Vobkent
111 J22 **Vác** *Ger.* Waitzen. Pest, N Hungary 47°46′N 19°08′E
61 I14 **Vacaria** Rio Grande do Sul, S Brazil 28°31′S 50°52′W
35 N7 **Vacaville** California, W USA 38°21′N 121°59′W
103 R15 **Vaccarès, Étang de** ◎ SE France
44 L10 **Vache, Île à** *island* SW Haiti
173 Y16 **Vacoas** W Mauritius 20°18′S 57°29′E
32 G10 **Vader** Washington, NW USA 46°23′N 122°58′W
94 D12 **Vadheim** Sogn Og Fjordane, S Norway 61°12′N 05°48′E
154 D11 **Vadodara** *prev.* Baroda. Gujarāt, W India 22°19′N 73°14′E
92 M8 **Vadsø** *Fin.* Vesisaari. Finnmark, N Norway 70°07′N 29°47′E
95 L17 **Vadstena** Östergötland, S Sweden 58°26′N 14°55′E
108 I8 **Vaduz** ● (Liechtenstein) W Liechtenstein 47°08′N 09°32′E
Vág *see* Váh
125 N12 **Vaga** ≈ NW Russian Federation
94 G11 **Vågåmo** Oppland, S Norway 61°52′N 09°06′E
112 D12 **Vaganski Vrh** ▲ W Croatia 44°24′N 15°32′E
95 A19 **Vágar** *Dan.* Vågø. *island* W Faeroe Islands
Vágbeszterce *see* Považská Bystrica
95 L19 **Vaggeryd** Jönköping, S Sweden 57°30′N 14°10′E
137 T12 **Vagharshapat** *var.* Ejmiadzin, Ejmiatsin, Etchmiadzin, *Rus.* Echmiadzin. W Armenia 40°10′N 44°17′E
95 O16 **Vagnhärad** Södermanland, C Sweden 58°57′N 17°32′E
Vågø *see* Vágar
104 G7 **Vagos** Aveiro, N Portugal 40°33′N 08°42′W
Vágsellye *see* Sal'a
92 H10 **Vågsfjorden** *fjord* N Norway
94 C10 **Vågsøy** *island* S Norway
Vágújhely *see* Nové Mesto nad Váhom
111 I21 **Váh** *Ger.* Waag, *Hung.* Vág. ≈ W Slovakia
93 K16 **Vähäkyrö** Länsi-Suomi, W Finland 63°04′N 22°05′E
191 X11 **Vahitahi** *atoll* Îles Tuamotu, E French Polynesia
Váhtjer *see* Gällivare
Vaidei *see* Vulcan
22 L4 **Vaiden** Mississippi, S USA 33°19′N 89°42′W
155 I23 **Vaigai** ≈ SE India
191 V16 **Vaihu** Easter Island, Chile, E Pacific Ocean 27°10′S 109°22′W
118 I6 **Väike Emajõgi** ≈ S Estonia
118 I4 **Väike-Maarja** *Ger.* Klein-Marien. Lääne-Virumaa, NE Estonia 59°07′N 26°16′E
Väike-Salatsi *see* Mazsalaca
37 R4 **Vail** Colorado, C USA 39°36′N 106°20′W
193 V15 **Vaina** Tongatapu, S Tonga 21°12′S 175°10′W
118 E5 **Väinameri** *prev.* Muhu Väin, *Ger.* Moon-Sund. *sea* E Baltic Sea
93 N18 **Vainikkala** Etelä-Suomi, SE Finland 60°54′N 28°18′E
118 D10 **Vaiņode** SW Latvia 56°25′N 21°52′E
155 H23 **Vaippār** ≈ SE India
191 W11 **Vairaatea** *atoll* Îles Tuamotu, C French Polynesia
191 R8 **Vairao** Tahiti, W French Polynesia 17°48′S 149°17′W
103 R14 **Vaison-la-Romaine** Vaucluse, SE France 44°15′N 05°04′E
190 G11 **Vaitupu** Île Uvea, E Wallis and Futuna 13°14′S 176°09′W
190 F7 **Vaitupu** *atoll* C Tuvalu
Vajdahunyad *see* Hunedoara
Vajdej *see* Vulcan
78 K12 **Vakaga** ◈ *prefecture* NE Central African Republic
114 H10 **Vakarel** Sofiya, W Bulgaria 42°35′N 23°40′E
Vakav *see* Ustrem
137 O11 **Vakfıkebir** Trabzon, NE Turkey 41°03′N 39°19′E
122 J10 **Vakh** ≈ C Russian Federation
Vakhon, Qatorkŭhi *see* Nicholas Range
147 P14 **Vakhsh** SW Tajikistan 37°46′N 68°48′E
147 Q12 **Vakhsh** ≈ SW Tajikistan
127 P1 **Vakhtan** Nizhegorodskaya Oblast', W Russian Federation 58°00′N 46°43′E
94 C13 **Vaksdal** Hordaland, S Norway 60°29′N 05°45′E
Valachia *see* Wallachia
108 D11 **Valais** *Ger.* Wallis. ◈ *canton* SW Switzerland
113 M21 **Valamarës, Mali i** ▲ SE Albania 40°48′N 20°31′E
127 S2 **Valamaz** Udmurtskaya Respublika, NW Russian Federation 57°36′N 52°07′E
113 Q19 **Valandovo** SE FYR Macedonia 41°20′N 22°33′E
111 I18 **Valašské Meziříčí** *Ger.* Wallachisch-Meseritsch, *Pol.* Wałeckie Międzyrzecze. Zlínský Kraj, E Czech Republic 49°29′N 17°57′E
115 I17 **Valáxa** *island* Vóreies Sporádes, Greece, Aegean Sea
95 K16 **Vålberg** Värmland, C Sweden 59°24′N 13°12′E
116 H12 **Vâlcea** *prev.* Vîlcea. ◈ *county* SW Romania
63 J16 **Valcheta** Río Negro, E Argentina 40°42′S 66°08′W
15 P12 **Valcourt** Québec, SE Canada 45°28′N 72°18′W
Valdai Hills *see* Valdayskaya Vozvyshennost'
104 M3 **Valdavia** ≈ N Spain
124 I15 **Valday** Novgorodskaya Oblast', W Russian Federation 57°57′N 33°20′E
124 I15 **Valdayskaya Vozvyshennost'** *var.* Valdai Hills. *hill range* W Russian Federation
104 L9 **Valdecañas, Embalse de** ▣ W Spain
118 E8 **Valdemārpils** *Ger.* Sassmacken. NW Latvia 57°23′N 22°36′E
95 N18 **Valdemarsvik** Östergötland, S Sweden 58°13′N 16°35′E
105 N8 **Valdemoro** Madrid, C Spain 40°12′N 03°40′W
105 O11 **Valdepeñas** Castilla-La Mancha, C Spain 38°46′N 03°24′W
104 L5 **Valderaduey** ≈ NE Spain
104 L5 **Valderas** Castilla y León, N Spain 42°05′N 05°27′W
105 T7 **Valderrobres** *var.* Vall-de-roures. Aragón, NE Spain 40°53′N 00°08′E
63 K17 **Valdés, Península** *peninsula* SE Argentina
56 C5 **Valdéz** *var.* Limones. Esmeraldas, NW Ecuador 01°13′N 79°00′W
39 S11 **Valdez** Alaska, USA 61°08′N 146°21′W
Valdia *see* Weldiya
103 U11 **Val d'Isère** Savoie, E France 45°23′N 07°03′E
63 G15 **Valdivia** Los Ríos, C Chile 39°50′S 73°13′W
Valdivia Bank *see* Valdivia Seamount
65 P17 **Valdivia Seamount** *var.* Valdivia Bank. *undersea feature* E Atlantic Ocean 26°15′S 06°25′E
103 N4 **Val-d'Oise** ◈ *department* N France
14 J8 **Val-d'Or** Québec, SE Canada 48°06′N 77°42′W
23 U8 **Valdosta** Georgia, SE USA 30°49′N 83°16′W
94 G13 **Valdres** *physical region* S Norway
32 L13 **Vale** Oregon, NW USA 43°59′N 117°15′W
116 F9 **Valea lui Mihai** *Hung.* Érmihályfalva. Bihor, NW Romania 47°31′N 22°08′E
11 N15 **Valemount** British Columbia, SW Canada 52°46′N 119°17′W
59 O17 **Valença** Bahia, E Brazil 13°22′S 39°06′W
104 F4 **Valença do Minho** Viana do Castelo, N Portugal 42°02′N 08°38′W
59 N14 **Valença do Piauí** Piauí, E Brazil 06°26′S 41°46′W
103 N8 **Valençay** Indre, C France 47°10′N 01°31′E
103 R13 **Valence** *anc.* Valentia, Valentia Julia, Ventia. Drôme, E France 44°56′N 04°54′E
105 S10 **Valencia** Valenciana, E Spain 39°29′N 00°24′W
54 K5 **Valencia** Carabobo, N Venezuela 10°12′N 68°02′W
105 R10 **Valencia** *Cat.* València. ◈ *province* Valenciana, E Spain
105 S10 **Valencia** ✈ Valencia, E Spain
104 I10 **Valencia de Alcántara** Extremadura, W Spain 39°25′N 07°14′W
104 L4 **Valencia de Don Juan** Castilla y León, N Spain 42°17′N 05°31′W
105 U9 **Valencia, Golfo de** *var.* Gulf of Valencia. *gulf* E Spain
Valencia, Gulf of *see* Valencia, Golfo de
97 A21 **Valencia Island** *Ir.* Dairbhre. *island* SW Ireland
105 R10 **Valenciana** *var.* Valencia, *Cat.* València; *anc.* Valentia. ◈ *autonomous community* NE Spain
Valencia/València *see* Valenciana
103 P2 **Valenciennes** Nord, N France 50°21′N 03°32′E
116 K13 **Vălenii de Munte** Prahova, SE Romania 45°11′N 26°02′E
Valentia *see* Valence, France
Valentia *see* Valenciana
Valentia Julia *see* Valence
103 T8 **Valentigney** Doubs, E France 47°27′N 06°49′E
28 M12 **Valentine** Nebraska, C USA 42°53′N 100°31′W
24 J10 **Valentine** Texas, SW USA 30°35′N 104°30′W
Valentine State *see* Oregon
106 C8 **Valenza** Piemonte, NW Italy 45°01′N 08°37′E
94 I13 **Våler** Hedmark, S Norway 60°39′N 11°52′E
54 I6 **Valera** Trujillo, NW Venezuela 09°21′N 70°38′W
192 M11 **Valerie Guyot** S Pacific Ocean 33°00′S 164°00′W
Valetta *see* Valletta
118 I7 **Valga** *Ger.* Walk, *Latv.* Valka. Valgamaa, S Estonia 57°48′N 26°04′E
118 I7 **Valgamaa** *var.* Valga Maakond. ◈ *province* S Estonia
Valga Maakond *see* Valgamaa
43 Q15 **Valiente, Península** *peninsula* NW Panama
103 X16 **Valinco, Golfe de** *gulf* Corse, France, C Mediterranean Sea
112 L12 **Valjevo** Serbia, W Serbia 44°17′N 19°54′E
Valjok *see* Válljohka
118 I7 **Valka** *Ger.* Walk. N Latvia 57°48′N 26°01′E
Valka *see* Valga
93 L18 **Valkeakoski** Länsi-Suomi, W Finland 61°17′N 24°05′E
93 M19 **Valkeala** Etelä-Suomi, S Finland 60°55′N 26°49′E
99 L18 **Valkenburg** Limburg, SE Netherlands 50°52′N 05°50′E
99 K15 **Valkenswaard** Noord-Brabant, S Netherlands 51°21′N 05°29′E
119 G15 **Valkininkai** Alytus, S Lithuania 54°22′N 24°51′E
117 U5 **Valky** Kharkivs'ka Oblast', E Ukraine 49°51′N 35°40′E
41 Y12 **Valladolid** Yucatán, SE Mexico 20°39′N 88°13′W
104 M5 **Valladolid** Castilla y León, NW Spain 41°39′N 04°45′W
104 L5 **Valladolid** ◈ *province* Castilla y León, N Spain
103 U15 **Vallauris** Alpes-Maritimes, SE France 43°34′N 07°03′E
Vall-de-roures *see* Valderrobres
Vall D'Uxó *see* La Vall d'Uixó
95 E16 **Valle** Aust-Agder, S Norway 59°13′N 07°33′E
105 N2 **Valle** Cantabria, N Spain 43°14′N 04°16′W
42 H8 **Valle** ◈ *department* S Honduras
105 N8 **Vallecas** Madrid, C Spain 40°23′N 03°37′W
37 Q8 **Vallecito Reservoir** ▣ Colorado, C USA
106 A7 **Valle d'Aosta** *Fr.* Vallée d'Aoste. ◈ *region* NW Italy
41 O14 **Valle de Bravo** México, S Mexico 19°19′N 100°08′W
55 N5 **Valle de Guanape** Anzoátegui, N Venezuela 09°54′N 65°41′W
54 M6 **Valle de La Pascua** Guárico, N Venezuela 09°15′N 66°00′W
54 B11 **Valle del Cauca** *off.* Departamento del Valle del Cauca. ◈ *province* W Colombia
Valle del Cauca, Departamento del *see* Valle del Cauca
41 N13 **Valle de Santiago** Guanajuato, C Mexico 20°25′N 101°15′W
40 J7 **Valle de Zaragoza** Chihuahua, N Mexico 27°25′N 105°50′W
54 G5 **Valledupar** Cesar, N Colombia 10°31′N 73°16′W
Vallée d'Aoste *see* Valle d'Aosta
76 G10 **Vallée de Ferlo** ≈ NW Senegal
57 M19 **Vallegrande** Santa Cruz, C Bolivia 18°30′S 64°06′W
41 P8 **Valle Hermoso** Tamaulipas, C Mexico 25°39′N 97°49′W
35 N8 **Vallejo** California, W USA 38°08′N 122°16′W
62 G8 **Vallenar** Atacama, N Chile 28°35′S 70°44′W
95 O15 **Vallentuna** Stockholm, C Sweden 59°32′N 18°05′E
121 P16 **Valletta** *prev.* Valetta. ● (Malta) E Malta 35°54′N 14°31′E
27 N6 **Valley Center** Kansas, C USA 37°49′N 97°22′W
29 Q5 **Valley City** North Dakota, N USA 46°57′N 97°58′W
32 I15 **Valley Falls** Oregon, NW USA 42°28′N 120°16′W
Valleyfield *see* Salaberry-de-Valleyfield
21 S4 **Valley Head** West Virginia, NE USA 38°33′N 80°01′W
25 T8 **Valley Mills** Texas, SW USA 31°36′N 97°27′W
75 W10 **Valley of the Kings** *ancient monument* E Egypt
29 R11 **Valley Springs** South Dakota, N USA 43°34′N 96°28′W
20 K5 **Valley Station** Kentucky, S USA 38°06′N 85°52′W
11 O13 **Valleyview** Alberta, W Canada 55°02′N 117°17′W
25 T5 **Valley View** Texas, SW USA 33°27′N 97°08′W
61 C21 **Vallimanca, Arroyo** ≈ E Argentina

◆ Country
● Country Capital
◇ Dependent Territory
○ Dependent Territory Capital
◈ Administrative Regions
✈ International Airport
▲ Mountain
⛰ Mountain Range
🌋 Volcano
≈ River
◎ Lake
▣ Reservoir

92 L9 **Válljohka** *var.* Valjok. Finnmark, N Norway 69°40′N 25°52′E
107 M19 **Vallo della Lucania** Campania, S Italy 40°13′N 15°15′E
108 B9 **Vallorbe** Vaud, W Switzerland 46°43′N 06°21′E
105 V6 **Valls** Cataluña, NE Spain 41°18′N 01°15′E
94 N11 **Vallsta** Gävleborg, C Sweden 61°30′N 16°25′E
94 N12 **Vallvik** Gävleborg, C Sweden 61°10′N 17°15′E
11 T17 **Val Marie** Saskatchewan, S Canada 49°15′N 107°44′W
118 H7 **Valmiera** *Est.* Volmari, *Ger.* Wolmar. N Latvia 57°34′N 25°26′E
105 N3 **Valnera** ▲ N Spain 43°08′N 03°39′W
102 J3 **Valognes** Manche, N France 49°31′N 01°28′W
Valona *see* Vlorë
Valona Bay *see* Vlorës, Gjiri i
104 G6 **Valongo** *var.* Valongo de Gaia. Porto, N Portugal 41°11′N 08°30′W
Valongo de Gaia *see* Valongo
104 M5 **Valoria la Buena** Castilla y León, N Spain 41°48′N 04°33′W
119 J15 **Valozhyn** *Pol.* Wołożyn, *Rus.* Volozhin. Minskaya Voblasts', C Belarus 54°05′N 26°32′E
104 I5 **Valpaços** Vila Real, N Portugal 41°36′N 07°17′W
62 G11 **Valparaíso** Valparaíso, C Chile 33°05′S 71°18′W
40 L11 **Valparaíso** Zacatecas, C Mexico 22°49′N 103°28′W
23 P8 **Valparaiso** Florida, SE USA 30°30′N 86°28′W
31 N11 **Valparaiso** Indiana, N USA 41°28′N 87°04′W
62 G11 **Valparaíso** *off.* Región de Valparaíso. ◐ *region* C Chile
Valparaíso, Región de *see* Valparaíso
Valpo *see* Valpovo
112 I9 **Valpovo** *Hung.* Valpo. Osijek-Baranja, E Croatia 45°40′N 18°25′E
103 R14 **Valréas** Vaucluse, SE France 44°22′N 05°00′E
Vals *see* Vals-Platz
154 D12 **Valsād** *prev.* Bulsar. Gujarāt, W India 20°40′N 72°55′E
Valsbaai *see* False Bay
171 T12 **Valse Pisang, Kepulauan** *island group* E Indonesia
108 H9 **Vals-Platz** *var.* Vals. Graubünden, S Switzerland 46°39′N 09°09′E
171 X16 **Vals, Tanjung** *headland* Papua, SE Indonesia 08°26′S 137°35′E
93 N15 **Valtimo** Itä-Suomi, E Finland 63°39′N 28°49′E
115 D17 **Váltou** ▲▲ C Greece
127 O12 **Valuyevka** Rostovskaya Oblast', SW Russian Federation 46°48′N 43°49′E
126 K9 **Valuyki** Belgorodskaya Oblast', W Russian Federation 50°11′N 38°07′E
36 L2 **Val Verda** Utah, W USA 40°51′N 111°53′W
64 N12 **Valverde** Hierro, Islas Canarias, Spain, NE Atlantic Ocean 27°48′N 17°55′W
104 I13 **Valverde del Camino** Andalucía, S Spain 37°35′N 06°45′W
95 G23 **Vamdrup** Syddanmark, C Denmark 55°26′N 09°18′E
94 L12 **Våmhus** Dalarna, C Sweden 61°07′N 14°30′E
93 K18 **Vammala** Länsi-Suomi, SW Finland 61°20′N 22°55′E
Vámosudvarhely *see* Odorheiu Secuiesc
137 S14 **Van** Van, E Turkey 38°30′N 43°23′E
25 V7 **Van** Texas, SW USA 32°31′N 95°38′W
137 T14 **Van** ◐ *province* E Turkey
137 T11 **Vanadzor** *prev.* Kirovakan. N Armenia 40°49′N 44°29′E
25 U5 **Van Alstyne** Texas, SW USA 33°25′N 96°34′W
33 W10 **Vananda** Montana, NW USA 46°22′N 106°58′W
116 I11 **Vânători** *Hung.* Héjjasfalva; *prev.* Vînători. Mureş, C Romania 46°14′N 24°56′E
191 W12 **Vanavana** *atoll* Îles Tuamotu, SE French Polynesia
Vana-Vändra *see* Vändra
122 M11 **Vanavara** Krasnoyarskiy Kray, C Russian Federation 60°19′N 102°19′E
15 Q8 **Van Bruyssel** Québec, SE Canada 47°56′N 72°08′W
27 R10 **Van Buren** Arkansas, C USA 35°28′N 94°25′W
19 S1 **Van Buren** Maine, NE USA 47°07′N 67°57′W
27 W7 **Van Buren** Missouri, C USA 37°00′N 91°00′W
19 T5 **Vanceboro** Maine, NE USA 45°31′N 67°25′W
21 W10 **Vanceboro** North Carolina, SE USA 35°16′N 77°06′W
21 O4 **Vanceburg** Kentucky, S USA 38°36′N 84°40′W
45 W10 **Vance W. Amory** ✈ Nevis, Saint Kitts and Nevis 17°08′N 62°36′W
Vanch *see* Vanj
10 L17 **Vancouver** British Columbia, SW Canada 49°13′N 123°06′W
32 G11 **Vancouver** Washington, NW USA 45°38′N 122°39′W
10 L17 **Vancouver** ✈ British Columbia, SW Canada 49°03′N 123°00′W
10 K16 **Vancouver Island** *island* British Columbia, SW Canada
Vanda *see* Vantaa
171 X13 **Van Daalen** ≈ Papua, E Indonesia
30 L15 **Vandalia** Illinois, N USA 38°57′N 89°05′W
27 V3 **Vandalia** Missouri, C USA 39°18′N 91°29′W
31 R13 **Vandalia** Ohio, N USA 39°53′N 84°12′W
25 U13 **Vanderbilt** Texas, SW USA 28°45′N 96°37′W
31 Q10 **Vandercook Lake** Michigan, N USA 42°11′N 84°23′W
10 L14 **Vanderhoof** British Columbia, SW Canada 53°54′N 124°00′W
18 K8 **Vanderwhacker Mountain** ▲ New York, NE USA 43°54′N 74°06′W
181 P1 **Van Diemen Gulf** *gulf* Northern Territory, N Australia
Van Diemen's Land *see* Tasmania
118 H5 **Vändra** *Ger.* Fennern; *prev.* Vana-Vändra. Pärnumaa, SW Estonia 58°39′N 25°00′E
Vandsburg *see* Więcbork
34 L4 **Van Duzen River** ≈ California, W USA
118 F13 **Vandžiogala** Kaunas, C Lithuania 55°07′N 23°55′E
41 N10 **Vanegas** San Luis Potosí, C Mexico 23°53′N 100°55′W
Vaner, Lake *see* Vänern
95 K17 **Vänern** *Eng.* Lake Vaner; *prev.* Lake Vener. ◎ S Sweden
95 J18 **Vänersborg** Västra Götaland, S Sweden 58°16′N 12°22′E
94 F12 **Vang** Oppland, S Norway 61°07′N 08°34′E
172 I7 **Vangaindrano** Fianarantsoa, SE Madagascar 23°21′S 47°35′E
137 S14 **Van Gölü** *Eng.* Lake Van; *anc.* Thospitis. *salt lake* E Turkey
186 L9 **Vangunu** *island* New Georgia Islands, NW Solomon Islands
24 J9 **Van Horn** Texas, SW USA 31°03′N 104°51′W
187 Q11 **Vanikolo** *var.* Vanikoro. *island* Santa Cruz Islands, E Solomon Islands
Vanikoro *see* Vanikolo
186 A5 **Vanimo** Sandaun, NW Papua New Guinea 02°40′S 141°17′E
123 T13 **Vanino** Khabarovskiy Kray, SE Russian Federation 49°10′N 140°18′E
155 G19 **Vānīvilāsa Sāgara** ◎ SW India
147 S13 **Vanj** *Rus.* Vanch. S Tajikistan 38°22′N 71°27′E
116 G14 **Vânju Mare** *prev.* Vînju Mare. Mehedinţi, SW Romania 44°25′N 22°52′E
15 N12 **Vankleek Hill** Ontario, SE Canada 45°32′N 74°39′W
Van, Lake *see* Van Gölü
93 I16 **Vännäs** Västerbotten, N Sweden 63°54′N 19°43′E
93 I15 **Vännäsby** Västerbotten, N Sweden 63°55′N 19°53′E
102 H7 **Vannes** *anc.* Dariorigum. Morbihan, NW France 47°40′N 02°45′W
92 I8 **Vannøya** *island* N Norway
103 T12 **Vanoise, Massif de la** ▲▲ E France
83 E24 **Vanrhynsdorp** Western Cape, SW South Africa 31°36′S 18°45′E
21 P7 **Vansant** Virginia, NE USA 37°13′N 82°03′W
94 L13 **Vansbro** Dalarna, C Sweden 60°32′N 14°15′E
95 D18 **Vanse** Vest-Agder, S Norway 58°04′N 06°40′E
9 P7 **Vansittart Island** *island* Nunavut, NE Canada
93 M20 **Vantaa** *Swe.* Vanda. Etelä-Suomi, S Finland 60°18′N 25°01′E
93 L19 **Vantaa** ✈ (Helsinki) Etelä-Suomi, S Finland 60°18′N 25°01′E
32 J9 **Vantage** Washington, NW USA 46°55′N 119°55′W
187 Z14 **Vanua Balavu** *prev.* Vanua Mbalavu. *island* Lau Group, E Fiji
187 R12 **Vanua Lava** *island* Banks Islands, N Vanuatu
187 Y13 **Vanua Levu** *island* N Fiji
Vanua Mbalavu *see* Vanua Balavu
187 R12 **Vanuatu** *off.* Republic of Vanuatu; *prev.* New Hebrides. ◆ *republic* SW Pacific Ocean
175 P8 **Vanuatu** *island group* SW Pacific Ocean
Vanuatu, Republic of *see* Vanuatu
31 Q12 **Van Wert** Ohio, N USA 40°52′N 84°34′W
187 Q17 **Vao** Province Sud, S New Caledonia 22°40′S 167°29′E
Vapincum *see* Gap
117 N7 **Vapnyarka** Vinnyts'ka Oblast', C Ukraine 48°31′S 28°44′E
103 T15 **Var** ◐ *department* SE France
103 U14 **Var** ≈ SE France
95 J18 **Vara** Västra Götaland, S Sweden 58°16′N 12°57′E
Varadinska Županija *see* Varaždin
118 J10 **Varakļāni** C Latvia 56°36′N 26°40′E
106 C7 **Varallo** Piemonte, NE Italy 45°51′N 08°16′E
143 O5 **Varāmīn** *var.* Veramin. Tehrān, N Iran 35°19′N 51°40′E
153 N14 **Vārānasi** *prev.* Banaras, Benares, *hist.* Kasi. Uttar Pradesh, N India 25°20′N 83°E
125 T3 **Varandey** Nenetskiy Avtonomnyy Okrug, NW Russian Federation 68°48′N 57°54′E
92 M8 **Varangerbotn** *Lapp.* Vuonnabahta. Finnmark, N Norway 70°09′N 28°28′E
92 M8 **Varangerfjorden** *Lapp.* Várjjatvuotna. *fjord* N Norway
92 M8 **Varangerhalvøya** *Lapp.* Várnjárga. *peninsula* N Norway
Varannó *see* Vranov nad Topl'ou
107 M15 **Varano, Lago di** ◎ SE Italy
118 J13 **Varapayeva** *Rus.* Voropayevo. Vitsyebskaya Voblasts', NW Belarus 55°09′N 27°13′E
Varasd *see* Varaždin
112 E7 **Varaždin** *Ger.* Warasdin, *Hung.* Varasd. Varaždin, N Croatia 46°18′N 16°21′E
112 E7 **Varaždin** *off.* Varadinska Županija. ◐ *province* N Croatia
106 C10 **Varazze** Liguria, NW Italy 44°21′N 08°35′E
95 J20 **Varberg** Halland, S Sweden 57°06′N 12°15′E
113 Q19 **Vardar** *Gk.* Axiós. ≈ FYR Macedonia/Greece *see also* Axiós
Vardar *see* Axiós
95 F23 **Varde** Syddtjylland, W Denmark 55°38′N 08°31′E
137 V12 **Vardenis** E Armenia 40°11′N 45°43′E
92 N8 **Vardø** *Fin.* Vuoreija. Finnmark, N Norway 70°22′N 31°06′E
115 E18 **Vardoúsia** ▲▲ C Greece
Vareia *see* Logroño
100 G10 **Varel** Niedersachsen, NW Germany 53°24′N 08°07′E
119 G15 **Varėna** *Pol.* Orany. Alytus, S Lithuania 54°13′N 24°35′E
15 O12 **Varennes** Québec, SE Canada 45°42′N 73°25′W
103 P10 **Varennes-sur-Allier** Allier, C France 46°17′N 03°24′E
112 I12 **Vareš** Federacija Bosna I Hercegovina, E Bosnia and Herzegovina 44°12′N 18°19′E
106 D7 **Varese** Lombardia, N Italy 45°49′N 08°50′E
116 J12 **Vârful Moldoveanu** *var.* Moldoveanul; *prev.* Vîrful Moldoveanu. ▲ C Romania 45°35′N 24°48′E
Varganzi *see* Warganza
95 J18 **Vårgårda** Västra Götaland, S Sweden 58°00′N 12°49′E
54 L4 **Vargas** *off.* Estado Vargas. ◐ *state* N Venezuela
95 J18 **Vargön** Västra Götaland, S Sweden 58°21′N 12°22′E
95 C17 **Varhaug** Rogaland, S Norway 58°37′N 05°39′E
Várjjatvuotna *see* Varangerfjorden
93 N17 **Varkaus** Itä-Suomi, C Finland 62°20′N 27°50′E
92 J2 **Varmahlidh** Nordhurland Vestra, N Iceland 65°32′N 19°33′W
95 J15 **Värmland** ◐ *county* C Sweden
95 K16 **Värmlandsnäs** *peninsula* S Sweden
114 N8 **Varna** *prev.* Stalin; *anc.* Odessus. Varna, E Bulgaria 43°14′N 27°56′E
114 N8 **Varna** ◐ *province* E Bulgaria
114 N8 **Varna** ✈ Varna, E Bulgaria 43°16′N 27°52′E
95 L20 **Värnamo** Jönköping, S Sweden 57°11′N 14°03′E
114 N8 **Varnenski Zaliv** *prev.* Stalinski Zaliv. *bay* E Bulgaria
114 N8 **Varnensko Ezero** *estuary* E Bulgaria
118 D11 **Varniai** Telšiai, W Lithuania 55°45′N 22°22′E
Várnjárga *see* Varangerhalvøya
Varnoús *see* Baba
111 D14 **Varnsdorf** *Ger.* Warnsdorf. Ústecký Kraj, NW Czech Republic 50°57′N 14°35′E
111 I23 **Várpalota** Veszprém, W Hungary 47°12′N 18°08′E
Varshava *see* Warszawa
118 K6 **Värska** Põlvamaa, SE Estonia 57°58′N 27°37′E
98 N12 **Varsseveld** Gelderland, E Netherlands 51°55′N 06°28′E
115 D19 **Vartholomió** *prev.* Vartholomión. Dytikí Elláda, S Greece 37°52′N 21°12′E
Vartholomión *see* Vartholomió
137 Q14 **Varto** Muş, E Turkey 39°10′N 41°28′E
95 K18 **Vartofta** Västra Götaland, S Sweden 58°06′N 13°40′E
93 O17 **Värtsilä** Itä-Suomi, E Finland 62°10′N 30°35′E
Värtsilä *see* Vyartsilya
117 R4 **Varva** Chernihivs'ka Oblast', NE Ukraine 50°31′N 32°43′E
59 H18 **Várzea Grande** Mato Grosso, SW Brazil 15°39′S 56°08′W
106 D9 **Varzi** Lombardia, N Italy 44°51′N 09°13′E
Varzimanor Ayni *see* Ayní
124 K5 **Varzuga** ≈ NW Russian Federation
103 P8 **Varzy** Nièvre, C France 47°22′N 03°22′E
111 G23 **Vas** *off.* Vas Megye. ◐ *county* W Hungary
Vasa *see* Vaasa
190 A9 **Vasafua** *island* Funafuti Atoll, C Tuvalu
111 O21 **Vásárosnamény** Szabolcs-Szatmár-Bereg, E Hungary 48°10′N 22°18′E
104 H13 **Vascão, Ribeira de** ≈ S Portugal
116 G10 **Vaşcău** *Hung.* Vaskoh. Bihor, NE Romania 46°28′N 22°30′E
Vascongadas, Provincias *see* País Vasco
Vashess Bay *see* Vaskess Bay
125 O8 **Vashka** ≈ NW Russian Federation
Väsht *see* Khāsh
Vasilevichi *see* Vasilyevichy
115 G14 **Vasiliká** Kentrikí Makedonía, NE Greece 40°28′N 23°08′E
115 C18 **Vasilikí** Lefkáda, Iónia Nisiá, Greece, C Mediterranean Sea 38°36′N 20°37′E
115 K25 **Vasilikí** Kríti, Greece, E Mediterranean Sea 35°04′N 25°49′E
119 G16 **Vasilishki** *Pol.* Wasiliszki. Hrodzyenskaya Voblasts', W Belarus 53°47′N 24°51′E
Vasil Kolarov *see* Pamporovo
Vasil'kov *see* Vasyl'kiv
119 N19 **Vasilyevichy** *Rus.* Vasilevichi. Homyel'skaya Voblasts', SE Belarus 52°15′N 29°50′E
191 Y3 **Vaskess Bay** *var.* Vashess Bay. *bay* Kiritimati, E Kiribati
Vaskoh *see* Vaşcău
Vaskohsziklás *see* Ştei
116 M10 **Vaslui** Vaslui, C Romania 46°38′N 27°44′E
116 L11 **Vaslui** ◐ *county* NE Romania
Vas Megye *see* Vas
31 R8 **Vassar** Michigan, N USA 43°22′N 83°34′W
95 E15 **Vassdalsegga** ▲ S Norway 59°47′N 07°07′E
60 P9 **Vassouras** Rio de Janeiro, SE Brazil 22°24′S 43°38′W
95 N15 **Västerås** Västmanland, C Sweden 59°37′N 16°33′E
93 G15 **Västerbotten** ◐ *county* N Sweden
94 K12 **Västerdalälven** ≈ C Sweden
95 O16 **Västerhaninge** Stockholm, C Sweden 59°07′N 18°06′E
94 M10 **Västernorrland** ◐ *county* C Sweden
95 N19 **Västervik** Kalmar, S Sweden 57°44′N 16°40′E
95 M15 **Västmanland** ◐ *county* C Sweden
107 L15 **Vasto** *anc.* Histonium. Abruzzo, C Italy 42°07′N 14°43′E
95 J19 **Västra Götaland** ◐ *county* S Sweden
95 J16 **Västra Silen** ◎ S Sweden
111 G23 **Vasvár** *Ger.* Eisenburg. Vas, W Hungary 47°03′N 16°48′E
117 U9 **Vasylivka** Zaporiz'ka Oblast', SE Ukraine 47°26′N 35°18′E
117 O5 **Vasyl'kiv** *var.* Vasil'kov. Kyyivs'ka Oblast', N Ukraine 50°12′N 30°18′E
117 V8 **Vasyl'kivka** Dnipropetrovs'ka Oblast', E Ukraine 48°12′N 36°00′E
122 I11 **Vasyugan** ≈ C Russian Federation
103 N8 **Vatan** Indre, C France 47°06′N 01°49′E
Vaté *see* Efate
115 C18 **Vathy** *prev.* Itháki. Itháki, Iónia Nisiá, Greece, C Mediterranean Sea 38°22′N 20°43′E
107 G15 **Vatican City** *off.* Vatican City. ◆ *papal state* S Europe
Vatican City *see* Vatican City
107 M22 **Vaticano, Capo** *headland* S Italy 38°37′N 15°49′E
92 K3 **Vatnajökull** *glacier* SE Iceland
95 P15 **Vätö** Stockholm, C Sweden 59°48′N 18°55′E
187 Z16 **Vatoa** *island* Lau Group, SE Fiji
172 J5 **Vatomandry** Toamasina, E Madagascar 19°20′S 48°58′E
116 J9 **Vatra Dornei** *Ger.* Dorna Watra. Suceava, NE Romania 47°20′N 25°21′E
116 J9 **Vatra Moldoviţei** Suceava, NE Romania 47°37′N 25°36′E
Vatter, Lake *see* Vättern
95 L18 **Vättern** *Eng.* Lake Vatter; *prev.* Lake Vetter. ◎ S Sweden
187 X5 **Vatulele** *island* SW Fiji
117 P7 **Vatutine** Cherkas'ka Oblast', C Ukraine 49°01′N 31°04′E
187 W15 **Vatu Vara** *island* Lau Group, E Fiji
103 R14 **Vaucluse** ◐ *department* SE France
103 S5 **Vaucouleurs** Meuse, NE France 48°37′N 05°38′E
108 B9 **Vaud** *Ger.* Waadt. ◐ *canton* SW Switzerland
15 N12 **Vaudreuil** Québec, SE Canada 45°24′N 74°01′W
37 T12 **Vaughn** New Mexico, SW USA 34°36′N 105°12′W
54 I14 **Vaupés** *off.* Comisaría del Vaupés. ◐ *province* SE Colombia
Vaupés, Comisaría del *see* Vaupés
54 J13 **Vaupés, Río** *var.* Rio Uaupés. ≈ Brazil/Colombia *see also* Uaupés, Rio
Vaupés, Río *see* Uaupés, Rio
103 Q15 **Vauvert** Gard, S France 43°42′N 04°16′E
11 R17 **Vauxhall** Alberta, SW Canada 50°05′N 112°09′W
99 K23 **Vaux-sur-Sûre** Luxembourg, SE Belgium 49°55′N 05°34′E
172 J4 **Vavatenina** Toamasina, E Madagascar 17°25′S 49°11′E
193 Y14 **Vava'u Group** *island group* N Tonga
76 M16 **Vavoua** W Ivory Coast 07°23′N 06°29′W
127 S2 **Vavozh** Udmurtskaya Respublika, NW Russian Federation 56°48′N 51°53′E
155 K23 **Vavuniya** Northern Province, N Sri Lanka 08°45′N 80°30′E
119 G17 **Vawkavysk** *Pol.* Wołkowysk, *Rus.* Volkovysk. Hrodzyenskaya Voblasts', W Belarus 53°10′N 24°28′E
119 F17 **Vawkavyskaye Wzvyshsha** *Rus.* Volkovyskiye Vysoty. *hill range* W Belarus
95 P15 **Vaxholm** Stockholm, C Sweden 59°25′N 18°21′E
95 L21 **Växjö** *var.* Vexiö. Kronoberg, S Sweden 56°52′N 14°50′E
125 T1 **Vaygach, Ostrov** *island* NW Russian Federation
137 V13 **Vayk'** *prev.* Azizbekov. SE Armenia 39°41′N 45°28′E
Vazáš *see* Vittangi
125 P8 **Vazhgort** *prev.* Chasovo. Respublika Komi, NW Russian Federation 64°06′N 46°44′E
45 V10 **V. C. Bird** ✈ (St. John's) Antigua, Antigua and Barbuda 17°07′N 61°49′W
167 R13 **Veal Renh** *prev.* Phumĭ Veal Renh. Kâmpôt, SW Cambodia 10°43′N 103°49′E
29 Q7 **Veblen** South Dakota, N USA 45°50′N 97°17′W
98 N9 **Vecht** *Ger.* Vechte. ≈ Germany/Netherlands *see also* Vechte
Vecht *see* Vechte
100 G12 **Vechta** Niedersachsen, NW Germany 52°44′N 08°16′E
100 E12 **Vechte** *Dut.* Vecht. ≈ Germany/Netherlands *see also* Vecht
Vechte *see* Vecht
118 I8 **Vecpiebalga** C Latvia 57°03′N 25°47′E
118 G9 **Vecumnieki** C Latvia 56°36′N 24°30′E
95 C16 **Vedavågen** Rogaland, S Norway 59°18′N 5°13′E
Vedāvati *see* Hagari
95 J20 **Veddige** Halland, S Sweden 57°16′N 12°19′E
116 J15 **Vedea** ≈ S Romania
127 P16 **Vedeno** Chechenskaya Respublika, SW Russian Federation 42°57′N 46°02′E
95 C16 **Vedvågen** Rogaland, S Norway 59°18′N 05°13′E
98 O6 **Veendam** Groningen, NE Netherlands 53°05′N 06°53′E
98 K12 **Veenendaal** Utrecht, C Netherlands 52°03′N 05°33′E
99 E14 **Veere** Zeeland, SW Netherlands 51°33′N 03°40′E
24 M2 **Vega** Texas, SW USA 35°14′N 102°26′W
92 E13 **Vega** *island* C Norway
45 T5 **Vega Baja** C Puerto Rico 18°27′N 66°23′W
38 D17 **Vega Point** *headland* Kiska Island, Alaska, USA 51°49′N 177°19′E
95 F17 **Vegår** ◎ S Norway
99 K14 **Veghel** Noord-Brabant, S Netherlands 51°37′N 05°33′E
Veglia *see* Krk
114 E13 **Vegorítida, Límni** *var.* Límni Vegorítis. ◎ N Greece
Vegorítis, Límni *see* Vegorítida, Límni
11 Q14 **Vegreville** Alberta, SW Canada 53°30′N 112°02′W
95 K21 **Veinge** Halland, S Sweden 56°33′N 13°04′E
61 B21 **Veinticinco de Mayo** *var.* 25 de Mayo. Buenos Aires, E Argentina 35°27′S 60°11′W
63 I14 **Veinticinco de Mayo** La Pampa, C Argentina 37°45′S 67°40′W
119 F15 **Veisiejai** Alytus, S Lithuania 54°06′N 23°42′E
95 F23 **Vejen** Syddtjylland, W Denmark 55°29′N 09°13′E
104 K16 **Vejer de la Frontera** Andalucía, S Spain 36°15′N 05°58′W
95 G23 **Vejle** Syddanmark, C Denmark 55°43′N 09°33′E
Vejle Amt *see* Syddanmark
114 M7 **Vekilski** Shumen, NE Bulgaria 43°33′N 27°19′E
54 G3 **Vela, Cabo de la** *headland* NE Colombia 12°14′N 72°13′W
Vela Goa *see* Goa
113 F15 **Vela Luka** Dubrovnik-Neretva, S Croatia 42°57′N 16°43′E
61 G19 **Velázquez** Rocha, E Uruguay 34°05′S 54°16′W
101 E15 **Velbert** Nordrhein-Westfalen, W Germany 51°22′N 07°03′E
109 S9 **Velden** Kärnten, S Austria 46°37′N 13°59′E
Veldes *see* Bled
99 K15 **Veldhoven** Noord-Brabant, S Netherlands 51°24′N 05°24′E
112 C11 **Velebit** ▲▲ C Croatia
114 N11 **Veleka** ≈ SE Bulgaria
109 V10 **Velenje** *Ger.* Wöllan. N Slovenia 46°22′N 15°07′E
190 E12 **Vele, Pointe** *headland* Île Futuna, S Wallis and Futuna
113 O18 **Veles** *Turk.* Köprülü. C FYR Macedonia 41°43′N 21°49′E
113 M20 **Velešta** SW FYR Macedonia 41°16′N 20°37′E
115 F16 **Velestíno** *prev.* Velestínon. Thessalía, C Greece 39°23′N 22°45′E
Velestínon *see* Velestíno
Velevshchina *see* Vyelyewshchyna
54 F9 **Vélez** Santander, C Colombia 06°02′N 73°43′W
105 Q13 **Vélez Blanco** Andalucía, S Spain 37°43′N 02°07′W
104 M17 **Vélez de la Gomera, Peñon de** *island group* S Spain
105 N15 **Vélez-Málaga** Andalucía, S Spain 36°47′N 04°06′W
105 Q13 **Vélez Rubio** Andalucía, S Spain 37°39′N 02°04′W
Velha Goa *see* Goa
Velho *see* Porto Velho
112 E8 **Velika Gorica** Zagreb, N Croatia 45°43′N 16°03′E
112 C9 **Velika Kapela** ▲▲ NW Croatia
Velika Kikinda *see* Kikinda
112 D10 **Velika Kladuša** Federacija Bosna I Hercegovina, NW Bosnia and Herzegovina 45°10′N 15°48′E
112 N11 **Velika Morava** *var.* Glavn'a Morava, Morava, *Ger.* Grosse Morava. ≈ C Serbia
112 N12 **Velika Plana** Serbia, C Serbia 44°20′N 21°01′E
109 U10 **Velika Raduha** ▲ N Slovenia 46°24′N 14°46′E
123 V7 **Velikaya** ≈ NE Russian Federation
124 F15 **Velikaya** ≈ W Russian Federation
Velikaya Berestovitsa *see* Vyalikaya Byerastavitsa
Velikaya Lepetikha *see* Velyka Lepetykha
Veliki Bečkerek *see* Zrenjanin
112 P12 **Veliki Krš** *var.* Stol. ▲ E Serbia 44°10′N 22°09′E
114 L8 **Veliki Preslav** *prev.* Preslav. Shumen, NE Bulgaria 43°09′N 26°50′E
112 B9 **Veliki Risnjak** ▲ NW Croatia 45°30′N 14°31′E
109 T13 **Veliki Snežnik** *Ger.* Schneeberg, *It.* Monte Nevoso. ▲ SW Slovenia 45°36′N 14°25′E
112 J13 **Veliki Stolac** ▲ E Bosnia and Herzegovina 43°55′N 19°15′E
Velikiy Bor *see* Vyaliki Bor
124 G16 **Velikiye Luki** Pskovskaya Oblast', W Russian Federation 56°20′N 30°27′E
124 H14 **Velikiy Novgorod** *prev.* Novgorod. Novgorodskaya Oblast', W Russian Federation 58°32′N 31°15′E
125 P12 **Velikiy Ustyug** Vologodskaya Oblast', NW Russian Federation 60°46′N 46°18′E
112 N11 **Veliko Gradište** Serbia, NE Serbia 44°46′N 21°28′E
155 I18 **Velikonda Range** ▲▲ SE India
114 K9 **Veliko Tŭrnovo** *prev.* Tirnovo, Trnovo, Tŭrnovo. Veliko Tŭrnovo, N Bulgaria 43°05′N 25°40′E
114 K8 **Veliko Tŭrnovo** ◐ *province* N Bulgaria
Velikovec *see* Völkermarkt
125 R5 **Velikovisochnoye** Nenetskiy Avtonomnyy Okrug, NW Russian Federation 67°13′N 52°00′E
76 H12 **Vélingara** C Senegal 15°00′N 14°39′W
76 H11 **Vélingara** S Senegal 13°12′N 14°05′W
114 H11 **Velingrad** Pazardzhik, C Bulgaria 42°01′N 24°00′E
126 H3 **Velizh** Smolenskaya Oblast', W Russian Federation 55°30′N 31°06′E
111 F16 **Velká Deštná** *var.* Deštná, Grosskoppe, *Ger.* Deschnaer Koppe. ▲ NE Czech Republic 50°18′N 16°25′E
111 F18 **Velké Meziříčí** *Ger.* Grossmeseritsch. Vysočina, C Czech Republic 49°22′N 16°02′E
92 N1 **Velkomstpynten** *headland* NW Svalbard 79°51′N 11°37′E
111 K21 **Vel'ký Krtíš** Banskobystrický Kraj, C Slovakia 48°13′N 19°21′E
186 J8 **Vella Lavella** *var.* Mbilua. *island* New Georgia Islands, NW Solomon Islands
107 I15 **Velletri** Lazio, C Italy 41°41′N 12°47′E
95 K23 **Vellinge** Skåne, S Sweden 55°29′N 13°00′E
155 I19 **Vellore** Tamil Nādu, SE India 12°56′N 79°09′E
Velobriga *see* Viana do Castelo
115 G21 **Velopoúla** *island* S Greece
98 M12 **Velp** Gelderland, SE Netherlands 52°00′N 05°59′E
Velsen *see* Velsen-Noord
98 H9 **Velsen-Noord** *var.* Velsen. Noord-Holland, W Netherlands 52°27′N 04°40′E
125 N12 **Vel'sk** *var.* Velsk. Arkhangel'skaya Oblast', NW Russian Federation 61°03′N 42°01′E
Velsuna *see* Orvieto
98 K10 **Veluwemeer** *lake channel* C Netherlands
28 M3 **Velva** North Dakota, N USA 48°03′N 100°55′W
Velvendos/Velvendós *see* Velventós
115 E14 **Velventós** *var.* Velvendos, Velvendós. Dytikí Makedonía, N Greece 40°15′N 22°04′E
117 S5 **Velyka Bahachka** Poltavs'ka Oblast', C Ukraine 49°46′N 33°44′E
117 S9 **Velyka Lepetykha** *Rus.* Velikaya Lepetikha. Khersons'ka Oblast', S Ukraine 47°09′N 33°59′E
117 O10 **Velyka Mykhaylivka** Odes'ka Oblast', SW Ukraine 47°07′N 29°49′E
117 W8 **Velyka Novosilka** Donets'ka Oblast', E Ukraine 47°49′N 36°49′E
117 S9 **Velyka Oleksandrivka** Khersons'ka Oblast', S Ukraine 47°17′N 33°16′E
117 T4 **Velyka Pysarivka** Sums'ka Oblast', NE Ukraine 50°25′N 35°28′E
116 G6 **Velykyy Bereznyy** Zakarpats'ka Oblast', W Ukraine 48°54′N 22°27′E
117 W4 **Velykyy Burluk** Kharkivs'ka Oblast', E Ukraine 50°04′N 37°25′E
Velykyy Tokmak *see* Tokmak
173 P7 **Vema Fracture Zone** *tectonic feature* W Indian Ocean
65 P18 **Vema Seamount** *undersea feature* SW Indian Ocean 31°38′S 08°19′E
93 F17 **Vemdalen** Jämtland, C Sweden 62°26′N 13°50′E
95 N19 **Vena** Kalmar, S Sweden 57°31′N 16°00′E
41 N11 **Venado** San Luis Potosí, C Mexico 22°56′N 101°05′W
62 L11 **Venado Tuerto** Entre Ríos, E Argentina 33°45′S 61°56′W
61 A19 **Venado Tuerto** Santa Fe, C Argentina 33°46′S 61°57′W
107 K16 **Venafro** Molise, C Italy 41°28′N 14°03′E
55 Q9 **Venamo, Cerro** ▲ E Venezuela 05°56′N 61°25′W
106 B8 **Venaria** Piemonte, NW Italy 45°09′N 07°40′E
103 U15 **Vence** Alpes-Maritimes, SE France 43°45′N 07°07′E
104 H5 **Venda Nova** Vila Real, N Portugal 41°40′N 07°58′W
104 G11 **Vendas Novas** Évora, S Portugal 38°41′N 08°27′W
102 J9 **Vendée** ◐ *department* NW France
103 Q6 **Vendeuvre-sur-Barse** Aube, NE France 48°08′N 04°17′E
102 M7 **Vendôme** Loir-et-Cher, C France 47°48′N 01°04′E
Venedig *see* Venezia
Vener, Lake *see* Vänern
106 I8 **Veneta, Laguna** *lagoon* NE Italy
Venetia *see* Venezia
39 S7 **Venetie** Alaska, USA 67°00′N 146°25′W
106 H8 **Veneto** *var.* Venezia Euganea. ◐ *region* NE Italy
114 M7 **Venets** Shumen, NE Bulgaria 43°33′N 26°56′E
126 L5 **Venev** Tul'skaya Oblast', W Russian Federation 54°18′N 38°16′E
106 I8 **Venezia** *Eng.* Venice, *Fr.* Venise, *Ger.* Venedig; *anc.* Venetia. Veneto, NE Italy 45°26′N 12°20′E
Venezia Euganea *see* Veneto
Venezia, Golfo di *see* Venice, Gulf of
Venezia Tridentina *see* Trentino-Alto Adige
54 K8 **Venezuela** *off.* Republic of Venezuela; *prev.* Estados Unidos de Venezuela, United States of Venezuela. ◆ *republic* N South America
Venezuela, Cordillera de *see* Costa, Cordillera de la
Venezuela, Estados Unidos de *see* Venezuela
54 I4 **Venezuela, Golfo de** *Eng.* Gulf of Maracaibo, Gulf of Venezuela. *gulf* NW Venezuela
Venezuela, Gulf of *see* Venezuela, Golfo de
64 F11 **Venezuelan Basin** *undersea feature* E Caribbean Sea
Venezuela, Republic of *see* Venezuela
Venezuela, United States of *see* Venezuela
155 D16 **Vengurla** Mahārāshtra, W India 15°55′N 73°39′E
39 O15 **Veniaminof, Mount** ▲ Alaska, USA 56°12′N 159°24′W
23 V14 **Venice** Florida, SE USA 27°06′N 82°27′W
22 L10 **Venice** Louisiana, S USA 29°15′N 89°20′W
Venice *see* Venezia
106 J8 **Venice, Gulf of** *It.* Golfo di Venezia, *Slvn.* Beneški Zaliv. *gulf* N Adriatic Sea
Venise *see* Venezia
94 K13 **Venjan** Dalarna, C Sweden 60°58′N 13°55′E
94 K13 **Venjanssjön** ◎ C Sweden
155 J18 **Venkatagiri** Andhra Pradesh, E India 14°00′N 79°39′E
99 M15 **Venlo** *prev.* Venloo. Limburg, SE Netherlands 51°22′N 06°11′E
Venloo *see* Venlo
95 E18 **Vennesla** Vest-Agder, S Norway 58°15′N 08°00′E
107 M17 **Venosa** *anc.* Venusia. Basilicata, S Italy 40°57′N 15°49′E
Venoste, Alpi *see* Ötztaler Alpen
Venraij *see* Venray
99 M14 **Venray** *var.* Venraij. Limburg, SE Netherlands 51°32′N 05°59′E
118 C8 **Venta** *Ger.* Windau. ≈ Latvia/Lithuania
Venta Belgarum *see* Winchester
40 G9 **Ventana, Punta Arena de la** *var.* Punta de la Ventana. *headland* NW Mexico 24°03′N 109°49′W
Ventana, Punta de la *see* Ventana, Punta Arena de la
61 B23 **Ventana, Sierra de la** *hill range* E Argentina
Ventia *see* Valence
191 S11 **Vent, Îles du** *var.* Windward Islands. *island group* Archipel de la Société, W French Polynesia
191 R10 **Vent, Îles Sous le** *var.* Leeward Islands. *island group* Archipel de la Société, W French Polynesia
106 B11 **Ventimiglia** Liguria, NW Italy 43°47′N 07°37′E
97 M24 **Ventnor** S England, United Kingdom 50°36′N 01°11′W
18 J17 **Ventnor City** New Jersey, NE USA 39°19′N 74°27′W
103 S14 **Ventoux, Mont** ▲ SE France 44°12′N 05°21′E
118 C8 **Ventspils** *Ger.* Windau. NW Latvia 57°22′N 21°34′E
54 M10 **Ventuari, Río** ≈ S Venezuela
35 R15 **Ventura** California, W USA 34°15′N 119°18′W
182 F8 **Venus Bay** South Australia 33°15′S 134°42′E
Venusia *see* Venosa
191 P7 **Vénus, Pointe** *var.* Pointe Tataaihoa. *headland* Tahiti, W French Polynesia 17°28′S 149°29′W
41 V16 **Venustiano Carranza** Chiapas, SE Mexico 16°21′N 92°33′W
41 N7 **Venustiano Carranza, Presa** ⊠ NE Mexico
61 B15 **Vera** Santa Fe, C Argentina 29°28′S 60°10′W
105 Q14 **Vera** Andalucía, S Spain 37°15′N 01°51′W
63 K18 **Vera, Bahía** *bay* E Argentina
41 R14 **Veracruz** *var.* Veracruz Llave. Veracruz-Llave, E Mexico 19°10′N 96°09′W
Veracruz *see* Veracruz-Llave
41 Q13 **Veracruz-Llave** *var.* Veracruz. ◐ *state* E Mexico
Veracruz Llave *see* Veracruz
43 Q16 **Veraguas** *off.* Provincia de Veraguas. ◐ *province* W Panama
Veraguas, Provincia de *see* Veraguas
Veramin *see* Varāmīn
154 B12 **Verāval** Gujarāt, W India 20°54′N 70°22′E
106 C6 **Verbania** Piemonte, NW Italy 45°56′N 08°34′E
107 N20 **Verbicaro** Calabria, SW Italy 39°44′N 15°51′E
108 D11 **Verbier** Valais, SW Switzerland 46°06′N 07°14′E
Vercellae *see* Vercelli
106 C8 **Vercelli** *anc.* Vercellae. Piemonte, NW Italy 45°19′N 08°25′E
103 S13 **Vercors** *physical region* E France
Verdal *see* Verdalsøra
93 E16 **Verdalsøra** *var.* Verdal. Nord-Trøndelag, C Norway 63°47′N 11°27′E
Verde, Cabo *see* Cape Verde
44 J5 **Verde, Cape** *headland* Long Island, C Bahamas 22°51′N 75°50′W
104 M2 **Verde, Costa** *coastal region* N Spain
Verde Grande, Río/Verde Grande y de Belem, Río *see* Verde, Río
100 H11 **Verden** Niedersachsen, NW Germany 52°55′N 09°14′E
57 P16 **Verde, Río** ≈ Bolivia/Brazil
59 J19 **Verde, Rio** ≈ SE Brazil
40 M12 **Verde, Río** *var.* Río Verde Grande, Río Verde Grande y de Belem. ≈ C Mexico
41 Q16 **Verde, Río** ≈ SE Mexico
36 L13 **Verde River** ≈ Arizona, SW USA
Verdhikoúsa/Verdhikoússa *see* Verdikoússa
27 Q8 **Verdigris River** ≈ Kansas/Oklahoma, C USA
115 E15 **Verdikoússa** *var.* Verdhikoúsa, Verdhikoússa. Thessalía, C Greece 39°47′N 21°59′E
103 S15 **Verdon** ≈ SE France
15 O12 **Verdun** Québec, SE Canada 45°27′N 73°36′W
103 S4 **Verdun** *var.* Verdun-sur-Meuse; *anc.* Verodunum. Meuse, NE France 49°09′N 05°25′E
Verdun-sur-Meuse *see* Verdun
83 J21 **Vereeniging** Gauteng, NE South Africa 26°41′S 27°56′E
Veremeyki *see* Vyeramyeyki

◆ Country ● Country Capital ◇ Dependent Territory ○ Dependent Territory Capital ◐ Administrative Regions ✈ International Airport ▲ Mountain ▲▲ Mountain Range Volcano ≈ River ◎ Lake ⊠ Reservoir

125 T14 **Vereshchagino** Permskiy Kray, NW Russian Federation 58°06′N 54°38′E
76 G14 **Verga, Cap** *headland* W Guinea 10°12′N 14°27′W
61 G18 **Vergara** Treinta y Tres, E Uruguay 32°58′S 53°54′W
108 G11 **Vergeletto** Ticino, S Switzerland 46°13′N 08°34′E
18 L8 **Vergennes** Vermont, NE USA 44°09′N 73°13′W
Veria *see* Véroia
104 I5 **Verín** Galicia, NW Spain 41°55′N 07°26′W
Verin T'alin *see* T'alin
118 K6 **Veriora** Põlvamaa, SE Estonia 57°57′N 27°23′E
117 T7 **Verkhivtseve** Dnipropetrovs'ka Oblast', E Ukraine 48°27′N 34°15′E
Verkhnedvinsk *see* Vyerkhnyadzvinsk
122 K10 **Verkhneimbatsk** Krasnoyarskiy Kray, N Russian Federation 63°06′N 88°03′E
124 I3 **Verkhnetulomskiy** Murmanskaya Oblast', NW Russian Federation 68°37′N 31°46′E
124 I3 **Verkhnetulomskoye Vodokhranilishche** ⊠ NW Russian Federation
Verkhneudinsk *see* Ulan-Ude
123 P10 **Verkhnevilyuysk** Respublika Sakha (Yakutiya), NE Russian Federation 63°44′N 119°59′E
127 W5 **Verkhniy Avzyan** Respublika Bashkortostan, W Russian Federation 53°31′N 57°26′E
127 Q11 **Verkhniy Baskunchak** Astrakhanskaya Oblast', SW Russian Federation 48°14′N 46°43′E
127 W3 **Verkhniye Kigi** Respublika Bashkortostan, W Russian Federation 55°25′N 58°40′E
117 T9 **Verkhniy Rohachyk** Khersons'ka Oblast', S Ukraine 47°16′N 34°16′E
123 Q11 **Verkhnyaya Amga** Respublika Sakha (Yakutiya), NE Russian Federation 59°34′N 127°07′E
125 V6 **Verkhnyaya Inta** Respublika Komi, NW Russian Federation 65°55′N 60°07′E
125 O10 **Verkhnyaya Toyma** Arkhangel'skaya Oblast', NW Russian Federation 62°12′N 44°57′E
126 K6 **Verkhov'ye** Orlovskaya Oblast', W Russian Federation 52°49′N 37°20′E
116 I8 **Verkhovyna** Ivano-Frankivs'ka Oblast', W Ukraine 48°09′N 24°48′E
123 P8 **Verkhoyanskiy Khrebet** ▲▲ NE Russian Federation
117 T7 **Verkn'odniprovs'k** Dnipropetrovs'ka Oblast', E Ukraine 48°40′N 34°17′E
101 G14 **Verl** Nordrhein-Westfalen, NW Germany 51°52′N 08°30′E
92 N1 **Verlegenhuken** *headland* N Svalbard 80°03′N 16°15′E
82 A9 **Vermelha, Ponta** *headland* NW Angola 05°40′S 12°09′E
103 P7 **Vermenton** Yonne, C France 47°40′N 03°43′E
11 R14 **Vermilion** Alberta, SW Canada 53°21′N 110°52′W
31 T11 **Vermilion** Ohio, N USA 41°25′N 82°21′W
22 I10 **Vermilion Bay** *bay* Louisiana, S USA
29 V4 **Vermilion Lake** ◎ Minnesota, N USA
14 F9 **Vermilion River** ≈ Ontario, S Canada
30 L12 **Vermilion River** ≈ Illinois, N USA
29 R12 **Vermillion** South Dakota, N USA 42°46′N 96°55′W
29 R12 **Vermillion River** ≈ South Dakota, N USA
15 O9 **Vermillon, Rivière** ≈ Québec, SE Canada
115 E14 **Vérmio** ▲▲ N Greece
18 L8 **Vermont** *off.* State of Vermont, *also known as* Green Mountain State. ◐ *state* NE USA
113 K16 **Vermosh** *var.* Vermoshi. Shkodër, N Albania 42°37′N 19°42′E
Vermoshi *see* Vermosh
37 O3 **Vernal** Utah, W USA 40°27′N 109°31′W
14 G11 **Verner** Ontario, S Canada 46°24′N 80°04′W
102 M5 **Verneuil-sur-Avre** Eure, N France 48°44′N 00°55′E
114 D13 **Vérno** ▲▲ N Greece
11 N17 **Vernon** British Columbia, SW Canada 50°17′N 119°19′W
102 M4 **Vernon** Eure, N France 49°04′N 01°28′E
23 N3 **Vernon** Alabama, S USA 33°45′N 88°06′W
31 P15 **Vernon** Indiana, N USA 38°59′N 85°39′W
25 Q4 **Vernon** Texas, SW USA 34°11′N 99°17′W
32 G10 **Vernonia** Oregon, NW USA 45°51′N 123°11′W
14 G12 **Vernon, Lake** ◎ Ontario, S Canada
22 G7 **Vernon Lake** ⊠ Louisiana, S USA
23 Y13 **Vero Beach** Florida, SE USA 27°38′N 80°24′W
Verőcze *see* Virovitica
Verodunum *see* Verdun
115 E14 **Véroia** *var.* Veria, Vérroia, *Turk.* Karaferiye. Kentrikí Makedonía, N Greece 40°32′N 22°11′E
106 E8 **Verolanuova** Lombardia, N Italy 45°20′N 10°06′E
14 K14 **Verona** Ontario, SE Canada 44°30′N 76°42′W
106 G8 **Verona** Veneto, NE Italy 45°27′N 11°E
29 P6 **Verona** North Dakota, N USA 46°19′N 98°03′W
30 L9 **Verona** Wisconsin, N USA 42°59′N 89°33′W
61 E20 **Verónica** Buenos Aires, E Argentina 35°25′S 57°16′W
22 J9 **Verret, Lake** ◎ Louisiana, S USA
Vérroia *see* Véroia
103 N5 **Versailles** Yvelines, N France 48°48′N 02°08′E
31 P15 **Versailles** Indiana, N USA 39°04′N 85°16′W
20 M5 **Versailles** Kentucky, S USA 38°02′N 84°45′W
27 U5 **Versailles** Missouri, C USA 38°25′N 92°51′W
31 Q13 **Versailles** Ohio, N USA 40°13′N 84°28′W
Versecz *see* Vršac
108 A10 **Versoix** Genève, SW Switzerland 46°17′N 06°10′E
15 Z6 **Verte, Pointe** *headland* Québec, SE Canada 48°36′N 64°10′W
111 I22 **Vértes** ▲▲ NW Hungary
44 G6 **Vertientes** Camagüey, C Cuba 21°18′N 78°11′W
114 G13 **Vertískos** ▲▲ N Greece
102 I8 **Vertou** Loire-Atlantique, NW France 47°10′N 01°28′W
Verulamium *see* St Albans
99 L19 **Verviers** Liège, E Belgium 50°36′N 05°52′E
103 Y14 **Vescovato** Corse, France, C Mediterranean Sea 42°30′N 09°27′E
99 L20 **Vesdre** ≈ E Belgium
117 U10 **Vesele** *Rus.* Veseloye. Zaporiz'ka Oblast', S Ukraine 47°00′N 34°52′E
111 D18 **Veselí nad Lužnicí** *var.* Weseli an der Lainsitz, *Ger.* Frohenbruck. Jihočeský Kraj, S Czech Republic 49°11′N 14°40′E
114 M9 **Veselinovo** Shumen, NE Bulgaria 43°01′N 27°02′E
126 L12 **Veselovskoye Vodokhranilishche** ⊠ SW Russian Federation
Veseloye *see* Vesele
117 Q9 **Veselynove** Mykolayivs'ka Oblast', S Ukraine 47°21′N 31°15′E
Veseya *see* Vyasyeya
126 M10 **Veshenskaya** Rostovskaya Oblast', SW Russian Federation 49°37′N 41°43′E
127 Q5 **Veshkayma** Ul'yanovskaya Oblast', W Russian Federation 54°04′N 47°06′E
Vesisaari *see* Vadsø
Vesontio *see* Besançon
103 T7 **Vesoul** *anc.* Vesulium, Vesulum. Haute-Saône, E France 47°37′N 06°09′E
95 J20 **Vessigebro** Halland, S Sweden 56°58′N 12°40′E
95 D17 **Vest-Agder** ◐ *county* S Norway
23 P4 **Vestavia Hills** Alabama, S USA 33°27′N 86°47′W
84 F6 **Vesterålen** *island* NW Norway
92 G10 **Vesterålen** *island group* N Norway
87 V3 **Vestervig** Midtjylland, NW Denmark 56°46′N 08°20′E
92 H2 **Vestfirdhir** ◐ *region* NW Iceland
92 G11 **Vestfjorden** *fjord* C Norway
95 G16 **Vestfold** ◐ *county* S Norway
Vestmanhavn *see* Vestmanna
95 B18 **Vestmanna** *Dan.* Vestmanhavn. Streymoy, N Faeroe Islands 62°09′N 07°11′W
92 I4 **Vestmannaeyjar** Sudhurland, S Iceland 63°26′N 20°14′W
94 E9 **Vestnes** Møre og Romsdal, S Norway 62°39′N 07°00′E
92 H3 **Vesturland** ◐ *region* W Iceland
92 G11 **Vestvågøya** *island* C Norway
Vesulium/Vesulum *see* Vesoul
Vesuna *see* Périgueux
107 K17 **Vesuvio** *Eng.* Vesuvius. ⛰ S Italy 40°48′N 14°29′E
Vesuvius *see* Vesuvio
124 K14 **Ves'yegonsk** Tverskaya Oblast', W Russian Federation 58°40′N 37°13′E
111 I23 **Veszprém** *Ger.* Veszprim. Veszprém, W Hungary 47°06′N 17°54′E
111 H23 **Veszprém** *off.* Veszprém Megye. ◐ *county* W Hungary
Veszprém Megye *see* Veszprém
Veszprim *see* Veszprém
Vetka *see* Vyetka
95 M19 **Vetlanda** Jönköping, S Sweden 57°26′N 15°05′E
127 P1 **Vetluga** Nizhegorodskaya Oblast', W Russian Federation 57°51′N 45°45′E
125 P14 **Vetluga** ≈ NW Russian Federation
125 O14 **Vetluzhskiy** Kostromskaya Oblast', NW Russian Federation 58°21′N 45°25′E
127 P2 **Vetluzhskiy** Nizhegorodskaya Oblast', W Russian Federation 57°10′N 45°07′E
114 K7 **Vetovo** Ruse, N Bulgaria 43°42′N 26°16′E
107 H14 **Vetralla** Lazio, C Italy 42°18′N 12°03′E
Vetrino *see* Vyetryna
122 L7 **Vetrovaya, Gora** ▲ N Russian Federation 73°54′N 95°00′E
Vetter, Lake *see* Vättern
106 J13 **Vettore, Monte** ▲ C Italy 42°49′N 13°15′E
99 A17 **Veurne** *var.* Furnes. West-Vlaanderen, W Belgium 51°04′N 02°40′E
31 Q15 **Vevay** Indiana, N USA 38°45′N 85°08′W
108 C10 **Vevey** *Ger.* Vivis; *anc.* Vibiscum. Vaud, SW Switzerland 46°28′N 06°51′E
Vexiö *see* Växjö
103 S13 **Veynes** Hautes-Alpes, SE France 44°33′N 05°51′E
103 N11 **Vézère** ≈ W France
114 I9 **Vezhen** ▲ C Bulgaria 42°45′N 24°22′E
136 K11 **Vezirköprü** Samsun, N Turkey 41°09′N 35°27′E
57 J18 **Viacha** La Paz, W Bolivia 16°40′S 68°17′W
27 R10 **Vian** Oklahoma, C USA 35°30′N 94°56′W
Viana de Castelo *see* Viana do Castelo
104 H12 **Viana do Alentejo** Évora, S Portugal 38°20′N 08°00′W
104 I4 **Viana do Bolo** Galicia, NW Spain 42°10′N 07°06′W
104 G5 **Viana do Castelo** *var.* Viana de Castelo; *anc.* Velobriga. Viana do Castelo, NW Portugal 41°41′N 08°50′W
104 G5 **Viana do Castelo** *var.* Viana de Castelo. ◐ *district* N Portugal
98 J12 **Vianen** Utrecht, C Netherlands 52°N 05°06′E
167 Q8 **Viangchan** *Eng./Fr.* Vientiane. ● (Laos) C Laos 17°58′N 102°38′E
167 P6 **Viangphoukha** *var.* Vieng Pou Kha. Louang Namtha, N Laos 20°41′N 101°03′E
104 K13 **Viar** ≈ SW Spain
106 E11 **Viareggio** Toscana, C Italy 43°52′N 10°15′E
103 O14 **Viaur** ≈ S France
Vibiscum *see* Vevey
95 G21 **Viborg** Midtjylland, NW Denmark 56°28′N 09°25′E
29 R12 **Viborg** South Dakota, N USA 43°10′N 97°04′W
Viborg Amt *see* Midtjylland
107 N22 **Vibo Valentia** *prev.* Monteleone di Calabria; *anc.* Hipponium. Calabria, SW Italy 38°40′N 16°06′E
105 W5 **Vic** *var.* Vich; *anc.* Ausa, Vicus Ausonensis. Cataluña, NE Spain 41°56′N 02°16′E
102 K16 **Vic-en-Bigorre** Hautes-Pyrénées, S France 43°23′N 00°04′E
40 K10 **Vicente Guerrero** Durango, C Mexico 23°30′N 104°24′W
41 P10 **Vicente Guerrero, Presa** *var.* Presa de las Adjuntas. ⊠ NE Mexico
Vicentia *see* Vicenza
106 G8 **Vicenza** *anc.* Vicentia. Veneto, NE Italy 45°32′N 11°31′E
Vich *see* Vic
54 J10 **Vichada** *off.* Comisaría del Vichada. ◐ *province* E Colombia
Vichada, Comisaría del *see* Vichada
54 K10 **Vichada, Río** ≈ E Colombia
61 G17 **Vichadero** Rivera, NE Uruguay 31°45′S 54°41′W
Vichegda *see* Vychegda
124 M16 **Vichuga** Ivanovskaya Oblast', W Russian Federation 57°13′N 41°51′E
103 P10 **Vichy** Allier, C France 46°08′N 03°26′E
26 K9 **Vici** Oklahoma, C USA 36°09′N 99°18′W
95 I19 **Vickan** Halland, S Sweden 57°25′N 12°00′E
31 P10 **Vicksburg** Michigan, N USA 42°07′N 85°31′W
22 J5 **Vicksburg** Mississippi, S USA 32°21′N 90°52′W
103 O12 **Vic-sur-Cère** Cantal, C France 45°00′N 02°36′E
59 I21 **Víctor** Mato Grosso do Sul, SW Brazil 21°39′S 53°21′W
29 X14 **Victor** Iowa, C USA 41°45′N 92°18′W
182 I10 **Victor Harbor** South Australia 35°33′S 138°37′E
61 C18 **Victoria** Entre Ríos, E Argentina 32°40′S 60°10′W
10 L17 **Victoria** *province capital* Vancouver Island, British Columbia, SW Canada 48°25′N 123°22′W
45 R14 **Victoria** NW Grenada 12°12′N 61°42′W
42 H6 **Victoria** Yoro, NW Honduras 15°01′N 87°28′W
121 O15 **Victoria** *var.* Rabat. Gozo, NW Malta 36°02′N 14°14′E
116 I12 **Victoria** *Ger.* Viktoriastadt. Braşov, C Romania 45°44′N 24°41′E
172 H17 **Victoria** ● (Seychelles) Mahé, SW Seychelles 04°38′S 28°28′E
25 U13 **Victoria** Texas, SW USA 28°47′N 96°59′W
183 N12 **Victoria** ◐ *state* SE Australia
174 K7 **Victoria** ≈ Western Australia
Victoria *see* Labuan, East Malaysia
Victoria *see* Masvingo, Zimbabwe
Victoria Bank *see* Vitória Seamount
11 Y15 **Victoria Beach** Manitoba, S Canada 50°40′N 96°30′W
Victoria de Durango *see* Durango
Victoria de las Tunas *see* Las Tunas
83 I16 **Victoria Falls** Matabeleland North, W Zimbabwe 17°55′S 25°51′E
83 I16 **Victoria Falls** *waterfall* Zambia/Zimbabwe
83 I16 **Victoria Falls** ✈ Matabeleland North, W Zimbabwe 18°03′S 25°48′E
Victoria Falls *see* Iguaçu, Salto do
63 F19 **Victoria, Isla** *island* Archipiélago de los Chonos, S Chile
8 K6 **Victoria Island** *island* Northwest Territories/ Nunavut, NW Canada
182 L8 **Victoria, Lake** ◎ New South Wales, SE Australia
68 I12 **Victoria, Lake** *var.* Victoria Nyanza. ◎ E Africa
195 S13 **Victoria Land** *physical region* Antarctica
187 X14 **Victoria, Mount** ▲ Viti Levu, W Fiji 17°37′S 178°00′E
166 L5 **Victoria, Mount** ▲ W Burma (Myanmar) 21°13′N 93°53′E
186 E9 **Victoria, Mount** ▲ S Papua New Guinea 08°51′S 147°36′E
81 F17 **Victoria Nile** *var.* Somerset Nile. ≈ C Uganda
Victoria Nyanza *see* Victoria, Lake
42 G3 **Victoria Peak** ▲ SE Belize 16°50′N 88°38′W
185 H16 **Victoria Range** ▲▲ South Island, New Zealand
181 O3 **Victoria River** ≈ Northern Territory, N Australia
181 P3 **Victoria River Roadhouse** Northern Territory, N Australia 15°37′S 131°07′E
15 Q11 **Victoriaville** Québec, SE Canada 46°04′N 71°57′W
Victoria-Wes *see* Victoria West
83 G24 **Victoria West** *Afr.* Victoria-Wes. Northern Cape, W South Africa 31°25′S 23°08′E
62 J13 **Victorica** La Pampa, C Argentina 36°15′S 65°25′W
Victor, Mount *see* Dronning Fabiolafjella
35 U14 **Victorville** California, W USA 34°32′N 117°17′W
62 G9 **Vicuña** Coquimbo, N Chile 30°00′S 70°44′W
62 K11 **Vicuña Mackenna** Córdoba, C Argentina 33°53′S 64°25′W
Vicus Ausonensis *see* Vic
Vicus Elbii *see* Viterbo
33 X7 **Vida** Montana, NW USA 47°52′N 105°30′W
23 V6 **Vidalia** Georgia, SE USA 32°13′N 82°24′W
22 J7 **Vidalia** Louisiana, S USA 31°34′N 91°25′W
95 F22 **Videbæk** Midtjylland, C Denmark 56°08′N 08°38′E
60 I13 **Videira** Santa Catarina, S Brazil 27°00′S 51°08′W
116 J14 **Videle** Teleorman, S Romania 44°15′N 25°27′E
Videm-Krško *see* Krško
Vídeň *see* Wien
104 H12 **Vidigueira** Beja, S Portugal 38°12′N 07°48′W
114 J9 **Vidima** ≈ N Bulgaria
114 G7 **Vidin** *anc.* Bononia. Vidin, NW Bulgaria 44°00′N 22°52′E
114 F8 **Vidin** ◐ *province* NW Bulgaria
154 H10 **Vidisha** Madhya Pradesh, C India 23°30′N 77°50′E
25 Y10 **Vidor** Texas, SW USA 30°07′N 94°01′W
95 L20 **Vidöstern** ◎ S Sweden
92 J13 **Vidsel** Norrbotten, N Sweden 65°49′N 20°31′E
118 H9 **Vidzemes Augstiene** ▲▲ C Latvia
118 J12 **Vidzy** Vitsyebskaya Voblasts', NW Belarus 55°24′N 26°38′E
63 L16 **Viedma** Río Negro, E Argentina 40°50′S 62°58′W
63 H22 **Viedma, Lago** ◎ S Argentina
45 O11 **Vieille Case** *var.* Itassi. N Dominica 15°36′N 61°24′W
104 M2 **Vieja, Peña** ▲ N Spain 43°09′N 04°47′W
24 J10 **Vieja, Sierra** ▲▲ Texas, SW USA
40 E4 **Viejo, Cerro** ▲ NW Mexico 30°16′N 112°18′W
56 B9 **Viejo, Cerro** ▲ N Peru 04°54′S 79°24′W
118 E10 **Viekšniai** Telšiai, NW Lithuania 56°14′N 22°33′E
105 U3 **Vielha** *var.* Viella. Cataluña, NE Spain 42°41′N 00°47′E
Viella *see* Vielha
99 L21 **Vielsalm** Luxembourg, E Belgium 50°17′N 05°55′E
Vieng Pou Kha *see* Viangphoukha
23 T6 **Vienna** Georgia, SE USA 32°05′N 83°48′W
30 L17 **Vienna** Illinois, N USA 37°24′N 88°55′W
27 V5 **Vienna** Missouri, C USA 38°12′N 91°59′W
21 Q3 **Vienna** West Virginia, NE USA 39°19′N 81°33′W
Vienna *see* Wien, Austria
Vienna *see* Vienne, France
103 R11 **Vienne** *anc.* Vienna. Isère, E France 45°32′N 04°53′E
102 L10 **Vienne** ◐ *department* W France
102 L9 **Vienne** ≈ W France
Vientiane *see* Viangchan
Vientos, Paso de los *see* Windward Passage
45 V6 **Vieques** *var.* Isabel Segunda. E Puerto Rico 18°08′N 65°25′W
45 V6 **Vieques, Isla de** *island* E Puerto Rico
45 V6 **Vieques, Pasaje de** *passage* E Puerto Rico
45 V5 **Vieques, Sonda de** *sound* E Puerto Rico
Vierdörfer *see* Săcele
93 M15 **Vieremä** Itä-Suomi, C Finland 63°42′N 27°02′E
99 M14 **Vierlingsbeek** Noord-Brabant, SE Netherlands 51°36′N 06°01′E
101 G20 **Viernheim** Hessen, W Germany 49°32′N 08°35′E
101 D15 **Viersen** Nordrhein-Westfalen, W Germany 51°16′N 06°24′E
108 G8 **Vierwaldstätter See** *Eng.* Lake of Lucerne. ◎ C Switzerland
103 N8 **Vierzon** Cher, C France 47°13′N 02°04′E
40 L8 **Viesca** Coahuila, NE Mexico 25°25′N 102°45′W
118 H10 **Viesīte** *Ger.* Eckengraf. S Latvia 56°21′N 25°30′E
107 N15 **Vieste** Puglia, SE Italy 41°52′N 16°11′E
167 T8 **Vietnam** *off.* Socialist Republic of Vietnam, *Vtn.* Công Hoa Xa Hôi Chu Nghia Viêt Nam. ◆ *republic* SE Asia
Vietnam, Socialist Republic of *see* Vietnam
167 S5 **Việt Quang** Ha Giang, N Vietnam 22°24′N 104°48′E
Vietri *see* Viêt Tri
167 S6 **Viêt Tri** *var.* Vietri. Vinh Phu, N Vietnam 21°20′N 105°26′E
30 L4 **Vieux Desert, Lac** ◎ Michigan/Wisconsin, N USA
45 Y13 **Vieux Fort** S Saint Lucia 13°43′N 60°57′W
45 X6 **Vieux-Habitants** Basse Terre, SW Guadeloupe 16°04′N 61°45′W
119 G14 **Vievis** Vilnius, S Lithuania 54°46′N 24°51′E
171 N2 **Vigan** Luzon, N Philippines 17°34′N 102°21′E
106 D8 **Vigevano** Lombardia, N Italy 45°19′N 08°51′E
107 N18 **Viggiano** Basilicata, S Italy 40°21′N 15°54′E
58 L12 **Vigia** Pará, NE Brazil 0°50′S 48°07′W
41 Y12 **Vigía Chico** Quintana Roo, SE Mexico 19°49′N 87°31′W
45 T11 **Vigie** *prev.* George F L Charles. ✈ (Castries) NE Saint Lucia 14°01′N 60°59′W
102 K17 **Vignemale** *var.* Pic de Vignemale. ▲ France/Spain 42°48′N 00°06′W
Vignemale, Pic de *see* Vignemale
106 G10 **Vignola** Emilia-Romagna, C Italy 44°28′N 11°00′E
104 G4 **Vigo** Galicia, NW Spain 42°15′N 08°44′W
104 G4 **Vigo, Ría de** *estuary* NW Spain
94 D9 **Vigra** *island* S Norway
95 C17 **Vigrestad** Rogaland, S Norway 58°34′N 05°42′E
93 L15 **Vihanti** Oulu, C Finland 64°29′N 25°E
149 U10 **Vihāri** Punjab, E Pakistan 30°03′N 72°32′E
102 K8 **Vihiers** Maine-et-Loire, NW France 47°09′N 00°37′W
111 O19 **Vihorlat** ▲ E Slovakia 48°54′N 22°09′E
93 L19 **Vihti** Etelä-Suomi, S Finland 60°25′N 24°16′E
Viipuri *see* Vyborg
93 M16 **Viitasaari** Länsi-Suomi, C Finland 63°05′N 25°52′E
118 K3 **Viivikonna** Ida-Virumaa, NE Estonia 59°19′N 27°41′E
155 K16 **Vijayawāda** *prev.* Bezwada. Andhra Pradesh, SE India 16°34′N 80°40′E
Vijosa/Vijosë *see* Aóos, Albania/Greece
Vijosa/Vijosë *see* Vjosës, Lumi i, Albania/Greece
92 J4 **Vík** Sudhurland, S Iceland 63°25′N 18°58′W
Vik *see* Vikøyri
94 L13 **Vika** Dalarna, C Sweden 60°55′N 14°30′E
92 L12 **Vikajärvi** Lappi, N Finland 66°37′N 26°10′E
94 L13 **Vikarbyn** Dalarna, C Sweden 60°57′N 15°00′E
95 J22 **Viken** Skåne, S Sweden 56°09′N 12°36′E
95 L17 **Viken** ◎ C Sweden
95 G15 **Vikersund** Buskerud, S Norway 59°58′N 09°59′E
114 G11 **Vikhren** ▲ SW Bulgaria 41°45′N 23°24′E
11 R15 **Viking** Alberta, SW Canada 53°07′N 111°50′W
84 E7 **Viking Bank** *undersea feature* N North Sea 60°35′N 02°35′E
95 M14 **Vikmanshyttan** Dalarna, C Sweden 60°19′N 15°55′E
94 D12 **Vikøyri** *var.* Vik. Sogn Og Fjordane, S Norway 61°04′N 06°34′E
93 H17 **Viksjö** Västernorrland, C Sweden 62°45′N 17°30′E
Viktoriastadt *see* Victoria
Vila *see* Port-Vila
Vila Arriaga *see* Bibala
Vila Artur de Paiva *see* Cubango
Vila Baleira *see* Porto Santo
Vila Bela da Santissima Trindade *see* Mato Grosso
58 B12 **Vila Bittencourt** Amazonas, NW Brazil 01°25′S 69°24′W
Vila da Ponte *see* Cubango
64 O2 **Vila da Praia da Vitória** Terceira, Azores, Portugal, NE Atlantic Ocean 38°44′N 27°04′W
Vila de Aljustrel *see* Cangamba
Vila de Almoster *see* Chiange
Vila de João Belo *see* Xai-Xai
Vila de Macia *see* Macia
Vila de Manhiça *see* Manhiça
Vila de Manica *see* Manica
Vila de Mocímboa da Praia *see* Mocímboa da Praia
83 N16 **Vila de Sena** *var.* Sena. Sofala, C Mozambique 17°25′S 34°59′E
104 F14 **Vila do Bispo** Faro, S Portugal 37°05′N 08°53′W
104 G6 **Vila do Conde** Porto, NW Portugal 41°21′N 08°45′W
Vila do Maio *see* Maio
64 P3 **Vila do Porto** Santa Maria, Azores, Portugal, NE Atlantic Ocean 36°57′N 25°10′W
83 K15 **Vila do Zumbo** *prev.* Vila do Zumbu, Zumbo. Tete, NW Mozambique 15°36′S 30°30′E
Vila do Zumbu *see* Vila do Zumbo
105 T8 **Vilafamés** *prev.* Villafamés. Valenciana, E Spain 40°07′N 00°03′W
104 I6 **Vila Flor** *var.* Vila Flôr. Bragança, N Portugal 41°18′N 07°09′W
105 V6 **Vilafranca del Penedès** *var.* Villafranca del Panadés. Cataluña, NE Spain 41°21′N 01°42′E
104 F10 **Vila Franca de Xira** *var.* Vilafranca de Xira. Lisboa, C Portugal 38°57′N 08°59′W
Vila Gago Coutinho *see* Lumbala N'Guimbo
104 G3 **Vilagarcía** *var.* Villagarcía de Arosa. Galicia, NW Spain 42°35′N 08°45′W
Vila General Machado *see* Camacupa
Vila Henrique de Carvalho *see* Saurimo
102 I7 **Vilaine** ≈ NW France
Vila João de Almeida *see* Chibia
118 K8 **Viļaka** *Ger.* Marienhausen. NE Latvia 57°12′N 27°43′E
104 I2 **Vilalba** Galicia, NW Spain 43°17′N 07°41′W
Vila Marechal Carmona *see* Uíge
Vila Mariano Machado *see* Ganda
172 G3 **Vilanandro, Tanjona** *prev./Fr.* Cap Saint-André. *headland* W Madagascar 16°10′S 44°27′E
Vilanculos *see* Vilankulo
118 J10 **Viļāni** E Latvia 56°33′N 26°55′E
83 N19 **Vilankulo** *var.* Vilanculos. Inhambane, E Mozambique 22°01′S 35°19′E
Vila Norton de Matos *see* Balombo
104 G6 **Vila Nova de Famalicão** *var.* Vila Nova de Famalicao. Braga, N Portugal 41°24′N 08°31′W
104 I6 **Vila Nova de Foz Côa** *var.* Vila Nova de Fozcôa. Guarda, N Portugal 41°05′N 07°09′W
Vila Nova de Fozcôa *see* Vila Nova de Foz Côa
104 F6 **Vila Nova de Gaia** Porto, NW Portugal 41°08′N 08°37′W
Vila Nova de Portimão *see* Portimão
105 V6 **Vilanova i La Geltru** Cataluña, NE Spain 41°15′N 01°42′E
Vila Pereira de Eça *see* N'Giva
104 H6 **Vila Pouca de Aguiar** Vila Real, N Portugal 41°30′N 07°38′W
104 H6 **Vila Real** *var.* Vila Rial. Vila Real, N Portugal 41°17′N 07°45′W
105 T9 **Vila-real** *var.* Vila-real de los Infantes; *prev.* Villarreal. Valenciana, E Spain 39°56′N 00°08′W
104 H6 **Vila Real** ◐ *district* N Portugal
Vila-real de los Infantes *see* Vila-real
104 H14 **Vila Real de Santo António** Faro, S Portugal 37°12′N 07°25′W
104 J7 **Vilar Formoso** Guarda, N Portugal 40°37′N 06°50′W
Vila Rial *see* Vila Real
59 J15 **Vila Rica** Mato Grosso, W Brazil 09°52′S 50°44′W
Vila Robert Williams *see* Caála
Vila Salazar *see* N'Dalatando
Vila Serpa Pinto *see* Menongue
Vila Teixeira da Silva *see* Bailundo
Vila Teixeira de Sousa *see* Luau
104 H9 **Vila Velha de Ródão** Castelo Branco, C Portugal 39°39′N 07°40′W
104 G5 **Vila Verde** Braga, N Portugal 41°39′N 08°27′W
104 H11 **Vila Viçosa** Évora, S Portugal 38°46′N 07°25′W
57 G15 **Vilcabamba, Cordillera de** ▲▲ C Peru
Vîlcea *see* Vâlcea
122 J4 **Vil'cheka, Zemlya** *Eng.* Wilczek Land. *island* Zemlya Frantsa-Iosifa, NW Russian Federation
95 F22 **Vildbjerg** Midtjylland, C Denmark 56°12′N 08°47′E
Vileyka *see* Vilyeyka
93 H15 **Vilhelmina** Västerbotten, N Sweden 64°38′N 16°40′E
59 F17 **Vilhena** Rondônia, W Brazil 12°40′S 60°08′W
115 G19 **Vília** Attikí, C Greece 38°09′N 23°21′E
119 I14 **Viliya** *Lith.* Neris. ≈ W Belarus
Viliya *see* Neris
118 H5 **Viljandi** *Ger.* Fellin. Viljandimaa, S Estonia 58°22′N 25°30′E
118 H5 **Viljandimaa** *var.* Viljandi Maakond. ◐ *province* SW Estonia
Viljandi Maakond *see* Viljandimaa
119 E14 **Vilkaviškis** *Pol.* Wyłkowyszki. Marijampolė, SW Lithuania 54°39′N 23°03′E
118 F13 **Vilkija** Kaunas, C Lithuania 55°02′N 23°36′E
197 V9 **Vil'kitskogo, Proliv** *strait* N Russian Federation
Vilkovo *see* Vylkove
57 L21 **Villa Abecia** Chuquisaca, S Bolivia 21°00′S 65°18′W
41 N5 **Villa Acuña** *var.* Ciudad Acuña. Coahuila, NE Mexico 29°18′N 100°58′W
40 J4 **Villa Ahumada** Chihuahua, N Mexico 30°38′N 106°30′W
45 O9 **Villa Altagracia** C Dominican Republic 18°43′N 70°13′W
56 L13 **Villa Bella** El Beni, N Bolivia 10°21′S 65°25′W
104 J3 **Villablino** Castilla y León, N Spain 42°55′N 06°21′W
54 K6 **Villa Bruzual** Portuguesa, N Venezuela 09°20′N 69°06′W
105 O9 **Villacañas** Castilla-La Mancha, C Spain 39°38′N 03°20′W
105 O12 **Villacarrillo** Andalucía, S Spain 38°07′N 03°05′W
104 M7 **Villacastín** Castilla y León, N Spain 40°46′N 04°25′W
Villa Cecilia *see* Ciudad Madero
109 S9 **Villach** *Slvn.* Beljak. Kärnten, S Austria 46°36′N 13°49′E
107 B20 **Villacidro** Sardegna, Italy, C Mediterranean Sea 39°28′N 08°43′E
Villa Concepción *see* Concepción
104 L4 **Villada** Castilla y León, N Spain 42°15′N 04°59′W
40 M10 **Villa de Cos** Zacatecas, C Mexico 23°20′N 102°20′W
54 L5 **Villa de Cura** *var.* Cura. Aragua, N Venezuela 10°00′N 67°30′W
Villa del Nevoso *see* Ilirska Bistrica
Villa del Pilar *see* Pilar
104 M13 **Villa del Río** Andalucía, S Spain 37°59′N 04°17′W
Villa de Méndez *see* Méndez
42 H6 **Villa de San Antonio** Comayagua, W Honduras 14°24′N 87°37′W
105 N4 **Villadiego** Castilla y León, N Spain 42°31′N 04°01′W
Villafamés *see* Vilafamés
41 U16 **Villa Flores** Chiapas, SE Mexico 16°12′N 93°16′W
104 J3 **Villafranca del Bierzo** Castilla y León, N Spain 42°36′N 06°49′W
105 S8 **Villafranca del Cid** Valenciana, E Spain 40°25′N 00°15′W
104 J11 **Villafranca de los Barros** Extremadura, W Spain 38°34′N 06°20′W
105 N10 **Villafranca de los Caballeros** Castilla-La Mancha, C Spain 39°26′N 03°21′W
Villafranca del Panadés *see* Vilafranca del Penedès
106 F8 **Villafranca di Verona** Veneto, NE Italy 45°22′N 10°51′E
107 J23 **Villafrati** Sicilia, Italy, C Mediterranean Sea 37°53′N 13°30′E
Villagarcía de Arosa *see* Vilagarcía
41 O9 **Villagrán** Tamaulipas, C Mexico 24°29′N 99°30′W
61 C17 **Villaguay** Entre Ríos, E Argentina 31°55′S 59°01′W
62 O6 **Villa Hayes** Presidente Hayes, S Paraguay 25°05′S 57°25′W
41 U15 **Villahermosa** *prev.* San Juan Bautista. Tabasco, SE Mexico 17°56′N 92°50′W
105 O11 **Villahermosa** Castilla-La Mancha, C Spain 38°46′N 02°52′W
64 O11 **Villahermoso** Gomera, Islas Canarias, Spain, NE Atlantic Ocean 38°46′N 02°52′W
Villa Hidalgo *see* Hidalgo
105 T12 **Villajoyosa** *Cat.* La Vila Joíosa. Valenciana, E Spain 38°31′N 00°14′W
Villa Juárez *see* Juárez
Villalba *see* Collado Villalba
41 N8 **Villaldama** Nuevo León, NE Mexico 26°29′N 100°27′W
104 L5 **Villalón de Campos** Castilla y León, N Spain 42°05′N 05°03′W
61 A25 **Villalonga** Buenos Aires, E Argentina 39°55′S 62°35′W
104 L5 **Villalpando** Castilla y León, N Spain 41°51′N 05°25′W
40 K9 **Villa Madero** *var.* Francisco I. Madero. Durango, C Mexico 24°28′N 104°20′W
41 O9 **Villa Mainero** Tamaulipas, C Mexico 24°32′N 99°39′W
Villamaña *see* Villamañán
104 L4 **Villamañán** *var.* Villamaña. Castilla y León, N Spain 42°19′N 05°35′W
62 L10 **Villa María** Córdoba, C Argentina 32°23′S 63°15′W
61 C17 **Villa María Grande** Entre Ríos, E Argentina 31°39′S 59°54′W
57 K21 **Villa Martín** Potosí, SW Bolivia 20°46′S 67°45′W
104 K15 **Villamartin** Andalucía, S Spain 36°52′N 05°38′W
62 J8 **Villa Mazán** La Rioja, NW Argentina 28°43′S 66°25′W
62 J11 **Villa Mercedes** *var.* Mercedes. San Luis, C Argentina 33°40′S 65°25′W
Villamil *see* Puerto Villamil
Villa Nador *see* Nador
54 G5 **Villanueva** La Guajira, N Colombia 10°37′N 72°58′W
42 H5 **Villanueva** Cortés, NW Honduras 15°14′N 88°00′W
40 L11 **Villanueva** Zacatecas, C Mexico 22°24′N 102°53′W
42 I9 **Villa Nueva** Chinandega, NW Nicaragua 12°58′N 86°46′W
37 T11 **Villanueva** New Mexico, SW USA 35°18′N 105°20′W
104 M12 **Villanueva de Córdoba** Andalucía, S Spain 38°20′N 04°38′W
105 O12 **Villanueva del Arzobispo** Andalucía, S Spain 38°10′N 03°00′W
104 K11 **Villanueva de la Serena** Extremadura, W Spain 38°58′N 05°48′W
104 L5 **Villanueva del Campo** Castilla y León, N Spain 41°59′N 05°25′W
105 O11 **Villanueva de los Infantes** Castilla-La Mancha, C Spain 38°45′N 03°01′W
61 C14 **Villa Ocampo** Santa Fe, C Argentina 28°28′S 59°22′W
40 J8 **Villa Ocampo** Durango, C Mexico 26°29′N 105°30′W
40 J7 **Villa Orestes Pereyra** Durango, C Mexico 26°30′N 105°38′W
105 N3 **Villarcayo** Castilla y León, N Spain 42°56′N 03°34′W
104 L5 **Villardefrades** Castilla y León, N Spain 41°43′N 05°15′W
105 S9 **Villar del Arzobispo** Valenciana, E Spain 39°44′N 00°50′W
105 Q6 **Villaroya de la Sierra** Aragón, NE Spain 41°28′N 01°46′W
Villarreal *see* Vila-real
62 P6 **Villarrica** Guairá, SE Paraguay 25°45′S 56°28′W
63 G15 **Villarrica, Volcán** ⛰ S Chile 39°28′S 71°57′W
105 P10 **Villarrobledo** Castilla-La Mancha, C Spain 39°16′N 02°36′W
105 N10 **Villarrubia de los Ojos** Castilla-La Mancha, C Spain 39°14′N 03°36′W
18 J17 **Villas** New Jersey, NE USA 39°01′N 74°54′W
105 O3 **Villasana de Mena** Castilla y León, N Spain 43°05′N 03°16′W
107 M23 **Villa San Giovanni** Calabria, S Italy 38°12′N 15°39′E
61 D18 **Villa San José** Entre Ríos, E Argentina 32°01′S 58°20′W
Villa Sanjurjo *see* Al-Hoceïma
105 P6 **Villasayas** Castilla y León, N Spain 41°19′N 02°36′W
107 C20 **Villasimius** Sardegna, Italy, C Mediterranean Sea 39°10′N 09°30′E
41 N6 **Villa Unión** Coahuila, NE Mexico 28°18′N 100°43′W
40 K10 **Villa Unión** Durango, C Mexico 23°59′N 104°01′W
40 J10 **Villa Unión** Sinaloa, C Mexico 23°10′N 106°12′W
62 K12 **Villa Valeria** Córdoba, C Argentina 34°21′S 64°56′W
105 N8 **Villaverde** Madrid, C Spain 40°21′N 03°43′W
54 F10 **Villavicencio** Meta, C Colombia 04°09′N 73°38′W
104 L2 **Villaviciosa** Asturias, N Spain 43°29′N 05°26′W
104 L12 **Villaviciosa de Córdoba** Andalucía, S Spain 38°04′N 05°00′W
57 L22 **Villazón** Potosí, S Bolivia 22°05′S 65°35′W
14 J8 **Villebon, Lac** ◎ Québec, SE Canada
Ville de Kinshasa *see* Kinshasa
102 J5 **Villedieu-les-Poêles** Manche, N France 48°51′N 01°12′W
Villefranche *see* Villefranche-sur-Saône
103 N16 **Villefranche-de-Lauragais** Haute-Garonne, S France 43°24′N 01°42′E
103 N14 **Villefranche-de-Rouergue** Aveyron, S France 44°21′N 02°02′E

◆ Country
● Country Capital
◇ Dependent Territory
○ Dependent Territory Capital
◐ Administrative Regions
✈ International Airport
▲ Mountain
▲▲ Mountain Range
⛰ Volcano
≈ River
◎ Lake
⊠ Reservoir

103 R10 **Villefranche-sur-Saône** *var.* Villefranche. Rhône, E France 46°00′N 04°40′E
14 H9 **Ville-Marie** Québec, SE Canada 47°21′N 79°26′W
102 M15 **Villemur-sur-Tarn** Haute-Garonne, S France 43°50′N 01°32′E
105 S11 **Villena** Valenciana, E Spain 38°39′N 00°52′W
Villeneuve-d'Agen *see* Villeneuve-sur-Lot
102 L13 **Villeneuve-sur-Lot** *var.* Villeneuve-d'Agen, *hist.* Gajac. Lot-et-Garonne, SW France 44°24′N 00°43′E
103 P6 **Villeneuve-sur-Yonne** Yonne, C France 48°04′N 03°21′E
22 H8 **Ville Platte** Louisiana, S USA 30°41′N 92°16′W
103 R11 **Villeurbanne** Rhône, E France 45°46′N 04°54′E
101 G23 **Villingen-Schwenningen** Baden-Württemberg, S Germany 48°04′N 08°27′E
29 T15 **Villisca** Iowa, C USA 40°55′N 94°58′W
Villmanstrand *see* Lappeenranta
Vilna *see* Vilnius
119 H14 **Vilnius** *Pol.* Wilno, *Ger.* Wilna; *prev. Rus.* Vilna. ● (Lithuania) Vilnius, SE Lithuania 54°41′N 25°20′E
119 H14 **Vilnius** ✕ Vilnius, SE Lithuania 54°33′N 25°17′E
117 S7 **Vil'nohirs'k** Dnipropetrovs'ka Oblast', E Ukraine 48°31′N 34°01′E
117 U8 **Vil'nyans'k** Zaporiz'ka Oblast', SE Ukraine 47°56′N 35°22′E
93 L17 **Vilppula** Länsi-Suomi, W Finland 62°02′N 24°30′E
101 M20 **Vils** ≈ SE Germany
118 C5 **Vilsandi** *island* W Estonia
117 P8 **Vil'shanka** *Rus.* Olshanka. Kirovohrads'ka Oblast', C Ukraine 48°12′N 30°54′E
101 O22 **Vilshofen** Bayern, SE Germany 48°36′N 13°10′E
155 J20 **Viluppuram** Tamil Nādu, SE India 12°54′N 79°40′E
113 J16 **Vilusi** W Montenegro 42°44′N 18°34′E
99 G18 **Vilvoorde** *Fr.* Vilvorde. Vlaams Brabant, C Belgium 50°56′N 04°25′E
Vilvorde *see* Vilvoorde
119 J14 **Vilyeyka** *Pol.* Wilejka, *Rus.* Vileyka. Minskaya Voblasts', NW Belarus 54°30′N 26°55′E
122 V11 **Vilyuchinsk** Kamchatskiy Kray, E Russian Federation 52°55′N 158°28′E
123 P10 **Vilyuy** ≈ NE Russian Federation
123 P10 **Vilyuysk** Respublika Sakha (Yakutiya), NE Russian Federation 63°42′N 121°20′E
123 N10 **Vilyuyskoye Vodokhranilishche** ⊞ NE Russian Federation
104 G2 **Vimianzo** Galicia, NW Spain 43°06′N 09°03′W
95 M19 **Vimmerby** Kalmar, S Sweden 57°40′N 15°50′E
102 L5 **Vimoutiers** Orne, N France 48°56′N 00°10′E
93 L16 **Vimpeli** Länsi-Suomi, W Finland 63°10′N 23°50′E
79 G14 **Vina** ≈ Cameroon/Chad
62 G11 **Viña del Mar** Valparaíso, C Chile 33°02′S 71°35′W
19 R8 **Vinalhaven Island** *island* Maine, NE USA
105 T8 **Vinaròs** Valenciana, E Spain 40°29′N 00°28′E
Vînători *see* Vânători
31 N15 **Vincennes** Indiana, N USA 38°42′N 87°30′W
195 Y12 **Vincennes Bay** *bay* Antarctica
25 O7 **Vincent** Texas, SW USA 32°30′N 101°10′W
95 H24 **Vindeby** Syddtjylland, C Denmark 54°55′N 11°09′E
93 I15 **Vindeln** Västerbotten, N Sweden 64°11′N 19°45′E
95 F21 **Vinderup** Midtjylland, C Denmark 56°29′N 08°48′E
Vindhya Mountains *see* Vindhya Range
153 N14 **Vindhya Range** *var.* Vindhya Mountains. ▲▲ N India
Vindobona *see* Wien
20 K6 **Vine Grove** Kentucky, S USA 37°48′N 85°58′W
18 J17 **Vineland** New Jersey, NE USA 39°29′N 75°02′W
116 E11 **Vinga** Arad, W Romania 46°00′N 21°14′E
95 M16 **Vingåker** Södermanland, C Sweden 59°02′N 15°52′E
167 S8 **Vinh** Nghê An, N Vietnam 18°42′N 105°41′E
104 I5 **Vinhais** Bragança, N Portugal 41°50′N 07°00′W
Vinh Linh *see* Hô Xa
Vinh Loi *see* Bac Liêu
167 S14 **Vinh Long** *var.* Vinhlong. Vinh Long, S Vietnam 10°15′N 105°59′E
Vinhlong *see* Vinh Long
113 Q18 **Vinica** NE FYR Macedonia 41°53′N 22°30′E
109 V13 **Vinica** SE Slovenia 45°28′N 15°12′E
114 G8 **Vinishte** Montana, NW Bulgaria 43°30′N 23°04′E
27 Q8 **Vinita** Oklahoma, C USA 36°38′N 95°09′W
Vinju Mare *see* Vânju Mare
98 I11 **Vinkeveen** Utrecht, C Netherlands 52°13′N 04°55′E
116 L6 **Vin'kivtsi** Khmel'nyts'ka Oblast', W Ukraine 49°02′N 27°13′E
112 I10 **Vinkovci** *Ger.* Winkowitz, *Hung.* Vinkovcze. Vukovar-Srijem, E Croatia 45°18′N 18°45′E
Vinkovcze *see* Vinkovci
Vinnitsa *see* Vinnytsya
Vinnitskaya Oblast'/Vinnytsya *see* Vinnyts'ka Oblast'
116 M7 **Vinnyts'ka Oblast'** *var.* Vinnytsya, *Rus.* Vinnitskaya Oblast'. ◈ *province* C Ukraine
117 N6 **Vinnytsya** *Rus.* Vinnitsa. Vinnyts'ka Oblast', C Ukraine 49°14′N 28°30′E
117 N6 **Vinnytsya** ✕ Vinnyts'ka Oblast', N Ukraine 49°13′N 28°40′E
Vinogradov *see* Vynohradiv
194 L8 **Vinson Massif** ▲ Antarctica 78°45′S 85°19′W
94 G11 **Vinstra** Oppland, S Norway 61°36′N 09°45′E
116 K12 **Vintilă Vodă** Buzău, SE Romania 45°28′N 26°43′E
29 X13 **Vinton** Iowa, C USA 42°10′N 92°01′W
22 F9 **Vinton** Louisiana, S USA 30°10′N 93°37′W
155 J17 **Vinukonda** Andhra Pradesh, E India 16°03′N 79°41′E
Vioara *see* Ocnele Mari
83 E23 **Vioolsdrif** Northern Cape, SW South Africa 28°50′S 17°38′E
82 M13 **Viphya Mountains** ▲▲ C Malawi
171 Q4 **Virac** Catanduanes Island, N Philippines 13°39′N 124°17′E
124 K8 **Virandozero** Respublika Kareliya, NW Russian Federation 63°59′N 36°00′E
137 P16 **Viranşehir** Şanlıurfa, SE Turkey 37°13′N 39°32′E
154 D13 **Virār** Mahārāshtra, W India 19°30′N 72°48′E
11 W16 **Virden** Manitoba, S Canada 49°50′N 100°57′W
30 K14 **Virden** Illinois, N USA 39°30′N 89°46′W
Virdois *see* Virrat
102 J5 **Vire** Calvados, N France 48°50′N 00°53′W
102 J4 **Vire** ≈ N France
83 A15 **Virei** Namibe, SW Angola 15°43′S 12°54′E
Vîrful Moldoveanu *see* Vârful Moldoveanu
35 R5 **Virginia Peak** ▲ Nevada, W USA 39°46′N 119°26′W
45 U9 **Virgin Gorda** *island* C British Virgin Islands
83 I22 **Virginia** Free State, C South Africa 28°06′S 26°53′E
30 K13 **Virginia** Illinois, N USA 39°57′N 90°12′W
29 W4 **Virginia** Minnesota, N USA 47°31′N 92°32′W
21 T6 **Virginia** *off.* Commonwealth of Virginia, *also known as* Mother of Presidents, Mother of States, Old Dominion. ◈ *state* NE USA
21 Y7 **Virginia Beach** Virginia, NE USA 36°51′N 75°59′W
33 R11 **Virginia City** Montana, NW USA 45°17′N 111°54′W
35 Q6 **Virginia City** Nevada, W USA 39°19′N 119°39′W
14 H8 **Virginiatown** Ontario, S Canada 48°09′N 79°35′W
Virgin Islands *see* British Virgin Islands
45 T9 **Virgin Islands (US)** *var.* Virgin Islands of the United States; *prev.* Danish West Indies. ◇ *US unincorporated territory* E West Indies
Virgin Islands of the United States *see* Virgin Islands (US)
45 T9 **Virgin Passage** *passage* Puerto Rico/Virgin Islands (US)
35 Y10 **Virgin River** ≈ Nevada/Utah, W USA
Virihaur *see* Virihaure
92 H12 **Virihaure** *Lapp.* Virihávrre, *var.* Virihaur. ◎ N Sweden
Virihávrre *see* Virihaure
167 T11 **Virôchey** Rôtânôkiri, NE Cambodia 13°59′N 106°49′E
93 N19 **Virolahti** Etelä-Suomi, S Finland 60°33′N 27°37′E
30 J8 **Viroqua** Wisconsin, N USA 43°33′N 90°54′W
112 G8 **Virovitica** *Ger.* Virovititz, *Hung.* Verőcze; *prev. Ger.* Werowitz. Virovitica-Podravina, NE Croatia 45°49′N 17°25′E
112 G8 **Virovitica-Podravina** *off.* Virovitičko-Podravska Županija. ◈ *province* NE Croatia
Virovitičko-Podravska Županija *see* Virovitica-Podravina
Virovititz *see* Virovitica
113 J17 **Virpazar** S Montenegro 42°15′N 19°06′E
93 L17 **Virrat** *Swe.* Virdois. Länsi-Suomi, W Finland 62°14′N 23°50′E
95 M20 **Virserum** Kalmar, S Sweden 57°17′N 15°18′E
99 K25 **Virton** Luxembourg, SE Belgium 49°34′N 05°32′E
118 F5 **Virtsu** *Ger.* Werder. Läänemaa, W Estonia 58°35′N 23°33′E
56 C12 **Virú** La Libertad, C Peru 08°24′S 78°40′W
Virudhunagar *see* Virudunagar
155 H23 **Virudunagar** *var.* Virudhunagar; *prev.* Virudupatti. Tamil Nādu, SE India 09°35′N 77°57′E
Virudupatti *see* Virudunagar
118 I3 **Viru-Jaagupi** *Ger.* Sankt-Jakobi. Lääne-Virumaa, NE Estonia 59°14′N 26°29′E
57 N19 **Viru-Viru** *var.* Santa Cruz. ✕ (Santa Cruz) Santa Cruz, C Bolivia 17°49′S 63°12′W
113 E15 **Vis** *It.* Lissa; *anc.* Issa. *island* S Croatia
Vis *see* Fish
118 I12 **Visaginas** *prev.* Sniečkus. Utena, E Lithuania 55°36′N 26°22′E
155 M15 **Visākhapatnam** *var.* Vishakhapatnam. Andhra Pradesh, SE India 17°45′N 83°19′E
35 R11 **Visalia** California, W USA 36°19′N 119°19′W
Višāu *see* Vișeu
95 P19 **Visby** *Ger.* Wisby. Gotland, SE Sweden 57°37′N 18°20′E
197 N9 **Viscount Melville Sound** *prev.* Melville Sound. *sound* Northwest Territories, N Canada
99 L19 **Visé** Liège, E Belgium 50°44′N 05°42′E
112 K13 **Višegrad** Republika Srpska, SE Bosnia and Herzegovina 43°46′N 19°18′E
58 L12 **Viseu** Pará, NE Brazil 01°10′S 46°09′W
104 H7 **Viseu** *prev.* Vizeu. Viseu, N Portugal 40°40′N 07°55′W
104 H7 **Viseu** *var.* Vizeu. ◈ *district* N Portugal
116 I8 **Vișeu** *Hung.* Visó; *prev.* Vișău. ≈ NW Romania
116 I8 **Vișeu de Sus** *var.* Vișeul de Sus, *Ger.* Oberwischau, *Hung.* Felsővisó. Maramureș, N Romania 47°43′N 23°24′E
Vișeul de Sus *see* Vișeu de Sus
Vishakhapatnam *see* Visākhapatnam
125 R10 **Vishera** ≈ NW Russian Federation
95 J19 **Viskafors** Västra Götaland, S Sweden 57°37′N 12°50′E
95 J20 **Viskan** ≈ S Sweden
95 L21 **Vislanda** Kronoberg, S Sweden 56°46′N 14°30′E
Vislinskiy Zaliv *see* Vistula Lagoon
Visó *see* Vișeu
112 H13 **Visoko** ◈ Federacija Bosna I Hercegovina, C Bosnia and Herzegovina
106 A9 **Viso, Monte** ▲ NW Italy 44°42′N 07°04′E
108 E10 **Visp** Valais, SW Switzerland 46°18′N 07°53′E
108 E10 **Vispa** ≈ S Switzerland
95 M21 **Vissefjärda** Kalmar, S Sweden 56°31′N 15°34′E
100 I11 **Visselhövede** Niedersachsen, NW Germany 52°58′N 09°36′E
95 G23 **Vissenbjerg** Syddtjylland, C Denmark 55°23′N 10°08′E
35 U17 **Vista** California, W USA 33°12′N 117°14′W
58 C11 **Vista Alegre** Amazonas, NW Brazil 01°23′N 68°13′W
114 J13 **Vistonída, Límni** ◎ NE Greece
Vistula *see* Wisła
119 A14 **Vistula Lagoon** *Ger.* Frisches Haff, *Pol.* Zalew Wiślany, *Rus.* Vislinskiy Zaliv. *lagoon* Poland/Russian Federation
114 I8 **Vit** ≈ NW Bulgaria
Vitebsk *see* Vitsyebsk
Vitebskaya Oblast' *see* Vitsyebskaya Voblasts'
107 H14 **Viterbo** *anc.* Vicus Elbii. Lazio, C Italy 42°25′N 12°08′E
112 H12 **Vitez** Federacija Bosna I Hercegovina, C Bosnia and Herzegovina 44°08′N 17°47′E
167 S14 **Vi Thanh** Cân Thơ, S Vietnam 09°45′N 105°28′E
Viti *see* Fiji
186 E7 **Vitiaz Strait** *strait* NE Papua New Guinea
104 J7 **Vitigudino** Castilla y León, N Spain 41°00′N 06°26′W
175 Q9 **Viti Levu** *island* W Fiji
187 W15 **Viti Levu** *island* W Fiji
123 O11 **Vitim** ≈ C Russian Federation
123 O12 **Vitimskiy** Irkutskaya Oblast', C Russian Federation 58°12′N 113°10′E
109 V2 **Vitis** Niederösterreich, N Austria 48°45′N 15°09′E
59 O20 **Vitória** *state capital* Espírito Santo, SE Brazil 20°19′S 40°21′W
Vitoria *see* Vitoria-Gasteiz
Vitoria Bank *see* Vitória Seamount
59 N18 **Vitória da Conquista** Bahia, E Brazil 14°53′S 40°52′W
105 P3 **Vitoria-Gasteiz** *var.* Vitoria, *Eng.* Vittoria. País Vasco, N Spain 42°51′N 02°40′W
65 J16 **Vitória Seamount** *var.* Victoria Bank, Vitoria Bank. *undersea feature* C Atlantic Ocean 18°48′S 37°24′W
112 F13 **Vitorog** ▲ SW Bosnia and Herzegovina 44°06′N 17°03′E
102 J6 **Vitré** Ille-et-Vilaine, NW France 48°07′N 01°12′W
103 R5 **Vitry-le-François** Marne, N France 48°43′N 04°36′E
114 D13 **Vítsi** *var.* Vítsoi. ▲ N Greece 40°39′N 21°23′E
Vítsoi *see* Vítsi
118 N13 **Vitsyebsk** *Rus.* Vitebsk. Vitsyebskaya Voblasts', NE Belarus 55°11′N 30°10′E
118 K13 **Vitsyebskaya Voblasts'** *prev. Rus.* Vitebskaya Oblast'. ◈ *province* N Belarus
92 J11 **Vittangi** *Lapp.* Vazáš. Norrbotten, N Sweden 67°40′N 21°39′E
103 R8 **Vitteaux** Côte d'Or, C France 47°24′N 04°31′E
103 S6 **Vittel** Vosges, NE France 48°13′N 05°57′E
95 N15 **Vittinge** Västmanland, C Sweden 59°52′N 17°04′E
107 K25 **Vittoria** Sicilia, Italy, C Mediterranean Sea 36°56′N 14°30′E
Vittoria *see* Vitoria-Gasteiz
106 I7 **Vittorio Veneto** Veneto, NE Italy 45°59′N 12°18′E
175 Q7 **Vityaz Trench** *undersea feature* W Pacific Ocean
108 G8 **Vitznau** Luzern, W Switzerland 47°01′N 08°28′E
104 I1 **Viveiro** Galicia, NW Spain 43°39′N 07°35′W
105 S9 **Viver** Valenciana, E Spain 39°55′N 00°36′W
103 Q13 **Viverais, Monts du** ▲▲ C France
122 L9 **Vivi** ≈ N Russian Federation
22 F4 **Vivian** Louisiana, S USA 32°52′N 93°59′W
29 N10 **Vivian** South Dakota, N USA 43°53′N 100°16′W
103 R13 **Viviers** Ardèche, E France 44°31′N 04°40′E
Vivis *see* Vevey
83 K19 **Vivo** Limpopo, NE South Africa 22°58′S 29°13′E
102 L10 **Vivonne** Vienne, W France 46°25′N 00°15′E
Vizakna *see* Ocna Sibiului
105 O2 **Vizcaya** *Basq.* Bizkaia. ◈ *province* País Vasco, N Spain
Vizcaya, Golfo de *see* Biscay, Bay of
136 C10 **Vize** Kırklareli, NW Turkey 41°34′N 27°45′E
122 K4 **Vize, Ostrov** *island* Severnaya Zemlya, N Russian Federation
Vizeu *see* Viseu
155 M15 **Vizianagaram** *var.* Vizianagram. Andhra Pradesh, E India 18°07′N 83°25′E
Vizianagram *see* Vizianagaram
103 S12 **Vizille** Isère, E France 45°05′N 05°46′E
125 R11 **Vizinga** Respublika Komi, NW Russian Federation 61°06′N 50°09′E
116 M13 **Viziru** Brăila, SE Romania 45°00′N 27°43′E
113 K21 **Vjosës, Lumi i** *var.* Vijosa, Vijosë, *Gk.* Aóos. ≈ Albania/Greece *see also* Aóos
Vjosës, Lumi i *see* Aóos
99 H18 **Vlaams Brabant** ◈ *province* C Belgium
99 G18 **Vlaanderen** *Eng.* Flanders, *Fr.* Flandre. *cultural region* Belgium/France
98 G12 **Vlaardingen** Zuid-Holland, SW Netherlands 51°55′N 04°21′E
116 F10 **Vlădeasa, Vârful** *prev.* Vîrful Vlădeasa. ▲ NW Romania 46°45′N 22°46′E
Vlădeasa, Vîrful *see* Vlădeasa, Vârful
113 P16 **Vladičin Han** Serbia, SE Serbia 42°44′N 22°04′E
127 O16 **Vladikavkaz** *prev.* Dzaudzhikau, Ordzhonikidze. Respublika Severnaya Osetiya, SW Russian Federation 42°58′N 44°41′E
126 M3 **Vladimir** Vladimirskaya Oblast', W Russian Federation 56°09′N 40°21′E
Vladimirets *see* Volodymyrets'
144 M7 **Vladimirovka** Kostanay, N Kazakhstan 53°30′N 64°02′E
Vladimirovka *see* Yuzhno-Sakhalinsk
126 L3 **Vladimirskaya Oblast'** ◈ *province* W Russian Federation
126 I3 **Vladimirskiy Tupik** Smolenskaya Oblast', W Russian Federation 55°45′N 33°25′E
Vladimir-Volynskiy *see* Volodymyr-Volyns'kyy
123 Q7 **Vladivostok** Primorskiy Kray, SE Russian Federation 43°09′N 131°53′E
117 U13 **Vladyslavivka** Avtonomna Respublika Krym, S Ukraine 45°09′N 35°25′E
98 P6 **Vlagtwedde** Groningen, NE Netherlands 53°02′N 07°07′E
Vlajna *see* Kukavica
112 J12 **Vlasenica** ◈ Republika Srpska, E Bosnia and Herzegovina
112 G12 **Vlašić** ▲ C Bosnia and Herzegovina 44°18′N 17°40′E
111 D17 **Vlašim** *Ger.* Wlaschim. Středočeský Kraj, C Czech Republic 49°42′N 14°54′E
113 P15 **Vlasotince** Serbia, SE Serbia 42°58′N 22°07′E
123 Q7 **Vlasovo** Respublika Sakha (Yakutiya), NE Russian Federation 70°41′N 134°49′E
98 I11 **Vleuten** Utrecht, C Netherlands 52°07′N 05°01′E
98 I5 **Vlieland** *Fris.* Flylân. *island* Waddeneilanden, N Netherlands
98 I5 **Vliestroom** *strait* NW Netherlands
99 J14 **Vlijmen** Noord-Brabant, S Netherlands 51°42′N 05°14′E
99 E15 **Vlissingen** *Eng.* Flushing, *Fr.* Flessingue. Zeeland, SW Netherlands 51°26′N 03°34′E
Vlodava *see* Włodawa
Vlonë/Vlora *see* Vlorë
113 K22 **Vlorë** *prev.* Vlonë, *It.* Valona, Vlora. Vlorë, SW Albania 40°28′N 19°31′E
113 K22 **Vlorë** ◈ *district* SW Albania
113 K22 **Vlorës, Gjiri i** *var.* Valona Bay. *bay* SW Albania
Vlotslavsk *see* Włocławek
111 C16 **Vltava** *Ger.* Moldau. ≈ W Czech Republic
126 K3 **Vnukovo** ✕ (Moskva) Gorod Moskva, W Russian Federation 55°30′N 36°52′E
146 L11 **Vobkent** *Rus.* Vabkent. Buxoro Viloyati, C Uzbekistan 40°01′N 64°25′E
25 Q9 **Voca** Texas, SW USA 30°58′N 99°09′W
109 R5 **Vöcklabruck** Oberösterreich, NW Austria 48°01′N 13°38′E
112 D13 **Vodice** Šibenik-Knin, S Croatia 43°46′N 15°46′E
124 K10 **Vodlozero, Ozero** ◎ NW Russian Federation
112 A10 **Vodnjan** *It.* Dignano d'Istria. Istra, NW Croatia 44°57′N 13°51′E
125 S9 **Vodnyy** Respublika Komi, NW Russian Federation 63°31′N 53°21′E
145 V15 **Vodokhranilishche Kapshagay** *Kaz.* Qapshagay Böyeni; *prev.* Kapchagayskoye Vodokhranilishche. ⊞ SE Kazakhstan
124 I6 **Vodokhranilishche, Kumskoye** ◎ NW Russian Federation
95 G20 **Vodskov** Nordjylland, N Denmark 57°07′N 10°02′E
92 H4 **Vogar** Sudurnes, SW Iceland 63°58′N 22°20′W
Vogelkop *see* Doberai, Jazirah
77 X15 **Vogel Peak** *prev.* Dimlang. ▲ E Nigeria 08°16′N 11°44′E
101 H17 **Vogelsberg** ▲▲ C Germany
106 D8 **Voghera** Lombardia, N Italy 44°59′N 09°01′E
112 I13 **Vogošća** Federacija Bosna I Hercegovina, SE Bosnia and Herzegovina 43°55′N 18°20′E
101 M17 **Vogtland** *historical region* E Germany
125 V12 **Vogul'skiy Kamen', Gora** ▲ NW Russian Federation 60°10′N 58°41′E
187 P16 **Voh** Province Nord, C New Caledonia 20°57′S 164°41′E
Vohémar *see* Iharaña
172 H8 **Vohimena, Tanjona** *Fr.* Cap Sainte Marie. *headland* S Madagascar 25°20′S 45°06′E
172 J6 **Vohipeno** Fianarantsoa, SE Madagascar 22°21′S 47°51′E
118 H5 **Võhma** *Ger.* Wöchma. Viljandimaa, S Estonia 58°37′N 25°34′E
81 J20 **Voi** Coast, S Kenya 03°23′S 38°35′E
76 K15 **Voinjama** N Liberia 08°25′N 09°42′W
103 S12 **Voiron** Isère, E France 45°22′N 05°35′E
109 V8 **Voitsberg** Steiermark, SE Austria 47°04′N 15°09′E
95 F24 **Vojens** *Ger.* Woyens. Syddanmark, SW Denmark 55°15′N 09°19′E
112 K9 **Vojvodina** *Ger.* Wojwodina. Vojvodina, N Serbia
15 S6 **Volant** ≈ Québec, SE Canada
Volaterrae *see* Volterra
43 P15 **Volcán** *var.* Hato del Volcán. Chiriquí, W Panama 08°45′N 82°38′W
Volcano Islands *see* Kazan-rettō
Volchansk *see* Vovchans'k
Volchya *see* Vovcha
94 D10 **Volda** Møre og Romsdal, S Norway 62°07′N 06°04′E
116 K3 **Voldymyerets'** *Russ.* Vladimirets. Rivnens'ka Oblast', NW Ukraine 51°24′N 25°52′E
98 J9 **Volendam** Noord-Holland, C Netherlands 52°30′N 05°04′E
124 L15 **Volga** Yaroslavskaya Oblast', W Russian Federation 57°56′N 38°23′E
29 R10 **Volga** South Dakota, N USA 44°19′N 96°55′W
122 C11 **Volga** ≈ NW Russian Federation
Volga-Baltic Waterway *see* Volgo-Baltiyskiy Kanal
Volga Uplands *see* Privolzhskaya Vozvyshennost'
124 L13 **Volgo-Baltiyskiy Kanal** *var.* Volga-Baltic Waterway. *canal* NW Russian Federation
126 M12 **Volgodonsk** Rostovskaya Oblast', SW Russian Federation 47°35′N 42°03′E
127 O10 **Volgograd** *prev.* Stalingrad, Tsaritsyn. Volgogradskaya Oblast', SW Russian Federation 48°42′N 44°29′E
127 N9 **Volgogradskaya Oblast'** ◈ *province* SW Russian Federation
127 P10 **Volgogradskoye Vodokhranilishche** ⊞ SW Russian Federation
101 J19 **Volkach** Bayern, C Germany 49°51′N 10°15′E
109 U9 **Völkermarkt** *Slvn.* Velikovec. Kärnten, S Austria 46°40′N 14°38′E
124 I12 **Volkhov** Leningradskaya Oblast', NW Russian Federation 59°56′N 32°19′E
101 D20 **Völklingen** Saarland, SW Germany 49°15′N 06°51′E
Volkovysk *see* Vawkavysk
Volkovyskiye Vysoty *see* Vawkavyskaye Wzvyshsha
83 K22 **Volksrust** Mpumalanga, E South Africa 27°22′S 29°54′E
98 L8 **Vollenhove** Overijssel, N Netherlands 52°40′N 05°58′E
119 L16 **Volma** ≈ C Belarus
Volmari *see* Valmiera
117 W9 **Volnovakha** Donets'ka Oblast', SE Ukraine 47°36′N 37°32′E
116 K6 **Volochys'k** Khmel'nyts'ka Oblast', W Ukraine 49°32′N 26°14′E
117 O6 **Volodarka** Kyyivs'ka Oblast', N Ukraine 49°31′N 29°55′E
117 W9 **Volodars'ke** Donets'ka Oblast', E Ukraine 47°11′N 37°19′E
127 R13 **Volodarskiy** Astrakhanskaya Oblast', SW Russian Federation 46°23′N 48°39′E
Volodarskoye *see* Saumalkol'
117 N8 **Volodars'k-Volyns'kyy** Zhytomyrs'ka Oblast', N Ukraine 50°37′N 28°28′E
116 I3 **Volodymyr-Volyns'kyy** *Pol.* Włodzimierz, *Rus.* Vladimir-Volynskiy. Volyns'ka Oblast', NW Ukraine 50°51′N 24°19′E
124 L14 **Vologda** Vologodskaya Oblast', W Russian Federation 59°10′N 39°55′E
124 L12 **Vologodskaya Oblast'** ◈ *province* NW Russian Federation
126 K3 **Volokolamsk** Moskovskaya Oblast', W Russian Federation 56°03′N 35°57′E
126 K9 **Volokonovka** Belgorodskaya Oblast', W Russian Federation 50°30′N 37°54′E
115 G16 **Vólos** Thessalía, C Greece 39°21′N 22°58′E
124 M11 **Voloshka** Arkhangel'skaya Oblast', NW Russian Federation 61°19′N 40°06′E
Vološinovo *see* Novi Bečej
116 H7 **Volovets'** Zakarpats'ka Oblast', W Ukraine 48°42′N 23°12′E
Volozhin *see* Valozhyn
127 Q7 **Vol'sk** Saratovskaya Oblast', W Russian Federation 52°04′N 47°20′E
77 Q17 **Volta** ≈ SE Ghana
Volta Blanche *see* White Volta
77 P16 **Volta, Lake** ⊞ SE Ghana
Volta Noire *see* Black Volta
60 O9 **Volta Redonda** Rio de Janeiro, SE Brazil 22°31′S 44°05′W
Volta Rouge *see* Red Volta
106 F12 **Volterra** *anc.* Volaterrae. Toscana, C Italy 43°23′N 10°52′E
107 K17 **Volturno** ≈ S Italy
113 I15 **Volujak** ▲▲ NW Montenegro
Volunteer Island *see* Starbuck Island
65 F24 **Volunteer Point** *headland* East Falkland, Falkland Islands 51°32′S 57°44′W
114 H13 **Vólvi, Límni** ◎ N Greece
Volyn *see* Volyns'ka Oblast'
116 I3 **Volyns'ka Oblast'** *var.* Volyn, *Rus.* Volynskaya Oblast'. ◈ *province* NW Ukraine
Volynskaya Oblast' *see* Volyns'ka Oblast'
127 Q3 **Volzhsk** Respublika Mariy El, W Russian Federation 55°53′N 48°21′E
127 O10 **Volzhskiy** Volgogradskaya Oblast', SW Russian Federation 48°49′N 44°40′E
172 I7 **Vondrozo** Fianarantsoa, SE Madagascar 22°50′S 47°20′E
39 P10 **Von Frank Mountain** ▲ Alaska, USA 63°36′N 154°29′W
115 C17 **Vónitsa** Dytikí Elláda, W Greece 38°55′N 20°53′E
118 J6 **Võnnu** *Ger.* Wendau. Tartumaa, SE Estonia 58°17′N 27°06′E
98 G12 **Voorburg** Zuid-Holland, W Netherlands 52°04′N 04°22′E
98 H11 **Voorschoten** Zuid-Holland, W Netherlands 52°08′N 04°26′E
98 M11 **Voorst** Gelderland, E Netherlands 52°10′N 06°10′E
98 K11 **Voorthuizen** Gelderland, C Netherlands 52°12′N 05°36′E
92 L2 **Vopnafjördhur** Austurland, E Iceland 65°45′N 14°51′W
92 L2 **Vopnafjördhur** *bay* E Iceland
Vora *see* Vorë
119 H15 **Voranava** *Pol.* Werenów, *Rus.* Voronovo. Hrodzyenskaya Voblasts', W Belarus 54°09′N 25°19′E
108 I8 **Vorarlberg** *off.* Land Vorarlberg. ◈ *state* W Austria
Vorarlberg, Land *see* Vorarlberg
109 X7 **Vorau** Steiermark, E Austria 47°22′N 15°55′E
98 N11 **Vorden** Gelderland, E Netherlands 52°07′N 06°18′E
108 H9 **Vorderrhein** ≈ SE Switzerland
92 J2 **Vordhufell** ▲ N Iceland 65°42′N 18°45′W
95 I24 **Vordingborg** Sjælland, SE Denmark 55°01′N 11°55′E
113 K19 **Vorë** *var.* Vora. Tiranë, W Albania 41°23′N 19°37′E
115 H17 **Vóreies Sporádes** *var.* Vóreioi Sporádes, Vórioi Sporádhes, *Eng.* Northern Sporades. *island group* E Greece
Vóreioi Sporádes *see* Vóreies Sporádes
115 J17 **Vóreion Aigaíon** *Eng.* Aegean North. ◈ *region* SE Greece
115 G18 **Vóreios Evvoïkós Kólpos** *var.* Vóreios Evvoïkós Kólpos. *gulf* E Greece
197 S16 **Voring Plateau** *undersea feature* N Norwegian Sea 67°00′N 04°00′E
Vórioi Sporádhes *see* Vóreies Sporádes
125 W4 **Vorkuta** Respublika Komi, NW Russian Federation 67°27′N 64°E
95 I14 **Vorma** ≈ S Norway
118 E4 **Vormsi** *var.* Vormsi Saar, *Ger.* Worms, *Swed.* Ormsö. *island* W Estonia
Vormsi Saar *see* Vormsi
127 N7 **Vorona** ≈ W Russian Federation
126 L7 **Voronezh** Voronezhskaya Oblast', W Russian Federation 51°40′N 39°13′E
126 L7 **Voronezh** ≈ W Russian Federation
126 K8 **Voronezhskaya Oblast'** ◈ *province* W Russian Federation
Voronovitsya *see* Voronovytsya
Voronovo *see* Voranava
117 N6 **Voronovytsya** *Rus.* Voronovitsya. Vinnyts'ka Oblast', C Ukraine 49°06′N 28°49′E
122 K7 **Vorontsovo** Krasnoyarskiy Kray, N Russian Federation 71°45′N 83°31′E
124 K3 **Voron'ya** ≈ NW Russian Federation
Voropayevo *see* Varapayeva
Voroshilov *see* Ussuriysk
Voroshilovgrad *see* Luhans'ka Oblast', Ukraine
Voroshilovgrad *see* Luhans'k, Ukraine
Voroshilovgradskaya Oblast' *see* Luhans'ka Oblast'
Voroshilovsk *see* Stavropol', Russian Federation
Voroshilovsk *see* Alchevs'k
137 V13 **Vorotan** *Az.* Bärgușad. ≈ Armenia/Azerbaijan
127 P3 **Vorotynets** Nizhegorodskaya Oblast', W Russian Federation 56°06′N 46°06′E
117 S3 **Vorozhba** Sums'ka Oblast', NE Ukraine 51°10′N 34°15′E
117 T5 **Vorskla** ≈ Russian Federation/Ukraine
99 I17 **Vorst** Antwerpen, N Belgium 51°06′N 05°01′E
83 G21 **Vorstershoop** North-West, N South Africa 25°46′S 22°57′E
118 H6 **Võrtsjärv** *Ger.* Wirz-See. ◎ SE Estonia
118 J7 **Võru** *Ger.* Werro. Võrumaa, SE Estonia 57°51′N 27°01′E
147 R11 **Vorukh** N Tajikistan 39°51′N 70°34′E
118 I7 **Võrumaa** *off.* Võru Maakond. ◈ *province* SE Estonia
Võru Maakond *see* Võrumaa
83 G24 **Vosburg** Northern Cape, W South Africa 30°35′S 22°52′E
147 Q14 **Vose'** *Rus.* Vose; *prev.* Aral. SW Tajikistan 37°51′N 69°31′E
103 S6 **Vosges** ◈ *department* NE France
103 U6 **Vosges** ▲▲ NE France
124 K13 **Voskresenkoye** Vologodskaya Oblast', NW Russian Federation 59°25′N 37°56′E
126 L4 **Voskresensk** Moskovskaya Oblast', W Russian Federation 55°19′N 38°42′E
127 P2 **Voskresenskoye** Nizhegorodskaya Oblast', W Russian Federation 57°00′N 45°33′E
127 V6 **Voskresenskoye** Respublika Bashkortostan, W Russian Federation 53°07′N 56°07′E
94 D13 **Voss** Hordaland, S Norway 60°38′N 06°25′E
94 D13 **Voss** *physical region* S Norway
99 I16 **Vosselaar** Antwerpen, N Belgium 51°19′N 04°55′E
94 D13 **Vosso** ≈ S Norway
Vostochno-Kazakhstanskaya Oblast' *see* Vostochnyy Kazakhstan
123 S5 **Vostochno-Sibirskoye More** *Eng.* East Siberian Sea. *sea* Arctic Ocean
145 X10 **Vostochnyy Kazakhstan** *off.* Vostochno-Kazakhstanskaya Oblast', *var.* East Kazakhstan, *Kaz.* Shyghys Qazaqstan Oblysy. ◈ *province* E Kazakhstan
122 L13 **Vostochnyy Sayan** *Eng.* Eastern Sayans, *Mong.* Dzüün Soyonï Nuruu. ▲▲ Mongolia/Russian Federation
Vostock Island *see* Vostok Island
195 U10 **Vostok** *Russian research station* Antarctica 77°18′S 105°32′E
191 X5 **Vostok Island** *var.* Vostock Island; *prev.* Stavers Island. *island* Line Islands, SE Kiribati
127 T2 **Votkinsk** Udmurtskaya Respublika, NW Russian Federation 57°04′N 54°00′E
125 U15 **Votkinskoye Vodokhranilishche** *var.* Votkinsk Reservoir. ⊞ NW Russian Federation
Votkinsk Reservoir *see* Votkinskoye Vodokhranilishche
60 J7 **Votuporanga** São Paulo, S Brazil 20°26′S 49°53′W
104 H7 **Vouga, Rio** ≈ N Portugal
115 E14 **Voúrinos** ▲ N Greece
115 G24 **Voúxa, Akrotírio** *headland* Kríti, Greece, E Mediterranean Sea 35°37′N 23°34′E
103 R4 **Vouziers** Ardennes, N France 49°24′N 04°42′E
117 V7 **Vovcha** *Rus.* Volchya. ≈ E Ukraine
117 V4 **Vovchans'k** *Rus.* Volchansk. Kharkivs'ka Oblast', E Ukraine 50°19′N 36°55′E
103 N6 **Voves** Eure-et-Loir, C France 48°18′N 01°39′E
79 M14 **Vovodo** ≈ S Central African Republic
94 M12 **Voxna** Gävleborg, C Sweden 61°21′N 15°35′E
94 L11 **Voxnan** ≈ C Sweden
114 F7 **Voynishka Reka** ≈ NW Bulgaria
125 T9 **Voyvozh** Respublika Komi, NW Russian Federation 62°54′N 54°52′E
124 M12 **Vozhega** Vologodskaya Oblast', NW Russian Federation 60°27′N 40°11′E
124 L12 **Vozhe, Ozero** ◎ NW Russian Federation
117 Q9 **Voznesens'k** *Rus.* Voznesensk. Mykolayivs'ka Oblast', S Ukraine 47°34′N 31°21′E
124 J12 **Voznesen'ye** Leningradskaya Oblast', NW Russian Federation 61°00′N 35°24′E
144 J14 **Vozrozhdeniya, Ostrov** *Uzb.* Wozrojdeniye Oroli. *island* Kazakhstan/Uzbekistan
95 G20 **Vrå** *var.* Vraa. Nordjylland, N Denmark 57°21′N 09°57′E
Vraa *see* Vrå
114 H9 **Vrachesh** Sofiya, W Bulgaria 42°52′N 23°45′E
115 C19 **Vrachíonas** ▲ Zákynthos, Iónia Nisiá, Greece, C Mediterranean Sea 37°49′N 20°43′E
117 P8 **Vradiyivka** Mykolayivs'ka Oblast', S Ukraine 47°51′N 30°37′E
113 G14 **Vran** ▲ SW Bosnia and Herzegovina 43°35′N 17°30′E
116 K12 **Vrancea** ◈ *county* E Romania
147 T14 **Vrang** SE Tajikistan 37°03′N 72°26′E
123 T4 **Vrangelya, Ostrov** *Eng.* Wrangel Island. *island* NE Russian Federation
112 H13 **Vranica** ▲ C Bosnia and Herzegovina 43°57′N 17°43′E
113 O16 **Vranje** Serbia, SE Serbia 42°33′N 21°55′E
Vranov *see* Vranov nad Topl'ou
111 N19 **Vranov nad Topl'ou** *var.* Vranov, *Hung.* Varannó. Prešovský Kraj, E Slovakia 48°54′N 21°41′E
114 H8 **Vratsa** Vratsa, NW Bulgaria 43°13′N 23°34′E
114 H8 **Vratsa** ◈ *province* NW Bulgaria
114 F10 **Vrattsa** *prev.* Mirovo. Kyustendil, W Bulgaria 42°15′N 22°33′E
112 G11 **Vrbanja** ≈ NW Bosnia and Herzegovina
112 K9 **Vrbas** Vojvodina, NW Serbia 45°34′N 19°39′E
112 G13 **Vrbas** ≈ N Bosnia and Herzegovina
112 E8 **Vrbovec** Zagreb, N Croatia 45°53′N 16°24′E
112 C9 **Vrbovsko** Primorje-Gorski Kotar, NW Croatia 45°22′N 15°06′E
111 E15 **Vrchlabí** *Ger.* Hohenelbe. Královéhradecký Kraj, N Czech Republic 50°38′N 15°35′E
83 J22 **Vrede** Free State, E South Africa 27°25′S 29°10′E
100 E13 **Vreden** Nordrhein-Westfalen, NW Germany 52°01′N 06°50′E
83 E25 **Vredenburg** Western Cape, SW South Africa 32°55′S 18°00′E
99 I23 **Vresse-sur-Semois** Namur, SE Belgium 49°52′N 04°56′E
95 L16 **Vretstorp** Örebro, C Sweden 59°03′N 14°51′E
113 G15 **Vrgorac** *prev.* Vrhgorac. Split-Dalmacija, SE Croatia 43°10′N 17°24′E
Vrhgorac *see* Vrgorac
109 T12 **Vrhnika** *Ger.* Oberlaibach. W Slovenia 45°57′N 14°18′E
155 I21 **Vriddhachalam** Tamil Nādu, SE India 11°33′N 79°18′E
98 N6 **Vries** Drenthe, NE Netherlands 53°04′N 06°34′E
98 O10 **Vriezenveen** Overijssel, E Netherlands 52°25′N 06°37′E
95 L20 **Vrigstad** Jönköping, S Sweden 57°19′N 14°30′E
108 H9 **Vrin** Graubünden, S Switzerland 46°40′N 09°06′E
112 E13 **Vrlika** Split-Dalmacija, S Croatia 43°54′N 16°24′E
113 M14 **Vrnjačka Banja** Serbia, C Serbia 43°36′N 20°55′E
Vrondádhes/Vrondados *see* Vrontádos

◆ Country
● Country Capital
◇ Dependent Territory
○ Dependent Territory Capital
◈ Administrative Regions
✕ International Airport
▲ Mountain
▲▲ Mountain Range
Ѫ Volcano
≈ River
◎ Lake
⊞ Reservoir

115 L18 **Vrontádos** var. Vrondados; prev. Vrondádhes. Chíos, E Greece 38°25′N 26°08′E
98 N9 **Vroomshoop** Overijssel, E Netherlands 52°28′N 06°35′E
112 N10 **Vršac** Ger. Werschetz, Hung. Versecz. Vojvodina, NE Serbia 45°08′N 21°18′E
112 M10 **Vršački Kanal** canal N Serbia
83 H21 **Vryburg** North-West, N South Africa 26°57′S 24°44′E
83 K22 **Vryheid** KwaZulu/Natal, E South Africa 27°45′S 30°48′E
111 I18 **Vsetín** Ger. Wsetin. Zlínský Kraj, E Czech Republic 49°21′N 17°57′E
111 J20 **Vtáčnik** Hung. Madaras, Ptacsnik; prev. Ptačnik. ▲ W Slovakia 48°38′N 18°38′E
Vuadil' see Wodil
114 I11 **Vŭcha** ≈ SW Bulgaria
Vučitrn see Vushtrri
99 J14 **Vught** Noord-Brabant, S Netherlands 51°37′N 05°19′E
117 W8 **Vuhledar** Donets'ka Oblast', E Ukraine 47°48′N 37°11′E
112 I9 **Vuka** ≈ E Croatia
113 K17 **Vukël** var. Vukli. Shkodër, N Albania 42°29′N 19°39′E
Vukli see Vukël
112 J9 **Vukovar** Hung. Vukovár. Vukovar-Srijem, E Croatia 45°18′N 18°45′E
Vukovarsko-Srijemska Županija see Vukovar-Srijem
112 I10 **Vukovar-Srijem** off. Vukovarsko-Srijemska Županija. ◈ province E Croatia
125 U8 **Vuktyl** Respublika Komi, NW Russian Federation 63°49′N 57°07′E
11 Q17 **Vulcan** Alberta, SW Canada 50°27′N 113°12′W
116 G12 **Vulcan** Ger. Wulkan, Hung. Zsilyvajdevulkán; prev. Crivadia Vulcanului, Vaidei, Hung. Sily-Vajdej, Vajdej. Hunedoara, W Romania 45°22′N 23°16′E
116 M12 **Vulcănești** Rus. Vulkaneshty. S Moldova 45°41′N 28°25′E
107 L22 **Vulcano, Isola** island Isole Eolie, S Italy
114 G7 **Vŭlchedrŭm** Montana, NW Bulgaria 43°42′N 23°25′E
114 N8 **Vŭlchidol** prev. Kurt-Dere. Varna, E Bulgaria 43°25′N 27°33′E
Vulkaneshty see Vulcănești
123 V11 **Vulkannyy** Kamchatskiy Kray, E Russian Federation 53°01′N 158°26′E
36 J13 **Vulture Mountains** ▲▲ Arizona, SW USA
167 T14 **Vung Tau** prev. Fr. Cape Saint Jacques, Cap Saint-Jacques. Ba Ria-Vung Tau, S Vietnam 10°21′N 107°04′E
187 X15 **Vunisea** Kadavu, SE Fiji 19°04′S 178°10′E
Vuohčču see Vuotso
93 N15 **Vuokatti** Oulu, C Finland 64°08′N 28°16′E
93 M15 **Vuolijoki** Oulu, C Finland 64°09′N 27°00′E
Vuolleriebme see Vuollerim
92 J13 **Vuollerim** Lapp. Vuolleriebme. Norrbotten, N Sweden 66°24′N 20°36′E
Vuonnabahta see Varangerbotn
Vuoreija see Vardø
92 L10 **Vuotso** Lapp. Vuohčču. Lappi, N Finland 68°04′N 27°05′E
114 J11 **Vŭrbitsa** prev. Filevo. Khaskovo, S Bulgaria 42°02′N 25°25′E
114 J12 **Vŭrbitsa** ≈ S Bulgaria
127 Q4 **Vurnary** Chuvashskaya Respublika, W Russian Federation 55°30′N 46°59′E
114 G8 **Vŭrshets** Montana, NW Bulgaria 43°14′N 23°20′E
Vusan see Busan
113 N16 **Vushtrri** Serb. Vučitrn. N Kosovo 42°49′N 21°00′E
119 F17 **Vyalikaya Byerastavitsa** Pol. Brzostowica Wielka, Rus. Bol'shaya Berëstovitsa; prev. Velikaya Berestovitsa. Hrodzyenskaya Voblasts', SW Belarus 53°12′N 24°03′E
119 N20 **Vyaliki Bor** Rus. Velikiy Bor. Homyel'skaya Voblasts', SE Belarus 52°02′N 29°56′E
119 J18 **Vyaliki Rozhan** Rus. Bol'shoy Rozhan. Minskaya Voblasts', S Belarus 52°46′N 27°07′E
124 H10 **Vyartsilya** Fin. Värtsilä. Respublika Kareliya, NW Russian Federation 62°07′N 30°43′E
119 K17 **Vyasyeya** Rus. Veseya. Minskaya Voblasts', C Belarus 53°04′N 27°41′E
125 R15 **Vyatka** ≈ NW Russian Federation
Vyatka see Kirov
125 S16 **Vyatskiye Polyany** Kirovskaya Oblast', NW Russian Federation 56°15′N 51°06′E
123 S14 **Vyazemskiy** Khabarovskiy Kray, SE Russian Federation 47°28′N 134°39′E
126 I4 **Vyaz'ma** Smolenskaya Oblast', W Russian Federation 55°09′N 34°20′E
127 N3 **Vyazniki** Vladimirskaya Oblast', W Russian Federation 56°15′N 42°06′E
127 O8 **Vyazovka** Volgogradskaya Oblast', SW Russian Federation 50°57′N 43°57′E
119 J14 **Vyazyn'** Minskaya Voblasts', NW Belarus 54°25′N 27°10′E
124 G11 **Vyborg** Fin. Viipuri. Leningradskaya Oblast', NW Russian Federation 60°44′N 28°47′E
125 P11 **Vychegda** var. Vichegda. ≈ NW Russian Federation
119 L14 **Vyelyewshchyna** Rus. Velevshchina. Vitsyebskaya Voblasts', N Belarus 54°44′N 28°35′E
119 P16 **Vyeramyeyki** Rus. Veremeyki. Mahilyowskaya Voblasts', E Belarus 53°46′N 31°17′E
118 K11 **Vyerkhnyadzvinsk** Rus. Verkhnedvinsk. Vitsyebskaya Voblasts', N Belarus 55°47′N 27°56′E
119 P18 **Vyetka** Rus. Vetka. Homyel'skaya Voblasts', SE Belarus 52°33′N 31°10′E
118 L12 **Vyetryna** Rus. Vetrino. Vitsyebskaya Voblasts', N Belarus 55°25′N 28°28′E
Vygonovskoye, Ozero see Vyhanashchanskaye, Vozyera
124 J9 **Vygozero, Ozero** ◎ NW Russian Federation
119 I18 **Vyhanashchanskaye, Vozyera** prev. Vozyera Vyhanawskaye, Rus. Ozero Vygonovskoye. ◎ SW Belarus
Vyhanawskaye, Vozyera see Vyhanashchanskaye, Vozyera
127 N4 **Vyksa** Nizhegorodskaya Oblast', W Russian Federation 55°21′N 42°10′E
117 O12 **Vylkove** Rus. Vilkovo. Odes'ka Oblast', SW Ukraine 45°24′N 29°37′E
125 R9 **Vym'** ≈ NW Russian Federation
116 H8 **Vynohradiv** Cz. Sevluš, Hung. Nagyszöllős, Rus. Vinogradov; prev. Sevlyush. Zakarpats'ka Oblast', W Ukraine 48°09′N 23°01′E
124 G13 **Vyritsa** Leningradskaya Oblast', NW Russian Federation 59°25′N 30°20′E
97 J19 **Vyrnwy** Wel. Afon Efyrnwy. ≈ E Wales, United Kingdom
145 X9 **Vyshe Ivanovskiy Belak, Gora** ▲ E Kazakhstan 50°16′N 83°46′E
117 P4 **Vyshhorod** Kyyivs'ka Oblast', N Ukraine 50°36′N 30°28′E
124 I15 **Vyshniy Volochek** Tverskaya Oblast', W Russian Federation 57°37′N 34°33′E
111 G18 **Vyškov** Ger. Wischau. Jihomoravský Kraj, SE Czech Republic 49°17′N 17°01′E
111 E18 **Vysočina** prev. Jihlavský Kraj. ◈ region N Czech Republic
119 E19 **Vysokaye** Rus. Vysokoye. Brestskaya Voblasts', SW Belarus 52°20′N 23°18′E
111 F17 **Vysoké Mýto** Ger. Hohenmauth. Pardubický Kraj, C Czech Republic 49°57′N 16°10′E
117 S9 **Vysokopillya** Khersons'ka Oblast', S Ukraine 47°28′N 33°30′E
126 K3 **Vysokovsk** Moskovskaya Oblast', W Russian Federation 56°12′N 36°42′E
Vysokoye see Vysokaye
124 K12 **Vytegra** Vologodskaya Oblast', NW Russian Federation 60°59′N 36°27′E
116 J8 **Vyzhnytsya** Chernivets'ka Oblast', W Ukraine 48°14′N 25°10′E

W

77 O14 **Wa** NW Ghana 10°07′N 02°28′W
Waadt see Vaud
Waag see Váh
Waagbistritz see Považská Bystrica
Waagneustadtl see Nové Mesto nad Váhom
81 M16 **Waajid** Gedo, SW Somalia 03°37′N 43°19′E
98 L13 **Waal** ≈ S Netherlands
187 O16 **Waala** Province Nord, W New Caledonia 19°46′S 163°41′E
99 I14 **Waalwijk** Noord-Brabant, S Netherlands 51°42′N 05°04′E
99 E16 **Waarschoot** Oost-Vlaanderen, NW Belgium 51°09′N 03°35′E
186 C7 **Wabag** Enga, W Papua New Guinea 05°28′S 143°40′E
15 N7 **Wabano** ≈ Québec, SE Canada
11 P11 **Wabasca** ≈ Alberta, SW Canada
31 P12 **Wabash** Indiana, N USA 40°47′N 85°48′W
29 X9 **Wabasha** Minnesota, N USA 44°22′N 92°01′W
31 N13 **Wabash River** ≈ N USA
14 C7 **Wabatongushi Lake** ◎ Ontario, S Canada
81 L15 **Wabē Gestro Wenz** ≈ SE Ethiopia
14 B9 **Wabos** Ontario, S Canada 46°48′N 84°06′W
11 W13 **Wabowden** Manitoba, C Canada 54°57′N 98°38′W
110 J9 **Wąbrzeźno** Kujawsko-pomorskie, C Poland 53°18′N 18°55′E
21 U12 **Waccamaw River** ≈ South Carolina, SE USA
23 U11 **Waccasassa Bay** bay Florida, SE USA
99 F16 **Wachtebeke** Oost-Vlaanderen, NW Belgium 51°10′N 03°52′E
25 T8 **Waco** Texas, SW USA 31°33′N 97°10′W
26 M3 **Waconda Lake** var. Great Elder Reservoir. ⊠ Kansas, C USA
Wadai see Ouaddaï
Wad Al-Hajarah see Guadalajara
164 I12 **Wadayama** Hyōgo, Honshū, SW Japan 35°19′N 134°51′E
80 D10 **Wad Banda** Southern Kordofan, C Sudan 13°08′N 27°56′E
75 P9 **Waddān** NW Libya 29°10′N 16°08′E
98 J4 **Waddeneilanden** Eng. West Frisian Islands. island group N Netherlands
98 J6 **Waddenzee** var. Wadden Zee. sea SE North Sea
Wadden Zee see Waddenzee
10 L16 **Waddington, Mount** ▲ British Columbia, SW Canada 51°17′N 125°16′W
98 H12 **Waddinxveen** Zuid-Holland, C Netherlands 52°03′N 04°38′E
11 U15 **Wadena** Saskatchewan, S Canada 51°57′N 103°48′W
29 T6 **Wadena** Minnesota, N USA 46°27′N 95°07′W
108 G7 **Wädenswil** Zürich, N Switzerland 47°14′N 08°41′E
21 S11 **Wadesboro** North Carolina, SE USA 34°59′N 80°03′W
155 G16 **Wādi** Karnātaka, C India 17°00′N 76°58′E
138 G10 **Wādī as Sīr** var. Wadi es Sir. 'Ammān, NW Jordan 31°57′N 35°49′E
Wadi es Sir see Wādī as Sīr
80 F5 **Wadi Halfa** var. Wādī Ḥalfā'. Northern, N Sudan 21°46′N 31°17′E
138 G13 **Wādī Mūsā** var. Petra. Ma'ān, S Jordan 30°19′N 35°29′E
23 V4 **Wadley** Georgia, SE USA 32°52′N 82°24′W
Wad Madanī see Wad Medani
80 G10 **Wad Medani** var. Wad Madanī. Gezira, C Sudan 14°24′N 33°30′E
80 F10 **Wad Nimr** White Nile, C Sudan 14°32′N 32°10′E
165 U16 **Wadomari** Kagoshima, Okinoerabu-jima, SW Japan 27°25′N 128°40′E
111 K17 **Wadowice** Małopolskie, S Poland 49°54′N 19°29′E
35 R5 **Wadsworth** Nevada, W USA 39°39′N 119°16′W
31 T12 **Wadsworth** Ohio, N USA 41°01′N 81°43′W
25 T11 **Waelder** Texas, SW USA 29°42′N 97°16′W
Waereghem see Waregem
163 U13 **Wafangdian** var. Fuxian, Fu Xian. Liaoning, NE China 39°36′N 122°00′E
171 R13 **Waflia** Pulau Buru, E Indonesia 03°10′S 126°05′E
98 K12 **Wageningen** Gelderland, SE Netherlands 51°58′N 05°40′E
55 V9 **Wageningen** Nickerie, NW Surinam 05°44′N 56°45′W
9 O8 **Wager Bay** inlet Nunavut, N Canada
183 P10 **Wagga Wagga** New South Wales, SE Australia 35°11′S 147°22′E
180 J13 **Wagin** Western Australia 33°16′S 117°26′E
108 H8 **Wägitaler See** ◎ SW Switzerland
29 P12 **Wagner** South Dakota, N USA 43°04′N 98°17′W
27 Q9 **Wagoner** Oklahoma, C USA 35°58′N 95°23′W
37 U10 **Wagon Mound** New Mexico, SW USA 36°00′N 104°42′W
32 J14 **Wagontire** Oregon, NW USA 43°15′N 119°51′W
110 H10 **Wągrowiec** Wielkopolskie, C Poland 52°49′N 17°11′E
149 U6 **Wāh** Punjab, NE Pakistan 33°50′N 72°44′E
171 S13 **Wahai** Pulau Seram, E Indonesia 02°48′S 129°29′E
169 V10 **Wahau, Sungai** ≈ Borneo, C Indonesia
Wahaybah, Ramlat Al see Wahībah, Ramlat Āl
80 D13 **Wahda** var. Unity State. ◈ state N South Sudan
38 D9 **Wahiawā** var. Wahiawa. O'ahu, Hawaii, USA, C Pacific Ocean 21°30′N 158°01′W
Wahībah, Ramlat Ahl see Wahībah, Ramlat Āl
141 Y9 **Wahībah, Ramlat Āl** var. Ramlat Ahl Wahībah, Ramlat Al Wahaybah, Eng. Wahibah Sands. desert N Oman
Wahībah Sands see Wahībah, Ramlat Āl
101 E16 **Wahn** ✈ (Köln) Nordrhein-Westfalen, W Germany 50°51′N 07°09′E
29 R15 **Wahoo** Nebraska, C USA 41°12′N 96°37′W
29 R6 **Wahpeton** North Dakota, N USA 46°16′N 96°36′W
Wahran see Oran
36 J6 **Wah Wah Mountains** ▲▲ Utah, W USA
38 D9 **Waialua** O'ahu, Hawaii, USA, C Pacific Ocean 21°34′N 158°07′W
38 D9 **Wai'anae** var. Waianae. O'ahu, Hawaii, USA, C Pacific Ocean 21°26′N 158°11′W
184 Q8 **Waiapu** ≈ North Island, New Zealand
185 I17 **Waiau** Canterbury, South Island, New Zealand 42°39′S 173°03′E
185 I17 **Waiau** ≈ South Island, New Zealand
185 B23 **Waiau** ≈ South Island, New Zealand
101 H21 **Waiblingen** Baden-Württemberg, S Germany 48°49′N 09°19′E
Waidhofen see Waidhofen an der Ybbs, Niederösterreich, Austria
Waidhofen see Waidhofen an der Thaya, Niederösterreich, Austria
109 V2 **Waidhofen an der Thaya** var. Waidhofen. Niederösterreich, NE Austria 48°49′N 15°17′E
109 U5 **Waidhofen an der Ybbs** var. Waidhofen. Niederösterreich, E Austria 47°58′N 14°47′E
171 T11 **Waigeo, Pulau** island Maluku, E Indonesia
184 L5 **Waiheke Island** island N New Zealand
184 M7 **Waihi** Waikato, North Island, New Zealand 37°22′S 175°51′E
185 C20 **Waihou** ≈ North Island, New Zealand
Waikaboebak see Waikabubak
171 N17 **Waikabubak** prev. Waikaboebak. Pulau Sumba, C Indonesia 09°40′S 119°25′E
185 D23 **Waikaia** ≈ South Island, New Zealand
185 D23 **Waikaka** Southland, South Island, New Zealand 45°55′S 168°59′E
184 L13 **Waikanae** Wellington, North Island, New Zealand 40°52′S 175°03′E
184 M7 **Waikare, Lake** ◎ North Island, New Zealand
184 O9 **Waikaremoana, Lake** ◎ North Island, New Zealand
185 I17 **Waikari** Canterbury, South Island, New Zealand 42°50′S 172°41′E
184 L8 **Waikato** off. Waikato Region. ◈ region North Island, New Zealand
184 M8 **Waikato** ≈ North Island, New Zealand
Waikato Region see Waikato
182 J9 **Waikerie** South Australia 34°12′S 139°57′E
185 F23 **Waikouaiti** Otago, South Island, New Zealand 45°36′S 170°39′E
38 H11 **Wailea** Hawaii, USA, C Pacific Ocean 19°53′N 155°07′W
38 F10 **Wailuku** Maui, Hawaii, USA, C Pacific Ocean 20°53′N 156°30′W
185 H18 **Waimakariri** ≈ South Island, New Zealand
38 D9 **Waimānalo Beach** var. Waimanalo Beach. O'ahu, Hawaii, USA, C Pacific Ocean 21°20′N 157°42′W
185 G15 **Waimangaroa** West Coast, South Island, New Zealand 41°41′S 171°49′E
185 G21 **Waimate** Canterbury, South Island, New Zealand 44°44′S 171°03′E
38 G11 **Waimea** var. Kamuela. Hawaii, USA, C Pacific Ocean 20°02′N 155°20′W
38 D9 **Waimea** var. Maunawai. O'ahu, Hawaii, USA, C Pacific Ocean 21°39′N 158°04′W
38 B8 **Waimea** Kaua'i, Hawaii, USA, C Pacific Ocean 21°57′N 159°40′W
99 M20 **Waimes** Liège, E Belgium 50°25′N 06°10′E
154 J11 **Wainganga** var. Wain River. ≈ C India
Waingapoe see Waingapu
171 N17 **Waingapu** prev. Waingapoe. Pulau Sumba, C Indonesia 09°40′S 120°16′E
55 S7 **Waini** ≈ N Guyana
55 S7 **Waini Point** headland NW Guyana 08°24′N 59°48′W
Wain River see Wainganga
11 R15 **Wainwright** Alberta, SW Canada 52°50′N 110°51′W
39 O5 **Wainwright** Alaska, USA 70°38′N 160°02′W
184 K4 **Waiotira** Northland, North Island, New Zealand 35°56′S 174°11′E
184 M11 **Waiouru** Manawatu-Wanganui, North Island, New Zealand 39°28′S 175°41′E
171 W14 **Waipa** Papua, E Indonesia 03°47′S 136°16′E
184 L8 **Waipa** ≈ North Island, New Zealand
184 P9 **Waipaoa** ≈ North Island, New Zealand
185 D25 **Waipapa Point** headland South Island, New Zealand 46°39′S 168°51′E
185 I18 **Waipara** Canterbury, South Island, New Zealand 43°04′S 172°45′E
184 N12 **Waipawa** Hawke's Bay, North Island, New Zealand 39°57′S 176°36′E
184 K4 **Waipu** Northland, North Island, New Zealand 35°58′S 174°25′E
184 N12 **Waipukurau** Hawke's Bay, North Island, New Zealand 40°01′S 176°34′E
171 U14 **Wair** Pulau Kai Besar, E Indonesia 05°16′S 133°09′E
Wairakai see Wairakei
184 N9 **Wairakei** var. Wairakai. Waikato, North Island, New Zealand 38°37′S 176°05′E
185 M14 **Wairarapa, Lake** ◎ North Island, New Zealand
185 J15 **Wairau** ≈ South Island, New Zealand
184 P10 **Wairoa** Hawke's Bay, North Island, New Zealand 39°03′S 177°26′E
184 P10 **Wairoa** ≈ North Island, New Zealand
184 J4 **Wairoa** ≈ North Island, New Zealand
184 N9 **Waitahanui** Waikato, North Island, New Zealand 38°48′S 176°04′E
184 M6 **Waitakaruru** Waikato, North Island, New Zealand 37°14′S 175°22′E
185 F21 **Waitaki** ≈ South Island, New Zealand
184 K10 **Waitara** Taranaki, North Island, New Zealand 39°01′S 174°14′E
184 M7 **Waitoa** Waikato, North Island, New Zealand 37°36′S 175°37′E
184 L8 **Waitomo Caves** Waikato, North Island, New Zealand 38°17′S 175°06′E
184 L11 **Waitotara** Taranaki, North Island, New Zealand 39°49′S 174°43′E
184 L11 **Waitotara** ≈ North Island, New Zealand
32 L10 **Waitsburg** Washington, NW USA 46°16′N 118°09′W
Waitzen see Vác
184 L6 **Waiuku** Auckland, North Island, New Zealand 37°15′S 174°45′E
164 L10 **Wajima** var. Wazima. Ishikawa, Honshū, SW Japan 37°23′N 136°53′E
81 K17 **Wajir** North Eastern, NE Kenya 01°46′N 40°05′E
79 J17 **Waka** Equateur, NW Dem. Rep. Congo 01°04′N 20°11′E
81 I14 **Waka** Southern Nationalities, S Ethiopia 07°12′N 37°19′E
14 D9 **Wakami Lake** ◎ Ontario, S Canada
164 I12 **Wakasa** Tottori, Honshū, SW Japan 35°18′N 134°25′E
164 J12 **Wakasa-wan** bay C Japan
185 C22 **Wakatipu, Lake** ◎ South Island, New Zealand
11 T15 **Wakaw** Saskatchewan, S Canada 52°40′N 105°45′W
164 I14 **Wakayama** Wakayama, Honshū, SW Japan 34°12′N 135°09′E
164 I15 **Wakayama** off. Wakayama-ken. ◈ prefecture Honshū, SW Japan
Wakayama-ken see Wakayama
26 K4 **Wa Keeney** Kansas, C USA 39°02′N 99°53′W
185 I14 **Wakefield** Tasman, South Island, New Zealand 41°24′S 173°03′E
97 M17 **Wakefield** N England, United Kingdom 53°42′N 01°29′W
27 O4 **Wakefield** Kansas, C USA 39°12′N 97°00′W
30 L4 **Wakefield** Michigan, N USA 46°27′N 89°55′W
21 U9 **Wake Forest** North Carolina, SE USA 35°58′N 78°30′W
Wakeham Bay see Kangiqsujuaq
189 Y11 **Wake Island** ◇ US unincorporated territory NW Pacific Ocean
189 Y12 **Wake Island** ✈ NW Pacific Ocean
189 Y12 **Wake Island** atoll NW Pacific Ocean
189 X12 **Wake Lagoon** lagoon Wake Island, NW Pacific Ocean
166 L8 **Wakema** Ayeyarwady, SW Burma (Myanmar) 16°36′N 95°11′E
Wakhan see Khandūd
164 H14 **Waki** Tokushima, Shikoku, SW Japan 34°04′N 134°10′E
165 T1 **Wakkanai** Hokkaidō, NE Japan 45°25′N 141°39′E
83 K22 **Wakkerstroom** Mpumalanga, E South Africa 27°21′S 30°10′E
14 C10 **Wakomata Lake** ◎ Ontario, S Canada
183 N10 **Wakool** New South Wales, SE Australia 35°30′S 144°22′E
Wakra see Al Wakrah
Waku Kungo see Uaco Cungo
186 J7 **Wakunai** Bougainville Island, NE Papua New Guinea 05°52′S 155°10′E
Walachei/Walachia see Wallachia
155 K26 **Walawe Ganga** ≈ S Sri Lanka
111 F15 **Wałbrzych** Ger. Waldenburg, Waldenburg in Schlesien. Dolnośląskie, SW Poland 50°45′N 16°20′E
183 T6 **Walcha** New South Wales, SE Australia 31°01′S 151°38′E
101 K24 **Walchensee** ◎ SE Germany
99 D14 **Walcheren** island SW Netherlands
29 Z14 **Walcott** Iowa, C USA 41°34′N 90°46′W
33 W16 **Walcott** Wyoming, C USA 41°46′N 106°46′W
99 G21 **Walcourt** Namur, S Belgium 50°16′N 04°26′E
110 G9 **Wałcz** Ger. Deutsch Krone. Zachodnio-pomorskie, NW Poland 53°17′N 16°29′E
108 H7 **Wald** Zürich, N Switzerland 47°17′N 08°56′E
109 U3 **Waldaist** ≈ N Austria
180 I9 **Waldburg Range** ▲▲ Western Australia
37 R3 **Walden** Colorado, C USA 40°43′N 106°16′W
18 K13 **Walden** New York, NE USA 41°35′N 74°09′W
Waldenburg/Waldenburg in Schlesien see Wałbrzych
11 T15 **Waldheim** Saskatchewan, S Canada 52°38′N 106°35′W
Waldia see Weldiya
101 M23 **Waldkraiburg** Bayern, SE Germany 48°10′N 12°23′E
27 T14 **Waldo** Arkansas, C USA 33°21′N 93°18′W
23 V9 **Waldo** Florida, SE USA 29°47′N 82°07′W
19 R7 **Waldoboro** Maine, NE USA 44°06′N 69°22′W
21 W4 **Waldorf** Maryland, NE USA 38°36′N 76°54′W
32 F12 **Waldport** Oregon, NW USA 44°25′N 124°04′W
27 S11 **Waldron** Arkansas, C USA 34°54′N 94°09′W
195 Y13 **Waldron, Cape** headland Antarctica 66°08′S 116°00′E
101 F24 **Waldshut-Tiengen** Baden-Württemberg, S Germany 47°37′N 08°13′E
171 P12 **Walea, Selat** strait Sulawesi, C Indonesia
Wałeckie Międzyrzecze see Valašské Meziříčí
108 H8 **Walensee** ◎ NW Switzerland
38 L8 **Wales** Alaska, USA 65°36′N 168°03′W
97 J20 **Wales** Wel. Cymru. ◈ national region Wales, United Kingdom
9 O7 **Wales Island** island Nunavut, NE Canada
77 P14 **Walewale** N Ghana 10°21′N 00°48′W
99 M24 **Walferdange** Luxembourg, C Luxembourg 49°39′N 06°08′E
183 Q5 **Walgett** New South Wales, SE Australia 30°02′S 148°14′E
194 K10 **Walgreen Coast** physical region Antarctica
29 Q2 **Walhalla** North Dakota, N USA 48°55′N 97°55′W
21 O11 **Walhalla** South Carolina, SE USA 34°46′N 83°05′W
79 O19 **Walikale** Nord-Kivu, E Dem. Rep. Congo 01°29′S 28°05′E
Walk see Valga, Estonia
Walk see Valka, Latvia
29 U5 **Walker** Minnesota, N USA 47°06′N 94°35′W
15 V4 **Walker, Lac** ◎ Québec, SE Canada
35 S7 **Walker Lake** ◎ Nevada, W USA
35 R6 **Walker River** ≈ Nevada, W USA
28 K10 **Wall** South Dakota, N USA 43°58′N 102°12′W
173 U9 **Wallaby Plateau** undersea feature E Indian Ocean
33 N8 **Wallace** Idaho, NW USA 47°28′N 115°55′W
21 V11 **Wallace** North Carolina, SE USA 34°42′N 77°59′W
14 D17 **Wallaceburg** Ontario, S Canada 42°34′N 82°22′W
22 F5 **Wallace Lake** ⊠ Louisiana, S USA
11 P13 **Wallace Mountain** ▲ Alberta, W Canada 54°50′N 115°57′W
116 J14 **Wallachia** var. Walachia, Ger. Walachei, Rom. Valachia. cultural region S Romania
Wallachisch-Meseritsch see Valašské Meziříčí
183 U4 **Wallangarra** New South Wales, SE Australia 28°56′S 151°57′E
182 I8 **Wallaroo** South Australia 33°56′S 137°38′E
32 L10 **Walla Walla** Washington, NW USA 46°03′N 118°20′W
101 H19 **Walldürn** Baden-Württemberg, SW Germany 49°34′N 09°22′E
100 F12 **Wallenhorst** Niedersachsen, NW Germany 52°21′N 08°01′E
Wallenthal see Haţeg
109 S4 **Wallern** Oberösterreich, N Austria 48°13′N 13°58′E
Wallern see Wallern im Burgenland
109 Z5 **Wallern im Burgenland** var. Wallern. Burgenland, E Austria 47°44′N 16°57′E
18 M9 **Wallingford** Vermont, NE USA 43°27′N 72°56′W
25 V11 **Wallis** Texas, SW USA 29°38′N 96°05′W
Wallis see Valais
192 K9 **Wallis and Futuna** Fr. Territoire de Wallis et Futuna. ◇ French overseas territory C Pacific Ocean
108 G7 **Wallisellen** Zürich, N Switzerland 47°25′N 08°36′E
Wallis et Futuna, Territoire de see Wallis and Futuna
190 H11 **Wallis, Îles** island group N Wallis and Futuna
99 G20 **Wallonia** cultural region SW Belgium
31 Q5 **Walloon Lake** ◎ Michigan, N USA
32 K10 **Wallula** Washington, NW USA 46°03′N 118°54′W
32 K10 **Wallula, Lake** ◎ Washington, NW USA
21 S8 **Walnut Cove** North Carolina, SE USA 36°18′N 80°08′W
35 N8 **Walnut Creek** California, W USA 37°52′N 122°04′W
26 K5 **Walnut Creek** ≈ Kansas, C USA
27 W9 **Walnut Ridge** Arkansas, C USA 36°06′N 90°56′W
25 S7 **Walnut Springs** Texas, SW USA 32°05′N 97°42′W
182 L10 **Walpeup** Victoria, SE Australia 35°09′S 142°01′E
187 R17 **Walpole, Île** island SE New Caledonia
39 N13 **Walrus Islands** island group Alaska, USA
97 L19 **Walsall** C England, United Kingdom 52°35′N 01°58′W
37 T7 **Walsenburg** Colorado, C USA 37°37′N 104°46′W
11 S17 **Walsh** Alberta, SW Canada 49°58′N 110°03′W
37 W7 **Walsh** Colorado, C USA 37°20′N 102°17′W
100 I11 **Walsrode** Niedersachsen, N Germany 52°52′N 09°36′E
Waltenberg see Zalău
21 R14 **Walterboro** South Carolina, SE USA 32°54′N 80°21′W
Walter F.George Lake see Walter F. George Reservoir
23 R6 **Walter F. George Reservoir** var. Walter F.George Lake. ⊠ Alabama/Georgia, SE USA
26 M12 **Walters** Oklahoma, C USA 34°22′N 98°18′W
101 J16 **Waltershausen** Thüringen, C Germany 50°53′N 10°33′E
173 N10 **Walters Shoal** var. Walters Shoals. reef S Madagascar
Walters Shoals see Walters Shoal
22 M3 **Walthall** Mississippi, S USA 33°36′N 89°16′W
20 M4 **Walton** Kentucky, S USA 38°52′N 84°36′W
18 J11 **Walton** New York, NE USA 42°10′N 75°07′W
79 O20 **Walungu** Sud-Kivu, E Dem. Rep. Congo 02°40′S 28°37′E
Walvisbaai see Walvis Bay
83 C19 **Walvis Bay** Afr. Walvisbaai. Erongo, NW Namibia 22°59′S 14°31′E
83 B19 **Walvis Bay** bay NW Namibia
Walvish Ridge see Walvis Ridge
65 O17 **Walvis Ridge** var. Walvish Ridge. undersea feature E Atlantic Ocean 28°00′S 03°00′E
171 X16 **Wamal** Papua, E Indonesia 08°00′S 139°06′E
171 U15 **Wamar, Pulau** island Kepulauan Aru, E Indonesia
79 O17 **Wamba** Orientale, NE Dem. Rep. Congo 02°10′N 27°59′E
77 V15 **Wamba** Nassarawa, C Nigeria 08°57′N 08°35′E
79 H22 **Wamba** var. Uamba. ≈ Angola/Dem. Rep. Congo
27 P4 **Wamego** Kansas, C USA 39°12′N 96°18′W
18 I10 **Wampsville** New York, NE USA 43°03′N 75°40′W
42 K6 **Wampú, Río** ≈ E Honduras
171 X16 **Wan** Papua, E Indonesia 08°15′S 138°00′E
Wan see Anhui
183 N4 **Wanaaring** New South Wales, SE Australia 29°42′S 144°07′E
185 D21 **Wanaka** Otago, South Island, New Zealand 44°42′S 169°09′E
185 D20 **Wanaka, Lake** ◎ South Island, New Zealand
171 W14 **Wanapiri** Papua, E Indonesia 04°21′S 135°52′E
14 F9 **Wanapitei** ≈ Ontario, S Canada
14 F10 **Wanapitei Lake** ◎ Ontario, S Canada
18 K14 **Wanaque** New Jersey, NE USA 41°02′N 74°17′W
171 U12 **Wanau** Papua, E Indonesia 01°20′S 132°40′E
185 F22 **Wanbrow, Cape** headland South Island, New Zealand 45°07′S 170°59′E
Wancheng see Wanning
Wanchuan see Zhangjiakou
171 W13 **Wandai** var. Komeyo. Papua, E Indonesia 03°35′S 136°15′E
163 Z8 **Wanda Shan** ▲▲ NE China
197 R11 **Wandel Sea** sea Arctic Ocean
160 D13 **Wanding** var. Wandingzhen. Yunnan, SW China 24°01′N 98°00′E
Wandingzhen see Wanding
99 H20 **Wanfercée-Baulet** Hainaut, S Belgium 50°27′N 04°37′E
184 L12 **Wanganui** Manawatu-Wanganui, North Island, New Zealand 39°56′S 175°02′E
184 L11 **Wanganui** ≈ North Island, New Zealand
183 P11 **Wangaratta** Victoria, SE Australia 36°22′S 146°17′E
160 J8 **Wangcang** var. Donghe; prev. Fengjiaba, Hongjiang. Sichuan, C China 32°15′N 106°16′E
Wangda see Zogang
101 I24 **Wangen im Allgäu** Baden-Württemberg, S Germany 47°40′N 09°49′E
Wangerin see Węgorzyno
100 F9 **Wangerooge** island NW Germany
171 W13 **Wanggar** Papua, E Indonesia 03°22′S 135°15′E
160 J13 **Wangmo** var. Fuxing. Guizhou, S China 25°08′N 106°08′E
Wangolodougou see Ouangolodougou
161 S9 **Wangpan Yang** sea E China
163 Y10 **Wangqing** Jilin, NE China 43°19′N 129°42′E
167 P8 **Wang Saphung** Loei, C Thailand 17°18′N 101°45′E
167 O6 **Wan Hsa-la** Shan State, E Burma (Myanmar) 20°27′N 98°39′E
55 W9 **Wanica** ◈ district N Surinam
79 M18 **Wanie-Rukula** Orientale, C Dem. Rep. Congo 0°13′N 25°34′E
Wankie see Hwange
Wanki, Río see Coco, Río
81 N17 **Wanlaweyn** var. Wanle Weyn, It. Uanle Uen. Shabeellaha Hoose, SW Somalia 02°36′N 44°47′E
Wanle Weyn see Wanlaweyn
180 I12 **Wanneroo** Western Australia 31°40′S 115°35′E
160 L17 **Wanning** var. Wancheng. Hainan, S China 18°55′N 110°27′E
167 Q8 **Wanon Niwat** Sakon Nakhon, E Thailand 17°39′N 103°45′E
155 H16 **Wanparti** Andhra Pradesh, C India 16°19′N 78°06′E
Wansen see Wiązów
160 L11 **Wanshan** Guizhou, S China 27°45′N 109°12′E
99 M14 **Wanssum** Limburg, SE Netherlands 51°31′N 06°04′E
184 N12 **Wanstead** Hawke's Bay, North Island, New Zealand 40°09′S 176°31′E
Wanxian see Wanzhou
188 F16 **Wanyaan** Yap, Micronesia
160 K8 **Wanyuan** Sichuan, C China 32°05′N 108°08′E
161 O11 **Wanzai** var. Kangle. Jiangxi, S China 28°06′N 114°27′E
99 J20 **Wanze** Liège, E Belgium 50°32′N 05°16′E
160 K9 **Wanzhou** var. Wanxian. Chongqing Shi, C China 30°48′N 108°21′E
31 R12 **Wapakoneta** Ohio, N USA 40°34′N 84°11′W
12 D7 **Wapaseese** ≈ Ontario, C Canada
32 I10 **Wapato** Washington, NW USA 46°27′N 120°25′W
29 Y15 **Wapello** Iowa, C USA 41°10′N 91°13′W
11 N13 **Wapiti** ≈ Alberta/British Columbia, SW Canada
27 X7 **Wappapello Lake** ⊠ Missouri, C USA
18 K13 **Wappingers Falls** New York, NE USA 41°36′N 73°54′W
29 X13 **Wapsipinicon River** ≈ Iowa, C USA
14 L9 **Wapus** ≈ Québec, SE Canada
160 H7 **Waqên** Sichuan, C China 33°05′N 102°34′E
21 Q7 **War** West Virginia, NE USA 37°18′N 81°39′W
155 J15 **Warangal** Andhra Pradesh, C India 18°N 79°35′E
Warasdin see Varaždin
183 O16 **Waratah** Tasmania, SE Australia 41°28′S 145°34′E
183 O14 **Waratah Bay** bay Victoria, SE Australia
101 H15 **Warburg** Nordrhein-Westfalen, W Germany 51°30′N 09°11′E
182 I1 **Warburton Creek** seasonal river South Australia
180 M9 **Warburton** Western Australia 26°17′S 126°18′E
99 M20 **Warche** ≈ E Belgium
Wardag/Wardak see Wardak
149 P5 **Wardak** prev. Wardag, Pash. Wardag. ◈ province E Afghanistan
32 K9 **Warden** Washington, NW USA 46°58′N 119°02′W
154 I12 **Wardha** Mahārāshtra, W India 20°41′N 78°40′E
Wardija Point see Wardija, Ras il-
121 N15 **Wardija, Ras il-** var. Ras il- Wardija, Wardija Point. headland Gozo, NW Malta 36°03′N 14°11′E
Wardija, Ras il- see Wardija, Ras il-
139 P3 **Wardīyah** Nīnawá, N Iraq 36°18′N 41°45′E
185 E19 **Ward, Mount** ▲ South Island, New Zealand 43°49′S 169°54′E
10 L11 **Ware** British Columbia, W Canada 57°26′N 125°41′W
99 D18 **Waregem** var. Waereghem. West-Vlaanderen, W Belgium 50°53′N 03°26′E
99 J19 **Waremme** Liège, E Belgium 50°41′N 05°15′E

◆ Country
● Country Capital
◇ Dependent Territory
○ Dependent Territory Capital
◈ Administrative Regions
✈ International Airport
▲ Mountain
▲▲ Mountain Range
Volcano
≈ River
◎ Lake
⊠ Reservoir

100 *N10* **Waren** Mecklenburg-Vorpommern, N Germany 53°32′N 12°42′E
171 *W13* **Waren** Papua, E Indonesia 02°13′S 136°21′E
101 *F14* **Warendorf** Nordrhein-Westfalen, W Germany 51°57′N 08°00′E
21 *P12* **Ware Shoals** South Carolina, SE USA 34°24′N 82°15′W
98 *N4* **Warffum** Groningen, NE Netherlands 53°22′N 06°34′E
81 *O15* **Wargalo** Mudug, E Somalia 06°06′N 47°40′E
146 *M12* **Warganza** *Rus.* Varganzi. Qashqadaryo Viloyati, S Uzbekistan 39°18′N 66°00′E
Wargla *see* Ouargla
183 *T4* **Warialda** New South Wales, SE Australia 29°34′S 150°35′E
154 *F13* **Wāri Godri** Mahārāshtra, C India 19°28′N 75°43′E
167 *R10* **Warin Chamrap** Ubon Ratchathani, E Thailand 15°11′N 104°51′E
25 *R11* **Waring** Texas, SW USA 29°56′N 98°48′W
39 *O8* **Waring Mountains** ▲ Alaska, USA
110 *M12* **Warka** Mazowieckie, E Poland 51°45′N 21°12′E
184 *L5* **Warkworth** Auckland, North Island, New Zealand 36°23′S 174°42′E
171 *U12* **Warmandi** Papua, E Indonesia 0°21′S 132°38′E
83 *E22* **Warmbad** Karas, S Namibia 28°29′S 18°41′E
98 *H8* **Warmenhuizen** Noord-Holland, NW Netherlands 52°43′N 04°45′E
110 *M8* **Warmińsko-Mazurskie** ◆ *province* C Poland
97 *L22* **Warminster** S England, United Kingdom 51°13′N 02°12′W
18 *I15* **Warminster** Pennsylvania, NE USA 40°11′N 75°04′W
35 *V8* **Warm Springs** Nevada, W USA 38°10′N 116°21′W
32 *H12* **Warm Springs** Oregon, NW USA 44°51′N 121°24′W
21 *S5* **Warm Springs** Virginia, NE USA 38°03′N 79°48′W
100 *M8* **Warnemünde** Mecklenburg-Vorpommern, NE Germany 54°10′N 12°03′E
27 *Q10* **Warner** Oklahoma, C USA 35°29′N 95°18′W
35 *Q2* **Warner Mountains** ▲ California, W USA
23 *T5* **Warner Robins** Georgia, SE USA 32°38′N 83°38′W
57 *N18* **Warnes** Santa Cruz, C Bolivia 17°30′S 63°11′W
100 *M9* **Warnow** ∽ NE Germany
Warnsdorf *see* Varnsdorf
98 *M11* **Warnsveld** Gelderland, E Netherlands 52°08′N 06°14′E
154 *I13* **Warora** Mahārāshtra, C India 20°12′N 79°01′E
182 *L11* **Warracknabeal** Victoria, SE Australia 36°17′S 142°26′E
183 *O13* **Warragul** Victoria, SE Australia 38°11′S 145°55′E
80 *D13* **Warrap** Warrap, W South Sudan 08°08′N 28°37′E
81 *D14* **Warrap** ◆ *state* W South Sudan
183 *O4* **Warrego River** *seasonal river* New South Wales/ Queensland, E Australia
183 *Q6* **Warren** New South Wales, SE Australia 31°41′S 147°51′E
11 *X16* **Warren** Manitoba, S Canada 50°05′N 97°33′W
27 *V14* **Warren** Arkansas, C USA 33°38′N 92°05′W
31 *S10* **Warren** Michigan, N USA 42°29′N 83°02′W
29 *R3* **Warren** Minnesota, N USA 48°12′N 96°46′W
31 *U11* **Warren** Ohio, N USA 41°14′N 80°49′W
18 *D12* **Warren** Pennsylvania, NE USA 41°52′N 79°09′W
25 *X10* **Warren** Texas, SW USA 30°33′N 94°24′W
97 *G16* **Warrenpoint** *Ir.* An Pointe. SE Northern Ireland, United Kingdom 54°07′N 06°16′W
27 *S4* **Warrensburg** Missouri, C USA 38°46′N 93°44′W
83 *H22* **Warrenton** Northern Cape, N South Africa 28°07′S 24°51′E
23 *U4* **Warrenton** Georgia, SE USA 33°24′N 82°39′W
27 *W4* **Warrenton** Missouri, C USA 38°48′N 91°08′W
21 *V8* **Warrenton** North Carolina, SE USA 36°24′N 78°11′W
21 *V4* **Warrenton** Virginia, NE USA 38°43′N 77°48′W
77 *U17* **Warri** Delta, S Nigeria 05°26′N 05°34′E
97 *L18* **Warrington** C England, United Kingdom 53°24′N 02°37′W
23 *O9* **Warrington** Florida, SE USA 30°22′N 87°16′W
23 *P3* **Warrior** Alabama, S USA 33°49′N 86°49′W
182 *L13* **Warrnambool** Victoria, SE Australia 38°23′S 142°30′E
29 *T2* **Warroad** Minnesota, N USA 48°55′N 95°18′W
183 *S6* **Warrumbungle Range** ▲ New South Wales, SE Australia
154 *J12* **Wārsa** Mahārāshtra, C India 20°42′N 79°58′E
31 *P11* **Warsaw** Indiana, N USA 41°13′N 85°52′W
20 *L4* **Warsaw** Kentucky, S USA 38°47′N 84°55′W
27 *T5* **Warsaw** Missouri, C USA 38°14′N 93°23′W
18 *E10* **Warsaw** New York, NE USA 42°44′N 78°06′W
21 *V10* **Warsaw** North Carolina, SE USA 35°00′N 78°05′W
21 *X5* **Warsaw** Virginia, NE USA 37°57′N 76°46′W
Warsaw/Warschau *see* Warszawa
81 *N17* **Warshiikh** Shabeellaha Dhexe, C Somalia 02°22′N 45°52′E
101 *G15* **Warstein** Nordrhein-Westfalen, W Germany 51°27′N 08°21′E
110 *M11* **Warszawa** *Eng.* Warsaw, *Ger.* Warschau, *Rus.* Varshava. ● (Poland) Mazowieckie, C Poland 52°15′N 21°E
110 *J13* **Warta** Sieradz, C Poland 51°43′N 18°37′E
110 *D11* **Warta** *Ger.* Warthe. ∽ W Poland
Wartberg *see* Senec
20 *M9* **Wartburg** Tennessee, S USA 36°08′N 84°37′W
108 *J7* **Warth** Vorarlberg, NW Austria 47°16′N 10°11′E
Warthe *see* Warta
169 *U12* **Waru** Borneo, C Indonesia 01°24′S 116°37′E
171 *T13* **Waru** Pulau Seram, E Indonesia 03°24′S 130°38′E
139 *N6* **Wa'r, Wādī al** *dry watercourse* E Syria
183 *U3* **Warwick** Queensland, E Australia 28°12′S 152°E
15 *Q11* **Warwick** Québec, SE Canada 45°55′N 72°00′W
97 *M20* **Warwick** C England, United Kingdom 52°17′N 01°34′W
18 *K13* **Warwick** New York, NE USA 41°15′N 74°21′W
29 *P4* **Warwick** North Dakota, N USA 47°49′N 98°42′W
19 *O12* **Warwick** Rhode Island, NE USA 41°40′N 71°21′W
97 *L20* **Warwickshire** *cultural region* C England, United Kingdom
14 *G14* **Wasaga Beach** Ontario, S Canada 44°30′N 80°00′W
77 *U13* **Wasagu** Kebbi, NW Nigeria 11°25′N 05°48′E
36 *M2* **Wasatch Range** ▲ W USA
35 *R12* **Wasco** California, W USA 35°34′N 119°20′W
29 *V10* **Waseca** Minnesota, N USA 44°04′N 93°30′W
14 *H13* **Washago** Ontario, S Canada 44°46′N 78°48′W
19 *S2* **Washburn** Maine, NE USA 46°46′N 68°08′W
28 *M5* **Washburn** North Dakota, N USA 47°15′N 101°02′W
30 *K3* **Washburn** Wisconsin, N USA 46°41′N 90°53′W
31 *S14* **Washburn Hill** *hill* Ohio, N USA
154 *H13* **Wāshīm** Mahārāshtra, C India 20°06′N 77°08′E
97 *M14* **Washington** NE England, United Kingdom 54°54′N 01°31′W
23 *U3* **Washington** Georgia, SE USA 33°44′N 82°44′W
30 *L12* **Washington** Illinois, N USA 40°42′N 89°24′W
31 *N15* **Washington** Indiana, N USA 38°40′N 87°10′W
29 *X15* **Washington** Iowa, C USA 41°18′N 91°41′W
27 *O3* **Washington** Kansas, C USA 39°49′N 97°03′W
27 *W5* **Washington** Missouri, C USA 38°31′N 91°01′W
21 *X9* **Washington** North Carolina, SE USA 35°33′N 77°04′W
18 *B15* **Washington** Pennsylvania, NE USA 40°11′N 80°16′W
25 *V10* **Washington** Texas, SW USA 30°18′N 96°08′W
36 *J8* **Washington** Utah, W USA 37°07′N 113°30′W
21 *V4* **Washington** Virginia, NE USA 38°43′N 78°11′W
32 *I9* **Washington** *off.* State of Washington, *also known as* Chinook State, Evergreen State. ◆ *state* NW USA
Washington *see* Washington Court House
31 *S14* **Washington Court House** *var.* Washington. Ohio, NE USA 39°32′N 83°29′W
21 *W4* **Washington DC** ● (USA) District of Columbia, NE USA 38°54′N 77°02′W
31 *O5* **Washington Island** *island* Wisconsin, N USA
Washington Island *see* Teraina
19 *O7* **Washington, Mount** ▲ New Hampshire, NE USA 44°16′N 71°18′W
26 *M11* **Washita River** ∽ Oklahoma/Texas, C USA
97 *O18* **Wash, The** *inlet* E England, United Kingdom
32 *L9* **Washtucna** Washington, NW USA 46°44′N 118°19′W
Wasiliszki *see* Vasilishki
110 *P9* **Wasilków** Podlaskie, NE Poland 53°12′N 23°15′E
39 *R11* **Wasilla** Alaska, USA 61°34′N 149°26′W
55 *U9* **Wasjabo** Sipaliwini, NW Surinam 05°09′N 57°09′W
12 *I10* **Waskaganish** *prev.* Fort Rupert, Rupert House. Québec, SE Canada 51°30′N 79°45′W
11 *X11* **Waskaiowaka Lake** ◎ Manitoba, C Canada
11 *T14* **Waskesiu Lake** Saskatchewan, C Canada 53°56′N 106°05′W
25 *X7* **Waskom** Texas, SW USA 32°28′N 94°03′W
110 *G13* **Wąsosz** Dolnośląskie, SW Poland 51°36′N 16°30′E
42 *M6* **Waspam** *var.* Waspán. Región Autónoma Atlántico Norte, NE Nicaragua 14°41′N 84°04′W
Waspán *see* Waspam
165 *T3* **Wassamu** Hokkaidō, NE Japan 44°01′N 142°25′E
108 *G9* **Wassen** Uri, C Switzerland 46°42′N 08°34′E
98 *G11* **Wassenaar** Zuid-Holland, W Netherlands 52°09′N 04°23′E
99 *N24* **Wasserbillig** Grevenmacher, E Luxembourg 49°43′N 06°30′E
Wasserburg *see* Wasserburg am Inn
101 *M23* **Wasserburg am Inn** *var.* Wasserburg. Bayern, SE Germany 48°02′N 12°12′E
101 *I17* **Wasserkuppe** ▲ C Germany 50°30′N 09°55′E
103 *R5* **Wassy** Haute-Marne, N France 48°32′N 04°54′E
171 *N14* **Watampone** *var.* Bone. Sulawesi, C Indonesia 04°33′S 120°20′E
171 *R13* **Watawa** Pulau Buru, E Indonesia 03°36′S 127°13′E
Watenstedt-Salzgitter *see* Salzgitter
18 *M13* **Waterbury** Connecticut, NE USA 41°33′N 73°01′W
21 *R11* **Wateree Lake** ▣ South Carolina, SE USA
21 *R12* **Wateree River** ∽ South Carolina, SE USA
97 *E20* **Waterford** *Ir.* Port Láirge. Waterford, S Ireland 52°15′N 07°08′W
31 *S9* **Waterford** Michigan, N USA 42°42′N 83°24′W
97 *E20* **Waterford** *Ir.* Port Láirge. *cultural region* S Ireland
97 *E21* **Waterford Harbour** *Ir.* Cuan Phort Láirge. *inlet* S Ireland
98 *G12* **Wateringen** Zuid-Holland, W Netherlands 52°02′N 04°16′E
99 *G19* **Waterloo** Walloon Brabant, C Belgium 50°43′N 04°24′E
14 *F16* **Waterloo** Ontario, S Canada 43°28′N 80°32′W
15 *P12* **Waterloo** Québec, SE Canada 45°20′N 72°28′W
30 *K16* **Waterloo** Illinois, N USA 38°20′N 90°09′W
29 *X13* **Waterloo** Iowa, C USA 42°31′N 92°16′W
18 *G10* **Waterloo** New York, NE USA 42°54′N 76°51′W
30 *L4* **Watersmeet** Michigan, N USA 46°16′N 89°10′W
23 *V9* **Watertown** Florida, SE USA 30°11′N 82°36′W
18 *I8* **Watertown** New York, NE USA 43°37′N 75°56′W
29 *R9* **Watertown** South Dakota, N USA 44°54′N 97°07′W
30 *M8* **Watertown** Wisconsin, N USA 43°12′N 88°44′W
22 *L3* **Water Valley** Mississippi, S USA 34°09′N 89°37′W
27 *O3* **Waterville** Kansas, C USA 39°41′N 96°45′W
17 *V6* **Waterville** Maine, NE USA 44°34′N 69°41′W
29 *V10* **Waterville** Minnesota, N USA 44°13′N 93°34′W
18 *I10* **Waterville** New York, NE USA 42°55′N 75°18′W
14 *E16* **Watford** Ontario, S Canada 42°57′N 81°51′W
97 *N21* **Watford** E England, United Kingdom 51°39′N 00°24′W
28 *K4* **Watford City** North Dakota, N USA 47°48′N 103°16′W
141 *X12* **Wāṭif** S Oman 18°34′N 56°31′E
18 *G11* **Watkins Glen** New York, NE USA 42°23′N 76°53′W
Watlings Island *see* San Salvador
171 *U15* **Watnil** Pulau Kai Kecil, E Indonesia 05°45′S 132°39′E
26 *M10* **Watonga** Oklahoma, C USA 35°52′N 98°26′W
11 *T16* **Watrous** Saskatchewan, S Canada 51°40′N 105°29′W
37 *T10* **Watrous** New Mexico, SW USA 35°48′N 104°58′W
79 *P16* **Watsa** Orientale, NE Dem. Rep. Congo 03°00′N 29°31′E
31 *N12* **Watseka** Illinois, N USA 40°46′N 87°44′W
79 *J19* **Watsikengo** Equateur, C Dem. Rep. Congo 0°49′S 20°34′E
182 *C5* **Watson** South Australia 30°32′S 131°29′E
11 *U15* **Watson** Saskatchewan, S Canada 52°13′N 104°30′W
195 *O10* **Watson Escarpment** ▲ Antarctica
10 *K9* **Watson Lake** Yukon Territory, W Canada 60°05′N 128°47′W
35 *N10* **Watsonville** California, W USA 36°53′N 121°43′W
167 *Q8* **Wattay** ✈ (Viangchan) Viangchan, C Laos 18°03′N 102°36′E
109 *N7* **Wattens** Tirol, W Austria 47°18′N 11°37′E
20 *M9* **Watts Bar Lake** ▣ Tennessee, S USA
108 *H7* **Wattwil** Sankt Gallen, NE Switzerland 47°18′N 09°06′E
171 *T14* **Watubela, Kepulauan** *island group* E Indonesia
101 *N24* **Watzmann** ▲ SE Germany 47°32′N 12°56′E
186 *E8* **Wau** Morobe, C Papua New Guinea 07°22′S 146°40′E
81 *D14* **Wau** *var.* Wāw. Western Bahr el Ghazal, W South Sudan 07°43′N 28°01′E
29 *Q8* **Waubay** South Dakota, N USA 45°19′N 97°18′W
29 *Q8* **Waubay Lake** ◎ South Dakota, N USA
183 *U7* **Wauchope** New South Wales, SE Australia 31°30′S 152°46′E
23 *W13* **Wauchula** Florida, SE USA 27°33′N 81°48′W
30 *M10* **Wauconda** Illinois, N USA 42°15′N 88°08′W
182 *J7* **Waukaringa** South Australia 32°19′S 139°27′E
31 *N10* **Waukegan** Illinois, N USA 42°21′N 87°50′W
30 *M9* **Waukesha** Wisconsin, N USA 43°01′N 88°14′W
29 *X11* **Waukon** Iowa, C USA 43°16′N 91°28′W
30 *L8* **Waunakee** Wisconsin, N USA 43°13′N 89°28′W
30 *L7* **Waupaca** Wisconsin, N USA 44°23′N 89°04′W
30 *M8* **Waupun** Wisconsin, N USA 43°40′N 88°43′W
26 *M13* **Waurika** Oklahoma, C USA 34°10′N 98°00′W
26 *M12* **Waurika Lake** ▣ Oklahoma, C USA
30 *L6* **Wausau** Wisconsin, N USA 44°58′N 89°40′W
31 *R11* **Wauseon** Ohio, N USA 41°33′N 84°08′W
30 *L7* **Wautoma** Wisconsin, N USA 44°05′N 89°17′W
30 *M9* **Wauwatosa** Wisconsin, N USA 43°03′N 88°03′W
22 *L9* **Waveland** Mississippi, S USA 30°17′N 89°22′W
97 *Q20* **Waveney** ∽ E England, United Kingdom
184 *L11* **Waverley** Taranaki, North Island, New Zealand 39°45′S 174°35′E
29 *W12* **Waverly** Iowa, C USA 42°43′N 92°28′W
27 *T4* **Waverly** Missouri, C USA 39°12′N 93°31′W
29 *R15* **Waverly** Nebraska, C USA 40°56′N 96°27′W
18 *G12* **Waverly** New York, NE USA 42°00′N 76°33′W
20 *H8* **Waverly** Tennessee, S USA 36°04′N 87°49′W
21 *W7* **Waverly** Virginia, NE USA 37°02′N 77°06′W
99 *H19* **Wavre** Walloon Brabant, C Belgium 50°43′N 04°37′E
166 *M8* **Waw** Bago, SW Burma (Myanmar) 17°26′N 96°40′E
Wāw *see* Wau
14 *B7* **Wawa** Ontario, S Canada 47°59′N 84°43′W
77 *T14* **Wawa** Niger, W Nigeria 09°52′N 04°33′E
75 *Q11* **Wāw al Kabīr** S Libya 25°21′N 16°41′E
43 *N7* **Wawa, Río** *var.* Rio Huahua. ∽ NE Nicaragua
186 *B8* **Wawoi** ∽ SW Papua New Guinea
25 *T7* **Waxahachie** Texas, SW USA 32°23′N 96°52′W
158 *L9* **Waxxari** Xinjiang Uygur Zizhiqu, NW China 38°43′N 87°11′E
Wayaobu *see* Zichang
23 *V7* **Waycross** Georgia, SE USA 31°13′N 82°21′W
180 *K10* **Way, Lake** ◎ Western Australia
31 *P9* **Wayland** Michigan, N USA 42°40′N 85°38′W
29 *R13* **Wayne** Nebraska, C USA 42°13′N 97°01′W
18 *K14* **Wayne** New Jersey, NE USA 40°57′N 74°16′W
21 *P5* **Wayne** West Virginia, NE USA 38°14′N 82°27′W
23 *V4* **Waynesboro** Georgia, SE USA 33°04′N 82°01′W
22 *M7* **Waynesboro** Mississippi, S USA 31°40′N 88°39′W
20 *H10* **Waynesboro** Tennessee, S USA 35°20′N 87°49′W
21 *U5* **Waynesboro** Virginia, NE USA 38°04′N 78°54′W
18 *B16* **Waynesburg** Pennsylvania, NE USA 39°51′N 80°10′W
27 *U6* **Waynesville** Missouri, C USA 37°48′N 92°11′W
21 *O10* **Waynesville** North Carolina, SE USA 35°29′N 82°59′W
26 *L8* **Waynoka** Oklahoma, C USA 36°36′N 98°53′W
Wazan *see* Ouazzane
Wazima *see* Wajima
149 *V7* **Wazīrābād** Punjab, NE Pakistan 32°28′N 74°04′E
Wazzan *see* Ouazzane
110 *I8* **Wda** *var.* Czarna Woda, *Ger.* Schwarzwasser. ∽ N Poland
187 *Q16* **Wé** Province des Îles Loyauté, E New Caledonia 20°55′S 167°15′E
97 *O23* **Weald, The** *lowlands* SE England, United Kingdom
186 *A9* **Weam** Western, SW Papua New Guinea 08°33′S 141°10′E
97 *L15* **Wear** ∽ N England, United Kingdom
Wearmouth *see* Sunderland
26 *L10* **Weatherford** Oklahoma, C USA 35°31′N 98°42′W
25 *S6* **Weatherford** Texas, SW USA 32°47′N 97°48′W
34 *M3* **Weaverville** California, W USA 40°42′N 122°57′W
27 *R7* **Webb City** Missouri, C USA 37°07′N 94°28′W
192 *G8* **Weber Basin** *undersea feature* S Ceram Sea
Webfoot State *see* Oregon
18 *F9* **Webster** New York, NE USA 43°12′N 77°25′W
29 *Q8* **Webster** South Dakota, N USA 45°19′N 97°31′W
29 *V13* **Webster City** Iowa, C USA 42°28′N 93°49′W
27 *X5* **Webster Groves** Missouri, C USA 38°32′N 90°20′W
21 *S4* **Webster Springs** *var.* Addison. West Virginia, NE USA 38°29′N 80°52′W
171 *S11* **Weda, Teluk** *bay* Pulau Halmahera, E Indonesia
65 *B25* **Weddell Island** *var.* Isla de San Jorge. *island* W Falkland Islands
65 *K22* **Weddell Plain** *undersea feature* SW Atlantic Ocean 65°00′S 40°00′W
65 *K23* **Weddell Sea** *sea* SW Atlantic Ocean
65 *B25* **Weddell Settlement** Weddell Island, W Falkland Islands 52°53′S 60°54′W
182 *M11* **Wedderburn** Victoria, SE Australia 36°26′S 143°37′E
100 *I9* **Wedel** Schleswig-Holstein, N Germany 53°35′N 09°42′E
92 *N3* **Wedel Jarlsberg Land** *physical region* SW Svalbard
100 *I12* **Wedemark** Niedersachsen, NW Germany 52°33′N 09°43′E
10 *M17* **Wedge Mountain** ▲ British Columbia, SW Canada 50°10′N 122°43′W
23 *R4* **Wedowee** Alabama, S USA 33°16′N 85°28′W
171 *U15* **Weduar** Pulau Kai Besar, E Indonesia 05°55′S 132°51′E
35 *N2* **Weed** California, W USA 41°26′N 122°24′W
15 *Q12* **Weedon Centre** Québec, SE Canada 45°40′N 71°28′W
18 *E13* **Weedville** Pennsylvania, NE USA 41°15′N 78°28′W
100 *F10* **Weener** Niedersachsen, NW Germany 53°09′N 07°19′E
29 *S16* **Weeping Water** Nebraska, C USA 40°52′N 96°08′W
99 *L16* **Weert** Limburg, SE Netherlands 51°15′N 05°43′E
98 *I10* **Weesp** Noord-Holland, C Netherlands 52°18′N 05°03′E
183 *S5* **Wee Waa** New South Wales, SE Australia 30°16′S 149°27′E
110 *N7* **Węgorzewo** *Ger.* Angerburg. Warmińsko-Mazurskie, NE Poland 54°12′N 21°49′E
110 *E9* **Węgorzyno** *Ger.* Wangerin. Zachodnio-pomorskie, NW Poland 53°34′N 15°35′E
110 *N11* **Węgrów** *Ger.* Bingerau. Mazowieckie, C Poland 52°22′N 22°00′E
98 *N5* **Wehe-Den Hoorn** Groningen, NE Netherlands 53°20′N 06°29′E
98 *M12* **Wehl** Gelderland, E Netherlands 51°58′N 06°13′E
Wehlau *see* Znamensk
168 *F7* **Weh, Pulau** *island* NW Indonesia
Wei *see* Weifang
161 *P1* **Weichang** *prev.* Zhuizishan. Hebei, E China 41°55′N 117°45′E
Weichang *see* Weishan
Weichsel *see* Wisła
101 *M16* **Weida** Thüringen, C Germany 50°46′N 12°05′E
Weiden *see* Weiden in der Oberpfalz
101 *M19* **Weiden in der Oberpfalz** *var.* Weiden. Bayern, SE Germany 49°40′N 12°10′E
161 *Q4* **Weifang** *var.* Wei, Wei-fang; *prev.* Weihsien. Shandong, E China 36°44′N 119°10′E
161 *S4* **Weihai** Shandong, E China 37°30′N 122°04′E
160 *K6* **Wei He** ∽ C China
Weihsien *see* Weifang
101 *G17* **Weilburg** Hessen, W Germany 50°31′N 08°18′E
101 *K24* **Weilheim in Oberbayern** Bayern, SE Germany 47°50′N 11°09′E
183 *P4* **Weilmoringle** New South Wales, SE Australia 29°13′S 146°51′E
101 *L16* **Weimar** Thüringen, C Germany 50°59′N 11°20′E
25 *U11* **Weimar** Texas, SW USA 29°42′N 96°46′W
160 *L6* **Weinan** Shaanxi, C China 34°30′N 109°30′E
108 *H6* **Weinfelden** Thurgau, NE Switzerland 47°33′N 09°09′E
101 *I24* **Weingarten** Baden-Württemberg, S Germany 47°49′N 09°37′E
101 *G20* **Weinheim** Baden-Württemberg, SW Germany 49°33′N 08°40′E
160 *H11* **Weining** *var.* Caohai, Weining Yizu Huizu Miaozu Zizhixian. Guizhou, S China 26°51′N 104°16′E
Weining Yizu Huizu Miaozu Zizhixian *see* Weining
181 *V2* **Weipa** Queensland, NE Australia 12°43′S 142°01′E
11 *Y11* **Weir River** Manitoba, C Canada 56°44′N 94°06′W
21 *R1* **Weirton** West Virginia, NE USA 40°24′N 80°37′W
32 *M13* **Weiser** Idaho, NW USA 44°15′N 116°58′W
160 *F12* **Weishan** *var.* Weichang. Yunnan, SW China 25°22′N 100°19′E
161 *P6* **Weishan Hu** ◎ E China
101 *M15* **Weisse Elster** *Eng.* White Elster. ∽ Czech Republic/ Germany
Weisse Körös/Weisse Kreisch *see* Crişul Alb
108 *L7* **Weissenbach am Lech** Tirol, W Austria 47°27′N 10°39′E
Weissenburg *see* Wissembourg, France
Weissenburg *see* Alba Iulia, Romania
101 *K21* **Weissenburg in Bayern** Bayern, SE Germany 49°02′N 10°59′E
101 *M15* **Weissenfels** *var.* Weißenfels. Sachsen-Anhalt, C Germany 51°12′N 11°58′E
109 *R9* **Weissensee** ◎ S Austria
Weissenstein *see* Paide
108 *E11* **Weisshorn** *var.* Flüela Wisshorn. ▲ SW Switzerland 46°06′N 07°43′E
Weisskirchen *see* Bela Crkva
23 *R3* **Weiss Lake** ▣ Alabama, S USA
101 *Q14* **Weisswasser** *Lus.* Běla Woda. Sachsen, E Germany 51°30′N 14°37′E
99 *M22* **Weiswampach** Diekirch, N Luxembourg 50°08′N 06°05′E
109 *U2* **Weitra** Niederösterreich, N Austria 48°41′N 14°54′E
161 *O4* **Weixian** *var.* Wei Xian. Hebei, E China 36°59′N 115°15′E
Wei Xian *see* Weixian
159 *V11* **Weiyuan** *var.* Qingyuan. Gansu, C China 35°07′N 104°12′E
Weiyuan *see* Shuangjiang
160 *F14* **Weiyuan Jiang** ∽ SW China
109 *W7* **Weiz** Steiermark, SE Austria 47°13′N 15°38′E
Weizhou *see* Wenchuan
160 *K16* **Weizhou Dao** *island* S China
110 *I6* **Wejherowo** Pomorskie, NW Poland 54°36′N 18°12′E
27 *Q8* **Welch** Oklahoma, C USA 36°52′N 95°06′W
24 *M6* **Welch** Texas, SW USA 32°52′N 102°06′W
21 *Q6* **Welch** West Virginia, NE USA 37°26′N 81°36′W
45 *O14* **Welchman Hall** C Barbados 13°10′N 59°34′W
80 *J11* **Weldiya** *var.* Waldia, *It.* Valdia. Āmara, N Ethiopia 11°45′N 39°39′E
21 *W8* **Weldon** North Carolina, SE USA 36°25′N 77°36′W
25 *V9* **Weldon** Texas, SW USA 31°00′N 95°33′W
99 *M19* **Welkenraedt** Liège, E Belgium 50°40′N 05°58′E
193 *O2* **Welker Seamount** *undersea feature* N Pacific Ocean 55°07′N 140°18′W
83 *I22* **Welkom** Free State, C South Africa 27°59′S 26°44′E
14 *H16* **Welland** Ontario, S Canada 42°59′N 79°14′W
14 *G16* **Welland** ∽ Ontario, S Canada
97 *O19* **Welland** ∽ C England, United Kingdom
14 *H17* **Welland Canal** *canal* Ontario, S Canada
155 *K25* **Wellawaya** Uva Province, SE Sri Lanka 06°44′N 81°07′E
Welle *see* Uele
181 *T4* **Wellesley Islands** *island group* Queensland, N Australia
99 *J22* **Wellin** Luxembourg, SE Belgium 50°06′N 05°05′E
97 *N20* **Wellingborough** C England, United Kingdom 52°19′N 00°42′W
183 *R7* **Wellington** New South Wales, SE Australia 32°33′S 148°59′E
14 *J15* **Wellington** Ontario, SE Canada 43°59′N 77°21′W
185 *L14* **Wellington** ● Wellington, North Island, New Zealand 41°17′S 174°47′E
83 *E26* **Wellington** Western Cape, SW South Africa 33°39′S 19°00′E
37 *T2* **Wellington** Colorado, C USA 40°42′N 105°00′W
27 *N7* **Wellington** Kansas, C USA 37°17′N 97°25′W
35 *R7* **Wellington** Nevada, W USA 38°45′N 119°22′W
31 *T11* **Wellington** Ohio, N USA 41°10′N 82°13′W
25 *P3* **Wellington** Texas, SW USA 34°52′N 100°13′W
36 *M4* **Wellington** Utah, W USA 39°31′N 110°45′W
185 *M14* **Wellington** *off.* Wellington Region. ◆ *region* (New Zealand) North Island, New Zealand
185 *L14* **Wellington** ✈ Wellington, North Island, New Zealand 41°19′S 174°48′E
Wellington *see* Wellington, Isla
63 *F22* **Wellington, Isla** *var.* Wellington. *island* S Chile
183 *P12* **Wellington, Lake** ◎ Victoria, SE Australia
Wellington Region *see* Wellington
29 *X14* **Wellman** Iowa, C USA 41°27′N 91°50′W
24 *M6* **Wellman** Texas, SW USA 33°03′N 102°25′W
97 *K22* **Wells** SW England, United Kingdom 51°13′N 02°39′W
29 *V11* **Wells** Minnesota, N USA 43°45′N 93°43′W
35 *X2* **Wells** Nevada, W USA 41°07′N 114°58′W
25 *W8* **Wells** Texas, SW USA 31°28′N 94°54′W
18 *F12* **Wellsboro** Pennsylvania, NE USA 41°43′N 77°39′W
21 *R1* **Wellsburg** West Virginia, NE USA 40°15′N 80°37′W
184 *K4* **Wellsford** Auckland, North Island, New Zealand 36°17′S 174°30′E
180 *L9* **Wells, Lake** ◎ Western Australia
181 *N4* **Wells, Mount** ▲ Western Australia 17°39′S 127°08′E
97 *P18* **Wells-next-the-Sea** E England, United Kingdom 52°58′N 00°48′E
31 *T15* **Wellston** Ohio, N USA 39°07′N 82°31′W
27 *O10* **Wellston** Oklahoma, C USA 35°41′N 97°03′W
18 *E11* **Wellsville** New York, NE USA 42°06′N 77°55′W
31 *V12* **Wellsville** Ohio, N USA 40°36′N 80°39′W
36 *L1* **Wellsville** Utah, W USA 41°38′N 111°55′W
36 *I14* **Wellton** Arizona, SW USA 32°40′N 114°09′W
109 *S4* **Wels** *anc.* Ovilava. Oberösterreich, N Austria 48°10′N 14°02′E
99 *K15* **Welschap** ✈ (Eindhoven) Noord-Brabant, S Netherlands 51°27′N 05°22′E
100 *P10* **Welse** ∽ NE Germany
22 *H9* **Welsh** Louisiana, S USA 30°12′N 92°49′W
97 *K19* **Welshpool** *Wel.* Y Trallwng. E Wales, United Kingdom 52°38′N 03°06′W
97 *O21* **Welwyn Garden City** E England, United Kingdom 51°48′N 00°13′W
79 *K18* **Wema** Equateur, NW Dem. Rep. Congo 0°25′S 21°33′E
81 *G21* **Wembere** ∽ C Tanzania
11 *N13* **Wembley** Alberta, W Canada 55°07′N 119°12′W
12 *I9* **Wemindji** *prev.* Nouveau-Comptoir , Paint Hills. Québec, C Canada 53°00′N 78°42′W
99 *G18* **Wemmel** Vlaams Brabant, C Belgium 50°54′N 04°18′E
32 *J8* **Wenatchee** Washington, NW USA 47°50′N 120°48′W
160 *M17* **Wenchang** Hainan, S China 19°34′N 110°46′E
161 *R11* **Wencheng** *var.* Daxue. Zhejiang, SE China 27°48′N 120°01′E
77 *P16* **Wenchi** W Ghana 07°45′N 02°02′W
Wen-chou/Wenchow *see* Wenzhou
160 *H8* **Wenchuan** *var.* Weizhou. Sichuan, C China 31°29′N 103°39′E
Wendau *see* Võnnu
Wenden *see* Cēsis
161 *S4* **Wendeng** Shandong, E China 37°10′N 122°00′E
81 *J14* **Wendo** Southern Nationalities, S Ethiopia 06°34′N 38°28′E
36 *J2* **Wendover** Utah, W USA 40°41′N 114°00′W
14 *D9* **Wenebegon** ∽ Ontario, S Canada
14 *D8* **Wenebegon Lake** ◎ Ontario, S Canada
108 *E9* **Wengen** Bern, W Switzerland 46°38′N 07°57′E
161 *O13* **Wengyuan** *var.* Longxian. Guangdong, S China 24°22′N 114°06′E
189 *P15* **Weno** *prev.* Moen. Chuuk, C Micronesia
189 *V12* **Weno** *prev.* Moen. *atoll* Chuuk Islands, C Micronesia
158 *N13* **Wenquan** Qinghai, C China 33°16′N 91°44′E
159 *H4* **Wenquan** *var.* Arixang, Bogeda'er. Xinjiang Uygur Zizhiqu, NW China 45°00′N 81°02′E
Wenquan *see* Yingshan
160 *H14* **Wenshan** *var.* Kaihua. Yunnan, SW China 23°22′N 104°21′E
158 *H6* **Wensu** Xinjiang Uygur Zizhiqu, W China 41°15′N 80°11′E
182 *L8* **Wentworth** New South Wales, SE Australia 34°04′S 141°53′E
27 *W4* **Wentzville** Missouri, C USA 38°48′N 90°51′W
159 *V12* **Wenxian** *var.* Wen Xian. Gansu, C China 32°57′N 104°42′E
Wen Xian *see* Wenxian
161 *S10* **Wenzhou** *var.* Wen-chou, Wenchow. Zhejiang, SE China 28°02′N 120°36′E
34 *L4* **Weott** California, W USA 40°19′N 123°57′W
99 *I20* **Wépion** Namur, SE Belgium 50°24′N 04°53′E
100 *O11* **Werbellinsee** ◎ NE Germany
99 *L21* **Werbomont** Liège, E Belgium 50°22′N 05°43′E
83 *G20* **Werda** Kgalagadi, S Botswana 25°13′S 23°16′E
81 *N14* **Werdēr** Sumalē, E Ethiopia 06°59′N 45°20′E
Werder *see* Virtsu
Werenów *see* Voranava
171 *U13* **Weri** Papua, E Indonesia 03°10′S 132°39′E
98 *I13* **Werkendam** Noord-Brabant, S Netherlands 51°48′N 04°54′E
101 *M20* **Wernberg-Köblitz** Bayern, SE Germany 49°31′N 12°10′E
101 *J18* **Werneck** Bayern, C Germany 50°00′N 10°06′E
101 *K14* **Wernigerode** Sachsen-Anhalt, C Germany 51°51′N 10°48′E
Werowitz *see* Virovitica
101 *J16* **Werra** ∽ C Germany
183 *N12* **Werribee** Victoria, SE Australia 37°55′S 144°39′E
183 *T6* **Werris Creek** New South Wales, SE Australia 31°22′S 150°40′E
Werro *see* Võru
Werschetz *see* Vršac
101 *K23* **Wertach** ∽ S Germany
101 *I19* **Wertheim** Baden-Württemberg, SW Germany 49°45′N 09°31′E
98 *J8* **Wervershoof** Noord-Holland, NW Netherlands 52°43′N 05°09′E
Wervicq *see* Wervik
99 *C18* **Wervik** *var.* Wervicq, Werwick. West-Vlaanderen, W Belgium 50°47′N 03°03′E
Werwick *see* Wervik
101 *D14* **Wesel** Nordrhein-Westfalen, W Germany 51°39′N 06°37′E
Weseli an der Lainsitz *see* Veselí nad Lužnicí
Wesenberg *see* Rakvere
100 *H12* **Weser** ∽ NW Germany
Wes-Kaap *see* Western Cape
25 *S17* **Weslaco** Texas, SW USA 26°09′N 97°59′W
14 *J13* **Weslemkoon Lake** ◎ Ontario, SE Canada
181 *R1* **Wessel Islands** *island group* Northern Territory, N Australia
29 *P9* **Wessington** South Dakota, N USA 44°27′N 98°40′W
29 *P10* **Wessington Springs** South Dakota, N USA 44°02′N 98°33′W
25 *T8* **West** Texas, SW USA 31°48′N 97°05′W
West *see* Ouest
30 *M9* **West Allis** Wisconsin, N USA 43°01′N 88°00′W
182 *E8* **Westall, Point** *headland* South Australia 32°54′S 134°04′E
194 *M10* **West Antarctica** *prev.* Lesser Antarctica. *physical region* Antarctica
14 *G11* **West Arm** Ontario, S Canada 46°16′N 80°25′W
West Australian Basin *see* Wharton Basin
West Azerbaijan *see* Āzarbāyjān-e Gharbī
11 *N17* **Westbank** British Columbia, SW Canada 49°50′N 119°37′W
138 *F10* **West Bank** *disputed region* SW Asia
14 *E11* **West Bay** Manitoulin Island, Ontario, S Canada 45°48′N 82°09′W
22 *L11* **West Bay** *bay* Louisiana, S USA
30 *M8* **West Bend** Wisconsin, N USA 43°26′N 88°13′W
153 *R16* **West Bengal** ◆ *state* NE India
West Borneo *see* Kalimantan Barat
29 *Y14* **West Branch** Iowa, C USA 41°40′N 91°21′W
31 *R7* **West Branch** Michigan, N USA 44°16′N 84°14′W
18 *F13* **West Branch Susquehanna River** ∽ Pennsylvania, NE USA
97 *L20* **West Bromwich** C England, United Kingdom 52°29′N 01°59′W
19 *P8* **Westbrook** Maine, NE USA 43°42′N 70°21′W
29 *T10* **Westbrook** Minnesota, N USA 44°02′N 95°26′W
29 *Y15* **West Burlington** Iowa, C USA 40°49′N 91°09′W
96 *L2* **West Burra** *island* NE Scotland, United Kingdom
30 *J8* **Westby** Wisconsin, N USA 43°39′N 90°52′W
44 *L6* **West Caicos** *island* W Turks and Caicos Islands
185 *A24* **West Cape** *headland* South Island, New Zealand 45°51′S 166°26′E
174 *L4* **West Caroline Basin** *undersea feature* SW Pacific Ocean 04°00′N 138°00′E
18 *I16* **West Chester** Pennsylvania, NE USA 39°56′N 75°35′W
185 *E18* **West Coast** *off.* West Coast Region. ◆ *region* South Island, New Zealand
West Coast Region *see* West Coast
25 *V12* **West Columbia** Texas, SW USA 29°08′N 95°39′W
29 *W10* **West Concord** Minnesota, N USA 44°09′N 92°54′W

◆ Country
● Country Capital
◇ Dependent Territory
○ Dependent Territory Capital
◆ Administrative Regions
✈ International Airport
▲ Mountain
▲ Mountain Range
Volcano
∽ River
◎ Lake
▣ Reservoir

29 V14 **West Des Moines** Iowa, C USA 41°33′N 93°42′W
37 Q6 **West Elk Peak** ▲ Colorado, C USA 38°43′N 107°12′W
44 F1 **West End** Grand Bahama Island, N Bahamas 26°36′N 78°55′W
44 F1 **West End Point** headland Grand Bahama Island, N Bahamas 26°40′N 78°58′W
98 O7 **Westerbork** Drenthe, NE Netherlands 52°49′N 06°36′E
98 N3 **Westereems** strait Germany/Netherlands
98 O9 **Westerhaar-Vriezenveensewijk** Overijssel, E Netherlands 52°28′N 06°38′E
100 G6 **Westerland** Schleswig-Holstein, N Germany 54°54′N 08°19′E
99 I17 **Westerlo** Antwerpen, N Belgium 51°05′N 04°55′E
19 N13 **Westerly** Rhode Island, NE USA 41°22′N 71°45′W
81 G18 **Western** ◈ province W Kenya
153 N11 **Western** ◈ zone C Nepal
186 A8 **Western** ◈ province SW Papua New Guinea
186 K9 **Western** ◈ province S Solomon Islands
186 J8 **Western** off. Western Province. ◈ province NW Solomon Islands
155 J26 **Western** ◈ province SW Sri Lanka
83 G15 **Western** ◈ province W Zambia
180 K8 **Western Australia** ◈ state W Australia
80 A13 **Western Bahr el Ghazal** ◈ state W South Sudan
Western Bug see Bug
83 F25 **Western Cape** off. Western Cape Province, Afr. Wes-Kaap. ◈ province SW South Africa
Western Cape Province see Western Cape
80 A11 **Western Darfur** ◈ state W Sudan
Western Desert see Şaḥrā' al Gharbīyah
118 G9 **Western Dvina** Bel. Dzvina, Ger. Düna, Latv. Daugava, Rus. Zapadnaya Dvina. ~ W Europe
81 D15 **Western Equatoria** ◈ state SW South Sudan
155 E16 **Western Ghats** ▲▲ SW India
186 C7 **Western Highlands** ◈ province C Papua New Guinea
Western Isles see Outer Hebrides
21 T3 **Westernport** Maryland, NE USA 39°29′N 79°03′W
Western Province see Western
Western Punjab see Punjab
74 B10 **Western Sahara** ◇ disputed territory N Africa
Western Samoa see Samoa
Western Sayans see Zapadnyy Sayan
Western Scheldt see Westerschelde
Western Sierra Madre see Madre Occidental, Sierra
99 E15 **Westerschelde** Eng. Western Scheldt; prev. Honte. inlet S North Sea
31 S13 **Westerville** Ohio, N USA 40°07′N 82°55′W
101 F17 **Westerwald** ▲▲ W Germany
65 C25 **West Falkland** var. Gran Malvina, Isla Gran Malvina. island W Falkland Islands
29 R5 **West Fargo** North Dakota, N USA 46°49′N 96°51′W
188 M15 **West Fayu Atoll** atoll Caroline Islands, C Micronesia
18 C11 **Westfield** New York, NE USA 42°18′N 79°34′W
30 L7 **Westfield** Wisconsin, N USA 43°56′N 89°31′W
West Flanders see West-Vlaanderen
27 S10 **West Fork** Arkansas, C USA 35°55′N 94°11′W
29 P16 **West Fork Big Blue River** ~ Nebraska, C USA
29 U12 **West Fork Des Moines River** ~ Iowa/Minnesota, C USA
25 S5 **West Fork Trinity River** ~ Texas, SW USA
30 L16 **West Frankfort** Illinois, N USA 37°54′N 88°55′W
98 I8 **West-Friesland** physical region NW Netherlands
West Frisian Islands see Waddeneilanden
19 T5 **West Grand Lake** ◎ Maine, NE USA
18 M12 **West Hartford** Connecticut, NE USA 41°44′N 72°45′W
18 M13 **West Haven** Connecticut, NE USA 41°16′N 72°57′W
27 X12 **West Helena** Arkansas, C USA 34°33′N 90°38′W
28 M2 **Westhope** North Dakota, N USA 48°54′N 101°01′W
195 Y8 **West Ice Shelf** ice shelf Antarctica
47 R2 **West Indies** island group SE North America
West Irian see Papua
West Irian Jaya see Papua Barat
West Java see Jawa Barat
36 L3 **West Jordan** Utah, W USA 40°37′N 111°55′W
West Kalimantan see Kalimantan Barat
99 D14 **Westkapelle** Zeeland, SW Netherlands 51°32′N 03°26′E
West Kazakhstan see Zapadnyy Kazakhstan
31 O13 **West Lafayette** Indiana, N USA 40°24′N 86°54′W
31 T13 **West Lafayette** Ohio, N USA 40°16′N 81°45′W
West Lake see Kagera
29 Y14 **West Liberty** Iowa, C USA 41°34′N 91°15′W
21 O5 **West Liberty** Kentucky, S USA 37°56′N 83°16′W
Westliche Morava see Zapadna Morava
10 J13 **Westlock** Alberta, SW Canada 54°12′N 113°50′W
14 E17 **West Lorne** Ontario, S Canada 42°36′N 81°35′W
96 J12 **West Lothian** cultural region S Scotland, United Kingdom
99 H16 **Westmalle** Antwerpen, N Belgium 51°18′N 04°40′E
192 G6 **West Mariana Basin** var. Perece Vela Basin. undersea feature W Pacific Ocean 15°00′N 137°00′E
97 E17 **Westmeath** Ir. An Iarmhí, Na H-Iarmhidhe. cultural region C Ireland
27 Y11 **West Memphis** Arkansas, C USA 35°09′N 90°11′W
21 W2 **Westminster** Maryland, NE USA 39°34′N 77°00′W
21 O11 **Westminster** South Carolina, SE USA 34°39′N 83°06′W
22 I5 **West Monroe** Louisiana, S USA 32°31′N 92°09′W
18 D15 **Westmont** Pennsylvania, NE USA 40°16′N 78°55′W
27 O3 **Westmoreland** Kansas, C USA 39°23′N 96°30′W
35 W17 **Westmorland** California, W USA 33°02′N 115°37′W
186 E6 **West New Britain** ◈ province E Papua New Guinea
West New Guinea see Papua
83 K18 **West Nicholson** Matabeleland South, S Zimbabwe 21°06′S 29°25′E
29 T14 **West Nishnabotna River** ~ Iowa, C USA
175 P11 **West Norfolk Ridge** undersea feature W Pacific Ocean
25 P12 **West Nueces River** ~ Texas, SW USA
West Nusa Tenggara see Nusa Tenggara Barat
29 T11 **West Okoboji Lake** ◎ Iowa, C USA
33 R16 **Weston** Idaho, NW USA 42°01′N 119°29′W
21 R4 **Weston** West Virginia, NE USA 39°03′N 80°28′W
97 J22 **Weston-super-Mare** SW England, United Kingdom 51°21′N 02°59′W
23 Z14 **West Palm Beach** Florida, SE USA 26°43′N 80°03′W
West Papua see Papua
188 E9 **West Passage** passage Babeldaob, N Palau
23 O9 **West Pensacola** Florida, SE USA 30°25′N 87°16′W
27 V8 **West Plains** Missouri, C USA 36°44′N 91°51′W
35 P7 **West Point** California, W USA 38°21′N 120°33′W
23 R5 **West Point** Georgia, SE USA 32°52′N 85°10′W
22 M3 **West Point** Mississippi, S USA 33°36′N 88°39′W
29 R14 **West Point** Nebraska, C USA 41°50′N 96°42′W
21 X6 **West Point** Virginia, NE USA 37°31′N 76°48′W
182 G10 **West Point** headland South Australia 35°01′S 135°58′E
65 B24 **Westpoint Island Settlement** Westpoint Island, NW Falkland Islands 51°21′S 60°41′W
23 R4 **West Point Lake** ▣ Alabama/Georgia, SE USA
97 B16 **Westport** Ir. Cathair na Mart. Mayo, W Ireland 53°48′N 09°32′W
185 G15 **Westport** West Coast, South Island, New Zealand 41°46′S 171°37′E
32 F10 **Westport** Oregon, NW USA 46°07′N 123°22′W
32 F9 **Westport** Washington, NW USA 46°53′N 124°06′W
31 S15 **West Portsmouth** Ohio, N USA 38°45′N 83°01′W
West Punjab see Punjab
11 V14 **Westray** Manitoba, C Canada 53°30′N 101°19′W
96 J4 **Westray** island NE Scotland, United Kingdom
14 F9 **Westree** Ontario, S Canada 47°25′N 81°32′W
97 L16 **West Riding** cultural region N England, United Kingdom
West River see Xi Jiang
30 J7 **West Salem** Wisconsin, N USA 43°54′N 91°04′W
65 H21 **West Scotia Ridge** undersea feature W Scotia Sea
West Sepik see Sandaun
173 N4 **West Sheba Ridge** undersea feature W Indian Ocean 12°45′N 48°15′E
West Siberian Plain see Zapadno-Sibirskaya Ravnina
31 S11 **West Sister Island** island Ohio, N USA
West-Skylge see West-Terschelling
West Sumatra see Sumatera Barat
98 J5 **West-Terschelling** Fris. West-Skylge. Fryslân, N Netherlands 53°23′N 05°15′E
64 J7 **West Thulean Rise** undersea feature N Atlantic Ocean
29 X12 **West Union** Iowa, C USA 42°57′N 91°48′W
31 R15 **West Union** Ohio, N USA 38°47′N 83°33′W
21 R3 **West Union** West Virginia, NE USA 39°18′N 80°47′W
31 N13 **Westville** Illinois, N USA 40°02′N 87°38′W
21 R3 **West Virginia** off. State of West Virginia, also known as Mountain State. ◈ state NE USA
99 A17 **West-Vlaanderen** Eng. West Flanders. ◈ province W Belgium
35 R7 **West Walker River** ~ California/Nevada, W USA
35 P4 **Westwood** California, W USA 40°18′N 121°02′W
183 P9 **West Wyalong** New South Wales, SE Australia 33°56′S 147°10′E
171 Q16 **Wetar, Pulau** island Kepulauan Damar, E Indonesia
Wetar, Selat see Wetar Strait
171 R16 **Wetar Strait** var. SelatWetar. strait Nusa Tenggara, S Indonesia
11 Q15 **Wetaskiwin** Alberta, SW Canada 52°57′N 113°20′W
81 K21 **Wete** Pemba, E Tanzania 05°03′S 39°41′E
166 M4 **Wetlet** Sagaing, C Burma (Myanmar) 22°43′N 95°22′E
37 T6 **Wet Mountains** ▲▲ Colorado, C USA
101 E15 **Wetter** Nordrhein-Westfalen, W Germany 51°22′N 07°24′E
101 H17 **Wetter** ~ W Germany
99 F17 **Wetteren** Oost-Vlaanderen, NW Belgium 51°06′N 03°59′E
108 F7 **Wettingen** Aargau, N Switzerland 47°28′N 08°20′E
27 P11 **Wetumka** Oklahoma, C USA 35°14′N 96°14′W
23 Q5 **Wetumpka** Alabama, S USA 32°32′N 86°12′W
108 G7 **Wetzikon** Zürich, N Switzerland 47°19′N 08°48′E
101 G17 **Wetzlar** Hessen, W Germany 50°33′N 08°30′E
99 C18 **Wevelgem** West-Vlaanderen, W Belgium 50°48′N 03°12′E
38 M6 **Wevok** var. Wewuk. Alaska, USA 68°52′N 166°05′W
23 R9 **Wewahitchka** Florida, SE USA 30°06′N 85°12′W
186 C6 **Wewak** East Sepik, NW Papua New Guinea 03°35′S 143°35′E
27 O11 **Wewoka** Oklahoma, C USA 35°09′N 96°30′W
Wewuk see Wevok
97 F20 **Wexford** Ir. Loch Garman. SE Ireland 52°21′N 06°31′W
97 F20 **Wexford** Ir. Loch Garman. cultural region SE Ireland
30 L7 **Weyauwega** Wisconsin, N USA 44°16′N 88°54′W
11 U17 **Weyburn** Saskatchewan, S Canada 49°39′N 103°51′W
Weyer see Weyer Markt
109 U5 **Weyer Markt** var. Weyer. Oberösterreich, N Austria 47°52′N 14°39′E
100 H11 **Weyhe** Niedersachsen, NW Germany 53°00′N 08°52′E
97 L24 **Weymouth** S England, United Kingdom 50°36′N 02°28′W
19 P11 **Weymouth** Massachusetts, NE USA 42°13′N 70°56′W
99 H18 **Wezembeek-Oppem** Vlaams Brabant, C Belgium 50°51′N 04°28′E
98 M9 **Wezep** Gelderland, E Netherlands 52°28′N 06°E
184 M9 **Whakamaru** Waikato, North Island, New Zealand 38°27′S 175°48′E
184 O8 **Whakatane** Bay of Plenty, North Island, New Zealand 37°58′S 177°E
184 O8 **Whakatane** ~ North Island, New Zealand
9 O9 **Whale Cove** var. Tikirarjuaq. Nunavut, C Canada 62°14′N 92°10′W
96 M2 **Whalsay** island NE Scotland, United Kingdom
184 L11 **Whangaehu** ~ North Island, New Zealand
184 M6 **Whangamata** Waikato, North Island, New Zealand 37°13′S 175°54′E
184 Q9 **Whangara** Gisborne, North Island, New Zealand 38°34′S 178°12′E
184 K3 **Whangarei** Northland, North Island, New Zealand 35°44′S 174°18′E
184 K3 **Whangaruru Harbour** inlet North Island, New Zealand
25 V12 **Wharton** Texas, SW USA 29°19′N 96°08′W
173 U8 **Wharton Basin** var. West Australian Basin. undersea feature E Indian Ocean
185 E18 **Whataroa** West Coast, South Island, New Zealand 43°17′S 170°20′E
8 K10 **Wha Ti** prev. Lac la Martre. Northwest Territories, W Canada 63°10′N 117°12′W
8 J9 **Wha Ti** Northwest Territories, W Canada 63°10′N 117°12′W
184 K6 **Whatipu** Auckland, North Island, New Zealand 37°17′S 174°44′E
33 Y16 **Wheatland** Wyoming, C USA 42°03′N 104°57′W
14 D18 **Wheatley** Ontario, S Canada 42°06′N 82°27′W
30 M10 **Wheaton** Illinois, N USA 41°52′N 88°06′W
29 R7 **Wheaton** Minnesota, N USA 45°48′N 96°30′W
37 T4 **Wheat Ridge** Colorado, C USA 39°44′N 105°06′W
25 P2 **Wheeler** Texas, SW USA 35°26′N 100°17′W
23 O2 **Wheeler Lake** ▣ Alabama, S USA
35 Y6 **Wheeler Peak** ▲ Nevada, W USA 39°00′N 114°17′W
37 T9 **Wheeler Peak** ▲ New Mexico, SW USA 36°34′N 105°25′W
31 S15 **Wheelersburg** Ohio, N USA 38°43′N 82°51′W
21 R2 **Wheeling** West Virginia, NE USA 40°05′N 80°43′W
97 L16 **Whernside** ▲ N England, United Kingdom 54°13′N 02°27′W
182 F9 **Whidbey, Point** headland South Australia 34°36′S 135°08′E
180 I7 **Whim Creek** Western Australia 20°51′S 117°54′E
10 L17 **Whistler** British Columbia, SW Canada 50°07′N 122°57′W
21 W8 **Whitakers** North Carolina, SE USA 36°06′N 77°43′W
14 H15 **Whitby** Ontario, S Canada 43°52′N 78°56′W
97 N15 **Whitby** N England, United Kingdom 54°29′N 00°37′W
10 G6 **White** ~ Yukon Territory, W Canada
13 T11 **White Bay** bay Newfoundland, Newfoundland and Labrador, E Canada
20 I8 **White Bluff** Tennessee, S USA 36°06′N 87°13′W
28 J6 **White Butte** ▲ North Dakota, N USA 46°23′N 103°18′W
19 R5 **White Cap Mountain** ▲ Maine, NE USA 45°33′N 69°15′W
22 J9 **White Castle** Louisiana, S USA 30°10′N 91°09′W
182 M5 **White Cliffs** New South Wales, SE Australia 30°52′S 143°04′E
31 P8 **White Cloud** Michigan, N USA 43°34′N 85°47′W
11 P14 **Whitecourt** Alberta, SW Canada 54°10′N 115°38′W
25 O2 **White Deer** Texas, SW USA 35°26′N 101°10′W
White Elster see Weisse Elster
24 M5 **Whiteface** Texas, SW USA 33°36′N 102°36′W
18 K7 **Whiteface Mountain** ▲ New York, NE USA 44°22′N 73°54′W
29 W5 **Whiteface Reservoir** ▣ Minnesota, N USA
33 O7 **Whitefish** Montana, NW USA 48°24′N 114°20′W
31 N9 **Whitefish Bay** Wisconsin, N USA 43°09′N 87°54′W
31 Q3 **Whitefish Bay** lake bay Canada/USA
14 E11 **Whitefish Falls** Ontario, S Canada 46°06′N 81°42′W
14 B7 **Whitefish Lake** ◎ Ontario, S Canada
29 U6 **Whitefish Lake** ◎ Minnesota, C USA
31 Q3 **Whitefish Point** headland Michigan, N USA 46°46′N 84°57′W
31 O4 **Whitefish River** ~ Michigan, N USA
25 O4 **Whiteflat** Texas, SW USA 34°06′N 100°55′W
27 V12 **White Hall** Arkansas, C USA 34°18′N 92°05′W
30 K14 **White Hall** Illinois, N USA 39°26′N 90°24′W
31 O8 **Whitehall** Michigan, N USA 43°24′N 86°21′W
18 L9 **Whitehall** New York, NE USA 43°33′N 73°24′W
31 S13 **Whitehall** Ohio, N USA 39°58′N 82°53′W
30 J7 **Whitehall** Wisconsin, N USA 44°22′N 91°19′W
97 J15 **Whitehaven** NW England, United Kingdom 54°33′N 03°35′W
10 I8 **Whitehorse** territory capital Yukon Territory, W Canada 60°41′N 135°08′W
184 O7 **White Island** island NE New Zealand
14 K13 **White Lake** ◎ Ontario, SE Canada
22 H10 **White Lake** ◎ Louisiana, S USA
186 G7 **Whiteman Range** ▲▲ New Britain, E Papua New Guinea
183 Q15 **Whitemark** Tasmania, SE Australia 40°10′S 148°01′E
35 S9 **White Mountains** ▲▲ California/Nevada, W USA
19 N7 **White Mountains** ▲▲ Maine/New Hampshire, NE USA
80 F11 **White Nile** ◈ state C Sudan
81 E14 **White Nile** Ar. Al Baḥr al Abyaḍ, An Nīl al Abyaḍ, Bahr el Jebel. ~ NE South Sudan
67 U7 **White Nile** var. Bahr el Jebel. ~ S Sudan
25 W5 **White Oak Creek** ~ Texas, SW USA
10 H9 **White Pass** pass Canada/USA
32 I9 **White Pass** pass Washington, NW USA
21 O9 **White Pine** Tennessee, S USA 36°06′N 83°17′W
18 K14 **White Plains** New York, NE USA 41°01′N 73°45′W
37 N13 **Whiteriver** Arizona, SW USA 33°50′N 109°57′W
28 M11 **White River** South Dakota, N USA 43°34′N 100°45′W
27 W12 **White River** ~ Arkansas, SE USA
37 P3 **White River** ~ Colorado/Utah, C USA
31 N15 **White River** ~ Indiana, N USA
31 O8 **White River** ~ Michigan, N USA
28 K11 **White River** ~ South Dakota, N USA
25 O5 **White River** ~ Texas, SW USA
18 M8 **White River** ~ Vermont, NE USA
25 O5 **White River Lake** ▣ Texas, SW USA
32 H11 **White Salmon** Washington, NW USA 45°43′N 121°29′W
18 I10 **Whitesboro** New York, NE USA 43°07′N 75°17′W
25 T5 **Whitesboro** Texas, SW USA 33°39′N 96°54′W
21 O7 **Whitesburg** Kentucky, S USA 37°07′N 82°52′W
White Sea see Beloye More
White Sea-Baltic Canal/White Sea Canal see Belomorsko-Baltiyskiy Kanal
63 I25 **Whiteside, Canal** channel S Chile
33 S10 **White Sulphur Springs** Montana, NW USA 46°33′N 110°54′W
21 R6 **White Sulphur Springs** West Virginia, NE USA 37°48′N 80°18′W
20 J6 **Whitesville** Kentucky, S USA 37°40′N 86°48′W
32 I10 **White Swan** Washington, NW USA 46°22′N 120°46′W
21 U12 **Whiteville** North Carolina, SE USA 34°20′N 78°42′W
20 F10 **Whiteville** Tennessee, S USA 35°19′N 89°09′W
77 Q13 **White Volta** var. Nakambé, Fr. Volta Blanche. ~ Burkina/Ghana
30 M9 **Whitewater** Wisconsin, N USA 42°51′N 88°43′W
37 P14 **Whitewater Baldy** ▲ New Mexico, SW USA 33°19′N 108°38′W
23 X17 **Whitewater Bay** bay Florida, SE USA
31 Q14 **Whitewater River** ~ Indiana/Ohio, N USA
11 V16 **Whitewood** Saskatchewan, S Canada 50°19′N 102°16′W
28 J9 **Whitewood** South Dakota, N USA 44°27′N 103°38′W
25 U5 **Whitewright** Texas, SW USA 33°30′N 96°23′W
97 I15 **Whithorn** S Scotland, United Kingdom 54°44′N 04°26′W
184 M6 **Whitianga** Waikato, North Island, New Zealand 36°50′S 175°42′E
19 N11 **Whitinsville** Massachusetts, NE USA 42°06′N 71°40′W
20 M8 **Whitley City** Kentucky, S USA 36°45′N 84°29′W
21 Q11 **Whitmire** South Carolina, SE USA 34°30′N 81°36′W
31 R10 **Whitmore Lake** Michigan, N USA 42°26′N 83°44′W
195 N9 **Whitmore Mountains** ▲▲ Antarctica
14 I12 **Whitney** Ontario, SE Canada 45°29′N 78°11′W
25 T8 **Whitney** Texas, SW USA 31°56′N 97°20′W
25 S8 **Whitney, Lake** ▣ Texas, SW USA
35 S11 **Whitney, Mount** ▲ California, W USA 37°45′N 119°55′W
181 Y6 **Whitsunday Group** island group Queensland, E Australia
25 S6 **Whitt** Texas, SW USA 32°55′N 98°01′W
29 U12 **Whittemore** Iowa, C USA 43°03′N 94°25′W
39 R12 **Whittier** Alaska, USA 60°46′N 148°40′W
35 T15 **Whittier** California, W USA 33°58′N 118°01′W
83 I25 **Whittlesea** Eastern Cape, S South Africa 32°08′S 26°51′E
20 K10 **Whitwell** Tennessee, S USA 35°12′N 85°31′W
8 L10 **Wholdaia Lake** ◎ Northwest Territories, NW Canada
182 H7 **Whyalla** South Australia 33°04′S 137°34′E
Whydah see Ouidah
14 F13 **Wiarton** Ontario, S Canada 44°44′N 81°10′W
171 O13 **Wiau** Sulawesi, C Indonesia 03°08′S 121°22′E
111 H15 **Wiązów** Ger. Wansen. Dolnośląskie, SW Poland 50°49′N 17°13′E
33 Y8 **Wibaux** Montana, NW USA 46°57′N 104°11′W
27 N6 **Wichita** Kansas, C USA 37°42′N 97°20′W
25 R5 **Wichita Falls** Texas, SW USA 33°55′N 98°30′W
26 L11 **Wichita Mountains** ▲▲ Oklahoma, C USA
25 R5 **Wichita River** ~ Texas, SW USA
96 K6 **Wick** N Scotland, United Kingdom 58°26′N 03°06′W
36 K13 **Wickenburg** Arizona, SW USA 33°57′N 112°41′W
24 L8 **Wickett** Texas, SW USA 31°34′N 103°00′W
180 I7 **Wickham** Western Australia 20°40′S 117°11′E
182 M14 **Wickham, Cape** headland Tasmania, SE Australia 39°36′S 143°55′E
20 G7 **Wickliffe** Kentucky, S USA 36°58′N 89°04′W
97 G19 **Wicklow** Ir. Cill Mhantáin. E Ireland 52°59′N 06°03′W
97 F19 **Wicklow** Ir. Cill Mhantáin. cultural region E Ireland
97 G19 **Wicklow Head** Ir. Ceann Chill Mhantáin. headland E Ireland 52°57′N 06°00′W
97 F18 **Wicklow Mountains** Ir. Sléibhte Chill Mhantáin. ▲▲ E Ireland
14 H10 **Wicksteed Lake** ◎ Ontario, S Canada
Wida see Ouidah
65 G15 **Wideawake Airfield** ✈ (Georgetown) SW Ascension Island
97 K18 **Widnes** NW England, United Kingdom 53°22′N 02°44′W
110 H9 **Więcbork** Ger. Vandsburg. Kujawsko-pomorskie, C Poland 53°21′N 17°31′E
101 E17 **Wied** ~ W Germany
101 F16 **Wiehl** Nordrhein-Westfalen, W Germany 50°57′N 07°33′E
111 L17 **Wieliczka** Małopolskie, S Poland 50°N 20°02′E
110 H12 **Wielkopolskie** ◈ province SW Poland
111 J14 **Wieluń** Sieradz, C Poland 51°14′N 18°33′E
109 X4 **Wien** Eng. Vienna, Hung. Bécs, Slvk. Vídeň, Slvn. Dunaj; anc. Vindobona. ● (Austria) Wien, NE Austria 48°13′N 16°22′E
109 X4 **Wien** off. Land Wien, Eng. Vienna. ◈ state NE Austria
109 X5 **Wiener Neustadt** Niederösterreich, E Austria 47°49′N 16°08′E
Wien, Land see Wien
110 G7 **Wieprza** Ger. Wipper. ~ NW Poland
98 O10 **Wierden** Overijssel, E Netherlands 52°22′N 06°35′E
98 I7 **Wieringerwerf** Noord-Holland, NW Netherlands 52°51′N 05°01′E
Wieruschow see Wieruszów
111 I14 **Wieruszów** Ger. Wieruschow. Łódzkie, C Poland 51°18′N 18°09′E
109 V9 **Wies** Steiermark, SE Austria 46°40′N 15°16′E
Wiesbachhorn see Grosses Wiesbachhorn
101 G18 **Wiesbaden** Hessen, W Germany 50°06′N 08°14′E
Wieselburg and Ungarisch-Altenburg/Wieselburg-Ungarisch-Altenburg see Mosonmagyaróvár
Wiesenhof see Ostrołęka
101 G20 **Wiesloch** Baden-Württemberg, SW Germany 49°18′N 08°42′E
100 F10 **Wiesmoor** Niedersachsen, NW Germany 53°22′N 07°46′E
110 I7 **Wieżyca** Ger. Turmberg. hill Pomorskie, N Poland
97 L17 **Wigan** NW England, United Kingdom 53°33′N 02°38′W
37 U3 **Wiggins** Colorado, C USA 40°11′N 104°03′W
22 M8 **Wiggins** Mississippi, S USA 30°50′N 89°09′W
Wigorna Ceaster see Worcester
97 I14 **Wigtown** S Scotland, United Kingdom 54°53′N 04°27′W
97 H14 **Wigtown** cultural region SW Scotland, United Kingdom
97 I15 **Wigtown Bay** bay SW Scotland, United Kingdom
98 L13 **Wijchen** Gelderland, SE Netherlands 51°48′N 05°44′E
92 N1 **Wijdefjorden** fjord NW Svalbard
98 M10 **Wijhe** Overijssel, E Netherlands 52°22′N 06°07′E
98 J12 **Wijk bij Duurstede** Utrecht, C Netherlands 51°58′N 05°21′E
98 J13 **Wijk en Aalburg** Noord-Brabant, S Netherlands 51°46′N 05°06′E
99 H16 **Wijnegem** Antwerpen, N Belgium 51°13′N 04°32′E
14 E11 **Wikwemikong** Manitoulin Island, Ontario, S Canada 45°46′N 81°43′W
108 H7 **Wil** Sankt Gallen, NE Switzerland 47°28′N 09°03′E
29 R16 **Wilber** Nebraska, C USA 40°28′N 96°57′W
32 K8 **Wilbur** Washington, NW USA 47°45′N 118°42′W
27 Q11 **Wilburton** Oklahoma, C USA 34°57′N 95°20′W
182 M6 **Wilcannia** New South Wales, SE Australia 31°34′S 143°23′E
18 D12 **Wilcox** Pennsylvania, NE USA 41°34′N 78°40′W
Wilczek Land see Vil'cheka, Zemlya
109 U6 **Wildalpen** Steiermark, E Austria 47°40′N 14°54′E
31 O13 **Wildcat Creek** ~ Indiana, N USA
108 L9 **Wilde Kreuzspitze** It. Picco di Croce. ▲ Austria/Italy 46°53′N 11°51′E
Wildenschwert see Ústí nad Orlicí
98 O6 **Wildervank** Groningen, NE Netherlands 53°04′N 06°52′E
100 G11 **Wildeshausen** Niedersachsen, NW Germany 52°54′N 08°26′E
108 D10 **Wildhorn** ▲ SW Switzerland 46°21′N 07°22′E
11 R17 **Wild Horse** Alberta, SW Canada 49°00′N 110°19′W
27 N12 **Wildhorse Creek** ~ Oklahoma, C USA
28 L14 **Wild Horse Hill** ▲ Nebraska, C USA 41°52′N 101°56′W
109 W8 **Wildon** Steiermark, SE Austria 46°53′N 15°29′E
24 M2 **Wildorado** Texas, SW USA 35°12′N 102°10′W
29 R6 **Wild Rice River** ~ Minnesota/North Dakota, N USA
Wilejka see Vilyeyka
195 Y9 **Wilhelm II Coast** physical region Antarctica
195 X9 **Wilhelm II Land** physical region Antarctica
55 U11 **Wilhelmina Gebergte** ▲ C Surinam
18 B13 **Wilhelm, Lake** ▣ Pennsylvania, NE USA
92 O2 **Wilhelmøya** island C Svalbard
Wilhelm-Pieck-Stadt see Guben
109 W4 **Wilhelmsburg** Niederösterreich, E Austria 48°07′N 15°37′E
100 G10 **Wilhelmshaven** Niedersachsen, NW Germany 53°31′N 08°07′E
Wilia/Wilja see Neris
18 H13 **Wilkes Barre** Pennsylvania, NE USA 41°15′N 75°50′W
21 R9 **Wilkesboro** North Carolina, SE USA 36°08′N 81°09′W
195 W15 **Wilkes Coast** physical region Antarctica
189 W12 **Wilkes Island** island N Wake Island
195 X12 **Wilkes Land** physical region Antarctica
11 S15 **Wilkie** Saskatchewan, S Canada 52°27′N 108°42′W
194 I6 **Wilkins Ice Shelf** ice shelf Antarctica
182 D4 **Wilkinsons Lakes** salt lake South Australia
Wiłkomierz see Ukmergė
182 K11 **Willalooka** South Australia 36°24′S 140°20′E
32 G11 **Willamette River** ~ Oregon, NW USA
183 O8 **Willandra Billabong Creek** seasonal river New South Wales, SE Australia
32 F9 **Willapa Bay** inlet Washington, NW USA
27 T7 **Willard** Missouri, C USA 37°18′N 93°25′W
37 S12 **Willard** New Mexico, SW USA 34°36′N 106°01′W
31 S12 **Willard** Ohio, N USA 41°03′N 82°43′W
36 L1 **Willard** Utah, W USA 41°23′N 112°01′W
186 G6 **Willaumez Peninsula** headland New Britain, E Papua New Guinea 05°03′S 150°04′E
37 N15 **Willcox** Arizona, SW USA 32°13′N 109°49′W
37 N16 **Willcox Playa** salt flat Arizona, SW USA
99 G17 **Willebroek** Antwerpen, C Belgium 51°04′N 04°22′E
45 P16 **Willemstad** ○ Curaçao 12°07′N 68°54′W
99 G14 **Willemstad** Noord-Brabant, S Netherlands 51°40′N 04°27′E
11 S11 **William** ~ Saskatchewan, C Canada
23 O6 **William "Bill" Dannelly Reservoir** ▣ Alabama, S USA
182 G3 **William Creek** South Australia 28°55′S 136°23′E
181 T15 **William, Mount** ▲ South Australia
36 K11 **Williams** Arizona, SW USA 35°15′N 112°11′W
29 X14 **Williamsburg** Iowa, C USA 41°39′N 92°00′W
20 M8 **Williamsburg** Kentucky, S USA 36°44′N 84°10′W
31 R15 **Williamsburg** Ohio, N USA 39°00′N 84°02′W
21 X6 **Williamsburg** Virginia, NE USA 37°17′N 76°43′W
10 M15 **Williams Lake** British Columbia, SW Canada 52°08′N 122°09′W
21 P6 **Williamson** West Virginia, NE USA 37°42′N 82°16′W
31 N13 **Williamsport** Indiana, N USA 40°18′N 87°18′W
18 G13 **Williamsport** Pennsylvania, NE USA 41°16′N 77°03′W
21 W9 **Williamston** North Carolina, SE USA 35°53′N 77°05′W
21 P11 **Williamston** South Carolina, SE USA 34°37′N 82°28′W
20 M4 **Williamstown** Kentucky, S USA 38°39′N 84°32′W
18 L10 **Williamstown** Massachusetts, NE USA 42°41′N 73°11′W
18 J16 **Willingboro** New Jersey, NE USA 40°01′N 74°52′W
11 Q14 **Willingdon** Alberta, SW Canada 53°49′N 112°08′W
25 W10 **Willis** Texas, SW USA 30°25′N 95°28′W
108 F8 **Willisau** Luzern, W Switzerland 47°07′N 08°00′E
83 F24 **Williston** Northern Cape, W South Africa 31°20′S 20°52′E
23 V10 **Williston** Florida, SE USA 29°23′N 82°27′W
28 J3 **Williston** North Dakota, N USA 48°07′N 103°37′W
21 Q13 **Williston** South Carolina, SE USA 33°24′N 81°25′W
10 L12 **Williston Lake** ▣ British Columbia, W Canada
34 L5 **Willits** California, W USA 39°24′N 123°22′W
29 T8 **Willmar** Minnesota, N USA 45°07′N 95°02′W
10 K11 **Will, Mount** ▲ British Columbia, W Canada 57°31′N 128°48′W
31 T11 **Willoughby** Ohio, N USA 41°38′N 81°24′W
11 U17 **Willow Bunch** Saskatchewan, S Canada 49°30′N 105°41′W
32 J11 **Willow Creek** ~ Oregon, NW USA
39 R11 **Willow Lake** Alaska, USA 61°44′N 150°02′W
8 I9 **Willowlake** ~ Northwest Territories, NW Canada
83 H25 **Willowmore** Eastern Cape, S South Africa 33°18′S 23°30′E
30 L5 **Willow Reservoir** ▣ Wisconsin, N USA
35 N5 **Willows** California, W USA 39°28′N 122°12′W
27 V7 **Willow Springs** Missouri, C USA 36°59′N 91°58′W
182 I7 **Wilmington** South Australia 32°42′S 138°08′E
21 Y2 **Wilmington** Delaware, NE USA 39°45′N 75°33′W
21 V12 **Wilmington** North Carolina, SE USA 34°14′N 77°55′W
31 R14 **Wilmington** Ohio, N USA 39°27′N 83°49′W
20 M6 **Wilmore** Kentucky, S USA 37°51′N 84°39′W
29 R8 **Wilmot** South Dakota, N USA 45°24′N 96°51′W
Wilna/Wilno see Vilnius
101 G16 **Wilnsdorf** Nordrhein-Westfalen, W Germany 50°49′N 08°06′E
99 G16 **Wilrijk** Antwerpen, N Belgium 51°11′N 04°25′E
100 I10 **Wilseder Berg** hill NW Germany
67 Z12 **Wilshaw Ridge** undersea feature W Indian Ocean 17°30′S 56°30′E
21 V9 **Wilson** North Carolina, SE USA 35°43′N 77°56′W
25 N5 **Wilson** Texas, SW USA 33°21′N 101°44′W
182 A7 **Wilson Bluff** headland South Australia/Western Australia 31°41′S 129°01′E
35 Y7 **Wilson Creek Range** ▲▲ Nevada, W USA
23 O1 **Wilson Lake** ▣ Alabama, S USA
26 M4 **Wilson Lake** ▣ Kansas, C USA
37 P7 **Wilson, Mount** ▲ Colorado, C USA 37°50′N 107°59′W
183 P13 **Wilsons Promontory** peninsula Victoria, SE Australia
29 Y14 **Wilton** Iowa, C USA 41°35′N 91°01′W
19 P7 **Wilton** Maine, NE USA 44°35′N 70°15′W
28 M5 **Wilton** North Dakota, N USA 47°09′N 100°46′W
97 L22 **Wiltshire** cultural region S England, United Kingdom
99 M23 **Wiltz** Diekirch, NW Luxembourg 49°58′N 05°56′E
180 K9 **Wiluna** Western Australia 26°34′S 120°14′E
99 M23 **Wilwerwiltz** Diekirch, NE Luxembourg 49°59′N 06°00′E
29 P5 **Wimbledon** North Dakota, N USA 47°08′N 98°25′W
42 K7 **Wina** var. Güina. Jinotega, N Nicaragua 14°00′N 85°14′W
31 O12 **Winamac** Indiana, N USA 41°03′N 86°37′W
81 G19 **Winam Gulf** var. Kavirondo Gulf. gulf SW Kenya
83 I22 **Winburg** Free State, C South Africa 28°31′S 27°01′E
19 N10 **Winchendon** Massachusetts, NE USA 42°41′N 72°01′W
14 M13 **Winchester** Ontario, SE Canada 45°07′N 75°19′W
97 M23 **Winchester** hist. Wintanceaster, Lat. Venta Belgarum. S England, United Kingdom 51°04′N 01°19′W
32 M10 **Winchester** Idaho, NW USA 46°13′N 116°35′W
30 J14 **Winchester** Illinois, N USA 39°38′N 90°28′W
31 Q13 **Winchester** Indiana, N USA 40°11′N 84°57′W
20 M5 **Winchester** Kentucky, S USA 38°00′N 84°10′W
18 M10 **Winchester** New Hampshire, NE USA 42°46′N 72°21′W
20 K10 **Winchester** Tennessee, S USA 35°11′N 86°06′W
21 V3 **Winchester** Virginia, NE USA 39°11′N 78°12′W
99 L22 **Wincrange** Diekirch, NW Luxembourg 50°03′N 05°55′E
10 I5 **Wind** ~ Yukon Territory, NW Canada

◆ Country ● Country Capital ◇ Dependent Territory ○ Dependent Territory Capital ◈ Administrative Regions ✈ International Airport ▲ Mountain ▲▲ Mountain Range Volcano ~ River ◎ Lake ▣ Reservoir

183 *S8* **Windamere, Lake** ◎ New South Wales, SE Australia
Windau *see* Ventspils, Latvia
Windau *see* Venta, Latvia/ Lithuania
18 *D15* **Windber** Pennsylvania, NE USA *40°12′N 78°47′W*
23 *T3* **Winder** Georgia, SE USA *33°59′N 83°43′W*
97 *K15* **Windermere** NW England, United Kingdom *54°24′N 02°54′W*
14 *C7* **Windermere Lake** ◎ Ontario, S Canada
31 *U11* **Windham** Ohio, N USA *41°14′N 81°03′W*
83 *D19* **Windhoek** *Ger.* Windhuk. ● (Namibia) Khomas, C Namibia *22°34′S 17°06′E*
83 *D20* **Windhoek** ✈ Khomas, C Namibia *22°31′S 17°04′E*
Windhuk *see* Windhoek
15 *O8* **Windigo** Québec, SE Canada *47°45′N 73°19′W*
15 *O8* **Windigo** ≈ Québec, SE Canada
Windischfeistritz *see* Slovenska Bistrica
109 *T6* **Windischgarsten** Oberösterreich, W Austria *47°42′N 14°21′E*
Windischgraz *see* Slovenj Gradec
37 *T16* **Wind Mountain** ▲ New Mexico, SW USA *32°01′N 105°35′W*
29 *T10* **Windom** Minnesota, N USA *43°52′N 95°07′W*
37 *Q7* **Windom Peak** ▲ Colorado, C USA *37°37′N 107°35′W*
181 *U9* **Windorah** Queensland, C Australia *25°25′S 142°41′E*
37 *O10* **Window Rock** Arizona, SW USA *35°40′N 109°03′W*
31 *N9* **Wind Point** *headland* Wisconsin, N USA *42°46′N 87°46′W*
33 *U14* **Wind River** ≈ Wyoming, C USA
13 *P15* **Windsor** Nova Scotia, SE Canada *45°00′N 64°09′W*
14 *C17* **Windsor** Ontario, S Canada *42°18′N 83°W*
15 *Q12* **Windsor** Québec, SE Canada *45°34′N 72°00′W*
97 *N22* **Windsor** S England, United Kingdom *51°29′N 00°39′W*
37 *T3* **Windsor** Colorado, C USA *40°28′N 104°54′W*
18 *M12* **Windsor** Connecticut, NE USA *41°51′N 72°38′W*
27 *T5* **Windsor** Missouri, C USA *38°31′N 93°31′W*
21 *X9* **Windsor** North Carolina, SE USA *36°00′N 76°57′W*
18 *M12* **Windsor Locks** Connecticut, NE USA *41°55′N 72°37′W*
25 *R5* **Windthorst** Texas, SW USA *33°34′N 98°26′W*
45 *Z14* **Windward Islands** *island group* E West Indies
Windward Islands *see* Barlavento, Ilhas de, Cape Verde
Windward Islands *see* Vent, Îles du, Archipel de la Société, French Polynesia
44 *K8* **Windward Passage** *Sp.* Paso de los Vientos. *channel* Cuba/Haiti
55 *T9* **Wineperu** C Guyana *06°10′N 58°34′W*
23 *O3* **Winfield** Alabama, S USA *33°55′N 87°49′W*
29 *Y15* **Winfield** Iowa, C USA *41°07′N 91°26′W*
27 *O7* **Winfield** Kansas, C USA *37°14′N 97°00′W*
25 *W6* **Winfield** Texas, SW USA *33°10′N 95°06′W*
21 *Q4* **Winfield** West Virginia, NE USA *38°30′N 81°54′W*
29 *N5* **Wing** North Dakota, N USA *47°06′N 100°16′W*
183 *U7* **Wingham** New South Wales, SE Australia *31°52′S 152°24′E*
12 *G16* **Wingham** Ontario, S Canada *43°54′N 81°19′W*
33 *T8* **Winifred** Montana, NW USA *47°33′N 109°26′W*
12 *E9* **Winisk Lake** ◎ Ontario, C Canada
24 *L8* **Wink** Texas, SW USA *31°45′N 103°09′W*
36 *M14* **Winkelman** Arizona, SW USA *32°59′N 110°46′W*
11 *X17* **Winkler** Manitoba, S Canada *49°12′N 97°55′W*
109 *Q9* **Winklern** Tirol, W Austria *46°54′N 12°54′E*
Winkowitz *see* Vinkovci
32 *G9* **Winlock** Washington, NW USA *46°29′N 122°56′W*
77 *P17* **Winneba** SE Ghana *05°22′N 00°38′W*
29 *U11* **Winnebago** Minnesota, N USA *43°46′N 94°10′W*
29 *R13* **Winnebago** Nebraska, C USA *42°14′N 96°28′W*
30 *M7* **Winnebago, Lake** ◎ Wisconsin, N USA
30 *M7* **Winneconne** Wisconsin, N USA *44°07′N 88°44′W*
35 *T3* **Winnemucca** Nevada, W USA *40°59′N 117°44′W*
35 *R4* **Winnemucca Lake** ◎ Nevada, W USA
101 *H21* **Winnenden** Baden-Württemberg, SW Germany *48°52′N 09°22′E*
29 *N11* **Winner** South Dakota, N USA *43°22′N 99°51′W*
33 *U9* **Winnett** Montana, NW USA *47°00′N 108°18′W*
14 *I9* **Winneway** Québec, SE Canada *47°35′N 78°33′W*
22 *H6* **Winnfield** Louisiana, S USA *31°55′N 92°38′W*
29 *U4* **Winnibigoshish, Lake** ◎ Minnesota, N USA
25 *X11* **Winnie** Texas, SW USA *29°49′N 94°22′W*
11 *Y16* **Winnipeg** *province capital* Manitoba, S Canada *49°53′N 97°10′W*
11 *X16* **Winnipeg** ✈ Manitoba, S Canada *49°56′N 97°16′W*
0 *J8* **Winnipeg** ≈ Manitoba, S Canada
11 *X16* **Winnipeg Beach** Manitoba, S Canada *50°25′N 96°59′W*
11 *W14* **Winnipeg, Lake** ◎ Manitoba, C Canada
11 *W15* **Winnipegosis** Manitoba, S Canada *51°36′N 99°59′W*
11 *W15* **Winnipegosis, Lake** ◎ Manitoba, C Canada
19 *O8* **Winnipesaukee, Lake** ◎ New Hampshire, NE USA
22 *I6* **Winnsboro** Louisiana, S USA *32°09′N 91°43′W*
21 *R12* **Winnsboro** South Carolina, SE USA *34°22′N 81°05′W*
25 *W6* **Winnsboro** Texas, SW USA *33°01′N 95°16′W*
29 *X10* **Winona** Minnesota, N USA *44°03′N 91°37′W*
22 *L4* **Winona** Mississippi, S USA *33°30′N 89°42′W*
27 *W7* **Winona** Missouri, C USA *37°00′N 91°19′W*
25 *W7* **Winona** Texas, SW USA *32°29′N 95°10′W*
18 *M7* **Winooski River** ≈ Vermont, NE USA
98 *P6* **Winschoten** Groningen, NE Netherlands *53°09′N 07°03′E*
100 *J10* **Winsen** Niedersachsen, N Germany *53°22′N 10°13′E*
36 *M11* **Winslow** Arizona, SW USA *35°01′N 110°42′W*
19 *Q7* **Winslow** Maine, NE USA *44°33′N 69°35′W*
18 *M12* **Winsted** Connecticut, NE USA *41°55′N 73°03′W*
32 *F14* **Winston** Oregon, NW USA *43°07′N 123°24′W*
21 *S9* **Winston Salem** North Carolina, SE USA *36°06′N 80°15′W*
98 *N5* **Winsum** Groningen, NE Netherlands *53°20′N 06°31′E*
Wintanceaster *see* Winchester
23 *W11* **Winter Garden** Florida, SE USA *28°34′N 81°35′W*
10 *J16* **Winter Harbour** Vancouver Island, British Columbia, SW Canada *50°28′N 128°03′W*
23 *W12* **Winter Haven** Florida, SE USA *28°01′N 81°43′W*
23 *X11* **Winter Park** Florida, SE USA *28°36′N 81°20′W*
25 *P8* **Winters** Texas, SW USA *31°57′N 99°57′W*
29 *U15* **Winterset** Iowa, C USA *41°19′N 94°00′W*
98 *O12* **Winterswijk** Gelderland, E Netherlands *51°58′N 06°44′E*
108 *G6* **Winterthur** Zürich, NE Switzerland *47°30′N 08°43′E*
29 *U9* **Winthrop** Minnesota, N USA *44°32′N 94°22′W*
32 *J7* **Winthrop** Washington, NW USA *48°28′N 120°13′W*
181 *V7* **Winton** Queensland, E Australia *22°22′S 143°04′E*
185 *C24* **Winton** Southland, South Island, New Zealand *46°08′S 168°20′E*
21 *X8* **Winton** North Carolina, SE USA *36°24′N 76°57′W*
101 *K15* **Wipper** ≈ C Germany
101 *K14* **Wipper** ≈ C Germany
Wipper *see* Wieprza
182 *G6* **Wirraminna** South Australia *31°10′S 136°13′E*
182 *F4* **Wirrida** South Australia *29°34′S 134°33′E*
182 *F7* **Wirrulla** South Australia *32°27′S 134°33′E*
Wirsitz *see* Wyrzysk
Wirz-See *see* Võrtsjärv
97 *O19* **Wisbech** E England, United Kingdom *52°39′N 00°08′E*
Wisby *see* Visby
19 *Q8* **Wiscasset** Maine, NE USA *44°01′N 69°41′W*
Wischau *see* Vyškov
30 *J5* **Wisconsin** *off.* State of Wisconsin, ***also known as*** Badger State. ◐ *state* N USA
30 *L8* **Wisconsin Dells** Wisconsin, N USA *43°37′N 89°43′W*
30 *L8* **Wisconsin, Lake** ⊠ Wisconsin, N USA
30 *L7* **Wisconsin Rapids** Wisconsin, N USA *44°24′N 89°50′W*
30 *L7* **Wisconsin River** ≈ Wisconsin, N USA
33 *P11* **Wisdom** Montana, NW USA *45°36′N 113°27′W*
21 *P7* **Wise** Virginia, NE USA *37°00′N 82°36′W*
39 *Q7* **Wiseman** Alaska, USA *67°24′N 150°06′W*
96 *J12* **Wishaw** W Scotland, United Kingdom *55°47′N 03°56′W*
29 *O6* **Wishek** North Dakota, N USA *46°12′N 99°33′W*
32 *I11* **Wishram** Washington, NW USA *45°40′N 120°53′W*
111 *J17* **Wisła** Śląskie, S Poland *49°39′N 18°50′E*
110 *K11* **Wisła** *Eng.* Vistula, *Ger.* Weichsel. ≈ C Poland
Wiślany, Zalew *see* Vistula Lagoon
111 *M16* **Wisłoka** ≈ SE Poland
100 *L9* **Wismar** Mecklenburg-Vorpommern, N Germany *53°54′N 11°28′E*
29 *R14* **Wisner** Nebraska, C USA *41°59′N 96°54′W*
103 *V4* **Wissembourg** *var.* Weissenburg. Bas-Rhin, NE France *49°03′N 07°57′E*
30 *J6* **Wissota, Lake** ⊠ Wisconsin, N USA
97 *O18* **Witham** ≈ E England, United Kingdom
97 *O17* **Withernsea** E England, United Kingdom *53°46′N 00°01′W*
37 *Q13* **Withington, Mount** ▲ New Mexico, SW USA *33°52′N 107°29′W*
23 *U8* **Withlacoochee River** ≈ Florida/Georgia, SE USA
110 *H11* **Witkowo** Wielkopolskie, C Poland *52°27′N 17°49′E*
97 *M21* **Witney** S England, United Kingdom *51°47′N 01°30′W*
101 *E15* **Witten** Nordrhein-Westfalen, W Germany *51°25′N 07°19′E*
101 *N14* **Wittenberg** Sachsen-Anhalt, E Germany *51°53′N 12°39′E*
30 *L6* **Wittenberg** Wisconsin, N USA *44°53′N 89°20′W*
100 *L11* **Wittenberge** Brandenburg, N Germany *52°59′N 11°45′E*
103 *U7* **Wittenheim** Haut-Rhin, NE France *47°49′N 07°19′E*
180 *I7* **Wittenoom** Western Australia *22°17′S 118°22′E*
Wittingau *see* Třeboň
100 *K12* **Wittingen** Niedersachsen, C Germany *52°42′N 10°43′E*
101 *E18* **Wittlich** Rheinland-Pfalz, SW Germany *49°59′N 06°54′E*
100 *F9* **Wittmund** Niedersachsen, NW Germany *53°34′N 07°46′E*
100 *M10* **Wittstock** Brandenburg, NE Germany *53°10′N 12°29′E*
186 *F6* **Witu Islands** *island group* E Papua New Guinea
110 *O7* **Wiżajny** Podlaskie, NE Poland *54°22′N 22°51′E*
55 *W10* **W. J. van Blommesteinmeer** ⊠ E Surinam
110 *L11* **Wkra** *Ger.* Soldau. ≈ C Poland
110 *I6* **Władysławowo** Pomorskie, N Poland *54°48′N 18°25′E*
Wlaschim *see* Vlašim
111 *E14* **Wleń** *Ger.* Lähn. Dolnośląskie, SW Poland *51°00′N 15°39′E*
110 *J11* **Włocławek** *Ger./Rus.* Vlotslavsk. Kujawsko-pomorskie, C Poland *52°39′N 19°03′E*
110 *P13* **Włodawa** *Rus.* Vlodava. Lubelskie, SE Poland *51°33′N 23°31′E*
Włodzimierz *see* Volodymyr-Volyns'kyy
111 *K15* **Włoszczowa** Świętokrzyskie, C Poland *50°51′N 19°58′E*
83 *C19* **Wlotzkasbaken** Erongo, W Namibia *22°26′S 14°30′E*
15 *R12* **Woburn** Québec, SE Canada *45°22′N 70°52′W*
19 *O11* **Woburn** Massachusetts, NE USA *42°28′N 71°09′W*
Wocheiner Feistritz *see* Bohinjska Bistrica
Wöchma *see* Võhma
147 *S11* **Wodil** *var.* Vuadil'. Farg'ona Viloyati, E Uzbekistan *40°10′N 71°43′E*
181 *V14* **Wodonga** Victoria, SE Australia *36°11′S 146°55′E*
111 *I17* **Wodzisław Śląski** *Ger.* Loslau. Śląskie, S Poland *49°59′N 18°27′E*
98 *I11* **Woerden** Zuid-Holland, C Netherlands *52°06′N 04°54′E*
98 *I8* **Wognum** Noord-Holland, NW Netherlands *52°40′N 05°01′E*
Wohlau *see* Wołów
108 *F7* **Wohlen** Aargau, NW Switzerland *47°21′N 08°17′E*
195 *R2* **Wohlthat Massivet** *Eng.* Wohlthat Mountains. ▲▲ Antarctica
Wohlthat Mountains *see* Wohlthat Massivet
Wojerecy *see* Hoyerswerda
Wōjjā *see* Wotje Atoll
Wojwodina *see* Vojvodina
171 *V15* **Wokam, Pulau** *island* Kepulauan Aru, E Indonesia
97 *N22* **Woking** SE England, United Kingdom *51°20′N 00°34′W*
Woldenberg Neumark *see* Dobiegniew
188 *K15* **Woleai Atoll** *atoll* Caroline Islands, W Micronesia
Woleu *see* Uolo, Río
79 *E17* **Woleu-Ntem** *off.* Province du Woleu-Ntem, *var.* Le Woleu-Ntem. ◐ *province* W Gabon
Woleu-Ntem, Province du *see* Woleu-Ntem
32 *F15* **Wolf Creek** Oregon, NW USA *42°40′N 123°22′W*
26 *K9* **Wolf Creek** ≈ Oklahoma/ Texas, SW USA
37 *R7* **Wolf Creek Pass** *pass* Colorado, C USA
19 *O9* **Wolfeboro** New Hampshire, NE USA *43°34′N 71°10′W*
25 *U5* **Wolfe City** Texas, SW USA *33°22′N 96°04′W*
14 *L15* **Wolfe Island** *island* Ontario, SE Canada
101 *M14* **Wolfen** Sachsen-Anhalt, E Germany *51°40′N 12°16′E*
100 *J13* **Wolfenbüttel** Niedersachsen, C Germany *52°10′N 10°33′E*
109 *T4* **Wolfern** Oberösterreich, N Austria *48°06′N 14°16′E*
109 *Q6* **Wolfgangsee** *var.* Abersee, St Wolfgangsee. ◎ N Austria
39 *P9* **Wolf Mountain** ▲ Alaska, USA *65°20′N 154°08′W*
33 *X7* **Wolf Point** Montana, NW USA *48°05′N 105°40′W*
22 *L8* **Wolf River** ≈ Mississippi, S USA
30 *M7* **Wolf River** ≈ Wisconsin, N USA
109 *U9* **Wolfsberg** Kärnten, SE Austria *46°50′N 14°50′E*
100 *K12* **Wolfsburg** Niedersachsen, N Germany *52°25′N 10°47′E*
57 *B17* **Wolf, Volcán** 🌋 Galapagos Islands, Ecuador, E Pacific Ocean *0°01′N 91°22′W*
100 *O8* **Wolgast** Mecklenburg-Vorpommern, NE Germany *54°04′N 13°47′E*
108 *F8* **Wolhusen** Luzern, W Switzerland *47°04′N 08°06′E*
110 *D8* **Wolin** *Ger.* Wollin. Zachodnio-pomorskie, NW Poland *53°52′N 14°35′E*
109 *Y3* **Wolkersdorf** Niederösterreich, NE Austria *48°24′N 16°31′E*
Wołkowysk *see* Vawkavysk
Wöllan *see* Velenje
8 *J6* **Wollaston, Cape** *headland* Victoria Island, Northwest Territories, NW Canada *71°00′N 118°21′W*
63 *J25* **Wollaston, Isla** *island* S Chile
11 *U11* **Wollaston Lake** Saskatchewan, C Canada *58°05′N 103°38′W*
11 *T10* **Wollaston Lake** ◎ Saskatchewan, C Canada
8 *J6* **Wollaston Peninsula** *peninsula* Victoria Island, Northwest Territories/ Nunavut NW Canada
Wollin *see* Wolin
183 *S9* **Wollongong** New South Wales, SE Australia *34°25′S 150°52′E*
Wolmar *see* Valmiera
100 *L13* **Wolmirstedt** Sachsen-Anhalt, C Germany *52°15′N 11°37′E*
110 *M11* **Wołomin** Mazowieckie, C Poland *52°20′N 21°11′E*
110 *G!3* **Wołów** *Ger.* Wohlau. Dolnośląskie, SW Poland *51°21′N 16°40′E*
Wołożyn *see* Valozhyn
14 *G11* **Wolseley Bay** Ontario, S Canada *46°05′N 80°16′W*
29 *P10* **Wolsey** South Dakota, N USA *44°22′N 98°28′W*
110 *F12* **Wolsztyn** Wielkopolskie, C Poland *52°07′N 16°07′E*
98 *M7* **Wolvega** *Fris.* Wolvegea. Fryslân, N Netherlands *52°53′N 06°E*
Wolvegea *see* Wolvega
97 *K19* **Wolverhampton** C England, United Kingdom *52°36′N 02°08′W*
Wolverine State *see* Michigan
99 *G18* **Wolvertem** Vlaams Brabant, C Belgium *50°55′N 04°19′E*
99 *H16* **Wommelgem** Antwerpen, N Belgium *51°12′N 04°32′E*
186 *D7* **Wonenara** *var.* Wonerara. Eastern Highlands, C Papua New Guinea *06°46′S 145°54′E*
Wonerara *see* Wonenara
Wongalara Lake *see* Wongalarroo Lake
183 *N6* **Wongalarroo Lake** *var.* Wongalara Lake. *seasonal lake* New South Wales, SE Australia
163 *Y15* **Wonju** *Jap.* Genshū; ***prev.*** Wŏnju. N South Korea *37°21′N 127°57′E*
Wŏnju *see* Wonju
10 *M12* **Wonowon** British Columbia, W Canada *56°46′N 121°54′W*
163 *X13* **Wŏnsan** SE North Korea *39°11′N 127°21′E*
183 *O13* **Wonthaggi** Victoria, SE Australia *38°38′S 145°37′E*
23 *N2* **Woodall Mountain** ▲ Mississippi, S USA *34°47′N 88°14′W*
23 *W7* **Woodbine** Georgia, SE USA *30°58′N 81°43′W*
29 *S14* **Woodbine** Iowa, C USA *41°44′N 95°42′W*
18 *J17* **Woodbine** New Jersey, NE USA *39°12′N 74°47′W*
21 *W4* **Woodbridge** Virginia, NE USA *38°40′N 77°17′W*
183 *V4* **Woodburn** New South Wales, SE Australia *29°07′S 153°23′E*
32 *G11* **Woodburn** Oregon, NW USA *45°08′N 122°51′W*
20 *K9* **Woodbury** Tennessee, S USA *35°49′N 86°06′W*
183 *V5* **Wooded Bluff** *headland* New South Wales, SE Australia *29°24′S 153°22′E*
183 *V3* **Woodenbong** New South Wales, SE Australia *28°24′S 152°39′E*
35 *R11* **Woodlake** California, W USA *36°24′N 119°06′W*
35 *N7* **Woodland** California, W USA *38°41′N 121°46′W*
19 *T5* **Woodland** Maine, NE USA *45°10′N 67°25′W*
32 *G10* **Woodland** Washington, NW USA *45°54′N 122°44′W*
37 *T5* **Woodland Park** Colorado, C USA *38°59′N 105°03′W*
186 *I9* **Woodlark Island** *var.* Murua Island. *island* SE Papua New Guinea
Woodle Island *see* Kuria
11 *T17* **Wood Mountain** ▲▲ Saskatchewan, S Canada
30 *K15* **Wood River** Illinois, N USA *38°51′N 90°06′W*
29 *P16* **Wood River** Nebraska, C USA *40°48′N 98°33′W*
39 *R9* **Wood River** ≈ Alaska, USA
39 *O13* **Wood River Lakes** *lakes* Alaska, USA
182 *C1* **Woodroffe, Mount** ▲ South Australia *26°19′S 131°42′E*
21 *P11* **Woodruff** South Carolina, SE USA *34°44′N 82°02′W*
30 *K4* **Woodruff** Wisconsin, N USA *45°55′N 89°41′W*
25 *T14* **Woodsboro** Texas, SW USA *28°14′N 97°19′W*
31 *U13* **Woodsfield** Ohio, N USA *39°45′N 81°07′W*
181 *P4* **Woods, Lake** ◎ Northern Territory, N Australia
11 *Z16* **Woods, Lake of the** *Fr.* Lac des Bois. ◎ Canada/USA
25 *Q6* **Woodson** Texas, SW USA *33°00′N 99°01′W*
13 *N14* **Woodstock** New Brunswick, SE Canada *46°10′N 67°38′W*
14 *F16* **Woodstock** Ontario, S Canada *43°07′N 80°46′W*
30 *M10* **Woodstock** Illinois, N USA *42°18′N 88°27′W*
18 *M9* **Woodstock** Vermont, NE USA *43°37′N 72°33′W*
21 *U4* **Woodstock** Virginia, NE USA *38°55′N 78°31′W*
19 *N8* **Woodsville** New Hampshire, NE USA *44°08′N 72°02′W*
184 *M12* **Woodville** Manawatu-Wanganui, North Island, New Zealand *40°22′S 175°59′E*
22 *J7* **Woodville** Mississippi, S USA *31°06′N 91°18′W*
25 *X9* **Woodville** Texas, SW USA *30°47′N 94°26′W*
26 *K9* **Woodward** Oklahoma, C USA *36°26′N 99°25′W*
29 *O5* **Woodworth** North Dakota, N USA *47°06′N 99°19′W*
171 *W12* **Wool** Papua, E Indonesia *01°38′S 135°34′E*
183 *V5* **Woolgoolga** New South Wales, E Australia *30°04′S 153°09′E*
182 *H6* **Woomera** South Australia *31°12′S 136°52′E*
19 *O12* **Woonsocket** Rhode Island, NE USA *41°58′N 71°27′W*
29 *P10* **Woonsocket** South Dakota, N USA *44°03′N 98°16′W*
31 *T12* **Wooster** Ohio, N USA *40°48′N 81°56′W*
80 *L12* **Woqooyi Galbeed** *off.* Gobolka Woqooyi Galbeed. ◐ *region* NW Somalia
Woqooyi Galbeed, Gobolka *see* Woqooyi Galbeed
108 *E8* **Worb** Bern, C Switzerland *46°54′N 07°36′E*
83 *F26* **Worcester** Western Cape, SW South Africa *33°41′S 19°22′E*
97 *L20* **Worcester** *hist.* Wigorna Ceaster. W England, United Kingdom *52°11′N 02°13′W*
19 *N11* **Worcester** Massachusetts, NE USA *42°17′N 71°48′W*
97 *L20* **Worcestershire** *cultural region* C England, United Kingdom
32 *H16* **Worden** Oregon, NW USA *42°04′N 121°50′W*
109 *O6* **Wörgl** Tirol, W Austria *47°29′N 12°04′E*
171 *V15* **Workai, Pulau** *island* Kepulauan Aru, E Indonesia
97 *J15* **Workington** NW England, United Kingdom *54°39′N 03°33′W*
98 *K7* **Workum** Fryslân, N Netherlands *52°58′N 05°25′E*
33 *V13* **Worland** Wyoming, C USA *44°01′N 107°57′W*
see São João de Cortes
Wormatia *see* Worms
99 *N25* **Wormeldange** Grevenmacher, E Luxembourg *49°37′N 06°25′E*
98 *I9* **Wormer** Noord-Holland, C Netherlands *52°30′N 04°50′E*
101 *G19* **Worms** *anc.* Augusta Vangionum, Borbetomagus, Wormatia. Rheinland-Pfalz, SW Germany *49°38′N 08°22′E*
Worms *see* Vormsi
101 *K21* **Wörnitz** ≈ S Germany
25 *U8* **Wortham** Texas, SW USA *31°47′N 96°27′W*
101 *G21* **Wörth am Rhein** Rheinland-Pfalz, SW Germany *49°04′N 08°16′E*
109 *S9* **Wörther See** ◎ S Austria
97 *O23* **Worthing** SE England, United Kingdom *50°48′N 00°23′W*
29 *S11* **Worthington** Minnesota, N USA *43°37′N 95°37′W*
31 *S13* **Worthington** Ohio, N USA *40°05′N 83°01′W*
35 *W8* **Worthington Peak** ▲ Nevada, W USA *37°57′N 115°32′W*
171 *Y13* **Wosi** Papua, E Indonesia *03°55′S 138°54′E*
171 *V13* **Wosimi** Papua, E Indonesia *02°44′S 134°34′E*
189 *R5* **Wotho Atoll** *var.* Wōtto. *atoll* Ralik Chain, W Marshall Islands
189 *V5* **Wotje Atoll** *var.* Wōjjā. *atoll* Ratak Chain, E Marshall Islands
Wotoe *see* Wotu
Wottawa *see* Otava
Wōtto *see* Wotho Atoll
171 *O13* **Wotu** *prev.* Wotoe. Sulawesi, C Indonesia *02°34′S 120°46′E*
98 *K11* **Woudenberg** Utrecht, C Netherlands *52°05′N 05°25′E*
98 *I13* **Woudrichem** Noord-Brabant, S Netherlands *51°49′N 05°E*
43 *N8* **Wounta** *var.* Huaunta. Región Autónoma Atlántico Norte, NE Nicaragua *13°30′N 83°32′W*
171 *P14* **Wowoni, Pulau** *island* C Indonesia
81 *J17* **Woyamdero Plain** *plain* E Kenya
Woyens *see* Vojens
Wozrojdeniye Oroli *see* Vozrozhdeniya, Ostrov
Wrangel Island *see* Vrangelya, Ostrov
39 *Y13* **Wrangell** Wrangell Island, Alaska, USA *56°28′N 132°22′W*
38 *C15* **Wrangell, Cape** *headland* Attu Island, Alaska, USA *52°55′N 172°28′E*
39 *S11* **Wrangell, Mount** ▲ Alaska, USA *62°00′N 144°01′W*
39 *T11* **Wrangell Mountains** ▲▲ Alaska, USA
197 *S7* **Wrangel Plain** *undersea feature* Arctic Ocean
96 *H6* **Wrath, Cape** *headland* N Scotland, United Kingdom *58°37′N 05°01′W*
37 *W3* **Wray** Colorado, C USA *40°01′N 102°12′W*
44 *K13* **Wreck Point** *headland* C Jamaica *17°50′N 76°55′W*
83 *C23* **Wreck Point** *headland* W South Africa *28°52′S 16°17′E*
23 *V4* **Wrens** Georgia, SE USA *33°12′N 82°23′W*
97 *K18* **Wrexham** NE Wales, United Kingdom *53°03′N 03°W*
27 *R13* **Wright City** Oklahoma, C USA *34°03′N 95°00′W*
194 *J12* **Wright Island** *island* Antarctica
13 *N9* **Wright, Mont** ▲ Québec, E Canada *52°36′N 67°40′W*
25 *X5* **Wright Patman Lake** ⊠ Texas, SW USA
36 *M16* **Wrightson, Mount** ▲ Arizona, SW USA *31°42′N 110°51′W*
23 *U5* **Wrightsville** Georgia, SE USA *32°43′N 82°43′W*
21 *W12* **Wrightsville Beach** North Carolina, SE USA *34°12′N 77°48′W*
35 *T15* **Wrightwood** California, W USA *34°21′N 117°37′W*
8 *H9* **Wrigley** Northwest Territories, W Canada *63°16′N 123°39′W*
111 *G14* **Wrocław** *Eng./Ger.* Breslau. Dolnośląskie, SW Poland *51°07′N 17°01′E*
110 *F10* **Wronki** *Ger.* Fronicken. Wielkopolskie, C Poland *52°42′N 16°22′E*
110 *H11* **Września** Wielkopolskie, C Poland *52°19′N 17°34′E*
110 *F12* **Wschowa** Lubuskie, W Poland *51°49′N 16°15′E*
Wsetin *see* Vsetín
161 *O5* **Wu'an** Hebei, E China *36°45′N 114°12′E*
180 *I12* **Wubin** Western Australia *30°05′S 116°43′E*
163 *W9* **Wuchang** Heilongjiang, NE China *44°55′N 127°13′E*
Wuchang *see* Wuhan
Wu-chou/Wuchow *see* Wuzhou
160 *M16* **Wuchuan** *var.* Meilu. Guangdong, S China *21°28′N 110°49′E*
160 *K10* **Wuchuan** *var.* Duru, Gelaozu Miaozu Zhizhixian. Guizhou, S China *28°40′N 108°04′E*
163 *O13* **Wuchuan** Nei Mongol Zizhiqu, N China *41°04′N 111°28′E*
163 *V6* **Wudalianchi** *var.* Qingshan; ***prev.*** Dedu. Heilongjiang, NE China *48°40′N 126°06′E*
159 *O11* **Wudaoliang** Qinghai, C China *35°16′N 93°03′E*
141 *Q13* **Wuday'ah** *spring/well* S Saudi Arabia *17°03′N 47°06′E*
77 *V13* **Wudil** Kano, N Nigeria *11°46′N 08°49′E*
160 *G12* **Wuding** *var.* Jincheng. Yunnan, SW China *25°30′N 102°21′E*
182 *G8* **Wudinna** South Australia *33°06′S 135°30′E*
Wudu *see* Longnan
160 *L9* **Wufeng** Hubei, C China *30°09′N 110°31′E*
161 *O11* **Wugong Shan** ▲▲ S China
157 *P7* **Wuhai** *var.* Haibowan. Nei Mongol Zizhiqu, N China *39°40′N 106°48′E*
161 *O9* **Wuhan** *var.* Han-kou, Han-k'ou, Hanyang, Wuchang, Wu-han; ***prev.*** Hankow. *province capital* Hubei, C China *30°35′N 114°19′E*
Wu-han *see* Wuhan
161 *Q7* **Wuhe** Anhui, E China *33°05′N 117°55′E*
Wuhsien *see* Suzhou
Wuhsi/Wu-his *see* Wuxi
161 *Q8* **Wuhu** *var.* Wu-na-mu. Anhui, E China *31°23′N 118°25′E*
Wūjae *see* Ujae Atoll
160 *K11* **Wu Jiang** ≈ C China
158 *L5* **Wujiaqu** Xinjiang Uygur Zizhiqu, NW China *44°11′N 87°30′E*
Wujlān *see* Ujelang Atoll
77 *W15* **Wukari** Taraba, E Nigeria *07°51′N 09°49′E*
Wulan *see* Jingyuan
152 *H4* **Wular Lake** ◎ NE India
162 *M13* **Wulashan** Nei Mongol Zizhiqu, N China *40°43′N 108°45′E*
160 *H11* **Wulian Feng** ▲▲ SW China
160 *F13* **Wuliang Shan** ▲▲ SW China
160 *K11* **Wuling Shan** ▲▲ S China
109 *Y5* **Wulka** ≈ E Austria
Wulkan *see* Vulcan
109 *T3* **Wullowitz** Oberösterreich, N Austria *48°37′N 14°27′E*
Wu-lu-k'o-mu-shi/Wu-lu-mu-ch'i *see* Ürümqi
79 *D14* **Wum** Nord-Ouest, NE Cameroon *06°24′N 10°04′E*
160 *H12* **Wumeng Shan** ▲▲ SW China
160 *K14* **Wuming** Guangxi Zhuangzu Zizhiqu, S China *23°12′N 108°11′E*
100 *I10* **Wümme** ≈ NW Germany
Wu-na-mu *see* Wuhu
171 *X13* **Wunen** Papua, E Indonesia *03°40′S 138°31′E*
12 *D9* **Wunnummin Lake** ◎ Ontario, C Canada
80 *D13* **Wun Rog** Warap, W South Sudan *09°00′N 28°20′E*
101 *M18* **Wunsiedel** Bayern, E Germany *50°02′N 12°00′E*
100 *I12* **Wunstorf** Niedersachsen, NW Germany *52°25′N 09°25′E*
166 *M3* **Wuntho** Sagaing, N Burma (Myanmar) *23°52′N 95°43′E*
101 *F15* **Wupper** ≈ W Germany
101 *E15* **Wuppertal** *prev.* Barmen-Elberfeld. Nordrhein-Westfalen, W Germany *51°16′N 07°12′E*
160 *K5* **Wuqi** Shaanxi, C China *36°57′N 108°15′E*
158 *E7* **Wuqia** Xinjiang Uygur Zizhiqu, NW China *39°50′N 75°19′E*
161 *P4* **Wuqiao** *var.* Sangyuan. Hebei, E China *37°40′N 116°21′E*
101 *L23* **Würm** ≈ SE Germany
77 *T12* **Wurno** Sokoto, NW Nigeria *13°15′N 05°24′E*
101 *I19* **Würzburg** Bayern, SW Germany *49°48′N 09°56′E*
101 *N15* **Wurzen** Sachsen, E Germany *51°21′N 12°48′E*
160 *L9* **Wu Shan** ▲▲ C China
158 *G7* **Wushi** *var.* Uqturpan. Xinjiang Uygur Zizhiqu, NW China *41°07′N 79°09′E*
Wusih *see* Wuxi
65 *N18* **Wüst Seamount** *undersea feature* S Atlantic Ocean *32°00′S 00°06′E*
Wusuli Jiang/Wusuri *see* Ussuri
161 *N3* **Wutai Shan** *var.* Beitai Ding. ▲ C China *39°00′N 114°00′E*
160 *H10* **Wutongqiao** Sichuan, C China *29°21′N 103°48′E*
159 *P6* **Wutongwozi Quan** *spring* NW China
99 *H15* **Wuustwezel** Antwerpen, N Belgium *51°24′N 04°34′E*
186 *B4* **Wuvulu Island** *island* NW Papua New Guinea
159 *U9* **Wuwei** *var.* Liangzhou. Gansu, C China *37°58′N 102°40′E*
161 *R8* **Wuxi** *var.* Wuhsi, Wu-hsi, Wusih. Jiangsu, E China *31°35′N 120°19′E*
Wuxing *see* Huzhou
160 *L14* **Wuxuan** Guangxi Zhuangzu Zizhiqu, S China *23°40′N 109°41′E*
Wuyang *see* Zhenyuan
160 *K11* **Wuyang He** ≈ S China
163 *X6* **Wuyiling** Heilongjiang, NE China *48°36′N 129°24′E*
161 *Q11* **Wuyishan** *prev.* Chong'an. Fujian, SE China *27°48′N 118°03′E*
157 *T12* **Wuyi Shan** ▲▲ SE China
162 *M13* **Wuyuan** Nei Mongol Zizhiqu, N China *41°05′N 108°15′E*
160 *L17* **Wuzhishan** *prev.* Tongshi. Hainan, S China *18°37′N 109°34′E*
160 *L17* **Wuzhi Shan** ▲ S China *18°52′N 109°36′E*
159 *W8* **Wuzhong** Ningxia, N China *37°58′N 106°09′E*
160 *M14* **Wuzhou** *var.* Wu-chou, Wuchow. Guangxi Zhuangzu Zizhiqu, S China *23°30′N 111°21′E*
18 *H12* **Wyalusing** Pennsylvania, NE USA *41°40′N 76°13′W*
182 *M10* **Wycheproof** Victoria, SE Australia *36°06′S 143°13′E*
97 *K21* **Wye** *Wel.* Gwy. ≈ England/ Wales, United Kingdom
Wyłkowyszki *see* Vilkaviškis
97 *P19* **Wymondham** E England, United Kingdom *52°29′N 01°10′E*
29 *R17* **Wymore** Nebraska, C USA *40°07′N 96°39′W*
182 *E5* **Wynbring** South Australia *30°34′S 133°27′E*
181 *N3* **Wyndham** Western Australia *15°28′S 128°08′E*
29 *R6* **Wyndmere** North Dakota, N USA *46°16′N 97°07′W*
27 *X11* **Wynne** Arkansas, C USA *35°14′N 90°48′W*
27 *N12* **Wynnewood** Oklahoma, C USA *34°39′N 97°09′W*
183 *O15* **Wynyard** Tasmania, SE Australia *40°57′S 145°33′E*
11 *U15* **Wynyard** Saskatchewan, S Canada *51°46′N 104°10′W*
33 *V11* **Wyola** Montana, NW USA *45°07′N 107°23′W*
182 *A4* **Wyola Lake** *salt lake* South Australia
31 *P9* **Wyoming** Michigan, N USA *42°54′N 85°42′W*
33 *V14* **Wyoming** *off.* State of Wyoming, ***also known as*** Equality State. ◐ *state* C USA
33 *S15* **Wyoming Range** ▲▲ Wyoming, C USA
183 *T8* **Wyong** New South Wales, SE Australia *33°18′S 151°27′E*
110 *G9* **Wyrzysk** *Ger.* Wirsitz. Wielkopolskie, C Poland *53°09′N 17°15′E*
Wysg *see* Usk
110 *O10* **Wysokie Mazowieckie** Łomża, E Poland *52°54′N 22°34′E*
110 *M11* **Wyszków** *Ger.* Probstberg. Mazowieckie, NE Poland *52°36′N 21°28′E*
110 *L11* **Wyszogród** Mazowieckie, C Poland *52°24′N 20°14′E*
21 *R7* **Wytheville** Virginia, NE USA *36°57′N 81°07′W*
111 *L15* **Wyżyna Małopolska** *plateau*

X

80 *Q12* **Xaafuun** *It.* Hafun. Bari, NE Somalia *10°25′N 51°17′E*
80 *Q12* **Xaafuun, Raas** *var.* Ras Hafun. *cape* NE Somalia
Xabia *see* Jávea
42 *C4* **Xaclbal, Río** *var.* Xalbal. ≈ Guatemala/Mexico
137 *Y10* **Xaçmaz** *Rus.* Khachmas. N Azerbaijan *41°26′N 48°47′E*
80 *O12* **Xadeed** *var.* Haded. *physical region* N Somalia
159 *O14* **Xagquka** Xizang Zizhiqu, W China *31°47′N 92°46′E*
Xai *see* Oudômxai
158 *F10* **Xaidulla** Xinjiang Uygur Zizhiqu, W China *36°27′N 77°46′E*
167 *Q7* **Xaignabouli** *prev.* Muang Xaignabouri, *Fr.* Sayaboury. Xaignabouli, N Laos *19°16′N 101°43′E*
167 *R7* **Xai Lai Leng, Phou** ▲ Laos/ Vietnam *19°13′N 104°09′E*
158 *L15* **Xainza** Xizang Zizhiqu, W China *30°54′N 88°36′E*
158 *L16* **Xaitongmoin** Xizang Zizhiqu, W China *29°27′N 88°13′E*
83 *F17* **Xaixai** *var.* Caecae. North-West, NW Botswana *19°52′S 21°04′E*
83 *M20* **Xai-Xai** *prev.* João Belo, Vila de João Belo. Gaza, S Mozambique *25°01′S 33°37′E*
Xalbal *see* Xaclbal, Río
80 *P13* **Xalin** Sool, N Somalia *09°16′N 49°00′E*
146 *H7* **Xalqobod** *Rus.* Khalkabad. Qoraqalpog'iston Respublikasi, W Uzbekistan *42°42′N 59°46′E*
160 *F11* **Xamgyi'nyilha** *var.* Jiantang; ***prev.*** Zhongdian. Yunnan, SW China *27°48′N 99°41′E*
167 *R6* **Xam Nua** *var.* Sam Neua. Houaphan, N Laos *20°24′N 104°03′E*
82 *D11* **Xá-Muteba** *Port.* Cinco de Outubro. Lunda Norte, NE Angola *09°34′S 17°50′E*
Xangda *see* Nangqên
83 *C16* **Xangongo** *Port.* Rocadas. Cunene, SW Angola *16°43′S 15°01′E*
137 *W12* **Xankändi** *Rus.* Khankendi; ***prev.*** Stepanakert. SW Azerbaijan *39°50′N 46°44′E*
114 *J13* **Xánthi** Anatolikí Makedonía kai Thráki, NE Greece *41°09′N 24°54′E*
60 *H13* **Xanxerê** Santa Catarina, S Brazil *26°52′S 52°25′W*
81 *O15* **Xarardheere** Mudug, E Somalia *04°45′N 47°54′E*
137 *Z11* **Xärä Zirä Adasi** *Rus.* Ostrov Bulla. *Island* E Azerbaijan
162 *K13* **Xar Burd** *prev.* Bayan Nuru. Nei Mongol Zizhiqu, N China *40°09′N 104°48′E*
163 *T11* **Xar Moron** ≈ NE China
163 *T11* **Xar Moron** ≈ N China
Xarra *see* Xarrë
113 *L23* **Xarrë** *var.* Xarra. Vlorë, S Albania *39°45′N 20°01′E*
82 *D12* **Xassengue** Lunda Sul, NW Angola *10°28′S 18°32′E*
105 *S11* **Xàtiva** *Cas.* Xátiva, *var.* Jativa; ***anc.*** Setabis. Valenciana, E Spain *39°N 00°32′W*
Xauen *see* Chefchaouen
60 *K10* **Xavantes, Represa de** *var.* Represa de Chavantes. ⊠ S Brazil
158 *I7* **Xayar** Xinjiang Uygur Zizhiqu, W China *41°16′N 82°52′E*

◆ Country ● Country Capital ◇ Dependent Territory ○ Dependent Territory Capital ◐ Administrative Regions ✈ International Airport ▲ Mountain ▲▲ Mountain Range 🌋 Volcano ≈ River ◎ Lake ⊠ Reservoir

Xäzär Dänizi see Caspian Sea
167 S8 Xé Bangfai ≈ C Laos
167 T9 Xé Banghiang var. Bang Hieng. ≈ S Laos
Xêgar see Tingri
167 T10 Xékong var. Lamam. Xékong, S Laos 15°22′N 106°40′E
31 R14 Xenia Ohio, N USA 39°40′N 83°55′W
Xeres see Jerez de la Frontera
115 E15 Xeriás ≈ C Greece
115 G17 Xeró ▲ Évvoia, C Greece 38°52′N 23°18′E
Xhumo see Cum
161 N15 Xiachuan Dao island S China
Xiacun see Rushan
Xiaguan see Dali
159 U11 Xiahe var. Labrang. Gansu, C China 35°12′N 102°28′E
161 Q13 Xiamen var. Hsia-men; prev. Amoy. Fujian, SE China 24°28′N 118°05′E
160 L6 Xi'an var. Changan, Sian, Signan, Siking, Singan, Xian. province capital Shaanxi, C China 34°16′N 108°54′E
160 L10 Xianfeng var. Gaoleshan. Hubei, C China 29°45′N 109°10′E
Xiang see Hunan
161 N7 Xiangcheng Henan, C China 33°51′N 113°27′E
160 F10 Xiangcheng var. Sampê, Tib. Qagchêng. Sichuan, C China 28°52′N 99°45′E
160 M8 Xiangfan var. Xiangyang. Hubei, C China 32°07′N 112°00′E
Xianggang see Hong Kong
161 N10 Xiang Jiang ≈ S China
Xiangkhoang see Phônsaven
167 Q7 Xiangkhoang, Plateau de var. Plain of Jars. plateau N Laos
161 N11 Xiangtan var. Hsiang-t'an, Siangtan. Hunan, S China 27°53′N 112°55′E
161 N11 Xiangxiang Hunan, S China 27°50′N 112°31′E
Xiangyang see Xiangfan
161 S10 Xianju Zhejiang, SE China 28°53′N 120°41′E
Xianshui see Dawu
160 F8 Xianshui He ≈ C China
161 N9 Xiantao var. Mianyang. Hubei, C China 30°20′N 113°31′E
161 R10 Xianxia Ling ▲▲ SE China
160 K6 Xianyang Shaanxi, C China 34°26′N 118°40′E
158 L5 Xiaocaohu Xinjiang Uygur Zizhiqu, W China 45°44′N 90°07′E
161 O9 Xiaogan Hubei, C China 30°55′N 113°54′E
Xiaogang see Dongxiang
163 W6 Xiao Hinggan Ling Eng. Lesser Khingan Range. ▲▲ NE China
160 M6 Xiao Shan ▲▲ C China
160 M12 Xiao Shui ≈ S China
Xiaoxi see Pinghe
161 P6 Xiaoxian var. Longcheng, Xiao Xian. Anhui, E China 34°11′N 116°56′E
Xiao Xian see Xiaoxian
160 G11 Xichang Sichuan, C China 27°52′N 102°16′E
41 P11 Xicoténcatl Tamaulipas, C Mexico 22°59′N 98°54′W
Xieng Khouang see Phônsaven
Xieng Ngeun see Muong Xiang Ngeun
160 J11 Xifeng var. Yongjing. Guizhou, S China 27°15′N 106°44′E
Xifeng see Qingcheng
Xigang see Helan
158 L16 Xigazê var. Jih-k'a-tse, Shigatse, Xigaze. Xizang Zizhiqu, W China 29°18′N 88°50′E
159 W11 Xihe var. Hanyuan. Gansu, C China 34°00′N 105°24′E
160 I8 Xi He ≈ C China
Xihuachi see Heshui
159 W10 Xiji Ningxia, N China 36°02′N 105°33′E
160 M14 Xi Jiang var. Hsi Chiang, Eng. West River. ≈ S China
159 Q7 Xijian Quan spring NW China
160 K15 Xijin Shuiku ⊠ S China
Xilaganí see Xylaganí
Xiligou see Ulan
160 I13 Xilin var. Bada. Guangxi Zhuangzu Zizhiqu, S China 24°30′N 105°00′E
163 Q10 Xilinhot var. Silinhot. Nei Mongol Zizhiqu, N China 43°58′N 116°07′E
Xilinji see Mohe
Xilokastro see Xylókastro
Xin see Xinjiang Uygur Zizhiqu
Xin'an see Anlong
Xin'anjiang Shuiku see Qiandao Hu
Xin'anzhen see Xinyi
Xin Barag Youqi see Altan Emel
Xin Barag Zuoqi see Amgalang
163 W12 Xinbin var. Xinbin Manzu Zizhixian. Liaoning, NE China 41°44′N 125°02′E
Xinbin Manzu Zizhixian see Xinbin
161 O7 Xincai Henan, C China 32°47′N 114°58′E
Xincheng see Zhaojue
Xindu see Luhuo
161 O13 Xinfeng var. Jiading. Jiangxi, S China 25°23′N 114°48′E
161 O14 Xinfengjiang Shuiku ⊠ S China
Xing'an see Ankang
Xingba see Lhünzê
163 T13 Xingcheng Liaoning, NE China 40°38′N 120°47′E
Xingcheng see Xingning
82 E11 Xinge Lunda Norte, NE Angola 09°44′S 19°10′E
161 P12 Xingguo var. Lianjiang. Jiangxi, S China 26°25′N 115°22′E
159 S11 Xinghai var. Ziketan. Qinghai, C China 35°12′N 102°28′E
161 R7 Xinghua Jiangsu, E China 32°54′N 119°48′E
Xingkai Hu see Khanka, Lake
161 P13 Xingning prev. Xingcheng. Guangdong, S China 24°05′N 115°47′E
160 I13 Xingren Guizhou, S China 25°26′N 105°08′E
161 O4 Xingtai Hebei, E China 37°08′N 114°29′E
59 J14 Xingu, Rio ≈ C Brazil
159 P6 Xingxingxia Xinjiang Uygur Zizhiqu, NW China 41°48′N 95°01′E
160 I13 Xingyi Guizhou, S China 25°04′N 104°51′E
158 I6 Xinhe var. Toksu. Xinjiang Uygur Zizhiqu, NW China 41°32′N 82°39′E
163 Q10 Xin Hot Nei Mongol Zizhiqu, N China 43°58′N 114°59′E
Xinhua see Funing
163 T12 Xinhui var. Aohan Qi. Nei Mongol Zizhiqu, N China 42°12′N 119°57′E
159 T10 Xining var. Hsining, Hsi-ning, Sining. province capital Qinghai, C China 36°37′N 101°46′E
161 O4 Xinji prev. Shulu. Hebei, E China 37°55′N 115°14′E
161 P10 Xinjian Jiangxi, S China 28°37′N 115°46′E
Xinjiang see Xinjiang Uygur Zizhiqu
162 D8 Xinjiang Uygur Zizhiqu var. Sinkiang, Sinkiang Uighur Autonomous Region, Xin, Xinjiang. ◆ autonomous region NW China
160 H9 Xinjin var. Meixing, Tib. Zainlha. Sichuan, C China 30°27′N 103°46′E
Xinjin see Pulandian
Xinjing see Jingxi
163 U12 Xinmin Liaoning, NE China 41°58′N 122°51′E
160 M12 Xinning var. Jinshi. Hunan, S China 26°34′N 110°57′E
Xinning see Ningxian
Xinning see Fusui
Xinpu see Lianyungang
Xinshan see Anyuan
161 P5 Xintai Shandong, E China 35°54′N 117°44′E
Xinwen see Suncun
Xin Xian see Xinzhou
161 N6 Xinxiang Henan, C China 35°13′N 113°48′E
161 O8 Xinyang var. Hsin-yang, Sinyang. Henan, C China 32°09′N 114°04′E
161 Q6 Xinyi var. Xin'anzhen. Jiangsu, E China 34°17′N 118°14′E
161 Q6 Xinyi He ≈ E China
161 S14 Xinying var. Sinying, Jap. Shinei; prev. Hsinying. C Taiwan 23°12′N 120°15′E
161 O11 Xinyu Jiangxi, S China 27°51′N 115°00′E
158 I5 Xinyuan var. Künes. Xinjiang Uygur Zizhiqu, NW China 43°25′N 83°12′E
Xinyuan see Tianjun
162 M13 Xinzhao Shan ▲ N China 39°37′N 107°51′E
161 N3 Xinzhou var. Xin Xian. Shanxi, C China 38°24′N 112°43′E
Xinzhou see Longlin
161 S13 Xinzhu var. Hsinchu. N Taiwan 24°48′N 120°59′E
104 H4 Xinzo de Limia Galicia, NW Spain 42°05′N 07°45′W
Xions see Książ Wielkopolski
161 O7 Xiping Henan, C China 33°22′N 114°00′E
Xiping see Songyang
159 T11 Xiqing Shan ▲▲ C China
59 N16 Xique-Xique Bahia, E Brazil 10°47′S 42°44′W
Xireg see Ulan
115 E14 Xirovoúni ▲ N Greece 40°31′N 21°58′E
162 M13 Xishanzui prev. Urad Qianqi. Nei Mongol Zizhiqu, N China 40°43′N 108°41′E
160 J11 Xishui var. Donghuang. Guizhou, S China 28°24′N 106°09′E
Xi Ujimqin Qi see Bayan Ul
160 K11 Xiushan var. Zhonghe. Chongqing Shi, C China 28°23′N 108°52′E
Xiushan see Tonghai
161 O10 Xiu Shui ≈ S China
Xiuyan see Qingjian
146 H9 Xiva Rus. Khiva, Khiwa. Xorazm Viloyati, W Uzbekistan 41°22′N 60°22′E
158 J16 Xixabangma Feng ▲ W China 28°25′N 85°47′E
160 M7 Xixia Henan, C China 33°30′N 111°25′E
Xixón see Gijón
Xixona see Jijona
Xizang see Xizang Zizhiqu
Xizang Gaoyuan see Qingzang Gaoyuan
160 E9 Xizang Zizhiqu var. Thibet, Tibetan Autonomous Region, Xizang, Eng. Tibet. ◆ autonomous region W China
163 U14 Xizhong Dao island N China
Xoi see Qüxü
146 H8 Xo'jayli Rus. Khodzheyli. Qoraqalpog'iston Respublikasi, W Uzbekistan 42°23′N 59°27′E
Xolotlán see Managua, Lago de
147 I9 Xonqa var. Khonqa, Rus. Khanka. Xorazm Viloyati, W Uzbekistan 41°31′N 60°39′E
146 H9 Xorazm Viloyati Rus. Khorezmskaya Oblast'. ◆ province W Uzbekistan
159 N9 Xorkol Xinjiang Uygur Zizhiqu, NW China 38°45′N 91°07′E
147 P11 Xovos var. Ursat'yevskaya, Rus. Khavast. Sirdaryo Viloyati, E Uzbekistan 40°14′N 68°46′E
41 X14 Xpujil Quintana Roo, E Mexico 18°30′N 89°24′W
161 Q8 Xuancheng var. Xuanzhou. Anhui, E China 30°57′N 118°53′E
167 T9 Xuân Đuc Quang Binh, C Vietnam 17°19′N 106°38′E
160 L9 Xuan'en var. Zhushan. Hubei, C China 30°03′N 109°26′E
160 K8 Xuanhan Sichuan, C China 31°25′N 107°41′E
161 O2 Xuanhua Hebei, E China 40°36′N 115°01′E
161 P4 Xuanhui He ≈ E China
167 T8 Xuan Sơn Quang Binh, C Vietnam 17°42′N 105°58′E
H12 Xuanwei Yunnan, China 26°08′N 104°04′E
Xuanzhou see Xuancheng
161 N7 Xuchang Henan, C China 34°03′N 113°48′E
Xucheng see Xuwen
137 X10 Xudat Rus. Khudat. NE Azerbaijan 41°37′N 48°39′E
81 M16 Xuddur var. Hudur, It. Oddur. Bakool, SW Somalia 04°07′N 43°47′E
80 O13 Xudun Sool, N Somalia 09°12′N 47°34′E
160 L11 Xuefeng Shan ▲▲ S China
161 S13 Xue Shan prev. Hsüeh Shan. ▲ N Taiwan
147 O13 Xufar Surkhondaryo Viloyati, S Uzbekistan 38°31′N 67°45′E
Xulun Hobot Qagan see Qagan Nur
42 F2 Xunantunich ruins Cayo, W Belize
163 W6 Xun He ≈ NE China
160 L7 Xun He ≈ C China
160 L14 Xun Jiang ≈ S China
163 W5 Xunke var. Bianjiang; prev. Qike. Heilongjiang, NE China 49°35′N 128°27′E
161 P13 Xunwu var. Changning. Jiangxi, S China 24°59′N 115°33′E
161 O3 Xushui Hebei, E China 39°01′N 115°38′E
160 L16 Xuwen var. Xucheng. Guangdong, S China 20°21′N 110°09′E
160 I11 Xuyong var. Yongning. Sichuan, C China 28°17′N 105°21′E
161 P6 Xuzhou var. Hsu-chou, Suchow, Tongshan; prev. T'ung-shan. Jiangsu, E China 34°17′N 117°09′E
114 K13 Xylaganí var. Xilaganí. Anatolikí Makedonía kai Thráki, NE Greece 40°58′N 25°27′E
115 F19 Xylókastro var. Xilokastro. Pelopónnisos, S Greece 38°04′N 22°36′E

Y

160 H9 Ya'an var. Yaan. Sichuan, C China 30°N 102°57′E
182 L10 Yaapeet Victoria, SE Australia 35°48′S 142°03′E
79 D15 Yabassi Littoral, W Cameroon 04°30′N 09°59′E
81 J15 Yabēlo Oromīya, C Ethiopia 04°53′N 38°01′E
114 H9 Yablanitsa Lovech, N Bulgaria 43°01′N 24°06′E
43 N7 Yablis Región Autónoma Atlántico Norte, NE Nicaragua 14°08′N 83°44′W
123 O14 Yablonovyy Khrebet ▲▲ S Russian Federation
162 J14 Yabrai Shan ▲▲ NE China
45 U6 Yabucoa E Puerto Rico 18°02′N 65°53′W
160 J11 Yachi He ≈ S China
32 H10 Yacolt Washington, NW USA 45°49′N 122°22′W
54 M10 Yacuaray Amazonas, S Venezuela 04°12′N 66°30′W
57 M22 Yacuiba Tarija, S Bolivia 22°00′S 63°43′W
57 K16 Yacuma, Río ≈ C Bolivia
155 H16 Yādgīr Karnātaka, C India 16°46′N 77°09′E
21 R8 Yadkin River ≈ North Carolina, SE USA
21 R9 Yadkinville North Carolina, SE USA 36°07′N 80°40′W
127 P3 Yadrin Chuvashskaya Respublika, W Russian Federation 55°55′N 46°10′E
Yaegama-shotō see Yaeyama-shotō
Yaeme-saki see Paimi-saki
165 O16 Yaeyama-shotō var. Yaegama-shotō. island group SW Japan
75 O8 Yafran NW Libya 32°04′N 12°31′E
165 S2 Yagashiri-tō island NE Japan
65 H21 Yaghan Basin undersea feature SE Pacific Ocean
123 S9 Yagodnoye Magadanskaya Oblast', E Russian Federation 62°37′N 149°18′E
Yagotin see Yahotyn
78 G12 Yagoua Extrême-Nord, NE Cameroon 10°23′N 15°13′E
159 Q11 Yagradagzê Shan ▲ C China 35°06′N 95°41′E
Yaguachi see Yaguachi Nuevo
56 B7 Yaguachi Nuevo var. Yaguachi. Guayas, W Ecuador 02°06′S 79°43′W
Yaguarón, Río see Jaguarão, Rio
117 Q11 Yahorlyts'kyy Lyman bay S Ukraine
117 Q5 Yahotyn Rus. Yagotin. Kyyivs'ka Oblast', N Ukraine 50°15′N 31°48′E
40 L12 Yahualica Jalisco, SW Mexico 21°11′N 102°29′W
79 L17 Yahuma Orientale, N Dem. Rep. Congo 01°12′N 23°00′E
136 K15 Yahyalı Kayseri, C Turkey 38°08′N 35°23′E
167 N15 Yai, Khao ▲ SW Thailand 08°45′N 99°32′E
164 M14 Yaizu Shizuoka, Honshū, S Japan 34°52′N 138°20′E
160 G9 Yajiang var. Hekou, Tib. Nyagquka. Sichuan, C China 30°05′N 100°57′E
119 O14 Yakawlyevichi Rus. Yakovlevichi. Vitsyebskaya Voblasts', NE Belarus 54°20′N 30°31′E
163 S6 Yakeshi Nei Mongol Zizhiqu, N China 49°16′N 120°42′E
32 I9 Yakima Washington, NW USA 46°36′N 120°30′W
32 J10 Yakima River ≈ Washington, NW USA
Yakkabag see Yakkabog'
147 N12 Yakkabog' Rus. Yakkabag. Qashqadaryo Viloyati, S Uzbekistan 38°57′N 66°35′E
148 L12 Yakmach Baluchistān, SW Pakistan 28°48′N 63°48′E
77 O12 Yako W Burkina 12°59′N 02°15′W
39 W13 Yakobi Island island Alexander Archipelago, Alaska, USA
79 K16 Yakoma Equateur, N Dem. Rep. Congo 04°04′N 22°23′E
114 H11 Yakoruda Blagoevgrad, SW Bulgaria 42°01′N 23°40′E
Yakovlevichi see Yakawlyevichi
127 T2 Yakshur-Bod'ya Udmurtskaya Respublika, NW Russian Federation 57°10′N 53°10′E
165 Q5 Yakumo Hokkaidō, NE Japan 42°18′N 140°15′E
164 B17 Yaku-shima island Nansei-shotō, SW Japan
39 V12 Yakutat Alaska, USA 59°33′N 139°44′W
39 U12 Yakutat Bay inlet Alaska, USA
Yakutia/Yakutiya/Yakutiya, Respublika see Sakha (Yakutiya), Respublika
123 Q10 Yakutsk Respublika Sakha (Yakutiya), NE Russian Federation 62°10′N 129°50′E
167 O17 Yala Yala, SW Thailand 06°32′N 101°19′E
182 D6 Yalata South Australia 31°30′S 131°53′E
31 S9 Yale Michigan, N USA 43°07′N 82°45′W
180 I11 Yalgoo Western Australia 28°23′S 116°43′E
114 O12 Yalıköy İstanbul, NW Turkey 41°29′N 28°19′E
79 L14 Yalinga Haute-Kotto, C Central African Republic 06°47′N 23°09′E
119 M17 Yalizava Rus. Yelizovo. Mahilyowskaya Voblasts', E Belarus 53°24′N 29°01′E
44 L13 Yallahs Hill ▲ E Jamaica 17°53′N 76°31′W
22 L3 Yalobusha River ≈ Mississippi, S USA
79 H15 Yaloké Ombella-Mpoko, W Central African Republic 05°15′N 17°02′E
160 E7 Yalong Jiang ≈ C China
136 E11 Yalova Yalova, NW Turkey 40°40′N 29°17′E
136 E11 Yalova ◆ province NW Turkey
Yaloveny see Ialoveni
Yalpug see Ialpug
Yalpug, Ozero see Yalpuh, Ozero
117 N12 Yalpuh, Ozero Rus. Ozero Yalpug. ◎ SW Ukraine
117 T14 Yalta Avtonomna Respublika Krym, S Ukraine 44°30′N 34°09′E
163 W12 Yalu Chin. Yalu Jiang, Jap. Oryokko, Kor. Amnok-kang. ≈ China/North Korea
Yalu Jiang see Yalu
136 F14 Yalvaç Isparta, SW Turkey 38°16′N 31°09′E
165 R9 Yamada Iwate, Honshū, C Japan 39°27′N 141°56′E
165 D14 Yamaga Kumamoto, Kyūshū, SW Japan 33°02′N 130°41′E
165 P10 Yamagata Yamagata, Honshū, C Japan 38°15′N 140°19′E
165 P9 Yamagata off. Yamagata-ken. ◆ prefecture Honshū, C Japan
Yamagata-ken see Yamagata
164 C16 Yamagawa Kagoshima, Kyūshū, SW Japan 31°12′N 130°37′E
164 E13 Yamaguchi var. Yamaguti. Yamaguchi, Honshū, SW Japan 34°11′N 131°26′E
164 E13 Yamaguchi off. Yamaguchi-ken, var. Yamaguti. ◆ prefecture Honshū, SW Japan
Yamaguchi-ken see Yamaguchi
Yamaguti see Yamaguchi
125 X5 Yamalo-Nenetskiy Avtonomnyy Okrug ◆ autonomous district N Russian Federation
122 J7 Yamal, Poluostrov peninsula N Russian Federation
165 N13 Yamanashi off. Yamanashi-ken, var. Yamanasi. ◆ prefecture Honshū, S Japan
Yamanashi-ken see Yamanashi
Yamanasi see Yamanashi
Yamanīyah, Al Jumhūrīyah al see Yemen
127 W5 Yamantau ▲ W Russian Federation 53°11′N 57°30′E
Yamasaki see Yamazaki
15 P12 Yamaska ≈ Québec, SE Canada
192 G4 Yamato Ridge undersea feature S Sea of Japan 39°20′N 135°00′E
164 I13 Yamazaki var. Yamasaki. Hyōgo, Honshū, SW Japan 35°00′N 134°31′E
183 V5 Yamba New South Wales, SE Australia 29°28′S 153°22′E
81 D16 Yambio var. Yambiyo. Western Equatoria, S South Sudan 04°34′N 28°21′E
Yambiyo see Yambio
114 L10 Yambol Turk. Yanboli. Yambol, E Bulgaria 42°29′N 26°30′E
114 M11 Yambol ◆ province E Bulgaria
79 M17 Yambuya Orientale, N Dem. Rep. Congo 01°22′N 24°21′E
171 T15 Yamdena, Pulau prev. Jamdena. island Kepulauan Tanimbar, E Indonesia
165 O14 Yame Fukuoka, Kyūshū, SW Japan 33°14′N 130°32′E
166 M6 Yamethin Mandalay, C Burma (Myanmar) 20°24′N 96°08′E
186 C6 Yaminbot East Sepik, NW Papua New Guinea 04°34′S 143°56′E
181 U9 Yamma Yamma, Lake ◎ Queensland, C Australia
76 M16 Yamoussoukro ● (Ivory Coast) C Ivory Coast 06°51′N 05°21′W
37 P3 Yampa River ≈ Colorado, C USA
117 S2 Yampil' Sums'ka Oblast', NE Ukraine 51°57′N 33°49′E
116 M8 Yampil' Vinnyts'ka Oblast', C Ukraine 48°15′N 28°18′E
123 T9 Yamsk Magadanskaya Oblast', E Russian Federation 59°33′N 154°04′E
152 J8 Yamuna prev. Jumna. ≈ N India
152 I9 Yamunānagar Haryāna, N India 30°07′N 77°17′E
Yamundá see Nhamundá, Rio
145 U8 Yamyshevo Pavlodar, NE Kazakhstan 51°49′N 77°28′E
159 N16 Yamzho Yumco ◎ W China
123 Q8 Yana ≈ NE Russian Federation
186 H9 Yanaba Island island SE Papua New Guinea
155 L16 Yanam var. Yanaon. Pondicherry, E India 16°45′N 82°16′E
160 L5 Yan'an var. Yanan. Shaanxi, C China 36°35′N 109°27′E
Yanaon see Yanam
127 U3 Yanaul ▲ Respublika Bashkortostan, W Russian Federation 56°15′N 54°57′E
118 O12 Yanavichy Rus. Yanovichi. Vitsyebskaya Voblasts', NE Belarus 55°17′N 30°42′E
Yanboli see Yambol
140 K8 Yanbu' al Baḩr Al Madīnah, W Saudi Arabia 24°07′N 38°03′E
21 T8 Yanceyville North Carolina, SE USA 36°25′N 79°22′W
161 R7 Yancheng Jiangsu, E China 33°28′N 120°10′E
159 W8 Yanchi Ningxia, N China 37°49′N 107°24′E
160 L5 Yanchuan Shaanxi, C China 36°54′N 110°04′E
183 O10 Yanco Creek seasonal river New South Wales, SE Australia
183 O6 Yanda Creek seasonal river New South Wales, SE Australia
182 K4 Yandama Creek seasonal river New South Wales/South Australia
161 S11 Yandang Shan ▲▲ SE China
159 O6 Yandun Xinjiang Uygur Zizhiqu, W China 42°24′N 94°08′E
76 L13 Yanfolila Sikasso, SW Mali 11°08′N 08°12′W
79 M18 Yangambi Orientale, N Dem. Rep. Congo 0°46′N 24°24′E
158 M15 Yangbajain Xizang Zizhiqu, W China 30°05′N 90°35′E
Yangcheng see Yangshan, Guangdong, S China
Yangchow see Yangzhou
160 M15 Yangchun var. Chuncheng. Guangdong, S China 22°16′N 111°49′E
161 N2 Yanggao var. Longquan. Shanxi, C China 40°24′N 113°51′E
Yanggeta see Yaqeta
Yangiabad see Yangiobod
Yangibazar see Dzhany-Bazar, Kyrgyzstan
Yangi-Bazar see Kofarnihon, Tajikistan
Yangiklshak see Yangiqishloq
146 M13 Yangi-Nishon Rus. Yany-Nishan. Qashqadaryo Viloyati, S Uzbekistan 38°37′N 65°39′E
147 Q9 Yangiobod Rus. Yangiabad. Toshkent Viloyati, E Uzbekistan 41°10′N 70°10′E
147 O10 Yangiqishloq Rus. Yangiklshak. Jizzax Viloyati, C Uzbekistan 40°27′N 67°06′E
147 P11 Yangiyer Sirdaryo Viloyati, E Uzbekistan 40°19′N 68°48′E
147 P9 Yangiyo'l Rus. Yangiyul'. Toshkent Viloyati, E Uzbekistan 41°12′N 69°05′E
Yangiyul' see Yangiyo'l
160 M15 Yangjiang Guangdong, S China 21°50′N 112°02′E
Yangku see Taiyuan
Yang-Nishan see Yangi-Nishon
166 L8 Yangon Eng. Rangoon. Yangon, S Burma (Myanmar) 16°50′N 96°11′E
166 M8 Yangon Eng. Rangoon. ◆ division SW Burma (Myanmar)
161 N4 Yangquan Shanxi, C China 37°52′N 113°29′E
161 N13 Yangshan var. Yangcheng. Guangdong, S China 24°32′N 112°36′E
167 U12 Yang Sin, Chu ▲ S Vietnam 12°23′N 108°25′E
Yangtze see Chang Jiang/Jinsha Jiang
Yangtze see Chang Jiang
Yangtze Kiang see Chang Jiang
161 R7 Yangzhou var. Yangchow. Jiangsu, E China 32°22′N 119°22′E
160 L5 Yan He ≈ C China
163 Y10 Yanji Jilin, NE China 42°54′N 129°31′E
Yanji see Longjing
Yanjing see Yanyuan
29 Q12 Yankton South Dakota, N USA 42°52′N 97°24′W
161 O12 Yanling prev. Lingxian, Ling Xian. Hunan, S China 26°32′N 113°48′E
Yannina see Ioánnina
123 Q7 Yano-Indigirskaya Nizmennost' plain NE Russian Federation
Yanovichi see Yanavichy
155 K24 Yan Oya ≈ N Sri Lanka
158 K6 Yanqi var. Yanqi Huizu Zizhixian. Xinjiang Uygur Zizhiqu, NW China 42°04′N 86°32′E
Yanqi Huizu Zizhixian see Yanqi
161 Q10 Yanshan var. Hekou. Jiangxi, S China 28°18′N 117°43′E
160 H14 Yanshan var. Jiangna. Yunnan, SW China 23°36′N 104°20′E
161 P2 Yan Shan ▲▲ E China
163 X8 Yanshou Heilongjiang, NE China 45°27′N 128°19′E
123 Q7 Yanskiy Zaliv bay N Russian Federation
183 O4 Yantabulla New South Wales, SE Australia 29°22′S 145°00′E
161 R4 Yantai var. Yan-t'ai; prev. Chefoo, Chih-fu. Shandong, E China 37°30′N 121°22′E
118 A13 Yantarnyy Ger. Palmnicken. Kaliningradskaya Oblast', W Russian Federation 54°53′N 19°59′E
114 J9 Yantra Gabrovo, N Bulgaria 42°58′N 25°19′E
114 K9 Yantra ≈ N Bulgaria
160 G11 Yanyuan var. Yanjing. Sichuan, C China 27°30′N 101°22′E
161 P5 Yanzhou Shandong, E China 35°35′N 116°53′E
79 E16 Yaoundé var. Yaunde. ● (Cameroon) Centre, S Cameroon 03°51′N 11°31′E
188 I14 Yap ◆ state W Micronesia
188 F16 Yap island Caroline Islands, W Micronesia
57 M18 Yapacani, Rio ≈ C Bolivia
171 W14 Yapa Kopra Papua, E Indonesia 04°18′S 135°05′E
Yapan see Yapen, Selat
Yapanskoye More see East Sea/Japan, Sea of
77 P15 Yapei N Ghana 09°10′N 01°08′W
12 M10 Yapeitso, Mont ▲ Québec, E Canada 52°18′N 70°24′W
171 W12 Yapen, Pulau prev. Japen. island E Indonesia
171 W12 Yapen, Selat var. Yapan. strait Papua, E Indonesia
61 E15 Yapeyú Corrientes, NE Argentina 29°28′S 56°50′W
136 I11 Yapraklı Çankırı, N Turkey 40°45′N 33°46′E
174 M3 Yap Trench var. Yap Trough. undersea feature SE Philippine Sea 08°30′N 138°00′E
Yap Trough see Yap Trench
Yapurá see Caquetá, Río, Brazil/Colombia
Yapurá see Japurá, Rio, Brazil/Colombia
197 I12 Yaqaga island N Fiji
197 H12 Yaqeta prev. Yanggeta. island Yasawa Group, NW Fiji
40 G6 Yaqui Sonora, NW Mexico 27°21′N 109°59′W
32 E12 Yaquina Bay bay Oregon, NW USA
40 G6 Yaqui, Río ≈ NW Mexico
54 K5 Yaracuy off. Estado Yaracuy. ◆ state NW Venezuela
Yaracuy, Estado see Yaracuy
146 E13 Yarajy Rus. Yaradzhi. Ahal Welaýaty, C Turkmenistan 38°12′N 57°40′E
Yaradzhi see Yarajy
125 Q15 Yaransk Kirovskaya Oblast', NW Russian Federation 57°18′N 47°52′E
136 F17 Yardımcı Burnu headland SW Turkey 36°10′N 30°25′E
97 Q19 Yare ≈ E England, United Kingdom
125 S9 Yarega Respublika Komi, NW Russian Federation 63°27′N 53°28′E
116 I7 Yaremcha Ivano-Frankivs'ka Oblast', W Ukraine 48°27′N 24°34′E
189 Q9 Yaren (district) ● (Nauru) SW Nauru 0°33′S 166°54′E
125 Q10 Yarensk Arkhangel'skaya Oblast', NW Russian Federation 62°09′N 49°03′E
155 F16 Yargatti Karnātaka, W India 16°07′N 75°11′E
164 M12 Yariga-take ▲ Honshū, S Japan 36°20′N 137°38′E
141 O15 Yarīm W Yemen 14°15′N 44°23′E
54 F14 Yarí, Río ≈ SW Colombia
54 K5 Yaritagua Yaracuy, N Venezuela 10°05′N 69°07′W
Yarkand see Yarkant He
Yarkant see Shache
158 E9 Yarkant He var. Yarkand. ≈ NW China
149 U3 Yarkhūn ≈ NW Pakistan
Yarlung Zangbo Jiang see Brahmaputra
116 L6 Yarmolyntsi Khmel'nyts'ka Oblast', W Ukraine 49°13′N 26°53′E
13 O16 Yarmouth Nova Scotia, SE Canada 43°53′N 66°09′W
Yarmouth see Great Yarmouth
Yaroslav see Jarosław
124 L15 Yaroslavl' Yaroslavskaya Oblast', W Russian Federation 57°38′N 39°53′E
124 K14 Yaroslavskaya Oblast' ◆ province W Russian Federation
123 N11 Yaroslavskiy Respublika Sakha (Yakutiya), NE Russian Federation 60°10′N 114°12′E
183 P13 Yarram Victoria, SE Australia 38°36′S 146°40′E
183 O11 Yarrawonga Victoria, SE Australia 36°04′S 145°58′E
182 L4 Yarriarraburra Swamp wetland New South Wales, SE Australia
122 I8 Yar-Sale Yamalo-Nenetskiy Avtonomnyy Okrug, N Russian Federation 66°52′N 70°42′E
122 K11 Yartsevo Krasnoyarskiy Kray, C Russian Federation 60°15′N 90°09′E
126 I4 Yartsevo Smolenskaya Oblast', W Russian Federation 55°03′N 32°46′E
54 E8 Yarumal Antioquia, NW Colombia 06°59′N 75°25′W
187 W14 Yasawa Group island group NW Fiji
77 V12 Yashi Katsina, N Nigeria 12°21′N 07°56′E
77 S14 Yashikera Kwara, W Nigeria 09°40′N 03°19′E
147 T14 Yashilkŭl Rus. Ozero Yashil'kul'. ◎ SE Tajikistan
Yashil'kul', Ozero see Yashilkŭl
165 P9 Yashima Akita, Honshū, C Japan 39°10′N 140°10′E
127 P13 Yashkul' Respublika Kalmykiya, SW Russian Federation 46°09′N 45°22′E
146 F13 Yashlyk Ahal Welaýaty, C Turkmenistan 37°46′N 58°51′E
Yasinovataya see Yasynuvata
114 N10 Yasna Polyana Burgas, E Bulgaria 42°18′N 27°35′E
167 R10 Yasothon Yasothon, E Thailand 15°46′N 104°12′E
183 R10 Yass New South Wales, SE Australia 34°52′S 148°55′E
Yassy see Iaşi
164 H12 Yasugi Shimane, Honshū, SW Japan 35°25′N 133°12′E
143 N10 Yāsūj var. Yesuj; prev. Tal-e Khosravī. Kohkīlūyeh va Būyer AḨmad, C Iran 30°40′N 51°34′E
136 M11 Yasun Burnu headland N Turkey 41°07′N 37°40′E
117 X8 Yasynuvata Rus. Yasinovataya. Donets'ka Oblast', SE Ukraine 48°05′N 37°57′E
136 C15 Yatağan Muğla, SW Turkey 37°22′N 28°08′E
165 Q7 Yatate-tōge pass Honshū, C Japan
187 Q17 Yaté Province Sud, S New Caledonia 22°10′S 166°56′E
27 P6 Yates Center Kansas, C USA 37°54′N 95°44′W
185 B21 Yates Point headland South Island, New Zealand 44°30′S 167°49′E
9 N9 Yathkyed Lake ◎ Nunavut, NE Canada
171 T16 Yatoke Pulau Babar, E Indonesia 07°51′S 129°49′E
79 M18 Yatolema Orientale, N Dem. Rep. Congo 0°25′N 24°35′E
164 C15 Yatsushiro var. Yatusiro. Kumamoto, Kyūshū, SW Japan 32°30′N 130°34′E
164 C15 Yatsushiro-kai bay SW Japan
138 F11 Yatta var. Yuta. S West Bank 31°29′N 35°10′E
81 J20 Yatta Plateau plateau SE Kenya
Yatusiro see Yatsushiro
57 F17 Yauca, Río ≈ SW Peru
45 S6 Yauco W Puerto Rico 18°02′N 66°51′W
Yaunde see Yaoundé
Yavan see Yovon
Yavarí see Javari, Rio
56 G9 Yavari Mirim, Río ≈ NE Peru
40 G7 Yavaros Sonora, NW Mexico 26°40′N 109°32′W
154 I13 Yavatmāl Mahārāshtra, C India 20°22′N 78°11′E
54 M9 Yaví, Cerro ▲ C Venezuela 05°43′N 65°51′W
43 W16 Yaviza Darién, SE Panama 08°09′N 77°41′W
138 F10 Yavne Central, W Israel 31°52′N 34°45′E
116 H5 Yavoriv Pol. Jaworów, Rus. Yavorov. L'vivs'ka Oblast', NW Ukraine 49°57′N 23°22′E
Yavorov see Yavoriv
164 F14 Yawatahama Ehime, Shikoku, SW Japan 33°27′N 132°24′E
Ya Xian see Sanya
136 L17 Yayladağı Hatay, S Turkey 35°55′N 36°00′E
125 V13 Yayva Permskiy Kray, NW Russian Federation 59°19′N 57°15′E
125 V12 Yayva ≈ NW Russian Federation
143 Q9 Yazd var. Yezd. Yazd, C Iran 31°55′N 54°22′E
143 Q8 Yazd off. Ostān-e Yazd, var. Yezd. ◆ province C Iran
Yazd, Ostān-e see Yazd
Yazgulemskiy Khrebet see Yazgulom, Qatorkŭhi
147 S13 Yazgulom, Qatorkŭhi Rus. Yazgulemskiy Khrebet. ▲▲ S Tajikistan
22 K5 Yazoo City Mississippi, S USA 32°51′N 90°24′W
22 K5 Yazoo River ≈ Mississippi, S USA
Yazovir Georgi Traykov see Tsonevo, Yazovir
127 Q5 Yazykovka Ul'yanovskaya Oblast', W Russian Federation 54°19′N 47°22′E
109 U4 Ybbs Niederösterreich, NE Austria 48°10′N 15°03′E
109 U4 Ybbs ≈ C Austria
95 G22 Yding Skovhøj hill C Denmark
115 G20 Ýdra var. Ídhra, Idra. Ýdra, S Greece 37°20′N 23°28′E
115 G21 Ýdra var. Ídhra. island Ýdra, S Greece
115 G20 Ýdras, Kólpos strait S Greece
167 N10 Ye Mon State, S Burma (Myanmar) 15°15′N 97°50′E
183 O12 Yea Victoria, SE Australia 37°15′S 145°27′E
167 P13 Yeay Sên prev. Phumĭ Yeay Sên. Kaôh Kŏng, SW Cambodia 11°09′N 103°09′E
Yebaishou see Jianping
78 I5 Yebbi-Bou Borkou-Ennedi-Tibesti, N Chad 21°12′N 17°55′E
158 F9 Yecheng var. Kargilik. Xinjiang Uygur Zizhiqu, NW China 37°54′N 77°26′E
105 R11 Yecla Murcia, SE Spain 38°36′N 01°07′W
40 H6 Yécora Sonora, NW Mexico 28°23′N 108°56′W
Yedintsy see Edineţ
124 J13 Yefimovskiy Leningradskaya Oblast', NW Russian Federation 59°32′N 34°34′E
126 K6 Yefremov Tul'skaya Oblast', W Russian Federation 53°10′N 38°02′E
159 T11 Yêgainnyin var. Henan Mongolzu Zizhixian. Qinghai, C China 34°42′N 101°36′E
137 U12 Yegbhegis Rus. Yekhegis. ≈ C Armenia

◆ Country ● Country Capital ◇ Dependent Territory ○ Dependent Territory Capital ◆ Administrative Regions ✈ International Airport ▲ Mountain ▲▲ Mountain Range ♆ Volcano ≈ River ◎ Lake ⊠ Reservoir

137 U12 **Yeghegnadzor** C Armenia 39°45′N 45°20′E
145 T10 **Yegindybulak** *Kaz.* Egindibulaq. Karaganda, C Kazakhstan 49°45′N 75°45′E
126 L4 **Yegor'yevsk** Moskovskaya Oblast', W Russian Federation 55°29′N 39°03′E
Yehuda, Haré *see* Judaean Hills
81 E15 **Yei** S South Sudan
161 P8 **Yeji** *var.* Yejiaji. Anhui, E China 31°52′N 115°58′E
Yejiaji *see* Yeji
122 G10 **Yekaterinburg** *prev.* Sverdlovsk. Sverdlovskaya Oblast', C Russian Federation 56°52′N 60°35′E
Yekaterinodar *see* Krasnodar
Yekaterinoslav *see* Dnipropetrovs'k
123 R13 **Yekaterinoslavka** Amurskaya Oblast', SE Russian Federation 50°23′N 129°03′E
127 O7 **Yekaterinovka** Saratovskaya Oblast', W Russian Federation 52°01′N 44°11′E
76 K16 **Yekepa** NE Liberia 07°35′N 08°32′W
Yekhegis *see* Yegbhegis
145 T8 **Yekibastuz** *prev.* Ekibastuz. Pavlodar, NE Kazakhstan 51°42′N 75°22′E
127 T3 **Yelabuga** Respublika Tatarstan, W Russian Federation 55°46′N 52°07′E
Yela Island *see* Rossel Island
127 O8 **Yelan'** Volgogradskaya Oblast', SW Russian Federation 51°00′N 43°40′E
117 Q9 **Yelanets'** *Rus.* Yelanets. Mykolayivs'ka Oblast', S Ukraine 47°40′N 31°51′E
144 I9 **Yelek** *Kaz.* Elek; *prev.* Ilek. Kazakhstan/Russian Federation
126 L7 **Yelets** Lipetskaya Oblast', W Russian Federation 52°37′N 38°29′E
125 W4 **Yeletskiy** Respublika Komi, NW Russian Federation 67°03′N 64°05′E
76 J11 **Yélimané** Kayes, W Mali 15°06′N 10°43′W
Yelisavetpol *see* Gäncä
Yelizavetgrad *see* Kirovohrad
123 T12 **Yelizavety, Mys** *headland* SE Russian Federation 54°20′N 142°39′E
Yelizovo *see* Yalizava
127 S5 **Yelkhovka** Samarskaya Oblast', W Russian Federation 53°51′N 50°16′E
96 M1 **Yell** *island* NE Scotland, United Kingdom
155 E17 **Yellāpur** Karnātaka, W India 15°06′N 74°50′E
11 U17 **Yellow Grass** Saskatchewan, S Canada 49°51′N 104°09′W
Yellowhammer State *see* Alabama
11 O15 **Yellowhead Pass** *pass* Alberta/British Columbia, SW Canada
8 K10 **Yellowknife** *territory capital* Northwest Territories, W Canada 62°30′N 114°29′W
8 K9 **Yellowknife** Northwest Territories, NW Canada
23 P8 **Yellow River** Alabama/Florida, S USA
30 K7 **Yellow River** Wisconsin, N USA
30 J6 **Yellow River** Wisconsin, N USA
30 I4 **Yellow River** Wisconsin, N USA
Yellow River *see* Huang He
157 V8 **Yellow Sea** *Chin.* Huang Hai, *Kor.* Hwang-Hae. *sea* E Asia
33 S13 **Yellowstone Lake** Wyoming, C USA
33 T13 **Yellowstone National Park** *national park* Wyoming, NW USA
33 Y8 **Yellowstone River** Montana/Wyoming, NW USA
96 L1 **Yell Sound** *strait* N Scotland, United Kingdom
27 U9 **Yellville** Arkansas, C USA 36°12′N 92°41′W
122 K10 **Yeloguy** C Russian Federation
Yëloten *see* Yolöten
119 M20 **Yel'sk** Homyel'skaya Voblasts', SE Belarus 51°48′N 29°09′E
77 T13 **Yelwa** Kebbi, W Nigeria 10°52′N 04°46′E
21 R15 **Yemassee** South Carolina, SE USA 32°41′N 80°51′W
141 O15 **Yemen** *off.* Republic of Yemen, *Ar.* Al Jumhuriyah al Yamaniyah, Al Yaman. ◆ *republic* SW Asia
Yemen, Republic of *see* Yemen
116 M4 **Yemil'chyne** Zhytomyrs'ka Oblast', N Ukraine 50°51′N 27°49′E
124 M10 **Yemtsa** Arkhangel'skaya Oblast', NW Russian Federation 63°04′N 40°18′E
124 M10 **Yemtsa** NW Russian Federation
125 R10 **Yemva** *prev.* Zheleznodorozhnyy. Respublika Komi, NW Russian Federation 62°38′N 50°59′E
77 U17 **Yenagoa** Bayelsa, S Nigeria 4°58′N 6°16′E
117 X7 **Yenakiyeve** *Rus.* Yenakiyevo; *prev.* Ordzhonikidze, Rykovo. Donets'ka Oblast', E Ukraine 48°13′N 38°13′E
Yenakiyevo *see* Yenakiyeve
166 L6 **Yenangyaung** Magway, W Burma (Myanmar) 20°28′N 94°54′E
167 S5 **Yên Bai** Yên Bai, N Vietnam 21°43′N 104°54′E
183 P9 **Yenda** New South Wales, SE Australia 34°16′S 146°15′E
77 Q14 **Yendi** NE Ghana 09°30′N 00°01′W
Yêndum *see* Zhag'yab
158 E8 **Yengisar** Xinjiang Uygur Zizhiqu, NW China 38°50′N 76°11′E
136 H11 **Yenice Çayı** *var.* Filyos Çayı. N Turkey
121 R1 **Yenierenköy** *var.* Yialousa, *Gk.* Agialoúsa. NE Cyprus 35°33′N 34°13′E
Yenipazar *see* Novi Pazar
136 E12 **Yenişehir** Bursa, NW Turkey 40°17′N 29°38′E
Yenisei Bay *see* Yeniseyskiy Zaliv
122 K12 **Yeniseysk** Krasnoyarskiy Kray, C Russian Federation 58°23′N 92°06′E
197 W10 **Yeniseyskiy Zaliv** *var.* Yenisei Bay. *bay* N Russian Federation
127 Q12 **Yenotayevka** Astrakhanskaya Oblast', SW Russian Federation 47°16′N 47°01′E
124 L4 **Yenozero, Ozero** NW Russian Federation
Yenping *see* Nanping
39 Q11 **Yentna River** Alaska, USA
180 M10 **Yeo, Lake** *salt lake* Western Australia
163 Z15 **Yeongcheon** *Jap.* Eisen; *prev.* Yŏngch'ŏn. SE South Korea 35°56′N 128°55′E
163 Y15 **Yeongju** *Jap.* Eishū; *prev.* Yŏngju. C South Korea 36°48′N 128°37′E
163 Y17 **Yeosu** *Jap.* Reisui; *prev.* Yŏsu. S South Korea 34°45′N 127°41′E
183 R7 **Yeoval** New South Wales, SE Australia 32°45′S 148°39′E
97 K23 **Yeovil** SW England, United Kingdom 50°57′N 02°39′W
40 H6 **Yepachic** Chihuahua, N Mexico 28°27′N 108°25′W
181 Y8 **Yeppoon** Queensland, E Australia 23°05′S 150°42′E
126 M5 **Yeraktur** Ryazanskaya Oblast', W Russian Federation 54°45′N 41°09′E
Yeraliyev *see* Kuryk
146 F12 **Yerbent** Ahal Welaýaty, C Turkmenistan 39°19′N 58°34′E
123 N11 **Yerbogachën** Irkutskaya Oblast', C Russian Federation 61°07′N 108°03′E
137 T12 **Yerevan** *Eng.* Erivan. ● (Armenia) C Armenia 40°12′N 44°31′E
137 U12 **Yerevan** ✕ C Armenia 40°07′N 44°34′E
145 R9 **Yereymentau** *var.* Jermentau, *Kaz.* Ereymentaū. Akmola, C Kazakhstan 51°38′N 73°10′E
145 R9 **Yereymentau, Gory** *prev.* Gory Yermentau. C Kazakhstan
127 O12 **Yergeni** *hill range* SW Russian Federation
Yeriho *see* Jericho
35 R6 **Yerington** Nevada, W USA 38°58′N 119°10′W
136 J13 **Yerköy** Yozgat, C Turkey 39°39′N 34°28′E
114 L13 **Yerlisu** Edirne, NW Turkey 40°45′N 26°38′E
Yermak *see* Aksu
Yermentau, Gory *see* Yereymentau, Gory
125 R5 **Yërmitsa** Respublika Komi, NW Russian Federation 66°57′N 52°15′E
35 V14 **Yermo** California, W USA 34°54′N 116°49′W
123 P13 **Yerofey Pavlovich** Amurskaya Oblast', SE Russian Federation 53°58′N 121°49′E
99 F15 **Yerseke** Zeeland, SW Netherlands 51°30′N 04°03′E
127 Q8 **Yershov** Saratovskaya Oblast', W Russian Federation 51°18′N 48°16′E
145 S7 **Yertis** *Kaz.* Ertis; *prev.* Irtyshsk. Pavlodar, NE Kazakhstan 53°21′N 75°27′E
129 R5 **Yertis** *var.* Irtish, *Kaz.* Ertis; *prev.* Irtysh. C Asia
125 P9 **Yërtom** Respublika Komi, NW Russian Federation 63°27′N 47°52′E
56 D13 **Yerupaja, Nevado** ▲ C Peru 10°23′S 76°58′W
Yerushalayim *see* Jerusalem
105 R4 **Yesa, Embalse de** NE Spain
144 F11 **Yesbol** *prev.* Kulagino. Atyrau, W Kazakhstan 48°30′N 51°33′E
144 F9 **Yesensay** Zapadnyy Kazakhstan, NW Kazakhstan 49°59′N 51°19′E
144 F9 **Yesensay** Zapadnyy Kazakhstan, NW Kazakhstan 49°58′N 51°19′E
145 V15 **Yesik** *Kaz.* Esik; *prev.* Issyk. Almaty, SE Kazakhstan 42°23′N 77°25′E
145 O8 **Yesil'** *Kaz.* Esil. Akmola, C Kazakhstan 51°58′N 66°24′E
129 R6 **Yesil'** *Kaz.* Esil. Kazakhstan/Russian Federation
136 K15 **Yeşilhisar** Kayseri, C Turkey 38°22′N 35°08′E
136 L11 **Yeşilırmak** *var.* Iris. N Turkey
37 U12 **Yeso** New Mexico, SW USA 34°25′N 104°36′W
Yeso *see* Hokkaidō
127 N15 **Yessentuki** Stavropol'skiy Kray, SW Russian Federation 44°06′N 42°51′E
122 M9 **Yessey** Krasnoyarskiy Kray, N Russian Federation 68°18′N 101°49′E
105 P12 **Yeste** Castilla-La Mancha, C Spain 38°21′N 02°18′W
Yesuj *see* Yāsūj
183 T4 **Yetman** New South Wales, SE Australia 28°56′S 150°47′E
76 L4 **Yetti** *physical region* N Mauritania
166 M4 **Ye-u** Sagaing, C Burma (Myanmar) 22°49′N 95°26′E
102 H9 **Yeu, Île d'** *island* NW France
Yevlakh *see* Yevlax
137 W11 **Yevlax** *Rus.* Yevlakh. C Azerbaijan 40°36′N 47°10′E
117 S13 **Yevpatoriya** Avtonomna Respublika Krym, S Ukraine 45°12′N 33°23′E
Ye Xian *see* Laizhou
126 K12 **Yeya** SW Russian Federation
158 I10 **Yeyik** Xinjiang Uygur Zizhiqu, W China 36°44′N 83°14′E
126 K12 **Yeysk** Krasnodarskiy Kray, SW Russian Federation 46°41′N 38°15′E
Yezd *see* Yazd
Yezerishche *see* Yezyaryshcha
Yezhou *see* Jianshi
Yezo *see* Hokkaidō
118 N11 **Yezyaryshcha** *Rus.* Yezerishche. Vitsyebskaya Voblasts', NE Belarus 55°50′N 29°59′E
Yialí *see* Gyalí
Yialousa *see* Yenierenköy
163 V7 **Yi'an** Heilongjiang, NE China 47°52′N 125°13′E
Yiannitsá *see* Giannitsá
160 I10 **Yibin** Sichuan, C China 28°50′N 104°35′E
158 K13 **Yibug Caka** W China
160 M9 **Yichang** Hubei, C China 30°37′N 111°02′E
160 L5 **Yichuan** *var.* Danzhou. Shaanxi, C China 36°05′N 110°02′E
157 W3 **Yichun** Heilongjiang, NE China 47°41′N 129°10′E
161 O11 **Yichun** Jiangxi, S China 27°45′N 114°22′E
160 M9 **Yidu** *prev.* Zhicheng. Hubei, C China 30°21′N 111°27′E
Yidu *see* Qingzhou
188 C15 **Yigo** NE Guam 13°33′N 144°53′E
161 Q5 **Yi He** E China
163 X8 **Yilan** Heilongjiang, NE China 46°18′N 129°36′E
136 C9 **Yıldız Dağları** ▲ NW Turkey
136 L13 **Yıldızeli** Sivas, N Turkey 39°52′N 36°37′E
163 U4 **Yilehuli Shan** ▲ NE China
163 S7 **Yimin He** NE China
159 W8 **Yinchuan** *var.* Yinch'uan, Yin-ch'uan, Yinchwan. *province capital* Ningxia, N China 38°30′N 106°19′E
Yinchwan *see* Yinchuan
Yindu He *see* Indus
Yingcheng *see* Yingde
161 N14 **Yingde** *var.* Yingcheng. Guangdong, S China 24°08′N 113°21′E
163 U13 **Yingkou** *var.* Ying-k'ou, Yingkow; *prev.* Newchwang, Niuchwang. Liaoning, NE China 40°40′N 122°17′E
Yingkow *see* Yingkou
161 P9 **Yingshan** *var.* Wenquan. Hubei, C China 30°45′N 115°41′E
161 Q10 **Yingtan** Jiangxi, S China 28°17′N 117°03′E
Yin-hsien *see* Ningbo
158 H5 **Yining** *var.* I-ning, *Uigh.* Gulja, Kuldja. Xinjiang Uygur Zizhiqu, NW China 43°53′N 81°18′E
160 K11 **Yinjiang** *var.* Yinjiang Tujiazu Miaozu Zizhixian. Guizhou, S China 28°22′N 108°07′E
Yinjiang Tujiazu Miaozu Zizhixian *see* Yinjiang
166 L4 **Yinmabin** Sagaing, C Burma (Myanmar) 22°05′N 94°57′E
163 N13 **Yin Shan** ▲ N China
Yinshan *see* Guangshui
Yin-tu Ho *see* Indus
159 P15 **Yi'ong Zangbo** W China
Yioúra *see* Gyáros
81 J14 **Yirga 'Alem** *It.* Irgalem. Southern Nationalities, S Ethiopia 06°43′N 38°24′E
61 E19 **Yí, Río** C Uruguay
81 E14 **Yirol** El Buhayrat, C South Sudan 06°34′N 30°33′E
163 S8 **Yirshi** *var.* Yirxie. Nei Mongol Zizhiqu, N China 47°16′N 119°51′E
Yirxie *see* Yirshi
Yishan *see* Guanyun
Yishi *see* Linyi
161 Q5 **Yishui** Shandong, E China 35°50′N 118°39′E
Yisrael/Yisra'el *see* Israel
Yithion *see* Gýtheio
Yitiaoshan *see* Jingtai
163 W10 **Yitong** *var.* Yitong Manzu Zizhixian. Jilin, NE China 43°23′N 125°19′E
Yitong Manzu Zizhixian *see* Yitong
159 P5 **Yiwu** *var.* Aratürük. Xinjiang Uygur Zizhiqu, NW China 43°16′N 94°38′E
163 U12 **Yiwulü Shan** ▲ N China
163 T12 **Yixian** *var.* Yizhou. Liaoning, NE China 41°29′N 121°21′E
159 R15 **Yixing** Jiangsu, China 31°14′N 119°18′E
161 N10 **Yiyang** Hunan, S China 28°39′N 112°10′E
161 Q10 **Yiyang** Jiangxi, S China 28°21′N 117°23′E
161 N13 **Yizhang** Hunan, S China 25°24′N 112°51′E
Yizhou *see* Yixian
93 K19 **Yläne** Länsi-Suomi, SW Finland 60°51′N 22°26′E
93 L14 **Yli-Ii** Oulu, C Finland 65°21′N 25°55′E
93 L14 **Ylikiiminki** Oulu, C Finland 65°00′N 26°10′E
92 N13 **Yli-Kitka** NE Finland
93 K17 **Ylistaro** Länsi-Suomi, W Finland 62°58′N 22°30′E
92 K13 **Ylitornio** Lappi, NW Finland 66°19′N 23°40′E
93 L15 **Ylivieska** Oulu, W Finland 64°05′N 24°30′E
93 L18 **Ylöjärvi** Länsi-Suomi, W Finland 61°31′N 23°37′E
95 N17 **Yngaren** C Sweden
25 T12 **Yoakum** Texas, SW USA 29°17′N 97°09′W
77 X13 **Yobe** ◆ *state* NE Nigeria
165 R3 **Yobetsu-dake** Hokkaidō, NE Japan 43°15′N 140°27′E
80 L11 **Yoboki** C Djibouti 11°30′N 42°04′E
22 M4 **Yockanookany River** Mississippi, S USA
22 L2 **Yocona River** Mississippi, S USA
171 Y15 **Yodom** Papua, E Indonesia 07°12′S 139°24′E
169 Q16 **Yogyakarta** *prev.* Djokjakarta, Jogjakarta, Jokyakarta. Jawa, C Indonesia 07°48′S 110°24′E
169 P17 **Yogyakarta** *off.* Daerah Istimewa Yogyakarta, *var.* Djokjakarta, Jogjakarta, Jokyakarta. ◆ *autonomous district* S Indonesia
Yogyakarta, Daerah Istimewa *see* Yogyakarta
165 Q3 **Yoichi** Hokkaidō, NE Japan 43°11′N 140°45′E
42 G6 **Yojoa, Lago de** NW Honduras
79 G16 **Yokadouma** Est, SE Cameroon 03°26′N 15°06′E
164 K13 **Yokkaichi** *var.* Yokkaiti. Mie, Honshū, SW Japan 34°58′N 136°38′E
Yokkaiti *see* Yokkaichi
79 E15 **Yoko** Centre, C Cameroon 05°29′N 12°19′E
165 V15 **Yokoate-jima** *island* Nansei-shotō, SW Japan
165 R6 **Yokohama** Aomori, Honshū, C Japan 41°04′N 141°14′E
165 O14 **Yokosuka** Kanagawa, Honshū, S Japan 35°18′N 139°39′E
164 G12 **Yokota** Shimane, Honshū, SW Japan 35°10′N 133°03′E
165 Q9 **Yokote** Akita, Honshū, C Japan 39°20′N 140°33′E
77 Y14 **Yola** Adamawa, E Nigeria 09°08′N 12°24′E
79 L19 **Yolombo** Equateur, C Dem. Rep. Congo 01°36′S 23°13′E
146 J14 **Ýolöten** *Rus.* Yëloten; *prev.* Iolotan'. Mary Welaýaty, S Turkmenistan 37°15′N 62°18′E
165 Y15 **Yome-jima** *island* Ogasawara-shotō, SE Japan
76 K16 **Yomou** SE Guinea 07°30′N 09°13′W
171 Y15 **Yomuka** Papua, E Indonesia 07°25′S 138°36′E
188 C16 **Yona** E Guam 13°24′N 144°46′E
164 H12 **Yonago** Tottori, Honshū, SW Japan 35°30′N 134°15′E
165 N16 **Yonaguni** Okinawa, SW Japan 24°29′N 123°00′E
165 N16 **Yonaguni-jima** *island* Nansei-shotō, SW Japan
165 T16 **Yonaha-dake** ▲ Okinawa, SW Japan 26°43′N 128°13′E
163 X14 **Yŏnan** SW North Korea 37°50′N 126°15′E
165 P10 **Yonezawa** Yamagata, Honshū, C Japan 37°56′N 140°06′E
161 Q12 **Yong'an** *var.* Yongan. Fujian, SE China 25°58′N 117°26′E
Yong'an *see* Fengjie
159 T9 **Yongchang** Gansu, N China 38°15′N 101°56′E
161 P7 **Yongcheng** Henan, C China 33°56′N 116°21′E
Yŏngch'ŏn *see* Yeongcheon
160 J10 **Yongchuan** Chongqing Shi, C China 29°27′N 105°56′E
159 U10 **Yongdeng** Gansu, C China 35°58′N 103°27′E
Yongding *see* Yongren
129 W9 **Yongding He** E China
161 P11 **Yongfeng** *var.* Enjiang. Jiangxi, S China 27°19′N 115°23′E
158 L5 **Yongfeng** *var.* Yongfengqu. Xinjiang Uygur Zizhiqu, W China 43°28′N 87°09′E
Yongfengqu *see* Yongfeng
160 L13 **Yongfu** Guangxi Zhuangzu Zizhiqu, S China 24°57′N 109°59′E
163 X13 **Yŏnghŭng** E North Korea 39°31′N 127°14′E
159 U10 **Yongjing** *var.* Liujiaxia. Gansu, C China 36°00′N 103°30′E
Yongjing *see* Xifeng
Yŏngju *see* Yeongju
Yongning *see* Xuyong
160 E12 **Yongping** Yunnan, SW China 25°30′N 99°28′E
160 G12 **Yongren** *var.* Yongding. Yunnan, SW China 26°09′N 101°40′E
160 L10 **Yongshun** *var.* Lingxi. Hunan, S China 29°02′N 109°46′E
161 P10 **Yongxiu** *var.* Tujiabu. Jiangxi, S China 29°09′N 115°47′E
Yongzhou *see* Lingling
Yongzhou *see* Zhishan
18 K14 **Yonkers** New York, NE USA 40°56′N 73°52′W
103 Q7 **Yonne** ◆ *department* C France
103 P6 **Yonne** C France
54 H9 **Yopal** *var.* El Yopal. Casanare, C Colombia 05°20′N 72°19′W
158 E8 **Yopurga** *var.* Yukuriawat. Xinjiang Uygur Zizhiqu, NW China 39°13′N 76°44′E
147 S11 **Yordon** *var.* Iordan, *Rus.* Jardan. Farg'ona Viloyati, E Uzbekistan 39°59′N 71°44′E
180 J12 **York** Western Australia 31°55′S 116°52′E
97 M16 **York** *anc.* Eboracum, Eburacum. N England, United Kingdom 53°58′N 01°05′W
23 N5 **York** Alabama, S USA 32°29′N 88°18′W
29 Q15 **York** Nebraska, C USA 40°52′N 97°35′W
18 G16 **York** Pennsylvania, NE USA 39°57′N 76°44′W
21 R11 **York** South Carolina, SE USA 34°59′N 81°14′W
14 J13 **York** Ontario, SE Canada
15 X6 **York** Québec, SE Canada
181 V1 **York, Cape** *headland* Queensland, NE Australia 10°40′S 142°36′E
182 I9 **Yorke Peninsula** *peninsula* South Australia
182 I9 **Yorketown** South Australia 35°01′S 137°38′E
19 P9 **York Harbor** Maine, NE USA 43°10′N 70°37′W
York, Kap *see* Innaanganeq
21 X6 **York River** Virginia, NE USA
97 M16 **Yorkshire** *cultural region* N England, United Kingdom
97 L16 **Yorkshire Dales** *physical region* N England, United Kingdom
11 V16 **Yorkton** Saskatchewan, S Canada 51°12′N 102°29′W
25 T12 **Yorktown** Texas, SW USA 28°58′N 97°30′W
21 X6 **Yorktown** Virginia, NE USA 37°14′N 76°32′W
30 M11 **Yorkville** Illinois, N USA 41°38′N 88°27′W
42 I5 **Yoro** Yoro, C Honduras 15°08′N 87°10′W
42 H5 **Yoro** ◆ *department* N Honduras
165 T16 **Yoron-jima** *island* Nansei-shotō, SW Japan
77 N13 **Yorosso** Sikasso, S Mali 12°21′N 04°47′W
35 R8 **Yosemite National Park** *national park* California, W USA
127 Q3 **Yoshkar-Ola** Respublika Mariy El, W Russian Federation 56°38′N 47°54′E
Yösönbulag *see* Altay
162 K8 **Yösöndzüyl** *var.* Mönhbulag. Övörhangay, C Mongolia 46°48′N 103°25′E
171 Y16 **Yos Sudarso, Pulau** *var.* Pulau Dolak, Pulau Kolepom; *prev.* Jos Sudarso. *island* E Indonesia
Yŏsu *see* Yeosu
165 R4 **Yōtei-zan** Hokkaidō, NE Japan 42°50′N 140°46′E
97 D21 **Youghal** *Ir.* Eochaill. Cork, S Ireland 51°57′N 07°50′W
97 D21 **Youghal Bay** *Ir.* Cuan Eochaille. *inlet* S Ireland
18 C15 **Youghiogheny River** Pennsylvania, NE USA
160 K14 **You Jiang** S China
183 Q9 **Young** New South Wales, SE Australia 34°19′S 148°20′E
11 T15 **Young** Saskatchewan, S Canada 51°44′N 105°44′W
61 E18 **Young** Río Negro, W Uruguay 32°44′S 57°36′W
182 G5 **Younghusband, Lake** *salt lake* South Australia
182 J10 **Younghusband Peninsula** *peninsula* South Australia
184 Q10 **Young Nicks Head** *headland* North Island, New Zealand 39°38′S 177°03′E
185 D20 **Young Range** ▲ South Island, New Zealand
191 Q15 **Young's Rock** *island* Pitcairn Island, Pitcairn Islands
11 R16 **Youngstown** Alberta, SW Canada 51°32′N 111°12′W
31 V12 **Youngstown** Ohio, N USA 41°06′N 80°39′W
159 N9 **Youshashan** Qinghai, C China 38°12′N 90°58′E
Youth, Isle of *see* Juventud, Isla de la
77 N11 **Youvarou** Mopti, C Mali 15°19′N 04°15′W
160 K10 **Youyang** *var.* Zhongduo. Chongqing Shi, C China 28°48′N 108°48′E
163 Y7 **Youyi** Heilongjiang, NE China 46°51′N 131°54′E
147 P13 **Yovon** *Rus.* Yavan. SW Tajikistan 38°19′N 69°02′E
136 J13 **Yozgat** Yozgat, C Turkey 39°49′N 34°48′E
136 K13 **Yozgat** ◆ *province* C Turkey
62 O6 **Ypacaraí** *var.* Ypacaray. Central, S Paraguay 25°23′S 57°16′W
Ypacaray *see* Ypacaraí
62 P5 **Ypané, Río** C Paraguay
Ypres *see* Ieper
114 I13 **Ypsário** *var.* Ipsario. ▲ Thásos, E Greece 40°43′N 24°39′E
31 R10 **Ypsilanti** Michigan, N USA 42°12′N 83°36′W
34 M1 **Yreka** California, W USA 41°43′N 122°39′W
Yrendagüé *see* General Eugenio A. Garay
144 L11 **Yrghyz** *prev.* Irgiz. Aktyubinsk, C Kazakhstan 48°36′N 61°14′E
186 G5 **Ysabel Channel** *channel* N Papua New Guinea
14 K8 **Yser, Lac** Québec, SE Canada
147 Y8 **Yshtyk** Issyk-Kul'skaya Oblast', E Kyrgyzstan 41°34′N 78°21′E
Yssel *see* IJssel
103 Q12 **Yssingeaux** Haute-Loire, C France 45°09′N 04°07′E
95 K23 **Ystad** Skåne, S Sweden 55°25′N 13°51′E
Ysyk-Köl *see* Issyk-Kul', Ozero
Ysyk-Köl *see* Balykchy
Ysyk-Köl Oblasty *see* Issyk-Kul'skaya Oblast'
96 L8 **Ythan** NE Scotland, United Kingdom
Y Trallwng *see* Welshpool
94 C13 **Ytre Arna** Hordaland, S Norway 60°28′N 05°25′E
94 B12 **Ytre Sula** *island* S Norway
93 G17 **Ytterhogdal** Jämtland, C Sweden 62°10′N 14°55′E
Yu *see* Henan
Yuan *see* Red River
Yuancheng *see* Heyuan, Guangdong, S China
Yuan Jiang *see* Red River
161 S13 **Yuanlin** *Jap.* Inrin; *prev.* Yüanlin. C Taiwan 23°57′N 120°33′E
161 N3 **Yuanping** Shanxi, C China 38°26′N 112°42′E
Yuanquan *see* Anxi
Yuanshan *see* Lianping
161 O11 **Yuan Shui** S China
35 O6 **Yuba City** California, W USA 39°07′N 121°40′W
35 O6 **Yuba River** California, W USA
80 H13 **Yubdo** Oromiya, C Ethiopia 09°05′N 35°28′E
41 X12 **Yucatán** ◆ *state* SE Mexico
47 O3 **Yucatan Basin** *var.* Yucatan Deep. *undersea feature* N Caribbean Sea 20°00′N 84°00′W
Yucatán, Canal de *see* Yucatan Channel
41 Y10 **Yucatan Channel** *Sp.* Canal de Yucatán. *channel* Cuba/Mexico
Yucatan Deep *see* Yucatan Basin
Yucatan Peninsula *see* Yucatán, Península de
41 X13 **Yucatán, Península de** *Eng.* Yucatan Peninsula. *peninsula* Guatemala/Mexico
36 I11 **Yucca** Arizona, SW USA 34°49′N 114°06′W
35 V15 **Yucca Valley** California, W USA 34°06′N 116°30′W
161 P4 **Yucheng** Shandong, E China 37°01′N 116°37′E
Yuci *see* Jinzhong
129 X5 **Yudoma** E Russian Federation
161 P12 **Yudu** *var.* Gongjiang. Jiangxi, C China 26°02′N 115°24′E
Yue *see* Guangdong
Yuecheng *see* Yuexi
160 M12 **Yuecheng Ling** ▲ S China
Yuegai *see* Qumarlêb
Yuegaitan *see* Qumarlêb
181 P7 **Yuendumu** Northern Territory, N Australia 22°19′S 131°51′E
Yue Shan, Tai *see* Lantau Island
160 H10 **Yuexi** *var.* Yuecheng. Sichuan, C China 28°50′N 102°36′E
161 N10 **Yueyang** Hunan, S China 29°24′N 113°08′E
125 U14 **Yug** Permskiy Kray, NW Russian Federation 57°49′N 56°08′E
125 P13 **Yug** NW Russian Federation
123 R10 **Yugorënok** Respublika Sakha (Yakutiya), NE Russian Federation 59°46′N 137°36′E
122 H9 **Yugorsk** Khanty-Mansiyskiy Avtonomnyy Okrug-Yugra, C Russian Federation 61°17′N 63°25′E
122 H7 **Yugorskiy Poluostrov** *peninsula* NW Russian Federation
Yugoslavia *see* Serbia
146 K14 **Yugo-Vostochnyye Garagumy** *prev.* Yugo-Vostochnyye Karakumy. *desert* E Turkmenistan
Yugo-Vostochnyye Karakumy *see* Yugo-Vostochnyye Garagumy
Yuhu *see* Eryuan
161 S10 **Yuhuan Dao** *island* SE China
160 L14 **Yu Jiang** S China
Yujin *see* Qianwei
159 P9 **Yuka** Qinghai, W China 38°03′N 94°45′E
123 S7 **Yukagirskoye Ploskogor'ye** *plateau* NE Russian Federation
159 P8 **Yuke He** C China
118 L11 **Yukhavichy** *Rus.* Yukhovichi. Vitsyebskaya Voblasts', N Belarus 56°02′N 28°39′E
126 J4 **Yukhnov** Kaluzhskaya Oblast', W Russian Federation 54°43′N 35°15′E
Yukhovichi *see* Yukhavichy
79 J20 **Yuki** *var.* Yuki Kengunda. Bandundu, W Dem. Rep. Congo 03°57′S 19°30′E
Yuki Kengunda *see* Yuki
26 M10 **Yukon** Oklahoma, C USA 35°30′N 97°45′W
0 F4 **Yukon** Canada/USA
Yukon *see* Yukon Territory
39 S7 **Yukon Flats** *salt flat* Alaska, USA
Yukon, Territoire du *see* Yukon Territory
10 I5 **Yukon Territory** *var.* Yukon, *Fr.* Territoire du Yukon. ◆ *territory* NW Canada
137 T16 **Yüksekova** Hakkâri, SE Turkey 37°35′N 44°17′E
123 N10 **Yukta** Krasnoyarskiy Kray, C Russian Federation 63°16′N 106°04′E
165 O13 **Yukuhashi** *var.* Yukuhasi. Fukuoka, Kyūshū, SW Japan 33°41′N 131°00′E
Yukuhasi *see* Yukuhashi
Yukuriawat *see* Yopurga
125 O9 **Yula** NW Russian Federation
181 P8 **Yulara** Northern Territory, N Australia 25°15′S 130°57′E
127 W6 **Yuldybayevo** Respublika Bashkortostan, W Russian Federation 52°22′N 57°55′E
23 W8 **Yulee** Florida, SE USA 30°37′N 81°36′W
158 K7 **Yuli** *var.* Lopnur. Xinjiang Uygur Zizhiqu, NW China 41°24′N 86°12′E
161 T14 **Yuli** *prev.* Yüli. C Taiwan 23°23′N 121°18′E
160 L15 **Yulin** Guangxi Zhuangzu Zizhiqu, S China 22°37′N 110°08′E
160 L4 **Yulin** Shaanxi, C China 38°14′N 109°48′E
161 T14 **Yuli Shan** *prev.* Yüli Shan. ▲ E Taiwan 23°23′N 121°14′E
160 F11 **Yulong Xueshan** ▲ SW China 27°09′N 100°10′E
36 H14 **Yuma** Arizona, SW USA 32°40′N 114°38′W
37 W3 **Yuma** Colorado, C USA 40°07′N 102°43′W
54 K5 **Yumare** Yaracuy, N Venezuela 10°37′N 68°41′W
63 G14 **Yumbel** Bío Bío, C Chile 37°05′S 72°40′W
79 N19 **Yumbi** Maniema, E Dem. Rep. Congo 01°14′S 26°14′E
159 Q7 **Yumendong** *prev.* Yumenzhen. Gansu, N China 40°19′N 97°12′E
159 R8 **Yumendong** *prev.* Laojunmiao. Gansu, N China 39°49′N 97°47′E
Yumenzhen *see* Yumendong
158 J3 **Yumin** *var.* Karabura. Xinjiang Uygur Zizhiqu, NW China 46°14′N 82°52′E
Yun *see* Yunnan
136 G14 **Yunak** Konya, W Turkey 38°50′N 31°42′E
45 O8 **Yuna, Río** E Dominican Republic
38 I17 **Yunaska Island** *island* Aleutian Islands, Alaska, USA
160 M6 **Yuncheng** Shanxi, C China 35°07′N 110°45′E
Yuncheng *see* Yunfu
161 N14 **Yunfu** *var.* Yuncheng. Guangdong, S China 22°56′N 112°02′E
57 L18 **Yungas** *physical region* E Bolivia
Yungki *see* Jilin
Yung-ning *see* Nanning
160 I12 **Yungui Gaoyuan** *plateau* SW China
Yunjinghong *see* Jinghong
160 M15 **Yunkai Dashan** ▲ S China
Yunki *see* Jilin
160 E11 **Yun Ling** ▲ SW China
Yunling *see* Yunxiao
161 N9 **Yunmeng** Hubei, C China 31°04′N 113°45′E
157 N14 **Yunnan** *var.* Yun, Yunnan Sheng, Yünnan, Yun-nan. ◆ *province* SW China
Yunnan *see* Kunming
Yunnan Sheng *see* Yunnan
Yünnan/Yun-nan *see* Yunnan
165 P15 **Yunomae** Kumamoto, Kyūshū, SW Japan 32°16′N 131°00′E
161 N8 **Yun Shui** C China
182 J7 **Yunta** South Australia 32°37′S 139°33′E
161 Q14 **Yunxiao** *var.* Yunling. Fujian, SE China 23°56′N 117°16′E
160 K9 **Yunyang** Sichuan, C China 31°03′N 109°43′E
Yunzhong *see* Huairen
193 S9 **Yupanqui Basin** *undersea feature* E Pacific Ocean
Yuping *see* Libo, Guizhou, China
Yuping *see* Pingbian, Yunnan, China
Yuratishki *see* Yuratsishki
119 I15 **Yuratsishki** *Pol.* Juraciszki, *Rus.* Yuratishki. Hrodzyenskaya Voblasts', W Belarus 54°02′N 25°56′E
Yurev *see* Tartu
122 J12 **Yurga** Kemerovskaya Oblast', S Russian Federation 55°42′N 84°59′E
Yurihonjō *see* Honjō
56 E10 **Yurimaguas** Loreto, N Peru 05°54′S 76°07′W
127 P3 **Yurino** Respublika Mariy El, W Russian Federation 56°19′N 46°15′E
41 N13 **Yuriria** Guanajuato, C Mexico 20°12′N 101°09′W
125 T13 **Yurla** Komi-Permyatskiy Okrug, NW Russian Federation 59°18′N 54°19′E
Yuruá, Río *see* Juruá, Rio
114 M13 **Yürük** Tekirdağ, NW Turkey 40°58′N 27°09′E
158 G10 **Yurungkax He** W China
125 Q14 **Yur'ya** *var.* Jarja. Kirovskaya Oblast', NW Russian Federation 59°01′N 49°22′E
Yur'ev *see* Tartu
125 N16 **Yur'yevets** Ivanovskaya Oblast', W Russian Federation 57°19′N 43°01′E
126 M3 **Yur'yev-Pol'skiy** Vladimirskaya Oblast', W Russian Federation 56°28′N 39°39′E
117 V7 **Yur"yivka** Dnipropetrovs'ka Oblast', E Ukraine 48°45′N 36°01′E
42 I7 **Yuscarán** El Paraíso, S Honduras 13°55′N 86°51′W
161 P12 **Yu Shan** ▲ S China
124 I7 **Yushkozero** Respublika Kareliya, NW Russian Federation 64°46′N 32°13′E
124 I7 **Yushkozerskoye Vodokhranilishche** *var.* Ozero Kujto. NW Russian Federation
169 W9 **Yushu** Jilin, China E Asia 44°48′N 126°55′E
159 R13 **Yushu** *var.* Gyêgu. Qinghai, C China 33°04′N 97°E
127 P12 **Yusta** Respublika Kalmykiya, SW Russian Federation 47°06′N 46°16′E
124 I10 **Yustozero** Respublika Kareliya, NW Russian Federation 62°44′N 33°31′E
137 Q11 **Yusufeli** Artvin, NE Turkey 40°50′N 41°31′E
164 F14 **Yusuhara** Kōchi, Shikoku, SW Japan 33°22′N 132°52′E
125 T14 **Yus'va** Permskiy Kray, NW Russian Federation 58°48′N 54°59′E
Yuta *see* Yatta
161 P2 **Yutian** Hebei, E China 39°52′N 117°44′E
158 H10 **Yutian** *var.* Keriya, Mugalla. Xinjiang Uygur Zizhiqu, NW China 36°49′N 81°31′E
62 K5 **Yuto** Jujuy, NW Argentina 23°35′S 64°28′W
62 P7 **Yuty** Caazapá, S Paraguay 26°31′S 56°20′W
160 G13 **Yuxi** Yunnan, SW China 24°22′N 102°28′E
161 O2 **Yuxian** *prev.* Yu Xian. Hebei, E China 39°50′N 114°33′E
Yu Xian *see* Yuxian
165 Q9 **Yuzawa** Akita, Honshū, C Japan 39°11′N 140°29′E
125 N16 **Yuzha** Ivanovskaya Oblast', W Russian Federation 56°34′N 42°00′E
Yuzhno-Alichurskiy Khrebet *see* Alichuri Janubí, Qatorkŭhi
Yuzhno-Kazakhstanskaya Oblast' *see* Yuzhnyy Kazakhstan
123 T13 **Yuzhno-Sakhalinsk** *Jap.* Toyohara; *prev.* Vladimirovka. Ostrov Sakhalin, Sakhalinskaya Oblast', SE Russian Federation 46°58′N 142°45′E
127 P14 **Yuzhno-Sukhokumsk** Respublika Dagestan, SW Russian Federation 44°43′N 45°32′E
145 Z10 **Yuzhnyy Altay, Khrebet** ▲ E Kazakhstan
Yuzhnyy Bug *see* Pivdennyy Buh
145 O15 **Yuzhnyy Kazakhstan** *off.* Yuzhno-Kazakhstanskaya Oblast', *Eng.* South Kazakhstan, *Kaz.* Ongtüstik Qazaqstan Oblysy; *prev.* Chimkentskaya Oblast'. ◆ *province* S Kazakhstan

◆ Country
● Country Capital
◇ Dependent Territory
○ Dependent Territory Capital
◆ Administrative Regions
✕ International Airport
▲ Mountain
▲ Mountain Range
Volcano
River
Lake
Reservoir

123 U10 **Yuzhnyy, Mys** *headland* E Russian Federation 57°44′N 156°49′E
122 H6 **Yuzhnyy, Ostrov** *island* NW Russian Federation
127 W6 **Yuzhnyy Ural** *var.* Southern Urals. ▲▲ W Russian Federation
159 V10 **Yuzhong** Gansu, C China 35°52′N 104°09′E
Yuzhou *see* Chongqing
103 N5 **Yvelines** ◐ *department* N France
108 B9 **Yverdon** *var.* Yverdon-les-Bains, *Ger.* Iferten; *anc.* Eborodunum. Vaud, W Switzerland 46°47′N 06°38′E
Yverdon-les-Bains *see* Yverdon
102 M3 **Yvetot** Seine-Maritime, N France 49°37′N 00°48′E
Ýylanly *see* Gurbansoltan Eje

Z

147 T12 **Zaalayskiy Khrebet** *Taj.* Qatorkŭhi Pasi Oloy. ▲▲ Kyrgyzstan/Tajikistan
Zaamin *see* Zomin
Zaandam *see* Zaanstad
98 I10 **Zaanstad** *prev.* Zaandam. Noord-Holland, C Netherlands 52°27′N 04°49′E
Zabadani *see* Az Zabdānī
Zabalatstsye *see* Zabalotstsye
112 L9 **Žabalj** *Ger.* Josefsdorf, *Hung.* Zsablya; *prev.* Józseffalva. Vojvodina, N Serbia 45°22′N 20°01′E
119 L18 **Zabalotstsye** *prev.* Zabalatstsye, *Rus.* Zabolot'ye. Homyel'skaya Voblasts', SE Belarus 52°40′N 28°34′E
Zāb aş Şaghīr, Nahraz *see* Little Zab
123 P14 **Zabaykal'sk** Zabaykal'skiy Kray, S Russian Federation 49°37′N 117°20′E
123 O12 **Zabaykal'skiy Kray** ◐ *province* S Russian Federation
Zāb-e Kūchek, Rūdkhāneh-ye *see* Little Zab
Zabeln *see* Sabile
Zabéré *see* Zabré
Zabern *see* Saverne
141 N16 **Zabīd** W Yemen 14°N 43°E
141 O16 **Zabīd, Wādī** *dry watercourse* SW Yemen
Žabinka *see* Zhabinka
Ząbkowice *see* Ząbkowice Śląskie
111 G15 **Ząbkowice Śląskie** *var.* Ząbkowice, *Ger.* Frankenstein, Frankenstein in Schlesien. Dolnośląskie, SW Poland 50°35′N 16°48′E
110 P10 **Zabłudów** Podlaskie, NE Poland 53°00′N 23°21′E
112 D8 **Zabok** Krapina-Zagorje, N Croatia 46°00′N 15°48′E
143 W9 **Zābol** *var.* Shahr-i-Zabul, Zabul; *prev.* Nasratabad. Sīstān va Balūchestān, E Iran 31°N 61°32′E
Zābol *see* Zābul
143 W13 **Zābolī** Sīstān va Balūchestān, SE Iran 27°09′N 61°32′E
Zabolot'ye *see* Zabalotstsye
77 Q13 **Zabré** *var.* Zabéré. S Burkina 11°13′N 00°34′W
111 G17 **Zábřeh** *Ger.* Hohenstadt. Olomoucký Kraj, E Czech Republic 49°52′N 16°53′E
111 J16 **Zabrze** *Ger.* Hindenburg, Hindenburg in Oberschlesien. Śląskie, S Poland 50°18′N 18°47′E
149 O7 **Zābul** *prev.* Zābol. ◐ *province* SE Afghanistan
Zabul/Zābul *see* Zābol
42 E6 **Zacapa** Zacapa, E Guatemala 14°59′N 89°33′W
42 A3 **Zacapa** *off.* Departamento de Zacapa. ◐ *department* E Guatemala
Zacapa, Departamento de *see* Zacapa
40 M14 **Zacapú** Michoacán, SW Mexico 19°49′N 101°48′W
41 V14 **Zacatal** Campeche, SE Mexico 18°40′N 91°52′W
40 M11 **Zacatecas** Zacatecas, C Mexico 22°46′N 102°33′W
40 L10 **Zacatecas** ◐ *state* C Mexico
42 F8 **Zacatecoluca** La Paz, S El Salvador 13°29′N 88°51′W
41 P15 **Zacatepec** Morelos, S Mexico 18°40′N 99°11′W
41 Q13 **Zacatlán** Puebla, S Mexico 19°56′N 97°58′W
144 F8 **Zachagansk** *Kaz.* Zashaghan. Zapadnyy Kazakhstan, NW Kazakhstan 51°04′N 51°13′E
115 D20 **Zacháro** *var.* Zaharo, Zakháro. Dytikí Elláda, S Greece 37°29′N 21°40′E
22 J8 **Zachary** Louisiana, S USA 30°39′N 91°09′W
117 U6 **Zachepylivka** Kharkivs'ka Oblast', E Ukraine 49°13′N 35°15′E
Zachist'ye *see* Zachystsye
110 E9 **Zachodnio-pomorskie** ◐ *province* NW Poland
119 L14 **Zachystsye** *Rus.* Zachist'ye. Minskaya Voblasts', NW Belarus 54°24′N 28°45′E
40 L13 **Zacoalco** *var.* Zacoalco de Torres. Jalisco, SW Mexico 20°14′N 103°33′W
Zacoalco de Torres *see* Zacoalco
41 P13 **Zacualtipán** Hidalgo, C Mexico 20°39′N 98°42′W
112 C12 **Zadar** *It.* Zara; *anc.* Iader. Zadar, SW Croatia 44°07′N 15°15′E
112 C12 **Zadar** *off.* Zadarsko-Kninska Županija, Zadar-Knin. ◐ *province* SW Croatia
Zadar-Knin *see* Zadar
Zadarsko-Kninska Županija *see* Zadar
166 M14 **Zadetkyi Kyun** *var.* St.Matthew's Island. *island* Mergui Archipelago, S Burma (Myanmar)
67 Q9 **Zadié** *var.* Djadié. ≈ NE Gabon
159 Q13 **Zadoi** *var.* Qapugtang. Qinghai, C China 32°56′N 95°21′E
126 L7 **Zadonsk** Lipetskaya Oblast', W Russian Federation 52°25′N 38°55′E
Za'farâna *see* Za'farānah
75 X8 **Za'farānah** *var.* Za'farâna. E Egypt 29°06′N 32°34′E
149 W7 **Zafarwāl** Punjab, E Pakistan 32°20′N 74°53′E
121 Q1 **Zafer Burnu** *var.* Cape Andreas, Cape Apostolas Andreas, *Gk.* Akrotíri Apostólou Andréa. *cape* NE Cyprus
107 J23 **Zafferano, Capo** *headland* Sicilia, Italy, C Mediterranean Sea 38°06′N 13°31′E
114 M7 **Zafirovo** Silistra, NE Bulgaria 44°00′N 26°51′E
Záfora *see* Sofraná
104 J12 **Zafra** Extremadura, W Spain 38°25′N 06°27′W
110 E13 **Żagań** *var.* Zagań, Żegań, *Ger.* Sagan. Lubuskie, W Poland 51°37′N 15°20′E
118 F10 **Žagarė** *Pol.* Żagory. Šiaulai, N Lithuania 56°22′N 23°16′E
Zagazig *see* Az Zaqāzīq
74 M5 **Zaghouan** *var.* Zaghwān. NE Tunisia 36°26′N 10°05′E
Zaghwān *see* Zaghouan
115 G16 **Zagorá** Thessalía, C Greece 39°27′N 23°06′E
Zagorod'ye *see* Zaharoddzye
Żagory *see* Žagarė
Zágráb *see* Zagreb
112 E8 **Zagreb** *Ger.* Agram, *Hung.* Zágráb. ● (Croatia) Zagreb, N Croatia 45°48′N 15°58′E
112 E8 **Zagreb** *prev.* Grad Zagreb. ◐ *province* N Croatia
142 L7 **Zāgros, Kūhhā-ye** *Eng.* Zagros Mountains. ▲▲ W Iran
Zagros Mountains *see* Zāgros, Kūhhā-ye
112 O12 **Žagubica** Serbia, E Serbia 44°13′N 21°47′E
Zagunao *see* Lixian
111 L22 **Zagyva** ≈ N Hungary
Zaharo *see* Zacháro
119 G19 **Zaharoddzye** *Rus.* Zagorod'ye. *physical region* SW Belarus
143 W11 **Zāhedān** *var.* Zahidan; *prev.* Duzdab. Sīstān va Balūchestān, SE Iran 29°31′N 60°51′E
Zahidan *see* Zāhedān
Zaḩlah *see* Zahlé
138 H7 **Zahlé** *var.* Zaḩlah. C Lebanon 33°51′N 35°54′E
146 J14 **Zähmet** *Rus.* Zakhmet. Mary Welaýaty, C Turkmenistan 37°48′N 62°33′E
111 O20 **Záhony** Szabolcs-Szatmár-Bereg, NE Hungary 48°26′N 22°11′E
141 N13 **Ẓahrān** 'Asīr, S Saudi Arabia 17°48′N 43°28′E
139 R12 **Ẓahrat al Baṭn** *hill range* S Iraq
120 H11 **Zahrez Chergui** *var.* Zahrez Chergúi. *marsh* N Algeria
Zainlha *see* Xinjin
127 S4 **Zainsk** Respublika Tatarstan, W Russian Federation 55°12′N 52°01′E
82 A10 **Zaire** *prev.* Congo. ◐ *province* NW Angola
Zaire *see* Congo (river)
Zaire *see* Congo (Democratic Republic of)
112 P13 **Zaječar** Serbia, E Serbia 43°54′N 22°16′E
83 L18 **Zaka** Masvingo, E Zimbabwe 20°20′S 31°29′E
122 M14 **Zakamensk** Respublika Buryatiya, S Russian Federation 50°18′N 102°57′E
116 G7 **Zakarpats'ka Oblast'** *Eng.* Transcarpathian Oblast, *Rus.* Zakarpatskaya Oblast'. ◐ *province* W Ukraine
Zakarpatskaya Oblast' *see* Zakarpats'ka Oblast'
Zakataly *see* Zaqatala
Zakháro *see* Zacháro
Zakhidnyy Buh/Zakhodni Buh *see* Bug
Zakhmet *see* Zähmet
139 Q1 **Zākhō** *var.* Zākhū. Dahūk, N Iraq 37°09′N 42°40′E
Zākhū *see* Zākhō
Zákinthos *see* Zákynthos
111 L18 **Zakopane** Małopolskie, S Poland 49°17′N 19°57′E
78 J12 **Zakouma** Salamat, S Chad 10°47′N 19°51′E
115 L25 **Zákros** Kríti, Greece, E Mediterranean Sea 35°06′N 26°12′E
115 C19 **Zákynthos** *var.* Zákinthos. Zákynthos, W Greece 37°47′N 20°54′E
115 C20 **Zákynthos** *var.* Zákinthos, *It.* Zante. *island* Iónia Nísoi, Greece, C Mediterranean Sea
115 C19 **Zakýnthou, Porthmós** *strait* SW Greece
111 G24 **Zala** *off.* Zala Megye. ◐ *county* W Hungary
111 G24 **Zala** ≈ W Hungary
138 M4 **Zalābiyah** Dayr az Zawr, C Syria 35°39′N 39°51′E
111 G24 **Zalaegerszeg** Zala, W Hungary 46°51′N 16°49′E
104 K11 **Zalamea de la Serena** Extremadura, W Spain 38°38′N 05°37′W
104 J13 **Zalamea la Real** Andalucía, S Spain 37°41′N 06°40′W
Zala Megye *see* Zala
163 U7 **Zalantun** *var.* Butha Qi. Nei Mongol Zizhiqu, N China 47°58′N 122°44′E
111 G23 **Zalaszentgrót** Zala, SW Hungary 46°57′N 17°05′E
Zalatna *see* Zlatna
116 G9 **Zalău** *Ger.* Waltenberg, *Hung.* Zilah; *prev. Ger.* Zillenmarkt. Sălaj, NW Romania 47°11′N 23°03′E
109 V10 **Žalec** *Ger.* Sachsenfeld. C Slovenia 46°15′N 15°08′E
110 K8 **Zalewo** *Ger.* Saalfeld. Warmińsko-Mazurskie, NE Poland 53°54′N 19°39′E
141 N9 **Ẓalim** Makkah, W Saudi Arabia 22°46′N 42°12′E
80 A11 **Zalingei** *var.* Zalinje. Western Darfur, W Sudan 12°51′N 23°29′E
Zalinje *see* Zalingei
116 K7 **Zalishchyky** Ternopil's'ka Oblast', W Ukraine 48°40′N 25°43′E
Zallah *see* Zillah
98 J13 **Zaltbommel** Gelderland, C Netherlands 51°49′N 05°15′E
124 H15 **Zaluch'ye** Novgorodskaya Oblast', NW Russian Federation 57°40′N 31°45′E
Zamak *see* Zamakh
141 Q14 **Zamakh** *var.* Zamak. N Yemen 16°26′N 47°35′E
136 K15 **Zamantı Irmağı** ≈ C Turkey
Zambesi/Zambeze *see* Zambezi
83 G14 **Zambezi** North Western, W Zambia 13°34′S 23°08′E
83 K15 **Zambezi** *var.* Zambesi, *Port.* Zambeze. ≈ S Africa
83 O15 **Zambézia** *off.* Província da Zambézia. ◐ *province* C Mozambique
Zambézia, Província da *see* Zambézia
83 I14 **Zambia** *off.* Republic of Zambia; *prev.* Northern Rhodesia. ◆ *republic* S Africa
Zambia, Republic of *see* Zambia
171 O8 **Zamboanga** *off.* Zamboanga City. Mindanao, S Philippines 06°56′N 122°03′E
Zamboanga City *see* Zamboanga
54 E5 **Zambrano** Bolívar, N Colombia 09°45′N 74°50′W
110 N10 **Zambrów** Łomża, E Poland 52°59′N 22°14′E
83 L14 **Zâmbuè** Tete, NW Mozambique 15°03′S 30°49′E
77 T13 **Zamfara** ≈ NW Nigeria
Zamkog *see* Zamtang
56 C9 **Zamora** Zamora Chinchipe, S Ecuador 04°04′S 78°52′W
104 K6 **Zamora** Castilla y León, NW Spain 41°30′N 05°45′W
104 K5 **Zamora** ◐ *province* Castilla y León, NW Spain
Zamora *see* Barinas
56 A13 **Zamora Chinchipe** ◐ *province* S Ecuador
40 M13 **Zamora de Hidalgo** Michoacán, SW Mexico 20°N 102°18′W
111 P15 **Zamość** *Rus.* Zamoste. Lubelskie, E Poland 50°44′N 23°16′E
Zamoste *see* Zamość
160 G7 **Zamtang** *var.* Zamkog; *prev.* Gamba. Sichuan, C China 32°19′N 100°55′E
75 O8 **Zamzam, Wādī** *dry watercourse* NW Libya
79 F20 **Zanaga** Lékoumou, S Congo 02°50′S 13°53′E
41 T16 **Zanatepec** Oaxaca, SE Mexico 16°28′N 94°24′W
105 P9 **Záncara** ≈ C Spain
Zancle *see* Messina
158 G14 **Zanda** Xizang Zizhiqu, W China 31°29′N 79°50′E
98 H10 **Zandvoort** Noord-Holland, W Netherlands 52°22′N 04°31′E
39 P8 **Zane Hills** *hill range* Alaska, USA
31 T13 **Zanesville** Ohio, N USA 39°55′N 82°02′W
Zanga *see* Hrazdan
Zangoza *see* Sangüesa
142 L4 **Zanjān** *var.* Zenjan, Zinjan. Zanjān, NW Iran 36°40′N 48°30′E
142 L4 **Zanjān** *off.* Ostān-e Zanjān, *var.* Zenjan, Zinjan. ◐ *province* NW Iran
Zanjān, Ostān-e *see* Zanjān
Zante *see* Zákynthos
81 J22 **Zanzibar** Zanzibar, E Tanzania 06°10′S 39°12′E
81 J22 **Zanzibar** ◐ *region* E Tanzania
81 J22 **Zanzibar** *Swa.* Unguja. *island* E Tanzania
81 J22 **Zanzibar Channel** *channel* E Tanzania
161 N8 **Zaoyang** Hubei, C China 32°10′N 112°45′E
165 P10 **Zaō-zan** ▲ Honshū, C Japan 38°06′N 140°27′E
124 J2 **Zaozërsk** Murmanskaya Oblast', NW Russian Federation 69°25′N 32°25′E
161 Q6 **Zaozhuang** Shandong, E China 34°53′N 117°38′E
28 L4 **Zap** North Dakota, N USA 47°18′N 101°55′W
112 L13 **Zapadna Morava** *Ger.* Westliche Morava. ≈ C Serbia
124 H16 **Zapadnaya Dvina** Tverskaya Oblast', W Russian Federation 56°17′N 32°03′E
Zapadnaya Dvina *see* Western Dvina
Zapadno-Kazakhstanskaya Oblast' *see* Zapadnyy Kazakhstan
122 I9 **Zapadno-Sibirskaya Ravnina** *Eng.* West Siberian Plain. *plain* C Russian Federation
Zapadnyy Bug *see* Bug
144 E9 **Zapadnyy Kazakhstan** *off.* Zapadno-Kazakhstanskaya Oblast', *Eng.* West Kazakhstan, *Kaz.* Batys Qazaqstan Oblysy; *prev.* Ural'skaya Oblast'. ◐ *province* NW Kazakhstan
122 K13 **Zapadnyy Sayan** *Eng.* Western Sayans. ▲▲ S Russian Federation
63 H15 **Zapala** Neuquén, W Argentina 38°54′S 70°06′W
62 I4 **Zapaleri, Cerro** *var.* Cerro Sapaleri. ▲ N Chile 22°51′S 67°10′W
25 Q16 **Zapata** Texas, SW USA 26°57′N 99°17′W
44 D5 **Zapata, Península de** *peninsula* W Cuba
61 G19 **Zapicán** Lavalleja, S Uruguay 33°31′S 54°55′W
65 J19 **Zapiola Ridge** *undersea feature* SW Atlantic Ocean
65 L19 **Zapiola Seamount** *undersea feature* S Atlantic Ocean 38°15′S 26°15′W
124 I2 **Zapolyarnyy** Murmanskaya Oblast', NW Russian Federation 69°24′N 30°53′E
117 U8 **Zaporizhzhya** *Rus.* Zaporozh'ye; *prev.* Aleksandrovsk. Zaporiz'ka Oblast', SE Ukraine 47°47′N 35°12′E
Zaporizhzhya *see* Zaporiz'ka Oblast'
117 U9 **Zaporiz'ka Oblast'** *var.* Zaporizhzhya, *Rus.* Zaporozhskaya Oblast'. ◐ *province* SE Ukraine
Zaporozhskaya Oblast' *see* Zaporiz'ka Oblast'
Zaporozh'ye *see* Zaporizhzhya
40 L14 **Zapotiltic** Jalisco, SW Mexico 19°40′N 103°29′W
158 G13 **Zapug** Xizang Zizhiqu, W China
137 V10 **Zaqatala** *Rus.* Zakataly. NW Azerbaijan 41°38′N 46°38′E
159 P13 **Zaqên** Qinghai, W China 33°23′N 94°31′E
159 Q13 **Za Qu** ≈ C China
136 M13 **Zara** Sivas, C Turkey 39°55′N 37°44′E
Zara *see* Zadar
Zarafshan *see* Zarafshon
147 P12 **Zarafshon** *Rus.* Zeravshan. W Tajikistan 39°12′N 68°36′E
146 L9 **Zarafshon** *Rus.* Zarafshan. Navoiy Viloyati, N Uzbekistan 41°33′N 64°09′E
Zarafshon *see* Zeravshan
147 O12 **Zarafshon, Qatorkŭhi** *Rus.* Zeravshanskiy Khrebet, *Uzb.* Zarafshon Tizmasi. ▲▲ Tajikistan/Uzbekistan
Zarafshon Tizmasi *see* Zarafshon, Qatorkŭhi
54 E7 **Zaragoza** Antioquia, N Colombia 07°30′N 74°52′W
40 I5 **Zaragoza** Chihuahua, N Mexico 29°36′N 107°41′W
41 N6 **Zaragoza** Coahuila, NE Mexico 28°31′N 100°54′W
41 O10 **Zaragoza** Nuevo León, NE Mexico 23°59′N 99°49′W
105 R5 **Zaragoza** *Eng.* Saragossa; *anc.* Caesaraugusta, Salduba. Aragón, NE Spain 41°39′N 00°54′W
105 R6 **Zaragoza** ◐ *province* Aragón, NE Spain
105 R5 **Zaragoza** ✈ Aragón, NE Spain 41°38′N 00°53′W
143 S10 **Zarand** Kermān, C Iran 30°50′N 56°35′E
148 J9 **Zaranj** Nīmrōz, SW Afghanistan 30°59′N 61°54′E
118 I11 **Zarasai** Utena, E Lithuania 55°44′N 26°17′E
62 N12 **Zárate** *prev.* General José F.Uriburu. Buenos Aires, E Argentina 34°06′S 59°03′W
105 Q2 **Zarautz** *var.* Zarauz. País Vasco, N Spain 43°17′N 02°10′W
Zarauz *see* Zarautz
Zaravecchia *see* Biograd na Moru
Zarāyīn *see* Zarēn
126 L4 **Zaraysk** Moskovskaya Oblast', W Russian Federation 54°48′N 38°54′E
55 N6 **Zaraza** Guárico, N Venezuela 09°23′N 65°20′W
Zarbdar *see* Zarbdor
147 P11 **Zarbdor** *Rus.* Zarbdar. Jizzax Viloyati, C Uzbekistan 40°04′N 68°10′E
142 M8 **Zard Kūh** ▲ SW Iran 32°19′N 50°03′E
124 I5 **Zarechensk** Murmanskaya Oblast', NW Russian Federation 66°39′N 31°27′E
127 P6 **Zarechnyy** Penzenskaya Oblast', W Russian Federation 53°12′N 45°12′E
Zareh Sharan *see* Sharan
39 Y14 **Zarembo Island** *island* Alexander Archipelago, Alaska, USA
139 V4 **Zarēn** *var.* Zarāyīn. As Sulaymānīyah, E Iraq 35°16′N 45°43′E
149 Q7 **Zarghūn Shahr** *var.* Katawaz. Paktīkā, SE Afghanistan 32°40′N 68°20′E
77 V13 **Zaria** Kaduna, C Nigeria 11°06′N 07°42′E
116 K2 **Zarichne** Rivnens'ka Oblast', NW Ukraine 51°49′N 26°09′E
122 J13 **Zarinsk** Altayskiy Kray, S Russian Federation 53°34′N 85°22′E
116 J12 **Zărneşti** *Hung.* Zernest. Braşov, C Romania 45°34′N 25°18′E
115 J25 **Zarós** Kríti, Greece, E Mediterranean Sea 35°08′N 24°54′E
100 O9 **Zarow** ≈ NE Germany
Zarqa *see* Az Zarqā'
Zarqa/Muḩāfaẓat az Zarqā' *see* Az Zarqā'
111 G20 **Záruby** ▲ W Slovakia 48°30′N 17°24′E
56 B8 **Zaruma** El Oro, SW Ecuador 03°46′S 79°38′W
110 E13 **Żary** *Ger.* Sorau, Sorau in der Niederlausitz. Lubuskie, W Poland 51°44′N 15°09′E
54 D10 **Zarzal** Valle del Cauca, W Colombia 04°24′N 76°01′W
42 I7 **Zarzalar, Cerro** ▲ S Honduras 14°15′N 86°49′W
Zashaghan *see* Zachagansk
152 I5 **Zāskār** ≈ NE India
152 I5 **Zāskār Range** ▲▲ NE India
119 K15 **Zaslawye** Minskaya Voblasts', C Belarus 54°01′N 27°16′E
116 K7 **Zastavna** Chernivets'ka Oblast', W Ukraine 48°30′N 25°51′E
111 B16 **Žatec** *Ger.* Saaz. Ústecký Kraj, NW Czech Republic 50°20′N 13°35′E
Zaumgarten *see* Chrzanów
Zaunguzskiye Garagumy *see* Üngüz Angyrsyndaky Garagum
25 X9 **Zavalla** Texas, SW USA 31°09′N 94°25′W
99 H18 **Zaventem** Vlaams Brabant, C Belgium 50°53′N 04°28′E
99 H18 **Zaventem** ✈ (Brussel/Bruxelles) Vlaams Brabant, C Belgium 50°55′N 04°28′E
Zavertse *see* Zawiercie
114 L7 **Zavet** Razgrad, NE Bulgaria 43°46′N 26°40′E
127 O12 **Zavetnoye** Rostovskaya Oblast', SW Russian Federation 47°10′N 43°54′E
156 M3 **Zavhan Gol** ≈ W Mongolia
112 H12 **Zavidovići** Federacija Bosna I Hercegovina, N Bosnia and Herzegovina 44°26′N 18°07′E
123 R13 **Zavitinsk** Amurskaya Oblast', SE Russian Federation 50°23′N 128°57′E
Zawia *see* Az Zāwiyah
111 K15 **Zawiercie** *Rus.* Zavertse. Śląskie, S Poland 50°29′N 19°24′E
75 P11 **Zawīlah** *var.* Zuwaylah, *It.* Zueila. C Libya 26°10′N 15°07′E
138 I4 **Zāwīyah, Jabal az** ▲▲ NW Syria
109 Y3 **Zaya** ≈ NE Austria
166 M8 **Zayatkyi** Bago, C Burma (Myanmar) 17°48′N 96°27′E
145 Y11 **Zaysan** Vostochnyy Kazakhstan, E Kazakhstan 47°30′N 84°55′E
Zaysan Köl *see* Zaysan, Ozero
145 Y11 **Zaysan, Ozero** *Kaz.* Zaysan Köl. ◎ E Kazakhstan
159 R16 **Zayü** *var.* Gyigang. Xizang Zizhiqu, W China 28°36′N 97°25′E
Zayyq *see* Zhayyk
44 F6 **Zaza** ≈ C Cuba
116 K5 **Zbarazh** Ternopil's'ka Oblast', W Ukraine 49°40′N 25°47′E
116 J5 **Zboriv** Ternopil's'ka Oblast', W Ukraine 49°40′N 25°07′E
111 F18 **Zbraslav** Jihomoravský Kraj, SE Czech Republic 49°13′N 16°19′E
116 K6 **Zbruch** ≈ W Ukraine
Žd'ár *see* Žd'ár nad Sázavou
111 F17 **Žd'ár nad Sázavou** *Ger.* Saar in Mähren; *prev.* Žd'ár. Vysočina, C Czech Republic 49°34′N 16°00′E
116 K4 **Zdolbuniv** *Pol.* Zdolbunów, *Rus.* Zdolbunov. Rivnens'ka Oblast', NW Ukraine 50°33′N 26°15′E
Zdolbunov/Zdolbunów *see* Zdolbuniv
110 J13 **Zduńska Wola** Sieradz, C Poland 51°37′N 18°57′E
117 O4 **Zdvizh** ≈ N Ukraine
Zdzięciół *see* Dzyatlava
111 I16 **Zdzieszowice** *Ger.* Odertal. Opolskie, SW Poland 50°24′N 18°06′E
Zealand *see* Sjælland
188 K6 **Zealandia Bank** *undersea feature* C Pacific Ocean
63 H20 **Zeballos, Monte** ▲ S Argentina 47°04′S 71°32′W
83 K20 **Zebediela** Limpopo, NE South Africa 24°16′S 29°21′E
113 L18 **Zebës, Mali i** *var.* Mali i Zebës. ▲ NE Albania 41°57′N 20°16′E
Zebës, Mali i *see* Zebës, Mali i
21 V9 **Zebulon** North Carolina, SE USA 35°49′N 78°19′W
112 K8 **Žednik** *Hung.* Bácsjózseffalva. Vojvodina, N Serbia 45°58′N 19°40′E
99 C15 **Zeebrugge** West-Vlaanderen, NW Belgium 51°20′N 03°13′E
183 N16 **Zeehan** Tasmania, SE Australia 41°54′S 145°19′E
99 L14 **Zeeland** Noord-Brabant, SE Netherlands 51°42′N 05°40′E
29 N7 **Zeeland** North Dakota, N USA 45°57′N 99°49′W
99 E14 **Zeeland** ◐ *province* SW Netherlands
83 I21 **Zeerust** North-West, N South Africa 25°33′S 26°06′E
98 K10 **Zeewolde** Flevoland, C Netherlands 52°20′N 05°32′E
Zefat *see* Tsefat
Żegań *see* Żagań
Zehden *see* Cedynia
100 O11 **Zehdenick** Brandenburg, NE Germany 52°58′N 13°19′E
Zē-i Bādīnān *see* Great Zab
Zeiden *see* Codlea
146 M14 **Zeidskoye Vodokhranilishche** ⊠ E Turkmenistan
Zē-i Kōya *see* Little Zab
181 P7 **Zeil, Mount** ▲ Northern Territory, C Australia 23°31′S 132°41′E
98 J12 **Zeist** Utrecht, C Netherlands 52°05′N 05°15′E
101 M16 **Zeitz** Sachsen-Anhalt, E Germany 51°03′N 12°08′E
159 T11 **Zêkog** *var.* Zequ; *prev.* Sonag. Qinghai, C China 35°03′N 101°30′E
Zelaya Norte *see* Atlántico Norte, Región Autónoma
Zelaya Sur *see* Atlántico Sur, Región Autónoma
99 F17 **Zele** Oost-Vlaanderen, NW Belgium 51°04′N 04°02′E
110 N12 **Żelechów** Lubelskie, E Poland 51°49′N 21°57′E
113 H14 **Zelena Glava** ▲ SE Bosnia and Herzegovina 43°32′N 17°55′E
113 P20 **Zelen Breg** ▲ S Macedonia 41°10′N 22°14′E
113 I14 **Zelengora** ▲▲ S Bosnia and Herzegovina
124 I5 **Zelenoborskiy** Murmanskaya Oblast', NW Russian Federation 66°52′N 32°25′E
127 R3 **Zelenodol'sk** Respublika Tatarstan, W Russian Federation 55°52′N 48°49′E
117 S9 **Zelenodols'k** Dnipropetrovs'ka Oblast', E Ukraine 47°38′N 33°41′E
122 J12 **Zelenogorsk** Krasnoyarskiy Kray, C Russian Federation 56°08′N 94°29′E
126 K3 **Zelenograd** Moskovskaya Oblast', W Russian Federation 56°02′N 37°08′E
118 B13 **Zelenogradsk** *Ger.* Cranz, Kranz. Kaliningradskaya Oblast', W Russian Federation 54°58′N 20°30′E
127 O15 **Zelenokumsk** Stavropol'skiy Kray, SW Russian Federation 44°22′N 43°48′E
165 X4 **Zelënyy, Ostrov** *var.* Shibotsu-jima. *island* NE Russian Federation
Železna Kapela *see* Eisenkappel
Železna Vrata *see* Demir Kapija
112 L11 **Železniki** Serbia, N Serbia 44°45′N 20°23′E
98 N12 **Zelhem** Gelderland, E Netherlands 52°00′N 06°21′E
113 N18 **Želino** NW FYR Macedonia 42°00′N 21°06′E
113 M14 **Željin** ▲▲ C Serbia
101 K17 **Zella-Mehlis** Thüringen, C Germany 50°40′N 10°40′E
109 P7 **Zell am See** *var.* Zell-am-See. Salzburg, S Austria 47°19′N 12°47′E
Zell-am-See *see* Zell am See
109 N7 **Zell am Ziller** Tirol, W Austria 47°13′N 11°52′E
Zelle *see* Celle
109 W2 **Zellerndorf** Niederösterreich, NE Austria 48°40′N 15°57′E
109 U7 **Zeltweg** Steiermark, S Austria 47°12′N 14°46′E
119 G17 **Zel'va** *Pol.* Zelwa. Hrodzyenskaya Voblasts', W Belarus 53°09′N 24°49′E
118 H13 **Želva** Vilnius, C Lithuania 55°13′N 25°07′E
Zelwa *see* Zel'va
99 E16 **Zelzate** *var.* Selzaete. Oost-Vlaanderen, NW Belgium 51°12′N 03°49′E
118 E11 **Žemaičių Aukštumas** *physical region* W Lithuania
118 C12 **Žemaičių Naumiestis** Klaipėda, SW Lithuania 55°22′N 21°39′E
119 L14 **Zembin** *var.* Zyembin. Minskaya Voblasts', C Belarus 54°22′N 28°13′E
127 N6 **Zemetchino** Penzenskaya Oblast', W Russian Federation 53°31′N 42°35′E
79 M15 **Zémio** Haut-Mbomou, E Central African Republic 05°04′N 25°07′E
41 R16 **Zempoaltepec, Cerro** ▲ SE Mexico 17°04′N 95°54′W
99 G17 **Zemst** Vlaams Brabant, C Belgium 50°59′N 04°28′E
112 L11 **Zemun** Serbia, N Serbia 44°52′N 20°25′E
Zendajan *see* Zindah Jān
Zendeh Jān *see* Zindah Jān
Zengg *see* Senj
112 H12 **Zenica** Federacija Bosna I Hercegovina, C Bosnia and Herzegovina 44°12′N 17°53′E
Zenjan *see* Zanjān
Zen'kov *see* Zin'kiv
Zenshū *see* Jeonju
Zenta *see* Senta
82 B11 **Zenza do Itombe** Cuanza Norte, NW Angola 09°22′S 14°10′E
112 H12 **Žepče** Federacija Bosna I Hercegovina, N Bosnia and Herzegovina 44°26′N 18°00′E
23 W12 **Zephyrhills** Florida, SE USA 28°13′N 82°10′W
158 F9 **Zepu** *var.* Poskam. Xinjiang Uygur Zizhiqu, NW China 38°10′N 77°18′E
Zequ *see* Zêkog
147 Q12 **Zeravshan** *Taj./Uzb.* Zarafshon. ≈ Tajikistan/Uzbekistan
Zeravshan *see* Zarafshon
Zeravshanskiy Khrebet *see* Zarafshon, Qatorkŭhi
101 M14 **Zerbst** Sachsen-Anhalt, E Germany 51°57′N 12°05′E
Zerenda *see* Zerendy
145 P8 **Zerendy** *prev.* Zerenda. Akmola, N Kazakhstan 52°56′N 69°09′E
110 H12 **Żerków** Wielkopolskie, C Poland 52°03′N 17°33′E
108 E11 **Zermatt** Valais, SW Switzerland 46°00′N 07°45′E
Zernest *see* Zărneşti
108 J9 **Zernez** Graubünden, SE Switzerland 46°42′N 10°06′E
126 L12 **Zernograd** Rostovskaya Oblast', SW Russian Federation 46°52′N 40°13′E
Zestafoni *see* Zest'aponi
137 S9 **Zest'aponi** *Rus.* Zestafoni; *prev.* Zestap'oni. C Georgia 42°09′N 43°00′E
Zestap'oni *see* Zest'aponi
98 H12 **Zestienhoven** ✈ (Rotterdam) Zuid-Holland, SW Netherlands 51°57′N 04°30′E
113 J16 **Zeta** ≈ C Montenegro
8 L6 **Zeta Lake** ◎ Victoria Island, Northwest Territories, N Canada
98 L12 **Zetten** Gelderland, SE Netherlands 51°55′N 05°43′E
101 M17 **Zeulenroda** Thüringen, C Germany 50°40′N 11°58′E
100 H10 **Zeven** Niedersachsen, NW Germany 53°17′N 09°16′E
98 M12 **Zevenaar** Gelderland, SE Netherlands 51°55′N 06°05′E
99 H14 **Zevenbergen** Noord-Brabant, S Netherlands 51°39′N 04°36′E
129 X6 **Zeya** ≈ SE Russian Federation
Zeya Reservoir *see* Zeyskoye Vodokhranilishche
143 T11 **Zeynalābād** Kermān, C Iran 29°56′N 57°29′E
123 R12 **Zeyskoye Vodokhranilishche** *Eng.* Zeya Reservoir. ⊠ SE Russian Federation
104 H8 **Zêzere, Rio** ≈ C Portugal
Zgerzh *see* Zgierz
138 H6 **Zgharta** N Lebanon 34°24′N 35°54′E
110 K12 **Zgierz** *Ger.* Neuhof, *Rus.* Zgerzh. Łódź, C Poland 51°55′N 19°20′E
111 E14 **Zgorzelec** *Ger.* Görlitz. Dolnośląskie, SW Poland 51°10′N 15°E
119 F19 **Zhabinka** *Pol.* Żabinka. Brestskaya Voblasts', SW Belarus 52°12′N 24°01′E
Zhaggo *see* Luhuo
159 R15 **Zhag'yab** *var.* Yêndum. Xizang Zizhiqu, W China 30°42′N 97°33′E
Zhailma *see* Zhayylma
145 N14 **Zhalagash** *prev.* Dzhalagash. Kzylorda, S Kazakhstan 45°06′N 64°40′E
145 V16 **Zhalanash** Almaty, SE Kazakhstan 43°04′N 78°08′E
145 S7 **Zhalauly, Ozero** ◎ NE Kazakhstan
145 W10 **Zhalgyztobe** *prev.* Zhangiztobe. Vostochnyy Kazakhstan, E Kazakhstan 49°15′N 81°16′E
144 E9 **Zhalpaktal** *Kaz.* Zhalpaqtal; *prev.* Furmanovo. Zapadnyy Kazakhstan, W Kazakhstan 49°43′N 49°28′E
Zhalpaqtal *see* Zhalpaktal
119 G16 **Zhaludok** *Rus.* Zheludok. Hrodzyenskaya Voblasts', W Belarus 53°36′N 24°59′E
Zhaman-Akkol', Ozero *see* Akkol', Ozero
145 Q14 **Zhambyl** *off.* Zhambylskaya Oblast', *Kaz.* Zhambyl Oblysy; *prev.* Dzhambulskaya Oblast'. ◐ *province* S Kazakhstan
Zhambyl *see* Taraz
Zhambyl Oblysy/Zhambylskaya Oblast' *see* Zhambyl
Zhamo *see* Bomi
145 S12 **Zhamshy** ≈ C Kazakhstan
144 M15 **Zhanadariya** *prev.* Zhanadar'ya. Kzylorda, S Kazakhstan 44°41′N 64°39′E
Zhanadar'ya *see* Zhanadariya
144 E10 **Zhanakazan** *prev.* Novaya Kazanka. Zapadnyy Kazakhstan, W Kazakhstan 48°57′N 49°34′E
145 O15 **Zhanakorgan** *Kaz.* Zhangaqorghan. Kzylorda, S Kazakhstan 43°57′N 67°14′E
159 N16 **Zhanang** *var.* Chatang. Xizang Zizhiqu, W China 29°15′N 91°20′E
145 T12 **Zhanaortalyk** Karaganda, C Kazakhstan 47°31′N 75°42′E
144 F15 **Zhanaozen** *Kaz.* Zhangaözen; *prev.* Novyy Uzen'. Mangistau, W Kazakhstan 43°22′N 52°50′E
145 Q16 **Zhanatas** Zhambyl, S Kazakhstan 43°36′N 69°43′E
Zhangaözen *see* Zhanaozen
Zhangaqazaly *see* Ayteke Bi
Zhangaqorghan *see* Zhanakorgan
161 O2 **Zhangbei** Hebei, E China 41°13′N 114°43′E
Zhang-chia-k'ou *see* Zhangjiakou
Zhangdian *see* Zibo
Zhanggu *see* Danba
163 X9 **Zhangguangcai Ling** ▲▲ NE China
161 S13 **Zhanghua** *Jap.* Shōka; *prev.* Changhua. C Taiwan 24°06′N 120°31′E
Zhangiztobe *see* Zhalgyztobe
159 W11 **Zhangjiachuan** Gansu, N China 34°55′N 106°26′E
160 L10 **Zhangjiajie** *var.* Dayong. Hunan, S China 29°10′N 110°22′E
161 O2 **Zhangjiakou** *var.* Changkiakow, Zhang-chia-k'ou, *Eng.* Kalgan; *prev.* Wanchuan. Hebei, E China 40°48′N 114°51′E
161 Q13 **Zhangping** Fujian, SE China 25°21′N 117°29′E
161 Q13 **Zhangpu** *var.* Sui'an. Fujian, SE China 24°08′N 117°36′E
163 U11 **Zhangwu** Liaoning, NE China 42°21′N 122°32′E
159 S8 **Zhangye** *var.* Ganzhou. Gansu, N China 38°58′N 100°30′E
161 Q13 **Zhangzhou** Fujian, SE China 24°31′N 117°40′E
163 W6 **Zhan He** ≈ NE China
Zhänibek *see* Dzhanibek
160 L16 **Zhanjiang** *var.* Chanchiang, Chan-chiang, *Cant.* Tsamkong, *Fr.* Fort-Bayard. Guangdong, S China 21°10′N 110°20′E
145 V14 **Zhansugirov** *prev.* Dzhansugurov. Almaty, SE Kazakhstan 45°23′N 79°29′E
163 V8 **Zhaodong** Heilongjiang, NE China 46°03′N 125°58′E
Zhaoge *see* Qixian
160 H11 **Zhaojue** *var.* Xincheng. Sichuan, C China 28°03′N 102°50′E
161 N14 **Zhaoqing** Guangdong, S China 23°08′N 112°26′E
Zhaoren *see* Changwu
158 H5 **Zhaosu** *var.* Mongolküre. Xinjiang Uygur Zizhiqu, NW China 43°09′N 81°07′E
160 H11 **Zhaotong** Yunnan, SW China 27°20′N 103°29′E
163 V9 **Zhaoyuan** Heilongjiang, NE China 45°30′N 125°05′E
163 V9 **Zhaozhou** Heilongjiang, NE China 45°42′N 125°11′E
145 X13 **Zharbulak** Vostochnyy Kazakhstan, E Kazakhstan 46°04′N 82°05′E
158 J15 **Zhari Namco** ◎ W China
144 I12 **Zharkamys** *Kaz.* Zharqamys. Aktyubinsk, W Kazakhstan 47°58′N 56°33′E
145 W15 **Zharkent** *prev.* Panfilov. Taldykorgan, SE Kazakhstan 44°10′N 80°01′E
124 H17 **Zharkovskiy** Tverskaya Oblast', W Russian Federation 55°51′N 32°19′E
145 W11 **Zharma** Vostochnyy Kazakhstan, E Kazakhstan 48°48′N 80°55′E
144 F14 **Zharmysh** Mangistau, SW Kazakhstan 44°12′N 52°27′E
Zharqamys *see* Zharkamys
118 L13 **Zhary** Vitsyebskaya Voblasts', N Belarus 55°05′N 28°40′E

◆ Country
● Country Capital
◇ Dependent Territory
○ Dependent Territory Capital
◐ Administrative Regions
✈ International Airport
▲ Mountain
▲▲ Mountain Range
⛰ Volcano
≈ River
◎ Lake
⊠ Reservoir

Zhaslyk *see* Jasliq
158 *J14* **Zhaxi Co** ◎ W China
127 *X6* **Zhayyk** *Kaz.* Zayyq, *var.* Ural. ≋ Kazakhstan/Russian Federation
144 *L9* **Zhayylma** *prev.* Zhailma. Kostanay, N Kazakhstan *51°34′N 61°39′E*
Zhdanov *see* Beyläqan
Zhdanov *see* Mariupol'
Zhe *see* Zhejiang
161 *R10* **Zhejiang** *var.* Che-chiang, Chekiang, Zhe, Zhejiang Sheng. ◐ *province* SE China
Zhejiang Sheng *see* Zhejiang
145 *S7* **Zhelezinka** Pavlodar, N Kazakhstan *53°35′N 75°16′E*
119 *C14* **Zheleznodorozhnyy** *Ger.* Gerdauen. Kaliningradskaya Oblast', W Russian Federation *54°21′N 21°17′E*
Zheleznodorozhnyy *see* Yemva
122 *K12* **Zheleznogorsk** Krasnoyarskiy, C Russian Federation *56°20′N 93°36′E*
126 *J7* **Zheleznogorsk** Kurskaya Oblast', W Russian Federation *52°22′N 35°21′E*
127 *N15* **Zheleznovodsk** Stavropol'skiy Kray, SW Russian Federation *44°12′N 43°01′E*
Zhëltyye Vody *see* Zhovti Vody
Zheludok *see* Zhaludok
144 *H12* **Zhem** *prev.* Emba. ≋ W Kazakhstan
160 *K7* **Zhenba** Shaanxi, C China *32°42′N 107°55′E*
160 *I13* **Zhenfeng** *var.* Mingu. Guizhou, S China *25°27′N 105°38′E*
Zhengjiatun *see* Shuangliao
159 *X10* **Zhengning** *var.* Shanhe. Gansu, N China *35°29′N 108°21′E*
Zhengxiangbai Qi *see* Qagan Nur
161 *N6* **Zhengzhou** *var.* Ch'eng-chou, Chengchow; *prev.* Chenghsien. *province capital* Henan, C China *34°45′N 113°38′E*
161 *R8* **Zhenjiang** *var.* Chenkiang. Jiangsu, E China *32°08′N 119°30′E*
163 *U9* **Zhenlai** Jilin, NE China *45°52′N 123°11′E*
160 *I11* **Zhenxiong** Yunnan, SW China *27°31′N 104°52′E*
160 *K11* **Zhenyuan** *var.* Wuyang. Guizhou, S China *27°07′N 108°33′E*
161 *R11* **Zherong** *var.* Shuangcheng. Fujian, SE China *27°16′N 119°54′E*
145 *U15* **Zhetigen** *prev.* Nikolayevka. Almaty, SE Kazakhstan *43°39′N 77°10′E*
Zhetiqara *see* Zhitikara
144 *F15* **Zhetybay** Mangistau, SW Kazakhstan *43°35′N 52°05′E*
145 *P17* **Zhetysay** *var.* Dzhetysay. Yuzhnyy Kazakhstan *40°45′N 68°18′E*
145 *W14* **Zhetysuskiy Alatau** *prev.* Dzhungarskiy Alatau. ▲▲ China/Kazakhstan
160 *M11* **Zhexi Shuiku** ⊠ C China
145 *O12* **Zhezdy** Karaganda, C Kazakhstan *48°06′N 67°01′E*
145 *O12* **Zhezkazgan** *Kaz.* Zhezqazghan; *prev.* Dzhezkazgan. Karaganda, C Kazakhstan *47°49′N 67°44′E*
Zhezqazghan *see* Zhezkazgan
Zhicheng *see* Yidu
Zhidachov *see* Zhydachiv
159 *Q12* **Zhidoi** *var.* Gyaijêpozhanggê. Qinghai, C China *33°55′N 95°39′E*
122 *M13* **Zhigalovo** Irkutskaya Oblast', S Russian Federation *54°47′N 105°00′E*
127 *R6* **Zhigulevsk** Samarskaya Oblast', W Russian Federation *53°24′N 49°30′E*
118 *D13* **Zhilino** *Ger.* Schillen. Kaliningradskaya Oblast', W Russian Federation *54°55′N 21°54′E*
Zhiloy, Ostrov *see* Çilov Adası
127 *O8* **Zhirnovsk** Volgogradskaya Oblast', SW Russian Federation *51°01′N 44°49′E*
160 *M12* **Zhishan** *prev.* Yongzhou. Hunan, S China *26°12′N 111°36′E*
Zhishan *see* Lingling
144 *L8* **Zhitikara** *Kaz.* Zhetiqara; *prev.* Džetygara. Kostanay, NW Kazakhstan *52°14′N 61°12′E*
Zhitkovichi *see* Zhytkavichy
Zhitomir *see* Zhytomyr
Zhitomirskaya Oblast' *see* Zhytomyrs'ka Oblast'
126 *J5* **Zhizdra** Kaluzhskaya Oblast', W Russian Federation *53°38′N 34°39′E*
119 *N18* **Zhlobin** Homyel'skaya Voblasts', SE Belarus *52°53′N 30°01′E*
Zhmerinka *see* Zhmerynka
116 *M7* **Zhmerynka** *Rus.* Zhmerinka. Vinnyts'ka Oblast', C Ukraine *49°00′N 28°02′E*
149 *R9* **Zhob** *var.* Fort Sandeman. Baluchistān, SW Pakistan *31°21′N 69°31′E*
149 *R8* **Zhob** ≋ C Pakistan
Zhodino *see* Zhodzina
119 *L15* **Zhodzina** *Rus.* Zhodino. Minskaya Voblasts', C Belarus *54°06′N 28°21′E*
123 *Q5* **Zhokhova, Ostrov** *island* Novosibirskiye Ostrova, NE Russian Federation
Zholkev/Zholkva *see* Zhovkva
Zhondor *see* Jondor
158 *I15* **Zhongba** *var.* Tuoji. Xizang Zizhiqu, W China *29°37′N 84°11′E*
Zhongba *see* Jiangyou
Zhongdian *see* Xamgyi'nyilha
Zhongduo *see* Youyang
Zhonghe *see* Xiushan
Zhonghua Renmin Gongheguo *see* China
159 *V9* **Zhongning** Ningxia, N China *37°26′N 105°40′E*
Zhongping *see* Huize
161 *N15* **Zhongshan** Guangdong, S China *22°30′N 113°20′E*
195 *X7* **Zhongshan** *Chinese research station* Antarctica *69°23′S 76°34′E*
160 *M6* **Zhongtiao Shan** ▲▲ C China
159 *V9* **Zhongwei** Ningxia, N China *37°31′N 105°10′E*
160 *K9* **Zhongxian** *var.* Zhongzhou. Chongqing Shi, C China *30°16′N 108°03′E*
161 *N9* **Zhongxiang** Hubei, C China *31°12′N 112°35′E*
Zhongzhou *see* Zhongxian
144 *M14* **Zhosaly** *prev.* Dzhusaly. Kzylorda, SW Kazakhstan *45°29′N 64°04′E*
161 *O7* **Zhoukou** *var.* Zhoukouzhen. Henan, C China *33°32′N 114°40′E*
Zhoukouzhen *see* Zhoukou
161 *S9* **Zhoushan** Zhejiang, S China
Zhoushan Islands *see* Zhoushan Qundao
161 *S9* **Zhoushan Qundao** *Eng.* Zhoushan Islands. *island group* SE China
116 *I5* **Zhovkva** *Pol.* Żółkiew, *Rus.* Zholkev, Zholkva; *prev.* Nesterov. L'vivs'ka Oblast', NW Ukraine *50°04′N 24°E*
117 *S7* **Zhovti Vody** *Rus.* Zhëltyye Vody. Dnipropetrovs'ka Oblast', E Ukraine *48°24′N 33°30′E*
117 *Q10* **Zhovtneve** *Rus.* Zhovtnevoye. Mykolayivs'ka Oblast', S Ukraine *46°50′N 32°00′E*
Zhovtnevoye *see* Zhovtneve
Zhi Qu *see* Tongtian He
114 *K9* **Zhrebchevo, Yazovir** ⊠ C Bulgaria
163 *V13* **Zhuanghe** Liaoning, NE China *39°42′N 123°00′E*
159 *W11* **Zhuanglang** *var.* Shuiluo; *prev.* Shuilocheng. Gansu, C China *35°06′N 106°21′E*
145 *P15* **Zhuantobe** *Kaz.* Zhūantöbe. Yuzhnyy Kazakhstan, S Kazakhstan *44°45′N 68°50′E*
161 *Q5* **Zhucheng** Shandong, E China *35°58′N 119°24′E*
159 *V12* **Zhugqu** Gansu, C China *33°51′N 104°14′E*
161 *N15* **Zhuhai** Guangdong, S China *22°16′N 113°30′E*
Zhuizishan *see* Weichang
Zhuji *see* Shangqiu
126 *I5* **Zhukovka** Bryanskaya Oblast', W Russian Federation *53°33′N 33°48′E*
161 *N7* **Zhumadian** Henan, C China *32°58′N 114°03′E*
161 *S13* **Zhunan** *prev.* Chunan. N Taiwan *24°44′N 120°51′E*
Zhuo Xian *see* Zhuozhou
161 *O3* **Zhuozhou** *prev.* Zhuo Xian. Hebei, E China *39°22′N 115°40′E*
162 *L14* **Zhuozi Shan** ▲ N China *39°28′N 106°58′E*
113 *M17* **Zhur** *Serb.* Žur. S Kosovo *42°10′N 20°37′E*
Zhuravichi *see* Zhuravichy
119 *O17* **Zhuravichy** *Rus.* Zhuravichi. Homyel'skaya Voblasts', SE Belarus *53°15′N 30°33′E*
145 *Q8* **Zhuravlevka** Akmola, N Kazakhstan *52°00′N 69°59′E*
117 *Q4* **Zhurivka** Kyyivs'ka Oblast', N Ukraine *50°28′N 31°48′E*
144 *J11* **Zhuryn** Aktyubinsk, W Kazakhstan *49°13′N 57°36′E*
145 *T15* **Zhusandala, Step'** *grassland* SE Kazakhstan
160 *L8* **Zhushan** Hubei, C China *32°11′N 110°05′E*
Zhushan *see* Xuan'en
Zhuyang *see* Dazhu
161 *N11* **Zhuzhou** Hunan, S China *27°52′N 112°52′E*
116 *I6* **Zhydachiv** *Pol.* Żydaczów, *Rus.* Zhidachov. L'vivs'ka Oblast', NW Ukraine *49°20′N 24°08′E*
144 *G9* **Zhympity** *Kaz.* Zhympīty; *prev.* Dzhambeyty. Zapadnyy, W Kazakhstan *50°16′N 52°34′E*
119 *K19* **Zhytkavichy** *Rus.* Zhitkovichi. Homyel'skaya Voblasts', SE Belarus *52°14′N 27°52′E*
117 *N4* **Zhytomyr** *Rus.* Zhitomir. Zhytomyrs'ka Oblast', NW Ukraine *50°17′N 28°40′E*
Zhytomyr *see* Zhytomyrs'ka Oblast'
116 *M4* **Zhytomyrs'ka Oblast'** *var.* Zhytomyr, *Rus.* Zhitomirskaya Oblast'. ◐ *province* N Ukraine
153 *U15* **Zia** ✕ (Dhaka) Dhaka, C Bangladesh
111 *J20* **Žiar nad Hronom** *var.* Sväty Kríž nad Hronom, *Ger.* Heiligenkreuz, *Hung.* Garamszentkereszt. Banskobystrický Kraj, C Slovakia *48°36′N 18°52′E*
161 *Q4* **Zibo** *var.* Zhangdian. Shandong, E China *36°51′N 118°01′E*
160 *L4* **Zichang** *prev.* Wayaobu. Shaanxi, C China *37°08′N 109°40′E*
Zichenau *see* Ciechanów
111 *G15* **Ziębice** *Ger.* Münsterberg in Schlesien. Dolnośląskie, SW Poland *50°37′N 17°01′E*
Ziebingen *see* Cybinka
Ziegenhais *see* Głuchołazy
110 *E12* **Zielona Góra** *Ger.* Grünberg, Grünberg in Schlesien, Grüneberg. Lubuskie, W Poland *51°56′N 15°31′E*
99 *F14* **Zierikzee** Zeeland, SW Netherlands *51°39′N 03°55′E*
160 *I10* **Zigong** *var.* Tzekung. Sichuan, C China *29°20′N 104°48′E*
76 *G12* **Ziguinchor** SW Senegal *12°34′N 16°20′W*
41 *N16* **Zihuatanejo** Guerrero, S Mexico *17°39′N 101°33′W*
Ziketan *see* Xinghai
Zilah *see* Zalău
127 *W7* **Zilair** Respublika Bashkortostan, W Russian Federation *52°12′N 57°15′E*
136 *L12* **Zile** Tokat, N Turkey *40°18′N 35°52′E*
111 *J18* **Žilina** *Ger.* Sillein, *Hung.* Zsolna. Zlínský Kraj, N Slovakia *49°13′N 18°44′E*
111 *J19* **Žilinský Kraj** ◐ *region* N Slovakia
75 *Q9* **Zillah** *var.* Zallah. C Libya *28°30′N 17°33′E*
Zillenmarkt *see* Zalău
109 *N7* **Ziller** ≋ W Austria
Zillertal Alps *see* Zillertaler Alpen
109 *N8* **Zillertaler Alpen** *Eng.* Zillertal Alps, *It.* Alpi Aurine. ▲▲ Austria/Italy
118 *K10* **Zilupe** *Ger.* Rosenhof. E Latvia *56°10′N 28°06′E*
41 *O13* **Zimapán** Hidalgo, C Mexico *20°45′N 99°21′W*
83 *I16* **Zimba** Southern, S Zambia *17°20′S 26°11′E*
83 *J17* **Zimbabwe** *off.* Republic of Zimbabwe; *prev.* Rhodesia. ◆ *republic* S Africa
Zimbabwe, Republic of *see* Zimbabwe
116 *H10* **Zimbor** *Hung.* Magyarzsombor. Sălaj, NW Romania *47°00′N 23°16′E*
Zimmerbude *see* Svetlyy
116 *J15* **Zimnicea** Teleorman, S Romania *43°39′N 25°21′E*
114 *L9* **Zimnitsa** Yambol, E Bulgaria *42°34′N 26°37′E*
127 *N12* **Zimovniki** Rostovskaya Oblast', SW Russian Federation *47°07′N 42°29′E*
148 *J5* **Zindah Jān** *var.* Zendajan, Zindajān; *prev.* Zendeh Jān. Herāt, NW Afghanistan *34°55′N 61°53′E*
Zindajān *see* Zindah Jān
77 *V12* **Zinder** Zinder, S Niger *13°47′N 09°02′E*
77 *W11* **Zinder** ◐ *department* S Niger
77 *P12* **Ziniaré** C Burkina *12°35′N 01°18′W*
Zinjan *see* Zanjān
141 *P16* **Zinjibār** SW Yemen *13°08′N 45°23′E*
117 *T4* **Zin'kiv** *var.* Zen'kov. Poltavs'ka Oblast', NE Ukraine *50°11′N 34°22′E*
Zinov'yevsk *see* Kirovohrad
Zintenhof *see* Sindi
31 *N10* **Zion** Illinois, N USA *42°27′N 87°49′W*
54 *F10* **Zipaquirá** Cundinamarca, C Colombia *05°03′N 74°01′W*
Zipser Neudorf *see* Spišská Nová Ves
111 *H23* **Zirc** Veszprém, W Hungary *47°16′N 17°52′E*
113 *D14* **Žirje** *It.* Zuri. *island* S Croatia
Zirknitz *see* Cerknica
108 *M7* **Zirl** Tirol, W Austria *47°17′N 11°16′E*
101 *K20* **Zirndorf** Bayern, SE Germany *49°27′N 10°57′E*
160 *M11* **Zi Shui** ≋ C China
109 *Y3* **Zistersdorf** Niederösterreich, NE Austria *48°32′N 16°45′E*
41 *O14* **Zitácuaro** Michoacán, SW Mexico *19°28′N 100°21′W*
Zito *see* Lhorong
101 *Q16* **Zittau** Sachsen, E Germany *50°53′N 14°48′E*
112 *I12* **Živinice** Federacija Bosna I Hercegovina, E Bosnia and Herzegovina *44°26′N 18°39′E*
Ziwa Magharibi *see* Kagera
81 *J14* **Ziway Hāyk'** ◎ C Ethiopia
161 *N12* **Zixing** Hunan, S China *26°01′N 113°25′E*
127 *W7* **Ziyanchurino** Orenburgskaya Oblast', W Russian Federation *51°36′N 56°58′E*
160 *K8* **Ziyang** Shaanxi, C China *32°33′N 108°27′E*
111 *I20* **Zlaté Moravce** *Hung.* Aranyosmarót. Nitriansky Kraj, SW Slovakia *48°24′N 18°20′E*
112 *K13* **Zlatibor** ▲▲ W Serbia
114 *L9* **Zlati Voyvoda** Sliven, C Bulgaria *42°36′N 26°13′E*
116 *G11* **Zlatna** *Ger.* Kleinschlatten, *Hung.* Zalatna; *prev. Ger.* Goldmarkt. Alba, C Romania *46°08′N 23°11′E*
114 *I8* **Zlatna Panega** Lovech, N Bulgaria *43°07′N 24°09′E*
114 *N8* **Zlatni Pyasŭtsi** Dobrich, NE Bulgaria *43°19′N 28°03′E*
122 *F11* **Zlatoust** Chelyabinskaya Oblast', C Russian Federation *55°12′N 59°33′E*
111 *M19* **Zlatý Stôl** *Ger.* Goldener Tisch, *Hung.* Aranyosasztal. ▲ C Slovakia *48°45′N 20°39′E*
113 *P18* **Zletovo** NE FYR Macedonia *42°00′N 22°14′E*
111 *H18* **Zlín** *prev.* Gottwaldov. Zlínský Kraj, E Czech Republic *49°14′N 17°40′E*
111 *H19* **Zlínský Kraj** ◐ *region* E Czech Republic
75 *O7* **Zliṭan** W Libya *32°28′N 14°34′E*
110 *F9* **Złocieniec** *Ger.* Falkenburg in Pommern. Zachodnio-pomorskie, NW Poland *53°31′N 16°01′E*
110 *J13* **Złoczew** Sieradz, S Poland *51°24′N 18°36′E*
Złoczów *see* Zolochiv
111 *F14* **Złotoryja** *Ger.* Goldberg. Dolnośląskie, W Poland *51°08′N 15°57′E*
110 *G9* **Złotów** Wielkopolskie, C Poland *53°22′N 17°02′E*
110 *G13* **Żmigród** *Ger.* Trachenberg. Dolnośląskie, SW Poland *51°31′N 16°55′E*
126 *J6* **Zmiyevka** Orlovskaya Oblast', W Russian Federation *52°39′N 36°20′E*
117 *V5* **Zmiyiv** Kharkivs'ka Oblast', E Ukraine *49°40′N 36°22′E*
Zna *see* Tsna
Znaim *see* Znojmo
126 *M7* **Znamenka** Tambovskaya Oblast', W Russian Federation *52°24′N 42°28′E*
Znamenka *see* Znam"yanka
119 *C14* **Znamens** Astrakhanskaya Oblast', W Russian Federation *54°37′N 21°13′E*
127 *P10* **Znamensk** *Ger.* Wehlau. Kaliningradskaya Oblast', W Russian Federation *48°33′N 46°18′E*
117 *R7* **Znam"yanka** *Rus.* Znamenka. Kirovohrads'ka Oblast', C Ukraine *48°41′N 32°40′E*
110 *H10* **Żnin** Kujawsko-pomorskie, C Poland *52°50′N 17°41′E*
111 *F19* **Znojmo** *Ger.* Znaim. Jihomoravský Kraj, SE Czech Republic *48°52′N 16°04′E*
79 *N16* **Zobia** Orientale, N Dem. Rep. Congo *02°57′N 25°55′E*
83 *N15* **Zóbuè** Tete, NW Mozambique *15°36′S 34°26′E*
98 *G12* **Zoetermeer** Zuid-Holland, W Netherlands *52°04′N 04°30′E*
108 *E7* **Zofingen** Aargau, N Switzerland *47°18′N 07°57′E*
159 *R15* **Zogang** *var.* Wangda. Xizang Zizhiqu, W China *29°41′N 97°54′E*
106 *E7* **Zogno** Lombardia, N Italy *45°49′N 09°42′E*
142 *M10* **Zohreh, Rūd-e** ≋ SW Iran
160 *H7* **Zoigê** *var.* Dagcagoin. Sichuan, C China *33°44′N 102°57′E*
Żółkiew *see* Zhovkva
108 *D8* **Zollikofen** Bern, W Switzerland *47°00′N 07°24′E*
Zolochev *see* Zolochiv
117 *U4* **Zolochiv** *Rus.* Zolochev. Kharkivs'ka Oblast', E Ukraine *50°16′N 35°58′E*
116 *J5* **Zolochiv** *Pol.* Złoczów, *var.* Zolochev. L'vivs'ka Oblast', W Ukraine *49°48′N 24°51′E*
117 *X7* **Zolote** *Rus.* Zolotoye. Luhans'ka Oblast', E Ukraine *48°42′N 38°33′E*
117 *Q6* **Zolotonosha** Cherkas'ka Oblast', C Ukraine *49°39′N 32°05′E*
Zolotoye *see* Zolote
Zólyom *see* Zvolen
83 *N15* **Zomba** Southern, S Malawi *15°22′S 35°23′E*
Zombor *see* Sombor
99 *D17* **Zomergem** Oost-Vlaanderen, NW Belgium *51°07′N 03°31′E*
147 *P11* **Zomin** *Rus.* Zaamin. Jizzax Viloyati, C Uzbekistan *39°56′N 68°16′E*
79 *I15* **Zongo** Equateur, N Dem. Rep. Congo *04°18′N 18°42′E*
136 *G10* **Zonguldak** Zonguldak, NW Turkey *41°26′N 31°47′E*
136 *H10* **Zonguldak** ◐ *province* NW Turkey
99 *K17* **Zonhoven** Limburg, NE Belgium *50°59′N 05°22′E*
142 *J2* **Zonūz** Āzarbāyjān-e Khāvarī, NW Iran *38°32′N 45°54′E*
103 *Y16* **Zonza** Corse, France, C Mediterranean Sea *41°49′N 09°13′E*
Zoppot *see* Sopot
Zorgho *see* Zorgo
77 *Q13* **Zorgo** *var.* Zorgho. C Burkina *12°15′N 00°37′W*
104 *K10* **Zorita** Extremadura, W Spain *39°18′N 05°42′W*
147 *U14* **Zorkŭl** *Rus.* Ozero Zorkul'. ◎ SE Tajikistan
Zorkul', Ozero *see* Zorkŭl
56 *A8* **Zorritos** Tumbes, N Peru *03°43′S 80°42′W*
111 *J16* **Żory** *var.* Zory, *Ger.* Sohrau. Śląskie, S Poland *50°04′N 18°42′E*
76 *K15* **Zorzor** N Liberia *07°46′N 09°28′W*
99 *E18* **Zottegem** Oost-Vlaanderen, NW Belgium *50°52′N 03°49′E*
77 *R15* **Zou** ≋ S Benin
78 *H6* **Zouar** Borkou-Ennedi-Tibesti, N Chad *20°25′N 16°28′E*
76 *J6* **Zouérat** *var.* Zouérate, Zouîrât. Tiris Zemmour, N Mauritania *22°44′N 12°29′W*
Zouérate *see* Zouérat
Zoug *see* Zug
Zouîrât *see* Zouérat
76 *M16* **Zoukougbeu** C Ivory Coast *09°47′N 06°50′W*
98 *M5* **Zoutkamp** Groningen, NE Netherlands *53°22′N 06°17′E*
99 *J18* **Zoutleeuw** *Fr.* Leau. Vlaams Brabant, C Belgium *50°49′N 05°06′E*
112 *L9* **Zrenjanin** *prev.* Petrovgrad, Veliki Bečkerek, *Ger.* Grossbetschkerek, *Hung.* Nagybecskerek. Vojvodina, N Serbia *45°23′N 20°24′E*
112 *E10* **Zrinska Gora** ▲▲ C Croatia
Zsablya *see* Žabalj
101 *N16* **Zschopau** ≋ E Germany
Zsebely *see* Jebel
Zsibó *see* Jibou
Zsilyvajdevulkán *see* Vulcan
Zsil/Zsily *see* Jiu
Zsolna *see* Žilina
Zsombolya *see* Jimbolia
Zsupanya *see* Županja
55 *N7* **Zuata** Anzoátegui, NE Venezuela *08°24′N 65°13′W*
105 *N14* **Zubia** Andalucía, S Spain *37°10′N 03°36′W*
65 *P16* **Zubov Seamount** *undersea feature* E Atlantic Ocean *20°45′S 08°45′E*
124 *I16* **Zubtsov** Tverskaya Oblast', W Russian Federation *56°10′N 34°34′E*
108 *M8* **Zuckerhütl** ▲ SW Austria *46°57′N 11°07′E*
Zueila *see* Zawīlah
76 *M16* **Zuénoula** C Ivory Coast *07°26′N 06°03′W*
105 *S5* **Zuera** Aragón, NE Spain *41°52′N 00°47′W*
141 *V13* **Ẓufār** *Eng.* Dhofar. *physical region* SW Oman
108 *G8* **Zug** *Fr.* Zoug. Zug, C Switzerland *47°11′N 08°31′E*
108 *G8* **Zug** *Fr.* Zoug. ◐ *canton* C Switzerland
137 *R9* **Zugdidi** W Georgia *42°30′N 41°52′E*
108 *G8* **Zuger See** ◎ NW Switzerland
101 *K25* **Zugspitze** ▲ S Germany *47°25′N 10°58′E*
117 *X8* **Zuhres** *Rus.* Shakhtërsk. Donets'ka Oblast', SE Ukraine *48°01′N 38°16′E*
99 *E15* **Zuid-Beveland** *var.* South Beveland. *island* SW Netherlands
98 *K10* **Zuidelijk-Flevoland** *polder* C Netherlands
Zuider Zee *see* IJsselmeer
98 *G12* **Zuid-Holland** *Eng.* South Holland. ◐ *province* W Netherlands
98 *N5* **Zuidhorn** Groningen, NE Netherlands *53°15′N 06°25′E*
98 *O6* **Zuidlaardermeer** ◎ NE Netherlands
98 *O6* **Zuidlaren** Drenthe, NE Netherlands *53°06′N 06°41′E*
99 *K14* **Zuid-Willemsvaart Kanaal** *canal* S Netherlands
98 *N8* **Zuidwolde** Drenthe, NE Netherlands *52°40′N 06°25′E*
Zuitai/Zuitaizi *see* Kangxian
105 *O14* **Zújar** Andalucía, S Spain *37°33′N 02°52′W*
104 *L11* **Zújar** ≋ W Spain
104 *L11* **Zújar, Embalse del** ⊠ W Spain
80 *J9* **Zula** E Eritrea *15°19′N 39°40′E*
54 *G6* **Zulia** *off.* Estado Zulia. ◐ *state* NW Venezuela
Zulia, Estado *see* Zulia
Zullapara *see* Maungdaw
Züllichau *see* Sulechów
105 *P3* **Zumárraga** País Vasco, N Spain *43°05′N 02°19′W*
112 *D8* **Žumberačko Gorje** *var.* Gorjanči, Uskocke Planine, Žumberak, *Ger.* Uskokengebirge; *prev.* Sichelburger Gerbirge. ▲ Croatia/Slovenia *see also* Gorjanci
Žumberak *see* Gorjanci/ Žumberačko Gorje
194 *K7* **Zumberge Coast** *coastal feature* Antarctica
Zumbo *see* Vila do Zumbo
29 *W10* **Zumbro Falls** Minnesota, N USA *44°15′N 92°25′W*
29 *W10* **Zumbro River** ≋ Minnesota, N USA
29 *W10* **Zumbrota** Minnesota, N USA *44°18′N 92°37′W*
99 *H15* **Zundert** Noord-Brabant, S Netherlands *51°28′N 04°40′E*
Zungaria *see* Dzungaria
77 *U14* **Zungeru** Niger, C Nigeria *09°49′N 06°10′E*
161 *P2* **Zunhua** Hebei, E China *40°10′N 117°58′E*
37 *O11* **Zuni** New Mexico, SW USA *35°03′N 108°52′W*
37 *P11* **Zuni Mountains** ▲▲ New Mexico, SW USA
160 *J11* **Zunyi** Guizhou, S China *27°40′N 106°56′E*
160 *J15* **Zuo Jiang** ≋ China/ Vietnam
Zuoqi *see* Gegan Gol
108 *J9* **Zuoz** Graubünden, SE Switzerland *46°37′N 09°58′E*
112 *I10* **Županja** *Hung.* Zsupanya. Vukovar-Srijem, E Croatia *45°03′N 18°42′E*
Žur *see* Zhur
127 *T2* **Zura** Udmurtskaya Respublika, NW Russian Federation *57°36′N 53°19′E*
139 *V8* **Zurbāṭīyah** Wāsiṭ, E Iraq *33°13′N 46°07′E*
Zuri *see* Žirje
108 *F7* **Zürich** *Eng./Fr.* Zurich, *It.* Zurigo. Zürich, N Switzerland *47°23′N 08°33′E*
108 *G6* **Zürich** *Eng./Fr.* Zurich. ◐ *canton* N Switzerland
Zurich, Lake *see* Zürichsee
108 *G7* **Zürichsee** *Eng.* Lake Zurich. ◎ NE Switzerland
Zurigo *see* Zürich
149 *V1* **Zŭrkŭl** *Pash.* Sarī Qūl, *Rus.* Ozero Zurkul'. ◎ Afghanistan/Tajikistan *see also* Sarī Qūl
Zŭrkŭl *see* Sarī Qūl
Zurkul', Ozero *see* Sarī Qūl/ Zŭrkŭl
110 *K10* **Żuromin** Mazowieckie, C Poland *53°00′N 19°54′E*
108 *J8* **Zürs** Vorarlberg, W Austria *47°11′N 10°11′E*
77 *T13* **Zuru** Kebbi, W Nigeria *11°28′N 05°13′E*
108 *F6* **Zurzach** Aargau, N Switzerland *47°33′N 08°21′E*
101 *J22* **Zusam** ≋ S Germany
98 *M11* **Zutphen** Gelderland, E Netherlands *52°09′N 06°12′E*
75 *N7* **Zuwārah** NW Libya *32°56′N 12°06′E*
Zuwaylah *see* Zawīlah
125 *R14* **Zuyevka** Kirovskaya Oblast', NW Russian Federation *58°24′N 51°08′E*
161 *N10* **Zuzhou** Hunan, S China *27°52′N 113°00′E*
Zvenigorodka *see* Zvenyhorodka
117 *P6* **Zvenyhorodka** *Rus.* Zvenigorodka. Cherkas'ka Oblast', C Ukraine *49°05′N 30°58′E*
123 *N12* **Zvezdnyy** Irkutskaya Oblast', C Russian Federation *56°43′N 106°22′E*
125 *U14* **Zvëzdnyy** Permskiy Kray, NW Russian Federation *57°45′N 56°20′E*
83 *K18* **Zvishavane** *prev.* Shabani. Matabeleland South, S Zimbabwe *20°20′S 30°02′E*
111 *J20* **Zvolen** *Ger.* Altsohl, *Hung.* Zólyom. Banskobystrický Kraj, C Slovakia *48°35′N 19°06′E*
112 *J12* **Zvornik** E Bosnia and Herzegovina *44°24′N 19°07′E*
98 *M5* **Zwaagwesteinde** *Fris.* De Westerein. Fryslân, N Netherlands *53°16′N 06°08′E*
98 *H10* **Zwanenburg** Noord-Holland, C Netherlands *52°22′N 04°44′E*
98 *L8* **Zwarte Meer** ◎ N Netherlands
98 *M9* **Zwarte Water** ≋ N Netherlands
98 *M8* **Zwartsluis** Overijssel, E Netherlands *52°39′N 06°04′E*
76 *L17* **Zwedru** *var.* Tchien. E Liberia *06°04′N 08°07′W*
98 *O8* **Zweeloo** Drenthe, NE Netherlands *52°48′N 06°45′E*
101 *E20* **Zweibrücken** *Fr.* Deux-Ponts, *Lat.* Bipontium. Rheinland-Pfalz, SW Germany *49°15′N 07°22′E*
108 *D9* **Zweisimmen** Fribourg, W Switzerland *46°33′N 07°22′E*
101 *M15* **Zwenkau** Sachsen, E Germany *51°11′N 12°19′E*
109 *V3* **Zwettl** Wien, NE Austria *48°28′N 14°17′E*
109 *T3* **Zwettl an der Rodl** Oberösterreich, N Austria *48°28′N 14°17′E*
99 *D18* **Zwevegem** West-Vlaanderen, W Belgium *50°48′N 03°20′E*
101 *M17* **Zwickau** Sachsen, E Germany *50°43′N 12°31′E*
101 *N16* **Zwickauer Mulde** ≋ E Germany
101 *O21* **Zwiesel** Bayern, SE Germany *49°02′N 13°14′E*
98 *H13* **Zwijndrecht** Zuid-Holland, SW Netherlands *51°49′N 04°39′E*
Zwischenwässern *see* Medvode
Zwittau *see* Svitavy
110 *N13* **Zwoleń** Mazowieckie, SE Poland *51°21′N 21°37′E*
98 *M9* **Zwolle** Overijssel, E Netherlands *52°31′N 06°06′E*
22 *G6* **Zwolle** Louisiana, S USA *31°37′N 93°38′W*
110 *K12* **Żychlin** Łódzkie, C Poland *52°15′N 19°38′E*
Żydaczów *see* Zhydachiv
Zyembin *see* Zembin
Zyôetu *see* Jōetsu
110 *L12* **Żyrardów** Mazowieckie, C Poland *52°02′N 20°28′E*
123 *S8* **Zyryanka** Respublika Sakha (Yakutiya), NE Russian Federation *65°45′N 150°43′E*
145 *Y9* **Zyryanovsk** Vostochnyy Kazakhstan, E Kazakhstan *49°45′N 84°16′E*

◆ Country
● Country Capital
◇ Dependent Territory
○ Dependent Territory Capital
◐ Administrative Regions
✕ International Airport
▲ Mountain
▲▲ Mountain Range
Volcano
≋ River
◎ Lake
⊠ Reservoir

Picture Credits

Dorling Kindersley would like to express their thanks to the following individuals, companies, and institutions for their help in preparing this atlas.

Earth Resource Mapping Ltd., Egham, Surrey
Brian Groombridge, World Conservation Monitoring Centre, Cambridge
The British Library, London
British Library of Political and Economic Science, London
The British Museum, London
The City Business Library, London
King's College, London
National Meteorological Library and Archive, Bracknell
The Printed Word, London
The Royal Geographical Society, London
University of London Library
Paul Beardmore
Philip Boyes
Hayley Crockford
Alistair Dougal
Reg Grant
Louise Keane
Zoe Livesley
Laura Porter
Jeff Eidenshink
Chris Hornby
Rachelle Smith
Ray Pinchard
Robert Meisner
Fiona Strawbridge

Every effort has been made to trace the copyright holders and we apologize in advance for any unintentional omissions. We would be pleased to insert the appropriate acknowledgment in any subsequent edition of this publication.

Adams Picture Library: 86CLA; **G Andrews:** 186CR; **Ardea London Ltd:** K Ghana 150C; M Iljima 132TC; R Waller 148TR; Art Directors **Aspect Picture Library:** P Carmichael 160TR; 131CR(below); G Tompkinson 190TRB; **Axiom:** C Bradley 148CA, 158CA; J Holmes xivCRA, xxivBCR, xxviiCRB, 150TCR, 166TL, J Morris 75TL, 77CRB, J Spaull 134BL; **Bridgeman Art Library, London / New York:** Collection of the Earl of Pembroke, Wilton House xxBC; **The J. Allan Cash Photolibrary:** xlBR, xliiCLA, xlivCL, 10BC, 60CL, 69CLB, 70CL, 72CLB, 75BR, 76BC, 87BL, 109BR, 138BCL, 141TL, 154CR, 178BR, 181TR; **Bruce Coleman Ltd:** 86BC, 98CL, 100TC; S Alden 192BC(below); Atlantide xxviTCR, 138BR; E Bjurstrom 141BR; S Bond 96CRB; T Buchholz xvCL, 92TR, 123TCL; J Burton xxiiiC; J Cancalosi 181TRB; B J Coates xxvBL, 192CL; B Coleman 63TL; B & C Colhoun 2TR, 36CB; A Compost xxiiiCBR; Dr S Coyne 45TL; G Cubitt xviTCL, 169BR, 178TR, 184TR; P Davey xxviiCLB, 121TL(below); N Devore 189CBL; S J Doylee xxiiCRR; H Flygare xviiCRA; M P L Fogden 17C(above) ; Jeff Foott Productions xxiiiCRB, 11CRA; M Freeman 91BRA; P van Gaalen 86TR; G Gualco 140C; B Henderson 194CR; Dr C Henneghien 69C; HPH Photography, H Van den Berg 69CR; C Hughes 69BCL; C James xxxixTC; J Johnson 39CR, 197TR; J Jurka 91CA; S C Kaufman 28C; S J Krasemann 33TR; H Lange 10TRB, 68CA; C Lockwood 32BC; L C Marigo xxiiBC, xxviiCLA, 49CRA, 59BR; M McCoy 187TR; D Meredith 3CR; J Murray xvCR, 179BR; Orion Press 165CR(above); Orion Services & Trading Co. Inc. 164CR; C Ott 17BL; Dr E Pott 9TR, 40CL, 87C, 93TL, 194CLB; F Prenzel 186BC, 193BC; M Read 42BR, 43CRB; H Reinhard xxiiCR, xxviiTR, 194BR; L Lee Rue III 151BCL; J Shaw xixTL; K N Swenson 194BC; P Terry 115CR; N Tomalin 54BCL; P Ward 78TC; S Widstrand 57TR; K Wothe 91C, 173TCL; J T Wright 127BR; **Colorific:** Black Star / L Mulvehil 156CL; Black Star / R Rogers 57BR; Black Star / J Rupp 161BCR; Camera Tres / C. Meyer 59BRA; R Caputo / Matrix 78CL; J. Hill 117CLB; M Koene 55TR; G Satterley xliiCLAR; M Yamashita 156BL, 167CR(above); **Comstock:** 108CRB; Corbis UK Ltd: 170TR, 170BL; **D Cousens:** 147 CRA; **Corbis:** Bob Daemmrich 6BL; Bryan Denton xxxCBL; Julie Dermansky / Julie Dermansky xxviiiTC; Everett Kennedy Brown / Epa 165CB; Kimimasa Mayama / Reuters 168CL(above); mosaaberizing / Demotix xxxCBR; Ocean 60BL; Ocean 135CL; Sucheta DAS / Reuters xxviBCR; Rob Widdis / epa 30CA; **Sue Cunningham Photographic:** 51CR; S Alden 192BC(below) **James Davis Travel Photography:** xxxviTCB, xxxviTR, xxxviCL, 13CA, 19BC, 49TLB, 56BCR, 57CLA, 61BCL, 93BC, 94TC, 102TR, 120CB, 158BC, 179CRA, 191BR; **Dorling Kindersley:** Paul Harris xxiiTR; Nigel Hicks xxiiBM; Jamie Marshall 181TR; Bharath Ramamrutham 155BR; Colin Sinclair 133BMR; George Dunnet: 124CA; **Environmental Picture Library:** Chris Westwood 126C; **Eye Ubiquitous:** xlCA; L. Fordyce 12CLA; L Johnstone 6CRA, 28BLA, 30CB; S. Miller xxiCA; M Southern 73BLA; **Chris Fairclough Colour Library:** xliBR; **Ffotograff:** N. Tapsell 158CL; **FLPA -Images of nature:** 123TR; **Geoscience Features:** xviBCR, xviBR, 102CL, 108BC, 122BR; Solar Film 64TC; **Getty Images:** Kim Steele 161BCL; **gettyone stone**: 131BC, 133BR, 164CR(above); G Johnson 130BL; R Passmore 120TR; D Austen 187CL; G Allison 186CL; L Ulrich 17TL; M Vines 17BL; R Wells 193BL; **Robert Harding Picture Library:** xviiTC, xxivCR, xxxC, xxxvTC, 2TLB, 3CA, 15CRB, 15CR, 37BC, 38CRA, 50BL, 95BR, 99CR, 114CR, 122BL, 131CLA, 142CB, 143TL, 147TR, 168TR, 168CA, 166BR; P G. Adam 13TCB; D Atchison-Jones 70BLA; J Bayne 72BCL; B Schuster 80CR; C Bowman 50BR, 53CA, 62CL, 70CRL; C Campbell xxiBC; G Corrigan 159CRB, 161CRB; P Craven xxxvBL; R Cundy 69BR; Delu 79BC; A Durand 111BR; Financial Times 142BR; R Frerck 51BL; T Gervis 3BCL, 7CR; I Griffiths xxxCL, 77TL; T Hall 166CRA; D Harney 142CA; S Harris xliiiBCL; G Hellier xvCRB, 135BL; F Jackson 137BCR; Jacobs xxxviiTL; P Koch 139TR; F Joseph Land 122TR; Y Marcoux 9BR; S Massif xvBC; A Mills 88CLB; L Murray 114TR; R Rainford xlivBL; G Renner 74CB, 194C; C Rennie 48CL, 116BR; R Richardson 118CL; P Van Riel 48BR; E Rooney 124TR; Sassoon xxivCL, 148CLB; Jochen Schlenker 193CL; P Scholey 176TR; M Short 137TL; E Simanor xxviiCR; V Southwell 139CR; J Strachan 42TR, 111BL, 132BCR; C Tokeley 131CLA; A C Waltham 161C; T Waltham xviiBL, xxiiCLLL, 138CRB; Westlight 37CR; N Wheeler 139BL; A Williams xxxviiiBR, xlTR; A Woolfitt 95BRA; Paul Harris: 168TC; **Hutchison Library:** 131CR (above) 6BL; P. Collomb 137CR; C. Dodwell 130TR; S Errington 70BCL; P. Hellyer 142BC; J. Horner xxxiTC; R. Ian Lloyd 134CRA; J.Nowell 135CLB, 143TC; A Zvoznikov xxiiCL; **Image Bank:** 87BR; J Banagan 190BCA; A Becker xxivBCL; M Khansa 121CR, M Isy-Schwart 193CR(above), 191CL; Khansa K Forest 163TR; Lomeo xxivTCR; T Madison 170TL(below); C Molyneux xxiiCRRR; C Navajas xviiiTR; Ocean Images Inc. 192CLB; J van Os xviiTCR; S Proehl 6CL; T Rakke xixTC, 64CL; M Reitz 196CA; M Romanelli 166CL(below); G A Rossi 151BCR, 176BLA; B Roussel 109TL; S Satushek xviiBCR; Stock Photos / J M Spielman xxivTRL; **Images Colour Library:** xxiiCLL, xxxixTR, xliCR, xliiiBL, 3BR, 19BR, 37TL, 44TL, 62TC, 91BR, 102CLB, 103CR, 150CL, 180CA; 164BC, 165TL; **Impact Photos:** J & G Andrews 186BL; C. Bluntzer 156BR; Cosmos / G. Buthaud 65BC; S Franklin 126BL; A. le Garsmeur 131C; C Jones xxxiCB, 70BL; V. Nemirousky 137BR; J Nicholl 76TCR; C. Penn 187C(below); G Sweeney xviiBR, 196CB, 196TR, J & G Andrews 186TR; **JVZ Picture Library:** T Nilson 135TC; **Frank Lane Picture Agency:** xxiTCR, xxiiiBL, 93TR; A Christiansen 58CRA; J Holmes xivBL; S. McCutcheon 3C; Silvestris 173TCR; D Smith xxiiBCL; W Wisniewsli 195BR; **Leeds Castle Foundation:** xxxviiBC; **Magnum:** Abbas 83CR, 136CA; S Franklin 134CRB; D Hurn 4BCL; P. Jones-Griffiths 191BL; H Kubota xviBCL, 156CLB; F Maver xviBL; S McCurry 73CL, 133BCR; G. Rodger 74TR; C Steele Perkins 72BL; **Mountain Camera / John Cleare:** 153TR; C Monteath 153CR; **Nature Photographers:** E.A. Janes 112CL; **Natural Science Photos:** M Andera 110C; **Network Photographers Ltd.:** C Sappa / Rapho 119BL; **N.H.P.A.:** N. J. Dennis xxiiiCL; D Heuchlin xxiiiCLA; S Krasemann 15BL, 25BR, 38TC; K Schafer 49CB; R Tidman 160CLB; D Tomlinson 145CR; M Wendler 48TR; **Nottingham Trent University:** T Waltham xivCL, xvBR; **Novosti:** 144BLA; **Oxford Scientific Films:** D Allan xxiiTR; H R Bardarson xviiiBC; D Bown xxiiiCBLL; M Brown 140BL; M Colbeck 147CAR; W Faidley 3TL; L Gould xxiiiTRB; D Guravich xxiiiTR; P Hammerschmidy / Okapia 87CLA; M Hill 57TL, 195TR; C Menteath ; J Netherton 2CRB; S Osolinski 82CA; R Packwood 72CA; M Pitts 179TC; N Rosing xxiiiCBL, 9TR, 197BR; D Simonson 57C; Survival Anglia / C Catton 137TR; R Toms xxiiiBR; K Wothe xxiBL, xviiCLA; **Panos Pictures:** B Aris 133C; P Barker xxivBR; T Bolstao 153BR; N Cooper 82CB, 153TC; J-L Dugast 166C(below), 167BR; J Hartley 73CA, 90CL; J Holmes 149BC; J Morris 76CLB; M Rose 146TR; D Sansoni 155CL; C Stowers 163TL; **Edward Parker:** 49TL, 49CLB; **Pictor International:** xivBR, xvBRA, xixTCL, xxCL, 3CLA, 17BR, 20TR, 20CRB, 23BCA, 23CL, 26CB, 27BC, 33TRB, 34BC, 34BR, 34CR, 38CB, 38CL, 43CL, 63BR, 65TC, 82CL, 83CLB, 99BR, 107CLA, 166TR, 171CL(above), 180CLB, 185TL; **Pictures Colour Library:** xxiBCL, xxiiBR, xxviBCL, 6BR, 15TR, 8TR, 16CL(above), 19TL, 20BL, 24C, 24CLA, 27TR, 32TRB, 36BC, 41CA, 43CRA, 68BL, 90TCB, 94BL, 99BL, 106CA, 107CLB, 107CR, 107BR, 117BL, 164BC, 192BL, K Forest 165TL(below); **Planet Earth Pictures:** 193CR(below); D Barrett 148CB, 184CA; R Coomber 16BL; G Douwma 172BR; E Edmonds 173BR; J Lythgoe 196BL; A Mounter 172CR; M Potts 6CA; P Scoones xxTR; J Walencik 110TR; J Waters 53BCL; **Popperfoto:** Reuters / J Drake xxxiiCLA; **Rex Features:** 165CR; Antelope xxxiiCLB; M Friedel xxiCR; J Shelley xxxCR; Sipa Press xxxCR; Sipa Press / Chamussy 176BL; **Robert Harding Picture Library:** C. Tokeley 131TL; J Strachan 132BL; Franz Joseph Land 122TR; Franz Joseph Land 364/7088 123BL, 169C(above), 170C(above), Tony Waltham 186CR(below), Y Marcoux 9BR; **Russia & Republics Photolibrary:** M Wadlow 118CR, 119CL, 124BC, 124CL, 125TL, 125BR, 126TCR; **Science Photo Library:** Earth Satellite Corporation xixTRB, xxxiCR, 49BCL; F Gohier xiCR; J Heseltine xviTCB; K Kent xvBLA; P Menzell xvBL; N.A.S.A. xBC; D Parker xivBC; University of Cambridge Collection Air Pictures 87CLB; RJ Wainscoat / P Arnold, Inc. xiBC; D Weintraub xiBL; **South American Pictures:** 57BL, 62TR; R Francis 52BL; Guyana Space Centre 50TR; T Morrison 49CRB, 49BL, 50CR, 52TR, 54TR, 61C; **Southampton Oceanography:** xviiiBL; **Sovofoto / Eastfoto:** xxxiiCBR; **Spectrum Colour Library:** 50BC, 160BC; J King 145BR; **Frank Spooner Pictures:** Gamma-Liason/Vogel 131CL(above); 26CRB; E. Baitel xxxiiBC; Bernstein xxxiCL; Contrast 112CR; Diard / Photo News 113CL; Liaison / C. Hires xxxiiTCB; Liaison / Nickelsberg xxxiiTR; Marleen 113TL; Novosti 116CA; P. Piel xxxCA; H Stucke 188CLB, 190CA; Torrengo / Figaro 78BR; A Zamur 113BL; **Still Pictures:** C Caldicott 77TC; A Crump 189CL; M & C Denis-Huot xxiiBL, 78CR, 81BL; M Edwards xxiCRL, 53BL, 64CR, 69BLA, 155BR; J Frebet 53CLB; H Giradet 53TC; E Parker 52CL; M Gunther 121BC; **Tony Stone Images:** xxviTR, 4CA 7BL, 7CL, 13CRB, 39BR, 58C, 97BC, 101BR, 106TR 109CL, 109CRB, 164CLB, 165C,180CB, 181BR, 188BC, 192TR; G Allison 18TR, 31CRB, 187CRB; D Armand 14TCB; D Austen 180TR, 186CL, 187CL; J Beatty 74CL; O Benn xxviBR; K Biggs xxiTL; R Bradbury 44BR; R A Butcher xxviTL; J Callahan xxviiCRA; P Chesley 185BCL, 188C; W Clay 30BL, 31CRA; J Cornish 96BL, 107TL; C Condina 41CB; T Craddock xxivTR; P Degginger 36CLB; Demetric 5BR; N DeVore xxivBC; A Diesendruck 60BR; S Egan 87CRA, 96BR; R Elliot xxiiBCR; S Elmore 19C; J Garrett 73CR; S Grandadam 14BR; R Grosskopf 28BL; D Hanson 104BC; C Harvey 69TL G Hellier 110BL, 165CR; S Huber 103CRB; D Hughs xxxiBR; A Husmo 91TR; G Irvine 31BC; J Jangoux 58CL; D Johnston xviiTR; A Kehr 113C; R Koskas xviTR; J Lamb 96CRA; J Lawrence 75CRA; L Lefkowitz 7CA; M Lewis 45CLA; S Mayman 55BR; Murray & Associates 45CR; G Norways 104CA; N Parfitt xxviiCL, 68TCR, 81TL; R Passmore 121TR; N Press xviBCA; E Pritchard 88CA, 90CLR; T Raymond 21BL, 29TR; L Resnick 74BR; M Rogers 80BR; A Sacks 28TCB; C Saule 90CR; S Schulhof xxivTC; P Seaward 34CL; M Sega 32BL; V Shenai 152CL; R Sherman 26CL; H Sitton 136CR; R Smith xxvBLA, 56C; S Studd 108CLA; H Strand 49BR, 63TR; P Tweedie 177CR; L Ulrich 17BL; M Vines 17TC; A B Wadham 60CR; J Warden 63CLB; R Wells 23CRA, 193BL; G Yeowell 34BL; **Telegraph Colour Library:** 61CRB, 61TCR, 157TL R Antrobus xxxixBR; J Sims 26BR; **Topham Picturepoint:** xxxiCBL, 162BR, 168TR, 168BC; **Travel Ink:** A Cowin 88TR; **Trip:** 140BR, 144CA, 155CRA; B Ashe 159TR; D Cole 190BCL, 190CR; D Davis 89BL; I Deineko xxxiTR; J Dennis 22BL; Dinodia 154CL; Eye Ubiquitous / L Fordyce 2CLB; A Gasson 149CR; W Jacobs 43TL, 54BL, 177BC, 178CLA, 185BCR, 186BL; P Kingsbury 112C; K Knight 177BR; V Kolpakov 147BL; T Noorits 87TL, 119BR, 146CL; R Power 41TR; N Ray 166BL, 168TC; C Rennie 116CLB; V Sidoropolev 145TR; E Smith 183BC, 183TL; **Woodfin Camp & Associates:** 92BLR; **World Pictures:** xvCRA, xviiCRA, 9CRB, 22CL, 23BC, 24BL, 35BL, 40TR, 51TR, 71BR, 80TCR, 82TR, 83BL, 86BCR, 96TC, 98BL, 100CR, 101CR, 103BC, 105TC, 157BL, 161BCL, 162CLB, 172CLB, 172BC, 179BL, 182CB, 183C, 184CL, 185CR; 121BR, 121TT; **Zefa Picture Library:** xviBLR, xviiBCL, xviiiCL, 3CL, 8BC, 8CT, 9CR, 13BC, 14TC, 16TR, 21TL, 22CRB, 25BL, 32TCR, 36BCR, 59BCL, 65TCL, 69CLA, 79TL, 81BR, 87CRB, 92C, 98C, 99TL, 100BL, 107TR, 118CRB, 120BL; 122C(below), 124CLA, 164BR, 183TR; Anatol 113BR; Barone 114BL; Brandenburg 5C; A J Brown 44TR; H J Clauss 55CLB; Damm 71BC; Evert 92BL; W Felger 3BL; J Fields 189CRA; R Frerck 4BL; G Heil 56BR; K Heibig 115BR; Heilman 28BC; Hunter 8C; Kitchen 10TR, 8CL, 8BL, 9TR; Dr H Kramarz 7BLA, 123CR(below); Mehlio 155BL; J F Raga 24TR; Rossenbach 105BR; Streichan 89TL; T Stewart 13TR, 19CR; Sunak 54BR, 162TR; D H Teuffen 95TL; B Zaunders 40BC **Additional Photography:** Geoff Dann; Rob Reichenfeld; H Taylor; Jerry Young.

Map Credits

World Population Density map, page xxiv:

Source:LandScanTM Global Population Database. Oak Ridge, TN; Oak Ridge National Laboratory. Available at http://www.ornl.gov/landscan/.

NORTH AMERICA

CANADA
Pages 8–15

UNITED STATES OF AMERICA
Pages 16–39

MEXICO
Pages 40–41

BELIZE
Pages 42–43

COSTA RICA
Pages 42–43

EL SALVADOR
Pages 42–43

GUATEMALA
Pages 42–43

HONDURAS
Pages 42–43

GRENADA
Pages 44–45

HAITI
Pages 44–45

JAMAICA
Pages 44–45

ST KITTS & NEVIS
Pages 44–45

ST LUCIA
Pages 44–45

ST VINCENT & THE GRENADINES
Pages 44–45

TRINIDAD & TOBAGO
Pages 44–45

SOUTH AMERIC

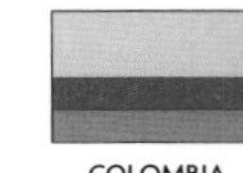
COLOMBIA
Pages 54–55

URUGUAY
Pages 60–61

CHILE
Pages 62–63

PARAGUAY
Pages 62–63

AFRICA

ALGERIA
Pages 74–75

EGYPT
Pages 74–75

LIBYA
Pages 74–75

MOROCCO
Pages 74–75

TUNISIA
Pages 74–75

LIBERIA
Pages 76–77

MALI
Pages 76–77

MAURITANIA
Pages 76–77

NIGER
Pages 76–77

NIGERIA
Pages 76–77

SENEGAL
Pages 76–77

SIERRA LEONE
Pages 76–77

TOGO
Pages 76–77

BURUNDI
Pages 80–81

DJIBOUTI
Pages 80–81

ERITREA
Pages 80–81

ETHIOPIA
Pages 80–81

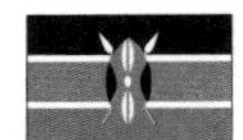
KENYA
Pages 80–81

RWANDA
Pages 80–81

SOMALIA
Pages 80–81

SUDAN
Pages 80–81

NAMIBIA
Pages 82–83

SOUTH AFRICA
Pages 82–83

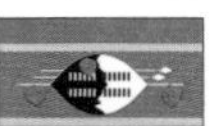
SWAZILAND
Pages 82–83

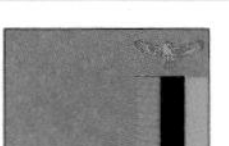
ZAMBIA
Pages 82–83

ZIMBABWE
Pages 82–83

COMOROS
Pages 172–173

MADAGASCAR
Pages 172–173

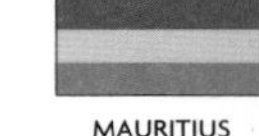
MAURITIUS
Pages 172–173

LUXEMBOURG
Pages 98–99

NETHERLANDS
Pages 98–99

GERMANY
Pages 100–101

FRANCE
Pages 102–103

MONACO
Pages 102–103

ANDORRA
Pages 104–105

PORTUGAL
Pages 104–105

SPAIN
Pages 104–105

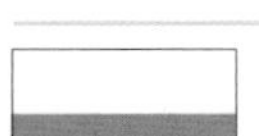
POLAND
Pages 110–111

SLOVAKIA
Pages 110–111

ALBANIA
Pages 112–113

BOSNIA & HERZEGOVINA
Pages 112–113

CROATIA
Pages 112–113

KOSOVO (disputed)
Pages 112–113

MACEDONIA
Pages 112–113

MONTENEGRO
Pages 112–113

LATVIA
Pages 118–119

LITHUANIA
Pages 118–119

CYPRUS
Pages 120–121

MALTA
Pages 120–121

RUSSIAN FEDERATION
Pages 122–127

ASIA

ARMENIA
Pages 136–137

AZERBAIJAN
Pages 136–137

GEORGIA
Pages 136–137

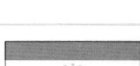

TURKEY
Pages 136–137/114–115

QATAR
Pages 140–143

SAUDI ARABIA
Pages 140–141

UNITED ARAB EMIRATES
Pages 140–143

YEMEN
Pages 140–141

IRAN
Pages 142–143

KAZAKHSTAN
Pages 144–145

KYRGYZSTAN
Pages 146–147

TAJIKISTAN
Pages 146–147

CHINA
Pages 156–163

MONGOLIA
Pages 156–157/162–163

NORTH KOREA
Pages 156–157/162–163

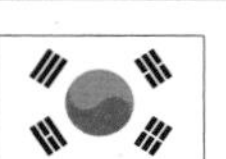
SOUTH KOREA
Pages 156–157/162–163

TAIWAN
Pages 156–157/160–161

JAPAN
Pages 164–165

MYANMAR
Pages 166–167

CAMBODIA
Pages 166–167

AUSTRALASIA & OCEANIA

SINGAPORE
Pages 168–169

MALDIVES
Pages 172–173

AUSTRALIA
Pages 180–183

NEW ZEALAND
Pages 184–185

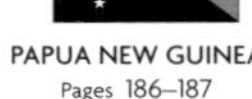
PAPUA NEW GUINEA
Pages 186–187

FIJI
Pages 186–187

SOLOMON ISLANDS
Pages 186–187

VANUATU
Pages 186–187